THIS HOLY BIBLE IS PRESENTED TO

BY

ON

YOUR WORD IS A LAMP FOR MY FEET,
A LIGHT ON MY PATH.

PSALM 119:105

NEW INTERNATIONAL VERSION

NIV ZONDERVAN STUDY BIBLE

NEW INTERNATIONAL VERSION

NIV ZONDERVAN STUDY BIBLE

Built on the Truth of Scripture and Centered on the Gospel Message

D. A. CARSON
GENERAL EDITOR

ZONDERVAN®

Published by Zondervan
Grand Rapids, Michigan, USA

www.zondervan.com

Library of Congress Catalog Card Number 2015932390

Printed in China N120712

15 16 17 18 19 20 21 22 23 24 25 /CTC/ 15 14 13 12 11 10 9 8 7 6 5 4 3 2

QUICK START GUIDE

WHAT IS THIS STUDY BIBLE?

The *NIV Zondervan Study Bible* is an all new study Bible built on the truth of Scripture and centering on "biblical theology"—the ways in which many important themes work their way through Scripture and come to a focus in Jesus Christ. It's a comprehensive combination of newly crafted study notes, articles, book introductions and study tools.

WHAT DO THE FEATURES OF THIS STUDY BIBLE OFFER ME?

Book introductions: When was this book written? Why was it written? How does the book fit with the rest of Scripture? What is in it? Nearly every book of the Bible begins with an introduction that offers helpful information about the book. The book introductions answer questions you may have about the book, and each book introduction provides an outline of the book.

Cross reference system: Where does this word or term appear in other parts of the Bible? A cross reference system enables you to search the Scriptures for terms, ideas, and themes that reappear in various books.

Study notes: What is the Bible saying here? God's Word was written down many years ago by different authors in different settings. The study notes at the bottom of each page explain or give background on words, phrases, and the flow of the argument to aid you in better understanding what God is saying in his Word. Each note was thoughtfully crafted to guide you in more clearly comprehending the Word of God.

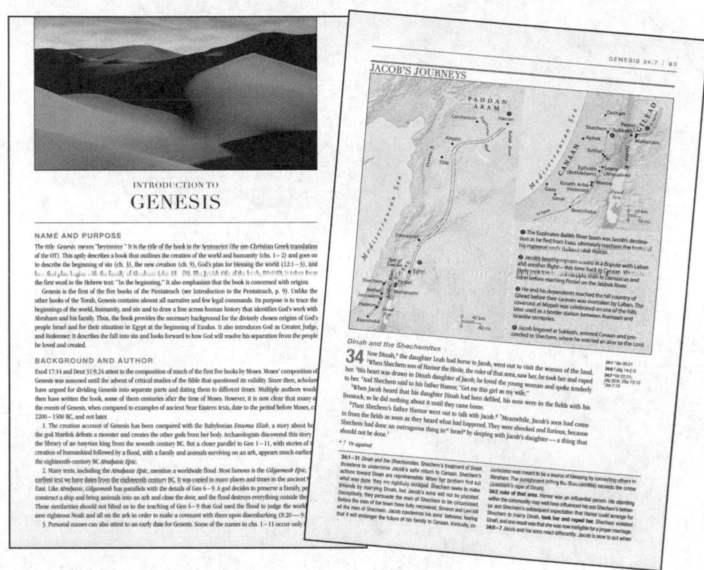

Maps, charts, illustrations, photos: Where did this happen? What else was going on during this time? The easy-to-use maps and charts will shed light on the Bible, its places, and its times. Illustrations and photos provide images that will enrich your experience with God's Word and give you rich insight to aid your study, for example, by demonstrating or illustrating the many events in the Bible that are anchored in ancient history.

Articles: What does the Bible say about . . . ? At the end of the Bible is a library of biblical-theological articles covering topics such as "The Bible and Theology," "Law," "The Gospel," and "Justice." Their purpose is to help you trace major biblical themes throughout the canon.

Concordance: A concordance to the New International Version text is located at the back of the Bible. It will help you find the location of words or phrases that are found in the Scripture text.

> *"All Scripture is God-breathed and is useful for teaching, rebuking, correcting and training in righteousness, so that the servant of God may be thoroughly equipped for every good work" (2 Timothy 3:16–17).*

TABLE OF CONTENTS

THE NEW TESTAMENT

MAPS

CHARTS

ILLUSTRATIONS

ARTICLES

ABBREVIATIONS AND TRANSLITERATIONS

ABBREVIATIONS

General

ASV	*American Standard Version*
ca.	*about, approximately*
cf.	*compare, confer*
ch., chs.	*chapter, chapters*
e.g.	*for example*
etc.	*and so forth*
ESV	*English Standard Version*
GNT	*Good News Translation*
i.e.	*that is*
KJV	*King James (Authorized) Version*
lit.	*literally, literal*
NASB	*New American Standard Version*
NEB	*New English Bible*
NRSV	*New Revised Standard Version*
NT	*New Testament*
OT	*Old Testament*
P	*papyrus*
p., pp.	*page, pages*
REB	*Revised English Version*
v., vv.	*verse, verses (in the chapter being commented on)*

Standard abbreviations of month names are also sometimes used, as well as a few other common abbreviations.

The following OT and NT abbreviations reflect the cross reference and concordance abbreviation first, followed by the abbreviation used elsewhere if different.

The Old Testament

Genesis	Ge, Gen
Exodus	Ex, Exod
Leviticus	Lev
Numbers	Nu, Num
Deuteronomy	Dt, Deut
Joshua	Jos, Josh
Judges	Jdg, Judg
Ruth	Ru, Ruth
1 Samuel	1Sa, 1 Sam
2 Samuel	2Sa, 2 Sam
1 Kings	1Ki, 1 Kgs
2 Kings	2Ki, 2 Kgs
1 Chronicles	1Ch, 1 Chr
2 Chronicles	2Ch, 2 Chr
Ezra	Ezr, Ezra
Nehemiah	Ne, Neh
Esther	Est, Esth
Job	Job
Psalms	Ps, Ps/Pss
Proverbs	Pr, Prov
Ecclesiastes	Ecc, Eccl
Song of Songs	SS, Song
Isaiah	Isa
Jeremiah	Jer
Lamentations	La, Lam
Ezekiel	Eze, Ezek
Daniel	Da, Dan
Hosea	Hos
Joel	Joel
Amos	Am, Amos
Obadiah	Ob, Obad
Jonah	Jnh, Jonah
Micah	Mic
Nahum	Na, Nah
Habakkuk	Hab
Zephaniah	Zep, Zeph
Haggai	Hag
Zechariah	Zec, Zech
Malachi	Mal

The New Testament

Matthew	Mt, Matt
Mark	Mk, Mark
Luke	Lk, Luke
John	Jn, John
Acts	Ac, Acts
Romans	Ro, Rom
1 Corinthians	1Co, 1 Cor
2 Corinthians	2Co, 2 Cor
Galatians	Gal
Ephesians	Eph
Philippians	Php, Phil
Colossians	Col
1 Thessalonians	1Th, 1 Thess
2 Thessalonians	2Th, 2 Thess
1 Timothy	1Ti, 1 Tim
2 Timothy	2Ti, 2 Tim
Titus	Titus
Philemon	Phm, Phlm
Hebrews	Heb
James	Jas
1 Peter	1Pe, 1 Pet
2 Peter	2Pe, 2 Pet
1 John	1Jn, 1 John
2 John	2Jn, 2 John
3 John	3Jn, 3 John
Jude	Jude
Revelation	Rev

TRANSLITERATIONS

A simplified system has been used for transliterating words from ancient Biblical languages into English. The only transliterations calling for comment are these:

Transliteration	*Pronunciation*
’	Glottal stop
ḥ	Similar to the “ch” in the German word *Buch*
ṭ	Similar to the “t” in the verb “tear”
‘	Similar to the glottal stop
ṣ	Similar to the “ts” in “hits”
ś	Similar to the “s” in “sing”

ACKNOWLEDGMENTS

The publication of a study Bible is possible only because scores of people have contributed to the work. All of us involved in this project first want to thank God for the immeasurable privilege of spending so many hours studying the Bible and writing notes on it for the good of the people of God around the world. The hard work has been both privilege and pleasure.

The three associate editors, T. D. Alexander, Douglas J. Moo, and Richard S. Hess, have labored tirelessly and with outstanding scholarship and scrupulous attention to the biblical text. All of them have worked through all the notes, as well as the articles at the end of the volume, and commented extensively. The first two editors focused special attention on biblical theology; Richard Hess's expertise has been invaluable in the messy domains of archaeology, geography, and chronology.

Andrew David Naselli, the assistant editor, not only provided thousands of comments on individual details, but served as the administrator of the project, keeping a genial eye on our master chart, keeping the bits and pieces flowing to the right people at the right time, as parts were edited, rewritten, checked again, edited by the folk at Zondervan, and so forth. Geeks and others who read these lines may be interested to learn that not a single piece of paper was passed around the writers and editors. All of the work was done digitally.

All the editors want to express thanks for all the writers. Some wrote relatively short pieces; others were responsible for much lengthier contributions, the equivalent of a good-sized book. The value of this *NIV Zondervan Study Bible* is largely a reflection of their knowledge and skill. Some of them worked under very tight deadlines; all of them had to put up with incessant suggestions from the editors, as we struggled to impose a certain consistency of format and style on the submitted notes and articles. Each writer responded with singular grace.

It would not be possible to mention by name all the people at Zondervan who have contributed to the production of this *NIV Zondervan Study Bible*. But it would be ungrateful and boorish not to mention the initial invitation to edit this study Bible that came to me from Maureen Girkins when she was CEO of Zondervan. In addition to her leadership, Chip Brown, Stan Gundry and Mark Schoenwald helped guide the Bible through its various stages. Similarly, the superior skills and good humor of Senior Editor Shari Vanden Berg and copyeditor Natalie J. Block place them at the very top of their profession. Senior Production Editor at Large Verlyn D. Verbrugge ably mediated the suggestions of the final review group, with his characteristic blend of careful scholarship and immaculate courtesy. Mike Vander Klipp, Kim Tanner, and Melinda Bouma lent their skills in a variety of capacities.

These names mean much to those of us who worked on this study Bible, but none of us will object in the slightest if you, the readers of this volume, forget our names, provided that as a result of this work you understand and love the Bible better, and recall the words of the living God: "These are the ones I look on with favor: those who are humble and contrite in spirit, and who tremble at my word" (Isaiah 66:2).

Soli Deo gloria.

D. A. Carson

EDITORIAL TEAM

The following people comprise the Executive Editorial Team, which developed the concept, selected the contributors, and provided general oversight and final approval of the *NIV Zondervan Study Bible* content and design.

General Editor:

D. A. Carson
Trinity Evangelical Divinity School
PhD, University of Cambridge

Associate Editor: Old Testament, Archaeology, and Maps

Richard S. Hess
Denver Seminary
PhD, Hebrew Union College

Associate Editor: Old Testament and Biblical Theology

T. D. Alexander
Union Theological College (Belfast)
PhD, The Queen's University of Belfast

Associate Editor: New Testament and Biblical Theology

Douglas J. Moo
Wheaton College
PhD, University of St. Andrews

Assistant Editor:

Andrew David Naselli
Bethlehem College & Seminary
PhD, Bob Jones University; PhD, Trinity Evangelical Divinity School

STUDY NOTE CONTRIBUTORS

The following people were responsible for writing the *NIV Zondervan Study Bible* notes for the corresponding books of the Bible. In some cases specific books had more than one writer; in every case the notes for each of the books involved several review and editorial stages. The notes that appear in the *NIV Zondervan Study Bible* are therefore the result of a collaborative editorial process, and may occasionally include content that differs from those of the primary contributors.

Introduction to the Old Testament

T. D. Alexander
Union Theological College (Belfast)
PhD, The Queen's University of Belfast

Introduction to the Pentateuch

T. D. Alexander
Union Theological College (Belfast)
PhD, The Queen's University of Belfast

Genesis

Richard S. Hess (especially Gen 1:1 — 11:26)
Denver Seminary
PhD, Hebrew Union College

T. D. Alexander (especially Gen 11:27 — 50:26)
Union Theological College (Belfast)
PhD, The Queen's University of Belfast

Exodus
Paul R. Williamson
Moore College
PhD, The Queen's University of Belfast

Leviticus
Richard E. Averbeck
Trinity Evangelical Divinity School
PhD, Dropsie College

Numbers
Jay A. Sklar
Covenant Theological Seminary
PhD, University of Gloucestershire

Deuteronomy
Stephen G. Dempster
Crandall University
PhD, University of Toronto

Introduction to the Historical Books
Richard S. Hess
Denver Seminary
PhD, Hebrew Union College

Joshua
Richard S. Hess
Denver Seminary
PhD, Hebrew Union College

Judges
K. Lawson Younger Jr.
Trinity Evangelical Divinity School
PhD, Sheffield University

Ruth
Robert L. Hubbard
North Park Theological Seminary
PhD, Claremont Graduate University

1–2 Samuel
John D. Currid
Reformed Theological Seminary (Charlotte)
PhD, University of Chicago

1 Kings
Robert L. Hubbard
North Park Theological Seminary
PhD, Claremont Graduate University

2 Kings
Todd Bolen
The Master's College
PhD, Dallas Theological Seminary

1–2 Chronicles
Frederick J. Mabie
Fireside Community Church, Dana Point, CA
PhD, University of California, Los Angeles

Ezra–Nehemiah
Robert S. Fyall
Cornhill Training Course (Scotland)
PhD, University of Edinburgh

Esther
Karen H. Jobes
Wheaton College
PhD, Westminster Theological Seminary

Introduction to the Wisdom and Lyrical Books
T. D. Alexander
Union Theological College (Belfast)
PhD, The Queen's University of Belfast

Job
C. Hassell Bullock
Wheaton College
PhD, Hebrew Union College-Jewish Institute of Religion

Psalms
David M. Howard Jr.
Bethel Seminary (St. Paul)
PhD, The University of Michigan

Michael K. Snearly (coauthored notes on Psalms: Books 4–5)
Red Hill Church (San Anselmo, CA)
PhD, Golden Gate Baptist Theological Seminary

Proverbs
Bruce K. Waltke
Knox Theological Seminary
ThD, Dallas Theological Seminary; PhD, Harvard University

Christopher B. Ansberry
Oak Hill College
PhD, Wheaton College

Ecclesiastes
Craig G. Bartholomew
Redeemer University College
PhD, University of Bristol

Song of Songs
Richard S. Hess
Denver Seminary
PhD, Hebrew Union College

Introduction to the Prophetic Books
Richard S. Hess
Denver Seminary
PhD, Hebrew Union College

Isaiah
John N. Oswalt
Asbury Theological Seminary
PhD, Brandeis University

Jeremiah
Iain M. Duguid
Westminster Theological Seminary
PhD, University of Cambridge

Lamentations
David J. Reimer
University of Edinburgh
DPhil, University of Oxford

Ezekiel
Donna Lee Petter
Gordon-Conwell Theological Seminary
PhD, University of Toronto

Daniel
Tremper Longman III
Westmont College
PhD, Yale University

Hosea
Douglas K. Stuart
Gordon-Conwell Theological Seminary
PhD, Harvard University

Joel
David W. Baker
Ashland Theological Seminary
PhD, University of London

Amos
M. Daniel Carroll R.
Denver Seminary
PhD, University of Sheffield

Obadiah
David W. Baker
Ashland Theological Seminary
PhD, University of London

Jonah
T. D. Alexander
Union Theological College (Belfast)
PhD, The Queen's University of Belfast

Micah
Bruce K. Waltke
Knox Theological Seminary
ThD, Dallas Theological Seminary; PhD, Harvard University

Nahum
V. Philips Long
Regent College
PhD, University of Cambridge

Habakkuk
Elmer A. Martens
Mennonite Brethren Biblical Seminary
PhD, Claremont Graduate University

Zephaniah
Jason S. DeRouchie
Bethlehem College & Seminary
PhD, The Southern Baptist Theological Seminary

Haggai
Anthony R. Petterson
Morling College
PhD, The Queen's University of Belfast

Zechariah
Anthony R. Petterson
Morling College
PhD, The Queen's University of Belfast

Malachi
Andrew E. Hill
Wheaton College
PhD, University of Michigan

The Time Between the Testaments
Douglas J. Moo
Wheaton College
PhD, University of St. Andrews

Introduction to the New Testament
Douglas J. Moo
Wheaton College
PhD, University of St. Andrews

Introduction to the Gospels and Acts
D. A. Carson
Trinity Evangelical Divinity School
PhD, University of Cambridge

Matthew
Craig L. Blomberg
Denver Seminary
PhD, University of Aberdeen

Mark
Rikk E. Watts
Regent College
PhD, University of Cambridge

Luke
David W. Pao
Trinity Evangelical Divinity School
PhD, Harvard University

John
D. A. Carson
Trinity Evangelical Divinity School
PhD, University of Cambridge

Andrew David Naselli
Bethlehem College & Seminary
PhD, Bob Jones University; PhD, Trinity Evangelical Divinity School

Acts
Mark L. Strauss
Bethel Seminary (San Diego)
PhD, University of Aberdeen

Introduction to the Letters and Revelation
Douglas J. Moo
Wheaton College
PhD, University of St. Andrews

Romans
Douglas J. Moo
Wheaton College
PhD, University of St. Andrews

1 Corinthians
Eckhard J. Schnabel
Gordon-Conwell Theological Seminary
PhD, University of Aberdeen

2 Corinthians
Murray J. Harris
Emeritus Professor of New Testament, Trinity Evangelical Divinity School
PhD, University of Manchester

Galatians
Stephen Westerholm
McMaster University
DTh, Lund University

Ephesians
Te-Li Lau
Trinity Evangelical Divinity School
PhD, Emory University

Philippians
Simon J. Gathercole
University of Cambridge
PhD, University of Durham

Colossians
David E. Garland
Baylor University
PhD, The Southern Baptist Theological Seminary

1–2 Thessalonians
Jeffrey A. D. Weima
Calvin Theological Seminary
PhD, University of Toronto

1–2 Timothy, Titus
Robert W. Yarbrough
Covenant Theological Seminary
PhD, University of Aberdeen

Philemon
David E. Garland
Baylor University
PhD, The Southern Baptist Theological Seminary

Hebrews
Buist M. Fanning
Dallas Theological Seminary
DPhil, University of Oxford

James
Douglas J. Moo
Wheaton College
PhD, University of St. Andrews

1 Peter
Karen H. Jobes
Wheaton College
PhD, Westminster Theological Seminary

2 Peter
Douglas J. Moo
Wheaton College
PhD, University of St. Andrews

Andrew David Naselli
Bethlehem College & Seminary
PhD, Bob Jones University; PhD, Trinity Evangelical Divinity School

1–3 John
Colin G. Kruse
Melbourne School of Theology
PhD, Fuller Theological Seminary

Jude
Douglas J. Moo
Wheaton College
PhD, University of St. Andrews

Andrew David Naselli
Bethlehem College & Seminary
PhD, Bob Jones University; PhD, Trinity Evangelical Divinity School

Revelation

Brian J. Tabb
Bethlehem College & Seminary
PhD, London School of Theology

ARTICLE CONTRIBUTORS

The Story of the Bible: How the Good News About Jesus Is Central

Timothy Keller
Redeemer Presbyterian Church (Manhattan)
DMin, Westminster Theological Seminary

The Bible and Theology

D. A. Carson
Trinity Evangelical Divinity School
PhD, University of Cambridge

A Biblical-Theological Overview of the Bible

D. A. Carson
Trinity Evangelical Divinity School
PhD, University of Cambridge

The Glory of God

James M. Hamilton Jr.
The Southern Baptist Theological Seminary
PhD, The Southern Baptist Theological Seminary

Creation

Henri A. G. Blocher
Former Gunther H. Knoedler Professor of Systematic Theology, Wheaton College
Faculté Libre de Théologie Protestante of Paris
Diplôme d'Etudes Supérieures de Théologie

Sin

Kevin DeYoung
University Reformed Church (Lansing, MI)
PhD candidate, University of Leicester

Covenant

Paul R. Williamson
Moore College
PhD, The Queen's University of Belfast

Law

T. D. Alexander
Union Theological College (Belfast)
PhD, The Queen's University of Belfast

Temple

T. D. Alexander
Union Theological College (Belfast)
PhD, The Queen's University of Belfast

Priest

Dana M. Harris
Trinity Evangelical Divinity School
PhD, Trinity Evangelical Divinity School

Sacrifice

Jay A. Sklar
Covenant Theological Seminary
PhD, University of Gloucestershire

Exile and Exodus

Thomas Richard Wood
Christ Fellowship Church, Deer Lodge, MT
PhD, Trinity Evangelical Divinity School

The Kingdom of God

T. D. Alexander
Union Theological College (Belfast)
PhD, The Queen's University of Belfast

Sonship

D. A. Carson
Trinity Evangelical Divinity School
PhD, University of Cambridge

The City of God

T. D. Alexander
Union Theological College (Belfast)
PhD, The Queen's University of Belfast

Prophets and Prophecy

Sam Storms
Bridgeway Church (Oklahoma City)
PhD, University of Texas

Death and Resurrection

Philip S. Johnston
Hughes Hall, University of Cambridge
PhD, University of Cambridge

People of God

Moisés Silva
Private Scholar
PhD, University of Manchester

Wisdom

Daniel J. Estes
Cedarville University
PhD, University of Cambridge

Holiness

Andrew David Naselli
Bethlehem College & Seminary
PhD, Bob Jones University; PhD, Trinity Evangelical Divinity School

Justice
Brian S. Rosner
Ridley College
PhD, University of Cambridge

Wrath
Christopher W. Morgan
California Baptist University
PhD, Mid-America Baptist Theological Seminary

Love and Grace
Graham A. Cole
Beeson Divinity School
ThD, Australian College of Theology

The Gospel
Greg D. Gilbert
Third Avenue Baptist Church (Louisville)
MDiv, The Southern Baptist Theological Seminary

Worship
David G. Peterson
Moore Theological College
PhD, University of Manchester

Mission
Andreas J. Köstenberger
Southeastern Baptist Theological Seminary
PhD, Trinity Evangelical Divinity School

Shalom
Timothy Keller
Redeemer Presbyterian Church (Manhattan)
DMin, Westminster Theological Seminary

The Consummation
Douglas J. Moo
Wheaton College
PhD, University of St. Andrews

EDITOR'S PREFACE

English-speaking people have no shortage of study Bibles. I have more than a dozen in front of me as I write these lines. All study Bibles have certain features in common. They bring together in one fat volume the complete text of the English Bible, and, on the same page, explanatory notes, maps, illustrations, etc. to help readers understand what they are reading. There is a danger in this, of course: we would not want any reader to confuse the authority and reliability of the biblical text with the notes and commentary that we provide. Although we have tried our best to provide true and faithful comments, our added features never claim the inspiration that belongs to Scripture alone. But provided readers avoid the danger by being careful not to confuse the biblical words and the words of the accompanying notes, study Bibles have a great advantage: in one volume readers have both the text of Scripture and some basic aids to help them understand what they are reading.

That such helps are necessary should not come as a surprise, for the Bible itself depicts the importance of teaching the words of Scripture to others. When Philip sees the Ethiopian eunuch reading the book of Isaiah, he boldly asks him, "Do you understand what you are reading?" (Acts 8:30). " 'How can I,' he said, 'unless someone explains it to me?' " (8:31), which is exactly what Philip proceeded to do. That is how Paul understood his own ministry; his concern was to teach people "the word of God," which is variously identified with the gospel and with Scripture itself. For example, "Paul stayed in Corinth for a year and a half, teaching them the word of God" (Acts 18:11). When Nehemiah and Ezra and others led the Israelites in reformation, "They read from the Book of the Law of God, making it clear and giving the meaning so that the people understood what was being read" (Neh 8:8).

Although all study Bibles have certain things in common, they vary quite a lot. Some are written by scholars who do not revere Scripture as the word of God, while others affirm Scripture as inspired. Different study Bibles are based on a variety of English translations. Some are long, detailed, and occasionally verbose; others aim for crisp brevity. Some add many maps, charts, and illustrations; others provide integrative theological essays.

So what characterizes this *NIV Zondervan Study Bible*? First, in common with the best study Bibles, all our contributors revere Scripture as the Word of God and joyfully bow to its authority. Our desire is not so much to be masters of the Word, as to be mastered by it. That shapes how we approach the text and how we write about it. Our aim is to bring glory to God by helping people think his thoughts after him, and to bring understanding and edification to his people as they do so.

Second, this study Bible is based on the NIV, which continues to be the best-selling, most widely circulated modern English version of the Bible in the world. This version excels in idiomatic accuracy. It remembers that not only the words of the original languages — Hebrew, Aramaic, Greek — are inspired by God, but so also are the phrases, the sentences, the idioms, the kinds of writing that make up the Bible, and all must be taken into account and worked through to generate a smooth and faithful translation.

Third, this study Bible aims to provide enough detail to answer the questions that many readers raise when they read the Bible without indulging in all the details that might be better left to separate commentaries.

Fourth, in addition to the notes on the biblical text, this study Bible provides an excellent collection of charts, maps, brief essays providing the historical circumstances when each biblical book was written, and many photos and illustrations.

Finally, this study Bible emphasizes biblical theology. By this we mean that instead of focusing primary attention on how the Bible as a whole addresses many questions (which is what many people mean by "systematic theology"), we have tried to highlight the way various themes develop within the Bible across time. Nowhere is this clearer than in the 28 articles at the end of the Bible, which survey the way certain themes develop in the Bible, taking us to their climax in the book of Revelation — such themes as temple, for instance, and sacrifice, Jerusalem, kingship, Messiah, and many more. In this way we hope to encourage readers of the Bible to spot these themes for themselves as they read their Bibles, becoming adept at tracing them throughout the Scriptures. Such biblical theology enables readers to follow the Bible's themes in the terms and categories that the Bible itself uses.

All of us who have worked on this project will be satisfied if readers come away from the Bible with increased understanding, greater grasp of the gospel, greater confidence in Scripture, more love for the Lord Jesus, renewed fear of sin and renewed love for the church, and greater joy in God.

Soli Deo gloria.

D. A. Carson

PREFACE

The goal of the New International Version (NIV) is to enable English-speaking people from around the world to read and hear God's eternal Word in their own language. Our work as translators is motivated by our conviction that the Bible is God's Word in written form. We believe that the Bible contains the divine answer to the deepest needs of humanity, sheds unique light on our path in a dark world and sets forth the way to our eternal well-being. Out of these deep convictions, we have sought to recreate as far as possible the experience of the original audience — blending transparency to the original text with accessibility for the millions of English speakers around the world. We have prioritized accuracy, clarity and literary quality with the goal of creating a translation suitable for public and private reading, evangelism, teaching, preaching, memorizing and liturgical use. We have also sought to preserve a measure of continuity with the long tradition of translating the Scriptures into English.

The complete NIV Bible was first published in 1978. It was a completely new translation made by over a hundred scholars working directly from the best available Hebrew, Aramaic and Greek texts. The translators came from the United States, Great Britain, Canada, Australia and New Zealand, giving the translation an international scope. They were from many denominations and churches — including Anglican, Assemblies of God, Baptist, Brethren, Christian Reformed, Church of Christ, Evangelical Covenant, Evangelical Free, Lutheran, Mennonite, Methodist, Nazarene, Presbyterian, Wesleyan and others. This breadth of denominational and theological perspective helped to safeguard the translation from sectarian bias. For these reasons, and by the grace of God, the NIV has gained a wide readership in all parts of the English-speaking world.

The work of translating the Bible is never finished. As good as they are, English translations must be regularly updated so that they will continue to communicate accurately the meaning of God's Word. Updates are needed in order to reflect the latest developments in our understanding of the biblical world and its languages and to keep pace with changes in English usage. Recognizing, then, that the NIV would retain its ability to communicate God's Word accurately only if it were regularly updated, the original translators established the Committee on Bible Translation (CBT). The Committee is a self-perpetuating group of biblical scholars charged with keeping abreast of advances in biblical scholarship and changes in English and issuing periodic updates to the NIV. The CBT is an independent, self-governing body and has sole responsibility for the NIV text. The Committee mirrors the original group of translators in its diverse international and denominational makeup and in its unifying commitment to the Bible as God's inspired Word.

In obedience to its mandate, the Committee has issued periodic updates to the NIV. An initial revision was released in 1984. A more thorough revision process was completed in 2005, resulting in the separately published TNIV. The updated NIV you now have in your hands builds on both the original NIV and the TNIV and represents the latest effort of the Committee to articulate God's unchanging Word in the way the original authors might have said it had they been speaking in English to the global English-speaking audience today.

Translation Philosophy

The Committee's translating work has been governed by three widely accepted principles about the way people use words and about the way we understand them.

First, the meaning of words is determined by the way that users of the language actually use them at any given time. For the biblical languages, therefore, the Committee utilizes the best and most recent scholarship on the way Hebrew, Aramaic and Greek words were being used in biblical times. At the same time, the Committee carefully studies the state of modern English. Good translation is like good communication: one must know the target audience so that the appropriate choices can be made about which English words to use to represent the original words of Scripture. From its inception, the NIV has had as its target the general English-speaking population all over the world, the "International" in its title reflecting this concern. The aim of the Committee is to put the Scriptures into natural English that will communicate effectively with the broadest possible audience of English speakers.

Modern technology has enhanced the Committee's ability to choose the right English words to convey the meaning of the original text. The field of computational linguistics harnesses the power of computers to provide broadly applicable and current data about the state of the language. Translators can now access huge databases of modern English to better understand the current meaning and usage of key words. The Committee utilized this resource in preparing the 2011 edition of the NIV. An area of especially rapid and significant change in English is the way certain nouns and pronouns are used to refer to human beings. The Committee therefore requested experts in computational linguistics at Collins Dictionaries to pose some key questions about this usage to its database of English — the largest in the world, with over 4.4 billion words, gathered from several English-speaking countries and including both spoken and written English. (The Collins Study, called "The Development and

Use of Gender Language in Contemporary English," can be accessed at ***http://www.thenivbible.com/about-the-niv/about-the-2011-edition/***.) The study revealed that the most popular words to describe the human race in modern U.S. English were "humanity," "man" and "mankind." The Committee then used this data in the updated NIV, choosing from among these three words (and occasionally others also) depending on the context.

A related issue creates a larger problem for modern translations: the move away from using the third-person masculine singular pronouns—"he/him/his"—to refer to men and women equally. This usage does persist in some forms of English, and this revision therefore occasionally uses these pronouns in a generic sense. But the tendency, recognized in day-to-day usage and confirmed by the Collins study, is away from the generic use of "he," "him" and "his." In recognition of this shift in language and in an effort to translate into the natural English that people are actually using, this revision of the NIV generally uses other constructions when the biblical text is plainly addressed to men and women equally. The reader will encounter especially frequently a "they," "their" or "them" to express a generic singular idea. Thus, for instance, Mark 8:36 reads: "What good is it for someone to gain the whole world, yet forfeit their soul?" This generic use of the "distributive" or "singular" "they/them/their" has been used for many centuries by respected writers of English and has now become established as standard English, spoken and written, all over the world.

A second linguistic principle that feeds into the Committee's translation work is that meaning is found not in individual words, as vital as they are, but in larger clusters: phrases, clauses, sentences, discourses. Translation is not, as many people think, a matter of word substitution: English word *x* in place of Hebrew word *y*. Translators must first determine the meaning of the words of the biblical languages in the context of the passage and then select English words that accurately communicate that meaning to modern listeners and readers. This means that accurate translation will not always reflect the exact structure of the original language. To be sure, there is debate over the degree to which translators should try to preserve the "form" of the original text in English. From the beginning, the NIV has taken a mediating position on this issue. The manual produced when the translation that became the NIV was first being planned states: "If the Greek or Hebrew syntax has a good parallel in modern English, it should be used. But if there is no good parallel, the English syntax appropriate to the meaning of the original is to be chosen." It is fine, in other words, to carry over the form of the biblical languages into English—but not at the expense of natural expression. The principle that meaning resides in larger clusters of words means that the Committee has not insisted on a "word-for-word" approach to translation. We certainly believe that every word of Scripture is inspired by God and therefore to be carefully studied to determine what God is saying to us. It is for this reason that the Committee labors over every single word of the original texts, working hard to determine how each of those words contributes to what the text is saying. Ultimately, however, it is how these individual words function in combination with other words that determines meaning.

A third linguistic principle guiding the Committee in its translation work is the recognition that words have a spectrum of meaning. It is popular to define a word by using another word, or "gloss," to substitute for it. This substitute word is then sometimes called the "literal" meaning of a word. In fact, however, words have a range of possible meanings. Those meanings will vary depending on the context, and words in one language will usually not occupy the same semantic range as words in another language. The Committee therefore studies each original word of Scripture in its context to identify its meaning in a particular verse and then chooses an appropriate English word (or phrase) to represent it. It is impossible, then, to translate any given Hebrew, Aramaic or Greek word with the same English word all the time. The Committee does try to translate related occurrences of a word in the original languages with the same English word in order to preserve the connection for the English reader. But the Committee generally privileges clear natural meaning over a concern with consistency in rendering particular words.

Textual Basis

For the Old Testament the standard Hebrew text, the Masoretic Text as published in the latest edition of *Biblia Hebraica*, has been used throughout. The Masoretic Text tradition contains marginal notations that offer variant readings. These have sometimes been followed instead of the text itself. Because such instances involve variants within the Masoretic tradition, they have not been indicated in the textual notes. In a few cases, words in the basic consonantal text have been divided differently than in the Masoretic Text. Such cases are usually indicated in the textual footnotes. The Dead Sea Scrolls contain biblical texts that represent an earlier stage of the transmission of the Hebrew text. They have been consulted, as have been the Samaritan Pentateuch and the ancient scribal traditions concerning deliberate textual changes. The translators also consulted the more important early versions. Readings from these versions, the Dead Sea Scrolls and the scribal traditions were occasionally followed where the Masoretic Text seemed doubtful and where accepted principles of textual criticism showed that one or more of these textual witnesses appeared to provide the correct reading. In rare cases, the translators have emended the Hebrew text where it appears to have become corrupted at an even earlier stage of its transmission. These departures from the

Masoretic Text are also indicated in the textual footnotes. Sometimes the vowel indicators (which are later additions to the basic consonantal text) found in the Masoretic Text did not, in the judgment of the translators, represent the correct vowels for the original text. Accordingly, some words have been read with a different set of vowels. These instances are usually not indicated in the footnotes.

The Greek text used in translating the New Testament has been an eclectic one, based on the latest editions of the Nestle-Aland/United Bible Societies' Greek New Testament. The translators have made their choices among the variant readings in accordance with widely accepted principles of New Testament textual criticism. Footnotes call attention to places where uncertainty remains.

The New Testament authors, writing in Greek, often quote the Old Testament from its ancient Greek version, the Septuagint. This is one reason why some of the Old Testament quotations in the NIV New Testament are not identical to the corresponding passages in the NIV Old Testament. Such quotations in the New Testament are indicated with the footnote "(see Septuagint)."

Footnotes and Formatting

Footnotes in this version are of several kinds, most of which need no explanation. Those giving alternative translations begin with "Or" and generally introduce the alternative with the last word preceding it in the text, except when it is a single-word alternative. When poetry is quoted in a footnote a slash mark indicates a line division.

It should be noted that references to diseases, minerals, flora and fauna, architectural details, clothing, jewelry, musical instruments and other articles cannot always be identified with precision. Also, linear measurements and measures of capacity can only be approximated (see the Table of Weights and Measures). Although *Selah*, used mainly in the Psalms, is probably a musical term, its meaning is uncertain. Since it may interrupt reading and distract the reader, this word has not been kept in the English text, but every occurrence has been signaled by a footnote.

As an aid to the reader, sectional headings have been inserted. They are not to be regarded as part of the biblical text and are not intended for oral reading. It is the Committee's hope that these headings may prove more helpful to the reader than the traditional chapter divisions, which were introduced long after the Bible was written.

Sometimes the chapter and/or verse numbering in English translations of the Old Testament differs from that found in published Hebrew texts. This is particularly the case in the Psalms, where the traditional titles are included in the Hebrew verse numbering. Such differences are indicated in the footnotes at the bottom of the page. In the New Testament, verse numbers that marked off portions of the traditional English text not supported by the best Greek manuscripts now appear in brackets, with a footnote indicating the text that has been omitted (see, for example, Matthew 17:[21]).

Mark 16:9–20 and John 7:53—8:11, although long accorded virtually equal status with the rest of the Gospels in which they stand, have a questionable standing in the textual history of the New Testament, as noted in the bracketed annotations with which they are set off. A different typeface has been chosen for these passages to indicate their uncertain status.

Basic formatting of the text, such as lining the poetry, paragraphing (both prose and poetry), setting up of (administrative-like) lists, indenting letters and lengthy prayers within narratives and the insertion of sectional headings, has been the work of the Committee. However, the choice between single-column and double-column formats has been left to the publishers. Also the issuing of "red-letter" editions is a publisher's choice—one that the Committee does not endorse.

The Committee has again been reminded that every human effort is flawed—including this revision of the NIV. We trust, however, that many will find in it an improved representation of the Word of God, through which they hear his call to faith in our Lord Jesus Christ and to service in his kingdom. We offer this version of the Bible to him in whose name and for whose glory it has been made.

The Committee on Bible Translation

OLD TESTAMENT CHRONOLOGY

Creation
Gen 1–2

Fall
Gen 3

Flood
Gen 6–9

Babel
Gen 11

?

?

?

?

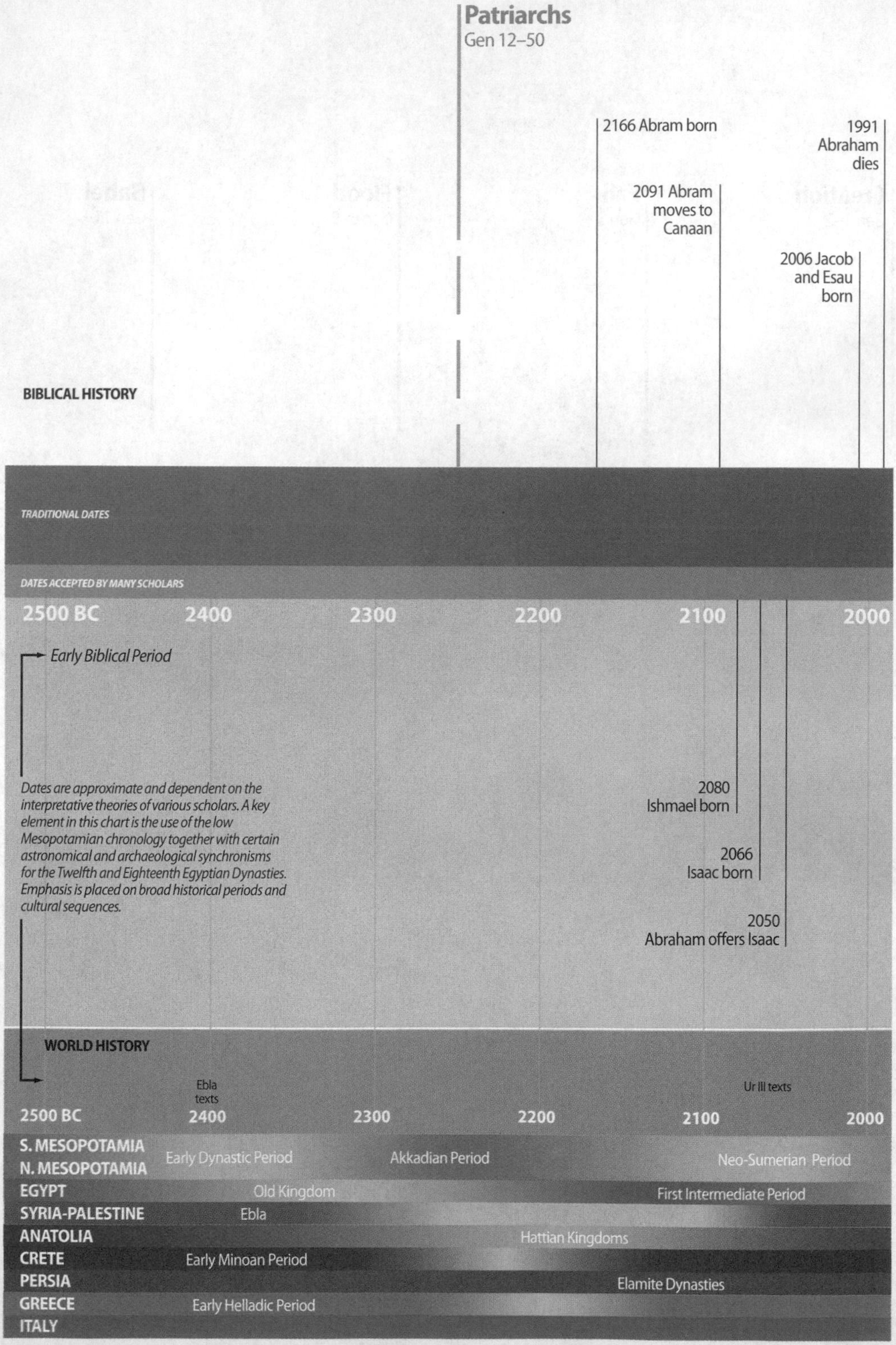

Patriarchs
Gen 12–50

2166 Abram born

1991 Abraham dies

2091 Abram moves to Canaan

2006 Jacob and Esau born

BIBLICAL HISTORY

TRADITIONAL DATES

DATES ACCEPTED BY MANY SCHOLARS

2500 BC | 2400 | 2300 | 2200 | 2100 | 2000

Early Biblical Period

Dates are approximate and dependent on the interpretative theories of various scholars. A key element in this chart is the use of the low Mesopotamian chronology together with certain astronomical and archaeological synchronisms for the Twelfth and Eighteenth Egyptian Dynasties. Emphasis is placed on broad historical periods and cultural sequences.

2080 Ishmael born

2066 Isaac born

2050 Abraham offers Isaac

WORLD HISTORY

Ebla texts

Ur III texts

2500 BC | 2400 | 2300 | 2200 | 2100 | 2000

S. MESOPOTAMIA / N. MESOPOTAMIA: Early Dynastic Period; Akkadian Period; Neo-Sumerian Period

EGYPT: Old Kingdom; First Intermediate Period

SYRIA-PALESTINE: Ebla

ANATOLIA: Hattian Kingdoms

CRETE: Early Minoan Period

PERSIA: Elamite Dynasties

GREECE: Early Helladic Period

ITALY

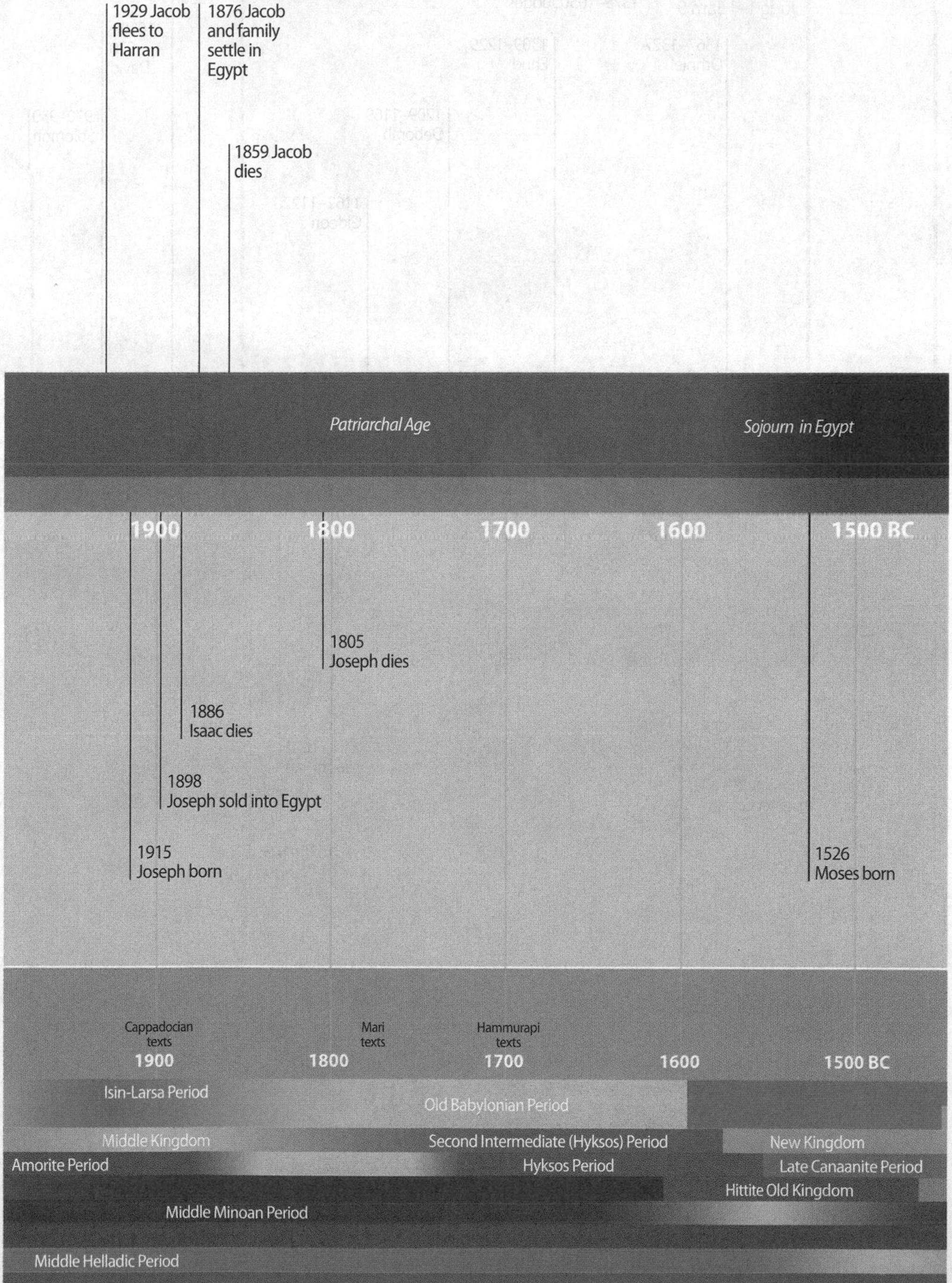

1929 Jacob flees to Harran

1876 Jacob and family settle in Egypt

1859 Jacob dies

Patriarchal Age

Sojourn in Egypt

1900 1800 1700 1600 1500 BC

1805 Joseph dies

1886 Isaac dies

1898 Joseph sold into Egypt

1915 Joseph born

1526 Moses born

Cappadocian texts

Mari texts

Hammurapi texts

1900 1800 1700 1600 1500 BC

Isin-Larsa Period

Old Babylonian Period

Middle Kingdom

Second Intermediate (Hyksos) Period

New Kingdom

Amorite Period

Hyksos Period

Late Canaanite Period

Hittite Old Kingdom

Middle Minoan Period

Middle Helladic Period

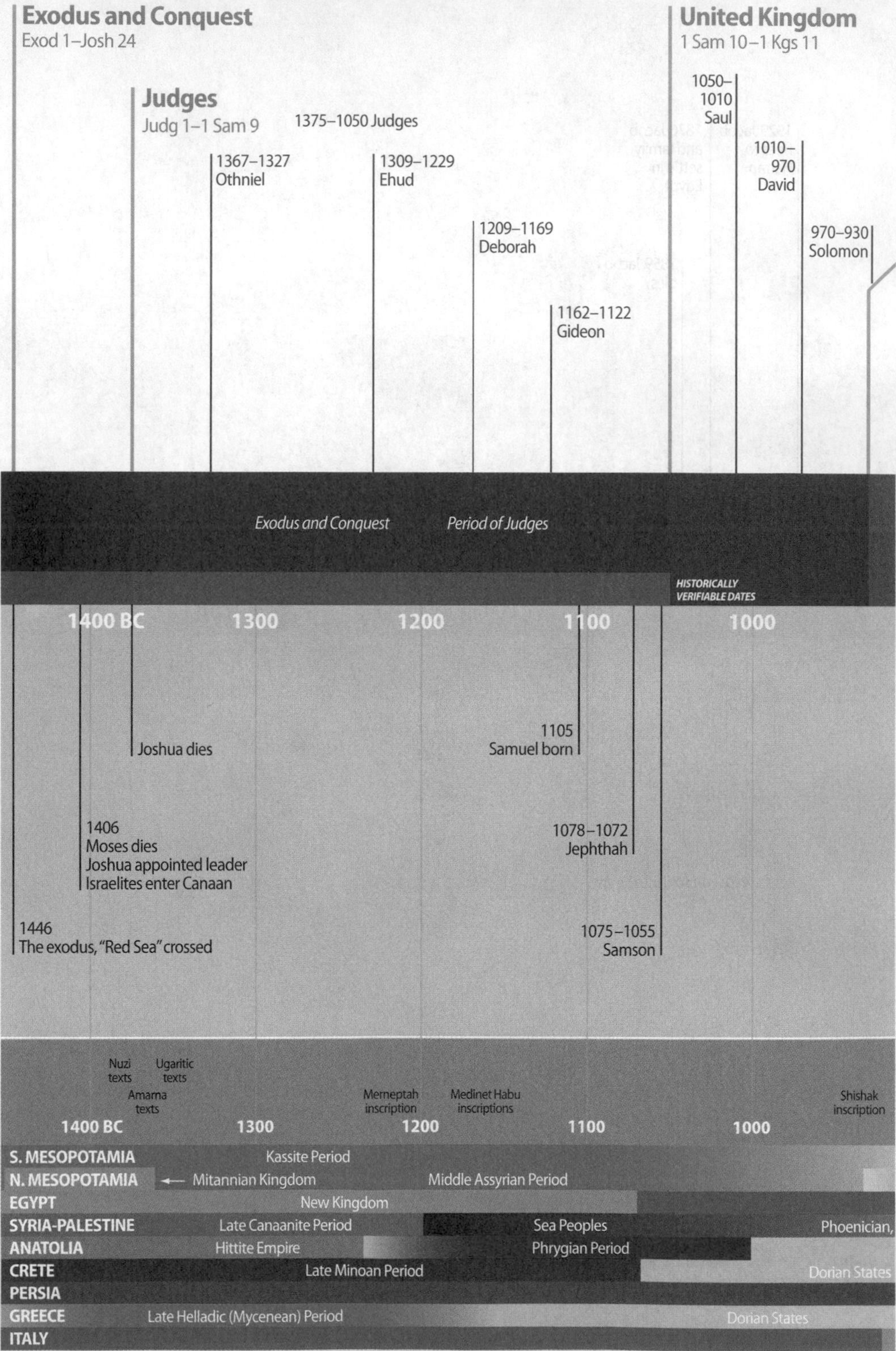
Exodus and Conquest
Exod 1–Josh 24
Judges
Judg 1–1 Sam 9
1375–1050 Judges
1367–1327
Othniel
1309–1229
Ehud
1209–1169
Deborah
1162–1122
Gideon
United Kingdom
1 Sam 10–1 Kgs 11
1050–
1010
Saul
1010–
970
David
970–930
Solomon
Exodus and Conquest
Period of Judges
HISTORICALLY
VERIFIABLE DATES
1400 BC
1300
1200
1100
1000
Joshua dies
1105
Samuel born
1406
Moses dies
Joshua appointed leader
Israelites enter Canaan
1078–1072
Jephthah
1446
The exodus, "Red Sea" crossed
1075–1055
Samson
Nuzi
texts
Ugaritic
texts
Amarna
texts
Merneptah
inscription
Medinet Habu
inscriptions
Shishak
inscription
1400 BC
1300
1200
1100
1000
S. MESOPOTAMIA
Kassite Period
N. MESOPOTAMIA
← Mitannian Kingdom
Middle Assyrian Period
EGYPT
New Kingdom
SYRIA-PALESTINE
Late Canaanite Period
Sea Peoples
Phoenician,
ANATOLIA
Hittite Empire
Phrygian Period
CRETE
Late Minoan Period
Dorian States
PERSIA
GREECE
Late Helladic (Mycenean) Period
Dorian States
ITALY

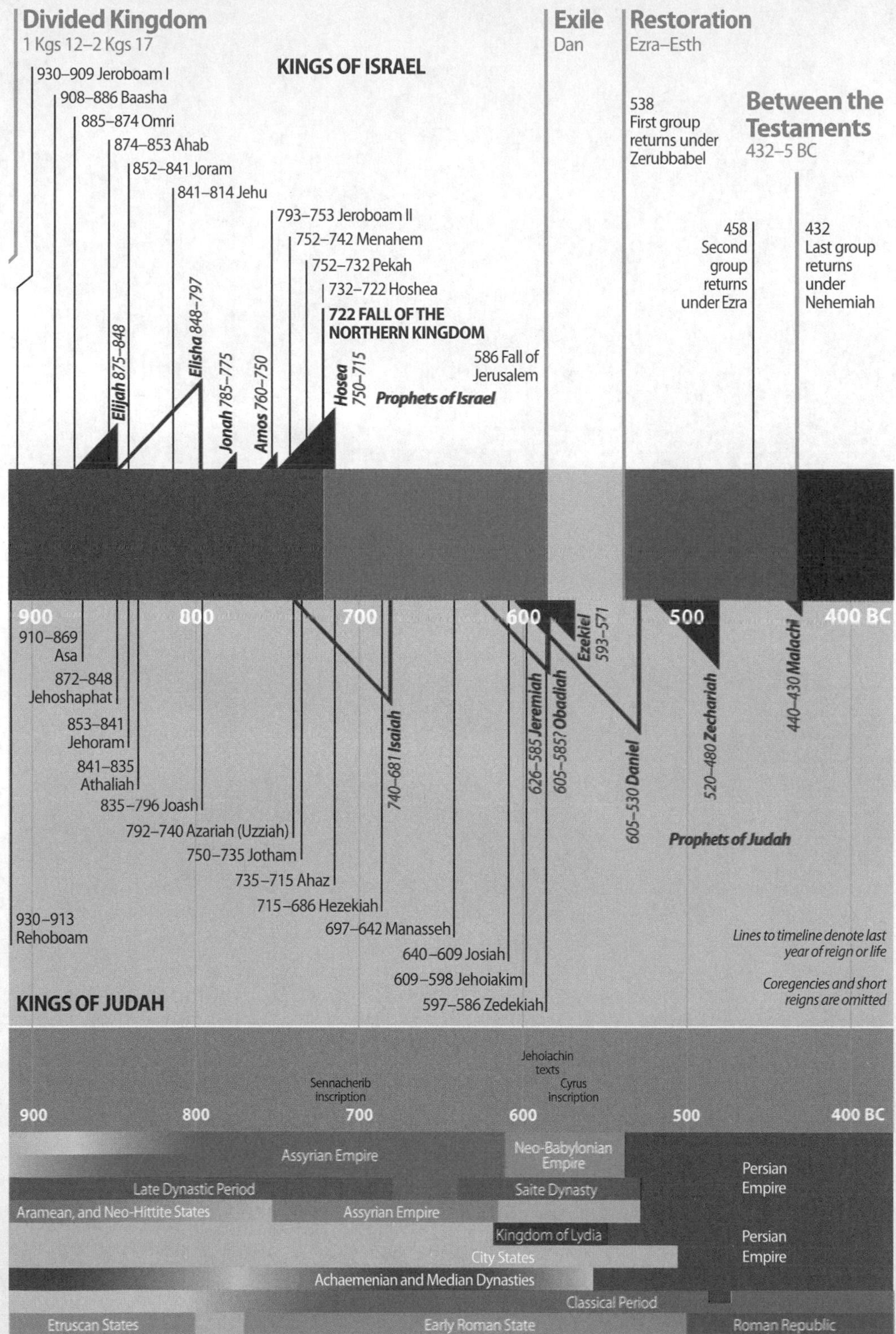
Divided Kingdom
1 Kgs 12–2 Kgs 17
KINGS OF ISRAEL
930–909 Jeroboam I
908–886 Baasha
885–874 Omri
874–853 Ahab
852–841 Joram
841–814 Jehu
793–753 Jeroboam II
752–742 Menahem
752–732 Pekah
732–722 Hoshea
722 FALL OF THE NORTHERN KINGDOM
Elijah 875–848
Elisha 848–797
Jonah 785–775
Amos 760–750
Hosea 750–715
Prophets of Israel
586 Fall of Jerusalem
Exile
Dan
Restoration
Ezra–Esth
538 First group returns under Zerubbabel
Between the Testaments
432–5 BC
458 Second group returns under Ezra
432 Last group returns under Nehemiah
900
800
700
600
500
400 BC
910–869 Asa
872–848 Jehoshaphat
853–841 Jehoram
841–835 Athaliah
835–796 Joash
792–740 Azariah (Uzziah)
750–735 Jotham
735–715 Ahaz
715–686 Hezekiah
697–642 Manasseh
640–609 Josiah
609–598 Jehoiakim
597–586 Zedekiah
930–913 Rehoboam
KINGS OF JUDAH
740–681 Isaiah
626–585 Jeremiah
605–585? Obadiah
Ezekiel 593–571
605–530 Daniel
520–480 Zechariah
440–430 Malachi
Prophets of Judah
Lines to timeline denote last year of reign or life
Coregencies and short reigns are omitted
Sennacherib inscription
Jehoiachin texts
Cyrus inscription
900
800
700
600
500
400 BC
Assyrian Empire
Neo-Babylonian Empire
Persian Empire
Late Dynastic Period
Saite Dynasty
Aramean, and Neo-Hittite States
Assyrian Empire
Kingdom of Lydia
Persian Empire
City States
Achaemenian and Median Dynasties
Classical Period
Etruscan States
Early Roman State
Roman Republic

THE OLD TESTAMENT

INTRODUCTION TO THE OLD TESTAMENT

T. D. Alexander

The 39 books of the OT are an integral and vital part of the Christian Bible. As a unique collection of religious documents, mostly written in the first millennium BC, they comprise about 75 percent of the Bible. The OT stands on a par with the NT, being equally inspired by God and essential for Christian teaching and practice (see 2 Tim 3:14–17).

Canon of the Old Testament

Although the evidence is sparse and open to debate, on balance it seems likely that the canon (i.e., the authoritative list of books) of the OT was closed well before the time of Jesus. While some scholars contend that the library of OT books remained fluid until the latter part of the first century AD, the earliest surviving evidence suggests that the books of the OT, or the Hebrew Bible as it is sometimes called, were viewed as an authoritative collection of writings by about 150 BC at the latest. In the prologue of Ecclesiasticus (in the Apocrypha), a Greek translation of a Hebrew book known as Sirach, the translator, writing about 132 BC, refers to the OT using the following expressions: "the Law and the Prophets and the others that followed them"; "the Law and the Prophets and the other books of our ancestors"; "the Law itself, the Prophecies, and the rest of the books." This threefold division reflects the later Jewish custom of referring to the Hebrew Bible as the Law, Prophets, and Writings. Unfortunately, no ancient texts survive to explain how the process of canonization happened and what criteria were used to determine which books should be included. The process itself may well have occurred in stages over several centuries, and individual books were probably viewed as special long before the different sections of the canon were finally closed. Although some Christian traditions hold that various other Jewish writings should be viewed as canonical, the earliest evidence, including the authoritative testimony of the NT, suggests that only those books that comprise the Hebrew Bible are divinely inspired. On the inspiration and authority of the NT, see Introduction to the New Testament, p. 1909.

Contents of the Old Testament

As a highly select library of religious writings, the OT has a rich variety of contents. Although we have become accustomed to viewing the books as ordered in a fixed way, the order differs in Jewish and Christian Bibles. Whereas Jewish tradition divides the OT into three sections, Christian tradition has favored four:

1. the Law, or Pentateuch: Genesis, Exodus, Leviticus, Numbers, Deuteronomy (see Introduction to the Pentateuch, p. 9);
2. the Historical Books: Joshua, Judges, Ruth, 1 and 2 Samuel, 1 and 2 Kings, 1 and 2 Chronicles, Ezra, Nehemiah, Esther (see Introduction to the Historical Books, p. 373);
3. the Wisdom and Lyrical Books: Job, Psalms, Proverbs, Ecclesiastes, Song of Songs (see Introduction to the Wisdom and Lyrical Books, p. 895); and
4. the Prophetic Books: the Major Prophets include Isaiah, Jeremiah, Lamentations, Ezekiel, and Daniel, and the Minor Prophets include Hosea through Malachi (see Introduction to the Prophetic Books, p. 1299).

Old Testament Story

The Bible is built around a grand story that starts in Genesis with the divine creation of the earth and ends in Revelation by anticipating the coming of a new earth. The OT contributes to this story by explaining the origin and nature of the human predicament, which, in essence, is our alienation from God. From the early chapters of Genesis onward, the OT describes how God sets about redeeming and restoring creation after the tragic rebellion of Adam and Eve in the Garden of Eden. Not only is God's redemptive activity evident throughout the OT, but by pointing forward to Jesus Christ, the OT introduces the ultimate means by which the tragic consequences of human sin will be reversed.

Fourth-century fresco of Adam and Eve. The OT describes how God sets about redeeming and restoring creation after the tragic rebellion of Adam and Eve in the Garden of Eden.

Roman, (4th century AD)/Cimitero dei SS. Marcellino e Pietro, Rome, Italy/De Agostini Picture Library/Bridgeman Images

To understand the grand story that underlies the OT, it is important to appreciate the flow of events that shape the main plot of the story. We must recognize, however, that although various OT books, especially the Wisdom and Lyrical Books, say little directly about the OT story, they complement it by addressing important theological issues. The same is partly true for most of the Prophetic Books, but their contents are usually tied more closely to the OT story.

Primeval Era

Gen 1–11 record a small number of highly significant episodes that belong to the early history of the world from creation up to about 2000 BC. These chapters describe how humanity becomes estranged from God, leading to a world dominated by violence due to the corruption of human nature. While Adam and Eve's betrayal of God has horrific consequences for all of earth's creatures, God promises that one of Eve's offspring will eventually crush the head of the mysterious, but clearly evil, serpent (Gen 3:15). Gen 4–11 trace this offspring from Adam (through Seth) to Noah and then onward (through Shem) to Abraham.

Patriarchal Period

Divided by genealogies, Gen 11:27—50:26 falls into three main sections that focus chiefly on (1) Abraham (chs. 12–24), (2) Isaac and his son Jacob (chs. 25–36), and (3) Joseph (chs. 37–50). God promises Abraham, who initially is both childless and landless, that his descendants will become a great nation in the land of Canaan and that a future descendant will mediate God's blessing to the nations of the earth. These promises link the divine redemption of humanity to a royal line descended from Abraham (cf. Matt 1:1–17). Gen 37–48 trace this potential royal line through Joseph and his son Ephraim. Anticipating later developments, Joseph's unexpected rise to prominence in Egypt results in blessing for many nations; this foreshadows the much greater blessing that will eventually come through Jesus Christ.

Deliverance From Oppression

Moses' birth and death frame the books of Exodus through Deuteronomy. Events move geographically from Egypt, via Mount Sinai, to the eastern bank of the Jordan River in the land of Moab.

The early chapters of Exodus recount the enslavement of the Israelites in Egypt. After God commissions him, Moses leads the Israelites out of Egypt. This involves a series of signs and wonders that emphasize God's authority over nature. When these extraordinary events climax in the death of the Egyptian firstborn males, God spares the Israelite firstborn when the Israelites observe a special "Passover" ritual. The Passover encapsulates the process of divine salvation whereby God redeems his people from slavery and ransoms them from death in order to create a holy nation. The subsequent destruction of the Egyptian army in the "Red Sea" confirms the Lord as savior of his people.

After rescuing the Israelites, God graciously invites them to submit to him as their sole sovereign by entering into a unique covenant relationship. God places distinctive obligations upon the Israelites, the most important being the Ten Commandments (Exod 20). The covenant ratified at Mount Sinai prepares the way for God to come and dwell among the Israelites. To facilitate this, the people construct a special tabernacle in which God will reside (Exod 25–31,35–40).

Leviticus addresses how the Israelites should maintain their newly acquired status as a holy nation. In particular, it describes the measures necessary to atone for sin, cleanse defilement, and promote holy living.

The Israelites' journey from Mount Sinai to the land of Canaan, recorded in the book of Numbers, is marked by a series of damaging events that demonstrate their lack of trust in God. Consequently, God punishes them: they must remain in the wilderness for 40 years. Only after the adults who left Egypt die does God permit their children to enter the promised land.

According to Deuteronomy, after arriving at the eastern border of Canaan, Moses delivers a valedictory address to the Israelites, reminding them of their covenant relationship with God and summoning them to greater loyalty. Moses pronounces that God will reward them with blessing for obedience but punish them for disobedience, resulting ultimately in exile from the land of Canaan.

Taking the Land

Joshua replaces Moses as the leader of the people and brings them safely into the land of Canaan. While only the tribes of Judah, Ephraim, and Manasseh actually take possession of territory in Canaan during Joshua's lifetime, this initial phase of occupation progresses well with God's support.

After Joshua's death, the Israelites enter into a period of moral and spiritual decline that results in their enemies gaining the upper hand. The book of Judges underscores how the Israelites spiral downward as they disregard their obligations to God under the Sinai covenant. Only the divine provision of Spirit-empowered leaders, traditionally known as judges, provides periods of relief. Significantly, the tribe of Ephraim, which had been privileged with leadership of the nation, rightly receives the harshest criticism for its apostasy. Ephraim's failure to lead the people prepares the way for the establishment of a monarchy drawn from the tribe of Judah.

The Early Monarchy

The books of Samuel record how Israel moves from a tribal system of government to a monarchy. The account of

Third-century painting from Dura-Europos shows Samuel anointing David as king. David is one of the kings during the early monarchy of Israel.

Z. Radovan/www.BibleLandPictures.com

the transition is complex, but it ultimately results in David from the tribe of Judah being appointed by God as the head of a dynasty that reigns from the city of Jerusalem. According to Ps 78:59 – 72, God chose David and Jerusalem (Zion) after rejecting Ephraim as the royal tribe and the city of Shiloh as the location of the central sanctuary.

The enthronement of David and the choice of Jerusalem as his capital city begin a process that leads to David's son Solomon building a temple (or divine palace) that transforms Jerusalem into the earthly residence of the divine King. Unfortunately, Solomon fails to adhere to the instructions for kings that Deut 17 lays out, resulting in his kingdom being partitioned in two.

The Two Kingdoms

The unity of the Israelites shatters after the death of Solomon when only two tribes remain faithful to his son Rehoboam. The other ten tribes appoint Jeroboam, an Ephraimite, as their king. This creates two kingdoms, Israel in the north and Judah in the south. Under a succession of short-lived dynasties, the northern kingdom becomes more and more apostate. Eventually, God punishes its population when the Assyrian king Sargon II decimates the kingdom in 722 BC.

While God's commitment to the Davidic dynasty offers some stability to the southern kingdom of Judah, it too comes under divine judgment due to the sinfulness of its monarchy and people. After a series of invasions, the Babylonians destroy Jerusalem in 586 BC, demolish the temple, and deport the Davidic monarchy into exile. These events mark the start of the Babylonian exile, a period of deep soul-searching as the people of Judah reflect on the catastrophic events that have led to their humiliation and punishment by God.

The Babylonian Exile

Although the Babylonians raze Jerusalem in 586 BC, they previously deported Judahites to Babylon in 605 BC (see Dan 1:1) and 597 BC (see note on Dan 1:2). The displacement and subjugation of Judahites creates a period of uncertainty for the exiles as they contemplate the theological significance of these events. Little survived of all that God did for them in the past. In spite of this, prophets spoke words of comfort and promised restoration to those in exile.

The Restoration

When the Babylonian Empire falls to the Persians in 539 BC, the conquering king, Cyrus the Great (559 – 530 BC), permits Judahite exiles to return to Jerusalem in order to reconstruct the temple. The work is eventually completed in 516 or 515 BC (Ezra 1 – 6; see note on Ezra 4:4). Although the returning exiles lack the resources to replicate the earlier temple, the process of restoration reassures the people that God has not abandoned them completely. Subsequently, the walls of Jerusalem are repaired under the guidance of Ezra (from 458 BC) and Nehemiah (from 445 BC). With the temple and city restored, the people are

The Cyrus Cylinder, ca. 539 – 530 BC. When the Babylonian Empire falls to the Persians in 539 BC, Cyrus the Great permits Judahite exiles to return to Jerusalem in order to reconstruct the temple.

encouraged to anticipate the reinstatement of the Davidic monarchy. This, however, remains unfulfilled during the OT period. What the OT anticipates, the NT brings to fulfillment with the coming of Jesus Christ.

While the grand story of the OT moves through a series of distinctive stages, these stages are closely linked to one another as God's plan of redemption unfolds. From the Garden of Eden to the return of the exiles from Babylon, God is at work, seeking to restore to himself an alienated humanity and to reclaim the earth from the powers of evil. In all of this, the OT prepares for events that come to fulfillment in Jesus Christ. With good reason the NT cannot be fully understood without an intimate knowledge of the OT.

Text of the Old Testament

With the modern proliferation of English Bibles, it is easy to forget that in the time of Jesus a copy of the Hebrew Bible consisted of numerous scrolls, each handwritten by a copyist. Although between the second and sixth centuries AD codices (i.e., book forms) gradually replaced scrolls, all biblical texts continued to be copied by hand. Only with the invention of the printing press in the mid-fifteenth century AD did it become possible to mass-produce identical copies of the Bible.

Not surprisingly, over a period of at least 1,500 years, copyists occasionally made minor errors as they produced new copies of biblical books one at a time. Even the best of scribes could make mistakes. Since no original manuscripts existed by which later manuscripts could be corrected, scribes replicated errors each time they made new copies. Consequently, few surviving manuscripts are completely identical. By identifying and rectifying scribal errors, modern scholars attempt to reconstruct the earliest text of the OT. This is a highly specialized field of study that relies heavily on gleaning information from the somewhat disparate manuscripts that have survived.

Before 1947, the oldest known manuscripts of the Hebrew OT were the Codex Cairensis (AD 895/96), the Aleppo Codex (ca. AD 925) and the Codex Leningradensis (AD 1008/09). With the unexpected discovery in 1947 of ancient scrolls in caves near Khirbet Qumran on the northwestern shore of the Dead Sea, scholars gained access to the remains of over 200 biblical scrolls copied between ca. 250 BC and AD 70. Among the first scrolls discovered at Qumran were a complete manuscript and a partial manuscript of the text of Isaiah in Hebrew.

Regrettably, due to the fragmentary nature of the surviving scrolls, the evidence from Qumran is not complete. Nevertheless, the scrolls confirm that the medieval codices preserve accurately the text of the Hebrew Bible. When the book of Isaiah in the medieval codices was compared with the manuscripts from Qumran, scholars concluded that only a dozen or so copyist errors need to be removed from the medieval text of Isaiah. Almost all of these changes involve correcting only one or two letters in Hebrew.

In addition to relying on the Dead Sea Scrolls, experts on OT manuscripts compare early translations of the Hebrew OT into other languages (e.g., Aramaic, Greek, Syriac). Some of these date to at least the third century BC, although only later copies have survived. The earliest and almost complete Greek translation of the OT is the fourth-century AD Codex Vaticanus. Unfortunately, the quality of translation varies among the different OT books.

Early Aramaic translations of the OT became necessary because more and more Jews spoke Aramaic as their first language. In the OT itself, half of the book of Daniel is written in Aramaic rather than Hebrew. Unfortunately, the surviving Aramaic translations tend to be paraphrases enhanced with interpretative comments. For this reason they offer only limited help in reconstructing the earliest text of the Hebrew Bible.

Although textual critics continue to explore the process by which the books of the OT were preserved and translated, we may, with a high degree of confidence, be certain that our English Bibles, allowing for translation, accurately reflect the original text of the biblical books.

The Great Isaiah Scroll of the Dead Sea Scrolls.
Wikimedia Commons

Reading the Old Testament

For most people the OT is distant geographically, historically, linguistically, and culturally. Some or all of these factors may present major barriers to how modern readers understand the OT.

1. *Geographic distance.* The OT books are located in the world of the Middle East; they deal with events that took place in the countries that we now refer to as Israel-Palestine, Egypt, Jordan, Syria, Turkey, and Iraq. The geography of the region impacts what we read. For example, harvest time for cereal crops occurs in the spring or early summer. The semi-arid nature of parts of this region means that references to rain are often positive.

2. *Historical distance.* The writing of all of the OT originates before the time of Christ. The world was a very different place then.

3. *Linguistic distance.* Almost all of the OT was composed in Hebrew, with a few passages in Aramaic. While modern English translations enable us to comprehend what the writers were saying, we should never forget that no translation can convey fully and accurately all the nuances of the original language. Resources like this study Bible are often helpful in addressing this issue.

4. *Cultural distance.* The OT frequently addresses situations far removed from the lifestyle of modern societies. When we read OT texts, we need to interpret them in the light of the customs and practices that existed in the past. We must be careful not to read the text against the background of our own culture.

Reading the OT is more alien than most people suppose. If we are to make sense of it, we need to overcome the distance that exists between it and us.

Importance of the Old Testament

History itself confirms the importance of the OT. In spite of fierce criticism from opponents, few documents can rival its prominence and popularity throughout the centuries. Three factors may begin to account for this.

1. The OT recounts a remarkable story that uniquely explains life as we experience it. Offering a very realistic view of human nature and society, warts and all, it provides an unexpected explanation for humanity's predicament. Most of all, it offers hope by reimagining a very different kind of world and by pointing readers to the God-given solution.

2. The OT has the potential to transform lives. It contains a wealth of moral teaching. It shapes our lives by its moral instructions and stories.

3. Most important, the OT provides unique insights into the nature of God. The books of the OT variously focus on the divine-human experience through stories, reports of divine messages given to earlier generations, songs of worship, and prayers. This God-orientated dimension causes the OT, alongside the NT, to transcend all other literature.

Chronology/Dating

Sometimes we can identify the events of the Bible with other events outside of the Bible and correlate those with known dates. For example, the Assyrian records of kings mention an eclipse in 763 BC, and the OT also mentions those kings. This process of correlating events yields exact dates, BC and AD. On this basis, scholars generally agree on the dating scheme for events from the time of David and Solomon onward, and we provide a single timeline for them. However, there exist two sets of dates for earlier events. These dates depend largely on how one interprets the dating scheme in the book of Judges and when one dates Israel's exodus from Egypt. We provide both options here. ■

INTRODUCTION TO

THE PENTATEUCH

GENESIS

EXODUS

LEVITICUS

NUMBERS

DEUTERONOMY

THE PENTATEUCH

T. D. Alexander

Designation

The Pentateuch consists of the five books of Genesis, Exodus, Leviticus, Numbers, and Deuteronomy. The English title "Pentateuch" comes from the Greek term *pentateuchos*, which means "five-volume work," a title that can be traced back to the third century AD. While Christians have tended to prefer the designation "Pentateuch," Jews have traditionally referred to these books by the title "*Torah*," a Hebrew term usually translated "law," although a better translation might be "instruction." The designation "law" goes back before the time of Jesus; the prologue of Ecclesiasticus in the Apocrypha (written about 132 BC) uses "Law" to denote the first five books of the OT.

While the use of the term "law" for the Pentateuch has a long history, in earlier times references to the "Book of the Law" (e.g., 2 Kgs 22:8,11; 2 Chr 17:9; cf. 2 Chr 34:14) and "the Law" (e.g., 2 Kgs 21:8; 2 Chr 25:4) probably refer to material now preserved in Deut 5 – 26 (or Deut 5 – 30). According to the book of Deuteronomy, the elderly Moses gave the Israelites "the law" that was to shape their lifestyle in the land of Canaan. This material extends from Deut 5:1 to 26:19 (or 30:20). Moses then entrusted a written copy of this law to the priests (Deut 31:9), who were to place it beside the ark of the covenant (Deut 31:26). Josh 1:7 – 8 mentions this same "Book of the Law." Various titles closely associated with Moses denote this "Book of the Law": the "Book of the Law of Moses" (e.g., Josh 8:31; 23:6; 2 Kgs 14:6; Neh 8:1), the "Law of Moses" (e.g., 1 Kgs 2:3; 2 Kgs 23:25; 2 Chr 23:18; 30:16; Ezra 3:2; 7:6; Dan 9:11,13), and the "Book of Moses" (e.g., 2 Chr 25:4; 35:12; Ezra 6:18; Neh 13:1). At some stage in the postexilic period, the title "Law" was applied to the whole of the Pentateuch.

Overview

The five books of Genesis to Deuteronomy narrate a remarkable story that consists of several distinctive chronological stages.

Primeval Era (Gen 1 – 11)

Gen 1 – 11, often called the primeval era, records a number of selective episodes in the early history of humanity. These events are highly significant because they shape the rest of the biblical story (see "Creation," p. 2642; "Sin," p. 2644).

Patriarchal Period (Gen 12 – 50)

Gen 12 – 50 is often referred to as the patriarchal period. The lives of three men dominate it: Abraham, his grandson Jacob, and his great-grandson Joseph. Abraham's son Isaac also plays an important part in the story, as do Joseph's brothers, especially Judah. The special role this family has in God's purposes explains the prominence that Gen 12 – 50 gives them (see "People of God," p. 2672). God gives them — promises that anticipate (1) the creation of a nation that will take possession of the land of Canaan and (2) the coming of a future king, descended from Abraham, who will mediate God's blessing to the nations of the earth (see "Covenant," p. 2646; "The Kingdom of God," p. 2662). Through this promised king, God will reverse the consequences of Adam and Eve's expulsion from the Garden of Eden. These two principal promises determine the direction for the rest of the story in Exodus to 2 Kings and beyond.

From Egypt to Sinai (Exod 1:1 — Num 10:10)

The book of Exodus jumps forward to a time when a succession of pharaohs in Egypt enslave and harshly treat Abraham's ever-increasing descendants. Moses' birth and death frame the books of Exodus to Deuteronomy. As the one

Byzantine mosaic in the Basilica of St. Vitalis in Ravenna, Italy shows Moses receiving the Ten Commandments.

LOCATIONS IN THE PENTATEUCH

Black Sea
Caspian Sea
Tigris R.
Harran
Nineveh
MESOPOTAMIA
Mari
Syrian Desert
Euphrates R.
Mediterranean Sea
Damascus
Babylon
Jerusalem
Beersheba
Hebron
Ur
Persian Gulf
Arabian Desert
Red Sea
Genesis
Exodus
Leviticus
Numbers
Deuteronomy
0 100 km.
0 100 mi.

whom God chose to lead the Israelites out of Egypt, Moses takes center stage in these books.

Exod 1 – 15 focuses on God's deliver ance of the Israelites from Egypt, ending in a victory song (see "Exile and Exodus," p. 2659), and chs. 16 – 18 briefly describe their journey to Mount Sinai. Then the pace of the narrative slows down. The story gives attention to the unique covenant relationship that God establishes with the Israelites. Reporting this event and its immediate consequences dominates Exod 19 – 40, all of Leviticus, and Num 1:1 — 10:10. The creation of this covenant relationship is marked by (1) listing various obligations (e.g., the Ten Commandments) that the Israelites must fulfill and (2) constructing a tent, or tabernacle, that will become God's dwelling place among his chosen people (see "Law," p. 2649; "Sacrifice," p. 2656; "Temple," p. 2652). By living among them, the Lord transforms the Israelites into a holy nation. The implications of this are set out more fully in the book of Leviticus, which places special emphasis on how the Israelites must live holy lives (see "Holiness," p. 2676).

From Sinai to Moab (Num 10:11 — Deut 34:12)

After a period of almost one year, the Israelites leave Mount Sinai and journey through the wilderness toward the land of Canaan (Num 10:11 — 36:13). Unfortunately, the people's faith in God wilts. When fear of the nations living in Canaan causes them to rebel against God, God punishes them, and they spend 40 years in the wilderness. Only after the death of the adults who had left Egypt does it become possible for the next generation of Israelites to enter the land of Canaan. Whereas much of Numbers concentrates on

Fifteenth-century Hebrew manuscript shows Moses leading the children of Israel across the Red Sea.

Moses leads the Children of Israel across the Red Sea from a Jewish Prayer Book, Hamburg, 1427, German School/Staats-und Universitatsbibliothek, Hamburg, Germany/Bridgeman Images

the failures of the Israelites, the final chapters of the book prepare them for life in the promised land. The book of Deuteronomy further develops this theme.

As Deuteronomy begins, the Israelites are camped to the east of the Jordan River near Jericho. Moses, close to death, encourages the people to renew the covenant that God initiated at Mount Sinai. Moses reviews the covenant obligations and reminds the people that obeying them will bring God's blessing and that disobeying them will lead to death. After setting out this challenge, the book of Deuteronomy ends by reporting the death of Moses in the land of Moab. While this brings to an end the period of Moses' leadership, the Pentateuch is an unfinished story. The Israelites are still outside the promised land, and God's promises to the patriarchs remain unfulfilled.

While people often view it as a self-contained section of the Bible, the Pentateuch is very closely linked to that which follows. The books of Genesis to Kings form one continuous account, with every subsequent book presupposing everything the previous books recount. Therefore, we should interpret the individual books of the Pentateuch in light of this larger whole, which in turn needs to be read in the light of the whole Bible.

Author

Given the prominence of Moses in the books of Exodus to Deuteronomy, it is no surprise that he should be associated with the composition of the Pentateuch. In the various expressions for the Pentateuch, the name of Moses occurs frequently. Jesus himself refers to the Pentateuch as "the Book of Moses" (Mark 12:26), "the Law of Moses" (Luke 24:44; see John 1:45), and simply "Moses" (Luke 16:29; cf. Luke 24:27; 2 Cor 3:15). Not surprisingly, in view of the prominence these titles give Moses and the high standing in which later generations held him, Moses is an obvious candidate to be the author of the Pentateuch. Further support for this comes from the Pentateuch itself, which directly credits Moses with writing down sections of the material, most notably the "Book of the Covenant" in Exod 20:22 — 23:33 (see Exod 24:4,7), and the "Book of the Law" in Deut 5 – 26 or Deut 5 – 30 (see Deut 31:9,26). In the absence of obvious contenders, there is much to commend the view that Moses composed the Pentateuch.

Post-Mosaic Evidence

While the evidence in favor of Mosaic authorship is persuasive, some features of the Pentateuch may point to a different conclusion. Certain details presuppose a knowledge of events that occur after Moses' lifetime. Among some of the more obvious examples are these: Gen 13:7 seems to be written from the perspective of an author who lived at a time when there were no Canaanites or Perizzites living in the land of Canaan; Gen 14:14 refers to the city of Dan, but this name was given to the town of

Mount Nebo, where Moses gave his speech to the Israelites (Deut 32:49).

Laish only after the tribe of Dan captured it (Judg 18:29); and Gen 36:31 possibly alludes to the existence of an Israelite monarchy. Another feature that weighs against Moses' authorship is the manner in which the Pentateuch normally refers to him in the third person. Num 12:3 possibly presents the greatest difficulty: "Now Moses was a very humble man, more humble than anyone else on the face of the earth." Would the most humble man on the earth write this? (By placing this verse in parentheses, the NIV implies that someone other than Moses wrote this.) And Deut 34 reports Moses' death. These and similar observations should caution against an overly dogmatic belief that Moses penned absolutely everything in the Pentateuch. At the very least we must allow for the possibility of editorial updating or explanatory additions. Moreover, at no point does the Pentateuch plainly state that Moses composed everything contained within these five books. As regards the book of Genesis, Moses may have taken over already existing written materials.

Modern Critical Scholarship

In the world of academic scholarship, the consensus of opinion largely dismisses the idea that Moses wrote the Pentateuch. The seeds for such an outlook may trace back to the end of the eighteenth century, when the Enlightenment concept of evolution or progress was applied to the development of religious ideas. Rejecting the biblical account of how Israelite religion began, a few scholars constructed their own theories based on the assumption that all religions evolve from a primitive to a more advanced form. In applying this philosophy to the Bible, these scholars argued that most biblical books were composed of materials from different chronological periods. Eventually, the German scholar Julius Wellhausen championed with considerable success a theory now known as the Documentary Hypothesis.

Wellhausen's *Prolegomena to the History of Israel* (English translation published in 1885) offers a radically different way of viewing the history of Israelite religion. He rejects the Mosaic authorship of the Pentateuch, arguing that four authors, now commonly referred to as the Yahwist, the Elohist, the Deuteronomist, and the Priestly Writer, wrote most of the materials that comprise the books of Genesis to Deuteronomy. In terms of dating the work of these authors, Wellhausen places the Yahwist at about 840 BC, the Elohist at about 700 BC, the Deuteronomist at about 623 BC, and the Priestly Writer at about 500–450 BC. By redating different sections of the Pentateuch in this way, Wellhausen rejects the longstanding tradition that Hebrew religion originated largely in the time of Moses. Rather, Wellhausen proposes that the true founders of Israelite religion were the prophets of the late ninth and eighth centuries BC. They were the men who inspired ethical monotheism (i.e., belief in one God linked to high ethical standards).

Although the story of the Pentateuch seems far removed from modern readers both chronologically and culturally and may frequently appear remote and obscure, it authoritatively explains the initial stages of God's redemptive activity in the world.

Although Wellhausen's Documentary Hypothesis dominated OT studies throughout the twentieth century and still enjoys some support, an increasing number of scholars have openly questioned its methodology and conclusions. While alternative theories have been proposed to explain how the Pentateuch was composed, this remains an issue of open debate. Unfortunately, the presuppositions of the Documentary Hypothesis still continue to influence OT scholarship.

A Literary Collage

The issue of authorship is complex because the materials that comprise the Pentateuch are not uniform in nature. The books of Genesis to Deuteronomy contain a rich blend of materials that reflect different literary forms. There are, for example, narratives of differing lengths and complexities, genealogies of varying kinds, paternal blessings in poetic style, songs, covenant obligations, case laws, instructions for the construction of cultic items, and directives for undertaking religious activities. If Moses shaped the Pentateuch as we know it, he probably took over materials that others composed, especially for the book of Genesis. Notwithstanding the variety of literary forms in the Pentateuch, these materials are skillfully blended together according to an overall plan. The Pentateuch is a literary collage in which different materials produce a remarkably rich and vibrant story.

The question of who wrote the Pentateuch must never divert attention from the more important task of understanding its message. Although many modern readers find the contents of the Pentateuch remote and obscure, the books of Genesis to Deuteronomy lay the foundation upon which the whole of Scripture rests. Without an awareness of these books, we cannot understand the rest of the Bible.

The Pentateuch From a Biblical Theology Perspective

Although the story of the Pentateuch is far removed from modern readers both chronologically and culturally and may frequently appear remote and obscure, it authoritatively explains the initial stages of God's redemptive activity in the world. It explains why our world displays every sign of being both ordered and chaotic at the same time, and it points forward in hope to a time when God will make all things right through Jesus Christ.

God's Creation Purpose

Genesis begins with God creating the world and appointing human beings to rule on his behalf over all other earthly creatures (see "Creation," p. 2642). Underlying this commission is the expectation that God's vice-regents will fill the earth, extending the sanctuary of Eden in order to make the whole world into a divine residence (see "Temple," p. 2652). Implicit in all of this is the creation of a holy city where God will live surrounded by those who affectionately serve and worship him (see "The City of God," p. 2666).

Betrayal and Rebellion

Against this background, the early chapters of Genesis record how an extraordinary serpent tempts Adam and Eve into betraying God. Having been instructed to rule over all other creatures, they fail to exercise authority over the serpent, and by their actions they submit to its authority rather than God's (see "Sin," p. 2644). Their behavior has dire consequences: they are alienated from God and expelled from the Garden of Eden (see "Wrath," p. 2681). Although humanity retains its capacity to rule, it no longer does so as God intended. Violence is the hallmark of humanity's presence on the earth, resulting eventually in divine punishment through a devastating flood. In spite of this, even after the flood humanity remains defiant. Gen 11 records another incident of human hubris as people conspire in unity to construct a city with a tower that might give them access to heaven itself. The name "Babel" becomes synonymous with humanity's desire to replace God and rule both earth and heaven. Not surprisingly, their efforts fall far short of their arrogance as God comes down and causes the people to babble in confusion.

A Promised Savior

While the dominant theme of Gen 3–11 is humanity's rebellion against

Life-size replica of the tabernacle.
Todd Bolen/www.BiblePlaces.com

Artist's representation of the New Jerusalem on a fourteenth-century tapestry. As the final chapters of Revelation anticipate, God will bring to perfect completion his purpose in creating this world, when the greenfield site of Eden is transformed into the New Jerusalem.

The New Jerusalem, number 80 from 'The Apocalypse of Angers', 1373 – 87, Bataille, Nicolas/Musee des Tapisseries, Angers, France/Giraudon/Bridgeman Images

God and its tragic consequences for the earth, these chapters are not without a glimmer of hope. In his condemnation of the serpent, God pronounces a judgment that contains an important element of hope. God warns the serpent, "I will put enmity between you and the woman, and between your offspring and hers; he will crush your head, and you will strike his heel" (Gen 3:15). The expectation that one of the woman's descendants will crush the serpent introduces a theme that runs throughout the book of Genesis and beyond. As we anticipate the woman's offspring, Gen 4 begins by focusing on how Eve's son Cain kills his brother Abel. The tragedy of this event is underscored by Cain's descendants appearing to follow in their father's footsteps. By the seventh generation, Lamech boasts of killing a man for striking him (Gen 4:23). Then, remarkably, the narrative jumps back in time to note that Adam and Eve had another son, Seth (Gen 4:25). Seth, Abel's replacement, keeps alive the hope that the serpent may yet be overcome.

A genealogy in Gen 5 highlights Seth's importance and ends with the birth of Noah, "a righteous man, blameless among the people of his time" who "walked faithfully with God" (Gen 6:9). From Noah, another genealogy in Gen 11 leads on to Abram. Against the background of humanity's estrangement from God, the Lord indicates that through Abram "all peoples on earth will be blessed" (Gen 12:3). The extent of the narrative devoted to Abram/Abraham underlines his importance in God's redemptive purposes (Gen 11:27 — 25:11). He is to be "the father of many nations" (Gen 17:4), but not only in a biological sense. Abraham's offspring will be those who exercise faith in God as Abraham does. Furthermore, God promises that his blessing will come to "all nations on earth" through one of Abraham's descendants (Gen 22:18). This expectation builds upon God's earlier promise regarding the offspring of the woman in Gen 3:15 and traces beyond Abraham to his son Isaac and grandson Jacob. God blesses them all, and they in turn mediate God's blessing to others. After Jacob, Joseph is the one who carries the mantle of blessing since his father appointed him firstborn over his older brothers (1 Chr 5:1 – 2). Although Genesis traces the line of "firstborn" sons from Abraham to Ephraim (Gen 48:17 – 20), Gen 38 unexpectedly focuses on the line of Judah, particularly his son Perez, who at birth breaks out in front of his "firstborn" twin brother, Zerah. Later, when Jacob blesses his 12 sons, he links future royalty to the tribe of Judah. God rejects the tribe of Ephraim as the royal tribe in the time of Samuel, and the tribe of Judah replaces it with David, son of Jesse, anointed king (Ps 78:67 – 72). Eventually, David's royal line leads to Jesus Christ, through whom God fulfills his promises to Abraham (Acts 3:22 – 26; Gal 3:16).

A Paradigm of Salvation

Whereas Genesis is especially interested in tracing the woman's offspring, the books of Exodus to Deuteronomy build on the expectation that Abraham's descendants will take possession of the land of Canaan, where God will reside among them. With this end in view, Exodus describes how God redeems the people of Israel from oppression in Egypt, ransoming from death their firstborn males. The account of the Passover provides a paradigm for divine salvation as God sanctifies the Israelites in order that they may become a royal priesthood and a holy nation. God subsequently ratifies a covenant with them before coming to reside in a newly constructed tabernacle in the middle of the Israelite camp (see "Temple," p. 2652). Not only does this series of events partially reverse the estrangement caused by Adam and Eve's rebellion against God in the Garden of Eden, but more important, it prefigures a much greater exodus that will come through Jesus Christ (see "Exile and Exodus," p. 2659).

A Holy Nation

In the light of God's presence among the Israelites, Leviticus emphasizes how the Israelites must reflect God's holy nature. In various ways, they are taught to associate holiness with wholeness and life, whereas uncleanness is associated with imperfection and death. Leviticus underlines that holiness requires moral perfection, not merely the performance of cultic rituals (see "Holiness," p. 2676).

The death of the exodus generation in the wilderness serves as a serious warning of the importance of continually trusting and obeying God. As the apostle Paul observes, "These things ... were written down as warnings for us" (1 Cor 10:11). Building on how God has punished the Israelites, in the book of Deuteronomy Moses emphasizes how the Israelites must demonstrate exclusive loyalty to God in order to enjoy the benefits of being God's chosen people. Having been rescued from slavery by God and after freely committing themselves to obey him fully and exclusively, God will judge the Israelites accordingly. Unfortunately, the remaining books of the OT witness in large measure to the failure of the Israelites, but they also look forward in anticipation to a time when God will institute a new covenant to replace the one ratified at Mount Sinai (see "Covenant," p. 2646).

From a biblical theology perspective, the Pentateuch is an essential component of Scripture. Not only does it explain the cause of the human predicament, but more important it points forward in hope to how God will address this issue through Jesus Christ. Ultimately, as the final chapters of Revelation anticipate, God will bring to perfect completion his purpose in creating this world, when the greenfield site of Eden is transformed into the new Jerusalem (see "Consummation," p. 2695). ■

INTRODUCTION TO GENESIS

NAME AND PURPOSE

The title, Genesis, means "beginning." It is the title of the book in the Septuagint (the pre-Christian Greek translation of the OT). This aptly describes a book that outlines the creation of the world and humanity (chs. 1–2) and goes on to describe the beginning of sin (ch. 3), the new creation (ch. 9), God's plan for blessing the world (12:1–3), and how that plan begins with the family of Abraham (chs. 12–50). The Jewish title of the book, *Bĕrē'šît*, is taken from the first word in the Hebrew text: "In the beginning." It also emphasizes that the book is concerned with origins.

Genesis is the first of the five books of the Pentateuch (see Introduction to the Pentateuch, p. 9). Unlike the other books of the Torah, Genesis contains almost all narrative and few legal commands. Its purpose is to trace the beginnings of the world, humanity, and sin and to draw a line across human history that identifies God's work with Abraham and his family. Thus, the book provides the necessary background for the divinely chosen origins of God's people Israel and for their situation in Egypt at the beginning of Exodus. It also introduces God as Creator, Judge, and Redeemer. It describes the fall into sin and looks forward to how God will resolve his separation from the people he loved and created.

BACKGROUND AND AUTHOR

Exod 17:14 and Deut 31:9,24 attest to the composition of much of the first five books by Moses. Moses' composition of Genesis was assumed until the advent of critical studies of the Bible that questioned its validity. Since then, scholars have argued for dividing Genesis into separate parts and dating them to different times. Multiple authors would then have written the book, some of them centuries after the time of Moses. However, it is now clear that many of the events of Genesis, when compared to examples of ancient Near Eastern texts, date to the period before Moses, ca. 2200–1500 BC, and not later.

1. The creation account of Genesis has been compared with the Babylonian *Enuma Elish*, a story about how the god Marduk defeats a monster and creates the other gods from her body. Archaeologists discovered this story in the library of an Assyrian king from the seventh century BC. But a closer parallel to Gen 1–11, with stories of the creation of humankind followed by a flood, with a family and animals surviving on an ark, appears much earlier in the eighteenth-century BC *Atraḫasis Epic*.

2. Many texts, including the *Atraḫasis Epic*, mention a worldwide flood. Most famous is the *Gilgamesh Epic*. The earliest text we have dates from the eighteenth century BC. It was copied in many places and times in the ancient Near East. Like *Atraḫasis*, *Gilgamesh* has parallels with the details of Gen 6–9. A god decides to preserve a family, people construct a ship and bring animals into an ark and close the door, and the flood destroys everything outside the ark. These similarities should not blind us to the teaching of Gen 6–9 that God used the flood to judge the world and save righteous Noah and all on the ark in order to make a covenant with them upon disembarking (8:20—9:17).

3. Personal names can also attest to an early date for Genesis. Some of the names in chs. 1–11 occur only in the

SETTING OF GENESIS

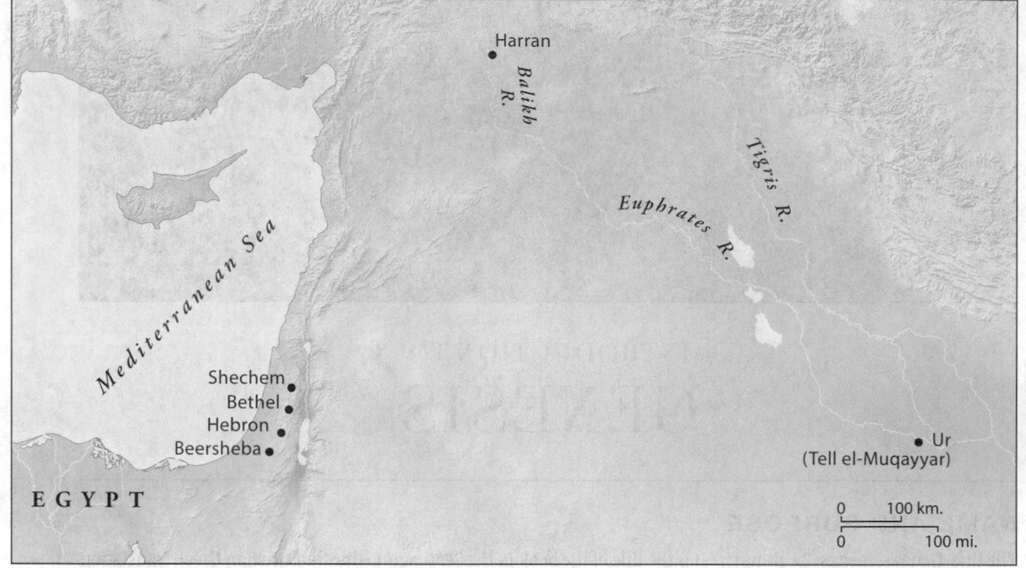

earlier period of the ancient Near East. Methushael, Methuselah, Jabal, Jubal, and Tubal-Cain appear only in the earlier second millennium BC, not later. In chs. 12–50 other names with forms such as Isaac, Ishmael, Jacob, and Joseph appear frequently in the early second millennium BC, but much less in the later second millennium BC and hardly at all in the first millennium BC. How would the author(s) of Genesis have known how to use these names that are authentic to the early period and not the later?

4. Gen 14 describes a war involving international armies from across the ancient Near East. Many of the names of the invaders in 14:1,9 occur only in the second millennium BC: Amraphel the Babylonian, Arioch the Hurrian (from northern Syria), and Tidal the Hittite (from modern Turkey). They do not appear later in the ancient Near Eastern texts. Only in this period (2000–1500 BC) was it possible for armies to move across the entire Holy Land with relative freedom as they do here. Only in this early period (the time of Abram, Isaac, Jacob, and Joseph) do the Elamites appear in texts as far west as they do in Gen 14.

5. Customs from the early second millennium BC recur later, but their concentration in Genesis is unique. Examples include the stipulation that a surrogate mother could be used in cases where the wife remains barren for a period of seven years (16:1–4) and the betrothal gift that allows the bridegroom to marry (34:12).

6. The city of Harran (11:31–32; 12:4; 27:43; 28:10; 29:4) appears in the accounts of Abram and his descendants. Ancient Near Eastern texts attest to the site as a well-populated city during the early second millennium BC, occupied by large tribal coalitions of Amorites.

7. In 37:12–17, Joseph's brothers graze the family's flocks some 60 miles (96.5 kilometers) north of their home in Hebron. Only in the early second millennium BC do we have records of similar shepherds (Amorites in north Syria) grazing their flocks and herds more than a hundred miles (160 kilometers) from their homes, where their families remained. In the biblical account of later shepherds such as David, there is no mention of grazing in such distant pastures.

8. Benjamin is the only son of Jacob named after the family migrates south to the area of Bethlehem (35:16–19). This name is identical to the eighteenth-century BC southern tribal confederation in Syria known as the Binu-Yamina. The name refers to the south. Along with Asher and Zebulon, these proper names were known in the second millennium BC.

9. Joseph's brothers sell him for 20 silver shekels (37:28). This price for a young male slave pertains only to the early second millennium BC.

These points provide evidence for the origin of the Genesis accounts early in the second millennium BC. How were they passed along to the time of Moses and later? We are not told. Perhaps this occurred through oral tradition among the decendants of Abraham. Alternatively, the discovery of a cuneiform tablet written in the early or middle second millennium BC and preserved in Hebron, where Abraham lived (13:18; 23:2), gives evidence of authorship in Abraham's day and in one of his places of residence.

The evidence allows for the origins of the accounts preserved in much of Genesis to be dated to the early second millennium BC. It counters critical scholarship that attempts to date the Genesis narratives a thousand years later to the middle of the first millennium BC. Some scholars argue that the composition of Genesis became a means to tell stories about where some customs and names originated, e.g. why do Jews in the fifth century BC not eat the meat around the hip of an animal? Because their ancestor Jacob wrestled with someone who touched the socket of his hip and caused him to limp (32:25 – 32). This approach is sometimes called tradition history: although the event is recorded in the Bible, some critical scholars maintain that the account is a fabrication of a later author.

Another critical approach is to divide the biblical text into layers that form sources written at different times in Israel's history. This is sometimes called source criticism or the Documentary Hypothesis. The sources reflect different concerns. Thus, 1:1 — 2:3 emphasizes the Sabbath (2:1 – 3), and priests wrote it in the fifth century BC because they were interested in enforcing laws such as the Sabbath. At another time, an individual who was interested in tracing God's plan through history wrote 2:4 – 25 to emphasize that God was involved in the lives of people. This person created a history that extends beyond the Pentateuch and ultimately demonstrates how God chose David as king.

But note that in this example from the Documentary Hypothesis, Gen 1 – 2 do not need to be understood as coming from two separate writers. Instead, they represent two different emphases:

- 1:1 — 2:3 describes God as the creator of the cosmos. Its themes focus on God's sovereignty as Lord over all: the importance of Sabbath rest, humanity's rulership over creation, and the creation of abundant life.
- 2:4 – 25 emphasizes different themes: the creation of man, his home, his partner, and his work. At the beginning of all, God is both the transcendent Creator who is sovereign over all and the imminent Lord providing a world in full harmony with himself and the people he has created.

Thus, significant evidence exists for the antiquity of the book. Attestations of a single author from Israel's earliest period are not explicit but can be inferred as providing the necessary background for the opening chapters of Exodus. Joseph dies in Gen 50 with his extended family blessed and living in Egypt. Exod 1:1 – 7 repeats this information and goes on to introduce Israel's oppressed condition and the birth of its deliverer, Moses.

STRUCTURE

The book can be naturally divided into two parts: the world before Abram (chs. 1 – 11) and the world of Abraham and his descendants (chs. 12 – 50). Genealogies divide the book into subsections, each beginning with "the account of": "the heavens and the earth" (2:4); "Adam's family line" (5:1); "Noah and his family" (6:9); "Shem, Ham and Japheth, Noah's sons" (10:1); "Shem's family line" (11:10); "Terah's family line" (11:27); "the family line of Abraham's son Ishmael" (25:12); "the family line of Abraham's son Isaac" (25:19); "the family line of Esau" (36:1,9); and "Jacob's family line" (37:2). The genealogies tend to form groups of two: Noah's three sons and the line of Shem (chs. 10 – 11); Ishmael and Isaac (ch. 25); Esau and Jacob (ch. 36; 37:2, where Jacob's line is mentioned). In each of these cases, the first of the two is identified and described principally by the names of the descendants. The second line of the doublet (Shem, Isaac, and Jacob) goes on to deal with a single line of descendants with much greater development of the narratives surrounding the key figures through whom God will work specific promises. This is also true of the two major divisions of the entire book: chs. 1 – 11 and chs. 12 – 50. The first part deals with the world as a whole. It ends with humanity's failure in the tower of Babel and with the decision of God to work with a single descendant in Shem's line and with his offspring. The story of the second part of the book of Genesis thus emerges out of ch. 11.

These two major divisions depict the following theological themes:

1. God chooses again and again to focus his attention on a single individual or family and to work through them to accomplish his purpose. He is revealed as a personal God who relates to his people in a manner that suggests intimacy.

2. The same God remains sovereign in each generation and for all the families of the earth. This is clear from ch. 10, which identifies all people of the known world by tracing their origins to Noah and his sons. Therefore, all bear God's image (9:6).

3. The God who speaks the world into being in ch. 1 is the same God who saves Noah in chs. 6 – 9. He is the same God who calls Abram from his land and gives him promises of blessing (12:1 – 3). He is the same God who provides Isaac and sustains Abram/Abraham's line through Jacob/Israel and his 12 sons in Egypt. This God remains alive and active in each generation from the beginning of creation until the present one.

GENESIS AND SCIENCE

The contemporary reader of Genesis should strive to read the text as it was originally intended to be read by the ancient reader — not to presume that one can carry into this ancient writing all the assumptions and questions that we might have today. This requires care and knowledge of the purpose for which Moses wrote the text. We should exercise care to read the Bible in a manner that remains sensitive to the literary clues and nuances that the writer intended. This approach is possible but requires study and the guidance of the Spirit of God.

The question of the age of the earth is not automatically resolved with the use of the seven days in 1:1 — 2:3. In 2:4, Moses uses the same Hebrew word for "day" to summarize all the work of creation: "In the day when God created the heavens and the earth." Of course, this does not mean that the term "day" cannot refer to a 24-hour day in the seven days of creation. But it may also serve other purposes. For one, the use of days builds up to the final climactic seventh day of Sabbath rest. This forms one of the major theological emphases of the creation account. The Sabbath rest is built into creation and forms the goal of world history from its beginning. Another reason for the seven days may be connected with "the account of" in 2:4. While this term often precedes the genealogical lines, it can also fall in the midst of longer accounts of individuals and their families. This is true in the case of the last mention of this in Genesis, in the account of Jacob's family line (37:2). Much of the story has already been told. The same may be true of 2:4. How do the heaven and earth have a "family line"? There are no parents or children, only the beginning of the human race. Using a metaphor in which the sun and moon bring forth the earth would only confuse the reader in a strictly monotheistic world where these created things have no personhood and should not be worshiped. Instead, the author may have used the sequence of days to parallel the sequences of generations in the later family lines. Each day prepares for and gives way to the next day just as each generation prepares for and gives way to the next generation. This emphasizes the logical development of God's creation more than it pinpoints the chronological development.

A second area concerns the expression "according to its/their kind(s)." This describes the plants (1:11 – 12), the fish of the sea (1:21), the land creatures (1:24 – 25), and all these as well as the birds (7:14). It is sometimes taken to mean that the text must describe exact reproduction and cannot allow for the gradual development of various forms of species. However, in Ezek 47:10 this same phrase refers to fish "of many kinds." If that is the case in Genesis, then it does not emphasize limitation of each life form to it specific species but emphasizes the diversity of each general life form: fish of many kinds, land creatures of many kinds, etc.

The role of Adam and Eve as the first human couple appears in chs. 2 – 4. While some may argue that these figures represent a symbolic or metaphoric story that has no relation to the early history of humanity, they must address the explicit presentation of the Hebrew text. The syntax of the text resembles that of later books such as 2 Kings, Ezra, and Nehemiah. All readers understand that the authors of these books intended readers to accept them as history. The same should be true of a text such as ch. 3. Indeed, this becomes the witness of the memories of Genesis in the later biblical text (see Introduction: Genesis and History; Genesis and the New Testament).

GENESIS AND HISTORY

Modern journalism requires the testimony of independent sources to demonstrate the historical reliability of a report. We are not often blessed with multiple witnesses for Genesis. Nevertheless, evidence shows that the figures and events of chs. 12 – 50 fit into the world of the early second millennium BC and not a later time (see Introduction: Background and Author). If Gen 12 – 50 witnesses an authentic and ancient heritage in places where they can be tested, what can one say about the world of Genesis before Abram? As noted, some of the names in these genealogies are attested in the earliest sources for names of the West Semitic peoples, of whom Abram and his family formed a part.

Further, the occurrence of a divinely sent flood with universal impact on the human race is also preserved in some of the earliest texts recounting the primeval times (such as the eighteenth-century BC Old Babylonian *Atraḫasis Epic*). At times the detailed agreement of these accounts (see also the story in the Old Babylonian version of and in later versions of *Gilgamesh*) suggests more than an independent witness to an ancient event. It may imply borrowing from a common source.

When we examine the account of the Sumerian King List from ca. 2000 BC, we find two important features that Gen 1 – 11 also shares: (1) A flood ended the cities named from earlier times (cf. 4:17), but survivors rebuilt cities after the flood. (2) The kings who ruled before the flood reigned for unusually long periods of time, often more than 10,000 years. This may preserve a memory of the actual event recorded in Gen 5, where those in Seth's line each lived for hundreds of years.

Examples such as these demonstrate the historical value of the early chapters of Genesis. They witness God's ongoing presence and work among the people of the world, especially with the line of promise as traced through Seth and Shem. But this does not mean it is possible to date the specific times when these events took place. As is true of all human history, the Bible selects those events and peoples that serve its purposes in recounting the advance of God's kingdom and his work on earth. It reports these accurately but does not provide a complete record. Thus, when 10:24 asserts that "Arphaxad was the father of Shelah," this may mean that he was the grandfather or ancestor of Shelah. (Luke 3:35–36 inserts the name of Cainan between these two men in its genealogy.)

GENESIS AND THEOLOGY

God

While the key themes of creation, sin, judgment, and salvation permeate the book of Genesis, the first three chapters express this in the most concentrated way in Scripture. God asserts his lordship over the world by speaking it into existence and then pronouncing each day's work as "good." It is good in that it perfectly agrees with God's will. "Very good" (1:31) signals the end of the creation work and God's blessing upon it by setting apart the next and final day for rest (2:1–3). The end of ch. 2 shows God's design in terms of the harmony of relationships among God, his creation, and Adam and Eve. When sin (which God's holiness cannot tolerate) enters the human race, God punishes the couple with expulsion from his presence and from the garden (3:23–24). But he also provides a way to continue his relationship with them, and he promises that a time would come when he would deal the serpent a mortal blow (3:15). When violence on the earth increases, God sends the judgment of the flood (chs. 6–9). Although the human race seeks to advance without God, he disperses them across the earth (11:1–9).

Faith

God calls one man, Abram, to come away from his home and move to a land that God will show him. In doing so, God promises land, seed, and blessing for Abram and his offspring (12:1–3; 13:14–17). They will become instruments of blessing for everyone. As Abraham exercises faith, God is able to work through him and to magnify the promises and blessings. God not only promises offspring to Abraham (ch. 15), but he brings it about when Abraham and Sarah are far beyond the age to have children (21:1–5). Yet Abraham does not hold back when God demands that he sacrifice his son Isaac (ch. 22). With his knife raised, he was ready to kill his son, but the angel of the Lord intervenes, for now Abraham has demonstrated that he will trust God even with his most precious possession. For this reason God extends the promise beyond the land to occupation of the cities in the land (22:17). Abraham has trusted God and knows him to be just (18:25).

Grace

Isaac also receives the promise from God (26:3,24). God exercises his sovereignty in granting to Isaac's son Jacob the birthright, even though this overturns custom. Esau is the firstborn but God favors Jacob (25:21–34; 27:1–30). He chooses to bless Jacob with the promises given to his father and grandfather (28:13–15). Jacob's time with his uncle Laban involves one trick after another in which Laban seeks to get the better of Jacob and to profit by him (chs. 29–30). Nevertheless, God blesses Jacob at every step so that Jacob gains much wealth and a large family. God protects him from the anger of both his uncle Laban and his brother Esau. He confirms Jacob's blessing by changing Jacob's name to Israel (32:28). In his later life, however, Jacob would see his own sons trick him (ch. 37) as they sell their brother Joseph into slavery and return home to tell their father that a wild animal killed him.

While God has worked with Abraham and Isaac through direct visits and has spoken with Jacob in dreams, he chooses to work behind the scenes with Joseph. Although God gives Joseph (a younger son of Jacob) the ability to interpret dreams, Joseph does not enjoy direct appearances from God. Whether resisting the temptation of Potiphar's wife or languishing in prison, Joseph serves responsibly, and God rewards him for it. Eventually, through his skill in interpreting dreams, Joseph is able to interpret the dreams of Pharaoh, who raises Joseph to second in command over Egypt (ch. 41). As Joseph gathers grain during the years of plenty, he is able to sell it in the famine years. He later reveals himself to his brothers and delivers his family from famine in Canaan, but that is only part of his work. God enables Joseph to provide grain for all of Canaan and Egypt (47:13–26), thereby preserving alive both the Egyptians who would later enslave Israel and the Canaanites who would lead Israel away from God. Joseph recognizes all of this. While his brothers meant to harm him, God worked it out for the good of Joseph and for the saving of many lives (50:19–20). God took his promise to Abraham to bless the nations of the world through him (12:2–3) and embodies it in Joseph as much as any of his predecessors.

Humanity

Three theological themes play important roles in the lives of major characters in Genesis: the image of God, the spread of sin, and the covenant. These three themes relate to the doctrine of humanity.

God creates humans in his image in 1:26–28. Although he commands them to reproduce like the plants and animals, he reserves a unique role for the human race. God appoints them, as those created in his image, to be leaders and rulers of his finished creation: God places the man in the Garden of Eden to take care to it, i.e., to maximize its life-giving potential (2:15). God reaffirms this image after the initial sin of Adam and Eve and the judgment of the flood (5:1; 9:6), and it becomes the basis for the prohibition of violence against and murder of others (9:6). As human society grows, God calls out Abram and his successors so that they reflect this image throughout the world and thereby bless the nations around them: Abram/Abraham gives Melchizedek, the king of Salem, a tenth of all he had with him (14:20). Later, Abraham intercedes for Sodom and Gomorrah (18:20–33). Jacob enriches Laban while working for him (30:27,30; 31:38–41). God uses Joseph to bless Potiphar and the prison warden through his administrative skills (39:2–5,22–23). God provides Joseph with the opportunity to collect grain during years of bountiful harvests and to sell it during a famine (41:48–49,56–57). Joseph's provision for the starving multitudes leads to the salvation of his own family, of Egypt, and of Canaan (47:13–27). Joseph confesses that God accomplished the salvation of many lives (50:20). In this manner, the blessing of God was reflected through the lives of those who bore God's image faithfully.

In opposition to the work of God in the world, the spread of sin becomes a major theme in Genesis. Human sin begins in the Garden of Eden when the man and woman follow their own desires rather than the will of God (3:1–7). It grows as Cain murders his brother (4:1–8) and his descendant Lamech kills out of vengeance (4:23–24). Finally, there comes a time when evil controls every thought of every person, with the exception of Noah (6:5,8). Violence has corrupted the earth (6:11). The flood wipes out that sinful generation, but it does not end the rebellion in the hearts of people. Righteous Noah became drunk, and his son saw his nakedness (9:20–22). The builders of the tower of Babel thought only of themselves and their glory (11:1–8). Even Abram lies about Sarai his wife, bringing about diseases in Pharaoh's household (12:10–20; cf. Abraham and Abimelek in ch. 20 and Isaac and Abimelek in 26:7–11). Abram's nephew Lot chooses the well-watered but wicked land around Sodom (13:10–13) and, like Noah, became drunk and was seduced by his own daughters (19:30–38). God judges the wicked cities of Sodom and Gomorrah and the other cities of that plain. He destroys them with fire when not even ten righteous can be found in Sodom (18:20—19:29). The deception of Jacob and Laban (chs. 29–31) and the betrayal of Joseph by his brothers (37:12–28) provide further examples of sin.

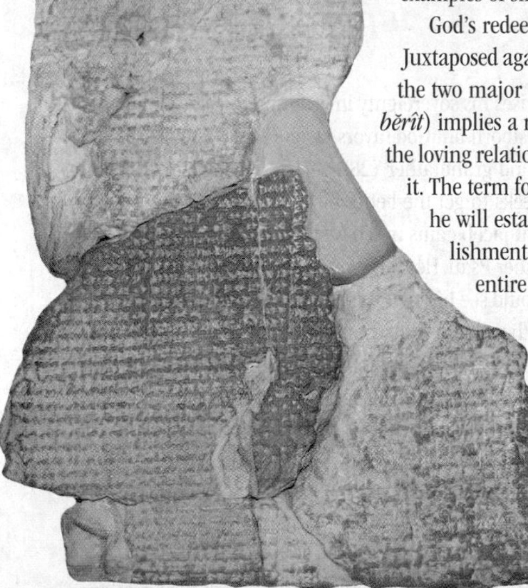

The Atrahasis Epic, ca. seventeenth century BC, contains stories of creation and the flood in a sequence similar to that of Genesis.

God's redeeming love and grace are always at work in the midst of this sin. Juxtaposed against some of the greatest descriptions of sin and judgment appear the two major covenants that Genesis describes. The term "covenant" (Hebrew *bĕrît*) implies a relationship with God. Through a covenant God seeks to recreate the loving relationship that he had with Adam and Eve before human sin destroyed it. The term for "covenant" first occurs in 6:18, where God promises Noah that he will establish a covenant that will benefit all life. God confirms its establishment in 9:9,11. The promise is that God will never again destroy the entire world with a flood. In 12:1–3, God begins to create a covenant with Abram (see Introduction: Genesis and Theology [Faith]). Abram believes God when God says that Abram will father a great nation (15:6). God makes the most solemn promise possible (15:1–21). He instructs Abram to divide the carcasses of various animals. At that point, Abram falls into a deep sleep, and in a dream God symbolically passes between the carcasses. In doing so, God swears by his own life that if his promises do not come true, he will be killed just like the animals were. The sign of the first covenant with Noah was the rainbow (9:13). The sign of the covenant God makes with Abraham is circumcision (17:11). This sign is related to the great increase in numbers that God promises he will give to Abraham and to his descendants (17:1–8).

GENESIS AND THE NEW TESTAMENT

Genesis lays the foundation for salvation history. It is no surprise, therefore, that the text has numerous connections with the NT. Four stand out. First, Paul repeatedly describes the sin and judgments of Gen 3 and applies them to the redeeming work of Christ. This is clearest in Rom 5:12–21: the sin and death that one man's (Adam's) transgression brought contrasts with the justification, righteousness, and life that one man (Jesus Christ) brings through his sacrifice on the cross for our sins. Jesus is a second Adam, succeeding where the first Adam failed.

Second, Gen 14:18–20 is a brief account about Melchizedek, the priest-king of Salem who blesses Abram by God Most High and receives from Abram a tithe of what Abram had captured. This account forms the background for designating the Messianic king of Ps 110 as one who is also a priest "in the order of Melchizedek" (Ps 110:4). The NT book of Hebrews mentions Melchizedek nine times to connect Jesus' priestly ministry with the order of Melchizedek (Heb 5:6,10; 6:20; 7:1,10,11,15,17). Because Abram gave a tithe to Melchizedek, so did all his descendants. This included Aaron and the priestly line of the tribe of Levi. Thus, this line of priests honored Melchizedek as superior. Jesus, the Messianic king, is in this priesthood (Ps 110), and therefore his priesthood surpasses that of Aaron and his line.

A third focus for the appearance of Genesis in the NT is the book of Revelation. The first book in the Bible describes how the serpent deceives the woman, and how her offspring consequently struggles with the serpent (Gen 3:1–15), and the last book describes how the serpent seeks to destroy the woman and her child (Rev 12:1–17). The serpent is ultimately defeated and is explicitly identified as Satan in the NT (Rev 20:2). The first Eden had an abundance of water and a tree of life that gave life to those who ate its fruit (Gen 2:10–14; 3:22). The new Eden of the restored world, the new Jerusalem, will have the river of the water of life with the tree of life growing on both sides of the river. The leaves of the tree will heal the nations (Rev 22:1–3). The curse of the ground (Gen 3:17) will no longer be present (Rev 22:3). Instead, the bounty of the Garden of Eden will return.

A final focus of Genesis in the NT appears in John 1:1–4, which consciously imitates the opening verses of Genesis. Theses verses refer to the Word, or Christ, who was present at the beginning and involved in the creation of the world. This parallels Gen 1:1 and identifies Jesus Christ with God and the Creator of the world. The light was present in Christ (John 1:4–5), parallel to the creation of light in Gen 1:3. Finally, the Gospel of John emphasizes life (see notes on John 1:1–18; 1:4), modeling one of the great themes of Gen 1, God's creation of abundant life and his blessing of that life.

OUTLINE

I. The Primeval History (1:1—11:26)

A. In the Beginning (1:1—2:3)
B. Adam and Eve (2:4–25)
C. The Fall (3:1–24)
D. Cain and Abel (4:1–26)
E. From Adam to Noah (5:1–32)
F. Wickedness in the World (6:1–8)
G. Noah and the Flood (6:9—8:22)
H. God's Covenant With Noah (9:1–17)
I. The Sons of Noah (9:18–29)
J. The Table of Nations (10:1–32)
K. The Tower of Babel (11:1–9)
L. From Shem to Abram (11:10–26)

II. The Family of Abraham (11:27—25:18)

A. Abram's Family (11:27–32)
B. The Call of Abram (12:1–9)
C. Abram in Egypt (12:10–20)
D. Abram and Lot Separate (13:1–18)
E. Abram Rescues Lot (14:1–24)
F. The Lord's Covenant With Abram (15:1–21)
G. Hagar and Ishmael (16:1–16)
H. The Covenant of Circumcision (17:1–27)
I. The Three Visitors (18:1–15)

J. Abraham Pleads for Sodom (18:16–33)
K. Sodom and Gomorrah Destroyed (19:1–29)
L. Lot and His Daughters (19:30–38)
M. Abraham and Abimelek (20:1–18)
N. The Birth of Isaac (21:1–7)
O. Hagar and Ishmael Sent Away (21:8–21)
P. The Treaty at Beersheba (21:22–34)
Q. Abraham Tested (22:1–19)
R. Nahor's Sons (22:20–24)
S. The Death of Sarah (23:1–20)
T. Isaac and Rebekah (24:1–67)
U. The Death of Abraham (25:1–11)
V. Ishmael's Sons (25:12–18)

III. The Family of Isaac (25:19—36:43)

A. Jacob and Esau (25:19–34)
B. Isaac and Abimelek (26:1–33)
C. Jacob Takes Esau's Blessing (26:34—28:9)
D. Jacob's Dream at Bethel (28:10–22)
E. Jacob Arrives in Paddan Aram (29:1–14)
F. Jacob Marries Leah and Rachel (29:15–30)
G. Jacob's Children (29:31—30:24)
H. Jacob's Flocks Increase (30:25–43)
I. Jacob Flees From Laban (31:1–21)
J. Laban Pursues Jacob (31:22–55)
K. Jacob Prepares to Meet Esau (32:1–21)
L. Jacob Wrestles With God (32:22–32)
M. Jacob Meets Esau (33:1–20)
N. Dinah and the Shechemites (34:1–31)
O. Jacob Returns to Bethel (35:1–15)
P. The Deaths of Rachel and Isaac (35:16–29)
Q. Esau's Descendants (36:1–30)
R. The Rulers of Edom (36:31–43)

IV. The Family of Jacob (37:1—50:26)

A. Joseph's Dreams (37:1–11)
B. Joseph Sold by His Brothers (37:12–36)
C. Judah and Tamar (38:1–30)
D. Joseph and Potiphar's Wife (39:1–23)
E. The Cupbearer and the Baker (40:1–23)
F. Pharaoh's Dreams (41:1–40)
G. Joseph in Charge of Egypt (41:41–57)
H. Joseph's Brothers Go to Egypt (42:1–38)
I. The Second Journey to Egypt (43:1–34)
J. A Silver Cup in a Sack (44:1–34)
K. Joseph Makes Himself Known (45:1–28)
L. Jacob Goes to Egypt (46:1—47:12)
M. Joseph and the Famine (47:13–31)
N. Manasseh and Ephraim (48:1–22)
O. Jacob Blesses His Sons (49:1–28)
P. The Death of Jacob (49:29—50:14)
Q. Joseph Reassures His Brothers (50:15–21)
R. The Death of Joseph (50:22–26)

GENESIS

The Beginning

1 In the beginning[a] God created the heavens and the earth.[b] 2 Now the earth was formless and
empty,[c] darkness was over the surface of the deep, and the Spirit of God[d] was hovering over the
waters.

3 And God said,[e] "Let there be light," and there was light.[f] 4 God saw that the light was good, and he
separated the light from the darkness. 5 God called the light "day," and the darkness he called
"night."[g] And there was evening, and there was morning—the first day.

1:1 [a] Jn 1:1-2 [b] Job 38:4; Ps 90:2; Isa 42:5; 44:24; 45:12,18; Ac 17:24; Heb 11:3; Rev 4:11
1:2 [c] Jer 4:23 [d] Ps 104:30
1:3 [e] Ps 33:6,9; 148:5; Heb 11:3 [f] 2Co 4:6*
1:5 [g] Ps 74:16

1:1—11:26 *The Primeval History.* The Bible begins by telling the story of how the world began, how humanity fell into sin, and how God began to address that sin. This story describes God's creation of the world and all of life, the harmony that was in the world, the sin that destroyed that perfect harmony between God and his creation, the spiral of sin and violence, the judgment and salvation in the flood, the covenant that resulted, the common heritage of all people, the tower of Babel, and the family line to Abram. The cycle begins: God creates, and humanity sins. As the violence of humanity increases, God punishes people with a flood and delivers Noah and his family. Humans continue to sin. Yet God does not give up but brings hope in the family line that leads to Abram.

1:1—2:25 The opening chapters of Genesis contain two complementary descriptions of creation: one panoramic, one close-up. The first creation account (1:1—2:3) describes God as the creator of the universe and of all life in it. The second account (2:4–25) focuses on God's creation of the man and woman and their home. While it is possible that the account in ch. 2 continues the story of ch. 1, it may be that these are two creation accounts from different perspectives. Compare, e.g., the fact that each of the four Gospels has its own particular emphasis. Setting Gen 1 and Gen 2 side by side, we see God at once as sovereign Creator and as personally involved with the first people. The more general creation of the world is followed by the more specific focus on the first man and woman. The term "account" in 2:4a suggests that the creation accounts are related to the "accounts" of the lines of Cain and Seth (chs. 4–5) and of Noah's sons (chs. 10–11). In each case the accounts appear as a pair, where the second account tends to zoom in on a specific line and move the story forward.

1:1—2:3 *In the Beginning.* The biblical account of creation presents the one God as Creator of all. It emphasizes how God creates life, establishes rest, and forms humanity in his image. The scientific information as to how this came about is not in the text.

1:1 In the beginning. This single Hebrew word (*bĕrēšît*) denotes the start of a sequence of events (cf. Isa 46:10). **God.** Hebrew *ʾĕlōhîm*, used of Israel's deity and of other gods. It describes divinity, power, and the object of worship; it is the only word for God in ch. 1, which emphasizes God's power as creator of the universe. **created.** God is the subject of this verb every time it appears in the Bible (e.g., 1:21,27; 2:3–4). This is something that only God does. Although creation out of nothing is implicit in Gen 1, for more complete statements see Isa 45:7–18; Rom 11:36; Col 1:16–17. **the heavens and the earth.** Describes all creation by identifying the extremes, i.e., from the heavens above to the earth below, and everything between them. God creates the heavens and the earth, and he will create the new heavens and the new earth. Isaiah repeatedly stresses that the heavens and earth are created by God (Isa 40:12,22; 42:5; 45:12,18; 51:13,16), who will also form the new heavens and the new earth that will never pass away (Isa 65:17; 66:22). For some, Gen 1:1 summarizes the account that follows; therefore, v. 2 is not subsequent to the events of v. 1 but is the first point in the unfolding of the creation. Others understand it as the creation of an unformed and empty heavens and earth that God forms and fills in the remaining verses of ch. 1.

1:2 the earth. The focus of God's creation in ch. 1. **formless and empty.** This phrase occurs elsewhere only in Jer 4:23, where it identifies the judgment of God so that the land is unproductive, out of order, and incapable of fulfilling its purpose of producing life-sustaining food. Gen 1 is less concerned with the production of things and more concerned with the creation of life. This expression describes the world before the creation of life, before there was even a background or context in which life could flourish. In days 1–3, God creates the structure of that background, while in days 4–6, he fills this world with living creatures. **darkness was over the surface of the deep, and the Spirit of God was hovering over the waters.** Further portrays this time before creation in a pictorial manner. **darkness.** Anticipates the coming light. **deep.** This is a common noun in Hebrew that describes the deep waters. Elsewhere, it parallels the waters or seas (Job 38:16). These waters portray the potential of one of the mightiest destructive powers that the ancient world knew (Gen 7:11; 8:2). **Spirit of God was hovering over.** The Spirit hovers over all potential threats as God prepares to create life. **Spirit.** Identical to the word for "wind" in both the OT and NT. God's Spirit appears at this first act of creation and is found again at the beginning of the great creative and redemptive acts of God through history: the turning of the destructive flood waters ("wind," 8:1), at the "birth" of Israel in crossing the Red Sea (Exod 14:21; 15:8,10), the coming of the day of the Lord (Joel 2:28–29), the conception of Jesus

1:6 [h] Jer 10:12
1:7 [i] Job 38:8-11,16; Ps 148:4
1:9 [j] Job 38:8-11; Ps 104:6-9; Pr 8:29; Jer 5:22; 2Pe 3:5
1:11 [k] Ps 65:9-13; 104:14
1:14 [l] Ps 74:16 [m] Jer 10:2 [n] Ps 104:19
1:16 [o] Ps 136:8 [p] Ps 136:9 [q] Job 38:7, 31-32; Ps 8:3; Isa 40:26

6 And God said, "Let there be a vault[h] between the waters to separate water from water." 7 So God made
the vault and separated the water under the vault from the water above it.[i] And it was so. 8 God
called the vault "sky." And there was evening, and there was morning — the second day.
9 And God said, "Let the water under the sky be gathered to one place,[j] and let dry ground appear."
And it was so. 10 God called the dry ground "land," and the gathered waters he called "seas." And
God saw that it was good.
11 Then God said, "Let the land produce vegetation:[k] seed-bearing plants and trees on the land
that bear fruit with seed in it, according to their various kinds." And it was so. 12 The land produced vegetation: plants bearing seed according to their kinds and trees bearing fruit with seed
in it according to their kinds. And God saw that it was good. 13 And there was evening, and there
was morning — the third day.
14 And God said, "Let there be lights[l] in the vault of the sky to separate the day from the night, and
let them serve as signs[m] to mark sacred times,[n] and days and years, 15 and let them be lights in
the vault of the sky to give light on the earth." And it was so. 16 God made two great lights — the
greater light to govern[o] the day and the lesser light to govern[p] the night. He also made the stars.[q]

(Matt 1:18,20; Luke 1:35), the act of coming to God the Father (John 3:5,8), and the advent of the church at Pentecost (Acts 2:1–4,16–21). Although the term "Holy Spirit" occurs only a few times in the OT (Ps 51:11; Isa 63:10–11), his creative and redemptive activity associate the Spirit of God with the NT Holy Spirit.

1:3 God said. All of creation and each part of it begins with the Word of God as in John 1:1–4, which also connects creation with light (both spiritual and physical). John's identification of the Word of God with Jesus Christ (John 1:14) draws out a doctrine that is not explicit in this text. **Let there be light.** Although God does not explicitly create light by using the terms "created," "formed," and "made" (as in the remainder of the six days), see Isa 45:7 for God creating light. **and there was light.** This response repeats the words of the command. Here, and throughout ch. 1 where the phrase, "there was" recurs, creation completely obeys God's command.

1:4 God saw. This describes the notice God takes of his own acts, as well of those of others (1:10,12,18,21,25,31; 6:2,12; Jonah 3:10). The quality of the light being "good" implies more than an aesthetic or moral judgment. The creation is good (1:10,12,18,21,25) because its creator is good (Pss 34:8; 100:5; Jer 33:11; Nah 1:7; 1 Pet 2:3). It follows God's plan exactly. **he separated the light from the darkness.** This characterizes the first three days of creation. Separating involves both distinguishing and purifying. God distinguishes between different items (here light and darkness) and thereby gives them an identity and integrity of their own. With light and darkness, the created order has daytime and nighttime.

1:5 called. This action repeatedly occurs in the accounts of creation (1:8,10; 2:19–20,23). **"day."** Here, as elsewhere, the name given identifies the purpose of the object (or person) so named even as the Creator God establishes its purpose by his authority. With light and darkness, this means that the day and night do not occur simultaneously, but in a sequence. Further, day does not intrude into night and vice versa. In this way time begins on the first day with "evening" (followed by night) and "morning" (followed by day). Time is logically the first element or dimension necessary for creating the world and for life to exist in it. The sun and moon are created on day four. **first day.** Or "day one." The term can be used interchangeably with "first" to denote the initial element in an assumed sequence, especially a sequence denoting days (e.g., Ezra 3:6; 10:16–17; Neh 8:2; Hag 1:1). The Hebrew word for "day" can refer to a 24-hour period or a larger period of time. For example, Gen 2:4 uses the same Hebrew word for "day" when it refers to the "account" of the heavens and the earth, that is, "on the day when they were created." Thus, seven days become one day. On the other hand, the Hebrew word "day" often refers to a 24-hour period (e.g., 7:11,13; 8:4–5,14).

1:6 vault. Has the root idea of a beaten metal plate; can also be translated "expanse" or "firmament." The Hebrew noun customarily carries the sense of the heavens or sky, where the sun, moon, and stars are found (vv. 14–17; Ps 19:1; Dan 12:3) and across which the birds fly (v. 20). The heavens also serve as the place where God lives (Ps 150:1) and as what lies above this world but beneath the divine throne (Ezek 1:22–26; 10:1). At the time Genesis was written, people thought the sky resembled a great dome or vault stretching from horizon to horizon.

1:7 separated. The act of separation on the second day is between "the water under the vault" and "the water above it." While God will again address the water under the sky, the water above this vault will not recur until 7:11.

1:9–10 water under the sky ... dry ground ... "land" ... "seas." God creates the second (land) and third (seas) domains that will support life. **gathered.** The term emphasizes that the seas and dry ground are distinct. This recalls the destructive power of these waters to flood coastal towns and cities, and the limits that God has imposed. This boundary completes the three separate domains: sky, seas, and land. These are the three arenas in which movement and life take place.

1:11–13 These verses describe the last preparations for the coming of animal and human life. Producing the food that the living creatures will consume (vv. 29–30) forms the final element in the great landscape that the divine artist has created.

1:11 seed-bearing plants and trees ... fruit with seed in it. God enables plant life to reproduce. On the one hand, plants bear food not because people use the correct magic rituals to invoke gods of storm (e.g., Baal) and goddesses of fertility (e.g., Asherah). Rather, God creates food with its own power to reproduce within his world, so it does not run out. This envisions abundant food to provide for all the life that God creates (cf. the garden in chs. 2–3). **according to their various kinds.** This may refer either to each species, or "kind," of plant reproducing in accordance with its parent plant (e.g., beans do not produce corn) or to "many kinds" of plants and trees (e.g., "many kinds" in Ezek 47:10).

1:14–19 The creation of the sun, moon, and stars continues the theme of the first day (separating day from night), but here the purpose is "to mark sacred times, and days and years" (v. 14). The emphasis now shifts from providing the background domains in which created things can move to filling these domains. Thus, "fill" is not used for vegetation in vv. 11–13, but it appears in vv. 22,28 to describe the creation of animals and people. Beginning with the domain that is farthest away, God fills the sky with the sun, moon, and stars. A second purpose is to "give light on the earth" (v. 15).

1:16 two great lights. The sun and moon. The ancients worshiped the sun and moon as divine, so this creation account distinguishes the God of the Bible as the one who created and controls the sun and moon.

17 God set them in the vault of the sky to give light on the earth, 18 to govern the day and the night,[r]
and to separate light from darkness. And God saw that it was good. 19 And there was evening, and
there was morning — the fourth day.
20 And God said, "Let the water teem with living creatures, and let birds fly above the earth across the
vault of the sky." 21 So God created the great creatures of the sea and every living thing with which
the water teems and that moves about in it,[s] according to their kinds, and every winged bird according to its kind. And God saw that it was good. 22 God blessed them and said, "Be fruitful and
increase in number and fill the water in the seas, and let the birds increase on the earth."[t] 23 And
there was evening, and there was morning — the fifth day.
24 And God said, "Let the land produce living creatures according to their kinds: the livestock, the creatures that move along the ground, and the wild animals, each according to its kind." And it was so.
25 God made the wild animals[u] according to their kinds, the livestock according to their kinds, and
all the creatures that move along the ground according to their kinds. And God saw that it was good.
26 Then God said, "Let us[v] make mankind in our image,[w] in our likeness, so that they may rule[x]
over the fish in the sea and the birds in the sky, over the livestock and all the wild animals,[a] and
over all the creatures that move along the ground."

27 So God created mankind in his own image,[y]
in the image of God he created them;
male and female[z] he created them.

28 God blessed them and said to them, "Be fruitful and increase in number; fill the earth[a] and
subdue it. Rule over the fish in the sea and the birds in the sky and over every living creature that
moves on the ground."

1:18 [r] Jer 33:20,25
1:21 [s] Ps 104:25-26
1:22 [t] ver 28; Ge 8:17
1:25 [u] Jer 27:5
1:26 [v] Ps 100:3 [w] Ge 9:6; Jas 3:9 [x] Ps 8:6-8
1:27 [y] 1Co 11:7 [z] Ge 5:2; Mt 19:4*; Mk 10:6*
1:28 [a] Ge 9:1,7; Lev 26:9

[a] *26* Probable reading of the original Hebrew text (see Syriac); Masoretic Text *the earth*

1:17 set them in the vault of the sky to give light. A further manifestation of God's sovereignty. He controls where they are and what they do. God — not the sun and moon as gods — is responsible for the days, months, and years.

1:20–23 It is only on the fifth day, after God produces the necessary backgrounds, that living creatures appear. The fifth day corresponds to the sky and waters on the second day: God fills the sky with birds and the waters with fish.

1:20 teem. It points to a key element of this creation account: life is abundant and fills the world.

1:21 the great creatures of the sea. May refer to snakes (Exod 7:9–12) or sea monsters (Ps 74:13; Isa 27:1). **creatures.** Plural in Hebrew, but the rest of ch. 1 collectively uses the Hebrew singular to identify entire groups: plant and tree (v. 11); living creature and bird (v. 20); domestic animal, creature that moves along the ground, and wild animal (v. 24). Perhaps "creatures" refers not to a large group but to a few specific animals such as large and more feared sea creatures. God creates them and has complete power over them. **according to their kinds.** As in vv. 11–12 (see note on v. 11), this can describe all kinds of creatures.

1:22 Be fruitful and increase. God creates life and wants it to fill the earth.

1:24–25 God creates land animals on the sixth day, which corresponds to dry land appearing on the third day. The animals fit in three categories: "the livestock, the creatures that move along the ground, and the wild animals" (v. 24). The first and third categories distinguish domestic and wild animals. The second group includes insects, reptiles, and other animals that remain close to the ground.

1:26–27 This last act of God's creative work is the climax.

1:26 us ... our ... our. "Us" portrays God deliberating in the midst of his court just as a king might have a court and discuss his plans among them (2 Kgs 22; Job 1–2; Ps 82; Isa 6). But "our" cannot be so easily explained in the context of the ancient world. No evidence exists for the creation of people in both the image of God and the image of his angels. Only the image of God appears in v. 27. It seems more likely that "us" and "our" imply a greater complexity to God's nature as already suggested by the Spirit of God (v. 2; see note on 11:7). **mankind.** Hebrew *'ādām.* This is used in ch. 1 for the human species just as every other creature (except "the great creatures of the sea" in v. 21; see note there) created in ch. 1 appears in the Hebrew singular and describes a class of animals (e.g., "bird" translated "birds," "wild animal" translated "wild animals"). In ch. 2, *'ādām* appears with a definite article ("the man") to describe the man placed in the garden. The personal name, Adam, has the same spelling. Ch. 1 does not focus on a single male (see the parallel "male and female" in 1:27) nor even on the first couple, but it focuses on the whole human race. **image ... likeness.** These are synonyms. Daniel 3:1 describes the statue of Nebuchadnezzar with the same Hebrew term for image; the statue represents the authority and power of the king and elicits obedience and worship from the multitude. Elsewhere in the ancient world, the same is true of this word "image," which appears alongside "likeness." A text from ancient Gozan contains both words, "image" and "likeness," and translates them into Assyrian by using the same word, meaning "statue" or a symbol of authority. Thus, in this context to be made in the image of God means to rule over the life in the three domains that God created. This rulership is a stewardship. It is illustrated in ch. 2, where the man takes care of the garden (2:15) and names the animals (2:20). In this context God placed humanity on earth to continue his rulership after he finished the work of creation. With the coming of Jesus Christ as the perfect image of God (Col 1:15), Christians are re-created (2 Cor 5:17) and become conformed to Christ as an expression of his image (Rom 8:29), with righteousness, holiness, and knowledge (Eph 4:24; Col 3:10).

1:28 Be fruitful ... increase ... fill. God also commanded the animals to do this (v. 22), so it represents the creaturely basis of humanity. **subdue ... Rule over.** God commanded only humans to do this because only they are made in the image of God. The repetition of this idea (v. 26) underlines its importance.

1:29 [b]Ps 104:14
1:30 [c]Ps 104:14,27; 145:15
1:31 [d]Ps 104:24 [e]1Ti 4:4
2:2 [f]Ex 20:11; 31:17; Heb 4:4*
2:3 [g]Lev 23:3; Isa 58:13
2:5 [h]Ge 1:11 [i]Ps 65:9-10

29 Then God said, "I give you every seed-bearing plant on the face of the whole earth and every
tree that has fruit with seed in it. They will be yours for food.[b] 30 And to all the beasts of the earth
and all the birds in the sky and all the creatures that move along the ground — everything that
has the breath of life in it — I give every green plant for food.[c]" And it was so.
31 God saw all that he had made,[d] and it was very good.[e] And there was evening, and there was
morning — the sixth day.

2 Thus the heavens and the earth were completed in all their vast array.

2 By the seventh day God had finished the work he had been doing; so on the seventh day he rested
from all his work.[f] 3 Then God blessed the seventh day and made it holy,[g] because on it he rested
from all the work of creating that he had done.

Adam and Eve

4 This is the account of the heavens and the earth when they were created, when the LORD God made
the earth and the heavens.

5 Now no shrub had yet appeared on the earth[a] and no plant had yet sprung up,[h] for the LORD God
had not sent rain on the earth[i] and there was no one to work the ground, 6 but streams[b] came up from
the earth and watered the whole surface of the ground. 7 Then the LORD God formed a man[c] from the

[a] 5 Or *land*; also in verse 6 [b] 6 Or *mist* [c] 7 The Hebrew for *man (adam)* sounds like and may be related to the Hebrew for *ground (adamah)*; it is also the name *Adam* (see verse 20).

1:29–30 God gives plants "for food" (v. 29) to sustain human and animal life. Vegetables and fruits form the foundation of the food chain for both herbivores and carnivores. Ch. 1 emphasizes abundant life; God provides abundant food, whose seeds guarantee that food will continue throughout the history of the world.
1:31 With the work of creation finished on the sixth day, all is now in perfect harmony with God's will. The result is more than good; it is "very good."
2:1 This verse concludes what the summary statement of 1:1 envisions. The same expressions for the heavens and for the earth appear in both verses, now adding all the elements ("all their vast array") that have been added since 1:1.
2:2 The creation "week" of seven days has been leading up to this point. The repeated phrases identifying the evening, morning, and ordinal number of each day finish and climax at "the seventh day." **God had finished the work.** Of creation. It is a day of rest, not one of further creative work. **finished.** The same Hebrew verb as the passive form translated "were completed" in v. 1. **rested.** God does not require rest because he is tired; he chooses to stop working because his creation is complete. The Hebrew root of "rested" forms the noun "Sabbath," and it carries the sense of stopping or ceasing.
2:3 made it holy. God's rest on the seventh day makes it different from the other days of the week. Although the law requiring Israel to observe the Sabbath comes later, the week is built into creation from the beginning. The seventh day as a time of rest climaxes God's work in ch. 1. All creation moves toward it. Both accounts of the Ten Commandments require Israel to observe the Sabbath (Exod 20:8–11; Deut 5:12–15), and Exod 20:11 explicitly relates it to the seven days of creation and indeed to all special days and years in Israel's sacred calendars. If the Sabbath is the climax of creation, it is also the goal of the redeemed community and cosmos (Heb 4:9–11). Remembering the Sabbath every week contributes to idea that seven days, not months or years, describe the creation account.
2:4–25 *Adam and Eve.* The rest of ch. 2 reviews all that happens with the creation of the man and his home, his tasks, and his companion. The account contrasts with ch. 1 by focusing on the people rather than the cosmos.
2:4 This verse moves from the previous account and introduces the creation story of ch. 2. The creation of the heavens and the earth is explicitly described in 1:1—2:1, but the ongoing life of humanity in the world that God created begins its history in 2:4 and continues through the rest of Genesis. **account.** This term that stands between the two creation accounts also introduces the family lines of Seth (5:1,3), of Noah (6:9), and of Shem (11:10), where it refers to a family history or genealogy. The repetitive style of the seven days resembles the repetitive style of the genealogies. Thus, the story begins with the beginning of creation and God's word (1:1–4), which connects it with all the family histories through Genesis. The word of God that created the world continues in each generation and remains the same word down to the present. **LORD.** Translates the Hebrew name Yahweh, the personal and covenant name of God ("Jehovah" in the ASV). The Greek term for "Lord" translates this name in the earliest Greek translation of the OT. The meaning of Yahweh is unknown, but it sounds like a form of the verb "to be, become" (see Exod 3:14 and note). **God.** *ʾĕlōhîm*, a title for deity (see note on 1:1) and the name of God used up to this point in Genesis. In ch. 1, *ʾĕlōhîm* emphasizes God's power and majesty as the Creator of the universe. The rest of Genesis retains that title but adds God's personal name. "LORD" reflects the changed tone, which becomes more personal and is concerned with God's relationship with the man and woman. **the earth and the heavens.** This reverses the order of "the heavens and the earth" as found in the beginning of the verse (see also 1:1; 2:1). It forms a "mirror" in Hebrew poetry in which the elements between the two references become important. The two phrases repeat the same idea in the fashion of a poetic couplet: "when they were created, / when the LORD God made." The first line uses "created," the special verb applied only to God and appropriately emphasizing the cosmic creation of ch. 1 (where it occurs three times; it does not appear at all in the rest of chs. 2–4). The second line focuses on God's personal role in his relation to people, which ch. 2 emphasizes.
2:5 no shrub ... no plant. Plants, essential for the life of animals and people (1:29–30), are not present because rain and humans are absent. This resembles ch. 1, which also begins with the absence of life and the material to sustain it (1:2).
2:6 streams. God provides water to create the food.
2:7 man ... ground ... life ... living. Not only does the Hebrew for "man" (*ʾādām*) sound like the Hebrew for "ground" (*ʾădāmâ*), but the

dust[j] of the ground[k] and breathed into his nostrils the breath[l] of life,[m] and the man became a living
being.[n]
8 Now the LORD God had planted a garden in the east, in Eden;[o] and there he put the man he had
formed. 9 The LORD God made all kinds of trees grow out of the ground — trees that were pleasing to
the eye and good for food. In the middle of the garden were the tree of life[p] and the tree of the knowledge of good and evil.[q]
10 A river watering the garden flowed from Eden; from there it was separated into four headwaters.
11 The name of the first is the Pishon; it winds through the entire land of Havilah, where there is gold.
12 (The gold of that land is good; aromatic resin[a] and onyx are also there.) 13 The name of the second
river is the Gihon; it winds through the entire land of Cush.[b] 14 The name of the third river is the Tigris;[r]
it runs along the east side of Ashur. And the fourth river is the Euphrates.
15 The LORD God took the man and put him in the Garden of Eden to work it and take care of it. 16 And
the LORD God commanded the man, "You are free to eat from any tree in the garden; 17 but you must not
eat from the tree of the knowledge of good and evil, for when you eat from it you will certainly die."[s]
18 The LORD God said, "It is not good for the man to be alone. I will make a helper suitable for him."[t]
19 Now the LORD God had formed out of the ground all the wild animals[u] and all the birds in the
sky. He brought them to the man to see what he would name them; and whatever the man called each
living creature,[v] that was its name. 20 So the man gave names to all the livestock, the birds in the sky
and all the wild animals.
But for Adam[c] no suitable helper was found. 21 So the LORD God caused the man to fall into a deep
sleep; and while he was sleeping, he took one of the man's ribs[d] and then closed up the place with flesh.
22 Then the LORD God made a woman from the rib[e][w] he had taken out of the man, and he brought her
to the man.

2:7 [j] Ge 3:19 [k] Ps 103:14 [l] Job 33:4 [m] Ac 17:25 [n] 1Co 15:45*
2:8 [o] Ge 3:23,24; Isa 51:3
2:9 [p] Ge 3:22,24; Rev 2:7; 22:2,14,19 [q] Eze 47:12
2:14 [r] Da 10:4
2:17 [s] Dt 30:15,19; Ro 5:12; 6:23; Jas 1:15
2:18 [t] 1Co 11:9
2:19 [u] Ps 8:7 [v] Ge 1:24
2:22 [w] 1Co 11:8,9,12

[a] *12* Or *good; pearls* [b] *13* Possibly southeast Mesopotamia [c] *20* Or *the man* [d] *21* Or *took part of the man's side* [e] *22* Or *part*

Hebrew for "life" (*ḥayyîm*) sounds like the Hebrew for "living" (*ḥayyâ*). This identifies the two stages and components that construct the human person: the dirt of creation and the breath of God. The man is between the Lord God and the created world (Ps 8:4–8); he is a ruler, yet he is under authority (Gen 1:26–28).

2:8–9 God creates a home for the man.

2:8 garden. A place for plants and thus food and work (v. 5). **the east.** The first of many hints in this chapter that the garden, as a sacred place where people meet with God, foreshadows the tabernacle and the Jerusalem temple, which both face eastward. **Eden.** Often thought to mean paradise, it may mean well-watered, abundant in streams. **there he put the man.** God takes the initiative with the man and guides him throughout the chapter.

2:9 the tree of life. This appears again in Genesis only in 3:22, just before the couple are banished from Eden, and it recurs in Rev 2:7; 22:2,14,19, where it heals all who come to it. **the tree of the knowledge of good and evil.** This forms the center for the one command that the Lord God gives to the first couple (v. 17). "Good" and "evil" represent moral and ethical categories. God designed this tree to teach the man and woman the difference between right and wrong, but first they must learn this by obeying what he has commanded.

2:10–14 This section describes how much water was available in Eden and names the connected rivers. The Tigris and the Euphrates Rivers are the best known. The name "Gihon" was also given to the underground spring beneath Jerusalem. It means "gusher" and could refer to another stream with this characteristic. "Cush" in the Bible is often connected with Africa but here may refer to an area in the Zagros Mountains east of the Tigris River, and thus east of Ashur, the name for the kingdom of Assyria. The Pishon River and land of Havilah are not otherwise known but may describe parts of central Saudi Arabia where gold has been located as well as a prehistoric riverbed that can be traced to the confluence of the Tigris and Euphrates at the head of the Persian Gulf. This may be the site of Eden, but it is not so easy to understand how the water flows from it (rather than into it). These descriptions also look forward to another place where God meets his people: the temple in Jerusalem with its great "Sea" that holds the water in front of it (1 Kgs 7:23–44), with the Gishon spring beneath it, and with much gold and precious stones, such as onyx, within it (1 Chr 29:2).

2:15 to work it and take care of it. Similar verbs describe the role of the priests and Levites in the tabernacle and temple (e.g., Num 3:7–8; 8:26). These verbs, however, can also be translated "serve" and "guard." The man has a priestly role to protect the garden sanctuary (Gen 1:26). When he fails to do this and is expelled from Eden, the task of guarding the garden is given to cherubim (3:24).

2:16–17 You are free to eat from any tree … but. In the Lord God's first words to the man in ch. 2, he graciously supplies abundant food and the freedom to eat it. As is customary in Hebrew speech, this general offer is followed by a specific exception: "but you must not eat from the tree of the knowledge of good and evil." The single forbidden tree contrasts with the many that are not forbidden. The reason for the prohibition is not explained. **you will certainly die.** This warning introduces death for the first time. If creation of life was "very good" (1:31) because it obeyed God perfectly, then the man's disobedience can bring death, the opposite of the life that God has given so freely.

2:18 not good. The opposite of the good creation of ch. 1. **helper.** The Lord God seeks a "helper" for the man so that he is not alone. The Hebrew term (but as a verb) is found later in 49:25, where God "helps" (is a helper for) Israel.

2:19–20 God's search for a helper involves the man's naming the animals. The man here discerns the purpose of the animals and so calls the creatures according to their role in creation. He exercises dominion over creation in general (see notes on 1:26,28).

2:22 rib. Always means "side" where it occurs elsewhere. As always, the Lord God initiates the action and takes from the man's side so that the woman is in every way human (*ʾādām*; see 1:26; 2:7 and notes), just like the man.

2:23 [x] Ge 29:14; Eph 5:28-30
2:24 [y] Mal 2:15 [z] Mt 19:5*; Mk 10:7-8*; 1Co 6:16*; Eph 5:31*
2:25 [a] Ge 3:7,10-11
3:1 [b] 2Co 11:3; Rev 12:9; 20:2
3:4 [c] Jn 8:44; 2Co 11:3
3:5 [d] Isa 14:14; Eze 28:2
3:6 [e] Jas 1:14-15; 1Jn 2:16 [f] 1Ti 2:14

23 The man said,

"This is now bone of my bones
and flesh of my flesh;[x]
she shall be called 'woman,'
for she was taken out of man."

24 That is why a man leaves his father and mother and is united[y] to his wife, and they become one flesh.[z]
25 Adam and his wife were both naked,[a] and they felt no shame.

The Fall

3 Now the serpent[b] was more crafty than any of the wild animals the LORD God had made. He said to
the woman, "Did God really say, 'You must not eat from any tree in the garden'?"
2 The woman said to the serpent, "We may eat fruit from the trees in the garden, 3 but God did say,
'You must not eat fruit from the tree that is in the middle of the garden, and you must not touch it,
or you will die.'"
4 "You will not certainly die," the serpent said to the woman.[c] 5 "For God knows that when you eat
from it your eyes will be opened, and you will be like God,[d] knowing good and evil."
6 When the woman saw that the fruit of the tree was good for food and pleasing to the eye, and also
desirable[e] for gaining wisdom, she took some and ate it. She also gave some to her husband, who was
with her, and he ate it.[f] 7 Then the eyes of both of them were opened, and they realized they were naked;
so they sewed fig leaves together and made coverings for themselves.

2:23 bone of my bones. The man recognizes that the woman originates from himself. **"woman" … man.** Hebrew *ʾiššâ … ʾiš*. Like *ʾādām* (masculine word for humans and the man) and *ʾădāmâ* (feminine word for ground) in v. 7 that connect man with the ground (see note on v. 7), these words sound similar and connect man with woman.

2:24 why a man leaves his father and mother and is united to his wife. The physical creation of the woman by taking her from the man implies a natural relationship that is restored when the man and woman become "one flesh" by physically reuniting.

2:25 naked … felt no shame. The two are in perfect harmony. There are no barriers and no shame from the absence of barriers. Ch. 2 ends with harmony between God and creation, between God and the human couple, between the couple and creation, and between the man and the woman (cf. 3:7).

3:1–24 *The Fall.* Continuing the creation account, the biblical story recounts what went wrong with the perfect harmony of ch. 2 and how sin changed everything so that the world has become the corrupted place that we know.

3:1 serpent. People in the ancient world considered snakes to be sources of long life, healing, and wisdom, but Israelites who were familiar with the food regulations of Leviticus would associate the serpent with unclean animals (Lev 11:42) and be suspicious. **crafty.** Hebrew *ʿārûm*. This rare Hebrew word, consistent with the snake's reputation for wisdom, sounds like the Hebrew for "naked" in 2:25 (*ʿămrûummîm*). The wordplay suggests that the serpent's craftiness will overturn the innocence symbolized by the couple's nakedness. **Did God really say …?** God invites the man to eat from "any tree" (2:16), but the serpent denies what God says by adding the word "not." Such lies characterize the serpent's speech (3:4). Genesis does not explicitly identify the serpent as Satan, but the NT describes the devil as "a liar and the father of lies" (John 8:44) and "that ancient serpent" (Rev 12:9; 20:2). If everything was "very good" in 1:31, then evil has now entered the world. The source of this evil is not given, but it existed before Adam and Eve disobeyed God. Something was already amiss in the world.

3:2 We may eat fruit from the trees. The woman correctly qualifies the serpent's charge, but she diminishes God's grace by not emphasizing that they are "free" to eat from "any" tree (2:16).

3:3 the tree that is in the middle of the garden. She omits the name of the tree, which contains the rationale for not eating from it. **you must not touch it.** A statement that God apparently never made. The effect creates an arbitrary command (God just chose any tree) and trivializes the offense in contrast to the punishment (death for touching fruit!). God originally spoke this command only to the man. Although the man is present in this exchange (v. 6), the woman speaks. How did she know what God said? We are not told whether God told her directly or whether the man passed the words along to her. The result indicts both the man and the woman in this transgression.

3:4 You will not certainly die. The snake lies, again quoting God's words (2:17) and placing a negative ("not") in front of them (see 3:1 and note).

3:5 God knows. Satan accuses God of selfish motives (cf. Job 1:9–11; 2:4–5). **your eyes will be opened … knowing good and evil.** This seems to coincide with the tree's purpose. The man and woman both become aware of their nakedness (v. 7). But this knowledge does not exclude the punishment that God promised. So the serpent denies the sin's punishment but glorifies its reward. The lure is to "be like God" in a manner different from God's intent. Ironically, the human couple have been made in the "image of God" (1:27). They are to be like God by ruling over the earth on his behalf. God has provided a way in the garden (through obedience) and will ultimately provide another way (through the sacrifice of Christ; see 2 Pet 1:4), but God's way lacks the attractive false promise of the serpent's seemingly easier way.

3:6 good. God created everything "good" (ch. 1). All the food in the garden was good, but the woman thought only of this food and made what God had said was not good (to eat) into something that seemed good. **pleasing.** The Hebrew word also occurs in Num 11:4, where the Israelites "crave" meat, rebel, and are judged. **desirable.** The Hebrew root for "covet" (*ḥāmad*). The same form appears in the Ten Commandments (Exod 20:17: Deut 5:21), where God also forbids desiring what is not yours. **saw … took … ate … gave … he ate.** The rapid-fire series of verbs suggests that everything happens quickly, so that the couple do not consider the consequences. By failing to rule over the serpent, the human couple betray God and permit evil to enter the garden.

3:7 realized they were naked. Their nakedness symbolizes their innocence (2:25), but now they have lost that innocence. So the first barrier is set up, symbolized by the fig leaves that separate them from each other, from the garden, and from God. The harmony has been lost.

8 Then the man and his wife heard the sound of the LORD God as he was walking[g] in the garden in
the cool of the day, and they hid[h] from the LORD God among the trees of the garden. 9 But the LORD God
called to the man, "Where are you?"
10 He answered, "I heard you in the garden, and I was afraid because I was naked; so I hid."
11 And he said, "Who told you that you were naked? Have you eaten from the tree that I commanded
you not to eat from?"
12 The man said, "The woman you put here with me — she gave me some fruit from the tree, and
I ate it."
13 Then the LORD God said to the woman, "What is this you have done?"
The woman said, "The serpent deceived me,[i] and I ate."
14 So the LORD God said to the serpent, "Because you have done this,

"Cursed[j] are you above all livestock
  and all wild animals!
You will crawl on your belly
  and you will eat dust[k]
  all the days of your life.
15 And I will put enmity
  between you and the woman,
  and between your offspring[a][l] and hers;[m]
he will crush[b] your head,[n]
  and you will strike his heel."

16 To the woman he said,

"I will make your pains in childbearing very severe;
  with painful labor you will give birth to children.
Your desire will be for your husband,
  and he will rule over you.[o]"

17 To Adam he said, "Because you listened to your wife and ate fruit from the tree about which I
commanded you, 'You must not eat from it,'

[a] *15* Or *seed* [b] *15* Or *strike*

3:8 [g] Dt 23:14 [h] Job 31:33; Ps 139:7-12; Jer 23:24
3:13 [i] 2Co 11:3; 1Ti 2:14
3:14 [j] Dt 28:15-20 [k] Isa 65:25; Mic 7:17
3:15 [l] Jn 8:44; Ac 13:10; 1Jn 3:8 [m] Isa 7:14; Mt 1:23; Rev 12:17 [n] Ro 16:20; Heb 2:14
3:16 [o] 1Co 11:3; Eph 5:22

3:8 the cool of the day. The evening (when the heat of the sun and the cool of the coming darkness create currents of wind). **they hid.** Their sin separates them from God.
3:9 the LORD God called to the man. The man is addressed first.
3:10 I was afraid. The man confesses his fear due to the shame of nakedness.
3:11 Who told you . . . ? God is not ignorant but elicits open and honest confession so he can address the sin. A major theme of the Bible is that although people sin, God seeks them out in order to bring them to repentance. Ultimately, Jesus "came to seek and to save the lost" (Luke 19:10).
3:12–13 Instead of admitting their own guilt and responsibility, the man blames the woman, and the woman blames the serpent.
3:14 God said. God first addresses the serpent, who spoke first. **Cursed.** Among living creatures, only the serpent is cursed. **crawl.** Whatever the serpent may have been before this moment, he would now crawl. Falling down on one's stomach is an act of self-humiliation before a king or leader. Under the laws of Leviticus, crawling animals were designated as ritually unclean (Lev 11:42). **dust.** Symbolizes humiliation (18:27; Job 30:19; 42:6; Ps 72:9; Isa 49:23; 65:25; Mic 7:17).
3:15 "Enmity." Extends beyond the woman and the snake to all future generations. **your offspring and hers.** Or "your seed and her seed" (see NIV text note). It is rare to refer to a woman's "seed." Genesis traces the line of seed from the woman (4:25). **crush . . . strike.** These words translate the same Hebrew verb. The snake's attack at the heel of the woman is painful but not necessarily mortal, but the same action by the woman and her seed against the snake's head will be mortal. This promise anticipates Rev 12 (especially 12:9) and the victory in Rev 19–20 (especially 20:2), where the dragon, "that ancient serpent," represents Satan, and the woman represents the mother of Jesus, who is her seed. Jesus' death and resurrection secures the final victory over Satan and death. His victory begins with his coming into the world at the incarnation (John 1:1–14) and will culminate when he returns. In Christian history, v. 15 has been called the Protoevangelium, the first announcement of the gospel. At both the beginning and the end, the Bible pictures Satan as a snake or dragon at war with God for the dominion of the earth and the human race.
3:16 make your pains in childbearing very severe. The Hebrew word for "pains" is identical to the "painful toil" assigned to the man in v. 17. **desire.** The Hebrew occurs elsewhere only in Song 7:10 and in Gen 4:7, which says that sin "desires" to control Cain but that Cain "must rule over it." That verse uses the same language as here and describes a struggle between sin and Cain. Here there is a breakdown in the original harmonious relationship between the man and the woman. Ideals such as care for one another (1 Pet 3:5–8) give way to conflict. As the NT suggests, this is not irreversible. The love that Song 7:10 suggests ("his desire is for me") can be restored. The reconciliation that Jesus Christ brought to the world by the forgiveness of sins (2 Cor 5:19) can restore the ideal harmony of the relationship that existed between the man and the woman before the fall.
3:17 Because you listened to your wife. The man followed his wife rather than God in this instance. 1 Tim 2:14 states that the woman was

3:17 [p]Ge 5:29; Ro 8:20-22 [q]Job 5:7; 14:1; Ecc 2:23
3:18 [r]Ps 104:14
3:19 [s]2Th 3:10 [t]Ge 2:7; Ps 90:3; 104:29; Ecc 12:7
3:22 [u]Rev 22:14
3:23 [v]Ge 2:8 [w]Ge 4:2
3:24 [x]Ex 25:18-22 [y]Ps 104:4 [z]Ge 2:9
4:2 [a]Lk 11:51
4:3 [b]Nu 18:12
4:4 [c]Lev 3:16 [d]Ex 13:2, 12 [e]Heb 11:4

"Cursed[p] is the ground because of you;
    through painful toil you will eat food from it
    all the days of your life.[q]
18 It will produce thorns and thistles for you,
    and you will eat the plants of the field.[r]
19 By the sweat of your brow
    you will eat your food[s]
until you return to the ground,
    since from it you were taken;
for dust you are
    and to dust you will return."[t]

20 Adam*[a]* named his wife Eve,*[b]* because she would become the mother of all the living.
21 The Lord God made garments of skin for Adam and his wife and clothed them. 22 And the Lord God
said, "The man has now become like one of us, knowing good and evil. He must not be allowed to reach
out his hand and take also from the tree of life[u] and eat, and live forever." 23 So the Lord God banished
him from the Garden of Eden[v] to work the ground[w] from which he had been taken. 24 After he drove the
man out, he placed on the east side*[c]* of the Garden of Eden cherubim[x] and a flaming sword[y] flashing
back and forth to guard the way to the tree of life.[z]

Cain and Abel

4 Adam*[a]* made love to his wife Eve, and she became pregnant and gave birth to Cain.*[d]* She said,
"With the help of the Lord I have brought forth*[e]* a man." 2 Later she gave birth to his brother Abel.[a]
Now Abel kept flocks, and Cain worked the soil. 3 In the course of time Cain brought some of the fruits
of the soil as an offering to the Lord.[b] 4 And Abel also brought an offering — fat portions[c] from some of
the firstborn of his flock.[d] The Lord looked with favor on Abel and his offering,[e] 5 but on Cain and his
offering he did not look with favor. So Cain was very angry, and his face was downcast.

[a] 20,1 Or *The man* *[b] 20* *Eve* probably means *living.* *[c] 24* Or *placed in front* *[d] 1* *Cain* sounds like the Hebrew for *brought forth* or *acquired.* *[e] 1* Or *have acquired*

deceived, but not the man. **Cursed.** God does not curse the man or woman, but he does curse the snake (v. 14) and the ground (here). The man (Hebrew *ʾādām*) and the ground (Hebrew *ʾădāmâ*) are connected by more than similar sound (see 2:7 and note). The cursed ground is no longer in harmony with the man; it does not respond to his desire for food with immediate abundance. Outside the garden, the man and woman will in the future "eat the plants of the field" (v. 18), where "thorns and thistles" (v. 18) threaten to destroy food and require toil. **painful toil.** Uses the same Hebrew noun as in v. 16 (see note there) and includes the accompanying frustration and difficulty of bringing forth a harvest.

3:19 return to the ground. The result of physical death (cf. 2:7). Spiritual death began with the sin of v. 6 (1 Cor 15:22). These judgments on the woman and the man describe how life will be. The world has changed because of sin. While humans rightly do what they can to ameliorate the tragic consequences of the fall, ultimately it is God who will create a new heavens and a new earth (see 1:1 and note).

3:20 Adam names the woman after hearing God's judgment against her (v. 16). **Eve.** The name (Hebrew *ḥawwâ*) suggests the woman's unique role since it sounds like the Hebrew word that means to "give life" (Hebrew *ḥawâ*).

3:21 garments of skin. They protect Adam and Eve in the harsh world outside the garden. They also mark a separation and shame that the loss of innocence has brought. God had to kill some of the animals he created to make these garments. Although this text does not mention forgiveness or blood, as do Levitical texts (e.g., Lev 17:11; see Heb 9:22), it is understandable that many find here an anticipation of animal sacrifices for the forgiveness of sins (Lev 1; 3–7) and even of Christ's sacrifice on the cross.

3:22 The man has now become like one of us. This affirms what the serpent predicted (v. 5). **tree of life.** God judges the couple with death and banishes them from the garden, denying them access to the tree of life, a blessing that God's people receive again in the new creation (cf. 2:9; Rev 2:7; 22:2,14,19).

3:23 banished. The sin's punishment includes removal from God's presence. Thus, sin disrupts the harmony of all parts of creation: between the ground and people, between one person and another, and between God and people. The couple forfeit their special relationship with God.

3:24 east side ... cherubim. This final scene further associates Eden with the later tabernacle and temple, which faced east and contained cherubim. **sword.** It points in every direction so that there is no way to enter the garden. By guarding the garden, the cherubim take on the role that previously had been delegated to the man (2:15).

4:1–26 *Cain and Abel.* The sin that Adam and Eve brought into the world passes on to their son Cain. In ch. 4 it leads to envy and violence that results in the murder of one brother by another. As the generations progress, the violence escalates so that Lamech, the last in Cain's line, commits murder to be avenged 11 times more than his ancestor, Cain.

4:2 Abel. Hebrew *hebel,* meaning "breath" or what passes away without leaving anything significant. It is a commentary on the short life of Abel and his lack of children and heirs.

4:3–5 If there is any hint as to the reason the Lord prefers Abel's sacrifice over Cain's, it may be that Abel offers the "fat portions" (v. 4), considered the best part of animals (Lev 3:16–17) from the "firstborn" (v. 4). Cain offers "some of the fruits of the soil" (v. 3), with no reference to their quality. Heb 11:4 attests to Abel's faith.

Two cherubs guarding a sacred tree, ca. 1400 BC, Cyprus. The author of Genesis uses similar imagery in Gen 3:24.
Z. Radovan/www.BibleLandPictures.com

6Then the LORD said to Cain, "Why are you angry? Why is your face downcast? 7If you do what is
right, will you not be accepted? But if you do not do what is right, sin is crouching at your door;[f] it
desires to have you, but you must rule over it.[g]"
8Now Cain said to his brother Abel, "Let's go out to the field."[a] While they were in the field, Cain
attacked his brother Abel and killed him.[h]
9Then the LORD said to Cain, "Where is your brother Abel?"
"I don't know," he replied. "Am I my brother's keeper?"
10The LORD said, "What have you done? Listen! Your brother's blood cries out to me from the ground.[i]
11Now you are under a curse and driven from the ground, which opened its mouth to receive your
brother's blood from your hand. 12When you work the ground, it will no longer yield its crops for you.
You will be a restless wanderer on the earth."
13Cain said to the LORD, "My punishment is more than I can bear. 14Today you are driving me from
the land, and I will be hidden from your presence;[j] I will be a restless wanderer on the earth, and whoever finds me will kill me."[k]
15But the LORD said to him, "Not so[b]; anyone who kills Cain[l] will suffer vengeance seven times over.[m]"
Then the LORD put a mark on Cain so that no one who found him would kill him. 16So Cain went out
from the LORD's presence and lived in the land of Nod,[c] east of Eden.[n]
17Cain made love to his wife, and she became pregnant and gave birth to Enoch. Cain was then

4:7 [f] Nu 32:23 [g] Ro 6:16
4:8 [h] Mt 23:35; 1Jn 3:12
4:10 [i] Ge 9:5; Nu 35:33; Heb 12:24; Rev 6:9-10
4:14 [j] 2Ki 17:18; Ps 51:11; 139:7-12; Jer 7:15; 52:3 [k] Ge 9:6; Nu 35:19,21,27,33
4:15 [l] Eze 9:4,6 [m] ver 24; Ps 79:12
4:16 [n] Ge 2:8

[a] 8 Samaritan Pentateuch, Septuagint, Vulgate and Syriac; Masoretic Text does not have *"Let's go out to the field."* [b] 15 Septuagint, Vulgate and Syriac; Hebrew *Very well* [c] 16 *Nod* means *wandering* (see verses 12 and 14).

4:7 sin. Named here for the first time in the Bible, it is personified as someone lying in wait for Cain. **it desires to have you, but you must rule over it.** A conflict of wills, just as in 3:16, where the same words and structure appear.
4:8 Sin escalates to one brother murdering another. This first violent act between two people anticipates the increase in violence in Cain's line (vv. 23–24) and the violence that brings the flood in judgment (6:11–13).
4:9 Am I my brother's keeper? Cain's callous and deceptive response contrasts with Adam and Eve's naive and evasive responses (3:10–13).
4:10 blood cries out ... from the ground. The shedding of innocent blood pollutes the ground (Num 35:33–34). **cries out.** Abel represents the first of a long line of faithful people who die and cry out for vengeance (Matt 23:35; Luke 11:51); in contrast, Jesus' innocent blood provides mercy (Heb 12:24).
4:11 under a curse. The Lord curses Cain in relation to the ground (Deut 27:24). **driven from the ground.** Cain has polluted the land and cannot remain there. Adam and Eve were driven from the garden; Cain is driven from all "ground."
4:12,14 restless wanderer. Cain must be on the move and leave nothing that will last.
4:12 it will no longer yield its crops. Cain works the ground (v. 2), so this punishment deprives him of his livelihood (v. 13).
4:14 whoever finds me will kill me. The penalty for murdering the innocent is death (Deut 19:11–13).
4:15 mark. The text does not say what the mark is, but it is readily visible and enables anyone to see that God marked Cain for his safety (see Ezek 9:4 for another protective mark).
4:16 Nod. Means "wandering," from the same Hebrew root in "restless wanderer" (vv. 12,14).
4:17–18 Cain ... Enoch ... Irad ... Mehujael ... Methushael ... Lamech. Together with Adam the genealogy of seven generations symbolizes the completion of the line. As seven symbolizes completeness, here it leads to a completeness of violence in Lamech's poem in vv. 23–24.
4:17 wife. Perhaps Cain's sister. **city.** Could be any settlement.

4:17 [o]Ps 49:11
4:23 [p]Ex 20:13; Lev 19:18
4:24 [q]Dt 32:35 [r]ver 15
4:25 [s]Ge 5:3 [t]ver 8
4:26 [u]Ge 12:8; 1Ki 18:24; Ps 116:17; Joel 2:32; Zep 3:9; Ac 2:21; 1Co 1:2
5:1 [v]Ge 1:27; Eph 4:24; Col 3:10
5:2 [w]Ge 1:27; Mt 19:4; Mk 10:6; Gal 3:28
5:3 [x]Ge 1:26; 1Co 15:49
5:5 [y]Ge 3:19

building a city, and he named it after his son[o] Enoch. 18 To Enoch was born Irad, and Irad was the father
of Mehujael, and Mehujael was the father of Methushael, and Methushael was the father of Lamech.
19 Lamech married two women, one named Adah and the other Zillah. 20 Adah gave birth to Jabal; he
was the father of those who live in tents and raise livestock. 21 His brother's name was Jubal; he was the
father of all who play stringed instruments and pipes. 22 Zillah also had a son, Tubal-Cain, who forged
all kinds of tools out of[a] bronze and iron. Tubal-Cain's sister was Naamah.
23 Lamech said to his wives,

"Adah and Zillah, listen to me;
wives of Lamech, hear my words.
I have killed[p] a man for wounding me,
a young man for injuring me.
24 If Cain is avenged[q] seven times,[r]
then Lamech seventy-seven times."

25 Adam made love to his wife again, and she gave birth to a son and named him Seth,[b][s] saying,
"God has granted me another child in place of Abel, since Cain killed him."[t] 26 Seth also had a son, and
he named him Enosh.
At that time people began to call on[c] the name of the LORD.[u]

From Adam to Noah

5 This is the written account of Adam's family line.

When God created mankind, he made them in the likeness of God.[v] 2 He created them male and female[w] and blessed them. And he named them "Mankind"[d] when they were created.
3 When Adam had lived 130 years, he had a son in his own likeness, in his own image;[x] and he named
him Seth. 4 After Seth was born, Adam lived 800 years and had other sons and daughters. 5 Altogether,
Adam lived a total of 930 years, and then he died.[y]

[a] 22 Or *who instructed all who work in* [b] 25 *Seth* probably means *granted.* [c] 26 Or *to proclaim*
[d] 2 Hebrew *adam*

4:18 Enoch … Irad. May be related to Erech and Eridu, two of the earliest cities in the south of ancient Mesopotamia (modern Iraq).
4:19 married two women. Genesis often mentions polygamy, which tends to end badly for those involved. **Adah … Zillah.** Could mean "ornament" and "cymbal," suggesting the cultural activities in this family history.
4:20–22 tents … livestock … stringed instruments and pipes … tools … bronze and iron. In ancient Mesopotamian lore, there were a group of sages, one for each generation of kings in the age before the flood. They introduce major aspects of human culture. The Bible teaches that these inventors came from the line of Cain. Although their work could be used for good, in this case it seems to have led to greater violence.
4:22 Tubal-Cain. Like his ancestor Cain, his name means "metalsmith," another aspect of civilization (see note on vv. 20–22).
4:23 killed a man for wounding me. This is not the later "eye for eye" of the law (Exod 21:23–25; Lev 24:20; Deut 19:21–22) but is inciting violence.
4:24 seventy-seven times. The anger is spelled out. As God promised sevenfold vengeance for any who tried to kill Cain (v. 15), Lamech's arrogance increases the vengeance another ten times in addition to the first seven. Cf. Matt 18:22, where Jesus transforms vengeance into forgiveness and uses the same number for how many times one must forgive.
4:25 Seth. The word sounds like the Hebrew of "granted" in the phrase "granted me another child in place of Abel." In chs. 4–5, two lines of descendants are contrasted—one negative, the other positive. One is associated with violence, which links with the reason for the flood. The other leads to Noah. The positive comments associated with the birth of Seth—another seed in place of Abel—suggest some connection with the seed of the woman (see 3:15 and note).
4:26 Enosh. Hebrew for "man," similar to a meaning of Adam. God provides a new line of hope. **call on the name of the LORD.** An expression used elsewhere for prayer (12:8; 26:25; 1 Kgs 18:24; 2 Kgs 5:11; Joel 2:32).
5:1–32 *From Adam to Noah.* In contrast with the line of Cain (4:17–24), the regularity of Seth's line, its positive notes of God's blessing—Enoch (vv. 21–24) and Lamech (vv. 28–31)—and its extension beyond the seventh generation to Noah identify this as the line of hope.
5:1 account. See note on 2:4. These headings structure Genesis (2:4; here; 6:9; 10:1; 11:10,27; 25:12,19; 36:1,9; 37:2). **the likeness of God.** This reaffirms the presence of God's image in humanity (see 1:26–28 and note on 1:26), despite the sin that has taken place since humanity's creation. It anticipates 9:6, which expands the sense of the image of God.
5:2–3 Mankind … Adam. "Mankind" and "Adam" translate the same Hebrew word (*ʾādām*). See note on 1:26.
5:5 930 years. Adam's life span and the life spans of others mentioned in this line far exceed today's human life span. Whether the long life spans are literal or serve a literary purpose, or both, the life spans of Enoch and Lamech may be symbolic (see notes on vv. 23,31). The ten names in this genealogy may suggest a selection of the line as in ch. 11 (cf. Luke 3:36, where the name Cainan is added to the line in Gen 11). Three kings listed in the Sumerian King List as ruling before the flood have reigns that add up to 72,000 years, and thus exaggerate these numbers. The connection with the line of hope (and not with Cain's line) suggests that God's blessing was on this line.

6 When Seth had lived 105 years, he became the father[a] of Enosh. 7 After he became the father of
Enosh, Seth lived 807 years and had other sons and daughters. 8 Altogether, Seth lived a total of 912
years, and then he died.
9 When Enosh had lived 90 years, he became the father of Kenan. 10 After he became the father of
Kenan, Enosh lived 815 years and had other sons and daughters. 11 Altogether, Enosh lived a total of
905 years, and then he died.
12 When Kenan had lived 70 years, he became the father of Mahalalel. 13 After he became the father
of Mahalalel, Kenan lived 840 years and had other sons and daughters. 14 Altogether, Kenan lived a total
of 910 years, and then he died.
15 When Mahalalel had lived 65 years, he became the father of Jared. 16 After
he became the father of Jared, Mahalalel lived 830 years and had other sons
and daughters. 17 Altogether, Mahalalel lived a total of 895 years, and then
he died.
18 When Jared had lived 162 years, he became the father of Enoch.[z] 19 After
he became the father of Enoch, Jared lived 800 years and had other sons and
daughters. 20 Altogether, Jared lived a total of 962 years, and then he died.
21 When Enoch had lived 65 years, he became the father of Methuselah. 22 After he became the father of Methuselah, Enoch walked faithfully with God[a] 300
years and had other sons and daughters. 23 Altogether, Enoch lived a total of
365 years. 24 Enoch walked faithfully with God;[b] then he was no more, because
God took him away.[c]
25 When Methuselah had lived 187 years, he became the father of Lamech.
26 After he became the father of Lamech, Methuselah lived 782 years and had
other sons and daughters. 27 Altogether, Methuselah lived a total of 969 years,
and then he died.
28 When Lamech had lived 182 years, he had a son. 29 He named him Noah[b]
and said, "He will comfort us in the labor and painful toil of our hands caused
by the ground the LORD has cursed.[d]" 30 After Noah was born, Lamech lived 595
years and had other sons and daughters. 31 Altogether, Lamech lived a total of
777 years, and then he died.
32 After Noah was 500 years old, he became the father of Shem, Ham and
Japheth.

Wickedness in the World

6 When human beings began to increase in number on the earth[e] and daughters were born to them, 2 the sons of God saw that the daughters of humans

[a] *6 Father* may mean *ancestor*; also in verses 7-26. [b] *29 Noah* sounds like the Hebrew for *comfort.*

5:18 [z] Jude 1:14
5:22 [a] ver 24; Ge 6:9; 17:1; 48:15; Mic 6:8; Mal 2:6
5:24 [b] ver 22 [c] 2Ki 2:1, 11; Heb 11:5
5:29 [d] Ge 3:17; Ro 8:20
6:1 [e] Ge 1:28

Sumerian King List, ca. 1800 BC, records kings who reigned tens of thousands of years "Before the Flood." Gen 5 also records ancient ancestors.

Sumerian King List giving rulers from 'before the Flood' to King Sin-magir of Isin (ca.1827 – 17 BC) inscribed in cuneiform script, probably from Larsa, Iraq, Sumerian/ Ashmolean Museum, University of Oxford, UK/Bridgeman Images

5:9 Kenan. Means "little Cain."

5:12 Mahalalel. Means "praising God."

5:15 Jared. Means "(God) has descended (from heaven)." This name given at birth may confess God's aid in a safe delivery.

5:18 Enoch. Means "dedicate; dedication."

5:21 Methuselah. Means perhaps "man/devotee of the spear/missile."

5:23 365 years. There are also 365 days in a solar year. Enoch became famous for his faithfulness to God and as one who knew much about God (Jude 14–15).

5:24 God took him. The seventh from Adam does not die like the others (cf. the seventh day of creation [2:2–3], which does not end like the other six days). Enoch's acceptance by God gives hope to his contemporaries as well as those who read this account.

5:25 Lamech. Meaning unknown. Like the Lamech of Cain's line, this Lamech brings the genealogy to an end with a statement. Whereas Cain's Lamech looks backward and stresses vengeance and violence (4:23–24), this Lamech looks forward to one who will bring "comfort" (5:29), which in Hebrew sounds like "Noah."

5:27 969 years. Methuselah, the longest living person in the Bible, dies in the year of the flood (see 5:25,28; 7:6, where 187 + 182 + 600 = 969).

5:31 777 years. This lifespan, composed of the number "7," symbolizes a perfect and complete number of years.

6:1–8 *Wickedness in the World.* Violence continues to grow (cf. ch. 4) and leads to continual thoughts and acts of evil that bring God's judgment on the world.

6:1 increase. Humans continue to "increase in number" as God commanded (1:28), but they are corrupt.

6:2 sons of God. Four options explain this phrase: (1) They are angels. This is what the phrase refers to elsewhere in the OT (see Job 1:6; 2:1; 38:7 and NIV text notes; cf. Pss 29:1; 89:6) except for a related expression in Hos 1:10. Mark 12:25 may suggest that angels do not marry, but

6:3 [f]Isa 57:16 [g]Ps 78:39
6:4 [h]Nu 13:33
6:5 [i]Ge 8:21; Ps 14:1-3
6:6 [j]1Sa 15:11,35; Isa 63:10
6:8 [k]Ge 19:19; Ex 33:12, 13,17; Lk 1:30; Ac 7:46
6:9 [l]Ge 7:1; Eze 14:14, 20; Heb 11:7; 2Pe 2:5 [m]Ge 5:22
6:10 [n]Ge 5:32
6:11 [o]Eze 7:23; 8:17
6:12 [p]Ps 14:1-3
6:13 [q]ver 17; Eze 7:2-3
6:14 [r]Heb 11:7; 1Pe 3:20 [s]Ex 2:3

were beautiful, and they married any of them they chose. 3Then the LORD said, "My Spirit will not contend
with[a] humans forever,[f] for they are mortal[b];[g] their days will be a hundred and twenty years."
4The Nephilim[h] were on the earth in those days—and also afterward—when the sons of God went
to the daughters of humans and had children by them. They were the heroes of old, men of renown.
5The LORD saw how great the wickedness of the human race had become on the earth, and that
every inclination of the thoughts of the human heart was only evil all the time.[i] 6The LORD regretted[j]
that he had made human beings on the earth, and his heart was deeply troubled. 7So the LORD said, "I
will wipe from the face of the earth the human race I have created—and with them the animals, the
birds and the creatures that move along the ground—for I regret that I have made them." 8But Noah
found favor in the eyes of the LORD.[k]

Noah and the Flood

9This is the account of Noah and his family.

Noah was a righteous man, blameless among the people of his time,[l] and he walked faithfully with
God.[m] 10Noah had three sons: Shem, Ham and Japheth.[n]
11Now the earth was corrupt in God's sight and was full of violence.[o] 12God saw how corrupt the earth
had become, for all the people on earth had corrupted their ways.[p] 13So God said to Noah, "I am going
to put an end to all people, for the earth is filled with violence because of them. I am surely going to
destroy both them and the earth.[q] 14So make yourself an ark of cypress[c] wood;[r] make rooms in it and
coat it with pitch[s] inside and out. 15This is how you are to build it: The ark is to be three hundred cubits

[a] *3* Or *My spirit will not remain in* [b] *3* Or *corrupt* [c] *14* The meaning of the Hebrew for this word is uncertain.

Mark 12 refers to angels who are in heaven fulfilling their roles, not in a fallen state. (Compare 2 Pet 2:4–5, Jude 5–6, and the tradition of these angels as "Watchers" in some strands of Judaism.) (2) They are sons of Cain. But given how ch. 4 describes them, it is surprising that they would be called "sons of God." (3) They are sons of Seth. (4) They are otherwise unknown kings. But why call them "sons of God"? Some commentators combine two or more explanations.

6:3 a hundred and twenty years. God limits the life span of humans because of their increasing sin and increasing numbers so that they cannot do more violence. If Abraham lived 175 years (25:7) and Isaac lived 180 years (35:28), how can this statement be true? Either it describes the number of years remaining to the flood and the destruction of all of that sinful generation or it is a general observation about human life spans (and not true in every case).

6:4 Nephilim. The Hebrew word means "fallen ones." They also appear much later (Num 13:33). They are not an ethnic group but a social group of warriors, usually past "heroes" of legendary power. Here they illustrate the extent of violence in the world.

6:5 This concisely describes total depravity, which continues after the flood (8:21).

6:6 regretted. Does sin cause God to change his mind? Elsewhere the answer is no (Mal 3:6; Heb 6:17; Jas 1:17). Yet some passages suggest the opposite (1 Sam 15:11 [but see v. 29]; Jonah 3:10). God is involved personally with humanity. While his final purpose for humanity does not change, his means to carry that purpose forward may.

6:8 Ezekiel twice mentions Noah first in a list of righteous men who, despite the enormity of their merit, could not prevent the city of Jerusalem from facing judgment (Ezek 14:14,20). **favor.** Of the dozens of times that the Bible mentions favor or grace, this is the first (see "Love and Grace," p. 2684). Noah represents the minority who remain righteous despite evil all around; he was the first, but not the last. It is this small group of believers that God calls out in each generation—Abram (Gen 12:1–3), Israel (Exod 1–19), faithful exiles (2 Kgs 19; Isa 10:20–22)—until the coming of Christ, who though abandoned by his disciples remains faithful to death.

6:9—8:22 *Noah and the Flood.* The story of the flood has many parallels with ancient Babylonian accounts. Agreement in details (e.g., a single man and his family rescued, a window, birds sent from the ark, the sequence in a larger narrative) make coincidence unlikely to explain the relationship. There was a memory of a great flood, but the reasoning for it in the fictional stories of Babylonia have to do with divine decisions to deal with too much human noise and overpopulation. In contrast, the biblical account connects the flood with God's judgment for sin, especially violence. In some ways the flood story resembles the opening account of creation and may be viewed as a re-creation of the earth after it has been cleansed from the defilement of human sin.

6:9–22 Righteous Noah (v. 9; 7:1) explicitly obeys God's detailed commands (6:22). He saves his family through faith and is heir to the righteousness that comes by faith (Heb 11:7).

6:9–10 account. This "account" of Noah and his sons and all their families as they survive the flood signals an important new unit in Genesis by describing a major event rather than listing a genealogy.

6:11 violence. The fundamental nature of harmful and destructive corruption (cf. 9:6).

Artistic representation of the size of the ark (see Gen 6:15).

long, fifty cubits wide and thirty cubits high.[a] 16Make a roof for it, leaving below the roof an opening
one cubit[b] high all around.[c] Put a door in the side of the ark and make lower, middle and upper decks.
17I am going to bring floodwaters on the earth to destroy all life under the heavens, every creature that
has the breath of life in it. Everything on earth will perish.[t] 18But I will establish my covenant with
you,[u] and you will enter the ark[v]—you and your sons and your wife and your sons' wives with you.
19You are to bring into the ark two of all living creatures, male and female, to keep them alive with you.
20Two[w] of every kind of bird, of every kind of animal and of every kind of creature that moves along
the ground will come to you to be kept alive. 21You are to take every kind of food that is to be eaten and
store it away as food for you and for them."

22Noah did everything just as God commanded him.[x]

7 The LORD then said to Noah, "Go into the ark, you and your whole family,[y] because I have found
you righteous[z] in this generation. 2Take with you seven pairs of every kind of clean[a] animal, a
male and its mate, and one pair of every kind of unclean animal, a male and its mate, 3and also seven
pairs of every kind of bird, male and female, to keep their various kinds alive throughout the earth.
4Seven days from now I will send rain on the earth for forty days and forty nights, and I will wipe from
the face of the earth every living creature I have made."

5And Noah did all that the LORD commanded him.[b]

6Noah was six hundred years old when the floodwaters came on the earth. 7And Noah and his sons
and his wife and his sons' wives entered the ark to escape the waters of the flood. 8Pairs of clean and
unclean animals, of birds and of all creatures that move along the ground, 9male and female, came
to Noah and entered the ark, as God had commanded Noah. 10And after the seven days the floodwaters
came on the earth.

11In the six hundredth year of Noah's life, on the seventeenth day of the second month—on that
day all the springs of the great deep[c] burst forth, and the floodgates of the heavens[d] were opened. 12And
rain fell on the earth forty days and forty nights.[e]

13On that very day Noah and his sons, Shem, Ham and Japheth, together with his wife and the wives
of his three sons, entered the ark. 14They had with them every wild animal according to its kind, all
livestock according to their kinds, every creature that moves along the ground according to its kind and
every bird according to its kind, everything with wings. 15Pairs of all creatures that have the breath of
life in them came to Noah and entered the ark.[f] 16The animals going in were male and female of every
living thing, as God had commanded Noah. Then the LORD shut him in.

17For forty days[g] the flood kept coming on the earth, and as the waters increased they lifted the ark
high above the earth. 18The waters rose and increased greatly on the earth, and the ark floated on the
surface of the water. 19They rose greatly on the earth, and all the high mountains under the entire

6:17 [t] Ge 7:4,21-23; 2Pe 2:5
6:18 [u] Ge 9:9-16 [v] Ge 7:1, 7,13
6:20 [w] Ge 7:15
6:22 [x] Ge 7:5,9,16
7:1 [y] Mt 24:38 [z] Ge 6:9; Eze 14:14
7:2 [a] ver 8; Ge 8:20; Lev 10:10; 11:1-47
7:5 [b] Ge 6:22
7:11 [c] Eze 26:19 [d] Ge 8:2
7:12 [e] ver 4
7:15 [f] Ge 6:19
7:17 [g] ver 4

a 15 That is, about 450 feet long, 75 feet wide and 45 feet high or about 135 meters long, 23 meters wide and 14 meters high *b 16* That is, about 18 inches or about 45 centimeters *c 16* The meaning of the Hebrew for this clause is uncertain.

6:15 Noah would build a rectangular ark, six times longer than it was wide and ten times longer than it was high. Estimates suggest that all the land animals could be accommodated in the ark with more than half of it remaining for other uses.

6:18 covenant. Hebrew *bĕrît*. This is its first occurrence in the Bible. God here prophesies the covenant of 9:8–17. As with the later covenants, God promises salvation and preservation. See "Covenant," p. 2646.

6:22 did everything just as God commanded him. Noah models perfect obedience (7:5).

7:2 seven pairs ... clean ... one pair ... unclean. The additional clean animals might be used for sacrifice (8:20) or food (9:2–4). Although details about clean and unclean animals occur later (Lev 11; Deut 14), there was early awareness of the correct animals for proper sacrifices (Gen 22:13).

7:4 forty days and forty nights. Forty years characterizes a generation of wilderness wandering (Num 14:33–34; 32:13) and rulership over Israel (David, 2 Sam 5:4; Solomon, 1 Kgs 11:42; cf. Judg 3:11; 5:31; 8:28; 1 Sam 4:18; 2 Kgs 12:1), and forty days characterizes important events like the reception of the law (Deut 9:11) and the temptation of Jesus (Matt 4:2).

7:11 In the six hundredth year. The numbers identify when key events occur. The general chronology continues a theme already mentioned in 1:1—2:4 (see Introduction: Structure, 3; see also note on 2:4) that the same God who created and worked in each generation (including Noah's) continues to work today for creative and redemptive purposes.

7:16 the LORD shut him in. The security of Noah and his family within the Lord's provision contrasts with the danger faced by those outside.

7:19 all the high mountains ... were covered. If this includes Mount Ararat (in the Urartian mountain range in eastern Turkey), then the waters need to rise above 16,854 feet (5,137 meters). A natural reading suggests a global flood, and some find this in 2 Pet 2:5; 3:6. The reference may also imply a regional flood (nevertheless possessing tremendous severity) with impact affecting the whole human race, who may have remained in one area (Gen 11:1–9). In 41:57, "all the world" refers to the eastern Mediterranean lands, so in chs. 6–8 the flood may have covered only the part of the earth where people lived.

7:19 [h]Ps 104:6
7:21 [i]Ge 6:7,13
7:22 [j]Ge 1:30
7:23 [k]Mt 24:39; Lk 17:27; 1Pe 3:20; 2Pe 2:5 [l]Heb 11:7
7:24 [m]Ge 8:3
8:1 [n]Ge 9:15; 19:29; Ex 2:24; 1Sa 1:11,19 [o]Ex 14:21
8:2 [p]Ge 7:11

heavens were covered.[h] 20The waters rose and covered the mountains to a depth of more than fifteen
cubits.[a,b] 21Every living thing that moved on land perished—birds, livestock, wild animals, all the
creatures that swarm over the earth, and all mankind.[i] 22Everything on dry land that had the breath of
life[j] in its nostrils died. 23Every living thing on the face of the earth was wiped out; people and animals
and the creatures that move along the ground and the birds were wiped from the earth.[k] Only Noah
was left, and those with him in the ark.[l]

24The waters flooded the earth for a hundred and fifty days.[m]

8 But God remembered[n] Noah and all the wild animals and the livestock that were with him in the
ark, and he sent a wind over the earth,[o] and the waters receded. 2Now the springs of the deep and
the floodgates of the heavens[p] had been closed, and the rain had stopped falling from the sky. 3The water receded steadily from the earth. At the end of the hundred and fifty days the water had gone down,
4and on the seventeenth day of the seventh month the ark came to rest on the mountains of Ararat.
5The waters continued to recede until the tenth month, and on the first day of the tenth month the tops
of the mountains became visible.

6After forty days Noah opened a window he had made in the ark 7and sent out a raven, and it kept
flying back and forth until the water had dried up from the earth. 8Then he sent out a dove to see if the
water had receded from the surface of the ground. 9But the dove could find nowhere to perch because
there was water over all the surface of the earth; so it returned to Noah in the ark. He reached out his
hand and took the dove and brought it back to himself in the ark. 10He waited seven more days and
again sent out the dove from the ark. 11When the dove returned to him in the evening, there in its beak
was a freshly plucked olive leaf! Then Noah knew that the water had receded from the earth. 12He
waited seven more days and sent the dove out again, but this time it did not return to him.

[a] *20* That is, about 23 feet or about 6.8 meters [b] *20* Or *rose more than fifteen cubits, and the mountains were covered*

7:23 Every living thing. Foreshadows the coming judgment of the cosmos by fire in 2 Pet 3:6–7.
7:24 a hundred and fifty days. Identical to 8:3. Rain comes in the first forty days (7:4,17), and the mountain tops become visible during the final forty days (8:5).
8:1 But God remembered Noah. At this turning point in the flood is the first use of the verb "remember." When God remembers, he acts for judgment (Rev 16:19) or blessing (Gen 30:22; 1 Sam 1:19–20). Here he saves faithful Noah and those with him. Judgment is over and a new creation lies ahead. **wind.** See note on 1:2.
8:4 mountains of Ararat. Mountain range in modern eastern Turkey. Today Mount Ararat is the highest peak, but the wording of the text refers to the range.

CHRONOLOGY OF NOAH'S TIME IN THE ARK

Dates are in the form of month, day, and Noah's year, as given in the text. Hence, 2/10/600 means the tenth day of the second month in Noah's 600th year. Months are calculated at 30 days each. Dates in parentheses are extrapolations from dates explicitly given in the text.

	REFERENCE	EVENT	DATE
Waters prevail: 150-day period	7:7,9,13	Noah, family, and animals enter ark	(2/10/600)
	7:10–11	Flood begins	2/17/600
	7:12	40 days of rain	(3/27/600)
	8:3–4	Waters present 150 days until ark rests on dry ground	7/17/600
Waters abate: 150-day period	8:5	Mountaintops visible	10/1/600
	8:6–7	Raven sent out 40 days later	(11/10/600)
	8:8	Dove sent out	(11/17/600)
	8:10	Dove's second flight	(11/24/600)
	8:12	Dove does not return	(12/1/600)
	8:3	Waters fully abated after 150 days	(12/17/600)
Earth dries: 70-day period	8:13	Noah opens the ark	1/1/601
	8:14–19	Earth dried out; Noah leaves ark	2/27/601
Total time in ark: 370 days			

13By the first day of the first month of Noah's six hundred and first year, the water had dried up from
the earth. Noah then removed the covering from the ark and saw that the surface of the ground was dry.
14By the twenty-seventh day of the second month the earth was completely dry.
15Then God said to Noah, 16"Come out of the ark, you and your wife and your sons and their wives.[q]
17Bring out every kind of living creature that is with you—the birds, the animals, and all the creatures that move along the ground—so they can multiply on the earth and be fruitful and increase
in number on it."[r]
18So Noah came out, together with his sons and his wife and his sons' wives. 19All the animals and all
the creatures that move along the ground and all the birds—everything that moves on land—came
out of the ark, one kind after another.
20Then Noah built an altar to the LORD[s] and, taking some of all the clean animals and clean[t] birds,
he sacrificed burnt offerings[u] on it. 21The LORD smelled the pleasing aroma[v] and said in his heart:
"Never again will I curse the ground[w] because of humans, even though[a] every inclination of the human heart is evil from childhood.[x] And never again will I destroy all living creatures,[y] as I have done.

22"As long as the earth endures,
seedtime and harvest,
cold and heat,
summer and winter,
day and night
will never cease."[z]

God's Covenant With Noah

9 Then God blessed Noah and his sons, saying to them, "Be fruitful and increase in number and fill
the earth.[a] 2The fear and dread of you will fall on all the beasts of the earth, and on all the birds
in the sky, on every creature that moves along the ground, and on all the fish in the sea; they are given
into your hands. 3Everything that lives and moves about will be food for you.[b] Just as I gave you the
green plants, I now give you everything.
4"But you must not eat meat that has its lifeblood still in it.[c] 5And for your lifeblood I will surely demand an accounting. I will demand an accounting from every animal.[d] And from each human being,
too, I will demand an accounting for the life of another human being.[e]

6"Whoever sheds human blood,
by humans shall their blood be shed;[f]
for in the image of God[g]
has God made mankind.

8:16 [q] Ge 7:13
8:17 [r] Ge 1:22
8:20 [s] Ge 12:7-8; 13:18; 22:9 [t] Ge 7:8; Lev 11:1-47 [u] Ge 22:2, 13; Ex 10:25
8:21 [v] Lev 1:9,13; 2Co 2:15 [w] Ge 3:17 [x] Ge 6:5; Ps 51:5; Jer 17:9 [y] Ge 9:11,15; Isa 54:9
8:22 [z] Ge 1:14; Jer 33:20,25
9:1 [a] Ge 1:22
9:3 [b] Ge 1:29
9:4 [c] Lev 3:17; 17:10-14; Dt 12:16,23-25; 1Sa 14:33
9:5 [d] Ex 21:28-32 [e] Ge 4:10
9:6 [f] Ge 4:14; Ex 21:12, 14; Lev 24:17; Mt 26:52 [g] Ge 1:26

[a] 21 Or *humans, for*

8:17 multiply ... be fruitful and increase. See 1:22,28, where God gave this command to animals and humans after creating them. God repeats it here as a new world begins, with the land having been cleansed from the defilement caused by the spilling of blood due to human violence.

8:20 altar. Almost always a place of animal sacrifice (though later some altars were used to burn incense).

8:21 Never again will I curse the ground. This promise may refer to the flood, or it may fulfill Lamech's promise that Noah would bring relief from the toil caused by the cursed ground (5:29). The effects of the curse (weeds and thistles, 3:18) remain, but for Noah, a man of the ground (9:20), the soil is productive. **evil from childhood.** God frankly acknowledges the human condition that will not be remedied by this judgment. **as I have done.** God will not again destroy life on earth by a flood, but he will continue to judge people (Matt 24:37–39; Luke 17:27–29), and he will move forward his plan of redemption for all (Gen 12:1–3).

8:22 This beautiful poem of promise launches the new world.

9:1–17 *God's Covenant With Noah.* God's salvation of Noah leads to the command to preserve human life and not destroy people who are created in God's image. The sign of the covenant is the rainbow, by which God's promise is guaranteed.

9:1,7 Be fruitful and increase. See note on 8:17. This command is an "envelope" because the paragraph begins and ends with it.

9:3 food. The first explicit statement of a carnivorous diet. Although the olive leaf (8:11) signifies the return of agricultural life, it cannot provide Noah's children with sufficient food, especially in the first months after departing from the ark, when the harvest season has not yet begun (8:22).

9:4,5 lifeblood. Blood is the God-given sign of life (Lev 17:11). God forbids his people to eat blood as a way of recognizing that life belongs to him (Lev 17:10–14). This remains a regulation through the OT and into the NT (Acts 15:20).

9:5 I will demand an accounting. God will hold responsible "each human being" who takes the life of another.

9:6 by humans shall their blood be shed. In the context of the law, God bans the vendetta and commands death for shedding innocent blood (Exod 21:12–13; Deut 21:1–9) while recognizing different levels

9:7 [h]Ge 1:22
9:9 [i]Ge 6:18
9:11 [j]ver 16; Isa 24:5 [k]Ge 8:21; Isa 54:9
9:12 [l]ver 17; Ge 17:11
9:15 [m]Ex 2:24; Lev 26:42,45; Dt 7:9; Eze 16:60
9:16 [n]ver 11; Ge 17:7, 13,19; 2Sa 7:13; 23:5
9:17 [o]ver 12; Ge 17:11
9:18 [p]ver 25-27; Ge 10:6,15
9:19 [q]Ge 10:32
9:25 [r]ver 18 [s]Ge 25:23; Jos 9:23

7 As for you, be fruitful and increase in number; multiply on the earth and increase upon it."[h]
8 Then God said to Noah and to his sons with him: 9 "I now establish my covenant with you[i] and with
your descendants after you 10 and with every living creature that was with you — the birds, the livestock
and all the wild animals, all those that came out of the ark with you — every living creature on earth.
11 I establish my covenant[j] with you: Never again will all life be destroyed by the waters of a flood; never
again will there be a flood to destroy the earth.[k]"
12 And God said, "This is the sign of the covenant[l] I am making between me and you and every living
creature with you, a covenant for all generations to come: 13 I have set my rainbow in the clouds, and
it will be the sign of the covenant between me and the earth. 14 Whenever I bring clouds over the earth
and the rainbow appears in the clouds, 15 I will remember my covenant[m] between me and you and all
living creatures of every kind. Never again will the waters become a flood to destroy all life. 16 Whenever
the rainbow appears in the clouds, I will see it and remember the everlasting covenant[n] between God
and all living creatures of every kind on the earth."
17 So God said to Noah, "This is the sign of the covenant[o] I have established between me and all life
on the earth."

The Sons of Noah

18 The sons of Noah who came out of the ark were Shem, Ham and Japheth. (Ham was the father of
Canaan.)[p] 19 These were the three sons of Noah, and from them came the people who were scattered
over the whole earth.[q]
20 Noah, a man of the soil, proceeded[a] to plant a vineyard. 21 When he drank some of its wine, he became drunk and lay uncovered inside his tent. 22 Ham, the father of Canaan, saw his father naked and
told his two brothers outside. 23 But Shem and Japheth took a garment and laid it across their shoulders;
then they walked in backward and covered their father's naked body. Their faces were turned the other
way so that they would not see their father naked.
24 When Noah awoke from his wine and found out what his youngest son had done to him, 25 he said,

"Cursed be Canaan![r]
  The lowest of slaves
  will he be to his brothers.[s]"

26 He also said,

"Praise be to the LORD, the God of Shem!
  May Canaan be the slave of Shem.

[a] 20 Or *soil, was the first*

of intention in planning a murder and adjusting the punishment accordingly. **in the image of God.** See note on 1:26. Because human beings are formed in God's image, human life is so valuable that taking innocent life can only be paid for by the life of the one who took it in the first place.
9:9,11 my covenant. The new world after the flood is characterized by covenants (6:18; see "Covenant," p. 2646). This covenant is for all of Noah's family, that is, for all the world (9:19; 10:1–32).
9:10 and with every living creature. This is God's only OT covenant with the animal kingdom.
9:11 Never again. This repeats the promise of 8:21–22 in the context of a covenant.
9:12–13 sign ... rainbow. Every major covenant that God makes in the Pentateuch has a sign: Abraham's covenant has circumcision (ch. 17) and Israel's covenant has the Sabbath (Exod 20:8–11; 31:13,17; Deut 5:12–15). The sign assures us that God remembers his covenant (see note on 8:1) and acts on our behalf.
9:16 This verse ends the paragraph (vv. 12–16) as it begins, with an "envelope" emphasizing the sign and the parties involved — God and all life. See vv. 1–7 and note on 9:1,7.
9:18–29 *The Sons of Noah.* Even one so righteous as Noah (6:9) is subject to the temptations of sin. The sin of Noah's son Ham and the acts of Ham's brothers to preserve Noah's honor lead to a prophecy about the descendants of Noah's three sons.
9:18 Ham was the father of Canaan. This anticipates Canaan's coming role in the curse of vv. 25–27 and in the subsequent condemnation of the Canaanites (15:16–21; Deut 20:17).
9:21 he became drunk and lay uncovered. As in 19:30–38, drunkenness is connected with sexual immorality.
9:22 saw his father naked. The curse (v. 25) suggests that Ham does more than see his father naked. "Uncover the nakedness" refers to dishonoring a close relative by having incestuous relations, which God condemns (Lev 18:6–18; 20:11–12,17,19–21). This text and the events in this passage are extremely difficult to interpret.
9:23 covered. Shem and Japheth's action respects their father.
9:25 Cursed be Canaan! Why does Noah single out Canaan rather than Canaan's father, Ham? There are various views. If Canaan is the fruit of some sort of sexual immorality, Noah could have cursed this symbol of his shame. This also may anticipate the future role of the Canaanites under Joshua and under David and Solomon.
9:26 the LORD, the God of Shem. Shem's line leads to Abram (11:10–26) and ultimately to Jesus Christ (Matt 1:1).

MAJOR COVENANTS IN THE OLD TESTAMENT

COVENANTS	REFERENCE	TYPE	PARTICIPANT	DESCRIPTION
NOAHIC	Gen 9:8–17	Royal Grant	Made with righteous (6:9) Noah and his descendants and every living thing on earth—all life that is subject to human jurisdiction	An unconditional divine promise never to destroy all earthly life with some natural catastrophe, the covenant "sign" (9:13,17) being the rainbow in the storm cloud
ABRAHAMIC A	Gen 15:6–21	Royal (land) Grant	Made with "righteous" Abram (his faith was "credited … to him as righteousness," v. 6) and his descendants, v. 16	An unconditional divine promise to fulfill the grant of the land; a self-maledictory oath symbolically enacted it (15:18; see note on vv. 18–21)
ABRAHAMIC B	Gen 17	Suzerain-vassal	Made with Abraham as patriarchal head of his household	A conditional divine pledge to be Abraham's God and the God of his descendants (cf. "as for me," v. 4; "as for you," v. 9); the condition: total consecration to the Lord as symbolized by circumcision
SINAITIC	Exod 19–24	Suzerain-vassal	Made with Israel as the descendants of Abraham, Isaac and Jacob, and as the people the Lord had redeemed from bondage to an earthly power	A conditional divine pledge to be Israel's God (as its protector and the guarantor of its blessed destiny); the condition: Israel's total consecration to the Lord as his people (his kingdom) who live by his rule and serve his purposes in history
PHINEHAS	Num 25:10–13	Royal Grant	Made with the zealous priest Phinehas	An unconditional divine promise to maintain the family of Phinehas in a "lasting priesthood" (v. 13; implicitly a pledge to Israel to provide it forever with a faithful priesthood)
DAVIDIC	2 Sam 7:5–16	Royal Grant	Made with faithful King David after his devotion to God as Israel's king and the Lord's anointed vassal had come to special expression (v. 2)	An unconditional divine promise to establish and maintain the Davidic dynasty on the throne of Israel (implicitly a pledge to Israel) to provide it forever with a godly king like David and through that dynasty to do for it what he had done through David—bring it into rest in the promised land (1 Kgs 4:20–21; 5:3–4)
NEW	Jer 31:31–34	Royal Grant	Promised to rebellious Israel as it is about to be expelled from the promised land in actualization of the most severe covenant curse (Lev 26:27–39; Deut 28:36–37, 45–68)	An unconditional divine promise to unfaithful Israel to forgive it sins and establish his relationship with it on a new basis by writing his law "on their hearts" (v. 33)—a covenant of pure grace

MAJOR TYPES OF ROYAL COVENANTS/TREATIES IN THE ANCIENT NEAR EAST

ROYAL GRANT (UNCONDITIONAL)	PARITY	SUZERAIN-VASSAL (CONDITIONAL)
A king's grant (of land or some other benefit) to a loyal servant for faithful or exceptional service. The grant was normally perpetual and unconditional, but the servant's heirs benefited from it only as they continued in their father's loyalty and service. (Cf. 1 Sam 8:14; 22:7; 27:6; Esth 8:1.)	A covenant between equals, binding them to mutual friendship or at least to mutual respect for each other's spheres and interests. Participants called each other "brother." (Cf. Gen 21:27; 26:31; 31:44–54; 1 Kgs 5:12; 15:19; 20:32–34; Amos 1:9.)	A covenant regulating the relationship between a great king and one of his subject kings. The great king claimed absolute right of sovereignty, demanded total loyalty and service (the vassal must "love" his suzerain) and pledged protection of the subject's realm and dynasty, conditional on the vassal's faithfulness and loyalty to him. The vassal pledged absolute loyalty to his suzerain—whatever service his suzerain demanded—and exclusive reliance on the suzerain's protection. Participants called each other "lord" and "servant" or "father" and "son." (Cf. Josh 9:6,8; Ezek 17:13–18; Hos 12:1.)

Commitments made in these covenants were accompanied by self-maledictory oaths (made orally, ceremonially, or both). The gods were called upon to witness the covenants and implement the curses of the oaths if the covenants were violated.

10:1 [t]Ge 2:4
10:2 [u]Eze 38:6
[v]Eze 38:2; Rev 20:8
[w]Isa 66:19
10:3 [x]Jer 51:27
[y]Eze 27:14; 38:6
10:4 [z]Eze 27:12,25;
Jnh 1:3
10:6 [a]ver 15; Ge 9:18

27 May God extend Japheth's[a] territory;
may Japheth live in the tents of Shem,
and may Canaan be the slave of Japheth."

28 After the flood Noah lived 350 years. 29 Noah lived a total of 950 years, and then he died.

The Table of Nations

10 This is the account[t] of Shem, Ham and Japheth, Noah's sons, who themselves had sons after the flood.

The Japhethites

10:2-5pp — 1Ch 1:5-7

2 The sons[b] of Japheth:
Gomer,[u] Magog,[v] Madai, Javan, Tubal,[w] Meshek and Tiras.
3 The sons of Gomer:
Ashkenaz,[x] Riphath and Togarmah.[y]
4 The sons of Javan:
Elishah, Tarshish,[z] the Kittites and the Rodanites.[c] 5 (From these the maritime peoples spread
out into their territories by their clans within their nations, each with its own language.)

The Hamites

10:6-20pp — 1Ch 1:8-16

6 The sons of Ham:
Cush, Egypt, Put and Canaan.[a]
7 The sons of Cush:
Seba, Havilah, Sabtah, Raamah and Sabteka.
The sons of Raamah:
Sheba and Dedan.

8 Cush was the father[d] of Nimrod, who became a mighty warrior on the earth. 9 He was a mighty
hunter before the LORD; that is why it is said, "Like Nimrod, a mighty hunter before the LORD."

[a] *27 Japheth* sounds like the Hebrew for *extend.* [b] *2 Sons* may mean *descendants* or *successors* or *nations*; also in verses 3, 4, 6, 7, 20-23, 29 and 31. [c] *4* Some manuscripts of the Masoretic Text and Samaritan Pentateuch (see also Septuagint and 1 Chron. 1:7); most manuscripts of the Masoretic Text *Dodanites*
[d] *8 Father* may mean *ancestor* or *predecessor* or *founder*; also in verses 13, 15, 24 and 26.

9:27 extend Japheth's territory. Japheth in Hebrew means "to (cause to) open." His descendants are most distant from the land of Israel (10:2–5); they include people whom Abram's offspring would bless (12:1–3), some of whom David and Solomon may rule ("live in the tents of Shem"), and people who would become the object of Christian mission (Matt 28:18–20; Acts 1:8).

10:1–32 *The Table of Nations.* This chapter divides into three groups according to the three sons of Noah (10:1). Although terms such as "sons of" and "father of" point to ethnic relations, some connections are surprising (e.g., Canaanites are not usually considered to be related to Egyptians as descendants of one ancestor — Ham). These names come to us as people groups; they may have migrated by the time they appear in historical records outside the Bible. All the people of the known world come from Noah. They are all made in God's image (9:6), and thus they are all equal before God. In contrast to past attempts to justify the enslavement of Africans by misinterpreting 9:25–27, ch. 10 celebrates the common origin and community of humanity.

10:1 account. See note on 2:4.

10:2 sons of Japheth. See note on 9:27. Japheth's descendants live in the most distant places from the land of Israel, particularly north and northwest. Most of the sons named may be connected with similar-sounding names of places known from ancient sources. **Gomer.** Cimmerians from the Caucasus region who moved south to eastern Turkey and Armenia. **Magog.** Unknown; likely related to Gomer. **Madai.** Lived in northwestern Iran. **Javan.** Ionia, Greek cities in western Turkey. **Tubal, Meshek.** Tabal and Mushki, Phyrgian kingdoms in Cappadocia (modern central Turkey). **Tiras.** Could refer to the Etruscans, who migrated from Lydia to Italy in the eighth century BC.

10:3 Ashkenaz. Could refer to the Scythians, first encountered when coming from the north into the region of eastern Turkey. **Riphath.** Unknown. **Togarmah.** Til-garimmu, modern Gurun on the Upper Euphrates.

10:4 Elishah. Alashia on the south coast of Cyprus. **Tarshish.** Tarsus in Cilicia, the Adana region of modern Turkey. **Kittites.** Kition in Cyprus. **Rodanites.** Associated with the Greek island of Rhodes.

10:6 sons of Ham. These include Egypt and Canaan, areas south of the land of Israel. **Cush.** Sudan. **Put.** Coastal Libya.

10:7 Seba, Havilah, Sabtah, Raamah and Sabteka ... Sheba and Dedan. On the southern tip of the Arabian peninsula or across the straits in Eritria and Djibouti. Raamah includes the western coastal area of Arabia, with Sheba in the south (1 Kgs 10:1–13; 2 Chr 9:1–12) and Dedan in the north.

10:8 Nimrod. In Hebrew this name uses a verbal form meaning "to rebel." He is connected with warfare, hunting, and ruling cities in Mesopotamia (modern Iraq). He is a mighty hunter and kingdom

[10]The first centers of his kingdom were Babylon,[b] Uruk, Akkad and Kalneh, in[a] Shinar.[bc] [11]From that
land he went to Assyria,[d] where he built Nineveh,[e] Rehoboth Ir,[c] Calah [12]and Resen, which is between
Nineveh and Calah — which is the great city.

[13] Egypt was the father of
the Ludites, Anamites, Lehabites, Naphtuhites, [14]Pathrusites, Kasluhites (from whom the Philistines[f] came) and Caphtorites.
[15] Canaan[g] was the father of
Sidon[h] his firstborn,[d] and of the Hittites,[i] [16]Jebusites,[j] Amorites, Girgashites, [17]Hivites, Arkites,
Sinites, [18]Arvadites, Zemarites and Hamathites.

Later the Canaanite[k] clans scattered [19]and the borders of Canaan[l] reached from Sidon[m] toward Gerar as far as Gaza, and then toward Sodom, Gomorrah, Admah and Zeboyim, as far as Lasha.
[20]These are the sons of Ham by their clans and languages, in their territories and nations.

The Semites

10:21-31pp — Ge 11:10-27; 1Ch 1:17-27

[21]Sons were also born to Shem, whose older brother was[e] Japheth; Shem was the ancestor of all the
sons of Eber.[n]

[22] The sons of Shem:
Elam,[o] Ashur, Arphaxad,[p] Lud and Aram.
[23] The sons of Aram:
Uz,[q] Hul, Gether and Meshek.[f]
[24] Arphaxad was the father of[g] Shelah,
and Shelah the father of Eber.[r]
[25] Two sons were born to Eber:
One was named Peleg,[h] because in his time the earth was divided; his brother was named
Joktan.

[a] 10 Or *Uruk and Akkad — all of them in* [b] 10 That is, Babylonia [c] 11 Or *Nineveh with its city squares* [d] 15 Or *of the Sidonians, the foremost* [e] 21 Or *Shem, the older brother of* [f] 23 See Septuagint and 1 Chron. 1:17; Hebrew *Mash.* [g] 24 Hebrew; Septuagint *father of Cainan, and Cainan was the father of* [h] 25 *Peleg* means *division.*

10:10 [b] Ge 11:9 [c] Ge 11:2
10:11 [d] Ps 83:8; Mic 5:6 [e] Jnh 1:2; 4:11; Na 1:1
10:14 [f] Ge 21:32,34; 26:1,8
10:15 [g] ver 6; Ge 9:18 [h] Eze 28:21 [i] Ge 23:3,20
10:16 [j] 1Ch 11:4
10:18 [k] Ge 12:6; Ex 13:11
10:19 [l] Ge 11:31; 13:12; 17:8 [m] ver 15
10:21 [n] ver 24; Nu 24:24
10:22 [o] Jer 49:34 [p] Lk 3:36
10:23 [q] Job 1:1
10:24 [r] ver 21

builder (vv. 9 – 12), and his name may suggest that he is "against Yahweh." Later, both the Assyrians and the Babylonians are responsible for the destruction of Israel and Judah, respectively. In the light of how violence is picked up in the early chapters of Genesis, Nimrod appears to be the antithesis of what God wants, using power to build cities and kingdoms that stand in opposition to God's kingdom and city.

10:10 Nimrod's lordship of Babylon and Shinar (the ancient name for Babylonia) may suggest a connection with the tower of Babel (11:2,9; see note on 11:9). **Uruk [Erech], Akkad and Kalneh.** The region of Babylon along the southern Euphrates River.

10:11 Assyria. Along the Tigris River north of Uruk, Akkad, and Kalneh. **Nineveh.** A capital of Assyria. **Rehoboth Ir.** The Hebrew means "squares/spaces of (the) city" (see NIV text note). **Calah.** An Assyrian city.

10:12 Resen. Unknown.

10:13 – 14 The names are organized according to the number of consonants they contain rather than any geographic relationship. **Ludites.** Lydia in western Turkey. **Anamites.** Unknown. **Lehabites.** May be Libyans, though the name is spelled differently elsewhere (2 Chr 12:3; 16:8; Isa 66:19; Ezek 30:5; Dan 11:43; Nah 3:9). **Naphtuhites, Pathrusites, Kasluhites.** Associated with the delta, southern Egypt, and elsewhere in northern Egypt (before Kasluhites moved to Greek islands, possibly where the Philistines came from). **Caphtorites.** Cretans.

10:15 – 19 Sidon. A coastal Lebanese city; Sidonians is another name for Phoenicians. **Hittites, Jebusites, Amorites, Girgashites, Hivites.** Inhabitants of Canaan who are to be removed when God gives the land to Israel (Deut 7:1; Josh 3:10). They probably originated in south Turkey (the Hittites were a kingdom in Turkey) and northwest Syria (if the Amorites are Amurru [Josh 13:4] and not the inhabitants of the hill country near the Jordan River [Deut 1:4,7]). **Arkites, Sinites, Arvadites, Zemarites and Hamathites.** Kingdoms in northwest Syria. **Canaan.** An area known in Egyptian records of the second millennium BC and in early biblical texts (Num 13:17,21 – 22; 34:3 – 12; Josh 1:4) but not later. **Gaza.** Ancient and modern city at the southern boundary of Canaan along the Mediterranean. The eastern border of Canaan is the Jordan Valley, with Sodom, Gomorrah, Admah and Zeboyim (14:2,8) southward and Lasha (Israelite Dan; Judg 18:29) in the north.

10:21 – 31 Ch. 11 repeats these descendants except for Joktan, the brother of Peleg (whose name means "divide, division"; see v. 25). Most of the places are east of the land of Israel.

10:22 sons of Shem. Shem is the origin of the term Semite. **Elam.** At the Persian Gulf. **Ashur.** A capital of Assyria (see v. 11 and note). **Aram.** The Arameans north and east of the land of Israel.

10:23 Uz. Job's land (Job 1:1). **Hul, Gether.** Appear elsewhere only in 1 Chr 1:17. **Meshek.** See note on v. 2.

10:25 Eber. This is the name from which the term "Hebrew" is derived. **the earth was divided.** This may refer to the division of people in 11:1 – 9 (see 10:8 – 12 and notes).

10:32 [s] ver 1 [t] Ge 9:19
11:2 [u] Ge 10:10
11:3 [v] Ex 1:14 [w] Ge 14:10
11:4 [x] Dt 1:28; 9:1 [y] Ge 6:4 [z] Dt 4:27
11:5 [a] ver 7; Ge 18:21; Ex 3:8; 19:11,18,20
11:7 [b] Ge 1:26 [c] Ge 42:23
11:8 [d] Ge 9:19; Lk 1:51
11:9 [e] Ge 10:10

26 Joktan was the father of
Almodad, Sheleph, Hazarmaveth, Jerah, 27 Hadoram, Uzal, Diklah, 28 Obal, Abimael, Sheba,
29 Ophir, Havilah and Jobab. All these were sons of Joktan.

30 The region where they lived stretched from Mesha toward Sephar, in the eastern hill country.
31 These are the sons of Shem by their clans and languages, in their territories and nations.

32 These are the clans of Noah's sons,[s] according to their lines of descent, within their nations. From
these the nations spread out over the earth[t] after the flood.

The Tower of Babel

11 Now the whole world had one language and a common speech. 2 As people moved eastward,[a]
they found a plain in Shinar[b][u] and settled there.
3 They said to each other, "Come, let's make bricks[v] and bake them thoroughly." They used brick
instead of stone, and tar[w] for mortar. 4 Then they said, "Come, let us build ourselves a city, with a tower
that reaches to the heavens,[x] so that we may make a name[y] for ourselves; otherwise we will be scattered
over the face of the whole earth."[z]
5 But the LORD came down[a] to see the city and the tower the people were building. 6 The LORD said,
"If as one people speaking the same language they have begun to do this, then nothing they plan to
do will be impossible for them. 7 Come, let us[b] go down and confuse their language so they will not
understand each other."[c]
8 So the LORD scattered them from there over all the earth,[d] and they stopped building the city. 9 That
is why it was called Babel[c][e] — because there the LORD confused the language of the whole world. From
there the LORD scattered them over the face of the whole earth.

a 2 Or *from the east*; or *in the east* *b* 2 That is, Babylonia *c* 9 That is, Babylon; *Babel* sounds like the Hebrew for *confused*.

10:26 Joktan. Most of the descendants of Joktan are unknown.
10:27 Hadoram. Related to Syrian Hamath (v. 18; 1 Chr 18:9–10). **Uzal.** Associated with Danites and Greeks (Ezek 27:19 "Izal").
10:28 Sheba. See v. 7 and note.
10:29 Ophir. Coastal land famous for gold (1 Kgs 9:28; 10:11; 22:48). **Havilah.** See v. 7; 2:10–14 and notes. **Jobab.** The name of an Edomite king (36:33; 1 Chr 1:44) and a king of Madon, north of the land of Israel (Josh 11:1).
10:30 Mesha ... Sephar. Unknown.
10:32 the nations spread out. This does not happen until after the tower of Babel incident (11:1–9), so this verse does not follow chronological order.
11:1–9 *The Tower of Babel.* The people of the earth want to make a name for themselves, even if this means opposing God. God's creation of the many languages of the human race leads them to spread across the earth and give up their defiant plans.
11:2 people moved eastward. In the eastern part of the Fertile Crescent, the waters of the Persian Gulf receded in the fourth millennium BC. There is archaeological evidence that people lived there. People who have not yet "spread out over the earth" (10:32) settle in Shinar (i.e., Babylon, 10:10). They band together for security.
11:3 bake them thoroughly. Mud bricks can simply dry in the heat of the sun, but the strongest ones were fired in kilns. Oven-fired bricks were more expensive and used only for the facades of special buildings. **brick instead of stone.** Brick is characteristic building material in Mesopotamia, where it is far more abundant than building stone.
11:4 tower. Hebrew *migdāl.* It usually refers to a fortress and emphasizes security. Here it may be associated with the pyramid-shaped ziggurats that humans in early Mesopotamian cities used to access the divine world of the god they worshiped. In some views, the ziggurat was primarily a staircase for the god; the temple was near the bottom of the stairs that went up the side of the ziggurat. The city was built to house the ziggurat, the temple, and other buildings for the priests, king, and army. **a name.** A reputation guaranteeing that one would be honored after death. This account intentionally contrasts with Abram and the "name" God promises him (12:1–3) by calling him out from the same urban environment and into a "backwater" land with little promise for security and worldly success. Because the people feared being "scattered" and were vulnerable, they planned to unite and build a powerful fortress that would allow them to call down their god to protect them and their descendants.
11:5 the LORD came down to see. The builders constructed their tower to the heavens. Ironically, God had to descend to reach them.
11:6 nothing they plan to do will be impossible. It will not be beyond their reach. The tower is a central fortress that opposes God's plans. Cities, though at times blessed by God (e.g., Jerusalem) and centers for the expansion of the gospel (as in Acts), can also be evil centers of rebellion against God.
11:7 us. The plural pronoun may reflect the divine court, where decisions are made that overturn the deliberations of any human court, or it may suggest God's self-reflection as a deity far more complex in personhood than other gods (see note on 1:26). **confuse.** Hebrew *n-b-l*, a wordplay on "brick" (Hebrew *l-b-n*). This does not permanently remove the danger of the city, but it mitigates the threat of a one-world government where no alternative worship is allowed.
11:9 Babel. Babylon (see 10:8–10 and notes). Babel (Hebrew *b-b-l*) is a wordplay on "confused" (Hebrew *n-b-l*; see note on v. 7). The name "Babel" is translated as "Babylon" everywhere else in the OT. Babylon becomes symbolic of human opposition to God and the antithesis of the city that God desires to have constructed for his glory on the earth.

From Shem to Abram

11:10-27pp — Ge 10:21-31; 1Ch 1:17-27

10 This is the account of Shem's family line.

Two years after the flood, when Shem was 100 years old, he became the father[a] of Arphaxad. 11 And
after he became the father of Arphaxad, Shem lived 500 years and had other sons and daughters.
12 When Arphaxad had lived 35 years, he became the father of Shelah.[f] 13 And after he became the
father of Shelah, Arphaxad lived 403 years and had other sons and daughters.[b]
14 When Shelah had lived 30 years, he became the father of Eber. 15 And after he became the father of
Eber, Shelah lived 403 years and had other sons and daughters.
16 When Eber had lived 34 years, he became the father of Peleg. 17 And after he became the father of
Peleg, Eber lived 430 years and had other sons and daughters.
18 When Peleg had lived 30 years, he became the father of Reu. 19 And after he became the father of
Reu, Peleg lived 209 years and had other sons and daughters.
20 When Reu had lived 32 years, he became the father of Serug.[g] 21 And after he became the father of
Serug, Reu lived 207 years and had other sons and daughters.
22 When Serug had lived 30 years, he became the father of Nahor. 23 And after he became the father
of Nahor, Serug lived 200 years and had other sons and daughters.
24 When Nahor had lived 29 years, he became the father of Terah.[h] 25 And after he became the father
of Terah, Nahor lived 119 years and had other sons and daughters.
26 After Terah had lived 70 years, he became the father of Abram,[i] Nahor[j] and Haran.

Abram's Family

27 This is the account of Terah's family line.

Terah became the father of Abram, Nahor and Haran. And Haran became the father of Lot.[k] 28 While
his father Terah was still alive, Haran died in Ur of the Chaldeans,[l] in the land of his birth. 29 Abram and
Nahor both married. The name of Abram's wife was Sarai,[m] and the name of Nahor's wife was Milkah;[n]
she was the daughter of Haran, the father of both Milkah and Iskah. 30 Now Sarai was childless because
she was not able to conceive.[o]

11:12 [f] Lk 3:35
11:20 [g] Lk 3:35
11:24 [h] Lk 3:34
11:26 [i] Lk 3:34 [j] Jos 24:2
11:27 [k] ver 31; Ge 12:4; 14:12; 19:1; 2Pe 2:7
11:28 [l] ver 31; Ge 15:7
11:29 [m] Ge 17:15 [n] Ge 22:20
11:30 [o] Ge 16:1; 18:11

[a] *10 Father* may mean *ancestor*; also in verses 11-25. [b] *12,13* Hebrew; Septuagint (see also Luke 3:35, 36 and note at Gen. 10:24) *35 years, he became the father of Cainan. 13 And after he became the father of Cainan, Arphaxad lived 430 years and had other sons and daughters, and then he died. When Cainan had lived 130 years, he became the father of Shelah. And after he became the father of Shelah, Cainan lived 330 years and had other sons and daughters*

11:10–26 *From Shem to Abram.* This genealogy forms the most direct line in Genesis, with no notes or glosses. It is regular and formulaic, suggesting an interest only in recording the line to show the connection between Shem and Abram. The life spans of these patriarchs before Abram's grandfather remain unusually long, gradually descending from 500 to 200 years. Perhaps this demonstrates the effects of sin on even the best of the human race. See 6:3 and note.
11:10 account. See note on 2:4. **Shem.** Means "name," perhaps related to the "name" the Babel builders wanted and the "name" God promised Abram (see v. 4; 12:2 and notes).
11:18 Reu. The name means "friend" or "shepherd." Cf. Reuel, "friend of God" (Exod 2:18).
11:20–26 Serug ... Nahor ... Terah. Also place-names in the region of Harran in northern Mesopotamia. The homeland for Abram was in this region. Ur may have been a branch of the "family business" (Josh 24:2).
11:27—25:18 *The Family of Abraham.* A new heading introduces the next major narrative section in Genesis. Almost every episode in 11:27—25:18 involves Abraham, who plays a very significant role in the outworking of God's redemptive plan.
11:27–32 *Abram's Family.* These verses provide background information essential for understanding the subsequent story: the death of Abram's brother, Haran, the father of Lot; the barrenness of Abram's wife, Sarai; the relocation of Terah's family to northern Mesopotamia.
11:27 This is the account of. Marks the start of a new section in Genesis. The heading introduces Terah's immediate family. **Abram.** God later renames him Abraham (17:5).
11:28 Ur of the Chaldeans. The remains of the ancient city of Ur, located at Tell el-Muqayyar in Iraq, were excavated by Leonard Woolley from 1922 to 1934. His investigations revealed the existence of a well-developed urban culture at the end of the third millennium and the start of the second millennium BC, around the time that Terah's family lived there. To distinguish it from other cities with the same name, Ur is associated with the Chaldeans. The Kaldu people settled in southern Babylon about 1200 BC, giving their name to the region. The designation "of the Chaldeans" probably belongs to the period 1000–500 BC and is anachronistic, reflecting, like some other place-names in Genesis, geographic knowledge from a later time when the text of Genesis was updated. See Introduction to the Pentateuch, pp. 12–13.
11:29 Sarai. Later renamed Sarah (17:15).
11:30 childless. Sarai's inability to have children is a major obstacle to the fulfillment of God's promise that Abram will have many descendants and become a great nation (12:2). The same problem recurs with Rebekah (25:21) and Rachel (29:31). In each case, God enables a son to

11:31 [p]Ge 15:7; Ne 9:7; Ac 7:4 [q]Ge 10:19
12:1 [r]Ac 7:3*; Heb 11:8
12:2 [s]Ge 15:5; 17:2,4; 18:18; 22:17; Dt 26:5 [t]Ge 24:1,35
12:3 [u]Ge 27:29; Ex 23:22; Nu 24:9 [v]Ge 18:18; 22:18; 26:4; Ac 3:25; Gal 3:8*
12:4 [w]Ge 11:31
12:5 [x]Ge 14:14; 17:23
12:6 [y]Heb 11:9 [z]Ge 35:4; Dt 11:30 [a]Ge 10:18
12:7 [b]Ge 17:1; 18:1; Ex 6:3 [c]Ge 13:15,17; 15:18; 17:8; Ps 105:9-11 [d]Ge 13:4

31 Terah took his son Abram, his grandson Lot son of Haran, and his daughter-in-law Sarai, the wife
of his son Abram, and together they set out from Ur of the Chaldeans[p] to go to Canaan.[q] But when they
came to Harran, they settled there.
32 Terah lived 205 years, and he died in Harran.

The Call of Abram

12 The LORD had said to Abram, "Go from your country, your people and your father's household
to the land I will show you.[r]

2 "I will make you into a great nation,[s]
and I will bless you;[t]
I will make your name great,
and you will be a blessing.[a]
3 I will bless those who bless you,
and whoever curses you I will curse;[u]
and all peoples on earth
will be blessed through you."[v][b]

4 So Abram went, as the LORD had told him; and Lot went with him. Abram was seventy-five years old
when he set out from Harran.[w] 5 He took his wife Sarai, his nephew Lot, all the possessions they had
accumulated and the people[x] they had acquired in Harran, and they set out for the land of Canaan,
and they arrived there.
6 Abram traveled through the land[y] as far as the site of the great tree of Moreh[z] at Shechem. At that
time the Canaanites[a] were in the land. 7 The LORD appeared to Abram[b] and said, "To your offspring[c] I
will give this land."[c] So he built an altar there to the LORD,[d] who had appeared to him.

[a] 2 Or *be seen as blessed* [b] 3 Or *earth / will use your name in blessings* (see 48:20) [c] 7 Or *seed*

be born who becomes an important link in the unique family line traced throughout Genesis.

11:31 Terah's family moves from southern to northern Mesopotamia. **Harran.** Located in Turkey at Eskiharran, the modern name meaning "old Harran." In Hebrew script the place-name Harran differs markedly from the name of Lot's father (Haran).

11:32 205 years. Taking into account the numbers given in v. 26 and 12:4, Terah would have been 145 years old when Abram left Harran. If Terah lived for 205 years, he would have died long after Abram's departure for Canaan. Yet in Acts 7:4 Stephen states that Abram departed from Harran after Terah's death. Stephen's remark corresponds with the text of the Samaritan Pentateuch, a very early version of Genesis through Deuteronomy, which claims that Terah died when he was 145 years old. The figure of 205 years may be due to a mistake by an early copyist.

12:1–9 *The Call of Abram.* Having set the scene in 11:27–32, the account of Abram's relationship with God begins with a significant agenda-setting speech that will influence both Abram's immediate future and the long-term future of all humanity.

12:1–3 God's invitation to Abram is a key passage in the book of Genesis. It places Abram at the heart of God's plans to reverse all that has gone wrong since Adam and Eve were expelled from the Garden of Eden (3:22–24). Adam and Eve's disobedience resulted in divine displeasure and curses; Abram's obedience will bring blessing. God's call requires Abram to exercise tremendous faith. He must first abandon the security of family and country and then travel to a foreign land, confidently believing that God will give him both descendants and land, essential ingredients in order to become a "great nation" (12:2). At the time of his call, Abram and Sarai are childless (11:30).

12:2 name great. The promise that God will make Abram famous comes in the wake of the failed ambitions of the city-builders of Babel (11:4–8) and possibly has royal connotations (2 Sam 7:9). While God's promises have an explicit national dimension, this is subservient to the international aspect that marks the climax of the speech.

12:3 bless those who bless you. The theme of God's blessing others through Abram later links to the line of descendants traced initially through Isaac and Jacob (22:18; 26:4; 27:29; 28:14). In the NT Paul sees in this promise of blessing an advance announcement of the gospel (Gal 3:8), the blessing coming ultimately through Jesus Christ, the "seed" of Abraham (Gal 3:16; see Gen 22:18 and NIV text note). The apostle Peter likewise associates Jesus Christ with the fulfillment of God's promise to bless the families of the earth (Acts 3:25–26). Although the initial promises of nationhood and international blessing are conditional upon Abram's obedience, God later guarantees these by making two covenants with Abram (chs. 15; 17). See "Covenant," p. 2646.

12:4 Abram went. In faith Abram obeys God's call (Heb 11:8). **Lot.** Although he is sufficiently wealthy to have remained in Harran (13:5–6), since his father is dead (11:28), Lot decides that his future will be served best by accompanying Abram, his uncle. This too is an act of faith on the part of Lot.

12:5 people they had acquired. Abram appears to have had a substantial number of men attached to his household; some were bought from foreigners (17:12) and some were born in his household. Gen 14:14 refers to 318 trained men. Lot also had a separate retinue of men (13:7).

12:6 traveled through the land. Abram's journey brings him to Shechem in Canaan. His lifestyle as a seminomadic herdsman involved living in a tent away from urban settlements. Occasionally large trees identify the locations of his encampments (13:18). Heb 11:8–16 emphasizes that Abram intentionally lived in a tent because he anticipated the creation of a city designed and built by God. This hope distinguishes him from the God-defiant city-builders of Babel (11:1–9). **Canaanites were in the land.** Although God promises Abram the land of Canaan, it is already occupied.

12:7 The LORD appeared. Genesis records a number of occasions when God appeared to the patriarchs. God pledges to transform Abram's present circumstances; at this stage Abram is both childless and landless.

[8]From there he went on toward the hills east of Bethel[e] and pitched his tent, with Bethel on the west
and Ai on the east. There he built an altar to the LORD and called on the name of the LORD.
[9]Then Abram set out and continued toward the Negev.[f]

12:8 [e] Ge 13:3
12:9 [f] Ge 13:1,3

Abram in Egypt

12:10-20Ref — Ge 20:1-18; 26:1-11

[10]Now there was a famine in the land, and Abram went down to Egypt to live there for a while because the famine was severe. [11]As he was about to enter Egypt, he said to his wife Sarai, "I know what a
beautiful woman you are. [12]When the Egyptians see you, they will say, 'This is his wife.' Then they will

12:8 Bethel. Means "house of God" in Hebrew. **built an altar.** The religious practices of the patriarchs predate the construction of the tabernacle and later the temple. The altars built by the patriarchs anticipate a future time when God will dwell on the earth permanently. Although they did not view God as residing at these altars, they could encounter him there (Exod 20:24). Their existence served as reminders of the patriarch's special relationship with God and the promise of land.

12:9 Negev. Means "south" in Hebrew. See map, p. 2866. Abram moves southward from Shechem, eventually coming by stages to the Negev.

12:10–20 *Abram in Egypt.* Egypt was better equipped than Canaan to withstand famine caused by drought because of irrigation along the banks of the Nile River. Given Abram's southward trek from Harran to Canaan, Egypt was a natural place to seek refuge.

12:11–13 Rather than trusting in God's protection, Abram selfishly devises a cunning ruse.

INTEGRATED CHRONOLOGY OF THE PATRIARCHS

Abraham

AGE	Event
75	To Canaan*
100	Birth of Isaac*
140	
160	
175	Abraham's death*

Isaac

AGE	Event
40	Isaac's marriage*
60	Births of Esau and Jacob*
75	
100	
137	
151	
157	
168	
180	Isaac's death*

Jacob

AGE	Event
15	
40	Esau's marriage*
77	Jacob to Paddan Aram
91	Birth of JOSEPH
97	Jacob's return to Canaan
108	
120	
121	
130	Jacob to Egypt*
147	Jacob's death*

JOSEPH

AGE	Event
6	
17	Joseph to Egypt*
29	
30	Joseph enters Pharaoh's service*
39	
56	
110	Joseph's death*

Note: The ages marked with (*) are expressly given.

12:13 [g]Ge 20:2; 26:7
12:17 [h]1Ch 16:21
12:18 [i]Ge 20:9; 26:10
13:1 [j]Ge 12:9
13:3 [k]Ge 12:8
13:4 [l]Ge 12:7

kill me but will let you live. [13]Say you are my sister,[g] so that I will be treated well for your sake and my
life will be spared because of you."
[14]When Abram came to Egypt, the Egyptians saw that Sarai was a very beautiful woman. [15]And when
Pharaoh's officials saw her, they praised her to Pharaoh, and she was taken into his palace. [16]He treated
Abram well for her sake, and Abram acquired sheep and cattle, male and female donkeys, male and
female servants, and camels.
[17]But the LORD inflicted serious diseases on Pharaoh and his household[h] because of Abram's wife
Sarai. [18]So Pharaoh summoned Abram. "What have you done to me?"[i] he said. "Why didn't you tell me
she was your wife? [19]Why did you say, 'She is my sister,' so that I took her to be my wife? Now then, here
is your wife. Take her and go!" [20]Then Pharaoh gave orders about Abram to his men, and they sent him
on his way, with his wife and everything he had.

Abram and Lot Separate

13 So Abram went up from Egypt to the Negev,[j] with his wife and everything he had, and Lot went
with him. [2]Abram had become very wealthy in livestock and in silver and gold.
[3]From the Negev he went from place to place until he came to Bethel,[k] to the place between Bethel
and Ai where his tent had been earlier [4]and where he had first built an altar.[l] There Abram called on
the name of the LORD.
[5]Now Lot, who was moving about with Abram, also had flocks and herds and tents. [6]But the land
could not support them while they stayed together, for their possessions were so great that they were

12:16 camels. It is often stated that references to camels in Genesis are anachronistic because camels were not domesticated until the end of the second millennium BC. Archaeological evidence for the early domestication of camels is understandably limited given their use in desert regions. Even in Genesis they are usually mentioned in contexts involving long-distance travel close to deserts (e.g., 24:10–64; 31:17,34; 37:25). Recent research, however, suggests that people used camels as early as the third millennium BC. Genesis tends to mention them at the very end of lists of possessions (30:43; 32:7), possibly suggesting that they were the least numerous of the animals the patriarchs owned.

12:17 serious diseases. A minimum of detail is given regarding Pharaoh's punishment. There is no reason to assume that these are related to any of the diseases recorded in Exod 7–12.

13:1–18 *Abram and Lot Separate.* After they return to Canaan, a conflict over pastureland causes Abram to give his nephew Lot first choice of the land. However, after the two men part company, God reiterates his promise to Abram that his descendants will possess all of Canaan.

13:6 land could not support them. The hill country to the east of Bethel (v. 3) provides inadequate pasture for all the livestock Abram and Lot own.

ABRAM'S TRAVELS

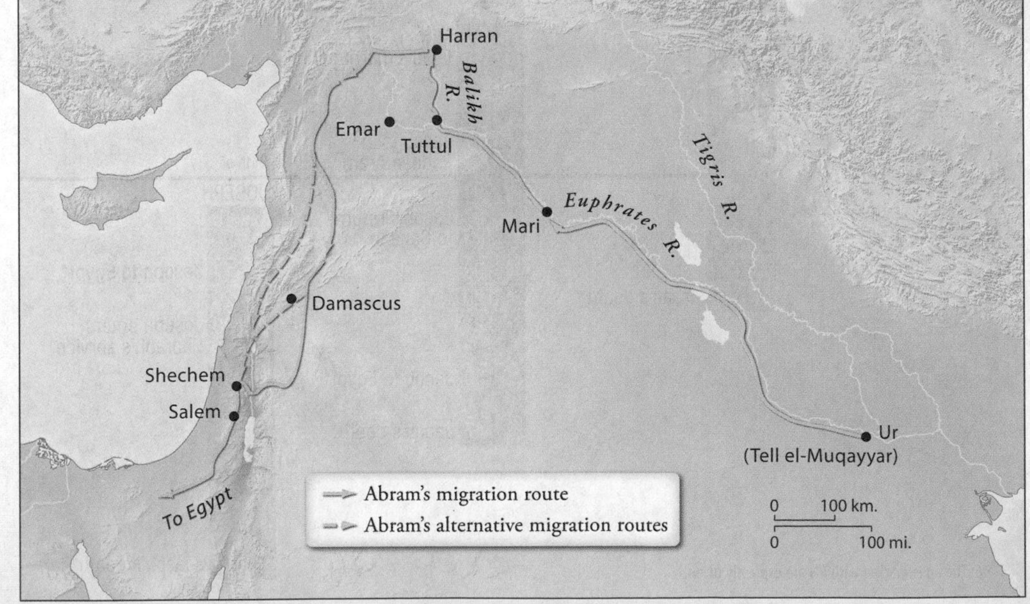

not able to stay together.[m] 7And quarreling[n] arose between Abram's herders and Lot's. The Canaanites
and Perizzites were also living in the land[o] at that time.
8So Abram said to Lot, "Let's not have any quarreling between you and me,[p] or between your herders
and mine, for we are close relatives.[q] 9Is not the whole land before you? Let's part company. If you go
to the left, I'll go to the right; if you go to the right, I'll go to the left."
10Lot looked around and saw that the whole plain of the Jordan toward Zoar[r] was well watered,
like the garden of the LORD,[s] like the land of Egypt. (This was before the LORD destroyed Sodom and
Gomorrah.)[t] 11So Lot chose for himself the whole plain of the Jordan and set out toward the east. The
two men parted company: 12Abram lived in the land of Canaan, while Lot lived among the cities of the
plain[u] and pitched his tents near Sodom.[v] 13Now the people of Sodom were wicked and were sinning
greatly against the LORD.[w]
14The LORD said to Abram after Lot had parted from him, "Look around from where you are, to the
north and south, to the east and west.[x] 15All the land that you see I will give to you and your offspring[a]
forever.[y] 16I will make your offspring like the dust of the earth, so that if anyone could count the dust,
then your offspring could be counted. 17Go, walk through the length and breadth of the land,[z] for I
am giving it to you."
18So Abram went to live near the great trees of Mamre[a] at Hebron,[b] where he pitched his tents. There
he built an altar to the LORD.[c]

Abram Rescues Lot

14 At the time when Amraphel was king of Shinar,[b][d] Arioch king of Ellasar, Kedorlaomer king of
Elam and Tidal king of Goyim, 2these kings went to war against Bera king of Sodom, Birsha
king of Gomorrah, Shinab king of Admah, Shemeber king of Zeboyim,[e] and the king of Bela (that is,
Zoar).[f] 3All these latter kings joined forces in the Valley of Siddim (that is, the Dead Sea Valley[g]). 4For
twelve years they had been subject to Kedorlaomer, but in the thirteenth year they rebelled.
5In the fourteenth year, Kedorlaomer and the kings allied with him went out and defeated the Rephaites[h] in Ashteroth Karnaim, the Zuzites in Ham, the Emites[i] in Shaveh Kiriathaim 6and the Horites[j]
in the hill country of Seir,[k] as far as El Paran[l] near the desert. 7Then they turned back and went to

13:6 [m]Ge 36:7
13:7 [n]Ge 26:20,21 [o]Ge 12:6
13:8 [p]Pr 15:18; 20:3 [q]Ps 133:1
13:10 [r]Ge 19:22,30 [s]Ge 2:8-10; Isa 51:3 [t]Ge 14:8; 19:17-29
13:12 [u]Ge 19:17,25,29 [v]Ge 14:12
13:13 [w]Ge 18:20; Eze 16:49-50; 2Pe 2:8
13:14 [x]Ge 28:14; Dt 3:27
13:15 [y]Ge 12:7; Gal 3:16*
13:17 [z]ver 15; Nu 13:17-25
13:18 [a]Ge 14:13,24; 18:1 [b]Ge 35:27 [c]Ge 8:20
14:1 [d]Ge 10:10
14:2 [e]Ge 10:19 [f]Ge 13:10
14:3 [g]Nu 34:3,12; Dt 3:17; Jos 3:16; 15:2,5
14:5 [h]Ge 15:20; Dt 2:11, 20 [i]Dt 2:10
14:6 [j]Dt 2:12,22 [k]Dt 2:1, 5,22 [l]Ge 21:21; Nu 10:12

[a] *15* Or *seed*; also in verse 16 [b] *1* That is, Babylonia; also in verse 9

13:7 Canaanites and Perizzites. The presence of other inhabitants probably also limited the pastureland available to the livestock of Abram and Lot.

13:10 well watered. An abundance of water made the Jordan Valley an obvious choice for Lot, especially after the famine mentioned in 12:10. But the fertility of the land masks a hidden danger. **Sodom and Gomorrah.** Linked in 10:19 to Canaan, Noah's grandson, whom Noah cursed (9:25–27). The brief remark about their destruction anticipates the fuller description in ch. 19. The original location of these cities is unknown, although they were probably situated near the southern end of the Dead Sea.

13:11–12 Separating from Abram, Lot camps near Sodom. When we next read of him, he has settled within the city (14:12; see 19:3–11). In sharp contrast to Abram, the men of Sodom are antagonistic toward the Lord. As subsequent events reveal, Lot's choice seriously endangers his well-being on two occasions (chs. 14; 19).

13:16 like the dust of the earth. Although Abram remains childless, the Lord promises him that his descendants will be numerous. Elsewhere, God compares Abram's descendants to the stars in the sky and the sand on the seashore (22:17; see 15:5).

13:18 altar. The one built by Abraham near Hebron was located relatively close to those mentioned in 12:6–8. All three altars were constructed in what would later be the central regions of the kingdoms of Israel and Judah.

14:1–24 *Abram Rescues Lot.* When a foreign confederation of four kings defeats an alliance of five Canaanite kings, they take captive Abram's nephew Lot. After Abram returns from successfully rescuing Lot and other captives, the kings of Sodom and Salem greet him. Abram's different responses to the two kings are exceptionally important, revealing how Abram rejects the spoils of battle in order to enhance his own standing within the land of Canaan. Although his defeat of the invading kings provides Abram with an opportunity to enrich himself further, he places his future hope in God, affirming through the gift of a tithe the truthfulness of Melchizedek's remarks. The events of this chapter portray Abram as worthy of royal status.

14:1–4 A dispute between two groups of kings results in a conflict in the Jordan Valley, where Lot is living. For 12 years the local kings have been subject to a foreign coalition composed of kings from the region of Mesopotamia and beyond. Although these kings are not known in existing extrabiblical sources, their names are typical of the territories associated with them.

14:1 Shinar. Region of southern Mesopotamia, later known as Babylonia (10:10; see Josh 7:21 and NIV text note). **Ellasar.** Possibly northern Mesopotamia, the name "Arioch" having been found in ancient texts from Mari and Nuzi. **Elam.** Region to the east of southern Mesopotamia. Only in the early second millennium BC is there evidence of Elamite armies advancing westward into Mesopotamia and possibly onward to Canaan. **Tidal.** The name may be of Hittite origin. The insertion of explanatory names in vv. 1–8 (e.g., Zoar [vv. 2,8] and Kadesh [v. 7]) point to the antiquity of this account.

14:5–7 Before they arrive in the Jordan Valley, the foreign coalition defeats various tribal groups whose territories lie along the King's Highway in Transjordan. After reaching the Gulf of Aqabah, they travel northward to Hazezon Tamar, known as En Gedi in 2 Chr 20:2.

14:7 [m]2Ch 20:2
14:8 [n]Ge 13:10; 19:17-29 [o]Dt 29:23
14:10 [p]Ge 19:17,30
14:13 [q]ver 24; Ge 13:18
14:14 [r]Ge 15:3 [s]Dt 34:1; Jdg 18:29
14:17 [t]2Sa 18:18
14:18 [u]Ps 110:4; Heb 5:6 [v]Ps 76:2; Heb 7:2
14:19 [w]Heb 7:6 [x]ver 22
14:20 [y]Ge 24:27 [z]Ge 28:22; Dt 26:12; Heb 7:4
14:22 [a]Ex 6:8; Da 12:7; Rev 10:5-6

En Mishpat (that is, Kadesh), and they conquered the whole territory of the Amalekites, as well as the
Amorites who were living in Hazezon Tamar.[m]
8 Then the king of Sodom, the king of Gomorrah,[n] the king of Admah, the king of Zeboyim[o] and
the king of Bela (that is, Zoar) marched out and drew up their battle lines in the Valley of Siddim
9 against Kedorlaomer king of Elam, Tidal king of Goyim, Amraphel king of Shinar and Arioch king of
Ellasar—four kings against five. 10 Now the Valley of Siddim was full of tar pits, and when the kings
of Sodom and Gomorrah fled, some of the men fell into them and the rest fled to the hills.[p] 11 The four
kings seized all the goods of Sodom and Gomorrah and all their food; then they went away. 12 They also
carried off Abram's nephew Lot and his possessions, since he was living in Sodom.
13 A man who had escaped came and reported this to Abram the Hebrew. Now Abram was living near
the great trees of Mamre[q] the Amorite, a brother[a] of Eshkol and Aner, all of whom were allied with
Abram. 14 When Abram heard that his relative had been taken captive, he called out the 318 trained
men born in his household[r] and went in pursuit as far as Dan.[s] 15 During the night Abram divided his
men to attack them and he routed them, pursuing them as far as Hobah, north of Damascus. 16 He recovered all the goods and brought back his relative Lot and his possessions, together with the women
and the other people.
17 After Abram returned from defeating Kedorlaomer and the kings allied with him, the king of
Sodom came out to meet him in the Valley of Shaveh (that is, the King's Valley).[t]
18 Then Melchizedek[u] king of Salem[v] brought out bread and wine. He was priest of God Most High,
19 and he blessed Abram,[w] saying,

"Blessed be Abram by God Most High,
Creator of heaven and earth.[x]
20 And praise be to God Most High,[y]
who delivered your enemies into your hand."

Then Abram gave him a tenth of everything.[z]
21 The king of Sodom said to Abram, "Give me the people and keep the goods for yourself."
22 But Abram said to the king of Sodom, "With raised hand[a] I have sworn an oath to the LORD, God

[a] *13* Or *a relative*; or *an ally*

14:8–11 Unable to repel the invading coalition, the local kings flee in disarray, leaving the cities of Sodom and Gomorrah to be plundered.
14:13 Hebrew. Against the background of all the different ethnic groups mentioned in the first part of this chapter, Abram is designated a Hebrew. This is the first occurrence of this term in the Bible. It may be associated with the name Eber, first mentioned in 10:21, from whom the Israelites are descended. Although similar sounding, the name Hebrew is not associated with the people referred to as *habiru/hapiru* in the el-Amarna tablets of the fourteenth century BC.
14:14 trained men. This translates a rare Hebrew word that possibly refers to those who have had some form of military training. Through a surprise attack at night, Abram's relatively small force successfully routs their opponents, who flee northward toward their own territories (v. 15). **Dan.** The name that the Israelites gave to the city of Laish after they captured it (Judg 18:27–29). See Introduction to the Pentateuch, p. 9.
14:17–24 The different responses of the kings of Salem and Sodom to Abram's victory contrast a God-centered approach to life with a human-centered one. Recognizing God's place in human affairs, Abram is not prepared to enhance his own status within the land of Canaan by taking what belonged to others, even when it is captured in battle. Abram distances himself from the "winner takes all" attitude of the king of Sodom. Abram will not use the military power available to him to take control of the land of Canaan; rather, he waits on God to reward him (cf. 15:1). Genesis condemns the misuse of violence as a perversion of humanity's divinely given authority over the earth.
14:17 Valley of Shaveh. Later known as the King's Valley (2 Sam 18:18), it was east of Jerusalem.
14:18 Melchizedek. This form of name was common among second-millennium BC Canaanites. Scholars debate its original meaning; it could possibly mean "Melek is just," "Zedek is my king," or "My king is just" (cf. Malkiel, meaning "El is my king," in 46:17), where Melek and Zedek are divine names. By NT times, the name was understood to mean "king of righteousness" (Heb 7:2). Although little is known of him, as a priest-king of Jerusalem associated with both righteousness and peace, Melchizedek became a figure of special significance (see Ps 110:4). The author of Hebrews argues that Jesus Christ is a priest belonging to the "order of Melchizedek" (Heb 5:6,10; 6:20; 7:11,17); because Abram gives him a tithe, Melchizedek's priestly order is superior to the priests associated with the tribe of Levi (see Heb 5:5–10; 6:20—7:28 and notes). **Salem.** A shortened form of Jerusalem (Ps 76:2). "Salem" also resembles the Hebrew word for peace (Heb 7:2). **God Most High.** This is one of several designations Genesis uses for God in which various attributes qualify "El," the common Semitic term for God (e.g., *ʾēl rŏʾî*, "the God who sees me" [16:13]; *ʾēl šadday*, "God Almighty" [17:1]; *ʾēl ʿôlām*, "the Eternal God" [21:33]).
14:19 Creator of heaven and earth. Melchizedek's description of God implies that God is more than simply the creator of everything. He is also its possessor, a striking affirmation in the light of the human conflict over territory in the opening part of this chapter. Rejecting God's ownership of the earth lies at the heart of human sin.
14:20 a tenth. In order to affirm Melchizedek's remarks, Abram gives him a tithe, or tenth, of the recovered goods.
14:22–24 Abram swiftly dismisses the king of Sodom's offer. He will not become indebted to the king of Sodom in order to fulfill God's plan that he become a "great nation" (12:2). Although Abram has demonstrated that he is more than the equal of earthly kings, he recognizes

Most High, Creator of heaven and earth,[b] 23that I will accept nothing belonging to you,[c] not even a thread or the strap of a sandal, so that you will never be able to say, 'I made Abram rich.' 24I will accept nothing but what my men have eaten and the share that belongs to the men who went with me — to Aner, Eshkol and Mamre. Let them have their share."

The Lord's Covenant With Abram

15 After this, the word of the LORD came to Abram[d] in a vision:

"Do not be afraid,[e] Abram.
I am your shield,[a][f]
your very great reward.[b]"

2But Abram said, "Sovereign LORD, what can you give me since I remain childless[g] and the one who will inherit[c] my estate is Eliezer of Damascus?" 3And Abram said, "You have given me no children; so a servant[h] in my household will be my heir."

4Then the word of the LORD came to him: "This man will not be your heir, but a son who is your own flesh and blood will be your heir.[i]" 5He took him outside and said, "Look up at the sky and count the stars[j] — if indeed you can count them." Then he said to him, "So shall your offspring[d] be."[k]

6Abram believed the LORD, and he credited it to him as righteousness.[l]

7He also said to him, "I am the LORD, who brought you out of Ur of the Chaldeans to give you this land to take possession of it."

8But Abram said, "Sovereign LORD, how can I know[m] that I will gain possession of it?"

9So the LORD said to him, "Bring me a heifer, a goat and a ram, each three years old, along with a dove and a young pigeon."

10Abram brought all these to him, cut them in two and arranged the halves opposite each other;[n] the birds, however, he did not cut in half.[o] 11Then birds of prey came down on the carcasses, but Abram drove them away.

12As the sun was setting, Abram fell into a deep sleep,[p] and a thick and dreadful darkness came over him. 13Then the LORD said to him, "Know for certain that for four hundred years[q] your descendants will be strangers in a country not their own and that they will be enslaved[r] and mistreated there. 14But I will punish the nation they serve as slaves, and afterward they will come out[s] with great possessions.[t] 15You,

[a] *1* Or *sovereign* [b] *1* Or *shield; / your reward will be very great* [c] *2* The meaning of the Hebrew for this phrase is uncertain. [d] *5* Or *seed*

14:22 [b] ver 19
14:23 [c] 2Ki 5:16
15:1 [d] Da 10:1 [e] Ge 21:17; 26:24; 46:3; 2Ki 6:16; Ps 27:1; Isa 41:10,13-14 [f] Dt 33:29; 2Sa 22:3,31; Ps 3:3
15:2 [g] Ac 7:5
15:3 [h] Ge 24:2,34
15:4 [i] Gal 4:28
15:5 [j] Ps 147:4; Jer 33:22 [k] Ge 12:2; 22:17; Ex 32:13; Ro 4:18*; Heb 11:12
15:6 [l] Ps 106:31; Ro 4:3*, 20-24*; Gal 3:6*; Jas 2:23*
15:8 [m] Lk 1:18
15:10 [n] ver 17; Jer 34:18 [o] Lev 1:17
15:12 [p] Ge 2:21
15:13 [q] ver 16; Ex 12:40; Ac 7:6,17 [r] Ex 1:11
15:14 [s] Ac 7:7* [t] Ex 12:32-38

that such greatness comes from God and is not the product of merely human effort.

15:1–21 *The Lord's Covenant With Abram.* The related issues of descendants and land dominate this chapter; both are essential to the future creation of a great nation. Whereas vv. 1–6 focus on Abram's childlessness, vv. 7–21 address the issue of how Abram can be certain that his descendants will possess the land of Canaan. The earlier conditional promise of nationhood (12:2) is now strengthened by a covenant that guarantees unconditionally a future fulfillment centuries after Abram's death.

15:1 very great reward. The events of ch. 15 are a sequel to Abram's rejection of the plunder taken from the cities of Sodom and Gomorrah. Rather than place his hope in wealth acquired by force, Abram looks to God. Possibly, Abram's vision occurs at night, for v. 5 indicates that numerous stars are visible.

15:2 Eliezer of Damascus. His identity is uncertain; he is mentioned by name only here. He is highly trusted by Abram and is perhaps a slave who came originally from Damascus. During his journey to Canaan, Abram probably acquired men to look after his herds and flocks (17:23,27). Ancient Near Eastern texts provide examples of childless couples adopting a member of their household to be their heir. Because the meaning of the Hebrew text is slightly obscure (see NIV text note), the interpretation of this verse should be approached cautiously.

15:6 This verse is highly significant within the episode. Descriptive comments like this are very rare in OT narratives and are all the more important when they occur. Abram's trust in God becomes the basis upon which God views him as righteous. Only later is Abram circumcised (17:23–27). The concept of righteousness based on faith becomes an important biblical principle for how people are brought into a right relationship with God. In the NT Paul quotes this verse three times (Rom 4:3,22; Gal 3:6) to argue that Gentile Christians can be righteous through faith without being circumcised (Rom 4:1–25; Gal 3:1–9). The apostle James observes that Abram's faith later expresses itself in good works (Jas 2:21–24).

15:9–17 The ritual described here has been interpreted in different ways. Based on possible parallels with Jer 34:18–19, this may be a self-curse in which God indicates that he will become like the dead animals if he breaks his promise to Abram. Alternatively, the "smoking firepot" (v. 17) may represent God; the animals, Abram's descendants; and the birds of prey, their enemies. If we adopt the symbolism of this second alternative, this unusual event anticipates the future presence of God among the Israelites after their exodus from Egypt.

15:13 four hundred years. God indicates clearly to Abram that his descendants will take possession of the land of Canaan only after a long period of time has elapsed. This figure, which may refer to all of the time spent in the foreign land and not just the period of oppression, is probably best understood as a round number, equivalent to the expression "four centuries" in English. Although Exod 12:40 states that the Israelites were in Egypt for 430 years, for at least 70 of these years they enjoyed protection from oppression while Joseph was still alive.

15:15 [u]Ge 25:8
15:16 [v]1Ki 21:26
15:17 [w]ver 10
15:18 [x]Ge 12:7 [y]Nu 34:5
16:1 [z]Ge 11:30; Gal 4:24-25 [a]Ge 21:9
16:2 [b]Ge 30:3-4,9-10
16:3 [c]Ge 12:5
16:5 [d]Ge 31:53
16:7 [e]Ge 21:17; 22:11, 15; 31:11 [f]Ge 20:1
16:10 [g]Ge 13:16; 17:20

however, will go to your ancestors in peace and be buried at a good old age.[u] 16 In the fourth generation
your descendants will come back here, for the sin of the Amorites[v] has not yet reached its full measure."
17 When the sun had set and darkness had fallen, a smoking firepot with a blazing torch appeared and
passed between the pieces.[w] 18 On that day the LORD made a covenant with Abram and said, "To your descendants I give this land,[x] from the Wadi[a] of Egypt[y] to the great river, the Euphrates— 19 the land of the Kenites,
Kenizzites, Kadmonites, 20 Hittites, Perizzites, Rephaites, 21 Amorites, Canaanites, Girgashites and Jebusites."

Hagar and Ishmael

16 Now Sarai, Abram's wife, had borne him no children.[z] But she had an Egyptian slave[a] named
Hagar; 2 so she said to Abram, "The LORD has kept me from having children. Go, sleep with my
slave; perhaps I can build a family through her."[b]
Abram agreed to what Sarai said. 3 So after Abram had been living in Canaan[c] ten years, Sarai his
wife took her Egyptian slave Hagar and gave her to her husband to be his wife. 4 He slept with Hagar,
and she conceived.
When she knew she was pregnant, she began to despise her mistress. 5 Then Sarai said to Abram, "You
are responsible for the wrong I am suffering. I put my slave in your arms, and now that she knows she
is pregnant, she despises me. May the LORD judge between you and me."[d]
6 "Your slave is in your hands," Abram said. "Do with her whatever you think best." Then Sarai mistreated Hagar; so she fled from her.
7 The angel of the LORD[e] found Hagar near a spring in the desert; it was the spring that is beside the
road to Shur.[f] 8 And he said, "Hagar, slave of Sarai, where have you come from, and where are you going?"
"I'm running away from my mistress Sarai," she answered.
9 Then the angel of the LORD told her, "Go back to your mistress and submit to her." 10 The angel
added, "I will increase your descendants so much that they will be too numerous to count."[g]
11 The angel of the LORD also said to her:

> "You are now pregnant
> and you will give birth to a son.

[a] 18 Or *river*

15:16 the sin of the Amorites. The population of Canaan consisted of various ethnic groups, among whom the Amorites appear to have been well established (vv. 19–21), especially in the hill country where the Israelites settled first (Num 13:29; Deut 1:7). God will dispossess the Amorites of their territory because of their immoral behavior. While God displays patience in not punishing them immediately, he will not tolerate their immorality forever. Later, the populations of both the northern kingdom of Israel and the southern kingdom of Judah will experience similar punishment for living immorally and disregarding their covenant commitments to God.
15:17 Assuming that vv. 1–6 are set during the night, Abram must have taken most of the day to prepare the animals. **a smoking firepot with a blazing torch.** After sunset this passes between the pieces. Since God's presence is frequently linked directly to fire (e.g., Exod 3:2; 13:21–22; 14:24; 19:18), it may be assumed that he is the one who passes between the divided animals.
15:18–21 The chapter concludes with a summary confirming that God made a covenant through which he pledged unconditionally to give to Abram's descendants the land of Canaan. This covenant guarantees that God will fulfill his earlier promise to make Abram into a great nation (12:2). All that is solemnly pledged here comes to fulfillment for a brief period during the reign of Solomon (1 Kgs 4:21). The boundaries of the land extend from the Euphrates in the north to the Wadi of Egypt in the south (see v. 18 and note).
15:18 Wadi of Egypt. May refer to the eastern branch of the Nile (although this is not the usual Hebrew word for the Nile). Alternatively, it may refer to the Wadi el Arish, which lies to the east of the Nile.
16:1–16 *Hagar and Ishmael.* Sarai's desire to provide an heir for Abram prompts her to adopt a custom referred to in a few ancient Near Eastern texts. Sarai offers her Egyptian maidservant Hagar to Abram in the hope that Hagar will bear a son on her behalf. After Hagar conceives, friction develops between the two women, causing Hagar to run away. In the end God sees Hagar's plight and persuades her to return. Perhaps Abram mistakenly assumes that Ishmael is the heir God promised.
16:3 wife. Hagar's status changes from servant to wife, although she still has a secondary position within the household in relation to Sarai (25:6). Abram's taking a second wife does not indicate that God sanctions bigamy. This was not something God required in order to fulfill his promises. Abram's actions hinder rather than help the outworking of God's plan for Abram. Scripture always portrays taking additional wives as problematic and less than the ideal.
16:5–6 Responding to the rift that develops between the two women, Abram acquiesces to Sarai's demand. As a result, Sarai treats Hagar harshly. Of Egyptian descent, Hagar flees toward her homeland.
16:7 angel of the LORD. The Hebrew word for "angel" may also denote a "messenger," and angels may have the appearance of human beings (18:2). While the expression "angel of the LORD" may denote a creature other than the Lord, it seems more likely in this instance, as sometimes elsewhere (e.g., Exod 3:2–4), that this is God himself. Not only does the angel speak with divine authority, but afterward Hagar refers to her experience in terms of having seen God (v. 13).
16:10 As a reward, the angel promises Hagar numerous descendants. This may have encouraged Abram to see Hagar's child as the divinely promised heir.
16:11 Ishmael. Hagar calls her son "God hears" (see NIV text note) in recognition of God's intervention.

You shall name him Ishmael,[a]
for the LORD has heard of your misery.[h]
12 He will be a wild donkey of a man;
his hand will be against everyone
and everyone's hand against him,
and he will live in hostility
toward[b] all his brothers.[i]"

13 She gave this name to the LORD who spoke to her: "You are the God who sees me," for she said,
"I have now seen[c] the One who sees me."[j] 14 That is why the well was called Beer Lahai Roi[d]; it is still
there, between Kadesh and Bered.

15 So Hagar bore Abram a son,[k] and Abram gave the name Ishmael to the son she had borne. 16 Abram
was eighty-six years old when Hagar bore him Ishmael.

The Covenant of Circumcision

17 When Abram was ninety-nine years old, the LORD appeared to him and said, "I am God Almighty[e];[l] walk before me faithfully and be blameless.[m] 2 Then I will make my covenant between
me and you[n] and will greatly increase your numbers."

3 Abram fell facedown, and God said to him, 4 "As for me, this is my covenant with you:[o] You will
be the father of many nations.[p] 5 No longer will you be called Abram[f]; your name will be Abraham,[g][q]
for I have made you a father of many nations.[r] 6 I will make you very fruitful;[s] I will make nations of
you, and kings will come from you.[t] 7 I will establish my covenant as an everlasting covenant between

[a] *11 Ishmael* means *God hears.* [b] *12* Or *live to the east / of* [c] *13* Or *seen the back of* [d] *14 Beer Lahai Roi* means *well of the Living One who sees me.* [e] *1* Hebrew *El-Shaddai* [f] *5 Abram* means *exalted father.* [g] *5 Abraham* probably means *father of many.*

16:11 [h] Ex 2:24; 3:7,9
16:12 [i] Ge 25:18
16:13 [j] Ge 32:30
16:15 [k] Gal 4:22
17:1 [l] Ge 28:3; Ex 6:3 [m] Dt 18:13
17:2 [n] Ge 15:18
17:4 [o] Ge 15:18 [p] ver 16; Ge 12:2; 35:11; 48:19
17:5 [q] ver 15; Ne 9:7 [r] Ro 4:17*
17:6 [s] Ge 35:11 [t] Mt 1:6

16:12 Although the angel commands Hagar to submit to Sarai (v. 9), he states that her son's independent spirit will bring him into conflict with others.

16:13–14 God's unexpected intervention makes a deep impression on Hagar. His concern for her plight causes her to name him "El Roi" ("the God who sees me") and the well "Beer Lahai Roi" (see NIV text note). Not only does God see her, but she has also seen him.

16:15 After Hagar returns to Abram's household and her son is born, Abram names him. Recognizing Ishmael as his heir, Abram must have believed that here was God's solution to the continuation of his family and the fulfillment of the divine promise of nationhood. Regrettably, Ishmael was not the promised son that God intended Abram and Sarai to have. Their attempt to fulfill God's plan by human effort ultimately fails. As the ongoing story of Abram's life reveals, in his time God enables Sarai to give birth to Isaac. The contrast between the son of promise and the son of the slave woman is later used by Paul in his letter to the Galatians to illustrate the distinction between acquiring salvation through faith in Christ and failing to merit salvation through human endeavor (Gal 4:21–31).

17:1–27 *The Covenant of Circumcision.* Having previously made a covenant with Abram to guarantee the divine promise of nationhood (ch. 15), the Lord now appears to Abram in order to either establish another covenant or develop further the one already made in Gen 15. Coming 13 years after the birth of Ishmael, this covenant involves the birth of Sarai's son, with whom God will establish the covenant in the next generation. At the heart of this covenant is God's promise to bless the nations of the earth (12:3), which the change of Abram's name to Abraham reflects. God's speech to Abraham moves from God's part (vv. 4–8) to that of Abraham (vv. 9–14) and then to Sarah (vv. 15–16).

17:1 God Almighty. God introduces himself to Abram as *El Shaddai* (see NIV text note). While the precise meaning of *Shaddai* is debated, the designation most likely underlines God's power, anticipating God's promise to provide Abram a son through Sarai, who is now 89 years old. **walk before me.** Elsewhere those who "walk with" God display a positive, consistent relationship with him (e.g., Enoch [5:22]; Noah [6:9]). **blameless.** The Hebrew elsewhere denotes sacrificial animals that are without blemish. Abram must resemble Noah (6:9), with whom God also made an everlasting covenant (9:1–17).

17:2 Then I will make my covenant. Unlike the covenant in ch. 15, the establishment of this covenant is conditional based upon Abram remaining faithful to God.

17:4,5 father of many nations. Repeated for emphasis, this phrase encapsulates the covenant.

17:5 By changing the patriarch's name from Abram to Abraham (see NIV text notes), God conveys the purpose of this covenant. **father.** Although this term usually points to a biological relationship, here it is metaphoric, picking up God's earlier promise that through Abram "all peoples on earth will be blessed" (12:3). As the spiritual father of many nations, Abraham will bring God's blessing to them. For this reason, the males circumcised in 17:27 include those who are not Abraham's offspring (see v. 12). Later in Genesis, Joseph, who brings blessing to the nations, states that God made him "father to Pharaoh" (45:8; see Judg 17:10 for another metaphoric use of "father"). **many nations.** The international dimension of this covenant is important and indicates that circumcision was not originally about merely defining ethnic Israel. For this reason the apostle Paul views the "offspring" of Abraham as including Gentiles who share Abraham's faith (Rom 4:16–17; 15:8–12; Gal 3:6–9,29; cf. Rom 9:6–7).

17:6 I will make you very fruitful. This promise recalls God's blessing of humanity at creation (1:28), which was later renewed with Noah (9:1). Through Abraham God will eventually fulfill his plan to fill the earth with people who will live in harmony with their Creator. **I will make nations of you.** This underlines the international nature of the covenant, for Abraham was the biological father of only a few nations. **kings will come from you.** This possibly looks backward to the theme of ruling mentioned in 1:26–28 and looks forward to the establishment of a monarchy within Israel.

17:7 everlasting. This covenant looks toward the future and will be established with future generations of Abraham's descendants, beginning with Isaac (v. 21).

17:7 [u]Ex 29:45,46 [v]Ro 9:8; Gal 3:16
17:8 [w]Ps 105:9,11 [x]Ge 23:4; 28:4; Ex 6:4 [y]Ge 12:7
17:10 [z]ver 23; Ge 21:4; Jn 7:22; Ac 7:8; Ro 4:11
17:11 [a]Ex 12:48; Dt 10:16 [b]Ro 4:11
17:12 [c]Lev 12:3; Lk 2:21
17:14 [d]Ex 4:24-26
17:16 [e]Ge 18:10 [f]Ge 35:11; Gal 4:31
17:17 [g]Ge 18:12; 21:6
17:19 [h]Ge 18:14; 21:2 [i]Ge 26:3
17:20 [j]Ge 16:10 [k]Ge 25:12-16 [l]Ge 21:18

me and you and your descendants after you for the generations to come, to be your God[u] and the God
of your descendants after you.[v] 8The whole land of Canaan,[w] where you now reside as a foreigner,[x] I
will give as an everlasting possession to you and your descendants after you;[y] and I will be their God."
9Then God said to Abraham, "As for you, you must keep my covenant, you and your descendants
after you for the generations to come. 10This is my covenant with you and your descendants after you,
the covenant you are to keep: Every male among you shall be circumcised.[z] 11You are to undergo
circumcision,[a] and it will be the sign of the covenant[b] between me and you. 12For the generations to
come every male among you who is eight days old must be circumcised,[c] including those born in your
household or bought with money from a foreigner — those who are not your offspring. 13Whether born
in your household or bought with your money, they must be circumcised. My covenant in your flesh is
to be an everlasting covenant. 14Any uncircumcised male, who has not been circumcised in the flesh,
will be cut off from his people;[d] he has broken my covenant."
15God also said to Abraham, "As for Sarai your wife, you are no longer to call her Sarai; her name
will be Sarah. 16I will bless her and will surely give
you a son by her.[e] I will bless her so that she will be
the mother of nations;[f] kings of peoples will come
from her."
17Abraham fell facedown; he laughed[g] and said
to himself, "Will a son be born to a man a hundred years old? Will Sarah bear a child at the age of
ninety?" 18And Abraham said to God, "If only Ishmael might live under your blessing!"
19Then God said, "Yes, but your wife Sarah will
bear you a son,[h] and you will call him Isaac.[a] I will
establish my covenant with him[i] as an everlasting
covenant for his descendants after him. 20And as for
Ishmael, I have heard you: I will surely bless him; I
will make him fruitful and will greatly increase his
numbers.[j] He will be the father of twelve rulers,[k]
and I will make him into a great nation.[l] 21But my

[a] *19 Isaac* means *he laughs.*

A detail of a relief in the tomb of Ankhmahor at Saqqara depicting a priest performing ritual circumcision, ca. 2600 BC.
Werner Forman Archive/Glow Images

17:10–14 Certain covenants have signs associated with them (e.g., the rainbow [9:12–13]; the Sabbath [Exod 31:16–17]). Circumcision is the distinctive sign of this covenant.
17:10 circumcised. This required cutting the foreskin off of the penis. Associating this covenant with the male reproductive organ draws attention to the special offspring of Abraham through whom the benefits of the covenant will be mediated to others. In the first instance, the covenant will be established with Isaac, but not Ishmael, even though Ishmael is circumcised.
17:12–14 Every male within Abraham's household must be circumcised, including those bought as slaves from foreigners. Given the international aspect of the covenant, circumcision is not restricted to only those who are the biological descendants of Abraham.
17:14 will be cut off from his people. Applies to those who are not circumcised. While the precise nature of this cutting off is unclear, it undoubtedly implies exclusion from the community, if not death. To refuse circumcision would have been perceived as rejecting the significance of God's promises to Abraham. Much later, when these promises are being fulfilled in Jesus Christ, the apostle Paul insists that the circumcision of the heart is more important than circumcision of the foreskin (Rom 2:25–29; cf. 1 Cor 7:18–19; Gal 6:15). For Paul, "righteousness" comes through faith in Christ, the one to whom circumcision pointed.
17:15 Sarah. Sarai's name is changed to Sarah; both forms mean "princess."
17:16 bless her. Although Sarah has been childless for many years (11:30), God states that he will bless her with a son. God's blessing, however, is not restricted to a son. Sarah will produce "nations," as well as "kings of peoples" (cf. 17:6). Once again this chapter underscores the international aspect of this covenant.
17:19 Isaac. Since Abraham laughed when God announced that Sarah will have a son (v. 17), it is ironic that their son should be called "he laughs" (see NIV text note). Later, when Sarah overhears that she will have a son, she also laughs (18:12–15). In both instances the laughter of Abraham and Sarah probably reflects their disbelief, given their ages (17:17). The motif of laughter recurs in the account of Isaac's birth (21:6). **establish my covenant.** Although Abraham considers Ishmael to be his son, God stresses that his covenant will be linked specifically to Isaac. While Ishmael and the other male members of Abraham's household will be circumcised before Isaac is born, God does not establish the covenant with them. **descendants after him.** God indicates that the covenant will pass from Abraham to Isaac and then on through Isaac to future generations. This links the blessing of the nations to the unique line of offspring descended from Abraham via Isaac and then Jacob. Ultimately this special lineage leads to Jesus Christ (Matt 1:1–17).
17:20 the father of twelve rulers. In spite of being passed over in favor of his yet-to-be-born brother, Ishmael's family will be important in its own right (25:12–18).

covenant I will establish with Isaac, whom Sarah will bear to you by this time next year."[m] 22When he had finished speaking with Abraham, God went up from him.

23On that very day Abraham took his son Ishmael and all those born in his household or bought with his money, every male in his household, and circumcised them, as God told him. 24Abraham was ninety-nine years old when he was circumcised,[n] 25and his son Ishmael was thirteen; 26Abraham and his son Ishmael were both circumcised on that very day. 27And every male in Abraham's household, including those born in his household or bought from a foreigner, was circumcised with him.

The Three Visitors

18 The LORD appeared to Abraham near the great trees of Mamre[o] while he was sitting at the entrance to his tent in the heat of the day. 2Abraham looked up and saw three men[p] standing nearby. When he saw them, he hurried from the entrance of his tent to meet them and bowed low to the ground.

3He said, "If I have found favor in your eyes, my lord,[a] do not pass your servant by. 4Let a little water be brought, and then you may all wash your feet[q] and rest under this tree. 5Let me get you something to eat,[r] so you can be refreshed and then go on your way—now that you have come to your servant."

"Very well," they answered, "do as you say."

6So Abraham hurried into the tent to Sarah. "Quick," he said, "get three seahs[b] of the finest flour and knead it and bake some bread."

7Then he ran to the herd and selected a choice, tender calf and gave it to a servant, who hurried to prepare it. 8He then brought some curds and milk and the calf that had been prepared, and set these before them.[s] While they ate, he stood near them under a tree.

9"Where is your wife Sarah?" they asked him.

"There, in the tent," he said.

10Then one of them said, "I will surely return to you about this time next year, and Sarah your wife will have a son."[t]

Now Sarah was listening at the entrance to the tent, which was behind him. 11Abraham and Sarah were already very old,[u] and Sarah was past the age of childbearing.[v] 12So Sarah laughed[w] to herself as she thought, "After I am worn out and my lord[x] is old, will I now have this pleasure?"

13Then the LORD said to Abraham, "Why did Sarah laugh and say, 'Will I really have a child, now that I am old?' 14Is anything too hard for the LORD?[y] I will return to you at the appointed time next year, and Sarah will have a son."

[a] *3* Or *eyes, Lord* [b] *6* That is, probably about 36 pounds or about 16 kilograms

17:21 [m] Ge 21:2
17:24 [n] Ro 4:11
18:1 [o] Ge 13:18; 14:13
18:2 [p] ver 16,22; Ge 32:24; Jos 5:13; Jdg 13:6-11; Heb 13:2
18:4 [q] Ge 19:2; 43:24
18:5 [r] Jdg 13:15
18:8 [s] Ge 19:3
18:10 [t] Ro 9:9*
18:11 [u] Ge 17:17 [v] Ro 4:19
18:12 [w] Ge 17:17; 21:6 [x] 1Pe 3:6
18:14 [y] Jer 32:17,27; Zec 8:6; Mt 19:26; Lk 1:37; Ro 4:21

17:23–27 Abraham confirms that he accepts everything God has said by circumcising all the males in his household.

18:1—19:38 The three episodes that comprise this section center on Lot's dramatic rescue when God destroys Sodom. By comparing Lot's hospitality with Abraham's, the narrative explains why God saves Lot and his family. However, God punishes the remaining inhabitants of the city for their immorality.

18:1–15 *The Three Visitors.* Responding generously to the unexpected arrival of three "men" at his tent, Abraham graciously offers them hospitality that extends from washing their feet to providing a freshly prepared meal. While the text describes all three visitors as "men," one of them is the Lord (v. 1), and the others are angels (19:1). They disclose the purpose of their encounter with Abraham only when they set out to journey on to Sodom (vv. 16–21).

18:1 the great trees of Mamre. As a seminomadic herdsman and tent-dweller, Abraham may have regularly camped at this location (13:18).

18:2 three men. See note on vv. 1–15. Abraham must have viewed them as important visitors, for he runs to meet them and bows down to the ground before them. An elderly, wealthy herdsman would not normally greet visitors like this.

18:3–5 While Abraham treats all the visitors with respect, his initial word of invitation indicates that he views one of the men as more important than the others.

18:3 my lord. May be used to indicate respect for an important person (e.g., 23:6 ["Sir"]) or to address God in prayer (e.g., 20:4). From what is said, it is difficult to tell at what point Abraham recognized the special visitor as the Lord (see NIV text note).

18:5 something to eat. Abraham sets about preparing a lavish meal for his visitors. Abraham's actions underline his desire to satisfy his guests as best he can. He even stands (v. 8), waiting on them, while they eat the food. Stressing the importance of hospitality, Heb 13:2 possibly alludes to this occasion and also Lot's actions in Gen 19:1–3.

18:9–15 As the meal proceeds, the Lord promises that Sarah will bear Abraham a son in 12 months (v. 10).

18:11–12 Since Sarah has passed the age of bearing children, she laughs disbelievingly at the thought of giving birth to a son. Her reaction resembles that of Abraham in 17:17. Nothing, however, is "too hard for the LORD" (18:14).

18:17 [z]Am 3:7 [a]Ge 19:24
18:18 [b]Gal 3:8*
18:19 [c]Dt 4:9-10; 6:7 [d]Jos 24:15; Eph 6:4
18:21 [e]Ge 11:5
18:22 [f]Ge 19:1
18:23 [g]Nu 16:22
18:24 [h]Jer 5:1
18:25 [i]Job 8:3,20; Ps 58:11; 94:2; Isa 3:10-11; Ro 3:6
18:26 [j]Jer 5:1
18:27 [k]Ge 2:7; 3:19; Job 30:19; 42:6
18:32 [l]Jdg 6:39 [m]Jer 5:1

15 Sarah was afraid, so she lied and said, "I did not laugh."
But he said, "Yes, you did laugh."

Abraham Pleads for Sodom

16 When the men got up to leave, they looked down toward Sodom, and Abraham walked along with
them to see them on their way. 17 Then the LORD said, "Shall I hide from Abraham[z] what I am about
to do?[a] 18 Abraham will surely become a great and powerful nation,[b] and all nations on earth will be
blessed through him.[a] 19 For I have chosen him, so that he will direct his children[c] and his household
after him to keep the way of the LORD[d] by doing what is right and just, so that the LORD will bring about
for Abraham what he has promised him."
20 Then the LORD said, "The outcry against Sodom and Gomorrah is so great and their sin so grievous 21 that I will go down[e] and see if what they have done is as bad as the outcry that has reached me.
If not, I will know."
22 The men turned away and went toward Sodom,[f] but Abraham remained standing before the LORD.[b]
23 Then Abraham approached him and said: "Will you sweep away the righteous with the wicked?[g]
24 What if there are fifty righteous people in the city? Will you really sweep it away and not spare[c] the
place for the sake of the fifty righteous people in it?[h] 25 Far be it from you to do such a thing—to kill
the righteous with the wicked, treating the righteous and the wicked alike. Far be it from you! Will not
the Judge of all the earth do right?"[i]
26 The LORD said, "If I find fifty righteous people in the city of Sodom, I will spare the whole place
for their sake.[j]"
27 Then Abraham spoke up again: "Now that I have been so bold as to speak to the Lord, though I
am nothing but dust and ashes,[k] 28 what if the number of the righteous is five less than fifty? Will you
destroy the whole city for lack of five people?"
"If I find forty-five there," he said, "I will not destroy it."
29 Once again he spoke to him, "What if only forty are found there?"
He said, "For the sake of forty, I will not do it."
30 Then he said, "May the Lord not be angry, but let me speak. What if only thirty can be found there?"
He answered, "I will not do it if I find thirty there."
31 Abraham said, "Now that I have been so bold as to speak to the Lord, what if only twenty can be
found there?"
He said, "For the sake of twenty, I will not destroy it."
32 Then he said, "May the Lord not be angry, but let me speak just once more.[l] What if only ten can
be found there?"
He answered, "For the sake of ten,[m] I will not destroy it."
33 When the LORD had finished speaking with Abraham, he left, and Abraham returned home.

[a] *18* Or *will use his name in blessings* (see 48:20) [b] *22* Masoretic Text; an ancient Hebrew scribal tradition *but the LORD remained standing before Abraham* [c] *24* Or *forgive*; also in verse 26

18:16–33 *Abraham Pleads for Sodom.* Perhaps out of concern for his nephew Lot (although he does not specifically mention Lot), Abraham questions the Lord about the forthcoming destruction of Sodom. The text already mentioned that Sodom's inhabitants are wicked (13:13), a point underlined by how Melchizedek contrasts with the king of Sodom (14:17–24). Abraham's concern centers on the possibility that the total destruction of the city may include people who are righteous. Cautiously, Abraham presents various scenarios to God, reducing by stages the number of righteous people in the city. Eventually, God reassures Abraham that he will not destroy Sodom if there are ten righteous people within the city.

18:18 all nations on earth. God's remarks emphasize the important role that Abraham will have in mediating God's blessing to the whole world. This recalls God's earlier promise in 12:2–3 and the covenant in ch. 17, which portrays Abraham as the "father of many nations" (17:5; see note there).

18:20–21 God does not take lightly his decision to destroy Sodom and Gomorrah. The Lord's visit demonstrates that the destruction is punishment for their wrongdoing. There is no reason to assume on the basis of these verses that God's knowledge of all that occurs on earth is somehow limited. Before God punishes, he scrutinizes the situation with the utmost rigor.

18:23–26 Seizing the opportunity, Abraham questions the Lord regarding the fate of the righteous in Sodom. Will God treat the good and the bad in the same way? Abraham seeks reassurance that God will not act unfairly. See "Justice," p. 2679.

18:27–32 Acknowledging the inappropriateness of questioning God on this issue (v. 27), Abraham boldly ventures to do so, gradually reducing the number of righteous from fifty (v. 28) to ten (v. 32). In all likelihood, Abraham stops at ten because God has established the principle that the righteous will not be punished alongside the wicked, and reducing the number yet further seems petty or unbelieving. In the light of this, it is noteworthy that in ch. 19 only Lot and two of his daughters escape from the city when the angels warn them of its destruction.

Sodom and Gomorrah Destroyed

19 The two angels arrived at Sodom[n] in the evening, and Lot was sitting in the gateway of the city.[o]
When he saw them, he got up to meet them and bowed down with his face to the ground. 2“My
lords,” he said, “please turn aside to your servant’s house. You can wash your feet[p] and spend the night
and then go on your way early in the morning.”

“No,” they answered, “we will spend the night in the square.”

3But he insisted so strongly that they did go with him and entered his house. He prepared a meal for
them, baking bread without yeast, and they ate.[q] 4Before they had gone to bed, all the men from every
part of the city of Sodom—both young and old—surrounded the house. 5They called to Lot, “Where
are the men who came to you tonight? Bring them out to us so that we can have sex with them.”[r]

6Lot went outside to meet them[s] and shut the door behind him 7and said, “No, my friends. Don’t do
this wicked thing. 8Look, I have two daughters who have never slept with a man. Let me bring them
out to you, and you can do what you like with them. But don’t do anything to these men, for they have
come under the protection of my roof.”[t]

9“Get out of our way,” they replied. “This fellow came here as a foreigner, and now he wants to play
the judge![u] We’ll treat you worse than them.” They kept bringing pressure on Lot and moved forward
to break down the door.

10But the men inside reached out and pulled Lot back into the house and shut the door. 11Then they
struck the men who were at the door of the house, young and old, with blindness[v] so that they could
not find the door.

12The two men said to Lot, “Do you have anyone else here—sons-in-law, sons or daughters, or anyone else in the city who belongs to you?[w] Get them out of here, 13because we are going to destroy this
place. The outcry to the LORD against its people is so great that he has sent us to destroy it.”[x]

14So Lot went out and spoke to his sons-in-law, who were pledged to marry[*a*] his daughters. He said,
“Hurry and get out of this place, because the LORD is about to destroy the city![y]” But his sons-in-law
thought he was joking.[z]

15With the coming of dawn, the angels urged Lot, saying, “Hurry! Take your wife and your two
daughters who are here, or you will be swept away[a] when the city is punished.[b]”

16When he hesitated, the men grasped his hand and the hands of his wife and of his two daughters
and led them safely out of the city, for the LORD was merciful to them. 17As soon as they had brought
them out, one of them said, “Flee for your lives![c] Don’t look back,[d] and don’t stop anywhere in the
plain! Flee to the mountains or you will be swept away!”

18But Lot said to them, “No, my lords,[*b*] please! 19Your[*c*] servant has found favor in your[*c*] eyes, and
you[*c*] have shown great kindness to me in sparing my life. But I can’t flee to the mountains; this disaster
will overtake me, and I’ll die. 20Look, here is a town near enough to run to, and it is small. Let me flee
to it—it is very small, isn’t it? Then my life will be spared.”

19:1 [n] Ge 18:22 [o] Ge 18:1
19:2 [p] Ge 18:4; Lk 7:44
19:3 [q] Ge 18:6
19:5 [r] Jdg 19:22; Isa 3:9; Ro 1:24-27
19:6 [s] Jdg 19:23
19:8 [t] Jdg 19:24
19:9 [u] Ex 2:14; Ac 7:27
19:11 [v] Dt 28:28-29; 2Ki 6:18; Ac 13:11
19:12 [w] Ge 7:1
19:13 [x] 1Ch 21:15
19:14 [y] Nu 16:21 [z] Ex 9:21; Lk 17:28
19:15 [a] Nu 16:26 [b] Rev 18:4
19:17 [c] Jer 48:6 [d] ver 26

[*a*] 14 Or *were married to* [*b*] 18 Or *No, Lord*; or *No, my lord* [*c*] 19 The Hebrew is singular.

19:1–29 *Sodom and Gomorrah Destroyed.* Although Sodom is destroyed, Lot escapes with two of his daughters due to the intervention of the angels. Lot’s desire to protect his “visitors” from being sexually abused by the men of Sodom sets him apart from the rest of the population. His hospitality and protection of the men is an indicator of his righteousness (2 Pet 2:7–8).

19:1–3 Lot previously camped “near Sodom” (13:12), but now he lives within the city. His hospitable response to the visitors closely resembles Abraham’s in 18:1–5. The similarities indicate that Lot by nature resembles Abraham. His subsequent protection of the men further indicates his righteousness (2 Pet 2:7–8). Lot’s wife, unlike Sarah, plays no obvious role in preparing the meal for the strangers.

19:4 from every part of the city … both young and old. The assault on Lot’s house involves all the men of Sodom.

19:5 have sex with them. Their desire to have homosexual relations with the two visitors indicates their depravity (Jude 7); the term “sodomy” derives from this episode. See note on Rom 1:26.

19:6–11 When Lot tries unsuccessfully to placate the men of Sodom, rather than hand over his guests, he offers the mob his unmarried daughters. In this ancient context, a host was obliged to protect his guests from all harm, a cultural imperative that drove him to this extreme suggestion. In 2 Pet 2:7 Lot is called a “righteous man, who was distressed by the depraved conduct of the lawless”; this statement is difficult to understand apart from this ancient code of honor. Lot’s offer also sheds light on the mob itself: These men of Sodom were determined to have sexual relations with Lot’s two guests. Their wickedness was pervasive and persistent.

19:12–16 Lot’s sons-in-law greet the announcement of Sodom’s destruction with ridicule. Even Lot himself is reluctant to leave and has to be physically led out of the city (v. 16).

19:17–23 In spite of being instructed to leave the valley, Lot begs for permission to go to another settlement in the valley appropriately called Zoar, which means “small.”

19:24 [e] Dt 29:23; Isa 1:9; 13:19 [f] Lk 17:29; 2Pe 2:6; Jude 7
19:25 [g] Ps 107:34; Eze 16:48
19:26 [h] ver 17 [i] Lk 17:32
19:27 [j] Ge 18:22
19:28 [k] Rev 9:2; 18:9
19:29 [l] 2Pe 2:7
19:30 [m] ver 19
19:37 [n] Dt 2:9
19:38 [o] Dt 2:19
20:1 [p] Ge 18:1 [q] Ge 26:1,6,17
20:2 [r] ver 12; Ge 12:13; 26:7 [s] Ge 12:15

[21]He said to him, "Very well, I will grant this request too; I will not overthrow the town you speak of. [22]But flee there quickly, because I cannot do anything until you reach it." (That is why the town was called Zoar.[a])

[23]By the time Lot reached Zoar, the sun had risen over the land. [24]Then the LORD rained down burning sulfur on Sodom and Gomorrah[e]—from the LORD out of the heavens.[f] [25]Thus he overthrew those cities and the entire plain, destroying all those living in the cities—and also the vegetation in the land.[g] [26]But Lot's wife looked back,[h] and she became a pillar of salt.[i]

[27]Early the next morning Abraham got up and returned to the place where he had stood before the LORD.[j] [28]He looked down toward Sodom and Gomorrah, toward all the land of the plain, and he saw dense smoke rising from the land, like smoke from a furnace.[k]

[29]So when God destroyed the cities of the plain, he remembered Abraham, and he brought Lot out of the catastrophe[l] that overthrew the cities where Lot had lived.

Lot and His Daughters

[30]Lot and his two daughters left Zoar and settled in the mountains,[m] for he was afraid to stay in Zoar. He and his two daughters lived in a cave. [31]One day the older daughter said to the younger, "Our father is old, and there is no man around here to give us children—as is the custom all over the earth. [32]Let's get our father to drink wine and then sleep with him and preserve our family line through our father."

[33]That night they got their father to drink wine, and the older daughter went in and slept with him. He was not aware of it when she lay down or when she got up.

[34]The next day the older daughter said to the younger, "Last night I slept with my father. Let's get him to drink wine again tonight, and you go in and sleep with him so we can preserve our family line through our father." [35]So they got their father to drink wine that night also, and the younger daughter went in and slept with him. Again he was not aware of it when she lay down or when she got up.

[36]So both of Lot's daughters became pregnant by their father. [37]The older daughter had a son, and she named him Moab[b]; he is the father of the Moabites[n] of today. [38]The younger daughter also had a son, and she named him Ben-Ammi[c]; he is the father of the Ammonites[d][o] of today.

Abraham and Abimelek

20:1-18Ref — Ge 12:10-20; 26:1-11

20 Now Abraham moved on from there[p] into the region of the Negev and lived between Kadesh and Shur. For a while he stayed in Gerar,[q] [2]and there Abraham said of his wife Sarah, "She is my sister."[r] Then Abimelek king of Gerar sent for Sarah and took her.[s]

[a] *22 Zoar* means *small.* [b] *37 Moab* sounds like the Hebrew for *from father.* [c] *38 Ben-Ammi* means *son of my father's people.* [d] *38* Hebrew *Bene-Ammon*

19:24–25 God destroys Sodom and Gomorrah using burning sulfur that rains down from the sky. The unusual nature of this exceptional event underlines that it is an act of divine punishment. Subsequently, the cities of Sodom and Gomorrah become synonymous with human depravity (e.g., Isa 1:9; Lam 4:6; Zeph 2:9; Matt 11:23–24; Rev 11:8). Against this background, Lot's rescue emphasizes God's concern for the righteous in the midst of a world that stands condemned for its sinfulness (2 Pet 2:6–9).
19:26 a pillar of salt. For disobeying the instruction not to look back (v. 17), Lot's wife becomes petrified. Her action suggests that she identified with the people of Sodom, of whom she may have been one. Her failure to flee from God's punishment becomes a vivid warning to others (Luke 17:32).
19:27–29 Looking down on the plain, Abraham witnesses what has happened to Sodom and Gomorrah. By linking Lot's rescue to the Lord remembering Abraham (v. 29), the narrator alludes to the recurring motif that through Abraham others will be divinely blessed. This is the second occasion when Abraham has come to the rescue of Lot (14:14–16).
19:30–38 *Lot and His Daughters.* Genesis records one further brief episode in Lot's life, revealing how through incestuous relations with his daughters he becomes the ancestor of the Moabites and Ammonites.
19:30 lived in a cave. Fear causes Lot to abandon Zoar and live in a cave. The ravines and cliffs around the Dead Sea contain numerous caves; archaeological evidence reveals that these were sometimes used for shelter from danger.
19:31–36 Lot's decision to live in the mountains has unexpected consequences. Given their isolated existence, his daughters have no one with which to have children. A childless woman in this time period had an insecure future. Thus, the daughters plot to become pregnant through having intercourse with their father. By getting Lot drunk with wine, they succeed in having sex with him, though he is entirely unaware of what has happened. As in the case of Noah (9:21–24), sexual immorality is associated with alcohol abuse.
19:37–38 Moab ... Ben-Ammi. These names possibly reflect the circumstances by which the boys are conceived (see NIV text notes). In explaining the origin of the Moabites and Ammonites, this episode clearly casts them in a negative light. Later generations of Israelites may well have been suspicious of these nations.
20:1–18 *Abraham and Abimelek.* Sarah's abduction by the king of Gerar threatens to undermine God's promise that she will bear Abraham a son. Building on the earlier account of Sarah being taken by Pharaoh (12:10–20), this episode stresses that Abimelek did not touch Sarah, an important consideration in the light of Isaac's subsequent birth (21:1–7).
20:1 This episode opens by describing how Abraham moves to a loca-

3 But God came to Abimelek in a dream[t] one night and said to him, "You are as good as dead because of the woman you have taken; she is a married woman."[u]

4 Now Abimelek had not gone near her, so he said, "Lord, will you destroy an innocent nation?[v] 5 Did he not say to me, 'She is my sister,' and didn't she also say, 'He is my brother'? I have done this with a clear conscience and clean hands."

6 Then God said to him in the dream, "Yes, I know you did this with a clear conscience, and so I have kept[w] you from sinning against me. That is why I did not let you touch her. 7 Now return the man's wife, for he is a prophet, and he will pray for you[x] and you will live. But if you do not return her, you may be sure that you and all who belong to you will die."

8 Early the next morning Abimelek summoned all his officials, and when he told them all that had happened, they were very much afraid. 9 Then Abimelek called Abraham in and said, "What have you done to us? How have I wronged you that you have brought such great guilt upon me and my kingdom? You have done things to me that should never be done.[y]" 10 And Abimelek asked Abraham, "What was your reason for doing this?"

11 Abraham replied, "I said to myself, 'There is surely no fear of God[z] in this place, and they will kill me because of my wife.'[a] 12 Besides, she really is my sister, the daughter of my father though not of my mother; and she became my wife. 13 And when God had me wander from my father's household, I said to her, 'This is how you can show your love to me: Everywhere we go, say of me, "He is my brother."'"

14 Then Abimelek brought sheep and cattle and male and female slaves and gave them to Abraham,[b] and he returned Sarah his wife to him. 15 And Abimelek said, "My land is before you; live wherever you like."[c] 16 To Sarah he said, "I am giving your brother a thousand shekels[a] of silver. This is to cover the offense against you before all who are with you; you are completely vindicated."

17 Then Abraham prayed to God,[d] and God healed Abimelek, his wife and his female slaves so they could have children again, 18 for the LORD had kept all the women in Abimelek's household from conceiving because of Abraham's wife Sarah.[e]

The Birth of Isaac

21 Now the LORD was gracious to Sarah[f] as he had said, and the LORD did for Sarah what he had promised.[g] 2 Sarah became pregnant and bore a son[h] to Abraham in his old age,[i] at the very time God had promised him. 3 Abraham gave the name Isaac[b][j] to the son Sarah bore him. 4 When his son Isaac was eight days old, Abraham circumcised him,[k] as God commanded him. 5 Abraham was a hundred years old when his son Isaac was born to him.

20:3 [t] Job 33:15; Mt 27:19 [u] Ps 105:14
20:4 [v] Ge 18:25
20:6 [w] 1Sa 25:26,34
20:7 [x] ver 17; 1Sa 7:5; Job 42:8
20:9 [y] Ge 12:18; 26:10; 34:7
20:11 [z] Ge 42:18; Ps 36:1 [a] Ge 12:12; 26:7
20:14 [b] Ge 12:16
20:15 [c] Ge 13:9
20:17 [d] Job 42:9
20:18 [e] Ge 12:17
21:1 [f] 1Sa 2:21 [g] Ge 8:1; 17:16,21; Gal 4:23
21:2 [h] Ge 17:19 [i] Gal 4:22; Heb 11:11
21:3 [j] Ge 17:19
21:4 [k] Ge 17:10,12; Ac 7:8

a *16* That is, about 25 pounds or about 12 kilograms   *b* *3* *Isaac* means *he laughs.*

tion where he and Sarah are unknown. **Gerar.** Located in the south of what became known as Israel (see map, p. 2865).
20:2 Because they are unknown in Gerar, Abraham is able to claim that Sarah is his sister. The narrator provides no explanation as to why Abraham makes this claim, presuming that the reader is already familiar with 12:11–13. Abraham's actions suggest that he lacks faith in God to protect him. **Abimelek.** Means "my father is king"; it was a common royal name (26:1; Ps 34 superscription).
20:3–5 God's intervention ensures that no harm comes to Sarah. Abimelek rightly proclaims his innocence. Such details underline that he did not have intercourse with Sarah, excluding the possibility that he could be the father of Isaac.
20:3 in a dream. This is the first occasion in the OT when God communicates in this way (see 28:12; 31:10–11; 37:5–9; 40:5–8; 41:1).
20:7 prophet. Abraham is the first person the OT designates as a prophet. God's comments emphasize how Abraham is able to intercede on behalf of others, which he previously did for the righteous in Sodom (18:16–33).
20:9 With justification Abimelek points to Abraham's deceptive behavior in calling Sarah his sister. **guilt.** May also be translated "sin." Canaanite texts designate adultery as a "great sin."
20:11 no fear of God in this place. As Abimelek's actions demonstrate, Abraham's expectations regarding the people of Gerar are mistaken.
20:12 Abraham looks to excuse his actions by noting that Sarah is his half sister. Abraham's use of this half-truth, however, has not prevented others from taking Sarah. But for God's intervention, Abimelek would not have returned Sarah to Abraham.
20:14–16 Although innocent, Abimelek makes restitution in public to Abraham for having taken Sarah. The king demonstrates that others should not attribute guilt to Sarah.
20:17–18 The healing of Abimelek, his wife, and his female slaves highlights God's ability to restore fertility. This anticipates the next episode, in which God restores to Sarah the ability to conceive and have a son. By noting that Abraham prayed for the restoration of Abimelek's household to normality, the narrator draws attention to the motif of others being blessed through Abraham (12:3). This is the first occasion in the Bible when healing is associated with intercessory prayer.
21:1–7 *The Birth of Isaac.* In her old age Sarah gives birth to Isaac in fulfillment of God's promise to Abraham and Sarah. God does what they had considered to be impossible.
21:1–2 God's earlier promises to Abraham and Sarah (17:16,19,21; 18:10,14) are now fulfilled.
21:3–4 Abraham obeys God's instructions by naming his son Isaac (17:19) and circumcising him (17:12).
21:5–7 Sarah's comments about laughter in v. 6 provide a further wordplay on the name Isaac, which means "he laughs" (17:17–19;

21:6 [l]Ge 17:17; Isa 54:1
21:9 [m]Ge 16:15 [n]Gal 4:29
21:10 [o]Gal 4:30*
21:11 [p]Ge 17:18
21:12 [q]Ro 9:7*; Heb 11:18*
21:13 [r]ver 18
21:14 [s]ver 31,32
21:17 [t]Ex 3:7
21:18 [u]ver 13
21:19 [v]Nu 22:31
21:20 [w]Ge 26:3,24; 28:15; 39:2,21,23
21:21 [x]Ge 24:4,38
21:23 [y]ver 31; Jos 2:12

6 Sarah said, "God has brought me laughter,[l] and everyone who hears about this will laugh with me." 7 And she added, "Who would have said to Abraham that Sarah would nurse children? Yet I have borne him a son in his old age."

Hagar and Ishmael Sent Away

8 The child grew and was weaned, and on the day Isaac was weaned Abraham held a great feast. 9 But Sarah saw that the son whom Hagar the Egyptian had borne to Abraham[m] was mocking,[n] 10 and she said to Abraham, "Get rid of that slave woman and her son, for that woman's son will never share in the inheritance with my son Isaac."[o]

11 The matter distressed Abraham greatly because it concerned his son.[p] 12 But God said to him, "Do not be so distressed about the boy and your slave woman. Listen to whatever Sarah tells you, because it is through Isaac that your offspring[a] will be reckoned.[q] 13 I will make the son of the slave into a nation[r] also, because he is your offspring."

14 Early the next morning Abraham took some food and a skin of water and gave them to Hagar. He set them on her shoulders and then sent her off with the boy. She went on her way and wandered in the Desert of Beersheba.[s]

15 When the water in the skin was gone, she put the boy under one of the bushes. 16 Then she went off and sat down about a bowshot away, for she thought, "I cannot watch the boy die." And as she sat there, she[b] began to sob.

17 God heard the boy crying,[t] and the angel of God called to Hagar from heaven and said to her, "What is the matter, Hagar? Do not be afraid; God has heard the boy crying as he lies there. 18 Lift the boy up and take him by the hand, for I will make him into a great nation.[u]"

19 Then God opened her eyes[v] and she saw a well of water. So she went and filled the skin with water and gave the boy a drink.

20 God was with the boy[w] as he grew up. He lived in the desert and became an archer. 21 While he was living in the Desert of Paran, his mother got a wife for him[x] from Egypt.

The Treaty at Beersheba

22 At that time Abimelek and Phicol the commander of his forces said to Abraham, "God is with you in everything you do. 23 Now swear[y] to me here before God that you will not deal falsely with me or my children or my descendants. Show to me and the country where you now reside as a foreigner the same kindness I have shown to you."

[a] *12* Or *seed* [b] *16* Hebrew; Septuagint *the child*

18:12–15). Laughter of disbelief now becomes laughter of joy as God provides the elderly couple with a son.

21:8–21 *Hagar and Ishmael Sent Away.* The departure of Ishmael from Abraham's household signals that he is no longer Abraham's main heir, something that would have been assumed as he is Abraham's firstborn son.

21:8 weaned. Isaac is possibly two or three years old.

21:9 Ishmael's attitude toward Isaac distresses Sarah. Ishmael, about 16 years old, mocks his younger brother (cf. Gal 4:29). **mocking.** The Hebrew term used probably implies here laughing in jest and is a further wordplay on the name Isaac (see note on vv. 5–7).

21:10 Offended by Ishmael's treatment of Isaac, Sarah demands that Abraham disinherit Ishmael, expelling both him and his mother, Hagar.

21:11 distressed. Abraham is distraught because he viewed Ishmael as his son (16:15; 17:18).

21:12–13 God intervenes, however, confirming Isaac's special status and reassuring Abraham again that Ishmael will become a nation (17:20).

21:12 offspring will be reckoned. In spite of Ishmael being Abraham's eldest son, God confirms that Abraham's descendants will be traced through Isaac. As in 17:19–21, the outworking of God's plan to bless the nations is linked to Isaac. Other biblical writers note that God chose Isaac over Ishmael. God's promise to establish his covenant with Isaac gives Abraham the confidence to believe that God, if necessary, will raise Isaac to life again (Heb 11:17–19). Paul draws on this verse to show that not all of Abraham's biological children are automatically "children of the promise" (Rom 9:8; see Rom 9:6–13). God is free to choose how he will fulfill his redemptive plan.

21:14–15 In obedience to God, Abraham sends Hagar and Ishmael off. When they run out of water in the desert region in the south of what became known as Israel, they collapse with exhaustion, anticipating that they will soon die. God, however, intervenes and reassures Hagar that he cares for both her and Ishmael. Although God has special plans for Isaac, he does not abandon Hagar and Ishmael. God previously intervened in Hagar's life and promised that she would be the mother of a great nation (16:10–12).

21:19 well of water. Wells were an important source of water in this region (26:18–22; see note on 21:25–26).

21:21 Desert of Paran. Lies in the northern part of Sinai, between Egypt and Canaan. See map, p. 2868.

21:22–34 *The Treaty at Beersheba.* Abimelek's desire to establish a friendship treaty with Abraham reflects Abraham's status as someone of importance. Abimelek's actions would be pointless if Abraham was merely an insignificant seminomadic herdsman.

21:22 God is with you in everything you do. Abimelek's opening words acknowledge the source of Abraham's power. Abimelek, king of Gerar (20:2), views Abraham as an equal.

24 Abraham said, "I swear it."
25 Then Abraham complained to Abimelek about a well of water that Abimelek's servants had seized.[z]
26 But Abimelek said, "I don't know who has done this. You did not tell me, and I heard about it only
today."
27 So Abraham brought sheep and cattle and gave them to Abimelek, and the two men made a treaty.[a]
28 Abraham set apart seven ewe lambs from the flock, 29 and Abimelek asked Abraham, "What is the
meaning of these seven ewe lambs you have set apart by themselves?"
30 He replied, "Accept these seven lambs from my hand as a witness[b] that I dug this well."
31 So that place was called Beersheba,[a][c] because the two men swore an oath there.
32 After the treaty had been made at Beersheba, Abimelek and Phicol the commander of his forces
returned to the land of the Philistines. 33 Abraham planted a tamarisk tree in Beersheba, and there he
called on the name of the LORD,[d] the Eternal God.[e] 34 And Abraham stayed in the land of the Philistines
for a long time.

Abraham Tested

22 Some time later God tested[f] Abraham. He said to him, "Abraham!"
"Here I am," he replied.
2 Then God said, "Take your son[g], your only son, whom you love — Isaac — and go to the region of
Moriah.[h] Sacrifice him there as a burnt offering on a mountain I will show you."
3 Early the next morning Abraham got up and loaded his donkey. He took with him two of his servants and his son Isaac. When he had cut enough wood for the burnt offering, he set out for the place
God had told him about. 4 On the third day Abraham looked up and saw the place in the distance. 5 He
said to his servants, "Stay here with the donkey while I and the boy go over there. We will worship and
then we will come back to you."
6 Abraham took the wood for the burnt offering and placed it on his son Isaac,[i] and he himself

[a] *31 Beersheba* can mean *well of seven* and *well of the oath.*

21:25 [z] Ge 26:15, 18, 20-22
21:27 [a] Ge 26:28, 31
21:30 [b] Ge 31:44, 47, 48, 50, 52
21:31 [c] Ge 26:33
21:33 [d] Ge 4:26 [e] Dt 33:27
22:1 [f] Dt 8:2, 16; Heb 11:17; Jas 1:12-13
22:2 [g] ver 12, 16; Jn 3:16; Heb 11:17; 1Jn 4:9 [h] 2Ch 3:1
22:6 [i] Jn 19:17

21:25–26 Since the treaty about to be sealed is designed to ensure harmony between the two men, Abraham seizes the opportunity to resolve a dispute over ownership of a well. Without Abimelek's knowledge, some of his servants took possession of a well Abraham had dug (26:18).
21:30 as a witness. In the process of ratifying the treaty, Abraham gives Abimelek seven lambs to confirm that he was responsible for digging the well.
21:31 Beersheba. The name of the well is associated with the covenant ceremony (see NIV text note). The Genesis narrative implies that in Abraham's time no permanent settlement existed at Beersheba. Later, when a town was established there, it became famous as the southern boundary of Israel (2 Sam 3:10; 17:11).
21:32 Philistines. The name usually denotes people from territories bordering the Aegean Sea who invaded southwest Canaan around 1180 BC. Since Abraham lived much earlier, some argue that this reference to Philistines is anachronistic. If this is so, "Philistines" may replace an older, less-known term so that readers of Genesis would easily understand the geographic detail. Such updating of names occurs elsewhere in Genesis (e.g., "Dan" in 14:14; see note there). It is also possible that even in Abraham's time some of the population in southwest Canaan may have originated from Crete and Cyprus. Aegean pottery from the first half of the second millennium BC has been found in the region of Beersheba. Later writers might well have considered these people to be Philistines, given their links with the Aegean region. See Introduction to the Pentateuch, pp. 12–13.
21:34 The treaty with Abimelek may explain Abraham's prolonged stay in the region of Beersheba.
22:1–19 *Abraham Tested.* God's request that Abraham sacrifice Isaac is highly remarkable, especially given the importance attached to Isaac's birth. This test of Abraham's obedience results, however, in a divine oath that guarantees the fulfillment of the promises God first gave to Abraham in 12:1–3. The events of ch. 22 form a fitting climax to the story of Abraham's relationship with God. While Abraham's faith in God has been evident from the time he left his family in Harran (12:1) and later led to God's crediting it to him as righteousness (15:6), this same faith, shown through obedience, brings to a special fulfillment Abraham's journey with God (Jas 2:21).
22:1 God tested Abraham. Faith in God, to be genuine, must be tested. On this occasion God seeks to determine Abraham's willingness to obey him by placing on him the ultimate challenge: he must kill his own son. This request is highly ironic given the importance placed upon the birth of Isaac in ch. 21 and the expectation that through him God will establish the covenant of circumcision (17:19). While God may test the obedience of people (e.g., Exod 15:25; 16:4), he never tempts anyone to do something wrong (Jas 1:13).
22:2 your son, your only son, whom you love. God's words underscore Abraham's special relationship with his son Isaac, especially given the departure of Ishmael (21:8–21). **Moriah.** The author of Chronicles places the later construction of the temple by Solomon at Mount Moriah (2 Chr 3:1). Although Gen 22 does not specifically identify the mountain, it is possible that it was located where Solomon constructed the temple. **Sacrifice him there as a burnt offering.** Although God demands that Abraham sacrifice Isaac, the outcome reveals that God never intended Abraham to fulfill this request. Rather, as the narrator highlights in his opening words, God intended to test Abraham's trust in him. God could have placed no greater demand on Abraham.
22:3–4 From Beersheba to the region of Moriah is about 45 miles (72 kilometers), a journey that would have taken several days.
22:5 we will come back to you. In spite of his mission, Abraham is confident that Isaac will return with him. According to the author of Hebrews, Abraham obeyed God, believing that in these circumstances God would restore Isaac to life again (Heb 11:17–19).

22:7 [j]Lev 1:10
22:9 [k]Heb 11:17-19; Jas 2:21
22:12 [l]1Sa 15:22; Jas 2:21-22 [m]ver 2; Jn 3:16
22:13 [n]Ro 8:32
22:14 [o]ver 8
22:16 [p]Lk 1:73; Heb 6:13
22:17 [q]Heb 6:14* [r]Ge 15:5 [s]Ge 26:24; 32:12 [t]Ge 24:60
22:18 [u]Ge 12:2,3; Ac 3:25*; Gal 3:8* [v]ver 10
22:20 [w]Ge 11:29

carried the fire and the knife. As the two of them went on together, [7]Isaac spoke up and said to his
father Abraham, "Father?"

"Yes, my son?" Abraham replied.

"The fire and wood are here," Isaac said, "but where is the lamb[j] for the burnt offering?"

[8]Abraham answered, "God himself will provide the lamb for the burnt offering, my son." And the
two of them went on together.

[9]When they reached the place God had told him about, Abraham built an altar there and arranged
the wood on it. He bound his son Isaac and laid him on the altar,[k] on top of the wood. [10]Then he
reached out his hand and took the knife to slay his son. [11]But the angel of the LORD called out to him
from heaven, "Abraham! Abraham!"

"Here I am," he replied.

[12]"Do not lay a hand on the boy," he said. "Do not do anything to him. Now I know that you fear
God,[l] because you have not withheld from me your son, your only son.[m]"

[13]Abraham looked up and there in a thicket he saw a ram[a] caught by its horns. He went over and
took the ram and sacrificed it as a burnt offering instead of his son.[n] [14]So Abraham called that place
The LORD Will Provide. And to this day it is said, "On the mountain of the LORD it will be provided.[o]"

[15]The angel of the LORD called to Abraham from heaven a second time [16]and said, "I swear by myself,[p] declares the LORD, that because you have done this and have not withheld your son, your only
son, [17]I will surely bless you and make your descendants[q] as numerous as the stars in the sky[r] and as
the sand on the seashore.[s] Your descendants will take possession of the cities of their enemies,[t] [18]and
through your offspring[b] all nations on earth will be blessed,[c][u] because you have obeyed me."[v]

[19]Then Abraham returned to his servants, and they set off together for Beersheba. And Abraham
stayed in Beersheba.

Nahor's Sons

[20]Some time later Abraham was told, "Milkah is also a mother; she has borne sons to your brother
Nahor:[w] [21]Uz the firstborn, Buz his brother, Kemuel (the father of Aram), [22]Kesed, Hazo, Pildash, Jid-

[a] *13* Many manuscripts of the Masoretic Text, Samaritan Pentateuch, Septuagint and Syriac; most manuscripts of the Masoretic Text *a ram behind him* [b] *18* Or *seed* [c] *18* Or *and all nations on earth will use the name of your offspring in blessings* (see 48:20)

22:8 God himself will provide the lamb. Up to this point, Abraham has apparently not disclosed to Isaac the full details of God's instructions. Abraham's reply to Isaac reflects either a profound trust in God that he will intervene or an attempt to conceal from Isaac the fate that awaits him.

22:11 angel of the LORD. See note on 16:7.

22:12 God intervenes because Abraham has shown through his obedience how much he reverences God. Previously, God reckoned Abraham righteous on the basis of his faith (15:6). That same faith is now made evident by what Abraham does (Jas 2:21–23).

22:13 ram. God not only intervenes to prevent Abraham from sacrificing Isaac, but he also provides an alternative sacrifice. Burnt offerings atone for human wrongdoing and are a reminder that obedience alone is insufficient to restore humanity's broken relationship with God. In this instance, the burnt offering precedes and prepares for a divine oath that confirms Abraham's unique place in God's plan for the redemption of humanity. The provision of the ram as a substitutionary offering in place of Isaac reflects a wider biblical understanding of sacrificial offerings. Animal sacrifice was commonly viewed as being substitutionary, i.e., the animal dies in the place of the worshiper. Jesus Christ is the ultimate, divinely provided substitute (Mark 10:45; John 1:29; Heb 7:27; 10:14; 1 Pet 3:18).

22:14 The LORD Will Provide. Echoing v. 8, this name reflects God's provision of a sacrifice. God later sends his Son to redeem humanity by dying sacrificially near the same location. **to this day.** Introduces a comment that probably comes from the time of the monarchy when the temple was functioning in Jerusalem. See Introduction to the Pentateuch, pp. 12–13. **the mountain of the LORD.** Alludes to the temple in Jerusalem (Isa 2:3).

22:15–18 The oath God swears links back to the call of Abraham in 12:1–3. The fulfillment of all that God promised Abraham in 12:1–3 was conditional upon the patriarch's obedience. Having passed the ultimate test of submission to God, Abraham now receives a solemn guarantee confirming that God will bring to completion everything that he promised Abraham (Heb 6:13–18). Whereas the first part of the divine oath affirms that Abraham will have many descendants, the final part indicates that through one of Abraham's offspring all nations on earth will be blessed. While some interpret the second half of the oath as referring to all of Abraham descendants, the book of Genesis as a whole associates blessing with a unique lineage that it traces from Abraham via Isaac and Jacob to Joseph. This family line anticipates the coming of a divinely chosen king who will mediate God's blessing to the nations. This divine oath to Abraham finds its fulfillment in Jesus Christ (Acts 3:25–26; Gal 3:16).

22:17 descendants. In the NIV, the final part of v. 17 refers to Abraham's many descendants. But it is possible that the Hebrew word denotes a single individual who will be victorious over his enemies. This singular reading could help explain the apostle Paul's claim that Jesus Christ is the ultimate descendant of Abraham (Gal 3:16).

22:20–24 *Nahor's Sons.* This short section lists the sons of Abraham's brother Nahor. This information is placed here to separate the main account of Abraham's life (chs. 12–22) from three episodes that bring closure to what has been recorded: reports of the death and burial of Sarah (23:1–20) and of Abraham (25:1–11) frame the lengthy report of how Rebekah becomes Isaac's wife (24:1–67).

laph and Bethuel." [23]Bethuel became the father of Rebekah.[x] Milkah bore these eight sons to Abraham's
brother Nahor. [24]His concubine, whose name was Reumah, also had sons: Tebah, Gaham, Tahash and
Maakah.

The Death of Sarah

23 Sarah lived to be a hundred and twenty-seven years old. [2]She died at Kiriath Arba[y] (that is,
Hebron)[z] in the land of Canaan, and Abraham went to mourn for Sarah and to weep over her.
[3]Then Abraham rose from beside his dead wife and spoke to the Hittites.[a] He said, [4]"I am a foreigner
and stranger[a] among you. Sell me some property for a burial site here so I can bury my dead."
[5]The Hittites replied to Abraham, [6]"Sir, listen to us. You are a mighty prince[b] among us. Bury your
dead in the choicest of our tombs. None of us will refuse you his tomb for burying your dead."
[7]Then Abraham rose and bowed down before the people of the land, the Hittites. [8]He said to them,
"If you are willing to let me bury my dead, then listen to me and intercede with Ephron son of Zohar[c]
on my behalf [9]so he will sell me the cave of Machpelah, which belongs to him and is at the end of his
field. Ask him to sell it to me for the full price as a burial site among you."
[10]Ephron the Hittite was sitting among his people and he replied to Abraham in the hearing of all
the Hittites who had come to the gate[d] of his city. [11]"No, my lord," he said. "Listen to me; I give[b][e] you
the field, and I give[b] you the cave that is in it. I give[b] it to you in the presence of my people. Bury your
dead."
[12]Again Abraham bowed down before the people of the land [13]and he said to Ephron in their hearing,
"Listen to me, if you will. I will pay the price of the field. Accept it from me so I can bury my dead there."
[14]Ephron answered Abraham, [15]"Listen to me, my lord; the land is worth four hundred shekels[c] of
silver,[f] but what is that between you and me? Bury your dead."
[16]Abraham agreed to Ephron's terms and weighed out for him the price he had named in the
hearing of the Hittites: four hundred shekels of silver,[g] according to the weight current among the
merchants.
[17]So Ephron's field in Machpelah near Mamre[h]—both the field and the cave in it, and all the trees
within the borders of the field—was deeded [18]to Abraham as his property in the presence of all the
Hittites who had come to the gate of the city. [19]Afterward Abraham buried his wife Sarah in the cave in
the field of Machpelah near Mamre (which is at Hebron) in the land of Canaan. [20]So the field and the
cave in it were deeded[i] to Abraham by the Hittites as a burial site.

[a] *3* Or *the descendants of Heth*; also in verses 5, 7, 10, 16, 18 and 20 [b] *11* Or *sell* [c] *15* That is, about 10 pounds or about 4.6 kilograms

22:23 [x] Ge 24:15
23:2 [y] Jos 14:15 [z] ver 19; Ge 13:18
23:4 [a] Ge 17:8; 1Ch 29:15; Ps 105:12; Heb 11:9,13
23:6 [b] Ge 14:14-16; 24:35
23:8 [c] Ge 25:9
23:10 [d] Ge 34:20-24; Ru 4:4
23:11 [e] 2Sa 24:23
23:15 [f] Eze 45:12
23:16 [g] Jer 32:9; Zec 11:12
23:17 [h] Ge 25:9; 49:30-32; 50:13; Ac 7:16
23:20 [i] Jer 32:10

22:23 Rebekah. A granddaughter of Nahor. This reference to her anticipates the events of ch. 24.

23:1–20 *The Death of Sarah.* The account of Sarah's death is significant because it results in Abraham buying a plot of land near the town of Hebron. As a burial site, the cave of Machpelah becomes the permanent property of Abraham's descendants, a reminder that their future will be closely tied to the land of Canaan, in fulfillment of God's promises (12:7; 13:14–17; 15:18–21; 17:8).

23:2 Kiriath Arba. This town was later renamed Hebron (Josh 14:15; Judg 1:10). Abraham's link with Hebron is first mentioned in 13:18.

23:3 Hittites. Here the term designates the inhabitants of Kiriath Arba (see NIV text note). This name appears to have been used of different people groups, the best known being the Hittites of Anatolia and Syria. It seems unlikely that the Hittites of Hebron are closely related to those of Anatolia and Syria.

23:4 a foreigner and stranger among you. Abraham recognizes that he has no legitimate claim to any land in Canaan. For 62 years he has adopted a seminomadic lifestyle, refusing to settle in any of the towns of Canaan. He now looks to make a permanent claim to some land by buying property close to Hebron. Heb 11:9–10 attributes Abraham's wandering lifestyle to his theological beliefs: "He was looking forward to the city with foundations, whose architect and builder is God" (v. 10).

23:6 Although Abraham plays down his status (v. 4), the Hittites view him as someone of standing, and they generously offer to let him bury Sarah in one of their own tombs. **mighty prince.** Or "prince of God"; the title is highly fitting in the light of the unique royal lineage that will come from Abraham (17:6; Matt 1:1–17).

23:7–9 Careful not to offend the Hittites in view of their generous offer, Abraham tactfully requests that he be permitted to buy a cave from its owner, Ephron. Abraham seeks permission from the Hittite population as a whole, possibly because selling property to a non-Hittite required communal approval. Without their support, Ephron would not have been able to sell the cave to Abraham.

23:10 gate. It was usual for transactions requiring public approval to take place at the entrance to the settlement (Ruth 4:1–11).

23:11–15 In spite of Ephron's willingness to give Abraham the cave and the field attached to it, Abraham insists on buying it for its full value. He wants to ensure that they will formally recognize the property as belonging to him and his descendants in perpetuity.

23:15 four hundred shekels of silver. Abraham readily agrees to what appears to be a substantial price (Jer 32:9). Later in Genesis, Joseph as a slave is valued at 20 shekels (37:28).

23:20 burial site. The cave of Machpelah was the burial site for Abraham (25:9) and Isaac (35:27–29; 49:29–31) and Jacob (49:29–30; 50:13).

24:1 [j]ver 35
24:2 [k]Ge 39:4-6 [l]ver 9; Ge 47:29
24:3 [m]Ge 14:19 [n]Ge 28:1; Dt 7:3 [o]Ge 10:15-19
24:4 [p]Ge 12:1; 28:2
24:7 [q]Gal 3:16* [r]Ge 12:7; 13:15 [s]Ex 23:20,23
24:9 [t]ver 2
24:11 [u]Ex 2:15 [v]ver 13; 1Sa 9:11
24:12 [w]ver 27,42,48; Ge 26:24; Ex 3:6,15,16
24:14 [x]Jdg 6:17,37
24:15 [y]ver 45 [z]Ge 22:23 [a]Ge 22:20 [b]Ge 11:29
24:16 [c]Ge 26:7
24:18 [d]ver 14
24:19 [e]ver 14
24:21 [f]ver 12
24:22 [g]ver 47

Isaac and Rebekah

24 Abraham was now very old, and the LORD had blessed him in every way.[j] 2He said to the senior
servant in his household, the one in charge of all that he had,[k] "Put your hand under my
thigh.[l] 3I want you to swear by the LORD, the God of heaven and the God of earth,[m] that you will not get
a wife for my son[n] from the daughters of the Canaanites,[o] among whom I am living, 4but will go to my
country and my own relatives[p] and get a wife for my son Isaac."
5The servant asked him, "What if the woman is unwilling to come back with me to this land? Shall
I then take your son back to the country you came from?"
6"Make sure that you do not take my son back there," Abraham said. 7"The LORD, the God of heaven,
who brought me out of my father's household and my native land and who spoke to me and promised
me on oath, saying, 'To your offspring[a][q] I will give this land'[r] — he will send his angel before you[s] so
that you can get a wife for my son from there. 8If the woman is unwilling to come back with you, then
you will be released from this oath of mine. Only do not take my son back there." 9So the servant put
his hand under the thigh[t] of his master Abraham and swore an oath to him concerning this matter.
10Then the servant left, taking with him ten of his master's camels loaded with all kinds of good
things from his master. He set out for Aram Naharaim[b] and made his way to the town of Nahor. 11He
had the camels kneel down near the well[u] outside the town; it was toward evening, the time the women
go out to draw water.[v]
12Then he prayed, "LORD, God of my master Abraham,[w] make me successful today, and show kindness to my master Abraham. 13See, I am standing beside this spring, and the daughters of the townspeople are coming out to draw water. 14May it be that when I say to a young woman, 'Please let down
your jar that I may have a drink,' and she says, 'Drink, and I'll water your camels too' — let her be
the one you have chosen for your servant Isaac. By this I will know[x] that you have shown kindness to
my master."
15Before he had finished praying,[y] Rebekah[z] came out with her jar on her shoulder. She was the
daughter of Bethuel son of Milkah,[a] who was the wife of Abraham's brother Nahor.[b] 16The woman was
very beautiful,[c] a virgin; no man had ever slept with her. She went down to the spring, filled her jar
and came up again.
17The servant hurried to meet her and said, "Please give me a little water from your jar."
18"Drink,[d] my lord," she said, and quickly lowered the jar to her hands and gave him a drink.
19After she had given him a drink, she said, "I'll draw water for your camels too,[e] until they have
had enough to drink." 20So she quickly emptied her jar into the trough, ran back to the well to draw
more water, and drew enough for all his camels. 21Without saying a word, the man watched her closely
to learn whether or not the LORD had made his journey successful.[f]
22When the camels had finished drinking, the man took out a gold nose ring[g] weighing a beka[c] and

[a] *7* Or *seed* [b] *10* That is, Northwest Mesopotamia [c] *22* That is, about 1/5 ounce or about 5.7 grams

24:1–67 *Isaac and Rebekah.* Reported in exceptional detail, the account of Rebekah becoming Isaac's wife not only underlines how God providentially directs Abraham's servant to her but also portrays Rebekah as following in Abraham's footsteps by leaving her family and country in order to settle permanently in Canaan.

24:1 the LORD had blessed him in every way. This opening statement confirms that God has fulfilled his earlier promise to bless Abraham (12:2).

24:2–8 Genesis usually describes the Canaanites negatively (9:25–27; 13:11–13); the inhabitants of Sodom (13:13) and Gomorrah are prime examples (18:20–32). For this reason, Abraham does not want Isaac to be influenced by a Canaanite wife. Too old to undertake the journey himself, he charges his most senior servant with the task of traveling to Abraham's homeland, Harran in northern Mesopotamia. While Abraham refers to this region as "my country" (v. 4), he prohibits Isaac from going there. Trusting in God's covenantal guarantee (15:18–21), Abraham is convinced that his future descendants will inhabit the land of Canaan. Moreover, he believes that God will enable his servant to successfully find a wife for Isaac.

24:9 put his hand under the thigh of his master Abraham. By placing his hand there, the servant formally commits himself to fulfilling Abraham's instructions. Jacob later uses this ritual to ensure that Joseph will bury him in Canaan (47:29–30).

24:10 camels. See note on 12:16. **Aram Naharaim.** Means "Aram of the rivers"; see NIV text note. Ancient texts from Mari mention a town called Nakhur situated close to Harran (see 11:31). **Nahor.** The name of both Abraham's grandfather and brother (11:25–27; 22:20). It is not unusual for individuals to be called after a place and vice versa. From Hebron to Harran is a journey of over 500 miles (800 kilometers).

24:12–14 Like Abraham, the servant is a man of faith. He asks God to guide him to the woman who will become Isaac's wife. Common sense informs his prayer for divine help. He seeks a woman who will be both hospitable and hardworking; ten camels (v. 10) would require a considerable quantity of water.

24:15–16 The narrator's description of Rebekah creates a sense of expectation; she is both a relative of Abraham and an attractive, unmarried woman. She has also come to the well to collect water.

24:17–21 Rebekah does everything that the servant mentioned in his prayer.

two gold bracelets weighing ten shekels.[a] 23Then he asked, "Whose daughter are you? Please tell me, is
there room in your father's house for us to spend the night?"
24She answered him, "I am the daughter of Bethuel, the son that Milkah bore to Nahor.[h]" 25And she
added, "We have plenty of straw and fodder, as well as room for you to spend the night."
26Then the man bowed down and worshiped the LORD,[i] 27saying, "Praise be to the LORD,[j] the God of
my master Abraham, who has not abandoned his kindness and faithfulness[k] to my master. As for me,
the LORD has led me on the journey[l] to the house of my master's relatives."[m]
28The young woman ran and told her mother's household about these things. 29Now Rebekah had a
brother named Laban,[n] and he hurried out to the man at the spring. 30As soon as he had seen the nose
ring, and the bracelets on his sister's arms, and had heard Rebekah tell what the man said to her, he went
out to the man and found him standing by the camels near the spring. 31"Come, you who are blessed by
the LORD,"[o] he said. "Why are you standing out here? I have prepared the house and a place for the camels."
32So the man went to the house, and the camels were unloaded. Straw and fodder were brought for
the camels, and water for him and his men to wash their feet.[p] 33Then food was set before him, but he
said, "I will not eat until I have told you what I have to say."
"Then tell us," Laban said.
34So he said, "I am Abraham's servant. 35The LORD has blessed my master abundantly,[q] and he has
become wealthy. He has given him sheep and cattle, silver and gold, male and female servants, and
camels and donkeys.[r] 36My master's wife Sarah has borne him a son in her old age,[s] and he has given
him everything he owns.[t] 37And my master made me swear an oath, and said, 'You must not get a wife
for my son from the daughters of the Canaanites, in whose land I live,[u] 38but go to my father's family
and to my own clan, and get a wife for my son.'[v]
39"Then I asked my master, 'What if the woman will not come back with me?'[w]
40"He replied, 'The LORD, before whom I have walked faithfully, will send his angel with you[x] and
make your journey a success, so that you can get a wife for my son from my own clan and from my
father's family. 41You will be released from my oath if, when you go to my clan, they refuse to give her
to you—then you will be released from my oath.'[y]
42"When I came to the spring today, I said, 'LORD, God of my master Abraham, if you will, please
grant success[z] to the journey on which I have come. 43See, I am standing beside this spring.[a] If a young
woman comes out to draw water and I say to her, "Please let me drink a little water from your jar,"[b]
44and if she says to me, "Drink, and I'll draw water for your camels too," let her be the one the LORD
has chosen for my master's son.'
45"Before I finished praying in my heart,[c] Rebekah came out, with her jar on her shoulder.[d] She
went down to the spring and drew water, and I said to her, 'Please give me a drink.'[e]
46"She quickly lowered her jar from her shoulder and said, 'Drink, and I'll water your camels too.'[f]
So I drank, and she watered the camels also.
47"I asked her, 'Whose daughter are you?'[g]
"She said, 'The daughter of Bethuel son of Nahor, whom Milkah bore to him.'[h]
"Then I put the ring in her nose and the bracelets on her arms,[i] 48and I bowed down and worshiped
the LORD.[j] I praised the LORD, the God of my master Abraham, who had led me on the right road to get
the granddaughter of my master's brother for his son.[k] 49Now if you will show kindness and faithfulness[l] to my master, tell me; and if not, tell me, so I may know which way to turn."
50Laban and Bethuel answered, "This is from the LORD;[m] we can say nothing to you one way or the

24:24 [h]ver 15
24:26 [i]ver 48,52; Ex 4:31
24:27 [j]Ex 18:10; Ru 4:14; 1Sa 25:32 [k]ver 49; Ge 32:10; Ps 98:3 [l]ver 21 [m]ver 12,48
24:29 [n]ver 4; Ge 29:5, 12,13
24:31 [o]Ge 26:29; Ru 3:10; Ps 115:15
24:32 [p]Ge 43:24; Jdg 19:21
24:35 [q]ver 1 [r]Ge 13:2
24:36 [s]Ge 21:2,10 [t]Ge 25:5
24:37 [u]ver 3
24:38 [v]ver 4
24:39 [w]ver 5
24:40 [x]ver 7
24:41 [y]ver 8
24:42 [z]ver 12
24:43 [a]ver 13 [b]ver 14
24:45 [c]1Sa 1:13 [d]ver 15 [e]ver 17
24:46 [f]ver 18-19
24:47 [g]ver 23 [h]ver 24 [i]Eze 16:11-12
24:48 [j]ver 26 [k]ver 27
24:49 [l]Ge 47:29; Jos 2:14
24:50 [m]Ps 118:23

a *22* That is, about 4 ounces or about 115 grams

24:24–27 When she identifies herself as the granddaughter of Nahor, Abraham's brother, the servant responds by worshiping God. Through divine guidance he has encountered Abraham's relatives.

24:29 After Rebekah rushes off to inform her family, her brother Laban comes to greet Abraham's servant. Laban's involvement (vv. 30–31,33,50,55–60) suggests that his father, Bethuel, is possibly old and frail. Bethuel is mentioned only once as an active participant in the events that unfold (v. 50). In marked contrast, there are several references to the involvement of Rebekah's mother (vv. 28,55,57–58).

24:34–49 The servant's speech rehearses closely the events that occur in vv. 1–27. The repetition underlines God's guidance in bringing the servant into contact with Rebekah. If Rebekah is to leave her family in order to marry Isaac, whom she has never met, she must be persuaded that this is God's will for her.

24:50 This is from the LORD. Rebekah's brother and father readily acknowledge that God intends Rebekah to marry Isaac.

24:50 [n]Ge 31:7, 24,29,42
24:52 [o]ver 26
24:53 [p]ver 10,22
24:54 [q]ver 56,59
24:59 [r]Ge 35:8
24:60 [s]Ge 17:16 [t]Ge 22:17
24:62 [u]Ge 16:14; 25:11 [v]Ge 20:1
24:63 [w]Ps 1:2; 77:12; 119:15,27,48,97,148; 143:5; 145:5
24:67 [x]Ge 25:20 [y]Ge 29:18,20 [z]Ge 23:1-2
25:2 [a]1Ch 1:32,33

other.[n] 51 Here is Rebekah; take her and go, and let her become the wife of your master's son, as the LORD has directed."

52 When Abraham's servant heard what they said, he bowed down to the ground before the LORD.[o] 53 Then the servant brought out gold and silver jewelry and articles of clothing and gave them to Rebekah; he also gave costly gifts[p] to her brother and to her mother. 54 Then he and the men who were with him ate and drank and spent the night there.

When they got up the next morning, he said, "Send me on my way[q] to my master."

55 But her brother and her mother replied, "Let the young woman remain with us ten days or so; then you[a] may go."

56 But he said to them, "Do not detain me, now that the LORD has granted success to my journey. Send me on my way so I may go to my master."

57 Then they said, "Let's call the young woman and ask her about it." 58 So they called Rebekah and asked her, "Will you go with this man?"

"I will go," she said.

59 So they sent their sister Rebekah on her way, along with her nurse[r] and Abraham's servant and his men. 60 And they blessed Rebekah and said to her,

> "Our sister, may you increase
> to thousands upon thousands;[s]
> may your offspring possess
> the cities of their enemies."[t]

61 Then Rebekah and her attendants got ready and mounted the camels and went back with the man. So the servant took Rebekah and left.

62 Now Isaac had come from Beer Lahai Roi,[u] for he was living in the Negev.[v] 63 He went out to the field one evening to meditate,[b][w] and as he looked up, he saw camels approaching. 64 Rebekah also looked up and saw Isaac. She got down from her camel 65 and asked the servant, "Who is that man in the field coming to meet us?"

"He is my master," the servant answered. So she took her veil and covered herself.

66 Then the servant told Isaac all he had done. 67 Isaac brought her into the tent of his mother Sarah, and he married Rebekah.[x] So she became his wife, and he loved her;[y] and Isaac was comforted after his mother's death.[z]

The Death of Abraham

25:1-4pp — 1Ch 1:32-33

25 Abraham had taken another wife, whose name was Keturah. 2 She bore him Zimran, Jokshan, Medan, Midian, Ishbak and Shuah.[a] 3 Jokshan was the father of Sheba and Dedan; the descendants of Dedan were the Ashurites, the Letushites and the Leummites. 4 The sons of Midian were Ephah, Epher, Hanok, Abida and Eldaah. All these were descendants of Keturah.

[a] 55 Or *she* [b] 63 The meaning of the Hebrew for this word is uncertain.

24:53 As a token of the commitment they have made, the servant gives gifts to Rebekah and members of her family. Marriage arrangements usually involved gifts of money to the bride's family.

25:55–58 Rebekah's willingness to go immediately with Abraham's servant reveals a deep faith in God. She is prepared to leave her family and country to marry a man she has never met. Her actions parallel closely those of Abraham (12:1), suggesting that she is indeed a suitable wife for Isaac.

24:60 The blessing resembles God's oath to Abraham in 22:17. **your offspring.** Could refer to an individual or group of people. Everything points to Rebekah being a perfect match for Isaac.

24:65 took her veil and covered herself. Probably a sign that she was betrothed. Having seen Isaac, she indicates her willingness to marry him.

25:1–11 *The Death of Abraham.* This concludes the account of Abraham's life, which started in 11:27. For completeness, it records additional family details.

25:1 another wife. See note on 16:3. The author provides few details about Abraham's relationship with Keturah and does not view her sons as being on a par with Isaac. Although Abraham provides for these sons during his lifetime, they do not inherit anything when he dies; everything goes to Isaac (vv. 5–6). Given how Abraham treats Keturah's sons, it seems likely that he viewed both Keturah and Hagar as concubines. Certain OT contexts portray such women as married, being "second" wives, but not necessarily of equal status to the "first" wife. Hagar, e.g., continued to be Sarah's maidservant after the birth of Ishmael (16:1–3; 21:10,12; cf. 29:24,29; 30:4,9). While 25:1–6 highlights the identity of various people groups descended from Abraham, it carefully distinguishes these descendants from Isaac. He alone is Abraham's heir.

[5]Abraham left everything he owned to Isaac.[b] [6]But while he was still living, he gave gifts to the sons
of his concubines[c] and sent them away from his son Isaac[d] to the land of the east.
[7]Abraham lived a hundred and seventy-five years. [8]Then Abraham breathed his last and died at a
good old age,[e] an old man and full of years; and he was gathered to his people.[f] [9]His sons Isaac and
Ishmael buried him[g] in the cave of Machpelah near Mamre, in the field of Ephron son of Zohar the
Hittite,[h] [10]the field Abraham had bought from the Hittites.[a][i] There Abraham was buried with his wife
Sarah. [11]After Abraham's death, God blessed his son Isaac, who then lived near Beer Lahai Roi.[j]

Ishmael's Sons

25:12-16pp — 1Ch 1:29-31

[12]This is the account of the family line of Abraham's son Ishmael, whom Sarah's slave, Hagar[k] the
Egyptian, bore to Abraham.[l]

[13]These are the names of the sons of Ishmael, listed in the order of their birth: Nebaioth the firstborn of
Ishmael, Kedar, Adbeel, Mibsam, [14]Mishma, Dumah, Massa, [15]Hadad, Tema, Jetur, Naphish and Kedemah.
[16]These were the sons of Ishmael, and these are the names of the twelve tribal rulers[m] according to their settlements and camps. [17]Ishmael lived a hundred and thirty-seven years. He breathed his last and died, and
he was gathered to his people.[n] [18]His descendants settled in the area from Havilah to Shur, near the eastern
border of Egypt, as you go toward Ashur. And they lived in hostility toward[b] all the tribes related to them.[o]

Jacob and Esau

[19]This is the account of the family line of Abraham's son Isaac.

Abraham became the father of Isaac, [20]and Isaac was forty years old[p] when he married Rebekah[q]
daughter of Bethuel the Aramean from Paddan Aram[c] and sister of Laban[r] the Aramean.
[21]Isaac prayed to the LORD on behalf of his wife, because she was childless. The LORD answered his
prayer,[s] and his wife Rebekah became pregnant. [22]The babies jostled each other within her, and she
said, "Why is this happening to me?" So she went to inquire of the LORD.[t]
[23]The LORD said to her,

"Two nations[u] are in your womb,
and two peoples from within you will be separated;
one people will be stronger than the other,
and the older will serve the younger.[v]"

25:5 [b]Ge 24:36
25:6 [c]Ge 22:24 [d]Ge 21:10,14
25:8 [e]Ge 15:15 [f]ver 17; Ge 35:29; 49:29,33
25:9 [g]Ge 35:29 [h]Ge 50:13
25:10 [i]Ge 23:16
25:11 [j]Ge 16:14
25:12 [k]Ge 16:1 [l]Ge 16:15
25:16 [m]Ge 17:20
25:17 [n]ver 8
25:18 [o]Ge 16:12
25:20 [p]ver 26; Ge 26:34 [q]Ge 24:67 [r]Ge 24:29
25:21 [s]1Ch 5:20; 2Ch 33:13; Ezr 8:23; Ps 127:3; Ro 9:10
25:22 [t]1Sa 9:9; 10:22
25:23 [u]Ge 17:4 [v]Ge 27:29,40; Mal 1:3; Ro 9:11-12*

[a] *10* Or *the descendants of Heth* [b] *18* Or *lived to the east of* [c] *20* That is, Northwest Mesopotamia

25:8 he was gathered to his people. This expression may indicate belief in life after death. It occurs elsewhere in Genesis in conjunction with the deaths of Ishmael (v. 17), Isaac (35:28–29), and Jacob (49:33). Abraham was buried in the cave of Machpelah (v. 9), which he had bought from Ephron (23:1–20).

25:12–18 *Ishmael's Sons.* While the main story focuses on Isaac and his sons, Genesis also includes some information about Ishmael's family.

25:12 This is the account of the family line of. A formulaic heading that introduces new sections of material in Genesis (see note on 2:4).

25:18 they lived in hostility toward. Regardless of how this phrase is translated (see NIV text note), it confirms what God predicted in 16:12.

25:19—36:43 *The Family of Isaac.* This is the next main narrative section in Genesis. It concentrates mainly on Isaac's twin sons, highlighting how the younger brother Jacob takes precedence over his older twin Esau. The entire story is skillfully composed, with the motifs of birthright and blessing being especially significant.

25:19–34 *Jacob and Esau.* The strained relationship between the twin sons of Isaac and Rebekah comes to the fore in chs. 25–36. Even before they are born, the boys struggle with each other (vv. 22–23), anticipating a greater struggle that will eventually result in Jacob fleeing for his life (27:41—28:5). At the heart of this struggle is the issue of who will be heir to the promises God gave to Abraham. While the birthright belongs to Esau, he dismisses it as unimportant, being willing to sell it to his brother for a bowl of stew (vv. 29–34). Jacob, however, is keen to have the benefits that accompany the status of firstborn.

25:19 This is the account of the family line of. This formula marks the start of a new section in Genesis (25:19—35:29). See note on 2:4.

25:20 Paddan Aram. The roots of Abraham's family go back to this location in Northwest Mesopotamia (see NIV text note); for this reason Abraham is later designated a "wandering Aramean" (Deut 26:5).

25:21 childless. Like Sarah before her (11:30) and Rachel after her (29:31), Rebekah is unable to have children. The motif of childlessness in Genesis draws attention to how God ensures the continuation of the unique family lineage through which the nations of the earth will be blessed.

25:22–23 When Rebekah asks God to explain the struggle that is happening inside her womb, she learns that her twins will produce two nations.

25:23 the older will serve the younger. Contrary to the custom of that time. This prediction provides the first indication that the special family line that Genesis traces will continue through Jacob rather than Esau. The struggle between the unborn babies recalls how throughout Genesis, beginning with Cain and Abel, conflict between brothers is a recurring motif. Such conflict threatens the survival of the unique lineage

25:25 [w] Ge 27:11
25:26 [x] Hos 12:3 [y] Ge 27:36
25:27 [z] Ge 27:3,5
25:28 [a] Ge 27:19 [b] Ge 27:6
25:33 [c] Ge 27:36; Heb 12:16
26:1 [d] Ge 12:10 [e] Ge 20:1
26:2 [f] Ge 12:7; 17:1; 18:1 [g] Ge 12:1
26:3 [h] Ge 20:1; 28:15 [i] Ge 12:2; 22:16-18 [j] Ge 12:7; 13:15; 15:18
26:4 [k] Ge 15:5; 22:17; Ex 32:13 [l] Ge 12:3; 22:18; Gal 3:8
26:5 [m] Ge 22:16
26:7 [n] Ge 12:13; 20:2, 12; Pr 29:25

24 When the time came for her to give birth, there were twin boys in her womb. 25 The first to come out was red, and his whole body was like a hairy garment;[w] so they named him Esau.[a] 26 After this, his brother came out, with his hand grasping Esau's heel;[x] so he was named Jacob.[b][y] Isaac was sixty years old when Rebekah gave birth to them.

27 The boys grew up, and Esau became a skillful hunter, a man of the open country,[z] while Jacob was content to stay at home among the tents. 28 Isaac, who had a taste for wild game,[a] loved Esau, but Rebekah loved Jacob.[b]

29 Once when Jacob was cooking some stew, Esau came in from the open country, famished. 30 He said to Jacob, "Quick, let me have some of that red stew! I'm famished!" (That is why he was also called Edom.[c])

31 Jacob replied, "First sell me your birthright."

32 "Look, I am about to die," Esau said. "What good is the birthright to me?"

33 But Jacob said, "Swear to me first." So he swore an oath to him, selling his birthright[c] to Jacob.

34 Then Jacob gave Esau some bread and some lentil stew. He ate and drank, and then got up and left.

So Esau despised his birthright.

Isaac and Abimelek

26:1-11Ref — Ge 12:10-20; 20:1-18

26 Now there was a famine in the land[d] — besides the previous famine in Abraham's time — and Isaac went to Abimelek king of the Philistines in Gerar.[e] 2 The LORD appeared[f] to Isaac and said, "Do not go down to Egypt; live in the land where I tell you to live.[g] 3 Stay in this land for a while,[h] and I will be with you and will bless you.[i] For to you and your descendants I will give all these lands[j] and will confirm the oath I swore to your father Abraham. 4 I will make your descendants as numerous as the stars in the sky[k] and will give them all these lands, and through your offspring[d] all nations on earth will be blessed,[e][l] 5 because Abraham obeyed me[m] and did everything I required of him, keeping my commands, my decrees and my instructions." 6 So Isaac stayed in Gerar.

7 When the men of that place asked him about his wife, he said, "She is my sister,[n]" because he was afraid to say, "She is my wife." He thought, "The men of this place might kill me on account of Rebekah, because she is beautiful."

[a] *25 Esau* may mean *hairy*. [b] *26 Jacob* means *he grasps the heel*, a Hebrew idiom for *he deceives*. [c] *30 Edom* means *red*. [d] *4* Or *seed* [e] *4* Or *and all nations on earth will use the name of your offspring in blessings* (see 48:20)

through which the nations will be blessed. The apostle Paul quotes from this verse to show that God is free to act as he pleases in the process of accomplishing his plan of salvation (Rom 9:10–13).

25:25–26 The names of both Jacob and Esau derive from features associated with their births (see NIV text notes). A person who grasps another person by the heel was a way to describe a deceiver. The motif of deception reappears throughout Jacob's life.

25:26 Isaac was sixty years old. If Isaac was this age when the twins were born, then Abraham was still alive. Not all events in Genesis are in strict chronological order; see vv. 7–10, where Abraham's death is recorded.

25:27–28 As the two boys grow into manhood, they differ significantly in their interests and character (see note on vv. 29–34). Esau favors outdoor activities, while Jacob prefers a more domesticated lifestyle. Their differing interests not only cause Isaac and Rebekah to favor different sons, but they set the scene for the events in the episodes that follow.

25:29–34 Although Jacob's desire to buy his brother's birthright demonstrates his grasping nature, Esau's attitude comes in for particular criticism. By selling for a bowl of stew the benefits associated with his firstborn status, Esau displays contempt for all that God promised to Abraham and his family line. What Esau despises (v. 34), Jacob desires. Jacob recognizes the value of the birthright, even though his method of attaining it is hardly commendable. This short episode casts a long shadow over the rest of the Jacob-Esau story, building on the earlier prediction in v. 23 that "the older will serve the younger."

26:1–33 *Isaac and Abimelek.* The next stage in the story of Jacob and Esau's struggle with each other occurs when their father Isaac is close to death (26:34 — 28:9). Meanwhile, ch. 26 records various incidents involving Isaac. Remarkably, these incidents have much in common with events involving Abraham. Not only do Isaac's actions closely parallel those of his father, but Isaac receives the promises God made to Abraham.

26:1 famine. Abraham went to Egypt during a famine (12:10–20), but God instructs Isaac to remain in Gerar (v. 2). **Abimelek.** Possibly the king chs. 20–21 mention; more likely, he is a son or grandson of that Abimelek. **Philistines.** See note on 21:32.

26:3–5 God accompanies his instructions to Isaac with assurances that resonate with the promises he gave to Abraham. Through Isaac God will "confirm the oath" (v. 3) that he swore to Abraham (22:16–18). Since Isaac was present when God made that oath, he would easily recall the occasion. By associating this oath with Abraham's obedience and by underlining that Abraham kept God's commands, decrees, and instructions, God encourages Isaac to obey him. Obeying God takes many forms.

26:7 Famine forces Isaac to relocate to a new region (see v. 1). Like Abraham (12:10–20; 20:1–18), Isaac pretends that his wife is his sister in order to safeguard his own life. Isaac's behavior implies that the region was far from peaceful. It also reflects his lack of trust in God.

8When Isaac had been there a long time, Abimelek king of the Philistines looked down from a window and saw Isaac caressing his wife Rebekah. 9So Abimelek summoned Isaac and said, "She is really
your wife! Why did you say, 'She is my sister'?"
Isaac answered him, "Because I thought I might lose my life on account of her."
10Then Abimelek said, "What is this you have done to us?[o] One of the men might well have slept with
your wife, and you would have brought guilt upon us."
11So Abimelek gave orders to all the people: "Anyone who harms[p] this man or his wife shall surely
be put to death."
12Isaac planted crops in that land and the same year reaped a hundredfold, because the LORD blessed
him.[q] 13The man became rich, and his wealth continued to grow until he became very wealthy.[r] 14He
had so many flocks and herds and servants[s] that the Philistines envied him.[t] 15So all the wells[u] that
his father's servants had dug in the time of his father Abraham, the Philistines stopped up,[v] filling
them with earth.
16Then Abimelek said to Isaac, "Move away from us; you have become too powerful for us.[w]"
17So Isaac moved away from there and encamped in the Valley of Gerar, where he settled. 18Isaac
reopened the wells[x] that had been dug in the time of his father Abraham, which the Philistines had
stopped up after Abraham died, and he gave them the same names his father had given them.
19Isaac's servants dug in the valley and discovered a well of fresh water there. 20But the herders
of Gerar quarreled with those of Isaac and said, "The water is ours!"[y] So he named the well Esek,[a]
because they disputed with him. 21Then they dug another well, but they quarreled over that one
also; so he named it Sitnah.[b] 22He moved on from there and dug another well, and no one quarreled
over it. He named it Rehoboth,[c] saying, "Now the LORD has given us room and we will flourish[z] in
the land."
23From there he went up to Beersheba. 24That night the LORD appeared to him and said, "I am the
God of your father Abraham.[a] Do not be afraid,[b] for I am with you; I will bless you and will increase
the number of your descendants[c] for the sake of my servant Abraham."[d]
25Isaac built an altar[e] there and called on the name of the LORD. There he pitched his tent, and there
his servants dug a well.
26Meanwhile, Abimelek had come to him from Gerar, with Ahuzzath his personal adviser and Phicol
the commander of his forces.[f] 27Isaac asked them, "Why have you come to me, since you were hostile
to me and sent me away?[g]"
28They answered, "We saw clearly that the LORD was with you;[h] so we said, 'There ought to be a sworn
agreement between us'—between us and you. Let us make a treaty with you 29that you will do us no
harm, just as we did not harm you but always treated you well and sent you away peacefully. And now
you are blessed by the LORD."[i]
30Isaac then made a feast[j] for them, and they ate and drank. 31Early the next morning the men swore
an oath[k] to each other. Then Isaac sent them on their way, and they went away peacefully.
32That day Isaac's servants came and told him about the well they had dug. They said, "We've found
water!" 33He called it Shibah,[d] and to this day the name of the town has been Beersheba.[e][l]

[a] *20 Esek* means *dispute.* [b] *21 Sitnah* means *opposition.* [c] *22 Rehoboth* means *room.*
[d] *33 Shibah* can mean *oath* or *seven.* [e] *33 Beersheba* can mean *well of the oath* and *well of seven.*

26:10 [o] Ge 20:9
26:11 [p] Ps 105:15
26:12 [q] ver 3; Job 42:12
26:13 [r] Pr 10:22
26:14 [s] Ge 24:36 [t] Ge 37:11
26:15 [u] Ge 21:30 [v] Ge 21:25
26:16 [w] Ex 1:9
26:18 [x] Ge 21:30
26:20 [y] Ge 21:25
26:22 [z] Ge 17:6; Ex 1:7
26:24 [a] Ge 24:12; Ex 3:6 [b] Ge 15:1 [c] ver 4 [d] Ge 17:7
26:25 [e] Ge 12:7,8; 13:4, 18; Ps 116:17
26:26 [f] Ge 21:22
26:27 [g] ver 16
26:28 [h] Ge 21:22
26:29 [i] Ge 24:31; Ps 115:15
26:30 [j] Ge 19:3
26:31 [k] Ge 21:31
26:33 [l] Ge 21:14

26:8–11 When Abimelek discovers Isaac's deception, he acts with integrity, fearful that unknowingly he and his people may become guilty of adultery. Abimelek's reaction contrasts sharply with what Isaac expected. This incident parallels Abraham's earlier ruse (20:1–18; cf. 12:10–20).

26:12 the LORD blessed him. God's favor or blessing is associated with those who belong to the unique lineage Genesis traces. Like Abraham, Isaac prospers materially (v. 13).

26:14–16 Isaac's prosperity causes the Philistines to become envious and fearful of Isaac, so Isaac moves away.

26:17–23 Isaac's move brings him to a location where earlier Abraham dug wells. Since the Philistines subsequently stopped up these wells (presumably to discourage seminomadic herdsmen from settling there), Isaac reopens them (v. 18). Unfortunately, his actions provoke protests (vv. 20–21), which eventually cause him to move further away from Gerar (vv. 22–23).

26:26–31 When Isaac relocates to Beersheba, Abimelek comes to him seeking to make a treaty. This event recalls 21:22–32, which records that Abraham and the king of Gerar made a similar peace treaty in Beersheba.

26:32–33 Digging a new well and discovering water coincides with ratifying the treaty. Isaac calls the well Shibah (see NIV text note), possibly because of circumstances surrounding Abraham's treaty with Abimelek (21:30–31; cf. v. 18).

26:34 [m]Ge 25:20 [n]Ge 28:9; 36:2
26:35 [o]Ge 27:46
27:1 [p]Ge 48:10; 1Sa 3:2 [q]Ge 25:25
27:2 [r]Ge 47:29
27:3 [s]Ge 25:27
27:4 [t]ver 10,25,31; Ge 49:28; Dt 33:1; Heb 11:20
27:6 [u]Ge 25:28
27:8 [v]ver 13,43
27:11 [w]Ge 25:25
27:12 [x]ver 22
27:13 [y]Mt 27:25 [z]ver 8
27:15 [a]ver 27
27:19 [b]ver 4
27:20 [c]Ge 24:12
27:21 [d]ver 12

Jacob Takes Esau's Blessing

34 When Esau was forty years old,[m] he married Judith daughter of Beeri the Hittite, and also Basemath daughter of Elon the Hittite.[n] 35 They were a source of grief to Isaac and Rebekah.[o]

27 When Isaac was old and his eyes were so weak that he could no longer see,[p] he called for Esau
his older son[q] and said to him, "My son."

"Here I am," he answered.

2 Isaac said, "I am now an old man and don't know the day of my death.[r] 3 Now then, get your equipment — your quiver and bow — and go out to the open country[s] to hunt some wild game for me.
4 Prepare me the kind of tasty food I like and bring it to me to eat, so that I may give you my blessing[t]
before I die."

5 Now Rebekah was listening as Isaac spoke to his son Esau. When Esau left for the open country to
hunt game and bring it back, 6 Rebekah said to her son Jacob,[u] "Look, I overheard your father say to
your brother Esau, 7 'Bring me some game and prepare me some tasty food to eat, so that I may give
you my blessing in the presence of the LORD before I die.' 8 Now, my son, listen carefully and do what I
tell you:[v] 9 Go out to the flock and bring me two choice young goats, so I can prepare some tasty food
for your father, just the way he likes it. 10 Then take it to your father to eat, so that he may give you his
blessing before he dies."

11 Jacob said to Rebekah his mother, "But my brother Esau is a hairy man[w] while I have smooth skin.
12 What if my father touches me?[x] I would appear to be tricking him and would bring down a curse on
myself rather than a blessing."

13 His mother said to him, "My son, let the curse fall on me.[y] Just do what I say;[z] go and get them for me."

14 So he went and got them and brought them to his mother, and she prepared some tasty food, just
the way his father liked it. 15 Then Rebekah took the best clothes[a] of Esau her older son, which she had
in the house, and put them on her younger son Jacob. 16 She also covered his hands and the smooth
part of his neck with the goatskins. 17 Then she handed to her son Jacob the tasty food and the bread
she had made.

18 He went to his father and said, "My father."

"Yes, my son," he answered. "Who is it?"

19 Jacob said to his father, "I am Esau your firstborn. I have done as you told me. Please sit up and
eat some of my game, so that you may give me your blessing."[b]

20 Isaac asked his son, "How did you find it so quickly, my son?"

"The LORD your God gave me success,[c]" he replied.

21 Then Isaac said to Jacob, "Come near so I can touch you,[d] my son, to know whether you really
are my son Esau or not."

26:34 — 28:9 *Jacob Takes Esau's Blessing.* This section gives considerable attention to how Jacob deceives his father Isaac into giving him the blessing due to the firstborn son. This incident, which is full of subtle observations regarding the family members, further develops Jacob's ambition to be heir to the promises God gave to Abraham and Isaac. While Jacob's actions are central to the deception, the narrator highlights the shortcomings of both Isaac and Esau and depicts Rebekah as the deception's prime instigator. In the light of the blessing Isaac gives to Jacob (27:28 – 29) and Isaac's subsequent reluctance to denounce Jacob (27:37), this fulfills what God predicted in 25:23, for Isaac says to Esau, "You will serve your brother" (27:40). Having previously sold his birthright to Jacob, Esau now witnesses the final stage in the process by which Jacob receives Isaac's deathbed blessing. In the Hebrew text, a striking wordplay links the concepts of blessing (*bĕrākâ*) and birthright (*bĕkōrâ*). The association of Jacob with blessing recalls what God promised Abraham in 12:1 – 3 (cf. 27:29).

26:35 a source of grief to Isaac and Rebekah. The story gives few details regarding this phrase, but a significant factor may be the Hittite origin of Esau's wives. Unlike his father, Isaac, Esau did not look for a wife from among his own relatives, suggesting that he did not fully embrace the beliefs of his parents.

27:1 – 4 Nearing death, Isaac summons Esau in order to make arrangements to formally bless him as his firstborn son. This blessing would confirm Esau as Isaac's principal heir, making him the one through whom the family line associated with God's redemptive plan would continue. By noting that Isaac was blind (v. 1), the narrator anticipates later developments in the story and may also indicate that Isaac failed to see clearly Esau's true nature. By highlighting Isaac's desire for "tasty food" (v. 4), the narrator possibly implies that selfishness motivated Isaac's decision to bless Esau.

27:5 – 13 As the one who overhears Isaac speaking to Esau, Rebekah both instigates and oversees Jacob's deception of Isaac. When Jacob voices anxiety about Isaac finding him out, Rebekah states that she will bear full responsibility: "My son, let the curse fall on me" (v. 13). While Rebekah's scheming probably reflects her particular love for Jacob (25:28), God's prediction that the older would serve the younger (25:23) and her own assessment of Esau's character may also have influenced her.

27:15 – 16 Rebekah cunningly disguises Jacob as Esau, even using goatskins to make Jacob appear hairy like Esau (v. 11; 25:25).

27:18 – 22 Although Isaac is blind, he is initially suspicious when Jacob claims to be Esau. Sensing that the voice is that of Jacob, he touches Jacob in order to be certain.

22 Jacob went close to his father Isaac, who touched him and said, "The voice is the voice of Jacob, but
the hands are the hands of Esau." 23 He did not recognize him, for his hands were hairy like those of his
brother Esau;[e] so he proceeded to bless him. 24 "Are you really my son Esau?" he asked.
"I am," he replied.
25 Then he said, "My son, bring me some of your game to eat, so that I may give you my blessing."[f]
Jacob brought it to him and he ate; and he brought some wine and he drank. 26 Then his father Isaac
said to him, "Come here, my son, and kiss me."
27 So he went to him and kissed him[g]. When Isaac caught the smell of his clothes,[h] he blessed him
and said,

"Ah, the smell of my son
  is like the smell of a field
  that the LORD has blessed.[i]
28 May God give you heaven's dew[j]
  and earth's richness[k]—
  an abundance of grain and new wine.[l]
29 May nations serve you
  and peoples bow down to you.[m]
Be lord over your brothers,
  and may the sons of your mother bow down to you.[n]
May those who curse you be cursed
  and those who bless you be blessed.[o]"

30 After Isaac finished blessing him, and Jacob had scarcely left his father's presence, his brother
Esau came in from hunting. 31 He too prepared some tasty food and brought it to his father. Then
he said to him, "My father, please sit up and eat some of my game, so that you may give me your
blessing."[p]
32 His father Isaac asked him, "Who are you?"[q]
"I am your son," he answered, "your firstborn, Esau."
33 Isaac trembled violently and said, "Who was it, then, that hunted game and brought it to me? I ate
it just before you came and I blessed him—and indeed he will be blessed!"[r]
34 When Esau heard his father's words, he burst out with a loud and bitter cry[s] and said to his father,
"Bless me—me too, my father!"
35 But he said, "Your brother came deceitfully[t] and took your blessing."
36 Esau said, "Isn't he rightly named Jacob[a]?[u] This is the second time he has taken advantage of
me: He took my birthright,[v] and now he's taken my blessing!" Then he asked, "Haven't you reserved
any blessing for me?"
37 Isaac answered Esau, "I have made him lord over you and have made all his relatives his servants, and I have sustained him with grain and new wine.[w] So what can I possibly do for you, my
son?"

[a] *36 Jacob* means *he grasps the heel*, a Hebrew idiom for *he takes advantage of* or *he deceives*.

27:23 [e] ver 16
27:25 [f] ver 4
27:27 [g] Heb 11:20 [h] SS 4:11 [i] Ps 65:9-13
27:28 [j] Dt 33:13 [k] ver 39 [l] Ge 45:18; Nu 18:12; Dt 33:28
27:29 [m] Isa 45:14,23; 49:7,23 [n] Ge 9:25; 25:23; 37:7 [o] Ge 12:3; Nu 24:9; Zep 2:8
27:31 [p] ver 4
27:32 [q] ver 18
27:33 [r] ver 29; Ge 28:3, 4; Ro 11:29
27:34 [s] Heb 12:17
27:35 [t] Jer 9:4; 12:6
27:36 [u] Ge 25:26 [v] Ge 25:33
27:37 [w] ver 28

27:27–29 Immediately prior to blessing Jacob, Isaac smells him in order to be convinced that this is indeed Esau. The outdoor scent of Esau's clothing, which Jacob has put on, reassures Isaac. While Isaac prays that God will bless Jacob materially, his aspirations for his firstborn son lead him to request that "nations" and "peoples" (v. 29) serve him, as well as his closest family members. Isaac's prayer is exceptionally ambitious given that he and his family are relative newcomers to the land of Canaan and Isaac himself has previously feared for his own life (26:7). His expectations regarding his firstborn son, however, are grounded in God's promises to Abraham; he assures Jacob that God will bless him, echoing what God said to Abraham (12:2).

27:30–40 Esau is furious when he learns that Jacob deceived Isaac and that Isaac gave Jacob the blessing he intended for Esau. Recalling that the name Jacob means "deceiver" (see NIV text note on v. 36), Esau charges Jacob with having exploited him on two occasions: Jacob has taken Esau's birthright (25:29–34) and his blessing. The patriarchal stories of Genesis give special attention to those who receive the blessing of the firstborn because through them God will fulfill his promise to bless the nations of the earth. When Esau pleads with his father for a blessing, Isaac states that he cannot revoke what he has requested for Jacob (v. 37). As God predicted in 25:23, Esau will serve Jacob. However, by way of consoling Esau, Isaac pronounces that although Esau will serve his brother, eventually he will "throw [off] his yoke" (v. 40). While Isaac's words seem to refer to Esau's own lifetime, in line with other paternal deathbed blessings, they include Esau's descendants. In the light of this, later history reveals that the relationship between Jacob's descendants (the Israelites) and Esau's descendants (the Edomites) was sometimes anything but brotherly (see Obad 1–21).

27:38 [x]Heb 12:17
27:39 [y]ver 28
27:40 [z]2Sa 8:14 [a]Ge 25:23 [b]2Ki 8:20-22
27:41 [c]Ge 37:4 [d]Ge 32:11 [e]Ge 50:4,10 [f]Ob 10
27:43 [g]ver 8 [h]Ge 24:29 [i]Ge 11:31
27:44 [j]Ge 31:38,41
27:45 [k]ver 35
27:46 [l]Ge 26:35
28:1 [m]Ge 24:3
28:2 [n]Ge 25:20
28:3 [o]Ge 17:1 [p]Ge 17:6
28:4 [q]Ge 12:2,3 [r]Ge 17:8
28:5 [s]Hos 12:12 [t]Ge 24:29
28:6 [u]ver 1

38 Esau said to his father, "Do you have only one blessing, my father? Bless me too, my father!" Then
Esau wept aloud.[x]
39 His father Isaac answered him,

"Your dwelling will be
  away from the earth's richness,
  away from the dew[y] of heaven above.
40 You will live by the sword
  and you will serve[z] your brother.[a]
But when you grow restless,
  you will throw his yoke
  from off your neck.[b]"

41 Esau held a grudge[c] against Jacob[d] because of the blessing his father had given him. He said to
himself, "The days of mourning[e] for my father are near; then I will kill my brother Jacob."[f]
42 When Rebekah was told what her older son Esau had said, she sent for her younger son Jacob
and said to him, "Your brother Esau is planning to avenge himself by killing you. 43 Now then, my
son, do what I say:[g] Flee at once to my brother Laban[h] in Harran.[i] 44 Stay with him for a while[j] until your brother's fury subsides. 45 When your brother is no longer angry with you and forgets what
you did to him,[k] I'll send word for you to come back from there. Why should I lose both of you in
one day?"
46 Then Rebekah said to Isaac, "I'm disgusted with living because of these Hittite women. If Jacob
takes a wife from among the women of this land, from Hittite women like these, my life will not be
worth living."[l]

28 So Isaac called for Jacob and blessed him. Then he commanded him: "Do not marry a Canaanite woman.[m] 2 Go at once to Paddan Aram,[*a*] to the house of your mother's father Bethuel.[n]
Take a wife for yourself there, from among the daughters of Laban, your mother's brother. 3 May God
Almighty[*b*][o] bless you and make you fruitful[p] and increase your numbers until you become a community of peoples. 4 May he give you and your descendants the blessing given to Abraham,[q] so that you
may take possession of the land where you now reside as a foreigner,[r] the land God gave to Abraham."
5 Then Isaac sent Jacob on his way, and he went to Paddan Aram,[s] to Laban son of Bethuel the Aramean,
the brother of Rebekah,[t] who was the mother of Jacob and Esau.
6 Now Esau learned that Isaac had blessed Jacob and had sent him to Paddan Aram to take a wife
from there, and that when he blessed him he commanded him, "Do not marry a Canaanite woman,"[u]

[*a*] *2* That is, Northwest Mesopotamia; also in verses 5, 6 and 7 [*b*] *3* Hebrew *El-Shaddai*

27:41–45 Unwilling to forgive his brother, Esau plots to kill Jacob once his father is dead. When Rebekah learns of Esau's intention, she tells Jacob to take refuge with her brother Laban in Harran (24:29).

27:46 Having decided that Jacob should flee to Harran, Rebekah looks to persuade Isaac that this would be best by highlighting the difficulties Esau's Hittite wives created (see 26:34–35). **life will not be worth living.** Rebekah bluntly states how devastated she would be if Jacob also were to marry a native of Canaan.

28:1–2 Because he also dislikes Esau's wives (26:35), Isaac instructs Jacob to go to Paddan Aram in order to find a wife. While Abraham had sent a servant to do this on behalf of Isaac (24:2–4), Jacob himself must go.

28:1 Canaanite woman. Whereas Rebekah speaks of "Hittite women" (27:46), Isaac uses the broader designation "Canaanite woman." On the basis of 10:15, Hittites were considered to be a subgroup of Canaanites (see note on 23:3).

28:2 Paddan Aram. See note on 25:20.

28:3–4 The second half of Isaac's speech abounds with expressions that recall God's promises to Abraham, whom Isaac names twice. Strikingly, Isaac stresses the divine promises of numerous descendants and possession of the land of Canaan. These promises take on added significance in the light of Esau's threat to kill his brother and Jacob's departure to Paddan Aram to find a wife. The fulfillment of the promises anticipates Jacob's safe return to the land of Canaan. Throughout the patriarchal stories, the promises of numerous descendants and possession of the land of Canaan connect to 1:28. Through the patriarchs and their descendants, God will eventually fulfill his purpose in creating people to inhabit the earth. By stating that Jacob will become a "community of peoples" (v. 3; see 35:11), Isaac alludes to the covenant involving circumcision, in which God promised that Abraham would become the father of many nations (17:4–6). While the creation of Israel as a nation fulfills God's promises to the patriarchs, that is not the sole purpose for which God chose Abraham and his descendants. Through all that occurs, God desires to bless all the families/nations of the earth.

28:6–9 In a belated attempt to gain his parent's approval, Esau marries a daughter of "Ishmael son of Abraham" (v. 9; see 16:15). Ironically, Esau's link with the family of Ishmael—Nebaioth (Esau's brother-in-law) is Ishmael's firstborn son (25:13)—further signals that God will not fulfill his promises through Esau, for God passed over Ishmael in favor of Isaac.

7and that Jacob had obeyed his father and mother and had gone to Paddan Aram. 8Esau then realized
how displeasing the Canaanite women[v] were to his father Isaac;[w] 9so he went to Ishmael and married
Mahalath, the sister of Nebaioth[x] and daughter of Ishmael son of Abraham, in addition to the wives
he already had.[y]

Jacob's Dream at Bethel

10Jacob left Beersheba and set out for Harran.[z] 11When he reached a certain place, he stopped for the
night because the sun had set. Taking one of the stones there, he put it under his head and lay down to
sleep. 12He had a dream[a] in which he saw a stairway resting on the earth, with its top reaching to heaven,
and the angels of God were ascending and descending on it.[b] 13There above it[a] stood the LORD,[c] and he
said: "I am the LORD, the God of your father Abraham and the God of Isaac.[d] I will give you and your
descendants the land[e] on which you are lying. 14Your descendants will be like the dust of the earth, and
you[f] will spread out to the west and to the east, to the north and to the south.[g] All peoples on earth will
be blessed through you and your offspring.[bh] 15I am with you[i] and will watch over you[j] wherever you go,
and I will bring you back to this land. I will not leave you[k] until I have done what I have promised you."[l]

16When Jacob awoke from his sleep, he thought, "Surely the LORD is in this place, and I was not
aware of it." 17He was afraid and said, "How awesome is this place![m] This is none other than the house
of God; this is the gate of heaven."

18Early the next morning Jacob took the stone he had placed under his head and set it up as a pillar[n] and poured oil on top of it.[o] 19He called that place Bethel,[c] though the city used to be called Luz.[p]

20Then Jacob made a vow,[q] saying, "If God will be with me and will watch over me[r] on this journey
I am taking and will give me food to eat and clothes to wear 21so that I return safely[s] to my father's
household, then the LORD[d] will be my God[t] 22and[e] this stone that I have set up as a pillar will be God's
house,[u] and of all that you give me I will give you a tenth.[v]"

28:8 [v]Ge 24:3 [w]Ge 26:35
28:9 [x]Ge 25:13 [y]Ge 26:34
28:10 [z]Ge 11:31
28:12 [a]Ge 20:3 [b]Jn 1:51
28:13 [c]Ge 12:7; 35:7,9; 48:3 [d]Ge 26:24 [e]Ge 13:15; 35:12
28:14 [f]Ge 26:4 [g]Ge 13:14 [h]Ge 12:3; 18:18; 22:18; Gal 3:8
28:15 [i]Ge 26:3; 48:21 [j]Nu 6:24; Ps 121:5,7-8 [k]Dt 31:6,8 [l]Nu 23:19
28:17 [m]Ex 3:5; Jos 5:15
28:18 [n]Ge 35:14 [o]Lev 8:11
28:19 [p]Jdg 1:23,26
28:20 [q]Ge 31:13; Jdg 11:30; 2Sa 15:8 [r]ver 15
28:21 [s]Jdg 11:31 [t]Dt 26:17
28:22 [u]Ge 35:7,14 [v]Ge 14:20; Lev 27:30

[a] 13 Or *There beside him* [b] 14 Or *will use your name and the name of your offspring in blessings* (see 48:20) [c] 19 *Bethel* means *house of God.* [d] 20,21 Or *Since God . . . father's household, the LORD* [e] 21,22 Or *household, and the LORD will be my God, 22then*

28:8 Canaanite women. See note on v. 1.

28:10–22 *Jacob's Dream at Bethel.* Jacob experiences two encounters with God that occur at significant points in his life: (1) in this nighttime experience when he is about to leave the land of Canaan and (2) when he returns to Canaan (32:22–32). God's speech to Jacob recalls his earlier promises to Abraham and Isaac, and he concludes by promising to protect Jacob. The whole experience transforms Jacob's understanding of God and is part of the process by which God changes him.

28:10 Harran. See note on 11:31.

28:12 stairway. While the Hebrew term *sullām* is often translated "ladder," it probably denotes here a flight of stairs like those constructed on ancient ziggurats. Linking heaven to earth, this stairway vividly reminds Jacob that God intends to reside on the earth, so Jacob calls the location Bethel (see NIV text note on v. 19). See note on John 1:51.

28:13–15 Jacob's father has blessed him, and now God gives Jacob similar assurances that his descendants will take possession of the land of Canaan and that all peoples on earth will be blessed through Jacob and his offspring. This not only echoes how Isaac blessed Jacob prior to his departure for Paddan Aram (vv. 3–4), but the wording closely resembles God's promises to Abraham (12:2–3,7; 13:14–17; 17:7–8; 18:18; 22:17–18) and Isaac (26:3–4). God reassures Jacob that he will accompany him on his journey.

28:13 above it. See NIV text note. When speaking to Jacob, God is standing either (1) in heaven at the top of the stairway or (2) on the earth beside Jacob, looking down on him as he lies on the ground.

28:16–17 For Jacob, his experience is more than a dream. He is filled with a sense of awe as he contemplates the significance of what has happened. His vision convinces him that this location is part of "the house of God" (v. 17), the entrance to heaven itself. This adds considerably to the significance of the promise of land in v. 13. God promises Jacob and his descendants land that includes "the gate of heaven" (v. 17).

28:18 pillar ... poured oil on top of it. The method Jacob uses to mark his experience. This is apparently a Canaanite practice that Deut 16:22 later prohibits. Interestingly, while Jacob continues the custom during his stay in Paddan Aram (31:45,51–52) and after he returns to Canaan (35:14,20), following his next encounter with God at Peniel (32:22–32) he constructs altars (33:20; 35:1–7), as Abraham (12:7–8; 13:4,18; 22:9) and Isaac (26:25) did, one of these being located at Bethel. The shift to making altars may indicate that Jacob has undergone a deep spiritual experience.

28:19 Bethel ... Luz. Jacob's vision of God probably took place outside the city of Luz (Josh 16:2). Although he names the location Bethel, the nearby city of Luz retained its name until the Israelites settled there after their exodus from Egypt (Josh 18:13; Judg 1:23,26).

28:20–21 If ... then. Jacob's vow possibly suggests that he is still less than fully committed to serving the Lord. He rests his future commitment to God on God's bringing him back safely to his father's household. His words suggest that he lacks a truly personal faith in God. This ambivalence may suggest why Jacob's next encounter with God at Peniel (32:22–32) is especially significant.

28:22 Having named the location Bethel (see NIV text note on v. 19), Jacob appears to suggest that on his return he will use the stone he has consecrated to construct a temple. While Jacob does not build a permanent temple at Bethel, he builds an altar (35:1–7), which he may have viewed as forming part of a temporary sanctuary. **I will give you a tenth.** The gift of a tithe to God became a regular feature of Israelite worship (Lev 27:30,32; Num 18:26; Deut 14:22–23). Previously, Abraham gave a tenth to Melchizedek to recognize God's role in helping him rescue Lot (14:20).

29:1 [w]Jdg 6:3,33
29:4 [x]Ge 28:10
29:9 [y]Ex 2:16
29:10 [z]Ex 2:17
29:11 [a]Ge 33:4
29:12 [b]Ge 13:8; 14:14, 16 [c]Ge 24:28
29:13 [d]Ge 24:29
29:14 [e]Ge 2:23; Jdg 9:2; 2Sa 19:12-13
29:18 [f]Hos 12:12
29:20 [g]SS 8:7; Hos 12:12
29:21 [h]Jdg 15:1
29:22 [i]Jdg 14:10; Jn 2:1-2

Jacob Arrives in Paddan Aram

29 Then Jacob continued on his journey and came to the land of the eastern peoples.[w] 2 There he saw a well in the open country, with three flocks of sheep lying near it because the flocks were watered from that well. The stone over the mouth of the well was large. 3 When all the flocks were gathered there, the shepherds would roll the stone away from the well's mouth and water the sheep. Then they would return the stone to its place over the mouth of the well.

4 Jacob asked the shepherds, "My brothers, where are you from?"

"We're from Harran,[x]" they replied.

5 He said to them, "Do you know Laban, Nahor's grandson?"

"Yes, we know him," they answered.

6 Then Jacob asked them, "Is he well?"

"Yes, he is," they said, "and here comes his daughter Rachel with the sheep."

7 "Look," he said, "the sun is still high; it is not time for the flocks to be gathered. Water the sheep and take them back to pasture."

8 "We can't," they replied, "until all the flocks are gathered and the stone has been rolled away from the mouth of the well. Then we will water the sheep."

9 While he was still talking with them, Rachel came with her father's sheep,[y] for she was a shepherd. 10 When Jacob saw Rachel daughter of his uncle Laban, and Laban's sheep, he went over and rolled the stone away from the mouth of the well and watered his uncle's sheep.[z] 11 Then Jacob kissed Rachel and began to weep aloud.[a] 12 He had told Rachel that he was a relative[b] of her father and a son of Rebekah. So she ran and told her father.[c]

13 As soon as Laban[d] heard the news about Jacob, his sister's son, he hurried to meet him. He embraced him and kissed him and brought him to his home, and there Jacob told him all these things. 14 Then Laban said to him, "You are my own flesh and blood."[e]

Jacob Marries Leah and Rachel

After Jacob had stayed with him for a whole month, 15 Laban said to him, "Just because you are a relative of mine, should you work for me for nothing? Tell me what your wages should be."

16 Now Laban had two daughters; the name of the older was Leah, and the name of the younger was Rachel. 17 Leah had weak[a] eyes, but Rachel had a lovely figure and was beautiful. 18 Jacob was in love with Rachel and said, "I'll work for you seven years in return for your younger daughter Rachel."[f]

19 Laban said, "It's better that I give her to you than to some other man. Stay here with me." 20 So Jacob served seven years to get Rachel, but they seemed like only a few days to him because of his love for her.[g]

21 Then Jacob said to Laban, "Give me my wife. My time is completed, and I want to make love to her.[h]"

22 So Laban brought together all the people of the place and gave a feast.[i] 23 But when evening came,

[a] *17* Or *delicate*

29:1–14 *Jacob Arrives in Paddan Aram.* Jacob's meeting with Rachel at a well recalls the earlier account of Abraham's servant meeting Rebekah at a well (24:10–20). On this occasion, the roles are reversed: Jacob waters the flock that Rachel brings to the well. As previously, when Laban hears what has happened, he hurries to meet the new arrival.

29:1 land of the eastern peoples. This is an unusual expression to designate Northwest Mesopotamia. However, Abraham's family was originally from Ur in southeastern Mesopotamia (see 11:28 and note). Terah and his sons migrated to Harran (11:31). Other families may also have moved in the same direction, settling in the region of Harran. This might explain the designation "eastern peoples."

29:6 sheep. The Hebrew term *ṣō'n* means flock. Jacob's family in Paddan Aram keep sheep and goats, like Abraham and Isaac. The family's dependency upon these animals may explain why Laban named his daughter Rachel (meaning "ewe"). Normally men would shepherd the animals. Possibly Laban's sons are still too young to undertake this duty (cf. 30:35; 31:1).

29:10 rolled the stone away ... and watered [the] sheep. Jacob's actions suggest that his presence would be an asset to Laban's family.

29:14 my own flesh and blood. On learning that Jacob is Rebekah's son, Laban embraces him as a close relative.

29:15–30 *Jacob Marries Leah and Rachel.* Having been sent to Paddan Aram to find a wife, Jacob is captivated by Rachel's beauty. He readily works seven years in order to earn the bride-price necessary to marry Rachel. However, in a deception that is highly ironic in the light of how Jacob treated Esau, Laban substitutes his older daughter Leah in place of his younger daughter Rachel. To have Rachel, Jacob must serve Laban for an additional seven years.

29:17 Leah ... Rachel. Although the descriptions of both are exceptionally brief, they sufficiently explain why Jacob is attracted to Rachel rather than Leah (v. 30; but see vv. 31–35).

29:19 Marriage arrangements in the ancient Near East normally required that a prospective husband give a gift of money, technically known as the bride-price, to the father of the bride. Since Jacob has arrived in Paddan Aram with no means of paying the bride-price, he offers to work for Laban without wages for seven years.

29:23 In the darkness of the evening and without artificial lighting,

he took his daughter Leah and brought her to Jacob, and Jacob made love to her. [24]And Laban gave his
servant Zilpah to his daughter as her attendant.
[25]When morning came, there was Leah! So Jacob said to Laban, "What is this you have done to me?[j]
I served you for Rachel, didn't I? Why have you deceived me?[k]"
[26]Laban replied, "It is not our custom here to give the younger daughter in marriage before the
older one. [27]Finish this daughter's bridal week;[l] then we will give you the younger one also, in return
for another seven years of work."
[28]And Jacob did so. He finished the week with Leah, and then Laban gave him his daughter Rachel
to be his wife. [29]Laban gave his servant Bilhah[m] to his daughter Rachel as her attendant.[n] [30]Jacob
made love to Rachel also, and his love for Rachel was greater than his love for Leah.[o] And he worked
for Laban another seven years.[p]

Jacob's Children

[31]When the LORD saw that Leah was not loved,[q] he enabled her to conceive,[r] but Rachel remained
childless. [32]Leah became pregnant and gave birth to a son. She named him Reuben,[a] for she said, "It
is because the LORD has seen my misery.[s] Surely my husband will love me now."
[33]She conceived again, and when she gave birth to a son she said, "Because the LORD heard that I
am not loved, he gave me this one too." So she named him Simeon.[b][t]
[34]Again she conceived, and when she gave birth to a son she said, "Now at last my husband will become attached to me,[u] because I have borne him three sons." So he was named Levi.[c][v]
[35]She conceived again, and when she gave birth to a son she said, "This time I will praise the LORD."
So she named him Judah.[d][w] Then she stopped having children.

30 When Rachel saw that she was not bearing Jacob any children,[x] she became jealous of her
sister.[y] So she said to Jacob, "Give me children, or I'll die!"
[2]Jacob became angry with her and said, "Am I in the place of God, who has kept you from having
children?"[z]
[3]Then she said, "Here is Bilhah, my servant. Sleep with her so that she can bear children for me and
I too can build a family through her."[a]

[a] *32 Reuben* sounds like the Hebrew for *he has seen my misery*; the name means *see, a son*. [b] *33 Simeon* probably means *one who hears*. [c] *34 Levi* sounds like and may be derived from the Hebrew for *attached*. [d] *35 Judah* sounds like and may be derived from the Hebrew for *praise*.

29:25 [j]Ge 12:18 [k]Ge 27:36
29:27 [l]Jdg 14:12
29:29 [m]Ge 30:3 [n]Ge 16:1
29:30 [o]ver 16 [p]Ge 31:41
29:31 [q]Dt 21:15-17 [r]Ge 11:30; 30:1; Ps 127:3
29:32 [s]Ge 16:11; 31:42; Ex 4:31; Dt 26:7; Ps 25:18
29:33 [t]Ge 34:25; 49:5
29:34 [u]Ge 30:20; 1Sa 1:2-4 [v]Ge 49:5-7
29:35 [w]Ge 49:8; Mt 1:2-3
30:1 [x]Ge 29:31; 1Sa 1:5-6 [y]Lev 18:18
30:2 [z]Ge 16:2; 20:18; 29:31
30:3 [a]Ge 16:2

Jacob does not recognize that his veiled bride is Leah (cf. 24:65). Perhaps after a day's feasting, Jacob is somewhat inebriated.

29:24 Zilpah. She later becomes a surrogate mother for Leah (30:9–13).

29:26 Laban justifies deceiving Jacob on the basis that a firstborn daughter should take precedence in marriage over other daughters. His remark recalls how Jacob deceived his own firstborn brother. Although Laban's actions are wrong, there is an element of poetic justice.

29:27 bridal week. To appease Jacob, Laban offers him Rachel on two conditions: Jacob must finish the wedding celebrations with Leah and commit to serving Laban for another seven years. Accepting these conditions, Jacob marries Rachel immediately after marrying Leah.

29:29 Bilhah. She later becomes a surrogate mother for Rachel (30:3–8).

29:30 his love for Rachel was greater than his love for Leah. This becomes a source of considerable friction between the two women. Many of the stories in Genesis involve tensions between family members, reflecting the consequences of Adam and Eve's rebellion against God. Polygamy adds another dimension to these family disputes (see note on 16:3).

29:31—30:24 *Jacob's Children.* The tension between Leah and Rachel impacts the process by which they bear children for Jacob. Although Jacob loves Leah less than Rachel, God enables Leah to bear four sons: Reuben, Simeon, Levi, and Judah. While Rachel remains childless, out of jealousy she gives her servant Bilhah to Jacob. Subsequently, Bilhah gives birth to Dan and Naphtali. In response Leah gives her servant Zilpah to Jacob, and she bears Gad and Asher. Afterward Leah has two more sons, Issachar and Zebulun, and a daughter, Dinah. Finally, Rachel conceives and gives birth to Joseph. While Jacob's family increases in size, with so many different women involved, the internal dynamics of the family are far from harmonious. In all this, the women perceive the hand of God at work in giving them children.

29:31 Leah was not loved. While the peculiar circumstances of Jacob's marriage to Leah explain why he does not love her as he does Rachel (v. 30), the way he treats Leah is nevertheless inappropriate. In Genesis the human tendency to favor one person over another frequently causes tension. In such circumstances God often acts on behalf of the underdog.

29:32–35 The Lord's enabling Leah to conceive (v. 31) accounts for how she names her first three sons. Significantly, the motif of Jacob not loving Leah repeats with the births of Reuben, Simeon, and Levi (see NIV text notes on vv. 32–34). However, there is no mention of it with Judah's birth (see NIV text note on v. 35). Possibly this implies that by this stage Jacob has started to love Leah on account of the sons that she has borne him. Most appropriately Leah praises God for the birth of Judah, the ancestor of the Messianic lineage (Matt 1:1–16). See note on 49:8–12.

30:1–2 Jealous of her sister, Rachel vents her frustration, accusing Jacob of not giving her children. Jacob blames Rachel's childlessness on God. Unlike Isaac in 25:21, the text does not say that Jacob prayed for his barren wife.

30:3–8 Like Sarah (16:1–4), Rachel proposes that her maidservant become a surrogate mother. When Bilhah bears Dan and Naphtali, Rachel

30:4 [b]ver 9,18 [c]Ge 16:3-4
30:6 [d]Ps 35:24; 43:1; La 3:59 [e]Ge 49:16-17
30:8 [f]Hos 12:3-4 [g]Ge 49:21
30:9 [h]ver 4
30:11 [i]Ge 49:19
30:13 [j]Ps 127:3 [k]Pr 31:28; Lk 1:48 [l]Ge 49:20
30:14 [m]SS 7:13
30:15 [n]Nu 16:9,13
30:17 [o]Ge 25:21
30:18 [p]Ge 49:14
30:20 [q]Ge 35:23; 49:13; Mt 4:13
30:22 [r]Ge 8:1; 1Sa 1:19-20 [s]Ge 29:31
30:23 [t]ver 6 [u]Isa 4:1; Lk 1:25
30:24 [v]Ge 35:24; 37:2; 39:1; 49:22-26 [w]Ge 35:17
30:25 [x]Ge 24:54
30:26 [y]Ge 29:20,30; Hos 12:12
30:27 [z]Ge 26:24; 39:3,5
30:28 [a]Ge 29:15

4 So she gave him her servant Bilhah as a wife.[b] Jacob slept with her,[c] 5 and she became pregnant and
bore him a son. 6 Then Rachel said, "God has vindicated me;[d] he has listened to my plea and given me
a son." Because of this she named him Dan.[a][e]

7 Rachel's servant Bilhah conceived again and bore Jacob a second son. 8 Then Rachel said, "I have
had a great struggle with my sister, and I have won."[f] So she named him Naphtali.[b][g]

9 When Leah saw that she had stopped having children, she took her servant Zilpah and gave her to
Jacob as a wife.[h] 10 Leah's servant Zilpah bore Jacob a son. 11 Then Leah said, "What good fortune!"[c] So
she named him Gad.[d][i]

12 Leah's servant Zilpah bore Jacob a second son. 13 Then Leah said, "How happy I am! The women
will call me[j] happy."[k] So she named him Asher.[e][l]

14 During wheat harvest, Reuben went out into the fields and found some mandrake plants,[m] which
he brought to his mother Leah. Rachel said to Leah, "Please give me some of your son's mandrakes."

15 But she said to her, "Wasn't it enough[n] that you took away my husband? Will you take my son's
mandrakes too?"

"Very well," Rachel said, "he can sleep with you tonight in return for your son's mandrakes."

16 So when Jacob came in from the fields that evening, Leah went out to meet him. "You must sleep
with me," she said. "I have hired you with my son's mandrakes." So he slept with her that night.

17 God listened to Leah,[o] and she became pregnant and bore Jacob a fifth son. 18 Then Leah said, "God
has rewarded me for giving my servant to my husband." So she named him Issachar.[f][p]

19 Leah conceived again and bore Jacob a sixth son. 20 Then Leah said, "God has presented me with
a precious gift. This time my husband will treat me with honor, because I have borne him six sons."
So she named him Zebulun.[g][q]

21 Some time later she gave birth to a daughter and named her Dinah.

22 Then God remembered Rachel;[r] he listened to her and enabled her to conceive.[s] 23 She became
pregnant and gave birth to a son[t] and said, "God has taken away my disgrace."[u] 24 She named him Joseph,[h][v] and said, "May the LORD add to me another son."[w]

Jacob's Flocks Increase

25 After Rachel gave birth to Joseph, Jacob said to Laban, "Send me on my way[x] so I can go back to
my own homeland. 26 Give me my wives and children, for whom I have served you,[y] and I will be on my
way. You know how much work I've done for you."

27 But Laban said to him, "If I have found favor in your eyes, please stay. I have learned by divination
that the LORD has blessed me because of you."[z] 28 He added, "Name your wages,[a] and I will pay them."

[a] 6 *Dan* here means *he has vindicated.* [b] 8 *Naphtali* means *my struggle.* [c] 11 Or *"A troop is coming!"* [d] 11 *Gad* can mean *good fortune* or *a troop.* [e] 13 *Asher* means *happy.* [f] 18 *Issachar* sounds like the Hebrew for *reward.* [g] 20 *Zebulun* probably means *honor.* [h] 24 *Joseph* means *may he add.*

names them, indicating in this particular context that they belong to her. The boys' names reflect Rachel's desire to outdo her sister: God has vindicated her, and she has won (see NIV text notes on vv. 6,8). Rachel's struggle with her sister recalls the struggle between Jacob and Esau.

30:9–13 Responding to Rachel, Leah gives her maidservant Zilpah to Jacob. The births of Gad and Asher bring joy to Leah, as their names indicate (see NIV text notes on vv. 11,13).

30:14–16 Jacob's relationships with Rachel and with Leah are dysfunctional. Their dispute becomes so twisted that Rachel is prepared to sell Leah a night with Jacob for the price of some mandrake plants that Reuben has collected. Rachel's behavior is reminiscent of Esau selling his birthright for a bowl of stew (25:29–34).

30:17–21 Although it appeared that Leah had stopped having children (v. 9), Leah becomes pregnant not once but three more times. She bears two sons, Issachar and Zebulun, once again acknowledging God's role in their births (see NIV text notes on vv. 18,20), and a daughter, Dinah. The brief mention of Dinah's birth prepares for the events in ch. 34.

30:22–24 After her sister Leah has given birth to six sons and a daughter, Rachel's prayer is eventually answered by God, and she gives birth to Joseph. The threefold reference to God in these verses underlines that he is the one who enables the matriarchs to have children. Childlessness in Genesis is an important motif, especially in the light of God's promise in 3:15 that salvation will come through the offspring of Eve. The divine gift of children to those who are barren takes on added significance, which is reflected in the importance of Isaac, Jacob, and Joseph in the Genesis story.

30:25–43 *Jacob's Flocks Increase.* After a period of at least 14 years, Jacob makes plans to return to Canaan. However, his father-in-law, Laban, does not want him to go, for Jacob's presence has been a source of blessing. As the patriarchal stories reflect elsewhere, the "firstborn" members of the family lineage mediate God's blessing. Laban yet again acts deceitfully toward Jacob and pays the consequences.

30:27 by divination. Laban discovers that God has blessed him because of Jacob. Later, God bans the practice of divination (Deut 18:10) because it uses inappropriate means (e.g., reading omens) to interpret present events or discern the future. **the LORD has blessed me.** Laban readily acknowledges Jacob's role in this. The motif of blessing is impor-

29 Jacob said to him, "You know how I have worked for you[b] and how your livestock has fared under my care.[c] 30 The little you had before I came has increased greatly, and the LORD has blessed you wherever I have been. But now, when may I do something for my own household?[d]"

31 "What shall I give you?" he asked.

"Don't give me anything," Jacob replied. "But if you will do this one thing for me, I will go on tending your flocks and watching over them: 32 Let me go through all your flocks today and remove from them every speckled or spotted sheep, every dark-colored lamb and every spotted or speckled goat.[e] They will be my wages. 33 And my honesty will testify for me in the future, whenever you check on the wages you have paid me. Any goat in my possession that is not speckled or spotted, or any lamb that is not dark-colored, will be considered stolen."

34 "Agreed," said Laban. "Let it be as you have said." 35 That same day he removed all the male goats that were streaked or spotted, and all the speckled or spotted female goats (all that had white on them) and all the dark-colored lambs, and he placed them in the care of his sons.[f] 36 Then he put a three-day journey between himself and Jacob, while Jacob continued to tend the rest of Laban's flocks.

37 Jacob, however, took fresh-cut branches from poplar, almond and plane trees and made white stripes on them by peeling the bark and exposing the white inner wood of the branches. 38 Then he placed the peeled branches in all the watering troughs, so that they would be directly in front of the flocks when they came to drink. When the flocks were in heat and came to drink, 39 they mated in front of the branches. And they bore young that were streaked or speckled or spotted. 40 Jacob set apart the young of the flock by themselves, but made the rest face the streaked and dark-colored animals that belonged to Laban. Thus he made separate flocks for himself and did not put them with Laban's animals. 41 Whenever the stronger females were in heat, Jacob would place the branches in the troughs in front of the animals so they would mate near the branches, 42 but if the animals were weak, he would not place them there. So the weak animals went to Laban and the strong ones to Jacob. 43 In this way the man grew exceedingly prosperous and came to own large flocks, and female and male servants, and camels and donkeys.[g]

Jacob Flees From Laban

31 Jacob heard that Laban's sons were saying, "Jacob has taken everything our father owned and has gained all this wealth from what belonged to our father." 2 And Jacob noticed that Laban's attitude toward him was not what it had been.

3 Then the LORD said to Jacob, "Go back[h] to the land of your fathers and to your relatives, and I will be with you."[i]

4 So Jacob sent word to Rachel and Leah to come out to the fields where his flocks were. 5 He said to them, "I see that your father's attitude toward me is not what it was before, but the God of my father has been with me.[j] 6 You know that I've worked for your father with all my strength,[k] 7 yet your father has cheated me by changing my wages ten times.[l] However, God has not allowed him to harm me.[m] 8 If

30:29 [b] Ge 31:6 [c] Ge 31:38-40
30:30 [d] 1Ti 5:8
30:32 [e] Ge 31:8,12
30:35 [f] Ge 31:1
30:43 [g] ver 30; Ge 12:16; 13:2; 24:35; 26:13-14
31:3 [h] ver 13; Ge 32:9 [i] Ge 21:22; 26:3; 28:15
31:5 [j] Ge 21:22; 26:3
31:6 [k] Ge 30:29
31:7 [l] ver 41; Job 19:3 [m] ver 52; Ps 37:28; 105:14

tant in Genesis, especially in view of how humanity comes under God's disfavor because of their sinfulness. Having received the blessing of the "firstborn," Jacob brings blessing to others.

30:31–34 The sheep and goats in Laban's flocks would have been variously colored, with only some being speckled or spotted.

30:35 Although Laban agrees to Jacob's proposal, he deliberately removes from his flock all the animals that should have belonged to Jacob, giving them to his own sons. Laban's self-seeking attitude is very much a match to Jacob's, for Jacob deceived his own father through the use of goatskins (27:1–29, especially v. 16).

30:38 peeled branches. How these influenced the outcome of the breeding is not immediately apparent.

30:39 streaked or speckled or spotted. By manipulating the breeding activity of Laban's flock (vv. 37–39), Jacob succeeds in creating for himself a large flock of animals.

30:40–42 By selective breeding Jacob ensures that the strongest animals in Laban's flocks produce streaked or dark-colored animals. Although Laban deliberately attempted to keep Jacob's wages to a minimum, Jacob succeeds in becoming very wealthy. Having arrived in Paddan Aram with little (32:10), he now has abundant possessions, resembling those of Abraham (12:16; 24:35).

31:1–21 *Jacob Flees From Laban.* Tension arises when Laban's sons become jealous of Jacob's prosperity. Against this background, the Lord instructs Jacob to return to Canaan. Speaking privately to his wives, Rachel and Leah, Jacob emphasizes how God has actively enriched him and invites them to join him as he returns to Canaan. Acknowledging that their father has also mistreated them, they willingly agree to flee from their homeland with Jacob.

31:3 the land of your fathers. God's brief instruction to Jacob highlights that Canaan is the homeland of his fathers. This was not so when God called Abraham (12:1).

31:7 your father has cheated me. Jacob explains to Rachel and Leah that their father has repeatedly changed his terms of employment. On every occasion, however, God has intervened, preventing Laban from harming Jacob. Consequently, Jacob has received more and more of Laban's livestock. The outcome reflects what Isaac said when he blessed Jacob: those who curse him will be cursed, and those who bless him will be blessed (27:29; cf. 12:3).

31:8 [n]Ge 30:32
31:9 [o]ver 1,16; Ge 30:42
31:11 [p]Ge 16:7; 48:16
31:12 [q]Ex 3:7
31:13 [r]Ge 28:10-22 [s]ver 3; Ge 32:9
31:15 [t]Ge 29:20
31:18 [u]Ge 35:27 [v]Ge 10:19
31:19 [w]ver 30,32, 34-35; Ge 35:2; Jdg 17:5; 1Sa 19:13; Hos 3:4
31:20 [x]Ge 27:36 [y]ver 27
31:21 [z]Ge 37:25
31:24 [a]Ge 20:3; Job 33:15 [b]Ge 24:50
31:26 [c]Ge 27:36 [d]1Sa 30:2-3
31:27 [e]Ex 15:20 [f]Ge 4:21
31:28 [g]ver 55
31:29 [h]ver 7

he said, 'The speckled ones will be your wages,' then all the flocks gave birth to speckled young; and if
he said, 'The streaked ones will be your wages,'[n] then all the flocks bore streaked young. 9 So God has
taken away your father's livestock and has given them to me.[o]

10 "In breeding season I once had a dream in which I looked up and saw that the male goats mating
with the flock were streaked, speckled or spotted. 11 The angel of God[p] said to me in the dream, 'Jacob.'
I answered, 'Here I am.' 12 And he said, 'Look up and see that all the male goats mating with the flock
are streaked, speckled or spotted, for I have seen all that Laban has been doing to you.[q] 13 I am the God
of Bethel,[r] where you anointed a pillar and where you made a vow to me. Now leave this land at once
and go back to your native land.[s]' "

14 Then Rachel and Leah replied, "Do we still have any share in the inheritance of our father's estate?
15 Does he not regard us as foreigners? Not only has he sold us, but he has used up what was paid for
us.[t] 16 Surely all the wealth that God took away from our father belongs to us and our children. So do
whatever God has told you."

17 Then Jacob put his children and his wives on camels, 18 and he drove all his livestock ahead of
him, along with all the goods he had accumulated in Paddan Aram,[a] to go to his father Isaac[u] in the
land of Canaan.[v]

19 When Laban had gone to shear his sheep, Rachel stole her father's household gods.[w] 20 Moreover,
Jacob deceived[x] Laban the Aramean by not telling him he
was running away.[y] 21 So he fled with all he had, crossed the
Euphrates River, and headed for the hill country of Gilead.[z]

Household gods similar to those Rachel stole (Gen 31:19).

Z. Radovan/www.BibleLandPictures.com

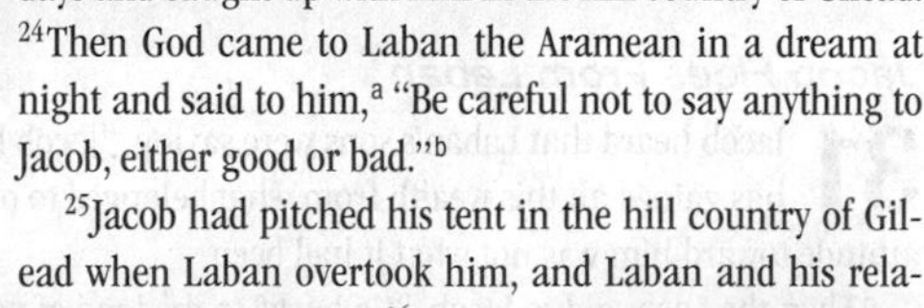

Laban Pursues Jacob

22 On the third day Laban was told that Jacob had fled.
23 Taking his relatives with him, he pursued Jacob for seven
days and caught up with him in the hill country of Gilead.
24 Then God came to Laban the Aramean in a dream at
night and said to him,[a] "Be careful not to say anything to
Jacob, either good or bad."[b]

25 Jacob had pitched his tent in the hill country of Gilead when Laban overtook him, and Laban and his relatives camped there too. 26 Then Laban said to Jacob, "What
have you done? You've deceived me,[c] and you've carried
off my daughters like captives in war.[d] 27 Why did you run
off secretly and deceive me? Why didn't you tell me, so I could send you away with joy and singing to
the music of timbrels[e] and harps?[f] 28 You didn't even let me kiss my grandchildren and my daughters
goodbye.[g] You have done a foolish thing. 29 I have the power to harm you;[h] but last night the God of

[a] *18* That is, Northwest Mesopotamia

31:14–16 For once Rachel and Leah agree. Their future will be best served by going with Jacob, especially since God has been with him.

31:19–20 Rachel stole … Jacob deceived. Although it is not immediately obvious from most English translations, these verses describe two thefts. The Hebrew text of v. 20 says, "Jacob stole the heart of Laban"; in Hebrew the idiom "to steal someone's heart" means to deceive or trick a person (see vv. 26–27). While Jacob steals Laban's heart (i.e., deceives him), Rachel steals her father's gods. Later, Laban accuses Jacob of stealing everything that Jacob now possesses (v. 43).

31:19 household gods. The objects Rachel steals may be small figurines that resemble certain gods. Worshipers thought that the gods were present in these images or idols, hence Laban speaks of them as "my gods" (v. 30). Perhaps Rachel steals these household gods because she hopes that possessing them will bring her good fortune and deprive her father of such benefit. If so, she has not fully broken free from her polytheistic upbringing (see 35:2; Josh 24:2). She may also have taken the items for their monetary value if they were made of precious metals.

31:21 Jacob travels south from Paddan Aram toward Canaan. **hill country of Gilead.** Located southeast of the Sea of Galilee, about 400 miles (645 kilometers) south of Harran.

31:22–55 *Laban Pursues Jacob.* Distrust and deception run deep within Laban's family. Jacob departs for Canaan when Laban is away. However, Jacob's father-in-law eventually overtakes Jacob and his retinue. After a heated encounter, the two men make a treaty guaranteeing not to harm each other.

31:22–23 Jacob and his family have journeyed for ten days before Laban overtakes them. By pursuing them so far, Laban demonstrates his determination to confront Jacob.

31:26–29 Laban portrays Jacob's actions as deceptive. Laban says that he, on the other hand, would have willingly and joyfully celebrated Jacob's departure for Canaan. In the light of his previous actions, Laban's words sound hollow.

31:29 the God of your father said to me. Laban himself has his own gods (v. 30), for he accuses Jacob of stealing them.

your father[i] said to me, 'Be careful not to say anything to Jacob, either good or bad.' 30 Now you have
gone off because you longed to return to your father's household. But why did you steal my gods?[j]"
31 Jacob answered Laban, "I was afraid, because I thought you would take your daughters away from
me by force. 32 But if you find anyone who has your gods, that person shall not live.[k] In the presence of
our relatives, see for yourself whether there is anything of yours here with me; and if so, take it." Now
Jacob did not know that Rachel had stolen the gods.
33 So Laban went into Jacob's tent and into Leah's tent and into the tent of the two female servants,
but he found nothing. After he came out of Leah's tent, he entered Rachel's tent. 34 Now Rachel had
taken the household gods and put them inside her camel's saddle and was sitting on them. Laban
searched[l] through everything in the tent but found nothing.
35 Rachel said to her father, "Don't be angry, my lord, that I cannot stand up in your presence;[m] I'm
having my period." So he searched but could not find the household gods.
36 Jacob was angry and took Laban to task. "What is my crime?" he asked Laban. "How have I
wronged you that you hunt me down? 37 Now that you have searched through all my goods, what have
you found that belongs to your household? Put it here in front of your relatives[n] and mine, and let
them judge between the two of us.
38 "I have been with you for twenty years now. Your sheep and goats have not miscarried, nor have I
eaten rams from your flocks. 39 I did not bring you animals torn by wild beasts; I bore the loss myself.
And you demanded payment from me for whatever was stolen by day or night.[o] 40 This was my situation: The heat consumed me in the daytime and the cold at night, and sleep fled from my eyes. 41 It
was like this for the twenty years I was in your household. I worked for you fourteen years for your
two daughters[p] and six years for your flocks, and you changed my wages ten times.[q] 42 If the God of
my father,[r] the God of Abraham and the Fear of Isaac,[s] had not been with me,[t] you would surely have
sent me away empty-handed. But God has seen my hardship and the toil of my hands,[u] and last night
he rebuked you."
43 Laban answered Jacob, "The women are my daughters, the children are my children, and the
flocks are my flocks. All you see is mine. Yet what can I do today about these daughters of mine, or
about the children they have borne? 44 Come now, let's make a covenant,[v] you and I, and let it serve as
a witness between us."[w]
45 So Jacob took a stone and set it up as a pillar.[x] 46 He said to his relatives, "Gather some stones."
So they took stones and piled them in a heap, and they ate there by the heap. 47 Laban called it Jegar
Sahadutha, and Jacob called it Galeed.[a]
48 Laban said, "This heap is a witness between you and me today." That is why it was called Galeed.
49 It was also called Mizpah,[b][y] because he said, "May the LORD keep watch between you and me when we
are away from each other. 50 If you mistreat my daughters or if you take any wives besides my daughters,
even though no one is with us, remember that God is a witness[z] between you and me."

[a] 47 The Aramaic *Jegar Sahadutha* and the Hebrew *Galeed* both mean *witness heap.* [b] 49 *Mizpah* means *watchtower.*

31:29 [i] ver 53
31:30 [j] ver 19; Jdg 18:24
31:32 [k] Ge 44:9
31:34 [l] ver 37; Ge 44:12
31:35 [m] Ex 20:12; Lev 19:3,32
31:37 [n] ver 23
31:39 [o] Ex 22:13
31:41 [p] Ge 29:30 [q] ver 7
31:42 [r] ver 5; Ex 3:15; 1Ch 12:17 [s] ver 53; Isa 8:13 [t] Ps 124:1-2 [u] Ge 29:32
31:44 [v] Ge 21:27; 26:28 [w] Jos 24:27
31:45 [x] Ge 28:18
31:49 [y] Jdg 11:29; 1Sa 7:5-6
31:50 [z] Jer 29:23; 42:5

31:32 that person shall not live. Unwittingly, Jacob's response to Laban places Rachel's life in danger. Members of this dysfunctional family act both deceptively and secretly.
31:34 camel's saddle. Rachel prevents Laban from finding his household gods by sitting on them. Rachel's actions suggest that she does not revere these gods.
31:36–42 Jacob turns on Laban, stressing both his innocence and the hardships that he endured in shepherding Laban's flocks.
31:42 the God of Abraham and the Fear of Isaac. Using two different names to refer to the one deity, Jacob attributes his prosperity to God. Perhaps Jacob designates God as "the Fear of Isaac" in order to subdue Laban. In contrast to Laban, who has lost his own gods, Jacob speaks of the need to respect the God who has guarded him. Jacob possibly alludes to how God's presence with Abraham and Isaac caused others to respect them (21:22–34; 26:26–33; cf. 20:11).
31:43 All you see is mine. Although Laban is reluctant to drop his claim of ownership, he proposes that the two men "make a covenant" (v. 44), committing them to live in harmony with each other.
31:44 covenant. The Hebrew word could equally be translated "treaty" (see 21:32).
31:45–49 The report of how they ratify the treaty concentrates on the element of witnesses. In ancient Near Eastern treaties the witnesses were usually deities; Jacob's stone pillar and his relatives' heap of stones probably reflect this practice. Jacob's single stone reflects his monotheistic outlook and contrasts with the polytheistic religion of his relatives (see Josh 24:2).
31:47 Jegar Sahadutha ... Galeed. The names associated with the treaty highlight the motif of witnesses (see NIV text note). The narrator may emphasize this because the two parties to the treaty will live about 400 miles (645 kilometers) apart.
31:49 Mizpah. This later becomes the name of a town in Gilead associated especially with the judge Jephthah (Judg 11:29).

31:51 [a] Ge 28:18
31:52 [b] Ge 21:30 [c] ver 7; Ge 26:29
31:53 [d] Ge 28:13 [e] Ge 16:5 [f] Ge 21:23,27 [g] ver 42
31:55 [h] ver 28 [i] Ge 18:33; 30:25
32:1 [j] Ge 16:11; 2Ki 6:16-17; Ps 34:7; 91:11; Heb 1:14
32:2 [k] Ge 28:17 [l] 2Sa 2:8,29
32:3 [m] Ge 27:41-42 [n] Ge 25:30; 36:8,9
32:5 [o] Ge 12:16; 30:43 [p] Ge 33:8,10,15
32:6 [q] Ge 33:1
32:7 [r] ver 11
32:9 [s] Ge 28:13; 31:42 [t] Ge 31:13
32:10 [u] Ge 24:27
32:11 [v] Ps 59:2 [w] Ge 27:41
32:12 [x] Ge 22:17 [y] Ge 28:13-15; Hos 1:10; Ro 9:27

51 Laban also said to Jacob, "Here is this heap, and here is this pillar[a] I have set up between you and me. 52 This heap is a witness, and this pillar is a witness,[b] that I will not go past this heap to your side to harm you and that you will not go past this heap and pillar to my side to harm me.[c] 53 May the God of Abraham[d] and the God of Nahor, the God of their father, judge between us."[e]

So Jacob took an oath[f] in the name of the Fear of his father Isaac.[g] 54 He offered a sacrifice there in the hill country and invited his relatives to a meal. After they had eaten, they spent the night there.

55 Early the next morning Laban kissed his grandchildren and his daughters[h] and blessed them. Then he left and returned home.[a][i]

Jacob Prepares to Meet Esau

32 [b] Jacob also went on his way, and the angels of God[j] met him. 2 When Jacob saw them, he said, "This is the camp of God!"[k] So he named that place Mahanaim.[c][l]

3 Jacob sent messengers ahead of him to his brother Esau[m] in the land of Seir, the country of Edom.[n] 4 He instructed them: "This is what you are to say to my lord Esau: 'Your servant Jacob says, I have been staying with Laban and have remained there till now. 5 I have cattle and donkeys, sheep and goats, male and female servants.[o] Now I am sending this message to my lord, that I may find favor in your eyes.[p]'"

6 When the messengers returned to Jacob, they said, "We went to your brother Esau, and now he is coming to meet you, and four hundred men are with him."[q]

7 In great fear[r] and distress Jacob divided the people who were with him into two groups,[d] and the flocks and herds and camels as well. 8 He thought, "If Esau comes and attacks one group,[e] the group[e] that is left may escape."

9 Then Jacob prayed, "O God of my father Abraham, God of my father Isaac,[s] LORD, you who said to me, 'Go back to your country and your relatives, and I will make you prosper,'[t] 10 I am unworthy of all the kindness and faithfulness[u] you have shown your servant. I had only my staff when I crossed this Jordan, but now I have become two camps. 11 Save me, I pray, from the hand of my brother Esau, for I am afraid he will come and attack me,[v] and also the mothers with their children.[w] 12 But you have said, 'I will surely make you prosper and will make your descendants like the sand[x] of the sea, which cannot be counted.[y]'"

[a] *55* In Hebrew texts this verse (31:55) is numbered 32:1. [b] In Hebrew texts 32:1-32 is numbered 32:2-33.
[c] *2* *Mahanaim* means *two camps.* [d] *7* Or *camps* [e] *8* Or *camp*

32:1–21 *Jacob Prepares to Meet Esau.* Twenty years have passed since Jacob fled from Esau. Having made peace with Laban, he now prays that God will enable him to be reconciled with his estranged brother.

32:1–2 Jacob is reassured of God's presence when the angels of God meet him and he sees the camp of God. This encounter recalls his earlier dream at Bethel, when he also saw "the angels of God" (28:12), an expression the OT uses nowhere else. Whereas Bethel, which means the "house of God," suggests a static residence for God, God's "camp" implies something mobile. God accompanies Jacob as he travels to Canaan.

32:2 Mahanaim. Means "two camps" (see NIV text note). Jacob probably alludes to the presence of God's camp alongside his own. Possibly the image of two camps inspires Jacob to divide his own camp into two sections prior to meeting Esau (vv. 7–10).

32:3 messengers. Having witnessed God's angels, Jacob sends messengers to Esau. The two events are connected by a wordplay involving the Hebrew noun *mal'ākîm*, which denotes both angels and messengers: God sends angels from his camp to meet Jacob, and Jacob sends messengers from his camp to meet Esau. **Seir.** This name resembles the Hebrew word for "hairy," which describes Esau in 25:25. Esau apparently settled in this region. **the country of Edom.** This expression not only recalls how Esau was known as Edom (25:30) but also echoes 25:27: Esau was "a man of the open country." The Hebrew term translated "open country" in 25:27 is rendered "country" here. Seir and Esau were well matched. Designating Edom as Esau suggests that Jacob is free to take possession of the land of Canaan.

32:4 my lord ... Your servant. Jacob's message to Esau expresses considerable humility. His language contrasts sharply with God's prediction that the older would serve the younger (25:23) and with Isaac's blessing, which speaks of Jacob being lord over his brothers (27:29). Having alienated himself from Esau, Jacob is keen to regain his brother's favor (33:8).

32:6 four hundred men. Jacob becomes exceptionally fearful when he hears that Esau is coming to meet him with a large number of men. With a force of 318 men, Abraham defeated the combined forces of four kings (14:14–16).

32:7 Jacob responds by dividing his camp into "two groups." His action recalls his earlier vision of God's camp (see v. 2 and note), but it implies that he has forgotten God's protective presence with him.

32:9 God of my father Abraham, God of my father Isaac, LORD. Jacob invokes God in prayer using three designations. The first two underline the importance of the family line, for both Abraham and Isaac have known God in a special way. "LORD" translates God's personal name (see 2:4 and note), which Jacob uses here for the first time.

32:10 kindness and faithfulness. By associating these characteristics with the Lord, Jacob's prayer anticipates how God himself declares his nature in Exod 34:6 (see note there).

13He spent the night there, and from what he had with him he selected a gift[z] for his brother Esau:
14two hundred female goats and twenty male goats, two hundred ewes and twenty rams, 15thirty female
camels with their young, forty cows and ten bulls, and twenty female donkeys and ten male donkeys.
16He put them in the care of his servants, each herd by itself, and said to his servants, "Go ahead of me,
and keep some space between the herds."

17He instructed the one in the lead: "When my brother Esau meets you and asks, 'Who do you
belong to, and where are you going, and who owns all these animals in front of you?' 18then you are
to say, 'They belong to your servant[a] Jacob. They are a gift sent to my lord Esau, and he is coming
behind us.' "

19He also instructed the second, the third and all the others who followed the herds: "You are to say
the same thing to Esau when you meet him. 20And be sure to say, 'Your servant Jacob is coming behind
us.' " For he thought, "I will pacify him with these gifts I am sending on ahead; later, when I see him,
perhaps he will receive me."[b] 21So Jacob's gifts went on ahead of him, but he himself spent the night
in the camp.

Jacob Wrestles With God

22That night Jacob got up and took his two wives, his two female servants and his eleven sons and
crossed the ford of the Jabbok.[c] 23After he had sent them across the stream, he sent over all his possessions. 24So Jacob was left alone, and a man[d] wrestled with him till daybreak. 25When the man saw that
he could not overpower him, he touched the socket of Jacob's hip[e] so that his hip was wrenched as he
wrestled with the man. 26Then the man said, "Let me go, for it is daybreak."

But Jacob replied, "I will not let you go unless you bless me."[f]

27The man asked him, "What is your name?"

"Jacob," he answered.

28Then the man said, "Your name will no longer be Jacob, but Israel,[a][g] because you have struggled
with God and with humans and have overcome."

29Jacob said, "Please tell me your name."[h]

But he replied, "Why do you ask my name?"[i] Then he blessed[j] him there.

30So Jacob called the place Peniel,[b] saying, "It is because I saw God face to face,[k] and yet my life
was spared."

31The sun rose above him as he passed Peniel,[c] and he was limping because of his hip. 32Therefore
to this day the Israelites do not eat the tendon attached to the socket of the hip, because the socket of
Jacob's hip was touched near the tendon.

[a] *28 Israel* probably means *he struggles with God.* [b] *30 Peniel* means *face of God.* [c] *31* Hebrew *Penuel*, a variant of *Peniel*

32:13 [z] Ge 43:11,15,25, 26; Pr 18:16
32:18 [a] Ge 18:3
32:20 [b] Ge 33:10; Pr 21:14
32:22 [c] Dt 2:37; 3:16; Jos 12:2
32:24 [d] Ge 18:2
32:25 [e] ver 32
32:26 [f] Hos 12:4
32:28 [g] Ge 17:5; 35:10; 1Ki 18:31
32:29 [h] Jdg 13:17 [i] Jdg 13:18 [j] Ge 35:9
32:30 [k] Ge 16:13; Ex 24:11; Nu 12:8; Jdg 6:22; 13:22

32:13–21 To placate his brother, Jacob generously sends herds of animals to Esau as a gift. To afford such a gift, Jacob must have become exceptionally wealthy during his stay in Paddan Aram.

32:22–32 *Jacob Wrestles With God.* Jacob's nighttime face-to-face encounter with God at Peniel remarkably transforms Jacob. Jacob previously met God when he left Canaan, and he encounters him again on his return (see note on 28:10–22). The events at Bethel and Peniel are exceptionally important milestones in Jacob's life.

32:22 Jabbok. This river flows into the Jordan Valley from the east. After seeing his family and possessions safely across, Jacob remains alone on the northern bank of the river.

32:24 a man. The unexpected introduction of a mysterious man who wrestles with Jacob during the night creates an element of suspense. Only at the end of the episode does the reader learn that Jacob has wrestled with God (v. 30). The Hebrew narrative displays the author's literary skill through alliteration, involving the words "Jacob" (Hebrew *ya'ăqōb*), "Jabbok" (Hebrew *yabbōq*) and "wrestles" (Hebrew *yē'ābēq*). The renaming of Jacob indicates that this event is an important turning point in his life.

32:25–26 Though his powerful opponent dislocates Jacob's hip, Jacob persistently continues to struggle with him, determined that the man bless him. Having previously struggled with Esau in order to gain the birthright and paternal blessing, Jacob now wrestles with God in order to gain his blessing.

32:28 Israel. Probably means "he struggles with God" (see NIV text note) but could mean "God struggles." By replacing Jacob's name with Israel, God acknowledges that Jacob has "struggled with God" and "overcome." Jacob begins a new relationship with God. The face-to-face struggle with God changes Jacob, "the deceiver," into Israel, the man who wrestles with God and survives, although not without personal injury.

32:30 Peniel. See NIV text note. The name captures the significance of Jacob's encounter with God and recalls Jacob's meeting with God face to face. Jacob has seen God and survived. Jacob's experience is similar to Abraham's in 18:1–15, when God appeared in human form. These encounters with God contrast with Moses' encounter with God at Mount Sinai, which involves seeing God in all his glory (Exod 33:20).

32:32 do not eat. As a memorial to this exceptionally important life-changing encounter with God, the Israelites adopt the custom of not eating "the tendon attached to the socket of the hip."

33:1 [l]Ge 32:6
33:3 [m]Ge 18:2; 42:6
33:4 [n]Ge 45:14-15
33:5 [o]Ge 48:9; Ps 127:3; Isa 8:18
33:8 [p]Ge 32:14-16 [q]Ge 24:9; 32:5
33:10 [r]Ge 16:13 [s]Ge 32:20
33:11 [t]1Sa 25:27 [u]Ge 30:43
33:14 [v]Ge 32:3
33:15 [w]Ge 34:11; 47:25; Ru 2:13
33:17 [x]Jos 13:27; Jdg 8:5,6,8,14-16; Ps 60:6
33:18 [y]Ge 25:20; 28:2 [z]Jos 24:1; Jdg 9:1
33:19 [a]Jos 24:32 [b]Jn 4:5

Jacob Meets Esau

33 Jacob looked up and there was Esau, coming with his four hundred men;[l] so he divided the
children among Leah, Rachel and the two female servants. 2 He put the female servants and
their children in front, Leah and her children next, and Rachel and Joseph in the rear. 3 He himself went
on ahead and bowed down to the ground[m] seven times as he approached his brother.
4 But Esau ran to meet Jacob and embraced him; he threw his arms around his neck and kissed him. And
they wept.[n] 5 Then Esau looked up and saw the women and children. "Who are these with you?" he asked.
Jacob answered, "They are the children God has graciously given your servant.[o]"
6 Then the female servants and their children approached and bowed down. 7 Next, Leah and her
children came and bowed down. Last of all came Joseph and Rachel, and they too bowed down.
8 Esau asked, "What's the meaning of all these flocks and herds I met?"[p]
"To find favor in your eyes, my lord,"[q] he said.
9 But Esau said, "I already have plenty, my brother. Keep what you have for yourself."
10 "No, please!" said Jacob. "If I have found favor in your eyes, accept this gift from me. For to see
your face is like seeing the face of God,[r] now that you have received me favorably.[s] 11 Please accept the
present[t] that was brought to you, for God has been gracious to me[u] and I have all I need." And because
Jacob insisted, Esau accepted it.
12 Then Esau said, "Let us be on our way; I'll accompany you."
13 But Jacob said to him, "My lord knows that the children are tender and that I must care for the
ewes and cows that are nursing their young. If they are driven hard just one day, all the animals will
die. 14 So let my lord go on ahead of his servant, while I move along slowly at the pace of the flocks and
herds before me and the pace of the children, until I come to my lord in Seir.[v]"
15 Esau said, "Then let me leave some of my men with you."
"But why do that?" Jacob asked. "Just let me find favor in the eyes of my lord."[w]
16 So that day Esau started on his way back to Seir. 17 Jacob, however, went to Sukkoth,[x] where he
built a place for himself and made shelters for his livestock. That is why the place is called Sukkoth.[a]
18 After Jacob came from Paddan Aram,[b][y] he arrived safely at the city of Shechem[z] in Canaan and
camped within sight of the city. 19 For a hundred pieces of silver,[c] he bought from the sons of Hamor,
the father of Shechem,[a] the plot of ground[b] where he pitched his tent. 20 There he set up an altar and
called it El Elohe Israel.[d]

[a] *17 Sukkoth* means *shelters.* [b] *18* That is, Northwest Mesopotamia [c] *19* Hebrew *hundred kesitahs*; a kesitah was a unit of money of unknown weight and value. [d] *20 El Elohe Israel* can mean *El is the God of Israel* or *mighty is the God of Israel.*

33:1–20 *Jacob Meets Esau.* The narrator recounts Jacob's encounter with Esau in the light of his nighttime wrestling with God (32:22–32). Jacob's remark that seeing Esau's face "is like seeing the face of God" (v. 10; see note there) closely connects the two events. To Jacob's surprise, Esau lovingly embraces him.
33:2 Rachel and Joseph in the rear. Jacob arranges his wives and children in order of ascending importance. As the only son the text specifically names, Joseph is set apart from his brothers. Joseph's special standing within Jacob's family becomes an important motif of the rest of Genesis.
33:3 bowed down. When Jacob received the paternal blessing, Isaac said that Jacob's brothers would bow down to him (27:29). Here Jacob bows down seven times to Esau and repeatedly calls Esau "my lord" (vv. 8,13,14,15). After striving to be superior to his brother, Jacob's attitude is now one of humble submission.
33:4 embraced him. Esau's embrace of Jacob signals a remarkable change of heart on the part of Esau; Jacob fled because Esau wanted to kill him (27:41).
33:10 to see your face is like seeing the face of God. Jacob compares his reunion with Esau with his experience at Peniel (32:22–32). Jacob's remark does not mean that Esau's appearance resembled God's. Rather, by embracing Jacob and forgiving him, Esau's actions resemble God's. Esau treats Jacob in a way that Jacob does not deserve.
33:11 present. Hebrew *bĕrākâ*, which is also the word for "blessing" (see note on 26:34—28:9). Having deceived Esau out of his blessing, Jacob now looks to make restitution by returning to Esau a "blessing."
33:13–14 Jacob declines Esau's invitation in a way that shows Esau the utmost respect.
33:17 Jacob travels the short distance from Peniel to Sukkoth, following the Jabbok River as it flows down to the Jordan River. Here Jacob rests his flocks and herds. **shelters.** Sukkoth is named after the shelters that Jacob erects for his livestock. The shelters were probably temporary, as was the case when later the Israelites celebrated the Festival of Tabernacles (see Lev 23:33–43).
33:18 Shechem. Lies about 20 miles (32 kilometers) to the west of Sukkoth. Possibly, Jacob traveled from Sukkoth to Seir, as he promised Esau (v. 14), before moving on to Shechem. The land of Seir lay to the southeast of Sukkoth. By camping close to Shechem, Jacob followed in Abraham's footsteps (12:6). While Abraham was at Shechem, God promised to give the land to his descendants (12:7).
33:19–20 Jacob buys a plot of ground in Shechem. He also sets up an altar, possibly reconstructing the one that Abraham made there (12:7). Shechem and his father, Hamor, figure prominently in the next episode.
33:20 El Elohe Israel. By naming the altar (see NIV text note), Jacob indicates that he is intimately connected to this God, the God who named him Israel at Peniel (32:28). No longer does Jacob refer to God simply as the God of his fathers.

JACOB'S JOURNEYS

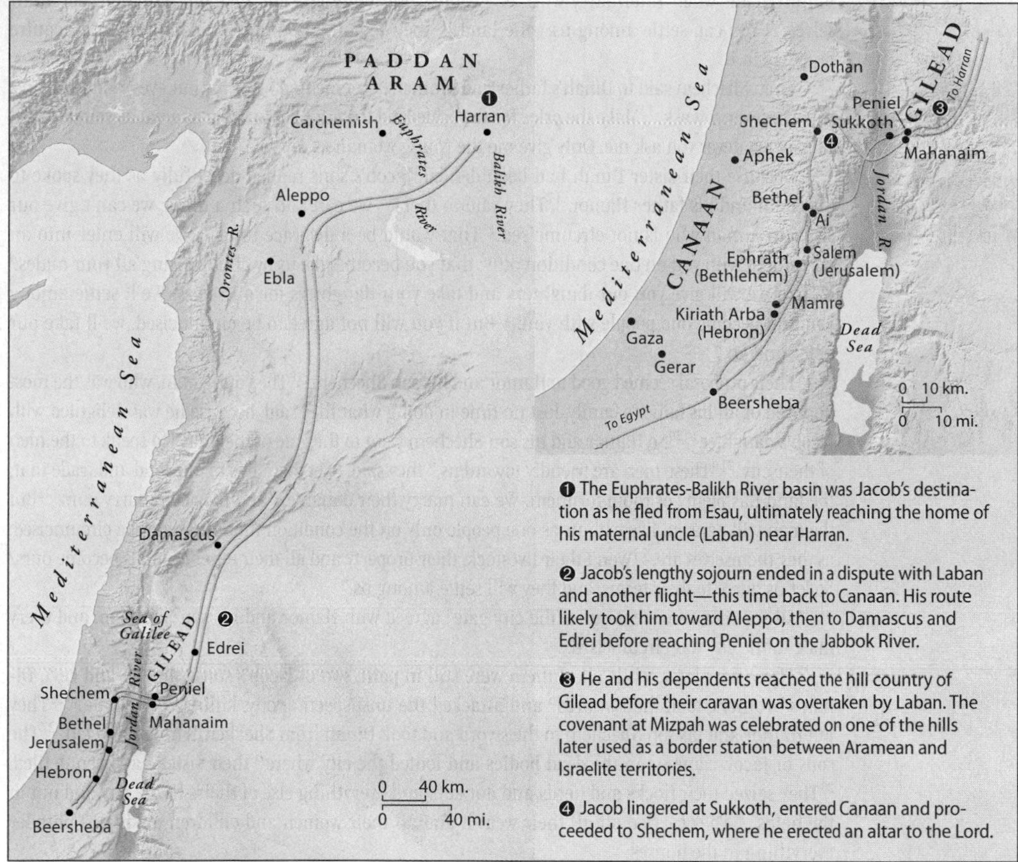

❶ The Euphrates-Balikh River basin was Jacob's destination as he fled from Esau, ultimately reaching the home of his maternal uncle (Laban) near Harran.

❷ Jacob's lengthy sojourn ended in a dispute with Laban and another flight—this time back to Canaan. His route likely took him toward Aleppo, then to Damascus and Edrei before reaching Peniel on the Jabbok River.

❸ He and his dependents reached the hill country of Gilead before their caravan was overtaken by Laban. The covenant at Mizpah was celebrated on one of the hills later used as a border station between Aramean and Israelite territories.

❹ Jacob lingered at Sukkoth, entered Canaan and proceeded to Shechem, where he erected an altar to the Lord.

Dinah and the Shechemites

34 Now Dinah,[c] the daughter Leah had borne to Jacob, went out to visit the women of the land.
2When Shechem son of Hamor the Hivite, the ruler of that area, saw her, he took her and raped
her. 3His heart was drawn to Dinah daughter of Jacob; he loved the young woman and spoke tenderly
to her. 4And Shechem said to his father Hamor, "Get me this girl as my wife."

5When Jacob heard that his daughter Dinah had been defiled, his sons were in the fields with his
livestock; so he did nothing about it until they came home.

6Then Shechem's father Hamor went out to talk with Jacob.[d] 7Meanwhile, Jacob's sons had come
in from the fields as soon as they heard what had happened. They were shocked and furious, because
Shechem had done an outrageous thing in[a] Israel[e] by sleeping with Jacob's daughter — a thing that
should not be done.[f]

34:1 [c] Ge 30:21
34:6 [d] Jdg 14:2-5
34:7 [e] Dt 22:21; Jdg 20:6; 2Sa 13:12 [f] Jos 7:15

[a] 7 Or *against*

34:1–31 *Dinah and the Shechemites.* Shechem's treatment of Dinah threatens to undermine Jacob's safe return to Canaan. Shechem's actions toward Dinah are reprehensible. When her brothers find out what was done, they are rightfully enraged. Shechem seeks to make amends by marrying Dinah, but Jacob's sons will not be placated. Deceptively, they persuade the men of Shechem to be circumcised. Before the men of the town have fully recovered, Simeon and Levi kill all the men of Shechem. Jacob condemns his sons' behavior, fearing that it will endanger the future of his family in Canaan. Ironically, circumcision was meant to be a source of blessing by connecting others to Abraham. The punishment (killing the Shechemites) exceeds the crime (Shechem's rape of Dinah).

34:2 ruler of that area. Hamor was an influential person. His standing within the community may well have influenced his son Shechem's behavior and Shechem's subsequent expectation that Hamor could arrange for Shechem to marry Dinah. **took her and raped her.** Shechem violated Dinah, and one result was that she was now ineligible for a proper marriage.

34:5–7 Jacob and his sons react differently: Jacob is slow to act when

34:10 [g] Ge 47:6,27 [h] Ge 13:9; 20:15 [i] Ge 42:34
34:12 [j] Ex 22:16; Dt 22:29; 1Sa 18:25
34:14 [k] Ge 17:14; Jdg 14:3
34:15 [l] Ex 12:48
34:19 [m] ver 3
34:20 [n] Ru 4:1; 2Sa 15:2
34:24 [o] Ge 23:10
34:25 [p] Ge 49:5 [q] Ge 49:7
34:30 [r] Ex 5:21; 1Sa 13:4 [s] Ge 13:7 [t] Ge 46:27; 1Ch 16:19; Ps 105:12

8 But Hamor said to them, "My son Shechem has his heart set on your daughter. Please give her to him as his wife. 9 Intermarry with us; give us your daughters and take our daughters for yourselves. 10 You can settle among us;[g] the land is open to you.[h] Live in it, trade[a] in it,[i] and acquire property in it."

11 Then Shechem said to Dinah's father and brothers, "Let me find favor in your eyes, and I will give you whatever you ask. 12 Make the price for the bride[j] and the gift I am to bring as great as you like, and I'll pay whatever you ask me. Only give me the young woman as my wife."

13 Because their sister Dinah had been defiled, Jacob's sons replied deceitfully as they spoke to Shechem and his father Hamor. 14 They said to them, "We can't do such a thing; we can't give our sister to a man who is not circumcised.[k] That would be a disgrace to us. 15 We will enter into an agreement with you on one condition only: that you become like us by circumcising all your males.[l] 16 Then we will give you our daughters and take your daughters for ourselves. We'll settle among you and become one people with you. 17 But if you will not agree to be circumcised, we'll take our sister and go."

18 Their proposal seemed good to Hamor and his son Shechem. 19 The young man, who was the most honored of all his father's family, lost no time in doing what they said, because he was delighted with Jacob's daughter.[m] 20 So Hamor and his son Shechem went to the gate of their city[n] to speak to the men of their city. 21 "These men are friendly toward us," they said. "Let them live in our land and trade in it; the land has plenty of room for them. We can marry their daughters and they can marry ours. 22 But the men will agree to live with us as one people only on the condition that our males be circumcised, as they themselves are. 23 Won't their livestock, their property and all their other animals become ours? So let us agree to their terms, and they will settle among us."

24 All the men who went out of the city gate[o] agreed with Hamor and his son Shechem, and every male in the city was circumcised.

25 Three days later, while all of them were still in pain, two of Jacob's sons, Simeon and Levi, Dinah's brothers, took their swords[p] and attacked the unsuspecting city, killing every male.[q] 26 They put Hamor and his son Shechem to the sword and took Dinah from Shechem's house and left. 27 The sons of Jacob came upon the dead bodies and looted the city where[b] their sister had been defiled. 28 They seized their flocks and herds and donkeys and everything else of theirs in the city and out in the fields. 29 They carried off all their wealth and all their women and children, taking as plunder everything in the houses.

30 Then Jacob said to Simeon and Levi, "You have brought trouble on me by making me obnoxious[r] to the Canaanites and Perizzites, the people living in this land.[s] We are few in number,[t] and if they join forces against me and attack me, I and my household will be destroyed."

31 But they replied, "Should he have treated our sister like a prostitute?"

[a] *10* Or *move about freely*; also in verse 21   [b] *27* Or *because*

he learns Shechem defiled Dinah, but Shechem's actions enrage Dinah's brothers. In the events that follow, Jacob's sons take the initiative, acting both deceitfully and without their father's approval.

34:8–10 Hamor attempts to get permission for Shechem to marry Dinah by offering Jacob's family the opportunity to integrate with the local community and become permanent residents.

34:12 the price for the bride. In line with ancient Near Eastern custom, Shechem offers Jacob and his sons a gift of money. This was a normal part of arranging a marriage. When Jacob was with Laban, he paid a bride-price equivalent to seven years labor. Shechem is obviously determined to have Dinah as his wife.

34:13 deceitfully. The Hebrew term conveys a strong sense of malice; Isaac uses the same word to describe Jacob's taking Esau's blessing (27:35). Unwilling to forgive Shechem, the sons of Jacob "the deceiver" respond "deceitfully."

34:14 not circumcised. In ch. 17 circumcision is the sign of the covenant that God establishes with Abraham. This covenant, which centers on Abraham being the father of many nations, is about Abraham and his descendants mediating God's blessing to others. While Jacob's sons correctly see circumcision as a means by which others may become part of Abraham's family, they have no desire to bring God's blessing to the people of Shechem.

34:21–23 Duped by Jacob's sons, Hamor and Shechem persuade the men of their city to be circumcised.

34:25 Simeon and Levi. Full brothers of Dinah. They slaughter the men of Shechem, who are still recovering after being circumcised. Shechem's crime, while serious, did not warrant such brutal retaliation. This punishment far exceeds Shechem's crime. Consequently, Jacob condemns it (v. 30) and continues to hold it against Simeon and Levi until his death (49:5–7). Although Simeon and Levi do the killing, their brothers join them in looting the city. The whole event is a shameful episode for Abraham's descendants.

34:30 brought trouble on me. As immigrants living in a hostile environment, Jacob fears for the future safety of his whole family.

34:31 The narrator gives the final word to Simeon and Levi, a possible reminder that Jacob's failure to intervene at an earlier stage may have contributed to the outcome.

Jacob Returns to Bethel

35 Then God said to Jacob, "Go up to Bethel[u] and settle there, and build an altar there to God, who
appeared to you when you were fleeing from your brother Esau."[v]
2So Jacob said to his household[w] and to all who were with him, "Get rid of the foreign gods[x] you have
with you, and purify yourselves and change your clothes.[y] 3Then come, let us go up to Bethel, where
I will build an altar to God, who answered me in the day of my distress[z] and who has been with me
wherever I have gone.[a]" 4So they gave Jacob all the foreign gods they had and the rings in their ears,
and Jacob buried them under the oak at Shechem.[b] 5Then they set out, and the terror of God[c] fell on
the towns all around them so that no one pursued them.

6Jacob and all the people with him came to Luz[d] (that is, Bethel) in the land of Canaan. 7There he
built an altar, and he called the place El Bethel,[a] because it was there that God revealed himself to him[e]
when he was fleeing from his brother.

8Now Deborah, Rebekah's nurse,[f] died and was buried under the oak outside Bethel. So it was named
Allon Bakuth.[b]

9After Jacob returned from Paddan Aram,[c] God appeared to him again and blessed him.[g] 10God said
to him, "Your name is Jacob,[d] but you will no longer be called Jacob; your name will be Israel.[e]"[h] So
he named him Israel.

11And God said to him, "I am God Almighty[f];[i] be fruitful and increase in number. A nation[j] and a
community of nations will come from you, and kings will be among your descendants.[k] 12The land I
gave to Abraham and Isaac I also give to you, and I will give this land to your descendants after you.[l]"[m]
13Then God went up from him[n] at the place where he had talked with him.

14Jacob set up a stone pillar at the place where God had talked with him, and he poured out a drink
offering on it; he also poured oil on it.[o] 15Jacob called the place where God had talked with him Bethel.[g][p]

[a] 7 *El Bethel* means *God of Bethel.* [b] 8 *Allon Bakuth* means *oak of weeping.* [c] 9 That is, Northwest Mesopotamia; also in verse 26 [d] 10 *Jacob* means *he grasps the heel*, a Hebrew idiom for *he deceives*. [e] 10 *Israel* probably means *he struggles with God.* [f] 11 Hebrew *El-Shaddai* [g] 15 *Bethel* means *house of God.*

35:1 [u] Ge 28:19 [v] Ge 27:43
35:2 [w] Ge 18:19; Jos 24:15 [x] Ge 31:19 [y] Ex 19:10,14
35:3 [z] Ge 32:7 [a] Ge 28:15,20-22; 31:3,42
35:4 [b] Jos 24:25-26
35:5 [c] Ex 15:16; 23:27; Jos 2:9
35:6 [d] Ge 28:19; 48:3
35:7 [e] Ge 28:13
35:8 [f] Ge 24:59
35:9 [g] Ge 32:29
35:10 [h] Ge 17:5
35:11 [i] Ge 17:1; Ex 6:3 [j] Ge 28:3; 48:4 [k] Ge 17:6
35:12 [l] Ge 13:15; 28:13 [m] Ge 12:7; 26:3
35:13 [n] Ge 17:22
35:14 [o] Ge 28:18
35:15 [p] Ge 28:19

35:1 – 15 *Jacob Returns to Bethel.* The events at Shechem possibly prompt God to instruct Jacob to relocate to Bethel. Jacob returns to where God appeared to him when he first fled from Canaan to go to Paddan Aram (28:10 – 22).
35:1 build an altar there. Jacob previously erected a pillar at Bethel (28:18). God now instructs him to return to Bethel, an event that will confirm God's faithfulness to Jacob's promises (28:20 – 22).
35:2 – 3 Recognizing that Bethel is the "house of God" (see NIV text note on 28:19), Jacob prepares his family for their encounter with God. At this stage some members of the family appear to be polytheists, worshiping a number of gods. Rachel, e.g., took her father's household gods (31:19). Jacob insists that they must abandon these gods in favor of God, who has faithfully cared for him. Additionally, Jacob demands that his family get rid of any defilement caused by worshiping other deities. After washing to purify themselves, they must change their clothes, further symbolizing their transformation from polytheism to monotheism.
35:3 in the day of my distress. Not just one particular day, but every occasion when Jacob was in difficulty.
35:4 rings in their ears. Possibly the idols, rather than the people, wore these. By burying these cultic objects, a known second millennium BC practice for disposing of images, Jacob placed them beyond further use. Their burial at Shechem may be symbolically significant, implying that the violent actions of Simeon and Levi reflect the influence of polytheism. Later, also at Shechem, Joshua challenges his fellow Israelites to throw away the gods that their ancestors worshiped (Josh 24:14,23).
35:5 the terror of God. An appropriate fear of God may restrain people's actions. "Fear of God" is a significant motif in Genesis (e.g., 20:8,11); God himself is even known by the title "the Fear of Isaac" (31:42,53).
35:6 Luz (that is, Bethel). See note on 28:19.
35:7 El Bethel. See NIV text note. The name draws attention to how God revealed himself at this location. Altars sometimes mark where God appeared to the patriarchs (12:7). They may also form a temporary sanctuary in the hope that God would make himself known at them (33:20).
35:8 Deborah. This brief note regarding the burial of Rebekah's nurse (24:59) under the oak called Allon Bakuth (see NIV text note) contrasts sharply with the mention of Jacob burying the foreign gods under the oak of Shechem (v. 4). They mourn for Deborah with weeping but shed no tears for the buried gods at Shechem.
35:9 – 10 This recalls how God blessed Jacob at Peniel (32:29), changing his name to Israel to signal his transformation (see note on 32:28). God has blessed Jacob like Abraham (24:1) and Isaac (25:11).
35:11 – 12 God speaks once more to Jacob at Bethel (see 28:13 – 15), using expressions that recall his previous promises to Abraham and Isaac.
35:11 God Almighty. This is how God revealed himself to Abraham (17:1) before promising numerous descendants, nations, and kings (17:6). Isaac highlighted the same concepts when he blessed Jacob (28:3 – 4; see 27:29). God now affirms that Jacob is heir to the covenant he initially made with Abraham and later established with Isaac. **be fruitful and increase in number.** God's plans for the patriarchs involve fulfilling what he originally intended when he created humanity (1:28). Through Abraham, Isaac, and Jacob, God sets in motion a process that will bring to completion his purposes in creating the world. **a community of nations will come from you.** This reflects God's earlier promise to Abraham that he would be the father of many nations (17:4 – 5), an idea Isaac echoed when he blessed Jacob (28:3). **kings will be among your descendants.** This again links to Abraham, whose descendants will be kings (17:6,16). As a whole, the book of Genesis follows a unique family line associated with future royalty. This royal expectation reappears in Joseph's dreams (37:6 – 10). God's promise of land to Abraham (e.g., 12:7; 13:15 – 17; 15:18 – 21) and Isaac (26:3 – 4) passes on to Jacob.
35:14 stone pillar. See note on 28:18. **drink offering.** Mentioned only here in Genesis, this may involve wine (see Exod 29:40).

35:17 [q] Ge 30:24
35:19 [r] Ge 48:7; Ru 1:1, 19; Mic 5:2; Mt 2:16
35:20 [s] 1Sa 10:2
35:22 [t] Ge 49:4; 1Ch 5:1 [u] Ge 29:29; Lev 18:8
35:23 [v] Ge 46:8 [w] Ge 29:35 [x] Ge 30:20
35:24 [y] Ge 30:24 [z] ver 18
35:25 [a] Ge 30:8
35:26 [b] Ge 30:11 [c] Ge 30:13
35:27 [d] Ge 13:18; 18:1 [e] Jos 14:15
35:28 [f] Ge 25:7,20
35:29 [g] Ge 25:8; 49:33 [h] Ge 15:15 [i] Ge 25:9
36:1 [j] Ge 25:30
36:2 [k] Ge 28:8-9 [l] Ge 26:34 [m] ver 25

The Deaths of Rachel and Isaac

35:23-26pp — 1Ch 2:1-2

16 Then they moved on from Bethel. While they were still some distance from Ephrath, Rachel began
to give birth and had great difficulty. 17 And as she was having great difficulty in childbirth, the midwife said to her, "Don't despair, for you have another son."[q] 18 As she breathed her last — for she was
dying — she named her son Ben-Oni.[a] But his father named him Benjamin.[b]
19 So Rachel died and was buried on the way to Ephrath (that is, Bethlehem[r]). 20 Over her tomb Jacob
set up a pillar, and to this day that pillar marks Rachel's tomb.[s]
21 Israel moved on again and pitched his tent beyond Migdal Eder. 22 While Israel was living in that
region, Reuben went in and slept with his father's concubine[t] Bilhah,[u] and Israel heard of it.

Jacob had twelve sons:

23 The sons of Leah:
Reuben the firstborn[v] of Jacob,
Simeon, Levi, Judah,[w] Issachar and Zebulun.[x]
24 The sons of Rachel:
Joseph[y] and Benjamin.[z]
25 The sons of Rachel's servant Bilhah:
Dan and Naphtali.[a]
26 The sons of Leah's servant Zilpah:
Gad[b] and Asher.[c]

These were the sons of Jacob, who were born to him in Paddan Aram.

27 Jacob came home to his father Isaac in Mamre,[d] near Kiriath Arba[e] (that is, Hebron), where Abraham and Isaac had stayed. 28 Isaac lived a hundred and eighty years.[f] 29 Then he breathed his last and
died and was gathered to his people,[g] old and full of years.[h] And his sons Esau and Jacob buried him.[i]

Esau's Descendants

36:10-14pp — 1Ch 1:35-37
36:20-28pp — 1Ch 1:38-42

36 This is the account of the family line of Esau (that is, Edom).[j]

2 Esau took his wives from the women of Canaan:[k] Adah daughter of Elon the Hittite,[l] and
Oholibamah daughter of Anah[m] and granddaughter of Zibeon the Hivite — 3 also Basemath
daughter of Ishmael and sister of Nebaioth.

[a] 18 *Ben-Oni* means *son of my trouble.* [b] 18 *Benjamin* means *son of my right hand.*

35:16–29 *The Deaths of Rachel and Isaac.* From Bethel, Jacob moves southward in the direction of Hebron to where Isaac, his father, is living (v. 27). Tragically, Rachel dies when giving birth.

35:16 Ephrath. A name associated with the town of Bethlehem (v. 19; Ruth 1:2; Mic 5:2).

35:18 Ben-Oni. Rachel's name for her son recalls her difficult labor (see NIV text note). **Benjamin.** Jacob's name for his son (see NIV text note); the name may also mean "son of the south," a suitable name since all of Jacob's other sons were born in the north.

35:20 that pillar marks Rachel's tomb. Rachel's burial place remained known centuries later during the time of Moses and early Israel (1 Sam 10:2).

35:21 Migdal Eder. The precise site is unknown. Since Migdal means "tower" and Eder means "flock/herd," perhaps this location had a tower that shepherds used.

35:22 Reuben … slept with … Bilhah. This brief report concerning Reuben has important implications for his standing within Jacob's family. While Reuben may have intentionally slept with Bilhah in order to establish his position as firstborn and principal heir (see 2 Sam 16:20–23), it has the opposite result. Jacob bestows on Joseph the status of firstborn (1 Chr 5:1–2; see note on Gen 49:3–4), and Reuben's later attempt to regain his father's favor fails (see 37:21–22 and note). **concubine.** See note on 25:1.

35:27 Mamre, near Kiriath Arba (that is, Hebron). See 13:18; 23:2 and note. Jacob follows in the footsteps of Abraham and Isaac. As ch. 35 reveals, Jacob is the one through whom God's promises to the patriarchs will move toward fulfillment. Isaac witnesses the return of Jacob to Hebron, having sent him away to Paddan Aram 20 years previously.

35:28–29 This report of Isaac's death and burial (see also 49:29–31) concludes 25:19 — 35:29.

36:1–30 *Esau's Descendants.* Before recounting events associated mainly with Jacob's sons, this passage provides some further information concerning Esau and his descendants. Genesis sometimes gives information about less important figures first (e.g., 4:17–24; 25:12–18).

36:1 This is the account of the family line of. See note on 2:4. Esau (that is, Edom). See 25:30.

36:2–3 The names of Esau's wives differ from those recorded in 26:34; 28:9. A variety of explanations may account for the variations: (1) the same woman may have been known by different names, (2) different women may have shared the same name, and (3) Esau may have had more than three wives.

4 Adah bore Eliphaz to Esau, Basemath bore Reuel,[n] 5 and Oholibamah bore Jeush, Jalam and
Korah. These were the sons of Esau, who were born to him in Canaan.

6 Esau took his wives and sons and daughters and all the members of his household, as well as
his livestock and all his other animals and all the goods he had acquired in Canaan,[o] and moved
to a land some distance from his brother Jacob. 7 Their possessions were too great for them to
remain together; the land where they were staying could not support them both because of their
livestock.[p] 8 So Esau[q] (that is, Edom) settled in the hill country of Seir.[r]

9 This is the account of the family line of Esau the father of the Edomites in the hill country of
Seir.

10 These are the names of Esau's sons:

Eliphaz, the son of Esau's wife Adah, and Reuel, the son of Esau's wife Basemath.

11 The sons of Eliphaz:[s]

Teman,[t] Omar, Zepho, Gatam and Kenaz.

12 Esau's son Eliphaz also had a concubine named Timna, who bore him Amalek.[u] These were
grandsons of Esau's wife Adah.[v]

13 The sons of Reuel:

Nahath, Zerah, Shammah and Mizzah. These were grandsons of Esau's wife Basemath.

14 The sons of Esau's wife Oholibamah daughter of Anah and granddaughter of Zibeon, whom she
bore to Esau:

Jeush, Jalam and Korah.

15 These were the chiefs[w] among Esau's descendants:

The sons of Eliphaz the firstborn of Esau:

Chiefs Teman,[x] Omar, Zepho, Kenaz, 16 Korah,[a] Gatam and Amalek. These were the chiefs descended from Eliphaz in Edom; they were grandsons of Adah.[y]

17 The sons of Esau's son Reuel:[z]

Chiefs Nahath, Zerah, Shammah and Mizzah. These were the chiefs descended from Reuel in
Edom; they were grandsons of Esau's wife Basemath.

18 The sons of Esau's wife Oholibamah:

Chiefs Jeush, Jalam and Korah. These were the chiefs descended from Esau's wife Oholibamah
daughter of Anah.

19 These were the sons of Esau (that is, Edom),[a] and these were their chiefs.

20 These were the sons of Seir the Horite,[b] who were living in the region:

Lotan, Shobal, Zibeon, Anah, 21 Dishon, Ezer and Dishan. These sons of Seir in Edom were
Horite chiefs.

22 The sons of Lotan:

Hori and Homam.[b] Timna was Lotan's sister.

23 The sons of Shobal:

Alvan, Manahath, Ebal, Shepho and Onam.

24 The sons of Zibeon:

Aiah and Anah. This is the Anah who discovered the hot springs[c] in the desert while he was
grazing the donkeys of his father Zibeon.

[a] *16* Masoretic Text; Samaritan Pentateuch (also verse 11 and 1 Chron. 1:36) does not have *Korah*.
[b] *22* Hebrew *Hemam,* a variant of *Homam* (see 1 Chron. 1:39) [c] *24* Vulgate; Syriac *discovered water;* the meaning of the Hebrew for this word is uncertain.

36:4 [n] 1Ch 1:35
36:6 [o] Ge 12:5
36:7 [p] Ge 13:6; 17:8; 28:4
36:8 [q] Dt 2:4 [r] Ge 32:3
36:11 [s] ver 15-16; Job 2:11 [t] Am 1:12; Hab 3:3
36:12 [u] Ex 17:8,16; Nu 24:20; 1Sa 15:2 [v] ver 16
36:15 [w] Ex 15:15 [x] Job 2:11
36:16 [y] ver 12
36:17 [z] 1Ch 1:37
36:19 [a] Ge 25:30
36:20 [b] Ge 14:6; Dt 2:12, 22; 1Ch 1:38

36:6–8 The reason for Esau's separation from Jacob echoes the earlier account of Abraham and Lot parting company (13:5–6).
36:9 This is the account of. Although this duplicates the heading that introduces ch. 36, this verse underlines in particular Esau's association with the hill country of Seir, which lay to the east of the Arabah.
36:12 concubine. See note on 25:1. **Timna.** Also mentioned in v. 22, she was a native of Seir and a sister of various tribal leaders.
36:15 chiefs. This emphasizes the identity of the tribal leaders descended from Esau. Esau has five sons and ten grandchildren (vv. 9–14), from whom 14 tribes descend (vv. 15–29).
36:20–30 Including details about the original inhabitants of Seir is surprising. There are seven tribal leaders (v. 29), suggesting that Esau's 14 tribes gained ascendancy in the hill country of Seir (see Deut 2:12,22).

36:31 [c] Ge 17:6; 1Ch 1:43
36:33 [d] Jer 49:13,22
36:34 [e] Eze 25:13
36:35 [f] Ge 19:37; Nu 22:1; Dt 1:5; Ru 1:1,6
37:1 [g] Ge 17:8 [h] Ge 10:19
37:2 [i] Ps 78:71 [j] Ge 35:25 [k] Ge 35:26 [l] 1Sa 2:24

25 The children of Anah:
Dishon and Oholibamah daughter of Anah.
26 The sons of Dishon[a]:
Hemdan, Eshban, Ithran and Keran.
27 The sons of Ezer:
Bilhan, Zaavan and Akan.
28 The sons of Dishan:
Uz and Aran.
29 These were the Horite chiefs:
Lotan, Shobal, Zibeon, Anah, 30 Dishon, Ezer and Dishan. These were the Horite chiefs, according to their divisions, in the land of Seir.

The Rulers of Edom

36:31-43pp — 1Ch 1:43-54

31 These were the kings who reigned in Edom before any Israelite king[c] reigned:
32 Bela son of Beor became king of Edom. His city was named Dinhabah.
33 When Bela died, Jobab son of Zerah from Bozrah[d] succeeded him as king.
34 When Jobab died, Husham from the land of the Temanites[e] succeeded him as king.
35 When Husham died, Hadad son of Bedad, who defeated Midian in the country of Moab,[f] succeeded him as king. His city was named Avith.
36 When Hadad died, Samlah from Masrekah succeeded him as king.
37 When Samlah died, Shaul from Rehoboth on the river succeeded him as king.
38 When Shaul died, Baal-Hanan son of Akbor succeeded him as king.
39 When Baal-Hanan son of Akbor died, Hadad[b] succeeded him as king. His city was named Pau, and his wife's name was Mehetabel daughter of Matred, the daughter of Me-Zahab.

40 These were the chiefs descended from Esau, by name, according to their clans and regions:
Timna, Alvah, Jetheth, 41 Oholibamah, Elah, Pinon, 42 Kenaz, Teman, Mibzar, 43 Magdiel and Iram. These were the chiefs of Edom, according to their settlements in the land they occupied.

This is the family line of Esau, the father of the Edomites.

Joseph's Dreams

37 Jacob lived in the land where his father had stayed,[g] the land of Canaan.[h]

2 This is the account of Jacob's family line.

Joseph, a young man of seventeen, was tending the flocks[i] with his brothers, the sons of Bilhah[j] and the sons of Zilpah,[k] his father's wives, and he brought their father a bad report[l] about them.

[a] *26* Hebrew *Dishan,* a variant of *Dishon* [b] *39* Many manuscripts of the Masoretic Text, Samaritan Pentateuch and Syriac (see also 1 Chron. 1:50); most manuscripts of the Masoretic Text *Hadar*

36:31–43 *The Rulers of Edom.* This section begins by listing various kings who reigned in Edom. Since the kings are linked to different towns, this list probably reflects the existence of a series of dynasties associated with towns, which in different periods exercised authority over the region of Seir.

36:31 before any Israelite king reigned. The observation that there were kings in Edom before there were kings in Israel implies that the author of this passage either anticipated or knew of an Israelite monarch. The movement in Edom from tribal leaders or chiefs to kings also occurred later in Israel.

36:40–43 A further list of Edomite chiefs links to Esau. While several of the names overlap with the chiefs in vv. 15–19, new clans probably come into being that are associated with particular locations. This list of chiefs also occurs in 1 Chr 1:51–54.

37:1—50:26 *The Family of Jacob.* The final narrative section in the book of Genesis gives special attention to Joseph because the continuation of the promised royal line traces to his son Ephraim. However, future kingship is also linked to the lineage of Judah, anticipating later developments when God rejects the line of Joseph in favor of David from the tribe of Judah (see Ps 78:67–72).

37:1–11 *Joseph's Dreams.* Although he is one of the younger sons of Jacob, special attention is given to Joseph. Favored by his father, he has two dreams in which he sees his brothers bowing down to him. Various indicators within this section suggest that Joseph will be the one through whom the promised line of royalty will continue.

37:1 Attention switches from the hill country of Seir, where Esau's descendants live, to Canaan, where Jacob settles.

37:2 This is the account of. This heading, the last in a long series (see note on 2:4), introduces the final part of Genesis. **Joseph.** The youngest of Jacob's sons (apart from Benjamin). Israel/Jacob gives Joseph the

3Now Israel loved Joseph more than any of his other sons,[m] because he had been born to him in his old age;[n] and he made an ornate[a] robe[o] for him. 4When his brothers saw that their father loved him more than any of them, they hated him[p] and could not speak a kind word to him.

5Joseph had a dream,[q] and when he told it to his brothers, they hated him all the more. 6He said to them, "Listen to this dream I had: 7We were binding sheaves of grain out in the field when suddenly my sheaf rose and stood upright, while your sheaves gathered around mine and bowed down to it."[r]

8His brothers said to him, "Do you intend to reign over us? Will you actually rule us?"[s] And they hated him all the more because of his dream and what he had said.

9Then he had another dream, and he told it to his brothers. "Listen," he said, "I had another dream, and this time the sun and moon and eleven stars were bowing down to me."

10When he told his father as well as his brothers,[t] his father rebuked him and said, "What is this dream you had? Will your mother and I and your brothers actually come and bow down to the ground before you?"[u] 11His brothers were jealous of him,[v] but his father kept the matter in mind.[w]

Joseph Sold by His Brothers

12Now his brothers had gone to graze their father's flocks near Shechem, 13and Israel said to Joseph, "As you know, your brothers are grazing the flocks near Shechem. Come, I am going to send you to them."

"Very well," he replied.

14So he said to him, "Go and see if all is well with your brothers and with the flocks, and bring word back to me." Then he sent him off from the Valley of Hebron.[x]

When Joseph arrived at Shechem, 15a man found him wandering around in the fields and asked him, "What are you looking for?"

16He replied, "I'm looking for my brothers. Can you tell me where they are grazing their flocks?"

17"They have moved on from here," the man answered. "I heard them say, 'Let's go to Dothan.'[y]"

So Joseph went after his brothers and found them near Dothan. 18But they saw him in the distance, and before he reached them, they plotted to kill him.[z]

19"Here comes that dreamer!" they said to each other. 20"Come now, let's kill him and throw him into one of these cisterns[a] and say that a ferocious animal devoured him. Then we'll see what comes of his dreams."[b]

37:3 [m]Ge 25:28 [n]Ge 44:20 [o]2Sa 13:18-19
37:4 [p]Ge 27:41; 49:22-23; Ac 7:9
37:5 [q]Ge 20:3; 28:12
37:7 [r]Ge 42:6,9; 43:26, 28; 44:14; 50:18
37:8 [s]Ge 49:26
37:10 [t]ver 5 [u]ver 7; Ge 27:29
37:11 [v]Ac 7:9 [w]Lk 2:19,51
37:14 [x]Ge 13:18; 35:27
37:17 [y]2Ki 6:13
37:18 [z]1Sa 19:1; Mk 14:1; Ac 23:12
37:20 [a]Jer 38:6,9 [b]Ge 50:20

[a] *3* The meaning of the Hebrew for this word is uncertain; also in verses 23 and 32.

---

status of firstborn, a special privilege that sets Joseph apart from his brothers (1 Chr 5:1–2). **bad report.** By reporting on his brothers, Joseph alienates himself from them. His action suggests that his attitude toward moral behavior differed from that of his older brothers, something that the subsequent narrative largely confirms.

37:3 Israel loved Joseph more than any of his other sons. Jacob may have favored Joseph over Joseph's brothers because Joseph was Rachel's older son (see 33:2) and apart from Benjamin, the youngest. **ornate robe.** This gift signals Joseph's special standing within the family. The precise style of the cloak is unknown; it is not necessarily multicolored (an idea that the earliest Greek translation of this passage introduces). 2 Sam 13:18 associates such distinctive clothing with royalty.

37:4 they hated him. Joseph's privileged position becomes a source of deep hatred within the family. His brothers despise him.

37:5 a dream. While the narrator does not disclose the source of Joseph's dream, throughout Genesis dreams are revelations from God (20:3; 28:12; 31:10–13; 40:5–8; 41:1,15–16).

37:8 reign over us. The image of Joseph's brothers' sheaves bowing down to Joseph's sheaf (v. 7) provokes a hostile reaction from Joseph's brothers. In light of God's promises to Abraham (17:6) and Jacob (35:11) that kings would come from them, as well as the special attention that Genesis gives to tracing a unique family lineage, Joseph's dream suggests that he will be the one through whom royalty will come. Set alongside his father's desire to dress him as a prince (see note on 37:3), the motif of royalty takes on added significance. The idea that Joseph might reign over his brothers fuels their hatred of him. The dream is later fulfilled on several occasions (42:6; 43:26; 44:14; 50:18).

37:9–11 Joseph's second dream reinforces the idea that he will rule over the members of his family. Including his father and mother among those who will bow down to him causes his father to rebuke him.

37:10 your mother. Leah, since Rachel is already dead (35:16–19).

37:11 his father kept the matter in mind. This remark suggests that Jacob did not dismiss the idea entirely. Jacob may well have recalled how his father Isaac had blessed him, promising that his brothers would bow down to him (27:29).

37:12–36 *Joseph Sold by His Brothers.* Filled with jealousy toward their younger brother, Joseph's brothers seize an opportunity to sell Joseph into slavery. As events develop, Reuben sees the assault on Joseph as providing a way of regaining his father's favor by restoring Joseph to him. In marked contrast Judah sees the possibility of enriching himself and his brothers through trading Joseph as a slave to passing merchants. The callous behavior of the brothers recalls how earlier in Genesis, Cain killed his brother Abel (4:1–16).

37:12–17 As shepherds, Jacob's sons take their flocks northward from Hebron to search for better grazing.

37:17 Dothan. About 13 miles (21 kilometers) north of Shechem.

37:18–20 Joseph's brothers conspire to kill him. See note on vv. 12–36.

Egyptian (at Beni Hasan) wall painting of western Semites such as Abraham and Joseph traveling to Egypt (nineteenth century BC). Note the ornate robes.

Beni-Hasan Necropolis. Tomb of Khnumhotep III. Detail: mural painting depicting an Asiatic caravan. Middle Kingdom/De Agostini Picture Library/G. Sioen/Bridgeman Images

37:21 [c] Ge 42:22
37:24 [d] Jer 41:7
37:25 [e] Ge 43:11 [f] ver 28
37:26 [g] ver 20; Ge 4:10
37:27 [h] Ge 42:21
37:28 [i] Ge 25:2; Jdg 6:1-3 [j] Ge 45:4-5; Ps 105:17; Ac 7:9
37:29 [k] ver 34; Ge 44:13; Job 1:20
37:30 [l] ver 22; Ge 42:13,36
37:31 [m] ver 3,23
37:33 [n] ver 20 [o] Ge 44:20,28
37:34 [p] ver 29 [q] 2Sa 3:31 [r] Ge 50:3,10,11
37:35 [s] Ge 42:38; 44:22,29,31

21 When Reuben heard this, he tried to rescue him from their hands. "Let's not take his life," he said.[c]
22 "Don't shed any blood. Throw him into this cistern here in the wilderness, but don't lay a hand on
him." Reuben said this to rescue him from them and take him back to his father.

23 So when Joseph came to his brothers, they stripped him of his robe — the ornate robe he was
wearing — 24 and they took him and threw him into the cistern.[d] The cistern was empty; there was
no water in it.

25 As they sat down to eat their meal, they looked up and saw a caravan of Ishmaelites coming from
Gilead. Their camels were loaded with spices, balm and myrrh,[e] and they were on their way to take
them down to Egypt.[f]

26 Judah said to his brothers, "What will we gain if we kill our brother and cover up his blood?[g]
27 Come, let's sell him to the Ishmaelites and not lay our hands on him; after all, he is our brother,[h] our
own flesh and blood." His brothers agreed.

28 So when the Midianite[i] merchants came by, his brothers pulled Joseph up out of the cistern and
sold him for twenty shekels[a] of silver to the Ishmaelites, who took him to Egypt.[j]

29 When Reuben returned to the cistern and saw that Joseph was not there, he tore his clothes.[k] 30 He
went back to his brothers and said, "The boy isn't there! Where can I turn now?"[l]

31 Then they got Joseph's robe,[m] slaughtered a goat and dipped the robe in the blood. 32 They took the
ornate robe back to their father and said, "We found this. Examine it to see whether it is your son's robe."

33 He recognized it and said, "It is my son's robe! Some ferocious animal[n] has devoured him. Joseph
has surely been torn to pieces."[o]

34 Then Jacob tore his clothes,[p] put on sackcloth[q] and mourned for his son many days.[r] 35 All his sons
and daughters came to comfort him, but he refused to be comforted. "No," he said, "I will continue to
mourn until I join my son in the grave.[s]" So his father wept for him.

[a] *28* That is, about 8 ounces or about 230 grams

37:21–22 Reuben's intervention is probably motivated by a desire to regain his father's favor rather than out of compassion for Joseph. Reuben hopes that Jacob will reinstate him as firstborn son (see 35:22 and note). Subsequent events, however, prevent him from rescuing Joseph (v. 29).

37:25 eat their meal. After throwing Joseph into a dry cistern, the brothers hard-heartedly begin to eat a meal. As they do, they observe a group of traders, whom they take to be Ishmaelites, traveling southward in the direction of Egypt. **camels.** See note on 12:16.

37:26–27 Revealing something of his selfish nature, Judah proposes that they sell Joseph as a slave. He cloaks his greed by suggesting that this will be an act of compassion on the part of the brothers.

37:28 Midianite merchants. When the traders get closer, they are identified more accurately. They may have been a subgroup within the broader category of Ishmaelites (v. 25). **twenty shekels of silver.** Early second-millennium BC documents indicate that slaves normally sold for 15–30 shekels.

37:29 tore his clothes. Reuben's response indicates his deep frustration at not being able to return Joseph to Jacob.

37:30 Where can I turn now? Reuben's concern is primarily about redeeming himself rather than about Joseph (see note on vv. 21–22).

37:31 Joseph's robe. There is an element of irony in how Jacob's sons deceive Jacob with the robe covered in goat's blood. Previously, Jacob deceived his father by wearing Esau's clothes and goatskins (27:15–16).

37:34 sackcloth. Attire appropriate to convey grief and personal loss. **many days.** Because of his special love for Joseph, Jacob mourns for a considerable period of time.

37:35 grave. Hebrew *šᵉʾōl* (see note on Ps 6:5).

[36]Meanwhile, the Midianites[a] sold Joseph in Egypt to Potiphar, one of Pharaoh's officials, the captain of the guard.[t]

Judah and Tamar

38 At that time, Judah left his brothers and went down to stay with a man of Adullam named Hirah. [2]There Judah met the daughter of a Canaanite man named Shua.[u] He married her and
made love to her; [3]she became pregnant and gave birth to a son, who was named Er.[v] [4]She conceived
again and gave birth to a son and named him Onan. [5]She gave birth to still another son and named
him Shelah. It was at Kezib that she gave birth to him.
[6]Judah got a wife for Er, his firstborn, and her name was Tamar. [7]But Er, Judah's firstborn, was
wicked in the LORD's sight; so the LORD put him to death.[w]
[8]Then Judah said to Onan, "Sleep with your brother's wife and fulfill your duty to her as a brother-
in-law to raise up offspring for your brother."[x] [9]But Onan knew that the child would not be his; so
whenever he slept with his brother's wife, he spilled his semen on the ground to keep from providing offspring for his brother. [10]What he did was wicked in the LORD's sight; so the LORD put him to death also.[y]
[11]Judah then said to his daughter-in-law Tamar, "Live as a widow in your father's household until
my son Shelah grows up."[z] For he thought, "He may die too, just like his brothers." So Tamar went to
live in her father's household.
[12]After a long time Judah's wife, the daughter of Shua, died. When Judah had recovered from his
grief, he went up to Timnah,[a] to the men who were shearing his sheep, and his friend Hirah the Adullamite went with him.
[13]When Tamar was told, "Your father-in-law is on his way to Timnah to shear his sheep," [14]she took
off her widow's clothes, covered herself with a veil to disguise herself, and then sat down at the entrance
to Enaim, which is on the road to Timnah. For she saw that, though Shelah[b] had now grown up, she
had not been given to him as his wife.
[15]When Judah saw her, he thought she was a prostitute, for she had covered her face. [16]Not realizing
that she was his daughter-in-law,[c] he went over to her by the roadside and said, "Come now, let me
sleep with you."
"And what will you give me to sleep with you?" she asked.
[17]"I'll send you a young goat[d] from my flock," he said.

37:36 [t] Ge 39:1
38:2 [u] 1Ch 2:3
38:3 [v] ver 6; Ge 46:12; Nu 26:19
38:7 [w] ver 10; Ge 46:12; 1Ch 2:3
38:8 [x] Dt 25:5-6; Mt 22:24-28
38:10 [y] Ge 46:12; Dt 25:7-10
38:11 [z] Ru 1:13
38:12 [a] ver 14; Jos 15:10,57
38:14 [b] ver 11
38:16 [c] Lev 18:15; 20:12
38:17 [d] Eze 16:33

[a] *36* Samaritan Pentateuch, Septuagint, Vulgate and Syriac (see also verse 28); Masoretic Text *Medanites*

37:36 Potiphar, one of Pharaoh's officials, the captain of the guard. Although the exact nature of Potiphar's post is uncertain, he was probably responsible for overseeing the detention of other important officials when Pharaoh imprisoned them (see 40:1–3). This probably explains why Potiphar later imprisons Joseph alongside those whom the king of Egypt has detained in prison (39:20).

38:1–30 *Judah and Tamar.* Although ch. 38 abruptly interrupts the story of Joseph in Egypt, it is an essential component within the overall story. It accounts for a remarkable transformation in the character of Judah, anticipating the positive role that he plays when later he and his brothers journey to Egypt in search of food. Additionally, and of equal importance, ch. 38 describes the continuation of Judah's family line, concluding with the birth of twins, when remarkably the "firstborn"—marked by the scarlet thread—is pushed aside by his sibling. Given the significance of similar events in Genesis involving "firstborn" sons, the birth of Perez is noteworthy, all the more so because he is the ancestor of the royal line of David (Ruth 4:18–22).

38:1–2 Judah's relocation to Adullam parallels Joseph's departure to Egypt. Judah's subsequent marriage to a Canaanite woman reinforces the impression that he cares little for his own family. The patriarchs discouraged marrying foreigners (24:3; 26:34–35; 28:1).

38:6–7 With minimal detail, the narrator presents Er as "wicked" (v. 7), and God punishes him by death. The twofold reference to him as "firstborn" is noteworthy in a book that is especially interested in tracing the assumed rights of firstborns.

38:8 Since Tamar is a childless widow, Judah arranges for his second-born son, Onan, to marry her, an arrangement known as levirate marriage (see Deut 25:5–10; Ruth 1:11–13; Matt 22:24–25; Luke 20:28).

38:9 he spilled his semen on the ground. The narrator does not fully explain the reason for Onan's action. Perhaps Onan despised his deceased brother and did not want Tamar's child to have Er's share of Judah's inheritance. Not only would this reduce Onan's portion of his father's possessions but, as firstborn heir, "Er's son" would receive a double portion.

38:11 The deaths of Er and Onan make Judah highly protective of Shelah. Out of self-interest, Judah sends Tamar back to her own family, giving little thought to her future well-being.

38:12 The death of Judah's wife sets the stage for an unexpected development.

38:13–14 Observing that Judah has not kept his promise regarding Shelah (v. 11), Tamar takes unusual steps to become pregnant by Judah. By hiding her face with a veil, Tamar disguises herself as a "shrine prostitute" (v. 21; see note there). Given Judah's inability to recognize Tamar, the name of the location where she waits for Judah is somewhat ironic: Enaim means "two springs" or "a pair of eyes." Its precise location is unknown.

38:15–18 Taking Tamar to be a prostitute, Judah, now a widower, looks to gratify his sexual desires. This further evidences his self-centered approach to life. Tamar, knowing that Judah is untrustworthy, asks for a guarantee that he will pay her with a young goat from his flock.

38:17 [e]ver 20
38:18 [f]ver 25
38:19 [g]ver 14
38:21 [h]Lev 19:29; Hos 4:14
38:24 [i]Lev 21:9; Dt 22:21,22
38:25 [j]ver 18
38:26 [k]1Sa 24:17 [l]ver 11
38:27 [m]Ge 25:24
38:29 [n]Ge 46:12; Nu 26:20,21; Ru 4:12, 18; 1Ch 2:4; Mt 1:3
38:30 [o]1Ch 2:4
39:1 [p]Ge 37:36 [q]Ge 37:25; Ps 105:17
39:2 [r]Ge 21:20,22; Ac 7:9
39:3 [s]Ge 21:22; 26:28 [t]Ps 1:3
39:4 [u]ver 8,22; Ge 24:2

"Will you give me something as a pledge[e] until you send it?" she asked.
18 He said, "What pledge should I give you?"
"Your seal[f] and its cord, and the staff in your hand," she answered. So he gave them to her and
slept with her, and she became pregnant by him. 19 After she left, she took off her veil and put on her
widow's clothes[g] again.
20 Meanwhile Judah sent the young goat by his friend the Adullamite in order to get his pledge back
from the woman, but he did not find her. 21 He asked the men who lived there, "Where is the shrine
prostitute[h] who was beside the road at Enaim?"
"There hasn't been any shrine prostitute here," they said.
22 So he went back to Judah and said, "I didn't find her. Besides, the men who lived there said, 'There
hasn't been any shrine prostitute here.'"
23 Then Judah said, "Let her keep what she has, or we will become a laughingstock. After all, I did
send her this young goat, but you didn't find her."
24 About three months later Judah was told, "Your daughter-in-law Tamar is guilty of prostitution,
and as a result she is now pregnant."
Judah said, "Bring her out and have her burned to death!"[i]
25 As she was being brought out, she sent a message to her father-in-law. "I am pregnant by the man
who owns these," she said. And she added, "See if you recognize whose seal and cord and staff these are."[j]
26 Judah recognized them and said, "She is more righteous than I,[k] since I wouldn't give her to my
son Shelah.[l]" And he did not sleep with her again.
27 When the time came for her to give birth, there were twin boys in her womb.[m] 28 As she was giving
birth, one of them put out his hand; so the midwife took a scarlet thread and tied it on his wrist and
said, "This one came out first." 29 But when he drew back his hand, his brother came out, and she said,
"So this is how you have broken out!" And he was named Perez.[a][n] 30 Then his brother, who had the
scarlet thread on his wrist, came out. And he was named Zerah.[b][o]

Joseph and Potiphar's Wife

39 Now Joseph had been taken down to Egypt. Potiphar, an Egyptian who was one of Pharaoh's officials, the captain of the guard,[p] bought him from the Ishmaelites who had taken him there.[q]
2 The LORD was with Joseph[r] so that he prospered, and he lived in the house of his Egyptian master.
3 When his master saw that the LORD was with him[s] and that the LORD gave him success in everything
he did,[t] 4 Joseph found favor in his eyes and became his attendant. Potiphar put him in charge of his
household, and he entrusted to his care everything he owned.[u] 5 From the time he put him in charge

[a] *29 Perez* means *breaking out.* [b] *30 Zerah* can mean *scarlet* or *brightness.*

38:18 seal and its cord. This may have been a necklace that consisted of a small cylinder seal that produced an impression unique to the owner.
38:20 his friend the Adullamite. Hirah (v. 12).
38:21 shrine prostitute. Occurs infrequently in the OT (Deut 23:17; Hos 4:14). Fertility rituals were an accepted part of Canaanite religious practices but played no part in orthodox Israelite worship.
38:24 have her burned to death! Judah's condemnation of Tamar is exceptionally hypocritical and shows little compassion for his daughter-in-law.
38:25–26 Judah acknowledges his own guilt in keeping Shelah from marrying Tamar. Not only does this justify Tamar's unconventional conduct, but it marks a turning point in Judah's life. From this point onward in the narrative, his behavior is very different. Without knowledge of this event, it would be difficult to explain why Judah, having sold Joseph into slavery in Egypt, is later prepared to sacrifice his own freedom in order to take the place of Benjamin as a slave.
38:27–30 To identify the firstborn son, the midwife ties a scarlet thread on the wrist of Zerah (see NIV text note on v. 30). Yet before Zerah is born, Perez breaks out in front of him (see NIV text note on v. 29). Genesis has recorded a series of incidents in which younger brothers usurp firstborn sons. Centuries later, in the time of Samuel, the lineage of Perez will replace the firstborn lineage of Joseph/Ephraim, leading to the creation of the Davidic dynasty (see Ps 78:67–72). The events of ch. 38 take on great significance when viewed in the light of God's plan to redeem humanity through an offspring descended from Eve through the line of Abraham, Isaac, and Jacob. Ultimately, this is fulfilled in Jesus Christ (Matt 1:1–16).
39:1–23 *Joseph and Potiphar's Wife.* God is with Joseph, in spite of his enslavement in Egypt. Joseph's loyalty to God, reflected in his personal integrity, results in blessing for Potiphar. This continues a pattern of God's mediating his blessing to others through the line of patriarchs, beginning with Abraham. However, Joseph's integrity results in Potiphar's wife falsely accusing him. Joseph is once more the victim of injustice.
39:1 By echoing 37:36, this verse resumes the story of the Midianites selling Joseph into slavery in Egypt. **one of Pharaoh's officials, the captain of the guard.** See note on 37:36.
39:2–5 The frequent references to the "LORD" underscore that Joseph's success comes from God. The "LORD" prospers both Joseph and those whom he serves. In light of God's earlier promises to bless others (12:3; 18:18; 22:18; 26:4), this presents Joseph as the "firstborn" heir to Abraham, Isaac, and Jacob.

of his household and of all that he owned, the LORD blessed the household of the Egyptian because of
Joseph.[v] The blessing of the LORD was on everything Potiphar had, both in the house and in the field.
6So Potiphar left everything he had in Joseph's care; with Joseph in charge, he did not concern himself
with anything except the food he ate.

Now Joseph was well-built and handsome,[w] 7and after a while his master's wife took notice of Joseph
and said, "Come to bed with me!"[x]

8But he refused.[y] "With me in charge," he told her, "my master does not concern himself with anything in the house; everything he owns he has entrusted to my care. 9No one is greater in this house
than I am.[z] My master has withheld nothing from me except you, because you are his wife. How then
could I do such a wicked thing and sin against God?"[a] 10And though she spoke to Joseph day after day,
he refused to go to bed with her or even be with her.

11One day he went into the house to attend to his duties, and none of the household servants was
inside. 12She caught him by his cloak[b] and said, "Come to bed with me!" But he left his cloak in her
hand and ran out of the house.

13When she saw that he had left his cloak in her hand and had run out of the house, 14she called
her household servants. "Look," she said to them, "this Hebrew has been brought to us to make sport
of us! He came in here to sleep with me, but I screamed.[c] 15When he heard me scream for help, he left
his cloak beside me and ran out of the house."

16She kept his cloak beside her until his master came home. 17Then she told him this story:[d] "That
Hebrew slave you brought us came to me to make sport of me. 18But as soon as I screamed for help, he
left his cloak beside me and ran out of the house."

19When his master heard the story his wife told him, saying, "This is how your slave treated me,"
he burned with anger.[e] 20Joseph's master took him and put him in prison,[f] the place where the king's
prisoners were confined.

But while Joseph was there in the prison, 21the LORD was with him; he showed him kindness and granted
him favor in the eyes of the prison warden.[g] 22So the warden put Joseph in charge of all those held in
the prison, and he was made responsible for all that was done there.[h] 23The warden paid no attention to
anything under Joseph's care, because the LORD was with Joseph and gave him success in whatever he did.[i]

The Cupbearer and the Baker

40 Some time later, the cupbearer[j] and the baker of the king of Egypt offended their master,
the king of Egypt. 2Pharaoh was angry[k] with his two officials, the chief cupbearer and
the chief baker, 3and put them in custody in the house of the captain of the guard,[l] in the same

39:5 [v] Ge 26:24; 30:27
39:6 [w] 1Sa 16:12
39:7 [x] 2Sa 13:11; Pr 7:15-18
39:8 [y] Pr 6:23-24
39:9 [z] Ge 41:33,40 [a] Ge 20:6; 42:18; 2Sa 12:13
39:12 [b] Pr 7:13
39:14 [c] Dt 22:24,27
39:17 [d] Ex 23:1,7; Ps 101:5
39:19 [e] Pr 6:34
39:20 [f] Ge 40:3; Ps 105:18
39:21 [g] Ex 3:21
39:22 [h] ver 4
39:23 [i] ver 3
40:1 [j] Ne 1:11
40:2 [k] Pr 16:14,15
40:3 [l] Ge 39:20

39:6–10 Potiphar's wife is attracted to Joseph because he is handsome and successfully manages her husband's household. However, Joseph's loyalty to his master, Potiphar, prevents him from yielding to the sexual advances of Potiphar's wife. His faith in God clearly influences his moral stance; to commit adultery would involve sinning "against God" (v. 9). Joseph does not exploit the trust Potiphar placed in him, nor does he succumb to the temptation of sexual gratification. He recognizes that all wrongdoing offends God (Ps 51:4).
39:11–18 This is the second time (see 37:31–33) in this short story of Joseph's life that someone uses one of Joseph's cloaks to deceive others. Potiphar's wife exploits the situation to the maximum. She emphasizes Joseph's foreign status by describing him as a "Hebrew" (vv. 14,17; see note on 14:13). She presents Joseph's assault on her as an assault on the entire household, persuading her servants to support her cause. The vehemence with which Potiphar's wife condemns Joseph is a chilling reminder of how vengeful human nature can be.
39:17 you brought. Subtly she places part of the blame on her husband because he was responsible for bringing Joseph into their household (see also "your slave" in v. 19). **make sport of.** The Hebrew word elsewhere describes Ishmael "mocking" his younger brother Isaac (21:9) and Isaac "caressing" his wife Rebekah (26:8).
39:19–20 Accepting his wife's accusation, Potiphar puts Joseph in prison. As captain of the guard (v. 1), Potiphar is well-placed to ensure Joseph's swift imprisonment (see note on 37:36).
39:20 where the king's prisoners were confined. This anticipates later developments in the story.
39:21–23 As in Potiphar's house, the Lord is with Joseph (vv. 2–5), so the warden entrusts Joseph with responsibility for all that happens within the prison.
40:1–23 *The Cupbearer and the Baker.* Through being imprisoned, Joseph comes into contact with two former members of the Egyptian royal household. As both officials await their fate in prison, Joseph's ability to interpret their dreams paves the way for later developments in his life.
40:1 cupbearer ... baker. Important positions within the royal household. Both men had regular access to the king. Their duties were not those of lowly domestic servants. **offended their master, the king of Egypt.** The reason they now find themselves imprisoned alongside Joseph. All three men share the same experience, although the outcome for one of them will be very different.
40:2 officials. The same Hebrew term denotes Potiphar (37:36; 39:1), who was a man of some wealth, having both slaves and fields.
40:3 captain of the guard. Potiphar held this position (37:36; 39:1), and he may have assigned Joseph to attend both officials.

40:4 [m]Ge 39:4
40:5 [n]Ge 41:11
40:7 [o]Ne 2:2
40:8 [p]Ge 41:8,15 [q]Ge 41:16; Da 2:22,28,47
40:12 [r]Ge 41:12,15,25; Da 2:36; 4:19
40:14 [s]Lk 23:42 [t]Jos 2:12; 1Sa 20:14,42; 1Ki 2:7
40:15 [u]Ge 37:26-28
40:18 [v]ver 12
40:19 [w]ver 13
40:20 [x]Mt 14:6-10 [y]Mk 6:21
40:21 [z]ver 13
40:22 [a]ver 19 [b]Ps 105:19
40:23 [c]Job 19:14; Ecc 9:15
41:1 [d]Ge 20:3
41:2 [e]ver 26 [f]Isa 19:6

prison where Joseph was confined. 4 The captain of the guard assigned them to Joseph,[m] and he
attended them.

After they had been in custody for some time, 5 each of the two men — the cupbearer and the baker
of the king of Egypt, who were being held in prison — had a dream the same night, and each dream
had a meaning of its own.[n]

6 When Joseph came to them the next morning, he saw that they were dejected. 7 So he asked Pharaoh's officials who were in custody with him in his master's house, "Why do you look so sad today?"[o]

8 "We both had dreams," they answered, "but there is no one to interpret them."[p]

Then Joseph said to them, "Do not interpretations belong to God?[q] Tell me your dreams."

9 So the chief cupbearer told Joseph his dream. He said to him, "In my dream I saw a vine in front of
me, 10 and on the vine were three branches. As soon as it budded, it blossomed, and its clusters ripened
into grapes. 11 Pharaoh's cup was in my hand, and I took the grapes, squeezed them into Pharaoh's cup
and put the cup in his hand."

12 "This is what it means,[r]" Joseph said to him. "The three branches are three days. 13 Within three days
Pharaoh will lift up your head and restore you to your position, and you will put Pharaoh's cup in his
hand, just as you used to do when you were his cupbearer. 14 But when all goes well with you, remember
me[s] and show me kindness;[t] mention me to Pharaoh and get me out of this prison. 15 I was forcibly carried
off from the land of the Hebrews,[u] and even here I have done nothing to deserve being put in a dungeon."

16 When the chief baker saw that Joseph had given a favorable interpretation, he said to Joseph, "I
too had a dream: On my head were three baskets of bread.[a] 17 In the top basket were all kinds of baked
goods for Pharaoh, but the birds were eating them out of the basket on my head."

18 "This is what it means," Joseph said. "The three baskets are three days.[v] 19 Within three days Pharaoh will lift off your head[w] and impale your body on a pole. And the birds will eat away your flesh."

20 Now the third day was Pharaoh's birthday,[x] and he gave a feast for all his officials.[y] He lifted up the
heads of the chief cupbearer and the chief baker in the presence of his officials: 21 He restored the chief
cupbearer to his position, so that he once again put the cup into Pharaoh's hand[z] — 22 but he impaled
the chief baker,[a] just as Joseph had said to them in his interpretation.[b]

23 The chief cupbearer, however, did not remember Joseph; he forgot him.[c]

Pharaoh's Dreams

41 When two full years had passed, Pharaoh had a dream:[d] He was standing by the Nile, 2 when
out of the river there came up seven cows, sleek and fat,[e] and they grazed among the reeds.[f]
3 After them, seven other cows, ugly and gaunt, came up out of the Nile and stood beside those on

[a] *16* Or *three wicker baskets*

40:5 Like Joseph as a teenager (37:5 – 11), the two men have intriguing dreams. However, because they are imprisoned, they cannot ask priests and wise men to interpret their dreams (cf. 41:8).

40:8 interpretations belong to God. This may not have surprised the two men since Egyptians consulted their temple priests for interpretations (see note on 41:8). However, by offering to explain their dreams, Joseph indicates that he has a special God-given ability.

40:9 – 11 The cupbearer's dream reflects something of what his normal duties entailed.

40:13 will lift up your head. This same motif comes later in v. 19, where it applies to the baker. However, although Pharaoh will lift up the heads of both men (v. 20), the results are very different.

40:14 remember me. In spite of Joseph's request, the cupbearer quickly forgets about him (v. 23).

40:15 dungeon. The Hebrew term is translated "cistern" in 37:24. In both Canaan and Egypt, Joseph finds himself unjustly imprisoned. While he declares his innocence, the cupbearer quickly forgets his plea.

40:16 – 17 The chief baker recounts his dream, hopeful of a positive interpretation.

40:19 will lift off your head. Whereas Pharaoh's lifting up the cupbearer's head reinstates him, the same idiom describes an ominous outcome for the chief baker. The idiom may not necessarily describe his decapitation, but Pharaoh impales the baker's body outdoors, permitting birds of carrion to gorge on it.

40:20 – 22 Joseph's interpretations of their dreams come to fruition.

40:20 Pharaoh's birthday. The anniversary of either his birth or his ascension to the throne of Egypt. **lifted up.** The heads of both men are raised (see note on v. 13) with very different consequences for them (see note on v. 19).

40:23 he forgot him. Joseph had asked the chief cupbearer to mention him to Pharaoh (v. 14).

41:1 – 40 *Pharaoh's Dreams.* After two years, the cupbearer recalls Joseph's ability to interpret dreams and tells Pharaoh about Joseph. When Joseph subsequently explains Pharaoh's dreams, Pharaoh dramatically exalts him from a prisoner to second-in-command to Pharaoh himself. This unexpected transformation prepares for later developments in the story involving Joseph's brothers. Joseph consistently credits God as both the source and interpreter of Pharaoh's dreams (vv. 16,25,28,32), and Pharaoh perceives that Joseph is unique (v. 38).

41:1 – 7 Pharaoh's dreams are the last of three pairs that the Joseph story records. Both of Pharaoh's dreams share common elements: seven fat heads of grain and seven thin ones parallel seven fat cows and seven thin ones; the seven thin items consume the seven fat ones.

41:1 two full years had passed. This is the time gap between the

the riverbank. 4And the cows that were ugly and gaunt ate up the seven sleek, fat cows. Then Pharaoh woke up.

5He fell asleep again and had a second dream: Seven heads of grain, healthy and good, were growing on a single stalk. 6After them, seven other heads of grain sprouted — thin and scorched by the east wind. 7The thin heads of grain swallowed up the seven healthy, full heads. Then Pharaoh woke up; it had been a dream.

8In the morning his mind was troubled,[g] so he sent for all the magicians[h] and wise men of Egypt. Pharaoh told them his dreams, but no one could interpret them for him.

9Then the chief cupbearer said to Pharaoh, "Today I am reminded of my shortcomings. 10Pharaoh was once angry with his servants,[i] and he imprisoned me and the chief baker in the house of the captain of the guard.[j] 11Each of us had a dream the same night, and each dream had a meaning of its own.[k] 12Now a young Hebrew was there with us, a servant of the captain of the guard. We told him our dreams, and he interpreted them for us, giving each man the interpretation of his dream.[l] 13And things turned out exactly as he interpreted them to us: I was restored to my position, and the other man was impaled.[m]"

14So Pharaoh sent for Joseph, and he was quickly brought from the dungeon.[n] When he had shaved and changed his clothes, he came before Pharaoh.

15Pharaoh said to Joseph, "I had a dream, and no one can interpret it. But I have heard it said of you that when you hear a dream you can interpret it."[o]

16"I cannot do it," Joseph replied to Pharaoh, "but God will give Pharaoh the answer he desires."[p]

17Then Pharaoh said to Joseph, "In my dream I was standing on the bank of the Nile, 18when out of the river there came up seven cows, fat and sleek, and they grazed among the reeds. 19After them, seven other cows came up — scrawny and very ugly and lean. I had never seen such ugly cows in all the land of Egypt. 20The lean, ugly cows ate up the seven fat cows that came up first. 21But even after they ate them, no one could tell that they had done so; they looked just as ugly as before. Then I woke up.

22"In my dream I saw seven heads of grain, full and good, growing on a single stalk. 23After them, seven other heads sprouted — withered and thin and scorched by the east wind. 24The thin heads of grain swallowed up the seven good heads. I told this to the magicians, but none of them could explain it to me.[q]"

25Then Joseph said to Pharaoh, "The dreams of Pharaoh are one and the same. God has revealed to Pharaoh what he is about to do.[r] 26The seven good cows[s] are seven years, and the seven good heads of grain are seven years; it is one and the same dream. 27The seven lean, ugly cows that came up afterward are seven years, and so are the seven worthless heads of grain scorched by the east wind: They are seven years of famine.[t]

28"It is just as I said to Pharaoh: God has shown Pharaoh what he is about to do. 29Seven years of great abundance[u] are coming throughout the land of Egypt, 30but seven years of famine[v] will follow them. Then all the abundance in Egypt will be forgotten, and the famine will ravage the land.[w] 31The abundance in the land will not be remembered, because the famine that follows it will be so severe. 32The reason the dream was given to Pharaoh in two forms is that the matter has been firmly decided[x] by God, and God will do it soon.

33"And now let Pharaoh look for a discerning and wise man[y] and put him in charge of the land of Egypt. 34Let Pharaoh appoint commissioners over the land to take a fifth[z] of the harvest of Egypt during

41:8 [g]Da 2:1,3; 4:5,19 [h]Ex 7:11,22; Da 1:20; 2:2,27; 4:7
41:10 [i]Ge 40:2 [j]Ge 39:20
41:11 [k]Ge 40:5
41:12 [l]Ge 40:12
41:13 [m]Ge 40:22
41:14 [n]Ps 105:20; Da 2:25
41:15 [o]Da 5:16
41:16 [p]Ge 40:8; Da 2:30; Ac 3:12; 2Co 3:5
41:24 [q]ver 8
41:25 [r]Da 2:45
41:26 [s]ver 2
41:27 [t]Ge 12:10; 2Ki 8:1
41:29 [u]ver 47
41:30 [v]ver 54; Ge 47:13 [w]ver 56
41:32 [x]Nu 23:19; Isa 46:10-11
41:33 [y]ver 39
41:34 [z]1Sa 8:15

cupbearer's release and Pharaoh's dreams. Joseph has remained in prison during this period.

41:8 The repetition of the common pattern in his dreams fills Pharaoh with unease; he realizes that these are no ordinary dreams, so he seeks an interpretation. **magicians.** Priests linked to Egyptians temples. Among their various duties, Egyptian priests interpreted omens and signs. Pharaoh may have expected these sorcerer-priests, along with the wise men, to explain his dreams.

41:12 Hebrew. See note on 14:13. Joseph's ethnic origin distinguished him from others (see note on 39:11–18).

41:14 dungeon. May refer to a "pit" (see note on 40:15). **shaved.** Egyptians tended to be smooth-shaven in contrast to some other ethnic groups (cf. 2 Sam 10:4).

41:16 Joseph emphatically identifies God as the one who interprets dreams. He downplays his own ability in order to give God his rightful place.

41:24 magicians. See note on v. 8.

41:25–32 Joseph explains Pharaoh's dreams, underlining that they reveal what God is "about to do" (v. 25).

41:33–36 Joseph goes beyond interpreting Pharaoh's dreams to offering a plan of action for addressing the forthcoming situation.

41:34 a fifth of the harvest. This probably takes into account loss due

41:34 [a] ver 48
41:35 [b] ver 48
41:36 [c] ver 56
41:37 [d] Ge 45:16
41:38 [e] Nu 27:18; Job 32:8; Da 4:8-9,18; 5:11,14
41:40 [f] Ps 105:21-22; Ac 7:10
41:41 [g] Ge 42:6; Da 6:3
41:42 [h] Est 3:10 [i] Da 5:7, 16,29
41:43 [j] Est 6:9
41:44 [k] Ps 105:22
41:45 [l] ver 50; Ge 46:20,27
41:46 [m] Ge 37:2 [n] 1Sa 16:21; Da 1:19
41:50 [o] Ge 46:20; 48:5
41:51 [p] Ge 48:14,18,20
41:52 [q] Ge 48:1,5; 50:23 [r] Ge 17:6; 28:3; 49:22
41:54 [s] ver 30; Ps 105:11; Ac 7:11
41:55 [t] Dt 32:24 [u] ver 41
41:56 [v] Ge 12:10
41:57 [w] Ge 42:5; 47:15

the seven years of abundance.[a] 35 They should collect all the food of these good years that are coming
and store up the grain under the authority of Pharaoh, to be kept in the cities for food.[b] 36 This food
should be held in reserve for the country, to be used during the seven years of famine that will come
upon Egypt,[c] so that the country may not be ruined by the famine."

37 The plan seemed good to Pharaoh and to all his officials.[d] 38 So Pharaoh asked them, "Can we find
anyone like this man, one in whom is the spirit of God*[a]*?"[e]

39 Then Pharaoh said to Joseph, "Since God has made all this known to you, there is no one so discerning and wise as you. 40 You shall be in charge of my palace, and all my people are to submit to your
orders.[f] Only with respect to the throne will I be greater than you."

Joseph in Charge of Egypt

41 So Pharaoh said to Joseph, "I hereby put you in charge of the whole land of Egypt."[g] 42 Then Pharaoh
took his signet ring[h] from his finger and put it on Joseph's finger. He dressed him in robes of fine linen and
put a gold chain around his neck.[i] 43 He had him ride in a chariot as his second-in-command,*[b]* and people
shouted before him, "Make way*[c]*!"[j] Thus he put him in charge of the whole land of Egypt.

44 Then Pharaoh said to Joseph, "I am Pharaoh, but without your word no one will lift hand or foot
in all Egypt."[k] 45 Pharaoh gave Joseph the name Zaphenath-Paneah and gave him Asenath daughter of
Potiphera, priest of On,*[d]* to be his wife.[l] And Joseph went throughout the land of Egypt.

46 Joseph was thirty years old[m] when he entered the service[n] of Pharaoh king of Egypt. And Joseph
went out from Pharaoh's presence and traveled throughout Egypt. 47 During the seven years of abundance the land produced plentifully. 48 Joseph collected all the food produced in those seven years of
abundance in Egypt and stored it in the cities. In each city he put the food grown in the fields surrounding it. 49 Joseph stored up huge quantities of grain, like the sand of the sea; it was so much that
he stopped keeping records because it was beyond measure.

50 Before the years of famine came, two sons were born to Joseph by Asenath daughter of Potiphera,
priest of On.[o] 51 Joseph named his firstborn[p] Manasseh*[e]* and said, "It is because God has made me forget
all my trouble and all my father's household." 52 The second son he named Ephraim*[f]*[q] and said, "It is
because God has made me fruitful[r] in the land of my suffering."

53 The seven years of abundance in Egypt came to an end, 54 and the seven years of famine began,[s]
just as Joseph had said. There was famine in all the other lands, but in the whole land of Egypt there was
food. 55 When all Egypt began to feel the famine,[t] the people cried to Pharaoh for food. Then Pharaoh
told all the Egyptians, "Go to Joseph and do what he tells you."[u]

56 When the famine had spread over the whole country, Joseph opened all the storehouses and sold
grain to the Egyptians, for the famine[v] was severe throughout Egypt. 57 And all the world came to Egypt
to buy grain from Joseph,[w] because the famine was severe everywhere.

a 38 Or *of the gods* *b* 43 Or *in the chariot of his second-in-command*; or *in his second chariot*
c 43 Or *Bow down* *d* 45 That is, Heliopolis; also in verse 50 *e* 51 *Manasseh* sounds like and may be derived from the Hebrew for *forget.* *f* 52 *Ephraim* sounds like the Hebrew for *twice fruitful.*

---

to their storing harvested grain "in reserve for the country" (v. 36) over a longer period of time.

41:38 Joseph deeply impresses Pharaoh. **in whom is the spirit of God.** See NIV text note. This does not necessarily refer to the Holy Spirit, although God's Spirit may well have enabled Joseph to interpret dreams. Pharaoh's remark may be of a more general nature, recognizing Joseph's God-orientated nature. Readers of Genesis, however, may have interpreted Pharaoh's remark as consistent with how God empowered particular individuals by his Spirit to undertake special duties on his behalf, especially those in positions of leadership (Judg 3:10; 6:34; 1 Sam 16:13).

41:41–57 *Joseph in Charge of Egypt.* This short passage covers seven years, from Joseph's appointment as Pharaoh's deputy to the start of the famine in Egypt.

41:42–43 Pharaoh dresses and honors Joseph as befits Joseph's new status as Pharaoh's "second-in-command" (v. 43).

41:45 Zaphenath-Paneah. The process of integrating Joseph, a Hebrew, into the mainstream of Egyptian life involves renaming him. His marriage to the daughter of a prominent priest would also have assisted Joseph's integration. The text does not indicate, however, that Joseph's marriage involved any religious compromise on his part. Toward the end of his life, he clearly identifies with the spiritual aspirations of Abraham and his descendants (50:24–25).

41:46 thirty years old. Joseph has been in Egypt for 12 or 13 years (see 37:2).

41:50–52 The birth of Joseph's sons coincides with the fruitful years.

41:51 Manasseh. Conveys the idea of "forget" (see NIV text note). Joseph wants to forget past events involving his affliction and the betrayal of his own brothers.

41:52 Ephraim. Means "twice fruitful" (see NIV text note); Joseph sees the birth of two sons as a sign of fruitfulness, an important motif in Genesis (e.g., 1:28; 17:6; 28:3; 35:11; 47:27).

41:53–57 Repeated references to Joseph underscore his role in providing food as famine grips Egypt and surrounding countries.

Joseph's Brothers Go to Egypt

42 When Jacob learned that there was grain in Egypt,[x] he said to his sons, "Why do you just keep
looking at each other?" 2 He continued, "I have heard that there is grain in Egypt. Go down
there and buy some for us, so that we may live and not die."[y]
3 Then ten of Joseph's brothers went down to buy grain from Egypt. 4 But Jacob did not send Benjamin, Joseph's brother, with the others, because he was afraid that harm might come to him.[z] 5 So Israel's
sons were among those who went to buy grain,[a] for there was famine in the land of Canaan also.[b]
6 Now Joseph was the governor of the land,[c] the person who sold grain to all its people. So when
Joseph's brothers arrived, they bowed down to him with their faces to the ground.[d] 7 As soon as Joseph
saw his brothers, he recognized them, but he pretended to be a stranger and spoke harshly to them.[e]
"Where do you come from?" he asked.
"From the land of Canaan," they replied, "to buy food."
8 Although Joseph recognized his brothers, they did not recognize him.[f] 9 Then he remembered
his dreams[g] about them and said to them, "You are spies! You have come to see where our land is
unprotected."
10 "No, my lord," they answered. "Your servants have come to buy food. 11 We are all the sons of one
man. Your servants are honest men, not spies."
12 "No!" he said to them. "You have come to see where our land is unprotected."
13 But they replied, "Your servants were twelve brothers, the sons of one man, who lives in the land
of Canaan. The youngest is now with our father, and one is no more."[h]
14 Joseph said to them, "It is just as I told you: You are spies! 15 And this is how you will be tested: As
surely as Pharaoh lives,[i] you will not leave this place unless your youngest brother comes here. 16 Send
one of your number to get your brother; the rest of you will be kept in prison, so that your words may be
tested to see if you are telling the truth.[j] If you are not, then as surely as Pharaoh lives, you are spies!"
17 And he put them all in custody[k] for three days.
18 On the third day, Joseph said to them, "Do this and you will live, for I fear God:[l] 19 If you are honest
men, let one of your brothers stay here in prison, while the rest of you go and take grain back for your
starving households. 20 But you must bring your youngest brother to me,[m] so that your words may be
verified and that you may not die." This they proceeded to do.
21 They said to one another, "Surely we are being punished because of our brother.[n] We saw how
distressed he was when he pleaded with us for his life, but we would not listen; that's why this distress[o]
has come on us."
22 Reuben replied, "Didn't I tell you not to sin against the boy?[p] But you wouldn't listen! Now we
must give an accounting[q] for his blood."[r] 23 They did not realize that Joseph could understand them,
since he was using an interpreter.
24 He turned away from them and began to weep, but then came back and spoke to them again. He
had Simeon taken from them and bound before their eyes.[s]

42:1 [x] Ac 7:12
42:2 [y] Ge 43:8
42:4 [z] ver 38
42:5 [a] Ge 41:57 [b] Ge 12:10; Ac 7:11
42:6 [c] Ge 41:41 [d] Ge 37:7-10
42:7 [e] ver 30
42:8 [f] Ge 37:2
42:9 [g] Ge 37:7
42:13 [h] Ge 37:30,33; 44:20
42:15 [i] 1Sa 17:55
42:16 [j] ver 11
42:17 [k] Ge 40:4
42:18 [l] Ge 20:11; Lev 25:43
42:20 [m] ver 15,34; Ge 43:5; 44:23
42:21 [n] Ge 37:26-28 [o] Hos 5:15
42:22 [p] Ge 37:21-22 [q] Ge 9:5 [r] 1Ki 2:32; 2Ch 24:22; Ps 9:12
42:24 [s] ver 13; Ge 43:14, 23; 45:14-15

42:1–38 *Joseph's Brothers Go to Egypt.* The impact of the famine causes Jacob to send his sons to Egypt. Having sold Joseph into slavery 20 years previously, the brothers have no reason to imagine that Joseph now oversees the government of Egypt. By accusing his brothers of spying, Joseph sets up a series of events that eventually result in dramatically reuniting Jacob's family, but not before Joseph discovers how much the guilt troubles his brothers.

42:1–5 The famine is widespread, causing food shortages in Canaan.

42:6 they bowed down to him. This recalls the dreams Joseph had 20 years previously as a teenager (37:5–11). His brothers unknowingly fulfill those dreams.

42:7–12 Joseph disguises his true identity from his brothers by using an interpreter (v. 23). Over 20 years have passed since the brothers were last together; at that time Joseph was only 17 years old. Now almost 40 years old, Joseph is dressed as a wealthy Egyptian administrator. Not surprisingly, his brothers do not recognize him. In order to discern something of their character, he charges them with being spies sent to determine the strength of Egyptian defenses.

42:13 one is no more. The brothers' short response ends ironically by alluding to Joseph.

42:17 custody for three days. Joseph places them under arrest. Maintaining his accusation that they are spies, Joseph demands that his brothers prove their honesty.

42:18–20 When Joseph addresses his brothers after three days, he reverses his prior decision to retain all the brothers in Egypt, apart from one. Joseph keeps one of them hostage, and he permits the other brothers to go to Canaan to bring Benjamin back to prove their honesty. By allowing most of the brothers to return to Canaan, they will be able to take grain back for their starving households. Joseph justifies this change of heart on the basis that he fears God (v. 18).

42:21–23 The brothers view their "misfortune" as God's punishment for treating Joseph callously. They are unaware that Joseph understands what they are saying, and he is moved to tears but hides them from his brothers.

42:25 [t] Ge 43:2 [u] Ge 44:1, 8 [v] Ro 12:17,20-21
42:27 [w] Ge 43:21-22
42:28 [x] Ge 43:23
42:30 [y] ver 7
42:31 [z] ver 11
42:33 [a] ver 19,20
42:34 [b] Ge 34:10
42:35 [c] Ge 43:12,15,18
42:36 [d] Ge 43:14
42:38 [e] Ge 37:33 [f] ver 4 [g] Ge 37:35 [h] Ge 44:29,34
43:1 [i] Ge 12:10; 41:56-57
43:3 [j] Ge 42:15; 44:23
43:5 [k] Ge 42:15; 2Sa 3:13
43:7 [l] ver 27 [m] Ge 42:13
43:8 [n] Ge 42:2; Ps 33:18-19

25 Joseph gave orders to fill their bags with grain,[t] to put each man's silver back in his sack,[u] and
to give them provisions for their journey.[v] After this was done for them, 26 they loaded their grain on
their donkeys and left.

27 At the place where they stopped for the night one of them opened his sack to get feed for his donkey, and he saw his silver in the mouth of his sack.[w] 28 "My silver has been returned," he said to his
brothers. "Here it is in my sack."

Their hearts sank and they turned to each other trembling and said, "What is this that God has
done to us?"[x]

29 When they came to their father Jacob in the land of Canaan, they told him all that had happened to them. They said, 30 "The man who is lord over the land spoke harshly to us[y] and treated us
as though we were spying on the land. 31 But we said to him, 'We are honest men; we are not spies.[z]
32 We were twelve brothers, sons of one father. One is no more, and the youngest is now with our father in Canaan.'

33 "Then the man who is lord over the land said to us, 'This is how I will know whether you are honest men: Leave one of your brothers here with me, and take food for your starving households and go.[a]
34 But bring your youngest brother to me so I will know that you are not spies but honest men. Then I
will give your brother back to you, and you can trade[a] in the land.[b]' "

35 As they were emptying their sacks, there in each man's sack was his pouch of silver! When they
and their father saw the money pouches, they were frightened.[c] 36 Their father Jacob said to them, "You
have deprived me of my children. Joseph is no more and Simeon is no more, and now you want to take
Benjamin.[d] Everything is against me!"

37 Then Reuben said to his father, "You may put both of my sons to death if I do not bring him back
to you. Entrust him to my care, and I will bring him back."

38 But Jacob said, "My son will not go down there with you; his brother is dead[e] and he is the only
one left. If harm comes to him[f] on the journey you are taking, you will bring my gray head down to
the grave[g] in sorrow.[h]"

The Second Journey to Egypt

43 Now the famine was still severe in the land.[i] 2 So when they had eaten all the grain they had
brought from Egypt, their father said to them, "Go back and buy us a little more food."

3 But Judah said to him, "The man warned us solemnly, 'You will not see my face again unless your
brother is with you.'[j] 4 If you will send our brother along with us, we will go down and buy food for you.
5 But if you will not send him, we will not go down, because the man said to us, 'You will not see my face
again unless your brother is with you.[k]' "

6 Israel asked, "Why did you bring this trouble on me by telling the man you had another brother?"

7 They replied, "The man questioned us closely about ourselves and our family. 'Is your father still
living?'[l] he asked us. 'Do you have another brother?'[m] We simply answered his questions. How were we
to know he would say, 'Bring your brother down here'?"

8 Then Judah said to Israel his father, "Send the boy along with me and we will go at once, so that
we and you and our children may live and not die.[n] 9 I myself will guarantee his safety; you can hold

[a] 34 Or *move about freely*

42:25–28 Unexpectedly discovering in a sack one of the payments they brought for the grain fills the men with apprehension. Trembling, they attribute this to divine providence, sensing that this may bring them additional trouble. Even after 20 years, their treatment of Joseph troubles their consciences.

42:35 Discovering the money pouches dismays Jacob and his sons. It appears that the brothers have not paid for the Egyptian grain.

42:36–37 The unfolding sequence of events appears ominous. Reuben's willingness to put to death his own sons fails to reassure Jacob. Benjamin is unlikely to be safe in the care of someone who would even consider killing his own sons. Unjustly, the punishment for Reuben's failure would fall more heavily on his sons than on Reuben himself.

42:38 Jacob emphatically rejects Reuben's offer. **grave.** See note on 37:35.

43:1–34 *The Second Journey to Egypt.* The pressing threat of starvation causes Jacob's sons to return to Egypt to buy more grain. Joseph unexpectedly invites them to eat at his house, causing the brothers to suspect that some terrible fate awaits them.

43:3–10 Unlike Reuben, who failed to persuade his father (42:37–38), Judah successfully convinces Jacob to entrust Benjamin into his care. In his speech, Judah emphasizes that he personally will bear the blame should anything happen to Benjamin. Judah displays qualities of leadership that are later reflected in his descendants, which include the royal lineage of David. See note on 49:8–12.

me personally responsible for him. If I do not bring him back to you and set him here before you, I
will bear the blame before you all my life.[o] 10As it is, if we had not delayed, we could have gone and
returned twice."

11Then their father Israel said to them, "If it must be, then do this: Put some of the best products
of the land in your bags and take them down to the man as a gift[p]—a little balm[q] and a little honey,
some spices[r] and myrrh, some pistachio nuts and almonds. 12Take double the amount of silver with
you, for you must return the silver that was put back into the mouths of your sacks.[s] Perhaps it was a
mistake. 13Take your brother also and go back to the man at once. 14And may God Almighty[a][t] grant
you mercy before the man so that he will let your other brother and Benjamin come back with you.[u]
As for me, if I am bereaved, I am bereaved."[v]

15So the men took the gifts and double the amount of silver, and Benjamin also. They hurried[w] down
to Egypt and presented themselves[x] to Joseph. 16When Joseph saw Benjamin with them, he said to the
steward of his house,[y] "Take these men to my house, slaughter an animal and prepare a meal;[z] they
are to eat with me at noon."

17The man did as Joseph told him and took the men to Joseph's house. 18Now the men were frightened[a] when they were taken to his house. They thought, "We were brought here because of the silver
that was put back into our sacks the first time. He wants to attack us and overpower us and seize us as
slaves and take our donkeys."

19So they went up to Joseph's steward and spoke to him at the entrance to the house. 20"We beg your
pardon, our lord," they said, "we came down here the first time to buy food.[b] 21But at the place where
we stopped for the night we opened our sacks and each of us found his silver—the exact weight—in
the mouth of his sack. So we have brought it back with us.[c] 22We have also brought additional silver
with us to buy food. We don't know who put our silver in our sacks."

23"It's all right," he said. "Don't be afraid. Your God, the God of your father, has given you treasure
in your sacks;[d] I received your silver." Then he brought Simeon out to them.[e]

24The steward took the men into Joseph's house,[f] gave them water to wash their feet[g] and provided
fodder for their donkeys. 25They prepared their gifts for Joseph's arrival at noon, because they had heard
that they were to eat there.

26When Joseph came home, they presented to him the gifts[h] they had brought into the house, and
they bowed down before him to the ground.[i] 27He asked them how they were, and then he said, "How is
your aged father you told me about? Is he still living?"[j]

28They replied, "Your servant our father is still alive and well." And they bowed down, prostrating
themselves before him.[k]

29As he looked about and saw his brother Benjamin, his own mother's son, he asked, "Is this your
youngest brother, the one you told me about?"[l] And he said, "God be gracious to you,[m] my son."
30Deeply moved[n] at the sight of his brother, Joseph hurried out and looked for a place to weep. He went
into his private room and wept[o] there.

31After he had washed his face, he came out and, controlling himself,[p] said, "Serve the food."

32They served him by himself, the brothers by themselves, and the Egyptians who ate with him by
themselves, because Egyptians could not eat with Hebrews,[q] for that is detestable to Egyptians.[r] 33The

43:9 [o] Ge 42:37; 44:32; Phm 1:18-19
43:11 [p] Ge 32:20; Pr 18:16 [q] Ge 37:25; Jer 8:22 [r] 1Ki 10:2
43:12 [s] Ge 42:25
43:14 [t] Ge 17:1; 28:3; 35:11 [u] Ge 42:24 [v] Est 4:16
43:15 [w] Ge 45:9,13 [x] Ge 47:2,7
43:16 [y] Ge 44:1,4,12 [z] ver 31; Lk 15:23
43:18 [a] Ge 42:35
43:20 [b] Ge 42:3
43:21 [c] ver 15; Ge 42:27,35
43:23 [d] Ge 42:28 [e] Ge 42:24
43:24 [f] ver 16 [g] Ge 18:4; 24:32
43:26 [h] Mt 2:11 [i] Ge 37:7,10
43:27 [j] ver 7
43:28 [k] Ge 37:7
43:29 [l] Ge 42:13 [m] Nu 6:25; Ps 67:1
43:30 [n] Jn 11:33,38 [o] Ge 42:24; 45:2,14,15; 46:29
43:31 [p] Ge 45:1
43:32 [q] Gal 2:12 [r] Ge 46:34; Ex 8:26

a 14 Hebrew *El-Shaddai*

43:11–14 Without knowing Joseph's true identity, Jacob sends gifts to honor him.
43:14 may God Almighty grant you mercy. Conscious of the potential danger awaiting his sons in Egypt, Jacob prays that God will be merciful to them. God subsequently answers his prayer when Joseph forgives his brothers.
43:15–18 The unanticipated invitation to Joseph's house alarms his brothers. Ironically, they fear that Joseph, the one they sold into slavery, will enslave them.
43:19–22 Describing how they discovered the silver in their sacks, the brothers are openly honest with Joseph's steward.
43:23 The steward's reply attributes the silver in the sacks to divine intervention, probably knowing that Joseph was responsible for this (42:25).
43:26 they bowed down. For a second time (see 42:6), Joseph's brothers fulfill his dreams (37:5–11) by prostrating themselves before him.
43:30 Seeing Benjamin after 20 years apart, Joseph struggles to control his feelings.
43:32–34 For cultural reasons Egyptians and Hebrews did not eat together. However, Joseph ensures that his younger brother Benjamin is especially privileged. Joseph may have done this to see how his brothers would react toward Benjamin. Would they be jealous of Benjamin as they had been jealous of him when their father had favored him (37:4)?

43:34 [s] Ge 37:3; 45:22
44:1 [t] Ge 42:25
44:4 [u] Ps 35:12
44:5 [v] Ge 30:27; Dt 18:10-14
44:8 [w] Ge 42:25; 43:21
44:9 [x] Ge 31:32
44:12 [y] ver 2
44:13 [z] Ge 37:29; Nu 14:6; 2Sa 1:11
44:14 [a] Ge 37:7,10
44:15 [b] ver 5; Ge 30:27
44:16 [c] ver 9; Ge 43:18 [d] ver 2

men had been seated before him in the order of their ages, from the firstborn to the youngest; and they looked at each other in astonishment. 34 When portions were served to them from Joseph's table, Benjamin's portion was five times as much as anyone else's.[s] So they feasted and drank freely with him.

A Silver Cup in a Sack

44 Now Joseph gave these instructions to the steward of his house: "Fill the men's sacks with as much food as they can carry, and put each man's silver in the mouth of his sack.[t] 2 Then put my cup, the silver one, in the mouth of the youngest one's sack, along with the silver for his grain." And he did as Joseph said.

3 As morning dawned, the men were sent on their way with their donkeys. 4 They had not gone far from the city when Joseph said to his steward, "Go after those men at once, and when you catch up with them, say to them, 'Why have you repaid good with evil?[u] 5 Isn't this the cup my master drinks from and also uses for divination?[v] This is a wicked thing you have done.' "

6 When he caught up with them, he repeated these words to them. 7 But they said to him, "Why does my lord say such things? Far be it from your servants to do anything like that! 8 We even brought back to you from the land of Canaan the silver we found inside the mouths of our sacks.[w] So why would we steal silver or gold from your master's house? 9 If any of your servants is found to have it, he will die;[x] and the rest of us will become my lord's slaves."

10 "Very well, then," he said, "let it be as you say. Whoever is found to have it will become my slave; the rest of you will be free from blame."

11 Each of them quickly lowered his sack to the ground and opened it. 12 Then the steward proceeded to search, beginning with the oldest and ending with the youngest. And the cup was found in Benjamin's sack.[y] 13 At this, they tore their clothes.[z] Then they all loaded their donkeys and returned to the city.

14 Joseph was still in the house when Judah and his brothers came in, and they threw themselves to the ground before him.[a] 15 Joseph said to them, "What is this you have done? Don't you know that a man like me can find things out by divination?[b]"

16 "What can we say to my lord?" Judah replied. "What can we say? How can we prove our innocence? God has uncovered your servants' guilt. We are now my lord's slaves[c] — we ourselves and the one who was found to have the cup.[d]"

17 But Joseph said, "Far be it from me to do such a thing! Only the man who was found to have the cup will become my slave. The rest of you, go back to your father in peace."

44:1–34 *A Silver Cup in a Sack.* Joseph instigates a plan to determine how his older brothers view their youngest brother, Benjamin. Will they treat him as callously as they had Joseph? How will they react when Benjamin is accused of misappropriating Joseph's silver cup? Remarkably, Judah not only pleads at length for Benjamin's release but willingly offers to become Joseph's slave so that Benjamin may return home safely to Canaan. Judah's intervention contrasts sharply with his earlier willingness to sell Joseph into slavery (37:26–27).

44:1–2 steward. This unnamed individual held a position of considerable importance within Joseph's house and was worthy of respect (see vv. 7–10). Joseph issues similar instructions to those that he gave when his brothers previously left Egypt (42:25). In addition, he commands that his own silver cup be placed in Benjamin's sack.

44:4–5 As part of the ruse by which Joseph intends to discern the attitude of his brothers, he sends his steward after them.

44:5 for divination. Possibly with a sense of irony, Joseph describes his cup as one used for gaining knowledge by supernatural means. It seems unlikely that Joseph practiced divination, something God later prohibited (Deut 18:10; see 2 Kgs 17:17; Jer 14:14; see note on 30:27). However, he obviously wished to make his brothers believe that he could discern things supernaturally (v. 15). Ironically, the cup becomes the means by which he gains an insight into the present inner nature of his brothers.

44:9–10 Joseph's steward imposes a less demanding punishment than the brothers suggest. He, unlike them, is fully aware of the ruse. Their proposal that the guilty party be put to death is their way of claiming that they, being innocent, have nothing to fear from the charge made against them.

44:13 tore their clothes. A visible demonstration of their grief as they contemplate Benjamin's fate.

44:14 Judah and his brothers. The narrator anticipates the special role that Judah will play in mediating Benjamin's release. **they threw themselves to the ground before him.** Joseph's brothers fulfill his dreams a third time (see note on 43:26).

44:15 find things out by divination. Joseph's steward described the silver cup as what Joseph "uses for divination" (v. 5). However, having orchestrated all that occurred, Joseph did not need to rely on divination to discover what happened. This reference to divination is another part of the ruse. By emphasizing his own ability to know things that are hidden, Joseph puts his brothers under pressure to speak the truth.

44:16 God has uncovered your servants' guilt. Judah's response is striking, probably alluding to how they earlier treated Joseph. What they did in the past places them under divine judgment. Because they sold their brother into slavery, their punishment is to be enslaved also. Remarkably, in light of Joseph's earlier dreams (37:5–11), Judah declares that he and his brothers are "now my lord's slaves."

44:17 In spite of how his brothers treated him, Joseph does not seek vengeance. Rather, he will let his older brothers return to Canaan, keeping only Benjamin as a slave. No doubt Joseph is especially keen to see how Judah and his brother will respond to this proposal. Will they place their own well-being above Benjamin's?

18Then Judah went up to him and said: "Pardon your servant, my lord, let me speak a word to my lord. Do not be angry[e] with your servant, though you are equal to Pharaoh himself. 19My lord asked his servants, 'Do you have a father or a brother?'[f] 20And we answered, 'We have an aged father, and there is a young son born to him in his old age.[g] His brother is dead,[h] and he is the only one of his mother's sons left, and his father loves him.'[i]

21"Then you said to your servants, 'Bring him down to me so I can see him for myself.'[j] 22And we said to my lord, 'The boy cannot leave his father; if he leaves him, his father will die.'[k] 23But you told your servants, 'Unless your youngest brother comes down with you, you will not see my face again.'[l] 24When we went back to your servant my father, we told him what my lord had said.

25"Then our father said, 'Go back and buy a little more food.'[m] 26But we said, 'We cannot go down. Only if our youngest brother is with us will we go. We cannot see the man's face unless our youngest brother is with us.'

27"Your servant my father said to us, 'You know that my wife bore me two sons.[n] 28One of them went away from me, and I said, "He has surely been torn to pieces."[o] And I have not seen him since. 29If you take this one from me too and harm comes to him, you will bring my gray head down to the grave in misery.'[p]

30"So now, if the boy is not with us when I go back to your servant my father, and if my father, whose life is closely bound up with the boy's life,[q] 31sees that the boy isn't there, he will die. Your servants will bring the gray head of our father down to the grave in sorrow. 32Your servant guaranteed the boy's safety to my father. I said, 'If I do not bring him back to you, I will bear the blame before you, my father, all my life!'[r]

33"Now then, please let your servant remain here as my lord's slave[s] in place of the boy,[t] and let the boy return with his brothers. 34How can I go back to my father if the boy is not with me? No! Do not let me see the misery that would come on my father."[u]

Joseph Makes Himself Known

45 Then Joseph could no longer control himself[v] before all his attendants, and he cried out, "Have everyone leave my presence!" So there was no one with Joseph when he made himself known to his brothers. 2And he wept[w] so loudly that the Egyptians heard him, and Pharaoh's household heard about it.[x]

3Joseph said to his brothers, "I am Joseph! Is my father still living?"[y] But his brothers were not able to answer him,[z] because they were terrified at his presence.

4Then Joseph said to his brothers, "Come close to me." When they had done so, he said, "I am your brother Joseph, the one you sold into Egypt![a] 5And now, do not be distressed[b] and do not be angry with yourselves for selling me here,[c] because it was to save lives that God sent me ahead of you.[d] 6For two years now there has been famine in the land, and for the next five years there will be no plowing and reaping. 7But God sent me ahead of you to preserve for you a remnant[e] on earth and to save your lives by a great deliverance.[a][f]

[a] 7 Or *save you as a great band of survivors*

44:18 [e] Ge 18:30; Ex 32:22
44:19 [f] Ge 43:7
44:20 [g] Ge 37:3 [h] Ge 37:33 [i] Ge 42:13
44:21 [j] Ge 42:15
44:22 [k] Ge 37:35
44:23 [l] Ge 43:5
44:25 [m] Ge 43:2
44:27 [n] Ge 46:19
44:28 [o] Ge 37:33
44:29 [p] Ge 42:38
44:30 [q] 1Sa 18:1
44:32 [r] Ge 43:9
44:33 [s] Ge 43:18 [t] Jn 15:13
44:34 [u] Est 8:6
45:1 [v] Ge 43:31
45:2 [w] Ge 29:11 [x] ver 16; Ge 46:29
45:3 [y] Ac 7:13 [z] ver 15
45:4 [a] Ge 37:28
45:5 [b] Ge 42:21 [c] Ge 42:22 [d] ver 7-8; Ge 50:20; Ps 105:17
45:7 [e] 2Ki 19:4,30,31; Isa 10:20,21; Mic 4:7; Zep 2:7 [f] Ex 15:2; Est 4:14; Isa 25:9

44:18–34 Judah's speech to Joseph is lengthy; most human speeches in Genesis are short. Humbly acknowledging Joseph's special status as "equal to Pharaoh" (v. 18), Judah pleads passionately for the release of Benjamin, outlining in some detail how the loss of Benjamin would severely affect his father. Having guaranteed the safe return of Benjamin, Judah offers himself as a slave in his place. More than anything else, Judah wants to prevent his father from suffering further grief. Judah's impassioned appeal to Joseph sharply contrasts with his previous proposal to sell Joseph into slavery (37:26–27). Now Judah himself is prepared to suffer loss of freedom and great hardship in order that Benjamin not be enslaved in Egypt.

45:1–28 *Joseph Makes Himself Known.* Although Joseph has successfully concealed his identity from his brothers, Judah's speech changes everything. Joseph can no longer hold back his feelings. With tears, he discloses his true identity to his brothers. In doing so, he refrains from condemning them, pointing rather to the providential nature of all that has occurred. In spite of all that he has suffered, Joseph can see God at work in everything that has happened. Building on this, he urges his brothers to return to Canaan in order that Jacob's whole family may migrate to Egypt to avoid the five years of famine that remain.

45:1–3 While Joseph dismisses his Egyptian attendants, they cannot but overhear their distraught and emotional master as he reveals his identity to his brothers. With good reason, Joseph's brothers are both speechless and fearful.

45:4–8 Joseph does his utmost to calm his fearful brothers. While he could have with justification pointed to their cruelty and deceit, he concentrates rather on how God transformed his tragic personal circumstances into an opportunity to help others. Twice in these verses Joseph refers to the concept of saving the lives of others. While this has a physical dimension, Joseph's actions foreshadow the greater salvation that will come through Jesus Christ, the one in whom is fulfilled everything associated with the divine promises linked to a royal descendant of Abraham.

45:8 [g] Jdg 17:10 [h] Ge 41:41
45:9 [i] Ge 43:10
45:10 [j] Ge 46:28,34; 47:1
45:11 [k] Ge 47:12
45:13 [l] Ac 7:14
45:15 [m] Lk 15:20 [n] ver 3
45:16 [o] Ac 7:13
45:18 [p] Ge 27:28; 46:34; 47:6,11,27; Nu 18:12, 29 [q] Ps 37:19
45:19 [r] Ge 46:5
45:21 [s] Ge 42:25
45:22 [t] Ge 37:3; 43:34
45:24 [u] Ge 42:21-22
45:26 [v] Ge 44:28
45:27 [w] ver 19

8"So then, it was not you who sent me here, but God. He made me father[g] to Pharaoh, lord of his entire household and ruler of all Egypt.[h] 9Now hurry back to my father and say to him, 'This is what your son Joseph says: God has made me lord of all Egypt. Come down to me; don't delay.[i] 10You shall live in the region of Goshen[j] and be near me—you, your children and grandchildren, your flocks and herds, and all you have. 11I will provide for you there,[k] because five years of famine are still to come. Otherwise you and your household and all who belong to you will become destitute.'

12"You can see for yourselves, and so can my brother Benjamin, that it is really I who am speaking to you. 13Tell my father about all the honor accorded me in Egypt and about everything you have seen. And bring my father down here quickly.[l]"

REGION OF GOSHEN

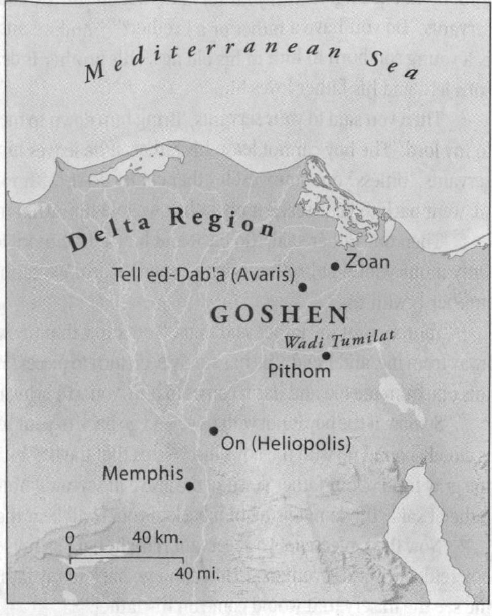

14Then he threw his arms around his brother Benjamin and wept, and Benjamin embraced him, weeping. 15And he kissed[m] all his brothers and wept over them. Afterward his brothers talked with him.[n]

16When the news reached Pharaoh's palace that Joseph's brothers had come,[o] Pharaoh and all his officials were pleased. 17Pharaoh said to Joseph, "Tell your brothers, 'Do this: Load your animals and return to the land of Canaan, 18and bring your father and your families back to me. I will give you the best of the land of Egypt[p] and you can enjoy the fat of the land.'[q]

19"You are also directed to tell them, 'Do this: Take some carts[r] from Egypt for your children and your wives, and get your father and come. 20Never mind about your belongings, because the best of all Egypt will be yours.'"

21So the sons of Israel did this. Joseph gave them carts, as Pharaoh had commanded, and he also gave them provisions for their journey.[s] 22To each of them he gave new clothing, but to Benjamin he gave three hundred shekels[a] of silver and five sets of clothes.[t] 23And this is what he sent to his father: ten donkeys loaded with the best things of Egypt, and ten female donkeys loaded with grain and bread and other provisions for his journey. 24Then he sent his brothers away, and as they were leaving he said to them, "Don't quarrel on the way!"[u]

25So they went up out of Egypt and came to their father Jacob in the land of Canaan. 26They told him, "Joseph is still alive! In fact, he is ruler of all Egypt." Jacob was stunned; he did not believe them.[v] 27But when they told him everything Joseph had said to them, and when he saw the carts[w] Joseph had

[a] *22* That is, about 7 1/2 pounds or about 3.5 kilograms

45:8 father to Pharaoh. Joseph's description of himself recalls how God previously covenanted with Abraham that he would be the "father of many nations" (17:4–5). Since Jacob gave Joseph the status of "firstborn" in place of Reuben (see 1 Chr 5:1–2), Joseph is heir to the special covenant God established with Abraham, Isaac, and Jacob.

45:9–13 Joseph gives instructions for the rest of his family to move to Egypt so that they may avoid the hardship of the famine that will last for five more years.

45:10 Goshen. Although its exact location is uncertain, it possibly lay in the eastern delta region of the Nile River, close to the city of Rowaty, which later became known as Avaris and then Pi-Rameses (see 47:11).

45:16–20 Pharaoh's reaction to the news that Joseph's brothers had come reflects Joseph's good standing with him.

45:21–23 Having arrived in Egypt as a slave, Joseph has become exceptionally wealthy.

45:22 three hundred shekels of silver and five sets of clothes. Whereas he was sold as a slave for 20 shekels (37:28), Joseph generously gives his younger brother Benjamin gifts of considerable value.

45:25–28 Jacob responds with incredulity, since his sons had deceived him 20 years earlier by telling him that Joseph was dead (37:31–35).

sent to carry him back, the spirit of their father Jacob revived. 28 And Israel said, "I'm convinced! My
son Joseph is still alive. I will go and see him before I die."

Jacob Goes to Egypt

46 So Israel set out with all that was his, and when he reached Beersheba,[x] he offered sacrifices
to the God of his father Isaac.[y]
2 And God spoke to Israel in a vision at night[z] and said, "Jacob! Jacob!"
"Here I am,"[a] he replied.
3 "I am God, the God of your father,"[b] he said. "Do not be afraid to go down to Egypt, for I will make
you into a great nation[c] there.[d] 4 I will go down to Egypt with you, and I will surely bring you back
again.[e] And Joseph's own hand will close your eyes."[f]
5 Then Jacob left Beersheba, and Israel's sons took their father Jacob and their children and their wives
in the carts[g] that Pharaoh had sent to transport him. 6 So Jacob and all his offspring went to Egypt,[h] taking with them their livestock and the possessions they had acquired in Canaan. 7 Jacob brought with him
to Egypt his sons and grandsons and his daughters and granddaughters—all his offspring.[i]

8 These are the names of the sons of Israel[j] (Jacob and his descendants) who went to Egypt:

Reuben the firstborn of Jacob.
9 The sons of Reuben:[k]
Hanok, Pallu, Hezron and Karmi.
10 The sons of Simeon:[l]
Jemuel,[m] Jamin, Ohad, Jakin, Zohar and Shaul the son of a Canaanite woman.
11 The sons of Levi:[n]
Gershon, Kohath and Merari.
12 The sons of Judah:[o]
Er, Onan, Shelah, Perez and Zerah (but Er and Onan had died in the land of Canaan).
The sons of Perez:[p]
Hezron and Hamul.
13 The sons of Issachar:[q]
Tola, Puah,[a][r] Jashub[b] and Shimron.
14 The sons of Zebulun:[s]
Sered, Elon and Jahleel.

a 13 Samaritan Pentateuch and Syriac (see also 1 Chron. 7:1); Masoretic Text *Puvah* *b 13* Samaritan Pentateuch and some Septuagint manuscripts (see also Num. 26:24 and 1 Chron. 7:1); Masoretic Text *Iob*

46:1 [x] Ge 21:14; 28:10 [y] Ge 26:24; 28:13; 31:42
46:2 [z] Ge 15:1; Job 33:14-15 [a] Ge 22:1; 31:11
46:3 [b] Ge 28:13 [c] Ge 12:2; Dt 26:5 [d] Ex 1:7
46:4 [e] Ge 28:15; 48:21; Ex 3:8 [f] Ge 50:1,24
46:5 [g] Ge 45:19
46:6 [h] Dt 26:5; Jos 24:4; Ps 105:23; Isa 52:4; Ac 7:15
46:7 [i] Ge 45:10
46:8 [j] Ex 1:1; Nu 26:4
46:9 [k] 1Ch 5:3
46:10 [l] Ge 29:33; Nu 26:14 [m] Ex 6:15
46:11 [n] Ge 29:34; Nu 3:17
46:12 [o] Ge 29:35 [p] 1Ch 2:5; Mt 1:3
46:13 [q] Ge 30:18 [r] 1Ch 7:1
46:14 [s] Ge 30:20

46:1—47:12 *Jacob Goes to Egypt.* The account of Jacob's journey to Egypt has four parts: (1) At Beersheba God permits Jacob to relocate to Egypt (vv. 1–7). (2) A list of the names of those who went to Egypt (vv. 8–27). (3) Jacob encounters Joseph (vv. 28–30). (4) Joseph prepares the way for his father to meet Pharaoh, conscious of the Egyptians' strong antipathy toward shepherds (46:31—47:12).

46:1 Possibly leaving from Hebron (see 37:14), Jacob travels southward. **Beersheba.** Where previously both Abraham and Isaac settled for some time (21:22–34; 26:23–33).

46:2–4 Through a nighttime vision, God authorizes Jacob to go to Egypt. This contrasts with a previous occasion when God prohibited Jacob's father, Isaac, from going to Egypt during a famine (26:1–5). Remarkably, it will be in Egypt that God transforms Abraham's descendants into a great nation, fulfilling his promise to Abraham (12:2). Later, in the book of Exodus, the remarkable growth of the Israelites eventually leads to their expulsion from Egypt and return to the land of Canaan. Through this entire process, God promises to be with Jacob.

46:4 I will surely bring you back again. The "you" is singular and refers to Jacob. While Jacob subsequently dies in Egypt (49:33), Joseph arranges to bury Jacob in Canaan alongside Abraham and Isaac (50:4–13). Burying the patriarchs at Hebron reflects God's commitment to give the land of Canaan to their descendants. Although the fulfillment of God's promises lies well beyond their lifetime, the patriarchs anticipated an ongoing relationship with God even after death (Heb 11:12–16,39). In the future they would share in the results of God's redemptive work in the world.

46:5–7 Jacob's entire family, with all their possessions, relocates to Egypt, a journey of about 150 miles (240 kilometers). They leave no living family member in Canaan.

46:8–27 A list of Jacob's family interrupts the report of Jacob's journey. It is arranged on the basis of his two wives and their two maidservants: Leah's children (vv. 8–15), Zilpah's children (vv. 16–18), Rachel's children (vv. 19–22), and Bilhah's children (vv. 23–25). A concluding summary follows the lists of names (vv. 26–27). This register includes all of Jacob's offspring, not just those who accompanied him down to Egypt (e.g., Er and Onan [v. 12] died in Canaan, and Joseph and his sons [v. 20] were already in Egypt).

46:8–15 Those associated with Leah comprise six sons, one daughter, 25 grandchildren, and two great-grandsons, for a total of 34 (but see v. 15 and note).

46:8 Reuben the firstborn of Jacob. Placed at the start of the list, reflecting that he was the first son born to Jacob (29:32). However, due to Reuben's inappropriate relationship with Bilhah (35:22), Jacob gave the privileged status of firstborn to Joseph (1 Chr 5:1–2).

46:16 [t] Ge 30:11 [u] Nu 26:15
46:17 [v] Ge 30:13; 1Ch 7:30-31
46:18 [w] Ge 30:10 [x] Ge 29:24
46:19 [y] Ge 44:27
46:20 [z] Ge 41:51 [a] Ge 41:52
46:21 [b] Nu 26:38-41; 1Ch 7:6-12; 8:1
46:25 [c] Ge 30:8 [d] Ge 29:29
46:26 [e] ver 5-7; Ex 1:5; Dt 10:22
46:27 [f] Ac 7:14
46:28 [g] Ge 45:10
46:29 [h] Ge 45:14-15; Lk 15:20

15 These were the sons Leah bore to Jacob in Paddan Aram,[a] besides his daughter Dinah. These sons
and daughters of his were thirty-three in all.

16 The sons of Gad:[t]
Zephon,[b][u] Haggi, Shuni, Ezbon, Eri, Arodi and Areli.
17 The sons of Asher:[v]
Imnah, Ishvah, Ishvi and Beriah.
Their sister was Serah.
The sons of Beriah:
Heber and Malkiel.
18 These were the children born to Jacob by Zilpah,[w] whom Laban had given to his daughter Leah[x] —
sixteen in all.

19 The sons of Jacob's wife Rachel:
Joseph and Benjamin.[y] 20 In Egypt, Manasseh[z] and Ephraim[a] were born to Joseph by Asenath
daughter of Potiphera, priest of On.[c]
21 The sons of Benjamin:[b]
Bela, Beker, Ashbel, Gera, Naaman, Ehi, Rosh, Muppim, Huppim and Ard.
22 These were the sons of Rachel who were born to Jacob — fourteen in all.

23 The son of Dan:
Hushim.
24 The sons of Naphtali:
Jahziel, Guni, Jezer and Shillem.
25 These were the sons born to Jacob by Bilhah,[c] whom Laban had given to his daughter Rachel[d] —
seven in all.

26 All those who went to Egypt with Jacob — those who were his direct descendants, not counting his
sons' wives — numbered sixty-six persons.[e] 27 With the two sons[d] who had been born to Joseph in Egypt,
the members of Jacob's family, which went to Egypt, were seventy[e] in all.[f]

28 Now Jacob sent Judah ahead of him to Joseph to get directions to Goshen.[g] When they arrived in the
region of Goshen, 29 Joseph had his chariot made ready and went to Goshen to meet his father Israel. As
soon as Joseph appeared before him, he threw his arms around his father[f] and wept for a long time.[h]

[a] *15* That is, Northwest Mesopotamia [b] *16* Samaritan Pentateuch and Septuagint (see also Num. 26:15); Masoretic Text *Ziphion* [c] *20* That is, Heliopolis [d] *27* Hebrew; Septuagint *the nine children* [e] *27* Hebrew (see also Exodus 1:5 and note); Septuagint (see also Acts 7:14) *seventy-five* [f] *29* Hebrew *around him*

46:15 thirty-three. The list names 34 people, not 33 (see note on vv. 8–15). This somewhat obvious discrepancy is not easy to explain. Ohad (v. 10) is missing from similar lists in Num 26:12–13; 1 Chr 4:24. Consequently, some scholars suggest that his name should be deleted here. Another possible explanation is that Dinah (v. 15), as the only woman listed, should be excluded from the total. Yet, v. 15 specifically refers to "sons and daughters." To complicate the picture further, Er and Onan (v. 12) died in Canaan (38:2–10) and should not be counted among those who migrate to Egypt. Additionally, Perez's two sons, Hezron and Hamul (v. 12), were probably born in Egypt.
46:18 Zilpah. Leah's maidservant (29:24); she became a surrogate mother when Leah appeared unable to have more children (30:9–12; 35:26).
46:19 Joseph. He is included in the list even though he and his family were already in Egypt (see note on vv. 8–27).
46:22 Rachel. Although she was Jacob's favorite wife (29:18–20,30–31), she was initially unable to have children and was jealous of her sister Leah (30:1).
46:25 Bilhah. Rachel's maidservant (29:29); she became a surrogate mother when Rachel was unable to have children (30:3–8).
46:26–27 This summary concludes the list of names in vv. 8–25.
46:26 sixty-six. This total, which excludes Jacob's sons' wives, who were not "his direct descendants," does not tally exactly with the totals in vv. 8–25 (i.e., 33+16+14+7=70). Nothing obvious explains how this was calculated to give the total 66. The second total of "seventy" (v. 27) is probably based on 66 plus Jacob, Joseph, and Joseph's two sons, Manasseh and Ephraim. To add to the complexity of these figures, the earliest Greek translation of Genesis records the number of Joseph's sons as nine (see first NIV text note on v. 27), giving a total of 75 (see second NIV text note on v. 27; see also Acts 7:14) rather than 70. In the process of copying manuscripts, mistakes occasionally can arise with numbers. Something like this may have occurred at an early stage in the transmission of the text of Genesis.
46:28 Joseph had already advised Jacob that the region of Goshen would be the most suitable location for Jacob's family (45:10), so Jacob entrusts Judah with getting directions from Joseph. In the later part of his life, Judah stands apart from his brothers as a trustworthy son. The exceptional blessing that Jacob later gives Judah reflects his faith in Judah (49:8–12).

30 Israel said to Joseph, "Now I am ready to die, since I have seen for myself that you are still alive."

31 Then Joseph said to his brothers and to his father's household, "I will go up and speak to Pharaoh and will say to him, 'My brothers and my father's household, who were living in the land of Canaan, have come to me.[i] 32 The men are shepherds; they tend livestock, and they have brought along their flocks and herds and everything they own.' 33 When Pharaoh calls you in and asks, 'What is your occupation?'[j] 34 you should answer, 'Your servants have tended livestock from our boyhood on, just as our fathers did.' Then you will be allowed to settle in the region of Goshen,[k] for all shepherds are detestable to the Egyptians.[l]"

47 Joseph went and told Pharaoh, "My father and brothers, with their flocks and herds and everything they own, have come from the land of Canaan and are now in Goshen."[m] 2 He chose five of his brothers and presented them before Pharaoh.

3 Pharaoh asked the brothers, "What is your occupation?"[n]

"Your servants are shepherds," they replied to Pharaoh, "just as our fathers were." 4 They also said to him, "We have come to live here for a while,[o] because the famine is severe in Canaan[p] and your servants' flocks have no pasture. So now, please let your servants settle in Goshen."[q]

5 Pharaoh said to Joseph, "Your father and your brothers have come to you, 6 and the land of Egypt is before you; settle your father and your brothers in the best part of the land.[r] Let them live in Goshen. And if you know of any among them with special ability,[s] put them in charge of my own livestock."

7 Then Joseph brought his father Jacob in and presented him before Pharaoh. After Jacob blessed[a] Pharaoh,[t] 8 Pharaoh asked him, "How old are you?"

9 And Jacob said to Pharaoh, "The years of my pilgrimage are a hundred and thirty.[u] My years have been few and difficult,[v] and they do not equal the years of the pilgrimage of my fathers.[w]" 10 Then Jacob blessed[b] Pharaoh[x] and went out from his presence.

11 So Joseph settled his father and his brothers in Egypt and gave them property in the best part of the land, the district of Rameses,[y] as Pharaoh directed. 12 Joseph also provided his father and his brothers and all his father's household with food, according to the number of their children.[z]

Joseph and the Famine

13 There was no food, however, in the whole region because the famine was severe; both Egypt and Canaan wasted away because of the famine.[a] 14 Joseph collected all the money that was to be found in

[a] 7 Or *greeted* [b] 10 Or *said farewell to*

46:31 [i] Ge 47:1
46:33 [j] Ge 47:3
46:34 [k] Ge 45:10 [l] Ge 43:32; Ex 8:26
47:1 [m] Ge 46:31
47:3 [n] Ge 46:33
47:4 [o] Ge 15:13; Dt 26:5 [p] Ge 43:1 [q] Ge 46:34
47:6 [r] Ge 45:18 [s] Ex 18:21,25
47:7 [t] ver 10; 2Sa 14:22
47:9 [u] Ge 25:7 [v] Heb 11:9,13 [w] Ge 35:28
47:10 [x] ver 7
47:11 [y] Ex 1:11; 12:37
47:12 [z] Ge 45:11
47:13 [a] Ge 41:30; Ac 7:11

46:32–34 In spite of knowing how the Egyptians detest shepherds (see note on v. 34), Joseph instructs his brothers to declare before Pharaoh that their occupation is tending flocks and herds. This will ensure that they will be located in the region of Goshen. By retaining their traditional way of life, the Israelites will remain apart from mainstream Egyptian society.

46:34 all shepherds are detestable to the Egyptians. The precise reason for this dislike is not clear. Differing religious practices may have motivated it (see Exod 8:26). The refusal of Egyptians to share a meal with Hebrews possibly reflects it (43:32).

47:1–6 Through tactful diplomacy Joseph gains permission from Pharaoh for his family to settle in Goshen. Pharaoh's willingness to entrust his own livestock to Joseph's brothers shows Joseph's good standing in the Egyptian court.

47:7–10 This brief scene begins and ends with Jacob blessing Pharaoh. Although these blessings may be merely part of the formalities of meeting and parting, they take on a greater significance when set against the background of the blessing Isaac bestowed on Jacob (27:29), which in turn echoes God's promise to Abraham in 12:3. The developing Genesis narrative closely ties God's blessing to the unique family line that descends from Abraham. Jacob blesses Pharaoh for showing respect to Abraham's descendants.

47:9 My years have been few and difficult. According to the chronological information in Genesis, Jacob is now 130 years old. While this is exceptional by modern standards, Abraham and Isaac lived to be 175 and 180 years old, respectively. They viewed such lengthy years as a sign of God's blessing. Jacob, however, alludes to the difficulties that have marked his life (e.g., his forced exile to Paddan Aram; his loss of Joseph as a much loved son). **the pilgrimage of my fathers.** Jacob refers to the seminomadic lifestyle of Abraham and Isaac, which meant that they had no permanent residence. The patriarchs deliberately adopted this lifestyle because they anticipated a city God designed and built (Heb 11:9–16). Jacob identifies with his immediate forefathers by speaking of his own pilgrimage.

47:11 district of Rameses. Probably a prime location within the larger region of Goshen (v. 6). While the name Rameses may have been in use in Joseph's time, it is more often associated with the famous Egyptian king Rameses II, who lived in the thirteenth century BC. Rameses was possibly the name of this region in the time of the author.

47:13–31 *Joseph and the Famine.* This section emphasizes Joseph's role in keeping the Egyptians alive during the years of famine. After exhausting all other options to pay for their food, the Egyptians sell their land to Pharaoh. Subsequently, Pharaoh receives from the people one-fifth of their produce. A similar pattern exists when the Israelites settle in

47:14 [b]Ge 41:56
47:15 [c]ver 19; Ex 16:3
47:17 [d]Ex 14:9
47:22 [e]Dt 14:28-29; Ezr 7:24
47:24 [f]Ge 41:34
47:25 [g]Ge 32:5
47:26 [h]ver 22
47:27 [i]Ge 17:6; 46:3; Ex 1:7
47:28 [j]Ps 105:23
47:29 [k]Dt 31:14 [l]Ge 24:2 [m]Ge 24:49
47:30 [n]Ge 49:29-32; 50:5,13; Ac 7:15-16
47:31 [o]Ge 21:23 [p]Ge 24:3 [q]Heb 11:21 *fn*; 1Ki 1:47

Egypt and Canaan in payment for the grain they were buying, and he brought it to Pharaoh's palace.[b]
15 When the money of the people of Egypt and Canaan was gone, all Egypt came to Joseph and said,
"Give us food. Why should we die before your eyes?[c] Our money is all gone."
16 "Then bring your livestock," said Joseph. "I will sell you food in exchange for your livestock, since
your money is gone." 17 So they brought their livestock to Joseph, and he gave them food in exchange
for their horses,[d] their sheep and goats, their cattle and donkeys. And he brought them through that
year with food in exchange for all their livestock.
18 When that year was over, they came to him the following year and said, "We cannot hide from
our lord the fact that since our money is gone and our livestock belongs to you, there is nothing
left for our lord except our bodies and our land. 19 Why should we perish before your eyes — we
and our land as well? Buy us and our land in exchange for food, and we with our land will be
in bondage to Pharaoh. Give us seed so that we may live and not die, and that the land may not
become desolate."
20 So Joseph bought all the land in Egypt for Pharaoh. The Egyptians, one and all, sold their fields,
because the famine was too severe for them. The land became Pharaoh's, 21 and Joseph reduced the people to servitude,[a] from one end of Egypt to the other. 22 However, he did not buy the land of the priests,
because they received a regular allotment from Pharaoh and had food enough from the allotment[e]
Pharaoh gave them. That is why they did not sell their land.
23 Joseph said to the people, "Now that I have bought you and your land today for Pharaoh, here is
seed for you so you can plant the ground. 24 But when the crop comes in, give a fifth[f] of it to Pharaoh.
The other four-fifths you may keep as seed for the fields and as food for yourselves and your households
and your children."
25 "You have saved our lives," they said. "May we find favor in the eyes of our lord;[g] we will be in
bondage to Pharaoh."
26 So Joseph established it as a law concerning land in Egypt — still in force today — that a
fifth of the produce belongs to Pharaoh. It was only the land of the priests that did not become
Pharaoh's.[h]
27 Now the Israelites settled in Egypt in the region of Goshen. They acquired property there and were
fruitful and increased greatly in number.[i]
28 Jacob lived in Egypt[j] seventeen years, and the years of his life were a hundred and forty-seven.
29 When the time drew near for Israel to die,[k] he called for his son Joseph and said to him, "If I have
found favor in your eyes, put your hand under my thigh[l] and promise that you will show me kindness
and faithfulness.[m] Do not bury me in Egypt, 30 but when I rest with my fathers, carry me out of Egypt
and bury me where they are buried."[n]
"I will do as you say," he said.
31 "Swear to me,"[o] he said. Then Joseph swore to him,[p] and Israel worshiped as he leaned on the
top of his staff.[b][q]

a 21 Samaritan Pentateuch and Septuagint (see also Vulgate); Masoretic Text *and he moved the people into the cities* *b 31* Or *Israel bowed down at the head of his bed*

the land of Canaan. There, however, they must give God only one-tenth of their harvest to recognize that he owns the land.

47:15–17 Joseph plays a central role in keeping the population of Egypt alive. His administrative skills are God-given (41:38).

47:18–26 Although the Egyptians are prepared to sell themselves into slavery in order to survive the famine, Joseph introduces a scheme whereby the people remain largely independent and self-sufficient. While they must give one-fifth of their harvest to Pharaoh, they readily acknowledge that Joseph has saved their lives (v. 25). This portrays Joseph as a fair and just administrator who does not exploit a tragic situation for his own benefit.

47:27 were fruitful and increased greatly in number. The numerical growth of the Israelites in Egypt echoes a motif that runs throughout Genesis, first introduced when God blesses humanity (1:28). Associating population growth with divine blessing is common (e.g., 9:1,7; 17:20; 28:3; 35:11; 48:4). The motif of being fruitful and multiplying plays an important role at the start of the book of Exodus (Exod 1:7); the large population of Israelites prompts a new pharaoh to oppress the Israelites (Exod 1:8–10).

47:28–30 As he nears death, Jacob's desire to be buried in Canaan recalls God's promises to Abraham and Isaac that their descendants will eventually possess the land of Canaan. Joseph later fulfills his commitment to Jacob (49:29—50:14).

47:29 put your hand under my thigh. A formal means of swearing an oath (see also 24:9 and note).

47:31 worshiped as he leaned on the top of his staff. Either Israel bowed down out of respect for Joseph, a motif that would be in keeping with Joseph's earlier dream (37:9–10), or Israel worshiped God in thankfulness for Joseph's response to his request to be buried in Canaan.

Manasseh and Ephraim

48 Some time later Joseph was told, "Your father is ill." So he took his two sons Manasseh and Ephraim[r] along with him. 2When Jacob was told, "Your son Joseph has come to you," Israel rallied his strength and sat up on the bed.

3Jacob said to Joseph, "God Almighty[a] appeared to me at Luz[s] in the land of Canaan, and there he blessed me[t] 4and said to me, 'I am going to make you fruitful and increase your numbers.[u] I will make you a community of peoples, and I will give this land as an everlasting possession to your descendants after you.'

5"Now then, your two sons born to you in Egypt[v] before I came to you here will be reckoned as mine; Ephraim and Manasseh will be mine,[w] just as Reuben and Simeon are mine. 6Any children born to you after them will be yours; in the territory they inherit they will be reckoned under the names of their brothers. 7As I was returning from Paddan,[b] to my sorrow Rachel died in the land of Canaan while we were still on the way, a little distance from Ephrath. So I buried her there beside the road to Ephrath" (that is, Bethlehem).[x]

8When Israel saw the sons of Joseph, he asked, "Who are these?"

9"They are the sons God has given me here,"[y] Joseph said to his father.

Then Israel said, "Bring them to me so I may bless[z] them."

10Now Israel's eyes were failing because of old age, and he could hardly see.[a] So Joseph brought his sons close to him, and his father kissed them[b] and embraced them.

11Israel said to Joseph, "I never expected to see your face again, and now God has allowed me to see your children too."[c]

12Then Joseph removed them from Israel's knees and bowed down with his face to the ground. 13And Joseph took both of them, Ephraim on his right toward Israel's left hand and Manasseh on his left toward Israel's right hand,[d] and brought them close to him. 14But Israel reached out his right hand and put it on Ephraim's head, though he was the younger, and crossing his arms, he put his left hand on Manasseh's head, even though Manasseh was the firstborn.[e]

15Then he blessed[f] Joseph and said,

"May the God before whom my fathers
  Abraham and Isaac walked faithfully,
the God who has been my shepherd[g]
  all my life to this day,

[a] 3 Hebrew *El-Shaddai* [b] 7 That is, Northwest Mesopotamia

48:1 [r] Ge 41:52
48:3 [s] Ge 28:19 [t] Ge 28:13; 35:9-12
48:4 [u] Ge 17:6
48:5 [v] Ge 41:50-52; 46:20 [w] 1Ch 5:1; Jos 14:4
48:7 [x] Ge 35:19
48:9 [y] Ge 33:5 [z] Ge 27:4
48:10 [a] Ge 27:1 [b] Ge 27:27
48:11 [c] Ge 50:23; Ps 128:6
48:13 [d] Ps 110:1
48:14 [e] Ge 41:51
48:15 [f] Ge 17:1 [g] Ge 49:24

48:1–22 *Manasseh and Ephraim.* Nearing death, Jacob blesses all of his sons. He begins with Joseph's two sons, Manasseh and Ephraim, before proceeding to bless his own children (49:1–28). Although these deathbed blessings all occur at the same time, Joseph's sons are distinguished from everyone else. They are the only grandchildren Jacob blesses, and Jacob bestows on Ephraim, not Manasseh, the blessing of the firstborn. The unique lineage that runs throughout Genesis continues through Ephraim and his descendants. This line later includes Joshua (1 Chr 7:20,27), who leads the Israelites into the promised land. Only in the time of David does God reject the Ephraimite line due to its sinfulness and replace it with one linked to the tribe of Judah (see Ps 78:67–71).
48:1–2 The opening report of Joseph bringing his sons to see his elderly father contains no hint of what is about to happen.
48:3–7 Although Jacob's speech centers on Joseph's sons, Ephraim and Manasseh, Jacob begins by recalling how God appeared to him at Luz (see 28:13–15 and note on 28:19). Jacob highlights the divine promises he received. Involving both numerous descendants and land, these promises are a common motif throughout Genesis (e.g., 12:7; 13:14–17; 15:5,18–21).
48:5 will be reckoned as mine. This unusual claim subsequently means that Ephraim and Manasseh are listed alongside Jacob's other sons as ancestors of the 12 tribes of Israel. This also means that Joseph, who is not usually listed as one of the 12 tribes, receives through his two sons twice as much territory in the land of Canaan as his brothers. (Because of their special connection with the tabernacle, the tribe of Levi does not receive territory like the other tribes.) This is in keeping with the idea that Jacob gives Joseph the status of firstborn in place of Reuben (1 Chr 5:1–2). Moreover, by reversing the order of the names, Ephraim coming before Manasseh (see the expected order in v. 1), Jacob appears to have already decided that he will bless the younger son, Ephraim, as firstborn in place of Manasseh, Ephraim's older brother (see vv. 13–19). As if to justify his special treatment of Joseph's sons, Jacob recalls how Rachel, Joseph's mother, died after their return to Canaan (35:16–20).
48:7 Paddan. Short for Paddan Aram (see note on 25:20). **Ephrath.** Earlier name for Bethlehem; later, David is known as an Ephrathite (1 Sam 17:12).
48:8–10 Jacob, like his father Isaac (27:1), had poor eyesight in old age.
48:13–20 Manasseh was the older of the two brothers (41:51–52). However, Jacob deliberately crosses over his hands in order to give Ephraim the firstborn blessing. Previously, Jacob received the firstborn blessing in place of his older brother Esau (27:1–29). In spite of Joseph's objection, Jacob persists in giving Ephraim this blessing. As the story of Israel's descendants continues, the tribe of Ephraim enjoys particular prominence with Joshua, an Ephraimite (Num 13:8,16), leading the Israelites into the land of Canaan after their time of slavery in Egypt.

48:16 [h] Heb 11:21
[i] Ge 28:13
48:17 [j] ver 14
48:19 [k] Ge 17:20
[l] Ge 25:23
48:20 [m] Nu 2:18
[n] Nu 2:20; Ru 4:11
48:21 [o] Ge 26:3; 46:4
[p] Ge 28:13; 50:24
48:22 [q] Jos 24:32; Jn 4:5
[r] Ge 37:8
49:1 [s] Nu 24:14; Jer 23:20
49:2 [t] Ps 34:11
49:3 [u] Ge 29:32
[v] Dt 21:17; Ps 78:51
49:4 [w] Isa 57:20
[x] Ge 35:22; Dt 27:20
49:5 [y] Ge 34:25; Pr 4:17

16 the Angel who has delivered me from all harm
    —may he bless these boys.[h]
May they be called by my name
    and the names of my fathers Abraham and Isaac,[i]
and may they increase greatly
    on the earth."

17 When Joseph saw his father placing his right hand on Ephraim's head[j] he was displeased; so he
took hold of his father's hand to move it from Ephraim's head to Manasseh's head.
18 Joseph said to him,
"No, my father, this one is the firstborn; put your right hand on his head."
19 But his father refused and said, "I know, my son, I know. He too will become a people, and he too
will become great.[k] Nevertheless, his younger brother will be greater than he,[l] and his descendants will
become a group of nations."
20 He blessed them that day and said,

"In your[a] name will Israel pronounce this blessing:
    'May God make you like Ephraim[m] and Manasseh.[n]'"

So he put Ephraim ahead of Manasseh.
21 Then Israel said to Joseph, "I am about to die, but God will be with you[b][o] and take you[b] back to the
land of your[b] fathers.[p]
22 And to you I give one more ridge of land[c][q] than to your brothers,[r] the ridge I
took from the Amorites with my sword and my bow."

Jacob Blesses His Sons

49:1-28Ref — Dt 33:1-29

49 Then Jacob called for his sons and said: "Gather around so I can tell you what will happen to
you in days to come.[s]

2 "Assemble and listen, sons of Jacob;
    listen to your father Israel.[t]

3 "Reuben, you are my firstborn,[u]
    my might, the first sign of my strength,[v]
    excelling in honor, excelling in power.
4 Turbulent as the waters,[w] you will no longer excel,
    for you went up onto your father's bed,
    onto my couch and defiled it.[x]

5 "Simeon and Levi are brothers—
    their swords[d] are weapons of violence.[y]

a 20 The Hebrew is singular. *b 21* The Hebrew is plural. *c 22* The Hebrew for *ridge of land* is identical with the place name Shechem. *d 5* The meaning of the Hebrew for this word is uncertain.

48:21–22 Jacob expresses confidence that God will bring his descendants back to the land God promised to his fathers, Abraham and Isaac.
48:22 one more ridge of land. Jacob uses the Hebrew term *šěkem* (see NIV text note). Later, Joseph's bones are buried at Shechem (Josh 24:32), where Jacob lived for a period of time (33:19—34:31).
49:1–28 *Jacob Blesses His Sons.* After blessing Joseph's sons, Jacob blesses his 12 sons in order of their birth, apart from placing Zebulun before Issachar. These blessings are more than simply predictions of what will happen in the future. They assess each son's character based on what they have done in the past. These judgments in turn influence what will happen in the future. Consequently, Jacob anticipates that Judah and Joseph will be preeminent among his sons; their blessings are the longest and most positive. Due to the poetic nature of the blessings and the use of wordplays, Jacob's statements may in places be interpreted in different ways. However, it undoubtedly makes sense to understand these blessings in line with how the unified story that runs through the books of Genesis through Kings presents the history of each tribe.
49:1 in days to come. Jacob does more than merely predict the future. His blessings have the power to shape what will happen to his descendants. For this reason, Jacob himself was prepared to deceive his own father in order to get the blessing of the firstborn (27:1–29).
49:3–4 As firstborn, Reuben ought to have enjoyed preeminence over his brothers. However, due to his inappropriate relationship with Bilhah (v. 4; see 35:22 and note), Jacob gave Reuben's status as firstborn to Joseph (1 Chr 5:1–2).
49:5–7 Jacob addresses Simeon and Levi together, reflecting their violent, joint action against the Shechemites after Shechem raped their sister Dinah (ch. 34). Denouncing their violent disposition, Jacob predicts that they will be scattered among the other tribes in order to dissipate their anger-fueled, warlike behavior (v. 7). After the Israelites settle in the land of Canaan, the Levites dwell mainly in 48 cities located throughout all of the tribal areas (Num 18:23–24; 35:1–8; Josh 21:1–45). God places the Simeonites within the territory of the more powerful tribe of Judah (Josh 19:1–9). This prevents the tribes of Simeon and Levi from jointly dominating others.

6 Let me not enter their council,
let me not join their assembly,[z]
for they have killed men in their anger[a]
and hamstrung oxen as they pleased.
7 Cursed be their anger, so fierce,
and their fury, so cruel!
I will scatter them in Jacob
and disperse them in Israel.[b]

8 "Judah,[a] your brothers will praise you;
your hand will be on the neck of your enemies;
your father's sons will bow down to you.[c]
9 You are a lion's[d] cub, Judah;[e]
you return from the prey, my son.
Like a lion he crouches and lies down,
like a lioness—who dares to rouse him?
10 The scepter will not depart from Judah,[f]
nor the ruler's staff from between his feet,[b]
until he to whom it belongs[c] shall come
and the obedience of the nations shall be his.[g]
11 He will tether his donkey to a vine,
his colt to the choicest branch;
he will wash his garments in wine,
his robes in the blood of grapes.
12 His eyes will be darker than wine,
his teeth whiter than milk.[d]

13 "Zebulun[h] will live by the seashore
and become a haven for ships;
his border will extend toward Sidon.

14 "Issachar[i] is a rawboned[e] donkey
lying down among the sheep pens.[f]

49:6 [z] Pr 1:15; Eph 5:11 [a] Ge 34:26
49:7 [b] Jos 19:1,9; 21:1-42
49:8 [c] Dt 33:7; 1Ch 5:2
49:9 [d] Nu 24:9; Eze 19:5; Mic 5:8 [e] Rev 5:5
49:10 [f] Nu 24:17,19; Ps 60:7 [g] Ps 2:9; Isa 42:1,4
49:13 [h] Ge 30:20; Dt 33:18-19; Jos 19:10-11
49:14 [i] Ge 30:18

[a] *8 Judah* sounds like and may be derived from the Hebrew for *praise.* [b] *10* Or *from his descendants* [c] *10* Or *to whom tribute belongs*; the meaning of the Hebrew for this phrase is uncertain. [d] *12* Or *will be dull from wine, / his teeth white from milk* [e] *14* Or *strong* [f] *14* Or *the campfires*; or *the saddlebags*

49:8–12 Jacob's positive blessing of Judah reflects the special standing that Judah enjoyed with Jacob's family after his transforming encounter with Tamar (ch. 38; see note on 38:25–26). Judah will receive the praise of his brothers (see NIV text note on v. 8) because his own personal qualities of leadership will permeate his future descendants. In the light of Joseph's associations with royalty, it is unexpected that Jacob links kingship to Judah's future descendants (see notes on vv. 8–10).
49:8–10 your father's sons will bow down to you ... the obedience of the nations shall be his. Recalls how Isaac blessed Jacob (27:29).
49:9 lion. This imagery enhances the royal image. Elsewhere the NT designates Jesus Christ as the "Lion of the tribe of Judah" (Rev 5:5), clearly alluding to this verse.
49:10 scepter ... ruler's staff. A further indication that Jacob anticipates a time when one of Judah's descendants will assume royal office and exercise universal authority. In later history, the Davidic dynasty comes from the tribe of Judah. Matthew's Gospel gives particular attention to how Jesus Christ becomes the heir to the Davidic throne (Matt 1:1–16; see Heb 7:14). **until he to whom it belongs shall come.** This translation is one of several suggestions (see NIV text note). Another possibility is "until Shiloh comes." The mention of Shiloh could foreshadow the time of Samuel when the Israelites take the ark of the covenant from Shiloh (1 Sam 4:3–4) and later when the newly enthroned David transports the ark to Jerusalem (2 Sam 6). These events associated with Shiloh mark the beginning of the process by which Israel's leadership moves from the tribe of Ephraim to the tribe of Judah (see Ps 78:59–72).
49:11 tether his donkey to a vine. This is the first of several lines that point forward to a time when the grape harvest will be exceptionally fruitful. This introduces the expectation that the reign of this king from the tribe of Judah will bring about the transformation of the natural environment, reversing the negative effects on creation that result from humanity's disobedience of God (cf. Ps 72:16; Amos 9:11–15).
49:13 Zebulun. Mentioning him before Issachar (v. 14–15) is unusual since Zebulun was born after Issachar (30:17–20). Jacob's blessing appears to anticipate a future time when Zebulun's territory will border the Mediterranean Sea. While the tribal district of Zebulun lay close to the sea, the border did not always extend to the coast.
49:14–15 Jacob likens the tribe of Issachar to a donkey that works hard because it is well-treated and enjoys good provisions.

49:16 [j] Ge 30:6; Dt 33:22; Jdg 18:26-27
49:17 [k] Jdg 18:27
49:18 [l] Ps 119:166,174
49:19 [m] Ge 30:11; Dt 33:20; 1Ch 5:18
49:20 [n] Ge 30:13; Dt 33:24
49:21 [o] Ge 30:8; Dt 33:23
49:22 [p] Ge 30:24; Dt 33:13-17
49:23 [q] Ge 37:24
49:24 [r] Ps 18:34 [s] Ps 132:2,5; Isa 1:24; 41:10 [t] Isa 28:16
49:25 [u] Ge 28:13 [v] Ge 27:28

15 When he sees how good is his resting place
and how pleasant is his land,
he will bend his shoulder to the burden
and submit to forced labor.

16 "Dan[a][j] will provide justice for his people
as one of the tribes of Israel.
17 Dan[k] will be a snake by the roadside,
a viper along the path,
that bites the horse's heels
so that its rider tumbles backward.

18 "I look for your deliverance, LORD.[l]

19 "Gad[b][m] will be attacked by a band of raiders,
but he will attack them at their heels.

20 "Asher's[n] food will be rich;
he will provide delicacies fit for a king.

21 "Naphtali[o] is a doe set free
that bears beautiful fawns.[c]

22 "Joseph[p] is a fruitful vine,
a fruitful vine near a spring,
whose branches climb over a wall.[d]
23 With bitterness archers attacked him;
they shot at him with hostility.[q]
24 But his bow remained steady,
his strong arms[r] stayed[e] limber,
because of the hand of the Mighty One of Jacob,[s]
because of the Shepherd, the Rock of Israel,[t]
25 because of your father's God,[u] who helps you,
because of the Almighty,[f] who blesses you
with blessings of the skies above,
blessings of the deep springs below,[v]
blessings of the breast and womb.
26 Your father's blessings are greater
than the blessings of the ancient mountains,
than[g] the bounty of the age-old hills.

[a] *16 Dan* here means *he provides justice.* [b] *19 Gad* sounds like the Hebrew for *attack* and also for *band of raiders.* [c] *21* Or *free; / he utters beautiful words* [d] *22* Or *Joseph is a wild colt, / a wild colt near a spring, / a wild donkey on a terraced hill* [e] *23,24* Or *archers will attack . . . will shoot . . . will remain . . . will stay* [f] *25* Hebrew *Shaddai* [g] *26* Or *of my progenitors, / as great as*

49:16–17 Jacob associates the tribe of Dan with justice, reflecting a wordplay on its name (see NIV text note on v. 16). While providing justice appears to be a positive attribute, describing Dan as a roadside "snake" (v. 17) suggests unexpected danger. Evidence of such behavior comes in the unprovoked assault that the tribe of Dan carried out in order to oust the residents of the city of Laish (Judg 18).

49:18 Jacob briefly petitions God, possibly due to the negative characteristics he has attributed to his descendants. Only through divine intervention can there be hope for the future.

49:19 Gad. Jacob's remarks concerning Gad's descendants involve wordplays on his name (see NIV text note). The tribal territory of Gad, in the region of Gilead to the east of the Jordan River, made them susceptible to attacks from raiders. Jacob anticipates that the Gadites will skillfully defend themselves.

49:20 By settling along the coastal plain of Akko (Josh 19:24–31), the tribe of Asher will prosper through both agriculture and maritime trade.

49:21 Naphtali. Jacob's brief remarks about Naphtali suggest that the tribe will flourish. They later settle in the fertile region of Upper Galilee.

49:22–26 Jacob's blessing of Joseph contrasts sharply with those immediately preceding it. While similar in length to the blessing given to Judah (vv. 8–12), Joseph's blessing is marked by a series of references to God, all affirming how God has protected and blessed Joseph abundantly. The frequent mention of blessing underlines the privileged position that Joseph has among Jacob's sons. Jacob's remarks suggest that Joseph's descendants will enjoy blessings that go beyond what his ancestors Abraham and Isaac experienced.

49:26 the prince among his brothers. The Hebrew word translated "prince" is *nāzîr*, a term associated with the concept of Nazirite (one

Let all these rest on the head of Joseph,
on the brow of the prince among[a] his brothers.[w]
27 "Benjamin[x] is a ravenous wolf;
in the morning he devours the prey,
in the evening he divides the plunder."

28 All these are the twelve tribes of Israel, and this is what their father said to them when he blessed
them, giving each the blessing appropriate to him.

The Death of Jacob

29 Then he gave them these instructions:[y] "I am about to be gathered to my people.[z] Bury me with
my fathers[a] in the cave in the field of Ephron the Hittite, 30 the cave in the field of Machpelah,[b] near
Mamre in Canaan, which Abraham bought along with the field[c] as a burial place from Ephron the Hittite. 31 There Abraham[d] and his wife Sarah[e] were buried, there Isaac and his wife Rebekah[f] were buried,
and there I buried Leah. 32 The field and the cave in it were bought from the Hittites.[b]"
33 When Jacob had finished giving instructions to his sons, he drew his feet up into the bed, breathed
his last and was gathered to his people.[g]

50 Joseph threw himself on his father and wept over him and kissed him.[h] 2 Then Joseph directed
the physicians in his service to embalm his father Israel. So the physicians embalmed him,[i]
3 taking a full forty days, for that was the time required for embalming. And the Egyptians mourned
for him seventy days.[j]
4 When the days of mourning had passed, Joseph said to Pharaoh's court, "If I have found favor in
your eyes, speak to Pharaoh for me. Tell him, 5 'My father made me swear an oath[k] and said, "I am
about to die; bury me in the tomb I dug for myself[l] in the land of Canaan."[m] Now let me go up and
bury my father; then I will return.'"
6 Pharaoh said, "Go up and bury your father, as he made you swear to do."
7 So Joseph went up to bury his father. All Pharaoh's officials accompanied him — the dignitaries
of his court and all the dignitaries of Egypt — 8 besides all the members of Joseph's household and his
brothers and those belonging to his father's household. Only their children and their flocks and herds
were left in Goshen. 9 Chariots and horsemen[c] also went up with him. It was a very large company.
10 When they reached the threshing floor of Atad, near the Jordan, they lamented loudly and
bitterly;[n] and there Joseph observed a seven-day period[o] of mourning for his father. 11 When the Canaanites who lived there saw the mourning at the threshing floor of Atad, they said, "The Egyptians

49:26 [w] Dt 33:15-16
49:27 [x] Ge 35:18; Jdg 20:12-13
49:29 [y] Ge 50:16 [z] Ge 25:8 [a] Ge 15:15; 47:30; 50:13
49:30 [b] Ge 23:9 [c] Ge 23:20
49:31 [d] Ge 25:9 [e] Ge 23:19 [f] Ge 35:29
49:33 [g] ver 29; Ge 25:8; Ac 7:15
50:1 [h] Ge 46:4
50:2 [i] ver 26; 2Ch 16:14
50:3 [j] Ge 37:34; Nu 20:29; Dt 34:8
50:5 [k] Ge 47:31 [l] 2Ch 16:14; Isa 22:16 [m] Ge 47:31
50:10 [n] 2Sa 1:17; Ac 8:2 [o] 1Sa 31:13; Job 2:13

[a] 26 Or *of the one separated from* [b] 32 Or *the descendants of Heth* [c] 9 Or *charioteers*

set apart from others; see second NIV text note; see also Num 6:1 – 21). The use of *nāzîr* in conjunction with Joseph may shed light on Matthew's remark concerning Jesus being a Nazarene (Matt 2:23).

49:27 Benjamin. The tribe, like a "ravenous wolf," will be known for its aggressive power (1 Chr 8:1,40; 12:2).

49:28 Jacob intends his blessings to be appropriate to the nature of each son. He clearly associates the tribes descended from Judah and Joseph with leadership within the nation of Israel. This reflects not only how chs. 37 – 50 portray Joseph and Judah, but it also anticipates how the tribes of Judah and Ephraim later take responsibility for leading the nation of Israel. While leadership is initially linked to Ephraim, eventually the tribe of Judah, through the Davidic dynasty, takes on prime responsibility for kingship within Israel (see Ps 78:67 – 72).

49:29 — 50:14 *The Death of Jacob.* With the death of Jacob, the book of Genesis moves toward a conclusion. Although Jacob dies in Egypt, he is confident that the future of his descendants lies in Canaan. For this reason, he requests that he be buried there.

49:29 – 32 cave in the field of Ephron ... bought from the Hittites. Abraham purchased this cave near Hebron (ch. 23), and both he and Isaac were buried there (v. 31; 25:8 – 10; 35:27 – 29). Jacob requests that he too be buried in the same tomb, having previously laid Leah to rest there (recorded only here in Genesis). Burying the patriarchs in Canaan underlines their claim to the land. Jacob's desire to be placed alongside his relatives reflects his belief that God will be true to his promise to give the land of Canaan to Abraham's descendants.

49:33 gathered to his people. Often describes an individual's death (e.g., 25:8,17; 35:29; Num 27:13). It possibly indicates belief in an afterlife when family members will be reunited.

50:2 embalm. Perhaps to delay the process of decomposition. Since this was not the normal custom of the Israelites, Egyptian physicians undertake the task. Joseph probably employs physicians, rather than priests, because of his father's commitment to worship only the Lord God.

50:3 seventy days. Typical of Egyptian practices; Israelites usually mourned between seven and thirty days.

50:7 Joseph's high standing in Egypt explains why court officials and other dignitaries accompany him.

50:10 the threshing floor of Atad. Location unknown, although the text places it "near the Jordan."

50:11 Abel Mizraim. The location is aptly named (see NIV text note) due to the unusual sight of Egyptians holding a seven-day mourning ritual in Canaan.

50:13 [p] Ge 23:20; Ac 7:16
50:15 [q] Ge 37:28; 42:21-22
50:18 [r] Ge 37:7 [s] Ge 43:18
50:19 [t] Ro 12:19; Heb 10:30
50:20 [u] Ge 37:20 [v] Mic 4:11-12 [w] Ro 8:28 [x] Ge 45:5
50:21 [y] Ge 45:11; 47:12
50:22 [z] Ge 25:7; Jos 24:29
50:23 [a] Job 42:16 [b] Nu 32:39,40
50:24 [c] Ge 48:21 [d] Ex 3:16-17 [e] Ge 15:14 [f] Ge 12:7; 26:3; 28:13; 35:12
50:25 [g] Ge 47:29-30; Ex 13:19; Jos 24:32; Heb 11:22
50:26 [h] ver 2

are holding a solemn ceremony of mourning." That is why that place near the Jordan is called Abel
Mizraim.[a]
12 So Jacob's sons did as he had commanded them: 13 They carried him to the land of Canaan and
buried him in the cave in the field of Machpelah, near Mamre, which Abraham had bought along with
the field[p] as a burial place from Ephron the Hittite. 14 After burying his father, Joseph returned to Egypt,
together with his brothers and all the others who had gone with him to bury his father.

Joseph Reassures His Brothers

15 When Joseph's brothers saw that their father was dead, they said, "What if Joseph holds a grudge
against us and pays us back for all the wrongs we did to him?"[q] 16 So they sent word to Joseph, saying,
"Your father left these instructions before he died: 17 'This is what you are to say to Joseph: I ask you
to forgive your brothers the sins and the wrongs they committed in treating you so badly.' Now please
forgive the sins of the servants of the God of your father." When their message came to him, Joseph wept.
18 His brothers then came and threw themselves down before him.[r] "We are your slaves,"[s] they said.
19 But Joseph said to them, "Don't be afraid. Am I in the place of God?[t] 20 You intended to harm me,[u]
but God intended[v] it for good[w] to accomplish what is now being done, the saving of many lives.[x] 21 So
then, don't be afraid. I will provide for you and your children.[y]" And he reassured them and spoke
kindly to them.

The Death of Joseph

22 Joseph stayed in Egypt, along with all his father's family. He lived a hundred and ten years[z] 23 and
saw the third generation[a] of Ephraim's children. Also the children of Makir[b] son of Manasseh were
placed at birth on Joseph's knees.[b]
24 Then Joseph said to his brothers, "I am about to die.[c] But God will surely come to your aid[d] and
take you up out of this land to the land[e] he promised on oath to Abraham, Isaac and Jacob."[f] 25 And
Joseph made the Israelites swear an oath and said, "God will surely come to your aid, and then you
must carry my bones up from this place."[g]
26 So Joseph died at the age of a hundred and ten. And after they embalmed him,[h] he was placed in
a coffin in Egypt.

[a] *11 Abel Mizraim* means *mourning of the Egyptians.* [b] *23* That is, were counted as his

50:13 Abraham had bought. See ch. 23.
50:15–21 *Joseph Reassures His Brothers.* After the death of their father, Joseph's brothers are deeply concerned that Joseph will take revenge for their earlier mistreatment of him. Joseph swiftly reassures them that he has forgiven their treachery.
50:15 Joseph's brothers are still troubled by their past actions and fear that Joseph will repay them for what they did in selling him into slavery (37:23–36).
50:16–17 Their guilt prevents the brothers from addressing Joseph directly; instead, they send a message seeking forgiveness for their past actions. Their confession moves Joseph deeply.
50:18–21 Joseph's reaction opens the way for his brothers to come to him.
50:18 threw themselves down before him. For a fourth time (see 42:6; 43:26; 44:14), Joseph's brothers fulfill his dreams as a teenager (37:5–11) by bowing down before him. **We are your slaves.** Sharply contrasts with how they previously sold Joseph into slavery (37:23–28).
50:19–21 Appreciating how God has guided his circumstances, Joseph boldly affirms that what has happened has resulted in "the saving of many lives" (v. 20; see 45:5–8). Joseph's sensitivity to God's providential activity enables him graciously to forgive his brothers. Joseph's experience demonstrates how God can overturn evil actions and through them bring salvation to people. The ultimate example of this is the crucifixion of Jesus (Act 2:22–24; 3:13–26).
50:22–26 *The Death of Joseph.* After the death and burial of Jacob, the narrative jumps forward about 60 years to the death of Joseph. While the report of Joseph's death is clearly important, preparing for the continuation of the story in the book of Exodus, the narrator lessens the sense of loss by looking optimistically to the future. Apart from mentioning the birth of great-grandchildren, Joseph anticipates with confidence that the Israelites will eventually leave Egypt to return to Canaan. This expectation rests in his belief that God will fulfill his promises to the patriarchs.
50:22–23 Joseph outlives his father Jacob by 60 years, surviving long enough to see his great-grandchildren.
50:24–26 Although Joseph does not ask to be buried at Machpelah, like his father Jacob, he does request that his descendants take his remains from Egypt to Canaan when God brings the Israelites back into the land he promised to the patriarchs. To facilitate this, Joseph's body is embalmed (see note on v. 2) and placed in a coffin. When the Israelites later leave Egypt, Moses ensures that they fulfill Joseph's wish (Exod 13:19). After the Israelites settle in Canaan, Joseph's remains are buried at Shechem (Josh 24:32; see Gen 48:21–22 and note on 48:22).

INTRODUCTION TO EXODUS

TITLE

Exodus, which means "exit" or "departure," derives from the word that the Greek translation of the OT uses to describe Israel's release from enslavement in Egypt. The narrative it unpacks is the sequel to the story that begins in Genesis (see Gen 46:8) and continues in the books that follow.

AUTHOR

Exodus makes no direct claims regarding authorship, but traditionally Moses has been identified as the author of the first five books of the OT (see Introduction to the Pentateuch, p. 12). According to explicit statements in the text (17:14; 24:4; 34:27 – 28), Moses wrote down at least some of the material recorded in Exodus. The fact that he was the only eyewitness to several recorded events may also indicate a significant input to the book's contents. This is further suggested by NT texts that link Exodus passages to Moses (e.g., Mark 7:10; 12:26; Luke 2:22 – 23). From this it seems reasonable to conclude that Moses played a key role in the compilation of Exodus, even though its canonical form reflects some measure of subsequent updating (e.g., 16:36).

MIDIAN WITH TRADITIONAL SITE OF MOUNT SINAI

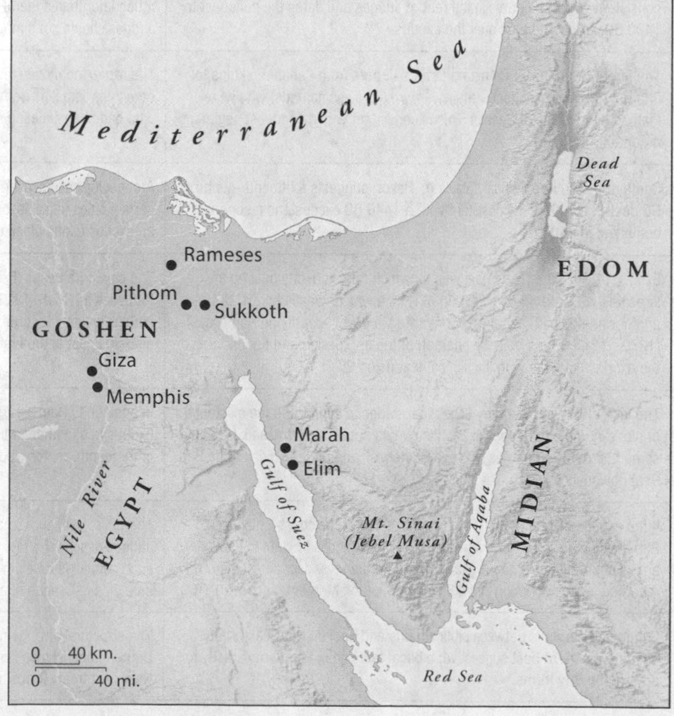

THE DATE OF THE EXODUS

Some contemporary scholars question whether or not the exodus happened at all, pointing to its absence in Egyptian records and the lack of archaeological support. However, neither objection is strong: (1) Official Egyptian records, like most ancient texts, emphasize military success rather than humiliating defeat. Thus, Egypt's official annals typically would not record an event like the exodus or would describe the historical circumstances very differently. (2) The climate in the eastern Nile delta and the Sinai wilderness is not conducive to the long-term survival of material remains. It is thus unreasonable to expect such evidence of a people, however numerous, who dwelt mainly in perishable tents.

Moreover, there are also good reasons for concluding that the biblical account is reliable: (1) It is most unlikely that any people would invent such a story of their national origins: as slaves oppressed by a powerful neighbor. (2) The Egyptians employed Semitic slave labor in the second millennium BC to make bricks for their building projects. (3) Authentic place-names (e.g., Rameses) are unlikely to have been remembered centuries later. (4) Tent-shrines, such as the tabernacle, are attested to in Egypt and Canaan from the second millennium BC.

While these observations do not prove that the biblical account is true, they certainly suggest that the skepticism reflected in some circles today is not based on unanswerable questions.

However, even those who believe the biblical account differ over the date of the events described; some date these events in the fifteenth century BC, whereas others prefer a later date, in the thirteenth century BC. The issue is quite complex and not easily resolved. The main arguments (and counterarguments) in support of the early and late dates are set out in "Dates in Exodus," this page.

As is clear from "Dates in Exodus," there are good arguments for either dating, and the archaeological evidence

DATES IN EXODUS

EARLY OR FIFTEENTH-CENTURY BC DATE (ca. 1446 BC)	**LATE OR THIRTEENTH-CENTURY BC DATE (ca. 1260 BC)**
1 Kgs 6:1 states that the construction of Solomon's temple began in Solomon's fourth year (ca. 966 BC), which is identified as the 480th year after the exodus. This places the exodus at 1446 BC.	The figure of 480 years mentioned in 1 Kgs 6:1 is not intended to be taken literally. Rather, it is symbolic (a multiple of 12), perhaps meaning 12 "idealized generations" of 40 years each. Generations were in reality much shorter (about 25 years), suggesting a date of ca. 1266 BC for the exodus.
In Judg 11:26 Jephthah asserts in a message to the Ammonite king (ca. 1100 BC) that Israel had already lived in Canaan for 300 years, which is consistent with the figures in the rest of Judges and dates the conquest to 1400 BC, some 40 years after the exodus.	Jephthah's claim may be mistaken or inflated. In any case, if (as is likely) he made this claim about 1070 BC, it would date the exodus around 1410, much later than a literal reading of 1 Kgs 6:1 suggests. The figures in Judges should not simply be added up, since there is significant overlap.
The fifteenth-century BC Amarna Letters (letters from Canaanite kings to Pharaoh) ask for assistance against *'apiru* (landless nomads) who were "taking over" parts of Canaan. This is consistent with a conquest beginning around 1406 BC.	The *'apiru* mentioned in the Amarna correspondence probably refer to other, non-Israelite, Semitic invaders, such as the Hyksos, Semitic invaders who had been expelled from Egypt centuries before the exodus.
Some of the archaeological data (e.g., Hazor) suggests a fifteenth-century BC destruction. This is consistent with a 1446 BC exodus and a conquest beginning in 1406 BC.	Archaeological discoveries in Canaan reflect the complete destruction of certain cities (e.g., Hazor) in the late thirteenth century. This accords with an exodus taking place ca. 1260 BC.
Exod 1:11 uses the name Rameses by which this store city built by the Israelites was later known (cf. Gen 47:11). It was originally known by another name, such as Rowaty or Avaris. Moreover, identifying Rameses II (1279–1213 BC) as both the pharaoh of the oppression and the pharaoh of the exodus conflicts with the biblical text (Exod 2:23; 4:19).	The city of Rameses (Exod 1:11), known also as Pi-Rameses, was built by Rameses II (1279–1213 BC) in 1270 BC. This city is not mentioned in any earlier Egyptian records; therefore, the Israelites who built it must have still been in Egypt in the first part of the thirteenth century BC.
The lack of fifteenth-century BC textual evidence supporting the existence of place-names mentioned in Exodus should not be overstressed. Possibly some had different names (such as Rameses), and others (such as the Red Sea) obviously existed.	In addition to Rameses, several other geographic sites mentioned in Exodus (e.g., Pithom, Migdol, and the Red Sea [*Yam Suf*]) are all attested in thirteenth-century (but not fifteenth-century) BC Egyptian texts.
If the exodus were dated 80 years (Exod 7:7) after the construction of Rameses (Exod 1:11), this would be 1190 BC, which is too late to explain an Egyptian military triumph over Israel in Canaan two decades earlier and recorded in an inscription of the Egyptian pharaoh Merneptah (ca. 1207 BC).	The Bible mentions almost no conflict with Egypt in either Joshua or Judges despite the fact that Egypt controlled Canaan in 1406 BC. However, such conflict is noted in the Merneptah stele (ca. 1207 BC), and Egyptian influence in Canaan diminished after 1200 BC.
Suggested parallels between biblical texts and ancient Near East treaty documents are at best suggestive; biblical texts do not conform exactly to any such treaty forms.	The structural arrangement of covenant material in Exodus and Deuteronomy shows significant correspondence with the typical ancient Near East treaty forms of the thirteenth century BC.

is, unfortunately, inconclusive. This conundrum might have been avoided if even one of the Egyptian kings involved had been named. However, even the royal title (Pharaoh) applied to these kings reflects later usage and so offers no help in resolving this ongoing scholarly debate. For the author and readers of this book, however, what really matters is not *when* the exodus took place, but *why*.

THEOLOGICAL FOCUS

While a major topic of the book is Israel's "exodus," or departure, from Egypt, this is really only the beginning of the story and is covered in the first third of the book (1:1 — 15:21); the majority of the book (15:22 — 40:38) concentrates on what happens next: Israel's journey to Sinai and what transpires once the Israelites arrive there. But what unites all the material is the focus on the divine-human relationship between "the LORD" (see notes on 3:13 – 15) and Israel, Abraham's offspring and heirs to God's promises. This unique relationship with Israel's ancestors motivates the Lord's gracious response (2:24 – 25; 6:5 – 8; 32:13 – 14), and his special relationship with Israel explains both his treatment of Pharaoh (4:22 – 23; 9:17 – 18) and the goal of the exodus (29:46). But this relationship is not an end in itself; it is a means to the Lord's greater objective: to make himself known. Thus, his actions are not simply for the benefit of Egypt (7:5,17; 8:10,22; 9:14,29; 11:7; 14:4,18) and Israel (6:7; 10:2; 16:6,8,12; 29:46; 31:13) but are also for the rest of the nations (9:16; 15:14; 33:16; 34:10) who would be blessed through Abraham and his seed (Gen 12:1 – 3; cf. Exod 19:6).

Exod 1:1 — 2:25, in which God seems largely absent, highlights God's faithfulness to the covenant promises he made to Israel's ancestors (Gen 15:13). Exod 3:1 — 15:21 emphasizes this still further by the measures the Lord takes to punish the oppressive regime and emancipate Abraham's descendants (Gen 15:14). Through word and action, the Lord makes himself known as the holy and incomparable God, sovereign over history and creation, far superior to the deities others worship (12:12; 15:11). Exod 15:22 — 18:27 further underlines this: the Lord demonstrates his incredible ability to sustain and protect the people he rescued, which culminates in Jethro, Moses' non-Israelite father-in-law, recognizing the Lord's supremacy (18:11).

The first half of the book shows the Israelites *why* the Lord, as savior, deserves their service and worship; the second half reveals *how* the Israelites should serve and worship him exclusively as their divine king. The strict preparations necessary before God's appearance on Mount Sinai again underscore God's holiness (ch. 19; cf. 3:5). Direct access to God is highly restricted: Israel must initially approach the Lord through a designated mediator. In the first instance, this mediator is Moses, through whom the Lord makes known Israel's covenant obligations and how to apply them (chs. 20 – 23). These covenant obligations are Israel's grateful response to the Lord's saving work (19:4; 20:2). However, they are also a means by which Israel's unique status as the Lord's special people is made evident (19:5 – 6). The Lord's presence among the Israelites also reflects this (29:45 – 46; 33:15 – 16), so God's imperfect people need an appropriate structure to accommodate such close proximity to a holy God. In contrast to the golden calf that Aaron and the Israelites devised, the divinely decreed means of worship involves a special tent (the tabernacle) and consecrated personnel (Aaron and his sons). This mandate enables Israel to live with the Lord among them and expresses their unique relationship with him.

BIBLICAL-THEOLOGICAL TRAJECTORIES

As noted in Introduction: Title, Exodus is part of the unfolding theological account that began in Genesis and continues in the books that follow. In terms of the promise-fulfillment theme that pervades the Bible, Exodus is therefore of key importance. Not only does God begin to fulfill his promises to Abraham in Exodus, but the book is foundational for several theological trajectories that run throughout the rest of Scripture. Three examples will suffice:

1. Israel's deliverance from Egypt becomes the major paradigm of salvation in the OT. It is therefore not surprising that later OT books anticipate a new exodus after Israel again ends up in exile (Isa 11:10 – 16; Jer 23:1 – 8) — this time because they sinfully rebel against God. Consequently, God's physical deliverance of Israel from Pharaoh's oppressive regime foreshadows God's spiritually delivering his people in the NT: Jesus is the ultimate Passover lamb (John 1:29; 1 Cor 5:7) through whom people are redeemed (1 Pet 1:18 – 19) from the sin that enslaves them (John 8:34 – 36; Rom 6:6,17,20).

2. The Sinai covenant establishes the framework for the divine-human relationship reflected in the rest of the OT. Despite their initial enthusiasm and avowed commitment (19:8; 24:3,7), the Israelites fail to keep this covenant — not just as God officially hands over the tablets of the Ten Commandments (ch. 32) but throughout the OT. Such perennial failure and its tragic consequences lead to the hope of a new covenant — one in which people internalize God's covenant requirements (Jer 31:33) by the work of his Spirit (Ezek 36:27). Jesus inaugurates this new covenant; the echo of Exod 24:8 in the Last Supper accounts implicitly reflects this (Matt 26:28; Mark 14:24; Luke 22:20;

1 Cor 11:25), and various letters explicitly underline it (e.g., 2 Cor 3; Heb 8–10). Consequentially, Christians are required to keep not the obligations of the Sinai covenant but the obligations of the new covenant.

3. The goal of the exodus — the Lord's dwelling among his people in the tabernacle — is subsequently expressed through Solomon's temple, but it is jeopardized when the nation's rebellion and idolatry eventually force the Lord to abandon this earthly dwelling and destroy it. Nevertheless, the OT never abandons the prospect of the Lord's dwelling among his people; the prophetic hope is an even more glorious temple to come (Ezek 37:28; 43:7). Once again, Jesus fulfills this hope (John 1:14), and God's people constitute his dwelling place (2 Cor 6:16), a reality that will ultimately be experienced in the new heaven and new earth (Rev 21:3).

When read in its literary and theological context, Exodus is much more than a story of miraculous deliverance or divine action on behalf of an oppressed people. Rather, it recounts a significant stage in the fulfillment of God's promises to Israel's ancestors — promises through which God eventually realizes his purpose for creation. This book as a whole and its opening chapters in particular are concerned primarily with these promises.

OUTLINE

I. Israel in Egypt (1:1 — 13:16)

- A. Egyptian Oppression and the Prospect of Deliverance (1:1 — 4:31)
  1. The Israelites Oppressed (1:1–22)
  2. The Birth of Moses (2:1–10)
  3. Moses Flees to Midian (2:11–25)
  4. Moses and the Burning Bush (3:1–22)
  5. Signs for Moses (4:1–17)
  6. Moses Returns to Egypt (4:18–31)
- B. Pharaoh's Hardness of Heart and the Lord's Mighty Acts (5:1 — 11:10)
  1. Bricks Without Straw (5:1–21)
  2. God Promises Deliverance (5:22 — 6:12)
  3. Family Record of Moses and Aaron (6:13–27)
  4. Aaron to Speak for Moses (6:28 — 7:7)
  5. Aaron's Staff Becomes a Snake (7:8–13)
  6. The Plague of Blood (7:14–24)
  7. The Plague of Frogs (7:25 — 8:15)
  8. The Plague of Gnats (8:16–19)
  9. The Plague of Flies (8:20–32)
  10. The Plague on Livestock (9:1–7)
  11. The Plague of Boils (9:8–12)
  12. The Plague of Hail (9:13–35)
  13. The Plague of Locusts (10:1–20)
  14. The Plague of Darkness (10:21–29)
  15. The Plague on the Firstborn (11:1–10)
- C. Redemption and Consecration of Israel's Firstborn (12:1 — 13:16)
  1. The Passover and the Festival of Unleavened Bread (12:1–30)
  2. The Exodus (12:31–42)
  3. Passover Restrictions (12:43–51)
  4. Consecration of the Firstborn (13:1–16)

II. From Egypt to Sinai (13:17 — 18:27)

- A. Israel's Rescue and Egypt's Punishment at the Red Sea (13:17 — 15:21)
  1. Crossing the Sea (13:17 — 14:31)
  2. The Song of Moses and Miriam (15:1–21)
- B. Divine Provision and Instruction in the Wilderness (15:22 — 17:7)
  1. The Waters of Marah and Elim (15:22–27)
  2. Manna and Quail (16:1–36)
  3. Water From the Rock (17:1–7)

- C. The Amalekites Defeated (17:8–16)
- D. Jethro Visits Moses (18:1–27)

III. Israel at Sinai (19:1—40:38)

- A. At Mount Sinai (19:1–25)
- B. Israel's Covenant Obligations Disclosed (20:1—23:33)
  1. The Ten Commandments (20:1–21)
  2. Idols and Altars (20:22—21:1)
  3. Hebrew Servants (21:2–11)
  4. Personal Injuries (21:12–36)
  5. Protection of Property (22:1–15)
  6. Social Responsibility (22:16–31)
  7. Laws of Justice and Mercy (23:1–9)
  8. Sabbath Laws (23:10–13)
  9. The Three Annual Festivals (23:14–19)
  10. God's Angel to Prepare the Way (23:20–33)
- C. The Covenant Confirmed (24:1–18)
- D. Instructions for Israel's Worship (25:1—31:18)
  1. Offerings for the Tabernacle (25:1–9)
  2. The Ark (25:10–22)
  3. The Table (25:23–30)
  4. The Lampstand (25:31–40)
  5. The Tabernacle (26:1–37)
  6. The Altar of Burnt Offering (27:1–8)
  7. The Courtyard (27:9–19)
  8. Oil for the Lampstand (27:20–21)
  9. The Priestly Garments (28:1–43)
  10. Consecration of the Priests (29:1–46)
  11. The Altar of Incense (30:1–10)
  12. Atonement Money (30:11–16)
  13. Basin for Washing (30:17–21)
  14. Anointing Oil and Incense (30:22–38)
  15. Bezalel and Oholiab (31:1–11)
  16. The Sabbath (31:12–18)
- E. The Covenant Broken and Reestablished (32:1—34:35)
  1. The Golden Calf (32:1—33:6)
  2. The Tent of Meeting (33:7–11)
  3. Moses and the Glory of the Lord (33:12–23)
  4. The New Stone Tablets (34:1–28)
  5. The Radiant Face of Moses (34:29–35)
- F. Construction and Consecration of the Tabernacle (35:1—40:38)
  1. Sabbath Regulations (35:1–3)
  2. Materials for the Tabernacle (35:4–29)
  3. Bezalel and Oholiab (35:30—36:7)
  4. The Tabernacle Constructed (36:8—38:31)
  5. The Priestly Garments Made (39:1–31)
  6. Moses Inspects the Work (39:32–43)
  7. Setting Up the Tabernacle (40:1–33)
  8. The Glory of the Lord (40:34–38)

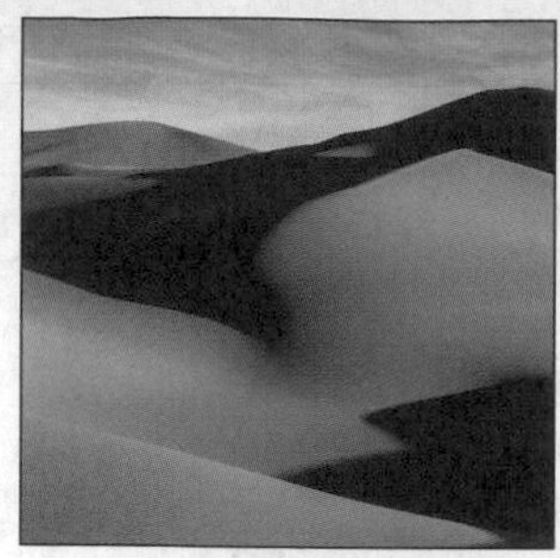

EXODUS

1:1 [a]Ge 46:8
1:5 [b]Ge 46:26
1:6 [c]Ge 50:26
1:7 [d]Ge 46:3; Dt 26:5; Ac 7:17
1:9 [e]Ps 105:24-25
1:10 [f]Ps 83:3 [g]Ac 7:17-19
1:11 [h]Ex 3:7 [i]Ge 15:13; Ex 2:11; 5:4; 6:6-7

The Israelites Oppressed

1 These are the names of the sons of Israel[a] who went to Egypt with Jacob, each with his family:
2 Reuben, Simeon, Levi and Judah; 3 Issachar, Zebulun and Benjamin; 4 Dan and Naphtali; Gad and
Asher. 5 The descendants of Jacob numbered seventy[*a*] in all;[b] Joseph was already in Egypt.
6 Now Joseph and all his brothers and all that generation died,[c] 7 but the Israelites were exceedingly
fruitful; they multiplied greatly, increased in numbers[d] and became so numerous that the land was
filled with them.
8 Then a new king, to whom Joseph meant nothing, came to power in Egypt. 9 "Look," he said to his
people, "the Israelites have become far too numerous[e] for us. 10 Come, we must deal shrewdly[f] with
them or they will become even more numerous and, if war breaks out, will join our enemies, fight
against us and leave the country."[g]
11 So they put slave masters[h] over them to oppress them with forced labor,[i] and they built Pithom and

a 5 Masoretic Text (see also Gen. 46:27); Dead Sea Scrolls and Septuagint (see also Acts 7:14 and note at Gen. 46:27) *seventy-five*

1:1—13:16 *Israel in Egypt.* The first section of the book recounts Israel's oppression in Egypt (1:1–22), the early life of Moses and his divine commission (2:1—4:31), the protracted conflict between the Lord and Pharaoh (5:1—11:10), and the death of Egypt's firstborn and Israel's deliverance (12:1—13:16). The total period covered is 430 years (12:40), although most of the material covers an 80-year period from Moses' birth (2:1–2) to Israel's departure (7:7).

1:1—4:31 *Egyptian Oppression and the Prospect of Deliverance.* Chs. 1–4 describe how a new regime ruthlessly attempted to control Jacob's descendants and anticipate the deliverance that God promises to bring about through a most unlikely and reluctant agent.

1:1–22 *The Israelites Oppressed.* The proliferation of Jacob's descendants in Egypt and a change in political leadership precipitate a crisis for the Israelites. The deliverance Joseph predicted (Gen 50:24–25) has not yet materialized. The opening chapter thus sets the scene for Israel's anticipated exodus by describing the circumstances that Jacob's descendants now face.

1:1–5 This flashback begins with the exact first words of Gen 46:8. Those listed (vv. 2–4; cf. Gen 46:8–25) and the quotation from Gen 46:27 ("seventy in all") in v. 5 further reinforce continuity with Genesis.

1:5 seventy. May be a round or symbolic figure. "Seventy-five" (see NIV text note) is almost certainly a later attempt to incorporate the immediate descendants of Ephraim and Manasseh.

1:7 exceedingly fruitful ... multiplied greatly ... the land was filled with them. God's promises (Gen 13:16; 15:5; 17:2,6; 22:17) are coming to fruition as Jacob's family in Egypt grows prolifically. Exodus thus opens on a very positive note: the mandate that God gave humans at creation (Gen 1:28), that was reiterated to Noah after the flood (Gen 9:1,7), and that became a promise to Abraham and his offspring (Gen 17:6) is now being realized.

1:8 new king. The identity of this king who instigated the oppression of the Israelites is unclear. For just over a century (ca. 1650–1550 BC) the northern part of Egypt, including Goshen (Gen 47:27), was ruled by Semitic invaders referred to by the Egyptians as Hyksos ("shepherd kings"). It is possible that the Israelites were somehow associated with these foreigners and so would have come under close scrutiny by the new rulers (Egypt's Eighteenth Dynasty) after the Hyksos were expelled by Ahmose I (1550–1525 BC). This new king may be one of his successors, possibly Thutmose I (1504–1491 BC) or Thutmose II (1491–1479 BC). Others associate this new regime with that of Seti I (1294–1279 BC) and his son, Rameses II (1279–1213 BC). See Introduction: The Date of the Exodus. **Joseph meant nothing.** This new ruler was under no obligation to maintain the special status that his predecessors conferred on the Hebrews. Like other pharaohs in this book, this king remains nameless. This may possibly be following the contemporary Egyptian custom of not naming their enemies. In any case, since the narrator did not consider such information essential, the identity of this pharaoh/dynasty should not distract us from the main focus.

1:10 deal shrewdly. Pharaoh thought he was being shrewd (cf. Gen 11:3–4), but attempting to thwart the fulfillment of God's set plan and purpose was an act of folly, setting the stage for the ensuing struggle between the Lord and the gods of Egypt. **leave the country.** While Israel's ethnic and political allegiance were an obvious worry, subsequent developments show that the chief concern was that Israel might leave the country.

1:11 slave masters. They were Egyptian, but they later delegated some

Rameses[j] as store cities[k] for Pharaoh. [12]But the more they were oppressed, the more they multiplied and
spread; so the Egyptians came to dread the Israelites [13]and worked them ruthlessly.[l] [14]They made their
lives bitter with harsh labor in brick and mortar and with all kinds of work in the fields; in all their
harsh labor the Egyptians worked them ruthlessly.[m]

[15]The king of Egypt said to the Hebrew midwives, whose names were Shiphrah and Puah, [16]"When
you are helping the Hebrew women during childbirth on the delivery stool, if you see that the baby is a
boy, kill him; but if it is a girl, let her live." [17]The midwives, however, feared[n] God and did not do what
the king of Egypt had told them to do;[o] they let the boys live. [18]Then the king of Egypt summoned the
midwives and asked them, "Why have you done this? Why have you let the boys live?"

[19]The midwives answered Pharaoh, "Hebrew women are not like Egyptian women; they are vigorous
and give birth before the midwives arrive."[p]

1:11 [j] Ge 47:11 [k] 1Ki 9:19; 2Ch 8:4
1:13 [l] Dt 4:20
1:14 [m] Ex 2:23; 6:9; Nu 20:15; Ps 81:6; Ac 7:19
1:17 [n] ver 21; Pr 16:6 [o] Da 3:16-18; Ac 4:18-20; 5:29
1:19 [p] Jos 2:4-6; 2Sa 17:20

responsibilities to Israelite overseers (5:14). **forced labor.** This is the first of several attempts at population control. But this oppressive and brutal treatment was anticipated by God (cf. Gen 15:13). Not surprisingly, therefore, this policy failed; brutal oppression seemed only to exacerbate the problem of population control (v. 12). **Pithom and Rameses.** Their precise locations and nature have generated significant archaeological debate, but presumably these two "store cities" were strategically located somewhere in the eastern Nile delta, close to Goshen (see map, p. 113), where the Israelites lived (Gen 45:10). **Pithom.** May have been located at Tell el-Retabeh, some 30 miles (48 kilometers) west of Lake Timsah. The name "Rameses" is probably linked to Rameses II, a pharaoh renowned for his building enterprises in the region, but it may be employed here for a location that previously had been known as Rowaty, then Avaris, and then possibly Peru-nefer. So this text does not indisputably settle the question of the date of these events.

1:13–14 worked ... labor ... work ... labor ... worked. Introduces a key motif. Serving and worshiping the Lord would eventually displace harsh labor in Egypt. The exploitive and demoralizing activity Pharaoh imposed sharply contrasts not only to work as God intended (cf. Gen 2:15) but to the service the Lord would demand of Israel. God's creative and redemptive purposes are thus both under assault here as Egyptian animosity toward Abraham's descendants intensifies.

1:15–21 Egypt's king introduces an even more radical strategy: he conscripts Hebrew midwives to implement a crude form of "birth control."

1:15 Shiphrah and Puah. It is not immediately obvious why these two midwives are named since neither is mentioned again. Perhaps these Semitic names simply make their nationality clear. This may contrast these women and the nameless pharaohs: unlike those who despised Abraham's offspring and brought God's curse upon themselves and their families (cf. Gen 12:3), these women are blessed, and posterity remember their names.

1:16,22 boy. Use of this word, which can also be translated "son," draws attention to a significant theme in chs. 1–15. To prevent Israel's rebellion and departure, Hebrew sons are sentenced to death by Pharaoh. The Israelites are subsequently described as God's "firstborn son" (4:22), and Pharaoh's refusal to release them will result in the death of Egypt's "firstborn son" (4:23). This happens as a result of the tenth plague (12:29–30), after which Israel is finally permitted to leave Egypt.

1:16 delivery stool. Comprised of two bricks, which women squatted on while giving birth. **kill him.** In keeping with the military threat previously envisaged (v. 10), Egypt's king selects Hebrew males for extermination.

1:17 The midwives courageously refuse to comply with Pharaoh's plan because they "feared God" more than Egypt's king. Human authority has limitations (cf. Dan 3; 6; Acts 4:19).

1:19 Perhaps there is some truth to this explanation. After all, if these Israelites were multiplying (v. 7) and there were only two midwives for the entire population, then many women could well have given birth before a midwife arrived. But the text does not rule out misinformation (it is unlikely they were late for all such births), nor does it suggest that God blessed these women because of their deceitfulness. God blessed them because they "feared God" (v. 21).

Fields with Tell ed-Daba (Rameses) in the background. Tell ed-Daba is a possible location of ancient Rameses (Exod 1:11).

Todd Bolen/www.BiblePlaces.com

1:20 [q]ver 12; Pr 11:18; Isa 3:10
1:21 [r]1Sa 2:35; 2Sa 7:11,27-29; 1Ki 11:38
1:22 [s]Ac 7:19
2:1 [t]Ex 6:20; Nu 26:59
2:2 [u]Ac 7:20; Heb 11:23
2:4 [v]Ex 15:20; Nu 26:59
2:5 [w]Ex 7:15; 8:20

20 So God was kind to the midwives[q] and the people increased and became even more numerous.
21 And because the midwives feared God, he gave them families[r] of their own.
22 Then Pharaoh gave this order to all his people: "Every Hebrew boy that is born you must throw
into the Nile, but let every girl live."[s]

The Birth of Moses

2 Now a man of the tribe of Levi married a Levite woman,[t] 2 and she became pregnant and gave
birth to a son. When she saw that he was a fine child, she hid him for three months.[u] 3 But when
she could hide him no longer, she got a papyrus basket[a] for him and coated it with tar and pitch. Then
she placed the child in it and put it among the reeds along the bank of the Nile. 4 His sister[v] stood at a
distance to see what would happen to him.
5 Then Pharaoh's daughter went down to the Nile to bathe, and her attendants were walking along
the riverbank.[w] She saw the basket among the reeds and sent her female slave to get it. 6 She opened it
and saw the baby. He was crying, and she felt sorry for him. "This is one of the Hebrew babies," she said.
7 Then his sister asked Pharaoh's daughter, "Shall I go and get one of the Hebrew women to nurse
the baby for you?"
8 "Yes, go," she answered. So the girl went and got the baby's mother. 9 Pharaoh's daughter said to
her, "Take this baby and nurse him for me, and I will pay you." So the woman took the baby and nursed
him. 10 When the child grew older, she took him to Pharaoh's daughter and he became her son. She
named him Moses,[b] saying, "I drew him out of the water."

[a] *3* The Hebrew can also mean *ark*, as in Gen. 6:14. [b] *10* *Moses* sounds like the Hebrew for *draw out.*

1:21 If these midwives were themselves Hebrews (see note on v. 15), the irony should not be missed: God blessed them with the very thing that Pharaoh was seeking to deny (v. 10). In any case, rather than Pharaoh thwarting God's plan, God thwarts Pharaoh's plan.

1:22 Pharaoh's final solution was state-imposed infanticide. While the dominant Hebrew text does not specify the ethnicity of the victims, English versions are undoubtedly correct in identifying them as "Hebrew" newborns. The opening chapter ends on an ominous note, but the thread of fulfillment running through it implies that Israel's future is nevertheless secure.

2:1–22 It is into this perilous context (1:22) that Moses, the human agent of Israel's deliverance, is born. Against all odds, he not only survives Pharaoh's murderous decree but also finds shelter and protection within the royal household. God's providential hand is evidently at work, even though the biblical narrator passes over this in silence. Other than the passing reference in 1:20, Exodus does not explicitly mention God until vv. 23–25, after Moses' prospects have apparently been jeopardized by an act of folly (vv. 11–14), leading to his own mini-exodus and self-imposed exile in Midian (vv. 15–22).

2:1–10 *The Birth of Moses.* Pharaoh's murderous efforts are foiled yet again, and interestingly, women again are involved: first the fertile Hebrew women; then the deceptive midwives; finally the child's mother, sister, and ironically, Pharaoh's daughter!

2:1–2 This new episode begins with the birth of a son to an unnamed Levite couple (see note on 6:20). Levites were the tribal descendants of Levi (Gen 29:34) and were later set apart as tabernacle officials (Exod 32:28–29; 38:21; Num 1:47–53). Nothing about this birth is unusual had it been under normal circumstances, but in view of Pharaoh's edict (1:22), this child's future seems grim.

2:2 saw … fine. Along with 1:7 (see note), this may possibly allude to the creation story (see Gen 1:31; the same Hebrew word translated "good" in Gen 1:31 is here translated "fine"), further depicting the unfolding events in terms of new creation—the creation of Israel as a nation. In any case, recognizing that he was "no ordinary child" (Acts 7:20; Heb 11:23), Moses' mother takes steps that would preserve not only the life of her son but also, and more important, the life of Israel.

2:3 papyrus basket. The way this container is described further indicates that God's saving purposes are at stake here. This is the only time the Hebrew noun translated "ark" in the flood story appears outside Genesis, where a much larger vessel is similarly waterproofed (Gen 6:14). Like the flood survivors, the baby is thus protected by an "ark." Ironically, however, this ark is deposited at the very river of execution (1:22). **the reeds.** Ominously foreshadow the later drowning of the Egyptians in the "Sea of Reeds" in ch. 14 (see note on 10:19).

2:5–9 It may seem ominous that Pharaoh's daughter discovers the ark, but unlike her father, she has compassion and thus ignores the royal edict. In an extraordinary turn of events, the child's older sister (presumably Miriam; see 15:20 and note) organizes a foster home. Pharaoh's daughter hires Moses' mother as Moses' wet-nurse, and Pharaoh ends up supporting one of those he condemned—the one through whom God would bring about what Pharaoh sought to prevent: the mass exodus of the Israelites from Egypt (1:10).

2:10 Moses. With a play on the boy's Egyptian name (cf. the second element, meaning "born of," in pharaonic names linked with the name of a deity such as Ah*mose*, Thut*mose*, and Ra*meses*) emphasizing his providential rescue from a watery grave, this rescued child is at last named, and thus, for an Israelite audience at least, he is hereby identified as

MOSES' LIFE

AGE	EVENT	REFERENCES
Birth	Moses is rescued by midwives	1:15–22
3 months	Moses is adopted by Pharaoh's daughter	2:1–10
40 years	Moses kills an Egyptian and flees to Midian	2:11–22; Acts 7:23–29
80	God commissions Moses; Israel is rescued from Egypt	7:7; Acts 7:30–36
120	Moses dies on Mount Nebo in Moab	Deut 34:1–8

Moses Flees to Midian

11One day, after Moses had grown up, he went out to where his own people[x] were and watched them
at their hard labor. He saw an Egyptian beating a Hebrew, one of his own people. 12Looking this way and
that and seeing no one, he killed the Egyptian and hid him in the sand. 13The next day he went out and
saw two Hebrews fighting. He asked the one in the wrong, "Why are you hitting your fellow Hebrew?"[y]
14The man said, "Who made you ruler and judge over us?[z] Are you thinking of killing me as you
killed the Egyptian?" Then Moses was afraid and thought, "What I did must have become known."
15When Pharaoh heard of this, he tried to kill Moses, but Moses fled from Pharaoh and went to live
in Midian,[a] where he sat down by a well. 16Now a priest of Midian[b] had seven daughters, and they came
to draw water[c] and fill the troughs to water their father's flock. 17Some shepherds came along and drove
them away, but Moses got up and came to their rescue and watered their flock.[d]
18When the girls returned to Reuel[e] their father, he asked them, "Why have you returned so early
today?"
19They answered, "An Egyptian rescued us from the shepherds. He even drew water for us and watered the flock."
20"And where is he?" Reuel asked his daughters. "Why did you leave him? Invite him to have something to eat."[f]
21Moses agreed to stay with the man, who gave his daughter Zipporah[g] to Moses in marriage. 22Zip-
porah gave birth to a son, and Moses named him Gershom,[a] saying, "I have become a foreigner[h] in
a foreign land."

2:11 [x]Ac 7:23; Heb 11:24-26
2:13 [y]Ac 7:26
2:14 [z]Ac 7:27*
2:15 [a]Ac 7:29; Heb 11:27
2:16 [b]Ex 3:1 [c]Ge 24:11
2:17 [d]Ge 29:10
2:18 [e]Nu 10:29
2:20 [f]Ge 31:54
2:21 [g]Ex 18:2
2:22 [h]Ex 18:3-4; Heb 11:13

[a] 22 *Gershom* sounds like the Hebrew for *a foreigner there.*

the human instrument God chose to deliver his people from captivity. Moses' deliverance from the reeds of the Nile River foreshadows an even greater deliverance from the "Sea of Reeds" (see ch. 14; see also note on 10:19) as well as the rescue of God's ultimate deliverer from death at the hands of Herod (Matt 2:13).

2:11–25 *Moses Flees to Midian.* Some 40 years elapse before this next episode takes place (Acts 7:23). According to Jewish tradition, during this time Moses received an Egyptian education (Acts 7:22; Philo and Josephus concur, adding that Moses surpassed all his peers and started to carve out a major political career). But these formative years are not important to include in Exodus, which skips over them without comment. The storyline resumes when the boy has grown up and is about to make some career-changing decisions.

2:11 went out. Moses is embarking here on his own mini-exodus, leaving the palace and exposing his personal sympathies. Moses thus takes the first tentative steps toward refusing "to be known as the son of Pharaoh's daughter [and choosing] to be mistreated along with the people of God" (Heb 11:24–25).

2:12 There are various explanations for Moses' action: (1) It was a rash, impulsive blow not intended to kill. (2) It was a deliberate, albeit reluctant, judicial act. (3) It was premeditated homicide. The text nowhere implies that Moses regretted his use of extreme force, and the proposal that he was looking around for someone else to intervene seems contrived. Fear of reprisal best explains Moses' actions, and the overall impression is that Moses did exactly as he intended (Acts 7:24–25). He "strikes" a blow for the oppressed, just as later their oppressors would "strike" them and God himself would in turn "strike" their oppressors. At this stage, however, Moses was clearly acting prematurely and without any explicit divine commission (cf. chs. 3–4).

2:14 Who made you ruler and judge over us? Ironically, this is precisely the role to which the Lord subsequently calls Moses (18:13–26; Acts 7:35). The dismissive response here foreshadows the subsequent negativity Moses experiences some 40 years later (6:9; 14:10–12; 16:2–3; 17:3–4), when the Israelites further and repeatedly challenge Moses' authority over them (Acts 7:39).

2:15 Pharaoh. Not necessarily the same pharaoh who instigated the oppression (1:8); therefore, there is no reason to insist on a reign of over 40 years for this particular pharaoh (see 2:23; 4:19; Acts 7:23). His identification again depends on which chronology is adopted for the exodus (see Introduction: The Date of the Exodus). **fled.** Moses instantly lost state protection when he became a fugitive. The NT appears to suggest that faith, not fear, motivated him (Heb 11:27), although that may allude to subsequent events at the time of the exodus (thus understood, Heb 11:28–29 expands on Heb 11:27 rather than reflecting a chronological sequence of events). **Midian.** Located in the northwestern part of the Arabian peninsula, including the southern part of the Negev (where "Midianite" ware has been found) and some of the Sinai peninsula. Midian was dry, uncultivated land, very different from the Nile delta. Significantly, the escape route chosen by Moses anticipates that of the exodus. Presumably this southeastern itinerary was chosen in order to avoid the chain of Egyptian forts along the more traveled northeastern routes and because there were no oases directly east. Although the Midianites, a nomadic people, were distant relatives of the Israelites (Gen 25:2–4), kinship was probably not a factor here (cf. Gen 27:42–45).

2:16 priest of Midian. Refers to Reuel (see note on v. 18).

2:17 came to their rescue. For the third time within a few verses (vv. 11–12,13–14), Moses demonstrates concern for the oppressed, a concern God himself shares (v. 25). This nomadic dispute over watering rights was evidently a frequent, if not daily, occurrence.

2:18 Reuel. Means "God's friend." He is a priest of Midian and later becomes Moses' father-in-law. Some infer that Reuel (also called Jethro; see note on 3:1) significantly influences Israel's subsequent faith. But Exodus suggests that Moses and his testimony of what the Lord has done for Israel influences Jethro's faith (18:9–12).

2:19 Egyptian. Moses' mistaken identity—presumably on account of his appearance and language—reflects his assimilation to Egyptian culture.

2:22 Gershom. The play on this name (see NIV text note) encapsulates Moses' resignation to refugee status. **I have become a foreigner in a foreign land.** While possibly alluding to Moses' previous status in Egypt (i.e., "I have been a foreigner in a foreign land"), it more likely describes his current status. Perhaps, however, the ambiguity is intended; whether in Egypt (see 23:9) or in Midian, Moses is an alien: his true home is the land God promised Abraham (Heb 11:26).

2:23 [i]Ac 7:30 [j]Ex 3:7,9; Dt 26:7; Jas 5:4
2:24 [k]Ex 6:5; Ps 105:10,42
2:25 [l]Ex 3:7; 4:31
3:1 [m]Ex 2:18 [n]1Ki 19:8 [o]Ex 18:5
3:2 [p]Ge 16:7 [q]Dt 33:16; Mk 12:26; Ac 7:30
3:5 [r]Ge 28:17; Jos 5:15; Ac 7:33*
3:6 [s]Ex 4:5; Mt 22:32*; Mk 12:26*; Lk 20:37*; Ac 7:32*

23During that long period,[i] the king of Egypt died. The Israelites groaned in their slavery and cried
out, and their cry[j] for help because of their slavery went up to God. 24God heard their groaning and he
remembered his covenant[k] with Abraham, with Isaac and with Jacob. 25So God looked on the Israelites
and was concerned[l] about them.

Moses and the Burning Bush

3 Now Moses was tending the flock of Jethro[m] his father-in-law, the priest of Midian, and he led the
flock to the far side of the wilderness and came to Horeb,[n] the mountain[o] of God. 2There the angel
of the LORD[p] appeared to him in flames of fire from within a bush.[q] Moses saw that though the bush
was on fire it did not burn up. 3So Moses thought, "I will go over and see this strange sight—why the
bush does not burn up."

4When the LORD saw that he had gone over to look, God called to him from within the bush, "Moses!
Moses!"

And Moses said, "Here I am."

5"Do not come any closer," God said. "Take off your sandals, for the place where you are standing is
holy ground."[r] 6Then he said, "I am the God of your father,[a] the God of Abraham, the God of Isaac and
the God of Jacob."[s] At this, Moses hid his face, because he was afraid to look at God.

[a] 6 Masoretic Text; Samaritan Pentateuch (see Acts 7:32) *fathers*

2:23–25 This transitional paragraph switches the focus back to the situation in Egypt and signals the most significant change in Israel's circumstances thus far.

2:23 long period. The story again passes over an undisclosed period of time (but see Acts 7:30) in relative silence. While Moses is making a new life for himself in Midian, oppression in Egypt continues—even after the death of the pharaoh. **cried out.** For the first time, the story mentions Israelites reacting to their enslavement.

2:24–25 God heard ... remembered ... looked ... was concerned. Finally the tension is relieved. Other than the passing reference in 1:20, this is the first explicit mention of God, who now becomes the central character in the plot. At long last God acknowledges the Israelites' distress and remembers (i.e., begins to act upon) the covenant (i.e., his sworn promises) he made with Israel's ancestors (Gen 15:18–21; 17:8; 26:2–5; 28:13–15; 35:11–12). Thus, for the reader at least, this renews hope.

3:1–22 *Moses and the Burning Bush.* According to Stephen (see Acts 7:23,30), the next incident took place when Moses was around 80 years old (cf. Exod 7:7), after having lived in Midian some 40 years. Over this period little has changed for Moses; he is still dependent on his father-in-law for his livelihood but seems quite content with his nomadic lifestyle, however alien it once was. He apparently has no intention of returning to Egypt, but this is about to change as God puts the next stage of his plan into action (see Gen 15:14).

3:1 Jethro. Unless this is some kind of title or clan name, Moses' father-in-law apparently had more than one name (other biblical examples include Abram/Abraham, Jacob/Israel, Joseph/Zaphenath-Paneah, Gideon/Jerub-Baal, Uzziah/Azariah, and Saul/Paul). **led the flock.** Here the actions of Moses again foreshadow the subsequent experience of the Israelites, whom Moses would likewise shepherd and lead to Mount Sinai. **Horeb, the mountain of God.** Horeb, meaning "desert" or "desolation," has been interpreted by some scholars either as just another name for Mount Sinai (19:11,18–23; cf. v. 12) or as a different mountain peak in close proximity. Biblical usage, however, implies that Horeb refers to a wide area, whereas Sinai refers to both a specific mountain and a specific region within Horeb. It becomes known as "the mountain of God" because God manifests his presence there—first to Moses (chs. 3–4) and subsequently to Israel (chs. 19–40). There is no suggestion that God actually dwells on this mountain (see note on 15:13). The precise location of this mountain is unknown. Its traditional site (Jebel Musa) is in the central southern region of the Sinai peninsula, but more northerly sites (Jebel Serbal and Jebel Sin Bishar) and even a mountain in northwest Saudi Arabia have also been suggested (see map, p. 147).

3:2 angel of the LORD. As elsewhere in the OT (e.g., Gen 22:11–18; Judg 13), this character is closely identified with God himself, reflected here in the interchangeable use of "the LORD" (vv. 4,7) and "God" (vv. 4,5,6) that immediately follows. His manifestation in flames of fire forms a strong link with the sign of God's presence elsewhere in the book: the pillar of fire and cloud (13:21–22; 14:24), the fire and cloud on Mount Sinai (19:18; 24:15–17), and the fire in the cloud over the tabernacle (40:38). At the Red Sea this angel protects the fleeing Israelites from the pursuing Egyptians (14:19), and presumably it is this same angel that God promises to send ahead of the Israelites into Canaan (23:20–23; 33:2).

3:3 strange sight. As in most biblical theophanies (divine appearances), flames of fire were a medium of such revelation—on this occasion appearing "within a bush" (v. 2). Attempts to explain the phenomenon naturalistically, however ingenious, strangely miss the point: this sight is so unusual that it catches this seasoned shepherd's attention and draws him closer to investigate.

3:4 God called. Significantly, it is "the LORD" who sees and calls to Moses "from within the bush." This could imply that the angel in v. 2 refers simply to the divine manifestation as flames of fire. In any case, from this point onward it is God who converses with Moses.

3:5 Do not come any closer. As was later true for the Israelites (ch. 19), Moses must maintain a safe distance and take appropriate action before approaching a holy God. **Take off your sandals.** The same instructions are later given to Joshua, Moses' successor, when he has a similar heavenly encounter (Josh 5:15). As the explanation offered in both texts implies, the removal of footwear was probably to avoid contaminating holy space; significantly, priests may have served barefoot, as the absence of prescribed footwear (28:1–43) strongly implies. **holy ground.** Not intrinsically sacred but "separated" or "set apart" from other ground because of God's presence. As elsewhere in Exodus, it is the Lord who makes or declares places and people to be holy, and such a status derives from their association with him, the holy God.

3:6 father. The singular (not "fathers") is unusual (see also 15:2). Perhaps it refers to Moses' biological father. In any case, explicitly mentioning Abraham, Isaac, and Jacob makes it clear that the God of his ancestors is addressing him, and Moses knows that standing in his presence is fraught with danger (cf. Gen 32:30). See note on 33:20.

[7]The LORD said, "I have indeed seen the misery of my people in Egypt. I have heard them crying
out because of their slave drivers, and I am concerned[t] about their suffering. [8]So I have come down[u]
to rescue them from the hand of the Egyptians and to bring them up out of that land into a good and
spacious land, a land flowing with milk and honey[v]—the home of the Canaanites, Hittites, Amorites,
Perizzites, Hivites and Jebusites.[w] [9]And now the cry of the Israelites has reached me, and I have seen
the way the Egyptians are oppressing[x] them. [10]So now, go. I am sending you to Pharaoh to bring my
people the Israelites out of Egypt."[y]
[11]But Moses said to God, "Who am I[z] that I should go to Pharaoh and bring the Israelites out of
Egypt?"
[12]And God said, "I will be with you.[a] And this will be the sign to you that it is I who have sent you:
When you have brought the people out of Egypt, you[a] will worship God on this mountain."
[13]Moses said to God, "Suppose I go to the Israelites and say to them, 'The God of your fathers has
sent me to you,' and they ask me, 'What is his name?' Then what shall I tell them?"
[14]God said to Moses, "I AM WHO I AM.[b] This is what you are to say to the Israelites: 'I AM[b] has sent me
to you.'"
[15]God also said to Moses, "Say to the Israelites, 'The LORD,[c] the God of your fathers—the God of
Abraham, the God of Isaac and the God of Jacob—has sent me to you.'

"This is my name[c] forever,
the name you shall call me
from generation to generation.

3:7 [t]Ex 2:25
3:8 [u]Ge 50:24 [v]ver 17; Ex 13:5; Dt 1:25 [w]Ge 15:18-21
3:9 [x]Ex 1:14; 2:23
3:10 [y]Mic 6:4
3:11 [z]Ex 6:12,30; 1Sa 18:18
3:12 [a]Ge 31:3; Jos 1:5; Ro 8:31
3:14 [b]Ex 6:2-3; Jn 8:58; Heb 13:8
3:15 [c]Ps 135:13; Hos 12:5

[a] *12* The Hebrew is plural. [b] *14* Or *I WILL BE WHAT I WILL BE* [c] *15* The Hebrew for *LORD* sounds like and may be related to the Hebrew for *I AM* in verse 14.

3:7–8 God makes his intentions clear, fleshing out what it means that God "remembered his covenant" (2:24): his plan involves emancipating his people from Egyptian oppression (see Gen 15:14) and sending them to the promised land (Gen 15:16).
3:8 God describes the promised land in terms of a herder's dream and delineates its parameters with a representative list of its indigenous inhabitants (Gen 13:7; 15:19–21; Num 13:29; Deut 7:1). **milk and honey.** This is the first occurrence of this phrase, covering both horticultural and pastoral activity, for the fertility of Canaan. **milk.** Refers to goat's milk as well as that of cattle. **honey.** Could be sweet syrup from grapes, dates, and figs, as well as honey from bees.
3:10 Pharaoh. Either Thutmose III (1479–1425) or Rameses II (1279–1213), depending on the precise historical setting (see Introduction: The Date of the Exodus).
3:11 Who am I . . . ? Moses is incredulous of God's commission, especially since Moses is focusing on himself and not factoring in the most important detail: God will help him (see v. 12 and note).
3:12 I will be with you. Foreshadows the divine name in vv. 14–15, so the outcome will succeed (the rescued people "will worship God on this mountain"). **sign.** This "sign" may seem a strange means of reassurance, but it is best thought of as a fulfillment sign designed to bolster faith both in the present and future. Its anticipatory nature, however, readily explains why on this occasion it fails to eradicate Moses' doubts and fears. **worship.** The Hebrew word can also be translated "serve," and is used for both the "labor/work" imposed by Pharaoh (1:13–14; 5:18) and the "service/worship" of the Lord (7:16; 8:1,20; 9:1,13; 10:3). Its use highlights that both Pharaoh and the Lord were vying for sovereignty over Israel, making a face-off inevitable.
3:13 What is his name? The context suggests that much more is at stake here than merely knowing God's name, even if that name had possibly fallen into disuse during Israel's slavery in Egypt. After all, mere acquaintance with God's name would not prove that a theophany occurred (less incredible explanations are conceivable), still less that God sent Moses on this errand. Even more problematic is the idea that God had not disclosed his name to anyone before now (see notes on 6:2–8). Apart from difficulties in accounting for all the occurrences of "the LORD" (Hebrew *YHWH*) in Genesis (e.g., Gen. 4:26; 9:26; 12:8; 22:14; 26:25; 28:16; 30:27), this fails to explain how Moses could validate his prophetic credentials by presenting himself in the name of a deity hitherto unknown. But what, then, are we to make of Moses' question? The answer may possibly be found in the interrogative used: Rather than the idiomatic "Who . . . ?" (cf. Judg 13:17), Moses asks, "What . . . ?" He is probably inquiring about God's character, not merely his name or title (cf. Neh 9:10; see note on 3:14). This is further suggested by the fact that in ancient cultures, names conveyed essential information and were more than simply a means of identification. Thus understood, whether Moses and his fellow Israelites were familiar with God's name or not, what both are asking for is further information about this God who has appeared to Moses.
3:14 Rather than simply answering, "My name is the LORD" (as would suffice if Moses asked for only a name), God explains his name to some extent. **I AM WHO I AM.** This is how most English versions render it; alternatively, "I WILL BE WHAT I WILL BE" (see NIV text note). God's response is somewhat cryptic and has been interpreted in a variety of ways: (1) God is a self-existent and independent being. (2) God is the creator and sustainer of everything. (3) God is unchangeable and so always reliable. (4) God is eternal in his existence. While such observations about God are certainly true, the immediate context suggests that God's explanation of his name primarily serves to bolster Israel's confidence in the message that Moses will deliver. Accordingly, the rest of God's answer (vv. 16–22) is a statement of his faithfulness in the past and a revelation of what he will do in the future. The Lord's "name" therefore invites God's people to trust him fully in anticipation of the fuller revelation of God that Moses and Israel are about to experience through the things they will see the Lord do. **I AM.** The divine name is now shortened to just one Hebrew word, the verbal form previously used in v. 12 ("*I will be* with you"). This is then replaced in v. 15 (see note there) with the more familiar form of the divine name, Yahweh, used throughout the OT.
3:15 The LORD. See NIV text note. Like most English versions, the NIV follows the practice of translating the Hebrew word (*yhwh*) here as "the LORD" (using "small caps" to distinguish it from another Hebrew word often translated "Lord"). The practice of translating *yhwh* as "LORD"

3:16 [d]Ex 4:29
3:17 [e]Ge 15:16; Jos 24:11
3:18 [f]Ex 4:1,8,31 [g]Ex 5:1,3
3:19 [h]Ex 4:21; 5:2
3:20 [i]Ex 6:1,6; 9:15 [j]Dt 6:22; Ne 9:10; Ac 7:36 [k]Ex 12:31-33
3:21 [l]Ex 12:36 [m]Ps 105:37
3:22 [n]Ex 11:2 [o]Eze 39:10
4:1 [p]Ex 3:18; 6:30
4:2 [q]ver 17,20
4:5 [r]Ex 19:9
4:6 [s]Nu 12:10; 2Ki 5:1,27
4:7 [t]Nu 12:13-15; Dt 32:39; 2Ki 5:14; Mt 8:3

16"Go, assemble the elders[d] of Israel and say to them, 'The LORD, the God of your fathers — the God
of Abraham, Isaac and Jacob — appeared to me and said: I have watched over you and have seen what
has been done to you in Egypt. 17And I have promised to bring you up out of your misery in Egypt[e]
into the land of the Canaanites, Hittites, Amorites, Perizzites, Hivites and Jebusites — a land flowing
with milk and honey.'
18"The elders of Israel will listen[f] to you. Then you and the elders are to go to the king of Egypt and
say to him, 'The LORD, the God of the Hebrews, has met with us. Let us take a three-day journey into the
wilderness to offer sacrifices[g] to the LORD our God.' 19But I know that the king of Egypt will not let you
go unless a mighty hand[h] compels him. 20So I will stretch out my hand[i] and strike the Egyptians with
all the wonders[j] that I will perform among them. After that, he will let you go.[k]
21"And I will make the Egyptians favorably disposed[l] toward this people, so that when you leave you
will not go empty-handed.[m] 22Every woman is to ask her neighbor and any woman living in her house
for articles of silver and gold[n] and for clothing, which you will put on your sons and daughters. And so
you will plunder[o] the Egyptians."

Signs for Moses

4 Moses answered, "What if they do not believe me or listen[p] to me and say, 'The LORD did not appear to you'?"
2Then the LORD said to him, "What is that in your hand?"
"A staff,"[q] he replied.
3The LORD said, "Throw it on the ground."
Moses threw it on the ground and it became a snake, and he ran from it. 4Then the LORD said to him,
"Reach out your hand and take it by the tail." So Moses reached out and took hold of the snake and it
turned back into a staff in his hand. 5"This," said the LORD, "is so that they may believe[r] that the LORD, the
God of their fathers — the God of Abraham, the God of Isaac and the God of Jacob — has appeared to you."
6Then the LORD said, "Put your hand inside your cloak." So Moses put his hand into his cloak, and
when he took it out, the skin was leprous[a] — it had become as white as snow.[s]
7"Now put it back into your cloak," he said. So Moses put his hand back into his cloak, and when he
took it out, it was restored,[t] like the rest of his flesh.

[a] 6 The Hebrew word for *leprous* was used for various diseases affecting the skin.

derives from the earliest pre-Christian Greek translation of the OT (the Septuagint) in the third century BC. This significantly influenced the NT, not only in its use of *kyrios* ("Lord") in OT quotations but also in the use of this term for Jesus, thus identifying him with the God of the OT. The divine name is also alluded to in the "I am" sayings of Jesus, correctly interpreted by the Jews as a claim to deity (see notes on John 8:58,59). **sent.** The Lord emphasizes that he, their ancestral deity, has sent Moses (see also v. 14).

3:16–22 God further unpacks his character and his saving intent that is forever bound up in his name as he reiterates and amplifies Moses' commission. Through Moses, Israel will actually discover much more about the Lord: he has actually "appeared" (v. 16) as such to Moses (cf. 4:1; 6:2–3), and he not only speaks but saves.

3:16 elders. Recognized leaders in many societies of the ancient world (cf. Gen 50:7 ["dignitaries"]; Num 22:7). They earned respect by their life experience and maturity as well as their position as heads of their tribe, clan, or household.

3:18 the God of the Hebrews. Such a depiction, however ridiculous it would seem to the mighty king of Egypt who had enslaved this people, associates the Lord with the weak and oppressed — those who are utterly dependent on him for deliverance. This is an important idea throughout the Bible. **three-day journey.** This may seem disingenuous in view of their ultimate destination (vv. 8,17). Perhaps this was a conventional expression for a short journey, possibly with Egyptian sensitivities in view (8:26), or it may have been a bartering technique, making a fairly small request to determine how much (or little) Pharaoh would concede. **to offer sacrifices to … our God.** Here and throughout the following account (7:16; 8:1,20; 9:1,13; 10:3), Israel's freedom from Egypt has a theological objective: the worship and service of God, their true king, whose relationship with them supersedes all other claims, including Pharaoh's.

3:19 unless a mighty hand compels him. Mere words will not compel Pharaoh, so God will deliver Israel by striking the Egyptians (cf. 2:12) and performing wonders (see v. 20 and note).

3:20 wonders. The subsequent disasters, or "plagues."

3:22 plunder. This alludes to the goods that victors take in battle. As well as being emancipated, the Israelite slaves will be enabled by God to receive some measure of compensation for their service (cf. 1:13).

4:1–17 *Signs for Moses.* Moses continues to focus on how the Israelites *might* respond to his extraordinary claims, prompting God to validate his testimony with the help of some supernatural phenomena.

4:2–5 The first of these "signs" (vv. 8–9) involves Moses' staff (see note on v. 2). Transforming this staff into a snake demonstrates that the Lord is sovereign over a creature that Egypt reveres and even uses as a symbol of Pharaoh's authority. And along with the following two signs (vv. 6–9), it subtly reminds others that the Lord not only has the power to transform but also has authority over life and death.

4:2 staff. A normal shepherd's crook that becomes "the staff of God" (v. 20) in the sense that God uses this instrument to bolster the Israelites' faith and demonstrate his power to the Egyptians in the subsequent account of the plagues and the exodus.

[8]Then the LORD said, "If they do not believe you or pay attention to the first sign, they may believe
the second. [9]But if they do not believe these two signs or listen to you, take some water from the Nile
and pour it on the dry ground. The water you take from the river will become blood[u] on the ground."
[10]Moses said to the LORD, "Pardon your servant, Lord. I have never been eloquent, neither in the past
nor since you have spoken to your servant. I am slow of speech and tongue."[v]
[11]The LORD said to him, "Who gave human beings their mouths? Who makes them deaf or mute?
Who gives them sight or makes them blind?[w] Is it not I, the LORD? [12]Now go; I will help you speak and
will teach you what to say."[x]
[13]But Moses said, "Pardon your servant, Lord. Please send someone else."
[14]Then the LORD's anger burned against Moses and he said, "What about your brother, Aaron the
Levite? I know he can speak well. He is already on his way to meet[y] you, and he will be glad to see you.
[15]You shall speak to him and put words in his mouth;[z] I will help both of you speak and will teach
you what to do. [16]He will speak to the people for you, and it will be as if he were your mouth[a] and as
if you were God to him. [17]But take this staff[b] in your hand so you can perform the signs[c] with it."

4:9 [u]Ex 7:17-21
4:10 [v]Ex 6:12; Jer 1:6
4:11 [w]Ps 94:9; Mt 11:5
4:12 [x]Isa 50:4; Jer 1:9; Mt 10:19-20; Mk 13:11; Lk 12:12; 21:14-15
4:14 [y]ver 27
4:15 [z]Nu 23:5,12,16
4:16 [a]Ex 7:1-2
4:17 [b]ver 2 [c]Ex 7:9-21
4:19 [d]Ex 2:15 [e]Ex 2:23
4:20 [f]Ex 17:9; Nu 20:8-9,11

Moses Returns to Egypt

[18]Then Moses went back to Jethro his father-in-law and said to him, "Let me return to my own people
in Egypt to see if any of them are still alive."
Jethro said, "Go, and I wish you well."
[19]Now the LORD had said to Moses in Midian, "Go back to Egypt, for all those who wanted to kill[d] you
are dead.[e]" [20]So Moses took his wife and sons, put them on a donkey and started back to Egypt. And he
took the staff[f] of God in his hand.
[21]The LORD said to Moses, "When you return to Egypt, see that you perform before Pharaoh all the

4:9 water ... will become blood. Possibly a graphic description of the water's extreme discoloration as clean water was poured out upon the ground (i.e., the water turned blood-red in color); the Hebrew word is sometimes used to describe something that simply looked like blood (cf. Gen 49:11; Deut 32:14; 2 Kgs 3:22; Joel 2:31). In any case, only something extraordinary could possibly have the desired persuasive effect on the target audience. This third phenomenon is later used against Pharaoh, albeit on a much larger scale (7:14–24).
4:10 slow of speech and tongue. Moses again appears to shift his focus from the Lord and the Israelites to himself and his personal inadequacies (v. 1; 3:11,13)—this time his inability to communicate. According to Stephen, before leaving Egypt Moses had been "powerful in speech and action" (Acts 7:22), which makes it unlikely that "slow of speech and tongue" refers to a speech impediment (cf. 6:12,30). Rather, Moses considers his communication skills inadequate because of a perceived lack of eloquence or quick-wittedness (see Paul's description of himself in 2 Cor 10:10); he thus perceives that he is not equipped for the task. But whatever the exact problem, Moses is essentially repeating his earlier mistake—focusing on his own abilities rather than the Lord's.
4:11–12 The rhetorical questions redirect Moses' gaze to the one who gives human beings their faculties and who is thus able to use whatever faculties are at his disposal.
4:13 send someone else. Excuses exhausted, Moses finally exposes his underlying reason for objecting: he simply does not want to go.
4:14–17 While Moses clearly wants a replacement, the Lord has already dispatched Moses' older brother (7:7), Aaron the Levite, to assist Moses (v. 27). Aaron's designation ("the Levite") probably anticipates the later significance of both him and his tribe in Israel's worship (28:1; 32:28–29). In the immediate future, however, Aaron will serve as Moses' mouthpiece, or "prophet" (7:1), and Moses will be like God to Aaron (see v. 16 and note). Moses and Aaron will communicate God's message together, but God will do the actual work of persuasion (v. 17).
4:14 the LORD's anger burned. Human disobedience—especially by God's chosen people (cf. 32:10)—is serious. Though God is "slow to anger" (34:6), disobedience inevitably evokes his wrath, as the Israelites later discover.
4:16 as if you were God to him. Moses will communicate God's thoughts and will.
4:18–31 *Moses Returns to Egypt.* While the issue of communication skills later resurfaces after Moses initially fails to persuade Pharaoh (6:12,30), Moses is finally ready to comply with the Lord's instructions and return to Egypt.
4:18 Let me return. Moses secures an amicable parting by observing typical etiquette (cf. Gen 31:26–28). **my own people.** Moses may seem somewhat vague about the goal of his mission (cf. 3:7–10,16–22), but his words probably allude to his failed attempt to rescue the Israelites, which also began with him going to see "his own people" (2:11). Moses intends to finish the task he previously initiated.
4:19 had said. The past perfect translation is certainly possible, in which case this is a literary flashback. However, since the explanation offered to Moses at this point is new, God may be further nudging Moses along lest he procrastinate. **are dead.** As well as suggesting that it is now safe for Moses to return since all his enemies are dead, God's point may be that he has already begun the process of deliverance.
4:20 sons. Although the text has mentioned only one son (2:22) and the enigmatic incident that follows mentions only one son (vv. 24–26), Moses and Zipporah have two sons (18:2–4). Moses sends them back with Zipporah to Jethro at some stage between his "near-death experience" (vv. 24–26) and the family reunion in ch.18. **staff of God.** As instructed (v. 17), Moses takes with him what becomes the symbol of his divine authority. This staff was used to unleash God's power, first before the Israelites (v. 30; cf. vv. 1–9) and then against the Egyptians—during which Aaron apparently retained possession of it (7:8–12,19; 8:5,16; cf. 7:17; 9:23; 10:13; 14:16). But whether it is associated with Moses or Aaron, it is probably this one staff that is referred to throughout.
4:21 wonders. The extraordinary phenomena that will culminate in the death of Egypt's firstborn (3:20; 7:8—11:10). There is evidently some overlap with the sign-acts that Moses performs before the Israelites

HARDENED HEART

SUBJECT AND MEANING OF "HARDEN"/"HARDENED"	PREDICTION	ACTION	SITUATION
The Lord makes Pharaoh's heart:			
firm/strong	4:21; 14:4	9:12; 10:20,27; 11:10; 14:8 (cf. 14:17)	
heavy		10:1	
difficult	7:3		
Pharaoh makes his heart:			
firm/strong		13:15 (heart implied)	
heavy		8:15,32; 9:34	
Pharaoh's heart is:			
firm/strong			7:13,22; 8:19; 9:35
heavy/unyielding			7:14; 9:7

4:21 [g] Ex 3:19,20 [h] Ex 7:3,13; 9:12,35; 14:4,8; Dt 2:30; Isa 63:17; Jn 12:40; Ro 9:18
4:22 [i] Isa 63:16; 64:8; Jer 31:9; Hos 11:1; Ro 9:4
4:23 [j] Ex 5:1; 7:16 [k] Ex 11:5; 12:12,29
4:24 [l] Nu 22:22
4:25 [m] Ge 17:14; Jos 5:2,3
4:27 [n] Ex 3:1 [o] ver 14
4:28 [p] ver 8-9,16
4:29 [q] Ex 3:16

wonders[g] I have given you the power to do. But I will harden his heart[h] so that he will not let the people
go. 22 Then say to Pharaoh, 'This is what the LORD says: Israel is my firstborn son,[i] 23 and I told you, "Let
my son go,[j] so he may worship me." But you refused to let him go; so I will kill your firstborn son.' "[k]
24 At a lodging place on the way, the LORD met Moses[a] and was about to kill[l] him. 25 But Zipporah took
a flint knife, cut off her son's foreskin[m] and touched Moses' feet with it.[b] "Surely you are a bridegroom
of blood to me," she said. 26 So the LORD let him alone. (At that time she said "bridegroom of blood,"
referring to circumcision.)
27 The LORD said to Aaron, "Go into the wilderness to meet Moses." So he met Moses at the mountain[n]
of God and kissed[o] him. 28 Then Moses told Aaron everything the LORD had sent him to say,[p] and also
about all the signs he had commanded him to perform.
29 Moses and Aaron brought together all the elders[q] of the Israelites, 30 and Aaron told them every-

[a] 24 Hebrew *him* [b] 25 The meaning of the Hebrew for this clause is uncertain.

(see note on 7:3). **I will harden his heart.** The first mention of a recurring theme in chs. 4–14, for which three different Hebrew verbs are used, with different subjects and in a variety of ways, as reflected in "Hardened Heart," this page.

These data are possibly best explained in terms of a disposition of Pharaoh's that became his undoing when God stiffened Pharaoh's resolve (from 9:12) not to let Israel go. And so an inflexible, insensitive, and unresponsive king became even more resistant to the Lord's will while at the same time ensuring that God's purpose for Pharaoh (9:16) would indeed be realized. But however we resolve the problem of Pharaoh's heart, two important points must be remembered: (1) The main concern in this section of the book is to demonstrate that the Lord, not Pharaoh, is ultimately in control, as indicated by the recurring phrase "as the LORD had said" (7:13; 8:15,19; 9:12,35). (2) God's sovereign control of these affairs does not absolve Pharaoh of blame because, like all sinners, he remains fully responsible for his refusal to obey God (Rom 9:16–18).

4:22–23 firstborn son. This speech appears to rehearse what God (through Moses) will declare to Pharaoh *at the climax* of the conflict (ch. 11), just prior to the final blow in the series: the death of Egypt's firstborn to punish them for refusing to release Israel, figuratively described as the Lord's "firstborn son." This draws attention to Israel's special relationship with God (Jer 31:9; Hos 11:1), which was formalized through the covenant made with Abraham (Gen 15:12–21). Since this relationship obviously predates Israel's time in Egypt, God's claims over Israel supersede any claims Egypt could possibly have had to Israel's service. As God's "firstborn son," Israel, and their Davidic king in particular (Pss 2:7; 89:26–28), foreshadows God's unique Son (Matt 2:14–15; Rom 1:3), in whom God's plans for Israel are perfectly realized.

4:24–26 This incident is enigmatic. The Lord seeks to kill Moses (cf. v. 19) and/or his son (see note on v. 24), apparently because Moses neglected the covenant sign of circumcision (Gen 17:1–14). Zipporah's decisive action averts tragedy.

4:24 lodging place. Most likely a nomadic campsite near an oasis. **him.** Seems to refer to Moses; the original text is ambiguous. It could also refer to Gershom (Moses' firstborn).

4:25–26 Zipporah resolves the problem by circumcising Gershom and atoning for Moses' negligence.

4:25 feet. May be a euphemism for genitalia. **bridegroom of blood.** Understood by some as a derogatory statement expressing Zipporah's revulsion over the rite of circumcision, but the precise connotation is uncertain. This incident highlights the importance of circumcision for being counted among Israel, God's firstborn son, and thus escaping the judgment that Egypt's firstborn will later experience (v. 23). Circumcision becomes a symbol of the inward spiritual change that generates true faith and obedience (Deut 30:6; Rom 2:28–29; Col 2:11).

4:27 This could possibly be a flashback (see v. 14). The reunion takes place at Horeb/Sinai (3:1), evidently located in the wilderness between Midian and Egypt (i.e., somewhere in the Sinai peninsula; see note on 3:1; see also map, p. 113).

4:29–31 As Moses anticipated, the Israelites need convincing, but belief and grateful adoration quickly displace their initial incredulity.

thing the LORD had said to Moses. He also performed the signs before the people, 31 and they believed.[r]
And when they heard that the LORD was concerned[s] about them and had seen their misery, they bowed
down and worshiped.

Bricks Without Straw

5 Afterward Moses and Aaron went to Pharaoh and said, "This is what the LORD, the God of Israel,
says: 'Let my people go, so that they may hold a festival[t] to me in the wilderness.'"
2 Pharaoh said, "Who is the LORD,[u] that I should obey him and let Israel go? I do not know the LORD
and I will not let Israel go."[v]
3 Then they said, "The God of the Hebrews has met with us. Now let us take a three-day journey into
the wilderness to offer sacrifices to the LORD our God, or he may strike us with plagues[w] or with the
sword."
4 But the king of Egypt said, "Moses and Aaron, why are you taking the people away from their labor?[x]
Get back to your work!" 5 Then Pharaoh said, "Look, the people of the land are now numerous,[y] and
you are stopping them from working."
6 That same day Pharaoh gave this order to the slave drivers and overseers in charge of the people:
7 "You are no longer to supply the people with straw for making bricks; let them go and gather their own
straw. 8 But require them to make the same number of bricks as before; don't reduce the quota. They
are lazy; that is why they are crying out, 'Let us go and sacrifice to our God.' 9 Make the work harder for
the people so that they keep working and pay no attention to lies."
10 Then the slave drivers and the overseers went out and said to the people, "This is what Pharaoh
says: 'I will not give you any more straw. 11 Go and get your own straw wherever you can find it, but
your work will not be reduced at all.'" 12 So the people scattered all over Egypt to gather stubble to use
for straw. 13 The slave drivers kept pressing them, saying, "Complete the work required of you for each
day, just as when you had straw." 14 And Pharaoh's slave drivers beat the Israelite overseers they had
appointed,[z] demanding, "Why haven't you met your quota of bricks yesterday or today, as before?"
15 Then the Israelite overseers went and appealed to Pharaoh: "Why have you treated your servants
this way? 16 Your servants are given no straw, yet we are told, 'Make bricks!' Your servants are being
beaten, but the fault is with your own people."
17 Pharaoh said, "Lazy, that's what you are—lazy![a] That is why you keep saying, 'Let us go and
sacrifice to the LORD.' 18 Now get to work. You will not be given any straw, yet you must produce your
full quota of bricks."
19 The Israelite overseers realized they were in trouble when they were told, "You are not to reduce

4:31 [r] ver 8; Ex 3:18 [s] Ex 2:25
5:1 [t] Ex 3:18
5:2 [u] 2Ki 18:35; Job 21:15 [v] Ex 3:19
5:3 [w] Ex 3:18
5:4 [x] Ex 1:11
5:5 [y] Ex 1:7,9
5:14 [z] Isa 10:24
5:17 [a] ver 8

5:1—11:10 *Pharaoh's Hardness of Heart and the Lord's Mighty Acts.* In this passage a prolonged conflict takes place between the Lord and Pharaoh. Pharaoh sees no reason why he should concede to any of the Lord's demands, but he and his officials are gradually persuaded by a series of disasters that culminate in the death of Egyptian firstborn.

5:1–21 *Bricks Without Straw.* The stage is now set for the initial confrontation between the Lord and Pharaoh. The positive responses concluding ch. 4 sharply contrast with Pharaoh's negative response.

5:1 Pharaoh. See note on 3:10.

5:2 Who is the LORD ...? Pharaoh's confessed ignorance of the Lord becomes a major theme in the ensuing narrative: the Lord makes himself known (the possible consequences of disobedience in v. 3 allude to this). Pharaoh clearly misses this implicit warning.

5:3 See note on 3:18.

5:4–5 For Pharaoh, all this talk of the Lord and his demands is simply impeding the royal construction project.

5:6–9 Intensifying their workload was probably a clever ploy to drive a wedge between the Israelites and Moses (vv. 19–21). In any case, by misconstruing their "crying out" (v. 8; cf. 2:23; 3:7) as a symptom of laziness and by dismissing their truthful claims as mere "lies" (v. 9), Pharaoh diabolically dismisses Moses' claims and Israel's hopes as false, and he sets himself in direct conflict with the God who has claimed this people as his own.

5:6 slave drivers. Such officials were previously described as "slave masters" (1:11). **overseers.** These appear to be Israelite supervisors appointed by the Egyptian slave drivers (see v. 14). Possibly, however, the "overseers" mentioned here and in v. 10 are Egyptian and therefore distinguished from the "Israelite overseers" referred to in vv. 14–16. This would explain why the latter requested information from Pharaoh (vv. 15–16) that he had already disclosed to those officially charged with carrying out his edict (vv. 6–9).

5:7 straw. A binding agent to reinforce clay bricks.

5:10 This is what Pharaoh says. This prophetic announcement formula deliberately echoes v. 1 (see also 4:22), further highlighting the competing claims of sovereignty underlying this struggle.

5:15 appealed. Or "cried out." Once again Israel's "cries" (see v. 8) come to Pharaoh, who, unlike God (2:23–25), is unmoved by their suffering.

5:18 get to work. The Hebrew could be translated "Go! Serve!" Pharaoh will repeat these exact words later, but in a different tone and with a different focal point (10:8,24; 12:31).

5:19–21 The Israelites (including Moses, v. 23) did not anticipate such a hostile Egyptian reaction. So in one sense, the way the overseers respond is understandable, however misguided: Moses' actions may have led to even more intense suffering, but Pharaoh and the Egyptians are responsible for it.

5:21 [b]Ge 34:30 [c]Ex 14:11
5:22 [d]Nu 11:11
5:23 [e]Jer 4:10
6:1 [f]Ex 3:19 [g]Ex 3:20 [h]Ex 12:31,33,39
6:3 [i]Ge 17:1 [j]Ps 68:4; 83:18; Isa 52:6 [k]Ex 3:14
6:4 [l]Ge 15:18 [m]Ge 28:4,13
6:5 [n]Ex 2:23
6:6 [o]Dt 7:8; 1Ch 17:21 [p]Dt 26:8
6:7 [q]Dt 4:20; 2Sa 7:24 [r]Ex 16:12; Isa 41:20

the number of bricks required of you for each day." [20]When they left Pharaoh, they found Moses and
Aaron waiting to meet them, [21]and they said, "May the LORD look on you and judge you! You have made
us obnoxious[b] to Pharaoh and his officials and have put a sword in their hand to kill us."[c]

God Promises Deliverance

[22]Moses returned to the LORD and said, "Why, Lord, why have you brought trouble on this people?[d]
Is this why you sent me? [23]Ever since I went to Pharaoh to speak in your name, he has brought trouble
on this people, and you have not rescued[e] your people at all."

6 Then the LORD said to Moses, "Now you will see what I will do to Pharaoh: Because of my mighty
hand[f] he will let them go;[g] because of my mighty hand he will drive them out of his country."[h]
[2]God also said to Moses, "I am the LORD. [3]I appeared to Abraham, to Isaac and to Jacob as God Almighty,[a][i] but by my name[j] the LORD[b][k] I did not make myself fully known to them. [4]I also established my
covenant[l] with them to give them the land of Canaan, where they resided as foreigners.[m] [5]Moreover, I
have heard the groaning[n] of the Israelites, whom the Egyptians are enslaving, and I have remembered
my covenant.
[6]"Therefore, say to the Israelites: 'I am the LORD, and I will bring you out from under the yoke of the
Egyptians. I will free you from being slaves to them, and I will redeem[o] you with an outstretched arm[p]
and with mighty acts of judgment. [7]I will take you as my own people, and I will be your God.[q] Then you
will know[r] that I am the LORD your God, who brought you out from under the yoke of the Egyptians.

[a] 3 Hebrew *El-Shaddai*   [b] 3 See note at 3:15.

5:22—6:12 *God Promises Deliverance.* In view of what God had already disclosed to Moses (3:19–20; 4:21), we might expect Moses' response to be quite different from the negativity of the disillusioned Israelites. Instead, Moses appears simply to follow suit: as the Israelite overseers blame Moses and Aaron (v. 21), so Moses now blames the Lord. Further divine reassurance is thus necessary.

5:22 returned to the LORD. Presumably Moses does not return to Mount Sinai but simply goes somewhere private where he can commune with God (cf. the tent of meeting, 33:7–11).

5:23 Moses never imagined that Israel's circumstances in Egypt might actually deteriorate.

6:1 my mighty hand ... my mighty hand. The Lord will deliver Israel not by mere words (4:20–21). Israel could be sure that Pharaoh would eventually capitulate to the Lord's demands.

6:2–8 To drive home the point of v. 1, the Lord reminds Moses and the Israelites of his covenant commitment to their ancestors. The deity with whom they are dealing, who is assuring them that he will deliver them from Egypt, is none other than "the LORD," the one who revealed himself to Israel's ancestors and made a sworn agreement (covenant) to give them the land of Canaan. The time has come for the Lord to fulfill these covenant promises, and thus Moses must assure the Israelites that emancipation from Egyptian bondage is imminent, the Lord is about to formalize his special relationship with them, and he is about to fulfill his territorial promise.

6:3 The interpretation of this verse is controversial: Did God make himself known to Israel's ancestors as "the LORD" (Yahweh) or simply as "God Almighty" (El-Shaddai)? As illustrated by "The Contribution of Exodus 6:3 to the Revelation of God's Name," this page, four significantly different approaches to this issue have been proposed.

The traditional solution is the least complicated, and makes perfectly good sense within the immediate and wider context. Thus understood, in keeping with 3:14, v. 3 is referring not to the revelation of a new name but rather to the way in which God discloses the meaning/significance of his name much more fully in the events of Exodus.

6:6–8 I am the LORD ... I am the LORD. Brackets the anticipated fulfillment of these covenant promises. Israel will appreciate much more about the Lord through what he is about to do for them ("bring ... free ... redeem ... take ... give") and to Egypt ("mighty acts of judgment").

6:6 redeem. This verb links to the concept of guardian-redeemer—implying that a relative seeks justice. See note on 15:13.

6:7 I will take you as my own people, and I will be your God. This

THE CONTRIBUTION OF EXODUS 6:3 TO THE REVELATION OF GOD'S NAME

A. YAHWEH = A NEW NAME REVEALED FIRST TO MOSES	B. YAHWEH = A KNOWN NAME GIVEN NEW MEANING/ SIGNIFICANCE
Source critical solution:	**Traditional solution:**
Yahweh is a new name in the "Elohist" (Exod 3:13–15) and "Priestly" sources (Exod 6:3) but not in the "Yahwist" material (the source behind Genesis occurrences, such as Gen 4:26). See Introduction to the Pentateuch: Author; Modern Critical Scholarship.	Yahweh's name was known, but in Exodus it is being/about to be given previously unknown meaning and significance.
Non-traditional solution:	**Grammatical solution:**
Yahweh is a new name disclosed to Moses. Genesis occurrences are theologically motivated: to highlight that the God of the patriarchs was either similar to or even identical with the God of Moses/Israel.	Exod 6:3 was originally a strong assertion ("not" should be read as "indeed," a quite similar word in Hebrew) or a rhetorical question ("but by my name was I not known to them?").

[8]And I will bring you to the land[s] I swore with uplifted hand[t] to give to Abraham, to Isaac and to Jacob.[u]
I will give it to you as a possession. I am the LORD.' "
[9]Moses reported this to the Israelites, but they did not listen to him because of their discouragement
and harsh labor.
[10]Then the LORD said to Moses, [11]"Go, tell Pharaoh king of Egypt to let the Israelites go out of his
country."
[12]But Moses said to the LORD, "If the Israelites will not listen to me, why would Pharaoh listen to me,
since I speak with faltering lips[a]?"[v]

6:8 [s]Ge 15:18; 26:3 [t]Ge 14:22 [u]Ps 136:21-22
6:12 [v]ver 30; Ex 4:10; Jer 1:6
6:14 [w]Ge 46:9
6:15 [x]Ge 46:10; 1Ch 4:24
6:16 [y]Ge 46:11 [z]Nu 3:17
6:17 [a]1Ch 6:17
6:18 [b]1Ch 6:2,18
6:19 [c]Nu 3:20,33; 1Ch 6:19; 23:21
6:20 [d]Ex 2:1-2; Nu 26:59
6:21 [e]1Ch 6:38
6:22 [f]Lev 10:4; Nu 3:30

Family Record of Moses and Aaron

[13]Now the LORD spoke to Moses and Aaron about the Israelites and Pharaoh king of Egypt, and he
commanded them to bring the Israelites out of Egypt.
[14]These were the heads of their families[b]:[w]

The sons of Reuben the firstborn son of Israel were Hanok and Pallu, Hezron and Karmi. These were the clans of Reuben.

[15]The sons of Simeon[x] were Jemuel, Jamin, Ohad, Jakin, Zohar and Shaul the son of a Canaanite woman. These were the clans of Simeon.
[16]These were the names of the sons of Levi according to their records: Gershon,[y] Kohath and
Merari.[z] Levi lived 137 years.
[17]The sons of Gershon, by clans, were Libni and Shimei.[a]
[18]The sons of Kohath were Amram, Izhar, Hebron and Uzziel.[b] Kohath lived 133 years.
[19]The sons of Merari were Mahli and Mushi.[c]

These were the clans of Levi according to their records.

[20]Amram married his father's sister Jochebed, who bore him Aaron and Moses.[d] Amram lived
137 years.
[21]The sons of Izhar[e] were Korah, Nepheg and Zikri.
[22]The sons of Uzziel were Mishael, Elzaphan[f] and Sithri.

[a] *12* Hebrew *I am uncircumcised of lips*; also in verse 30 [b] *14* The Hebrew for *families* here and in verse 25 refers to units larger than clans.

oft-repeated divine promise articulates the essence of God's covenant relationship with his people (Lev 26:12; Deut 29:13; Jer 31:33; Ezek 37:27; Rev 21:3).

6:8 I swore with uplifted hand. An expression of a solemn promise or oath. See Gen 14:22.

6:9 Circumstances blind the Israelites in unbelief. It seems they too need to be persuaded by more than mere words (see 14:10,21).

6:10—7:7 Exod 6:10–12 may conclude the previous unit, but it could also be read as the introduction to the following section: together with 6:28—7:7, these verses would thus be part of the frame that surrounds the genealogy in 6:13–27. The almost identical 6:10–12 and 6:28–30 serve as a bracketing device, isolating the genealogy in 6:13–27. Most significant, however, is the shift in focus in this unit from what Moses must say to Israel to what he must say to Pharaoh (7:1–5).

6:10–12 The adverse response of the demoralized Israelites (v. 9) evidently brushes off on Moses himself, who again focuses on himself and his perceived inadequacies.

6:12 faltering lips. See NIV text note. Refers simply to Moses' lack of eloquence or his tendency to get tongue-tied (see note on 4:10). Whatever the particular concern, it explains and necessitates the role of Aaron.

6:13–27 *Family Record of Moses and Aaron.* This genealogy may seem to disrupt the narrative, but it serves largely to establish Aaron's credentials and legitimacy as a leader alongside Moses. Such is clear from the introduction (v. 13) and conclusion (vv. 26–27): the usual sequence ("Moses and Aaron," vv. 13,27) reverses ("Aaron and Moses," vv. 20,26) after the genealogy ends. The genealogy mentions Reuben and Simeon only in passing to get to Jacob's third-born son, Levi, and it quickly zooms in on his descendants. However, it terminates not with Moses but with the high priestly descendants of Aaron; including both spouses and offspring in vv. 23,25 (cf. v. 20) highlights this. This again shifts the primary focus to Aaron. Other descendants of Kohath (i.e., Korah and his sons, and Aaron's grandson Phinehas) are probably included because of their later significance (cf. Korah's rebellion in Num 16 with Phinehas's act of faithfulness in Num 25). In any case, the genealogy's main objective is to demonstrate Aaron's legitimacy as the mediator of Moses' words.

6:20 Amram married ... Jochebed. The fact that Jochebed was Amram's paternal aunt attests to the text's historicity; such a marriage was later prohibited (Lev 18:12; 20:19), so it would not have been "invented" by later storytellers. **bore him Aaron and Moses.** Kohath, born at least 350 years before Moses (Gen 46:11; cf. Exod 12:40–41), is too old to have been Moses' grandfather, which this verse might otherwise imply (cf. Num 26:59; 1 Chr 6:3). For this reason, it seems likely that some generations are skipped over between v. 18 and v. 20, which may be further suggested by the break signaled at v. 19b. Thus understood, Amram refers to two different people in this genealogy, which has omitted less significant generations in between these two individuals—a practice which is also reflected in some other biblical genealogies (e.g., Matt 1:1–16, where two generations between David and Jesus are clearly omitted [see Matt 1:8,11 and note on v. 8]).

6:23 [g]Ru 4:19,20 [h]Lev 10:1 [i]Nu 3:2,32 [j]Nu 26:60
6:24 [k]Nu 26:11
6:25 [l]Nu 25:7,11; Jos 24:33; Ps 106:30
6:26 [m]Ex 7:4; 12:17,41,51
6:29 [n]ver 11; Ex 7:2
6:30 [o]ver 12; Ex 4:10
7:1 [p]Ex 4:16
7:3 [q]Ex 4:21; 11:9
7:4 [r]Ex 11:9 [s]Ex 3:20; 6:6
7:5 [t]ver 17; Ex 8:19,22 [u]Ex 3:20
7:6 [v]ver 2
7:7 [w]Dt 31:2; 34:7; Ac 7:23,30
7:9 [x]Isa 7:11; Jn 2:18 [y]Ex 4:2-5

23 Aaron married Elisheba, daughter of Amminadab[g] and sister of Nahshon, and she bore him Nadab and Abihu,[h] Eleazar[i] and Ithamar.[j]

24 The sons of Korah[k] were Assir, Elkanah and Abiasaph. These were the Korahite clans.

25 Eleazar son of Aaron married one of the daughters of Putiel, and she bore him Phinehas.[l]

These were the heads of the Levite families, clan by clan.

26 It was this Aaron and Moses to whom the LORD said, "Bring the Israelites out of Egypt by their divisions."[m] 27 They were the ones who spoke to Pharaoh king of Egypt about bringing the Israelites out of Egypt—this same Moses and Aaron.

Aaron to Speak for Moses

28 Now when the LORD spoke to Moses in Egypt, 29 he said to him, "I am the LORD.[n] Tell Pharaoh king of Egypt everything I tell you."

30 But Moses said to the LORD, "Since I speak with faltering lips,[o] why would Pharaoh listen to me?"

7 Then the LORD said to Moses, "See, I have made you like God[p] to Pharaoh, and your brother Aaron will be your prophet. 2 You are to say everything I command you, and your brother Aaron is to tell Pharaoh to let the Israelites go out of his country. 3 But I will harden Pharaoh's heart,[q] and though I multiply my signs and wonders in Egypt, 4 he will not listen[r] to you. Then I will lay my hand on Egypt and with mighty acts of judgment[s] I will bring out my divisions, my people the Israelites. 5 And the Egyptians will know that I am the LORD[t] when I stretch out my hand[u] against Egypt and bring the Israelites out of it."

6 Moses and Aaron did just as the LORD commanded[v] them. 7 Moses was eighty years old[w] and Aaron eighty-three when they spoke to Pharaoh.

Aaron's Staff Becomes a Snake

8 The LORD said to Moses and Aaron, 9 "When Pharaoh says to you, 'Perform a miracle,'[x] then say to Aaron, 'Take your staff and throw it down before Pharaoh,' and it will become a snake."[y]

10 So Moses and Aaron went to Pharaoh and did just as the LORD commanded. Aaron threw his staff down in front of Pharaoh and his officials, and it became a snake. 11 Pharaoh then summoned wise men

---

6:28—7:7 *Aaron to Speak for Moses.* The repetition of 6:10–12 in 6:28–30 signals a return to the main story line, which continues with God's solution to both the communication issue that Moses raised and the more significant problems ahead.

7:1 like God. Moses is like God to Pharaoh as Moses is like God to Aaron (see 4:16 and note). **prophet.** Aaron assumes the role of a prophet by transmitting the divine message to the intended audience (see note on 4:14–17).

7:3–5 Speaking with such divine authority does not guarantee a receptive audience, for God intends to "harden Pharaoh's heart" (v. 3; 4:21) so that God might make himself known through "mighty acts of judgment" (v. 4) that culminate in God's striking down Egypt's firstborn and then destroying Egypt's elite chariot force. Thus, despite what Pharaoh or others may think, Pharaoh's refusal to comply ensures that the Lord's ultimate plans materialize.

7:3 my signs and wonders. Refer to the transformation of Aaron's staff (vv. 8–12) and in particular, the sequence of phenomena that follow (7:13—10:29; 11:10). Although there is clearly some overlap with the "signs" that Moses had earlier performed before the Israelites (4:1–9,30), the latter were clearly designed to stimulate faith, whereas these extraordinary events, demonstrating the supremacy of the Lord and the impotence of Egyptian deities such as Pharaoh, primarily function as acts of judgment designed to induce repentance.

7:5 the Egyptians will know that I am the LORD. Addressing Pharaoh's earlier question and professed ignorance in 5:2 ("Who is the LORD ...? I do not know the LORD"), this repeated statement (see 7:17; 8:10,22; 14:4,18) explains the rationale behind God's "signs and wonders" (7:3) and "mighty acts of judgment" (7:4): they were so that God might make himself known to the Egyptians, as well as to the Israelites (6:6–7; 10:2), as Israel's covenant God (3:14–15; 6:2–8). Centuries afterward, in the context of the Babylonian exile and the prospect of a new exodus, Ezekiel similarly uses the phrase in relation to the Lord's later acts of judgment and salvation (e.g., Ezek 28:22; 36:23), foreshadowing the personal knowledge (John 17; see Heb 8:10–12) and acknowledgement (Phil 2:9–11) of the Lord that comes through God's final self-revelation in Jesus.

7:8–13 *Aaron's Staff Becomes a Snake.* Though distinct from the following series of phenomena traditionally called "plagues," this first "wonder" that Moses and Aaron perform before Pharaoh serves as a prelude: the Lord demonstrates his great power, but Pharaoh foolishly refuses to learn from it.

7:9–12 snake ... snake ... snake. This translates a different Hebrew word than that translated "snake" in v. 15 and 4:3; the term used in 7:9–12 is apparently a more terrifying reptile, possibly a crocodile. It is most often associated with primordial monsters of chaos (Job 7:12; Pss 74:13; 148:7; Isa 27:1; 51:9), but on two occasions it symbolizes Pharaoh's own despotic power (Ezek 29:3; 32:2).

7:11 magicians. They are the "wise men and sorcerers," not a subgroup (cf. Gen 41:8). In Egypt, religious practices were closely linked to magic, and temple libraries included ritual and magical texts studied by the priests. According to the NT, two of these professionals summoned by Pharaoh—Jannes and Jambres (2 Tim 3:8)—seem to have played a leading role. **their secret arts.** Whether this alludes to magical deception (i.e., sleight of hand) or genuine occult activity is beside the point:

and sorcerers, and the Egyptian magicians[z] also did the same things by their secret arts:[a] 12Each one
threw down his staff and it became a snake. But Aaron's staff swallowed up their staffs. 13Yet Pharaoh's
heart[b] became hard and he would not listen to them, just as the LORD had said.

The Plague of Blood

14Then the LORD said to Moses, "Pharaoh's heart is unyielding;[c] he refuses to let the people go.
15Go to Pharaoh in the morning as he goes out to the river. Confront him on the bank of the Nile,
and take in your hand the staff that was changed into a snake. 16Then say to him, 'The LORD, the
God of the Hebrews, has sent me to say to you: Let my people go, so that they may worship[d] me in the
wilderness. But until now you have not listened. 17This is what the LORD says: By this you will know
that I am the LORD:[e] With the staff that is in my hand I will strike the water of the Nile, and it will be
changed into blood.[f] 18The fish in the Nile will die, and the river will stink; the Egyptians will not be
able to drink its water.' "[g]
19The LORD said to Moses, "Tell Aaron, 'Take your staff and stretch out your hand[h] over the waters
of Egypt — over the streams and canals, over the ponds and all the reservoirs — and they will turn to
blood.' Blood will be everywhere in Egypt, even in vessels[a] of wood and stone."

a 19 Or *even on their idols*

7:11 [z] Ge 41:8; 2Ti 3:8 [a] ver 22; Ex 8:7,18
7:13 [b] Ex 4:21
7:14 [c] Ex 8:15,32; 10:1,20,27
7:16 [d] Ex 3:18; 5:1,3
7:17 [e] Ex 5:2 [f] Ex 4:9; Rev 11:6; 16:4
7:18 [g] ver 21,24
7:19 [h] Ex 8:5-6,16; 9:22; 10:12,21; 14:21

Aaron's staff swallowing up their staffs (v. 12) demonstrates that the Lord is superior. It is a portent of the Lord's ultimate triumph over Pharaoh when the earth swallows up Pharaoh's army (15:12).

7:13 as the LORD had said. A recurring refrain in the plague narrative (v. 22; 8:15,19; 9:12,35). It further emphasizes that the Lord is sovereign over Pharaoh.

7:14—10:29 God's striking of the Egyptians, which he anticipates in 3:20, begins with the ten "plagues" (9:14; 11:1). The first nine of these are arranged in three groups of three: 7:14—8:19; 8:20—9:12; 9:13—10:29. The accounts of some of the signs omit certain details, assuming that the reader will fill in these "narrative gaps" from the general pattern described. The first disaster in each group (i.e., the first, the fourth, and the seventh plagues) is introduced by a warning delivered to Pharaoh in the morning as he went out to the Nile (7:15; 8:20; 9:13), whereas the last disaster in each group (i.e., the third, the sixth, and the ninth plagues) comes without any warning to Pharaoh. The trajectory of each group, and of the unit as a whole, thus signals that the Lord's patience with Pharaoh will run out. See "Structural Features of the 'Signs and Wonders' Narratiave," this page.

The catastrophes demonstrate that the Lord, not Pharaoh, is sovereign over Egypt, and they constitute judgment on the Egyptians for refusing to submit to God's demands. Explanations of their chronology in terms of sequentially related natural disasters (e.g., red silt washed into the Nile River, starting a domino effect on Egypt's ecology) invariably undermine the miraculous nature and theological significance attached to these events in the biblical account, and they are deeply flawed if the objective is in any way to bolster the text's historical credibility.

7:14–24 *The Plague of Blood.* The first plague strikes at the very heart of Egypt's life and economy: the Nile River.

7:14 Then the LORD said to Moses. All the disasters in the following sequence begin with this phrase (8:1,16,20; 9:1,8,13; 10:1,21; see 11:1), signifying that each of them is governed by God's word to Moses.

7:15 in the morning. See "Structural Features of the 'Signs and Wonders' Narratiave," this page.

7:17 you will know. See notes on 5:2; 7:5. See also 8:10,22; 9:14,29; 11:7. **changed into blood.** See note on 4:9. Unlike the Israelites (see 4:1–9,29–31), who were persuaded when similar signs were performed before them (staff to reptile; water to blood), Pharaoh is unimpressed by this ecological crisis that severely impacts Egypt's fresh water supply (v. 24).

7:18,21,24 Egyptians. May imply that the Israelites were somehow sheltered from the immediate effects of this plague. Although 8:22 explicitly mentions such discrimination for the first time, this may not necessarily be a new development; as the impact of the strikes/plagues increases, the issue of discrimination becomes more important.

STRUCTURAL FEATURES OF THE "SIGNS AND WONDERS" NARRATIVE

SIGN/WONDER	WARNING	TIMING	INSTRUCTION	DISTINCTION MADE FOR ISRAELITES
1. bloody water (7:14–25)	yes	morning	confront Pharaoh	implicit (7:24)
2. frogs (8:1–15)	yes	?	go to Pharaoh	implicit (8:3–4,8,11)
3. gnats (8:16–19)	no	?	none	?
4. flies (8:20–32)	yes	morning	confront Pharaoh	explicit (8:22–23)
5. livestock (9:1–7)	yes	?	go to Pharaoh	explicit (9:4,6–7)
6. boils (9:8–12)	no	?	none	implicit (9:11)
7. hail (9:13–35)	yes	morning	confront Pharaoh	explicit (9:26)
8. locusts (10:1–20)	yes	?	go to Pharaoh	implicit (10:1–2,6)
9. darkness (10:21–29)	no	?	none	explicit (10:23)

7:20 [i]Ex 17:5 [j]Ps 78:44; 105:29
7:22 [k]ver 11
8:1 [l]Ex 3:12,18; 4:23
8:3 [m]Ex 10:6
8:5 [n]Ex 7:19
8:6 [o]Ps 78:45; 105:30
8:7 [p]Ex 7:11
8:8 [q]ver 28; Ex 9:28; 10:17 [r]ver 25
8:10 [s]Ex 9:14; Dt 4:35; 33:26; 2Sa 7:22; 1Ch 17:20; Ps 86:8; Isa 46:9; Jer 10:6
8:15 [t]Ex 7:14

20 Moses and Aaron did just as the LORD had commanded. He raised his staff in the presence of
Pharaoh and his officials and struck the water of the Nile,[i] and all the water was changed into blood.[j]
21 The fish in the Nile died, and the river smelled so bad that the Egyptians could not drink its water.
Blood was everywhere in Egypt.
22 But the Egyptian magicians did the same things by their secret arts,[k] and Pharaoh's heart became
hard; he would not listen to Moses and Aaron, just as the LORD had said. 23 Instead, he turned and went
into his palace, and did not take even this to heart. 24 And all the Egyptians dug along the Nile to get
drinking water, because they could not drink the water of the river.

The Plague of Frogs

8[a] 25 Seven days passed after the LORD struck the Nile. 1 Then the LORD said to Moses, "Go to Pharaoh
and say to him, 'This is what the LORD says: Let my people go, so that they may worship[l] me. 2 If
you refuse to let them go, I will send a plague of frogs on your whole country. 3 The Nile will teem with
frogs. They will come up into your palace and your bedroom and onto your bed, into the houses of your
officials and on your people,[m] and into your ovens and kneading troughs. 4 The frogs will come up on
you and your people and all your officials.' "
5 Then the LORD said to Moses, "Tell Aaron, 'Stretch out your hand with your staff[n] over the streams
and canals and ponds, and make frogs come up on the land of Egypt.' "
6 So Aaron stretched out his hand over the waters of Egypt, and the frogs[o] came up and covered the
land. 7 But the magicians did the same things by their secret arts;[p] they also made frogs come up on
the land of Egypt.
8 Pharaoh summoned Moses and Aaron and said, "Pray[q] to the LORD to take the frogs away from me
and my people, and I will let your people go to offer sacrifices[r] to the LORD."
9 Moses said to Pharaoh, "I leave to you the honor of setting the time for me to pray for you and
your officials and your people that you and your houses may be rid of the frogs, except for those that
remain in the Nile."
10 "Tomorrow," Pharaoh said.
Moses replied, "It will be as you say, so that you may know there is no one like the LORD our God.[s]
11 The frogs will leave you and your houses, your officials and your people; they will remain only in
the Nile."
12 After Moses and Aaron left Pharaoh, Moses cried out to the LORD about the frogs he had brought
on Pharaoh. 13 And the LORD did what Moses asked. The frogs died in the houses, in the courtyards
and in the fields. 14 They were piled into heaps, and the land reeked of them. 15 But when Pharaoh
saw that there was relief, he hardened his heart[t] and would not listen to Moses and Aaron, just as the
LORD had said.

[a] In Hebrew texts 8:1-4 is numbered 7:26-29, and 8:5-32 is numbered 8:1-28.

7:20 Moses and Aaron readily obey God (cf. vv. 6,10), sharply contrasting with Pharaoh's defiance.
7:22–24 As before (vv. 11–13), the magicians' actions foster Pharaoh's resistance.
7:24 Apparently only the water of the Nile River was unusable.
7:25—8:15 *The Plague of Frogs.* The scale of the second plague is again widespread: frogs encroach everywhere and on everyone. While the magicians are apparently able to replicate this phenomenon also (8:7), Pharaoh's reaction is more conciliatory (8:8)—at least until the crisis ends.
7:25 Seven days passed. Pharaoh is graciously given time to repent before further judgment, but he squanders the opportunity (cf. Rev 9:20–21; 16:10–11).
8:2–4 Presumably the frogs abandon the Nile River because it is so contaminated.
8:5–7 As before, the onset of the plague swiftly follows its announcement. While possibly a narrative gap, more probably this indicates that Pharaoh has no intention of changing his mind.
8:8 Rather than hardening his resolve (as previously), Pharaoh for the first time acknowledges the Lord's power—indeed, his request is a tacit admission of Egyptian impotence (v. 9). **I will let your people go.** For the first time, Pharaoh mentions the possibility of emancipation, but his subsequent actions do not match his words.
8:9–11 To remove any doubt about this phenomenon and thus the Lord's supremacy, Moses gives Pharaoh the "honor" (v. 9) of deciding when it should end.
8:12–15 Significantly, when Moses cries out to the Lord on Pharaoh's behalf, the Lord responds to Pharaoh's request immediately.
8:13,31 the LORD did what Moses asked. See Gen 20:7; Jas 5:16.
8:13 The frogs died. Clearly as a result of the Lord's action, whether or not environmental circumstances were used to bring this about.
8:15 he hardened his heart. See note on 4:21 and "Hardened Heart," p. 126. This is the first text that explicitly says that Pharaoh hardens his heart (see also v. 32; 9:34).

The Plague of Gnats

16 Then the LORD said to Moses, "Tell Aaron, 'Stretch out your staff and strike the dust of the ground,' and throughout the land of Egypt the dust will become gnats." 17 They did this, and when Aaron stretched out his hand with the staff and struck the dust of the ground, gnats[u] came on people and animals. All the dust throughout the land of Egypt became gnats. 18 But when the magicians[v] tried to produce gnats by their secret arts,[w] they could not.

Since the gnats were on people and animals everywhere, 19 the magicians said to Pharaoh, "This is the finger[x] of God." But Pharaoh's heart was hard and he would not listen, just as the LORD had said.

The Plague of Flies

20 Then the LORD said to Moses, "Get up early in the morning[y] and confront Pharaoh as he goes to the river and say to him, 'This is what the LORD says: Let my people go, so that they may worship[z] me. 21 If you do not let my people go, I will send swarms of flies on you and your officials, on your people and into your houses. The houses of the Egyptians will be full of flies; even the ground will be covered with them.

22 " 'But on that day I will deal differently with the land of Goshen, where my people live;[a] no swarms of flies will be there, so that you will know[b] that I, the LORD, am in this land. 23 I will make a distinction[*a*] between my people and your people. This sign will occur tomorrow.' "

24 And the LORD did this. Dense swarms of flies poured into Pharaoh's palace and into the houses of his officials; throughout Egypt the land was ruined by the flies.[c]

25 Then Pharaoh summoned[d] Moses and Aaron and said, "Go, sacrifice to your God here in the land."

26 But Moses said, "That would not be right. The sacrifices we offer the LORD our God would be detestable to the Egyptians.[e] And if we offer sacrifices that are detestable in their eyes, will they not stone us? 27 We must take a three-day journey into the wilderness to offer sacrifices[f] to the LORD our God, as he commands us."

28 Pharaoh said, "I will let you go to offer sacrifices to the LORD your God in the wilderness, but you must not go very far. Now pray[g] for me."

29 Moses answered, "As soon as I leave you, I will pray to the LORD, and tomorrow the flies will leave Pharaoh and his officials and his people. Only let Pharaoh be sure that he does not act deceitfully[h] again by not letting the people go to offer sacrifices to the LORD."

30 Then Moses left Pharaoh and prayed to the LORD,[i] 31 and the LORD did what Moses asked. The flies left Pharaoh and his officials and his people; not a fly remained. 32 But this time also Pharaoh hardened his heart[j] and would not let the people go.

a 23 Septuagint and Vulgate; Hebrew *will put a deliverance*

8:17 [u]Ps 105:31
8:18 [v]Ex 9:11; Da 5:8 [w]Ex 7:11
8:19 [x]Ex 7:5; 10:7; Ps 8:3; Lk 11:20
8:20 [y]Ex 7:15; 9:13 [z]ver 1; Ex 3:18
8:22 [a]Ex 9:4,6,26; 10:23; 11:7 [b]Ex 7:5; 9:29
8:24 [c]Ps 78:45; 105:31
8:25 [d]ver 8; Ex 9:27
8:26 [e]Ge 43:32; 46:34
8:27 [f]Ex 3:18
8:28 [g]ver 8; Ex 9:28; 1Ki 13:6
8:29 [h]ver 15
8:30 [i]ver 12
8:32 [j]ver 8,15; Ex 4:21

8:16–19 *The Plague of Gnats.* It is impossible to determine what biting insect this is. It is possibly some form of lice. The impact is clearly extensive (vv. 16b,17b).

8:19 finger of God. For the first time, the Egyptian magicians cannot duplicate the wonder, and thus they acknowledge its divine source using a figure of speech that elsewhere refers to God's miraculous power (31:18; Luke 11:20). See also the similar use of the Lord's "hand" (3:19–20; 7:4–5; 9:3,15; 13:3) and the Lord's "arm" (6:6; 15:16). While the Egyptians' use of this phrase is arguably a clever attempt to avoid offending Pharaoh, their divine king, whose hand is all-powerful, it seems more likely that they are conceding that their own expertise and supernatural powers are manifestly inferior to that exercised by Aaron. **would not listen.** Despite this significant concession by his magicians, Pharaoh remains adamant. But the author reminds us that such obstinacy only amplifies the extent of the Lord's dominion.

8:20–32 *The Plague of Flies.* This is the first disaster that explicitly mentions the Lord discriminating between the Egyptians and the Israelites, limiting this infestation to areas that the Egyptians occupy.

8:22 Goshen. The region enjoys immunity, a distinction that cogently illustrates the Lord's presence in the land as well as his ability to protect his people while judging his enemies (cf. Ezek 9; 2 Pet 2:4–9).

8:24 For the first time in this sequence of wonders, there is no mention of any human agency.

8:25–27 Pharaoh subtly reduces their demand to merely performing religious ritual that they could carry out anywhere. It is ill-conceived in terms of Egyptian sensitivities (the precise nature of which are debatable; see Gen 43:32; 46:34), but more important, it is contrary to what the Lord expressly demands.

8:28 in the wilderness. Pharaoh makes a further concession but still attempts to control the Israelites' movements. **pray for me.** Pharaoh is clearly acting out of self-interest: he desires immediate relief from the flies.

8:30–32 As expected, Pharaoh's accommodating attitude dissipates as soon as the immediate crisis passes. For the second time in the sequence (v. 15), Pharaoh himself hardens his heart in response to the relief the Lord graciously grants.

9:1 [k]Ex 8:1
9:3 [l]Ex 7:4
9:4 [m]ver 26; Ex 8:22
9:6 [n]ver 19-21; Ex 11:5 [o]Ps 78:48-50
9:7 [p]Ex 7:14; 8:32
9:9 [q]Dt 28:27,35; Rev 16:2
9:11 [r]Ex 8:18
9:12 [s]Ex 4:21
9:13 [t]Ex 8:20
9:14 [u]Ex 8:10 [v]2Sa 7:22; 1Ch 17:20; Ps 86:8; Isa 46:9; Jer 10:6
9:15 [w]Ex 3:20
9:16 [x]Pr 16:4 [y]Ro 9:17*
9:18 [z]ver 23

The Plague on Livestock

9 Then the LORD said to Moses, "Go to Pharaoh and say to him, 'This is what the LORD, the God of the Hebrews, says: "Let my people go, so that they may worship[k] me." [2]If you refuse to let them go and continue to hold them back, [3]the hand[l] of the LORD will bring a terrible plague on your livestock in the field — on your horses, donkeys and camels and on your cattle, sheep and goats. [4]But the LORD will make a distinction between the livestock of Israel and that of Egypt,[m] so that no animal belonging to the Israelites will die.' "

[5]The LORD set a time and said, "Tomorrow the LORD will do this in the land." [6]And the next day the LORD did it: All the livestock[n] of the Egyptians died,[o] but not one animal belonging to the Israelites died. [7]Pharaoh investigated and found that not even one of the animals of the Israelites had died. Yet his heart was unyielding and he would not let the people go.[p]

The Plague of Boils

[8]Then the LORD said to Moses and Aaron, "Take handfuls of soot from a furnace and have Moses toss it into the air in the presence of Pharaoh. [9]It will become fine dust over the whole land of Egypt, and festering boils[q] will break out on people and animals throughout the land."

[10]So they took soot from a furnace and stood before Pharaoh. Moses tossed it into the air, and festering boils broke out on people and animals. [11]The magicians[r] could not stand before Moses because of the boils that were on them and on all the Egyptians. [12]But the LORD hardened Pharaoh's heart[s] and he would not listen to Moses and Aaron, just as the LORD had said to Moses.

The Plague of Hail

[13]Then the LORD said to Moses, "Get up early in the morning, confront Pharaoh and say to him, 'This is what the LORD, the God of the Hebrews, says: Let my people go, so that they may worship[t] me, [14]or this time I will send the full force of my plagues against you and against your officials and your people, so you may know[u] that there is no one like[v] me in all the earth. [15]For by now I could have stretched out my hand and struck you and your people[w] with a plague that would have wiped you off the earth. [16]But I have raised you up[a] for this very purpose,[x] that I might show you my power[y] and that my name might be proclaimed in all the earth. [17]You still set yourself against my people and will not let them go. [18]Therefore, at this time tomorrow I will send the worst hailstorm[z] that has ever fallen on Egypt, from

[a] *16* Or *have spared you*

9:1–7 *The Plague on Livestock.* The intensity and seriousness of these disasters now appear to increase. Previously these have been little more than a gross inconvenience or irritation. This plague, however, results in the death of Egyptian livestock.

9:1–2 The announcement of the fifth plague again begins with the Lord's basic demand (see v. 13; 5:1; 7:16; 8:1,20; 10:3) followed by a conditional threat. A phrase here uniquely augments the conditional element: "continue to hold them back" (see v. 2 and note).

9:2 hold them back. This possibly alludes to Pharaoh's hardened heart, because different forms of the same Hebrew word describe the hardening of Pharaoh's heart 12 times (vv. 12,35; 4:21; 7:13,22; 8:19; 10:20,27; 11:10; 14:4,8,17).

9:3 hand of the LORD. The first mention since 7:4 (cf. 8:19). This verse uniquely describes the imminent disaster as a "terrible" plague.

9:4 See note on 8:22.

9:5 Tomorrow. Now the Lord sets the time (cf. 8:9–10), suggesting that Pharaoh is losing what little control he exercised.

9:6 All the livestock ... died. Possibly just those outside (see v. 3, which stipulates "in the field"), since the subsequent account (vv. 20–21) clearly shows that at least some Egyptian livestock survive. The main point is that, unlike the Lord, Pharaoh cannot preserve the livestock of his people. This contrast is even more pronounced when it comes to protecting their respective people from death.

9:8–12 *The Plague of Boils.* In some respects this disaster foreshadows the tenth, seriously impacting both humans and animals.

9:11 could not stand before. The Egyptian magicians, who previously "opposed Moses" (2 Tim 3:8), cannot protect *themselves* from these boils, still less the Egyptian population as a whole. Their inability further underlines their impotence. Despite this, Pharaoh remains indifferent (v. 12).

9:12 the LORD hardened Pharaoh's heart. In explicit fulfillment of the earlier declarations (4:21; 7:3), perhaps further indicating that Pharaoh's reaction is both irrational and unnatural. In any case, events are working out exactly as the Lord planned.

9:13–35 *The Plague of Hail.* The final triad of plagues is the longest, due mainly to the increased level of interaction between the parties involved. The first of the three also contains additional information about Pharaoh's role in the plan and purposes of God.

9:14 full force of my plagues. The prospect of fully unleashing the Lord's wrath against Egypt intensifies the threat. He "could have" (v. 15) already annihilated Egypt.

9:16 This explains why the Lord has not annihilated Egypt (v. 15). **I have raised you up.** Or "I have caused you to stand." The ambiguity of the verb allows two interpretations: (1) "I have raised you up" (cf. Rom 9:17), meaning the Lord sovereignly ordains Pharaoh's circumstances. (2) "I have spared you" (see NIV text note). In either translation, the Lord has not exercised lethal force against Egypt thus far so that he might personally disclose his mighty power and so that his name would be globally proclaimed.

9:17–19 The opportunity given to shelter potential victims from this unprecedented hailstorm highlights not only the escalating scale of

the day it was founded till now.[a] 19 Give an order now to bring your livestock and everything you have in the field to a place of shelter, because the hail will fall on every person and animal that has not been brought in and is still out in the field, and they will die.'"

20 Those officials of Pharaoh who feared[b] the word of the LORD hurried to bring their slaves and their livestock inside. 21 But those who ignored the word of the LORD left their slaves and livestock in the field.

22 Then the LORD said to Moses, "Stretch out your hand toward the sky so that hail will fall all over Egypt—on people and animals and on everything growing in the fields of Egypt." 23 When Moses stretched out his staff toward the sky, the LORD sent thunder[c] and hail,[d] and lightning flashed down to the ground. So the LORD rained hail on the land of Egypt; 24 hail fell and lightning flashed back and forth. It was the worst storm in all the land of Egypt since it had become a nation. 25 Throughout Egypt hail struck everything in the fields—both people and animals; it beat down everything growing in the fields and stripped every tree.[e] 26 The only place it did not hail was the land of Goshen,[f] where the Israelites were.[g]

27 Then Pharaoh summoned Moses and Aaron. "This time I have sinned,"[h] he said to them. "The LORD is in the right,[i] and I and my people are in the wrong. 28 Pray[j] to the LORD, for we have had enough thunder and hail. I will let you go;[k] you don't have to stay any longer."

29 Moses replied, "When I have gone out of the city, I will spread out my hands[l] in prayer to the LORD. The thunder will stop and there will be no more hail, so you may know that the earth[m] is the LORD's. 30 But I know that you and your officials still do not fear the LORD God."

31 (The flax and barley[n] were destroyed, since the barley had headed and the flax was in bloom. 32 The wheat and spelt, however, were not destroyed, because they ripen later.)

33 Then Moses left Pharaoh and went out of the city. He spread out his hands toward the LORD; the thunder and hail stopped, and the rain no longer poured down on the land. 34 When Pharaoh saw that the rain and hail and thunder had stopped, he sinned again: He and his officials hardened their hearts. 35 So Pharaoh's heart[o] was hard and he would not let the Israelites go, just as the LORD had said through Moses.

The Plague of Locusts

10 Then the LORD said to Moses, "Go to Pharaoh, for I have hardened his heart[p] and the hearts of his officials so that I may perform these signs[q] of mine among them 2 that you may tell your children[r] and grandchildren how I dealt harshly with the Egyptians and how I performed my signs among them, and that you may know that I am the LORD."

3 So Moses and Aaron went to Pharaoh and said to him, "This is what the LORD, the God of the Hebrews, says: 'How long will you refuse to humble[s] yourself before me? Let my people go, so that they may worship me. 4 If you refuse to let them go, I will bring locusts[t] into your country tomorrow. 5 They will cover the face of the ground so that it cannot be seen. They will devour what little you have left[u] after the hail, including every tree that is growing in your fields. 6 They will fill your houses and those of all

9:18 [a] ver 24
9:20 [b] Pr 13:13
9:23 [c] Ps 18:13 [d] Jos 10:11; Ps 78:47; 105:32; Isa 30:30; Eze 38:22; Rev 8:7; 16:21
9:25 [e] Ps 105:32-33
9:26 [f] ver 4 [g] Ex 8:22; 10:23; 11:7; 12:13
9:27 [h] Ex 10:16 [i] 2Ch 12:6; Ps 129:4; La 1:18
9:28 [j] Ex 10:17 [k] Ex 8:8
9:29 [l] 1Ki 8:22,38; Ps 143:6; Isa 1:15 [m] Ex 19:5; Ps 24:1; 1Co 10:26
9:31 [n] Ru 1:22; 2:23
9:35 [o] Ex 4:21
10:1 [p] Ex 4:21 [q] Ex 7:3
10:2 [r] Ex 12:26-27; 13:8, 14; Dt 4:9; Ps 44:1; 78:4,5; Joel 1:3
10:3 [s] 1Ki 21:29; Jas 4:10; 1Pe 5:6
10:4 [t] Rev 9:3
10:5 [u] Ex 9:32; Joel 1:4

---

these disasters but also God's concern to preserve rather than extinguish life (see Ezek 18:32; 2 Pet 3:9)—including that of animals (Jonah 4:11).

9:20 The wise actions of a few of Pharaoh's officials show that some Egyptians are gradually recognizing that the Lord is supreme. This anticipates even greater capitulation (10:7).

9:22–26 As anticipated, the storm destroys everything in its wake. Only Goshen (cf. 8:22) escapes unscathed, further demonstrating that this hailstorm is no ordinary severe weather system or coincidental freak of nature but is an act of God.

9:25 everything. See note on vv. 31–32.

9:28 With his petition for prayer (cf. 8:28) and further promise of freedom, Pharaoh seems defeated. But Moses' critical appraisal (vv. 29–30) shows that the Lord does not yet give Moses any reason to believe Pharaoh (cf. 11:1).

9:29 spread out my hands. A common posture for prayer (1 Kgs 8:22; Ezra 9:5; Isa 1:15; 1 Tim 2:8). Archaeological excavations have uncovered statues of men praying with elevated arms.

9:31–32 This parenthetical note qualifies v. 25 and explains how the forthcoming locust invasion is so catastrophic even in the aftermath of the hail's destruction.

9:34 In keeping with the now-familiar pattern, once Moses secures relief, Pharaoh reneges on his promises (vv. 27–28) and transgresses. **officials.** Presumably those in v. 21 but possibly those in v. 20 as well. **hardened their hearts.** Further underlines Egyptian (not just Pharaoh's) culpability.

9:35 See note on 4:21.

10:1–20 *The Plague of Locusts.* Like the account of the previous disaster, this one is considerably longer than others. It further explains Pharaoh's obstinacy.

10:1–2 so that ... that ... that. The Lord hardens the hearts of Pharaoh and his officials for the three purposes mentioned in the text.

10:3 The rhetorical question highlights the underlying problem: Pharaoh refuses to acknowledge his proper place in the created order by asserting that he is sovereign over the Lord. This is the last time the Lord restates his core demand (5:1; 7:16; 8:1,20; 9:1,13), which further indicates that this struggle is approaching resolution.

10:5–6 The locust invasion's anticipated effects and unprecedented nature show that the plagues are escalating in their intensity.

10:7 [v]Ex 23:33; Jos 23:13; 1Sa 18:21; Ecc 7:26 [w]Ex 8:19
10:8 [x]Ex 8:8
10:12 [y]Ex 7:19
10:13 [z]Ps 105:34
10:14 [a]Ps 78:46; Joel 2:1-11,25
10:15 [b]ver 5; Ps 105:34-35
10:16 [c]Ex 9:27
10:17 [d]Ex 8:8
10:18 [e]Ex 8:30
10:20 [f]Ex 4:21; 11:10
10:21 [g]Dt 28:29

your officials and all the Egyptians—something neither your parents nor your ancestors have ever
seen from the day they settled in this land till now.'" Then Moses turned and left Pharaoh.
7 Pharaoh's officials said to him, "How long will this man be a snare[v] to us? Let the people go, so that
they may worship the LORD their God. Do you not yet realize that Egypt is ruined?"[w]
8 Then Moses and Aaron were brought back to Pharaoh. "Go, worship[x] the LORD your God," he said.
"But tell me who will be going."
9 Moses answered, "We will go with our young and our old, with our sons and our daughters, and
with our flocks and herds, because we are to celebrate a festival to the LORD."
10 Pharaoh said, "The LORD be with you—if I let you go, along with your women and children!
Clearly you are bent on evil.[a] 11 No! Have only the men go and worship the LORD, since that's what you
have been asking for." Then Moses and Aaron were driven out of Pharaoh's presence.
12 And the LORD said to Moses, "Stretch out your hand[y] over Egypt so that locusts swarm over the land
and devour everything growing in the fields, everything left by the hail."
13 So Moses stretched out his staff over Egypt, and the LORD made an east wind blow across the land
all that day and all that night. By morning the wind had brought the locusts;[z] 14 they invaded all Egypt
and settled down in every area of the country in great numbers. Never before had there been such a
plague of locusts,[a] nor will there ever be again. 15 They covered all the ground until it was black. They
devoured[b] all that was left after the hail—everything growing in the fields and the fruit on the trees.
Nothing green remained on tree or plant in all the land of Egypt.
16 Pharaoh quickly summoned Moses and Aaron and said, "I have sinned[c] against the LORD your God
and against you. 17 Now forgive my sin once more and pray[d] to the LORD your God to take this deadly
plague away from me."
18 Moses then left Pharaoh and prayed to the LORD.[e] 19 And the LORD changed the wind to a very
strong west wind, which caught up the locusts and carried them into the Red Sea.[b] Not a locust was left
anywhere in Egypt. 20 But the LORD hardened Pharaoh's heart,[f] and he would not let the Israelites go.

The Plague of Darkness

21 Then the LORD said to Moses, "Stretch out your hand toward the sky so that darkness[g] spreads over
Egypt—darkness that can be felt." 22 So Moses stretched out his hand toward the sky, and total dark-

[a] 10 Or *Be careful, trouble is in store for you!* [b] 19 Or *the Sea of Reeds*

10:7 How long ...? Ironically, Pharaoh's exasperated officials echo Moses' question in v. 3 before they reiterate the Lord's basic demand to Pharaoh. **Egypt is ruined.** Persistent rebellion against God has disastrous consequences for nations as well as individuals.
10:10 The LORD be with you. This bristles with sarcasm. **you are bent on evil.** Expresses Pharaoh's true sentiments.
10:11 only the men. Pharaoh's restriction is a clever ploy to ensure that they return to Egypt. **driven out.** Patience on either side is wearing increasingly thin (cf. v. 3).
10:13 east wind. Possibly explains how such a huge swarm of locusts came to be in Egypt (cf. v. 19). This may also anticipate the Lord's final victory over the Egyptians (14:21; 15:10). God's ability to control even the wind displays his sovereign power (see Ps 135:7; Jer 10:13; Matt 8:23–27).
10:14 Never before ... nor will there ever be again. This is an idiom meaning, "this is as bad as it gets." It further highlights the escalating scale of these disasters (cf. 9:18). The impact of this plague in the ancient world is barely imaginable.
10:16–17 The text implies but does not explicitly state that Pharaoh is willing to grant the Lord's wishes (cf. v. 20).
10:18 Moses does not warn Pharaoh (as in 8:29) or accuse him (as in 9:30) in return. This gives the impression that Moses is resigned to Pharaoh's stubbornness, which must run its course.
10:19 Red Sea. Behind this name is the Egyptian term for "reed" that was assimilated into the Hebrew of the OT to identify this body of water as the Reed Sea, or the Sea of Reeds (see NIV text note). Apparently not knowing how to translate this term, the Septuagint (the pre-Christian Greek translation of the OT) and later translators wrote "Red Sea." The Gulf of Suez and other bodies of water bordering the southern Sinai peninsula became known as the Red Sea. In Moses' time the waters of the Gulf of Suez extended farther north. That, combined with other lakes and man-made canals, formed a boundary between Egypt and the lands to the east. One or perhaps several of these lakes (for which there is no separate word in Hebrew; cf. "Sea of Galilee") made up the Red ("Reed") Sea that Israel would cross. It was known to the Egyptians of Moses' day as the Reed Sea. Whatever its exact location, it was a significant body of water—large (and deep) enough to drown the Egyptian army (ch. 14), which the fate of the locusts here seems to foreshadow.
10:21–29 *The Plague of Darkness.* Like the third and sixth plagues, the ninth is unannounced. But this one ends with an unexpected twist: Pharaoh bans Moses from any further audiences with him.
10:21 darkness. Egypt's chief deity, with the most expensive and influential temple (at Karnak), was the sun-god Amun Ra (or Re). Of all the first nine plagues, this one would have held the most obvious challenge to Egypt's religion. Its duration and intensity (vv. 22–23) suggest that (like the previous two plagues) this is an unprecedented experience in Egypt's history.
10:22 three days. It is unclear whether Pharaoh summons Moses during this period of darkness or after light is restored. Pharaoh's track record suggests the former, yet he does not ask Moses to remove the darkness nor does the text explicitly say that the Lord does so. Perhaps Pharaoh breaks off negotiations (v. 28) at the end of the three days once he sees that normality is restored.

ness[h] covered all Egypt for three days. 23 No one could see anyone else or move about for three days. Yet
all the Israelites had light in the places where they lived.[i]
24 Then Pharaoh summoned Moses and said, "Go, worship the LORD. Even your women and children[j]
may go with you; only leave your flocks and herds behind."
25 But Moses said, "You must allow us to have sacrifices and burnt offerings to present to the LORD
our God. 26 Our livestock too must go with us; not a hoof is to be left behind. We have to use some of
them in worshiping the LORD our God, and until we get there we will not know what we are to use to
worship the LORD."
27 But the LORD hardened Pharaoh's heart,[k] and he was not willing to let them go. 28 Pharaoh said to
Moses, "Get out of my sight! Make sure you do not appear before me again! The day you see my face
you will die."
29 "Just as you say," Moses replied. "I will never appear[l] before you again."

The Plague on the Firstborn

11 Now the LORD had said to Moses, "I will bring one more plague on Pharaoh and on Egypt. After
that, he will let you go from here, and when he does, he will drive you out completely. 2 Tell the
people that men and women alike are to ask their neighbors for articles of silver and gold."[m] 3 (The LORD
made the Egyptians favorably disposed toward the people, and Moses himself was highly regarded[n] in
Egypt by Pharaoh's officials and by the people.)
4 So Moses said, "This is what the LORD says: 'About midnight[o] I will go throughout Egypt. 5 Every
firstborn[p] son in Egypt will die, from the firstborn son of Pharaoh, who sits on the throne, to the firstborn son of the female slave, who is at her hand mill, and all the firstborn of the cattle as well. 6 There
will be loud wailing[q] throughout Egypt—worse than there has ever been or ever will be again. 7 But
among the Israelites not a dog will bark at any person or animal.' Then you will know that the LORD
makes a distinction[r] between Egypt and Israel. 8 All these officials of yours will come to me, bowing
down before me and saying, 'Go,[s] you and all the people who follow you!' After that I will leave." Then
Moses, hot with anger, left Pharaoh.
9 The LORD had said to Moses, "Pharaoh will refuse to listen[t] to you—so that my wonders may be
multiplied in Egypt." 10 Moses and Aaron performed all these wonders before Pharaoh, but the LORD
hardened Pharaoh's heart,[u] and he would not let the Israelites go out of his country.

10:22 [h] Ps 105:28; Rev 16:10
10:23 [i] Ex 8:22
10:24 [j] ver 8-10
10:27 [k] ver 20; Ex 4:21
10:29 [l] Heb 11:27
11:2 [m] Ex 3:21,22
11:3 [n] Dt 34:11
11:4 [o] Ex 12:29
11:5 [p] Ex 4:23; Ps 78:51
11:6 [q] Ex 12:30
11:7 [r] Ex 8:22
11:8 [s] Ex 12:31-33
11:9 [t] Ex 7:4
11:10 [u] Ex 4:21; 10:20,27

10:23 all the Israelites had light. This makes naturalistic explanations for the darkness (e.g., an extremely severe sandstorm or solar eclipse) problematic.

10:24–26 Pharaoh concedes a little more by allowing women and children to go (cf. v. 11). However, as Moses observes, Pharaoh's restrictions undermine and frustrate the major objective of their departure.

10:27 See note on 4:21. Pharaoh has lost any control over how this conflict with the Lord will work out.

10:28–29 Pharaoh's threat and Moses' response may seem strange since Moses does speak to Pharaoh in person in 11:4–8, and a further meeting between them is reported in 12:31–32; the problem of 11:4–8 is resolved by the use of the past perfect ("had said") in 11:1,9—interpreting the initial and concluding verses of ch. 11 as literary flashbacks. Accordingly, the words of 11:4–8 were actually spoken during the heated exchange of 10:24–29 rather than subsequently. It is also possible to make sense of the sequence without using the past perfect in 11:1. Since the instructions of 4:21 have been faithfully carried out, Moses is now being told (11:1–2) to implement the instructions of 4:22–23 and 3:22 (cf. 3:20–21). Whatever the case, this heated exchange clearly marks the end of formal negotiations between Pharaoh and Moses, and it demonstrates Pharaoh's continual disrespect for both Moses and God.

11:1–10 *The Plague on the Firstborn.* This announces the tenth plague, but its execution and consequences appear later (12:29–36). If vv. 1–3 and 9–10 are literary flashbacks (cf. 3:19–22; 4:21–23), the dialogue between Pharaoh and Moses in vv. 4–8 is simply the tail end of the conversation in 10:24–29 (see note on 10:28–29). Thus understood, having obeyed the instruction of 4:21, Moses now (i.e., as the final part of the conversation with which ch. 10 ends) carries out the instruction of 4:22–23 before negotiations break off entirely.

11:1 had said. Understood in the past perfect, vv. 1–2 reiterate what the Lord told Moses previously. Taken in the simple past, the Lord here announces that the sequence of wonders has run its course and it is now time for the final, deadly blow that had been anticipated from the outset (4:23).

11:2–3 See note on 3:22. For the fulfillment of this prediction (indicating Egypt's total capitulation and defeat), see 12:35–36.

11:4–8 The narrator returns to the conclusion of the conversation that seemingly ended with 10:29. In keeping with the Lord's earlier directive (4:21–23), the time has come for executing Egypt's firstborn. This last plague is retribution for the suffering that Egypt inflicted on Israel, God's firstborn son (4:22–23): Egypt's "wailing" (v. 6) echoes Israel's "crying out" (3:7; the same Hebrew verb is used). Pharaoh's supposed divinity is once more undermined here by the God who is sovereign over life and death.

11:7 The discriminating effect of this plague (like previous ones) highlights its extraordinary nature and theological significance.

11:8 The anticipated capitulation of Pharaoh's officials again highlights that the Lord is sovereign and Pharaoh is impotent. Pharaoh may still be issuing orders (cf. 10:28), but the Lord is in control.

11:9–10 A final summary of all that has transpired so far. Pharaoh's stubbornness has served God's sovereign purpose.

12:2 [v]Ex 13:4; Dt 16:1
12:5 [w]Lev 22:18-21; Heb 9:14
12:6 [x]Lev 23:5; Nu 9:1-3,5,11 [y]Ex 16:12; Dt 16:4,6
12:8 [z]Ex 34:25; Nu 9:12 [a]Dt 16:7 [b]Nu 9:11 [c]Dt 16:3-4; 1Co 5:8
12:10 [d]Ex 23:18; 34:25
12:11 [e]Dt 16:3 [f]ver 13, 21,27,43; Dt 16:1
12:12 [g]Ex 11:4; Am 5:17 [h]Nu 33:4 [i]Ex 6:2

The Passover and the Festival of Unleavened Bread

12:14-20pp — Lev 23:4-8; Nu 28:16-25; Dt 16:1-8

12 The LORD said to Moses and Aaron in Egypt, 2 "This month is to be for you the first month,[v]
the first month of your year. 3 Tell the whole community of Israel that on the tenth day of
this month each man is to take a lamb[a] for his family, one for each household. 4 If any household
is too small for a whole lamb, they must share one with their nearest neighbor, having taken into
account the number of people there are. You are to determine the amount of lamb needed in accordance with what each person will eat. 5 The animals you choose must be year-old males without
defect,[w] and you may take them from the sheep or the goats. 6 Take care of them until the fourteenth
day of the month,[x] when all the members of the community of Israel must slaughter them at twilight.[y] 7 Then they are to take some of the blood and put it on the sides and tops of the doorframes
of the houses where they eat the lambs. 8 That same night[z] they are to eat the meat roasted[a] over the
fire, along with bitter herbs,[b] and bread made without yeast.[c] 9 Do not eat the meat raw or boiled in
water, but roast it over a fire — with the head, legs and internal organs. 10 Do not leave any of it till
morning;[d] if some is left till morning, you must burn it. 11 This is how you are to eat it: with your
cloak tucked into your belt, your sandals on your feet and your staff in your hand. Eat it in haste;[e]
it is the LORD's Passover.[f]

12 "On that same night I will pass through[g] Egypt and strike down every firstborn of both people
and animals, and I will bring judgment on all the gods[h] of Egypt. I am the LORD.[i] 13 The blood will be a

[a] *3* The Hebrew word can mean *lamb* or *kid*; also in verse 4.

12:1 — 13:16 *Redemption and Consecration of Israel's Firstborn.* The material in ch. 11 is descriptive, containing information necessary to understand the story. Chs. 12 – 13 are largely prescriptive, focusing on the ritual involved in that first Passover night as well as the regular celebration of Passover/Unleavened Bread and the consecration of the firstborn by future generations.

12:1 – 30 *The Passover and the Festival of Unleavened Bread.* Between the announcement of the final plague and the execution of it are instructions concerning the Passover Festival. The first section (vv. 1 – 20) contains two subunits: vv. 1 – 13 relate primarily to the original Passover, and vv. 14 – 20 concern its annual commemoration. The second section (vv. 21 – 28) narrates Moses' communication of these instructions (at least in part) to the people via their elders, followed by a brief description of the scale of the actual destruction (vv. 29 – 30).

12:2 The exodus marks the start of the process by which Israel became a holy nation, and so it marks the beginning of the nation's religious calendar. **first month.** Aviv (13:4); the spring month (corresponding to March – April in the Western calendar); renamed Nisan after the exile (Esth 3:7).

12:3 lamb. The sacrificial animal can be either a lamb or a kid (see NIV text note). Small households are to share an animal (v. 4), which ensures adequate provision without unnecessary waste.

12:5 without defect. While not explained here, this stipulation is elucidated elsewhere in terms of the animal's acceptability as a sacrifice (Lev 22:18 – 25; Mal 1:6 – 14). This requirement clearly foreshadows the sinless perfection of Jesus, the ultimate Passover Lamb, whose death was a substitutionary atonement for human sin (John 1:29; 1 Cor 5:7; 1 Pet 1:19.). Although the connection between the Passover sacrifice and either sin or atonement is not made explicit in Exodus, its substitutionary nature clearly implies that the death of the Passover animal, like that of Jesus, had atoning significance for Israel. This is further suggested by the fact that, unlike in the preceding disasters, God does not simply exempt his people from this destruction. Like Pharaoh, Israel's sin had to be addressed by a holy God, either through punishment or atonement.

12:6 at twilight. Or "between the evenings"; the period between either (1) early evening and sunset or (2) sunset and nightfall — which has given rise to disputes about when the Sabbath and other holy days begin. Some scholars hold that in the preexilic period the day was reckoned as starting in the morning, but this changes to evening in the postexilic period due to Babylonian influence.

12:7 blood. Represents life (Lev 17:11), thus deliverance through the blood of the Passover animal denotes its substitutionary nature; its life was given in exchange for another. Elsewhere in Exodus blood is used for both atonement (30:10) and consecration (29:19 – 21; cf. 24:6 – 8). Both concepts are probably included here: the blood both atones for Israel's sin (Heb 9:22) and consecrates each household by purifying it with this distinguishing mark. Deliverance through the blood of a lamb prefigures the eternal salvation secured through the Lamb of God by his death (John 1:29).

12:8 – 9 Regulations governing the meat's consumption distinguish this rite from analogous rituals in Canaanite practice.

12:8 bitter herbs. A side salad requiring little preparation and not necessarily carrying any theological significance — despite the earlier use of the same word for Israel's "bitter" service (1:14) and the subsequent association of these two texts in later practice. **bread made without yeast.** Unleavened bread reflects their hasty departure (vv. 11,39).

12:10 Do not leave any of it till morning. This regulation, reiterated in 23:18, was probably to prevent using the consecrated meat for normal consumption.

12:11 cloak ... sandals ... staff. The Israelites are to eat the meat dressed and ready to leave because there will be little time to pack or prepare for the journey (v. 39). **Passover.** Refers primarily to the victim, secondarily to the festival. The word is explained by the fact that the Lord "passed over" (v. 27; see vv. 13,23) Israelite households marked by the sign of the animal's blood.

12:12 In executing Egypt's firstborn, the Lord brought "judgment on all the gods of Egypt." Some infer a subtle critique of Egyptian gods and beliefs throughout the plague narrative. While certain plagues may implicitly expose the impotency of particular Egyptian deities, the text focuses much more on how they demonstrate the Lord's supremacy over Pharaoh, an unwitting instrument in God's plan and purposes (Rom 9:17,22 – 24).

12:13 sign. Marks the Israelites' special status as God's people, those the Lord chose to redeem rather than judge (8:23).

sign for you on the houses where you are, and when I see the blood, I will pass over you. No destructive
plague will touch you when I strike Egypt.
14"This is a day you are to commemorate;[j] for the generations to come you shall celebrate it as a
festival to the LORD—a lasting ordinance.[k] 15For seven days you are to eat bread made without yeast.[l]
On the first day remove the yeast from your houses, for whoever eats anything with yeast in it from the
first day through the seventh must be cut off[m] from Israel. 16On the first day hold a sacred assembly,
and another one on the seventh day. Do no work at all on these days, except to prepare food for everyone to eat; that is all you may do.
17"Celebrate the Festival of Unleavened Bread, because it was on this very day that I brought your
divisions out of Egypt.[n] Celebrate this day as a lasting ordinance for the generations to come. 18In
the first month[o] you are to eat bread made without yeast, from the evening of the fourteenth day
until the evening of the twenty-first day. 19For seven days no yeast is to be found in your houses.
And anyone, whether foreigner or native-born, who eats anything with yeast in it must be cut off
from the community of Israel. 20Eat nothing made with yeast. Wherever you live, you must eat unleavened bread."
21Then Moses summoned all the elders of Israel and said to them, "Go at once and select the animals
for your families and slaughter the Passover[p] lamb. 22Take a bunch of hyssop, dip it into the blood in
the basin and put some of the blood[q] on the top and on both sides of the doorframe. None of you shall
go out of the door of your house until morning. 23When the
LORD goes through the land to strike down the Egyptians, he
will see the blood[r] on the top and sides of the doorframe and
will pass over[s] that doorway, and he will not permit the destroyer[t] to enter your houses and strike you down.
24"Obey these instructions as a lasting ordinance for you
and your descendants. 25When you enter the land that the
LORD will give you as he promised, observe this ceremony.
26And when your children[u] ask you, 'What does this ceremony mean to you?' 27then tell them, 'It is the Passover[v]
sacrifice to the LORD, who passed over the houses of the Israelites in Egypt and spared our homes when he struck down

Hyssop (Exod 12:22).
Eitan f/Wikimedia Commons, CC BY 3.0

12:14 [j]Ex 13:9 [k]ver 17, 24; Ex 13:5,10; 2Ki 23:21
12:15 [l]Ex 13:6-7; 23:15; 34:18; Lev 23:6; Dt 16:3 [m]Ge 17:14; Nu 9:13
12:17 [n]ver 41; Ex 13:3
12:18 [o]ver 2; Lev 23:5-8; Nu 28:16-25
12:21 [p]ver 11; Mk 14:12-16
12:22 [q]ver 7; Heb 11:28
12:23 [r]Rev 7:3 [s]ver 13 [t]1Co 10:10; Heb 11:28
12:26 [u]Ex 10:2; 13:8, 14-15; Jos 4:6
12:27 [v]ver 11

12:14 The focus shifts to how future generations should commemorate this event (cf. Num 9:1–5; Josh 5:10; 2 Kgs 23:21–23; Ezra 6:19–22; Matt 26:17–19; Luke 2:41; John 11:55).
12:15 without yeast. The dough for a day's bread was normally mixed and left to stand before being baked so that a small quantity of the fermented dough from the previous day's batch could "leaven" (raise) the new batch. In this instance the Israelites must remove such fermented dough or "leaven" on the first day; God imposes a total ban. Leaven/yeast thus becomes a symbol in the NT for sinful behavior (Luke 12:1; 1 Cor 5:6–8), which must likewise be eradicated, as far as is possible, from the life of the Christian community. **cut off.** Consuming leavened bread during this seven-day period was a serious matter; in the present context, "cut off from the community of Israel" (v. 19) may elaborate on "cut off from Israel"; i.e., it refers here to exclusion from the annual celebration rather than to some form of execution, as is plainly the case later in the book (see 31:14–15, where the same Hebrew verb is used).
12:17 Unleavened Bread. The name of this week-long (v. 15) festival. Here, as elsewhere in the Pentateuch, its rationale is explicitly tied to the exodus.
12:18 from the evening ... until the evening. This suggests that the Festival of Unleavened Bread begins on the evening of the 14th day and ceases on the evening of the 21st day. But other passages suggest it begins on the 15th day, the day after Passover (Lev 23:5–6; Num 28:16–17). The simplest solution to this crux is that the 15th day in the latter texts begins with sunrise rather than sunset (see note on v. 6); Lev 23:6 and Num 28:17 do not mention "twilight" or "evening." While the Jewish day began at sunset in the postexilic period, the dating formula in all Pentateuchal Passover texts could imply that the day starts at sunrise (as with the Egyptians). Thus understood, while Israelites are not to consume any leaven from the beginning of Passover at twilight on the 14th day, the Festival of Unleavened Bread officially begins on the morning of the 15th day and concludes on the evening of the 21st day by sacred assemblies.
12:21–28 Moses imparts the Lord's twofold set of directives—in the same sequence—to "all the elders of Israel" (v. 21; see note on 3:16). They are "all" involved only twice elsewhere in the book, and each instance is a particularly significant occasion (4:29; 18:12).
12:21 elders. See note on 3:16. **Go at once.** "Round up and select" possibly explains the idea here. **Passover lamb.** Jesus fulfills this OT type (see note on v. 5).
12:22 hyssop. This plant (probably from the mint family) had a straight stalk (John 19:29) that, along with the hairy texture of its leaves, made it a natural sprinkling device. Elsewhere in the Bible it is generally associated with purification rituals (Lev 14:4,6,49,51–52; Num 19:6,18; Heb 9:19; cf. Ps 51:7).
12:23 destroyer. Traditionally understood as a destroying angel (cf. 2 Sam 24:15–16; 2 Kgs 19:35; 1 Cor 10:10).
12:26 when your children ask. Cf. 13:14. Celebrating Passover and Unleavened Bread instructs future generations and helps them grasp its ongoing significance for them as the nation the Lord has redeemed.
12:27–28 The Israelites again respond positively to Moses' message (4:31). Evidently the Lord's signs and wonders in Egypt eradicated their

12:27 [w]Ex 4:31
12:29 [x]Ex 11:4 [y]Ex 4:23; Ps 78:51 [z]Ex 9:6
12:30 [a]Ex 11:6
12:31 [b]Ex 8:8
12:32 [c]Ex 10:9,26
12:33 [d]Ps 105:38
12:35 [e]Ex 3:22
12:36 [f]Ex 3:22
12:37 [g]Nu 33:3-5 [h]Ex 38:26; Nu 1:46; 11:13,21
12:38 [i]Nu 11:4
12:39 [j]ver 31-33; Ex 6:1; 11:1
12:40 [k]Ge 15:13; Ac 7:6; Gal 3:17
12:41 [l]ver 17; Ex 6:26 [m]Ex 3:10
12:42 [n]Ex 13:10; Dt 16:1,6
12:43 [o]ver 11 [p]ver 48; Nu 9:14
12:44 [q]Ge 17:12-13
12:45 [r]Lev 22:10

the Egyptians.' " Then the people bowed down and worshiped.[w] 28The Israelites did just what the LORD
commanded Moses and Aaron.
29At midnight[x] the LORD struck down all the firstborn[y] in Egypt, from the firstborn of Pharaoh, who
sat on the throne, to the firstborn of the prisoner, who was in the dungeon, and the firstborn of all the
livestock[z] as well. 30Pharaoh and all his officials and all the Egyptians got up during the night, and
there was loud wailing[a] in Egypt, for there was not a house without someone dead.

The Exodus

31During the night Pharaoh summoned Moses and Aaron and said, "Up! Leave my people, you and
the Israelites! Go, worship[b] the LORD as you have requested. 32Take your flocks and herds,[c] as you have
said, and go. And also bless me."
33The Egyptians urged the people to hurry and leave[d] the country. "For otherwise," they said, "we
will all die!" 34So the people took their dough before the yeast was added, and carried it on their shoulders in kneading troughs wrapped in clothing. 35The Israelites did as Moses instructed and asked the
Egyptians for articles of silver and gold[e] and for clothing. 36The LORD had made the Egyptians favorably
disposed toward the people, and they gave them what they asked for; so they plundered[f] the Egyptians.
37The Israelites journeyed from Rameses to Sukkoth.[g] There were about six hundred thousand men[h]
on foot, besides women and children. 38Many other people[i] went up with them, and also large droves
of livestock, both flocks and herds. 39With the dough the Israelites had brought from Egypt, they baked
loaves of unleavened bread. The dough was without yeast because they had been driven out[j] of Egypt
and did not have time to prepare food for themselves.
40Now the length of time the Israelite people lived in Egypt[a] was 430 years.[k] 41At the end of the 430
years, to the very day, all the LORD's divisions[l] left Egypt.[m] 42Because the LORD kept vigil that night to
bring them out of Egypt, on this night all the Israelites are to keep vigil to honor the LORD for the generations to come.[n]

Passover Restrictions

43The LORD said to Moses and Aaron, "These are the regulations for the Passover meal:[o]
"No foreigner[p] may eat it. 44Any slave you have bought may eat it after you have circumcised[q] him,
45but a temporary resident or a hired worker[r] may not eat it.

[a] 40 Masoretic Text; Samaritan Pentateuch and Septuagint *Egypt and Canaan*

fears and misgivings (cf. 6:9). The Israelites again serve as a foil to Pharaoh, whose negative response is a refrain throughout the plague narrative.

12:29 struck down. As promised, the Lord has already struck Egypt with several disasters (3:20); however, this blow is the most devastating. As anticipated (11:5), no Egyptian family enjoys immunity, regardless of their social status or category.

12:31–42 *The Exodus.* After the mixture of initial instructions and regulations for its subsequent celebration, the story of Israel's escape from Egypt resumes. The Lord makes good on both his threats and his promises.

12:31–32 In view of 10:28, there is some degree of irony here; Pharaoh now summons Moses and Aaron into his presence, despite his previous attempt to break off all communication with a threat of death. **as you have requested ... as you have said.** Just as God had predicted (3:20; 11:1), Pharaoh now capitulates entirely.

12:32 bless me. This is the closest Pharaoh comes to acknowledging the power of Israel's God, although even now he fails to confess the Lord's universal supremacy (cf. 15:11; 18:11) and displays the same desire for immediate respite that he has demonstrated throughout the plague narrative. Ironically, the blessing Pharaoh asks for might already have been experienced had he dealt with God's people differently (cf. Gen 12:3; 21:22–24; 26:28–31; 39:5).

12:36 The Egyptians' generosity contrasts with Pharaoh's earlier intransigence. Both are direct human responses to the Lord's dealings with Egypt, but whereas Pharaoh responds negatively to God's leniency, Pharaoh's subjects respond positively to God's severity.

12:37 six hundred thousand men. This number seems excessively large, projecting a total population of 2–3 million. Many, therefore, interpret this number as theological hyperbole or the result of subsequent scribal misunderstanding. No explanation is without difficulty, and there is no consensus on this thorny issue, but see note on 38:25–26.

12:38 Many other people. Those who participated in the exodus were ethnically diverse. Other ethnic groups apparently remained with the Israelites for some time (Num 11:4), and there was at least some degree of amalgamation (Num 12:1).

12:39 The Israelites had to eat unleavened bread (see v. 8) because there was insufficient time for the leaven to do its work on the dough.

12:40 430 years. This appears to be an exact figure as opposed to the round numbers mentioned elsewhere (see notes on Gen 15:13; Acts 7:6). The main point is that Yahweh keeps his promise to Abraham.

12:41 to the very day. A different reading is "on that same day" (cf. v. 17). Thus understood, it refers to the night of the Passover, making a smooth transition to the following verse with its focus on "that night" (v. 42). **divisions.** Rather than a military image, this term, first introduced in 6:26, simply portrays them leaving in orderly fashion, highlighting the dignity of Israel's departure.

12:43–51 *Passover Restrictions.* Verses 43–49 focus mainly on subsequent participation in the celebration of Passover; vv. 50–51 are a summary note highlighting Israel's obedience and deliverance.

46"It must be eaten inside the house; take none of the meat outside the house. Do not break any of
the bones.[s] 47The whole community of Israel must celebrate it.
48"A foreigner residing among you who wants to celebrate the LORD's Passover must have all the males
in his household circumcised; then he may take part like one born in the land.[t] No uncircumcised male
may eat it. 49The same law applies both to the native-born and to the foreigner[u] residing among you."
50All the Israelites did just what the LORD had commanded Moses and Aaron. 51And on that very day
the LORD brought the Israelites out of Egypt by their divisions.[v]

Consecration of the Firstborn

13 The LORD said to Moses, 2"Consecrate to me every firstborn male.[w] The first offspring of every
womb among the Israelites belongs to me, whether human or animal."
3Then Moses said to the people, "Commemorate this day, the day you came out of Egypt, out of the
land of slavery, because the LORD brought you out of it with a mighty hand.[x] Eat nothing containing
yeast.[y] 4Today, in the month of Aviv,[z] you are leaving. 5When the LORD brings you into the land of the
Canaanites, Hittites, Amorites, Hivites and Jebusites[a] — the land he swore to your ancestors to give you,
a land flowing with milk and honey — you are to observe this ceremony[b] in this month: 6For seven
days eat bread made without yeast and on the seventh day hold a festival[c] to the LORD. 7Eat unleavened
bread during those seven days; nothing with yeast in it is to be seen among you, nor shall any yeast
be seen anywhere within your borders. 8On that day tell your son,[d] 'I do this because of what the LORD
did for me when I came out of Egypt.' 9This observance will be for you like a sign on your hand and a
reminder on your forehead[e] that this law of the LORD is to be on your lips. For the LORD brought you out
of Egypt with his mighty hand. 10You must keep this ordinance[f] at the appointed time year after year.
11"After the LORD brings you into the land of the Canaanites and gives it to you, as he promised on
oath to you and your ancestors, 12you are to give over to the LORD the first offspring of every womb. All
the firstborn males of your livestock belong to the LORD.[g] 13Redeem with a lamb every firstborn donkey,
but if you do not redeem it, break its neck.[h] Redeem every firstborn among your sons.[i]
14"In days to come, when your son[j] asks you, 'What does this mean?' say to him, 'With a mighty
hand the LORD brought us out of Egypt, out of the land of slavery.[k] 15When Pharaoh stubbornly refused
to let us go, the LORD killed the firstborn of both people and animals in Egypt. This is why I sacrifice to
the LORD the first male offspring of every womb and redeem each of my firstborn sons.'[l] 16And it will be
like a sign on your hand and a symbol on your forehead[m] that the LORD brought us out of Egypt with
his mighty hand."

12:46 [s] Nu 9:12; Jn 19:36*
12:48 [t] Nu 9:14
12:49 [u] Nu 15:15-16,29; Gal 3:28
12:51 [v] ver 41; Ex 6:26
13:2 [w] ver 12,13,15; Ex 22:29; Nu 3:13; Dt 15:19; Lk 2:23*
13:3 [x] Ex 3:20; 6:1 [y] Ex 12:19
13:4 [z] Ex 12:2
13:5 [a] Ex 3:8 [b] Ex 12:25-26
13:6 [c] Ex 12:15-20
13:8 [d] ver 14; Ex 10:2; Ps 78:5-6
13:9 [e] ver 16; Dt 6:8; 11:18
13:10 [f] Ex 12:24-25
13:12 [g] Lev 27:26; Lk 2:23*
13:13 [h] Ex 34:20 [i] Nu 18:15
13:14 [j] Ex 10:2; 12:26-27; Dt 6:20 [k] ver 3,9
13:15 [l] Ex 12:29
13:16 [m] ver 9

12:46 These stipulations probably keep the consecrated meat from any profane use. **Do not break any of the bones.** Symbolically foreshadows the ultimate Passover lamb (John 19:36).

12:48 No uncircumcised male. Only those counted among Israel, God's covenant people (cf. 4:24–26), may participate, because only they experienced the redemption that Passover commemorates. Through circumcision non-Israelites could align themselves with God's covenant people; then they also could participate in the Passover. Likewise, participation in the Lord's Supper expresses the unity of believers through faith in Jesus (1 Cor 11:27–30).

12:51 divisions. See note on v. 41.

13:1–16 *Consecration of the Firstborn.* The final unit of this section repeats and expands the regulations relating to the Festival of Unleavened Bread (vv. 3–10); it is sandwiched between regulations concerning the consecration of Israel's firstborn (vv. 1–2,11–16).

13:2 Consecrate ... every firstborn male. This instruction is somewhat unexpected (12:3–20 does not mention it). Moses explains its rationale when he conveys the instruction to Israel: it reminds them that God ransomed the Israelite firstborn from death (vv. 11–16).

13:5 See note on 3:8. **swore to your ancestors.** This (and v. 11) describes Israel's territorial inheritance not only in terms of its present inhabitants but also in terms of the ancestral oath; this further reminds them that God is keeping his covenant promises.

13:6–7 See note on 12:18.

13:8 See note on 12:26. Like the consecration of the firstborn (vv. 1–2,11–16), the Festival of Unleavened Bread will inform future generations about the Lord's deliverance, so it is important to continue these traditions in the promised land (vv. 5,10; 12:25).

13:9 like a sign on your hand and a reminder on your forehead. In later history some interpret this figurative language literally (along with Deut 6:8), hence the Jewish use of phylacteries (see Matt 23:5 and note). But the Lord's intent is that this festival remind the Israelites of their commitment to him.

13:11–16 Attention reverts to the instructions concerning the firstborn begun in vv. 1–2.

13:12 give over to the LORD. This evidently involves ritual slaughter.

13:13 Redeem. Just as Israel's firstborn were redeemed with a Passover lamb (12:13), so all future firstborn (whether human or animal) must be either redeemed with a lamb, sacrificed, or slaughtered. Later the Levites become substitutes for the firstborn (Num 3:12,41,45; 8:15–18). Like the Passover sacrifice, the substitutionary death of the lamb foreshadows redemption through God's unique firstborn Son. **donkey.** Unlike sheep and cattle, donkeys could not be sacrificed. In such cases, the animal was simply to be killed.

13:17 [n]Ex 14:11; Nu 14:1-4; Dt 17:16
13:18 [o]Ps 136:16 [p]Jos 1:14
13:19 [q]Jos 24:32; Ac 7:16 [r]Ge 50:24-25
13:20 [s]Nu 33:6
13:21 [t]Ex 14:19,24; 33:9-10; Nu 9:16; Dt 1:33; Ne 9:12,19; Ps 78:14; 99:7; 105:39; Isa 4:5; 1Co 10:1
14:2 [u]Nu 33:7; Jer 44:1
14:4 [v]Ex 4:21 [w]Ro 9:17, 22-23 [x]Ex 7:5

Crossing the Sea

17 When Pharaoh let the people go, God did not lead them on the road through the Philistine country,
though that was shorter. For God said, "If they face war, they might change their minds and return to
Egypt."[n] 18 So God led[o] the people around by the desert road toward the Red Sea.[a] The Israelites went
up out of Egypt ready for battle.[p]
19 Moses took the bones of Joseph[q] with him because Joseph had made the Israelites swear an oath. He had
said, "God will surely come to your aid, and then you must carry my bones up with you from this place."[b][r]
20 After leaving Sukkoth they camped at Etham on the edge of the desert.[s] 21 By day the LORD went
ahead of them in a pillar of cloud[t] to guide them on their way and by night in a pillar of fire to give
them light, so that they could travel by day or night. 22 Neither the pillar of cloud by day nor the pillar
of fire by night left its place in front of the people.

14 Then the LORD said to Moses, 2 "Tell the Israelites to turn back and encamp near Pi Hahiroth,
between Migdol[u] and the sea. They are to encamp by the sea, directly opposite Baal Zephon. 3 Pharaoh will think, 'The Israelites are wandering around the land in confusion, hemmed in by the desert.' 4 And
I will harden Pharaoh's heart,[v] and he will pursue them. But I will gain glory[w] for myself through Pharaoh
and all his army, and the Egyptians will know that I am the LORD."[x] So the Israelites did this.
5 When the king of Egypt was told that the people had fled, Pharaoh and his officials changed their
minds about them and said, "What have we done? We have let the Israelites go and have lost their services!" 6 So he had his chariot made ready and took his army with him. 7 He took six hundred of the best

[a] *18* Or *the Sea of Reeds* [b] *19* See Gen. 50:25.

13:17—18:27 *From Egypt to Sinai.* The next major narrative block recounts the first leg of Israel's journey from Egypt to the promised land. The events in this section span approximately two and a half months. The first part (13:17—15:21) focuses on the exodus and the Lord's climactic victory over the Egyptians at the Red Sea. The second part (15:22—18:27) highlights key stages in Israel's journey from the Red Sea to their encampment at Rephidim (within the region of Horeb, but outside the wilderness of Sinai; see 18:5).

13:17—15:21 *Israel's Rescue and Egypt's Punishment at the Red Sea.* This section recounts the climactic act of divine judgment: the destruction of Pharaoh's army in the Red Sea. The theological implications of this are then expressed and celebrated.

13:17—14:31 *Crossing the Sea.* This resumes the account of Israel's itinerary from 12:37 (see 13:20). But before outlining the next stage of the journey, it provides the theological rationale for what might otherwise appear to be a strange route and thus sets the stage for Pharaoh's ultimate act of folly.

13:17 let … go. Now that Pharaoh has submitted to the Lord's demand (5:1), the story takes an unexpected twist: because the road through the Philistine country is so heavily fortified, the Lord leads Israel on a more circuitous route.

13:18 desert road. This led south, along the western coast of the Sinai peninsula. **Red Sea.** See note on 10:19. **ready for battle.** This refers to their orderly departure from Egypt, including their being ready for battle (see note on 12:41).

13:19 Moses took the bones of Joseph. The exodus story again connects with the patriarchal accounts (and hence, the covenant promises) in the book of Genesis, particularly the hope of future deliverance that Joseph held out (see note on Gen 50:24–26). See Josh 24:32; this symbolizes Israel in Egypt, on its journey, and at rest in the promised land.

13:20 Scholars disagree on the locations of several places mentioned in the text, including key sites such as Mount Sinai itself. It is difficult, therefore, to reconstruct Israel's precise itinerary from Egypt with absolute certainty. **Sukkoth.** Means "booths" or "shelters"; it may be a region or a specific location, possibly Tell el-Maskuta. **Etham.** A name possibly connected with the god Atum; it is located east of Tell el-Maskuta, close to the Egyptian border. **the desert.** Israel's direction of travel suggests that this is the northern part of the Sinai peninsula, in the vicinity of Lake Timsah (see map, p. 147).

13:21 pillar of cloud … fire. Presumably this is the same phenomenon viewed during daytime and nighttime, respectively. Like the burning bush (3:2–3) and the subsequent inferno on Mount Sinai (19:18; 24:17), it is clearly a theophany (a manifestation of God's presence) that leads and directs God's people on their journey.

14:2 Pi Hahiroth. Meaning "mouth of the canals," it may refer to the eastern frontier canal. It, Baal Zephon, and the "Red Sea" all appear on a thirteenth-century BC Egyptian papyrus as situated along the frontier at the Ballah lakes. **Migdol.** Meaning "tower," it may be attested in fourteenth-century BC texts and situated in this region. This suggests that the infamous body of water in this chapter is located at Lake Ballah, about 30 miles (48 kilometers) above the northern tip of the Gulf of Suez (see notes on 10:19; 13:20).

14:4 I will harden Pharaoh's heart. See note on 4:21. The Lord is laying the trap that will result in the climactic humiliation of Pharaoh. As before, Pharaoh's hardening seems to be a direct consequence of the Lord's activities (in this case, placing the Israelites in an apparently vulnerable position). Thus, again God's sovereignty (it is the Lord who controls these events) and human responsibility (it is Pharaoh who makes this treacherous decision) dovetail in such a way that the Lord's objectives are achieved through what takes place (cf. vv. 17–18). **I will gain glory.** God's glory, or "heaviness" (see "The Glory of God," p. 2640), will be manifest and acknowledged through what he does to Pharaoh and the Egyptian army (cf. v. 31). **the Egyptians will know that I am the LORD.** God's express goal throughout Exodus is to make himself known as "the LORD" (6:2–3,7; 7:5,17; 8:10,22; 9:14,16,29; 10:2; 29:46; 33:19; 34:10).

14:5 king … was told. This may seem strange in view of 12:31–32, but it probably alludes to a progress report. Whatever the explanation, socioeconomic realities prompt Pharaoh to set about recapturing his slaves—spurred on, no doubt, by the Israelites' apparent geographic confusion.

14:7–9 Chariots provided a kind of mobile firing platform for archers and represented the most technologically advanced weapons available. Egypt, the mightiest superpower of this period, now dispatches this elite task force after the fleeing Israelite slaves. This demonstrates

chariots, along with all the other chariots of Egypt, with officers over all of them. 8The LORD hardened
the heart[y] of Pharaoh king of Egypt, so that he pursued the Israelites, who were marching out boldly.[z]
9The Egyptians — all Pharaoh's horses and chariots, horsemen[a] and troops — pursued the Israelites
and overtook[a] them as they camped by the sea near Pi Hahiroth, opposite Baal Zephon.

10As Pharaoh approached, the Israelites looked up, and there were the Egyptians, marching after
them. They were terrified and cried[b] out to the LORD. 11They said to Moses, "Was it because there were
no graves in Egypt that you brought us to the desert to die?[c] What have you done to us by bringing us
out of Egypt? 12Didn't we say to you in Egypt, 'Leave us alone; let us serve the Egyptians'? It would have
been better for us to serve the Egyptians than to die in the desert!"

13Moses answered the people, "Do not be afraid.[d] Stand firm and you will see[e] the deliverance the
LORD will bring you today. The Egyptians you see today you will never see[f] again. 14The LORD will fight[g]
for you; you need only to be still."[h]

15Then the LORD said to Moses, "Why are you crying out to me? Tell the Israelites to move on. 16Raise
your staff[i] and stretch out your hand over the sea to divide the water[j] so that the Israelites can go through
the sea on dry ground. 17I will harden the hearts of the Egyptians so that they will go in after them.[k] And
I will gain glory through Pharaoh and all his army, through his chariots and his horsemen. 18The Egyptians will know that I am the LORD when I gain glory through Pharaoh, his chariots and his horsemen."

19Then the angel of God, who had been traveling in front of Israel's army, withdrew and went behind
them. The pillar of cloud[l] also moved from in front and stood behind them, 20coming between the armies of Egypt and Israel. Throughout the night the cloud brought darkness to the one side and light to
the other side; so neither went near the other all night long.

21Then Moses stretched out his hand over the sea, and all that night the LORD drove the sea back

a 9 Or *charioteers*; also in verses 17, 18, 23, 26 and 28

14:8 [y] ver 4; Ex 11:10 [z] Nu 33:3; Ac 13:17
14:9 [a] Ex 15:9
14:10 [b] Jos 24:7; Ne 9:9; Ps 34:17
14:11 [c] Ps 106:7-8
14:13 [d] Ge 15:1 [e] 2Ch 20:17; Isa 41:10, 13-14 [f] ver 30
14:14 [g] ver 25; Ex 15:3; Dt 1:30; 3:22; 2Ch 20:29 [h] Ps 37:7; 46:10; Isa 30:15
14:16 [i] Ex 4:17; Nu 20:8-9,11 [j] Isa 10:26
14:17 [k] ver 4
14:19 [l] Ex 13:21

Rameses II (1279 – 1213 BC) fighting from his chariot in a carving at Abu Simbel. The chariots used by Pharaoh to chase the Israelites (Exod 14:7) may have been similar.

how eager Pharaoh is to recapture his slaves, although it also reflects his folly; his conflict is really with the God who has laid claim to these Hebrews and who has amply demonstrated that no human force is any match for him.

14:7 officers. The precise connotation is unclear; it could be runners who keep pace with the chariots or the wealthy Egyptians who own and maintain such military carriages. Whatever the case, they are included among the Egyptians who perish in the Red Sea (15:4).

14:8 See note on 4:21.

14:9 Pi Hahiroth ... Baal Zephon. See note on v. 2.

14:10 – 12 Israelite confidence in the Lord and/or Moses (cf. 12:27 – 28,50) quickly dissipates in the face of this crisis, giving place to bitter recriminations. Such lack of faith in the light of all that preceded this is startling and a harbinger of things to come. The Israelites' natural tendency to grumble at every hurdle is a recurring motif in Exodus and beyond.

14:13 The Lord's word (vv. 2 – 4) bolsters Moses' faith. On this basis Moses confidently proclaims Israel's forthcoming deliverance and Egypt's imminent demise.

14:14 The LORD will fight for you. This is the first instance of a theme that becomes prominent in Israel's subsequent history and beyond: as divine warrior (15:3), the Lord fights on Israel's behalf — usually in a manner that secures him the exclusive glory (cf. 23:20 – 30; Hab 3:3 – 15; Hag 2:1 – 22; Zech 14:3 – 15; Rev 19:11 – 16). Thus, Israel need only to "be still" in the sense of "keep silent" (i.e., do nothing) in the context of the ensuing conflict.

14:15 Either there is a narrative gap here (i.e., Moses did indeed cry out to the Lord, but the narrator has skipped over this) or, more probably, Moses is so closely identified with Israel (the people he represents before God) that their guilt becomes his by association.

14:16 divide the water. However one explains the phenomenon (see note on vv. 21 – 22), the Israelites will traverse the sea on dry ground.

14:17 harden the hearts of the Egyptians. God will induce or give them courage (i.e., strengthen their hearts) to pursue the Israelites into this visibly precarious situation, and God will thus bring about his ultimate goal. **gain glory.** See note on v. 4.

14:19 angel of God. This divine messenger is closely associated with the pillar of cloud and fire, and thus with the Lord himself (13:21; see note on 3:2). **withdrew ... moved.** The almost identical description of the actions of the angel and the pillar of cloud possibly identifies these as a single phenomenon, although the different verbs used ("went"/"stood behind") could imply two separate entities; the angel's movement then precipitates the cloud's movement.

14:20 The details are unclear, but the cloud evidently serves the interests of the Israelites while thwarting the intentions of the Egyptians — possibly by supplying light to the former while simultaneously inflicting darkness on the latter. Its isolating effect protects the Israelites from immediate attack.

14:21 – 22 As with the series of wonders in Egypt, naturalistic explanations of this event inevitably undermine its theological significance. Whatever "natural" elements the Lord may have employed (as "a strong east wind" blowing all night might imply), the timing of

14:21 [m]Ex 15:8 [n]Ps 74:13; 114:5; Isa 63:12
14:22 [o]Ex 15:19; Ne 9:11; Ps 66:6; Heb 11:29
14:24 [p]Ex 13:21
14:25 [q]ver 14
14:27 [r]Jos 4:18 [s]Ex 15:1,21; Ps 78:53; 106:11
14:29 [t]ver 22
14:30 [u]Ps 106:8,10,21
14:31 [v]Ps 106:12; Jn 2:11
15:1 [w]Rev 15:3 [x]Ps 106:12
15:2 [y]Ps 59:17 [z]Ps 18:2, 46; Isa 12:2; Hab 3:18 [a]Ge 28:21 [b]Ex 3:6, 15-16; Isa 25:1
15:3 [c]Ex 14:14; Ps 24:8; Rev 19:11 [d]Ex 6:2-3, 7-8; Ps 83:18
15:4 [e]Ex 14:6-7

with a strong east wind[m] and turned it into dry land. The waters were divided,[n] [22]and the Israelites went
through the sea on dry ground,[o] with a wall of water on their right and on their left.
[23]The Egyptians pursued them, and all Pharaoh's horses and chariots and horsemen followed them
into the sea. [24]During the last watch of the night the LORD looked down from the pillar of fire and
cloud[p] at the Egyptian army and threw it into confusion. [25]He jammed[a] the wheels of their chariots so
that they had difficulty driving. And the Egyptians said, "Let's get away from the Israelites! The LORD is
fighting[q] for them against Egypt."
[26]Then the LORD said to Moses, "Stretch out your hand over the sea so that the waters may flow back
over the Egyptians and their chariots and horsemen." [27]Moses stretched out his hand over the sea, and
at daybreak the sea went back to its place.[r] The Egyptians were fleeing toward[b] it, and the LORD swept
them into the sea.[s] [28]The water flowed back and covered the chariots and horsemen — the entire army
of Pharaoh that had followed the Israelites into the sea. Not one of them survived.
[29]But the Israelites went through the sea on dry ground,[t] with a wall of water on their right and on
their left. [30]That day the LORD saved[u] Israel from the hands of the Egyptians, and Israel saw the Egyptians lying dead on the shore. [31]And when the Israelites saw the mighty hand of the LORD displayed
against the Egyptians, the people feared the LORD and put their trust[v] in him and in Moses his servant.

The Song of Moses and Miriam

15 Then Moses and the Israelites sang this song[w] to the LORD:

"I will sing[x] to the LORD,
  for he is highly exalted.
Both horse and driver
  he has hurled into the sea.

[2]"The LORD is my strength[y] and my defense[c];
  he has become my salvation.[z]
He is my God,[a] and I will praise him,
  my father's God, and I will exalt[b] him.
[3]The LORD is a warrior;[c]
  the LORD is his name.[d]
[4]Pharaoh's chariots and his army[e]
  he has hurled into the sea.

[a] *25* See Samaritan Pentateuch, Septuagint and Syriac; Masoretic Text *removed* [b] *27* Or *from*
[c] *2* Or *song*

this phenomenon, as well as its depiction both here and elsewhere (cf. 15:8,10; Pss 66:6; 106:9; 136:13–14; Isa 51:10; 63:11–13), suggests that it was a supernatural display of the Lord's "mighty hand" (14:31). As such, this was not a purely natural event, however unusual. Rather, God's ability to control this large body of water, like later similar events (e.g., Josh 3:14–17; 2 Kgs 2:8,14), demonstrates his lordship over creation. Such lordship is likewise reflected when Jesus calmed the storm and demonstrated that "even the winds and the water ... obey him" (Luke 8:25).

14:22 wall. A vivid description of the protection the piled up water provided (cf. 1 Sam 25:16; Ezra 9:9; Jer 15:20).

14:25 jammed the wheels. Ironically, a symbol of Egypt's strength — their chariots — becomes their downfall. Whether the wheels fall off (see NIV text note) or simply are bogged down in the silt, the chariots are somehow immobilized, thus offering no help to the panic-stricken Egyptians. **The LORD is fighting for them.** See note on v. 14.

14:27 toward. Or "from" (see NIV text note). **swept them into the sea.** Like the locusts (10:19).

14:28 the entire army of Pharaoh. Egypt suffers a devastating and humiliating defeat that the official annals typically do not record.

14:29–31 "The mighty hand of the LORD" (v. 31) saves Israel from "the hands of the Egyptians" (v. 30), a contrast more obvious in the original than in the English translation. Not surprisingly, this instills respect for the Lord as well as fresh confidence in his power and Moses' leadership.

15:1–21 *The Song of Moses and Miriam.* The "Song at the Sea" celebrates the Lord's climactic victory over the Egyptians at the Red Sea and looks to the future establishment of God's sanctuary on the earth. "Moses and the Israelites sang this song" (v. 1), and "Miriam sang" (v. 21). They probably sing antiphonally, with Miriam alternating with the rest. Alternatively, Miriam encourages others to join in singing Moses' song by rephrasing its opening line as an invocation. In any case, Miriam's exhortation invites all generations of God's people to share in this celebration.

15:1 The song initially focuses on the Lord's annihilation of the Egyptian chariot force in the sea, the theme that permeates vv. 1–11.

15:2 defense. Most translations have "song" (see NIV text note), but Hebrew parallelism ("strength") suggests that "defense" is more appropriate. **my father's God.** See note on 3:6. Possibly, however, this further alludes to the Lord's covenant faithfulness.

15:3 The LORD is a warrior. See note on 14:14. This concept adds specific content to the name by which the Lord has revealed himself (see 3:14,15 and notes).

15:4 officers. See note on 14:7. **Red Sea.** See note on 10:19.

The best of Pharaoh's officers
are drowned in the Red Sea.[a]
5 The deep waters have covered them;
they sank to the depths like a stone.[f]
6 Your right hand,[g] LORD,
was majestic in power.
Your right hand, LORD,
shattered the enemy.

7 "In the greatness of your majesty
you threw down those who opposed you.
You unleashed your burning anger;[h]
it consumed them like stubble.
8 By the blast of your nostrils[i]
the waters piled up.[j]
The surging waters stood up like a wall;[k]
the deep waters congealed in the heart of the sea.
9 The enemy boasted,
'I will pursue,[l] I will overtake them.
I will divide the spoils;[m]
I will gorge myself on them.
I will draw my sword
and my hand will destroy them.'
10 But you blew with your breath,
and the sea covered them.
They sank like lead
in the mighty waters.[n]
11 Who among the gods
is like you,[o] LORD?
Who is like you—
majestic in holiness,[p]
awesome in glory,[q]
working wonders?

12 "You stretch out your right hand,
and the earth swallows your enemies.
13 In your unfailing love you will lead[r]
the people you have redeemed.

[a] 4 Or *the Sea of Reeds*; also in verse 22

15:5 [f] ver 10; Ne 9:11
15:6 [g] Ps 118:15
15:7 [h] Ps 78:49-50
15:8 [i] Ex 14:21 [j] Ps 78:13 [k] Ex 14:22
15:9 [l] Ex 14:5-9 [m] Jdg 5:30; Isa 53:12
15:10 [n] ver 5; Ex 14:27-28
15:11 [o] Ex 8:10; Dt 3:24; Ps 77:13 [p] Isa 6:3; Rev 4:8 [q] Ps 8:1
15:13 [r] Ne 9:12; Ps 77:20

15:5 deep ... depths. While admittedly poetry, this implies that Pharaoh's elite chariot force did not drown in relatively shallow water such as that of a mudflat or marshy lagoon.
15:6 right hand ... right hand. Echoes the Lord's earlier words to Moses (3:19–20; 6:1; 7:4–5).
15:8 blast of your nostrils. A metaphor for the "east wind" (14:21), further highlighting the event's supernatural nature (cf. v. 10). **waters piled up ... like a wall.** Possibly another metaphor, although the terminology concurs with the prose description in 14:22. The imagery shows God's control over the most powerful natural force, the sea, side by side with his control over the most powerful human force, Pharaoh's army.
15:11 Who among the gods is like you ...? The Lord is unique, superior to every other deity (1 Sam 2:2; Pss 35:10; 71:19; 89:6; 113:5; Mic 7:18). This probably alludes to his humiliating "all the gods of Egypt" (12:12), which includes Pharaoh in particular. **majestic in holiness, awesome in glory, working wonders.** Distinctive attributes that set the Lord apart from all others.
15:12 This verse may mark the transition in the poem from the deliverance at the sea to events Israel is about to experience. **earth swallows your enemies.** Alludes either to the destruction of the Egyptians (in which case "earth" refers to the realm of death; see Pss 63:9; 71:20) or, looks ahead to the Korah incident (Num 16:28–34).
15:13–17 This clearly focuses on events subsequent to the Red Sea crossing. With the possible exception of v. 13, in the immediate context this section of the song is anticipating still future events associated with the rest of Israel's journey, which subsequent readers are also expected to celebrate.
15:13 people you have redeemed. See note on 13:13. **redeemed.** May simply be synonymous with "rescued" (cf. 6:6), but could also imply that the Lord is performing the role of Israel's guardian-redeemer (Lev 25:25; Ruth 3:9–13). Either way, the result is that Israel is free from Egyptian

15:13 [s]Ps 78:54
15:14 [t]Dt 2:25
15:15 [u]Ge 36:15 [v]Nu 22:3 [w]Jos 5:1
15:16 [x]Ex 23:27; Jos 2:9 [y]1Sa 25:37 [z]Ps 74:2
15:17 [a]Ps 44:2 [b]Ps 78:54,68
15:19 [c]Ex 14:28 [d]Ex 14:22
15:20 [e]Nu 26:59 [f]Jdg 4:4 [g]Jdg 11:34; 1Sa 18:6; Ps 30:11; 150:4
15:21 [h]ver 1; Ex 14:27

In your strength you will guide them
  to your holy dwelling.[s]
14 The nations will hear and tremble;[t]
  anguish will grip the people of Philistia.
15 The chiefs[u] of Edom will be terrified,
  the leaders of Moab will be seized with trembling,[v]
the people[*a*] of Canaan will melt[w] away;
16 terror[x] and dread will fall on them.
By the power of your arm
  they will be as still as a stone[y] —
until your people pass by, LORD,
  until the people you bought[*b*z] pass by.
17 You will bring them in and plant[a] them
  on the mountain[b] of your inheritance —
the place, LORD, you made for your dwelling,
  the sanctuary, Lord, your hands established.

18 "The LORD reigns
  for ever and ever."

19 When Pharaoh's horses, chariots and horsemen[*c*] went into the sea,[c] the LORD brought the waters
of the sea back over them, but the Israelites walked through the sea on dry ground.[d] 20 Then Miriam[e]
the prophet,[f] Aaron's sister, took a timbrel in her hand, and all the women followed her, with timbrels
and dancing.[g] 21 Miriam sang to them:

"Sing to the LORD,
  for he is highly exalted.
Both horse and driver
  he has hurled into the sea."[h]

The Waters of Marah and Elim

22 Then Moses led Israel from the Red Sea and they went into the Desert of Shur. For three days they
traveled in the desert without finding water. 23 When they came to Marah, they could not drink its water

a *15* Or *rulers* *b* *16* Or *created* *c* *19* Or *charioteers*

slavery. **dwelling.** The Hebrew term refers to a campsite where shepherds would rest, so this could possibly allude to Israel's present location or more probably to Mount Sinai, previously and subsequently described as sacred space (3:5; 19:23). This holy dwelling place is further reflected in the tabernacle Israel is commanded to construct, which foreshadows God's holy dwelling in the promised land, first at Shiloh and later in Jerusalem. But it also foreshadows God dwelling in the world through Jesus (John 1:14) and the Spirit (1 Cor 6:19; cf. 2 Cor 6:16), and what will finally be experienced forever in the new Jerusalem (Rev 21:2–3).
15:14–15 Philistia ... Edom ... Moab ... Canaan. The order in which these nations will hear about and/or encounter the Israelites (cf. 13:17).
15:16 bought. Or "created" (see NIV text note), but the parallelism with "redeemed" (v. 13) favors the idea of "purchased" or "acquired" (cf. Ps 74:2). See notes on v. 13; 13:13.
15:17 mountain ... sanctuary. See note on v. 13.
15:18 The song fittingly concludes by explicitly stating that the Lord is king. Its primary theme is that the Lord is supreme over all.
15:19 The summary statement in this verse, which echoes closely 14:28–29, takes the story line back to that point of time and provides the context for Miriam's exhortation in v. 21.
15:20 Miriam ... Aaron's sister. The first explicit mention of Miriam (cf. 2:4,7), Moses' elder sister (Num 26:59; 1 Chr 6:3). **prophet.** Num 12:1–2 alludes to Miriam's role as prophet (see note on Exod 7:1), possibly including her leadership role in calling Israel to worship as the prophet Elijah did on Mount Carmel. This might also explain why she is associated here with Aaron in particular. Other female prophets in Scripture include Deborah (Judg 4:4), Huldah (2 Kgs 22:14), Noadiah (Neh 6:14), Anna (Luke 2:36), and Philip's daughters (Acts 21:9). **dancing.** Probably a kind of folk dance.
15:21 Sing. Miriam summons all of the Israelites to worship.
15:22—17:7 *Divine Provision and Instruction in the Wilderness.* Sandwiched between victory over the Egyptians and victory over the Amalekites (17:8–16) are three accounts (15:22–27; 16:1–36; 17:1–7) of Israel's grumbling and the Lord's provision. The Lord responds to each crisis with amazing patience, grace, and compassion; he uses the crises to teach Israel more about himself.
15:22–27 *The Waters of Marah and Elim.* The first crisis relates to Israel's water supply. The people's negative reaction to finding only undrinkable water demonstrates their lack of faith in the Lord's ability to provide for them, and it calls into question whether they are willing to follow his directions.
15:22 Desert of Shur. Located east of Egypt (Gen 25:18; 1 Sam 15:7), probably in the northwestern part of the Sinai peninsula. The book of Numbers fills out details of Israel's itinerary and refers to "Shur" (Hebrew "wall") as "Etham" (Num 33:8), possibly its Egyptian equivalent or else one is enclosed within the other. **three days.** Despite their three-day journey (see note on 3:18), their initial destination is nowhere in sight.
15:23 Marah. This appropriately named oasis was probably one of the

POSSIBLE ROUTE OF THE EXODUS

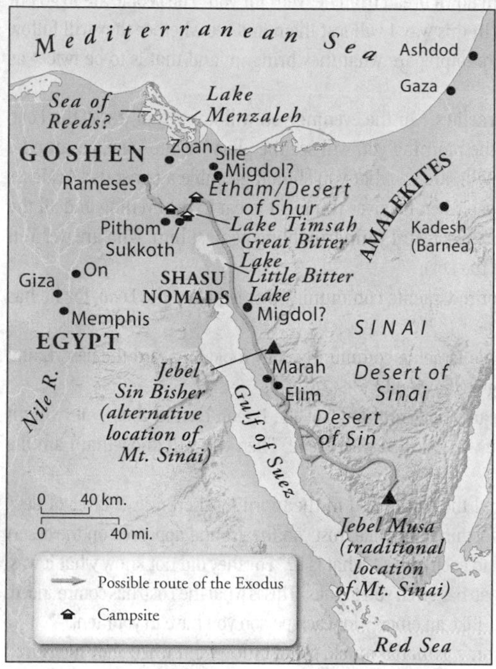

because it was bitter. (That is why the
place is called Marah.[a]) 24So the people grumbled[j] against Moses, saying,
"What are we to drink?"

25Then Moses cried out[k] to the
LORD, and the LORD showed him a
piece of wood. He threw it into the water, and the water became fit to drink.

There the LORD issued a ruling and
instruction for them and put them
to the test.[l] 26He said, "If you listen
carefully to the LORD your God and
do what is right in his eyes, if you pay
attention to his commands and keep
all his decrees,[m] I will not bring on
you any of the diseases[n] I brought on
the Egyptians, for I am the LORD, who
heals[o] you."

27Then they came to Elim, where
there were twelve springs and seventy
palm trees, and they camped[p] there
near the water.

Manna and Quail

16 The whole Israelite community set out from Elim and
came to the Desert of Sin,[q] which is
between Elim and Sinai, on the fifteenth day of the second month after they had come out of Egypt.
2In the desert the whole community grumbled[r] against Moses and Aaron. 3The Israelites said to them,

15:23 [i] Nu 33:8
15:24 [j] Ex 14:12; 16:2
15:25 [k] Ex 14:10 [l] Jdg 3:4
15:26 [m] Dt 7:12 [n] Dt 28:27,58-60 [o] Ex 23:25-26
15:27 [p] Nu 33:9
16:1 [q] Nu 33:11,12
16:2 [r] Ex 14:11; 15:24; 1Co 10:10

[a] *23 Marah* means *bitter.*

Bitter Lakes or else modern Hawarah, a well some 50 miles (80 kilometers) south of the northern tip of the Gulf of Suez (see map, this page).
15:24 grumbled. This is their default response to crises in the wilderness (16:2; 17:3; Num 14:2; 16:11,41). While ostensibly directed toward Moses (and Aaron), in reality such grumbling is against the Lord (16:7–8). God responds graciously here; later, however, after the people receive and accept their covenant obligations (Exod 20–24), he is much less tolerant (cf. Num 11:4–34; 14:26–35; 16:41–50). Their covenant relationship with God renders God's people more accountable. Accordingly, Paul strongly warns Christians not to engage in such behavior (1 Cor 10:10).
15:25 The Lord responds to this crisis with yet another water miracle—once again demonstrating that he controls nature. **piece of wood.** Whatever the chemical properties of the tree, log, or branch, this is not some "herbal remedy" that Moses discovered during his days as a nomadic shepherd. Rather, the Lord "showed" (i.e., instructed) Moses what to do. **water became fit to drink.** Just as he previously made palatable water undrinkable (7:14–21), God makes undrinkable water palatable. Possibly the "bitter" water (v. 23) alludes to Israel's own "bitter" experience in Egypt (1:14; see note on 12:8), highlighting the Lord's ability to deliver from both sorts of crises. **ruling and instruction.** Probably a single concept; v. 26 encapsulates this guiding principle. **put them to the test.** Relates to how Israel will respond (16:4; 20:20; Deut 8:2).
15:26 I am the LORD, who heals you. By keeping God's "commands" and "decrees" (clearly anticipating the covenant law that God will reveal at Sinai), the Israelites will avoid the "diseases" (i.e., plagues) that he inflicted on Egypt.
15:27 Elim. Means "large trees"; it is a much more satisfying oasis than Marah and sharply contrasts with the bitter experience there. **twelve springs and seventy palm trees.** Elim shows God's ability to provide for the Israelites had they been patient and trusting rather than complaining (v. 24). As such, it also anticipates the future blessing promised to Israel (23:25–26), which is ultimately found in Jesus (John 4:10–14; 6:35) and experienced in God's restored universe (Ezek 47:1–12; Rev 22:1–2).
16:1–36 *Manna and Quail.* Shortly after the exodus, Israel faces their next crisis. This one relates to food rather than water. Again they respond by grumbling, and again God turns the occasion into an opportunity to test them and develop their faith.
16:1 Desert of Sin. "Sin" should not be confused with the English word; here it is a geographic place-name, probably related to the word "Sinai." The "Desert of Sin" (here) and the "Desert of Sinai" (19:1–2) refer to distinct locations (Num 33:12,15). The Desert of Sinai may refer to a particular region within the much larger Desert of Sin (i.e., in the immediate vicinity of Horeb/Sinai) and was probably located in the southwestern part of the peninsula (see map, this page). **Sinai.** See note on 3:1.
16:2 grumbled. See note on 15:24.
16:3 pots of meat and ate all the food we wanted. While their Egyptian diet (Num 11:5) had been undoubtedly better than what they found in the wilderness (Num 20:5), their claim here almost certainly exaggerates how well-off they were in the past, as is typical of such a

16:3 [s]Ex 17:3 [t]Nu 11:4,34
16:4 [u]Dt 8:3; Jn 6:31*
16:5 [v]ver 22
16:6 [w]Ex 6:6
16:7 [x]ver 10; Isa 35:2; 40:5 [y]ver 12; Nu 14:2, 27,28 [z]Nu 16:11
16:8 [a]1Sa 8:7; Ro 13:2
16:10 [b]ver 7; Nu 16:19 [c]Ex 13:21; 1Ki 8:10
16:12 [d]ver 7
16:13 [e]Nu 11:31; Ps 78:27-28; 105:40 [f]Nu 11:9
16:14 [g]ver 31; Nu 11:7-9; Ps 105:40
16:15 [h]ver 4; Jn 6:31
16:16 [i]ver 32,36

"If only we had died by the LORD's hand in Egypt![s] There we sat around pots of meat and ate all the food[t] we wanted, but you have brought us out into this desert to starve this entire assembly to death."

4Then the LORD said to Moses, "I will rain down bread from heaven[u] for you. The people are to go out each day and gather enough for that day. In this way I will test them and see whether they will follow my instructions. 5On the sixth day they are to prepare what they bring in, and that is to be twice[v] as much as they gather on the other days."

6So Moses and Aaron said to all the Israelites, "In the evening you will know that it was the LORD who brought you out of Egypt,[w] 7and in the morning you will see the glory[x] of the LORD, because he has heard your grumbling[y] against him. Who are we, that you should grumble against us?"[z] 8Moses also said, "You will know that it was the LORD when he gives you meat to eat in the evening and all the bread you want in the morning, because he has heard your grumbling against him. Who are we? You are not grumbling against us, but against the LORD."[a]

9Then Moses told Aaron, "Say to the entire Israelite community, 'Come before the LORD, for he has heard your grumbling.' "

10While Aaron was speaking to the whole Israelite community, they looked toward the desert, and there was the glory[b] of the LORD appearing in the cloud.[c]

11The LORD said to Moses, 12"I have heard the grumbling[d] of the Israelites. Tell them, 'At twilight you will eat meat, and in the morning you will be filled with bread. Then you will know that I am the LORD your God.' "

13That evening quail[e] came and covered the camp, and in the morning there was a layer of dew[f] around the camp. 14When the dew was gone, thin flakes like frost[g] on the ground appeared on the desert floor. 15When the Israelites saw it, they said to each other, "What is it?" For they did not know what it was.

Moses said to them, "It is the bread[h] the LORD has given you to eat. 16This is what the LORD has commanded: 'Everyone is to gather as much as they need. Take an omer[a][i] for each person you have in your tent.' "

17The Israelites did as they were told; some gathered much, some little. 18And when they measured

[a] *16* That is, possibly about 3 pounds or about 1.4 kilograms; also in verses 18, 32, 33 and 36

complaining and unbelieving attitude. **starve.** Their situation is not as dire as they imply; they have considerable livestock with them, although consuming their future livelihood would be short-sighted.

16:4 bread from heaven. God will supply physical food to nourish and sustain Israel. As Moses later explains (Deut 8:3), this teaches an important spiritual lesson about relying on God and his word. In Jesus, "the true bread from heaven" (John 6:32; see John 6:33,35,48), God becomes "the living bread that came down from heaven" (John 6:51)—providing spiritual nourishment to his people and "life to the world" (John 6:33). **gather enough for that day.** God will supply the food one day at a time. The petition for "daily bread" in Jesus' model prayer probably alludes to this (Matt 6:11; Luke 11:3). **test.** This regular supply of manna will demonstrate whether or not Israel will indeed follow God's instructions (15:25–26). However, when the Israelites later test God (17:3,7), they question his commitment in a way that expresses unbelief.

16:5 sixth day ... twice as much. Facilitates rest on the Sabbath (see vv. 22–30), further anticipating what God will reveal at Sinai (cf. 15:26, "commands" and "decrees"). In this way God is teaching his people to live by faith and depend on him to supply their needs. This is a lesson the NT applies both physically and spiritually (2 Cor 9:8–11; Phil 4:19).

16:6 you will know. The evening supply of meat and the morning supply of bread (v. 8) will further acquaint Israel with their God (see note on 6:3).

16:7 you will see the glory of the LORD. The first reference in Exodus to God's "glory," which elsewhere refers to a visible manifestation of God's presence (v. 10; 24:16–17; 29:43; 33:12–23; 40:34–35). But here it apparently alludes to God's demonstrating his presence by means of the manna he supplies the next day.

16:8 meat ... and all the bread you want. Deliberately echoes Israel's complaint in v. 3.

16:10 glory of the LORD appearing in the cloud. See notes on v. 7; 13:21. The Lord manifests his glory (signifying his presence) in the cloud.

16:11–12 At this point the chronology of the passage is rather confusing. The Lord appears to repeat (to Moses) information that Moses already told Israel (vv. 6–8). This is possibly another literary flashback that fills in missing details from the Lord's earlier speech (vv. 4–5). Alternatively, this narrates a subsequent communication that focuses on *what* rather than *whom* (vv. 7–8) they were grumbling about.

16:13 quail. Small migrating birds; their presence in this region was apparently unusual (Num 11:31–32). The biblical account clearly suggests that the Lord was responsible for both the timing and scale of this miraculous supply. Here the quail seem to be of secondary significance—a temporary measure to tide the Israelites over until the regular provision of manna begins the next day. In Num 11, however, the literary and theological focus is reversed, and in this much later incident the quail become an instrument of judgment on a people who, now in covenant relationship with the Lord (Exod 19–24), should have known better.

16:14 dew ... thin flakes. Apparently the manna descends during the night and becomes visible only after the morning dew evaporates (cf. Num 11:9). Modern explanations for the manna include equating it with the sticky, sweet secretions of plant lice that solidify rapidly through evaporation. Such naturalistic explanations fail to take the biblical account seriously by implying that it is embellished folklore that massively exaggerates. Several facts, however, point to the manna's uniqueness: (1) The meaning of the word "manna" (see NIV text note on v. 31), as well as how it is described, implies that it was hitherto unknown. (2) Its year-round availability for the entire wilderness trek, as well as its nonappearance every seventh day, does not fit any naturally occurring phenomenon. (3) The preservation of a sample for future generations (vv. 33–34) implies that it was not something likely to be found after its regular supply ceased.

16:15 What is it? See v. 31 and NIV text note there.

16:16 an omer for each person. See NIV text note.

16:17–18 The prescribed measurement (an omer) ensures that every-

it by the omer, the one who gathered much did not have too much, and the one who gathered little did not have too little.[j] Everyone had gathered just as much as they needed.

19Then Moses said to them, "No one is to keep any of it until morning."[k]

20However, some of them paid no attention to Moses; they kept part of it until morning, but it was full of maggots and began to smell. So Moses was angry with them.

21Each morning everyone gathered as much as they needed, and when the sun grew hot, it melted away. 22On the sixth day, they gathered twice[l] as much—two omers[a] for each person—and the leaders of the community[m] came and reported this to Moses. 23He said to them, "This is what the LORD commanded: 'Tomorrow is to be a day of sabbath rest, a holy sabbath[n] to the LORD. So bake what you want to bake and boil what you want to boil. Save whatever is left and keep it until morning.'"

24So they saved it until morning, as Moses commanded, and it did not stink or get maggots in it. 25"Eat it today," Moses said, "because today is a sabbath to the LORD. You will not find any of it on the ground today. 26Six days you are to gather it, but on the seventh day, the Sabbath,[o] there will not be any."

27Nevertheless, some of the people went out on the seventh day to gather it, but they found none. 28Then the LORD said to Moses, "How long will you[b] refuse to keep my commands[p] and my instructions? 29Bear in mind that the LORD has given you the Sabbath; that is why on the sixth day he gives you bread for two days. Everyone is to stay where they are on the seventh day; no one is to go out." 30So the people rested on the seventh day.

31The people of Israel called the bread manna.[c][q] It was white like coriander seed and tasted like wafers made with honey. 32Moses said, "This is what the LORD has commanded: 'Take an omer of manna and keep it for the generations to come, so they can see the bread I gave you to eat in the wilderness when I brought you out of Egypt.'"

33So Moses said to Aaron, "Take a jar and put an omer of manna[r] in it. Then place it before the LORD to be kept for the generations to come."

34As the LORD commanded Moses, Aaron put the manna with the tablets of the covenant law,[s] so that it might be preserved. 35The Israelites ate manna[t] forty years,[u] until they came to a land that was settled; they ate manna until they reached the border of Canaan.[v]

36(An omer is one-tenth of an ephah.)

Water From the Rock

17 The whole Israelite community set out from the Desert of Sin,[w] traveling from place to place as the LORD commanded. They camped at Rephidim, but there was no water[x] for the people to drink. 2So they quarreled with Moses and said, "Give us water[y] to drink."

[a] *22* That is, possibly about 6 pounds or about 2.8 kilograms [b] *28* The Hebrew is plural. [c] *31 Manna* sounds like the Hebrew for *What is it?* (see verse 15).

16:18 [j] 2Co 8:15*
16:19 [k] ver 23; Ex 12:10; 23:18
16:22 [l] ver 5 [m] Ex 34:31
16:23 [n] Ge 2:3; Ex 20:8; 23:12; Lev 23:3
16:26 [o] Ex 20:9-10
16:28 [p] 2Ki 17:14; Ps 78:10; 106:13
16:31 [q] Nu 11:7-9
16:33 [r] Heb 9:4
16:34 [s] Ex 25:16,21,22; 40:20; Nu 17:4,10
16:35 [t] Jn 6:31,49 [u] Ne 9:21 [v] Jos 5:12
17:1 [w] Ex 16:1 [x] Nu 33:14
17:2 [y] Nu 20:2

one has just enough, however much manna they personally gather, and thus discourages greed by emphasizing equality of provision. Paul cites v. 18 and applies the principle to Christian giving (2 Cor 8:15).

16:19–20 Not storing manna requires the Israelites to trust God to provide daily. Not surprisingly, some find this prohibition too challenging and ignore it, foreshadowing even greater rebellion ahead (ch. 32).

16:23 See note on v. 5. **sabbath.** The people need to be taught to keep this, which suggests that it was not observed previously. The concept, however, appears in Gen 2:3, which God cites as a theological rationale for the fourth commandment (20:11; see 31:17).

16:28 How long will you refuse ...? Like Pharaoh, some of the Israelites are slow learners, hence this strong rebuke that echoes the question the Lord previously asked the stubborn Egyptian pharaoh (cf. 10:3). Such heady defiance does not bode well for people who will shortly obligate themselves to doing everything the Lord says (19:8; 24:3,7).

16:31–36 This chapter's final section focuses primarily on events that occur after God gives the tablets of the covenant law at Sinai (see v. 34) and possibly after Israel constructs the ark of the covenant (cf. 25:16; Heb 9:4).

16:31 For a slightly different description, see Num 11:7–8. Evidently, the manna is off-white (the color of "coriander seed"), has crisp texture ("like wafers"; see v. 14), and tastes sweet.

16:32–34 As a perpetual reminder of how the Lord provided for his redeemed people, Aaron, Israel's high priest, later preserves one person's daily ration of manna in a gold jar (Heb 9:4), which is placed "before the LORD" (i.e., in the ark of the covenant).

16:35 The manna ceases just after Israel's first Passover celebration in Canaan (Josh 5:10–12).

16:36 This information is clearly for the benefit of later readers, for whom an ephah was the standard unit of measurement. The term "omer" is not used elsewhere in the OT.

17:1–7 *Water From the Rock.* The last in this trio of grumbling stories is undoubtedly the most serious. Together with a similar episode in Num 20:1–13, it brackets Israel's wilderness period as a time of rebellion. Moreover, this event attains a measure of notoriety, serving as a severe warning in other parts of Scripture (Ps 95:7–11; Heb 3:7—4:13).

17:1 Desert of Sin. See note on 16:1. **as the LORD commanded.** A subtle reminder that, despite the forthcoming crisis, they are still on the right track. **Rephidim.** Israel's last stop before reaching Sinai, which is evidently nearby (19:2). For the difficulty in tying down this and other locations mentioned, see notes on 3:1; 10:19; 13:20; 16:1.

17:2 quarreled. May suggest a heated exchange. The Hebrew implies that one party has wronged the other. Moses is accused of acting

17:2 [z] Dt 6:16; Ps 78:18, 41; 1Co 10:9
17:3 [a] Ex 15:24; 16:2-3
17:4 [b] Nu 14:10; 1Sa 30:6
17:5 [c] Ex 7:20
17:6 [d] Nu 20:11; Ps 114:8; 1Co 10:4
17:7 [e] Nu 20:13,24; Ps 81:7
17:8 [f] Ge 36:12; Dt 25:17-19
17:9 [g] Ex 4:17
17:10 [h] Ex 24:14
17:11 [i] Jas 5:16
17:14 [j] Ex 24:4; 34:27; Nu 33:2 [k] 1Sa 15:3; 30:17-18

Moses replied, "Why do you quarrel with me? Why do you put the LORD to the test?"[z]
3 But the people were thirsty for water there, and they grumbled[a] against Moses. They said, "Why did
you bring us up out of Egypt to make us and our children and livestock die of thirst?"
4 Then Moses cried out to the LORD, "What am I to do with these people? They are almost ready to
stone[b] me."
5 The LORD answered Moses, "Go out in front of the people. Take with you some of the elders of Israel
and take in your hand the staff with which you struck the Nile,[c] and go. 6 I will stand there before you
by the rock at Horeb. Strike the rock, and water[d] will come out of it for the people to drink." So Moses
did this in the sight of the elders of Israel. 7 And he called the place Massah[a] and Meribah[b][e] because the
Israelites quarreled and because they tested the LORD saying, "Is the LORD among us or not?"

The Amalekites Defeated

8 The Amalekites[f] came and attacked the Israelites at Rephidim. 9 Moses said to Joshua, "Choose some
of our men and go out to fight the Amalekites. Tomorrow I will stand on top of the hill with the staff[g]
of God in my hands."
10 So Joshua fought the Amalekites as Moses had ordered, and Moses, Aaron and Hur[h] went to the top
of the hill. 11 As long as Moses held up his hands, the Israelites were winning,[i] but whenever he lowered
his hands, the Amalekites were winning. 12 When Moses' hands grew tired, they took a stone and put it
under him and he sat on it. Aaron and Hur held his hands up — one on one side, one on the other — so
that his hands remained steady till sunset. 13 So Joshua overcame the Amalekite army with the sword.
14 Then the LORD said to Moses, "Write[j] this on a scroll as something to be remembered and make
sure that Joshua hears it, because I will completely blot out the name of Amalek[k] from under heaven."

[a] 7 *Massah* means *testing.* [b] 7 *Meribah* means *quarreling.*

against the well-being of the Israelites. **put the LORD to the test.** See note on 16:4. By demanding that the Lord prove to them his presence and care (v. 7), these unbelieving Israelites were elevating themselves as judge over God (cf. John 6:30). They were also ignoring the revelation (both in Egypt and in the wilderness) they had already received (Ps 95:8–9).

17:3 grumbled. See note on 15:24.

17:5–6 Despite the people's very negative response to their circumstances (vv. 3–4), once again the Lord responds graciously.

17:5 elders. See note on 3:16. They accompany Moses as reliable witnesses. **staff.** See note on 4:2.

17:6 I will stand. The pillar of cloud presumably manifests the Lord's presence (Ps 81:7). **the rock.** The definite article ("the") suggests a rock face rather than a large boulder or free-standing rock. **at Horeb.** This does not appear to be Mount Sinai itself (unless Mount Sinai refers to a mountainous region, rather than a single peak); significantly, no particular "mountain" is mentioned here (cf. 3:1; 19:2–3), so this is possibly an outcropping of the mountain range. **water.** Both the timing and the means by which this water suddenly appears are extraordinary. Theologically, these "waters" of God's blessing anticipate what the Horeb/Sinai covenant will bring to Israel, thus this is a foretaste before Israel arrives at Mount Sinai. For Christians it foreshadows the blessing that flows to us through Jesus (John 7:38), whom Paul identifies with Israel's Rock (i.e., the Lord), the source of the blessings they experienced (1 Cor 10:3–4).

17:7 Massah and Meribah. See NIV text notes. Only here do both names describe this particular location, although on two occasions the names occur in poetic parallelism (Deut 33:8; Ps 95:8). In Deut 33:8 "Massah" refers to the present incident, whereas the expression "waters of Meribah" refers to Num 20:1–13. Ps 95:8 may be referring to only Exod 17 or to both Exod 17 and Num 20. By itself "Massah" refers to Exod 17 (see Deut 6:16; 9:22). With the possible exception of Ps 81:7, the other two references to "Meribah" (Num 27:14; Ps 106:32) allude to Num 20. Both names perpetually remind Israel that they intrinsically tend to disobey and not trust God.

17:8–16 *The Amalekites Defeated.* Unlike the three previous crises, this time there is no mention of grumbling or panic. Moses knows precisely what to do, and everyone falls into line. Moreover, the Lord does not explicitly appear until the crisis is over.

17:8 Amalekites. These seminomads were descendants of Esau (Gen 36:12,16), but this does not seem to be a factor in the animosity here; rather, these bedouin raiders were simply exploiting the opportunity to attack weak and defenseless members of Israel and take advantage of the nation when it was unprepared (cf. Deut 25:17–19; 1 Sam 15:2).

17:9 Joshua. Moses' aide (24:13; 33:11) and designated successor (Num 27:12–23) appears without formal introduction, which the original readers did not need. His role here is exclusively a military one. Fittingly, Joshua, the name Moses gave Hoshea (meaning "he saves"; Num 13:16) means "the LORD saves" and is the Hebrew equivalent of the name Jesus. **some of our men.** Rather than an elite fighting unit, some able-bodied men assemble for the ensuing conflict. **Tomorrow ... with the staff of God.** Evokes memories of the signs and wonders narrative: "tomorrow" was when the Lord punished Israel's enemies (8:23,29; 9:5,18; 10:4), and he used the staff to strike those who opposed him and his people (7:20; 8:5–6,17; 9:23; 10:13).

17:10 Hur. Mentioned here for the first time and without genealogy, implying that he is a well-known figure. He reappears in 24:14, where he and Aaron again assist Moses. If all these texts refer to the same Hur, he belongs to the tribe of Judah and is the grandfather of Bezalel (31:2; 35:30; 38:22; see 1 Chr 2:19–20).

17:11 held up his hands. Often interpreted as prayer; elevating the staff probably symbolizes the divine power that is key to Israel's military success (7:20; 14:16). It may also serve as some type of ensign, bolstering the faith and courage of those engaged in the fight below. In any case, it clearly focuses the reader's attention primarily on the hill and not on the battlefield, suggesting that this is where the victory is truly won. Like the earlier conflict with the Egyptians, Israel prevails through the Lord.

17:14 Write. The first explicit reference to Moses recording something at God's command (24:4; 34:27–28; Num 33:2; Deut 31:9,19,22,24).

15 Moses built an altar and called it The LORD is my Banner. 16 He said, "Because hands were lifted
up against[a] the throne of the LORD,[b] the LORD will be at war against the Amalekites from generation
to generation."

Jethro Visits Moses

18 Now Jethro, the priest of Midian[l] and father-in-law of Moses, heard of everything God had done
for Moses and for his people Israel, and how the LORD had brought Israel out of Egypt.
2 After Moses had sent away his wife Zipporah,[m] his father-in-law Jethro received her 3 and her two
sons.[n] One son was named Gershom,[c] for Moses said, "I have become a foreigner in a foreign land";[o]
4 and the other was named Eliezer,[d][p] for he said, "My father's God was my helper; he saved me from
the sword of Pharaoh."
5 Jethro, Moses' father-in-law, together with Moses' sons and wife, came to him in the wilderness,
where he was camped near the mountain[q] of God. 6 Jethro had sent word to him, "I, your father-in-law
Jethro, am coming to you with your wife and her two sons."
7 So Moses went out to meet his father-in-law and bowed down[r] and kissed[s] him. They greeted each
other and then went into the tent. 8 Moses told his father-in-law about everything the LORD had done to
Pharaoh and the Egyptians for Israel's sake and about all the hardships they had met along the way
and how the LORD had saved[t] them.
9 Jethro was delighted to hear about all the good things the LORD had done for Israel in rescuing
them from the hand of the Egyptians. 10 He said, "Praise be to the LORD,[u] who rescued you from the
hand of the Egyptians and of Pharaoh, and who rescued the people from the hand of the Egyptians.
11 Now I know that the LORD is greater than all other gods,[v] for he did this to those who had treated Israel arrogantly."[w] 12 Then Jethro, Moses' father-in-law, brought a burnt offering and other sacrifices

18:1 [l] Ex 2:16; 3:1
18:2 [m] Ex 2:21; 4:25
18:3 [n] Ex 4:20; Ac 7:29 [o] Ex 2:22
18:4 [p] 1Ch 23:15
18:5 [q] Ex 3:1
18:7 [r] Ge 43:28 [s] Ge 29:13
18:8 [t] Ex 15:6,16; Ps 81:7
18:10 [u] Ge 14:20; Ps 68:19-20
18:11 [v] Ex 12:12; 15:11; 2Ch 2:5 [w] Lk 1:51

[a] *16* Or *to* [b] *16* The meaning of the Hebrew for this clause is uncertain. [c] *3* *Gershom* sounds like the Hebrew for *a foreigner there.* [d] *4* *Eliezer* means *my God is helper.*

See Introduction: Author. **scroll.** A long, rolled-up strip of papyrus parchment used for recording information (usually in columns; Jer 36:23) on one or both sides (Ezek 2:10). **something to be remembered ... name.** There is a pun in the original between "memorial" and "memory." **make sure that Joshua hears it.** The rationale for recording this material and reading it out loud is so that Israel (and Joshua, their military leader, in particular) will mete out the divinely decreed punishment on the Amalekites, eradicating all memory of them (Deut 25:17–19).

17:15 Moses erects and names an altar to commemorate the victory. **The LORD is my Banner.** The Hebrew word for "banner" may simply refer to a pole (like a flagstaff; Num 21:8–9). Thus understood, the altar here may be more like an obelisk, symbolizing the role God (represented by Moses' staff) played in routing the Amalekites.

17:16 against the throne. See NIV text notes. Whatever the precise meaning of the clause, the rest of the verse highlights, for all subsequent generations, God's (and thus their) attitude toward the Amalekites, whose fate serves as a warning for all who dare to oppose the Lord and his people.

18:1–27 *Jethro Visits Moses.* Some scholars believe this chapter is out of chronological sequence because it seems to assume that (1) the Israelites are already encamped beside Mount Sinai (v. 5) and (2) God has already disclosed the Sinai legislation (v. 16). Neither argument is conclusive since the context places the Israelites *near* but not yet *at* the mountain of God (17:5–6; 19:2) and God disclosed some of his decrees and instructions prior to Sinai (12:24,49; 13:9; 16:4,28).

18:1–12 One possible reason the author preserves a detailed record of this family reunion (these verses mention that Jethro is Moses' "father-in-law" eight times) is that it contrasts so markedly with the previous incident. Jethro's response is more in keeping with the previously stated purpose of God's actions with Pharaoh (9:16). Also, emphasizing Jethro's status may bracket Moses' mission (4:18), which is about to reach the significant milestone to which 3:12 alludes (see 18:12).

18:1 Jethro. See notes on 2:16,18; 3:1. **everything God had done.** Travelers may have spread the news.

18:2 sent away. Zipporah and her sons may have returned to Jethro shortly after the circumcision incident (4:24–26), sometime between then and the exodus, or even more recently during Israel's journey toward Sinai. There is obviously a narrative gap here, so any suggestions and explanations are conjecture. Jethro is reuniting Moses with his sons and "wife" (vv. 5–6), and there is no indication that they returned with Jethro after this reunion (cf. v. 27).

18:3–4 Gershom ... Eliezer. See NIV text notes. The names of Moses' sons focus attention on the Lord's deliverance of Moses (2:11–15) and also the Israelites, since they now share in Moses' experience.

18:5 near the mountain of God. See note on 3:1. The reunion takes place at Rephidim (17:1; cf. vv. 5–6) prior to the last leg of Israel's journey to Sinai (19:2). Since Moses knows exactly where he is headed (3:12), he possibly prearranged this rendezvous near Sinai.

18:8 Moses' report to Jethro, like his earlier report to Aaron (4:28), focuses on the Lord's actions and possibly fills in some of the gaps in Jethro's knowledge (v. 1) with further testimony to the Lord's sustenance in the wilderness.

18:11 Now I know. Jethro fittingly responds to what Moses proclaims about the Lord (cf. 9:16), employing one of the book's recurring ideas (5:2; 6:7; 7:5; 8:10; 9:29). **greater than all other gods.** Jethro acknowledges what others (like Pharaoh) refused to acknowledge. On the lips of a non-Israelite, this confession about the Lord is particularly significant in view of the objective stated back in 9:16—that God's "name might be proclaimed in all the earth." It also foreshadows the fulfillment of God's global purpose—that his name "will be great among the nations" (Mal 1:11; see 1 Cor 1:2).

18:12 eat a meal ... in the presence of God. The text makes no mention of a covenant; some scholars have speculated that one occurred, but the evidence for this is weak. More likely, this was simply a

18:12 [x]Dt 12:7
18:15 [y]Nu 9:6,8; Dt 17:8-13
18:16 [z]Lev 24:12
18:18 [a]Nu 11:11,14,17
18:19 [b]Ex 3:12 [c]Nu 27:5
18:20 [d]Dt 5:1 [e]Ps 143:8 [f]Dt 1:18
18:21 [g]Ac 6:3 [h]Dt 16:19; Ps 15:5; Eze 18:8 [i]Dt 1:13,15; 2Ch 19:5-10
18:22 [j]Dt 1:17-18 [k]Nu 11:17
18:25 [l]Dt 1:13-15
18:26 [m]ver 22
18:27 [n]Nu 10:29-30
19:2 [o]Ex 17:1 [p]Ex 3:1

to God, and Aaron came with all the elders of Israel to eat a meal with Moses' father-in-law in the
presence[x] of God.
13The next day Moses took his seat to serve as judge for the people, and they stood around him from
morning till evening. 14When his father-in-law saw all that Moses was doing for the people, he said,
"What is this you are doing for the people? Why do you alone sit as judge, while all these people stand
around you from morning till evening?"
15Moses answered him, "Because the people come to me to seek God's will.[y] 16Whenever they have
a dispute, it is brought to me, and I decide between the parties and inform them of God's decrees and
instructions."[z]
17Moses' father-in-law replied, "What you are doing is not good. 18You and these people who come
to you will only wear yourselves out. The work is too heavy for you; you cannot handle it alone.[a] 19Lis-
ten now to me and I will give you some advice, and may God be with you.[b] You must be the people's
representative before God and bring their disputes[c] to him. 20Teach them his decrees and instructions,[d]
and show them the way they are to live[e] and how they are to behave.[f] 21But select capable men[g] from
all the people — men who fear God, trustworthy men who hate dishonest gain[h] — and appoint them
as officials[i] over thousands, hundreds, fifties and tens. 22Have them serve as judges for the people at all
times, but have them bring every difficult case[j] to you; the simple cases they can decide themselves. That
will make your load lighter, because they will share[k] it with you. 23If you do this and God so commands,
you will be able to stand the strain, and all these people will go home satisfied."
24Moses listened to his father-in-law and did everything he said. 25He chose capable men from all
Israel and made them leaders of the people, officials over thousands, hundreds, fifties and tens.[l] 26They
served as judges for the people at all times. The difficult cases they brought to Moses, but the simple
ones they decided themselves.[m]
27Then Moses sent his father-in-law on his way, and Jethro returned to his own country.[n]

At Mount Sinai

19 On the first day of the third month after the Israelites left Egypt — on that very day — they
came to the Desert of Sinai. 2After they set out from Rephidim,[o] they entered the Desert of Sinai,
and Israel camped there in the desert in front of the mountain.[p]

fellowship meal, through which Jethro expresses his affiliation with the Lord and the Israelites, as the participation of Aaron and Israel's elders further suggests. Even though Jethro chooses not to remain with Israel (v. 27), he embraces Israel's God, thus becoming an important model of hope for the nations (Gen 12:3).

18:13–27 The second half of ch. 18 anticipates developments at Mount Sinai. Similar episodes elsewhere (Num 11:16–17; Deut 1:9–18) seem to recount separate events that took place after Israel reached Mount Sinai. Perhaps, however, Moses implements Jethro's advice in stages (vv. 24–26), which would explain his absence in these otherwise similar episodes.

18:13–14 There is nothing unusual about Moses, as leader, assuming the role of legal arbiter. It is the logistics of his excessive case load rather than his role as judge that Jethro questions.

18:15 seek God's will. They were seeking an authoritative ruling on civil disputes.

18:16 God's decrees and instructions. Since most disputes are likely to be in some fashion unique, they require guidance as to how they should be resolved. Moses seeks this from God. Over time a pattern would develop and this could be taught to others who act as judges. Illustrative case laws for those who judge probably comprise some of the material in the Book of the Covenant (e.g., 20:22 — 23:33; see 24:7). Here Moses feels obliged to act alone, presumably on the basis of his unique role as mediator.

18:17–18 The text does not qualify Jethro's critical appraisal, which suggests that the current judicial procedure was not something God had disclosed.

18:19–22 Jethro addresses theological, not just logistical, concerns. Israel's judicial system must build upon God's "decrees and instructions" (v. 20), but to facilitate this, Moses must establish a hierarchy of suitably qualified (capable, God-fearing, honest, and reliable) assistants to handle "simple cases" (v. 22; i.e., those for which relevant legislation already exists), thus allowing Moses to focus on every "difficult case" (v. 22; i.e., those for which there is no explicit law or legal precedent).

18:23 and God so commands. This is a pious expression of hope (see also "may God be with you" in v. 19) rather than a bold theological assertion. In vv. 13–27 Jethro is referred to only as "Moses' father-in-law" (see note on vv. 1–12); this avoids the idea of foreign "priestly" (see note on 2:18) input into Israel's judicial procedure.

18:24 Moses listened ... and did everything he said. Jethro's advice evidently has divine approval, underlined by how vv. 25–26 report its implementation almost verbatim.

18:27 Jethro returned. Since this mentions only Jethro, presumably Zipporah, Gershom, and Eliezer remain with Moses. Zipporah is not mentioned again; Moses' Cushite wife is probably a second wife (Num 12:1). Gershom's descendants serve as illicit priests (Judg 18:30), and 1 Chr 23:16–17 lists the sons of both Gershom and Eliezer.

19:1 — 40:38 *Israel at Sinai.* The second half of Exodus focuses on what took place after Israel arrived at Mount Sinai: the creation of a special relationship preparing for God's coming to dwell among the Israelites. This includes: preparation of the people for the Lord's descent (19:1–25), revelation of Israel's covenant obligations (20:1 — 23:19), instructions for entering the land (23:20–33), confirmation of the covenant (24:1–18), instructions given to Moses for the tabernacle and its priests (25:1 — 31:18), breach and renewal of the covenant (32:1 — 34:35), communication and implementation of God's instructions for

3 Then Moses went up to God, and the LORD called[q] to him from the mountain and said, "This is what
you are to say to the descendants of Jacob and what you are to tell the people of Israel: 4 'You yourselves
have seen what I did to Egypt,[r] and how I carried you on eagles' wings[s] and brought you to myself.
5 Now if you obey me fully[t] and keep my covenant,[u] then out of all nations you will be my treasured
possession.[v] Although the whole earth[w] is mine, 6 you[a] will be for me a kingdom of priests[x] and a holy
nation.'[y] These are the words you are to speak to the Israelites."
7 So Moses went back and summoned the elders of the people and set before them all the words the
LORD had commanded him to speak. 8 The people all responded together, "We will do everything the
LORD has said."[z] So Moses brought their answer back to the LORD.
9 The LORD said to Moses, "I am going to come to you in a dense cloud,[a] so that the people will hear
me speaking[b] with you and will always put their trust in you." Then Moses told the LORD what the
people had said.
10 And the LORD said to Moses, "Go to the people and consecrate[c] them today and tomorrow. Have them
wash their clothes[d] 11 and be ready by the third day,[e] because on that day the LORD will come down on Mount
Sinai in the sight of all the people. 12 Put limits for the people around the mountain and tell them, 'Be careful
that you do not approach the mountain or touch the foot of it. Whoever touches the mountain is to be put
to death. 13 They are to be stoned[f] or shot with arrows; not a hand is to be laid on them. No person or animal
shall be permitted to live.' Only when the ram's horn sounds a long blast may they approach the mountain."
14 After Moses had gone down the mountain to the people, he consecrated them, and they washed
their clothes. 15 Then he said to the people, "Prepare yourselves for the third day. Abstain from sexual
relations."

19:3 [q] Ex 3:4; Ac 7:38
19:4 [r] Dt 29:2 [s] Isa 63:9
19:5 [t] Ex 15:26 [u] Dt 5:2 [v] Dt 14:2; Ps 135:4 [w] Ex 9:29; Dt 10:14
19:6 [x] 1Pe 2:5 [y] Dt 7:6; 26:19; Isa 62:12
19:8 [z] Ex 24:3,7; Dt 5:27
19:9 [a] ver 16; Ex 24:15-16 [b] Dt 4:12,36
19:10 [c] Lev 11:44; Heb 10:22 [d] Ge 35:2
19:11 [e] ver 16
19:13 [f] Heb 12:20*

[a] 5,6 Or *possession, for the whole earth is mine.* 6 *You*

the tabernacle (35:1—40:33), and consecration of the tabernacle by the Lord's visible presence (40:34–38).

19:1—24:18 This is an important milestone in Exodus. Israel finally arrives at the location anticipated back in 3:12, and the Lord begins to spell out his plans for Israel and elaborate on the service/worship to which 3:12 alluded. According to many scholars, this section dealing with the Mosaic covenant reflects the typical arrangement of ancient Near Eastern suzerainty-vassal treaties, in which the superior ("suzerain") promised to protect subject peoples ("vassals") who pledged loyalty to him. Like such treaties, this covenant was subject to subsequent renewals (e.g., ch. 34; Josh 24).

19:1–25 *At Mount Sinai.* See photos, pp. 191, 2520. This chapter reveals the Lord's plans for Israel more fully and highlights what Israel must do to survive a close-up encounter with a holy God.

19:1 Desert of Sinai. See note on 16:1.

19:2 Israel remained at Sinai for almost a year (Num 10:11–12).

19:4 what I did. Israel's covenant obligations respond to God's gracious acts of salvation; God saves his people based on his grace, not their works. See note on 20:2. **on eagles' wings.** A metaphor of the Lord's tender care, possibly comparing God's bringing Israel out of Egypt with eagles carrying their young on their backs (Deut 32:10–11). The key point is that Israel's rescue and survival were facilitated by the Lord's action, intervention, and protection.

19:5–6 if ... then. While the Mosaic covenant is clearly conditional, the obedience and covenant keeping that God encourages here is designed not to secure Israel's salvation (see v. 4 and note) but to enable Israel to serve in the special role that God intends. Everything God has done thus far (v. 4) has this objective in view.

19:5 treasured possession. Valued personal property (see 1 Chr 29:3; Eccl 2:8, where it refers to a king's private treasure), a metaphor showing how God values Israel (Deut 7:6; 14:2; 26:18; Ps 135:4; Mal 3:17) but also emphasizing Israel's election by God. In the ancient Near East a king (but never a whole people as here) is a treasured possession of his own god, and he is personally chosen, blessed, and protected by that deity.

19:6 Here God offers the Israelites both royal and priestly status. **kingdom of priests.** The expression is like "kingdom of David"; the second element (priests/David) points to those who reign; here Israel as a whole is referred to as "priests," those who will serve in the presence of God (cf. the more exclusive priestly ministry of Aaron and his sons in 28:1). **a holy nation.** As a kingdom of priests, Israel will be set apart from other nations in order to serve God, just as Aaron and his sons are later consecrated for a particular kind of service in the tabernacle (28:41; 40:12–15). Despite the commitment expressed in v. 8, Israel's persistent failure to keep this covenant meant forfeiting their exclusive status. However, through the new covenant established by Jesus, it is inherited by the whole people of God, including both Jews and Gentiles. Thus, NT authors apply the terms used here in v. 6 to the church (e.g., 1 Pet 2:5,9; Rev 1:6; 5:10; 20:6), which likewise has been "called ... out of darkness into [God's] wonderful light" (1 Pet 2:9).

19:8 We will do everything the LORD has said. Israel freely chooses to serve God and enter his covenant; the Israelites will reiterate this promise to keep the covenant after God more fully discloses their obligations (24:3,7).

19:9 The main purpose of the forthcoming theophany (divine appearance) is to authenticate Moses as covenant mediator.

19:10 consecrate. As the following clause suggests, and as v. 14 confirms, this entails washing their clothes in preparation for their meeting with a holy God (cf. 3:5). **wash their clothes.** Like the prohibition on sexual relations (v. 15), this is related to ceremonial uncleanness (Lev 11:25,32,40) and implies a change of status (Lev 16:26,28).

19:12 Put limits ... around the mountain. The closest the general populace may come is the foot of the mountain (v. 17), hence the strict limits imposed around it (v. 23). Similar restrictions, for the same reason, apply to the tabernacle (Num 3:10), where the Lord manifests his ongoing presence with Israel (40:36–38).

19:13 approach. Another possibility is "ascend," although this would imply less restrictive access to the mountain than the context suggests. Only Israel's representatives—Moses and Aaron (v. 24) or Moses, Aaron, Nadab, Abihu, and the 70 elders (24:1,9)—are subsequently invited to ascend part of the mountain.

19:15 Abstain from sexual relations. Not because sex is sinful but

19:16 [g] Heb 12:18-19; Rev 4:1 [h] Heb 12:21
19:18 [i] Ps 104:32 [j] Ex 3:2; 24:17; Dt 4:11; 2Ch 7:1; Ps 18:8; Heb 12:18 [k] Ge 19:28 [l] Jdg 5:5; Ps 68:8; Jer 4:24
19:19 [m] Ne 9:13 [n] Ps 81:7
19:21 [o] Ex 3:5; 1Sa 6:19
19:22 [p] Lev 10:3 [q] 2Sa 6:7
19:23 [r] ver 12
19:24 [s] Ex 24:1,9
20:2 [t] Ex 13:3
20:3 [u] Dt 6:14; Jer 35:15
20:4 [v] Lev 26:1; Dt 4:15-19,23; 27:15

16 On the morning of the third day there was thunder and lightning, with a thick cloud over the mountain, and a very loud trumpet blast.[g] Everyone in the camp trembled.[h] 17 Then Moses led the people out of the camp to meet with God, and they stood at the foot of the mountain. 18 Mount Sinai was covered with smoke,[i] because the LORD descended on it in fire.[j] The smoke billowed up from it like smoke from a furnace,[k] and the whole mountain[a] trembled[l] violently. 19 As the sound of the trumpet grew louder and louder, Moses spoke and the voice[m] of God answered[n] him.[b]

20 The LORD descended to the top of Mount Sinai and called Moses to the top of the mountain. So Moses went up 21 and the LORD said to him, "Go down and warn the people so they do not force their way through to see[o] the LORD and many of them perish. 22 Even the priests, who approach[p] the LORD, must consecrate themselves, or the LORD will break out against them."[q]

23 Moses said to the LORD, "The people cannot come up Mount Sinai, because you yourself warned us, 'Put limits[r] around the mountain and set it apart as holy.'"

24 The LORD replied, "Go down and bring Aaron[s] up with you. But the priests and the people must not force their way through to come up to the LORD, or he will break out against them."

25 So Moses went down to the people and told them.

The Ten Commandments

20:1-17pp — Dt 5:6-21

20 And God spoke all these words:

2 "I am the LORD your God, who brought you out of Egypt, out of the land of slavery.[t]

3 "You shall have no other gods before[c] me.[u]

4 "You shall not make for yourself an image[v] in the form of anything in heaven above or on the

[a] 18 Most Hebrew manuscripts; a few Hebrew manuscripts and Septuagint *and all the people* [b] 19 Or *and God answered him with thunder* [c] 3 Or *besides*

because it may result in ceremonial uncleanness (Lev 15:16–18; 1 Sam 21:4–5), thus excluding contact with a holy God. See note on v. 10.

19:16–19 An impressive audio-visual display heralds the Lord's descent upon the mountain. These special effects parallel those of the chief Canaanite god (Baal) and suggest that Israel would now know its supreme and only God. Sandwiched in the middle of two repetitive sections, this emphasizes that the preparation of Israel was essential for the holy God to be revealed in their midst. The awe-inspiring display culminates in the dialogue between Moses and God anticipated back in v. 9. In the NT this terrifying experience of Israel is set in bold relief to those who have heard God speak through the mediator of a new covenant and must likewise heed his warnings (Heb 12:18–29).

19:20–25 Unlike vv. 16–19, these verses emphasize the holiness of the mountain that has resulted from the Lord's descent (cf. 3:5). The main point is that the Lord is holy. Now that he is visibly present on Mount Sinai, the people must exercise even greater caution and restraint.

19:21–24 many of them perish ... break out against them ... break out against them. Trespassers previously faced execution by fellow Israelites (vv. 12–13), but now the Lord himself threatens to execute them (cf. Lev 10:1–2; 2 Sam 6:6–8).

19:22 priests. Arguably those who functioned as priests (cf. 24:5) before God instituted the Aaronic priesthood (28:1). But in view of the immediate context, it more likely anticipates the subsequent role of Aaron and his sons (24:1)—in particular, the incident involving Nadab and Abihu (Lev 10:1–2; 16:1).

19:24 bring Aaron up with you. This invitation probably relates not to the immediate situation but to a subsequent ascent (i.e., 24:9). The latter part of this verse thus refers only to unauthorized access: priests and people may approach but only when God invites them.

20:1—23:33 *Israel's Covenant Obligations Disclosed.* Other than a brief narrative section (20:18–21), this sets out Israel's covenant obligations: the general stipulations of "the Ten Commandments" (found in 20:1–17; see 34:28) and the more detailed requirements of "the Book of the Covenant" (found in 20:22—23:33; see 24:7).

20:1–21 *The Ten Commandments.* See also Deut 5:6–21. The Decalogue, or "ten words" (see 34:28; cf. Deut 4:13; 10:4), encompasses Israel's responsibilities to God (vv. 1–11) and to each other (vv. 12–17). This twin focus may explain why God uses two stone tablets (31:18). Alternatively, the two stone tablets reflect the ancient custom of having two identical copies of a treaty-type text. Rather than a legal code that human courts can enforce (e.g., see v. 17 and note), it establishes the core spiritual and socioethical principles that must undergird Israel's covenant life, and the stipulations are thus expressed using very general language to be as broad as possible in their application.

20:1 God spoke all these words. Perhaps stressing the importance of this communication; it is as direct as possible to Israel so there can be no doubt as to its source and authority (cf. Deut 5:22–26). **words.** A technical ancient Near Eastern term for "(covenant) stipulations" (cf. 24:3,8; 34:28). God's basic stipulations (i.e., the "ten words"; cf. 34:28; Deut 4:13; 10:4) for Israel are recorded in vv. 2–17.

20:2 The covenant stipulations are firmly grounded in who God is and how he has made himself known. A typical ancient Near Eastern treaty pattern is reflected in how the introductory preamble ("I am the LORD your God") and brief historical prologue ("who brought you out of Egypt") immediately precedes a statement of the general stipulations ("You shall have ..."). The Lord is being presented here as Israel's great king, whose action on Israel's behalf commands their gratitude and allegiance. God commands Israel to observe these stipulations not in order to become his people but because this is how his people, whom he has rescued from oppression, should respond. See note on 19:4.

20:3 no other gods. This forbids any form of religious pluralism: God demands exclusive loyalty from Israel (and from us; see Matt 6:24; 1 John 5:21). **before me.** The precise nuance is debated, but worshiping other gods as well as the Lord (rather than just "instead of" or "ahead of"; see NIV text note) is most likely in view (22:20; 23:13,24,33).

20:4 image in the form of anything. The first command (v. 3) excludes

earth beneath or in the waters below. [5]You shall not bow down to them or worship[w] them;
for I, the LORD your God, am a jealous God,[x] punishing the children for the sin of the
parents to the third and fourth generation[y] of those who hate me, [6]but showing love to a
thousand[z] generations of those who love me and keep my commandments.
[7] "You shall not misuse the name of the LORD your God, for the LORD will not hold anyone guiltless
who misuses his name.[a]
[8] "Remember the Sabbath[b] day by keeping it holy. [9]Six days you shall labor and do all your work,[c]
[10]but the seventh day is a sabbath to the LORD your God. On it you shall not do any work,
neither you, nor your son or daughter, nor your male or female servant, nor your animals,
nor any foreigner residing in your towns. [11]For in six days the LORD made the heavens and
the earth, the sea, and all that is in them, but he rested[d] on the seventh day. Therefore the
LORD blessed the Sabbath day and made it holy.
[12] "Honor your father and your mother,[e] so that you may live long in the land the LORD your God is
giving you.
[13] "You shall not murder.[f]
[14] "You shall not commit adultery.[g]
[15] "You shall not steal.[h]
[16] "You shall not give false testimony against your neighbor.[i]

20:5 [w] Isa 44:15,17,19 [x] Ex 34:14; Dt 4:24 [y] Nu 14:18; Jer 32:18
20:6 [z] Dt 7:9
20:7 [a] Lev 19:12; Mt 5:33
20:8 [b] Ex 31:13-16; Lev 26:2
20:9 [c] Ex 34:21; Lk 13:14
20:11 [d] Ge 2:2
20:12 [e] Mt 15:4*; Mk 7:10*; Eph 6:2
20:13 [f] Mt 5:21*; Ro 13:9*
20:14 [g] Mt 19:18*
20:15 [h] Lev 19:11,13; Mt 19:18*
20:16 [i] Ex 23:1,7; Mt 19:18*

worshiping any other deity; this second command may reinforce this by including all deities, or it may relate, in particular, to worshiping the Lord. Either way, God expressly forbids manufacturing and worshiping any idolatrous object, whether it is associated with the Lord or not. See Deut 4:15–18, which underlines the inherent difficulty involved in making an idol that can accurately represent the Lord. **heaven ... earth ... waters.** Correspond to the three areas of creation (Gen 1).

20:5–6 The incentive to obey is twofold: (1) the negative threat of cross-generational judgment and (2) the positive assurance of multi-generational love.

20:5 jealous. Often translated "zealous." Unlike human jealousy (so often a vice rather than a virtue), God's jealousy always expresses genuine love and informed concern for his exclusive rights, so he zealously protects his interests. **punishing the children.** This could be because an extended family unit living together shares the guilt (e.g., Num 16:31–34; Josh 7:24–25), but it may also attest to the long-term influence (and consequences) of sinful behavior. **third and fourth generation.** The largest conceivable extended family, but it may also define the extent of direct influence any individual might possibly have. The deliberate imbalance between this and "a thousand generations" (v. 6)—which can also mean "to thousands," emphasizing the breadth of God's love rather than its duration (cf. 34:6–7)—indicates what God desires. **those who hate me.** In covenant/treaty language, those who are disloyal to the king (God). This describes all those the Lord punishes, just as the positive counterpart ("those who love me and keep my commandments," v. 6) describes all those he loves.

20:7 misuse the name. Popularly interpreted as an irreverent use of God's name as an expletive or blasphemy, this third command probably relates in particular to invoking God's name to sanction inappropriate behavior or to endorse deceptive oaths. The NT insists on a strict honesty that renders any such language unnecessary (Matt 5:33–37; Jas 5:12).

20:8 Remember the Sabbath. This commandment (vv. 8–11) and the next (v. 12) are the only two in the series that are framed positively. As God gave all Israel its people and life but required that Israel acknowledge this by giving back the firstborn (13:1–2), so God gives Israel all its days but requires that Israel acknowledge this by giving back one in seven. The Lord's instructions for collecting manna (16:22–26) already established the sabbatical structure of Israel's week. The seventh day is exclusively for the Lord, so Israel must remember it "by keeping it holy," namely, by making this day distinct from all others: the entire Israelite community (including livestock and resident aliens) is to cease normal labor (v. 10).

20:11 For in six days the LORD made. Celebrating the Sabbath looks back to both creation (Gen 2:2–3) and redemption from slavery (Deut 5:15), and anticipates the experience of rest through faith in Christ (Heb 4:1–11; see note on 31:17).

20:12 Honor. This command (v. 12), like the previous one (vv. 8–11), is framed positively. Honoring parents involves showing them respect (Lev 19:3; Mal 1:6) and obeying them (Deut 21:18–21; Eph 6:1); it thus means not doing anything that would be disrespectful or harmful to parents (21:15,17; Lev 20:9), as well as acting positively to do them good (Mark 7:9–13; 1 Tim 5:4). **so that you may live long in the land.** This is the only commandment in 20:1–17 that includes a promise, but this promise is national rather than personal; the land in question is Canaan, where Israel's tenure was dependent on faithfulness to the covenant. Parents had an important role to play in communicating the covenant's requirements to their children (Deut 6:7,20–24), which also explains why Paul highlights the importance of this commandment in a Christian setting (Eph 6:1–3).

20:13 murder. The first of the purely moral commands with immediate civic implications, like the first of the "religious" commands, is of first importance. "Murder" is a more appropriate translation than "kill," even though the word occasionally refers to involuntary homicide. The wider OT context clearly shows that this prohibition does not apply to capital punishment, killing in war, or slaughtering animals. For Jesus' stricter ethic, see Matt 5:21–26.

20:14 adultery. Intercourse between a married or betrothed person and someone who is not their spouse (Lev 18:20; 20:10; Deut 22:22–27). It was a heinous offense in ancient times (Gen 12:18; 20:9; 39:9), and Israel executed both parties involved (Lev 20:10; Deut 22:23–24). The unfaithfulness involved in adultery makes it an appropriate metaphor for Israel's subsequent covenant unfaithfulness to the Lord (see the Prophets, particularly the book of Hosea). For Jesus' stricter ethic, see Matt 5:27–30.

20:15 steal. This relates to more than just capital offenses such as kidnapping (21:16); it encompasses all forms of theft, i.e., taking what God has entrusted to someone else (22:1–15).

20:16 give false testimony. Since people did not give testimony under oath in ancient Israel, the third commandment did not encompass "false testimony." But while this commandment suggests that a legal setting (i.e., testifying in court) is the primary focus, it may apply more generally

20:17 [j]Ro 7:7*; 13:9*; Eph 5:3
20:18 [k]Ex 19:16-19; Heb 12:18-19
20:19 [l]Dt 5:5,23-27; Gal 3:19
20:20 [m]Dt 4:10; Isa 8:13 [n]Pr 16:6
20:21 [o]Dt 5:22
20:22 [p]Ne 9:13
20:23 [q]ver 3 [r]Ex 32:4,8,31
20:24 [s]Dt 12:5; 16:6,11; 2Ch 6:6 [t]Ge 12:2
20:25 [u]Dt 27:5-6
21:1 [v]Dt 4:14
21:2 [w]Jer 34:8,14

17 "You shall not covet[j] your neighbor's house. You shall not covet your neighbor's wife, or his male or female servant, his ox or donkey, or anything that belongs to your neighbor."

18 When the people saw the thunder and lightning and heard the trumpet[k] and saw the mountain in smoke, they trembled with fear. They stayed at a distance
19 and said to Moses, "Speak to us yourself and we will listen. But do not have God speak to us or we will die."[l]

20 Moses said to the people, "Do not be afraid. God has come to test you, so that the fear[m] of God will be with you to keep you from sinning."[n]

21 The people remained at a distance, while Moses approached the thick darkness[o] where God was.

Idols and Altars

22 Then the LORD said to Moses, "Tell the Israelites this: 'You have seen for yourselves that I have spoken to you from heaven:[p]
23 Do not make any gods to be alongside me;[q] do not make for yourselves gods of silver or gods of gold.[r]

24 " 'Make an altar of earth for me and sacrifice on it your burnt offerings and fellowship offerings, your sheep and goats and your cattle. Wherever I cause my name[s] to be honored, I will come to you and bless[t] you.
25 If you make an altar of stones for me, do not build it with dressed stones, for you will defile it if you use a tool[u] on it.
26 And do not go up to my altar on steps, or your private parts may be exposed.'

21

"These are the laws[v] you are to set before them:

Hebrew Servants

21:2-6pp — Dt 15:12-18
21:2-11Ref — Lev 25:39-55

2 "If you buy a Hebrew servant, he is to serve you for six years. But in the seventh year, he shall go free,[w] without paying anything.
3 If he comes alone, he is to go free alone; but if he has a wife when he

to any use of dishonest or deceptive language (23:1). False testimony could have serious consequences (23:7); in such cases it became a capital offense (Deut 19:16–21).

20:17 covet. Unlike the preceding commandments, the tenth is more internally focused on the human heart/mind. "Covet" may be a morally neutral word, but here the connotation is obviously illicit desire (Deut 5:21) motivated by greed and selfishness that betrays a lack of trust in the Lord as provider. While this is clearly not an offense that any human court can prosecute, left unchecked it inevitably produces more visible fruit (Jas 1:14–15), such as breaking other commandments, including the very first—given its close association with greed, which Paul calls idolatry (Eph 5:5; Col 3:5). It is also a fundamental breach of the law of love (Rom 13:8–10).

20:18–21 The narrative returns now to Israel's response to the theophany (divine appearance) on Sinai (see also Deut 5:23–27).

20:19 Terrified by these events and unwilling to go up the mountain themselves (19:12–13; Deut 5:5), the Israelites ask Moses to act as mediator. Successive prophets "like [Moses]" (Deut 18:18) subsequently carry out the mediator role to which the people formally appoint Moses, until Jesus himself ultimately fulfills it (Matt 17:5; Acts 3:22–23; Heb 1:1–2; 8:6; 9:15; 12:24). One greater than Moses (Heb 3:1–6), Jesus becomes the sole Mediator between God and humanity (1 Tim 2:5), one who has supremely made God known (John 1:14–18) and whose voice dare not be ignored (Heb 12:25).

20:20 Do not be afraid ... the fear of God will be with you. Two kinds of fear explain this paradox: (1) an abject terror and (2) a godly fear that facilitates trust and obedience. God designs the theophany (divine appearance) to instill a "fear of God" that would keep Israel "from sinning," so the second kind of fear is an entirely appropriate response (Deut 5:23–29).

20:22—21:1 *Idols and Altars.* This introduction and the conclusion (23:20–33)—both of which highlight the exclusive allegiance that the Lord demands—bracket the more detailed covenant stipulations (21:2—23:19). In addition, 20:22–26 addresses the most likely way in which the Israelites would fail in their obligation to love God: by worshiping other gods and making images of God rather than using a simple altar to worship God. Similarly, 21:2–11 addresses the likely way the people would fail in their obligation to love their neighbor.

20:23 These two prohibitions echo the first two commands in the Decalogue and serve as a foil for the legitimate and acceptable way to worship the Lord that the following verses set out.

20:24–26 These altar laws appear to prepare for the covenant ratification ritual that is carried out in 24:4b–8; they involve both erecting an altar and performing these two types of sacrifice.

20:24 altar of earth. They may use only clumps of earth (or naturally shaped rocks; v. 25) as a platform for burning sacrifices. **burnt offerings ... fellowship offerings.** See notes on Lev 1; 3. **Wherever I cause my name to be honored.** This refers to temporary places of worship, such as those used after Israel entered Canaan (Josh 8:30–31; Judg 6:24; 21:4; 1 Sam 7:17; 2 Sam 24:25; 1 Kgs 18:30).

20:25 tool. These altars were meant to be of a temporary nature and not meant to become cultic shrines, hence the prohibition of defiling them by using sharp instruments.

20:26 exposed. Although Israel's priests later served at stepped altars (Lev 9:22; cf. Ezek 43:17), the linen undergarments they wore (Exod 28:42–43; Lev 6:10; 16:3–4; cf. Ezek 44:17–18) prevented such exposure.

21:1 laws. Social policy (judgments) that could be used in a judicial setting. This verse functions as the heading for the following section (21:2—22:20), which is the only segment containing clearly stated punishments.

21:2—23:19 This is a carefully arranged collection of material that applies the general stipulations in a more particular manner. While it does not exhaustively explain or apply the Decalogue, the legisla-

comes, she is to go with him. [4]If his master gives him a wife and she bears him sons or daughters, the
woman and her children shall belong to her master, and only the man shall go free.
[5]"But if the servant declares, 'I love my master and my wife and children and do not want to go
free,'[x] [6]then his master must take him before the judges.[a][y] He shall take him to the door or the doorpost
and pierce his ear with an awl. Then he will be his servant for life.[z]
[7]"If a man sells his daughter as a servant, she is not to go free as male servants do. [8]If she does not
please the master who has selected her for himself,[b] he must let her be redeemed. He has no right to
sell her to foreigners, because he has broken faith with her. [9]If he selects her for his son, he must grant
her the rights of a daughter. [10]If he marries another woman, he must not deprive the first one of her
food, clothing and marital rights.[a] [11]If he does not provide her with these three things, she is to go free,
without any payment of money.

Personal Injuries

[12]"Anyone who strikes a person with a fatal blow is to be put to death.[b] [13]However, if it is not done
intentionally, but God lets it happen, they are to flee to a place[c] I will designate. [14]But if anyone schemes
and kills someone deliberately,[d] that person is to be taken from my altar and put to death.[e]
[15]"Anyone who attacks[c] their father or mother is to be put to death.
[16]"Anyone who kidnaps someone is to be put to death,[f] whether the victim has been sold[g] or is still
in the kidnapper's possession.
[17]"Anyone who curses their father or mother is to be put to death.[h]
[18]"If people quarrel and one person hits another with a stone or with their fist[d] and the victim does
not die but is confined to bed, [19]the one who struck the blow will not be held liable if the other can get
up and walk around outside with a staff; however, the guilty party must pay the injured person for any
loss of time and see that the victim is completely healed.
[20]"Anyone who beats their male or female slave with a rod must be punished if the slave dies as a

[a] *6* Or *before God* [b] *8* Or *master so that he does not choose her* [c] *15* Or *kills* [d] *18* Or *with a tool*

21:5 [x]Dt 15:16
21:6 [y]Ex 22:8-9 [z]Ne 5:5
21:10 [a]1Co 7:3-5
21:12 [b]Ge 9:6; Mt 26:52
21:13 [c]Nu 35:10-34; Dt 19:2-13; Jos 20:9; 1Sa 24:4,10,18
21:14 [d]Heb 10:26 [e]Dt 19:11-12; 1Ki 2:28-34
21:16 [f]Ex 22:4; Dt 24:7 [g]Ge 37:28
21:17 [h]Lev 20:9-10; Mt 15:4*; Mk 7:10*

tion clearly reflects its two main emphases: love for God and love for neighbor. Despite some similarities with other ancient law codes (most famously that of Hammurapi, king of Babylon, ca. 1750 BC), in some respects it is significantly different (e.g., it values human life and does not discriminate between classes). God designed it to reflect and proclaim his distinctiveness and values to the surrounding nations.

21:2–11 *Hebrew Servants.* The social laws follow the religious laws (20:22–26) and begin in the area in which the Israelites were most likely to go astray in regard to loving their neighbor: indentured servants, the most vulnerable part of society. Indentured service differs markedly from forced labor or human trafficking, which God forbids (v. 16). Israelites sold themselves (and/or family members) into such a contractual arrangement in order to survive extreme financial crisis. The legislation intends to prevent exploitation, although some Israelites subsequently ignored it (Jer 34:8–16). Significantly, to have this material protecting the rights of servants (rather than chiefly those of their masters) makes this legislation distinct from other ancient Near Eastern legal collections, and it suggests that these servants should be treated as human beings rather than as mere personal property (v. 21). This may also explain the absence of servants from the property laws in 22:1–15.

21:2–3 Such restriction on the length any servant could be expected to serve is not found in other ancient Near Eastern law collections and is the first example in these laws that resists permanent class distinctions between people, an ideal realized (with respect to our spiritual status) in the Christian gospel (Gal 3:28).

21:6 before the judges. As the NIV text notes on this verse and 22:8,9,28 indicate, this may refer to either "judges" or "God." The context here may suggest that God is more appropriate, as in 22:28. **pierce his ear with an awl.** This ear piercing is not a cruel act but a voluntary rite by which the servant symbolizes his desire to remain a servant. Ps 40:6 may apply this metaphorically.

21:12–36 *Personal Injuries.* The laws in this section all relate to attacks on people (intentional or otherwise) and prescribe the appropriate penalty or compensation to impose. The material is arranged mainly in descending order as regards the punishments prescribed. The severity of the punishments reflects the nature of the assault and the death or injury caused by it.

21:12–14 As in the second half of the Decalogue, homicide begins the social laws as the most important such law, because the transcendent value of human life cannot be compromised by anything on this earth.

21:13 not done intentionally. Alternative descriptions include "accidentally" (Num 35:11; Josh 20:3,9), "without enmity" (Num 35:22), "not an enemy" and "no harm was intended" (Num 35:23), and "without malice aforethought" (Deut 4:42; 19:4,6; Josh 20:5). All these distinguish unintentional homicide (manslaughter) from premeditated murder; only the latter automatically incurs capital punishment (Gen 9:6). **a place I will designate.** Alludes to subsequently establishing "cities of refuge" (Num 35:6; Deut 4:41–43; 19:1–13; Josh 20:1–9).

21:14 taken from my altar. The horns of the altar were a place of refuge (1 Kgs 1:50–51; 2:28), symbolic of God's mercy (Amos 3:14).

21:15 attacks. As the preceding material and the NIV text note suggest, this possibly means "kills"; thus understood, the focus shifts here from homicide in society to homicide in the family.

21:16–17 These laws relate to other serious offenses that are related to murder in seeking to destroy or devalue human life, which explains why these also are capital offenses. As in vv. 12–15, the law in society (v. 16) is followed by the family law (v. 17).

21:16 kidnaps. In relation to forced labor or human trafficking.

21:18–27 Inflicting injury on others carries physical or financial consequences. The assailant must compensate the incapacitated person.

21:20 Beating a slave to death must be "punished," a practice unique to Hebrew law in the ancient world.

21:21 [i]Lev 25:44-46
21:22 [j]ver 30; Dt 22:18-19
21:23 [k]Lev 24:19; Dt 19:21
21:24 [l]Mt 5:38*
21:28 [m]ver 32; Ge 9:5
21:30 [n]ver 22; Nu 35:31
21:32 [o]Zec 11:12-13; Mt 26:15; 27:3,9
22:1 [p]2Sa 12:6; Pr 6:31; Lk 19:8
22:2 [q]Mt 6:19-20; 24:43 [r]Nu 35:27
22:3 [s]Ex 21:2; Mt 18:25
22:4 [t]Ge 43:12

direct result, 21but they are not to be punished if the slave recovers after a day or two, since the slave is their property.[i]

22"If people are fighting and hit a pregnant woman and she gives birth prematurely[a] but there is no serious injury, the offender must be fined whatever the woman's husband demands[j] and the court allows. 23But if there is serious injury, you are to take life for life,[k] 24eye for eye, tooth for tooth,[l] hand for hand, foot for foot, 25burn for burn, wound for wound, bruise for bruise.

26"An owner who hits a male or female slave in the eye and destroys it must let the slave go free to compensate for the eye. 27And an owner who knocks out the tooth of a male or female slave must let the slave go free to compensate for the tooth.

28"If a bull gores a man or woman to death, the bull is to be stoned to death,[m] and its meat must not be eaten. But the owner of the bull will not be held responsible. 29If, however, the bull has had the habit of goring and the owner has been warned but has not kept it penned up and it kills a man or woman, the bull is to be stoned and its owner also is to be put to death. 30However, if payment is demanded, the owner may redeem his life by the payment of whatever is demanded.[n] 31This law also applies if the bull gores a son or daughter. 32If the bull gores a male or female slave, the owner must pay thirty shekels[b][o] of silver to the master of the slave, and the bull is to be stoned to death.

33"If anyone uncovers a pit or digs one and fails to cover it and an ox or a donkey falls into it, 34the one who opened the pit must pay the owner for the loss and take the dead animal in exchange.

35"If anyone's bull injures someone else's bull and it dies, the two parties are to sell the live one and divide both the money and the dead animal equally. 36However, if it was known that the bull had the habit of goring, yet the owner did not keep it penned up, the owner must pay, animal for animal, and take the dead animal in exchange.

Protection of Property

22 [c] "Whoever steals an ox or a sheep and slaughters it or sells it must pay back[p] five head of cattle for the ox and four sheep for the sheep.

2"If a thief is caught breaking in[q] at night and is struck a fatal blow, the defender is not guilty of bloodshed;[r] 3but if it happens after sunrise, the defender is guilty of bloodshed.

"Anyone who steals must certainly make restitution, but if they have nothing, they must be sold[s] to pay for their theft. 4If the stolen animal is found alive in their possession—whether ox or donkey or sheep—they must pay back double.[t]

[a] *22* Or *she has a miscarriage* [b] *32* That is, about 12 ounces or about 345 grams [c] In Hebrew texts 22:1 is numbered 21:37, and 22:2-31 is numbered 22:1-30.

21:21 their property. The word "property" is elsewhere often translated "silver"; it implies the slave's labor, consistent with vv. 2–11.

21:22 This has generated considerable controversy, especially in view of the modern abortion debate. It is unclear whether premature birth or miscarriage is in view (see NIV text note), and we are not told explicitly who suffers the "serious injury"—the mother or her baby. However, the wording and application of the principle of moral equivalence (see note on vv. 23–24) may imply that both victims (mother and child) were taken into account. Accordingly, this law protects all human life, including life in the womb, and is obviously in keeping with the Scripture's subsequent attribution of human personhood to the unborn child (Pss 51:5–6; 139:13–16; Luke 1:44).

21:23–24 life for life ... bruise for bruise. This principle of moral equivalence curtails retaliatory action by ensuring that punishment does not exceed the crime; it does not encourage or validate barbaric revenge, but controls the clan vendetta by ensuring that no revenge exceeds the original offense. The immediate and wider context suggests that Israel does not apply it literally in terms of physical mutilation; rather, people make appropriate compensation (vv. 26–27,30). For Jesus' teaching on retaliation and revenge, see Matt 5:38–42 (cf. Rom 12:17–21).

21:26–27 Less severe beatings of slaves (those not resulting in death) do not invoke the death penalty (vv. 20–21), but the principle of vv. 23–24 requires that the slave should go free. Again this distinguishes this collection of sample laws from other ancient Near Eastern ones, which determine punishment by social class.

21:28–36 These laws deal mainly with cases of criminal negligence: loss of human or animal life resulting from lack of due diligence and care. Where a rogue animal is responsible for human death, its life is forfeit (Gen 9:5). This highlights the intrinsic value of human life. But where criminal negligence is involved, the life of the offender is forfeited unless they pay appropriate compensation. In the case of a slave, there is a set amount (v. 32) for this ransom payment (see note on 30:12), possibly suggesting that the victim's intrinsic value determines the compensation demanded in other cases.

21:32 thirty shekels of silver. See NIV text note. Apparently the standard price for a slave.

22:1–15 *Protection of Property.* After dealing with bodily injuries, the focus moves to issues concerning property—in particular, the appropriate compensation for stolen, lost, or damaged property. While this section arguably extends to include vv. 16–17, the latter verses deal with a very different kind of financial loss.

22:1–4 This focuses on theft and the punitive and compensatory damages it incurs. The damages correlate to the value of what is lost and whether such loss is permanent or temporary.

22:2–3 Exploiting the darkness for nefarious purposes such as burglary

5“If anyone grazes their livestock in a field or vineyard and lets them stray and they graze in someone else’s field, the offender must make restitution from the best of their own field or vineyard.
6“If a fire breaks out and spreads into thornbushes so that it burns shocks of grain or standing grain
or the whole field, the one who started the fire must make restitution.
7“If anyone gives a neighbor silver or goods for safekeeping and they are stolen from the neighbor’s house, the thief, if caught, must pay back double.[u] 8But if the thief is not found, the owner of
the house must appear before the judges,[v] and they must[a] determine whether the owner of the house
has laid hands on the other person’s property. 9In all cases of illegal possession of an ox, a donkey, a
sheep, a garment, or any other lost property about which somebody says, ‘This is mine,’ both parties
are to bring their cases before the judges.[b][w] The one whom the judges declare[c] guilty must pay back
double to the other.
10“If anyone gives a donkey, an ox, a sheep or any other animal to their neighbor for safekeeping
and it dies or is injured or is taken away while no one is looking, 11the issue between them will be settled by the taking of an oath[x] before the LORD that the neighbor did not lay hands on the other person’s
property. The owner is to accept this, and no restitution is required. 12But if the animal was stolen from
the neighbor, restitution must be made to the owner. 13If it was torn to pieces by a wild animal, the
neighbor shall bring in the remains as evidence and shall not be required to pay for the torn animal.[y]
14“If anyone borrows an animal from their neighbor and it is injured or dies while the owner is not
present, they must make restitution. 15But if the owner is with the animal, the borrower will not have
to pay. If the animal was hired, the money paid for the hire covers the loss.

Social Responsibility

16“If a man seduces a virgin[z] who is not pledged to be married and sleeps with her, he must pay the
bride-price, and she shall be his wife. 17If her father absolutely refuses to give her to him, he must still
pay the bride-price for virgins.
18“Do not allow a sorceress[a] to live.
19“Anyone who has sexual relations with an animal[b] is to be put to death.
20“Whoever sacrifices to any god other than the LORD must be destroyed.[d][c]
21“Do not mistreat or oppress a foreigner,[d] for you were foreigners[e] in Egypt.

[a] 8 Or *before God, and he will* [b] 9 Or *before God* [c] 9 Or *whom God declares* [d] 20 The Hebrew term refers to the irrevocable giving over of things or persons to the LORD, often by totally destroying them.

22:7 [u] ver 4
22:8 [v] Ex 21:6; Dt 17:8-9; 19:17
22:9 [w] ver 28; Dt 25:1
22:11 [x] Heb 6:16
22:13 [y] Ge 31:39
22:16 [z] Dt 22:28
22:18 [a] Lev 20:27; Dt 18:11; 1Sa 28:3
22:19 [b] Lev 18:23; Dt 27:21
22:20 [c] Dt 17:2-5
22:21 [d] Lev 19:33 [e] Dt 10:19

could cost intruders their life. This presumably functions here as a deterrent; the context certainly suggests a focus on the thief rather than the occupant (who acts with impunity before sunrise).

22:5–6 These are two further examples of negligence (21:28–36) rather than acts with criminal intent. The compensation is simply to equal the loss because the offender did not intend harm.

22:6 thornbushes. Used as hedges around fields (Mic 7:4).

22:7–15 Attention shifts to property lost or damaged when entrusted to another. Where theft is involved, the thief must pay appropriate damages, i.e., “pay back double” (vv. 7,9; cf. Lev 6:2–5, where, if one confesses one’s sin of theft—rather than being caught as here in Exodus—the penalty is restitution plus 20 percent). If an animal is injured or dies while borrowed, the borrower must make restitution (i.e., pay for the animal) unless the owner is actually present or the animal is contracted for hire. Thus, where no criminal intent or negligence is involved, no one is held responsible.

22:16–31 *Social Responsibility.* This section addresses various kinds of inappropriate behavior. While all these offenses constitute breaches of Israel’s covenant obligations, some are clearly more serious than others, as reflected in the associated punishments.

22:16–17 While the case law framework is connected with the preceding material (dealing with the protection of property), the nature of the “property” and “theft” envisaged here is rather different. For this reason, it is often grouped with the social offenses that follow (vv. 18–31). The scenario appears to involve consent (“seduces”) rather than rape. This discourages such premarital intercourse by making men liable to pay a substantial sum (“the bride-price,” which was normally paid by the groom to the girl’s father; see Gen 24:53; 34:12), whether or not the girl’s father gives consent to a subsequent marriage. In this and similar laws in Deut 22, no dowry or wedding gift (1 Kgs 9:16) is envisaged from the family of the bride.

22:18–20 These three capital crimes are incompatible with the Lord’s and Israel’s holy status, and they exemplify the behavior for which the Canaanites would be judged (Lev 18:3,21,23; 19:31; 20:2–6,23). Sorcery (v. 18) seems to encompass any manipulation of power that belongs exclusively to the Lord (7:11; Deut 18:10). Bestiality (v. 19) not only defiles the offender but perverts natural sexual relations (Lev 18:23). Sacrificing to other gods (v. 20) utterly disregards the Lord’s covenant commands and thus invokes the same judgment that is subsequently meted out on the Canaanites (Deut 7:1–2; 20:17).

22:21—23:9 The material in this section differs from the judgments that precede it. No punishments are listed that could be applied by a human court.

22:21 Israel’s experience as oppressed foreigners should discourage them from oppressing others in that way. The reiteration of this particular prohibition in 23:9 suggests that 22:21—23:9 forms a discrete section within the Book of the Covenant (cf. 24:7). This seems to be confirmed by the contents of these verses, which affirm behavior that goes beyond that which may be controlled by legislation.

22:22 [f] Dt 24:6,10,12,17
22:23 [g] Lk 18:7 [h] Dt 15:9; Ps 18:6
22:24 [i] Ps 69:24; 109:9
22:25 [j] Lev 25:35-37; Dt 23:20; Ps 15:5
22:26 [k] Dt 24:6
22:27 [l] Ex 34:6
22:28 [m] Lev 24:11,16 [n] Ecc 10:20; Ac 23:5*
22:29 [o] Ex 23:15,16,19 [p] Ex 13:2
22:30 [q] Ex 13:12; Dt 15:19 [r] Lev 22:27
22:31 [s] Lev 19:2 [t] Eze 4:14
23:1 [u] Ex 20:16; Ps 101:5 [v] Ps 35:11; Ac 6:11
23:2 [w] Dt 16:19
23:4 [x] Dt 22:1-3
23:5 [y] Dt 22:4
23:6 [z] ver 2
23:7 [a] Eph 4:25
23:8 [b] Dt 10:17; 16:19; Pr 15:27
23:9 [c] Ex 22:21

22 "Do not take advantage of the widow or the fatherless.[f] 23 If you do and they cry out[g] to me, I will
certainly hear their cry.[h] 24 My anger will be aroused, and I will kill you with the sword; your wives will
become widows and your children fatherless.[i]

25 "If you lend money to one of my people among you who is needy, do not treat it like a business
deal; charge no interest.[j] 26 If you take your neighbor's cloak as a pledge,[k] return it by sunset, 27 because
that cloak is the only covering your neighbor has. What else can they sleep in? When they cry out to
me, I will hear, for I am compassionate.[l]

28 "Do not blaspheme God[a][m] or curse the ruler of your people.[n]

29 "Do not hold back offerings[o] from your granaries or your vats.[b]

"You must give me the firstborn of your sons.[p] 30 Do the same with your cattle and your sheep.[q] Let
them stay with their mothers for seven days, but give them to me on the eighth day.[r]

31 "You are to be my holy people.[s] So do not eat the meat of an animal torn by wild beasts;[t] throw
it to the dogs.

Laws of Justice and Mercy

23 "Do not spread false reports.[u] Do not help a guilty person by being a malicious witness.[v]
2 "Do not follow the crowd in doing wrong. When you give testimony in a lawsuit, do not
pervert justice[w] by siding with the crowd, 3 and do not show favoritism to a poor person in a lawsuit.

4 "If you come across your enemy's ox or donkey wandering off, be sure to return it.[x] 5 If you see the
donkey[y] of someone who hates you fallen down under its load, do not leave it there; be sure you help
them with it.

6 "Do not deny justice[z] to your poor people in their lawsuits. 7 Have nothing to do with a false charge[a]
and do not put an innocent or honest person to death, for I will not acquit the guilty.

8 "Do not accept a bribe,[b] for a bribe blinds those who see and twists the words of the innocent.

9 "Do not oppress a foreigner;[c] you yourselves know how it feels to be foreigners, because you were
foreigners in Egypt.

Sabbath Laws

10 "For six years you are to sow your fields and harvest the crops, 11 but during the seventh year let the
land lie unplowed and unused. Then the poor among your people may get food from it, and the wild
animals may eat what is left. Do the same with your vineyard and your olive grove.

[a] *28* Or *Do not revile the judges* [b] *29* The meaning of the Hebrew for this phrase is uncertain.

22:22–24 The Lord's special concern for widows and orphans (i.e., defenseless people), coupled with the threat of retribution, should have deterred Israel from exploiting the vulnerable members of their society. Unfortunately, they subsequently ignore this despite frequent reiterations of God's concern (e.g., Lev 19:9–10; Deut 10:18; 14:28–29; Pss 10:17–18; 68:5; Isa 10:1–2; Jer 22:3; Ezek 22:29), so the threat here became a reality (Lam 5:3). Such negligence continued even after the exile (Zech 7:10; Mal 3:5) and remains the antithesis of "religion that God ... accepts" (Jas 1:27; cf. Matt 5:2–4; 1 John 3:17).

22:25–27 Both examples of mistreatment concern financial relief for the poor: (1) charging interest for charitable loans and (2) putting one's own (financial) interests above an impoverished neighbor's well-being. The Lord's compassion for such people should motivate a loving response and discourage any selfish lack of concern. Jesus encourages even greater generosity (Luke 6:34–35).

22:28 Do not blaspheme God. See NIV text note; see also note on 21:6. **curse the ruler of your people.** Paul applies this in terms of verbal insult (Acts 23:4–5).

22:29 You must give me the firstborn. See note on 13:13.

22:30 eighth day. The seven-day delay is not simply on compassionate grounds but could also relate to its unacceptability (Lev 22:27) due to ritual uncleanness, which may be inferred from the timing of circumcision (Gen 17:12), purification after male childbirth (Lev 12:2–3), and other purification regulations (Lev 15:13–14,24,28–29).

22:31 As God's holy people, the Israelites must abstain from foods that would ritually defile them, such as an animal not properly drained of blood (see Lev 17:13–14, where the context explicitly relates to not eating blood).

23:1–9 *Laws of Justice and Mercy.* These stipulations (see note on 22:21—23:9) focus primarily on perverting justice by offering false testimony (vv. 1–2), showing partiality (v. 3), making false allegations (v. 7), or accepting a bribe (v. 8).

23:3 to a poor person. While the weight of the law and of prophetic indictment is certainly against favoritism shown to the rich and powerful, any sort of favoritism, even to the poor, is forbidden.

23:4–5 The Israelites are not merely to refrain from hurting others; they must help others, even their adversaries. The NT likewise encourages such active love, not simply passive restraint (Luke 6:27–36; Rom 12:14,20).

23:10–13 *Sabbath Laws.* The principle enshrined in the weekly Sabbath is now more broadly applied in terms of sabbatical years and humanitarian concerns.

23:10–12 The sabbatical year, like the weekly Sabbath on which it is patterned (20:8–11), expresses humanitarian and ecological concern; it is not primarily an attempt to maximize productivity, even though it may

12“Six days do your work,[d] but on the seventh day do not work, so that your ox and your donkey may
rest, and so that the slave born in your household and the foreigner living among you may be refreshed.
13“Be careful[e] to do everything I have said to you. Do not invoke the names of other gods; do not let
them be heard on your lips.

The Three Annual Festivals

14“Three times[f] a year you are to celebrate a festival to me.
15“Celebrate the Festival of Unleavened Bread;[g] for seven days eat bread made without yeast, as I
commanded you. Do this at the appointed time in the month of Aviv, for in that month you came out
of Egypt.
“No one is to appear before me empty-handed.[h]
16“Celebrate the Festival of Harvest with the firstfruits[i] of the crops you sow in your field.
“Celebrate the Festival of Ingathering at the end of the year, when you gather in your crops from
the field.[j]
17“Three times[k] a year all the men are to appear before the Sovereign LORD.
18“Do not offer the blood of a sacrifice to me along with anything containing yeast.[l]
“The fat of my festival offerings must not be kept until morning.[m]
19“Bring the best of the firstfruits[n] of your soil to the house of the LORD your God.
“Do not cook a young goat in its mother’s milk.[o]

God’s Angel to Prepare the Way

20“See, I am sending an angel[p] ahead of you to guard you along the way and to bring you to
the place I have prepared.[q] 21Pay attention to him and listen[r] to what he says. Do not rebel against
him; he will not forgive your rebellion,[s] since my Name is in him. 22If you listen carefully to what
he says and do all that I say, I will be an enemy[t] to your enemies and will oppose those who oppose
you. 23My angel will go ahead of you and bring you into the land of the Amorites, Hittites, Perizzites,
Canaanites, Hivites and Jebusites,[u] and I will wipe them out. 24Do not bow down before their gods or
worship[v] them or follow their practices.[w] You must demolish[x] them and break their sacred stones
to pieces. 25Worship the LORD your God,[y] and his blessing[z] will be on your food and water. I will take
away sickness[a] from among you, 26and none will miscarry or be barren[b] in your land. I will give
you a full life span.[c]

23:12 [d] Ex 20:9
23:13 [e] 1Ti 4:16
23:14 [f] Ex 34:23,24
23:15 [g] Ex 12:17 [h] Ex 34:20
23:16 [i] Ex 34:22 [j] Dt 16:13
23:17 [k] Dt 16:16
23:18 [l] Ex 34:25 [m] Dt 16:4
23:19 [n] Ex 22:29; Dt 26:2,10 [o] Dt 14:21
23:20 [p] Ex 14:19; 32:34 [q] Ex 15:17
23:21 [r] Nu 14:11; Dt 18:19 [s] Ps 78:8,40,56
23:22 [t] Ge 12:3; Dt 30:7
23:23 [u] ver 20; Jos 24:8,11
23:24 [v] Ex 20:5 [w] Dt 12:30-31 [x] Ex 34:13; Nu 33:52
23:25 [y] Dt 6:13; Mt 4:10 [z] Dt 7:12-15; 28:1-14 [a] Ex 15:26
23:26 [b] Dt 7:14; Mal 3:11 [c] Job 5:26

also facilitate such due to nutrient replenishment and because God has built the Sabbath into the created order (Gen 2:1–3).

23:13 Do not invoke the names of other gods. In the immediate context, this may prohibit worshiping Canaan’s fertility deities, which the Israelites may be tempted to do in order to secure good harvests. However, use of the plural “you” in this verse sets it apart from its context, so a more general prohibition could also be intended.

23:14–19 *The Three Annual Festivals.* See 34:18–26; Lev 23:4–44; Num 28:16—29:40; Deut 16:1–17. The first festival is explicitly related to the exodus, and the latter two are implicitly associated with God’s gift of the land. By making these pilgrimages and bringing these offerings, Israel acknowledges the Lord as the God who provides.

23:15 Unleavened Bread. See notes on 12:17,18.

23:16 Harvest. Also called “Weeks” (34:22) or “Pentecost” (Acts 2:1; 20:16); celebrated seven weeks (on the 50th day) after the Festival of Unleavened Bread, after the wheat harvest. **Ingathering.** Also called “Tabernacles” (Lev 23:34). Occurring at the end of the agricultural year, it celebrated the fruit harvest and involved reenacting Israel’s temporary shelters following the exodus (Lev 23:42–43; Neh 8:13–17).

23:18–19 These four instructions concerning food and offerings (cf. 34:25–26) formally conclude the specific obligations of the covenant; they apply particularly (if not exclusively) to Passover (v. 18b; cf. 12:9–10), Unleavened Bread (vv. 15a,18a; cf. 12:15–16), and Harvest (v. 19; cf. v. 16).

23:18 fat … morning. As fat was otherwise burnt in meat offerings, this prohibition must relate exclusively to the Passover.

23:19 firstfruits. This representative portion acknowledges that the entire harvest is the Lord’s gift and belongs to him. **in its mother’s milk.** The reason for this taboo is unclear. It may simply violate the natural order because the mother’s milk sustains the life of its offspring; the speculative idea that it was a Canaanite fertility ritual has no firm evidence.

23:20–33 *God’s Angel to Prepare the Way.* The “Book of the Covenant” (24:7) concludes by exhorting Israel, focusing primarily on their journeying to and possessing the promised land.

23:23 My angel. See notes on 3:2; 14:19. As in ch. 3, this angel is closely identified with God himself; such is particularly clear from God’s instructions: “Do not rebel against him; he will not forgive your rebellion, since my Name is in him” (v. 21). Moreover, to obey this angel is to obey God (v. 22). Even after Israel’s idolatry (ch. 32) has jeopardized the construction of the tabernacle, the promise here is not withdrawn (32:34; 33:2). It seems to be fulfilled by the “commander of the army of the LORD” who appears to Joshua (Josh 5:13–15) and says almost exactly what God previously told Moses at the burning bush (3:5).

23:24–26 Blessing in the land likewise depends on whether Israel worships the Lord exclusively, so they must eradicate every vestige of the Canaanite fertility cult.

23:27 [d]Ex 15:14; Dt 2:25 [e]Dt 7:23
23:28 [f]Dt 7:20; Jos 24:12
23:29 [g]Dt 7:22
23:31 [h]Ge 15:18 [i]Jos 21:44; 24:12,18
23:32 [j]Ex 34:12; Dt 7:2
23:33 [k]Dt 7:16; Ps 106:36
24:1 [l]Ex 6:23; Lev 10:1-2 [m]Nu 11:16
24:3 [n]Ex 19:8; Dt 5:27
24:4 [o]Dt 31:9 [p]Ge 28:18
24:6 [q]Heb 9:18
24:7 [r]Heb 9:19

[27]"I will send my terror[d] ahead of you and throw into confusion[e] every nation you encounter. I will make all your enemies turn their backs and run. [28]I will send the hornet[f] ahead of you to drive the Hivites, Canaanites and Hittites out of your way. [29]But I will not drive them out in a single year, because the land would become desolate and the wild animals[g] too numerous for you. [30]Little by little I will drive them out before you, until you have increased enough to take possession of the land.

[31]"I will establish your borders from the Red Sea[a] to the Mediterranean Sea,[b] and from the desert to the Euphrates River.[h] I will give into your hands the people who live in the land, and you will drive them out[i] before you. [32]Do not make a covenant[j] with them or with their gods. [33]Do not let them live in your land or they will cause you to sin against me, because the worship of their gods will certainly be a snare[k] to you."

The Covenant Confirmed

24 Then the LORD said to Moses, "Come up to the LORD, you and Aaron, Nadab and Abihu,[l] and seventy of the elders[m] of Israel. You are to worship at a distance, [2]but Moses alone is to approach the LORD; the others must not come near. And the people may not come up with him."

[3]When Moses went and told the people all the LORD's words and laws, they responded with one voice, "Everything the LORD has said we will do."[n] [4]Moses then wrote[o] down everything the LORD had said.

He got up early the next morning and built an altar at the foot of the mountain and set up twelve stone pillars[p] representing the twelve tribes of Israel. [5]Then he sent young Israelite men, and they offered burnt offerings and sacrificed young bulls as fellowship offerings to the LORD. [6]Moses took half of the blood[q] and put it in bowls, and the other half he splashed against the altar. [7]Then he took the Book of the Covenant[r] and read it to the people. They responded, "We will do everything the LORD has said; we will obey."

[a] *31* Or *the Sea of Reeds* [b] *31* Hebrew *to the Sea of the Philistines*

23:27–30 The Lord himself will secure the conquest of Canaan. He will spread terror and confusion among Israel's enemies.

23:28 hornet. The meaning of the Hebrew noun is uncertain; it could refer either to some agent God will send to terrify Canaan's inhabitants or to the ensuing panic itself. Either way, it will seriously affect their ability to resist Israel's invasion.

23:29–30 Gradually displacing the indigenous population, the Israelites are implicitly responsible to subdue the land and rule over the wild animals (cf. Gen 1:26–28).

23:31 Israel's western territorial border extends "from the Red Sea to the Mediterranean Sea" (see NIV text notes), and its eastern border runs "from the desert [the southern or Negev wilderness] to the Euphrates River" in the north. This encompasses all the territory between Egypt and northern Mesopotamia (Gen 15:18; 1 Kgs 4:21).

23:33 snare to you. Graphically warns of impending disaster (cf. 10:7) that Israel subsequently ignores, eventually leading to their own expulsion from the land.

24:1–18 *The Covenant Confirmed.* These verses describe three stages in confirming the covenant: (1) an oath ritually ratifies it (vv. 3–8), (2) the Israelite leaders eat an extraordinary meal in God's presence (vv. 9–11), and (3) God formally invites Moses to receive the tablets of stone (vv. 12–18).

24:1 For the next ascent, God instructs Moses to include a representative group of Israel's civil and religious leadership. **Nadab and Abihu.** Aaron's oldest sons (6:23; 28:1), who later seal their fate when they offer unauthorized fire before the Lord (Lev 10:1–2; Num 3:4). **seventy.** May signify the inclusiveness of this representative group (v. 5). **elders.** See note on 3:16.

24:2 Like the tabernacle soon to be constructed, this meeting place is segregated, reflecting different gradations of holiness. At its base, where the Israelites are encamped, is its outer court; further up, where this delegation will ascend to worship God, is its Holy Place; and right at the top, where the glory of God settles (v. 16), or tabernacles, is its Most Holy Place.

24:3–4a Once again (19:8), the people commit themselves unreservedly to what the Lord said, so Moses duly records the terms of the covenant before they formally ratify it by means of a ritual oath.

24:4b–8 Covenant ratification takes the form of an elaborate ceremony involving an altar, 12 pillars, sacrifices, and the ritual sprinkling of blood.

24:4b altar. Represents the Lord in the ensuing ceremony. **twelve stone pillars.** Represent the 12 tribes of Israel, the Lord's covenant partner. The prohibition against using such cultic objects (23:24) applies only if they are associated with some pagan ritual.

24:5 young Israelite men. See note on 19:22. **burnt offerings ... fellowship offerings.** See notes on Lev 1; 3. The use of such offerings is associated with the consecration of the Aaronic priests (29:10–46). The Israelites are to become a "kingdom of priests" (19:6).

24:6–8 This blood-sprinkling ritual might also be part of an ordination ritual for Israel, akin to that of the Aaronic priesthood. But in the ancient world, covenants were often sealed with blood. The dual sprinkling (some on the altar, some on the people), separated by the recitation of the covenant obligations and Israel's assent (v. 7), suggests such a significance here. The splattered blood is an enacted oath symbolizing the death of the covenant makers if they become covenant breakers (see Gen 15:8–17; see also notes on Gen 15:9–17,18–21). The blood also purifies the people so that they enter the covenant with their sin atoned for and begin a new relationship with God (e.g., 30:10; Lev 6:30; 8:15; 16:14–18; 17:11). Accordingly, the NT suggests that the blood sprinkled on the altar foreshadows Jesus' atonement for human sin through his death (Matt 26:28; see Heb 9:15–28; 1 Pet 1:2).

24:7 Book of the Covenant. Usually understood as containing only the material in 20:22—23:33.

8 Moses then took the blood, sprinkled it on the people and said, "This is the blood of the covenant[s]
that the LORD has made with you in accordance with all these words."
9 Moses and Aaron, Nadab and Abihu, and the seventy elders[t] of Israel went up 10 and saw[u] the God
of Israel. Under his feet was something like a pavement made of lapis lazuli,[v] as bright blue as the
sky.[w] 11 But God did not raise his hand against these leaders of the Israelites; they saw[x] God, and they
ate and drank.
12 The LORD said to Moses, "Come up to me on the mountain and stay here, and I will give you the
tablets of stone[y] with the law and commandments I have written for their instruction."
13 Then Moses set out with Joshua[z] his aide, and Moses went up on the mountain[a] of God. 14 He said
to the elders, "Wait here for us until we come back to you. Aaron and Hur are with you, and anyone
involved in a dispute can go to them."
15 When Moses went up on the mountain, the cloud[b] covered it, 16 and the glory[c] of the LORD settled
on Mount Sinai. For six days the cloud covered the mountain, and on the seventh day the LORD called
to Moses from within the cloud.[d] 17 To the Israelites the glory of the LORD looked like a consuming fire[e]
on top of the mountain. 18 Then Moses entered the cloud as he went on up the mountain. And he stayed
on the mountain forty[f] days and forty nights.[g]

24:8 [s] Heb 9:20*; 1Pe 1:2
24:9 [t] ver 1
24:10 [u] Mt 17:2; Jn 1:18; 6:46 [v] Eze 1:26 [w] Rev 4:3
24:11 [x] Ge 32:30; Ex 19:21
24:12 [y] Ex 32:15-16
24:13 [z] Ex 17:9 [a] Ex 3:1
24:15 [b] Ex 19:9
24:16 [c] Ex 16:10 [d] Ps 99:7
24:17 [e] Ex 3:2; Dt 4:36; Heb 12:18,29
24:18 [f] Dt 9:9 [g] Ex 34:28
25:2 [h] Ex 35:21; 1Ch 29:5,7,9; Ezr 2:68; 2Co 8:11-12; 9:7

Offerings for the Tabernacle

25:1-7pp — Ex 35:4-9

25 The LORD said to Moses, 2 "Tell the Israelites to bring me an offering. You are to receive the
offering for me from everyone whose heart prompts[h] them to give. 3 These are the offerings
you are to receive from them: gold, silver and bronze; 4 blue, purple and scarlet yarn and fine linen;

24:9–11 Having sealed the covenant in blood, Israel's leaders ascend the mountain as God instructed (v. 1), and they experience an extraordinary encounter with God.

24:10–11 saw the God of Israel ... they saw God. Perhaps they lifted their gaze no higher than the bright blue platform on which God stood (cf. Ezek 1:22–28), but whatever they saw was clearly different from seeing God's "face" (33:20,23). Even so, the experience here was clearly exceptional (v. 11; cf. 3:6) and foreshadows the full and complete vision of God the NT promises to the people of God (Matt 5:8; Rev 22:4).

24:11 ate and drank. This fellowship or covenant meal (cf. Gen 26:30; 31:54) celebrates the formal ratification of the covenant (vv. 3–8) and expresses Israel's unique relationship with God. As such, this unique occasion in Israel's history foreshadows the Lord's Supper, which celebrates the new covenant ratified by Christ's death and the fellowship with God experienced in Christ (1 Cor 11:23–26). Both meals also anticipate the final Messianic banquet (Rev 19:9).

24:12–18 The ancient Near Eastern suzerain-vassal treaty may partly explain Moses' next ascent. The final stage in the ratification of such a treaty normally involved depositing the agreement in the respective temples of each treaty partner. This is possibly why two stone tablets are necessary (31:18) and why God presents these tablets to Moses only after the tabernacle instructions, which begin with the ark where the engraved tablets will be deposited (25:16). While certainly not the main purpose for the tabernacle's construction, this is clearly an important function of "the ark of the covenant law" (25:22).

24:12 stay here. Moses anticipates a significant absence, so he temporarily delegates some of his authority (v. 14). This is the second time that Joshua, Aaron, and Hur assist Moses (17:10–13). But here their roles are reversed: Joshua ascends with Moses, while Aaron and Hur remain to handle any disputes among the people. **tablets of stone.** These two tablets (31:18), inscribed on both sides (32:15), were probably not large or heavy since Moses carried them unassisted (32:19). In this unique situation, both tablets were deposited in the temple (i.e., tabernacle) shared by both parties. **law and commandments.** The "law" (i.e., "Torah") essentially means "teaching," whereas "commandments" is more specific.

24:16–17 glory of the LORD ... glory of the LORD. See note on 16:7.

24:16 settled. Lit. "tabernacled." This foreshadows the manifestation of the Lord's presence in the tabernacle (40:34–38), in the temple (1 Kgs 8:10–11), and ultimately in Jesus (John 1:14) and in the new creation (Rev 21:3).

24:17 consuming fire. See Heb 12:18–29.

25:1—40:38 The last major block of material focuses primarily on the special tent that will accomodate the Lord's presence among his people after they leave Mount Sinai and continue their journey to the promised land. God instructs Moses regarding its construction and personnel (chs. 25–31), and Moses then implements those instructions (chs. 35–40). The golden calf episode interrupts the account of the tabernacle's construction and, among other things, highlights how the Lord's presence will be made known to his people; it also sets inappropriate worship in bold contrast to the worship that the Lord demands from those who serve him (chs. 32–34). The actual construction of the tabernacle indicated that God's plans to dwell with his people were intact, as he further demonstrates by filling the tabernacle and by the associated cloud directing Israel's travels in the closing verses of the book. Throughout their subsequent history, the Israelites continue to jeopardize having the presence of a holy God among them; finally their covenant rebellion results in the destruction of God's later dwelling place, the Jerusalem temple, and the expulsion of Israel from the land they had defiled by their rebellious acts. But even this did not permanently disrupt God's plans. Rather, God graciously restored Israel to the land; and the temple, the symbol of his presence, was rebuilt. Like the tabernacle, however, the temple merely foreshadowed the fullness of God's presence that came to earth through Jesus (Matt 1:23; John 1:14) and that will be experienced forever in the new heaven and the new earth (Rev 21:3,22; 22:4).

25:1—31:18 *Instructions for Israel's Worship.* Like observing the Sabbath (31:12–17; 35:1–3), the tabernacle was designed to reflect God's continuing presence (or "glory"; 24:16), fellowship, and blessing with Israel as they move forward. Not surprisingly, therefore, the space devoted to this movable sanctuary (both here and in chs. 35–40) underscores its importance.

25:6 [i]Ex 27:20; 30:22-32
25:7 [j]Ex 28:4,6-14
[k]Ex 28:15-30
25:8 [l]Ex 36:1-5;
Heb 9:1-2 [m]Ex 29:45;
1Ki 6:13; 2Co 6:16;
Rev 21:3
25:9 [n]ver 40; Ac 7:44;
Heb 8:5
25:10 [o]Dt 10:1-5;
Heb 9:4
25:15 [p]1Ki 8:8
25:16 [q]Dt 31:26; Heb 9:4
25:17 [r]Ro 3:25
25:20 [s]1Ki 8:7;
1Ch 28:18; Heb 9:5
25:21 [t]Ex 26:34 [u]ver 16
25:22 [v]Nu 7:89; 1Sa 4:4;
2Sa 6:2; 2Ki 19:15;
Ps 80:1; Isa 37:16
[w]Ex 29:42-43
25:23 [x]Heb 9:2

goat hair; 5ram skins dyed red and another type of durable leather[a]; acacia wood; 6olive oil[i] for the
light; spices for the anointing oil and for the fragrant incense; 7and onyx stones and other gems to be
mounted on the ephod[j] and breastpiece.[k]
8"Then have them make a sanctuary[l] for me, and I will dwell[m] among them. 9Make this tabernacle
and all its furnishings exactly like the pattern[n] I will show you.

The Ark

25:10-20pp — Ex 37:1-9

10"Have them make an ark[b][o] of acacia wood — two and a half cubits long, a cubit and a half wide,
and a cubit and a half high.[c] 11Overlay it with pure gold, both inside and out, and make a gold molding
around it. 12Cast four gold rings for it and fasten them to its four feet, with two rings on one side and
two rings on the other. 13Then make poles of acacia wood and overlay them with gold. 14Insert the poles
into the rings on the sides of the ark to carry it. 15The poles are to remain in the rings of this ark; they
are not to be removed.[p] 16Then put in the ark the tablets of the covenant law,[q] which I will give you.
17"Make an atonement cover[r] of pure gold — two and a half cubits long and a cubit and a half
wide. 18And make two cherubim out of hammered gold at the ends of the cover. 19Make one cherub on
one end and the second cherub on the other; make the cherubim of one piece with the cover, at the
two ends. 20The cherubim are to have their wings spread upward, overshadowing[s] the cover with them.
The cherubim are to face each other, looking toward the cover. 21Place the cover on top of the ark[t] and
put in the ark the tablets of the covenant law[u] that I will give you. 22There, above the cover between
the two cherubim[v] that are over the ark of the covenant law, I will meet[w] with you and give you all my
commands for the Israelites.

The Table

25:23-29pp — Ex 37:10-16

23"Make a table[x] of acacia wood — two cubits long, a cubit wide and a cubit and a half high.[d]
24Overlay it with pure gold and make a gold molding around it. 25Also make around it a rim a handbreadth[e] wide and put a gold molding on the rim. 26Make four gold rings for the table and fasten them
to the four corners, where the four legs are. 27The rings are to be close to the rim to hold the poles used

[a] *5* Possibly the hides of large aquatic mammals [b] *10* That is, a chest [c] *10* That is, about 3 3/4 feet long and 2 1/4 feet wide and high or about 1.1 meters long and 68 centimeters wide and high; similarly in verse 17 [d] *23* That is, about 3 feet long, 1 1/2 feet wide and 2 1/4 feet high or about 90 centimeters long, 45 centimeters wide and 68 centimeters high [e] *25* That is, about 3 inches or about 7.5 centimeters

25:1 — 27:21 This focuses on the design of the tabernacle and its constituent parts.

25:1 – 9 *Offerings for the Tabernacle.* Presumably most of the raw materials, which the Israelites voluntarily donate to the Lord, came from the Egyptians (12:35 – 36). In any case, these "freewill offerings" (35:29; 36:3) exceed requirements (36:5 – 7).

25:4 blue, purple and scarlet. Royal colors. **yarn and fine linen.** Rather than referring to two different materials, the colored "yarn" may have been spun from "fine linen" (similarly in 26:1). Expertise for weaving such fabric could have developed in Egypt, renowned for its fine linen.

25:7 ephod. See note on 28:6 – 14.

25:9 Manufacturing the tabernacle and its furnishings must conform to God's blueprint, a "pattern" (i.e., construction plan) that God is about to disclose (v. 40; 26:30; 27:8).

25:10 – 22 *The Ark.* The ark is a gold-plated rectangular chest that subsequently houses "the tablets of the covenant law" (v. 16; see 31:18). It is the only furniture in the Most Holy Place (40:20 – 21), and it symbolizes the footstool of the Lord's throne (1 Chr 28:2; see 1 Sam 4:4; 2 Sam 6:2), a description that links the earthly dwelling of God with the heavenly one.

25:12 – 15 Israel transported the ark using two gold-plated poles inserted through rings on its feet, presumably to avoid any direct contact that might defile it (2 Sam 6:6 – 7).

25:16 See notes on v. 22; 24:12 – 18.

25:17 atonement cover. The chest's lid is a solid slab of gold decorated with an image of two cherubim (see note on v. 18).

25:18 two cherubim. Awesome heavenly creatures that Ezekiel more fully describes (Ezek 1:5 – 14; 10:1 – 22). Their posture on the ark is one of reverent awe in the presence of the Lord himself (v. 22).

25:22 ark of the covenant law. So called because it contained the two stone "tablets of the covenant law" (v. 16). It is more commonly described simply as the "ark of the covenant" (e.g., Josh 3:6). **I will meet with you.** The tabernacle's main purpose is to provide a place where the Lord can formally meet and communicate with his people; hence, it is later called "the tent of meeting" (e.g., 27:21; 29:42 – 43). This must not be confused with the temporary "tent of meeting" that was used by Moses prior to the construction of the tabernacle (33:7; the NIV uses quotation marks to distinguish this temporary tent of meeting from the tabernacle). Only 33:7 names this alternative tent as such. Every other reference to the tent of meeting is to the tabernacle.

25:23 – 30 *The Table.* The table and lampstand (vv. 31 – 40) are for the Holy Place. Like the ark, the table is made of gold-plated acacia wood and similarly designed to be carried by gold-plated poles on either side. The decorative molding around the edges keeps its utensils (plates, dishes, pitchers, and bowls) from sliding off the table.

in carrying the table. 28 Make the poles of acacia wood, overlay them with gold and carry the table with
them. 29 And make its plates and dishes of pure gold, as well as its pitchers and bowls for the pouring
out of offerings.[y] 30 Put the bread of the Presence[z] on this table to be before me at all times.

25:29 [y] Nu 4:7
25:30 [z] Lev 24:5-9
25:31 [a] 1Ki 7:49; Zec 4:2; Heb 9:2; Rev 1:12

The Lampstand

25:31-39pp — Ex 37:17-24

31 "Make a lampstand[a] of pure gold. Hammer out its base and shaft, and make its flowerlike cups,
buds and blossoms of one piece with them. 32 Six branches are to extend from the sides of the lampstand — three on one side and three on the other. 33 Three cups shaped like almond flowers with buds
and blossoms are to be on one branch, three on the next branch, and the same for all six branches
extending from the lampstand. 34 And on the lampstand there are to be four cups shaped like almond
flowers with buds and blossoms. 35 One bud shall be under the first pair of branches extending from

25:30 bread of the Presence. In this phrase, "Presence" refers to the Lord's presence (as in 33:14–15). The bread, part of the priests' consecrated food (Lev 24:8–9), was in fact 12 loaves (Lev 24:5), one for each tribe. This was a perpetual offering by which the fruit of Israel's labors was consecrated to God and by which the nation also acknowledged the Lord as the sole provider of such blessings. See Lev 24:5–9; see also 1 Sam 21:4–6; Matt 12:3–4.

25:31–40 *The Lampstand.* Like the atonement cover, this is hammered out of pure gold. Three branches, each featuring three cups shaped like almond flowers, extend from each side of the central stand, which itself has four such cups: one at the base and one above each pair of extending branches. The traditional form of the lampstand (the seven-pronged menorah) comes from the time of Herod the Great and may be seen on the Arch of Titus in Rome. It depicts a flowering almond tree, most likely symbolizing the tree of life in Eden. The people were to supply the necessary fuel (olive oil) to keep these seven lamps burning throughout the night (Lev 24:2–4). As with the bread, the light indicated that the Lord was resident in his tent. Significantly, it is in such a setting (the temple courts) that Jesus claims to be "the light of the world" (John 8:12–20).

TABERNACLE FURNISHINGS

The symbolism of God's redemptive covenant was preserved in the tabernacle, making each element an object lesson for the worshiper. Likely reconstructions of the furnishings are based on the detailed descriptions and precise measurements recorded in Exod 25–40. (The bronze basin is not shown here.)

❶ ARK OF THE COVENANT
The ark of the covenant compares with the roughly contemporary shrine and funerary furniture of Tutankhamun (ca. 1300 BC), which, along with the Nimrud and Samaria ivories from a later period, have been used to guide the graphic interpretation of the text. Both sources show the conventional way of depicting extreme reverence, with facing winged guardians shielding a sacred place.

❷ INCENSE ALTAR

❸ LAMPSTAND
The traditional form of the lampstand is not attested archaeologically until much later.

❹ TABLE
The table holding the bread of the Presence was made of wood overlaid with thin sheets of gold. All of the objects were portable and were fitted with rings and carrying poles, practices typical of Egyptian ritual processions as early as the Old Kingdom period.

❺ BRONZE ALTAR
The altar of burnt offering was made of wood overlaid with bronze. The size, five cubits square and three cubits high, matches that of an altar found at Arad from the time of Solomon.

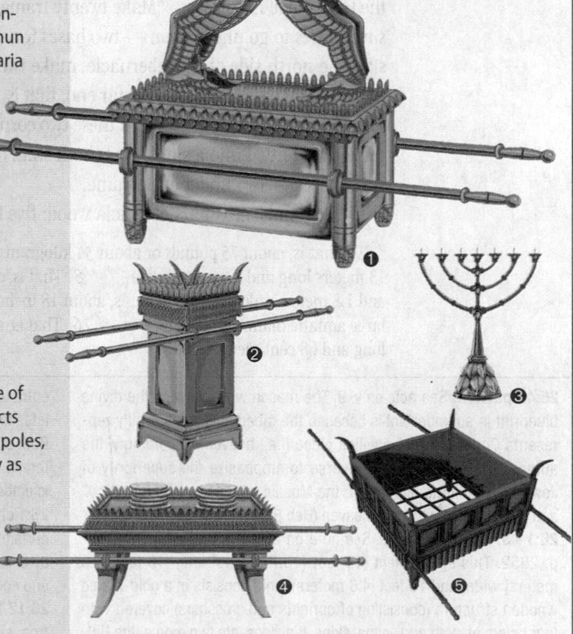

25:37 [b] Ex 27:21; Lev 24:3-4; Nu 8:2
25:40 [c] Ex 26:30; Nu 8:4; Ac 7:44; Heb 8:5*
26:14 [d] Ex 36:19; Nu 4:25

the lampstand, a second bud under the second pair, and a third bud under the third pair—six
branches in all. [36]The buds and branches shall all be of one piece with the lampstand, hammered
out of pure gold.
[37]"Then make its seven lamps[b] and set them up on it so that they light the space in front of it.
[38]Its wick trimmers and trays are to be of pure gold. [39]A talent[a] of pure gold is to be used for the
lampstand and all these accessories. [40]See that you make them according to the pattern[c] shown you
on the mountain.

The Tabernacle

26:1-37pp — Ex 36:8-38

26 "Make the tabernacle with ten curtains of finely twisted linen and blue, purple and
scarlet yarn, with cherubim woven into them by a skilled worker. [2]All the curtains are
to be the same size—twenty-eight cubits long and four cubits wide.[b] [3]Join five of the curtains
together, and do the same with the other five. [4]Make loops of blue material along the edge of the
end curtain in one set, and do the same with the end curtain in the other set. [5]Make fifty loops
on one curtain and fifty loops on the end curtain of the other set, with the loops opposite each
other. [6]Then make fifty gold clasps and use them to fasten the curtains together so that the tabernacle is a unit.
[7]"Make curtains of goat hair for the tent over the tabernacle—eleven altogether. [8]All eleven
curtains are to be the same size—thirty cubits long and four cubits wide.[c] [9]Join five of the curtains
together into one set and the other six into another set. Fold the sixth curtain double at the front
of the tent. [10]Make fifty loops along the edge of the end curtain in one set and also along the edge
of the end curtain in the other set. [11]Then make fifty bronze clasps and put them in the loops to
fasten the tent together as a unit. [12]As for the additional length of the tent curtains, the half curtain
that is left over is to hang down at the rear of the tabernacle. [13]The tent curtains will be a cubit[d]
longer on both sides; what is left will hang over the sides of the tabernacle so as to cover it. [14]Make
for the tent a covering of ram skins dyed red, and over that a covering of the other durable leather.[e][d]
[15]"Make upright frames of acacia wood for the tabernacle. [16]Each frame is to be ten cubits long
and a cubit and a half wide,[f] [17]with two projections set parallel to each other. Make all the frames of
the tabernacle in this way. [18]Make twenty frames for the south side of the tabernacle [19]and make forty
silver bases to go under them—two bases for each frame, one under each projection. [20]For the other
side, the north side of the tabernacle, make twenty frames [21]and forty silver bases—two under each
frame. [22]Make six frames for the far end, that is, the west end of the tabernacle, [23]and make two frames
for the corners at the far end. [24]At these two corners they must be double from the bottom all the way to
the top and fitted into a single ring; both shall be like that. [25]So there will be eight frames and sixteen
silver bases—two under each frame.
[26]"Also make crossbars of acacia wood: five for the frames on one side of the tabernacle, [27]five for

[a] *39* That is, about 75 pounds or about 34 kilograms [b] *2* That is, about 42 feet long and 6 feet wide or about 13 meters long and 1.8 meters wide [c] *8* That is, about 45 feet long and 6 feet wide or about 13.5 meters long and 1.8 meters wide [d] *13* That is, about 18 inches or about 45 centimeters [e] *14* Possibly the hides of large aquatic mammals (see 25:5) [f] *16* That is, about 15 feet long and 2 1/4 feet wide or about 4.5 meters long and 68 centimeters wide

25:40 pattern. See note on v. 9. The reason why following the divine blueprint is so important is because the tabernacle symbolically represents God's spiritual dwelling place (i.e., heaven). Accordingly, the author of Hebrews cites this verse to emphasize the superiority of Jesus, the ultimate high priest; the Mosaic tabernacle is but a "copy" and "shadow" of what is in heaven (Heb 8:5).

26:1–37 *The Tabernacle.* See note on 25:1—40:38 and "Temple," p. 2652. This special tent (45 feet [13.7 meters] long, 15 feet [4.6 meters] wide, and 15 feet [4.6 meters] high) consists of a gold-plated wooden structure (consisting of uprights and crossbars) covered with four layers of cloth and animal skins. It divides into two rooms (the Holy Place and the Most Holy Place; v. 33) and has two curtains: one is the entrance to the Holy Place (the Lord's guest room), and the other isolates the Most Holy Place (the Lord's throne room) from the Holy Place. Both curtains are made of linen woven from blue, purple, and scarlet thread (see note on 25:4), but only the curtain into the Most Holy Place is embroidered with cherubim (see vv. 31–35 and note).

26:1 cherubim. See note on 25:18. They are embroidered on the inner curtain to remind Israel of the holiness of the one who has chosen to dwell among them (cf. Gen 3:22–24). **skilled worker.** See 31:1–11 and note on 31:6.

26:12 The surplus curtain material shuts off the rear of the tabernacle from external view.

those on the other side, and five for the frames on the west, at the far end of the tabernacle. [28]The center
crossbar is to extend from end to end at the middle of the frames. [29]Overlay the frames with gold and
make gold rings to hold the crossbars. Also overlay the crossbars with gold.
[30]"Set up the tabernacle according to the plan[e] shown you on the mountain.
[31]"Make a curtain[f] of blue, purple and scarlet yarn and finely twisted linen, with cherubim[g]
woven into it by a skilled worker. [32]Hang it with gold hooks on four posts of acacia wood overlaid
with gold and standing on four silver bases. [33]Hang the curtain from the clasps and place the ark of
the covenant law behind the curtain.[h] The curtain will separate the Holy Place from the Most Holy
Place.[i] [34]Put the atonement cover[j] on the ark of the covenant law in the Most Holy Place. [35]Place
the table[k] outside the curtain on the north side of the tabernacle and put the lampstand[l] opposite
it on the south side.
[36]"For the entrance to the tent make a curtain of blue, purple and scarlet yarn and finely twisted
linen — the work of an embroiderer. [37]Make gold hooks for this curtain and five posts of acacia wood
overlaid with gold. And cast five bronze bases for them.

26:30 [e] Ex 25:9,40; Ac 7:44; Heb 8:5
26:31 [f] 2Ch 3:14; Mt 27:51; Heb 9:3 [g] Ex 36:35
26:33 [h] Ex 40:3,21; Lev 16:2 [i] Heb 9:2-3
26:34 [j] Ex 25:21; 40:20; Heb 9:5
26:35 [k] Heb 9:2 [l] Ex 40:22,24

26:30 plan. See note on 25:9. Because the information provided in the text lacks sufficient detail, any reconstruction of the tabernacle is necessarily tentative. It possibly had a flat (rather than a ridged) roof, with the coverings drawn to each side like awnings.

26:31 – 35 These instructions relate to the curtain isolating the Most Holy Place from the Holy Place and barring access to all except the high priest, who entered only on the Day of Atonement (Lev 16), prefiguring how only Jesus could secure access to God (Heb 9:7 – 14; 10:19 – 22). The inner curtain may be equivalent to the curtain that tore in Herod's temple when Jesus died (Mark 15:38), signifying that, unlike Israel, God's people under the new covenant have direct access to God's presence (Heb 10:19 – 22).

THE TABERNACLE

The new religious observances, taught by Moses in the wilderness, centered on rituals connected with the tabernacle and amplified Israel's sense of separateness, purity, and oneness under the lordship of Yahweh.

Desert shrines have been found in the Sinai region, notably the tent shrine in the Timna Valley, dating from the era of the exodus.

Specific cultural antecedents to portable shrines carried on poles and covered with thin sheets of gold can be found in ancient Egypt as early as the Old Kingdom (ca. 2800 – 2250 BC), but they were especially prominent in the Eighteenth and Nineteenth Dynasties (1570 – 1180). The best examples come from the fabulous tomb of Tutankhamun, ca. 1300 BC.

Comparisons of construction details in the text of Exod 25 – 40 with the frames, shrines, poles, sheathing, draped fabric covers, gilt rosettes, and winged protective figures from the shrine of Tutankhamun are instructive. The period, the Late Bronze Age, is equivalent in all dating systems to the era of Moses and the exodus.

27:1 [m]Eze 43:13
27:2 [n]Ps 118:27
27:8 [o]Ex 25:9,40
27:21 [p]Ex 28:43
[q]Ex 26:31,33

The Altar of Burnt Offering

27:1-8pp — Ex 38:1-7

27 "Build an altar[m] of acacia wood, three cubits[a] high; it is to be square, five cubits long and five cubits wide.[b] [2]Make a horn[n] at each of the four corners, so that the horns and the altar are of one piece, and overlay the altar with bronze. [3]Make all its utensils of bronze — its pots to remove the ashes, and its shovels, sprinkling bowls, meat forks and firepans. [4]Make a grating for it, a bronze network, and make a bronze ring at each of the four corners of the network. [5]Put it under the ledge of the altar so that it is halfway up the altar. [6]Make poles of acacia wood for the altar and overlay them with bronze. [7]The poles are to be inserted into the rings so they will be on two sides of the altar when it is carried. [8]Make the altar hollow, out of boards. It is to be made just as you were shown[o] on the mountain.

The Courtyard

27:9-19pp — Ex 38:9-20

[9]"Make a courtyard for the tabernacle. The south side shall be a hundred cubits[c] long and is to have curtains of finely twisted linen, [10]with twenty posts and twenty bronze bases and with silver hooks and bands on the posts. [11]The north side shall also be a hundred cubits long and is to have curtains, with twenty posts and twenty bronze bases and with silver hooks and bands on the posts.

[12]"The west end of the courtyard shall be fifty cubits[d] wide and have curtains, with ten posts and ten bases. [13]On the east end, toward the sunrise, the courtyard shall also be fifty cubits wide. [14]Curtains fifteen cubits[e] long are to be on one side of the entrance, with three posts and three bases, [15]and curtains fifteen cubits long are to be on the other side, with three posts and three bases.

[16]"For the entrance to the courtyard, provide a curtain twenty cubits[f] long, of blue, purple and scarlet yarn and finely twisted linen — the work of an embroiderer — with four posts and four bases. [17]All the posts around the courtyard are to have silver bands and hooks, and bronze bases. [18]The courtyard shall be a hundred cubits long and fifty cubits wide,[g] with curtains of finely twisted linen five cubits[h] high, and with bronze bases. [19]All the other articles used in the service of the tabernacle, whatever their function, including all the tent pegs for it and those for the courtyard, are to be of bronze.

Oil for the Lampstand

27:20-21pp — Lev 24:1-3

[20]"Command the Israelites to bring you clear oil of pressed olives for the light so that the lamps may be kept burning. [21]In the tent of meeting,[p] outside the curtain that shields the ark of the covenant law,[q]

[a] *1* That is, about 4 1/2 feet or about 1.4 meters [b] *1* That is, about 7 1/2 feet or about 2.3 meters long and wide [c] *9* That is, about 150 feet or about 45 meters; also in verse 11 [d] *12* That is, about 75 feet or about 23 meters; also in verse 13 [e] *14* That is, about 23 feet or about 6.8 meters; also in verse 15 [f] *16* That is, about 30 feet or about 9 meters [g] *18* That is, about 150 feet long and 75 feet wide or about 45 meters long and 23 meters wide [h] *18* That is, about 7 1/2 feet or about 2.3 meters

27:1–8 *The Altar of Burnt Offering.* The altar has a square wooden frame overlaid with bronze. A bronze network grating (v. 4) is inserted halfway up the altar with rings at each corner of the network so the altar could be transported using bronze-overlaid poles. Measuring 7.5 feet (2.3 meters) long and wide and 4.5 feet (1.4 meters) high, it is essentially a grill for roasting offerings (38:1). Sacrifice on this altar was required for access to God (Lev 4:10), foreshadowing the necessity of Christ's sacrifice (Heb 9:12–14).

27:2 horns. The purpose of these horns is not explained. Theological significance is implied by the fact that blood was put on them (e.g., 29:12; Lev 4:25,30,34). The atoning significance of this (Lev 8:15; 9:9; 16:18) may explain why both Adonijah and Joab took hold of them in order to seek refuge from Solomon (1 Kgs 1:50; 2:28).

27:3 meat forks. Presumably for turning or extracting cooked meat for human consumption.

27:7 poles … rings. See note on 25:12–15.

27:8 just as you were shown. See note on 25:9.

27:9–19 *The Courtyard.* A rectangular courtyard, 150 feet (45.7 meters) long and 75 feet (22.9 meters) wide, surrounds the tabernacle. It has twenty evenly spaced posts on each side, ten along the back, and three on either side of the entrance at the front. These bronze-overlaid wooden posts support the plain (off-white) linen curtains that stand 7.5 feet (2.3 meters) high and form the tabernacle's perimeter fence. Four more posts support the colored curtain that provides access into the enclosure (26:36).

27:13 Like the Garden of Eden (Gen 3:24), the tabernacle was entered from the east.

27:20–21 *Oil for the Lampstand.* Top-quality oil (pressed rather than crushed olives) fuels the tabernacle lamps (presumably the menorah; see 25:31–40 and note) that light the Holy Place throughout the night (1 Sam 3:3). This is a natural segue into the following material, which focuses on the priests who move between the outer court and the Holy Place.

27:21 tent of meeting. See note on 25:22.

Aaron and his sons are to keep the lamps[r] burning before the LORD from evening till morning. This is to be a lasting ordinance[s] among the Israelites for the generations to come.

The Priestly Garments

28 "Have Aaron[t] your brother brought to you from among the Israelites, along with his sons Nadab and Abihu, Eleazar and Ithamar, so they may serve me as priests.[u] 2 Make sacred garments[v] for your brother Aaron to give him dignity and honor. 3 Tell all the skilled workers[w] to whom I have given wisdom[x] in such matters that they are to make garments for Aaron, for his consecration, so he may serve me as priest. 4 These are the garments they are to make: a breastpiece,[y] an ephod, a robe,[z] a woven tunic,[a] a turban and a sash. They are to make these sacred garments for your brother Aaron and his sons, so they may serve me as priests. 5 Have them use gold, and blue, purple and scarlet yarn, and fine linen.

The Ephod

28:6-14pp — Ex 39:2-7

6 "Make the ephod of gold, and of blue, purple and scarlet yarn, and of finely twisted linen — the work of skilled hands. 7 It is to have two shoulder pieces attached to two of its corners, so it can be fastened. 8 Its skillfully woven waistband is to be like it — of one piece with the ephod and made with gold, and with blue, purple and scarlet yarn, and with finely twisted linen.

9 "Take two onyx stones and engrave on them the names of the sons of Israel 10 in the order of their birth — six names on one stone and the remaining six on the other. 11 Engrave the names of the sons of Israel on the two stones the way a gem cutter engraves a seal. Then mount the stones in gold filigree settings 12 and fasten them on the shoulder pieces of the ephod as memorial stones for the sons of Israel. Aaron is to bear the names on his shoulders as a memorial before the LORD. 13 Make gold filigree settings 14 and two braided chains of pure gold, like a rope, and attach the chains to the settings.

The Breastpiece

28:15-28pp — Ex 39:8-21

15 "Fashion a breastpiece for making decisions — the work of skilled hands. Make it like the ephod: of gold, and of blue, purple and scarlet yarn, and of finely twisted linen. 16 It is to be square — a span[a] long and a span wide — and folded double. 17 Then mount four rows of precious stones on it. The first row shall be carnelian, chrysolite and beryl; 18 the second row shall be turquoise, lapis lazuli and emerald; 19 the third row shall be jacinth, agate and amethyst; 20 the fourth row shall be topaz, onyx and jasper.[b] Mount them in gold filigree settings. 21 There are to be twelve stones, one for each of the names of the sons of Israel, each engraved like a seal with the name of one of the twelve tribes.

27:21 [r]Ex 25:37; 30:8; 1Sa 3:3; 2Ch 13:11 [s]Ex 29:9; Lev 3:17; 16:34; Nu 18:23; 19:21
28:1 [t]Heb 5:4 [u]Nu 18:1-7; Heb 5:1
28:2 [v]Ex 29:5,29; 31:10; 39:1; Lev 8:7-9,30
28:3 [w]Ex 31:6; 36:1 [x]Ex 31:3
28:4 [y]ver 15-30 [z]ver 31-35 [a]ver 39

[a] *16* That is, about 9 inches or about 23 centimeters [b] *20* The precise identification of some of these precious stones is uncertain.

28:1 – 43 *The Priestly Garments.* This section focuses on the priests' garments, particularly the high priest's special clothing (vv. 3 – 39).
28:1 Nadab and Abihu, Eleazar and Ithamar. Their grouping in pairs (cf. 6:23) may anticipate subsequent events (Num 3:4; see note on 24:1).
28:2 – 5 The high priest's garments are manufactured with the same fabrics (except for the additional strands of gold; 39:2 – 3) as the tabernacle curtains.
28:2 dignity and honor. The garments reflect the holy status of the priests.
28:3 skilled workers. See note on 31:6.
28:4 The design and function of these six items (as well as the priests' linen underwear) are elaborated on in vv. 6 – 43.
28:6 – 14 The ephod is an ornate apron-like outer garment the high priest wears. It is held on by two shoulder pieces and a waistband (vv. 7 – 8), which suggests that it extends at least to the upper thighs. Two onyx stones, each engraved with a chronological list of six of Israel's tribes, attach to the shoulder pieces (vv. 9 – 12a), symbolizing Aaron's representative role for all Israel (v. 12b). Two braided chains of pure gold are attached (vv. 13 – 14) to hold the "breastpiece" (vv. 15 – 30) in place.
28:15 – 30 The breastpiece is a folded piece of ornate fabric about nine inches (about 23 centimeters) square decorated with four rows of precious stones (each engraved with a tribal name) mounted in gold lace settings (vv. 15 – 21). Braided chains of pure gold on the breastpiece are attached with blue cord to their counterparts on the ephod to keep the chains in place (vv. 22 – 28). The theological rationale (v. 29) is similar to before (v. 12b): it symbolizes Aaron's representative role before the Lord.

28:29 [b]ver 12
28:30 [c]Lev 8:8; Nu 27:21; Dt 33:8; Ezr 2:63; Ne 7:65
28:36 [d]Zec 14:20
28:38 [e]Lev 10:17; 22:9,16; Nu 18:1; Heb 9:28; 1Pe 2:24
28:40 [f]ver 4; Ex 39:41
28:41 [g]Ex 29:7; Lev 10:7 [h]Ex 29:7-9; 30:30; 40:15; Lev 8:1-36; Heb 7:28
28:42 [i]Lev 6:10; 16:4, 23; Eze 44:18
28:43 [j]Ex 27:21 [k]Ex 20:26 [l]Lev 17:7

22 “For the breastpiece make braided chains of pure gold, like a rope. 23 Make two gold rings for
it and fasten them to two corners of the breastpiece. 24 Fasten the two gold chains to the rings at the
corners of the breastpiece, 25 and the other ends of the chains to the two settings, attaching them to
the shoulder pieces of the ephod at the front. 26 Make two gold rings and attach them to the other
two corners of the breastpiece on the inside edge next to the ephod. 27 Make two more gold rings and
attach them to the bottom of the shoulder pieces on the front of the ephod, close to the seam just
above the waistband of the ephod. 28 The rings of the breastpiece are to be tied to the rings of the
ephod with blue cord, connecting it to the waistband, so that the breastpiece will not swing out from
the ephod.

29 “Whenever Aaron enters the Holy Place,[b] he will bear the names of the sons of Israel over his heart
on the breastpiece of decision as a continuing memorial before the LORD. 30 Also put the Urim and the
Thummim[c] in the breastpiece, so they may be over Aaron’s heart whenever he enters the presence of
the LORD. Thus Aaron will always bear the means of making decisions for the Israelites over his heart
before the LORD.

Other Priestly Garments

28:31-43pp — Ex 39:22-31

31 “Make the robe of the ephod entirely of blue cloth, 32 with an opening for the head in its center.
There shall be a woven edge like a collar[a] around this opening, so that it will not tear. 33 Make pomegranates of blue, purple and scarlet yarn around the hem of the robe, with gold bells between them.
34 The gold bells and the pomegranates are to alternate around the hem of the robe. 35 Aaron must wear
it when he ministers. The sound of the bells will be heard when he enters the Holy Place before the LORD
and when he comes out, so that he will not die.

36 “Make a plate of pure gold and engrave on it as on a seal: HOLY TO THE LORD.[d] 37 Fasten a blue cord
to it to attach it to the turban; it is to be on the front of the turban. 38 It will be on Aaron’s forehead, and
he will bear the guilt[e] involved in the sacred gifts the Israelites consecrate, whatever their gifts may be.
It will be on Aaron’s forehead continually so that they will be acceptable to the LORD.

39 “Weave the tunic of fine linen and make the turban of fine linen. The sash is to be the work of an
embroiderer. 40 Make tunics, sashes and caps for Aaron’s sons[f] to give them dignity and honor. 41 After
you put these clothes on your brother Aaron and his sons, anoint[g] and ordain them. Consecrate them
so they may serve me as priests.[h]

42 “Make linen undergarments[i] as a covering for the body, reaching from the waist to the thigh.
43 Aaron and his sons must wear them whenever they enter the tent of meeting[j] or approach the altar
to minister in the Holy Place, so that they will not incur guilt and die.[k]

“This is to be a lasting ordinance[l] for Aaron and his descendants.

[a] *32* The meaning of the Hebrew for this word is uncertain.

28:29 breastpiece of decision. The breastpiece’s association with decision making explains why the breastpiece is folded double (v. 16): it forms a pouch for the Urim and Thummim (see note on v. 30).

28:30 the Urim and the Thummim. Israel’s only legitimate means of divination (Num 27:21; Deut 33:8; 1 Sam 14:41–42; 28:6; Ezra 2:63). Urim may mean “lights,” while Thummim may relate to a word meaning “complete, perfect.” Perhaps these were gems that might in some way provide divine guidance when thrown by the priest.

28:31–35 Priests wear a blue robe directly underneath the ephod. It has a hole in the middle (like a pullover), and a woven edge reinforces it to prevent tearing (vv. 31–32). Braided pomegranates interspersed with functional gold bells decorate its hem, which probably extends to the lower legs (vv. 33–34). The practical function of these bells (v. 35) emphasizes the inherent danger involved in approaching the Lord, and it may implicitly warn that any unauthorized tabernacle service will certainly result in death (cf. Lev 10).

28:36–38 The engraved gold “plate,” which attaches with blue cord to the front of the linen turban (v. 37), is associated with the high priest’s role: he “will bear the guilt” in relation to Israel’s “sacred gifts” (v. 38). The inscription (“HOLY TO THE LORD”) reminds Israel of the holy status of the high priest, who has been consecrated to God. Only someone who is holy to the Lord can bear guilt for others — in this case those who inadvertently bring a gift that might otherwise be unacceptable. As such, the high priest symbolically foreshadows the work of the ultimate high priest: Jesus, who is uniquely holy (Heb 7:26) and so offered to God a perfect sacrifice on behalf of others (1 Pet 1:19).

28:39–41 An embroidered sash around the priest’s waist ties the robe and the long linen tunic (worn under the robe; 29:5). Similar, although plainer, items designed for Aaron’s sons (vv. 40–41) have the same distinguishing purpose (v. 2).

28:42 linen undergarments. Basically underwear that further reduced any risk of exposure as they carried out their priestly activities in the presence of God (cf. 20:26). Just as Adam and Eve had to be clothed after the fall (Gen 3:21), so any exposure of genitalia in the Lord’s presence was strictly forbidden.

Consecration of the Priests

29:1-37pp — Lev 8:1-36

29 "This is what you are to do to consecrate them, so they may serve me as priests: Take a young bull and two rams without defect. 2And from the finest wheat flour make round loaves without yeast, thick loaves without yeast and with olive oil mixed in, and thin loaves without yeast and brushed with olive oil.[m] 3Put them in a basket and present them along with the bull and the two rams. 4Then bring Aaron and his sons to the entrance to the tent of meeting and wash them with water.[n] 5Take the garments[o] and dress Aaron with the tunic, the robe of the ephod, the ephod itself and the breastpiece. Fasten the ephod on him by its skillfully woven waistband.[p] 6Put the turban on his head and attach the sacred emblem[q] to the turban. 7Take the anointing oil[r] and anoint him by pouring it on his head. 8Bring his sons and dress them in tunics 9and fasten caps on them. Then tie sashes on Aaron and his sons.[a][s] The priesthood is theirs by a lasting ordinance.[t]

"Then you shall ordain Aaron and his sons.

10"Bring the bull to the front of the tent of meeting, and Aaron and his sons shall lay their hands on its head. 11Slaughter it in the LORD's presence at the entrance to the tent of meeting. 12Take some of the bull's blood and put it on the horns[u] of the altar with your finger, and pour out the rest of it at the base of the altar. 13Then take all the fat[v] on the internal organs, the long lobe of the liver, and both kidneys with the fat on them, and burn them on the altar. 14But burn the bull's flesh and its hide and its intestines outside the camp.[w] It is a sin offering.[b]

15"Take one of the rams, and Aaron and his sons shall lay their hands on its head. 16Slaughter it and take the blood and splash it against the sides of the altar. 17Cut the ram into pieces and wash the internal organs and the legs, putting them with the head and the other pieces. 18Then burn the entire ram on the altar. It is a burnt offering to the LORD, a pleasing aroma,[x] a food offering presented to the LORD.

19"Take the other ram,[y] and Aaron and his sons shall lay their hands on its head. 20Slaughter it, take some of its blood and put it on the lobes of the right ears of Aaron and his sons, on the thumbs of their right hands, and on the big toes of their right feet. Then splash blood against the sides of the altar. 21And take some blood[z] from the altar and some of the anointing oil[a] and sprinkle it on Aaron and his garments and on his sons and their garments. Then he and his sons and their garments will be consecrated.[b]

22"Take from this ram the fat, the fat tail, the fat on the internal organs, the long lobe of the liver, both kidneys with the fat on them, and the right thigh. (This is the ram for the ordination.) 23From the basket of bread made without yeast, which is before the LORD, take one round loaf, one thick loaf with olive oil mixed in, and one thin loaf. 24Put all these in the hands of Aaron and his sons and have them wave them before the LORD as a wave offering.[c] 25Then take them from their hands and burn them on the altar along with the burnt offering for a pleasing aroma to the LORD, a food offering presented to the LORD. 26After you take the breast of the ram for Aaron's ordination, wave it before the LORD as a wave offering, and it will be your share.[d]

29:2 [m]Lev 2:1,4; 6:19-23
29:4 [n]Ex 40:12; Heb 10:22
29:5 [o]Ex 28:2; Lev 8:7 [p]Ex 28:8
29:6 [q]Lev 8:9
29:7 [r]Ex 30:25,30,31; Lev 8:12; 21:10; Nu 35:25; Ps 133:2
29:9 [s]Ex 28:40 [t]Ex 40:15; Nu 3:10; 18:7; 25:13; Dt 18:5
29:12 [u]Ex 27:2
29:13 [v]Lev 3:3,5,9
29:14 [w]Lev 4:11-12,21; Heb 13:11
29:18 [x]Ge 8:21
29:19 [y]ver 3
29:21 [z]Heb 9:22 [a]Ex 30:25,31 [b]ver 1
29:24 [c]Lev 7:30
29:26 [d]Lev 7:31-34

[a] 9 Hebrew; Septuagint *on them* [b] 14 Or *purification offering*; also in verse 36

29:1–46 *Consecration of the Priests.* This focuses on the consecration of the priests, altar, and sanctuary.

29:1 consecrate. To make holy. **a young bull and two rams.** Required for the ritual consecration of the priests, which involves a purification offering (vv. 10–14), a burnt offering (vv. 15–18), and a fellowship offering (vv. 19–34).

29:4 wash them with water. Symbolizes removing ritual defilement. Other OT passages apply the imagery to the eradication of moral defilement (e.g., Ps 51:2,7; Ezek 36:25; Zech 13:1), which the NT applies to the spiritual cleansing God offers through Jesus (1 Cor 6:11; Titus 3:5; Heb 10:22).

29:7 anointing oil. See note on 30:22–38.

29:10–14 The young bull (v. 1) is used as a sin offering (v. 14; Lev 8:14); as such, it has an atoning function (vv. 36–37; Lev 4:20,26,31,35).

29:10,15,19 lay their hands on its head. They personally identify with the sin or purification offering (v. 14) and symbolically transfer guilt.

29:14 burn ... outside the camp. Due to association with sin/impurity, carcasses of sacrificial animals were removed from the community; the same principle explains why Jesus died outside Jerusalem (Heb 13:11–12).

29:15–18 The first of the two rams (v. 1) is a burnt offering (Lev 1; 6:8–13). This was totally consumed on the altar, which signifies total dedication to God. Thus, the priests, having had their sins atoned for by means of the purification offering (vv. 10–14), now dedicate themselves to God.

29:19–34 The second ram (v. 1), a fellowship offering, serves a different purpose: ordination (v. 22). It involves a distinct ritual: (1) Moses smears some of its blood on the priests (v. 20), and he sprinkles some of the blood that splashed on the altar, together with anointing oil, on the priests and their garments to consecrate them (v. 21). (2) The priests offer to the Lord (v. 25) only parts of the ram (v. 22), together with a loaf of each kind of bread (vv. 23–25; see v. 2). The breast is for Moses (v. 26; Lev 8:29).

29:24 wave offering. This was a means of drawing attention to the part of the sacrifice that would be consumed by the priests, most likely for the sake of transparency (v. 27).

29:27 [e]Lev 7:31,34; Dt 18:3
29:28 [f]Lev 10:15
29:29 [g]Nu 20:26,28
29:30 [h]Nu 20:28
29:32 [i]Mt 12:4
29:33 [j]Lev 10:14; 22:10,13
29:34 [k]Ex 12:10
29:36 [l]Heb 10:11 [m]Ex 40:10
29:37 [n]Ex 30:28-29; 40:10; Mt 23:19
29:38 [o]Nu 28:3-8; 1Ch 16:40; Da 12:11
29:39 [p]Eze 46:13-15
29:42 [q]Ex 30:8 [r]Ex 25:22
29:43 [s]1Ki 8:11
29:44 [t]Lev 21:15
29:45 [u]Ex 25:8; Lev 26:12; Zec 2:10; Jn 14:17 [v]2Co 6:16; Rev 21:3
29:46 [w]Ex 20:2
30:1 [x]Ex 37:25 [y]Rev 8:3
30:2 [z]Ex 27:2

27 "Consecrate those parts of the ordination ram that belong to Aaron and his sons:[e] the breast that was waved and the thigh that was presented. 28 This is always to be the perpetual share from the Israelites for Aaron and his sons. It is the contribution the Israelites are to make to the LORD from their fellowship offerings.[f]

29 "Aaron's sacred garments will belong to his descendants so that they can be anointed and ordained in them.[g] 30 The son[h] who succeeds him as priest and comes to the tent of meeting to minister in the Holy Place is to wear them seven days.

31 "Take the ram for the ordination and cook the meat in a sacred place. 32 At the entrance to the tent of meeting, Aaron and his sons are to eat the meat of the ram and the bread[i] that is in the basket. 33 They are to eat these offerings by which atonement was made for their ordination and consecration. But no one else may eat[j] them, because they are sacred. 34 And if any of the meat of the ordination ram or any bread is left over till morning,[k] burn it up. It must not be eaten, because it is sacred.

35 "Do for Aaron and his sons everything I have commanded you, taking seven days to ordain them. 36 Sacrifice a bull each day[l] as a sin offering to make atonement. Purify the altar by making atonement for it, and anoint it to consecrate[m] it. 37 For seven days make atonement for the altar and consecrate it. Then the altar will be most holy, and whatever touches it will be holy.[n]

38 "This is what you are to offer on the altar regularly each day:[o] two lambs a year old. 39 Offer one in the morning and the other at twilight.[p] 40 With the first lamb offer a tenth of an ephah[a] of the finest flour mixed with a quarter of a hin[b] of oil from pressed olives, and a quarter of a hin of wine as a drink offering. 41 Sacrifice the other lamb at twilight with the same grain offering and its drink offering as in the morning—a pleasing aroma, a food offering presented to the LORD.

42 "For the generations to come[q] this burnt offering is to be made regularly at the entrance to the tent of meeting, before the LORD. There I will meet you and speak to you;[r] 43 there also I will meet with the Israelites, and the place will be consecrated by my glory.[s]

44 "So I will consecrate the tent of meeting and the altar and will consecrate Aaron and his sons to serve me as priests.[t] 45 Then I will dwell[u] among the Israelites and be their God.[v] 46 They will know that I am the LORD their God, who brought them out of Egypt so that I might dwell among them. I am the LORD their God.[w]

The Altar of Incense

30:1-5pp — Ex 37:25-28

30 "Make an altar[x] of acacia wood for burning incense.[y] 2 It is to be square, a cubit long and a cubit wide, and two cubits high[c]—its horns[z] of one piece with it. 3 Overlay the top and all the sides and the horns with pure gold, and make a gold molding around it. 4 Make two gold rings for

[a] *40* That is, probably about 3 1/2 pounds or about 1.6 kilograms [b] *40* That is, probably about 1 quart or about 1 liter [c] *2* That is, about 1 1/2 feet long and wide and 3 feet high or about 45 centimeters long and wide and 90 centimeters high

---

29:27–28 This aside highlights how the normal practice of donating the breast and right thigh of fellowship offerings to the priests (Lev 7:28–36) carries on from this ordination rite in which only the breast was given to Moses (vv. 22,26).

29:29–30 This seems to be another aside (see note on vv. 27–28), again looking beyond the initial ordination ceremony of Aaron and his sons. The issue is high priestly succession.

29:31–34 These verses describe how the priests, as offerers, have a share of the fellowship offering offered at the time of their consecration (vv. 27–28). This pattern of forgiveness of sins (sin offering), dedication to God (burnt offering), and fellowship with God (fellowship offering) is followed (in part or in whole) in other sacrifice sequences (e.g., Lev 16) and forms the basis for the apostolic teaching concerning the life of Christian discipleship (Rom 5:1; 12:1; Heb 10:19–25).

29:35 The ordination process lasts seven days, during which Aaron and his sons must remain at the entrance of the tent (Lev 8:33–35). What happens each day is unclear, but it seems unlikely that they repeat the ritual daily. Possibly the entire process takes several days to complete, as purifying the altar does (vv. 36–37).

29:38–43 Attention shifts here to the priestly responsibility of presenting sacrifices twice daily, which God requires for the tent to function as a meeting place between himself and humans. These burnt offerings do not consecrate the tent of meeting (v. 43) but facilitate regular communion with a holy God by atoning for sin.

29:45–46 See note on 6:7. The tabernacle is not an addendum to God's delivering Israel from Egypt. Rather, God delivered Israel from Egypt so that, by dwelling among them, they might be a priestly kingdom and a holy nation (19:6).

30:1–10 *The Altar of Incense.* While similar in design to the bronze altar (27:1–8), the incense altar is a third the size of the bronze altar, is overlaid with pure gold, and is located just outside the Most Holy Place.

30:1 For the recipe of this unique incense, see vv. 34–38. Its significance is not made explicit, but its fragrant smoke is used elsewhere as a symbol for the prayers of God's people (Ps 141:2; Luke 1:10; Rev 5:8; 8:3–4), so it may prefigure Christ's heavenly intercession (Heb 7:25).

30:2 horns. See note on 27:2.

30:4 rings ... poles. See note on 25:12–15.

the altar below the molding—two on each of the opposite sides—to hold the poles used to carry it. [5]Make the poles of acacia wood and overlay them with gold. [6]Put the altar in front of the curtain that shields the ark of the covenant law—before the atonement cover[a] that is over the tablets of the covenant law—where I will meet with you.

[7]"Aaron must burn fragrant incense[b] on the altar every morning when he tends the lamps. [8]He must burn incense again when he lights the lamps at twilight so incense will burn regularly before the LORD for the generations to come. [9]Do not offer on this altar any other incense[c] or any burnt offering or grain offering, and do not pour a drink offering on it. [10]Once a year Aaron shall make atonement[d] on its horns. This annual atonement must be made with the blood of the atoning sin offering[a] for the generations to come. It is most holy to the LORD."

Atonement Money

[11]Then the LORD said to Moses, [12]"When you take a census[e] of the Israelites to count them, each one must pay the LORD a ransom[f] for his life at the time he is counted. Then no plague[g] will come on them when you number them. [13]Each one who crosses over to those already counted is to give a half shekel,[b] according to the sanctuary shekel,[h] which weighs twenty gerahs. This half shekel is an offering to the LORD. [14]All who cross over, those twenty years old or more, are to give an offering to the LORD. [15]The rich are not to give more than a half shekel and the poor are not to give less[i] when you make the offering to the LORD to atone for your lives. [16]Receive the atonement money from the Israelites and use it for the service of the tent of meeting.[j] It will be a memorial for the Israelites before the LORD, making atonement for your lives."

Basin for Washing

[17]Then the LORD said to Moses, [18]"Make a bronze basin,[k] with its bronze stand, for washing. Place it between the tent of meeting and the altar, and put water in it. [19]Aaron and his sons are to wash their hands and feet[l] with water[m] from it. [20]Whenever they enter the tent of meeting, they shall wash with water so that they will not die. Also, when they approach the altar to minister by presenting a food offering to the LORD, [21]they shall wash their hands and feet so that they will not die. This is to be a lasting ordinance[n] for Aaron and his descendants for the generations to come."

Anointing Oil

[22]Then the LORD said to Moses, [23]"Take the following fine spices: 500 shekels[c] of liquid myrrh,[o] half as much (that is, 250 shekels) of fragrant cinnamon, 250 shekels[d] of fragrant calamus, [24]500 shekels of cassia[p]—all according to the sanctuary shekel—and a hin[e] of olive oil. [25]Make these into a sacred anointing oil, a fragrant blend, the work of a perfumer.[q] It will be the sacred anointing oil.[r] [26]Then use it to anoint[s] the tent of meeting, the ark of the covenant law, [27]the table and all its articles, the lampstand and its accessories, the altar of incense, [28]the altar of burnt offering and all its utensils, and

30:6 [a]Ex 25:22; 26:34
30:7 [b]ver 34-35; Ex 27:21; 1Sa 2:28
30:9 [c]Lev 10:1
30:10 [d]Lev 16:18-19,30
30:12 [e]Ex 38:25; Nu 1:2, 49; 2Sa 24:1 [f]Nu 31:50; Mt 20:28 [g]2Sa 24:13
30:13 [h]Nu 3:47; Mt 17:24
30:15 [i]Pr 22:2; Eph 6:9
30:16 [j]Ex 38:25-28
30:18 [k]Ex 38:8; 40:7,30
30:19 [l]Ex 40:31-32; Isa 52:11 [m]Ps 26:6
30:21 [n]Ex 27:21; 28:43
30:23 [o]Ge 37:25
30:24 [p]Ps 45:8
30:25 [q]Ex 37:29 [r]Ex 40:9
30:26 [s]Ex 40:9; Lev 8:10; Nu 7:1

[a] *10* Or *purification offering* [b] *13* That is, about 1/5 ounce or about 5.8 grams; also in verse 15 [c] *23* That is, about 12 1/2 pounds or about 5.8 kilograms; also in verse 24 [d] *23* That is, about 6 1/4 pounds or about 2.9 kilograms [e] *24* That is, probably about 1 gallon or about 3.8 liters

30:10 Once a year. Annually, on the Day of Atonement (Lev 16), the high priest purifies this altar with the blood of the purification offering.
30:11–16 *Atonement Money.* This poll tax provides some of the raw materials for the tabernacle (38:25–28). It becomes the basis for the later tax for repairing and maintaining the temple (2 Chr 24:8–12; Matt 17:24–27). But this tax also symbolizes that the Israelites belong to God and owe their lives to him.
30:12 ransom. Previously, a redemption payment (21:30); related terminology includes "atonement cover" (25:17) and "make atonement" (32:30). The Greek equivalent describes the purpose of Christ's death in Mark 10:45.
30:14 twenty years old. Of military age (Num 1:3).
30:16 atonement money. Prefigures how Christians are redeemed by the blood of Jesus (1 Pet 1:18–19).
30:17–21 *Basin for Washing.* The bronze basin, set up in the courtyard between the altar and the tent, holds the water with which the priests must wash their hands and feet (whether ritually, practically, or both) before entering the tent or burning food on the altar. For the source of the raw material, see 38:8.
30:18 washing. See note on 29:4.
30:22–38 *Anointing Oil and Incense.* The fragrant oil used to "consecrate" (i.e., make holy) the tent and its furniture (vv. 26–29), as well as its priests (v. 30), is itself "sacred" (i.e., set apart) in that it has a unique recipe (vv. 23–25) and an exclusive use (vv. 31–33). The incense that burns inside the tent (vv. 1–9) is a unique blend of materials that the priests use exclusively for cultic purposes; thus, it is "holy to the LORD" (v. 37).
30:23 myrrh. See Song 1:13 and note. **calamus.** See Jer 6:20 and note.

30:29 [t]Ex 29:37
30:30 [u]Ex 29:7; Lev 8:2,12,30
30:32 [v]ver 25,37
30:33 [w]ver 38; Ge 17:14
30:35 [x]ver 25
30:36 [y]ver 32; Ex 29:37; Lev 2:3
30:37 [z]ver 32
30:38 [a]ver 33
31:2 [b]Ex 36:1,2; 1Ch 2:20
31:3 [c]1Ki 7:14
31:7 [d]Ex 36:8-38 [e]Ex 37:1-5 [f]Ex 37:6
31:8 [g]Ex 37:10-16 [h]Ex 37:17-24
31:10 [i]Ex 28:2; 39:1,41
31:11 [j]Ex 30:22-32
31:13 [k]Ex 20:8; Lev 19:3,30 [l]Eze 20:12, 20 [m]Lev 11:44
31:14 [n]Nu 15:32-36
31:15 [o]Ex 20:8-11 [p]Ge 2:3; Ex 16:23

the basin with its stand. [29]You shall consecrate them so they will be most holy, and whatever touches them will be holy.[t]

[30]"Anoint Aaron and his sons and consecrate[u] them so they may serve me as priests. [31]Say to the Israelites, 'This is to be my sacred anointing oil for the generations to come. [32]Do not pour it on anyone else's body and do not make any other oil using the same formula. It is sacred, and you are to consider it sacred.[v] [33]Whoever makes perfume like it and puts it on anyone other than a priest must be cut off[w] from their people.' "

Incense

[34]Then the LORD said to Moses, "Take fragrant spices—gum resin, onycha and galbanum—and pure frankincense, all in equal amounts, [35]and make a fragrant blend of incense, the work of a perfumer.[x] It is to be salted and pure and sacred. [36]Grind some of it to powder and place it in front of the ark of the covenant law in the tent of meeting, where I will meet with you. It shall be most holy[y] to you. [37]Do not make any incense with this formula for yourselves; consider it holy[z] to the LORD. [38]Whoever makes incense like it to enjoy its fragrance must be cut off[a] from their people."

Bezalel and Oholiab

31:2-6pp — Ex 35:30-35

31 Then the LORD said to Moses, [2]"See, I have chosen Bezalel[b] son of Uri, the son of Hur, of the tribe of Judah, [3]and I have filled him with the Spirit of God, with wisdom, with understanding, with knowledge and with all kinds of skills[c]— [4]to make artistic designs for work in gold, silver and bronze, [5]to cut and set stones, to work in wood, and to engage in all kinds of crafts. [6]Moreover, I have appointed Oholiab son of Ahisamak, of the tribe of Dan, to help him. Also I have given ability to all the skilled workers to make everything I have commanded you: [7]the tent of meeting,[d] the ark of the covenant law[e] with the atonement cover[f] on it, and all the other furnishings of the tent— [8]the table[g] and its articles, the pure gold lampstand[h] and all its accessories, the altar of incense, [9]the altar of burnt offering and all its utensils, the basin with its stand— [10]and also the woven garments[i], both the sacred garments for Aaron the priest and the garments for his sons when they serve as priests, [11]and the anointing oil[j] and fragrant incense for the Holy Place. They are to make them just as I commanded you."

The Sabbath

[12]Then the LORD said to Moses, [13]"Say to the Israelites, 'You must observe my Sabbaths.[k] This will be a sign[l] between me and you for the generations to come, so you may know that I am the LORD, who makes you holy.[m]

[14]" 'Observe the Sabbath, because it is holy to you. Anyone who desecrates it is to be put to death;[n] those who do any work on that day must be cut off from their people. [15]For six days work[o] is to be done, but the seventh day is a day of sabbath rest,[p] holy to the LORD. Whoever does any work on the Sabbath day is to be put to death. [16]The Israelites are to observe the Sabbath, celebrating it for the generations

---

31:1–11 *Bezalel and Oholiab.* The two artisans Bezalel and Oholiab, along with suitably trained assistants, are responsible for all the skilled labor involved in constructing the tabernacle.

31:1 Hur. See note on 17:10.

31:3 filled ... with the Spirit. This is the first time in the Bible that someone is filled with the Spirit, here for the creative task of an artisan. In both the OT and NT, being filled with the Spirit generally refers to a God-given ability to perform some action in service to God (Deut 34:9; Mic 3:8; Luke 1:15,67; Acts 2:4; 4:8,31; 13:9). Bezalel is proficient in "all kinds of skills" not simply because he has natural abilities but because God gave him wisdom, understanding, and knowledge (28:3; 35:31; cf. Prov 3:19–20, where the same terminology is used of God creating the earth). In 1 Cor 3, Paul sees himself as performing a similar function to Bezalel as regards laying the foundations for the church as God's temple.

31:6 Oholiab. Possibly Bezalel's protégé. In any case, both men pass on their expertise to others (35:34), and thus God equips "all the skilled workers" for this special assignment (35:35—36:1).

31:12–18 *The Sabbath.* This section concludes the instructions given to Moses on the mountaintop (24:12–18) and stresses the importance of observing the Sabbath as a perpetual covenant sign.

31:13 observe my Sabbaths. See notes on 20:8,11. **sign.** A visible symbol not of the Lord's power (cf. 3:12; 4:8; 7:3) but of the special relationship he formed with Israel. **who makes you holy.** The Sabbath is a symbol and perpetual reminder of Israel's status. Just as the Lord set one day apart from all the others, so also he set one people apart from all others.

31:14,15 put to death. Desecrating the Sabbath denies Israel's holy status and thus invokes the death penalty (35:2).

31:16 covenant. Probably means "covenant " sign (cf. Gen 17:9–11). By emulating their Creator in observing the weekly Sabbaths, the Israelites regularly recall and express their special relationship with him.

to come as a lasting covenant. 17It will be a sign[q] between me and the Israelites forever, for in six days
the LORD made the heavens and the earth, and on the seventh day he rested and was refreshed.[r]"
18When the LORD finished speaking to Moses on Mount Sinai, he gave him the two tablets of the
covenant law, the tablets of stone[s] inscribed by the finger of God.[t]

The Golden Calf

32 When the people saw that Moses was so long in coming down from the mountain,[u] they gathered around Aaron and said, "Come, make us gods[a] who will go before us. As for this fellow
Moses who brought us up out of Egypt, we don't know what has happened to him."[v]
2Aaron answered them, "Take off the gold earrings[w] that your wives, your sons and your daughters
are wearing, and bring them to me." 3So all the people took off their earrings and brought them to
Aaron. 4He took what they handed him and made it into an idol cast in the shape of a calf,[x] fashioning
it with a tool. Then they said, "These are your gods,[b] Israel, who brought you up out of Egypt."
5When Aaron saw this, he built an altar in front of the calf and announced, "Tomorrow there will
be a festival[y] to the LORD." 6So the next day the people rose early and sacrificed burnt offerings and presented fellowship offerings.[z] Afterward they sat down to eat and drink and got up to indulge in revelry.[a]
7Then the LORD said to Moses, "Go down, because your people, whom you brought up out of Egypt,[b]
have become corrupt.[c] 8They have been quick to turn away from what I commanded them and have
made themselves an idol[d] cast in the shape of a calf. They have bowed down to it and sacrificed[e] to it
and have said, 'These are your gods, Israel, who brought you up out of Egypt.'[f]
9"I have seen these people," the LORD said to Moses, "and they are a stiff-necked[g] people. 10Now leave
me alone so that my anger may burn against them and that I may destroy them. Then I will make you
into a great nation."[h]

31:17 [q]ver 13 [r]Ge 2:2-3
31:18 [s]Ex 24:12 [t]Ex 32:15-16; 34:1,28; Dt 4:13; 5:22
32:1 [u]Ex 24:18; Dt 9:9-12 [v]Ac 7:40*
32:2 [w]Ex 35:22
32:4 [x]Dt 9:16; Ne 9:18; Ps 106:19; Ac 7:41
32:5 [y]Lev 23:2,37; 2Ki 10:20
32:6 [z]Nu 25:2; Ac 7:41 [a]ver 17-19; 1Co 10:7*
32:7 [b]ver 4,11 [c]Ge 6:11-12; Dt 9:12
32:8 [d]Ex 20:4 [e]Ex 22:20 [f]1Ki 12:28
32:9 [g]Ex 33:3,5; 34:9; Isa 48:4; Ac 7:51
32:10 [h]Nu 14:12; Dt 9:14

[a] *1* Or *a god;* also in verses 23 and 31 [b] *4* Or *This is your god;* also in verse 8

31:17 for in six days the LORD made. See note on 20:11. **on the seventh day he rested and was refreshed.** The Lord rested not because he was tired or out of breath but because he had completed his creative work. By imitating the Lord's "creation rest" in observing his Sabbaths, the Israelites foreshadow his creative and redemptive goal: a divine-human relationship through which humanity shares in the blessing of God's rest (Heb 4:1–11).

31:18 two tablets. These are not necessarily large or heavy. They are engraved front and back (32:15) with the ten "words" (34:1,28; see note on 20:1–21). **finger of God.** A bold metaphor (cf. 8:19; Luke 11:20) highlighting the divine inspiration of the covenant obligations; it may not literally describe the engraving process (34:1,27–28). Deut 4:13, 5:22, and 10:4 imply that God did the writing, but this may simply be a way of emphasizing the ultimate source of the tablets (24:12).

32:1—34:35 *The Covenant Broken and Reestablished.* The focus now shifts to events in the camp during Moses' absence (32:1; see 24:18). Israel's idolatry with the golden calf (ch. 32) flagrantly breaches the covenant. Only after the consequences of Israel's folly are spelled out and Moses persistently intercedes on Israel's behalf (ch. 33) is the covenant graciously renewed (ch. 34).

32:1—33:6 *The Golden Calf.* This incident, which essentially describes Israel's fall (cf. Gen 3), raises grave concerns regarding Israel's future.

32:1 they. Presumably representatives and leaders, not the entire community. **gods.** See NIV text note. The repeated use of plural verb forms in the Hebrew may suggest that the Israelites are flagrantly breaching the first and second commandments (but see note on v. 5). **who will go before us.** They effectively replace the Lord's leadership and protection with a dumb idol they can control. **Moses who brought us up out of Egypt.** Ignoring God, they credit exclusively Moses for the exodus (cf. 20:2; 29:46).

32:2 gold earrings. Rather than use this gold for the tabernacle, they use it for a rival system of worship ironically designed to reflect the Lord's presence in the camp.

32:4 idol. See note on 20:4. See photo, p. 331. **calf.** A bull-calf symbolized power and fertility. Whether this is a carved wooden calf with gold plating or a solid gold image refined by a craftsman's tool (v. 20), Aaron's handiwork is stamped all over it (cf. v. 35). **These are your gods.** See note on v. 1. Significantly, the same phrase occurs centuries later to describe the golden calves Jeroboam I sets up in Dan and Bethel (1 Kgs 12:28). God was thought to be present in the idol.

32:5 altar in front of the calf. Somewhat ironic in view of 20:22–25. Aaron seems determined to give this worship some vestige of authenticity by declaring "a festival to the LORD." For Aaron at least, the golden calf *represents* the Lord and therefore does not break the first commandment. But while this may explain his involvement, it does not exonerate him (32:21).

32:6 burnt offerings ... fellowship offerings. See notes on Lev 1; 3. Despite similarities with legitimate worship, what Aaron organizes is a parody of the real thing and quickly degenerates into something altogether different (v. 25). **revelry.** May allude to promiscuous sexual activity (the same Hebrew verb has sexual connotations in Gen 26:8 ["caressing"]; 39:14,17 ["make sport"]), which was often featured in ancient pagan worship. Because of the serious consequences (1 Cor 10:5), Paul warns Christians not to emulate Israel's idolatrous behavior (1 Cor 10:7).

32:7 your people, whom you brought up. By calling them "your people" (cf. 3:10) and crediting Moses with Israel's exodus (cf. 32:1), the Lord is effectively disowning them. **corrupt.** Through engaging in this act of folly (Ps 106:20), Israel sins and becomes ripe for judgment (cf. Gen 6:11–13).

32:9 stiff-necked. Used here for the first time, it alludes to Israel's natural propensity to disobey God's explicit commands (Deut 10:16; 31:27; Neh 9:16; Jer 19:15).

32:10 destroy them. Israel's future is in jeopardy; God will fulfill his promises (Gen 12:2) through Moses. The Lord would presumably have done so had Moses not responded as he did (Ps 106:23). Nevertheless, the Lord is clearly prompting Moses into action here; thus, the unfolding events neither take the Lord by surprise nor are they contrary to his sovereign plan and purpose.

32:11 [i] Dt 9:18 [j] Dt 9:26 **32:12** [k] Nu 14:13-16; Dt 9:28 **32:13** [l] Ex 2:24 [m] Ge 22:16; Heb 6:13 [n] Ge 15:5; 26:4 [o] Ge 12:7 **32:14** [p] 2Sa 24:16; Ps 106:45 **32:15** [q] Ex 31:18 [r] Dt 9:15 **32:16** [s] Ex 31:18 **32:19** [t] Dt 9:16 [u] Dt 9:17 **32:20** [v] Dt 9:21 **32:22** [w] Dt 9:24 **32:23** [x] ver 1 **32:24** [y] ver 4

11 But Moses sought the favor[i] of the LORD his God. "LORD," he said, "why should your anger burn
against your people, whom you brought out of Egypt with great power and a mighty hand?[j] 12 Why
should the Egyptians say, 'It was with evil intent that he brought them out, to kill them in the mountains and to wipe them off the face of the earth'?[k] Turn from your fierce anger; relent and do not bring
disaster on your people. 13 Remember[l] your servants Abraham, Isaac and Israel, to whom you swore by
your own self:[m] 'I will make your descendants as numerous as the stars[n] in the sky and I will give your
descendants all this land[o] I promised them, and it will be their inheritance forever.' " 14 Then the LORD
relented[p] and did not bring on his people the disaster he had threatened.

15 Moses turned and went down the mountain with the two tablets of the covenant law[q] in his hands.[r]
They were inscribed on both sides, front and back. 16 The tablets were the work of God; the writing was
the writing of God, engraved on the tablets.[s]

17 When Joshua heard the noise of the people shouting, he said to Moses, "There is the sound of war
in the camp."

18 Moses replied:

"It is not the sound of victory,
    it is not the sound of defeat;
    it is the sound of singing that I hear."

19 When Moses approached the camp and saw the calf[t] and the dancing, his anger burned and he
threw the tablets out of his hands, breaking them to pieces[u] at the foot of the mountain. 20 And he took
the calf the people had made and burned it in the fire; then he ground it to powder, scattered it on the
water[v] and made the Israelites drink it.

21 He said to Aaron, "What did these people do to you, that you led them into such great sin?"

22 "Do not be angry, my lord," Aaron answered. "You know how prone these people are to evil.[w]
23 They said to me, 'Make us gods who will go before us. As for this fellow Moses who brought us up out
of Egypt, we don't know what has happened to him.'[x] 24 So I told them, 'Whoever has any gold jewelry,
take it off.' Then they gave me the gold, and I threw it into the fire, and out came this calf!"[y]

25 Moses saw that the people were running wild and that Aaron had let them get out of control and so
become a laughingstock to their enemies. 26 So he stood at the entrance to the camp and said, "Whoever
is for the LORD, come to me." And all the Levites rallied to him.

27 Then he said to them, "This is what the LORD, the God of Israel, says: 'Each man strap a sword to

32:11–13 In response to what the Lord just told him (vv. 7–10), Moses employs three persuasive arguments: (1) It makes no sense for God to destroy Israel because they belong to him ("your people" [v. 11]; cf. v. 7) and he has rescued them from Egypt (v. 11). (2) The Egyptians would misinterpret the Lord's annihilating Israel and thus malign God (v. 12; cf. Deut 9:28). (3) Annihilating Israel (v. 10) is not in keeping with the spirit of the Lord's promise to multiply the descendants of Israel (v. 13).
32:14 relented. The basic idea is "felt sorrow" or "had compassion." Thus, God tempers his wrath with mercy. Moses' intercession as mediator averts the first crisis—the immediate threat of annihilation—and foreshadows the ongoing intercessory work of the risen and ascended Jesus (Heb 7:25), an important aspect of his role as mediator (1 Tim 2:5).
32:15–16 See note on 31:18. Focusing on these unique tablets anticipates the impact of Israel's great sin on their covenant with the Lord, as is clear from Moses' subsequent action (v. 19).
32:17 Joshua. See notes on 17:9; 24:12. At some unspecified stage Moses and Joshua reunite and descend the rest of the way together.
32:19 anger burned. Moses reacts like the Lord did (v. 10). **breaking them.** Destroying the tablets symbolizes the end of the covenant relationship, which Israel broke.
32:20 Destroying the calf reflects standard procedure for desecrating such an image in the ancient world: Moses (1) "burned it," (2) "ground it to powder," and (3) "scattered it" on the water supply (Deut 9:21; cf. 2 Kgs 23:15). In a thirteenth-century BC myth from Western Semitic Ugarit, the war goddess Anat burns, grinds to dust, and scatters the god Mot in a field. This represents complete destruction of the god. If this were a true god, a mortal like Moses could not so destroy him. The threefold ritual thus highlights the folly of worshiping such an object.
32:21 great sin. This was an ancient Near Eastern expression used of adultery. Its repeated use to describe Israel's idolatry (vv. 30,31) further underlines how serious this incident is. Like Adam, Israel flouted God's prohibition and jeopardized the divine-human relationship for which God created them.
32:22–24 Aaron's assessment of the people may be true, but he minimizes his own involvement and culpability: he begins almost verbatim with the earlier report (v. 1), but when it comes to his own role, he departs noticeably from the narrator's perspective (cf. v. 4; see v. 35).
32:24 out came this calf! See note on v. 4. Like Adam (Gen 3:12), Aaron indulges in the blame game. Like Israel (v. 10), he would be in serious trouble if Moses did not seek God's mercy (Deut 9:20).
32:25 running wild ... out of control. Both expressions reflect the same Hebrew verb, meaning "let go" or "cast off restraint" (Prov 29:18). See note on v. 6.
32:26 Whoever is for the LORD, come to me. This is an opportunity to repent and demonstrate allegiance to the Lord (cf. Josh 24:15; 1 Kgs 18:21). **all the Levites.** See note on 2:1–2. Only the Levites (or a majority thereof; see note on Deut 33:9) declare themselves unequivocally for the Lord.
32:27–28 This is probably not random slaughter but a "surgical strike," targeting a relatively small number ("about three thousand," v. 28) who

his side. Go back and forth through the camp from one end to the other, each killing his brother and
friend and neighbor.' "[z] 28The Levites did as Moses commanded, and that day about three thousand of
the people died. 29Then Moses said, "You have been set apart to the LORD today, for you were against
your own sons and brothers, and he has blessed you this day."

30The next day Moses said to the people, "You have committed a great sin.[a] But now I will go up to
the LORD; perhaps I can make atonement[b] for your sin."

31So Moses went back to the LORD and said, "Oh, what a great sin these people have committed![c]
They have made themselves gods of gold.[d] 32But now, please forgive their sin — but if not, then blot
me[e] out of the book[f] you have written."

33The LORD replied to Moses, "Whoever has sinned against me I will blot out[g] of my book. 34Now go,
lead the people to the place[h] I spoke of, and my angel[i] will go before you. However, when the time comes
for me to punish,[j] I will punish them for their sin."

35And the LORD struck the people with a plague because of what they did with the calf[k] Aaron had
made.

33 Then the LORD said to Moses, "Leave this place, you and the people you brought up out of Egypt,
and go up to the land I promised on oath to Abraham, Isaac and Jacob, saying, 'I will give it to
your descendants.'[l] 2I will send an angel[m] before you and drive out the Canaanites, Amorites, Hittites,
Perizzites, Hivites and Jebusites.[n] 3Go up to the land flowing with milk and honey.[o] But I will not go with
you, because you are a stiff-necked[p] people and I might destroy[q] you on the way."

4When the people heard these distressing words, they began to mourn[r] and no one put on any ornaments. 5For the LORD had said to Moses, "Tell the Israelites, 'You are a stiff-necked people. If I were
to go with you even for a moment, I might destroy you. Now take off your ornaments and I will decide
what to do with you.' " 6So the Israelites stripped off their ornaments at Mount Horeb.

The Tent of Meeting

7Now Moses used to take a tent and pitch it outside the camp some distance away, calling it the
"tent of meeting."[s] Anyone inquiring of the LORD would go to the tent of meeting outside the camp.

32:27 [z] Nu 25:3,5; Dt 33:9
32:30 [a] 1Sa 12:20 [b] Lev 1:4; Nu 25:13
32:31 [c] Dt 9:18 [d] Ex 20:23
32:32 [e] Ro 9:3 [f] Ps 69:28; Da 12:1; Php 4:3; Rev 3:5; 21:27
32:33 [g] Dt 29:20; Ps 9:5
32:34 [h] Ex 3:17 [i] Ex 23:20 [j] Dt 32:35; Ps 99:8; Ro 2:5-6
32:35 [k] ver 4
33:1 [l] Ge 12:7
33:2 [m] Ex 32:34 [n] Ex 23:27-31; Jos 24:11
33:3 [o] Ex 3:8 [p] Ex 32:9 [q] Ex 32:10
33:4 [r] Nu 14:39
33:7 [s] Ex 29:42-43

refused to repent and possibly persisted in the aforementioned revelry (v. 6; cf. Num 25:5–9). In any case, loyalty to God trumps all other loyalties, including loyalty to family (cf. Matt 10:37; Luke 14:26).

32:29 Because the Levites restore order to the camp, the Lord sets them apart to himself and blesses them. They are to assist Aaron and the priests, primarily by transporting the tabernacle and its furnishings (Num 1:47–53; 3:5–9,12,41,45; 4:2–3,15,18–33).

32:30–32 While Moses' earlier intercession secured Israel's survival (v. 14), the Lord has said nothing about forgiving Israel's "great sin." It is to this that Moses now turns his attention.

32:30 perhaps I can make atonement. This entails primarily interceding before the Lord as covenant mediator rather than offering some form of atoning sacrifice.

32:32 blot me out. Not some form of penal substitutionary atonement (see note on v. 30). Rather, Moses is categorically rejecting the Lord's earlier offer (v. 10) by identifying fully with Israel (i.e., he is also willing to perish with Israel should their sin not be forgiven). Even so, Moses' example here foreshadows the Mediator who uniquely demonstrated self-sacrificial love (Phil 2:5–8); Jesus gave his life as an atoning sacrifice for the sins of others (Heb 9:15; 1 John 2:1) and, by doing so, he secured for them forgiveness (Eph 1:7) and eternal life (John 3:16). **book you have written.** Alludes to a heavenly register of the living (Ps 69:28; Isa 4:3; Dan 12:1), akin to ancient census records. Mal 3:16 refers to a "scroll of remembrance" listing the faithful remnant, and this may be the basis for the NT concept of the "book of life" (Phil 4:3; Rev 3:5; 20:12,15; 21:27; see Luke 10:20), a metaphoric record of God's elect.

32:33 Whoever has sinned … I will blot out. While not committing himself to forgiveness, the Lord is unwilling to punish anyone except the guilty (Gen 18:20–33; Deut 24:16; Ezek 18:4). All Moses has secured at this stage is another stay of execution.

32:34 place I spoke of. The promised land (3:8,17; 23:23; 33:1–3a). **my angel.** See note on 23:23. **I will punish.** While Israel's future prospects have improved (cf. v. 10), the Lord reserves the right to punish them for their sin.

32:35 plague. Either immediately fulfills the punishment just anticipated (v. 34) or alludes to some subsequent punishment of the exodus generation. 1 Cor 10:8 appears to refer to this punishment.

33:1–3 The Lord ostensibly begins on a positive note with instructions to leave Sinai and go to the promised land, but it quickly becomes evident that a major problem remains unresolved: Israel's sinfulness is impeding the Lord's plan to accompany them (v. 3b). Given the tabernacle's express purpose (25:8; 29:44–46), the plans to erect it have thus been shelved.

33:1 The Lord's covenant promise of land remains intact, but he has suspended the prospect of his dwelling in Israel's midst because of the inherent dangers for these "stiff-necked people" (v. 3; see note on 32:9).

33:2 angel. Cf. 32:34 and note. **Canaanites … Jebusites.** The indigenous inhabitants of the promised land.

33:4–6 Grieving and removing their "ornaments" (i.e., the kind of jewelry used to make the golden calf; 32:2–4) were signs of repentance.

33:7–11 *The Tent of Meeting.* This material is arguably a literary flashback outlining the circumstances that prevailed prior to Israel's "great sin" (see 32:21 and note) and the crisis over the Lord's continuing presence. It provides significant insight into the special relationship between the Lord and Moses and the role it played in resolving the current crisis.

33:7 "tent of meeting." A temporary arrangement used by Moses prior to the erection of the tabernacle (see note on 25:22). In light of the people's sinful behavior, this may now be the only such tent Israel is ever likely to have. But while very inferior to the tabernacle, it serves a similar function: it is a meeting place where the Lord can manifest his presence and communicate with Israel.

33:8 [t]Nu 16:27 **33:9** [u]Ex 13:21 [v]Ex 31:18; Ps 99:7 **33:11** [w]Nu 12:8; Dt 34:10 **33:12** [x]Ex 3:10 [y]ver 17; Jn 10:14-15; 2Ti 2:19 **33:13** [z]Ps 25:4; 86:11; 119:33 [a]Ex 34:9; Dt 9:26,29 **33:14** [b]Isa 63:9 [c]Jos 21:44; 22:4 **33:16** [d]Nu 14:14 [e]Ex 34:10

8And whenever Moses went out to the tent, all the people rose and stood at the entrances to their tents,[t]
watching Moses until he entered the tent. 9As Moses went into the tent, the pillar of cloud[u] would come
down and stay at the entrance, while the LORD spoke[v] with Moses. 10Whenever the people saw the pillar
of cloud standing at the entrance to the tent, they all stood and worshiped, each at the entrance to their
tent. 11The LORD would speak to Moses face to face,[w] as one speaks to a friend. Then Moses would return
to the camp, but his young aide Joshua son of Nun did not leave the tent.

Moses and the Glory of the LORD

12Moses said to the LORD, "You have been telling me, 'Lead these people,'[x] but you have not let me
know whom you will send with me. You have said, 'I know you by name[y] and you have found favor with
me.' 13If you are pleased with me, teach me your ways[z] so I may know you and continue to find favor
with you. Remember that this nation is your people."[a]

14The LORD replied, "My Presence[b] will go with you, and I will give you rest."[c]

15Then Moses said to him, "If your Presence does not go with us, do not send us up from here. 16How
will anyone know that you are pleased with me and with your people unless you go with us?[d] What else
will distinguish me and your people from all the other people on the face of the earth?"[e]

17And the LORD said to Moses, "I will do the very thing you have asked, because I am pleased with
you and I know you by name."

18Then Moses said, "Now show me your glory."

19And the LORD said, "I will cause all my goodness to pass in front of you, and I will proclaim my
name, the LORD, in your presence. I will have mercy on whom I will have mercy, and I will have com-

33:10 pillar of cloud. See note on 13:21. **stood and worshiped.** Acknowledges that the Lord is visibly manifesting his presence and is communicating to Moses in the tent.

33:11 face to face, as one speaks to a friend. As covenant mediator, Moses is unique among the prophets (Num 12:6–8), enjoying a more personal encounter with God (see note on v. 20). Thus, there is hope for Israel, despite the present crisis, so long as they have such a mediator. **Joshua ... did not leave the tent.** Presumably to prevent unauthorized access.

33:12–23 *Moses and the Glory of the Lord.* Picks up where vv. 1–6 leave off; the threat of the Lord's absence is particularly in focus. While Moses initiates the conversation (cf. 32:31), this intercession is not changing God's eternal plans or purpose; rather, by responding to God as he does, Moses plays a significant role (i.e., through prayer) in how God's sovereign will is put into effect. See note on 32:10.

33:12 you have not let me know whom you will send with me. While the Lord's angel would still go before Israel (32:34; 33:2; cf. 23:20,23), Moses is not content with this: he wants to know who will actually accompany them. Moreover, it is clear from what follows that only the Lord will do. **I know you by name.** This, along with the following phrase, alludes to Moses' special relationship with the Lord (see v. 11 and note), the basis for the following appeal and its successful outcome (v. 17). **found favor.** A recurring emphasis in these verses; the same expression is also translated "pleased with" in vv. 13,16,17.

33:13 teach me your ways so I may know you. True knowledge of God depends on his self-revelation. For the answer to this petition, see 34:6–7. **Remember that this nation is your people.** The crux of Moses' petition is for the Lord to demonstrate his grace to Israel.

33:14 My Presence will go. The Lord grants Moses' request, reversing his earlier decision to send them alone (v. 3). **rest.** Secure settlement in the promised land (Deut 3:20; 25:19; Josh 22:4; 23:1; 2 Sam 7:1,11; cf. Ps 95:11). This foreshadows the spiritual "rest" found in Christ (Matt 11:28–29; Heb 4:1–11; Rev 14:13b). See note on 20:11.

33:15–16 Reinforces the importance of the divine presence. God's presence distinguishes Israel from other nations.

33:15 If your Presence does not go with us. This response is somewhat surprising, given what the Lord just promised (v. 14). But Moses is probably insisting that God's promise to accompany them take effect immediately. In particular, he may have in mind what God revealed concerning the tabernacle (25:8; 29:44–46). This is how the Lord's grace to Moses and Israel, as well as Israel's unique status, will be most obvious.

33:17 because I am pleased with you. See note on v. 12. How much more will the Lord Jesus, with whom God is "well pleased" (Matt 17:5), intercede for us (Heb 7:25) as one greater than Moses (Heb 3:1–6).

33:18–23 Despite the Lord's concessions, the issue of how a holy God can accompany this sinful people without destroying them (33:3; see note on v. 1) still remains unsettled (34:9). In view of this, Moses' new petition (v. 18) is not a request for something more personal but is for a visible demonstration of God's assurance in v. 17.

33:18 show me your glory. The Lord manifested his glory in the pillar of cloud (16:10) and in the fiery cloud that descended on Sinai (24:15–17). Moreover, he promised that this glory would sanctify the tabernacle (29:43), and this is precisely what happens (40:34–35). Verses 7–11 explicitly connect the presence of the pillar of cloud with the Lord speaking to Moses "face to face" (v. 11), and ch. 34 concludes by highlighting the glorious effect that speaking directly with the Lord has on Moses' face (34:29–35). So Moses is probably requesting an experience similar to that which he enjoyed previously. The Lord's immediate response seems to confirm this: God will manifest his glory, although he must shelter Moses from full exposure to it (vv. 19–23).

33:19–23 In response to Moses' request, the Lord promises to manifest his glory (v. 22) and provide further insight into his character by proclaiming his name. Whatever the difference between full exposure (v. 20) and partial exposure (v. 23) to the Lord's glory (v. 22), the Lord accedes to the spirit of Moses' request.

33:19 all my goodness. Emphasizes the Lord's character rather than his glory. This is what Moses (and Israel) most need, hence the further insight into God's "name"—what he is really like (see notes on 3:13,14). **I will have mercy on whom I will have mercy, and I will have compassion on whom I will have compassion.** Expands on the name "the LORD" (see notes on 3:13–15). In the context of Israel's rebellion, the Lord reserves the right to be merciful and compassionate on whomever he chooses. Paul quotes these words in Rom 9:15 to illustrate God's sovereign choice with respect to salvation.

passion on whom I will have compassion.[f] 20But," he said, "you cannot see my face, for no one may
see[g] me and live."

21Then the LORD said, "There is a place near me where you may stand on a rock. 22When my glory
passes by, I will put you in a cleft in the rock and cover you with my hand[h] until I have passed by. 23Then
I will remove my hand and you will see my back; but my face must not be seen."

The New Stone Tablets

34 The LORD said to Moses, "Chisel out two stone tablets like the first ones, and I will write on
them the words that were on the first tablets,[i] which you broke.[j] 2Be ready in the morning,
and then come up on Mount Sinai.[k] Present yourself to me there on top of the mountain. 3No one is
to come with you or be seen anywhere on the mountain;[l] not even the flocks and herds may graze in
front of the mountain."

4So Moses chiseled out two stone tablets like the first ones and went up Mount Sinai early in the
morning, as the LORD had commanded him; and he carried the two stone tablets in his hands. 5Then
the LORD came down in the cloud and stood there with him and proclaimed his name, the LORD.[m] 6And
he passed in front of Moses, proclaiming, "The LORD, the LORD, the compassionate[n] and gracious God,
slow to anger,[o] abounding in love[p] and faithfulness,[q] 7maintaining love to thousands,[r] and forgiving
wickedness, rebellion and sin.[s] Yet he does not leave the guilty unpunished;[t] he punishes the children
and their children for the sin of the parents to the third and fourth generation."

8Moses bowed to the ground at once and worshiped. 9"Lord," he said, "if I have found favor in your
eyes, then let the Lord go with us.[u] Although this is a stiff-necked people, forgive our wickedness and
our sin, and take us as your inheritance."[v]

10Then the LORD said: "I am making a covenant[w] with you. Before all your people I will do wonders
never before done in any nation in all the world.[x] The people you live among will see how awesome
is the work that I, the LORD, will do for you. 11Obey what I command you today. I will drive out before you the Amorites, Canaanites, Hittites, Perizzites, Hivites and Jebusites.[y] 12Be careful not to make

33:19 [f]Ro 9:15*
33:20 [g]Ge 32:30; Isa 6:5
33:22 [h]Ps 91:4
34:1 [i]Dt 10:2,4 [j]Ex 32:19
34:2 [k]Ex 19:11
34:3 [l]Ex 19:12-13,21
34:5 [m]Ex 33:19
34:6 [n]Ps 86:15 [o]Nu 14:18; Ro 2:4 [p]Ne 9:17; Ps 103:8; Joel 2:13 [q]Ps 108:4
34:7 [r]Ex 20:6 [s]Ps 103:3; 130:4,8; Da 9:9; 1Jn 1:9 [t]Job 10:14; Na 1:3
34:9 [u]Ex 33:15 [v]Ps 33:12
34:10 [w]Dt 5:2-3 [x]Ex 33:16; Dt 4:32
34:11 [y]Ex 33:2

33:20 face. His full, *unmediated* glory. A mediated revelation is found in Jesus (John 1:14–18; cf. Matt 17:2). **no one may see me and live.** While it is clearly possible to see some manifestation of God and survive (3:6; 24:9–11), this is clearly exceptional (Gen 16:13; 32:30; Judg 6:22–23; 13:22; Isa 6:5); it seems likely that it was such an experience that produced the radiant face of Moses (34:29–35). However, no mortal being has ever seen God (John 1:18; 6:46; 1 Tim 6:16; 1 John 4:12) or could survive seeing God's "face" (here; v. 23).
33:23 my back. Like the Lord's "face" (v. 20), we should not interpret this literally.
34:1–28 *The New Stone Tablets.* Divine forgiveness does not annul the covenant obligations. By reissuing such obligations the covenant is now renewed.
34:1 two stone tablets. See note on 31:18. **you broke.** See 32:19 and note.
34:2–3 These instructions echo those given before the earlier theophany (19:12,20–24), but they exclude others from coming up with Moses, suggesting that another theophany (divine appearance) is about to occur.
34:5–7 This is the theophany (divine appearance) that 33:19–23 anticipates, but what Moses hears (vv. 6b–7) almost totally eclipses what he sees (vv. 5–6a). Here the Lord more fully reveals his character, as anticipated in 33:19 (see note there). His self-description (vv. 6–7) becomes an important OT statement of God's nature (Num 14:18; 2 Chr 30:9; Neh 9:17,31; Pss 86:5,15; 103:8; 145:8; Joel 2:13; Jonah 4:2; Nah 1:3).
34:6 The LORD. See note on 3:15. The repetition here suggests that God is more fully explaining his name's significance (see note on 3:14). **compassionate and gracious.** Together emphasize God's tender and generous character: he sees our needs and responds benevolently. **slow to anger.** The Hebrew idiom is the opposite of "burning with anger" (4:14; 11:8); God lets his anger cool before responding to human sin (32:10–14,33–35). **abounding in love and faithfulness.** Two key covenant concepts: (1) God's steadfast or persistent love and (2) God's faithfulness or trustworthiness. Both terms stress God's reliability as covenant partner.
34:7 maintaining love to thousands. See note on 20:5. This may also be translated as "a thousand generations"; but here thousands of Israelites already need such reassurance of God's steadfast love. **forgiving ... sin.** Israel's most pressing need (v. 9; 32:32). **wickedness, rebellion and sin.** The use of the three major OT words for sin emphasizes that God is willing to forgive all kinds of sin/sinners. **Yet ... unpunished.** God's forgiveness is never at the expense of his justice; the guilty cannot simply be acquitted. **punishes ... generation.** See note on 20:5. There is no such thing as sin without consequences, which here, as in 20:5, impacts successive generations. The implicit tensions of vv. 6–7 are only partially resolved by the various judgments of Israel's sin that culminated with the exile; but they are fully resolved in the death of Jesus, which was both the ultimate expression of God's love and a full expression of God's wrath (Rom 3:25–26).
34:8–9 Capitalizing on the Lord's self-proclamation, Moses asks the Lord to forgive Israel and so fulfill his original intentions.
34:10–35 After the prolonged and intense dialogue that occupies most of chs. 32–33, these verses describe the resolution to this crisis: God reestablishes the covenant that Israel's apostasy obliterated.
34:10 I am making a covenant. The Lord persists with his original plans; he begins by renewing or remaking the broken covenant.
34:11–26 Abridges "the Book of the Covenant" (see 24:7 and note) and focuses mainly on Israel's cultic obligations. This is especially pertinent in a context in which Israel adopted worship practices typical of other nations. Thus understood, these commands emphasize Israel's covenant obligation to worship the Lord only as he prescribes.
34:12 treaty. Or covenant. Israel's only covenant was to be exclusively with the Lord.

34:12 [z] Ex 23:32-33
34:13 [a] Ex 23:24; Dt 12:3; 2Ki 18:4
34:14 [b] Ex 20:3 [c] Ex 20:5; Dt 4:24
34:15 [d] Jdg 2:17 [e] Nu 25:2; 1Co 8:4
34:16 [f] Dt 7:3 [g] 1Ki 11:4
34:17 [h] Ex 32:8
34:18 [i] Ex 12:17 [j] Ex 12:15 [k] Ex 12:2
34:19 [l] Ex 13:2
34:20 [m] Ex 13:13,15 [n] Ex 23:15; Dt 16:16
34:21 [o] Ex 20:9; Lk 13:14
34:22 [p] Ex 23:16
34:23 [q] Ex 23:14
34:24 [r] Ex 23:28; 33:2; Ps 78:55
34:25 [s] Ex 23:18 [t] Ex 12:8,10
34:26 [u] Ex 23:19
34:27 [v] Ex 17:14; 24:4
34:28 [w] Ge 7:4; Ex 24:18; Mt 4:2 [x] ver 1; Ex 31:18 [y] Dt 4:13; 10:4
34:29 [z] Ex 32:15 [a] Ps 34:5; Mt 17:2; 2Co 3:7,13

a treaty with those who live in the land where you are going, or they will be a snare[z] among you. 13 Break down their altars, smash their sacred stones and cut down their Asherah poles.[a][a] 14 Do not worship any other god,[b] for the LORD, whose name is Jealous, is a jealous God.[c]

15 "Be careful not to make a treaty with those who live in the land; for when they prostitute[d] themselves to their gods and sacrifice to them, they will invite you and you will eat their sacrifices.[e] 16 And when you choose some of their daughters as wives[f] for your sons and those daughters prostitute themselves to their gods,[g] they will lead your sons to do the same.

Possible image of Asherah (Exod 34:13) tree on Taanach cult stand, tenth century BC.

Z. Radovan/www.BibleLandPictures.com

17 "Do not make any idols.[h]

18 "Celebrate the Festival of Unleavened Bread.[i] For seven days eat bread made without yeast,[j] as I commanded you. Do this at the appointed time in the month of Aviv,[k] for in that month you came out of Egypt.

19 "The first offspring[l] of every womb belongs to me, including all the firstborn males of your livestock, whether from herd or flock. 20 Redeem the firstborn donkey with a lamb, but if you do not redeem it, break its neck.[m] Redeem all your firstborn sons.

"No one is to appear before me empty-handed.[n]

21 "Six days you shall labor, but on the seventh day you shall rest;[o] even during the plowing season and harvest you must rest.

22 "Celebrate the Festival of Weeks with the firstfruits of the wheat harvest, and the Festival of Ingathering[p] at the turn of the year.[b] 23 Three times[q] a year all your men are to appear before the Sovereign LORD, the God of Israel. 24 I will drive out nations[r] before you and enlarge your territory, and no one will covet your land when you go up three times each year to appear before the LORD your God.

25 "Do not offer the blood of a sacrifice to me along with anything containing yeast,[s] and do not let any of the sacrifice from the Passover Festival remain until morning.[t]

26 "Bring the best of the firstfruits of your soil to the house of the LORD your God.

"Do not cook a young goat in its mother's milk."[u]

27 Then the LORD said to Moses, "Write[v] down these words, for in accordance with these words I have made a covenant with you and with Israel." 28 Moses was there with the LORD forty days and forty nights[w] without eating bread or drinking water. And he wrote on the tablets[x] the words of the covenant—the Ten Commandments.[y]

The Radiant Face of Moses

29 When Moses came down from Mount Sinai with the two tablets of the covenant law in his hands,[z] he was not aware that his face was radiant[a] because he had spoken with the LORD. 30 When Aaron and all the

[a] *13* That is, wooden symbols of the goddess Asherah [b] *22* That is, in the autumn

34:13 Asherah poles. See NIV text note. Asherah was the name of the wife of El, the chief Canaanite deity. Wooden poles, possibly carved images of Asherah, were set up in her honor beside related idolatrous objects (Judg 6:25).
34:14 name is Jealous. See notes on 3:13; 20:5.
34:15 prostitute themselves. A frequent OT metaphor for Israel's covenant unfaithfulness. By establishing his covenant with Israel, the Lord had metaphorically become Israel's "husband" (Isa 54:5–6; Jer 3:14; 31:32; Hos 2:2,7,16; cf. Jer 2:2; 3:1,14,20; Ezek 16:8,32,45; 23:4,37). Israel's unfaithfulness was commonly expressed by crediting other gods (called "lovers"; e.g., Ezek 16:33,36; Hos 2:5,13) with the protection or provision that the Lord alone could supply. **eat their sacrifices.** Like the fellowship offering involved eating and communion with the true God, eating the sacrifices of false gods involved communion with them. For Israel, such participation demonstrates an unacceptable degree of cultural and religious assimilation (cf. 1 Cor 8; 10:18–21).
34:17 idols. Such as the golden calf (32:4), described by the same Hebrew word that means "cast metal." Idolatry is one of Israel's persistent sins, leading eventually to exile (2 Kgs 22:17). While modern-day idol worship may be more sophisticated, the covenant established by Jesus likewise prohibits all idolatry (Col 3:5; 1 Pet 4:3; 1 John 5:21).
34:18–26 See notes on 23:14–19.
34:27 Write down. See note on 31:18. **these words.** Possibly not just the preceding summary but also "the Ten Commandments" (v. 28).
34:28 he wrote. See note on 31:18.
34:29–35 *The Radiant Face of Moses.* The rays emanating from Moses' face are a visible sign not only of the Lord's restored presence with Israel but also of the divine authority with which this mediator of the old

Israelites saw Moses, his face was radiant, and they were afraid to come near him. [31]But Moses called to them;
so Aaron and all the leaders of the community came back to him, and he spoke to them. [32]Afterward all the
Israelites came near him, and he gave them all the commands[b] the LORD had given him on Mount Sinai.
[33]When Moses finished speaking to them, he put a veil[c] over his face. [34]But whenever he entered
the LORD's presence to speak with him, he removed the veil until he came out. And when he came out
and told the Israelites what he had been commanded, [35]they saw that his face was radiant. Then Moses
would put the veil back over his face until he went in to speak with the LORD.

Sabbath Regulations

35 Moses assembled the whole Israelite community and said to them, "These are the things the
LORD has commanded[d] you to do: [2]For six days, work is to be done, but the seventh day shall
be your holy day, a day of sabbath[e] rest to the LORD. Whoever does any work on it is to be put to death.
[3]Do not light a fire in any of your dwellings on the Sabbath day.[f]"

Materials for the Tabernacle

35:4-9pp — Ex 25:1-7
35:10-19pp — Ex 39:32-41

[4]Moses said to the whole Israelite community, "This is what the LORD has commanded: [5]From what
you have, take an offering for the LORD. Everyone who is willing is to bring to the LORD an offering of
gold, silver and bronze; [6]blue, purple and scarlet yarn and fine linen; goat hair; [7]ram skins dyed red and
another type of durable leather[a]; acacia wood; [8]olive oil for the light; spices for the anointing oil and
for the fragrant incense; [9]and onyx stones and other gems to be mounted on the ephod and breastpiece.
[10]"All who are skilled among you are to come and make everything the LORD has commanded:[g] [11]the
tabernacle[h] with its tent and its covering, clasps, frames, crossbars, posts and bases; [12]the ark[i] with its
poles and the atonement cover and the curtain that shields it; [13]the table[j] with its poles and all its articles
and the bread of the Presence; [14]the lampstand[k] that is for light with its accessories, lamps and oil for
the light; [15]the altar[l] of incense with its poles, the anointing oil[m] and the fragrant incense;[n] the curtain
for the doorway at the entrance to the tabernacle; [16]the altar[o] of burnt offering with its bronze grating,
its poles and all its utensils; the bronze basin with its stand; [17]the curtains of the courtyard with its posts
and bases, and the curtain for the entrance to the courtyard;[p] [18]the tent pegs for the tabernacle and for
the courtyard, and their ropes; [19]the woven garments worn for ministering in the sanctuary — both the
sacred garments[q] for Aaron the priest and the garments for his sons when they serve as priests."
[20]Then the whole Israelite community withdrew from Moses' presence, [21]and everyone who was
willing and whose heart moved them came and brought an offering to the LORD for the work on the
tent of meeting, for all its service, and for the sacred garments. [22]All who were willing, men and women
alike, came and brought gold jewelry of all kinds: brooches, earrings, rings and ornaments. They all

34:32 [b]Ex 24:3
34:33 [c]2Co 3:13
35:1 [d]Ex 34:32
35:2 [e]Ex 20:9-10; 34:21; Lev 23:3
35:3 [f]Ex 16:23
35:10 [g]Ex 31:6
35:11 [h]Ex 26:1-37
35:12 [i]Ex 25:10-22
35:13 [j]Ex 25:23-30; Lev 24:5-6
35:14 [k]Ex 25:31
35:15 [l]Ex 30:1-6 [m]Ex 30:25 [n]Ex 30:34-38
35:16 [o]Ex 27:1-8
35:17 [p]Ex 27:9
35:19 [q]Ex 28:2; 31:10; 39:1

[a] 7 Possibly the hides of large aquatic mammals; also in verse 23

covenant speaks — both now and subsequently (vv. 34–35). This experience of Moses and what it signifies is probably the basis for the priestly blessing (Num 6:24–26) and the refrain of Ps 80:3,7,19. It is also key to understanding the significance of Jesus' transfiguration (Matt 17:2–5); the temporary brilliance of Christ's transfigured face helps identify Jesus as the new Moses (Deut 18:15; Matt 17:5) who uniquely reveals God's glory and makes him known (John 1:14–18; 2 Cor 4:6).

34:33 veil over his face. The radiant face of Moses intimidated the Israelites (v. 30) and was apparently not something they could continue to look at (2 Cor 3:7); therefore, this veil was used to shelter the Israelites from prolonged exposure to the reflected glory of God.

34:34–35 The use of this veil established a regular pattern of activity described by these two verses. By removing the veil in God's presence and then communicating the Lord's instructions with unveiled face, Moses ensured that Israel was regularly reminded of the instructions' divine source and authority. However, the veil also hid from the Israelites the passing nature of Moses' radiant face, a fact that Paul exploits in 2 Cor 3:7–18 to contrast the transient glory of the old (i.e., Mosaic) covenant (which, by letters on stone, issues in death and condemnation) with the surpassing and lasting glory of the new covenant (which, by the Spirit, issues in life and righteousness).

35:1 — 40:38 *Construction and Consecration of the Tabernacle.* Most of this material repeats, almost verbatim, material from chs. 25–28; 30:1–5; 31:1–11. It differs only in the order it discusses the items and in the use of past-tense rather than future-tense verbs. Repetition was a common feature of ancient Near Eastern literature and was designed to fix details firmly in readers' minds. The repetition here emphasizes that the tabernacle is important, that Israel must carefully obey the divine instructions (see the repeated refrain "as the LORD commanded"), and most important, that God's plans for Israel are back on track (25:8; 29:45–46).

35:1–3 *Sabbath Regulations.* This brief repetition of the Sabbath regulations further highlights that the covenant has been reestablished and that maintaining Israel's holy status is a priority. See notes on 31:12–18.

35:4–29 *Materials for the Tabernacle.* Assembling the raw materials

35:23 [r]1Ch 29:8
35:25 [s]Ex 28:3
35:27 [t]1Ch 29:6; Ezr 2:68
35:28 [u]Ex 25:6
35:29 [v]ver 21; 1Ch 29:9 [w]ver 4-9; Ex 25:1-7; 36:3; 2Ki 12:4
35:31 [x]ver 35; 2Ch 2:7,14
35:34 [y]Ex 31:6 [z]2Ch 2:14
35:35 [a]ver 31; Ex 31:3, 6; 1Ki 7:14
36:1 [b]Ex 28:3 [c]Ex 25:8
36:2 [d]Ex 31:2 [e]Ex 31:6 [f]Ex 25:2; 35:21,26; 1Ch 29:5
36:3 [g]Ex 35:29
36:5 [h]2Ch 24:14; 31:10; 2Co 8:2-3
36:7 [i]1Ki 7:47
36:13 [j]ver 18

presented their gold as a wave offering to the LORD. [23]Everyone who had blue, purple or scarlet yarn[r] or fine linen, or goat hair, ram skins dyed red or the other durable leather brought them. [24]Those presenting an offering of silver or bronze brought it as an offering to the LORD, and everyone who had acacia wood for any part of the work brought it. [25]Every skilled woman[s] spun with her hands and brought what she had spun — blue, purple or scarlet yarn or fine linen. [26]And all the women who were willing and had the skill spun the goat hair. [27]The leaders[t] brought onyx stones and other gems to be mounted on the ephod and breastpiece. [28]They also brought spices and olive oil for the light and for the anointing oil and for the fragrant incense.[u] [29]All the Israelite men and women who were willing[v] brought to the LORD freewill offerings[w] for all the work the LORD through Moses had commanded them to do.

Bezalel and Oholiab

35:30-35pp — Ex 31:2-6

[30]Then Moses said to the Israelites, "See, the LORD has chosen Bezalel son of Uri, the son of Hur, of the tribe of Judah, [31]and he has filled him with the Spirit of God, with wisdom, with understanding, with knowledge and with all kinds of skills[x] — [32]to make artistic designs for work in gold, silver and bronze, [33]to cut and set stones, to work in wood and to engage in all kinds of artistic crafts. [34]And he has given both him and Oholiab[y] son of Ahisamak, of the tribe of Dan, the ability to teach[z] others. [35]He has filled them with skill to do all kinds of work[a] as engravers, designers, embroiderers in blue, purple and scarlet yarn and fine linen, and weavers — all of them skilled workers and designers.

36 [1]So Bezalel, Oholiab and every skilled person[b] to whom the LORD has given skill and ability to know how to carry out all the work of constructing the sanctuary[c] are to do the work just as the LORD has commanded."

[2]Then Moses summoned Bezalel[d] and Oholiab[e] and every skilled person to whom the LORD had given ability and who was willing[f] to come and do the work. [3]They received from Moses all the offerings[g] the Israelites had brought to carry out the work of constructing the sanctuary. And the people continued to bring freewill offerings morning after morning. [4]So all the skilled workers who were doing all the work on the sanctuary left what they were doing [5]and said to Moses, "The people are bringing more than enough[h] for doing the work the LORD commanded to be done."

[6]Then Moses gave an order and they sent this word throughout the camp: "No man or woman is to make anything else as an offering for the sanctuary." And so the people were restrained from bringing more, [7]because what they already had was more[i] than enough to do all the work.

The Tabernacle

36:8-38pp — Ex 26:1-37

[8]All those who were skilled among the workers made the tabernacle with ten curtains of finely twisted linen and blue, purple and scarlet yarn, with cherubim woven into them by expert hands. [9]All the curtains were the same size — twenty-eight cubits long and four cubits wide.[a] [10]They joined five of the curtains together and did the same with the other five. [11]Then they made loops of blue material along the edge of the end curtain in one set, and the same was done with the end curtain in the other set. [12]They also made fifty loops on one curtain and fifty loops on the end curtain of the other set, with the loops opposite each other. [13]Then they made fifty gold clasps and used them to fasten the two sets of curtains together so that the tabernacle was a unit.[j]

[14]They made curtains of goat hair for the tent over the tabernacle — eleven altogether. [15]All eleven

[a] 9 That is, about 42 feet long and 6 feet wide or about 13 meters long and 1.8 meters wide

for the project (see 25:1 – 7 and note on 25:1 – 9) involves sacrificially donating both possessions (vv. 5 – 9) and expertise (vv. 10 – 19). The community's voluntary response (vv. 20 – 29) is overwhelming (36:2 – 7).

35:30 — 36:7 *Bezalel and Oholiab.* See 31:1 – 11 and notes. An undesignated number of apprentices, to whom the Lord has given the requisite skills (35:10; 36:1 – 2), assist Bezalel and Oholiab. Along with moving the peoples' hearts, this divine empowerment with skills highlights that constructing the tabernacle is more than just a human endeavor.

36:3 – 7 The community's generosity (such that Moses must restrain their giving) is a fitting response to God's amazing grace that they experienced (cf. 2 Cor 8:9).

36:8 — 38:31 *The Tabernacle Constructed.* Focuses on the tabernacle and its furnishings, ending with an inventory of the gold, silver, and bronze involved. It implements the instructions in 26:1 – 37 and differs only in the person and tense of the verbs. It follows a more logical sequence: work on the tabernacle prefaces work on its furniture (cf. chs. 25 – 26).

36:10 They. Rightly gives the impression that this is a collaborative enterprise. But here and throughout the following verses the person doing the

curtains were the same size — thirty cubits long and four cubits wide.[a] 16They joined five of the curtains into one set and the other six into another set. 17Then they made fifty loops along the edge of the
end curtain in one set and also along the edge of the end curtain in the other set. 18They made fifty
bronze clasps to fasten the tent together as a unit.[k] 19Then they made for the tent a covering of ram
skins dyed red, and over that a covering of the other durable leather.[b]
20They made upright frames of acacia wood for the tabernacle. 21Each frame was ten cubits long and
a cubit and a half wide,[c] 22with two projections set parallel to each other. They made all the frames of
the tabernacle in this way. 23They made twenty frames for the south side of the tabernacle 24and made
forty silver bases to go under them — two bases for each frame, one under each projection. 25For the
other side, the north side of the tabernacle, they made twenty frames 26and forty silver bases — two
under each frame. 27They made six frames for the far end, that is, the west end of the tabernacle, 28and
two frames were made for the corners of the tabernacle at the far end. 29At these two corners the frames
were double from the bottom all the way to the top and fitted into a single ring; both were made alike.
30So there were eight frames and sixteen silver bases — two under each frame.
31They also made crossbars of acacia wood: five for the frames on one side of the tabernacle, 32five for
those on the other side, and five for the frames on the west, at the far end of the tabernacle. 33They made
the center crossbar so that it extended from end to end at the middle of the frames. 34They overlaid the
frames with gold and made gold rings to hold the crossbars. They also overlaid the crossbars with gold.
35They made the curtain[l] of blue, purple and scarlet yarn and finely twisted linen, with cherubim
woven into it by a skilled worker. 36They made four posts of acacia wood for it and overlaid them with
gold. They made gold hooks for them and cast their four silver bases. 37For the entrance to the tent
they made a curtain of blue, purple and scarlet yarn and finely twisted linen — the work of an embroiderer;[m] 38and they made five posts with hooks for them. They overlaid the tops of the posts and their
bands with gold and made their five bases of bronze.

The Ark

37:1-9pp — Ex 25:10-20

37 Bezalel[n] made the ark[o] of acacia wood — two and a half cubits long, a cubit and a half wide,
and a cubit and a half high.[d] 2He overlaid it with pure gold,[p] both inside and out, and made a
gold molding around it. 3He cast four gold rings for it and fastened them to its four feet, with two rings
on one side and two rings on the other. 4Then he made poles of acacia wood and overlaid them with
gold. 5And he inserted the poles into the rings on the sides of the ark to carry it.
6He made the atonement cover[q] of pure gold — two and a half cubits long and a cubit and a half
wide. 7Then he made two cherubim[r] out of hammered gold at the ends of the cover. 8He made one
cherub on one end and the second cherub on the other; at the two ends he made them of one piece
with the cover. 9The cherubim had their wings spread upward, overshadowing[s] the cover with them.
The cherubim faced each other, looking toward the cover.[t]

The Table

37:10-16pp — Ex 25:23-29

10They[e] made the table[u] of acacia wood — two cubits long, a cubit wide and a cubit and a half high.[f]
11Then they overlaid it with pure gold[v] and made a gold molding around it. 12They also made around it

36:18 [k] ver 13
36:35 [l] Ex 39:38; Mt 27:51; Lk 23:45; Heb 9:3
36:37 [m] Ex 27:16
37:1 [n] Ex 31:2 [o] Ex 30:6; 39:35; Dt 10:3
37:2 [p] ver 11,26
37:6 [q] Ex 26:34; 31:7; Heb 9:5
37:7 [r] Eze 41:18
37:9 [s] Heb 9:5 [t] Dt 10:3
37:10 [u] Heb 9:2
37:11 [v] ver 2

[a] *15* That is, about 45 feet long and 6 feet wide or about 14 meters long and 1.8 meters wide [b] *19* Possibly the hides of large aquatic mammals (see 35:7) [c] *21* That is, about 15 feet long and 2 1/4 feet wide or about 4.5 meters long and 68 centimeters wide [d] *1* That is, about 3 3/4 feet long and 2 1/4 feet wide and high or about 1.1 meters long and 68 centimeters wide and high; similarly in verse 6 [e] *10* Or *He*; also in verses 11-29 [f] *10* That is, about 3 feet long, 1 1/2 feet wide and 2 1/4 feet high or about 90 centimeters long, 45 centimeters wide and 68 centimeters high

work is described as "he" in the Hebrew (see the alternative reading in the NIV text notes on 37:10 (the first text note); 38:1; 39:2), presumably referring to Bezalel (37:1), who supervised the work (35:30–34).

37:1–9 Bezalel oversees the production of the ark. The main difference with the original instructions (25:10–20) relates to the verbal forms and the necessary postponement of the final part (25:21–22) until the tabernacle is initially set up (40:20–21). The ark reflects the Lord's presence and is the legitimate alternative to the idolatrous golden calf.

37:10–16 While not mentioned explicitly (see the first NIV text note on v. 10; see also note on 36:10), Bezalel also oversees the construction of the table.

37:14 [w] ver 27
37:17 [x] Heb 9:2; Rev 1:12
37:22 [y] ver 17; Nu 8:4
37:23 [z] Ex 40:4,25
37:25 [a] Ex 30:34-36; Lk 1:11; Heb 9:4; Rev 8:3 [b] Ex 27:2; Rev 9:13
37:27 [c] ver 14
37:28 [d] Ex 25:13
37:29 [e] Ex 31:11 [f] Ex 30:1,25; 39:38
38:2 [g] 2Ch 1:5
38:3 [h] Ex 31:9
38:8 [i] Ex 30:18; 40:7 [j] Dt 23:17; 1Sa 2:22; 1Ki 14:24

a rim a handbreadth[a] wide and put a gold molding on the rim. 13 They cast four gold rings for the table
and fastened them to the four corners, where the four legs were. 14 The rings[w] were put close to the rim
to hold the poles used in carrying the table. 15 The poles for carrying the table were made of acacia wood
and were overlaid with gold. 16 And they made from pure gold the articles for the table—its plates and
dishes and bowls and its pitchers for the pouring out of drink offerings.

The Lampstand

37:17-24pp — Ex 25:31-39

17 They made the lampstand[x] of pure gold. They hammered out its base and shaft, and made its flowerlike cups, buds and blossoms of one piece with them. 18 Six branches extended from the sides of the
lampstand—three on one side and three on the other. 19 Three cups shaped like almond flowers with
buds and blossoms were on one branch, three on the next branch and the same for all six branches
extending from the lampstand. 20 And on the lampstand were four cups shaped like almond flowers with
buds and blossoms. 21 One bud was under the first pair of branches extending from the lampstand, a
second bud under the second pair, and a third bud under the third pair—six branches in all. 22 The
buds and the branches were all of one piece with the lampstand, hammered out of pure gold.[y]
23 They made its seven lamps,[z] as well as its wick trimmers and trays, of pure gold. 24 They made the
lampstand and all its accessories from one talent[b] of pure gold.

The Altar of Incense

37:25-28pp — Ex 30:1-5

25 They made the altar of incense[a] out of acacia wood. It was square, a cubit long and a cubit wide
and two cubits high[c]—its horns[b] of one piece with it. 26 They overlaid the top and all the sides and
the horns with pure gold, and made a gold molding around it. 27 They made two gold rings[c] below the
molding—two on each of the opposite sides—to hold the poles used to carry it. 28 They made the poles
of acacia wood and overlaid them with gold.[d]
29 They also made the sacred anointing oil[e] and the pure, fragrant incense[f]—the work of a perfumer.

The Altar of Burnt Offering

38:1-7pp — Ex 27:1-8

38 They[d] built the altar of burnt offering of acacia wood, three cubits[e] high; it was square, five
cubits long and five cubits wide.[f] 2 They made a horn at each of the four corners, so that the
horns and the altar were of one piece, and they overlaid the altar with bronze.[g] 3 They made all its utensils[h] of bronze—its pots, shovels, sprinkling bowls, meat forks and firepans. 4 They made a grating for
the altar, a bronze network, to be under its ledge, halfway up the altar. 5 They cast bronze rings to hold
the poles for the four corners of the bronze grating. 6 They made the poles of acacia wood and overlaid
them with bronze. 7 They inserted the poles into the rings so they would be on the sides of the altar for
carrying it. They made it hollow, out of boards.

The Basin for Washing

8 They made the bronze basin[i] and its bronze stand from the mirrors of the women[j] who served at
the entrance to the tent of meeting.

[a] *12* That is, about 3 inches or about 7.5 centimeters [b] *24* That is, about 75 pounds or about 34 kilograms
[c] *25* That is, about 1 1/2 feet long and wide and 3 feet high or about 45 centimeters long and wide and 90 centimeters high [d] *1* Or *He*; also in verses 2-9 [e] *1* That is, about 4 1/2 feet or about 1.4 meters
[f] *1* That is, about 7 1/2 feet or about 2.3 meters long and wide

He follows the instructions of 25:23–29 but postpones placing the table in the tent and showcasing the bread of the Presence (25:30; 40:22–23).
37:17–24 See note on 25:31–40. Like the other items of sacred furniture, this is subsequently set up in the tent as God directed (40:24–25).
37:25–29 The construction of the incense altar is logically placed alongside other internal tabernacle furniture (cf. 30:1–5). Verse 29 mentions the anointing oil (30:22–33) and incense (30:34–38).
38:1–7 The focus shifts to constructing items placed outside the tent in the courtyard. Constructing the curtains for the courtyard immediately follows (vv. 9–20). For the altar of burnt offering and its usage, see notes on 27:1–8.
38:8 bronze basin. See note on 30:17–21. **mirrors.** Highly polished bronze was used in ancient times as a mirror. **women who served.** The service they performed is not explained.

The Courtyard

38:9-20pp — Ex 27:9-19

9Next they made the courtyard. The south side was a hundred cubits[a] long and had curtains of finely twisted linen, 10with twenty posts and twenty bronze bases, and with silver hooks and bands on the posts. 11The north side was also a hundred cubits long and had twenty posts and twenty bronze bases, with silver hooks and bands on the posts.

12The west end was fifty cubits[b] wide and had curtains, with ten posts and ten bases, with silver hooks and bands on the posts. 13The east end, toward the sunrise, was also fifty cubits wide. 14Curtains fifteen cubits[c] long were on one side of the entrance, with three posts and three bases, 15and curtains fifteen cubits long were on the other side of the entrance to the courtyard, with three posts and three bases. 16All the curtains around the courtyard were of finely twisted linen. 17The bases for the posts were bronze. The hooks and bands on the posts were silver, and their tops were overlaid with silver; so all the posts of the courtyard had silver bands.

18The curtain for the entrance to the courtyard was made of blue, purple and scarlet yarn and finely twisted linen — the work of an embroiderer. It was twenty cubits[d] long and, like the curtains of the courtyard, five cubits[e] high, 19with four posts and four bronze bases. Their hooks and bands were silver, and their tops were overlaid with silver. 20All the tent pegs[k] of the tabernacle and of the surrounding courtyard were bronze.

The Materials Used

21These are the amounts of the materials used for the tabernacle, the tabernacle of the covenant law,[l] which were recorded at Moses' command by the Levites under the direction of Ithamar[m] son of Aaron, the priest. 22(Bezalel[n] son of Uri, the son of Hur, of the tribe of Judah, made everything the LORD commanded Moses; 23with him was Oholiab[o] son of Ahisamak, of the tribe of Dan — an engraver and designer, and an embroiderer in blue, purple and scarlet yarn and fine linen.) 24The total amount of the gold from the wave offering used for all the work on the sanctuary[p] was 29 talents and 730 shekels,[f] according to the sanctuary shekel.[q]

25The silver obtained from those of the community who were counted in the census[r] was 100 talents[g] and 1,775 shekels,[h] according to the sanctuary shekel — 26one beka per person,[s] that is, half a shekel,[i] according to the sanctuary shekel,[t] from everyone who had crossed over to those counted, twenty years old or more,[u] a total of 603,550 men.[v] 27The 100 talents of silver were used to cast the bases[w] for the sanctuary and for the curtain — 100 bases from the 100 talents, one talent for each base. 28They used the 1,775 shekels to make the hooks for the posts, to overlay the tops of the posts, and to make their bands.

29The bronze from the wave offering was 70 talents and 2,400 shekels.[j] 30They used it to make the bases for the entrance to the tent of meeting, the bronze altar with its bronze grating and all its utensils, 31the bases for the surrounding courtyard and those for its entrance and all the tent pegs for the tabernacle and those for the surrounding courtyard.

[a] *9* That is, about 150 feet or about 45 meters [b] *12* That is, about 75 feet or about 23 meters [c] *14* That is, about 22 feet or about 6.8 meters [d] *18* That is, about 30 feet or about 9 meters [e] *18* That is, about 7 1/2 feet or about 2.3 meters [f] *24* The weight of the gold was a little over a ton or about 1 metric ton. [g] *25* That is, about 3 3/4 tons or about 3.4 metric tons; also in verse 27 [h] *25* That is, about 44 pounds or about 20 kilograms; also in verse 28 [i] *26* That is, about 1/5 ounce or about 5.7 grams [j] *29* The weight of the bronze was about 2 1/2 tons or about 2.4 metric tons.

38:20 [k]Ex 35:18
38:21 [l]Nu 1:50,53; 8:24; 9:15; 10:11; 17:7; 1Ch 23:32; 2Ch 24:6; Ac 7:44; Rev 15:5 [m]Nu 4:28,33
38:22 [n]Ex 31:2
38:23 [o]Ex 31:6
38:24 [p]Ex 30:16 [q]Ex 30:13; Lev 27:25; Nu 3:47; 18:16
38:25 [r]Ex 30:12
38:26 [s]Ex 30:12 [t]Ex 30:13 [u]Ex 30:14 [v]Ex 12:37; Nu 1:46
38:27 [w]Ex 26:19

38:9–20 The final step in creating the Lord's sacred tent is enclosing the courtyard with a perimeter fence. Again, these verses implement previous instructions (27:9–19), but they also supply additional information regarding the height of the entrance curtain (v. 18) and the silver caps on its posts (v. 19).

38:21–31 This inventory elucidates the more general description of the community's generosity, with which the account begins (35:4–29), and thus functions as a bracket around manufacturing the tabernacle and its furniture.

38:21 tabernacle of the covenant law. This unique description highlights another aspect of its covenantal significance: it serves as the vault for Israel's covenant obligations.

38:25–26 A census (see note on 30:11–16) taken at some undisclosed point prior to the tabernacle's construction provides the silver used in its posts. Unlike the freewill offerings in 35:4–29, this is a compulsory poll tax for each adult male (v. 26). The huge amount collected (v. 25) tallies with the 603,550 men mentioned in v. 26 (see 12:37 and note).

39:1 [x]Ex 35:23 [y]Ex 35:19 [z]ver 41; Ex 28:2
39:7 [a]Lev 24:7; Jos 4:7
39:8 [b]Lev 8:8
39:14 [c]Rev 21:12

The Priestly Garments

39 From the blue, purple and scarlet yarn[x] they made woven garments for ministering in the sanctuary.[y] They also made sacred garments[z] for Aaron, as the LORD commanded Moses.

The Ephod

39:2-7pp — Ex 28:6-14

2 They[a] made the ephod of gold, and of blue, purple and scarlet yarn, and of finely twisted linen. 3 They hammered out thin sheets of gold and cut strands to be worked into the blue, purple and scarlet yarn and fine linen — the work of skilled hands. 4 They made shoulder pieces for the ephod, which were attached to two of its corners, so it could be fastened. 5 Its skillfully woven waistband was like it — of one piece with the ephod and made with gold, and with blue, purple and scarlet yarn, and with finely twisted linen, as the LORD commanded Moses.

6 They mounted the onyx stones in gold filigree settings and engraved them like a seal with the names of the sons of Israel. 7 Then they fastened them on the shoulder pieces of the ephod as memorial[a] stones for the sons of Israel, as the LORD commanded Moses.

The Breastpiece

39:8-21pp — Ex 28:15-28

8 They fashioned the breastpiece[b] — the work of a skilled craftsman. They made it like the ephod: of gold, and of blue, purple and scarlet yarn, and of finely twisted linen. 9 It was square — a span[b] long and a span wide — and folded double. 10 Then they mounted four rows of precious stones on it. The first row was carnelian, chrysolite and beryl; 11 the second row was turquoise, lapis lazuli and emerald; 12 the third row was jacinth, agate and amethyst; 13 the fourth row was topaz, onyx and jasper.[c] They were mounted in gold filigree settings. 14 There were twelve stones, one for each of the names of the sons of Israel, each engraved like a seal with the name of one of the twelve tribes.[c]

15 For the breastpiece they made braided chains of pure gold, like a rope. 16 They made two gold filigree settings and two gold rings, and fastened the rings to two of the corners of the breastpiece. 17 They fastened the two gold chains to the rings at the corners of the breastpiece, 18 and the other ends of the chains to the two settings, attaching them to the shoulder pieces of the ephod at the front. 19 They made two gold rings and attached them to the other two corners of the breastpiece on the inside edge next to the ephod. 20 Then they made two more gold rings and attached them to the bottom of the shoulder pieces on the front of the ephod, close to the seam just above the waistband of the ephod. 21 They tied the rings of the breastpiece to the rings of the ephod with blue cord, connecting it to the waistband so that the breastpiece would not swing out from the ephod — as the LORD commanded Moses.

Other Priestly Garments

39:22-31pp — Ex 28:31-43

22 They made the robe of the ephod entirely of blue cloth — the work of a weaver — 23 with an opening in the center of the robe like the opening of a collar,[d] and a band around this opening, so that it would not tear. 24 They made pomegranates of blue, purple and scarlet yarn and finely twisted linen around the hem of the robe. 25 And they made bells of pure gold and attached them around the hem between the pomegranates. 26 The bells and pomegranates alternated around the hem of the robe to be worn for ministering, as the LORD commanded Moses.

[a] *2* Or *He*; also in verses 7, 8 and 22 [b] *9* That is, about 9 inches or about 23 centimeters
[c] *13* The precise identification of some of these precious stones is uncertain. [d] *23* The meaning of the Hebrew for this word is uncertain.

39:1–31 *The Priestly Garments Made.* The focus once again shifts (see ch. 28) from manufacturing the tabernacle to the special garments of its priests. As previously noted (see note on 36:10), the skilled artisans apparently work under the supervision of Bezalel (see NIV text note on v. 2). The refrain "as the LORD commanded Moses" occurs eight times (vv. 1,5,7,21,26,29,31,32): Israel successfully completes the component parts and complies with the Lord's design.

39:3 Explains how they accomplish the unusual blend of fabrics and gold that 28:6–8 commands.

27For Aaron and his sons, they made tunics of fine linen[d]—the work of a weaver— 28and the turban[e] of fine linen, the linen caps and the undergarments of finely twisted linen. 29The sash was made
of finely twisted linen and blue, purple and scarlet yarn—the work of an embroiderer—as the LORD
commanded Moses.
30They made the plate, the sacred emblem, out of pure gold and engraved on it, like an inscription
on a seal: HOLY TO THE LORD. 31Then they fastened a blue cord to it to attach it to the turban, as the LORD
commanded Moses.

Moses Inspects the Tabernacle

39:32-41pp — Ex 35:10-19

32So all the work on the tabernacle, the tent of meeting, was completed. The Israelites did everything
just as the LORD commanded Moses.[f] 33Then they brought the tabernacle to Moses: the tent and all its
furnishings, its clasps, frames, crossbars, posts and bases; 34the covering of ram skins dyed red and the
covering of another durable leather[a] and the shielding curtain; 35the ark of the covenant law[g] with its
poles and the atonement cover; 36the table with all its articles and the bread of the Presence; 37the pure
gold lampstand[h] with its row of lamps and all its accessories, and the olive oil for the light; 38the gold
altar,[i] the anointing oil, the fragrant incense, and the curtain[j] for the entrance to the tent; 39the bronze
altar with its bronze grating, its poles and all its utensils; the basin with its stand; 40the curtains of the
courtyard with its posts and bases, and the curtain for the entrance to the courtyard;[k] the ropes and
tent pegs for the courtyard; all the furnishings for the tabernacle, the tent of meeting; 41and the woven
garments worn for ministering in the sanctuary, both the sacred garments for Aaron the priest and the
garments for his sons when serving as priests.
42The Israelites had done all the work just as the LORD had commanded Moses.[l] 43Moses inspected
the work and saw that they had done it just as the LORD had commanded. So Moses blessed[m] them.

Setting Up the Tabernacle

40 Then the LORD said to Moses: 2"Set up the tabernacle, the tent of meeting,[n] on the first day of
the first month.[o] 3Place the ark[p] of the covenant law in it and shield the ark with the curtain.
4Bring in the table and set out what belongs on it.[q] Then bring in the lampstand[r] and set up its lamps.
5Place the gold altar[s] of incense in front of the ark of the covenant law and put the curtain at the entrance to the tabernacle.
6"Place the altar of burnt offering in front of the entrance to the tabernacle, the tent of meeting;
7place the basin[t] between the tent of meeting and the altar and put water in it. 8Set up the courtyard
around it and put the curtain at the entrance to the courtyard.
9"Take the anointing oil and anoint[u] the tabernacle and everything in it; consecrate it and all its
furnishings, and it will be holy. 10Then anoint the altar of burnt offering and all its utensils; consecrate[v]
the altar, and it will be most holy. 11Anoint the basin and its stand and consecrate them.
12"Bring Aaron and his sons to the entrance to the tent of meeting and wash them with water.[w]
13Then dress Aaron in the sacred garments,[x] anoint him and consecrate[y] him so he may serve me as
priest. 14Bring his sons and dress them in tunics. 15Anoint them just as you anointed their father, so
they may serve me as priests. Their anointing will be to a priesthood that will continue throughout their
generations.[z]" 16Moses did everything just as the LORD commanded him.

a 34 Possibly the hides of large aquatic mammals

39:27 [d] Lev 6:10
39:28 [e] Ex 28:4
39:32 [f] ver 42-43; Ex 25:9
39:35 [g] Ex 30:6
39:37 [h] Ex 25:31
39:38 [i] Ex 30:1-10 [j] Ex 36:35
39:40 [k] Ex 27:9-19
39:42 [l] Ex 25:9
39:43 [m] Lev 9:22,23; Nu 6:23-27; 2Sa 6:18; 1Ki 8:14,55; 2Ch 30:27
40:2 [n] Nu 1:1 [o] ver 17; Ex 12:2
40:3 [p] ver 21; Nu 4:5; Ex 26:33
40:4 [q] Ex 25:30 [r] ver 22-25; Ex 26:35
40:5 [s] ver 26; Ex 30:1
40:7 [t] ver 30; Ex 30:18
40:9 [u] Ex 30:26; Lev 8:10
40:10 [v] Ex 29:36
40:12 [w] Lev 8:1-13
40:13 [x] Ex 28:41 [y] Lev 8:12
40:15 [z] Ex 29:9; Nu 25:13

39:32–43 *Moses Inspects the Work.* After they complete all the preliminary work as instructed (v. 32), Moses inspects it to ensure that everything is manufactured according to the Lord's explicit design (25:9). Once satisfied, Moses blesses the people (v. 43), echoing God's blessing of the seventh day after his work of creation (Gen 2:3). Along with 1:7, v. 43 would mark the events recorded in Exodus as a very significant stage in God's plan for a new creation.

40:1–33 *Setting Up the Tabernacle.* With everything now ready, Moses sets up the tabernacle and consecrates it (i.e., sets it apart) for sacred use, along with its furnishings and priests.

40:2 first day of the first month. Almost a year after the exodus and nine months after Israel arrived at Sinai.

40:12–15 Lev 8 describes this ordination service in detail.

40:16–33 Verses 17–35 concisely summarize events that transpire over several days.

40:16 as the LORD commanded. This refrain occurs eight times regarding the making of the priestly garments (see note on 39:1–31), and the repeated refrain appears eight more times regarding the setting up of the tabernacle (vv. 16,19,21,23,25,27,29,32). The repetition emphasizes that Israel obeys the Lord's commands in contrast with their earlier

40:17 [a]Nu 7:1 [b]ver 2
40:20 [c]Ex 16:34; 25:16; Dt 10:5; 1Ki 8:9; Heb 9:4
40:21 [d]Ex 26:33
40:22 [e]Ex 26:35
40:23 [f]ver 4
40:24 [g]Ex 26:35
40:25 [h]ver 4; Ex 25:37
40:26 [i]ver 5; Ex 30:6
40:27 [j]Ex 30:7
40:28 [k]Ex 26:36
40:29 [l]ver 6; Ex 29:38-42
40:30 [m]ver 7
40:32 [n]Ex 30:20
40:33 [o]Ex 27:9 [p]ver 8
40:34 [q]Nu 9:15-23; 1Ki 8:12
40:35 [r]1Ki 8:11; 2Ch 5:13-14
40:36 [s]Nu 9:17-23; 10:13; Ne 9:19
40:38 [t]Ex 13:21; Nu 9:15; 1Co 10:1

17 So the tabernacle[a] was set up on the first day of the first month[b] in the second year. 18 When Moses
set up the tabernacle, he put the bases in place, erected the frames, inserted the crossbars and set up
the posts. 19 Then he spread the tent over the tabernacle and put the covering over the tent, as the LORD
commanded him.
20 He took the tablets of the covenant law[c] and placed them in the ark, attached the poles to the
ark and put the atonement cover over it. 21 Then he brought the ark into the tabernacle and hung the
shielding curtain[d] and shielded the ark of the covenant law, as the LORD commanded him.
22 Moses placed the table[e] in the tent of meeting on the north side of the tabernacle outside the curtain 23 and set out the bread[f] on it before the LORD, as the LORD commanded him.
24 He placed the lampstand[g] in the tent of meeting opposite the table on the south side of the tabernacle 25 and set up the lamps[h] before the LORD, as the LORD commanded him.
26 Moses placed the gold altar[i] in the tent of meeting in front of the curtain 27 and burned fragrant
incense on it, as the LORD commanded[j] him.
28 Then he put up the curtain[k] at the entrance to the tabernacle. 29 He set the altar of burnt offering
near the entrance to the tabernacle, the tent of meeting, and offered on it burnt offerings and grain
offerings,[l] as the LORD commanded him.
30 He placed the basin[m] between the tent of meeting and the altar and put water in it for washing,
31 and Moses and Aaron and his sons used it to wash their hands and feet. 32 They washed whenever they
entered the tent of meeting or approached the altar,[n] as the LORD commanded Moses.
33 Then Moses set up the courtyard[o] around the tabernacle and altar and put up the curtain[p] at the
entrance to the courtyard. And so Moses finished the work.

The Glory of the LORD

34 Then the cloud[q] covered the tent of meeting, and the glory of the LORD filled the tabernacle. 35 Moses could not enter the tent of meeting because the cloud had settled on it, and the glory of the LORD
filled the tabernacle.[r]
36 In all the travels of the Israelites, whenever the cloud lifted from above the tabernacle, they would
set out;[s] 37 but if the cloud did not lift, they did not set out—until the day it lifted. 38 So the cloud[t] of
the LORD was over the tabernacle by day, and fire was in the cloud by night, in the sight of all the Israelites during all their travels.

---

apostasy involving the golden calf (ch. 32). The tabernacle's architecture and the design and location of each item of furniture precisely follow the divine blueprint (25:40).

40:17–38 The word "tabernacle" occurs 13 times in these verses. It refers to the most significant part, the tent of meeting (v. 21), rather than to the entire enclosure, which includes the courtyard (v. 33).

40:30–32 Ritual washing symbolizes that humans must be pure before they can enter the presence of a holy God (cf. 3:5; 19:14). See 1 Cor 6:11; Heb 10:22; Rev 7:14; 21:27. See "The Tabernacle," p. 167.

40:34–38 *The Glory of the Lord.* The cloud that previously descended on top of Mount Sinai (24:15–18) now descends on the tabernacle and fills it with the glory of the Lord, barring access even to Moses (v. 35). Thereafter the cloud dictated Israel's travel itinerary (vv. 36–38; cf. 13:21). All this not only seals the tabernacle construction with the Lord's approval but, more important, it answers Moses' petition (33:15–18) and concretely expresses the ultimate goal of the exodus: Israel is to be a holy nation in relationship with God, a kingdom of priests who serve in his presence (29:44–46). Thus, a book that begins with God's apparent absence ends with his glorious and ongoing presence in the midst of his redeemed people.

INTRODUCTION TO
LEVITICUS

The end of Exodus details the construction of the tabernacle (Exod 25 – 40). The first part of Numbers recounts the arrangements made for Israel's journey from Sinai to the promised land with the tabernacle in the midst of the camp (Num 1 – 9). Leviticus stands between these two, listing the regulations for the tabernacle of the Lord's presence and for the Israelite community that surrounded it.

AUTHOR AND DATE

The date and authorship of Leviticus are bound up with that of the Pentateuch as a whole, especially Exodus through Deuteronomy (see Introduction to the Pentateuch, p. 12). Exodus and Deuteronomy explicitly state that Moses himself wrote down certain substantial portions of the Pentateuch (e.g., Exod 17:14; 24:4,7; 34:27; Deut 31:9,19,22,24 – 26). There is no such statement anywhere in Leviticus, but there does exist a constant stream of references throughout the book stating that God spoke these regulations and stories to and through Moses (sometimes along with Aaron); see, e.g., 1:1; 4:1; 5:14; 6:1,8,19,24; 7:22,28. Moreover, the final notices refer to Moses as the mediator of the revelation at Sinai (26:46; 27:34; cf. 16:34b).

MAJOR THEOLOGICAL THEMES

The theological focal point of Leviticus is God's presence in the midst of Israel. Sinai was "the mountain of God" (see Exod 3:1 and note; 4:27; 18:5; 24:13), and the tabernacle was his tent. As the tent of the Lord, the tabernacle went with the Israelites in the midst of their tents. Along with God's presence, of course, comes the need for holiness, purity, and atonement, all of which are also key theological themes in Leviticus.

The Lord's Presence

After almost a year at Sinai, the tabernacle was erected (Exod 40) and the glory cloud of the Lord so filled the tabernacle that Moses could not even enter the tent (Exod 40:34 – 35). Therefore, the Lord spoke the tabernacle sacrificial regulations in Lev 1 – 7 to Moses "from the tent of meeting" (1:1). The glory cloud of the Lord's presence (with fire in it by night) had led them from Egypt to Sinai (Exod 13:20 – 22; 14:19 – 20,24; 16:10), and now it would lead them from Sinai through the wilderness and eventually to the promised land (Exod 40:36 – 38). Num 1 – 9 recounts the preparations of the camp and concludes in 9:15 – 23 with an extended reference back to the pillar of cloud and fire occupying the tabernacle in Exod 40:34 – 38. When the glory cloud finally lifted up over the tabernacle and set out for the promised land, the camp followed (Num 10:11 – 13). Centuries later the same glory cloud of the Lord's presence would occupy Solomon's temple (1 Kgs 8:10 – 11; 2 Chr 5:11 – 14; 7:1 – 3).

The Lord said in the blessings of the covenant, "I will put my dwelling place among you, and I will not abhor you. I will walk among you and be your God, and you will be my people" (26:11 – 12). His presence among them was a key factor in their identity as the people of God. It was a promise Moses had depended on since the burning bush (Exod 3:12) and through some especially difficult times (e.g., the golden calf incident in Exod 33:15 – 16).

Unfortunately, by the time of the Babylonian captivity, the Israelites had so desecrated and defiled the temple that the glory cloud (presence) of the Lord actually departed from it, abandoning it to destruction (Ezek 8:2–4; 10:3–4,18–19; 11:22–25).

The NT develops the themes of the tabernacle and the temple and God's glory and presence in them by noting their fulfillment in Jesus Christ, in the church, and in the believer. John 1:14 says, "The Word became flesh and made his dwelling [i.e., pitched his tent or tabernacled] among us. We have seen his glory, the glory of the one and only Son, who came from the Father, full of grace and truth." And Jesus himself prayed to the Father just before he went to the cross that the world would also see his glorious presence in the unity of believers (John 17:22–23a).

Paul develops this theme on the level of both the individual Christian (1 Cor 6:18–20; 2 Cor 6:14–18) and the Christian community, the body of believers. He treats the latter most extensively in Eph 2–3 (cf. 1 Cor 3:9–17). We are all "fellow citizens ... [and] members of [God's] household ... a holy temple in the Lord ... being built together to become a dwelling in which God lives by his Spirit" (Eph 2:19–22). In Eph 3:14–21 Paul returns to the theme of the church as the temple of the Holy Spirit filled with God's glory. Paul wants believers to be "filled to the measure of all the fullness of God" (Eph 3:19; recalls the glory cloud filling the tabernacle and temple) so that there will be "glory in the church and in Christ Jesus throughout all generations, for ever and ever! Amen" (Eph 3:21). See "Temple," p. 2652.

Holiness and Purity

After the Lord consumed Nadab and Abihu with fire on the tabernacle inauguration day (10:1–2), he instructed the priests to "distinguish between the holy and the common, between the unclean and the clean" (10:10; cf. Ezek 22:26; 42:20; 44:23; 48:14–15). The two polarities—holy versus common (i.e., holiness) and clean versus unclean (i.e., purity)—are core issues in the theology of Leviticus precisely because the Lord was present, dwelling with them in the tabernacle. Neither holiness nor purity was limited to the tabernacle, of course, since the people themselves were a "holy nation" (Exod 19:6), and holiness and purity were to be maintained in the community as well, but the main concern was that no impurity from the community accrue to the tabernacle (Lev 15:31). (See "Holiness and Purity," this page, and the explanation that follows.) Along with holiness and purity, 10:17 adds "atonement" as a third essential element: the sin offering "is most holy" because "it was given to you [the priests] to take away the guilt of the community by making atonement for them before the LORD." Atonement was the means by which they would deal with problems that arose in the realms of holiness and purity.

HOLINESS AND PURITY

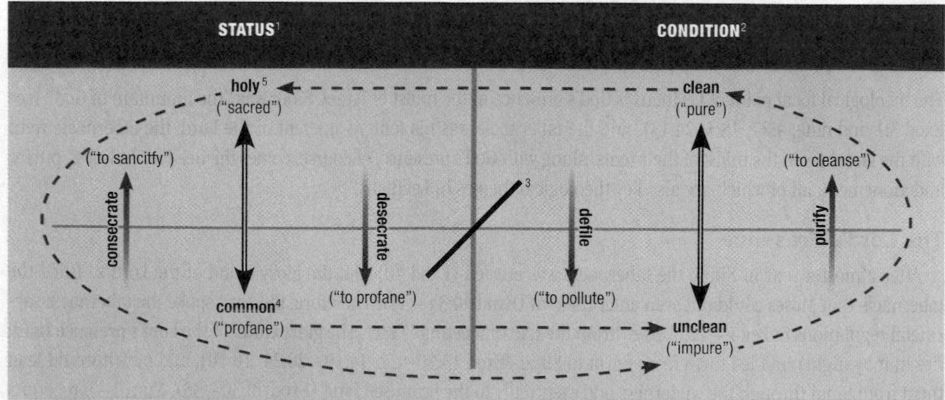

Numerals 1–5 on the chart above correspond to (1) the "status" of a person, place, or thing as either "holy" or "common" (see the left side of the chart; Lev 10:10a), (2) the "condition" of a person, place, or thing as either "clean" or "unclean" (see the right side of the chart; Lev 10:10b), (3) the main concern that nothing unclean come into direct contact with that which is holy (the diagonal bar through the middle of the chart blocking the way between holy and unclean), and (4–5) whenever either a holy or a common person becomes unclean they must first ritually "purify" (= "cleanse") their body before they approach that which is holy (see the arrowed lines going from both holy and common to unclean and from there to clean).

Jebel Musa (traditional site of Mount Sinai) from the southwest.

Todd Bolen/www.BiblePlaces.com

As for holiness (see "holy" versus "common" in 10:10a), since God is most holy and he dwelled in the tabernacle, the central place of holiness in Israel was the tabernacle, and the holy priests officiated there (8:10–15,30; 10:3,12–13,17–18; 16:19,24). In this sense and on this level, the priests had a holy status that the common people as a whole did not have. The noun "common" is sometimes translated "profane," but the latter word has negative connotations in English that are not necessarily included in the Hebrew term. There was nothing essentially negative about being a common person, for example. It was the normal status of regular people. However, if someone or something was holy, to treat him, her, or it as if they were common would "profane" them (sometimes translated "defile," "degrade," "desecrate," or "treat with contempt"; see 19:8; 21:4,7,9,12,14–15,23; 22:9,15–16; Ezek 7:21–22; 20:9,14,22; 23:39). Holiness was "graded" so that, e.g., the innermost cella (chamber) of the tabernacle (where the ark of the covenant was located) was the "Most Holy Place," whereas the next cella leading into it was the "Holy Place" (Exod 26:33–35; cf. Lev 16:2,16–17; see "Tabernacle Floor Plan," p. 192). Again, the Aaronic priests were holy as compared to the common Israelites, but the common Israelites were holy as compared to non-Israelites (Exod 19:6). So, e.g., the Lord commanded his people, "Be holy because I, the LORD your God, am holy" (19:2), so no one should "degrade" their daughter by making her a prostitute (19:29).

Purity (see "unclean" versus "clean" in 10:10b), on the other hand, was essential for approaching this holy God in whose presence they dwelled. This was a matter of the person's condition, i.e., whether their body was ritually clean or unclean. If unclean, they must not enter the tabernacle lest they pollute it with uncleanness. This was most important (15:31). If a person was unclean, they should also avoid contact with other holy things lest they pollute them (e.g., 7:19–21). They should even avoid contact with other (holy or common) people lest uncleanness spread in the camp. Moreover, if they made any object unclean, a clean person who touched it became unclean (e.g., 13:45–46; 15:1–12). Avoidance of such people or objects was intended to prevent spreading uncleanness throughout the camp (cf. Hag 2:11–13). There was nothing essentially wrong with becoming "unclean" as long as one handled it properly. In fact, becoming unclean could hardly be avoided. Even priests became unclean (e.g., they could marry and have sexual intercourse, which would make them unclean for that day, 15:16–18). An unclean priest could not enter the tabernacle to worship or serve there. However, even in their unclean condition their status as holy was maintained. They did not need to be reconsecrated to serve as a priest again the next day. Similarly, a common person could be either clean or unclean, but they could only enter the tabernacle in a clean condition.

Probably the best way to understand the ritual purification laws is to recall the manifest visible presence of God in the OT tabernacle and later in the temple (see Introduction: Major Theologial Themes [The Lord's Presence]). This place of visible presence was precisely the focus of the priestly worldview and the theology with which the book of Leviticus is concerned. The ritual purity laws correspond to the visible presence of the Lord in the tabernacle. Since God was visibly present, the people needed to be ritually pure in his presence.

In the NT church, God is present with his people in a different way—by the individual and corporate indwelling of the Holy Spirit (see Introduction: Major Theological Themes [The Lord's Presence]). There is no tent or building over which the cloud of God's presence appears in a pillar of cloud by day and a pillar of fire by night. The concern for purity shifts to the spiritual level since that is the level of the presence. Thus, we have passages like 1 Pet 1:22, "Now that you have purified yourselves [lit. "your souls"] by obeying the truth so that you have sincere love for each other, love one another deeply, from the heart" (cf. Matt 15:1–20). The purity needs to function on the same level as the presence. Thus, in the OT system there were physical washings. Of course, where God is present in a visible way, he is also present spiritually. Thus, the physical cleansing terminology is sometimes used for spiritual purity and cleansing even in the OT (e.g., Ps 51:2,6–7,10,12,16–17). Purity and holiness terminology therefore continues from the OT into the NT. Compare, e.g., how the woman was made "ceremonially clean" from her flow of blood after childbirth in 12:7 (cf. Luke 2:22) with Peter's statement in the Jerusalem council: "He did not discriminate between us and them [i.e., Jews and Gentiles], for he purified their hearts by faith" (Acts 15:9). The ritual procedures for physical purity do not come through into the NT, but purity of the heart does (cf. Heb 9:13–14; 1 Pet 1:22). See "Holiness," p. 2676.

Offerings, Sacrifices, and Atonement

The offerings and sacrifices were above all a means of worshiping the God who dwelled in the midst of Israel. Leviticus is concerned with the details of which offerings Israelites should make to God and how they should offer them. Atonement was the means God designed for them to deal properly with their sins and impurities and thereby avoid violating God's holiness and purity. Lev 15:31 is particularly clear on this matter: "You must keep the Israelites separate from things that make them unclean, so they will not die in their uncleanness for defiling my dwelling place, which is among them." The next chapter (ch. 16), highlights the importance of the Day of Atonement for cleansing the tabernacle from pollutions.

The English word "atonement" comes from combining the preposition "at" with Middle English "onement" (i.e., bringing together as one). Basically, it is concerned with making reconciliation. The Hebrew verb itself (*kipper*) means primarily to purge or wipe away, but the overall effect of doing this was indeed reconciliation. Therefore, the Hebrew verb and other forms of the same word group can mean "to ransom" (= to make a payment to appease; e.g., ***kōper*** ["ransom"], ***kipper*** ["to atone"], and ***kippurîm*** ["atonement"] in Exod 30:11–16). The same Hebrew verb appears numerous times in the sin and guilt offering regulations (4:1—6:7) precisely because the actual focus of those two offerings was on making atonement for the various kinds of holiness and purity issues that would arise.

The purpose of the Day of Atonement was to cleanse the tabernacle. It was the culmination of the sacrificial procedures for the year that went before it. There were three sin offering animals on that day: a bull for the priests and two goats for the sin offering of the people; one of the goats was slaughtered, and the other was sent away as a scapegoat (16:5–10; both goats are included in the "sin offering" in v. 5 even though the scapegoat was not to be slaughtered). The slaughtered sin offerings for the priests and the people purged the tabernacle itself from its impurities all the way into the Most Holy Place, where the ark of the covenant was behind the veil, and out to the burnt offering altar near the entrance to the tabernacle (16:11–19; cf. 16:32–33; see "Tabernacle Floor Plan," this page). Then the high

TABERNACLE FLOOR PLAN

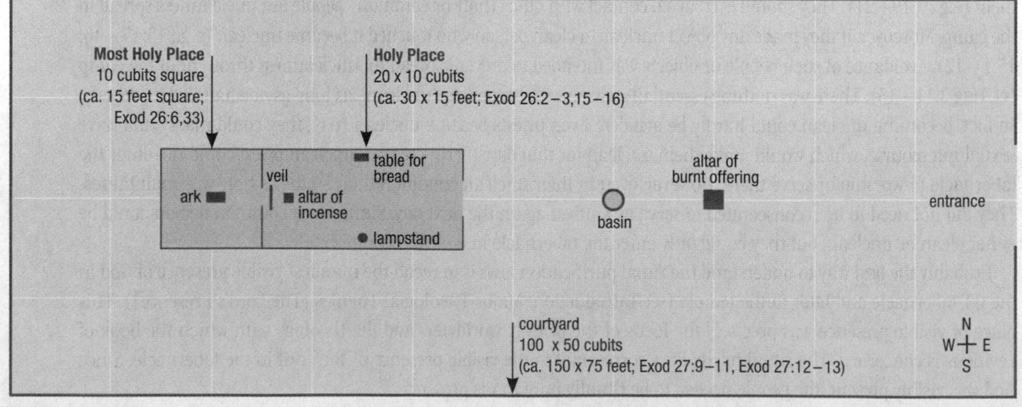

priest loaded the iniquities of the whole community onto the live scapegoat so that it could take them as far away as possible from the Israelite community, thus removing the iniquities into the wilderness, never to return (16:20–22). Both the tabernacle and the community, therefore, had a new start for the upcoming year.

In the NT sacrifice of Jesus Christ, he himself made atonement for those who put their faith in him as their Savior (Rom 3:24–26). The priests applied the blood of the OT sacrifices to the tabernacle on earth (see "Tabernacle Floor Plan," p. 192), but the blood of Jesus was applied to the tabernacle in heaven, the very throne room of God (Heb 9:6–14,23–24). Furthermore, in the OT the people had to continue offering their sacrifices year after year, but in the NT Jesus offered himself as the sacrifice on our behalf "once for all" (Heb 9:25—10:4). Jesus is the ultimate "sin offering" (Rom 8:3) and the new covenant ratification sacrifice (Luke 22:19–20). The point is this: Jesus fulfilled all the sacrificial requirements for us.

Many of the basic principles of the sacrificial system apply not only to Christ but also to the life of the Christian. If we are going to be like Christ, we need to give ourselves as sacrifices, like he did. The burnt offering, e.g., is the primary background for Rom 12:1: "Offer your bodies as a living sacrifice, holy and pleasing to God—this is your true and proper worship." We are "a holy priesthood, offering spiritual sacrifices acceptable to God through Jesus Christ" (1 Pet 2:5b). Our worship of God and our good works for him are our "sacrifices" (Heb 13:15–16; cf. Phil 4:18). Paul also uses sacrificial terminology to describe the fruits of his ministry of the gospel (Rom 15:16; Phil 2:17). See "Sacrifice," p. 2656.

OUTLINE

Leviticus divides naturally into two major sections, chs. 1–16 and chs. 17–27. The first half focuses primarily on regulations for the tabernacle; the second half focuses on the importance of purity in the community that surrounded the tabernacle. Ch. 16 binds the two halves together by concluding the first half and leading into the second.

- **I. Laws of the Tabernacle (1:1—16:34)**
  - A. Sacrifices and Offerings (1:1—7:38)
    - 1. Description of the Rituals (1:1—6:7)
    - 2. Distribution of the Sacrificial Portions (6:8—7:38)
  - B. The Ordination of Aaron and His Sons (8:1–36)
  - C. The Priests Begin Their Ministry (9:1—10:20)
  - D. Purity Regulations (11:1—15:33)
  - E. The Day of Atonement (16:1–34)
- **II. Laws of the Community (17:1—27:34)**
  - A. Eating Blood Forbidden (17:1–16)
  - B. Laws of Community Holiness (18:1—26:46)
    - 1. Unlawful Sexual Relations, Various Laws, and Punishments for Sin (18:1—20:27)
    - 2. Rules for the Priests and Unacceptable Sacrifices (21:1—22:33)
    - 3. The Appointed Festivals, Sabbath Year, and Year of Jubilee (23:1—25:55)
    - 4. Reward for Obedience and Punishment for Disobedience (26:1–46)
  - C. Redeeming What Is the Lord's (27:1–34)

LEVITICUS

1:1 [a]Ex 19:3; 25:22 [b]Nu 7:89
1:2 [c]Lev 22:18-19
1:3 [d]Ex 12:5; Dt 15:21; Heb 9:14; 1Pe 1:19 [e]Lev 17:9

The Burnt Offering

1 The LORD called to Moses[a] and spoke to him from the tent of meeting.[b] He said, 2"Speak to the
Israelites and say to them: 'When anyone among you brings an offering to the LORD, bring as your
offering an animal from either the herd or the flock.[c]
3" 'If the offering is a burnt offering from the herd, you are to offer a male without defect.[d] You must
present it at the entrance to the tent[e] of meeting so that it will be acceptable to the LORD. 4You are to lay your

1:1—16:34 *Laws of the Tabernacle.* Chs. 1–16 focus primarily on regulations for the tabernacle in the midst of the community and the importance of purity in the community that surrounded the tabernacle. Chs. 1–7 serve as a manual for the various kinds of sacrificial procedures. Chs. 8–10 recount the consecration of the priests and the inauguration of their service in the tabernacle. Chs. 11–15 detail the purity regulations for the community, and ch. 16 concludes the section with the Day of Atonement procedures.

1:1—7:38 *Sacrifices and Offerings.* Chs. 1–7 detail (1) the regulations for the five main types of offerings in the tabernacle (burnt, grain, fellowship, sin, and guilt offerings [1:3—6:7; 1:1–2 introduces the whole section]; see "Major OT Offerings and Sacrifices," p. 197, which describes the basic regulations concerning them) and (2) the specific regulations for the priests and their portions from the offerings (6:8—7:38).

1:1—6:7 *Description of the Rituals.* After an introduction to the section (1:1–2), there are three main units: (1) the burnt, grain, and fellowship offerings (1:3—3:17); (2) the sin offering (4:1—5:13); and (3) the guilt offering (5:14—6:7). The first three sacrifices are grouped together as a unit because there is no new introductory note in 2:1 and 3:1 as there is in 4:1 and 5:14 ("The LORD said to Moses").

1:1 from the tent of meeting. Directly connects back to the end of Exodus. The glory cloud of the Lord's presence had so completely filled the tent that Moses could not enter (Exod 40:34–35). **tent of meeting.** The tabernacle (Exod 26). "Tabernacle" refers to the tent as a dwelling place, while "tent of meeting" focuses on the same tent as a place where the Israelites could meet with the Lord. It was set up in the middle of the camp (Num 2:2) and served as the Lord's residence until the temple was built in the days of Solomon (1 Kgs 8:4–6; 2 Chr 5:5–7). It is not to be confused with the other "tent of meeting" that stood outside the camp (Exod 33:7–8); this other "tent of meeting" was for revelation, not sacrifice, and the Lord did not dwell in this tent but came and spoke to Moses at the entrance (see Exod 33:9–11 and note on 33:7). There is some uncertainty about whether certain other passages refer to this tent outside the camp or the tabernacle in the midst of the camp (e.g., Num 11:24–26,30; 12:4–5; and perhaps Deut 31:14–15).

1:2 Speak to the Israelites and say to them. Moses was to speak not just to the priests but also to the Israelites as a whole (cf. 10:11). These were not secret texts intended only for the priests, as is the case with many ancient ritual texts. **offering.** The Hebrew word, pronounced "korban," refers to "something brought near." Jesus used this Hebrew word when he rebuked Jewish religious leaders for allowing offerings to be used as an excuse for not providing for one's parents (see Mark 7:11–13 and note). **animal.** A general word for four-footed herd or flock animals. This verse does not mention birds in spite of the regulations for them in vv. 14–17 probably because they are not pasture animals and were allowed to be offered largely as a concession to the poor (e.g., 5:7–10; 12:8; 14:21–32). **herd.** Cattle (vv. 3,5). **flock.** Sheep or goats (v. 10).

1:3–17 This section on the burnt offering divides into three subsections: burnt offerings (1) from the herd (vv. 3–9), (2) from the flock (vv. 10–13), and (3) of birds (vv. 14–17). See "Major OT Offerings and Sacrifices," p. 197; cf. 6:8–13. A burnt offering was offered every morning and evening in the tabernacle (Exod 29:38–42; Num 28:3–4); this was doubled on the Sabbath day (Num 28:9–10), and extra burnt offerings were offered on festival days (Num 28–29). The NT reflects the background of the burnt offering when it urges believers to "offer [their] bodies" to God as a "living sacrifice, holy and pleasing to God"—the kind God will find acceptable—which is their "true and proper worship" (Rom 12:1).

1:3 male. A bull, not a female cow, was the first option for the burnt offering (cf. v. 10). A male was required perhaps because it was more dominant than the female, and perhaps also because the male was more expendable, not being able to produce milk or offspring. A bull was often offered by more prominent members of the community (vv. 3–9); a common person would offer a sheep or goat (vv. 10–13), and a poor person would offer a bird (vv. 14–17). **without defect ... acceptable to the LORD.** It would be offensive to offer a defective animal to the Lord since such an animal was less valuable and showed disrespect (e.g., Mal 1:6–14; cf. 1 Pet 1:19). **entrance to the tent of meeting.** At the east end. The slaughtering took place in the northeast section (v. 11). The waste heap was in the southeast section (v. 16). See "Tabernacle Floor Plan," p. 192.

1:4 lay your hand on the head. The offerer identified the offering as belonging to him and, at the same time, dedicated it for the purpose(s) for which he brought it. Some say this action transferred the offerer's sin to the offering, but that would defile the altar and tabernacle, the opposite of atonement (15:31). The Day of Atonement hand-laying was very different, and that animal was not offered on the altar (see 16:21,22 and notes).

hand on the head[f] of the burnt offering, and it will be accepted on your behalf to make atonement[g] for you.
5You are to slaughter[h] the young bull before the LORD, and then Aaron's sons the priests shall bring the blood
and splash it against the sides of the altar[i] at the entrance to the tent of meeting. 6You are to skin[j] the burnt
offering and cut it into pieces. 7The sons of Aaron the priest are to put fire on the altar and arrange wood[k]
on the fire. 8Then Aaron's sons the priests shall arrange the pieces, including the head and the fat,[l] on the
wood that is burning on the altar. 9You are to wash the internal organs and the legs with water, and the
priest is to burn all of it on the altar.[m] It is a burnt offering, a food offering, an aroma pleasing to the LORD.[n]
10" 'If the offering is a burnt offering from the flock, from either the sheep or the goats,[o] you are to
offer a male without defect. 11You are to slaughter it at the north side of the altar before the LORD, and
Aaron's sons the priests shall splash its blood against the sides of the altar.[p] 12You are to cut it into pieces, and the priest shall arrange them, including the head and the fat, on the wood that is burning on
the altar. 13You are to wash the internal organs and the legs with water, and the priest is to bring all of
them and burn them on the altar. It is a burnt offering, a food offering, an aroma pleasing to the LORD.
14" 'If the offering to the LORD is a burnt offering of birds, you are to offer a dove or a young pigeon.[q]
15The priest shall bring it to the altar, wring off the head and burn it on the altar; its blood shall be
drained out on the side of the altar.[r] 16He is to remove the crop and the feathers[a] and throw them down
east of the altar where the ashes[s] are. 17He shall tear it open by the wings, not dividing it completely,[t]
and then the priest shall burn it on the wood[u] that is burning on the altar. It is a burnt offering, a food
offering, an aroma pleasing to the LORD.

1:4 [f]Ex 29:10,15; Lev 3:2 [g]2Ch 29:23-24
1:5 [h]Lev 3:2,8 [i]Heb 12:24; 1Pe 1:2
1:6 [j]Lev 7:8
1:7 [k]Lev 6:12
1:8 [l]ver 12
1:9 [m]Ex 29:18 [n]ver 13; Ge 8:21; Nu 15:8-10; Eph 5:2
1:10 [o]ver 3; Ex 12:5
1:11 [p]ver 5
1:14 [q]Ge 15:9; Lev 5:7; Lk 2:24
1:15 [r]Lev 5:9
1:16 [s]Lev 6:10
1:17 [t]Ge 15:10 [u]Lev 5:8
2:1 [v]Lev 6:14-18 [w]Nu 15:4
2:2 [x]Lev 5:11 [y]Lev 6:15; Isa 66:3

The Grain Offering

2 " 'When anyone brings a grain offering[v] to the LORD, their offering is to be of the finest flour.
They are to pour olive oil[w] on it, put incense on it 2and take it to Aaron's sons the priests. The
priest shall take a handful of the flour[x] and oil, together with all the incense,[y] and burn this as a

[a] *16* Or *crop with its contents*; the meaning of the Hebrew for this word is uncertain.

atonement. See Introduction: Major Theological Themes (Offerings, Sacrifices, and Atonement). The atonement in the burnt offering ritual was about ransom (payment) and propitiation (appeasement), not expiation (removal of sin or impurity, for which see especially the sin offering [ch. 4]). The blood, representing the life of the animal (17:11), was splashed all around on the sides of the altar (v. 5) as part of offering the whole animal on the altar (vv. 8–9). The offerings that made atonement were the burnt, sin, and guilt offerings, not the fellowship offering or grain offering, except when the latter was a sin offering concession to the poor (5:11–13).

1:5 You. The offerer. **blood.** Especially important because it represented the life of the animal (17:11). In this way, not only the dead carcass but also the life of the animal was given over to the Lord as a substitute for the life of the offerer. Jesus Christ became the sacrificial mediator of the new covenant when he shed his blood and thus gave his life for those who would believe in him (Heb 9:11–15,22).

1:6 skin. Given to the priest who performed the priestly duties for the particular burnt offering (7:8). Not all priests actively served at the altar at the same time.

1:8 The offerer slaughtered the offering (v. 5), but the priests placed the parts of the slaughtered animal on the altar. Only the priests—not ordinary Israelites—could come into direct contact with the altar.

1:9 food offering. The whole carcass of the burnt offering was consumed on the altar as a food offering (but not the hide, see v. 6 and note). The other offerings were only partially consumed on the altar. Some take this term (Hebrew *ʾiššeh*) to mean "an offering [made] by fire" because it is thought to derive from the Hebrew word for "fire" (Hebrew *ʾēš*). However, the way the same term is used in other ancient texts and the fact that in the Bible it sometimes refers to offerings that are not burned up on the altar (e.g., 24:9) suggests the NIV rendering. **an aroma pleasing to the LORD.** Suits the purpose(s) of the offering, which was to present a pleasing food gift to the Lord (cf. Gen 8:21), even though the Lord himself does not "eat" food (Ps 50:7–15).

1:14–17 The burnt offering procedures for birds naturally differ from those for herd and flock animals (vv. 3–13) because birds are smaller and have a different kind of anatomy.

1:14 young pigeon. Either a young pigeon or perhaps one from the various species of pigeons.

1:16 crop. The enlarged part of a bird's gullet that serves as a pouch for storing food before full digestion. **feathers.** See NIV text note. The whole expression could also mean "remove its entrails by [cutting off] its tail feathers." **east of the altar.** Where they took the waste from slaughtered animals (e.g., the crop) and the ashes from the burnt offering after the animal was consumed on the altar (6:10–11).

1:17 not dividing it completely. Birds were not split in two or cut up into various parts like the other animals were when they were placed on the altar. They were so small that the whole carcass could easily burn up without such severing.

2:1 grain offering. See "Major OT Offerings and Sacrifices," p. 197; cf. 6:14–23; 7:9–10. The instructions for the grain offering divide into four subsections: (1) general regulations (vv. 1–3), (2) kinds of grain offerings (vv. 4–10), (3) yeast and salt (vv. 11–13), and (4) firstfruits grain offerings (vv. 14–16). A grain offering generally accompanied a burnt or fellowship offering to supplement the meat with bread (cf. Num 15:1–10; 28:12–13; 29:3–4); a drink offering of wine (Lev 23:13) was also offered, thus completing the "food offering" to the Lord (see note on 1:9). It could make atonement either along with the burnt offering (14:20) or alone as a sin offering for the poor (5:11–13). In some instances the Hebrew word for grain offering is used for either a meat or a grain offering to God (Gen 4:3–5), a gift to another person (Gen 32:13,20–21), or tribute to a king (Judg 3:17–18). **finest flour.** Finely ground wheat flour as opposed to barley; but also possibly "grits," not so finely ground. **incense.** Frankincense, a white gum substance from trees of the genus *Boswellia,* native to Sheba in South Arabia.

2:2 all the incense. They did not eat incense. Its purpose here was to

2:2 [z]ver 9,16; Lev 5:12; 6:15; 24:7; Ac 10:4
2:3 [a]ver 10; Lev 6:16; 10:12,13
2:4 [b]Ex 29:2
2:7 [c]Lev 7:9
2:9 [d]ver 2 [e]Ex 29:18; Lev 6:15
2:10 [f]ver 3
2:11 [g]Ex 23:18; 34:25; Lev 6:16
2:12 [h]Lev 7:13; 23:10
2:13 [i]Nu 18:19; Eze 43:24
2:14 [j]Lev 23:10
2:16 [k]ver 2
3:1 [l]Lev 7:11-34 [m]Lev 1:3; 22:21
3:2 [n]Ex 29:10,15 [o]Lev 1:5
3:3 [p]Ex 29:13
3:5 [q]Lev 7:29-34 [r]Ex 29:13,38-42
3:6 [s]ver 1
3:7 [t]Lev 17:8-9
3:8 [u]ver 2; Lev 1:5

memorial[a] portion[z] on the altar, a food offering, an aroma pleasing to the LORD. 3The rest of the grain offering belongs to Aaron and his sons;[a] it is a most holy part of the food offerings presented to the LORD.

4" 'If you bring a grain offering baked in an oven, it is to consist of the finest flour: either thick loaves made without yeast and with olive oil mixed in or thin loaves made without yeast and brushed with olive oil.[b] 5If your grain offering is prepared on a griddle, it is to be made of the finest flour mixed with oil, and without yeast. 6Crumble it and pour oil on it; it is a grain offering. 7If your grain offering is cooked in a pan,[c] it is to be made of the finest flour and some olive oil. 8Bring the grain offering made of these things to the LORD; present it to the priest, who shall take it to the altar. 9He shall take out the memorial portion[d] from the grain offering and burn it on the altar as a food offering, an aroma pleasing to the LORD.[e] 10The rest of the grain offering belongs to Aaron and his sons;[f] it is a most holy part of the food offerings presented to the LORD.

11" 'Every grain offering you bring to the LORD must be made without yeast,[g] for you are not to burn any yeast or honey in a food offering presented to the LORD. 12You may bring them to the LORD as an offering of the firstfruits,[h] but they are not to be offered on the altar as a pleasing aroma. 13Season all your grain offerings with salt. Do not leave the salt of the covenant[i] of your God out of your grain offerings; add salt to all your offerings.

14" 'If you bring a grain offering of firstfruits[j] to the LORD, offer crushed heads of new grain roasted in the fire. 15Put oil and incense on it; it is a grain offering. 16The priest shall burn the memorial portion[k] of the crushed grain and the oil, together with all the incense, as a food offering presented to the LORD.

The Fellowship Offering

3 " 'If your offering is a fellowship offering,[l] and you offer an animal from the herd, whether male or female, you are to present before the LORD an animal without defect.[m] 2You are to lay your hand on the head[n] of your offering and slaughter it[o] at the entrance to the tent of meeting. Then Aaron's sons the priests shall splash the blood against the sides of the altar. 3From the fellowship offering you are to bring a food offering to the LORD: the internal organs and all the fat[p] that is connected to them, 4both kidneys with the fat on them near the loins, and the long lobe of the liver, which you will remove with the kidneys. 5Then Aaron's sons[q] are to burn it on the altar on top of the burnt offering[r] that is lying on the burning wood; it is a food offering, an aroma pleasing to the LORD.

6" 'If you offer an animal from the flock as a fellowship offering[s] to the LORD, you are to offer a male or female without defect. 7If you offer a lamb, you are to present it before the LORD,[t] 8lay your hand on its head and slaughter it[u] in front of the tent of meeting. Then Aaron's sons shall splash its blood against the sides of the altar. 9From the fellowship offering you are to bring a food offering to the LORD: its fat, the entire fat tail cut off close to the backbone, the internal organs and all the fat that is connected to them, 10both kidneys with the fat on them near the loins, and the long lobe of the liver,

[a] 2 Or *representative*; also in verses 9 and 16

give off a fine fragrance to the Lord when burnt on the altar along with the handful of grain and oil. **memorial portion.** Intended to memorialize the offerer's specific reason for bringing the offering to the Lord.
2:3 most holy. Only the consecrated priests could eat the rest of the grain offering, and they were to eat it within the sanctuary courtyard. It was their payment for performing the service at the altar on behalf of the people (cf. 6:16–18).
2:4 thick loaves. Either "ring-shaped" or perhaps "perforated."
2:5 prepared on a griddle. Producing something like a pancake made on a plate of iron.
2:7 cooked in a pan. Suggests that the olive oil in the pan was used for deep-frying, perhaps like making a donut.
2:11 yeast. Anything having a "leavening" effect on the bread.
2:12 firstfruits. Given to the priests as payment for their service to the Lord, so they were not offered on the altar (Num 18:12–13).
2:13 salt of the covenant. Appears only two other places in the OT: for the Lord's covenant with the priests (Num 18:19) and his covenant with David (2 Chr 13:5). **salt.** Its character suggests the enduring nature of the covenant-bond between the Lord and his people.

3:1 your offering is a fellowship offering. See "Major OT Offerings and Sacrifices," p. 197; cf. 7:11–34. Either "sacrifice offering" or "fellowship offering" can designate the fellowship offering, or they can occur in combination. Both terms refer to offerings of which the worshipers ate the meat as part of a banquet in fellowship with God and one another. The fellowship offering occurs throughout the OT for eating meals together as part of making covenants, whether between God and people (Exod 24:5–11) or between two (groups of) people (Gen 31:51–54). The term for the fellowship offering is related to the well-known Hebrew word for "peace" or "well-being" (*šālôm*), so this offering is often called the "peace offering," which is appropriate for making, renewing, and practicing covenant relationships. This is the kind of covenant sacrifice offering Jesus alluded to at the Last Supper (Luke 22:19–20; 1 Cor 11:24–25; cf. Jer 31:31–37). Compare, e.g., what Moses says about the blood in Exod 24:8 with what Jesus says about his own blood in Luke 22:20. **male or female.** Unlike the burnt offering, in which only a male animal was acceptable (1:3,10). **without defect.** See note on 1:3.

MAJOR OLD TESTAMENT OFFERINGS AND SACRIFICES

NAME	PRIMARY REFERENCES	MATERIALS	ASSOCIATED OFFERING(S)	BLOOD MANIPULATION	PORTION(S) BURNT ON THE ALTAR	PORTION(S) EATEN	PURPOSE(S)
Burnt offering	**Lev 1**; Gen 8:20–21; Lev 6:8–13; 22:18–20; Num 15:1–16	(1) Male of the herd or flock (2) Dove or pigeon (Lev 1)	(1) Regularly accompanied by a grain offering and libation (Num 15:1–16) (2) Offered with fellowship and/or sin offerings (Exod 24:5; Lev 5:7–10; Num 6:14)	Splashed against the sides of the altar (Lev 1:5)	Complete carcass except: (1) the hide of herd animals (Lev 7:8) (2) "the crop and the feathers" of birds (Lev 1:16)	None	A gift to make "atonement … an aroma pleasing to the LORD" (Lev 1:4,9): (1) a votive or freewill offering (Lev 22:18–20) (2) for prayer and supplication (1 Sam 7:9–10) (3) for regular offerings (Num 28–29)
Grain offering (the same Hebrew term is used as a general word for "offering" in Gen 4:3–5 and elsewhere)	**Lev 2**; 6:14–23; 7:9–14; Num 15:4,6,9,11–16	(1) Grain that is raw, baked, cooked, fried, or otherwise prepared plus oil and incense (Lev 2:1–7) with salt (Lev 2:13), but without yeast (leaven) or honey (Lev 2:11) (2) On a few esp. solemn occasions, without oil or incense (Lev 5:11–13 [as a sin offering for the poor]; Num 5:15)	Usually offered with a libation as a supplement to the burnt or fellowship offering (Lev 7:12–14; Num 15:1–16)	None	(1) Normally its "memorial portion" of incense, oil, and a small portion of flour (Lev 2:2) (2) The whole grain offering of the priests (Lev 6:23)	(1) Worshipers: none (except the extra loaves made with yeast in Lev 7:13–14) (2) Priests: all that is left over from the worshiper's grain offering after the memorial portion (Lev 2:3; 6:16–18; 10:12–13)	(1) Accompanied a burnt or fellowship offering to supplement the meat with bread (see also the libation; Num 15:1–16) (2) Made atonement, along with the burnt offering (Lev 14:20), or alone as a sin offering for the poor (Lev 5:11–13)
Fellowship offering (or "peace" offering)	**Lev 3**; Exod 24:5–8; Lev 7:11–34; 17:10–14; 22:21–30; Num 15:1–16	Male or female of the herd, flock, or goats (Lev 3)	Grain offering and libation (Num 15:1–16)	(1) Splashed against the sides of the altar (Lev 3:2) (2) For ordination (fellowship) offering for priests, applied to the right ear lobe, thumb, and big toe (Exod 29:19–21; Lev 8:22–24)	All the fat, the kidneys, and the "long lobe of the liver" (Lev 3:3–5); for sheep, also the fat tail (Lev 3:9)	(1) Worshipers: all the meat (Lev 7:15–21) except the portions that go to the priests (2) Priests: the "breast" as a "wave offering" for all the priests and their families (Lev 7:30–31); and the "right thigh" as a "contribution" for the officiating priest and his family (Lev 7:32–34)	(1) Primarily to enact fellowship between God and people (fat and blood go to the Lord on the altar; meat is eaten by the people) (2) Specifically, it could serve as: a "thank offering" (Lev 7:11–15), an "offering" to fulfill a "vow" (Lev 7:16–18), or a "freewill offering" (Lev 7:16–18)
Sin offering	**Lev 4:1—5:13**; 6:24–30 (cf. vv. 17–23); 8:14–17; 10:16–20; 16:11–22	(1) Bull of the herd for a priest or the whole community (Lev 4:3–21) (2) Male goat for a community leader (Lev 4:22–26) (3) Female goat or lamb for a commoner (Lev 4:27–35; 5:6); (4) Two doves or two pigeons or a grain offering for a poor commoner (Lev 5:7–13)	Normally offered first in a series followed by a burnt offering (Lev 5:7–11; 16:11–25), and possibly also a fellowship offering (Lev 9:8–22)	(1) For a priest or the whole community, "sprinkled" seven times in front of the curtain of the sanctuary and applied to the horns of the incense altar (Lev 4:3,6–7,17–18) (2) For a leader or commoner, applied to the horns of the burnt offering altar (Lev 4:22,25,30,34)	Same as the fellowship offering (Lev 4:8–10)	(1) Worshipers: none (2) Priests: the meat of the sin offering of a leader or commoner (Lev 6:24–29) but *not* the meat of the sin offering of a priest or the whole community (Lev 4:12,21; 6:30)	To be forgiven of sin or cleansed from ritual physical impurity, making atonement (Lev 4:20,26,31; 12:7–8), in order to consecrate or maintain the purity of the tabernacle and community (Lev 8:15; 15:31; 16:29–34)
Guilt offering	**Lev 5:14—6:7**; 7:1–7; 14:12–18; 19:20–22; Num 5:5–10; 6:12; 1 Sam 6:3–9,17–18	Normally a ram of the flock, but convertible into silver/money (Lev 5:15)	Offered alone or in a series with sin, burnt and/or grain offerings (Lev 14:12–20)	(1) Splashed against the sides of the altar (Lev 7:2) (2) Applied to the right ear lobe, thumb, and big toe (Lev 14:12–18)	Same as the fellowship offering (Lev 7:3–5)	(1) Worshipers: none (2) Priests: same as the sin offering (see above; Lev 7:7)	To atone for violating the Lord's holy things or the property of others in the community (Lev 5:1—6:7), usually accompanied by restitution—replacing what was violated plus one fifth its value (Lev 5:16; 6:5)

3:11 [v]ver 5 [w]ver 16; Lev 21:6,17
3:13 [x]Ex 24:6
3:16 [y]1Sa 2:16
3:17 [z]Lev 6:18; 17:7 [a]Ge 9:4; Lev 7:25-26; 17:10-16; Dt 12:16; Ac 15:20
4:2 [b]Lev 5:15-18; Ps 19:12; Heb 9:7
4:3 [c]ver 14; Ps 66:15 [d]Lev 9:2-22; Heb 9:13-14
4:4 [e]Lev 1:3

which you will remove with the kidneys. [11]The priest shall burn them on the altar[v] as a food offering[w]
presented to the LORD.

[12]" 'If your offering is a goat, you are to present it before the LORD, [13]lay your hand on its head and
slaughter it in front of the tent of meeting. Then Aaron's sons shall splash[x] its blood against the sides
of the altar. [14]From what you offer you are to present this food offering to the LORD: the internal organs
and all the fat that is connected to them, [15]both kidneys with the fat on them near the loins, and the
long lobe of the liver, which you will remove with the kidneys. [16]The priest shall burn them on the altar
as a food offering, a pleasing aroma. All the fat is the LORD's.[y]

[17]" 'This is a lasting ordinance for the generations to come,[z] wherever you live: You must not eat
any fat or any blood.[a]' "

The Sin Offering

4 The LORD said to Moses, [2]"Say to the Israelites: 'When anyone sins unintentionally[b] and does what
is forbidden in any of the LORD's commands—

[3]" 'If the anointed priest sins, bringing guilt on the people, he must bring to the LORD a young bull[c]
without defect as a sin offering[a][d] for the sin he has committed. [4]He is to present the bull at the entrance
to the tent of meeting before the LORD.[e] He is to lay his hand on its head and slaughter it there before the

[a] *3* Or *purification offering*; here and throughout this chapter

3:2 lay your hand on the head of your offering. See note on 1:4. **entrance.** See note on 1:3.
3:11 as a food offering. This does not mean that God was actually eating the "food" (Ps 50:7–15).
3:17 You must not eat any fat or any blood. A permanent prohibition repeated in 7:22–27, also in the context of regulations for the fellowship offering. This is the only kind of offering of which regular worshipers could eat some of the meat, so it was the only offering that required accompanying warnings against eating the fat or blood. **fat.** Considered the finest part of the animal. Even "the finest of wheat" (Ps 147:14) is literally "the fat of wheat" (cf. Gen 45:18; Num 18:12). Because they preferred fat as the finest part of the animal, the corrupt sons of Eli came to the sacrifice "even before the fat was burned" and took their priestly portion from it raw with the fat (1 Sam 2:15). **blood.** Not eaten because it stands for the life of the animal, and life belongs only to God (see 17:11 and note; cf. Gen 9:4–5; Deut 12:23–24).
4:1—5:13 This section is a single, long, complex unit of regulations for the "sin offering," sometimes translated "purification offering" because its purpose was to purify. This section includes a short introduction (4:1–2), the sin offering for the priest (4:3–12), the sin offering for the whole Israelite community (4:13–21), the sin offering for the tribal leader (4:22–26), the sin offering for any other member of the community (4:27–35), a list of certain kinds of sins involved (5:1–6), and sin offerings for the poor (5:7–13). The Hebrew word for "sin offering" is the same as the Hebrew word for "sin." Which rendering is intended can only be determined by the context. See, e.g., 4:3, where the priest is to bring "a sin offering [Hebrew *ḥaṭṭā'ṯ*] for the sin [*ḥaṭṭā'ṯ*] he has committed." The sin offering consecrated (i.e., "de-sinned") or restored the purity of the tabernacle and/or community (8:15; 16:29–34). The Israelites were to avoid contaminating the tabernacle (i.e., the tent of God's special presence in their midst) with sin or impurity lest God's wrath come against them (15:31). The sin offering made atonement to gain either forgiveness of sin (4:20,26,31,35; 5:10,13) or purification from uncleanness (12:7–8; 14:20,31; 15:15,30; 16:19). In the latter case it was not a matter of sin in any moral sense but a matter of ceremonial impurity (see Introduction: Major Theological Themes [Holiness and Purity]). See "Major OT Offerings and Sacrifices," p. 197.

In the NT Jesus is sometimes referred to as the sin offering for the people of the new covenant (see Introduction: Major Theological Themes [Offerings, Sacrifices, and Atonement]). Rom 8:3 says God sent Jesus "to be a sin offering," or to be sin (see NIV text note); and 2 Cor 5:21 says God made Jesus "to be sin," or "to be a sin offering," for us (see NIV text note).
4:1 The LORD said to Moses. Introduces the section (see note on 1:1—6:7) that ends at 5:13.
4:2 unintentionally. This word occurs regularly in the sections on the sin offering (vv. 13,22,27) and guilt offering (5:15,18). Num 15:27–31 contrasts sinning "unintentionally" with sinning "defiantly" (or "with a raised hand"); those sinning defiantly raise their fist, so to speak, and presumptuously defy the Lord. Such a person "blasphemes the LORD" (Num 15:30), so they must be "cut off from their people" (see note on 7:20,21). They have "despised the LORD's word and broken his commands" (Num 15:31). One could not bring an offering for such sin. Unintentional sin was another matter. It was straying from the Lord's commands either through ignorance, inattention, or human frailty, not through defiance or blasphemy (see 22:14–16 and note on 22:14). Forgiveness was available for unintentional sin through the sin offering. **what is forbidden in any of the LORD's commands.** Prohibitive commands in the Mosaic law—what one must *not* do. Some would restrict these commands to those given in the tabernacle and community regulations here in Leviticus. The term "any," however, suggests that it would also include the numerous prohibitions that the Lord had already pronounced at Sinai—whether, e.g., in the Ten Commandments (Exod 20:1–17) or in the Book of the Covenant (Exod 20:22—23:33). To violate any of them and not deal with them according to the regulations given in the law itself would be to sin against either God, the people, or both. This would generate impurity that would defile the tabernacle. For example, a person sinned if they did not come forward in a legal dispute in which they were a witness, if they handled uncleanness improperly, or if they did not fulfill a vow; these kinds of violation required confession and a sin offering (see 5:1–6 and notes there).
4:3 anointed priest. Refers either to only the high priest (cf. 8:12; Exod 29:7) or to any of the anointed priests (cf. Exod 40:15). **bringing guilt on the people.** The effect on the people as a whole when the anointed priest sinned. All priests sinned. This is why they needed to bring a sin offering for themselves, e.g., on the Day of Atonement (16:6,11–14). The only exception is Jesus Christ, our sinless high priest (Heb 4:15), who offered himself once for all so that "sacrifice for sin is no longer necessary" (Heb 10:18; cf. Heb 9:11—10:18). **he must bring.** Burnt, grain, and fellowship offerings were voluntary on some occasions (see 7:12–18 and note) but required on other occasions (see 16:23–25). The sin and guilt offerings were always required.

LORD. 5 Then the anointed priest shall take some of the bull's blood[f] and carry it into the tent of meeting. 6 He is to dip his finger into the blood and sprinkle some of it seven times before the LORD, in front of the curtain of the sanctuary. 7 The priest shall then put some of the blood on the horns of the altar of fragrant incense that is before the LORD in the tent of meeting. The rest of the bull's blood he shall pour out at the base of the altar[g] of burnt offering[h] at the entrance to the tent of meeting. 8 He shall remove all the fat[i] from the bull of the sin offering — all the fat that is connected to the internal organs, 9 both kidneys with the fat on them near the loins, and the long lobe of the liver, which he will remove with the kidneys[j] — 10 just as the fat is removed from the ox[a] sacrificed as a fellowship offering. Then the priest shall burn them on the altar of burnt offering. 11 But the hide of the bull and all its flesh, as well as the head and legs, the internal organs and the intestines[k] — 12 that is, all the rest of the bull — he must take outside the camp[l] to a place ceremonially clean,[m] where the ashes are thrown, and burn it there in a wood fire on the ash heap.

13 " 'If the whole Israelite community sins unintentionally[n] and does what is forbidden in any of the LORD's commands, even though the community is unaware of the matter, when they realize their guilt 14 and the sin they committed becomes known, the assembly must bring a young bull[o] as a sin offering[p] and present it before the tent of meeting. 15 The elders of the community are to lay their hands on the bull's head[q] before the LORD, and the bull shall be slaughtered before the LORD. 16 Then the anointed priest is to take some of the bull's blood[r] into the tent of meeting. 17 He shall dip his finger into the blood and sprinkle it before the LORD[s] seven times in front of the curtain. 18 He is to put some of the blood on the horns of the altar that is before the LORD[t] in the tent of meeting. The rest of the blood he shall pour out at the base of the altar of burnt offering at the entrance to the tent of meeting. 19 He shall remove all the fat[u] from it and burn it on the altar, 20 and do with this bull just as he did with the bull for the sin offering. In this way the priest will make atonement[v] for the community, and they will be forgiven.[w] 21 Then he shall take the bull outside the camp and burn it as he burned the first bull. This is the sin offering for the community.[x]

22 " 'When a leader[y] sins unintentionally[z] and does what is forbidden in any of the commands of the LORD his God, when he realizes his guilt 23 and the sin he has committed becomes known, he must bring as his offering a male goat without defect. 24 He is to lay his hand on the goat's head and slaughter it at

a *10* The Hebrew word can refer to either male or female.

4:5 [f]Lev 16:14
4:7 [g]ver 34; Lev 8:15 [h]ver 18,30; Lev 5:9; 9:9; 16:18
4:8 [i]Lev 3:3-5
4:9 [j]Lev 3:4
4:11 [k]Ex 29:14; Lev 9:11; Nu 19:5
4:12 [l]Heb 13:11 [m]Lev 6:11
4:13 [n]ver 2; Lev 5:2-4, 17; Nu 15:24-26
4:14 [o]ver 3 [p]ver 23,28
4:15 [q]Lev 1:4; 8:14,22; Nu 8:10
4:16 [r]ver 5
4:17 [s]ver 6
4:18 [t]ver 7
4:19 [u]ver 8
4:20 [v]Heb 10:10-12 [w]Nu 15:25
4:21 [x]Lev 16:5,15
4:22 [y]Nu 31:13 [z]ver 2

4:5 The manipulation of the blood for the sin offering was different than that for the burnt, fellowship, and guilt offerings (1:5; 3:2; 7:2). **into the tent of meeting.** Into the tent itself, not just to the altar of burnt offering that was out near the entrance to the tabernacle complex (see "Tabernacle Floor Plan," p. 192).

4:6 seven times. The number seven suggests complete purification (cf. 8:11; 14:7; 16:14,19; Num 19:4), like the cycle of seven days completes the week (Exod 20:9–10). **curtain.** Separated the front room of the tabernacle (the Holy Place) from the back room (the Most Holy Place), where the ark of the covenant was. The curtain stretched not only in front of the ark but also, like a canopy, over the top of the ark.

4:7 horns. Protruded from the altar's four corners (Exod 30:1–3). **altar of fragrant incense.** Stood right in front of the curtain just opposite the ark of the covenant, which was on the other side of the curtain (see "Tabernacle Floor Plan," p. 192). Sprinkling the blood in front of the curtain (v. 6) along with smearing it on the horns of the altar signified purification of the entire tent from the ritual pollution caused by the priest's sin.

4:12 outside the camp. When the sin offering was offered for the priest or for the Israelite community as a whole (vv. 3–21), the blood was applied in the Holy Place (vv. 5–7,16–18) and the body of the animal was burned up in a fire outside the camp, not eaten by the priests (6:30). The meat of the sin offering for a regular Israelite or a leader was most holy (see note on 2:3), so it would be eaten by the priests (6:24–26; see note on 4:25). As our sin offering, Jesus was crucified outside Jerusalem (Heb 13:11–12). **a place ceremonially clean.** A place where there was nothing ritually unclean, such as carcasses of dead animals.

4:13 the whole Israelite community. Includes all the people and the priests as well. For this reason the blood was applied inside the tent of meeting as it was for the priest (cf. vv. 5–7 with vv. 16–18; see note on v. 16).

4:16 into the tent of meeting. See note on v. 13 and recall that the priests would enter into the tent of meeting every day for ministry purposes (24:1–4). The blood was therefore applied here because the ritual impurity caused by the sin of the priests had reached this far into the tabernacle (contrast vv. 25,30,34; see note on v. 25).

4:22–23 when he realizes his guilt and the sin he has committed becomes known. There are difficulties here in the translation, which are reflected in the diverse renderings of modern English versions. First, the NIV renders the end of v. 22 as "realizes his guilt"; another possible translation would be "incurs guilt" (i.e., by committing the sin). Second, the Hebrew text at the beginning of v. 23 may suggest that this is a second possible situation in which the leader knows about his guilt through being informed by someone else or through being convicted of his guilt by legal action. Cf. vv. 27–28.

4:22 leader. Perhaps one of the elders of a clan or tribe (Exod 16:22; Num 1:16,44; Josh 9:15,18).

4:23 a male goat. This was a less expensive offering than the bull brought for the priest or the whole Israelite community (vv. 3,14), but it was more valuable than the female goat or lamb brought for a regular member of the community (vv. 28,32).

4:25 [a] ver 7,18,30,34; Lev 9:9
4:26 [b] Lev 5:10
4:27 [c] ver 2; Nu 15:27
4:28 [d] ver 23 [e] ver 3
4:29 [f] ver 4,24 [g] Lev 1:4
4:30 [h] ver 7
4:31 [i] Ge 8:21
4:32 [j] ver 28
4:33 [k] ver 29
4:34 [l] ver 7
4:35 [m] ver 26,31
5:1 [n] Pr 29:24 [o] ver 17
5:2 [p] Lev 11:11,24-40; Dt 14:8
5:3 [q] Nu 19:11-16
5:4 [r] Nu 30:6,8
5:5 [s] Lev 16:21; 26:40; Nu 5:7; Pr 28:13

the place where the burnt offering is slaughtered before the LORD. It is a sin offering. 25 Then the priest
shall take some of the blood of the sin offering with his finger and put it on the horns of the altar of
burnt offering and pour out the rest of the blood at the base of the altar.[a] 26 He shall burn all the fat on
the altar as he burned the fat of the fellowship offering. In this way the priest will make atonement for
the leader's sin, and he will be forgiven.[b]

27 " 'If any member of the community sins unintentionally[c] and does what is forbidden in any
of the LORD's commands, when they realize their guilt 28 and the sin they have committed becomes
known, they must bring as their offering[d] for the sin they committed a female goat[e] without defect.
29 They are to lay their hand on the head[f] of the sin offering[g] and slaughter it at the place of the burnt
offering. 30 Then the priest is to take some of the blood with his finger and put it on the horns of the
altar of burnt offering[h] and pour out the rest of the blood at the base of the altar. 31 They shall remove
all the fat, just as the fat is removed from the fellowship offering, and the priest shall burn it on the
altar as an aroma pleasing to the LORD.[i] In this way the priest will make atonement for them, and
they will be forgiven.

32 " 'If someone brings a lamb as their sin offering, they are to bring a female without defect.[j] 33 They
are to lay their hand on its head and slaughter it for a sin offering at the place where the burnt offering
is slaughtered.[k] 34 Then the priest shall take some of the blood of the sin offering with his finger and
put it on the horns of the altar of burnt offering and pour out the rest of the blood at the base of the
altar.[l] 35 They shall remove all the fat, just as the fat is removed from the lamb of the fellowship offering,
and the priest shall burn it on the altar[m] on top of the food offerings presented to the LORD. In this way
the priest will make atonement for them for the sin they have committed, and they will be forgiven.

5 " 'If anyone sins because they do not speak up when they hear a public charge to testify[n] regarding
something they have seen or learned about, they will be held responsible.[o]

2 " 'If anyone becomes aware that they are guilty—if they unwittingly touch anything ceremonially unclean (whether the carcass of an unclean animal, wild or domestic, or of any unclean creature
that moves along the ground)[p] and they are unaware that they have become unclean, but then they
come to realize their guilt; 3 or if they touch human uncleanness[q] (anything that would make them
unclean) even though they are unaware of it, but then they learn of it and realize their guilt; 4 or if
anyone thoughtlessly takes an oath[r] to do anything, whether good or evil (in any matter one might
carelessly swear about) even though they are unaware of it, but then they learn of it and realize their
guilt— 5 when anyone becomes aware that they are guilty in any of these matters, they must confess[s]

4:25 on the horns of the altar of burnt offering. For the first time in the chapter the blood is manipulated on the altar of burnt offering near the entrance to the tabernacle complex, not at the altar of incense inside the tabernacle tent itself (contrast vv. 5–6,16–17; see notes on vv. 12,16). The meat was therefore eaten by the priests (6:24–29).

4:27–28 See note on vv. 22–23.

4:31 an aroma pleasing to the LORD. Like burning the meat and fat of the burnt offering (1:9,13,17; see note on 1:9) and like the fat of the fellowship offering (3:5,16). This is significant because, in principle, it tells us that the sin offering procedure included within it both a "sin offering" (the blood manipulation) and a "burnt offering" (the burning of the fat). This is confirmed by the sin offering of the poor, who could bring two birds, "one for a sin offering and the other for a burnt offering" (5:7). **make atonement.** Both the blood manipulation and the burning of the fat contributed to making atonement (see note on 1:4).

5:1 do not speak up when they hear a public charge to testify. The person had "seen" or otherwise "learned about" the case but did not come forward as a witness as they were required to do when the public call for witnesses was made. The reason for not coming forward is not given, and it did not matter. It was then too late to step forward in the court case. **they will be held responsible.** See note on 10:17.

5:2 ceremonially unclean. Touching the carcass of an unclean animal made the person unclean (see ch. 11 for clean and unclean animals). **they are unaware.** Here the person was not aware that they had become unclean, so they had not handled their uncleanness in a proper and timely way (see 11:28,40 for the required procedure). They had therefore spread uncleanness to the tabernacle in the midst of the community. This was especially worrisome (15:31).

5:3 human uncleanness. Caused by an unclean bodily flow of some sort (15:4–12,21–24) or by touching a human corpse (Num 19:11–20). **they are unaware.** See note on v. 2. For the regular required procedures, see 15:5–6,13–15.

5:4 thoughtlessly. A person might carelessly, foolishly, or in the heat of the moment speak a promissory oath. Nevertheless, they would need to fulfill the vow (cf. Num 30:6–8 for more on rash vows; see also Deut 23:21–23). Jephthah's vow was one kind of rash vow, but he knew that he had made the vow (Judg 11:30–31) and everyone knew that he needed to fulfill it (Judg 11:35–36). **but then they learn of it.** Sometimes in emotional situations a person might say things that they were unaware of and that they really did not mean. If they made an oath in this state of mind, they might not even remember it as such, so time might pass without their fulfilling the oath. If after that time they learned that they had made the oath, they were guilty of breaking it. **realize their guilt.** Or "incurs guilt." See note on 4:22–23.

5:5 they must confess. Since the four violators described in vv. 1–4 had either concealed their violation or it had been concealed from them, they needed to confess their sin to bring it to light before God and others.

in what way they have sinned. 6As a penalty for the sin they have committed, they must bring to the LORD a female lamb or goat from the flock as a sin offering[a];[t] and the priest shall make atonement for them for their sin.

7"'Anyone who cannot afford[u] a lamb is to bring two doves or two young pigeons to the LORD as a penalty for their sin—one for a sin offering and the other for a burnt offering. 8They are to bring them to the priest, who shall first offer the one for the sin offering. He is to wring its head from its neck,[v] not dividing it completely,[w] 9and is to splash some of the blood of the sin offering against the side of the altar; the rest of the blood must be drained out at the base of the altar.[x] It is a sin offering. 10The priest shall then offer the other as a burnt offering in the prescribed way[y] and make atonement for them for the sin they have committed, and they will be forgiven.[z]

11"'If, however, they cannot afford two doves or two young pigeons, they are to bring as an offering for their sin a tenth of an ephah[b] of the finest flour[a] for a sin offering. They must not put olive oil or incense on it, because it is a sin offering. 12They are to bring it to the priest, who shall take a handful of it as a memorial[c] portion and burn it on the altar on top of the food offerings presented to the LORD. It is a sin offering. 13In this way the priest will make atonement[b] for them for any of these sins they have committed, and they will be forgiven. The rest of the offering will belong to the priest,[c] as in the case of the grain offering.'"

The Guilt Offering

14The LORD said to Moses: 15"When anyone is unfaithful to the LORD by sinning unintentionally in regard to any of the LORD's holy things, they are to bring to the LORD as a penalty[d] a ram[e] from the flock, one without defect and of the proper value in silver, according to the sanctuary shekel.[d][f] It is a guilt offering. 16They must make restitution[g] for what they have failed to do in regard to the holy things, pay an additional penalty of a fifth of its value[h] and give it all to the priest. The priest will make atonement for them with the ram as a guilt offering, and they will be forgiven.

17"If anyone sins and does what is forbidden in any of the LORD's commands, even though they do not know it,[i] they are guilty and will be held responsible. 18They are to bring to the priest as a guilt

5:6 [t] Lev 4:28
5:7 [u] Lev 12:8; 14:21
5:8 [v] Lev 1:15 [w] Lev 1:17
5:9 [x] Lev 4:7,18
5:10 [y] Lev 1:14-17 [z] Lev 4:26
5:11 [a] Lev 2:1
5:13 [b] Lev 4:26 [c] Lev 2:3
5:15 [d] Lev 22:14 [e] Nu 5:8 [f] Ex 30:13
5:16 [g] Lev 6:4 [h] Lev 22:14; Nu 5:7
5:17 [i] ver 15; Lev 4:2

[a] *6* Or *purification offering*; here and throughout this chapter [b] *11* That is, probably about 3 1/2 pounds or about 1.6 kilograms [c] *12* Or *representative* [d] *15* That is, about 2/5 ounce or about 12 grams

5:6 sin offering. After they confessed their guilt (v. 5), they needed to make atonement with a sin offering since they had, in the meantime, polluted the tabernacle in their midst.
5:7 Anyone who cannot afford a lamb. For a sin offering. The regulations in vv. 7–10 are a concession to the poor. The Hebrew term used for "lamb" here refers to any flock animal, whether a sheep or a goat, as distinguished from the larger herd animals (see note on 1:2).
5:10 prescribed way. Following the basic regulations for birds as the burnt offering (see 1:14–17).
5:11 a tenth of an ephah. Although the measurements are debated, the grain offered here probably amounts to two quarts (2 liters), approximately the size of one daily ration. Alternatively, it may be understood as a measure of weight rather than volume. See NIV text note. **finest flour.** See note on 2:1. **because it is a sin offering.** Not a regular grain offering, so "they must not put olive oil or incense on it" (cf. 2:1). This was a concession to the poor and should not be construed as a contradiction to Heb 9:22: "Without the shedding of blood there is no forgiveness." Here the "finest flour" was a substitute for the bloody sin offerings prescribed previously.
5:14—6:7 This section on the guilt offering falls into three parts: the guilt offering for (1) trespassing on the Lord's holy things (5:14–16), (2) an unknown suspected violation (5:17–19), and (3) trespassing upon a neighbor's property (6:1–7). The sin offering made atonement for defiling the tabernacle with impurities, whether through sin or ritual impurity (see 4:1—5:13), whereas the guilt offering made atonement for desecration of the Lord's holy things by trespassing on whatever had been devoted to him. For that reason the guilt offering is sometimes called the "trespass offering." In addition to the guilt offering, the violator needed to make restitution plus pay a fine of a fifth of the value (see 5:16; 6:5; see also Introduction: Major Theological Themes [Holiness and Purity]). A guilt offering was necessary for something as simple as unintentionally eating an animal that had been specifically devoted to the Lord, like a firstborn animal (Lev 22:14–16; Exod 13:1–2,11–16). The guilt offering was also required when an Israelite violated the property of another Israelite through some kind of fraud (6:1–7). See "Major OT Offerings and Sacrifices," p. 197; see also notes on 5:15—6:2.
5:15 proper value in silver. The value of the ram that was offered. Alternatively, this might suggest that the guilt offering could be presented in the form of money. **sanctuary shekel.** See NIV text note.
5:16 make restitution. Replace the holy thing that they violated. **fifth.** A 20 percent fine was added to the restitution to compensate for the violation, even though unintentional, of something that was holy (see v. 15; contrast Exod 22:4,7,9, where a thief had to pay back double what he had stolen).
5:17 do not know it. It seems that they did not know what they had done wrong and never came to know it, so this is a "suspected violation." Another interpretation is that the offender did not originally know what their violation was but then they came to know it; however, there is no indication in the passage that they ever came to know it. No restitution and no fine of 20 percent could be made because the offender only suspected they had done something wrong but did not know what it was. This kind of suspicion and fear of having violated the holy things is also known from elsewhere in the ancient world.

5:18 [j] ver 15
6:2 [k] Nu 5:6; Ac 5:4; Col 3:9 [l] Pr 24:28 [m] Ex 22:7
6:3 [n] Dt 22:1-3
6:4 [o] Lk 19:8
6:5 [p] Nu 5:7 [q] Lev 5:15
6:6 [r] Lev 5:15
6:7 [s] Lev 4:26
6:10 [t] Ex 28:39-42, 43; 39:28
6:11 [u] Lev 4:12
6:14 [v] Lev 2:1; 15:4
6:15 [w] Lev 2:9 [x] Lev 2:2
6:16 [y] Lev 2:3 [z] Eze 44:29 [a] Lev 2:11 [b] Lev 10:13
6:17 [c] ver 29; Ex 40:10; Nu 18:9, 10
6:18 [d] ver 29; Nu 18:9-10 [e] ver 27

offering a ram from the flock, one without defect and of the proper value. In this way the priest will
make atonement for them for the wrong they have committed unintentionally, and they will be forgiven.[j] 19 It is a guilt offering; they have been guilty of[a] wrongdoing against the LORD."

6 [b] The LORD said to Moses: 2 "If anyone sins and is unfaithful to the LORD[k] by deceiving a neighbor[l]
about something entrusted to them or left in their care[m] or about something stolen, or if they
cheat their neighbor, 3 or if they find lost property and lie about it,[n] or if they swear falsely about any
such sin that people may commit — 4 when they sin in any of these ways and realize their guilt, they
must return[o] what they have stolen or taken by extortion, or what was entrusted to them, or the lost
property they found, 5 or whatever it was they swore falsely about. They must make restitution[p] in full,
add a fifth of the value to it and give it all to the owner on the day they present their guilt offering.[q]
6 And as a penalty they must bring to the priest, that is, to the LORD, their guilt offering,[r] a ram from
the flock, one without defect and of the proper value. 7 In this way the priest will make atonement[s] for
them before the LORD, and they will be forgiven for any of the things they did that made them guilty."

The Burnt Offering

8 The LORD said to Moses: 9 "Give Aaron and his sons this command: 'These are the regulations for the
burnt offering: The burnt offering is to remain on the altar hearth throughout the night, till morning,
and the fire must be kept burning on the altar. 10 The priest shall then put on his linen clothes, with
linen undergarments next to his body,[t] and shall remove the ashes of the burnt offering that the fire
has consumed on the altar and place them beside the altar. 11 Then he is to take off these clothes and
put on others, and carry the ashes outside the camp to a place that is ceremonially clean.[u] 12 The fire
on the altar must be kept burning; it must not go out. Every morning the priest is to add firewood and
arrange the burnt offering on the fire and burn the fat of the fellowship offerings on it. 13 The fire must
be kept burning on the altar continuously; it must not go out.

The Grain Offering

14 " 'These are the regulations for the grain offering:[v] Aaron's sons are to bring it before the LORD,
in front of the altar. 15 The priest is to take a handful of the finest flour and some olive oil, together
with all the incense on the grain offering,[w] and burn the memorial[c] portion[x] on the altar as an aroma
pleasing to the LORD. 16 Aaron and his sons[y] shall eat the rest[z] of it, but it is to be eaten without yeast[a]
in the sanctuary area;[b] they are to eat it in the courtyard of the tent of meeting. 17 It must not be baked
with yeast; I have given it as their share of the food offerings presented to me. Like the sin offering[d]
and the guilt offering, it is most holy.[c] 18 Any male descendant of Aaron may eat it.[d] For all generations
to come it is his perpetual share of the food offerings presented to the LORD. Whatever touches them
will become holy.[e][e]' "

[a] *19* Or *offering; atonement has been made for their* [b] In Hebrew texts 6:1-7 is numbered 5:20-26, and 6:8-30 is numbered 6:1-23. [c] *15* Or *representative* [d] *17* Or *purification offering*; also in verses 25 and 30 [e] *18* Or *Whoever touches them must be holy*; similarly in verse 27

6:1 Cf. 5:14. This introduces vv. 2–7 as a second subsection of the guilt offering section (5:14—6:7).
6:2 sins and is unfaithful to the LORD by deceiving a neighbor. Like in 5:15, the violation was a trespass upon property, but here it was the property of a neighbor (i.e., a member of the Israelite community) rather than the property of the Lord (see the parallel law in Num 5:5–10). After all, the people of Israel belonged to the Lord as his "holy nation" (Exod 19:6) and were therefore part of the Lord's "holy" things.
6:8—7:38 *Distribution of the Sacrificial Portions.* These regulations are addressed first to Aaron and his sons (6:8—7:21) and then to all the Israelites (7:22–36). They refer to the same five kinds of offerings as in 1:1—6:7, but here the concern is the distribution of the various parts of the offerings, whether to the Lord on the altar or to the priests or people.
6:10 linen clothes. The outer layer. **linen undergarments.** Possibly leggings, underwear, shorts, or some kind of apron worn under the linen clothes. They reached from a priest's waist to his thighs, and priests wore them whenever they ministered in the tabernacle tent or at the altar of burnt offering "so that they [did] not incur guilt and die" (Exod 28:43). The undergarments prevented their private parts from being exposed as they were ministering (Exod 20:26).
6:11 a place that is ceremonially clean. Cf. 4:12; see note there.
6:18 Whatever touches them will become holy. There are two possible translations and interpretations here. The main text of the NIV has "will become holy," indicating that the "most holy" grain offering (v. 17) would transfer holiness to anyone who touched it (cf. v. 27; Exod 29:37; 30:29). Ezek 46:20 would seem to support this view. The NIV text note has "must be holy," which would prohibit anyone who was not consecrated as a priest from touching the holy food, but this rendering does not suggest that holiness would transfer to the person who touched it. Hag 2:11–13 could be taken to support this rendering: uncleanness was transferable by touch, but holiness was not. But Haggai is not referring specifically to "most holy" food, which this verse and Ezek 46:20 do, so the rendering in the NIV main text is preferable. Food that was "holy" did not transfer holiness but "most holy" (vv. 17–18) food did.

19The LORD also said to Moses, 20"This is the offering Aaron and his sons are to bring to the LORD on
the day he[a] is anointed: a tenth of an ephah[b][f] of the finest flour as a regular grain offering,[g] half of
it in the morning and half in the evening. 21It must be prepared with oil on a griddle;[h] bring it well-
mixed and present the grain offering broken[c] in pieces as an aroma pleasing to the LORD. 22The son
who is to succeed him as anointed priest shall prepare it. It is the LORD's perpetual share and is to be
burned completely. 23Every grain offering of a priest shall be burned completely; it must not be eaten."

The Sin Offering

24The LORD said to Moses, 25"Say to Aaron and his sons: 'These are the regulations for the sin offering: The sin offering is to be slaughtered before the LORD[i] in the place[j] the burnt offering is slaughtered;
it is most holy. 26The priest who offers it shall eat it; it is to be eaten in the sanctuary area,[k] in the
courtyard[l] of the tent of meeting. 27Whatever touches any of the flesh will become holy,[m] and if any of
the blood is spattered on a garment, you must wash it in the sanctuary area. 28The clay pot[n] the meat
is cooked in must be broken; but if it is cooked in a bronze pot, the pot is to be scoured and rinsed with
water. 29Any male in a priest's family may eat it;[o] it is most holy.[p] 30But any sin offering whose blood
is brought into the tent of meeting to make atonement in the Holy Place[q] must not be eaten; it must
be burned up.[r]

The Guilt Offering

7 " 'These are the regulations for the guilt offering,[s] which is most holy: 2The guilt offering is to be
slaughtered in the place where the burnt offering is slaughtered, and its blood is to be splashed
against the sides of the altar. 3All its fat[t] shall be offered: the fat tail and the fat that covers the internal
organs, 4both kidneys with the fat on them near the loins, and the long lobe of the liver, which is to
be removed with the kidneys. 5The priest shall burn them on the altar as a food offering presented to
the LORD. It is a guilt offering. 6Any male in a priest's family may eat it,[u] but it must be eaten in the
sanctuary area; it is most holy.[v]

7" 'The same law applies to both the sin offering[d] and the guilt offering: They belong to the priest[w]
who makes atonement with them. 8The priest who offers a burnt offering for anyone may keep its hide
for himself. 9Every grain offering baked in an oven or cooked in a pan or on a griddle[x] belongs to the
priest who offers it, 10and every grain offering, whether mixed with olive oil or dry, belongs equally to
all the sons of Aaron.

The Fellowship Offering

11" 'These are the regulations for the fellowship offering anyone may present to the LORD:

12" 'If they offer it as an expression of thankfulness, then along with this thank offering[y] they are
to offer thick loaves made without yeast and with olive oil mixed in, thin loaves[z] made without yeast
and brushed with oil, and thick loaves of the finest flour well-kneaded and with oil mixed in. 13Along
with their fellowship offering of thanksgiving they are to present an offering with thick loaves of bread

6:20 [f] Ex 16:36 [g] Ex 29:2
6:21 [h] Lev 2:5
6:25 [i] Lev 1:3 [j] Lev 1:5,11
6:26 [k] ver 16 [l] Lev 10:17-18
6:27 [m] Ex 29:37
6:28 [n] Lev 11:33; 15:12
6:29 [o] ver 18 [p] ver 17
6:30 [q] Lev 4:18 [r] Lev 4:12
7:1 [s] Lev 5:14-6:7
7:3 [t] Ex 29:13; Lev 3:4,9
7:6 [u] Lev 6:18; Nu 18:9-10 [v] Lev 2:3
7:7 [w] Lev 6:17,26; 1Co 9:13
7:9 [x] Lev 2:5
7:12 [y] ver 13,15 [z] Lev 2:4; Nu 6:15

[a] *20* Or *each* [b] *20* That is, probably about 3 1/2 pounds or about 1.6 kilograms [c] *21* The meaning of the Hebrew for this word is uncertain. [d] *7* Or *purification offering*; also in verse 37

6:30 blood … brought into the tent of meeting. Sin offerings for the anointed priest and for the whole Israelite community (4:3–21). The meat was burned up outside the camp, not eaten by the priests (see note on 4:12).

7:2 its blood is to be splashed. Unlike that of the sin offering (see 4:5–7,25 and notes), the blood of the guilt offering was handled the same way as that of the burnt and fellowship offerings (1:5; 3:2). Here the blood was not used to cleanse the tabernacle from impurity but to make amends for the trespass violation of other things that were holy (see note on 5:14—6:7).

7:7 They belong to the priest. Like the meat of the sin offering, the meat of the guilt offering was "most holy" (6:25; see notes on 6:18; 27:28).

7:12–18 There are three major kinds of fellowship offerings: thank offerings (vv. 12–15), vow offerings (vv. 16–18), and freewill offerings (vv. 16–18). Thus, one could bring a fellowship offering for various purposes. Sometimes a person was especially thankful for something the Lord had done in their life; sometimes a person needed to fulfill a vow they had made (e.g., Gen 28:20–22; Num 30:1–2; Deut 23:21–23); and sometimes a person simply wanted to freely express their love and worship of the Lord with a freewill offering. The freewill offering was the least regulated since, by definition, it was offered freely, without any kind of specific obligation attached (vv. 15–17; 22:23).

7:12 without yeast. These breads were unleavened (cf. 2:11–12) because a memorial portion from them (see note on 2:2) would be offered on the altar.

7:13 with yeast. Contrast v. 12. No memorial portion was given from these loaves, so they could be made with yeast (cf. 2:11–12).

7:13 [a]Lev 23:17; Am 4:5
7:15 [b]Lev 22:30
7:16 [c]Lev 19:5-8
7:18 [d]Lev 19:7 [e]Nu 18:27
7:20 [f]Lev 22:3-7
7:21 [g]Lev 5:2; 11:24,28
7:23 [h]Lev 3:17; 17:13-14
7:24 [i]Ex 22:31
7:26 [j]Ge 9:4
7:27 [k]Lev 17:10-24; Ac 15:20,29
7:30 [l]Ex 29:24; Nu 6:20

made with yeast.[a] 14They are to bring one of each kind as an offering, a contribution to the LORD; it
belongs to the priest who splashes the blood of the fellowship offering against the altar. 15The meat of
their fellowship offering of thanksgiving must be eaten on the day it is offered; they must leave none
of it till morning.[b]

16" 'If, however, their offering is the result of a vow or is a freewill offering, the sacrifice shall be
eaten on the day they offer it, but anything left over may be eaten on the next day.[c] 17Any meat of the
sacrifice left over till the third day must be burned up. 18If any meat of the fellowship offering is eaten
on the third day, the one who offered it will not be accepted.[d] It will not be reckoned[e] to their credit, for
it has become impure; the person who eats any of it will be held responsible.

19" 'Meat that touches anything ceremonially unclean must not be eaten; it must be burned up. As
for other meat, anyone ceremonially clean may eat it. 20But if anyone who is unclean eats any meat
of the fellowship offering belonging to the LORD, they must be cut off from their people.[f] 21Anyone who
touches something unclean[g]—whether human uncleanness or an unclean animal or any unclean
creature that moves along the ground[a]—and then eats any of the meat of the fellowship offering
belonging to the LORD must be cut off from their people.' "

Eating Fat and Blood Forbidden

22The LORD said to Moses, 23"Say to the Israelites: 'Do not eat any of the fat of cattle, sheep or goats.[h]
24The fat of an animal found dead or torn by wild animals[i] may be used for any other purpose, but you
must not eat it. 25Anyone who eats the fat of an animal from which a food offering may be[b] presented
to the LORD must be cut off from their people. 26And wherever you live, you must not eat the blood[j] of
any bird or animal. 27Anyone who eats blood[k] must be cut off from their people.' "

The Priests' Share

28The LORD said to Moses, 29"Say to the Israelites: 'Anyone who brings a fellowship offering to the
LORD is to bring part of it as their sacrifice to the LORD. 30With their own hands they are to present the
food offering to the LORD; they are to bring the fat, together with the breast, and wave the breast before
the LORD as a wave offering.[l] 31The priest shall burn the fat on the altar, but the breast belongs to Aaron

[a] *21* A few Hebrew manuscripts, Samaritan Pentateuch, Syriac and Targum (see 5:2); most Hebrew manuscripts *any unclean, detestable thing* [b] *25* Or *offering is*

7:14 contribution. What was set aside from the offerings to the Lord as payment for the officiating priests (vv. 28–36).
7:15 eaten on the day it is offered. Some argue that this rule was required so the meal would be shared with others and not selfishly hoarded. Others argue that the distinction between the thank offering (all eaten on the first day) and the votive and freewill offerings (eaten on the first and second day [vv. 16–18]) reflects the higher level of gratitude owed to the Lord in the thank offering.
7:18 not be accepted. Voided the benefit of the offering altogether. **It will not be reckoned to their credit.** Whatever recognition the worshiper would have received from the Lord for the offering was canceled. **impure.** Cf. 19:7–8. In Isa 65:4 this term stands parallel to the flesh of pigs (an unclean animal), and in Ezek 4:14 it is parallel to the meat of animals found dead or killed by wild animals. It may refer here to the spoiling of the meat after two days, but the main point is simply that this holy meat had become desecrated by eating from it beyond the prescribed period of two days. **held responsible.** For violating these regulations.
7:19–21 Uncleanness was contagious (cf. Hag 2:11–13), so it was important that no thing (or person) that was unclean touch (or eat) the holy dedicated meat of the fellowship offering, rendering the meat unclean (cf. 22:3–8).
7:20,21 cut off from their people. This penalty clause seems to indicate varying consequences in different contexts. It may refer to execution either by the community (e.g., 20:2–3; Exod 31:14–15; and perhaps Num 15:30–36) or by the Lord himself (e.g., 20:4–5, which may include also terminating the violator's line of descent [extirpation]). The similar expression in Num 19:13 refers to excommunication from the covenant community so that the impure person would not defile the tabernacle.
7:24 This extends the prohibition against eating fat (vv. 23,25; cf. 3:17) to that of "an animal found dead or torn by wild animals" (cf. 17:15–16). They could use it, however, for other purposes and for daily needs such as oil for lamps.
7:26–27 The fat of wild game that had been hunted and killed could be eaten, but even then the blood needed to be poured out on the ground—no blood could ever be eaten (Deut 12:15–16). The origin of this prohibition goes back to Gen 9:4–5, the rationale being that blood represents the life of the animal, and life belongs only to the Lord himself (see note on 17:11). Its importance is stressed even in the letter to the Gentile churches in Acts 15:20,29.
7:29 bring part of it as their sacrifice to the LORD. The worshipers ate most of the meat of the fellowship offering (see ch. 3), but the parts referred to here (vv. 30–34) were to be given to the priests to eat.
7:30 fat. See note on 3:17. **breast.** Went to the priests as payment for their priestly services. **wave.** Probably a special lifting up of the fat and the breast as a way of presenting them to the Lord. According to Num 8:11, however, Aaron was to "present ['wave'] the Levites before the LORD as a wave offering." Obviously he did not take them on his hands and literally "wave" them. **wave offering.** Refers specifically to the part(s) of the offering that the priests did not put on the altar and the offerer did not eat.
7:31 belongs to Aaron and his sons. The wave offering went to all the priests and their families as a benefit to them (10:14–15; 22:10–16; Num 18:18–19).

and his sons.[m] 32You are to give the right thigh of your fellowship offerings to the priest as a contribution.[n] 33The son of Aaron who offers the blood and the fat of the fellowship offering shall have the right thigh as his share. 34From the fellowship offerings of the Israelites, I have taken the breast that is waved and the thigh[o] that is presented and have given them to Aaron the priest and his sons[p] as their perpetual share from the Israelites.' "

35This is the portion of the food offerings presented to the LORD that were allotted to Aaron and his sons on the day they were presented to serve the LORD as priests. 36On the day they were anointed,[q] the LORD commanded that the Israelites give this to them as their perpetual share for the generations to come.

37These, then, are the regulations for the burnt offering,[r] the grain offering,[s] the sin offering, the guilt offering, the ordination offering[t] and the fellowship offering, 38which the LORD gave Moses at Mount Sinai in the Desert of Sinai on the day he commanded the Israelites to bring their offerings to the LORD.[u]

The Ordination of Aaron and His Sons

8:1-36pp — Ex 29:1-37

8 The LORD said to Moses, 2"Bring Aaron and his sons, their garments, the anointing oil,[v] the bull for the sin offering,[a] the two rams and the basket containing bread made without yeast,[w] 3and gather the entire assembly[x] at the entrance to the tent of meeting." 4Moses did as the LORD commanded him, and the assembly gathered at the entrance to the tent of meeting.

5Moses said to the assembly, "This is what the LORD has commanded to be done." 6Then Moses brought Aaron and his sons forward and washed them with water.[y] 7He put the tunic on Aaron, tied the sash around him, clothed him with the robe and put the ephod on him. He also fastened the ephod with a decorative waistband, which he tied around him.[z] 8He placed the breastpiece on him and put the Urim and Thummim[a] in the breastpiece. 9Then he placed the turban on Aaron's head and set the gold plate, the sacred emblem,[b] on the front of it, as the LORD commanded Moses.

10Then Moses took the anointing oil[c] and anointed[d] the tabernacle and everything in it, and so consecrated them. 11He sprinkled some of the oil on the altar seven times, anointing the altar and all its utensils and the basin with its stand, to consecrate them.[e] 12He poured some of the anointing oil on Aaron's head and anointed[f] him to consecrate him.[g] 13Then he brought Aaron's sons forward, put tunics on them, tied sashes around them and fastened caps on them, as the LORD commanded Moses.

14He then presented the bull[h] for the sin offering,[i] and Aaron and his sons

Artist's rendition of the priestly garments (Lev 8:2; Exod 28).
Public Domain

[a] 2 Or *purification offering*; also in verse 14

7:31 [m] ver 34
7:32 [n] ver 34; Lev 9:21; Nu 6:20
7:34 [o] Lev 10:15 [p] Ex 29:27; Nu 18:18-19
7:36 [q] Ex 40:13,15; Lev 8:12,30
7:37 [r] Lev 6:9 [s] Lev 6:14 [t] ver 1,11
7:38 [u] Lev 1:2
8:2 [v] Ex 30:23-25,30 [w] Ex 29:2-3
8:3 [x] Nu 8:9
8:6 [y] Ex 29:4; 30:19; Ps 26:6; Ac 22:16; 1Co 6:11; Eph 5:26
8:7 [z] Ex 28:4
8:8 [a] Ex 28:30
8:9 [b] Ex 28:36
8:10 [c] ver 2 [d] Ex 30:26
8:11 [e] Ex 30:29
8:12 [f] Lev 21:10,12 [g] Ex 30:30
8:14 [h] Lev 4:3 [i] Ps 66:15; Eze 43:19

7:32 right thigh. For the priest who presided over an offering (v. 33). **contribution.** Translated "heave offering" in some earlier versions because it comes from a Hebrew verb that means "raise" or "lift" (heave = to lift or push something heavy). But in Leviticus the same Hebrew verb describes priests or offerers *removing* or *taking out* a certain portion from the offering to use it for a specific purpose (2:9; 4:8,10,19) such as to make a "contribution" to the officiating priest.

7:35 This. Either refers to the priestly portions described by all the regulations in 6:8 — 7:34 or only the breast and right thigh of the fellowship offering described by the regulations in vv. 28 – 34.

8:1 – 36 *The Ordination of Aaron and His Sons.* Moses ordained the priests according to the regulations set forth in Exod 29 and as the Lord directed him in Exod 40:12 – 15. This is the first time in Leviticus that the offerings and sacrifices prescribed in chs. 1 – 7 are actually performed.

8:2 garments. See vv. 7 – 9; see also Exod 28 and notes; see further the illustration of the priestly garments, this page; cf. Exod 39:1 – 31. **without yeast.** Because one of each kind of loaf was to be burned up on the altar (vv. 26,28) and nothing made with yeast could ever be offered on the altar (2:11 – 12).

8:7 – 9 See notes on Exod 28.

8:10 anointing oil. A special recipe sprinkled or poured on only the tabernacle and the priests (Exod 30:22 – 33). **consecrated.** Made holy or sacred, putting them into the category of holy/sacred as opposed to common/profane (see 10:10 and note; see also Introduction: Major Theological Themes [Holiness and Purity]). See "Holiness," p. 2676.

8:13 Cf. Exod 28:40; 29:8 – 9; 39:27 – 29. The priestly garments of Aaron's sons are compared to those of Aaron the high priest (vv. 7 – 9). **tunics ... sashes.** The same as for Aaron (v. 7). **fastened.** Tied on the head, possibly by some kind of strap. **caps.** Different than Aaron's "turban" (v. 9); the Hebrew word is related to the word for "cup," which suggests that it is perhaps more like a regular cap placed on the head.

8:15 [j]Lev 4:7 [k]Heb 9:22 [l]Eze 43:20
8:17 [m]Lev 4:11 [n]Lev 4:12
8:18 [o]ver 2
8:22 [p]ver 2
8:24 [q]Heb 9:18-22
8:29 [r]Lev 7:31-34
8:30 [s]Ex 28:2 [t]Nu 3:3
8:34 [u]Heb 7:16
8:35 [v]Nu 3:7; 9:19; Dt 11:1; 1Ki 2:3; Eze 48:11
9:1 [w]Eze 43:27

laid their hands on its head. 15 Moses slaughtered the bull and took some of the blood, and with his finger he put it on all the horns of the altar[j] to purify the altar.[k] He poured out the rest of the blood at the base of the altar. So he consecrated it to make atonement for it.[l] 16 Moses also took all the fat around the internal organs, the long lobe of the liver, and both kidneys and their fat, and burned it on the altar. 17 But the bull with its hide and its flesh and its intestines[m] he burned up outside the camp,[n] as the LORD commanded Moses.

18 He then presented the ram[o] for the burnt offering, and Aaron and his sons laid their hands on its head. 19 Then Moses slaughtered the ram and splashed the blood against the sides of the altar. 20 He cut the ram into pieces and burned the head, the pieces and the fat. 21 He washed the internal organs and the legs with water and burned the whole ram on the altar. It was a burnt offering, a pleasing aroma, a food offering presented to the LORD, as the LORD commanded Moses.

22 He then presented the other ram, the ram for the ordination,[p] and Aaron and his sons laid their hands on its head. 23 Moses slaughtered the ram and took some of its blood and put it on the lobe of Aaron's right ear, on the thumb of his right hand and on the big toe of his right foot. 24 Moses also brought Aaron's sons forward and put some of the blood on the lobes of their right ears, on the thumbs of their right hands and on the big toes of their right feet. Then he splashed blood against the sides of the altar.[q] 25 After that, he took the fat, the fat tail, all the fat around the internal organs, the long lobe of the liver, both kidneys and their fat and the right thigh. 26 And from the basket of bread made without yeast, which was before the LORD, he took one thick loaf, one thick loaf with olive oil mixed in, and one thin loaf, and he put these on the fat portions and on the right thigh. 27 He put all these in the hands of Aaron and his sons, and they waved them before the LORD as a wave offering. 28 Then Moses took them from their hands and burned them on the altar on top of the burnt offering as an ordination offering, a pleasing aroma, a food offering presented to the LORD. 29 Moses also took the breast, which was his share of the ordination ram,[r] and waved it before the LORD as a wave offering, as the LORD commanded Moses.

30 Then Moses took some of the anointing oil and some of the blood from the altar and sprinkled them on Aaron and his garments[s] and on his sons and their garments. So he consecrated[t] Aaron and his garments and his sons and their garments.

31 Moses then said to Aaron and his sons, "Cook the meat at the entrance to the tent of meeting and eat it there with the bread from the basket of ordination offerings, as I was commanded: 'Aaron and his sons are to eat it.' 32 Then burn up the rest of the meat and the bread. 33 Do not leave the entrance to the tent of meeting for seven days, until the days of your ordination are completed, for your ordination will last seven days. 34 What has been done today was commanded by the LORD[u] to make atonement for you. 35 You must stay at the entrance to the tent of meeting day and night for seven days and do what the LORD requires,[v] so you will not die; for that is what I have been commanded."

36 So Aaron and his sons did everything the LORD commanded through Moses.

The Priests Begin Their Ministry

9 On the eighth day[w] Moses summoned Aaron and his sons and the elders of Israel. 2 He said to Aaron, "Take a bull calf for your sin offering[a] and a ram for your burnt offering, both without defect, and present them before the LORD. 3 Then say to the Israelites: 'Take a male goat for a sin offering,

[a] 2 Or *purification offering*; here and throughout this chapter

8:15 purify. "De-sin" or decontaminate the altar. **for.** Either the sin offering made atonement "for" the altar so that it became consecrated on this ordination day, or by purifying it so that the altar became a consecrated place upon which atonement could be made then and into the future.

8:22 ordination. This Hebrew term derives from the expression in v. 33 "your ordination will last seven days," which can be translated "seven days he will fill your hands." It refers to putting the priestly responsibilities (or possibly the portions of the offerings that went to the priests) into their hands. The ordination offering was a kind of fellowship offering.

8:23 took ... put. The same terms as those used in v. 15 for applying the blood to the horns of the altar of burnt offering to purify and consecrate it. The lobe of the right ear, the thumb on the right hand, and the big toe on the right foot probably correspond to the "horns" of the altar: they protrude from the human body like the horns from the four corners of the altar (Exod 27:2). Thus, Moses purified and consecrated the priests like he did the altar.

8:30 consecrated. By taking some of the oil and blood that was on the altar and sprinkling it on the priests, Moses bound the priests to the altar as those who were of the same level of holiness and purity as the altar. This qualified them to actually touch the altar so that they could minister there on behalf of the people.

9:1—10:20 *The Priests Begin Their Ministry.* The priests ordained in ch. 8 begin their ministry in chs. 9–10, the inauguration day of tabernacle worship. All that happens in chs. 9–10 takes place "on the eighth day" (9:1), the day after the seven-day ordination of the tabernacle and the priests in ch. 8.

9:2–4 The combination of offerings for the priests first (vv. 2,8–14) and then for the people (vv. 3–4,15–21) appears again on the Day of Atone-

a calf and a lamb — both a year old and without defect — for a burnt offering, 4 and an ox[a] and a ram for a fellowship offering to sacrifice before the LORD, together with a grain offering mixed with olive oil. For today the LORD will appear to you.[x]"

5 They took the things Moses commanded to the front of the tent of meeting, and the entire assembly came near and stood before the LORD. 6 Then Moses said, "This is what the LORD has commanded you to do, so that the glory of the LORD[y] may appear to you."

7 Moses said to Aaron, "Come to the altar and sacrifice your sin offering and your burnt offering and make atonement for yourself and the people; sacrifice the offering that is for the people and make atonement for them, as the LORD has commanded.[z]"

8 So Aaron came to the altar and slaughtered the calf as a sin offering[a] for himself. 9 His sons brought the blood to him,[b] and he dipped his finger into the blood and put it on the horns of the altar; the rest of the blood he poured out at the base of the altar.[c] 10 On the altar he burned the fat, the kidneys and the long lobe of the liver from the sin offering, as the LORD commanded Moses; 11 the flesh and the hide[d] he burned up outside the camp.[e]

12 Then he slaughtered the burnt offering. His sons handed him the blood, and he splashed it against the sides of the altar. 13 They handed him the burnt offering piece by piece, including the head, and he burned them on the altar.[f] 14 He washed the internal organs and the legs and burned them on top of the burnt offering on the altar.

15 Aaron then brought the offering that was for the people.[g] He took the goat for the people's sin offering and slaughtered it and offered it for a sin offering as he did with the first one.

16 He brought the burnt offering and offered it in the prescribed way.[h] 17 He also brought the grain offering, took a handful of it and burned it on the altar in addition to the morning's burnt offering.[i]

18 He slaughtered the ox and the ram as the fellowship offering for the people.[j] His sons handed him the blood, and he splashed it against the sides of the altar. 19 But the fat portions of the ox and the ram — the fat tail, the layer of fat, the kidneys and the long lobe of the liver — 20 these they laid on the breasts, and then Aaron burned the fat on the altar. 21 Aaron waved the breasts and the right thigh before the LORD as a wave offering,[k] as Moses commanded.

22 Then Aaron lifted his hands toward the people and blessed them.[l] And having sacrificed the sin offering, the burnt offering and the fellowship offering, he stepped down.

23 Moses and Aaron then went into the tent of meeting. When they came out, they blessed the people; and the glory of the LORD[m] appeared to all the people. 24 Fire[n] came out from the presence of the LORD and consumed the burnt offering and the fat portions on the altar. And when all the people saw it, they shouted for joy and fell facedown.[o]

The Death of Nadab and Abihu

10 Aaron's sons Nadab and Abihu[p] took their censers, put fire in them[q] and added incense; and they offered unauthorized fire before the LORD, contrary to his command.[r] 2 So fire came out from the presence of the LORD and consumed them,[s] and they died before the LORD. 3 Moses then said to Aaron, "This is what the LORD spoke of when he said:

[a] *4* The Hebrew word can refer to either male or female; also in verses 18 and 19.

9:4 [x] Ex 29:43
9:6 [y] ver 23; Ex 24:16
9:7 [z] Heb 5:1,3; 7:27
9:8 [a] Lev 4:1-12
9:9 [b] ver 12,18 [c] Lev 4:7
9:11 [d] Lev 4:11 [e] Lev 4:12; 8:17
9:13 [f] Lev 1:8
9:15 [g] Lev 4:27-31
9:16 [h] Lev 1:1-13
9:17 [i] Lev 2:1-2; 3:5
9:18 [j] Lev 3:1-11
9:21 [k] Ex 29:24,26; Lev 7:30-34
9:22 [l] Nu 6:23; Dt 21:5; Lk 24:50
9:23 [m] ver 6
9:24 [n] Jdg 6:21; 2Ch 7:1 [o] 1Ki 18:39
10:1 [p] Ex 24:1; Nu 3:2-4; 26:61 [q] Lev 16:12 [r] Ex 30:9
10:2 [s] Nu 3:4; 16:35; 26:61

ment (ch. 16). The sequence of offerings is important: first, the sin offering for purification (vv. 8–11,15); second, the burnt offering as a dedicatory gift to the Lord (vv. 12–14,16–17); and finally, the fellowship offering to enact the relationship between God and his people (vv. 18–21).

9:4 today the LORD will appear to you. The rationale for these offerings on this occasion. They anticipated the appearance of the glory of the Lord (vv. 6,23) and the fire that came out from the Lord and consumed the inauguration-day offerings on the altar (v. 24).

9:6 so that the glory of the LORD may appear to you. See note on v. 4. This refers to the same glory cloud that occupied the tabernacle in Exod 40:34–35. See Introduction: Major Theological Themes (The Lord's Presence); see also "The Glory of God," p. 2640.

9:17 in addition to the morning's burnt offering. The regular morning burnt and grain offerings had already been placed on the altar before the inaugural burnt and grain offerings referred to here (Exod 29:18–42; 40:29).

9:21 wave offering. See note on 7:30. The right thigh was the normal contribution to the officiating priest and his family (see note on 7:32). It could be presented as a wave offering along with the breasts, which were given to all the priests and their families, which is the case here (cf. 8:27,29; 10:15).

9:23 glory of the LORD. See note on v. 6; cf. 16:2; Exod 40:34–38; Num 9:15–23; 10:11–12.

9:24 shouted for joy. The Hebrew word may mean either that the people shouted for joy or shouted out of fear (cf. Exod 19:16; 20:18–21).

10:1–20 See note on 9:1—10:20.

10:1 unauthorized. This may have involved any (or a combination) of the following: (1) using coals taken from someplace other than the

10:3 [t]Ex 19:22 [u]Ex 30:29; Lev 21:6; Eze 28:22 [v]Isa 49:3
10:4 [w]Ex 6:22 [x]Ex 6:18 [y]Ac 5:6,9,10
10:5 [z]Lev 8:13
10:6 [a]Lev 21:10 [b]Nu 1:53; 16:22; Jos 7:1; 22:18; 2Sa 24:1
10:7 [c]Ex 28:41; Lev 21:12
10:9 [d]Hos 4:11 [e]Pr 20:1; Isa 28:7; Eze 44:21; Lk 1:15; Eph 5:18; 1Ti 3:3; Titus 1:7
10:10 [f]Lev 11:47; 20:25; Eze 22:26
10:11 [g]Mal 2:7 [h]Dt 24:8
10:12 [i]Lev 6:14-18; 21:22
10:14 [j]Ex 29:24,26-27; Lev 7:31,34; Nu 18:11
10:15 [k]Lev 7:34
10:16 [l]Lev 9:3

" 'Among those who approach me[t]
I will be proved holy;[u]
in the sight of all the people
I will be honored.[v]' "

Aaron remained silent.

[4]Moses summoned Mishael and Elzaphan,[w] sons of Aaron's uncle Uzziel,[x] and said to them, "Come
here; carry your cousins outside the camp,[y] away from the front of the sanctuary." [5]So they came and
carried them, still in their tunics,[z] outside the camp, as Moses ordered.

[6]Then Moses said to Aaron and his sons Eleazar and Ithamar, "Do not let your hair become unkempt[a][a] and do not tear your clothes, or you will die and the LORD will be angry with the whole community.[b] But your relatives, all the Israelites, may mourn for those the LORD has destroyed by fire. [7]Do
not leave the entrance to the tent of meeting or you will die, because the LORD's anointing oil[c] is on
you." So they did as Moses said.

[8]Then the LORD said to Aaron, [9]"You and your sons are not to drink wine[d] or other fermented drink[e]
whenever you go into the tent of meeting, or you will die. This is a lasting ordinance for the generations
to come, [10]so that you can distinguish between the holy and the common, between the unclean and the
clean,[f] [11]and so you can teach[g] the Israelites all the decrees the LORD has given them through Moses.[h]"

[12]Moses said to Aaron and his remaining sons, Eleazar and Ithamar, "Take the grain offering left
over from the food offerings prepared without yeast and presented to the LORD and eat it beside the
altar,[i] for it is most holy. [13]Eat it in the sanctuary area, because it is your share and your sons' share
of the food offerings presented to the LORD; for so I have been commanded. [14]But you and your sons
and your daughters may eat the breast that was waved and the thigh that was presented. Eat them in a
ceremonially clean place;[j] they have been given to you and your children as your share of the Israelites'
fellowship offerings. [15]The thigh[k] that was presented and the breast that was waved must be brought
with the fat portions of the food offerings, to be waved before the LORD as a wave offering. This will be
the perpetual share for you and your children, as the LORD has commanded."

[16]When Moses inquired about the goat of the sin offering[b][l] and found that it had been burned up,

[a] 6 Or *Do not uncover your heads* [b] 16 Or *purification offering*; also in verses 17 and 19

altar of burnt offering (16:12); (2) using the wrong kind of incense (Exod 30:34–38); (3) performing an incense offering at a time not prescribed; or (4) entering the Most Holy Place at an inappropriate time (16:1–2). For another possible violation, see note on v. 9.

10:2 fire came out from the presence of the LORD and consumed. As in 9:24. **died.** This too took place on the inauguration day (see note on 10:16). This was a terrible catastrophe, but v. 3 tells us why the Lord responded this way to their violation.

10:3 be proved holy. Or "be treated as holy" or "show myself holy." In the immediate situation the Lord himself indeed showed himself to be holy by how he responded to the illegitimate incense offering in v. 1. Nadab and Abihu did not treat the Lord as holy, so the Lord acted on his own behalf to demonstrate his holiness in a way that would emphasize the importance of it. See "Holiness," p. 2676. Similar demonstrations of the Lord's holiness occurred at the beginning of the conquest of the land (the Achan incident, Josh 7), when they brought the ark up to Jerusalem (Uzzah's death, 2 Sam 6:1–7), and at the beginning of the church (the death of Ananias and Sapphira, Acts 5:1–11).

10:8 the LORD said to Aaron. Normally the Lord spoke to and through Moses. In fact, in Leviticus this is the only time God spoke to Aaron alone. In this catastrophic moment for Aaron and his family, the Lord emphasized to Aaron and his remaining sons the serious nature and dangers of the priestly ministry (see notes on vv. 3,9; cf. 15:31; 16:2).

10:9 not to drink wine or other fermented drink. This warning stands out in isolation here, which suggests that perhaps Nadab and Abihu had offered the unauthorized fire because they were under the influence of alcohol and therefore did not follow the incense regulations carefully (see note on v. 1).

10:10 holy ... common. A person, place, thing, or time was either consecrated and, therefore, had holy status, or was not consecrated and, therefore, had common status. There were certain regulations for each (see note on v. 11). There was nothing inherently wrong with being common as long as the rules for that status were maintained. For example, a common person (i.e., not a holy priest) was never to come into contact with the altar in the tabernacle since it was a holy thing. **unclean ... clean.** A person, place, or thing could be in a condition of being either clean or unclean. For example, even a holy priest could become unclean, but once he purified himself he could return to his work in the holy sanctuary. These are the basic underlying principles of the entire priestly ritual system in the tabernacle (see Introduction: Major Theological Themes [Holiness and Purity]).

10:11 all the decrees. All the commands God gave through Moses, including and especially the various regulations that went with the core concerns underlined in v. 10. The priests were to instruct all Israel in the principles and practices of walking with God and one another. The priests were the custodians of the law in ancient Israel (Deut 17:8–13,18).

10:12–15 Summarizes regulations for payments to the priests from "the food offerings" (v. 13; see note on 1:9; cf. 6:8—7:36).

10:16–18 Follows naturally after the payments to the priests reiterated in vv. 12–15 because this was a "most holy" (v. 17) portion for only the priests to eat and only "in the sanctuary area" (v. 17; cf. 6:24–29).

10:16 goat of the sin offering. Earlier that day Aaron had offered it for the people (9:15). **angry.** Because they burned the offering instead of eating it in the prescribed manner (v. 18; cf. 6:24–29). Moses was concerned that once again they had violated the tabernacle regulations, similar to what Nadab and Abihu had done (vv. 1–2).

he was angry with Eleazar and Ithamar, Aaron's remaining sons, and asked, 17"Why didn't you eat the
sin offering[m] in the sanctuary area? It is most holy; it was given to you to take away the guilt of
the community by making atonement for them before the LORD. 18Since its blood was not taken into the
Holy Place,[n] you should have eaten the goat in the sanctuary area, as I commanded."
19Aaron replied to Moses, "Today they sacrificed their sin offering and their burnt offering[o] before
the LORD, but such things as this have happened to me. Would the LORD have been pleased if I had eaten
the sin offering today?" 20When Moses heard this, he was satisfied.

10:17 [m]Lev 6:24-30
10:18 [n]Lev 6:26,30
10:19 [o]Lev 9:12
11:2 [p]Ac 10:12-14
11:7 [q]Isa 65:4; 66:3,17
11:8 [r]Isa 52:11; Heb 9:10

Clean and Unclean Food

11:1-23pp — Dt 14:3-20

11 The LORD said to Moses and Aaron, 2"Say to the Israelites: 'Of all the animals that live on land,
these are the ones you may eat:[p] 3You may eat any animal that has a divided hoof and that
chews the cud.
4" 'There are some that only chew the cud or only have a divided hoof, but you must not eat them.
The camel, though it chews the cud, does not have a divided hoof; it is ceremonially unclean for you.
5The hyrax, though it chews the cud, does not have a divided hoof; it is unclean for you. 6The rabbit,
though it chews the cud, does not have a divided hoof; it is unclean for you. 7And the pig,[q] though it
has a divided hoof, does not chew the cud; it is unclean for you. 8You must not eat their meat or touch
their carcasses; they are unclean for you.[r]

10:17 to take away the guilt. Part of the priestly mediatorial role. Some argue that the priests did this by eating the meat of the sin offering. This is not likely. The priests received their portions from the offerings (such as the meat of the sin offerings of the people here), as well as their share of the tithe, as payment for the work they did "to bear the responsibility for offenses connected with the sanctuary" (Num 18:1). Since the priests bore the iniquities of the congregation on themselves, the high priest could confess them and so lay them on the scapegoat to completely remove them from the community on the Day of Atonement (see 16:21–22 and note on 16:21). In fact, the verses just previous (10:12–15) focus on such provisions for the priests.

10:19 Eating the meat of the sin offering was a provision for the priests; it provided a celebratory banquet for them before the Lord. But this was not a day for celebration because Aaron had lost his two sons, Nadab and Abihu, that very day (vv. 1–2). Aaron argued that this was an exception to the general rule. That was why Aaron had broken the regulations for eating the sin offering.

10:20 satisfied. Moses thought Aaron made a good argument for not following the regulations on this occasion.

11:1—15:33 *Purity Regulations.* According to 16:1, "The LORD spoke to Moses after the death of the two sons of Aaron who died when they approached the LORD," referring back to ch. 10. The purity laws are inserted as a unit between 10:20 and 16:1. Chs. 11–15 focus on the importance of holiness and purity in Israel (see note on 10:10), focusing specifically on clean and unclean animals (ch. 11); purification after childbirth (ch. 12); regulations about defiling skin diseases and defiling molds (ch.13); cleansing from defiling skin diseases and defiling molds (ch. 14); and discharges causing uncleanness (ch. 15). See note on 15:31, which connects all these regulations to the Day of Atonement (ch. 16) and the issue of tabernacle purity and purification. See Introduction: Major Theological Themes (Holiness and Purity).

11:1–47 The rationale for distinguishing between clean and unclean food is not altogether clear and is debated among scholars. Nevertheless, some of the basic principles are quite clear. Verse 46 lists four general categories of living creatures, and v. 47 gives this chapter's purpose, i.e., to set forth what the Israelites could and could not eat. The terminology for the animal world is essentially the same as for days five and six in Gen 1:20–25; this is as close as we come to broad categories of zoology in ancient Israel. Whether a species is clean or unclean has a good deal to do with its means of locomotion and whether it is appropriate to the sphere in which it lives and moves (land, water, or sky). Another consideration is the animal's diet. Animals that eat the flesh of other animals eat their meat with the blood in it. Therefore, scavenger birds, e.g., are unclean (vv. 13–19) as are land animals that do not chew the cud (see note on v. 3). Not only were the Israelites not to eat meat with the blood in it (7:26–27; 17:10–12; cf. Gen 9:4–5), they were also to avoid eating the meat of animals that eat the meat of other animals with the blood in it. Another stated purpose of the clean and unclean animal laws was to separate Jews from Gentiles (see notes on vv. 44,45; cf. 20:22–26). If Jews had dietary laws that kept them from eating with Gentiles, they would be less likely to have meaningful relationships with Gentiles. This is one of the main reasons the clean and unclean animal laws are set aside in the NT. The "barrier" or "dividing wall of hostility" between Jews and Gentiles has been broken down by Christ (Eph 2:14); therefore, regulations that kept Jews separate from Gentiles needed to be set aside in favor of the unity of the church (Acts 10:9–16; 10:44—11:18; Gal 2:11–21). Of course, underlying all this is the fact that, as Jesus put it, the things that enter into a person are not what defiles them, but what comes out of them from their heart is what defiles them (Mark 7:18–23; note especially v. 19: "In saying this, Jesus declared all foods clean").

11:2 animals. Land animals that walk on four legs (vv. 2–7). God created them from the ground in the first part of day six (Gen 1:24–25), and ch. 11 treats them first because they are closest to the world of humans.

11:3 You may eat. Thus, clean animals. **divided hoof.** A split hoof is naturally good for walking on pasture, so these are largely pastoral animals. This also eliminates animals with paws rather than hooves (cf. v. 27). Cattle, goats, sheep, and pigs, e.g., have divided hooves, while horses and donkeys do not. **chews the cud.** Eats only grass and other fodder. These animals eat and swallow their food and then later, at their leisure, regurgitate it and chew it more thoroughly and swallow it again as part of their digestive process. They cannot digest meat, so they cannot eat blood or the meat of animals with the blood still in it. Cattle, goats, and sheep, e.g., chew the cud. Pigs have a divided hoof but do not chew the cud, so they were unclean. Similarly, camels chew the cud but do not have a divided hoof, so they were unclean.

11:4–7 Edible animals had both features, not just one of them (see v. 3 and note).

11:5 hyrax. A relatively small rodent-like animal that lives in rocky areas and eats plants (e.g., the rock badger).

11:8 touch their carcasses. Not only was it unacceptable to eat

11:10 [s]Lev 7:18
11:20 [t]Ac 10:14
11:22 [u]Mt 3:4; Mk 1:6
11:25 [v]Lev 14:8,47; 15:5 [w]ver 40; Nu 31:24
11:29 [x]Isa 66:17
11:32 [y]Lev 15:12
11:33 [z]Lev 6:28; 15:12

9" 'Of all the creatures living in the water of the seas and the streams you may eat any that have fins
and scales. 10But all creatures in the seas or streams that do not have fins and scales—whether among
all the swarming things or among all the other living creatures in the water—you are to regard as
unclean.[s] 11And since you are to regard them as unclean, you must not eat their meat; you must regard their carcasses as unclean. 12Anything living in the water that does not have fins and scales is to
be regarded as unclean by you.

13" 'These are the birds you are to regard as unclean and not eat because they are unclean: the
eagle,[a] the vulture, the black vulture, 14the red kite, any kind of black kite, 15any kind of raven, 16the
horned owl, the screech owl, the gull, any kind of hawk, 17the little owl, the cormorant, the great owl,
18the white owl, the desert owl, the osprey, 19the stork, any kind of heron, the hoopoe and the bat.

20" 'All flying insects that walk on all fours are to be regarded as unclean by you.[t] 21There are, however, some flying insects that walk on all fours that you may eat: those that have jointed legs for hopping on the ground. 22Of these you may eat any kind of locust,[u] katydid, cricket or grasshopper. 23But
all other flying insects that have four legs you are to regard as unclean.

24" 'You will make yourselves unclean by these; whoever touches their carcasses will be unclean till
evening. 25Whoever picks up one of their carcasses must wash their clothes,[v] and they will be unclean
till evening.[w]

26" 'Every animal that does not have a divided hoof or that does not chew the cud is unclean for you;
whoever touches the carcass of any of them will be unclean. 27Of all the animals that walk on all fours,
those that walk on their paws are unclean for you; whoever touches their carcasses will be unclean till
evening. 28Anyone who picks up their carcasses must wash their clothes, and they will be unclean till
evening. These animals are unclean for you.

29" 'Of the animals that move along the ground, these are unclean for you: the weasel, the rat,[x] any
kind of great lizard, 30the gecko, the monitor lizard, the wall lizard, the skink and the chameleon. 31Of
all those that move along the ground, these are unclean for you. Whoever touches them when they are
dead will be unclean till evening. 32When one of them dies and falls on something, that article, whatever its use, will be unclean, whether it is made of wood, cloth, hide or sackcloth.[y] Put it in water; it
will be unclean till evening, and then it will be clean. 33If one of them falls into a clay pot, everything
in it will be unclean, and you must break the pot.[z] 34Any food you are allowed to eat that has come into
contact with water from any such pot is unclean, and any liquid that is drunk from such a pot is unclean. 35Anything that one of their carcasses falls on becomes unclean; an oven or cooking pot must be
broken up. They are unclean, and you are to regard them as unclean. 36A spring, however, or a cistern
for collecting water remains clean, but anyone who touches one of these carcasses is unclean. 37If a
carcass falls on any seeds that are to be planted, they remain clean. 38But if water has been put on the
seed and a carcass falls on it, it is unclean for you.

[a] *13* The precise identification of some of the birds, insects and animals in this chapter is uncertain.

unclean animals, but the Israelites were not to even touch their carcasses (v. 26). If they touched such a carcass, they were unclean until evening; if they picked it up, they needed to wash their clothes and were unclean until evening (v. 28). As an unclean person, they could not enter the tabernacle lest they defile it, and they could not eat anything that required a person to be clean (7:20–21).

11:9 creatures living in the water. Those that have fins and scales belong to the category of normal; they were considered edible fish. Those that do not have these features are by and large scavengers, bottom feeders that eat flesh with the blood in it (lobster, catfish, etc.; see note on vv. 1–47); they were not to be eaten (see note on v. 10).

11:10 you are to regard as unclean. Or "they are detestable to you"; the regular Hebrew word for "unclean" does not occur here (nor does it occur in vv. 11–13,20,23,41–42). The inedible land animals (vv. 2–8) were "unclean," while inedible fish, birds, and most flying insects were worse than unclean; they were detestable or repugnant (vv. 11–13,20,23). This corresponds to the distinction between fifth-day water and sky creatures (Gen 1:20–23) versus sixth-day land animals (Gen 1:24–25). The sixth-day land animals belong to the primary world of humans, having been created on the same day, while the fifth-day animals do not. The term "detestable" also describes creeping and crawling land creatures (see notes on vv. 41,43).

11:13–19 This list of unclean birds does not identify them by features of the body, which is true of the land animals and fish in vv. 2–12. Rather, these are exclusively scavenger birds that eat flesh with the blood in it. They were detestable (see note on v. 10).

11:20–23 The only four-legged flying insects they could eat were those with "jointed legs for hopping on the ground" (v. 21). This made the four-legged flying insects something like the four-legged animals they could eat (vv. 2–8). John the Baptist, e.g., ate a diet of "locusts and wild honey" (Matt 3:4).

11:29–40 Animals that moved along the ground fell into two main categories: (1) unclean (vv. 29–40) and (2) not only unclean but detestable (vv. 41–43; see notes on vv. 10,43). For the eight in the first category, their dead carcasses would defile a person or thing if touched (v. 31). These were the kinds of creatures they might find lying dead in their homes (vv. 32–38).

[39]" 'If an animal that you are allowed to eat dies, anyone who touches its carcass will be unclean
till evening. [40]Anyone who eats some of its carcass must wash their clothes, and they will be unclean
till evening.[a] Anyone who picks up the carcass must wash their clothes, and they will be unclean till
evening.

[41]" 'Every creature that moves along the ground is to be regarded as unclean; it is not to be eaten.
[42]You are not to eat any creature that moves along the ground, whether it moves on its belly or walks
on all fours or on many feet; it is unclean. [43]Do not defile yourselves by any of these creatures.[b] Do not
make yourselves unclean by means of them or be made unclean by them. [44]I am the LORD your God;[c]
consecrate yourselves[d] and be holy,[e] because I am holy.[f] Do not make yourselves unclean by any creature that moves along the ground. [45]I am the LORD, who brought you up out of Egypt[g] to be your God;[h]
therefore be holy, because I am holy.[i]

[46]" 'These are the regulations concerning animals, birds, every living thing that moves about in the
water and every creature that moves along the ground. [47]You must distinguish between the unclean and
the clean, between living creatures that may be eaten and those that may not be eaten.[j] "

Purification After Childbirth

12 The LORD said to Moses, [2]"Say to the Israelites: 'A woman who becomes pregnant and gives
birth to a son will be ceremonially unclean for seven days, just as she is unclean during
her monthly period.[k] [3]On the eighth day the boy is to be circumcised.[l] [4]Then the woman must wait
thirty-three days to be purified from her bleeding. She must not touch anything sacred or go to the
sanctuary until the days of her purification are over. [5]If she gives birth to a daughter, for two weeks
the woman will be unclean, as during her period. Then she must wait sixty-six days to be purified
from her bleeding.

11:40 [a]Lev 17:15; 22:8; Eze 44:31
11:43 [b]Lev 20:25
11:44 [c]Ex 6:2,7; Isa 43:3; 51:15 [d]Lev 20:7 [e]Ex 19:6 [f]Lev 19:2; Ps 99:3; Eph 1:4; 1Th 4:7; 1Pe 1:15,16*
11:45 [g]Lev 25:38,55; Ex 6:7; 20:2 [h]Ge 17:7 [i]Ex 19:6; 1Pe 1:16*
11:47 [j]Lev 10:10
12:2 [k]Lev 15:19; 18:19
12:3 [l]Ge 17:12; Lk 1:59; 2:21

11:41 unclean. Detestable (see note on v. 10).

11:43 defile yourselves. Or "make yourselves detestable." **by any of these creatures.** By eating any of these detestable creeping and crawling creatures (vv. 41–43). See note on v. 10.

11:44 be holy, because I am holy. This is the first instance of the expression in the Bible. The same basic expression with some variations is found also in v. 45; 19:2; 20:7,26; 21:8 (see note on 18:1—26:46). In the present context this holiness formula is sandwiched between commands that the Israelites not make themselves unclean by the unclean ("detestable," see note on v. 10) creatures referred to in vv. 41–43 (cf. v. 43b with 44b; cf. also 20:25–26). Elsewhere in the book the holiness formula emphasizes the importance of moral holiness (19:2; 20:7) and the need for priests to maintain their holiness as those who served their holy Lord in the tabernacle (21:8). In other places God's holiness is a matter of his overwhelming majesty, purity, or both (Isa 6:3–5). Peter cites this formula in 1 Pet 1:16 in support of the holiness and purity of those who believe in Jesus Christ (see note on 1 Pet 1:15–16).

11:45 I am the LORD. This is the covenant name of God proclaimed to Moses at the burning bush (see Exod 3:14–15 and notes there) when he commissioned Moses to lead Israel out of Egypt. **who brought you up out of Egypt to be your God.** The Lord's claim is that by delivering the Israelites from Egypt they were now bound to worship and serve him as their one and only God. This refrain appears repeatedly with variations in Leviticus (8 more times: 19:36; 22:33; 23:43; 25:38,42,55; 26:13,45), and nearly 60 times in 18 other OT books. **holy.** See note on v. 44. Faithful obedience to these clean and unclean animal laws would keep them holy, separated from the worship of other gods because worshiping the gods of the peoples around them would require violating their own regulations about clean and unclean animals. They could not worship with people if they could not eat with them. Eating was then, and still is today, central to social, political, and religious relations (see note on 20:25). See "Holiness," p. 2676.

11:46–47 These verses summarize ch. 11. See note on vv. 1–47.

12:2 gives birth to a son. A woman was ceremonially unclean after giving birth to a son because of the flow of blood during and after the birth. For the longer period of time after the birth of a daughter, see v. 5 and note. **seven days, just as she is unclean during her monthly period.** As during her monthly period, she was unclean for seven days and her uncleanness could be contracted by anyone who had physical contact with her or with anything on which she lay or sat. Her husband would become impure for seven days if he had sexual intercourse with her during this time (15:19–24). The flow of blood was ceremonially unclean in the first place because of the problems with hygiene and, in the case of childbirth, especially because of the danger of sickness or death from loss of blood.

12:3 circumcised. For the original institution of circumcision of the male child in ancient Israel, see Gen 17:9–14 and notes.

12:4 thirty-three. Number of days required to be purified from her bleeding (in addition to the seven days in v. 2). **must not touch anything sacred or go to the sanctuary.** If she did so during this time, she would defile it. However, during this 33-day period she was no longer contagious like she had been during the first seven days (v. 2), so she could engage in normal everyday life, including sexual intercourse, without fear of contaminating anyone. After these 33 days, blood atonement was made for her purification from her blood flow so that she could be pronounced "clean" by the priest (vv. 6–8).

12:5 gives birth to a daughter … two weeks … sixty-six days. Doubling the time after the birth of a female child is puzzling. What stands out about the passage, however, are the doublings of 7 to 14 and 33 to 66, adding up to 40 days for the son and 80 days for the daughter. The mention of circumcision on the eighth day for the boy child (v. 3) may also be of help here. First, a male baby had to be circumcised on the eighth day, so the contagious impurity of the mother could not last beyond the first seven days lest it interfere with the circumcision rite (cf. Luke 2:21–24). Of course, this did not apply to the female baby. Second, one would expect that the increased severity of the blood flow after childbirth, as compared to that of a woman's monthly period, would call for a longer period of impurity than the normal seven days (see note on v. 2). The initial 14-day impurity period for the female baby would have

12:6 [m]Lk 2:22 [n]Ex 29:38; Lev 23:12; Nu 6:12,14; 7:15 [o]Lev 5:7
12:8 [p]Ge 15:9; Lev 14:22 [q]Lev 5:7; Lk 2:22-24* [r]Lev 4:26
13:2 [s]ver 10,19,28,43 [t]ver 4,38,39; Lev 14:56 [u]ver 3,9,15; Ex 4:6; Lev 14:3,32; Nu 5:2; Dt 24:8 [v]Dt 24:8
13:3 [w]ver 8,11,20,30; Lev 21:1; Nu 9:6
13:4 [x]ver 2 [y]ver 5,21, 26,33,46; Lev 14:38; Nu 12:14,15; Dt 24:9
13:5 [z]Lev 14:9 [a]ver 27,32,34,51
13:6 [b]ver 13,17,23,28, 34; Mt 8:3; Lk 5:12-14 [c]Lev 11:25 [d]Lev 11:25; 14:8,9,20,48; 15:8; Nu 8:7
13:7 [e]Lk 5:14
13:11 [f]Ex 4:6; Lev 14:8; Nu 12:10; Mt 8:2

6" 'When the days of her purification for a son or daughter are over,[m] she is to bring to the priest at
the entrance to the tent of meeting a year-old lamb[n] for a burnt offering and a young pigeon or a dove
for a sin offering.[a][o] 7He shall offer them before the LORD to make atonement for her, and then she will
be ceremonially clean from her flow of blood.

" 'These are the regulations for the woman who gives birth to a boy or a girl. 8But if she cannot afford a lamb, she is to bring two doves or two young pigeons,[p] one for a burnt offering and the other for
a sin offering.[q] In this way the priest will make atonement for her, and she will be clean.[r] ' "

Regulations About Defiling Skin Diseases

13 The LORD said to Moses and Aaron, 2"When anyone has a swelling[s] or a rash or a shiny spot[t]
on their skin that may be a defiling skin disease,[b][u] they must be brought to Aaron the priest[v]
or to one of his sons[c] who is a priest. 3The priest is to examine the sore on the skin, and if the hair in
the sore has turned white and the sore appears to be more than skin deep, it is a defiling skin disease.
When the priest examines that person, he shall pronounce them ceremonially unclean.[w] 4If the shiny
spot[x] on the skin is white but does not appear to be more than skin deep and the hair in it has not
turned white, the priest is to isolate the affected person for seven days.[y] 5On the seventh day[z] the priest
is to examine them,[a] and if he sees that the sore is unchanged and has not spread in the skin, he is to
isolate them for another seven days. 6On the seventh day the priest is to examine them again, and if the
sore has faded and has not spread in the skin, the priest shall pronounce them clean;[b] it is only a rash.
They must wash their clothes,[c] and they will be clean.[d] 7But if the rash does spread in their skin after
they have shown themselves to the priest to be pronounced clean, they must appear before the priest
again.[e] 8The priest is to examine that person, and if the rash has spread in the skin, he shall pronounce
them unclean; it is a defiling skin disease.

9"When anyone has a defiling skin disease, they must be brought to the priest. 10The priest is to examine them, and if there is a white swelling in the skin that has turned the hair white and if there is
raw flesh in the swelling, 11it is a chronic skin disease[f] and the priest shall pronounce them unclean.
He is not to isolate them, because they are already unclean.

12"If the disease breaks out all over their skin and, so far as the priest can see, it covers all the skin
of the affected person from head to foot, 13the priest is to examine them, and if the disease has covered
their whole body, he shall pronounce them clean. Since it has all turned white, they are clean. 14But
whenever raw flesh appears on them, they will be unclean. 15When the priest sees the raw flesh, he

[a] *6* Or *purification offering*; also in verse 8 [b] *2* The Hebrew word for *defiling skin disease*, traditionally translated "leprosy," was used for various diseases affecting the skin; here and throughout verses 3-46. [c] *2* Or *descendants*

been more appropriate. But this had to be shortened for the male baby precisely because of circumcision. The second set of days is handled proportionately (i.e., 33 becomes 66).

12:6 sin offering. See note on 4:1—5:13. Its purpose was to purge impurities from the tabernacle. In this case, the woman had not sinned by having a child. Even Mary brought such offerings for giving birth to Jesus (Luke 2:22–24), though she certainly did not sin in giving birth to the Messiah.

12:7 she will be ceremonially clean. The result of bringing the "sin offering" was that the mother was pronounced "clean" (vv. 7–8), not forgiven (see note on v. 6).

13:1—14:57 Chs. 13–14 deal with defiling skin diseases and defiling molds: first, the diagnosis (ch. 13) and second, purification procedures if or when the person/fabric/house recovered (ch. 14). The summary statement at the end of the section lays out the main categories of such diseases (14:54–57). Regarding defiling skin diseases, they could occur (1) as a swelling, rash or shiny spot on the body (14:56; cf. 13:2–28,38–44); (2) as a sore on the head or chin (14:54b; cf. 13:29–37); or (3) as a defiling mold either in fabric (14:55; cf. 13:47–59) or in a house (14:55; cf. 14:33–53).

13:2 Some of the terms for disease or symptoms of disease in ch. 13 present difficulties for translators. **swelling.** Could derive from a verb that means "to rise up." **rash.** Exact meaning unknown; some versions translate it "scab" or "flaking skin" or "eruption." **defiling skin disease.** See NIV text note. The regulations are concerned with any diseases that are observable on the surface of the skin or penetrate below the surface of the skin (vv. 3–4) or spread further across the surface of the skin (vv. 5–8).

13:3 unclean. See also vv. 8,11,15,20 and throughout the chapter. The primary concern of ch. 13 is that these diseases make a person ceremonially unclean. These were actual diseases from which a person could be physically healed (14:3), but even then the focus became the ceremonial cleansing procedures that followed (14:4–20).

13:4 isolate the affected person. Because it might take time for the priest to determine whether the mark indicated a defiling skin disease.

13:11 chronic skin disease. An old, enduring disease that keeps on developing or recurring. **not to isolate.** See note on v. 4. Since it is already clear that the disease is infectious, there is no need to isolate them for seven days to find that out. For the full and enduring quarantine required, see note on v. 46.

13:13–14 If it had all turned white, it was dried up and healing (cf. vv. 16–17), but if there was raw flesh, the disease was still active (vv. 10–11).

shall pronounce them unclean. The raw flesh is unclean; they have a defiling disease.[g] 16 If the raw
flesh changes and turns white, they must go to the priest. 17 The priest is to examine them, and if the
sores have turned white, the priest shall pronounce the affected person clean;[h] then they will be clean.
18 "When someone has a boil[i] on their skin and it heals, 19 and in the place where the boil was, a
white swelling or reddish-white[j] spot[k] appears, they must present themselves to the priest. 20 The priest
is to examine it, and if it appears to be more than skin deep and the hair in it has turned white, the
priest shall pronounce that person unclean. It is a defiling skin disease[l] that has broken out where the
boil was. 21 But if, when the priest examines it, there is no white hair in it and it is not more than skin
deep and has faded, then the priest is to isolate them for seven days. 22 If it is spreading in the skin, the
priest shall pronounce them unclean; it is a defiling disease. 23 But if the spot is unchanged and has not
spread, it is only a scar from the boil, and the priest shall pronounce them clean.[m]
24 "When someone has a burn on their skin and a reddish-white or white spot appears in the raw
flesh of the burn, 25 the priest is to examine the spot, and if the hair in it has turned white, and it appears to be more than skin deep, it is a defiling disease that has broken out in the burn. The priest shall
pronounce them unclean; it is a defiling skin disease.[n] 26 But if the priest examines it and there is no
white hair in the spot and if it is not more than skin deep and has faded, then the priest is to isolate
them for seven days.[o] 27 On the seventh day the priest is to examine that person,[p] and if it is spreading
in the skin, the priest shall pronounce them unclean; it is a defiling skin disease. 28 If, however, the spot
is unchanged and has not spread in the skin but has faded, it is a swelling from the burn, and the priest
shall pronounce them clean; it is only a scar from the burn.[q]
29 "If a man or woman has a sore on their head[r] or chin, 30 the priest is to examine the sore, and if
it appears to be more than skin deep and the hair in it is yellow and thin, the priest shall pronounce
them unclean; it is a defiling skin disease on the head or chin. 31 But if, when the priest examines the
sore, it does not seem to be more than skin deep and there is no black hair in it, then the priest is to
isolate the affected person for seven days.[s] 32 On the seventh day the priest is to examine the sore,[t] and
if it has not spread and there is no yellow hair in it and it does not appear to be more than skin deep,
33 then the man or woman must shave themselves, except for the affected area, and the priest is to keep
them isolated another seven days. 34 On the seventh day the priest is to examine the sore,[u] and if it has
not spread in the skin and appears to be no more than skin deep, the priest shall pronounce them clean.
They must wash their clothes, and they will be clean.[v] 35 But if the sore does spread in the skin after they
are pronounced clean, 36 the priest is to examine them, and if he finds that the sore has spread in the
skin, he does not need to look for yellow hair; they are unclean.[w] 37 If, however, the sore is unchanged
so far as the priest can see, and if black hair has grown in it, the affected person is healed. They are
clean, and the priest shall pronounce them clean.
38 "When a man or woman has white spots on the skin, 39 the priest is to examine them, and if the
spots are dull white, it is a harmless rash that has broken out on the skin; they are clean.
40 "A man who has lost his hair and is bald[x] is clean. 41 If he has lost his hair from the front of his
scalp and has a bald forehead, he is clean. 42 But if he has a reddish-white sore on his bald head or
forehead, it is a defiling disease breaking out on his head or forehead. 43 The priest is to examine him,
and if the swollen sore on his head or forehead is reddish-white like a defiling skin disease, 44 the man
is diseased and is unclean. The priest shall pronounce him unclean because of the sore on his head.
45 "Anyone with such a defiling disease must wear torn clothes,[y] let their hair be unkempt,[a] cover
the lower part of their face[z] and cry out, 'Unclean! Unclean!'[a] 46 As long as they have the disease they
remain unclean. They must live alone; they must live outside the camp.[b]

[a] *45* Or *clothes, uncover their head*

13:15 [g] ver 2
13:17 [h] ver 6
13:18 [i] Ex 9:9
13:19 [j] ver 24, 42; Lev 14:37 [k] ver 2
13:20 [l] ver 2
13:23 [m] ver 6
13:25 [n] ver 11
13:26 [o] ver 4
13:27 [p] ver 5
13:28 [q] ver 2
13:29 [r] ver 43, 44
13:31 [s] ver 4
13:32 [t] ver 5
13:34 [u] ver 5 [v] Lev 11:25
13:36 [w] ver 30
13:40 [x] Lev 21:5; 2Ki 2:23; Isa 3:24; 15:2; 22:12; Eze 27:31; 29:18; Am 8:10; Mic 1:16
13:45 [y] Lev 10:6 [z] Eze 24:17, 22; Mic 3:7 [a] Lev 5:2; La 4:15; Lk 17:12
13:46 [b] Nu 5:1-4; 12:14; 2Ki 7:3; 15:5; Lk 17:12

13:26 isolate. See note on v. 4.

13:45 wear torn clothes, let their hair be unkempt, cover the lower part of their face. All these practices were associated with funerary mourning rites (10:6; 21:10; Ezek 24:17,22; Mic 3:7). In Num 12:10–12 Miriam, the sister of Moses and Aaron, was punished with a skin disease. Aaron associated it with death when he begged the Lord, "Do not let her be like a stillborn infant coming from its mother's womb with its flesh half eaten away" (Num 12:12). The close association with death explains why such diseases were so defiling and required such extreme measures to ensure that the defilement did not spread (cf. Num 19:11–13). In a sense, the person was considered dead by the community. **cry out, 'Unclean! Unclean!'** See Lam 4:15; Luke 17:12–13. The purpose was to announce their uncleanness so people would not touch them or even come near them.

13:46 They must live alone; they must live outside the camp. This is different from the period of "isolation," the purpose of which was to

13:49 [c]Mk 1:44
13:50 [d]Eze 44:23
13:51 [e]ver 5 [f]Lev 14:44
13:52 [g]ver 55,57
14:2 [h]Mt 8:2-4; Mk 1:40-44; Lk 5:12-14; 17:14
14:3 [i]Lev 13:46
14:4 [j]ver 6,49,51,52; Nu 19:6; Ps 51:7
14:6 [k]ver 4
14:7 [l]2Ki 5:10,14; Isa 52:15; Eze 36:25

Regulations About Defiling Molds

47“As for any fabric that is spoiled with a defiling mold — any woolen or linen clothing, 48any woven
or knitted material of linen or wool, any leather or anything made of leather — 49if the affected area
in the fabric, the leather, the woven or knitted material, or any leather article, is greenish or reddish,
it is a defiling mold and must be shown to the priest.[c] 50The priest is to examine the affected area[d] and
isolate the article for seven days. 51On the seventh day he is to examine it,[e] and if the mold has spread
in the fabric, the woven or knitted material, or the leather, whatever its use, it is a persistent defiling
mold; the article is unclean.[f] 52He must burn the fabric, the woven or knitted material of wool or linen,
or any leather article that has been spoiled; because the defiling mold is persistent, the article must
be burned.[g]

53“But if, when the priest examines it, the mold has not spread in the fabric, the woven or knitted
material, or the leather article, 54he shall order that the spoiled article be washed. Then he is to isolate
it for another seven days. 55After the article has been washed, the priest is to examine it again, and if the
mold has not changed its appearance, even though it has not spread, it is unclean. Burn it, no matter
which side of the fabric has been spoiled. 56If, when the priest examines it, the mold has faded after
the article has been washed, he is to tear the spoiled part out of the fabric, the leather, or the woven or
knitted material. 57But if it reappears in the fabric, in the woven or knitted material, or in the leather
article, it is a spreading mold; whatever has the mold must be burned. 58Any fabric, woven or knitted
material, or any leather article that has been washed and is rid of the mold, must be washed again.
Then it will be clean.”

59These are the regulations concerning defiling molds in woolen or linen clothing, woven or knitted
material, or any leather article, for pronouncing them clean or unclean.

Cleansing From Defiling Skin Diseases

14 The LORD said to Moses, 2“These are the regulations for any diseased person at the time of their
ceremonial cleansing, when they are brought to the priest:[h] 3The priest is to go outside the
camp and examine them.[i] If they have been healed of their defiling skin disease,[a] 4the priest shall order
that two live clean birds and some cedar wood, scarlet yarn and hyssop be brought for the person to be
cleansed.[j] 5Then the priest shall order that one of the birds be killed over fresh water in a clay pot. 6He
is then to take the live bird and dip it, together with the cedar wood, the scarlet yarn and the hyssop,
into the blood of the bird that was killed over the fresh water.[k] 7Seven times he shall sprinkle[l] the one
to be cleansed of the defiling disease, and then pronounce them clean. After that, he is to release the
live bird in the open fields.

[a] *3* The Hebrew word for *defiling skin disease*, traditionally translated “leprosy,” was used for various diseases affecting the skin; also in verses 7, 32, 54 and 57.

determine whether the disease was active or not (see vv. 4,10–11 and notes). Here the presence of active disease had already been confirmed, so a quarantine was imposed. No matter how long it took, the person needed to be healed from the disease (14:3) before they could start the required ritual purification procedures (14:4–20) and eventually move back into the camp. The primary purpose of the quarantine was to prevent the spread of ceremonial impurity in the camp and to the tabernacle (see note on v. 3; cf. 15:31). Of course, it would also help prevent the spread of the actual disease if it was contagious, but many of the people with such diseases were not contagious, so that was not the main point.

13:47–48 defiling mold. Translates the same term rendered “defiling skin disease” in v. 2. **woolen or linen ... leather.** Defiling mold could appear and spread on any such materials. The regulations that follow are in many ways parallel to the way defiling skin diseases were to be diagnosed and dealt with (cf. vv. 1–46).

14:3 go outside the camp. The person could not reenter the camp until (1) they were purified by the priest through certain special rituals (vv. 4–7), (2) the priest declared them “clean” (v. 7), and (3) they washed their clothes, shaved off all their hair, and bathed their bodies (v. 8). After that, they could reenter the camp but had to live outside their tent for seven days (v. 8). To make sure they were rid of the skin disease, on the seventh day they once again washed their clothes, shaved off all their hair, and bathed their bodies; then they were “clean” (v. 9). On the eighth day they performed sacrificial rituals for atonement and final purification (vv. 10–20).

14:4 cedar wood, scarlet yarn. Both the reddish color of the cedar wood and the scarlet-colored fabric seem to correspond to the color of blood and may therefore symbolize either “life,” which is in the blood, or the use of blood to “make atonement” (17:11; see Gen 9:4). **hyssop.** A spice and herb that grew out of walls in the Holy Land (1 Kgs 4:33). It was particularly leafy and therefore especially useful for sprinkling the purifying liquid (cf. vv. 6–7).

14:5–7 This ritual procedure probably symbolized the renewed life of the diseased person and displayed it publicly for all to see. It was preparatory to the sacrificial rituals that followed (vv. 10–20, especially vv. 18–20). The nature of this ritual and its obvious similarity to the scapegoat ritual in 16:20–22 suggests that the person’s uncleanness was removed far away so that they were free from its effects both personally and communally.

8"The person to be cleansed must wash their clothes,[m] shave off all their hair and bathe with water;[n] then they will be ceremonially clean.[o] After this they may come into the camp,[p] but they must
stay outside their tent for seven days. 9On the seventh day they must shave off all their hair; they must
shave their head, their beard, their eyebrows and the rest of their hair. They must wash their clothes
and bathe themselves with water, and they will be clean.
10"On the eighth day[q] they must bring two male lambs and one ewe lamb a year old, each without
defect, along with three-tenths of an ephah[a] of the finest flour mixed with olive oil for a grain offering,[r]
and one log[b] of oil.[s] 11The priest who pronounces them clean shall present both the one to be cleansed
and their offerings before the LORD at the entrance to the tent of meeting.
12"Then the priest is to take one of the male lambs and offer it as a guilt offering,[t] along with the
log of oil; he shall wave them before the LORD as a wave offering.[u] 13He is to slaughter the lamb in the
sanctuary area[v] where the sin offering[c] and the burnt offering are slaughtered. Like the sin offering,
the guilt offering belongs to the priest;[w] it is most holy. 14The priest is to take some of the blood of the
guilt offering and put it on the lobe of the right ear of the one to be cleansed, on the thumb of their right
hand and on the big toe of their right foot.[x] 15The priest shall then take some of the log of oil, pour it
in the palm of his own left hand, 16dip his right forefinger into the oil in his palm, and with his finger
sprinkle some of it before the LORD seven times. 17The priest is to put some of the oil remaining in his
palm on the lobe of the right ear of the one to be cleansed, on the thumb of their right hand and on the
big toe of their right foot, on top of the blood of the guilt offering. 18The rest of the oil in his palm the
priest shall put on the head of the one to be cleansed and make atonement for them before the LORD.
19"Then the priest is to sacrifice the sin offering and make atonement for the one to be cleansed from
their uncleanness. After that, the priest shall slaughter the burnt offering 20and offer it on the altar,
together with the grain offering, and make atonement for them, and they will be clean.[y]
21"If, however, they are poor[z] and cannot afford these,[a] they must take one male lamb as a guilt offering to be waved to make atonement for them, together with a tenth of an ephah[d] of the finest flour
mixed with olive oil for a grain offering, a log of oil, 22and two doves or two young pigeons,[b] such as
they can afford, one for a sin offering and the other for a burnt offering.
23"On the eighth day they must bring them for their cleansing to the priest at the entrance to the tent
of meeting, before the LORD.[c] 24The priest is to take the lamb for the guilt offering,[d] together with the log
of oil,[e] and wave them before the LORD as a wave offering.[f] 25He shall slaughter the lamb for the guilt
offering and take some of its blood and put it on the lobe of the right ear of the one to be cleansed, on
the thumb of their right hand and on the big toe of their right foot.[g] 26The priest is to pour some of the
oil into the palm of his own left hand,[h] 27and with his right forefinger sprinkle some of the oil from his
palm seven times before the LORD. 28Some of the oil in his palm he is to put on the same places he put
the blood of the guilt offering—on the lobe of the right ear of the one to be cleansed, on the thumb of
their right hand and on the big toe of their right foot. 29The rest of the oil in his palm the priest shall
put on the head of the one to be cleansed, to make atonement for them before the LORD.[i] 30Then he shall
sacrifice the doves or the young pigeons, such as the person can afford,[j] 31one as a sin offering and the
other as a burnt offering,[k] together with the grain offering. In this way the priest will make atonement
before the LORD on behalf of the one to be cleansed."

14:8 [m]Lev 11:25; 13:6 [n]ver 9 [o]ver 20 [p]Nu 5:2, 3; 12:14,15; 2Ch 26:21
14:10 [q]Mt 8:4; Mk 1:44; Lk 5:14 [r]Lev 2:1 [s]ver 12, 15,21,24
14:12 [t]Lev 5:18; 6:6-7 [u]Ex 29:24
14:13 [v]Ex 29:11 [w]Lev 6:24-30; 7:7
14:14 [x]Ex 29:20; Lev 8:23
14:20 [y]ver 8
14:21 [z]Lev 5:7; 12:8 [a]ver 22,32
14:22 [b]Lev 5:7
14:23 [c]ver 10,11
14:24 [d]Nu 6:14 [e]ver 10 [f]ver 12
14:25 [g]ver 14; Ex 29:20
14:26 [h]ver 15
14:29 [i]ver 18
14:30 [j]Lev 5:7
14:31 [k]ver 22; Lev 5:7; 15:15,30 [l]ver 18,19

[a] *10* That is, probably about 11 pounds or about 5 kilograms [b] *10* That is, about 1/3 quart or about 0.3 liter; also in verses 12, 15, 21 and 24 [c] *13* Or *purification offering*; also in verses 19, 22 and 31
[d] *21* That is, probably about 3 1/2 pounds or about 1.6 kilograms

14:8 ceremonially clean … they may come into the camp. The outcome of the ritual procedures in vv. 4–7 and the washing and shaving in v. 8 (cf. 13:46). But they had to undergo further cleansing rituals and pronouncements in the tabernacle (vv. 10–20).

14:12 guilt offering. The primary purpose of the guilt offering was to make atonement for desecration of the Lord's "holy" things, whether they were his sacred objects or his sacred people (see note on 5:14—6:7). Israel was "a kingdom of priests and a holy nation" to the Lord (Exod 19:6), and the skin-diseased person was a member of the "holy nation." Therefore, being expelled from the community was desecration—that which was holy had been treated as not holy. **wave offering.** See notes on 7:30,31.

14:14–17 See the similarities of the manipulation of blood and oil here to that for the consecration of the Aaronic priests (see 8:22–24,30 and notes; Exod 29:19–21). All the Israelites were consecrated to worship and serve the Lord.

14:18 make atonement. Also in vv. 18,19,21,31,53; see notes on 16:20–22; 17:11; see also NIV text note on Rom 3:25.

14:21–22 Concessions to the poor allowed them to bring less expensive offerings (cf. 5:7–13; see notes on 5:7,11), but the procedures in vv. 23–31 are virtually the same as those in vv. 14–20.

14:32 [m]Lev 13:2 [n]ver 21
14:34 [o]Ge 12:5; Ex 6:4; Nu 13:2 [p]Ge 17:8; 48:4; Nu 27:12; 32:22; Dt 3:27; 7:1; 32:49
14:37 [q]Lev 13:19
14:38 [r]Lev 13:4
14:39 [s]Lev 13:5
14:40 [t]ver 45
14:44 [u]Lev 13:51
14:46 [v]Lev 11:24
14:47 [w]Lev 11:25
14:48 [x]Lev 13:6
14:49 [y]ver 4; 1Ki 4:33; ver 4
14:50 [z]ver 5
14:51 [a]ver 6; Ps 51:7 [b]ver 4,7
14:53 [c]ver 7 [d]ver 20
14:54 [e]Lev 13:2,30
14:55 [f]Lev 13:47-52
14:56 [g]Lev 13:2
14:57 [h]Lev 10:10
15:2 [i]ver 16,32; Lev 22:4; Nu 5:2; 2Sa 3:29; Mt 9:20
15:5 [j]Lev 11:25 [k]Lev 14:8

32 These are the regulations for anyone who has a defiling skin disease[m] and who cannot afford the regular offerings[n] for their cleansing.

Cleansing From Defiling Molds

33 The LORD said to Moses and Aaron, 34 "When you enter the land of Canaan,[o] which I am giving you as your possession,[p] and I put a spreading mold in a house in that land, 35 the owner of the house must go and tell the priest, 'I have seen something that looks like a defiling mold in my house.' 36 The priest is to order the house to be emptied before he goes in to examine the mold, so that nothing in the house will be pronounced unclean. After this the priest is to go in and inspect the house. 37 He is to examine the mold on the walls, and if it has greenish or reddish[q] depressions that appear to be deeper than the surface of the wall, 38 the priest shall go out the doorway of the house and close it up for seven days.[r] 39 On the seventh day[s] the priest shall return to inspect the house. If the mold has spread on the walls, 40 he is to order that the contaminated stones be torn out and thrown into an unclean place outside the town.[t] 41 He must have all the inside walls of the house scraped and the material that is scraped off dumped into an unclean place outside the town. 42 Then they are to take other stones to replace these and take new clay and plaster the house.

43 "If the defiling mold reappears in the house after the stones have been torn out and the house scraped and plastered, 44 the priest is to go and examine it and, if the mold has spread in the house, it is a persistent defiling mold; the house is unclean.[u] 45 It must be torn down—its stones, timbers and all the plaster—and taken out of the town to an unclean place.

46 "Anyone who goes into the house while it is closed up will be unclean till evening.[v] 47 Anyone who sleeps or eats in the house must wash their clothes.[w]

48 "But if the priest comes to examine it and the mold has not spread after the house has been plastered, he shall pronounce the house clean,[x] because the defiling mold is gone. 49 To purify the house he is to take two birds and some cedar wood, scarlet yarn and hyssop.[y] 50 He shall kill one of the birds over fresh water in a clay pot.[z] 51 Then he is to take the cedar wood, the hyssop,[a] the scarlet yarn and the live bird, dip them into the blood of the dead bird and the fresh water, and sprinkle the house seven times.[b] 52 He shall purify the house with the bird's blood, the fresh water, the live bird, the cedar wood, the hyssop and the scarlet yarn. 53 Then he is to release the live bird in the open fields[c] outside the town. In this way he will make atonement for the house, and it will be clean.[d]"

54 These are the regulations for any defiling skin disease,[e] for a sore, 55 for defiling molds[f] in fabric or in a house, 56 and for a swelling, a rash or a shiny spot,[g] 57 to determine when something is clean or unclean.

These are the regulations for defiling skin diseases and defiling molds.[h]

Discharges Causing Uncleanness

15 The LORD said to Moses and Aaron, 2 "Speak to the Israelites and say to them: 'When any man has an unusual bodily discharge,[i] such a discharge is unclean. 3 Whether it continues flowing from his body or is blocked, it will make him unclean. This is how his discharge will bring about uncleanness:

4 " 'Any bed the man with a discharge lies on will be unclean, and anything he sits on will be unclean. 5 Anyone who touches his bed must wash their clothes[j] and bathe with water,[k] and they will be unclean

14:34 I put. Reflects the reality that such things are from the Lord too. **spreading mold.** As in 13:47–48 (see note there), the term is the same as that for a "defiling skin disease" in 13:2.

14:48–53 The rituals for the house that the priest pronounced clean are virtually the same as those for the recovered person (see 14:4–7 and notes).

14:54–57 See note on 13:1—14:57.

15:1–33 See the summary in vv. 32–33. Here the concern is discharges from a man or woman's body, specifically those from the sexual organs: (1) a male's emission of semen, even in regular sexual intercourse (vv. 16–18); (2) a woman's monthly period (vv. 19–23); (3) an irregular discharge from the sexual organs of a man (vv. 1–15) or a woman (vv. 25–30). There is also a regulation for a man who had sexual relations with a woman who was ceremonially unclean because of her monthly period (v. 24). For the rationale of ceremonial uncleanness, see note on 11:1—15:33; see also Introduction: Major Theological Themes (Holiness and Purity).

15:2 unusual bodily discharge. In ch. 15, the terms "flesh" and "body" are usually euphemisms for the male or female genitals.

15:4 lies … sits. Uncleanness was contagious (see Hag 2:11–13), so those who were unclean had to be cleansed, and others needed to avoid physical contact with them or anything to which the person's uncleanness had been transferred.

15:5 unclean. Also vv. 6–11. The person could not, e.g., eat holy food

till evening.[l] 6 Whoever sits on anything that the man with a discharge sat on must wash their clothes and bathe with water, and they will be unclean till evening.

7 " 'Whoever touches the man[m] who has a discharge[n] must wash their clothes and bathe with water, and they will be unclean till evening.

8 " 'If the man with the discharge spits[o] on anyone who is clean, they must wash their clothes and bathe with water, and they will be unclean till evening.

9 " 'Everything the man sits on when riding will be unclean, 10 and whoever touches any of the things that were under him will be unclean till evening; whoever picks up those things[p] must wash their clothes and bathe with water, and they will be unclean till evening.

11 " 'Anyone the man with a discharge touches without rinsing his hands with water must wash their clothes and bathe with water, and they will be unclean till evening.

12 " 'A clay pot[q] that the man touches must be broken, and any wooden article[r] is to be rinsed with water.

13 " 'When a man is cleansed from his discharge, he is to count off seven days[s] for his ceremonial cleansing; he must wash his clothes and bathe himself with fresh water, and he will be clean.[t] 14 On the eighth day he must take two doves or two young pigeons[u] and come before the LORD to the entrance to the tent of meeting and give them to the priest. 15 The priest is to sacrifice them, the one for a sin offering[a][v] and the other for a burnt offering.[w] In this way he will make atonement before the LORD for the man because of his discharge.[x]

16 " 'When a man has an emission of semen,[y] he must bathe his whole body with water, and he will be unclean till evening.[z] 17 Any clothing or leather that has semen on it must be washed with water, and it will be unclean till evening. 18 When a man has sexual relations with a woman and there is an emission of semen,[a] both of them must bathe with water, and they will be unclean till evening.

19 " 'When a woman has her regular flow of blood, the impurity of her monthly period[b] will last seven days, and anyone who touches her will be unclean till evening.

20 " 'Anything she lies on during her period will be unclean, and anything she sits on will be unclean. 21 Anyone who touches her bed will be unclean; they must wash their clothes and bathe with water, and they will be unclean till evening.[c] 22 Anyone who touches anything she sits on will be unclean; they must wash their clothes and bathe with water, and they will be unclean till evening. 23 Whether it is the bed or anything she was sitting on, when anyone touches it, they will be unclean till evening.

24 " 'If a man has sexual relations with her and her monthly flow[d] touches him, he will be unclean for seven days; any bed he lies on will be unclean.

25 " 'When a woman has a discharge of blood for many days at a time other than her monthly period[e] or has a discharge that continues beyond her period, she will be unclean as long as she has the discharge, just as in the days of her period. 26 Any bed she lies on while her discharge continues will be unclean, as is her bed during her monthly period, and anything she sits on will be unclean, as during her period. 27 Anyone who touches them will be unclean; they must wash their clothes and bathe with water, and they will be unclean till evening.

28 " 'When she is cleansed from her discharge, she must count off seven days, and after that she will be ceremonially clean. 29 On the eighth day she must take two doves or two young pigeons[f] and bring them to the priest at the entrance to the tent of meeting. 30 The priest is to sacrifice one for a sin offering and the other for a burnt offering. In this way he will make atonement for her before the LORD for the uncleanness of her discharge.[g]

31 " 'You must keep the Israelites separate from things that make them unclean, so they will not die in their uncleanness for defiling my dwelling place,[b][h] which is among them.' "

15:5 [l] Lev 11:24
15:7 [m] ver 19; Lev 22:5 [n] ver 16; Lev 22:4
15:8 [o] Nu 12:14
15:10 [p] Nu 19:10
15:12 [q] Lev 6:28 [r] Lev 11:32
15:13 [s] Lev 8:33 [t] ver 5
15:14 [u] Lev 14:22
15:15 [v] Lev 5:7 [w] Lev 14:31 [x] Lev 14:18,19
15:16 [y] ver 2; Lev 22:4; Dt 23:10 [z] ver 5; Dt 23:11
15:18 [a] 1Sa 21:4
15:19 [b] ver 24; Lev 12:2
15:21 [c] ver 27
15:24 [d] ver 19; Lev 12:2; 18:19; 20:18; Eze 18:6
15:25 [e] Mt 9:20; Mk 5:25; Lk 8:43
15:29 [f] Lev 14:22
15:30 [g] Lev 5:10; 14:20, 31; 18:19; 2Sa 11:4; Mk 5:25; Lk 8:43
15:31 [h] Lev 20:3; Nu 5:3; 19:13,20; 2Sa 15:25; 2Ki 21:7; Ps 33:14; 74:7; 76:2; Eze 5:11; 23:38

[a] *15* Or *purification offering*; also in verse 30 [b] *31* Or *my tabernacle*

or enter the tabernacle until their uncleanness was cleansed lest they contaminate it (cf. 7:20–21). **till evening.** From 23:32 it is clear that the day went from evening to evening. So if a person became unclean for the day, they needed to do cleansing procedures (i.e., wash their body and clothes) and consider themselves unclean until the coming evening, which was the beginning of the next day.

15:16–18 Whether in sexual intercourse or not, an emission of semen caused ceremonial uncleanness. This does not imply that there is anything sinful about sex or sexual relations between a husband and wife. When a sin offering was presented for such uncleanness, it always resulted in cleansing, not forgiveness (see notes on 4:1—5:13; 12:6,7).

15:31 separate. Translates a Hebrew word from the same root used for the "Nazirite" vow (Num 6), a special vow of holy separation unto God. Here it refers to the need to prevent contamination of the tabernacle in their midst. **so they will not die in their uncleanness.** This was a matter of life and death. Nadab and Abihu are examples of such a

15:32 [i]ver 2
15:33 [j]ver 19,24,25
16:1 [k]Lev 10:1
16:2 [l]Ex 30:10; Heb 9:7 [m]Heb 9:25; 10:19 [n]Ex 25:22 [o]Ex 40:34
16:3 [p]Heb 9:24,25
16:4 [q]Ex 28:39 [r]Ex 28:42 [s]ver 24; Heb 10:22
16:5 [t]Lev 4:13-21 [u]2Ch 29:23
16:6 [v]Lev 9:7; Heb 5:3; 7:27; 9:7,12
16:10 [w]Isa 53:4-10; Ro 3:25; 1Jn 2:2
16:11 [x]Heb 7:27; 9:7
16:12 [y]Lev 10:1 [z]Ex 30:34-38
16:13 [a]Ex 28:43; Lev 22:9
16:14 [b]Lev 4:5; Heb 9:7, 13,25 [c]Lev 4:6
16:15 [d]Heb 9:7,12 [e]Heb 9:3
16:16 [f]Ex 29:36

32 These are the regulations for a man with a discharge, for anyone made unclean by an emission of
semen,[i] 33 for a woman in her monthly period, for a man or a woman with a discharge, and for a man
who has sexual relations with a woman who is ceremonially unclean.[j]

The Day of Atonement

16:2-34pp — Lev 23:26-32; Nu 29:7-11

16 The LORD spoke to Moses after the death of the two sons of Aaron who died when they approached the LORD.[k] 2 The LORD said to Moses: "Tell your brother Aaron that he is not to come
whenever he chooses[l] into the Most Holy Place[m] behind the curtain in front of the atonement cover on
the ark, or else he will die. For I will appear[n] in the cloud[o] over the atonement cover.

3 "This is how Aaron is to enter the Most Holy Place:[p] He must first bring a young bull for a sin offering[a] and a ram for a burnt offering. 4 He is to put on the sacred linen tunic, with linen undergarments
next to his body; he is to tie the linen sash around him and put on the linen turban.[q] These are sacred
garments;[r] so he must bathe himself with water[s] before he puts them on. 5 From the Israelite community[t] he is to take two male goats[u] for a sin offering and a ram for a burnt offering.

6 "Aaron is to offer the bull for his own sin offering to make atonement for himself and his household.[v] 7 Then he is to take the two goats and present them before the LORD at the entrance to the tent of
meeting. 8 He is to cast lots for the two goats — one lot for the LORD and the other for the scapegoat.[b]
9 Aaron shall bring the goat whose lot falls to the LORD and sacrifice it for a sin offering. 10 But the goat
chosen by lot as the scapegoat shall be presented alive before the LORD to be used for making atonement[w] by sending it into the wilderness as a scapegoat.

11 "Aaron shall bring the bull for his own sin offering to make atonement for himself and his household,[x] and he is to slaughter the bull for his own sin offering. 12 He is to take a censer full of burning
coals[y] from the altar before the LORD and two handfuls of finely ground fragrant incense[z] and take them
behind the curtain. 13 He is to put the incense on the fire before the LORD, and the smoke of the incense
will conceal the atonement cover above the tablets of the covenant law, so that he will not die.[a] 14 He
is to take some of the bull's blood[b] and with his finger sprinkle it on the front of the atonement cover;
then he shall sprinkle some of it with his finger seven times before the atonement cover.[c]

15 "He shall then slaughter the goat for the sin offering for the people[d] and take its blood behind the
curtain[e] and do with it as he did with the bull's blood: He shall sprinkle it on the atonement cover and
in front of it. 16 In this way he will make atonement[f] for the Most Holy Place because of the uncleanness

[a] *3* Or *purification offering*; here and throughout this chapter [b] *8* The meaning of the Hebrew for this word is uncertain; also in verses 10 and 26.

catastrophe (10:1 – 2), and the purity laws in chs. 11 – 15 are set forth right after that incident occurred to instruct the people in this regard (see 10:10 – 11 and notes). **for defiling my dwelling place.** This key verse states the purpose of the purity regulations in chs. 11 – 15.

15:32 – 33 A summary of ch. 15. See note on vv. 1 – 33.

16:1 – 34 *The Day of Atonement.* The Day of Atonement (Yom Kippur; Hebrew *yōm hakkippurîm*; cf. 23:26 – 32; 25:9; Exod 30:10; Num 29:7 – 11) was the capstone of the tabernacle sacrificial procedures for the year. It was the annual day of purification for the whole tabernacle, including even the Most Holy Place (see note on 15:31). It provided a complete ceremonial cleansing for the whole community of Israel (vv. 29 – 31) and for the tabernacle for the coming year (see vv. 32 – 33 and note on v. 33). It included both sin offerings (vv. 3,5 – 22) and burnt offerings (vv. 3,5,23 – 25). There was a sin offering for the high priest and his household (vv. 6,11 – 14) and two sin offerings for the people: the slaughtered sin offering (vv. 9,15 – 19) and the scapegoat sin offering (vv. 10,20 – 22). There was also a burnt offering for the high priest and his household as well as one for the whole community (vv. 3,5,23 – 25).

16:2 atonement cover. Served as the lid for the ark of the covenant and was the site of the most important atonement procedures on the Day of Atonement. For Jesus Christ as our "atonement cover" (i.e., place of atonement), see NIV text note on Rom 3:25.

16:6 Aaron needed to make atonement for himself and his whole household first (cf. vv. 11 – 14); only after that could he mediate for the rest of Israel (vv. 7 – 10,15 – 19). That the priest needed to bring such offerings for himself from year to year stands in contrast to Jesus, our high priest, who offered himself once for all and thereby put an end to the need for sacrifice (Heb 9:25 — 10:14; cf. Heb 4:15; 5:1 – 3; 7:26 – 28).

16:8,10,26 scapegoat. Hebrew *ʿăzāʾzēl*, occurs four times in the OT — all in ch. 16 (v. 8, v. 10 (twice), v. 26); see NIV text note on v. 8. Its meaning is debated: (1) It may derive from a combination of the words for "goat" (*ʿēz*) and "go away" (*ʾāzal*): "the goat that departs." This would suit the ritual practice of sending the so-called scapegoat away into the wilderness (vv. 10,21 – 22,26). (2) It may mean "rough ground," describing the wilderness area to which the goat was dispatched. (3) It may be the name of a particular demon associated with the wilderness desert regions (see 17:7 and note). But even if a demon or the demonic realm is the source for the name, there is no intention here of appeasing the demons. The goal is to remove impurity and iniquity from the community (vv. 21 – 22) in order to avoid offending the Lord and the repercussions of it (see note on 15:31).

16:14 atonement cover. See note on v. 2.

16:16 uncleanness and rebellion ... whatever their sins have been ... uncleanness. The focus here is on "uncleanness" (the first term, and then repeated at the end of the verse). This uncleanness attached itself to the tabernacle and its furniture and so defiled them (see chs. 11 – 15

and rebellion of the Israelites, whatever their sins have been. He is to do the same for the tent of meeting, which is among them in the midst of their uncleanness. [17]No one is to be in the tent of meeting
from the time Aaron goes in to make atonement in the Most Holy Place until he comes out, having
made atonement for himself, his household and the whole community of Israel.

[18]"Then he shall come out to the altar[g] that is before the LORD and make atonement for it. He shall
take some of the bull's blood and some of the goat's blood and put it on all the horns of the altar.[h] [19]He
shall sprinkle some of the blood on it with his finger seven times to cleanse it and to consecrate it from
the uncleanness of the Israelites.[i]

[20]"When Aaron has finished making atonement for the Most Holy Place, the tent of meeting and
the altar, he shall bring forward the live goat. [21]He is to lay both hands on the head of the live goat
and confess[j] over it all the wickedness and rebellion of the Israelites — all their sins — and put them
on the goat's head. He shall send the goat away into the wilderness in the care of someone appointed
for the task. [22]The goat will carry on itself all their sins[k] to a remote place; and the man shall release
it in the wilderness.

[23]"Then Aaron is to go into the tent of meeting and take off the linen garments he put on before
he entered the Most Holy Place, and he is to leave them there.[l] [24]He shall bathe himself with water in
the sanctuary area and put on his regular garments.[m] Then he shall come out and sacrifice the burnt
offering for himself and the burnt offering for the people, to make atonement for himself and for the
people. [25]He shall also burn the fat of the sin offering on the altar.

[26]"The man who releases the goat as a scapegoat must wash his clothes[n] and bathe himself with
water; afterward he may come into the camp. [27]The bull and the goat for the sin offerings, whose blood
was brought into the Most Holy Place to make atonement, must be taken outside the camp;[o] their hides,
flesh and intestines are to be burned up. [28]The man who burns them must wash his clothes and bathe
himself with water; afterward he may come into the camp.

[29]"This is to be a lasting ordinance for you: On the tenth day of the seventh month you must
deny yourselves[a][p] and not do any work — whether native-born or a foreigner residing among you —

[a] *29* Or *must fast*; also in verse 31

16:18 [g]Lev 4:7 [h]Lev 4:25
16:19 [i]Eze 43:20
16:21 [j]Lev 5:5
16:22 [k]Isa 53:12
16:23 [l]Eze 42:14; 44:19
16:24 [m]ver 3-5
16:26 [n]Lev 11:25
16:27 [o]Lev 4:12,21; Heb 13:11
16:29 [p]Lev 23:27,32; Nu 29:7; Isa 58:3

and notes on 10:10; 15:31). The atonement made by means of the slaughtered sin offerings purged the tabernacle and its furniture of such uncleanness (contrast note on v. 21). In the NT the sacrifice of Jesus Christ is sometimes specifically referred to as a sin offering for us so that we can be cleansed and forgiven of our sins (see, e.g., Rom 8:3; 2 Cor 5:21 [see NIV text note]; see also note on 4:1 — 5:13). Heb 9:6 – 14 and 9:23 — 10:4 draw on these sin offerings on the Day of Atonement to explain that Christ cleansed the tabernacle in heaven for us once for all so that we can enter directly and boldly into the heavenly throne room of God (Heb 4:14 – 16; 10:19 – 22; note also the tearing of the curtain from top to bottom in Matt 27:51; Mark 15:38; Luke 23:45).

16:20 making atonement for. Summarizes the work that had been accomplished so far (vv. 11 – 19). The Most Holy Place, the tent of meeting, and the altar are all the direct objects of the verb. The basic meaning of the Hebrew verb translated "make atonement for" is "purge" or "wipe clean," and this comes to the forefront here. All the various kinds of uncleanness have been purged from the sanctuary (see note on v. 16). That was the goal of the slaughtered sin offerings — the bull for the priest and the goat for the people — on this day. See note on v. 33.

16:21 lay both hands on the head of the live goat and confess over it. See note on vv. 8,10,26. Previously and normally in Leviticus, the offerer laid a hand (but not both hands; cf. 3:2,8,13; 4:4,15,24) on the head of the sacrificial animal to identify the offering as belonging to them, and, at the same time, dedicated it for the purpose(s) for which they had brought the offering. No confession of sin is mentioned, and there was no transfer of sin to the animal (see note on 1:4). Here in ch. 16, however, the high priest explicitly transferred the sins of the people to the scapegoat by the laying on of the hands with confession. As their substitute, therefore, the goat bore the sins of the people on itself and took them away (v. 22). It was the high priest who would "confess over" the goat the wickedness of the people and thereby put it on the goat's head because the high priest and his sons were the mediators for the Israelites: the priests were to "bear the responsibility for offenses connected with the sanctuary" (Num 18:1; see note on Lev 10:17). **all the wickedness and rebellion of the Israelites — all their sins.** The scapegoat referred to here was never slain, and "uncleanness" is never mentioned here. The key term and the main concern is the actual sinful and rebellious "wickedness" of the people. Thus, on the Day of Atonement both the tabernacle and the community were "cleansed" from all the "sins" of the people (see v. 30 and note), whether they consisted of "uncleanness" (vv. 16 – 19) or "wickedness" (v. 21).

16:22 carry on itself all their sins to a remote place ... in the wilderness. The scapegoat was never slain. It carried all the "wickedness" away from the community — away from all the people and the camp (vv. 21 – 22). It was released alive in the wilderness, never to return to the camp. Thus, all the sins of the whole community were completely removed and eliminated.

16:24 burnt offering ... to make atonement for himself and for the people. Burnt offerings made atonement as a gift offered up on the altar to the Lord, unlike the sin offerings in vv. 3 – 23, which were offered to cleanse the tabernacle. See note on 1:4; see also Introduction: Major Theological Themes (Offerings, Sacrifices, and Atonement).

16:27 taken outside the camp ... to be burned up. See notes of 4:12; 6:30. Whenever the blood of a sin offering was applied inside the tabernacle tent, as it was here (vv. 14 – 17), and not just out at the altar of burnt offering in the court of the tabernacle, the carcass of the animal was burned outside the camp. This principle also applied to Christ, who "suffered outside the city gate" (Heb 13:12).

16:29 tenth day of the seventh month. The last month of the annual agricultural cycle (September/October). They planted grain crops in

16:30 [q]Jer 33:8; Eph 5:26
16:31 [r]Isa 58:3,5
16:32 [s]ver 4; Nu 20:26,28
16:33 [t]ver 11,16-18
16:34 [u]Heb 9:7,25
17:4 [v]Dt 12:5-21 [w]Ge 17:14
17:6 [x]Lev 3:2 [y]Nu 18:17
17:7 [z]Ex 22:20; 2Ch 11:15 [a]Ex 32:8; 34:15; Dt 32:17; 1Co 10:20
17:9 [b]ver 4
17:10 [c]Ge 9:4; Lev 3:17; Dt 12:16,23; 1Sa 14:33
17:11 [d]ver 14; Ge 9:4 [e]Heb 9:22

30because on this day atonement will be made for you, to cleanse you. Then, before the LORD, you will
be clean from all your sins.[q] 31It is a day of sabbath rest, and you must deny yourselves;[r] it is a lasting
ordinance. 32The priest who is anointed and ordained to succeed his father as high priest is to make
atonement. He is to put on the sacred linen garments[s] 33and make atonement for the Most Holy Place,
for the tent of meeting and the altar, and for the priests and all the members of the community.[t]
34"This is to be a lasting ordinance for you: Atonement is to be made once a year[u] for all the sins
of the Israelites."

And it was done, as the LORD commanded Moses.

Eating Blood Forbidden

17 The LORD said to Moses, 2"Speak to Aaron and his sons and to all the Israelites and say to them:
'This is what the LORD has commanded: 3Any Israelite who sacrifices an ox,[a] a lamb or a goat
in the camp or outside of it 4instead of bringing it to the entrance to the tent of meeting to present it as
an offering to the LORD in front of the tabernacle of the LORD[v]—that person shall be considered guilty
of bloodshed; they have shed blood and must be cut off from their people.[w] 5This is so the Israelites
will bring to the LORD the sacrifices they are now making in the open fields. They must bring them to
the priest, that is, to the LORD, at the entrance to the tent of meeting and sacrifice them as fellowship
offerings. 6The priest is to splash the blood against the altar of the LORD[x] at the entrance to the tent of
meeting and burn the fat as an aroma pleasing to the LORD.[y] 7They must no longer offer any of their
sacrifices to the goat idols[b][z] to whom they prostitute themselves.[a] This is to be a lasting ordinance for
them and for the generations to come.'

8"Say to them: 'Any Israelite or any foreigner residing among them who offers a burnt offering or
sacrifice 9and does not bring it to the entrance to the tent of meeting[b] to sacrifice it to the LORD must
be cut off from the people of Israel.

10" 'I will set my face against any Israelite or any foreigner residing among them who eats blood,[c]
and I will cut them off from the people. 11For the life of a creature is in the blood,[d] and I have given it to
you to make atonement for yourselves on the altar; it is the blood that makes atonement for one's life.[c][e]

a 3 The Hebrew word can refer to either male or female. *b 7* Or *the demons* *c 11* Or *atonement by the life in the blood*

the fall season and harvested them in the spring. **deny yourselves.** See NIV text note; see also v. 31. Refers to various forms of self-denial, which includes but is not limited to fasting (see the emphasis in 23:27,29,32; cf. Ps 35:13; Isa 58:3,10). Later Jewish tradition lists abstentions from food and drink, bathing, using oil as an unguent to moisten the skin, wearing leather sandals, and sexual intercourse (cf. 2 Sam 12:16–17,20).

16:30 clean from all your sins. The full effect of the Day of Atonement. Nothing was left to hinder their relationship with the Lord. Sin was the source of both the uncleanness (vv. 14–19) and the wickedness (vv. 21–22) dealt with (vv. 16,21).

16:33 make atonement for the Most Holy Place, for the tent of meeting and the altar. "Make atonement" basically means "purge" or "wipe clean." The high priest purged all the uncleanness from the sanctuary on this day. This was the goal of the slaughtered sin offerings—the bull for the priest and his household and the goat for the people. **for the priests and all the members of the community.** The high priest purged the sanctuary (v. 33a) on behalf of the priests and the people (v. 33b).

17:1—27:34 *Laws of the Community.* The internal structure of the second half of Leviticus is more difficult to discern than that of chs. 1–16. In general, the focus shifts from the holiness and purity of the tabernacle, culminating in the Day of Atonement (ch. 16), to the holiness and purity of the community of Israel surrounding the tabernacle. As the pivotal chapter, ch. 16 actually looks both ways with its concern for both tabernacle and community holiness and purity (see note on 16:21). See note on 18:1—26:46.

17:1–16 *Eating Blood Forbidden.* On the one hand, ch. 17 looks back to chs. 1–16 in the sense that it emphasizes making offerings in the tabernacle (vv. 1–9) along with blood "atonement," which therefore includes the prohibition against eating blood (vv. 10–16). On the other hand, the primary goal of the regulations in ch. 17 is to introduce one of the major concerns of chs. 18–26: the absolute exclusivity of Yahweh worship.

17:3–4 Slaughter at the tabernacle was to be under the supervision of the Aaronic priests (e.g., 1:5; 3:2; 4:5–7), so the sacrifice would be offered properly.

17:4 to the LORD. Contrast v. 7; see note there. **bloodshed.** Illegitimately shedding animal blood, similar to shedding the blood of an innocent human being (e.g., Deut 19:10; cf. Gen 9:4–6).

17:7 goat idols. May refer to demons (see NIV text note). Apparently they occupied the wilderness regions. Lev 16:8 says, "One lot [was] for the LORD and the other for the scapegoat," which suggests that "Azazel" may be the proper name of one of the major goat idols in the wilderness (see note on 16:8,10,26). **prostitute themselves.** While on their way to the promised land, they needed to avoid worshiping other gods or demons. The same Hebrew term occurs in chs. 18–20 for Molek worship and for turning to mediums and spiritists (20:5–6; cf. 18:21; 19:31; 20:27). This would become a danger, especially after they occupied the land of Canaan, where such practices were common.

17:8–9 See note on vv. 3–4.

17:10 eats blood. Refers to eating blood or meat with the blood still in it (not properly drained out). See Gen 9:4; Deut 12:23–25.

17:11 the life of a creature is in the blood. This is a key verse for blood atonement in the Bible. The close association between the blood and the life of a creature is first noted in Gen 9:2–5 (if not Gen 4:10–11), where the Lord affirms the eating of meat, but with a warning: "You must not eat meat that has its lifeblood still in it" (Gen 9:4; see note on v. 10; see also notes on 3:17; 7:26–27). Blood is sacred because life is sacred,

12 Therefore I say to the Israelites, "None of you may eat blood, nor may any foreigner residing among
you eat blood."
13 " 'Any Israelite or any foreigner residing among you who hunts any animal or bird that may be
eaten must drain out the blood and cover it with earth,[f] 14 because the life of every creature is its blood.
That is why I have said to the Israelites, "You must not eat the blood of any creature, because the life
of every creature is its blood; anyone who eats it must be cut off."[g]
15 " 'Anyone, whether native-born or foreigner, who eats anything found dead or torn by wild animals[h] must wash their clothes and bathe with water, and they will be ceremonially unclean till evening;
then they will be clean. 16 But if they do not wash their clothes and bathe themselves, they will be held
responsible.' "

Unlawful Sexual Relations

18 The LORD said to Moses, 2 "Speak to the Israelites and say to them: 'I am the LORD your God.[i]
3 You must not do as they do in Egypt, where you used to live, and you must not do as they do
in the land of Canaan, where I am bringing you. Do not follow their practices.[j] 4 You must obey my laws
and be careful to follow my decrees. I am the LORD your God.[k] 5 Keep my decrees and laws, for the person
who obeys them will live by them.[l] I am the LORD.
6 " 'No one is to approach any close relative to have sexual relations. I am the LORD.
7 " 'Do not dishonor your father[m] by having sexual relations with your mother.[n] She is your mother;
do not have relations with her.
8 " 'Do not have sexual relations with your father's wife;[o] that would dishonor your father.[p]
9 " 'Do not have sexual relations with your sister,[q] either your father's daughter or your mother's
daughter, whether she was born in the same home or elsewhere.
10 " 'Do not have sexual relations with your son's daughter or your daughter's daughter; that would
dishonor you.
11 " 'Do not have sexual relations with the daughter of your father's wife, born to your father; she
is your sister.

17:13 [f] Lev 7:26; Dt 12:16
17:14 [g] ver 11; Ge 9:4
17:15 [h] Ex 22:31; Dt 14:21
18:2 [i] Ex 6:7; Lev 11:44; Eze 20:5
18:3 [j] ver 24-30; Ex 23:24; Lev 20:23
18:4 [k] ver 2
18:5 [l] Eze 20:11; Ro 10:5*; Gal 3:12*
18:7 [m] Lev 20:11 [n] Eze 22:10
18:8 [o] 1Co 5:1 [p] Lev 20:11
18:9 [q] Lev 20:17

---

and the blood represents the life of the animal. In the NT the blood of Christ is what provides our eternal redemption (Heb 9:12). Heb 9:22 says, "Without the shedding of blood there is no forgiveness." **it is the blood that makes atonement for one's life.** This could mean either that the blood makes atonement for the life of the one who brings the offering, or perhaps the blood makes atonement by means of the life that is in it, since it represents the life of the animal (see NIV text note).

17:12–14 See note on v. 11.

17:15 anything found dead or torn by wild animals. The people could eat the meat of such animals, but doing so would make them ceremonially unclean for the remainder of the day (see note on 7:24).

17:16 they will be held responsible. If a person did not perform the prescribed cleansing procedures that day, they would not become clean that evening; they themselves would bear the consequences of their uncleanness (see note on 10:17). They would be responsible for spreading uncleanness in the camp, could not enter the tabernacle in their unclean condition, and could not eat sacrificial offerings in their unclean state (see note on 7:19–21) lest they be cut off from their people (see note on 7:20,21).

18:1—26:46 *Laws of Community Holiness.* Chs. 17–26 are often called the "Holiness Code" because of the repeated formula: "Be holy because I, the LORD your God, am holy" (19:2; see also 20:7,26; 21:6–8). It is the general principle of the Holiness Code. The recurring short form "I am the LORD (your God)," which occurs 47 times in these chapters, keeps the holiness principle active as the main point throughout (18:2,4,5,6,21,30; 19:3,4, etc., ending at 26:45; for the name "LORD," see notes on Exod 3:14,15).

18:1—20:27 *Unlawful Sexual Relations, Various Laws, and Punishments for Sin.* The correspondence between the introduction (18:1–5) and conclusion (20:22–27) sets this off as a distinct unit. The intervening statutes and ordinances, if Israel followed them, would distinguish them morally from the other nations. Ch. 18 focuses on boundaries for marriage and sexual relations; ch. 19 gives moral guidance that corresponds well to that of the Ten Commandments (Exod 20:1–17); ch. 20 includes penalties for various violations of the moral code.

18:2 I am the LORD your God. See note on 18:1—26:46.

18:5 live. A common OT theme is that keeping the Lord's commands leads to a good life lived under God's favor in the land. See, e.g., 26:3–13; Exod 20:12; Deut 4:1; Ezek 20:11. But keeping the law was never a way of eternal salvation for the lost (Rom 10:4–5,10; Gal 3:10–12, where this verse is cited).

18:6 close relative. This general statement prohibiting sexual intercourse between close relatives serves as an opening summary statement for the following section, especially vv. 7–18.

18:8 your father's wife. Not the man's mother but another wife of the man's father. The laws in the Pentateuch sometimes assumed the possibility that a man might have more than one wife (cf. Deut 21:15–17). Though not the ideal (Gen 2:24), it was not forbidden. The Lord's concern was to manage polygamy in a way that did not devastate immediate or extended families, which it historically tended to do (see, e.g., Gen 16; 21; 29:28—30:24; 1 Sam 1:2–8).

18:9,11 your sister. Verse 9 includes half sisters in the category of "sister," so they were not marriageable. Verse 11 includes a daughter born to the father's wife from a previous marriage as a sister, even though she was not a blood half sister. Though there were instances of marriage to a half sister before the giving of this law at Sinai (Gen 20:12), it was now prohibited. Sexual relations with one's sister was, of course, prohibited (Ezek 22:11).

18:12 [r] Lev 20:19
18:14 [s] Lev 20:20
18:15 [t] Lev 20:12
18:16 [u] Lev 20:21
18:17 [v] Lev 20:14
18:19 [w] Lev 15:24; 20:18
18:20 [x] Ex 20:14; Lev 20:10; Mt 5:27,28; 1Co 6:9; Heb 13:4
18:21 [y] Dt 12:31 [z] Lev 20:2-5 [a] Lev 19:12; 21:6; Eze 36:20
18:22 [b] Lev 20:13; Dt 23:18; Ro 1:27
18:23 [c] Ex 22:19; Lev 20:15; Dt 27:21
18:24 [d] ver 3,27,30 [e] Dt 18:12
18:25 [f] Lev 20:23; Dt 9:5; 18:12 [g] ver 28; Lev 20:22
18:30 [h] Dt 11:1 [i] ver 2
19:2 [j] 1Pe 1:16*; Lev 11:44
19:3 [k] Ex 20:12 [l] Lev 11:44

12 “ ‘Do not have sexual relations with your father’s sister;[r] she is your father’s close relative.
13 “ ‘Do not have sexual relations with your mother’s sister, because she is your mother’s close relative.
14 “ ‘Do not dishonor your father’s brother by approaching his wife to have sexual relations; she is
your aunt.[s]
15 “ ‘Do not have sexual relations with your daughter-in-law.[t] She is your son’s wife; do not have
relations with her.
16 “ ‘Do not have sexual relations with your brother’s wife;[u] that would dishonor your brother.
17 “ ‘Do not have sexual relations with both a woman and her daughter.[v] Do not have sexual relations
with either her son’s daughter or her daughter’s daughter; they are her close relatives. That is wickedness.
18 “ ‘Do not take your wife’s sister as a rival wife and have sexual relations with her while your wife is living.
19 “ ‘Do not approach a woman to have sexual relations during the uncleanness of her monthly period.[w]
20 “ ‘Do not have sexual relations with your neighbor’s wife[x] and defile yourself with her.
21 “ ‘Do not give any of your children[y] to be sacrificed to Molek,[z] for you must not profane the name
of your God.[a] I am the LORD.
22 “ ‘Do not have sexual relations with a man as one does with a woman;[b] that is detestable.
23 “ ‘Do not have sexual relations with an animal and defile yourself with it. A woman must not present herself to an animal to have sexual relations with it; that is a perversion.[c]
24 “ ‘Do not defile yourselves in any of these ways, because this is how the nations that I am going to
drive out before you[d] became defiled.[e] 25 Even the land was defiled; so I punished it for its sin,[f] and the
land vomited out its inhabitants.[g] 26 But you must keep my decrees and my laws. The native-born and
the foreigners residing among you must not do any of these detestable things, 27 for all these things were
done by the people who lived in the land before you, and the land became defiled. 28 And if you defile the
land, it will vomit you out as it vomited out the nations that were before you.
29 “ ‘Everyone who does any of these detestable things—such persons must be cut off from their
people. 30 Keep my requirements[h] and do not follow any of the detestable customs that were practiced
before you came and do not defile yourselves with them. I am the LORD your God.[i] ’ ”

Various Laws

19 The LORD said to Moses, 2 “Speak to the entire assembly of Israel and say to them: ‘Be holy because I, the LORD your God, am holy.[j]
3 “ ‘Each of you must respect your mother and father,[k] and you must observe my Sabbaths. I am the
LORD your God.[l]

18:17 wickedness. The Hebrew term almost always carries a connotation of shameful deeds cunningly devised. It is closely associated with sexual and religious infidelity (cf. 19:29; 20:14; Job 31:11; Ezek 16:27; 22:9).
18:18 sister ... rival wife. See the marriage of Jacob to two sisters, Leah and Rachel (Gen 29:16–30). Such marriages were naturally quarrelsome (see note on v. 8).
18:19 uncleanness of her monthly period. She was ceremonially unclean for seven days, and her uncleanness was ritually contagious (15:19–24). For a fuller discussion of ritual ceremonial impurity, see Introduction: Major Theological Themes (The Lord’s Presence; Holiness and Purity). Maintaining the purity of the Lord’s tabernacle required maintaining the ceremonial purity of the community that surrounded the tabernacle (see 15:31 and note).
18:21 children ... sacrificed to Molek. This involved not only dedicating the child to Molek, which was idolatry, but perhaps also burning the child in sacrifice to Molek (or Baal in some instances). As here, this prohibition sometimes occurs in the midst of prohibitions about incest and other sexual violations because there is a natural connection between sexual relations and having children. **profane.** To treat someone or something that was holy as if it were common (see note on 10:10).
18:22 sexual relations with a man. This verse prohibits homosexual intercourse for men (cf. 1 Cor 6:9–10). Rom 1:26–27 describes unnatural homosexual intercourse for women and for men. Lev 20:13 prescribes the death penalty for such acts. **detestable.** Refers to repugnant practices, whether from the viewpoint of other peoples toward the Hebrews (Gen 43:32; 46:34; Exod 8:26) or from the viewpoint of the Lord toward the Israelites (cf. 20:13; Deut 14:3; 24:4; Isa 41:24) or other peoples (Lev 18:26–27,29–30). All the practices forbidden in ch. 18 are repugnant according to the summary of the chapter (vv. 26–27,29–30). Within ch. 18, however, the Hebrew term is used only here in v. 22, emphasizing how repulsive and shameful such sexual acts are. These acts are at odds with the basic creation design (Gen 2:18–25).
18:23 perversion. Related to a Hebrew verb that means “mix” or “confuse.” It refers to illegitimate mixtures of species or violation of the natural order of things. In 20:12 the term refers to incest with one’s daughter-in-law. For bestiality, see also 20:16.
18:24–28 Concludes the regulations in vv. 6–23. Verses 26–28 apply v. 25 as a lesson to the Israelites.
18:29 cut off. See note on 7:20,21.
19:2 Be holy because I, the LORD your God, am holy. See notes on 11:44; 18:1—26:46.
19:3–18 The numerous parallels to the Ten Commandments suggest that ch. 19 focuses on the primary concerns of the covenant. Practices such as revering one’s father and mother, keeping the Sabbath, leaving the gleanings after the harvest, dealing justly in court, and loving your neighbor as yourself contributed to community holiness in ancient Israel.
19:3 See Exod 20:8–12.

4 “ ‘Do not turn to idols or make metal gods for yourselves.[m] I am the LORD your God.

5 “ ‘When you sacrifice a fellowship offering to the LORD, sacrifice it in such a way that it will be accepted on your behalf. 6 It shall be eaten on the day you sacrifice it or on the next day; anything left over until the third day must be burned up. 7 If any of it is eaten on the third day, it is impure and will not be accepted. 8 Whoever eats it will be held responsible because they have desecrated what is holy to the LORD; they must be cut off from their people.

9 “ ‘When you reap the harvest of your land, do not reap to the very edges of your field or gather the gleanings of your harvest.[n] 10 Do not go over your vineyard a second time or pick up the grapes that have fallen. Leave them for the poor and the foreigner. I am the LORD your God.

11 “ ‘Do not steal.[o]

“ ‘Do not lie.[p]

“ ‘Do not deceive one another.

12 “ ‘Do not swear falsely by my name[q] and so profane the name of your God. I am the LORD.

13 “ ‘Do not defraud or rob your neighbor.[r]

“ ‘Do not hold back the wages of a hired worker overnight.[s]

14 “ ‘Do not curse the deaf or put a stumbling block in front of the blind,[t] but fear your God. I am the LORD.

15 “ ‘Do not pervert justice;[u] do not show partiality[v] to the poor or favoritism to the great, but judge your neighbor fairly.

16 “ ‘Do not go about spreading slander[w] among your people.

“ ‘Do not do anything that endangers your neighbor’s life.[x] I am the LORD.

17 “ ‘Do not hate a fellow Israelite in your heart.[y] Rebuke your neighbor frankly[z] so you will not share in their guilt.

18 “ ‘Do not seek revenge[a] or bear a grudge[b] against anyone among your people, but love your neighbor as yourself.[c] I am the LORD.

19 “ ‘Keep my decrees.

“ ‘Do not mate different kinds of animals.

“ ‘Do not plant your field with two kinds of seed.[d]

“ ‘Do not wear clothing woven of two kinds of material.[e]

20 “ ‘If a man sleeps with a female slave who is promised to another man but who has not been

19:4 [m] Ex 20:4,23; 34:17; Lev 26:1; Ps 96:5; 115:4-7
19:9 [n] Lev 23:10,22; Dt 24:19-22
19:11 [o] Ex 20:15 [p] Eph 4:25
19:12 [q] Ex 20:7; Mt 5:33
19:13 [r] Ex 22:15,25-27 [s] Dt 24:15; Jas 5:4
19:14 [t] Dt 27:18
19:15 [u] Ex 23:2,6 [v] Dt 1:17
19:16 [w] Ps 15:3; Eze 22:9 [x] Ex 23:7
19:17 [y] 1Jn 2:9; 3:15 [z] Mt 18:15; Lk 17:3
19:18 [a] Ro 12:19 [b] Ps 103:9 [c] Mt 5:43*; 19:16*; 22:39*; Mk 12:31*; Lk 10:27*; Jn 13:34; Ro 13:9*; Gal 5:14*; Jas 2:8*
19:19 [d] Dt 22:9 [e] Dt 22:11

19:4 See Exod 20:3–6.

19:5–8 See 7:15–21 and notes.

19:8 held responsible. See 5:1 and note on 10:17. **cut off.** See note on 7:20,21.

19:10 foreigner. A person from another land who took up residence among the Israelites. Although not a native Israelite, they were accepted as a member of the host community, often a relatively disadvantaged member (vv. 33–34; cf. 23:22).

19:11–13 Do not steal. The eighth commandment (Exod 20:15). There are multiple ways to “steal,” whether by lying, deceiving, giving a false oath, fraud, robbery, or holding back someone’s wages overnight when they needed them for their daily provisions.

19:15 Do not pervert justice. Heads a series of prohibitions against such things as false testimony (Exod 20:16), which perverts justice by showing partiality to the poor or favoritism to the rich. Its concern is perjury in the law court (Exod 23:1,6–7; Deut 17:6–7; 19:16–21).

19:16 spreading slander. Possibly cutthroat business dealings or spying on someone.

19:18 bear a grudge. Retain or maintain vengeful feelings toward someone (cf. Nah 1:2). **love your neighbor as yourself.** Do what is good for others just as you naturally love doing what is good for yourself. Such love contrasts with taking vengeance or bearing a grudge against someone. Therefore, v. 18 probably does not imply that people need to learn to love themselves in order to love their neighbors. Instead, in NT terms it amounts to fulfilling the “Golden Rule” (Matt 7:12). Do good for your neighbor since that is the way you would want them to treat you. This is the source for the second of Jesus’ two great commandments in Matt 22:36–40 and Mark 12:28–31. In Luke 10:25–37 Jesus clarifies that “neighbor” includes those whom a person does not know personally—even those with whom a person would not normally associate. Lev 19:34 anticipates this when it calls for such love toward the “foreigner” who lived among them, not just the native Israelite, and then supports this by reminding them that they were “foreigners” in Egypt. They would have wanted to be treated well there, so they should treat the foreigners among them well.

19:19 mate ... plant ... wear. These three “decrees” have a principle in common: do not mix two different “kinds” of animals, seeds, or clothing fabrics. Deut 22:11 uses the same terminology to prohibit weaving linen and wool together in a garment. The rationale for these prohibitions is uncertain. Such mixtures may violate God’s creation order, e.g., when he separated out the various species or “kinds” (Gen 1:11–12,21,24–25). Or these prohibitions may belong to the sacred sphere, not to the world of the common Israelite (see note on 10:10). The priestly garments and the tabernacle fabric, e.g., were a mixture of linen and wool (Exod 26:1), and cherubim (composite beings with a human form but with wings) were woven into the tabernacle curtains (Exod 28:6–8).

19:20 promised to another man. Betrothed but not yet married; therefore, still belonging to her master. **due punishment.** Damages and compensation determined by an investigation of the facts; e.g., in that day a man paid a bride-price for marrying a woman, but the bride-price

19:21 [f] Lev 5:15
19:24 [g] Pr 3:9
19:26 [h] Lev 17:10 [i] Dt 18:10
19:27 [j] Lev 21:5
19:29 [k] Dt 23:18
19:30 [l] Lev 26:2
19:31 [m] Lev 20:6; Isa 8:19
19:32 [n] 1Ti 5:1
19:34 [o] Ex 12:48 [p] Dt 10:19
19:36 [q] Dt 25:13-15
20:3 [r] Lev 15:31 [s] Lev 18:21

ransomed or given her freedom, there must be due punishment.[a] Yet they are not to be put to death,
because she had not been freed. 21 The man, however, must bring a ram to the entrance to the tent of
meeting for a guilt offering to the Lord.[f] 22 With the ram of the guilt offering the priest is to make atonement for him before the Lord for the sin he has committed, and his sin will be forgiven.

23 " 'When you enter the land and plant any kind of fruit tree, regard its fruit as forbidden.[b] For
three years you are to consider it forbidden[b]; it must not be eaten. 24 In the fourth year all its fruit will
be holy,[g] an offering of praise to the Lord. 25 But in the fifth year you may eat its fruit. In this way your
harvest will be increased. I am the Lord your God.

26 " 'Do not eat any meat with the blood still in it.[h]

" 'Do not practice divination or seek omens.[i]

27 " 'Do not cut the hair at the sides of your head or clip off the edges of your beard.[j]

28 " 'Do not cut your bodies for the dead or put tattoo marks on yourselves. I am the Lord.

29 " 'Do not degrade your daughter by making her a prostitute,[k] or the land will turn to prostitution
and be filled with wickedness.

30 " 'Observe my Sabbaths and have reverence for my sanctuary. I am the Lord.[l]

31 " 'Do not turn to mediums or seek out spiritists,[m] for you will be defiled by them. I am the Lord your God.

32 " 'Stand up in the presence of the aged, show respect for the elderly[n] and revere your God. I am
the Lord.

33 " 'When a foreigner resides among you in your land, do not mistreat them. 34 The foreigner residing among you must be treated as your native-born.[o] Love them as yourself, for you were foreigners in
Egypt.[p] I am the Lord your God.

35 " 'Do not use dishonest standards when measuring length, weight or quantity. 36 Use honest scales
and honest weights, an honest ephah[c] and an honest hin.[d][q] I am the Lord your God, who brought
you out of Egypt.

37 " 'Keep all my decrees and all my laws and follow them. I am the Lord.' "

Punishments for Sin

20 The Lord said to Moses, 2 "Say to the Israelites: 'Any Israelite or any foreigner residing in Israel
who sacrifices any of his children to Molek is to be put to death. The members of the community are to stone him. 3 I myself will set my face against him and will cut him off from his people; for
by sacrificing his children to Molek, he has defiled my sanctuary[r] and profaned my holy name.[s] 4 If the
members of the community close their eyes when that man sacrifices one of his children to Molek and

[a] *20* Or *be an inquiry* [b] *23* Hebrew *uncircumcised* [c] *36* An ephah was a dry measure having the capacity of about 3/5 of a bushel or about 22 liters. [d] *36* A hin was a liquid measure having the capacity of about 1 gallon or about 3.8 liters.

for marrying a virgin was more than that for marrying a non-virgin (see Exod 22:16–17; cf. Deut 22:13–21). **not to be put to death.** There was no execution for adultery in this case because she was a slave, not a free woman (cf. Deut 22:23–27).

19:21 ram ... for a guilt offering. In addition to the damages in v. 20 because the man violated another's property (see 6:1–7 and note on 6:2).

19:26 Do not eat any meat with the blood still in it. See notes on 3:17; 17:11. This may refer to some kind of sacrificial practice related to divination with links to necromancy (i.e., communication with the dead). If so, this regulation closely relates to the following ones. **practice divination or seek omens.** For a more complete list of forbidden occult practices, see Deut 18:9–14. These terms occur together also in Deut 18:10; 2 Kgs 21:6; 2 Chr 33:6. Deut 18:9–14 prohibits such practices in favor of seeking a word from the Lord through his prophet (Deut 18:15–22). **practice divination.** Seems to indicate attempting to read signs from the surrounding environment. **seek omens.** May be a more active form of divination, but it is difficult to isolate the exact means by which they would do so.

19:27 cut ... clip off. Based on Deut 14:1; perhaps this refers to certain kinds of pagan mourning practices. This fits the context of the occult practices in v. 26b.

19:28 cut your bodies for the dead. Another pagan mourning practice (see note on v. 27; cf. 1 Kgs 18:28). **tattoo.** Includes "writing," so it refers to writing or inscribing some kind of "marks" on the body. The context suggests it is another pagan mourning practice of that day or perhaps a means of warding off the spirits of the dead (cf. 21:5).

19:29 degrade. Elsewhere translated "profane" (v. 12; 18:21) and "desecrated" (v. 8). The main theme of ch. 19 is: "Be holy because I, the Lord your God, am holy" (v. 2). To "degrade" (or desecrate or profane) one's daughter by making her a prostitute was the opposite of maintaining her as "holy" (see notes on 10:10; 18:21).

19:31 turn to mediums or seek out spiritists. Seek special knowledge through the spirits of the dead, whether the dead in general or dead relatives in particular (i.e., familiar spirits). Cf. 20:6,27.

19:33,34 foreigner. See note on v. 10.

19:34 Love them as yourself. See v. 18 and note.

20:1–27 See note on 18:1—20:27. The severe penalties given here underline the seriousness of these offenses.

20:2 Molek. See note on 18:21.

20:3 cut ... off. See note on 7:20,21.

if they fail to put him to death,[t] 5 I myself will set my face against him and his family and will cut them
off from their people together with all who follow him in prostituting themselves to Molek.
6 " 'I will set my face against anyone who turns to mediums and spiritists to prostitute themselves by
following them, and I will cut them off from their people.[u]
7 " 'Consecrate yourselves and be holy,[v] because I am the LORD your God. 8 Keep my decrees and follow
them. I am the LORD, who makes you holy.[w]
9 " 'Anyone who curses their father or mother[x] is to be put to death.[y] Because they have cursed their
father or mother, their blood will be on their own head.[z]
10 " 'If a man commits adultery with another man's wife[a]—with the wife of his neighbor—both
the adulterer and the adulteress are to be put to death.
11 " 'If a man has sexual relations with his father's wife, he has dishonored his father.[b] Both the man
and the woman are to be put to death; their blood will be on their own heads.
12 " 'If a man has sexual relations with his daughter-in-law,[c] both of them are to be put to death.
What they have done is a perversion; their blood will be on their own heads.
13 " 'If a man has sexual relations with a man as one does with a woman, both of them have done
what is detestable.[d] They are to be put to death; their blood will be on their own heads.
14 " 'If a man marries both a woman and her mother,[e] it is wicked. Both he and they must be burned
in the fire, so that no wickedness will be among you.[f]
15 " 'If a man has sexual relations with an animal,[g] he is to be put to death, and you must kill the animal.
16 " 'If a woman approaches an animal to have sexual relations with it, kill both the woman and the
animal. They are to be put to death; their blood will be on their own heads.
17 " 'If a man marries his sister[h], the daughter of either his father or his mother, and they have sexual relations, it is a disgrace. They are to be publicly removed from their people. He has dishonored his
sister and will be held responsible.
18 " 'If a man has sexual relations with a woman during her monthly period,[i] he has exposed the
source of her flow, and she has also uncovered it. Both of them are to be cut off from their people.
19 " 'Do not have sexual relations with the sister of either your mother or your father,[j] for that would
dishonor a close relative; both of you would be held responsible.
20 " 'If a man has sexual relations with his aunt,[k] he has dishonored his uncle. They will be held
responsible; they will die childless.
21 " 'If a man marries his brother's wife,[l] it is an act of impurity; he has dishonored his brother. They
will be childless.
22 " 'Keep all my decrees and laws and follow them, so that the land[m] where I am bringing you to
live may not vomit you out. 23 You must not live according to the customs of the nations[n] I am going to
drive out before you.[o] Because they did all these things, I abhorred them. 24 But I said to you, "You will
possess their land; I will give it to you as an inheritance, a land flowing with milk and honey."[p] I am
the LORD your God, who has set you apart from the nations.[q]
25 " 'You must therefore make a distinction between clean and unclean animals and between unclean

20:4 [t] Dt 17:2-5
20:6 [u] Lev 19:31
20:7 [v] Eph 1:4; 1Pe 1:16*
20:8 [w] Ex 31:13
20:9 [x] Dt 27:16 [y] Ex 21:17; Mt 15:4*; Mk 7:10* [z] ver 11; 2Sa 1:16
20:10 [a] Ex 20:14; Dt 5:18; 22:22
20:11 [b] Lev 18:7; Dt 27:23
20:12 [c] Lev 18:15
20:13 [d] Lev 18:22
20:14 [e] Lev 18:17 [f] Dt 27:23
20:15 [g] Lev 18:23
20:17 [h] Lev 18:9
20:18 [i] Lev 15:24; 18:19
20:19 [j] Lev 18:12-13
20:20 [k] Lev 18:14
20:21 [l] Lev 18:16
20:22 [m] Lev 18:25-28
20:23 [n] Lev 18:3 [o] Lev 18:24,27,30
20:24 [p] Ex 3:8; 13:5; 33:3 [q] Ex 33:16

20:6 mediums and spiritists. See note on 19:31.
20:7–8 See 19:2 and notes on 11:44; 18:1—26:46.
20:10–21 These regulations add penalties to the prohibitions in ch. 18.
20:10 See 18:20; Deut 22:22.
20:11 See 18:8 and note. **their blood will be on their own heads.** The shedding of blood brought guilt on the one who shed it illegitimately (including even the blood of animals shed illegitimately, see notes on 17:3–4; cf. the background of Gen 4:10–11; 9:4–6). If the community performed a legitimate execution, the blood guilt rested on the person who had been legitimately executed.
20:12 See 18:15. **perversion.** This kind of sexual activity brought confusion to the community.
20:13 detestable. See 18:22 and note.
20:14 See 18:17. **wicked.** Equals "wickedness" in 18:17 (see note there). **burned in the fire.** An especially severe penalty. Perhaps they were executed before their corpses were burned (Josh 7:25; cf. Deut 13:15–16; Josh 6:21,24).
20:15–16 See 18:23.
20:17 publicly removed. See 18:9,29; see note on 7:20,21. **held responsible.** He did not have the benefit of the priestly sacrificial system to make atonement and receive forgiveness for this act (see note on 10:17).
20:18 See 18:19.
20:19 See 18:12–13. **held responsible.** See note on v. 17.
20:20 See 18:14.
20:21 See 18:16.
20:22–23 See 18:24–28.
20:23 abhorred. Felt repugnance or disgust; especially suitable for a context in which the land might "vomit" out its inhabitants (v. 22).
20:24–26 set you apart ... set you apart. Translates the same Hebrew verb rendered "make a distinction" in v. 25.
20:25 clean and unclean animals ... birds. See note on 11:1–47. Because God distinguished them from the other peoples around them, the Israelites were to distinguish between clean and unclean creatures.

20:25 [r] Lev 11:1-47; Dt 14:3-21
20:26 [s] Lev 19:2
20:27 [t] Lev 19:31
21:1 [u] Eze 44:25
21:5 [v] Eze 44:20 [w] Lev 19:28; Dt 14:1
21:6 [x] Lev 18:21 [y] Lev 3:11
21:7 [z] ver 13,14 [a] Eze 44:22
21:8 [b] ver 6
21:9 [c] Ge 38:24; Lev 19:29
21:10 [d] Lev 16:32 [e] Lev 10:6
21:11 [f] Nu 19:11,13,14 [g] Lev 19:28
21:12 [h] Ex 29:6-7; Lev 10:7
21:13 [i] Eze 44:22
21:17 [j] ver 6
21:18 [k] Lev 22:19-25
21:20 [l] Dt 23:1; Isa 56:3
21:22 [m] 1Co 9:13

and clean birds.[r] Do not defile yourselves by any animal or bird or anything that moves along the
ground — those that I have set apart as unclean for you. 26 You are to be holy to me because I, the LORD,
am holy,[s] and I have set you apart from the nations to be my own.
27 " 'A man or woman who is a medium or spiritist among you must be put to death.[t] You are to stone
them; their blood will be on their own heads.' "

Rules for Priests

21 The LORD said to Moses, "Speak to the priests, the sons of Aaron, and say to them: 'A priest must
not make himself ceremonially unclean for any of his people who die,[u] 2 except for a close
relative, such as his mother or father, his son or daughter, his brother, 3 or an unmarried sister who is
dependent on him since she has no husband — for her he may make himself unclean. 4 He must not
make himself unclean for people related to him by marriage,[a] and so defile himself.
5 " 'Priests must not shave their heads or shave off the edges of their beards[v] or cut their bodies.[w]
6 They must be holy to their God and must not profane the name of their God.[x] Because they present
the food offerings to the LORD,[y] the food of their God, they are to be holy.
7 " 'They must not marry women defiled by prostitution or divorced from their husbands,[z] because
priests are holy to their God.[a] 8 Regard them as holy,[b] because they offer up the food of your God. Consider them holy, because I the LORD am holy — I who make you holy.
9 " 'If a priest's daughter defiles herself by becoming a prostitute, she disgraces her father; she must
be burned in the fire.[c]
10 " 'The high priest, the one among his brothers who has had the anointing oil poured on his head
and who has been ordained to wear the priestly garments,[d] must not let his hair become unkempt[b] or
tear his clothes.[e] 11 He must not enter a place where there is a dead body.[f] He must not make himself
unclean,[g] even for his father or mother, 12 nor leave the sanctuary of his God or desecrate it, because he
has been dedicated by the anointing oil[h] of his God. I am the LORD.
13 " 'The woman he marries must be a virgin.[i] 14 He must not marry a widow, a divorced woman, or
a woman defiled by prostitution, but only a virgin from his own people, 15 so that he will not defile his
offspring among his people. I am the LORD, who makes him holy.' "
16 The LORD said to Moses, 17 "Say to Aaron: 'For the generations to come none of your descendants
who has a defect may come near to offer the food of his God.[j] 18 No man who has any defect[k] may
come near: no man who is blind or lame, disfigured or deformed; 19 no man with a crippled foot or
hand, 20 or who is a hunchback or a dwarf, or who has any eye defect, or who has festering or running
sores or damaged testicles.[l] 21 No descendant of Aaron the priest who has any defect is to come near to
present the food offerings to the LORD. He has a defect; he must not come near to offer the food of his
God. 22 He may eat the most holy food of his God,[m] as well as the holy food; 23 yet because of his defect,

[a] 4 Or *unclean as a leader among his people* [b] 10 Or *not uncover his head*

This was one way the Lord made Israel a holy nation, separate from the other nations. Not being able to eat with other peoples made it difficult for the Israelites to establish and maintain marital and other social relations with them.

21:1 — 22:33 *Rules for the Priests and Unacceptable Sacrifices.* Chs. 21 – 22 are addressed to the priests. Variations of the holiness formula throughout this unit refer not to the sanctity of the community at large but to that of the priests (21:1,8,15), the precincts of the tabernacle (21:23), and the sacred offerings (22:9,16). The unit then concludes with another reference to the entire nation as a holy nation that the Lord himself sanctified (22:32 – 33; see note on 18:1 — 26:46).

21:1 people who die. A corpse was severely defiling to the point that anyone who touched it would be "unclean for seven days" (Num 19:11). They needed to wash their body with the water containing the ashes of the red heifer on the third and seventh days to purify their body from the uncleanness (Num 19:12) so that they did not "defile the LORD's tabernacle" (Num 19:13). Death was incompatible with holiness.

21:5 See notes on 19:27,28.

21:7 not marry women defiled by prostitution or divorced. This kept priests holy to their God; i.e., set apart from any kind of desecration or defilement sexually (see note on 19:29).

21:10 hair ... unkempt or tear ... clothes. Regular and accepted mourning rites for the death of friends and relatives (cf. 10:6). The high priest's head had been anointed, so it was not to be unkempt, and his garments were special priestly garments so they were not to be torn.

21:11 a place where there is a dead body. The high priest's position did not allow him to participate in mourning rites, not even for his father or mother (contrast the other priests, v. 2).

21:12 desecrate. See notes on 10:10; 19:29.

21:13,14 a virgin. The marriage regulations for the high priest were even more strict than those for the other priests (see v. 7 and note).

21:15 defile. See note on 19:29.

21:17 defect. Any birth defect or physical injury listed in vv. 18 – 20. The same Hebrew term describes animals that must not be offered to the Lord (22:20 – 25). Holiness was symbolized by wholeness.

he must not go near the curtain or approach the altar, and so desecrate my sanctuary. I am the LORD,
who makes them holy.' "
[24]So Moses told this to Aaron and his sons and to all the Israelites.
22 The LORD said to Moses, [2]"Tell Aaron and his sons to treat with respect the sacred offerings the
Israelites consecrate to me, so they will not profane my holy name. I am the LORD.
[3]"Say to them: 'For the generations to come, if any of your descendants is ceremonially unclean and
yet comes near the sacred offerings that the Israelites consecrate to the LORD, that person must be cut
off from my presence.[n] I am the LORD.
[4]" 'If a descendant of Aaron has a defiling skin disease[a] or a bodily discharge,[o] he may not eat
the sacred offerings until he is cleansed. He will also be unclean if he touches something defiled by a
corpse[p] or by anyone who has an emission of semen, [5]or if he touches any crawling thing[q] that makes
him unclean, or any person[r] who makes him unclean, whatever the uncleanness may be. [6]The one
who touches any such thing will be unclean till evening. He must not eat any of the sacred offerings
unless he has bathed himself with water. [7]When the sun goes down, he will be clean, and after that he
may eat the sacred offerings, for they are his food.[s] [8]He must not eat anything found dead[t] or torn by
wild animals,[u] and so become unclean[v] through it. I am the LORD.
[9]" 'The priests are to perform my service in such a way that they do not become guilty and die[w] for
treating it with contempt. I am the LORD, who makes them holy.
[10]" 'No one outside a priest's family may eat the sacred offering, nor may the guest of a priest or his
hired worker eat it. [11]But if a priest buys a slave with money, or if slaves are born in his household, they
may eat his food.[x] [12]If a priest's daughter marries anyone other than a priest, she may not eat any of
the sacred contributions. [13]But if a priest's daughter becomes a widow or is divorced, yet has no children, and she returns to live in her father's household as in her youth, she may eat her father's food.
No unauthorized person, however, may eat it.
[14]" 'Anyone who eats a sacred offering by mistake must make restitution to the priest for the offering
and add a fifth of the value[y] to it. [15]The priests must not desecrate the sacred offerings the Israelites present to the LORD[z] [16]by allowing them to eat the sacred offerings and so bring upon them guilt requiring
payment.[a] I am the LORD, who makes them holy.' "

Unacceptable Sacrifices

[17]The LORD said to Moses, [18]"Speak to Aaron and his sons and to all the Israelites and say to them:
'If any of you—whether an Israelite or a foreigner residing in Israel—presents a gift[b] for a burnt
offering to the LORD, either to fulfill a vow or as a freewill offering, [19]you must present a male without
defect[c] from the cattle, sheep or goats in order that it may be accepted on your behalf. [20]Do not bring
anything with a defect,[d] because it will not be accepted on your behalf. [21]When anyone brings from
the herd or flock a fellowship offering[e] to the LORD to fulfill a special vow or as a freewill offering, it
must be without defect or blemish to be acceptable. [22]Do not offer to the LORD the blind, the injured
or the maimed, or anything with warts or festering or running sores. Do not place any of these on the
altar as a food offering presented to the LORD. [23]You may, however, present as a freewill offering an
ox[b] or a sheep that is deformed or stunted, but it will not be accepted in fulfillment of a vow. [24]You
must not offer to the LORD an animal whose testicles are bruised, crushed, torn or cut.[f] You must not

a *4* The Hebrew word for *defiling skin disease*, traditionally translated "leprosy," was used for various diseases affecting the skin. *b* *23* The Hebrew word can refer to either male or female.

22:3 [n]Lev 7:20,21; Nu 19:13
22:4 [o]Lev 14:1-32; 15:2-15 [p]Lev 11:24-28,39
22:5 [q]Lev 11:24-28,43 [r]Lev 15:7
22:7 [s]Nu 18:11
22:8 [t]Lev 11:39 [u]Ex 22:31; Lev 17:15 [v]Lev 11:40
22:9 [w]ver 16; Ex 28:43
22:11 [x]Ge 17:13; Ex 12:44
22:14 [y]Lev 5:15
22:15 [z]Nu 18:32
22:16 [a]ver 9
22:18 [b]Lev 1:2
22:19 [c]Lev 1:3
22:20 [d]Dt 15:21; 17:1; Mal 1:8,14; Heb 9:14; 1Pe 1:19
22:21 [e]Lev 3:6; Nu 15:3,8
22:24 [f]Lev 21:20

22:3 ceremonially unclean. See vv. 4–8. **cut off from my presence.** Could no longer function as a priest in the tabernacle of the Lord's presence. One of the main concerns was that someone might defile the Lord's dwelling place in the midst of the people (see 15:31 and note). **22:9 perform my service.** Priests needed to be more careful about contracting and cleansing uncleanness because they performed the service of the Lord and, therefore, had more occasion to defile the tabernacle or the sacred offerings, which was to be avoided at all cost (see v. 3 and note). **become guilty and die.** See notes on 10:2,3. **treating it with contempt.** The same Hebrew term as "profane" (18:21) and "desecrate" (21:12). Holy things were to be treated in holy ways (see note on 10:10).
22:10 guest. Someone who lodged with the priest. The consecrated food was only for priests and their families.
22:14 by mistake. Translates the same Hebrew term rendered "unintentionally" elsewhere (see note on 4:2). A person might make such a mistake, e.g., by confusing a firstborn (and therefore consecrated animal, Exod 13:2) with one that was not. **make restitution.** The replacement of the offering plus one-fifth of its value could be made as a monetary payment (see notes on 5:15,16).

22:25 [g] Lev 21:6
22:27 [h] Ex 22:30
22:28 [i] Dt 22:6,7
22:29 [j] Lev 7:12; Ps 107:22
22:30 [k] Lev 7:15
22:31 [l] Dt 4:2,40; Ps 105:45
22:32 [m] Lev 18:21 [n] Lev 10:3
22:33 [o] Lev 11:45
23:2 [p] ver 4,37,44; Nu 29:39 [q] ver 21,27
23:3 [r] Ex 20:9 [s] Ex 20:10; 31:13-17; Lev 19:3; Dt 5:13; Heb 4:9,10
23:5 [t] Ex 12:18-19; Nu 28:16-17; Dt 16:1-8
23:7 [u] ver 3,8

do this in your own land, 25 and you must not accept such animals from the hand of a foreigner and
offer them as the food of your God.[g] They will not be accepted on your behalf, because they are deformed and have defects.' "

26 The LORD said to Moses, 27 "When a calf, a lamb or a goat is born, it is to remain with its mother
for seven days.[h] From the eighth day on, it will be acceptable as a food offering presented to the LORD.
28 Do not slaughter a cow or a sheep and its young on the same day.[i]

29 "When you sacrifice a thank offering[j] to the LORD, sacrifice it in such a way that it will be accepted
on your behalf. 30 It must be eaten that same day; leave none of it till morning.[k] I am the LORD.

31 "Keep[l] my commands and follow them. I am the LORD. 32 Do not profane my holy name,[m] for I must
be acknowledged as holy by the Israelites.[n] I am the LORD, who made you holy 33 and who brought you
out of Egypt to be your God.[o] I am the LORD."

The Appointed Festivals

23 The LORD said to Moses, 2 "Speak to the Israelites and say to them: 'These are my appointed
festivals,[p] the appointed festivals of the LORD, which you are to proclaim as sacred assemblies.[q]

The Sabbath

3 " 'There are six days when you may work,[r] but the seventh day is a day of sabbath rest,[s] a day of
sacred assembly. You are not to do any work; wherever you live, it is a sabbath to the LORD.

The Passover and the Festival of Unleavened Bread

23:4-8pp — Ex 12:14-20; Nu 28:16-25; Dt 16:1-8

4 " 'These are the LORD's appointed festivals, the sacred assemblies you are to proclaim at their appointed times: 5 The LORD's Passover begins at twilight on the fourteenth day of the first month.[t] 6 On
the fifteenth day of that month the LORD's Festival of Unleavened Bread begins; for seven days you must
eat bread made without yeast. 7 On the first day hold a sacred assembly[u] and do no regular work. 8 For
seven days present a food offering to the LORD. And on the seventh day hold a sacred assembly and do
no regular work.' "

22:27–28 remain with its mother ... seven days ... eighth day. The young animal is nursed by its mother for seven days, so it would not be accepted on the altar until the eighth day. A period of seven days is a full cycle, like the seven-day week ending with a Sabbath (Exod 20:8–11; cf. also other "sevens," e.g., see 4:6 and note).

22:28 its young ... same day. The compassionate treatment of animals is a regular theme in the OT law (e.g., Exod 23:5,11–12; Deut 25:4), including the prohibition of taking a mother when killing her young ones for food (e.g., Deut 22:6–7). Some would apply the same principle to the interpretation of the rule "Do not cook a young goat in its mother's milk" (Exod 23:19b; Deut 14:21b).

23:1—25:55 *The Appointed Festivals, Sabbath Year, and Year of Jubilee.* "Holy" or "sacred" repeatedly refers to the sabbatical regulations in chs. 23 and 25. Legislation about the weekly Sabbath and yearly festivals begins in ch. 23; the regulations about the sabbatical year and the Year of Jubilee conclude the sabbatical legislation in ch. 25. In between, ch. 24 emphasizes the daily and weekly practice of the presence of the Lord in the tabernacle and, in light of that, the importance of treating both the name of the Lord (24:10–16,23) and his people (24:17–22) with due respect.

23:2 appointed festivals. Set forth in ch. 23. **sacred assemblies.** Although actual assembly may be included, the primary concern is that the Israelites set the day aside to sanctify it to the Lord by not doing any (regular) work on that day (e.g., on the weekly Sabbath day, v. 3). It sometimes fit within the context of a larger festival (e.g., the first and last days of Passover were sacred assemblies, vv. 7–8).

23:4 the LORD's appointed festivals. See "The Lord's Appointed Festivals," p. 229.

23:5 Passover. Jesus was crucified during the Passover Festival. He ate the Passover with his disciples and instituted the Lord's Supper earlier on the same evening he was betrayed to be crucified (Luke 22:14–22). **twilight.** Designates the time between the setting of the sun and the true darkness of night.

23:6 Festival of Unleavened Bread. Belongs together with the Passover (indicated by the close sequence in vv. 5–6 and the next new introduction formula ["the LORD said to Moses"] not appearing until v. 9). **bread made without yeast.** Derives from the haste in leaving Egypt on the eve of the exodus, which allowed no time for the bread dough to rise in the leavening process (Exod 12:39). Rabbinic literature elaborates in great detail on the need to rid the Jewish household of leaven/yeast before the arrival of Passover (Exod 12:14–20). It is an important element in commemorating the exodus from Egypt. Jesus ate the Passover with his disciples the same evening he was betrayed to be crucified (see note on v. 5). As it relates to the church, Jesus, our "Passover lamb," has already been sacrificed, so the church must rid themselves of any "old yeast" (1 Cor 5:7). See note on Num 28:17.

23:7,8 sacred assembly. On both the first day and last day of the Festival of Unleavened Bread. See note on v. 2. **regular.** Refers to daily labor of the normal work day, whether agricultural work or other work by which they made their living. In other words, this was not to be treated as a regular work day; however, the more specific regulations for what one could or could not do on the weekly seventh day (the Sabbath) were not applied to these particular days of sacred assembly. For rules concerning the Sabbath, see, e.g., Exod 35:2–3; Num 15:32–36, where the point is that one could not even gather wood or light a fire to use for basic food preparation on the Sabbath. The food to be eaten on the Sabbath was to be prepared the previous day.

Offering the Firstfruits

[9]The LORD said to Moses, [10]"Speak to the Israelites and say to them: 'When you enter the land I am
going to give you and you reap its harvest, bring to the priest a sheaf[v] of the first grain you harvest. [11]He
is to wave the sheaf before the LORD[w] so it will be accepted on your behalf; the priest is to wave it on the
day after the Sabbath. [12]On the day you wave the sheaf, you must sacrifice as a burnt offering to the

23:10 [v] Ex 23:16,19; 34:26
23:11 [w] Ex 29:24

23:10 the first grain you harvest. Barley, not wheat (v. 16); see "The Lord's Appointed Festivals," this page. Barley is a light grain that ripens earlier than wheat, which is a heavier grain that takes longer to grow and mature. So the barley harvest comes first (Ruth 1:22) and then the wheat harvest (Ruth 2:23). The climate in Israel is too dry for such grain crops to grow through the summer months (June–August), so they are planted in the fall (October) and grow through the rainy seasons, which come during the winter months (November–March). The grain is ready for harvest in the spring and early summer (May and June).
23:11 wave the sheaf. To dedicate the whole barley harvest to the

THE LORD'S APPOINTED FESTIVALS

APPOINTED FESTIVAL	BIBLICAL REFERENCES	TIME OF YEAR: OT	TIME OF YEAR: MODERN	SIGNIFICANCE CELEBRATED	SPECIAL REQUIREMENTS
(1) Weekly Sabbath	**OT:** Exod 20:8–11; 31:12–17; Lev 23:3; Deut 5:12–15 **NT:** Matt 12:1–14; 28:1; Mark 2:23—3:6; Luke 4:16; 6:1–11; 14:1; John 5:9–18; Acts 13:42; Col 2:16; Heb 4:1–11	7th day of every week	Same	Rest as sign of the covenant (Exod 31:12–17)	No work for people or animals
(2) Passover **and**	**OT:** Exod 12:11–14; Lev 23:5; Num 28:16 **NT:** Matt 26:17–29; Mark 14:12–26; Luke 22:7–20; John 2:13; 11:55; 1 Cor 5:7; 11.23–20, Heb 11.28	1st month (Aviv/Nisan) 14th day (1 day)	March/April [2nd Passover is one month later, Num 9:10–11]	Exodus from Egypt	No regular work on days 1 and 7; males go to the sanctuary
Unleavened Bread	**OT:** Exod 12:15–20; Lev 23:6–8; Num 28:17–25; Deut 16:1–8 **NT:** Mark 14:1,12; Acts 12:3; 1 Cor 5:6–8	15th–21st days length: 7 days			
(3) Firstfruits of barley **and**	**OT:** Lev 23:9–14 (cf. Exod 23:16; 34:26)	Day after the Sabbath of Unleavened Bread week	March/April	Dedication of the barley harvest to the Lord	Must not eat any of the new crop until after this dedication
Firstfruits of wheat	**OT:** Lev 23:15–17 **NT:** Rom 8:23; 1 Cor 15:20–23	Day after the Sabbath 7 weeks later (see Festival of Weeks [Pentecost])	May/June	Dedication of the wheat harvest to the Lord	No regular work on this day
(4) Weeks (Pentecost)	**OT:** Lev 23:15–22; Num 28:26–31; Deut 16:9–12 **NT:** Acts 2:1–4; 20:16; 1 Cor 16:8	3rd month (Sivan); 7 weeks after Unleavened Bread week	May/June	Dedication of the harvest to the Lord	No regular work on this day; males go to the sanctuary
(5) Trumpets	**OT:** Lev 23:23–25; Num 29:1–6	7th month (Ethanim/Tishri); 1st day of the month	September/October	New Year (agricultural)	No regular work on this day
(6) Day of Atonement (Yom Kippur)	**OT:** Lev 16; 23:26–32; Num 29:7–11 **NT:** Rom 3:24–26; Heb 9:7–14; 9:23—10:4,19–22	7th month (Ethanin/Tishri); 10th day of the month	September/October	Making atonement for sins of priests and people	No work on this day; deny (afflict) oneself, fasting
(7) Tabernacles (Booths) (Sukkoth)	**OT:** Lev 23:33–36,39–43; Num 29:12–38; Deut 16:13–15 **NT:** John 7:2,8,11,14,37–38	7th month (Ethanim/Tishri): 15th day of the month length: 8 days	September/October	Harvest	No regular work on 1st and 8th days; males go to the sanctuary
[NOT IN LEVITICUS 23] (8) Purim	**OT:** Esth 9:18–32	12th month (Adar)	February/March	National deliverance in time of Esther	Day of joy, feasting, and giving gifts
[NOT IN LEVITICUS 23] (9) Dedication (Lights) (Hanukkah)	**Apocrypha:** 1 Maccabees 4:36–61 **NT:** John 10:22	9th month (Kislev); 25th day of the month length: 8 days	November/December	Restoration of the temple and dedication of the altar (165/164 BC)	Days of joy and gladness

23:13 [x]Lev 2:14-16; 6:20
23:14 [y]Ex 34:26 [z]Nu 15:21
23:16 [a]Nu 28:26; Ac 2:1
23:17 [b]Ex 34:22; Lev 2:12
23:21 [c]ver 2 [d]ver 3
23:22 [e]Lev 19:9 [f]Lev 19:10; Dt 24:19-21; Ru 2:15
23:24 [g]Lev 25:9; Nu 10:9,10; 29:1
23:25 [h]ver 21
23:27 [i]Lev 16:29 [j]Ex 30:10 [k]Nu 29:7
23:29 [l]Ge 17:14; Nu 5:2
23:30 [m]Lev 20:3

LORD a lamb a year old without defect, 13together with its grain offering[x] of two-tenths of an ephah[a] of
the finest flour mixed with olive oil — a food offering presented to the LORD, a pleasing aroma — and
its drink offering of a quarter of a hin[b] of wine. 14You must not eat any bread, or roasted or new grain,
until the very day you bring this offering to your God.[y] This is to be a lasting ordinance for the generations to come,[z] wherever you live.

The Festival of Weeks
23:15-22pp — Nu 28:26-31; Dt 16:9-12

15" 'From the day after the Sabbath, the day you brought the sheaf of the wave offering, count off
seven full weeks. 16Count off fifty days up to the day after the seventh Sabbath,[a] and then present an
offering of new grain to the LORD. 17From wherever you live, bring two loaves made of two-tenths of an
ephah of the finest flour, baked with yeast, as a wave offering of firstfruits[b] to the LORD. 18Present with
this bread seven male lambs, each a year old and without defect, one young bull and two rams. They
will be a burnt offering to the LORD, together with their grain offerings and drink offerings — a food
offering, an aroma pleasing to the LORD. 19Then sacrifice one male goat for a sin offering[c] and two
lambs, each a year old, for a fellowship offering. 20The priest is to wave the two lambs before the LORD
as a wave offering, together with the bread of the firstfruits. They are a sacred offering to the LORD for
the priest. 21On that same day you are to proclaim a sacred assembly[c] and do no regular work.[d] This is
to be a lasting ordinance for the generations to come, wherever you live.

22" 'When you reap the harvest[e] of your land, do not reap to the very edges of your field or gather
the gleanings of your harvest.[f] Leave them for the poor and for the foreigner residing among you. I
am the LORD your God.' "

The Festival of Trumpets
23:23-25pp — Nu 29:1-6

23The LORD said to Moses, 24"Say to the Israelites: 'On the first day of the seventh month you are to
have a day of sabbath rest, a sacred assembly commemorated with trumpet blasts.[g] 25Do no regular
work,[h] but present a food offering to the LORD.' "

The Day of Atonement
23:26-32pp — Lev 16:2-34; Nu 29:7-11

26The LORD said to Moses, 27"The tenth day of this seventh month[i] is the Day of Atonement.[j] Hold a
sacred assembly[k] and deny yourselves,[d] and present a food offering to the LORD. 28Do not do any work
on that day, because it is the Day of Atonement, when atonement is made for you before the LORD your
God. 29Those who do not deny themselves on that day must be cut off from their people.[l] 30I will destroy
from among their people[m] anyone who does any work on that day. 31You shall do no work at all. This is

[a] *13* That is, probably about 7 pounds or about 3.2 kilograms; also in verse 17 [b] *13* That is, about 1 quart or about 1 liter [c] *19* Or *purification offering* [d] *27* Or *and fast*; similarly in verses 29 and 32

Lord (see note on 7:30). **sheaf.** A bundle of stalks of grain that could be held in one's hand. **the day after the Sabbath.** Either the day after the Sabbath day that followed immediately after Passover, during the week of Unleavened Bread (cf. v. 15), or the day after the Sabbath day at the end of the days of Unleavened Bread. The ambiguity may be intentional to allow for variations in the ripening of the crops from year to year.
23:13 two-tenths of an ephah. See NIV text note. The officiating priest consumed most of this grain (except a handful that was burned on the altar as the memorial portion) and the wine as payment for his work at the altar (see notes on 2:2,3). **hin.** See NIV text note.
23:16 day after the seventh Sabbath. A total of 50 days after they offered the firstfruits of the barley harvest (v. 10). The NT refers to this as Pentecost, meaning "fifty." **new grain.** From the wheat harvest (see note on v. 10).
23:21 sacred assembly. See note on v. 2.
23:22 gleanings of your harvest. See 19:9–10; Deut 24:19–22; Ruth 2. This was an important way of providing for the poor and foreigners in ancient Israel. The book of Ruth illustrates the importance of this provision.
23:24 seventh month. Particularly loaded with special occasions for the Lord and the people. **sacred assembly**. See note on v. 2. **trumpet blasts.** Probably from the *šôpār*, a trumpet made from a ram's horn. The loud blasts announced the coming of the seventh month as a special month in which they observed the Day of Atonement and the Festival of Tabernacles (vv. 26–43). The religious year and, therefore, the first month of the year for the Jewish people began in the spring of the year with the month of Aviv, or Nisan, because the exodus from Egypt occurred in that month (Exod 12:2).
23:25 regular work. See note on vv. 7,8.
23:26–32 See ch. 16 and notes.
23:27,29,32 deny yourselves/themselves. See note on 16:29.
23:29 cut off. See note on 7:20,21.

to be a lasting ordinance for the generations to come, wherever you live. [32]It is a day of sabbath rest for you, and you must deny yourselves. From the evening of the ninth day of the month until the following evening you are to observe your sabbath."

The Festival of Tabernacles

23:33-43pp — Nu 29:12-39; Dt 16:13-17

[33]The LORD said to Moses, [34]"Say to the Israelites: 'On the fifteenth day of the seventh month the LORD's Festival of Tabernacles[n] begins, and it lasts for seven days. [35]The first day is a sacred assembly; do no regular work. [36]For seven days present food offerings to the LORD, and on the eighth day hold a sacred assembly[o] and present a food offering to the LORD. It is the closing special assembly; do no regular work.

[37]("'These are the LORD's appointed festivals, which you are to proclaim as sacred assemblies for bringing food offerings to the LORD—the burnt offerings and grain offerings, sacrifices and drink offerings[p] required for each day. [38]These offerings are in addition to those for the LORD's Sabbaths[q] and[a] in addition to your gifts and whatever you have vowed and all the freewill offerings you give to the LORD.)

[39]"'So beginning with the fifteenth day of the seventh month, after you have gathered the crops of the land, celebrate the festival to the LORD for seven days;[r] the first day is a day of sabbath rest, and the eighth day also is a day of sabbath rest. [40]On the first day you are to take branches from luxuriant trees—from palms, willows and other leafy trees[s]—and rejoice before the LORD your God for seven days. [41]Celebrate this as a festival to the LORD for seven days each year. This is to be a lasting ordinance for the generations to come; celebrate it in the seventh month. [42]Live in temporary shelters[t] for seven days: All native-born Israelites are to live in such shelters [43]so your descendants will know[u] that I had the Israelites live in temporary shelters when I brought them out of Egypt. I am the LORD your God.'"

[44]So Moses announced to the Israelites the appointed festivals of the LORD.

Olive Oil and Bread Set Before the LORD

24:1-3pp — Ex 27:20-21

24 The LORD said to Moses, [2]"Command the Israelites to bring you clear oil of pressed olives for the light so that the lamps may be kept burning continually. [3]Outside the curtain that shields the ark of the covenant law in the tent of meeting, Aaron is to tend the lamps before the LORD from evening till morning, continually. This is to be a lasting ordinance for the generations to come. [4]The lamps on the pure gold lampstand[v] before the LORD must be tended continually.

[5]"Take the finest flour and bake twelve loaves of bread,[w] using two-tenths of an ephah[b] for each loaf. [6]Arrange them in two stacks, six in each stack, on the table of pure gold[x] before the LORD. [7]By each stack put some pure incense as a memorial[c] portion[y] to represent the bread and to be a food offering presented to the LORD. [8]This bread is to be set out before the LORD regularly,[z] Sabbath after Sabbath,[a] on behalf of the Israelites, as a lasting covenant. [9]It belongs to Aaron and his sons,[b] who are to eat it in the sanctuary area, because it is a most holy part of their perpetual share of the food offerings presented to the LORD."

[a] *38* Or *These festivals are in addition to the LORD's Sabbaths, and these offerings are* [b] *5* That is, probably about 7 pounds or about 3.2 kilograms [c] *7* Or *representative*

23:34 [n]Ex 23:16; Dt 16:13; Ezr 3:4; Ne 8:14; Zec 14:16; Jn 7:2
23:36 [o]2Ch 7:9; Ne 8:18; Jn 7:37
23:37 [p]ver 2,4
23:38 [q]Eze 45:17
23:39 [r]Ex 23:16; Dt 16:13
23:40 [s]Ne 8:14-17
23:42 [t]Ne 8:14-16
23:43 [u]Dt 31:13; Ps 78:5
24:4 [v]Ex 25:31; 31:8
24:5 [w]Ex 25:30
24:6 [x]Ex 25:23-30; 1Ki 7:48
24:7 [y]Lev 2:2
24:8 [z]Nu 4:7; 1Ch 9:32; 2Ch 2:4 [a]Mt 12:5
24:9 [b]Lev 8:31; Mt 12:4; Mk 2:26; Lk 6:4

23:34 Tabernacles. Not the same Hebrew term as that for the tabernacle of the Lord referred to in, e.g., Exod 25:9; 40:1–38. The Festival of Tabernacles commemorates the Israelites' journey to Sinai after they left Egypt, so "tabernacles" here refers to temporary shelters made from tree branches (vv. 42–43).
23:35 sacred assembly. See note on v. 2.
23:37–38 required for each day ... in addition to your gifts. This summary tells us that what has been listed as required offerings for the festival days in this chapter does not take into account the other offerings regularly required on the Lord's Sabbaths and offered throughout the year.
23:39 after you have gathered the crops of the land. All the work of harvesting for the whole agricultural year was to be finished by that time so they could truly celebrate the Lord's blessings at this festival (v. 41).
24:2,3,4 lamps. Seven lamps rested on top of the seven branches of the lampstand—one middle branch going straight up from the stem and three coming out from each side of the stem. They could be taken off the lampstand to add oil. **continually ... from evening till morning ... continually.** Through the night.
24:8 lasting covenant. Weekly exchanging the old loaves for new ones was part of their covenant obligations. The 12 loaves (symbolizing the 12 tribes) pointed to the actual presence of the Lord in the tabernacle, which is why they are sometimes called "the bread of the Presence" (Exod 25:30).
24:9 Since these loaves were to be edible after a week of sitting out on the table, they were most likely unleavened.

24:11 [c]Ex 3:15
24:12 [d]Ex 18:16; Nu 15:34
24:14 [e]Lev 20:27; Dt 13:9; 17:5,7; 21:21
24:15 [f]Ex 22:28
24:16 [g]1Ki 21:10,13; Mt 26:66
24:17 [h]Ge 9:6; Ex 21:12; Nu 35:30-31; Dt 27:24
24:18 [i]ver 21
24:20 [j]Ex 21:24; Mt 5:38*
24:21 [k]ver 17
24:22 [l]Ex 12:49 [m]Nu 9:14; 15:16
25:3 [n]Ex 23:10
25:6 [o]ver 20
25:9 [p]Lev 23:24
25:10 [q]Isa 61:1; Jer 34:8,15,17; Lk 4:19 [r]Nu 36:4

A Blasphemer Put to Death

[10]Now the son of an Israelite mother and an Egyptian father went out among the Israelites, and a fight broke out in the camp between him and an Israelite. [11]The son of the Israelite woman blasphemed the Name[c] with a curse; so they brought him to Moses. (His mother's name was Shelomith, the daughter of Dibri the Danite.) [12]They put him in custody until the will of the LORD should be made clear to them.[d]

[13]Then the LORD said to Moses: [14]"Take the blasphemer outside the camp. All those who heard him are to lay their hands on his head, and the entire assembly is to stone him.[e] [15]Say to the Israelites: 'Anyone who curses their God[f] will be held responsible; [16]anyone who blasphemes the name of the LORD is to be put to death.[g] The entire assembly must stone them. Whether foreigner or native-born, when they blaspheme the Name they are to be put to death.

[17]" 'Anyone who takes the life of a human being is to be put to death.[h] [18]Anyone who takes the life of someone's animal must make restitution[i] — life for life. [19]Anyone who injures their neighbor is to be injured in the same manner: [20]fracture for fracture, eye for eye, tooth for tooth.[j] The one who has inflicted the injury must suffer the same injury. [21]Whoever kills an animal must make restitution, but whoever kills a human being is to be put to death.[k] [22]You are to have the same law for the foreigner[l] and the native-born.[m] I am the LORD your God.' "

[23]Then Moses spoke to the Israelites, and they took the blasphemer outside the camp and stoned him. The Israelites did as the LORD commanded Moses.

The Sabbath Year

25 The LORD said to Moses at Mount Sinai, [2]"Speak to the Israelites and say to them: 'When you enter the land I am going to give you, the land itself must observe a sabbath to the LORD. [3]For six years sow your fields, and for six years prune your vineyards and gather their crops.[n] [4]But in the seventh year the land is to have a year of sabbath rest, a sabbath to the LORD. Do not sow your fields or prune your vineyards. [5]Do not reap what grows of itself or harvest the grapes of your untended vines. The land is to have a year of rest. [6]Whatever the land yields during the sabbath year[o] will be food for you — for yourself, your male and female servants, and the hired worker and temporary resident who live among you, [7]as well as for your livestock and the wild animals in your land. Whatever the land produces may be eaten.

The Year of Jubilee

25:8-38Ref — Dt 15:1-11
25:39-55Ref — Ex 21:2-11; Dt 15:12-18

[8]" 'Count off seven sabbath years — seven times seven years — so that the seven sabbath years amount to a period of forty-nine years. [9]Then have the trumpet[p] sounded everywhere on the tenth day of the seventh month; on the Day of Atonement sound the trumpet throughout your land. [10]Consecrate the fiftieth year and proclaim liberty[q] throughout the land to all its inhabitants. It shall be a jubilee[r]

24:11 blasphemed the Name with a curse. The exact meaning is uncertain. There are three main views: (1) he pronounced the name "Yahweh," (see Exod 3:14–15 and notes) in a way or with words that amounted to some sort of verbal aggression against Yahweh himself (v. 15); (2) he pronounced a curse against the man using the name "Yahweh"; or (3) he pronounced the name "Yahweh" and thereby blasphemed since "the Name" was never to be pronounced (a standard Jewish explanation). The offense violated the third commandment (Exod 20:7). The same verb for cursing is used explicitly in Exod 22:28 in a prohibition against "cursing" God (translated there as "blaspheme"; see also Lev 24:15).

24:14 lay their hands on his head. Two basic interpretations: (1) they testified against him or (2) they transferred their pollution back to the offender because they had become polluted by hearing the blasphemy.

24:16 Whether foreigner or native-born. See also v. 22. Whether blasphemy (vv. 13–16) or another offense such as murder, killing another person's animal, or some kind of bodily injury (vv. 17–21), the same punishment applied to both the foreigner and the native Israelite. The issue probably arose here because the blasphemy was committed by the son of an Israelite mother and Egyptian father (vv. 10–11). **they are to be put to death.** The punishment for blasphemy was death, whether for the foreigner or the native Israelite.

24:17–21 The punishment should match the crime — no more, no less. Cf. Exod 21:23–25, the so-called *lex talionis* (Latin for "the law of the talon/claw"). This principle also occurs elsewhere in ancient Near Eastern law.

25:1–55 Regulations about the sabbatical year and the Year of Jubilee conclude the sabbatical legislation that began in ch. 23. The principle of the sabbatical year is that people get a Sabbath every seven days, so the land gets a Sabbath every seven years (vv. 2–7). The pattern is important, and it extends further into the Jubilee, which the people were to celebrate every 50 years — after every seven-times-seven years (vv. 8–55; see note on vv. 24–55).

25:10 fiftieth year. Some would identify this as the same as the seventh sabbatical year in the cycle, while others would see it as the year after the seventh sabbatical year. **liberty.** Verses 11–34 detail this. There is

for you; each of you is to return to your family property and to your own clan. 11The fiftieth year shall
be a jubilee for you; do not sow and do not reap what grows of itself or harvest the untended vines. 12For
it is a jubilee and is to be holy for you; eat only what is taken directly from the fields.
13" 'In this Year of Jubilee[s] everyone is to return to their own property.
14" 'If you sell land to any of your own people or buy land from them, do not take advantage of each
other.[t] 15You are to buy from your own people on the basis of the number of years[u] since the Jubilee.
And they are to sell to you on the basis of the number of years left for harvesting crops. 16When the
years are many, you are to increase the price, and when the years are few, you are to decrease the price,[v]
because what is really being sold to you is the number of crops. 17Do not take advantage of each other,[w]
but fear your God.[x] I am the LORD your God.[y]
18" 'Follow my decrees and be careful to obey my laws, and you will live safely in the land.[z] 19Then
the land will yield its fruit,[a] and you will eat your fill and live there in safety. 20You may ask, "What will
we eat in the seventh year[b] if we do not plant or harvest our crops?" 21I will send you such a blessing[c]
in the sixth year that the land will yield enough for three years. 22While you plant during the eighth
year, you will eat from the old crop and will continue to eat from it until the harvest of the ninth year
comes in.[d]
23" 'The land must not be sold permanently, because the land is mine[e] and you reside in my land as
foreigners[f] and strangers. 24Throughout the land that you hold as a possession, you must provide for
the redemption of the land.
25" 'If one of your fellow Israelites becomes poor and sells some of their property, their nearest relative[g] is to come and redeem[h] what they have sold. 26If, however, there is no one to redeem it for them
but later on they prosper and acquire sufficient means to redeem it themselves, 27they are to determine
the value for the years since they sold it and refund the balance to the one to whom they sold it; they
can then go back to their own property. 28But if they do not acquire the means to repay, what was sold
will remain in the possession of the buyer until the Year of Jubilee. It will be returned in the Jubilee,
and they can then go back to their property.[i]
29" 'Anyone who sells a house in a walled city retains the right of redemption a full year after its
sale. During that time the seller may redeem it. 30If it is not redeemed before a full year has passed, the
house in the walled city shall belong permanently to the buyer and the buyer's descendants. It is not
to be returned in the Jubilee. 31But houses in villages without walls around them are to be considered
as belonging to the open country. They can be redeemed, and they are to be returned in the Jubilee.
32" 'The Levites always have the right to redeem their houses in the Levitical towns,[j] which they possess. 33So the property of the Levites is redeemable—that is, a house sold in any town they hold—and
is to be returned in the Jubilee, because the houses in the towns of the Levites are their property among
the Israelites. 34But the pastureland belonging to their towns must not be sold; it is their permanent
possession.[k]
35" 'If any of your fellow Israelites become poor[l] and are unable to support themselves among you,

25:13 [s] ver 10
25:14 [t] Lev 19:13; 1Sa 12:3,4
25:15 [u] Lev 27:18,23
25:16 [v] ver 27,51,52
25:17 [w] Pr 22:22; Jer 7:5,6; 1Th 4:6 [x] Lev 19:14 [y] Lev 19:32
25:18 [z] Lev 26:4,5; Dt 12:10; Ps 4:8; Jer 23:6
25:19 [a] Lev 26:4
25:20 [b] ver 4
25:21 [c] Dt 28:8,12; Hag 2:19; Mal 3:10
25:22 [d] Lev 26:10
25:23 [e] Ex 19:5 [f] Ge 23:4; 1Ch 29:15; Ps 39:12; Heb 11:13; 1Pe 2:11
25:25 [g] Ru 2:20; Jer 32:7 [h] Lev 27:13,19,31; Ru 4:4
25:28 [i] ver 10
25:32 [j] Nu 35:1-8; Jos 21:2
25:34 [k] Nu 35:2-5
25:35 [l] Dt 24:14,15

a good deal of background information for similar kinds of release from debts in the ancient Near Eastern world surrounding Israel. The goal was to relieve economic pressures that built up over time. Isa 61:1–2 uses some of the concepts from the Jubilee in Lev 25, and these come through into the NT as well in Luke 4:18–19. **jubilee.** Probably means "ram" and can refer to a "ram's horn." So the fiftieth year was called the "Jubilee" because of the associated sounding of the "ram's horn" (v. 9). **return ... family property.** As originally distributed to the various tribes when they first conquered the land (Josh 13–21; cf. Ruth 2:3; 4:3,5).

25:15 years since the Jubilee. The purchaser was actually buying only the crops that the land would produce until the next Jubilee, since the land would revert to the original owner at that time. The purchaser was not actually buying the land itself.

25:17 take advantage. To purchase the land permanently would be to "take advantage" of the people and families to whom God had granted it.

25:23 foreigners. Israel was attached to the Lord's household. They did not own the land and, in this regard, were like foreigners in the land (see note on 19:10).

25:24–55 The subject shifts from the Jubilee to the related subject of redemption of land (vv. 25–28), houses (vv. 29–34), and debt-slaves (vv. 35–53) during the time between Jubilee years. This "redemption" was about the right to buy (i.e., "redeem") these back when the money was available to do so (cf. Ruth 4:1–10). If the money to redeem them did not become available to the family before the next Jubilee, then they generally went free in the Jubilee year (vv. 28,31,33,40–41,54–55). The exception is the sale of houses in walled cities (v. 30). The same basic terminology is used for the Lord's redeeming Israel out of Egypt (e.g., Exod 6:6; 15:13), and this usage extends through the rest of the OT (e.g., Pss 74:2; 77:15) and into the NT for our "redemption" in Christ Jesus (Titus 2:14; 1 Pet 1:18–19).

25:25 redeem. There were multiple potential redeemers in the family, but only one was the nearest and responsible to do this if he had the resources to do so (Jer 32:6–15). In the case of Naomi and Ruth, the obligation to marry the widow and raise up a family in the deceased husband's name also applied (Deut 25:5–10; cf. Ruth 2:20; 3:12; 4:3,6,9–10).

25:35 [m]Dt 15:8; Ps 37:21,26; Lk 6:35
25:36 [n]Ex 22:25; Dt 23:19-20
25:38 [o]Ge 17:7; Lev 11:45
25:39 [p]Ex 21:2; Dt 15:12; 1Ki 9:22
25:41 [q]ver 28
25:43 [r]Ex 1:13; Eze 34:4; Col 4:1
25:48 [s]Ne 5:5
25:49 [t]ver 26
25:50 [u]Job 7:1; Isa 16:14; 21:16
26:1 [v]Ex 20:4; Lev 19:4; Dt 5:8 [w]Ex 23:24 [x]Nu 33:52
26:2 [y]Lev 19:30

help them[m] as you would a foreigner and stranger, so they can continue to live among you. 36Do not
take interest[n] or any profit from them, but fear your God, so that they may continue to live among you.
37You must not lend them money at interest or sell them food at a profit. 38I am the LORD your God, who
brought you out of Egypt to give you the land of Canaan and to be your God.[o]
39" 'If any of your fellow Israelites become poor and sell themselves to you, do not make them work
as slaves.[p] 40They are to be treated as hired workers or temporary residents among you; they are to
work for you until the Year of Jubilee. 41Then they and their children are to be released, and they will
go back to their own clans and to the property[q] of their ancestors. 42Because the Israelites are my servants, whom I brought out of Egypt, they must not be sold as slaves. 43Do not rule over them ruthlessly,[r]
but fear your God.
44" 'Your male and female slaves are to come from the nations around you; from them you may buy
slaves. 45You may also buy some of the temporary residents living among you and members of their
clans born in your country, and they will become your property. 46You can bequeath them to your children as inherited property and can make them slaves for life, but you must not rule over your fellow
Israelites ruthlessly.
47" 'If a foreigner residing among you becomes rich and any of your fellow Israelites become poor
and sell themselves to the foreigner or to a member of the foreigner's clan, 48they retain the right of
redemption after they have sold themselves. One of their relatives[s] may redeem them: 49An uncle or a
cousin or any blood relative in their clan may redeem them. Or if they prosper,[t] they may redeem themselves. 50They and their buyer are to count the time from the year they sold themselves up to the Year of
Jubilee. The price for their release is to be based on the rate paid to a hired worker[u] for that number of
years. 51If many years remain, they must pay for their redemption a larger share of the price paid for
them. 52If only a few years remain until the Year of Jubilee, they are to compute that and pay for their
redemption accordingly. 53They are to be treated as workers hired from year to year; you must see to it
that those to whom they owe service do not rule over them ruthlessly.
54" 'Even if someone is not redeemed in any of these ways, they and their children are to be released
in the Year of Jubilee, 55for the Israelites belong to me as servants. They are my servants, whom I
brought out of Egypt. I am the LORD your God.

Reward for Obedience

26 " 'Do not make idols[v] or set up an image or a sacred stone[w] for yourselves, and do not place a
carved stone[x] in your land to bow down before it. I am the LORD your God.
2" 'Observe my Sabbaths and have reverence for my sanctuary.[y] I am the LORD.

25:36 Do not take interest or any profit from them. They were to avoid taking advantage of another person's misfortune. See note on v. 38.
25:38 I am the LORD your God, who brought you out of Egypt. This had implications for all of life in the land, including how Israelites treated one another. Rather than take advantage of others, they were to take care of each other, especially through difficult circumstances.
25:39 sell themselves. As "debt-slaves" for a period of time. Some Israelites did this if they became destitute (cf. Exod 21:2–11; Deut 15:12–18). It was a way to pay off their debt and, in the meantime, they and their family were provided for by the master. When it was time to go free, the master was to make sure he gave them a good start on their own (Deut 15:13–15).
25:40 treated as hired workers. Israelite debt-slaves were to be treated not as permanent slaves but as hired workers (contrast vv. 44–46). **until the Year of Jubilee.** Even if the regular six years for the debt-slave were not yet completed (cf. Exod 21:2; Deut 15:12), when the Jubilee year came around, all debt-slaves were to return to their original family land (see vv. 8–11 and note on v. 10).
25:42 servants. See note on v. 55. **brought out of Egypt.** See note on 11:45.
25:43 See also vv. 46,53.
25:44 Your male and female slaves. The Israelites could have permanent slaves ("chattel") like all the other peoples of the ancient Near Eastern world, but they could not take their fellow Israelites as such slaves (see vv. 39–43 and the rationale in vv. 54–55). The two sources for permanent slaves in Israel were the nations around them (v. 44) and the non-Israelite temporary residents who lived among them (v. 45; see note on 19:10). Neither of these could own land permanently in ancient Israel, so they would not be included in the Jubilee return to the ancestral family land (see note on v. 10). Slaves were often refugees of war, for whom this was their only means of survival. The law includes protection for slaves (e.g., Exod 21:20–21; Deut 21:10–14; 23:15–16). The NT does not prohibit slavery either, but it instructs Christian slave owners to treat their Christian slaves as beloved brothers and sisters in Christ, not as slaves (Phlm 16). And the NT urges Christian slaves to be faithful to their masters and even be willing to suffer unjustly as Christ did on the cross as God's suffering servant (1 Pet 2:18–25; cf. Isa 53). This in no way justifies slavery as an institution, but it helped Christians know how to live well even in the midst of the fallen corrupt conditions of this world.
25:46 inherited property ... slaves for life. Permanent slaves did not go free in the seventh year like debt-slaves, and they could even be passed down to the next generation as family inheritance property.
25:55 servants. Or slaves.
26:1–46 *Reward for Obedience and Punishment for Disobedience.* Ch. 25 flows directly into 26; there is no new introduction or division

3“ ‘If you follow my decrees and are careful to obey[z] my commands, 4I will send you rain[a] in its season, and the ground will yield its crops and the trees their fruit.[b] 5Your threshing will continue until grape harvest and the grape harvest will continue until planting, and you will eat all the food you want[c] and live in safety in your land.[d]

6“ ‘I will grant peace in the land,[e] and you will lie down[f] and no one will make you afraid.[g] I will remove wild beasts[h] from the land, and the sword will not pass through your country. 7You will pursue your enemies, and they will fall by the sword before you. 8Five of you will chase a hundred, and a hundred of you will chase ten thousand, and your enemies will fall by the sword before you.[i]

9“ ‘I will look on you with favor and make you fruitful and increase your numbers,[j] and I will keep my covenant[k] with you. 10You will still be eating last year’s harvest when you will have to move it out to make room for the new.[l] 11I will put my dwelling place[a][m] among you, and I will not abhor you. 12I will walk[n] among you and be your God, and you will be my people.[o] 13I am the LORD your God, who brought you out of Egypt so that you would no longer be slaves to the Egyptians; I broke the bars of your yoke[p] and enabled you to walk with heads held high.

Punishment for Disobedience

14“ ‘But if you will not listen to me and carry out all these commands,[q] 15and if you reject my decrees and abhor my laws and fail to carry out all my commands and so violate my covenant, 16then I will do this to you: I will bring on you sudden terror, wasting diseases and fever[r] that will destroy your sight and sap your strength.[s] You will plant seed in vain, because your enemies will eat it.[t] 17I will set my face[u] against you so that you will be defeated by your enemies; those who hate you will rule over you,[v] and you will flee even when no one is pursuing you.[w]

18“ ‘If after all this you will not listen to me, I will punish you for your sins seven times over.[x] 19I will break down your stubborn pride[y] and make the sky above you like iron and the ground beneath you like bronze.[z] 20Your strength will be spent in vain,[a] because your soil will not yield its crops, nor will the trees of your land yield their fruit.[b]

21“ ‘If you remain hostile toward me and refuse to listen to me, I will multiply your afflictions seven times over,[c] as your sins deserve. 22I will send wild animals[d] against you, and they will rob you of your children, destroy your cattle and make you so few in number that your roads will be deserted.

23“ ‘If in spite of these things you do not accept my correction[e] but continue to be hostile toward me, 24I myself will be hostile toward you and will afflict you for your sins seven times over. 25And I will bring the sword on you to avenge the breaking of the covenant. When you withdraw into your cities, I will send a plague[f] among you, and you will be given into enemy hands. 26When I cut off your supply of bread,[g] ten women will be able to bake your bread in one oven, and they will dole out the bread by weight. You will eat, but you will not be satisfied.

27“ ‘If in spite of this you still do not listen to me but continue to be hostile toward me, 28then in my

[a] *11* Or *my tabernacle*

26:3 [z] Dt 7:12; 11:13,22; 28:1,9
26:4 [a] Dt 11:14 [b] Ps 67:6
26:5 [c] Dt 11:15; Joel 2:19,26; Am 9:13 [d] Lev 25:18
26:6 [e] Ps 29:11; 85:8; 147:14 [f] Ps 4:8 [g] Zep 3:13 [h] ver 22
26:8 [i] Dt 32:30; Jos 23:10
26:9 [j] Ge 17:6; Ne 9:23 [k] Ge 17:7
26:10 [l] Lev 25:22
26:11 [m] Ex 25:8; Ps 76:2; Eze 37:27
26:12 [n] Ge 3:8 [o] 2Co 6:16*
26:13 [p] Eze 34:27
26:14 [q] Dt 28:15-68; Mal 2:2
26:16 [r] Dt 28:22,35 [s] 1Sa 2:33 [t] Job 31:8
26:17 [u] Lev 17:10 [v] Ps 106:41 [w] ver 36,37; Dt 28:7,25; Ps 53:5
26:18 [x] ver 21
26:19 [y] Isa 25:11 [z] Dt 28:23
26:20 [a] Ps 127:1; Isa 17:11 [b] Dt 11:17
26:21 [c] ver 18
26:22 [d] Dt 32:24
26:23 [e] Jer 2:30; 5:3
26:25 [f] Nu 14:12; Eze 5:17
26:26 [g] Ps 105:16; Isa 3:1; Mic 6:14

between them. The Mosaic covenant was sealed in Exod 24:1–11, but then the Lord called Moses up on Sinai again (Exod 24:12–18) to give him further covenantal regulations regarding the construction of the tabernacle (Exod 25–31; 35–40), the functions within the tabernacle (Lev 1–16), and life in the community surrounding the tabernacle (chs. 17–27). It was normal in the ancient Near East to conclude covenants with blessings for obedience and curses for disobedience to the covenant stipulations. See Deut 28 for the blessings and curses of the covenant.

26:11–12 See Introduction: Major Theological Themes (The Lord’s Presence).

26:12 walk. The same word describes the Lord walking in the Garden of Eden (Gen 3:8), Enoch walking with God (Gen 5:22,24), Noah walking with God (Gen 6:9), and others walking with or before God (e.g., Gen 17:1; 24:40; Ps 56:13; Isa 38:3; cf. Deut 23:14). The Lord would “walk” right along with his people through life and history if they would remain faithful to their covenant commitments.

26:16–20 This neediness, warfare, and defeat contrasts with the prosperity, peace, and victory of vv. 4–12.

26:18 seven times over. Occurs four times in vv. 18–33 to emphasize the increasing intensity of punishments with which the Lord would afflict rebellious Israel (vv. 18,21,24,28). Their sin and rebellion led ultimately to their exile from the land and dispersion (vv. 33–39), which is the main substance of the fourth of the “seven times over” afflictions (vv. 29–33).

26:19 break down your stubborn pride. This is the goal and rationale of the “seven times over” punishments (see note on v. 18).

26:21 If you remain hostile. If they continued to be hostile to the Lord, he would be hostile in turn until he broke down their stubbornness (vv. 21,23–24,27–28). Things would go from bad to worse: from infertility of the land (vv. 19–20), to being overrun by wild animals (v. 22), to enemy attacks, plague, and hunger (vv. 25–26), to starvation, defeat, and devastation of the land, leading to exile and dispersion (vv. 29–33).

26:22 Contrasts with the removal of the wild beasts from the land in v. 6.

26:29 [h]Dt 28:53
26:30 [i]2Ch 34:3; Eze 6:3 [j]Eze 6:6 [k]Eze 6:13
26:31 [l]Ps 74:3-7
26:32 [m]Jer 9:11
26:33 [n]Dt 4:27; Eze 12:15; 20:23; Zec 7:14
26:34 [o]ver 43; 2Ch 36:21
26:36 [p]Eze 21:7
26:37 [q]Jos 7:12
26:38 [r]Dt 4:26
26:39 [s]Eze 4:17
26:40 [t]Jer 3:12-15; Lk 15:18; 1Jn 1:9
26:41 [u]Eze 44:7,9; Ac 7:51
26:42 [v]Ge 22:15-18; 28:15 [w]Ge 26:5
26:44 [x]Ro 11:2 [y]Dt 4:31; Jer 30:11 [z]Jer 33:26
26:45 [a]Ge 17:7 [b]Ex 6:8; Lev 25:38
26:46 [c]Lev 7:38; 27:34

anger I will be hostile toward you, and I myself will punish you for your sins seven times over. 29You will
eat the flesh of your sons and the flesh of your daughters.[h] 30I will destroy your high places,[i] cut down
your incense altars[j] and pile your dead bodies[a] on the lifeless forms of your idols,[k] and I will abhor
you. 31I will turn your cities into ruins and lay waste your sanctuaries,[l] and I will take no delight in
the pleasing aroma of your offerings. 32I myself will lay waste the land,[m] so that your enemies who live
there will be appalled. 33I will scatter you among the nations[n] and will draw out my sword and pursue
you. Your land will be laid waste, and your cities will lie in ruins. 34Then the land will enjoy its sabbath
years all the time that it lies desolate and you are in the country of your enemies;[o] then the land will
rest and enjoy its sabbaths. 35All the time that it lies desolate, the land will have the rest it did not have
during the sabbaths you lived in it.

36" 'As for those of you who are left, I will make their hearts so fearful in the lands of their enemies
that the sound of a windblown leaf will put them to flight.[p] They will run as though fleeing from the
sword, and they will fall, even though no one is pursuing them. 37They will stumble over one another
as though fleeing from the sword, even though no one is pursuing them. So you will not be able to
stand before your enemies.[q] 38You will perish among the nations; the land of your enemies will devour
you.[r] 39Those of you who are left will waste away in the lands of their enemies because of their sins;
also because of their ancestors' sins they will waste away.[s]

40" 'But if they will confess their sins and the sins of their ancestors[t]—their unfaithfulness
and their hostility toward me, 41which made me hostile toward them so that I sent them into the
land of their enemies—then when their uncircumcised hearts[u] are humbled and they pay for
their sin, 42I will remember my covenant with Jacob[v] and my covenant with Isaac[w] and my covenant with Abraham, and I will remember the land. 43For the land will be deserted by them and
will enjoy its sabbaths while it lies desolate without them. They will pay for their sins because
they rejected my laws and abhorred my decrees. 44Yet in spite of this, when they are in the land
of their enemies, I will not reject them or abhor[x] them so as to destroy them completely,[y] breaking my covenant[z] with them. I am the LORD their God. 45But for their sake I will remember[a] the
covenant with their ancestors whom I brought out of Egypt[b] in the sight of the nations to be their
God. I am the LORD.' "

46These are the decrees, the laws and the regulations that the LORD established at Mount Sinai between himself and the Israelites through Moses.[c]

[a] *30* Or *your funeral offerings*

26:34 Then the land will enjoy its sabbath years. Refers back to the sabbatical year plan for the land (25:2–7). Even though they did not give the land its sabbaths through the years, it would get its sabbaths all at once while the people were in exile. Since they would be out of the land, they would not be able to continually plant and harvest the land in violation of the sabbatical year regulation of rest for the land (v. 43).
26:40 if they will confess. Or "when they confess" or "they will confess." **their sins and the sins of their ancestors.** Verses 40–45 contrast with v. 39. **hostility.** See note on v. 21.
26:41 when their uncircumcised hearts are humbled. For the covenantal background of circumcision, see Gen 17:9–14. As indicated here, the figurative use in applying it to the human heart would mean that their hearts would become humble rather than arrogant and rebellious. This is the first time this figurative use appears in the Bible, but it appears elsewhere in Deut 10:16; 30:6; Jer 4:4; 9:25–26; Ezek 44:7,9). Rom 2:28–29 says "circumcision of the heart" is the work of the Holy Spirit in the heart of true believers—those in Christ (cf. Col 2:11).
26:42 covenant. See Gen 15:8–21; 17:1–14; 26:3–5; 28:13–15; Exod 2:24; 3:6. The concept of God "remembering" a covenant means that he will be faithful to it; e.g., the covenant in Gen 6:18–20 is remembered in Gen 8:1; the covenant in Gen 9:8–13 is remembered whenever the rainbow appears; Exod 2:24; 6:5 are about God remembering the Abrahamic covenant. See "Covenant," p. 2646. **I will remember the land.** Part of remembering the Abrahamic covenant (Gen 15:8–21). The land is especially significant here because of the importance of the sabbatical-year rest for the land.
26:43 See note on v. 34.
26:44 I will not reject them ... breaking my covenant with them. See note on v. 42. Although they would break their covenant with the Lord (which is why they would be exiled), the Lord would not break his side of the covenant. He would remain committed to them by virtue of his covenant with them.
26:45 covenant with their ancestors whom I brought out of Egypt in the sight of the nations. Refers to the Mosaic covenant made at Sinai (not the Abrahamic covenant mentioned in v. 42 [see note there]), since that was the covenant God made with them when they came out of Egypt (Exod 3–24).The Lord was committed not only to the Abrahamic covenant but also to the Mosaic covenant. This corresponds to the fact that the people of Israel who came out of Egypt were the descendants of Abraham—the Abrahamic family had grown into a nation. So the Abrahamic promises anticipated this people and the theocratic nation they would become at Sinai (Gen 15:13–14) as well as the blessing of all the nations through the Abrahamic seed (Gen 17:4,6). The "all Israel" of Rom 11:26 "are loved on account of the patriarchs, for God's gifts and his call are irrevocable" (Rom 11:28–29).

Redeeming What Is the Lord*'s*

27 The Lord said to Moses, 2“Speak to the Israelites and say to them: ‘If anyone makes a special
vow[d] to dedicate a person to the Lord by giving the equivalent value, 3set the value of a male
between the ages of twenty and sixty at fifty shekels[a] of silver, according to the sanctuary shekel[b],[e]
4for a female, set her value at thirty shekels[c]; 5for a person between the ages of five and twenty, set the
value of a male at twenty shekels[d] and of a female at ten shekels[e]; 6for a person between one month
and five years, set the value of a male at five shekels[f][f] of silver and that of a female at three shekels[g] of
silver; 7for a person sixty years old or more, set the value of a male at fifteen shekels[h] and of a female
at ten shekels. 8If anyone making the vow is too poor to pay[g] the specified amount, the person being
dedicated is to be presented to the priest, who will set the value[h] according to what the one making the
vow can afford.

9“ ‘If what they vowed is an animal that is acceptable as an offering to the Lord, such an animal
given to the Lord becomes holy. 10They must not exchange it or substitute a good one for a bad one, or
a bad one for a good one;[i] if they should substitute one animal for another, both it and the substitute
become holy. 11If what they vowed is a ceremonially unclean animal—one that is not acceptable as an
offering to the Lord—the animal must be presented to the priest, 12who will judge its quality as good
or bad. Whatever value the priest then sets, that is what it will be. 13If the owner wishes to redeem[j] the
animal, a fifth must be added to its value.

14“ ‘If anyone dedicates their house as something holy to the Lord, the priest will judge its quality
as good or bad. Whatever value the priest then sets, so it will remain. 15If the one who dedicates their
house wishes to redeem it,[k] they must add a fifth to its value, and the house will again become theirs.

16“ ‘If anyone dedicates to the Lord part of their family land, its value is to be set according to the
amount of seed required for it—fifty shekels of silver to a homer[i] of barley seed. 17If they dedicate a
field during the Year of Jubilee, the value that has been set remains. 18But if they dedicate a field after
the Jubilee, the priest will determine the value according to the number of years that remain[l] until
the next Year of Jubilee, and its set value will be reduced. 19If the one who dedicates the field wishes to
redeem it, they must add a fifth to its value, and the field will again become theirs. 20If, however, they
do not redeem the field, or if they have sold it to someone else, it can never be redeemed. 21When the
field is released in the Jubilee,[m] it will become holy, like a field devoted to the Lord;[n] it will become
priestly property.

22“ ‘If anyone dedicates to the Lord a field they have bought, which is not part of their family land,
23the priest will determine its value up to the Year of Jubilee, and the owner must pay its value on that
day as something holy to the Lord. 24In the Year of Jubilee the field will revert to the person from whom
it was bought,[o] the one whose land it was. 25Every value is to be set according to the sanctuary shekel,[p]
twenty gerahs[q] to the shekel.

26“ ‘No one, however, may dedicate the firstborn of an animal, since the firstborn already belongs
to the Lord;[r] whether an ox[j] or a sheep, it is the Lord's. 27If it is one of the unclean animals,[s] it may

27:2 [d] Nu 6:2
27:3 [e] Ex 30:13; Nu 3:47; 18:16
27:6 [f] Nu 18:16
27:8 [g] Lev 5:11 [h] ver 12,14
27:10 [i] ver 33
27:13 [j] ver 15,19; Lev 25:25
27:15 [k] ver 13,20
27:18 [l] Lev 25:15
27:21 [m] Lev 25:10 [n] ver 28; Nu 18:14; Eze 44:29
27:24 [o] Lev 25:28
27:25 [p] Ex 30:13; Nu 18:16 [q] Nu 3:47; Eze 45:12
27:26 [r] Ex 13:2,12
27:27 [s] ver 11

[a] *3* That is, about 1 1/4 pounds or about 575 grams; also in verse 16 [b] *3* That is, about 2/5 ounce or about 12 grams; also in verse 25 [c] *4* That is, about 12 ounces or about 345 grams [d] *5* That is, about 8 ounces or about 230 grams [e] *5* That is, about 4 ounces or about 115 grams; also in verse 7 [f] *6* That is, about 2 ounces or about 58 grams [g] *6* That is, about 1 1/4 ounces or about 35 grams [h] *7* That is, about 6 ounces or about 175 grams [i] *16* That is, probably about 300 pounds or about 135 kilograms [j] *26* The Hebrew word can refer to either male or female.

27:1–34 *Redeeming What Is the Lord's.* This section is a collection of regulations concerning the consecration and redemption of difficult vows and votive offerings (vv. 2–13), freewill offerings (vv. 14–25), firstborn animals (vv. 26–27), devoted things (vv. 28–29), and tithes (vv. 30–33).
27:2 special vow. Here, the special vow is the giving of a person as a special gift to God, arising out of special circumstances in the life of the worshiper. **the equivalent value.** As set forth in vv. 3–7. The money was given to God in place of the person dedicated.
27:16 dedicates. Consecrates; sets apart as holy. **part of their family land.** The rest of the field is not included in what the person dedicates.
27:20 if they have sold it to someone else. Probably the farmer decided not to redeem the (part of the) field he had dedicated to the Lord, but instead sold it to someone else.
27:21 devoted. See v. 28 and note. When the land was “released in the Jubilee” (see 25:25–34), that part of the field did not revert to the farmer who was the original owner but became permanently holy to the Lord.
27:27 one of the unclean animals. The firstborn of unclean animals also belonged to the Lord, but these could be redeemed by paying their value to the priests plus one-fifth its value. One-fifth was the regular compensation for buying back something that was consecrated to be holy to the Lord (see note on 5:16).

27:28 [t]Nu 18:14; Jos 6:17-19
27:30 [u]Ge 28:22; 2Ch 31:6; Mal 3:8
27:32 [v]Jer 33:13; Eze 20:37
27:33 [w]ver 10
27:34 [x]Lev 26:46; Dt 4:5

be bought back at its set value, adding a fifth of the value to it. If it is not redeemed, it is to be sold at
its set value.
28" 'But nothing that a person owns and devotes[a][t] to the LORD—whether a human being or an
animal or family land—may be sold or redeemed; everything so devoted is most holy to the LORD.
29" 'No person devoted to destruction[b] may be ransomed; they are to be put to death.
30" 'A tithe[u] of everything from the land, whether grain from the soil or fruit from the trees, belongs
to the LORD; it is holy to the LORD. 31Whoever would redeem any of their tithe must add a fifth of the
value to it. 32Every tithe of the herd and flock—every tenth animal that passes under the shepherd's
rod[v]—will be holy to the LORD. 33No one may pick out the good from the bad or make any substitution.[w] If anyone does make a substitution, both the animal and its substitute become holy and cannot
be redeemed.' "

34These are the commands the LORD gave Moses at Mount Sinai for the Israelites.[x]

[a] *28* The Hebrew term refers to the irrevocable giving over of things or persons to the LORD. [b] *29* The Hebrew term refers to the irrevocable giving over of things or persons to the LORD, often by totally destroying them.

27:28 devotes. See NIV text note. **most holy.** Things that are "dedicated" (i.e., "consecrated" or "set apart as holy") to the Lord are simply "holy" (e.g., vv. 30,32), which makes them both saleable and redeemable, unlike things that are "most holy."
27:29 devoted to destruction. Translates the same Hebrew term that v. 28 renders "devotes"; see NIV text note. The same Hebrew term is used when Saul sinned against the Lord by not totally destroying the Amalekites (1 Sam 15:3,8–9,15,18,20), and elsewhere it describes the complete destruction of the peoples who lived in the promised land when the Israelites entered it to conquer and inhabit it (e.g., Deut 3:6; 7:2; 20:17; Josh 2:10; 10:28; 11:12,21).
27:30–33 On the tithe system in Israel, see Num 18:8–32; Deut 14:22–29.
27:30 tithe. One-tenth (see Num 18:25–32; Deut 12:6–19; 14:22–29; 26:12). In Israel, the Lord was the king, and his royal court was made up of the Levites, to whom people paid the tithe. The Aaronic priests also belonged to the tribe of Levi and received a tithe from the Levites out of the tithe they received—a tithe of the tithe (Num 18:25–29). Some think there were three tithes (one to the Levites, Num 18:21–32; one consumed at the sanctuary, Deut 14:22–27; and one given every third year for the poor, Deut 14:28–29). Others think there are only two (one to the Levites, and one every third year to the poor). Still others think there was only one (but distributed locally in the third year, Deut 14:28–29). **grain … fruit.** The tithe was taken from the crops as well as from the animals (v. 32).
27:32 every tenth animal. The tenth animal that passed "under the shepherd's rod" as they were being counted. There was no latitude to "pick" the animal or substitute animals (v. 33). Since some animals were defective and, therefore, could not be offered on the altar (see note on 1:3), the herdsman might wish to add another animal to the tithe that was suitable to be offered on the altar as a substitute, but then both the substitute and the original animal still belonged to the tithe (v. 33).
27:34 commands. Cf. 26:46. Refers to all the regulations in Leviticus that Moses was commanded to mediate to the Israelites.

INTRODUCTION TO

NUMBERS

TITLE

Numbers is an unfortunate title for this book. It comes from the Septuagint (the pre-Christian Greek translation of the OT) and was likely inspired by the census-counts the book contains (chs. 1–4,26). Its Hebrew name, "In the wilderness," refers to the fifth Hebrew word contained in its opening verse (1:1). But neither title captures its focus. If length were not an issue, a more appropriate title might be "A Tale of Two Generations of Israelites, One Faithless and One Faithful."

AUTHOR

The book identifies Moses as writing down information recorded in the travel itinerary of 33:3–49 (33:2). In addition, the phrases "the LORD said (spoke) to Moses" and "the LORD commanded Moses" occur more than 60 times (e.g., 1:1; 2:1,33; 3:5). While these phrases are not explicit commands for him to write down the Lord's words, God elsewhere tells him to do so (Exod 17:14; 34:27), and it would have been natural for him to continue this practice. All this leads to the conclusion that Moses is responsible for the bulk of the book's material (while not denying that a final editor added some information, such as at 12:3). For further discussion, see Introduction to the Pentateuch, p. 12.

HISTORICAL SETTING

Numbers covers events that happened sometime between 1450 and 1240 BC (see "Dates in Exodus," p. 14). Geographically, the book opens at Mount Sinai, where the Israelites arrived in Exod 19. They remained there for the rest of Exodus (chs. 19–40), all of Leviticus, and the beginning of Numbers, finally breaking camp in Num 10:11–12. They arrived at the southern border of the promised land in 12:16 but rebelled against the Lord's command to enter (chs. 13–14). Because of this, they spent the next 38 years in the wilderness until finally arriving at the plains of Moab (22:1), just east of the promised land, where they would stay for the rest of Numbers (see "The Israelites' Location: Where and How Long," p. 246). It was here they received the book of Deuteronomy and awaited final orders to go into the promised land under Joshua (Josh 3).

THEOLOGICAL THEMES

Broadly speaking, Numbers tells this story: The Lord, the covenant God of the Israelites, provides them with final instructions for preparing to march into the land he has sworn to give to them (1:1—10:10). They could do so with confidence because the Lord himself would be going along in their midst (10:33–36). But the adult Israelites of the exodus generation continue to grumble and complain as they had done in the book of Exodus. Ultimately, they reject the Lord and the leaders he appointed, turn to other gods, and cause the leaders themselves to commit gross sin (10:11—25:18). The Lord punishes them but also responds repeatedly with mercy, refusing to treat the people as a whole as their sins deserve (chs. 14,21,25). Finally, after the exodus generation has died out, the Lord prepares the next generation of Israelites to enter the promised land and live there as his covenant people (chs. 26–36).

In the course of telling this story, Numbers emphasizes different theological themes, and these may be grouped under three headings: the Lord, the people, and the land. As part of the Pentateuch, Numbers focuses on the promises made to the patriarchs. These promises focus on *the Lord* calling a specific *people* (Israel) to himself and promising to give them a *land* (Hebrew *ʾereṣ*) where they could walk in fellowship with him (Gen 12:1–3,7; 17:1–8). What should not be missed is that these promises are in direct keeping with the Lord's intent for humanity from the very beginning. The Bible begins with the story of *the Lord* creating *people* (Adam and Eve) and commanding them to fill all the *earth* (Hebrew *ʾereṣ*) as they walked in fellowship with him and reflected his image to the world (Gen 1–2). The Lord's intent has always been to enjoy fellowship with his created people and to have them fill all the earth with his character—love, justice, mercy, goodness, and peace. To return to Numbers, this means that Israel's purpose is nothing less than to carry out the Lord's creational purpose for humanity: walking in close fellowship with their King as they live out his love, justice, and mercy, in this way filling all the land with his holy kingdom, in anticipation of the time when God's kingdom will fill the earth.

The Lord

Three themes focus on the Lord:

1. *The Lord's Presence.* The covenant-keeping King of Israel dwells in the midst of his covenant people. He does this in the tent of meeting, which serves as his portable royal residence (see note on 1:1). He appears there in a cloud of divine glory (see "The Glory of God," p. 2640), assuring the Israelites he is with them and will march before them into the promised land (10:33–36). The people are to respond to the Lord's presence among them by following him with bold confidence into the promised land (see notes on 21:1–3,21–35; 36:13) and by living holy lives (15:38–41).

EXODUS AND WILDERNESS WANDERINGS

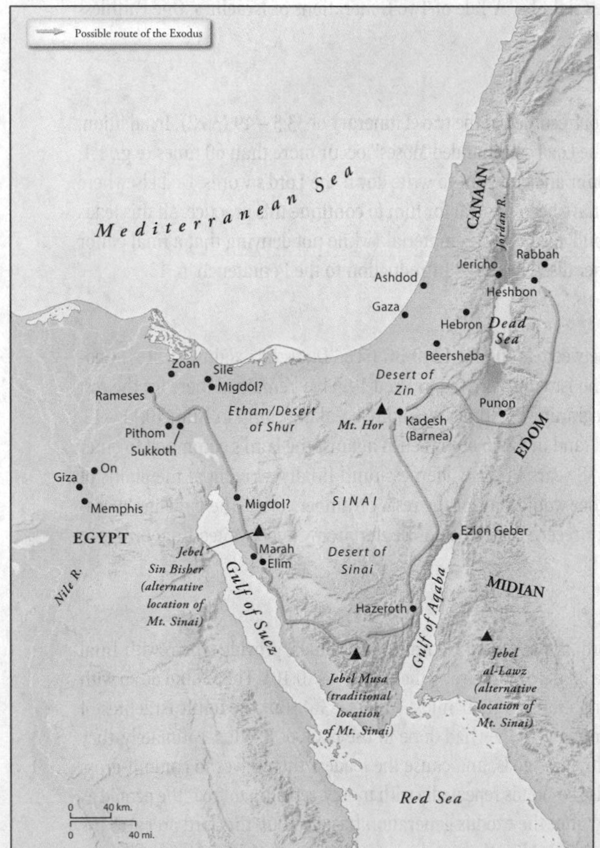

In terms of the larger biblical story, this theme of the Lord's presence among his people runs from one end of the Bible to the other. In the OT, it begins before Numbers (Gen 3:8; Exod 29:42–46; 40:34–38; etc.) and continues after it (Deut 31:6; Josh 1:9; 1 Kgs 8:10–12; Ps 46:7; Isa 43:5; etc.). In the NT, Jesus becomes the ultimate expression of God dwelling among his people (John 1:14), a presence that continues among us to this day (Rev 1:12–20) and will find its complete expression in the new heaven and the new earth (Rev 21:3–4). As in Numbers, the Lord's ongoing presence should fill his people today with bold confidence in carrying out his kingdom mission (Matt 28:18–20). It should also inspire us to live holy lives of reverence before him (2 Cor 7:1; Heb 12:18–29; see "Holiness," p. 2676), especially since God himself dwells within us by his Holy Spirit (1 Cor 6:19).

2. *The Lord's Faithfulness to His Covenant Promises.* The Lord has been and continues to be faithful to the covenant promises he made to Israel's forefathers: he will be their God (10:33–36; cf. Gen 17:7; 26:24), make them a great people (1:20–46; 22:2–4; cf. Gen 13:16; 15:5; 26:4), give them the promised land (21:1–3,21–35; cf. Gen 12:7; 15:18; 26:3), bless the nations through them (15:14–16; cf. Gen 12:3; 26:4), and generally, bless them (6:27; 23:7–10; 24:3–9; cf. Gen 12:2–3). "God is not

human, that he should lie, not a human being, that he should change his mind" (23:19a). Because he is faithful to his promises, the Israelites can follow him with full confidence that the blessings of the covenant will be theirs.

The Lord's faithfulness to his promises continues after Numbers as Israel experiences the blessings of the covenant, in particular, making it safely into the long-awaited promised land (see Joshua). The Lord's faithfulness gives the Israelites freedom to pursue covenant living boldly and wholeheartedly, knowing that the Lord's promises are certain and sure for those who trust in him. The NT applies this truth to those who follow Jesus, affirming they can have full confidence that the Lord will be faithful to his promises to them and will ensure that they receive all the blessings of the new covenant, particularly eternal life now and eternal fellowship with him in the far greater promised land to come (John 14:1–3; 1 Cor 1:4–9; 2 Cor 1:20–22; Phil 1:6; 1 Thess 5:23–24; Heb 6:13–20).

3. *The Lord's Patience, Mercy, and Justice.* The Lord is patient and merciful with his people, yet committed to justice. The Lord shows his patience and mercy again and again by forgiving his people and not unleashing on them the full fury their sins deserve (see notes on 14:13–19,20,22). But the Lord's patience does not mean that his justice never comes, and sometimes his punishment can be very severe (e.g., 11:33–34; 12:9–10; 15:32–36; 16:31–35,47–49). His judgment strongly warns Israel (and us!) not to rebel against the King and Creator. "It is a dreadful thing to fall into the hands of the living God" (Heb 10:31).

The Lord's patience and mercy toward his people continue throughout the OT (Pss 30:5; 103:1–18; Mic 7:18) and into the NT (Rev 2:21). They shine forth with greatest clarity in the death of Jesus on behalf of sinners (John 3:16; Rom 5:8; Eph 5:2; 1 John 4:9–10) and in the Lord's delay of ushering in final judgment (Rom 2:4; 2 Pet 3:9). (See "Love and Grace," p. 2684.) But the theme of the Lord's justice continues as well. It breaks out among the people of God (Acts 5:1–11; 1 Cor 11:30; Jas 5:16) and the nations (Acts 12:21–23), and it will do so at the final judgment for those without faith in Jesus (John 3:18,36; 5:24; 8:24; Acts 4:12; Rom 6:23). (See "Justice," p. 2679.) Again, this is a stark reminder that we must embrace the Lord, keeping his covenant and following him wholeheartedly.

The People

Five major themes focus on the Israelites (see "People of God," p. 2672):

1. *Unity.* The Lord's people are to be unified in order to carry out their kingdom mission together. Numbers emphasizes the Israelites' unity time and again: the census lists (they are "the sons of Israel" and therefore blood relatives [1:20–46; 26:4b–51]); the list of gifts at the tabernacle dedication (every tribe participated equally [7:10–88]); sending one spy from each tribe to scout the land (13:2); sending 1,000 from each tribe to fight Midian (31:4); and requiring that the tribes settling on the east side of the Jordan help the remaining tribes battle for Canaan on the west side (ch. 32).

The NT also focuses on the necessity of unity among the Lord's covenant people. In his longest recorded prayer, Jesus prays that his followers may have "complete unity" so that the world might know that his message is true (John 17:20–23). Paul pictures the unity of the Lord's people by describing Jesus as "the chief cornerstone" of "a holy temple" made up of the people of God (Eph 2:20–21). This is a temple "in which God lives by his Spirit" (Eph 2:22) and where the glory of God is made manifest in the earth (Eph 3:20–21; see "Temple," p. 2652), especially as his people show one another his love (Eph 4:1–6).

2. *Respecting Callings.* The Lord's people are to respect the different callings of the individuals among them. God called Moses to serve as the chief leader of the people (12:6–8), and he called Aaron and the priests to the special privilege of serving in his tabernacle (1:47–53; 3:5–39; 4:1–49; 16:1—17:11). As many of these references show, the first-generation Israelites often failed to respect these callings.

Believers today are likewise to respect the different callings of their brothers and sisters (1 Cor 12:4–31) as well as the authority structures the Lord has put in place (1 Thess 5:12–13; 1 Tim 5:17). Believers must respect their leaders (Heb 13:17) and provide for their material needs (1 Cor 9:14; Gal 6:6). The NT also emphasizes that Jesus is a leader incomparably greater than any who have gone before. While Moses was a faithful servant *in* God's house, Jesus is the ruling Son of God *over* God's house (Heb 3:1–6); while Aaron was a high priest who atoned for Israel's sins by means of sacrifices in a temporary way (Heb 10:1–4), Jesus is the great high priest who offered himself as a sacrifice that atones for sins once and for all (Heb 10:5–14; see "Sacrifice," The Day of Atonement, p. 2657). If the Israelites were to follow their leaders in Numbers, how much more are we to follow Jesus today (Heb 3:7–11)!

3. *Disobedience.* This theme occurs especially in the book's second section (10:11—25:18), where the first-generation Israelites doubt the Lord's provision (11:1–9; 14:1–10; 20:2–5; 21:4–5), question the authority structure he sets up (see Introduction: Theological Themes [The People, 2]), and go astray by worshiping other gods (25:1–3). This rebellion not only results in the Lord's judgment (see Introduction: Theological Themes [The Lord, 3]) but ultimately prevents that generation from receiving the covenant promise of land (14:22–23,28–35).

Kadesh Barnea.
Gary Pratico/www.BiblePlaces.com

Ps 95:7 – 11 and especially 1 Cor 10:1 – 13 and Heb 3:6 — 4:13 return to the theme of the Israelites' disobedience. These passages view the faithless generation in Numbers as a warning: hardening your heart against the Lord and turning away from him is extremely dangerous. The NT passages warn believers not to reject Jesus and therefore fail to receive the covenant promise of the eternal promised land awaiting those who follow him (see Heb 10:19 – 31,36).

4. *Need for a Mediator.* God's people need a mediator, especially when they rebel defiantly against the Lord. When the Israelites rebelled, there was no automatic forgiveness by means of sacrifice (see notes on 15:22 – 31), though it was possible that a mediator — such as Moses or Aaron or a priest — could either stand in the gap and carry out an act that atoned for the people (16:47; 25:7 – 13) or could plead for the Lord to be gracious and forgive (11:2; 12:13; 16:20 – 24; 21:7). (See "Sacrifice," Blood, p. 2657.)

Any mediation sinners could ever need has been accomplished fully and finally in Jesus, the "one mediator between God and mankind" (1 Tim 2:5), who is able to fulfill this role perfectly because he "gave himself as a ransom for all people" (1 Tim 2:6; see Heb 9:12). Jesus continues to mediate for believers to this day and is at this very moment "at the right hand of God ... interceding for us" (Rom 8:34; see Heb 7:23 – 25; 9:24; 1 John 2:1). For this reason, the repentant people of God should never fear losing God's love. Nothing and no one can "separate us from the love of God that is in Christ Jesus our Lord" (Rom 8:39; see Rom 8:34 – 38).

5. *Obedience.* This theme, which contrasts with the previous two, occurs especially with the exodus generation in the book's first section (1:54; 2:33 – 34; 4:49; 8:20,22; 9:5) and with the next generation in the book's final section (26:4 – 63; 31:7,31; 36:10). Not surprisingly, the Lord's judgment against them is absent in these sections. Instead, we see the Lord's covenant people enjoying his presence, demonstrating their faith by obediently living out their calling and privileges as his covenant people, and preparing to follow him into the promised land.

The NT also emphasizes that obedience is a necessary sign of faith and is required in order to have fellowship with the Lord (John 14:15,23 – 24; 15:1 – 8; Jas 2:14 – 26). In addition, Jesus emphasizes that to obey is to testify to the reality of our heavenly Father: "Let your light shine before others, that they may see your good deeds and glorify your Father in heaven" (Matt 5:16; cf. Deut 4:5 – 8). Our obedience is indeed for the sake of the nations.

The Land

Two themes concern the land:

1. *Inheritance.* The Israelites will one day inherit the land, i.e., Canaan, which the Lord earlier promised Israel's forefathers in his covenant with them (Gen 12:7; 15:18; 26:3; see map, p. 380; see also "Covenant," p. 2646). This is especially clear in the closing chapters of Numbers, which provide numerous laws to inform the Israelites how to live once they enter the land (33:50 — 36:13) and end with the Israelites on the land's border, ready to march in (36:13). The Lord has promised Israel this land, and they will one day live in it.

The theme of inheriting the physical land of Canaan begins to take place in the book of Joshua. But the NT also applies this theme to the eternal inheritance that awaits those who become God's children through faith in Jesus (Rom 8:1,12–17; Gal 4:4–7; Eph 1:13–14; Col 1:12–14; Heb 9:13–15; 1 Pet 1:3–6). This inheritance radically redefines how believers live since their focus is not on the things of this world but on the praise from their covenant King in the world to come (Matt 6:19–24).

2. *Mission.* Israel's land was to have a special place in the Lord's mission of filling the earth with his kingdom. In many ways the promised land was to function in the world the way the tabernacle functioned in Israel. (See "Temple," p. 2652.) For example, just as the tabernacle was to be kept pure and holy because the Lord lived there (Lev 15:31), so too was the land of Israel to be kept holy because the Lord lived there: "Do not defile the land where you live and where I dwell, for I, the LORD, dwell among the Israelites" (35:34; cf. Lev 18:24–30; 20:22–26; see "Holiness," p. 2676). And just as the Israelite priests functioned as priests at the tabernacle, so too the Israelites were to function as priests in the earth (Exod 19:6; see note on Num 15:37–41). In short, the land was to be a place where the nations could see the type of life the Lord intended for his creation: a holy people, enjoying covenant fellowship with their Creator and King, extending his kingdom of mercy, love, purity, and justice in all the earth.

While the actual land of Canaan was to be an area of sacred space in Numbers, the area of sacred space was never to be limited to the actual land of Canaan either in the OT (cf. Ps 67) or in the NT (Acts 1:8). What is more, the NT redefines sacred space in terms of the body of believers: wherever they are, it is a holy place, the temple of God (1 Cor 3:16; 2 Cor 6:16; Eph 2:20–22; 1 Pet 2:5). The church is given the mission to spread and fill the entire earth so that the temple of God encompasses everything. This is the very thing Jesus teaches us to pray: "your kingdom come, your will be done, on earth as it is in heaven" (Matt 6:10). We can have confidence to do this because Jesus is the supreme King, and he goes with us in this mission (Matt 28:18–20; see "Mission," p. 2691).

INTERPRETIVE ISSUES

Ch. 1 and ch. 26—which occur roughly 40 years apart—both contain a census of the Israelites "twenty years old or more" (1:18; 26:2). The totals are 603,550 (1:46) and 601,730 (26:51), with the Levites not included in these totals (1:47; cf. 3:14–39; 26:57–62). How these numbers should be understood is widely debated. Four main approaches may be briefly noted.

1. *The numbers are literal.* This is perhaps the most traditional approach, although it creates a difficulty. The difficulty is not whether the Lord could do the miraculous in multiplying the people so quickly (the Lord can do anything he desires); the difficulty is that taking these numbers at face value creates tension with other passages. In Josh 4:13, e.g., Israel has 40,000 fighting men, a number far fewer than the 603,550 given in Num 1:46 (cf. also Josh 8:3). In addition, an army of over half a million men would make Israel's army far larger than what we believe to have been true of other armies at the time, even though Israel is called "the fewest of all peoples" (Deut 7:7). This tension suggests finding a different approach.

2. *The numbers are symbolic.* This approach has two different versions. In the first, the symbolism may be unlocked using gematria, a system in which numbers correspond to letters of the alphabet and work as a code to spell out different words. In the second, the numbers are related to astronomical phenomena. For example, when Benjamin's total of 35,400 (1:37) is divided by 100, the number is the same as the number of days in a short lunar year: 354. Very few scholars have adopted either of these approaches because they either fail to explain all the data or can explain it only by complex (and many would say arbitrary) calculations.

3. *There is a misunderstanding of the Hebrew word* ʾelep. The Hebrew word *ʾelep* usually means "1,000" and has traditionally been translated this way in chs. 1; 26. But it can also mean "family" or "clan," and a word built on the same root can mean "tribal leader." Some scholars have therefore suggested that the text originally referred to one of these other meanings. For example, Reuben's total of 46,500 (1:21) represents 46 *families* (not 46 *thousand*) and these total 500 people. But such approaches either fail to explain the final totals in 1:46 and 26:51 (which understand *ʾelep* to mean "1,000" throughout these chapters) or explain them by means of complicated and conjectural textual emendations.

4. *The numbers are deliberate hyperbole.* The final approach has the fewest problems and thus the most to commend it. It understands the numbers as being intentionally inflated. Some who adopt this approach suggest that the numbers were inflated by a factor of 10, though others suggest that it is no longer possible to identify the way in which the numbers were inflated. At first glance, this is the least attractive approach to many moderns, who tend to believe that if numbers are not reported with scientific accuracy, they are misleading. But such was not the case in the ancient Near East. There is clear evidence that numbers were often inflated, particularly in a military context (as demonstrated by examples from Ugaritic and Assyrian texts dating from the fourteenth and thirteenth centuries

BC, the same general time period in which Numbers was written). It was neither unusual nor extraordinary. Indeed, the people to whom Numbers was written would have immediately been able to recognize that the numbers were inflated (in keeping with convention). There is no reason to believe that the original readers would have seen this as deceptive. Indeed, they may have seen it as a way of emphasizing what was true: the Lord had indeed been faithful to his covenant promise to make Abraham into a numerous people (Gen 12:2; 15:5).

Despite the lack of an interpretive consensus among scholars concerning the numbers themselves, it is likely that the numbering of the people tribe by tribe would have served, at the very least, to remind the Israelites that the Lord had fulfilled his promise to make them into a numerous people. And since he had been faithful to that covenant promise, he could also be trusted to fulfill his covenant promise to give them a land. They could march into Canaan with full confidence in their covenant King.

OUTLINE

I. The Death of the Exodus Generation in the Wilderness (1:1—25:18)
- A. Preparing to Enter the Promised Land (1:1—10:10)
  - 1. The Census of Israel and the Arrangement of the Tribal Camps (1:1—2:34)
    - a. The Census (1:1–54)
    - b. The Arrangement of the Tribal Camps (2:1–34)
  - 2. The Censuses of the Levites and Their Tabernacle Responsibilities (3:1—4:49)
    - a. The Tribe of Levi (3:1–51)
    - b. The Kohathites (4:1–20)
    - c. The Gershonites (4:21–28)
    - d. The Merarites (4:29–33)
    - e. The Numbering of the Levite Clans (4:34–49)
  - 3. Laws Related to the Camp's Purity and the Priests' Roles (5:1—6:27)
    - a. The Purity of the Camp (5:1–4)
    - b. Restitution for Wrongs; Priestly Portions (5:5–10)
    - c. The Test For a Wife Suspected of Adultery (5:11–31)
    - d. The Nazirite (6:1–21)
    - e. The Priestly Blessing (6:22–27)
  - 4. The Tabernacle's Dedication and Related Matters (7:1—9:14)
    - a. Offerings at the Dedication of the Tabernacle (7:1–89)
    - b. Setting Up the Lamps (8:1–4)
    - c. The Setting Apart of the Levites (8:5–26)
    - d. The Passover (9:1–14)
  - 5. Transition: Getting Ready to Depart for the Promised Land (9:15—10:10)
    - a. The Cloud Above the Tabernacle (9:15–23)
    - b. The Silver Trumpets (10:1–10)
- B. Rebellion Against the Lord and the Death of the Exodus Generation (10:11—25:18)
  - 1. The Israelites Leave Sinai (10:11–36)
  - 2. Initial Acts of Unbelief (11:1—12:16)
    - a. Fire From the Lord (11:1–3)
    - b. Quail From the Lord (11:4–35)
    - c. Miriam and Aaron Oppose Moses (12:1–16)
  - 3. Arrival at Kadesh, Full-Scale Rebellion, the Lord's Judgment (13:1—14:45)
    - a. Exploring Canaan (13:1–25)
    - b. Report on the Exploration (13:26–33)
    - c. The People Rebel (14:1–45)
  - 4. Further Laws, Emphasizing Especially the Need for Covenant Faithfulness (15:1–41)
    - a. Supplementary Offerings (15:1–21)
    - b. Offerings for Unintentional Sins (15:22–31)
    - c. The Sabbath-Breaker Put to Death (15:32–36)

- d. Tassels on Garments (15:37–41)
- 5. Challenging the Authority Structure Established by the Lord (16:1—18:32)
  - a. Korah, Dathan and Abiram (16:1–50)
  - b. The Budding of Aaron's Staff (17:1–13)
  - c. Duties of Priests and Levites (18:1–7)
  - d. Offerings for Priests and Levites (18:8–32)
- 6. The Water of Cleansing (19:1–22)
- 7. Further Rebellions, Initial Victories (20:1—21:35)
  - a. Water From the Rock (20:1–13)
  - b. Edom Denies Israel Passage (20:14–21)
  - c. The Death of Aaron (20:22–29)
  - d. Arad Destroyed (21:1–3)
  - e. The Bronze Snake (21:4–9)
  - f. The Journey to Moab (21:10–20)
  - g. Defeat of Sihon and Og (21:21–35)
- 8. The Story of Balak and Balaam (22:1—24:25)
  - a. Balak Summons Balaam (22:1–20)
  - b. Balaam's Donkey (22:21–41)
  - c. Balaam's First Message (23:1–12)
  - d. Balaam's Second Message (23:13–26)
  - e. Balaam's Third Message (23:27—24:14)
  - f. Balaam's Fourth Message (24:15–19)
  - g. Balaam's Fifth Message (24:20)
  - h. Balaam's Sixth Message (24:21–22)
  - i. Balaam's Seventh Message (24:23–25)
- 9. Moab Seduces Israel (25:1–18)

II. The Next Generation: A New Start for Israel on the Border of the Promised Land (26:1—36:13)

- A. The Second Census (26:1–65)
- B. Zelophehad's Daughters (27:1–11)
- C. Joshua to Succeed Moses (27:12–23)
- D. Offerings and Festivals (28:1—29:40)
  - 1. Daily Offerings (28:1–8)
  - 2. Sabbath Offerings (28:9–10)
  - 3. Monthly Offerings (28:11–15)
  - 4. The Passover (28:16–25)
  - 5. The Festival of Weeks (28:26–31)
  - 6. The Festival of Trumpets (29:1–6)
  - 7. The Day of Atonement (29:7–11)
  - 8. The Festival of Tabernacles (29:12–40)
- E. Vows (30:1–16)
- F. Vengeance on the Midianites (31:1–24)
- G. Dividing the Spoils (31:25–54)
- H. The Transjordan Tribes (32:1–42)
- I. Stages in Israel's Journey (33:1–56)
- J. Commands and Regulations for Life in the Promised Land (34:1—36:13)
  - 1. Boundaries of Canaan (34:1–29)
  - 2. Towns for the Levites (35:1–5)
  - 3. Cities of Refuge (35:6–34)
  - 4. Inheritance of Zelophehad's Daughters (36:1–13)

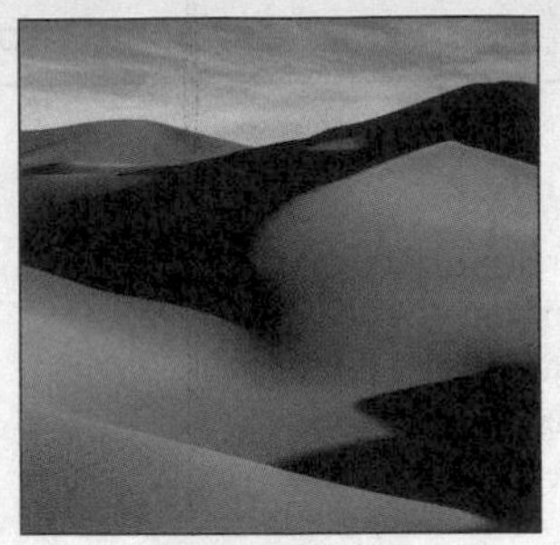

NUMBERS

1:1 [a]Ex 40:2 [b]Ex 19:1 [c]Ex 40:17
1:2 [d]Ex 30:11-16; Nu 26:2
1:3 [e]Ex 30:14
1:4 [f]ver 16 [g]Ex 18:21; Dt 1:15

The Census

1 The LORD spoke to Moses in the tent of meeting[a] in the Desert of Sinai[b] on the first day of the second
month[c] of the second year after the Israelites came out of Egypt. He said: 2“Take a census[d] of the
whole Israelite community by their clans and families, listing every man by name, one by one. 3You
and Aaron are to count according to their divisions all the men in Israel who are twenty years old or
more[e] and able to serve in the army. 4One man from each tribe, each of them the head of his family,[f]
is to help you.[g] 5These are the names of the men who are to assist you:

1:1—25:18 *The Death of the Exodus Generation in the Wilderness.* This section has two parts: 1:1—10:10 and 10:11—25:18. In the first part, the Israelites are faithful, obedient, and careful to do “just as the LORD commanded” (1:54; cf. 2:34; 4:49; 8:4,22; 9:5,23). In the second part, they disbelieve, disobey, and ultimately rebel against the Lord (14:1–10; cf. 11:1–9; 14:39–45; 16:1–14; 20:2–5; 25:1–3). This rebellion results in the Lord’s discipline: it will not be the exodus generation of Israelites that enters the promised land, but their children (14:26–35).
1:1—10:10 *Preparing to Enter the Promised Land.* As the book of Numbers opens, the Israelites are at Mount Sinai, where they have camped for 11 months (cf. Exod 19:1 with Num 1:1). Since their arrival in Exod 19, the text has focused on the question, What does it mean for the Israelites to be a kingdom of priests and a holy nation (Exod 19:4–6)? To answer this question, the text provides instructions and laws that guide the people in holy living (Exod 20–23; 34; Lev 11–27) and in holy worship (Exod 25–31; 35–40; Lev 1–10). Now the text begins to focus on the question, How do the Israelites prepare to march into battle in the promised land? It answers this question by describing various preparations that need to take place (1:1—10:10). The tone of this section is positive (see note on 1:1—25:18): the Israelites are faithful to do everything the Lord commands.
1:1—2:34 *The Census of Israel and the Arrangement of the Tribal Camps.* In order to prepare for the upcoming battles in the promised land, the Israelites needed to know the number of their troops (1:1–46) and what their war camp should look like when at rest or on the march (2:1–34).
1:1–54 *The Census.* After briefly describing the setting (v. 1), ch. 1 describes the preparation for the census (vv. 2–19), its results (vv. 20–46), and the duties of the one tribe (Levi) not counted in the census (vv. 47–53). Verse 54 is a conclusion.
1:1 Moses. See Introduction: Author. **tent of meeting.** Described in Exod 25–27; it stood within the sanctuary complex (see “The Tabernacle,” p. 167). It was the Lord’s portable royal palace, where he sat enthroned over the ark (2 Sam 6:2; 1 Chr 28:2). **Desert of Sinai.** Traditionally identified with an area in the south of the Sinai peninsula in modern-day Egypt (see note on Exod 16:1). The Israelites arrived here ten months earlier (see “The Israelites’ Location: Where and How Long,” this page). **second month.** Sometime in April or May. **out of Egypt.** A reminder from the very beginning of the book that the Lord is a God who delivers his people (see Exod 12–15; see “Exile and Exodus,” p. 2659); the Israelites need to embrace this with full faith as they head to battle in the promised land.
1:3 Armies preparing for battle need to know the extent of their resources.
1:4–16 Only Levi is not counted (see note on 1:47–53). The list still arrives at 12 tribes because Joseph’s tribe is counted as two tribes: Ephraim and Manasseh (v. 10; see Gen 48:1,5).

THE ISRAELITES’ LOCATION: WHERE AND HOW LONG

GEOGRAPHICAL LOCATION	DURATION
Deliverance from Egypt (Exod 3:1—15:21)	Several months (?)
Travel to Sinai (Exod 15:22—18:27)	2 months, 14 days (Exod 19:1)
Encamped at Sinai (Exod 19:1—Num 10:10) • from arrival to erecting the tent of meeting • from erecting the tent of meeting to the beginning of Numbers • from beginning of Numbers to departing Sinai	10 months and 19 days • 9 months (cf. Exod 19:1 with Exod 40:2) • 1 month (cf. Exod 40:2 with Num 1:1) • 19 days (cf. Num 1:1 with Num 10:11)
Travel to Kadesh (Num 10:11—12:16)	Several months (cf. at Num 13:20)
Travel to and stay at the plains of Moab (Num 15:1[?]—22:1)	38 years (cf. Deut 2:14)
Total	40 years (Num 32:13)

from Reuben,[h] Elizur son of Shedeur;
6 from Simeon, Shelumiel son of Zurishaddai;
7 from Judah,[i] Nahshon son of Amminadab;[j]
8 from Issachar,[k] Nethanel son of Zuar;
9 from Zebulun,[l] Eliab son of Helon;
10 from the sons of Joseph:
from Ephraim,[m] Elishama son of Ammihud;
from Manasseh, Gamaliel son of Pedahzur;
11 from Benjamin, Abidan son of Gideoni;
12 from Dan,[n] Ahiezer son of Ammishaddai;
13 from Asher,[o] Pagiel son of Okran;
14 from Gad, Eliasaph son of Deuel;[p]
15 from Naphtali,[q] Ahira son of Enan."

16 These were the men appointed from the community, the leaders[r] of their ancestral tribes. They
were the heads of the clans of Israel.[s]

17 Moses and Aaron took these men whose names had been specified,
18 and they called the whole
community together on the first day of the second month.[t] The people registered their ancestry[u] by
their clans and families, and the men twenty years old or more were listed by name, one by one,
19 as
the LORD commanded Moses. And so he counted them in the Desert of Sinai:

20 From the descendants of Reuben[v] the firstborn son of Israel:
All the men twenty years old or more who were able to serve in the army were listed by name,
one by one, according to the records of their clans and families.
21 The number from the tribe
of Reuben was 46,500.

22 From the descendants of Simeon:[w]
All the men twenty years old or more who were able to
serve in the army were counted and listed by name, one
by one, according to the records of their clans and families.
23 The number from the tribe of Simeon was 59,300.

24 From the descendants of Gad:[x]
All the men twenty years old or more who were able
to serve in the army were listed by name, according to
the records of their clans and families.
25 The number
from the tribe of Gad was 45,650.

26 From the descendants of Judah:[y]
All the men twenty years old or more who were able
to serve in the army were listed by name, according to
the records of their clans and families.
27 The number
from the tribe of Judah was 74,600.

28 From the descendants of Issachar:[z]
All the men twenty years old or more who were able
to serve in the army were listed by name, according to
the records of their clans and families.
29 The number
from the tribe of Issachar was 54,400.

1:5 [h] Ge 29:32; Dt 33:6; Rev 7:5
1:7 [i] Ge 29:35; Ps 78:68 [j] Ru 4:20; 1Ch 2:10; Lk 3:32
1:8 [k] Ge 30:18
1:9 [l] ver 30
1:10 [m] ver 32
1:12 [n] ver 38
1:13 [o] ver 40
1:14 [p] Nu 2:14
1:15 [q] ver 42
1:16 [r] Ex 18:25 [s] ver 4; Ex 18:21; Nu 7:2
1:18 [t] ver 1 [u] Ezr 2:59; Heb 7:3
1:20 [v] Nu 26:5-11; Rev 7:5
1:22 [w] Nu 26:12-14; Rev 7:7
1:24 [x] Ge 30:11; Nu 26:15-18; Rev 7:5
1:26 [y] Ge 29:35; Nu 26:19-22; Mt 1:2; Rev 7:5
1:28 [z] Nu 26:23-25; Rev 7:7

THE CENSUS RESULTS

TRIBE	NUM 1 CENSUS	NUM 26 CENSUS	PERCENT CHANGE
Reuben	46,500	43,730	- 6%
Simeon	59,300	22,200	- 63%
Gad	45,650	40,500	- 11%
Judah	74,600	76,500	+ 3%
Issachar	54,400	64,300	+ 18%
Zebulun	57,400	60,500	+ 5%
Manasseh (Joseph)	32,200	52,700	+ 64%
Ephraim (Joseph)	40,500	32,500	- 20%
Benjamin	35,400	45,600	+ 29%
Dan	62,700	64,400	+ 3%
Asher	41,500	53,400	+ 29%
Naphtali	53,400	45,400	- 15%
Total	603,550	601,730	- 0.3%

1:20–46 The census shows that the Lord had begun to fulfill his covenant promise to give Abraham many descendants (Gen 13:16; 15:5; 22:17; see "Covenant," p. 2646). God could therefore be trusted to fulfill his promise to give Abraham's descendants a land (Gen 12:7; 13:15; 15:18). As for the numbers, there is significant debate (see Introduction: Interpretive Issues). The Israelites are heirs of the Abrahamic covenant and jointly responsible for carrying out its mission of spreading God's kingdom (see notes on Gen 12:1–3; Exod 19:4–6). In place of 12 tribes, Jesus called 12 apostles, commanding them to carry out the new covenant's kingdom mission in the land of Israel (Luke 9:1–6) and beyond (Matt 28:18–20).

1:20 Israel. Abraham's grandson; also known as Jacob (Gen 32:28).

1:30 [a]Nu 26:26-27; Rev 7:8
1:32 [b]Nu 26:35-37
1:34 [c]Nu 26:28-34; Rev 7:6
1:36 [d]Nu 26:38-41; 2Ch 17:17; Rev 7:8
1:38 [e]Ge 30:6; Nu 26:42-43
1:40 [f]Nu 26:44-47; Rev 7:6
1:42 [g]Nu 26:48-50; Rev 7:6
1:44 [h]Nu 26:64
1:46 [i]Ex 12:37; 38:26; Nu 2:32; 26:51
1:47 [j]Nu 2:33; 26:57 [k]Nu 4:3,49
1:50 [l]Ex 38:21; Ac 7:44
1:51 [m]Nu 3:38; 4:1-33
1:52 [n]Nu 2:2; Ps 20:5

30 From the descendants of Zebulun:[a]

All the men twenty years old or more who were able to serve in the army were listed by name, according to the records of their clans and families. 31 The number from the tribe of Zebulun was 57,400.

32 From the sons of Joseph:
From the descendants of Ephraim:[b]

All the men twenty years old or more who were able to serve in the army were listed by name, according to the records of their clans and families. 33 The number from the tribe of Ephraim was 40,500.

34 From the descendants of Manasseh:[c]

All the men twenty years old or more who were able to serve in the army were listed by name, according to the records of their clans and families. 35 The number from the tribe of Manasseh was 32,200.

36 From the descendants of Benjamin:[d]

All the men twenty years old or more who were able to serve in the army were listed by name, according to the records of their clans and families. 37 The number from the tribe of Benjamin was 35,400.

38 From the descendants of Dan:[e]

All the men twenty years old or more who were able to serve in the army were listed by name, according to the records of their clans and families. 39 The number from the tribe of Dan was 62,700.

40 From the descendants of Asher:[f]

All the men twenty years old or more who were able to serve in the army were listed by name, according to the records of their clans and families. 41 The number from the tribe of Asher was 41,500.

42 From the descendants of Naphtali:[g]

All the men twenty years old or more who were able to serve in the army were listed by name, according to the records of their clans and families. 43 The number from the tribe of Naphtali was 53,400.

44 These were the men counted by Moses and Aaron[h] and the twelve leaders of Israel, each one representing his family. 45 All the Israelites twenty years old or more who were able to serve in Israel's army
were counted according to their families. 46 The total number was 603,550.[i]
47 The ancestral tribe of the Levites,[j] however, was not counted[k] along with the others. 48 The LORD
had said to Moses: 49 "You must not count the tribe of Levi or include them in the census of the other
Israelites. 50 Instead, appoint the Levites to be in charge of the tabernacle of the covenant law[l]—over all
its furnishings and everything belonging to it. They are to carry the tabernacle and all its furnishings;
they are to take care of it and encamp around it. 51 Whenever the tabernacle is to move, the Levites are
to take it down, and whenever the tabernacle is to be set up, the Levites shall do it.[m] Anyone else who
approaches it is to be put to death. 52 The Israelites are to set up their tents by divisions, each of them
in their own camp under their standard.[n] 53 The Levites, however, are to set up their tents around the

1:47–53 The tribe of Levi was not counted in the military census. They were not to fight but were to assist with the tabernacle and make sure that unauthorized people did not mishandle the holy property or trespass on it (1:48–53). Chs. 3–4 describe these responsibilities in greater detail.

1:50–51 carry ... take care of it ... take it down ... set up. Due to the tabernacle's holiness (Exod 30:26–29), the Levites went through a special purifying rite (Num 8:5–22) and were responsible for handling the tabernacle and its furnishings.

1:50 tabernacle. Means "dwelling place"; another name for the "tent of meeting" (v. 1). **covenant law.** In particular, the Ten Commandments, which were written on two stone tablets (Exod 31:18; 32:15; 34:28) and put in an ornate golden box (Exod 25:16,21; 40:20) called the "ark of the covenant law" (Exod 25:22). The ark sat within the Most Holy Place in the tabernacle (Exod 26:33–34).

1:51 put to death. Swift justice, perhaps by the priests or Levites themselves. For an unauthorized person to handle such holy property was a sign of great disrespect.

1:52 See ch. 2.

1:53 Levites ... set up their tents around the tabernacle. So that

tabernacle of the covenant law so that my wrath will not fall[o] on the Israelite community. The Levites are to be responsible for the care of the tabernacle of the covenant law.[p]"

54 The Israelites did all this just as the LORD commanded Moses.

The Arrangement of the Tribal Camps

2 The LORD said to Moses and Aaron: 2 "The Israelites are to camp around the tent of meeting some distance from it, each of them under their standard[q] and holding the banners of their family."

3 On the east, toward the sunrise, the divisions of the camp of Judah are to encamp under their standard. The leader of the people of Judah is Nahshon son of Amminadab.[r] 4 His division numbers 74,600.

5 The tribe of Issachar will camp next to them. The leader of the people of Issachar is Nethanel son of Zuar.[s] 6 His division numbers 54,400.

1:53 [o] Lev 10:6; Nu 16:46; 18:5 [p] Nu 18:2-4
2:2 [q] Nu 1:52; Ps 74:4; Isa 31:9
2:3 [r] Nu 10:14; Ru 4:20; 1Ch 2:10
2:5 [s] Nu 1:8

non-Levites did not trespass on the Lord's holy property (see note on 3:38). **wrath.** The Lord's just anger against rebellion (cf. Lev 10:1–3 with Lev 16:1–2; see "Wrath," p. 2681). The Lord draws near to his people in love, but he is still their King, and they must greatly revere him (cf. 2 Sam 6:7; Acts 5:1–5; Heb 12:18–29).
1:54 Obeying the Lord's commands is typical in the beginning of the book (1:1—10:10) and in the end (26:1—36:13) but not in the middle (10:11—25:18; see note on 10:11—25:18). Obedience is a necessary sign of embracing the covenant from the heart and therefore a sign of true faith (Deut 6:1–9; John 14:15,23–24; Jas 2:14–26).
2:1–34 *The Arrangement of the Tribal Camps.* Ch. 2 gives instructions regarding the arrangement of the tribes in the camp, whether at rest or on the march. See "The Camp of the Tribes of Israel," this page.
2:2 The Israelites are to camp around the tent of meeting some distance from it. To provide room for the Levites to camp immediately around it (3:23,29,35,38) and to protect themselves from inappropriate contact with it (see note on 1:53). The King (the Lord) is at the camp's center (the "tent of meeting"). This was the common practice of other ancient Near Eastern kings around this time (e.g., Ramses II, king of Egypt, 1200s BC). The theme of the Lord dwelling among his people goes from Genesis (3:8) to Revelation (21:3) and was perfectly fulfilled when Jesus, the God-man, "made his dwelling among us" (John 1:14). **banners.** Perhaps a flag or symbol mounted on a pole; these would help bring order to the camp.
2:3 east. A common way to orient oneself in the ancient Near East and thus the natural place to begin a list. **Judah.** Though not the firstborn, his tribe comes first in keeping with Jacob's prophetic blessing that placed Judah at the head of his brothers (Gen 49:8,10; cf. Gen 49:3–4). This blessing would find initial fulfillment in King David, who was of this tribe, and ultimate fulfillment in King Jesus, the Lord of all (Rev 19:16).
2:4 division. Translates a Hebrew word that elsewhere refers to an army (Judg 9:29), demonstrating the camp's military nature.
2:5–7 Issachar and Zebulun were Judah's two younger brothers (Gen 29:35; 30:18–20), perhaps explaining why these three tribes are placed together.

THE CAMP OF THE TRIBES OF ISRAEL

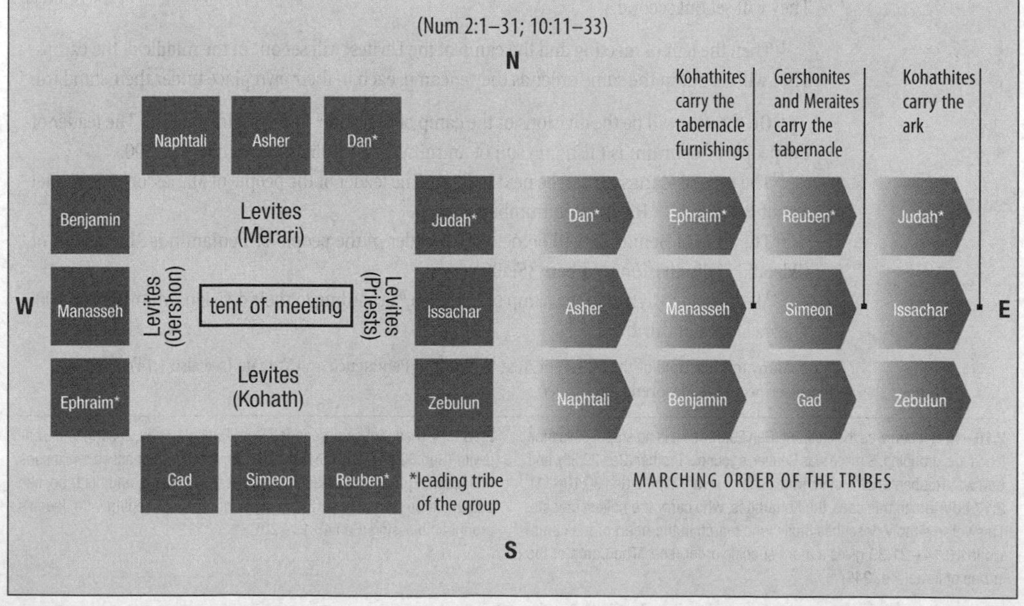

Artist's recreation of Rameses II's military camp based on thirteenth-century BC reliefs of the battle of Kadesh at Abu Simbel. The tabernacle in the camp of Moses and Israel resembles the two-part tent of Rameses II on the right side and surrounded by the camp. The two parts include an outer area similar to the Holy Place and an inner chamber (similar to the Most Holy Place) with the name of the pharaoh and two winged cherubs guarding the name.
Stephen C. Meyers

2:7 [t] Nu 1:9 **2:9** [u] Nu 10:14 **2:10** [v] Nu 1:5 **2:12** [w] Nu 1:6 **2:14** [x] Nu 1:14 **2:16** [y] Nu 10:18 **2:17** [z] Nu 1:53; 10:21 **2:18** [a] Ge 48:20; Jer 31:18-20 [b] Nu 1:10 **2:20** [c] Nu 1:10 **2:22** [d] Nu 1:11; Ps 68:27 **2:24** [e] Nu 10:22 [f] Ps 80:2

7 The tribe of Zebulun will be next. The leader of the people of Zebulun is Eliab son of Helon.[t]
8 His division numbers 57,400.
9 All the men assigned to the camp of Judah, according to their divisions, number 186,400.
They will set out first.[u]

10 On the south will be the divisions of the camp of Reuben under their standard. The leader of
the people of Reuben is Elizur son of Shedeur.[v] 11 His division numbers 46,500.
12 The tribe of Simeon will camp next to them. The leader of the people of Simeon is Shelumiel
son of Zurishaddai.[w] 13 His division numbers 59,300.
14 The tribe of Gad will be next. The leader of the people of Gad is Eliasaph son of Deuel.[a][x]
15 His division numbers 45,650.
16 All the men assigned to the camp of Reuben,[y] according to their divisions, number 151,450.
They will set out second.

17 Then the tent of meeting and the camp of the Levites[z] will set out in the middle of the camps.
They will set out in the same order as they encamp, each in their own place under their standard.

18 On the west will be the divisions of the camp of Ephraim[a] under their standard. The leader of
the people of Ephraim is Elishama son of Ammihud.[b] 19 His division numbers 40,500.
20 The tribe of Manasseh will be next to them. The leader of the people of Manasseh is Gamaliel
son of Pedahzur.[c] 21 His division numbers 32,200.
22 The tribe of Benjamin will be next. The leader of the people of Benjamin is Abidan son of
Gideoni.[d] 23 His division numbers 35,400.
24 All the men assigned to the camp of Ephraim,[e] according to their divisions, number 108,100.
They will set out third.[f]

[a] *14* Many manuscripts of the Masoretic Text, Samaritan Pentateuch and Vulgate (see also 1:14); most manuscripts of the Masoretic Text *Reuel*

2:10–16 Reuben was the firstborn (Gen 29:32), so it is no surprise his tribe leads this grouping. Simeon was Reuben's younger brother (Gen 29:33), and Gad was Reuben's half brother from Leah's servant Zilpah (Gen 30:10–11).
2:17 Levites. In this case, the Kohathites, who carry the holiest objects. This verse simply describes those who march in the heart of the camp, while 10:14–21,33 gives a more specific order (see "The Camp of the Tribes of Israel," p. 249).
2:18–24 These tribes descended from Rachel's sons, Joseph and Benjamin (Gen 30:22–24; 35:16–18). Ephraim and Manasseh were sons of Joseph. Ephraim, like Judah, was not the firstborn, and his tribe, like Judah's tribe (see note on 2:3), may come first in keeping with Jacob's prophetic blessing (Gen 48:13–20).

25 On the north will be the divisions of the camp of Dan under their standard. The leader of the
people of Dan is Ahiezer son of Ammishaddai.[g] 26 His division numbers 62,700.
27 The tribe of Asher will camp next to them. The leader of the people of Asher is Pagiel son of
Okran.[h] 28 His division numbers 41,500.
29 The tribe of Naphtali will be next. The leader of the people of Naphtali is Ahira son of Enan.[i]
30 His division numbers 53,400.
31 All the men assigned to the camp of Dan number 157,600. They will set out last,[j] under
their standards.

32 These are the Israelites, counted according to their families. All the men in the camps, by
their divisions, number 603,550.[k] 33 The Levites, however, were not counted[l] along with the other
Israelites, as the LORD commanded Moses.

34 So the Israelites did everything the LORD commanded Moses; that is the way they encamped under
their standards, and that is the way they set out, each of them with their clan and family.

The Levites

3 This is the account of the family of Aaron and Moses[m] at the time the LORD spoke to Moses at
Mount Sinai.
2 The names of the sons of Aaron were Nadab the firstborn and Abihu, Eleazar and Ithamar.[n] 3 Those
were the names of Aaron's sons, the anointed priests,[o] who were ordained to serve as priests. 4 Nadab
and Abihu, however, died before the LORD[p] when they made an offering with unauthorized fire before
him in the Desert of Sinai.[q] They had no sons, so Eleazar and Ithamar served as priests during the
lifetime of their father Aaron.[r]
5 The LORD said to Moses, 6 "Bring the tribe of Levi[s] and present them to Aaron the priest to assist him.[t]
7 They are to perform duties for him and for the whole community at the tent of meeting by doing the
work[u] of the tabernacle. 8 They are to take care of all the furnishings of the tent of meeting, fulfilling
the obligations of the Israelites by doing the work of the tabernacle. 9 Give the Levites to Aaron and his
sons;[v] they are the Israelites who are to be given wholly to him.[a] 10 Appoint Aaron and his sons to serve
as priests;[w] anyone else who approaches the sanctuary is to be put to death."[x]
11 The LORD also said to Moses, 12 "I have taken the Levites[y] from among the Israelites in place of the

2:25 [g] Nu 1:12
2:27 [h] Nu 1:13
2:29 [i] Nu 1:15
2:31 [j] Nu 10:25
2:32 [k] Ex 38:26; Nu 1:46
2:33 [l] Nu 1:47; 26:57-62
3:1 [m] Ex 6:27
3:2 [n] Ex 6:23; Nu 26:60
3:3 [o] Ex 28:41
3:4 [p] Lev 10:2 [q] Lev 10:1 [r] 1Ch 24:1
3:6 [s] Dt 10:8; 31:9; 1Ch 15:2 [t] Nu 8:6-22; 18:1-7; 2Ch 29:11
3:7 [u] Lev 8:35; Nu 1:50
3:9 [v] Nu 8:19; 18:6
3:10 [w] Ex 29:9 [x] Nu 1:51
3:12 [y] Mal 2:4

[a] *9* Most manuscripts of the Masoretic Text; some manuscripts of the Masoretic Text, Samaritan Pentateuch and Septuagint (see also 8:16) *to me*

2:25–31 Dan, Asher, and Naphtali were the remaining children of Leah's and Rachel's servants, Bilhah and Zilpah (Gen 30:5–8,12–13). Dan may come first because he was the firstborn of those servants or because of the leadership role given him in Jacob's prophetic blessing (Gen 49:16).
2:32 603,550. See Introduction: Interpretive Issues.
2:34 See note on 1:54.
3:1—4:49 *The Censuses of the Levites and Their Tabernacle Responsibilities.* This elaborates on the details that 1:47–53 summarizes. It describes the Levites' numbers, placement in the camp, and responsibilities. Here, as elsewhere, the Lord structures his people, giving everyone a certain role for the common good (cf. 1 Cor 12:4–7) and expecting everyone to respect the roles of others, especially that of the leaders (cf. Heb 13:17).
3:1–51 *The Tribe of Levi.* This tribe consisted of priestly Levites (Aaron and his family) and non-priestly Levites (males not in the family of Aaron; in Numbers, the term "Levites" often refers to this second group in particular). After a brief census of the priestly Levites (vv. 1–4), ch. 3 describes the non-priestly Levites (vv. 5–13), reports a census of them (vv. 14–39), and explains how to reconcile their total number and the total number of firstborn Israelite males (vv. 40–51).
3:1 Aaron and Moses. Brothers (Exod 6:20); they camp in the same place (v. 38).
3:2 sons of Aaron. They lead the Levites (vv. 9,32; 4:28,33).
3:3 anointed ... ordained. See note on Exod 30:22–38.
3:4 Nadab and Abihu. Aaron's oldest sons. **died before the LORD.** See Lev 10:1–3 and notes. Recalling this incident here emphasizes the importance of treating the Lord and his holy tent with utmost respect (see note on 1:47–53; see also 3:10,38; 4:15,18–20; cf. 16:1–35; 2 Sam 6:6–7). While the Lord's presence among his people is to fill them with joy, they must not forget to revere him as their holy King (Acts 5:1–11; 1 Cor 10:6–11).
3:5–10 In the tribe of Levi, only the priests (Aaron and his sons) could present sacrifices or go into the tent of meeting to minister (v. 10). There was other work to be done at the tent, but lay Israelites were not ceremonially pure enough to work in such a holy place (for ceremonial purity and impurity, see Introduction to Leviticus: Major Theological Themes [Holiness and Purity]). The Lord therefore required the non-priestly Levites to go through a special cleansing ceremony (8:5–22) that enabled them to assist the priests on behalf of the whole community.
3:11–13 By sparing the Israelites' firstborn during the last plague on Egypt (Exod 12:23–32), the Lord set them apart for himself. From that point on, every firstborn human or animal was dedicated to him (Exod 13:1–16). For firstborn children, this would mean serving in the tabernacle (cf. 1 Sam 1:11,22–28). However, instead of disrupting families like this, the Lord states that the Levites will serve in place of the firstborn. This leads to a counting of both the Levites (vv. 14–39) and the firstborn (vv. 40–43) to make sure there are enough Levites to serve as substitutes (vv. 44–48).

3:12 [z] ver 41; Nu 8:16,18 [a] Ex 13:2
3:13 [b] Ex 13:12
3:15 [c] ver 39 [d] Nu 26:62
3:17 [e] Ge 46:11 [f] Ex 6:16
3:18 [g] Ex 6:17
3:19 [h] Ex 6:18
3:20 [i] Ge 46:11 [j] Ex 6:19
3:21 [k] Ex 6:17
3:25 [l] Ex 25:9 [m] Ex 26:14 [n] Ex 26:36; Nu 4:25
3:26 [o] Ex 27:9 [p] Ex 35:18
3:27 [q] 1Ch 26:23
3:29 [r] Nu 1:53
3:31 [s] Ex 25:10-22 [t] Ex 25:23 [u] Ex 25:31 [v] Ex 27:1; 30:1 [w] Ex 26:33 [x] Nu 4:15

first male offspring[z] of every Israelite woman. The Levites are mine,[a] 13 for all the firstborn are mine.[b]
When I struck down all the firstborn in Egypt, I set apart for myself every firstborn in Israel, whether
human or animal. They are to be mine. I am the LORD."

14 The LORD said to Moses in the Desert of Sinai, 15 "Count[c] the Levites by their families and clans.
Count every male a month old or more."[d] 16 So Moses counted them, as he was commanded by the
word of the LORD.

17 These were the names of the sons of Levi:[e]
Gershon, Kohath and Merari.[f]
18 These were the names of the Gershonite clans:
Libni and Shimei.[g]
19 The Kohathite clans:
Amram, Izhar, Hebron and Uzziel.[h]
20 The Merarite clans:[i]
Mahli and Mushi.[j]
These were the Levite clans, according to their families.

21 To Gershon belonged the clans of the Libnites and Shimeites;[k] these were the Gershonite clans.
22 The number of all the males a month old or more who were counted was 7,500. 23 The Gershonite
clans were to camp on the west, behind the tabernacle. 24 The leader of the families of the Gershonites
was Eliasaph son of Lael. 25 At the tent of meeting the Gershonites were responsible for the care of the
tabernacle[l] and tent, its coverings,[m] the curtain at the entrance[n] to the tent of meeting, 26 the curtains
of the courtyard[o], the curtain at the entrance to the courtyard surrounding the tabernacle and altar,
and the ropes[p]—and everything related to their use.

27 To Kohath belonged the clans of the Amramites, Izharites, Hebronites and Uzzielites;[q] these were the
Kohathite clans. 28 The number of all the males a month old or more was 8,600.[a] The Kohathites were
responsible for the care of the sanctuary. 29 The Kohathite clans were to camp on the south side[r] of the
tabernacle. 30 The leader of the families of the Kohathite clans was Elizaphan son of Uzziel. 31 They were
responsible for the care of the ark,[s] the table,[t] the lampstand,[u] the altars,[v] the articles of the sanctuary used
in ministering, the curtain,[w] and everything related to their use.[x] 32 The chief leader of the Levites was Eleazar son of Aaron, the priest. He was appointed over those who were responsible for the care of the sanctuary.

[a] *28* Hebrew; some Septuagint manuscripts *8,300*

3:15 families. Verse 17 lists the three major ones. **clans.** Subgroups within these large family groupings (vv. 18–20).
3:21–37 See "Levite Numbers and Responsibilities," this page, and "The Camp of the Tribes of Israel," p. 249.
3:32 Eleazar. Mentioned with the Kohathites since he had special responsibilities among them (cf. 4:16) and perhaps also because that was his tribal family (Exod 6:18,20).

LEVITE NUMBERS AND RESPONSIBILITIES (Num 3–4)

	GERSHON (NUM 3:21–26)	KOHATH (NUM 3:27–32)	MERARI (NUM 3:33–37)
Clans	Libnites, Shimeites (3:21)	Amramites, Izharites, Hebronites, Uzzielites (3:27)	Mahlites, Mushites (3:33)
Number of males a month old or more	7,500 (3:22)	8,600 (3:28)	6,200 (3:34)
Males 30–50 years old	2,630 (4:40)	2,750 (4:36)	3,200 (4:44)
Placement in the camp	West side of the tabernacle (3:23)	South side of the tabernacle (3:29)	North side of the tabernacle (3:35)
Levitical leader	Eliasaph (3:24)	Elizaphan (3:30)	Zuriel (3:35)
Priestly leader	Ithamar (4:28)	Eleazar (4:16)	Ithamar (4:33)
Items of the tabernacle they transported	Mostly fabrics (4:24–26)	Mostly furniture and utensils (4:15)	Mostly structural elements (4:31–32)
How they did so	With two carts and four oxen (7:7)	By carrying them on their shoulders (7:9)	With four carts and eight oxen (7:8)

33 To Merari belonged the clans of the Mahlites and the Mushites;[y] these were the Merarite clans. 34 The number of all the males a month old or more who were counted was 6,200. 35 The leader of the families of the Merarite clans was Zuriel son of Abihail; they were to camp on the north side of the tabernacle.[z] 36 The Merarites were appointed[a] to take care of the frames of the tabernacle, its crossbars, posts, bases, all its equipment, and everything related to their use, 37 as well as the posts of the surrounding courtyard with their bases, tent pegs and ropes.

38 Moses and Aaron and his sons were to camp to the east[b] of the tabernacle, toward the sunrise, in front of the tent of meeting.[c] They were responsible for the care of the sanctuary[d] on behalf of the Israelites. Anyone else who approached the sanctuary was to be put to death.[e]

39 The total number of Levites counted at the LORD's command by Moses and Aaron according to their clans, including every male a month old or more, was 22,000.[f]

40 The LORD said to Moses, "Count all the firstborn Israelite males who are a month old or more[g] and make a list of their names. 41 Take the Levites for me in place of all the firstborn of the Israelites,[h] and the livestock of the Levites in place of all the firstborn of the livestock of the Israelites. I am the LORD."

42 So Moses counted all the firstborn of the Israelites, as the LORD commanded him. 43 The total number of firstborn males a month old or more, listed by name, was 22,273.[i]

44 The LORD also said to Moses, 45 "Take the Levites in place of all the firstborn of Israel, and the livestock of the Levites in place of their livestock. The Levites are to be mine. I am the LORD. 46 To redeem[j] the 273 firstborn Israelites who exceed the number of the Levites, 47 collect five shekels[a][k] for each one, according to the sanctuary shekel,[l] which weighs twenty gerahs.[m] 48 Give the money for the redemption of the additional Israelites to Aaron and his sons."

49 So Moses collected the redemption money from those who exceeded the number redeemed by the Levites. 50 From the firstborn of the Israelites he collected silver weighing 1,365 shekels,[b][n] according to the sanctuary shekel. 51 Moses gave the redemption money to Aaron and his sons, as he was commanded by the word of the LORD.

The Kohathites

4 The LORD said to Moses and Aaron: 2 "Take a census[o] of the Kohathite branch of the Levites by their clans and families. 3 Count all the men from thirty to fifty years of age[p] who come to serve in the work at the tent of meeting.

3:33 [y] Ex 6:19
3:35 [z] Nu 1:53; 2:25
3:36 [a] Nu 4:32
3:38 [b] Nu 2:3 [c] Nu 1:53 [d] ver 7; Nu 18:5 [e] ver 10; Nu 1:51
3:39 [f] Nu 26:62
3:40 [g] ver 15
3:41 [h] ver 12
3:43 [i] ver 39
3:46 [j] Ex 13:13; Nu 18:15
3:47 [k] Lev 27:6 [l] Ex 30:13 [m] Lev 27:25
3:50 [n] ver 46-48
4:2 [o] Ex 30:12
4:3 [p] ver 23; Nu 8:25; 1Ch 23:3,24,27; Ezr 3:8

[a] *47* That is, about 2 ounces or about 58 grams [b] *50* That is, about 35 pounds or about 16 kilograms

3:38 east of the tabernacle. Its entrance (see "The Camp of the Tribes of Israel," p. 249), enabling them to guard it to prevent illicit entry. **care.** Or perhaps more generally, the "obligations." **put to death.** The penalty for lay people who tried to perform priestly duties (see notes on 1:50 – 53). With Moses and Aaron and his sons on the east — and with the other Levites on the north, south, and west — priests and Levites encircled the tabernacle (see "The Camp of the Tribes of Israel," p. 249), acting as a protective barrier to prevent Israelites from illicit contact with the holy items (1:53).
3:39 22,000. The numbers in vv. 22,28,34 total 22,300, not 22,000. It seems likely that v. 28 contains a scribal error and should read 8,300 (as in other ancient translations; see NIV text note), not 8,600. In Hebrew, there is just one letter difference between the words for three and six.
3:40 – 51 There are 273 more firstborn Israelites (v. 43) than Levites (v. 39), and these must be redeemed (v. 46), which in this context refers to transferring them from the ownership of one party (the Lord) to that of another party (the parents; see note on vv. 11 – 13). This redemption is made by payment of money (vv. 47 – 48).
3:41 livestock. Perhaps unclean animals, which were redeemed instead of sacrificed (18:15).
3:43 22,273. See Introduction: Interpretive Issues.
3:48 Aaron and his sons. The Lord's representatives, who would use the money for the service of the tabernacle (Exod 30:16).
4:1 – 20 *The Kohathites.* In ch. 3, all the Levites were counted to see if there were enough of them to substitute for the Israelites' firstborn. In ch. 4, the Levites from 30 to 50 years old are counted to see how many are available for tabernacle service (vv. 34 – 45), especially for transporting the tabernacle (vv. 1 – 33). The Kohathites were counted first. Kohath was not the firstborn, but the Kohathites are mentioned first because they transported the tabernacle's most holy things (see "The Camp of the Tribes of Israel," p. 249; see also "Levite Numbers and Responsibilities," p. 252). Only those who were ceremonially holy (Aaron and his sons) could handle the holy things and therefore pack them (vv. 5 – 15; for ceremonial holiness, see Introduction to Leviticus: Major Theological Themes [Holiness and Purity]). Anyone else who touched (v. 15) or saw them (v. 20) showed great disrespect for the Lord's holiness and would die (see note on 1:53; cf. 1 Sam 6:19; 2 Sam 6:6 – 7). The Gershonites and Merarites did not need the priests' help in packing because the items they transported were not the most holy items (vv. 21 – 33; see "Levite Numbers and Responsibilities," p. 252).
4:3 thirty to fifty. Men strong enough to transport the tabernacle and mature enough to care for such holy items. **serve.** Like the Israelites

4:4 [q]ver 19
4:5 [r]Ex 26:31,33 [s]Ex 25:10,16
4:6 [t]Ex 25:13-15; 1Ki 8:7; 2Ch 5:8
4:7 [u]Ex 25:23,29; Lev 24:6 [v]Ex 25:30
4:9 [w]Ex 25:31,37,38
4:11 [x]Ex 30:1
4:13 [y]Ex 27:1-8
4:14 [z]2Ch 4:16 [a]Jer 52:18 [b]Ex 27:6
4:15 [c]Nu 7:9 [d]Nu 1:51; 2Sa 6:6,7
4:16 [e]Lev 10:6 [f]Ex 25:6 [g]Ex 29:41; Lev 6:14-23
4:19 [h]ver 15
4:20 [i]Ex 19:21; 1Sa 6:19
4:23 [j]ver 3; 1Ch 23:3,24,27
4:25 [k]Ex 27:10-18; Nu 3:26 [l]Nu 3:25 [m]Ex 26:14

4 “This is the work of the Kohathites at the tent of meeting: the care of the most holy things.[q] 5 When the camp is to move, Aaron and his sons are to go in and take down the shielding curtain[r] and put it over the ark of the covenant law.[s] 6 Then they are to cover the curtain with a durable leather,[a] spread a cloth of solid blue over that and put the poles[t] in place.

7 “Over the table of the Presence[u] they are to spread a blue cloth and put on it the plates, dishes and bowls, and the jars for drink offerings; the bread that is continually there[v] is to remain on it. 8 They are to spread a scarlet cloth over them, cover that with the durable leather and put the poles in place.

9 “They are to take a blue cloth and cover the lampstand that is for light, together with its lamps, its wick trimmers and trays,[w] and all its jars for the olive oil used to supply it. 10 Then they are to wrap it and all its accessories in a covering of the durable leather and put it on a carrying frame.

11 “Over the gold altar[x] they are to spread a blue cloth and cover that with the durable leather and put the poles in place.

12 “They are to take all the articles used for ministering in the sanctuary, wrap them in a blue cloth, cover that with the durable leather and put them on a carrying frame.

13 “They are to remove the ashes from the bronze altar[y] and spread a purple cloth over it. 14 Then they are to place on it all the utensils used for ministering at the altar, including the firepans, meat forks,[z] shovels and sprinkling bowls.[a] Over it they are to spread a covering of the durable leather and put the poles[b] in place.

15 “After Aaron and his sons have finished covering the holy furnishings and all the holy articles, and when the camp is ready to move, only then are the Kohathites to come and do the carrying.[c] But they must not touch the holy things or they will die.[d] The Kohathites are to carry those things that are in the tent of meeting.

16 “Eleazar[e] son of Aaron, the priest, is to have charge of the oil for the light,[f] the fragrant incense, the regular grain offering[g] and the anointing oil. He is to be in charge of the entire tabernacle and everything in it, including its holy furnishings and articles.”

17 The LORD said to Moses and Aaron, 18 “See that the Kohathite tribal clans are not destroyed from among the Levites. 19 So that they may live and not die when they come near the most holy things,[h] do this for them: Aaron and his sons are to go into the sanctuary and assign to each man his work and what he is to carry. 20 But the Kohathites must not go in to look[i] at the holy things, even for a moment, or they will die.”

The Gershonites

21 The LORD said to Moses, 22 “Take a census also of the Gershonites by their families and clans. 23 Count all the men from thirty to fifty years of age[j] who come to serve in the work at the tent of meeting.

24 “This is the service of the Gershonite clans in their carrying and their other work: 25 They are to carry the curtains of the tabernacle,[k] that is, the tent of meeting,[l] its covering[m] and its outer covering of durable leather, the curtains for the entrance to the tent of meeting, 26 the curtains of the courtyard surrounding the tabernacle and altar, the curtain for the entrance to the courtyard, the ropes and all the equipment used in the service of the tent. The Gershonites are to do all that needs to be done with these things. 27 All their service, whether carrying or doing other work, is to be done under the direction

[a] *6* Possibly the hides of large aquatic mammals; also in verses 8, 10, 11, 12, 14 and 25

in 1:3,20. All the tribes were obligated to serve the Lord in one way or another.

4:4–14 Aside from the bronze altar and its utensils (vv. 13–14), all items came from within the tabernacle. For descriptions, see Exod 25:10–40; 26:31–35; 27:1–8; 30:1–10. Most items received two coverings, but the ark and table received three, perhaps due to their holier nature. The coverings' colors (blue, scarlet, purple) are associated elsewhere with royalty (2 Sam 1:24; Esth 1:6; Ezek 23:6); the covered items belonged to the divine King. The ark's outer covering differed from the rest (v. 6; cf. vv. 8,10–12,14). The ark, the holiest item of all, was the footstool of the divine King (1 Chr 28:2) and required special attention.

4:15 carrying. With poles (vv. 6,8,11,14) or a frame (v. 12).

4:21–28 *The Gershonites.* Their duties focused on the tabernacle's fabrics (see “Levite Numbers and Responsibilities,” p. 252).

of Aaron and his sons. You shall assign to them as their responsibility all they are to carry. [28]This is the service of the Gershonite clans[n] at the tent of meeting. Their duties are to be under the direction of Ithamar son of Aaron, the priest.

The Merarites

[29]"Count the Merarites by their clans and families.[o] [30]Count all the men from thirty to fifty years of age who come to serve in the work at the tent of meeting. [31]As part of all their service at the tent, they are to carry the frames of the tabernacle, its crossbars, posts and bases,[p] [32]as well as the posts of the surrounding courtyard with their bases, tent pegs, ropes, all their equipment and everything related to their use. Assign to each man the specific things he is to carry. [33]This is the service of the Merarite clans as they work at the tent of meeting under the direction of Ithamar son of Aaron, the priest."

The Numbering of the Levite Clans

[34]Moses, Aaron and the leaders of the community counted the Kohathites[q] by their clans and families. [35]All the men from thirty to fifty years of age who came to serve in the work at the tent of meeting, [36]counted by clans, were 2,750. [37]This was the total of all those in the Kohathite clans[r] who served at the tent of meeting. Moses and Aaron counted them according to the LORD's command through Moses.

[38]The Gershonites[s] were counted by their clans and families. [39]All the men from thirty to fifty years of age who came to serve in the work at the tent of meeting, [40]counted by their clans and families, were 2,630. [41]This was the total of those in the Gershonite clans who served at the tent of meeting. Moses and Aaron counted them according to the LORD's command.

[42]The Merarites were counted by their clans and families. [43]All the men from thirty to fifty years of age who came to serve in the work at the tent of meeting, [44]counted by their clans, were 3,200. [45]This was the total of those in the Merarite clans.[t] Moses and Aaron counted them according to the LORD's command through Moses.

[46]So Moses, Aaron and the leaders of Israel counted all the Levites by their clans and families. [47]All the men from thirty to fifty years of age[u] who came to do the work of serving and carrying the tent of meeting [48]numbered 8,580.[v] [49]At the LORD's command through Moses, each was assigned his work and told what to carry.

Thus they were counted,[w] as the LORD commanded Moses.

The Purity of the Camp

5 The LORD said to Moses, [2]"Command the Israelites to send away from the camp anyone who has a defiling skin disease[a][x] or a discharge[y] of any kind, or who is ceremonially unclean[z] because of a dead body. [3]Send away male and female alike; send them outside the camp so they will not defile their camp, where I dwell among them.[a]" [4]The Israelites did so; they sent them outside the camp. They did just as the LORD had instructed Moses.

a 2 The Hebrew word for *defiling skin disease*, traditionally translated "leprosy," was used for various diseases affecting the skin.

4:28 [n] Nu 7:7
4:29 [o] Ge 46:11
4:31 [p] Nu 3:36
4:34 [q] ver 2
4:37 [r] Nu 3:27
4:38 [s] Ge 46:11
4:45 [t] ver 29
4:47 [u] ver 3
4:48 [v] Nu 3:39
4:49 [w] Nu 1:47
5:2 [x] Lev 13:46 [y] Lev 15:2; Mt 9:20 [z] Lev 13:3; Nu 9:6-10
5:3 [a] Lev 26:12; Nu 35:34; 2Co 6:16

4:29–33 *The Merarites.* Their duties focused on the tabernacle's structural elements (see "Levite Numbers and Responsibilities," p. 252).
4:34–49 *The Numbering of the Levite Clans.* Having described their tabernacle duties (vv. 1–33), a census is now taken of those old enough to perform these duties.
4:34 leaders. Listed in 1:5–16.
4:48 8,580. The number of Levites old enough for tabernacle service.
4:49 Emphasizes the theme of obedience (see note on 1:54).
5:1—6:27 *Laws Related to the Camp's Purity and the Priests' Roles.* These laws address themes from chs. 3–4. There are five main laws: the first four are for the Israelites (5:2,6,12; 6:2), and the fifth is for the priests (6:23).
5:1–4 *The Purity of the Camp.* Because the holy Lord dwelled among his people, he required their ceremonial purity (see Introduction to Leviticus: Major Theological Themes [Holiness and Purity]).
5:2 send away. Lest those suffering from one of three major ceremonial impurities spread them through the camp and defile the Lord's tent (Lev 15:31). They were not necessarily sent alone (2 Kgs 7:3). **defiling skin disease.** Ceremonially defiling (see NIV text note; see also note on Lev 13:3). **discharge.** Any abnormal genital discharge requiring sacrifice for cleansing (see note on Lev 15:1–33). **dead body.** Highly defiling (see note on 19:1–22).

5:6 [b]Lev 6:2 [c]Lev 5:14-6:7
5:7 [d]Lev 5:5; 26:40; Jos 7:19; Lk 19:8 [e]Lev 6:5
5:8 [f]Lev 6:6,7; 7:7
5:9 [g]Lev 6:17; 7:6-14
5:10 [h]Lev 10:13
5:12 [i]Ex 20:14
5:13 [j]Lev 18:20; 20:10
5:14 [k]Pr 6:34; SS 8:6
5:15 [l]Ex 16:36 [m]Lev 6:20 [n]Eze 29:16
5:18 [o]Lev 10:6; 1Co 11:6
5:19 [p]ver 12,29
5:20 [q]ver 12
5:21 [r]Jos 6:26; 1Sa 14:24; Ne 10:29

Restitution for Wrongs

5 The LORD said to Moses, 6 "Say to the Israelites: 'Any man or woman who wrongs another in any way[a] and so is unfaithful[b] to the LORD is guilty[c] 7 and must confess[d] the sin they have committed. They must make full restitution[e] for the wrong they have done, add a fifth of the value to it and give it all to the person they have wronged. 8 But if that person has no close relative to whom restitution can be made for the wrong, the restitution belongs to the LORD and must be given to the priest, along with the ram with which atonement is made for the wrongdoer.[f] 9 All the sacred contributions the Israelites bring to a priest will belong to him.[g] 10 Sacred things belong to their owners, but what they give to the priest will belong to the priest.[h]' "

The Test for an Unfaithful Wife

11 Then the LORD said to Moses, 12 "Speak to the Israelites and say to them: 'If a man's wife goes astray[i] and is unfaithful to him 13 so that another man has sexual relations with her,[j] and this is hidden from her husband and her impurity is undetected (since there is no witness against her and she has not been caught in the act), 14 and if feelings of jealousy[k] come over her husband and he suspects his wife and she is impure — or if he is jealous and suspects her even though she is not impure — 15 then he is to take his wife to the priest. He must also take an offering of a tenth of an ephah[b][l] of barley flour[m] on her behalf. He must not pour olive oil on it or put incense on it, because it is a grain offering for jealousy, a reminder-offering[n] to draw attention to wrongdoing.

16 " 'The priest shall bring her and have her stand before the LORD. 17 Then he shall take some holy water in a clay jar and put some dust from the tabernacle floor into the water. 18 After the priest has had the woman stand before the LORD, he shall loosen her hair[o] and place in her hands the reminder-offering, the grain offering for jealousy, while he himself holds the bitter water that brings a curse. 19 Then the priest shall put the woman under oath and say to her, "If no other man has had sexual relations with you and you have not gone astray[p] and become impure while married to your husband, may this bitter water that brings a curse not harm you. 20 But if you have gone astray[q] while married to your husband and you have made yourself impure by having sexual relations with a man other than your husband" — 21 here the priest is to put the woman under this curse[r] — "may the LORD cause you to become a curse[c] among your people when he makes your womb miscarry and your

[a] *6* Or *woman who commits any wrong common to mankind* [b] *15* That is, probably about 3 1/2 pounds or about 1.6 kilograms [c] *21* That is, may he cause your name to be used in cursing (see Jer. 29:22); or, may others see that you are cursed; similarly in verse 27.

5:5–10 *Restitution for Wrongs; Priestly Portions.* This summarizes the law in Lev 6:1–7 about stealing from others and then swearing a false oath, but it adds a new detail: restitution sometimes went to the priest (v. 8). Other priestly portions or sacred contributions were food items presented to the Lord, who then gave them to the priests and their households (vv. 9–10; 18:19). This freed the priests to lead the people in the things of God (cf. 1 Cor 9:13–14; Gal 6:6). Shepherds cannot care well for the sheep if their needs are not met (cf. Neh 13:10–11).

5:10 The Hebrew here is difficult. Some understand the second half of the verse to be emphasizing the first half: "Sacred things belong to their owners [i.e., to the priests]; what is given to the priest will belong to the priest."

5:11–31 *The Test for a Wife Suspected of Adultery.* Before paternity tests and with no witnesses, the only way to confirm adultery was to ask for divine aid. In a similar case in ancient Babylon, the woman had to throw herself into a river. If she lived, she was innocent (the gods had spared her); if she died, she was guilty. Naturally, many innocent wives died. Our passage poses no such risk for the innocent. What the wife drank was no more harmful than what swimmers at the beach swallow (vv. 17,23–24). If there was guilt, it was the Lord (not the water) that would bring harm (v. 21; cf. 1 Kgs 8:31–32). Indeed, this ritual was not primitive magic but an acted-out prayer that asked the Lord to rule directly. This assured accurate justice, and if the wife was innocent, her reputation was cleared before her husband and the public.

5:13 impurity. Sexual immorality, which resulted in a deep moral defilement and the Lord's judgment (see Lev 18:24–30 and context; cf. Rev 22:14–15). It was to have no place among the Lord's holy people (cf. 1 Cor 5:9–13).

5:14 feelings of jealousy. These may have been accurate ("she is impure") or inaccurate ("she is not impure"). Either way, this law prevented the husband from taking matters into his own hands; he was to let the Lord act as judge.

5:15 not pour olive oil ... incense. Forbidden perhaps because this was not to be an "aroma pleasing to the LORD" (Lev 2:2; cf. Lev 2:1–3). **reminder-offering.** A way of asking the Lord to act on any wrongdoing (Jer 14:10).

5:18 loosen her hair. May symbolize (1) shame or mourning (not because she was necessarily guilty, but because she had been accused of great wrong and was suffering socially) or (2) that she was not trying to hide anything. **bitter.** Perhaps not in taste as much as the result for the guilty (it "brings a curse").

5:21–22 womb ... abdomen ... abdomen ... womb. Matches the place of the crime: sinning with her womb and (potentially) conceiving in her abdomen. She would be unable to have children (v. 27).

5:21 become a curse. See NIV text note. Not having children was a severe consequence to an ancient Israelite woman (Gen 30:1).

abdomen swell. 22 May this water[s] that brings a curse[t] enter your body so that your abdomen swells or your womb miscarries."

" 'Then the woman is to say, "Amen. So be it.[u]"

23 " 'The priest is to write these curses on a scroll[v] and then wash them off into the bitter water. 24 He shall make the woman drink the bitter water that brings a curse, and this water that brings a curse and causes bitter suffering will enter her. 25 The priest is to take from her hands the grain offering for jealousy, wave it before the LORD[w] and bring it to the altar. 26 The priest is then to take a handful of the grain offering as a memorial[a] offering and burn it on the altar; after that, he is to have the woman drink the water. 27 If she has made herself impure and been unfaithful to her husband, this will be the result: When she is made to drink the water that brings a curse and causes bitter suffering, it will enter her, her abdomen will swell and her womb will miscarry, and she will become a curse.[x] 28 If, however, the woman has not made herself impure, but is clean, she will be cleared of guilt and will be able to have children.

29 " 'This, then, is the law of jealousy when a woman goes astray[y] and makes herself impure while married to her husband, 30 or when feelings of jealousy come over a man because he suspects his wife. The priest is to have her stand before the LORD and is to apply this entire law to her. 31 The husband will be innocent of any wrongdoing, but the woman will bear the consequences[z] of her sin.' "

5:22 [s]Ps 109:18 [t]ver 18 [u]Dt 27:15
5:23 [v]Jer 45:1
5:25 [w]Lev 8:27
5:27 [x]Isa 43:28; 65:15; Jer 26:6; 29:18; 42:18; 44:12,22; Zec 8:13
5:29 [y]ver 19
5:31 [z]Lev 5:1; 20:17
6:2 [a]Ge 28:20; Ac 21:23 [b]Jdg 13:5; 16:17; Am 2:11,12
6:3 [c]Lk 1:15 [d]Ru 2:14; Ps 69:21; Pr 10:26
6:5 [e]Ps 52:2; 57:4; 59:7; Isa 7:20; Eze 5:1 [f]1Sa 1:11
6:6 [g]Lev 21:1-3; Nu 19:11-22
6:7 [h]Nu 9:6
6:9 [i]ver 18 [j]Lev 14:9
6:10 [k]Lev 5:7; 14:22
6:11 [l]Ge 8:20 [m]Ex 29:36

The Nazirite

6 The LORD said to Moses, 2 "Speak to the Israelites and say to them: 'If a man or woman wants to make a special vow[a], a vow of dedication to the LORD as a Nazirite,[b] 3 they must abstain from wine[c] and other fermented drink and must not drink vinegar[d] made from wine or other fermented drink. They must not drink grape juice or eat grapes or raisins. 4 As long as they remain under their Nazirite vow, they must not eat anything that comes from the grapevine, not even the seeds or skins.

5 " 'During the entire period of their Nazirite vow, no razor[e] may be used on their head.[f] They must be holy until the period of their dedication to the LORD is over; they must let their hair grow long.

6 " 'Throughout the period of their dedication to the LORD, the Nazirite must not go near a dead body.[g] 7 Even if their own father or mother or brother or sister dies, they must not make themselves ceremonially unclean[h] on account of them, because the symbol of their dedication to God is on their head. 8 Throughout the period of their dedication, they are consecrated to the LORD.

9 " 'If someone dies suddenly in the Nazirite's presence, thus defiling the hair that symbolizes their dedication,[i] they must shave their head on the seventh day—the day of their cleansing.[j] 10 Then on the eighth day they must bring two doves or two young pigeons[k] to the priest at the entrance to the tent of meeting. 11 The priest is to offer one as a sin offering[b] and the other as a burnt offering[l] to make atonement[m] for the Nazirite because they sinned by being in the presence of the dead body. That same day they are to consecrate their head again. 12 They must rededicate themselves to the LORD for the

[a] 26 Or *representative* [b] 11 Or *purification offering*; also in verses 14 and 16

5:22 Amen. So be it. Shows her agreement to the curse (cf. Deut 27:15–26).

5:29–31 Though this law focuses on the woman, Israelite law is clear that both parties to an affair were to be punished (Lev 20:10; Deut 22:22). If the guilty man kept his sin hidden from the human court, it would not be hidden from the Lord (cf. Ps 90:8), and he should expect that his sin would find him out (cf. 32:23).

5:31 innocent. It was not wrong for him to ensure his wife's faithfulness. **bear the consequences.** If she was guilty.

6:1–21 *The Nazirite.* Someone became a Nazirite by taking a special vow (v. 2). Though a few people were lifelong Nazirites (Samson, Samuel, John the Baptist), a person usually vowed to be a Nazirite for a short period of time. Like priests, it seems Nazirites became ceremonially holy (v. 5) and thus visually reminded the Israelites to live as "a kingdom of priests and a holy nation" (Exod 19:6; cf. Rev 5:9–10; for ceremonial holiness, see Introduction to Leviticus: Major Theological Themes [Holiness and Purity]).

6:1–8 The three rules for a Nazirite vow: no alcohol (vv. 3–4), no cutting of their hair (v. 5), and no contact with a dead body, which caused them to become unclean (vv. 6–8).

6:2 dedication ... Nazirite. Share the same root word in Hebrew. Nazirites set themselves apart to the Lord in a special way.

6:3–4 Alcohol was forbidden to priests on duty so that it did not prevent them from properly doing their job (Lev 10:9–11). Nazirites were like priests who were perpetually on duty, so they must refrain from any fermented drink or anything that came from the grapevine.

6:5 head. Represents the entire person. **hair grow long.** Indicates their dedication to the Lord.

6:6–8 Nazirites were prohibited not from being sad but from mourning rites that made them ceremonially unclean (for similar prohibitions for the high priest, see Lev 21:10–11). This was incompatible with their holy status. Dedication to God took priority over every earthly loyalty (cf. Matt 10:37).

6:9 dies suddenly in the Nazirite's presence. Thus, the Nazirite did not mean to sin by being in the presence of a dead body (v. 11). Nonetheless, atonement was necessary for unintentional sins (cf. Lev 4:27–28,31b).

6:13 [n]Ac 21:26
6:14 [o]Lev 14:10; Nu 15:27
6:15 [p]Nu 15:1-7 [q]Ex 29:2; Lev 2:4
6:18 [r]ver 9; Ac 21:24
6:20 [s]Ecc 9:7
6:23 [t]Dt 21:5; 1Ch 23:13
6:24 [u]Dt 28:3-6; Ps 28:9 [v]1Sa 2:9; Ps 17:8

same period of dedication and must bring a year-old male lamb as a guilt offering. The previous days do not count, because they became defiled during their period of dedication.

13 " 'Now this is the law of the Nazirite when the period of their dedication is over.[n] They are to be brought to the entrance to the tent of meeting. 14 There they are to present their offerings to the LORD: a year-old male lamb without defect for a burnt offering, a year-old ewe lamb without defect for a sin offering,[o] a ram without defect for a fellowship offering, 15 together with their grain offerings and drink offerings,[p] and a basket of bread made with the finest flour and without yeast—thick loaves with olive oil mixed in, and thin loaves brushed with olive oil.[q]

16 " 'The priest is to present all these before the LORD and make the sin offering and the burnt offering. 17 He is to present the basket of unleavened bread and is to sacrifice the ram as a fellowship offering to the LORD, together with its grain offering and drink offering.

18 " 'Then at the entrance to the tent of meeting, the Nazirite must shave off the hair that symbolizes their dedication.[r] They are to take the hair and put it in the fire that is under the sacrifice of the fellowship offering.

19 " 'After the Nazirite has shaved off the hair that symbolizes their dedication, the priest is to place in their hands a boiled shoulder of the ram, and one thick loaf and one thin loaf from the basket, both made without yeast. 20 The priest shall then wave these before the LORD as a wave offering; they are holy and belong to the priest, together with the breast that was waved and the thigh that was presented. After that, the Nazirite may drink wine.[s]

21 " 'This is the law of the Nazirite who vows offerings to the LORD in accordance with their dedication, in addition to whatever else they can afford. They must fulfill the vows they have made, according to the law of the Nazirite.' "

The Priestly Blessing

22 The LORD said to Moses, 23 "Tell Aaron and his sons, 'This is how you are to bless[t] the Israelites. Say to them:

24 " ' "The LORD bless you[u]
and keep you;[v]

A form of the blessing in Num 6:24–26 was found on two small silver scrolls in a burial cave near Jerusalem. The burial dates to ca. 600 BC; the scrolls were written 50–100 years earlier. This is the earliest copy of a biblical text that has been discovered.

Z. Radovan/www.BibleLandPictures.com

6:13–20 At the vow's completion, the Nazirite offered sacrifices.
6:14 year-old. Younger animals may have been more valued because of the tastiness of their meat (like today's veal). **without defect.** See note on Lev 1:3; cf. Lev 22:18–25.
6:15 grain offerings ... drink offerings. See notes on 15:4–5; see also "Grain and Drink Offerings That Accompany Animal Sacrifices," p. 273.
6:18 put it in the fire. To destroy what was holy (cf. Lev 7:17), express full dedication to the Lord, or both.
6:19 The ram's shoulder and the loaves were given to the priest in addition to the priest's regular fellowship offering portion of the right thigh and the breast (see Lev 7:28–34 and notes; see also note on Lev 9:21). Thus, the Nazirite received less of the sacrifice than an offerer normally received, perhaps emphasizing the vow's costliness.
6:20 wave. A ritual action by which something was dedicated to the Lord by waving it back and forth (see Lev 7:30,31 and notes). **wave offering.** See note on Lev 9:21.
6:22–27 *The Priestly Blessing.* Blessings were spoken prayers (2 Chr 30:27). In vv. 24–26, each verse identifies two aspects of blessing. The repetition of the divine name ("the LORD") throughout makes clear that the source of all blessing is God. He created people for blessing (Gen 1:27–28), entered into covenant relationship to bless (Gen 12:1–3), and sent Jesus to bring ultimate blessing to the world (Acts 3:26; Gal 3:14). (A form of the blessing in vv. 24–26 was found on two small silver scrolls in a burial cave near Jerusalem. The burial dates to ca. 600 BC; the scrolls were written 50–100 years earlier. This is the earliest copy yet of a biblical text.)
6:24 bless. Show good favor in every sphere of life (Lev 26:4–12). **keep.** Protect from harm of any kind (Ps 121:3–8).

25 the LORD make his face shine on you[w]
and be gracious to you;[x]
26 the LORD turn his face[y] toward you
and give you peace.[z]" '

27 "So they will put my name[a] on the Israelites, and I will bless them."

Offerings at the Dedication of the Tabernacle

7 When Moses finished setting up the tabernacle,[b] he anointed and consecrated it and all its furnishings.[c] He also anointed and consecrated the altar and all its utensils.[d] 2 Then the leaders of
Israel,[e] the heads of families who were the tribal leaders in charge of those who were counted, made
offerings. 3 They brought as their gifts before the LORD six covered carts and twelve oxen — an ox from
each leader and a cart from every two. These they presented before the tabernacle.
4 The LORD said to Moses, 5 "Accept these from them, that they may be used in the work at the tent of
meeting. Give them to the Levites as each man's work requires."
6 So Moses took the carts and oxen and gave them to the Levites. 7 He gave two carts and four oxen
to the Gershonites,[f] as their work required, 8 and he gave four carts and eight oxen to the Merarites,[g] as
their work required. They were all under the direction of Ithamar son of Aaron, the priest. 9 But Moses
did not give any to the Kohathites, because they were to carry on their shoulders[h] the holy things, for
which they were responsible.
10 When the altar was anointed,[i] the leaders brought their offerings for its dedication[j] and presented
them before the altar. 11 For the LORD had said to Moses, "Each day one leader is to bring his offering
for the dedication of the altar."

12 The one who brought his offering on the first day was Nahshon son of Amminadab of the tribe of
Judah.
13 His offering was one silver plate weighing a hundred and thirty shekels[a] and one silver sprinkling bowl weighing seventy shekels,[b] both according to the sanctuary shekel,[k] each filled with
the finest flour mixed with olive oil as a grain offering;[l] 14 one gold dish weighing ten shekels,[c]

6:25 [w] Job 29:24; Ps 31:16; 80:3; 119:135 [x] Ge 43:29; Ps 25:16; 86:16
6:26 [y] Ps 4:6; 44:3 [z] Ps 29:11; 37:11,37; Jn 14:27
6:27 [a] Dt 28:10; 2Sa 7:23; 2Ch 7:14; Ne 9:10; Jer 25:29
7:1 [b] Ex 40:17 [c] Ex 40:9 [d] ver 84,88; Ex 40:10
7:2 [e] Nu 1:5-16
7:7 [f] Nu 4:24-26,28
7:8 [g] Nu 4:31-33
7:9 [h] Nu 4:15
7:10 [i] ver 1 [j] 2Ch 7:9
7:13 [k] Ex 30:13; Nu 3:47 [l] Lev 2:1

[a] *13* That is, about 3 1/4 pounds or about 1.5 kilograms; also elsewhere in this chapter [b] *13* That is, about 1 3/4 pounds or about 800 grams; also elsewhere in this chapter [c] *14* That is, about 4 ounces or about 115 grams; also elsewhere in this chapter

6:25 Cf. Ps 67:1. **shine.** "Beam" with delight, showing you special favor (Pss 4:6; 31:16; 80:19; cf. Prov 16:15). **gracious.** Mercifully help you and hear your prayers (Gen 33:5; Pss 25:16–18; 111:4–5; 116:5–6).
6:26 turn his face toward. Pay attention to you and your needs (Ps 34:15). **peace.** Not only the absence of evil (war, sickness), but also the presence of good (well-being, health) and ultimately fellowship with God (Lev 26:3–12). It is the state of favor for which people were created and that is definitively established by Jesus (John 14:27; Phil 4:7; Col 1:20). See "Shalom," p. 2693.
6:27 put my name on. Identify them as the Lord's and thus those who will receive his blessing (Deut 28:9–10). **bless.** And so be faithful to all his covenant promises to those who embrace his covenant from the heart (cf. Lev 26:3 with 26:4–13). The Hebrew emphasizes the word "I," again showing that the source of all blessing is the Lord. Such blessing also had a missional goal: the nations were to see it and be drawn to Israel's God (Ps 67).
7:1 — 9:14 *The Tabernacle's Dedication and Related Matters.* The events of this section take place the month before the events of chs. 1–6 (cf. 1:1 with 7:1 and Exod 40:2–11). Chronologically, this section belongs closer to Exod 40 than to Num 1–6, but thematically, it fits well here. See notes on 7:1–89; 8:1–4,5–26; 9:1–14.
7:1–89 *Offerings at the Dedication of the Tabernacle.* The next major event in Numbers is the departure of the Israelites from Sinai (10:11). Before that happens, the Levites dismantle and move the tabernacle, and they need carts and oxen to do so. Ch. 7 describes how the Israelites provide these carts and oxen, along with many other precious items, at the tabernacle's dedication.
7:1 anointed and consecrated. With the holy anointing oil (see note on Exod 30:22–38).
7:2–8 The Gershonites and Merarites used carts to transport most of the tabernacle's (heavy and bulky) fabrics and structural elements (4:24–26,31–32).
7:9 The Kohathites did not use carts to transport the tabernacle's furniture, for the pieces were not only lighter but also most holy and thus worthy of special care. **on their shoulders.** With poles and frames (4:4–15).
7:10–88 Describes the offerings that each of the 12 tribes gave at the tabernacle's dedication. (Israelites used the altar to present offerings to the Lord. It was therefore at the heart of their worship and probably represented the entire tabernacle.) The nearly identical descriptions may strike modern readers as tedious, but the repetitions make an important point: all tribes participated equally in worshiping the Lord and providing for the tabernacle's ministry (cf. 1 Cor 9:3–14). The details show that their worship was costly, an appropriate response to the divine King's gracious redemption (cf. Rom 12:1).
7:13–14 plate ... bowl ... dish. To use in tabernacle matters (cf. Exod 25:29; 27:3).
7:13 grain offering. Often accompanied burnt and fellowship offerings (15:8–10; see notes on Lev 2).

7:14 [m]Ex 30:34
7:15 [n]Ex 24:5; 29:3; Nu 28:11 [o]Lev 1:3
7:16 [p]Lev 4:3,23
7:17 [q]Lev 3:1 [r]Nu 1:7
7:18 [s]Nu 1:8
7:20 [t]ver 14
7:24 [u]Nu 1:9
7:30 [v]Nu 1:5
7:36 [w]Nu 1:6
7:42 [x]Nu 1:14
7:48 [y]Nu 1:10

filled with incense;[m] 15 one young bull,[n] one ram and one male lamb a year old for a burnt offering;[o] 16 one male goat for a sin offering[a];[p] 17 and two oxen, five rams, five male goats and five
male lambs a year old to be sacrificed as a fellowship offering.[q] This was the offering of Nahshon
son of Amminadab.[r]

18 On the second day Nethanel son of Zuar,[s] the leader of Issachar, brought his offering.
19 The offering he brought was one silver plate weighing a hundred and thirty shekels and one silver sprinkling bowl weighing seventy shekels, both according to the sanctuary shekel, each filled
with the finest flour mixed with olive oil as a grain offering; 20 one gold dish[t] weighing ten shekels,
filled with incense; 21 one young bull, one ram and one male lamb a year old for a burnt offering;
22 one male goat for a sin offering; 23 and two oxen, five rams, five male goats and five male lambs
a year old to be sacrificed as a fellowship offering. This was the offering of Nethanel son of Zuar.

24 On the third day, Eliab son of Helon,[u] the leader of the people of Zebulun, brought his offering.
25 His offering was one silver plate weighing a hundred and thirty shekels and one silver sprinkling bowl weighing seventy shekels, both according to the sanctuary shekel, each filled with the
finest flour mixed with olive oil as a grain offering; 26 one gold dish weighing ten shekels, filled
with incense; 27 one young bull, one ram and one male lamb a year old for a burnt offering; 28 one
male goat for a sin offering; 29 and two oxen, five rams, five male goats and five male lambs a year
old to be sacrificed as a fellowship offering. This was the offering of Eliab son of Helon.

30 On the fourth day Elizur son of Shedeur,[v] the leader of the people of Reuben, brought his offering.
31 His offering was one silver plate weighing a hundred and thirty shekels and one silver sprinkling bowl weighing seventy shekels, both according to the sanctuary shekel, each filled with the
finest flour mixed with olive oil as a grain offering; 32 one gold dish weighing ten shekels, filled
with incense; 33 one young bull, one ram and one male lamb a year old for a burnt offering; 34 one
male goat for a sin offering; 35 and two oxen, five rams, five male goats and five male lambs a
year old to be sacrificed as a fellowship offering. This was the offering of Elizur son of Shedeur.

36 On the fifth day Shelumiel son of Zurishaddai,[w] the leader of the people of Simeon, brought his
offering.
37 His offering was one silver plate weighing a hundred and thirty shekels and one silver sprinkling bowl weighing seventy shekels, both according to the sanctuary shekel, each filled with the
finest flour mixed with olive oil as a grain offering; 38 one gold dish weighing ten shekels, filled
with incense; 39 one young bull, one ram and one male lamb a year old for a burnt offering; 40 one
male goat for a sin offering; 41 and two oxen, five rams, five male goats and five male lambs a year
old to be sacrificed as a fellowship offering. This was the offering of Shelumiel son of Zurishaddai.

42 On the sixth day Eliasaph son of Deuel,[x] the leader of the people of Gad, brought his offering.
43 His offering was one silver plate weighing a hundred and thirty shekels and one silver sprinkling bowl weighing seventy shekels, both according to the sanctuary shekel, each filled with the
finest flour mixed with olive oil as a grain offering; 44 one gold dish weighing ten shekels, filled
with incense; 45 one young bull, one ram and one male lamb a year old for a burnt offering; 46 one
male goat for a sin offering; 47 and two oxen, five rams, five male goats and five male lambs a
year old to be sacrificed as a fellowship offering. This was the offering of Eliasaph son of Deuel.

48 On the seventh day Elishama son of Ammihud,[y] the leader of the people of Ephraim, brought his
offering.
49 His offering was one silver plate weighing a hundred and thirty shekels and one silver sprinkling bowl weighing seventy shekels, both according to the sanctuary shekel, each filled with the
finest flour mixed with olive oil as a grain offering; 50 one gold dish weighing ten shekels, filled

[a] 16 Or *purification offering*; also elsewhere in this chapter

7:15–16 burnt offering ... sin offering. To atone for sin and impurity (see notes on Lev 1:3–17; 4:1—5:13).

7:17 fellowship offering. To celebrate their covenant fellowship with the Lord (see notes on Lev 3). The large number of animals was necessary to provide enough meat for the tribe (or its representatives) to eat.

with incense; 51 one young bull, one ram and one male lamb a year old for a burnt offering; 52 one
male goat for a sin offering; 53 and two oxen, five rams, five male goats and five male lambs a year
old to be sacrificed as a fellowship offering. This was the offering of Elishama son of Ammihud.[z]

54 On the eighth day Gamaliel son of Pedahzur,[a] the leader of the people of Manasseh, brought his
offering.

55 His offering was one silver plate weighing a hundred and thirty shekels and one silver sprinkling bowl weighing seventy shekels, both according to the sanctuary shekel, each filled with the
finest flour mixed with olive oil as a grain offering; 56 one gold dish weighing ten shekels, filled
with incense; 57 one young bull, one ram and one male lamb a year old for a burnt offering; 58 one
male goat for a sin offering; 59 and two oxen, five rams, five male goats and five male lambs a year
old to be sacrificed as a fellowship offering. This was the offering of Gamaliel son of Pedahzur.

60 On the ninth day Abidan son of Gideoni,[b] the leader of the people of Benjamin, brought his offering.

61 His offering was one silver plate weighing a hundred and thirty shekels and one silver sprinkling bowl weighing seventy shekels, both according to the sanctuary shekel, each filled with the
finest flour mixed with olive oil as a grain offering; 62 one gold dish weighing ten shekels, filled
with incense; 63 one young bull, one ram and one male lamb a year old for a burnt offering; 64 one
male goat for a sin offering; 65 and two oxen, five rams, five male goats and five male lambs a
year old to be sacrificed as a fellowship offering. This was the offering of Abidan son of Gideoni.

66 On the tenth day Ahiezer son of Ammishaddai,[c] the leader of the people of Dan, brought his offering.

67 His offering was one silver plate weighing a hundred and thirty shekels and one silver sprinkling bowl weighing seventy shekels, both according to the sanctuary shekel, each filled with the
finest flour mixed with olive oil as a grain offering; 68 one gold dish weighing ten shekels, filled
with incense; 69 one young bull, one ram and one male lamb a year old for a burnt offering; 70 one
male goat for a sin offering; 71 and two oxen, five rams, five male goats and five male lambs a year
old to be sacrificed as a fellowship offering. This was the offering of Ahiezer son of Ammishaddai.

72 On the eleventh day Pagiel son of Okran,[d] the leader of the people of Asher, brought his offering.

73 His offering was one silver plate weighing a hundred and thirty shekels and one silver sprinkling bowl weighing seventy shekels, both according to the sanctuary shekel, each filled with the
finest flour mixed with olive oil as a grain offering; 74 one gold dish weighing ten shekels, filled
with incense; 75 one young bull, one ram and one male lamb a year old for a burnt offering; 76 one
male goat for a sin offering; 77 and two oxen, five rams, five male goats and five male lambs a
year old to be sacrificed as a fellowship offering. This was the offering of Pagiel son of Okran.

78 On the twelfth day Ahira son of Enan,[e] the leader of the people of Naphtali, brought his offering.

79 His offering was one silver plate weighing a hundred and thirty shekels and one silver sprinkling bowl weighing seventy shekels, both according to the sanctuary shekel, each filled with the
finest flour mixed with olive oil as a grain offering; 80 one gold dish weighing ten shekels, filled
with incense; 81 one young bull, one ram and one male lamb a year old for a burnt offering; 82 one
male goat for a sin offering; 83 and two oxen, five rams, five male goats and five male lambs a year
old to be sacrificed as a fellowship offering. This was the offering of Ahira son of Enan.

84 These were the offerings of the Israelite leaders for the
dedication of the altar when it was anointed:[f] twelve silver plates, twelve silver sprinkling bowls[g] and twelve gold
dishes.[h] 85 Each silver plate weighed a hundred and thirty
shekels, and each sprinkling bowl seventy shekels. Altogether, the silver dishes weighed two thousand four hundred
shekels,[a] according to the sanctuary shekel. 86 The twelve
gold dishes filled with incense weighed ten shekels each, according to the sanctuary shekel. Altogether, the gold dishes

7:53 [z] Nu 1:10
7:54 [a] Nu 1:10; 2:20
7:60 [b] Nu 1:11
7:66 [c] Nu 1:12; 2:25
7:72 [d] Nu 1:13
7:78 [e] Nu 1:15; 2:29
7:84 [f] ver 1,10 [g] Nu 4:14 [h] ver 14

DISHES PRESENTED

DISH (SEE NUM 7:84 – 86)	BIBLICAL WEIGHT	APPROXIMATE MODERN EQUIVALENT
12 silver plates	1,560 shekels	39 pounds (17.9 kilograms)
12 silver sprinkling bowls	840 shekels	21 pounds (9.7 kilograms)
12 gold dishes	120 shekels	3 pounds (1.4 kilograms)

a 85 That is, about 60 pounds or about 28 kilograms

7:88 [i]ver 1,10
7:89 [j]Ex 25:21,22; 33:9,11 [k]Ps 80:1; 99:1
8:2 [l]Ex 25:37; Lev 24:2,4
8:4 [m]Ex 25:18,36; 25:18 [n]Ex 25:9
8:6 [o]Lev 22:2; Isa 1:16; 52:11
8:7 [p]Nu 19:9,17 [q]Lev 14:9; Dt 21:12 [r]Lev 14:8
8:8 [s]Lev 2:1; Nu 15:8-10
8:9 [t]Ex 40:12 [u]Lev 8:3
8:10 [v]Ac 6:6
8:11 [w]Lev 7:30
8:12 [x]Ex 29:10 [y]Ex 29:36
8:14 [z]Nu 3:12
8:15 [a]Ex 29:24

weighed a hundred and twenty shekels.[a] 87 The total number of animals for the burnt offering came to twelve young bulls, twelve rams and twelve male lambs a year old, together with their grain offering. Twelve male goats were used for the sin offering. 88 The total number of animals for the sacrifice of the fellowship offering came to twenty-four oxen, sixty rams, sixty male goats and sixty male lambs a year old. These were the offerings for the dedication of the altar after it was anointed.[i]

ANIMALS OFFERED

OFFERING	ANIMALS (NUM 7:87–88)
burnt	12 young bulls, 12 rams, 12 year-old male lambs
sin	12 male goats
fellowship	24 oxen, 60 rams, 60 male goats, 60 year-old male lambs

89 When Moses entered the tent of meeting to speak with the LORD,[j] he heard the voice speaking to him from between the two cherubim above the atonement cover[k] on the ark of the covenant law. In this way the LORD spoke to him.

Setting Up the Lamps

8 The LORD said to Moses, 2 "Speak to Aaron and say to him, 'When you set up the lamps, see that all seven light up the area in front of the lampstand.[l]' "

3 Aaron did so; he set up the lamps so that they faced forward on the lampstand, just as the LORD commanded Moses. 4 This is how the lampstand was made: It was made of hammered gold[m]—from its base to its blossoms. The lampstand was made exactly like the pattern[n] the LORD had shown Moses.

The Setting Apart of the Levites

5 The LORD said to Moses: 6 "Take the Levites from among all the Israelites and make them ceremonially clean.[o] 7 To purify them, do this: Sprinkle the water of cleansing[p] on them; then have them shave their whole bodies[q] and wash their clothes.[r] And so they will purify themselves. 8 Have them take a young bull with its grain offering of the finest flour mixed with olive oil;[s] then you are to take a second young bull for a sin offering.[b] 9 Bring the Levites to the front of the tent of meeting[t] and assemble the whole Israelite community.[u] 10 You are to bring the Levites before the LORD, and the Israelites are to lay their hands on them.[v] 11 Aaron is to present the Levites before the LORD as a wave offering[w] from the Israelites, so that they may be ready to do the work of the LORD.

12 "Then the Levites are to lay their hands on the heads of the bulls,[x] using one for a sin offering to the LORD and the other for a burnt offering, to make atonement[y] for the Levites. 13 Have the Levites stand in front of Aaron and his sons and then present them as a wave offering to the LORD. 14 In this way you are to set the Levites apart from the other Israelites, and the Levites will be mine.[z]

15 "After you have purified the Levites and presented them as a wave offering,[a] they are to come to do their work at the tent of meeting. 16 They are the Israelites who are to be given wholly to me. I have

[a] *86* That is, about 3 pounds or about 1.4 kilograms [b] *8* Or *purification offering*; also in verse 12

7:89 The Lord indeed came to dwell in this newly built and consecrated tabernacle (cf. Exod 25:22). **atonement cover.** See note on Exod 25:17. **ark.** See note on Exod 25:10–22.

8:1–4 *Setting Up the Lamps.* Describes what Aaron did when the tabernacle was set up (ch. 7 describes what the tribes did).

8:2 area in front. The entire Holy Place (see "Tabernacle Floor Plan," p. 192). **lampstand.** See Exod 25:31–40 and note. It was to be kept burning continually (Exod 27:20–21), probably signifying the Lord's continual presence among his people (when the lights are on, someone is home). Jesus is the ultimate expression of this presence (John 1:14; 14:9), and he assures his disciples he is always with them (Matt 28:20; cf. Rev 1:12—2:1).

8:4 Emphasizes obedience (see note on 1:54; cf. Exod 25:31–40).

8:5–26 *The Setting Apart of the Levites.* Describes how to set the Levites apart to ceremonial purity, so they could take part in tabernacle service (see 3:5–10 and note; for ceremonial purity and impurity, see Introduction to Leviticus: Major Theological Themes [Holiness and Purity]). This prepares the Levites for moving the tabernacle (10:11). The ceremony occurs in three main stages: (1) an initial purification through sprinkling, shaving, and washing (v. 7); (2) presenting the Levites to the Lord on the Israelites' behalf (vv. 9–11; vv. 13–14 probably summarize the same event); and (3) a final purification (vv. 12,21). The section concludes by discussing age restrictions for the Levites working at the tabernacle (vv. 23–26).

8:7 Sprinkle. Often associated with cleansing or consecrating (19:19; Lev 8:11,30; 16:14–19). **water of cleansing.** Likely the water described in 19:1–10. **shave.** Closely scraping the skin symbolizes a very complete cleansing. **wash their clothes.** Symbolizes cleansing.

8:10 the Israelites. Perhaps Israelite leaders in particular. **lay their hands on them.** In this way identifying the Levites as their substitutes (cf. vv. 16,18).

8:11 wave offering. Aaron may have simply waved his hands over them to indicate they were dedicated to the Lord (see 6:20 and note).

8:16–19 The rationale for this ceremony (see notes on 3:5–10,11–13).

taken them as my own in place of the firstborn, the first male offspring[b] from every Israelite woman.
17 Every firstborn male in Israel, whether human or animal,[c] is mine. When I struck down all the firstborn in Egypt, I set them apart for myself.[d] 18 And I have taken the Levites in place of all the firstborn
sons in Israel.[e] 19 From among all the Israelites, I have given the Levites as gifts to Aaron and his sons[f]
to do the work at the tent of meeting on behalf of the Israelites[g] and to make atonement for them[h] so
that no plague will strike the Israelites when they go near the sanctuary."

20 Moses, Aaron and the whole Israelite community did with the Levites just as the LORD commanded
Moses. 21 The Levites purified themselves and washed their clothes.[i] Then Aaron presented them as a
wave offering before the LORD and made atonement for them to purify them.[j] 22 After that, the Levites
came to do their work at the tent of meeting under the supervision of Aaron and his sons. They did with
the Levites just as the LORD commanded Moses.

23 The LORD said to Moses, 24 "This applies to the Levites: Men twenty-five years old or more[k] shall
come to take part in the work at the tent of meeting,[l] 25 but at the age of fifty, they must retire from
their regular service and work no longer. 26 They may assist their brothers in performing their duties
at the tent of meeting, but they themselves must not do the work. This, then, is how you are to assign
the responsibilities of the Levites."

8:16 [b] Nu 3:12
8:17 [c] Ex 4:23 [d] Ex 13:2; Lk 2:23
8:18 [e] Nu 3:12
8:19 [f] Nu 3:9 [g] Nu 1:53 [h] Nu 16:46
8:21 [i] ver 7 [j] ver 12
8:24 [k] 1Ch 23:3 [l] Ex 38:21; Nu 4:3
9:1 [m] Ex 40:2 [n] Nu 1:1
9:3 [o] Ex 12:2-11,43-49; Lev 23:5-8; Dt 16:1-8
9:5 [p] Ex 12:1-13; Jos 5:10
9:6 [q] Lev 5:3 [r] Ex 18:15; Nu 27:2
9:8 [s] Ex 18:15; Nu 27:5, 21; Ps 85:8
9:10 [t] 2Ch 30:2
9:11 [u] Ex 12:8
9:12 [v] Ex 12:10,43 [w] Ex 12:46; Jn 19:36*

The Passover

9 The LORD spoke to Moses in the Desert of Sinai in the first month[m] of the second year after they
came out of Egypt.[n] He said, 2 "Have the Israelites celebrate the Passover at the appointed time.
3 Celebrate it at the appointed time, at twilight on the fourteenth day of this month, in accordance with
all its rules and regulations.[o]"

4 So Moses told the Israelites to celebrate the Passover, 5 and they did so in the Desert of Sinai at
twilight on the fourteenth day of the first month.[p] The Israelites did everything just as the LORD commanded Moses.

6 But some of them could not celebrate the Passover on that day because they were ceremonially
unclean[q] on account of a dead body. So they came to Moses and Aaron[r] that same day 7 and said to
Moses, "We have become unclean because of a dead body, but why should we be kept from presenting
the LORD's offering with the other Israelites at the appointed time?"

8 Moses answered them, "Wait until I find out what the LORD commands concerning you."[s]

9 Then the LORD said to Moses, 10 "Tell the Israelites: 'When any of you or your descendants are unclean because of a dead body or are away on a journey, they are still to celebrate[t] the LORD's Passover,
11 but they are to do it on the fourteenth day of the second month at twilight. They are to eat the lamb,
together with unleavened bread and bitter herbs.[u] 12 They must not leave any of it till morning[v] or
break any of its bones.[w] When they celebrate the Passover, they must follow all the regulations. 13 But
if anyone who is ceremonially clean and not on a journey fails to celebrate the Passover, they must be

8:19 make atonement for them. By serving at the tabernacle on the Israelites' behalf and thus rescuing them from defiling the Lord's holy property and thereby experiencing his wrath (see note on 1:53). **plague.** See note on 16:46.

8:20–22 Emphasizes obedience (see note on 1:54).

8:24 twenty-five. In ch. 4, which records events that happen after events in ch. 8 (see note on 7:1—9:14), the age is 30 (4:3,23,30). Why was the age raised? Perhaps (1) it was not raised but a five-year apprenticeship began at age 25 or (2) it was raised in response to the actions of Nadab and Abihu (Lev 10:1–3) to emphasize the maturity needed when handling the holy things. **work at the tent of meeting.** Possibly the heavy work of tearing down and setting up the tent.

8:26 duties at the tent of meeting. Possibly less heavy work (see note on v. 24) done at the tent when it was set up.

9:1–14 *The Passover.* For details on the Passover, see Exod 12:1–11,43–50 and notes. This law fits here chronologically: Num 7:1 mentions the setting up of the tabernacle, which happened on the first day of the first month (Exod 40:2); the Passover was to be celebrated on the fourteenth day of that same month (9:3, cf. Exod 12:2,6). This was the second Passover, held here at Sinai one year after the first Passover was held in Egypt (Exod 12). The Passover was a time for the Israelites to remember how the Lord spared them from judgment and brought them out of the land of slavery (Exod 12:25–27,42). The ultimate Passover sacrifice is Jesus (1 Cor 5:7), whose death delivers us from the Lord's judgment (1 Thess 1:10) and brings us out of sin's slavery and into adoption as God's children (John 1:12; Eph 1:5; cf. Exod 4:22). See "Sacrifice," p. 2656.

9:1–3 first month ... fourteenth day. The Passover's date (cf. Exod 12:2,6).

9:5 Emphasizes the Israelites' obedience (see note on 1:54).

9:6–12 Two practical issues might cause someone to miss the Passover: being ceremonially unclean (in which case they could not eat sacrificial meat [Lev 7:20–21]) or being away on a journey.

9:6 on account of a dead body. See 19:11.

9:7 Israelites longed to be with their covenant family when they were celebrating the Lord's mighty acts of deliverance.

9:11–12 See note on Exod 12:46.

9:13 fails to celebrate. Refusing to eat the Passover was equal to denying what it celebrated: the Lord's salvation and deliverance. Jesus

9:13 [x]Ge 17:14; Ex 12:15
9:14 [y]Ex 12:48,49
9:15 [z]Ex 40:34 [a]Ex 13:21
9:17 [b]Ex 40:36-38; Nu 10:11,12; 1Co 10:1
10:2 [c]Ne 12:35; Ps 47:5 [d]Jer 4:5,19; 6:1; Hos 5:8; Joel 2:1,15; Am 3:6
10:4 [e]Ex 18:21; Nu 1:16; 7:2
10:5 [f]ver 14
10:6 [g]ver 18
10:7 [h]Eze 33:3; Joel 2:1 [i]1Co 14:8
10:8 [j]Nu 31:6
10:9 [k]Jdg 2:18; 6:9; 1Sa 10:18; Ps 106:42 [l]Ge 8:1

cut off from their people[x] for not presenting the LORD's offering at the appointed time. They will bear
the consequences of their sin.
14“ ‘A foreigner[y] residing among you is also to celebrate the LORD's Passover in accordance with its
rules and regulations. You must have the same regulations for both the foreigner and the native-born.’ ”

The Cloud Above the Tabernacle

15On the day the tabernacle, the tent of the covenant law, was set up, the cloud[z] covered it. From
evening till morning the cloud above the tabernacle looked like fire.[a] 16That is how it continued to be;
the cloud covered it, and at night it looked like fire. 17Whenever the cloud lifted from above the tent,
the Israelites set out; wherever the cloud settled, the Israelites encamped.[b] 18At the LORD's command the
Israelites set out, and at his command they encamped. As long as the cloud stayed over the tabernacle,
they remained in camp. 19When the cloud remained over the tabernacle a long time, the Israelites
obeyed the LORD's order and did not set out. 20Sometimes the cloud was over the tabernacle only a
few days; at the LORD's command they would encamp, and then at his command they would set out.
21Sometimes the cloud stayed only from evening till morning, and when it lifted in the morning, they
set out. Whether by day or by night, whenever the cloud lifted, they set out. 22Whether the cloud stayed
over the tabernacle for two days or a month or a year, the Israelites would remain in camp and not set
out; but when it lifted, they would set out. 23At the LORD's command they encamped, and at the LORD's
command they set out. They obeyed the LORD's order, in accordance with his command through Moses.

The Silver Trumpets

10 The LORD said to Moses: 2“Make two trumpets[c] of hammered silver, and use them for calling
the community[d] together and for having the camps set out. 3When both are sounded, the whole
community is to assemble before you at the entrance to the tent of meeting. 4If only one is sounded,
the leaders[e] — the heads of the clans of Israel — are to assemble before you. 5When a trumpet blast is
sounded, the tribes camping on the east are to set out.[f] 6At the sounding of a second blast, the camps
on the south are to set out.[g] The blast will be the signal for setting out. 7To gather the assembly, blow
the trumpets,[h] but not with the signal for setting out.[i]
8“The sons of Aaron, the priests, are to blow the trumpets. This is to be a lasting ordinance for you
and the generations to come.[j] 9When you go into battle in your own land against an enemy who is
oppressing you,[k] sound a blast on the trumpets. Then you will be remembered[l] by the LORD your God

instituted communion as the new covenant meal celebrating his salvation (Mark 14:12–26), and the NT emphasizes the importance of properly partaking in it (1 Cor 11:23–30). **cut off.** Removed from the covenant community, either through exile or death (see note on Lev 7:20,21).

9:14 Non-Israelites wanting to celebrate the Passover had to apply the covenant sign (circumcision) to all the males in their household (Exod 12:48). This showed they were embracing the Lord's covenant. The presence of this requirement also shows that the blessings God promised Abraham and Israel were indeed to spread to “all peoples on earth” (Gen 12:3).

9:15—10:10 *Transition: Getting Ready to Depart for the Promised Land.* This addresses two matters related to Israel's departure from Sinai: the Lord's guidance in their travels by means of the cloud (9:15–23) and the silver trumpets that will help them break camp in an orderly way (10:1–10).

9:15–23 *The Cloud Above the Tabernacle.* No person could see the Lord directly and live (Exod 33:20), so God concealed his glorious presence in a cloud whenever he descended among his people. The cloud first appeared as the Lord led his people out of Egypt (Exod 13:21) and appeared again as he descended on Mount Sinai to give Moses the covenant law (Exod 19:16—31:18). After the tabernacle was set up, the Lord descended there in the cloud to show that he was now dwelling among his covenant people (Exod 40:34–38). The tabernacle was now like a portable Mount Sinai since the Lord gave his law there (Lev 1:1, “tent of meeting”), while the cloud that covered it was the means by which he once again guided Israel in the wilderness. The Israelites could march forward with bold confidence, knowing their covenant Lord dwelled among them. The passage before us is fairly repetitious, which gives it a poetic feel and, most important, emphasizes again that the people are obeying the Lord (see note on 1:54). The NT alludes to the cloud passages when it describes Jesus as the one who “made his dwelling among us” and showed us his “glory” (John 1:14). Jesus was the ultimate expression of the Lord among us.

10:1–10 *The Silver Trumpets.* These served two functions. First, they directed the Israelites in the camp (vv. 1–7). Trumpet signals were a common way to communicate with large groups of people. Some signals called the whole community or the heads of the clans of Israel to the tent of meeting (vv. 3–4), perhaps to receive instructions (1:16) or to participate in worship or special services (8:9). Other signals indicated the order in which the tribes were to set out (vv. 5–6). Second, the trumpets were blown at times of battle (v. 9) as well as over the Israelites' offerings at various festivals (v. 10) as a way of offering a musical prayer to the Lord that requested his favor and care. The priests, the Lord's representatives, blew the trumpets (v. 8), indicating that the Lord was ultimately the one leading his people.

10:2 trumpets. No description is given, though an Egyptian trumpet from this general time period has been found; it was a slender tube, almost two feet (0.6 meters) in length, with a flared end.

10:9 remembered. The language of remembrance describes the Lord's favor and care toward his people (Gen 30:22; Ps 20:2–3; see note on Lev 26:42).

and rescued from your enemies.[m] 10Also at your times of rejoicing — your appointed festivals and New
Moon feasts[n] — you are to sound the trumpets[o] over your burnt offerings and fellowship offerings, and
they will be a memorial for you before your God. I am the LORD your God."

The Israelites Leave Sinai

11On the twentieth day of the second month of the second year,[p] the cloud lifted[q] from above the
tabernacle of the covenant law. 12Then the Israelites set out from the Desert of Sinai and traveled from
place to place until the cloud came to rest in the Desert of Paran. 13They set out, this first time, at the
LORD's command through Moses.[r]

14The divisions of the camp of Judah went first, under their standard.[s] Nahshon son of Amminadab[t]
was in command. 15Nethanel son of Zuar was over the division of the tribe of Issachar, 16and Eliab son
of Helon was over the division of the tribe of Zebulun. 17Then the tabernacle was taken down, and the
Gershonites and Merarites, who carried it, set out.[u]

18The divisions of the camp of Reuben went next, under their standard.[v] Elizur son of Shedeur was in
command. 19Shelumiel son of Zurishaddai was over the division of the tribe of Simeon, 20and Eliasaph
son of Deuel was over the division of the tribe of Gad. 21Then the Kohathites set out, carrying the holy
things.[w] The tabernacle was to be set up before they arrived.[x]

22The divisions of the camp of Ephraim[y] went next, under their standard. Elishama son of Ammihud
was in command. 23Gamaliel son of Pedahzur was over the division of the tribe of Manasseh, 24and
Abidan son of Gideoni was over the division of the tribe of Benjamin.

25Finally, as the rear guard[z] for all the units, the divisions of the camp of Dan set out under their
standard. Ahiezer son of Ammishaddai was in command. 26Pagiel son of Okran was over the division
of the tribe of Asher, 27and Ahira son of Enan was over the division of the tribe of Naphtali. 28This was
the order of march for the Israelite divisions as they set out.

29Now Moses said to Hobab[a] son of Reuel[b] the Midianite, Moses' father-in-law,[c] "We are setting out
for the place about which the LORD said, 'I will give it to you.'[d] Come with us and we will treat you well,
for the LORD has promised good things to Israel."

30He answered, "No, I will not go;[e] I am going back to my own land and my own people."

31But Moses said, "Please do not leave us. You know where we should camp in the wilderness, and you
can be our eyes.[f] 32If you come with us, we will share with you[g] whatever good things the LORD gives us.[h]"

33So they set out[i] from the mountain of the LORD and traveled for three days. The ark of the covenant
of the LORD[j] went before them during those three days to find them a place to rest. 34The cloud of the
LORD was over them by day when they set out from the camp.[k]

35Whenever the ark set out, Moses said,

"Rise up, LORD!
May your enemies be scattered;[l]
may your foes flee before you.[m]"

10:9 [m] Ps 106:4
10:10 [n] Ps 81:3 [o] Lev 23:24
10:11 [p] Ex 40:17 [q] Nu 9:17
10:13 [r] Dt 1:6
10:14 [s] Nu 2:3-9 [t] Nu 1:7
10:17 [u] Nu 4:21-32
10:18 [v] Nu 2:10-16
10:21 [w] Nu 4:20 [x] ver 17
10:22 [y] Nu 2:24
10:25 [z] Nu 2:31; Jos 6:9
10:29 [a] Jdg 4:11 [b] Ex 2:18 [c] Ex 3:1 [d] Ge 12:7
10:30 [e] Mt 21:29
10:31 [f] Job 29:15
10:32 [g] Dt 10:18 [h] Ps 22:27-31; 67:5-7
10:33 [i] ver 12; Dt 1:33 [j] Jos 3:3
10:34 [k] Nu 9:15-23
10:35 [l] Ps 68:1 [m] Dt 7:10; 32:41; Ps 68:2; Isa 17:12-14

10:11 — 25:18 *Rebellion Against the Lord and the Death of the Exodus Generation.* After spending almost a year at Mount Sinai (see note on 10:11), the Israelites now depart for the promised land. Disaster quickly strikes. The Israelites are faithful to the Lord in 1:1 — 10:10, but they are unfaithful to him in 10:11 — 25:18 (see note on 1:1 — 25:18). In particular, their refusing to enter the promised land results in a punishment that fits the crime: they will die before reaching it (ch. 14). Their disobedience stands as a strong warning to believers of the danger of hardening their hearts to the Lord and turning away from him (see note on 14:1 – 45; cf. Ps 95:7 – 11; 1 Cor 10:1 – 13; Heb 3:6 — 4:13). By the end of this section, the exodus generation has died and the next generation is camped on the plains of Moab, opposite Jericho, ready to march into the land (26:1 – 4).

10:11 – 36 *The Israelites Leave Sinai.* They march toward the promised land (see map, p. 240). They begin their journey obediently (10:11 – 36) but soon show disbelief (11:1 – 20,31 – 35; 12:1 – 16).

10:11 second month. Sometime in April or May. The Israelites depart 10 months and 19 days after arriving at Sinai (see "The Israelites' Location: Where and How Long," p. 246).

10:12 Summarizes the journey that 10:11 — 12:16 describes (cf. 12:16).

10:13 – 28 The marching order follows the pattern set forth in ch. 2 (see "The Camp of the Tribes of Israel," p. 249). Among the Levites, the Gershonites and Merarites (who carry the tabernacle's structural elements) set out first so they can set up the tabernacle before the Kohathites arrive with the objects that go inside it (vv. 17 – 21).

10:29 Hobab. Moses' brother-in-law. **Reuel.** Moses' father-in-law Jethro (see note on Exod 3:1). **promised.** Moses' deep faith in the Lord's promises (see also v. 32) sharply contrasts with the Israelites' actions in chs. 11 – 12; 14.

10:31 Hobab was familiar with the desert and could provide practical advice related to camping in the best spot (e.g., finding pasture or springs near the camping site). He apparently agreed to go (cf. Judg 1:16).

10:33 While the rest of the tabernacle furniture was in the middle of the march (v. 21), the Lord's ark led the march. The Israelites' covenant King was leading them and would fight for them.

10:35 Rise up, LORD! It is he who fights for Israel (Ps 68).

10:36 [n]Isa 63:17 [o]Dt 1:10
11:1 [p]Lev 10:2
11:2 [q]Nu 21:7
11:3 [r]Dt 9:22
11:4 [s]Ex 12:38 [t]Ps 78:18; 1Co 10:6
11:5 [u]Ex 16:3
11:7 [v]Ex 16:31 [w]Ge 2:12
11:9 [x]Ex 16:13
11:11 [y]Ex 5:22
11:12 [z]Isa 40:11; 49:23 [a]Ex 13:5
11:13 [b]Jn 6:5-9
11:14 [c]Ex 18:18
11:15 [d]Ex 32:32; 1Ki 19:4; Jnh 4:3
11:17 [e]ver 25,29; 1Sa 10:6; 2Ki 2:9,15; Joel 2:28 [f]Ex 18:18
11:18 [g]Ex 19:10

36 Whenever it came to rest, he said,

> "Return,[n] LORD,
> to the countless thousands of Israel.[o]"

Fire From the LORD

11 Now the people complained about their hardships in the hearing of the LORD, and when he heard them his anger was aroused. Then fire from the LORD burned among them[p] and consumed some of the outskirts of the camp. 2 When the people cried out to Moses, he prayed to the LORD[q] and the fire died down. 3 So that place was called Taberah,[a][r] because fire from the LORD had burned among them.

Quail From the LORD

4 The rabble with them began to crave other food,[s] and again the Israelites started wailing[t] and said, "If only we had meat to eat! 5 We remember the fish we ate in Egypt at no cost—also the cucumbers, melons, leeks, onions and garlic.[u] 6 But now we have lost our appetite; we never see anything but this manna!"

7 The manna was like coriander seed[v] and looked like resin.[w] 8 The people went around gathering it, and then ground it in a hand mill or crushed it in a mortar. They cooked it in a pot or made it into loaves. And it tasted like something made with olive oil. 9 When the dew[x] settled on the camp at night, the manna also came down.

10 Moses heard the people of every family wailing at the entrance to their tents. The LORD became exceedingly angry, and Moses was troubled. 11 He asked the LORD, "Why have you brought this trouble on your servant? What have I done to displease you that you put the burden of all these people on me?[y] 12 Did I conceive all these people? Did I give them birth? Why do you tell me to carry them in my arms, as a nurse carries an infant,[z] to the land you promised on oath to their ancestors?[a] 13 Where can I get meat for all these people?[b] They keep wailing to me, 'Give us meat to eat!' 14 I cannot carry all these people by myself; the burden is too heavy for me.[c] 15 If this is how you are going to treat me, please go ahead and kill me[d]—if I have found favor in your eyes—and do not let me face my own ruin."

16 The LORD said to Moses: "Bring me seventy of Israel's elders who are known to you as leaders and officials among the people. Have them come to the tent of meeting, that they may stand there with you. 17 I will come down and speak with you there, and I will take some of the power of the Spirit that is on you and put it on them.[e] They will share the burden of the people with you so that you will not have to carry it alone.[f]

18 "Tell the people: 'Consecrate yourselves[g] in preparation for tomorrow, when you will eat meat.

[a] 3 *Taberah* means *burning*.

10:36 countless thousands. The Lord's covenant promises to Abraham have begun to be fulfilled (Gen 22:17; cf. Gen 24:60).

11:1—12:16 *Initial Acts of Unbelief.* The three stories in this section introduce the themes of 11:1—25:18: the Israelites' unbelief and rebellion.

11:1–3 *Fire From the Lord.* Though short, this section emphasizes the dangers of rebelling against the Lord.

11:1 complained. They did not trust the Lord for guidance and provision (Ps 78:21–22). **fire from the LORD.** Elsewhere, a sign of his judgment (16:35; Lev 10:2). **outskirts.** But not within the camp—a merciful warning to an unfaithful people.

11:2 Moses, the people's mediator, frequently appeases the Lord's just wrath against the people (14:13–20; 16:22; Exod 32:11–14). Jesus acts as a far greater mediator on our behalf (1 Tim 2:5–6).

11:3 Taberah. See NIV text note.

11:4–35 *Quail From the Lord.* There is a contrast here between the Israelites' sinful complaint about having no food and Moses' earnest request that the Lord help him provide meat and bear the burden of this people.

11:4–9 The Lord previously provided quail for the people (Exod 16:3,12–13). Instead of asking for more in faith, they complained about the Lord's current provision (manna) and implied that life in Egypt was far better (vv. 4–6). This blasphemously rejected the Lord and his deliverance (v. 20; cf. Pss 78:20b–22; 106:13–15).

11:4 rabble. See note on Exod 12:38. **again.** See vv. 1–3 and perhaps also Exod 16:3.

11:5 fish ... cucumbers ... garlic. Rich variety when compared to the manna (v. 6). What they do not mention is the severe hardship that went along with these things (Exod 2:23).

11:7 manna. First described in Exod 16:13–15,31, it was a miraculous and wonderful provision from God. Jesus applied this image to himself: "it is my Father who gives you the true bread from heaven ... I am the bread of life ... Whoever eats this bread will live forever" (John 6:32,35,51).

11:8 like something made with olive oil. Thus, rich and tasty (cf. Exod 16:31; Ps 78:24–25).

11:10–15 Moses complains in the face of the hardship he experiences as a leader, but unlike the people, he brings his complaints to the Lord in an earnest plea for mercy and help.

11:16 seventy. The same number (though not necessarily the same elders) represented the people in Exod 24:1.

11:17 I will take some of the power of the Spirit. Just as the Lord had given Moses a special anointing of his Spirit for service, he would do the same for these elders.

11:18–20 In a punishment that fits the crime, the people will come to loathe the very meat they crave.

11:18 Consecrate yourselves. See Exod 19:10–15 and notes. This command implies that the Lord is about to perform a miracle.

The LORD heard you when you wailed,[h] "If only we had meat to eat! We were better off in Egypt!"[i] Now the LORD will give you meat, and you will eat it. 19You will not eat it for just one day, or two days, or five, ten or twenty days, 20but for a whole month—until it comes out of your nostrils and you loathe it[j]—because you have rejected the LORD,[k] who is among you, and have wailed before him, saying, "Why did we ever leave Egypt?" ' "

21But Moses said, "Here I am among six hundred thousand men[l] on foot, and you say, 'I will give them meat to eat for a whole month!' 22Would they have enough if flocks and herds were slaughtered for them? Would they have enough if all the fish in the sea were caught for them?"[m]

23The LORD answered Moses, "Is the LORD's arm too short?[n] Now you will see whether or not what I say will come true for you.[o]"

24So Moses went out and told the people what the LORD had said. He brought together seventy of their elders and had them stand around the tent. 25Then the LORD came down in the cloud[p] and spoke with him,[q] and he took some of the power of the Spirit[r] that was on him and put it on the seventy elders.[s] When the Spirit rested on them, they prophesied[t]—but did not do so again.

26However, two men, whose names were Eldad and Medad, had remained in the camp. They were listed among the elders, but did not go out to the tent. Yet the Spirit also rested on them, and they prophesied in the camp. 27A young man ran and told Moses, "Eldad and Medad are prophesying in the camp."

28Joshua son of Nun, who had been Moses' aide[u] since youth, spoke up and said, "Moses, my lord, stop them!"[v]

29But Moses replied, "Are you jealous for my sake? I wish that all the LORD's people were prophets[w] and that the LORD would put his Spirit on them!" 30Then Moses and the elders of Israel returned to the camp.

31Now a wind went out from the LORD and drove quail[x] in from the sea. It scattered them up to two cubits[a] deep all around the camp, as far as a day's walk in any direction. 32All that day and night and all the next day the people went out and gathered quail. No one gathered less than ten homers.[b] Then they spread them out all around the camp. 33But while the meat was still between their teeth[y] and before it could be consumed, the anger of the LORD burned against the people, and he struck them with a severe plague.[z] 34Therefore the place was named Kibroth Hattaavah,[c][a] because there they buried the people who had craved other food.

35From Kibroth Hattaavah the people traveled to Hazeroth[b] and stayed there.

Miriam and Aaron Oppose Moses

12 Miriam and Aaron began to talk against Moses because of his Cushite wife,[c] for he had married a Cushite. 2"Has the LORD spoken only through Moses?" they asked. "Hasn't he also spoken through us?"[d] And the LORD heard this.[e]

3(Now Moses was a very humble man,[f] more humble than anyone else on the face of the earth.)

a 31 That is, about 3 feet or about 90 centimeters *b 32* That is, possibly about 1 3/4 tons or about 1.6 metric tons *c 34* *Kibroth Hattaavah* means *graves of craving.*

11:18 [h]Ex 16:7 [i]ver 5; Ac 7:39
11:20 [j]Ps 78:29; 106:14, 15 [k]Jos 24:27; 1Sa 10:19
11:21 [l]Ex 12:37
11:22 [m]Mt 15:33
11:23 [n]Isa 50:2; 59:1 [o]Nu 23:19; Eze 12:25; 24:14
11:25 [p]Nu 12:5 [q]ver 17 [r]1Sa 10:6 [s]Ac 2:17 [t]1Sa 10:10
11:28 [u]Ex 33:11; Jos 1:1 [v]Mk 9:38-40
11:29 [w]1Co 14:5
11:31 [x]Ex 16:13; Ps 78:26-28
11:33 [y]Ps 78:30 [z]Ps 106:15
11:34 [a]Dt 9:22
11:35 [b]Nu 33:17
12:1 [c]Ex 2:21
12:2 [d]Nu 16:3 [e]Nu 11:1
12:3 [f]Mt 11:29

11:20 rejected the LORD. See note on vv. 4–9.
11:21–22 Moses is hesitant to announce such an amazing provision of food.
11:23 arm. The very one with which he redeemed Israel in power (cf. Exod 3:20, where the same Hebrew word is translated "hand"). **too short.** Unable to achieve what it is trying to do (cf. Isa 50:2; 59:1). **what I say.** Or "my word" (cf. Isa 55:11).
11:24–25 See vv. 16–17 and notes.
11:25 prophesied. Perhaps by giving ecstatic expression in word or deed, thus showing that the Spirit rested on them (see note on 1 Sam 10:5–6). **did not do so again.** Implying that they did not continue in a prophetic role; their prophesying on this one occasion served to establish them as leaders empowered by the Spirit and enabled to help Moses.
11:26–30 Demonstrates Moses' great humility (cf. 12:3). While Joshua, Moses' aide (Exod 33:11), wanted to guard Moses' prestige, Moses' greatest desire was for all the people to experience this special anointing for the Lord's service. The Lord's greatest leaders always look for ways to spread his glory, not their own (see John 3:22–30).
11:34 Kibroth Hattaavah. See NIV text note.
12:1–16 *Miriam and Aaron Oppose Moses.* This chapter introduces a form of unbelief that is one of the themes of 10:11—25:18: rejecting the leadership structure the Lord set in place (see also chs. 16–17).
12:1 Miriam. Moses' and Aaron's sister (26:59). It is rare to list a woman's name first; this suggests that she was the chief complainer (and thus bore the chief penalty, vv. 10–15). **Cushite wife.** Mentioned only here. Possibly (1) Zipporah from Midian (Exod 2:16–21; Cushan may refer to Midian [Hab 3:7]) or (2) a second wife (Cush refers elsewhere to Sudan, see Gen 10:6 and note). The text does not say why Miriam and Aaron complained about her, though it suggests this was simply an excuse for their real complaint in v. 2.
12:2 A complaint that Moses was selfishly taking the lead. **through us.** Miriam was a prophet (Exod 15:20), and the Lord had elsewhere addressed Aaron directly (see Lev 10:8 and note; 11:1; 13:1).
12:3 humble. Moses was not proud and did not seek his own glory;

12:5 [g]Nu 11:25
12:6 [h]Ge 15:1; 46:2 [i]Ge 31:10; 1Ki 3:5; Heb 1:1
12:7 [j]Jos 1:1-2; Ps 105:26 [k]Heb 3:2,5
12:8 [l]Dt 34:10 [m]Ex 20:4; Ps 17:15
12:9 [n]Ge 17:22
12:10 [o]Ex 4:6; Dt 24:9 [p]2Ki 5:1,27
12:11 [q]2Sa 19:19; 24:10
12:13 [r]Isa 30:26; Jer 17:14
12:14 [s]Dt 25:9; Job 17:6; 30:9-10; Isa 50:6 [t]Lev 13:46; Nu 5:2-3
12:16 [u]Nu 11:35
13:2 [v]Dt 1:22

4 At once the LORD said to Moses, Aaron and Miriam, "Come out to the tent of meeting, all three of
you." So the three of them went out. 5 Then the LORD came down in a pillar of cloud;[g] he stood at the
entrance to the tent and summoned Aaron and Miriam. When the two of them stepped forward, 6 he
said, "Listen to my words:

> "When there is a prophet among you,
> I, the LORD, reveal myself to them in visions,[h]
> I speak to them in dreams.[i]
> 7 But this is not true of my servant Moses;[j]
> he is faithful in all my house.[k]
> 8 With him I speak face to face,
> clearly and not in riddles;[l]
> he sees the form of the LORD.[m]
> Why then were you not afraid
> to speak against my servant Moses?"

9 The anger of the LORD burned against them, and he left them.[n]
10 When the cloud lifted from above the tent, Miriam's skin was leprous[a]—it became as white as
snow.[o] Aaron turned toward her and saw that she had a defiling skin disease,[p] 11 and he said to Moses,
"Please, my lord, I ask you not to hold against us the sin we have so foolishly committed.[q] 12 Do not let
her be like a stillborn infant coming from its mother's womb with its flesh half eaten away."
13 So Moses cried out to the LORD, "Please, God, heal her!"[r]
14 The LORD replied to Moses, "If her father had spit in her face,[s] would she not have been in disgrace for
seven days? Confine her outside the camp[t] for seven days; after that she can be brought back." 15 So Miriam
was confined outside the camp for seven days, and the people did not move on till she was brought back.
16 After that, the people left Hazeroth[u] and encamped in the Desert of Paran.

Exploring Canaan

13 The LORD said to Moses, 2 "Send some men to explore[v] the land of Canaan, which I am giving
to the Israelites. From each ancestral tribe send one of its leaders."
3 So at the LORD's command Moses sent them out from the Desert of Paran. All of them were leaders
of the Israelites. 4 These are their names:

[a] *10* The Hebrew for *leprous* was used for various diseases affecting the skin.

he recognized the Lord's greatness and sought to follow him in dependence and with meekness (cf. Prov 18:12; 22:4; Zeph 2:3). This comment, perhaps made by a final editor (see Introduction: Author), makes clear that Moses had not sought out this leadership position. The complaint of Miriam and Aaron was simply wrong.

12:4–5 The divine King summons them to his tent, where he holds court and issues decrees (cf. 16:16–18), and calls forward the guilty parties (Aaron and Miriam).

12:7 faithful in all my house. Just as a servant may be trusted as a faithful manager of a household (cf. Gen 39:4), so Moses is the trusted and faithful manager of God's household, the people of Israel. Moses is therefore to be heeded (v. 8). With Jesus, it is even more so, since he is not simply a servant "in" the household of the Lord's people but a son "over" it (Heb 3:1–12).

12:8 face to face ... sees the form of the LORD. Moses hears from the Lord directly (cf. Exod 33:11). This does not mean that he sees God completely as he is; that is impossible (Exod 33:20). Moses has special access to, and intimacy with, the Lord (as the elders did in Exod 24:9–11). Others should listen to such a servant as the master's representative. **riddles.** Parables (see, e.g., Ezek 17:2–10). Most prophets hear from the Lord in visions or dreams (v. 6).

12:10 leprous. See NIV text note. **white as snow.** Either because of the skin's color, or because it was flaking off, or both.

12:11 Please, my lord. Aaron's language now acknowledges Moses' chief leadership role.

12:14 spit in her face. Implies that a father might do this when his child wronged him (cf. Deut 25:9), in which case the child would bear disgrace "for seven days," as Miriam does here (v. 15). The point is that Miriam must respect the Lord's leader, Moses.

12:15 brought back. Presumably the Lord healed her (otherwise she could not have returned). She would need to go through the cleansing procedures of Lev 14.

12:16 Desert of Paran. Kadesh in particular (13:26; see map, p. 2868).

13:1—14:45 *Arrival at Kadesh, Full-Scale Rebellion, the Lord's Judgment.* The Israelites should be marching into the promised land with full faith in the Lord. Instead, they continue in disbelief (chs. 11–12) with a full-scale revolt against the Lord. Those who reject the Lord's covenant promises will not enjoy his covenant blessings (cf. 1 Cor 10:1–13; Heb 3:7—4:13).

13:1–25 *Exploring Canaan.* The Lord promised a land "flowing with milk and honey" (Exod 13:5; Lev 20:24): having everything necessary and desirable for abundant living (Deut 8:7–10). He commands Moses to send 12 spies into the land in order to confirm his promise (cf. v. 27) and collect information helpful for waging war.

13:2 land of Canaan. See map, p. 380. Egyptian sources at this time also speak of "the land of Canaan." **I am giving.** A reminder of God's promise (cf. Gen 12:7).

13:3–16 Emphasizes Israel's unity: the spies represent all 12 military tribes. The Levites were not a military tribe (see note on 1:47–53).

from the tribe of Reuben, Shammua son of Zakkur;
[5]from the tribe of Simeon, Shaphat son of Hori;
[6]from the tribe of Judah, Caleb son of Jephunneh;[w]
[7]from the tribe of Issachar, Igal son of Joseph;
[8]from the tribe of Ephraim, Hoshea son of Nun;
[9]from the tribe of Benjamin, Palti son of Raphu;
[10]from the tribe of Zebulun, Gaddiel son of Sodi;
[11]from the tribe of Manasseh (a tribe of Joseph), Gaddi son of Susi;
[12]from the tribe of Dan, Ammiel son of Gemalli;
[13]from the tribe of Asher, Sethur son of Michael;
[14]from the tribe of Naphtali, Nahbi son of Vophsi;
[15]from the tribe of Gad, Geuel son of Maki.

[16]These are the names of the men Moses sent to explore the land. (Moses gave Hoshea son of Nun[x] the
name Joshua.)[y]

[17]When Moses sent them to explore Canaan, he said, "Go up through the Negev[z] and on into the hill
country.[a] [18]See what the land is like and whether the people who live there are strong or weak, few or
many. [19]What kind of land do they live in? Is it good or bad? What kind of towns do they live in? Are they
unwalled or fortified? [20]How is the soil? Is it fertile or poor? Are there trees in it or not? Do your best to
bring back some of the fruit of the land.[b]" (It was the season for the first ripe grapes.)

[21]So they went up and explored the land from the Desert of Zin[c] as far as Rehob,[d] toward Lebo Hamath.[e] [22]They went up through the Negev and came to Hebron, where Ahiman, Sheshai and Talmai,[f]
the descendants of Anak,[g] lived. (Hebron had been built seven years before Zoan in Egypt.)[h] [23]When
they reached the Valley of Eshkol,[a] they cut off a branch bearing a single cluster of grapes. Two of them
carried it on a pole between them, along with some pomegranates and figs. [24]That place was called the
Valley of Eshkol because of the cluster of grapes the Israelites cut off there. [25]At the end of forty days
they returned from exploring the land.

Report on the Exploration

[26]They came back to Moses and Aaron and the whole Israelite community at Kadesh in the Desert of
Paran. There they reported to them[i] and to the whole assembly and showed them the fruit of the land.
[27]They gave Moses this account: "We went into the land to which you sent us, and it does flow with milk
and honey![j] Here is its fruit.[k] [28]But the people who live there are powerful, and the cities are fortified and
very large.[l] We even saw descendants of Anak there. [29]The Amalekites live in the Negev; the Hittites, Jebusites and Amorites live in the hill country; and the Canaanites live near the sea and along the Jordan."

[30]Then Caleb silenced the people before Moses and said, "We should go up and take possession of
the land, for we can certainly do it."

[31]But the men who had gone up with him said, "We can't attack those people; they are stronger

[a] *23 Eshkol* means *cluster*; also in verse 24.

13:6 [w] ver 30; Nu 14:6, 24; 34:19; Jdg 1:12-15
13:16 [x] ver 8 [y] Dt 32:44
13:17 [z] Ge 12:9 [a] Jdg 1:9
13:20 [b] Dt 1:25
13:21 [c] Nu 20:1; 27:14; 33:36; Jos 15:1 [d] Jos 19:28 [e] Jos 13:5
13:22 [f] Jos 15:14 [g] Jos 15:13 [h] Ps 78:12, 43; Isa 19:11,13
13:26 [i] Nu 32:8
13:27 [j] Ex 3:8 [k] Dt 1:25
13:28 [l] Dt 1:28; 9:1,2

13:8,16 Hoshea. Means "he saves." In v. 16 Moses gives him the name Joshua, which means "the LORD saves." Salvation comes from the Lord alone (cf. Pss 3:8; 37:39; Hos 13:4). See NIV text note on Matt 1:21 (cf. Acts 4:10–12).
13:17–20 Moses' questions focus on the land (Is this indeed a land flowing with milk and honey?) and the people (Who is it we are up against in the coming battles?).
13:20 season for the first ripe grapes. Sometime in July, roughly two to three months after leaving Sinai (see note on 10:11).
13:21 The spies' route took them from the very south to the very north of the land (see map, p. 380).
13:22 Hebron. The site of Abraham's only property (Gen 23:17–20) and where the patriarchs were buried (Gen 25:9; 35:27–29; 50:13). It was a foretaste of the Lord's promise to give this land to Israel and should therefore encourage them to march into it boldly. **descendants of Anak.** Known for their height (Deut 2:10).
13:23 The land was incredibly fruitful.
13:26–33 *Report on the Exploration.* The majority of the spies acknowledge the land's fruitfulness (v. 27) but focus on the people's strength, cities, and size (vv. 28–29). They claim that the Israelites face an impossible task (v. 31).
13:26 Kadesh. Also called Kadesh Barnea (32:8; see map, p. 147). **Desert of Paran.** Perhaps bordering Kadesh southward. The Desert of Zin also bordered on Kadesh (13:21; 20:1; see map, p. 2868).
13:30 Caleb. One of two spies who has faith that the Lord can give the Israelites the land. Joshua is the other (14:6–9). Caleb does not deny the difficulty before them but has faith that the Lord is even greater. The Lord rewards Caleb's deep faith (14:24; Josh 14:6–15).
13:31–33 The unfaithful spies give a "bad report" (v. 32), focusing on (and exaggerating) the inhabitants' strength.

13:31 [m] Dt 1:28; 9:1; Jos 14:8
13:32 [n] Nu 14:36,37 [o] Eze 36:13,14 [p] Am 2:9
13:33 [q] Ge 6:4 [r] Dt 1:28
14:2 [s] Nu 11:1
14:4 [t] Ne 9:17
14:5 [u] Nu 16:4,22,45
14:7 [v] Nu 13:27; Dt 1:25
14:8 [w] Dt 10:15 [x] Nu 13:27
14:9 [y] Dt 1:26; 9:7,23,24 [z] Dt 1:21; 7:18; 20:1
14:10 [a] Ex 17:4 [b] Lev 9:23
14:11 [c] Ps 78:22; 106:24
14:12 [d] Ex 32:10

than we are."[m] 32 And they spread among the Israelites a
bad report[n] about the land they had explored. They said,
"The land we explored devours[o] those living in it. All the
people we saw there are of great size.[p] 33 We saw the Nephilim[q] there (the descendants of Anak[r] come from the Nephilim). We seemed like grasshoppers in our own eyes, and
we looked the same to them."

Twelfth-century BC image of a "Canaanite" on a glazed tile from the palace of pharaoh Rameses III.
Z. Radovan/www.BibleLandPictures.com

The People Rebel

14 That night all the members of the community
raised their voices and wept aloud. 2 All the Israelites grumbled against Moses and Aaron, and the whole
assembly said to them, "If only we had died in Egypt! Or in
this wilderness![s] 3 Why is the LORD bringing us to this land
only to let us fall by the sword? Our wives and children will
be taken as plunder. Wouldn't it be better for us to go back
to Egypt?" 4 And they said to each other, "We should choose
a leader and go back to Egypt.[t]"

5 Then Moses and Aaron fell facedown[u] in front of the
whole Israelite assembly gathered there. 6 Joshua son of
Nun and Caleb son of Jephunneh, who were among those
who had explored the land, tore their clothes 7 and said to
the entire Israelite assembly, "The land we passed through
and explored is exceedingly good.[v] 8 If the LORD is pleased
with us,[w] he will lead us into that land, a land flowing
with milk and honey,[x] and will give it to us. 9 Only do not
rebel[y] against the LORD. And do not be afraid of the people
of the land,[z] because we will devour them. Their protection
is gone, but the LORD is with us. Do not be afraid of them."

10 But the whole assembly talked about stoning[a] them. Then the glory of the LORD[b] appeared at the
tent of meeting to all the Israelites. 11 The LORD said to Moses, "How long will these people treat me with
contempt? How long will they refuse to believe in me,[c] in spite of all the signs I have performed among
them? 12 I will strike them down with a plague and destroy them, but I will make you into a nation[d]
greater and stronger than they."

13 Moses said to the LORD, "Then the Egyptians will hear about it! By your power you brought these

13:32 All. Earlier they said that only *some* were "descendants of Anak" (v. 28; see note on v. 22).

13:33 Nephilim. Renowned warriors. See Gen 6:4 and note.

14:1–45 *The People Rebel.* The Israelites' disbelief climaxes: they completely reject the Lord and his promises and decide to return to the land of slavery (Egypt) rather than enter the land of promise (Canaan). With a punishment that fits the crime, the Lord declares that those who have rejected the land he has promised will die without receiving it. Heb 3:7—4:13 uses this as a strong warning: Do not reject Jesus and thereby fail to enter the eternal promised land awaiting those who follow him.

14:1–4 Because of the faithless spies' report, the people are convinced that entering the land will result in the men dying and their wives and children being taken as plunder (v. 3). They decide to go back to Egypt (v. 4), which is to reject the promise of the covenant (Gen 12:7) and thus the covenant Lord (cf. v. 11).

14:5 fell facedown. Perhaps in prayer, asking the Lord immediately for help (cf. 20:6).

14:6 tore their clothes. A sign of deep grief (Gen 37:29).

14:7 exceedingly good. The opposite report of the faithless spies (cf. 13:31–33).

14:8 If the LORD is pleased with us. A statement not of doubt (see also v. 9b) but of respect: the Lord sovereignly does whatever he pleases. **milk and honey.** Absent in the faithless spies' "bad report" (13:32; cf. 13:27).

14:9 rebel. As against a king (2 Kgs 18:7). **we will devour them.** Contrast 13:32. **the LORD is with us.** Therefore they need not fear to obey him and fulfill his kingdom mission. Cf. Matt 28:18–20.

14:10–12 The people respond to Joshua and Caleb, and the Lord responds to the people (cf. Exod 32:7–10).

14:10 stoning. Has judicial overtones (cf. 15:36), as though Joshua and Caleb are guilty of a crime. **the glory of the LORD appeared.** Probably means that the cloud at the tent lit up with fire (cf. Exod 24:15–18), an event so spectacular it demonstrated the Lord was worthy of being glorified (cf. 1 Kgs 18:36–39).

14:11 believe in me. Accept his word as true and obey it (cf. Jas 2:17–26). **signs.** Even miracles fail to penetrate hearts hardened in unbelief (cf. v. 22; John 11:43–48).

14:12 The Lord said similar words after the people rebelled with the golden calf (Exod 32:10). **destroy.** Disinherit; they will no longer be the Lord's people. **make you into a nation.** And thus become the new Abraham.

14:13–19 Moses' response to the Lord is in two parts: (1) If the Lord

people up from among them.[e] 14And they will tell the inhabitants of this land about it. They have already heard[f] that you, LORD, are with these people and that you, LORD, have been seen face to face, that your cloud stays over them, and that you go before them in a pillar of cloud by day and a pillar of fire by night.[g] 15If you put all these people to death, leaving none alive, the nations who have heard this report about you will say, 16"The LORD was not able to bring these people into the land he promised them on oath, so he slaughtered them in the wilderness.'[h]

17"Now may the Lord's strength be displayed, just as you have declared: 18'The LORD is slow to anger, abounding in love and forgiving sin and rebellion.[i] Yet he does not leave the guilty unpunished; he punishes the children for the sin of the parents to the third and fourth generation.'[j] 19In accordance with your great love, forgive[k] the sin of these people,[l] just as you have pardoned them from the time they left Egypt until now."[m]

20The LORD replied, "I have forgiven them,[n] as you asked. 21Nevertheless, as surely as I live[o] and as surely as the glory of the LORD fills the whole earth,[p] 22not one of those who saw my glory and the signs I performed in Egypt and in the wilderness but who disobeyed me and tested me ten times[q] — 23not one of them will ever see the land I promised on oath[r] to their ancestors. No one who has treated me with contempt will ever see it.[s] 24But because my servant Caleb has a different spirit and follows me wholeheartedly,[t] I will bring him into the land he went to, and his descendants will inherit it.[u] 25Since the Amalekites and the Canaanites are living in the valleys, turn[v] back tomorrow and set out toward the desert along the route to the Red Sea.[a]"

26The LORD said to Moses and Aaron: 27"How long will this wicked community grumble against me? I have heard the complaints of these grumbling Israelites.[w] 28So tell them, 'As surely as I live,[x] declares the LORD, I will do to you the very thing I heard you say: 29In this wilderness your bodies will fall[y] — every one of you twenty years old or more[z] who was counted in the census and who has grumbled against me. 30Not one of you will enter the land I swore with uplifted hand to make your home, except Caleb son of Jephunneh and Joshua son of Nun. 31As for your children that you said would be taken as plunder, I will bring them in to enjoy the land you have rejected.[a] 32But as for you, your bodies will fall[b] in this wilderness. 33Your children will be shepherds here for forty years, suffering for your unfaithfulness, until the last of your bodies lies in the wilderness. 34For forty years — one year for each of the forty days you explored the land[c] — you will suffer for your sins and know what it is like to have me against you.' 35I, the LORD, have spoken, and I will surely do these things[d] to this whole wicked community, which has banded together against me. They will meet their end in this wilderness; here they will die."

36So the men Moses had sent[e] to explore the land, who returned and made the whole community grumble against him by spreading a bad report[f] about it — 37these men who were responsible for spreading the bad report[g] about the land were struck down and died of a plague[h] before the LORD. 38Of the men who went to explore the land, only Joshua son of Nun and Caleb son of Jephunneh survived.[i]

39When Moses reported this to all the Israelites, they mourned[j] bitterly. 40Early the next morning

14:13 [e] Ex 32:11-14; Ps 106:23
14:14 [f] Ex 15:14 [g] Ex 13:21
14:16 [h] Jos 7:7
14:18 [i] Ex 34:6; Ps 145:8; Jnh 4:2 [j] Ex 20:5
14:19 [k] Ex 34:9 [l] Ps 106:45 [m] Ps 78:38
14:20 [n] Ps 106:23; Mic 7:18-20
14:21 [o] Dt 32:40; Isa 49:18 [p] Ps 72:19; Isa 6:3; Hab 2:14
14:22 [q] Ex 14:11; 32:1; 1Co 10:5
14:23 [r] Nu 32:11 [s] Heb 3:18
14:24 [t] ver 6-9; Jos 14:8, 14 [u] Nu 32:12
14:25 [v] Dt 1:40
14:27 [w] Ex 16:12
14:28 [x] ver 21
14:29 [y] Nu 26:65 [z] Nu 1:45
14:31 [a] Ps 106:24
14:32 [b] 1Co 10:5
14:34 [c] Nu 13:25
14:35 [d] Nu 23:19
14:36 [e] Nu 13:4-16 [f] Nu 13:32
14:37 [g] 1Co 10:10 [h] Nu 16:49
14:38 [i] Jos 14:6
14:39 [j] Ex 33:4

[a] 25 Or *the Sea of Reeds*

destroys Israel, the nations will conclude he is a weak god who cannot keep his promises (vv. 13–16). Moses prays instead that the Lord bring Israel into the land so the nations will see the Lord's strength (v. 17; cf. Isa 48:9,11; Ezek 36:22–23). (2) The Lord's love is great, so he can forgive his people yet again (vv. 18–19).

14:18 Summarizes Exod 34:6–7. **punishes the children.** See note on v. 33.

14:20–35 The Lord responds to Moses in summary form (vv. 20–25) and more detail (vv. 26–35). The punishment fits the crime (v. 28): they will die in the wilderness (v. 29), just as they wished (v. 2). Ironically, their children will not be plunder (v. 3) but will enjoy the land (v. 31).

14:20 I have forgiven them. The Lord will not carry out the deserved punishment: immediate death and disinheritance as his people (v. 12).

14:21 Nevertheless. There will still be discipline. **as I live.** People swear by the Lord (Judg 8:19) because he is greater than they are; the Lord swears by himself (Gen 22:16) because "there [is] no one greater for him to swear by" (Heb 6:13). **glory … fills the whole earth.** A reference to the Lord's mighty work, which causes those who see it to give him glory (cf. Ps 72:18–19; Rev 15:3–4).

14:22 ten times. Perhaps a way of saying "many" (cf. Gen 31:7). Cf. "dozen" in the phrase "I've told you a dozen times."

14:24,30 See Josh 14:6–15; 19:49–50.

14:29,32 See 1 Cor 10:5; Heb 3:17.

14:33 Because families are so interconnected, even the children suffer when their parents' unfaithfulness is punished (cf. v. 18b, but see also v. 31).

14:37 God holds those in positions of authority to higher account for their sin (cf. Luke 12:47–48; Heb 13:17; Jas 3:1). **plague.** See note on 16:46.

14:40 we have sinned! Recognizing their wrong, the people decide to enter the land. Ironically, this is now a disobedient act (v. 41; cf. v. 25) and will not work because the Lord is not with them (v. 42).

14:40 [k]Dt 1:41
14:41 [l]2Ch 24:20
14:42 [m]Dt 1:42
14:44 [n]Dt 1:43 [o]Nu 31:6
14:45 [p]Nu 21:3; Dt 1:44; Jdg 1:17
15:2 [q]Lev 23:10
15:3 [r]Lev 1:2 [s]ver 24; Ge 8:21; Ex 29:18 [t]Nu 28:19,27 [u]Lev 22:18,21; Ezr 1:4 [v]Lev 23:1-44
15:4 [w]Lev 2:1; 6:14
15:5 [x]Nu 28:7,14
15:6 [y]Lev 5:15 [z]Nu 28:12 [a]Eze 46:14
15:8 [b]Lev 1:3; 3:1
15:9 [c]Lev 14:10
15:13 [d]Lev 16:29
15:15 [e]ver 29; Nu 9:14
15:16 [f]Nu 9:14

they set out for the highest point in the hill country, saying, "Now we are ready to go up to the land the LORD promised. Surely we have sinned![k]"

[41]But Moses said, "Why are you disobeying the LORD's command? This will not succeed![l] [42]Do not go up, because the LORD is not with you. You will be defeated by your enemies,[m] [43]for the Amalekites and the Canaanites will face you there. Because you have turned away from the LORD, he will not be with you and you will fall by the sword."

[44]Nevertheless, in their presumption they went up[n] toward the highest point in the hill country, though neither Moses nor the ark of the LORD's covenant moved from the camp.[o] [45]Then the Amalekites and the Canaanites who lived in that hill country came down and attacked them and beat them down all the way to Hormah.[p]

Supplementary Offerings

15 The LORD said to Moses, [2]"Speak to the Israelites and say to them: 'After you enter the land I am giving you[q] as a home [3]and you present to the LORD food offerings from the herd or the flock,[r] as an aroma pleasing to the LORD[s]—whether burnt offerings[t] or sacrifices, for special vows or freewill offerings[u] or festival offerings[v]— [4]then the person who brings an offering shall present to the LORD a grain offering[w] of a tenth of an ephah[a] of the finest flour mixed with a quarter of a hin[b] of olive oil. [5]With each lamb for the burnt offering or the sacrifice, prepare a quarter of a hin of wine[x] as a drink offering.

[6]" 'With a ram[y] prepare a grain offering[z] of two-tenths of an ephah[c] of the finest flour mixed with a third of a hin[d] of olive oil,[a] [7]and a third of a hin of wine as a drink offering. Offer it as an aroma pleasing to the LORD.

[8]" 'When you prepare a young bull as a burnt offering or sacrifice, for a special vow or a fellowship offering[b] to the LORD, [9]bring with the bull a grain offering of three-tenths of an ephah[e][c] of the finest flour mixed with half a hin[f] of olive oil, [10]and also bring half a hin of wine as a drink offering. This will be a food offering, an aroma pleasing to the LORD. [11]Each bull or ram, each lamb or young goat, is to be prepared in this manner. [12]Do this for each one, for as many as you prepare.

[13]" 'Everyone who is native-born[d] must do these things in this way when they present a food offering as an aroma pleasing to the LORD. [14]For the generations to come, whenever a foreigner or anyone else living among you presents a food offering as an aroma pleasing to the LORD, they must do exactly as you do. [15]The community is to have the same rules for you and for the foreigner residing among you; this is a lasting ordinance for the generations to come.[e] You and the foreigner shall be the same before the LORD: [16]The same laws and regulations will apply both to you and to the foreigner residing among you.[f]' "

[17]The LORD said to Moses, [18]"Speak to the Israelites and say to them: 'When you enter the land to

[a] *4* That is, probably about 3 1/2 pounds or about 1.6 kilograms [b] *4* That is, about 1 quart or about 1 liter; also in verse 5 [c] *6* That is, probably about 7 pounds or about 3.2 kilograms [d] *6* That is, about 1 1/3 quarts or about 1.3 liters; also in verse 7 [e] *9* That is, probably about 11 pounds or about 5 kilograms [f] *9* That is, about 2 quarts or about 1.9 liters; also in verse 10

14:44 Moses ... the ark of the LORD's covenant. Both represent the Lord's presence.
14:45 Hormah. Means "destruction"; located south in the land and west of the Dead Sea. See map, p. 2869.
15:1–41 *Further Laws, Emphasizing Especially the Need for Covenant Faithfulness.* The next generation will receive the land that the Lord promised (vv. 2,18; cf. ch. 14), but they must be faithful to the covenant (vv. 30–41).
15:1–21 *Supplementary Offerings.* Israelites often thought of sacrifices as meals (see notes on v. 3; Lev 3:1,11). The offerings of vv. 1–16 made the "meal" complete by adding bread (a grain offering) and wine (a drink offering) to the meat (the animal sacrifice). The size of these offerings increased with the size of the animal sacrificed.
15:2 After you enter the land. Coming after the rebellion of ch. 14, this is a wonderful affirmation that the Lord has not abandoned his promises to Israel (see v. 18).
15:3 aroma pleasing to the LORD. Not because the Lord was "hungry" (Ps 50:12–13) but because these offerings were like meals by which the Israelites honored him (see note on Lev 3:17) or confirmed their covenant relationship with him. **burnt offerings.** See Lev 1:3–9 and notes. **sacrifices.** Fellowship offerings (cf. v. 8; see Lev 3:1–5 and note on 3:1). **special vows.** See note on Lev 27:2. **freewill offerings.** Brought voluntarily, not because of a vow. **festival offerings.** See Lev 23:4–38 and notes.
15:4 grain offering. See Lev 2:1–16 and notes.
15:5 drink offering. Poured out on the altar (Exod 29:41; cf. Exod 30:9), perhaps over the animal sacrifice.
15:14–16 This is one way that God will fulfill his promise to bless the nations through Abraham's descendants: foreigners will be joining their ranks to worship the Lord (Gen 12:3). This promise reaches its final fulfillment as the nations put their faith in Abraham's ultimate descendant, Jesus (Gal 3:8).
15:17–21 By presenting these offerings, the Israelites gratefully acknowledge that the Lord has blessed them with the crops they need to survive (Deut 26:10).

GRAIN AND DRINK OFFERINGS THAT ACCOMPANY ANIMAL SACRIFICES

	GRAIN OFFERING		DRINK OFFERING	
	BIBLICAL MEASURE	***MODERN EQUIVALENT***	***BIBLICAL MEASURE***	***MODERN EQUIVALENT***
lamb	1/10 ephah flour + 1/4 hin oil	3.5 pounds (1.6 kilograms) + 1 quart (1 liter)	1/4 hin wine	1 quart (1 liter)
ram	2/10 ephah flour + 1/3 hin oil	7 pounds (3.2 kilograms) + 1.3 quarts (1.3 liters)	1/3 hin wine	1.3 quarts (1.3 liters)
bull	3/10 ephah flour + 1/2 hin oil	11 pounds (5 kilograms) + 2 quarts (1.9 liters)	1/2 hin wine	2 quarts (1.9 liters)

which I am taking you 19 and you eat the food of the land,[g] present a portion as an offering to the LORD.
20 Present a loaf from the first of your ground meal[h] and present it as an offering from the threshing
floor.[i] 21 Throughout the generations to come you are to give this offering to the LORD from the first of
your ground meal.[j]

Offerings for Unintentional Sins

22 " 'Now if you as a community unintentionally fail to keep any of these commands the LORD gave
Moses[k] — 23 any of the LORD's commands to you through him, from the day the LORD gave them and
continuing through the generations to come — 24 and if this is done unintentionally without the community being aware of it,[l] then the whole community is to offer a young bull for a burnt offering[m] as
an aroma pleasing to the LORD, along with its prescribed grain offering and drink offering, and a male
goat for a sin offering.[a][n] 25 The priest is to make atonement for the whole Israelite community, and they
will be forgiven,[o] for it was not intentional and they have presented to the LORD for their wrong a food
offering and a sin offering. 26 The whole Israelite community and the foreigners residing among them
will be forgiven, because all the people were involved in the unintentional wrong.[p]

27 " 'But if just one person sins unintentionally,[q] that person must bring a year-old female goat for
a sin offering. 28 The priest is to make atonement before the LORD for the one who erred by sinning
unintentionally, and when atonement has been made, that person will be forgiven.[r] 29 One and the
same law applies to everyone who sins unintentionally, whether a native-born Israelite or a foreigner
residing among you.

30 " 'But anyone who sins defiantly,[s] whether native-born or foreigner,[t] blasphemes the LORD and
must be cut off from the people of Israel. 31 Because they have despised the LORD's word and broken his
commands,[u] they must surely be cut off; their guilt remains on them.[v] ' "

The Sabbath-Breaker Put to Death

32 While the Israelites were in the wilderness, a man was found gathering wood on the Sabbath
day.[w] 33 Those who found him gathering wood brought him to Moses and Aaron and the whole

[a] 24 Or *purification offering*; also in verses 25 and 27

15:19 [g] Jos 5:11,12
15:20 [h] Ex 34:26; Lev 23:14; Dt 26:2,10 [i] Lev 2:14
15:21 [j] Ro 11:16
15:22 [k] Lev 4:2
15:24 [l] Lev 5:15 [m] Lev 4:14 [n] Lev 4:3
15:25 [o] Lev 4:20; Ro 3:25; Heb 2:17
15:26 [p] ver 24
15:27 [q] Lev 4:27
15:28 [r] Lev 4:35
15:30 [s] Nu 14:40-44; Dt 1:43; 17:13; Ps 19:13 [t] ver 14
15:31 [u] 2Sa 12:9; Ps 119:126; Pr 13:13 [v] Lev 5:1; Eze 18:20
15:32 [w] Ex 31:14,15; 35:2,3

15:20 from the first. The firstfruits are the harvest's best (18:12). Giving them to the Lord displays that he is worthy of one's very best.
15:22–31 *Offerings for Unintentional Sins.* The King of heaven graciously provides an automatic means of atonement for those who break his laws unintentionally — sacrifice (vv. 22–29). But for those who commit outright treason against him, he describes a penalty: being cut off (vv. 30–31; see note on 9:13).
15:22–26 Requires more sacrificial animals than Lev 4:13–20, perhaps to emphasize the costliness of community sin in light of ch. 14.
15:22 as a community. A possible example is Josh 9:3–15. **unintentionally fail.** Because one is either (1) unaware of a law or (2) aware of a law but unaware they are breaking it (Gen 20:2–7).
15:27 just one person. A possible example: an individual not realizing they are ritually unclean and eating the meat of the fellowship offering (cf. Lev 7:20).
15:30–31 A strong warning never to commit defiant sin (cf. Heb 10:26–31). **defiantly ... blasphemes ... despised ... broken.** Apostasy: high treason against the heavenly King.
15:31 cut off. See note on 9:13. In some cases, defiant sin could be forgiven after a mediator acted on the sinner's behalf (14:13–20; cf. Exod 32:11–14; see 1 Tim 2:5–6 for Jesus as both mediator and sacrifice). But the discipline that followed could be severe (14:22–23).
15:32–36 *The Sabbath-Breaker Put to Death.* These verses illustrate the seriousness of what is said in vv. 30–31. The Sabbath was like a

15:34 [x]Nu 9:8
15:35 [y]Ex 31:14,15; Dt 21:21 [z]Lev 20:2; 24:14; Ac 7:58
15:38 [a]Dt 22:12; Mt 23:5
15:39 [b]Dt 4:23; 6:12; Ps 73:27
15:40 [c]Lev 11:44; Ro 12:1; Col 1:22; 1Pe 1:15
16:1 [d]Jude 1:11 [e]Nu 26:8; Dt 11:6
16:2 [f]Nu 1:16; 26:9
16:3 [g]ver 7; Ps 106:16 [h]Ex 19:6 [i]Nu 14:14 [j]Nu 12:2
16:4 [k]Nu 14:5
16:5 [l]Lev 10:3; 2Ti 2:19* [m]Nu 17:5; Ps 65:4
16:9 [n]Nu 3:6; Dt 10:8
16:10 [o]Nu 3:10; 18:7
16:11 [p]1Co 10:10 [q]Ex 16:7
16:13 [r]Nu 14:2 [s]Ac 7:27,35

assembly, 34 and they kept him in custody, because it was not clear what should be done to him.[x]
35 Then the LORD said to Moses, "The man must die.[y] The whole assembly must stone him outside the
camp.[z]" 36 So the assembly took him outside the camp and stoned him to death, as the LORD commanded Moses.

Tassels on Garments

37 The LORD said to Moses, 38 "Speak to the Israelites and say to them: 'Throughout the generations to
come you are to make tassels on the corners of your garments,[a] with a blue cord on each tassel. 39 You
will have these tassels to look at and so you will remember[b] all the commands of the LORD, that you
may obey them and not prostitute yourselves by chasing after the lusts of your own hearts and eyes.
40 Then you will remember to obey all my commands and will be consecrated to your God.[c] 41 I am the
LORD your God, who brought you out of Egypt to be your God. I am the LORD your God.'"

Korah, Dathan and Abiram

16 Korah[d] son of Izhar, the son of Kohath, the son of Levi, and certain Reubenites—Dathan and
Abiram, sons of Eliab,[e] and On son of Peleth—became insolent[a] 2 and rose up against Moses.
With them were 250 Israelite men, well-known community leaders who had been appointed members
of the council.[f] 3 They came as a group to oppose Moses and Aaron[g] and said to them, "You have gone
too far! The whole community is holy,[h] every one of them, and the LORD is with them.[i] Why then do you
set yourselves above the LORD's assembly?"[j]

4 When Moses heard this, he fell facedown.[k] 5 Then he said to Korah and all his followers: "In the
morning the LORD will show who belongs to him and who is holy,[l] and he will have that person come
near him. The man he chooses[m] he will cause to come near him. 6 You, Korah, and all your followers
are to do this: Take censers 7 and tomorrow put burning coals and incense in them before the LORD. The
man the LORD chooses will be the one who is holy. You Levites have gone too far!"

8 Moses also said to Korah, "Now listen, you Levites! 9 Isn't it enough for you that the God of Israel has
separated you from the rest of the Israelite community and brought you near himself to do the work
at the LORD's tabernacle and to stand before the community and minister to them?[n] 10 He has brought
you and all your fellow Levites near himself, but now you are trying to get the priesthood too.[o] 11 It is
against the LORD that you and all your followers have banded together. Who is Aaron that you should
grumble[p] against him?[q]"

12 Then Moses summoned Dathan and Abiram, the sons of Eliab. But they said, "We will not come!
13 Isn't it enough that you have brought us up out of a land flowing with milk and honey to kill us in
the wilderness?[r] And now you also want to lord it over us![s] 14 Moreover, you haven't brought us into a

[a] *1* Or *Peleth—took men*

wedding ring: it symbolized the covenant relationship between Israel and the Lord (Exod 31:13–17). To break it was to reject the covenant partner (like throwing away your wedding ring). This was rank apostasy, and God punished it as such.

15:37–41 *Tassels on Garments.* They were to contain blue (v. 38), a royal color (Esth 1:6; 8:15), and were therefore associated with the heavenly King's home (the tabernacle [Exod 26:1]) and his servants (the priests [Exod 28:6,8,33]). The tassels were thus a good reminder for the Israelites to be a "kingdom of priests and a holy nation" (Exod 19:6) and to obey all the King's commands.

15:39 The Lord elsewhere requires visual reminders of his commandments (cf. Deut 6:8–9 and note).

16:1—18:32 *Challenging the Authority Structure Established by the Lord.* The people rebel against the Lord's leaders (ch. 16; cf. chs. 12; 14), and the Lord responds with judgment (ch. 16), a miraculous sign (ch. 17), and instruction (ch. 18), making it clear that he himself has chosen these leaders.

16:1–50 *Korah, Dathan and Abiram.* Korah's rebellion focuses on the priesthood (vv. 10–11), and Dathan and Abiram's rebellion focuses on Moses (vv. 13–14). In both rebellions, the Lord's leader is rejected.

16:1 Korah. The group's leader (cf. v. 5).

16:2 leaders. Had great influence in the community.

16:3 The whole community is holy ... the LORD is with them. They mistake the Lord's grace to live among his sinful people as a sign that anyone could approach him as a priest. Cf. 3:10,38; 4:5–15. **set yourselves above.** Ironically, Moses tried to refuse his leadership role (Exod 3). This leadership arrangement was the Lord's doing (cf. Heb 5:4).

16:4 fell facedown. Perhaps to pray (see note on 14:5), after which he knew what to do (vv. 5–11).

16:5–7 Aaron, Korah, and Korah's followers will perform a priestly duty (presenting incense) to see whom the Lord accepts in this role (cf. v. 40; 2 Chr 26:16–20).

16:10 Korah was claiming that anyone—or at least any Levite—could be a priest.

16:11 against the LORD. Because he had set the priests apart.

16:13–14 Dathan and Abiram blasphemously (1) call Egypt the "land flowing with milk and honey" (thus describing their former slave house as the promised land), (2) claim that Moses brought them out of Egypt to kill them (cf. 14:13–19), and (3) assassinate Moses' character as a deceptive promise-breaker.

land flowing with milk and honey[t] or given us an inheritance of fields and vineyards.[u] Do you want to
treat these men like slaves[a]?[v] No, we will not come!"
15 Then Moses became very angry and said to the LORD, "Do not accept their offering. I have not taken
so much as a donkey[w] from them, nor have I wronged any of them."
16 Moses said to Korah, "You and all your followers are to appear before the LORD tomorrow—you
and they and Aaron.[x] 17 Each man is to take his censer and put incense in it—250 censers in all—and
present it before the LORD. You and Aaron are to present your censers also." 18 So each of them took his
censer, put burning coals and incense in it, and stood with Moses and Aaron at the entrance to the tent
of meeting. 19 When Korah had gathered all his followers in opposition to them[y] at the entrance to the
tent of meeting, the glory of the LORD[z] appeared to the entire assembly. 20 The LORD said to Moses and
Aaron, 21 "Separate yourselves from this assembly so I can put an end to them at once."[a]
22 But Moses and Aaron fell facedown[b] and cried out, "O God, the God who gives breath to all living
things,[c] will you be angry with the entire assembly when only one man sins?"[d]
23 Then the LORD said to Moses, 24 "Say to the assembly, 'Move away from the tents of Korah, Dathan
and Abiram.' "
25 Moses got up and went to Dathan and Abiram, and the elders of Israel followed him. 26 He warned
the assembly, "Move back from the tents of these wicked men![e] Do not touch anything belonging to
them, or you will be swept away[f] because of all their sins." 27 So they moved away from the tents of
Korah, Dathan and Abiram. Dathan and Abiram had come out and were standing with their wives,
children and little ones at the entrances to their tents.
28 Then Moses said, "This is how you will know that the LORD has sent me[g] to do all these things and
that it was not my idea: 29 If these men die a natural death and suffer the fate of all mankind, then the
LORD has not sent me.[h] 30 But if the LORD brings about something totally new, and the earth opens its
mouth and swallows them, with everything that belongs to them, and they go down alive into the realm
of the dead,[i] then you will know that these men have treated the LORD with contempt."
31 As soon as he finished saying all this, the ground under them split apart[j] 32 and the earth opened
its mouth and swallowed them[k] and their households, and all those associated with Korah, together
with their possessions. 33 They went down alive into the realm of the dead, with everything they owned;
the earth closed over them, and they perished and were gone from the community. 34 At their cries, all
the Israelites around them fled, shouting, "The earth is going to swallow us too!"
35 And fire came out from the LORD[l] and consumed[m] the 250 men who were offering the incense.
36 The LORD said to Moses, 37 "Tell Eleazar son of Aaron, the priest, to remove the censers from the
charred remains and scatter the coals some distance away, for the censers are holy— 38 the censers
of the men who sinned at the cost of their lives.[n] Hammer the censers into sheets to overlay the altar,
for they were presented before the LORD and have become holy. Let them be a sign[o] to the Israelites."
39 So Eleazar the priest collected the bronze censers brought by those who had been burned to death,
and he had them hammered out to overlay the altar, 40 as the LORD directed him through Moses. This
was to remind the Israelites that no one except a descendant of Aaron should come to burn incense[p]
before the LORD,[q] or he would become like Korah and his followers.[r]
41 The next day the whole Israelite community grumbled against Moses and Aaron. "You have killed
the LORD's people," they said.

16:14 [t] Lev 20:24 [u] Ex 22:5; 23:11; Nu 20:5 [v] Jdg 16:21; 1Sa 11:2
16:15 [w] 1Sa 12:3
16:16 [x] ver 6
16:19 [y] ver 42 [z] Ex 16:7; Nu 14:10; 20:6
16:21 [a] Ex 32:10
16:22 [b] Nu 14:5 [c] Nu 27:16; Job 12:10; Heb 12:9 [d] Ge 18:23
16:26 [e] Isa 52:11 [f] Ge 19:15
16:28 [g] Ex 3:12; Jn 5:36; 6:38
16:29 [h] Ecc 3:19
16:30 [i] ver 33; Ps 55:15
16:31 [j] Mic 1:3-4
16:32 [k] Nu 26:11; Dt 11:6; Ps 106:17
16:35 [l] Nu 11:1-3; 26:10 [m] Lev 10:2
16:38 [n] Pr 20:2 [o] Nu 26:10; Eze 14:8; 2Pe 2:6
16:40 [p] Ex 30:7-10; Nu 1:51 [q] 2Ch 26:18 [r] Nu 3:10

[a] 14 Or *to deceive these men*; Hebrew *Will you gouge out the eyes of these men*

16:15 not taken ... a donkey. As a bribe (cf. 1 Sam 12:3).
16:19 glory of the LORD. See note on 14:10.
16:22 Moses and Aaron plead for the Lord to focus his justice on the rebellion's leaders, not on the entire people.
16:24–27 The rebels are isolated from the covenant community.
16:31–33 The judgment was so miraculous it was clearly the Lord's doing (cf. vv. 29–30).
16:32 and their households. Due to the interconnectedness of families, the parents' sin affects their children (see note on 14:33). While there is not strong hope for the eternal destiny of the parents (who are presented as apostates), the same is not true of their covenant children (who are not apostates; cf. Luke 18:15–16). **those associated with Korah.** Not the 250 men (cf. v. 35) or Korah's entire household (cf. 26:11), but others who stood with him in support.
16:35 fire ... consumed. Just as it did for others who presented an illicit incense offering (see Lev 10:1,2 and notes; cf. Jude 11).
16:38 altar. For burnt offerings; every Israelite would see the altar when coming into the tabernacle courtyard (see "Tabernacle Floor Plan," p. 192). **sign.** A visible reminder (v. 40) that only priests could do priestly work. (For "signs" as reminders, see Exod 31:13; Deut 6:8; Josh 4:7.)
16:41 Moses and Aaron. The very ones who saved them earlier (vv. 21–22) and will save them again (vv. 46–50). **You have killed.** Cf. vv. 28–30,35; it was clearly the Lord's judgment.

16:42 [s] ver 19; Nu 20:6
16:46 [t] Lev 10:6
[u] Nu 18:5; 25:13; Dt 9:22
[v] Nu 8:19; Ps 106:29
16:47 [w] Nu 25:6-8
16:48 [x] Nu 25:8; Ps 106:30
16:49 [y] ver 32
17:3 [z] Nu 1:3
17:4 [a] ver 7 [b] Ex 25:22
17:5 [c] Nu 16:5
17:7 [d] Ex 38:21; Ac 7:44
17:8 [e] Eze 17:24; Heb 9:4
17:10 [f] Dt 9:24
17:12 [g] Isa 6:5
17:13 [h] Nu 1:51
18:1 [i] Ex 28:38

42 But when the assembly gathered in opposition[s] to Moses and Aaron and turned toward the tent of
meeting, suddenly the cloud covered it and the glory of the LORD appeared. 43 Then Moses and Aaron
went to the front of the tent of meeting, 44 and the LORD said to Moses, 45 "Get away from this assembly
so I can put an end to them at once." And they fell facedown.

46 Then Moses said to Aaron, "Take your censer and put incense in it, along with burning coals from
the altar, and hurry to the assembly[t] to make atonement[u] for them. Wrath has come out from the LORD;
the plague[v] has started." 47 So Aaron did as Moses said, and ran into the midst of the assembly. The
plague had already started among the people,[w] but Aaron offered the incense and made atonement for
them. 48 He stood between the living and the dead, and the plague stopped.[x] 49 But 14,700 people died
from the plague, in addition to those who had died because of Korah.[y] 50 Then Aaron returned to Moses
at the entrance to the tent of meeting, for the plague had stopped.[a]

The Budding of Aaron's Staff

17 [b] The LORD said to Moses, 2 "Speak to the Israelites and get twelve staffs from them, one from
the leader of each of their ancestral tribes. Write the name of each man on his staff. 3 On the
staff of Levi write Aaron's name,[z] for there must be one staff for the head of each ancestral tribe. 4 Place
them in the tent of meeting in front of the ark of the covenant law,[a] where I meet with you.[b] 5 The staff
belonging to the man I choose[c] will sprout, and I will rid myself of this constant grumbling against
you by the Israelites."

6 So Moses spoke to the Israelites, and their leaders gave him twelve staffs, one for the leader of each
of their ancestral tribes, and Aaron's staff was among them. 7 Moses placed the staffs before the LORD in
the tent of the covenant law.[d]

8 The next day Moses entered the tent and saw that Aaron's staff, which represented the tribe of Levi,
had not only sprouted but had budded, blossomed and produced almonds.[e] 9 Then Moses brought out
all the staffs from the LORD's presence to all the Israelites. They looked at them, and each of the leaders
took his own staff.

10 The LORD said to Moses, "Put back Aaron's staff in front of the ark of the covenant law, to be kept
as a sign to the rebellious.[f] This will put an end to their grumbling against me, so that they will not
die." 11 Moses did just as the LORD commanded him.

12 The Israelites said to Moses, "We will die! We are lost, we are all lost![g] 13 Anyone who even comes
near the tabernacle of the LORD will die.[h] Are we all going to die?"

Duties of Priests and Levites

18 The LORD said to Aaron, "You, your sons and your family are to bear the responsibility for
offenses connected with the sanctuary,[i] and you and your sons alone are to bear the responsibility for offenses connected with the priesthood. 2 Bring your fellow Levites from your ancestral tribe

[a] *50* In Hebrew texts 16:36-50 is numbered 17:1-15. [b] In Hebrew texts 17:1-13 is numbered 17:16-28.

16:42 glory of the LORD. See note on 14:10.
16:46–47 The Lord accepts Aaron's incense, confirming Aaron's role as priest (cf. v. 35).
16:46 Wrath. The Lord's just anger against rebellion (see note on 1:53). **plague.** An unidentified but deadly punishment (vv. 47–49).
16:47 Another instance of a mediator atoning for the people by means of intercession (see note on 11:2).
17:1–13 *The Budding of Aaron's Staff.* The Lord had already clearly shown Aaron to be his chosen priest (ch. 16), but he gives another sign to rebellious Israel to prove it: Aaron's budding staff.
17:2 staffs. This word in Hebrew is also translated "tribe" (e.g., 1:4) and "scepter" (e.g., Ps 110:2). A staff represents authority to rule and is the perfect symbol to show which tribe should lead.
17:4 in front of the ark. In the Most Holy Place (cf. Exod 16:33–34), the Lord's throne room (see notes on Exod 25:10–22; 26:1–37).
17:5 the man I choose. To serve God as priest and enter into God's throne room (like that man's staff). **sprout.** Often a metaphor for those who flourish because of the Lord's favor (Ps 92:12; Prov 11:28; Isa 27:6). **myself … you.** Their grumbling against Moses was grumbling against the Lord (cf. 16:11,30).
17:8 produced almonds. A miracle: budding or blossoming might happen in a night, but not this. The Lord's choice of Aaron is clear. **almonds.** Translates a Hebrew word that sounds like the Hebrew word for "watch" or "guard," perhaps symbolizing Aaron's duty to guard the Lord's tent from improper entry (18:1; cf. the same play on words in Jer 1:11–12 [see NIV text note on Jer 1:12]).
17:9 They looked at them. To confirm that these were the same staffs put in the tent the day before.
17:10 sign to the rebellious. Just like the plating for the altar (see 16:38 and note). In this case, the sign is a reminder that the only ones who may enter the tent are those belonging to the one whose name was on the staff: Aaron. Cf. Heb 10:19–39.
17:12–13 The Israelites, finally convinced they may not be priests, conclude that they will die if they even go near the tabernacle. This is not the case as long as they follow the proper guidelines (18:1–7).
18:1–7 *Duties of Priests and Levites.* Four guidelines: (1) Aaron, his sons,

THE PRIESTS' SHARE IN THE OFFERINGS

OFFERING TYPE (NUM 18)	CEREMONIAL STATUS OF THE OFFERING	EXAMPLES	WHO COULD EAT IT
most holy offerings (vv. 9–10)	most holy	grain, sin, and guilt offerings	priests
wave offerings (v. 11)	holy	breast of fellowship offering (Lev 7:29–30)	priestly households (person had to be ceremonially clean)
firstfruits (vv. 12–13)	holy	olive oil, new wine, grain	priestly households (person had to be ceremonially clean)
devoted items (v. 14)	most holy (Lev 27:28)	cows, sheep, goats (cf. Lev 27:28)	not stated (priests only?)
firstborn (vv. 15–18)	holy	cows, sheep, goats	priestly households (person had to be ceremonially clean)

to join you and assist you when you and your sons minister[j] before the tent of the covenant law. 3They
are to be responsible to you and are to perform all the duties of the tent,[k] but they must not go near
the furnishings of the sanctuary or the altar. Otherwise both they and you will die.[l] 4They are to join
you and be responsible for the care of the tent of meeting—all the work at the tent—and no one else
may come near where you are.
5"You are to be responsible for the care of the sanctuary and the altar,[m] so that my wrath will not fall
on the Israelites again. 6I myself have selected your fellow Levites from among the Israelites as a gift
to you,[n] dedicated to the LORD to do the work at the tent of meeting. 7But only you and your sons may
serve as priests in connection with everything at the altar and inside the curtain.[o] I am giving you the
service of the priesthood as a gift.[p] Anyone else who comes near the sanctuary is to be put to death.[q]"

Offerings for Priests and Levites

8Then the LORD said to Aaron, "I myself have put you in charge of the offerings presented to me; all
the holy offerings the Israelites give me I give to you and your sons as your portion, your perpetual
share.[r] 9You are to have the part of the most holy offerings that is kept from the fire. From all the gifts
they bring me as most holy offerings, whether grain[s] or sin[a][t] or guilt offerings,[u] that part belongs to
you and your sons. 10Eat it as something most holy; every male shall eat it.[v] You must regard it as holy.
11"This also is yours: whatever is set aside from the gifts of all the wave offerings[w] of the Israelites.
I give this to you and your sons and daughters as your perpetual share. Everyone in your household
who is ceremonially clean[x] may eat it.
12"I give you all the finest olive oil and all the finest new wine and grain they give the LORD as the
firstfruits of their harvest.[y] 13All the land's firstfruits that they bring to the LORD will be yours.[z] Everyone
in your household who is ceremonially clean may eat it.

[a] 9 Or *purification*

18:2 [j] Nu 3:10
18:3 [k] Nu 1:51 [l] ver 7; Nu 4:15
18:5 [m] Nu 16:46
18:6 [n] Nu 3:9
18:7 [o] Heb 9:3,6 [p] ver 20; Ex 29:9 [q] Nu 3:10
18:8 [r] Lev 6:16; 7:6, 31-34,36
18:9 [s] Lev 2:1 [t] Lev 6:25 [u] Lev 5:15; 7:7
18:10 [v] Lev 6:16
18:11 [w] Ex 29:26 [x] Lev 22:1-16
18:12 [y] Ex 23:19; Ne 10:35
18:13 [z] Ex 22:29; 23:19

and his family (perhaps the Kohathites) must guard against people having improper contact with the sanctuary (or perhaps "the holy things," 10:21). They are responsible for any offense (v. 1a). (2) Aaron and his sons must guard against other people doing priestly duties (vv. 1b,5,7). They are responsible for any offense (v. 3). (3) The Levites must assist Aaron and his sons with tabernacle matters (vv. 2–4,6) but must not perform priestly duties (v. 3b). (4) No one else (whether Levite or layman) may do priestly duties, lest they be put to death—presumably by the priests (vv. 4,7). By following these guidelines, the Israelites may come and worship without fearing the Lord's wrath (v. 5). (For the difference between priests and Levites, see note on 3:1–51.)

18:8–32 *Offerings for Priests and Levites.* Since the priests and Levites did not inherit large tracts of land for farming, these offerings provided for their practical needs and let them focus on matters related to leading in the Lord's worship at the tabernacle. The NT carries on the principle of providing practically for the leaders of the Lord's people (1 Cor 9:13–14; Gal 6:6). When this does not happen, the Lord's worship suffers (Neh 13:10–11).

18:8–20 Most of the Israelites' gifts and offerings to the Lord were not completely burned up on the altar; this section explains what portions belonged to the priests and their families. These portions were all considered holy or most holy and were to be eaten only by the priests, or in some cases, by those in the priestly household.

18:9 most holy. See notes on Lev 2:3; 27:28.

18:10 male. Priests, who were ceremonially holy and could therefore partake of "most holy" food (cf. v. 11; for ceremonial holiness, see Introduction to Leviticus: Major Theological Themes [Holiness and Purity]).

18:11 wave offerings. See notes on Exod 29:24; Lev 7:30.

18:12 finest. See notes on 15:17–21; Lev 3:17.

18:13 firstfruits. See Deut 26:1–11 for the ceremony in which they were presented.

18:14 [a]Lev 27:28
18:15 [b]Ex 13:2 [c]Nu 3:46 [d]Ex 13:13
18:16 [e]Lev 27:6 [f]Ex 30:13
18:17 [g]Dt 15:19 [h]Lev 3:2
18:18 [i]Lev 7:30
18:19 [j]Lev 2:13; 2Ch 13:5
18:20 [k]Dt 12:12 [l]Dt 10:9; 14:27; 18:1-2; Jos 13:33; Eze 44:28
18:21 [m]Dt 14:22; Mal 3:8 [n]Lev 27:30-33; Heb 7:5
18:22 [o]Lev 22:9; Nu 1:51
18:23 [p]ver 20
18:26 [q]ver 21 [r]Ne 10:38
18:28 [s]Mal 3:8
18:30 [t]ver 27
18:32 [u]Lev 22:15 [v]Lev 19:8
19:2 [w]Ge 15:9; Heb 9:13 [x]Lev 22:19-25 [y]Dt 21:3; 1Sa 6:7
19:3 [z]Nu 3:4 [a]Lev 4:12, 21; Heb 13:11

14“Everything in Israel that is devoted*[a]* to the LORD[a] is yours. 15The first offspring of every womb,
both human and animal, that is offered to the LORD is yours.[b] But you must redeem[c] every firstborn
son and every firstborn male of unclean animals.[d] 16When they are a month old, you must redeem
them at the redemption price set at five shekels*[b]*[e] of silver, according to the sanctuary shekel,[f] which
weighs twenty gerahs.

17“But you must not redeem the firstborn of a cow, a sheep or a goat; they are holy.[g] Splash their
blood[h] against the altar and burn their fat as a food offering, an aroma pleasing to the LORD. 18Their
meat is to be yours, just as the breast of the wave offering[i] and the right thigh are yours. 19Whatever
is set aside from the holy offerings the Israelites present to the LORD I give to you and your sons and
daughters as your perpetual share. It is an everlasting covenant of salt[j] before the LORD for both you
and your offspring.”

20The LORD said to Aaron, “You will have no inheritance in their land, nor will you have any share
among them;[k] I am your share and your inheritance[l] among the Israelites.

21“I give to the Levites all the tithes[m] in Israel as their inheritance[n] in return for the work they do
while serving at the tent of meeting. 22From now on the Israelites must not go near the tent of meeting,
or they will bear the consequences of their sin and will die.[o] 23It is the Levites who are to do the work
at the tent of meeting and bear the responsibility for any offenses they commit against it. This is a
lasting ordinance for the generations to come. They will receive no inheritance[p] among the Israelites.
24Instead, I give to the Levites as their inheritance the tithes that the Israelites present as an offering to
the LORD. That is why I said concerning them: ‘They will have no inheritance among the Israelites.’ ”

25The LORD said to Moses, 26“Speak to the Levites and say to them: ‘When you receive from the Israelites the tithe I give you[q] as your inheritance, you must present a tenth of that tithe as the LORD’s
offering.[r] 27Your offering will be reckoned to you as grain from the threshing floor or juice from the
winepress. 28In this way you also will present an offering to the LORD from all the tithes[s] you receive
from the Israelites. From these tithes you must give the LORD’s portion to Aaron the priest. 29You must
present as the LORD’s portion the best and holiest part of everything given to you.’

30“Say to the Levites: ‘When you present the best part, it will be reckoned to you as the product of
the threshing floor or the winepress.[t] 31You and your households may eat the rest of it anywhere, for it
is your wages for your work at the tent of meeting. 32By presenting the best part[u] of it you will not be
guilty in this matter; then you will not defile the holy offerings[v] of the Israelites, and you will not die.’ ”

The Water of Cleansing

19 The LORD said to Moses and Aaron: 2“This is a requirement of the law that the LORD has commanded: Tell the Israelites to bring you a red heifer[w] without defect or blemish[x] and that has
never been under a yoke.[y] 3Give it to Eleazar[z] the priest; it is to be taken outside the camp[a] and slaugh-

a 14 The Hebrew term refers to the irrevocable giving over of things or persons to the LORD. *b 16* That is, about 2 ounces or about 58 grams

18:14 devoted. See NIV text note; see also notes on Lev 27:28,29.
18:15 first offspring. See note on 3:11–13. **redeem every firstborn.** See note on 3:40–51. **unclean animals.** Such as a donkey (Exod 13:13), which could not be sacrificed.
18:19 covenant of salt. “Everlasting” and therefore permanent (see note on Lev 2:13).
18:20 I am your share and your inheritance. The priests experience this by serving at the Lord’s tabernacle and eating his food (vv. 1–18). The priests thus serve as a sign that a person’s ultimate inheritance is the Lord (cf. Ps 73:25–26). The NT uses the language of “inheritance” to describe eternal life in God’s kingdom through faith in Jesus (Eph 1:13–14; Heb 9:15; 1 Pet 1:3–5; see also Introduction: Theological Themes [The Land, 1]).
18:21–24 The Israelites were to give the tithes of their harvest to the Levites (Lev 27:30), in this way providing for the Levites and their households (cf. v. 31).
18:25–32 The tithe given to the Levites counted as their wages (v. 31), so the Levites had to tithe as well, with their tithe going to the priests (v. 28). Tithing acknowledged that the Lord provides (Gen 28:22) and owns (Lev 25:23) all one has.
18:28 to Aaron the priest. And thus to his whole family (cf. vv. 1,8), in this way helping to supplement the priests’ income and diet.
19:1–22 *The Water of Cleansing.* People must not defile the Lord’s tabernacle (vv. 13,20; cf. 18:1,7,22). Those who touched corpses (vv. 11–13,16) or came into a tent where a human corpse was (v. 14) became ceremonially unclean with a major uncleanness (for ceremonial purity and impurity, see Introduction to Leviticus: Major Theological Themes [Holiness and Purity]). This type of uncleanness appears to have defiled the sanctuary from afar (v. 20), though this was not held against the Israelites if they properly cleansed themselves (and thus the sanctuary as well). This chapter explains how to go about such cleansing. If the Israelites did not follow this cleansing procedure, they showed total disrespect to the Lord’s holy tabernacle and therefore the Lord himself.
19:1–10 A person with a major uncleanness was normally expected to offer a sin offering (see Lev 12:6–8; 15:13–15; see note on Lev 4:1—5:13). However, when a whole family became unclean through

tered in his presence. [4]Then Eleazar the priest is to take some of its blood on his finger and sprinkle[b] it
seven times toward the front of the tent of meeting. [5]While he watches, the heifer is to be burned—its
hide, flesh, blood and intestines.[c] [6]The priest is to take some cedar wood, hyssop[d] and scarlet wool[e] and
throw them onto the burning heifer. [7]After that, the priest must wash his clothes and bathe himself with
water.[f] He may then come into the camp, but he will be ceremonially unclean till evening. [8]The man
who burns it must also wash his clothes and bathe with water, and he too will be unclean till evening.
[9]"A man who is clean shall gather up the ashes of the heifer[g] and put them in a ceremonially clean
place outside the camp. They are to be kept by the Israelite community for use in the water of cleansing;[h] it is for purification from sin. [10]The man who gathers up the ashes of the heifer must also wash his
clothes, and he too will be unclean till evening. This will be a lasting ordinance both for the Israelites
and for the foreigners residing among them.
[11]"Whoever touches a human corpse[i] will be unclean for seven days.[j] [12]They must purify themselves
with the water on the third day and on the seventh day;[k] then they will be clean. But if they do not purify themselves on the third and seventh days, they will not be clean. [13]If they fail to purify themselves
after touching a human corpse,[l] they defile the LORD's tabernacle.[m] They must be cut off from Israel.[n]
Because the water of cleansing has not been sprinkled on them, they are unclean;[o] their uncleanness
remains on them.
[14]"This is the law that applies when a person dies in a tent: Anyone who enters the tent and anyone
who is in it will be unclean for seven days, [15]and every open container without a lid fastened on it will
be unclean.
[16]"Anyone out in the open who touches someone who has been killed with a sword or someone
who has died a natural death,[p] or anyone who touches a human bone or a grave,[q] will be unclean for
seven days.
[17]"For the unclean person, put some ashes[r] from the burned purification offering into a jar and
pour fresh water over them. [18]Then a man who is ceremonially clean is to take some hyssop,[s] dip it in
the water and sprinkle the tent and all the furnishings and the people who were there. He must also
sprinkle anyone who has touched a human bone or a grave or anyone who has been killed or anyone
who has died a natural death. [19]The man who is clean is to sprinkle those who are unclean on the
third and seventh days, and on the seventh day he is to purify them.[t] Those who are being cleansed
must wash their clothes and bathe with water, and that evening they will be clean. [20]But if those who
are unclean do not purify themselves, they must be cut off from the community, because they have
defiled the sanctuary of the LORD. The water of cleansing has not been sprinkled on them, and they are
unclean. [21]This is a lasting ordinance for them.

19:4 [b]Lev 4:17
19:5 [c]Ex 29:14
19:6 [d]ver 18; Ps 51:7 [e]Lev 14:4
19:7 [f]Lev 11:25; 16:26, 28; 22:6
19:9 [g]Heb 9:13 [h]ver 13; Nu 8:7
19:11 [i]Lev 21:1; Nu 5:2 [j]Nu 31:19
19:12 [k]ver 19; Nu 31:19
19:13 [l]Lev 20:3 [m]Lev 15:31; 2Ch 36:14 [n]Lev 7:20; 22:3 [o]Hag 2:13
19:16 [p]Nu 31:19 [q]Mt 23:27
19:17 [r]ver 9
19:18 [s]ver 6
19:19 [t]Eze 36:25; Heb 10:22

contact with the body of a deceased loved one, it would have been a severe financial burden if each person had to offer a sacrifice. The Lord therefore describes how to prepare the water of cleansing, central to which were the ashes of a female animal without defect, the very type of animal required for an individual's sin offering (cf. Lev 4:28; a heifer is perhaps used in Numbers instead of a goat in order to provide the maximum amount of ashes). The water thus had the same result as a sin offering when sprinkled on the unclean: cleansing them of their ceremonial defilement. The NT contrasts this with Jesus, who by his sacrifice cleanses us from moral defilement (Heb 9:13–14; 1 John 1:7).

19:2 red. Central to this rite, perhaps because it was a reminder of blood, the most powerful cleansing agent in ancient Israel. **without defect.** See note on Lev 1:3; cf. Lev 22:18–25. **never been under a yoke.** And therefore not used for common purposes (cf. Deut 15:19).

19:4 seven times. Symbolizes complete cleansing (see note on 29:12–34; cf. Lev 16:19). **toward … the tent of meeting.** Perhaps to indicate the rite's purpose (maintaining the tent's purity) or to set apart the animal for holy use.

19:6 cedar wood, hyssop and scarlet wool. See note on Lev 14:4.

19:7–8,10 Cf. Lev 16:26–28.

19:9 water of cleansing. Sprinkled on the unclean to cleanse them. **purification from sin.** Or a "purification offering" (v. 17; see 8:8 and NIV text note), which purified them from their ceremonial uncleanness.

19:11–22 The uncleanness lasted seven days (vv. 11,14,16), the standard length of a major uncleanness (cf. Lev 14:8–9; 15:13). A ceremonially clean person would sprinkle the unclean with the water for cleansing on the third and seventh days (v. 19). Those being cleansed would then wash their clothes and bodies and be clean on the evening of the seventh day (v. 19).

19:12 purify themselves. Probably by following the instructions in vv. 17–19.

19:13 defile the LORD's tabernacle. See note on vv. 1–22. **cut off.** Removed from the covenant community, either through exile or death (see note on Lev 7:20,21). In this case, the latter method may be in view (cf. Lev 15:31).

19:14–15 The impurity is like a gas that fills the room and defiles everything in it.

19:17 fresh. The Israelites may have considered this water especially purifying; it is called for only in the context of major impurities (Lev 14:5–7,50–52; 15:13). **them.** The ashes.

19:18 hyssop. See note on Lev 14:4 (cf. Exod 12:22). **sprinkle.** Often associated with cleansing (Lev 4:5–6; 8:11).

19:19 wash … bathe. Typical cleansing rites, along with waiting until evening (Lev 15:5; 17:15).

19:21 Cf. Lev 16:26–28.

19:22 [u]Lev 5:2; Hag 2:13,14
20:1 [v]Nu 13:21 [w]Nu 33:36 [x]Ex 15:20
20:2 [y]Ex 17:1 [z]Nu 16:19
20:3 [a]Ex 17:2 [b]Nu 14:2; 16:31-35
20:4 [c]Ex 14:11; 17:3; Nu 14:3; 16:13
20:5 [d]Nu 16:14
20:6 [e]Nu 14:5 [f]Nu 16:19
20:8 [g]Ex 4:17,20 [h]Ex 17:6; Isa 43:20
20:9 [i]Nu 17:10
20:10 [j]Ps 106:32,33
20:11 [k]Ex 17:6; Dt 8:15; Ps 78:16; Isa 48:2; 1Co 10:4
20:12 [l]Nu 27:14 [m]ver 24; Dt 1:37; 3:27
20:13 [n]Ex 17:7 [o]Dt 33:8; Ps 95:8; 106:32
20:14 [p]Jdg 11:16-17 [q]Dt 2:4 [r]Jos 2:11; 9:9
20:15 [s]Ge 46:6 [t]Ge 15:13; Ex 12:40 [u]Ex 1:11; Dt 26:6
20:16 [v]Ex 2:23; 3:7 [w]Ex 14:19

"The man who sprinkles the water of cleansing must also wash his clothes, and anyone who touches the water of cleansing will be unclean till evening. 22 Anything that an unclean[u] person touches becomes unclean, and anyone who touches it becomes unclean till evening."

Water From the Rock

20 In the first month the whole Israelite community arrived at the Desert of Zin,[v] and they stayed at Kadesh.[w] There Miriam[x] died and was buried.

2 Now there was no water for the community,[y] and the people gathered in opposition[z] to Moses and Aaron. 3 They quarreled[a] with Moses and said, "If only we had died when our brothers fell dead before the LORD![b] 4 Why did you bring the LORD's community into this wilderness, that we and our livestock should die here?[c] 5 Why did you bring us up out of Egypt to this terrible place? It has no grain or figs, grapevines or pomegranates.[d] And there is no water to drink!"

6 Moses and Aaron went from the assembly to the entrance to the tent of meeting and fell facedown,[e] and the glory of the LORD[f] appeared to them. 7 The LORD said to Moses, 8 "Take the staff,[g] and you and your brother Aaron gather the assembly together. Speak to that rock before their eyes and it will pour out its water.[h] You will bring water out of the rock for the community so they and their livestock can drink."

9 So Moses took the staff from the LORD's presence,[i] just as he commanded him. 10 He and Aaron gathered the assembly together in front of the rock and Moses said to them, "Listen, you rebels, must we bring you water out of this rock?"[j] 11 Then Moses raised his arm and struck the rock twice with his staff. Water[k] gushed out, and the community and their livestock drank.

12 But the LORD said to Moses and Aaron, "Because you did not trust in me enough to honor me as holy[l] in the sight of the Israelites, you will not bring this community into the land I give them."[m]

13 These were the waters of Meribah,[a][n] where the Israelites quarreled[o] with the LORD and where he was proved holy among them.

Edom Denies Israel Passage

14 Moses sent messengers from Kadesh[p] to the king of Edom,[q] saying:

> "This is what your brother Israel says: You know[r] about all the hardships that have come on us. 15 Our ancestors went down into Egypt,[s] and we lived there many years.[t] The Egyptians mistreated[u] us and our ancestors, 16 but when we cried out to the LORD, he heard our cry[v] and sent an angel[w] and brought us out of Egypt.

[a] 13 *Meribah* means *quarreling.*

20:1—21:35 *Further Rebellions, Initial Victories.* These chapters begin a transition. This is the 40th year (see note on 20:1), so most of the exodus generation has died. The next generation begins their journey to the promised land and ends up in sight of it (22:1). Along the way, various victories anticipate the victories they will have in the promised land.
20:1–13 *Water From the Rock.* This is the story of two rebellions, one by the Israelites (vv. 2–5) and one by Moses and Aaron (vv. 9–12).
20:1 first month. Of the 40th year (cf. vv. 22–29 with 33:38–39). **Desert of Zin ... Kadesh.** See note on 13:26.
20:2–5 The Lord had provided in a similar situation (Exod 17:1–7), but instead of looking to him in faith, the Israelites "gathered in opposition" against his leaders (cf. 16:3,42). These trials were meant not to harm the Israelites but to strengthen their faith (Deut 8:3,16; cf. Jas 1:2–4).
20:6 fell facedown. In dependent prayer (cf. 16:22).
20:9 staff from the LORD's presence. Most likely a reference to the staff that budded (17:8–10); using it emphasizes the authority of the Lord's leaders (see notes on 17:2,10).
20:10 must we bring you water. Moses focuses the peoples' attention on himself and Aaron, not the Lord. Cf. Ps 106:32–33.
20:11 raised his arm. Emphasizes the rebellious nature of Moses' action because this translates the same Hebrew words that 15:30 renders "defiantly." **struck the rock.** But did not "speak" to it, as commanded (v. 8; cf. Exod 17:6), thus making his disobedience clear.
20:12 did not trust in me. The same Hebrew phrase describes the rebellious Israelites in 14:11; Moses and Aaron are imitating them: to disobey is to disbelieve and rebel (v. 24; cf. Deut 9:23). **honor me as holy.** Acknowledge the Lord's greatness through obedience. Instead, they honored themselves (see v. 10 and note). **you will not bring this community into the land.** Moses and Aaron joined in the Israelites' rebellion and so will share in their punishment. Cf. Luke 12:47–48; Heb 13:17; Jas 3:1.
20:13 Meribah. Means "quarreling," the same name given to a different location 38 years earlier (Exod 17:7). **quarreled.** Cf. 16:3–11; 17:1–5. **proved holy.** By providing water, by judging Moses and Aaron, or by both. See note on Lev 10:3.
20:14–21 *Edom Denies Israel Passage.* The Israelites are headed to the promised land and will enter it from northeast of the Dead Sea. The quickest way there was by taking the King's Highway through Edom's territory. Because Edom denied Israel passage, Israel had to take a longer route, skirting Edom to the east (Judg 11:18; see map, p. 147, for possible route taken).
20:14 brother. A general term for a relative. The Edomites were descendants of Esau (Gen 36:1), the brother of Jacob/Israel, the Israelites' forefather (cf. Gen 32:3,28).
20:16 angel. See Exod 14:19; 23:20; 32:34.

[16]"Now we are here at Kadesh, a town on the edge of your territory. [17]Please let us pass through your country. We will not go through any field or vineyard, or drink water from any well. We will travel along the King's Highway and not turn to the right or to the left until we have passed through your territory.[x]"

[18]But Edom answered:

"You may not pass through here; if you try, we will march out and attack you with the sword."

[19]The Israelites replied:

"We will go along the main road, and if we or our livestock[y] drink any of your water, we will pay for it.[z] We only want to pass through on foot — nothing else."

[20]Again they answered:

"You may not pass through."

Then Edom came out against them with a large and powerful army. [21]Since Edom refused to let them go through their territory, Israel turned away from them.[a]

20:17 [x]Nu 21:22
20:19 [y]Ex 12:38 [z]Dt 2:6,28
20:21 [a]Dt 2:8; Jdg 11:18
20:22 [b]Nu 33:37
20:23 [c]Nu 33:37
20:24 [d]Ge 25:8 [e]ver 10
20:25 [f]Nu 33:38
20:26 [g]ver 24
20:28 [h]Ex 29:29 [i]Nu 33:38; Dt 10:6; 32:50
20:29 [j]Dt 34:8
21:1 [k]Nu 33:40; Jos 12:14 [l]Jdg 1:9,16
21:4 [m]Nu 20:22 [n]Dt 2:8; Jdg 11:18
21:5 [o]Ps 78:19

The Death of Aaron

[22]The whole Israelite community set out from Kadesh and came to Mount Hor.[b] [23]At Mount Hor, near the border of Edom,[c] the LORD said to Moses and Aaron, [24]"Aaron will be gathered to his people.[d] He will not enter the land I give the Israelites, because both of you rebelled against my command[e] at the waters of Meribah. [25]Get Aaron and his son Eleazar and take them up Mount Hor.[f] [26]Remove Aaron's garments and put them on his son Eleazar, for Aaron will be gathered to his people;[g] he will die there."

[27]Moses did as the LORD commanded: They went up Mount Hor in the sight of the whole community. [28]Moses removed Aaron's garments and put them on his son Eleazar.[h] And Aaron died there[i] on top of the mountain. Then Moses and Eleazar came down from the mountain, [29]and when the whole community learned that Aaron had died, all the Israelites mourned for him[j] thirty days.

Arad Destroyed

21 When the Canaanite king of Arad,[k] who lived in the Negev,[l] heard that Israel was coming along the road to Atharim, he attacked the Israelites and captured some of them. [2]Then Israel made this vow to the LORD: "If you will deliver these people into our hands, we will totally destroy[a] their cities." [3]The LORD listened to Israel's plea and gave the Canaanites over to them. They completely destroyed them and their towns; so the place was named Hormah.[b]

The Bronze Snake

[4]They traveled from Mount Hor[m] along the route to the Red Sea,[c] to go around Edom. But the people grew impatient on the way;[n] [5]they spoke against God[o] and against Moses, and said, "Why have

[a] 2 The Hebrew term refers to the irrevocable giving over of things or persons to the LORD, often by totally destroying them; also in verse 3. [b] 3 *Hormah* means *destruction.* [c] 4 Or *the Sea of Reeds*

20:21 The Lord forbade the Israelites from engaging Edom in battle (Deut 2:4–5); his focus of judgment was on the horrendous sins of the Canaanites (Gen 15:16; Lev 18:24–25).
20:22–29 *The Death of Aaron.* Like the passing of a crown to a new king after the death of the old king, Aaron's garments pass to his son so that all the people know that Eleazar is now the high priest. Unlike Aaron, Jesus' priestly intercession for his people continues to this very day, for he lives forever (Heb 7:23–25).
20:22 Mount Hor. See map, p. 240.
20:24 both of you rebelled. See vv. 10–12 and notes.
20:29 mourned for him thirty days. Indicating that he was a leader of great importance to them (cf. Deut 34:8).
21:1–3 *Arad Destroyed.* This is the Israelites' first victory over the Canaanites. It strongly contrasts with their first defeat 38 years earlier—also involving a place called Hormah (14:45). This victory signifies to the next generation that as they look to the Lord in faith, he will deliver all the Canaanites into their hands.
21:1 An unprovoked attack initiated by the king of Arad.
21:2 totally destroy. See NIV text note. This is what God will command the Israelites to do with all the Canaanites (Deut 7:1–2). See Introduction to Deuteronomy: Themes and Theology (Holy War).
21:4–9 *The Bronze Snake.* In previous rebellions, the Israelites complained first against the leaders (14:2; 16:2–3,41–42; 20:2); here they complain first against God (v. 5). To make matters worse, they combine many of their previous complaints into one (cf. 11:4–6; 14:2–3; 20:3–5). As in previous episodes, the Lord's judgment comes (v. 6), Moses intercedes (v. 7), and the Lord responds with mercy (vv. 8–9; cf. 11:2–3; 14:11–20).
21:4 go around Edom. See note on 20:14–21.

21:5 [p]Nu 14:2,3 [q]Nu 11:6
21:6 [r]Dt 8:15; Jer 8:17 [s]1Co 10:9
21:7 [t]Ps 78:34; Hos 5:15 [u]Ex 8:8; Ac 8:24 [v]Nu 11:2
21:8 [w]Jn 3:14
21:9 [x]2Ki 18:4 [y]Jn 3:14-15
21:10 [z]Nu 33:43
21:11 [a]Nu 33:44
21:12 [b]Dt 2:13,14
21:13 [c]Nu 22:36; Jdg 11:13,18
21:15 [d]ver 28; Dt 2:9,18
21:16 [e]Jdg 9:21
21:17 [f]Ex 15:1
21:21 [g]Dt 1:4; 2:26-27; Jdg 11:19-21
21:22 [h]Nu 20:17
21:23 [i]Nu 20:21 [j]Dt 2:32; Jdg 11:20

you brought us up out of Egypt to die in the wilderness?[p] There is no bread! There is no water! And we
detest this miserable food!"[q]
[6]Then the LORD sent venomous snakes[r] among them; they bit the people and many Israelites died.[s]
[7]The people came to Moses[t] and said, "We sinned when we spoke against the LORD and against you. Pray
that the LORD[u] will take the snakes away from us." So Moses prayed[v] for the people.
[8]The LORD said to Moses, "Make a snake and put it up on a pole;[w] anyone who is bitten can look at
it and live." [9]So Moses made a bronze snake[x] and put it up on a pole. Then when anyone was bitten by
a snake and looked at the bronze snake, they lived.[y]

The Journey to Moab

[10]The Israelites moved on and camped at Oboth.[z] [11]Then they set out from Oboth and camped in
Iye Abarim, in the wilderness that faces Moab[a] toward the sunrise. [12]From there they moved on and
camped in the Zered Valley.[b] [13]They set out from there and camped alongside the Arnon[c], which is in
the wilderness extending into Amorite territory. The Arnon is the border of Moab, between Moab and
the Amorites. [14]That is why the Book of the Wars of the LORD says:

"... Zahab[a] in Suphah and the ravines,
the Arnon [15]and[b] the slopes of the ravines
that lead to the settlement of Ar[d]
and lie along the border of Moab."

[16]From there they continued on to Beer,[e] the well where the LORD said to Moses, "Gather the people
together and I will give them water."
[17]Then Israel sang this song:[f]

"Spring up, O well!
Sing about it,
[18]about the well that the princes dug,
that the nobles of the people sank—
the nobles with scepters and staffs."

Then they went from the wilderness to Mattanah, [19]from Mattanah to Nahaliel, from Nahaliel to Bamoth, [20]and from Bamoth to the valley in Moab where the top of Pisgah overlooks the wasteland.

Defeat of Sihon and Og

[21]Israel sent messengers to say to Sihon[g] king of the Amorites:

[22]"Let us pass through your country. We will not turn aside into any field or vineyard, or drink
water from any well. We will travel along the King's Highway until we have passed through your
territory.[h]"

[23]But Sihon would not let Israel pass through his territory.[i] He mustered his entire army and
marched out into the wilderness against Israel. When he reached Jahaz,[j] he fought with Israel. [24]Israel,

[a] 14 Septuagint; Hebrew *Waheb* [b] 14,15 Or *"I have been given from Suphah and the ravines / of the Arnon [15]to*

21:8–9 While this strikes many moderns as some form of ancient magic, the text is clear that it is actually the Lord's solution and works only because of his power. By having the Israelites look at the very symbol of their judgment, the Lord is having them acknowledge, "This is the judgment that you, Lord, have justly brought upon us, and only you can deliver us from it." Jesus uses this event to explain his death on the cross (see John 3:14–15 and note).

21:10–20 *The Journey to Moab.* Many of the places mentioned in this passage are hard to identify with certainty (cf. note on 33:1–56). See map, p. 147, for possible route.

21:14 Book of the Wars of the LORD. Not mentioned elsewhere. Its name implies it was a record of the Lord's victories over Israel's enemies (cf. 32:21) and was perhaps a collection of songs (note the poetic nature of vv. 14–15).

21:20 Pisgah. Perhaps a mountain range of which Mount Nebo was a part (Deut 34:1). This was the place from which Balaam would bless Israel (23:14) and Moses would see the promised land (Deut 34:1–4).

21:21–35 *Defeat of Sihon and Og.* Verses 21–32 focus on Sihon and vv. 33–35 on Og. These battles happened on the way to "the valley in Moab" (v. 20). They are a foretaste of the victories the Lord will give the Israelites in Canaan itself. After the battles are over, the Israelites possess land on the east side of the Jordan that extends from the Arnon River in the south to the area of Mount Hermon in the north (see map,

however, put him to the sword[k] and took over his land from the Arnon to the Jabbok, but only as far
as the Ammonites,[l] because their border was fortified. 25 Israel captured all the cities of the Amorites[m]
and occupied them, including Heshbon and all its surrounding settlements. 26 Heshbon was the city of
Sihon[n] king of the Amorites, who had fought against the former king of Moab and had taken from him
all his land as far as the Arnon.
27 That is why the poets say:

> "Come to Heshbon and let it be rebuilt;
> let Sihon's city be restored.
>
> 28 "Fire went out from Heshbon,
> a blaze from the city of Sihon.[o]
> It consumed Ar[p] of Moab,
> the citizens of Arnon's heights.[q]
> 29 Woe to you, Moab![r]
> You are destroyed, people of Chemosh![s]
> He has given up his sons as fugitives[t]
> and his daughters as captives[u]
> to Sihon king of the Amorites.
>
> 30 "But we have overthrown them;
> Heshbon's dominion has been destroyed all the way to Dibon.[v]
> We have demolished them as far as Nophah,
> which extends to Medeba."

31 So Israel settled in the land of the Amorites.
32 After Moses had sent spies to Jazer,[w] the Israelites captured its surrounding settlements and drove
out the Amorites who were there. 33 Then they turned and went up along the road toward Bashan[x],[y] and
Og king of Bashan and his whole army marched out to meet them in battle at Edrei.[z]
34 The LORD said to Moses, "Do not be afraid of him, for I have delivered him into your hands, along
with his whole army and his land. Do to him what you did to Sihon king of the Amorites, who reigned
in Heshbon.[a]"
35 So they struck him down, together with his sons and his whole army, leaving them no survivors.
And they took possession of his land.

Balak Summons Balaam

22 Then the Israelites traveled to the plains of Moab and camped along the Jordan across from
Jericho.[b]
2 Now Balak son of Zippor[c] saw all that Israel had done to the Amorites, 3 and Moab was terrified because there were so many people. Indeed, Moab was filled with dread[d] because of the Israelites.
4 The Moabites said to the elders of Midian, "This horde is going to lick up everything around us, as
an ox licks up the grass of the field."

21:24 [k] Dt 2:33; Ps 135:10-11; Am 2:9 [l] Dt 2:37
21:25 [m] Nu 13:29; Jdg 10:11; Am 2:10
21:26 [n] Dt 29:7; Ps 135:11
21:28 [o] Jer 48:45 [p] ver 15 [q] Nu 22:41; Isa 15:2
21:29 [r] Isa 25:10; Jer 48:46 [s] Jdg 11:24; 1Ki 11:7,33; 2Ki 23:13; Jer 48:7,46 [t] Isa 15:5 [u] Isa 16:2
21:30 [v] Nu 32:3; Isa 15:2; Jer 48:18,22
21:32 [w] Nu 32:1,3,35; Jer 48:32
21:33 [x] Dt 3:3 [y] Dt 3:4 [z] Dt 1:4; 3:1,10; Jos 13:12,31
21:34 [a] Dt 3:2
22:1 [b] Nu 33:48
22:2 [c] Jdg 11:25
22:3 [d] Ex 15:15

p. 2866; cf. Deut 3:8–10; Josh 12:1–6). This land will belong to the Reubenites, Gadites, and half-tribe of Manasseh (Josh 12:1–6).

21:27–30 This poem recounts Heshbon's history. Moabites had controlled it until Sihon, king of the Amorites, captured it.

21:29 Chemosh. A god the Moabites worshiped.

21:33–35 See Deut 3:1–11.

22:1—24:25 *The Story of Balak and Balaam.* Because the Moabites and Midianites fear the Israelites, they seek help from Balaam, a pagan from Mesopotamia (Deut 23:4, see NIV text note). It is true that he speaks God's word (23:5; 24:2–3a) and at times sounds holy (22:18,38; 23:12), but a careful reading of this section shows that he is presented very negatively as a money-hungry seer who does his work using ways that the Lord clearly prohibited and whose donkey is more morally upright than he is (see notes on 22:7,8,18,22,29,30,37; cf. 2 Pet 2:15–16). Later verses make clear he was an enemy to Israel (31:8,15–16; cf. Rev 2:14). Although Balaam was paid to curse the Israelites, the Lord causes him to bless them instead (Deut 23:4–5), repeating over them the Abrahamic promises and blessings (see especially 24:3–9). If God is for Israel, no one can stand against them.

22:1–20 *Balak Summons Balaam.* Balak wants Balaam to curse the Israelites so he can defeat them in battle.

22:1 plains of Moab. The Israelites arrive here after leaving the "valley in Moab" (21:20). From here they could see the long-awaited promised land (see map, p. 380). They remain here for the rest of Numbers (cf. 36:13).

22:2 done to the Amorites. See 21:21–32.

22:3 so many people. See 23:10. The Lord's promise that Abraham would have many descendants has begun to be fulfilled (Gen 13:16; 15:5; 22:17).

22:4 Midian. Midianites lived east of the Jordan in the same general area as the plains of Moab (cf. Judg 6–7).

22:5 [e]Dt 23:4; Jos 13:22; 24:9; Ne 13:2; Mic 6:5; 2Pe 2:15
22:6 [f]ver 12,17; Nu 23:7,11,13
22:7 [g]Nu 23:23; 24:1
22:8 [h]ver 19
22:9 [i]Ge 20:3 [j]ver 20
22:12 [k]Ge 12:2; 22:17; Nu 23:20
22:17 [l]ver 37; Nu 24:11 [m]ver 6
22:18 [n]ver 38; Nu 23:12, 26; 24:13; 1Ki 22:14; 2Ch 18:13; Jer 42:4
22:19 [o]ver 8
22:20 [p]Ge 20:3 [q]ver 35, 38; Nu 23:5,12,16,26; 24:13; 2Ch 18:13
22:22 [r]Ex 4:14 [s]Ge 16:7; Ex 23:20; Jdg 13:3,6,13
22:23 [t]Jos 5:13 [u]ver 25,27

So Balak son of Zippor, who was king of Moab at that time, [5]sent messengers to summon Balaam son of Beor,[e] who was at Pethor, near the Euphrates River, in his native land. Balak said:

> "A people has come out of Egypt; they cover the face of the land and have settled next to me. [6]Now come and put a curse[f] on these people, because they are too powerful for me. Perhaps then I will be able to defeat them and drive them out of the land. For I know that whoever you bless is blessed, and whoever you curse is cursed."

[7]The elders of Moab and Midian left, taking with them the fee for divination.[g] When they came to Balaam, they told him what Balak had said.

[8]"Spend the night here," Balaam said to them, "and I will report back to you with the answer the LORD gives me.[h]" So the Moabite officials stayed with him.

[9]God came to Balaam[i] and asked,[j] "Who are these men with you?"

[10]Balaam said to God, "Balak son of Zippor, king of Moab, sent me this message: [11]'A people that has come out of Egypt covers the face of the land. Now come and put a curse on them for me. Perhaps then I will be able to fight them and drive them away.'"

[12]But God said to Balaam, "Do not go with them. You must not put a curse on those people, because they are blessed.[k]"

[13]The next morning Balaam got up and said to Balak's officials, "Go back to your own country, for the LORD has refused to let me go with you."

[14]So the Moabite officials returned to Balak and said, "Balaam refused to come with us."

[15]Then Balak sent other officials, more numerous and more distinguished than the first. [16]They came to Balaam and said:

> "This is what Balak son of Zippor says: Do not let anything keep you from coming to me, [17]because I will reward you handsomely[l] and do whatever you say. Come and put a curse[m] on these people for me."

[18]But Balaam answered them, "Even if Balak gave me all the silver and gold in his palace, I could not do anything great or small to go beyond the command of the LORD my God.[n] [19]Now spend the night here so that I can find out what else the LORD will tell me.[o]"

[20]That night God came to Balaam[p] and said, "Since these men have come to summon you, go with them, but do only what I tell you."[q]

Balaam's Donkey

[21]Balaam got up in the morning, saddled his donkey and went with the Moabite officials. [22]But God was very angry[r] when he went, and the angel of the LORD[s] stood in the road to oppose him. Balaam was riding on his donkey, and his two servants were with him. [23]When the donkey saw the angel of the LORD standing in the road with a drawn sword[t] in his hand, it turned off the road into a field. Balaam beat it[u] to get it back on the road.

[24]Then the angel of the LORD stood in a narrow path through the vineyards, with walls on both sides. [25]When the donkey saw the angel of the LORD, it pressed close to the wall, crushing Balaam's foot against it. So he beat the donkey again.

22:7 divination. Seeking secret knowledge. It is often associated with magic, using supernatural power to do something (such as call down supernatural curses on someone). To use divination or magic is to take the place of God, who therefore strictly forbids it (Deut 18:10–11).

22:8 the LORD. Balaam refers to God by his personal name and later speaks of "the LORD my God" (v. 18) as if to say that he really knows God. The narrator uses the more general term "God" (vv. 9,10,12,20) as if to say that Balaam does not know "the LORD." This indicates Balaam's deceitful character.

22:12 blessed. By the Lord; therefore they may not be cursed (cf. Gen 12:2–3).

22:18 Balaam acts as though he cares not about money but only about what "the LORD my God" commands. The surrounding context suggests this is not at all the case (see note on 22:22).

22:21–41 *Balaam's Donkey.* The Lord uses the donkey as a living parable to warn and rebuke Balaam for his wrong (see notes on vv. 28–30).

22:22 very angry. If God permitted Balaam to go (v. 20), why was he angry when Balaam went? Verse 35 provides the clue: Balaam must "speak only what" the Lord tells him, which suggests that Balaam had been ready to do whatever Balak paid him to do (cf. 2 Pet 2:15). **angel of the LORD.** Carried out the Lord's judgment (cf. Exod 33:2). For his identity, see note on Exod 3:2.

22:23 Ironically, while Balaam claims to know the Lord (see note on v. 8), only the donkey can see the Lord's angel. Balaam's donkey is more spiritually discerning than he is.

26 Then the angel of the LORD moved on ahead and stood in a narrow place where there was no room to turn, either to the right or to the left. 27 When the donkey saw the angel of the LORD, it lay down under Balaam, and he was angry[v] and beat it with his staff. 28 Then the LORD opened the donkey's mouth,[w] and it said to Balaam, "What have I done to you to make you beat me these three times?[x]"

29 Balaam answered the donkey, "You have made a fool of me! If only I had a sword in my hand, I would kill you right now.[y]"

30 The donkey said to Balaam, "Am I not your own donkey, which you have always ridden, to this day? Have I been in the habit of doing this to you?"

"No," he said.

31 Then the LORD opened Balaam's eyes,[z] and he saw the angel of the LORD standing in the road with his sword drawn. So he bowed low and fell facedown.

32 The angel of the LORD asked him, "Why have you beaten your donkey these three times? I have come here to oppose you because your path is a reckless one before me.[a] 33 The donkey saw me and turned away from me these three times. If it had not turned away, I would certainly have killed you by now,[a] but I would have spared it."

34 Balaam said to the angel of the LORD, "I have sinned.[b] I did not realize you were standing in the road to oppose me. Now if you are displeased, I will go back."

35 The angel of the LORD said to Balaam, "Go with the men, but speak only what I tell you." So Balaam went with Balak's officials.

36 When Balak heard that Balaam was coming, he went out to meet him at the Moabite town on the Arnon[c] border, at the edge of his territory. 37 Balak said to Balaam, "Did I not send you an urgent summons? Why didn't you come to me? Am I really not able to reward you?"

38 "Well, I have come to you now," Balaam replied. "But I can't say whatever I please. I must speak only what God puts in my mouth."[d]

39 Then Balaam went with Balak to Kiriath Huzoth. 40 Balak sacrificed cattle and sheep,[e] and gave some to Balaam and the officials who were with him. 41 The next morning Balak took Balaam up to Bamoth Baal,[f] and from there he could see the outskirts of the Israelite camp.[g]

Balaam's First Message

23 Balaam said, "Build me seven altars here, and prepare seven bulls and seven rams[h] for me." 2 Balak did as Balaam said, and the two of them offered a bull and a ram on each altar.[i]

3 Then Balaam said to Balak, "Stay here beside your offering while I go aside. Perhaps the LORD will come to meet with me.[j] Whatever he reveals to me I will tell you." Then he went off to a barren height.

[a] *32* The meaning of the Hebrew for this clause is uncertain.

22:27 [v] Nu 11:1; Jas 1:19
22:28 [w] 2Pe 2:16 [x] ver 32
22:29 [y] Dt 25:4; Pr 12:10; 27:23-27; Mt 15:19
22:31 [z] Ge 21:19
22:33 [a] ver 29
22:34 [b] Ge 39:9; Nu 14:40; 1Sa 15:24,30; 2Sa 12:13; 24:10; Job 33:27; Ps 51:4
22:36 [c] Nu 21:13
22:38 [d] Nu 23:5,16,26
22:40 [e] Nu 23:1,14,29; Eze 45:23
22:41 [f] Nu 21:28 [g] Nu 23:13
23:1 [h] Nu 22:40
23:2 [i] ver 14,30
23:3 [j] ver 15

22:28 the LORD opened the donkey's mouth. A miracle. Every Israelite knew that donkeys do not talk.

22:29 You have made a fool of me! By disobeying Balaam's commands—the very thing Balaam was about to do concerning the Lord's command to him (cf. v. 20). **I would kill you.** The appropriate penalty for those who play the fool with a master and the very thing the Lord's angel is getting ready to do to Balaam. Balaam has pronounced his own sentence.

22:30 The donkey is a picture of what Balaam should be: faithful to his master's commands.

22:35 speak only what I tell you. The real issue: God requires absolute obedience.

22:36 To be greeted by a king was a great honor. **at the edge of his territory.** A royal reception at the border guaranteed this foreigner's safety.

22:37 reward. Balak again mentions financial reward (v. 17).

22:38 Balaam has apparently learned his lesson (cf. 23:12,26; 24:12–13). Sadly, this does not stop him from later acting as Israel's enemy (31:8,15–16; cf. Rev 2:14).

22:41 Bamoth Baal. Location unknown, but presumably in the mountain range at the northeastern end of the Dead Sea near Pisgah (cf. 23:14; see note on 21:20). The name means "the high places of Baal," which puts these activities in a negative light. **outskirts.** Not the whole camp (cf. 23:13), which emphasizes how numerous the people are; the Lord's promise to give Abraham many descendants has begun to be fulfilled (Gen 13:16; 15:5; 22:17).

23:1–12 *Balaam's First Message.* Balaam's message focuses on the Israelites' great numbers (v. 10) and the favor the Lord shows them (v. 8), both of which were part of the Abrahamic promises (Gen 12:1–3). The story has five sections: preparing to receive the message (vv. 1–3); receiving the message (vv. 4–5); delivering the message (vv. 6–10); Balak's response (v. 11); and Balaam's counter-response (v. 12). The next two stories follow the same pattern (vv. 13–26; 23:27—24:14) and will have the same theme: the Lord will indeed bless the Israelites and fulfill his covenant promises to them (see note on 24:3–9).

23:1 seven altars. Apparently a standard way at that time for some pagans to approach a deity.

23:3 Stay. Perhaps to pray while Balaam went to do his work. A pagan diviner from Mesopotamia would normally use divination to receive a message from God (cf. 24:1).

23:4 [k]ver 16
23:5 [l]Dt 18:18; Jer 1:9 [m]Nu 22:20
23:6 [n]ver 17
23:7 [o]Nu 22:5 [p]ver 18; Nu 24:3,21 [q]Nu 22:6; Dt 23:4
23:8 [r]Nu 22:12
23:9 [s]Ex 33:16; Dt 32:8; 33:28
23:10 [t]Ge 13:16 [u]Ps 116:15; Isa 57:1 [v]Ps 37:37
23:11 [w]Nu 24:10; Ne 13:2
23:12 [x]Nu 22:20,38
23:14 [y]ver 2
23:16 [z]Nu 22:38
23:19 [a]Isa 55:9; Hos 11:9 [b]1Sa 15:29; Mal 3:6; Titus 1:2; Jas 1:17

4 God met with him,[k] and Balaam said, "I have prepared seven altars, and on each altar I have offered a bull and a ram."
5 The LORD put a word in Balaam's mouth[l] and said, "Go back to Balak and give him this word."[m]
6 So he went back to him and found him standing beside his offering, with all the Moabite officials.[n]
7 Then Balaam[o] spoke his message:[p]

"Balak brought me from Aram,
the king of Moab from the eastern mountains.
'Come,' he said, 'curse Jacob for me;
come, denounce Israel.'[q]
8 How can I curse
those whom God has not cursed?[r]
How can I denounce
those whom the LORD has not denounced?
9 From the rocky peaks I see them,
from the heights I view them.
I see a people who live apart
and do not consider themselves one of the nations.[s]
10 Who can count the dust of Jacob[t]
or number even a fourth of Israel?
Let me die the death of the righteous,[u]
and may my final end be like theirs![v]"

11 Balak said to Balaam, "What have you done to me? I brought you to curse my enemies, but you
have done nothing but bless them!"[w]
12 He answered, "Must I not speak what the LORD puts in my mouth?"[x]

Balaam's Second Message

13 Then Balak said to him, "Come with me to another place where you can see them; you will not
see them all but only the outskirts of their camp. And from there, curse them for me." 14 So he took
him to the field of Zophim on the top of Pisgah, and there he built seven altars and offered a bull and
a ram on each altar.[y]
15 Balaam said to Balak, "Stay here beside your offering while I meet with him over there."
16 The LORD met with Balaam and put a word in his mouth[z] and said, "Go back to Balak and give
him this word."
17 So he went to him and found him standing beside his offering, with the Moabite officials. Balak
asked him, "What did the LORD say?"
18 Then he spoke his message:

"Arise, Balak, and listen;
hear me, son of Zippor.
19 God is not human,[a] that he should lie,
not a human being, that he should change his mind.[b]

23:7 Aram. Another name for the area of Mesopotamia where Balaam is from (see Deut 23:4 and NIV text note).

23:8 God is not opposed to Israel, an important point in light of the divine punishment of the adults of the exodus generation. Verses 9–10 make clear that God has in fact blessed Israel (cf. v. 20).

23:9 The Israelites themselves understand that God has set them apart (cf. Exod 19:4–6; Deut 7:6–8).

23:10 dust. Israel's vast numbers are a beginning of the fulfillment of the Lord's promises to Abraham (Gen 13:16; 15:5; 22:17). **righteous.** They are in right relationship with God. **may my final end be like theirs.** Cf. Gen 12:3. Sadly, Balaam will not join Israel's faith so that this may occur (cf. 31:8,16).

23:11 Balak believes that he can manipulate the gods to do whatever he wants as long as he has the right person (Balaam) to do the manipulating. He is therefore angry that Balaam has done the opposite of what Balak asked him to do.

23:12 Balaam has learned that the Lord is a sovereign God whom people cannot manipulate (cf. v. 26; 24:12–13).

23:13–26 *Balaam's Second Message.* This focuses on the Lord's faithfulness to bless his people (vv. 19–20), his presence with them (v. 21), and the strength they have because of him (vv. 22–24). For the story's structure, see note on 23:1–12.

23:13 not see them all ... outskirts. See note on 22:41.

23:14 top of Pisgah. See note on 21:20.

23:19 lie ... change his mind. Contrary to what Balak thinks, the Lord is not like pagan gods, who are comparable to capricious and fickle

Does he speak and then not act?
Does he promise and not fulfill?
20 I have received a command to bless;
he has blessed,[c] and I cannot change it.[d]

21 "No misfortune is seen in Jacob,[e]
no misery observed[a] in Israel.[f]
The LORD their God is with them;[g]
the shout of the King[h] is among them.
22 God brought them out of Egypt;[i]
they have the strength of a wild ox.[j]
23 There is no divination against[b] Jacob,
no evil omens[k] against[b] Israel.
It will now be said of Jacob
and of Israel, 'See what God has done!'
24 The people rise like a lioness;[l]
they rouse themselves like a lion[m]
that does not rest till it devours its prey
and drinks the blood of its victims."

25 Then Balak said to Balaam, "Neither curse them at all nor bless them at all!"
26 Balaam answered, "Did I not tell you I must do whatever the LORD says?"

Balaam's Third Message

27 Then Balak said to Balaam, "Come, let me take you to another place.[n] Perhaps it will please God
to let you curse them for me from there." 28 And Balak took Balaam to the top of Peor,[o] overlooking
the wasteland.
29 Balaam said, "Build me seven altars here, and prepare seven bulls and seven rams for me." 30 Balak
did as Balaam had said, and offered a bull and a ram on each altar.

24 Now when Balaam saw that it pleased the LORD to bless Israel, he did not resort to divination[p]
as at other times, but turned his face toward the wilderness.[q] 2 When Balaam looked out and
saw Israel encamped tribe by tribe, the Spirit of God came on him[r] 3 and he spoke his message:

"The prophecy of Balaam son of Beor,
the prophecy of one whose eye sees clearly,
4 the prophecy of one who hears the words of God,[s]
who sees a vision from the Almighty,[c][t]
who falls prostrate, and whose eyes are opened:

[a] *21* Or *He has not looked on Jacob's offenses / or on the wrongs found* [b] *23* Or *in* [c] *4* Hebrew *Shaddai*; also in verse 16

23:20 [c] Ge 22:17; Nu 22:12 [d] Isa 43:13
23:21 [e] Ps 32:2,5; Ro 4:7-8 [f] Isa 40:2; Jer 50:20 [g] Ex 29:45,46; Ps 145:18 [h] Dt 33:5; Ps 89:15-18
23:22 [i] Nu 24:8 [j] Dt 33:17; Job 39:9
23:23 [k] Nu 24:1; Jos 13:22
23:24 [l] Na 2:11 [m] Ge 49:9
23:27 [n] ver 13
23:28 [o] Ps 106:28
24:1 [p] Nu 23:23 [q] Nu 23:28
24:2 [r] Nu 11:25,26; 1Sa 10:10; 19:20; 2Ch 15:1
24:4 [s] Nu 22:20 [t] Ge 15:1

human beings and who could therefore be asked to break their promises. **Does he speak and then not act?** The Lord does what he says, which in this case is to bless Israel (v. 20). He is always faithful to his covenant promises (cf. Titus 1:2).
23:21 God is with them ... the King is among them. This is the basis of all that follows: their redemption from Egypt (v. 22), their immunity to pagan divination and omens (v. 23), and their success in battle (v. 24).
23:27—24:14 *Balaam's Third Message.* This message focuses on several Abrahamic promises (see note on 24:3–9). Balaam receives this message differently (24:1–2), and there is a new focus on its prophetic nature (24:3–4). For the story's structure, see note on 23:1–12.
23:27 Perhaps. Completely ignores the Lord's message in vv. 19–20,23.
24:1 turned his face toward the wilderness. Set out to see Israel's encampment (perhaps to bless them).
24:2 the Spirit of God came on him. Not to indicate he was now redeemed but to give him a prophetic message.
24:3–9 The first two messages describe present realities; this one describes future realities. It focuses on five elements of the Abrahamic promises: (1) the fruitfulness of the people (cf. Gen 13:16; 15:5; 22:17), who are like well-watered gardens and mighty cedars (v. 6; cf. Pss 1:3; 92:12; Isa 58:11; 61:3); (2) their king's might (v. 7; cf. Gen 17:6; 49:10; see note on v. 17); (3) the strength of their kingdom (v. 7)—Israel will defeat all their enemies with God's help (vv. 8–9; cf. Gen 22:17); (4) Israel's relationship with God (v. 8; cf. Gen 17:7); (5) blessing comes to those who bless Israel and cursing to those who curse them (v. 9; cf. Gen 12:3; 27:29). Balak has been warned. He would be wise to bless this people and worship their God.

24:6 [u]Ps 45:8 [v]Ps 1:3; 104:16 **24:7** [w]2Sa 15:8 [x]2Sa 5:12; 1Ch 14:2; Ps 145:11-13 **24:8** [y]Ps 2:9; Jer 50:17 [z]Ps 45:5 **24:9** [a]Ge 49:9; Nu 23:24 [b]Ge 12:3 **24:10** [c]Eze 21:14 [d]Nu 23:11 [e]Ne 13:2 **24:11** [f]Nu 22:17 **24:12** [g]Nu 22:18 **24:13** [h]Nu 22:18 [i]Nu 22:20 **24:14** [j]Ge 49:1; Nu 31:8, 16; Da 2:28; Mic 6:5 **24:17** [k]Rev 1:7 [l]Mt 2:2 [m]Ge 49:10

5 "How beautiful are your tents, Jacob,
your dwelling places, Israel!

6 "Like valleys they spread out,
like gardens beside a river,
like aloes[u] planted by the LORD,
like cedars beside the waters.[v]
7 Water will flow from their buckets;
their seed will have abundant water.

"Their king will be greater than Agag;[w]
their kingdom will be exalted.[x]

8 "God brought them out of Egypt;
they have the strength of a wild ox.
They devour hostile nations
and break their bones in pieces;[y]
with their arrows they pierce them.[z]
9 Like a lion they crouch and lie down,
like a lioness[a] — who dares to rouse them?

"May those who bless you be blessed
and those who curse you be cursed!"[b]

10 Then Balak's anger burned against Balaam. He struck his hands together[c] and said to him, "I
summoned you to curse my enemies, but you have blessed them[d] these three times.[e] 11 Now leave at once
and go home! I said I would reward you handsomely,[f] but the LORD has kept you from being rewarded."
12 Balaam answered Balak, "Did I not tell the messengers you sent me,[g] 13 'Even if Balak gave me all
the silver and gold in his palace, I could not do anything of my own accord, good or bad, to go beyond
the command of the LORD[h] — and I must say only what the LORD says'?[i] 14 Now I am going back to my
people, but come, let me warn you of what this people will do to your people in days to come."[j]

Balaam's Fourth Message

15 Then he spoke his message:

"The prophecy of Balaam son of Beor,
the prophecy of one whose eye sees clearly,
16 the prophecy of one who hears the words of God,
who has knowledge from the Most High,
who sees a vision from the Almighty,
who falls prostrate, and whose eyes are opened:

17 "I see him, but not now;
I behold him, but not near.[k]
A star will come out of Jacob;[l]
a scepter will rise out of Israel.[m]

24:7 Agag. Not mentioned elsewhere but apparently known for his great power. The Agag in 1 Sam 15:32–33 comes later. In the ancient Near East, multiple kings used the same name (e.g., five different Assyrian kings are named Shalmaneser).

24:10 Balak utterly rejects Balaam and his message. He is not thankful for learning the truth. **struck his hands together.** Perhaps as an act of derision or scorn (cf. Lam 2:15).

24:11 Balak (perhaps mockingly) throws Balaam's explanation back in his face: "Blame the LORD, not me, that you're not getting paid!" (cf. 22:38; 23:12,26).

24:15–19 *Balaam's Fourth Message.* While the previous three messages focused on the blessings that will come to Israel, the next four focus on the ruin that will come to other nations (vv. 15–24). This suggests that these are nations that will not bless Israel (v. 9).

24:17–18 Moab ... Edom. See map, p. 2868.

24:17 star ... scepter. Language that describes a king (cf. Gen 49:10; Isa 14:12). **Jacob.** Forefather of the nation of Israel. Israel's king would come from Judah (Gen 49:10), suggesting that this prophecy finds the beginning of its fulfillment in David (cf. 2 Sam 8:2,14) and its final fulfillment in Jesus (Rev 5:5; 22:16; see note on Rev 5:5). Jesus is the far greater Davidic King, who rules over all people (Acts 2:29–36; Phil 2:9–11; Heb 1:3).

He will crush the foreheads of Moab,[n]
the skulls[a] of[b] all the people of Sheth.[c]
18 Edom[o] will be conquered;
Seir, his enemy, will be conquered,
but Israel will grow strong.
19 A ruler will come out of Jacob[p]
and destroy the survivors of the city."

Balaam's Fifth Message

20 Then Balaam saw Amalek[q] and spoke his message:

"Amalek was first among the nations,
but their end will be utter destruction."

Balaam's Sixth Message

21 Then he saw the Kenites[r] and spoke his message:

"Your dwelling place is secure,
your nest is set in a rock;
22 yet you Kenites will be destroyed
when Ashur[s] takes you captive."

Balaam's Seventh Message

23 Then he spoke his message:

"Alas! Who can live when God does this?[d]
24 Ships will come from the shores of Cyprus;[t]
they will subdue Ashur and Eber,[u]
but they too will come to ruin.[v]"

25 Then Balaam[w] got up and returned home, and Balak went his own way.

Moab Seduces Israel

25 While Israel was staying in Shittim,[x] the men began to indulge in sexual immorality[y] with
Moabite women,[z] 2 who invited them to the sacrifices[a] to their gods.[b] The people ate the sacrificial meal and bowed down before these gods. 3 So Israel yoked themselves to the Baal of Peor.[c] And
the LORD's anger burned against them.

24:17 [n] Nu 21:29; Isa 15:1-16:14
24:18 [o] Am 9:12
24:19 [p] Ge 49:10; Mic 5:2
24:20 [q] Ex 17:14
24:21 [r] Ge 15:19
24:22 [s] Ge 10:22
24:24 [t] Ge 10:4 [u] Ge 10:21 [v] ver 20
24:25 [w] Nu 31:8
25:1 [x] Jos 2:1; Mic 6:5 [y] 1Co 10:8; Rev 2:14 [z] Nu 31:16
25:2 [a] Ex 34:15 [b] Ex 20:5; Dt 32:38; 1Co 10:20
25:3 [c] Ps 106:28; Hos 9:10

[a] *17* Samaritan Pentateuch (see also Jer. 48:45); the meaning of the word in the Masoretic Text is uncertain.
[b] *17* Or possibly *Moab, / batter* [c] *17* Or *all the noisy boasters* [d] *23* Masoretic Text; with a different word division of the Hebrew *The people from the islands will gather from the north.*

24:20 *Balaam's Fifth Message.* This message concerns the people descended from Amalek. See map, p. 322.

24:20 first among the nations. In status, chronology (Exod 17:8–16), or both. **end will be utter destruction.** For trying to destroy Israel (Exod 17:8–16). See also 1 Sam 15:1–33; 30:1–18; 1 Chr 4:42–43.

24:21–22 *Balaam's Sixth Message.* This message concerns the Kenites, who were apparently a tribal group that lived in the general region that Judah would inherit (Judg 1:16; cf. 1 Sam 15:6; see map, p. 412).

24:22 Ashur. Perhaps a people who lived nearby in the north Sinai region (Gen 25:3,18).

24:23–25 *Balaam's Seventh Message.* This message appears to refer to a people coming from the west (perhaps the Sea Peoples who invaded Canaan ca. 1200 BC) who will defeat others and then be defeated.

24:25 Although Balaam departs here, he will play a part in the events of ch. 25 (see 31:16; see also note on 31:8).

25:1–18 *Moab Seduces Israel.* While staying on the plains of Moab, the Israelites commit sexual immorality with foreign women and worship foreign gods (vv. 1–5). The Lord brings a plague that kills many of the people and is stopped when a priest shows zeal for the Lord's honor by performing an act of judgment against the sin (vv. 6–18).

25:1 Shittim. On the plains of Moab where Israel is encamped (22:1). They will depart from here for the promised land (Josh 3:1; see map, p. 380). **sexual immorality.** Sex outside the marriage covenant. The Hebrew word used here also describes a severe form of covenant unfaithfulness to the Lord: idolatry (Jer 3:6–9). Here the sexual immorality and idolatry seem related.

25:3 yoked themselves. In a double yoke: Israel on one side and Baal on the other. Israel should have been "yoked" to the Lord alone (cf. Matt 11:28–30). **Baal of Peor.** Apparently a local nature spirit of the region of Peor who was thought to control its fertility (Judg 2:12b–13). **the LORD's anger burned against them.** Idolatry was a very serious sin (cf. Deut 4:3–4; Ps 106:28–29).

4The LORD said to Moses, "Take all the leaders of these people, kill them and expose them in broad
daylight before the LORD,[d] so that the LORD's fierce anger[e] may turn away from Israel."
5So Moses said to Israel's judges, "Each of you must put to death[f] those of your people who have
yoked themselves to the Baal of Peor."
6Then an Israelite man brought into the camp a Midianite woman right before the eyes of Moses
and the whole assembly of Israel while they were weeping at the entrance to the tent of meeting. 7When
Phinehas son of Eleazar, the son of Aaron, the priest, saw this, he left the assembly, took a spear in his
hand 8and followed the Israelite into the tent. He drove the spear into both of them, right through the
Israelite man and into the woman's stomach. Then the plague against the Israelites was stopped;[g] 9but
those who died in the plague[h] numbered 24,000.[i]
10The LORD said to Moses, 11"Phinehas son of Eleazar, the son of Aaron, the priest, has turned my
anger away from the Israelites.[j] Since he was as zealous for my honor[k] among them as I am, I did not
put an end to them in my zeal. 12Therefore tell him I am making my covenant of peace[l] with him. 13He
and his descendants will have a covenant of a lasting priesthood,[m] because he was zealous for the honor
of his God and made atonement[n] for the Israelites."
14The name of the Israelite who was killed with the Midianite woman was Zimri son of Salu, the
leader of a Simeonite family. 15And the name of the Midianite woman who was put to death was Kozbi[o]
daughter of Zur, a tribal chief of a Midianite family.[p]
16The LORD said to Moses, 17"Treat the Midianites[q] as enemies and kill them. 18They treated you
as enemies when they deceived you in the Peor incident[r] involving their sister Kozbi, the daughter
of a Midianite leader, the woman who was killed when the plague came as a result of that
incident."

The Second Census

26 After the plague the LORD said to Moses and Eleazar son of Aaron, the priest, 2"Take a census[s] of
the whole Israelite community by families—all those twenty years old or more who are able
to serve in the army[t] of Israel." 3So on the plains of Moab[u] by the Jordan across from Jericho,[v] Moses

25:4 [d]Dt 4:3 [e]Dt 13:17
25:5 [f]Ex 32:27
25:8 [g]Nu 16:46-48; Ps 106:30
25:9 [h]Nu 14:37; 1Co 10:8 [i]Nu 31:16
25:11 [j]Ps 106:30 [k]Ex 20:5; Dt 32:16,21; Ps 78:58
25:12 [l]Isa 54:10; Eze 34:25; Mal 2:4,5
25:13 [m]Ex 29:9 [n]Nu 16:46
25:15 [o]ver 18 [p]Nu 31:8; Jos 13:21
25:17 [q]Nu 31:1-3
25:18 [r]Nu 31:16
26:2 [s]Ex 30:11-16; 38:25-26; Nu 1:2 [t]Nu 1:3
26:3 [u]Nu 33:48 [v]Nu 22:1

25:4 leaders. Involved in the idolatry (or at least approving of it). They are held to a higher standard and therefore singled out for judgment (cf. Luke 12:47–48; Heb 13:17; Jas 3:1). **in broad daylight.** A shameful way to die (cf. 1 Sam 31:8–13).

25:5 judges. Responsible for executing judgment (Exod 18:21–26). **put to death.** Cf. Exod 32:27.

25:6–15 Like his grandfather Aaron, Phinehas the priest makes atonement for the Israelites and stops a plague among them (vv. 7–9; cf. 16:47–49).

25:6 brought into the camp. For sex (see v. 8 and note). **Midianite woman.** The Midianites lived in this region (22:4,7). **before the eyes.** Publicly, with no shame. **weeping.** Perhaps because of the Lord's pronouncement (v. 4) and the plague (v. 9).

25:8 tent. Not the tent of meeting; this translates a different Hebrew word. **drove the spear into both of them.** Perhaps suggesting they were having sex; they died together in their rebellious act. **plague.** See note on 16:46.

25:11 as zealous ... as I am. Phinehas did what God called priests to do: protect God's honor and reflect his holy character to the world (Ps 106:30; cf. John 2:13–17).

25:12 covenant of peace. A promise of life and peace that flows from being in relationship with God (cf. Isa 54:10; Ezek 37:26; Mal 2:5).

25:13 lasting priesthood. The Lord would watch over the life and peace of Phinehas's descendants (cf. Ps 106:30–31). **made atonement.** Fulfilling his priestly duties and thereby showing his worthiness of the priestly office. Sadly, atonement was not made here by slaughtering an animal for sinners but by slaughtering the sinners themselves.

25:14–15 The man and woman involved were people from leading families of these nations (cf. 31:8); this emphasizes the gravity of the sin.

25:16–18 From the beginning, the Midianites were involved with the Moabites in trying to harm Israel (22:4,7). The punishment the Lord commands for them fits the crime: they treated the Israelites as enemies, purposely deceiving them into a harmful situation by leading them astray into idolatry (e.g., Kozbi [25:15]). They will now get what they asked for: they will be treated as enemies by the Israelites (see ch. 31; Judg 6–8).

26:1—36:13 *The Next Generation: A New Start for Israel on the Border of the Promised Land.* The story of Israel's exodus generation began with censuses (chs. 1–4) and then further preparations for marching into the promised land (5:1—10:10). The story of the next generation also starts with a census (ch. 26) and then further preparations for marching into the promised land (chs. 27–36). While the exodus generation was characterized by disobedience to the Lord's commands and was shut out of the promised land (see note on 10:11—25:18), the next generation is characterized by obedience (31:7,31; 36:10; see note on 1:54) and is now at the border of the promised land awaiting the Lord's command to enter it (see note on 36:13).

26:1–65 *The Second Census.* With the faithless exodus generation now dead (26:64–65), the faithful next generation takes their own military census as they prepare to do battle in the promised land.

26:1 After the plague. See 25:9. **Eleazar.** Replaced Aaron (cf. 1:3; see 20:22–29).

26:2 serve in the army. See note on 1:3. The conquest of the promised land is directly ahead.

26:3 plains of Moab ... Jericho. See map, p. 380. Jericho is the first city in which they will do battle in the promised land (Josh 6).

and Eleazar the priest spoke with them and said, [4]"Take a census of the men twenty years old or more, as the LORD commanded Moses."

These were the Israelites who came out of Egypt:

[5]The descendants of Reuben, the firstborn son of Israel, were:
through Hanok,[w] the Hanokite clan;
through Pallu,[x] the Palluite clan;
[6]through Hezron, the Hezronite clan;
through Karmi, the Karmite clan.
[7]These were the clans of Reuben; those numbered were 43,730.
[8]The son of Pallu was Eliab, [9]and the sons of Eliab[y] were Nemuel, Dathan and Abiram. The same Dathan and Abiram were the community[z] officials who rebelled against Moses and Aaron and were among
Korah's followers when they rebelled against the LORD.[a] [10]The earth opened its mouth and swallowed
them along with Korah, whose followers died when the fire devoured the 250 men. And they served as
a warning sign.[b] [11]The line of Korah,[c] however, did not die out.[d]

[12]The descendants of Simeon by their clans were:
through Nemuel, the Nemuelite clan;
through Jamin,[e] the Jaminite clan;
through Jakin, the Jakinite clan;
[13]through Zerah,[f] the Zerahite clan;
through Shaul, the Shaulite clan.
[14]These were the clans of Simeon; those numbered were 22,200.[g]

[15]The descendants of Gad by their clans were:
through Zephon,[h] the Zephonite clan;
through Haggi, the Haggite clan;
through Shuni, the Shunite clan;
[16]through Ozni, the Oznite clan;
through Eri, the Erite clan;
[17]through Arodi,[a] the Arodite clan;
through Areli, the Arelite clan.
[18]These were the clans of Gad;[i] those numbered were 40,500.

[19]Er and Onan were sons of Judah, but they died[j] in Canaan.
[20]The descendants of Judah by their clans were:
through Shelah,[k] the Shelanite clan;
through Perez, the Perezite clan;
through Zerah, the Zerahite clan.[l]
[21]The descendants of Perez were:
through Hezron,[m] the Hezronite clan;
through Hamul, the Hamulite clan.
[22]These were the clans of Judah;[n] those numbered were 76,500.

[a] *17* Samaritan Pentateuch and Syriac (see also Gen. 46:16); Masoretic Text *Arod*

26:5 [w]Ge 46:9 [x]1Ch 5:3
26:9 [y]Nu 16:1 [z]Nu 1:16 [a]Nu 16:2
26:10 [b]Nu 16:35,38
26:11 [c]Ex 6:24 [d]Nu 16:33; Dt 24:16
26:12 [e]1Ch 4:24
26:13 [f]Ge 46:10
26:14 [g]Nu 1:23
26:15 [h]Ge 46:16
26:18 [i]Nu 1:25; Jos 13:24-28
26:19 [j]Ge 38:2-10; 46:12
26:20 [k]1Ch 2:3 [l]Jos 7:17
26:21 [m]Ru 4:19; 1Ch 2:9
26:22 [n]Nu 1:27

26:4–51 For each tribe, a standard formula is used: the tribe, its main clans (see note on 3:15), and its total number (see "The Census Results," p. 247; see also Introduction: Interpretive Issues). "Clans" are perhaps mentioned because of their role in the land allotments (vv. 52–57 cf. Josh 19:1,10).

26:8–11 Recalls the story of ch. 16. Since Dathan and Abiram were Reubenites, their story fits here logically. It also explains why their lines did not continue.

26:10 warning. If any of the Israelites act like them, they will have no part in Israel.

26:11 line. Perhaps they survived because they disagreed with their father's actions and did not stand with him in support (see note on 16:32).

26:14 22,200. Down from 59,300 (1:23). Perhaps this tribe was especially involved in the sin at Shittim (cf. 25:14) and was therefore decimated by the plague (25:9).

26:19 Er and Onan ... died. See Gen 38:7–10.

26:22 76,500. The largest number, in keeping with the earlier blessing-prophecy of Judah's future success (Gen 49:8–12). From this tribe came King David and the far greater Davidic King, Jesus (Matt 1:2–16).

26:23 [o]Ge 46:13; 1Ch 7:1
26:24 [p]Ge 46:13
26:25 [q]Nu 1:29
26:27 [r]Nu 1:31
26:29 [s]Jos 17:1 [t]Jdg 11:1
26:30 [u]Jos 17:2; Jdg 6:11
26:33 [v]Nu 27:1 [w]Nu 36:11
26:34 [x]Nu 1:35
26:37 [y]Nu 1:33
26:38 [z]Ge 46:21; 1Ch 7:6
26:40 [a]Ge 46:21; 1Ch 8:3

23 The descendants of Issachar by their clans were:
through Tola,[o] the Tolaite clan;
through Puah, the Puite[a] clan;
24 through Jashub,[p] the Jashubite clan;
through Shimron, the Shimronite clan.
25 These were the clans of Issachar;[q] those numbered were 64,300.

26 The descendants of Zebulun by their clans were:
through Sered, the Seredite clan;
through Elon, the Elonite clan;
through Jahleel, the Jahleelite clan.
27 These were the clans of Zebulun;[r] those numbered were 60,500.

28 The descendants of Joseph by their clans through Manasseh and Ephraim were:
29 The descendants of Manasseh:
through Makir,[s] the Makirite clan (Makir was the father of Gilead[t]);
through Gilead, the Gileadite clan.
30 These were the descendants of Gilead:
through Iezer,[u] the Iezerite clan;
through Helek, the Helekite clan;
31 through Asriel, the Asrielite clan;
through Shechem, the Shechemite clan;
32 through Shemida, the Shemidaite clan;
through Hepher, the Hepherite clan.
33 (Zelophehad[v] son of Hepher had no sons; he had only daughters, whose names were Mahlah, Noah, Hoglah, Milkah and Tirzah.)[w]
34 These were the clans of Manasseh; those numbered were 52,700.[x]

35 These were the descendants of Ephraim by their clans:
through Shuthelah, the Shuthelahite clan;
through Beker, the Bekerite clan;
through Tahan, the Tahanite clan.
36 These were the descendants of Shuthelah:
through Eran, the Eranite clan.
37 These were the clans of Ephraim;[y] those numbered were 32,500.

These were the descendants of Joseph by their clans.

38 The descendants of Benjamin[z] by their clans were:
through Bela, the Belaite clan;
through Ashbel, the Ashbelite clan;
through Ahiram, the Ahiramite clan;
39 through Shupham,[b] the Shuphamite clan;
through Hupham, the Huphamite clan.
40 The descendants of Bela through Ard[a] and Naaman were:
through Ard,[c] the Ardite clan;
through Naaman, the Naamite clan.

[a] *23* Samaritan Pentateuch, Septuagint, Vulgate and Syriac (see also 1 Chron. 7:1); Masoretic Text *through Puvah, the Punite* [b] *39* A few manuscripts of the Masoretic Text, Samaritan Pentateuch, Vulgate and Syriac (see also Septuagint); most manuscripts of the Masoretic Text *Shephupham* [c] *40* Samaritan Pentateuch and Vulgate (see also Septuagint); Masoretic Text does not have *through Ard.*

26:33 Prepares readers for 27:1 – 11.
26:34 52,700. Up from 32,200 (1:35). The reason for the large increase is not known.

[41]These were the clans of Benjamin;[b] those numbered were 45,600.

[42]These were the descendants of Dan by their clans:
through Shuham,[c] the Shuhamite clan.
These were the clans of Dan: [43]All of them were Shuhamite clans; and those numbered were 64,400.

[44]The descendants of Asher by their clans were:
through Imnah, the Imnite clan;
through Ishvi, the Ishvite clan;
through Beriah, the Beriite clan;
[45]and through the descendants of Beriah:
through Heber, the Heberite clan;
through Malkiel, the Malkielite clan.
[46](Asher had a daughter named Serah.)
[47]These were the clans of Asher;[d] those numbered were 53,400.

[48]The descendants of Naphtali[e] by their clans were:
through Jahzeel, the Jahzeelite clan;
through Guni, the Gunite clan;
[49]through Jezer, the Jezerite clan;
through Shillem, the Shillemite clan.
[50]These were the clans of Naphtali;[f] those numbered were 45,400.

[51]The total number of the men of Israel was 601,730.[g]

[52]The LORD said to Moses, [53]"The land is to be allotted to them as an inheritance based on the number of names.[h] [54]To a larger group give a larger inheritance, and to a smaller group a smaller one;
each is to receive its inheritance according to the number[i] of those listed. [55]Be sure that the land is distributed by lot.[j] What each group inherits will be according to the names for its ancestral tribe. [56]Each
inheritance is to be distributed by lot among the larger and smaller groups."

[57]These were the Levites[k] who were counted by their clans:
through Gershon, the Gershonite clan;
through Kohath, the Kohathite clan;
through Merari, the Merarite clan.
[58]These also were Levite clans:
the Libnite clan,
the Hebronite clan,
the Mahlite clan,
the Mushite clan,
the Korahite clan.
(Kohath was the forefather of Amram;[l] [59]the name of Amram's wife was Jochebed,[m] a descendant
of Levi, who was born to the Levites[a] in Egypt. To Amram she bore Aaron, Moses[n] and their sister
Miriam. [60]Aaron was the father of Nadab and Abihu, Eleazar and Ithamar.[o] [61]But Nadab and
Abihu[p] died when they made an offering before the LORD with unauthorized fire.)[q]

[62]All the male Levites a month old or more numbered 23,000.[r] They were not counted[s] along with the
other Israelites because they received no inheritance[t] among them.[u]

[a] 59 Or *Jochebed, a daughter of Levi, who was born to Levi*

26:41 [b]Nu 1:37
26:42 [c]Ge 46:23
26:47 [d]Nu 1:41
26:48 [e]Ge 46:24; 1Ch 7:13
26:50 [f]Nu 1:43
26:51 [g]Ex 12:37; 38:26; Nu 1:46; 11:21
26:53 [h]Jos 11:23; 14:1; Eze 45:8
26:54 [i]Nu 33:54
26:55 [j]Nu 34:14
26:57 [k]Ge 46:11; Ex 6:16-19
26:58 [l]Ex 6:20
26:59 [m]Ex 2:1 [n]Ex 6:20
26:60 [o]Nu 3:2
26:61 [p]Lev 10:1-2 [q]Nu 3:4
26:62 [r]Nu 3:39 [s]Nu 1:47 [t]Nu 18:23 [u]Nu 2:33; Dt 10:9

26:46 Serah. Perhaps mentioned because she, like Zelophehad's daughters (v. 33), will inherit land (cf. ch. 27).
26:52–56 The land is to be divided proportionately (vv. 53–54), so the census numbers are very important. There is also an emphasis on distributing the land by lot (vv. 55–56; cf. 33:54; Josh 14–19). Since the lot's decision is from the Lord (Prov 16:33), no tribe can complain about their inheritance. See note on 18:20 for the NT use of inheritance language.
26:57–62 The Levites are not listed with the rest of the Israelites because they will not receive large plots of land, only cities to live in (35:1–8), and because they will not take part in battle (see note on 1:47–53).
26:58–61 Further details on the all-important priestly line.
26:61 See Lev 10:1–3. Presumably this helps explain why their descendants do not carry on in Israel. It is also enshrined in the priestly genealogy as a warning to all priests.
26:62 no inheritance. See note on 18:20.

26:63 [v] ver 3
26:64 [w] Nu 14:29; Dt 2:14-15; Heb 3:17
26:65 [x] Nu 14:28; 1Co 10:5 [y] Jos 14:6-10
27:1 [z] Nu 26:33 [a] Jos 17:2,3 [b] Nu 36:1
27:3 [c] Nu 26:65 [d] Nu 16:2 [e] Nu 26:33
27:5 [f] Ex 18:19 [g] Nu 9:8
27:7 [h] Job 42:15 [i] Jos 17:4
27:11 [j] Nu 35:29
27:12 [k] Nu 33:47; Jer 22:20 [l] Dt 3:23-27; 32:48-52
27:13 [m] Nu 31:2 [n] Nu 20:28
27:14 [o] Nu 20:12 [p] Ex 17:7; Dt 32:51; Ps 106:32
27:16 [q] Nu 16:22
27:17 [r] Dt 31:2; 1Ki 22:17; Eze 34:5; Zec 10:2; Mt 9:36; Mk 6:34

63 These are the ones counted by Moses and Eleazar the priest when they counted the Israelites on
the plains of Moab[v] by the Jordan across from Jericho. 64 Not one of them was among those counted[w] by
Moses and Aaron the priest when they counted the Israelites in the Desert of Sinai. 65 For the LORD had
told those Israelites they would surely die in the wilderness,[x] and not one of them was left except Caleb
son of Jephunneh and Joshua son of Nun.[y]

Zelophehad's Daughters

27:1-11pp — Nu 36:1-12

27 The daughters of Zelophehad[z] son of Hepher,[a] the son of Gilead, the son of Makir,[b] the son of
Manasseh, belonged to the clans of Manasseh son of Joseph. The names of the daughters were
Mahlah, Noah, Hoglah, Milkah and Tirzah. They came forward 2 and stood before Moses, Eleazar the
priest, the leaders and the whole assembly at the entrance to the tent of meeting and said, 3 "Our father
died in the wilderness.[c] He was not among Korah's followers, who banded together against the LORD,[d]
but he died for his own sin and left no sons.[e] 4 Why should our father's name disappear from his clan
because he had no son? Give us property among our father's relatives."

5 So Moses brought their case[f] before the LORD,[g] 6 and the LORD said to him, 7 "What Zelophehad's
daughters are saying is right. You must certainly give them property as an inheritance[h] among their
father's relatives and give their father's inheritance to them.[i]

8 "Say to the Israelites, 'If a man dies and leaves no son, give his inheritance to his daughter. 9 If he
has no daughter, give his inheritance to his brothers. 10 If he has no brothers, give his inheritance to
his father's brothers. 11 If his father had no brothers, give his inheritance to the nearest relative in his
clan, that he may possess it. This is to have the force of law[j] for the Israelites, as the LORD commanded
Moses.' "

Joshua to Succeed Moses

12 Then the LORD said to Moses, "Go up this mountain in the Abarim Range[k] and see the land[l] I have
given the Israelites. 13 After you have seen it, you too will be gathered to your people,[m] as your brother
Aaron[n] was, 14 for when the community rebelled at the waters in the Desert of Zin, both of you disobeyed
my command to honor me as holy[o] before their eyes." (These were the waters of Meribah[p] Kadesh, in
the Desert of Zin.)

15 Moses said to the LORD, 16 "May the LORD, the God who gives breath to all living things,[q] appoint
someone over this community 17 to go out and come in before them, one who will lead them out and
bring them in, so the LORD's people will not be like sheep without a shepherd."[r]

26:63–65 The Lord's judgment indeed came to pass (see 14:20–35 and note).

26:65 except Caleb … and Joshua. Cf. 13:30; 14:6–9,24,30; Josh 14:6–14; 19:49–50.

27:1–11 *Zelophehad's Daughters.* Num 26:52–56 mentions dividing the promised land among the Israelites. In Israelite society, the man who was head of a family unit received the land. After his death, the land passed to his sons who would carry on his line. Daughters could also receive inheritance in the form of a dowry, a wedding gift from their father (Gen 29:24,29; Judg 1:13–15). This story answers the question, If a man has daughters, but no sons, and then dies, to whom does the land go at his death? The text affirms that the daughters should indeed inherit the land (Num 27:7). It also makes clear how to keep family land within the clan and tribe if a man has no surviving children (vv. 8–11), thus maintaining equity among the tribes in terms of property holdings.

27:3 not among Korah's followers. So his name should not be blotted out from Israel (see note on 26:8–11). **died for his own sin.** He was part of the rebellious generation of ch. 14, whose descendants would nonetheless inherit the land.

27:4 disappear. Come to an end. **Give us.** Giving property to the daughters presumably prevents the father's name from disappearing because if the daughters marry (presumably within the father's tribe, cf. 36:5–10), a grandson can carry on their father's name and inherit the property (cf. Deut 25:5–6). See ch. 36 for an appendix to this account.

27:12–23 *Joshua to Succeed Moses.* While Moses could see the promised land (v. 12), he would not lead Israel into it (vv. 13–14; cf. 20:12; Deut 34). Joshua will do so when Moses is gone (vv. 15–23).

27:12 Go up this mountain. Mount Nebo (Deut 32:49), from which the land was visible (see map, p. 380). Moses fulfills this command in Deut 34.

27:14 disobeyed my command to honor me as holy. They instead sought their own glory (see notes on 20:9–12).

27:16–17 Moses requests a leader for Israel because he cares for and loves the Lord's people.

27:16 God who gives breath to all. So he knows them intimately and can choose the best leader.

27:17 sheep. Many texts use this image to describe the Lord's people, sometimes to critique current leaders for not taking care of them (Jer 23:1–3; Ezek 34:1–10; Matt 9:36) and sometimes to describe the Lord's care for them (see Ps 23:1 and note). Jesus is described as the ultimate good shepherd who loves his sheep so much that he lays his life down for them (John 10:11–15).

18 So the LORD said to Moses, "Take Joshua son of Nun, a man in whom is the spirit of leadership,[a][s] and lay your hand on him.[t] 19 Have him stand before Eleazar the priest and the entire assembly and commission him[u] in their presence.[v] 20 Give him some of your authority so the whole Israelite community will obey him.[w] 21 He is to stand before Eleazar the priest, who will obtain decisions for him by inquiring[x] of the Urim[y] before the LORD. At his command he and the entire community of the Israelites will go out, and at his command they will come in."

22 Moses did as the LORD commanded him. He took Joshua and had him stand before Eleazar the priest and the whole assembly. 23 Then he laid his hands on him and commissioned him, as the LORD instructed through Moses.

Daily Offerings

28 The LORD said to Moses, 2 "Give this command to the Israelites and say to them: 'Make sure that you present to me at the appointed time my food[z] offerings, as an aroma pleasing to me.' 3 Say to them: 'This is the food offering you are to present to the LORD: two lambs a year old without defect, as a regular burnt offering each day.[a] 4 Offer one lamb in the morning and the other at twilight, 5 together with a grain offering of a tenth of an ephah[b] of the finest flour mixed with a quarter of a hin[c] of oil[b] from pressed olives. 6 This is the regular burnt offering instituted at Mount Sinai[c] as a pleasing aroma, a food offering presented to the LORD. 7 The accompanying drink offering[d] is to be a quarter of a hin of fermented drink with each lamb. Pour out the drink offering to the LORD at the sanctuary.[e] 8 Offer the second lamb at twilight, along with the same kind of grain offering and drink offering that you offer in the morning. This is a food offering, an aroma pleasing to the LORD.[f]

Sabbath Offerings

9 " 'On the Sabbath[g] day, make an offering of two lambs a year old without defect, together with its drink offering and a grain offering of two-tenths of an ephah[d][h] of the finest flour mixed with olive oil. 10 This is the burnt offering for every Sabbath, in addition to the regular burnt offering[i] and its drink offering.

Monthly Offerings

11 " 'On the first of every month,[j] present to the LORD a burnt offering of two young bulls, one ram and seven male lambs a year old, all without defect.[k] 12 With each bull there is to be a grain offering[l] of three-tenths of an ephah[e][m] of the finest flour mixed with oil; with the ram, a grain offering of two-tenths of an ephah of the finest flour mixed with oil; 13 and with each lamb, a grain offering[n] of a tenth of an ephah of the finest flour mixed with oil. This is for a burnt offering, a pleasing aroma, a

a *18* Or *the Spirit* *b* *5* That is, probably about 3 1/2 pounds or about 1.6 kilograms; also in verses 13, 21 and 29 *c* *5* That is, about 1 quart or about 1 liter; also in verses 7 and 14 *d* *9* That is, probably about 7 pounds or about 3.2 kilograms; also in verses 12, 20 and 28 *e* *12* That is, probably about 11 pounds or about 5 kilograms; also in verses 20 and 28

27:18 [s]Ge 41:38; Nu 11:25-29 [t]ver 23; Dt 34:9
27:19 [u]Dt 3:28; 31:14, 23 [v]Dt 31:7
27:20 [w]Jos 1:16,17
27:21 [x]Jos 9:14 [y]Ex 28:30
28:2 [z]Lev 3:11
28:3 [a]Ex 29:38
28:5 [b]Lev 2:1; Nu 15:4
28:6 [c]Ex 19:3
28:7 [d]Ex 29:41 [e]Lev 3:7
28:8 [f]Lev 1:9
28:9 [g]Ex 20:10 [h]Lev 23:13
28:10 [i]ver 3
28:11 [j]Nu 10:10 [k]Lev 1:3
28:12 [l]Nu 15:6 [m]Nu 15:9
28:13 [n]Lev 6:14

27:18 Joshua. Moses' assistant since Mount Sinai (Exod 33:11); he has proven leadership experience (Exod 17:8–13) and proven faithfulness (Num 14:6–9). **the spirit of leadership.** Or "spirit," referring either to courage for leadership (cf. Josh 2:11; 5:1, where "courage" translates the Hebrew word for "spirit") or to a God-given gift for leadership (cf. Exod 28:3).
27:19–20 The public nature of this event aids the leadership transition by making clear that Joshua is now the one the Israelites are to obey.
27:21 Urim. The Urim and the Thummim were in the high priest's breastpiece (Exod 28:30) and appear to have been lots used to inquire of the Lord (1 Sam 14:41–42; see note on Exod 28:30).
28:1—29:40 *Offerings and Festivals.* Chs. 28–29 describe what Israel's worship should look like in the promised land. This section focuses on the sacrifices required at set times throughout the year as opposed to sacrifices brought to fulfill a vow or as freewill offerings (29:39). It lists the sacrifices by frequency: daily (28:2–8), weekly (28:9–10), monthly (28:11–15), and yearly (28:16—29:38, listed chronologically). Through these offerings and festivals, the people maintain and strengthen their relationship with the Lord and with each other. They acknowledge their need for the Lord's forgiveness and help, celebrate what he has done for them in the past and what he promises to do for them in the future, and affirm that they are brothers and sisters in one covenant family. See "The Lord's Appointed Festivals," p. 229.
28:1–8 *Daily Offerings.* See note on Exod 29:38–43. Cf. Heb 7:17; 10:11–14.
28:2 appointed time. Detailed in chs. 28–29. **food offerings ... aroma pleasing to me.** See note on 15:3.
28:3 year old without defect. See note on 6:14.
28:5–7 grain offering ... drink offering. For these offerings, which are mentioned many times in chs. 28–29, see notes on 15:4,5 and "Grain and Drink Offerings That Accompany Animal Sacrifices," p. 273.
28:9–10 *Sabbath Offerings.* The daily offerings were doubled, setting this day apart as special.
28:11–15 *Monthly Offerings.* Israel celebrated "on the first of every month" (v. 11), which came at the new moon (v. 14). There were as many offerings at this festival as at the important Festival of Weeks (cf. 28:26–31).

28:14 [o]Nu 15:7 [p]Ezr 3:5
28:15 [q]ver 3,23,24 [r]Lev 4:3
28:16 [s]Ex 12:6,18; Lev 23:5; Dt 16:1
28:17 [t]Ex 12:19 [u]Ex 23:15; 34:18; Lev 23:6; Dt 16:3-8
28:18 [v]Ex 12:16; Lev 23:7
28:20 [w]Lev 14:10
28:22 [x]Ro 8:3 [y]Nu 15:28
28:26 [z]Ex 34:22 [a]Ex 23:16 [b]ver 18; Dt 16:10
28:29 [c]ver 13
28:31 [d]ver 3,19
29:1 [e]Lev 23:24
29:2 [f]Nu 28:2 [g]Nu 28:3

food offering presented to the LORD. [14]With each bull there is to be a drink offering[o] of half a hin[a] of wine; with the ram, a third of a hin[b]; and with each lamb, a quarter of a hin. This is the monthly burnt offering to be made at each new moon[p] during the year. [15]Besides the regular burnt offering[q] with its drink offering, one male goat is to be presented to the LORD as a sin offering.[cr]

The Passover

28:16-25pp — Ex 12:14-20; Lev 23:4-8; Dt 16:1-8

[16]" 'On the fourteenth day of the first month the LORD's Passover[s] is to be held. [17]On the fifteenth day of this month there is to be a festival; for seven days[t] eat bread made without yeast.[u] [18]On the first day hold a sacred assembly and do no regular work.[v] [19]Present to the LORD a food offering consisting of a burnt offering of two young bulls, one ram and seven male lambs a year old, all without defect. [20]With each bull offer a grain offering of three-tenths of an ephah[w] of the finest flour mixed with oil; with the ram, two-tenths; [21]and with each of the seven lambs, one-tenth. [22]Include one male goat as a sin offering[x] to make atonement for you.[y] [23]Offer these in addition to the regular morning burnt offering. [24]In this way present the food offering every day for seven days as an aroma pleasing to the LORD; it is to be offered in addition to the regular burnt offering and its drink offering. [25]On the seventh day hold a sacred assembly and do no regular work.

The Festival of Weeks

28:26-31pp — Lev 23:15-22; Dt 16:9-12

[26]" 'On the day of firstfruits,[z] when you present to the LORD an offering of new grain during the Festival of Weeks,[a] hold a sacred assembly and do no regular work.[b] [27]Present a burnt offering of two young bulls, one ram and seven male lambs a year old as an aroma pleasing to the LORD. [28]With each bull there is to be a grain offering of three-tenths of an ephah of the finest flour mixed with oil; with the ram, two-tenths; [29]and with each of the seven lambs, one-tenth.[c] [30]Include one male goat to make atonement for you. [31]Offer these together with their drink offerings, in addition to the regular burnt offering[d] and its grain offering. Be sure the animals are without defect.

The Festival of Trumpets

29:1-6pp — Lev 23:23-25

29 " 'On the first day of the seventh month hold a sacred assembly and do no regular work.[e] It is a day for you to sound the trumpets. [2]As an aroma pleasing to the LORD,[f] offer a burnt offering of one young bull, one ram and seven male lambs a year old, all without defect.[g] [3]With the bull offer a grain offering of three-tenths of an ephah[d] of the finest flour mixed with olive oil; with the ram,

[a] *14* That is, about 2 quarts or about 1.9 liters [b] *14* That is, about 1 1/3 quarts or about 1.3 liters [c] *15* Or *purification offering*; also in verse 22 [d] *3* That is, probably about 11 pounds or about 5 kilograms; also in verses 9 and 14

28:16–25 *The Passover.* See note on 9:1–14.
28:17 festival ... bread made without yeast. The Festival of Unleavened Bread. This was one of three festivals to be celebrated by all Israelite males at the sanctuary (Exod 23:14–17). As its name implies, only unleavened bread (bread without yeast, Exod 12:15) could be eaten during this time (see note on Exod 12:15). It began the day after the Passover and had the same purpose: to remember how the Lord delivered the Israelites from slavery (Exod 12:17; Deut 16:3). Because Passover and the Festival of Unleavened Bread took place in the first month (v. 16), the Israelites began their year by declaring and celebrating the Lord's deliverance and remembering to trust in his power to rescue and save. It is thus appropriate that Jesus' death and resurrection—the ultimate displays of the Lord's deliverance and power to save—happened at this same time in the Jewish calendar (cf. Matt 26:17; 27:15–26,62–66; 28:1–10).
28:18 sacred assembly. The people assembled together and set the day apart as holy to the Lord, especially by stopping regular work and observing any rites connected to the holiday (vv. 25–26; 29:1,12). **regular work.** Such as farming; other work, such as food preparation, was allowed (Exod 12:16; cf. Lev 23:3,28).
28:19 two young bulls, one ram. Reverses the number in Lev 23:18 because of either different traditions or a scribal error in one of the passages.
28:26–31 *The Festival of Weeks.* So called because it took place seven weeks after the firstfruits of the barley harvest were offered (see note on Lev 23:16; cf. Exod 34:22; Deut 16:9–10). Also known as the Festival of Harvest (see note on Exod 23:16) and as Pentecost (see note on Acts 2:1). Like the Festival of Unleavened Bread, it was also one of three festivals to be celebrated by all Israelite males at the sanctuary (Deut 16:16; Deut 16:11 suggests entire families often went). It was a time to celebrate the Lord's provision in the harvest and in this way remember that the Lord could be trusted to provide for their physical needs (Deut 26:10; see Ps 145:15–16; Matt 6:19–34; cf. Hos 2:8–9).
29:1–6 *The Festival of Trumpets.* See note on Lev 23:24.
29:1 sound the trumpets. See note on 10:1–10.

two-tenths[a]; 4 and with each of the seven lambs, one-tenth.[b] 5 Include one male goat[h] as a sin offering[c]
to make atonement for you. 6 These are in addition to the monthly[i] and daily burnt offerings[j] with
their grain offerings and drink offerings as specified. They are food offerings presented to the LORD, a
pleasing aroma.

The Day of Atonement

29:7-11pp — Lev 16:2-34; 23:26-32

7 " 'On the tenth day of this seventh month hold a sacred assembly. You must deny yourselves[d][k] and
do no work.[l] 8 Present as an aroma pleasing to the LORD a burnt offering of one young bull, one ram and
seven male lambs a year old, all without defect. 9 With the bull offer a grain offering[m] of three-tenths
of an ephah of the finest flour mixed with oil; with the ram, two-tenths; 10 and with each of the seven
lambs, one-tenth.[n] 11 Include one male goat as a sin offering, in addition to the sin offering for atonement and the regular burnt offering[o] with its grain offering, and their drink offerings.

The Festival of Tabernacles

29:12-39pp — Lev 23:33-43; Dt 16:13-17

12 " 'On the fifteenth day of the seventh[p] month,[q] hold a sacred assembly and do no regular work.
Celebrate a festival to the LORD for seven days. 13 Present as an aroma pleasing to the LORD a food offering
consisting of a burnt offering of thirteen young bulls, two rams and fourteen male lambs a year old, all
without defect. 14 With each of the thirteen bulls offer a grain offering[r] of three-tenths of an ephah of
the finest flour mixed with oil; with each of the two rams, two-tenths; 15 and with each of the fourteen
lambs, one-tenth. 16 Include one male goat as a sin offering, in addition to the regular burnt offering
with its grain offering and drink offering.[s]

17 " 'On the second day[t] offer twelve young bulls, two rams and fourteen male lambs a year old, all
without defect.[u] 18 With the bulls, rams and lambs, offer their grain offerings[v] and drink offerings[w] according to the number specified.[x] 19 Include one male goat as a sin offering,[y] in addition to the regular
burnt offering with its grain offering, and their drink offerings.

20 " 'On the third day offer eleven bulls, two rams and fourteen male lambs a year old, all without defect.[z] 21 With the bulls, rams and lambs, offer their grain offerings and drink offerings according to the
number specified.[a] 22 Include one male goat as a sin offering, in addition to the regular burnt offering
with its grain offering and drink offering.

23 " 'On the fourth day offer ten bulls, two rams and fourteen male lambs a year old, all without de
fect. 24 With the bulls, rams and lambs, offer their grain offerings and drink offerings according to the
number specified. 25 Include one male goat as a sin offering, in addition to the regular burnt offering
with its grain offering and drink offering.

26 " 'On the fifth day offer nine bulls, two rams and fourteen male lambs a year old, all without defect.

29:5 [h] Nu 28:15
29:6 [i] Nu 28:11 [j] Nu 28:3
29:7 [k] Ac 27:9 [l] Ex 31:15; Lev 16:29; 23:26-32
29:9 [m] ver 3,18
29:10 [n] Nu 28:13
29:11 [o] Lev 16:3; Nu 28:3
29:12 [p] 1Ki 8:2 [q] Lev 23:24
29:14 [r] ver 3
29:16 [s] ver 6
29:17 [t] Lev 23:36 [u] Nu 28:3
29:18 [v] ver 9 [w] Nu 28:7 [x] Nu 15:4-12
29:19 [y] Nu 28:15
29:20 [z] ver 17
29:21 [a] ver 18

[a] *3* That is, probably about 7 pounds or about 3.2 kilograms; also in verses 9 and 14 [b] *4* That is, probably about 3 1/2 pounds or about 1.6 kilograms; also in verses 10 and 15 [c] *5* Or *purification offering*; also elsewhere in this chapter [d] *7* Or *must fast*

29:7–11 *The Day of Atonement.* See note on Lev 16:1–34; see also "Sacrifice," p. 2656, for further details.
29:7 deny yourselves. At least by fasting (see NIV text note; cf. Ps 35:13) and possibly by other forms of self-denial such as not using ointments (cf. Dan 10:2–3 with Dan 10:12; see also note on Lev 16:29). Such self-denial was often an outward sign of a humble, repentant heart (cf. 1 Sam 7:6; Dan 9:3–5). This day's rites mattered little if the Israelites did not acknowledge their sins and turn from them (see Lev 16:29–31 and note on v. 30; cf. Ps 51:3,17; Isa 1:11–17). **do no work.** Not even "regular work" (28:18; see note); as on the Sabbath, all work is forbidden (cf. Lev 23:3).
29:8–10 In addition to the offerings in Lev 16.
29:11 sin offering for atonement. See Lev 16:3,5.
29:12–40 *The Festival of Tabernacles.* This was a harvest festival also known as the Festival of Ingathering (Exod 23:16b). Like the Festivals of Unleavened Bread and Weeks, it was to be celebrated by all Israelite males at the sanctuary (Deut 16:16; Deut 16:14 suggests entire families often went). The name "Tabernacles" (or "Booths") comes from the temporary shelters the Israelites would live in during the festival (Lev 23:42), the same type of shelters the Israelites lived in when the Lord brought them out of Egypt (Lev 23:43). By doing this as they feasted on the harvest, the Israelites reminded themselves—and taught their descendants—that the Lord was their powerful redeemer as well as their gracious provider. See Neh 8:13–18 for a narrative example of this festival.
29:12–34 The number seven, which often represents completion or perfection (cf. the complete judgment of Lev 26:18,21,24,28), is central throughout the ceremony, which occurs in the seventh month and is seven days long. The various animal offerings are also divisible by seven (70 bulls, 14 rams, 98 lambs, 7 male goats). These were required from the community as a whole, not from each individual.

29:35 [b]Lev 23:36
29:36 [c]Lev 1:9 [d]ver 2
29:39 [e]Nu 6:2 [f]Lev 23:2 [g]Lev 1:3; 1Ch 23:31; 2Ch 31:3
30:1 [h]Nu 1:4
30:2 [i]Dt 23:21-23; Jdg 11:35; Job 22:27; Ps 22:25; 50:14; 116:14; Pr 20:25; Ecc 5:4,5; Jnh 1:16
30:4 [j]ver 7
30:6 [k]Lev 5:4
30:8 [l]Ge 3:16

27 With the bulls, rams and lambs, offer their grain offerings and drink offerings according to the number specified. 28 Include one male goat as a sin offering, in addition to the regular burnt offering with its grain offering and drink offering.

29 " 'On the sixth day offer eight bulls, two rams and fourteen male lambs a year old, all without defect. 30 With the bulls, rams and lambs, offer their grain offerings and drink offerings according to the number specified. 31 Include one male goat as a sin offering, in addition to the regular burnt offering with its grain offering and drink offering.

32 " 'On the seventh day offer seven bulls, two rams and fourteen male lambs a year old, all without defect. 33 With the bulls, rams and lambs, offer their grain offerings and drink offerings according to the number specified. 34 Include one male goat as a sin offering, in addition to the regular burnt offering with its grain offering and drink offering.

35 " 'On the eighth day hold a closing special assembly[b] and do no regular work. 36 Present as an aroma pleasing to the LORD[c] a food offering consisting of a burnt offering of one bull, one ram and seven male lambs a year old,[d] all without defect. 37 With the bull, the ram and the lambs, offer their grain offerings and drink offerings according to the number specified. 38 Include one male goat as a sin offering, in addition to the regular burnt offering with its grain offering and drink offering.

39 " 'In addition to what you vow[e] and your freewill offerings, offer these to the LORD at your appointed festivals:[f] your burnt offerings,[g] grain offerings, drink offerings and fellowship offerings.' "

40 Moses told the Israelites all that the LORD commanded him.[a]

Vows

30 [b] Moses said to the heads of the tribes of Israel:[h] "This is what the LORD commands: 2 When a man makes a vow to the LORD or takes an oath to obligate himself by a pledge, he must not break his word but must do everything he said.[i]

3 "When a young woman still living in her father's household makes a vow to the LORD or obligates herself by a pledge 4 and her father hears about her vow or pledge but says nothing to her, then all her vows and every pledge by which she obligated herself will stand.[j] 5 But if her father forbids her when he hears about it, none of her vows or the pledges by which she obligated herself will stand; the LORD will release her because her father has forbidden her.

6 "If she marries after she makes a vow[k] or after her lips utter a rash promise by which she obligates herself 7 and her husband hears about it but says nothing to her, then her vows or the pledges by which she obligated herself will stand. 8 But if her husband[l] forbids her when he hears about it, he nullifies the vow that obligates her or the rash promise by which she obligates herself, and the LORD will release her.

9 "Any vow or obligation taken by a widow or divorced woman will be binding on her.

10 "If a woman living with her husband makes a vow or obligates herself by a pledge under oath 11 and her husband hears about it but says nothing to her and does not forbid her, then all her vows or

[a] *40* In Hebrew texts this verse (29:40) is numbered 30:1. [b] In Hebrew texts 30:1-16 is numbered 30:2-17.

29:39 vow ... freewill. Additional offerings they could make at any point in the year, including at these festivals. These did not replace the offerings that chs. 28–29 require.

30:1–16 *Vows.* Ch. 30 is a logical place to discuss questions related to vows, not only because 29:39 mentions them but also because someone who vowed to offer a sacrifice might carry it out during one of the festivals of chs. 28–29 (cf. 1 Sam 1:21). This chapter answers whether there are any exceptions to fulfilling vows, especially when the person making the vow is under the authority of someone else.

30:2 vow. A promise to the Lord to perform something, such as a sacrifice. People took vows to emphasize how serious their prayer request was and to ensure they would appropriately express thanksgiving if the Lord answered their prayer (1 Sam 1:11; 2:1–10; Ps 116:14–19). **pledge.** A promise of some sort to the Lord (see v. 13 and note on 29:7). People took pledges to emphasize the seriousness of their prayer request and their need of the Lord's help (1 Sam 14:24) and/or to commit themselves to fulfill a task (Ps 132:2–5). Since vows and pledges were very easy to make (it simply involved uttering the vow or pledge), people sometimes made them rashly (v. 6; cf. Prov 20:25). **break.** Vows and pledges were considered holy because they involved a promise to the Lord. People did not dare break their word to God (Deut 23:21–23; Eccl 5:4–7; Mal 1:14).

30:3–8 In ancient Israel, a father bore ultimate economic responsibility for any promises made by his young, unmarried daughters (vv. 3–5), and a husband bore the responsibility for his wife's promises (vv. 6–8). These laws allow the men to protect their families economically from any excessive promises while at the same time affirming the women's right to make promises to the Lord.

30:6 rash promise. Apparently a common problem with vows and pledges (see note on v. 2). If a wife made such a promise, she would undoubtedly consider it a blessing that her husband could nullify it.

30:9 widow or divorced woman. She is not under the authority of another, so there is no one to nullify her promise to the Lord.

30:10–15 Similar to vv. 6–8 except the woman is already married.

the pledges by which she obligated herself will stand. 12But if her husband nullifies them when he hears about them, then none of the vows or pledges that came from her lips will stand.[m] Her husband has nullified them, and the LORD will release her. 13Her husband may confirm or nullify any vow she makes or any sworn pledge to deny herself.[a] 14But if her husband says nothing to her about it from day to day, then he confirms all her vows or the pledges binding on her. He confirms them by saying nothing to her when he hears about them. 15If, however, he nullifies them some time after he hears about them, then he must bear the consequences of her wrongdoing."

16These are the regulations the LORD gave Moses concerning relationships between a man and his wife, and between a father and his young daughter still living at home.

Vengeance on the Midianites

31 The LORD said to Moses, 2"Take vengeance on the Midianites[n] for the Israelites. After that, you will be gathered to your people.[o]"

3So Moses said to the people, "Arm some of your men to go to war against the Midianites so that they may carry out the LORD's vengeance[p] on them. 4Send into battle a thousand men from each of the tribes of Israel." 5So twelve thousand men armed for battle, a thousand from each tribe, were supplied from the clans of Israel. 6Moses sent them into battle, a thousand from each tribe, along with Phinehas son of Eleazar, the priest, who took with him articles from the sanctuary[q] and the trumpets[r] for signaling.

7They fought against Midian, as the LORD commanded Moses, and killed every man.[s] 8Among their victims were Evi, Rekem, Zur, Hur and Reba[t]—the five kings of Midian.[u] They also killed Balaam son of Beor with the sword.[v] 9The Israelites captured the Midianite women and children and took all the Midianite herds, flocks and goods as plunder. 10They burned all the towns where the Midianites had settled, as well as all their camps.[w] 11They took all the plunder and spoils, including the people and animals,[x] 12and brought the captives, spoils and plunder to Moses and Eleazar the priest and the Israelite assembly[y] at their camp on the plains of Moab, by the Jordan across from Jericho.

13Moses, Eleazar the priest and all the leaders of the community went to meet them outside the camp. 14Moses was angry with the officers of the army[z]—the commanders of thousands and commanders of hundreds—who returned from the battle.

15"Have you allowed all the women to live?" he asked them. 16"They were the ones who followed Balaam's advice[a] and enticed the Israelites to be unfaithful to the LORD in the Peor incident,[b] so that a plague struck the LORD's people. 17Now kill all the boys. And kill every woman who has slept with a man,[c] 18but save for yourselves every girl who has never slept with a man.

19"Anyone who has killed someone or touched someone who was killed[d] must stay outside the camp

a 13 Or *to fast*

30:12 [m] Eph 5:22; Col 3:18
31:2 [n] Ge 25:2 [o] Nu 20:26; 27:13
31:3 [p] Jdg 11:36; 1Sa 24:12; 2Sa 4:8; 22:48; Ps 94:1; 149:7
31:6 [q] Nu 14:44 [r] Nu 10:9
31:7 [s] Dt 20:13; Jdg 21:11; 1Ki 11:15,16
31:8 [t] Jos 13:21 [u] Nu 25:15 [v] Jos 13:22
31:10 [w] Ge 25:16; 1Ch 6:54; Ps 69:25; Eze 25:4
31:11 [x] Dt 20:14
31:12 [y] Nu 27:2
31:14 [z] ver 48; Ex 18:21; Dt 1:15
31:16 [a] 2Pe 2:15; Rev 2:14 [b] Nu 25:1-9
31:17 [c] Dt 7:2; 20:16-18; Jdg 21:11
31:19 [d] Nu 19:16

30:13 deny herself. See note on 29:7.

30:15 some time after. If a husband wants to nullify his wife's vow or pledge, he must do so the first time he hears about it, not later (when perhaps he realizes how costly it will be). **bear the consequences of her wrongdoing.** Her failure to fulfill the vow or pledge will fall on his shoulders, not hers, since he is the one who prevents her from carrying out a promise that has been ratified before the Lord.

30:16 the regulations. Those concerning vows.

31:1–24 *Vengeance on the Midianites.* The Israelites fulfill the Lord's earlier command (see 25:16–18 and note). This victory is another foretaste of the victories the Lord will give them in the promised land (see notes on 21:1–3,21–35).

31:2 vengeance. Not sinful revenge (cf. Rom 12:19) but carrying out the Lord's punishment on a guilty people (v. 3).

31:3 carry out the LORD's vengeance. The Lord at times uses one nation to punish another. Sometimes he uses Israel to do this (as here), sometimes he uses a nation to punish Israel (see Habakkuk), and sometimes Israel is not involved (Isa 13:17–22). The people of God today are no longer a national theocracy, so they do not do this as a military body. But they do exercise discipline in the context of the local church (1 Cor 5).

31:6 Phinehas. Known for his zeal for the Lord's honor (25:11). **articles from the sanctuary.** Represent the Lord's presence with Israel.

31:8 Zur. Father of Kozbi (25:15). **five kings.** In those days a king was often a leader who ruled a small area (cf. Josh 10:1–5). **Balaam.** Advised Midian on their treacherous strategy (v. 16). He seems to have gone home after advising Balak (24:25), suggesting he later returned to Midian, perhaps to try to make money (see note on 22:1—24:25).

31:13–24 Midian tried to destroy Israel, but the Lord in his justice determined that Midian be destroyed. (The Lord also executed severe punishments on his own people [14:35–37; 16:46–49; 25:9]; his justice shows no favoritism.)

31:16 See 25:1–3.

31:17–18 In the ancient world, sons and the wives who bore them carried on the male line. If a man died without sons, his wife might remarry and the firstborn would then carry on the former husband's name (Deut 25:5–6.) The Israelites were thus to kill males and wives (lest they propagate more Midianites) but not unmarried girls, who would marry an Israelite and carry on his line (see Deut 21:10–14 for the dignity with which the Israelites must treat these women). When an entire nation is punished, the innocent within it (such as young boys in this case) often suffer as well (see note on 14:33).

31:19–24 Since those who had contact with a dead body experienced

31:19 [e]Nu 19:12
31:20 [f]Nu 19:19
31:22 [g]Jos 6:19; 22:8
31:23 [h]1Co 3:13 [i]Nu 19:9,17
31:24 [j]Lev 11:25
31:26 [k]Nu 1:19
31:27 [l]Jos 22:8; 1Sa 30:24
31:28 [m]Nu 18:21
31:30 [n]Nu 3:7; 18:3
31:37 [o]ver 38-41
31:41 [p]Nu 5:9; 18:8
31:49 [q]Jer 23:4
31:50 [r]Ex 30:16
31:53 [s]Dt 20:14
31:54 [t]Ex 28:12

seven days. On the third and seventh days you must purify yourselves[e] and your captives. [20]Purify every
garment[f] as well as everything made of leather, goat hair or wood."

[21]Then Eleazar the priest said to the soldiers who had gone into battle, "This is what is required by
the law that the LORD gave Moses: [22]Gold, silver, bronze, iron,[g] tin, lead [23]and anything else that can
withstand fire must be put through the fire,[h] and then it will be clean. But it must also be purified with
the water of cleansing.[i] And whatever cannot withstand fire must be put through that water. [24]On the
seventh day wash your clothes and you will be clean.[j] Then you may come into the camp."

Dividing the Spoils

[25]The LORD said to Moses, [26]"You and Eleazar the priest and the family heads of the community are
to count all the people[k] and animals that were captured. [27]Divide[l] the spoils equally between the soldiers
who took part in the battle and the rest of the community. [28]From the soldiers who fought in the battle,
set apart as tribute for the LORD[m] one out of every five hundred, whether people, cattle, donkeys or sheep.
[29]Take this tribute from their half share and give it to Eleazar the priest as the LORD's part. [30]From the
Israelites' half, select one out of every fifty, whether people, cattle, donkeys, sheep or other animals. Give
them to the Levites, who are responsible for the care of the LORD's tabernacle.[n]" [31]So Moses and Eleazar
the priest did as the LORD commanded Moses.

[32]The plunder remaining from the spoils that the soldiers took was 675,000 sheep, [33]72,000 cattle,
[34]61,000 donkeys [35]and 32,000 women who had never slept with a man.

[36]The half share of those who fought in the battle was:

337,500 sheep, [37]of which the tribute for the LORD[o] was 675;
[38]36,000 cattle, of which the tribute for the LORD was 72;
[39]30,500 donkeys, of which the tribute for the LORD was 61;
[40]16,000 people, of whom the tribute for the LORD was 32.

[41]Moses gave the tribute to Eleazar the priest as the LORD's part,[p] as the LORD commanded Moses.

[42]The half belonging to the Israelites, which Moses set apart from that of the fighting men— [43]the
community's half—was 337,500 sheep, [44]36,000 cattle, [45]30,500 donkeys [46]and 16,000 people. [47]From
the Israelites' half, Moses selected one out of every fifty people and animals, as the LORD commanded
him, and gave them to the Levites, who were responsible for the care of the LORD's tabernacle.

[48]Then the officers who were over the units of the army—the commanders of thousands and commanders of hundreds—went to Moses [49]and said to him, "Your servants have counted the soldiers
under our command, and not one is missing.[q] [50]So we have brought as an offering to the LORD the
gold articles each of us acquired—armlets, bracelets, signet rings, earrings and necklaces—to make
atonement for ourselves[r] before the LORD."

[51]Moses and Eleazar the priest accepted from them the gold—all the crafted articles. [52]All the gold
from the commanders of thousands and commanders of hundreds that Moses and Eleazar presented as
a gift to the LORD weighed 16,750 shekels.[a] [53]Each soldier had taken plunder[s] for himself. [54]Moses and
Eleazar the priest accepted the gold from the commanders of thousands and commanders of hundreds
and brought it into the tent of meeting as a memorial[t] for the Israelites before the LORD.

[a] 52 That is, about 420 pounds or about 190 kilograms

a major uncleanness (see note on 19:1–22), the army had to cleanse themselves and all they carried before coming back into the camp (see 5:2 and note; see also note on 5:1–4; for the cleansing procedures, see 19:11–22; Lev 11:32).

31:25–54 *Dividing the Spoils.* This section provides direction for how to divide the plunder (vv. 25–31), lists the plunder itself (vv. 32–47), and describes a special offering of the plunder made by the soldiers (vv. 48–54).

31:27–30 The spoil was divided evenly between the soldiers and the people. The soldiers then gave a tribute of 0.2 percent to the priests, and the people gave a tribute of 2 percent to the Levites. Because there were far fewer priests than Levites, this difference makes sense and also allows the soldiers to keep a larger share than the people in recognition of their service in battle.

31:40,47 people. Perhaps they became servants for the tabernacle (cf. Josh 9:21–27).

31:49 counted. Taking a census in ancient Israel was dangerous, especially when the Lord did not explicitly command it (see 2 Sam 24:1–10). **not one is missing.** Demonstrates that the Lord fought for them.

31:50 A ransom payment was needed to atone for those in the census (Exod 30:11–16).

31:52 The soldiers give an average of 1.4 shekels per person, almost three times the required amount (cf. Exod 30:13), perhaps to express thanksgiving for the Lord's help in battle.

The Transjordan Tribes

32 The Reubenites and Gadites, who had very large herds and flocks, saw that the lands of Jazer[u] and Gilead were suitable for livestock.[v] 2So they came to Moses and Eleazar the priest and to the leaders of the community, and said, 3"Ataroth,[w] Dibon, Jazer, Nimrah,[x] Heshbon, Elealeh,[y] Sebam, Nebo and Beon[z] — 4the land the LORD subdued[a] before the people of Israel — are suitable for livestock,[b] and your servants have livestock. 5If we have found favor in your eyes," they said, "let this land be given to your servants as our possession. Do not make us cross the Jordan."

6Moses said to the Gadites and Reubenites, "Should your fellow Israelites go to war while you sit here? 7Why do you discourage the Israelites from crossing over into the land the LORD has given them?[c] 8This is what your fathers did when I sent them from Kadesh Barnea to look over the land.[d] 9After they went up to the Valley of Eshkol[e] and viewed the land, they discouraged the Israelites from entering the land the LORD had given them. 10The LORD's anger was aroused[f] that day and he swore this oath: 11'Because they have not followed me wholeheartedly, not one of those who were twenty years old or more[g] when they came up out of Egypt will see the land I promised on oath[h] to Abraham, Isaac and Jacob[i] — 12not one except Caleb son of Jephunneh the Kenizzite and Joshua son of Nun, for they followed the LORD wholeheartedly.'[j] 13The LORD's anger burned against Israel[k] and he made them wander in the wilderness forty years, until the whole generation of those who had done evil in his sight was gone.[l]

14"And here you are, a brood of sinners, standing in the place of your fathers and making the LORD even more angry with Israel.[m] 15If you turn away from following him, he will again leave all this people in the wilderness, and you will be the cause of their destruction.[n]"

16Then they came up to him and said, "We would like to build pens here for our livestock[o] and cities for our women and children. 17But we will arm ourselves for battle[a] and go ahead of the Israelites[p] until we have brought them to their place.[q] Meanwhile our women and children will live in fortified cities, for protection from the inhabitants of the land. 18We will not return to our homes until each of the Israelites has received their inheritance.[r] 19We will not receive any inheritance with them on the other side of the Jordan, because our inheritance has come to us on the east side of the Jordan."[s]

20Then Moses said to them, "If you will do this — if you will arm yourselves before the LORD for battle[t] 21and if all of you who are armed cross over the Jordan before the LORD until he has driven his enemies out before him — 22then when the land is subdued before the LORD, you may return[u] and be free from your obligation to the LORD and to Israel. And this land will be your possession before the LORD.[v]

23"But if you fail to do this, you will be sinning against the LORD; and you may be sure that your sin will find you out.[w] 24Build cities for your women and children, and pens for your flocks,[x] but do what you have promised.[y]"

25The Gadites and Reubenites said to Moses, "We your servants will do as our lord commands. 26Our children and wives, our flocks and herds will remain here in the cities of Gilead.[z] 27But your servants, every man who is armed for battle, will cross over to fight before the LORD, just as our lord says."

28Then Moses gave orders about them[a] to Eleazar the priest and Joshua son of Nun and to the family

32:1 [u]Nu 21:32 [v]Ex 12:38
32:3 [w]ver 34 [x]ver 36 [y]ver 37; Isa 15:4; 16:9; Jer 48:34 [z]ver 38; Jos 13:17; Eze 25:9
32:4 [a]Nu 21:34 [b]Ex 12:38
32:7 [c]Nu 13:27-14:4
32:8 [d]Nu 13:3,26; Dt 1:19-25
32:9 [e]Nu 13:23; Dt 1:24
32:10 [f]Nu 11:1
32:11 [g]Ex 30:14 [h]Nu 14:23 [i]Nu 14:28-30
32:12 [j]Nu 14:24,30; Dt 1:36; Ps 63:8
32:13 [k]Ex 4:14 [l]Nu 14:28-35; 26:64,65
32:14 [m]ver 10; Dt 1:34; Ps 78:59
32:15 [n]Dt 30:17-18; 2Ch 7:20
32:16 [o]Ex 12:38; Dt 3:19
32:17 [p]Jos 4:12,13 [q]Nu 22:4; Dt 3:20
32:18 [r]Jos 22:1-4
32:19 [s]Jos 12:1
32:20 [t]Dt 3:18
32:22 [u]Jos 22:4 [v]Dt 3:18-20
32:23 [w]Ge 4:7; 44:16; Isa 59:12
32:24 [x]ver 1,16 [y]Nu 30:2
32:26 [z]Jos 1:14
32:28 [a]Dt 3:18-20; Jos 1:13

[a] 17 Septuagint; Hebrew *will be quick to arm ourselves*

32:1–42 *The Transjordan Tribes.* While most of Israel's tribes eventually settled west of the Jordan River, the tribes of Reuben, Gad, and half of Manasseh settled east of it (see map, p. 412). This chapter describes how that came about.

32:1 To the east of the Jordan River is a plateau whose slopes receive sufficient amounts of rainfall to produce vegetation, the very thing Gad and Reuben need.

32:3 For possible locations of some of these cities, see map, p. 2869.

32:5 The request to inherit east of the Jordan was not necessarily sinful. The Lord had promised that Israel's land would stretch from Egypt to Assyria (Gen 15:18). This land on the east side of the Jordan was well within those bounds.

32:6–15 The two and a half tribes make no mention of helping to fight for the rest of the promised land, and Moses provides an appropriate rebuke.

32:7 discourage. If part of the army refused to go into battle, the rest of the soldiers would quickly lose hope. The end result would be the same as what happened in ch. 14: the Israelites refusing to enter the promised land and experiencing the Lord's judgment (vv. 8–15).

32:17 go ahead of the Israelites. Not only fight with them, but take the lead.

32:20–22 That Moses accepts their proposal is further proof that their desire for land east of the Jordan is not wrong.

32:21 before the LORD. Perhaps the troops march in front of the Lord's ark (Josh 6:7). **he has driven his enemies out.** "The battle is the LORD's" (1 Sam 17:47).

32:22 See Josh 22:1–9.

32:23 your sin. The punishment it deserves. **will find you out.** Because the sovereign Lord justly judges sin (Gen 44:16; Gal 6:7–9).

32:25,27 See Josh 4:12–13; 22:1–9.

32:28–32 Since Moses will soon die (27:12–14; 31:2), he makes sure the other leaders are aware of the arrangement.

32:31 [b]ver 29
32:33 [c]Jos 13:24-28; 1Sa 13:7 [d]Dt 2:26 [e]Nu 21:24; Jos 12:6
32:34 [f]Dt 2:36; Jdg 11:26
32:35 [g]ver 3
32:36 [h]ver 3
32:38 [i]ver 3; Isa 15:2; Jer 48:1,22
32:39 [j]Ge 50:23
32:40 [k]Dt 3:15; Jos 17:1
32:41 [l]Dt 3:14; Jos 13:30; Jdg 10:4; 1Ch 2:23
32:42 [m]2Sa 18:18; Ps 49:11
33:1 [n]Mic 6:4 [o]Ps 77:20
33:3 [p]Ex 13:4 [q]Ex 14:8
33:4 [r]Ex 12:12
33:5 [s]Ex 12:37
33:6 [t]Ex 13:20
33:7 [u]Ex 14:9 [v]Ex 14:2
33:8 [w]Ex 14:22 [x]Ex 15:23

heads of the Israelite tribes. 29 He said to them, "If the Gadites and Reubenites, every man armed for
battle, cross over the Jordan with you before the LORD, then when the land is subdued before you, you
must give them the land of Gilead as their possession. 30 But if they do not cross over with you armed,
they must accept their possession with you in Canaan."

31 The Gadites and Reubenites answered, "Your servants will do what the LORD has said.[b] 32 We will cross
over before the LORD into Canaan armed, but the property we inherit will be on this side of the Jordan."

33 Then Moses gave to the Gadites,[c] the Reubenites and the half-tribe of Manasseh son of Joseph the
kingdom of Sihon king of the Amorites[d] and the kingdom of Og king of Bashan — the whole land with
its cities and the territory around them.[e]

34 The Gadites built up Dibon, Ataroth, Aroer,[f] 35 Atroth Shophan, Jazer,[g] Jogbehah, 36 Beth Nimrah[h]
and Beth Haran as fortified cities, and built pens for their flocks. 37 And the Reubenites rebuilt Heshbon,
Elealeh and Kiriathaim, 38 as well as Nebo[i] and Baal Meon (these names were changed) and Sibmah.
They gave names to the cities they rebuilt.

39 The descendants of Makir[j] son of Manasseh went to Gilead, captured it and drove out the Amorites
who were there. 40 So Moses gave Gilead to the Makirites,[k] the descendants of Manasseh, and they settled there. 41 Jair, a descendant of Manasseh, captured their settlements and called them Havvoth Jair.[a][l]
42 And Nobah captured Kenath and its surrounding settlements and called it Nobah after himself.[m]

Stages in Israel's Journey

33 Here are the stages in the journey of the Israelites when they came out of Egypt[n] by divisions
under the leadership of Moses and Aaron.[o] 2 At the LORD's command Moses recorded the stages
in their journey. This is their journey by stages:

3 The Israelites set out from Rameses on the fifteenth day of the first month, the day after the
Passover.[p] They marched out defiantly[q] in full view of all the Egyptians, 4 who were burying all
their firstborn, whom the LORD had struck down among them; for the LORD had brought judgment on their gods.[r]

5 The Israelites left Rameses and camped at Sukkoth.[s]

6 They left Sukkoth and camped at Etham, on the edge of the desert.[t]

7 They left Etham, turned back to Pi Hahiroth, to the east of Baal Zephon,[u] and camped near
Migdol.[v]

8 They left Pi Hahiroth[b] and passed through the sea[w] into the desert, and when they had traveled for three days in the Desert of Etham, they camped at Marah.[x]

[a] *41* Or *them the settlements of Jair* [b] *8* Many manuscripts of the Masoretic Text, Samaritan Pentateuch and Vulgate; most manuscripts of the Masoretic Text *left from before Hahiroth*

32:33–42 These verses describe the property inherited by the two and a half tribes; Josh 13:8–33 does so in more detail.
32:33 half-tribe. Half the tribe of Manasseh settled on the east side of the Jordan and half on the west side (see map, p. 412). This tribe was not part of the original request (v. 1), but certain of its members captured land east of the Jordan (vv. 39–42), so this verse mentions the tribe here with the others that settled east of the Jordan.
33:1–56 *Stages in Israel's Journey.* Ch. 33 summarizes the 40-year journey that brought the Israelites from Egypt to this point on the plains of Moab. They will shortly march from here into the promised land. This itinerary lists 42 travel stations, many of which were not cities that left ruins behind but simply encampments and thus are difficult to identify with certainty. This itinerary overlaps with other itineraries (21:10–20; Deut 1–3), though there are differences, perhaps in part because not one of these itineraries is complete. The locations remind the Israelites of their faithlessness, the Lord's justice, and the Lord's mercy and faithfulness in bringing them to this point. The people of God must always remember who the Lord has shown himself to be in the past and then act in light of that in the present (cf. Deut 8:1–18; 9:7; Rom 12:1). For further details on some of the places and events listed in this itinerary, see the following table:

STAGES IN ISRAEL'S JOURNEY

NUMBERS 33			
vv. 3–4	Exod 12:1–36	v. 17	Num 11:35
v. 5	Exod 12:37	v. 36	Num 20:1
v. 6	Exod 13:20	vv. 37–39	Num 20:22–29
vv. 7–8	Exod 14:2—15:26	v. 40	Num 21:1–3
v. 9	Exod 15:27	v. 41	Num 21:4
vv. 10–11	Exod 16:1	v. 43	Num 21:10
v. 14	Exod 17:1–7	v. 44	Num 21:11
v. 15	Exod 19:2	vv. 48–49	Num 22–25
v. 16	Num 10:11—11:34		

[9]They left Marah and went to Elim, where there were twelve springs and seventy palm trees,
and they camped[y] there.
[10]They left Elim and camped by the Red Sea.[a]
[11]They left the Red Sea and camped in the Desert of Sin.[z]
[12]They left the Desert of Sin and camped at Dophkah.
[13]They left Dophkah and camped at Alush.
[14]They left Alush and camped at Rephidim, where there was no water for the people to drink.
[15]They left Rephidim[a] and camped in the Desert of Sinai.[b]
[16]They left the Desert of Sinai and camped at Kibroth Hattaavah.[c]
[17]They left Kibroth Hattaavah and camped at Hazeroth.[d]
[18]They left Hazeroth and camped at Rithmah.
[19]They left Rithmah and camped at Rimmon Perez.
[20]They left Rimmon Perez and camped at Libnah.[e]
[21]They left Libnah and camped at Rissah.
[22]They left Rissah and camped at Kehelathah.
[23]They left Kehelathah and camped at Mount Shepher.
[24]They left Mount Shepher and camped at Haradah.
[25]They left Haradah and camped at Makheloth.
[26]They left Makheloth and camped at Tahath.
[27]They left Tahath and camped at Terah.
[28]They left Terah and camped at Mithkah.
[29]They left Mithkah and camped at Hashmonah.
[30]They left Hashmonah and camped at Moseroth.[f]
[31]They left Moseroth and camped at Bene Jaakan.
[32]They left Bene Jaakan and camped at Hor Haggidgad.
[33]They left Hor Haggidgad and camped at Jotbathah.[g]
[34]They left Jotbathah and camped at Abronah.
[35]They left Abronah and camped at Ezion Geber.[h]
[36]They left Ezion Geber and camped at Kadesh, in the Desert of Zin.[i]
[37]They left Kadesh and camped at Mount Hor,[j] on the border of Edom.[k] [38]At the LORD's command Aaron the priest went up Mount Hor, where he died[l] on the first day of the fifth month of
the fortieth year after the Israelites came out of Egypt.[m] [39]Aaron was a hundred and twenty-three
years old when he died on Mount Hor.
[40]The Canaanite king of Arad,[n] who lived in the Negev of Canaan, heard that the Israelites
were coming.
[41]They left Mount Hor and camped at Zalmonah.
[42]They left Zalmonah and camped at Punon.
[43]They left Punon and camped at Oboth.[o]
[44]They left Oboth and camped at Iye Abarim, on the border of Moab.[p]
[45]They left Iye Abarim and camped at Dibon Gad.
[46]They left Dibon Gad and camped at Almon Diblathaim.
[47]They left Almon Diblathaim and camped in the mountains of Abarim,[q] near Nebo.
[48]They left the mountains of Abarim and camped on the plains of Moab by the Jordan across
from Jericho.[r] [49]There on the plains of Moab they camped along the Jordan from Beth Jeshimoth
to Abel Shittim.[s]

[50]On the plains of Moab by the Jordan across from Jericho the LORD said to Moses, [51]"Speak to the
Israelites and say to them: 'When you cross the Jordan into Canaan,[t] [52]drive out all the inhabitants of

[a] *10* Or *the Sea of Reeds*; also in verse 11

33:9 [y]Ex 15:27
33:11 [z]Ex 16:1
33:15 [a]Ex 17:1 [b]Ex 19:1
33:16 [c]Nu 11:34
33:17 [d]Nu 11:35
33:20 [e]Jos 10:29
33:30 [f]Dt 10:6
33:33 [g]Dt 10:7
33:35 [h]Dt 2:8; 1Ki 9:26; 22:48
33:36 [i]Nu 20:1
33:37 [j]Nu 20:22 [k]Nu 20:16; 21:4
33:38 [l]Dt 10:6 [m]Nu 20:25-28
33:40 [n]Nu 21:1
33:43 [o]Nu 21:10
33:44 [p]Nu 21:11
33:47 [q]Nu 27:12
33:48 [r]Nu 22:1
33:49 [s]Nu 25:1
33:51 [t]Jos 3:17

33:50–56 Now that the Israelites are on the cusp of the promised land, the Lord reissues commands that emphasize the importance of dispossessing the land of its inhabitants and their idolatrous practices (cf. Exod 23:24; 34:12–14; Lev 18:24–27). Once again, full obedience to his commands is of utmost importance.

33:52 drive out. Other texts make clear that this would happen when

33:52 [u]Ex 23:24; 34:13; Lev 26:1; Dt 7:2,5; 12:3; Jos 11:12; Ps 106:34-36
33:53 [v]Dt 11:31; Jos 21:43
33:54 [w]Nu 26:54
33:55 [x]Jos 23:13; Jdg 2:3; Ps 106:36
34:2 [y]Ge 17:8; Dt 1:7-8; Ps 78:54-55 [z]Eze 47:15
34:3 [a]Jos 15:1-3 [b]Ge 14:3
34:4 [c]Jos 15:3 [d]Nu 32:8
34:5 [e]Ge 15:18; Jos 15:4
34:7 [f]Eze 47:15-17
34:8 [g]Nu 13:21; Jos 13:5
34:11 [h]2Ki 23:33; Jer 39:5 [i]Dt 3:17; Jos 11:2; 13:27
34:13 [j]Jos 14:1-5
34:14 [k]Nu 32:33; Jos 14:3
34:17 [l]Jos 14:1
34:18 [m]Nu 1:4,16
34:19 [n]Nu 26:65 [o]Ge 29:35; Dt 33:7
34:20 [p]Ge 49:5

the land before you. Destroy all their carved images and their cast idols, and demolish all their high places.[u] 53Take possession of the land and settle in it, for I have given you the land to possess.[v] 54Distribute the land by lot, according to your clans.[w] To a larger group give a larger inheritance, and to a smaller group a smaller one. Whatever falls to them by lot will be theirs. Distribute it according to your ancestral tribes.

55" 'But if you do not drive out the inhabitants of the land, those you allow to remain will become barbs in your eyes and thorns[x] in your sides. They will give you trouble in the land where you will live. 56And then I will do to you what I plan to do to them.' "

Boundaries of Canaan

34 The LORD said to Moses, 2"Command the Israelites and say to them: 'When you enter Canaan, the land that will be allotted to you as an inheritance[y] is to have these boundaries:[z]

3" 'Your southern side will include some of the Desert of Zin[a] along the border of Edom. Your southern boundary will start in the east from the southern end of the Dead Sea,[b] 4cross south of Scorpion Pass,[c] continue on to Zin and go south of Kadesh Barnea.[d] Then it will go to Hazar Addar and over to Azmon, 5where it will turn, join the Wadi of Egypt[e] and end at the Mediterranean Sea.

6" 'Your western boundary will be the coast of the Mediterranean Sea. This will be your boundary on the west.

7" 'For your northern boundary,[f] run a line from the Mediterranean Sea to Mount Hor 8and from Mount Hor to Lebo Hamath.[g] Then the boundary will go to Zedad, 9continue to Ziphron and end at Hazar Enan. This will be your boundary on the north.

10" 'For your eastern boundary, run a line from Hazar Enan to Shepham. 11The boundary will go down from Shepham to Riblah[h] on the east side of Ain and continue along the slopes east of the Sea of Galilee.[a][i] 12Then the boundary will go down along the Jordan and end at the Dead Sea.

" 'This will be your land, with its boundaries on every side.' "

13Moses commanded the Israelites: "Assign this land by lot as an inheritance.[j] The LORD has ordered that it be given to the nine and a half tribes, 14because the families of the tribe of Reuben, the tribe of Gad and the half-tribe of Manasseh have received their inheritance.[k] 15These two and a half tribes have received their inheritance east of the Jordan across from Jericho, toward the sunrise."

16The LORD said to Moses, 17"These are the names of the men who are to assign the land for you as an inheritance: Eleazar the priest and Joshua[l] son of Nun. 18And appoint one leader from each tribe to help[m] assign the land. 19These are their names:

Caleb[n] son of Jephunneh,
from the tribe of Judah;[o]
20 Shemuel son of Ammihud,
from the tribe of Simeon;[p]

[a] *11* Hebrew *Kinnereth*

the Lord drove out the nations in terror (Exod 23:27–28) or gave them over to Israel to be destroyed in warfare (Deut 7:1–2; 20:16–18). See Introduction to Deuteronomy: Themes and Theology (Holy War); see also Introduction to Joshua: Theological Themes (Genocide?). **Destroy.** The land was the Lord's, and he alone was to be worshiped in it; this is also true of the earth as a whole (cf. Pss 24:1–2; 67:1–7).

33:54 Distribute the land by lot. See note on 26:52–56.

33:55 barbs ... thorns ... trouble. The inhabitants would lead Israel into the same types of wickedness they engaged in, and the Lord would punish Israel with the same type of judgment the inhabitants would suffer (v. 56; cf. Exod 34:11–17; Lev 18:24–30; Deut 7:1–5; 12:29–31).

34:1 — 36:13 *Commands and Regulations for Life in the Promised Land.* This is a fitting way to close the book; Israel will be marching into the land very soon.

34:1–29 *Boundaries of Canaan.* Since Israel is about to inherit the promised land, this chapter describes its borders: southern (vv. 3–5), western (v. 6), northern (vv. 7–9), and eastern (vv. 10–12). These borders match descriptions of Canaan in Egyptian sources from the second half of the second millennium BC, the exact time period Israel is getting ready to enter the land (and therefore evidence for the antiquity of this list). Since two and a half tribes have already claimed their inheritance east of the Jordan, this land will be for the remaining nine and a half tribes (vv. 13–15). See map, p. 412. (The northern and northeastern borders are less than certain due to the difficulty of identifying many of the sites.)

34:16–29 Now that the land's borders have been described (vv. 3–12), this section identifies who will help properly apportion it. The main leaders are Eleazar and Joshua (v. 17); the leaders from the nine and a half tribes are listed more or less in their tribes' geographic order from south to north (vv. 18–28).

34:17 assign the land. By lot; see note on 26:52–56. **Eleazar ... Joshua.** They will lead in place of Aaron and Moses.

34:19 Caleb. See note on 13:30.

[21]Elidad son of Kislon,
from the tribe of Benjamin;[q]
[22]Bukki son of Jogli,
the leader from the tribe of Dan;
[23]Hanniel son of Ephod,
the leader from the tribe of Manasseh son of Joseph;
[24]Kemuel son of Shiphtan,
the leader from the tribe of Ephraim son of Joseph;
[25]Elizaphan son of Parnak,
the leader from the tribe of Zebulun;
[26]Paltiel son of Azzan,
the leader from the tribe of Issachar;
[27]Ahihud son of Shelomi,
the leader from the tribe of Asher;[r]
[28]Pedahel son of Ammihud,
the leader from the tribe of Naphtali."

[29]These are the men the LORD commanded to assign the inheritance to the Israelites in the land of Canaan.

34:21 [q]Ge 49:27; Ps 68:27
34:27 [r]Nu 1:40
35:2 [s]Lev 25:32-34; Jos 14:3,4
35:6 [t]Jos 20:7-9; 21:3,13

Towns for the Levites

35 On the plains of Moab by the Jordan across from
Jericho, the LORD said to Moses, [2]"Command the
Israelites to give the Levites towns to live in[s] from the inheritance the Israelites will possess. And give them pasturelands around the towns. [3]Then they will have towns to live in
and pasturelands for the cattle they own and all their other
animals.
[4]"The pasturelands around the towns that you give the
Levites will extend a thousand cubits[a] from the town wall.
[5]Outside the town, measure two thousand cubits[b] on the east
side, two thousand on the south side, two thousand on the
west and two thousand on the north, with the town in the
center. They will have this area as pastureland for the towns.

PASTURELANDS

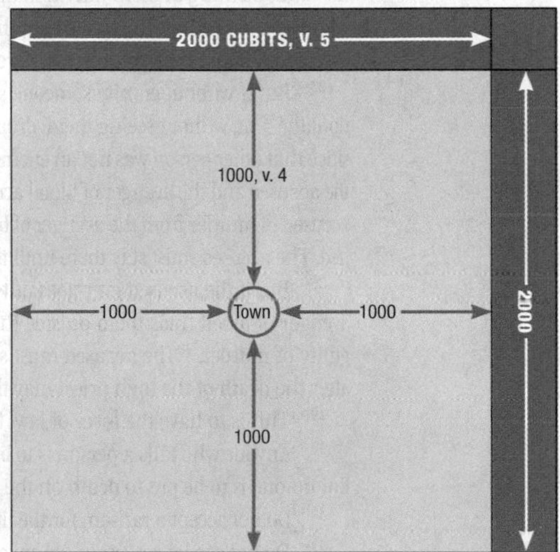

Cities of Refuge

35:6-34Ref — Dt 4:41-43; 19:1-14; Jos 20:1-9

[6]"Six of the towns you give the Levites will be cities of refuge, to which a person who has killed someone may flee.[t] In addition, give them forty-two other towns. [7]In all you must give the Levites forty-eight
towns, together with their pasturelands. [8]The towns you give the Levites from the land the Israelites

[a] *4* That is, about 1,500 feet or about 450 meters [b] *5* That is, about 3,000 feet or about 900 meters

35:1–5 *Towns for the Levites.* In contrast to the other tribes (ch. 34), the Levites do not inherit large tracts of land (18:21–24) and therefore receive cities in which to live (Josh 21; see also map, p. 412).
35:4–5 While there is some debate, many understand the 1,000 cubits (1,500 feet or about 450 meters) to be the distance from the wall of the city to the edge of the pasturelands (v. 4), and the 2,000 cubits (3,000 feet or about 900 meters) to be the length of the outer edge of the pasturelands when thought of as a square. See "Pasturelands," this page.
35:6–34 *Cities of Refuge.* Three important facts shed light on how these cities functioned. (1) Anyone who murdered another person was to be put to death. Humans bear God's image and are worthy of great respect. To destroy human life was therefore to commit a great crime and to be subject to the greatest penalty: death (Gen 9:5–6). (2) Atonement was necessary for unintentional sins (cf. Lev 4:27–28,31b). Normally a sacrificial animal's blood could atone for unintentional sin (e.g., Lev 4:2–3; see 17:11), but when a person accidentally killed another person (manslaughter), only human blood would do—namely, that of the guilty party (v. 33). But for manslaughter there was a way of escape: the guilty party could go to a city of refuge and wait until the high priest's death (vv. 25,28,32), at which point the guilty party could go free. Apparently, the high priest's death substituted for the death of the guilty party. The author of Hebrews describes Jesus as the ultimate high priest who gives his own lifeblood to atone for people's sins (Heb 7:26–27; 9:11–14). (3) To stay in the city was to acknowledge the sin and its seriousness and to follow the God-appointed way of dealing with it. Failing to stay in the city was to deny the sin and its seriousness and thus leave oneself open to God's justice (see note on v. 12).

35:8 [u]Nu 26:54; 33:54; Jos 21:1-42
35:10 [v]Jos 20:2
35:11 [w]ver 22-25 [x]Ex 21:13; Dt 19:1-13
35:12 [y]Dt 19:6; Jos 20:3
35:16 [z]Ex 21:12; Lev 24:17
35:19 [a]ver 21
35:20 [b]Ge 4:8; Ex 21:14; Dt 19:11; 2Sa 3:27; 20:10
35:22 [c]ver 11; Ex 21:13
35:24 [d]ver 12; Jos 20:6
35:25 [e]Ex 29:7
35:29 [f]Nu 27:11
35:30 [g]ver 16; Dt 17:6; 19:15; Mt 18:16; Jn 7:51; 2Co 13:1; Heb 10:28
35:33 [h]Ge 9:6; Ps 106:38; Mic 4:11
35:34 [i]Lev 18:24,25 [j]Ex 29:45
36:1 [k]Nu 26:29 [l]Nu 27:2

possess are to be given in proportion to the inheritance of each tribe: Take many towns from a tribe that has many, but few from one that has few."[u]

9Then the LORD said to Moses: 10"Speak to the Israelites and say to them: 'When you cross the Jordan into Canaan,[v] 11select some towns to be your cities of refuge, to which a person who has killed someone[w] accidentally[x] may flee. 12They will be places of refuge from the avenger,[y] so that anyone accused of murder may not die before they stand trial before the assembly. 13These six towns you give will be your cities of refuge. 14Give three on this side of the Jordan and three in Canaan as cities of refuge. 15These six towns will be a place of refuge for Israelites and for foreigners residing among them, so that anyone who has killed another accidentally can flee there.

16" 'If anyone strikes someone a fatal blow with an iron object, that person is a murderer; the murderer is to be put to death.[z] 17Or if anyone is holding a stone and strikes someone a fatal blow with it, that person is a murderer; the murderer is to be put to death. 18Or if anyone is holding a wooden object and strikes someone a fatal blow with it, that person is a murderer; the murderer is to be put to death. 19The avenger of blood shall put the murderer to death; when the avenger comes upon the murderer, the avenger shall put the murderer to death.[a] 20If anyone with malice aforethought shoves another or throws something at them intentionally[b] so that they die 21or if out of enmity one person hits another with their fist so that the other dies, that person is to be put to death; that person is a murderer. The avenger of blood shall put the murderer to death when they meet.

22" 'But if without enmity someone suddenly pushes another or throws something at them unintentionally[c] 23or, without seeing them, drops on them a stone heavy enough to kill them, and they die, then since that other person was not an enemy and no harm was intended, 24the assembly[d] must judge between the accused and the avenger of blood according to these regulations. 25The assembly must protect the one accused of murder from the avenger of blood and send the accused back to the city of refuge to which they fled. The accused must stay there until the death of the high priest, who was anointed with the holy oil.[e]

26" 'But if the accused ever goes outside the limits of the city of refuge to which they fled 27and the avenger of blood finds them outside the city, the avenger of blood may kill the accused without being guilty of murder. 28The accused must stay in the city of refuge until the death of the high priest; only after the death of the high priest may they return to their own property.

29" 'This is to have the force of law[f] for you throughout the generations to come, wherever you live.

30" 'Anyone who kills a person is to be put to death as a murderer only on the testimony of witnesses. But no one is to be put to death on the testimony of only one witness.[g]

31" 'Do not accept a ransom for the life of a murderer, who deserves to die. They are to be put to death.

32" 'Do not accept a ransom for anyone who has fled to a city of refuge and so allow them to go back and live on their own land before the death of the high priest.

33" 'Do not pollute the land where you are. Bloodshed pollutes the land,[h] and atonement cannot be made for the land on which blood has been shed, except by the blood of the one who shed it. 34Do not defile the land[i] where you live and where I dwell,[j] for I, the LORD, dwell among the Israelites.' "

Inheritance of Zelophehad's Daughters

36:1-12pp — Nu 27:1-11

36 The family heads of the clan of Gilead[k] son of Makir, the son of Manasseh, who were from the clans of the descendants of Joseph, came and spoke before Moses and the leaders,[l] the heads of the Israelite families. 2They said, "When the LORD commanded my lord to give the land as an

35:12 avenger. The person who carried out the Lord's justice (execution), usually understood to be a close relative of the deceased (called the "avenger of blood" in vv. 19,21,24,25,27). **stand trial.** Have his day in court and therefore be protected from blood vengeance (cf. v. 25).
35:13 six towns. See Josh 20:7–8 and map, p. 412.
35:16–21 Examples of murder.
35:22–23 Examples of manslaughter (cf. Deut 19:5).
35:25 send the accused back to the city of refuge. Apparently, the accused stood trial at some place outside the city, perhaps in the original place of the crime or perhaps at the city limits.
35:30 testimony of witnesses. Ensures that one person alone cannot falsely accuse another (Deut 17:6; 19:15).
35:31 ransom. A payment of money.
35:33 Bloodshed pollutes the land. With a stain that could only be removed by the life (i.e., the blood) of the guilty party (or the high priest in cases of manslaughter). A ransom (v. 31) cannot remove the stain; the land would remain defiled, which would lead to the Lord's punishment (Lev 18:24–28).
35:34 dwell among the Israelites. In the tabernacle (Exod 29:42–46).
36:1–13 *Inheritance of Zelophehad's Daughters.* This chapter returns to

inheritance to the Israelites by lot, he ordered you to give the inheritance of our brother Zelophehad[m]
to his daughters. 3Now suppose they marry men from other Israelite tribes; then their inheritance will
be taken from our ancestral inheritance and added to that of the tribe they marry into. And so part of
the inheritance allotted to us will be taken away. 4When the Year of Jubilee[n] for the Israelites comes,
their inheritance will be added to that of the tribe into which they marry, and their property will be
taken from the tribal inheritance of our ancestors."

5Then at the LORD's command Moses gave this order to the Israelites: "What the tribe of the descendants of Joseph is saying is right. 6This is what the LORD commands for Zelophehad's daughters: They
may marry anyone they please as long as they marry within their father's tribal clan. 7No inheritance[o]
in Israel is to pass from one tribe to another, for every Israelite shall keep the tribal inheritance of their
ancestors. 8Every daughter who inherits land in any Israelite tribe must marry someone in her father's
tribal clan,[p] so that every Israelite will possess the inheritance of their ancestors. 9No inheritance may
pass from one tribe to another, for each Israelite tribe is to keep the land it inherits."

10So Zelophehad's daughters did as the LORD commanded Moses. 11Zelophehad's daughters — Mahlah, Tirzah, Hoglah, Milkah and Noah[q] — married their cousins on their father's side. 12They married
within the clans of the descendants of Manasseh son of Joseph, and their inheritance remained in their
father's tribe and clan.

13These are the commands and regulations the LORD gave through Moses[r] to the Israelites on the
plains of Moab by the Jordan across from Jericho.[s]

36:2 [m] Nu 26:33; 27:1,7
36:4 [n] Lev 25:10
36:7 [o] 1Ki 21:3
36:8 [p] 1Ch 23:22
36:11 [q] Nu 26:33; 27:1
36:13 [r] Lev 26:46; 27:34 [s] Nu 22:1

the story of ch. 27 (see note on 27:1–11 for background). In doing so, it links together chs. 27–36 (with ch. 26 introducing the whole section).
36:3 The leaders correctly assume that if a daughter marries someone from outside her tribe, the land would pass to her husband's tribe (thus diminishing the land inheritance of the original tribe).
36:4 Year of Jubilee. When land normally returned to its original owner and therefore to the original tribe (see note on Lev 25:10). But in this case, the land would not return to its original tribe because the Jubilee laws applied only to land that people leased, not to inherited land.
36:5–9 Helped ensure that all tribes in Israel kept the land the Lord gave them and therefore that all his people had an inheritance in the promised land.
36:10–12 Many clan-based societies encourage marriage within the clan, perhaps to strengthen clan ties and to safeguard clan property. So marrying one's cousin was not unusual. But even within the clan, they considered certain relatives too close for sexual relations (see Lev 18:6–18).
36:13 The concluding verse looks backward and forward. **the plains of Moab.** Looks back at least to 33:50 (and ties together six different sections with commands and regulations relating to life in the promised land) and at most to 22:1 (and ties together chs. 22–36 as one unit, describing what Israel did and learned while waiting on those plains). **Jericho.** Since it is in the promised land, this looks forward to the coming conquest of that land as the people of Israel march forward with bold faith in the covenant Lord who has promised it to them. This was to be for them a land of rest (Lev 25:4–5), a return to Eden, where they could live securely in a fruitful land with all their needs met, walk in obedient fellowship with the Lord, and extend his holy kingdom throughout the earth (Exod 19:5–6; Lev 26:3–12). The NT applies this picture to Christians, exhorting them to enter the eternal promised land of rest by holding fast to their faith in Jesus (Heb 3:6,12–14; 4:8–11), the one who has atoned for their sins so that they can enter into a final and perfect Eden and walk in perfect fellowship with God (Rev 5:9–10; 21:1–5; 22:1–5). This is exceedingly good news, and Jesus commands his followers to share it with all peoples so that they too may enter into his kingdom and the eternal rest that he has won for them (Matt 28:18–20; cf. 1 John 2:2; Rev 7:9–10).

INTRODUCTION TO DEUTERONOMY

Deuteronomy is both the climax of the Pentateuch (the five books of Moses that the Bible begins with) and the introduction to the historical books, particularly Joshua, Judges, 1 – 2 Samuel, and 1 – 2 Kings. The historical books view Israel's past through the lens provided by the book of Deuteronomy, particularly the blessings and curses of chs. 27 – 28.

The Greek translators mistakenly entitled this book "Deuteronomy," meaning "second (*deutero*) law (*nomos*)." This was based on a translation of the Hebrew word for "copy" in 17:18, where the king is commanded to make a copy of the law as a guide for his life. But Deuteronomy is not a second law; it is an exposition of the meaning of the first law given at Horeb, which is found in sections of Exodus, Leviticus, and Numbers, particularly the "Ten Words" (the "Ten Commandments") in Exod 20:1 – 17. For Jews and Christians, Deuteronomy has always been an important book. The central liturgical text in Judaism — the *Shema* (Hebrew *šěmaʿ*; 6:4 – 9; cf. 11:18 – 20; Num 15:37 – 41), which contains the foremost theological truth of God's oneness and the accompanying ethic of a total love for this one God — stems from this book. Jesus agrees with this assessment (Mark 12:29 – 30). But his is not just a formal agreement. He must have meditated on this book so much during his life that its fundamental themes of trust and obedience became the overarching motivation of his life. As an indication of its significance for him, he cited the book more than any other OT book. At the beginning of his ministry when he was tested in the wilderness for 40 days, he cited texts from Deuteronomy three times to defeat the tempter (Matt 4:4,7,10). He thus paralleled Israel's 40-year period of testing in the OT; but by relying on the word of God, he succeeded where Israel failed.

Deuteronomy comes after an entire generation has died in the wilderness as a result of disobedience. The book powerfully renews the covenant to ancient Israel and attempts to show the Israelites the heart of the covenant. Israel is called to consider the meaning of its call and election, the blessing of Abraham, the exodus, and the imminent gift of the land. Will God's project for the world — that Israel bless the nations through the seed of Abraham — fail? This book ultimately teaches that the greatest obstacle to this project will not be the Egyptians or the Canaanites but the human heart. And God will solve that problem.

AUTHOR AND DATE

The book presents Moses' last address to a new generation of Israelites as they are about to enter the promised land in fulfillment of some of the promises to the patriarchs. It functions as Moses' last will and testament to Israel as he prepares to die. He represents the last of the old generation that has died in the wilderness because of unbelief as he passes on the torch of faith to the new generation on the plains of Moab. Between a short introduction (1:1 – 5) and a brief conclusion (34:1 – 12), the book consists of four major sections that are largely made up of speeches looking to the past (1:6 — 4:43), present (4:44 — 28:68), and future (29:1 — 32:52), followed by a final benediction (33:1 – 29). In the second and third sections the structure is complex. Ch. 27 provides a narrative interlude before the climax of the second speech (ch. 28), indicating how the people will ratify the covenant when they enter the land of Canaan. In the third section, after the major speech (29:1 — 30:20), there are a number of speeches by Moses and God (ch. 31), followed by a long poem of witness against the people (32:1 – 43).

The ever-present Mosaic stamp on this book has testified to its authorship for generations of believers. The book essentially presents itself as a collection of speeches given by this great Israelite leader. If Moses did not speak them, then who in the history of Israel did? Even the great Moses could not have written about his own death (ch. 34), and there are many other places within the present book where an editor's hand can be detected since Moses is written about in the third person (1:1 – 5; 2:10 – 12,20 – 23; 3:9,11,13 – 14; 4:41 — 5:1a; 10:6 – 9; 27:1a,9a,11; 29:1 – 2a; 31:1,7a, 9 – 10a,14a,14c – 16a,22 – 23a,24 – 25,30; 32:44 – 45,48; 33:1; 34:1 – 4a,5 – 12). Sometimes it is clear that the wording comes from a much later period, such as the assumption that the conquest by Israel is now a distant memory (2:12). Moreover, the final epitaph on Moses' life suggests that many prophets have come and gone but none has equaled his stature (34:10 – 12). At the same time, these points should not detract from the important contribution of Moses in the same way that an editor of a modern book only enhances an author's work. This is particularly the case when it is updated for another audience.

PARTICULAR CHALLENGES

Literary Fiction

Beginning in the eighteenth century with the rise of modern biblical criticism, many scholars severed the historical bond between Moses and Deuteronomy. Stylistic comparisons linking the book with the historical section from Joshua – 2 Kings and the book of Jeremiah (whose final forms are dated to the sixth century BC), as well as other factors, led to the view that Deuteronomy was produced by scribes in the late seventh century BC who "planted" it in the temple to be "discovered" by those renovating the temple (2 Kgs 22:8 – 20). It thus became the basis for a wide-ranging reform, aiding Josiah, the king of Judah, in his attempt to establish his nation's independence. The book was no more than a pious forgery, supplying the literary fiction of Mosaic authorship to bolster political reform with theological authority. While many scholars would not accept the theory in this form any longer, the consensus of critical scholarship still views the book as being far removed from Mosaic times of the second millennium BC.

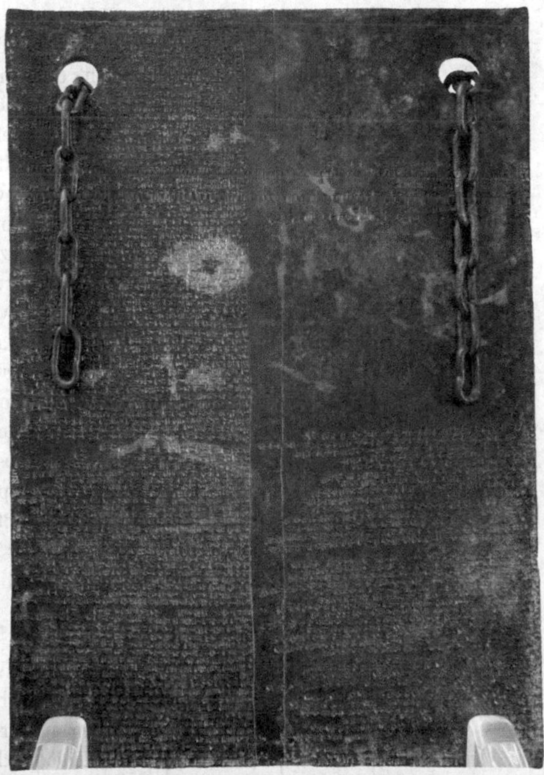

Bronze tablet (1235 BC) testifying to the treaty between Tudhaliya IV (Egyptian) and Kurunta of Tarhuntassa (Hittite), which promises the sovereignty of Tarhuntassa and another territory to Kurunta and his sons for the future. Hittite vassal treaties of the fifteenth to thirteenth centuries BC exhibit the same order of contents and many similarities as God's covenant with Israel in Deuteronomy. This text also contains boundary descriptions resembling those of Josh 13 – 19.
© Baker Publishing Group and Dr. James C. Martin, courtesy of the Museum of Anatolian Civilizations, Ankara, Turkey

Within the last century, significant archaeological discoveries have elucidated both the covenantal structure of the book and its antiquity. The basic structure of the book parallels the genre of an ancient treaty form. Hittite treaties of the second millennium BC and Assyrian treaties from the first millennium BC exhibit many similarities to Deuteronomy. These "suzerainty" treaties were made between two parties, a sovereign and a vassal state, and consisted of six elements: (1) preamble (identifying the parties), (2) historical prologue, (3) stipulations (a list of the vassal's obligations), (4) document deposit (an accessible copy of the treaty), (5) sanctions imposed for stipulations, and (6) witnesses to the proceedings. First-millennium treaties omit historical prologues and contain only curses for sanctions, while second-millennium pacts have historical sections and a list of blessings for loyalty. It is difficult to escape the conclusion that Deuteronomy reflects the second-millennium treaty structure: (1) preamble (1:1 – 5), (2) historical prologue (1:6 — 3:29), (3) stipulations (chs. 5 – 28), (4) document deposit (31:9 – 13), (5) sanctions — both curses and blessings (chs. 7 – 30), and (6) list of witnesses (31:28; 32:1). In ancient Near Eastern treaties, witnesses consisted of numerous gods, whereas the monotheism of Deuteronomy required the elimination of these "divine witnesses" and the substitution in their place of "the heavens and the earth" (31:28).

Nevertheless, Deuteronomy is more than a treaty document; it is too lengthy, and its rhetorical and urgent style is aimed mainly to persuade. Even its purely legal sections are replete with motivations. The use of treaty elements within this rhetorical *tour de force* points to the theological genius of the author. A genre of common political currency was modified and adapted to communicate a profound theological truth during a critical time. Israel is the servant of a divine Suzerain with obligations of love and loyalty and must remember this regularly in a public ceremony (31:10–13). The urgent, sermonic quality of the book combined with ancient treaty features point toward an ancient leader transmitting important truths to a new generation before he dies. These support the book's claim that its author was none other than the great prophet Moses, a person uniquely familiar with all the wisdom of Egypt (Acts 7:22)—and presumably also its legal documents. The later editing of the prophet's words shows them being used to speak to every generation.

Central Sanctuary

In line with the book's focus on God as the center of Israel's life and devotion, there is the call for a central worship site for offering sacrifices and tithes (ch. 12). This particular place is never identified within the book since, from its perspective, Israel has not entered the land. It is known as "the place the LORD your God will choose" (12:5; cf. 12:14). However, centralizing worship seems to conflict with other passages in the OT that describe the existence of open-air altars at other worship sites (Exod 20:24–25; Josh 8:30; 24:1,26; Judg 2:5; 6:26; 13:16,19; 1 Sam 7:9,17; 9:12–14; 14:35; 2 Sam 15:7,12,32; 1 Kgs 18:30; 19:10,14; Ps 74:8). Thus, many scholars understand this to be further evidence for the literary fiction of Deuteronomy: Josiah's concern to centralize worship in Jerusalem had Mosaic roots. Of course the pious forgers were not able to erase the evidence of noncentralization from the historical record.

But the issue is fraught with complexity. Most interpreters who argue that the centralization legislation is much later also believe that "the place the LORD your God will choose" (12:5) is a coded expression for Jerusalem. Yet Deuteronomy never mentions that name, and there is provision for a sacrificial altar in Shechem (ch. 27)! Similarly, legislation in Deuteronomy assumes the construction of other altars (16:21). This coheres with earlier Pentateuchal legislation that allows for stone altars other than the bronze altar at the central sanctuary (Exod 20:24–26; 27:1–8). Thus, the central sanctuary is the exclusive gathering for national holy days and, for the most part, for the offerings of tithes and sacrifices. This central sanctuary did not have a permanent location until the temple was built in Jerusalem. It existed earlier at Shiloh (Josh 18:1; 1 Sam 1:3) and also perhaps at Bethel, Shechem (Josh 24), and Gilgal (Josh 4:18—5:12). Other altars would have been a necessity in a large and spacious land; otherwise, the practice of regular formal worship would have been a practical impossibility for most people.

In later Israelite history, some of these altars seemed to compete for centralization (Josh 22:10–34; 1 Kgs 13) or became contaminated by foreign religious practices. Thus, there is the later concern to eliminate such sanctuaries, which were often described as "high places." Such high places became the locus of religious syncretism within the kingdom of Israel. They were also tolerated by the kings of Judah with three exceptions: Jehoshaphat (2 Chr 17:6; cf. 1 Kgs 22:43), Hezekiah (2 Kgs 18:2–4), and Josiah (2 Kgs 22:1—23:25). God's ideal was to have one central sanctuary and one main sacrificial site, but this was hard to achieve in reality.

PLACE OF COMPOSITION AND DESTINATION

The core of the book was first spoken on the plains of Moab, and its literary form was stored beside the ark of the covenant, which was to be placed in the central sanctuary in the land of Canaan (31:24–26). But its ultimate destination was meant to be the lives of the Israelites, written on their individual hearts, the doorposts of their homes, and their city gates throughout the land (6:6,9). A final edition of the book, emphasizing the end of prophecy and the eschatological hope for a prophet like Moses (34:10–12), was eventually incorporated into the Genesis to Kings history.

THEMES AND THEOLOGY

The Unity and Centrality of God

The dominant theme of the book is that the one God, the Creator, has acted in history and called out a people, rescued them from slavery, and entered into a covenant with them, calling them to love him with all their being. All other allegiances are subordinate. The theological heart of the book is 6:4–9, the Shema, which Orthodox Jews recite every morning and evening: "Hear [Hebrew *šĕmaʿ*], O Israel: The LORD our God, the LORD is one ..."

The Unity of the People

Matching the centrality of God and the centrality of a national worship site is the oneness of the people of Israel. The gatherings for public worship at the various national festivals celebrate not only the oneness of God but also the unity of the people. The people are often depicted in all their diversity—adults, children, servants, Levites, foreigners—rejoicing before the Lord and celebrating as one people in their annual pilgrimages. The book frequently uses the Hebrew word *'aḥ* (47 times), which is a kinship term meaning "relative," "brother," or "fellow Israelite," and its frequent use indicates the filial regard that the people are to express for one another. They are all members of one family, whether or not they live close to one another or know one another (cf. 22:1–3). This unity means that even the king is simply a fellow Israelite (17:20) and as family members, God's people must be kind to one another, especially the economically destitute (ch. 15).

The Name, Word, and Image of God

Another theme in Deuteronomy is the transcendence of God. Even when God appeared in the fire on Mount Sinai (usually named "Horeb" in Deuteronomy), Israel did not see any divine form. God was audible but invisible. God came near in his words. One could not make a divine image, but one could clearly discern God's will and presence. He was present in his words and name, which represent his character.

God places his name in his dwelling place at the central sanctuary (12:5,11). The name is a personal identity card, indicating God's presence and character and his stamp of ownership. To know God's name is to know God's character and his way of acting in the world. It is the fundamental sign of his presence. God revealed his name at the burning bush (Exod 3:12–15) and then more fully at the burning mountain (Exod 34:5–7). It is this God who has drawn near to the Israelites in the burning fire and placed his name among them. The speaking God has no man-made or artificial image. The tablets of stone on which God inscribed his words were to be transferred to human hearts not with ink but with the Holy Spirit (2 Cor 3:2). This is one way the invisible God becomes clearly visible.

Holy War

One cannot read Deuteronomy for long without encountering violence and war. What makes it worse is that these wars are divinely sanctioned (7:1–26; 20:16–18). All the Canaanites must be wiped out. Biblical interpreters have tried to address this troubling teaching in at least four ways:

1. Israel misunderstood the divine command, hearing it in the context of an often violent ancient Near Eastern culture. Thus, e.g., it would have been natural in the ancient world for people to slaughter their enemies and legitimize the violence by claiming divine sanction. There are many examples outside Israel of this feature of ancient culture. For example, Mesha, the Moabite king in the time of Omri, claimed that his god, Chemosh, commanded him to annihilate the Israelites in the town of Nebo (Moabite Stone, lines 14–16). It would have been natural, so the argument goes, for Israel to have had the same mistaken assumptions about their God and his will for their enemies. They thus confused their "cultural" will with God's will.

2. God accommodated his commands to ancient Israel's understanding, gradually helping his people move beyond their bloodthirsty cultural roots to a more humane level of civilization. Thus, God "got his hands dirty," accepting the basic cultural framework of the Israelites and issuing commands that he would not otherwise give in order eventually to lead the Israelites beyond the violent wars (in which they must destroy the enemy) to the ethic of the Sermon on the Mount (in which they must love the enemy).

3. The language is more rhetoric than reality, in line with ancient Near Eastern conventions, basically emphasizing intolerance for religious compromise. After all, after ordering the destruction of the enemy populations (e.g., 7:2), the text forbids intermarriage with them (e.g., 7:3). Why would the latter command even be necessary if the former was carried out?

4. This was an act of God's judging people who deserved it (cf. Gen 15:16). In some ways it was no different than the flood and the destruction of Sodom and Gomorrah; the only difference in the case of the conquest of Canaan was that human beings were the agents of destruction.

First, while there are elements of truth in the second and third views, it is difficult to avoid the clear teaching of Deuteronomy and the rest of the Bible: God's judgment is a reality. In many ways what God commanded Israel to do was no different than what other nations had done when God guided them to execute his judgment upon other groups by conquering them (2:10–12,20–23).

Second, the text constantly refers to the abominations of the Canaanites and mentions some of their barbaric practices (12:31; 18:9–12; cf. Gen 15:16).

Third, the Israelites were to be just as ruthless in eliminating religious apostates from their own community (13:12 – 17) as they were in destroying apostate nations. At the conquest of Jericho, a Canaanite woman and her family were spared destruction because of faith in the Lord, while an Israelite man and his family were destroyed for breaking the covenant (Josh 6:17; 7:18 – 26). The Canaanite woman, Rahab, was included in the genealogy of Jesus, whose purpose in coming was ultimately to be a worldwide blessing. Rahab is but one example of people spared divine judgment because of faith. There were probably others (cf. Josh 9; Judg 1:23 – 28).

Fourth, the wars of military conquest were limited to the land of Canaan, where God's holy presence was to dwell, and they were one-time actions, foreshadowing final judgment when the world will be cleansed from all evil (2 Pet 3:11 – 14; Rev 21:1 – 8). In the meantime, the constant concern is that Israelite faith would be contaminated and destroyed if Canaanite idolatry were allowed to coexist with it. Without that faith intact, God's salvation-project — to bless the nations through Israel — would be in jeopardy (Gen 12:3). Thus, in a very real sense, God had to be against the Canaanites in a particular, limited time in order to be for them in the long run.

Fifth, the covenantal context of these wars is striking. After a city was defeated in the wars of conquest, the enemy king's corpse was taken outside the city and hung on a tree until sundown, thus indicating that the king and people were under the curse of judgment for violating God's law (21:22 – 23; Josh 8:29; 10:26 – 27). In the fullness of time, in order that the entire world would be blessed, the holy Son of God bore the judgment of God's curse by being crucified outside the holy city, hanging upon a tree until sundown. With his resurrection a new world has begun in which everyone by faith in the "cursed" Messiah might be blessed, for "now is the day of salvation" for universal blessing (2 Cor 6:2). The Valley of Achor has now become "a door of hope" (Hos 2:15). But for those who remain intransigent in their sin and evil, a judgment day is coming compared to which the Canaanite judgment is a pale imitation (2 Thess 2:7 – 10).

Sixth, because of this new world order that has begun, Christians in the meantime are called to engage in spiritual warfare, fighting the principalities and powers of the old age that remain hostile to God's will through spiritual weapons and not material swords and spears (Eph 6:10 – 20). They are called to go not into Canaan but into all the world with the message of Christ (Matt 28:18 – 20). Their weapons are not "the weapons of the world" (2 Cor 10:4); the latter have been transformed into pruning hooks and plowshares with the coming of the Messiah (Isa 2:1 – 5). The spiritual weapons of prayer, the word of God, faith, and proclamation of the gospel attack every spiritual stronghold that would set itself up against the knowledge of God (2 Cor 10:5) until the kingdom of God has finally come.

The Nature of the Law and Its Fundamental Spirit

Most of the legislation in Deuteronomy applies the Ten Commandments to the new conditions of Israelite settlement in the land of Canaan. The "Ten Words" that the Lord directly spoke are the fundamental moral directives for this new life upon which everything is based. In terms of modern legal systems, the Ten Commandments function like the constitution of ancient Israel: all other laws apply this policy to the situations in ancient Israel. As a constitution reflects the basic values of the nation that creates it, the constitution of Israel reflects God's character. What kind of God would forbid other gods and idols? A God committed to truth and reality. What kind of God would forbid violating his name and identity? A God committed to his own holiness. What kind of God would command a Sabbath law? A God committed to the re-creation of his world and the liberty and rest of his creatures. While there certainly are exceptions, the Ten Commandments provide a basic, general framework for the organization of the many laws in chs. 12 – 26. The initial two commandments, which forbid the worship of other gods and idolatry, find expression in the command to destroy Canaanite sanctuaries throughout the land (12:1 – 3). The third commandment, which forbids violating the holiness of the name of God, is reflected in the concern for the Israelites to live holy lives (ch. 14), particularly in their distinct diet. The fourth commandment, the command to observe the Sabbath, is expressed in the command to observe the sabbatical year in order to provide economic relief for the poor (ch. 15). Thus, the Ten Commandments consist of broad principles, not narrow laws, and their interpretation should not be restricted to a wooden literalism. Consequently the sixth commandment, which forbids murder, can result in a building code concerned for safety (22:8), and the seventh commandment, which forbids adultery, also addresses sexual purity, even before marriage (22:13 – 21). Deuteronomic law, like biblical law in the Pentateuch and ancient Near Eastern law, is exemplary rather than comprehensive, but this exemplary nature points to its wide-ranging application. Such examples show the concern for a life of total obedience aimed at the transformation of the heart.

This sermon on the plains of Moab demonstrates the implications of the covenant at Mount Sinai and may be compared to the Sermon on the Mount. Like Jesus' sermon, it takes the words of God delivered on Mount Sinai and shows what obedience to God should look like in the new land of Canaan. More than any other book in the OT,

Deuteronomy expresses the demand for total obedience to the divine will. It indicates that the first commandment is not just negatively a matter of not worshiping other gods but is positively a matter of loving the one, true God with everything in one's being. This is impossible without divine help.

The Importance of Decision: Now and in the Future

The urgent need for the present generation to make a decision for the Lord is one of the main concerns in the book. Repeatedly (48 times) the word "today" sounds in the ears of the people as they stand on the plains of Moab. The word calls for decision *now*— not yesterday, not tomorrow, but today! The previous generation failed to obey, and they ended up wandering in the wilderness for 40 years before they all perished (1:41–46; 2:14–15). The situation is urgent. Israel must obey today!

Similarly, the revelation of God cannot be confined to the past. Even though most of the generation on the plains of Moab was not at Horeb to witness the theophany, God made the covenant with them and not with their parents (5:2–3), speaking with them "face to face" (5:4). The time between the moment then and the moment now has been erased as the people hear the word of God directly and immediately. The same experience must also be communicated to the next generation (4:9–10,40; 5:29; 6:2; 11:19,21; 12:25,28; 29:11,22,29; 30:2,19; 31:13; 32:46). The people must embody the covenant in rituals and habits that will be such a part of ordinary life that their children will naturally ask about the meaning of such things (6:4–9,20). When this opportunity arises, the parents will respond with "gospel": "We were slaves of Pharaoh in Egypt, but the LORD brought us out of Egypt with a mighty hand . . . The LORD commanded us to obey all these decrees and to fear the LORD our God" (6:21–24). Faith is not just a privatized concern for individual salvation but also involves an intentional decision to shape future generations.

The Eschatological Hope and a New Covenant

As Moses presides over covenant renewal, he is aware of the eventual apostasy of his people. Israel will be a witness to the nations that human beings— despite the best advantages— cannot do the will of God without God's help (4:25–28; 29:22–28; 30:1–10; 31:14–29; 32:15–38). Deuteronomy bears witness to the hope that the Lord will someday do for Israel what it could not do for itself: circumcise the peoples' hearts so that keeping the law was as natural as breathing (30:6; cf. 10:16; 30:14). The prophets were influenced by this hope and called it the new covenant— a covenant by which the Lord would forgive the sins of his people and write the law on their hearts (Jer 31:31–34; cf. Isa 54–55). Paul said that such a day finally arrived in Christ, who perfectly kept the law while suffering its curses— not for himself but for covenant-breakers. Now when such sinners confess Jesus as Lord, they are fully justified by God and empowered to do his will (Rom 10:6–10; cf. Deut 30:11–14).

The Arnon Gorge on the northern border of Moab (Deut 2:24).

OCCASION AND PURPOSE

The book addresses a new generation of Israelites on the verge of entering the land God promised to the patriarchs. Moses, as the last of the previous generation (with the exception of Caleb and Joshua), is presenting his final words to the new generation before he dies. His speeches aim to interpret the law given at Horeb for the new generation, and as such there is an air of dire urgency and importance. The previous generation failed because they did not believe the divine word. Though the book has often been seen as a covenant renewal document, it also points forward to an ultimate resolution of the problem of evil in the human heart (30:1 – 14). God promised the seeds of such a solution long before in the Abrahamic covenant (4:31). The book's primary purpose as the word of God is to reveal clearly the unflinching demands of a holy God and his provision of radical grace. Consequently, the book inspired far-reaching renewal in the later history of Israel during the reigns of Jehoshaphat, Hezekiah, and Josiah, as well as in the later history of the church.

GENRE AND STRUCTURE

The hortatory, repetitive nature of the book, with its core of legislation (chs. 12 – 26) and treaty elements, has been organized into six sections, the heart of which contains a number of motivational speeches (or "sermons"), the aim of which is to renew the covenant at Horeb. Each speech is introduced with a formal rubric (1:1 – 5; 4:44 – 49; 29:1; 33:1), and the speeches move in staircase-like fashion, finally climaxing in a pronouncement of blessing on the tribes (33:2 – 29). There is a narrative interlude at the end of the second speech (ch. 27), followed by a list of blessings and curses (ch. 28).

Section 1 (1:1 – 5) is a short introduction to the book. Section 2 begins with an initial speech that recapitulates the history from the covenant made at Horeb until the present time with Israel now on the doorstep of Canaan (1:6 — 3:29) and concludes with the implications of the revelation at Horeb (4:1 – 43).

Section 3 begins with the second speech (4:44 — 26:19; 28:1 – 68), which resumes the last main point of the first speech (the revelation at the mountain) and hammers home repeatedly the significance of the Ten Commandments and the importance of obedience (5:1 — 11:32). Then it applies the Ten Commandments to the life of the nation (chs. 12 – 26) along with the consequences of blessings for obedience and curses for disobedience (ch. 28). Ch. 27 briefly interrupts the speech with a narrative in order to provide instructions for a covenant ratification ceremony when Israel enters the land.

Section 4 begins with the third speech (29:1 — 30:20). Moses addresses the last main point of the second speech — the problem of the inevitability of the curses for disobedience — and promises eschatological hope, "the secret things" (29:29), as an ultimate solution (30:1 – 10). Ch. 31 introduces Section 5 with a narrative depicting the transition of leadership to Joshua, which is followed by a prediction of Israel's future rebellion and a song of witness against Israel. This song provides an entire mini-history of Israel in its election, judgment, and final salvation, and it reinforces Israel's future hope (32:1 – 47). This is followed by a final address by God to Moses (32:48 – 52).

Section 6, the last section, reinforces the final note of blessing predicted for Israel's future in the previous two sections; that blessing is now elaborated and extended to all the tribes, envisioned now throughout the land of Canaan (33:1 – 29). As Jacob delivered a deathbed benediction to his sons (Gen 49), so Moses does the same for Israel. An epilogue (ch. 34) describes Moses' final vision of the land before his death and burial and then notes the transition of leadership to Joshua.

THE APPLICATION OF THE TEN COMMANDMENTS TO LIFE IN THE LAND OF CANAAN

After presenting the fundamental call to allegiance to the one God in his second address to the Israelites, Moses then delivers the core of the speech in chs. 12 – 26. While there are some significant exceptions, the laws found here are not arranged haphazardly but generally reflect the order of the Ten Commandments.

These decrees and laws creatively apply the fundamental values embodied in the Ten Commands in sermonic form with many motivations. For example, one of the first concerns for the application of the Sabbath law is relief from debt slavery during the sabbatical year (ch. 15), and the command to honor parents expresses concern for the right attitude with regard to authority in general (16:18 — 18:22). Moses is thus interpreting the law — opening it up instead of shutting down its relevance through a woodenly literal understanding — and trying to persuade the Israelites to keep the commands for various reasons. They are ultimately words of "life" (32:47). The Ten Commandments are not so much a law code as they are broad principles that underlie the decrees and laws Moses is about to expound to the people in chs. 12 – 26. Moreover, these decrees and laws are far from exhaustive; they are paradigms of how to interpret the Ten Commandments. This requires wisdom, which is what the law is all about (4:6 – 8).

CANONICITY

There has never been any doubt about the canonicity of Deuteronomy. Many OT scholars argue that the process of canonization began with Deuteronomy. Its concepts were recognized as authoritative for the historical books; and from its inception as the "Book of the Law," it was placed alongside the "Ten Words" by the ark of the covenant. With the "Ten Words" Deuteronomy formed a seminal canon that would evolve to include more and more books until the canon was finally closed. The first evidence of a canonical formula in the Bible occurs in Deuteronomy (4:2; 12:32), and the last time it occurs in Scripture is, appropriately, at the end of the Bible (Rev 22:18–19).

THE ORDER OF THE TEN COMMANDMENTS

COMMANDMENT	SEQUENCE IN CHS. 12–26	TOPIC
1–3	12:1—14:29	proper worship and holiness
4	15:1—16:17	holy time
5	16:18—18:22	respect for authority
6	19:1—22:12	destruction of human life
7	22:13—23:14	sexuality
8	23:15—24:7	theft and various laws
9	24:8—25:4	justice/truth and various laws
10	25:5—26:15	covetousness

OUTLINE

I. Introduction (1:1–5)

II. The First Speech: Keep the Law (1:6—4:43)

A. The Command to Leave Horeb (1:6–8)
B. The Appointment of Leaders (1:9–18)
C. Spies Sent Out (1:19–25)
D. Rebellion Against the Lord (1:26–46)
E. Wanderings in the Wilderness (2:1–23)
F. Defeat of Sihon King of Heshbon (2:24–37)
G. Defeat of Og King of Bashan (3:1–11)
H. Division of the Land (3:12–20)
I. Moses Forbidden to Cross the Jordan (3:21–29)
J. Obedience Commanded (4:1–14)
K. Idolatry Forbidden (4:15–31)
L. The Lord Is God (4:32–40)
M. Cities of Refuge (4:41–43)

III. The Second Speech: The First Priority Is Absolute Allegiance to the Lord (4:44—28:68)

A. Introduction to the Law (4:44–49)
B. The Ten Commandments (5:1–33)
C. Love the Lord Your God (6:1–25)
D. Driving Out the Nations (7:1–26)
E. Do Not Forget the Lord (8:1–20)
F. Not Because of Israel's Righteousness (9:1–6)
G. The Golden Calf (9:7–29)
H. Tablets Like the First Ones (10:1–11)
I. Fear the Lord (10:12–22)
J. Love and Obey the Lord (11:1–32)
K. The One Place of Worship (12:1–32)
L. Worshiping Other Gods (13:1–18)
M. Holiness (14:1–29)
  1. Clean and Unclean Food (14:1–21)
  2. Tithes (14:22–29)
N. The Year for Canceling Debts (15:1–11)
O. Freeing Servants (15:12–18)

P. The Firstborn Animals (15:19–23)
Q. The Passover (16:1–8)
R. The Festival of Weeks (16:9–12)
S. The Festival of Tabernacles (16:13–17)
T. Judges (16:18–20)
U. Worshiping Other Gods (16:21—17:7)
V. Law Courts (17:8–13)
W. The King (17:14–20)
X. Offerings for Priests and Levites (18:1–8)
Y. Occult Practices (18:9–13)
Z. The Prophet (18:14–22)
AA. Cities of Refuge (19:1–14)
BB. Witnesses (19:15–21)
CC. Going to War (20:1–20)
DD. Atonement for an Unsolved Murder (21:1–9)
EE. Marrying a Captive Woman (21:10–14)
FF. The Right of the Firstborn (21:15–17)
GG. A Rebellious Son (21:18–21)
HH. Various Laws (21:22—22:12)
II. Marital and Spiritual Fidelity (22:13—23:14)
   1. Marriage Violations (22:13–30)
   2. Exclusion From the Assembly (23:1–8)
   3. Uncleanness in the Camp (23:9–14)
JJ. Miscellaneous Laws (23:15—25:19)
KK. Firstfruits and Tithes (26:1–15)
LL. Follow the Lord's Commands (26:16–19)
MM. The Altar on Mount Ebal (27:1–8)
NN. Curses From Mount Ebal (27:9–26)
OO. Blessings and Curses (28:1–68)
   1. Blessings for Obedience (28:1–14)
   2. Curses for Disobedience (28:15–68)

IV. The Third Speech: Covenant Ratification, Failure, and Future Hope (29:1—30:20)
A. Renewal of the Covenant (29:1–29)
B. Prosperity After Turning to the Lord (30:1–10)
C. The Offer of Life or Death (30:11–20)

V. Planning for the Future (31:1—32:52)
A. Joshua to Succeed Moses (31:1–8)
B. Public Reading of the Law (31:9–13)
C. Israel's Rebellion Predicted (31:14–29)
D. The Song of Moses (31:30—32:47)
E. Moses to Die on Mount Nebo (32:48–52)

VI. Benediction and Burial (33:1—34:12)
A. Moses Blesses the Tribes (33:1–29)
B. The Death of Moses (34:1–12)

DEUTERONOMY

The Command to Leave Horeb

1 These are the words Moses spoke to all Israel in the wilderness east of the Jordan — that is, in the
Arabah — opposite Suph, between Paran and Tophel, Laban, Hazeroth and Dizahab. 2(It takes
eleven days to go from Horeb[a] to Kadesh Barnea[b] by the Mount Seir road.)
3In the fortieth year,[c] on the first day of the eleventh month, Moses proclaimed[d] to the Israelites all that
the LORD had commanded him concerning them. 4This was after he had defeated Sihon[e] king of the Amorites, who reigned in Heshbon,[f] and at Edrei had defeated Og[g] king of Bashan, who reigned in Ashtaroth.
5East of the Jordan in the territory of Moab, Moses began to expound this law, saying:

6The LORD our God said to us[h] at Horeb,[i] "You have stayed long enough at this mountain. 7Break
camp and advance into the hill country of the Amorites; go to all the neighboring peoples in the Arabah,

1:2 [a]Ex 3:1 [b]Nu 13:26; Dt 9:23
1:3 [c]Nu 33:38 [d]Dt 4:1-2
1:4 [e]Nu 21:21-26 [f]Nu 21:25 [g]Nu 21:33-35; Jos 13:12
1:6 [h]Nu 10:13 [i]Ex 3:1

1:1–5 *Introduction.* Deuteronomy represents Moses' last words to Israel as the people prepare to enter the land promised to their ancestors and become an established nation. This introduction to the book provides background information while resuming the storyline from Genesis to Numbers. Verse 1 links with the last verse of Numbers (Num 36:13). Israel is on the doorstep of Canaan with the wilderness behind them and the land of promise before them. Theologically it is a critical place. Deuteronomy is also in a strategic place in the Bible's storyline as it ends an old era and begins a new one. It functions as the capstone of the Pentateuch and the foundation of the subsequent historical books. It thus faces in both directions — backward to the past and forward to the future.
1:1 the words Moses spoke. These are no ordinary words. Even though Moses is teaching and instructing, his words have a note of divine authority. They are the words God spoke to him (v. 3). The book begins with Moses speaking the words of the Lord and ends by describing Moses as the unsurpassed prophet (34:10–12). **east of the Jordan.** Moses and Israel are outside the promised land. The location is further clarified as "the territory of Moab" (v. 5), and other place-names suggest that it is the destination of a journey that began at Mount Horeb, an alternate name for Sinai. Deuteronomy uses "Horeb" consistently with one exception (33:2). **Suph ... Paran ... Tophel, Laban, Hazeroth and Dizahab.** Places along the route from Horeb to Moab.
1:2 eleven days. The time it should take to travel the distance between Horeb and the southern limit of the promised land, Kadesh Barnea, where the Israelites failed to enter the land 40 years earlier (cf. Num 13–14).
1:3 fortieth year. A journey that should have taken 11 days has taken 40 years! There have been no major physical barriers, only spiritual ones (29:3–4). **eleventh month.** January-February. Moses has little time left as the 40-year period is almost finished. Will the new generation inherit the promises and enter the land successfully, or will they turn back to the wilderness and Egypt?

Crossing the Jordan is a major turning point in Scripture. It is a crossing over into the place of promised blessing — the land. The waters will soon open up for Israel to cross the Jordan into the promised land (Josh 3–4) as the spirit of Moses is passed on to Joshua (his name means "the LORD saves"). Later, the same waters divide for Elisha (his name means "my God saves") as Elijah gives him a double portion of the Spirit (2 Kgs 2). Still later, John baptizes Jesus (his name means "the LORD saves") at the Jordan as the heavens open and the Holy Spirit descends on him (Mark 1:9–11); and Jesus later baptizes his followers with the Holy Spirit at Pentecost and sends them out to inherit the entire world (Acts 1–2).
1:5 expound. Occurs in two other places in the Bible (27:8; Hab 2:2), where it means "write plainly or legibly." It has the sense here of clarifying the meaning of the law. This accounts for the sermonic quality of the speeches. **law.** The Hebrew word includes the broader meanings of "instruction" or "teaching."
1:6—4:43 *The First Speech: Keep the Law.* Moses begins his first long speech, which functions as a lengthy history lesson (1:6—3:29) with a sharp theological point (4:1–43): How can history help Israel understand the present moment?
1:6–8 *The Command to Leave Horeb.* God initiates the journey of the Israelites from Horeb to the land of Canaan and describes the land in all its rich variety as the fulfillment of his promises to Abraham.
1:6 Moses takes Israel back to their time at Mount Sinai when God organized them as a new society under his rule and ordered them to move to the land of promise. These are the first words that Moses speaks, and they are definitive for Israel. **LORD.** A personal name, further identified as "our God"; the Lord had revealed his name (and thus his personal presence and character) only to Israel. Together, "the LORD your God" and "the LORD our God" occur almost 300 times in Deuteronomy, in addition to the many times that "LORD" is used alone or in other combinations (see notes on 28:58; Gen 2:4; Exod 3:14,15; 6:3). **You have stayed long enough.** The holy mountain was not a destination but an important point on the journey to the promised land. The people had to move on to the

1:7 [j]Jos 10:40 [k]Dt 11:24
1:8 [l]Ge 12:7; 15:18; 17:7-8; 26:4; 28:13
1:9 [m]Ex 18:18
1:10 [n]Ge 15:5 [o]Dt 10:22; 28:62
1:11 [p]Ge 22:17; Ex 32:13
1:13 [q]Ex 18:21
1:15 [r]Ex 18:25
1:16 [s]Dt 16:18; Jn 7:24 [t]Lev 24:22
1:17 [u]Lev 19:15; Dt 16:19; Pr 24:23; Jas 2:1 [v]2Ch 19:6 [w]Ex 18:26
1:19 [x]Dt 8:15; Jer 2:2,6 [y]ver 2; Nu 13:26
1:21 [z]Jos 1:6,9,18

in the mountains, in the western foothills, in the Negev[j] and along the coast, to the land of the Canaanites and to Lebanon,[k] as far as the great river, the Euphrates. 8See, I have given you this land. Go
in and take possession of the land the LORD swore[l] he would give to your fathers — to Abraham, Isaac
and Jacob — and to their descendants after them."

The Appointment of Leaders

9At that time I said to you, "You are too heavy a burden for me to carry alone.[m] 10The LORD your
God has increased your numbers so that today you are as numerous[n] as the stars in the sky.[o] 11May the
LORD, the God of your ancestors, increase you a thousand times and bless you as he has promised![p] 12But
how can I bear your problems and your burdens and your disputes all by myself? 13Choose some wise,
understanding and respected men[q] from each of your tribes, and I will set them over you."
14You answered me, "What you propose to do is good."
15So I took[r] the leading men of your tribes, wise and respected men, and appointed them to have
authority over you — as commanders of thousands, of hundreds, of fifties and of tens and as tribal officials. 16And I charged your judges at that time, "Hear the disputes between your people and judge fairly,[s]
whether the case is between two Israelites or between an Israelite and a foreigner residing among you.[t]
17Do not show partiality[u] in judging; hear both small and great alike. Do not be afraid of anyone,[v] for
judgment belongs to God. Bring me any case too hard for you, and I will hear it."[w] 18And at that time
I told you everything you were to do.

Spies Sent Out

19Then, as the LORD our God commanded us, we set out from Horeb and went toward the hill country
of the Amorites through all that vast and dreadful wilderness[x] that you have seen, and so we reached
Kadesh Barnea.[y] 20Then I said to you, "You have reached the hill country of the Amorites, which the
LORD our God is giving us. 21See, the LORD your God has given you the land. Go up and take possession
of it as the LORD, the God of your ancestors, told you. Do not be afraid;[z] do not be discouraged."

place of the fulfillment of promise. The circle of holiness must enlarge not only to surround Sinai but to fill Canaan and eventually the world.

1:7 The geographic terms express the variety and extent of the land of promise, the borders of which match the first general description of the promise to Abraham (Gen 15:18–21). **hill country of the Amorites.** Generally designates the central part of the land between the west and east; it (along with "land of the Canaanites") reminds the Israelites of obstacles in their path; it also perhaps alludes to the coming judgment of the Amorites (Gen 15:16). **Arabah.** The Jordan Valley and the valley that continues south of the Dead Sea to Elath (2:8). It is east of the Jordan River (4:49) as well as west. **mountains.** The central "backbone" of Israel, where most of the Israelite population would later reside. **western foothills.** From the perspective of those living in mountains; they slope down to the coastal plain, which meets the Mediterranean Sea. **Negev.** The Beersheba valley in the region of that city and Arad. **to Lebanon, as far as the great river, the Euphrates.** Israel never did realize these borders from Egypt to the Euphrates in their history, suggesting a failure to reach their destiny.

1:8 land the LORD swore he would give to your fathers. The book's first explicit reference to the promises God made to Abraham, Isaac, and Jacob. A similar passage suitably ends the book (34:4). Land is a central theme of this book, and it means much more than a physical location: it is the truest sense of place, where one is oriented rightly to God and to God's creation. This possession is not just another ambitious landgrab by a militaristic nation but is a part of the salvation-project God initiated when he chose Abraham (Gen 12:1–3,7). God gives Israel the land, yet Israel must take it, showing the seamless compatibility between divine sovereignty and human agency.

1:9–18 *The Appointment of Leaders.* Cf. 16:18–20; Exod 18:13–26. While not digressing from the theme of the land, this new section reminds Israel that God has already been faithful in fulfilling the Abrahamic promise of numerous descendants. Before the actual departure from the mount can take place, leadership is needed. In Exodus, the same event is depicted *before* the making of the covenant (Exod 18). But the sermonic and pastoral nature of Deuteronomy assumes knowledge of the story and is not concerned with chronological precision.

1:9–13 The extravagant fulfillment of the promise of descendants to the ancestors requires more leadership to help Moses.

1:10 as the stars in the sky. Cf. the promise to Abraham of numerous descendants (Gen 15:5). Having just exhorted Israel regarding the promise of land in Gen 15:18–21 (a promise yet to be fulfilled), Moses refers to a promise already fulfilled in order to stir up Israel's faith that God will keep the promise of land.

1:13 Moses highlights the role of the people themselves in choosing leaders who have character and wisdom.

1:16–17 judge fairly ... Do not show partiality in judging. Before the journey to the promised land begins, Israel is a nation that is a community, a family, committed to justice. This justice is to distinguish the Israelite nation, a point emphasized throughout Deuteronomy, so that it will be a beacon of light to the nations (4:6–8). By having such leadership the nation will be committed to walk in "the way of the LORD" (Gen 18:19), the way of true social justice.

1:19–25 *Spies Sent Out.* Moses skips over incidents on the journey from the holy mountain to the promised land (Num 10–12) in order to get to the heart of the matter: the previous generation failed to inherit the promises because of their unbelief. This same account is more detailed in Num 13–14.

1:21 Do not be afraid; do not be discouraged. The first time these commands occur in Deuteronomy; similar injunctions appear throughout the text at critical junctures (v. 29; 3:2,22; 7:18; 20:1,3; 31:6,8). They assume a present danger that needs to be overcome by placing faith in the Lord. Canaanite power is feeble when compared to divine strength.

[22]Then all of you came to me and said, "Let us send men ahead to spy out the land for us and bring back a report about the route we are to take and the towns we will come to."

[23]The idea seemed good to me; so I selected[a] twelve of you, one man from each tribe. [24]They left and went up into the hill country, and came to the Valley of Eshkol[b] and explored it. [25]Taking with them some of the fruit of the land, they brought it down to us and reported,[c] "It is a good land that the LORD our God is giving us."

Rebellion Against the LORD

[26]But you were unwilling to go up;[d] you rebelled against the command of the LORD your God. [27]You grumbled[e] in your tents and said, "The LORD hates us; so he brought us out of Egypt to deliver us into the hands of the Amorites to destroy us. [28]Where can we go? Our brothers have made our hearts melt in fear. They say, 'The people are stronger and taller[f] than we are; the cities are large, with walls up to the sky. We even saw the Anakites[g] there.' "

[29]Then I said to you, "Do not be terrified; do not be afraid of them. [30]The LORD your God, who is going before you, will fight[h] for you, as he did for you in Egypt, before your very eyes, [31]and in the wilderness. There you saw how the LORD your God carried[i] you, as a father carries his son, all the way you went until you reached this place."

[32]In spite of this, you did not trust[j] in the LORD your God, [33]who went ahead of you on your journey, in fire by night and in a cloud by day,[k] to search[l] out places for you to camp and to show you the way you should go.

[34]When the LORD heard what you said, he was angry and solemnly swore:[m] [35]"No one from this evil generation shall see the good land[n] I swore to give your ancestors, [36]except Caleb son of Jephunneh. He will see it, and I will give him and his descendants the land he set his feet on, because he followed the LORD wholeheartedly.[o]"

[37]Because of you the LORD became angry[p] with me also and said, "You shall not enter[q] it, either. [38]But your assistant, Joshua[r] son of Nun, will enter it. Encourage[s] him, because he will lead[t] Israel to inherit it. [39]And the little ones that you said would be taken captive,[u] your children who do not yet know[v] good from bad — they will enter the land. I will give it to them and they will take possession of it. [40]But as for you, turn around and set out toward the desert along the route to the Red Sea.[a][w]"

[41]Then you replied, "We have sinned against the LORD. We will go up and fight, as the LORD our God commanded us." So every one of you put on his weapons, thinking it easy to go up into the hill country.

[42]But the LORD said to me, "Tell them, 'Do not go up and fight, because I will not be with you. You will be defeated by your enemies.' "[x]

1:23 [a] Nu 13:1-3
1:24 [b] Nu 13:21-25
1:25 [c] Nu 13:27
1:26 [d] Nu 14:1-4
1:27 [e] Dt 9:28; Ps 106:25
1:28 [f] Nu 13:32 [g] Nu 13:33; Dt 9:1-3
1:30 [h] Ex 14:14; Dt 3:22; Ne 4:20
1:31 [i] Dt 32:10-12; Isa 46:3-4; 63:9; Hos 11:3; Ac 13:18
1:32 [j] Ps 106:24; Jude 1:5
1:33 [k] Ex 13:21; Ps 78:14 [l] Nu 10:33
1:34 [m] Nu 14:23,28-30
1:35 [n] Ps 95:11
1:36 [o] Nu 14:24; Jos 14:9
1:37 [p] Dt 3:26; 4:21 [q] Nu 20:12
1:38 [r] Nu 14:30 [s] Dt 31:7 [t] Dt 3:28
1:39 [u] Nu 14:3 [v] Isa 7:15-16
1:40 [w] Nu 14:25
1:42 [x] Nu 14:41-43

[a] *40* Or *the Sea of Reeds*

1:22 Let us send men ahead to spy. By first emphasizing the request of the Israelites to scout out the land before invading it and by omitting the unfavorable "majority report" until the end (v. 28), Moses emphasizes their lack of faith. Without faith the conquest would be doomed from the start.

1:24 Eshkol. Located near Hebron. Moses focuses on the one location in the journey of the spies that describes the bounty of the land (cf. Num 13:23), thereby showing God's goodness.

1:25 God's goodness contrasts with the people's rebellion.

1:26–46 *Rebellion Against the Lord.* In this section Israel fails to understand God's great love and rebels.

1:27 The LORD hates us. Israel's disbelief distorts reality completely and produces horrific heresy: the people reverse salvation history.

1:28 Anakites. Merely mentioning the name of this race of giants created terror (2:10–11; Gen 6:1–4; Num 13:31–33). They were part of a group called the Rephaites (2:11), who seem to be associated with the giant Og, king of Bashan, whose "bed" (3:11) was about 14 feet (4 meters) long and 6 feet (1.8 meters) wide. The remnants of this race may be reflected in the story of Goliath (1 Sam 17; see also 2 Sam 21:15–22).

1:29–31 The antidote to terror is faith in the Lord. Moses reminds Israel of the Lord's power in conquering the formidable Egyptians and his personal provision of fatherly care in the wilderness. God did not hate his people but passionately loved them. Verse 31 is the second time the OT explicitly describes God as a "father" to his people (cf. Exod 4:22). This is the beginning of a spiritual journey that will end with disciples from all nations calling God "*Abba*, Father" (Rom 8:15).

1:32 Moses' correction of heresy registered no impact. Israel had no faith.

1:34–36 The Lord angrily barred the entire adult population from entering the land of promise except Caleb (v. 36), who alone stood against the majority with his faith, and Joshua (v. 38).

1:35 this evil generation. Jesus uses a similar phrase to describe groups of unbelieving people (Matt 12:45; 16:4; Mark 8:38), including his own disciples (Matt 17:17).

1:37 Because of you. God barred Moses from entering the land because of the sins of the Israelites, but this did not exclude Moses' own responsibility (32:51; cf. Num 20:2–13; Ps 106:32–33). Moses' sin was a failure to honor the Lord at Meribah (Num 20:9–13) when he struck the rock twice in exasperation because of the Israelites' disbelief. Here the Israelites' provocation of Moses is mentioned (cf. 3:26; 4:21). Later Moses' own culpability is noted (32:51).

1:41 The people changed their minds, but it was too late. Delayed obedience becomes disobedience.

1:44 [y]Ps 118:12
1:46 [z]Nu 20:1; Jdg 11:17
2:1 [a]Nu 21:4
2:4 [b]Nu 20:14-21
2:5 [c]Ge 36:8; Jos 24:4
2:7 [d]Dt 8:2-4
2:8 [e]1Ki 9:26 [f]Jdg 11:18
2:9 [g]Nu 21:15 [h]Ge 19:36-38
2:10 [i]Ge 14:5 [j]Nu 13:22,33
2:12 [k]ver 22
2:14 [l]Nu 13:26 [m]Nu 14:29-35 [n]Dt 1:34-35
2:15 [o]Ps 106:26
2:19 [p]Ge 19:38 [q]ver 9
2:21 [r]ver 10
2:22 [s]Ge 36:8
2:23 [t]Jos 13:3

43 So I told you, but you would not listen. You rebelled against the LORD's command and in your arrogance you marched up into the hill country. 44 The Amorites who lived in those hills came out against
you; they chased you like a swarm of bees[y] and beat you down from Seir all the way to Hormah. 45 You
came back and wept before the LORD, but he paid no attention to your weeping and turned a deaf ear to
you. 46 And so you stayed in Kadesh[z] many days — all the time you spent there.

Wanderings in the Wilderness

2 Then we turned back and set out toward the wilderness along the route to the Red Sea,[a][a] as the
LORD had directed me. For a long time we made our way around the hill country of Seir.
2 Then the LORD said to me, 3 "You have made your way around this hill country long enough; now turn
north. 4 Give the people these orders:[b] 'You are about to pass through the territory of your relatives the descendants of Esau, who live in Seir. They will be afraid of you, but be very careful. 5 Do not provoke them to
war, for I will not give you any of their land, not even enough to put your foot on. I have given Esau the hill
country of Seir as his own.[c] 6 You are to pay them in silver for the food you eat and the water you drink.' "
7 The LORD your God has blessed you in all the work of your hands. He has watched[d] over your journey through this vast wilderness. These forty years the LORD your God has been with you, and you have
not lacked anything.
8 So we went on past our relatives the descendants of Esau, who live in Seir. We turned from the Arabah road, which comes up from Elath and Ezion Geber,[e] and traveled along the desert road of Moab.[f]
9 Then the LORD said to me, "Do not harass the Moabites or provoke them to war, for I will not give
you any part of their land. I have given Ar[g] to the descendants of Lot[h] as a possession."
10 (The Emites[i] used to live there — a people strong and numerous, and as tall as the Anakites.[j]
11 Like the Anakites, they too were considered Rephaites, but the Moabites called them Emites. 12 Horites
used to live in Seir, but the descendants of Esau drove them out. They destroyed the Horites from before
them and settled in their place, just as Israel did[k] in the land the LORD gave them as their possession.)
13 And the LORD said, "Now get up and cross the Zered Valley." So we crossed the valley.
14 Thirty-eight years passed from the time we left Kadesh Barnea[l] until we crossed the Zered Valley.
By then, that entire generation[m] of fighting men had perished from the camp, as the LORD had sworn to
them.[n] 15 The LORD's hand was against them until he had completely eliminated[o] them from the camp.
16 Now when the last of these fighting men among the people had died, 17 the LORD said to me, 18 "Today you are to pass by the region of Moab at Ar. 19 When you come to the Ammonites,[p] do not harass
them or provoke them to war, for I will not give you possession of any land belonging to the Ammonites.
I have given it as a possession to the descendants of Lot.[q] "
20 (That too was considered a land of the Rephaites, who used to live there; but the Ammonites called
them Zamzummites. 21 They were a people strong and numerous, and as tall as the Anakites.[r] The LORD
destroyed them from before the Ammonites, who drove them out and settled in their place. 22 The LORD
had done the same for the descendants of Esau, who lived in Seir,[s] when he destroyed the Horites from
before them. They drove them out and have lived in their place to this day. 23 And as for the Avvites[t]

[a] *1* Or *the Sea of Reeds*

2:1–23 *Wanderings in the Wilderness.* The Israelites begin to move again to the promised land, avoiding hostilities with their ancient relatives — the Edomites (Gen 25:22–34) and the Moabites and the Ammonites (Gen 19:30–38) — because God had allotted them their land, just as he was giving Israel the land of Canaan. Moses omits the account of Edomite and Moabite hostility toward Israel (Num 20:14–21; Judg 11:14–18) to focus on God's provision for these nations and thus his future provision for his people.
2:1 For a long time we made our way around the hill country of Seir. Only one sentence summarizes about 40 years of wandering because it is a history of disobedience. **Seir.** The Edomite territory south of the Dead Sea.
2:3 You have made your way around this hill country long enough. Echoes 1:6, indicating the beginning of a new start for the people.
2:10–12 This is an editorial comment written much later as a parenthesis to confirm that Israel's Gentile neighbors conquered intimidating, gigantic nations just as the Israelites did (see note on Gen 14:14). Merely mentioning the names of these peoples, especially when headed by a group whose name literally means "terrors," would inspire later readers to have confidence. All of these terrifying peoples are now "history" because of the divine Judge.
2:11 Rephaites. See note on 1:28.
2:15 The journey continues until the first generation of Israelites dies as divine judgment. **eliminated.** Translates a Hebrew word used in holy war contexts to describe God's fighting against Israel's enemies (Exod 14:24 ["threw … into confusion"]; 23:27 ["throw into confusion"]; Josh 10:10 ["threw … into confusion"]; Judg 4:15 ["routed"]). Here God fights against his own people.
2:20–23 This is another parenthetical note (cf. vv. 10–12 and note) listing nations that once inspired terror and that are now historical footnotes.
2:20 Zamzummites. The ominous sound of the name adds to the terror.
2:23 Avvites. Derives from a Hebrew word meaning "distortion" or

who lived in villages as far as Gaza, the Caphtorites[u] coming out from Caphtor[a][v] destroyed them and
settled in their place.)

Defeat of Sihon King of Heshbon

24“Set out now and cross the Arnon Gorge.[w] See, I have given into your hand Sihon the Amorite, king
of Heshbon, and his country. Begin to take possession of it and engage him in battle. 25This very day I
will begin to put the terror[x] and fear[y] of you on all the nations under heaven. They will hear reports of
you and will tremble[z] and be in anguish because of you.”
26From the Desert of Kedemoth I sent messengers to Sihon king of Heshbon offering peace and
saying, 27“Let us pass through your country. We will stay on the main road; we will not turn aside to
the right or to the left.[a] 28Sell us food to eat and water to drink for their price in silver. Only let us pass
through on foot[b]— 29as the descendants of Esau, who live in Seir, and the Moabites, who live in Ar,
did for us—until we cross the Jordan into the land the LORD our God is giving us.” 30But Sihon king of
Heshbon refused to let us pass through. For the LORD[c] your God had made his spirit stubborn[d] and his
heart obstinate in order to give him into your hands, as he has now done.
31The LORD said to me, “See, I have begun to deliver Sihon and his country over to you. Now begin
to conquer and possess his land.”[e]
32When Sihon and all his army came out to meet us in battle[f] at Jahaz, 33the LORD our God delivered
him over to us and we struck him down,[g] together with his sons and his whole army. 34At that time we
took all his towns and completely destroyed[b][h] them—men, women and children. We left no survivors. 35But the livestock and the plunder from the towns we had captured we carried off for ourselves.
36From Aroer[i] on the rim of the Arnon Gorge, and from the town in the gorge, even as far as Gilead, not
one town was too strong for us. The LORD our God gave[j] us all of them. 37But in accordance with the
command of the LORD our God,[k] you did not encroach on any of the land of the Ammonites,[l] neither
the land along the course of the Jabbok[m] nor that around the towns in the hills.

Defeat of Og King of Bashan

3 Next we turned and went up along the road toward Bashan, and Og king of Bashan with his whole
army marched out to meet us in battle at Edrei.[n] 2The LORD said to me, “Do not be afraid[o] of him,
for I have delivered him into your hands, along with his whole army and his land. Do to him what you
did to Sihon king of the Amorites, who reigned in Heshbon.”

a 23 That is, Crete *b 34* The Hebrew term refers to the irrevocable giving over of things or persons to the LORD, often by totally destroying them.

2:23 [u]Ge 10:14 [v]Am 9:7
2:24 [w]Nu 21:13-14; Jdg 11:13,18
2:25 [x]Dt 11:25 [y]Jos 2:9, 11 [z]Ex 15:14-16
2:27 [a]Nu 21:21-22
2:28 [b]Nu 20:19
2:30 [c]Jos 11:20 [d]Ex 4:21; Nu 21:23; Ro 9:18
2:31 [e]Dt 1:8
2:32 [f]Nu 21:23
2:33 [g]Dt 29:7
2:34 [h]Dt 3:6; 7:2
2:36 [i]Dt 3:12; 4:48; Jos 13:9 [j]Ps 44:3
2:37 [k]ver 18-19 [l]Nu 21:24 [m]Ge 32:22; Dt 3:16
3:1 [n]Nu 21:33
3:2 [o]Nu 21:34

“ruin.” These historical asides show that Israel’s God is the Sovereign Lord of history and that the Canaanite conquest that happened under Israel was fully justified, eliminating “terrors” from the land.

2:24–37 *Defeat of Sihon King of Heshbon.* Israel begins its occupation of the land by moving into the territory of Heshbon, located between Moab and Ammon. A similar account also occurs in Num 21:21–31, but here Moses provides theological perspective. Sihon’s refusal to allow Israel through his land has its origin not only in human intransigence but also in divine sovereignty. Sihon may be an Amorite, but he is regarded as just another stubborn king like Pharaoh whose heart God hardened in order to judge him and save Israel (Exod 4:21; 14:4). Moses thus views the conquest as the deliverance from oppression initiated by the exodus.

2:24 Arnon Gorge. The northern border of Moab. By crossing the Arnon Gorge, Israel experiences a defining moment. The conquest has officially begun.

2:25 God guarantees supernatural aid. The Canaanites will soon experience this fear (see Josh 2:9).

2:26 Kedemoth. Desert area north of the Arnon Gorge.

2:32 Jahaz. A city located just north of the Arnon Gorge. The Moabite Stone, a text dating from the ninth century BC, mentions Jahaz.

2:34 completely destroyed. See NIV text note. This is the first practice of the “ban” in Deuteronomy, an important ritual in holy war in the ancient world. The defiled enemy had to be removed from the human world and transferred to the divine world. The victors renounced all claim on the enemy. Destruction of people and things made them useless to the conquerors but put them in the hands of God. So the Hebrew term is sometimes translated “destroyed” and sometimes “devoted” (Num 18:14; Josh 6:17). If the ban was total (see 1 Sam 15:3), all the possessions of the enemy were confiscated and destroyed, but items of precious metal were purged with fire (Num 31:22–23) and removed to a special zone for use by God (Josh 6:24). Sometimes the ban was restricted to combatants, as in this case. In similar military contexts Deuteronomy sometimes speaks of nations being driven out instead of being destroyed, which suggests that the ban applied to those fighting against Israel rather than those who fled (9:3; 11:23; 18:12).

3:1–11 *Defeat of Og King of Bashan.* Right after the Israelites deal with Sihon, they face the gigantic Og, king of Bashan, from the northeast. Much description is given to the formidable size of Og’s cities (v. 5) and his own gigantic stature, which for a later audience could be verified since his iron “bed”—perhaps a sarcophagus (cf. “bier” in 2 Sam 3:31)—was still to be seen in Ammon’s capital city of Rabbah (v. 11). The iron may have been used as ornamentation. As Israel moves closer to its own conquest of the land of Canaan, Moses encourages them by noting their triumph over formidable obstacles.

3:1 Edrei. Modern Dera. The first battle took place about 60 miles (about

3:3 [p]Nu 21:35
3:4 [q]1Ki 4:13
3:6 [r]Dt 2:24,34
3:9 [s]Dt 4:48; Ps 29:6 [t]1Ch 5:23
3:10 [u]Jos 13:11
3:11 [v]Ge 14:5 [w]2Sa 12:26; Jer 49:2
3:12 [x]Nu 32:32-38; Dt 2:36; Jos 13:8-13
3:14 [y]Nu 32:41; 1Ch 2:22
3:15 [z]Nu 32:39-40
3:16 [a]Nu 21:24

3 So the LORD our God also gave into our hands Og king of Bashan and all his army. We struck them
down, leaving no survivors.[p] 4 At that time we took all his cities. There was not one of the sixty cities
that we did not take from them — the whole region of Argob, Og's kingdom in Bashan.[q] 5 All these cities were fortified with high walls and with gates and bars, and there were also a great many unwalled
villages. 6 We completely destroyed[a] them, as we had done with Sihon king of Heshbon, destroying[a][r]
every city — men, women and children. 7 But all the livestock and the plunder from their cities we
carried off for ourselves.

8 So at that time we took from these two kings of the Amorites the territory east of the Jordan, from
the Arnon Gorge as far as Mount Hermon. 9 (Hermon is called Sirion[s] by the Sidonians; the Amorites
call it Senir.)[t] 10 We took all the towns on the plateau, and all Gilead, and all Bashan as far as Salekah[u]
and Edrei, towns of Og's kingdom in Bashan. 11 (Og king of Bashan was the last of the Rephaites.[v] His
bed was decorated with iron and was more than nine cubits long and four cubits wide.[b] It is still in
Rabbah[w] of the Ammonites.)

Division of the Land

12 Of the land that we took over at that time, I gave the Reubenites and the Gadites the territory north
of Aroer[x] by the Arnon Gorge, including half the hill country of Gilead, together with its towns. 13 The
rest of Gilead and also all of Bashan, the kingdom of Og, I gave to the half-tribe of Manasseh. (The
whole region of Argob in Bashan used
to be known as a land of the Rephaites.
14 Jair,[y] a descendant of Manasseh, took
the whole region of Argob as far as the
border of the Geshurites and the Maakathites; it was named after him, so that to
this day Bashan is called Havvoth Jair.[c])
15 And I gave Gilead to Makir.[z] 16 But to
the Reubenites and the Gadites I gave
the territory extending from Gilead
down to the Arnon Gorge (the middle
of the gorge being the border) and out
to the Jabbok River,[a] which is the border
of the Ammonites. 17 Its western border

THE BATTLES OF SIHON AND OG

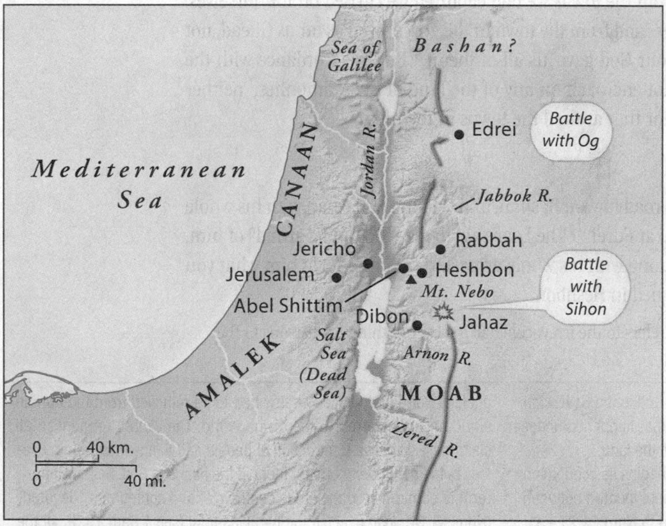

[a] *6* The Hebrew term refers to the irrevocable giving over of things or persons to the LORD, often by totally destroying them. [b] *11* That is, about 14 feet long and 6 feet wide or about 4 meters long and 1.8 meters wide [c] *14* Or *called the settlements of Jair*

100 kilometers) to the north of Jahaz at the southern border of Bashan, a land noted for its fertility and prize cattle.

3:4 Argob. Another name for Og's kingdom in Bashan.

3:8 Mount Hermon. The highest mountain in the area at over 9,000 feet (2,750 meters) in elevation.

3:9 Sirion ... Senir. Other names for Hermon, to which ancient texts attest.

3:10 Salekah. City on the eastern border of Bashan.

3:11 This aside about Og — written for a later audience — provides Israel with an object lesson for contemporary faith. No opponent is invincible, no matter how intimidating.

3:12–20 *Division of the Land.* Cf. Num 32; 34:13–15. Moses divided the conquered land on the east side of the Jordan among Reuben, Gad, and one-half of the tribe of Manasseh, not mentioning the request of these tribes to settle in this area (Num 32). Even though they have inherited their own territory in the promised land, they must also help their fellow Israelites since Israel is a united community. The northern part of the conquered land is distributed to Manasseh, and the southern part to the tribes of Reuben and Gad.

3:12 Aroer. A city just north of the northern border of Moab. **Gilead.** Originally Gilead was the name of Makir's son, from the tribe of Manasseh (Num 26:29; Josh 17:1). The powerful clan of Gilead gave its name to virtually the entire conquered land east of the Jordan, but its territory here is restricted to the hilly central Transjordan region, north and south of the Jabbok River.

3:14 Jair. Cf. Num 32:41. **Argob.** See note on v. 4. **Geshurites ... Maakathites.** People of two small states north of Bashan. Geshur is just east of the Sea of Galilee, and it extends north. Maakah is north near Lake Huleh. Much later, Maakah the daughter of the king of Geshur married King David; she was the mother of Absalom and Tamar (2 Sam 3:3; 13:1).

3:17 Kinnereth. A small region on the northwestern plain of the Sea of Galilee. By extension the name sometimes applies to the sea (see Num

was the Jordan in the Arabah, from Kinnereth[b] to the Sea of the Arabah (that is, the Dead Sea[c]), below
the slopes of Pisgah.
18 I commanded you at that time: "The LORD your God has given you this land to take possession
of it. But all your able-bodied men, armed for battle, must cross over ahead of the other Israelites.[d]
19 However, your wives, your children and your livestock (I know you have much livestock) may stay
in the towns I have given you, 20 until the LORD gives rest to your fellow Israelites as he has to you, and
they too have taken over the land that the LORD your God is giving them across the Jordan. After that,
each of you may go back to the possession I have given you."

Moses Forbidden to Cross the Jordan

21 At that time I commanded Joshua: "You have seen with your own eyes all that the LORD your God
has done to these two kings. The LORD will do the same to all the kingdoms over there where you are
going. 22 Do not be afraid[e] of them; the LORD your God himself will fight[f] for you."
23 At that time I pleaded with the LORD: 24 "Sovereign LORD, you have begun to show to your servant
your greatness[g] and your strong hand. For what god[h] is there in heaven or on earth who can do the
deeds and mighty works[i] you do?[j] 25 Let me go over and see the good land[k] beyond the Jordan — that
fine hill country and Lebanon."
26 But because of you the LORD was angry[l] with me and would not listen to me. "That is enough,"
the LORD said. "Do not speak to me anymore about this matter. 27 Go up to the top of Pisgah and look
west and north and south and east. Look at the land with your own eyes, since you are not going to
cross this Jordan.[m] 28 But commission[n] Joshua, and encourage and strengthen him, for he will lead this
people across[o] and will cause them to inherit the land that you will see." 29 So we stayed in the valley
near Beth Peor.[p]

Obedience Commanded

4 Now, Israel, hear the decrees and laws I am about to teach you. Follow them so that you may live[q]
and may go in and take possession of the land the LORD, the God of your ancestors, is giving you.
2 Do not add[r] to what I command you and do not subtract from it, but keep the commands of the LORD
your God that I give you.

3:17 [b] Nu 34:11; Jos 13:27 [c] Ge 14:3; Jos 12:3
3:18 [d] Nu 32:17
3:22 [e] Dt 1:29 [f] Ex 14:14; Dt 20:4
3:24 [g] Dt 11:2 [h] Ex 15:11; Ps 86:8 [i] Ps 71:16,19 [j] 2Sa 7:22
3:25 [k] Dt 4:22
3:26 [l] Dt 1:37; 31:2
3:27 [m] Nu 27:12
3:28 [n] Nu 27:18-23 [o] Dt 31:3,23
3:29 [p] Dt 4:46; 34:6
4:1 [q] Dt 5:33; 8:1; 16:20; 30:15-20; Eze 20:11; Ro 10:5
4:2 [r] Dt 12:32; Jos 1:7; Rev 22:18-19

34:11 and NIV text note there) and may be related to the Hebrew word for "harp" (*kinnôr*), since the sea's shape resembles a harp.

3:20 rest. A rich theological term; this is the first time Deuteronomy refers to it. The Transjordanian tribes now have rest, but rest is for all the tribes. The essence of Israel's rest: when all the Israelites are living in the land, safe and secure, and worshiping and rejoicing before the Lord as one people. It is intimately related to the Hebrew word *šālôm* ("peace"); see "Shalom," p. 2693. The book of Hebrews mentions that Israel never obtained final rest in Canaan (Heb 4:1 – 11).

3:21 – 29 *Moses Forbidden to Cross the Jordan.* Cf. Num 20:12; 27:12 – 23. Moses ends the history lesson that began in 1:6 by encouraging the new leader, Joshua, to learn the faith lessons of the recent conquests. Moses also reports how he failed to persuade the Lord to let him experience "rest" in the land.

3:21 The LORD will do the same. Joshua can expect the same divine aid for future battles that God provided for past ones.

3:22 Do not be afraid. People new to leadership are often intimidated by the daunting nature of the task. Faith is the antidote to fear.

3:24 Sovereign LORD. One of two times this divine title occurs in the book to initiate a passionate request. Moses appeals to God's great power in order to enter the land, just as he passionately asked God to forgive his people (9:26).

3:26 because of you. See note on 1:37. Moses is a sterling example of a leader suffering for his people. **That is enough.** Even as great a leader as Moses cannot alter God's decision.

3:27 God lets Moses see the promised land. Yet the failure of Moses to gain entry to the land emphasizes the importance of obedience to Moses' audience. **Pisgah.** This mountain is part of the Abarim Range. It is sometimes called Nebo because of the town by that name at its base (32:49; 34:1; Num 27:12).

3:29 Beth Peor. At this place many Israelites died on the verge of entering the promised land (Num 25). Merely mentioning this name would have shattered complacency.

4:1 – 14 *Obedience Commanded.* The history lesson is now over, and Israel is called to ponder its implications in order to avoid exile. The passage centers on the meaning of the covenant at Horeb, where God spoke from the fire. Israel must obey God's instructions at all costs. The invisible God was present in this unique historical event, so they must totally reject idolatry. Idolatry will lead to the sure judgment of exile due to God's wrath, but repentance can evoke God's mercy. Judgment does not have to be the final word.

4:1 Now, Israel. This indicates an important transition from the history lesson to the meaning of that lesson for present life (cf. 10:12). **hear.** This command signifies not only physical hearing but hearing that leads to action, i.e., obedience. Moses does not leave the previous history lesson in the realm of abstract theory but applies it. Thus, the people must obey "the decrees and laws" given at Horeb. **decrees and laws.** This two-part designation for divine revelation expands the single term "law" (v. 44; 1:5) and probably refers to the entire corpus of divine instruction. "Decrees" often refer to laws that have been inscribed permanently (but cf. "ordinance" in Exod 12:24), whereas "laws" refer to decisions rendered for certain cases (cf. "judgment" in 1:17). "Stipulations" (v. 45) may refer to the two tablets of stone on which the Ten Commandments were written.

4:2 Do not add ... do not subtract. These commands describe the unique divine authority of the revelation; they would be diluted by addition and diminished by subtraction. The canon of Scripture both

4:3 [s]Nu 25:1-9; Ps 106:28
4:6 [t]Dt 30:19-20; Ps 19:7; Pr 1:7 [u]Job 28:28
4:7 [v]2Sa 7:23 [w]Ps 46:1; Isa 55:6
4:9 [x]Pr 4:23 [y]Ge 18:19; Eph 6:4 [z]Ps 78:5-6
4:10 [a]Ex 19:9,16
4:11 [b]Ex 19:18; Heb 12:18-19
4:12 [c]Ex 20:22; Dt 5:4,22
4:13 [d]Dt 9:9,11 [e]Ex 24:12; 31:18; 34:28
4:15 [f]Isa 40:18 [g]Jos 23:11
4:16 [h]Ex 20:4-5; 32:7; Dt 5:8; Ro 1:23
4:19 [i]Dt 17:3; Job 31:26 [j]2Ki 17:16; 21:3; Ro 1:25
4:20 [k]1Ki 8:51; Jer 11:4 [l]Ex 19:5; Dt 9:29
4:21 [m]Nu 20:12; Dt 1:37

3You saw with your own eyes what the LORD did at Baal Peor.[s] The LORD your God destroyed from among you everyone who followed the Baal of Peor, 4but all of you who held fast to the LORD your God are still alive today.

5See, I have taught you decrees and laws as the LORD my God commanded me, so that you may follow them in the land you are entering to take possession of it. 6Observe them carefully, for this will show your wisdom[t] and understanding to the nations, who will hear about all these decrees and say, "Surely this great nation is a wise and understanding people."[u] 7What other nation is so great[v] as to have their gods near[w] them the way the LORD our God is near us whenever we pray to him? 8And what other nation is so great as to have such righteous decrees and laws as this body of laws I am setting before you today?

9Only be careful,[x] and watch yourselves closely so that you do not forget the things your eyes have seen or let them fade from your heart as long as you live. Teach[y] them to your children[z] and to their children after them. 10Remember the day you stood before the LORD your God at Horeb,[a] when he said to me, "Assemble the people before me to hear my words so that they may learn to revere me as long as they live in the land and may teach them to their children." 11You came near and stood at the foot of the mountain while it blazed with fire[b] to the very heavens, with black clouds and deep darkness. 12Then the LORD spoke[c] to you out of the fire. You heard the sound of words but saw no form; there was only a voice. 13He declared to you his covenant,[d] the Ten Commandments,[e] which he commanded you to follow and then wrote them on two stone tablets. 14And the LORD directed me at that time to teach you the decrees and laws you are to follow in the land that you are crossing the Jordan to possess.

Idolatry Forbidden

15You saw no form[f] of any kind the day the LORD spoke to you at Horeb out of the fire. Therefore watch yourselves very carefully,[g] 16so that you do not become corrupt and make for yourselves an idol,[h] an image of any shape, whether formed like a man or a woman, 17or like any animal on earth or any bird that flies in the air, 18or like any creature that moves along the ground or any fish in the waters below. 19And when you look up to the sky and see the sun,[i] the moon and the stars—all the heavenly array[j]—do not be enticed into bowing down to them and worshiping things the LORD your God has apportioned to all the nations under heaven. 20But as for you, the LORD took you and brought you out of the iron-smelting furnace,[k] out of Egypt, to be the people of his inheritance,[l] as you now are.

21The LORD was angry with me[m] because of you, and he solemnly swore that I would not cross the

restricts and liberates. It is only the divine word that demands obedience; all other words lack the same authority (12:32; Prov 30:5–6; Gal 3:15–16; Rev 22:18–19).

4:3 You saw with your own eyes. Deut 3:21 uses the evidence of eyesight as encouragement; this verse uses it as warning. **Baal Peor.** Many Israelites died as a result of worshiping the Baal of Peor, known as the god of Mount Peor (Num 25:1–3). Adding to God's word proved fatal for those who, on the very edge of the promised land, followed Baal, while those "who held fast to the LORD" (v. 4) survived. The same Hebrew root for "held fast" describes both the physical bond of marriage (Gen 2:24 in which a couple is united) and a welding of two metals by an artisan (Isa 41:7). Here it means to attach oneself permanently to God and his word.

4:6 this will show your wisdom and understanding to the nations. Obedience will attract the attention of the nations, who will then proclaim the incomparability of Israel. God originally called Abraham to mediate blessing to the nations (Gen 12:3), and part of this mediation involved demonstrating an appropriate human-divine relationship by means of obedience (Gen 18:19).

4:8 righteous. Normally describes people, but here it describes the law of God.

4:9–13 Moses again marshals empirical evidence to warn Israel not to forget the vision at Horeb (Sinai) when God spoke from the fire. The people saw no form but heard words, which were then transcribed on two tablets of stone—the essence of the Horeb covenant. The text captured this unique experience and now permanently brings God's presence near to every generation.

4:9 Teach them to your children. Israel must extend the covenant through time by intentionally transmitting it to the next generation.

4:10 Remember the day you stood. Most in the audience were not at Horeb, but in a sense they were there since God made a covenant with *the nation* (cf. 5:2).

4:14 decrees and laws. Here probably a reference to the Book of the Covenant (Exod 20:22—23:33), which applied the Ten Commandments (Exod 20:1–17) to the life of the nation.

4:15–31 *Idolatry Forbidden.* Israel is to "connect the theological dots" from the revelation at Horeb: God forbids idolatry in whatever form it might take, whether it involves worshiping human beings or animals or even celestial bodies. Created things cannot represent the Creator. Paul also regards such idolatry as the primal sin (Rom 1:23). God will judge the sin of idolatry severely.

4:16–19 The list of possible options for idolatry is based on the creation account in Gen 1 in inverse order: from humanity (the crown of creation) to inanimate celestial phenomena. One of the results of idolatry is to invert the created order. Ironically, idolatry (the activity of worshiping the creature rather than the Creator) dehumanizes human beings.

4:19 has apportioned to all the nations under heaven. Moses criticizes the idolatry of the nations. They have deified the simple elements of nature.

4:20 In contrast to the nations, Israel is "the people of his inheritance." **inheritance.** Implies that Israel has a unique relationship with God (cf. Exod 4:22).

Jordan and enter the good land the LORD your God is giving you as your inheritance. 22 I will die in this
land; I will not cross the Jordan; but you are about to cross over and take possession of that good land.[n]
23 Be careful not to forget the covenant[o] of the LORD your God that he made with you; do not make for
yourselves an idol[p] in the form of anything the LORD your God has forbidden. 24 For the LORD your God
is a consuming fire,[q] a jealous God.

25 After you have had children and grandchildren and have lived in the land a long time—if you
then become corrupt and make any kind of idol, doing evil[r] in the eyes of the LORD your God and arousing his anger, 26 I call the heavens and the earth as witnesses against you[s] this day that you will quickly
perish from the land that you are crossing the Jordan to possess. You will not live there long but will
certainly be destroyed. 27 The LORD will scatter[t] you among the peoples, and only a few of you will survive among the nations to which the LORD will drive you. 28 There you will worship man-made gods[u] of
wood and stone, which cannot see or hear or eat or smell.[v] 29 But if from there you seek[w] the LORD your
God, you will find him if you seek him with all your heart[x] and with all your soul.[y] 30 When you are in
distress and all these things have happened to you, then in later days[z] you will return to the LORD your
God and obey him. 31 For the LORD your God is a merciful[a] God; he will not abandon or destroy you or
forget the covenant with your ancestors, which he confirmed to them by oath.

The LORD Is God

32 Ask[b] now about the former days, long before your time, from the day God created human beings on
the earth;[c] ask from one end of the heavens to the other.[d] Has anything so great as this ever happened,
or has anything like it ever been heard of? 33 Has any other people heard the voice of God[a] speaking out
of fire, as you have, and lived?[e] 34 Has any god ever tried to take for himself one nation out of another
nation,[f] by testings, by signs[g] and wonders,[h] by war, by a mighty hand and an outstretched arm,[i] or by
great and awesome deeds,[j] like all the things the LORD your God did for you in Egypt before your very eyes?

35 You were shown these things so that you might know that the LORD is God; besides him there is no
other.[k] 36 From heaven he made you hear his voice[l] to discipline you. On earth he showed you his great
fire, and you heard his words from out of the fire. 37 Because he loved[m] your ancestors and chose their
descendants after them, he brought you out of Egypt by his Presence and his great strength,[n] 38 to drive
out before you nations greater and stronger than you and to bring you into their land to give it to you
for your inheritance,[o] as it is today.

39 Acknowledge and take to heart this day that the LORD is God in heaven above and on the earth
below. There is no other.[p] 40 Keep[q] his decrees and commands, which I am giving you today, so that it

[a] 33 Or *of a god*

4:22 [n] Dt 3:25
4:23 [o] ver 9,16 [p] Ex 20:4
4:24 [q] Ex 24:17; Dt 9:3; Heb 12:29
4:25 [r] 2Ki 17:2,17
4:26 [s] Dt 30:18-19; Isa 1:2; Mic 6:2
4:27 [t] Lev 26:33; Dt 28:36,64; Ne 1:8
4:28 [u] Dt 28:36,64; 1Sa 26:19; Jer 16:13 [v] Ps 115:4-8; 135:15-18
4:29 [w] 2Ch 15:4; Isa 55:6 [x] Jer 29:13 [y] Dt 30:1-3,10
4:30 [z] Dt 31:29; Jer 23:20; Hos 3:5
4:31 [a] 2Ch 30:9; Ne 9:31; Ps 116:5; Jnh 4:2
4:32 [b] Dt 32:7; Job 8:8 [c] Ge 1:27 [d] Mt 24:31
4:33 [e] Ex 20:22; Dt 5:24-26
4:34 [f] Ex 6:6 [g] Ex 7:3 [h] Dt 7:19; 26:8 [i] Ex 13:3 [j] Dt 34:12
4:35 [k] Dt 32:39; 1Sa 2:2; Isa 45:5,18
4:36 [l] Ex 19:9,19
4:37 [m] Dt 10:15 [n] Ex 13:3,9,14
4:38 [o] Dt 7:1; 9:5
4:39 [p] ver 35; Jos 2:11
4:40 [q] Lev 22:31; Dt 5:33

4:24 a consuming fire. This description of God can be traced back to Abraham's vision of God (Gen 15:17), the burning bush (Exod 3:1–5), the pillar of fire by night (Exod 13:21), the fiery mountain (Exod 19–24), the fire of judgment that destroyed Nadab and Abihu (Lev 10), and the Israelites in the wilderness (Num 11:1–3). Fire frequently accompanies theophanies (manifestations of God's presence) in the OT (Exod 3:1–6; Lev 9:24; 1 Kgs 18:38). In the NT, John the Baptist sees the coming Messiah bringing the fire of judgment to burn up sinners (Matt 3:11–12). Jesus describes his own mission as coming to cast fire down on the earth, and he experiences a baptism by fire on the cross (Luke 12:49–51). His disciples are baptized with this fire at Pentecost and are miraculously not consumed; rather, they declare the mighty works of God (Acts 2:1–11). It is this divine fire that will someday transform the heavens and the earth in judgment and redemption (2 Pet 3:10–13). **a jealous God.** Cf. 6:15; Exod 20:5; 34:14. A husband's passionate claim on his wife's fidelity begins to capture what this means. It is the healthy counterpart of love. Divine jealousy is the response when God is robbed of his rightful place, so it occurs mainly in contexts of idolatry, the theological equivalent of adultery.

4:28 There you will worship man-made gods. In exile the people will experience the consequences of idolatry: the impotence of false gods.

4:30 later days. May refer to the indefinite future or to a special time near the end of history when God decisively intervenes to manifest his kingship in the world, i.e., the Messianic era (cf. Num 24:14; Isa 2:1–5; Heb 1:3).

4:31 a merciful God. God is a consuming fire (see note on v. 24), but he is also merciful (Exod 34:6). He will not forget his covenant with the patriarchs. This tension between justice and mercy runs throughout the OT. By repenting, human beings can resolve this tension and experience God's mercy, but God's justice still requires a price to be paid. Paul sees the divine resolution to this tension in the cross, where God's justice and mercy perfectly meet, demonstrating God "to be just and the one who justifies those who have faith in Jesus" (Rom 3:26).

4:32–40 *The Lord Is God.* A flurry of rhetorical questions signals the end of this long speech. This is not just a history lesson that began at Horeb. Moses surveys the entire scope of human history from the creation of the world to his own time to the exodus and to the revelation at Horeb. There is no historical equivalent to the covenant at Horeb. World history finds an important event in Horeb, where the living God speaks directly to his people. The divine motivation is love and fidelity (v. 37). Election is rooted in the mystery of divine love that will climactically be expressed in the new covenant (cf. 7:7–8; Matt 26:26–29; Eph 1:4–8a).

4:40 Keep his decrees and commands. The final point of the history

4:40 [r]Dt 5:16 [s]Dt 6:3, 18; Eph 6:2-3
4:46 [t]Nu 21:26; Dt 3:29
4:48 [u]Dt 2:36 [v]Dt 3:9
5:2 [w]Ex 19:5
5:3 [x]Heb 8:9
5:4 [y]Dt 4:12,33,36
5:5 [z]Gal 3:19 [a]Ex 20:18,21

may go well[r] with you and your children after you and that you may live long[s] in the land the LORD your God gives you for all time.

Cities of Refuge

4:41-43Ref — Nu 35:6-34; Dt 19:1-14; Jos 20:1-9

[41]Then Moses set aside three cities east of the Jordan, [42]to which anyone who had killed a person could flee if they had unintentionally killed a neighbor without malice aforethought. They could flee into one of these cities and save their life. [43]The cities were these: Bezer in the wilderness plateau, for the Reubenites; Ramoth in Gilead, for the Gadites; and Golan in Bashan, for the Manassites.

Introduction to the Law

[44]This is the law Moses set before the Israelites. [45]These are the stipulations, decrees and laws Moses gave them when they came out of Egypt [46]and were in the valley near Beth Peor east of the Jordan, in the land of Sihon[t] king of the Amorites, who reigned in Heshbon and was defeated by Moses and the Israelites as they came out of Egypt. [47]They took possession of his land and the land of Og king of Bashan, the two Amorite kings east of the Jordan. [48]This land extended from Aroer[u] on the rim of the Arnon Gorge to Mount Sirion[a][v] (that is, Hermon), [49]and included all the Arabah east of the Jordan, as far as the Dead Sea,[b] below the slopes of Pisgah.

The Ten Commandments

5:6-21pp — Ex 20:1-17

5 Moses summoned all Israel and said:

Hear, Israel, the decrees and laws I declare in your hearing today. Learn them and be sure to follow them. [2]The LORD our God made a covenant[w] with us at Horeb. [3]It was not with our ancestors[c] that the LORD made this covenant, but with us, with all of us who are alive here today.[x] [4]The LORD spoke[y] to you face to face out of the fire on the mountain. [5](At that time I stood between[z] the LORD and you to declare to you the word of the LORD, because you were afraid[a] of the fire and did not go up the mountain.) And he said:

[6]"I am the LORD your God, who brought you out of Egypt, out of the land of slavery.

[7]"You shall have no other gods before[d] me.

[a] *48* Syriac (see also 3:9); Hebrew *Siyon* [b] *49* Hebrew *the Sea of the Arabah* [c] *3* Or *not only with our parents* [d] *7* Or *besides*

lesson is that they are to respond in love in order to make the invisible God visible: they are to show the world what God is really like.

4:41–43 *Cities of Refuge.* The text supplies an addendum to the first speech of Moses by echoing the concern for justice, which is the first topic of the speech (1:9–18). Providing sanctuary for those guilty of accidental homicide is accomplished by appointing three cities of refuge in central locations in Transjordan (cf. Num 35:6–34; Josh 20). Bloodshed must not contaminate the land.

4:44—28:68 *The Second Speech: The First Priority Is Absolute Allegiance to the Lord.* Moses sets the divine instruction before the Israelites. This speech continues to expound the covenant obligations, first in general terms (4:44—11:32) and then in specific stipulations (12:1—26:19). Then a narrative describes how the covenant should be ratified in the land of Canaan (ch. 27). The speech concludes with a list of blessings and curses (ch. 28). The Ten Commandments are central to the law; the rest is commentary.

4:44–49 *Introduction to the Law.* This section sets the scene for the second speech and duplicates some of the introduction to the first speech (1:1–5). Such repetition is not unusual in Hebrew, and Moses probably repeats it because of the extraordinary length of the second speech.

4:44–45 God's will can be expressed with one word ("law" [v. 44], i.e., instruction), a two-part phrase ("decrees and laws"; see note on v. 1), or a three-part expression ("stipulations, decrees and laws," v. 45). These different words to describe the divine revelation point to different types of material that will be used to instruct the people.

5:1–33 *The Ten Commandments.* Moses rehearses the divine encounter experienced at Horeb and the resulting covenant summarized in the Ten Commandments. The encounter was to establish a relationship realized in obedience and blessing (vv. 32–33). "Hear" (4:1) was the key verb in the revelation at Horeb (ch. 4), and this first part of the second speech develops that theme. Ch. 5 begins with the command to "hear" God's words (5:1), and this verb occurs eight more times (see vv. 23–28, "heard," "hear," "listen") after the thunderous pronouncements. As in Exod 20:2–7, where the object of the verb "spoke" is "all these words" (i.e., the Ten Commandments), here in Deut 5 the same Ten Commandments—the first object of "hearing"—are placed before all the additional laws and decrees. This shows the central importance of the Commandments.

5:1 Hear. The second time (cf. 4:1) this command occurs in Deuteronomy, signaling the dramatic importance of the information about to be presented (cf. 6:3,4; 9:1; 20:3).

5:2 not with our ancestors … but with us. The covenant transcends time. Most of those listening to Moses were not present at Horeb, but it is as if they were. The Lord's covenant love lasts forever (7:9; Ps 136).

5:4 face to face out of the fire. "Face to face" is an idiom meaning "directly," i.e., without a mediator (Exod 33:11; cf. 20:18–19); therefore, this is not to be understood literally. It expresses an intimate personal encounter since the Israelites saw no form of God at the mountain.

5:6–21 See notes on Exod 20:2–17. The Ten Commandments are the central stipulations of God's covenant with Israel. It is impossible to overestimate the influence of these laws on subsequent history.

[8]"You shall not make for yourself an image in the form of anything in heaven above or on the
earth beneath or in the waters below. [9]You shall not bow down to them or worship them; for
I, the LORD your God, am a jealous God, punishing the children for the sin of the parents to
the third and fourth generation of those who hate me,[b] [10]but showing love to a thousand
generations of those who love me and keep my commandments.[c]

[11]"You shall not misuse the name of the LORD your God, for the LORD will not hold anyone guiltless
who misuses his name.[d]

[12]"Observe the Sabbath day by keeping it holy,[e] as the LORD your God has commanded you. [13]Six
days you shall labor and do all your work, [14]but the seventh day[f] is a sabbath to the LORD
your God. On it you shall not do any work, neither you, nor your son or daughter, nor
your male or female servant, nor your ox, your donkey or any of your animals, nor any
foreigner residing in your towns, so that your male and female servants may rest, as you
do. [15]Remember that you were slaves in Egypt and that the LORD your God brought you out
of there with a mighty hand and an outstretched arm.[g] Therefore the LORD your God has
commanded you to observe the Sabbath day.

[16]"Honor your father and your mother,[h] as the LORD your God has commanded you, so that you
may live long[i] and that it may go well with you in the land the LORD your God is giving you.

[17]"You shall not murder.[j]

[18]"You shall not commit adultery.[k]

[19]"You shall not steal.

[20]"You shall not give false testimony against your neighbor.

[21]"You shall not covet your neighbor's wife. You shall not set your desire on your neighbor's house
or land, his male or female servant, his ox or donkey, or anything that belongs to your
neighbor."[l]

[22]These are the commandments the LORD proclaimed in a loud voice to your whole assembly there
on the mountain from out of the fire, the cloud and the deep darkness; and he added nothing more.
Then he wrote them on two stone tablets[m] and gave them to me.

[23]When you heard the voice out of the darkness, while the mountain was ablaze with fire, all the
leaders of your tribes and your elders came to me. [24]And you said, "The LORD our God has shown
us his glory and his majesty, and we have heard his voice from the fire. Today we have seen that a
person can live even if God speaks with them.[n] [25]But now, why should we die? This great fire will
consume us, and we will die if we hear the voice of the LORD our God any longer.[o] [26]For what mortal
has ever heard the voice of the living God speaking out of fire, as we have, and survived?[p] [27]Go near

5:9 [b]Ex 34:7
5:10 [c]Jer 32:18
5:11 [d]Lev 19:12; Mt 5:33-37
5:12 [e]Ex 20:8
5:14 [f]Ge 2:2; Heb 4:4
5:15 [g]Dt 4:34
5:16 [h]Ex 20:12; Lev 19:3; Dt 27:16; Eph 6:2-3*; Col 3:20 [i]Dt 4:40
5:17 [j]Mt 5:21-22*
5:18 [k]Mt 5:27-30; Lk 18:20*; Jas 2:11*
5:21 [l]Ro 7:7*; 13:9*
5:22 [m]Ex 24:12; 31:18; Dt 4:13
5:24 [n]Ex 19:19
5:25 [o]Dt 18:16
5:26 [p]Dt 4:33

They provide the foundation for morality throughout the Western world and concisely summarize God's expectations for his people. Moses rehearses the Ten Commandments given in Exod 20:2–17 with a few changes to highlight some features for the Moab generation. For example, the last five commands are linked more tightly in Deuteronomy than in Exodus, which treats these commands as a single group emphasizing concern for one's neighbor. As a whole, the commands are not arbitrary but reveal that God is characterized by mercy and justice, which is expressed in zeal for his own honor (commandments 1–3) and concern for the welfare of all his creatures (commandments 4–10). These "words" are the heart of the covenant and thus the "constitution" of Israel. All other legislation concretely applies the Ten Commandments in daily life. Commandments 1–4 and 10 are unique in the ancient world.

5:12 Observe. This variation (rather than "remember" in Exod 20:8) emphasizes action and may suggest previous laxity. **as the LORD your God has commanded you.** An addition to the original command in Exod 20:8, indicating its temporal priority 40 years earlier.

5:14 nor your ox, your donkey or any of your animals. The need to expand the list of animals given in Exod 20:10 suggests that the Israelites may have violated the original spirit of the Sabbath law.

5:15 Remember that you were slaves in Egypt. Moses provides an alternative motivation to the original command in Exod 20:11. Sabbath rest must be enacted weekly as a reminder of not only creation but also redemption from bondage in Egypt, where oppressive work dominated life. Israel must incorporate this pattern of remembering redemption in its weekly life as a reminder of the rest that God intends for all creation.

5:16 that it may go well with you. This is missing from the parallel in Exod 20:12, and it points out that the life the Lord desires for his people is not to be measured simply in terms of longevity.

5:21 wife ... house. In contrast to the same law in Exod 20:17, here the neighbor's wife is not included with the house, i.e., the possessions. She is distinguished here by being an object of a different expression (the verb "covet" versus "set your desire on").

5:22 he wrote them. See note on Exod 31:18. **two stone tablets.** Each of the tablets probably contained the Ten Commandments. The practice of making two copies of a treaty document in the ancient world was common, one copy for the servant vassal and one copy for his lord. Here both documents are placed inside the ark of the covenant (10:5); the remainder of Israel's law was written on a scroll and placed beside the ark (31:24–26).

5:23–27 Moses recounts the awesome impact that God's revelation had upon Israel. Unlike Adam and Eve before the fall, Israel could not bear God's immediate presence and urged Moses to be a mediator.

5:27–29 Moses compares Israel's eagerness to obey the Lord ("We

5:28 [q]Dt 18:17
5:29 [r]Ps 81:8,13 [s]Dt 11:1; Isa 48:18 [t]Dt 4:1,40
5:31 [u]Ex 24:12
5:32 [v]Dt 17:11,20; 28:14; Jos 1:7; 23:6; Pr 4:27
5:33 [w]Jer 7:23 [x]Dt 4:40
6:2 [y]Ex 20:20; Dt 10:12-13
6:3 [z]Dt 5:33 [a]Ex 3:8
6:4 [b]Mk 12:29*; 1Co 8:4
6:5 [c]Mt 22:37*; Mk 12:30*; Lk 10:27* [d]Dt 10:12
6:6 [e]Dt 11:18

and listen to all that the LORD our God says. Then
tell us whatever the LORD our God tells you. We
will listen and obey."

[28]The LORD heard you when you spoke to me, and
the LORD said to me, "I have heard what this people
said to you. Everything they said was good.[q] [29]Oh,
that their hearts would be inclined to fear me[r] and
keep all my commands[s] always, so that it might go
well with them and their children forever![t]

[30]"Go, tell them to return to their tents. [31]But
you stay here[u] with me so that I may give you all
the commands, decrees and laws you are to teach
them to follow in the land I am giving them to
possess."

[32]So be careful to do what the LORD your God has
commanded you; do not turn aside to the right or
to the left.[v] [33]Walk in obedience to all that the LORD
your God has commanded you,[w] so that you may
live and prosper and prolong your days[x] in the land
that you will possess.

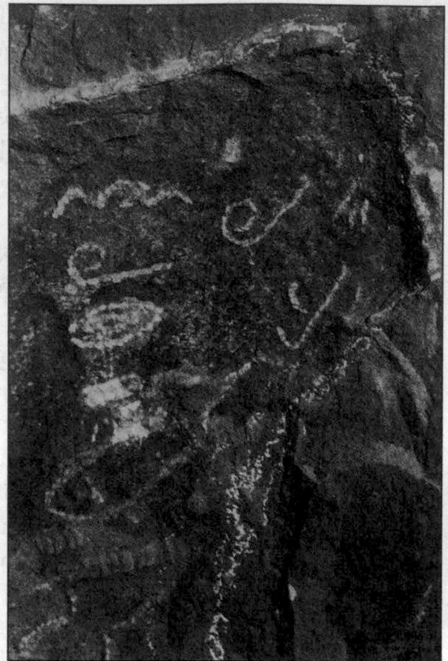

Semitic writing at Serabit el-Khadim similar in style, date, and location (western Sinai peninsula) to that of Moses.
Z. Radovan/www.BibleLandPictures.com

Love the LORD Your God

6 These are the commands, decrees and laws the
LORD your God directed me to teach you to observe in the land that you are crossing the Jordan to
possess, [2]so that you, your children and their children after them may fear[y] the LORD your God as long
as you live by keeping all his decrees and commands that I give you, and so that you may enjoy long life.
[3]Hear, Israel, and be careful to obey so that it may go well with you and that you may increase greatly[z]
in a land flowing with milk and honey,[a] just as the LORD, the God of your ancestors, promised you.

[4]Hear, O Israel: The LORD our God, the LORD is one.[a][b] [5]Love[c] the LORD your God with all your heart
and with all your soul and with all your strength.[d] [6]These commandments that I give you today are to
be on your hearts.[e] [7]Impress them on your children. Talk about them when you sit at home and when

[a] 4 Or *The LORD our God is one LORD*; or *The LORD is our God, the LORD is one*; or *The LORD is our God, the LORD alone*

will listen and obey," v. 27) to God's awareness of the nation's limitations ("Oh, that their hearts would be inclined to fear me," v. 29). It is ultimately a matter of the heart. Moses recognizes later that God will someday rectify the problem (30:6; cf. Jer 31:33).

6:1–25 *Love the Lord Your God.* Moses expounds the fundamental significance of the Decalogue (the "Ten Words," i.e., the Ten Commandments). God's people must love the one God with their whole being (v. 5). To ensure this, Israel must avoid three dangers, which will be discussed in later chapters: paganism (ch. 7), materialism (ch. 8), and egotism (chs. 9–10). The one God demands a complete love that unites all the facets of the personality, inculcating the next generation with this vision of life through teaching (v. 7), action (vv. 8–9), memory (v. 12), worship (v. 13), ritual (v. 20), and story (vv. 21–23).

6:3 Hear, Israel, and be careful to obey. The English word-pair "hear and heed" better captures the alliteration of the two Hebrew words that these commands translate, drawing attention to the command to obey.

6:4–9 These verses constitute the foremost text in Judaism identified as the *Shema* (Hebrew *šĕma*ʿ, "hear") because of its initial word in Hebrew. It is one of the three texts in Orthodox Judaism to be recited every day (cf. 11:18–21; Num 15:37–41). Jesus agreed that this particular text was the most important commandment (Mark 12:29–30).

6:4 The LORD ... the LORD. This double use of the divine name is unique in the OT except for Exod 34:6, where Moses alludes to and explains in more detail the meaning of the name. **one.** The Lord is not just God for Israel; he is God for all (cf. Zech 14:9). This is the principle of monotheism. The Lord is one of a kind, absolutely unique (32:39; Isa 44:8; 45:6). In contrast in the ancient world polytheism—the belief in many gods—was prevalent.

6:5 From the oneness of God flows a oneness in love: one must love God with the entirety of one's being—one's heart (mind), soul (life force or breath), and strength. Thus, what is involved here is not a love that can be reduced to a feeling or sentiment but a love for God that commands the entire personality.

6:6 These commandments that I give you today. All the teaching that Moses is giving (not just v. 4), although in principle the commands can be reduced to v. 4.

6:7 Impress. From a Hebrew word that means "repeat." This is a rare word and may also have the meaning of "engrave." Thus, by repeating something often enough, the teacher can "engrave" the meaning on the mind. **Talk about them.** The commandments should be the topic of conversation in daily life.

you walk along the road, when you lie down and when you get up.[f] 8Tie them as symbols on your hands
and bind them on your foreheads.[g] 9Write them on the doorframes of your houses and on your gates.[h]
10When the LORD your God brings you into the land he swore to your fathers, to Abraham, Isaac and
Jacob, to give you—a land with large, flourishing cities you did not build,[i] 11houses filled with all kinds
of good things you did not provide, wells you did not dig, and vineyards and olive groves you did not
plant—then when you eat and are satisfied,[j] 12be careful that you do not forget the LORD, who brought
you out of Egypt, out of the land of slavery.
13Fear the LORD[k] your God, serve him only[l] and take your oaths in his name. 14Do not follow other
gods, the gods of the peoples around you; 15for the LORD your God[m], who is among you, is a jealous God
and his anger will burn against you, and he will destroy you from the face of the land. 16Do not put the
LORD your God to the test[n] as you did at Massah. 17Be sure to keep the commands of the LORD your God
and the stipulations and decrees he has given you.[o] 18Do what is right and good in the LORD's sight, so
that it may go well[p] with you and you may go in and take over the good land the LORD promised on oath
to your ancestors, 19thrusting out all your enemies before you, as the LORD said.
20In the future, when your son asks you,[q] "What is the meaning of the stipulations, decrees and laws
the LORD our God has commanded you?" 21tell him: "We were slaves of Pharaoh in Egypt, but the LORD
brought us out of Egypt with a mighty hand. 22Before our eyes the LORD sent signs and wonders—great
and terrible—on Egypt and Pharaoh and his whole household. 23But he brought us out from there
to bring us in and give us the land he promised on oath to our ancestors. 24The LORD commanded us
to obey all these decrees and to fear the LORD our God,[r] so that we might always prosper and be kept
alive, as is the case today.[s] 25And if we are careful to obey all this law before the LORD our God, as he has
commanded us, that will be our righteousness.[t]"

6:7 [f]Dt 4:9; 11:19; Eph 6:4
6:8 [g]Ex 13:9,16; Dt 11:18
6:9 [h]Dt 11:20
6:10 [i]Jos 24:13
6:11 [j]Dt 8:10
6:13 [k]Dt 10:20 [l]Mt 4:10*; Lk 4:8*
6:15 [m]Dt 4:24
6:16 [n]Ex 17:7; Mt 4:7*; Lk 4:12*
6:17 [o]Dt 11:22; Ps 119:4
6:18 [p]Dt 4:40
6:20 [q]Ex 13:14
6:24 [r]Dt 10:12; Jer 32:39 [s]Ps 41:2
6:25 [t]Dt 24:13; Ro 10:3,5
7:1 [u]Dt 31:3; Ac 13:19
7:2 [v]Ex 23:32

Driving Out the Nations

7 When the LORD your God brings you into the land you are entering to possess and drives out before
you many nations[u]—the Hittites, Girgashites, Amorites, Canaanites, Perizzites, Hivites and Jebusites, seven nations larger and stronger than you— 2and when the LORD your God has delivered them
over to you and you have defeated them, then you must destroy them totally.[a] Make no treaty[v] with

[a] 2 The Hebrew term refers to the irrevocable giving over of things or persons to the LORD, often by totally destroying them; also in verse 26.

6:8–9 Tie them ... Write them. Probably not literally, although it later became the practice of Jews to bind the commands to their bodies. There is evidence of this at Qumran and in the NT (see note on Matt 23:5). Jews also placed passages of Scripture in small wooden or metal containers called mezuzot and attached them to the doorframes of their houses. The commands, however, were to affect behavior—to dominate action ("on your hands") and vision ("on your foreheads") and to be an integral part of one's home ("on the doorframes of your houses") and one's town ("on your gates"). The commands written on stone must not stay there; they must also be written on the *individual* heart, the *family* homestead, and the *societal* gathering place. For further support for a figurative interpretation of this command, see 11:18–20; Exod 13:9,16.

6:10–19 This unit describes the gift of the land in all its abundance along with its peculiar temptations.

6:10–11 you did not build ... did not provide ... did not dig ... did not plant. The bountiful land is a picture of pure grace. Israel certainly did not earn these gifts. The abundance of God's grace virtually whets the appetite in anticipation of the gift of land. But these generous gifts come accompanied by a warning not to forget their Giver. Affluence can often lead to this kind of amnesia.

6:13 The Hebrew sentence structure emphasizes the priority of God by putting him at the initial grammatical position of each clause in this verse. He must never be demoted to second place. When Jesus was in the desert, Satan sought to derail his mission, but Jesus countered the attempt with this verse (Matt 4:10; Luke 4:8).

6:16 Do not put the LORD your God to the test. Jesus rebuffed Satan with these words when he was tempted to presume on divine power to perform miracles in order to prove that he was the Messiah (Matt 4:7; Luke 4:12). The Israelites are to trust rather than test God.

6:20 In the future, when your son asks you. Natural opportunities to teach children will occur if children see the importance of their parents' faith. Such faith responds with the essential story of salvation. The children can then "own" the faith of their parents.

6:25 that will be our righteousness. Righteousness is equivalent to being in a right standing with God because of obedience to the covenant. If understood in isolation, this verse suggests that righteousness can be earned, but it is clear from the context that exodus salvation (v. 23) precedes the command to obey (v. 24). Similarly Abraham believed (Gen 15:6) before he received the command to be circumcised (Gen 17:10).

7:1–26 *Driving Out the Nations.* This warns of an immediate danger that would compromise the complete devotion of the Israelites that ch. 6 demands: pagan religions in the promised land. Ch. 7 begins and ends on the same note: the Israelites must eliminate every vestige of Canaanite religion. The middle of the chapter reflects on Israel's unique status as the people of God and their special responsibilities.

7:1 seven nations. Of the 27 lists of pre-Israelite peoples in Canaan, only three lists have seven members (cf. Josh 3:10; 24:11). The number suggests completeness. **larger and stronger than you.** Israelite victory was dependent on divine help.

7:2–5 you must destroy them totally ... Make no treaty with them ... Do not intermarry ... Break down their altars. While the Israelites were to destroy the Canaanites, most of the attention is devoted to eliminating any possibility of sharing their religion, which is the issue addressed by these commands. See Introduction: Themes and Theology (Holy War).

7:2 [w] Dt 13:8
7:3 [x] Ex 34:15-16; Ezr 9:2
7:4 [y] Dt 6:15
7:5 [z] Ex 23:24; Dt 12:2-3
7:6 [a] Ex 19:5-6; 1Pe 2:9 [b] Ps 50:5; Jer 2:3 [c] Dt 14:2
7:7 [d] Dt 10:22
7:8 [e] Dt 10:15 [f] Ex 32:13 [g] Ex 13:14
7:9 [h] Dt 4:35 [i] 1Co 1:9; 2Ti 2:13 [j] Ne 1:5; Da 9:4
7:12 [k] Lev 26:3-13; Dt 28:1-14; Ps 105:8-9
7:13 [l] Jn 14:21 [m] Dt 28:4
7:14 [n] Ex 23:26
7:15 [o] Ex 15:26
7:16 [p] ver 2; Ex 23:33 [q] Jdg 8:27
7:17 [r] Nu 33:53
7:18 [s] Dt 31:6 [t] Ps 105:5
7:19 [u] Dt 4:34
7:20 [v] Ex 23:28; Jos 24:12
7:21 [w] Jos 3:10 [x] Dt 10:17; Ne 9:32
7:22 [y] Ex 23:28-30
7:24 [z] Jos 23:9

them, and show them no mercy.[w] 3 Do not intermarry with them.[x] Do not give your daughters to their sons or take their daughters for your sons, 4 for they will turn your children away from following me to serve other gods, and the LORD's anger will burn against you and will quickly destroy[y] you. 5 This is what you are to do to them: Break down their altars, smash their sacred stones, cut down their Asherah poles[a] and burn their idols in the fire.[z] 6 For you are a people holy[a] to the LORD your God.[b] The LORD your God has chosen[c] you out of all the peoples on the face of the earth to be his people, his treasured possession.

7 The LORD did not set his affection on you and choose you because you were more numerous than other peoples, for you were the fewest of all peoples.[d] 8 But it was because the LORD loved[e] you and kept the oath he swore[f] to your ancestors that he brought you out with a mighty hand and redeemed you from the land of slavery,[g] from the power of Pharaoh king of Egypt. 9 Know therefore that the LORD your God is God;[h] he is the faithful God,[i] keeping his covenant of love[j] to a thousand generations of those who love him and keep his commandments. 10 But

> those who hate him he will repay to their face by destruction;
> he will not be slow to repay to their face those who hate him.

11 Therefore, take care to follow the commands, decrees and laws I give you today.

12 If you pay attention to these laws and are careful to follow them, then the LORD your God will keep his covenant of love with you, as he swore to your ancestors.[k] 13 He will love you and bless you[l] and increase your numbers. He will bless the fruit of your womb, the crops of your land—your grain, new wine and olive oil—the calves of your herds and the lambs of your flocks in the land he swore to your ancestors to give you.[m] 14 You will be blessed more than any other people; none of your men or women will be childless, nor will any of your livestock be without young.[n] 15 The LORD will keep you free from every disease.[o] He will not inflict on you the horrible diseases you knew in Egypt, but he will inflict them on all who hate you. 16 You must destroy all the peoples the LORD your God gives over to you. Do not look on them with pity[p] and do not serve their gods, for that will be a snare[q] to you.

17 You may say to yourselves, "These nations are stronger than we are. How can we drive them out?"[r] 18 But do not be afraid[s] of them; remember well what the LORD your God did to Pharaoh and to all Egypt.[t] 19 You saw with your own eyes the great trials, the signs and wonders, the mighty hand and outstretched arm, with which the LORD your God brought you out. The LORD your God will do the same to all the peoples you now fear.[u] 20 Moreover, the LORD your God will send the hornet[v] among them until even the survivors who hide from you have perished. 21 Do not be terrified by them, for the LORD your God, who is among you,[w] is a great and awesome God.[x] 22 The LORD your God will drive out those nations before you, little by little.[y] You will not be allowed to eliminate them all at once, or the wild animals will multiply around you. 23 But the LORD your God will deliver them over to you, throwing them into great confusion until they are destroyed. 24 He will give their kings into your hand, and you will wipe out their names from under heaven. No one will be able to stand up against you;[z] you will destroy them. 25 The images of

[a] 5 That is, wooden symbols of the goddess Asherah; here and elsewhere in Deuteronomy

---

7:6 Moses applies Exod 19:5–6 to the Israelites. They are a holy people, dedicated to the Lord, called out by him to be his treasured possession—like a personal cache of wealth a king treasures for his private use (1 Chr 29:3).

7:8 because the LORD loved you. Moses traces back the mystery of Israel's election to God's love.

7:9 keeping his covenant of love. A rich theological phrase. See 1 Kgs 8:23; 2 Chr 6:14; see also Pss 89:28; 106:45. This is a covenant God makes with his people to demonstrate his unfailing love for them in such a way that all his promises to them are fulfilled. The identity of God is not in doubt; he is a God of faithful love for a thousand generations of those who follow him (v. 9) but a God who repays quickly those who hate him (v. 10). Cf. Exod 34:6–7, where the accent on God's love is much stronger (thousands [of generations]) than his anger (three/four generations).

7:12–15 This is the first extended description of the blessings for obedience in the land (elaborated in 28:1–14; 30:1–10). Obedience will lead to extraordinary fertility and good health.

7:16–26 Moses returns to the original topic: the Canaanites and their idolatry.

7:16 snare. Associating with the Canaanites will lead to religious entrapment and ruin.

7:17–19 Moses anticipates objections (v. 17) but swiftly overrules them with object lessons from history (vv. 18–19).

7:20 hornet. A further elaboration of Exod 23:28 (see note there; cf. Josh 24:12).

7:22 little by little. The conquest will be protracted because God wishes to spare his people from the dangers associated with the multiplication of wild animals.

7:23 the LORD your God will deliver them over to you. The first description of the Lord's help in the future conquest.

7:25 Do not covet the silver and gold on them. Anticipates the story of Achan, who did not heed this warning and contaminated his family (Josh 6:17–19; 7:1,20–25; cf. Acts 5:1–10).

Eighteenth-century BC bronze calf god from Ashkelon covered with silver on head and legs. The author of Deuteronomy commands the people to burn their gods in the fire instead of coveting the silver and gold on them (Deut 7:25). The gold calf that Israel worshiped at Mount Sinai (Exod 32) may have resembled this.

their gods you are to burn[a] in the fire. Do not covet[b]
the silver and gold on them, and do not take it for
yourselves, or you will be ensnared[c] by it, for it is
detestable[d] to the LORD your God. 26 Do not bring a
detestable thing into your house or you, like it, will
be set apart for destruction.[e] Regard it as vile and
utterly detest it, for it is set apart for destruction.

Do Not Forget the LORD

8 Be careful to follow every command I am
giving you today, so that you may live[f] and
increase and may enter and possess the land the
LORD promised on oath to your ancestors. 2 Remember how the LORD your God led[g] you all the
way in the wilderness these forty years, to humble
and test you in order to know what was in your
heart, whether or not you would keep his commands. 3 He humbled you, causing you to hunger
and then feeding you with manna,[h] which neither
you nor your ancestors had known, to teach you
that man does not live on bread alone but on every word that comes from the mouth of the LORD.[i]
4 Your clothes did not wear out and your feet did
not swell during these forty years.[j] 5 Know then in
your heart that as a man disciplines his son, so the
LORD your God disciplines you.[k]
6 Observe the commands of the LORD your God,
walking in obedience to him and revering him.[l] 7 For the LORD your God is bringing you into a good
land — a land with brooks, streams, and deep springs gushing out into the valleys and hills;[m] 8 a land with
wheat and barley, vines and fig trees, pomegranates, olive oil and honey; 9 a land where bread will not be
scarce and you will lack nothing; a land where the rocks are iron and you can dig copper out of the hills.
10 When you have eaten and are satisfied,[n] praise the LORD your God for the good land he has given
you. 11 Be careful that you do not forget the LORD your God, failing to observe his commands, his laws
and his decrees that I am giving you this day. 12 Otherwise, when you eat and are satisfied, when you
build fine houses and settle down,[o] 13 and when your herds and flocks grow large and your silver and
gold increase and all you have is multiplied, 14 then your heart will become proud and you will forget[p]
the LORD your God, who brought you out of Egypt, out of the land of slavery. 15 He led you through the
vast and dreadful wilderness,[q] that thirsty and waterless land, with its venomous snakes[r] and scorpions.
He brought you water out of hard rock.[s] 16 He gave you manna to eat in the wilderness, something your
ancestors had never known,[t] to humble and test you so that in the end it might go well with you. 17 You
may say to yourself,[u] "My power and the strength of my hands have produced this wealth for me." 18 But

7:25 [a] Ex 32:20; 1Ch 14:12 [b] Jos 7:21 [c] Jdg 8:27 [d] Dt 17:1
7:26 [e] Lev 27:28-29
8:1 [f] Dt 4:1
8:2 [g] Am 2:10
8:3 [h] Ex 16:12,14,35 [i] Ex 16:2-3; Mt 4:4*; Lk 4:4*
8:4 [j] Dt 29:5; Ne 9:21
8:5 [k] 2Sa 7:14; Pr 3:11-12; Heb 12:5-11; Rev 3:19
8:6 [l] Dt 5:33
8:7 [m] Dt 11:9-12
8:10 [n] Dt 6:10-12
8:12 [o] Hos 13:6
8:14 [p] Ps 106:21
8:15 [q] Jer 2:6 [r] Nu 21:6 [s] Nu 20:11; Ps 78:15; 114:8
8:16 [t] Ex 16:15
8:17 [u] Dt 9:4,7,24

8:1–20 *Do Not Forget the Lord.* After conquering the enemy, Israel faces another danger: the material abundance of the land could lead to affluence, which could lead to spiritual amnesia. If idolatry distorts devotion (ch. 7), affluence could cause it to be forgotten. Beginning with God's supernatural provision in the wilderness, Moses describes God's natural provision in Canaan and warns of the dangers of affluence.

8:3 man does not live on bread alone. Biblical texts in themselves rarely provide a systematic doctrine of humanity, but this verse provides one in abbreviated form. Human beings need bread, but, more important, they need a word from God; the Israelites in the wilderness learned that God's daily decree provided the bread itself. Jesus cited this verse when Satan tempted him in the desert (Matt 4:4, Luke 4:4).

8:7–9 The first extended description of the natural wealth of the land: water, grains, wine, and minerals such as iron and copper. The land is like the Garden of Eden, abounding in wealth and fertility. The mountains of southern Lebanon and the regions east of the Sea of Galilee and south of the Dead Sea also contain iron. Both iron and copper were abundant in the Arabah south of the Dead Sea.

8:9 bread will not be scarce. Unlike the wilderness, where God provided supernaturally. Whether by supernatural or natural methods, God still provides.

8:13–14 This is also why the king must not multiply wealth (17:14–20).

8:17 My ... my ... for me. A focus on oneself rather than God. Amnesia has become complete. Israel in such a state is much like the rich fool in Luke 12:16–20.

8:18 [v]Pr 10:22; Hos 2:8
8:19 [w]Dt 4:26; 30:18
9:1 [x]Dt 4:38; 11:23,31 [y]Dt 1:28
9:2 [z]Nu 13:22,28,32-33
9:3 [a]Dt 31:3; Jos 3:11 [b]Dt 4:24; Heb 12:29 [c]Ex 23:31; Dt 7:23-24
9:4 [d]Dt 8:17 [e]Lev 18:21, 24-30; Dt 18:9-14
9:5 [f]Titus 3:5 [g]Ge 12:7; 13:15; 15:7; 17:8; 26:4
9:6 [h]ver 13; Ex 32:9; Dt 31:27
9:8 [i]Ex 32:7-10; Ps 106:19
9:9 [j]Ex 24:12, 15,18; 34:28
9:10 [k]Ex 31:18; Dt 4:13
9:12 [l]Ex 32:7-8; Dt 31:29 [m]Jdg 2:17

remember the LORD your God, for it is he who gives you the ability to produce wealth,[v] and so confirms his covenant, which he swore to your ancestors, as it is today.

19 If you ever forget the LORD your God and follow other gods and worship and bow down to them, I testify against you today that you will surely be destroyed.[w] 20 Like the nations the LORD destroyed before you, so you will be destroyed for not obeying the LORD your God.

Not Because of Israel's Righteousness

9 Hear, Israel: You are now about to cross the Jordan to go in and dispossess nations greater and stronger than you,[x] with large cities that have walls up to the sky.[y] 2 The people are strong and tall—Anakites! You know about them and have heard it said: "Who can stand up against the Anakites?"[z] 3 But be assured today that the LORD your God is the one who goes across ahead of you[a] like a devouring fire.[b] He will destroy them; he will subdue them before you. And you will drive them out and annihilate them quickly,[c] as the LORD has promised you.

4 After the LORD your God has driven them out before you, do not say to yourself,[d] "The LORD has brought me here to take possession of this land because of my righteousness." No, it is on account of the wickedness of these nations[e] that the LORD is going to drive them out before you. 5 It is not because of your righteousness or your integrity[f] that you are going in to take possession of their land; but on account of the wickedness of these nations, the LORD your God will drive them out before you, to accomplish what he swore[g] to your fathers, to Abraham, Isaac and Jacob. 6 Understand, then, that it is not because of your righteousness that the LORD your God is giving you this good land to possess, for you are a stiff-necked people.[h]

The Golden Calf

7 Remember this and never forget how you aroused the anger of the LORD your God in the wilderness. From the day you left Egypt until you arrived here, you have been rebellious against the LORD. 8 At Horeb you aroused the LORD's wrath so that he was angry enough to destroy you.[i] 9 When I went up on the mountain to receive the tablets of stone, the tablets of the covenant that the LORD had made with you, I stayed on the mountain forty days and forty nights; I ate no bread and drank no water.[j] 10 The LORD gave me two stone tablets inscribed by the finger of God.[k] On them were all the commandments the LORD proclaimed to you on the mountain out of the fire, on the day of the assembly.

11 At the end of the forty days and forty nights, the LORD gave me the two stone tablets, the tablets of the covenant. 12 Then the LORD told me, "Go down from here at once, because your people whom you brought out of Egypt have become corrupt.[l] They have turned away quickly[m] from what I commanded them and have made an idol for themselves."

8:19–20 If they forget God and engage in idolatry, Israel will be destroyed like the nations before them.

9:1–6 *Not Because of Israel's Righteousness.* The third danger, egotism leading to self-righteousness (see note on 6:1–25), was perhaps the most lethal of all the spiritual perils. Moses begins by focusing on the formidable size of their enemies and the coming demise of their enemies at the hands of the Lord. The temptation of self-righteousness will set in after the conquest and settlement. The Israelites might reach the false conclusion that God gave them victory because they are morally superior. Moses punctures this illusion with a vivid history lesson that extends through 10:11: they have been rebellious from the beginning.

9:4 because of my righteousness. In the ancient world victory battle was viewed frequently as a reward for righteousness in the eyes of the gods. Moses completely decimates this claim. **on account of the wickedness of these nations.** The first evidence to counter any claim of self-righteousness. The nations are so wicked that they are ripe for judgment (cf. Gen 15:16).

9:5 Second (see note on v. 4), to discourage a belief in relative righteousness, Moses shows that the conquest fulfills God's promise to the patriarchs. Israel's election was grounded in divine love and nothing more (7:8).

9:6 you are a stiff-necked people. The third piece of evidence contradicting the delusion of self-righteousness (see notes on vv. 4,5). The metaphor suggests unnatural stubbornness. Moses will now complete this initial sketch of Israel's character in great historical detail.

9:7–29 *The Golden Calf.* Israel violates the covenant as soon as it has been enacted.

9:7 Moses points out their rebellious nature from the beginning of the nation's salvation (the exodus) up to the present moment.

9:8–21 Moses focuses on the golden calf episode at Mount Horeb to illustrate dramatically the people's rebellion; this account is a free retelling of Exod 24:12–18; 32:1–35; 34:1–35. The covenant had hardly been made when the people rebelled by breaking the first two commandments—something like a spouse committing adultery on the wedding night. The account here is highly rhetorical, serving mainly to illustrate Israel's sinful propensities. The people—even Aaron the high priest—owed their survival to Moses' intercession (Exod 32:7–14,31–35).

9:9 forty days and forty nights. See Exod 24:18; cf. 32:1. **forty.** A prolonged period of time often representing a period of testing (Num 13:25; Jonah 3:4; Matt 4:2).

13 And the LORD said to me, "I have seen this people[n], and they are a stiff-necked people indeed! 14 Let me alone,[o] so that I may destroy them and blot out[p] their name from under heaven. And I will make you into a nation stronger and more numerous than they."

15 So I turned and went down from the mountain while it was ablaze with fire. And the two tablets of the covenant were in my hands.[q] 16 When I looked, I saw that you had sinned against the LORD your God; you had made for yourselves an idol cast in the shape of a calf.[r] You had turned aside quickly from the way that the LORD had commanded you. 17 So I took the two tablets and threw them out of my hands, breaking them to pieces before your eyes.

18 Then once again I fell[s] prostrate before the LORD for forty days and forty nights; I ate no bread and drank no water, because of all the sin you had committed, doing what was evil in the LORD's sight and so arousing his anger. 19 I feared the anger and wrath of the LORD, for he was angry enough with you to destroy you.[t] But again the LORD listened to me.[u] 20 And the LORD was angry enough with Aaron to destroy him, but at that time I prayed for Aaron too. 21 Also I took that sinful thing of yours, the calf you had made, and burned it in the fire. Then I crushed it and ground it to powder as fine as dust and threw the dust into a stream that flowed down the mountain.[v]

22 You also made the LORD angry at Taberah,[w] at Massah[x] and at Kibroth Hattaavah.[y]

23 And when the LORD sent you out from Kadesh Barnea, he said, "Go up and take possession of the land I have given you." But you rebelled against the command of the LORD your God. You did not trust[z] him or obey him. 24 You have been rebellious against the LORD ever since I have known you.[a]

25 I lay prostrate before the LORD those forty days and forty nights because the LORD had said he would destroy you.[b] 26 I prayed to the LORD and said, "Sovereign LORD, do not destroy your people, your own inheritance that you redeemed by your great power and brought out of Egypt with a mighty hand.[c] 27 Remember your servants Abraham, Isaac and Jacob. Overlook the stubbornness of this people, their wickedness and their sin. 28 Otherwise, the country from which you brought us will say, 'Because the LORD was not able to take them into the land he had promised them, and because he hated them, he brought them out to put them to death in the wilderness.'[d] 29 But they are your people, your inheritance[e] that you brought out by your great power and your outstretched arm.[f]"

Tablets Like the First Ones

10 At that time the LORD said to me, "Chisel out two stone tablets[g] like the first ones and come up to me on the mountain. Also make a wooden ark.[a] 2 I will write on the tablets the words that were on the first tablets, which you broke. Then you are to put them in the ark."[h]

3 So I made the ark out of acacia wood[i] and chiseled[j] out two stone tablets like the first ones, and I went up on the mountain with the two tablets in my hands. 4 The LORD wrote on these tablets what he had written before, the Ten Commandments he had proclaimed[k] to you on the mountain, out of the fire, on the day of the assembly. And the LORD gave them to me. 5 Then I came back down the mountain[l] and put the tablets in the ark[m] I had made, as the LORD commanded me, and they are there now.[n]

9:13 [n] ver 6; Ex 32:9; Dt 10:16
9:14 [o] Ex 32:10 [p] Nu 14:12; Dt 29:20
9:15 [q] Ex 19:18; 32:15
9:16 [r] Ex 32:19
9:18 [s] Ex 34:28
9:19 [t] Ex 32:10-11,14 [u] Dt 10:10
9:21 [v] Ex 32:20
9:22 [w] Nu 11:3 [x] Ex 17:7 [y] Nu 11:34
9:23 [z] Ps 106:24
9:24 [a] ver 7; Dt 31:27
9:25 [b] ver 18
9:26 [c] Ex 32:11
9:28 [d] Ex 32:12; Nu 14:16
9:29 [e] Dt 4:20; 1Ki 8:51 [f] Dt 4:34; Ne 1:10
10:1 [g] Ex 25:10; 34:1-2
10:2 [h] Ex 25:16,21; Dt 4:13
10:3 [i] Ex 25:5,10; 37:1-9 [j] Ex 34:4
10:4 [k] Ex 20:1
10:5 [l] Ex 34:29 [m] Ex 40:20 [n] 1Ki 8:9

[a] *1* That is, a chest

9:17–18 In Deuteronomy the smashing of the tablets symbolizes that the end of the covenant takes place before Moses intercedes (cf. Exod 32:11–19). This emphasizes the impact of the prolonged intercession of Moses. Sinful Israel is figuratively brought back from the dead by Moses' intercession.

9:20 I prayed for Aaron too. Not mentioned explicitly in Exodus. The retelling of this story stresses Israel's sin by indicating that even its high priest had to be delivered from judgment.

9:21 that sinful thing of yours. The first words Moses uses to describe the idol indicate its diabolical nature. Then he names it and obliterates it.

9:22 Cf. Exod 17:1–7; Num 11:1–3,31–34. After recalling the destruction of the idol, Moses' mind races from Horeb to a rapid succession of places; they are not necessarily in historical order since Massah occurred before the golden calf revolt.

9:23 Kadesh Barnea. The rebellion against God climaxes at this location, as is noted by the dense concentration of the language of spiritual revolt in vv. 23–24. Moses describes the second generation with the characteristics of the first.

9:25–29 Moses resumes his description of the golden calf fiasco to show that the people owed their survival to his intercession (vv. 26–29), God's covenant with their ancestors (v. 27), and God's concern for his own glory (vv. 28–29). Any righteousness of Israel was a myth.

10:1–11 *Tablets Like the First Ones.* Moses finishes the Horeb story not with the glorious revelation of Exod 34:5–7 but with the replacement of the broken tablets. Nevertheless, these two tablets of stone contain the divine glory because the words were spoken from the divine fire (v. 4). In the interest of brevity, Moses telescopes the original story here. Thus, he describes himself making the ark for the commandments (v. 5), whereas in Exodus Bezalel does not make it until much later (Exod 37:1–9).

10:6 [o] Nu 33:30-31,38 [p] Nu 20:25-28
10:7 [q] Nu 33:32-34
10:8 [r] Nu 3:6 [s] Dt 18:5 [t] Dt 21:5
10:9 [u] Nu 18:20; Dt 18:1-2; Eze 44:28
10:10 [v] Ex 33:17; 34:28; Dt 9:18-19,25
10:12 [w] Mic 6:8 [x] Dt 5:33; 6:13; Mt 22:37 [y] Dt 6:5
10:14 [z] 1Ki 8:27 [a] Ex 19:5
10:15 [b] Dt 4:37
10:16 [c] Jer 4:4 [d] Dt 9:6
10:17 [e] Jos 22:22; Da 2:47 [f] Ac 10:34; Ro 2:11; Eph 6:9
10:18 [g] Ps 68:5
10:19 [h] Lev 19:34
10:20 [i] Mt 4:10 [j] Dt 11:22 [k] Ps 63:11
10:21 [l] Ex 15:2; Jer 17:14 [m] Ps 106:21-22
10:22 [n] Ge 46:26-27 [o] Ge 15:5; Dt 1:10
11:1 [p] Dt 10:12 [q] Zec 3:7
11:2 [r] Dt 5:24; 8:5

6 (The Israelites traveled from the wells of Bene Jaakan to Moserah.[o] There Aaron died and was buried, and Eleazar his son succeeded him as priest.[p] 7 From there they traveled to Gudgodah and on to
Jotbathah, a land with streams of water.[q] 8 At that time the LORD set apart the tribe of Levi[r] to carry the
ark of the covenant of the LORD, to stand before the LORD to minister[s] and to pronounce blessings[t] in his
name, as they still do today. 9 That is why the Levites have no share or inheritance among their fellow
Israelites; the LORD is their inheritance,[u] as the LORD your God told them.)
10 Now I had stayed on the mountain forty days and forty nights, as I did the first time, and the LORD listened to me at this time also. It was not his will to destroy you.[v] 11 "Go," the LORD said to me, "and lead the
people on their way, so that they may enter and possess the land I swore to their ancestors to give them."

Fear the LORD

12 And now, Israel, what does the LORD your God ask of you[w] but to fear the LORD your God, to walk
in obedience to him, to love him,[x] to serve the LORD your God with all your heart[y] and with all your
soul, 13 and to observe the LORD's commands and decrees that I am giving you today for your own good?
14 To the LORD your God belong the heavens, even the highest heavens,[z] the earth and everything in it.[a]
15 Yet the LORD set his affection on your ancestors and loved[b] them, and he chose you, their descendants,
above all the nations—as it is today. 16 Circumcise[c] your hearts, therefore, and do not be stiff-necked[d] any
longer. 17 For the LORD your God is God of gods[e] and Lord of lords, the great God, mighty and awesome, who
shows no partiality[f] and accepts no bribes. 18 He defends the cause of the fatherless and the widow,[g] and
loves the foreigner residing among you, giving them food and clothing. 19 And you are to love those who are
foreigners, for you yourselves were foreigners in Egypt.[h] 20 Fear the LORD your God and serve him.[i] Hold fast[j]
to him and take your oaths in his name.[k] 21 He is the one you praise;[l] he is your God, who performed for
you those great and awesome wonders[m] you saw with your own eyes. 22 Your ancestors who went down into
Egypt were seventy in all,[n] and now the LORD your God has made you as numerous as the stars in the sky.[o]

Love and Obey the LORD

11 Love[p] the LORD your God and keep his requirements, his decrees, his laws and his commands
always.[q] 2 Remember today that your children were not the ones who saw and experienced
the discipline of the LORD your God:[r] his majesty, his mighty hand, his outstretched arm; 3 the signs he

10:6–9 A parenthetical section provides supplementary historical information at this point because of the focus on the ark of the covenant, Aaron, and the Levites. Aaron and the Israelites survived because of Moses' successful intercessory prayer.

10:10–11 Moses completes his speech regarding Israel's sinful nature. If he had not interceded, Israel would have been destroyed. They should now possess the land with the right attitude: humility.

10:12–22 *Fear the Lord.* After pointing out the three lethal temptations (see note on 6:1–25), Moses resumes his speech demanding complete love for God (ch. 6), which is really the heart of the Ten Commandments (ch. 5).

10:12–13 fear ... walk ... love ... serve ... observe. Moses piles up five concise requirements in which the central one is love. These related statements are all integrated around love.

10:12 And now, Israel. A transitional signal directing attention to the implications of the previous discourse (cf. 4:1). **what does the LORD your God ask of you ...?** In other words, what is the meaning of the previous speech? Cf. Mic 6:6–8. For the answer, see the note on vv. 12–13.

10:14–15 To the LORD your God ... and he chose you. The mystery and marvel of election.

10:16 Israel's history of rebellion points to the basic issue: a sinful heart. This is the Bible's first command to circumcise the heart (cf. Lev 26:41). Circumcision removes the skin of the male sexual organ, and circumcision of the heart removes the "skin" of a hard heart. Physical circumcision reminds people that they need spiritual circumcision (cf. 30:6; Jer 9:25; Rom 2:29).

10:17–19 God's activity in stooping down to care for the fatherless, widow, and foreigner graphically shows what will happen when the hearts of the Israelites are circumcised. Biblical law often displays concern for this "trio of the marginalized" (24:17–21; cf. Exod 22:21–22; Ps 146:9; Jer 7:6; Zech 7:10). The Israelites must replicate God's compassion in their own lives and behavior (vv. 18–19). They must love refugees from other lands, because they were once refugees in Egypt. As God had granted them an exodus to a new way of life, they are to do the same for others.

10:20 Moses returns to the theme of single-hearted devotion to God by essentially repeating 6:13.

10:21–22 The call to love the Lord is not arbitrary, and the call to praise him is not irrational since he liberated them from oppressive slavery in Egypt and made a mere 70 individuals into a great nation. He not only delivers from death; he gives abundant life.

11:1–32 *Love and Obey the Lord.* As Moses finishes this part of his speech, he points to the past to motivate obedience, to the future to encourage, and to the present to ensure longevity in the land. He sums up the speech by giving his people two choices.

11:1 In both the OT and NT, the way to love God is never vague and nebulous; it is inextricably connected to doing his will (cf. John 15:14; 1 John 5:2–3).

11:2–7 Moses always confronts the present generation with their responsibilities. Just as in 5:3 it was not the parents with whom the covenant was made but the children, now it is not the children who experienced God's discipline but the parents. There is no substitute for present obedience.

11:3–4 The most complete description thus far in Deuteronomy of

performed and the things he did in the heart of Egypt, both to Pharaoh king of Egypt and to his whole country; 4what he did to the Egyptian army, to its horses and chariots, how he overwhelmed them with the waters of the Red Sea[a][s] as they were pursuing you, and how the LORD brought lasting ruin on them. 5It was not your children who saw what he did for you in the wilderness until you arrived at this place, 6and what he did[t] to Dathan and Abiram, sons of Eliab the Reubenite, when the earth opened its mouth right in the middle of all Israel and swallowed them up with their households, their tents and every living thing that belonged to them. 7But it was your own eyes that saw all these great things the LORD has done.

8Observe therefore all the commands I am giving you today, so that you may have the strength to go in and take over the land that you are crossing the Jordan to possess,[u] 9and so that you may live long[v] in the land the LORD swore[w] to your ancestors to give to them and their descendants, a land flowing with milk and honey.[x] 10The land you are entering to take over is not like the land of Egypt, from which you have come, where you planted your seed and irrigated it by foot as in a vegetable garden. 11But the land you are crossing the Jordan to take possession of is a land of mountains and valleys that drinks rain from heaven.[y] 12It is a land the LORD your God cares for; the eyes[z] of the LORD your God are continually on it from the beginning of the year to its end.

13So if you faithfully obey[a] the commands I am giving you today—to love[b] the LORD your God and to serve him with all your heart and with all your soul— 14then I will send rain[c] on your land in its season, both autumn and spring rains,[d] so that you may gather in your grain, new wine and olive oil. 15I will provide grass[e] in the fields for your cattle, and you will eat and be satisfied.[f]

16Be careful, or you will be enticed to turn away and worship other gods and bow down to them.[g] 17Then the LORD's anger[h] will burn against you, and he will shut up[i] the heavens so that it will not rain and the ground will yield no produce, and you will soon perish[j] from the good land the LORD is giving you. 18Fix these words of mine in your hearts and minds; tie them as symbols on your hands and bind them on your foreheads.[k] 19Teach them to your children,[l] talking about them when you sit at home and when you walk along the road, when you lie down and when you get up.[m] 20Write them on the doorframes of your houses and on your gates,[n] 21so that your days and the days of your children may be many[o] in the land the LORD swore to give your ancestors, as many as the days that the heavens are above the earth.[p]

22If you carefully observe[q] all these commands I am giving you to follow—to love the LORD your God, to walk in obedience to him and to hold fast[r] to him— 23then the LORD will drive out all these nations before you, and you will dispossess nations larger and stronger than you.[s] 24Every place where you set your foot will be yours:[t] Your territory will extend from the desert to Lebanon, and from the Euphrates River to the Mediterranean Sea. 25No one will be able to stand against you. The LORD your God, as he promised you, will put the terror and fear of you on the whole land, wherever you go.[u]

26See, I am setting before you today a blessing and a curse[v]— 27the blessing[w] if you obey the commands of the LORD your God that I am giving you today; 28the curse if you disobey[x] the commands of

[a] 4 Or *the Sea of Reeds*

11:4 [s]Ex 14:27
11:6 [t]Nu 16:1-35
11:8 [u]Jos 1:7
11:9 [v]Dt 4:40; Pr 10:27 [w]Dt 9:5 [x]Ex 3:8
11:11 [y]Dt 8:7
11:12 [z]1Ki 9:3
11:13 [a]Dt 6:17 [b]Dt 10:12
11:14 [c]Lev 26:4; Dt 28:12 [d]Joel 2:23; Jas 5:7
11:15 [e]Ps 104:14 [f]Dt 6:11
11:16 [g]Dt 8:19; 29:18; Job 31:9,27
11:17 [h]Dt 6:15 [i]1Ki 8:35; 2Ch 6:26 [j]Dt 4:26
11:18 [k]Dt 6:6-8
11:19 [l]Dt 6:7 [m]Dt 4:9-10
11:20 [n]Dt 6:9
11:21 [o]Pr 3:2; 4:10 [p]Ps 72:5
11:22 [q]Dt 6:17 [r]Dt 10:20
11:23 [s]Dt 4:38; 9:1
11:24 [t]Ge 15:18; Ex 23:31; Jos 1:3; 14:9
11:25 [u]Ex 23:27; Dt 7:24
11:26 [v]Dt 30:1,15,19
11:27 [w]Dt 28:1-14
11:28 [x]Dt 28:15

God's power in destroying Egypt. Moses intends to impress the Israelites with the importance of *their* obedience.

11:6 Another historical reminder to instill obedience (cf. Num 16). As the sea overwhelmed the Egyptian rebels, the earth did the same for Israelite rebels in the desert.

11:8–9 After warning the Israelites with historical examples of ruin, Moses expounds on the gift coming to Israel: the land of Canaan.

11:10 not like the land of Egypt. Herodotus once called Egypt the "gift of the Nile." It was a strip of flat land irrigated by the Nile River. In contrast the promised land had rich geographic variety watered by dew and rainfall, making it much less dependent on human labor for irrigation.

11:13–15 if you faithfully obey ... then I will send ... I will provide. Obedience will lead to fertility. The autumn rains usually appear in October and are essential for fertility, while the spring rains normally begin in March-April. The former rains break the drought of summer and facilitate plowing and seeding, while the latter rains provide the final catalyst for a rich crop of "grain, new wine and olive oil" (v. 14; cf. Jer 5:24; Joel 2:23).

11:16 The nations in the land worshiped fertility gods (e.g., Baal was the rain-god). These gods, with their promise of material abundance, would be an alluring temptation for the Israelites.

11:18–21 Moses again reminds the people of his important words at the beginning (6:4–9). He has come now full circle, stressing the importance of the people intentionally placing God's will in the forefront of life through constant repetition so that it becomes a habit of the heart.

11:22–23 Moses again emphasizes the importance of obedience for the successful invasion of Canaan.

11:24 set your foot. A sign of ownership and a way of describing conquest and occupation of a territory (cf. Josh 1:3). The image occurs also in Gen 13:17, where God told Abraham to "Go, walk through the length and breadth of the land, for I am giving it to you."

11:26–28 The speech ends with a dramatic choice between life and

11:29 [y]Dt 27:12-13; Jos 8:33
11:30 [z]Ge 12:6 [a]Jos 4:19
11:31 [b]Dt 9:1; Jos 1:11
12:1 [c]Dt 4:9-10; 1Ki 8:40
12:2 [d]2Ki 16:4; 17:10
12:3 [e]Nu 33:52; Dt 7:5; Jdg 2:2
12:5 [f]ver 11,13; 2Ch 7:12,16
12:6 [g]Dt 14:22-23
12:7 [h]ver 12,18; Lev 23:40; Dt 14:26
12:10 [i]Dt 11:31
12:11 [j]ver 5; Dt 15:20; 16:2

the LORD your God and turn from the way that I command you today by following other gods, which
you have not known. 29When the LORD your God has brought you into the land you are entering to
possess, you are to proclaim on Mount Gerizim the blessings, and on Mount Ebal the curses.[y] 30As you
know, these mountains are across the Jordan, westward, toward the setting sun, near the great trees of
Moreh,[z] in the territory of those Canaanites living in the Arabah in the vicinity of Gilgal.[a] 31You are
about to cross the Jordan to enter and take possession[b] of the land the LORD your God is giving you.
When you have taken it over and are living there, 32be sure that you obey all the decrees and laws I am
setting before you today.

The One Place of Worship

12 These are the decrees and laws you must be careful to follow in the land that the LORD, the God of
your ancestors, has given you to possess—as long as you live in the land.[c] 2Destroy completely
all the places on the high mountains, on the hills and under every spreading tree,[d] where the nations you
are dispossessing worship their gods. 3Break down their altars, smash[e] their sacred stones and burn their
Asherah poles in the fire; cut down the idols of their gods and wipe out their names from those places.
4You must not worship the LORD your God in their way. 5But you are to seek the place the LORD your
God will choose from among all your tribes to put his Name there for his dwelling.[f] To that place you
must go; 6there bring your burnt offerings and sacrifices, your tithes[g] and special gifts, what you have
vowed to give and your freewill offerings, and the firstborn of your herds and flocks. 7There, in the presence of the LORD your God, you and your families shall eat and shall rejoice[h] in everything you have put
your hand to, because the LORD your God has blessed you.
8You are not to do as we do here today, everyone doing as they see fit, 9since you have not yet reached
the resting place and the inheritance the LORD your God is giving you. 10But you will cross the Jordan
and settle in the land the LORD your God is giving[i] you as an inheritance, and he will give you rest from
all your enemies around you so that you will live in safety. 11Then to the place the LORD your God will
choose as a dwelling for his Name[j]—there you are to bring everything I command you: your burnt

death, obedience and disobedience. Moses develops this at the very end of the second speech (chs. 27–28).

11:29 The first act of worship in Canaan will be a ceremony that formally depicts the crucial choice before the eyes of the entire nation. A fuller description of this ceremony is found in 27:1–14. **Mount Gerizim.** The fertile mountain symbolizes life. **Mount Ebal.** The barren mountain symbolizes death.

11:30 This is the general area of central Canaan, near Shechem, where Israelite faith had its formal beginning in the land when Abraham built his first altar to the Lord (Gen 12:6–7).

11:32 This recalls the first words of the speech (4:45; 5:1) and provides a bridge to the next section, which spells out the content of these decrees and laws (see 12:1).

12:1–32 *The One Place of Worship.* Moses now begins to apply the Ten Commandments to the new situation, when the Israelites are living in the land of Canaan.

12:1–7 The previous discourse (chs. 4–11) speaks of the oneness of God and the singleness of devotion required for worship. The first commandment forbids other gods. Now Moses practically applies this commandment. This law about the exclusivity of the divine name in the land of Israel and the elimination of all competitors will finally be realized when all creation will confess that Jesus Christ is Lord (Phil 2:10–11).

12:1 Links with 4:45; 5:1; 11:32.

12:2 Destroy completely. Every vestige of Canaanite religion had to go, particularly places of worship throughout the land, whether on mountains or hills or under trees, complete with their images, altars, sacred stones, and Asherah poles (v. 3).

12:3 Asherah poles. Carved images of a goddess or stylized fertility trees. **wipe out their names.** The Canaanite gods had names representing aspects of nature: e.g., Baal was the rain-god and storm-god; Dagan was a grain-god; Asherah was a female fertility goddess. The NT links idols with demonic presences behind the idols (1 Cor 10:19–20); to eliminate idols is to engage in spiritual warfare, which helps disempower demons.

12:5 the place. In contrast to the multiplicity of pagan worship centers, emphasizing a multiplicity of gods, there must be one central Israelite location for sacrifices and offerings. Deuteronomy never specifies that central location. In the history of Israel its location changed from time to time until it eventually became Jerusalem, and it did not necessarily exclude other legitimate altars used in special circumstances as long as God appointed them (cf. Exod 20:24–25; 23:17). **to put his Name there for his dwelling.** In contrast to the command to wipe out the name of the Canaanite gods (v. 3). This is the first appearance of what becomes a virtual idiom in the book (14:23; 16:6; 26:2). To put a name on something meant to declare ownership; it was also a sign of presence since the name represented the character, authority, and reputation of the person. Thus, ancient texts from Amarna describe a pre-Israelite ruler of Jerusalem appealing for military help to an Egyptian pharaoh who has "set his name" over Jerusalem. This theme of the placing of the divine name in Israel further develops the heart of the covenant, which declares that God will be with his people (Exod 6:7; Lev 26:12; Num 6:26). The theme develops further in the birth of Immanuel (Matt 1:23) and climaxes in the new heaven and new earth, where the divine name will be written on believers' foreheads (Rev 22:4).

12:8 everyone doing as they see fit. A surprising characterization of the Israelites; but Israel's history up to this point has been morally checkered. This same expression is also found in Judges (Judg 17:6; 21:25), where it also indicates a lack of moral discipline. Moses insists that this practice of everyone doing as they see fit must change as soon as the occupation of the new land occurs.

12:10 rest. See note on 3:20.

offerings and sacrifices, your tithes and special gifts, and all the choice possessions you have vowed to
the LORD. 12And there rejoice[k] before the LORD your God—you, your sons and daughters, your male and
female servants, and the Levites from your towns who have no allotment or inheritance[l] of their own.
13Be careful not to sacrifice your burnt offerings anywhere you please. 14Offer them only at the place
the LORD will choose[m] in one of your tribes, and there observe everything I command you.
15Nevertheless, you may slaughter your animals in any of your towns and eat as much of the meat
as you want, as if it were gazelle or deer,[n] according to the blessing the LORD your God gives you. Both
the ceremonially unclean and the clean may eat it. 16But you must not eat the blood;[o] pour it out on
the ground like water.[p] 17You must not eat in your own towns the tithe of your grain and new wine and
olive oil, or the firstborn of your herds and flocks, or whatever you have vowed to give, or your freewill
offerings or special gifts. 18Instead, you are to eat[q] them in the presence of the LORD your God at the
place the LORD your God will choose[r]—you, your sons and daughters, your male and female servants,
and the Levites from your towns—and you are to rejoice[s] before the LORD your God in everything you
put your hand to. 19Be careful not to neglect the Levites[t] as long as you live in your land.
20When the LORD your God has enlarged your territory[u] as he promised[v] you, and you crave meat and
say, "I would like some meat," then you may eat as much of it as you want. 21If the place where the LORD
your God chooses to put his Name is too far away from you, you may slaughter animals from the herds
and flocks the LORD has given you, as I have commanded you, and in your own towns you may eat as
much of them as you want. 22Eat them as you would gazelle or deer.[w] Both the ceremonially unclean
and the clean may eat. 23But be sure you do not eat the blood,[x] because the blood is the life, and you
must not eat the life with the meat. 24You must not eat the blood; pour it out on the ground like water.
25Do not eat it, so that it may go well[y] with you and your children after you, because you will be doing
what is right[z] in the eyes of the LORD.
26But take your consecrated things and whatever you have vowed to give,[a] and go to the place the
LORD will choose. 27Present your burnt offerings[b] on the altar of the LORD your God, both the meat and
the blood. The blood of your sacrifices must be poured beside the altar of the LORD your God, but you
may eat the meat. 28Be careful to obey all these regulations I am giving you, so that it may always go
well[c] with you and your children after you, because you will be doing what is good and right in the
eyes of the LORD your God.
29The LORD your God will cut off[d] before you the nations you are about to invade and dispossess. But
when you have driven them out and settled in their land, 30and after they have been destroyed before
you, be careful not to be ensnared by inquiring about their gods, saying, "How do these nations serve
their gods? We will do the same." 31You must not worship the LORD your God in their way, because in
worshiping their gods, they do all kinds of detestable things the LORD hates.[e] They even burn their sons[f]
and daughters in the fire as sacrifices to their gods.
32See that you do all I command you; do not add[g] to it or take away from it.[a]

12:12 [k] ver 7 [l] Dt 10:9; 14:29
12:14 [m] ver 11
12:15 [n] ver 20-23; Dt 14:5; 15:22
12:16 [o] Ge 9:4; Lev 7:26; 17:10-12 [p] Dt 15:23
12:18 [q] Dt 14:23 [r] ver 5 [s] ver 7,12
12:19 [t] Dt 14:27
12:20 [u] Dt 19:8 [v] Ge 15:18; Dt 11:24
12:22 [w] ver 15
12:23 [x] ver 16; Ge 9:4; Lev 17:11,14
12:25 [y] Dt 4:40; Isa 3:10 [z] Ex 15:26; Dt 13:18; 1Ki 11:38
12:26 [a] ver 17; Nu 5:9-10
12:27 [b] Lev 1:5,9,13
12:28 [c] ver 25; Dt 4:40
12:29 [d] Jos 23:4
12:31 [e] Dt 9:5 [f] Dt 18:10; Jer 32:35
12:32 [g] Dt 4:2; Jos 1:7; Rev 22:18-19

a 32 In Hebrew texts this verse (12:32) is numbered 13:1.

12:12 Formal worship is a time of celebration for *all* people, even for those with no tribal inheritance. It is fitting that fellowship among the people and the Lord takes place at a meal. The practice continued in the NT as Jesus was known as someone who had table fellowship with sinners (Luke 15:2) and wished to be remembered in the meal of the Eucharist (Matt 26:17–30). One of the last visions of the Bible is that of a wedding feast (Rev 19:9).

12:15 slaughter. Virtually always used for "sacrifice" in the OT, which suggests that a holy act is still taking place by a holy people wherever they are, although there is a special sanctity attributed to the central place. **in any of your towns.** For many Israelites wanting to eat meat in the new land, it would have been a great burden to have to sacrifice an animal at the central sanctuary or even another appointed altar. Some of the towns would be too far away, so an exception is made. Animals may be slaughtered at home as long as the blood is completely drained (v. 16).

12:22 gazelle or deer. Clean game animals that do not meet sacrificial regulations; Israelites may hunt and eat them as long as they drain the animal's blood (v. 24; cf. 14:5). **Both the ceremonially unclean and the clean may eat.** One had to be ceremonially clean to eat sacrificial meat (Lev 7:19–21), but one need not be ceremonially clean to eat this meat.

12:31 burn their sons and daughters in the fire. True and false worship have consequences, and human sacrifice was one such consequence of false worship in Canaan. Although there is no real extrabiblical evidence of child sacrifice in Canaan (aside from a possibility on the Merneptah relief of Ashkelon), there is evidence of such child sacrifices at Carthage in North Africa, a colony founded by the Phoenicians, who shared the religion of their Canaanite neighbors in Israel. Many urns containing the ashes of children have been discovered in a cemetery there, and these point to child sacrifice. Unfortunately the Israelites later succumbed to the worldview of their neighbors and ended up doing the same thing (cf. Judg 11:30–40; 2 Kgs 16:3; 17:17; 23:10; Mic 6:7).

12:32 do not add to it or take away from it. See note on 4:2. In the Hebrew Bible this verse more suitably begins ch. 13 rather than closing

13:1 [h]Mt 24:24; Mk 13:22; 2Th 2:9
13:2 [i]ver 6,13
13:3 [j]Dt 8:2,16
13:4 [k]2Ki 23:3; 2Ch 34:31 [l]Dt 10:20
13:5 [m]Dt 17:7,12; 1Co 5:13
13:6 [n]Dt 17:2-7; 29:18
13:8 [o]Pr 1:10
13:9 [p]Dt 17:5,7
13:11 [q]Dt 19:20
13:13 [r]ver 2,6; 1Jn 2:19
13:16 [s]Jos 6:24 [t]Jos 8:28; Jer 49:2

Worshiping Other Gods

13 [a] If a prophet,[h] or one who foretells by dreams, appears among you and announces to you a
sign or wonder, 2and if the sign or wonder spoken of takes place, and the prophet says, "Let us
follow other gods"[i] (gods you have not known) "and let us worship them," 3you must not listen to the
words of that prophet or dreamer. The LORD your God is testing[j] you to find out whether you love him
with all your heart and with all your soul. 4It is the LORD your God you must follow,[k] and him you must
revere. Keep his commands and obey him; serve him and hold fast[l] to him. 5That prophet or dreamer
must be put to death for inciting rebellion against the LORD your God, who brought you out of Egypt
and redeemed you from the land of slavery. That prophet or dreamer tried to turn you from the way the
LORD your God commanded you to follow. You must purge the evil[m] from among you.

6If your very own brother, or your son or daughter, or the wife you love, or your closest friend secretly
entices[n] you, saying, "Let us go and worship other gods" (gods that neither you nor your ancestors have
known, 7gods of the peoples around you, whether near or far, from one end of the land to the other),
8do not yield[o] to them or listen to them. Show them no pity. Do not spare them or shield them. 9You
must certainly put them to death.[p] Your hand must be the first in putting them to death, and then the
hands of all the people. 10Stone them to death, because they tried to turn you away from the LORD your
God, who brought you out of Egypt, out of the land of slavery. 11Then all Israel will hear and be afraid,[q]
and no one among you will do such an evil thing again.

12If you hear it said about one of the towns the LORD your God is giving you to live in 13that troublemakers[r] have arisen among you and have led the people of their town astray, saying, "Let us go
and worship other gods" (gods you have not known), 14then you must inquire, probe and investigate
it thoroughly. And if it is true and it has been proved that this detestable thing has been done among
you, 15you must certainly put to the sword all who live in that town. You must destroy it completely,[b]
both its people and its livestock. 16You are to gather all the plunder of the town into the middle of the
public square and completely burn the town and all its plunder as a whole burnt offering to the LORD
your God.[s] That town is to remain a ruin[t] forever, never to be rebuilt, 17and none of the condemned

[a] In Hebrew texts 13:1-18 is numbered 13:2-19. [b] *15* The Hebrew term refers to the irrevocable giving over of things or persons to the LORD, often by totally destroying them.

ch. 12 (13:1–19 in Hebrew texts is numbered 12:32—13:18 in English Bibles). Thus, in Hebrew texts it is a warning about adding to the divine revelation, whether by a miracle-working prophet, an intimate family member, or a large group. God's people must categorically reject such words, whatever the source.

13:1–18 *Worshiping Other Gods.* Moses continues to apply the initial commands of the Ten Commandments: God's people must forcefully resist the temptation to follow other gods.

13:1–5 The litmus test of prophecy, even if accompanied by a miraculous sign, is whether the prophet urges obedience to the first commandment. Another test is whether or not a prophecy is fulfilled (18:21–22).

13:2 gods you have not known. In contrast to the well-known God who redeemed Israel (v. 5).

13:3 whether you love him with all your heart. Links this command with the call to total devotion in 6:4–9; 11:18–21. God permits this "rebellion" (v. 5) for the purpose of testing Israel's commitment to the first commandment.

13:4 It is the LORD your God. The English word order, with its emphasis on "the LORD," reflects the importance of serving God alone.

13:5 put to death. False prophecy inciting rebellion against God was a capital crime (18:20; 1 Kgs 18:40; Jer 28:15–17). **purge the evil from among you.** The first time this expression occurs in the Bible; it occurs frequently in Deuteronomy as a motivation to execute a criminal for a heinous crime (17:7; 19:19; 21:21; 22:21,24; 24:7) or to atone for pollution of the land (19:13; 21:9). The land is holy and must not be defiled by evil, which has to be removed. Also, the punishment will act as a deterrent (19:20). This particular demand occurs similarly in the subsequent historical books (Judg 20:13; 2 Sam 4:11 ["rid the earth"]; 1 Kgs 22:46 ["rid the land"]; 2 Kgs 23:24 ["got rid of"]) and metaphorically in the NT as a motivation for church discipline (1 Cor 5:13 ["Expel"]).

13:6–11 If the first test warned the Israelites of spiritual seduction from nonfamily members (vv. 1–5), the second alerts them to a danger closer to home. Even if the person encouraging apostasy is an intimate family member or a best friend, that person must be exposed and executed. There can be no competition for absolute loyalty to God (cf. Matt 10:37).

13:9 Your hand must be the first. While the execution by stoning mentioned here is a corporate matter, the accuser/witness must take the lead (cf. 17:7; John 8:7).

13:12–18 The third example of apostasy arises as a result of troublemakers inciting a town to depart from the Lord. Even if the entire town apostatizes, Israel must wage holy war against it, condemning it to the same fate as the Canaanites.

13:13 troublemakers. This Hebrew term in the OT can describe rapists (Judg 19:22 ["wicked"]), despicable priests (1 Sam 2:12 ["scoundrels"]), and slanderers (1 Kgs 21:13 ["scoundrels"]). In the NT the Hebrew term used here (Belial) is another name for Satan (2 Cor 6:15), the father of evil.

13:14 you must inquire. An accusation cannot be based on hearsay. There must be a responsible investigation.

13:15 destroy it completely. See note on 7:2–5. When idolatry occurred among its ranks, Israel declared holy war on its own members. The first commandments transcend all other loyalties and commitments. Cf. Judg 19–20 for the use of similar language when Israel punished an apostate Israelite town, virtually annihilating the tribe of Benjamin. In his defense of the gospel, Paul pronounces a holy curse on anyone—even an angel from heaven—who would change the message of salvation (Gal 1:8–9).

things[a] are to be found in your hands. Then the LORD will turn from his fierce anger,[u] will show you
mercy, and will have compassion[v] on you. He will increase your numbers,[w] as he promised[x] on oath
to your ancestors— 18 because you obey the LORD your God by keeping all his commands that I am
giving you today and doing what is right[y] in his eyes.

Clean and Unclean Food

14:3-20pp — Lev 11:1-23

14 You are the children[z] of the LORD your God. Do not cut yourselves or shave the front of your
heads for the dead, 2 for you are a people holy to the LORD your God.[a] Out of all the peoples on
the face of the earth, the LORD has chosen you to be his treasured possession.[b]

3 Do not eat any detestable thing.[c] 4 These are the animals you may eat:[d] the ox, the sheep, the goat,
5 the deer, the gazelle, the roe deer, the wild goat, the ibex, the antelope and the mountain sheep.[b] 6 You
may eat any animal that has a divided hoof and that chews
the cud. 7 However, of those that chew the cud or that have a
divided hoof you may not eat the camel, the rabbit or the hyrax. Although they chew the cud, they do not have a divided
hoof; they are ceremonially unclean for you. 8 The pig is also
unclean; although it has a divided hoof, it does not chew the
cud. You are not to eat their meat or touch their carcasses.[e]

9 Of all the creatures living in the water, you may eat any
that has fins and scales. 10 But anything that does not have
fins and scales you may not eat; for you it is unclean.

11 You may eat any clean bird. 12 But these you may not
eat: the eagle, the vulture, the black vulture, 13 the red kite,
the black kite, any kind of falcon, 14 any kind of raven, 15 the

13:17 [u] Nu 25:4 [v] Dt 30:3 [w] Dt 7:13 [x] Ge 22:17; 26:4,24; 28:14
13:18 [y] Dt 12:25,28
14:1 [z] Lev 19:28; 21:5; Jer 16:6; 41:5; Ro 8:14; 9:8; Gal 3:26
14:2 [a] Lev 20:26 [b] Dt 7:6; 26:18-19
14:3 [c] Eze 4:14
14:4 [d] Lev 11:2-45; Ac 10:14
14:8 [e] Lev 11:26-27

Pig bones at Gath of the Philistines demonstrate that it was part of the diet of these contemporary non-Israelites. Deut 14:8 instructs God's people that pigs are unclean to eat.
Joshua Walton, courtesy of the Tell es-Safi excavations

[a] *17* The Hebrew term refers to the irrevocable giving over of things or persons to the LORD, often by totally destroying them.
[b] *5* The precise identification of some of the birds and animals in this chapter is uncertain.

14:1–29 *Holiness.* The entire chapter deals with the fundamental theme of holiness and thus may be loosely linked to a special concern for the divine name (the third commandment). God's name is holy and not to be profaned. God's people must embody that holiness, honoring the special name of God. The chapter begins with a prohibition of certain mourning practices involving laceration of the body and then focuses on bodily dietary restrictions; then there is a command for annual celebration and triennial provision for the economically vulnerable. The motivation for such legislation is the new identity of the people: they are children of God, a holy people. Holiness is not just for the realm of the spirit; it is also for the body. Being "holy" means being totally dedicated to God and, by implication, separated from everything else. Holiness is particularly associated with life and wholeness: the signs of death must not mark the bodies of Israelites (vv. 1–2), their diet (vv. 3–21), or their economic existence (vv. 22–29). See "Holiness," p. 2676.
14:1–21 *Clean and Unclean Food.* See Lev 11 and notes there. These laws demonstrated to Israel that their God was the Lord of all life, including their diet. For some of the possible reasons for the distinction between clean and unclean foods, see note on 14:3. The NT makes clear that these laws have been abrogated (Mark 7:19b; Acts 10:9–16). All foods are now "clean," and such distinctions between the various types of food have become obsolete with the arrival of the Messiah. They served their temporally defined purpose of helping Israel make important distinctions and showing the nation that the Lord is sovereign over all of life. Perhaps their obsolescence is a sign of the new world to come, where the creation itself has begun its transformation in Christ: all old distinctions between foods have been erased because everything has become new. Similarly, the distinction between the days in the calendar has vanished, and every day has become holy because of the coming of the Messiah (see Rom 14:5–6).
14:1 children of the LORD. Cf. 1:31; 8:5. Israel as an entire people, not just a select few, was the family of God. As Seth was the image of his father Adam (Gen 5:1–3), Israel was to be God's face (image) to the world. **cut yourselves.** It was common in other cultures to gash the body because of overwhelming grief. The Israelites, with their faith in the Lord, were to face death differently. For mutilation in the context of pagan worship, see 1 Kgs 18:28. **shave the front of your heads for the dead.** Shaving the forehead was a practice of mourners in Canaan. The children of God were not to deface their bodies.
14:2 a people holy to the LORD. See Exod 3:5 and note. **treasured possession.** See notes on 7:6; Exod 19:5.
14:3 Do not eat any detestable thing. Holiness must distinguish the Israelite's eating habits (vv. 3–21) as well as their mourning practices (vv. 1–2). In general, these eating practices considerably restrict the killing of animal life. Some suggest that the suitability of the animal to its habitat determines whether it could be eaten. For example, among marine animals, only those with fins and scales could be consumed. The various animals are characterized by their locomotion in the created spheres described in Gen 1, whether land (Gen 1:24–25), sea or air (Gen 1:20–23). When there is little difference in the physical appearance of the animals, e.g., in the case of various birds, those that prey on animals or that eat carrion are not to be eaten since they exemplify death.

14:21 [f] Lev 17:15; 22:8 [g] ver 2 [h] Ex 23:19; 34:26
14:22 [i] Lev 27:30; Dt 12:6,17; Ne 10:37
14:23 [j] Dt 12:5 [k] Dt 4:10
14:26 [l] Dt 12:7-8
14:27 [m] Dt 12:19 [n] Nu 18:20
14:28 [o] Dt 26:12
14:29 [p] ver 27 [q] Dt 26:12 [r] Dt 15:10; Mal 3:10
15:1 [s] Dt 31:10

horned owl, the screech owl, the gull, any kind of hawk, [16]the little owl, the great owl, the white owl,
[17]the desert owl, the osprey, the cormorant, [18]the stork, any kind of heron, the hoopoe and the bat.
[19]All flying insects are unclean to you; do not eat them. [20]But any winged creature that is clean you
may eat.
[21]Do not eat anything you find already dead.[f] You may give it to the foreigner residing in any of
your towns, and they may eat it, or you may sell it to any other foreigner. But you are a people holy to
the LORD your God.[g]
Do not cook a young goat in its mother's milk.[h]

Tithes

[22]Be sure to set aside a tenth[i] of all that your fields produce each year. [23]Eat the tithe of your grain,
new wine and olive oil, and the firstborn of your herds and flocks in the presence of the LORD your God at
the place he will choose as a dwelling for his Name,[j] so that you may learn[k] to revere the LORD your God
always. [24]But if that place is too distant and you have been blessed by the LORD your God and cannot carry
your tithe (because the place where the LORD will choose to put his Name is so far away), [25]then exchange
your tithe for silver, and take the silver with you and go to the place the LORD your God will choose. [26]Use
the silver to buy whatever you like: cattle, sheep, wine or other fermented drink, or anything you wish.
Then you and your household shall eat there in the presence of the LORD your God and rejoice.[l] [27]And
do not neglect the Levites[m] living in your towns, for they have no allotment or inheritance of their own.[n]
[28]At the end of every three years, bring all the tithes of that year's produce and store it in your towns,[o]
[29]so that the Levites (who have no allotment[p] or inheritance of their own) and the foreigners,[q] the fatherless and the widows who live in your towns may come and eat and be satisfied, and so that the LORD
your God may bless[r] you in all the work of your hands.

The Year for Canceling Debts

15:1-11Ref — Lev 25:8-38

15 At the end of every seven years you must cancel debts.[s] [2]This is how it is to be done: Every creditor shall cancel any loan they have made to a fellow Israelite. They shall not require payment
from anyone among their own people, because the LORD's time for canceling debts has been proclaimed.

14:21 Do not eat anything you find already dead. Since the blood was not properly drained. **Do not cook a young goat in its mother's milk.** Although this law became the basis for much later Jewish kosher legislation (milk and meat products are not to be eaten together), it more likely has a humanitarian thrust (20:19; 22:6; cf. Exod 23:19; 34:26). It was considered particularly cruel to use the life-giving milk of the mother to kill its young. This may also critique other religious practices.
14:22–29 *Tithes.* There is a smooth transition from diet to tithing as the Israelites are now commanded to have a yearly feast with their Lord, consuming their tithes in fellowship with him.
14:22 Cf. Num 18:21–29. Tithing (giving a tenth of one's income, mainly understood in the Bible as agricultural produce) was to be practiced once a year, regularly, and it was to be a time of celebration and joy. The people were to enjoy a feast of their firstborn clean animals and a tenth of their produce in an annual family celebration. If the sanctuary was too distant, the produce was to be converted to "cash" so that worshipers could purchase the food necessary for the "tithe" feast at the place of worship. The Israelites were being commanded to come to the Lord's house as a family to enjoy a meal and fellowship with their divine host (Ps 23).
14:27–29 A law distinctive to Deuteronomy (cf. Amos 4:4). Every three years the Israelites were to gather a tithe in the local villages and distribute it to those without natural means of support (i.e., land): Levites, foreigners (refugees), the fatherless, and widows. God wanted his people to remember the landless in the midst of plenty. He desired his people to enlarge the circle of celebration and fellowship to include this "quartet of the vulnerable." He attaches a special blessing to the tithe: "so that the LORD your God may bless you in all the work of your hands" (v. 29). Tithing required faith; it was a powerful temptation to use the tithe for one's own personal good, but that would mean forfeiting the divine blessing (26:12–15; cf. Mal 3:8–10).
15:1–11 *The Year for Canceling Debts.* Cf. Lev 25:8–28. This new section largely applies the fourth commandment (notice the repetition of the number "seven" in vv. 1,9; cf. v. 12), but it does not merely repeat it. It extends its principles deep into the structure of society. The Sabbath principle was to transform culture so that the ideal society would have regular periods of rest and relief from debt; in this way poverty might become obsolete. The principle stressed freedom, rest, generosity, and *šālôm* (see "Shalom," p. 2693). The previous tithing law with its concern for the marginalized is now broadened to include all society. Throughout this text there is a reminder that the Israelites are family members, not rivals. Such a Sabbath principle had been developed in the past through the Sabbath year for the land (Exod 23:10–11) and through the Year of Jubilee (Lev 25:8–55), and the prophets projected it into the future to describe an ultimate release for the entire world (Isa 61:1–3). Jesus announced such a year at the beginning of his ministry (Luke 4:16–21), and the early church embodied such a view (Acts 2:42–47).
15:1–6 In the ancient world a new king would occasionally proclaim a debt amnesty as an act of grace for the impoverished. The Lord, Israel's king, institutionalized this practice *every* seven years within Israel. Every Israelite creditor had to forgive debts to Israelite debtors at the beginning of the sabbatical year. This was understandably not required for foreigners, who were mainly temporary residents.

3 You may require payment from a foreigner,[t] but you must cancel any debt your fellow Israelite owes you. 4 However, there need be no poor people among you, for in the land the LORD your God is giving you to possess as your inheritance, he will richly bless[u] you, 5 if only you fully obey the LORD your God and are careful to follow[v] all these commands I am giving you today. 6 For the LORD your God will bless you as he has promised, and you will lend to many nations but will borrow from none. You will rule over many nations but none will rule over you.[w]

7 If anyone is poor among your fellow Israelites in any of the towns of the land the LORD your God is giving you, do not be hardhearted or tightfisted[x] toward them. 8 Rather, be openhanded[y] and freely lend them whatever they need. 9 Be careful not to harbor this wicked thought: "The seventh year, the year for canceling debts,[z] is near," so that you do not show ill will[a] toward the needy among your fellow Israelites and give them nothing. They may then appeal to the LORD against you, and you will be found guilty of sin.[b] 10 Give generously to them and do so without a grudging heart;[c] then because of this the LORD your God will bless[d] you in all your work and in everything you put your hand to. 11 There will always be poor people in the land. Therefore I command you to be openhanded toward your fellow Israelites who are poor and needy in your land.[e]

Freeing Servants

15:12-18pp — Ex 21:2-6
15:12-18Ref — Lev 25:38-55

12 If any of your people — Hebrew men or women — sell themselves to you and serve you six years, in the seventh year you must let them go free.[f] 13 And when you release them, do not send them away empty-handed. 14 Supply them liberally from your flock, your threshing floor and your winepress. Give to them as the LORD your God has blessed you. 15 Remember that you were slaves[g] in Egypt and the LORD your God redeemed you.[h] That is why I give you this command today.

16 But if your servant says to you, "I do not want to leave you," because he loves you and your family and is well off with you, 17 then take an awl and push it through his earlobe into the door, and he will become your servant for life. Do the same for your female servant.

18 Do not consider it a hardship to set your servant free, because their service to you these six years has been worth twice as much as that of a hired hand. And the LORD your God will bless you in everything you do.

The Firstborn Animals

19 Set apart for the LORD your God every firstborn male[i] of your herds and flocks. Do not put the firstborn of your cows to work, and do not shear the firstborn of your sheep. 20 Each year you and your family are to eat them in the presence of the LORD your God at the place he will choose.[j] 21 If an animal has a defect, is lame or blind, or has any serious flaw, you must not sacrifice it to the LORD your God.[k]

15:3 [t] Dt 23:20
15:4 [u] Dt 28:8
15:5 [v] Dt 28:1
15:6 [w] Dt 28:12-13,44
15:7 [x] 1Jn 3:17
15:8 [y] Mt 5:42; Lk 6:34
15:9 [z] ver 1 [a] Mt 20:15 [b] Dt 24:15
15:10 [c] 2Co 9:5 [d] Dt 14:29; 24:19
15:11 [e] Mt 26:11; Mk 14:7; Jn 12:8
15:12 [f] Ex 21:2; Lev 25:39; Jer 34:14
15:15 [g] Dt 5:15 [h] Dt 16:12
15:19 [i] Ex 13:2
15:20 [j] Dt 12:5-7,17,18; 14:23
15:21 [k] Lev 22:19-25

15:4 there need be no poor people among you. This contrasts the ideal vision of a poverty-free society with the reality of impoverishment. See note on v. 11.
15:6 you will lend to many nations. Individual acts of blessing for the poor have international significance as an obedient Israel will have worldwide influence.
15:7–11 The ideal vision is also realistic; thus a generous spirit is encouraged. Those who are "tightfisted" (v. 7) must become "openhanded" (v. 8).
15:11 There will always be poor people. The clash with v. 4 describes the actual situation versus the ideal one.
15:12–18 *Freeing Servants.* Cf. Exod 21:2–6; Lev 25:39–55. This law provides for landless Hebrews (see note on v. 12) who have been forced into servitude because of economic insolvency. In vv. 12–15 Sabbath rest is extended to slaves on the basis of the exodus from Egypt. They are also in need of a sabbatical, an economic exodus. In Exod 21 there is provision for allowing the freedom of a male slave, while here there is allowance for freedom of a female slave as well. Moreover, it is important to ensure the economic viability of the man and woman once released.
15:12 Hebrew. A term often used of a landless social class made up of those who had joined the Israelites, but it is more likely that here it distinguishes Israelites from non-Israelites.
15:14 Supply them liberally. This addition to the original law was probably necessary to show that the spirit of the law reflected the compassionate generosity of God.
15:15 Remember that you were slaves. Cf. Exod 22:21; 23:9. The law is thus to exemplify a mini-exodus based on compassion.
15:17 take an awl. If a debt-servant for some reason did not desire freedom, his ear was physically marked to indicate lifelong servitude.
15:18 Do not consider it a hardship to set your servant free. Contrasts with Pharaoh's hard heart when he would not release the Israelites (Exod 13:15).
15:19–23 *The Firstborn Animals.* There is a natural link from freedom of slaves (vv. 12–18) to the exodus from Egypt, which entailed deliverance of firstborn males. Verse 19 alludes to Exod 13:2,11–16; cf. Exod 22:29–30; Num 18:15–18. As God had delivered Israel's firstborn sons from Egypt, the people are to make an annual sacrifice of the firstborn males of their herds and flocks at the worship sanctuary.
15:21 If an animal has a defect. The principle of sacrifice excludes

15:22 [l]Dt 12:15,22
15:23 [m]Dt 12:16
16:1 [n]Ex 12:2; 13:4
16:2 [o]Dt 12:5,26
16:3 [p]Ex 12:8,39; 34:18 [q]Ex 12:11,15,19 [r]Ex 13:3,6-7
16:4 [s]Ex 12:10; 34:25
16:6 [t]Ex 12:6; Dt 12:5
16:7 [u]Ex 12:8; 2Ch 35:13
16:8 [v]Ex 12:16; 13:6; Lev 23:8
16:9 [w]Ex 34:22; Lev 23:15 [x]Ex 23:16; Nu 28:26
16:11 [y]Dt 12:7 [z]Dt 12:12
16:12 [a]Dt 15:15
16:13 [b]Lev 23:34 [c]Ex 23:16
16:14 [d]ver 11

22 You are to eat it in your own towns. Both the ceremonially unclean and the clean may eat it, as if it were gazelle or deer.[l] 23 But you must not eat the blood; pour it out on the ground like water.[m]

The Passover

16:1-8pp — Ex 12:14-20; Lev 23:4-8; Nu 28:16-25

16 Observe the month of Aviv[n] and celebrate the Passover of the LORD your God, because in the month of Aviv he brought you out of Egypt by night. 2 Sacrifice as the Passover to the LORD your God an animal from your flock or herd at the place the LORD will choose as a dwelling for his Name.[o] 3 Do not eat it with bread made with yeast, but for seven days eat unleavened bread, the bread of affliction,[p] because you left Egypt in haste[q]—so that all the days of your life you may remember the time of your departure from Egypt.[r] 4 Let no yeast be found in your possession in all your land for seven days. Do not let any of the meat you sacrifice on the evening of the first day remain until morning.[s]

5 You must not sacrifice the Passover in any town the LORD your God gives you 6 except in the place he will choose as a dwelling for his Name. There you must sacrifice the Passover in the evening, when the sun goes down, on the anniversary[a][t] of your departure from Egypt. 7 Roast[u] it and eat it at the place the LORD your God will choose. Then in the morning return to your tents. 8 For six days eat unleavened bread and on the seventh day hold an assembly[v] to the LORD your God and do no work.

The Festival of Weeks

16:9-12pp — Lev 23:15-22; Nu 28:26-31

9 Count off seven weeks[w] from the time you begin to put the sickle to the standing grain.[x] 10 Then celebrate the Festival of Weeks to the LORD your God by giving a freewill offering in proportion to the blessings the LORD your God has given you. 11 And rejoice[y] before the LORD your God at the place he will choose as a dwelling for his Name—you, your sons and daughters, your male and female servants, the Levites[z] in your towns, and the foreigners, the fatherless and the widows living among you. 12 Remember that you were slaves in Egypt,[a] and follow carefully these decrees.

The Festival of Tabernacles

16:13-17pp — Lev 23:33-43; Nu 29:12-39

13 Celebrate the Festival of Tabernacles for seven days after you have gathered the produce of your threshing floor[b] and your winepress.[c] 14 Be joyful[d] at your festival—you, your sons and daughters, your male and female servants, and the Levites, the foreigners, the fatherless and the widows who live in your towns. 15 For seven days celebrate the festival to the LORD your God at the place the LORD will

[a] 6 Or *down, at the time of day*

blemished animals (cf. 2 Sam 24:24; Mal 1:6–8), which could be consumed at home as long as they were drained of their blood.

16:1–17 Cf. Exod 23:14–19; 34:18–26; Lev 23:4–44; Num 28:16—29:40. The holy days of Passover, Festival of Weeks, and Festival of Tabernacles extend the sabbatical principle into the entire yearly calendar. As if to underline the significance of the Sabbath, the number seven is repeated (in the Hebrew) seven times (vv. 3,4,8,9 [twice in the Hebrew],13,15).

16:1–8 *The Passover.* The first of the great festivals at the beginning of the year. The new year was to begin on a note of freedom.

16:1 Aviv. The first month in the Hebrew calendar; it means "the month of the ears of grain," the time when the grain started sprouting.

16:2 at the place the LORD will choose. The Israelites are now to commemorate Passover at the central sanctuary as opposed to their own dwellings (Exod 12). This does not mention spattering the doorframes with the blood of the sacrificial animals (Exod 12:7), presumably because most worshipers are now pilgrims living in tents.

16:4 in all your land for seven days. Even though the formal worship occurs at the central sanctuary, yeast must be removed from the entire land. Worship thus envelops the whole nation.

16:7 return to your tents. Probably refers to their temporary dwellings during the festival since the assembly of the people seven days later assumes the location of the central sanctuary (v. 8).

16:9–12 *The Festival of Weeks.* This occurred seven weeks after Passover, 50 days after the first ripe sheaf of barley appeared. It was the time of the wheat harvest. "Pentecost" is the Greek name for this festival, meaning "fifty" (see Acts 2).

16:11 rejoice before the LORD. The note of joy is unmistakable. "Holy day" and "holiday" were synonymous in Israel. Verse 11b mentions no less than seven categories of people. This is a festival of total inclusion that will someday be fulfilled when there will be neither Jew nor Gentile, neither slave nor free, neither male nor female in the future thanksgiving celebrations in the Christian church (Gal 3:28).

16:12 Remember that you were slaves in Egypt. The memory of slavery was to provide the incentive for the celebration of freedom for everyone at the central sanctuary.

16:13–17 *The Festival of Tabernacles.* The third major festival, the fall fruit harvest. See note on Lev 23:34.

16:13 The Festival of Tabernacles was to be celebrated for seven days after the fruit harvest in the fall. Again the celebration is marked by radical inclusion (see note on v. 11).

choose. For the LORD your God will bless you in all your harvest and in all the work of your hands, and
your joy[e] will be complete.
[16]Three times a year all your men must appear before the LORD your God at the place he will choose:
at the Festival of Unleavened Bread, the Festival of Weeks and the Festival of Tabernacles.[f] No one should
appear before the LORD empty-handed:[g] [17]Each of you must bring a gift in proportion to the way the
LORD your God has blessed you.

Judges

[18]Appoint judges[h] and officials for each of your tribes in every town the LORD your God is giving you,
and they shall judge the people fairly. [19]Do not pervert justice[i] or show partiality.[j] Do not accept a bribe,[k]
for a bribe blinds the eyes of the wise and twists the words of the innocent. [20]Follow justice and justice
alone, so that you may live and possess the land the LORD your God is giving you.

Worshiping Other Gods

[21]Do not set up any wooden Asherah pole[l] beside the altar you build to the LORD your God,[m] [22]and
do not erect a sacred stone,[n] for these the LORD your God hates.

17 Do not sacrifice to the LORD your God an ox or a sheep that has any defect[o] or flaw in it, for
that would be detestable to him.[p]
[2]If a man or woman living among you in one of the towns the LORD gives you is found doing evil in the
eyes of the LORD your God in violation of his covenant,[q] [3]and contrary to my command[r] has worshiped other
gods, bowing down to them or to the sun[s] or the moon or the stars in the sky, [4]and this has been brought to
your attention, then you must investigate it thoroughly. If it is true and it has been proved that this detestable
thing has been done in Israel,[t] [5]take the man or woman who has done this evil deed to your city gate and
stone that person to death.[u] [6]On the testimony of two or three witnesses a person is to be put to death, but no
one is to be put to death on the testimony of only one witness.[v] [7]The hands of the witnesses must be the first in
putting that person to death, and then the hands of all the people. You must purge the evil[w] from among you.

Law Courts

[8]If cases come before your courts that are too difficult for you to judge—whether bloodshed, lawsuits or assaults[x]—take them to the place the LORD your God will choose.[y] [9]Go to the Levitical priests

16:15 [e]Lev 23:39
16:16 [f]Ex 23:14,16 [g]Ex 34:20
16:18 [h]Dt 1:16
16:19 [i]Ex 23:2,8 [j]Lev 19:15; Dt 1:17 [k]Ecc 7:7
16:21 [l]Dt 7:5 [m]Ex 34:13; 2Ki 17:16; 21:3; 2Ch 33:3
16:22 [n]Lev 26:1
17:1 [o]Mal 1:8,13 [p]Dt 15:21
17:2 [q]Dt 13:6-11
17:3 [r]Jer 7:22-23 [s]Job 31:26
17:4 [t]Dt 13:12-14
17:5 [u]Lev 24:14
17:6 [v]Nu 35:30; Dt 19:15; Jos 7:25; Mt 18:16; Jn 8:17; 2Co 13:1; 1Ti 5:19; Heb 10:28
17:7 [w]Dt 13:5,9
17:8 [x]2Ch 19:10 [y]Dt 12:5; Hag 2:11

16:15 your joy will be complete. Can also be translated "you will have nothing but joy!"
16:16–17 This summarizes the three festivals and their importance (cf. Exod 23:14–19). These pilgrimages of joy are not just nature festivals; they commemorate God's historical salvation of his people, so attendance helps form national identity. This trio of festivals began the new year on a note of salvation, and the year was to be continued on the notes of harvest and joy.
16:18—18:22 This section develops the principle underlying the command to honor parents (the fifth commandment): there is to be respect for authority in general, including the judicial, royal, sacral, and prophetic spheres.
16:18–20 *Judges.* Judges have a special position in Israelite society since they are mentioned here first among all the leaders.
16:18 Cf. Exod 18. The first leaders to be appointed are not kings but "judges" and legal "officials." These were the first leaders Moses appointed at Horeb (1:12–17). Israel was to be preeminently a just society with everyone being subject to the divine law and everyone having equal access to the judicial system.
16:19–20 Moses exhorts the elected officials to maintain law and order (Exod 23:6–8).
16:19 a bribe blinds the eyes. At a much later time, Rome had Lady Justice as one of its gods; she was blindfolded to ensure impartiality. For the Hebrews the judges must see reality clearly and make their decisions fairly and justly. At all costs, judges had to repudiate bribes since bribes destroyed vision.
16:20 Follow justice and justice alone. God's priority for Israel is justice, and his blessing is conditioned upon a just society.
16:21—17:7 *Worshiping Other Gods.* Though this seems like an intrusion between the appointment of judges and the administration of law courts, it naturally belongs to this section on justice because of the underlying theology. The root of all injustice is idolatry since it distorts reality. Whenever the true God does not occupy the center of worship, some aspect of his creation will take his place, and this false center cannot hold: other aspects of creation will be diminished or destroyed. Examples abound from the brutal tyrannies of the ancient world to those in our own contemporary societies. Only when all worship the one God will there be true peace and justice (Isa 2:1–5; 2 Pet 3:13).
16:21 God's people must not attempt to introduce pagan elements that might lead to syncretism, because the result will inevitably be injustice.
17:1 Using a defective animal does not properly honor God and therefore is implicit idolatry.
17:2–7 This textbook case of idolatry differs from its counterpart in 13:6–11 because of its concern for the proper legal procedure: detection ("investigate it thoroughly," v. 4), proof ("two or three witnesses," v. 6), conviction ("it has been proved," v. 4), and sentence ("death," v. 7). Also, in ch. 13 seduction to idolatry is the primary issue, while here it is covenant violation.
17:8–13 *Law Courts.* This is a provision for complex cases at the central sanctuary, where a higher court consisting of Levitical priests and an appointed judge adjudicated.

17:9 [z]Dt 19:17; Eze 44:24
17:11 [a]Dt 25:1
17:12 [b]Nu 15:30
17:13 [c]Dt 13:11; 19:20
17:14 [d]Dt 11:31; 1Sa 8:5,19-20
17:15 [e]Jer 30:21
17:16 [f]1Ki 4:26; 10:26 [g]Isa 31:1; Hos 11:5 [h]1Ki 10:28; Eze 17:15 [i]Ex 13:17
17:17 [j]1Ki 11:3
17:18 [k]Dt 31:22,24
17:19 [l]Jos 1:8
17:20 [m]1Ki 15:5 [n]Dt 5:32
18:1 [o]Dt 10:9; 1Co 9:13

and to the judge who is in office at that time. Inquire of them and they will give you the verdict.[z] 10You
must act according to the decisions they give you at the place the LORD will choose. Be careful to do
everything they instruct you to do. 11Act according to whatever they teach you and the decisions they
give you. Do not turn aside from what they tell you, to the right or to the left.[a] 12Anyone who shows
contempt[b] for the judge or for the priest who stands ministering there to the LORD your God is to be put
to death. You must purge the evil from Israel. 13All the people will hear and be afraid, and will not be
contemptuous again.[c]

The King

14When you enter the land the LORD your God is giving you and have taken possession of it and settled in it, and you say, "Let us set a king over us like all the nations around us,"[d] 15be sure to appoint
over you a king the LORD your God chooses. He must be from among your fellow Israelites.[e] Do not place
a foreigner over you, one who is not an Israelite. 16The king, moreover, must not acquire great numbers
of horses for himself[f] or make the people return to Egypt[g] to get more of them,[h] for the LORD has told
you, "You are not to go back that way again."[i] 17He must not take many wives,[j] or his heart will be led
astray. He must not accumulate large amounts of silver and gold.

18When he takes the throne of his kingdom, he is to write[k] for himself on a scroll a copy of this
law, taken from that of the Levitical priests. 19It is to be with him, and he is to read it all the days
of his life[l] so that he may learn to revere the LORD his God and follow carefully all the words of this
law and these decrees 20and not consider himself better than his fellow Israelites and turn from the
law[m] to the right or to the left.[n] Then he and his descendants will reign a long time over his kingdom in Israel.

Offerings for Priests and Levites

18 The Levitical priests—indeed, the whole tribe of Levi—are to have no allotment or inheritance with Israel. They shall live on the food offerings presented to the LORD, for that is their
inheritance.[o] 2They shall have no inheritance among their fellow Israelites; the LORD is their inheritance, as he promised them.

3This is the share due the priests from the people who sacrifice a bull or a sheep: the shoulder,

17:14–20 *The King.* This is one of the most radical laws in the ancient world. Kingship is accepted as a matter of fact, but this law transforms kingship by making the king a living, breathing *servant* of God and the people. This law finds its final expression in the coming of a fellow Israelite who is a Servant-King and not only washes the feet of his people (John 13:1–17) but lays down his life for them as well (John 10:11,17–18).

17:14 Let us set a king over us. The desire for a king comes from the people's concern to be "like all the nations." Kingship in Israel does not have an auspicious beginning since pagan notions of kingship could corrupt Israel. In contrast to the nations, Israel was to be a *kingdom* of priests marked by divine rule in which all its members were royal (Gen 1:26–28; but see 1 Sam 8:4–9). God accepts this desire of the Israelites but transforms kingship into something no longer recognizable.

17:15 a king the LORD your God chooses. God's election is paramount. **from among your fellow Israelites.** An Israelite is to be chosen because of the Israelite value system that sees God's law as central.

17:16 not acquire great numbers of horses. Horses were the ancient equivalent of rapid deployment military forces, thus emphasizing superior military power. This is how kings could enforce their will. Solomon flagrantly broke this command with his large military arsenal (1 Kgs 4:26). **You are not to go back that way again.** Egypt represented a former way of life, a life from which God redeemed Israel.

17:17 not take many wives. Royal marriages often ratified political alliances, increasing political power. In the ancient world kings married many wives to cement treaties with other nations, thus showing that politics was more important to them than theology and trust in God. Polygamy is neither prohibited nor sanctioned by this text. This command was intended to regulate the practice. Both David (2 Sam 5:13; 12:11) and Solomon (1 Kgs 11:3–4) ignored this warning to their own detriment and that of their nation. **not accumulate large amounts of silver and gold.** Economic power must not become a royal goal.

17:18–20 The king must make his own personal copy of the law of the Lord, read it daily, organize his life and the nation's life around the law, and be a humble servant to his people. The king is to be an ordinary Israelite whose mind is daily informed by the law of God (cf. Ps 1:1–3).

18:1–8 *Offerings for Priests and Levites.* The third group of authority figures in Israel were the priests and Levites, the priests being a special class within the tribe of Levi. The male members of the tribe were full-time religious professionals supported by the offerings and sacrifices of the people since the Levites had no land inheritance to cultivate. Some towns and pasturelands were set aside throughout the land for their use (Josh 21:41–42).

18:2 the LORD is their inheritance. The Levites' inheritance is a realization of the ultimate inheritance of the believer. Ps 16:6 reflects on the property boundary lines of the land being drawn up for the tribal allotments (Josh 15–19); the boundary lines for the Levites are drawn up around the Lord.

18:3–4 The portions of the sacrifices used here are different from those used in earlier legislation where the breast and right thigh were allocated for the priests (Lev 7:29–34). The difference may reflect different customs and traditions in Israel, or this legislation may institute a slight change.

the internal organs and the meat from the head.[p] 4You are to give them the firstfruits of your grain, new wine and olive oil, and the first wool from the shearing of your sheep,[q] 5for the LORD your God has chosen them[r] and their descendants out of all your tribes to stand and minister[s] in the LORD's name always.

6If a Levite moves from one of your towns anywhere in Israel where he is living, and comes in all earnestness to the place the LORD will choose,[t] 7he may minister in the name of the LORD his God like all his fellow Levites who serve there in the presence of the LORD. 8He is to share equally in their benefits, even though he has received money from the sale of family possessions.[u]

Occult Practices

9When you enter the land the LORD your God is giving you, do not learn to imitate[v] the detestable ways of the nations there. 10Let no one be found among you who sacrifices their son or daughter in the fire, who practices divination[w] or sorcery, interprets omens, engages in witchcraft,[x] 11or casts spells, or who is a medium or spiritist or who consults the dead. 12Anyone who does these things is detestable to the LORD; because of these same detestable practices the LORD your God will drive out those nations before you.[y] 13You must be blameless before the LORD your God.

The Prophet

14The nations you will dispossess listen to those who practice sorcery or divination. But as for you, the LORD your God has not permitted you to do so. 15The LORD your God will raise up for you a prophet like me from among you, from your fellow Israelites.[z] You must listen to him. 16For this is what you asked of the LORD your God at Horeb on the day of the assembly when you said, "Let us not hear the voice of the LORD our God nor see this great fire anymore, or we will die."[a]

17The LORD said to me: "What they say is good. 18I will raise up for them a prophet like you from among their fellow Israelites, and I will put my words[b] in his mouth. He will tell them everything I command him.[c] 19I myself will call to account[d] anyone who does not listen to my words that the prophet speaks in my name. 20But a prophet who presumes to speak in my name anything I have not commanded, or a prophet who speaks in the name of other gods,[e] is to be put to death."[f]

21You may say to yourselves, "How can we know when a message has not been spoken by the LORD?" 22If what a prophet proclaims in the name of the LORD does not take place or come true, that is a message the LORD has not spoken.[g] That prophet has spoken presumptuously,[h] so do not be alarmed.

Cities of Refuge

19:1-14Ref — Nu 35:6-34; Dt 4:41-43; Jos 20:1-9

19 When the LORD your God has destroyed the nations whose land he is giving you, and when you have driven them out and settled in their towns and houses,[i] 2then set aside for yourselves

18:3 [p]Lev 7:28-34
18:4 [q]Ex 22:29; Nu 18:12
18:5 [r]Ex 28:1 [s]Dt 10:8
18:6 [t]Nu 35:2-3
18:8 [u]2Ch 31:4; Ne 12:44,47
18:9 [v]Dt 12:29-31
18:10 [w]Dt 12:31 [x]Lev 19:31
18:12 [y]Lev 18:24; Dt 9:4
18:15 [z]Jn 1:21; Ac 3:22*; 7:37*
18:16 [a]Ex 20:19; Dt 5:23-27
18:18 [b]Isa 51:16; Jn 17:8 [c]Jn 4:25-26; 8:28; 12:49-50
18:19 [d]Ac 3:23*
18:20 [e]Jer 14:14 [f]Dt 13:1-5
18:22 [g]Jer 28:9 [h]ver 20
19:1 [i]Dt 12:29

18:9–13 *Occult Practices.* The fourth category of leader is the prophet. In order to emphasize the distinctive prophetic role, Moses forbids a virtually exhaustive list—the most complete list in the entire Bible—of occult practices used in the ancient world for understanding the world and predicting the future. Examples of such practices in the OT abound, from using child sacrifice for influencing the outcome of the future (2 Kgs 3:26–27) to inspecting the entrails of animals for discovering the future (Ezek 21:21) to consulting the dead for information (1 Sam 28:3–25). These practices were part of the religious and mental culture of the surrounding nations and had to be categorically rejected.

18:13 blameless. Not sinless but having integrity (cf. Noah in Gen 6:9; Job in Job 1:1) and rejecting occult practices for ascertaining the divine will.

18:14–22 *The Prophet.* The divine will is not to be found by searching desperately in the depths of animals' organs or in the grave or in the esoteric signs of nature, but it is found in intelligible speech. The Lord puts his words in the prophet's mouth.

18:15 a prophet like me. The context envisions a series of prophets who function like Moses to continue divine revelation after the Mount Sinai experience. This is therefore a collective reference to the prophets after Moses—a type of prophetic succession. But since no one equaled the great Moses (34:10), this text is the basis for a future Messianic expectation of a new Moses and receives a unique fulfillment in Jesus (see John 1:21,25,45; 5:46; 6:14; 7:40; Acts 3:22–26; 7:37).

18:17–18 Prophecy continues the Mount Sinai revelation, which was given when God spoke from the fire and Moses became his messenger. Moses is thus the preeminent prophet and will be followed by a line of prophets who will transmit the divine will to future generations.

19:1–14 *Cities of Refuge.* Cf. 4:41–43; Num 35:6–34; Josh 20:1–9. This series of laws develops the underlying sixth commandment, which forbids murder. A paramount concern of this legislation is to not pollute the land by shedding innocent blood. It deals with manslaughter, perjury, war, unsolved murder, building codes, etc. The land, like the people, must be holy.

19:2 set aside for yourselves three cities. Like their counterparts east

19:6 [j] Nu 35:12
19:9 [k] Jos 20:7-8
19:10 [l] Nu 35:33; Dt 21:1-9
19:11 [m] Nu 35:16
19:13 [n] Dt 7:2 [o] 1Ki 2:31
19:14 [p] Dt 27:17; Pr 22:28; Hos 5:10
19:15 [q] Nu 35:30; Dt 17:6; Mt 18:16*; Jn 8:17; 2Co 13:1*; 1Ti 5:19; Heb 10:28
19:16 [r] Ex 23:1; Ps 27:12
19:17 [s] Dt 17:9
19:19 [t] Pr 19:5,9
19:20 [u] Dt 17:13; 21:21
19:21 [v] ver 13 [w] Ex 21:24; Lev 24:20; Mt 5:38*

three cities in the land the LORD your God is giving you to possess. 3 Determine the distances involved and divide into three parts the land the LORD your God is giving you as an inheritance, so that a person who kills someone may flee for refuge to one of these cities.

4 This is the rule concerning anyone who kills a person and flees there for safety — anyone who kills a neighbor unintentionally, without malice aforethought. 5 For instance, a man may go into the forest with his neighbor to cut wood, and as he swings his ax to fell a tree, the head may fly off and hit his neighbor and kill him. That man may flee to one of these cities and save his life. 6 Otherwise, the avenger of blood[j] might pursue him in a rage, overtake him if the distance is too great, and kill him even though he is not deserving of death, since he did it to his neighbor without malice aforethought. 7 This is why I command you to set aside for yourselves three cities.

8 If the LORD your God enlarges your territory, as he promised on oath to your ancestors, and gives you the whole land he promised them, 9 because you carefully follow all these laws I command you today — to love the LORD your God and to walk always in obedience to him[k] — then you are to set aside three more cities. 10 Do this so that innocent blood will not be shed in your land, which the LORD your God is giving you as your inheritance, and so that you will not be guilty of bloodshed.[l]

11 But if out of hate someone lies in wait, assaults and kills a neighbor,[m] and then flees to one of these cities, 12 the killer shall be sent for by the town elders, be brought back from the city, and be handed over to the avenger of blood to die. 13 Show no pity.[n] You must purge from Israel the guilt of shedding innocent blood,[o] so that it may go well with you.

14 Do not move your neighbor's boundary stone set up by your predecessors in the inheritance you receive in the land the LORD your God is giving you to possess.[p]

Witnesses

15 One witness is not enough to convict anyone accused of any crime or offense they may have committed. A matter must be established by the testimony of two or three witnesses.[q]

16 If a malicious witness[r] takes the stand to accuse someone of a crime, 17 the two people involved in the dispute must stand in the presence of the LORD before the priests and the judges[s] who are in office at the time. 18 The judges must make a thorough investigation, and if the witness proves to be a liar, giving false testimony against a fellow Israelite, 19 then do to the false witness as that witness intended to do to the other party.[t] You must purge the evil from among you. 20 The rest of the people will hear of this and be afraid,[u] and never again will such an evil thing be done among you. 21 Show no pity:[v] life for life, eye for eye, tooth for tooth, hand for hand, foot for foot.[w]

---

of the Jordan (4:41 – 43), these cities would offer sanctuary throughout the land west of the Jordan for those who might kill someone unintentionally. The location of the cities allows for accessibility throughout the country.

19:6 avenger of blood. The closest family member, who must avenge the loss of innocent blood by shedding the blood of the guilty. One of the main points of the law is to prevent a vendetta.

19:9 set aside three more cities. Not mentioned anywhere else in the Bible. These three cities were to be added to the other six when the Israelites took full possession of the land (1:7; 11:23 – 24), something that never happened. This suggests that the promise was never fully attained because the people disobeyed.

19:13 Innocent blood that has been shed by murder cries out from the land for justice (cf. Gen 4:10). The guilt of the criminal must be addressed with his death. This concern resurfaces in later legislation (21:8; 27:25).

19:14 boundary stone. Indicated the borders of a person's land. Stones were usually moved to increase land holdings, but to do this unlawfully was a serious crime because of the inextricable relationship between land and life (27:17; Hos 5:10). Land had spiritual significance (the fulfillment of God's promises to the individual) and economic potential, so loss of land often meant loss of life, particularly for the vulnerable (Prov 15:25; 23:10).

19:15 – 21 *Witnesses.* The question of truth is also linked to the protection of life.

19:15 Two or three eyewitnesses in a court are required for a successful conviction (cf. 17:6).

19:16 malicious witness. Such a witness seeks to hurt a person rather than help and is ruthless (cf. Ps 35:11 – 12). One person presumably would have to enlist the support of another for a charge to be taken seriously.

19:17 in the presence of the LORD before the priests and the judges. The chief court in Israel, where difficult cases would be decided (cf. 17:8 – 12).

19:18 – 19 Judges take legal measures to establish truth; perjury is a deadly serious matter.

19:21 life for life, eye for eye, tooth for tooth. The first occurrence of the so-called *lex talionis* (law of retaliation/compensation) in Deuteronomy (cf. Exod 21:23 – 25; Lev 24:19 – 20). Modern popular culture usually considers this law barbaric, but its original context shows its concern to protect and enforce justice (cf. Exod 21:18 – 27; see note on Exod 21:23 – 24). The malicious witness will be judged according to his malice — no less and no more. This protects truth, which protects innocent life.

Going to War

20 When you go to war against your enemies and see horses and chariots and an army greater
than yours,[x] do not be afraid[y] of them,[z] because the LORD your God, who brought you up out
of Egypt, will be with you. 2When you are about to go into battle, the priest shall come forward and
address the army. 3He shall say: "Hear, Israel: Today you are going into battle against your enemies. Do
not be fainthearted[a] or afraid; do not panic or be terrified by them. 4For the LORD your God is the one
who goes with you to fight[b] for you against your enemies to give you victory."
5The officers shall say to the army: "Has anyone built a new house and not yet begun to live
in[c] it? Let him go home, or he may die in battle and someone else may begin to live in it. 6Has
anyone planted a vineyard and not begun to enjoy it? Let him go home, or he may die in battle
and someone else enjoy it. 7Has anyone become pledged to a woman and not married her? Let
him go home, or he may die in battle and someone else marry her.[d]" 8Then the officers shall add,
"Is anyone afraid or fainthearted? Let him go home so that his fellow soldiers will not become
disheartened too."[e] 9When the officers have finished speaking to the army, they shall appoint
commanders over it.
10When you march up to attack a city, make its people an offer of peace.[f] 11If they accept and open
their gates, all the people in it shall be subject to forced labor[g] and shall work for you. 12If they refuse
to make peace and they engage you in battle, lay siege to that city. 13When the LORD your God delivers it
into your hand, put to the sword all the men in it.[h] 14As for the women, the children, the livestock[i] and
everything else in the city, you may take these as plunder for yourselves. And you may use the plunder
the LORD your God gives you from your enemies. 15This is how you are to treat all the cities that are at
a distance from you and do not belong to the nations nearby.
16However, in the cities of the nations the LORD your God is giving you as an inheritance, do not
leave alive anything that breathes.[j] 17Completely destroy[*a*] them—the Hittites, Amorites, Canaanites,
Perizzites, Hivites and Jebusites—as the LORD your God has commanded you. 18Otherwise, they will
teach you to follow all the detestable things they do in worshiping their gods,[k] and you will sin[l] against
the LORD your God.
19When you lay siege to a city for a long time, fighting against it to capture it, do not destroy its trees
by putting an ax to them, because you can eat their fruit. Do not cut them down. Are the trees people,
that you should besiege them?[*b*] 20However, you may cut down trees that you know are not fruit trees
and use them to build siege works until the city at war with you falls.

a *17* The Hebrew term refers to the irrevocable giving over of things or persons to the LORD, often by totally destroying them. *b* *19* Or *down to use in the siege, for the fruit trees are for the benefit of people.*

20:1 [x] Ps 20:7; Isa 31:1 [y] Dt 31:6,8 [z] 2Ch 32:7-8
20:3 [a] Jos 23:10
20:4 [b] Dt 1:30; 3:22; Jos 23:10
20:5 [c] Ne 12:27
20:7 [d] Dt 24:5
20:8 [e] Jdg 7:3
20:10 [f] Lk 14:31-32
20:11 [g] 1Ki 9:21
20:13 [h] Nu 31:7
20:14 [i] Jos 8:2; 22:8
20:16 [j] Ex 23:31-33; Nu 21:2-3; Dt 7:2; Jos 11:14
20:18 [k] Ex 34:16; Dt 7:4; 12:30-31 [l] Ex 23:33

20:1–20 *Going to War.* War legitimizes killing, and thus this legislation is linked to the sixth commandment ("You shall not murder"). But just as there is the death penalty for capital crimes, killing is legalized in certain cases in war. Israel, of course, is preparing to go to war in Deuteronomy, and this particular legislation involving three texts (vv. 1–9,10–18,19–20) seeks to relate the command to war.

20:1–4 The entire section on war is prefaced with preparation procedures that prioritize faith rather than strenuous physical training. The enemy's military superiority is assumed, and thus Israel must depend on the Lord for victory.

20:2–4 Remarkably, charismatic military leaders are largely absent: it is the priest who is the first to speak. Far from being the equivalent of a timid chaplain, he rallies the troops by asserting that the antidote to fear is faith in the divine Warrior.

20:5–8 Surprisingly, the first instructions provide for exemptions from military duty. What kind of an army is this? This army is concerned that its members experience blessing. The first three exemptions ensure that war would not deprive a young soldier of the blessings of a new home, vineyard, or marriage. Cf. 28:30, where curses deprive people of such blessings. The last exemption is for the benefit of the army itself. Someone afraid in battle might demoralize other soldiers and thus lead to their deaths.

20:5 officers. Military officials responsible for organizing the troops.

20:9 appoint commanders. The real military organization is mentioned last.

20:10–18 This section lays out the rules of engagement for war outside the promised land versus war inside it.

20:10–15 Outside the promised land, a city that surrenders will be subject to forced labor. If it resists, an Israelite victory results in the destruction of the enemy soldiers and the capture of the rest of the city.

20:16–18 Inside the promised land, there must be a "take no prisoners" policy—not only the soldiers but also their families are to be devoted to destruction. Any survival of the enemy will result in learning the practices of these idolatrous nations, which will destroy Israelite faith. It is possible that vv. 16–18 are qualified by the offer of peace that is made to the far-off nations in v. 10, but if the near nation refuses, a complete ban results. This then would be similar to what happened east of the Jordan in Heshbon and Bashan (2:24—3:11).

20:19–20 In the midst of the horror of war, it is ironic that there is concern for the environment. But trees are not corrupt moral agents. When protracted sieges occur, Israel is to use only the wood of non-fruit-bearing trees for building siege ramps. Such a law was not always put into practice (2 Kgs 3:25).

21:5 [m] 1Ch 23:13 [n] Dt 17:8-11
21:6 [o] Mt 27:24
21:8 [p] Nu 35:33-34
21:9 [q] Dt 19:13
21:10 [r] Jos 21:44
21:12 [s] Lev 14:9; Nu 6:9
21:13 [t] Ps 45:10
21:14 [u] Ge 34:2
21:15 [v] Ge 29:33
21:16 [w] 1Ch 26:10

Atonement for an Unsolved Murder

21 If someone is found slain, lying in a field in the land the LORD your God is giving you to possess, and it is not known who the killer was, 2 your elders and judges shall go out and measure the distance from the body to the neighboring towns. 3 Then the elders of the town nearest the body shall take a heifer that has never been worked and has never worn a yoke 4 and lead it down to a valley that has not been plowed or planted and where there is a flowing stream. There in the valley they are to break the heifer's neck. 5 The Levitical priests shall step forward, for the LORD your God has chosen them to minister and to pronounce blessings[m] in the name of the LORD and to decide all cases of dispute and assault.[n] 6 Then all the elders of the town nearest the body shall wash their hands[o] over the heifer whose neck was broken in the valley, 7 and they shall declare: "Our hands did not shed this blood, nor did our eyes see it done. 8 Accept this atonement for your people Israel, whom you have redeemed, LORD, and do not hold your people guilty of the blood of an innocent person." Then the bloodshed will be atoned for,[p] 9 and you will have purged[q] from yourselves the guilt of shedding innocent blood, since you have done what is right in the eyes of the LORD.

Marrying a Captive Woman

10 When you go to war against your enemies and the LORD your God delivers them into your hands[r] and you take captives, 11 if you notice among the captives a beautiful woman and are attracted to her, you may take her as your wife. 12 Bring her into your home and have her shave her head,[s] trim her nails 13 and put aside the clothes she was wearing when captured. After she has lived in your house and mourned her father and mother for a full month,[t] then you may go to her and be her husband and she shall be your wife. 14 If you are not pleased with her, let her go wherever she wishes. You must not sell her or treat her as a slave, since you have dishonored her.[u]

The Right of the Firstborn

15 If a man has two wives, and he loves one but not the other, and both bear him sons but the firstborn is the son of the wife he does not love,[v] 16 when he wills his property to his sons, he must not give the rights of the firstborn to the son of the wife he loves in preference to his actual firstborn, the son of the wife he does not love.[w] 17 He must acknowledge the son of his unloved wife as the firstborn by

---

21:1–9 *Atonement for an Unsolved Murder.* No other law regarding human life shows the importance of eradicating blood guilt from the land more than this law does. If there is an unsolved murder, it is the responsibility of the elders of the community nearest in proximity to the murder to perform a ritual act to atone for the shedding of innocent blood. The ritual act is unique in the Bible and shows the connection between bloodshed and the land. The land is in some sense defiled until atonement can be made (cf. 2 Sam 21:1–9). If the murderer is found, his punishment (death) atones for the crime (Num 35:33), but in his absence, another means of atonement must be made.

21:3–4 While the heifer is not sacrificed (no blood or altar), its neck is broken, with no blood being spilled. The heifer's death is probably required as a substitute for the unknown criminal. The atonement rite consists of using elements that have been uncontaminated by contact with humanity (the heifer and the land); the flowing stream suggests the removal of sin from the community.

21:3 elders of the town. Legal responsibility of towns for their surrounding area was known in the ancient world.

21:5–8 Priests preside over the rite, giving it official status. The elders wash their hands in the flowing water of the brook. This act both asserts their innocence (cf. Ps 26:6) and perhaps removes any taint of sin from their community. Then they declare their innocence in the death of the man and offer the corpse of the animal, representing the criminal, as an atonement rite (cf. Gen 9:6).

21:10–14 *Marrying a Captive Woman.* This law relates to the previous commands dealing with human life and war and the following command regarding polygamous marriage. Both laws show the importance of respecting human life in compromising situations. The first law is striking in its limitation. A perennial problem in war is rape, but this was forbidden in Israel. If a soldier was attracted to a woman, he had to marry her, but he could do so only after she had lived with him in a state of humiliation and mourning for a month. If he changed his mind after they were married, she had to be granted her freedom. Her dignity had to be guarded, and she could not be treated like a slave. The fact that female prisoners of war could be taken as wives by the Israelites does not sanction the practice so much as regulate and transform an existing evil.

21:12–13 shave her head, trim her nails and put aside the clothes. More than just humiliation and mourning but indicating a complete break with her past to join a new community. By changing her clothes she symbolically embraced a new life.

21:14 dishonored. The Hebrew verb occurs 12 other times in the Bible and is used to refer to men forcing women to have sexual intercourse with them (22:24,29; Gen 34:2; Judg 19:24; 20:5; 2 Sam 13:12,14,32; Lam 5:11; Ezek 22:10–11).

21:15–17 *The Right of the Firstborn.* In a polygamous marriage, the right of the firstborn son had to be protected against favoritism. The inheritance—and thus life—was not to be determined by personal feeling but was an objective right and thus had to be protected. The firstborn son would receive a double portion of the inheritance. This probably also applied in the case of remarriage after the death of the first wife. Elisha's request for a double portion of the estate of Elijah—the Holy Spirit—showed figuratively that he was Elijah's firstborn son (2 Kgs 2:9).

giving him a double share of all he has. That son is the first sign of his father's strength.[x] The right of
the firstborn belongs to him.[y]

A Rebellious Son

18If someone has a stubborn and rebellious son who does not obey his father and mother[z] and will
not listen to them when they discipline him, 19his father and mother shall take hold of him and bring
him to the elders at the gate of his town. 20They shall say to the elders, "This son of ours is stubborn and
rebellious. He will not obey us. He is a glutton and a drunkard." 21Then all the men of his town are to
stone him to death. You must purge the evil[a] from among you. All Israel will hear of it and be afraid.[b]

Various Laws

22If someone guilty of a capital offense[c] is put to death and their body is exposed on a pole, 23you
must not leave the body hanging on the pole overnight.[d] Be sure to bury it that same day, because anyone who is hung on a pole is under God's curse.[e] You must not desecrate[f] the land the LORD your God
is giving you as an inheritance.

22 If you see your fellow Israelite's ox or sheep straying, do not ignore it but be sure to take it back
to its owner.[g] 2If they do not live near you or if you do not know who owns it, take it home with
you and keep it until they come looking for it. Then give it back. 3Do the same if you find their donkey
or cloak or anything else they have lost. Do not ignore it.

4If you see your fellow Israelite's donkey[h] or ox fallen on the road, do not ignore it. Help the owner
get it to its feet.

5A woman must not wear men's clothing, nor a man wear women's clothing, for the LORD your God
detests anyone who does this.

6If you come across a bird's nest beside the road, either in a tree or on the ground, and the mother is
sitting on the young or on the eggs, do not take the mother with the young.[i] 7You may take the young,
but be sure to let the mother go, so that it may go well with you and you may have a long life.[j]

8When you build a new house, make a parapet around your roof so that you may not bring the guilt
of bloodshed on your house if someone falls from the roof.

21:17 [x] Ge 49:3 [y] Ge 25:31
21:18 [z] Pr 1:8; Isa 30:1; Eph 6:1-3
21:21 [a] Dt 19:19; 1Co 5:13* [b] Dt 13:11
21:22 [c] Dt 22:26; Mk 14:64; Ac 23:29
21:23 [d] Jos 8:29; 10:27; Jn 19:31 [e] Gal 3:13* [f] Lev 18:25; Nu 35:34
22:1 [g] Ex 23:4-5
22:4 [h] Ex 23:5
22:6 [i] Lev 22:28
22:7 [j] Dt 4:40

21:18–21 *A Rebellious Son.* This law apparently deals with violating the fifth commandment; it appears here because of the concern with sons in the previous law. Firstborn status did not guarantee the son a license to do as he pleased. It was important to prohibit a type of disrespect and dishonor of parents that amounted to a form of killing. Unless checked, such an incorrigible ("stubborn and rebellious," vv. 18,20) son could turn out to be a grave danger to the entire community.
21:19 his father and mother. Both parents are involved in the decision, but it is not theirs alone; the entire community has a stake.
21:20 a glutton and a drunkard. Cf. similar terminology in Prov 23:20–22 in the context of parental obedience. Such a law is unique in the ancient world; however, it is important to remember that it deals not with a young child but with a much older son who has become a reprobate, bringing disgrace to the family and a threat to its continuity. Perhaps he also has struck and cursed his parents (cf. Exod 21:15,17). Capital punishment is taken out of the hands of the parents and delivered to the community. The son's execution is to provide a deterrent.
21:22—22:12 *Various Laws.* Some of these laws further develop the idea of the respect for life.
21:22 guilty of a capital offense. Probably murder given the context (cf. 19:6), but other capital offenses could be included. **exposed on a pole.** After execution, the body would be hung to show the accursed nature of the act and the shameful curse (death) the criminal incurred (cf. Gen 40:19; Josh 10:26–27; Esth 2:23).
21:23 overnight. Prolonged exposure desecrated the land; the corpse must be removed from the tree and buried the same day. This law combined with the previous two laws, the inheritance of the firstborn son (vv. 15–17) and the stubborn and rebellious son who is executed (vv. 18–21), certainly played a role in the apostle Paul's thought. His reflection on the disobedience of Israel as God's firstborn son and the execution of Jesus, the obedient son, on a tree connects the theological "dots" in these laws (Gal 3:10–13). Christ accepts the curse for a lost and rebellious humanity.
22:1–12 The regulations in this brief section continue the theme of stressing respect for life while perhaps expanding the seventh commandment (regarding adultery) with injunctions to respect God-ordained boundaries (vv. 9–12).
22:1–4 These two laws dealing with the loss of property and potential damage of property show the concern for the total welfare of the covenant community. Lost property cannot be confiscated but must be returned. Animals of neighbors that need help must not be ignored.
22:5 This law forbids cross-dressing (transvestism), which confuses the created categories of sexuality. The God-created differences between men and women are not to be disregarded (see Lev 18:22, 20:13). Transvestism may have been derived from Canaanite practices of cross-dressing in the context of the worship of pagan deities. This law would thus reflect the value of not crossing boundaries that God has established (see note on vv. 9–11).
22:6–7 The sixth commandment (regarding murder) applies also to the treatment of wildlife (cf. Prov 12:10). The means of life (the mother) must be respected. In other ancient cultures such respect and care for the creation was disregarded.
22:8 Ancient Israelite houses had flat roofs for relaxation and rest. This law is the equivalent of an ancient building code to protect residents and guests of the house.

Assyrian eunuchs bearing trophies of the royal hunt including bird nests with young in one hand and mother bird in the other; Israel is to be different, showing mercy to the creation for its Creator (Deut 22:6).

Kim Walton, taken at the British Museum

22:9 [k]Lev 19:19
22:10 [l]2Co 6:14
22:11 [m]Lev 19:19
22:12 [n]Nu 15:37-41; Mt 23:5
22:13 [o]Dt 24:1
22:18 [p]Ex 18:21

9 Do not plant two kinds of seed in your vineyard;[k] if you do, not only the crops you plant but also
the fruit of the vineyard will be defiled.[a]
10 Do not plow with an ox and a donkey yoked together.[l]
11 Do not wear clothes of wool and linen woven together.[m]
12 Make tassels on the four corners of the cloak you wear.[n]

Marriage Violations

13 If a man takes a wife and, after sleeping with her[o], dislikes her 14 and slanders her and gives
her a bad name, saying, "I married this woman, but when I approached her, I did not find proof of
her virginity," 15 then the young woman's father and mother shall bring to the town elders at the
gate proof that she was a virgin. 16 Her father will say to the elders, "I gave my daughter in marriage
to this man, but he dislikes her. 17 Now he has slandered her and said, 'I did not find your daughter
to be a virgin.' But here is the proof of my daughter's virginity." Then her parents shall display the
cloth before the elders of the town, 18 and the elders[p] shall take the man and punish him. 19 They
shall fine him a hundred shekels[b] of silver and give them to the young woman's father, because

[a] 9 Or *be forfeited to the sanctuary* [b] 19 That is, about 2 1/2 pounds or about 1.2 kilograms

22:9–11 Like the law on transvestism, creational categories are to be kept separate whether in planting gardens or plowing fields or wearing clothes. The symbolism is clear: it is dangerous to blur these boundaries.
22:12 This perhaps alludes to another command that makes the tassels a reminder of the covenant to protect against spiritual adultery (see Num 15:37–41, especially v. 39). Thus, this text is a segue to the next section, which deals with the theme of the seventh commandment. In contrast to the confusion of the creational categories in vv. 9–11, the tassels remind the Israelites that the Creator is to be so woven into their lives that he is part of the clothing they wear (cf. Rom 13:14).
22:13—23:14 *Marital and Spiritual Fidelity.* Linking these laws is a dominant theme of illicit sexuality. Consequently, they reflect the underlying principle of the seventh commandment: "You shall not commit adultery" (5:18). As God symbolically was to be woven into the Israelite's clothing (see note on 22:12), his revelation was woven into the ancient cultural context of Deuteronomy. Sadly, rape victims in the ancient Near East would not only have to endure the humiliation and degradation of the crime itself, but also the consequence in this culture would be shame, ostracism, and destitution. They frequently would be driven to prostitution for survival. Some of these laws were intended to protect the victim from such a fate. Similarly, arranged marriages, payments for the bride, and dowries given to the bride were inextricably connected to the culture. While customs vary from culture to culture, the following laws extrapolate the principle of the seventh commandment into ancient Israelite culture.
22:13–30 *Marriage Violations.* Laws dealing with sexual fidelity.
22:13–21 This law occurs at the beginning of this section because it involves a newly married couple, with the bride suspected of unfaithfulness before the marriage actually occurred. In ancient culture, it was a universal expectation that a bride be a virgin (except in the case of divorce and widowhood).
22:14 proof of her virginity. Perhaps a bloodstained wedding sheet from the night of their consummation. It is clearly a cloth of some sort (v. 17) that was customarily given to the parents.
22:19 a hundred shekels of silver. An expensive fine. Thus, an attempt to retrieve the original amount given to cement the marriage boomer-

this man has given an Israelite virgin a bad name. She shall continue to be his wife; he must not
divorce her as long as he lives.

[20]If, however, the charge is true and no proof of the young woman's virginity can be found, [21]she
shall be brought to the door of her father's house and there the men of her town shall stone her to
death. She has done an outrageous thing[q] in Israel by being promiscuous while still in her father's
house. You must purge the evil from among you.

[22]If a man is found sleeping with another man's wife, both the man who slept with her and the
woman must die.[r] You must purge the evil from Israel.

[23]If a man happens to meet in a town a virgin pledged to be married and he sleeps with her, [24]you
shall take both of them to the gate of that town and stone them to death — the young woman because
she was in a town and did not scream for help, and the man because he violated another man's wife.
You must purge the evil from among you.[s]

[25]But if out in the country a man happens to meet a young woman pledged to be married and rapes
her, only the man who has done this shall die. [26]Do nothing to the woman; she has committed no sin
deserving death. This case is like that of someone who attacks and murders a neighbor, [27]for the man
found the young woman out in the country, and though the betrothed woman screamed, there was no
one to rescue her.

[28]If a man happens to meet a virgin who is not pledged to be married and rapes her and they are

22:21 [q] Ge 34:7; Dt 13:5; 23:17-18; Jdg 20:6; 2Sa 13:12
22:22 [r] Lev 20:10; Jn 8:5
22:24 [s] ver 21-22; 1Co 5:13*

Israelite joint family compound with two pillared houses and various courtyard activities. Deut 22:8 instructs builders to make a parapet around the roof to keep people from falling off the roof.

angs, and the false accuser pays a costly penalty. **he must not divorce her.** The attempt to end the marriage results in no possibility of divorce.
22:21 promiscuous while still in her father's house. In the context, this woman who is "still in her father's house" was betrothed (viewed as a binding relationship) but had not yet been united to her husband. If in this context she was "promiscuous," the sexual sin was seen as adultery owing to the binding nature of betrothal.
22:22 The death penalty for both parties in adultery indicates that the woman was not simply the property of her husband. In the ancient Near East, the offended husband could reduce the sentence if he wished.
22:23 – 29 Betrothal was significant in ancient Israel; it was tantamount to marriage apart from consummation. The first example (vv. 23 – 24) assumes that adultery has taken place between consenting parties since the act happens in the city, where other people could hear a cry for help. Thus, the penalty is the same as in the previous law. The second case (vv. 25 – 27) assumes that rape has occurred since the act happened in the countryside, where no one would be able to hear a cry for help. Consequently, only the male offender must die. The third case (vv. 28 – 29) develops earlier legislation in Exod 22:16 – 17; if there is no betrothal and rape occurs, the woman becomes the wife of the offender with no provision of divorce.

22:28 [t]Ex 22:16
22:30 [u]Lev 18:8; 20:11; Dt 27:20; 1Co 5:1
23:3 [v]Ne 13:2
23:4 [w]Nu 22:5-6; 23:7; 2Pe 2:15
23:5 [x]Pr 26:2
23:6 [y]Ezr 9:12
23:7 [z]Ge 25:26; Ob 10, 12 [a]Ex 22:21; 23:9; Lev 19:34; Dt 10:19
23:10 [b]Lev 15:16
23:14 [c]Lev 26:12 [d]Ex 3:5

discovered,[t] 29 he shall pay her father fifty shekels[a] of silver. He must marry the young woman, for he
has violated her. He can never divorce her as long as he lives.
30 A man is not to marry his father's wife; he must not dishonor his father's bed.[b][u]

Exclusion From the Assembly

23 [c] 1 No one who has been emasculated by crushing or cutting may enter the assembly of the LORD.
2 No one born of a forbidden marriage[d] nor any of their descendants may enter the assembly
of the LORD, not even in the tenth generation.
3 No Ammonite or Moabite or any of their descendants may enter the assembly of the LORD, not even
in the tenth generation.[v] 4 For they did not come to meet you with bread and water on your way when
you came out of Egypt, and they hired Balaam[w] son of Beor from Pethor in Aram Naharaim[e] to pronounce a curse on you. 5 However, the LORD your God would not listen to Balaam but turned the curse[x]
into a blessing for you, because the LORD your God loves you. 6 Do not seek a treaty of friendship with
them as long as you live.[y]
7 Do not despise an Edomite, for the Edomites are related to you.[z] Do not despise an Egyptian, because you resided as foreigners in their country.[a] 8 The third generation of children born to them may
enter the assembly of the LORD.

Uncleanness in the Camp

9 When you are encamped against your enemies, keep away from everything impure. 10 If one of your
men is unclean because of a nocturnal emission, he is to go outside the camp and stay there.[b] 11 But as
evening approaches he is to wash himself, and at sunset he may return to the camp.
12 Designate a place outside the camp where you can go to relieve yourself. 13 As part of your equipment
have something to dig with, and when you relieve yourself, dig a hole and cover up your excrement. 14 For
the LORD your God moves[c] about in your camp to protect you and to deliver your enemies to you. Your
camp must be holy,[d] so that he will not see among you anything indecent and turn away from you.

[a] *29* That is, about 1 1/4 pounds or about 575 grams [b] *30* In Hebrew texts this verse (22:30) is numbered 23:1. [c] In Hebrew texts 23:1-25 is numbered 23:2-26. [d] *2* Or *one of illegitimate birth* [e] *4* That is, Northwest Mesopotamia

22:29 fifty shekels of silver. Not a bride-price, which in many cultures is a payment to the family of the bride. This is a serious fine. The implication is that the man would be indentured to the woman's family to pay off the debt.

22:30 father's wife. Probably not the son's mother (cf. the case of Reuben and Bilhah in Gen 35:22). The relationship is forbidden even if the father has died.

23:1–8 *Exclusion From the Assembly.* The assembly of the Lord is the dominant theme in this passage, which is concerned with formal worship. For the Israelite the transition from marriage legislation to laws dealing with formal worship is natural and anticipates a later prophetic theme of Israel as the bride of the Lord (Hos 1–3). The exclusion of both groups, the Ammonites and the Moabites, is due to their failure to provide Israel with the basic necessities in their sojourn in the desert and their hiring of Balaam to curse God's people (Num 22–24). The text here indicates that the Ammonites were also involved in the curse (vv. 3–4), a point not mentioned in Num 22–24. Provision is made for Edomites and Egyptians to enter into worship because of genetic bonds in the case of the former and generosity in the case of the latter, foreshadowing the inclusion of the nations in the blessing of Abraham (Gen 12:1–3).

23:1 emasculated. Castration was not practiced in Israel. Wholeness in health and holiness are related. This requirement for participation in formal worship is not unlike a requirement for the priest (Lev 21:17–20). Although eunuchs were excluded from formal worship in OT times, Isaiah looks forward to a time when this restriction will be removed (Isa 56:4–5); the Ethiopian eunuch's conversion in the book of Acts shows that this hope was realized (Acts 8:27,38–39). **assembly of the LORD.** A rare phrase since the more usual expression is "assembly of Israel." An equivalent phrase in Nehemiah is "assembly of God" (Neh 13:1).

23:2 born of a forbidden marriage. Born of an illicit union between an Israelite and a Canaanite (cf. 7:3–4) and thus a foreigner to Israel's ways (cf. Zech 9:6). **tenth generation.** Possibly "forever" since the phrase symbolizes completeness. The gospel does away with this restriction since the cross demolishes every barrier to radical inclusion (Gal 3:26–29).

23:3–4 The OT itself revokes this exclusion when Ruth showed love to Naomi, embraced her God, and became a full member of the Israelite community, even becoming the great-great-grandmother of David (see Ruth 1–4; but cf. a strict application in Neh 13:1–3).

23:7 Edomite ... Egyptian. Genetic bonds allow for including Edomites, and the generosity of the Egyptians permits their inclusion.

23:8 third generation. Shows the importance of socialization in faith since there must be two generations of exposure to the Israelite way of life before Edomites and Egyptians can become full members in the congregation.

23:9–14 *Uncleanness in the Camp.* These laws relate to God's presence and ritual purity (cf. 14:3–21; Lev 11–15). Nothing indecent is to be found in the relationship between Israel and their God; the expression "anything indecent" (23:14) occurs only one other time in the Bible, and it represents the only legitimate reason for a divorce in the OT (24:1; but cf. Neh 13:1–3). The military camp is to be kept ritually clean because of God's presence. The NT abounds with similar moral injunctions since the church must be a pure and spotless bride for her divine spouse (2 Cor 11:2; cf. Rev 14:4).

Miscellaneous Laws

15If a slave has taken refuge with you, do not hand them over to their master.[e] 16Let them live among
you wherever they like and in whatever town they choose. Do not oppress[f] them.
17No Israelite man[g] or woman is to become a shrine prostitute.[h] 18You must not bring the earnings of
a female prostitute or of a male prostitute[a] into the house of the LORD your God to pay any vow, because
the LORD your God detests them both.
19Do not charge a fellow Israelite interest, whether on money or food or anything else that may earn
interest.[i] 20You may charge a foreigner interest, but not a fellow Israelite, so that the LORD your God may
bless[j] you in everything you put your hand to in the land you are entering to possess.
21If you make a vow to the LORD your God, do not be slow to pay it, for the LORD your God will certainly demand it of you and you will be guilty of sin.[k] 22But if you refrain from making a vow, you will
not be guilty. 23Whatever your lips utter you must be sure to do, because you made your vow freely to
the LORD your God with your own mouth.
24If you enter your neighbor's vineyard, you may eat all the grapes you want, but do not put any in
your basket. 25If you enter your neighbor's grainfield, you may pick kernels with your hands, but you
must not put a sickle to their standing grain.[l]

24 If a man marries a woman who becomes displeasing to him[m] because he finds something indecent about her, and he writes her a certificate of divorce,[n] gives it to her and sends her from
his house, 2and if after she leaves his house she becomes the wife of another man, 3and her second
husband dislikes her and writes her a certificate of divorce, gives it to her and sends her from his house,
or if he dies, 4then her first husband, who divorced her, is not allowed to marry her again after she has
been defiled. That would be detestable in the eyes of the LORD. Do not bring sin upon the land the LORD[o]
your God is giving you as an inheritance.
5If a man has recently married, he must not be sent to war or have any other duty laid on him. For
one year he is to be free to stay at home and bring happiness to the wife he has married.[p]
6Do not take a pair of millstones—not even the upper one—as security for a debt, because that
would be taking a person's livelihood as security.

23:15 [e] 1Sa 30:15
23:16 [f] Ex 22:21
23:17 [g] Ge 19:25; 2Ki 23:7 [h] Lev 19:29; Dt 22:21
23:19 [i] Ex 22:25; Lev 25:35-37
23:20 [j] Dt 15:10; 28:12
23:21 [k] Nu 30:1-2; Ecc 5:4-5; Mt 5:33
23:25 [l] Mt 12:1; Mk 2:23; Lk 6:1
24:1 [m] Dt 22:13 [n] Mt 5:31*; 19:7-9; Mk 10:4-5
24:4 [o] Jer 3:1
24:5 [p] Dt 20:7

[a] 18 Hebrew *of a dog*

23:15—25:19 *Miscellaneous Laws.* The various laws in this grouping appear to be a miscellany, nonetheless there are some significant underlying themes. Although there are some exceptions, there are applications of the eighth commandment in 23:15—24:7, the ninth commandment in 24:8—25:4, and the tenth commandment in 25:5–19. In these cases, there is wide latitude as to how these commandments relate to life. For example, oppressive slave owners steal the dignity of their slaves (23:15–16); prostitutes steal money with their services (23:17–18); money lenders steal income with their interest charges (23:19–20). In addition, truth demands following commands (24:8), respecting privacy (24:10–11), paying for services (24:14–15), punishing the offender and not his child (24:16), and providing a descendant for a dead brother while not coveting his dead brother's property (25:5–10).

23:15–16 Runaway slaves must receive asylum and freedom. This does not indicate whether the slave is foreign or indigenous, but it probably does not matter. This extraordinary law is unique in the ancient world and implicitly critiques certain types of slavery. When slavery leads to oppression, Israel must grant an exodus.

23:17 shrine prostitute. Male and female prostitution was at times practiced in worship centers in Canaan due to the belief that this would increase fertility through sympathetic magic. Fees earned were donated to the religious institutions (v. 18). The practice was forbidden in Israel—not always with success (Mic 1:7).

23:19–20 Perhaps the financial profit from interest amounts to a type of theft, particularly given the exorbitant interest rates in the ancient world. This is an extraordinary law since this practice was institutionalized in ancient cultures, often extracting huge economic payments from needy debtors. International trade was exempt from the law forbidding interest (v. 20) since a foreign merchant would come into Israel for financial advantage.

23:21–23 Breaking a vow amounts to withholding from God a pledge, so it is important to either keep vows or not make them.

23:24–25 This remarkable law indicates that ultimately the Lord owns Israel's land. Israelites have a right to alleviate their hunger when in need (cf. Matt 12:1–8).

24:1–4 This is the only OT law that explicitly deals with divorce. The syntax ("If ... then") suggests that Israelite society accepted divorce. This law is intended to restrict a practice that could lead to treating women as a commodity. Cavalier divorce would rob the wife of not only her dignity but also her wealth. By divorcing his wife, a husband would acquire her dowry, which was her father's marriage present to her. Thus, the law protects the second marriage by imparting a solemn gravity to the first divorce.

24:1 something indecent. Probably implies something sexual since the Hebrew word translated "indecent" is usually translated as "nakedness." Jesus remarked that this law conceded to the hardness of the human heart; his disciples are called to a higher standard (see notes on Matt 19:1–12; 1 Cor 7:10–16).

24:5–7 This trio of laws may apply the principle of theft (the eighth commandment). (1) The military draft must not deprive a newly married wife of her husband (v. 5); she has the right to a first year of wedded bliss (cf. 20:7). (2) Collateral for loans must never affect a person's means of sustaining life, so taking a millstone used for grinding grain is a far worse crime than stealing the shirt from someone's back (v. 6). (3) Kidnapping (stealing human beings for human trafficking) is a

24:7 [q]Ex 21:16
24:8 [r]Lev 13:1-46; 14:2
24:9 [s]Nu 12:10
24:13 [t]Ex 22:26 [u]Dt 6:25; Da 4:27
24:14 [v]Lev 25:35-43; Dt 15:12-18
24:15 [w]Jer 22:13 [x]Lev 19:13 [y]Dt 15:9; Jas 5:4
24:16 [z]2Ki 14:6; 2Ch 25:4; Jer 31:29-30; Eze 18:20
24:17 [a]Dt 1:17; 10:17-18; 16:19
24:19 [b]Lev 19:9; 23:22 [c]Pr 19:17
24:20 [d]Lev 19:10
24:22 [e]ver 18
25:1 [f]Dt 19:17 [g]Dt 1:16-17
25:2 [h]Lk 12:47-48
25:3 [i]2Co 11:24 [j]Job 18:3
25:4 [k]Pr 12:10; 1Co 9:9*; 1Ti 5:18*

7 If someone is caught kidnapping a fellow Israelite and treating or selling them as a slave, the kidnapper must die.[q] You must purge the evil from among you.
8 In cases of defiling skin diseases,[a] be very careful to do exactly as the Levitical priests instruct you.
You must follow carefully what I have commanded them.[r] 9 Remember what the LORD your God did to
Miriam along the way after you came out of Egypt.[s]
10 When you make a loan of any kind to your neighbor, do not go into their house to get what is
offered to you as a pledge. 11 Stay outside and let the neighbor to whom you are making the loan bring
the pledge out to you. 12 If the neighbor is poor, do not go to sleep with their pledge in your possession.
13 Return their cloak by sunset[t] so that your neighbor may sleep in it. Then they will thank you, and it
will be regarded as a righteous act in the sight of the LORD your God.[u]
14 Do not take advantage of a hired worker who is poor and needy, whether that worker is a fellow
Israelite or a foreigner residing in one of your towns.[v] 15 Pay them their wages each day before sunset,
because they are poor[w] and are counting on it.[x] Otherwise they may cry to the LORD against you, and
you will be guilty of sin.[y]
16 Parents are not to be put to death for their children, nor children put to death for their parents;
each will die for their own sin.[z]
17 Do not deprive the foreigner or the fatherless of justice,[a] or take the cloak of the widow as a pledge.
18 Remember that you were slaves in Egypt and the LORD your God redeemed you from there. That is
why I command you to do this.
19 When you are harvesting in your field and you overlook a sheaf, do not go back to get it.[b] Leave it
for the foreigner, the fatherless and the widow, so that the LORD your God may bless[c] you in all the work
of your hands. 20 When you beat the olives from your trees, do not go over the branches a second time.[d]
Leave what remains for the foreigner, the fatherless and the widow. 21 When you harvest the grapes in
your vineyard, do not go over the vines again. Leave what remains for the foreigner, the fatherless and
the widow. 22 Remember that you were slaves in Egypt. That is why I command you to do this.[e]

25 When people have a dispute, they are to take it to court and the judges will decide the case,[f] acquitting the innocent and condemning the guilty.[g] 2 If the guilty person deserves to be beaten,[h]
the judge shall make them lie down and have them flogged in his presence with the number of lashes
the crime deserves, 3 but the judge must not impose more than forty lashes.[i] If the guilty party is flogged
more than that, your fellow Israelite will be degraded in your eyes.[j]
4 Do not muzzle an ox while it is treading out the grain.[k]
5 If brothers are living together and one of them dies without a son, his widow must not marry out-

[a] *8* The Hebrew word for *defiling skin diseases*, traditionally translated "leprosy," was used for various diseases affecting the skin.

particularly offensive crime and worthy of capital punishment (v. 7); it is the only theft law that requires death.

24:8—25:4 Some of these laws may apply the principle of truthfulness (the ninth commandment), but they mainly have to do with the powerless in society.

24:8 skin diseases. An infectious skin disease not to be identified with leprosy (see NIV text note; cf. Lev 13:1–46). **follow carefully.** Since the priests' instructions are trustworthy.

24:9 Miriam. An example of someone who slandered Moses by questioning his authority and ended up with a skin disease (Num 12:1–16).

24:10–15 Pledges and payments for services rendered must be honored, but the dignity of the debtor and employee must be respected (cf. Exod 22:26–27).

24:16 each will die for their own sin. This law was enforced during the time of Amaziah when he executed the assassins of his father, Joash, but not their children (2 Kgs 14:5–6). Ezekiel stresses the same principle (Ezek 18:1–4). This law is not to be viewed as being in conflict with the statement that God punishes the children for the sins of their parents (5:9). The former is a legal injunction; the latter, a divine prerogative. The latter probably means that God permits the consequences of sin to affect the extended family (for three to four generations).

24:17–22 These laws mainly deal with the socially marginalized and economically deprived. Twice within this short collection of laws, the Israelites are to remember their deliverance from oppression in Egypt to motivate them to show compassion to the poor (vv. 18,22).

25:1–4 Even the sentenced criminal has dignity. His punishment must be fair (cf. 2 Cor 11:24 for evidence that later Jewish tradition avoided breaking the law by requiring one less lash). Similarly the ox deserves its proper "wage" when performing its service (v. 4). The apostle Paul sees this law as an illustration of a larger principle of provision for labor in the church (1 Cor 9:9–10; 1 Tim 5:17–18).

25:5—26:15 Again, there are varied laws in this collection, some of which can be viewed as reflecting the underlying principle of the tenth commandment ("You shall not covet," 5:21).

25:5–10 In Israel there was provision for the redemption of family property (Lev 25:23–28), the life of a relative (Num 35:19), and a man's name, i.e., his descendants (Gen 38; Ruth 4). This last law, the right of levirate marriage, is linked to all three but in particular to the name. The refusal of a brother to perpetuate the name of his dead brother by marrying his dead brother's wife and producing an heir shows that he is more concerned with his own financial loss than the welfare of his dead brother's house. To marry his brother's widow would incur a substantial economic burden by providing for a widow, raising a child, and looking after his brother's land until his brother's "son" inherited it. Interestingly,

side the family. Her husband's brother shall take her and marry her and fulfill the duty of a brother-in-law to her.[l] 6 The first son she bears shall carry on the name of the dead brother so that his name will not be blotted out from Israel.[m]

7 However, if a man does not want to marry his brother's wife, she shall go to the elders at the town gate and say, "My husband's brother refuses to carry on his brother's name in Israel. He will not fulfill the duty of a brother-in-law to me."[n] 8 Then the elders of his town shall summon him and talk to him. If he persists in saying, "I do not want to marry her," 9 his brother's widow shall go up to him in the presence of the elders, take off one of his sandals,[o] spit in his face and say, "This is what is done to the man who will not build up his brother's family line." 10 That man's line shall be known in Israel as The Family of the Unsandaled.

11 If two men are fighting and the wife of one of them comes to rescue her husband from his assailant, and she reaches out and seizes him by his private parts, 12 you shall cut off her hand. Show her no pity.[p]

13 Do not have two differing weights in your bag — one heavy, one light.[q] 14 Do not have two differing measures in your house — one large, one small. 15 You must have accurate and honest weights and measures, so that you may live long[r] in the land the LORD your God is giving you. 16 For the LORD your God detests anyone who does these things, anyone who deals dishonestly.[s]

17 Remember what the Amalekites[t] did to you along the way when you came out of Egypt. 18 When you were weary and worn out, they met you on your journey and attacked all who were lagging behind; they had no fear of God.[u] 19 When the LORD your God gives you rest from all the enemies around you in the land he is giving you to possess as an inheritance, you shall blot out the name of Amalek[v] from under heaven. Do not forget!

Firstfruits and Tithes

26 When you have entered the land the LORD your God is giving you as an inheritance and have taken possession of it and settled in it, 2 take some of the firstfruits[w] of all that you produce from the soil of the land the LORD your God is giving you and put them in a basket. Then go to the place the LORD your God will choose as a dwelling for his Name[x] 3 and say to the priest in office at the time, "I declare today to the LORD your God that I have come to the land the LORD swore to our ancestors to give us." 4 The priest shall take the basket from your hands and set it down in front of the altar of the LORD your God. 5 Then you shall declare before the LORD your God: "My father was a wandering Aramean,[y] and he went down into Egypt with a few people[z] and lived there and became a great nation,

25:5 [l] Mt 22:24; Mk 12:19; Lk 20:28
25:6 [m] Ge 38:9; Ru 4:5,10
25:7 [n] Ru 4:1-2,5-6
25:9 [o] Ru 4:7-8,11
25:12 [p] Dt 19:13
25:13 [q] Lev 19:35-37; Pr 11:1; Eze 45:10; Mic 6:11
25:15 [r] Ex 20:12
25:16 [s] Pr 11:1
25:17 [t] Ex 17:8
25:18 [u] Ps 36:1; Ro 3:18
25:19 [v] 1Sa 15:2-3
26:2 [w] Ex 22:29; 23:16,19; Nu 18:13; Pr 3:9 [x] Dt 12:5
26:5 [y] Hos 12:12 [z] Ge 43:1-2; 45:7,11; 46:27; Dt 10:22

Onan's refusal to perform his sexual duty to his brother's widow in order to provide a descendant to carry on his brother's name may have been rooted in greed (Gen 38:9). If a child had been born, not only would Onan have had to provide for the mother and child, but he would *not* have acquired his brother's land. While he married his brother's widow, he refused to raise up a child to be the heir of his brother's property.

25:9 take off one of his sandals. The foot symbolized authority and ownership (cf. 11:24; Ps 8:6). Thus, Moses was to relinquish authority and ownership of the land near the burning bush by removing his shoes in the presence of God (Exod 3:1 – 5). **spit in his face.** A sign of gross contempt (cf. Num 12:14; Job 30:10).

25:10 The Family of the Unsandaled. The covetous brother was to be publicly insulted by having his household's name marked by homelessness. Since he brought an end to his brother's house through his refusal to marry the widow, his own house becomes a symbol of notoriety and shame.

25:11 – 12 These verses are linked to the previous command by the concern for posterity. Whereas the man refuses to provide children for his dead brother's wife in the previous example, now a living man's wife attacks his opponent's ability to bear children. She bears the shame of her attempted "castration" in her mutilated hand. This is the *only* law in the Bible in which mutilation functions as a punishment; this is in sharp contrast to its common occurrence in the ancient world.

25:13 – 16 Greedy merchants would use different weights and measures that were marked with the same measuring weight or capacity. Thus, one would be heavier or larger for buying and the other lighter or smaller for selling. The laws concerning fairness and equity in business dealings discourage theft by prohibiting even the *possession* of unjust weights and measures.

25:17 – 19 The Amalekites may be an example of the power of greed and covetousness, for they ambushed worn and weary stragglers for personal profit (cf. Exod 17:8 – 16; Num 14:45). Such behavior is rooted in the absence of the fear of God.

25:19 blot out. The Amalekites are to be eliminated not because of their race but because of their character. Saul was ordered to fulfill this command (1 Sam 15), and his descendant Mordecai completed the task (Esth 9:7 – 10; see notes on Esth 3:1; 8:11).

26:1 – 15 *Firstfruits and Tithes.* An antidote to covetousness is generosity, reflected in offerings and tithes. As the legislation draws to a close, this text echoes the importance of worship at the central sanctuary found in 12:1 – 18.

26:2 take some of the firstfruits. As a one-time offering at the central sanctuary and therefore distinct from a similar annual offering (18:4).

26:5 – 10 This recites a mini-history of salvation: election, oppression, exodus, and the gift of land. The first formal declaration of worship in the new land begins with recounting the old story of salvation. Thus, the offering springs from genuine gratitude. This identifies the current generation with previous ones through the use of the first person pronouns ("us," "we").

26:6 [a]Ex 1:11,14
26:7 [b]Ex 2:23-25 [c]Ex 3:9
26:8 [d]Dt 4:34
26:9 [e]Ex 3:8
26:11 [f]Dt 12:7 [g]Dt 16:11
26:12 [h]Lev 27:30 [i]Nu 18:24; Dt 14:28-29; Heb 7:5,9
26:13 [j]Ps 119:141, 153,176
26:14 [k]Lev 7:20; Hos 9:4
26:15 [l]Isa 63:15; Zec 2:13
26:16 [m]Dt 4:29
26:18 [n]Ex 6:7; 19:5; Dt 7:6; 14:2; 28:9
26:19 [o]Dt 4:7-8; 28:1, 13,44 [p]Ex 19:6; Dt 7:6; 1Pe 2:9
27:2 [q]Jos 8:31
27:3 [r]Dt 26:9

powerful and numerous. 6But the Egyptians mistreated us and made us suffer,[a] subjecting us to harsh
labor. 7Then we cried out to the LORD, the God of our ancestors, and the LORD heard our voice[b] and
saw[c] our misery, toil and oppression. 8So the LORD brought us out of Egypt with a mighty hand and an
outstretched arm, with great terror and with signs and wonders.[d] 9He brought us to this place and gave
us this land, a land flowing with milk and honey;[e] 10and now I bring the firstfruits of the soil that you,
LORD, have given me." Place the basket before the LORD your God and bow down before him. 11Then you
and the Levites[f] and the foreigners residing among you shall rejoice[g] in all the good things the LORD
your God has given to you and your household.

12When you have finished setting aside a tenth[h] of all your produce in the third year, the year of the
tithe,[i] you shall give it to the Levite, the foreigner, the fatherless and the widow, so that they may eat
in your towns and be satisfied. 13Then say to the LORD your God: "I have removed from my house the
sacred portion and have given it to the Levite, the foreigner, the fatherless and the widow, according to
all you commanded. I have not turned aside from your commands nor have I forgotten any of them.[j]
14I have not eaten any of the sacred portion while I was in mourning, nor have I removed any of it
while I was unclean,[k] nor have I offered any of it to the dead. I have obeyed the LORD my God; I have
done everything you commanded me. 15Look down from heaven,[l] your holy dwelling place, and bless
your people Israel and the land you have given us as you promised on oath to our ancestors, a land
flowing with milk and honey."

Follow the LORD's Commands

16The LORD your God commands you this day to follow these decrees and laws; carefully observe them
with all your heart and with all your soul.[m] 17You have declared this day that the LORD is your God and
that you will walk in obedience to him, that you will keep his decrees, commands and laws — that you
will listen to him. 18And the LORD has declared this day that you are his people, his treasured possession[n]
as he promised, and that you are to keep all his commands. 19He has declared that he will set you in
praise, fame and honor high above all the nations[o] he has made and that you will be a people holy[p] to
the LORD your God, as he promised.

The Altar on Mount Ebal

27 Moses and the elders of Israel commanded the people: "Keep all these commands that I give you
today. 2When you have crossed the Jordan into the land the LORD your God is giving you, set up
some large stones and coat them with plaster.[q] 3Write on them all the words of this law when you have
crossed over to enter the land the LORD your God is giving you, a land flowing with milk and honey,[r] just
as the LORD, the God of your ancestors, promised you. 4And when you have crossed the Jordan, set up

26:12–15 The three-year tithe is specifically directed to the "quartet of the vulnerable" — "the Levite, the foreigner, the fatherless and the widow," vv. 12,13 — and the Israelites must declare that nothing has been withheld (v. 14), perhaps as a means to counteract covetousness. A prayer for blessing suitably ends this section of the laws (v. 15).

26:16–19 *Follow the Lord's Commands.* A solemn conclusion to the paradigmatic application of the Ten Commandments in the life of the nation (12:1 — 26:15).

26:16 with all your heart. Obedience is not a matter of adhering to legalistic ritual requirements but is a matter of the heart (6:5).

26:17 You have declared. Evidence of a formal treaty ritual in which Israel has taken a solemn vow to keep the covenant. Both forms of the verb "declared" (here and in v. 18) are unique forms of the verb in the original text and emphasize a formalized, ritual vow, much like a modern-day marriage covenant. **the LORD is your God.** The heart of the covenant for Israel.

26:18 the LORD has declared. Evidence of a formal treaty ritual in which God has taken a solemn vow to keep the covenant (see note on v. 17). **you are his people, his treasured possession.** The heart of the covenant for the Lord.

26:19 praise, fame and honor high above all the nations. The accumulation of accolades shows the Lord's extraordinary desire to bless his people. This theme is resumed in 28:1, which concludes the speech with blessings and curses after the narrative interlude of ch. 27.

27:1–8 *The Altar on Mount Ebal.* This expands on an earlier command to renew the covenant upon entering the land of Canaan (11:29–32) and interrupts the second speech of Moses, which continues in ch. 28. Continuity between the formal declaration (26:17–18) and the future ratification ceremony in the land produces this narrative pause in the speech. The national task of erecting an altar in the land parallels the individual's presentation of firstfruits in the new land (26:1–11). Mount Ebal may have been one of the first places where the central sanctuary was set up, but the altar built here is different from the altar of the tabernacle, which suggests that such earthen altars could be erected for special purposes in the life of the nation (Exod 20:24–26; cf. Judg 6:24; 21:4; 1 Sam 7:17; 1 Kgs 18:30; 19:10,14). What makes this particular altar different from all others is that stones are set up nearby on which are inscribed the words of the covenant. Setting up stones inscribed with messages to be remembered was common in the ancient world.

27:2 large stones. Cf. vv. 6–7; Exod 20:24–26. **coat them with plaster.** Plastering for writing was an Egyptian custom.

27:4 Mount Ebal. Selected probably because Israelite faith began

these stones on Mount Ebal,[s] as I command you today, and coat
them with plaster. 5Build there an altar[t] to the LORD your God,
an altar of stones. Do not use any iron tool[u] on them. 6Build
the altar of the LORD your God with fieldstones and offer burnt
offerings on it to the LORD your God. 7Sacrifice fellowship offerings there, eating them and rejoicing in the presence of the
LORD your God. 8And you shall write very clearly all the words
of this law on these stones you have set up."

Twelfth-century BC image of a "Canaanite" on a glazed tile from the palace of Pharaoh Rameses III.

Guillaume Blanchard

Curses From Mount Ebal

9Then Moses and the Levitical priests said to all Israel, "Be
silent, Israel, and listen! You have now become the people of
the LORD your God.[v] 10Obey the LORD your God and follow his
commands and decrees that I give you today."

11On the same day Moses commanded the people:

12When you have crossed the Jordan, these tribes shall
stand on Mount Gerizim[w] to bless the people: Simeon, Levi,
Judah, Issachar, Joseph and Benjamin.[x] 13And these tribes
shall stand on Mount Ebal to pronounce curses: Reuben,
Gad, Asher, Zebulun, Dan and Naphtali.

14The Levites shall recite to all the people of Israel in a loud voice:

15"Cursed is anyone who makes an idol[y] — a thing detestable to the LORD, the work of skilled hands — and sets it up in secret."

Then all the people shall say, "Amen!"

16"Cursed is anyone who dishonors their father or mother."[z]

Then all the people shall say, "Amen!"

17"Cursed is anyone who moves their neighbor's boundary stone."[a]

Then all the people shall say, "Amen!"

18"Cursed is anyone who leads the blind astray on the road."[b]

Then all the people shall say, "Amen!"

19"Cursed is anyone who withholds justice from the foreigner,[c] the fatherless or the widow."[d]

Then all the people shall say, "Amen!"

20"Cursed is anyone who sleeps with his father's wife, for he dishonors his father's bed."[e]

Then all the people shall say, "Amen!"

27:4 [s] Dt 11:29
27:5 [t] Jos 8:31 [u] Ex 20:25
27:9 [v] Dt 26:18
27:12 [w] Dt 11:29 [x] Jos 8:35
27:15 [y] Ex 20:4; 34:17; Lev 19:4; 26:1; Dt 4:16, 23; 5:8; Isa 44:9
27:16 [z] Ex 20:12; 21:17; Lev 19:3; 20:9
27:17 [a] Dt 19:14; Pr 22:28
27:18 [b] Lev 19:14
27:19 [c] Ex 22:21; Dt 24:19 [d] Dt 10:18
27:20 [e] Lev 18:7; Dt 22:30

here in the new land. Abram built an altar in Shechem between the two mountains of Ebal and Gerizim when he first entered the land of promise (Gen 12:6–7). Shechem literally means "shoulders," which are represented in the geography of the two mountains.

27:5 iron tool. Dressed stones were forbidden probably because the stone could be defiled by an instrument that could also shed human blood, which would then desecrate the altar (cf. Exod 20:25). David could not be involved in building the temple because his hands had shed blood (1 Chr 22:8). Perhaps also there is a desire to use natural elements formed directly from the hand of the Creator.

27:6–7 Cf. Exod 20:24.

27:6 burnt offerings. Reserved totally for God; they are consumed by fire (see Lev 1 and note on 1:3–17).

27:7 fellowship offerings. Most of these could be shared between the priests and the worshipers (see Lev 3 and note on 3:1).

27:8 The focus on worship leads to "the words of this law." As each individual household is to have words of the law inscribed on its doorframes (6:9), so also is the national home or worship center. **words of this law.** Probably refers to the Ten Commandments.

27:9–26 *Curses From Mount Ebal.* Moses formally pronounces the covenant renewal and obligations to the new generation.

27:11–13 When the Israelites enter the land to formalize the covenant, they will not only have to build the altar at Mount Ebal but also to invoke the blessings and curses. Six tribes that have Rachel and Leah as their ancestral mothers are to stand on Mount Gerizim to pronounce the blessings for obedience, while six tribes that have Leah, Bilhah, and Zilpah as their mothers are to stand on Mount Ebal to pronounce the curses for disobedience (cf. Gen 29:31 — 30:24).

27:14–26 Remarkably there are no blessings mentioned here, only 12 curses. Since the list of blessings and curses found in 28:1–19 consists of six blessings (28:3–6) and six curses (28:16–19), it seems that before the tribes pronounce the blessings and curses, the Levites, who are to stand on Mount Gerizim, invoke 12 curses for covenant violations that predominantly have an air of secrecy (vv. 15,24) about them. These are followed by a comprehensive curse for any covenant violation (v. 26). The covenant is thus interested in self-censorship and, ultimately, heart transformation. This shows again Deuteronomy's concern for more than a strictly legal understanding of the law. A renovation of the heart is required to keep the law. While the list of curses is somewhat unusual, the underlying value system presented here assumes a concern for both God (v. 15) and neighbor (vv. 16–25).

27:21 [f] Lev 18:23
27:22 [g] Lev 18:9; 20:17
27:23 [h] Lev 20:14
27:24 [i] Lev 24:17; Nu 35:31
27:25 [j] Ex 23:7-8; Dt 10:17; Eze 22:12
27:26 [k] Jer 11:3; Gal 3:10*
28:1 [l] Ex 15:26; Lev 26:3; Dt 7:12-26 [m] Dt 26:19
28:2 [n] Zec 1:6
28:3 [o] Ps 128:1,4 [p] Ge 39:5
28:4 [q] Ge 49:25; Pr 10:22
28:6 [r] Ps 121:8
28:7 [s] Lev 26:8,17
28:9 [t] Ex 19:6; Dt 7:6
28:10 [u] 2Ch 7:14
28:11 [v] Dt 30:9; Pr 10:22
28:12 [w] Lev 26:4 [x] Dt 15:3,6
28:14 [y] Dt 5:32

21 “Cursed is anyone who has sexual relations with any animal.”[f]

Then all the people shall say, “Amen!”

22 “Cursed is anyone who sleeps with his sister, the daughter of his father or the daughter of
his mother.”[g]

Then all the people shall say, “Amen!”

23 “Cursed is anyone who sleeps with his mother-in-law.”[h]

Then all the people shall say, “Amen!”

24 “Cursed is anyone who kills[i] their neighbor secretly.”

Then all the people shall say, “Amen!”

25 “Cursed is anyone who accepts a bribe to kill an innocent person.”[j]

Then all the people shall say, “Amen!”

26 “Cursed is anyone who does not uphold the words of this law by carrying them out.”[k]

Then all the people shall say, “Amen!”

Blessings for Obedience

28 If you fully obey the LORD your God and carefully follow all his commands[l] I give you today,
the LORD your God will set you high above all the nations on earth.[m] 2 All these blessings will
come on you[n] and accompany you if you obey the LORD your God:

3 You will be blessed[o] in the city and blessed in the country.[p]
4 The fruit of your womb will be blessed, and the crops of your land and the young of your
livestock — the calves of your herds and the lambs of your flocks.[q]
5 Your basket and your kneading trough will be blessed.
6 You will be blessed when you come in and blessed when you go out.[r]

7 The LORD will grant that the enemies who rise up against you will be defeated before you. They will
come at you from one direction but flee from you in seven.[s]
8 The LORD will send a blessing on your barns and on everything you put your hand to. The LORD your
God will bless you in the land he is giving you.
9 The LORD will establish you as his holy people,[t] as he promised you on oath, if you keep the commands of the LORD your God and walk in obedience to him. 10 Then all the peoples on earth will see that
you are called by the name[u] of the LORD, and they will fear you. 11 The LORD will grant you abundant
prosperity — in the fruit of your womb, the young of your livestock and the crops of your ground — in
the land he swore to your ancestors to give you.[v]
12 The LORD will open the heavens, the storehouse of his bounty, to send rain[w] on your land in season
and to bless all the work of your hands. You will lend to many nations but will borrow from none.[x]
13 The LORD will make you the head, not the tail. If you pay attention to the commands of the LORD your
God that I give you this day and carefully follow them, you will always be at the top, never at the bottom.
14 Do not turn aside from any of the commands I give you today, to the right or to the left,[y] following
other gods and serving them.

27:26 Paul cites this text in Gal 3:10–14 to indict the entire human race before God. Since no one is able to keep the law fully (Jas 2:10; 1 John 1:8,10), no one can be justified by personal merits. Disobedience results in a curse (21:18–21), but the solution to this universal problem is that Jesus Christ, who was able to keep the law completely, bore the curse for humanity (cf. 21:22–23; Gal 3:13–14).

28:1–68 *Blessings and Curses.* Cf. Lev 26. After the narrative interlude of ch. 27, Moses resumes his second speech by picking up the last threads of the promise that God would set Israel high above all the nations if Israel obeys (cf. 26:19). The speech is continued with a flourish to hammer home the gravity of the choice set before Israel in the renewal of the covenant. The curses far outnumber the blessings in the speech. Perhaps this expresses Moses' ultimately negative view of Israel's ability to keep the law. But it is also a fact that Hittite treaties from the same time period have a much longer and colorful list of curses than blessings.

28:1–14 *Blessings for Obedience.* There are six specific blessings that presumably the six tribes on Mount Gerizim will pronounce. The word “bless” first occurs in Gen 1:22, where God blesses the marine life with the ability to reproduce and fill the waters with life. It refers to fullness of life. The six blessings (vv. 3–6) stress location (everywhere in the land), fertility (human, crops, livestock), fullness (plenty of food), and time (comprehensive).

28:1 high above all the nations. Signals that Moses is resuming the second speech (cf. 26:19).

28:7–12 Moses expands the original blessings (vv. 3–6) on the tribes for rhetorical effect, emphasizing success against enemies (v. 7) and the prospering of all of their activities and ways (vv. 8–12).

28:13–14 Blessing is contingent on obedience.

Curses for Disobedience

15 However, if you do not obey[z] the LORD your God and do not carefully follow all his commands and
decrees I am giving you today, all these curses will come on you and overtake you:[a]

16 You will be cursed in the city and cursed in the country.

17 Your basket and your kneading trough will be cursed.

18 The fruit of your womb will be cursed, and the crops of your land, and the calves of your
herds and the lambs of your flocks.

19 You will be cursed when you come in and cursed when you go out.

20 The LORD will send on you curses,[b] confusion and rebuke[c] in everything you put your hand to,
until you are destroyed and come to sudden ruin[d] because of the evil you have done in forsaking him.[*a*]
21 The LORD will plague you with diseases until he has destroyed you from the land you are entering to
possess.[e] 22 The LORD will strike you with wasting disease, with fever and inflammation, with scorching
heat and drought,[f] with blight and mildew, which will plague you until you perish.[g] 23 The sky over your
head will be bronze, the ground beneath you iron.[h] 24 The LORD will turn the rain of your country into
dust and powder; it will come down from the skies until you are destroyed.

25 The LORD will cause you to be defeated before your enemies. You will come at them from one
direction but flee from them in seven,[i] and you will become a thing of horror to all the kingdoms on
earth.[j] 26 Your carcasses will be food for all the birds and the wild animals, and there will be no one
to frighten them away.[k] 27 The LORD will afflict you with the boils of Egypt[l] and with tumors, festering
sores and the itch, from which you cannot be cured. 28 The LORD will afflict you with madness, blindness and confusion of mind. 29 At midday you will grope[m] about like a blind person in the dark. You
will be unsuccessful in everything you do; day after day you will be oppressed and robbed, with no
one to rescue you.

30 You will be pledged to be married to a woman, but another will take her and rape her.[n] You will
build a house, but you will not live in it.[o] You will plant a vineyard, but you will not even begin to enjoy
its fruit.[p] 31 Your ox will be slaughtered before your eyes, but you will eat none of it. Your donkey will be
forcibly taken from you and will not be returned. Your sheep will be given to your enemies, and no one
will rescue them. 32 Your sons and daughters will be given to another nation,[q] and you will wear out
your eyes watching for them day after day, powerless to lift a hand. 33 A people that you do not know will
eat what your land and labor produce, and you will have nothing but cruel oppression all your days.[r]
34 The sights you see will drive you mad. 35 The LORD will afflict your knees and legs with painful boils[s]
that cannot be cured, spreading from the soles of your feet to the top of your head.

36 The LORD will drive you and the king[t] you set over you to a nation unknown to you or your ancestors.[u] There you will worship other gods, gods of wood and stone.[v] 37 You will become a thing of horror,
a byword and an object of ridicule among all the peoples where the LORD will drive you.[w]
38 You will sow much seed in the field but you will harvest little,[x] because locusts will devour[y] it. 39 You
will plant vineyards and cultivate them but you will not drink the wine or gather the grapes, because
worms will eat them.[z] 40 You will have olive trees throughout your country but you will not use the oil,

a 20 Hebrew *me*

28:15 [z] Lev 26:14 [a] Jos 23:15; Da 9:11; Mal 2:2
28:20 [b] Mal 2:2 [c] Isa 51:20; 66:15 [d] Dt 4:26
28:21 [e] Lev 26:25; Jer 24:10
28:22 [f] Lev 26:16 [g] Am 4:9
28:23 [h] Lev 26:19
28:25 [i] Isa 30:17 [j] Jer 15:4; 24:9; Eze 23:46
28:26 [k] Jer 7:33; 16:4; 34:20
28:27 [l] ver 60-61; 1Sa 5:6
28:29 [m] Job 5:14; Isa 59:10
28:30 [n] Job 31:10; Jer 8:10 [o] Am 5:11 [p] Jer 12:13
28:32 [q] ver 41
28:33 [r] Jer 5:15-17
28:35 [s] ver 27
28:36 [t] 2Ki 17:4,6; 24:12,14; 25:7,11 [u] Jer 16:13 [v] Dt 4:28
28:37 [w] Jer 24:9
28:38 [x] Mic 6:15; Hag 1:6,9 [y] Joel 1:4
28:39 [z] Isa 5:10; 17:10-11

28:15–68 *Curses for Disobedience.* Disobedience leads to curses that are just as negative as the blessings are positive. As the blessings represent the fullness of life, the curses represent the opposite: the deprivation of life, the presence of death, disease, defeat, and exile. But these curses are multiplied far more than the blessings so that they never seem to end. Probably the tribes on Mount Ebal pronounce an initial group of curses (vv. 16–19) that reverses the initial group of blessings (vv. 3–6). This expands to include multiple curses in the land of Canaan (vv. 20–44), which then increases to include curses suffered under siege (vv. 45–63), followed by exile (vv. 64–67). This leads to an ultimate exile when Israel will return to Egypt in ships (v. 68). This return to Egypt by ordinary means completely reverses salvation history, in which Israel miraculously escaped Egypt by crossing the Red Sea on dry ground. It thus shows the full extent of Israel's damnation.

28:23–24 bronze … iron … dust and powder. The total absence of fertility as moisture is removed from the land.

28:26 carcasses. Exposed corpses were a particularly horrible fate in the ancient world.

28:27 boils of Egypt. Israel would experience one of the hardships brought by God upon the Egyptians (Exod 9:9).

28:29 unsuccessful. In contrast to the one who meditates on the law of God day and night (Ps 1:2–3).

28:30–33,38–42 A standard list of "futility curses" in the ancient Near East.

28:35 from the soles of your feet to the top of your head. They will experience sufferings like those Job suffered—but for a very different reason (cf. Job 2:7).

28:40 [a] Mic 6:15
28:41 [b] ver 32
28:43 [c] ver 13
28:44 [d] ver 12 [e] ver 13
28:45 [f] ver 15
28:46 [g] Isa 8:18; Eze 14:8
28:47 [h] Dt 32:15 [i] Ne 9:35
28:48 [j] Jer 28:13-14
28:49 [k] Jer 5:15; 6:22 [l] La 4:19; Hos 8:1
28:50 [m] Isa 47:6
28:51 [n] ver 33
28:52 [o] Jer 10:18; Zep 1:14-16,17
28:53 [p] Lev 26:29; 2Ki 6:28-29; Jer 19:9; La 2:20; 4:10
28:56 [q] ver 54
28:58 [r] Mal 1:14 [s] Ex 6:3
28:60 [t] ver 27
28:61 [u] Dt 4:25-26
28:62 [v] Dt 4:27; 10:22; Ne 9:23
28:63 [w] Jer 32:41 [x] Pr 1:26 [y] Jer 12:14; 45:4
28:64 [z] Lev 26:33; Dt 4:27 [a] Ne 1:8
28:65 [b] Lev 26:16,36

because the olives will drop off.[a] 41 You will have sons and daughters but you will not keep them, because they will go into captivity.[b] 42 Swarms of locusts will take over all your trees and the crops of your land.

43 The foreigners who reside among you will rise above you higher and higher, but you will sink lower and lower.[c] 44 They will lend to you, but you will not lend to them.[d] They will be the head, but you will be the tail.[e]

45 All these curses will come on you. They will pursue you and overtake you until you are destroyed,[f] because you did not obey the LORD your God and observe the commands and decrees he gave you. 46 They will be a sign and a wonder to you and your descendants forever.[g] 47 Because you did not serve[h] the LORD your God joyfully and gladly[i] in the time of prosperity, 48 therefore in hunger and thirst, in nakedness and dire poverty, you will serve the enemies the LORD sends against you. He will put an iron yoke[j] on your neck until he has destroyed you.

49 The LORD will bring a nation against you from far away, from the ends of the earth,[k] like an eagle[l] swooping down, a nation whose language you will not understand, 50 a fierce-looking nation without respect for the old[m] or pity for the young. 51 They will devour the young of your livestock and the crops of your land until you are destroyed. They will leave you no grain, new wine or olive oil, nor any calves of your herds or lambs of your flocks until you are ruined.[n] 52 They will lay siege to all the cities throughout your land until the high fortified walls in which you trust fall down. They will besiege all the cities throughout the land the LORD your God is giving you.[o]

53 Because of the suffering your enemy will inflict on you during the siege, you will eat the fruit of the womb, the flesh of the sons and daughters the LORD your God has given you.[p] 54 Even the most gentle and sensitive man among you will have no compassion on his own brother or the wife he loves or his surviving children, 55 and he will not give to one of them any of the flesh of his children that he is eating. It will be all he has left because of the suffering your enemy will inflict on you during the siege of all your cities. 56 The most gentle and sensitive[q] woman among you — so sensitive and gentle that she would not venture to touch the ground with the sole of her foot — will begrudge the husband she loves and her own son or daughter 57 the afterbirth from her womb and the children she bears. For in her dire need she intends to eat them secretly because of the suffering your enemy will inflict on you during the siege of your cities.

58 If you do not carefully follow all the words of this law, which are written in this book, and do not revere[r] this glorious and awesome name[s] — the LORD your God — 59 the LORD will send fearful plagues on you and your descendants, harsh and prolonged disasters, and severe and lingering illnesses. 60 He will bring on you all the diseases of Egypt[t] that you dreaded, and they will cling to you. 61 The LORD will also bring on you every kind of sickness and disaster not recorded in this Book of the Law, until you are destroyed.[u] 62 You who were as numerous as the stars in the sky[v] will be left but few in number, because you did not obey the LORD your God. 63 Just as it pleased[w] the LORD to make you prosper and increase in number, so it will please[x] him to ruin and destroy you. You will be uprooted[y] from the land you are entering to possess.

64 Then the LORD will scatter[z] you among all nations,[a] from one end of the earth to the other. There you will worship other gods — gods of wood and stone, which neither you nor your ancestors have known. 65 Among those nations you will find no repose, no resting place for the sole of your foot. There the LORD will give you an anxious mind, eyes weary with longing, and a despairing heart.[b] 66 You will live in constant suspense, filled with dread both night and day, never sure of your life.

28:45 – 48 This break from the avalanche of curses explains their cause: blatant disobedience.
28:47 Because you did not serve the LORD your God joyfully and gladly in the time of prosperity. Rather than joyously serving God and being grateful for his gifts of prosperity, Israel has only "served" God reluctantly and halfheartedly.
28:49 ends of the earth. A metaphor for distance. **like an eagle.** A simile for speed and power.
28:53 eat the fruit of the womb. Cannibalism could happen during prolonged sieges (cf. 2 Kgs 6:28 – 29). Desperate situations produce desperate measures.
28:58 This verse introduces a final flurry of curses. Israel's final disaster coincides with profaning God's majestic "name," which here uniquely emphasizes the gravity of the offense since God himself "signs off" on the coming annihilation with his own personal imprimatur.
28:60 diseases of Egypt. Cf. 7:15; Exod 15:26.
28:61 not recorded in this Book of the Law. The floodgates of possible curses are opened to any curse imaginable.
28:62 – 63 few in number ... uprooted from the land. This reverses the Abrahamic promise (Gen 13:15; 15:5,18). See "Covenant," p. 2646.

67 In the morning you will say, "If only it were evening!" and in the evening, "If only it were morning!" — because of the terror that will fill your hearts and the sights that your eyes will see.[c] 68 The
LORD will send you back in ships to Egypt on a journey I said you should never make again. There
you will offer yourselves for sale to your enemies as male and female slaves, but no one will buy you.

Renewal of the Covenant

29[a] These are the terms of the covenant the LORD commanded Moses to make with the Israelites
in Moab, in addition to the covenant he had made with them at Horeb.[d]
2 Moses summoned all the Israelites and said to them:

Your eyes have seen all that the LORD did in Egypt to Pharaoh, to all his officials and to all his land.[e]
3 With your own eyes you saw those great trials, those signs and great wonders.[f] 4 But to this day the
LORD has not given you a mind that understands or eyes that see or ears that hear.[g] 5 Yet the LORD says,
"During the forty years that I led you through the wilderness, your clothes did not wear out, nor did
the sandals on your feet.[h] 6 You ate no bread and drank no wine or other fermented drink. I did this so
that you might know that I am the LORD your God."[i]
7 When you reached this place, Sihon[j] king of Heshbon and Og king of Bashan came out to fight
against us, but we defeated them.[k] 8 We took their land and gave it as an inheritance to the Reubenites,
the Gadites and the half-tribe of Manasseh.[l]
9 Carefully follow[m] the terms of this covenant, so that you may prosper in everything you do.[n] 10 All
of you are standing today in the presence of the LORD your God — your leaders and chief men, your
elders and officials, and all the other men of Israel, 11 together with your children and your wives, and
the foreigners living in your camps who chop your wood and carry your water.[o] 12 You are standing here
in order to enter into a covenant with the LORD your God, a covenant the LORD is making with you this
day and sealing with an oath, 13 to confirm you this day as his people,[p] that he may be your God[q] as he
promised you and as he swore to your fathers, Abraham, Isaac and Jacob. 14 I am making this covenant,[r]
with its oath, not only with you 15 who are standing here with us today in the presence of the LORD our
God but also with those who are not here today.[s]
16 You yourselves know how we lived in Egypt and how we passed through the countries on the way
here. 17 You saw among them their detestable images and idols of wood and stone, of silver and gold.[t]
18 Make sure there is no man or woman, clan or tribe among you today whose heart turns away from

28:67 [c] ver 34; Job 7:4
29:1 [d] Dt 5:2-3
29:2 [e] Ex 19:4
29:3 [f] Dt 4:34; 7:19
29:4 [g] Isa 6:10; Ac 28:26-27; Ro 11:8*; Eph 4:18
29:5 [h] Dt 8:4
29:6 [i] Dt 8:3
29:7 [j] Dt 2:32; 3:1 [k] Nu 21:21-24,33-35
29:8 [l] Nu 32:33; Dt 3:12-13
29:9 [m] Dt 4:6; Jos 1:7 [n] 1Ki 2:3
29:11 [o] Jos 9:21,23,27
29:13 [p] Dt 28:9 [q] Ge 17:7; Ex 6:7
29:14 [r] Jer 31:31
29:15 [s] Ac 2:39
29:17 [t] Dt 28:36

[a] In Hebrew texts 29:1 is numbered 28:69, and 29:2-29 is numbered 29:1-28.

28:67 morning ... evening. God established this rhythm at creation; a world of blessing is now a world filled with anxiety and deprivation.
28:68 This completely reverses salvation history because of disobedience (see note on vv. 15–68).
29:1 — 30:20 *The Third Speech: Covenant Ratification, Failure, and Future Hope.* After presenting Israel's history to encourage present obedience (1:6 — 4:43), declaring the content of the obedience (4:44 — 26:15), stating the initial steps to formalize the covenant in the present (26:16–19) and in the new land (ch. 27), and listing the blessings and curses (ch. 28), the formal covenantal proceedings for the Moab generation are now finalized. The speech divides into three main sections: the Moab covenant (29:1–29), future hope (30:1–10 or 30:1–14), and final challenge (30:11–20 or 30:15–20). This covenant does not merely repeat the Horeb covenant, which revealed the failure of Israel to keep the law; it looks beyond such failure to a future solution that God himself provides. While renewing the covenant, God will finally deal with the intractable problem of the human heart and provide a new one. This is grounded in his covenant with Abraham (cf. 4:30–31).
29:1–29 *Renewal of the Covenant.* The finalizing of the Moab covenant has four discrete units: a history lesson (vv. 1–8), a covenantal ceremony (vv. 9–15), warnings (vv. 16–28), and a conclusion (v. 29).
29:1 This verse can be understood either as a concluding postscript for the previous speech (as in the Hebrew Bible) or as an introduction for the next speech (as in most English versions). Its opening words signal a new beginning in the rest of the book (cf. 1:1; 4:45; 12:1; 33:1). Whatever view is taken, the basic understanding is not affected since the covenant at Moab has been the subject of chs. 5–28, which revises the Sinai covenant for the new generation. **in addition to.** The covenant at Moab incorporates the Sinai covenant within its framework and seeks to spell out the covenant obligations in more detail. It sharpens and expands the demands of the covenant and points Israel to the future when God will fulfill his promise to the patriarchs (cf. 4:30–32; Lev 26:40–42) and help his people do his will as easily as they speak his words in their mouths (30:11–14).
29:4 The people have been spiritually obtuse and need new minds, eyes, and ears, just like the people in Isaiah's time (Isa 6:10–12). Paul later applies this passage to Israel's failure to receive the gospel (Rom 11:8).
29:9–15 Although there is no mention here of covenant ratification through a sacrifice (cf. Exod 24), this text presents a solemn ritual in which the people and the Lord are entering into a covenant so that they might have a new relationship. Moses has already provided instructions for a formal covenant renewal when the Israelites enter the land (cf. ch. 27). The covenant is also completely comprehensive. This list of various groups is the most complete in the OT, including even future generations not present (vv. 14–15).
29:16–21 A solemn warning to individuals, clans, or tribes who do not take the covenant seriously.

29:18 [u]Dt 11:16; Heb 12:15
29:20 [v]Eze 23:25 [w]Ps 74:1; 79:5 [x]Ex 32:33; Dt 9:14
29:22 [y]Jer 19:8
29:23 [z]Isa 34:9 [a]Jer 17:6 [b]Ge 19:24,25; Zep 2:9
29:24 [c]1Ki 9:8; Jer 22:8-9
29:27 [d]Da 9:11,13,14
29:28 [e]1Ki 14:15; 2Ch 7:20; Ps 52:5; Pr 2:22
30:1 [f]ver 15,19; Dt 11:26 [g]Lev 26:40-45; Dt 28:64; 29:28; 1Ki 8:47
30:2 [h]Dt 4:30; Ne 1:9
30:3 [i]Ps 126:4 [j]Ps 147:2; Jer 32:37; Eze 34:13 [k]Jer 29:14
30:4 [l]Ne 1:8-9; Isa 43:6
30:5 [m]Jer 29:14
30:6 [n]Dt 10:16; Jer 32:39
30:7 [o]Dt 7:15

the LORD our God to go and worship the gods of those nations; make sure there is no root among you
that produces such bitter poison.[u]
19 When such a person hears the words of this oath and they invoke a blessing on themselves, thinking, "I will be safe, even though I persist in going my own way," they will bring disaster on the watered
land as well as the dry. 20 The LORD will never be willing to forgive them; his wrath and zeal[v] will burn[w]
against them. All the curses written in this book will fall on them, and the LORD will blot[x] out their
names from under heaven. 21 The LORD will single them out from all the tribes of Israel for disaster,
according to all the curses of the covenant written in this Book of the Law.
22 Your children who follow you in later generations and foreigners who come from distant lands
will see the calamities that have fallen on the land and the diseases with which the LORD has afflicted
it.[y] 23 The whole land will be a burning waste[z] of salt[a] and sulfur — nothing planted, nothing sprouting, no vegetation growing on it. It will be like the destruction of Sodom and Gomorrah,[b] Admah and
Zeboyim, which the LORD overthrew in fierce anger. 24 All the nations will ask: "Why has the LORD done
this to this land?[c] Why this fierce, burning anger?"
25 And the answer will be: "It is because this people abandoned the covenant of the LORD, the God
of their ancestors, the covenant he made with them when he brought them out of Egypt. 26 They went
off and worshiped other gods and bowed down to them, gods they did not know, gods he had not given
them. 27 Therefore the LORD's anger burned against this land, so that he brought on it all the curses
written in this book.[d] 28 In furious anger and in great wrath the LORD uprooted[e] them from their land
and thrust them into another land, as it is now."
29 The secret things belong to the LORD our God, but the things revealed belong to us and to our children forever, that we may follow all the words of this law.

Prosperity After Turning to the LORD

30 When all these blessings and curses[f] I have set before you come on you and you take them
to heart wherever the LORD your God disperses you among the nations,[g] 2 and when you and
your children return[h] to the LORD your God and obey him with all your heart and with all your soul
according to everything I command you today, 3 then the LORD your God will restore your fortunes[a][i] and
have compassion on you and gather[j] you again from all the nations where he scattered you.[k] 4 Even if
you have been banished to the most distant land under the heavens, from there the LORD your God will
gather you and bring you back.[l] 5 He will bring[m] you to the land that belonged to your ancestors, and
you will take possession of it. He will make you more prosperous and numerous than your ancestors.
6 The LORD your God will circumcise your hearts and the hearts of your descendants,[n] so that you may
love him with all your heart and with all your soul, and live. 7 The LORD your God will put all these
curses on your enemies who hate and persecute you.[o] 8 You will again obey the LORD and follow all his

[a] 3 Or *will bring you back from captivity*

29:19 watered land … dry. Possibly metaphors for the righteous ("watered land") and wicked ("dry"). Private acts have public consequences.

29:20 Cf. the NT's severe warnings about such a resolve to sin (Mark 3:29; Heb 6:4–6; 12:16–17).

29:22–28 From the individual to the nation, the sin has spread and contaminated everything, leading to wholesale idolatry and apostasy. This is the most complete description of God's anger in the book. All the curses of the law are consequently invoked, and the country is turned into a vast burning wasteland like the cities of the plain in Gen 19:24–29. The survivors go into exile.

29:29 These famous words look back to the warnings about curses and exile (vv. 16–28) and look ahead to a future of hope (30:1–14). How could the nation continue to exist in light of its foretold destruction? Only God knows such "secret things." **secret things.** This expression links up with the inaccessible knowledge found in the heavens and beyond the seas (30:12–13) and probably pertains to the future. The people will never be able to gain knowledge of such mysterious matters, but they do have access to what God has clearly revealed in his word.

30:1–10 *Prosperity After Turning to the Lord.* Cf. Lev 26:40–45. Moses looks to the future, beyond the success and ultimate failure of the people to keep the requirements of the covenant, to show that the point of the Moab covenant (29:1) is to cast Israel upon the grace of the Lord, based on the Abrahamic covenant to which Moses has already alluded (4:25–31). Turning to the Lord (v. 10) and returning to him (v. 2) result in the Lord restoring his people (v. 3). These different English words—"turn," "return" and "restore"—translate the same Hebrew word that abounds in this passage. God turns to Israel when Israel turns to God.

30:1–4 The books of Joshua, Judges, Samuel, and Kings detail this fulfillment. But these words ensure that exile and curse are not the final word. In exile, Israel will consider the meaning of it all, repent, and be restored.

30:5–10 This will happen not because Israel has within itself the ability to do God's will but because the Lord himself will finally circumcise their hearts to enable Israel to love God completely (cf. Jer 4:4; Rom 4:1–12). The same imagery occurs in Lev 26:40–45, where an uncircumcised heart will be humbled in the exile.

commands I am giving you today. 9Then the LORD your God will make you most prosperous in all the work of your hands and in the fruit of your womb, the young of your livestock and the crops of your land.[p] The LORD will again delight in you and make you prosperous, just as he delighted in your ancestors, 10if you obey the LORD your God and keep his commands and decrees that are written in this Book of the Law and turn to the LORD your God with all your heart and with all your soul.[q]

The Offer of Life or Death

11Now what I am commanding you today is not too difficult for you or beyond your reach.[r] 12It is not up in heaven, so that you have to ask, "Who will ascend into heaven to get it and proclaim it to us so we may obey it?"[s] 13Nor is it beyond the sea, so that you have to ask, "Who will cross the sea to get it and proclaim it to us so we may obey it?" 14No, the word is very near you; it is in your mouth and in your heart so you may obey it.

15See, I set before you today life and prosperity, death and destruction.[t] 16For I command you today to love the LORD your God, to walk in obedience to him, and to keep his commands, decrees and laws; then you will live and increase, and the LORD your God will bless you in the land you are entering to possess.

17But if your heart turns away and you are not obedient, and if you are drawn away to bow down to other gods and worship them, 18I declare to you this day that you will certainly be destroyed.[u] You will not live long in the land you are crossing the Jordan to enter and possess.

19This day I call the heavens and the earth as witnesses against you[v] that I have set before you life and death, blessings and curses.[w] Now choose life, so that you and your children may live 20and that you may love[x] the LORD your God, listen to his voice, and hold fast to him. For the LORD is your life,[y] and he will give you many years in the land he swore to give to your fathers, Abraham, Isaac and Jacob.

Joshua to Succeed Moses

31 Then Moses went out and spoke these words to all Israel: 2"I am now a hundred and twenty years old[z] and I am no longer able to lead you.[a] The LORD has said to me, 'You shall not cross the Jordan.'[b] 3The LORD your God himself will cross[c] over ahead of you.[d] He will destroy these nations

30:9 [p] Dt 28:11; Jer 31:28; 32:41
30:10 [q] Dt 4:29
30:11 [r] Isa 45:19,23
30:12 [s] Ro 10:6*
30:15 [t] Dt 11:26
30:18 [u] Dt 8:19
30:19 [v] Dt 4:26 [w] ver 1
30:20 [x] Dt 6:5; 10:20 [y] Ps 27:1; Jn 11:25
31:2 [z] Dt 34:7 [a] Nu 27:17; 1Ki 3:7 [b] Dt 3:23,26
31:3 [c] Nu 27:18 [d] Dt 9:3

30:11–20 *The Offer of Life or Death.* Israel is now presented with two critical choices.

30:11–14 This text can be interpreted in different ways: (1) These verses begin a new section of discourse, with Moses returning to the present and challenging Israel to keep the covenant, reminding them that they can do it. (2) These verses continue Moses' prediction about Israel, pointing out that when their hearts are circumcised in the future, it will be easy to obey the law. The vast majority of interpreters (including those responsible for the divisions in the NIV text) hold to the first interpretation, while the second interpretation is a relatively recent one.

In the first interpretation the focus is on the present challenge to obey the law since it is not inaccessible (neither up in heaven nor across the sea, vv. 12–13) but has been given to be spoken in the mouths of the Israelites. It is thus in contrast to the "secret things" (29:29). The text is seen to be fulfilled when Jesus, the ultimate Word from God, becomes flesh and by faith becomes resident in the mouths and hearts of believers (Rom 10:6–9).

In the second interpretation, the verses are understood to continue the future prediction about Israel (30:1–10), with the major break occurring at v. 15, returning the discourse from the future to the present. Thus, when the Lord has circumcised the heart of the exiles, they will not find the law too difficult to obey. They will not have to go up to the mountain like Moses to bring it down or cross the Red Sea like Israel to have it revealed and then be unable to do it. Now it will be just as easy to do as it is to speak. Thus, Jeremiah's prophecy of a new covenant reinforces this passage: God's law will be written on the hearts of his people (Jer 31:31–34). Paul sees it fulfilled when people do not try to perform the law on their own but instead confess with their mouths that Jesus is Lord (Rom 10:7–10). Jesus is the goal of the law.

Of the two interpretations, the first reads more naturally, especially in the light of the use of the word "today" (v. 11), which suggests a shift from the future time of return from exile to the present time on the plains of Moab.

30:15–20 Depending on the interpretation (see note on vv. 11–14), either Moses continues the new discourse begun at v. 11 (the more natural reading), or he now returns to the present situation at Moab after discoursing about Israel in the future. In these verses Moses concludes his third speech by passionately presenting the two choices before the people: life or death.

30:19 the heavens and the earth as witnesses. Ancient Near Eastern treaties often invoked a plethora of gods as witnesses to the proceedings. But in a monotheistic worldview, apart from the one God, there could be no more comprehensive or enduring witnesses than heaven and earth. Here they witness to what Moses has done, not to the treaty itself (31:28). **choose life.** Moses does not present a detached description of the alternatives. He wants Israel to embrace life.

31:1—32:52 *Planning for the Future.* The material in chs. 31–34 is frequently treated as an appendix to the book since it wraps up a few details. But a structural marker at 33:1 (see note on 29:1) suggests that chs. 31–32 are part of the fourth section—underlining distinctive emphases in the speech of chs. 29–30 and bringing them to a climax with a prediction of apostasy (ch. 31) and a poem of witness (ch. 32)—which seeks to bring about the repentance necessary for the future heart-circumcision of Israel. However, because of its different genre, narrative and poetry, it is considered a separate section that further develops the themes of the fourth section, emphasizing planning for the future, culminating in a dramatic poem about Israel's future defection that results in judgment and then final salvation and atonement for the land (ch. 32). What is also important in this section is the provision for the leadership transition from Moses to Joshua. While Moses will soon

31:3 [e]Dt 3:28
31:5 [f]Dt 7:2
31:6 [g]Jos 10:25; 1Ch 22:13 [h]Dt 7:18 [i]Dt 1:29; 20:4 [j]Jos 1:5 [k]Heb 13:5*
31:7 [l]Dt 1:38; 3:28
31:8 [m]Ex 13:21; 33:14
31:9 [n]ver 25; Nu 4:15; Jos 3:3
31:10 [o]Dt 15:1 [p]Lev 23:34
31:11 [q]Dt 16:16 [r]Jos 8:34-35; 2Ki 23:2
31:12 [s]Dt 4:10
31:13 [t]Dt 11:2; Ps 78:6-7
31:14 [u]Nu 27:13; Dt 32:49-50
31:15 [v]Ex 33:9
31:16 [w]Jdg 2:12 [x]Jdg 10:6,13
31:17 [y]Jdg 2:14,20 [z]Jdg 6:13; 2Ch 15:2 [a]Dt 32:20; Isa 1:15; 8:17 [b]Nu 14:42
31:20 [c]Dt 6:10-12 [d]Dt 32:15-17 [e]ver 16
31:21 [f]ver 17 [g]Hos 5:3
31:22 [h]ver 19
31:23 [i]ver 7 [j]Jos 1:6

before you, and you will take possession of their land. Joshua also will cross[e] over ahead of you, as the LORD said. 4 And the LORD will do to them what he did to Sihon and Og, the kings of the Amorites, whom he destroyed along with their land. 5 The LORD will deliver[f] them to you, and you must do to them all that I have commanded you. 6 Be strong and courageous.[g] Do not be afraid or terrified[h] because of them, for the LORD your God goes with you;[i] he will never leave you[j] nor forsake[k] you."

7 Then Moses summoned Joshua and said[l] to him in the presence of all Israel, "Be strong and courageous, for you must go with this people into the land that the LORD swore to their ancestors to give them, and you must divide it among them as their inheritance. 8 The LORD himself goes before you and will be with you;[m] he will never leave you nor forsake you. Do not be afraid; do not be discouraged."

Public Reading of the Law

9 So Moses wrote down this law and gave it to the Levitical priests, who carried[n] the ark of the covenant of the LORD, and to all the elders of Israel. 10 Then Moses commanded them: "At the end of every seven years, in the year for canceling debts,[o] during the Festival of Tabernacles,[p] 11 when all Israel comes to appear[q] before the LORD your God at the place he will choose, you shall read this law[r] before them in their hearing. 12 Assemble the people—men, women and children, and the foreigners residing in your towns—so they can listen and learn[s] to fear the LORD your God and follow carefully all the words of this law. 13 Their children,[t] who do not know this law, must hear it and learn to fear the LORD your God as long as you live in the land you are crossing the Jordan to possess."

Israel's Rebellion Predicted

14 The LORD said to Moses, "Now the day of your death[u] is near. Call Joshua and present yourselves at the tent of meeting, where I will commission him." So Moses and Joshua came and presented themselves at the tent of meeting.

15 Then the LORD appeared at the tent in a pillar of cloud, and the cloud stood over the entrance to the tent.[v] 16 And the LORD said to Moses: "You are going to rest with your ancestors, and these people will soon prostitute[w] themselves to the foreign gods of the land they are entering. They will forsake[x] me and break the covenant I made with them. 17 And in that day I will become angry[y] with them and forsake[z] them; I will hide[a] my face from them, and they will be destroyed. Many disasters and calamities will come on them, and in that day they will ask, 'Have not these disasters come on us because our God is not with us?'[b] 18 And I will certainly hide my face in that day because of all their wickedness in turning to other gods.

19 "Now write down this song and teach it to the Israelites and have them sing it, so that it may be a witness for me against them. 20 When I have brought them into the land flowing with milk and honey, the land I promised on oath to their ancestors,[c] and when they eat their fill and thrive, they will turn to other gods[d] and worship them, rejecting me and breaking my covenant.[e] 21 And when many disasters and calamities come on them,[f] this song will testify against them, because it will not be forgotten by their descendants. I know what they are disposed to do,[g] even before I bring them into the land I promised them on oath." 22 So Moses wrote[h] down this song that day and taught it to the Israelites.

23 The LORD gave this command[i] to Joshua son of Nun: "Be strong and courageous,[j] for you will bring the Israelites into the land I promised them on oath, and I myself will be with you."

---

become absent physically, his words will continue to provide authoritative guidance.

31:1–8 *Joshua to Succeed Moses.* After the speech of chs. 29–30, the section returns to the imminent future and the conquest. Joshua will be the new leader, and Moses encourages him and the people for the task set before them. The defeats of Sihon and Og continue to be object lessons of God's power.

31:9–13 *Public Reading of the Law.* Moses commands that the law be read to the entire community every seven years.

31:9 When ancient treaties were ratified, a copy was often deposited in a sacred place before the gods of the covenant-makers. Moses similarly writes a copy of the law and gives it to the priests, who place it beside the ark (v. 26).

31:10 The priests are responsible for publicly reading the law to all Israel during the Festival of Tabernacles. **every seven years.** A seven-year period marked the release of debts; thus, reading this book at the end of such a period emphasizes liberation. The purpose of the public reading is worshiping God and educating the next generation.

31:14–29 *Israel's Rebellion Predicted.* Despite having every advantage, Israel will defect.

31:23 For the first time God speaks directly to Joshua, assuring Joshua of his presence (cf. Josh 1:1–9).

24 After Moses finished writing in a book the words of this law from beginning to end, 25 he gave
this command to the Levites who carried the ark of the covenant of the LORD: 26 "Take this Book of the
Law and place it beside the ark of the covenant of the LORD your God. There it will remain as a witness
against you.[k] 27 For I know how rebellious and stiff-necked[l] you are. If you have been rebellious against
the LORD while I am still alive and with you, how much more will you rebel after I die! 28 Assemble
before me all the elders of your tribes and all your officials, so that I can speak these words in their
hearing and call the heavens and the earth to testify against them.[m] 29 For I know that after my death
you are sure to become utterly corrupt[n] and to turn from the way I have commanded you. In days to
come, disaster[o] will fall on you because you will do evil in the sight of the LORD and arouse his anger
by what your hands have made."

31:26 [k] ver 19
31:27 [l] Ex 32:9; Dt 9:6,24
31:28 [m] Dt 4:26; 30:19; 32:1
31:29 [n] Dt 32:5; Jdg 2:19 [o] Dt 28:15
32:1 [p] Isa 1:2
32:2 [q] Isa 55:11 [r] Ps 72:6
32:3 [s] Ex 33:19 [t] Dt 3:24
32:4 [u] ver 15,18,30 [v] 2Sa 22:31 [w] Dt 7:9
32:5 [x] Dt 31:29
32:6 [y] Ps 116:12 [z] Ps 74:2 [a] Dt 1:31; Isa 63:16 [b] ver 15

The Song of Moses

30 And Moses recited the words of this song from beginning to end in the hearing of the whole assembly of Israel:

32

Listen, you heavens,[p] and I will speak;
hear, you earth, the words of my mouth.
2 Let my teaching fall like rain
and my words descend like dew,[q]
like showers[r] on new grass,
like abundant rain on tender plants.

3 I will proclaim the name of the LORD.[s]
Oh, praise the greatness[t] of our God!
4 He is the Rock,[u] his works are perfect,[v]
and all his ways are just.
A faithful God[w] who does no wrong,
upright and just is he.

5 They are corrupt and not his children;
to their shame they are a warped and crooked
generation.[x]
6 Is this the way you repay[y] the LORD,
you foolish and unwise people?[z]
Is he not your Father,[a] your Creator,[a]
who made you and formed you?[b]

7 Remember the days of old;
consider the generations long past.

[a] 6 Or *Father, who bought you*

31:26 The Levites must place the completed speeches beside the ark containing the Ten Commandments. In form and purpose, this law comes close to the Book of the Covenant in Exod 21–23, which expands on the Ten Commandments in Exodus. This book will serve as a second witness for the divine court.

31:28 the heavens and the earth. See note on 30:19. Here the heavens and the earth are the second pair of witnesses against Israel, matching the two literary ones, the Ten Commandments and the Book of the Law (v. 26).

31:30—32:47 *The Song of Moses.* This song, given by God and written down by Moses (cf. 31:19–22), looks back on Israel's history and forward to the future. It captures in inimitable poetry the story of Israel's rise, demise, and resurrection from death, which earlier parts of the book anticipate (4:25–31; 30:1–10). It frequently tells the story from the perspective of the divine parent, and it is filled with frustration and sadness. Israel had every advantage; it came from *nothing* to become "the apple of [God's] eye" (32:10), protected by a *hovering* mother eagle (32:11). This forcefully echoes creation language, which describes the beginning of the world as nothing but emptiness, with the Spirit of God hovering over the dark and wild waters (Gen 1:2). Such language shows what God had in mind with Israel: nothing less than a new creation. But the unfortunate result was idolatrous affluence, apostasy, and judgment. But judgment is not the end. This gives the audience a window into God's heart, showing his concern for his reputation and resolving to make atonement for his people and his land. This magnificent poem anticipates some of the main ideas of Paul's theology in the book of Romans because its themes include election, judgment, outreach to the nations, and the triumph of God's mercy in atoning for sin (Rom 9–11).

32:4 He is the Rock. The first time this metaphor for God is developed (cf. Gen 49:24, where a different Hebrew word is used). It signifies solidity, strength, and permanence. This poem uses it this way five times (vv. 4,15,18,30,31).

32:7 [c]Ex 13:14
32:8 [d]Ge 11:8; Ac 17:26
32:9 [e]Jer 10:16 [f]1Ki 8:51,53
32:10 [g]Jer 2:6 [h]Ps 17:8; Zec 2:8
32:11 [i]Ex 19:4
32:12 [j]ver 39
32:13 [k]Isa 58:14 [l]Job 29:6
32:14 [m]Ps 81:16; 147:14 [n]Ge 49:11
32:15 [o]Dt 31:20 [p]ver 6; Isa 1:4,28 [q]ver 4
32:16 [r]1Co 10:22 [s]Ps 78:58
32:17 [t]Dt 28:64 [u]Jdg 5:8
32:18 [v]Isa 17:10

Ask your father and he will tell you,
your elders, and they will explain to you.[c]
8 When the Most High gave the nations their
inheritance,
when he divided all mankind,[d]
he set up boundaries for the peoples
according to the number of the sons of Israel.[a]
9 For the LORD's portion[e] is his people,
Jacob his allotted inheritance.[f]

10 In a desert[g] land he found him,
in a barren and howling waste.
He shielded him and cared for him;
he guarded him as the apple of his eye,[h]
11 like an eagle that stirs up its nest
and hovers over its young,[i]
that spreads its wings to catch them
and carries them aloft.
12 The LORD alone led him;
no foreign god was with him.[j]

13 He made him ride on the heights[k] of the land
and fed him with the fruit of the fields.
He nourished him with honey from the rock,
and with oil[l] from the flinty crag,
14 with curds and milk from herd and flock
and with fattened lambs and goats,
with choice rams of Bashan
and the finest kernels of wheat.[m]
You drank the foaming blood of the grape.[n]

15 Jeshurun[b] grew fat[o] and kicked;
filled with food, they became heavy and sleek.
They abandoned[p] the God who made them
and rejected the Rock[q] their Savior.
16 They made him jealous[r] with their foreign gods
and angered[s] him with their detestable idols.
17 They sacrificed to false gods, which are not
God—
gods they had not known,[t]
gods that recently appeared,[u]
gods your ancestors did not fear.
18 You deserted the Rock, who fathered you;
you forgot[v] the God who gave you birth.

[a] 8 Masoretic Text; Dead Sea Scrolls (see also Septuagint) *sons of God* [b] 15 *Jeshurun* means *the upright one*, that is, Israel.

32:8 Most High. The only occurrence of this name for God in the book. **according to the number of the sons of Israel.** Israel is distinguished from the nations; its number becomes the figure by which the boundaries of the nations are determined. In Exod 1:5 the number of Israelites going down to Egypt is 70, which corresponds to the 70 nations in the great "table of nations" in Gen 10. The Septuagint, the pre-Christian Greek translation of the OT, offers a different reading of Deut 32:8: "When God separated the sons of man, he determined the boundaries of the nations according to the angels."

32:10 apple of his eye. The pupil, a delicate part of the eye that is essential for vision and must be protected at all costs.

32:13–14 A lush picture of prosperity with images suggesting a virtual cornucopia of blessing.

32:14 choice rams of Bashan. The fields of Bashan were noted for their fertility and their prized cattle and livestock (cf. Amos 4:1–2).

32:15 Jeshurun. See NIV text note. The name is used sarcastically here. **grew fat.** Has the same Hebrew root as "oil" in v. 13; it is ironic that the recipient of blessing becomes corrupted by it.

[19] The LORD saw this and rejected them[w]
because he was angered by his sons and daughters.[x]
[20] "I will hide my face[y] from them," he said,
"and see what their end will be;
for they are a perverse generation,[z]
children who are unfaithful.
[21] They made me jealous[a] by what is no god
and angered me with their worthless idols.[b]
I will make them envious by those who are not a people;
I will make them angry by a nation that has no
understanding.[c]
[22] For a fire will be kindled by my wrath,
one that burns down to the realm of the dead below.[d]
It will devour the earth and its harvests
and set afire the foundations of the mountains.

[23] "I will heap calamities[e] on them
and spend my arrows[f] against them.
[24] I will send wasting famine against them,
consuming pestilence[g] and deadly plague;[h]
I will send against them the fangs of wild beasts,[i]
the venom of vipers[j] that glide in the dust.
[25] In the street the sword will make them childless;
in their homes terror will reign.[k]
The young men and young women will perish,
the infants and those with gray hair.[l]
[26] I said I would scatter[m] them
and erase their name from human memory,[n]
[27] but I dreaded the taunt of the enemy,
lest the adversary misunderstand
and say, 'Our hand has triumphed;
the LORD has not done all this.' "[o]

[28] They are a nation without sense,
there is no discernment in them.
[29] If only they were wise and would understand this[p]
and discern what their end will be!
[30] How could one man chase a thousand,
or two put ten thousand to flight,[q]
unless their Rock had sold them,
unless the LORD had given them up?[r]
[31] For their rock is not like our Rock,
as even our enemies concede.
[32] Their vine comes from the vine of Sodom
and from the fields of Gomorrah.
Their grapes are filled with poison,
and their clusters with bitterness.

32:19 [w] Jer 44:21-23 [x] Ps 106:40
32:20 [y] Dt 31:17,29 [z] ver 5
32:21 [a] 1Co 10:22 [b] 1Ki 16:13,26 [c] Ro 10:19*
32:22 [d] Ps 18:7-8; Jer 15:14; La 4:11
32:23 [e] Dt 29:21 [f] Ps 7:13; Eze 5:16
32:24 [g] Dt 28:22 [h] Ps 91:6 [i] Lev 26:22 [j] Am 5:18-19
32:25 [k] Eze 7:15 [l] 2Ch 36:17; La 2:21
32:26 [m] Dt 4:27 [n] Ps 34:16
32:27 [o] Isa 10:13
32:29 [p] Dt 5:29; Ps 81:13
32:30 [q] Lev 26:8 [r] Ps 44:12

32:19–27 God speaks in the first person, revealing his plan to judge his people, make them jealous, and afflict them with a virtual avalanche of curses. He decides not to destroy them in order to stop the boasting of Israel's enemies.

32:21 Used in Rom 10:19 to explain Israel's rejection and the inclusion of the Gentiles. Israel provoked God's jealousy with idolatry, and God makes them jealous by including the Gentiles in the divine plan (cf. Rom 11:11,14).

32:23–25 The curses (cf. 28:15–68).

32:27 lest the adversary misunderstand. God's reputation is at stake, and concern for his reputation is the decisive reason for his intervention to save Israel (cf. 9:28; Exod 32:12–13).

32:29 wise. The essence of wisdom is being able to see the connection between choices and consequences.

32:33 [s]Ps 58:4
32:34 [t]Jer 2:22; Hos 13:12
32:35 [u]Ro 12:19*; Heb 10:30* [v]Jer 23:12 [w]Eze 7:8-9
32:36 [x]Dt 30:1-3; Ps 135:14; Joel 2:14
32:37 [y]Jdg 10:14; Jer 2:28
32:39 [z]Isa 41:4 [a]Isa 45:5 [b]1Sa 2:6; Ps 68:20 [c]Hos 6:1 [d]Ps 50:22
32:41 [e]Isa 34:6; 66:16; Eze 21:9-10 [f]Jer 50:29
32:42 [g]ver 23 [h]Jer 46:10,14
32:43 [i]Ro 15:10* [j]2Ki 9:7 [k]Ps 65:3; 85:1; Rev 19:2
32:44 [l]Nu 13:8,16

33 Their wine is the venom of serpents,
the deadly poison of cobras.[s]

34 "Have I not kept this in reserve
and sealed it in my vaults?[t]
35 It is mine to avenge; I will repay.[u]
In due time their foot will slip;[v]
their day of disaster is near
and their doom rushes upon them.[w]"

36 The LORD will vindicate his people
and relent concerning his servants[x]
when he sees their strength is gone
and no one is left, slave or free.[a]
37 He will say: "Now where are their gods,
the rock they took refuge in,[y]
38 the gods who ate the fat of their sacrifices
and drank the wine of their drink offerings?
Let them rise up to help you!
Let them give you shelter!

39 "See now that I myself am he![z]
There is no god besides me.[a]
I put to death and I bring to life,[b]
I have wounded and I will heal,[c]
and no one can deliver out of my hand.[d]
40 I lift my hand to heaven and solemnly swear:
As surely as I live forever,
41 when I sharpen my flashing sword[e]
and my hand grasps it in judgment,
I will take vengeance on my adversaries
and repay those who hate me.[f]
42 I will make my arrows drunk with blood,[g]
while my sword devours flesh:[h]
the blood of the slain and the captives,
the heads of the enemy leaders."

43 Rejoice,[i] you nations, with his people,[b,c]
for he will avenge the blood of his servants;[j]
he will take vengeance on his enemies
and make atonement for his land and people.[k]

44 Moses came with Joshua[d][l] son of Nun and spoke all the words of this song in the hearing of the
people. 45 When Moses finished reciting all these words to all Israel, 46 he said to them, "Take to heart all

[a] 36 Or *and they are without a ruler or leader* [b] 43 Or *Make his people rejoice, you nations*
[c] 43 Masoretic Text; Dead Sea Scrolls (see also Septuagint) *people, / and let all the angels worship him, /*
[d] 44 Hebrew *Hoshea*, a variant of *Joshua*

32:35–36 It is mine to avenge; I will repay ... The LORD will vindicate his people. God's judgment is final and inevitable. Paul quotes v. 35a in Rom 12:19 to show that only God has the right to judge finally; Heb 10:30 quotes this verse as a warning against rejecting the Son of God.

32:39 At the end of the song, the focus dramatically shifts to the Lord's transcendent power. Hannah (1 Sam 2:6) and Isaiah (Isa 45:5) later use similar language. God uses this unique power to save his people and judge their enemies. Someday he will even resurrect his people from death (cf. Hos 6:1–2).

32:43 Moses urges the nations to rejoice because their salvation is bound up with Israel's (Gen 12:3). The song ends with the theme of atonement (cf. 21:8). God's judgment also effects atonement, removing the guilt and sin from the land and people.

32:44–47 Moses, joined by Joshua, commands the people to keep the words of the law because they are life itself.

the words I have solemnly declared to you this day,[m] so that you may command your children to obey
carefully all the words of this law. [47]They are not just idle words for you — they are your life.[n] By them
you will live long in the land you are crossing the Jordan to possess."

Moses to Die on Mount Nebo

[48]On that same day the LORD told Moses, [49]"Go up into the Abarim[o] Range to Mount Nebo in Moab,
across from Jericho, and view Canaan, the land I am giving the Israelites as their own possession.
[50]There on the mountain that you have climbed you will die[p] and be gathered to your people, just as
your brother Aaron died on Mount Hor and was gathered to his people. [51]This is because both of you
broke faith with me in the presence of the Israelites at the waters of Meribah Kadesh in the Desert of
Zin[q] and because you did not uphold my holiness among the Israelites.[r] [52]Therefore, you will see the
land only from a distance;[s] you will not enter[t] the land I am giving to the people of Israel."

Moses Blesses the Tribes

33:1-29Ref — Ge 49:1-28

33 This is the blessing that Moses the man of God[u] pronounced on the Israelites before his death.
[2]He said:

"The LORD came from Sinai[v]
and dawned over them from Seir;[w]
he shone forth from Mount Paran.[x]
He came with[*a*] myriads of holy ones[y]
from the south, from his mountain slopes.[*b*]
[3]Surely it is you who love[z] the people;
all the holy ones are in your hand.[a]
At your feet they all bow down,[b]
and from you receive instruction,
[4]the law that Moses gave us,[c]
the possession of the assembly of Jacob.[d]
[5]He was king over Jeshurun[*c*]
when the leaders of the people assembled,
along with the tribes of Israel.

[6]"Let Reuben live and not die,
nor[*d*] his people be few."

[*a*] 2 Or *from* [*b*] 2 The meaning of the Hebrew for this phrase is uncertain. [*c*] 5 *Jeshurun* means *the upright one,* that is, Israel; also in verse 26. [*d*] 6 Or *but let*

32:46 [m]Eze 40:4
32:47 [n]Dt 30:20
32:49 [o]Nu 27:12
32:50 [p]Ge 25:8
32:51 [q]Nu 20:11-13 [r]Nu 27:14
32:52 [s]Dt 34:1-3 [t]Dt 1:37
33:1 [u]Jos 14:6
33:2 [v]Ex 19:18; Ps 68:8 [w]Jdg 5:4 [x]Hab 3:3 [y]Da 7:10; Ac 7:53; Rev 5:11
33:3 [z]Hos 11:1 [a]Dt 14:2 [b]Lk 10:39
33:4 [c]Jn 1:17 [d]Ps 119:111

32:48–52 *Moses to Die on Mount Nebo.* These verses explain why Moses will not enter the promised land.
32:51 Earlier Moses said that he was barred from the land because of the Israelite's sins (1:37; 3:26; 31:2). This verse is not a contradiction since the people's stubbornness contributed to Moses' public anger that dishonored God (Num 20:11).
33:1—34:12 *Benediction and Burial.* Moses pronounces a blessing on the tribes and then prepares for his death and burial.
33:1–29 *Moses Blesses the Tribes.* The sixth major section of Deuteronomy begins with Moses pronouncing a last blessing on the tribes of Israel just as Jacob had done before him (Gen 49). It is a fitting word of grace and blessing, the words of a dying "father" to his children. It is something like a last will and testament. The blessing ends with a promise that Israel will tread on its enemies (v. 29), perhaps alluding to the defeat of the ultimate enemy of humanity in Genesis (Gen 3:15). Despite the predicted long history of disobedience, the song of Moses concluded with God making atonement for the people and the land (32:43). Thus, blessing is a natural segue. This pattern of judgment followed by blessing continues a trajectory throughout the history of Israel, culminating in the resurrection of Christ, which follows the curse of his death to bring about atonement for the entire world.
33:1 man of God. The first use of this prophetic title to describe Moses the great prophet as he pronounces a benediction upon the people before his death.
33:2–3 The Lord's coming is depicted as a march through the wilderness from Sinai (the only time Deuteronomy calls Sinai/Horeb "Sinai") to Canaan. His fiery Sinaitic glory accompanied him. The use of "Seir" and "Paran" probably suggests a march to Canaan from Sinai through Edom (Seir) to the southern boundary of the promised land (Paran). See Judg 5:4–5; Hab 3:3.
33:4–5 God's rule is where God's law is proclaimed, suggesting that God, not Moses or others, "was king over Jeshurun" (v. 5). His kingship triumphs over Jeshurun's having grown "fat" (32:15).
33:6–25 The actual words of blessing are now pronounced over tribes and not sons (cf. Gen 49). Genesis ends with Jacob, the father of the nation of Israel, blessing his sons before he died. Now Moses does the same for the tribes of Israel at the end of Deuteronomy. The order of these two lists is slightly different. Jacob blessed all the sons of his first

33:7 [e] Ge 49:10
33:8 [f] Ex 28:30 [g] Ex 17:7
33:9 [h] Ex 32:26-29 [i] Mal 2:5
33:10 [j] Lev 10:11; Dt 31:9-13 [k] Ps 51:19
33:11 [l] 2Sa 24:23
33:12 [m] Dt 12:10 [n] Ex 28:12
33:13 [o] Ge 49:25 [p] Ge 27:28
33:15 [q] Hab 3:6

7 And this he said about Judah:[e]

"Hear, LORD, the cry of Judah;
  bring him to his people.
With his own hands he defends his cause.
  Oh, be his help against his foes!"

8 About Levi he said:

"Your Thummim and Urim[f] belong
  to your faithful servant.
You tested him at Massah;
  you contended with him at the waters of Meribah.[g]
9 He said of his father and mother,[h]
  'I have no regard for them.'
He did not recognize his brothers
  or acknowledge his own children,
but he watched over your word
  and guarded your covenant.[i]
10 He teaches your precepts to Jacob
  and your law to Israel.[j]
He offers incense before you
  and whole burnt offerings on your altar.[k]
11 Bless all his skills, LORD,
  and be pleased with the work of his hands.[l]
Strike down those who rise against him,
  his foes till they rise no more."

12 About Benjamin he said:

"Let the beloved of the LORD rest secure in him,[m]
  for he shields him all day long,
  and the one the LORD loves rests between his
    shoulders.[n]"

13 About Joseph[o] he said:

"May the LORD bless his land
  with the precious dew from heaven above
  and with the deep waters that lie below;[p]
14 with the best the sun brings forth
  and the finest the moon can yield;
15 with the choicest gifts of the ancient mountains[q]
  and the fruitfulness of the everlasting hills;

wife, Leah, at the beginning of his speech and the sons of his second wife, Rachel, at the end. Moses' blessing places the tribes of Rachel in the middle of those of Leah and omits the tribe of Simeon.

33:6 Reuben is still at the head of the tribes as firstborn, but there is an awareness that his numbers have been waning.

33:7 Judah has been moved up dramatically in this blessing (cf. Gen 49:8–12) into second place and is seen to be in a fight that requires divine help. The Messianic significance of Judah's blessing in Genesis is probably assumed here. Judah will encounter a serious challenge before attaining eventual supremacy. The anticipated Messianic ruler will come through Judah (cf. Gen 49:10, Ruth 4:18–22, Matt 1:1–16).

33:8 A dramatic reversal has taken place in Levi's fortunes (cf. Gen 49:5–7). Levi channeled its aggression in a godly direction. The blessings of Levi and Joseph constitute the longest blessings invoked upon the tribes. Levi's faithfulness in providing guidance through appointed means (Urim and Thummim) is noted first of all.

33:9 Placing God above family ties refers to the incident of the golden calf (Exod 32:27–29), when the Levites did not spare their own families. Consequently, the Levites were appointed the teachers of the word of God and the administrators of the sacrificial rites.

33:13–17 Joseph is blessed with incredible fertility by "him who dwelt in the burning bush." God first spoke to Moses out of the desert bush (Exod 3:1–6) to reveal his name and glory. The Hebrew term for "dwelt" can also mean "settle temporarily" and is used for God dwelling among his people (cf. Exod 24:16; 29:45). From such humble beginnings come great blessings. Some of these blessings closely echo Gen 49:26. See notes on Gen 49:22–26.

[16]with the best gifts of the earth and its fullness
and the favor of him who dwelt in the burning bush.[r]
Let all these rest on the head of Joseph,
on the brow of the prince among[a] his brothers.
[17]In majesty he is like a firstborn bull;
his horns are the horns of a wild ox.[s]
With them he will gore[t] the nations,
even those at the ends of the earth.
Such are the ten thousands of Ephraim;
such are the thousands of Manasseh."

[18]About Zebulun[u] he said:

"Rejoice, Zebulun, in your going out,
and you, Issachar, in your tents.
[19]They will summon peoples to the mountain[v]
and there offer the sacrifices of the righteous;[w]
they will feast on the abundance of the seas,[x]
on the treasures hidden in the sand."

[20]About Gad[y] he said:

"Blessed is he who enlarges Gad's domain!
Gad lives there like a lion,
tearing at arm or head.
[21]He chose the best land for himself;[z]
the leader's portion was kept for him.
When the heads of the people assembled,
he carried out the LORD's righteous will,[a]
and his judgments concerning Israel."

[22]About Dan[b] he said:

"Dan is a lion's cub,
springing out of Bashan."

[23]About Naphtali he said:

"Naphtali is abounding with the favor of the LORD
and is full of his blessing;
he will inherit southward to the lake."

[24]About Asher[c] he said:

"Most blessed of sons is Asher;
let him be favored by his brothers,
and let him bathe his feet in oil.[d]
[25]The bolts of your gates will be iron and bronze,
and your strength will equal your days.[e]

[26]"There is no one like the God of Jeshurun,[f]
who rides across the heavens to help you[g]
and on the clouds in his majesty.

33:16 [r]Ex 3:2
33:17 [s]Nu 23:22 [t]1Ki 22:11; Ps 44:5
33:18 [u]Ge 49:13-15
33:19 [v]Ex 15:17; Isa 2:3 [w]Ps 4:5 [x]Isa 60:5,11
33:20 [y]Ge 49:19
33:21 [z]Nu 32:1-5,31-32 [a]Jos 4:12; 22:1-3
33:22 [b]Ge 49:16
33:24 [c]Ge 49:21 [d]Ge 49:20; Job 29:6
33:25 [e]Dt 4:40; 32:47
33:26 [f]Ex 15:11 [g]Ps 104:3

[a] 16 Or *of the one separated from*

33:16 the prince among his brothers. Kingship is associated with the tribe of Joseph in Genesis. Joseph dreams that his brothers will bow down to him, and his dream comes true (Gen 37:9–10; 42:6–9).
33:26–33 This addresses God and his people as incomparable. There is no God like the God of Jeshurun, who provides transcendent help, and thus there is no people like Israel, who will tread on the "heights" of their enemies, perhaps referring to their final triumph over their adversaries.

33:27 [h]Ps 90:1 [i]Jos 24:18 [j]Dt 7:2
33:28 [k]Nu 23:9; Jer 23:6 [l]Ge 27:28
33:29 [m]Ps 144:15 [n]Ps 18:44 [o]2Sa 7:23 [p]Ps 115:9-11 [q]Dt 32:13
34:1 [r]Dt 32:49 [s]Dt 32:52
34:2 [t]Dt 11:24
34:3 [u]Jdg 1:16; 3:13; 2Ch 28:15
34:4 [v]Ge 28:13 [w]Ge 12:7 [x]Dt 3:27
34:5 [y]Nu 12:7 [z]Dt 32:50; Jos 1:1-2
34:6 [a]Dt 3:29 [b]Jude 1:9
34:7 [c]Dt 31:2 [d]Ge 27:1
34:8 [e]Ge 50:3,10; 2Sa 11:27
34:9 [f]Ge 41:38; Isa 11:2; Da 6:3 [g]Nu 27:18,23
34:10 [h]Dt 18:15,18 [i]Ex 33:11; Nu 12:6,8; Dt 5:4
34:11 [j]Dt 4:34 [k]Dt 7:19

27 The eternal God is your refuge,[h]
and underneath are the everlasting arms.
He will drive out your enemies before you,[i]
saying, 'Destroy them!'[j]
28 So Israel will live in safety;[k]
Jacob will dwell[a] secure
in a land of grain and new wine,
where the heavens drop dew.[l]
29 Blessed are you, Israel![m]
Who is like you,[n]
a people saved by the LORD?[o]
He is your shield and helper[p]
and your glorious sword.
Your enemies will cower before you,
and you will tread on their heights.[q]"

The Death of Moses

34 Then Moses climbed Mount Nebo from the plains of Moab to the top of Pisgah, across from
Jericho.[r] There the LORD showed[s] him the whole land—from Gilead to Dan, 2 all of Naphtali,
the territory of Ephraim and Manasseh, all the land of Judah as far as the Mediterranean Sea,[t] 3 the
Negev and the whole region from the Valley of Jericho, the City of Palms,[u] as far as Zoar. 4 Then the
LORD said to him, "This is the land I promised on oath[v] to Abraham, Isaac and Jacob when I said, 'I will
give it[w] to your descendants.' I have let you see it with your eyes, but you will not cross[x] over into it."
5 And Moses the servant of the LORD[y] died[z] there in Moab, as the LORD had said. 6 He buried him[b] in
Moab, in the valley opposite Beth Peor,[a] but to this day no one knows where his grave is.[b] 7 Moses was
a hundred and twenty years old[c] when he died, yet his eyes were not weak[d] nor his strength gone. 8 The
Israelites grieved for Moses in the plains of Moab thirty days, until the time of weeping and mourning[e]
was over.
9 Now Joshua son of Nun was filled with the spirit[c] of wisdom[f] because Moses had laid his hands on
him.[g] So the Israelites listened to him and did what the LORD had commanded Moses.
10 Since then, no prophet has risen in Israel like Moses,[h] whom the LORD knew face to face,[i] 11 who
did all those signs and wonders[j] the LORD sent him to do in Egypt—to Pharaoh and to all his officials[k]
and to his whole land. 12 For no one has ever shown the mighty power or performed the awesome deeds
that Moses did in the sight of all Israel.

[a] *28* Septuagint; Hebrew *Jacob's spring is* [b] *6* Or *He was buried* [c] *9* Or *Spirit*

34:1–12 *The Death of Moses.* After pronouncing his final blessing, Moses climbs Mount Nebo, where he receives a panoramic vision of the land before he dies.
34:4 the land I promised on oath. Links with God's initial promise to Abraham when he first set foot in the land (Gen 12:7).
34:5 the servant of the LORD. This is the first time the Bible calls someone by this title (though cf. Gen 26:24), but it is not the last. This title starts a trajectory that comes to expression in another servant who makes atonement for his people through death (Isa 42:1–4; 52:13—53:12, cf. John 13:1–17; Phil 2:6–11).
34:6 to this day no one knows. Reflects a much later time.
34:7 a hundred and twenty years old. An extremely old age. Joseph died at 110 (Gen 50:26). **his eyes were not weak nor his strength gone.** Moses was still healthy, indicating that his death was due to God's judgment.
34:8 grieved for Moses. One of Israel's last acts on the eastern side of the Jordan. **thirty days.** The time allotted to mourn for a distinguished figure (cf. Num 20:29).
34:9 Joshua is now the leader of Israel because Moses has transferred the divine authority to him. The new leader is thus filled with a spirit of wisdom to lead and guide the people.
34:10–12 The author of this section has looked back on Israel's history and has seen many prophets come and go, but none has matched Moses' prophetic power. Thus, this description of Moses' unequalled authority that closes Deuteronomy suggests the importance of the first five books of the OT within the canon of Scripture. But at the same time, there is a prophetic expectancy. There is the hope that someday a new Moses will appear (18:15); he will be accompanied by many signs and wonders and bring about liberation not just for one nation but for the entire world. The rest of the OT keeps such a hope alive (Mal 4:5–6). No prophet in the OT was superior to Moses. Finally Jesus came and fulfilled this prophecy. He radiated the face of God in a way that transcended Moses (Acts 3:22–26; 7:37; Heb 1:3; 3:1–6). Through great signs and wonders, he was able to accomplish a new and greater exodus for his people from the slavery of sin.

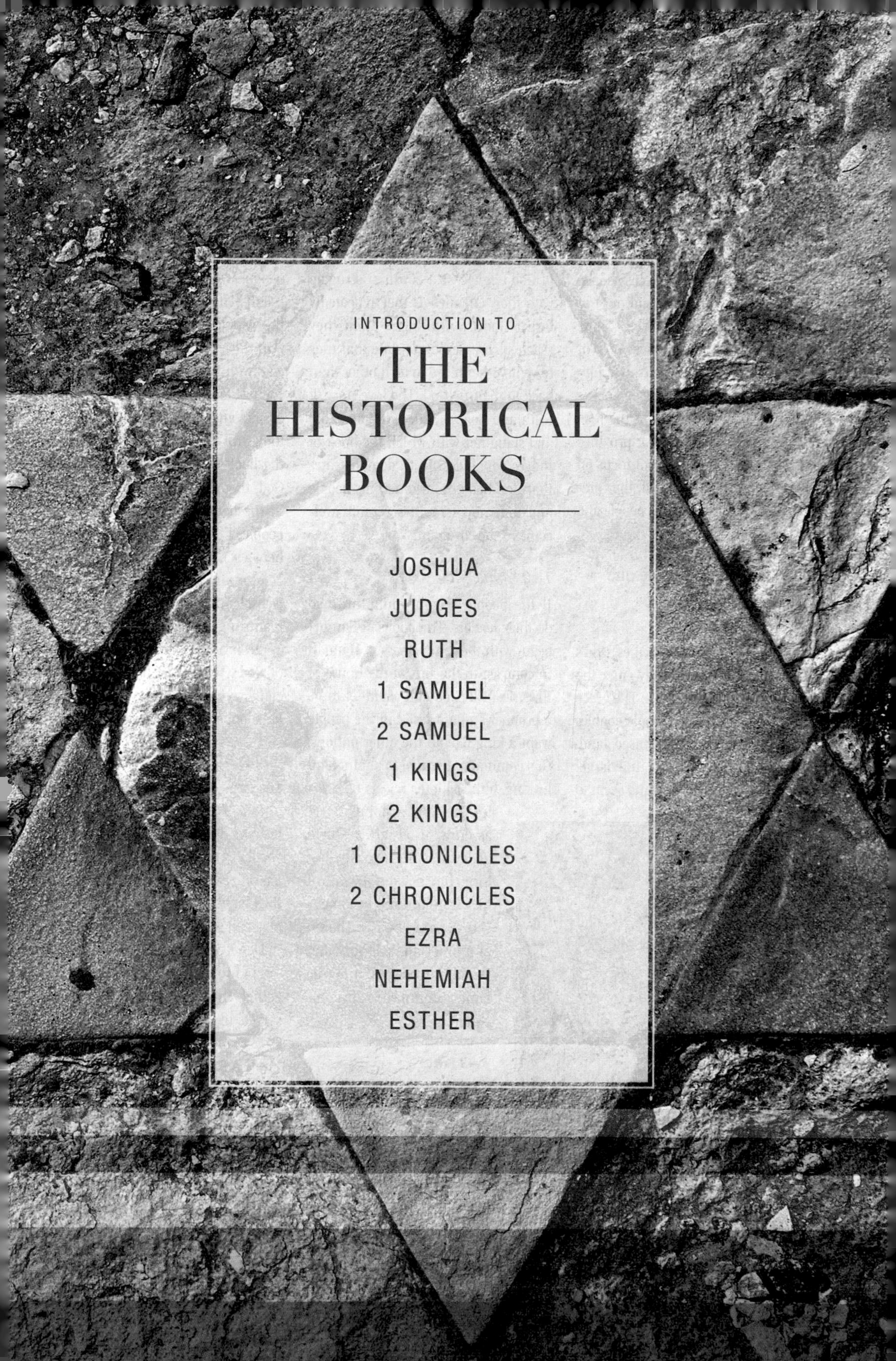

INTRODUCTION TO

THE HISTORICAL BOOKS

JOSHUA

JUDGES

RUTH

1 SAMUEL

2 SAMUEL

1 KINGS

2 KINGS

1 CHRONICLES

2 CHRONICLES

EZRA

NEHEMIAH

ESTHER

THE HISTORICAL BOOKS

Richard S. Hess

The Historical Books (Joshua–Esther) describe God's work among his people. They enable us to understand most of the OT's chronological order. These books outline the major events of Israel's history from its entrance into the land of Canaan until the end of the monarchy and the return of the Jews and rebuilding of the Jewish province in Israel. These books do not focus on a collection of facts. Instead, they present God's dealings with his people and their leaders.

The Story of God's Grace and Human Response

Joshua, Judges, Ruth

The book of Joshua describes God's gift of land to Israel as they enter the land of Canaan to possess it. The grace God pours out upon his people enables great victories in the promised land. The covenantal promises that Israel gives God at the end of Joshua seem to disappear in Judges. There the people of God engage in a constant struggle with their enemies as they repeatedly forget God's faithfulness. Then they reach such a desperate state that they have no other place to turn other than back to the true God. The love story of Ruth and Boaz balances the brutality and slaughter with which the book of Judges concludes. Ruth demonstrates that God has not forgotten his people and that non-Israelites remain welcome in the covenant.

1–2 Samuel

If the people become unfaithful, so do their leaders. The books of Samuel begin with the faithfulness of Hannah in contrast to the sins of the house of the priest Eli. God calls Samuel to be a prophet and a priest, but the people want a king like all the other nations. God commands Samuel to anoint Saul as king, but God later rejects unfaithful Saul and appoints David as king. God gives David an everlasting dynasty, but King David cannot control his desire for another man's wife (2 Sam 11–12). The sin of murder and adultery that David introduces into his family continues to affect his children.

Illuminated manuscript depicts scenes from the story of Ruth. On the top, Ruth meets Boaz as she gleans (Ruth 2:4–16). On the bottom, Ruth sleeps at Boaz's feet (Ruth 3:7).
Wikimedia Commons

1–2 Kings, 1–2 Chronicles, Ezra, Nehemiah, Esther

1–2 Kings display further examples of God's faithfulness among his people, preserving them in the midst of threats to destroy them. Nevertheless, the kings and the people depart from God's teaching and serve other gods and goddesses. In the end God allows foreign nations to conquer the kingdoms of Israel and Judah. These foreign nations deport the people, but the promise of the faithful God to preserve his people goes with them into exile. There God's compassion preserves the Jewish people despite attempts by powerful enemies to destroy them. This is illustrated in the book of Esther, a story in which God, though not mentioned by name in the book, works salvation for his people. Ezra and Nehemiah describe how a scribe and a governor lead the community of exiles who return to Jerusalem. They rebuild the walls and reaffirm the covenant God gave them. 1–2 Chronicles survey the great story of God's work with his people, especially with the people of the southern kingdom of Judah.

Books of History

The term "Historical Books" invites us to ask, "What are the books? What is history?" In ancient Israel each of these "books" would actually have been written on a scroll. These books appear in the Christian OT in the general chronological order of their content: Joshua, Judges, Ruth, 1–2 Samuel, 1–2 Kings, 1–2 Chronicles, Ezra, Nehemiah, and Esther. In the Hebrew Bible (as preserved in Judaism), Joshua, Judges, 1–2 Samuel, and 1–2 Kings constitute the Former Prophets. This section immediately follows the Torah (Genesis–Deuteronomy), as in Christian Bibles, and precedes Isaiah and the other prophetic books that constitute the Latter Prophets. The remaining historical books appear in the final section of the Hebrew Bible, called the Writings, with 1–2 Chronicles closing the Jewish Bible.

Although many books contain historic materials, the Historical

Relief (ca. 730–727 BC) of Tiglath-Pilesar III attacking a city. Tiglath-Pilesar III was one of the foreign kings God allowed to conquer the kings of Israel and Judah. These foreign nations deport God's people, but the promise of their faithful God to preserve them goes with them into exile.
Werner Forman Archive/Heritage Images/Glow Images

Books focus on history by presenting it in narrative form. In conveying the story of God's acts, they also use poetry (Judg 5), prophecy (2 Kgs 19), building descriptions (1 Kgs 6–8), prayers (1 Kgs 8; Neh 9), royal decrees (Ezra 6:3–12), boundary descriptions (Josh 13–19), covenants (Josh 24), and genealogies (1 Chr 1–9). Most often, however, they tell stories that describe God at work among his people. The form of language used to convey great examples of God's direct involvement to deliver his people (Josh 10; 2 Kgs 18–20; 2 Chr 20) is not different from that used to record history without the extraordinary miraculous intervention of God (Ruth; Ezra; Nehemiah). The two types of accounts flow together as different ways in which the same God works with his people to bring about his purposes. Nor does the narrative show privilege to those of high social status. Humble foreigners such as Rahab the Canaanite (Josh 2), Ruth the Moabite (Ruth 1), and the woman of Sidon (1 Kgs 17) play crucial roles in the salvation of Israel. They appear alongside the line of its divinely chosen kings as well as priestly and prophetic leaders.

Historical writing is always selective. For this reason, we may read two well-written histories that are both factually accurate, yet they portray the same events from different perspectives. One example of this can be found in the accounts of the invasion of Judah by the Assyrian king Sennacherib when Hezekiah was king in Jerusalem. Much of the same information in 2 Kgs 18–19 (see the parallel account in Isa 36–37) is repeated in 2 Chr 32. However, 2 Kgs 18:13–16 begins the story by making clear that Hezekiah paid tribute to Sennacherib, while 2 Chr 32:22–23 concludes the story with many people bringing offerings to God in Jerusalem and giving honor to Hezekiah because the Lord delivered his people. While 2 Kings emphasizes Hezekiah's innocence by recording that Hezekiah gave Sennacherib what he demanded, 2 Chronicles focuses on how much God did and how the people responded to God with worship. Much of the account in 2 Kings concerns the prophet Isaiah's involvement, while only one verse in 2 Chronicles (2 Chr 32:20) mentions Isaiah. The two accounts both present history, but they provide different theological emphases and concerns. Both emphasize how Hezekiah trusted in God and how God miraculously defeated Sennacherib's army.

A second example in this same context mentions how Sennacherib's own sons killed him while he was worshiping in the temple of his god (2 Kgs 19:36–37; 2 Chr 32:21). As Assyrian records show, this murder occurred 20 years after Sennacherib invaded Judah. The Bible does not indicate this length of time because it is not important to its purpose. Instead, it demonstrates the disgraceful end of the king who mocked God's ability to defend his people. Given its selective nature, accounts of history should be read with special attention to the author's purpose. In the historical books of the Bible, the focus remains on God's relationship with his people and the outworking of his covenants with them.

Covenant Themes

God established covenants with Abraham, with the people of Israel, and with David. Each of these covenants defines aspects of how God will act in Israel's history in accordance with Israel's beliefs and behavior. The Historical Books maintain a special concern for the events in Israel in light of the covenants and God's work through them.

Prisoners kneel before King Sennacherib at the siege of Lachish. 2 Kings and 2 Chronicles both give accounts of Sennacherib's invasion of Judah.

The Covenant With Abraham

God promised Abraham (1) a great nation, (2) a land, and (3) a means by which Abraham and his descendants would bless all peoples of the earth (Gen 12:1 – 3,7). By the time we encounter Israel in the book of Joshua, the people are becoming a great nation. This first book among the Historical Books establishes how Israel acquires some of the land. The possession of the promised land remains precarious in Judges, which describes many warring peoples seeking to destroy Israel (and ultimately the nation turns against itself in the civil war of Judg 19 – 21). This uncertainty continues in 1 Samuel as the Philistines threaten to remove the tribes from their land. However, the wars of David (2 Sam 5 – 10) establish the city of Jerusalem and the capital of a nation that stretches to the limits of that which God had promised to Abraham (Gen 15:18 – 21) Nevertheless, the faithlessness of the people of Israel prevents them from enjoying this prosperity for more than a generation. When Solomon dies, his son Rehoboam makes unwise choices that divide the kingdom and plunge much of it into the worship of other gods (1 Kgs 12 – 13). The varying fortunes of the northern kingdom of Israel and the southern kingdom of Judah exhibit the differences in attitude the Israelite people and their kings have toward their God. The destruction of the northern and southern kingdoms and the subsequent deportations of their inhabitants might suggest that God has forgotten his promise to Abraham. Instead, the promise of the return (already found in 2 Chr 36:20 – 23) comes to pass as the books of Ezra and Nehemiah demonstrate the faithfulness of God to increase Abraham's descendants and secure them in the land.

The third part of the promise to Abraham is that God will bless other nations through Abraham's descendants. The first miracle of the Historical Books occurs when God stops the Jordan River and Israel marches across on dry ground (Josh 3 – 4). God did this "so that all the peoples of the earth might know that the hand of the LORD is powerful" (Josh 4:24). This and the subsequent acts of God signify that the God of Israel is the true God; he alone is able to perform miracles. These actions bring many non-Israelite people into God's kingdom: Rahab (Josh 2; 6), the Gibeonites (Josh 9), Ruth (Ruth 1 – 4), the queen of Sheba (1 Kgs 10; 2 Chr 9), Naaman (2 Kgs 5). Even King Cyrus (2 Chr 36:23; Ezra 1:2) recognizes the greatness of Israel's God.

When Solomon dedicates the temple (1 Kgs 8), he describes how God's people may look to the temple and their God and pray to find salvation and relief in various circumstances of need and distress. His prayer turns to consider those outside the family of Israel (1 Kgs 8:41 – 43): Solomon asks God to "do whatever the foreigner asks" (1 Kgs 8:43b) if the foreigner comes and prays toward the temple. The foreigner need not be part of the people of God. Solomon specifies the purpose of his request to God: "so that all the peoples of the earth may know your name and fear you, as do your own people Israel" (1 Kgs 8:43c). Solomon requests that God might bless the peoples of the world, just as God promised Abraham, so that they might come to know God.

The Covenant on Mount Sinai

God's covenant with the nation of Israel provides a key to understanding major themes in the historical books. The covenant emphasizes the importance of worshiping God alone (Exod 20:3 – 6,22 – 23; Deut 4 – 13). Along with many specific laws, God also promises blessings for obedience and curses for disobedience (Deut 28). After details about suffering and barrenness, the curses conclude with God's warning that he will scatter Israel among the nations if they worship other gods (Deut 28:64 – 68).

God's promise of the land, and his warnings of expulsion from it, overshadow the major events of many of the historical books. God partially fulfills his promise of the land when Joshua acquires it. The difficulties of the following generations arise from their worshiping other gods and refusing to worship the true God (Judg 2:10 – 15). Contrast this with Ruth's confession (Ruth 1:16 – 17). The wickedness of the sons of Eli lead to the Philistine victory and the loss of the ark (1 Sam 2:12 — 4:18). Saul faces defeat at the hands of the Philistines as well. God's expanding the borders of Israel signifies his blessing of David and Solomon (2 Sam 6–10; 1 Kgs 3). Nevertheless, Solomon abandons the exclusive worship of God (1 Kgs 11:4,9), which leads to the kingdom's division.

In the northern kingdom of Israel, every ruler turned away from God and led their people in the worship of images and other deities. In 1–2 Kings, God sent many prophets, notably Elijah and his successor Elisha, to warn the people and their leaders (1 Kgs 18:1—2 Kgs 9:13; 2 Kgs 13:14–21). The people did not turn back to God. Because they refused to worship God alone, they were deported by the Assyrians (2 Kgs 17:1–23), who then resettled the northern kingdom with people from nations who practiced various forms of false worship (2 Kgs 17:24–41). Unlike the author of Kings, the writer of Chronicles ignores most of the events that took place in the northern kingdom, focusing instead on the southern kingdom of Judah as the place of hope for restoration.

The people of the southern kingdom were also inclined to serve other gods and goddesses. However, the rise of several good kings, such as Jehoshaphat, Hezekiah, and Josiah, reignited faith in the one true God of Israel. The books of Kings and Chronicles relate how the people celebrated the Passover in the time of Josiah (2 Kgs 23:21–23; 2 Chr 35:1–19), while 2 Chr 30 records the celebration of Passover nearly a century earlier in the time of Hezekiah. These historical books relate the building of the temple and its role in the worship of the people. 1 Kgs 6–9 summarizes the details of the building of the temple as part of the larger picture of the administration and reign of King Solomon. For 1–2 Chronicles, however, it is the centerpiece of the entire account. The temple dominates the legacy David leaves his son, from the details of its construction and personnel to its dedication by Solomon (1 Chr 22—2 Chr 8). Subsequently the temple appears in Chronicles nearly 90 times as a focus for the reforms by the good kings. The temple thus symbolizes God's presence among his people and their worship of him.

Both 2 Kgs 25:1–21 and 2 Chr 36:15–21 describe the Babylonian attack and destruction of Jerusalem and its temple as well as the deportation of much of the Jewish population. 2 Kgs 22:15–20 already explained this as God's judgment for their worship of other gods, a judgment that was postponed but could not be prevented. 2 Chr 36 reiterates that the loss of the land came because the people broke their covenant with God and worshiped other gods.

The final verses of both 2 Kings and 2 Chronicles indicate that this was not the end of the story. A Davidic king remained, although captive (2 Kgs 25:27–30); and a new Persian king, Cyrus, released the people to return and rebuild their land and temple (2 Chr 36:22–23; Ezra 1:1). Both themes continue in Ezra and Nehemiah, with special concern given to the need for Israel to confirm its role as God's people secure in the land he had given them and with emphasis on worshiping God alone.

These books outline the major events of Israel's history from its entrance into the land of Canaan until the end of the monarchy and the return of the Jews and rebuilding of the Jewish province in Israel.

The Covenant With David

2 Sam 7 describes the creation of the perpetual kingship of David and his descendants. Although the dynasties of Saul (1 Sam 9:15–17) and Jeroboam I (1 Kgs 11:34–39) might have known similar blessings, God rejected both due to the disobedience of the kings (1 Sam 13:13–14; 1 Kgs 14:7–11). God's promise to David alone remained and endured through the reign of his son Solomon and his descendants for the duration of the southern kingdom of Judah. However, God promised to punish those successors of David who sinned (2 Sam 7:14). Thus Solomon's sins in worshiping the gods and goddesses of the surrounding nations led to the removal of most of the kingdom from the rule of Solomon's son Rehoboam; there remained only the tribal area of Judah and Benjamin. Nevertheless, God promised that an heir would rule in Jerusalem as a "lamp" (1 Kgs 11:36). God repeated his promise several times in the history of the kings of Judah, especially during the reigns of those who sinned against God, such as Abijah (1 Kgs 15:4) and Jehoram (2 Kgs 8:19; 2 Chr 21:7). Even faithful rulers, such as Jehoshaphat (2 Chr 20), Hezekiah (2 Kgs 18:1—19:37; 2 Chr 32:1–23), and Josiah (2 Kgs 22:1—23:30; 2 Chr 34–35), committed sins before God (Jehoshaphat: 2 Chr 20:35–37; Hezekiah: 2 Kgs 20:12–19; 2 Chr 32:25–31; Josiah: 2 Chr 35:20–24). Among the worst of the kings of Judah was Manasseh. Despite his repentance later in his life (2 Chr 33:10–16), Manasseh's sins were so great that Josiah's later reforms could only postpone the judgment (2 Kgs 23:26; 24:3) that included the destruction of Jerusalem and Judah, and an end to the independent reign of the Davidic kings.

Despite the sin and punishment, 1–2 Kings ends on a hopeful note: the line of David, in the person of Jehoiachin, the last surviving king of Judah, remained alive in exile, and Jehoiachin ate from the table of the king of Babylon (2 Kgs 25:27–30). If Shenazzar (1 Chr 3:18), a descendant of Jehoiachin, is the Sheshbazzar of Ezra (Ezra 1:8,11; 5:14,16) who served as governor after the return from exile and who laid the foundations of the new temple in Jerusalem, then the line of David continued among the leadership that returned. We know that Zerubbabel, another descendant of Jehoiachin (1 Chr 3:19), also served as governor during the early period of rebuilding the temple in Jerusalem (Ezra 2:2; 3:2,8; 4:2–3; 5:2; Neh 7:7; 12:1,47). It is through this line that both Matthew (Matt 1:12–16) and Luke (Luke 3:23–27) trace David's greatest descendant: Jesus, who comes as the fulfillment of God's covenant with David.

The tree of Jesse from a thirteenth-century psalter. Jesus comes as the fulfillment of God's covenant with David.

Ms 21926 The Tree of Jesse from a psalter, English School, (13th century)/British Library, London, UK/Bridgeman Images

Chronology/Dating

For OT chronology, see Introduction to the Old Testament, p. 7. ■

INTRODUCTION TO
JOSHUA

TITLE

The name Joshua refers to the chief human character in the book. He leads the Israelites from the time of Moses' death until they enter and allot the promised land. Joshua's name in Greek is Jesus. It means "The LORD saves."

AUTHOR AND DATE

The author of the book is not identified; however, 24:26 attributes at least part of the book to Joshua himself. The date of the book is not clearly stated. Some scholars date the work very late, arguing that it serves the interests of Josiah (641/40 – 609 BC) or even Israel in the Persian period (539 – 333 BC). However, several points suggest that the book was written close to the time of Joshua. The phrase "to this day" appears 12 times (4:9; 5:9; 6:25; 7:26; 8:28,29; 9:27; 10:27; 13:13; 15:63; 16:10; 23:9). In 13:13 it refers to the people of Geshur, who are not mentioned after the time of David (2 Sam 14:32; 15:8). Rahab is said to live in Israel "to this day" (6:25), implying a time no later than the first generation after Joshua. Mention of the Book of Jashar (10:13) seems to argue that this account of Joshua was copied later, after the Book of Jashar was written. This Book of Jashar is mentioned in 2 Sam 1:18, suggesting that it was written as late as David's time. However, David might have used a later edition of that book. Josh 10:13 suggests an earlier edition of the Book of Jashar could have been written and referred to in the time of Joshua. Additional implications as to the antiquity of the book of Joshua (see Historical Setting) imply a date of composition, in a form similar to what we have, not later than the time of David and Solomon and possibly as early as the generation of Joshua.

THE FIGURE OF JOSHUA

Joshua first appears in Exod 17:8 – 13, where he serves as leader of Israel's army and defeats the Amalekites. He ascends part way up Mount Sinai (Exod 24:13 – 14) with Moses and hears of Israel's worship of the golden calf without actually participating in it (Exod 32:17). As Moses' "aide" (Josh 1:1), Joshua remained in the tent where Moses met with God (Exod 33:11). Joshua is there as God's Spirit settles on the elders outside the camp as well as on Eldad and Medad inside the camp (Num 11:24 – 30). Joshua tries to preserve Moses' honor by asking him to rebuke Eldad and Medad, but Moses responds to Joshua by underscoring how much more important the presence of the Spirit is (Num 11:24 – 29) than his own honor. Moses gives Hoshea (meaning "[He] has saved") the name Joshua (meaning "the LORD saves," Num 13:16). Joshua is most often remembered as one of 12 spies sent to explore Canaan (Num 13:1 – 25). He and Caleb were the only two to bring back a good report (Num 13:26 — 14:38), for which they were rewarded (see Josh 14:6 – 15; 19:49 – 51 and notes).

HISTORICAL SETTING

The book of Joshua chronicles the Israelites entering the promised land (chs. 1 – 5), defeating their enemies in the land (chs. 6 – 12), allotting the land to their tribes (chs. 13 – 21), and preparing to pass this inheritance on to future

CONQUEST OF CANAAN

① ENTRY INTO CANAAN

When the Israelite tribes approached Canaan after four decades of wilderness existence, they had to overcome two Amorite kingdoms on the Medeba plateau and in Bashan. Under Moses' leadership, they also subdued the Midianites in order to consolidate their control over the Transjordanian region.

The conquest of Canaan followed a course that in retrospect appears as though it had been planned by a brilliant military strategist. Taking Jericho gave Israel control of its strategic plains, fords, and roads as a base of operations. When Israel next gained control of the Bethel, Gibeon, and Upper Beth Horon regions, it dominated the center of the north-south Palestinian ridge. Subsequently, Israel was able to break the power of the allied urban centers in separate campaigns south and north (for the northern campaign, see map, p. 402).

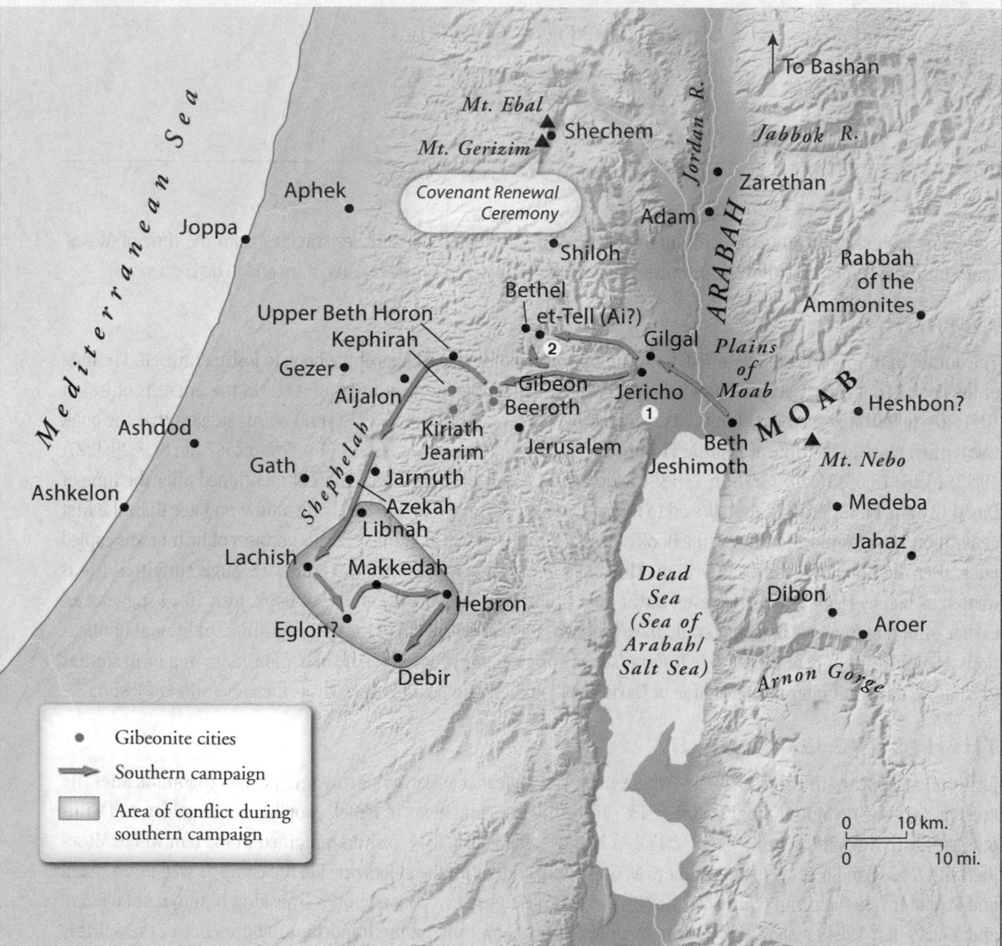

② THE SOUTHERN CAMPAIGN

The destruction of both Jericho and Ai led to a major victory against the Canaanites in the Valley of Aijalon — the battle of the long day (see Josh 10:12–14)—which then allowed Joshua to proceed against the cities of the western foothills.

Azekah, Libnah, Lachish, Eglon, and Debir were all captured by Joshua in his campaign against the southern coalition of Canaanite cities that was led by the king of Jerusalem.

Several of these towns, most notably Lachish, contain destruction evidence that might possibly be correlated with the Israelite conquest, but with Jericho and Ai the historical implications are not clear.

generations (chs. 22–24). The contents suggest that the events took place 40 years after the exodus, implying a date for the events of Joshua of either ca. 1406 BC or ca. 1220 BC, depending on whether one accepts an early or late date for the exodus (see Introduction to the Old Testament: Chronology/Dating, p. 7; see also Introduction to Exodus: The Date of the Exodus).

More important are the numerous pieces of evidence for an authentic second-millennium BC origin of the book. For example, virtually all the Canaanite personal names preserved in Joshua (2:1; 10:3,33; 11:1; 15:14) are found in the second millennium BC. Some occur only in the second millennium BC (Hoham, Piram, Japhia, Sheshai, and Talmai). It becomes difficult to explain how these names were correctly included if the book of Joshua was composed many hundreds of years later. The covenant of ch. 24 follows the elements of a second-millennium BC vassal treaty (see note on 24:1–28) and includes a clearly attested item (a historical prologue) not found in first-millennium BC treaties.

Some argue that the accounts of Joshua must be fictions created from a later time. However, those holding this view do not address the above matters. It is true that some of the places named in the allotments (chs. 13–19) were founded later. However, chs. 13–19 form a legal document that serves to define the tribal territories generation after generation (see note on 13:1—21:45). Thus, adding the names of later towns did not change these documents but further defined which towns belonged to which tribes. On the other hand, many of the towns that Joshua attacked and those where he assembled all Israel were well-known settlements in the second millennium BC.

THEOLOGICAL THEMES

The great themes of the book of Joshua include: the gift of the promised land, the sovereign presence of a holy and loving God, the covenant, and God's call to faithful obedience.

The Gift of the Promised Land

The promised land was part of God's covenant with Abraham (Gen 12:1–3,7; 13:15–17; 15:17–21; 17:8; 22:17) and his descendants (Gen 26:4; 28:4,13; 35:12). This is the land to which God directed the Israelites after they left Egypt (1:2; Exod 3:8,17; 34:24; Lev 20:24; Num 14:8; Deut 6:10; 9:5; 11:9; 26:1–3; 28:52). This land fulfills God's promise to Abraham, Isaac, and Jacob; it is the divine gift to the Israelites and belongs to them as they accept and obey the covenant (Deut 28). God's gift of the promised land provides the Israelites with all the blessings they require to live in prosperity and security. It is no accident that the form of the whole book of Joshua most closely resembles royal land grants in the ancient Near East. For example, the ca. eighteenth-century BC land grant of the city of Alalakh from Abbael king of Aleppo to Yarimlim contains all the major elements found in Joshua: a historical narrative of the battle that acquired Alalakh (cf. 6:1—12:24), a list of towns included in the grant (cf. 13:1—21:45), and the establishment of a covenant by oath that includes requirements for retaining the land grant (cf. 8:30–35; 23:1—24:27).

The promised rest (1:13,15) comes when the battles have ended and the victory has been won (11:23; 14:15; 21:44; 22:4; 23:1). No enemies remain to threaten the Israelites' occupation of the land and their worship of God. Such rest disappears in the following generations as the people turn away from God. The Hebrew word for "rest" never appears in the book of Judges. Only in David's time does Israel again have "rest" from its enemies (2 Sam 7:1,11). The generation of Joshua contrasts with the previous one, whose rebellions and faithlessness led God to deny them rest (Ps 95:11; Heb 3:11; 4:3,5). In a similar manner the author of Hebrews invites the members of the new covenant to enter into the true and complete Sabbath rest that Joshua did not give (Heb 4:8–11).

The Sovereign Presence of a Holy and Loving God

The sovereign presence of a holy and loving God is an essential theme of Joshua. God initiates the charge to Joshua (1:1–9), and Joshua then obeys by setting in motion the crossing of the Jordan River from Moab to Canaan. God promises his presence as a guarantee of faithfulness and success (1:5–9). It is God who chooses Joshua and who exalts him (3:7). The presence of God, represented by the ark of the covenant, leads Israel forward and overcomes the natural barriers of the Jordan River (chs. 3–4) and the human barriers of the walls of Jericho (ch. 6). It is God who orchestrates Canaan's fear of the Israelites (2:9,11,24) through these events (4:24; 5:1). It is God who topples Jericho's walls and preserves Rahab (ch. 6), enables the Israelites to defeat Ai (ch. 8), sends down hail on the southern coalition and lengthens the day to defeat them (ch. 10), gives Hazor and the north into Joshua's hands (ch. 11), guides the lot to determine the tribal lands (chs. 13–19), and renews his covenant partnership with Israel (ch. 24). If God is sovereign, he is holy. He demands Israel follow him in the signs of circumcision and Passover (ch. 5) and in covenant renewal (8:30–35; 24:1–28). God will not tolerate the theft of that which belongs to him (ch. 7) nor will

Aerial view of Jericho and the hills to the west. Josh 2 relates how the Israelite spies stayed at the home of Rahab, located in the wall of Jericho.

he allow the worship of anyone or anything else (chs. 22–24). Yet he is gracious and compassionate (Exod 34:6–7) in providing salvation for Rahab (2:1–21; 6:25), protecting Israel in their battles (chs. 6–11), providing grace for the Gibeonites (ch. 9), giving Caleb and Joshua allotments (14:6–15; 19:49–51), providing extra land for Israel to clear (17:14–18), caring for the unintentional killer (ch. 20), and providing for the tribeless Levites throughout the land (ch. 21).

The Covenant

Like the promised land, the covenant is God's gift to Israel. It is their means of life and success in the promised land (1:5–9). The ark of the covenant symbolizes God's presence. It is so named because the ark contains the physical text of the covenant document made at Mount Sinai (Exod 25:16,21; 40:20; Deut 10:2,5). Whoever violates the covenant is punished in the harshest manner (7:11–15; 23:16). This ancient document lies at the center of the covenant renewal (8:33), and it forms the basis for Joshua's final address and the people's oath of loyalty (chs. 23–24). If the gift of the promised land is God's response in the covenant, then the heart of the book—mapping and distributing the land (chs. 13–21)—uniquely and physically expresses the covenant that will connect each Israelite with God, wherever they live in that land.

God's Call to Faithful Obedience

Israel's correct response to God's covenant is obedience. From ch. 1 to ch. 24, God calls his people to obey him. Throughout the book the Israelites receive blessings when they respond faithfully and punishments when they disobey (see Theological Themes [The Gift of the Promised Land]).

But God's blessings are not for Israel alone. The mighty works of God's salvation proclaim that same hope to "all the peoples of the earth" (4:24). God designs his miracles to proclaim who he is, to bless the people of Israel, and to provide the means by which they can bless others (Gen 12:1–3; Exod 19:5–6). But it is a matter of decision. For Rahab, who confesses the works of God and responds by assisting Israel (ch. 2), there is salvation and blessing (6:25). For the kings of Canaan and their armies who respond by opposing God's work and will, there is destruction and cursing (chs. 6; 8; 10–11).

Genocide?

Perhaps the greatest challenge to belief in the God of the OT is found in Joshua. Many assume that under divine direction Joshua and the Israelites stormed great towns and cities and put to death noncombatants such as babies, children, and the elderly. It is clear that God does not tolerate the sins of people and that the consequence of sin is death (Rom 6:23) — to the point that the Israelites were commanded to let no one live (Deut 20:16–18). But this sort of total destruction is difficult to find in Joshua. Given the biblical descriptions and the (lack of) archaeological evidence for towns, it is reasonable to assume that Jericho and Ai were forts. Except for the role of Rahab and her family (see 2:1 and note), these were military garrisons (see chs. 2,6–8 and notes). For the unusual Hebrew construction translated "men and women," see note on 6:21. The remaining wars that all Israel fought (chs. 10–11) began as defensive battles. If Israel had not fought, it would have been wiped out. The kings and their armies were indeed destroyed. It is reasonable to assume that with their armies destroyed, the noncombatants would have fled (see 10:28–43 and note). We know that there were plenty of Canaanites around to lead the Israelites into sin in the following generation (Judg 2:11–13). Overall, the accusation of genocide is an unfounded myth (but see Introduction to Deuteronomy: Themes and Theology [Holy War]).

OUTLINE

I. The Promised Land Entered (1:1 — 5:12)
- A. Joshua Installed as Leader (1:1–18)
- B. Rahab and the Spies (2:1–24)
- C. Crossing the Jordan (3:1 — 5:1)
- D. Circumcision and Passover at Gilgal (5:2–12)

II. The Promised Land Taken (5:13 — 12:24)
- A. The Fall of Jericho (5:13 — 6:27)
- B. Achan's Sin (7:1–26)
- C. Ai Destroyed (8:1–29)
- D. The Covenant Renewed at Mount Ebal (8:30–35)
- E. The Gibeonite Deception (9:1–27)
- F. The Sun Stands Still (10:1–15)
- G. Five Amorite Kings Killed (10:16–27)
- H. Southern Cities Conquered (10:28–43)
- I. Northern Kings Defeated (11:1–23)
- J. List of Defeated Kings (12:1–24)

III. The Promised Land Allotted (13:1 — 21:45)
- A. Land Still to Be Taken (13:1–7)
- B. Division of the Land East of the Jordan (13:8–33)
- C. Division of the Land West of the Jordan (14:1–5)
- D. Allotment for Caleb (14:6–15)
- E. Allotment for Judah (15:1–63)
- F. Allotment for Ephraim and Manasseh (16:1 — 17:18)
- G. Division of the Rest of the Land (18:1–10)
- H. Allotment for Benjamin (18:11–28)
- I. Allotment for Simeon (19:1–9)
- J. Allotment for Zebulun (19:10–16)
- K. Allotment for Issachar (19:17–23)
- L. Allotment for Asher (19:24–31)
- M. Allotment for Naphtali (19:32–39)
- N. Allotment for Dan (19:40–48)
- O. Allotment for Joshua (19:49–51)
- P. Cities of Refuge (20:1–9)
- Q. Towns for the Levites (21:1–45)

IV. Israel United to Serve God in the Promised Land (22:1 — 24:33)
- A. Eastern Tribes Return Home (22:1–34)
- B. Joshua's Farewell to the Leaders (23:1–16)
- C. The Covenant Renewed at Shechem (24:1–28)
- D. Buried in the Promised Land (24:29–33)

JOSHUA

1:1 [a]Nu 12:7; Dt 34:5 [b]Ex 24:13; Dt 1:38
1:2 [c]ver 11
1:3 [d]Dt 11:24
1:4 [e]Ge 15:18 [f]Nu 34:2-12
1:5 [g]Dt 7:24

Joshua Installed as Leader

1 After the death of Moses the servant of the LORD,[a] the LORD said to Joshua[b] son of Nun, Moses'
aide: [2]"Moses my servant is dead. Now then, you and all these people, get ready to cross the
Jordan River[c] into the land I am about to give to them — to the Israelites. [3]I will give you every
place where you set your foot,[d] as I promised Moses. [4]Your territory will extend from the desert
to Lebanon, and from the great river, the Euphrates[e] — all the Hittite country — to the Mediterranean Sea in the west.[f] [5]No one will be able to stand against you[g] all the days of your life. As

1:1 — 5:12 *The Promised Land Entered.* The beginning of Joshua recounts the spiritual and physical preparations for the subsequent battles to acquire the land. God appoints Joshua as leader, and Joshua takes charge of all Israel. Rahab's confession of faith encourages the Israelites before God leads the people into the promised land through a miracle. Israel celebrates God's gift of the land with the sign of the Abrahamic covenant (circumcision) and the festival of God's redemption from Egypt (Passover).

1:1 – 18 *Joshua Installed as Leader.* God's vision for Israel consists of establishing Joshua as its leader and giving him promises (vv. 1 – 5a) and the means to accomplish them (vv. 5b – 9). The promises outline the contents of the book of Joshua, and the means to accomplish them place Israel in God's ongoing plan to bless his people and give them success (Gen 12:1 – 3). Joshua implements God's instructions for Israel (vv. 10 – 11) and faces a potential challenge to his leadership (vv. 12 – 18).

1:1 death of Moses. Described in the preceding chapter (Deut 34), thus connecting this book with the first five books of the Bible. Moses' death creates a vacuum in Israel's leadership. Joshua could not be leader while Moses was God's appointed head, but now he must become leader or Israel as a nation will be vulnerable to infighting and divisions over this concern. The book of Joshua begins with a need to replace the former leader, Moses, just as the book of Judges begins with the death Joshua (Judg 1:1; cf. Exod 1:6). **the servant of the LORD.** Although Moses was recognized as God's servant earlier (Exod 14:31), this title is first given to him at his death (Deut 34:5; then 13 times in Joshua); it will also be bestowed on Joshua at his death (24:29). It honors the leaders for a life of faithfulness. **Joshua son of Nun.** Nun was an Ephraimite (Num 13:8; see Jacob's choice of Ephraim over Manasseh in Gen 48:5 – 20). The full name identifies this figure with the Joshua of Exodus – Deuteronomy and the divinely chosen successor of Moses as leader of God's people (Deut 31:23; cf. Deut 3:28; 31:14). See Introduction: The Figure of Joshua. **Moses' aide.** Only Joshua has this role in Exodus – Deuteronomy (Exod 24:13; 33:11; Num 11:28).

1:2 all these people. The unity of God's people in faithfulness is key to success. When Israel is united in their faithfulness to God, they cannot be defeated (chs. 6; 8; 10 – 11; etc.). When they are divided, they do not win (7:3 – 5; much of Judges). The Hebrew word for "all" or "each" or "every" occurs 236 times in Joshua, inundating the book with the theme of a unified nation called to receive the whole land. The unity of God's people in their faithfulness to him remains key for winning Canaan and, in the NT, for winning the world (John 17:21). **cross the Jordan River.** This charge summarizes 1:1 — 5:12, describing the first major part of Israel's responsibility under Joshua. **cross.** The Hebrew word for "cross (over)" appears 32 times in the first five chapters, unifying many acts in these chapters as part of a greater movement into the promised land (e.g., "go through," 1:11; "go into," 3:11; "carried ... over," 4:8). **land I am about to give to them.** A promise God first made to Abraham (Gen 12:1 – 3,5 – 7; 15:18; etc.). **give.** The Hebrew word is used 89 times in Joshua; 78 times it refers to God's gift of all or part of the land and its occupants. The land is God's gift to his covenant people.

1:3 every place where you set your foot. By repeating Deut 11:24, this phrase informs Israel as to what it should do to occupy the land. It summarizes the second part of Joshua (5:13 — 12:24): Israel's acts of taking the land. **as I promised Moses.** Mentions Moses (Deut 34:1 – 4) rather than Abraham to indicate Joshua's role as successor. What God promised Moses, he promises Joshua; every promise will be fulfilled (23:14).

1:4 God identifies the areas and borders of the promised land, identical to Canaan (Gen 10:19; 15:18; Num 13:17 – 22; Deut 1:7) in the Bible and in ancient descriptions from Egypt at the time of Joshua. Although only David and Solomon would control all this land, the southern part is allotted to the tribes in 13:1 — 21:45. **desert.** The southern part of the promised land, including the "wilderness" (i.e., the desert region west of the Dead Sea) and the region around Bethel and Ai (8:15,20; 12:8; 15:61; 16:1; 18:12). **Lebanon.** The mountains of modern Lebanon that stretch into the northern part of the promised land. **Euphrates ... Mediterranean Sea.** The northeastern and western boundaries. **Hittite country.** The Hittites, a second-millennium BC empire in modern Turkey, extended their rule into Canaan. The area became known as "Hittite land" as early as Joshua.

1:5a No one will be able to stand against you all the days of your life. This promise anticipates Joshua's career and summarizes the last

I was with[h] Moses, so I will be with you; I will never leave you nor forsake[i] you. 6Be strong and
courageous, because you will lead these people to inherit the land I swore to their ancestors[j] to
give them.
7"Be strong and very courageous. Be careful to obey all the law my servant Moses gave you; do not
turn from it to the right or to the left,[k] that you may be successful wherever you go.[l] 8Keep this Book of
the Law always on your lips; meditate on it day and night, so that you may be careful to do everything
written in it. Then you will be prosperous and successful.[m] 9Have I not commanded you? Be strong and
courageous. Do not be afraid;[n] do not be discouraged, for the LORD your God will be with you wherever
you go."[o]
10So Joshua ordered the officers of the people: 11"Go through the camp and tell the people, 'Get your
provisions ready. Three days from now you will cross the Jordan here to go in and take possession[p] of
the land the LORD your God is giving you for your own.'"
12But to the Reubenites, the Gadites and the half-tribe of Manasseh,[q] Joshua said, 13"Remember the
command that Moses the servant of the LORD gave you after he said, 'The LORD your God will give you
rest[r] by giving you this land.' 14Your wives, your children and your livestock may stay in the land that
Moses gave you east of the Jordan, but all your fighting men, ready for battle, must cross over ahead of
your fellow Israelites. You are to help them 15until the LORD gives them rest, as he has done for you, and
until they too have taken possession of the land the LORD your God is giving them. After that, you may
go back and occupy your own land, which Moses the servant of the LORD gave you east of the Jordan
toward the sunrise."[s]
16Then they answered Joshua, "Whatever you have commanded us we will do, and wherever you send
us we will go. 17Just as we fully obeyed Moses, so we will obey you.[t] Only may the LORD your God be with
you as he was with Moses. 18Whoever rebels against your word and does not obey it, whatever you may
command them, will be put to death. Only be strong and courageous!"

1:5 [h] Jos 3:7; 6:27 [i] Dt 31:6-8
1:6 [j] Dt 31:23
1:7 [k] Dt 5:32; 28:14 [l] Jos 11:15
1:8 [m] Dt 29:9; Ps 1:1-3
1:9 [n] Ps 27:1 [o] ver 7; Dt 31:7-8; Jer 1:8
1:11 [p] Joel 3:2
1:12 [q] Nu 32:20-22
1:13 [r] Dt 3:18-20
1:15 [s] Jos 22:1-4
1:17 [t] ver 5,9

days of his life (chs. 23–24), when all Israel "presented themselves" (24:1, translating the same Hebrew verb behind "stand against") and Joshua reviewed all God had done.

1:5b–9 As I was with Moses, so I will be with you. This moves from God's promises (that summarize the book of Joshua) to explaining how this vision will be enacted. We can understand this by seeing the structure: the first and last phrases of vv. 5b–9 repeat one another (*a* / *a´*, *b* / *b´*, etc.) and the middle is the focus:

a I will never leave you nor forsake you.
b Be strong and courageous ...
c Be strong and very courageous.
d Be careful to obey all the law ...
e Keep this Book of the Law ...
e´ meditate on it day and night ...
d´ be careful to do everything written in it.
c´ Be strong and courageous.
b´ Do not be afraid; do not be discouraged ...
a´ God will be with you wherever you go.

Note that *a*, like *a´*, emphasizes God's presence as essential for accomplishing the vision; *b* and *c*, like *b´* and *c´*, repeat the charge to Israel and Joshua in Deut 31:6–8,23. "Be strong and courageous" appears three additional times in the OT (10:25; 1 Chr 28:20; 2 Chr 32:7), always to encourage God's people to a great mission (fighting on, building the temple, resisting the Assyrians).

1:6 inherit the land I swore to their ancestors. See vv. 3–4 and notes.

1:7 Be careful to obey all the law. See note on vv. 5b–9 where lines *d* and *e*, like *d´* and *e´* repeat the central emphasis on God's law as a guide for obedience and meditation.

1:8 Book of the Law. For Joshua, God's law consisted of the instruction found in Deuteronomy (cf. Deut 31:24–26) and possibly Genesis–Numbers. **always on your lips.** The ancients read aloud. **prosperous and successful.** This instruction (especially Deuteronomy) became the standard by which God judged Israel in the OT period. Verses 5 and 9 surround this command with God's promised presence. Joshua and Israel will be successful not because they obey God's word but because God is with them to enable them to obey his word—just as Jesus promises to be with his disciples in their mission (Matt 28:18–20). Joshua possessed the law of God as revealed in Genesis through Deuteronomy. Today we have all of God's Word in the Old and New Testaments. Those who study and obey God's Word (1 Tim 4:11–14) also succeed in God's mission.

1:10 ordered. Joshua enlists the others to assist in the implementation of the vision. **officers.** Civil leaders (3:2; 8:33; 23:2; 24:1; Exod 5:6–19; Deut 1:15; 20:5–9; 29:10; 31:28).

1:11 Three days. Sometimes this refers to a general period of time (9:16), but here it is likely three specific days (2:16,22; 3:2) that include a series of ceremonial actions (cf. 6:3,14).

1:12 Reubenites ... Gadites ... half-tribe of Manasseh. Having already received their land from Moses (Num 32; Deut 3:12–20), these tribes represent those most likely to reject Joshua's leadership and command to cross the Jordan and risk their lives. Joshua directly confronts this challenge to his God-given leadership.

1:13 Remember. God's leader quotes Deut 3:18–20, using Scripture (cf. 1:8–9) to make his case. As they followed Moses in receiving the land, they must now follow Joshua in fighting with all Israel. **give you rest.** See Introduction: Theological Themes (The Gift of the Promised Land).

1:16–17 Whatever ... wherever ... Just as we fully. This is a structured oath with three clauses, each beginning with the Hebrew word for "all" or "everything" to emphasize total commitment. Oaths would be taken pledging allegiance to a new leader.

1:17 Only may the LORD. This forms a blessing on Joshua.

1:18 rebels ... put to death. Capital crimes for Israel (Deut 1:26; 9:7,23–24; 31:27) and individuals (Deut 21:18–21). **be strong and courageous!** Cf. vv. 5b–9 (see note there).

2:1 [u]Jas 2:25 [v]Nu 25:1; Jos 3:1 [w]Heb 11:31
2:4 [x]2Sa 17:19-20
2:6 [y]Jas 2:25 [z]Ex 1:17, 19; 2Sa 17:19
2:9 [a]Ge 35:5; Ex 23:27; Dt 2:25
2:10 [b]Ex 14:21 [c]Nu 23:22 [d]Nu 21:21, 24,34-35
2:11 [e]Ex 15:14; Jos 5:1; 7:5; Ps 22:14; Isa 13:7 [f]Dt 4:39

Rahab and the Spies

2 Then Joshua son of Nun secretly sent two spies[u] from Shittim.[v] "Go, look over the land," he said,
"especially Jericho." So they went and entered the house of a prostitute named Rahab[w] and stayed
there.
2 The king of Jericho was told, "Look, some of the Israelites have come here tonight to spy out the
land." 3 So the king of Jericho sent this message to Rahab: "Bring out the men who came to you and
entered your house, because they have come to spy out the whole land."
4 But the woman had taken the two men and hidden them.[x] She said, "Yes, the men came to me, but
I did not know where they had come from. 5 At dusk, when it was time to close the city gate, they left. I
don't know which way they went. Go after them quickly. You may catch up with them." 6 (But she had
taken them up to the roof and hidden them under the stalks of flax[y] she had laid out on the roof.)[z] 7 So
the men set out in pursuit of the spies on the road that leads to the fords of the Jordan, and as soon as
the pursuers had gone out, the gate was shut.
8 Before the spies lay down for the night, she went up on the roof 9 and said to them, "I know that
the LORD has given you this land and that a great fear[a] of you has fallen on us, so that all who live in
this country are melting in fear because of you. 10 We have heard how the LORD dried up[b] the water of
the Red Sea[*a*] for you when you came out of Egypt,[c] and what you did to Sihon and Og,[d] the two kings
of the Amorites east of the Jordan, whom you completely destroyed.[*b*] 11 When we heard of it, our hearts
melted in fear and everyone's courage failed because of you,[e] for the LORD your God is God in heaven
above and on the earth[f] below.

a 10 Or *the Sea of Reeds* *b* 10 The Hebrew term refers to the irrevocable giving over of things or persons to the LORD, often by totally destroying them.

2:1–24 *Rahab and the Spies.* Rahab provides a Canaanite counterpart to Joshua. Rahab risks her life to hide the spies (vv. 1–8), confesses her faith in God's acts of redemption (vv. 9–11), and negotiates for her family's preservation (vv. 12–21). Using Rahab's words, the spies confess their faith that God has given the land to Israel (vv. 22–24).

2:1 two spies. Using spies was part of Israel's strategy (7:2–3; Num 13:1–33). Spies could both gather and disseminate information (2 Sam 15:10). Staying at Rahab's house, which was likely an inn, would enable them to gather information from travelers and military personnel and identify potential allies. **Shittim.** Means "Acacia trees," likely Tell Ḥammām, nine miles (14.5 kilometers) northeast of the Dead Sea and ten miles (16 kilometers) east of the Jordan in the plains of Moab (Num 22:1; 25:1–3). **Jericho.** Tell es-Sultan; with little archaeological evidence for occupation of the site at the time of Joshua, it may suggest a fort rather than a large city (contrast 10:2; 11:10, where large size is noted, unlike here). **house of a prostitute.** Ancient sources (e.g., Hammurabi's law code, #109) assume that innkeepers are female and warn against their hosting conspiracies. At Shittim Israel fell into the sin (Num 25:1–3) that Rahab abandons. Located on east-west and north-south trade routes, Jericho and Rahab's inn were strategic. For an inn at NT Jericho, cf. Luke 10:25–37. **Rahab.** The only Canaanite named from Jericho and Ai.

2:2–8 Repetition of phrases in this story emphasize Rahab's great risk (see notes on these verses).

2:2 king of Jericho. Canaan at this time was divided into small kingdoms such as Jericho. Or Jericho was a fort, and the "king" was a commander. If Jericho was a fort, it was garrisoned by "kings" of Jerusalem and Bethel, whose ancient roads ran directly to Jericho.

2:2,3 to spy out the [whole] land. If Rahab hides these spies, she is a traitor.

2:4,6 had taken the two men [them] ... and hidden them. A second repetition in this narrative.

2:4,5 I did not know ... I don't know. Rahab lies not because she is a Canaanite and doesn't know better but because no other response would protect the spies. The story does not dwell on the morality of lying but reports that this ruse was used to subvert certain death (cf. Exod 1:15–21; 1 Sam 16:2). Heb 11:31 and Jas 2:25 praise Rahab for hiding the spies.

2:5,7 gate. Shutting the city gate requires that the king's agents make an immediate decision. If they believe Rahab, they must leave at once without searching her house. But doing so also prevents Joshua's spies from escaping the way they entered Jericho. They are completely dependent on Rahab (cf. vv. 15,21).

2:6 This parenthesis (note the parentheses in the text) heightens the story's drama. The reader is not told whether the king's agents follow Rahab's advice until v. 7.

2:6,8 the roof. Farthest from the entrance and the public areas. Withholding nothing, Rahab opens the most secluded part of her house to the spies.

2:9–11 "I know" (v. 9) contrasts the "I did not [don't] know" of vv. 4,5. Rahab separates herself from Jericho's people and identifies with Israel. Beginning the longest biblical prose speech by a woman, this confession forms a concentric structure (cf. 1:5b–9; see note there):

a the LORD has given you this land ...
  b a great fear of you has fallen on us ...
    c all who live in this country are melting in fear because of you.
      d We have heard
        e how the LORD dried up the water of the Red Sea ...
        e´ what you did to Sihon and Og ...
      d´ When we heard of it,
    c´ our hearts melted in fear ...
  b´ everyone's courage failed because of you,
a´ for the LORD your God is God in heaven above and on the earth below.

In the structure above, *b* and *c* quote Exod 15:15b–16a, fulfilling the prophecy at the exodus of how Canaan would respond (see 5:1 and note; 10:2; 14:8); *e* and *e´* are God's historic acts of redemption at the beginning (Exod 14–15) and end (Num 21; Deut 3) of Israel's sojourn; similarly, the historic acts of redemption that Christians confess and believe are Christ's death and resurrection (Rom 10:9).

12"Now then, please swear to me by the LORD that you will show kindness to my family, because I have
shown kindness to you. Give me a sure sign[g] 13that you will spare the lives of my father and mother, my
brothers and sisters, and all who belong to them — and that you will save us from death."
14"Our lives for your lives!" the men assured her. "If you don't tell what we are doing, we will treat
you kindly and faithfully[h] when the LORD gives us the land."
15So she let them down by a rope through the window,[i] for the house she lived in was part of the city
wall. 16She said to them, "Go to the hills so the pursuers will not find you. Hide yourselves there three
days[j] until they return, and then go on your way."[k]
17Now the men had said to her, "This oath[l] you made us swear will not be binding on us 18unless,
when we enter the land, you have tied this scarlet cord in the window through which you let us down,
and unless you have brought your father and mother, your brothers and all your family[m] into your
house. 19If any of them go outside your house into the street, their blood will be on their own heads;[n]
we will not be responsible. As for those
who are in the house with you, their
blood will be on our head[o] if a hand
is laid on them. 20But if you tell what
we are doing, we will be released from
the oath you made us swear."
21"Agreed," she replied. "Let it be
as you say."
So she sent them away, and they
departed. And she tied the scarlet cord
in the window.
22When they left, they went into the
hills and stayed there three days, until
the pursuers had searched all along
the road and returned without finding them. 23Then the two men started
back. They went down out of the hills,
forded the river and came to Joshua son
of Nun and told him everything that
had happened to them. 24They said to
Joshua, "The LORD has surely given the
whole land into our hands;[p] all the people are melting in fear because of us."

Casemate wall at Hazor. It is possible that the wall of Jericho where Rahab lived was constructed this way.

Todd Bolen/www.BiblePlaces.com

2:12 [g]ver 18
2:14 [h]Jdg 1:24; Mt 5:7
2:15 [i]Ac 9:25
2:16 [j]Jas 2:25 [k]Heb 11:31
2:17 [l]Ge 24:8
2:18 [m]ver 12; Jos 6:23
2:19 [n]Eze 33:4 [o]Mt 27:25
2:24 [p]ver 9; Jos 6:2

2:12 kindness. Hebrew *hesed*; covenantal love and loyalty (Exod 15:13; Deut 7:9). "Show kindness" refers to future generations (Gen 24:12,49; Exod 20:6; Deut 5:10). Rahab's confession of faith leads on to petition. She expresses concern for her family (listing them in v. 13 but not naming herself) and their welfare. **my family.** Lit. "the household of my father"; the extended family (grandparents, their children, married sons and their families), the basic unit of Canaanite and Israelite societies. Rahab negotiates as leader of her extended family.

2:14 Our lives for your lives! These first recorded words of the spies consent to her request. By negotiating the means to preserve both Rahab and themselves, the spies recognize that Rahab has converted from Canaanite religion (which is to be eliminated, Deut 20:16–18) to Israelite faith (cf. vv. 9–11; 6:22–25).

2:15 she let them down by a rope. The discussion of vv. 16–21 does not take place with spies dangling on the wall or shouting from beneath Rahab's window; v. 15 introduces the scene, and v. 21 concludes by summarizing the action. **through the window.** Contrasts with the shut gate (vv. 5,7; 6:1); Rahab's openness to the spies in aiding them (ch. 2) contrasts with Jericho's resistance (ch. 6). **part of the city wall.** Either the wall consisted of houses joined end to end, or the wall was a "casemate" wall with two parallel walls joined by short connecting walls that formed sections filled in with rubble or that created living spaces.

2:16 Go to the hills. West of Jericho the hills rise dramatically out of the Jordan Valley. This direction is opposite that of the Jordan, where the king's agents searched. Rahab believes God, acts on that belief to preserve God's people, and advances the kingdom. **three days.** See note on 1:11.

2:18 scarlet cord in the window ... all your family into your house. Rahab had closed her door on the rest of Jericho and opened her window for the spies to return to the Israelite camp. The scarlet cord would show the Israelite forces that Rahab and her family had become identified with them. At the same time that Rahab and her family were anticipating the coming of Israel, Israel was celebrating Passover (5:10–12), during which the Israelites gathered as families (Exod 12:1–11,43).

2:24 The LORD has surely given. Summarizes Rahab's words that begin her confession (v. 9). As with Caleb's report (Num 14:30), this report emphasizes that following God will lead to success. Spies who instead evaluate the physical threat (Num 13:27–29,31–33) counsel in a way that leads to defeat.

3:1 [q]Jos 2:1
3:2 [r]Jos 1:11
3:3 [s]Nu 10:33 [t]Dt 31:9
3:5 [u]Ex 19:10,14; Lev 20:7; Jos 7:13; 1Sa 16:5; Joel 2:16
3:7 [v]Jos 4:14; 1Ch 29:25 [w]Jos 1:5
3:8 [x]ver 3
3:10 [y]Dt 5:26; 1Sa 17:26,36; 2Ki 19:4, 16; Hos 1:10; Mt 16:16; 1Th 1:9 [z]Ex 33:2; Dt 7:1
3:11 [a]ver 13; Job 41:11; Zec 6:5
3:12 [b]Jos 4:2,4
3:13 [c]ver 11 [d]ver 16 [e]Ex 15:8; Ps 78:13
3:14 [f]Ps 132:8 [g]Ac 7:44-45
3:15 [h]Jos 4:18; 1Ch 12:15
3:16 [i]Ps 66:6; 74:15 [j]1Ki 4:12; 7:46 [k]ver 13 [l]Dt 1:1 [m]Ge 14:3
3:17 [n]Ex 14:22,29

Crossing the Jordan

3 Early in the morning Joshua and all the Israelites set out from Shittim[q] and went to the Jordan, where they camped before crossing over. 2After three days the officers went throughout the camp,[r] 3giving orders to the people: "When you see the ark of the covenant[s] of the LORD your God, and the Levitical priests[t] carrying it, you are to move out from your positions and follow it. 4Then you will know which way to go, since you have never been this way before. But keep a distance of about two thousand cubits[a] between you and the ark; do not go near it."

5Joshua told the people, "Consecrate yourselves,[u] for tomorrow the LORD will do amazing things among you."

6Joshua said to the priests, "Take up the ark of the covenant and pass on ahead of the people." So they took it up and went ahead of them.

7And the LORD said to Joshua, "Today I will begin to exalt you[v] in the eyes of all Israel, so they may know that I am with you as I was with Moses.[w] 8Tell the priests[x] who carry the ark of the covenant: 'When you reach the edge of the Jordan's waters, go and stand in the river.'"

9Joshua said to the Israelites, "Come here and listen to the words of the LORD your God. 10This is how you will know that the living God[y] is among you and that he will certainly drive out before you the Canaanites, Hittites, Hivites, Perizzites, Girgashites, Amorites and Jebusites.[z] 11See, the ark of the covenant of the Lord of all the earth[a] will go into the Jordan ahead of you. 12Now then, choose twelve men[b] from the tribes of Israel, one from each tribe. 13And as soon as the priests who carry the ark of the LORD — the Lord of all the earth[c] — set foot in the Jordan, its waters flowing downstream[d] will be cut off and stand up in a heap.[e]"

14So when the people broke camp to cross the Jordan, the priests carrying the ark of the covenant[f] went ahead[g] of them. 15Now the Jordan is at flood stage[h] all during harvest. Yet as soon as the priests who carried the ark reached the Jordan and their feet touched the water's edge, 16the water from upstream stopped flowing.[i] It piled up in a heap a great distance away, at a town called Adam in the vicinity of Zarethan,[j] while the water flowing down[k] to the Sea of the Arabah[l] (that is, the Dead Sea[m]) was completely cut off. So the people crossed over opposite Jericho. 17The priests who carried the ark of the covenant of the LORD stopped in the middle of the Jordan and stood on dry ground, while all Israel passed by until the whole nation had completed the crossing on dry ground.[n]

a *4* That is, about 3,000 feet or about 900 meters

3:1—5:1 *Crossing the Jordan.* The Israelites approach the Jordan River (3:1). A holy God leads his consecrated people across the last natural barrier with a great miracle and a memorial for future generations (3:2–13). The ceremony focuses on the priests who carry the ark, the symbol of God's presence, into the riverbed and stand until all have crossed (3:14–17). The memorial of 12 stones evokes the unity of the nation before God (4:1–9,19–24), just as Israel's safe crossing fulfills the promise of bringing them into the promised land (4:10–13,15–18). Exalting Joshua remains central to God's purpose (4:14), and the enemy reacts with fear (5:1).

3:2 three days. This reference returns the reader to the events of 1:10–18 (see note on 1:11).

3:3 ark of the covenant. Constructed 40 years earlier at Sinai (Exod 25:10–22; 37:1–5), the ark is a gold-covered box that represents the special presence of God with his people and may be associated with the throne of God. It is where the high priest sprinkles blood to atone for the sins of the people (Lev 16). As God led the nation through the wilderness (Num 10:33–36), the ark will lead Israel into the promised land and come to rest in Jerusalem (1 Sam 4–6; 2 Sam 6).

3:5 Consecrate yourselves. At Sinai (Exod 19:10–15) Moses told the people to abstain from sex and wash their clothes to become consecrated. **amazing things.** Whether sending the Egyptian plagues (Exod 3:20) or holding back the Jordan River, God's power is apparent.

3:7 exalt. Israel will regard Joshua as they did Moses (1:1,3).

3:9 Come here and listen. Joshua commands the people to listen (cf. Deut 6:4–9) and be assured that they will win their battles (cf. 1:5). Israel will be assured by seeing evidence of God's presence (cf. 1:5–9) when the Jordan stops flowing (mentioned for the first time in v. 13).

3:10 living God. Describes God's closeness to his people and his amazing acts for them (cf. Pss 42:2; 84:2; Hos 1:10). **drive out.** The expression is often used of Israel's occupation of the land and suggests expulsion rather than annihilation (Num 14:24; 32:21; 33:52–53,55; Deut 4:38; 7:17; 9:4–5; 11:23). **Canaanites.** Deut 7:1 mentions the same seven nations of Canaan — seven being a full number. See variations of those included: 9:1; 12:8; Gen 15:19–21; Exod 3:8,17; 23:23; 33:2; 34:11; Deut 20:17; etc.

3:15 flood stage all during harvest. In the spring (the Passover of 5:10 is celebrated in March/April) the faster-flowing Jordan reaches 100 feet (30 meters) in width. **feet touched the water's edge.** Even at the river's edge, this dangerous act required obedient trust.

3:16 heap. See v. 13; it describes the Red Sea crossing (Exod 15:8; Ps 78:13). **Adam.** Ed-Damiye, where the Jabbok River joins from the east, about 18 miles (29 kilometers) north, indicating that the stoppage affected the lower part of the Jordan Valley.

3:17 all. Stresses the unity of the people of God (see 1:2 and note). **passed by.** Uses the key Hebrew *ʿābar* (translated "to cross" in 1:2), which occurs 23 times in 3:1—5:1 and emphasizes the key event: Israel's crossing of the Jordan River.

4 When the whole nation had finished crossing the Jordan,[o] the LORD said to Joshua, 2“Choose twelve
men[p] from among the people, one from each tribe, 3and tell them to take up twelve stones[q] from
the middle of the Jordan, from right where the priests are standing, and carry them over with you and
put them down at the place where you stay tonight.[r]”
4So Joshua called together the twelve men he had appointed from the Israelites, one from each tribe,
5and said to them, “Go over before the ark of the LORD your God into the middle of the Jordan. Each
of you is to take up a stone on his shoulder, according to the number of the tribes of the Israelites, 6to
serve as a sign among you. In the future, when your children ask you, ‘What do these stones mean?’[s]
7tell them that the flow of the Jordan was cut off[t] before the ark of the covenant of the LORD. When it
crossed the Jordan, the waters of the Jordan were cut off. These stones are to be a memorial[u] to the
people of Israel forever.”
8So the Israelites did as Joshua commanded them. They took twelve stones from the middle of the
Jordan, according to the number of the tribes of the Israelites, as the LORD had told Joshua;[v] and they
carried them over with them to their camp, where they put them down. 9Joshua set up the twelve
stones[w] that had been[a] in the middle of the Jordan at the spot where the priests who carried the ark of
the covenant had stood. And they are there to this day.
10Now the priests who carried the ark remained standing in the middle of the Jordan until everything
the LORD had commanded Joshua was done by the people, just as Moses had directed Joshua. The people
hurried over, 11and as soon as all of them had crossed, the ark of the LORD and the priests came to the
other side while the people watched. 12The men of Reuben, Gad and the half-tribe of Manasseh crossed
over, ready for battle, in front of the Israelites,[x] as Moses had directed them. 13About forty thousand
armed for battle crossed over before the LORD to the plains of Jericho for war.
14That day the LORD exalted[y] Joshua in the sight of all Israel; and they stood in awe of him all the
days of his life, just as they had stood in awe of Moses.
15Then the LORD said to Joshua, 16“Command the priests carrying the ark of the covenant law[z] to
come up out of the Jordan.”
17So Joshua commanded the priests, “Come up out of the Jordan.”
18And the priests came up out of the river carrying the ark of the covenant of the LORD. No sooner
had they set their feet on the dry ground than the waters of the Jordan returned to their place and ran
at flood stage[a] as before.

[a] 9 Or *Joshua also set up twelve stones*

4:1 [o] Dt 27:2
4:2 [p] Jos 3:12
4:3 [q] ver 20 [r] ver 19
4:6 [s] ver 21; Ex 12:26; 13:14
4:7 [t] Jos 3:13 [u] Ex 12:14
4:8 [v] ver 20
4:9 [w] Ge 28:18; Jos 24:26; 1Sa 7:12
4:12 [x] Nu 32:27
4:14 [y] Jos 3:7
4:16 [z] Ex 25:22
4:18 [a] Jos 3:15

4:3 twelve stones. Represents Israel's 12 tribes. **priests.** They carry the ark that remains in the riverbed and is blocking the waters (3:17). They remain close to God's presence, despite the danger. As Israel crosses the people witness the example of the priests who stand in the riverbed, dependent on God for their safety.

4:5–7 In v. 5 Joshua instructs the 12 men about what they are to do. Verses 6–7 form a concentric structure that describes the deed's significance (cf. 1:5b–9; 2:9–11; see notes there).

- *a* to serve as a sign among you. In the future, when your children ask you,
  - *b* "What do these stones mean?" tell them that
    - *c* the flow of the Jordan was cut off
      - *d* before the ark of the covenant of the LORD.
      - *d´* When it crossed the Jordan,
    - *c´* the waters of the Jordan were cut off.
  - *b´* These stones are to be
- *a´* a memorial to the people of Israel forever.

4:7 memorial. Used in conjunction with the exodus, the Passover, and the Festival of Unleavened Bread (Exod 12:14; 13:9), it also describes a military victory (Exod 17:14), priestly and cultic items (Exod 28:12,29; 30:16; 39:7; Num 16:38), and festivals, feasts, and offerings (Lev 23:24; Num 5:15,18; 10:10; 31:54). This is the first of seven stone memorials in the promised land that commemorate God's work among his people (7:26; 8:28–29,32; 10:27; 22:34; 24:26; cf. 1 Sam 7:12). The visual aid will remain and help future generations remember how God provisioned his people. The central emphasis is on the ark itself. No obstacle can stop the onward movement of God's presence, whether natural (e.g., the Jordan River) or man-made (e.g., Jericho, ch. 6).

4:9 There are three possibilities for interpreting this verse: (1) These stones were different from those of vv. 3,8. Those earlier stones, placed in the middle of the Jordan, may have been visible during the dry season. (2) The men took these stones *from* the Jordan to the riverbank. (3) Joshua *had* set a stone memorial in the middle of the Jordan and then had the men move it to the bank. Options 2 and 3 imply that this memorial and that of vv. 3,8 are the same.

4:13 About forty thousand. Seems far fewer than those mentioned in Num 26 for Reuben (43,730), Gad (40,500), and about half of Manasseh's forces (half of 52,700). Some may have stayed east of the Jordan to guard the land there. More likely, "thousand" (Hebrew *'elep*) can mean a military squad or unit (a "clan": Num 10:4; Judg 6:15; 1 Sam 10:19; see Introduction to Numbers: Interpretive Issues) so that these tribal units were reorganized to march together. Those who promised to follow Joshua (1:12–18) become an example of loyalty to Joshua and of courage to Israel.

4:14 exalted. God uses the miracle to exalt Joshua as a new Moses (see 3:7).

4:16 ark of the covenant law. See note on 3:3; see also Introduction: Theological Themes (The Sovereign Presence of a Holy and Loving God).

4:19 [b] Jos 5:9
4:20 [c] ver 3,8
4:21 [d] ver 6
4:22 [e] Jos 3:17
4:23 [f] Ex 14:21
4:24 [g] 1Ki 8:42-43; 2Ki 19:19; Ps 106:8; Jer 10:7 [h] Ex 15:16; 1Ch 29:12; Ps 89:13 [i] Ex 14:31
5:1 [j] Nu 13:29 [k] Jos 2:9-11
5:2 [l] Ex 4:25
5:4 [m] Dt 2:14
5:6 [n] Dt 2:7 [o] Nu 14:23, 29-35; Dt 2:14 [p] Ex 3:8
5:8 [q] Ge 34:25
5:10 [r] Ex 12:6

19On the tenth day of the first month the people went up from the Jordan and camped at Gilgal[b] on the eastern border of Jericho. 20And Joshua set up at Gilgal the twelve stones[c] they had taken out of the Jordan. 21He said to the Israelites, "In the future when your descendants ask their parents, 'What do these stones mean?'[d] 22tell them, 'Israel crossed the Jordan on dry ground.'[e] 23For the LORD your God dried up the Jordan before you until you had crossed over. The LORD your God did to the Jordan what he had done to the Red Sea[a] when he dried it up before us until we had crossed over.[f] 24He did this so that all the peoples of the earth might know[g] that the hand of the LORD is powerful[h] and so that you might always fear the LORD your God.[i]"

5 Now when all the Amorite kings west of the Jordan and all the Canaanite kings along the coast[j] heard how the LORD had dried up the Jordan before the Israelites until they[b] had crossed over, their hearts melted in fear[k] and they no longer had the courage to face the Israelites.

Circumcision and Passover at Gilgal

2At that time the LORD said to Joshua, "Make flint knives[l] and circumcise the Israelites again." 3So Joshua made flint knives and circumcised the Israelites at Gibeath Haaraloth.[c]

4Now this is why he did so: All those who came out of Egypt—all the men of military age—died in the wilderness on the way after leaving Egypt.[m] 5All the people that came out had been circumcised, but all the people born in the wilderness during the journey from Egypt had not. 6The Israelites had moved about in the wilderness forty years[n] until all the men who were of military age when they left Egypt had died, since they had not obeyed the LORD. For the LORD had sworn to them that they would not see the land he had solemnly promised their ancestors to give us,[o] a land flowing with milk and honey.[p] 7So he raised up their sons in their place, and these were the ones Joshua circumcised. They were still uncircumcised because they had not been circumcised on the way. 8And after the whole nation had been circumcised, they remained where they were in camp until they were healed.[q]

9Then the LORD said to Joshua, "Today I have rolled away the reproach of Egypt from you." So the place has been called Gilgal[d] to this day.

10On the evening of the fourteenth day of the month,[r] while camped at Gilgal on the plains of Jericho, the Israelites celebrated the Passover. 11The day after the Passover, that very day, they ate some of

[a] *23* Or *the Sea of Reeds* [b] *1* Another textual tradition *we* [c] *3 Gibeath Haaraloth* means *the hill of foreskins.* [d] *9 Gilgal* sounds like the Hebrew for *roll.*

4:19 tenth day of the first month. The day of preparation for the Passover (Exod 12:3). **went up from the Jordan.** The wilderness journey began (Exod 14–15) and here ends by passing through waters. **Gilgal.** Khirbet el-Mafjir lies about two miles (3 kilometers) northeast of OT Jericho.

4:24 all the peoples of the earth might know that the hand of the LORD is powerful. This missional goal to the world recalls the promise that Abram would be a blessing to all people on earth (Gen 12:1–3) and that Israel would become a priesthood (Exod 19:6).

5:1 Amorite ... Canaanite. While these two terms may overlap in this context, Amorites may refer to those in the hill country (10:6; 11:3; Num 13:29; Deut 1:7,19–20,44; Judg 1:34) and Canaanites to those in the valleys and plains (17:16; Num 13:29; 14:25; Deut 1:7). **their hearts melted in fear.** The proper response of "fear" (4:24) comes upon the leaders as a result of God's work for Israel. Israel is not attacked at this point.

5:2–12 *Circumcision and Passover at Gilgal.* Circumcision was the sign of God's covenant with Abraham (Gen 17:8–13). Passover recalls God's redemptive act of delivering the people from Egypt so that all Israel could become a covenant people (Exod 12:1–17). As Christian baptism (Col 2:11–12) and the Lord's Supper (Matt 26:26–29) symbolize faith and remembrance of Christ's redemption in the new covenant, so circumcision and Passover symbolize the Abrahamic covenant and Israel's covenant. Israel observes these symbols as it enters the land and begins to claim the fulfillment of God's covenantal promises.

5:2,3 flint knives. Likely obsidian, with a sharper (though more brittle) edge than metal. Obsidian was widely used for knives. Egyptians circumcised their males with such knives. Circumcision was required to celebrate the Passover (Exod 12:48).

5:2 circumcise ... again. Although the regulations of Leviticus refer to the circumcision of a recently born male (Lev 12:3), this is the first reference to its practice (cf. vv. 4–8) since before the exodus (Exod 4:26).

5:4–8 All ... all ... All ... all ... all ... whole. Contrasts Israel's first generation with the present one. Both generations were circumcised (although the second generation was not circumcised as children), but only the second generation followed God's covenant and saw the promised land.

5:6 milk and honey. Egyptians also were impressed with the herds and orchards of Canaan, which this faithful generation of Israel would see and taste.

5:9 rolled away the reproach of Egypt. Perhaps this describes the disgrace of slavery in Egypt. Alternatively, the obedience of the present generation (signaled by their practicing circumcision) contrasts with the disobedience of the first generation that left Egypt.

5:10 Gilgal on the plains of Jericho. Mention of these places looks back to the crossing and circumcision (Gilgal) and forward to the fall of Jericho (ch. 6). **Passover.** In Exod 12:25–27; 13:5, Israel is commanded to observe the Passover when they enter the promised land. This generation inherited the promises that the first generation had lost through disobedience. As the first generation celebrated the Passover and then crossed the Red Sea, the present generation crossed the Jordan River and celebrated this festival.

5:11 unleavened bread and roasted grain. They celebrate the Festival of Unleavened Bread the week following the Passover (Exod 12:17–20;

the produce of the land:[s] unleavened bread and roasted grain.[t] 12The manna stopped the day after[a]
they ate this food from the land; there was no longer any manna for the Israelites, but that year they
ate the produce of Canaan.[u]

The Fall of Jericho

13Now when Joshua was near Jericho, he looked up and saw a man[v] standing in front of him with
a drawn sword[w] in his hand. Joshua went up to him and asked, "Are you for us or for our enemies?"
14"Neither," he replied, "but as commander of the army of the LORD I have now come." Then Joshua
fell facedown[x] to the ground in reverence, and asked him, "What message does my Lord[b] have for his
servant?"
15The commander of the LORD's army replied, "Take off your sandals, for the place where you are
standing is holy."[y] And Joshua did so.

6 Now the gates of Jericho[z] were securely barred because of the Israelites. No one went out and no
one came in.
2Then the LORD said to Joshua, "See, I have delivered[a] Jericho into your hands, along with its king
and its fighting men. 3March around the city once with all the armed men. Do this for six days. 4Have
seven priests carry trumpets of rams' horns in front of the ark. On the seventh day, march around the
city seven times, with the priests blowing the trumpets.[b] 5When you hear them sound a long blast[c] on
the trumpets, have the whole army give a loud shout;[d] then the wall of the city will collapse and the
army will go up, everyone straight in."
6So Joshua son of Nun called the priests and said to them, "Take up the ark of the covenant of the

[a] 12 Or *the day* [b] 14 Or *lord*

5:11 [s] Nu 15:19 [t] Lev 23:14
5:12 [u] Ex 16:35
5:13 [v] Ge 18:2; 32:24 [w] Nu 22:23
5:14 [x] Ge 17:3
5:15 [y] Ex 3:5; Ac 7:33
6:1 [z] Jos 24:11
6:2 [a] Dt 7:24; Jos 2:9,24; 8:1
6:4 [b] Lev 25:9; Nu 10:8
6:5 [c] Ex 19:13 [d] ver 20; 1Sa 4:5; Ps 42:4; Isa 42:13

13:7; 23:15; Deut 16:3). It recalls Israel's hasty departure from Egypt, which allowed them no time to bake bread and wait for the yeast to work. These foods also reflect the barley harvest in the spring.

5:12 manna. This is the staple food of the wilderness as grains are the staple food of the promised land. The roasted grain forms a "down payment" on Israel's acquiring the whole land and all its blessings (24:13).

5:13—12:24 *The Promised Land Taken.* Initial entry through Jericho (ch. 6) and into the central hill country via Ai (chs. 7–8) leads to Israel's defeat of coalitions in the south (ch. 10) and north (ch. 11). Corresponding to this is the initial outworking of sin (Achan in ch. 7) that grows to include failure to seek God first (Gibeon in ch. 9), despite the renewed covenant at Mount Ebal (8:30–35). Nevertheless, God faithfully gives Israel the land (ch.12).

5:13—6:27 *The Fall of Jericho.* The commander of the Lord's army prepares Joshua for the battle that illustrates (1) how nothing can resist the advancement of God's people when led by him and (2) how much God is concerned for the salvation of those who have faith, such as Rahab and her family.

5:13–14 Like Jacob (Gen 32:22–32) and Moses (Exod 3:1—4:17), Joshua encounters the divine presence before he begins his mission. He immediately accepts his task and obeys.

5:13 drawn sword. Prepares to execute divine judgment (Num 22:23; 1 Chr 21:16).

5:14 commander of the army of the LORD. This is either an appearance of God (a theophany) or an angel representing God.

5:15 Take off your sandals ... holy. Echoing God's command to Moses (Exod 3:5), the holiness of the place demonstrates that God is meeting with Joshua. This, along with Joshua's worship of this figure (v. 14) and the continuing divine instructions (ch. 6), indicates that God is present here (cf. Gen 18; 22; 32; Exod 3). Joshua's acknowledgment of God's holiness leads to the charge of ch. 6. Cf. the emphasis on God's holiness followed by God's call to a mission for Isaiah (Isa 6), Ezekiel (Ezek 1), Mary (Luke 1:26–38), and Jesus at the transfiguration (Matt 17:1–13; Mark 9:2–13; Luke 9:28–36).

6:1 This verse appears out of place in the middle of God's charge to Joshua (5:14—6:5). It emphasizes the physical obstacle that prevents the onward movement of God's presence and people. Cf. 2:5,7. **Jericho.** See note on 2:1. Jericho means "moon" and may refer to the site as a center of moon worship. But its status at the time of Joshua is not known. Except for Rahab (see note on 2:15), Jericho shuts itself against God.

6:2 I have delivered Jericho. God has done the work (1:2; 2:8–11; 5:1; 10:8). Joshua and Israel need only believe (cf. Eph 2:8–9). God can give assurance before the battle (cf. Pss 18:43; 54:7; 56:13; 71:23; 86:13; 116:8). **its king and its fighting men.** This suggests that Jericho is a fortress occupied by a king/commander (see 2:1–2 and notes) and warriors.

6:3–4 six days ... seventh day. Takes place during the seven days of the Festival of Unleavened Bread (5:11). Like the Passover (see 5:10 and note), the festival takes on new meaning for Joshua's generation. The "seven days" also signals a special event for God (Gen 7:4,10; Exod 7:25; 29:37; 1 Sam 13:8; 1 Kgs 8:65; 2 Chr 30:22,23; Neh 8:18). The seven priests, trumpets, and marches also emphasize it (vv. 4,13,15,16). This march warns of Israel's hostile intent while it daily and publicly appeals to Jericho to open its city and yield or flee (cf. Rahab in 2:15 [see note]).

6:4–5 rams' horns ... long blast ... loud shout. Blowing the horns prepares Israel for sacred marches (Num 10:9). Loud noises proclaim victory in war and accompany the ark's processions (Num 10:2–6; 1 Sam 4:5–6; 2 Sam 6:15–16).

6:4 ark. Symbolizes God's presence in the ceremonial processions (see 3:3 and note) around Jericho and in its destruction.

6:5 whole army ... will go up ... straight in. Just as they crossed the Jordan after God stopped the waters (chs. 3–4), God again wins the victory; Israel need only walk in and take Jericho. **wall ... will collapse.** The shut gate (2:5,7; 6:1) and resistance for six days (6:3–4) climax in God's destroying Jericho's symbol of resistance. God's gracious offer to allow Jericho to yield ends. Nothing natural (chs. 3–4) or man-made (Jericho's walls) stops the advance of God's mission. The ark that was constructed at Mount Sinai will move forward until it reaches its resting place in Jerusalem (2 Sam 6).

6:6–15 These verses repeat the divine commands of vv. 3–5. Joshua

6:7 [e]Ex 14:15
6:9 [f]ver 13; Isa 52:12
6:10 [g]ver 20
6:15 [h]1Ki 18:44
6:17 [i]Lev 27:28; Dt 20:17 [j]Jos 2:4
6:18 [k]Jos 7:1 [l]Jos 7:12 [m]Jos 7:25,26
6:19 [n]ver 24; Nu 31:22
6:20 [o]Jdg 6:34; Jer 4:21; Am 2:2 [p]ver 5 [q]Heb 11:30
6:21 [r]Dt 20:16
6:22 [s]Jos 2:14; Heb 11:31
6:23 [t]Jos 2:13
6:24 [u]ver 19

LORD and have seven priests carry trumpets in front of it." 7And he ordered the army, "Advance[e]! March
around the city, with an armed guard going ahead of the ark of the LORD."
8When Joshua had spoken to the people, the seven priests carrying the seven trumpets before the
LORD went forward, blowing their trumpets, and the ark of the LORD's covenant followed them. 9The
armed guard marched ahead of the priests who blew the trumpets, and the rear guard[f] followed the
ark. All this time the trumpets were sounding. 10But Joshua had commanded the army, "Do not give a
war cry, do not raise your voices, do not say a word until the day I tell you to shout. Then shout![g]" 11So
he had the ark of the LORD carried around the city, circling it once. Then the army returned to camp
and spent the night there.
12Joshua got up early the next morning and the priests took up the ark of the LORD. 13The seven
priests carrying the seven trumpets went forward, marching before the ark of the LORD and blowing the
trumpets. The armed men went ahead of them and the rear guard followed the ark of the LORD, while
the trumpets kept sounding. 14So on the second day they marched around the city once and returned
to the camp. They did this for six days.
15On the seventh day, they got up at daybreak and marched around the city seven times in the same
manner, except that on that day they circled the city seven times.[h] 16The seventh time around, when
the priests sounded the trumpet blast, Joshua commanded the army, "Shout! For the LORD has given
you the city! 17The city and all that is in it are to be devoted[a][i] to the LORD. Only Rahab the prostitute
and all who are with her in her house shall be spared, because she hid[j] the spies we sent. 18But keep
away from the devoted things,[k] so that you will not bring about your own destruction by taking any
of them. Otherwise you will make the camp of Israel liable to destruction[l] and bring trouble[m] on it.
19All the silver and gold and the articles of bronze and iron[n] are sacred to the LORD and must go into
his treasury."
20When the trumpets sounded,[o] the army shouted, and at the sound of the trumpet, when the men
gave a loud shout,[p] the wall collapsed; so everyone charged straight in, and they took the city.[q] 21They
devoted the city to the LORD and destroyed[r] with the sword every living thing in it—men and women,
young and old, cattle, sheep and donkeys.
22Joshua said to the two men who had spied out the land, "Go into the prostitute's house and bring
her out and all who belong to her, in accordance with your oath to her.[s]" 23So the young men who
had done the spying went in and brought out Rahab, her father and mother, her brothers and sisters
and all who belonged to her.[t] They brought out her entire family and put them in a place outside the
camp of Israel.
24Then they burned the whole city and everything in it, but they put the silver and gold and the
articles of bronze and iron[u] into the treasury of the LORD's house. 25But Joshua spared Rahab the pros-

[a] *17* The Hebrew term refers to the irrevocable giving over of things or persons to the LORD, often by totally destroying them; also in verses 18 and 21.

leads Israel to obey (1:8; cf. Exod 19:8; 23:13; 24:7; 2 Kgs 21:8; 2 Chr 33:8; Jer 11:4).

6:9 armed guard ... priests ... rear guard. In this holy procession, the honor guard (all the army of Israel) surrounds the priests, whose horns announce the ark that follows them (cf. 3:1–17; Num 10:1–28; 2 Sam 6:12–17).

6:16–25 Saving Rahab's family interweaves with the story of Jericho's destruction. God's gracious saving of Rahab and his destruction of Jericho are equally important.

6:17 devoted to the LORD. See NIV text note; see also Introduction to Deuteronomy: Themes and Theology (Holy War). God commanded Israel to do to Canaan (Deut 20:17) what Israel had done to Sihon and Og (Josh 2:10; see Num 21:21–35; Deut 2:34; 3:6). Although this practice existed among Israel's neighbors (Mesha of Moab later uses it against Israel in the ninth century BC), Israel practiced it because of Canaan's sin (Gen 15:16) and to preserve their own holiness (worshiping God alone) from the seduction of living with those who worshiped other gods (Deut 20:18). Jericho's likely status as a fort (see notes on 2:1,2; 6:2) implies that Israel attacks an army, not civilians. **Rahab.** God does not devote to destruction those who devote themselves freely to him. They can, like Rahab, become heroes of faith (Heb 11:31; Jas 2:25). Rahab became part of the ancestral line of Jesus (Matt 1:5).

6:18 devoted things. Everything not destroyed is to go to the Lord's treasury for his use (v. 19), not to the Israelites for personal plunder. Jericho had turned away from God, and now God demands Jericho back, including all its property. It is either to be placed in God's treasury or sacrificed to him and burnt in the fire (v. 24). Joshua's warning anticipates Achan's sin and Israel's punishment (ch. 7).

6:21 men and women. The Hebrew has the idea "from man unto woman" (8:25; 1 Sam 15:3; 22:19; 2 Sam 6:19; 1 Chr 16:3; 2 Chr 15:13; Neh 8:2). The phrase regularly appears with the Hebrew for "all" as a stereotypical way to signify everyone. This formed part of the checklist, along with the animals, and indicated that outwardly (cf. ch. 7) Israel followed Joshua's command (v. 17). They killed any on the list who were found. However, the expression does not necessarily mean that noncombatants were present.

6:23 outside the camp. Rahab and her family remain temporarily (v. 25) in this unclean place.

titute,[v] with her family and all who belonged to her, because she hid the men Joshua had sent as spies
to Jericho[w]—and she lives among the Israelites to this day.
26At that time Joshua pronounced this solemn oath: "Cursed before the LORD is the one who undertakes to rebuild this city, Jericho:

> "At the cost of his firstborn son
> he will lay its foundations;
> at the cost of his youngest
> he will set up its gates."[x]

27So the LORD was with Joshua,[y] and his fame spread[z] throughout the land.

Achan's Sin

7 But the Israelites were unfaithful in regard to the devoted things[a];[a] Achan son of Karmi, the son
of Zimri,[b] the son of Zerah,[b] of the tribe of Judah, took some of them. So the LORD's anger burned
against Israel.
2Now Joshua sent men from Jericho to Ai, which is near Beth Aven[c] to the east of Bethel, and told
them, "Go up and spy out the region." So the men went up and spied out Ai.
3When they returned to Joshua, they said, "Not all the army will have to go up against Ai. Send two
or three thousand men to take it and do not weary the whole army, for only a few people live there." 4So
about three thousand went up; but they were routed by the men of Ai,[d] 5who killed about thirty-six of
them. They chased the Israelites from the city gate as far as the stone quarries and struck them down
on the slopes. At this the hearts of the people melted in fear[e] and became like water.
6Then Joshua tore his clothes[f] and fell facedown to the ground before the ark of the LORD, remaining
there till evening. The elders of Israel did the same, and sprinkled dust[g] on their heads. 7And Joshua
said, "Alas, Sovereign LORD, why did you ever bring this people across the Jordan to deliver us into the
hands of the Amorites to destroy us?[h] If only we had been content to stay on the other side of the Jordan! 8Pardon your servant, Lord. What can I say, now that Israel has been routed by its enemies? 9The
Canaanites and the other people of the country will hear about this and they will surround us and wipe
out our name from the earth.[i] What then will you do for your own great name?"
10The LORD said to Joshua, "Stand up! What are you doing down on your face? 11Israel has sinned;
they have violated my covenant,[j] which I commanded them to keep. They have taken some of the
devoted things; they have stolen, they have lied,[k] they have put them with their own possessions.

[a] *1* The Hebrew term refers to the irrevocable giving over of things or persons to the LORD, often by totally destroying them; also in verses 11, 12, 13 and 15. [b] *1* See Septuagint and 1 Chron. 2:6; Hebrew *Zabdi*; also in verses 17 and 18.

6:25 [v]Heb 11:31 [w]Jos 2:6
6:26 [x]1Ki 16:34
6:27 [y]Ge 39:2; Jos 1:5 [z]Jos 9:1
7:1 [a]Jos 6:18 [b]Jos 22:20
7:2 [c]Jos 18:12; 1Sa 13:5; 14:23
7:4 [d]Lev 26:17; Dt 28:25
7:5 [e]Lev 26:36; Jos 2:9, 11; Eze 21:7; Na 2:10
7:6 [f]Ge 37:29 [g]1Sa 4:12; 2Sa 13:19; Ne 9:1; Job 2:12; La 2:10; Rev 18:19
7:7 [h]Ex 5:22
7:9 [i]Ex 32:12; Dt 9:28
7:11 [j]Jos 6:17-19 [k]Ac 5:1-2

6:26 Cursed ... is the one. Deut 13:16 commands that any town destroyed for advocating the worship of other gods should never be inhabited again. This curse was fulfilled in 1 Kgs 16:34.
7:1–26 *Achan's Sin.* This story describes the effects of a single transgression that leads all Israel to sin and defeat (vv. 1–5). Its resolution requires turning to God (vv. 6–9) and a divinely led purification from the sin (vv. 10–26). Achan's departure from God's covenant with Israel contrasts with Rahab's embrace of that covenant (chs. 2; 6). God can forgive the nation, but the effects of this sin affect the attitudes of the surrounding nations (v. 9; cf. 5:1).
7:1 Israelites were unfaithful. Israel violated their obligations toward the "devoted things" (6:18). **son of Karmi.** This, the longest genealogy in Joshua, proves that Achan (a non-Hebrew name) is an Israelite and connects him and his sin with Israel.
7:2 Ai. Usually associated with et-Tell, this site guarded the middle of three roads from Jericho. The path to Ai led 15 miles (24 kilometers) westward and ascended 3,400 feet (1,035 meters). **Bethel.** Usually associated with Beitin, about two miles (3 kilometers) northwest of Ai. **spy out.** Cf. 2:1–2.
7:3 Not all the army. This decision breaks the unity of "all" the people (see 1:2 and note there).
7:4–5 This loss meant God was not with Israel.
7:5 melted in fear. The loss reversed the effect of the previous victories (2:11; 5:1). Instead of Canaan fearing Israel (see 2:24 and note), Israel feared Canaan.
7:6 tore his clothes. This sign of distress and mourning (Gen 37:34; 44:13; Judg 11:35) introduces the sorrow of Joshua and the elders. **sprinkled dust.** Another sign of sorrow (Job 2:12; Lam 2:10).
7:9 wipe out our name. Joshua foresees the Canaanites, who were emboldened by Israel's defeat, attacking Israel and reversing the great reputation that God promised Abram (Gen 12:2–3). **for your own great name.** Like Moses (Num 14:13–16; Deut 9:28–29), Joshua puts God's honor at the center of his plea.
7:11 Israel has sinned. God announces the reason for Israel's failure for the first time after Israel's day of prayer and sorrow. The sin of one affects all (22:20). Achan's disobedience compromises the integrity of Israel as a nation dedicated to God. They need to know how serious disobedience is. **violated.** Israel could not cross against its enemies because it crossed against (the same Hebrew term translated "crossed" is here translated "violated"; see note on 1:2) God and his covenant. **stolen ... lied.** The one act leads to sin in several areas (Exod 20:15–16; Deut 5:19–20).

7:12 [l]Nu 14:45; Jdg 2:14 [m]Jos 6:18
7:13 [n]Jos 3:5; 6:18
7:14 [o]Pr 16:33
7:15 [p]1Sa 14:39 [q]ver 11 [r]Ge 34:7
7:17 [s]Nu 26:20
7:19 [t]1Sa 6:5; Jer 13:16; Jn 9:24* [u]1Sa 14:43
7:21 [v]Dt 7:25; Eph 5:5; 1Ti 6:10
7:24 [w]ver 26; Jos 15:7
7:25 [x]Jos 6:18

12 That is why the Israelites cannot stand against their enemies;[l] they turn their backs and run because
they have been made liable to destruction.[m] I will not be with you anymore unless you destroy whatever
among you is devoted to destruction.
13 "Go, consecrate the people. Tell them, 'Consecrate yourselves[n] in preparation for tomorrow; for
this is what the LORD, the God of Israel, says: There are devoted things among you, Israel. You cannot
stand against your enemies until you remove them.
14 " 'In the morning, present yourselves tribe by tribe. The tribe the LORD chooses[o] shall come forward clan by clan; the clan the LORD chooses shall come forward family by family; and the family the
LORD chooses shall come forward man by man. 15 Whoever is caught with the devoted things shall be
destroyed by fire, along with all that belongs to him.[p] He has violated the covenant[q] of the LORD and
has done an outrageous thing in Israel!' "[r]
16 Early the next morning Joshua had Israel come forward by tribes, and Judah was chosen. 17 The
clans of Judah came forward, and the Zerahites were chosen.[s] He had the clan of the Zerahites come
forward by families, and Zimri was chosen. 18 Joshua had his family come forward man by man, and
Achan son of Karmi, the son of Zimri, the son of Zerah, of the tribe of Judah, was chosen.
19 Then Joshua said to Achan, "My son, give glory[t] to the LORD, the God of Israel, and honor him. Tell[u]
me what you have done; do not hide it from me."
20 Achan replied, "It is true! I have sinned against the LORD, the God of Israel. This is what I have
done: 21 When I saw in the plunder a beautiful robe from Babylonia,[a] two hundred shekels[b] of silver
and a bar of gold weighing fifty shekels,[c] I coveted[v] them and took them. They are hidden in the ground
inside my tent, with the silver underneath."
22 So Joshua sent messengers, and they ran to the tent, and there it was, hidden in his tent, with the
silver underneath. 23 They took the things from the tent, brought them to Joshua and all the Israelites
and spread them out before the LORD.
24 Then Joshua, together with all Israel, took Achan son of Zerah, the silver, the robe, the gold bar, his
sons and daughters, his cattle, donkeys and sheep, his tent and all that he had, to the Valley of Achor.[w]
25 Joshua said, "Why have you brought this trouble[x] on us? The LORD will bring trouble on you today."

[a] *21* Hebrew *Shinar* [b] *21* That is, about 5 pounds or about 2.3 kilograms [c] *21* That is, about 1 1/4 pounds or about 575 grams

7:12 devoted to destruction. God owns the "devoted things" from Jericho (see 6:18 and note there; see also 6:19,24). Until Israel rids itself of the one responsible for taking those "devoted things" (7:1), God will treat Israel as "devoted things."

7:13 Consecrate yourselves. See 3:5 and note.

7:14 tribe ... clan ... family. Israelite society was based on kinship relations. The extended "family" formed the basic unit (2:12), multiple families composed the clan, and multiple clans made up the tribe. The OT people of God were a large family; what affected one (as Achan's sin) affected all. **the LORD chooses.** While it is not stated here, the priest normally used the Urim and Thummim to determine God's will (1 Sam 10:20–21 ["lot"]; 14:41–42). These were associated with casting lots (see notes on Exod 28:30; Num 27:21).

7:15 destroyed by fire. As Israel devoted Jericho to the Lord by fire (6:24), so any who took the "devoted things" (see 6:18 and note there) must be devoted to him by fire. **outrageous thing.** A shockingly wicked and willful act against God's holiness (Deut 22:21; Judg 19:23–24; 20:6,10; 2 Sam 13:12).

7:18 Achan ... was chosen. Cf. v. 1. God discloses the identity of the sinner (Num 32:23).

7:19 give glory to the LORD. Speak the truth and so give glory to God (John 9:24). With the guilt established, Joshua instructs Achan to confess the sin so that Achan may honor God with his words and Joshua may restore the "devoted things" (v. 1) to God. Confession cannot avert the consequences of this sin, but it can begin to repair the broken relationships that dishonored God.

7:21 saw ... beautiful. Eve's sin is also described with these Hebrew words, translated "saw ... good" (see Gen 3:6 and note). **two hundred shekels of silver.** The value of a slave (perhaps representing a lifetime of labor) was 30 silver shekels (Exod 21:32).

7:23 spread them out before the LORD. Israel returned to God what was his.

7:24 all Israel. The sin affects all Israel. Everyone must participate in Achan's punishment in order to "purge the evil from among [them]" (Deut 17:7). **took Achan ... and all that he had.** They burn and so devote to God Achan, his property, and the goods he took. It is not clear if the silver and gold that the fire could not destroy remain in the pile of rocks or if it was returned to the tabernacle treasury. The family of Achan would have known what he had hidden in his tent (v. 22) and therefore shared his guilt (Prov 15:27). **Valley of Achor.** The Hebrew name is *ʿākar* ("trouble"). See NIV text note on v. 26.

7:25 trouble on us ... trouble on you. This wordplay with the Hebrew *ʿākar* ("trouble") sounds like "Achan" and becomes the name of the valley of Achan's execution as well as Achan's nickname (see 1 Chr 2:7 and NIV text note). **stoned.** Stoning punished idolatry, blasphemy, Sabbath breaking, and disobeying one's parents (Lev 20:2; 24:14; Num 15:35; Deut 21:21). The whole community participates in the punishment and purge the sin from their midst. **stoned the rest.** This "stoned" is a different Hebrew word (*sql*) than the first use of "stoned" in this verse (Hebrew *rgm*). In Hebrew, the clause follows "they burned them," which may suggest heaping up the pile of stones in v. 26. There is another possibility. In 2 Sam 16:6,13 *sql* is used to describe how Shimei threw stones at David. Perhaps after burning Achan's tent and his belongings, the Israelites drove away Achan's family and cattle by throwing stones at them. **burned.** Cf. 6:24, where Jericho is similarly "devoted to the LORD" (6:17).

Then all Israel stoned him,[y] and after they had stoned the rest, they burned them. 26Over Achan they heaped up a large pile of rocks, which remains to this day. Then the LORD turned from his fierce anger.[z] Therefore that place has been called the Valley of Achor[a][a] ever since.

Ai Destroyed

8 Then the LORD said to Joshua, "Do not be afraid;[b] do not be discouraged.[c] Take the whole army[d] with you, and go up and attack Ai. For I have delivered[e] into your hands the king of Ai, his people, his city and his land. 2You shall do to Ai and its king as you did to Jericho and its king, except that you may carry off their plunder and livestock for yourselves.[f] Set an ambush behind the city."

3So Joshua and the whole army moved out to attack Ai. He chose thirty thousand of his best fighting men and sent them out at night 4with these orders: "Listen carefully. You are to set an ambush behind the city. Don't go very far from it. All of you be on the alert. 5I and all those with me will advance on the city, and when the men come out against us, as they did before, we will flee from them. 6They will pursue us until we have lured them away from the city, for they will say, 'They are running away from us as they did before.' So when we flee from them, 7you are to rise up from ambush and take the city. The LORD your God will give it into your hand.[g] 8When you have taken the city, set it on fire.[h] Do what the LORD has commanded.[i] See to it; you have my orders."

9Then Joshua sent them off, and they went to the place of ambush[j] and lay in wait between Bethel and Ai, to the west of Ai—but Joshua spent that night with the people.

10Early the next morning[k] Joshua mustered his army, and he and the leaders of Israel[l] marched before them to Ai. 11The entire force that was with him marched up and approached the city and arrived in front of it. They set up camp north of Ai, with the valley between them and the city. 12Joshua had taken about five thousand men and set them in ambush between Bethel and Ai, to the west of the city. 13So the soldiers took up their positions—with the main camp to the north of the city and the ambush to the west of it. That night Joshua went into the valley.

14When the king of Ai saw this, he and all the men of the city hurried out early in the morning to meet Israel in battle at a certain place overlooking the Arabah.[m] But he did not know[n] that an ambush had been set against him behind the city. 15Joshua and all Israel let themselves be driven back[o] before them, and they fled toward the wilderness.[p] 16All the men of Ai were called to pursue them, and they pursued Joshua and were lured away[q] from the city. 17Not a man remained in Ai or Bethel who did not go after Israel. They left the city open and went in pursuit of Israel.

[a] 26 *Achor* means *trouble.*

7:25 [y] Dt 17:5
7:26 [z] Nu 25:4; Dt 13:17 [a] ver 24; Isa 65:10; Hos 2:15
8:1 [b] Dt 31:6 [c] Dt 1:21; 7:18; Jos 1:9 [d] Jos 10:7 [e] Jos 6:2
8:2 [f] ver 27; Dt 20:14
8:7 [g] Jdg 7:7; 1Sa 23:4
8:8 [h] Jdg 20:29-38 [i] ver 19
8:9 [j] 2Ch 13:13
8:10 [k] Ge 22:3 [l] Jos 7:6
8:14 [m] Dt 1:1 [n] Jdg 20:34
8:15 [o] Jdg 20:36 [p] Jos 15:61; 16:1; 18:12
8:16 [q] Jdg 20:31

7:26 pile. These stones recall those set up at the crossing of the Jordan (4:20). The circular pile would remind passersby that God demands holiness. **turned from.** The prophets use this verb to call Israel to repent, or turn from their sin, and return to God (e.g., Jer 3), so that God may turn from his anger. Here, at the beginning of their life in the promised land, the Israelites learn the terrible consequences of sin and the need to purge it, just as the young church would later learn (Acts 5:1–11). **Valley of Achor.** Probably Buqei'ah Valley, about eight miles (13 kilometers) south of Jericho; see note on v. 24.

8:1–29 *Ai Destroyed.* In part 2 of Ai's story (ch. 7 is part 1), success for the Israelites comes from obeying God's instructions.

8:1 the LORD said to Joshua. Contrast the lack of divine direction in 7:1–5. **Do not be afraid; do not be discouraged.** See 1:5b–9 and note. The second phrase is found in 1 Chr 22:13; 28:20 (cf. Deut 1:21), where David charges Solomon to build the temple. Here as well, these words encourage Joshua for a great mission from God. God mercifully gives Israel a second chance (ch. 7). **the whole army.** All Israel, not a fraction (7:3–4), is united before God (see 1:2 and note). **I have delivered.** See 6:2 and note. **king ... city.** Cf. 2:2; 6:2 (see notes there). **his land.** Israel could occupy this land, unlike cursed Jericho (6:26).

8:2 you may carry off their plunder and livestock. While Israel's destruction of Jericho allowed no plunder or livestock (cf. Deut 20:16–18) to be taken, here God gives these to Israel as food to sustain them. **Set an ambush.** While this has many parallels in the history of warfare, here it demonstrates God's use of strategy rather than an overt miracle (e.g., Jericho).

8:3 thousand. Hebrew *'elep*; it can also mean a military unit or squad, which would suggest a smaller size (cf. 4:13; 7:3,4; 8:12,25; see Introduction to Numbers: Interpretive Issues).

8:9–13 Joshua spent that night with the people ... That night Joshua went into the valley. As in the story of the spies (2:1–8), crossing the Jordan (chs. 3–4), and attacking Jericho (ch. 6), this story positions different groups in different places (30,000 in vv. 3–9; "his army" in vv. 10–11; 5,000 in vv. 12–13). The two phrases ("Joshua spent that night with the people" and "That night Joshua went into the valley") are identical in the Hebrew except for the addition of an additional letter at the end of the second phrase (Hebrew *'m* ["people"] versus *'mq* ["valley"]). The phrases bracket the section that describes the preparation for the battle. They also emphasize the main position of Israel ("the people") in "the valley" in front of Ai.

8:12 five thousand. The 30,000 of v. 3 (see note there) may have included the 5,000 of vv. 12–13 plus 25,000 others who are not mentioned. The 30,000 may include the entire fighting force, from which 5,000 were set apart for the ambush.

8:14 the king of Ai saw this. The armed force in the valley to the north was too large to be hidden in the morning light. **Arabah.** See Deut 1:1; see also note on Deut 1:7.

8:17 Bethel. Either Bethel was an ally or it garrisoned Ai to guard the

8:18 [r]Job 41:26; Ps 35:3 [s]Ex 4:2; 14:16; 17:9-12 [t]ver 26
8:19 [u]Jdg 20:33 [v]ver 8
8:20 [w]Jdg 20:40
8:22 [x]Dt 7:2; Jos 10:1
8:23 [y]1Sa 15:8
8:25 [z]Dt 20:16-18
8:26 [a]Nu 21:2 [b]Ex 17:12
8:27 [c]ver 2
8:28 [d]Nu 31:10 [e]Jos 7:2; Jer 49:3 [f]Dt 13:16; Jos 10:1 [g]Ge 35:20
8:29 [h]Dt 21:23; Jn 19:31 [i]2Sa 18:17
8:30 [j]Dt 11:29 [k]Ex 20:24
8:31 [l]Ex 20:25 [m]Dt 27:6-7
8:32 [n]Dt 27:8
8:33 [o]Dt 31:12 [p]Lev 16:29 [q]Dt 11:29; 27:11-14
8:34 [r]Dt 28:61; 31:11; Jos 1:8
8:35 [s]Ex 12:38; Dt 31:12

[18]Then the LORD said to Joshua, "Hold out toward Ai the javelin[r] that is in your hand,[s] for into your hand I will deliver the city." So Joshua held out toward the city the javelin that was in his hand.[t] [19]As soon as he did this, the men in the ambush rose quickly[u] from their position and rushed forward. They entered the city and captured it and quickly set it on fire.[v]

[20]The men of Ai looked back and saw the smoke of the city rising up into the sky,[w] but they had no chance to escape in any direction; the Israelites who had been fleeing toward the wilderness had turned back against their pursuers. [21]For when Joshua and all Israel saw that the ambush had taken the city and that smoke was going up from it, they turned around and attacked the men of Ai. [22]Those in the ambush also came out of the city against them, so that they were caught in the middle, with Israelites on both sides. Israel cut them down, leaving them neither survivors nor fugitives.[x] [23]But they took the king of Ai alive[y] and brought him to Joshua.

[24]When Israel had finished killing all the men of Ai in the fields and in the wilderness where they had chased them, and when every one of them had been put to the sword, all the Israelites returned to Ai and killed those who were in it. [25]Twelve thousand men and women fell that day—all the people of Ai.[z] [26]For Joshua did not draw back the hand that held out his javelin until he had destroyed[*a*][a] all who lived in Ai.[b] [27]But Israel did carry off for themselves the livestock and plunder of this city, as the LORD had instructed Joshua.[c]

[28]So Joshua burned[d] Ai[*b*][e] and made it a permanent heap of ruins,[f] a desolate place to this day.[g] [29]He impaled the body of the king of Ai on a pole and left it there until evening. At sunset,[h] Joshua ordered them to take the body from the pole and throw it down at the entrance of the city gate. And they raised a large pile of rocks[i] over it, which remains to this day.

The Covenant Renewed at Mount Ebal

[30]Then Joshua built on Mount Ebal[j] an altar[k] to the LORD, the God of Israel, [31]as Moses the servant of the LORD had commanded the Israelites. He built it according to what is written in the Book of the Law of Moses—an altar of uncut stones, on which no iron tool[l] had been used. On it they offered to the LORD burnt offerings and sacrificed fellowship offerings.[m] [32]There, in the presence of the Israelites, Joshua wrote on stones a copy of the law of Moses.[n] [33]All the Israelites, with their elders, officials and judges, were standing on both sides of the ark of the covenant of the LORD, facing the Levitical[o] priests who carried it. Both the foreigners living among them and the native-born[p] were there. Half of the people stood in front of Mount Gerizim and half of them in front of Mount Ebal,[q] as Moses the servant of the LORD had formerly commanded when he gave instructions to bless the people of Israel.

[34]Afterward, Joshua read all the words of the law—the blessings and the curses—just as it is written in the Book of the Law.[r] [35]There was not a word of all that Moses had commanded that Joshua did not read to the whole assembly of Israel, including the women and children, and the foreigners who lived among them.[s]

a *26* The Hebrew term refers to the irrevocable giving over of things or persons to the LORD, often by totally destroying them. *b* *28* *Ai* means *the ruin*.

---

road from the Jordan Valley (for Ai's "king" as a commander, see note on 2:2).

8:18 the LORD said. God directs when and where to accomplish his purpose. **Hold out ... the javelin.** The soldiers could have seen the upraised javelin in the morning light.

8:25 men and women. See 6:21 and note.

8:29 impaled the body of the king. This public spectacle bore witness to the success of God and Israel; it was less brutal and gruesome than practices of other countries (e.g., Assyria), which might impale an entire army alive. **take the body.** Cf. Deut 21:23. **large pile of rocks over it.** This second memorial (cf. 7:26) completes the story of Ai.

8:30–35 *The Covenant Renewed at Mount Ebal.* This occurred about 1406 or 1220 BC (for the two possible dates, see Introduction to the Old Testament: Chronology/Dating, p. 7). The external battles against Jericho (ch. 6) and Ai (8:1–29) alternate with events inside Israel: the Passover (ch. 5), dealing with Achan's sin (ch. 7), and the covenant at Mount Ebal (8:30–35). Israel prepares and consecrates itself before and after each battle. This renewal emphasizes the covenant, the participation of all Israel, and the obedience of Joshua.

8:30 Mount Ebal. The highest mountain in the region north of Shechem, where Abram built his first altar (Gen 12:6–7) as did Jacob on his return to the promised land (Gen 33:19).

8:31–32 uncut stones ... burnt offerings ... fellowship offerings ... Joshua wrote. Precisely follows Deut 27:4–8 (cf. Exod 24:1–8).

8:33 Half of the people stood in front of Mount Gerizim and half of them in front of Mount Ebal. Cf. Deut 27:12–13. Gerizim was south of Shechem, which does not appear in this text. Shechem may have joined Israel peacefully (but cf. 11:19), may have fled, or the battle was not recorded (cf. 21:21; 24:25,32).

8:34 blessings ... curses. These form an important part of OT covenants that motivate God's people to obedience (cf. Deut 27:14—28:68). **Book of the Law.** This identifies the laws (and blessings and curses) in Deuteronomy (Deut 28:61; 29:21; 30:10; 31:24,26). See note on 1:8.

An altar from Mount Ebal possibly dating to the time of Joshua.

© Hanan Isachar/Alamy

The Gibeonite Deception

9 Now when all the kings west of the Jordan heard about these things — the kings in the hill country,
in the western foothills, and along the entire coast of the Mediterranean Sea[t] as far as Lebanon
(the kings of the Hittites, Amorites, Canaanites, Perizzites, Hivites and Jebusites)[u] — 2they came together to wage war against Joshua and Israel.
3However, when the people of Gibeon[v] heard what Joshua had done to Jericho and Ai, 4they resorted
to a ruse: They went as a delegation whose donkeys were loaded[a] with worn-out sacks and old wineskins, cracked and mended. 5They put worn and patched sandals on their feet and wore old clothes.
All the bread of their food supply was dry and moldy. 6Then they went to Joshua in the camp at Gilgal[w]
and said to him and the Israelites, "We have come from a distant country; make a treaty with us."
7The Israelites said to the Hivites,[x] "But perhaps you live near us, so how can we make a treaty[y]
with you?"
8"We are your servants,[z]" they said to Joshua.

9:1 [t] Nu 34:6 [u] Ex 3:17; Jos 3:10
9:3 [v] ver 17; Jos 10:2; 2Sa 2:12; 2Ch 1:3; Isa 28:21
9:6 [w] Jos 5:10
9:7 [x] ver 1; Jos 11:19 [y] Ex 23:32; Dt 7:2
9:8 [z] Dt 20:11; 2Ki 10:5

[a] *4* Most Hebrew manuscripts; some Hebrew manuscripts, Vulgate and Syriac (see also Septuagint) *They prepared provisions and loaded their donkeys*

9:1–27 *The Gibeonite Deception.* This is the first of three chapters that describe Israel's taking the land of Canaan. Like Rahab (ch. 2), the Gibeonites negotiate with Israel. Similar to the Achan incident (ch. 7), Joshua leads the Israelites in repentance before God. Following the covenant renewal (8:30–35), Israel does not first seek God but seeks its own interests (cf. Achan [ch. 7] after the Passover [ch. 5]). Despite Israel's lack of faithfulness, God keeps his promises to give them the land.

9:1 in the hill country, in the western foothills, and along the entire coast. These three major north-south divisions (from east to west) form Israel's topography. Moving from east to west are the hill country, the foothills, and the Mediterranean coast. **Mediterranean … Lebanon … Hittites.** For the regions and borders given to Israel, see 1:4 and note. This reaches to Lebanon but omits the northernmost part that extends to the Euphrates (1:4), which is not involved in Joshua. **Hittites, Amorites, Canaanites, Perizzites, Hivites and Jebusites.** See 3:10 and note; 11:3; 12:8; 24:11; Deut 7:1; 20:17; they all concern Joshua and Israel's taking of the land. **Amorites, Canaanites.** See 5:1 and note. **Perizzites, Hivites and Jebusites.** They likely migrated into Canaan from north of Israel (modern Syria and Turkey). They are perhaps related to extrabiblical Hurrians and Hittites of the second millennium BC. **Hivites.** Include Gibeonites (v. 7; 11:19). **Jebusites.** Their territory includes Jerusalem (15:8; 18:16,28), anticipating major characters in chs. 9–10.

9:2 to wage war. This fulfills Joshua's prophecy (7:7–9). The kings learn of the initial defeat at Ai (7:1–5), and rather than being awed by God's great deeds of victory as had been true of Jericho's inhabitants earlier (2:10–11; 5:1), they are not fearful but wage war. Had Achan not sinned, perhaps the battles of chs. 10 and 11, as well as the loss of life, could have been avoided. As with the sin of Gen 3 and all sin (Rom 6:23), the consequences are more terrible than the sinners expected (see notes on 7:11,19,26).

9:3 Gibeon. El-Jîb, about six miles (9.5 kilometers) north of ancient Jerusalem; dozens of jar handles bearing the incised name of Gibeon have been found in a water shaft there (2 Sam 2:13).

9:4 ruse. The Gibeonites would trick Joshua just as he had tricked Ai (v. 3). The term "ruse" carries the sense of prudence (Prov 1:4; 8:5,12) rather than suggesting a malicious scheme as elsewhere (Exod 21:14).

9:6 distant country. So the Israelites could allow them to live as they were (Deut 20:10–18). **treaty.** Hebrew *bĕrît*; used of the covenant relationship between God and his people (see Gen 6:18; Exod 24:6–8 and notes).

9:7 Hivites. See v. 1 and note.

9:8 servants. The treaty (v. 6) is between the suzerain Israel and the

9:9 [a] Dt 20:15 [b] ver 24; Jos 2:9
9:10 [c] Nu 21:33 [d] Nu 21:24,35
9:14 [e] Nu 27:21
9:15 [f] Ex 23:32; Jos 11:19; 2Sa 21:2
9:17 [g] Jos 18:25 [h] 1Sa 7:1-2
9:18 [i] Ps 15:4 [j] Ex 15:24
9:21 [k] ver 15 [l] Dt 29:11
9:22 [m] ver 6 [n] ver 16
9:23 [o] Ge 9:25
9:24 [p] ver 9
9:25 [q] Ge 16:6
9:27 [r] Dt 12:5
10:1 [s] Jdg 1:7 [t] Jos 8:1 [u] Dt 20:16; Jos 8:22 [v] Jos 9:15

But Joshua asked, "Who are you and where do you come from?"
9 They answered: "Your servants have come from a very distant country[a] because of the fame of the
LORD your God. For we have heard reports[b] of him: all that he did in Egypt, 10 and all that he did to the
two kings of the Amorites east of the Jordan — Sihon king of Heshbon, and Og king of Bashan,[c] who
reigned in Ashtaroth.[d] 11 And our elders and all those living in our country said to us, 'Take provisions
for your journey; go and meet them and say to them, "We are your servants; make a treaty with us." '
12 This bread of ours was warm when we packed it at home on the day we left to come to you. But now
see how dry and moldy it is. 13 And these wineskins that we filled were new, but see how cracked they
are. And our clothes and sandals are worn out by the very long journey."
14 The Israelites sampled their provisions but did not inquire[e] of the LORD. 15 Then Joshua made a
treaty of peace[f] with them to let them live, and the leaders of the assembly ratified it by oath.
16 Three days after they made the treaty with the Gibeonites, the Israelites heard that they were
neighbors, living near them. 17 So the Israelites set out and on the third day came to their cities: Gibeon,
Kephirah, Beeroth[g] and Kiriath Jearim.[h] 18 But the Israelites did not attack them, because the leaders of
the assembly had sworn an oath[i] to them by the LORD, the God of Israel.
The whole assembly grumbled[j] against the leaders, 19 but all the leaders answered, "We have given
them our oath by the LORD, the God of Israel, and we cannot touch them now. 20 This is what we will do
to them: We will let them live, so that God's wrath will not fall on us for breaking the oath we swore to
them." 21 They continued, "Let them live,[k] but let them be woodcutters and water carriers[l] in the service
of the whole assembly." So the leaders' promise to them was kept.
22 Then Joshua summoned the Gibeonites and said, "Why did you deceive us by saying, 'We live a
long way[m] from you,' while actually you live near[n] us? 23 You are now under a curse:[o] You will never be
released from service as woodcutters and water carriers for the house of my God."
24 They answered Joshua, "Your servants were clearly told[p] how the LORD your God had commanded
his servant Moses to give you the whole land and to wipe out all its inhabitants from before you. So we
feared for our lives because of you, and that is why we did this. 25 We are now in your hands.[q] Do to us
whatever seems good and right to you."
26 So Joshua saved them from the Israelites, and they did not kill them. 27 That day he made the Gibeonites woodcutters and water carriers for the assembly, to provide for the needs of the altar of the LORD
at the place the LORD would choose.[r] And that is what they are to this day.

The Sun Stands Still

10 Now Adoni-Zedek king of Jerusalem[s] heard that Joshua had taken Ai[t] and totally destroyed[a][u] it,
doing to Ai and its king as he had done to Jericho and its king, and that the people of Gibeon
had made a treaty of peace[v] with Israel and had become their allies. 2 He and his people were very much

[a] *1* The Hebrew term refers to the irrevocable giving over of things or persons to the LORD, often by totally destroying them; also in verses 28, 35, 37, 39 and 40.

vassal Gibeon; it follows the international language of ancient diplomacy and anticipates Gibeon's role (vv. 21,27).
9:9–10 Egypt . . . Sihon . . . Og. This confession of God as Savior (like Rahab's confession in 2:9–11) leads Gibeon to submit to God and his people.
9:9 we have heard reports. These reports emphasize the historic acts of redemption. Contrast the kings of Canaan (see vv. 1–2 and note on v. 2).
9:14 Although initially suspicious (v. 7), Israel relies on its own ability to discern the truthfulness of the Gibeonites' story. The Gibeonites confess how God led Israel, but Israel ignores God's leadership!
9:15 peace. Hebrew *šālôm*; here it is the language of diplomacy (see v. 6 and note). **oath.** A covenant sworn before God (vv. 18–19) required obedience (Gen 26:26–31; Exod 20:7; Lev 19:12; Deut 5:11; 1 Sam 14:24; 20:8; 23:18 Ezek 16:59–60).
9:18 sworn an oath. See v. 15 and note. **grumbled.** The same word used of Israel's wilderness grumbling (Exod 15:24; 16:2; Num 14:2,27,36). The assembly's anger may come as much from the loss of Gibeonite booty as from any sin.
9:21 woodcutters and water carriers. In Deut 29:11 these are the activities of foreigners in Israel.
9:23 for the house of my God. Gibeonite service was devoted to God.
9:27 place the LORD would choose. Cf. Deut 12:5 (see note there). While later associated with Shiloh (1 Sam 4:3) and Jerusalem, the context places God's choice on Mount Ebal (8:30–35; cf. chs. 23–24) or, perhaps more likely, at Gilgal (4:19–20; 5:9–10).
10:1–15 *The Sun Stands Still.* In ch. 10 Israel responds to a threat to its ally Gibeon (vv. 1–9) with a conflict described in three accounts: vv. 12–15, vv. 16–27, and vv. 28–43. The first (following the summary of vv. 10–11) emphasizes God's assistance. As with the preceding miracles in Joshua, God provides everything needed, and Israel needs only walk across the land (1:3) and claim victory (vv. 16–43).
10:1 Adoni-Zedek. A Canaanite name that means "(my) lord is righteous"; similar to the earlier king Melchizedek (see Gen 14:18 and note). **Jerusalem.** This is its first mention in the Bible. See 9:1 and note ("Jebusites").
10:2 Gibeon was an important city, like one of the royal cities.

alarmed at this, because Gibeon was an important city, like one of the royal cities; it was larger than
Ai, and all its men were good fighters. [3]So Adoni-Zedek king of Jerusalem appealed to Hoham king of
Hebron,[w] Piram king of Jarmuth, Japhia king of Lachish[x] and Debir king of Eglon. [4]"Come up and help
me attack Gibeon," he said, "because it has made peace[y] with Joshua and the Israelites."

[5]Then the five kings of the Amorites[z] — the kings of Jerusalem, Hebron, Jarmuth, Lachish and Eglon — joined forces. They moved up with all their troops and took up positions against Gibeon and
attacked it.

[6]The Gibeonites then sent word to Joshua in the camp at Gilgal: "Do not abandon your servants.
Come up to us quickly and save us! Help us, because all the Amorite kings from the hill country have
joined forces against us."

[7]So Joshua marched up from Gilgal with his entire army,[a] including all the best fighting men. [8]The
LORD said to Joshua, "Do not be afraid[b] of them; I have given them into your hand. Not one of them
will be able to withstand you."

[9]After an all-night march from Gilgal, Joshua took them by surprise. [10]The LORD threw them into
confusion before Israel,[c] so Joshua and the Israelites defeated them completely at Gibeon. Israel pursued them along the road going up to Beth Horon[d] and cut them down all the way to Azekah[e] and
Makkedah. [11]As they fled before Israel on the road down from Beth Horon to Azekah, the LORD hurled
large hailstones[f] down on them, and more of them died from the hail than were killed by the swords
of the Israelites.

[12]On the day the LORD gave the Amorites[g] over to Israel, Joshua said to the LORD in the presence of
Israel:

"Sun, stand still over Gibeon,
  and you, moon, over the Valley of Aijalon.[h]"
[13]So the sun stood still,[i]
  and the moon stopped,
  till the nation avenged itself on[a] its enemies,

as it is written in the Book of Jashar.[j]

The sun stopped[k] in the middle of the sky and delayed going down about a full day. [14]There has never

[a] *13* Or *nation triumphed over*

10:3 [w]Ge 13:18 [x]2Ch 11:9; 25:27; Ne 11:30; Isa 36:2; 37:8; Jer 34:7; Mic 1:13
10:4 [y]Jos 9:15
10:5 [z]Nu 13:29
10:7 [a]Jos 8:1
10:8 [b]Dt 3:2; Jos 1:9
10:10 [c]Dt 7:23 [d]Jos 16:3,5 [e]Jos 15:35
10:11 [f]Ps 18:12; Isa 28:2,17
10:12 [g]Am 2:9 [h]Jdg 1:35; 12:12
10:13 [i]Hab 3:11 [j]2Sa 1:18 [k]Isa 38:8

Unlike Jericho and Ai, Gibeon was the center of its own kingdom (cf. Gath in 1 Sam 27:3–5). Israel's alliance threatens Jerusalem, Gibeon's southern neighbor (see note on 9:3), cutting off political and commercial access to the north.

10:3 Hoham ... Piram ... Japhia ... Debir. Names attested in Canaan in the second millennium BC. Hoham is a Hittite name; Piram, a Hurrian name. Both come from the north of Israel (see note on 9:1). Japhia and Debir are Canaanite names. **Hebron ... Jarmuth ... Lachish ... Eglon.** City-states south and west of Jerusalem (vv. 31–37).

10:5 Amorites. See 5:1 and note.

10:6 save. The verbal form of Joshua's name, which means "salvation." The Gibeonites' appeal to Joshua alone parallels and contrasts with Adoni-Zedek's appeal to "all the Amorite kings from the hill country" (see vv. 3–4). The size of the opposition is irrelevant where God is concerned.

10:8 Do not be afraid. Cf. 1:5b–9; 8:1 (see notes there). **I have given them.** God has decided the victory (see 1:2; 6:2 and notes). **into your hand.** Cf. v. 19. "Hand" symbolizes power.

10:9 all-night march from Gilgal. This well-known military tactic gave the Israelites the advantage of surprise as it required an arduous climb of 15 miles (24 kilometers), if this Gilgal is the same as that in 4:19.

10:10 confusion. In other ancient accounts, the victorious king causes the confusion. Here it is God who controls the battle (cf. Exod 14:24; 23:27; Deut 2:15; Judg 4:15; 1 Sam 7:10; 2 Chr 15:6). **Beth Horon.** This is the easiest pass from Jerusalem and Gibeon westward six miles (9.5 kilometers) to Upper and Lower Beth Horon and through the Aijalon Valley. **Azekah.** It is 15 miles (24 kilometers) south of Beth Horon; it guards the Elah Valley and is close to Jarmuth. **Makkedah.** Khirbet el-Qôm, about 15 miles (24 kilometers) south of Azekah at crossroads roughly six miles (9.5 kilometers) west to Lachish, ten miles (16 kilometers) east to Hebron, and four miles (6.5 kilometers) south to Eglon. These key positions opened to Israel the entire inland region south and west of Jerusalem. Details of this brief summary emphasize God's work (vv. 11–15) and Israel's activities (vv. 16–43).

10:11 Claims of divine intervention like this are known in other ancient battle accounts. Hittites, Egyptians, Assyrians, and Babylonians also asserted that their gods fought for them with hailstones. They saw it as supernatural, though some scholars view it as bragging and hyperbole. Israel's God defeats all the false gods using their own weapons. **hailstones.** Or "stones," but specifically "hailstones" here ("rocks" in v. 18); the term appears 22 times in Joshua. These weapons against the armies also become a sign of judgment against the kings (vv. 18,27). **more of them died.** As at Jericho (see 6:5 and note) God's miracles bring the victory, and Israel follows after the miracles.

10:12–13 stand still ... stood still ... stopped. Although scholars have proposed a variety of interpretations for this miracle (an eclipse, an omen, literary imagery, etc.), the third verb ("stopped, stood" from Hebrew *ʿmd*) is the clearest in meaning. It suggests that the sun "stood" still. What followed was likely a prolonged day that enabled Israel to complete its victory over its enemies.

10:13 Book of Jashar. A historical (poetic? — Jashar may mean "sings" or "is upright") source no longer available (cf. 2 Sam 1:18).

10:14 never been a day like it. This supports the traditional explanation

10:14 [l]ver 42; Ex 14:14; Dt 1:30; Ps 106:43; 136:24
10:15 [m]ver 43
10:20 [n]Dt 20:16
10:24 [o]Mal 4:3 [p]Ps 110:1
10:25 [q]Dt 31:6
10:27 [r]Dt 21:23; Jos 8:9,29
10:28 [s]Dt 20:16 [t]Jos 6:21

been a day like it before or since, a day when the LORD listened to a human being. Surely the LORD was fighting[l] for Israel!

15 Then Joshua returned with all Israel to the camp at Gilgal.[m]

Five Amorite Kings Killed

16 Now the five kings had fled and hidden in the cave at Makkedah. 17 When Joshua was told that the five kings had been found hiding in the cave at Makkedah, 18 he said, "Roll large rocks up to the mouth of the cave, and post some men there to guard it. 19 But don't stop; pursue your enemies! Attack them from the rear and don't let them reach their cities, for the LORD your God has given them into your hand."

20 So Joshua and the Israelites defeated them completely,[n] but a few survivors managed to reach their fortified cities. 21 The whole army then returned safely to Joshua in the camp at Makkedah, and no one uttered a word against the Israelites.

22 Joshua said, "Open the mouth of the cave and bring those five kings out to me." 23 So they brought the five kings out of the cave — the kings of Jerusalem, Hebron, Jarmuth, Lachish and Eglon. 24 When they had brought these kings to Joshua, he summoned all the men of Israel and said to the army commanders who had come with him, "Come here and put your feet[o] on the necks of these kings." So they came forward and placed their feet[p] on their necks.

25 Joshua said to them, "Do not be afraid; do not be discouraged. Be strong and courageous.[q] This is what the LORD will do to all the enemies you are going to fight." 26 Then Joshua put the kings to death and exposed their bodies on five poles, and they were left hanging on the poles until evening.

27 At sunset[r] Joshua gave the order and they took them down from the poles and threw them into the cave where they had been hiding. At the mouth of the cave they placed large rocks, which are there to this day.

Southern Cities Conquered

28 That day Joshua took Makkedah. He put the city and its king to the sword and totally destroyed everyone in it. He left no survivors.[s] And he did to the king of Makkedah as he had done to the king of Jericho.[t]

29 Then Joshua and all Israel with him moved on from Makkedah to Libnah and attacked it. 30 The LORD also gave that city and its king into Israel's hand. The city and everyone in it Joshua put to the sword. He left no survivors there. And he did to its king as he had done to the king of Jericho.

of a prolonged day (see vv. 12–13 and note; cf. 2 Kgs 20:9–11; Isa 38:8 for a different miracle with the sun).

10:15 As in v. 43, the return to Gilgal signals the end of the campaign (and ends the first description of the event; see note on vv. 1–15). Israel remains unified and without any recorded loss of life.

10:16–27 *Five Amorite Kings Killed.* Just as vv. 10–15 emphasize God's involvement in the account, so vv. 16–27 consider Israel's treatment of the captured kings under Joshua's authority.

10:16 Makkedah. See v. 10 and note.

10:18 large rocks. Mention of rocks begins and ends (v. 27) the story of the Amorite kings. See v. 11 and note.

10:19 pursue ... don't let them reach their cities. They are close to three of the five fortified enemy cities (see vv. 3,10 and notes), and Joshua tries to prevent any survivors. God promised Israel's victory (v. 8).

10:20 a few survivors managed to reach their fortified cities. In order to completely destroy the army, including these survivors, the systematic attack and dismantling of the fortified centers becomes necessary (vv. 28–42). No enemy is to be left alive in the cities (Deut 20:15–18).

10:21 no one uttered a word against the Israelites. No enemy is left to attack them verbally (or militarily).

10:24 put your feet on the necks. A public symbol of absolute power over the defeated. Cf. Ps 110:1; see photo, p. 1138.

10:25 Do not be afraid. Cf. v. 8. **do not be discouraged. Be strong and courageous.** Joshua passes on the charge that God gave to him (1:9) at a moment of victory. **what the LORD will do.** It is God's battle; Israel must act on faith.

10:26 exposed their bodies on five poles. See 8:29 and note. As with Ai's king, they are first executed.

10:27 large rocks. Cf. v. 18.

10:28–43 *Southern Cities Conquered.* This part of Israel's campaign (see the summary, v. 10; God's role, vv. 11–15; Israel's role, vv. 16–43) moves from executing the Amorite kings to dismantling their cities. In many cases, these "cities" were not where everyone lived but were fortified centers of power; archaeologists have found the palace, army barracks, storehouses for the taxed produce from the region, and the temple(s) to false gods. The general populace lived in unfortified villages and came to the city to do business and for protection when attacked — though probably not in this case since their armies had been destroyed. Likely they fled and returned to trouble Israel in the following generation (Judg 2:1–4,11–14). Deut 20:13–18 specifies the destruction of the cities, which served as centers of human and divine power (of other gods). The repetitive style of the destruction of city after city imitates the style of ancient conquest accounts and establishes God's sovereignty over all of southern Canaan.

10:28 no survivors. This fulfills the divine command (Deut 20:16–18) to eliminate the cities and their inhabitants.

31 Then Joshua and all Israel with him moved on from Libnah to Lachish; he took up positions
against it and attacked it. 32 The LORD gave Lachish into Israel's hands, and Joshua took it on the second day. The city and everyone in it he put to the sword, just as he had done to Libnah. 33 Meanwhile,
Horam king of Gezer[u] had come up to help Lachish, but Joshua defeated him and his army—until
no survivors were left.

34 Then Joshua and all Israel with him moved on from Lachish to Eglon; they took up positions
against it and attacked it. 35 They captured it that same day and put it to the sword and totally destroyed
everyone in it, just as they had done to Lachish.

36 Then Joshua and all Israel with him went up from Eglon to Hebron[v] and attacked it. 37 They took
the city and put it to the sword, together with its king, its villages and everyone in it. They left no survivors. Just as at Eglon, they totally destroyed it and everyone in it.

38 Then Joshua and all Israel with him turned around and attacked Debir.[w] 39 They took the city, its
king and its villages, and put them to the sword. Everyone in it they totally destroyed. They left no survivors. They did to Debir and its king as they had done to Libnah and its king and to Hebron.

40 So Joshua subdued the whole region, including the hill country, the Negev,[x] the western foothills
and the mountain slopes,[y] together with all their kings.[z] He left no survivors. He totally destroyed all
who breathed, just as the LORD, the God of Israel, had commanded.[a] 41 Joshua subdued them from Kadesh Barnea[b] to Gaza[c] and from the whole region of Goshen[d] to Gibeon. 42 All these kings and their
lands Joshua conquered in one campaign, because the LORD, the God of Israel, fought[e] for Israel.

43 Then Joshua returned with all Israel to the camp at Gilgal.[f]

Northern Kings Defeated

11 When Jabin[g] king of Hazor[h] heard of this, he sent word to Jobab king of Madon, to the kings of
Shimron[i] and Akshaph, 2 and to the northern kings who were in the mountains, in the Arabah[j]
south of Kinnereth,[k] in the western foothills and in Naphoth Dor[l] on the west; 3 to the Canaanites in the
east and west; to the Amorites, Hittites, Perizzites and Jebusites in the hill country; and to the Hivites[m]
below Hermon in the region of Mizpah.[n] 4 They came out with all their troops and a large number of
horses and chariots—a huge army, as numerous as the sand on the seashore.[o] 5 All these kings joined
forces[p] and made camp together at the Waters of Merom to fight against Israel.

6 The LORD said to Joshua, "Do not be afraid of them, because by this time tomorrow I will hand[q] all
of them, slain, over to Israel. You are to hamstring[r] their horses and burn their chariots."

10:33 [u] Jos 16:3,10; Jdg 1:29; 1Ki 9:15
10:36 [v] Jos 14:13; 15:13; Jdg 1:10
10:38 [w] Jos 15:15; Jdg 1:11
10:40 [x] Ge 12:9; Jos 12:8 [y] Dt 1:7 [z] Dt 7:24 [a] Dt 20:16-17
10:41 [b] Ge 14:7 [c] Ge 10:19 [d] Jos 11:16; 15:51
10:42 [e] ver 14
10:43 [f] ver 15; Jos 5:9
11:1 [g] Jdg 4:2,7,23 [h] ver 10; 1Sa 12:9 [i] Jos 19:15
11:2 [j] Jos 12:3 [k] Nu 34:11 [l] Jos 17:11; Jdg 1:27; 1Ki 4:11
11:3 [m] Dt 7:1; Jdg 3:3,5; 1Ki 9:20 [n] Ge 31:49; Jos 15:38; 18:26
11:4 [o] Jdg 7:12; 1Sa 13:5
11:5 [p] Jdg 5:19
11:6 [q] Jos 10:8 [r] 2Sa 8:4

10:33 Gezer. Of the seven cities listed in vv. 28–39, this is the fourth or middle one, suggesting an important site. Uniquely, Israel does not attack Gezer but defeats its king and army. Perhaps Gezer's role as the major Egyptian administrative city in the region at that time may have discouraged an attack on it (16:10; Judg 1:29). Centuries later, when the city had come under Canaanite rule, Pharaoh attacked and captured it and gave it to Solomon (1 Kgs 9:15–17).

10:38 Debir. Khirbet Rabud (also called Kiriath Sepher [15:15]); it is about five miles (8 kilometers) southwest of Hebron.

10:40 subdued. This does not mean that the Israelites settle this land but only that they defeat their enemies. **no survivors.** See note on v. 28. **totally destroyed all who breathed.** This summarizes the complete destruction of all the kings, their armies, and the cities from which they ruled (vv. 28–39).

10:41 Goshen. This is not the region in Egypt (Gen 47:27) but a town in the Negev in the southeastern part of the area covered by Israel's southern campaign (11:16; 15:51).

10:42 the LORD, the God of Israel, fought for Israel. Although God's role is emphasized in vv. 12–15, this summarizes God's role in the whole campaign as the key to Israel's survival and victory.

10:43 returned with all Israel to ... Gilgal. See v. 15 and note.

11:1–23 *Northern Kings Defeated.* Like ch. 10, Israel is attacked first (vv. 1–5) and must defend itself to survive. God's promise and command (vv. 6,15) set the context for Joshua to lead Israel to defeat the northern coalition (vv. 7–14). The summary (vv. 15–23) emphasizes the faithfulness of Joshua and Israel in the lengthy battles and the manner in which God prepared the hearts of the Canaanites so that they would not respond as the Gibeonites had (vv. 19–20).

11:1 Jabin. A different Jabin appears in Judg 4; the name may be dynastic. **Hazor.** The largest Canaanite city in the north (v. 10), covering about 175 acres (70 hectares), leads the region against Israel. Second-millennium BC texts from Hazor, Mari (eighteenth century BC), and Egypt (at Amarna, fourteenth century BC) attest to its importance.

11:2 Arabah. The Jordan Valley (Deut 1:1; see note on Deut 1:7). **Kinnereth.** The Sea of Galilee (but see Deut 3:17 and note). **Naphoth.** Uncertain; associated only with Dor (12:23; 17:11; 1 Kgs 4:11).

11:3 Amorites, Hittites, Perizzites and Jebusites ... Hivites. See 5:1; 9:1 and notes. **Mizpah.** This region may be the southern Lebanese valley of the Litani River.

11:4 horses and chariots. See photo, p. 143. As mobile firing platforms for archers, chariots were the most advanced weapon technology of the day and symbolized military power (Exod 14:9,23; Deut 11:4; 20:1; 1 Kgs 20:1,21). **sand on the seashore.** A large number of people (Gen 22:17; 1 Sam 13:5) or animals (Judg 7:12); emphasizes the power of the opposition, invincible from a human perspective.

11:5 Waters of Merom. May be Tel Qarnei Hattin, five miles (8 kilometers) west of the Sea of Galilee, a battle site known throughout recorded history.

11:6 hamstring their horses. Cutting the tendon above the ankle cripples the animal and also makes it unusable for Israel. Horses were used for military purposes. God's people were to trust in him, not in

11:8 [s]Jos 13:6
11:11 [t]Dt 20:16-17
11:12 [u]Nu 33:50-52; Dt 7:2
11:14 [v]Nu 31:11-12
11:15 [w]Ex 34:11; Jos 1:7
11:16 [x]Jos 10:41
11:17 [y]Jos 12:7 [z]Dt 7:24
11:19 [a]Jos 9:3

7 So Joshua and his whole army came against them suddenly at the Waters of Merom and attacked
them, 8 and the LORD gave them into the hand of Israel. They defeated them and pursued them all the
way to Greater Sidon, to Misrephoth Maim,[s] and to the Valley of Mizpah on the east, until no survivors
were left. 9 Joshua did to them as the LORD had directed: He hamstrung their horses and burned their
chariots.
10 At that time Joshua turned back and captured Hazor and put its king to the sword. (Hazor had
been the head of all these kingdoms.) 11 Everyone in it they put to the sword. They totally destroyed[a]
them, not sparing anyone that breathed,[t] and
he burned Hazor itself.
12 Joshua took all these royal cities and their
kings and put them to the sword. He totally destroyed them, as Moses the servant of the LORD
had commanded.[u] 13 Yet Israel did not burn any
of the cities built on their mounds — except
Hazor, which Joshua burned. 14 The Israelites
carried off for themselves all the plunder and
livestock of these cities, but all the people they
put to the sword until they completely destroyed
them, not sparing anyone that breathed.[v] 15 As
the LORD commanded his servant Moses, so Moses commanded Joshua, and Joshua did it; he
left nothing undone of all that the LORD commanded Moses.[w]
16 So Joshua took this entire land: the hill
country, all the Negev, the whole region of Goshen, the western foothills,[x] the Arabah and the
mountains of Israel with their foothills, 17 from
Mount Halak, which rises toward Seir, to Baal
Gad in the Valley of Lebanon[y] below Mount
Hermon. He captured all their kings and put
them to death.[z] 18 Joshua waged war against
all these kings for a long time. 19 Except for the
Hivites living in Gibeon,[a] not one city made a
treaty of peace with the Israelites, who took
them all in battle. 20 For it was the LORD himself

NORTHERN CAMPAIGN

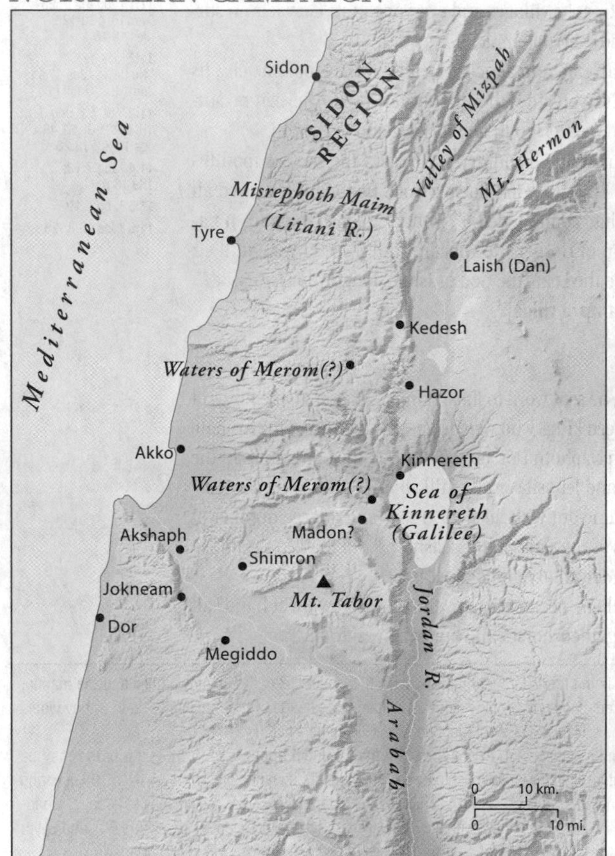

[a] 11 The Hebrew term refers to the irrevocable giving over of things or persons to the LORD, often by totally destroying them; also in verses 12, 20 and 21.

horses, for their victories (Deut 17:16). **burn their chariots.** Israel's trust in God would enable them to destroy these wooden instruments of war rather than use them.

11:8 Greater Sidon, to Misrephoth Maim, and to the Valley of Mizpah. Israel moves clockwise; from Merom (v. 5) west and north to the Mediterranean coast, and then east (see v. 3 and note). **Misrephoth Maim.** Uncertain but may relate to the Litani River ("Maim" means "waters") that formed a border south of Sidon and north of Tyre.

11:10 turned back. Israel moves from Mizpah (see v. 3 and note) in southern Lebanon south toward Hazor and the heart of their territory (chs. 5–10). **Hazor ... head of all these.** See v. 1 and note.

11:11 not sparing anyone that breathed. See note on 10:40. **burned Hazor.** Israel burns only Hazor after Ai (v. 13; 8:19). Multiple burn layers have been found at Hazor, attesting to its conflagration in the time of Joshua.

11:12 royal cities. See 10:2 and note. **destroyed.** See v. 20; 2:10; 6:18,21; 8:26; 10:1,28,35,37,39,40; see also notes on v. 20; 6:17, 18,21; 7:12,15; 10:28,40; see further Introduction to Deuteronomy: Themes and Theology (Holy War).

11:13 mounds. Hebrew *tēl* ("tell"); a hill formed by accumulated debris from previous settlements one on top of another on the same site. The levels of debris from previous generations attested to the importance of the city. Instead of burning these cities, conquerors would dismantle the cities' defenses.

11:15 Moses commanded Joshua. See 1:1–3 and notes; cf. Deut 34. **left nothing undone.** Joshua is successful because he obeys God's instructions in each campaign.

11:16 Goshen. See 10:41 and note.

11:18 a long time. See 14:7,10 and note.

11:19 Except for the Hivites living in Gibeon. See ch. 9.

11:20 hardened their hearts. See Exod 4:21 and note; 7:13. **exterminating.** Translates the same Hebrew word elsewhere translated "destroyed" (see v. 12 and note).

who hardened their hearts[b] to wage war against Israel, so that he might destroy them totally, exterminating them without mercy, as the LORD had commanded Moses.[c]

21 At that time Joshua went and destroyed the Anakites[d] from the hill country: from Hebron, Debir and Anab, from all the hill country of Judah, and from all the hill country of Israel. Joshua totally destroyed them and their towns. 22 No Anakites were left in Israelite territory; only in Gaza, Gath[e] and Ashdod[f] did any survive.

23 So Joshua took the entire land,[g] just as the LORD had directed Moses, and he gave it as an inheritance[h] to Israel according to their tribal divisions.[i] Then the land had rest from war.[j]

Hazor acropolis (ca. 1400–1250 BC) with its multi-chambered gate (foreground), palaces, and major Canaanite temple (protected by a modern roof) that may have been destroyed by Joshua and Israel.

Used by permission of Prof. Amnon Ben-Tor

List of Defeated Kings

12 These are the kings of the land whom the Israelites had defeated and whose territory they took over east of the Jordan, from the Arnon Gorge to Mount Hermon,[k] including all the eastern side of the Arabah:

2 Sihon king of the Amorites, who reigned in Heshbon.
He ruled from Aroer on the rim of the Arnon Gorge—from the middle of the gorge—to the
Jabbok River, which is the border of the Ammonites. This included half of Gilead.[l] 3 He also
ruled over the eastern Arabah from the Sea of Galilee[a][m] to the Sea of the Arabah (that is, the
Dead Sea), to Beth Jeshimoth,[n] and then southward below the slopes of Pisgah.

4 And the territory of Og king of Bashan,[o] one of the last of the Rephaites, who reigned in Ashtaroth[p] and Edrei.

5 He ruled over Mount Hermon, Salekah,[q] all of Bashan to the border of the people of Geshur[r] and Maakah,[s] and half of Gilead to the border of Sihon king of Heshbon.

6 Moses, the servant of the LORD, and the Israelites conquered them. And Moses the servant of the LORD gave their land to the Reubenites, the Gadites and the half-tribe of Manasseh to be their possession.[t]

7 Here is a list of the kings of the land that Joshua and the Israelites conquered on the west side of
the Jordan, from Baal Gad in the Valley of Lebanon[u] to Mount Halak, which rises toward Seir. Joshua

11:20 [b] Ex 14:17; Ro 9:18 [c] Dt 7:16; Jdg 14:4
11:21 [d] Nu 13:22,33; Dt 9:2
11:22 [e] 1Sa 17:4; 1Ki 2:39; 1Ch 8:13 [f] 1Sa 5:1; Isa 20:1
11:23 [g] Jos 21:43-45 [h] Dt 1:38; 12:9-10; 25:19 [i] Nu 26:53 [j] Jos 14:15
12:1 [k] Dt 3:8
12:2 [l] Dt 2:36
12:3 [m] Jos 11:2 [n] Jos 13:20
12:4 [o] Nu 21:21,33; Dt 3:11 [p] Dt 1:4
12:5 [q] Dt 3:10 [r] 1Sa 27:8 [s] Dt 3:14
12:6 [t] Nu 32:29,33; Jos 13:8
12:7 [u] Jos 11:17

[a] 3 Hebrew *Kinnereth*

11:22 Anakites. Leaders, warriors, and giants, the Anakites were the reason the Israelites had earlier feared to enter the land (Num 13:33). Now the victory includes their elimination. Compare the work of Caleb (15.14). The Anakites may appear in Egyptian records of the second millennium BC.
11:23 the land had rest from war. This ends Joshua's battles (14:15). **rest.** See Introduction: Theological Themes (The Gift of the Promised Land).
12:1–24 *List of Defeated Kings.* Ch. 12 explains 11:15–23, giving details of the places and towns defeated. It summarizes the victories under Moses east of the Jordan River (vv. 1–6) and under Joshua west of the Jordan River (vv. 7–24). This story begins not with Joshua but with Moses. Nevertheless, Joshua is the divinely appointed successor to Moses to acquire the promised land.
12:1 These are the kings of the land. The Hebrew behind the phrase is identical to the Hebrew in v. 7; it introduces each of the two parts of ch. 12. **took over.** Emphasizes possessing the land and anticipates its allotment (chs. 13–21). **Arnon Gorge.** Marked Moab's northern border and Israel's southern border. **Arabah.** See 11:2 and note; Deut 1:1; see also Deut 1:7 and note.
12:2 Heshbon. Probably not Tell Hesban, which was not inhabited until later, but a nearby site east of the Dead Sea. **from Aroer.** The area east of the Jordan River was divided into larger states comprising regions ruled by Sihon and Og. Contrast the area west of the Jordan that was comprised of cities and their immediate environs.
12:4 Rephaites. Legendary warriors; similar to the Anakites west of the Jordan River (see 11:22 and note; 17:15; Num 13:33). **Ashtaroth and Edrei.** Sites near the modern border of Syria and Jordan; mentioned in Ugaritic legends (thirteenth century BC) and related to ancient heroes. The picture emphasizes God's great work for Israel.
12:5 people of Geshur and Maakah. Kingdoms north and east of the Sea of Galilee and reaching into the Golan Heights.
12:7 Here is a list of the kings of the land. Cf. v. 1 (see note there). **from Baal Gad.** Cf. 11:2,17,21.

12:8 [v] Jos 11:16
12:9 [w] Jos 6:2 [x] Jos 8:29
12:10 [y] Jos 10:23
12:12 [z] Jos 10:33
12:14 [a] Nu 21:1
12:16 [b] Jos 7:2
12:17 [c] 1Ki 4:10
12:18 [d] Jos 13:4
12:20 [e] Jos 11:1
12:22 [f] Jos 19:37; 20:7; 21:32 [g] 1Sa 15:12
12:23 [h] Jos 11:2
12:24 [i] Ps 135:11; Dt 7:24
13:1 [j] Ge 24:1; Jos 14:10
13:3 [k] Jer 2:18 [l] Jdg 1:18

gave their lands as an inheritance to the tribes of Israel according to their tribal divisions. 8The lands
included the hill country, the western foothills, the Arabah, the mountain slopes, the wilderness and
the Negev.[v] These were the lands of the Hittites, Amorites, Canaanites, Perizzites, Hivites and Jebusites.
These were the kings:

9 the king of Jericho[w] one
the king of Ai[x] (near Bethel) one
10 the king of Jerusalem[y] one
the king of Hebron one
11 the king of Jarmuth one
the king of Lachish one
12 the king of Eglon one
the king of Gezer[z] one
13 the king of Debir one
the king of Geder one
14 the king of Hormah one
the king of Arad[a] one
15 the king of Libnah one
the king of Adullam one
16 the king of Makkedah one
the king of Bethel[b] one
17 the king of Tappuah one
the king of Hepher[c] one
18 the king of Aphek[d] one
the king of Lasharon one
19 the king of Madon one
the king of Hazor one
20 the king of Shimron Meron one
the king of Akshaph[e] one
21 the king of Taanach one
the king of Megiddo one
22 the king of Kedesh[f] one
the king of Jokneam in Carmel[g] one
23 the king of Dor (in Naphoth Dor[h]) one
the king of Goyim in Gilgal one
24 the king of Tirzah one
thirty-one kings in all.[i]

Land Still to Be Taken

13 When Joshua had grown old,[j] the LORD said to him, "You are now very old, and there are still
very large areas of land to be taken over.

2"This is the land that remains: all the regions of the Philistines and Geshurites, 3from the Shihor
River[k] on the east of Egypt to the territory of Ekron[l] on the north, all of it counted as Canaanite

12:8 Hittites ... Jebusites. See 3:10; 9:1 and notes.

12:9–24 This list resembles lists of defeated Canaanite kings (and their cities) found in contemporary Egyptian accounts. It generally follows the sequence in chs. 6–12, beginning with Jericho and Ai, turning south, and then listing northern towns. This list includes Hormah, Arad, Bethel, and many northern towns not found in the preceding chapters. It indicates that Joshua preserves select battle accounts rather than a record of every conflict. This is not merely history but also a statement about God's faithfulness and the response of this first generation of Israel in the land of promise. This list demonstrates the extent of the towns and their regions that God gave his people, including every part of the land that would become Israel.

12:23 Goyim in Gilgal. Cf. Harosheth Haggoyim (Judg 4:2,13,16), perhaps related.

13:1—21:45 *The Promised Land Allotted.* These chapters provide in much greater detail the allotments for which the summary of ch. 12 sets the background. Chapters 13–21 provide the general order of allotments (east of the Jordan and then overall south to north in the land west of the Jordan). The areas are described with town lists (cities and towns within the tribe) and boundary lists (lines running between towns and features

though held by the five Philistine rulers[m] in Gaza, Ashdod, Ashkelon, Gath and Ekron; the territory of the Avvites[n] 4on the south; all the land of the Canaanites, from Arah of the Sidonians as far as Aphek[o] and the border of the Amorites;[p] 5the area of Byblos;[q] and all Lebanon[r] to the east, from Baal Gad below Mount Hermon to Lebo Hamath.

6"As for all the inhabitants of the mountain regions from Lebanon to Misrephoth Maim,[s] that is, all the Sidonians, I myself will drive them out before the Israelites. Be sure to allocate this land to Israel for an inheritance, as I have instructed you,[t] 7and divide it as an inheritance[u] among the nine tribes and half of the tribe of Manasseh."

Division of the Land East of the Jordan

8The other half of Manasseh,[a] the Reubenites and the Gadites had received the inheritance that Moses had given them east of the Jordan, as he, the servant of the LORD, had assigned[v] it to them.

9It extended from Aroer[w] on the rim of the Arnon Gorge, and from the town in the middle of the gorge, and included the whole plateau[x] of Medeba as far as Dibon,[y] 10and all the towns of Sihon king of the Amorites, who ruled in Heshbon, out to the border of the Ammonites.[z] 11It also included Gilead, the territory of the people of Geshur and Maakah, all of Mount Hermon and all Bashan as far as Salekah[a]— 12that is, the whole kingdom of Og in Bashan,[b] who had reigned in Ashtaroth[c] and Edrei. (He was the last of the Rephaites.[d]) Moses had defeated them and taken over their land. 13But the Israelites did not drive out the people of Geshur[e] and Maakah,[f] so they continue to live among the Israelites to this day.

14But to the tribe of Levi he gave no inheritance, since the food offerings presented to the LORD, the God of Israel, are their inheritance, as he promised them.[g]

15This is what Moses had given to the tribe of Reuben, according to its clans:

16The territory from Aroer[h] on the rim of the Arnon Gorge, and from the town in the middle of the gorge, and the whole plateau past Medeba[i] 17to Heshbon and all its towns on the plateau, including Dibon,[j] Bamoth Baal, Beth Baal Meon,[k] 18Jahaz,[l] Kedemoth, Mephaath,[m] 19Kiriathaim,[n]

[a] 8 Hebrew *With it* (that is, with the other half of Manasseh)

13:3 [m] Jdg 3:3 [n] Dt 2:23
13:4 [o] Jos 12:18; 19:30 [p] Am 2:10
13:5 [q] 1Ki 5:18; Ps 83:7; Eze 27:9 [r] Jos 12:7
13:6 [s] Jos 11:8 [t] Nu 33:54
13:7 [u] Jos 11:23; Ps 78:55
13:8 [v] Jos 12:6
13:9 [w] ver 16; Jdg 11:26 [x] Jer 48:8,21 [y] Nu 21:30
13:10 [z] Nu 21:24
13:11 [a] Jos 12:5
13:12 [b] Dt 3:11 [c] Jos 12:4 [d] Ge 14:5
13:13 [e] Jos 12:5 [f] Dt 3:14
13:14 [g] ver 33; Dt 18:1-2
13:16 [h] ver 9; Jos 12:2 [i] Nu 21:30
13:17 [j] Nu 32:3 [k] 1Ch 5:8
13:18 [l] Nu 21:23 [m] Jer 48:21
13:19 [n] Nu 32:37

lying on the borders of a tribe). In a document that could be used to settle legal disputes about land ownership, these boundaries and town lists would have been updated as Israel populated the land and built more cities. Interspersed with the allotments are notes concerning specific divine blessings: Caleb's allotment and family (14:6–15; 15:13–19), the inheritance of Zelophehad's daughters (17:3–6), the need for more land for the Joseph tribes (17:14–18), mapping and allotting the land for the seven remaining tribes (18:1–10), Joshua's allotment (19:49–51), the cities of refuge (20:1–9), and Israel's returning to God a portion of what they have been given in the form of the Levitical towns (21:1–45). Outlined first, however, is the implicit judgment and warning in the form of a list of towns and lands not taken by Israel (13:1–7).

13:1–7 *Land Still to Be Taken.* Joshua's old age implies that the rest of the land would remain for a future, faithful generation to acquire control of the whole land. This awaits David's reign, when God gives Israel the entire promised land.

13:1 had grown old. The same Hebrew expression in 23:1 marks the end of the allotment and the beginning of Joshua's final charge to Israel and renewal of God's covenant with Israel (chs. 23–24); the same expression occurs in Gen 18:12,13; 24:1; 1 Kgs 1:1. In every case the expression follows a major task given to the person to move God's covenant forward to the next generation.

13:3 Shihor River. Here it is possibly the Wadi el-Arish. **Philistine rulers.** "Ruler" (Hebrew *seren*), associated with only Philistines, may relate to "tyrant" (Greek *tyrannos*), a word for a ruler in the Philistine homeland of the Aegean. **Gaza, Ashdod, Ashkelon, Gath and Ekron.** The Philistines lived in these five cities in the southwest part of the Holy Land after they arrived in the twelfth century BC (1 Sam 6:17).

13:4 all the land of the Canaanites. What follows describes the Mediterranean coastline north of Philistia to Byblos in northern Lebanon. **Amorites.** Elsewhere in the Bible, the term Amorites refers generally to the inhabitants of southern Canaan (see note on 5:1). Only here in the Bible does this term refer to the ancient kingdom of Amurru in northern Lebanon that disappeared from history after the thirteenth century BC.

13:5 Baal Gad. See note on 12:7. **Lebo Hamath.** Cf. Num 13:21.

13:6 Misrephoth Maim. See 11:8 and note. **I myself will drive them out.** See vv. 1–7 note.

13:8–33 *Division of the Land East of the Jordan.* These verses describe the allotments Moses made for the tribes that settled east of the Jordan River. Moving from south to north, vv. 9–13 repeat the summary of 12:1–5. Then vv. 16–32 move from south to north with towns allotted to Reuben and their western boundary (vv. 16–23), Gad (vv. 24–28), and the half-tribe of Manasseh (vv. 29–31). Notes within the text repeatedly identify Moses and his acts of leadership as responsible (Num 32:33–42; Deut 3:8–17) for these unusual allotments (vv. 8,12,15,21,24,29,32) that lie outside the promised land (see 1:4 and note). See map, p. 412.

13:8 Verse 7 ends God's command to allot the land west of the Jordan to the nine and a half tribes. Verses 8–33 constitute God's command to allot the land east of the Jordan. **The other half of Manasseh.** Emphasizes the large size of Manasseh (cf. 17:14–18) and reasserts the unity of Israel both east and west of the Jordan (see 1:2 and note).

13:14,33 tribe of Levi. Has a special position in relation to God. The Levites did not receive land (Deut 18:1–8), but these interspersed notes within the text anticipate their cities in this region (ch. 21).

13:20 [o] Dt 3:29
13:21 [p] Nu 25:15 [q] Nu 31:8
13:22 [r] Nu 22:5; 31:8
13:25 [s] Nu 21:32; Jos 21:39
13:26 [t] Nu 21:25; Jer 49:3 [u] Jos 10:3
13:27 [v] Ge 33:17 [w] Nu 34:11
13:28 [x] Nu 32:33
13:30 [y] Ge 32:2 [z] Nu 32:41
13:31 [a] Ge 50:23
13:33 [b] Nu 18:20 [c] ver 14; Jos 18:7
14:1 [d] Nu 34:17-18
14:2 [e] Nu 26:55
14:3 [f] Nu 32:33 [g] Jos 13:14
14:4 [h] Ge 41:52; 48:5
14:5 [i] Nu 34:13; 35:2; Jos 21:2
14:6 [j] Nu 13:6; 14:30 [k] Nu 13:26

Sibmah, Zereth Shahar on the hill in the valley, 20 Beth Peor,[o] the slopes of Pisgah, and Beth Jeshimoth — 21 all the towns on the plateau and the entire realm of Sihon king of the Amorites, who
ruled at Heshbon. Moses had defeated him and the Midianite chiefs,[p] Evi, Rekem, Zur, Hur and
Reba[q] — princes allied with Sihon — who lived in that country. 22 In addition to those slain in
battle, the Israelites had put to the sword Balaam son of Beor,[r] who practiced divination. 23 The
boundary of the Reubenites was the bank of the Jordan. These towns and their villages were the
inheritance of the Reubenites, according to their clans.

24 This is what Moses had given to the tribe of Gad, according to its clans:

25 The territory of Jazer,[s] all the towns of Gilead and half the Ammonite country as far as Aroer,
near Rabbah; 26 and from Heshbon[t] to Ramath Mizpah and Betonim, and from Mahanaim to the
territory of Debir;[u] 27 and in the valley, Beth Haram, Beth Nimrah, Sukkoth[v] and Zaphon with the
rest of the realm of Sihon king of Heshbon (the east side of the Jordan, the territory up to the end
of the Sea of Galilee[a][w]). 28 These towns and their villages were the inheritance of the Gadites,[x]
according to their clans.

29 This is what Moses had given to the half-tribe of Manasseh, that is, to half the family of the descendants of Manasseh, according to its clans:

30 The territory extending from Mahanaim[y] and including all of Bashan, the entire realm of Og
king of Bashan — all the settlements of Jair[z] in Bashan, sixty towns, 31 half of Gilead, and Ashtaroth and Edrei (the royal cities of Og in Bashan). This was for the descendants of Makir[a] son of
Manasseh — for half of the sons of Makir, according to their clans.

32 This is the inheritance Moses had given when he was in the plains of Moab across the Jordan east
of Jericho. 33 But to the tribe of Levi, Moses had given no inheritance; the LORD, the God of Israel, is their
inheritance,[b] as he promised them.[c]

Division of the Land West of the Jordan

14 Now these are the areas the Israelites received as an inheritance in the land of Canaan, which Eleazar the priest, Joshua son of Nun and the heads of the tribal clans of Israel allotted to them.[d] 2 Their
inheritances were assigned by lot[e] to the nine and a half tribes, as the LORD had commanded through Moses. 3 Moses had granted the two and a half tribes their inheritance east of the Jordan[f] but had not granted
the Levites an inheritance among the rest,[g] 4 for Joseph's descendants had become two tribes — Manasseh
and Ephraim.[h] The Levites received no share of the land but only towns to live in, with pasturelands for
their flocks and herds. 5 So the Israelites divided the land, just as the LORD had commanded Moses.[i]

Allotment for Caleb

6 Now the people of Judah approached Joshua at Gilgal, and Caleb son of Jephunneh[j] the Kenizzite
said to him, "You know what the LORD said to Moses the man of God at Kadesh Barnea[k] about you and

[a] 27 Hebrew *Kinnereth*

13:22 Balaam son of Beor. See Num 22–24. For his death in battle, see Num 31:8.

14:1–5 *Division of the Land West of the Jordan.* This introduction emphasizes how the Israelites follow God's instruction for dividing the land and allotting it to all the tribes. See map, p. 412.

14:1 Eleazar the priest. A son of Aaron (Exod 6:23,25; 28:1; Lev 10:6,12,16; Num 3:2) who became chief priest following the deaths of his brothers (Num 3:4,32). **heads.** Cf. Num 34:18–29.

14:2 lot. May be the Urim and Thummim (see 7:14 and note), indicating that God makes the decision (Prov 16:33). A distinction is drawn between the three tribes of Judah, Ephraim, and Manasseh and the other tribes. The first group has already taken possession of their territory. The other tribes still have to take possession of their land; this is why it is allotted to them by lot.

14:3–4 Levites ... Levites. See note on 13:14,33.

14:4 Manasseh and Ephraim. Joseph's sons adopted by Jacob as his sons (Gen 48:5) and thus two separate tribes. Because Jacob had elevated Joseph to firstborn status, Joseph receives a double portion of the inheritance.

14:6–15 *Allotment for Caleb.* Caleb and Joshua were the only two of the twelve spies sent from Kadesh Barnea who believed that God would give Israel the promised land (Num 13:30). God promised them that they, unlike the rest of their generation, would enter the land (Num 14:24,30,38; 26:65; 32:12). The inheritances of Caleb and Joshua (19:49–50) frame the allotments west of the Jordan.

14:6 Kenizzite. Of uncertain origin (Num 32:12); perhaps related to Kenites, a group of people who lived at Arad, south of Hebron (Judg 1:16; cf. 4:11,17; 5:24). If so, Caleb was not a full Israelite but a member of his father-in-law's tribe.

me. 7 I was forty years old when Moses the servant of the LORD sent me from Kadesh Barnea to explore
the land.[l] And I brought him back a report according to my convictions,[m] 8 but my fellow Israelites who
went up with me made the hearts of the people melt in fear.[n] I, however, followed the LORD my God
wholeheartedly.[o] 9 So on that day Moses swore to me, 'The land on which your feet have walked will
be your inheritance and that of your children[p] forever, because you have followed the LORD my God
wholeheartedly.'[a]

10 "Now then, just as the LORD promised,[q] he has kept me alive for forty-five years since the time he
said this to Moses, while Israel moved about in the wilderness. So here I am today, eighty-five years old!
11 I am still as strong[r] today as the day Moses sent me out; I'm just as vigorous to go out to battle now

[a] 9 Deut. 1:36

14:7 [l] Nu 13:17 [m] Nu 13:30; 14:6-9
14:8 [n] Nu 13:31 [o] Nu 14:24
14:9 [p] Nu 14:24; Dt 1:36
14:10 [q] Nu 14:30
14:11 [r] Dt 34:7

14:7–10 forty … forty-five … eighty-five. If Israel was in the wilderness for 40 years (5:6; Exod 16:35; Num 14:33,34; 32:13; Deut 8:2,4), then Israel had been in the promised land about five years when Caleb took control of Hebron, demonstrating that God preserved Caleb for this task (cf. 13:1; see note there).

14:8,9,14 followed the LORD … wholeheartedly. This threefold repetition emphasizes Caleb's commitment to God. Wholehearted faithfulness applies only to Joshua and Caleb (Num 32:12; Deut 1:36). Contrast Solomon (1 Kgs 11:6).

DISTANCES IN MILES BETWEEN OLD TESTAMENT CITIES

(1 mile = 1.6 kilometers)

	ASHKELON	BABYLON	BEERSHEBA	BETHEL	BETH SHAN	CARCHEMISH	DAMASCUS	DAN	HARRAN	HAZOR	HEBRON	JERICHO	JERUSALEM	JOPPA	LACHISH	MARI	MEGIDDO	MEMPHIS	NINEVEH	SAMARIA	SHECHEM	SIDON	SUSA	THEBES	TYRE	UR
Ashkelon		900	36	48	87	454	178	139	519	117	36	57	44	32	21	653	80	269	726	60	63	155	1118	601	133	1070
Babylon	900		930	869	823	479	724	764	442	783	901	869	880	868	907	251	824	1172	264	845	847	779	218	1504	792	170
Beersheba	36	930		58	104	484	206	166	549	147	28	61	47	62	25	679	116	259	752	80	78	190	1148	591	176	1100
Bethel	48	869	58		47	423	145	105	488	86	31	12	11	32	40	618	50	303	691	26	22	129	1087	635	115	1039
Beth Shan	87	823	104	47		377	92	59	442	40	78	45	57	59	86	572	21	349	645	27	26	82	1041	681	62	993
Carchemish	454	479	484	423	377		278	318	65	337	455	423	434	366	461	228	378	726	285	399	401	333	697	1058	346	649
Damascus	178	724	206	145	92	278		45	343	59	177	134	149	133	181	473	98	441	546	121	123	55	942	773	68	894
Dan	139	764	166	105	59	318	45		383	19	137	105	116	104	142	513	59	408	586	80	82	29	982	740	28	934
Harran	519	442	549	488	442	65	343	383		402	520	488	500	396	526	191	443	791	215	464	466	398	660	1123	411	612
Hazor	117	783	147	86	40	337	59	19	402		118	86	97	85	124	532	41	389	605	62	64	43	1001	721	29	953
Hebron	36	901	28	31	78	455	177	137	520	118		36	21	45	17	650	80	297	723	51	53	161	1119	629	147	1071
Jericho	57	869	61	12	45	423	134	105	488	86	36		15	43	44	618	54	307	691	32	26	129	1087	639	115	1039
Jerusalem	44	880	47	11	57	434	149	116	500	97	21	15		36	29	629	61	292	702	37	33	140	1098	624	126	1050
Joppa	32	868	62	32	59	366	133	104	396	85	45	43	36		37	372	53	301	548	31	36	112	1086	633	89	1038
Lachish	21	907	25	40	86	461	181	142	526	124	17	44	29	37		656	83	281	729	66	62	158	1125	613	136	1077
Mari	653	251	679	618	572	228	473	513	191	532	650	618	629	372	656		573	921	173	594	596	528	469	1253	541	421
Megiddo	80	824	116	50	21	378	98	59	443	41	80	54	61	53	83	573		348	646	25	29	75	1042	680	53	994
Memphis	269	1172	259	303	349	726	441	408	791	389	297	307	292	301	281	921	348		994	329	325	424	1390	332	402	1342
Nineveh	726	264	752	691	645	285	546	586	215	605	723	691	702	548	729	173	646	994		667	669	601	453	1326	614	434
Samaria	60	845	80	26	27	399	121	80	464	62	51	32	37	31	66	594	25	329	667		8	105	1063	661	77	1015
Shechem	63	847	78	22	26	401	123	82	466	64	53	26	33	36	62	596	29	325	669	8		107	1065	657	80	1017
Sidon	155	779	190	129	82	333	55	29	398	43	161	129	140	112	158	528	75	424	601	105	107		997	755	25	949
Susa	1118	218	1148	1087	1041	697	942	982	660	1001	1119	1087	1098	1086	1125	469	1042	1390	453	1063	1065	997		1722	1110	145
Thebes	601	1504	591	635	681	1058	773	740	1123	721	629	639	624	633	613	1253	680	332	1326	661	657	755	1722		733	1674
Tyre	133	792	176	115	62	346	68	28	411	29	147	115	126	89	136	541	53	402	614	77	80	25	1110	733		962
Ur	1070	170	1100	1039	993	649	894	934	612	953	1071	1039	1050	1038	1077	421	994	1342	434	1015	1017	949	145	1674	962	

Note: These distances are meant only as rough estimates. They do not take into account terrain obstacles, although they do, for the most part, follow ancient routes (e.g., around the Fertile Crescent rather than across the desert).

14:12 [s]Nu 13:33 [t]Nu 13:28
14:13 [u]Jos 22:6,7 [v]Jos 10:36 [w]Jdg 1:20; 1Ch 6:56
14:15 [x]Ge 23:2 [y]Jos 15:13 [z]Jos 11:23
15:1 [a]Nu 34:3 [b]Nu 33:36
15:3 [c]Nu 34:4
15:4 [d]Nu 34:5 [e]Ge 15:18
15:5 [f]Nu 34:10 [g]Jos 18:15-19
15:6 [h]Jos 18:19,21 [i]Jos 18:17
15:7 [j]Jos 7:24 [k]2Sa 17:17; 1Ki 1:9
15:8 [l]ver 63; Jos 18:16, 28; Jdg 1:21; 19:10
15:9 [m]Jos 18:15 [n]1Ch 13:6
15:10 [o]Ge 38:12; Jdg 14:1
15:11 [p]Jos 19:33
15:12 [q]Nu 34:6
15:13 [r]Jos 14:13-15
15:14 [s]Nu 13:33 [t]Nu 13:22 [u]Jdg 1:10,20

as I was then. 12 Now give me this hill country that the LORD promised me that day. You yourself heard then that the Anakites[s] were there and their cities were large and fortified,[t] but, the LORD helping me, I will drive them out just as he said."

13 Then Joshua blessed[u] Caleb son of Jephunneh and gave him Hebron[v] as his inheritance.[w] 14 So Hebron has belonged to Caleb son of Jephunneh the Kenizzite ever since, because he followed the LORD, the God of Israel, wholeheartedly. 15 (Hebron used to be called Kiriath Arba[x] after Arba,[y] who was the greatest man among the Anakites.)

Then the land had rest[z] from war.

Allotment for Judah

15:15-19pp — Jdg 1:11-15

15 The allotment for the tribe of Judah, according to its clans, extended down to the territory of Edom,[a] to the Desert of Zin[b] in the extreme south.

2 Their southern boundary started from the bay at the southern end of the Dead Sea, 3 crossed south of Scorpion Pass,[c] continued on to Zin and went over to the south of Kadesh Barnea. Then it ran past Hezron up to Addar and curved around to Karka. 4 It then passed along to Azmon[d] and joined the Wadi of Egypt,[e] ending at the Mediterranean Sea. This is their[a] southern boundary.

5 The eastern boundary[f] is the Dead Sea as far as the mouth of the Jordan.

The northern boundary[g] started from the bay of the sea at the mouth of the Jordan, 6 went up to Beth Hoglah[h] and continued north of Beth Arabah to the Stone of Bohan[i] son of Reuben. 7 The boundary then went up to Debir from the Valley of Achor[j] and turned north to Gilgal, which faces the Pass of Adummim south of the gorge. It continued along to the waters of En Shemesh and came out at En Rogel.[k] 8 Then it ran up the Valley of Ben Hinnom along the southern slope of the Jebusite[l] city (that is, Jerusalem). From there it climbed to the top of the hill west of the Hinnom Valley at the northern end of the Valley of Rephaim. 9 From the hilltop the boundary headed toward the spring of the waters of Nephtoah,[m] came out at the towns of Mount Ephron and went down toward Baalah[n] (that is, Kiriath Jearim). 10 Then it curved westward from Baalah to Mount Seir, ran along the northern slope of Mount Jearim (that is, Kesalon), continued down to Beth Shemesh and crossed to Timnah.[o] 11 It went to the northern slope of Ekron, turned toward Shikkeron, passed along to Mount Baalah and reached Jabneel.[p] The boundary ended at the sea.

12 The western boundary is the coastline of the Mediterranean Sea.[q]

These are the boundaries around the people of Judah by their clans.

13 In accordance with the LORD's command to him, Joshua gave to Caleb son of Jephunneh a portion in Judah — Kiriath Arba, that is, Hebron. (Arba was the forefather of Anak.)[r] 14 From Hebron Caleb drove out the three Anakites[s] — Sheshai, Ahiman and Talmai,[t] the sons of Anak.[u] 15 From there he marched against the people living in Debir (formerly called Kiriath Sepher). 16 And Caleb said, "I will

[a] 4 Septuagint; Hebrew *your*

14:12 Anakites. See note on 11:22.

14:13 Hebron. About 25 miles (40 kilometers) south of Jerusalem on the watershed of the central hill country.

14:15 Kiriath Arba. Means "town of Arba," which might mean "town of four" (quarters or districts). But Arba here is a proper name. As the burial place of Abraham, Sarah, and other patriarchal figures, it is significant that Israel takes possession of the land (Gen 23). **rest from war.** This ends Caleb's battles (cf. 11:23).

15:1 – 63 *Allotment for Judah.* A complete boundary description (vv. 1 – 12) is followed by lists of towns in 11 districts of Judah (vv. 20 – 63), with a note about the allotment of Hebron and Kiriath Sepher to Caleb and his family (vv. 13 – 19) bridging the two sections. This is the first, the most complete, and the most detailed of the allotments. It suggests a special recognition of Judah as blessed by God (Gen 49:8 – 10) and anticipates Judah's role in the line of David and Jesus Christ (Mic 5:2). This land has already been taken, perhaps reflecting Judah's commitment to God. Throughout Joshua and Judges the tribe of Judah is portrayed in a largely positive light, preparing for the appointment of David as king over Israel. See map, p. 412.

15:8 Jebusite. See note on 9:1.

15:13 – 19 See 14:6 – 15 and note.

15:14 Anakites. See note on 11:22. **Sheshai ... Talmai.** Northern names.

15:16 – 19 Aksah ... upper and lower springs. Cf. Judg 1:12 – 16. For Aksah approaching a member of her family, making a request, and obtaining something, compare Rebekah (Gen 24:55 – 67). Aksah's inheritance (cf. Zelophehad's daughters, 17:3 – 6) forms part of her dowry and remains in the family of Caleb and Othniel, and it witnesses to God's ongoing blessing for Caleb's faith.

give my daughter Aksah[v] in marriage to the man who attacks and captures Kiriath Sepher." 17 Othniel[w]
son of Kenaz, Caleb's brother, took it; so Caleb gave his daughter Aksah to him in marriage.
18 One day when she came to Othniel, she urged him[a] to ask her father for a field. When she got off
her donkey, Caleb asked her, "What can I do for you?"
19 She replied, "Do me a special favor. Since you have given me land in the Negev, give me also springs
of water." So Caleb gave her the upper and lower springs.

20 This is the inheritance of the tribe of Judah, according to its clans:

21 The southernmost towns of the tribe of Judah in the Negev toward the boundary of Edom were:
Kabzeel, Eder,[x] Jagur, 22 Kinah, Dimonah, Adadah, 23 Kedesh, Hazor, Ithnan, 24 Ziph,[y] Telem,
Bealoth, 25 Hazor Hadattah, Kerioth Hezron (that is, Hazor), 26 Amam, Shema, Moladah,[z] 27 Hazar
Gaddah, Heshmon, Beth Pelet, 28 Hazar Shual, Beersheba,[a] Biziothiah, 29 Baalah,[b] Iyim, Ezem,
30 Eltolad,[c] Kesil, Hormah, 31 Ziklag,[d] Madmannah, Sansannah, 32 Lebaoth, Shilhim, Ain and Rim-
mon[e]—a total of twenty-nine towns and their villages.

33 In the western foothills:
Eshtaol,[f] Zorah, Ashnah, 34 Zanoah,[g] En Gannim, Tappuah, Enam, 35 Jarmuth,[h] Adullam,[i] Sokoh, Azekah, 36 Shaaraim, Adithaim and Gederah[j] (or Gederothaim)[b]—fourteen towns and their
villages.
37 Zenan, Hadashah, Migdal Gad, 38 Dilean, Mizpah, Joktheel,[k] 39 Lachish,[l] Bozkath,[m] Eglon,
40 Kabbon, Lahmas, Kitlish, 41 Gederoth, Beth Dagon, Naamah and Makkedah[n]—sixteen towns
and their villages.
42 Libnah, Ether, Ashan,[o] 43 Iphtah, Ashnah, Nezib, 44 Keilah, Akzib[p] and Mareshah[q]—nine
towns and their villages.
45 Ekron, with its surrounding settlements and villages; 46 west of Ekron, all that were in the
vicinity of Ashdod, together with their villages; 47 Ashdod,[r] its surrounding settlements and villages; and Gaza, its settlements and villages, as far as the Wadi of Egypt[s] and the coastline of the
Mediterranean Sea.[t]

48 In the hill country:
Shamir, Jattir,[u] Sokoh, 49 Dannah, Kiriath Sannah (that is, Debir[v]), 50 Anab, Eshtemoh,[w] Anim,
51 Goshen,[x] Holon and Giloh—eleven towns and their villages.
52 Arab, Dumah,[y] Eshan, 53 Janim, Beth Tappuah, Aphekah, 54 Humtah, Kiriath Arba (that is,
Hebron) and Zior—nine towns and their villages.
55 Maon, Carmel,[z] Ziph, Juttah, 56 Jezreel,[a] Jokdeam, Zanoah, 57 Kain, Gibeah[b] and Timnah—
ten towns and their villages.
58 Halhul, Beth Zur,[c] Gedor, 59 Maarath, Beth Anoth and Eltekon—six towns and their villages.[c]
60 Kiriath Baal (that is, Kiriath Jearim[d]) and Rabbah[e]—two towns and their villages.

61 In the wilderness:
Beth Arabah, Middin, Sekakah, 62 Nibshan, the City of Salt and En Gedi[f]—six towns and their
villages.
63 Judah could not[g] dislodge the Jebusites[h], who were living in Jerusalem; to this day the Jebusites
live there with the people of Judah.

[a] *18* Hebrew and some Septuagint manuscripts; other Septuagint manuscripts (see also note at Judges 1:14) *Othniel, he urged her* [b] *36* Or *Gederah and Gederothaim* [c] *59* The Septuagint adds another district of eleven towns, including Tekoa and Ephrathah (Bethlehem).

15:16 [v] Jdg 1:12
15:17 [w] Jdg 3:9,11
15:21 [x] Ge 35:21
15:24 [y] 1Sa 23:14
15:26 [z] 1Ch 4:28
15:28 [a] Ge 21:31
15:29 [b] ver 9
15:30 [c] Jos 19:4
15:31 [d] 1Sa 27:6
15:32 [e] Jdg 20:45
15:33 [f] Jdg 13:25; 16:31
15:34 [g] 1Ch 4:18; Ne 3:13
15:35 [h] Jos 10:3 [i] 1Sa 22:1
15:36 [j] 1Ch 12:4
15:38 [k] 2Ki 14:7
15:39 [l] Jos 10:3; 2Ki 14:19 [m] 2Ki 22:1
15:41 [n] Jos 10:10
15:42 [o] 1Sa 30:30
15:44 [p] Jdg 1:31 [q] Mic 1:15
15:47 [r] Jos 11:22 [s] ver 4 [t] Nu 34:6
15:48 [u] 1Sa 30:27
15:49 [v] Jos 10:3
15:50 [w] Jos 21:14
15:51 [x] Jos 10:41; 11:16
15:52 [y] Ge 25:14
15:55 [z] Jos 12:22
15:56 [a] Jos 17:16
15:57 [b] Jos 18:28; Jdg 19:12
15:58 [c] 1Ch 2:45
15:60 [d] Jos 18:14 [e] Dt 3:11
15:62 [f] 1Sa 23:29
15:63 [g] Jdg 1:21 [h] 2Sa 5:6

15:17 Othniel. Links the generation of Joshua (and Caleb) with the period of the judges; Othniel, the first judge, continues the faith and courage of his father-in-law (Judg 3:7–11).
15:21–32 Many of these southern towns already taken by the tribe of Judah are later allotted to Simeon (19:1–9).
15:33 foothills. Lying between the Philistine coast and the hill country of Judah, these towns would exchange hands during the Philistine wars before David's kingship. Dan receives some of the towns (19:41–43).
15:48 hill country. The watershed area from Jerusalem south to the region of Hebron.
15:61 wilderness. The desert region west of the Dead Sea. **Sekakah.** Probably Khirbet Qumran, where the community that produced the Dead Sea Scrolls was later located.
15:63 could not dislodge the Jebusites. The first of several notes at the end of specific allotments about towns and areas not captured in the hill country (16:10; 17:12). Although commanded to take the whole land

16:1 [i]Jos 8:15; 18:12
16:2 [j]Jos 18:13
16:3 [k]2Ch 8:5 [l]Jos 10:33; 1Ki 9:15
16:4 [m]Jos 17:14
16:5 [n]Jos 18:13
16:6 [o]Jos 17:7
16:7 [p]1Ch 7:28
16:8 [q]Jos 17:9
16:10 [r]Jos 17:13; Jdg 1:28-29; 1Ki 9:16
17:1 [s]Ge 41:51 [t]Ge 50:23
17:2 [u]Nu 26:30; 1Ch 7:18
17:3 [v]Nu 27:1 [w]Nu 26:33
17:4 [x]Nu 27:5-7
17:7 [y]Jos 16:6 [z]Ge 12:6; Jos 21:21
17:8 [a]Jos 16:8
17:9 [b]Jos 16:8

Allotment for Ephraim and Manasseh

16 The allotment for Joseph began at the Jordan, east of the springs of Jericho, and went up from there through the desert[i] into the hill country of Bethel. 2It went on from Bethel (that is, Luz[j]),[a] crossed over to the territory of the Arkites in Ataroth, 3descended westward to the territory of the Japhletites as far as the region of Lower Beth Horon[k] and on to Gezer,[l] ending at the Mediterranean Sea.

4So Manasseh and Ephraim, the descendants of Joseph, received their inheritance.[m]

5This was the territory of Ephraim, according to its clans:

The boundary of their inheritance went from Ataroth Addar[n] in the east to Upper Beth Horon 6and continued to the Mediterranean Sea. From Mikmethath[o] on the north it curved eastward to Taanath Shiloh, passing by it to Janoah on the east. 7Then it went down from Janoah to Ataroth[p] and Naarah, touched Jericho and came out at the Jordan. 8From Tappuah the border went west to the Kanah Ravine[q] and ended at the Mediterranean Sea. This was the inheritance of the tribe of the Ephraimites, according to its clans. 9It also included all the towns and their villages that were set aside for the Ephraimites within the inheritance of the Manassites.

10They did not dislodge the Canaanites living in Gezer; to this day the Canaanites live among the people of Ephraim but are required to do forced labor.[r]

17 This was the allotment for the tribe of Manasseh as Joseph's firstborn,[s] that is, for Makir,[t] Manasseh's firstborn. Makir was the ancestor of the Gileadites, who had received Gilead and Bashan because the Makirites were great soldiers. 2So this allotment was for the rest of the people of Manasseh — the clans of Abiezer,[u] Helek, Asriel, Shechem, Hepher and Shemida. These are the other male descendants of Manasseh son of Joseph by their clans.

3Now Zelophehad son of Hepher,[v] the son of Gilead, the son of Makir, the son of Manasseh, had no sons but only daughters,[w] whose names were Mahlah, Noah, Hoglah, Milkah and Tirzah. 4They went to Eleazar the priest, Joshua son of Nun, and the leaders and said, "The LORD commanded Moses to give us an inheritance among our relatives." So Joshua gave them an inheritance along with the brothers of their father, according to the LORD's command.[x] 5Manasseh's share consisted of ten tracts of land besides Gilead and Bashan east of the Jordan, 6because the daughters of the tribe of Manasseh received an inheritance among the sons. The land of Gilead belonged to the rest of the descendants of Manasseh.

7The territory of Manasseh extended from Asher to Mikmethath[y] east of Shechem.[z] The boundary ran southward from there to include the people living at En Tappuah. 8(Manasseh had the land of Tappuah, but Tappuah[a] itself, on the boundary of Manasseh, belonged to the Ephraimites.) 9Then the boundary continued south to the Kanah Ravine.[b] There were towns belonging to

[a] 2 Septuagint; Hebrew *Bethel to Luz*

(see 1:2–4 and notes), the tribe of Judah does not succeed in Joshua's lifetime. Jerusalem is temporarily captured in Judg 1:8, but only under David would it become a permanent part of Israel (2 Sam 5:6–9).

16:1—17:18 *Allotment for Ephraim and Manasseh.* Moving north from the key southern tribe, Judah (ch. 15), one reaches Ephraim (16:5–10) and then Manasseh (17:1–13) as the two central tribes of the north. This concerns Manasseh's (half) tribal area west of the Jordan. For the half-tribe of Manasseh east of the Jordan, see 13:8–33 and note. See map, p. 412. Ephraim and Manasseh were both sons of Joseph. This land is largely taken by these tribes, but not as fully as that of Judah. Given that Joshua is an Ephraimite, we might have expected to see Ephraim taking the lead in seizing the land. This is not the case however.

16:4 See 14:3–4 and note on 14:4.

16:5 Ephraim. The lead tribe before the time of David's kingship. However, there are cracks already beginning to appear regarding their leadership in the time of Joshua (an Ephraimite). Shiloh, the location of the first permanent temple, is located in the tribal region of Ephraim (v. 6; 18:1–10).

16:10 Gezer. See note on 10:33. **forced labor.** A "tax" of human labor for building and other projects enacted under David and Solomon (2 Sam 12:31; 1 Kgs 4:6; 9:15,20–21).

17:1 Although Manasseh was Joseph's firstborn, Jacob chose Ephraim as firstborn when he adopted the two brothers as his own sons (Gen 48:14,19).

17:2–3 Manasseh's allotment does not appear to preserve any town lists. However, all the clans listed in v. 2 (except Hepher) and all the daughters in v. 3 represent towns (vv. 5–6) named in the Samaria ostraca, receipts from the eighth century BC found at the Israelite capital of Samaria. In contrast to Judah (see 15:1–63 and note), the difficulty of settlement (vv. 12–18) may have extended the time of occupying the land.

17:3 Zelophehad ... had no sons. Normally a daughter received a dowry as her inheritance when she moved (away from her parents' land) to her husband's family. But when a man had no sons, daughters could inherit (cf. 15:16–19 and note), as Moses decreed for Zelophehad's daughters (Num 27:1–11; 36:1–13). This would preserve the land, God's gift to each family of Israel for their livelihood, and prevent it from going to another tribe.

17:5 ten tracts of land. Distributed to the clans of Manasseh and to Zelophehad's daughters (see vv. 2–3 and note).

Ephraim lying among the towns of Manasseh, but the boundary of Manasseh was the northern
side of the ravine and ended at the Mediterranean Sea. 10On the south the land belonged to
Ephraim, on the north to Manasseh. The territory of Manasseh reached the Mediterranean Sea
and bordered Asher on the north and Issachar[c] on the east.
11Within Issachar and Asher, Manasseh also had Beth Shan,[d] Ibleam and the people of Dor,[e]
Endor,[f] Taanach and Megiddo,[g] together with their surrounding settlements (the third in the list
is Naphoth[a]).
12Yet the Manassites were not able[h] to occupy these towns, for the Canaanites were determined to live in
that region. 13However, when the Israelites grew stronger, they subjected the Canaanites to forced labor
but did not drive them out completely.[i]
14The people of Joseph said to Joshua, "Why have you given us only one allotment and one portion
for an inheritance? We are a numerous people, and the LORD has blessed us abundantly."[j]
15"If you are so numerous," Joshua answered, "and if the hill country of Ephraim is too small
for you, go up into the forest and clear land for yourselves there in the land of the Perizzites and
Rephaites.[k]"
16The people of Joseph replied, "The hill country is not enough for us, and all the Canaanites who
live in the plain have chariots fitted with iron,[l] both those in Beth Shan and its settlements and those
in the Valley of Jezreel."
17But Joshua said to the tribes of Joseph — to Ephraim and Manasseh — "You are numerous and
very powerful. You will have not only one allotment 18but the forested hill country as well. Clear it, and
its farthest limits will be yours; though the Canaanites have chariots fitted with iron[m] and though they
are strong, you can drive them out."

Division of the Rest of the Land

18 The whole assembly of the Israelites gathered at Shiloh[n] and set up the tent of meeting[o] there.
The country was brought under their control, 2but there were still seven Israelite tribes who
had not yet received their inheritance.
3So Joshua said to the Israelites: "How long will you wait before you begin to take possession of the
land that the LORD, the God of your ancestors, has given you? 4Appoint three men from each tribe. I will
send them out to make a survey of the land and to write a description of it, according to the inheritance
of each.[p] Then they will return to me. 5You are to divide the land into seven parts. Judah is to remain
in its territory on the south[q] and the tribes of Joseph in their territory on the north.[r] 6After you have
written descriptions of the seven parts of the land, bring them here to me and I will cast lots[s] for you
in the presence of the LORD our God. 7The Levites, however, do not get a portion among you, because
the priestly service of the LORD is their inheritance.[t] And Gad, Reuben and the half-tribe of Manasseh

[a] *11* That is, Naphoth Dor

17:10 [c] Ge 30:18
17:11 [d] 1Sa 31:10; 1Ki 4:12; 1Ch 7:29 [e] Jos 11:2 [f] 1Sa 28:7; Ps 83:10 [g] 1Ki 9:15
17:12 [h] Jdg 1:27
17:13 [i] Jos 16:10
17:14 [j] Nu 26:28-37
17:15 [k] Ge 14:5
17:16 [l] Jdg 1:19; 4:3,13
17:18 [m] ver 16
18:1 [n] Jos 19:51; 21:2; Jdg 18:31; 21:12,19; 1Sa 1:3; 4:3; Jer 7:12; 26:6 [o] Ex 27:21
18:4 [p] Mic 2:5
18:5 [q] Jos 15:1 [r] Jos 16:1-4
18:6 [s] Jos 14:2
18:7 [t] Jos 13:33

17:13 forced labor. See note on 16:10.
17:15 hill country of Ephraim. Reached into Manasseh's territory as well but retained the name Ephraim, perhaps due to Jacob's choice of Ephraim over Manasseh (see v. 1 and note). **clear land.** Israel exploited forested hill country by removing the Mediterranean scrubland vegetation and building terraces to retain the topsoil. The appearance of up to 300 villages in this region (ca. 1200 BC) attests to the success of this process. It set the stage for the dominant Israelite village and agricultural life found in the accounts of Judges, Ruth, and 1 Samuel. The villages were spaced so as to provide adequate farmland and grazing land. Terrace upkeep required significant labor and contributed to the value placed on large families (Ps 127:3–5). **Perizzites.** See note on 9:1. They may have inhabited some of the villages. **Rephaites.** See note on 12:4.
17:16,18 chariots fitted with iron. Likely iron axles that provided support for the chariot wheels (see note on 11:4).
17:18 you can drive them out. Although chariot warfare was confined to the lowlands, God provided a secure Israelite base in the hill country so that Israel, by trusting in God, could win battles against their more powerful enemy (Deut 20:1). Israel experienced both failure (Judg 1:19) and success (Judg 4:3–16) in their faith and in their battles.
18:1–10 *Division of the Rest of the Land.* From the strategic position of Shiloh in the central hill country, Joshua gathers all of Israel for the allotments of the remaining tribes (vv. 1–3,5,7). These tribes have yet to take possession of any territory at the time of the allocation. This explains why lots are used. This was not the case with Judah, Ephraim, and Manasseh. The repeated references to God's gift of the land (v. 3) and Joshua's casting lots in the Lord's presence (vv. 6,8,10) permeate the text with faith and divine guidance. Like the earlier tribal divisions, these are not uniform but follow the land's topography and allocate its resources by sometimes tracing the boundaries of earlier Canaanite city-states. See map, p. 412.
18:1 Shiloh. About ten miles (16 kilometers) northeast of Bethel, this sanctuary was close to the center of Israel's people and land in the tribal territory of Ephraim. God's tabernacle remained there until Eli died and Israel lost the ark (1 Sam 4).
18:6,8,10 cast lots. See 7:14; 14:2 and notes. Joshua may have supervised Eleazar the priest in casting the lots (19:51).

18:7 [u] Jos 13:8
18:8 [v] ver 1

have already received their inheritance on the east side of the Jordan. Moses the servant of the LORD
gave it to them.[u]"
[8]As the men started on their way to map out the land, Joshua instructed them, "Go and make a
survey of the land and write a description of it. Then return to me, and I will cast lots for you here at
Shiloh[v] in the presence of the LORD." [9]So the men left and went through the land. They wrote its description on a scroll, town by town, in seven parts, and returned to Joshua in the camp at Shiloh. [10]Joshua

DIVIDING THE LAND

Hebron Cities of refuge (underlined)
Levitical cities:
Towns received by Kohathite clans
Towns received by Gershonite clans
Towns received by Merarite clans

then cast lots[w] for them in Shiloh in the presence[x] of the LORD, and there he distributed the land to the Israelites according to their tribal divisions.[y]

Allotment for Benjamin

11The first lot came up for the tribe of Benjamin according to its clans. Their allotted territory lay between the tribes of Judah and Joseph:

12On the north side their boundary began at the Jordan, passed the northern slope of Jericho
and headed west into the hill country, coming out at the wilderness[z] of Beth Aven.[a] 13From there
it crossed to the south slope of Luz[b] (that is, Bethel[c]) and went down to Ataroth Addar[d] on the
hill south of Lower Beth Horon.

14From the hill facing Beth Horon[e] on the south the boundary turned south along the western
side and came out at Kiriath Baal (that is, Kiriath Jearim), a town of the people of Judah. This
was the western side.

15The southern side began at the outskirts of Kiriath Jearim on the west, and the boundary
came out at the spring of the waters of Nephtoah.[f] 16The boundary went down to the foot of the
hill facing the Valley of Ben Hinnom, north of the Valley of Rephaim. It continued down the Hinnom Valley[g] along the southern slope of the Jebusite city and so to En Rogel.[h] 17It then curved
north, went to En Shemesh, continued to Geliloth, which faces the Pass of Adummim, and ran
down to the Stone of Bohan[i] son of Reuben. 18It continued to the northern slope of Beth Arabah[a][j]
and on down into the Arabah. 19It then went to the northern slope of Beth Hoglah and came
out at the northern bay of the Dead Sea,[k] at the mouth of the Jordan in the south. This was the
southern boundary.

20The Jordan formed the boundary on the eastern side.

These were the boundaries that marked out the inheritance of the clans of Benjamin on all sides.[l]

21The tribe of Benjamin, according to its clans, had the following towns:

Jericho, Beth Hoglah, Emek Keziz, 22Beth Arabah, Zemaraim, Bethel,[m] 23Avvim, Parah, Ophrah,
24Kephar Ammoni, Ophni and Geba[n] — twelve towns and their villages.

25Gibeon,[o] Ramah,[p] Beeroth,[q] 26Mizpah,[r] Kephirah, Mozah, 27Rekem, Irpeel, Taralah, 28Zelah,[s] Haeleph, the Jebusite city[t] (that is, Jerusalem[u]), Gibeah[v] and Kiriath — fourteen towns and
their villages.

This was the inheritance of Benjamin for its clans.

Allotment for Simeon

19:2-10pp — 1Ch 4:28-33

19 The second lot came out for the tribe of Simeon according to its clans. Their inheritance lay within the territory of Judah.[w] 2It included:

Beersheba[x] (or Sheba),[b] Moladah, 3Hazar Shual, Balah, Ezem, 4Eltolad, Bethul, Hormah,
5Ziklag, Beth Markaboth, Hazar Susah, 6Beth Lebaoth and Sharuhen — thirteen towns and their
villages;

7Ain, Rimmon, Ether and Ashan[y] — four towns and their villages — 8and all the villages
around these towns as far as Baalath Beer (Ramah in the Negev).[z]

This was the inheritance of the tribe of the Simeonites, according to its clans. 9The inheritance of the
Simeonites was taken from the share of Judah,[a] because Judah's portion was more than they needed.
So the Simeonites received their inheritance within the territory of Judah.[b]

[a] *18* Septuagint; Hebrew *slope facing the Arabah* [b] *2* Or *Beersheba, Sheba*; 1 Chron. 4:28 does not have *Sheba*.

18:10 [w] Nu 34:13 [x] ver 1; Jer 7:12 [y] Nu 33:54; Jos 19:51
18:12 [z] Jos 16:1 [a] Jos 7:2
18:13 [b] Ge 28:19 [c] Jdg 1:23 [d] Jos 16:5
18:14 [e] Jos 10:10
18:15 [f] Jos 15:9
18:16 [g] Jos 15:8; 2Ki 23:10 [h] Jos 15:7
18:17 [i] Jos 15:6
18:18 [j] Jos 15:6
18:19 [k] Ge 14:3
18:20 [l] Jos 21:4,17; 1Sa 9:1
18:22 [m] Jos 16:1
18:24 [n] Isa 10:29
18:25 [o] Jos 9:3 [p] Jdg 4:5 [q] Jos 9:17
18:26 [r] Jos 11:3
18:28 [s] 2Sa 21:14 [t] Jos 15:8 [u] Jos 10:1 [v] Jos 15:57
19:1 [w] ver 9; Ge 49:7
19:2 [x] Ge 21:14; 1Ki 19:3
19:7 [y] Jos 15:42
19:8 [z] Jos 10:40
19:9 [a] Ge 49:7 [b] Eze 48:24

18:11–28 *Allotment for Benjamin.* Benjamin was the only full brother of Joseph (Gen 35:24), the father of Ephraim and Manasseh. Their territories had been allotted (chs. 16–17). Benjamin means "son of the right hand," where "right" is south and "left" is north in Hebrew directions. Thus, Benjamin's territory borders the Joseph tribes to their south. Situated between Judah to the south and Ephraim and Manasseh to the north, Benjamin plays a key role in Israel's history both before the monarchy (chs. 1–9; Judg 3:13–27) and during it (Saul was from the tribe of Benjamin, 1 Sam 9–31).

19:1–9 *Allotment for Simeon.* While some towns of Manasseh were in other tribal territories (17:11), Simeon had no contiguous territory, only towns in southern Judah (see 15:21–32 and note). Gen 49:5–7 prophesies that Simeon and Levi (Exod 32:26–29) would be warriors. Simeon may have defended the southern border of Judah and of all Israel.

19:10 [c]Jos 21:7,34
19:11 [d]Jos 12:22
19:13 [e]Jos 15:32
19:15 [f]Ge 35:19
19:16 [g]ver 10; Jos 21:7 [h]Eze 48:26
19:17 [i]Ge 30:18
19:18 [j]Jos 15:56 [k]1Sa 28:4; 2Ki 4:8
19:22 [l]Jdg 4:6,12; Ps 89:12 [m]Jos 15:10
19:23 [n]Jos 17:10 [o]Ge 49:15; Eze 48:25
19:24 [p]Jos 17:7
19:26 [q]Jos 12:22
19:27 [r]ver 10 [s]1Ki 9:13
19:28 [t]Jdg 1:31 [u]1Ch 6:76 [v]Ge 10:19; Jos 11:8
19:29 [w]Jos 18:25 [x]2Sa 5:11; 24:7; Isa 23:1; Jer 25:22; Eze 26:2 [y]Jdg 1:31
19:31 [z]Ge 30:13; Eze 48:2
19:35 [a]Jos 11:2
19:36 [b]Jos 18:25 [c]Jos 11:1
19:37 [d]Nu 21:33
19:39 [e]Dt 33:23; Eze 48:3
19:42 [f]Jdg 1:35
19:43 [g]Ge 38:12

Allotment for Zebulun

10 The third lot came up for Zebulun[c] according to its clans:

The boundary of their inheritance went as far as Sarid. 11 Going west it ran to Maralah,
touched Dabbesheth, and extended to the ravine near Jokneam.[d] 12 It turned east from Sarid
toward the sunrise to the territory of Kisloth Tabor and went on to Daberath and up to Japhia.
13 Then it continued eastward to Gath Hepher and Eth Kazin; it came out at Rimmon[e] and turned
toward Neah. 14 There the boundary went around on the north to Hannathon and ended at the
Valley of Iphtah El. 15 Included were Kattath, Nahalal, Shimron, Idalah and Bethlehem.[f] There
were twelve towns and their villages.

16 These towns and their villages were the inheritance of Zebulun,[g] according to its clans.[h]

Allotment for Issachar

17 The fourth lot came out for Issachar[i] according to its clans. 18 Their territory included:

Jezreel,[j] Kesulloth, Shunem,[k] 19 Hapharaim, Shion, Anaharath, 20 Rabbith, Kishion, Ebez,
21 Remeth, En Gannim, En Haddah and Beth Pazzez. 22 The boundary touched Tabor,[l] Sha-
hazumah and Beth Shemesh,[m] and ended at the Jordan. There were sixteen towns and their
villages.

23 These towns and their villages were the inheritance of the tribe of Issachar,[n] according to its clans.[o]

Allotment for Asher

24 The fifth lot came out for the tribe of Asher[p] according to its clans. 25 Their territory included:

Helkath, Hali, Beten, Akshaph, 26 Allammelek, Amad and Mishal. On the west the boundary
touched Carmel[q] and Shihor Libnath. 27 It then turned east toward Beth Dagon, touched Zebulun[r]
and the Valley of Iphtah El, and went north to Beth Emek and Neiel, passing Kabul[s] on the left.
28 It went to Abdon,[a] Rehob,[t] Hammon[u] and Kanah, as far as Greater Sidon.[v] 29 The boundary then
turned back toward Ramah[w] and went to the fortified city of Tyre,[x] turned toward Hosah and
came out at the Mediterranean Sea in the region of Akzib,[y] 30 Ummah, Aphek and Rehob. There
were twenty-two towns and their villages.

31 These towns and their villages were the inheritance of the tribe of Asher,[z] according to its clans.

Allotment for Naphtali

32 The sixth lot came out for Naphtali according to its clans:

33 Their boundary went from Heleph and the large tree in Zaanannim, passing Adami Nekeb
and Jabneel to Lakkum and ending at the Jordan. 34 The boundary ran west through Aznoth Tabor
and came out at Hukkok. It touched Zebulun on the south, Asher on the west and the Jordan[b]
on the east. 35 The fortified towns were Ziddim, Zer, Hammath, Rakkath, Kinnereth,[a] 36 Adamah,
Ramah,[b] Hazor,[c] 37 Kedesh, Edrei,[d] En Hazor, 38 Iron, Migdal El, Horem, Beth Anath and Beth Shemesh. There were nineteen towns and their villages.

39 These towns and their villages were the inheritance of the tribe of Naphtali, according to its clans.[e]

Allotment for Dan

40 The seventh lot came out for the tribe of Dan according to its clans. 41 The territory of their inheritance included:

Zorah, Eshtaol, Ir Shemesh, 42 Shaalabbin, Aijalon,[f] Ithlah, 43 Elon, Timnah,[g] Ekron, 44 Eltekeh,

a 28 Some Hebrew manuscripts (see also 21:30); most Hebrew manuscripts *Ebron* *b* 34 Septuagint; Hebrew *west, and Judah, the Jordan,*

19:10–16 *Allotment for Zebulun.* This territory lay in the southwest Galilean highlands around the fruitful Beit Netofah valley.
19:15 Bethlehem. Beit Lāḥem, not the Bethlehem of David and Jesus.
19:17–23 *Allotment for Issachar.* This territory included much of the strategically important and fertile Jezreel Valley, where Canaanite cities made settlement difficult.
19:24–31 *Allotment for Asher.* This territory lay along the Mediterranean coast and included the important harbor at Akko.
19:32–39 *Allotment for Naphtali.* Other than Zebulun in the southwest, Naphtali had most of the Galilean highlands.
19:40–48 *Allotment for Dan.* This territory included towns lying west of Benjamin to Joppa on the Mediterranean.

Gibbethon, Baalath, 45Jehud, Bene Berak, Gath Rimmon,[h] 46Me Jarkon and Rakkon, with the area facing Joppa.[i]

47(When the territory of the Danites was lost to them,[j] they went up and attacked Leshem[k], took it, put it to the sword and occupied it. They settled in Leshem and named it Dan after their ancestor.)[l] 48These towns and their villages were the inheritance of the tribe of Dan,[m] according to its clans.

Allotment for Joshua

49When they had finished dividing the land into its allotted portions, the Israelites gave Joshua son of Nun an inheritance among them, 50as the LORD had commanded. They gave him the town he asked for — Timnath Serah[a][n] in the hill country of Ephraim. And he built up the town and settled there.

51These are the territories that Eleazar the priest, Joshua son of Nun and the heads of the tribal clans of Israel assigned by lot at Shiloh in the presence of the LORD at the entrance to the tent of meeting. And so they finished dividing the land.[o]

Cities of Refuge

20:1-9Ref — Nu 35:9-34; Dt 4:41-43; 19:1-14

20 Then the LORD said to Joshua: 2"Tell the Israelites to designate the cities of refuge, as I instructed you through Moses, 3so that anyone who kills a person accidentally and unintentionally[p] may flee there and find protection from the avenger of blood.[q] 4When they flee to one of these cities, they are to stand in the entrance of the city gate[r] and state their case before the elders[s] of that city. Then the elders are to admit the fugitive into their city and provide a place to live among them. 5If the avenger of blood comes in pursuit, the elders must not surrender the fugitive, because the fugitive killed their neighbor unintentionally and without malice aforethought. 6They are to stay in that city until they have stood trial before the assembly[t] and until the death of the high priest who is serving at that time. Then they may go back to their own home in the town from which they fled."

7So they set apart Kedesh[u] in Galilee in the hill country of Naphtali, Shechem[v] in the hill country of Ephraim, and Kiriath Arba (that is, Hebron[w]) in the hill country of Judah.[x] 8East of the Jordan (on the other side from Jericho) they designated Bezer[y] in the wilderness on the plateau in the tribe of Reuben, Ramoth in Gilead[z] in the tribe of Gad, and Golan in Bashan in the tribe of Manasseh. 9Any of the Israelites or any foreigner residing among them who killed someone accidentally could flee to these designated cities and not be killed by the avenger of blood prior to standing trial before the assembly.[a]

a 50 Also known as *Timnath Heres* (see Judges 2:9)

19:45 [h] Jos 21:24; 1Ch 6:69
19:46 [i] 2Ch 2:16; Jnh 1:3
19:47 [j] Jdg 18:1 [k] Jdg 18:7,14 [l] Jdg 18:27,29
19:48 [m] Ge 30:6
19:50 [n] Jos 24:30
19:51 [o] Jos 14:1; 18:10; Ac 13:19
20:3 [p] Lev 4:2 [q] Nu 35:12
20:4 [r] Ru 4:1; Jer 38:7 [s] Jos 7:6
20:6 [t] Nu 35:12
20:7 [u] Jos 21:32; 1Ch 6:76 [v] Ge 12:6 [w] Jos 10:36; 21:11 [x] Lk 1:39
20:8 [y] Jos 21:36; 1Ch 6:78 [z] Jos 12:2
20:9 [a] Ex 21:13; Nu 35:15

19:47 Powerful Canaanites along the coast (see 17:15 – 18 and notes), as well as Amorites (Judg 1:34), possessed these towns. Philistine expansion may have also presented problems. See Judg 18 for the Danite migration and brutal destruction of Leshem (called Laish in Judg 18:29).

19:49 – 51 *Allotment for Joshua.* Caleb (see 14:6 – 15 and note; 15:13 – 19) and Joshua are the first recipients of allotments to clans and families within the tribal allotments. All of Israel's clans and families will receive an inheritance, but Joshua and Caleb are the only representatives of the previous generation who were faithful and whom God promised would come into the land and enjoy its blessings (Num 14:30; 26:65; 32:12). Unlike Caleb, whose son-in-law Othniel has a role in the next generation, Joshua has no named heir.

19:50 Timnath Serah. May be Khirbet Timnah, 16 miles (25.5 kilometers) southwest of Shechem.

19:51 by lot. See 7:14; 14:2; 18:6,8,10 and notes.

20:1 – 9 *Cities of Refuge.* Exod 21:12 – 14; Num 35:6 – 34; Deut 4:41 – 43; 19:1 – 14 (see notes) identify the purpose and places for the cities of refuge, as summarized here. Someone who kills another person unintentionally is not subject to the death penalty (Exod 21:12 – 13; Num 35:31) but nevertheless may face a vendetta from the victim's family (Num 35:27). Laws and customs elsewhere require the killer to flee the country. However, the land of Israel is God's gift to his people, and their lives should be there with him. Therefore, God uniquely provides for sanctuary within the promised land for those who are innocent.

20:3,5,9 avenger of blood. A close relative responsible for protecting the life and memory of the family members (see Num 35:21; Deut 19:6 and notes) and their inheritance (called "guardian-redeemers" [Ruth 2:20; 3:9 – 13; 4:1 – 8; see notes on Ruth 2:20; 3:9,10; 4:3 – 8]).

20:4 – 9 state their case ... standing trial. The elders functioned as judges ("the assembly" [v. 6]) for capital and other cases (Num 35:24 – 25).

20:7 Kedesh ... Shechem ... Hebron. Found in the land from north to south. If Israel fully obeyed and God enlarged their territory, then they would set aside three more cities (Deut 19:8 – 9).

20:8 Bezer ... Ramoth ... Golan. Listed from south to north.

20:9 Israelites or any foreigner. There is no distinction between persons in God's concern for justice (Exod 22:21; Lev 19:34; 24:22; Num 15:15; Deut 1:16; 10:18).

21:1 [b]Jos 14:1
21:2 [c]Jos 18:1 [d]Nu 35:2-3
21:4 [e]ver 19
21:5 [f]ver 26
21:6 [g]Ge 30:18
21:7 [h]Ex 6:16 [i]Jos 19:10
21:11 [j]Jos 15:13; 1Ch 6:55
21:13 [k]Jos 15:42; 1Ch 6:57
21:14 [l]Jos 15:48 [m]Jos 15:50
21:15 [n]Jos 15:51
21:16 [o]Jos 15:55 [p]Jos 15:10
21:17 [q]Jos 18:24
21:21 [r]Jos 17:7; 20:7
21:22 [s]Jos 10:10 [t]1Sa 1:1
21:24 [u]Jos 19:45
21:27 [v]Jos 12:5 [w]Nu 35:6

Towns for the Levites

21:4-39pp — 1Ch 6:54-80

21 Now the family heads of the Levites approached Eleazar the priest, Joshua son of Nun, and the heads of the other tribal families of Israel[b] 2 at Shiloh[c] in Canaan and said to them, "The LORD commanded through Moses that you give us towns to live in, with pasturelands for our livestock."[d] 3 So, as the LORD had commanded, the Israelites gave the Levites the following towns and pasturelands out of their own inheritance:

4 The first lot came out for the Kohathites, according to their clans. The Levites who were descendants of Aaron the priest were allotted thirteen towns from the tribes of Judah, Simeon and Benjamin.[e] 5 The rest of Kohath's descendants were allotted ten towns from the clans of the tribes of Ephraim, Dan and half of Manasseh.[f]

6 The descendants of Gershon were allotted thirteen towns from the clans of the tribes of Issachar,[g] Asher, Naphtali and the half-tribe of Manasseh in Bashan.

7 The descendants of Merari,[h] according to their clans, received twelve towns from the tribes of Reuben, Gad and Zebulun.[i]

8 So the Israelites allotted to the Levites these towns and their pasturelands, as the LORD had commanded through Moses.

9 From the tribes of Judah and Simeon they allotted the following towns by name 10 (these towns were assigned to the descendants of Aaron who were from the Kohathite clans of the Levites, because the first lot fell to them):

> 11 They gave them Kiriath Arba (that is, Hebron[j]), with its surrounding pastureland, in the hill country of Judah. (Arba was the forefather of Anak.) 12 But the fields and villages around the city they had given to Caleb son of Jephunneh as his possession.
>
> 13 So to the descendants of Aaron the priest they gave Hebron (a city of refuge for one accused of murder), Libnah,[k] 14 Jattir,[l] Eshtemoa,[m] 15 Holon,[n] Debir, 16 Ain, Juttah[o] and Beth Shemesh,[p] together with their pasturelands — nine towns from these two tribes.
>
> 17 And from the tribe of Benjamin they gave them Gibeon, Geba,[q] 18 Anathoth and Almon, together with their pasturelands — four towns.

19 The total number of towns for the priests, the descendants of Aaron, came to thirteen, together with their pasturelands.

20 The rest of the Kohathite clans of the Levites were allotted towns from the tribe of Ephraim:

> 21 In the hill country of Ephraim they were given Shechem[r] (a city of refuge for one accused of murder) and Gezer, 22 Kibzaim and Beth Horon,[s] together with their pasturelands — four towns.[t]
>
> 23 Also from the tribe of Dan they received Eltekeh, Gibbethon, 24 Aijalon and Gath Rimmon,[u] together with their pasturelands — four towns.
>
> 25 From half the tribe of Manasseh they received Taanach and Gath Rimmon, together with their pasturelands — two towns.

26 All these ten towns and their pasturelands were given to the rest of the Kohathite clans.

27 The Levite clans of the Gershonites were given:

> from the half-tribe of Manasseh,
> Golan in Bashan[v] (a city of refuge for one accused of murder[w]) and Be Eshterah, together with their pasturelands — two towns;

21:1–45 *Towns for the Levites.* This apportionment fulfills God's command (Num 35:1–8; 1 Chr 6:54–81). The Levites had no inheritance in the land, but God provided for them. As with the Sabbath (Exod 20:8–11; 31:14–15; Deut 5:12–15) and firstfruits offerings (Exod 23:19; Num 28:26; Deut 26:2,10), a token of God's blessing is returned to him to acknowledge God as the giver. Here it is a token of the land. Located in many previously Canaanite cities and in border towns, these towns would function as teaching centers where the Levites would carry out the priestly duties (Lev 10:10–11) of teaching God's instruction and covenant faith (cf. Acts 2:42–47; Rom 15:26–27; Phil 4:10–18). A concluding summary (vv. 43–45) reemphasizes the fulfillment of God's promises in giving Israel the land.

21:2 Shiloh. See note on 18:1.

21:10 descendants of Aaron. The priests (Num 18:1–6), whose towns were in the south near the later Jerusalem temple.

21:20–26 The Kohathites transported the ark and tabernacle furniture and held Levitical towns in the central hill country (Num 3:30–31; 4:15–20; 7:9) near Shiloh (see 18:1 and note).

21:27–33 The Gershonites transported the tabernacle textiles and received towns in the north (Num 3:25–26; 4:24–26).

[28]from the tribe of Issachar,[x]
Kishion, Daberath, [29]Jarmuth and En Gannim, together with their pasturelands — four towns;
[30]from the tribe of Asher,[y]
Mishal, Abdon, [31]Helkath and Rehob, together with their pasturelands — four towns;
[32]from the tribe of Naphtali,
Kedesh[z] in Galilee (a city of refuge for one accused of murder[a]), Hammoth Dor and Kartan, together with their pasturelands — three towns.
[33]The total number of towns of the Gershonite[b] clans came to thirteen, together with their pasturelands.

[34]The Merarite clans (the rest of the Levites) were given:
from the tribe of Zebulun,[c]
Jokneam, Kartah, [35]Dimnah and Nahalal, together with their pasturelands — four towns;
[36]from the tribe of Reuben,
Bezer,[d] Jahaz, [37]Kedemoth and Mephaath, together with their pasturelands — four towns;
[38]from the tribe of Gad,
Ramoth[e] in Gilead (a city of refuge for one accused of murder), Mahanaim,[f] [39]Heshbon and Jazer, together with their pasturelands — four towns in all.
[40]The total number of towns allotted to the Merarite clans, who were the rest of the Levites, came to twelve.

[41]The towns of the Levites in the territory held by the Israelites were forty-eight in all, together with their pasturelands.[g] [42]Each of these towns had pasturelands surrounding it; this was true for all these towns.

[43]So the LORD gave Israel all the land he had sworn to give their ancestors,[h] and they took possession[i] of it and settled there.[j] [44]The LORD gave them rest[k] on every side, just as he had sworn to their ancestors. Not one of their enemies[l] withstood them; the LORD gave all their enemies[m] into their hands.[n] [45]Not one of all the LORD's good promises[o] to Israel failed; every one was fulfilled.

Eastern Tribes Return Home

22 Then Joshua summoned the Reubenites, the Gadites and the half-tribe of Manasseh [2]and said to them, "You have done all that Moses the servant of the LORD commanded,[p] and you have obeyed me in everything I commanded. [3]For a long time now — to this very day — you have not deserted your fellow Israelites but have carried out the mission the LORD your God gave you. [4]Now that the LORD your God has given them rest as he promised, return to your homes[q] in the land that Moses the servant of the LORD gave you on the other side of the Jordan.[r] [5]But be very careful to keep the commandment[s] and the law that Moses the servant of the LORD gave you: to love the LORD your God, to walk in obedience to him, to keep his commands,[t] to hold fast to him and to serve him with all your heart and with all your soul.[u]"

[6]Then Joshua blessed[v] them and sent them away, and they went to their homes. [7](To the half-tribe

21:28 [x]Ge 30:18
21:30 [y]Jos 17:7
21:32 [z]Jos 12:22 [a]Nu 35:6; Jos 20:7
21:33 [b]ver 6
21:34 [c]Jos 19:10; 1Ch 6:77
21:36 [d]Jos 20:8
21:38 [e]Dt 4:43 [f]Ge 32:2
21:41 [g]Nu 35:7
21:43 [h]Dt 34:4 [i]Dt 11:31 [j]Dt 17:14
21:44 [k]Ex 33:14; Jos 1:13 [l]Dt 6:19 [m]Ex 23:31 [n]Dt 7:24; 21:10
21:45 [o]Jos 23:14; Ne 9:8
22:2 [p]Nu 32:25
22:4 [q]Nu 32:22; Dt 3:20 [r]Nu 32:18; Jos 1:13-15
22:5 [s]Isa 43:22 [t]Dt 5:29 [u]Dt 6:6,17
22:6 [v]Ex 39:43

21:34–40 The Merarites transported the tabernacle structures and received towns in Zebulun and Transjordan (Num 1:47–53; 3:33–37; 4:29–33).

21:43 the LORD gave Israel all the land. God has given all to Israel, and no one could withstand them. Yet Israel was not altogether faithful (chs. 7; 9), and land remained to be taken (13:1–7; 15:63; 16:10; 17:12). God graciously gave the gift but it remained necessary for Israel to receive fully what had been given. Divine sovereignty does not eliminate human responsibility.

22:1—24:33 *Israel United to Serve God in the Promised Land.* Throughout the book, God gave the promises and commands and then led Israel with miraculous signs (chs. 6; 8; 10; 11) and divine guidance through casting lots (chs. 7; 13–21). In every case, Israel was called to respond in faith. With some of the land taken and all of the land allotted, Israel must proceed by faith. Ch. 22 examines Israel's response in terms of unity and worship, and chs. 23–24 challenge the nation to a life of continuing faithfulness. The deaths of Joshua and Eleazar mark the end of the generation that saw God begin the process of giving all of the land to Israel, and the question of how Israel will respond is yet to be answered.

22:1–34 *Eastern Tribes Return Home.* The loyalty of the tribes east of the Jordan was examined in 1:12–18. Their oaths and subsequent service (4:12) confirmed their faith, but the land Moses gave them was not in the promised land (ch. 13). As these eastern tribes were the first group separated from all Israel in ch. 1, they become the last group examined before all Israel comes together in the final chapters. Ch. 22 addresses what is essential to the unity and holiness of Israel (properly worshiping God with an altar in the promised land) and what is peripheral (living in the promised land).

22:2–4 all that Moses ... commanded ... return to your homes. See 1:12–15 and notes.

22:5 love ... obedience. For the love of God as loyal service, see Deut 6:5 and note.

22:7 [w]Nu 32:33; Jos 12:5 [x]Jos 17:2,5
22:8 [y]Dt 20:14 [z]Nu 31:27 [a]Ge 49:27; 1Sa 30:16; Isa 9:3
22:9 [b]Nu 32:26,29
22:12 [c]Jos 18:1
22:13 [d]Nu 25:7 [e]Nu 3:32; Jos 24:33
22:14 [f]Nu 1:4
22:16 [g]Dt 13:14 [h]Dt 12:13-14
22:17 [i]Nu 25:1-9
22:18 [j]Lev 10:6; Nu 16:22
22:20 [k]Jos 7:1 [l]Ps 7:11 [m]Jos 7:5
22:22 [n]Dt 10:17 [o]Ps 50:1 [p]1Ki 8:39; Job 10:7; Ps 44:21; Jer 17:10
22:23 [q]Jer 41:5 [r]Dt 12:11; 18:19; 1Sa 20:16
22:27 [s]Ge 21:30; Jos 24:27

of Manasseh Moses had given land in Bashan,[w] and to the other half of the tribe Joshua gave land on
the west side[x] of the Jordan along with their fellow Israelites.) When Joshua sent them home, he blessed
them, 8saying, "Return to your homes with your great wealth—with large herds of livestock,[y] with
silver, gold, bronze and iron, and a great quantity of clothing—and divide[z] the plunder[a] from your
enemies with your fellow Israelites."

9So the Reubenites, the Gadites and the half-tribe of Manasseh left the Israelites at Shiloh in Canaan
to return to Gilead,[b] their own land, which they had acquired in accordance with the command of the
LORD through Moses.

10When they came to Geliloth near the Jordan in the land of Canaan, the Reubenites, the Gadites
and the half-tribe of Manasseh built an imposing altar there by the Jordan. 11And when the Israelites
heard that they had built the altar on the border of Canaan at Geliloth near the Jordan on the Israelite
side, 12the whole assembly of Israel gathered at Shiloh[c] to go to war against them.

13So the Israelites sent Phinehas[d] son of Eleazar,[e] the priest, to the land of Gilead—to Reuben, Gad
and the half-tribe of Manasseh. 14With him they sent ten of the chief men, one from each of the tribes
of Israel, each the head of a family division among the Israelite clans.[f]

15When they went to Gilead—to Reuben, Gad and the half-tribe of Manasseh—they said to them:
16"The whole assembly of the LORD says: 'How could you break faith[g] with the God of Israel like this?
How could you turn away from the LORD and build yourselves an altar in rebellion[h] against him now?
17Was not the sin of Peor[i] enough for us? Up to this very day we have not cleansed ourselves from that
sin, even though a plague fell on the community of the LORD! 18And are you now turning away from
the LORD?

" 'If you rebel against the LORD today, tomorrow he will be angry with the whole community[j] of
Israel. 19If the land you possess is defiled, come over to the LORD's land, where the LORD's tabernacle
stands, and share the land with us. But do not rebel against the LORD or against us by building an altar
for yourselves, other than the altar of the LORD our God. 20When Achan son of Zerah was unfaithful in
regard to the devoted things,[a][k] did not wrath[l] come on the whole community of Israel? He was not the
only one who died for his sin.' "[m]

21Then Reuben, Gad and the half-tribe of Manasseh replied to the heads of the clans of Israel: 22"The
Mighty One, God, the LORD! The Mighty One, God,[n] the LORD![o] He knows![p] And let Israel know! If this has
been in rebellion or disobedience to the LORD, do not spare us this day. 23If we have built our own altar
to turn away from the LORD and to offer burnt offerings and grain offerings,[q] or to sacrifice fellowship
offerings on it, may the LORD himself call us to account.[r]

24"No! We did it for fear that some day your descendants might say to ours, 'What do you have
to do with the LORD, the God of Israel? 25The LORD has made the Jordan a boundary between us and
you—you Reubenites and Gadites! You have no share in the LORD.' So your descendants might cause
ours to stop fearing the LORD.

26"That is why we said, 'Let us get ready and build an altar—but not for burnt offerings or sacrifices.' 27On the contrary, it is to be a witness[s] between us and you and the generations that follow, that

a *20* The Hebrew term refers to the irrevocable giving over of things or persons to the LORD, often by totally destroying them.

22:8 divide the plunder ... with your fellow Israelites. Foreseen by Moses (Num 31:25–27), God gave Israel the plunder of Ai (8:2,27) and that of its subsequent enemies (11:14). Equal sharing enhanced Israel's unity.
22:10 Geliloth. Probably near the Jordan (see 18:17; perhaps Araq ed-Deir). **imposing altar.** Placed prominently west of the Jordan, it would also be visible east of the Jordan.
22:12 gathered at Shiloh to go to war. The one God should have one altar, located at that time at Shiloh (see 18:1–10 and note on 18:1; Deut 12:4–14 and note on 12:5). Disobedience in this crucial matter meant war (Deut 13:12–18).
22:13 Phinehas. A priest was responsible for the altar and worship (Lev 1–7; Num 5:25–26; 1 Sam 2:28).
22:17 sin of Peor. The previous apostasy by all Israel; Phinehas stopped it (Num 25:1–9).
22:20 Achan ... was not the only one who died for his sin. Verse 18 anticipates that, like the fate of Achan's family (7:24–25), all Israel will experience God's anger, especially if it knows of sin and does nothing (Deut 13:6–15).
22:22 The Mighty One, God, the LORD! Can also be translated "The LORD, the greatest God." Its repetition signals the strongest of oaths.
22:26–27 an altar ... to be a witness. Most often a witness is someone who gives testimony (Exod 23:1), but stone heaps were sometimes used as witnesses between two people or groups to confirm the taking of an oath (Gen 31:44–48). Although these tribes live outside the promised land, this witness guarantees that they are united with Israel in worshiping God.

we will worship the LORD at his sanctuary with our burnt offerings, sacrifices and fellowship offerings.[t] Then in the future your descendants will not be able to say to ours, 'You have no share in the LORD.'

28“And we said, 'If they ever say this to us, or to our descendants, we will answer: Look at the replica of the LORD's altar, which our ancestors built, not for burnt offerings and sacrifices, but as a witness between us and you.'

29“Far be it from us to rebel[u] against the LORD and turn away from him today by building an altar for burnt offerings, grain offerings and sacrifices, other than the altar of the LORD our God that stands before his tabernacle.[v]”

30When Phinehas the priest and the leaders of the community—the heads of the clans of the Israelites—heard what Reuben, Gad and Manasseh had to say, they were pleased. 31And Phinehas son of Eleazar, the priest, said to Reuben, Gad and Manasseh, “Today we know that the LORD is with us,[w] because you have not been unfaithful to the LORD in this matter. Now you have rescued the Israelites from the LORD's hand.”

32Then Phinehas son of Eleazar, the priest, and the leaders returned to Canaan from their meeting with the Reubenites and Gadites in Gilead and reported to the Israelites. 33They were glad to hear the report and praised God.[x] And they talked no more about going to war against them to devastate the country where the Reubenites and the Gadites lived.

34And the Reubenites and the Gadites gave the altar this name: A Witness[y] Between Us—that the LORD is God.

Joshua's Farewell to the Leaders

23 After a long time had passed and the LORD had given Israel rest[z] from all their enemies around them, Joshua, by then a very old man,[a] 2summoned all Israel—their elders,[b] leaders, judges and officials[c]—and said to them: “I am very old. 3You yourselves have seen everything the LORD your God has done to all these nations for your sake; it was the LORD your God who fought for you.[d] 4Remember how I have allotted[e] as an inheritance for your tribes all the land of the nations that remain—the nations I conquered—between the Jordan and the Mediterranean Sea[f] in the west. 5The LORD your God himself will push them out for your sake. He will drive them out before you, and you will take possession of their land, as the LORD your God promised you.[g]

6“Be very strong; be careful to obey all that is written in the Book of the Law of Moses, without turning aside to the right or to the left.[h] 7Do not associate with these nations that remain among you; do not invoke the names of their gods or swear[i] by them. You must not serve them or bow down[j] to them. 8But you are to hold fast to the LORD[k] your God, as you have until now.

9“The LORD has driven out before you great and powerful nations;[l] to this day no one has been able to withstand you.[m] 10One of you routs a thousand,[n] because the LORD your God fights for you,[o] just as he promised. 11So be very careful to love the LORD[p] your God.

12“But if you turn away and ally yourselves with the survivors of these nations that remain among you and if you intermarry with them[q] and associate with them,[r] 13then you may be sure that the LORD your God will no longer drive out these nations before you. Instead, they will become snares[s] and traps

22:27 [t] Dt 12:6
22:29 [u] Jos 24:16 [v] Dt 12:13-14
22:31 [w] Lev 26:11-12; 2Ch 15:2
22:33 [x] 1Ch 29:20; Da 2:19; Lk 2:28
22:34 [y] Ge 21:30
23:1 [z] Dt 12:9; Jos 21:44 [a] Jos 13:1
23:2 [b] Jos 7:6 [c] Jos 24:1
23:3 [d] Ex 14:14
23:4 [e] Jos 19:51 [f] Nu 34:6
23:5 [g] Ex 23:30; Nu 33:53
23:6 [h] Dt 5:32; Jos 1:7
23:7 [i] Ex 23:13; Ps 16:4; Jer 5:7 [j] Ex 20:5
23:8 [k] Dt 10:20
23:9 [l] Dt 11:23 [m] Dt 7:24
23:10 [n] Lev 26:8 [o] Ex 14:14; Dt 3:22
23:11 [p] Jos 22:5
23:12 [q] Dt 7:3 [r] Ex 34:16; Ps 106:34-35
23:13 [s] Ex 23:33

22:28 replica. The same Hebrew word as the “pattern” God showed Israel of the tabernacle they were to build (Exod 25:9,40); it points to (but does not replace) the true altar and the true worship at Shiloh.

22:34 A Witness Between Us. See v. 27; see also note on vv. 26–27.

23:1–16 *Joshua's Farewell to the Leaders.* Like Jacob (Gen 48–49) and Moses (Deut 1–33), this faithful leader gives his final testament to God's people. Most of what Joshua says can be found in the Pentateuch, especially Deuteronomy. God has fulfilled his promises, as Israel witnessed. They must choose to continue to serve him.

23:1 After a long time. If Joshua died at 110 (24:29) and Caleb was 80 at the time of Israel's entrance into the promised land (see 14:7,10 and note), then Joshua was also likely nearly the same age when he entered the land. So about 30 years have elapsed. **the LORD had given Israel rest.** See 1:13,15; 11:23; 14:15. “Rest” involves the absence of any threat from neighbors and looks forward to (but does not replace) the promised rest of God's people with him (Heb 4:8; see Introduction: Theological Themes [The Gift of the Promised Land]). **very old man.** See 13:1 and note.

23:4–5 I have allotted ... The LORD your God himself will push them out. Joshua oversaw the allotment (see 13:1—21:45 and note; 14:1–5 and notes). But Judges describes how much work remains for Israel to secure the land and live there.

23:6 Be very strong. See 1:5b–9 and note. **be careful to obey.** See 1:7–8 and notes; 8:31.

23:7 do not invoke the names of their gods. The fundamental command against idolatry (Exod 20:3–6; Deut 5:7–10) becomes Israel's test of obedience to God's covenant.

23:11 love the LORD your God. For this recurring concern, see 22:5 and note.

23:13 until you perish from this good land. The context provides

23:13 [t]Nu 33:55
23:14 [u]1Ki 2:2 [v]Jos 21:45
23:15 [w]Lev 26:17; Dt 28:15
23:16 [x]Dt 4:25-26
24:1 [y]Jos 23:2
24:2 [z]Ge 11:32
24:3 [a]Ge 12:1 [b]Ge 15:5 [c]Ge 21:3
24:4 [d]Ge 25:26 [e]Dt 2:5 [f]Ge 46:5-6
24:5 [g]Ex 3:10
24:6 [h]Ex 14:9
24:7 [i]Ex 14:20 [j]Ex 14:28 [k]Dt 1:46
24:8 [l]Nu 21:31
24:9 [m]Nu 22:2 [n]Nu 22:6
24:10 [o]Nu 23:11; Dt 23:5
24:11 [p]Jos 3:16-17 [q]Jos 6:1 [r]Ex 23:23; Dt 7:1
24:12 [s]Ex 23:28; Dt 7:20; Ps 44:3,6-7
24:13 [t]Dt 6:10-11
24:14 [u]Dt 10:12; 18:13; 1Sa 12:24; 2Co 1:12 [v]ver 23

for you, whips on your backs and thorns in your eyes,[t] until you perish from this good land, which the
LORD your God has given you.
14 "Now I am about to go the way of all the earth.[u] You know with all your heart and soul that not
one of all the good promises the LORD your God gave you has failed. Every promise has been fulfilled;
not one has failed.[v] 15 But just as all the good things the LORD your God has promised you have come to
you, so he will bring on you all the evil things he has threatened, until the LORD your God has destroyed
you from this good land he has given you.[w] 16 If you violate the covenant of the LORD your God, which
he commanded you, and go and serve other gods and bow down to them, the LORD's anger will burn
against you, and you will quickly perish from the good land he has given you.[x]"

The Covenant Renewed at Shechem

24 Then Joshua assembled all the tribes of Israel at Shechem. He summoned the elders, leaders,
judges and officials of Israel,[y] and they presented themselves before God.
2 Joshua said to all the people, "This is what the LORD, the God of Israel, says: 'Long ago your ancestors, including Terah the father of Abraham and Nahor, lived beyond the Euphrates River and worshiped other gods.[z] 3 But I took your father Abraham from the land beyond the Euphrates and led him
throughout Canaan[a] and gave him many descendants.[b] I gave him Isaac,[c] 4 and to Isaac I gave Jacob
and Esau.[d] I assigned the hill country of Seir[e] to Esau, but Jacob and his family went down to Egypt.[f]
5 " 'Then I sent Moses and Aaron,[g] and I afflicted the Egyptians by what I did there, and I brought
you out. 6 When I brought your people out of Egypt, you came to the sea, and the Egyptians pursued
them with chariots and horsemen[a][h] as far as the Red Sea.[b] 7 But they cried to the LORD for help, and
he put darkness[i] between you and the Egyptians; he brought the sea over them and covered them.[j] You
saw with your own eyes what I did to the Egyptians. Then you lived in the wilderness for a long time.[k]
8 " 'I brought you to the land of the Amorites who lived east of the Jordan. They fought against you,
but I gave them into your hands. I destroyed them from before you, and you took possession of their
land.[l] 9 When Balak son of Zippor,[m] the king of Moab, prepared to fight against Israel, he sent for Balaam son of Beor to put a curse on you.[n] 10 But I would not listen to Balaam, so he blessed you[o] again
and again, and I delivered you out of his hand.
11 " 'Then you crossed the Jordan[p] and came to Jericho.[q] The citizens of Jericho fought against you,
as did also the Amorites, Perizzites, Canaanites, Hittites, Girgashites, Hivites and Jebusites, but I gave
them into your hands.[r] 12 I sent the hornet[s] ahead of you, which drove them out before you — also the
two Amorite kings. You did not do it with your own sword and bow. 13 So I gave you a land on which you
did not toil and cities you did not build; and you live in them and eat from vineyards and olive groves
that you did not plant.'[t]
14 "Now fear the LORD and serve him with all faithfulness.[u] Throw away the gods[v] your ancestors

[a] 6 Or *charioteers*   [b] 6 Or *the Sea of Reeds*

blessings for obedience (Lev 26:1–13; Deut 28:1–14) and curses for disobedience (Lev 26:14–46; Deut 28:15–68). Worshiping other gods leads to banishment from the land (vv. 15–16; 2 Kgs 17:7–8; 2 Chr 7:19–20).

24:1–28 *The Covenant Renewed at Shechem.* As Moses did at the end of his life (Deut 1–33), so Joshua at the end of his life renews God's covenant with Israel. These covenants (23:1–16; 24:1–28) closely resemble the vassal treaty structure used in the fourteenth and thirteenth centuries BC and preserved among the Hittites. The overlord makes a treaty with a vassal king and people. God transforms this medium to define his relationship (as the overlord) with his people (as the vassal). These second-millennium BC treaties always had five parts: (1) *Title.* Identifies the great king (v. 2b: "This is what the LORD, the God of Israel, says"). (2) *Historical Prologue.* Reviews the faithfulness of the great king in past relationships (extending back for generations) in order to motivate the vassal to future loyalty (vv. 2c–13). (3) *Stipulations.* Defines the relationship in terms of laws that the vassal must obey (vv. 14–21,23). Most often these emphasize exclusive loyalty to the overlord. (4) *Witnesses.* Deities of both the overlord and vassal enforce the treaty when the overlord is not present with the vassal. Israel has one God, and he cannot be witness because he is the overlord. Instead, Israel itself and a large stone under the oak at Shechem are witnesses (vv. 22,26–27). (5) *Curses and Blessings.* Results of disobedience and obedience (v. 20).

24:1 Shechem. Joshua had renewed the covenant at nearby Mount Ebal (8:30–35; see note on 8:30), also associated with Israel's first generations. Some identify the "fortress temple" found at the archaeological site (Tell Balatah) with the place of Joshua's covenant renewal (cf. Judg 9). It becomes Joseph's burial place (v. 32; Gen 49:26).

24:2 Terah ... worshiped other gods. Gen 11 assumes polytheism, but it is not explicit.

24:3 I took your father Abraham. Abraham's faith and Israel's history are all God's initiative (Gen 12).

24:12 the hornet. Cf. Exod 23:28 (see note); Deut 7:20. A symbol of the fear that God brings against Israel's enemies.

24:14 fear the LORD and serve him. Contrast "the hornet" to bring fear in v. 12. As the key response for God's people, "serve" (whether as a verb or in its noun form, "service, work") appears 16 times in ch. 24

worshiped beyond the Euphrates River and in Egypt,[w] and serve the LORD. 15But if serving the LORD seems undesirable to you, then choose for yourselves this day whom you will serve, whether the gods your ancestors served beyond the Euphrates, or the gods of the Amorites,[x] in whose land you are living. But as for me and my household, we will serve the LORD."[y]

16Then the people answered, "Far be it from us to forsake the LORD to serve other gods! 17It was the LORD our God himself who brought us and our parents up out of Egypt, from that land of slavery, and performed those great signs before our eyes. He protected us on our entire journey and among all the nations through which we traveled. 18And the LORD drove out before us all the nations, including the Amorites, who lived in the land. We too will serve the LORD, because he is our God."

19Joshua said to the people, "You are not able to serve the LORD. He is a holy God;[z] he is a jealous God.[a] He will not forgive your rebellion[b] and your sins. 20If you forsake the LORD[c] and serve foreign gods, he will turn[d] and bring disaster on you and make an end of you,[e] after he has been good to you."

21But the people said to Joshua, "No! We will serve the LORD."

22Then Joshua said, "You are witnesses against yourselves that you have chosen[f] to serve the LORD."

"Yes, we are witnesses," they replied.

23"Now then," said Joshua, "throw away the foreign gods[g] that are among you and yield your hearts[h] to the LORD, the God of Israel."

24And the people said to Joshua, "We will serve the LORD our God and obey him."[i]

25On that day Joshua made a covenant[j] for the people, and there at Shechem he reaffirmed for them decrees and laws.[k] 26And Joshua recorded these things in the Book of the Law of God.[l] Then he took a large stone[m] and set it up there under the oak near the holy place of the LORD.

27"See!" he said to all the people. "This stone will be a witness[n] against us. It has heard all the words the LORD has said to us. It will be a witness against you if you are untrue to your God."

28Then Joshua dismissed the people, each to their own inheritance.

Buried in the Promised Land

24:29-31pp — Jdg 2:6-9

29After these things, Joshua son of Nun, the servant of the LORD, died at the age of a hundred and ten.[o] 30And they buried him in the land of his inheritance, at Timnath Serah[a][p] in the hill country of Ephraim, north of Mount Gaash.

[a] 30 Also known as *Timnath Heres* (see Judges 2:9)

24:14 [w] Eze 23:3
24:15 [x] Jdg 6:10; Ru 1:15 [y] Ru 1:16; 1Ki 18:21
24:19 [z] Lev 19:2; 20:26 [a] Ex 20:5 [b] Ex 23:21
24:20 [c] 1Ch 28:9,20 [d] Ac 7:42 [e] Jos 23:15
24:22 [f] Ps 119:30,173
24:23 [g] ver 14 [h] 1Ki 8:58; Ps 119:36; 141:4
24:24 [i] Ex 19:8; 24:3,7; Dt 5:27
24:25 [j] Ex 24:8 [k] Ex 15:25
24:26 [l] Dt 31:24 [m] Ge 28:18
24:27 [n] Jos 22:27
24:29 [o] Jdg 2:8
24:30 [p] Jos 19:50

out of 40 occurrences in Joshua. **Throw away the gods.** Harran (Gen 11:31; 12:4) was an ancient tribal center where images of gods were brought from other regions. Egypt possessed many gods (Exod 12:12). At Shechem, Jacob buried the images that his family brought with them after fleeing from Laban (Gen 35:4).

24:15 choose ... as for me. To emphasize the decisive nature of this moment, Joshua gives Israel a choice and makes his own decision public. As a leader, he chooses first.

24:17 out of Egypt. This was God's historic act of redemption (see 2:9–11 and note).

24:19 You are not able ... He will not forgive. God's grace (Exod 34:6) cannot condone apostasy, whether among the Canaanites or the Israelites. The point is not that obedience is impossible in principle (Deut 30:11–14), but that before a God who is both holy and jealous, a cavalier attitude to obedience is an invitation to disastrous condemnation and judgment. A later biblical writer clarifies that what was "wrong" with the old covenant was not so much an intrinsic weakness within the covenant as that God "found fault with the people" (Heb 8:7–8). **holy God.** See Lev 11:44 and note. **jealous God.** See Exod 20:5 and note.

24:23–24 throw away the foreign gods ... We will serve the LORD. Joshua resembles Jacob at Shechem when Jacob commanded his family to rid themselves of pagan images (see note on v. 14; Gen 35:2). Jacob's family did so immediately (Gen 35:4), but Israel's response is to repeat their oath of loyalty. They never dispose of their gods. Words without actions are ominous (Jas 2:14–16); they anticipate the apostasy of Judg 2:11–13.

24:26–27 large stone ... a witness. See 4:3,9; 7:26; 8:29; 10:18,27; 22:26–27 and notes.

24:26 the Book of the Law of God. The law of Moses (1:8; 8:31–35; Neh 8:1,3), especially as found in Deuteronomy. The "law" refers to instruction or teaching. Joshua adds the covenant found in this chapter.

24:29–33 *Buried in the Promised Land.* Joshua's burial closes the story of the book of Joshua. Joseph's burial connects the generation that left the promised land for Egypt with the one that entered the promised land. Eleazar's burial makes way for Phinehas, the only member of the next generation identified. Verses 29–31 are repeated in Judg 2:7–9, which continues the account into the next generation.

24:29 servant of the LORD. As with Moses (Deut 34:5), first used here of Joshua at his death (cf. 1:1; see note there). **a hundred and ten.** Cf. Joseph's age (Gen 50:26). In Egypt this was an ideal lifespan. Unlike Joseph, none of Joshua's descendants are named (contrast Eleazar, v. 33). Nevertheless, there was expectation that future leadership should come from the tribe of Ephraim (as reflected, e.g., in Judg 12:1–6 when the Ephraimites assume that they should take the lead). The book of Joshua hints at and the book of Judges confirms that the waywardness of the Ephraimites results in their rejection as the "firstborn" tribe.

24:31 [q]Jdg 2:7
24:32 [r]Ge 50:25; Ex 13:19 [s]Ge 33:19; Jn 4:5; Ac 7:16
24:33 [t]Jos 22:13 [u]Ex 6:25

[31]Israel served the LORD throughout the lifetime of Joshua and of the elders[q] who outlived him and
who had experienced everything the LORD had done for Israel.
[32]And Joseph's bones, which the Israelites had brought up from Egypt,[r] were buried at Shechem in
the tract of land[s] that Jacob bought for a hundred pieces of silver[a] from the sons of Hamor, the father
of Shechem. This became the inheritance of Joseph's descendants.
[33]And Eleazar son of Aaron[t] died and was buried at Gibeah, which had been allotted to his son Phinehas[u] in the hill country of Ephraim.

[a] *32* Hebrew ***hundred kesitahs***; a kesitah was a unit of money of unknown weight and value.

24:32 Joseph's bones … buried. See Gen 50:25; Exod 13:19. **Hamor.** Cf. Gen 33:19–20; 34:2–26 (see notes).
24:33 Eleazar. Cf. Exod 6:23,25. His final role was overseeing Israel's allotments (14:1; 17:4; 19:51; 21:1). **Phinehas.** The priesthood would continue in a lineage (Exod 29:9).

INTRODUCTION TO JUDGES

TITLE OF THE BOOK AND ROLE OF THE JUDGES

The English title for the book of Judges derives from the Latin (*Liber Judicum*) titles. The English term implies the notion of persons who adjudicate legal disputes or decide criminal cases. But the Hebrew title of the book (*šōpĕṭîm*) implies something different. Judg 2:16–17a states, "Then the LORD raised up judges [Hebrew *šōpĕṭîm*], who saved them out of the hands of these raiders. Yet they would not listen to their judges but prostituted themselves to other gods and worshiped them."

Thus the judges were to be both "deliverers" or "saviors" of their people from their enemies and "catalysts" or "stimuli" for godly living. Their purpose was not judicial; they were saviors. The first two judges, Othniel (3:9) and Ehud (3:15), are specifically called "deliverers." Others are described through the use of the verb "save" or "deliver" (Shamgar, 3:31; Gideon, 6:15; 8:22; Tola, 10:1; Jephthah, 12:3; Samson, 13:5). But 2:17 implies that they were also to be spiritual and moral leaders. Therefore, the success of each judge is related to his success in delivering the people and his success in spurring the Israelites to live proper lives before God.

There are two types of judges, usually designated as "major" and "minor" judges. The functional distinctions between the two types should not be too sharply drawn since the differences seem to be due to the author's choice of whether or not to include and develop the "cycle" in the story.

AUTHOR AND DATE

The author of the book of Judges is unknown. The date of composition is also unknown, but it was probably written during the monarchy (although the precise time is impossible to determine). Some of the stories may have existed in oral or written form at an early stage before the monarchy, but none is attributed to any particular source. The reference in 18:30 to "the time of the captivity of the land" seems to refer to the exile of the northern kingdom (722 BC) and suggests that the final edition of the book, at the earliest, came from this period. However, some scholars understand this to refer to the taking of the ark (see note on 18:30).

CHRONOLOGY

The period of the judges extends from the death of Joshua to the coronation of Saul, so the book does not cover the entire period of the judges. It leaves out two judges whose stories are found in the book of Samuel: Eli and Samuel (cf. 1 Sam 1–7). Simply adding the lengths of rule of each judge with its preceding oppression gives a total that cannot fit into the time between Joshua and Saul. Therefore, some oppressions and judgeships overlapped. This is to be expected since many (if not all) of the judges were local tribal leaders operating in geographically limited portions of Israel. Since there is no link in the book to the external chronology of the ancient Near East, the degree of overlap is difficult to discern. Thus the precise chronology of the period of the judges is unknown (cf. 1 Sam 12:9–11). This chronology is also dependent on the date of the exodus and conquest; early dates would

THE JUDGES OF ISRAEL

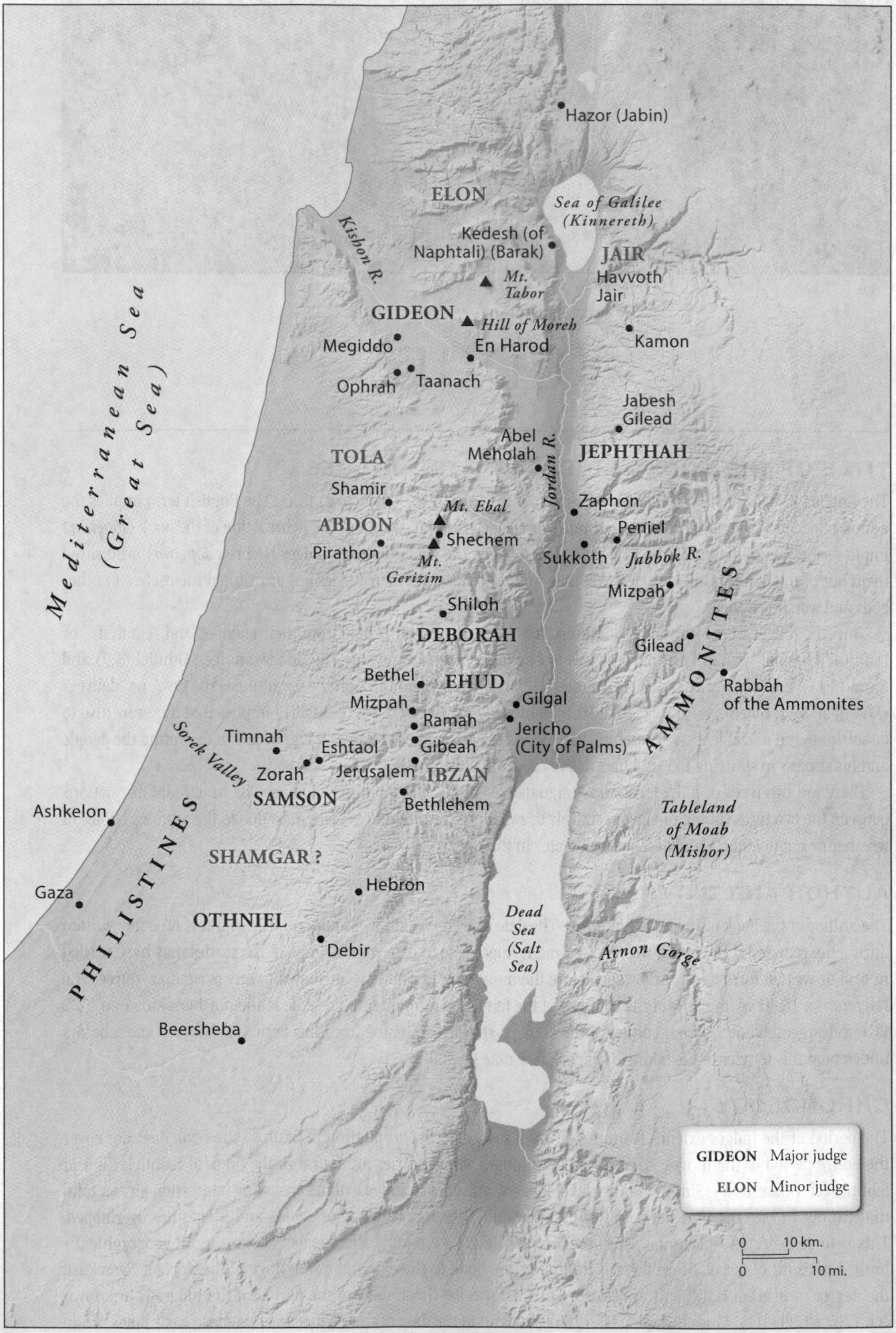

Hazor (Jabin)
ELON
Sea of Galilee (Kinnereth)
Kishon R.
Kedesh (of Naphtali) (Barak)
JAIR
Havvoth Jair
Mt. Tabor
Mediterranean Sea (Great Sea)
GIDEON
Hill of Moreh
Megiddo
En Harod
Kamon
Ophrah
Taanach
Jabesh Gilead
Abel Meholah
Jordan R.
JEPHTHAH
TOLA
Shamir
Mt. Ebal
Zaphon
ABDON
Shechem
Peniel
Pirathon
Mt. Gerizim
Sukkoth
Jabbok R.
Mizpah
AMMONITES
Shiloh
DEBORAH
Gilead
Bethel
EHUD
Rabbah of the Ammonites
Mizpah
Gilgal
Ramah
Sorek Valley
Timnah
Jericho (City of Palms)
Eshtaol
Gibeah
Zorah
Jerusalem
IBZAN
SAMSON
Bethlehem
Ashkelon
Tableland of Moab (Mishor)
PHILISTINES
SHAMGAR ?
Gaza
Hebron
Dead Sea (Salt Sea)
OTHNIEL
Debir
Arnon Gorge
Beersheba

GIDEON Major judge
ELON Minor judge

0 10 km.
0 10 mi.

be 1380–1050 BC; late dates would be ca. 1235–1050 BC (see Introduction to the Old Testament: Chronology/Dating, p. 7).

In addition, the book's use of numbers is not always clear. For example, the book may use the number 40 as a round number or figuratively to denote a generation. The first four major judges (Othniel, Ehud, Deborah, Gideon) are credited with 40 years of rest for the land (in the case of Ehud double 40, i.e., 80 [3:30]). The Philistine oppression (13:1) is 40 years. Samson's judgeship is 20 years (half 40), but mentioned twice (15:20; 16:31). The Canaanite oppression (4:3) is also 20 years.

The book does not include a complete historical presentation of any of the judges. In the case of the so-called minor judges, the writer chooses to give very limited information. For example, "Tola ... rose to save Israel" (10:1). But from whom? Had Israel done evil in the eyes of the Lord as in other cases? How did Tola "save" Israel? The information is not forthcoming. In addition, there is not a narration about every oppression during the judges' era. For example, in 10:11–14, the Lord refers to the oppressions of the Israelites by the Egyptians, Amorites, Sidonians, and Maonites. None of these is connected with a story of a judge who delivered the Israelites. The book's selective presentation is the way the author works his literary artistry and communicates with great clarity his theological message.

LITERARY ASPECTS AND MESSAGE

The book of Judges has three main parts: a double introduction (1:1—3:6), a double conclusion (17:1—21:25), and a main section commonly called the "cycles" section (3:7—16:31). See Outline.

The book has a coherent message concerning the consequences of disobedience to God with the resultant moral degeneration that characterized the history of Israel during this period. In a sense, it describes the degeneracy of Israel, its "Canaanization." The book is clearly designed to instruct the reader on the consequences of covenantal unfaithfulness to God and his law. Although Israel's degeneracy directly challenges God's rule, it cannot undo the Lord's sovereign kingship.

The book develops Israel's degeneracy from different perspectives: a ***historical/military*** perspective (1:1—2:5) and a ***religious*** perspective (2:6—3:6). The cycles section (3:7—16:31) uses the ***religious*** perspective traced in the individual lives of the judges themselves. The book's final section (17:1—21:25) represents both perspectives in which Israel as a nation expresses its fullest point of degeneracy by its corporate actions. While Samson is the climax and moral nadir of the cycles section, the full scope of degeneration is seen in chs. 17–21, which document Israel's deterioration into idolatry, civil war, and rape sanctioned by the leaders of Israel.

THE DOUBLE INTRODUCTION AND DOUBLE CONCLUSION

The double introduction is symmetrical to the double conclusion, framing the "cycles":

a Foreign wars with failure to apply the law of Deut 7 (*ḥērem*) (1:1—2:5)
　b Difficulties with foreign idols (2:6—3:6)
　b´ Difficulties with domestic idols (17:1—18:31)
a´ Domestic wars with misapplication of the law of Deut 7 (*ḥērem*) (19:1—21:25)

The first introduction (*a*) is balanced by the second conclusion (*a´*), and the second introduction (*b*) is balanced by the first conclusion (*b´*). On the law of the ban (Hebrew *ḥērem*), see Introduction to Deuteronomy: Themes and Theology (Holy War); Deut 7 and notes; Deut 20 and notes; Introduction to Joshua: Theological Themes (Genocide?); Josh 6 and notes; see also Theology on p. 429.

The double introduction (1:1—3:6) initiates two patterns that create literary expectations for the main "cycles" section. Judg 1:1—2:5 introduces the reader to the pattern of Israel's increasing failure to drive out the Canaanites—a pattern that will be mirrored in the degeneration of the "cycles" section. It also reveals the geographic sequence pattern of Judah to Dan reflected in the cycles (Othniel to Samson). Judg 2:6—3:6 introduces the reader to a second pattern, the all-important "cycles" pattern, the very framework of each of the six major cycles (see The Cycles Section).

The double conclusion (17:1—21:25) is not only linked with the double introduction (1:1—3:6), but it is itself unified by the four-time repetition of a distinctive refrain: "In those days Israel had no king; everyone did as they saw fit." The refrain occurs twice in full (at the beginning and end of the double conclusion: 17:6; 21:25) and twice with an ellipsis of the refrain's second line (in the middle of the double conclusion: 18:1; 19:1). This forms a concentric (chiastic) pattern—a (17:6)—b (18:1) / b´ (19:1)—a´ 21:25—that reinforces the theological significance of the refrain (see Theology).

THE CYCLES SECTION

The "cycles" section (3:7—16:31) contains six major judge cycles: Othniel (3:7–11), Ehud (3:12–30), Deborah and Barak (4:1—5:31), Gideon and Abimelek (6:1—9:57), Jephthah (10:6—12:7), and Samson (13:1—16:31). In the two center cycles there is a pairing of the judge with another person: Deborah (the prophetess, see note on 4:4) and Barak (the judge); Gideon (the judge) and Abimelek (the "king") (see notes on 6:1—9:57; 8:33—9:57). There are also six minor judge mini-narratives: Shamgar (3:31), Tola (10:1–2), Jair (10:3–5), Ibzan (12:8–10), Elon (12:11–12), and Abdon (12:13–15). These are interspersed among the major judge stories, occurring in a 1–2–3 sequence: (1) Shamgar, (2) Tola and Jair, (3) Ibzan, Elon, and Abdon.

The six major judge cycles are built around the following components (see generally ch. 2):

1. Israel does evil in the eyes of the Lord.
2. The Lord gives/sells them into the hands of oppressors.
3. Israel serves the oppressor for x years.
4. Israel cries out to the Lord.
5. The Lord raises up a deliverer (i.e., a judge).
6. The Spirit of the Lord is upon the deliverer.
7. The oppressor is subdued.
8. The land has peace ("rest") for x years.

It is very important to read the six major judge cycles (3:7–11; 3:12–30; 4:1—5:31; 6:1—9:57; 10:6—12:7; 13:1—16:31) within the larger narrative complex of 3:7—16:31 and to take into account the double introduction's paradigms that initiate the patterns of Israel's moral degeneration.

The cycle components vary in such a way as to contribute to the book's message. With each major judge, the cycle unravels. In turn, this unraveling reinforces the message of moral deterioration. The initial cycle (3:7–11), where all the components are present, portrays Othniel, who captured Debir by trusting in God (1:11–13), as the ideal judge: the text mentions no character flaws and calls him "a deliverer" (3:9). Ehud is also a "deliverer" (3:15) whom God raised up (3:12–30). But the Deborah-Barak cycle does not explicitly identify the "deliverer," and Barak's initial refusal to go reveals a problem. The people do not remain faithful to Yahweh during Gideon's lifetime; rather, Gideon's own construction of a golden ephod (that is worshiped as an idol) becomes a snare both to him and to his family. By the time of Jephthah, the list of Israel's apostasies is considerably expanded (10:6), and when the people first cry out, Yahweh ("the Lord") refuses to deliver them (10:14). Ironically Jephthah will offer his daughter as a burnt offering. Neither the Jephthah story nor the Samson story depicts the land as regaining peace ("rest"). By the time of Samson, the cycle has almost disappeared: the people of Samson's time do not even bother to cry to Yahweh, and Samson himself dies in captivity to the oppressor, only *beginning* the deliverance from the Philistines (see note on 13:5). Samson, who is more interested in loving foreign women than saving Israel, is a man motivated by self-gratification and personal revenge. Thus this unraveling of the cycle climaxes in the degeneracy of the last judge. This does not mean these individuals did not have faith; rather, it means God used these increasingly flawed men to accomplish his deliverances of the nation. With each cycle, God's grace is truly more amazing (see Theology).

The cycles section also divides into two parts: the in-group judges and the out-group judges. The in-group judges (Othniel, Ehud, Barak) come from outstanding or acceptable backgrounds. This in-group judge part ends with the Song of Deborah (5:1–31), the only positive celebration of Yahweh's victory in the book! In certain respects, it is the theological hub of the book (see Theology). While two of these in-group judge cycles (Ehud and Barak) manifest less than perfect characters, the out-group judges exhibit disturbing weaknesses, if not serious faults. The out-group judges (Gideon, Jephthah, and Samson) come from less than acceptable backgrounds: Gideon's father made a Baal altar and an Asherah pole in Gideon's hometown; Jephthah is the son of a prostitute and becomes a leader of a gang of criminals; and Samson is from the renegade tribe of Dan, and his parents reveal their spiritual dullness in the two theophanies prophesying his birth and mission.

Thus the Gideon cycle is pivotal as the beginning of the out-group judge cycles. In this out-group judge part, there is a notable religious deterioration: from Gideon-Abimelek (idolatry and the worship of Baal Berith) to Jephthah (human sacrifice) to Samson (doing what was right in his own eyes [see note on 14:3] and violating all of his Nazirite vows). Revenge is a major motif among the out-group judges: in the Gideon-Abimelek cycle it is severe revenge on the two towns of Sukkoth and Peniel, Jotham's prophetic allegory, Abimelek's retribution on the people of Shechem; in the Jephthah cycle it is vengeance on the Ephraimites; and in the Samson cycle it is revenge again and again on the Philistines, who are also motivated by revenge. This motif climaxes in the Samson cycle. Beginning with the outgroup judges, there is a movement toward civil war that eventually becomes a reality at the end of the book. From Gideon on, Israelite society seems to become more and more fractured and chaotic.

The Gideon narrative is also pivotal because it is the first time that Yahweh meets Israel's appeal with a stern rebuke rather than immediate assistance. Yahweh's response in the Jephthah cycle is even more severe: Yahweh is straightforwardly sarcastic in his response to Israel's continuing apostasy. In the Samson cycle, Israel does not appeal to Yahweh at all. From Gideon on, the major/cyclical judges show significant character flaws.

In the cycles about the in-group judges, things return basically to the status quo that was in effect at the beginning of the cycle. But in the cycles of the out-group judges, things are much worse in Israel at the end of each cycle than they were before the beginning of that cycle. By the end of the Gideon-Abimelek cycle, Israel has returned to worshiping the Baals and has begun to unravel internally. Jephthah reintroduces a situation of instability into Israel with the over-the-top slaughter of 42,000 Ephraimites (similar to Gideon's and Abimelek's actions). Finally, Samson has not delivered Israel (though he has killed a number of Philistines in his quests for personal revenge); he really only agitates the Philistines into making their oppression on Israel worse.

The motifs of fire and burning play an important role in the out-group judges. In the case of Gideon, there is the incineration of the sacrifice, the use of 300 torches, etc. Jephthah burns his daughter, and the Ephraimites threaten to burn Jephthah's house over him. In the Samson cycle, the Philistines threaten to burn Samson's wife and father-in-law if she doesn't get the answer to Samson's riddle; 300 foxes, released by Samson, burn the shocks, standing grain, vineyards, and olive groves; the Philistines burn Samson's wife and father-in-law; the ropes with which the Judahites tied Samson up became as "charred flax" in the presence of the Philistines (15:14); and the fresh bowstrings used in Delilah's first attempt to subdue Samson "snapped ... as easily as a piece of string snaps when it comes close to a flame" (16:9b).

The spiritual decline in the relationship between Israel and Yahweh can also be seen in the characterization of the women of the book. Aksah (Othniel's wife) is noted for her practical shrewdness and resourcefulness in seizing the blessings of God in the land (1:14–15). This is followed by other women noted for their commitments to the Lord (Deborah [4:1—5:31] and Jael [4:17–22]) or their use by God (9:53–54). Then follows the tragic story of the unnamed daughter of Jephthah (11:34–40), deteriorating to Delilah, who is willing to take the initiative to bring down her man (16:4–22), and culminating with the tragically silent women of chs. 19–21.

Another important observation is that the center cycles (Deborah-Barak and Gideon-Abimelek) manifest a propensity for pairs. Deborah and Barak are paired against Jabin and Sisera. The cycle of Gideon and Abimelek has many pairs. A few are: Gideon faces the pairs of Oreb and Zeeb (killed on the west side of the Jordan) and Zebah and Zalmunna (killed later on the east side of the Jordan); two altar and offering scenes; two names for the hero (Gideon and Jerub-Baal); two different reductions in the size of Gideon's military force; two battles with surprise attacks; two tests of God by fleece and dew; and two towns on which extreme reprisals are executed.

The Gideon-Abimelek cycle also has two climaxes (although nonparallel): the accounts of Gideon (6:1—8:35) and Abimelek (9:1–57). The Abimelek account prolongs the Gideon account, resolving a number of complications that the Gideon narrative spawns. While both narratives address the issue of the danger of kingship, neither condemns kingship as an institution. But they both demonstrate the significant dangers of the wrong kind of kingship: one that is not patterned according to God's law (Hebrew *tōrâ*), one that is Canaanite in its essence. They accomplish this from two different directions: the Gideon narrative is subtle and implicit; the Abimelek story is blunt and explicit. Even though Gideon attacked Baal worship and declared Yahweh's kingship, he subverted God's kingship with his own. Abimelek blatantly sets himself up as a king of a Canaanite city with the help of Baal/El.

Both accounts address the issue of infidelity: the Gideon narrative addresses infidelity to Yahweh (8:34), while the Abimelek narrative addresses infidelity to Gideon's family (8:35). Finally, in many ways, Jotham's act of challenging the people of Shechem concerning their allegiance to Abimelek is analogous to Gideon's act of destroying the Baal altar and challenging the people of Ophrah concerning their allegiance to Baal.

There are other clear links between the two center cycles. The Deborah-Barak cycle begins with a prophetess (Deborah) ministering to Israel and ends with a woman performing a mighty deed as an agent of Yahweh (Jael drives a tent peg into Sisera's skull). The Gideon-Abimelek cycle begins with an unnamed prophet challenging Israel (6:7–10) and ends with a woman performing a mighty deed as the agent of Yahweh (a woman smashes Abimelek's skull with an upper millstone). Both cycles demonstrate Yahweh's sovereign control over circumstances in order to bring about victory (over Sisera or Abimelek) and poetic justice (vis-à-vis Barak or Abimelek).

Besides this propensity for pairing in the two middle cyclical judge narratives, it is also clear that there is a set of three pairings among the major judges themselves. Othniel and Ehud form an initial pair. They exhibit the two most successful judges. They are also, by far, the two shortest narratives of the six major judges. They are the only two cycles that designate the judge by the term "savior" or "deliverer" (Hebrew *môšîaʿ*), and they do their delivering in the southern part of the country. The Deborah-Barak and Gideon-Abimelek cycles form the second pairing. They are the pivotal cycles, with Deborah-Barak being the last of the in-group judges and Gideon-Abimelek being the first of the out-group judges. They do their delivering in the northern part of the country. The third pairing is Jephthah and Samson. They demonstrate the most serious character flaws of the six major judges, and the oppressions they address are introduced together (10:6 – 8). They both feature agreements with leaders and vows to God, and each is undone by a female. In particular, this can be seen in the matter of vows. Jephthah ignorantly fulfills the manipulative, rash vow, but Samson callously breaks the God-ordained Nazirite vow.

Finally, the three pairings of the cyclical judges can be seen in the type of oppressors or opponents they are associated with:

Judge Cycle	Type of Oppressor(s)	Name(s)
1. Othniel	single, named	Cushan-Rishathaim (king)
2. Ehud	single, named	Eglon (king)
3. Deborah-Barak	pair, named	Jabin (king) / Sisera (commander/chief)
4. Gideon-Abimelek	pairs, named	Oreb and Zeeb (commanders/chiefs); Zebah and Zalmunna (kings); Jotham and Gaal
5. Jephthah	single, unnamed	________
6. Samson	multiple, unnamed	________

While each pairing has its own internal links, there are also strong links between the pairs themselves. For example, the Ehud and Deborah-Barak cycles witness a number of links, the most obvious of which is how each portrays the death scene of the oppressor (Eglon or Sisera). Ehud and Jael are painted in very similar colors as they execute the enemy leader. And there is great similarity between the discovery of Eglon by his Moabite guards and the discovery of Sisera by the pursuing Barak.

View of Beth Shemesh in the Valley of Sorek. Beth Shemesh is about 12 miles west of Jerusalem and is where the Philistines returned the ark of the covenant to the Israelites (1 Sam 6). The Valley of Sorek is also where Samson fell in love with Delilah (Judg 16:4).

William Schlegel/www.BiblePlaces.com

There are also very strong links between the Gideon-Abimelek cycle and the Jephthah cycle. Both open with a confrontation between Yahweh and Israel (6:7–10; 10:6–10). Both Gideon and Jephthah begin as nobodies, become heroes (both are characterized as *gibbôr ḥāyîl*, "mighty warrior"), and end as despots. Both are empowered by the Spirit of Yahweh, which results in the immediate mobilization of troops (6:34–35; 11:29). Both follow up the divine empowerment with expressions of doubt (6:36–40; 11:30–31). Both win great victories over the enemy (7:19–25; 11:32–33). Both must deal with confrontations with the jealous Ephraimites after the battle has been won (8:1–3; 12:1–3). Both brutalize their own countrymen (8:4–17; 12:4–6).

In addition, there are strong bonds between the Abimelek account and the Jephthah cycle. Both men are children of secondary women: a concubine and a prostitute (8:31; 11:1). Both are disinherited by their half brothers. Both recruit morally empty and reckless men to make up their armed gang (9:4; 11:3). Both are opportunists who negotiate their way into powerful leadership positions (9:1–6; 11:4–11). Both seal the agreement with their subjects in a formal ceremony at a sacred site (9:6; 11:11). Both turn out to be brutal rulers, slaughtering their own relatives (9:5; 11:34–40) and engaging their own countrymen in battle (9:26–57; 12:1–6). Both end up as tragic figures without descendants (9:50–57; 11:34–35). Jephthah is in many ways a composite of Gideon and Abimelek.

The short notices about the minor judges are integral to the message. The moral degeneration of the major cyclical judges is also perceptible in the minor noncyclical judges, especially in the concern for building power. The minor judges are presented in a 1–2–3 sequence: (1) Shamgar (3:31a), (2) Tola (10:1a), and Jair (10:3a); (3) Ibzan (12:8a), Elon (12:11a), and Abdon (12:13a). This 1–2–3 pattern is a purposeful way of moving the narrative to the climax in the Samson cycle.

Thus, in every way the cycles section of the book reflects a progressive degeneration. By the end of the story of Samson, the reader is left questioning the value of judgeship altogether. This is precisely what the narrator planned so that his double conclusion to the book (17:1—21:25) would be exactly the proper ending in which to highlight the issue of kingship.

THEOLOGY

The book of Judges is a literary masterpiece. However, all the literary structuring and thematic developments are in the service of communicating important theological teachings. The book of Judges portrays a sovereign God of incredible faithfulness to his covenant, who abounds in grace in spite of the great sinfulness of the Israelites and the individual judges.

The downward spiral is heightened by a focus on the covenantal disloyalty of both the people and their leaders, the judges. The depth of this depravity can only be truly perceived through the reader's familiarity with the law (the Torah), especially the book of Deuteronomy. The author assumes that his readers have some knowledge of the law.

An important example of this is the law of Deut 7 (the law concerning the *ḥērem*). Although the Hebrew word *ḥērem* ("totally destroy") only occurs in 1:17 (see NIV text note) and 21:11 (NIV "kill"), it is clearly the main issue in these passages. Deut 7 explains the law of the *ḥērem*: the Israelites are to "destroy totally" the inhabitants of Canaan (see Deut 7:2 and NIV text note there) and "set [material objects] apart for destruction" (Deut 7:26), i.e., "devote" the material objects to the Lord; they are not to make a covenant (treaty) with them; they are to show them no mercy; there should be no intermarriage between the Israelites and the Canaanites; and all Canaanite altars and idols are to be destroyed. The purpose of this *ḥērem* law was to "drive out" the Canaanites (Deut 7:22). Deut 7 stresses that love of Yahweh is demonstrated in the implementation of the *ḥērem*. Not implementing the law of Deut 7 in all of its aspects is considered covenantal disobedience and disloyalty to the Lord. In Judg 1:27, the Israelites "did not drive out" the Canaanites; instead, the Canaanites "live" among the Israelites, or worse, the Israelites live among the Canaanites (cf. Deut 12:29). In 2:1–5, the Lord condemns them specifically for not carrying out the law of Deut 7; they have made covenants (treaties) with the Canaanites and have not torn down the Canaanite altars. In chs. 20–21, the Israelites misapply the *ḥērem* law of Deut 7 for their own purposes! A reading of Deut 7 makes very clear that Israel did not obey this law (see Introduction to Deuteronomy: Themes and Theology [Holy War]). This is the beginning of Israel's spiritual and moral decline. That this is a predominant issue of covenantal unfaithfulness on the part of Israel is seen throughout the book. For example, at the beginning of the Gideon story, an altar to Baal and an Asherah pole have been set up by Gideon's father!

At the beginning of all six major judge cycles, the text states, "The Israelites did evil in the eyes of the LORD" (3:7; 3:12; 4:1; 6:1; 10:6; 13:1; introduced first in 2:11). The details of this evil are developed as the reader progresses through the book. A contrast is developed between God's righteousness and the Israelites' lack thereof (both in perception and deed). Not only do the Israelites do evil as the Lord sees it; they do what is right in their own eyes. The righteous deeds of Yahweh ("the victories of the LORD" [5:11]) are juxtaposed with the "evil" of the people and their leaders. In short, all the deliverances of Israel in the book are testimonies to the Lord's righteousness.

God chastens Israel for this disobedience ("evil") by giving them into the hands of oppressors. Israel cannot break the covenant without consequences. God disciplines his people.

Yet God graciously saves Israel, even though the character of the judges becomes increasingly flawed, and disobedience abounds. Thus by illustrating human sin in each successive story, the writer highlights the great lengths to which God goes in order to save his people. No matter how flawed or sinful the judge, God saves (or in the case of Samson, "begins to save" [see note on 13:5]). God demonstrates that he is gracious and long-suffering. Through each cycle, the writer emphasizes that God is sovereign; the disobedience of his people cannot thwart his plan. This absolute divine sovereignty comes together in Yahweh's roles as judge, divine warrior, and king. His righteousness and sovereignty in these roles make his graciousness and long-suffering very potent and effectual.

At this point, it is important to discuss the listing of some of the judges in the book of Hebrews. Heb 11:32,39 states: "And what more shall I say? I do not have time to tell about Gideon, Barak, Samson and Jephthah, about David and Samuel and the prophets ... These were all commended for their faith." The ordering is in pairs with the first in each pair in reverse chronological order to the second: so Gideon is listed first even though he followed Barak; so too with Samson and Jephthah and David and Samuel (Samuel, in fact, anointed David). The writer of Hebrews is doing this for rhetorical reasons, namely, in order to help the reader get his point: all these individuals were commended for their faith; therefore let believers lay aside everything that keeps them from living a godly life for the Lord (Heb 11:39 — 12:2). Clearly, the writer does not intend for his readers to conclude that all these individuals had the same spirituality, the same level of faith and maturity. By far the most developed in Hebrews 11 are Abraham (Heb 11:8 – 10,17 – 19) and Moses (Heb 11:24 – 28), and the writer hardly intends to equate Samson with them in spirituality issues. It is a mistake to read into the Judges passages redeeming features that the writer of the book of Judges is not stating or to interpret the character flaws as not being as serious as they are. So while all had faith, some had significant character flaws, while others had deeper walks with God (e.g., Othniel). Not all of these were the same sort of heroes of the faith. The point is not that all these individuals attained a "hall of fame" level of faith but that all, even to the smallest degree, demonstrated faith. Therefore, these judges really do have the character flaws and sins that the text of Judges attributes to them. But God's grace is greater than all these character flaws and sins (whether one speaks of the individual judges or the nation of Israel). God uses sinful humans — sometimes very sinful and spiritually immature humans — to accomplish his will.

Another important theological theme is woven into this: the attempt to manipulate God. God saves, but not because he has been manipulated. Attempts to manipulate God can be as simple as Barak's words, "If you [Deborah] go with me, I will go" (4:8), trying to guarantee God's presence. Or it can be as rash as Jephthah's vow (11:30 – 31). Israel's attempts to manipulate God through their crying out to him fail (the second element of the cycle). This crying out to God in the midst of the oppression is not due to repentance (as a study of the wording in the original Hebrew demonstrates). Obviously, true repentance is accepted by God. But in the book of Judges, Israel's cries are increasingly met with prophetic indictments and sarcastic ridicule of their worship of other gods (10:11 – 13). In every case, God demonstrates that he will not be manipulated by humans. The true and living God cannot be manipulated by finite creatures.

However, idols can be manipulated. The Israelites succumb first to the Canaanite deities (idols, 2:13) and then to those of their own making (8:27 – 28; 17:1 — 18:31). Instead of succeeding in manipulating God, the Israelites become ensnared by these idols, whether made by the Canaanites or by their own hands (2:3; 8:27; 17:4). In every attempt, God frustrates the Israelites when they do this by giving them into the hands of their enemies. So why is Israel saved from its oppressors? Not because of manipulation but because of God's faithfulness to his covenant. God has a plan for the redemption of the world; his will cannot be thwarted by his people's disobedience or attempted manipulations.

The issue of the covenant (treaty) permeates the book. For God, it is the primary issue (2:1 – 5), and the writer stresses that Israel's disobedience to the law is covenantal infidelity, spiritual prostitution (2:17; 8:27). Ironically, it is the judges themselves in the last three cycles who lead Israel down the path of covenantal unfaithfulness: Gideon makes a golden ephod to which all Israel prostitutes itself; Jephthah makes a foolish and manipulative vow that leads to child sacrifice just like those who worship Molek, and he engages in intertribal warfare; Samson does what is right in his own eyes (one of the strongest and most common forms of idolatry). This is true not only of his desire for women but also in his attitude in dealing with the Philistines (which is motivated by personal revenge).

Throughout the book, the issue of the covenant is linked to the issue of kingship. Israel's disobedience to the covenant is a constant attempt to undermine God's kingship. This issue becomes particularly acute with the Gideon-Abimelek cycle, but it dominates in the double conclusion, where there is no king in Israel — physically or spiritually. The refrain in the double conclusion is: "In those days Israel had no king; everyone did as they saw fit" (17:6; 21:25; cf. 18:1; 19:1). This is not simply a political statement expressing the desire for a king (in other words, a pro-monarchic and pro-Davidic wish). Rather, based on the second part of the refrain, "everyone did as they saw fit" (an alternate translation is: "each man did what was right in his own eyes") connects the refrain with the covenant. Thus the refrain is not as much about physical kingship as it is about spiritual kingship. It is not saying, "If we only had a king, things would be different." It is God's kingship that is being broken in all that Israel does! Physical kingship will not make a difference in this. Israel will still break the covenant, rebelling against God's kingship. Later, the whole intention of Israel in wanting a king is deemed by God himself to be rebellion (1 Sam 8:7b: "It is not you they have rejected, but they have rejected me as their king"). Gideon rightly told the Israelites that he would not rule over them, saying, "The LORD will rule over you" (8:23). Thus, the statement that "everyone did as they saw fit" highlights the fact that it is themselves they are serving and not the Lord. When the Israelites rebel against the Lord as their covenantal king, they have no king as envisioned by the covenant; and so everyone acts as their own king. In a real sense, the book of Judges is a prophetic call to acknowledge the kingship of the Lord, the true King and Judge of Israel.

The only song in the book, the Song of Deborah (5:1–31), is one of the most beautiful and emotive victory songs in the Bible: praising God for his deliverance, celebrating his use of nature and storm, his sovereign timing, and his justice over evil men and women (Sisera and his mother). Yet it also emphasizes the participation of the people of God in his kingdom, praising the non-Israelite Jael for her willingness to do what needed to be done for God's justice and rule. It is not by chance that the Song of Deborah comes at the end of the in-group judge cycles: God's covenantal kingship will be progressively more undermined from this point to the end of the book, when "everyone did as they saw fit" (21:25b). In many ways, the Song of Deborah is the theological hub of the book: here God is worshiped and praised with a wonderful focus on God's intervention on behalf of his people.

OUTLINE

I. The Double Introduction (1:1—3:6)
- A. Foreign Wars of Subjugation With Failure to Apply the Law of Deut 7 (*ḥērem*) — the Pre-Judge Political/Military Background — the Incomplete Conquest (1:1—2:5)
- B. Difficulties With Foreign Idols — the Thematic Summarizing Outline of the Spiritual Background — the Incomplete Faith (2:6—3:6)

II. Cycles of the Judges (3:7—16:31)
- A. Major Judge Cycle: Othniel (3:7–11)
- B. Major Judge Cycle: Ehud (3:12–30)
- C. Minor Judge: Shamgar (3:31)
- D. Major Judge Cycle: Deborah and Barak (4:1—5:31)
  1. The Narrative (4:1–24)
  2. The Poem: Song of Deborah (5:1–31c)
     - a. Introduction to the Poem (5:1)
     - b. Act A: Initial Call to Praise and Report of Need (5:2–8)
     - c. Act B: Renewal of the Call to Praise Because of the Volunteers (5:9–13)
     - d. Act C: Recognition of the Tribes That Did or Did Not Participate (5:14–18)
     - e. Act D: The Battle and the Curse of Meroz (5:19–23)
     - f. Act E: Jael's Deed and Sisera's Mother (5:24–31c)
  3. Concluding Framework Statement (5:31d)
- E. Major Judge Cycle: Gideon and Abimelek (6:1—9:57)
  1. The Gideon Narrative (6:1—8:32)
     - a. The Setting Before Gideon's Call (6:1–10)
     - b. The Call of Gideon (6:11–32)
     - c. Gideon's Struggle With Belief in God's Promise (6:33—7:18)

d. God Delivers Israel From the Midianites (7:19—8:21)
(1) Battle West of the Jordan (7:19—8:3)
(2) Pursuit and Battle East of the Jordan (8:4–21)
e. Conclusion to Gideon's Life After the Victory (8:22–32)
2. The Abimelek Narrative (8:33—9:57)
a. The Prologue to the Story (8:33–35)
b. Abimelek's Rise (9:1–24)
(1) Elimination of Rivals (9:1–6)
(2) Jotham's Fable and Curse (9:7–21)
(a) The Fable (9:7–15)
(b) The Fable Applied (9:16–21)
(3) The Narrator's Assessment of God's Involvement (9:22–24)
c. Abimelek's Decline (9:25–57)
F. Minor Judge: Tola (10:1–2)
G. Minor Judge: Jair (10:3–5)
H. Major Judge Cycle: Jephthah (10:6—12:7)
1. Introduction: Israel Versus the Lord (10:6–16)
2. The Ammonite Threat: The Elders' Choice of Jephthah (10:17—11:11)
3. Jephthah Versus the Ammonite King (11:12–28)
4. The Ammonite Defeat: Jephthah's Vow (11:29–40)
5. The Conclusion: Jephthah Versus the Ephraimites (12:1–7)
I. Minor Judge: Ibzan (12:8–10)
J. Minor Judge: Elon (12:11–12)
K. Minor Judge: Abdon (12:13–15)
L. Major Judge Cycle: Samson (13:1—16:31)
1. Samson's Birth (13:1–25)
2. Samson's Wedding (14:1–20)
3. Samson's Revenge (15:1–20)
4. Samson's Death (16:1–31)
a. The Incident With the Prostitute of Gaza (16:1–3)
b. The Delilah Incident (16:4–22)
c. Samson's Final Act of Vengeance (16:23–31)

III. The Double Conclusion: Specific Conditions During These Times (17:1—21:25)
A. Difficulties With Domestic Idols—the Origin of the Pre-Monarchic Sanctuary of Dan (17:1—18:31)
1. The Idolatry of Micah the Ephraimite (17:1–13)
a. The Shrine of Micah (17:1–6)
b. Micah's Priest (17:7–13)
2. The Migration of the Danites (18:1–31)
B. Domestic Wars With Misapplication of the Law of Deut 7 (*ḥērem*) Being Applied—the Benjamite Atrocity and the War (Chiastically Arranged) (19:1—21:25)
a The Rape of the Concubine (19:1–30)
b The Misapplication of the Law of Deut 7 (*ḥērem*) on Benjamin (20:1–48)
c The Oaths: Benjamin Threatened With Extinction (21:1–5)
b´ The Misapplication of the Law of Deut 7 (*ḥērem*) on Jabesh Gilead (21:6–14)
a´ The Rape of the Daughters of Shiloh (21:15–25)

JUDGES

Israel Fights the Remaining Canaanites

1:11-15pp — Jos 15:15-19

1 After the death[a] of Joshua, the Israelites asked the LORD, "Who of us is to go up first[b] to fight against the Canaanites?[c]"

[2]The LORD answered, "Judah[d] shall go up; I have given the land into their hands.[e]"
[3]The men of Judah then said to the Simeonites their fellow Israelites, "Come up with us into the territory allotted to us, to fight against the Canaanites. We in turn will go with you into yours." So the Simeonites[f] went with them.

[4]When Judah attacked, the LORD gave the Canaanites and Perizzites[g] into their hands, and they struck down ten thousand men at Bezek.[h] [5]It was there that they found Adoni-Bezek and fought against him, putting to rout the Canaanites and Perizzites. [6]Adoni-Bezek fled, but they chased him and caught him, and cut off his thumbs and big toes.

[7]Then Adoni-Bezek said, "Seventy kings with their thumbs and big toes cut off have picked up scraps under my table. Now God has paid me back[i] for what I did to them." They brought him to Jerusalem, and he died there.

[8]The men of Judah attacked Jerusalem[j] also and took it. They put the city to the sword and set it on fire.

1:1 [a]Jos 24:29 [b]Nu 27:21 [c]ver 27; Jdg 3:1-6
1:2 [d]Ge 49:8 [e]ver 4; Jdg 3:28
1:3 [f]ver 17
1:4 [g]Ge 13:7; Jos 3:10 [h]1Sa 11:8
1:7 [i]Lev 24:19
1:8 [j]ver 21; Jos 15:63

1:1 — 3:6 *The Double Introduction.* The book opens with a double introduction (see Introduction: The Double Introduction and Double Conclusion).
1:1 — 2:5 *Foreign Wars of Subjugation With Failure to Apply the Law of Deut 7 (ḥērem).* This first introduction utilizes materials from the book of Joshua (especially Josh 13 – 19), along with some expansions (e.g., stories not found in Josh 13 – 19). It describes the general success of Judah and the increasing failure of the other Israelite tribes, especially Dan, in the process of dispossessing the Canaanites from the individual tribal allotments. There are four stages in this declining success that are identified through the use of two notions: to "(not) drive out" and to "live among." These demonstrate the Israelites' increasing failure to apply the law of Deut 7 (*ḥērem*) (see Introduction: Theology; see also Introduction to Deuteronomy: Themes and Theology [Holy War]). They form the basis for the words of condemnation by the angel of the Lord in 2:1 – 5.
1:1 – 20 Stage 1: The general success of Judah is recounted through a number of very short stories. The Judahites, having enlisted the Simeonites as their allies, are able to "drive out" (see note on 1:1 — 2:5) the Canaanites everywhere except in the "plains" (v. 19). No Canaanites "live among" (see note on 1:1 — 2:5) the Judahites.
1:1 After the death of Joshua. This is a stylistic way of briefly recapitulating the previous book before beginning the narrative. Ch. 1 recapitulates the position of the book of Joshua (*How much* of the land would Israel occupy?) before going on to the central question of the book of Judges (*Why* couldn't they completely occupy the land?). **asked the LORD.** The high priest did this by using the Urim and Thummim to ascertain God's will (Exod 28:30; Num 27:21).
1:2 Judah shall go up. Judah was the first tribe in the order of march (Num 10:14) and the first tribe to receive an allotment in the land of Canaan (Josh 14:6; 15:1).
1:3 Simeonites. The tribe of Simeon, which played no significant role in the later history of Israel, was in time assimilated into Judah (Josh 19:9).
1:4 Canaanites and Perizzites. Probably a figurative reference to all the inhabitants of the land (urban and rural peoples). **ten thousand.** Likely figurative for a very large number, similar to how "million" is used today. **Bezek.** Location uncertain, perhaps north of Jerusalem (1 Sam 11:8).
1:5 Adoni-Bezek. Means "the lord of Bezek"; it is not a personal name but a title.
1:6 – 7 Judah captures, mutilates, and kills the lord of Bezek. This highlights the humiliation of the Canaanite ruler since it emphasizes retributive justice for the evil monarch. Physical mutilation of prisoners of war was common in the ancient Near East because it rendered them unable to serve in the military.
1:7 Seventy. Possibly a round number; however, this number is used symbolically in numerous ancient Near Eastern contexts, in which case it probably symbolizes this man's complete domination.
1:8 Jerusalem. Not an Israelite city here or in its only other appearance in Judges (19:10), where it is a Jebusite city (Josh 15:63). Several

1:9 [k]Nu 13:17 [l]Nu 21:1
1:10 [m]Ge 13:18 [n]Ge 35:27 [o]Jos 15:14
1:11 [p]Jos 15:15
1:16 [q]Nu 10:29 [r]Ge 15:19; Jdg 4:11 [s]Dt 34:3; Jdg 3:13 [t]Nu 21:1
1:17 [u]ver 3 [v]Nu 21:3
1:18 [w]Jos 11:22
1:19 [x]ver 2 [y]Jos 17:16
1:20 [z]Jos 14:9; 15:13-14 [a]ver 10; Jos 14:13
1:21 [b]Jos 15:63 [c]ver 8
1:23 [d]Ge 28:19
1:24 [e]Jos 2:12,14
1:25 [f]Jos 6:25
1:27 [g]Jos 17:11 [h]ver 1
1:29 [i]1Ki 9:16 [j]Jos 16:10

9 After that, Judah went down to fight against the Canaanites living in the hill country,[k] the Negev[l] and the western foothills. 10 They advanced against the Canaanites living in Hebron[m] (formerly called Kiriath Arba[n]) and defeated Sheshai, Ahiman and Talmai.[o] 11 From there they advanced against the people living in Debir[p] (formerly called Kiriath Sepher).

12 And Caleb said, "I will give my daughter Aksah in marriage to the man who attacks and captures Kiriath Sepher." 13 Othniel son of Kenaz, Caleb's younger brother, took it; so Caleb gave his daughter Aksah to him in marriage.

14 One day when she came to Othniel, she urged him[*a*] to ask her father for a field. When she got off her donkey, Caleb asked her, "What can I do for you?"

15 She replied, "Do me a special favor. Since you have given me land in the Negev, give me also springs of water." So Caleb gave her the upper and lower springs.

16 The descendants of Moses' father-in-law,[q] the Kenite,[r] went up from the City of Palms[*b*][s] with the people of Judah to live among the inhabitants of the Desert of Judah in the Negev near Arad.[t]

17 Then the men of Judah went with the Simeonites[u] their fellow Israelites and attacked the Canaanites living in Zephath, and they totally destroyed[*c*] the city. Therefore it was called Hormah.[*d*][v] 18 Judah also took[*e*] Gaza,[w] Ashkelon and Ekron — each city with its territory.

19 The LORD was with[x] the men of Judah. They took possession of the hill country, but they were unable to drive the people from the plains, because they had chariots fitted with iron.[y] 20 As Moses had promised, Hebron[z] was given to Caleb, who drove from it the three sons of Anak.[a] 21 The Benjamites, however, did not drive out[b] the Jebusites, who were living in Jerusalem;[c] to this day the Jebusites live there with the Benjamites.

22 Now the tribes of Joseph attacked Bethel, and the LORD was with them. 23 When they sent men to spy out Bethel (formerly called Luz),[d] 24 the spies saw a man coming out of the city and they said to him, "Show us how to get into the city and we will see that you are treated well.[e]" 25 So he showed them, and they put the city to the sword but spared[f] the man and his whole family. 26 He then went to the land of the Hittites, where he built a city and called it Luz, which is its name to this day.

27 But Manasseh did not drive out the people of Beth Shan or Taanach or Dor or Ibleam[g] or Megiddo and their surrounding settlements, for the Canaanites[h] were determined to live in that land. 28 When Israel became strong, they pressed the Canaanites into forced labor but never drove them out completely. 29 Nor did Ephraim drive out the Canaanites living in Gezer,[i] but the Canaanites continued to live there among them.[j] 30 Neither did Zebulun drive out the Canaanites living in Kitron or Nahalol, so these Canaanites lived among them, but Zebulun did subject them to forced labor. 31 Nor did Asher

a 14 Hebrew; Septuagint and Vulgate *Othniel, he urged her* *b* 16 That is, Jericho *c* 17 The Hebrew term refers to the irrevocable giving over of things or persons to the LORD, often by totally destroying them. *d* 17 *Hormah* means *destruction.* *e* 18 Hebrew; Septuagint *Judah did not take*

---

centuries later, David brings Jerusalem into Israelite possession (2 Sam 5:6–9).

1:9–16 Three reports of Judahite activities in the south: the capture of Hebron (vv. 9–10), the capture of Debir with the Othniel and Aksah story (vv. 11–15), and the movement of the Kenites (v. 16). These are stories dependent on Josh 15:13–19.

1:10 Hebron. About 20 miles (32 kilometers) south of Jerusalem.

1:11 Debir. Located at Khirbet Rabûd.

1:13 son of Kenaz. Othniel is of the Kenizzite clan like Caleb the "son of Jephunneh the Kenizzite" (Num 32:12; Josh 14:6). **younger brother.** Means "younger relative" ("brother" describes clan relationship [e.g., Ruth 4:3,10]). Othniel is later the first judge (3:7–11).

1:16 Kenite. The Kenites were relatives of Moses (4:11). This anticipates 4:11,17. **City of Palms.** See NIV text note (cf. 3:13).

1:17 destroyed ... Hormah. See NIV text notes. Hormah is derived from the Hebrew *ḥērem* ("total destruction"). See Introduction: Theology; see also Introduction to Deuteronomy: Themes and Theology (Holy War).

1:18 took. See NIV text note. **Gaza, Ashkelon and Ekron.** Three of the five principal cities of the Philistine confederation (see Josh 13:3). David later captures these Philistine cities.

1:19 chariots fitted with iron. Anticipates the chariots of Sisera in 4:3.

1:20 See Josh 14:9.

1:21–30 Stage 2: Benjamin, Manasseh, Ephraim, and Zebulun do not "drive out" the Canaanites, and the Canaanites "live among" them (see note on vv. 1–20), though some Canaanites are pressed into forced labor (v. 28; cf. Josh 16:10; 17:13).

1:21 Jerusalem. Located on the border between Judah and Benjamin (cf. Josh 15:63; 18:28).

1:22–26 The tribes of Joseph capture "Bethel" (means "house of God"), "formerly called Luz" (v. 23). The capture is accomplished through compromise and deceit, tainting this success of the Joseph tribes.

1:24 we will see that you are treated well. That is, "we will show you covenant loyalty (*ḥesed*)." Ironically, the Israelites show covenant loyalty (Hebrew *ḥesed*) to the man of Bethel instead of loyalty (*ḥesed*) to Yahweh's covenant. Even in carrying out the law of Deut 7 (*ḥērem*), the Joseph tribes, in effect, produce another Canaanite city ("Luz," v. 26).

1:26 land of the Hittites. Probably the Neo-Hittite or Hittite successor states in north Syria (cf. 2 Kgs 7:6).

1:31–33 Stage 3: Asher and Naphtali do not "drive out" the Canaanites, the inhabitants of the land, but instead these tribes "live among" the

drive out those living in Akko or Sidon or Ahlab or Akzib[k] or Helbah or Aphek or Rehob. 32The Asherites
lived among the Canaanite inhabitants of the land because they did not drive them out. 33Neither did
Naphtali drive out those living in Beth Shemesh or Beth Anath[l]; but the Naphtalites too lived among
the Canaanite inhabitants of the land, and those living in Beth Shemesh and Beth Anath became forced
laborers for them. 34The Amorites[m] confined the Danites to the hill country, not allowing them to come
down into the plain. 35And the Amorites were determined also to hold out in Mount Heres, Aijalon[n] and

1:31 [k] Jdg 10:6
1:33 [l] Jos 19:38
1:34 [m] Ex 3:17
1:35 [n] Jos 19:42

Canaanites (see note on vv. 1–20). A few Canaanites become forced laborers.
1:33 Beth Shemesh. Means "house/shrine of the sun-god"; located in Naphtali. **Beth Anath.** Means "house/shrine of the goddess Anat." The Israelites live in a land controlled by the Canaanites, who worship these deities.
1:34 Stage 4: There is no statement about "driving out" or "living among" (see note on vv. 1–20). Instead, the Amorites oppress or confine the Danites, not allowing them into the plain. The Danites' utter failure anticipates their move in ch. 18. **confined.** Translated "oppressing" in Exod 3:9, where the Egyptians "oppress" the Israelites. It anticipates 2:18; 4:3; 6:9; 10:12.
1:35–36 Conclusion: The Amorites were determined to live in the land. Ironically, theirs is the only border described, even though Joshua defeated them (Josh 10:5–13).

FIVE CITIES OF THE PHILISTINES

Gaza, Ashkelon, Ashdod, Ekron, and Gath comprise a list of familiar biblical names. Each of these cities was a commercial emporium with important connections both north (as far as Mesopotamia) and south (as far as Egypt) by way of the coastal highway that served as one of the major highways of the ancient world. Also the ships of Phoenicia, Cyprus, Crete, and the Aegean called at Philistia's seaports. Among these seaports was a place today called Tel Qasile on the Yarkon River (the "Kanah Ravine" of Josh16:8; 17:9) just north of modern Tel Aviv. A Philistine temple has been found at Tel Qasile.

The Philistine plain itself was an arid, loam-covered lowland between the Mediterranean Sea and the foothills of the Judahite plateau on the east. To the south lay a stretch of undulating sand dunes adjacent to the sea. No area in biblical history was more frequently contested than the western foothills, lying on the border between Judah and Philistia. Originally a part of Judah's tribal allotment, the coastal area was never totally wrested away from the Philistines. Beth Shemesh, Timnah, Azekah, and Ziklag were among the towns coveted by both Israelites and Philistines, and they figure in the stories of Samson, Goliath, and David. The area to the north of Philistia, the plain of Sharon, was also contested at various periods. During Saul's reign, the Philistines even held Beth Shan and the Valley of Jezreel. Later, from about the time of Baasha on, a long border war was conducted by the Israelites at Gibbethon.

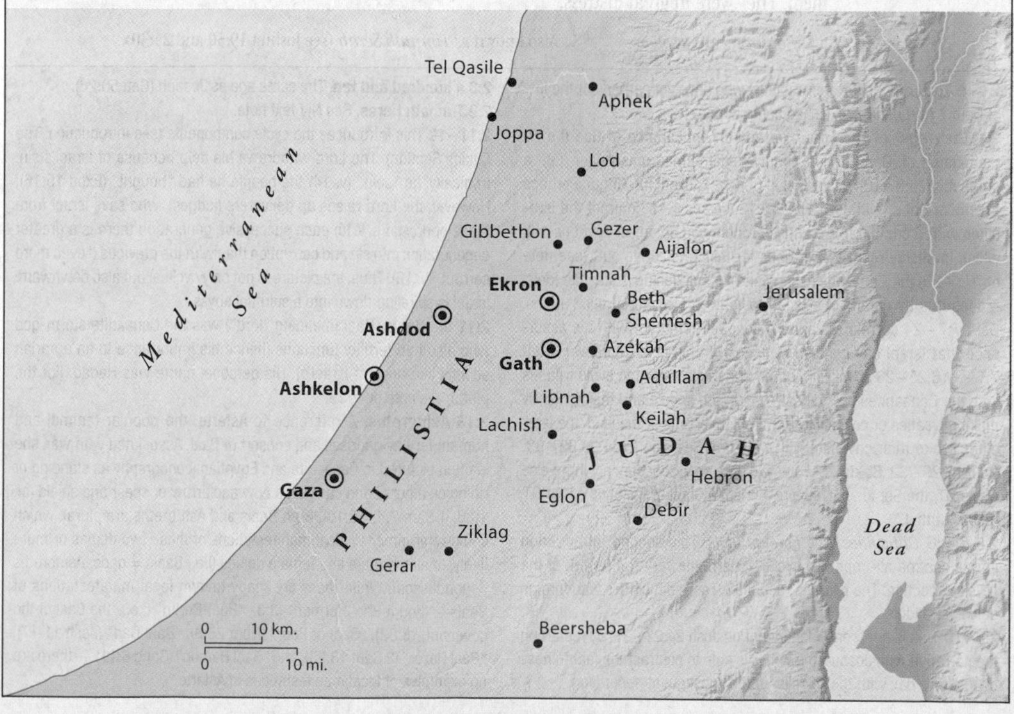

1:36 [o] Jos 15:3
2:1 [p] Jdg 6:11 [q] ver 5 [r] Ex 20:2 [s] Ge 17:8 [t] Lev 26:42-44; Dt 7:9
2:2 [u] Ex 23:32; 34:12; Dt 7:2 [v] Ex 34:13
2:3 [w] Jos 23:13 [x] Nu 33:55 [y] Dt 7:16; Jdg 3:6; Ps 106:36
2:9 [z] Jos 19:50
2:10 [a] Ex 5:2; 1Sa 2:12; 1Ch 28:9; Gal 4:8
2:11 [b] Jdg 3:12; 4:1; 6:1; 10:6 [c] Jdg 3:7; 8:33
2:12 [d] Ps 106:36 [e] Dt 31:16; Jdg 10:6
2:13 [f] Jdg 10:6
2:14 [g] Dt 31:17 [h] Ps 106:41 [i] Dt 32:30; Jdg 3:8 [j] Dt 28:25

Shaalbim, but when the power of the tribes of Joseph increased, they too were pressed into forced labor.
36 The boundary of the Amorites was from Scorpion Pass[o] to Sela and beyond.

The Angel of the LORD at Bokim

2 The angel of the LORD[p] went up from Gilgal to Bokim[q] and said, "I brought you up out of Egypt[r]
and led you into the land I swore to give to your ancestors.[s] I said, 'I will never break my covenant
with you,[t] 2 and you shall not make a covenant with the people of this land,[u] but you shall break down
their altars.'[v] Yet you have disobeyed me. Why have you done this? 3 And I have also said, 'I will not drive
them out before you;[w] they will become traps[x] for you, and their gods will become snares[y] to you.' "
4 When the angel of the LORD had spoken these things to all the Israelites, the people wept aloud, 5 and
they called that place Bokim.[a] There they offered sacrifices to the LORD.

Disobedience and Defeat

2:6-9pp — Jos 24:29-31

6 After Joshua had dismissed the Israelites, they went to take possession of the land, each to their
own inheritance. 7 The people served the LORD throughout the lifetime of Joshua and of the elders who
outlived him and who had seen all the great things the LORD had done for Israel.
8 Joshua son of Nun, the servant of the LORD, died at the age of a hundred and ten. 9 And they buried
him in the land of his inheritance, at Timnath Heres[b][z] in the hill country of Ephraim, north of Mount
Gaash.
10 After that whole generation had been gathered to their ancestors, another generation grew up
who knew neither the LORD nor what he had done for Israel.[a] 11 Then the Israelites did evil in the
eyes of the LORD[b] and served the Baals.[c] 12 They forsook the LORD, the God of their ancestors, who had
brought them out of Egypt. They followed and worshiped various gods[d] of the peoples around them.[e]
They aroused the LORD's anger 13 because they forsook him and served Baal and the Ashtoreths.[f] 14 In
his anger[g] against Israel the LORD gave them into the hands[h] of raiders who plundered them. He sold
them[i] into the hands of their enemies all around, whom they were no longer able to resist.[j] 15 Whenever
Israel went out to fight, the hand of the LORD was against them to defeat them, just as he had sworn to
them. They were in great distress.

[a] 5 *Bokim* means *weepers*. [b] 9 Also known as *Timnath Serah* (see Joshua 19:50 and 24:30)

2:1–5 The Lord indicts the Israelites, who have not carried out the law of Deut 7 (the *ḥērem*) as he had commanded.

2:1 The angel of the LORD. Perhaps an appearance of God (i.e., a theophany; cf. Gen 16:7) or simply God's human messenger (i.e., a prophet; cf. 6:8–10). See notes on Gen 16:7; Exod 3:2. **Gilgal.** Perhaps the important site of Josh 4:19–5:12. Verses 1–5 confront the Israelites with a comparable claim: "I brought you up out of Egypt (v. 1b), which implicitly rebukes the tribes for failing to "drive out" (see note on 1:1–20) the Canaanite nations and for worshiping Canaanite idols. It does this by means of allusion to Yahweh's covenant stipulations. Deut 7:7–24 correlate Yahweh's conquest of Egypt with his assurance that Israel can conquer Canaan with his help. Moreover, Deut 7:1–5,16,25–26 specifically command the Israelites to avoid treaties with the Canaanites and to destroy both the people and their idols. By making treaties or covenants with the inhabitants of the land, the Israelites broke their covenant with the Lord. See also Exod 23:32–33; Deut 12:29–32. **Bokim.** See NIV text note on v. 5; occurs nowhere else in the OT; the Septuagint, the pre-Christian Greek translation of the OT, reads "Bethel."

2:6 — 3:6 *Difficulties With Foreign Idols.* This second introduction introduces the all-important cyclic pattern, the very framework of the "cycles" section. The passage recounts Israel's difficulties with foreign deities and idols.

2:6–10 This is apparently dependent on Josh 24:28–31. By restarting the narrative with Joshua, the writer is able to contrast the faithfulness of Joshua's day with the infidelity of the subsequent generation.

2:8 a hundred and ten. The same age as Joseph (Gen 50:26).

2:9 Timnath Heres. See NIV text note.

2:11–19 This introduces the cycle components (see Introduction: The Cycles Section). The Lord withdraws his help because of Israel's sin. Ironically, he "sold" (v. 14) the people he had "bought" (Exod 15:16). However, the Lord raises up deliverers (judges), who save Israel from these oppressors. With each successive generation there is a greater degeneration into sin and corruption than with the previous ("even more corrupt," v. 19). Thus, the picture is not only cyclical but also downward. Israel is spiraling down into a spiritual abyss.

2:11 the Baals. Baal (meaning "lord") was the Canaanite storm-god who also had fertility functions (hence his importance to an agrarian society like ancient Israel's). His personal name was Hadad. For the plural, see note on v. 13.

2:13 Ashtoreths. A reference to Astarte, the popular (animal and human) fertility goddess and consort of Baal. Associated with war, she is often pictured in Canaanite and Egyptian iconography as standing or riding on a horse and carrying a bow and arrow or spear and shield (cf. 10:6; 1 Sam 7:4; 12:10). Both Baals and Ashtoreths are plural, which could refer either to local manifestations of these two deities or more likely, to all the male and female deities (i.e., Baals = gods; Ashtoreths = goddesses). While there are many known local manifestations of Baal — "Mount Baal Hermon" (3:3), "Baal-Berith" (i.e., "the Baal of the covenant," 8:33), "Baal of Peor" (Num 25:5), "Baal Gad" (Josh 11:17), "Baal Hazor" (2 Sam 13:23), and "Baal Hamon" (Song 8:11) — there are no examples of local manifestations of Astarte.

16 Then the LORD raised up judges,[a][k] who saved[l] them out of the hands of these raiders. 17 Yet they
would not listen to their judges but prostituted[m] themselves to other gods and worshiped them. They
quickly turned from the ways of their ancestors, who had been obedient to the LORD's commands.[n]
18 Whenever the LORD raised up a judge for them, he was with the judge and saved them out of the hands
of their enemies as long as the judge lived; for the LORD relented[o] because of their groaning[p] under those
who oppressed and afflicted them. 19 But when the judge died, the people returned to ways even more
corrupt[q] than those of their ancestors, following other gods and serving and worshiping them.[r] They
refused to give up their evil practices and stubborn ways.

20 Therefore the LORD was very angry[s] with Israel and said, "Because this nation has violated
the covenant I ordained for their ancestors and has not listened to me, 21 I will no longer drive
out[t] before them any of the nations Joshua left when he died. 22 I will use them to test[u] Israel and
see whether they will keep the way of the LORD and walk in it as their ancestors did." 23 The LORD
had allowed those nations to remain; he did not drive them out at once by giving them into the
hands of Joshua.

3 These are the nations the LORD left to test[v] all those Israelites who had not experienced any of the
wars in Canaan 2 (he did this only to teach warfare to the descendants of the Israelites who had not
had previous battle experience): 3 the five[w] rulers of the Philistines, all the Canaanites, the Sidonians,
and the Hivites living in the Lebanon mountains from Mount Baal Hermon to Lebo Hamath. 4 They
were left to test[x] the Israelites to see whether they would obey the LORD's commands, which he had given
their ancestors through Moses.

5 The Israelites lived[y] among the Canaanites, Hittites, Amorites, Perizzites, Hivites and Jebusites.
6 They took their daughters in marriage and gave their own daughters to their sons, and served their
gods.[z]

Othniel

7 The Israelites did evil in the eyes of the LORD; they forgot the LORD[a] their God and served the Baals and the Asherahs.[b] 8 The anger of the LORD burned against Israel so that he sold[c] them into the
hands of Cushan-Rishathaim king of Aram Naharaim,[b] to whom the Israelites were subject for eight
years. 9 But when they cried out[d] to the LORD, he raised up for them a deliverer, Othniel[e] son of Kenaz,
Caleb's younger brother, who saved them. 10 The Spirit of the LORD came on him,[f] so that he became
Israel's judge[c] and went to war. The LORD gave Cushan-Rishathaim king of Aram into the hands of
Othniel, who overpowered him. 11 So the land had peace for forty years, until Othniel son of Kenaz
died.

2:16 [k] Ac 13:20 [l] Ps 106:43
2:17 [m] Ex 34:15 [n] ver 7
2:18 [o] Dt 32:36; Jos 1:5 [p] Ps 106:44
2:19 [q] Jdg 3:12 [r] Jdg 4:1; 8:33
2:20 [s] ver 14; Jos 23:16
2:21 [t] Jos 23:13
2:22 [u] Dt 8:2,16; Jdg 3:1,14
3:1 [v] Jdg 2:21-22
3:3 [w] Jos 13:3
3:4 [x] Dt 8:2; Jdg 2:22
3:5 [y] Ps 106:35
3:6 [z] Ex 34:16; Dt 7:3-4
3:7 [a] Dt 4:9 [b] Ex 34:13; Jdg 2:11,13
3:8 [c] Jdg 2:14
3:9 [d] ver 15; Jdg 6:6,7; 10:10; Ps 106:44 [e] Jdg 1:13
3:10 [f] Nu 11:25,29; 24:2; Jdg 6:34; 11:29; 13:25; 14:6,19; 1Sa 11:6

[a] *16* Or *leaders*; similarly in verses 17-19 [b] *8* That is, Northwest Mesopotamia [c] *10* Or *leader*

2:16 See Introduction: Title of the Book and Role of the Judges.

2:20—3:4 The resultant conclusion to the cyclical, downward pattern. Due to Israel's disobedience and unfaithfulness and the Lord's consequent anger with them, the Lord determines that he will not drive out all the peoples in the land; instead, he will use them to test and discipline Israel.

3:5–6 This summary conclusion to the whole introduction stresses that the Israelites failed to keep the covenant: they (1) "lived among" the peoples of the land, (2) intermarried with them, and (3) "served their gods." Marriage outside the Israelite community leads to weakening Israel's bonds with the Lord. This ironically anticipates the Israelites' oath in 21:1–5 concerning marriage with the Benjamites, yet it contrasts with 1:12–13.

3:7—16:31 *Cycles of the Judges.* See Introduction: The Cycles Section.

3:7–11 *Major Judge Cycle: Othniel.* The hero of 1:12–15 appears here as Israel's first deliverer. Othniel stands as the model judge; the text highlights no character flaws (see Introduction: The Cycles Section). Nothing distracts the reader from the clear message of God's intervention through the deliverer he raises up.

3:7 The Israelites did evil in the eyes of the LORD. The opening formula for all the judge cycles. **the Baals and the Asherahs.** For the use of the plurals, see note on 2:13. For "Baals," see note on 2:11. Asherah was a female fertility deity, often worshiped with poles and sacred prostitution.

3:8 Cushan-Rishathaim. Means "dark, double wicked Cushan," likely a pejorative name created from the real name as a literary device meant to heighten Othniel's deliverance of Israel. **Aram Naharaim.** Means "Aram of the Two Rivers"; it is an area known as the Jezirah in modern eastern Syria. Naharaim was the earlier name of the area in second-millennium BC sources.

3:9 who saved them. Due to the syntax, there may be a purposeful ambiguity so that both the Lord and Othniel are seen as saving Israel in tandem.

3:10 The Spirit of the LORD came on. The Lord's Spirit is on Othniel in order to empower him to deliver Israel. Othniel used this empowerment in the right way. **gave ... into the hands of.** Only here in this cycle does this phrase describe Yahweh's delivering the oppressor into the hand of the judge. Normally it describes the Lord giving the Israelites into the hands of their enemies (e.g., v. 8). In this way, Othniel is uniquely described as accomplishing the complete reversal of Cushan-Rishathaim's oppression.

3:11 the land had peace. A component of the cycle (v. 30; 5:31; 8:28).

3:12 [g]Jdg 2:11,14 [h]1Sa 12:9
3:13 [i]Jdg 1:16
3:15 [j]ver 9; Ps 78:34; 107:13
3:17 [k]ver 12
3:24 [l]1Sa 24:3
3:25 [m]2Ki 2:17; 8:11
3:27 [n]Jdg 6:34; 1Sa 13:3
3:28 [o]Jdg 7:9,15 [p]Jos 2:7; Jdg 7:24; 12:5
3:30 [q]ver 11

Ehud

12 Again the Israelites did evil in the eyes of the LORD,[g] and because they did this evil the LORD gave
Eglon king of Moab[h] power over Israel. 13 Getting the Ammonites and Amalekites to join him, Eglon
came and attacked Israel, and they took possession of the City of Palms.[a][i] 14 The Israelites were subject
to Eglon king of Moab for eighteen years.

15 Again the Israelites cried out to the LORD, and he gave them a deliverer[j]—Ehud, a left-handed
man, the son of Gera the Benjamite. The Israelites sent him with tribute to Eglon king of Moab. 16 Now
Ehud had made a double-edged sword about a cubit[b] long, which he strapped to his right thigh under
his clothing. 17 He presented the tribute to Eglon king of Moab, who was a very fat man.[k] 18 After Ehud
had presented the tribute, he sent on their way those who had carried it. 19 But on reaching the stone
images near Gilgal he himself went back to Eglon and said, "Your Majesty, I have a secret message
for you."

The king said to his attendants, "Leave us!" And they all left.

20 Ehud then approached him while he was sitting alone in the upper room of his palace[c] and
said, "I have a message from God for you." As the king rose from his seat, 21 Ehud reached with his
left hand, drew the sword from his right thigh and plunged it into the king's belly. 22 Even the handle sank in after the blade, and his bowels discharged. Ehud did not pull the sword out, and the fat
closed in over it. 23 Then Ehud went out to the porch[d]; he shut the doors of the upper room behind
him and locked them.

24 After he had gone, the servants came and found the doors of the upper room locked. They said,
"He must be relieving himself[l] in the inner room of the palace." 25 They waited to the point of embarrassment,[m] but when he did not open the doors of the room, they took a key and unlocked them. There
they saw their lord fallen to the floor, dead.

26 While they waited, Ehud got away. He passed by the stone images and escaped to Seirah. 27 When
he arrived there, he blew a trumpet[n] in the hill country of Ephraim, and the Israelites went down with
him from the hills, with him leading them.

28 "Follow me," he ordered, "for the LORD has given Moab, your enemy, into your hands.[o]" So they
followed him down and took possession of the fords of the Jordan[p] that led to Moab; they allowed no
one to cross over. 29 At that time they struck down about ten thousand Moabites, all vigorous and strong;
not one escaped. 30 That day Moab was made subject to Israel, and the land had peace[q] for eighty years.

[a] *13* That is, Jericho [b] *16* That is, about 18 inches or about 45 centimeters [c] *20* The meaning of the Hebrew for this word is uncertain; also in verse 24. [d] *23* The meaning of the Hebrew for this word is uncertain.

3:12–30 *Major Judge Cycle: Ehud.* A regional oppression by Moab. The story is rich in humor, sarcasm, and irony. Through these the narrator chastens Israel because the oppression by Eglon and the Moabites is due to Israel's sin. But while Eglon and the Moabites oppressed Israel for 18 years, they were no match for a savior that Yahweh raised up.

3:12 did evil ... did this evil. Emphasis through repetition. **gave ... power over Israel.** The text commonly states that the Lord gave or sold the Israelites into the hands of their oppressors. Only here does the writer say that Yahweh actively *strengthened* or *empowered* the oppressor against Israel. **Eglon.** Means "young calf." **Moab.** The country immediately east of the Dead Sea, south of the Arnon River.

3:13 took possession. "Drove out" (cf. ch. 1). **the City of Palms.** See NIV text note; cf. 1:16. Ironically, the Moabites are seen as reversing the Israelite conquest of Jericho.

3:15 a left-handed man. The Hebrew could mean that he had great ability in the use of his left hand, not necessarily that he was left-handed (which is said another way in Hebrew). Perhaps this is ironic, since Benjamin means "son of the right hand or south." In any case, Ehud concealed his dagger on the side where it was not expected, and he used his left-handed ability to kill Eglon (v. 21).

3:16 sword about a cubit long. Recent scholarship has demonstrated that the Hebrew (*gōmed*) may indicate a short cubit, about 2/3 of a cubit, around 11.5 inches (29 centimeters).

3:17 a very fat man. Eglon's fattened physique was no doubt the result of the extorted tribute of agricultural produce from the Israelites.

3:19 stone images. Perhaps boundary stones that contained idolatrous symbols. **secret message.** The Hebrew term translated "message" can also mean "thing." Thus, while Eglon may be thinking of a "secret message," Ehud has in mind the dagger ("secret thing").

3:21 with his left hand, drew the sword from his right thigh. Concealing the dagger on his right thigh permitted Ehud to quickly grasp it with his left hand and stab Eglon.

3:22 The satirical tone presents Eglon as the fattened sacrifice: "the fat" is a sacrificial term used for the choicest parts, the entrails (see note on Lev 3:17). **his bowels discharged.** This explains the next verse (see note on vv. 24–25).

3:24–25 Eglon's guards conclude that he must be "relieving himself." While they wait, Ehud escapes. With a bit of satire, Eglon's guards wait behind locked doors "to the point of embarrassment," only to find their lord dead.

3:26–30 The Moabites, like their monarch, are sacrificially slaughtered so that Israel is delivered. The Ephraimites seize the fords of the Jordan River (cf. 7:24–25).

3:29 ten thousand. See note on 1:4.

Shamgar

31 After Ehud came Shamgar son of Anath,[r] who struck down six hundred[s] Philistines with an oxgoad. He too saved Israel.

Deborah

4 Again the Israelites did evil[t] in the eyes of the LORD, now that Ehud was dead. 2 So the LORD sold
them into the hands of Jabin king of Canaan, who reigned in Hazor.[u] Sisera,[v] the commander of
his army, was based in Harosheth Haggoyim. 3 Because he had nine hundred chariots fitted with iron[w]
and had cruelly oppressed[x] the Israelites for twenty years, they cried to the LORD for help.
4 Now Deborah, a prophet, the wife of Lappidoth, was leading[a] Israel at that time. 5 She held court
under the Palm of Deborah between Ramah and Bethel[y] in the hill country of Ephraim, and the Israelites went up to her to have their disputes decided. 6 She sent for Barak son of Abinoam[z] from Kedesh in
Naphtali and said to him, "The LORD, the God of Israel, commands you: 'Go, take with you ten thousand
men of Naphtali and Zebulun and lead them up to Mount Tabor. 7 I will lead Sisera, the commander
of Jabin's army, with his chariots and his troops to the Kishon River[a] and give him into your hands.' "
8 Barak said to her, "If you go with me, I will go; but if you don't go with me, I won't go."
9 "Certainly I will go with you," said Deborah. "But because of the course you are taking, the honor
will not be yours, for the LORD will deliver Sisera into the hands of a woman." So Deborah went with
Barak to Kedesh.[b] 10 There Barak summoned[c] Zebulun and Naphtali, and ten thousand men went up
under his command. Deborah also went up with him.
11 Now Heber the Kenite had left the other Kenites,[d] the descendants of Hobab,[e] Moses' brother-in-
law,[b] and pitched his tent by the great tree in Zaanannim[f] near Kedesh.

[a] 4 Traditionally *judging* [b] 11 Or *father-in-law*

3:31 [r] Jdg 5:6 [s] Jos 23:10
4:1 [t] Jdg 2:19
4:2 [u] Jos 11:1 [v] ver 13, 16; 1Sa 12:9; Ps 83:9
4:3 [w] Jdg 1:19 [x] Ps 106:42
4:5 [y] Ge 35:8
4:6 [z] Heb 11:32
4:7 [a] Ps 83:9
4:9 [b] ver 21; Jdg 2:14
4:10 [c] ver 14; Jdg 5:15,18
4:11 [d] Jdg 1:16 [e] Nu 10:29 [f] Jos 19:33

3:31 *Minor Judge: Shamgar.* Shamgar, the first of the six minor judges, saves Israel.
3:31 Shamgar. The name is not Israelite, probably not even Semitic. Hence, he was probably a non-Israelite (5:6) mercenary. He was a contemporary of Jael (5:6) and saved Israel with a mighty exploit against the Philistines (cf. 15:14–17; 2 Sam 23:8–23). **son of Anath.** Anath is not the name of his father (there is no evidence for this as a personal name); perhaps it is an indication that he was from the town of Beth Anath (1:33; Josh 19:38); but it is most likely, based on Egyptian and Canaanite evidence, the name of a military contingent of which he was a member. Anat was a Canaanite goddess of war (also worshiped in Egypt). **oxgoad.** A long wooden pole, sometimes having a metal tip, used for driving cattle (1 Sam 13:21). It was an improvised weapon, just like some others in the book (v. 16; 4:21–22; 7:20; 9:53; 15:15).
4:1—5:31 *Major Judge Cycle: Deborah and Barak.* The prose story in ch. 4 and the poetic account in ch. 5 complement one another. Both are needed in order to understand the story. Deborah is the prophetess who commissions Barak as judge (deliverer) (see note on 4:4).
4:1–24 *The Narrative.* This prose account uses the cycle components and is complemented by the poetic account (called The Song of Deborah [5:1–31]).
4:1–3 The prologue narrates the setting of the oppression.
4:1 the Israelites did evil in the eyes of the LORD. For the third time (cf. 3:7,12), Israel's disobedience leads to oppression.
4:2 Jabin. A different king with the same name as in Josh 11:1 (cf. Ps 83:9). He plays a role only in the story's prologue and epilogue. The name is most likely a shortened form for a name attested archaeologically at Hazor from an earlier period. **Hazor.** An important city in Galilee because of its proximity to trade routes; it is nine miles (14.5 kilometers) north of the Sea of Galilee. **Sisera.** A non-Semitic name (meaning unknown); a mercenary commander for Jabin. **Harosheth Haggoyim.** The town's precise location is unknown.
4:3 The number of chariots is great and reflects the situation's hopelessness. These chariots of iron (cf. 1:19) were a technology that Israel did not possess and posed a huge challenge to an army that only had infantry to fight a battle in the Jezreel Valley.
4:4–16 The call of Barak and the defeat of Sisera's army.
4:4 Deborah. Means "bee" (cf. 14:8; Deut 1:44). The verse seems to imply that Deborah was functioning as a judge; however, this is unlikely, since it is Barak, not Deborah, who is the designated deliverer and who ought to have served as the main character of the account. Thus, while she is serving in rendering judgments, she is a prophetess who called Barak to be the deliverer (i.e., judge). Her role as prophetess parallels that of the angel of the Lord in 6:11–16.
4:5 Palm of Deborah. A location relatively far away from Hazor in contrast to Barak's home in v. 6.
4:6–7 Deborah takes the initiative, sending for and commanding Barak. Deborah calls Barak to lead the army (a woman normally would not be a military leader in Israel).
4:6 Barak. Means "lightning" (cf. Heb 11:32). **ten thousand.** See note on 1:4. **Mount Tabor.** A lone mountain standing in the northeast corner of the Jezreel Valley.
4:7 Kishon River. A seasonal stream (wadi) that may have very little water flowing in it during the dry season but can overflow and flood in the rainy season. It flows northwestward through the Jezreel Valley to the Mediterranean. Sisera chose the Jezreel plain because his chariots would have a great military advantage; yet the text attributes the Lord with leading the Canaanites to this spot in order to destroy them.
4:8–9 To his discredit, Barak hesitated to lead the Israelites in battle (v. 8). His insistence that Deborah accompany him diminishes his heroic stature: the honor will go to a woman. Deborah agreed to go with him but predicted that the glory for the battle would go to a woman. At this point in the story, the only woman mentioned so far is Deborah, but the story will surprise us with another woman (v. 17).
4:10 Barak's deployment. **Zebulun and Naphtali.** Two tribes from Galilee.
4:11 Kenites. See note on 1:16. This anticipates vv. 17–22.

4:13 [g] ver 3
4:14 [h] Dt 9:3; 2Sa 5:24; Ps 68:7
4:15 [i] Jos 10:10; Ps 83:9-10
4:16 [j] Ps 83:9
4:19 [k] Jdg 5:25
4:21 [l] Jdg 5:26
4:23 [m] Ne 9:24; Ps 18:47
5:1 [n] Ex 15:1
5:2 [o] 2Ch 17:16; Ps 110:3 [p] ver 9

12 When they told Sisera that Barak son of Abinoam had gone up to Mount Tabor, 13 Sisera summoned from Harosheth Haggoyim to the Kishon River all his men and his nine hundred chariots fitted with iron.[g]

14 Then Deborah said to Barak, "Go! This is the day the LORD has given Sisera into your hands. Has not the LORD gone ahead[h] of you?" So Barak went down Mount Tabor, with ten thousand men following him. 15 At Barak's advance, the LORD routed[i] Sisera and all his chariots and army by the sword, and Sisera got down from his chariot and fled on foot.

16 Barak pursued the chariots and army as far as Harosheth Haggoyim, and all Sisera's troops fell by the sword; not a man was left.[j] 17 Sisera, meanwhile, fled on foot to the tent of Jael, the wife of Heber the Kenite, because there was an alliance between Jabin king of Hazor and the family of Heber the Kenite.

18 Jael went out to meet Sisera and said to him, "Come, my lord, come right in. Don't be afraid." So he entered her tent, and she covered him with a blanket.

19 "I'm thirsty," he said. "Please give me some water." She opened a skin of milk,[k] gave him a drink, and covered him up.

20 "Stand in the doorway of the tent," he told her. "If someone comes by and asks you, 'Is anyone in there?' say 'No.'"

21 But Jael, Heber's wife, picked up a tent peg and a hammer and went quietly to him while he lay fast asleep, exhausted. She drove the peg through his temple into the ground, and he died.[l]

22 Just then Barak came by in pursuit of Sisera, and Jael went out to meet him. "Come," she said, "I will show you the man you're looking for." So he went in with her, and there lay Sisera with the tent peg through his temple—dead.

23 On that day God subdued[m] Jabin king of Canaan before the Israelites. 24 And the hand of the Israelites pressed harder and harder against Jabin king of Canaan until they destroyed him.

The Song of Deborah

5 On that day Deborah and Barak son of Abinoam sang this song:[n]

2 "When the princes in Israel take the lead,
when the people willingly offer[o] themselves—
praise the LORD![p]

4:12–13 Sisera's deployment.
4:14 Deborah again commands Barak, giving him assurance of victory through the Lord. **gone ahead of you.** In the ancient Near East, deities were seen as going before the king and army in order to ensure protection and victory.
4:15 routed. The Lord threw Sisera, along with his chariots and army, into a panic before Barak (cf. Exod 14:24; 23:27; Deut 2:15; Josh 10:10; 1 Sam 7:10).
4:16 Barak expends tremendous effort in pursuing the enemy to Harosheth Haggoyim, but it is all for naught.
4:17–22 Jael kills Sisera.
4:17 Jael. Means "ibex" or "mountain goat." Like Shamgar, Jael is a non-Israelite, specifically a Kenite (v. 11; 1:16).
4:18–20 Jael demonstrates ancient Near Eastern hospitality, which disarms Sisera.
4:19 skin. Liquids were commonly kept in skins of goats or sheep. **milk.** See note on 5:25.
4:21 The text narrates Jael's killing of Sisera in the same vivid style as Ehud's killing of Eglon (3:21–22). She dispatches with a domestic implement the great warrior that Barak so feared.
4:22 Jael has in effect conquered both Sisera (by depriving him of his life) and Barak (by depriving him of the honor). The text pictures Barak in a similar fashion to Eglon's guards (3:24–25).
4:23–24 The oppression ends. The repetition of King Jabin of Canaan stresses the magnitude of the victory over the oppressor. Without his general Sisera, Jabin was no threat. The land "flowing with milk and honey" was saved by a "bee" and a "mountain goat" (see notes on vv. 4,17). While the phrase "flowing with milk and honey" does not occur in the book of Judges, it occurs so often in the law that it is in view here (see Exod 3:8,17; 13:5; 33:3; Lev 20:24; Num 13:27; 14:8; 16:13,14; Deut 6:3; 11:9; 26:9,15; 27:3; 31:20; Josh 5:6). See also 14:8.
5:1–31 *The Poem: Song of Deborah.* This poetic counterpart to the prose account (ch. 4) furnishes the emotional celebration of the victory over Sisera and the Canaanites. Many scholars believe that the song is one of the oldest parts of the Hebrew Bible. It also contains some obscure and difficult verses. But it clearly celebrates the Lord's role in the victory over Sisera through a sudden downpour that disabled his chariots in the battle, and it assesses the involvements of God's people in this enterprise for better (blessing) or worse (curse). Some other examples of Israelite victory songs are Exod 15:1–18,21; Num 21:27–30; Deut 32:1–43; 1 Sam 2:1–10. Traditionally the author of the song is understood to be Deborah (e.g., v. 7), though it is possible to understand the poem as speaking figuratively. Besides the narrative that frames the setting (v. 1) and conclusion (v. 31d), the poem itself has a complex structure. It is comprised of five acts or movements: Act A (vv. 2–8), Act B (vv. 9–13), Act C (vv. 14–18), Act D (vv. 23), and Act E (vv. 24–31c). While there are many other subdivisions, emphasis will be placed on the Acts. The song contains a narrowing shift in focus: from a focus on the nation (Acts A and B) to a focus on the ten tribes (Acts C and D) to a focus on two female individuals (Act E).
5:1 *Introduction to the Poem.* The context for the song is given.
5:2–8 *Act A: Initial Call to Praise and Report of Need.* While this corresponds to the concluding Act E (vv. 24–31c), it has a parallel structure to Act B. There is an invocation to praise (v. 2), an exhortation (v. 3), and two causes for praise and response of the people (vv. 4–8).
5:2 Act A opens with an invocation to praise Yahweh. **When the princes**

[3] "Hear this, you kings! Listen, you rulers!
I, even I, will sing to[a] the LORD;
I will praise the LORD, the God of Israel, in song.[q]

[4] "When you, LORD, went out from Seir,[r]
when you marched from the land of Edom,
the earth shook, the heavens poured,
the clouds poured down water.[s]
[5] The mountains quaked[t] before the LORD, the One of Sinai,
before the LORD, the God of Israel.

[6] "In the days of Shamgar son of Anath,[u]
in the days of Jael,[v] the highways[w] were abandoned;
travelers took to winding paths.
[7] Villagers in Israel would not fight;
they held back until I, Deborah, arose,
until I arose, a mother in Israel.
[8] God chose new leaders[x]
when war came to the city gates,
but not a shield or spear was seen
among forty thousand in Israel.
[9] My heart is with Israel's princes,
with the willing volunteers[y] among the people.
Praise the LORD!

[10] "You who ride on white donkeys,[z]
sitting on your saddle blankets,
and you who walk along the road,
consider [11] the voice of the singers[b] at the watering places.
They recite the victories[a] of the LORD,
the victories of his villagers in Israel.

5:3 [q] Ps 27:6
5:4 [r] Dt 33:2 [s] Ps 68:8
5:5 [t] Ex 19:18; Ps 68:8; 97:5; Isa 64:3
5:6 [u] Jdg 3:31 [v] Jdg 4:17 [w] Isa 33:8
5:8 [x] Dt 32:17
5:9 [y] ver 2
5:10 [z] Jdg 10:4; 12:14
5:11 [a] 1Sa 12:7; Mic 6:5

[a] *3* Or *of* [b] *11* The meaning of the Hebrew for this word is uncertain.

in Israel take the lead. The Hebrew of this verse is difficult to translate. Another possible translation could refer to unbound hair: "because hair was unbound in Israel" or "when locks were loosened in Israel." The term translated "princes" is translated "hair" in Num 6:5; Ezek 44:20. That could suggest the idea of dedication to the purposes of Yahweh: either a vow similar to that of a Nazirite or intense military dedication that results in unkempt, shaggy hair.

5:3 kings! … rulers! The exhortation to pay attention addresses royalty, probably foreign monarchs (cf. Ps 2:2,10). The Canaanite kings and princes are ordered to listen, but they are mere witnesses; they will certainly keep their mouths shut after the devastating defeat just suffered. **I, even I.** Emphasizes a shift from exhorting the audience to praise Yahweh (v. 2c) to Deborah's praising Yahweh herself.

5:4–8 Act A gives two causes for praise: (1) Yahweh's epiphany upon the earth (vv. 4–5) and (2) the state of affairs before the victory (vv. 6–8), which anticipates Yahweh's action in the storm.

5:4–5 The Lord's epiphany upon the earth is described in terms of storm and quake. A concentric pattern can be discerned in the poetry of this section: (a) Yahweh marched from Seir/Edom (v. 4a–b); (b) the earth shook (v. 4c1); (c) the heavens poured (v. 4c2); (c′) the clouds poured (v. 4d); (b′) the mountains quaked (v. 5a1); (a′) before Yahweh of Sinai, Israel's God (v. 5a2–b). **earth shook … mountains quaked.** Describes the storm's lightning and thunder.

5:4 Seir. Edom. The Lord comes from the barren regions of the southeast with an overwhelming storm.

5:5 the LORD, the God of Israel. The last line both here and in v. 3. The storm imagery is used polemically against the Canaanite storm-god, Baal (cf. Ps 68:7–8; Hab 3:3–12).

5:6 In the days of Shamgar … in the days of Jael. The parallelism shows that the events are contemporaneous (3:31; 4:17). These two non-Israelite heroes share the ability to fashion an improvised weapon to deliver Israel. At the time, due to the oppression, it was extremely difficult to travel.

5:7 Villagers. The term could also mean "warriors." **would not fight.** The picture is one of military weakness similar to that painted in v. 8b. Whatever the case, the oppression is in view. But Deborah documents God's actions behind the scenes.

5:8 God chose new leaders when war came to the city gates. This could be translated as "When they chose new gods, then war came to the city gates." Israel's choice of "new" gods brought military humiliation and servitude, including the lack of the very weapons of war ("shield" and "spear") necessary to overcome the oppression. This stresses the need for Yahweh's intervention.

5:9–13 *Act B: Renewal of the Call to Praise Because of the Volunteers.* There is an invocation to praise (v. 9), an exhortation (v. 10), and two causes for praise and response of the people (vv. 11–13). This parallels Act A (see note on vv. 2–8).

5:9–10 An invocation to praise the Lord with an exhortation to pay attention (cf. v. 3). Those who volunteered inspired the invocation.

5:11–13 Two causes for praise and response of the people: (1) The

5:11 [b]ver 8
5:12 [c]Ps 57:8 [d]Ps 68:18; Eph 4:8
5:14 [e]Jdg 3:13
5:15 [f]Jdg 4:10
5:16 [g]Nu 32:1
5:17 [h]Jos 19:29
5:18 [i]Jdg 4:6,10
5:19 [j]Jos 11:5; Jdg 4:13 [k]Jdg 1:27 [l]ver 30
5:20 [m]Jos 10:11

"Then the people of the LORD
went down to the city gates.[b]
12 'Wake up,[c] wake up, Deborah!
Wake up, wake up, break out in song!
Arise, Barak!
Take captive your captives,[d] son of Abinoam.'

13 "The remnant of the nobles came down;
the people of the LORD came down to me against the mighty.
14 Some came from Ephraim, whose roots were in Amalek;[e]
Benjamin was with the people who followed you.
From Makir captains came down,
from Zebulun those who bear a commander's[a] staff.
15 The princes of Issachar were with Deborah;[f]
yes, Issachar was with Barak,
sent under his command into the valley.
In the districts of Reuben
there was much searching of heart.
16 Why did you stay among the sheep pens[b]
to hear the whistling for the flocks?[g]
In the districts of Reuben
there was much searching of heart.
17 Gilead stayed beyond the Jordan.
And Dan, why did he linger by the ships?
Asher remained on the coast[h]
and stayed in his coves.
18 The people of Zebulun risked their very lives;
so did Naphtali on the terraced fields.[i]

19 "Kings came[j], they fought,
the kings of Canaan fought.
At Taanach, by the waters of Megiddo,[k]
they took no plunder of silver.[l]
20 From the heavens[m] the stars fought,
from their courses they fought against Sisera.

[a] *14* The meaning of the Hebrew for this word is uncertain. [b] *16* Or *the campfires*; or *the saddlebags*

"voice of the singers" recount the "victories" (or the righteous deeds) of the Lord and his warriors, stimulating the response: "then the people of the LORD went down to the city gates" (in order to do battle). (2) The leadership of Deborah and then Barak is invoked to conduct the campaign, stimulating the response: "the people of the LORD came down to me against the mighty." In the ancient Near East, only a victory song of the people of the Lord would extol the inferiority of its own army in the face of opposition.

5:14–18 *Act C: Recognition of the Tribes That Did or Did Not Participate.* This focal point of the song gives a full picture of the tribal mobilization. It assesses the tribes morally and spiritually. The evaluation is positive or negative, depending on whether or not they involve themselves in the battle: (1) Those who answered the call to arms are Ephraim, Benjamin, Makir (a subdivision of Manasseh, perhaps the part for the whole), Zebulun, and Issachar (vv. 14–15a). Deborah and Barak are paired once again (v. 15a). (2) Those who did not participate are Reuben, Gilead (i.e., Gad), Dan, and Asher (vv. 15b–17). The poem does not mention the tribes of Judah and Simeon, probably because the oppression was geographically limited. Levi is also not mentioned.

5:15 In the districts of Reuben there was much searching of heart. Repeated in v. 16b. It frames the particular taunt of Reuben (v. 16a). While there was some reflective concern expressed by the Reubenites as they tended their sheep, they were indifferent to the plight of the other tribes (v. 16a).

5:17 Dan and Asher were reluctant to join the fight, possibly because they did not want to jeopardize their economic position, which was dependent on Phoenician commerce and shipping. **Gilead.** Gad. They may have been simply apathetic, since being located in the Transjordan, they were some distance from the battle.

5:18 The song returns to praising the participating tribes of Zebulun and Naphtali, who were especially brave.

5:19–23 *Act D: The Battle and the Curse of Meroz.* This describes the battle (vv. 19–22) and presents a transition: the curse of Meroz (v. 23).

5:19 kings of Canaan. In the ancient Near East, an army was often composed of troops from numerous small vassal states with their kings or chiefs leading them. **Taanach ... Megiddo.** Cities that guarded two of the passes through the Carmel range. **took no plunder.** The Canaanite kings who joined Sisera fought without success.

5:20–21 This vividly and emotionally portrays divine intervention: a storm of epic proportions overwhelms the technologically superior

21 The river Kishon[n] swept them away,
the age-old river, the river Kishon.
March on, my soul; be strong!
22 Then thundered the horses' hooves —
galloping, galloping go his mighty steeds.
23 'Curse Meroz,' said the angel of the LORD.
'Curse its people bitterly,
because they did not come to help the LORD,
to help the LORD against the mighty.'

24 "Most blessed of women be Jael,[o]
the wife of Heber the Kenite,
most blessed of tent-dwelling women.
25 He asked for water, and she gave him milk;[p]
in a bowl fit for nobles she brought him curdled milk.
26 Her hand reached for the tent peg,
her right hand for the workman's hammer.
She struck Sisera, she crushed his head,
she shattered and pierced his temple.[q]
27 At her feet he sank,
he fell; there he lay.
At her feet he sank, he fell;
where he sank, there he fell — dead.

28 "Through the window peered Sisera's mother;
behind the lattice she cried out,[r]
'Why is his chariot so long in coming?
Why is the clatter of his chariots delayed?'
29 The wisest of her ladies answer her;
indeed, she keeps saying to herself,
30 'Are they not finding and dividing the spoils:[s]
a woman or two for each man,

5:21 [n] Jdg 4:7
5:24 [o] Jdg 4:17
5:25 [p] Jdg 4:19
5:26 [q] Jdg 4:21
5:28 [r] Pr 7:6
5:30 [s] Ex 15:9; 1Sa 30:24

Canaanite charioteers. The overflowing Kishon River "swept them away." The sudden flood of the wadi renders the Canaanite chariots useless (similar to the destruction of Pharaoh's chariots, Exod 15:4). The poetic combination of skies ("heavens") and water links back to the epiphany of Act A (see vv. 4–5 and note).
5:21 March on, my soul; be strong! Minimally describes Israelite involvement. The depiction allows all the glory to go to the Lord.
5:22 The final scene of the battle is that of chaos: the horses galloping wildly over the field, free of their chariots. Cavalry did not exist at this time.
5:23 Meroz. A nearby Israelite town. This is a curse for not joining in the battle (cf. Sukkoth and Peniel in 8:7,9,16–17). The curse provides the transition from the battle of the kings to the fleeing king, Sisera. Meroz did not aid Yahweh in the pursuit, but Jael (a non-Israelite) did, and she is "blessed" as fervently as Meroz is cursed (v. 24). Meroz represents those Israelites who have taken their stand on the side of the Canaanites; Jael represents those non-Israelites who have taken their stand on the side of Israel. **the angel of the LORD.** See 2:1 and note.
5:24–31 *Act E: Jael's Deed and Sisera's Mother.* The climactic conclusion to the song portrays the killing of Sisera by Jael (vv. 24–27) and a taunt of Sisera's mother (vv. 28–30).
5:24 Most blessed ... most blessed. Because Jael resourcefully and courageously slew Sisera. The only other object of blessing in this poem is God himself (vv. 2,9). The unrestrained praise of Jael is analogous to that of Mary in Luke 1:42.
5:25 Sisera ironically requested water, the very thing that had just destroyed his army. Jael instead gives him "curdled milk" (a type of curds/yogurt) in a bowl fit for nobility. Her motherly act of hospitality disarms her victim.
5:26 This poetic description ironically paints Jael in terms of the ancient Near Eastern tradition of a head-smashing, victorious monarch (especially known in Egyptian imagery).
5:27 The repetitions of the verbs "sank" and "fell" build the poetic scene to a climax: "dead" (cf. Eglon in 3:25).
5:28–30 The poem uses the conflicting emotions felt by the Canaanite women (especially Sisera's mother), who wait for the return of the Canaanite army to expose the evil intentions of Sisera and his mother.
5:28 The scene in the palace of Sisera's mother with her royal retainers starkly contrasts with Jael's tent. The questions not only reveal her emotions but also produce irony since the reader knows why Sisera is delayed.
5:29–30 The voice of the mother merges with the voice of her wisest attendant.
5:30 Are they not finding and dividing the spoils ...? The rhetorical question evokes an affirmative answer, but the reader knows the answer is negative. The fantasizing of the mother and her attendants about all the spoils and plunder reveals their orientation. **a woman or**

5:31 [t]2Sa 23:4; Ps 19:4; 89:36 [u]Jdg 3:11
6:1 [v]Jdg 2:11 [w]Nu 25:15-18; 31:1-3
6:2 [x]1Sa 13:6; Isa 8:21 [y]Heb 11:38
6:3 [z]Jdg 3:13
6:4 [a]Lev 26:16; Dt 28:30,51
6:5 [b]Jdg 7:12 [c]Jdg 8:10
6:6 [d]Jdg 3:9
6:8 [e]Jdg 2:1
6:9 [f]Ps 44:2
6:10 [g]2Ki 17:35 [h]Jer 10:2
6:11 [i]Ge 16:7 [j]Jos 17:2 [k]Heb 11:32
6:12 [l]Jos 1:5; Jdg 13:3; Lk 1:11,28

colorful garments as plunder for Sisera,
 colorful garments embroidered,
highly embroidered garments for my neck—
 all this as plunder?'

31 "So may all your enemies perish, LORD!
 But may all who love you be like the sun[t]
 when it rises in its strength."

Then the land had peace[u] forty years.

Gideon

6 The Israelites did evil in the eyes of the LORD,[v] and for seven years he gave them into the hands of
the Midianites.[w] 2Because the power of Midian was so oppressive,[x] the Israelites prepared shelters
for themselves in mountain clefts, caves and strongholds.[y] 3Whenever the Israelites planted their crops,
the Midianites, Amalekites[z] and other eastern peoples invaded the country. 4They camped on the land
and ruined the crops[a] all the way to Gaza and did not spare a living thing for Israel, neither sheep nor
cattle nor donkeys. 5They came up with their livestock and their tents like swarms of locusts.[b] It was
impossible to count them or their camels;[c] they invaded the land to ravage it. 6Midian so impoverished
the Israelites that they cried out[d] to the LORD for help.
7When the Israelites cried out to the LORD because of Midian, 8he sent them a prophet, who said,
"This is what the LORD, the God of Israel, says: I brought you up out of Egypt,[e] out of the land of
slavery. 9I rescued you from the hand of the Egyptians. And I delivered you from the hand of all your
oppressors; I drove them out before you and gave you their land.[f] 10I said to you, 'I am the LORD your
God; do not worship[g] the gods of the Amorites,[h] in whose land you live.' But you have not listened
to me."
11The angel of the LORD[i] came and sat down under the oak in Ophrah that belonged to Joash the
Abiezrite,[j] where his son Gideon[k] was threshing wheat in a winepress to keep it from the Midianites.
12When the angel of the LORD appeared to Gideon, he said, "The LORD is with you,[l] mighty warrior."
13"Pardon me, my lord," Gideon replied, "but if the LORD is with us, why has all this happened to us?

two for each man. The Canaanite women speaking reduce the Israelite women to mere items of plunder. **garments.** Spoils typically plundered from the defeated army's tents and dead bodies. The mother's greed for such treasure is unmistakable. Yet the last words of v. 27 ("dead") and v. 30 ("plunder") taunt Sisera, for he is unable to fulfill the expectations of his mother, because he himself has become the plunder.

5:31a–c The climactic conclusion appeals for justice over evil and blessing on the righteous in accordance with the covenant blessings and curses of Lev 26; Deut 28.

5:31d *Concluding Framework Statement.* This is the typical framework statement concerning the land having rest.

5:31d forty years. A conventional number for a generation.

6:1—9:57 *Major Judge Cycle: Gideon and Abimelek.* The major judge cycle about Gideon is incomplete until the sequel about his aberrant son Abimelek is finished. The text emphasizes the Lord's covenant with and kingship over Israel. This cycle is the pivotal cycle in the book since Gideon is the first "out-group" judge (see Introduction: The Cycles Section). It is the first time that Yahweh meets Israel's cry with a stern rebuke rather than immediate assistance, so it signals the beginning of a swifter moral degeneration in the cycles.

6:1—8:32 *The Gideon Narrative.* A hero of the tribe of Manasseh ends the oppression of his tribe by the Midianites, but before he dies he leads Israel into worshiping an idol of his own making.

6:1–10 *The Setting Before Gideon's Call.* This gives an introduction and setting that leads up to the appearance of Gideon. It demonstrates that God will not always simply deliver Israel whenever they cry to him.

6:1 Once again Israel does evil in the eyes of the Lord. **Midianites.** A seminomadic group from the south that Israel had fought before (Num 25:16–18; 31:1–54).

6:2–6 The severe oppression leads Israel to cry out to God.

6:3 Amalekites. A seminomadic group from the Sinai (Exod 17:8–15).

6:5 swarms of locusts. A vivid image of the oppressors. **camels.** The first OT mention of people using camels in warfare in the OT.

6:7–10 This time God answers Israel's cry by sending an unnamed prophet who rebukes them. While God is still gracious to Israel, he will not be manipulated, for he knows Israel's heart. The prophet enumerates all of God's mighty acts of deliverance on behalf of Israel, in spite of the Israelites' disregard for God's covenant. This section provides the basis for evaluating Gideon's words in v. 13. In the next cycle (Jephthah), the Lord himself rebukes Israel (10:11–14).

6:11–32 *The Call of Gideon.* This section relates God's plan of deliverance through the call of Gideon.

6:11–24 The Lord calls Gideon through an appearance of the angel of the Lord. Though characterized by extraordinary fearfulness and reluctance, Gideon ("hacker, cutter, thresher," an indication of his warring ability: the thresher of wheat will become a thresher of men) is the Lord's choice to save Israel (Deut 7:5; 12:3; see note on vv. 25–32).

6:11 angel of the LORD. See note on 2:1. **Abiezrite.** See Josh 17:2; 1 Chr 7:18. **threshing wheat in a winepress.** Normally grain was threshed on an elevated, exposed threshing floor (cf. Ruth 3:2–17).

6:12 mighty warrior. The Lord's words accurately describe what Gideon is and will be, in spite of his fear and reluctance at this moment.

6:13 A dull, cynical response to God's treatment of the nation, particularly in light of the prophet's words in vv. 8–10.

Where are all his wonders that our ancestors told[m] us about when they said, 'Did not the LORD bring us up out of Egypt?' But now the LORD has abandoned[n] us and given us into the hand of Midian."

14The LORD turned to him and said, "Go in the strength you have[o] and save Israel out of Midian's hand. Am I not sending you?"

15"Pardon me, my lord," Gideon replied, "but how can I save Israel? My clan is the weakest in Manasseh, and I am the least in my family.[p]"

16The LORD answered, "I will be with you[q], and you will strike down all the Midianites, leaving none alive."

17Gideon replied, "If now I have found favor in your eyes, give me a sign[r] that it is really you talking to me. 18Please do not go away until I come back and bring my offering and set it before you."

And the LORD said, "I will wait until you return."

19Gideon went inside, prepared a young goat, and from an ephah[a] of flour he made bread without yeast. Putting the meat in a basket and its broth in a pot, he brought them out and offered them to him under the oak.[s]

20The angel of God said to him, "Take the meat and the unleavened bread, place them on this rock,[t] and pour out the broth." And Gideon did so. 21Then the angel of the LORD touched the meat and the unleavened bread[u] with the tip of the staff that was in his hand. Fire flared from the rock, consuming the meat and the bread. And the angel of the LORD disappeared. 22When Gideon realized[v] that it was the angel of the LORD, he exclaimed, "Alas, Sovereign LORD! I have seen the angel of the LORD face to face!"[w]

23But the LORD said to him, "Peace! Do not be afraid.[x] You are not going to die."

24So Gideon built an altar to the LORD there and called[y] it The LORD Is Peace. To this day it stands in Ophrah[z] of the Abiezrites.

Assyrians using camels in warfare. Judg 6:5 is the first mention of camels being used in warfare in the OT.
Kim Walton, taken at the British Museum

25That same night the LORD said to him, "Take the second bull from your father's herd, the one seven years old.[b] Tear down your father's altar to Baal and cut down the Asherah pole[c][a] beside it. 26Then build a proper kind of[d] altar to the LORD your God on the top of this height. Using the wood of the Asherah pole that you cut down, offer the second[e] bull as a burnt offering."

27So Gideon took ten of his servants and did as the LORD told him. But because he was afraid of his family and the townspeople, he did it at night rather than in the daytime.

6:13 [m] Ps 44:1 [n] 2Ch 15:2
6:14 [o] Heb 11:34
6:15 [p] Ex 3:11; 1Sa 9:21
6:16 [q] Ex 3:12; Jos 1:5
6:17 [r] ver 36-37; Ge 24:14; Isa 38:7-8
6:19 [s] Ge 18:7-8
6:20 [t] Jdg 13:19
6:21 [u] Lev 9:24
6:22 [v] Jdg 13:16,21 [w] Ge 32:30; Ex 33:20; Jdg 13:22
6:23 [x] Da 10:19
6:24 [y] Ge 22:14 [z] Jdg 8:32
6:25 [a] Ex 34:13; Dt 7:5

[a] *19* That is, probably about 36 pounds or about 16 kilograms [b] *25* Or *Take a full-grown, mature bull from your father's herd* [c] *25* That is, a wooden symbol of the goddess Asherah; also in verses 26, 28 and 30 [d] *26* Or *build with layers of stone an* [e] *26* Or *full-grown*; also in verse 28

6:14 Am I not sending you? God persists in commissioning Gideon (cf. Exod 3:7–10).
6:17 Gideon's lack of faith is characterized by a need for signs.
6:19 As Manoah later does (13:15–23), Gideon attempts to detain God's emissary with an offering. The offering is not in accordance with any Levitical sacrifice. Based on the nature and size of the offering, it appears that Gideon is preparing a meal for a god.
6:21 In spite of Gideon's motives, the Lord accepts the sacrifice with miraculous fire coming from the rock, an outcome Gideon did not expect. God's actions are not just concerned with Gideon but are centered on delivering Israel. **Fire.** A motif that recurs throughout the Gideon-Abimelek cycle (v. 26; 7:16,20; 9:15,20,49).
6:22 Gideon's conclusion that he will die because he saw the angel of the Lord mirrors Manoah's false conclusion (cf. 13:22).
6:23 Only God's declaration of "peace" (Hebrew *šālôm*) and that Gideon will not die can relieve this highly emotional and illogical conclusion (cf. Manoah's wife's words in 13:23).
6:24 built an altar. The first of two altars. **The LORD Is Peace.** Given the circumstances, the name is quite appropriate. **Peace.** Hebrew *šālôm*.
6:25–32 Gideon destroys his father's Baal altar and Asherah pole. Ironically, Gideon's own family worships major Canaanite deities. God's command is nothing more than the covenantal expectation, namely, the destruction of altars to false deities (see Deut 7:5; 12:3—both of which use the verb form of Gideon's name ["to cut down, hack"]). There must not be an altar to the Lord and an altar to Baal in the same place. "No one can serve two masters" (Matt 6:24).
6:25 Baal. See note on 2:11. **Asherah.** See note on 3:7.

6:28 [b]1Ki 16:32
6:32 [c]Jdg 7:1; 8:29,35; 1Sa 12:11
6:33 [d]ver 3 [e]Jos 17:16
6:34 [f]Jdg 3:10; 1Ch 12:18; 2Ch 24:20 [g]Jdg 3:27
6:35 [h]Jdg 4:6
6:36 [i]ver 14
6:37 [j]Ex 4:3-7 [k]Ge 24:14
6:39 [l]Ge 18:32
7:1 [m]Jdg 6:32 [n]Ge 12:6
7:2 [o]Dt 8:17; 2Co 4:7
7:3 [p]Dt 20:8
7:4 [q]1Sa 14:6

[28]In the morning when the people of the town got up, there was Baal's altar,[b] demolished, with the Asherah pole beside it cut down and the second bull sacrificed on the newly built altar!
[29]They asked each other, "Who did this?"

When they carefully investigated, they were told, "Gideon son of Joash did it."

[30]The people of the town demanded of Joash, "Bring out your son. He must die, because he has broken down Baal's altar and cut down the Asherah pole beside it."

[31]But Joash replied to the hostile crowd around him, "Are you going to plead Baal's cause? Are you trying to save him? Whoever fights for him shall be put to death by morning! If Baal really is a god, he can defend himself when someone breaks down his altar." [32]So because Gideon broke down Baal's altar, they gave him the name Jerub-Baal[a][c] that day, saying, "Let Baal contend with him."

[33]Now all the Midianites, Amalekites and other eastern peoples[d] joined forces and crossed over the Jordan and camped in the Valley of Jezreel.[e] [34]Then the Spirit of the LORD came on[f] Gideon, and he blew a trumpet,[g] summoning the Abiezrites to follow him. [35]He sent messengers throughout Manasseh, calling them to arms, and also into Asher, Zebulun and Naphtali,[h] so that they too went up to meet them.

[36]Gideon said to God, "If you will save[i] Israel by my hand as you have promised— [37]look, I will place a wool fleece on the threshing floor.[j] If there is dew only on the fleece and all the ground is dry, then I will know[k] that you will save Israel by my hand, as you said." [38]And that is what happened. Gideon rose early the next day; he squeezed the fleece and wrung out the dew—a bowlful of water.

[39]Then Gideon said to God, "Do not be angry with me. Let me make just one more request.[l] Allow me one more test with the fleece, but this time make the fleece dry and let the ground be covered with dew."
[40]That night God did so. Only the fleece was dry; all the ground was covered with dew.

Gideon Defeats the Midianites

7 Early in the morning, Jerub-Baal[m] (that is, Gideon) and all his men camped at the spring of Harod. The camp of Midian was north of them in the valley near the hill of Moreh.[n] [2]The LORD said to Gideon, "You have too many men. I cannot deliver Midian into their hands, or Israel would boast against me, 'My own strength[o] has saved me.' [3]Now announce to the army, 'Anyone who trembles with fear may turn back and leave Mount Gilead.[p]' " So twenty-two thousand men left, while ten thousand remained.

[4]But the LORD said to Gideon, "There are still too many[q] men. Take them down to the water, and I will thin them out for you there. If I say, 'This one shall go with you,' he shall go; but if I say, 'This one shall not go with you,' he shall not go."

[5]So Gideon took the men down to the water. There the LORD told him, "Separate those who lap the water with their tongues as a dog laps from those who kneel down to drink." [6]Three hundred of them drank from cupped hands, lapping like dogs. All the rest got down on their knees to drink.

[a] 32 *Jerub-Baal* probably means *let Baal contend.*

6:30 The Israelites were so disloyal to God's covenant that they were willing to kill a fellow Israelite for the cause of Baal. Contrast Deut 13:6–10, where unfaithful Israelites were to be put to death.

6:32 Jerub-Baal. See NIV text note. Ironically, judge Gideon, the son of apostate Joash, wears this Baal-name with increasing frequency in chs. 7–8.

6:33—7:18 *Gideon's Struggle With Belief in God's Promise.* God's promise and Gideon's lack of faith are the crucial matters of tension in this section.

6:33–40 Gideon mobilizes his troops, but he seeks more reassuring signs through the fleece incidents.

6:34 came on. May also be translated "clothed." The wording is ironic because Gideon later made a piece of a clothing (a golden ephod) that Israel worshiped (8:27). This is not a comment on Gideon's spirituality; rather, the Spirit of the Lord empowers Gideon to deliver Israel.

6:36–40 Although God promised to save Israel through Gideon, Gideon is unwilling to take God at his word (i.e., have faith); instead, Gideon must have tangible signs in order to believe. The two signs involving the fleece that Gideon seeks are utterly unnecessary and speak to his unbelief. Ironically, Gideon is "clothed" by the Spirit (see note on v. 34) but must have tangible signs that involve a piece of clothing (a fleece). Gideon prefaces the request for signs by saying, "If you will save Israel by my hand as you have promised." Gideon is the first person in the Bible to request a sign from God. Normally, God initiates signs, and he does so not by request but by his design. Since God said he would save Israel, why does he perform the requested signs? God performed the signs with the fleece because he intended to save Israel; he will not let Gideon's unbelief derail his plan. No character in the book receives more divine assurance than Gideon, yet none displays more doubt.

7:1–8 Gideon wanted two signs; now God doubly reduces Gideon's force: (1) God tells Gideon to encourage the fearful Israelites to leave (vv. 2–3; cf. Deut 20:8), and (2) God tells Gideon to arbitrarily select men according to how they drink water (vv. 4–8). This is hardly a practical way to determine who should remain (it has not been practiced by any army throughout history). Only 300 men are left. The main point in the reductions is to reduce the possibility of ascribing the victory over Midian to human prowess (v. 2).

7:1 spring of Harod. At the foot of Mount Gilboa. **hill of Moreh.** A mountain to the north of Mount Gilboa in the Jezreel Valley.

7The LORD said to Gideon, "With the three hundred men that lapped I will save you and give the Midianites into your hands. Let all the others go home."[r] 8So Gideon sent the rest of the Israelites home but kept the three hundred, who took over the provisions and trumpets of the others.

Now the camp of Midian lay below him in the valley. 9During that night the LORD said to Gideon, "Get up, go down against the camp, because I am going to give it into your hands.[s] 10If you are afraid to attack, go down to the camp with your servant Purah 11and listen to what they are saying. Afterward, you will be encouraged to attack the camp." So he and Purah his servant went down to the outposts of the camp. 12The Midianites, the Amalekites[t] and all the other eastern peoples had settled in the valley, thick as locusts.[u] Their camels[v] could no more be counted than the sand on the seashore.[w]

13Gideon arrived just as a man was telling a friend his dream. "I had a dream," he was saying. "A round loaf of barley bread came tumbling into the Midianite camp. It struck the tent with such force that the tent overturned and collapsed."

14His friend responded, "This can be nothing other than the sword of Gideon son of Joash, the Israelite. God has given the Midianites and the whole camp into his hands."

15When Gideon heard the dream and its interpretation, he bowed down and worshiped.[x] He returned to the camp of Israel and called out, "Get up! The LORD has given the Midianite camp into your hands." 16Dividing the three hundred men[y] into three companies,[z] he placed trumpets and empty jars in the hands of all of them, with torches inside.

17"Watch me," he told them. "Follow my lead. When I get to the edge of the camp, do exactly as I do. 18When I and all who are with me blow our trumpets,[a] then from all around the camp blow yours and shout, 'For the LORD and for Gideon.' "

19Gideon and the hundred men with him reached the edge of the camp at the beginning of the middle watch, just after they had changed the guard. They blew their trumpets and broke the jars that were in their hands. 20The three companies blew the trumpets and smashed the jars. Grasping the torches in their left hands and holding in their right hands the trumpets they were to blow, they shouted, "A sword[b] for the LORD and for Gideon!" 21While each man held his position around the camp, all the Midianites ran, crying out as they fled.[c]

22When the three hundred trumpets sounded,[d] the LORD caused the men throughout the camp to turn on each other[e] with their swords. The army fled to Beth Shittah toward Zererah as far as the border of Abel Meholah[f] near Tabbath. 23Israelites from Naphtali, Asher and all Manasseh were called out,[g] and they pursued the Midianites. 24Gideon sent messengers throughout the hill country of Ephraim, saying, "Come down against the Midianites and seize the waters of the Jordan[h] ahead of them as far as Beth Barah."

So all the men of Ephraim were called out and they seized the waters of the Jordan as far as Beth Barah. 25They also captured two of the Midianite leaders, Oreb and Zeeb[i]. They killed Oreb at the rock of Oreb,[j] and Zeeb at the winepress of Zeeb. They pursued the Midianites and brought the heads of Oreb and Zeeb to Gideon, who was by the Jordan.[k]

Zebah and Zalmunna

8 Now the Ephraimites asked Gideon, "Why have you treated us like this? Why didn't you call us when you went to fight Midian?"[l] And they challenged him vigorously.[m]

2But he answered them, "What have I accomplished compared to you? Aren't the gleanings of

7:7 [r] 1Sa 14:6
7:9 [s] Jos 2:24; 10:8; 11:6
7:12 [t] Jdg 8:10 [u] Jdg 6:5 [v] Jer 49:29 [w] Jos 11:4
7:15 [x] 1Sa 15:31
7:16 [y] Ge 14:15 [z] 2Sa 18:2
7:18 [a] Jdg 3:27
7:20 [b] ver 14
7:21 [c] 2Ki 7:7
7:22 [d] Jos 6:20 [e] 1Sa 14:20; 2Ch 20:23 [f] 1Ki 4:12; 19:16
7:23 [g] Jdg 6:35
7:24 [h] Jdg 3:28
7:25 [i] Jdg 8:3; Ps 83:11 [j] Isa 10:26 [k] Jdg 8:4
8:1 [l] Jdg 12:1 [m] 2Sa 19:41

7:9–18 Gideon goes down to the enemy camp and overhears a Midianite relating a dream to a friend, who interprets it. Nothing in the dream necessarily points to the interpretation that is given, but the timing (i.e., the arrival just at the point to overhear the conversation), the dream itself, and its interpretation are quite extraordinary. Small wonder that Gideon worships the Lord. Gideon mobilizes his force of 300 for a surprise attack against the Midianites, fully confident in God's promise.

7:18 For the LORD and for Gideon. Gideon usurps God's glory (v. 2). By using a well-known form ("for god X and for king Y"), he lays the foundation for the offer in 8:22.

7:19—8:21 *God Delivers Israel From the Midianites.* There are two units in this section: 7:19—8:3 and 8:4–21. In each, a battle is fought and a pair of Midianite rulers is executed.

7:19—8:3 *Battle West of the Jordan.* A battle is fought west of the Jordan; two Midianite leaders are captured and executed.

7:19–25 Gideon's forces surprise the Midianites. The elimination of two Midianite leaders consolidates Gideon's victory.

7:24 hill country of Ephraim. The Ephraimites seize the fords of the Jordan, particularly at Beth Barah (location uncertain). Cf. 3:27–29.

7:25 Oreb. He is killed at a rock (cf. 6:20). **Zeeb.** He is killed at a winepress (cf. 6:11).

8:1–3 Gideon diplomatically handles the provocations of the Ephraimites. Contrast Jephthah's lack of diplomacy and the Ephraimite defeat

8:3 [n] Jdg 7:25; Pr 15:1
8:4 [o] Jdg 7:25
8:5 [p] Ge 33:17 [q] Ps 83:11
8:6 [r] 1Sa 25:11 [s] ver 15
8:7 [t] Jdg 7:15
8:8 [u] Ge 32:30; 1Ki 12:25
8:9 [v] ver 17
8:10 [w] Jdg 6:5; 7:12; Isa 9:4
8:11 [x] Nu 32:42 [y] Nu 32:35
8:15 [z] ver 6
8:16 [a] ver 7
8:17 [b] ver 9
8:18 [c] Jos 19:22; Jdg 4:6
8:21 [d] ver 26; Ps 83:11

Ephraim's grapes better than the full grape harvest of Abiezer? 3 God gave Oreb and Zeeb,[n] the Midianite
leaders, into your hands. What was I able to do compared to you?" At this, their resentment against
him subsided.
4 Gideon and his three hundred men, exhausted yet keeping up the pursuit, came to the Jordan[o] and
crossed it. 5 He said to the men of Sukkoth,[p] "Give my troops some bread; they are worn out, and I am
still pursuing Zebah and Zalmunna,[q] the kings of Midian."
6 But the officials of Sukkoth said, "Do you already have the hands of Zebah and Zalmunna in your
possession? Why should we give bread[r] to your troops?"[s]
7 Then Gideon replied, "Just for that, when the LORD has given Zebah and Zalmunna[t] into my hand,
I will tear your flesh with desert thorns and briers."
8 From there he went up to Peniel[a][u] and made the same request of them, but they answered as the
men of Sukkoth had. 9 So he said to the men of Peniel, "When I return in triumph, I will tear down
this tower."[v]
10 Now Zebah and Zalmunna were in Karkor with a force of about fifteen thousand men, all that
were left of the armies of the eastern peoples; a hundred and twenty thousand swordsmen had fallen.[w]
11 Gideon went up by the route of the nomads east of Nobah[x] and Jogbehah[y] and attacked the unsuspecting army. 12 Zebah and Zalmunna, the two kings of Midian, fled, but he pursued them and captured
them, routing their entire army.
13 Gideon son of Joash then returned from the battle by the Pass of Heres. 14 He caught a young
man of Sukkoth and questioned him, and the young man wrote down for him the names of the seventy-seven officials of Sukkoth, the elders of the town. 15 Then Gideon came and said to the men of
Sukkoth, "Here are Zebah and Zalmunna, about whom you taunted me by saying, 'Do you already
have the hands of Zebah and Zalmunna in your possession? Why should we give bread to your exhausted men?[z]' " 16 He took the elders of the town and taught the men of Sukkoth a lesson[a] by punishing them with desert thorns and briers. 17 He also pulled down the tower of Peniel and killed the
men of the town.[b]
18 Then he asked Zebah and Zalmunna, "What kind of men did you kill at Tabor?[c]"
"Men like you," they answered, "each one with the bearing of a prince."
19 Gideon replied, "Those were my brothers, the sons of my own mother. As surely as the LORD lives, if
you had spared their lives, I would not kill you." 20 Turning to Jether, his oldest son, he said, "Kill them!"
But Jether did not draw his sword, because he was only a boy and was afraid.
21 Zebah and Zalmunna said, "Come, do it yourself. 'As is the man, so is his strength.' " So Gideon
stepped forward and killed them, and took the ornaments[d] off their camels' necks.

[a] *8* Hebrew *Penuel,* a variant of *Peniel;* also in verses 9 and 17

---

in 12:1–6. Gideon successfully averts the threat of civil war by quelling the intertribal jealousies of the Ephraimites. His reply implies that they have accomplished much more than he and the other Israelites (v. 2). While this satisfies the Ephraimite contention, it is a psychological rather than a theological argument. He does not mention Yahweh's call of him as the leader to deliver Israel.

8:4–21 *Pursuit and Battle East of the Jordan.* There are no indications of the Lord's involvement in this second battle. Gideon is acting on his own. There is no participation by Yahweh and no reference to him, except by Gideon's own proclamation (vv. 7,19).

8:4–9 The cities of Sukkoth and Peniel, fearing Midianite reprisals, refuse to help Gideon. Gideon threatens them with his own severe punishment.

8:5 Sukkoth. A Transjordanian city on the Jabbok River. **Zebah and Zalmunna.** These names are likely pejorative names created from the real names as a literary device (see note on 3:8 [Cushan-Rishathaim]). Zebah means "sacrifice" or "offering," and Zalmunna sounds like "protection refused." Ironically, the Israelites fear these Midianite leaders who have, in fact, been oppressed by them. If the Israelites had feared God and walked with him, they would not have been oppressed or had a reason to fear now.

8:6 hands. One of the ways of counting the dead was to cut off the hands.

8:7 tear your flesh with desert thorns and briers. Threshing the skin, a terrible torture used by the ancient Assyrians. The victims die a gruesome death. Such action is strongly condemned in Amos 1:3.

8:8 Peniel. Located farther up the Jabbok River from Sukkoth. It was the place where Jacob wrestled God (Gen 32:30–31).

8:10–12 The second battle against the Midianites.

8:10 Karkor. Located about 113 miles (180 kilometers) southeast of Peniel in the Wadi Sirân.

8:13–21 Gideon takes reprisals against Sukkoth and Peniel, torturing and killing fellow Israelites for refusing to support his army. Gideon is the first judge to turn the sword against his fellow Israelites. This anticipates actions by Abimelek (9:46–49) and Jephthah (12:1–6).

8:14 wrote. This youth is apparently capable of writing all the names of the 77 chiefs and elders of Sukkoth—an important evidence of literacy in ancient Israel.

8:16 punishing them with desert thorns and briers. See note on v. 7.

8:18–19 Gideon reveals his motive: personal revenge for the death of his brothers. Gideon foreshadows Samson, who is motivated by personal revenge.

Gideon's Ephod

22The Israelites said to Gideon, "Rule over us — you, your son and your grandson — because you have saved us from the hand of Midian."

23But Gideon told them, "I will not rule over you, nor will my son rule over you. The LORD will rule[e] over you." 24And he said, "I do have one request, that each of you give me an earring from your share of the plunder." (It was the custom of the Ishmaelites[f] to wear gold earrings.)

25They answered, "We'll be glad to give them." So they spread out a garment, and each of them threw a ring from his plunder onto it. 26The weight of the gold rings he asked for came to seventeen hundred shekels,[a] not counting the ornaments, the pendants and the purple garments worn by the kings of Midian or the chains that were on their camels' necks. 27Gideon made the gold into an ephod,[g] which he placed in Ophrah, his town. All Israel prostituted themselves by worshiping it there, and it became a snare[h] to Gideon and his family.

Gideon's Death

28Thus Midian was subdued before the Israelites and did not raise its head again. During Gideon's lifetime, the land had peace[i] forty years.

29Jerub-Baal[j] son of Joash went back home to live. 30He had seventy sons[k] of his own, for he had many wives. 31His concubine, who lived in Shechem, also bore him a son, whom he named Abimelek.[l] 32Gideon son of Joash died at a good old age[m] and was buried in the tomb of his father Joash in Ophrah of the Abiezrites.

33No sooner had Gideon died than the Israelites again prostituted themselves to the Baals.[n] They set up Baal Berith[o] as their god[p] 34and did not remember[q] the LORD their God, who had rescued them from the hands of all their enemies on every side. 35They also failed to show any loyalty to the family of Jerub-Baal (that is, Gideon) in spite of all the good things he had done for them.[r]

a 26 That is, about 43 pounds or about 20 kilograms

8:23 [e] Ex 16:8; 1Sa 8:7; 10:19; 12:12
8:24 [f] Ge 25:13
8:27 [g] Jdg 17:5; 18:14 [h] Dt 7:16; Ps 106:39
8:28 [i] Jdg 5:31
8:29 [j] Jdg 7:1
8:30 [k] Jdg 9:2,5,18,24
8:31 [l] Jdg 9:1
8:32 [m] Ge 25:8
8:33 [n] Jdg 2:11,13,19 [o] Jdg 9:4 [p] Jdg 9:27,46
8:34 [q] Jdg 3:7; Dt 4:9; Ps 78:11,42
8:35 [r] Jdg 9:16

8:22–32 *Conclusion to Gideon's Life After the Victory.* This section narrates the events during the time between Gideon's victories and his death.

8:22–23 Gideon's refusal reflects the belief that only the Lord was to rule over Israel, but Gideon does not correct their error in attributing Israel's victory over the Midianites to the Lord. Theologically, Gideon is accurate: the Lord should rule over Israel (see Introduction: Theology). Unfortunately, Gideon's subsequent actions reveal his hypocrisy, since he is seduced by the lures of being king (vv. 23–32). Israel's disobedience to the covenant is a constant attempt to undermine God's kingship, and Gideon's actions speak louder than his words. By not correcting the Israelites' mistake regarding who saved them, Gideon allows the glory for the victory to accrue to him.

8:24 Ishmaelites. Used as a parallel designation for "the Midianites, Amalekites and other eastern peoples" (v. 10; 6:3,33; 7:12; cf. Gen 37:25–36; 39:1).

8:26 The weight of gold was about 43 pounds (20 kilograms), not including the kings' materials.

8:27 ephod. A garment worn primarily by the high priest (Exod 28:6–14; 39:2–7) but later also by King David (2 Sam 6:14; 1 Chr 15:27). It was sometimes associated with divining the will of God (1 Sam 23:9–10; 30:7–8; Hos 3:4). Archaeology has shown that this is a garment that also adorned male idols; therefore, it is likely used here as a euphemism for an idol, since all Israel "prostituted themselves" to it (i.e., worshiped it). Due to the amount of gold used, the "ephod" figuratively represents not only the garment that clothed a sacred image but also the image over which the garment was draped. Since Gideon was neither a priest nor a king, he had no business making an ephod. It was placed in Ophrah, his hometown, where his father's Baal altar and sacred ("Asherah") pole had been located. **All Israel prostituted themselves.** As the Israelites had prostituted themselves to the deity Baal (v. 33; 2:17), they prostituted themselves to the ephod made by Gideon. They worshiped an idol made by their own judge. **and it became a snare to Gideon and his family.** Tragically, Gideon enticed himself and his family away from the Lord with this idol (cf. Deut 12:30). Later, Micah also made an ephod and an image (17:5), which the Danites stole (18:14–20).

8:29–32 Gideon's private life contradicts his confession of the Lord's kingship. The accumulation of wives was common among ancient Near Eastern monarchs, but it is a specific violation of Deut 17:16–17. Gideon had to have many wives in order to have 70 sons (see note on v. 30). In order to support all these wives and sons, Gideon had to have the resources of a king.

8:30 seventy. The number may have been used as symbolic of an ideal royal household. Ahab had 70 sons (2 Kgs 10:1–11). In the case of Gideon, the number plays an actual role in the story (see 9:5). Gideon named one of his sons Abimelek ("my [divine] father is king"), though the implication of the name is borne out in the following narrative.

8:33—9:57 *The Abimelek Narrative.* This sequel resolves numerous issues of the Gideon story. Gideon's disinherited son seizes the kingship that Gideon publicly rejected but in fact, lived out. The story develops the theme of retribution: God causes the evil that Abimelek and the men of Shechem did to redound on their own heads (9:56–57). The issues of covenant and kingship are played out in this story. While the Lord should be Israel's king and Israel should be faithful to his covenant, on account of Israel's unfaithfulness to the covenant, Abimelek was Israel's king (9:6,22).

8:33–35 *The Prologue to the Story.* This section provides a context for understanding the complex story of Abimelek.

8:33 Baal-Berith. Means "lord of the covenant"; probably an epithet for the god El-Berith (9:46). Covenant faithfulness was the problem at the beginning of the cycle (cf. 6:7–10) and is still the problem after Gideon's death. Gideon's ephod prepared the Israelites for a rapid return to worshiping Baal. Ironically, Yahweh, not Baal, is the true Lord of the covenant.

9:1 [s]Jdg 8:31
9:2 [t]Ge 29:14; Jdg 8:30
9:4 [u]Jdg 8:33 [v]Jdg 11:3; 2Ch 13:7
9:5 [w]ver 2; Jdg 8:30 [x]2Ki 11:2
9:7 [y]Dt 11:29; 27:12; Jn 4:20
9:13 [z]Ecc 2:3
9:15 [a]Isa 30:2 [b]ver 20 [c]Isa 2:13
9:18 [d]ver 5-6; Jdg 8:30
9:20 [e]ver 15
9:23 [f]1Sa 16:14,23; 18:10; 1Ki 22:22; Isa 19:14; 33:1

Abimelek

9 Abimelek[s] son of Jerub-Baal went to his mother's brothers in Shechem and said to them and to all
his mother's clan, 2 "Ask all the citizens of Shechem, 'Which is better for you: to have all seventy of
Jerub-Baal's sons rule over you, or just one man?' Remember, I am your flesh and blood.[t]"
3 When the brothers repeated all this to the citizens of Shechem, they were inclined to follow Abimelek, for they said, "He is related to us." 4 They gave him seventy shekels[a] of silver from the temple of
Baal-Berith,[u] and Abimelek used it to hire reckless scoundrels,[v] who became his followers. 5 He went to
his father's home in Ophrah and on one stone murdered his seventy brothers,[w] the sons of Jerub-Baal.
But Jotham, the youngest son of Jerub-Baal, escaped by hiding.[x] 6 Then all the citizens of Shechem and
Beth Millo gathered beside the great tree at the pillar in Shechem to crown Abimelek king.
7 When Jotham was told about this, he climbed up on the top of Mount Gerizim[y] and shouted to them,
"Listen to me, citizens of Shechem, so that God may listen to you. 8 One day the trees went out to anoint
a king for themselves. They said to the olive tree, 'Be our king.'
9 "But the olive tree answered, 'Should I give up my oil, by which both gods and humans are honored,
to hold sway over the trees?'
10 "Next, the trees said to the fig tree, 'Come and be our king.'
11 "But the fig tree replied, 'Should I give up my fruit, so good and sweet, to hold sway over the trees?'
12 "Then the trees said to the vine, 'Come and be our king.'
13 "But the vine answered, 'Should I give up my wine,[z] which cheers both gods and humans, to hold
sway over the trees?'
14 "Finally all the trees said to the thornbush, 'Come and be our king.'
15 "The thornbush said to the trees, 'If you really want to anoint me king over you, come and take
refuge in my shade;[a] but if not, then let fire come out[b] of the thornbush and consume the cedars of
Lebanon!'[c]
16 "Have you acted honorably and in good faith by making Abimelek king? Have you been fair to
Jerub-Baal and his family? Have you treated him as he deserves? 17 Remember that my father fought for
you and risked his life to rescue you from the hand of Midian. 18 But today you have revolted against my
father's family. You have murdered his seventy sons[d] on a single stone and have made Abimelek, the son
of his female slave, king over the citizens of Shechem because he is related to you. 19 So have you acted
honorably and in good faith toward Jerub-Baal and his family today? If you have, may Abimelek be
your joy, and may you be his, too! 20 But if you have not, let fire come out[e] from Abimelek and consume
you, the citizens of Shechem and Beth Millo, and let fire come out from you, the citizens of Shechem
and Beth Millo, and consume Abimelek!"
21 Then Jotham fled, escaping to Beer, and he lived there because he was afraid of his brother
Abimelek.
22 After Abimelek had governed Israel three years, 23 God stirred up animosity[f] between Abimelek

[a] *4* That is, about 1 3/4 pounds or about 800 grams

9:1–24 *Abimelek's Rise.* The section narrates Abimelek's treacherous rise to kingship.

9:1–6 *Elimination of Rivals.* Abimelek eliminated all potential rivals and took the throne of Shechem (ironically, where the Israelite covenant assembly took place, cf. Josh 24:1–27). Excavations at Shechem have revealed a sacred area that the excavators have identified with the temple of Baal-Berith.

9:2 one man. Ironically, Abimelek's argument that it is better to have "one man" rule over them will be squashed by one woman and her upper millstone (v. 53).

9:4 seventy. Corresponds to the number of Gideon's 70 sons (8:30). **seventy shekels.** See NIV text note. **reckless scoundrels.** A vivid moral assessment (cf. 11:3).

9:5 The murders take place "on one stone." A single stone will kill Abimelek (v. 53). Only Jotham (meaning "Yahweh is blameless/has integrity") escapes. Ironically, in this passage rife with evil and treachery, the Lord is in fact blameless, maintaining his integrity.

9:6 great tree at the pillar. Cf. Josh 24:26.

9:7–21 *Jotham's Fable and Curse.* Jotham's four-part plant fable satirizes and rebukes the kingship of his half brother Abimelek, as well as the people of Shechem for their treachery.

9:7–15 *The Fable.* The trees (the Shechemites) go out to anoint a king over themselves, approaching four plants (the first three of which have significant agricultural value). Each is offered the kingship, but the first three — the olive tree (vv. 8–9), the fig tree (vv. 10–11), and the vine (vv. 12–13) — decline the offer. Only the thornbush, a useless plant (Abimelek), accepts the trees' (Shechemites') offer with an absurd condition: come and take refuge in my shade (the tall trees cannot possibly get under the tiny leaves of the thornbush).

9:7 Mount Gerizim. Just south of Shechem, opposite Mount Ebal.

9:16–21 *The Fable Applied.* Jotham applies the fable and flees.

9:22–24 *The Narrator's Assessment of God's Involvement.* God takes action against Abimelek to revenge the murder of Jerub-Baal's sons.

and the citizens of Shechem so that they acted treacherously against Abimelek. 24 God did this in order that the crime against Jerub-Baal's seventy sons, the shedding[g] of their blood, might be avenged[h] on their brother Abimelek and on the citizens of Shechem, who had helped him[i] murder his brothers. 25 In opposition to him these citizens of Shechem set men on the hilltops to ambush and rob everyone who passed by, and this was reported to Abimelek.

26 Now Gaal son of Ebed moved with his clan into Shechem, and its citizens put their confidence in him. 27 After they had gone out into the fields and gathered the grapes and trodden[j] them, they held a festival in the temple of their god.[k] While they were eating and drinking, they cursed Abimelek. 28 Then Gaal son of Ebed said, "Who[l] is Abimelek, and why should we Shechemites be subject to him? Isn't he Jerub-Baal's son, and isn't Zebul his deputy? Serve the family of Hamor,[m] Shechem's father! Why should we serve Abimelek? 29 If only this people were under my command![n] Then I would get rid of him. I would say to Abimelek, 'Call out your whole army!'"[a]

30 When Zebul the governor of the city heard what Gaal son of Ebed said, he was very angry. 31 Under cover he sent messengers to Abimelek, saying, "Gaal son of Ebed and his clan have come to Shechem and are stirring up the city against you. 32 Now then, during the night you and your men should come and lie in wait[o] in the fields. 33 In the morning at sunrise, advance against the city. When Gaal and his men come out against you, seize the opportunity to attack them.[p]"

34 So Abimelek and all his troops set out by night and took up concealed positions near Shechem in four companies. 35 Now Gaal son of Ebed had gone out and was standing at the entrance of the city gate just as Abimelek and his troops came out from their hiding place.[q]

36 When Gaal saw them, he said to Zebul, "Look, people are coming down from the tops of the mountains!"

Zebul replied, "You mistake the shadows of the mountains for men."

37 But Gaal spoke up again: "Look, people are coming down from the central hill,[b] and a company is coming from the direction of the diviners' tree."

38 Then Zebul said to him, "Where is your big talk now, you who said, 'Who is Abimelek that we should be subject to him?' Aren't these the men you ridiculed?[r] Go out and fight them!"

39 So Gaal led out[c] the citizens of Shechem and fought Abimelek. 40 Abimelek chased him all the way to the entrance of the gate, and many were killed as they fled. 41 Then Abimelek stayed in Arumah, and Zebul drove Gaal and his clan out of Shechem.

42 The next day the people of Shechem went out to the fields, and this was reported to Abimelek. 43 So he took his men, divided them into three companies[s] and set an ambush in the fields. When he saw the people coming out of the city, he rose to attack them. 44 Abimelek and the companies with him rushed forward to a position at the entrance of the city gate. Then two companies attacked those in the fields and struck them down. 45 All that day Abimelek pressed his attack against the city until he had captured it and killed its people. Then he destroyed the city[t] and scattered salt[u] over it.

46 On hearing this, the citizens in the tower of Shechem went into the stronghold of the temple[v] of El-Berith. 47 When Abimelek heard that they had assembled there, 48 he and all his men went up Mount Zalmon.[w] He took an ax and cut off some branches, which he lifted to his shoulders. He ordered the men with him, "Quick! Do what you have seen me do!" 49 So all the men cut branches and followed Abimelek. They piled them against the stronghold and set it on fire with the people still inside. So all the people in the tower of Shechem, about a thousand men and women, also died.

50 Next Abimelek went to Thebez[x] and besieged it and captured it. 51 Inside the city, however, was a strong tower, to which all the men and women—all the people of the city—had fled. They had locked

9:24 [g] Nu 35:33; 1Ki 2:32 [h] ver 56-57 [i] Dt 27:25
9:27 [j] Am 9:13 [k] Jdg 8:33
9:28 [l] 1Sa 25:10; 1Ki 12:16 [m] Ge 34:2,6
9:29 [n] 2Sa 15:4
9:32 [o] Jos 8:2
9:33 [p] 1Sa 10:7
9:35 [q] Ps 32:7; Jer 49:10
9:38 [r] ver 28-29
9:43 [s] Jdg 7:16
9:45 [t] ver 20; 2Ki 3:25 [u] Dt 29:23
9:46 [v] Jdg 8:33
9:48 [w] Ps 68:14
9:50 [x] 2Sa 11:21

[a] *29* Septuagint; Hebrew *him." Then he said to Abimelek, "Call out your whole army!"* [b] *37* The Hebrew for this phrase means *the navel of the earth.* [c] *39* Or *Gaal went out in the sight of*

9:24 Important theologically, it is God himself who begins the process of avenging the wrongs done by both Abimelek and the Shechemites. In this instance, God will use each to judge the other.

9:25–57 *Abimelek's Decline.* While Abimelek made himself king, God brings about his fall.

9:25–41 This section narrates the treachery against Abimelek. The Shechemites turn their loyalties to Gaal, another raw opportunist. But with Abimelek's military action, Gaal flees.

9:42–55 Abimelek carries out three acts of repression: he slaughters the Shechemites (vv. 42–45); he destroys the tower of Shechem (vv. 46–49); and he attacks the town of Thebez (vv. 50–52). These acts are like his father's against Sukkoth and Peniel (8:14–17).

9:53 [y] 2Sa 11:21
9:54 [z] 1Sa 31:4; 2Sa 1:9
9:57 [a] ver 20
10:1 [b] Ge 30:18
[c] Ge 46:13
[d] Jdg 2:16; 6:14
10:4 [e] Nu 32:41
10:6 [f] Jdg 2:11
[g] Jdg 2:13 [h] Jdg 2:12
[i] Dt 32:15
10:7 [j] Dt 31:17
[k] Dt 32:30; Jdg 2:14;
1Sa 12:9
10:10 [l] 1Sa 12:10
10:11 [m] Ex 14:30
[n] Nu 21:21; Jdg 3:13
[o] Jdg 3:31

themselves in and climbed up on the tower roof. 52 Abimelek went to the tower and attacked it. But as
he approached the entrance to the tower to set it on fire, 53 a woman dropped an upper millstone on
his head and cracked his skull.[y]

54 Hurriedly he called to his armor-bearer, "Draw your sword and kill me,[z] so that they can't say,
'A woman killed him.'" So his servant ran him through, and he died. 55 When the Israelites saw that
Abimelek was dead, they went home.

56 Thus God repaid the wickedness that Abimelek had done to his father by murdering his seventy
brothers. 57 God also made the people of Shechem pay for all their wickedness.[a] The curse of Jotham
son of Jerub-Baal came on them.

Tola

10 After the time of Abimelek, a man of Issachar[b] named Tola son of Puah,[c] the son of Dodo, rose
to save[d] Israel. He lived in Shamir, in the hill country of Ephraim. 2 He led[a] Israel twenty-three
years; then he died, and was buried in Shamir.

Jair

3 He was followed by Jair of Gilead, who led Israel twenty-two years. 4 He had thirty sons, who rode
thirty donkeys. They controlled thirty towns in Gilead, which to this day are called Havvoth Jair.[b][e]
5 When Jair died, he was buried in Kamon.

Jephthah

6 Again the Israelites did evil in the eyes of the LORD.[f] They served the Baals and the Ashtoreths,[g] and
the gods of Aram, the gods of Sidon, the gods of Moab, the gods of the Ammonites and the gods of the
Philistines.[h] And because the Israelites forsook the LORD[i] and no longer served him, 7 he became angry[j]
with them. He sold them[k] into the hands of the Philistines and the Ammonites, 8 who that year shattered
and crushed them. For eighteen years they oppressed all the Israelites on the east side of the Jordan in
Gilead, the land of the Amorites. 9 The Ammonites also crossed the Jordan to fight against Judah, Benjamin and Ephraim; Israel was in great distress. 10 Then the Israelites cried out to the LORD, "We have
sinned against you, forsaking our God and serving the Baals."[l]

11 The LORD replied, "When the Egyptians,[m] the Amorites, the Ammonites,[n] the Philistines,[o] 12 the Si-

[a] 2 Traditionally *judged*; also in verse 3 [b] 4 Or *called the settlements of Jair*

9:53–55 There is irony in that Abimelek is killed by a woman with a single upper millstone, for he had slaughtered his 70 half brothers, except for Jotham, on a single stone in order to secure his throne (cf. the "one stone" in v. 5).

9:53 upper. The smaller upper stone of a hand mill or saddle quern. The grain was placed on the bottom larger stone; the grinder knelt in front of the quern and moved the upper millstone back and forth, grinding the grain. Such an upper millstone made an ideal projectile (being ca. 12–15 pounds [5.5–6.8 kilograms]).

9:54 Abimelek's desire not to suffer the dishonor of being killed by a woman was not met (cf. 2 Sam 11:21).

9:56–57 It was God who brought retribution on Abimelek and the Shechemites. The Lord works vindication and justice (Pss 7:6; 9:16; 72:2; 99:4; 103:6; Isa 5:16).

10:1–2 *Minor Judge: Tola.* Tola is the second of the six minor judges. He, like the first minor judge (Shamgar, 3:31), saves Israel. Only Othniel, Shamgar, Deborah, and Tola are specifically described by the writer of the book as "saving" Israel, though in this case, the oppressor remains anonymous.

10:1 Tola ... Puah. Clan names in 1 Chr 7:1.

10:3–5 *Minor Judge: Jair.* Jair is the third of the six minor judges. He was a powerful man. To have 30 sons required a harem, and these sons ruled over 30 towns. Syro-Palestinian monarchs often rode on donkeys (2 Sam 13:29; 18:9; 1 Kgs 1:33; Matt 21:5). Jair was clearly building a power base in the region. Both Jair (here) and Ibzan (12:8–10) are contrasted with Jephthah (10:6—12:7). Thus with only one child (and a daughter at that), Jephthah is sandwiched between Jair with his 30 sons and Ibzan with his 30 sons and 30 daughters.

10:4 Havvoth Jair. See NIV text note; located in the Transjordanian region.

10:6—12:7 *Major Judge Cycle: Jephthah.* The Transjordanian setting is unique in Judges. The story unfolds as a series of crises. Jephthah, the son of a prostitute, a social outcast, and the leader of a gang of criminals, was hired by the elders of Gilead, who acted without inquiring of the Lord. Though Jephthah saved Israel, he faced a personal tragedy because of his ignorance of God's word.

10:6–16 *Introduction: Israel Versus the Lord.* Israel's problems resulted from its infidelity toward the Lord.

10:6 This lists seven groups of deities. Israel is giving itself over to the worship of all the gods of the surrounding nations.

10:7 Philistines. See note on 13:1. **Ammonites.** A Transjordanian people identified as descendants of Lot (Gen 19:38).

10:10 We have sinned. This verbal acknowledgment leads to an act of repentance in v. 16, the only such act in the book.

10:11 God did not send a prophet as in 6:7–10; he rebuked Israel himself. The book does not narrate all seven of these oppressors, indicating the selective nature of the account, which is geared to the book's central message. It is reminiscent of the seven-member stereotypical list of nations in Deut 7:1 (cf. 3:5).

donians, the Amalekites and the Maonites[a] oppressed you[p] and you cried to me for help, did I not save you from their hands? 13But you have forsaken me and served other gods, so I will no longer save you. 14Go and cry out to the gods you have chosen. Let them save you when you are in trouble![q]"

15But the Israelites said to the LORD, "We have sinned. Do with us whatever you think best,[r] but please rescue us now." 16Then they got rid of the foreign gods among them and served the LORD.[s] And he could bear Israel's misery[t] no longer.[u]

17When the Ammonites were called to arms and camped in Gilead, the Israelites assembled and camped at Mizpah.[v] 18The leaders of the people of Gilead said to each other, "Whoever will take the lead in attacking the Ammonites will be head[w] over all who live in Gilead."

11 Jephthah[x] the Gileadite was a mighty warrior.[y] His father was Gilead; his mother was a prostitute. 2Gilead's wife also bore him sons, and when they were grown up, they drove Jephthah away. "You are not going to get any inheritance in our family," they said, "because you are the son of another woman." 3So Jephthah fled from his brothers and settled in the land of Tob,[z] where a gang of scoundrels[a] gathered around him and followed him.

4Some time later, when the Ammonites[b] were fighting against Israel, 5the elders of Gilead went to get Jephthah from the land of Tob. 6"Come," they said, "be our commander, so we can fight the Ammonites."

7Jephthah said to them, "Didn't you hate me and drive me from my father's house?[c] Why do you come to me now, when you're in trouble?"

8The elders of Gilead said to him, "Nevertheless, we are turning to you now; come with us to fight the Ammonites, and you will be head[d] over all of us who live in Gilead."

9Jephthah answered, "Suppose you take me back to fight the Ammonites and the LORD gives them to me — will I really be your head?"

10The elders of Gilead replied, "The LORD is our witness;[e] we will certainly do as you say." 11So Jephthah went with the elders of Gilead, and the people made him head and commander over them. And he repeated all his words before the LORD in Mizpah.[f]

12Then Jephthah sent messengers to the Ammonite king with the question: "What do you have against me that you have attacked my country?"

13The king of the Ammonites answered Jephthah's messengers, "When Israel came up out of Egypt, they took away my land from the Arnon to the Jabbok,[g] all the way to the Jordan. Now give it back peaceably."

14Jephthah sent back messengers to the Ammonite king, 15saying:

"This is what Jephthah says: Israel did not take the land of Moab[h] or the land of the Ammonites.[i] 16But when they came up out of Egypt, Israel went through the wilderness to the Red Sea[b][j] and on to Kadesh.[k] 17Then Israel sent messengers[l] to the king of Edom, saying, 'Give us permission to go through your country,'[m] but the king of Edom would not listen. They sent also to the king of Moab, and he refused.[n] So Israel stayed at Kadesh.

[a] *12* Hebrew; some Septuagint manuscripts *Midianites* [b] *16* Or *the Sea of Reeds*

10:12 [p] Ps 106:42
10:14 [q] Dt 32:37
10:15 [r] 1Sa 3:18; 2Sa 15:26
10:16 [s] Jos 24:23; Jer 18:8 [t] Isa 63:9 [u] Dt 32:36; Ps 106:44-45
10:17 [v] Ge 31:49; Jdg 11:29
10:18 [w] Jdg 11:8,9
11:1 [x] Heb 11:32 [y] Jdg 6:12
11:3 [z] 2Sa 10:6,8 [a] Jdg 9:4
11:4 [b] Jdg 10:9
11:7 [c] Ge 26:27
11:8 [d] Jdg 10:18
11:10 [e] Ge 31:50; Jer 42:5
11:11 [f] Jos 11:3; Jdg 10:17; 20:1; 1Sa 10:17
11:13 [g] Ge 32:22; Nu 21:24
11:15 [h] Dt 2:9 [i] Dt 2:19
11:16 [j] Nu 14:25; Dt 1:40 [k] Nu 20:1
11:17 [l] Nu 20:14 [m] Nu 20:18,21 [n] Jos 24:9

10:13 God's refusal to deliver Israel showed the degree of Israel's failures. This was a harbinger of the tragedy to come, since God was no longer swayed by a claim of repentance.

10:14 God uses sarcasm to get Israel's attention.

10:17—11:11 *The Ammonite Threat: The Elders' Choice of Jephthah.* The Israelites considered their problem a military one, so they chose an accomplished military leader. Because of Jephthah's previous experience with the Gileadites (having been disinherited and banished), he accepted their commission only on his terms. A ritual at Mizpah sealed the commission.

10:18 head. The leaders of Gilead declare that their "head" will be whoever takes the initiative to lead Gilead against the Ammonites (see note on v. 7).

11:1–3 This is a parenthetical paragraph about Jephthah's background: he is the son of a prostitute; he is a mighty warrior; he was disinherited by his half brothers; he settled in Tob; he led "a gang of scoundrels" (cf. 9:4 and note).

11:5 Gilead. The territory east of the Jordan River and west of the Ammonite border.

11:6 The elders of Gilead attempted to get Jephthah cheap, offering him only the position of "commander."

11:11 commander. Hebrew *qāṣîn*; apparently a lesser title and probably less permanent than the title "head" (Hebrew *rōʾš*, see note on 10:18). While the elders attempted to get Jephthah cheap, he held out for both titles, especially that of "head" or "chief." **Mizpah.** A "watchtower" located in Transjordan, not Benjamin. Their ritual ceremony uses the Lord's name, but the Lord is absent from the process of raising up Jephthah. Just using the divine name does not mean that God is in it (cf. 17:1–13).

11:12–28 *Jephthah Versus the Ammonite King.* Religious beliefs and historical precedents were the basis of the claims of Jephthah and the counterclaims of the king of Ammon.

11:17 See Num 20:14–21.

11:18 [o] Nu 21:4 [p] Dt 2:8 [q] Nu 21:13
11:19 [r] Nu 21:21-22; Dt 2:26-27
11:20 [s] Nu 21:23; Dt 2:32
11:22 [t] Dt 2:36
11:24 [u] Nu 21:29; Jos 3:10; 1Ki 11:7
11:25 [v] Nu 22:2 [w] Jos 24:9
11:26 [x] Nu 21:25
11:27 [y] Ge 18:25 [z] Ge 16:5; 31:53; 1Sa 24:12,15
11:29 [a] Nu 11:25; Jdg 3:10; 6:34; 14:6,19; 15:14; 1Sa 11:6; 16:13; Isa 11:2
11:30 [b] Ge 28:20
11:33 [c] Eze 27:17
11:34 [d] Ex 15:20; Jer 31:4
11:35 [e] Nu 30:2; Ecc 5:2,4,5
11:36 [f] Lk 1:38 [g] 2Sa 18:19

18 "Next they traveled through the wilderness, skirted the lands of Edom[o] and Moab, passed along the eastern side[p] of the country of Moab, and camped on the other side of the Arnon.[q] They did not enter the territory of Moab, for the Arnon was its border.

19 "Then Israel sent messengers to Sihon king of the Amorites, who ruled in Heshbon, and said to him, 'Let us pass through your country to our own place.'[r] 20 Sihon, however, did not trust Israel[a] to pass through his territory. He mustered all his troops and encamped at Jahaz and fought with Israel.[s]

21 "Then the LORD, the God of Israel, gave Sihon and his whole army into Israel's hands, and they defeated them. Israel took over all the land of the Amorites who lived in that country, 22 capturing all of it from the Arnon to the Jabbok and from the desert to the Jordan.[t]

23 "Now since the LORD, the God of Israel, has driven the Amorites out before his people Israel, what right have you to take it over? 24 Will you not take what your god Chemosh[u] gives you? Likewise, whatever the LORD our God has given us, we will possess. 25 Are you any better than Balak son of Zippor,[v] king of Moab? Did he ever quarrel with Israel or fight with them?[w] 26 For three hundred years Israel occupied[x] Heshbon, Aroer, the surrounding settlements and all the towns along the Arnon. Why didn't you retake them during that time? 27 I have not wronged you, but you are doing me wrong by waging war against me. Let the LORD, the Judge,[y] decide[z] the dispute this day between the Israelites and the Ammonites."

28 The king of Ammon, however, paid no attention to the message Jephthah sent him.

29 Then the Spirit[a] of the LORD came on Jephthah. He crossed Gilead and Manasseh, passed through Mizpah of Gilead, and from there he advanced against the Ammonites. 30 And Jephthah made a vow[b] to the LORD: "If you give the Ammonites into my hands, 31 whatever comes out of the door of my house to meet me when I return in triumph from the Ammonites will be the LORD's, and I will sacrifice it as a burnt offering."

32 Then Jephthah went over to fight the Ammonites, and the LORD gave them into his hands. 33 He devastated twenty towns from Aroer to the vicinity of Minnith,[c] as far as Abel Keramim. Thus Israel subdued Ammon.

34 When Jephthah returned to his home in Mizpah, who should come out to meet him but his daughter, dancing to the sound of timbrels![d] She was an only child. Except for her he had neither son nor daughter. 35 When he saw her, he tore his clothes and cried, "Oh no, my daughter! You have brought me down and I am devastated. I have made a vow to the LORD that I cannot break.[e]"

36 "My father," she replied, "you have given your word to the LORD. Do to me just as you promised,[f] now that the LORD has avenged you of your enemies,[g] the Ammonites. 37 But grant me this one request," she said. "Give me two months to roam the hills and weep with my friends, because I will never marry."

38 "You may go," he said. And he let her go for two months. She and her friends went into the hills and wept because she would never marry. 39 After the two months, she returned to her father, and he did to her as he had vowed. And she was a virgin.

[a] 20 Or *however, would not make an agreement for Israel*

11:19–23 See Num 21:21–32.

11:24 Chemosh. The national god of the Moabites. Jephthah is in error: the god of the Ammonites was Milkom or Molek (1 Kgs 11:5–7). Jephthah is also in error about who gave the Ammonites their land: the Lord gave the Ammonites their allotment, according to Deut 2:19. And Jephthah is in error when he views the Lord giving land as being similar with other gods giving land (it was a common view of his pagan neighbors, but quite wrong).

11:25 Jephthah is in error about Balak quarreling or fighting with Israel (Num 22–24).

11:26 Jephthah may also be in error about how long the Israelites have lived in these cities, though his overall argument has validity.

11:28 The king of the Ammonites rejects all of Jephthah's arguments; he is determined to wage war.

11:29–40 *The Ammonite Defeat: Jephthah's Vow.* The centerpiece of this story is Jephthah's vow; the outcome of the battle with Ammon is almost an aside.

11:29 The coming of the Spirit of the Lord upon Jephthah (i.e., his empowerment) should have been the guarantee of victory; but his vow will undermine everything.

11:30–36 Jephthah's vow is manipulative, promising a burnt offering in exchange for victory. It is also rash in its qualification: "whatever comes out of the door of my house to meet me." Given the arrangement of homes with courtyards that housed domesticated animals, Jephthah may have intended that one of these animals be encountered first upon his return home. Nevertheless, it was a distinct possibility that it would be a human being.

11:37–38 Because a Hebrew woman could suffer no greater disgrace than to die childless, Jephthah's daughter asks for time to bewail her virginity. Similar pagan rites elsewhere were disapproved (Ezek 8:14).

11:39–40 The worship of Molek (see note on v. 24) involved child sacrifice (cf. Lev 18:21; 20:2–5). This is ironic because Jephthah had delivered the Israelites from the Ammonites, who sacrificed their

From this comes the Israelite tradition [40]that each year the young women of Israel go out for four days to commemorate the daughter of Jephthah the Gileadite.

Jephthah and Ephraim

12 The Ephraimite forces were called out, and they crossed over to Zaphon. They said to Jephthah, "Why did you go to fight the Ammonites without calling us to go with you?[h] We're going to burn down your house over your head."

[2]Jephthah answered, "I and my people were engaged in a great struggle with the Ammonites, and although I called, you didn't save me out of their hands. [3]When I saw that you wouldn't help, I took my life in my hands[i] and crossed over to fight the Ammonites, and the LORD gave me the victory over them. Now why have you come up today to fight me?"

[4]Jephthah then called together the men of Gilead and fought against Ephraim. The Gileadites struck them down because the Ephraimites had said, "You Gileadites are renegades from Ephraim and Manasseh." [5]The Gileadites captured the fords of the Jordan[j] leading to Ephraim, and whenever a survivor of Ephraim said, "Let me cross over," the men of Gilead asked him, "Are you an Ephraimite?" If he replied, "No," [6]they said, "All right, say 'Shibboleth.'" If he said, "Sibboleth," because he could not pronounce the word correctly, they seized him and killed him at the fords of the Jordan. Forty-two thousand Ephraimites were killed at that time.

[7]Jephthah led[a] Israel six years. Then Jephthah the Gileadite died and was buried in a town in Gilead.

Ibzan, Elon and Abdon

[8]After him, Ibzan of Bethlehem led Israel. [9]He had thirty sons and thirty daughters. He gave his daughters away in marriage to those outside his clan, and for his sons he brought in thirty young women as wives from outside his clan. Ibzan led Israel seven years. [10]Then Ibzan died and was buried in Bethlehem.

[11]After him, Elon the Zebulunite led Israel ten years. [12]Then Elon died and was buried in Aijalon in the land of Zebulun.

[13]After him, Abdon son of Hillel, from Pirathon, led Israel. [14]He had forty sons and thirty grandsons,[k] who rode on seventy donkeys.[l] He led Israel eight years. [15]Then Abdon son of Hillel died and was buried at Pirathon in Ephraim, in the hill country of the Amalekites.[m]

[a] 7 Traditionally *judged*; also in verses 8-14

12:1 [h] Jdg 8:1
12:3 [i] 1Sa 19:5; 28:21; Job 13:14
12:5 [j] Jos 22:11; Jdg 3:28
12:14 [k] Jdg 10:4 [l] Jdg 5:10
12:15 [m] Jdg 5:14

children to Molek, yet Jephthah sacrifices his daughter to the Lord, who does not accept human sacrifice. Unfortunately, other Israelites offered human sacrifices too (2 Kgs 16:3; 21:6; Ezek 20:25–26,31). Jephthah's ignorance of the law is compounded: he could have redeemed his daughter (Lev 27:1–8). While a vow was not to be broken (Num 30:2; Deut 23:21–23), God had provided the means for redemption of vows. Jephthah was apparently ignorant of this.

12:1–7 *The Conclusion: Jephthah Versus the Ephraimites.* The Ephraimites are depicted as upstarts who want to be included where they do not belong. Perhaps the Ephraimites are upset that they will miss out on some of the plunder from Jephthah's victory. Cf. their earlier complaint to Gideon (8:1–3).

12:1 The Ephraimites threaten to burn Jephthah's house over his "head" (Hebrew *rōʾš*). But tragically, Jephthah has just burned his only child and thus has no house(hold). "Head" plays cruelly on what Jephthah had so desired to be: the head or chief (Hebrew *rōʾš*, 11:11).

12:4 renegades. An insult to the Gileadites' legitimacy as Israelites (cf. Josh 22), a taunt particularly personal to Jephthah (11:1–2). The Lord's noninvolvement shows that this is an intertribal feud that God has not sanctioned. The episode anticipates the intertribal war of chs. 19–21.

12:6 Shibboleth. Its meaning is uncertain, possibly "ear of wheat" or (less likely) "current of water." The Gileadites chose the word not because of any significance inherent in its meaning but because it exposed the inability of the Ephraimites to pronounce it.

12:8–10 *Minor Judge: Ibzan.* He is the fourth of the six minor judges.

12:8 Bethlehem. Generally thought to refer to the northern Bethlehem of Josh 19:15, located on the Asher-Zebulun border.

12:9 After Jephthah's childlessness comes Ibzan's fecundity, which underscores the tragedy of 11:34–40. **thirty.** Recalls Jair (10:4). To have 60 children required a harem, so Ibzan lived as an ancient Near Eastern king. He arranged marriages for all his children to individuals outside his clan, securing his power base.

12:11–12 *Minor Judge: Elon.* He is the fifth of the six minor judges.

12:11 Elon. Also the name of a clan in the tribe of Zebulun (Gen 46:14; Num 26:26).

12:13–15 *Minor Judge: Abdon.* He is the sixth and the final minor judge.

12:14 forty ... thirty. Reminiscent of Gideon's "seventy" (8:30). **rode on ... donkeys.** Evidence of their royal-type power over the region (cf. 10:4 and note on 10:3–5). But Abdon extended the control to another generation.

12:15 buried ... in the hill country of the Amalekites. The mention of the hill country of the Amalekites, who were a major enemy of Israel, creates an irony: Whose land is this?

13:1 [n]Jdg 2:11; 1Sa 12:9
13:2 [o]Jos 15:33; 19:41
13:3 [p]ver 6,8; Jdg 6:12 [q]ver 10 [r]Lk 1:13
13:4 [s]ver 14; Nu 6:2-4; Lk 1:15
13:5 [t]Nu 6:5; 1Sa 1:11 [u]Nu 6:2,13 [v]1Sa 7:13
13:6 [w]ver 8; 1Sa 2:27; 9:6 [x]ver 17-18; Mt 28:3
13:14 [y]Nu 6:4 [z]ver 4

The Birth of Samson

13 Again the Israelites did evil in the eyes of the LORD, so the LORD delivered them into the hands of the Philistines[n] for forty years.

2 A certain man of Zorah,[o] named Manoah, from the clan of the Danites, had a wife who was childless, unable to give birth. 3 The angel of the LORD[p] appeared to her[q] and said, "You are barren and childless, but you are going to become pregnant and give birth to a son.[r] 4 Now see to it that you drink no wine or other fermented drink and that you do not eat anything unclean.[s] 5 You will become pregnant and have a son whose head is never to be touched by a razor[t] because the boy is to be a Nazirite,[u] dedicated to God from the womb. He will take the lead[v] in delivering Israel from the hands of the Philistines."

6 Then the woman went to her husband and told him, "A man of God[w] came to me. He looked like an angel of God,[x] very awesome. I didn't ask him where he came from, and he didn't tell me his name. 7 But he said to me, 'You will become pregnant and have a son. Now then, drink no wine or other fermented drink and do not eat anything unclean, because the boy will be a Nazirite of God from the womb until the day of his death.' "

8 Then Manoah prayed to the LORD: "Pardon your servant, Lord. I beg you to let the man of God you sent to us come again to teach us how to bring up the boy who is to be born."

9 God heard Manoah, and the angel of God came again to the woman while she was out in the field; but her husband Manoah was not with her. 10 The woman hurried to tell her husband, "He's here! The man who appeared to me the other day!"

11 Manoah got up and followed his wife. When he came to the man, he said, "Are you the man who talked to my wife?"

"I am," he said.

12 So Manoah asked him, "When your words are fulfilled, what is to be the rule that governs the boy's life and work?"

13 The angel of the LORD answered, "Your wife must do all that I have told her. 14 She must not eat anything that comes from the grapevine, nor drink any wine or other fermented drink[y] nor eat anything unclean.[z] She must do everything I have commanded her."

13:1—16:31 *Major Judge Cycle: Samson.* The final "deliverer" is the literary climax of the cycles section and the moral nadir of the major judges. In many ways, it is a tragedy: a man with a powerful gifting from God does not use it to the Lord's glory for most of his life. Samson broke his Nazirite vows, had intercourse with non-Israelite women, never associated with other Israelites in his conflicts with the Philistines, and did not deliver the Israelites from the Philistine oppression. After the initial statement in 13:1, Israel does not even cry out to the Lord! So the cycle itself devolves. Samson demonstrates faith, very specifically in the action surrounding his death (Heb 11:32). See Introduction: Theology.

13:1–25 *Samson's Birth.* The theophanies reveal God's plan for Samson's life.

13:1 Philistines. A people of Aegean origin, part of the larger "Sea People" movements at the beginning of the twelfth century BC. Prophetic tradition identifies Caphtor (Crete) as their precise place of origin (Jer 47:4; Amos 9:7).

13:2 Zorah. A town on the border between Judah and Dan (Josh 15:33; 19:41). **Danites.** A southern tribe here; chs. 17–18 describe the tribe's migration to the north. The Samson stories illustrate some of the reasons for the migration.

13:3–7 The angel of the Lord appears to Samson's mother, not his father Manoah, announcing the birth of a son to this barren and childless woman.

13:3 The angel of the LORD. Cf. 2:1–5; 6:11–24; see note on 2:1. This is the first theophany of the Lord to Samson's mother. Any Israelite, male or female, could take a Nazirite vow (Num 6:1–21), dedicating themselves to holiness to the Lord. This was normally voluntary and usually for a limited time. It involved three basic prohibitions: (1) consuming wine or other intoxicating drink, in fact anything from the vine; (2) cutting one's hair for the duration of the vow; and (3) coming into contact with a dead body. If the Nazirite became defiled by a corpse, they had to go to the tabernacle for a ritual cleansing. Samson's vow was not voluntary and was to be applied to his entire life. Samson broke all three prohibitions: he consumed wine and strong drink at his wedding feast (14:10–20); he came into contact with corpses (14:6–9; 15:15); and his hair was cut off (16:17,19).

13:4 The requirement that the Nazirite abstain from wine even becomes a requirement for Samson's mother while pregnant. (v. 7). In addition to the Nazirite prohibitions (see note on v. 3), the angel of the Lord added the prohibition for Samson's mother to consume any unclean food during her pregnancy. Since all Israelites were subject to this law, not just Nazirites, this testifies to the condition of the nation as a whole (apparently disregarding the covenantal stipulations).

13:5 He will take the lead in delivering. There could also be reference to Samson's "beginning" to deliver the people. God knows that Samson will not actually finish the job; Samson will only arouse Israel from its oppressive slumber. Samson did not save Israel from the Philistine oppression; he only started the process.

13:6–7 Samson's mother perceived this to be only a divine being, not the angel of the Lord, i.e., the Lord himself. Samson's father is incredulous, even cynical, about his wife's report.

13:8–23 The angel of the Lord comes again to Samson's mother—not to Samson's father, Manoah. Though Manoah demanded another appearance, this second appearance adds no new revelation about Samson. It was unnecessary and underscores Manoah's unbelief.

15 Manoah said to the angel of the LORD, "We would like you to stay until we prepare a young goat[a]
for you."
16 The angel of the LORD replied, "Even though you detain me, I will not eat any of your food. But
if you prepare a burnt offering,[b] offer it to the LORD." (Manoah did not realize that it was the angel of
the LORD.)
17 Then Manoah inquired of the angel of the LORD, "What is your name,[c] so that we may honor you
when your word comes true?"
18 He replied, "Why do you ask my name?[d] It is beyond understanding.[a]" 19 Then Manoah took a
young goat, together with the grain offering, and sacrificed it on a rock[e] to the LORD. And the LORD did
an amazing thing while Manoah and his wife watched: 20 As the flame[f] blazed up from the altar toward
heaven, the angel of the LORD ascended in the flame. Seeing this, Manoah and his wife fell with their
faces to the ground.[g] 21 When the angel of the LORD did not show himself again to Manoah and his wife,
Manoah realized[h] that it was the angel of the LORD.
22 "We are doomed[i] to die!" he said to his wife. "We have seen[j] God!"
23 But his wife answered, "If the LORD had meant to kill us, he would not have accepted a burnt offering and grain offering from our hands, nor shown us all these things or now told us this."[k]
24 The woman gave birth to a boy and named him Samson.[l] He grew[m] and the LORD blessed him,[n] 25 and
the Spirit of the LORD began to stir[o] him while he was in Mahaneh Dan,[p] between Zorah and Eshtaol.

Samson's Marriage

14 Samson went down to Timnah[q] and saw there a young Philistine woman. 2 When he returned,
he said to his father and mother, "I have seen a Philistine woman in Timnah; now get her for
me as my wife."[r]
3 His father and mother replied, "Isn't there an acceptable woman among your relatives or among
all our people?[s] Must you go to the uncircumcised[t] Philistines to get a wife?[u]"
But Samson said to his father, "Get her for me. She's the right one for me." 4 (His parents did not
know that this was from the LORD, who was seeking an occasion to confront the Philistines;[v] for at that
time they were ruling over Israel.)[w]
5 Samson went down to Timnah together with his father and mother. As they approached the vineyards of Timnah, suddenly a young lion came roaring toward him. 6 The Spirit of the LORD came powerfully upon him[x] so that he tore the lion apart with his bare hands as he might have torn a young
goat. But he told neither his father nor his mother what he had done. 7 Then he went down and talked
with the woman, and he liked her.
8 Some time later, when he went back to marry her, he turned aside to look at the lion's carcass, and

[a] 18 Or *is wonderful*

13:15 [a] ver 3; Jdg 6:19
13:16 [b] Jdg 6:20
13:17 [c] Ge 32:29
13:18 [d] Isa 9:6
13:19 [e] Jdg 6:20
13:20 [f] Lev 9:24 [g] 1Ch 21:16; Eze 1:28; Mt 17:6
13:21 [h] ver 16; Jdg 6:22
13:22 [i] Dt 5:26 [j] Ge 32:30; Jdg 6:22
13:23 [k] Ps 25:14
13:24 [l] Heb 11:32 [m] 1Sa 3:19 [n] Lk 1:80
13:25 [o] Jdg 3:10 [p] Jdg 18:12
14:1 [q] Ge 38:12
14:2 [r] Ge 21:21; 34:4
14:3 [s] Ge 24:4 [t] Dt 7:3 [u] Ex 34:16
14:4 [v] Jos 11:20 [w] Jdg 13:1
14:6 [x] Jdg 3:10; 13:25

13:15–23 Manoah's hospitality parallels Gideon's (6:11–24). However, Gideon, who feared death, was assured by the Lord himself, while Manoah, who feared for his life, received reassurance only from his wife, who chided him for not comprehending the purpose of the divine visit (v. 23).

13:18 beyond understanding. A Hebrew term used in similar revelatory contexts (Gen 18:14 ["hard"]; Isa 9:6 ["Wonderful"]).

13:24 Ironically, his mother names him Samson, a name related to the Hebrew word for sun (and the Canaanite sun-god). It is a pagan name. After two appearances of the Lord, one would expect a name with the name of Yahweh in it, e.g., Zechariah ("the LORD [Yahweh] remembered").

13:25 Mahaneh Dan. Its location is problematic. Here it is "between Zorah and Eshtaol"; in 18:12, it is "west of Kiriath Jearim" in Judah. It may not be a place-name but may simply mean "camp of Dan" (since Hebrew *maḥănēh* means "camp").

14:1–20 *Samson's Wedding.* The stories about Samson show that he was a judge who avenged only personal grievances and chased women instead of enemies.

14:1 Timnah. Perhaps Tell el-Batashi, four miles (6.5 kilometers) north of Beth-Shemesh.

14:2 Samson is a man dominated by his senses.

14:3 Samson's marriage to a Philistine causes all of the events of 14:5—15:19. **Get her for me.** Samson totally disregards God's covenant (Deut 7:3) and dishonors his father and mother. **She's the right one for me.** Hebrew may also be translated (more ambiguously) "She is right in my eyes." Israel has done evil in the eyes of the Lord (13:1); now there is a judge who does what is right in his own eyes. Little wonder that in chs. 17–21 everyone does what is right in their own eyes (see 17:6 and note; see also Introduction: The Cycles Section; Theology).

14:4 An editorial comment. **this was from the LORD.** God, who does not cause humans to sin, can nevertheless use human sin and folly to accomplish his divine purpose. In other words, God used Samson in spite of Samson's wrong motives and actions (cf. Gen 45:8; 50:20; 2 Chr 25:20; Acts 2:23; 4:28; Rom 8:28–29).

14:6 Empowered by the Spirit, Samson is able to do a great deed. **he told neither his father nor his mother.** Defilement caused by being in the presence of a dead body required an eight-day ritual (Num 6:6–12), which Samson did not want to do.

14:8–9 Samson flagrantly violates his Nazirite status and carelessly defiles his parents. Food from a corpse defiles.

14:12 [y] 1Ki 10:1; Eze 17:2 [z] Ge 29:27 [a] Ge 45:22; 2Ki 5:5
14:15 [b] Jdg 16:5; Ecc 7:26 [c] Jdg 15:6
14:16 [d] Jdg 16:15
14:17 [e] Est 1:5
14:18 [f] ver 14
14:19 [g] Nu 11:25; Jdg 3:10; 6:34; 11:29; 13:25; 15:14; 1Sa 11:6; 16:13; 1Ki 18:46; 2Ch 24:20; Isa 11:2 [h] 1Sa 11:6
14:20 [i] Jdg 15:2,6; Jn 3:29
15:1 [j] Ge 38:17
15:2 [k] Jdg 14:20

in it he saw a swarm of bees and some honey. 9 He scooped out the honey with his hands and ate as he went along. When he rejoined his parents, he gave them some, and they too ate it. But he did not tell them that he had taken the honey from the lion's carcass.

10 Now his father went down to see the woman. And there Samson held a feast, as was customary for young men. 11 When the people saw him, they chose thirty men to be his companions.

12 "Let me tell you a riddle,[y]" Samson said to them. "If you can give me the answer within the seven days of the feast,[z] I will give you thirty linen garments and thirty sets of clothes.[a] 13 If you can't tell me the answer, you must give me thirty linen garments and thirty sets of clothes."

"Tell us your riddle," they said. "Let's hear it."

14 He replied,

> "Out of the eater, something to eat;
> out of the strong, something sweet."

For three days they could not give the answer.

15 On the fourth[a] day, they said to Samson's wife, "Coax[b] your husband into explaining the riddle for us, or we will burn you and your father's household to death.[c] Did you invite us here to steal our property?"

16 Then Samson's wife threw herself on him, sobbing, "You hate me! You don't really love me.[d] You've given my people a riddle, but you haven't told me the answer."

"I haven't even explained it to my father or mother," he replied, "so why should I explain it to you?" 17 She cried the whole seven days[e] of the feast. So on the seventh day he finally told her, because she continued to press him. She in turn explained the riddle to her people.

18 Before sunset on the seventh day the men of the town said to him,

> "What is sweeter than honey?
> What is stronger than a lion?"[f]

Samson said to them,

> "If you had not plowed with my heifer,
> you would not have solved my riddle."

19 Then the Spirit of the LORD came powerfully upon him.[g] He went down to Ashkelon, struck down thirty of their men, stripped them of everything and gave their clothes to those who had explained the riddle. Burning with anger,[h] he returned to his father's home. 20 And Samson's wife was given to one of his companions[i] who had attended him at the feast.

Samson's Vengeance on the Philistines

15 Later on, at the time of wheat harvest, Samson took a young goat[j] and went to visit his wife. He said, "I'm going to my wife's room." But her father would not let him go in.

2 "I was so sure you hated her," he said, "that I gave her to your companion.[k] Isn't her younger sister more attractive? Take her instead."

3 Samson said to them, "This time I have a right to get even with the Philistines; I will really harm them." 4 So he went out and caught three hundred foxes and tied them tail to tail in pairs. He then fas-

[a] *15* Some Septuagint manuscripts and Syriac; Hebrew *seventh*

14:10–18 Philistine wedding feasts, like those of other people of the ancient Near East, included wine and beer. Drinking vessels of this type have been found in excavations of Philistine sites. The hostility between Samson and the Philistines flared up because of verbal jousting between Samson and his guests. Samson proposed a riddle they could not solve (or so he thought). Samson's bride betrayed him (anticipating Delilah's betrayal in ch. 16).

14:18 my heifer. This refers to Samson's wife (v. 15). Since heifers were not used for plowing, Samson is accusing them of unfairness.

14:19 Ashkelon. A Mediterranean coastal city, one of the five main Philistine cities. Samson murdered 30 men and robbed them of their clothing just to pay his debts to his wedding companions. His unbridled anger sets the stage for his bride being given to another.

15:1–20 *Samson's Revenge.* Samson's anger after his wife was given to another man led him to destroy the Philistines' grain crop. This began a cycle of revenge with escalating violence between Samson and the Philistines.

15:4–5 Though this was a truly great physical feat, it was purely for personal revenge and contrary to the law: "If a fire breaks out and spreads into thornbushes so that it burns shocks of grain or standing grain or the whole field, the one who started the fire must make restitution" (Exod 22:6).

tened a torch to every pair of tails, [5]lit the torches and let the foxes loose in the standing grain of the
Philistines. He burned up the shocks and standing grain, together with the vineyards and olive groves.
[6]When the Philistines asked, "Who did this?" they were told, "Samson, the Timnite's son-in-law,
because his wife was given to his companion."
So the Philistines went up and burned her and her father to death.[l] [7]Samson said to them, "Since
you've acted like this, I swear that I won't stop until I get my revenge on you." [8]He attacked them vi-
ciously and slaughtered many of them. Then he went down and stayed in a cave in the rock of Etam.
[9]The Philistines went up and camped in Judah, spreading out near Lehi.[m] [10]The people of Judah
asked, "Why have you come to fight us?"
"We have come to take Samson prisoner," they answered, "to do to him as he did to us."
[11]Then three thousand men from Judah went down to the cave in the rock of Etam and said to Samson, "Don't you realize that the Philistines are rulers over us?[n] What have you done to us?"
He answered, "I merely did to them what they did to me."
[12]They said to him, "We've come to tie you up and hand you over to the Philistines."
Samson said, "Swear to me that you won't kill me yourselves."
[13]"Agreed," they answered. "We will only tie you up and hand you over to them. We will not kill you."
So they bound him with two new ropes and led him up from the rock. [14]As he approached Lehi, the
Philistines came toward him shouting. The Spirit of the LORD came powerfully upon him.[o] The ropes on
his arms became like charred flax, and the bindings dropped from his hands. [15]Finding a fresh jawbone
of a donkey, he grabbed it and struck down a thousand men.[p]
[16]Then Samson said,

> "With a donkey's jawbone
> I have made donkeys of them.[a]
> With a donkey's jawbone
> I have killed a thousand men."

[17]When he finished speaking, he threw away the jawbone; and the place was called Ramath Lehi.[b]
[18]Because he was very thirsty, he cried out to the LORD,[q] "You have given your servant this great
victory. Must I now die of thirst and fall into the hands of the uncircumcised?" [19]Then God opened up
the hollow place in Lehi, and water came out of it. When Samson drank, his strength returned and he
revived.[r] So the spring was called En Hakkore,[c] and it is still there in Lehi.
[20]Samson led[d] Israel for twenty years[s] in the days of the Philistines.

Samson and Delilah

16 One day Samson went to Gaza, where he saw a prostitute. He went in to spend the night with her.
[2]The people of Gaza were told, "Samson is here!" So they surrounded the place and lay in wait
for him all night at the city gate.[t] They made no move during the night, saying, "At dawn we'll kill him."

[a] *16* Or *made a heap or two*; the Hebrew for *donkey* sounds like the Hebrew for *heap.* [b] *17* *Ramath Lehi* means *jawbone hill.* [c] *19* *En Hakkore* means *caller's spring.* [d] *20* Traditionally *judged*

15:6 [l] Jdg 14:15
15:9 [m] ver 14,17,19
15:11 [n] Jdg 13:1; 14:4; Ps 106:40-42
15:14 [o] Jdg 3:10; 14:19; 1Sa 11:6
15:15 [p] Lev 26:8; Jos 23:10; Jdg 3:31
15:18 [q] Jdg 16:28
15:19 [r] Ge 45:27; Isa 40:29
15:20 [s] Jdg 13:1; 16:31; Heb 11:32
16:2 [t] 1Sa 23:26; Ps 118:10-12; Ac 9:24

15:6 Ironically, Samson's arson leads to the incineration of his wife and father-in-law by the Philistines.

15:7 I won't stop until I get my revenge on you. Samson is motivated by personal revenge. God's people are not to seek vengeance; vengeance belongs to God (Lev 19:18; Deut 32:35; Prov 20:22; 24:29; Matt 7:12; Rom 12:17–21).

15:8 Etam. Location uncertain.

15:9–13 The people of Judah refuse to provide Samson with sanctuary. In fact, they apprehend Samson for the Philistines. For the Philistines, Judahites, and Samson, the only thing that matters is reprisal and counterprisal.

15:10–11 to do to him as he did to us ... I merely did to them what they did to me. Samson is no different than the Philistines; both are driven to get even (see note on v. 7).

15:14–17 Another great feat motivated by personal revenge (see note on vv. 4–5).

15:15 fresh jawbone of a donkey. An improvised weapon; it is not a normal weapon of war (cf. 3:31; 4:21). It was ritually unclean, so he again broke his Nazirite vow concerning corpses (see note on 14:6).

15:16 donkeys. See NIV text note; the couplet involves a pun; the same Hebrew word can mean both donkey and heap.

15:18–19 Samson's first prayer is a demand for water. Cf. Israel's demands in the wilderness (Exod 17:1–7; Num 20:2–13).

15:20 This comment by the narrator authenticates Samson as a judge.

16:1–31 *Samson's Death.* Samson's weakness for women led to his betrayal and death.

16:1–3 *The Incident With the Prostitute of Gaza.* Samson's spending the night with the prostitute demonstrates once again his lack of regard for God's law. This act endangers his life.

16:1 Gaza. Southernmost Philistine coastal city. Samson's going to this city is deliberate, i.e., for his own gratification.

This mosaic of Samson carrying the Gaza gate was found in 2013 at the fifth-century synagogue at Huqoq.

16:3 [u]Jos 10:36 16:4 [v]Ge 24:67 16:5 [w]Jos 13:3 [x]Ex 10:7; Jdg 14:15 [y]ver 18 16:9 [z]ver 12 16:10 [a]ver 13 16:11 [b]Jdg 15:13

3But Samson lay there only until the middle of the night. Then he got up and took hold of the doors
of the city gate, together with the two posts, and tore them loose, bar and all. He lifted them to his
shoulders and carried them to the top of the hill that faces Hebron.[u]
4Some time later, he fell in love[v] with a woman in the Valley of Sorek whose name was Delilah. 5The
rulers of the Philistines[w] went to her and said, "See if you can lure[x] him into showing you the secret of
his great strength and how we can overpower him so we may tie him up and subdue him. Each one of
us will give you eleven hundred shekels[a] of silver."[y]
6So Delilah said to Samson, "Tell me the secret of your great strength and how you can be tied up
and subdued."
7Samson answered her, "If anyone ties me with seven fresh bowstrings that have not been dried, I'll
become as weak as any other man."
8Then the rulers of the Philistines brought her seven fresh bowstrings that had not been dried, and
she tied him with them. 9With men hidden in the room,[z] she called to him, "Samson, the Philistines
are upon you!" But he snapped the bowstrings as easily as a piece of string snaps when it comes close
to a flame. So the secret of his strength was not discovered.
10Then Delilah said to Samson, "You have made a fool of me;[a] you lied to me. Come now, tell me
how you can be tied."
11He said, "If anyone ties me securely with new ropes[b] that have never been used, I'll become as
weak as any other man."

a 5 That is, about 28 pounds or about 13 kilograms

16:3 A third great exploit; like the other feats, it is based on personal motives, not to save Israel (see notes on 15:4–5,14–17). **city gate.** Gates for a city like Gaza were at least two stories high, and their heavy posts were set in firm sockets. The distance from Gaza to Hebron is roughly 40 miles (64 kilometers) and involves an ascent, so to haul this gate and its posts such a considerable distance is very impressive! Although here Samson escaped from Gaza, later he will be enslaved there (v. 21).

16:4–22 *The Delilah Incident.* The Philistines use the deception of Delilah to get revenge on Samson for his destruction of the gates of Gaza.

16:4 Valley of Sorek. Modern Wadi-es-Sarar; it begins 13 miles (21 kilometers) southwest of Jerusalem. **Delilah.** The name's meaning is uncertain. While the text does not say that she was a Philistine, Samson has demonstrated a distinct preference for "foreign," Philistine women, not Israelite women.

16:5 rulers. They make the most of this opportunity.

16:6–21 Four times Delilah unleashes a verbal attack on Samson in order to subdue him and receive her payment.

12 So Delilah took new ropes and tied him with them. Then, with men hidden in the room, she called
to him, "Samson, the Philistines are upon you!" But he snapped the ropes off his arms as if they were
threads.
13 Delilah then said to Samson, "All this time you have been making a fool of me and lying to me.
Tell me how you can be tied."

He replied, "If you weave the seven braids of my head into the fabric on the loom and tighten it with
the pin, I'll become as weak as any other man." So while he was sleeping, Delilah took the seven braids
of his head, wove them into the fabric 14 and[a] tightened it with the pin.

Again she called to him, "Samson, the Philistines are upon you!"[c] He awoke from his sleep and
pulled up the pin and the loom, with the fabric.

15 Then she said to him, "How can you say, 'I love you,'[d] when you won't confide in me? This is the
third time[e] you have made a fool of me and haven't told me the secret of your great strength.[f]" 16 With
such nagging she prodded him day after day until he was sick to death of it.

17 So he told her everything.[g] "No razor has ever been used on my head," he said, "because I have
been a Nazirite[h] dedicated to God from my mother's womb. If my head were shaved, my strength would
leave me, and I would become as weak as any other man."

18 When Delilah saw that he had told her everything, she sent word to the rulers of the Philistines[i],
"Come back once more; he has told me everything." So the rulers of the Philistines returned with the
silver in their hands. 19 After putting him to sleep on her lap, she called for someone to shave off the
seven braids of his hair, and so began to subdue him.[b] And his strength left him.[j]

20 Then she called, "Samson, the Philistines are upon you!"

He awoke from his sleep and thought, "I'll go out as before and shake myself free." But he did not
know that the LORD had left him.[k]

21 Then the Philistines[l] seized him, gouged out his eyes[m] and took him down to Gaza. Binding him
with bronze shackles, they set him to grinding grain[n] in the prison. 22 But the hair on his head began
to grow again after it had been shaved.

The Death of Samson

23 Now the rulers of the Philistines assembled to offer a great sacrifice to Dagon[o] their god and to
celebrate, saying, "Our god has delivered Samson, our enemy, into our hands."
24 When the people saw him, they praised their god,[p] saying,

> "Our god has delivered our enemy
> into our hands,[q]
> the one who laid waste our land
> and multiplied our slain."

25 While they were in high spirits,[r] they shouted, "Bring out Samson to entertain us." So they called
Samson out of the prison, and he performed for them.

When they stood him among the pillars, 26 Samson said to the servant who held his hand, "Put me
where I can feel the pillars that support the temple, so that I may lean against them." 27 Now the temple

16:14 [c] ver 9,20
16:15 [d] Jdg 14:16 [e] Nu 24:10 [f] ver 5
16:17 [g] Mic 7:5 [h] Nu 6:2,5; Jdg 13:5
16:18 [i] Jos 13:3; 1Sa 5:8
16:19 [j] Pr 7:26-27
16:20 [k] Nu 14:42; Jos 7:12; 1Sa 16:14; 18:12; 28:15
16:21 [l] Jer 47:1 [m] Nu 16:14 [n] Job 31:10; Isa 47:2
16:23 [o] 1Sa 5:2; 1Ch 10:10
16:24 [p] Da 5:4 [q] 1Sa 31:9; 1Ch 10:9
16:25 [r] Jdg 9:27; Ru 3:7; Est 1:10

[a] *13,14* Some Septuagint manuscripts; Hebrew *replied, "I can if you weave the seven braids of my head into the fabric on the loom." 14 So she* [b] *19* Hebrew; some Septuagint manuscripts *and he began to weaken*

16:17 As with his Timnite wife (14:15–17), Samson succumbs and reveals the truth.

16:18–21 The source of Samson's strength was ultimately the Lord. With the shaving of his hair, Samson's last Nazirite vow was broken and his strength left him. The Philistines humiliate Samson by blinding him and setting him to work grinding grain, work usually done by a slave or a woman. He suffers the consequences for the flippant revelation of his special giftedness and status with Yahweh.

16:22 the hair on his head began to grow again. This anticipates the events of the final story. With the regrowth of his hair, a new period of consecration could begin.

16:23–31 *Samson's Final Act of Vengeance.* Samson's prayer reveals a motive of vengeance; however, by his trust in the Lord to renew his strength, Samson proves that the glory belongs to the Lord, not the Philistine god Dagon.

16:23 Dagon. A Canaanite grain deity the Philistines adopted after migrating to Canaan.

16:24 they praised their god. The Philistines praise and credit Dagon with the demise of Samson, though it was the Lord who did this. The Lord will prove them wrong by strengthening Samson to destroy the temple of Dagon.

16:27 [s]Dt 22:8; Jos 2:8
16:28 [t]Jdg 15:18 [u]Jer 15:15
16:31 [v]Jdg 13:2 [w]Ru 1:1; 1Sa 4:18 [x]Jdg 15:20
17:1 [y]Jdg 18:2,13
17:2 [z]Ru 2:20; 1Sa 15:13; 2Sa 2:5
17:3 [a]Ex 20:4,23; 34:17; Lev 19:4
17:4 [b]Ex 32:4; Isa 17:8
17:5 [c]Isa 44:13; Eze 8:10 [d]Jdg 8:27 [e]Ge 31:19; Jdg 18:14 [f]Nu 16:10 [g]Ex 29:9; Jdg 18:24
17:6 [h]Jdg 18:1; 19:1; 21:25 [i]Dt 12:8

was crowded with men and women; all the rulers of the Philistines were there, and on the roof[s] were
about three thousand men and women watching Samson perform. [28]Then Samson prayed to the LORD,[t]
"Sovereign LORD, remember me. Please, God, strengthen me just once more, and let me with one blow
get revenge[u] on the Philistines for my two eyes." [29]Then Samson reached toward the two central pillars
on which the temple stood. Bracing himself against them, his right hand on the one and his left hand
on the other, [30]Samson said, "Let me die with the Philistines!" Then he pushed with all his might, and
down came the temple on the rulers and all the people in it. Thus he killed many more when he died
than while he lived.

[31]Then his brothers and his father's whole family went down to get him. They brought him back
and buried him between Zorah and Eshtaol in the tomb of Manoah[v] his father. He had led[aw] Israel
twenty years.[x]

Micah's Idols

17 Now a man named Micah[y] from the hill country of Ephraim [2]said to his mother, "The eleven
hundred shekels[b] of silver that were taken from you and about which I heard you utter a
curse—I have that silver with me; I took it."

Then his mother said, "The LORD bless you,[z] my son!"

[3]When he returned the eleven hundred shekels of silver to his mother, she said, "I solemnly consecrate my silver to the LORD for my son to make an image overlaid with silver.[a] I will give it back to you."

[4]So after he returned the silver to his mother, she took two hundred shekels[c] of silver and gave them
to a silversmith, who used them to make the idol.[b] And it was put in Micah's house.

[5]Now this man Micah had a shrine,[c] and he made an ephod[d] and some household gods[e] and installed[f] one of his sons as his priest.[g] [6]In those days Israel had no king;[h] everyone did as they saw fit.[i]

[a] *31* Traditionally *judged* [b] *2* That is, about 28 pounds or about 13 kilograms [c] *4* That is, about 5 pounds or about 2.3 kilograms

16:28 Samson's second and final prayer is for personal revenge (for his first prayer, see 15:18–19).

16:30 The excavation of a Philistine temple at Tel Qasile revealed a structure with a long room, the roof of which was originally supported by two wooden pillars set on round, well-made stone bases. The temple of Dagon in Gaza probably had a similar construction. Samson killed many more when he died, including the supposed god Dagon, than he killed while he lived. The victory is unquestionably Yahweh's, even though it is achieved through Samson's death. Samson's faith is clearly evident. This is why the author of Hebrews includes him in Heb 11:32 (see Introduction: Theology).

17:1—21:25 *The Double Conclusion.* The double conclusion is symmetrical with the double introduction (see Introduction: The Double Introduction and Double Conclusion). This describes the self-destructive actions by which the Israelites almost destroyed themselves during the period of the judges. Chs. 17–18, the first conclusion, describe the difficulties with domestic idols as Israel disintegrated religiously. Chs. 19–21, the second conclusion, describe a civil war that internally applied the *ḥērem.* The refrain repeated in 17:6; 18:1; 19:1; 21:25 unites the double conclusion (see Introduction: The Double Introduction and Double Conclusion). The double conclusion has other internal links. (1) In chs. 17–18, the story's coherence revolves around a Levite in *Judah* moving to the hill country of *Ephraim* and then on to Dan. In chs. 19–21, the story's coherence revolves around a Levite in *Ephraim* looking for his concubine in Bethlehem in *Judah.* Both passages end with a reference to Shiloh. (2) Both conclusions begin by narrating the actions of individual Israelites (Micah and his mother in ch. 17; the Levite and his concubine in ch. 19) that consequently expand events on the tribal or national level (Dan in ch. 18; all the Israelite tribes in chs. 20–21). (3) Both conclusions begin with a predicament (the curse of Micah's mother; the Levite's estrangement from his concubine) that seems to be solved almost immediately but turns out to have further complications and ramifications. Thus, these repeated patterns unify the chapters and demonstrate that everything narrated in this final section, though "right" in Israel's eyes, is wrong because it is in rebellion against Yahweh's kingship and covenantal rule.

17:1—18:31 *Difficulties With Domestic Idols.* The first conclusion should be read in the light of Deut 12:1—13:18. It is the thematic antithesis of that passage. The incredible corruption of Israelite worship is seen in Micah's idol that a Levite serves. In turn, this evil is multiplied by the Danites' theft and establishment of this idol in a place that was not part of this tribe's allotment.

17:1–13 *The Idolatry of Micah the Ephraimite.* This story demonstrates the Israelites' capacity to sink into idolatry; proper worship of God has been abandoned.

17:1–6 *The Shrine of Micah.* At the beginning of the period of the judges, the Israelites had difficulties with the worship of the foreign deities of the people of the land (2:6—3:6). Now the Israelites are shown to be perfectly capable of manufacturing their own idols.

17:1 Micah. Abbreviates a name that means "Who is like the LORD?" An Israelite with such a name built a shrine with an image not far from the tabernacle. **hill country of Ephraim.** The central highlands north of Bethel and south of Shechem. Shiloh, where the tabernacle was located, was in this region. The story begins with an ironic twist.

17:2–4 Obviously, Micah's theft of the silver broke two of the Ten Commandments: the fifth (dishonoring his mother, Exod 20:12) and the eighth (stealing, Exod 20:15). Ironically, the returned silver is used to make an idol. The production of an image for worship is an obvious violation of the second commandment (Exod 20:4; cf. Exod 20:23; 34:17; Lev 19:4) as well as the focus of a specific Deuteronomic curse (Deut 27:15).

17:5 He made an ephod. Like Gideon did (see note on 8:27). **household gods.** Hebrew *tĕrāpîm*; some type of household or personal deities used for divinatory purposes (Gen 31:19; Ezek 21:21; Zech 10:2). Installing someone other than a Levite as a priest violated the law (Exod 29:9; 1 Kgs 12:31).

17:6 The first occurrence of the refrain in full (see Introduction: The

7A young Levite from Bethlehem in Judah,[j] who had been living within the clan of Judah, 8left that town
in search of some other place to stay. On his way[a] he came to Micah's house in the hill country of Ephraim.
9Micah asked him, "Where are you from?"
"I'm a Levite from Bethlehem in Judah," he said, "and I'm looking for a place to stay."
10Then Micah said to him, "Live with me and be my father and priest,[k] and I'll give you ten shekels[b]
of silver a year, your clothes and your food." 11So the Levite agreed to live with him, and the young man
became like one of his sons to him. 12Then Micah installed[l] the Levite, and the young man became his
priest and lived in his house. 13And Micah said, "Now I know that the LORD will be good to me, since
this Levite has become my priest."

The Danites Settle in Laish

18 In those days Israel had no king.[m]
And in those days the tribe of the Danites was seeking a place of their own where they might
settle, because they had not yet come into an inheritance among the tribes of Israel.[n] 2So the Danites[o]
sent five of their leading men from Zorah and Eshtaol to spy out the land and explore it. These men
represented all the Danites. They told them, "Go, explore the land."[p]
So they entered the hill country of Ephraim and came to the house of Micah,[q] where they spent the
night. 3When they were near Micah's house, they recognized the voice of the young Levite; so they turned
in there and asked him, "Who brought you here? What are you doing in this place? Why are you here?"
4He told them what Micah had done for him, and said, "He has hired me and I am his priest.[r]"
5Then they said to him, "Please inquire of God[s] to learn whether our journey will be successful."
6The priest answered them, "Go in peace[t]. Your journey has the LORD's approval."
7So the five men left and came to Laish,[u] where they saw that the people were living in safety, like the
Sidonians, at peace and secure. And since their land lacked nothing, they were prosperous.[c] Also, they
lived a long way from the Sidonians[v] and had no relationship with anyone else.[d]
8When they returned to Zorah and Eshtaol, their fellow Danites asked them, "How did you find things?"
9They answered, "Come on, let's attack them! We have seen the land, and it is very good. Aren't you
going to do something? Don't hesitate to go there and take it over.[w] 10When you get there, you will
find an unsuspecting people and a spacious land that God has put into your hands, a land that lacks
nothing[x] whatever.[y]"
11Then six hundred men[z] of the Danites,[a] armed for battle, set out from Zorah and Eshtaol. 12On
their way they set up camp near Kiriath Jearim in Judah. This is why the place west of Kiriath Jearim
is called Mahaneh Dan[e][b] to this day. 13From there they went on to the hill country of Ephraim and
came to Micah's house.

[a] *8* Or *To carry on his profession* [b] *10* That is, about 4 ounces or about 115 grams [c] *7* The meaning of the Hebrew for this clause is uncertain. [d] *7* Hebrew; some Septuagint manuscripts *with the Arameans*
[e] *12* *Mahaneh Dan* means *Dan's camp.*

17:7 [j] Jdg 19:1; Ru 1:1-2; Mic 5:2; Mt 2:1
17:10 [k] Jdg 18:19
17:12 [l] Nu 16:10
18:1 [m] Jdg 17:6; 19:1 [n] Jos 19:47
18:2 [o] Jdg 13:25 [p] Jos 2:1 [q] Jdg 17:1
18:4 [r] Jdg 17:12
18:5 [s] 1Ki 22:5
18:6 [t] 1Ki 22:6
18:7 [u] Jos 19:47 [v] ver 28
18:9 [w] Nu 13:30; 1Ki 22:3
18:10 [x] ver 7,27; Dt 8:9 [y] 1Ch 4:40
18:11 [z] ver 16,17 [a] Jdg 13:2
18:12 [b] Jdg 13:25

Double Introduction and Double Conclusion; Theology). **everyone did as they saw fit.** See note on 14:3; see also Introduction: Theology.

17:7–13 *Micah's Priest.* An opportunistic Levite becomes Micah's priest (Num 16:8–11).

17:7 Bethlehem in Judah. Located just south of Jerusalem (cf. 12:8 and note). It was not a Levitical town (Josh 21:9–16), so it is unclear what the Levite was doing there (see note on v. 8).

17:8 in search of some other place to stay. Apparently, the Israelites were not providing for the Levites (contrary to the law of Deut 12:19; 18:1–8), resulting in their search for a place to survive.

17:10–11 The Levite accepts Micah's exceptional offer even though it means serving at a private, idolatrous shrine.

17:13 Now I know that the LORD will be good to me, since this Levite has become my priest. It is indeed ironic that Micah thinks the Lord will bless him because he has a real Levite as his priest; never mind that every part of the situation is contrary to the law of the Lord.

18:1–31 *The Migration of the Danites.* The story of the Danite migration starts with a partial repetition of the refrain. The ellipsis of the second line forces the reader to supply the thought (see 17:6 for the full refrain). The Danites could not control their allotment (1:34), so they abandoned it and migrated to the far north of Galilee.

18:1–6 The Danites seek an oracle from the Levite serving at Micah's shrine. The Levite's oracle to them assures them of the Lord's support, even though the Lord has not sanctioned any of this (the shrine, priest, or the Danite migration). Cf. Deut 18:20.

18:5 inquire of God. In context, a reference to divination.

18:7 Laish. Modern Tel Dan, a city at the foot of Mount Hermon. **Sidonians.** People from a Phoenician city along the Mediterranean. The city was too far from Laish to offer it effective protection. **at peace and secure.** Undefended. **had no relationship with anyone else.** Probably refers to Aram Rehob or Aram Zobah, just to the north of Laish in the Beqa Valley. Without proper defenses or effective alliances, Laish was easy prey.

18:11–26 On their way to Laish, the Danites stole Micah's cultic objects and induced his priest to join them.

18:11 six hundred men. Cf. 3:31.

18:14 [c] Ge 31:19; Jdg 17:5
18:16 [d] ver 11
18:17 [e] Ge 31:19; Mic 5:13
18:18 [f] Isa 46:2; Jer 43:11; Hos 10:5
18:19 [g] Job 21:5; 29:9; 40:4; Mic 7:16 [h] Jdg 17:10
18:26 [i] Ps 18:17; 35:10
18:27 [j] ver 7,10 [k] Ge 49:17; Jos 19:47
18:28 [l] ver 7 [m] Nu 13:21; 2Sa 10:6
18:29 [n] Ge 14:14 [o] Jos 19:47; 1Ki 15:20
18:30 [p] Ex 2:22; Jdg 17:3,5
18:31 [q] Jdg 19:18 [r] Jos 18:1; Jer 7:14
19:1 [s] Jdg 18:1 [t] Ru 1:1

14 Then the five men who had spied out the land of Laish said to their fellow Danites, "Do you know
that one of these houses has an ephod, some household gods and an image overlaid with silver?[c] Now
you know what to do." 15 So they turned in there and went to the house of the young Levite at Micah's
place and greeted him. 16 The six hundred Danites,[d] armed for battle, stood at the entrance of the gate.
17 The five men who had spied out the land went inside and took the idol, the ephod and the household
gods[e] while the priest and the six hundred armed men stood at the entrance of the gate.
18 When the five men went into Micah's house and took[f] the idol, the ephod and the household gods,
the priest said to them, "What are you doing?"
19 They answered him, "Be quiet![g] Don't say a word. Come with us, and be our father and priest.[h]
Isn't it better that you serve a tribe and clan in Israel as priest rather than just one man's household?"
20 The priest was very pleased. He took the ephod, the household gods and the idol and went along with
the people. 21 Putting their little children, their livestock and their possessions in front of them, they
turned away and left.
22 When they had gone some distance from Micah's house, the men who lived near Micah were called
together and overtook the Danites. 23 As they shouted after them, the Danites turned and said to Micah,
"What's the matter with you that you called out your men to fight?"
24 He replied, "You took the gods I made, and my priest, and went away. What else do I have? How can
you ask, 'What's the matter with you?' "
25 The Danites answered, "Don't argue with us, or some of the men may get angry and attack you,
and you and your family will lose your lives." 26 So the Danites went their way, and Micah, seeing that
they were too strong for him,[i] turned around and went back home.
27 Then they took what Micah had made, and his priest, and went on to Laish, against a people at
peace and secure.[j] They attacked them with the sword and burned down their city.[k] 28 There was no one
to rescue them because they lived a long way from Sidon[l] and had no relationship with anyone else.
The city was in a valley near Beth Rehob.[m]
The Danites rebuilt the city and settled there. 29 They named it Dan[n] after their ancestor Dan, who
was born to Israel—though the city used to be called Laish.[o] 30 There the Danites set up for themselves
the idol, and Jonathan son of Gershom,[p] the son of Moses,[a] and his sons were priests for the tribe of
Dan until the time of the captivity of the land. 31 They continued to use the idol Micah had made, all
the time the house of God[q] was in Shiloh.[r]

A Levite and His Concubine

19 In those days Israel had no king.
Now a Levite who lived in a remote area in the hill country of Ephraim[s] took a concubine from
Bethlehem in Judah.[t] 2 But she was unfaithful to him. She left him and went back to her parents' home

[a] *30* Many Hebrew manuscripts, some Septuagint manuscripts and Vulgate; many other Hebrew manuscripts and some other Septuagint manuscripts *Manasseh*

18:15–17 The Danites should have destroyed Micah's shrine (Deut 12:2–3); instead, they steal it.

18:18–20 The Levite joins the Danites, who make him a better offer. He serves not God but only his stomach.

18:27–31 The Danites take Laish, rename it, and install Micah's images and the Levite there. Israel's attempts at manipulating God through idolatry ensnare them (see Introduction: Theology).

18:30 A priest descended from Moses is associated with this illegitimate cult at Dan (Exod 2:22; 1 Chr 23:14–15). Some scholars think that "until the time of the captivity of the land" alludes to the taking of the ark by the Philistines. However, the second part of verse 30 is affirming that the descendants of this Levite served as priests for the tribe of Dan until the captivity of the land (not the ark) at the time of the exile. See Jer 1:3 for a similar construction. Thus, it most likely refers to the captivity of the northern kingdom.

18:31 This verse affirms that the Danites used the image that Micah made until the capture and destruction of Shiloh, when the ark of the covenant was captured by the Philistines (1 Sam 4:11–22). The ark had been at Shiloh since the subduing of the land (Josh 18:1). Dan became an important center of worship for the northern kingdom (1 Kgs 12:29).

19:1—21:25 *Domestic Wars With Misapplication of the Law of Deut 7 (ḥērem) Being Applied.* The second conclusion opens and closes with the partial (19:1) and full (21:25) refrain (see Introduction: The Double Introduction and Double Conclusion). The section reveals a concentric (or chiastic) structure:

- *a* The rape of the concubine (19:1–30)
  - *b* The misapplication of the law of Deut 7 (*ḥērem*) on Benjamin (20:1–48)
    - *c* The oaths: Benjamin threatened with extinction (21:1–5)
  - *b´* The misapplication of the law of Deut 7 (*ḥērem*) on Jabesh Gilead (21:6–14)
- *a´* The rape of the daughters of Shiloh (21:15–25)

19:1–30 *The Rape of the Concubine.* This incident sets up a conflict that eventually pits the tribal assembly against Benjamin.

19:2 The woman of Bethlehem was not the full legal wife of the Levite,

in Bethlehem, Judah. After she had been there four months, 3 her husband went to her to persuade her to return. He had with him his servant and two donkeys. She took him into her parents' home, and when her father saw him, he gladly welcomed him. 4 His father-in-law, the woman's father, prevailed on him to stay; so he remained with him three days, eating and drinking,[u] and sleeping there.

5 On the fourth day they got up early and he prepared to leave, but the woman's father said to his son-in-law, "Refresh yourself[v] with something to eat; then you can go." 6 So the two of them sat down to eat and drink together. Afterward the woman's father said, "Please stay tonight and enjoy yourself.[w]" 7 And when the man got up to go, his father-in-law persuaded him, so he stayed there that night. 8 On the morning of the fifth day, when he rose to go, the woman's father said, "Refresh yourself. Wait till afternoon!" So the two of them ate together.

9 Then when the man, with his concubine and his servant, got up to leave, his father-in-law, the woman's father, said, "Now look, it's almost evening. Spend the night here; the day is nearly over. Stay and enjoy yourself. Early tomorrow morning you can get up and be on your way home." 10 But, unwilling to stay another night, the man left and went toward Jebus[x] (that is, Jerusalem), with his two saddled donkeys and his concubine.

11 When they were near Jebus and the day was almost gone, the servant said to his master, "Come, let's stop at this city of the Jebusites[y] and spend the night."

12 His master replied, "No. We won't go into any city whose people are not Israelites. We will go on to Gibeah." 13 He added, "Come, let's try to reach Gibeah or Ramah[z] and spend the night in one of those places." 14 So they went on, and the sun set as they neared Gibeah in Benjamin.[a] 15 There they stopped to spend the night. They went and sat in the city square,[b] but no one took them in for the night.

16 That evening[c] an old man from the hill country of Ephraim,[d] who was living in Gibeah (the inhabitants of the place were Benjamites), came in from his work in the fields. 17 When he looked and saw the traveler in the city square, the old man asked, "Where are you going? Where did you come from?"[e]

18 He answered, "We are on our way from Bethlehem in Judah to a remote area in the hill country of Ephraim where I live. I have been to Bethlehem in Judah and now I am going to the house of the LORD.[a][f] No one has taken me in for the night. 19 We have both straw and fodder[g] for our donkeys and bread and wine[h] for ourselves your servants — me, the woman and the young man with us. We don't need anything."

20 "You are welcome at my house," the old man said. "Let me supply whatever you need. Only don't spend the night in the square." 21 So he took him into his house and fed his donkeys. After they had washed their feet, they had something to eat and drink.[i]

22 While they were enjoying themselves,[j] some of the wicked men[k] of the city surrounded the house. Pounding on the door, they shouted to the old man who owned the house, "Bring out the man who came to your house so we can have sex with him.[l]"

23 The owner of the house went outside[m] and said to them, "No, my friends, don't be so vile. Since this man is my guest, don't do this outrageous thing.[n] 24 Look, here is my virgin daughter,[o] and his concubine. I will bring them out to you now, and you can use them and do to them whatever you wish. But as for this man, don't do such an outrageous thing."

[a] 18 Hebrew, Vulgate, Syriac and Targum; Septuagint *going home*

19:4 [u] Ex 32:6
19:5 [v] ver 8; Ge 18:5
19:6 [w] ver 9,22; Jdg 16:25
19:10 [x] Ge 10:16; Jos 15:8; 1Ch 11:4-5
19:11 [y] Jos 3:10
19:13 [z] Jos 18:25
19:14 [a] 1Sa 10:26; Isa 10:29
19:15 [b] Ge 19:2
19:16 [c] Ps 104:23 [d] ver 1
19:17 [e] Ge 29:4
19:18 [f] Jdg 18:31
19:19 [g] Ge 24:25 [h] Ge 14:18
19:21 [i] Ge 24:32-33; Lk 7:44
19:22 [j] Jdg 16:25 [k] Dt 13:13 [l] Ge 19:4-5; Jdg 20:5; Ro 1:26-27
19:23 [m] Ge 19:6 [n] Ge 34:7; Lev 19:29; Dt 22:21; Jdg 20:6; 2Sa 13:12; Ro 1:27
19:24 [o] Ge 19:8; Dt 21:14

so the text calls her his "concubine" (v. 1). The woman initiated the separation. The Levite went to Bethlehem to recover his concubine. His father-in-law's hospitality borders on the excessive, a foil to Gibeah's inhospitality (vv. 10–30).

19:10–21 The Levite prefers to spend the night in an Israelite town rather than a Canaanite (or more precisely, Jebusite) one. Ironically, by seeking to avoid the potential inhospitality of a foreign city, the Levite and his concubine suffer a worse fate than inhospitality in Gibeah, the Israelite city.

19:12 Gibeah. Identified with Tell el-Ful, four miles (6.5 kilometers) north of Jerusalem. It became Saul's royal residence (1 Sam 15:34).

19:13 Ramah. Identified with er-Ram, five miles (eight kilometers) north of Jerusalem.

19:16–21 An old man from Ephraim finally shows hospitality and at first appears to be the model host.

19:22–26 The old man's actions are similar to those of Lot when Lot offered his two daughters to the men of Sodom (Gen 19:1–11). While the text initially touches on the issue of hospitality, it is clear from v. 22 that the wicked men of the city intended to carry out a homosexual gang rape of the Levite. The old man's response is appalling: he offers his own virgin daughter and the Levite's concubine (see note on v. 24). The men at the door refuse to listen to the old man. In order to forestall his own rape by the men of Gibeah, the Levite offers them his concubine. The old man and the Levite do what is right in their own eyes. When God's word is unknown or ignored, innocent people are victimized (cf. Jephthah's daughter in 11:39–40). This poor woman suffers gang rape and abuse, and she is then discarded. She collapses at the door of the old man's house.

19:24 you can use them and do to them whatever you wish. Alternate translation: "Rape them and do to them what is good in your eyes."

19:25 [p] 1Sa 31:4
19:29 [q] Ge 22:6 [r] Jdg 20:6; 1Sa 11:7
19:30 [s] Hos 9:9 [t] Jdg 20:7; Pr 13:10
20:1 [u] Jdg 21:5 [v] 1Sa 3:20; 2Sa 3:10; 1Ki 4:25 [w] 1Sa 11:7 [x] 1Sa 7:5
20:2 [y] Jdg 8:10
20:4 [z] Jos 15:57 [a] Jdg 19:15
20:5 [b] Jdg 19:22 [c] Jdg 19:25-26
20:6 [d] Jdg 19:29 [e] Jos 7:15; Jdg 19:23
20:7 [f] Jdg 19:30
20:9 [g] Lev 16:8
20:11 [h] ver 1

[25]But the men would not listen to him. So the man took his concubine and sent her outside to them,
and they raped her and abused her[p] throughout the night, and at dawn they let her go. [26]At daybreak
the woman went back to the house where her master was staying, fell down at the door and lay there
until daylight.
[27]When her master got up in the morning and opened the door of the house and stepped out to
continue on his way, there lay his concubine, fallen in the doorway of the house, with her hands on
the threshold. [28]He said to her, "Get up; let's go." But there was no answer. Then the man put her on
his donkey and set out for home.
[29]When he reached home, he took a knife[q] and cut up his concubine, limb by limb, into twelve parts
and sent them into all the areas of Israel.[r] [30]Everyone who saw it was saying to one another, "Such a
thing has never been seen or done, not since the day the Israelites came up out of Egypt.[s] Just imagine!
We must do something! So speak up!"[t]

The Israelites Punish the Benjamites

20 Then all Israel[u] from Dan to Beersheba[v] and from the land of Gilead came together as one[w]
and assembled[x] before the LORD in Mizpah. [2]The leaders of all the people of the tribes of Israel
took their places in the assembly of God's people, four hundred thousand men[y] armed with swords.
[3](The Benjamites heard that the Israelites had gone up to Mizpah.) Then the Israelites said, "Tell us
how this awful thing happened."
[4]So the Levite, the husband of the murdered woman, said, "I and my concubine came to Gibeah[z]
in Benjamin to spend the night.[a] [5]During the night the men of Gibeah came after me and surrounded
the house, intending to kill me.[b] They raped my concubine, and she died.[c] [6]I took my concubine, cut
her into pieces and sent one piece to each region of Israel's inheritance,[d] because they committed
this lewd and outrageous act[e] in Israel. [7]Now, all you Israelites, speak up and tell me what you have
decided to do.[f]"
[8]All the men rose up together as one, saying, "None of us will go home. No, not one of us will return
to his house. [9]But now this is what we'll do to Gibeah: We'll go up against it in the order decided by
casting lots.[g] [10]We'll take ten men out of every hundred from all the tribes of Israel, and a hundred
from a thousand, and a thousand from ten thousand, to get provisions for the army. Then, when the
army arrives at Gibeah[a] in Benjamin, it can give them what they deserve for this outrageous act done
in Israel." [11]So all the Israelites got together and united as one against the city.[h]
[12]The tribes of Israel sent messengers throughout the tribe of Benjamin, saying, "What about this

[a] *10* One Hebrew manuscript; most Hebrew manuscripts *Geba,* a variant of *Gibeah*

19:28 Get up; let's go. Rather than seeking the authorities to save his concubine, the Levite sleeps throughout the night. In the morning, he callously commands his concubine. Usually the OT states when a person is dead. Here it is ambiguous because the text says only that "there was no answer." Since it does not say that she is dead, there is some uncertainty as to when she dies.

19:29 After returning home, instead of giving her a proper burial (if she is dead), the Levite takes a knife and cuts her up limb by limb. He sends the parts to the 12 tribes in order to cause horror among them and muster them for war against Benjamin. Ultimately, this was to obtain his own personal revenge against the men of Gibeah. It is ironic that the one who issued such a call was himself so selfish and insensitive. Later, Saul calls up the tribes of Israel in a strikingly similar fashion, although he cuts up a pair of oxen (1 Sam 11:7).

20:1–48 *The Misapplication of the Law of Deut 7 (ḥērem) on Benjamin.* While the Israelites would not carry out the law of Deut 7 (the *ḥērem* of the Canaanites) in 1:1—2:5, they carry it out on a tribe of Israel, bringing it to near extinction. This is a misapplication of not only the law of Deut 7 but also of the law of Deut 13:12–18 (specifically v. 15).

20:1–11 It is truly ironic that this nameless Levite gets the greatest response from the greatest number of tribes in Israel in all of the book of Judges. The Levite, who calls the tribes to muster by the grotesque mutilation of his concubine, has become a self-appointed judge. He is the sole witness. Moreover, he bears false witness by heightening the crime of the men of Gibeah while downplaying his own guilt in sacrificing his concubine by pushing her out to the Gibeahites. Ironically, the Levite sacrificed his concubine to save himself and now is willing to sacrifice the sons of Israel to get his personal revenge on the Gibeahites. Without any additional testimony (contrary to the law that required two or more witnesses, Deut 19:15), the tribal assembly condemns the crime against the Levite's concubine and takes steps to punish the guilty. The Levite now disappears. All actions are based on tribally determined loyalties, regardless of moral questions. The only consideration was that he was a fellow tribe member. A proper theological view of justice, derived and implemented from God's law, should override such human preconceptions.

20:1 Dan. The northernmost Israelite city. **Beersheba.** The southernmost Israelite city. "From Dan to Beersheba" was a conventional way of describing all Israel from north to south. **Gilead.** The Transjordanian territories. **Mizpah.** Probably the Mizpah of Benjamin (Josh 18:26), identified with Tell en-Nasbeh, eight miles (13 kilometers) north of Jerusalem. (A few Israelite towns were named Mizpah.)

20:12–17 The Benjamites refused to subject themselves to the authority of the tribal assembly, and civil war ensued. Tribal integrity was more important to them than justice for a criminal act.

awful crime that was committed among you? [13]Now turn those wicked men[i] of Gibeah over to us so that
we may put them to death and purge the evil from Israel.[j]"
But the Benjamites would not listen to their fellow Israelites. [14]From their towns they came together at Gibeah to fight against the Israelites. [15]At once the Benjamites mobilized twenty-six thousand
swordsmen from their towns, in addition to seven hundred able young men from those living in Gibeah.
[16]Among all these soldiers there were seven hundred select troops who were left-handed,[k] each of whom
could sling a stone at a hair and not miss.
[17]Israel, apart from Benjamin, mustered four hundred thousand swordsmen, all of them fit for
battle.
[18]The Israelites went up to Bethel[a] and inquired of God.[l] They said, "Who of us is to go up first to
fight[m] against the Benjamites?"
The LORD replied, "Judah shall go first."
[19]The next morning the Israelites got up and pitched camp near Gibeah. [20]The Israelites went out to
fight the Benjamites and took up battle positions against them at Gibeah. [21]The Benjamites came out
of Gibeah and cut down twenty-two thousand Israelites[n] on the battlefield that day. [22]But the Israelites
encouraged one another and again took up their positions where they had stationed themselves the first
day. [23]The Israelites went up and wept before the LORD until evening,[o] and they inquired of the LORD.
They said, "Shall we go up again to fight[p] against the Benjamites, our fellow Israelites?"
The LORD answered, "Go up against them."
[24]Then the Israelites drew near to Benjamin the second day. [25]This time, when the Benjamites came
out from Gibeah to oppose them, they cut down another eighteen thousand Israelites,[q] all of them
armed with swords.
[26]Then all the Israelites, the whole army, went up to Bethel, and there they sat weeping before the
LORD.[r] They fasted that day until evening and presented burnt offerings and fellowship offerings to the
LORD.[s] [27]And the Israelites inquired of the LORD. (In those days the ark of the covenant of God[t] was there,
[28]with Phinehas son of Eleazar,[u] the son of Aaron, ministering before it.)[v] They asked, "Shall we go up
again to fight against the Benjamites, our fellow Israelites, or not?"
The LORD responded, "Go, for tomorrow I will give them into your hands.[w]"
[29]Then Israel set an ambush[x] around Gibeah. [30]They went up against the Benjamites on the third
day and took up positions against Gibeah as they had done before. [31]The Benjamites came out to meet
them and were drawn away[y] from the city. They began to inflict casualties on the Israelites as before,
so that about thirty men fell in the open field and on the roads—the one leading to Bethel and the
other to Gibeah. [32]While the Benjamites were saying, "We are defeating them as before,"[z] the Israelites
were saying, "Let's retreat and draw them away from the city to the roads."
[33]All the men of Israel moved from their places and took up positions at Baal Tamar, and the Israelite
ambush charged out of its place[a] on the west[b] of Gibeah.[c] [34]Then ten thousand of Israel's able young
men made a frontal attack on Gibeah. The fighting was so heavy that the Benjamites did not realize[b] how
near disaster was.[c] [35]The LORD defeated Benjamin[d] before Israel, and on that day the Israelites struck down
25,100 Benjamites, all armed with swords. [36]Then the Benjamites saw that they were beaten.
Now the men of Israel had given way[e] before Benjamin, because they relied on the ambush they had
set near Gibeah. [37]Those who had been in ambush made a sudden dash into Gibeah, spread out and put
the whole city to the sword.[f] [38]The Israelites had arranged with the ambush that they should send up a
great cloud of smoke[g] from the city, [39]and then the Israelites would counterattack.
The Benjamites had begun to inflict casualties on the Israelites (about thirty), and they said, "We are

20:13 [i]Dt 13:13; Jdg 19:22 [j]Dt 17:12
20:16 [k]Jdg 3:15; 1Ch 12:2
20:18 [l]ver 26-27; Nu 27:21 [m]ver 23,28
20:21 [n]ver 25
20:23 [o]Jos 7:6 [p]ver 18
20:25 [q]ver 21
20:26 [r]ver 23 [s]Jdg 21:4
20:27 [t]Jos 18:1
20:28 [u]Jos 24:33 [v]Dt 18:5 [w]Jdg 7:9
20:29 [x]Jos 8:2,4
20:31 [y]Jos 8:16
20:32 [z]ver 39
20:33 [a]Jos 8:19
20:34 [b]Jos 8:14 [c]Isa 47:11
20:35 [d]1Sa 9:21
20:36 [e]Jos 8:15
20:37 [f]Jos 8:19
20:38 [g]Jos 8:20

[a] *18* Or *to the house of God*; also in verse 26 [b] *33* Some Septuagint manuscripts and Vulgate; the meaning of the Hebrew for this word is uncertain. [c] *33* Hebrew *Geba,* a variant of *Gibeah*

20:16 left-handed. Cf. 3:15.

20:18–48 The Israelites attempt to subdue Benjamin in three battles: (1) they attack en masse but suffer a severe defeat (vv. 18–21); (2) they again attack en masse but suffer a severe defeat (vv. 22–25); and (3) they set an ambush and almost accomplish the *ḥērem* of the Benjamites: men, women, children, and animals—all except 600 men (vv. 26–48). Ironically, the determination and thoroughness surpasses anything evidenced in most of Israel's wars against the Canaanites elsewhere in Judges. Because the Israelites are doing what is right in their eyes, they come close to destroying one of their own tribes. Clearly, the punishment on Benjamin far exceeds the crime that was committed. In fact, the men of Gibeah who raped the concubine may be among the surviving 600.

20:18 Bethel. Once known as Luz, it had associations with both Abraham (Gen 12:8; 13:3) and Jacob (Gen 28:10–22).

20:39 [h] ver 32
20:40 [i] Jos 8:20
20:44 [j] Ps 76:5
20:45 [k] Jos 15:32; Jdg 21:13
20:48 [l] Jdg 21:23
21:1 [m] Jos 9:18 [n] Jdg 20:1 [o] ver 7,18
21:4 [p] Jdg 20:26; 2Sa 24:25
21:5 [q] Jdg 5:23; 20:1
21:7 [r] ver 1
21:8 [s] 1Sa 11:1; 31:11
21:11 [t] Nu 31:17-18
21:12 [u] Jos 18:1
21:13 [v] Dt 20:10 [w] Jdg 20:47

defeating them as in the first battle."[h] [40]But when the column of smoke began to rise from the city, the Benjamites turned and saw the whole city going up in smoke.[i] [41]Then the Israelites counterattacked, and the Benjamites were terrified, because they realized that disaster had come on them. [42]So they fled before the Israelites in the direction of the wilderness, but they could not escape the battle. And the Israelites who came out of the towns cut them down there. [43]They surrounded the Benjamites, chased them and easily[a] overran them in the vicinity of Gibeah on the east. [44]Eighteen thousand Benjamites fell, all of them valiant fighters.[j] [45]As they turned and fled toward the wilderness to the rock of Rimmon,[k] the Israelites cut down five thousand men along the roads. They kept pressing after the Benjamites as far as Gidom and struck down two thousand more.

[46]On that day twenty-five thousand Benjamite swordsmen fell, all of them valiant fighters. [47]But six hundred of them turned and fled into the wilderness to the rock of Rimmon, where they stayed four months. [48]The men of Israel went back to Benjamin and put all the towns to the sword, including the animals and everything else they found. All the towns they came across they set on fire.[l]

Wives for the Benjamites

21 The men of Israel had taken an oath[m] at Mizpah:[n] "Not one of us will give[o] his daughter in marriage to a Benjamite."

[2]The people went to Bethel,[b] where they sat before God until evening, raising their voices and weeping bitterly. [3]"LORD, God of Israel," they cried, "why has this happened to Israel? Why should one tribe be missing from Israel today?"

[4]Early the next day the people built an altar and presented burnt offerings and fellowship offerings.[p]

[5]Then the Israelites asked, "Who from all the tribes of Israel[q] has failed to assemble before the LORD?" For they had taken a solemn oath that anyone who failed to assemble before the LORD at Mizpah was to be put to death.

[6]Now the Israelites grieved for the tribe of Benjamin, their fellow Israelites. "Today one tribe is cut off from Israel," they said. [7]"How can we provide wives for those who are left, since we have taken an oath[r] by the LORD not to give them any of our daughters in marriage?" [8]Then they asked, "Which one of the tribes of Israel failed to assemble before the LORD at Mizpah?" They discovered that no one from Jabesh Gilead[s] had come to the camp for the assembly. [9]For when they counted the people, they found that none of the people of Jabesh Gilead were there.

[10]So the assembly sent twelve thousand fighting men with instructions to go to Jabesh Gilead and put to the sword those living there, including the women and children. [11]"This is what you are to do," they said. "Kill every male and every woman who is not a virgin.[t]" [12]They found among the people living in Jabesh Gilead four hundred young women who had never slept with a man, and they took them to the camp at Shiloh[u] in Canaan.

[13]Then the whole assembly sent an offer of peace[v] to the Benjamites at the rock of Rimmon.[w] [14]So the Benjamites returned at that time and were given the women of Jabesh Gilead who had been spared. But there were not enough for all of them.

[a] *43* The meaning of the Hebrew for this word is uncertain. [b] *2* Or *to the house of God*

21:1–5 *The Oaths: Benjamin Threatened With Extinction.* The inept handling of the Gibeah incident leads to the near extinction of the tribe of Benjamin.

21:1 The men of Israel had taken an oath at Mizpah. The Israelites create a dilemma. Because they have taken a rash oath that none of them will give their daughters to the Benjamites (cf. Jephthah's vow in 11:30–31), there is no way to ensure the survival of the tribe of Benjamin without breaking their oath. Ironically, the daughters of Benjamin have suffered the same fate as the Levite's concubine. In contrast, the Israelites gave their daughters to the Canaanites (3:5–6).

21:5 The Israelites had taken a second oath concerning nonparticipation in the war against Benjamin.

21:6–14 *The Misapplication of the Law of Deut 7 (ḥērem) on Jabesh Gilead.* In order to repopulate the tribe of Benjamin, the Israelites resort to applying the *ḥērem* on Jabesh Gilead, a town whose people had not supplied troops for the war against Benjamin. This is another misapplication of the law of Deut 7 and the law of Deut 13:12–18 (specifically *ḥērem* in v. 15; see note on 20:1–48). It is ironic that had the Israelites followed the law of Deut 13, they would have done what was right in the eyes of the Lord (v. 18).

21:9 none of the people of Jabesh Gilead were there. This was discovered through the pragmatics of a roll call, not through divine guidance (the Lord is silent). **Jabesh Gilead.** A town in the northern Transjordan region. Ironically, the Israelites destroy the town that Jephthah rescued from the Ammonites' threat (11:4–33), and later, after it is rebuilt, Saul (a Benjamite) rescues the people of Jabesh Gilead (1 Sam 11).

21:12–14 The Israelites spare 400 virgins and give them to the remaining Benjamites as wives.

21:12 Shiloh. About nine miles (14.5 kilometers) north of Bethel.

[15]The people grieved for Benjamin,[x] because the LORD had made a gap in the tribes of Israel. [16]And
the elders of the assembly said, "With the women of Benjamin destroyed, how shall we provide wives
for the men who are left? [17]The Benjamite survivors must have heirs," they said, "so that a tribe of Israel will not be wiped out. [18]We can't give them our daughters as wives, since we Israelites have taken
this oath: 'Cursed be anyone who gives[y] a wife to a Benjamite.' [19]But look, there is the annual festival
of the LORD in Shiloh,[z] which lies north of Bethel, east of the road that goes from Bethel to Shechem,
and south of Lebonah."

[20]So they instructed the Benjamites, saying, "Go and hide in the vineyards [21]and watch. When the
young women of Shiloh come out to join in the dancing,[a] rush from the vineyards and each of you
seize one of them to be your wife. Then return to the land of Benjamin. [22]When their fathers or brothers complain to us, we will say to them, 'Do us the favor of helping them, because we did not get wives
for them during the war. You will not be guilty of breaking your oath because you did not give[b] your
daughters to them.'"

[23]So that is what the Benjamites did. While the young women were dancing, each man caught one
and carried her off to be his wife. Then they returned to their inheritance and rebuilt the towns and
settled in them.[c]

[24]At that time the Israelites left that place and went home to their tribes and clans, each to his own
inheritance.

[25]In those days Israel had no king; everyone did as they saw fit.[d]

21:15 [x] ver 6
21:18 [y] ver 1
21:19 [z] Jos 18:1; Jdg 18:31; 1Sa 1:3
21:21 [a] Ex 15:20; Jdg 11:34
21:22 [b] ver 1,18
21:23 [c] Jdg 20:48
21:25 [d] Dt 12:8; Jdg 17:6; 18:1; 19:1

21:15–25 *The Rape of the Daughters of Shiloh.* The elders of Israel devise the second strategy for repopulating Benjamin, which is nothing short of another rape. The Benjamites are allowed to abduct unprotected dancers among the women of Shiloh without fear of reprisal. The annual festival of the Lord provides the context. That this occurs at a religious festival to Yahweh underlines how little respect the Israelites have for their covenant obligations.

21:22 The elders use the Mizpah oath against the girls' fathers. The rape of the daughters of Shiloh is an ironic counterpoint to the rape of the concubine (ch. 19).

21:25 The refrain that characterizes the double conclusion gives a final verdict on the events of chs. 19–21. Israel has broken the covenant. It has ignored God's kingship and hence done what is right in its own eyes (see Introduction: Theology).

INTRODUCTION TO RUTH

This is one of the Bible's most popular stories. Its clever, charming literary artistry makes the history a delight to read. It also illustrates one way in which God influences the lives of his people.

AUTHOR AND PLACE OF COMPOSITION

The OT offers no clue as to the author of the book of Ruth. Jewish tradition credits it to Samuel, but that seems unlikely because he died long before David became king. Clearly, the author is a superb storyteller with access to the history of David's family and to the royal archive in Jerusalem (cf. 4:18 – 22). If the date of the book proposed below holds, the author may have worked in Jerusalem on the staff of the royal court, perhaps as a scribe.

DATE

The book was probably written during Solomon's reign (ca. tenth century BC). Theologically, it compares to literature of that period, and so do its themes and purpose (see Occasion and Purpose; Themes).

View of Moab.

THE BOOK OF RUTH

Set in the dark and bloody days of the judges, the story of Ruth is silent about the underlying hostility and suspicion the two peoples—Judahites and Moabites—felt for each other. The original onslaught of the invading Israelite tribes against towns that were once Moabite had never been forgotten or forgiven, while the Hebrew prophets denounced Moab's pride and arrogance for trying to bewitch, seduce, and oppress Israel from t he time of Balaam on. The Mesha Stele (ca. 830 BC) boasts of the massacre of entire Israelite towns.

Moab encompassed the expansive, grain-rich plateau between the Dead Sea and the eastern desert on both sides of the enormous rift of the Arnon River gorge. Much of eastern Moab was steppe land—semi-arid wastes not profitable for cultivation, but excellent for grazing flocks of sheep and goats. The tribute Moab paid to Israel in the days of Ahab was 100,000 lambs and the wool of 100,000 rams (see 2 Kgs 3:4).

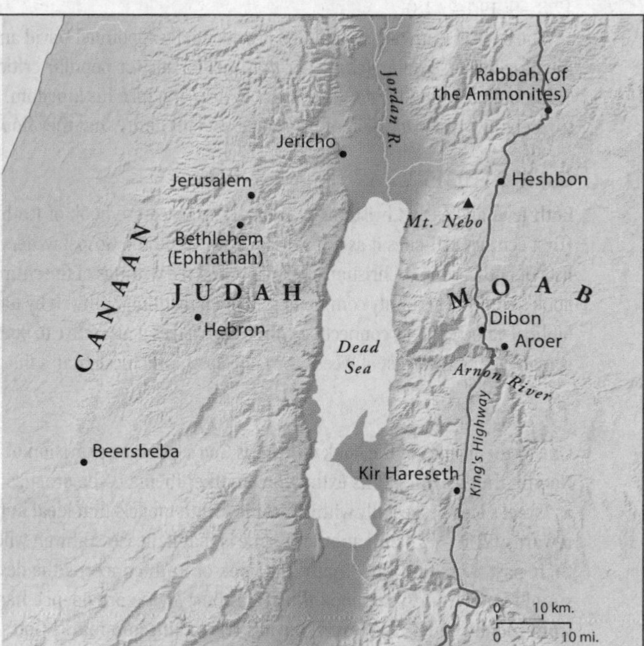

PARTICULAR CHALLENGES

The Israelite legal practices behind the book of Ruth pose a particular challenge for modern readers. Fortunately, other biblical narratives are helpful, showing how Israelite law applies in situations similar to those in Ruth. The widow who petitions the king to restore her house and land to her possession (2 Kgs 8:1 – 6) indicates that she either already owned them herself or served as their trustee on behalf of her son, the rightful heir. Similarly, as her husband's sole survivor, Naomi probably had the right to sell the land to close family.

The duty of a guardian-redeemer (Lev 25:23 – 55) helps explain the land's purchase by Boaz and also his marriage to Ruth. This law tasks close relatives, the guardian-redeemers (Hebrew *gōʾēl*), with buying back mortgaged clan property and freeing relatives from debt-slavery. Boaz, as a *gōʾēl*, buys the family land, marries Ruth to produce an heir for Naomi, and holds the land in trust on behalf of the hoped-for heir. The solution keeps Naomi's family line alive on its ancestral property. For more legal background, see the notes on 4:3,6.

GENRE

The book of Ruth is a short story penned by a master narrator. Structurally, the story has a beginning (1:1 – 5), middle (1:6 — 4:17), and end (4:18 – 22). It features characters that are ordinary people inhabiting a small town, not kings in capital cities. Readers easily identify with Naomi's bitter experience, and they fear for the safety of Ruth the Moabite. They also admire the noble Boaz. The dialogues between the characters dominate the story, driving its action forward and sounding key themes. Like any short story, it intends to instruct, but it does so in a very enthralling way. The author's literary devices include word repetition, word or sound plays, inclusios, pathos, allusions, flashbacks, occasional interpretive comments, surprise endings, and a concluding genealogy. In the hands of a master, these devices (and others) have produced a literary, historical, and theological gem.

OCCASION AND PURPOSE

The book ends with David (4:17b – 22), sounding the theme that David's rise to prominence culminated centuries of divine providence in his family. His kingship fulfills the promise given to the patriarchs (Gen 17:6,16; 35:11), and his advent was anticipated by Moses (Deut 17:14 – 20).

Theologically, the book of Ruth lays a bridge between the repeated longing for leadership at the end of Judges (17:6; 18:1; 19:1; 21:25) and God's provision of it in Saul and David (1 Sam 9; 16). It commends the exemplary faithfulness of Ruth and Boaz in Bethlehem over the compromise and misfortune of two earlier Bethlehemites (Judg 17:8–9; 19:1–2,18).

The book of Ruth asserts that God providentially appointed David and his descendants to rule Israel. Further, Ruth the Moabite's exemplary character may seek to answer popular criticism about the many foreign advisors whom Solomon had brought into the country to help organize his kingdom. Above all, the book's purpose is to extol God's sovereignty, loyal protection of his people, and his desire that they flourish as a nation.

CANONICITY

Both Jews and early Christians universally accepted the book of Ruth as canonical. The Jewish historian Josephus (first century AD) cites it as a historical book, as do the Gospel writers (Matt 1:5; Luke 3:32). The earliest canonical lists of both Jews and Christians include it, and the writings of the church fathers use it in Scriptural discussions. The book's contents certainly commend it: it often mentions Yahweh by name; its noble characters exemplify the best of biblical values; and its connection with David makes it attractive to both Jews and Christians. In Jewish worship, Ruth is read during the Feast of Weeks (or Pentecost), which celebrates the giving of the Torah at Mount Sinai.

THEMES

One of the themes of the book of Ruth is God's gracious provision of a son for the heirless family of Elimelek and Naomi, thus staving off its extinction. Another theme is the practice of *ḥesed* (Hebrew for "loyalty, compassion") as Israel's ideal, especially within families. Ruth models that ideal at its best (1:8; 3:10) and rightly earns Yahweh's rewards (2:11–12). Still another theme is that it pleases Yahweh when Israel welcomes foreigners who, whatever their past, worship him. Finally, the book of Ruth concerns the descent of David from Ruth and Boaz and the simple family story. The book illustrates how divine providence has shadowed and shepherded this family line from Judah (Gen 38) to David. David's rise to kingship marks God's provision of long-expected royal leadership for Israel's good.

THEOLOGY

The theological atmosphere in the book of Ruth is unique. Absent are the dramatic miracles and wonders of other biblical books. God never speaks at all. Center stage belongs to the human characters. At two key points, however, God

View of Moab looking across from the Judean desert.
Designpics/Glow Images

intervenes, renewing food production (1:6) and enabling Ruth to conceive (4:13). The former guides Naomi back to Judah, and the latter enables Ruth to provide Naomi's family with an heir. In between, "accidents" happen, hints that divine providence is quietly at work. Ruth "just happens" to glean in Boaz's field on the very day that Boaz "just happens" to visit. Boaz "just happens" to reach the city gate just as the relative he needs to see passes by. In retrospect, however, Naomi's friends credit Yahweh with everything — the direct interventions and the "accidents" (4:14).

Two theological beliefs shape the book: (1) Yahweh's sovereign activity is ongoing but hidden, and (2) Yahweh plays a cosmic role as a doer and rewarder of *ḥesed* (acts of loyalty, compassion, mercy). The second explains why the book links Naomi's childlessness and Ruth's familial devotion with later reversals of their fortunes. The reversals — divine rewards for their *ḥesed* — also comprise answers to earlier petitions (1:8; 2:12; 4:11 – 12). In Ruth's case, her rewards actually exceed expectations. In short, theologically the book of Ruth teaches that sometimes God's sovereignly works behind the scenes in and through human acts of *ḥesed*, especially when those actions serve some larger, divine purpose.

OUTLINE

I. Naomi Loses Her Husband and Sons (1:1 – 5)

II. Naomi and Ruth Return to Bethlehem (1:6 – 22)

III. Ruth Meets Boaz in the Grain Field (2:1 – 23)

IV. Ruth and Boaz at the Threshing Floor (3:1 – 18)

V. Boaz Marries Ruth (4:1 – 12)

VI. Naomi Gains a Son (4:13 – 17)

VII. The Genealogy of David (4:18 – 22)

RUTH

1:1 [a]Jdg 2:16-18 [b]Ge 12:10; Ps 105:16 [c]Jdg 3:30
1:2 [d]Ge 35:19
1:4 [e]Mt 1:5
1:6 [f]Ex 4:31; Jer 29:10; Zep 2:7 [g]Ps 132:15; Mt 6:11

Naomi Loses Her Husband and Sons

1 In the days when the judges ruled,[a][a] there was a famine in the land.[b] So a man from Bethlehem in Judah, together with his wife and two sons, went to live for a while in the country of
Moab.[c] 2 The man's name was Elimelek, his wife's name was Naomi, and the names of his two sons
were Mahlon and Kilion. They were Ephrathites from Bethlehem,[d] Judah. And they went to Moab
and lived there.
3 Now Elimelek, Naomi's husband, died, and she was left with her two sons. 4 They married Moabite
women, one named Orpah and the other Ruth.[e] After they had lived there about ten years, 5 both Mahlon and Kilion also died, and Naomi was left without her two sons and her husband.

Naomi and Ruth Return to Bethlehem

6 When Naomi heard in Moab that the Lord had come to the aid of his people[f] by providing food[g]
for them, she and her daughters-in-law prepared to return home from there. 7 With her two daughters-in-law she left the place where she had been living and set out on the road that would take them
back to the land of Judah.
8 Then Naomi said to her two daughters-in-law, "Go back, each of you, to your mother's home. May

[a] 1 Traditionally *judged*

1:1–5 *Naomi Loses Her Husband and Sons.* The book of Ruth opens with huge sadness that sets the scene for the story of a childless widow, Naomi (1:6—4:17). From the outset, the book's underlying question is "Where is God in all this?"
1:1 judges. The famous leaders who led Israel during the era that the book of Judges reports. **famine.** Often sent Israelites to nearby countries that had ample food, mainly Egypt and Philistia (Gen 12:10; 26:1; 2 Kgs 8:1–2). **live for a while.** The Hebrew word evokes the ancient tradition of hospitality and its legal protection of resident aliens, the status of Israel's patriarchs (Gen 12:10; 47:4). Mosaic law later established similar protection in Israel (Exod 23:9; Deut 10:18). **Moab.** Sits along the Dead Sea's lower east bank between the Arnon and Zered Rivers (Num 21:13). The Moabites descended from the son born from Lot's incestuous union with his older daughter (Gen 19:37).
1:2 Elimelek. Means "my God is king"; affirms God's royal sovereignty. **Naomi.** See note on v. 20. **Mahlon.** Ruth's husband (4:10); his name probably means "weakling" or "sickly person." **Kilion.** Probably means something like "frail person." Both names bode ill for their fates. **Ephrathites.** Cf. 4:11.
1:3 Elimelek's death suddenly reduces Naomi to widowhood with two sons to raise. The book offers no explanation for this tragedy. Israel's morality declined in the period of the judges, so Elimelek's death might be punishment for sin (i.e., for his leaving Judah rather than trusting God to provide during the famine).
1:4 Orpah. Means "obstinate" or "with thick hair." **Ruth.** Means "refreshment." **about ten years.** Implies "a good, long time," i.e., time enough for fertile wives to bear children (cf. Gen 16:3), but not in this case.
1:5 her two sons and her husband. Tallies up Naomi's cruel losses in reverse order; the tragic end of the family line now seems certain.
1:6–22 *Naomi and Ruth Return to Bethlehem.* The main story (1:6—4:17) begins with two brief scenes in which Naomi voices her anger and grief for the first time (vv. 8–18, 19–21). The word "return" (repeated 12 times)—back to Moab or back to Judah—brackets the section (vv. 6,22) and sounds its main theme. Naomi's powerful words reiterate the question "Where is God in all of this?"
1:6 come to the aid. Invokes a key Hebrew word for divine interventions (cf. Gen 21:1 ["was gracious to"]; Exod 3:16 ["have watched over"]; 20:5 ["punishing … for"]) to mark the first of only two reports in Ruth of God's direct intervention (4:13 for the second intervention).
1:8–18 Down the road, Naomi tries to persuade the two young widows to return to Moab rather than accompany her to Bethlehem. Orpah obeys and returns (v. 14), but Ruth's beautiful declaration of commitment (vv. 16–17) finally silences Naomi (v. 18).
1:8 mother's home. Probably where marriages were arranged (Gen 24:28,67; Song 3:4; 8:2). **kindness.** Hebrew *ḥesed,* meaning "compassion, commitment," one of the book's main themes (see Introduction: Themes; Theology). Naomi asks the Lord to repay the kindness of her two daughters-in-law with commensurate kindness (cf. 2:20; 3:10). The reward sought here is "rest" (v. 9).

the LORD show you kindness,[h] as you have shown kindness to your dead husbands[i] and to me. 9May the
LORD grant that each of you will find rest[j] in the home of another husband."
Then she kissed them goodbye and they wept aloud 10and said to her, "We will go back with you to
your people."
11But Naomi said, "Return home, my daughters. Why would you come with me? Am I going to have
any more sons, who could become your husbands?[k] 12Return home, my daughters; I am too old to
have another husband. Even if I thought there was still hope for me—even if I had a husband tonight
and then gave birth to sons— 13would you wait until they grew up? Would you remain unmarried
for them? No, my daughters. It is more bitter for me than for you, because the LORD's hand has turned
against me![l]"
14At this they wept aloud again. Then Orpah kissed her mother-in-law[m] goodbye, but Ruth clung
to her.[n]
15"Look," said Naomi, "your sister-in-law is going back to her people and her gods.[o] Go back with her."
16But Ruth replied, "Don't urge me to leave you[p] or to turn back from you. Where you go I will go,
and where you stay I will stay. Your people will be my people and your God my God.[q] 17Where you die
I will die, and there I will be buried. May the LORD deal with me, be it ever so severely,[r] if even death
separates you and me." 18When Naomi realized that Ruth was determined to go with her, she stopped
urging her.[s]
19So the two women went on until they came to Bethlehem. When they arrived in Bethlehem, the
whole town was stirred[t] because of them, and the women exclaimed, "Can this be Naomi?"
20"Don't call me Naomi,[a]" she told them. "Call me Mara,[b] because the Almighty[c][u] has made my
life very bitter.[v] 21I went away full, but the LORD has brought me back empty.[w] Why call me Naomi? The
LORD has afflicted[d] me; the Almighty has brought misfortune upon me."
22So Naomi returned from Moab accompanied by Ruth the Moabite, her daughter-in-law, arriving
in Bethlehem as the barley harvest[x] was beginning.[y]

Ruth Meets Boaz in the Grain Field

2 Now Naomi had a relative[z] on her husband's side, a man of standing from the clan of Elimelek,[a]
whose name was Boaz.[b]
2And Ruth the Moabite said to Naomi, "Let me go to the fields and pick up the leftover grain[c] behind
anyone in whose eyes I find favor."

1:8 [h] Ru 2:20; 2Ti 1:16 [i] ver 5
1:9 [j] Ru 3:1
1:11 [k] Ge 38:11; Dt 25:5
1:13 [l] Jdg 2:15; Job 4:5; 19:21; Ps 32:4
1:14 [m] Ru 2:11 [n] Pr 17:17; 18:24
1:15 [o] Jos 24:14; Jdg 11:24
1:16 [p] 2Ki 2:2 [q] Ru 2:11,12
1:17 [r] 1Sa 3:17; 25:22; 2Sa 19:13; 2Ki 6:31
1:18 [s] Ac 21:14
1:19 [t] Mt 21:10
1:20 [u] Ex 6:3 [v] ver 13; Job 6:4
1:21 [w] Job 1:21
1:22 [x] Ex 9:31; Ru 2:23 [y] 2Sa 21:9
2:1 [z] Ru 3:2,12 [a] Ru 1:2 [b] Ru 4:21
2:2 [c] ver 7; Lev 19:9; 23:22; Dt 24:19

[a] *20 Naomi* means *pleasant.* [b] *20 Mara* means *bitter.* [c] *20* Hebrew *Shaddai*; also in verse 21
[d] *21* Or *has testified against*

1:9 rest. Settle into a long, satisfying marriage (cf. 3:1).
1:11–12 Return home ... Return home. Naomi pleads with Orpah and Ruth to go where their best hopes for marriage and children lie: Why should they sacrifice their futures to share her hopeless one? The scene ends tenderly with Orpah's tearful goodbye and departure and Ruth's tearful, determined embrace of Naomi.
1:12–13 Naomi has in mind "levirate marriage," the marriage of a childless widow to her brother-in-law to provide her late husband an heir (cf. Gen 38; Deut 25:5–10).
1:12 too old. Naomi is postmenopausal, so the younger women are foolish to stick with her. She cannot provide them with new husbands to replace her dead sons.
1:13 LORD's hand. Symbolizes the Lord's great power. **turned against.** Pictures Naomi as "under attack."
1:15 Naomi's final tactic is an appeal to peer pressure: Ruth should follow Orpah's wise course.
1:16–17 Ruth renounces all her past ties in Moab to embrace Naomi's country, family, and faith in Bethlehem.
1:16 your God. Previously Ruth probably worshiped the Moabite god, Chemosh (Judg 11:24; 2 Kgs 23:13).
1:17 be buried. Ruth may allude to burial in a common family grave, an ancient practice attested by tombs at Beth Shemesh. **May the LORD.** Ruth's oath invokes Yahweh by name for the first time and confirms how serious her commitment is.
1:19–21 Arriving at the gate of Bethlehem, Naomi laments her bitter fate and accuses the cruel divine hand she deems behind it.
1:19 stirred. Pictures an excited city abuzz with conversations as news of Naomi's unexpected arrival spreads. **Can this be Naomi?** Women at the gate voice the town's stunned disbelief.
1:20 Naomi. Means "my pleasant one," an ironic insult (Naomi thinks) given her misery. **Mara.** Means "bitter." Naomi prefers this name because she thinks that God made her life "very bitter." **Almighty.** See note on Gen 17:1; cf. Gen 35:11; Job 5:17; 6:4,14.
1:21 full ... empty. Contrasts Naomi's situation at her departure (she had a husband and sons) and her return (she is a childless widow). **brought ... back.** A form of "return," the chapter's thematic key (see note on vv. 11–12). **afflicted ... brought misfortune.** Climactically Naomi holds God accountable for her tragic life, another chapter theme.
1:22 Naomi returned. This summary closes the section that v. 6 opened ("return"). **barley harvest.** Dates the widows' arrival to April and sets the scene for what comes next.
2:1–23 *Ruth Meets Boaz in the Grain Field.* The story takes a positive turn with the chance, first meeting of Ruth and Boaz. Ruth's work proposal (v. 2) and her report to Naomi (vv. 18–23) bracket the meeting

2:4 [d]Jdg 6:12; Lk 1:28; 2Th 3:16 [e]Ps 129:7-8
2:6 [f]Ru 1:22
2:10 [g]1Sa 25:23 [h]Ps 41:1 [i]Dt 15:3
2:11 [j]Ru 1:14 [k]Ru 1:16-17
2:12 [l]1Sa 24:19 [m]Ps 17:8; 36:7; 57:1; 61:4; 63:7; 91:4 [n]Ru 1:16
2:14 [o]ver 18

Naomi said to her, "Go ahead, my daughter." 3 So she went out, entered a field and began to glean
behind the harvesters. As it turned out, she was working in a field belonging to Boaz, who was from
the clan of Elimelek.
4 Just then Boaz arrived from Bethlehem and greeted the harvesters, "The LORD be with you![d]"
"The LORD bless you![e]" they answered.
5 Boaz asked the overseer of his harvesters, "Who does that young woman belong to?"
6 The overseer replied, "She is the Moabite[f] who came back from Moab with Naomi. 7 She said, 'Please
let me glean and gather among the sheaves behind the harvesters.' She came into the field and has
remained here from morning till now, except for a short rest in the shelter."
8 So Boaz said to Ruth, "My daughter, listen to me. Don't go and glean in another field and don't go
away from here. Stay here with the women who work for me. 9 Watch the field where the men are harvesting, and follow along after the women. I have told the men not to lay a hand on you. And whenever
you are thirsty, go and get a drink from the water jars the men have filled."
10 At this, she bowed down with her face to the ground.[g] She asked him, "Why have I found such favor
in your eyes that you notice me[h]—a foreigner?[i]"
11 Boaz replied, "I've been told all about what you have done for your mother-in-law[j] since the
death of your husband—how you left your father and mother and your homeland and came to
live with a people you did not know before.[k] 12 May the LORD repay you for what you have done. May
you be richly rewarded by the LORD,[l] the God of Israel, under whose wings[m] you have come to take
refuge.[n]"
13 "May I continue to find favor in your eyes, my lord," she said. "You have put me at ease by speaking
kindly to your servant—though I do not have the standing of one of your servants."
14 At mealtime Boaz said to her, "Come over here. Have some bread and dip it in the wine vinegar."
When she sat down with the harvesters, he offered her some roasted grain. She ate all she wanted
and had some left over.[o] 15 As she got up to glean, Boaz gave orders to his men, "Let her gather among

---

(vv. 3–17). In ch. 1 Naomi cried out against God, but ch. 2 shows subtle signs of kindly divine providence. The setting of Ruth 2–3 are the two main sites of the annual harvest, usually April for barley and May for wheat (1:22; 2:23). The first site, the harvest field proper (ch. 2), hosts the first three steps of the harvest: (1) *cutting* the grain stalks (usually done by men) with scythes or sickles and piling them along the edge of the field (Deut 16:9; Joel 3:13); (2) *tying* the reaped grain into bundles (usually done by women) to ready it for transport to the second site (v. 16); (3) *gleaning* (gathering) grain stalks left behind after the men and women have finished (vv. 7,17). Transporting the bundled grain from the field to the second site, the threshing floor (ch. 3; Amos 2:13), was done by donkeys or carts. For the steps taken at the threshing floor, see note on 3:1–18.

2:1 Now Naomi had. The opening sentence inaugurates a new scene and introduces a new character. **relative.** Identifies Boaz as family (cf. 3:2). **man of standing.** Wealthy and highly respected (1 Sam 9:1; 1 Kgs 11:28). **clan.** Designates the group midway between a "tribe" and a "family" (cf. v. 3). **Boaz.** Means "in him is strength"; his name commends him as just the person to benefit the two widows.

2:2 pick up the leftover grain. Mosaic law authorized Ruth's initiative to "glean" unharvested grain and grapes (Lev 19:9–10). This is step 3 in the harvesting process at the field (see note on vv. 1–23). In the field Ruth hopes to find unexpected kindness ("favor") rather than mere grudging legalism. Cf. vv. 10,13.

2:3 a field. Probably the large, flat acreage below the town's eastern slope. **As it turned out.** The Hebrew twice uses a word that can be translated "her chance chanced upon"; this is tongue-in-cheek hyperbole to highlight Ruth's "accidental" finding of Boaz's field amid a patchwork of unmarked parcels. Divine providence again shows its presence.

2:4 Just then. Signals more divine providence: the arrivals of Ruth and Boaz overlap. The exchange of greetings invoking the Lord hints at his presence with owner and workers—and with Ruth too.

2:5 that young woman. Boaz's question asks for Ruth's social location (i.e., family, employer, etc.), not her name.

2:7 She said. A brief flashback reports Ruth's activities that morning. This verse suggests that all three steps of the harvesting process at the field (see note on vv. 1–23) go on simultaneously.

2:8 My daughter. Boaz is probably Naomi's contemporary, i.e., much older than Ruth (3:10). **listen to me.** Emphatically, Boaz grants Ruth permission to glean, promises her protection ("not to lay a hand on you," v. 9; cf. vv. 15–16), and even provides her water (v. 9).

2:10 bowed down. Ruth recognizes Boaz's authority and has gratitude for his unexpected generosity. **found such favor.** This echo of Ruth's earlier wish (v. 2; cf. v. 13) signals that she has found exactly the person she was looking for! **notice me.** This phrase is a pun on the Hebrew word for "foreigner." Ruth's statement means "You've 'noticed' one usually 'unnoticed.'"

2:11 I've been told. Devotion to Naomi has earned Ruth a positive reputation in Bethlehem (cf. 3:11). His praise echoes both Naomi's wish (1:8) and Ruth's sweeping commitment (1:16).

2:12 richly rewarded. In employer-employee language, Boaz hopes that Yahweh will "repay" Ruth's actions "in full." Theologically, Boaz's words create expectations that if good things later come to Ruth, the Lord the "paymaster" is likely behind them. **wings.** As a bird's wings protect its young, so the Lord protects all who "take refuge" under his "wings" (Pss 36:7; 57:1; 61:4).

2:14 Boaz's invitation to lunch and his personal attention grant Ruth additional "favor." **left over.** Well satisfied herself, Ruth sets aside a portion to take home (cf. v. 18).

2:15–16 don't reprimand ... rebuke her. Rather than impede Ruth, Boaz's workers pull out extra stalks (v. 16) for her to glean. By providing Ruth plenty to glean, Boaz further shows his "favor" (v. 13) toward her.

2:15 sheaves. Piles of (reaped) grain left by reapers beside the field (see step 1 of the harvesting process at the field in the note on vv. 1–23).

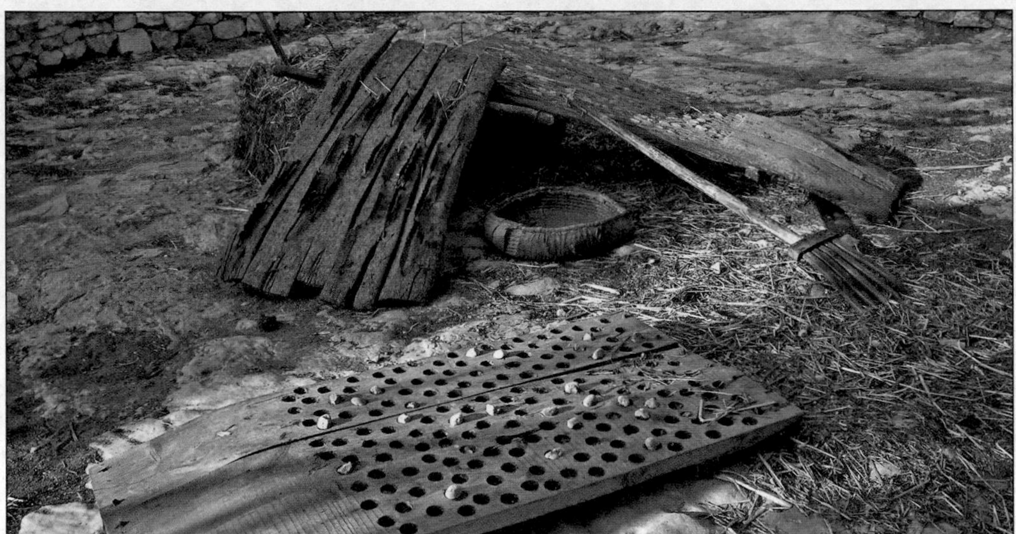

Threshing floor with sledges and winnowing fork. Ruth first meets Boaz in a grain field that is being harvested.
Todd Bolen/www.BiblePlaces.com

the sheaves and don't reprimand her. [16]Even pull out some stalks for her from the bundles and leave
them for her to pick up, and don't rebuke her."
[17]So Ruth gleaned in the field until evening. Then she threshed the barley she had gathered, and it
amounted to about an ephah.[a] [18]She carried it back to town, and her mother-in-law saw how much she
had gathered. Ruth also brought out and gave her what she had left over[p] after she had eaten enough.
[19]Her mother-in-law asked her, "Where did you glean today? Where did you work? Blessed be the
man who took notice of you![q]"
Then Ruth told her mother-in-law about the one at whose place she had been working. "The name
of the man I worked with today is Boaz," she said.
[20]"The LORD bless him!" Naomi said to her daughter-in-law. "He has not stopped showing his kindness[r] to the living and the dead." She added, "That man is our close relative; he is one of our guardian-redeemers.[b][s]"
[21]Then Ruth the Moabite said, "He even said to me, 'Stay with my workers until they finish harvesting all my grain.'"
[22]Naomi said to Ruth her daughter-in-law, "It will be good for you, my daughter, to go with the
women who work for him, because in someone else's field you might be harmed."

2:18 [p]ver 14
2:19 [q]ver 10; Ps 41:1
2:20 [r]Ru 3:10; 2Sa 2:5; Pr 17:17 [s]Ru 3:9,12; 4:1,14

[a] *17* That is, probably about 30 pounds or about 13 kilograms [b] *20* The Hebrew word for *guardian-redeemer* is a legal term for one who has the obligation to redeem a relative in serious difficulty (see Lev. 25:25-55).

2:16 bundles. Stacks of stalks tied up for transport to the threshing floor (see step 2 of the harvesting process at the field in the note on vv. 1–23).
2:17 ephah. See NIV text note; by any standard this is an amazing amount—food for about a week and a half—for one day of gleaning. Through Boaz, God has rewarded Ruth.
2:18 Naomi immediately notices the startling quantity of grain Ruth has brought home. Additionally, Ruth's leftover portion (v. 14) will feed Naomi today, further testimony to her daughter-in-law's devotion.
2:19 notice. Naomi's two quick questions and spontaneous blessing show excitement that someone has taken special notice of Ruth (cf. "notice" in v. 10; see note). **Boaz.** The author strings out the excitement by making the as-yet unspoken name the very last word.
2:20 He has not stopped showing. Probably refers to Yahweh, although possibly Boaz (cf. Gen 24:27). **kindness.** Hebrew *ḥesed* (see 1:8 and note; 3:10). **guardian-redeemers.** Hebrew *gōʾēl* (see NIV text note; cf. 4:14); it designates a group of close relatives responsible for getting family members out of difficulties. It also describes God as rescuer of Israel from Egyptian slavery (Exod 6:6 ["will redeem"]; 15:13 ["have redeemed"]) and Babylonian exile (Isa 43:1,14 ["have redeemed" and "Redeemer," respectively]). Both human and divine examples of kindness and protection anticipate the work of Christ, the Redeemer par excellence.
2:21 The permission to glean now extends into the wheat harvest (cf. v. 23), thus prolonging the contacts between Ruth and Boaz.
2:22 Just to be safe, Naomi asks that Ruth stay with Boaz's female workers (cf. 3:2). Concern for Ruth's safety recurs in ch. 2 (cf. vv. 9,15–16), no doubt because Ruth is a Moabite and because immorality was widespread during the period of the judges.

2:23 [t] Dt 16:9
3:1 [u] Ru 1:9
3:2 [v] Dt 25:5-10; Ru 2:1
3:3 [w] 2Sa 14:2
3:5 [x] Eph 6:1; Col 3:20
3:7 [y] Jdg 19:6,9,22; 2Sa 13:28; 1Ki 21:7; Est 1:10
3:9 [z] Eze 16:8 [a] ver 12; Ru 2:20

23 So Ruth stayed close to the women of Boaz to glean until the barley and wheat harvests[t] were finished. And she lived with her mother-in-law.

Ruth and Boaz at the Threshing Floor

3 One day Ruth's mother-in-law Naomi said to her, "My daughter, I must find a home[a][u] for you, where you will be well provided for. 2 Now Boaz, with whose women you have worked, is a relative[v] of ours. Tonight he will be winnowing barley on the threshing floor. 3 Wash, put on perfume,[w] and get dressed in your best clothes. Then go down to the threshing floor, but don't let him know you are there until he has finished eating and drinking. 4 When he lies down, note the place where he is lying. Then go and uncover his feet and lie down. He will tell you what to do."

5 "I will do whatever you say,"[x] Ruth answered. 6 So she went down to the threshing floor and did everything her mother-in-law told her to do.

7 When Boaz had finished eating and drinking and was in good spirits,[y] he went over to lie down at the far end of the grain pile. Ruth approached quietly, uncovered his feet and lay down. 8 In the middle of the night something startled the man; he turned—and there was a woman lying at his feet!

9 "Who are you?" he asked.

"I am your servant Ruth," she said. "Spread the corner of your garment[z] over me, since you are a guardian-redeemer[b][a] of our family."

[a] *1* Hebrew *find rest* (see 1:9) [b] *9* The Hebrew word for *guardian-redeemer* is a legal term for one who has the obligation to redeem a relative in serious difficulty (see Lev. 25:25-55); also in verses 12 and 13.

2:23 The end of spring harvests (April-May) ends Ruth's day-to-day contact with Boaz. Some further step is necessary to resume their connection and to pave the way for Yahweh to reward Ruth.

3:1–18 *Ruth and Boaz at the Threshing Floor.* Harvesting (see note on 2:1–23) gives way to threshing at the threshing floor (see note on v. 2). Naomi sends Ruth there to have a secret talk with Boaz about marriage. The final four steps of the harvest take place at the threshing floor: (1) *threshing*, separating the husk from the grain, requires either beating the husks with a stick or using a toothed threshing sledge (2:17; Isa 41:15; Amos 1:3) or crushing the husks under cattle hooves or the wheels of carts (Deut 25:4; Isa 28:28; Hos 10:11); (2) *winnowing*, throwing the threshed grain into the air with a special long-handled fork, uses the wind to blow the husk away, while the grain falls to the ground (3:2; Ps 1:4; Jer 15:7); (3) *sifting* removes any remaining unwanted matter from the winnowed grain (Amos 9:9); (4) *bagging* readies the grain for transport to the city to be consumed, sold, or bartered (Gen 42–44).

3:1–5 In 2:2, Ruth initiated the foray to the field, but here a revived Naomi, seizing what seems to be a golden opportunity, takes the initiative—and for a new purpose.

3:1 Ruth's gleaning initiative benefited Naomi (2:2); now Naomi's plan will benefit Ruth. **home.** The Hebrew word translated as "home" alludes to the "rest" Naomi wished for Ruth in 1:9. What Naomi earlier wished from Yahweh she will seek to arrange herself.

3:2 relative. Cf. 2:1 and note. **Tonight.** Boaz's plans and isolated location offer an opportunity not to be missed. **winnowing.** Tossing the kernel-chaff mix upward, causing the heavier grain to fall to the ground for collection, while the wind blows the chaff away (see step 2 of the harvesting process at the threshing floor in the note on vv. 1–18). **threshing floor.** A flat, large open space of exposed bedrock or hardened clay downhill east of the town (see note on v. 3), where the velocity of prevailing winds allows harvesters to beat or crush kernels to separate the edible grain from its husk (see step 1 of the harvesting process at the threshing floor in the note on vv. 1–18). Darkness and isolation will guard the secrecy and confidentiality of the proposed conversation.

3:3 Wash ... perfume ... best clothes. Naomi instructs Ruth to dress herself as a bride (Ezek 16:9–12) to be attractive to Boaz. Her bridal dress might also symbolize the end of her mourning period for her husband (2 Sam 12:20) and signal her openness to marry again. **go down.** Apparently downhill east of Bethlehem (see note on v. 2). **finished eating and drinking.** Naomi may have hoped that the meal would induce Boaz to sleep and postpone the conversation until everyone else had gone home or fallen asleep.

3:4 uncover his feet. Ruth is secretly to fold back the skirt of Boaz's long tunic, exposing the "area around the feet" (Hebrew *margĕlôt*), and "lie down" there. These proposed actions seem very forward but in fact involve no moral compromise by either Ruth or Boaz (cf. v. 11). The exposure of Boaz's feet to the night chill will awaken him at the best moment for a private conversation (see notes on vv. 3,8). More important, the gesture symbolizes Ruth's willingness to marry Boaz (cf. v. 9; Ezek 16:8). For the legal basis of her appeal, see note on v. 9. For a comparable situation involving Tamar and Judah, see Gen 38:13–30 (cf. Ruth 4:12). **tell you what to do.** Seeing the gesture, Boaz is to explain what Ruth is to do next.

3:6–15 Sometime after dark, Ruth descends from the town to the threshing floor and carries out Naomi's plan. Ruth's secret visit with Boaz runs serious risks for them both. If discovered, it could easily be misread as an illicit rendezvous, since prostitutes sometimes did business at threshing floors (Hos 9:1). Public embarrassment and tarnished reputations might hound them and complicate the family's acceptance of their marriage.

3:6 Once again the author summarizes an entire scene in advance (cf. 1:6; 2:3).

3:7 in good spirits. Due to the food and drink. **grain pile.** Grain already winnowed and almost ready for use or sale; steps 3 and 4 of the harvesting process at the threshing floor (see note on vv. 1–18) are still to follow. Providentially, Boaz lies at its "far end," a more secluded spot.

3:8 middle of the night. Other winnowers, if present, are probably asleep. The darkness obscures the identities of Boaz and Ruth; they become merely "the man" and "a woman." **something startled.** May mean that Boaz shivered from cold feet or vaguely sensed something amiss. **a woman lying at his feet.** This surprising discovery was the last thing Boaz expected.

3:9 Who are you? Boaz asks the name of the female figure before him (cf. 2:5), and Ruth supplies it. **Spread the corner ... over me.** The symbolic response to the uncovered feet signals agreement to marry (cf. Ezek 16:8). "Corner" plays on "wings" (of the Lord) in Boaz's earlier remark (2:12) about Ruth's finding refuge (both are forms of the same Hebrew word). Ruth's wordplay appeals to Boaz's godliness, asking him

[10]"The LORD bless you, my daughter," he replied. "This kindness is greater than that which you
showed earlier: You have not run after the younger men, whether rich or poor. [11]And now, my daughter,
don't be afraid. I will do for you all you ask. All the people of my town know that you are a woman of
noble character.[b] [12]Although it is true that I am a guardian-redeemer of our family,[c] there is another
who is more closely related than[d] I. [13]Stay here for the night, and in the morning if he wants to do his
duty as your guardian-redeemer,[e] good; let him redeem you. But if he is not willing, as surely as the
LORD lives[f] I will do it. Lie here until morning."
[14]So she lay at his feet until morning, but got up before anyone could be recognized; and he said,
"No one must know that a woman came to the threshing floor."[g]
[15]He also said, "Bring me the shawl you are wearing and hold it out." When she did so, he poured
into it six measures of barley and placed the bundle on her. Then he[a] went back to town.
[16]When Ruth came to her mother-in-law, Naomi asked, "How did it go, my daughter?"
Then she told her everything Boaz had done for her [17]and added, "He gave me these six measures of
barley, saying, 'Don't go back to your mother-in-law empty-handed.' "
[18]Then Naomi said, "Wait, my daughter, until you find out what happens. For the man will not rest
until the matter is settled today."[h]

3:11 [b]Pr 12:4; 31:10
3:12 [c]ver 9 [d]Ru 4:1
3:13 [e]Dt 25:5; Ru 4:5; Mt 22:24 [f]Jdg 8:19; Jer 4:2
3:14 [g]Ro 14:16; 2Co 8:21
3:18 [h]Ps 37:3-5
4:1 [i]Ru 3:12
4:2 [j]1Ki 21:8; Pr 31:23

Boaz Marries Ruth

4 Meanwhile Boaz went up to the town gate and sat down there just as the guardian-redeemer[b] he
had mentioned[i] came along. Boaz said, "Come over here, my friend, and sit down." So he went
over and sat down.
[2]Boaz took ten of the elders[j] of the town and said, "Sit here," and they did so. [3]Then he said to the

[a] *15* Most Hebrew manuscripts; many Hebrew manuscripts, Vulgate and Syriac *she* [b] *1* The Hebrew word for *guardian-redeemer* is a legal term for one who has the obligation to redeem a relative in serious difficulty (see Lev. 25:25-55); also in verses 3, 6, 8 and 14.

to provide her protection after Yahweh's example. **guardian-redeemer.** See note on 2:20. For marriage to a guardian-redeemer, see Introduction: Themes; Theology. The appeal to Boaz as guardian-redeemer (cf. 2:20) may be implicit in Naomi's plan, or it may be Ruth's own innovation; it invites him to agree to marriage by "covering" her (cf. v. 9; Ezek 16:8).

3:10 The LORD bless you. Boaz blesses Ruth for far outdoing her earlier, remarkable "kindness" (Hebrew *ḥesed*, see note on 1:8), alluding to 2:11 (cf. 1:8–9). Ruth chooses marriage to a guardian-redeemer, which benefits Naomi, rather than choosing to pursue "younger men." **my daughter.** See 2:8 and note.

3:11 I will do for you all you ask. Boaz promises to marry Ruth. **woman of noble character.** The only other occurrences of this phrase are in Prov 12:4; 31:10 ("wife"). It reflects Bethlehem's high regard for Ruth and compares her to the ideal woman. The phrase is parallel to the phrase about Boaz in 2:1 and reckons Ruth a good match for him.

3:12 Boaz reveals an unexpected complication in the situation: an even closer relative has a prior right to serve as Naomi's *gōʾēl*.

3:13 as surely as the LORD lives. A traditional oath backs up Boaz's promise to "redeem" (i.e., marry) Ruth.

3:14 Ruth's rising before dawn ("before anyone could be recognized") gets Boaz thinking ("he said" to himself, not aloud). **No one must know.** Lest the wild gossip tarnish Ruth's reputation and complicate Boaz's dealings with the other *gōʾēl* (cf. Hos 9:1).

3:15 shawl. Probably a large, sturdy head covering to go with Ruth's long tunic. **six measures.** About seven quarts (about 6.5 liters), a very generous gift—nearly three times what she gleaned her first day (2:17). The large amount requires Boaz's help in loading it. For the purpose of this gift, see 3:17. **he went back.** Boaz went back to town by himself rather than with Ruth to keep their visit a secret.

3:16–18 Ruth returns home alone to debrief an understandably excited Naomi about the night's events.

3:16 How did it go ...? The Hebrew is the same as that of Boaz's earlier question of Ruth in v. 9. Here, however, Naomi is not seeking to learn Ruth's identity (she recognizes Ruth!) but Ruth's present situation after meeting Boaz. Presumably, Ruth reports Boaz's promise concerning arranging their marriage.

3:17 Ruth quotes Boaz to explain that the barley is for Naomi. **six measures.** Symbolizes a magnificent reversal: Naomi now has plenty of food, and Ruth may soon provide her family line with an heir. **empty-handed.** Recurs from 1:21 ("empty"), where it describes the famine and death of Naomi's past.

3:18 Wait. Naomi counsels Ruth to be patient because Boaz "will not rest" until he settles the matter. Ruth's fate is in Boaz's very capable hands.

4:1–22 Two scenes and an epilogue—a genealogy—bring the book to a close. Boaz dominates the first scene (vv. 1–12) and his newborn child the second (vv. 13–17). Ruth is mentioned but is not present in either scene, and fittingly, in the second scene the moment belongs to Naomi.

4:1–12 *Boaz Marries Ruth.* This tells how Ruth became the wife of Boaz rather than that of the other guardian-redeemer. The other man waves his prior right; Boaz acquires both Ruth and Elimelek's land; and a brief ceremony celebrates public acceptance of the outcome.

4:1 town gate. A large open space between a town's outer and inner walls and their gates. It serves as the town courthouse, where trials and administrative hearings are held. The gate area at Dan illustrates the size and layout of this common ancient city entrance (see photo, p. 480). **just as.** Highlights the providential timing of Boaz's encounter with the man he wants to see (cf. 2:4). **"Come over here ..." So he went over.** The two apparently settle into one of the small alcoves along the walls and away from the foot traffic.

4:2 elders. Heads of the town's main families; they governed ancient towns as a kind of town council. The number of members varied (cf. Judg 8:14); "ten" may have been the minimum legal quorum required for this case. **Sit here.** Given the context, it may mean "Sit as a court."

4:3 Given the events of ch. 3, mentioning "Naomi" and her "piece of

Beersheba Iron Age gate with benches where people would sit to conduct business. It was at the "town gate" (Ruth 4:1) in Bethlehem where Boaz announced to the elders that he had bought Naomi's property and taken Ruth as his wife.

Todd Bolen/www.BiblePlaces.com

4:4 [k] Lev 25:25; Jer 32:7-8
4:5 [l] Ge 38:8; Dt 25:5-6; Ru 3:13; Mt 22:24
4:6 [m] Lev 25:25; Ru 3:13

guardian-redeemer, "Naomi, who has come back from Moab, is selling the piece of land that belonged
to our relative Elimelek. [4]I thought I should bring the matter to your attention and suggest that you
buy it in the presence of these seated here and in the presence of the elders of my people. If you will
redeem it, do so. But if you[a] will not, tell me, so I will know. For no one has the right to do it except
you,[k] and I am next in line."

"I will redeem it," he said.

[5]Then Boaz said, "On the day you buy the land from Naomi, you also acquire Ruth the Moabite, the[b]
dead man's widow, in order to maintain the name of the dead with his property."[l]

[6]At this, the guardian-redeemer said, "Then I cannot redeem[m] it because I might endanger my own
estate. You redeem it yourself. I cannot do it."

[7](Now in earlier times in Israel, for the redemption and transfer of property to become final, one

[a] *4* Many Hebrew manuscripts, Septuagint, Vulgate and Syriac; most Hebrew manuscripts *he* [b] *5* Vulgate and Syriac; Hebrew (see also Septuagint) *Naomi and from Ruth the Moabite, you acquire the*

land" seems a surprise. The subject had not come up before, but both "land" and "wife" may underlie his promise as *gō'ēl* to do "all you ask" (3:11). Boaz may also want, for now, to keep Naomi out front and Ruth in the background. **selling the … land.** Naomi's destitution may also require its sale for her financial survival. She offers it first to the family (i.e., a guardian-redeemer) before selling it to an outsider. Alternatively, the sale may concern only the right to redeem it. This assumes that Elimelek had already sold it to an outsider and that Naomi's poverty forces her to enlist a guardian-redeemer to return it to the family. For more legal background, see Introduction: Particular Challenges.

4:4 buy it in the presence of … redeem it. To "redeem" land is to return or retain it within the clan's inheritance by purchase through a public legal process. **no one … except you.** Boaz is the *gō'ēl* "next in line," not the closest relative (3:12). **I will redeem it.** The man understandably decides to do his duty. Since Naomi will have no more sons to claim the property, it will become his, free and clear.

4:5 the dead man's widow. Ruth. The introduction of Ruth gives the transaction a more specific purpose: to produce an heir to "maintain" the connection between the land and her late husband (v. 10). Unlike Naomi, Ruth may bear a son to claim ownership, preventing the *gō'ēl* from recouping his purchase price.

4:6 endanger my own estate. He may fear in the end having to divide his present holdings among both his own heirs and children born to him by Ruth after the birth of Naomi's heir. If the latter were to be his only heir, he may fear loss of his land to Elimelek's family (an outcome that Boaz might also face). Or perhaps he simply does not want to be bothered with such complexities. In any case, the man's refusal only underscores the kindness and generosity of Boaz toward two needy widows, much as Orpah's return to her home underscores Ruth's selfless devotion to Naomi (1:14).

4:7 The author's parenthetical comment (note the parentheses) explains the ancient sandal ceremony for any "redemption and transfer of property" to an audience probably unfamiliar with it. The Nuzi documents from Mesopotamia also mention this custom.

party took off his sandal and gave it to the other. This was the method of legalizing transactions in Israel.)[n]

[8]So the guardian-redeemer said to Boaz, "Buy it yourself." And he removed his sandal.

[9]Then Boaz announced to the elders and all the people, "Today you are witnesses that I have bought from Naomi all the property of Elimelek, Kilion and Mahlon. [10]I have also acquired Ruth the Moabite, Mahlon's widow, as my wife, in order to maintain the name of the dead with his property, so that his name will not disappear from among his family or from his hometown.[o] Today you are witnesses!"

[11]Then the elders and all the people at the gate said, "We are witnesses.[p] May the LORD make the woman who is coming into your home like Rachel and Leah,[q] who together built up the family of Israel. May you have standing in Ephrathah[r] and be famous in Bethlehem. [12]Through the offspring the LORD gives you by this young woman, may your family be like that of Perez,[s] whom Tamar bore to Judah."

Naomi Gains a Son

[13]So Boaz took Ruth and she became his wife. When he made love to her, the LORD enabled her to conceive,[t] and she gave birth to a son. [14]The women[u] said to Naomi: "Praise be to the LORD, who this day has not left you without a guardian-redeemer. May he become famous throughout Israel! [15]He will renew your life and sustain you in your old age. For your daughter-in-law, who loves you and who is better to you than seven sons,[v] has given him birth."

[16]Then Naomi took the child in her arms and cared for him. [17]The women living there said, "Naomi has a son!" And they named him Obed. He was the father of Jesse,[w] the father of David.

4:7 [n] Dt 25:7-9
4:10 [o] Dt 25:6
4:11 [p] Dt 25:9 [q] Ps 127:3; 128:3 [r] Ge 35:16
4:12 [s] ver 18; Ge 38:29
4:13 [t] Ge 29:31; 33:5; Ru 3:11
4:14 [u] Lk 1:58
4:15 [v] Ru 1:16-17; 2:11-12; 1Sa 1:8
4:17 [w] ver 22; 1Sa 16:1, 18; 1Ch 2:12,13

4:8 Buy it yourself. The sandal transfer to Boaz makes him the legal owner of the redemption right.
4:9 I have bought. Marks the moment of formal purchase from Naomi of "all the property."
4:10 as my wife. Declares that Ruth is now his wife and that the purpose of their marriage is to produce an heir for Mahlon (v. 5). **name will not disappear.** The hoped-for heir will ensure that both Mahlon's family and hometown remember him and honor his heir's property rights. **Today you are witnesses!** The customary legal formula to finalize matters.
4:11a We are witnesses. The crowd's reply voices official, public approval of everything (cf. Josh 24:22). Deal done!
4:11b–12 Two wishes for Ruth bracket two for Boaz.
4:11b standing. Cf. 2:1. **Ephrathah.** The ancient patriarchal name for Bethlehem, home of the Ephrathite clan (1:2; Gen 35:19; 48:7; Ps 132:6; cf. Mic 5:2). The crowd wishes Ruth the fertility of Israel's founding mothers, Rachel and Leah, to "build" Boaz a large, prominent family.
4:12 Perez. Son of Judah and Tamar (Gen 38:29); he founded the leading clan of Judah to which Boaz belongs (see vv. 18,21). Ruth parallels Tamar, another non-Jew: both take daring steps to continue a family line, and both in the end belong to a royal lineage that links David with Abraham, a connection Jesus' genealogy highlights (Matt 1:1,3,5,17). Taken together, the crowd's wishes affirm Ruth as, so to speak, "one of us."
4:13–17 *Naomi Gains a Son.* The story quickly moves from the public square to the wedding night and the later birth of a son (v. 13). The closing scene (vv. 14–17) finds Naomi and the town's women (but not Boaz and Ruth) welcoming Obed as Naomi's "son" (v. 17). It thus offers a happy reversal of the unhappy arrival scene (1:19–21).
4:13 enabled her to conceive. Boaz "made love" to Ruth, but she became pregnant because Yahweh intervened. This is the second of only two acts of direct divine intervention in the book (see 1:6). Such divine actions stamp the newborn with a special divine destiny (cf. Gen 21:1–2; 1 Sam 1:27; Luke 1:31–35).
4:14 Women, who once greeted "bitter" Naomi at Bethlehem's gate (1:19–20), now address "pleasant" Naomi with promises, not wishes (cf. vv. 11–12). The newborn gives Naomi the benefit of another *gōʾēl* besides Boaz (v. 15). This detail casts David and his descendants as a lineage of guardian-redeemers whose reigns are expected similarly to rescue Israel from enemies and to provide for Israel's needs. In David's line, the guardian-redeemer par excellence is Jesus Christ. The book of Ruth features human actions, but "praise be to the LORD" (cf. 2:4,19,20; 3:10) voices the author's view of providence: divine action through human action. **famous.** Expands the crowd's wishes (v. 11) beyond Bethlehem to "throughout Israel" and subtly anticipates the revelation of the newborn's revered descendant, David (v. 17b).
4:15 renew your life. The infant guardian-redeemer will remove Naomi's tragic grief, and her deceased husband's family line will continue. **sustain you.** He will also supply her daily food when "old age" prevents Naomi from doing so herself. Both mark reversals of ch. 1. **better ... than.** The women highly praise Ruth, a woman of remarkable love and devotion, for surpassing even the lofty ideal of "seven sons" (cf. 2:11; 3:10). **seven sons.** Israel especially valued sons as family protectors, and seven represented a family made complete (1 Sam 2:5; Job 1:2; Jer 15:9).
4:16 cared for him. The term for "nursing mother," "nanny," or "foster mother," i.e., one who cares for dependent children on behalf of or in the absence of parents (2 Sam 4:4; 2 Kgs 10:1,5; cf. Esth 2:7). The term implies that Naomi will be a hands-on mother caring for her "son."
4:17a said. The actual naming comes next ("they named him"). Probably means "proclaimed his significance [Hebrew *šēm*]"—i.e., "Naomi has a son!" The naming uses the traditional wording for a birth announcement (Job 3:3; Isa 9:6; Jer 20:15), here with a touch of special amazement and joy. **Obed.** Means "one who works/serves"; may anticipates the child's service for Naomi (cf. v. 15). Naomi has come full circle. She arrived from Moab "empty" (1:21)—a tragic, childless widow who asked to be called Mara ("bitter one") rather than Naomi ("my pleasant one") (see note on 1:20). But her newborn "son" has restored her from "empty" to "full" and from "bitter one" to a joyous "pleasant one."
4:17b He was. The story suddenly stops, and the narrator springs the biggest surprise: Obed turns out to be the grandfather of the great King David. God has rewarded Naomi's suffering and Ruth's devotion, fulfilling, if not exceeding, the "prayer" for Ruth made by both Boaz (2:12) and the crowd (vv. 11–12).

4:18 [x] Mt 1:3-6
4:19 [y] Ex 6:23
4:21 [z] Ru 2:1

The Genealogy of David

4:18-22pp — 1Ch 2:5-15; Mt 1:3-6; Lk 3:31-33

18 This, then, is the family line of Perez[x]:

Perez was the father of Hezron,
19 Hezron the father of Ram,
Ram the father of Amminadab,[y]
20 Amminadab the father of Nahshon,
Nahshon the father of Salmon,[a]
21 Salmon the father of Boaz,[z]
Boaz the father of Obed,
22 Obed the father of Jesse,
and Jesse the father of David.

[a] *20* A few Hebrew manuscripts, some Septuagint manuscripts and Vulgate (see also verse 21 and Septuagint of 1 Chron. 2:11); most Hebrew manuscripts *Salma*

4:18–22 *The Genealogy of David.* The genealogy formula "the family line of" (cf. Gen 10:1; 36:9) heads the list of ten names, a common schema in ancient royal genealogies (cf. 1 Chr 2:10–12; Matt 1:3b–6a). It spans the more than eight centuries between the patriarchs ("Perez") and the united monarchy of David. Like the closing credits of a movie, it lists names—a few known, but most not—of those who produced this memorable family. Its theme is the centuries-long divine providence that eventually gave Israel David.
4:20 Nahshon. The brother-in-law of Aaron (Exod 6:23); recalls the exodus-wilderness period when Judah emerged as a leading tribe under Nahshon's leadership (Num 2:3–4). The author makes the point that David descends from a family of leaders.
4:21 Obed. Known only in genealogies.
4:22 Jesse. Appears twice: 1 Sam 16:1–16; 17:12. **David.** Symbolizes the triumph of God's providence, a triumph that confirms his divine appointment as king. Thus, the book of Ruth links the family line in Genesis that cherished hopes of kingship with their realization in 1 Samuel through David. The book's portrait of David's righteous ancestral family also sharply contrasts the raucous unfaithfulness of the people in the book of Judges. It anticipates God's response in 1 Samuel to the repeated refrain hoping for a good king that echoes across Judg 17–21. From the ancient family line of Abraham descends a revered guardian-redeemer, David, from whom Jesus, the Son of David and guardian-redeemer par excellence, descends to redeem the world.

INTRODUCTION TO 1 SAMUEL

AUTHOR

The authorship of 1 – 2 Samuel is unknown. Jewish tradition, at least as far back as the Babylonian Talmud of the sixth century AD, believed the prophet Samuel to be the author. A major problem is that 1 Sam 25:1 and 28:3 record Samuel's death, and he obviously could not have written the material after his death. Some commentators argue that Samuel wrote much of the document up to that point and other prophets then took over the writing. They cite 1 Chr 29:29 as evidence: "As for the events of King David's reign, from beginning to end, they are written in the records of Samuel the seer, the records of Nathan the prophet and the records of Gad the seer."

The title "Samuel" refers to the prophet Samuel as the pivotal figure in the books of 1 – 2 Samuel. As Israel's final judge, Samuel is the transitional figure from a tribal confederacy in the period of the judges to a united monarchy; Samuel anointed Saul and then David as the first kings of Israel (1 Sam 10:1; 16:13). Samuel and his name, however, appear nowhere in 2 Samuel. The reason that 2 Samuel bears his name is because originally 1 – 2 Samuel were one book. The Septuagint, the pre-Christian Greek translation of the OT, is probably the first to divide "Samuel" into two separate books because of its length.

DATE

First Samuel begins with the birth and call of the prophet Samuel, which occurred in the eleventh century BC. 2 Samuel ends near the close of David's reign (ca. 1010 – 970 BC). However, the final form of 1 – 2 Samuel does not date from the time in which the events recorded took place. Some of the material does originate from the date of the event, such as David's eulogies for Saul and Jonathan (2 Sam 1:17 – 27) and his lament for Abner (2 Sam 3:33 – 34). Thus, the final composition relies on annals, poems, and stories that come from an earlier period.

The text itself provides adequate proof that the final composition of the books is later than the events recorded. First, the words "to this day" or similar expressions indicate that the author is narrating events that had occurred prior to his time (1 Sam 5:5; 6:18; 27:6; 30:25; 2 Sam 4:3; 6:8; 18:18). Second, 1 Sam 27:6 states, "So on that day Achish gave him Ziklag, and it has belonged to the kings of Judah ever since." This statement reflects both a situation in which a number of kings have ruled over Judah since the death of Solomon and the division of the united monarchy into two kingdoms. Third, 2 Sam 5:5 summarizes the length of David's reign: "In Hebron he reigned over Judah seven years and six months, and in Jerusalem he reigned over all Israel and Judah thirty-three years." At the close of 2 Samuel, however, David's reign is not yet completed. Fourth, the author explains customs of the early monarchic period because they are no longer used during his time (1 Sam 9:9; 2 Sam 13:18).

All evidence suggests that the final editing of the two books occurred after some of "the kings of Judah" reigned (1 Sam 27:6), that is, in the ninth – eighth centuries BC. It is certainly reasonable to believe that an official historian wrote 1 – 2 Samuel within one to two centuries of the events. There is no compelling reason to think that the two books were given a final form in the exilic or postexilic periods.

THE BOOKS OF SAMUEL

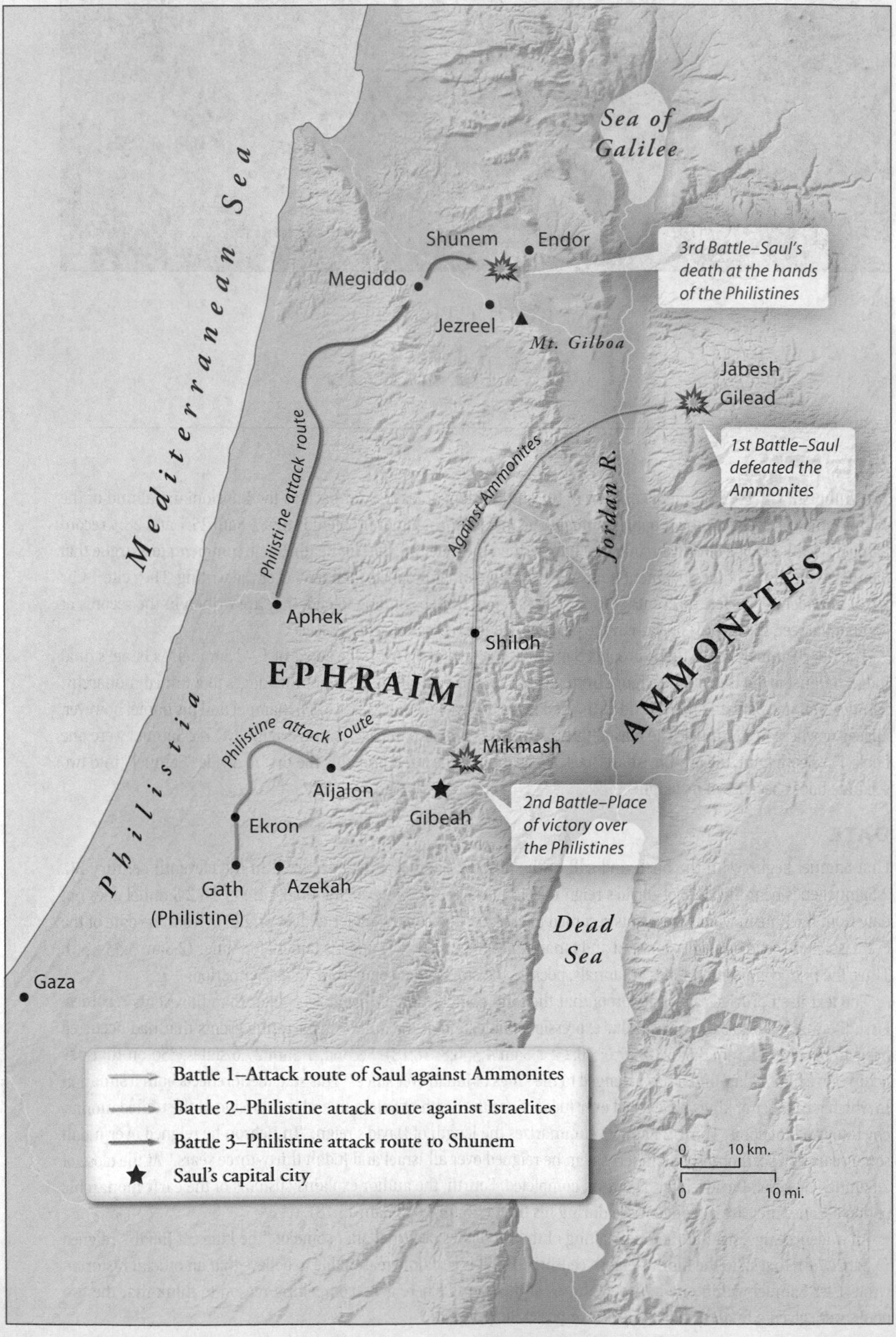

PURPOSE

The primary purpose of 1 – 2 Samuel is to record the establishment of the kingship in Israel. This event is a pivotal moment in the unfolding of God's revelational history.

The kingship is, in the first place, an initial fulfillment of ancient prophecy. God revealed to the patriarchs that kings would descend from them (Gen 17:6,16; 35:11). The great promise that Jacob gives to his son Judah and his descendants is that the scepter, the symbol of kingly rule, will not depart from the tribe of Judah. The kingship will reach its climax in a supreme ruler who will one day come from Judah (Gen 49:10). Instituting a monarchy in Israel is clearly consistent with God's plan and will for his people. The type of kingship that Israel is to have is a theocratic monarchy, in which Israel has a human king who obeys the Lord, the ultimate, sovereign king (Deut 17:14 – 20).

There is nothing intrinsically wrong with the elders requesting a king in 1 Sam 8. The problem is their desire for a king like the other nations have rather than for one who is part of a theocratic monarchy submitted to the Lord. By desiring an autonomous human king, the elders reject God as king (1 Sam 8:7). Samuel warns Israel that a king like those in the ancient Near Eastern nations around them will be oppressive, demanding, and self-centered (1 Sam 8:11 – 18). Saul, the first king of Israel, turns out to be the type of king that Samuel had warned against.

David's kingship initially fulfills what God promised his people. David is from Judah and is a man after God's own heart (1 Sam 13:14). God inaugurates and establishes David's dynasty in Israel, not Saul's (1 Sam 13:13 – 14; 15:28). Although David is a complicated figure and is sinful, he recognizes that God is the ultimate king in Israel (Pss 10:16; 24:8 – 10; 29:10).

David's kingship also points forward to the final Messianic king (Pss 2; 72; 110). The Lord promises David that his offspring would sit on the throne of Israel "forever" and that his son will build a temple for the Lord (2 Sam 7:12 – 16). This is a double prophecy: Solomon fulfills the first stage, and the Messianic king, "the son of David" (Matt 1:1) who builds a new temple (John 2:19 – 22), fulfills the second.

STYLE AND CONTENT

Like many books in the Bible, 1 – 2 Samuel contain a variety of literary genres. The primary genre is narrative, but non-narrative material often interrupts it: poetry (1 Sam 15:22 – 23), prophecy (2 Sam 7:4 – 17), prayer (1 Sam 2:1 – 10), lament (2 Sam 1:17 – 27; 3:33 – 34), chant (1 Sam 18:7; 21:11; 29:5), military catalog (2 Sam 8:1 – 14), lists of court officials (2 Sam 8:15 – 18; 20:23 – 26), parable (2 Sam 12:1 – 4), psalm/song (2 Sam 22:1 – 51), military lists (2 Sam 23:8 – 39).

The biblical writer does not provide a broad survey of the history of Israel during the judges and the early monarchic period but focuses on the three most prominent leaders of the day: Samuel, Saul, and David. 1 Sam 1 – 8 describes Samuel's birth, call, and judgeship. As the last judge of Israel, he transitions Israel from the period of the judges to the monarchic period of the kings of Israel. 1 Sam 9 – 31 concentrates on the failed rule of Saul, the first king of Israel. It narrates his call and anointing to the office of king, his good beginning as king, God's rejection of him because of his disobedience, the rise of David, and Saul's death at the hands of the Philistines on Mount Gilboa.

2 Samuel is a history of David's kingship. The first part (chs. 1 – 9) describes how David rises to the position of ruler over all Israel (2 Sam 2:1 — 5:5), consolidates power (2 Sam 5:6 — 7:29), and conquers the nations surrounding Israel (ch. 8). It sounds a high note: "The Lord gave David victory wherever he went" (2 Sam 8:14). The second major section narrates David's complacency and sin (chs. 10 – 12). The book's pivot is David's adultery with Bathsheba (2 Sam 11:1 — 12:25). The third major section of 2 Samuel almost exclusively describes how David deals with rebellion in his own kingdom (chs. 13 – 20).

The author deliberately contrasts the kingships of Saul and David. Their lives generally run parallel: they both start off well with strong military successes, and they win the favor of the people under their rule. However, their ascendancies are followed by grievous sins as they both disobey God's word. The similarity ends with how the two of them deal with their sin. Saul's sin leads to bitterness, vengeance, and hatred directed toward David and others, but David shows genuine sorrow and contrition for his sin (Ps 51). The Lord forgives David, although that does not remove his sin's severe temporal consequences. The Lord establishes David's dynasty, but not Saul's. It is through David's line that the Messianic king will appear: Saul, thus, serves as a foil to David in the plot of 1 – 2 Samuel.

PARTICULAR CHALLENGES

Text

The Hebrew Masoretic Text of 1 – 2 Samuel is loaded with difficulties, and it has suffered numerous scribal errors in written transmission from one generation to another. Perhaps the most difficult verse in regard to the text in all the OT appears in 1 Sam 13:1. The intensity of the degree of perplexity is reflected in the wide variety of English translations of the verse:

- "Saul was thirty years old when he became king, and he reigned over Israel forty-two years" (NIV).
- "Saul lived for one year and then became king, and when he had reigned for two years over Israel ..." (ESV).
- "Saul reigned one year; and when he had reigned two years over Israel ..." (KJV).
- "Saul was fifty years old when he became king, and he reigned over Israel for twenty-two years" (NEB).
- "Saul was *thirty* years old when he began to reign, and he reigned *forty* two years over Israel" (NASB, 1995).
- "Saul was thirty years old when he became king, and he reigned over Israel for twenty-two years" (REB).

The Septuagint, the pre-Christian Greek translation of the OT, simply omits the verse altogether. While no other verse in 1–2 Samuel is as textually difficult as 1 Sam 13:1, there are many others that are considerably hard to understand and interpret.

The Septuagint is notorious for its differences with the Masoretic Text of 1–2 Samuel. Many scholars assume that the Masoretic Text has been deeply corrupted through scribal errors in written transmission and that the Septuagint actually better reflects the original Hebrew text. Numerous scholarly attempts have been made to correct the corrupted Masoretic Text texts on the basis of the Septuagint. So for example, in the Masoretic Text, the story of David and Goliath contains 88 verses, and the Septuagint lacks 39 of those verses. Many commentators assume that the Septuagint preserves the earlier text and that the Masoretic Text adds a parallel account to it to make up the final story. The issue of which text reflects the earliest manuscript is actually quite complicated. The degree of difficulty is reflected in the following points:

1. The Dead Sea Scrolls of Samuel (second century BC to first century AD) support only some of the Septuagint readings, certainly not most of them.
2. The existing Septuagint manuscripts often differ among themselves in written transmission.
3. Parts of the Masoretic Text do reflect the earliest Hebrew texts. For example, the Septuagint of 1 Sam 1–2 appears to intentionally rewrite the earlier text preserved in the Masoretic Text.
4. The Septuagint at times makes deliberate literary changes to some verses by adding material to them (e.g., 1 Sam 5:3).

When all is said and done, one needs to be cautious and careful in regard to the textual problems of the Masoretic Text of 1–2 Samuel. The problems are not easily solved. However, for the most part, the Masoretic Text stands on fairly solid ground. The NIV translation follows it closely, although it occasionally agrees with the Septuagint (e.g., 1 Sam 8:16; 13:5,20; 14:41).

Parallel Passages

Another specific area of controversy regarding the interpretation of 1–2 Samuel is the appearance of numerous parallel passages elsewhere in Scripture. 1 Samuel has only a few parallels, but 2 Samuel has many in the book of 1 Chronicles. The parallels between the latter are extensive but often with many additions and subtractions. It has been widely accepted for a long time that the author of Chronicles uses Samuel as a major source in his writing. But his interpretation of history is different in that he emphasizes different things because of his peculiar historical and theological context. The Chronicler writes much later than the author of Samuel, and his audience is the people who have returned from exile in Babylon. The people return in order to rebuild the temple in Jerusalem, to worship, and to create a sense of national identity. The Chronicler encourages them in these tasks by recounting in detail the work of David and Solomon in regard to the sanctuary. He does not retell the stories of David's battles with Saul or his sin with Bathsheba. Such events do not fit into the Chronicler's purpose.

David's song in 2 Sam 22 is almost identical to Ps 18. There are minor variations between the two accounts; several involve the addition of a conjunction in the Hebrew in the psalm (vv. 13,15,17,27,42). Some differences are larger. For instance, in Ps 18, v. 1 adds the line "I love you, LORD, my strength" (when compared to 2 Sam 22:1), and v. 2 subtracts the line "my refuge and my savior — from violent people you save me" (when compared to 2 Sam 22:2–3). The title, or superscription, of Ps 18 fills out 2 Sam 22:1, and a musical notation is added that says, "For the director of music." That addition helps to highlight the fact that only this song, along with its superscription, appears *in toto* in two different places in the Bible. In 2 Sam 22, the song is an individual hymn of praise by King David; its appearance in the book of Psalms is as a public hymn for singing in the temple.

The wall excavated in 2012, located along the southern slope of Tell Shiloh. Shiloh was hometown of the priestly family of Eli and the location of the ark of the covenant (1 Sam 1:1–20).
www.HolyLandPhotos.org

THEMES AND THEOLOGY

Four of the key themes of 1–2 Samuel are kingship, kingdom, God's sovereignty over the world and, in particular, the affairs of humanity, and God's redemptive covenant.

1. *Kingship.* The institution of kingship is at the very heart of 1–2 Samuel. Appearing over 350 times, "king" is the leading word in 1–2 Samuel. In addition, the subject matter of 1–2 Samuel centers on the major leaders (e.g., Samuel), kings (Saul and David), and men who want to be king in Israel (e.g., Absalom). In other words, the books do not concentrate on the everyday lives of the common Israelite but picture the upper echelon of Israelite society, principally the leaders in the palace courts and the military.

The foundational pillar of the Hebrew conception of kingship is that God is King and that he always has been and always will be King. As the psalmist so forcefully declares, "The LORD is King for ever and ever" (Ps 10:16) and "the LORD is enthroned as King forever" (Ps 29:10). Before Israel captured the land of promise, God had declared to the people that they would have a king (Deut 17:14–20). This human king would be subject to God as king and fully dependent on God's word as the rule of the kingdom. The ultimate king of Israel is the Lord, and the human ruler is to serve as his deputy. When Israel chooses a ruler in 1 Sam 8, the elders reject this plan by choosing a king like all the surrounding nations. This king is autonomous. The Lord himself assesses that choice by saying, "They have rejected me as their king" (v. 7).

The prophet Samuel warns the people that they are seeking a king who will be self-centered and selfish (vv. 10–18). But they do not heed his warning; they demand a king like all the nations. And that is exactly what Israel gets with their first king, Saul. While God chooses Saul as the first king of Israel, Saul is corrupted by power and does not submit his kingship to the Lord. The biblical writer describes the demise of Saul and the rise of David in contrasting terms. David is a man after God's own heart, and he founds a dynasty that will last forever (2 Sam 7:16).

Although David is perhaps the greatest king to sit on the throne of Israel, his rule is deeply flawed and broken. By the second half of 2 Samuel, David's kingdom is in disarray. The rebellions of Absalom and Sheba have taken their toll, and David sins greatly by taking a census of his military. Although David is the prototype for the Messianic King, he is not the Messianic King. At the close of 2 Samuel, the reader is left yearning for the coming of the king who truly keeps the word of God (Deut 17:14–20). That figure arrives in the person of Jesus Christ, the Messianic King, who is the "Son of David" (Matt 12:23) and comes "from David's descendants and from Bethlehem, the town where David lived" (John 7:42).

2. *Kingdom.* One of the great promises that God gives to Israel at Mount Sinai is that they will become a kingdom under the rule of God. The Lord says to the people through Moses, "Although the whole earth is mine, you will be for me a kingdom of priests and a holy nation" (Exod 19:5b–6a). A kingdom is a territory with human subjects under the governmental rule or control of a monarch. After Sinai, God leads the people to the land of promise, and they conquer and secure that territory under the leadership of Joshua. A primary purpose of 1–2 Samuel is to establish

that territory under the authority and power of a king. Some commentators call this period the *kingdomization* of Israel. Saul's words to David in 1 Sam 24:20 reflect that: "I know that you will surely be king and that the kingdom of Israel will be established in your hands."

The kingdom of Israel, however, is never completely united under one king. Hostility between the northern tribes and southern tribes is ever present (2 Sam 2:10; 19:43; 20:1–2). This animosity eventually leads to the division of Israel into two kingdoms (1 Kgs 12:16–17), and invading foreign armies finally destroy both kingdoms.

Does this sad conclusion nullify God's promise that his people would be *kingdomized*? Certainly not. When the Messianic King, the son of David, came to the earth, he proclaimed "the good news of the kingdom" (Matt 4:23; 9:35). Jesus is the final and ultimate king (Matt 2:2; 21:5; 27:37,42). And in his coming to the earth, he inaugurates the final and ultimate kingdom. As Peter says to the people of God, "You are a chosen people, a royal priesthood, a holy nation, God's special possession" (1 Pet 2:9). This kingdom reaches its zenith in the new heavens and the new earth, which is "an inheritance that can never perish, spoil or fade. This inheritance is kept in heaven for you" (1 Pet 1:4).

3. *The sovereignty of God.* The doctrine of the sovereignty of God teaches that everything that occurs in heaven or on earth, from the greatest to the least, unfolds according to the purpose and plan of God. In other words, God has ordained whatever happens. There are simply no surprises for him because he established the plan from all eternity (Matt 25:34; Eph 1:4). Hannah's prayer offers a glimpse into the sovereignty of God with four merisms (a merism is a figure of two opposites that are all-inclusive):

> [1] The LORD brings death and makes alive;
>   [2] he brings down to the grave and raises up.
> [3] The LORD sends poverty and wealth;
>   [4] he humbles and he exalts.
> He raises the poor from the dust
>   and lifts the needy from the ash heap …
> For the foundations of the earth are the LORD's;
>   on them he has set the world. (1 Sam 2:6–7)

Although at times it may appear that God changes his mind or his plan, "He who is the Glory of Israel does not lie or change his mind; for he is not a human being, that he should change his mind" (1 Sam 15:29). Indeed, his sovereign will and plan are unshakable: "the plans of the LORD stand firm forever, the purposes of his heart through all generations" (Ps 33:11).

The books of 1–2 Samuel clearly reveal God's sovereignty in the seemingly minor events of everyday life. God orchestrates the ordinary, sometimes mundane, events in the books. For example, Kish tells his son Saul to go search for the family's lost donkeys (1 Sam 9). This ordinary circumstance leads to Saul's meeting with Samuel at Ramah and being anointed as king. God tells Samuel "the day before Saul came" what is about to happen (v. 15). The meeting is not a chance happening but unfolds according to God's will and word. Major events, such as the choosing of David as Saul's replacement, are also by God's predetermined plan (1 Sam 16:7).

4. *God's redemptive covenant.* The books of 1–2 Samuel fit into the larger picture of the unfolding of God's redemptive-historical plan. So for instance, the Lord's specific intervention to cause Hannah to give birth to Samuel (1 Sam 1:19–20) and her subsequent song of praise (1 Sam 2:1–10) are paradigms of the miraculous birth of Jesus and Mary's Magnificat (Luke 1:46–55). In addition, God's choosing David to be king and David's line to sit on the throne of Israel forever climaxes in the appearance of the Messianic King, who is the eternal ruler. Thus, God says to David through Nathan the prophet, "Your house and your kingdom will endure forever before me; your throne will be established forever" (2 Sam 7:16). This promise that God will establish David's house eternally is fully established only in the coming of Christ.

OUTLINE

I. Birth, Youth, and Call of the Prophet Samuel (1 Sam 1:1—4:1a)

- A. The Birth of Samuel (1:1–20)
- B. Hannah Dedicates Samuel (1:21–28)
- C. Hannah's Prayer (2:1–11)
- D. Eli's Wicked Sons (2:12–26)
- E. Prophecy Against the House of Eli (2:27–36)
- F. The Lord Calls Samuel (3:1—4:1a)

II. The Ark Narrative (4:1b — 7:2a)
- A. The Philistines Capture the Ark (4:1b – 11)
- B. Death of Eli (4:12 – 18)
- C. The Birth of Ichabod (4:19 – 22)
- D. The Ark in Ashdod and Ekron (5:1 – 12)
- E. The Ark Returned to Israel (6:1 — 7:2a)

III. Samuel Subdues the Philistines at Mizpah (7:2b – 17)

IV. Israel Asks for a King (8:1 – 22)

V. Choosing and Anointing a King (9:1 — 10:27)

VI. Saul Rescues the City of Jabesh (11:1 – 11)

VII. Saul Confirmed as King (11:12 – 15)

VIII. Samuel's Farewell Speech (12:1 – 25)
- A. Samuel's Plea of Innocence (12:1 – 5)
- B. Samuel's Lawsuit Against the People (12:6 – 19)
- C. A Final Warning (12:20 – 25)

IX. Saul's Kingship (13:1 — 15:35)
- A. Samuel Rebukes Saul (13:1 – 15)
- B. Israel Without Weapons (13:16 – 22)
- C. War Against the Philistines (13:23 — 14:46)
  1. Jonathan Attacks the Philistines (13:23 — 14:14)
  2. Israel Routs the Philistines (14:15 – 23)
  3. Jonathan Eats Honey (14:24 – 46)
- D. Summary of Saul's Kingship (14:47 – 52)
- E. The Lord Rejects Saul as King (15:1 – 35)

X. Saul's Fall and David's Rise (16:1 — 31:13)
- A. Samuel Anoints David (16:1 – 13)
- B. David in Saul's Service (16:14 – 23)
- C. David and Goliath (17:1 – 58)
  1. The Setting of War (17:1 – 11)
  2. David at Home (17:12 – 19)
  3. David in the Ranks of Israel (17:20 – 30)
  4. David Volunteers (17:31 – 39)
  5. The Fight (17:40 – 54)
  6. David's Pedigree Revealed to Saul (17:55 – 58)
- D. Saul's Growing Fear of David (18:1 – 30)
- E. Saul Tries to Kill David (19:1 – 24)
- F. David and Jonathan (20:1 – 42)
- G. David at Nob (21:1 – 9)
- H. David at Gath (21:10 – 15)
- I. David at Adullam and Mizpah (22:1 – 5)
- J. Saul Kills the Priests of Nob (22:6 – 23)
- K. David Delivers Keilah (23:1 – 6)
- L. Saul Pursues David (23:7 – 29)
- M. David Spares Saul's Life (24:1 – 22)
- N. David, Nabal, and Abigail (25:1 – 44)
- O. David Again Spares Saul's Life (26:1 – 25)
- P. David Among the Philistines (27:1 — 28:2)
- Q. Saul and the Medium at Endor (28:3 – 25)
- R. Achish Sends David Back to Ziklag (29:1 – 11)

S. David Destroys the Amalekites (30:1–31)
T. Saul Takes His Own Life (31:1–13)

XI. David's Early Success (2 Sam 1:1—10:19)
A. David Hears of Saul's Death (1:1–16)
B. David's Lament for Saul and Jonathan (1:17–27)
C. David Anointed King Over Judah (2:1–7)
D. War Between the Houses of David and Saul (2:8—3:5)
E. Abner Goes Over to David (3:6–21)
F. Joab Murders Abner (3:22–39)
G. Ish-Bosheth Murdered (4:1–12)
H. David Becomes King Over Israel (5:1–5)
I. David Conquers Jerusalem (5:6–16)
J. David Defeats the Philistines (5:17–25)
K. The Ark Brought to Jerusalem (6:1–23)
L. God's Promise to David (7:1–17)
M. David's Prayer (7:18–29)
N. David's Victories (8:1–14)
O. David's Officials (8:15–18)
P. David and Mephibosheth (9:1–13)
Q. David Defeats the Ammonites (10:1–19)

XII. David's Grievous Sins (11:1—12:31)
A. David and Bathsheba (11:1–27)
B. Nathan Rebukes David (12:1–31)

XIII. Later Years of David's Rule (13:1—24:25)
A. Amnon and Tamar (13:1–22)
B. Absalom Kills Amnon (13:23–39)
C. Absalom Returns to Jerusalem (14:1–33)
D. Absalom's Conspiracy (15:1–12)
E. David Flees (15:13–37)
F. David and Ziba (16:1–4)
G. Shimei Curses David (16:5–14)
H. The Advice of Ahithophel and Hushai (16:15–23)
I. Hushai's Advice Is Accepted (17:1–23)
J. Absalom's Death (17:24—18:18)
K. David Mourns (18:19—19:8)
L. David Returns to Jerusalem (19:9–43)
M. Sheba Rebels Against David (20:1–22)
N. David's Officials (20:23–26)
O. The Gibeonites Avenged (21:1–14)
P. Wars Against the Philistines (21:15–22)
Q. David's Song of Praise (22:1–51)
R. David's Last Words (23:1–7)
S. David's Mighty Warriors (23:8–39)
T. David Enrolls the Fighting Men (24:1–17)
U. David Builds an Altar (24:18–25)

1 SAMUEL

The Birth of Samuel

1 There was a certain man from Ramathaim, a Zuphite[a] from the hill country[a] of Ephraim, whose
name was Elkanah[b] son of Jeroham, the son of Elihu, the son of Tohu, the son of Zuph, an Ephraimite. 2He had two wives;[c] one was called Hannah and the other Peninnah. Peninnah had children,
but Hannah had none.
3Year after year[d] this man went up from his town to worship[e] and sacrifice to the LORD Almighty at
Shiloh,[f] where Hophni and Phinehas, the two sons of Eli, were priests of the LORD. 4Whenever the day came
for Elkanah to sacrifice,[g] he would give portions of the meat to his wife Peninnah and to all her sons and
daughters. 5But to Hannah he gave a double portion because he loved her, and the LORD had closed her
womb.[h] 6Because the LORD had closed Hannah's wombs, her rival kept provoking her in order to irritate her.[i]

[a] *1* See Septuagint and 1 Chron. 6:26-27,33-35; or *from Ramathaim Zuphim.*

1:1 [a]Jos 17:17-18 [b]1Ch 6:27,34
1:2 [c]Dt 21:15-17; Lk 2:36
1:3 [d]ver 21; Ex 23:14; 34:23; Lk 2:41 [e]Dt 12:5-7 [f]Jos 18:1
1:4 [g]Dt 12:17-18
1:5 [h]Ge 16:1; 30:2
1:6 [i]Job 24:21

1:1—4:1a *Birth, Youth, and Call of the Prophet Samuel.* This section transitions from the period of the judges to establishing the monarchy in Israel. Samuel himself is a transitional figure. He is often called the last judge in Israel. Samuel will oversee Israel's change from a tribal confederation to a monarchy.

1:1–20 *The Birth of Samuel.* These verses tell the story of Hannah, a woman of faith who is barren but eventually gives birth to Samuel. The "barren woman" motif is common in Scripture (Gen 11:27–30; 25:21; 29:31; Judg 13:2; Isa 54:1; Luke 1:7; Gal 4:27). In these scenes God intervenes miraculously to produce a deliverer or leader for his people. Samuel will be instrumental in leading God's people during the establishment of the Davidic monarchy.

1:1 Ramathaim. A town in Ephraim mentioned by this name only here in the OT. It is abbreviated in v. 19 and 2:11 as Ramah. Samuel later lives here (7:17; 8:4; 15:34; 25:1), and for a short time David lives with Samuel here (19:18–19). **Elkanah.** Samuel's father; he is from Ramathaim. He is mentioned only in chs. 1–2 and the genealogy of 1 Chr 6, which classifies him as a Levite and not an Ephraimite. Some explain this apparent contradiction by saying that the Chronicler is attempting to link Samuel to a Levitical ancestry and thereby legitimize his priestly office, although in reality he is an Ephraimite. However, nowhere in this verse does it say that Elkanah is an Ephraimite; the Hebrew text claims that he is literally an Ephrathite, which appears to designate a family or clan.

1:2 two wives. Monogamy predominates in the OT, and it is God's design for humanity (Gen 2:18–25). But there are a few instances of men having more than one wife, such as Abraham, Isaac, David, and Solomon (see notes on Gen 4:19; 16:3; 25:1). The latter may mostly be explained by political factors such as treaty marriages. Hannah is presumably Elkanah's first wife; because she is barren, Elkanah may have felt it necessary to take a second wife and continue the line of inheritance through her.

1:3 LORD Almighty. This is the first reference to this name for God in the Bible, and it appears also in v. 11; 4:4; 15:2; 17:45. The Hebrew name "Yahweh," God's covenantal name (Exod 3:14), is translated "LORD." "Yahweh" is thematically tied to "I am who I am" and expresses God's immutable and eternal nature. "Almighty" is literally "armies/hosts"; it may refer to all the heavenly armies that God has at his beck and call. Others assert the word gives the name of Yahweh the extended meaning of "the Almighty one." **Shiloh.** The tabernacle has been located here since the time of Joshua and the conquest of the land (Josh 18:1). The ancient site lies near the modern village of Sailun, approximately 20 miles (32 kilometers) north of Jerusalem in the tribal holdings of the Ephraimites. Excavations there have revealed a town that thrived during the period of the judges and the early monarchy. Religious festivals were held there yearly (Judg 21:19). Elkanah makes the annual trek to Shiloh to worship the Lord.

1:4 portions. This refers to parts of fellowship offerings for tabernacle sacrifices (Lev 3:1–17; 7:11–21). Levitical regulations require some of the fellowship offering to be sacrificed, some to be eaten by the priests, and some to be consumed by the worshiper who brings the offering. The fellowship offering is a joyous occasion in which those offering the sacrifice show gratitude to God for the many blessings God has given them.

1:5 double portion. Elkanah loves Hannah so much that he gives her a "double portion" of the sacrifice to eat. This act is comparable to the inheritance laws of the Torah in which the firstborn son receives a double portion of the goods of his father (Deut 21:17). **the LORD had closed her womb.** The Lord withholds children and he gives them (Gen 18:10; 29:31; 30:2,22).

1:6–7 Peninnah uses her fertility to lord it over Hannah. Peninnah's derision of Hannah is emphatic to the point that it is like the sound of thunder. Such mocking regarding fertility is nothing new to the Scriptures (Gen 16:4; 30:1–24).

1:8 [j]Ru 4:15
1:9 [k]1Sa 3:3
1:10 [l]Job 7:11
1:11 [m]Ge 8:1; 28:20; 29:32 [n]Nu 6:1-21; Jdg 13:5
1:15 [o]Ps 42:4; 62:8; La 2:19
1:17 [p]Jdg 18:6; 1Sa 25:35; 2Ki 5:19; Mk 5:34 [q]Ps 20:3-5
1:18 [r]Ru 2:13 [s]Ecc 9:7; Ro 15:13
1:19 [t]Ge 4:1; 30:22
1:20 [u]Ge 41:51-52; Ex 2:10,22; Mt 1:21
1:21 [v]ver 3 [w]Dt 12:11
1:22 [x]ver 11,28; Lk 2:22
1:23 [y]ver 17; Nu 30:7
1:24 [z]Nu 15:8-10; Dt 12:5; Jos 18:1

[7]This went on year after year. Whenever Hannah went up to the house of the LORD, her rival provoked her
till she wept and would not eat. [8]Her husband Elkanah would say to her, "Hannah, why are you weeping?
Why don't you eat? Why are you downhearted? Don't I mean more to you than ten sons?[j]"
[9]Once when they had finished eating and drinking in Shiloh, Hannah stood up. Now Eli the priest
was sitting on his chair by the doorpost of the LORD's house.[k] [10]In her deep anguish[l] Hannah prayed to
the LORD, weeping bitterly. [11]And she made a vow, saying, "LORD Almighty, if you will only look on your
servant's misery and remember[m] me, and not forget your servant but give her a son, then I will give
him to the LORD for all the days of his life, and no razor[n] will ever be used on his head."
[12]As she kept on praying to the LORD, Eli observed her mouth. [13]Hannah was praying in her heart,
and her lips were moving but her voice was not heard. Eli thought she was drunk [14]and said to her,
"How long are you going to stay drunk? Put away your wine."
[15]"Not so, my lord," Hannah replied, "I am a woman who is deeply troubled. I have not been drinking wine or beer; I was pouring[o] out my soul to the LORD. [16]Do not take your servant for a wicked
woman; I have been praying here out of my great anguish and grief."
[17]Eli answered, "Go in peace,[p] and may the God of Israel grant you what you have asked of him.[q]"
[18]She said, "May your servant find favor in your eyes.[r]" Then she went her way and ate something,
and her face was no longer downcast.[s]
[19]Early the next morning they arose and worshiped before the LORD and then went back to their
home at Ramah. Elkanah made love to his wife Hannah, and the LORD remembered[t] her. [20]So in the
course of time Hannah became pregnant and gave birth to a son. She named[u] him Samuel,[a] saying,
"Because I asked the LORD for him."

Hannah Dedicates Samuel

[21]When her husband Elkanah went up with all his family to offer the annual[v] sacrifice to the LORD
and to fulfill his vow,[w] [22]Hannah did not go. She said to her husband, "After the boy is weaned, I will
take him and present[x] him before the LORD, and he will live there always."[b]
[23]"Do what seems best to you," her husband Elkanah told her. "Stay here until you have weaned
him; only may the LORD make good[y] his[c] word." So the woman stayed at home and nursed her son
until she had weaned him.
[24]After he was weaned, she took the boy with her, young as he was, along with a three-year-old bull,[d][z]

[a] *20* *Samuel* sounds like the Hebrew for *heard by God.* [b] *22* Masoretic Text; Dead Sea Scrolls *always. I have dedicated him as a Nazirite—all the days of his life."* [c] *23* Masoretic Text; Dead Sea Scrolls, Septuagint and Syriac *your* [d] *24* Dead Sea Scrolls, Septuagint and Syriac; Masoretic Text *with three bulls*

1:8 Elkanah is concerned for Hannah's welfare, but he does not understand the depth of her despair. For many married women the inability to have children is a source of considerable grief. **ten.** Often signifies completion in Hebrew culture (e.g., ten plagues, ten commandments).

1:9 chair. This symbolizes Eli's authority; this same idea appears in the NT in which religious leaders sat in the seat of Moses (cf. Matt 23:2). The Talmud also mentions such a seat or throne. Chairs of this nature have been found in the excavations of the synagogues at Chorazin and Hammath-Tiberius.

1:10 deep anguish. Expresses despondency and despair (Job 7:11; 10:1; Isa 38:15; Ezek 27:31). Hannah responds by praying to the Lord and "weeping bitterly" (an emphatic expression in Hebrew).

1:11 made a vow. If Hannah bears a son, she vows to consecrate him to the Lord as a Nazirite. The Nazirites are men and women who are set apart to the Lord and are spiritual leaders. They express their devotion by abstaining from three things: strong drink, cutting their hair, and touching dead bodies (Num 6:2–8; Amos 2:11–12).

1:12–14 Eli believes Hannah has been drinking. To drink in the tabernacle precincts would be quite an offense. For a priest to do so in the tent of meeting would mean the sanction of death (Lev 10:9), and so priests are commanded not to enter the courts that way (Ezek 44:21).

1:15–16 Hannah responds to Eli politely and firmly. She has not been drinking but is "deeply troubled" (v. 15), which refers to Hannah's persistent prayer. Eli's charge is wrong; Hannah is showing true and deep emotion.

1:16 wicked woman. Lit. "a daughter of Belial." Belial refers to people who are good-for-nothings or worthless. Ironically, the Hebrew uses similar language to describe Eli's own sons ("scoundrels," 2:12).

1:17–18 Eli blesses Hannah, a common priestly function (see Lev 9:22; Num 6:22–27; Deut 21:5). Hannah hopes to find "favor" in Eli's sight. A pun: "favor" (Hebrew *hēn*) is related to the name Hannah (Hebrew *Hannâ*).

1:18 no longer downcast. Hannah returns with a changed demeanor, no longer showing her vexation and sadness.

1:19 the LORD remembered her. As Hannah asked in v. 11. The verb "remembered" is also used in the story of God opening Rachel's womb (Gen 30:22).

1:21–28 *Hannah Dedicates Samuel.* Hannah fulfills her vow (v. 11).

1:21–22 A year has elapsed since Elkanah and his family worshiped in Shiloh (v. 19). Elkanah now makes his annual trip to Shiloh, but Hannah does not go with him. She will make a special trip to the tabernacle when Samuel is weaned and then dedicate him. Then Samuel will be independent and able to stay at Shiloh permanently.

1:23 Elkanah supports Hannah's wishes and decision to remain in Ramah.

1:24–25 Hannah takes Samuel to Shiloh along with offerings for the dedicatory service. **three-year-old bull.** Lit. "three bulls" (see NIV text

an ephah[a] of flour and a skin of wine, and brought him to the house of the LORD at Shiloh. [25]When the
bull had been sacrificed, they brought the boy to Eli, [26]and she said to him, "Pardon me, my lord. As
surely as you live, I am the woman who stood here beside you praying to the LORD. [27]I prayed[a] for this
child, and the LORD has granted me what I asked of him. [28]So now I give him to the LORD. For his whole
life[b] he will be given over to the LORD." And he worshiped the LORD there.

Hannah's Prayer

2 Then Hannah prayed and said:[c]

"My heart rejoices[d] in the LORD;
in the LORD my horn[b][e] is lifted high.
My mouth boasts over my enemies,
for I delight in your deliverance.

[2]"There is no one holy[f] like the LORD;
there is no one besides you;
there is no Rock[g] like our God.

[3]"Do not keep talking so proudly
or let your mouth speak such arrogance,[h]
for the LORD is a God who knows,
and by him deeds[i] are weighed.[j]

[4]"The bows of the warriors are broken,[k]
but those who stumbled are armed with strength.
[5]Those who were full hire themselves out for food,
but those who were hungry are hungry no more.

1:27 [a]ver 11-13; Ps 66:19-20
1:28 [b]ver 11,22; Ge 24:26,52
2:1 [c]Lk 1:46-55 [d]Ps 9:14; 13:5 [e]Ps 89:17,24; 92:10; Isa 12:2-3
2:2 [f]Ex 15:11; Lev 19:2 [g]Dt 32:30-31; 2Sa 22:2,32
2:3 [h]Pr 8:13 [i]1Sa 16:7; 1Ki 8:39 [j]Pr 16:2; 24:11-12
2:4 [k]Ps 37:15

[a] *24* That is, probably about 36 pounds or about 16 kilograms [b] *1* *Horn* here symbolizes strength; also in verse 10.

note), which may be the case because she also brings "an ephah of flour" (v. 24). The Torah law requires sacrificing a bull to be accompanied by offering three-tenths of an ephah of flour (Num 15:9; 28:12,20,28). Hannah has a full ephah of flour, just over the required nine-tenths of an ephah for the offering of three bulls. An ephah, equal to 3/5 bushel (21 liters), is the most common dry measurement. A sacrifice of three bulls, an ephah of flour, and a jar of wine perhaps indicates that Elkanah is wealthy. If Hannah is offering one three-year-old bull, that would also be impressive because of the animal's value (Gen 15:9).

1:26–27 Hannah's excitement is evident as she calls Eli "my lord" twice in the Hebrew and then uses the common oath formula "as surely as you live" (2 Sam 11:11; 14:19). In the earlier episode, Eli blessed her, and now that blessing has occurred. **granted me what I asked of him.** Almost verbatim what Eli said to her in his blessing (v. 17). Samuel is the direct answer to her prayer and to Eli's blessing.

2:1–11 *Hannah's Prayer.* In response to God's marvelous work, Hannah gives this benedictory prayer. Hannah's prayer in poetic form anticipates the coming of a king anointed by God to reign over Israel, a significant theme developed in the books of 1 and 2 Samuel. Throughout church history it has been called the *Magnificat* because it principally magnifies the name of the Lord. Mary's prayer in Luke 1:46–55 is also called the *Magnificat*, and it echoes Hannah's prayer. The basic content and settings of both stories are similar: God intervenes by giving a son to each woman, and the son grows up to deliver God's people. The themes of the two prayers are the same, and Mary quotes Hannah's prayer in her own (e.g., v. 1 in Luke 1:46).

2:1 Hannah opens her prayer with adoration to God, the theme of the song. **horn.** Of an animal; symbolizes an animal's strength and power and can symbolize a human's victory (see Pss 89:17–18; 92:10). The Lord gave Hannah victory over barrenness. **lifted high.** Appears again in v. 10 ("exalt the horn") and thus serves as bookends to the passage. **mouth boasts over.** Or "mouth has widened against"; reflects loud derision of intent to destroy one's enemies. Hannah is so joyous because the Lord delivered her and because she belongs to the Lord.

2:2 Hannah proclaims God's incomparability: (1) No one is as "holy" (Hebrew *qādôš*); God is set apart, distinct, and wholly other. (2) The Lord alone is God, and there is "no one" like him — a confession of monotheism. (3) There is no "Rock" like God; God is a sure defense for his people (see Ps 31:3; Isa 17:10).

2:3 Hannah calls for humility from the boastful in light of the truth of vv. 1–2, leaving no room for human arrogance. This may be generally directed at Peninnah, who lorded her fertility over Hannah (1:6). The Lord weighs the deeds of all humans — likely related to the OT picture of God weighing the heart in judgment (Prov 16:2; 21:2; 24:12).

2:4–5 The Lord makes the strong weak and the weak strong. The first four lines follow a pattern: the strong become weak (lines 1 and 3), and the weak become strong (lines 2 and 4). The final two lines reverse the pattern: the weak become strong (line 5) and the strong become weak (line 6). This emphasizes the Lord's work for the weak, particularly his labors for the barren woman (line 5). **broken.** Picturing a warrior's armaments being broken is a common metaphor for the strong becoming weak (Pss 37:15; 46:9; Jer 49:35; Ezek 39:3). **seven children.** Symbolizes fulfillment and completion (cf. Ruth 4:15). **pines away.** A verb also used of a fisherman who has lost his trade (Isa 19:8). These metaphors apply to Hannah and Peninnah: Hannah bears six children (1 Sam 2:21), and Peninnah is never mentioned again in Scripture.

2:5 [l]Ps 113:9; Jer 15:9
2:6 [m]Dt 32:39 [n]Isa 26:19
2:7 [o]Dt 8:18 [p]Job 5:11; Ps 75:7
2:8 [q]Ps 113:7-8 [r]Job 36:7 [s]Job 38:4
2:9 [t]Ps 91:12 [u]Mt 8:12 [v]Ps 33:16-17
2:10 [w]Ps 2:9 [x]Ps 18:13 [y]Ps 96:13 [z]Ps 21:1 [a]Ps 89:24
2:11 [b]ver 18; 1Sa 3:1
2:12 [c]Jer 2:8; 9:6
2:13 [d]Lev 7:29-34

She who was barren[l] has borne seven children,
but she who has had many sons pines away.
6 "The LORD brings death and makes alive;[m]
he brings down to the grave and raises up.[n]
7 The LORD sends poverty and wealth;[o]
he humbles and he exalts.[p]
8 He raises[q] the poor from the dust
and lifts the needy from the ash heap;
he seats them with princes
and has them inherit a throne of honor.[r]

"For the foundations[s] of the earth are the LORD's;
on them he has set the world.
9 He will guard the feet[t] of his faithful servants,
but the wicked will be silenced in the place of darkness.[u]

"It is not by strength[v] that one prevails;
10 those who oppose the LORD will be broken.[w]
The Most High will thunder[x] from heaven;
the LORD will judge[y] the ends of the earth.

"He will give strength[z] to his king
and exalt the horn[a] of his anointed."

11 Then Elkanah went home to Ramah, but the boy ministered[b] before the LORD under Eli the priest.

Eli's Wicked Sons

12 Eli's sons were scoundrels; they had no regard[c] for the LORD. 13 Now it was the practice of the
priests that, whenever any of the people offered a sacrifice, the priest's servant would come with a
three-pronged fork in his hand while the meat[d] was being boiled 14 and would plunge the fork into the
pan or kettle or caldron or pot. Whatever the fork brought up the priest would take for himself. This is
how they treated all the Israelites who came to Shiloh. 15 But even before the fat was burned, the priest's
servant would come and say to the person who was sacrificing, "Give the priest some meat to roast; he
won't accept boiled meat from you, but only raw."

2:6–8 The Lord is sovereign over all things. Hannah begins with four *merisms* (a literary figure in which two polar opposites are all-inclusive): the Lord (1) rules over death and life; (2) brings a person down to the grave and raises up, which may carry a resurrection idea (cf. Job 19:25–26); (3) makes people poor or rich; and (4) humbles some and exalts others. God providentially raises the weak to positions of prominence, exactly what God did for Hannah and will do for Saul and David. And God can do these things because he created the world. He not only made the earth but set it on its "foundations"—God created all the physical order of the universe (cf. Job 9:6).

2:9–10 faithful ... wicked. The faithful shall prevail because they depend on God's power alone. The wicked rely on their own strength and end up being "silenced in the place of darkness," a metaphor for death (cf. Job 10:21–22; 15:22). **thunder from heaven.** The Lord's enemies will be shattered because he will thunder against them. The way the Lord responds to the proud and arrogant demonstrates ironic justice compared to how Peninnah treated Hannah (1:6).

2:10 his anointed. A royal designation parallel with "his king"; this is the first time this designation appears in the Bible, and it anticipates royalty because in Hannah's day "Israel had no king; everyone did as they saw fit" (Judg 21:25). Hannah concludes her song by pleading that God would "give strength" to his future king and that he would lift up the king's "horn" (see note on v. 1).

2:12–26 *Eli's Wicked Sons.* This section condemns Israel's priesthood while Eli was high priest, highlighting the abuses of the sacrificial practices. These abuses include extortion of quality meat and the priests' appropriation of the fat portion, which belonged to the Lord, for themselves. Particularly problematic is that Eli's two sons are at the forefront of the rebellion.

2:12 scoundrels. See note on 1:16. **they had no regard for the LORD.** A literal translation of the Hebrew text is actually much stronger. It says that "they did not know the LORD," which is the heart of the problem.

2:13–14 The priests in Eli's day practice extortion by taking the quality meat from the Israelites who sacrifice at Shiloh. According to God's instructions, the priests must receive the animal's breast, right thigh, shoulders, and internal organs along with meat from its head (Lev 7:28–36; Deut 18:3). At Shiloh, when the priest's servant sticks his fork in the pot, he gives whatever adheres to the fork to the priest, thereby taking the best meat and disregarding God. The weight of the offense is underscored by the statement that they do this to "all the Israelites" who come to sacrifice at Shiloh. It is widespread sin.

2:15–16 But even before. Indicates an additional abuse by the priests at Shiloh. The fat portion of the sacrifice must be burned on the altar to the Lord, not eaten (Lev 7:25,31; 17:6). At Shiloh, the attendant takes the meat with the fat portion and appropriates the Lord's portion of the sacrifice. If worshipers complain about that practice, they are threatened with physical violence.

16 If the person said to him, "Let the fat be burned first, and then take whatever you want," the servant would answer, "No, hand it over now; if you don't, I'll take it by force."
17 This sin of the young men was very great in the LORD's sight, for they[a] were treating the LORD's
offering with contempt.[e]
18 But Samuel was ministering[f] before the LORD—a boy wearing a linen ephod.[g] 19 Each year his
mother made him a little robe and took it to him when she went up with her husband to offer the annual[h] sacrifice. 20 Eli would bless Elkanah and his wife, saying, "May the LORD give you children by this
woman to take the place of the one she prayed[i] for and gave to[b] the LORD." Then they would go home.
21 And the LORD was gracious to Hannah;[j] she gave birth to three sons and two daughters. Meanwhile,
the boy Samuel grew[k] up in the presence of the LORD.
22 Now Eli, who was very old, heard about everything his sons were doing to all Israel and how they
slept with the women[l] who served at the entrance to the tent of meeting. 23 So he said to them, "Why
do you do such things? I hear from all the people about these wicked deeds of yours. 24 No, my sons;
the report I hear spreading among the LORD's people is not good. 25 If one person sins against another,
God[c] may mediate for the offender; but if anyone sins against the LORD, who will[m] intercede[n] for them?"
His sons, however, did not listen to their father's rebuke, for it was the LORD's will to put them to death.
26 And the boy Samuel continued to grow[o] in stature and in favor with the LORD and with people.

Prophecy Against the House of Eli

27 Now a man of God[p] came to Eli and said to him, "This is what the LORD says: 'Did I not clearly
reveal myself to your ancestor's family when they were in Egypt under Pharaoh? 28 I chose[q] your ancestor out of all the tribes of Israel to be my priest, to go up to my altar, to burn incense, and to wear
an ephod[r] in my presence. I also gave your ancestor's family all the food offerings presented by the
Israelites. 29 Why do you[d] scorn my sacrifice and offering[s] that I prescribed for my dwelling?[t] Why do
you honor your sons more than me by fattening yourselves on the choice parts of every offering made
by my people Israel?'
30 "Therefore the LORD, the God of Israel, declares: 'I promised that members of your family would
minister before me forever.[u]' But now the LORD declares: 'Far be it from me! Those who honor me I

2:17 [e] Mal 2:7-9
2:18 [f] ver 11; 1Sa 3:1 [g] ver 28
2:19 [h] 1Sa 1:3
2:20 [i] 1Sa 1:11,27-28; Lk 2:34
2:21 [j] Ge 21:1 [k] ver 26; Jdg 13:24; 1Sa 3:19; Lk 2:40
2:22 [l] Ex 38:8
2:25 [m] Nu 15:30; Jos 11:20 [n] Dt 1:17; 1Sa 3:14; Heb 10:26
2:26 [o] ver 21; Lk 2:52
2:27 [p] Ex 4:14-16; 1Ki 13:1
2:28 [q] Ex 28:1 [r] Lev 8:7-8
2:29 [s] ver 12-17 [t] Dt 12:5; Mt 10:37
2:30 [u] Ex 29:9

[a] *17* Dead Sea Scrolls and Septuagint; Masoretic Text *people* [b] *20* Dead Sea Scrolls; Masoretic Text *and asked from* [c] *25* Or *the judges* [d] *29* The Hebrew is plural.

2:18–26 The beginning and end of this section refer to Samuel as a "boy" (vv. 18,26). The same Hebrew word is used for the priest's "servant" (vv. 13,15) and for Eli's sons as "young men" (v. 17). They serve as a foil to Samuel, who is not involved in any extortion in the temple.
2:18–19 Samuel continues to minister in the tent of meeting at Shiloh.
2:18 linen ephod. Probably a simple tunic or apron; normally worn by priests (22:18) but at times worn by others as well, including David as he brought the ark to Jerusalem (2 Sam 6:14).
2:20–21 Eli blesses Elkanah and Hannah at the annual sacrifice, and he asks the Lord to grant them more children because they had dedicated Samuel to the Lord's service. Indeed Hannah bears five more children. Samuel's parents disappear from the story at this point.
2:22–24 Eli confronts his priestly sons regarding their "wicked deeds" (v. 23). In addition to the sacrificial abuses, the sons have taken advantage of their position by having sexual relations with women who labor at the entrance to the tent of meeting. There is no hard evidence that these women are cult prostitutes in the manner of the Canaanite religious practices.
2:25 While God can mediate between Eli's sons and the people they sin against, there is no one to mediate the sins the sons have perpetrated against God. The people need someone to intercede between God and themselves. The sons of Eli have no hope. And because they willfully reject the Lord, he brings a death sentence against them.
2:26 This section (vv. 18–26) begins and ends with Samuel, who contrasts with Eli's sons. Samuel continues to mature, and he is pleasing to both God and humans. The reader is left in no doubt as to who is under favor and who is under condemnation.
2:27–36 *Prophecy Against the House of Eli.* Eli is culpable for the impoverished priesthood at Shiloh. Because he honored his sons more than God by neglecting to discipline them, God will judge the house of Eli swiftly and surely, and it will be long lasting.
2:27 man of God. A title for a prophet (9:6–8; 1 Kgs 12:22; 13:5,11–12,14). **This is what the LORD says.** Resembles a common introductory formula in the ancient Near East when a prophet speaks the very words of a god or king. The spokesman must not alter the words in any way. **ancestor's family.** Refers to Eli's extended family that came out of Egypt. Eli descended from Ithamar, one of Aaron's sons (Exod 28:1), so this refers to the Levitical line.
2:28 The Lord specified three duties for Aaron: (1) **go up to my altar.** To present Israel's sacrifices. (2) **burn incense.** On the altar of incense in the Holy Place (Exod 30:1–10). (3) **wear an ephod.** Before the Lord. **wear.** Translates a Hebrew word that has the connotation "carry" or "lift." It likely refers to the ephod used in consultation (Exod 28:24–30) rather than to the basic linen garment worn by priests.
2:29 you scorn. "You" is plural, so it refers to Eli, his sons, and the priesthood. "Scorn" is a strong action verb in Hebrew that literally means to "kick" at something. These priests are not only rejecting the laws of sacrifice but are "fattening" themselves by taking the fat portions of the sacrificial animals (see note on vv.15–16).
2:30 God reverses what he promised to Eli's family because they broke the terms of the promise: they no longer "honor" God but "despise" him (cf. Lev 10:1–3). **Far be it from me!** An exclamation that strongly negates the previous statement (12:23; 2 Sam 23:17; Gen 44:17; Josh 24:16).

2:30 [v]Ps 50:23; 91:15 [w]Mal 2:9
2:31 [x]1Sa 4:11-18; 22:16-20
2:32 [y]1Ki 2:26-27; Zec 8:4
2:34 [z]1Sa 4:11 [a]1Ki 13:3
2:35 [b]1Sa 12:3; 1Ki 2:35 [c]1Sa 16:13; 2Sa 7:11, 27; 1Ki 11:38
2:36 [d]1Ki 2:27
3:1 [e]1Sa 2:11 [f]Ps 74:9 [g]Am 8:11
3:2 [h]1Sa 4:15
3:3 [i]Lev 24:1-4
3:4 [j]Isa 6:8
3:7 [k]Ac 19:12

will honor,[v] but those who despise[w] me will be disdained. 31 The time is coming when I will cut short
your strength and the strength of your priestly house, so that no one in it will reach old age,[x] 32 and
you will see distress in my dwelling. Although good will be done to Israel, no one in your family line
will ever reach old age.[y] 33 Every one of you that I do not cut off from serving at my altar I will spare
only to destroy your sight and sap your strength, and all your descendants will die in the prime of life.
34 " 'And what happens to your two sons, Hophni and Phinehas, will be a sign to you—they will both
die[z] on the same day.[a] 35 I will raise up for myself a faithful priest,[b] who will do according to what is in
my heart and mind. I will firmly establish his priestly house, and they will minister before my anointed[c]
one always. 36 Then everyone left in your family line will come and bow down before him for a piece of
silver and a loaf of bread and plead, "Appoint me to some priestly office so I can have food to eat.[d]" ' "

The Lord Calls Samuel

3 The boy Samuel ministered[e] before the Lord under Eli. In those days the word of the Lord was
rare;[f] there were not many visions.[g]
2 One night Eli, whose eyes[h] were becoming so weak that he could barely see, was lying down in his
usual place. 3 The lamp[i] of God had not yet gone out, and Samuel was lying down in the house of the
Lord, where the ark of God was. 4 Then the Lord called Samuel.
Samuel answered, "Here I am.[j]" 5 And he ran to Eli and said, "Here I am; you called me."
But Eli said, "I did not call; go back and lie down." So he went and lay down.
6 Again the Lord called, "Samuel!" And Samuel got up and went to Eli and said, "Here I am; you
called me."
"My son," Eli said, "I did not call; go back and lie down."
7 Now Samuel did not yet know the Lord: The word of the Lord had not yet been revealed[k] to him.
8 A third time the Lord called, "Samuel!" And Samuel got up and went to Eli and said, "Here I am;
you called me."
Then Eli realized that the Lord was calling the boy. 9 So Eli told Samuel, "Go and lie down, and if he
calls you, say, 'Speak, Lord, for your servant is listening.' " So Samuel went and lay down in his place.
10 The Lord came and stood there, calling as at the other times, "Samuel! Samuel!"

2:31–34 The penalties that will come on Eli's house are varied and severe. "The time is coming" (v. 31) is a prophetic eschatological formula to introduce future events. God will decimate Eli's house so that "no one ... will reach old age" (repeated for emphasis in vv. 31,32). All of Eli's descendants "will die in the prime of life" (v. 33). This prophecy is fulfilled when Saul massacres the priests of Nob (22:11–19). Verse 33 refers to Abiathar, the only priest to escape Saul's execution (22:20–23). Solomon later exiles Abiathar to Anathoth during a palace intrigue (1 Kgs 1:5–7; 2:26–27), which fulfills the prophecy against Eli's house. The concurrent deaths of Hophni and Phinehas will serve as a "sign" (1 Sam 2:34) to Eli that everything the man of God prophesied will certainly come to pass.

2:35 firmly establish his priestly house. Or "build for him a faithful house." The Hebrew term "faithful" describing the priest's house also describes the priest. This priest is probably Zadok, a descendant of Aaron through his son Eleazar (2 Sam 8:17; 1 Chr 24:3,31). In contrast to the line of Eli, the Zadokites will conform their priesthood to the Lord's commands. The survivors of Eli's line will perform the most menial labor for the Zadokites so that they might survive the ravages of God's judgment on them (v. 36). **my anointed.** Anticipates the future establishment of kingship in Israel.

3:1—4:1a *The Lord Calls Samuel.* The spiritual setting is a time when the word of the Lord is rarely heard (3:1). In a highly structured passage, God calls to Samuel four different times (3:4–14). It is a fine example of what linguists call a paneled sequence, which consists of repeated elements appearing in successive movements. There are four panels: the first three (3:4–5,6–7,8–9) include the Lord calling to Samuel, Samuel going to Eli, and Eli telling Samuel to go back to sleep; in the fourth panel, the Lord calls to Samuel but now Samuel responds to the Lord and receives his message (3:10–14). Paneling builds dramatic tension in a story. The text then repeats the judgment to come on the house of Eli (3:15–18). Samuel is established as a true prophet of the Lord, and he speaks God's word to all Israel (3:19—4:1a). In contrast to 3:1, the word of the Lord is no longer rare in the land.

3:1 The narrative returns to Samuel after the extended prophecy against Eli's house (2:27–36). He continues to perform his duties for the Lord under the oversight of Eli. **rare.** God's revelation to a prophet is uncommon; that is, God's word is absent, and God is displeased with his people (see Amos 8:12).

3:2–3 Eli is lying down in the precincts of the tent of meeting, and his eyes are dimming. In an ironic sense, Eli is one without vision (v. 1). **The lamp of God had not yet gone out.** The lamp, or menorah, is made of pure gold, and it sits inside the tent of meeting just outside the veil that separates the Holy Place from the Most Holy Place (Exod 25:31–39). The lamp is to burn without interruption every day from evening until morning (Exod 27:20–21). Thus the unfolding scene is taking place at nighttime while the lamp is yet burning. We are not told why Samuel lies down in the house of the Lord "where the ark of God was." This is the first time the book mentions the ark; its appearance here probably anticipates the ark narrative (4:1b—7:2a). See illustration, p. 165.

3:7 did not yet know the Lord. The text of 2:12 says, literally, that the sons of Eli "did not know the Lord" (see note on 2:12). The text of 3:7 says the same thing about Samuel except it adds the word "yet." It is anticipatory: Samuel will come to know God, and the word of God will be revealed through him.

3:10 The fourth time the Lord calls to Samuel is an intensive and heightened scene. **stood.** Commonly used in the OT when God appears in a theophany, a visible manifestation of God to humans (Gen 18:2; 28:13;

Then Samuel said, "Speak, for your servant is listening."
11 And the LORD said to Samuel: "See, I am about to do something in Israel that will make the ears
of everyone who hears about it tingle.[l] 12 At that time I will carry out against Eli everything[m] I spoke
against his family—from beginning to end. 13 For I told him that I would judge his family forever because of the sin he knew about; his sons blasphemed God,[a] and he failed to restrain[n] them. 14 Therefore
I swore to the house of Eli, 'The guilt of Eli's house will never be atoned[o] for by sacrifice or offering.' "
15 Samuel lay down until morning and then opened the doors of the house of the LORD. He was afraid
to tell Eli the vision, 16 but Eli called him and said, "Samuel, my son."
Samuel answered, "Here I am."
17 "What was it he said to you?" Eli asked. "Do not hide it from me. May God deal with you, be it ever
so severely,[p] if you hide from me anything he told you." 18 So Samuel told him everything, hiding nothing from him. Then Eli said, "He is the LORD; let him do what is good in his eyes."[q]
19 The LORD was with[r] Samuel as he grew[s] up, and he let none[t] of Samuel's words fall to the ground.
20 And all Israel from Dan to Beersheba[u] recognized that Samuel was attested as a prophet of the LORD.
21 The LORD continued to appear at Shiloh, and there he revealed[v] himself to Samuel through his word.
4 And Samuel's word came to all Israel.

The Philistines Capture the Ark

Now the Israelites went out to fight against the Philistines. The Israelites camped at Ebenezer,[w] and
the Philistines at Aphek.[x] 2 The Philistines deployed their forces to meet Israel, and as the battle spread,
Israel was defeated by the Philistines, who killed about four thousand of them on the battlefield. 3 When
the soldiers returned to camp, the elders of Israel asked, "Why[y] did the LORD bring defeat on us today
before the Philistines? Let us bring the ark[z] of the LORD's covenant from Shiloh, so that he may go with
us and save us from the hand of our enemies."
4 So the people sent men to Shiloh, and they brought back the ark of the covenant of the LORD

[a] 13 An ancient Hebrew scribal tradition (see also Septuagint); Masoretic Text *sons made themselves contemptible*

3:11 [l] 2Ki 21:12; Jer 19:3
3:12 [m] 1Sa 2:27-36
3:13 [n] 1Sa 2:12,17,22, 29-31
3:14 [o] Lev 15:30-31; 1Sa 2:25; Isa 22:14
3:17 [p] Ru 1:17; 2Sa 3:35
3:18 [q] Job 2:10; Isa 39:8
3:19 [r] Ge 21:22; 39:2 [s] 1Sa 2:21 [t] 1Sa 9:6
3:20 [u] Jdg 20:1
3:21 [v] ver 10
4:1 [w] 1Sa 7:12 [x] Jos 12:18; 1Sa 29:1
4:3 [y] Jos 7:7 [z] Nu 10:35; Jos 6:7

Num 22:22). For the first time, God calls to the boy twice ("Samuel! Samuel!"), a common Hebrew technique for emphasis (Exod 3:4). The drama is reaching a fevered pitch.

3:11–14 make the ears ... tingle. An expression later used regarding the destruction God will bring on Judah and Jerusalem by means of the Babylonians (2 Kgs 21:12; Jer 19:3). God is in the process of destroying Eli's house because "his sons blasphemed God" (v. 13).

3:12 from beginning to end. This is a *merism* (a rhetorical term in which two polar opposites are all-inclusive): the prophecy will happen fully from first to last.

3:13 his sons blasphemed God. Lit. "blasphemed themselves"; the difference between the word for "God" and the word for "themselves" is one letter in Hebrew. A common understanding is that the scribes purposefully left out one of the letters in the name of "God" so that they would not be guilty of blaspheming the name of God. See NIV text note.

3:17 Five times in this verse Eli uses nouns or verbs related to the Hebrew term "word." The word of the Lord thus receives great emphasis in a time when "the word of the LORD was rare" (v. 1). **May God deal with you.** A common formula in 1 Samuel (14:44; 20:13; 25:22).

3:18 Eli acknowledges that the Lord has spoken and that as the sovereign God he will do "what is good in his eyes."

3:19 The LORD was with Samuel. A common expression in the OT that reflects the status of a believer (16:18; 18:12,28; Gen 39:2–3,21). It contrasts Samuel to Eli's sons (2:12). **none of Samuel's words fall to the ground.** Samuel is a true prophet (Deut 18:21–22); the Lord fulfills all that he speaks through the prophet.

3:20 from Dan to Beersheba. This geographic marker is a merism (a literary figure in which two polar opposites are all-inclusive) that encapsulates the limits of all the land of Israel from north to south (2 Sam 3:10; 17:11; Judg 20:1).

3:21 Ch. 3 comes full circle with contrasting bookends: in v. 1, the word of God was rare in Israel and there were few visions; in v. 21, the Lord reveals himself to Samuel in Shiloh "through his word."

4:1b—7:2a *The Ark Narrative.* Samuel disappears from the story, but he returns as an older, mature prophet of the Lord in ch. 7. The focus turns to the ark of the covenant: the Philistines capture it, and the Israelites recover it. Israel loses two battles to the Philistines and loses the ark (4:1b–11). Eli dies (4:12–18), and Ichabod is born (4:19–22). The ark of God becomes an unwelcome guest in the land of the Philistines (5:1–12), so the Philistines return it to Israel (6:1—7:2a).

4:1b–11 *The Philistines Capture the Ark.* After the Philistines defeat Israel (vv. 1b–2), Israel transports the ark of the covenant from Shiloh to the battlefield (vv. 3–4). It initially encourages Israel, but the Philistines defeat them again and capture it (vv. 5–11).

4:1b Philistines. Part of the Sea Peoples, who are known as early as the fourteenth century BC. An inscription from the time of Rameses III (1194–1163 BC) from Medinet Habu describes a battle between Pharaoh and the Sea Peoples. Rameses III won the battle and repulsed the Sea Peoples, preventing them from capturing and settling in Egypt. Instead, the Philistines colonized the coastal plain of the land of Canaan. **Ebenezer.** Located at the modern site of Izbet Sartah. **Aphek.** About two miles (3.2 kilometers) west of Ebenezer.

4:3 ark of the LORD's covenant. Symbolizes the very presence of God with his people.

4:4 brought back. The proper way to transport the ark is to carry it on poles resting on the priests' shoulders (Num 4:15; 7:9; 10:21; 1 Chr 15:13–15). **is enthroned between the cherubim.** Cf. 2 Sam 6:2; Exod 25:22. In the first battle the Israelites lose about 4,000 men, prompting the soldiers to wonder why the Lord brought this loss upon them. The clear answer to them: the ark is not at the battle. Thus the elders

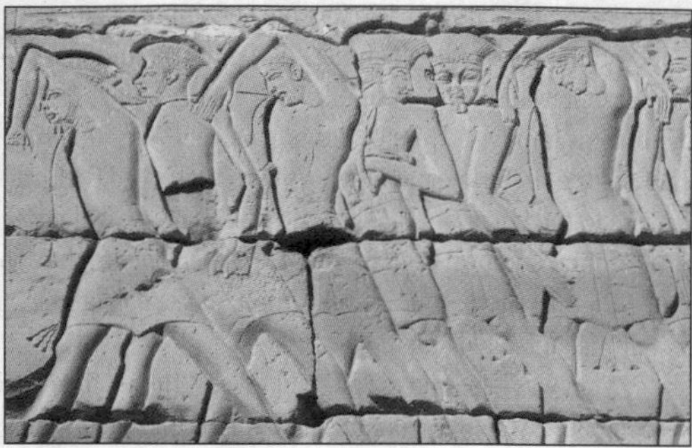

Depiction at Medinet Habu of the Philistines in the battle between the Sea Peoples and Rameses III.
left: Todd Bolen/www.BiblePlaces.com; *right:* (c) BasPhoto/Shutterstock

4:4 [a] Ex 25:22; 2Sa 6:2
4:5 [b] Jos 6:5,10
4:7 [c] Ex 15:14
4:9 [d] Jdg 13:1; 1Co 16:13
4:10 [e] ver 2; Dt 28:25; 2Sa 18:17; 2Ki 14:12
4:11 [f] 1Sa 2:34; Ps 78:61,64
4:12 [g] Jos 7:6; 2Sa 1:2; 15:32; Ne 9:1; Job 2:12
4:13 [h] ver 18; 1Sa 1:9

Almighty, who is enthroned between the cherubim.[a] And Eli's two sons, Hophni and Phinehas, were
there with the ark of the covenant of God.
5 When the ark of the LORD's covenant came into the camp, all Israel raised such a great shout[b] that
the ground shook. 6 Hearing the uproar, the Philistines asked, "What's all this shouting in the Hebrew
camp?"
When they learned that the ark of the LORD had come into the camp, 7 the Philistines were afraid.[c]
"A god has[a] come into the camp," they said. "Oh no! Nothing like this has happened before. 8 We're
doomed! Who will deliver us from the hand of these mighty gods? They are the gods who struck the
Egyptians with all kinds of plagues in the wilderness. 9 Be strong, Philistines! Be men, or you will be
subject to the Hebrews, as they[d] have been to you. Be men, and fight!"
10 So the Philistines fought, and the Israelites were defeated[e] and every man fled to his tent. The
slaughter was very great; Israel lost thirty thousand foot soldiers. 11 The ark of God was captured, and
Eli's two sons, Hophni and Phinehas, died.[f]

Death of Eli

12 That same day a Benjamite ran from the battle line and went to Shiloh with his clothes torn and
dust[g] on his head. 13 When he arrived, there was Eli[h] sitting on his chair by the side of the road, watching, because his heart feared for the ark of God. When the man entered the town and told what had
happened, the whole town sent up a cry.
14 Eli heard the outcry and asked, "What is the meaning of this uproar?"

[a] 7 Or *"Gods have* (see Septuagint)

hope that the presence of the ark will deliver Israel from their enemies. **Hophni and Phinehas.** Mentioning them anticipates their death in v. 11.
4:5 great shout. War cry.
4:6–8 The Philistines hear the shouting from the Israelite camp and respond in fear. The Philistines refer to the Israelites as "Hebrews" (vv. 6,9; 13:19; 14:11; 29:3), an ethnic term; "Israelites" reflects a national, geo-political identity. Perhaps the Philistines do this because they believe they are culturally superior. They refer to the Hebrews as polytheists ("gods," v. 8), but they are afraid because the God of Israel "has come" (a singular verb, v. 7) into the camp. The author may be mocking the Philistines for misunderstanding Israelite religion and monotheism. The Philistines have some knowledge of Israelite history, but they are confused. They proclaim that Israel's gods defeated Egypt with numerous plagues "in the wilderness" (v. 8). Of course, the Lord struck the Egyptians in Egypt, not in the wilderness.
4:9 fight. The Philistines encourage themselves to resist Israel in order to avoid slavery, as the Hebrews had been enslaved to them. The Israelites were under the oppressive hand of the Philistines prior to this time (Judg 10:7–8; 13:1).
4:10 The results of the second battle are much worse than the first. **every man fled to his tent.** The army disbanded (cf. 13:2; 2 Sam 18:17; 19:8; 20:1,22; Judg 7:8).
4:11 The text does not tell how Eli's sons died; we may assume the Philistines killed them. Their deaths fulfill prophecy (2:34).
4:12–18 *Death of Eli.* An escapee from the battle runs to Shiloh to bring tidings of the Israelite defeat. Eli and the entire city are anxiously awaiting news of the battle and, in particular, the fate of the ark of the covenant. When Eli hears the distressing news, he falls from his chair and breaks his neck. The influence of the house of Eli over the nation of Israel is coming to an end.
4:12 Benjamite. May subtly point to the leadership of Israel passing from the house of Eli to the kingship under Saul, a Benjamite. **went to Shiloh.** From Ebenezer to Shiloh is a distance of about 20 miles (32 kilometers) and mostly uphill. The man makes the distance in one day. **clothes torn and dust on his head.** Common signs of grief and despair (2 Sam 1:2,11; Job 1:20; 2:12).
4:13–15 The scene drips with ironic tragedy. Eli waits by the gate at Shiloh "watching" (v. 13) for a messenger, but "he could not see" (v. 15)—physically or spiritually.

The man hurried over to Eli, [15]who was ninety-eight years old and whose eyes[i] had failed so that he could not see. [16]He told Eli, "I have just come from the battle line; I fled from it this very day."

Eli asked, "What happened, my son?"

[17]The man who brought the news replied, "Israel fled before the Philistines, and the army has suffered heavy losses. Also your two sons, Hophni and Phinehas, are dead, and the ark of God has been captured."

[18]When he mentioned the ark of God, Eli fell backward off his chair by the side of the gate. His neck was broken and he died, for he was an old man, and he was heavy. He had led[a][j] Israel forty years.

[19]His daughter-in-law, the wife of Phinehas, was pregnant and near the time of delivery. When she heard the news that the ark of God had been captured and that her father-in-law and her husband were dead, she went into labor and gave birth, but was overcome by her labor pains. [20]As she was dying, the women attending her said, "Don't despair; you have given birth to a son." But she did not respond or pay any attention.

[21]She named the boy Ichabod,[b][k] saying, "The Glory[l] has departed from Israel"—because of the capture of the ark of God and the deaths of her father-in-law and her husband. [22]She said, "The Glory has departed from Israel, for the ark of God has been captured."

The Ark in Ashdod and Ekron

5 After the Philistines had captured the ark of God, they took it from Ebenezer[m] to Ashdod.[n] [2]Then they carried the ark into Dagon's temple and set it beside Dagon.[o] [3]When the people of Ashdod rose early the next day, there was Dagon, fallen[p] on his face on the ground before the ark of the LORD! They took Dagon and put him back in his place. [4]But the following morning when they rose, there was Dagon, fallen on his face on the ground before the ark of the LORD! His head and hands had been broken[q] off and were lying on the threshold; only his body remained. [5]That is why to this day neither the priests of Dagon nor any others who enter Dagon's temple at Ashdod step on the threshold.[r]

[6]The LORD's hand[s] was heavy on the people of Ashdod and its vicinity; he brought devastation[t] on them and afflicted them with tumors.[c][u] [7]When the people of Ashdod saw what was happening, they said, "The ark of the god of Israel must not stay here with us, because his hand is heavy on us and on

4:15 [i] 1Sa 3:2
4:18 [j] ver 13
4:21 [k] Ge 35:18 [l] Ps 26:8; Jer 2:11
5:1 [m] 1Sa 4:1; 7:12 [n] Jos 13:3
5:2 [o] Jdg 16:23
5:3 [p] Isa 19:1; 46:7
5:4 [q] Eze 6:6; Mic 1:7
5:5 [r] Zep 1:9
5:6 [s] ver 7; Ex 9:3; Ps 32:4; Ac 13:11 [t] ver 11; Ps 78:66 [u] Dt 28:27; 1Sa 6:5

[a] *18* Traditionally *judged* [b] *21* *Ichabod* means *no glory.* [c] *6* Hebrew; Septuagint and Vulgate *tumors. And rats appeared in their land, and there was death and destruction throughout the city*

4:17–18 The tragic news comes in three parts: (1) the Philistines soundly routed Israel; (2) Eli's two sons died; and (3) the Philistines captured the ark of the covenant. Eli is more concerned about the ark than his sons. **He had led Israel forty years.** Eli's service as a judge in Israel is summarized like the leaders in the book of Judges (Judg 12:7,9,14; 15:20; 16:31).

4:19–22 *The Birth of Ichabod.* This brief episode bridges the desperate unorthodoxy of Eli and the return of orthodoxy under Samuel. True religion is at a low point in Israel: the Philistines have captured the ark of God, and God's very presence has left his people.

4:21–22 Apparently in her dying gasp, the woman names the child Ichabod, which likely means "no glory" (see the NIV text note). The woman answers her own question: "The Glory has departed from Israel" (v. 21). The ark of the covenant has been taken to the land of the Philistines. **Glory.** Signals the very presence of God with his people (Ezek 10:18).

5:1–12 *The Ark in Ashdod and Ekron.* The Philistine army soundly thrashes Israel at Ebenezer, and they capture the ark of the covenant. The triumphant Philistines parade the ark to Ashdod, one of their pentapolis cities (see map, p. 435). God shows his power over the Philistines and their god Dagon in a most impressive way. The language in this episode is reminiscent of the exodus out of Egypt; the author is drawing a parallel between the two events.

5:1 Ebenezer to Ashdod. Approximately 35 miles (56 kilometers). **Ashdod.** One of five capital cities (pentapolis) of Philistia. Excavations at this site reveal a flourishing Philistine presence and culture during the twelfth to eleventh centuries BC.

5:2 The Philistines place the ark in the temple of Dagon right next to a statue of that god. **Dagon.** A main god of the Philistines; a god of agriculture. "Dagon" is related to a Hebrew word for "grain" (*dāgān*). It was once thought that he is a fish god because the Semitic word *dāg* means "fish," but this is a minority view today. **set it beside Dagon.** To symbolize that it submits to the Philistine deity.

5:3–4 In retaliation, Dagon is twice made to bow in submission to the God of Israel. The second time is more emphatic than the first because Dagon's head and hands are severed and lying at the doorstep of the temple. **fallen on his face on the ground ... His head ... had been broken off.** The same words describe Goliath's death (17:48–51). What happened to Dagon is what happened to his famous follower.

5:5 step on the threshold. Debasing Dagon led to a superstition at the temple of Dagon. The priests would no longer step on the threshold of the sanctuary because Dagon's severed head and hands fell there. Walking on the threshold became taboo for the priests.

5:6 The language of this verse is reminiscent of the exodus out of Egypt. **The LORD's hand.** Commonly used of God's strength in attacking the Egyptians (Exod 3:20; 6:1; 9:3). **heavy.** Echoes the Lord hardening the hearts of the Egyptians (Exod 10:1). **tumors.** Some historians believe this refers to bubonic plague, which is characterized by swelling of lymph glands and passed to people by mice or rats (cf. 6:5). Others think that it refers simply to something like hemorrhoids.

5:7 The continued presence of the ark in Ashdod is intolerable. The people are well aware that the hand of the Lord is "heavy" on them (v. 7), a term used of the Lord hardening Pharaoh's heart (Exod 7:3).

5:8 [v]ver 11
5:9 [w]ver 6,11; Dt 2:15; 1Sa 7:13; Ps 78:66
5:11 [x]ver 6,8-9
6:2 [y]Ge 41:8; Ex 7:11; Isa 2:6
6:3 [z]Ex 23:15; Dt 16:16 [a]Lev 5:15 [b]ver 9
6:4 [c]ver 17-18; Jos 13:3; Jdg 3:3
6:5 [d]1Sa 5:6-11 [e]Jos 7:19; Isa 42:12; Jn 9:24; Rev 14:7
6:6 [f]Ex 7:13; 8:15; 9:34; 14:17 [g]Ex 12:31,33
6:7 [h]2Sa 6:3 [i]Nu 19:2

Dagon our god." 8So they called together all the rulers of the Philistines and asked them, "What shall
we do with the ark of the god of Israel?"

They answered, "Have the ark of the god of Israel moved to Gath.[v]" So they moved the ark of the
God of Israel.

9But after they had moved it, the LORD's hand was against that city, throwing it into a great panic.[w]
He afflicted the people of the city, both young and old, with an outbreak of tumors.[a] 10So they sent the
ark of God to Ekron.

As the ark of God was entering Ekron, the people of Ekron cried out, "They have brought the ark of
the god of Israel around to us to kill us and our people." 11So they called together all the rulers[x] of the
Philistines and said, "Send the ark of the god of Israel away; let it go back to its own place, or it[b] will kill
us and our people." For death had filled the city with panic; God's hand was very heavy on it. 12Those
who did not die were afflicted with tumors, and the outcry of the city went up to heaven.

The Ark Returned to Israel

6 When the ark of the LORD had been in Philistine territory seven months, 2the Philistines called for
the priests and the diviners[y] and said, "What shall we do with the ark of the LORD? Tell us how we
should send it back to its place."

3They answered, "If you return the ark of the god of Israel, do not send it back to him without a gift;[z]
by all means send a guilt offering[a] to him. Then you will be healed, and you will know why his hand[b]
has not been lifted from you."

4The Philistines asked, "What guilt offering should we send to him?"

They replied, "Five gold tumors and five gold rats, according to the number[c] of the Philistine rulers,
because the same plague has struck both you and your rulers. 5Make models of the tumors[d] and of the
rats that are destroying the country, and give glory[e] to Israel's god. Perhaps he will lift his hand from you
and your gods and your land. 6Why do you harden[f] your hearts as the Egyptians and Pharaoh did? When
Israel's god dealt harshly with them, did they[g] not send the Israelites out so they could go on their way?

7"Now then, get a new cart[h] ready, with two cows that have calved and have never been yoked.[i] Hitch

[a] 9 Or *with tumors in the groin* (see Septuagint)   [b] 11 Or *he*

5:8 all the rulers of the Philistines. The five leaders of the pentapolis (6:4,17). **Gath.** A capital city, located at modern Tell es-Safi, approximately 12 miles (19 kilometers) east of Ashdod. David briefly seeks refuge from Saul in Gath (21:10–15). Goliath, the great Philistine warrior, is from Gath (17:23).
5:9 panic. A word used of the Egyptian army while God was destroying it in the Red Sea ("confusion," Exod 14:24). **outbreak.** Used only here in the Bible. It appears to be related to an Arabic word that means "to have cracked eyelids or lower lips," and it indicates that the disease is breaking the surface of the skin.
5:10–12 Ekron. The third Philistine capital city; located at Tel Miqne, some 19 miles (30.5 kilometers) inland and 12 miles (19.3 kilometers) northeast of Ashdod. It is the closest Philistine capital city to Israel. Extensive excavations here have uncovered a large Philistine temple. The Ekronites respond to the appearance of the ark with unbridled chaos. The Hebrew of these verses is oddly related in first person pronouns: v. 10 quotes the Ekronites as saying, literally, "They have brought to me the ark of the God of Israel to kill me and my people," and v. 11 repeats the phrase "kill me and my people." Some understand the first person to reflect a leader speaking for all the people or that each individual Ekronite is saying the same thing. This is the same wording that Pharaoh uses in Egypt when the Lord brings plagues on the Egyptians (Exod 8:8). This is further evidence that the ark narrative echoes the exodus pattern. **outcry ... to heaven.** This ironically reverses Exod 2:23, where the Israelites give an "outcry" up to the Lord because of the Egyptian oppression.
6:1—7:2a *The Ark Returned to Israel.* The Philistines reluctantly return the ark, and they do so with an offering to placate the God of Israel. Even so, the Philistines are not yet convinced that the plague was the work of the Lord, so they use the ark as a means of divination.
6:1 territory. This may suggest that the ark is purposefully kept away from urban population centers because of the devastation to Ashdod, Gath, and Ekron. **seven months.** May symbolize the completeness of havoc and chaos (cf. the "seven days" of the first plague in Egypt in Exod 7:25).
6:2 The Philistines admit defeat and determine to return the ark. **called for the priests and the diviners.** Reminiscent of the Egyptians in the plague account: they summoned their priests to deal with the pestilences (Exod 7:22; 8:7,18; 9:11).
6:3 guilt offering. Specifically treats a sin in which the holy things of the Lord have been misused (Lev 5:14–16) and atones for sins against the sanctuary and the objects within it.
6:4–5 Five gold tumors and five gold rats. An example of sympathetic magic in which one makes an image of what is threatening in order to ward off the danger; it is a means of controlling an adversary through replication. **plague.** Used commonly of the pestilences that the Lord brought on Egypt (Exod 9:14; 12:13). **both you and your rulers.** A further reminder of the plagues on Egypt (Exod 11:5).
6:6 This seals the parallel between the ark narrative and the exodus account. Both the Philistines and Egyptians are guilty of hardening their hearts. **dealt harshly.** Makes the tie between the two episodes tighter and clearer; this rare term of mockery, which reflects the idea of "making a toy" of Egypt, also appears in the plague account (Exod 10:2).
6:7–9 The cultic leaders give instructions regarding the ark's removal. The ark is to be carried back to Israel on a "new cart" (v. 7) led by two cows that have "never been yoked" (v. 7). Neither has been used in secular labor, but they are being set apart for ritual work. The gold images

the cows to the cart, but take their calves away and pen them up. [8]Take the ark of the LORD and put it
on the cart, and in a chest beside it put the gold objects you are sending back to him as a guilt offering.
Send it on its way, [9]but keep watching it. If it goes up to its own territory, toward Beth Shemesh,[j] then
the LORD has brought this great disaster on us. But if it does not, then we will know that it was not his
hand that struck us but that it happened to us by chance."

[10]So they did this. They took two such cows and hitched them to the cart and penned up their calves.
[11]They placed the ark of the LORD on the cart and along with it the chest containing the gold rats and
the models of the tumors. [12]Then the cows went straight up toward Beth Shemesh, keeping on the road
and lowing all the way; they did not turn to the right or to the left. The rulers of the Philistines followed
them as far as the border of Beth Shemesh.

[13]Now the people of Beth Shemesh were harvesting their wheat in the valley, and when they looked
up and saw the ark, they rejoiced at the sight. [14]The cart came to the field of Joshua of Beth Shemesh,
and there it stopped beside a large rock. The people chopped up the wood of the cart and sacrificed the
cows as a burnt offering[k] to the LORD. [15]The Levites[l] took down the ark of the LORD, together with the
chest containing the gold objects, and placed them on the large rock. On that day the people of Beth
Shemesh offered burnt offerings and made sacrifices to the LORD. [16]The five rulers of the Philistines saw
all this and then returned that same day to Ekron.

[17]These are the gold tumors the Philistines sent as a guilt offering to the LORD—one each[m] for Ashdod, Gaza, Ashkelon, Gath and Ekron. [18]And the number of the gold rats was according to the number
of Philistine towns belonging to the five rulers—the fortified towns with their country villages. The
large rock on which the Levites set the ark of the LORD is a witness to this day in the field of Joshua of
Beth Shemesh.

[19]But God struck down[n] some of the inhabitants of Beth Shemesh, putting seventy[a] of them to death
because they looked[o] into the ark of the LORD. The people mourned because of the heavy blow the LORD
had dealt them. [20]And the people of Beth Shemesh asked, "Who can stand[p] in the presence of the LORD,
this holy[q] God? To whom will the ark go up from here?"

[21]Then they sent messengers to the people of Kiriath Jearim,[r] saying, "The Philistines have returned
7 the ark of the LORD. Come down and take it up to your town." [1]So the men of Kiriath Jearim came and
took up the ark of the LORD. They brought it to Abinadab's[s] house on the hill and consecrated Eleazar
his son to guard the ark of the LORD. [2]The ark remained at Kiriath Jearim a long time—twenty years in all.

[a] *19* A few Hebrew manuscripts; most Hebrew manuscripts and Septuagint *50,070*

6:9 [j] ver 3; Jos 15:10; 21:16
6:14 [k] 2Sa 24:22; 1Ki 19:21
6:15 [l] Jos 3:3
6:17 [m] ver 4
6:19 [n] 2Sa 6:7 [o] Ex 19:21; Nu 4:5,15,20
6:20 [p] 2Sa 6:9; Mal 3:2; Rev 6:17 [q] Lev 11:45
6:21 [r] Jos 9:17; 15:9,60; 1Ch 13:5-6
7:1 [s] 2Sa 6:3

are to be included on the cart by the side of the ark. The Philistines are then to send the ark on its way. Divination is part and parcel of the ark's return. If the ark goes directly to the Israelite town of Beth Shemesh, then it is clearly the God of Israel who brought the plague on Philistia. If it goes another way, then the plague was a mere accidental happening. **Beth Shemesh.** Located approximately ten miles (16 kilometers) east of Ekron in the Sorek Valley. Excavations at the site have uncovered an Israelite village from this time period.

6:12 straight up ... on the road ... they did not turn. The description of the traveling cows is emphatic. **on the road.** The animals took the most direct route to Beth Shemesh. The rulers of the Philistines trail the ark to determine an answer to their divination. The answer is vivid and clear!

6:13–15 Because the people of Beth Shemesh are harvesting their grain, there are many workers in the field to see and greet the ark on its return. The cart stops in the field of a man named Joshua, and in the field is a stone that could serve as a natural altar. The Israelites are not to build any altars with tools (Exod 20:22–26), and so this altar at Beth Shemesh fits the bill. It appears to be a problem that the people sacrifice the cows as whole burnt offerings because the law requires such sacrifices to be males only (Lev 1:3; 22:19). The Levites, who remove the ark from the cart and place it on the great stone, are authorized to do this work (Num 4:5–15). **Beth Shemesh.** See note on vv. 7–9. It is one of the Levitical cities (Josh 21:16).

6:17–18 The five gold tumors each represent one of the Philistine pentapolis cities, indicating the ark's total victory over the Philistines. Each of the five gold mice represents one of the pentapolis cities and all the territory under the rulership of each city. This again demonstrates the total submission of Philistine land to the God of Israel. **large rock.** Where all the sacrificial activity takes place; it stands as a witness to the submission of Philistia even to the writer's day. Stones as monuments to great events are common in the OT, especially in the book of Joshua (Josh 4:20; 7:26; 8:28–29,32; 10:27; 24:27).

6:19 God struck down. This reminds the Israelites not to be presumptuous regarding the ark of the Lord. Because some of the men of Beth Shemesh gazed into the ark, the Lord strikes down some of their number. Even the priests are not to look at the holy objects "even for a moment, or they will die" (Num 4:20). **seventy.** See NIV text note.

6:20—7:2a The people at Beth Shemesh sound like the Ashdodites in 5:7–8. They want the ark to leave them because of the divine outburst against them. So they send messengers to Kiriath Jearim, and they demand that the ark be taken there.

6:21 Kiriath Jearim. Located nearly ten miles (16 kilometers) east of Beth Shemesh in the Sorek Valley. It is one of the Gibeonite cities (Josh 9:17), and perhaps the Israelites thought this would be a neutral site to house the ark. The ark will remain here for almost 20 years until the time when King David recovers it and brings it to Jerusalem (2 Sam 6).

7:2b–17 *Samuel Subdues the Philistines at Mizpah.* Samuel is the last judge of Israel. Judg 2:11–19 provides a macro-structure for the time period of the judges. It is a pattern and a cycle, a monotonous refrain

7:3 [t]Dt 30:10; Isa 55:7; Hos 6:1 [u]Ge 35:2; Jos 24:14 [v]Jdg 2:12-13; 1Sa 31:10 [w]Joel 2:12 [x]Dt 6:13; Mt 4:10; Lk 4:8
7:5 [y]Jdg 20:1
7:6 [z]Ps 62:8; La 2:19 [a]Jdg 10:10; Ne 9:1; Ps 106:6
7:7 [b]1Sa 17:11
7:8 [c]1Sa 12:19,23; Isa 37:4; Jer 15:1
7:9 [d]Ps 99:6 [e]Jer 15:1
7:10 [f]1Sa 2:10; 2Sa 22:14-15 [g]Jos 10:10
7:12 [h]Ge 35:14; Jos 4:9
7:13 [i]Jdg 13:1,5; 1Sa 13:5
7:15 [j]ver 6; 1Sa 12:11

Samuel Subdues the Philistines at Mizpah

Then all the people of Israel turned back to the LORD. [3]So Samuel said to all the Israelites, "If you are
returning[t] to the LORD with all your hearts, then rid[u] yourselves of the foreign gods and the Ashtoreths[v]
and commit[w] yourselves to the LORD and serve him only,[x] and he will deliver you out of the hand of the
Philistines." [4]So the Israelites put away their Baals and Ashtoreths, and served the LORD only.
[5]Then Samuel said, "Assemble all Israel at Mizpah,[y] and I will intercede with the LORD for you."
[6]When they had assembled at Mizpah, they drew water and poured[z] it out before the LORD. On that day
they fasted and there they confessed, "We have sinned against the LORD." Now Samuel was serving as
leader[a][a] of Israel at Mizpah.
[7]When the Philistines heard that Israel had assembled at Mizpah, the rulers of the Philistines came
up to attack them. When the Israelites heard of it, they were afraid[b] because of the Philistines. [8]They
said to Samuel, "Do not stop crying[c] out to the LORD our God for us, that he may rescue us from the
hand of the Philistines." [9]Then Samuel[d] took a suckling lamb and sacrificed it as a whole burnt offering to the LORD. He cried out to the LORD on Israel's behalf, and the LORD answered him.[e]
[10]While Samuel was sacrificing the burnt offering, the Philistines drew near to engage Israel in
battle. But that day the LORD thundered[f] with loud thunder against the Philistines and threw them into
such a panic[g] that they were routed before the Israelites. [11]The men of Israel rushed out of Mizpah and
pursued the Philistines, slaughtering them along the way to a point below Beth Kar.
[12]Then Samuel took a stone[h] and set it up between Mizpah and Shen. He named it Ebenezer,[b] saying,
"Thus far the LORD has helped us."
[13]So the Philistines were subdued[i] and they stopped invading Israel's territory. Throughout Samuel's
lifetime, the hand of the LORD was against the Philistines. [14]The towns from Ekron to Gath that the Philistines had captured from Israel were restored to Israel, and Israel delivered the neighboring territory
from the hands of the Philistines. And there was peace between Israel and the Amorites.
[15]Samuel[j] continued as Israel's leader all the days of his life. [16]From year to year he went on a circuit from Bethel to Gilgal to Mizpah, judging Israel in all those places. [17]But he always went back to

[a] *6* Traditionally *judge*; also in verse 15 [b] *12 Ebenezer* means *stone of help.*

that fixes Israel's history at this time. The first part of the pattern is Israel's idolatry (Judg 2:11–13), which is followed by the Lord's anger and judgment against Israel (Judg 2:14–15). The Lord then gives the people into the hands of their enemies. The people cry out to the Lord for help, and he raises up a judge to deliver them for a season (Judg 2:16). After a time, however, the nation returns to its ways of apostasy (Judg 2:17), and thus the cycle begins again. These elements are evident in the present story of Samuel's judgeship.

7:2b turned back. Has a negative aspect to it, bearing the idea of the people "wailing" or "moaning bitterly" (Ezek 32:18; Mic 2:4).

7:3 The people are crying out to God because of "the hand of the Philistines" oppressing them. Israel is in the midst of apostasy, and because of her idolatry she is under severe ill-treatment. Samuel calls the people to repentance and reformation. They must (1) get rid of their idols, (2) commit to the Lord, and (3) serve him only. If they truly repent, then God will deliver the people from Philistine mastery.

7:4 put away. The same Hebrew verb is translated "rid" in v. 3. **Ashtoreths.** Canaanite fertility goddesses. **served the LORD only.** These repetitions indicate that the people did exactly as Samuel instructed.

7:5–6 Mizpah. See note on vv. 15–17. Samuel responds by summoning all Israel to Mizpah for a ritual of confession. Samuel will intercede for Israel at this time; elsewhere in the OT he is pictured as an intercessor for the people (12:19; Ps 99:6; Jer 15:1). The Israelites appear to truly repent: they (1) present a drink offering that represents their sorrow and repentance (cf. 2 Sam 23:14–17), (2) fast as a sign of mourning, and (3) confess their sin against the Lord.

7:7 When the Philistines hear that Israel is gathered at Mizpah, their armies take the field against Israel. Perhaps they thought it would be a good opportunity to destroy all Israel in one fell swoop. This military incursion evokes great fear in the people of God.

7:8–9 The Israelites want God to listen to and act upon their demands. Samuel complies by offering a nursing lamb as a whole burnt offering. A lamb is to remain with its mother for the first seven days of life, but it is acceptable for sacrifice after that time (Lev 22:27).

7:9 whole burnt offering. It is totally consumed on the altar (Lev 8:18–21), and its purpose is atonement for sin (Lev 1:4). The Lord answers Samuel, although the content of his answer is not given until the following verses.

7:10–11 Concurrent with Samuel's sacrifices, the Philistine army forms a battle line against Israel. The Lord responds by leading the battle on Israel's behalf: he thunders against the Philistines, and he throws them into a panic. **panic.** Describes what God had done to the Egyptian army at the Red Sea (Exod 14:24) and what he promises to do to all his enemies (1 Sam 2:10; Exod 23:27). Israel mops up and chases the Philistines back in the direction of the coastal plain. **Beth Kar.** Location uncertain.

7:12 stone. Samuel sets up a rock as a memorial to the victory over the Philistines (see note on 6:17–18). **Ebenezer.** Means "rock of help"; it is a testimony to the help God gave Israel in battle.

7:13 subdued. Commonly used in the book of Judges when Israel overthrows their oppressors by the hand of a judge (Judg 3:30 ["made subject"]; 8:28; 11:33).

7:14 Ekron … Gath. Easternmost cities of the Philistines. They were Philistine capital cities, so they would have received any conquered land in Israel. Israel annexes the territory that the Philistine capital cities of Ekron and Gath had taken from them. **Amorites.** A generic term referring to the inhabitants of the land of Canaan before Israel or the Philistines entered and conquered it. They were a major group in the region that threatened Israel's security.

7:15–17 As a judge, Samuel has a yearly circuit that he travels to per-

Ramah,[k] where his home was, and there he also held court for Israel. And he built an altar[l] there to
the LORD.

Israel Asks for a King

8 When Samuel grew old, he appointed[m] his sons as Israel's leaders.[a] 2The name of his firstborn
was Joel and the name of his second was Abijah, and they served at Beersheba.[n] 3But his sons did
not follow his ways. They turned aside after dishonest gain and accepted bribes[o] and perverted justice.
4So all the elders of Israel gathered together and came to Samuel at Ramah.[p] 5They said to him,
"You are old, and your sons do not follow your ways; now appoint a king[q] to lead[b] us, such as all the
other nations have."
6But when they said, "Give us a king to lead us," this displeased[r] Samuel; so he prayed to the LORD.
7And the LORD told him: "Listen to all that the people are saying to you; it is not you they have rejected,
but they have rejected me as their king.[s] 8As they have done from the day I brought them up out of
Egypt until this day, forsaking me and serving other gods, so they are doing to you. 9Now listen to
them; but warn them solemnly and let them know[t] what the king who will reign over them will claim
as his rights."
10Samuel told all the words of the LORD to the people who were asking him for a king. 11He said,
"This is what the king who will reign over you will claim as his rights: He will take[u] your sons and
make them serve with his chariots and horses, and they will run in front of his chariots.[v] 12Some he
will assign to be commanders[w] of thousands and commanders of fifties, and others to plow his ground
and reap his harvest, and still others to make weapons of war and equipment for his chariots. 13He will
take your daughters to be perfumers and cooks and bakers. 14He will take the best of your[x] fields and

7:17 [k] 1Sa 1:19; 8:4 [l] Jdg 21:4
8:1 [m] Dt 16:18-19
8:2 [n] Ge 22:19; 1Ki 19:3; Am 5:4-5
8:3 [o] Ex 23:8; Dt 16:19; Ps 15:5
8:4 [p] 1Sa 7:17
8:5 [q] Dt 17:14-20
8:6 [r] 1Sa 15:11
8:7 [s] Ex 16:8; 1Sa 10:19
8:9 [t] ver 11-18; 1Sa 10:25
8:11 [u] 1Sa 10:25; 14:52 [v] Dt 17:16; 2Sa 15:1
8:12 [w] 1Sa 22:7
8:14 [x] Eze 46:18

[a] *1* Traditionally *judges* [b] *5* Traditionally *judge*; also in verses 6 and 20

form his duty. His home base is Ramah, and from there he journeys to Bethel, Gilgal, and Mizpah. All four of these towns are located on a heavily trafficked road known as the Central Ridge Route or the "spine" that traverses the hill country north to south from Shechem to Hebron. The four towns of Samuel's circuit lie within a range of 12 miles (19 kilometers) from one another, a limited area considering Samuel is judge for all Israel. Ramah is the southernmost site, lying 5 miles (8 kilometers) north of Jerusalem, and Gilgal is the northernmost town (at modern Jiljulieh), some 17 miles (28 kilometers) north of Jerusalem.

8:1–22 *Israel Asks for a King.* The concept of kingship in Israel is not a bad one. God willed that institution for his people even from the patriarchal period (Gen 17:16; 35:11; 49:10). Israel itself was founded as a kingdom (Exod 19:6). God tells his people as they are dwelling in the plains of Moab that when they cross into Canaan they may indeed have a king. Deut 17:14–20 outlines what type of king Israel must have over them: he must be a Hebrew (v. 15); he must not be greedy or desire to turn to the way of paganism (vv. 16–17); Scripture must be his guiding principle and light (vv. 18–19). God directs Israel to have a theocratic monarchy in which a human king obeys the divine king. Establishing kingship also corrects the dominant relativism of the period of the judges, a time when "Israel had no king; everyone did as they saw fit" (Judg 21:25). Thus, there is nothing intrinsically wrong with the elders' request for a human king. The problem is twofold: (1) The people desire to have a king "as all the other nations have" (1 Sam 8:5)—vastly different from the king of Deut 17. (2) The people are moved by a sense of military insecurity. They want a king to lead them in battle. After Samuel soberly warns them what the king will exact from them, the Israelites refuse to relent from their request, and God accedes to their demands.

8:1 leaders. Or "judges" (see NIV text note), indicating that they are to succeed Samuel as judge. The text does not state why Samuel does this, but the act hints at nepotism. Judgeship in Israel is not based on hereditary succession. The judge Gideon makes a strong case against hereditary succession (Judg 8:22–23). So it appears that Samuel himself helps set the stage for a monarchy.

8:2–3 Beersheba. Located at the modern site of Tell es-Seba, 45 miles (72 kilometers) south of Jerusalem. The territory of ancient Israel is commonly described with the formula "from Dan to Beersheba," which describes the northern and southern limits, respectively, of the land of Israel. Samuel's two sons are profaning their judgeships on the territorial fringes of the land of Israel and thus away from the prying eyes of their father. They are engaged in the worst possible behavior for judges. **dishonest gain.** Ironically, Samuel's two sons are much like Eli's.

8:6 displeased Samuel. While personal rejection is a component, Samuel is also concerned about the request for a king "as all the other nations have." In response, Samuel goes to the Lord in prayer.

8:7–9 The people are, in fact, opposing Samuel and his judgeship, but more serious is that they are rejecting God as king. They are laying aside the idea of a theocratic monarchy (God is the ultimate king) in place of an earthly kingship. Israel's pattern has been to reject the Lord from the time of the exodus out of Egypt until now. God then commands Samuel to warn the people what the earthly king will demand from them.

8:10–17 take. The Hebrew verb appears four times in this section (vv. 11,13,14,16). This key word defines the worldly king as a taker. He confiscates property and uses it for his own ends, sometimes corruptly (v. 14). Throughout this section the property that the ruler appropriates occurs in the first position of the Hebrew sentence for the purpose of emphasis. Israel's desire for a king will be costly.

8:11 take your sons. The king will conscript some of the sons of Israel to be his footmen and "run in front of his chariots." Both Absalom and Adonijah secure for themselves chariots and horses, and they have "fifty men" to run ahead of them (2 Sam 15:1; 1 Kgs 1:5). The men are used simply for pomp and circumstance to highlight the status and importance of royalty.

8:12–13 Because the Israelites want a king who will lead them in war, the monarch will conscript their children to take care of the army's needs. Some will serve in the military as officers; some will grow crops to sustain the army; some will prepare the food; some will make the weapons of warfare.

8:14–15 The king's taxation of the people will be 10 percent of their

8:14 [y] 1Ki 21:7,15
8:18 [z] Pr 1:28; Isa 1:15; Mic 3:4
8:19 [a] Isa 66:4; Jer 44:16
8:20 [b] ver 5
8:21 [c] Jdg 11:11
8:22 [d] ver 7
9:1 [e] 1Sa 14:51; 1Ch 8:33; 9:39
9:2 [f] 1Sa 10:24 [g] 1Sa 10:23
9:4 [h] Jos 24:33 [i] 2Ki 4:42
9:5 [j] 1Sa 1:1 [k] 1Sa 10:2
9:6 [l] Dt 33:1; 1Ki 13:1 [m] 1Sa 3:19
9:7 [n] 1Ki 14:3; 2Ki 5:5,15; 8:8

vineyards[y] and olive groves and give them to his attendants. 15 He will take a tenth of your grain and of
your vintage and give it to his officials and attendants. 16 Your male and female servants and the best
of your cattle[a] and donkeys he will take for his own use. 17 He will take a tenth of your flocks, and you
yourselves will become his slaves. 18 When that day comes, you will cry out for relief from the king you
have chosen, but the LORD will not answer[z] you in that day."

19 But the people refused[a] to listen to Samuel. "No!" they said. "We want a king over us. 20 Then we
will be like all the other nations,[b] with a king to lead us and to go out before us and fight our battles."
21 When Samuel heard all that the people said, he repeated[c] it before the LORD. 22 The LORD answered,
"Listen[d] to them and give them a king."

Then Samuel said to the Israelites, "Everyone go back to your own town."

Samuel Anoints Saul

9 There was a Benjamite, a man of standing, whose name was Kish[e] son of Abiel, the son of Zeror,
the son of Bekorath, the son of Aphiah of Benjamin. 2 Kish had a son named Saul, as handsome a
young man as could be found[f] anywhere in Israel, and he was a head taller[g] than anyone else.

3 Now the donkeys belonging to Saul's father Kish were lost, and Kish said to his son Saul, "Take one
of the servants with you and go and look for the donkeys." 4 So he passed through the hill[h] country of
Ephraim and through the area around Shalisha,[i] but they did not find them. They went on into the
district of Shaalim, but the donkeys were not there. Then he passed through the territory of Benjamin,
but they did not find them.

5 When they reached the district of Zuph,[j] Saul said to the servant who was with him, "Come, let's go
back, or my father will stop thinking about the donkeys and start worrying[k] about us."

6 But the servant replied, "Look, in this town there is a man of God;[l] he is highly respected, and everything[m] he says comes true. Let's go there now. Perhaps he will tell us what way to take."
7 Saul said to his servant, "If we go, what can we give the man? The food in our sacks is gone. We
have no gift[n] to take to the man of God. What do we have?"

8 The servant answered him again. "Look," he said, "I have a quarter of a shekel[b] of silver. I will give

[a] *16* Septuagint; Hebrew *young men* [b] *8* That is, about 1/10 ounce or about 3 grams

agricultural holdings. The proceeds from the tax will then be redistributed to the loyal subjects of the king and to his military officers. This is an unjust activity that helps to centralize the king's power. Saul attempts to keep his kingship through these very means (22:7–8).

8:16–17 The king will conscript the Israelites as forced labor for his building projects (1 Kgs 5:13). **you yourselves will become his slaves.** The climax of Samuel's warning; the heart of the issue.

8:18 cry out. Commonly appears in the book of Judges when the people bewail a foreign king's oppression (Judg 3:9,15; 4:3; 6:7). The Israelites will respond the same way to their own king.

8:19–20 Despite the solemn warning, the Israelites continue to demand a king. In the Hebrew of these two verses, the pronouns "we," "our," and "us" appear seven times; their demand is self-centered and self-serving.

8:20 like all the other nations. Appears also in v. 5; these two references bracket the entire episode of Israel asking for a king. A primary problem in this story is that Israel rejects the theocratic monarchy in favor of an earthly monarchy.

8:22 The Lord agrees to the request of the elders. Samuel then dismisses the people, each person to his hometown. This is a dramatic ending as the reader now awaits the appointment of Israel's first king.

9:1—10:27 *Choosing and Anointing a King.* This story begins seemingly by coincidence, with mundane events of ordinary life. A man has lost his donkeys, so he sends his son to find them. But the Lord is orchestrating these events to bring Saul to the city of Ramah, Samuel's hometown. The Lord tells Samuel before Saul's arrival that Saul is the chosen one to be king. Samuel then prepares to anoint Saul as the first monarch over Israel.

9:1–2 A genealogy of six generations of Benjamites introduces Saul. Saul's ancestors obviously survived the Israelite civil war that almost annihilated the tribe of Benjamin (Judg 20:48). **a man of standing.** Used elsewhere in the OT to portray one who is wealthy and has upright character (Ruth 2:1). Saul's physical appearance and stature is also impressive (cf. 1 Sam 10:23).

9:3–5 Kish's donkeys have simply wandered off, so he commands his son to go find them. Saul goes on a three-day search (v. 20), and he begins traveling through the highlands of the tribal inheritance of Ephraim, located directly to the north of Benjamin. He and his servant also scout out the land of Benjamin, but they come up empty. As they arrive in the land of Zuph, which lies on the border between the two tribes, Saul is on the verge of giving up the quest.

9:6 everything he says comes true. A sign of a true prophet of the Lord (Deut 18:21–22).

9:7 gift. It is customary to take a gift to a seer (1 Kgs 14:2–3; 2 Kgs 4:42; 5:15; 8:8).

9:8 shekel. A weight of silver and not a coin. Inscribed shekel weights have been found in large numbers at various sites in the Holy Land, such as Lachish, Samaria, and Gezer. They weigh anywhere from 8 to 12 grams. Different shekel systems operated in Hebrew culture simultaneously. Gen 23:16 mentions "shekels of silver, according to the weight current among the merchants." The merchant/trader appears to have had two sets of weights, a light set for purchasing and a heavy set for selling (Deut 25:13). The Pentateuch also mentions a "sanctuary shekel" (Exod 30:13,24; 38:24–26; Lev 5:15; 27:3,25), and the Historical Books speak of a "royal standard" (2 Sam 14:26).

it to the man of God so that he will tell us what way to take.” 9 (Formerly in Israel, if someone went to
inquire of God, they would say, “Come, let us go to the seer,” because the prophet of today used to be
called a seer.)[o]
10 “Good,” Saul said to his servant. “Come, let’s go.” So they set out for the town where the man of
God was.
11 As they were going up the hill to the town, they met some young women coming out to draw[p] water,
and they asked them, “Is the seer here?”
12 “He is,” they answered. “He’s ahead of you. Hurry now; he has just come to our town today, for the
people have a sacrifice[q] at the high place.[r] 13 As soon as you enter the town, you will find him before he
goes up to the high place to eat. The people will not begin eating until he comes, because he must bless
the sacrifice; afterward, those who are invited will eat. Go up now; you should find him about this time.”
14 They went up to the town, and as they were entering it, there was Samuel, coming toward them
on his way up to the high place.
15 Now the day before Saul came, the LORD had revealed this to Samuel: 16 “About this time tomorrow
I will send you a man from the land of Benjamin. Anoint[s] him ruler over my people Israel; he will deliver[t] them from the hand of the Philistines. I have looked on my people, for their cry has reached me.”
17 When Samuel caught sight of Saul, the LORD said to him, “This[u] is the man I spoke to you about;
he will govern my people.”
18 Saul approached Samuel in the gateway and asked, “Would you please tell me where the seer’s
house is?”
19 “I am the seer,” Samuel replied. “Go up ahead of me to the high place, for today you are to eat with
me, and in the morning I will send you on your way and will tell you all that is in your heart. 20 As for
the donkeys[v] you lost three days ago, do not worry about them; they have been found. And to whom is
all the desire[w] of Israel turned, if not to you and your whole family line?”
21 Saul answered, “But am I not a Benjamite, from the smallest tribe[x] of Israel, and is not my clan
the least of all the clans of the tribe of Benjamin?[y] Why do you say such a thing to me?”
22 Then Samuel brought Saul and his servant into the hall and seated them at the head of those who
were invited—about thirty in number. 23 Samuel said to the cook, “Bring the piece of meat I gave you,
the one I told you to lay aside.”
24 So the cook took up the thigh[z] with what was on it and set it in front of Saul. Samuel said, “Here is
what has been kept for you. Eat, because it was set aside for you for this occasion from the time I said,
‘I have invited guests.’ ” And Saul dined with Samuel that day.
25 After they came down from the high place to the town, Samuel talked with Saul on the roof[a] of his
house. 26 They rose about daybreak, and Samuel called to Saul on the roof, “Get ready, and I will send
you on your way.” When Saul got ready, he and Samuel went outside together. 27 As they were going
down to the edge of the town, Samuel said to Saul, “Tell the servant to go on ahead of us”—and the
servant did so—“but you stay here for a while, so that I may give you a message from God.”

9:9 [o] 2Sa 24:11; 2Ki 17:13; 1Ch 9:22; 26:28; 29:29; Isa 30:10; Am 7:12
9:11 [p] Ge 24:11,13
9:12 [q] Nu 28:11-15; 1Sa 7:17 [r] Ge 31:54; 1Sa 10:5; 1Ki 3:2
9:16 [s] 1Sa 10:1 [t] Ex 3:7-9
9:17 [u] 1Sa 16:12
9:20 [v] ver 3 [w] 1Sa 8:5; 12:13
9:21 [x] 1Sa 15:17 [y] Jdg 20:35,46
9:24 [z] Lev 7:32-34; Nu 18:18
9:25 [a] Dt 22:8; Ac 10:9

9:9 seer. Refers to Samuel 8 of the 12 times it appears in the OT. It does not seem to be a separate office from the prophet, but is synonymous with it. The term occurs primarily before the monarchy’s establishment and rarely during it.
9:11–12 A frequent scene in the OT is the chance meeting with women on their way to draw water (Gen 24:15–20; 29:1–12; Exod 2:11–22). These appear to be random encounters, but God providentially orchestrates them. Here, the seer comes to the city at the same time that Saul arrives; the timing is perfect.
9:12 high place. Seems to have been a legitimate place for sacrifice prior to establishing the temple in Jerusalem (1 Kgs 3:4–5).
9:16 I will send you a man. Accentuates the reality that this episode is not happenstance.
9:19–20 Samuel identifies himself as the seer and then tells Saul to go up to the high place to share a meal. He also promises that he will answer every question of Saul’s heart the next morning. What is on Saul’s heart? Is it merely the whereabouts of the donkeys? Almost as an afterthought Samuel relates to Saul that the animals have been found. **to whom is all the desire of Israel.** Can be read in two ways: (1) Israel desires a king, and Saul is the answer to that yearning; or (2) all the desirable things of Israel—tax money, agricultural produce, servants, etc.—will belong to Saul as king. Either way, Samuel calls Saul the chosen one.
9:21 the smallest tribe. Benjamin. Saul understands Samuel, and he is greatly surprised because he is from the tribe of Benjamin. The tribe is small because of the civil war (Judg 19–21). The other tribes massacred the Benjamites at Gibeah (Judg 20:20; 21:6), Saul’s hometown (1 Sam 10:26), because of the great immorality.
9:22–24 This scene is perhaps a pre-coronation sacrifice and banquet (cf. 2 Sam 15:10–12). **thirty.** Perhaps anticipates the Thirty, i.e., the 30 mighty men who surround and protect David as king (2 Sam 23:13–39). **set aside for you.** Saul receives a set-apart portion of meat from the sacrifice because God has set him apart for a special function.

10:1 [b]1Sa 16:13; 2Ki 9:1,3,6 [c]Ps 2:12 [d]Dt 32:9; Ps 78:62,71
10:2 [e]Ge 35:20 [f]1Sa 9:4 [g]1Sa 9:5
10:3 [h]Ge 28:22; 35:7-8
10:5 [i]1Sa 13:3 [j]1Sa 9:12 [k]2Ki 3:15 [l]1Sa 19:20; 1Co 14:1
10:6 [m]ver 10; Nu 11:25; 1Sa 19:23-24
10:7 [n]Ecc 9:10 [o]Jos 1:5; Jdg 6:12; Heb 13:5
10:8 [p]1Sa 11:14-15
10:9 [q]ver 6
10:10 [r]ver 5-6; 1Sa 19:20
10:11 [s]Mt 13:54; Jn 7:15 [t]1Sa 19:24
10:14 [u]1Sa 14:50
10:16 [v]1Sa 9:20

10 Then Samuel took a flask[b] of olive oil and poured it on Saul's head and kissed him, saying,
"Has not the LORD anointed[c] you ruler over his inheritance?[a][d] 2 When you leave me today, you
will meet two men near Rachel's tomb,[e] at Zelzah on the border of Benjamin. They will say to you, 'The
donkeys[f] you set out to look for have been found. And now your father has stopped thinking about them
and is worried[g] about you. He is asking, "What shall I do about my son?"'
3 "Then you will go on from there until you reach the great tree of Tabor. Three men going up to
worship God at Bethel[h] will meet you there. One will be carrying three young goats, another three loaves
of bread, and another a skin of wine. 4 They will greet you and offer you two loaves of bread, which you
will accept from them.
5 "After that you will go to Gibeah of God, where there is a Philistine outpost.[i] As you approach the
town, you will meet a procession of prophets coming down from the high place[j] with lyres, timbrels,
pipes and harps[k] being played before them, and they will be prophesying.[l] 6 The Spirit[m] of the LORD will
come powerfully upon you, and you will prophesy with them; and you will be changed into a different
person. 7 Once these signs are fulfilled, do whatever[n] your hand finds to do, for God is with[o] you.
8 "Go down ahead of me to Gilgal.[p] I will surely come down to you to sacrifice burnt offerings and
fellowship offerings, but you must wait seven days until I come to you and tell you what you are to do."

Saul Made King

9 As Saul turned to leave Samuel, God changed[q] Saul's heart, and all these signs were fulfilled that
day. 10 When he and his servant arrived at Gibeah, a procession of prophets met him; the Spirit of God
came powerfully upon him, and he joined in their prophesying.[r] 11 When all those who had formerly
known him saw him prophesying with the prophets, they asked each other, "What is this[s] that has
happened to the son of Kish? Is Saul also among the prophets?"[t]
12 A man who lived there answered, "And who is their father?" So it became a saying: "Is Saul also
among the prophets?" 13 After Saul stopped prophesying, he went to the high place.
14 Now Saul's uncle[u] asked him and his servant, "Where have you been?"
"Looking for the donkeys," he said. "But when we saw they were not to be found, we went to Samuel."
15 Saul's uncle said, "Tell me what Samuel said to you."
16 Saul replied, "He assured us that the donkeys[v] had been found." But he did not tell his uncle what
Samuel had said about the kingship.

[a] *1* Hebrew; Septuagint and Vulgate *over his people Israel? You will reign over the LORD's people and save them from the power of their enemies round about. And this will be a sign to you that the LORD has anointed you ruler over his inheritance:*

10:1–16 The prophet Samuel anoints Saul as king in a private ceremony. He then prophesies that Saul will receive three signs to confirm that God is with him and that he is set apart to be king. After the confirmation, Saul goes home, but he does not reveal his anointing as king. This sets up the subsequent account when the people themselves proclaim Saul to be king.

10:1 oil. Pouring oil on the head of one set apart as king was common (16:13; 2 Kgs 9:1–3). **kissed him.** A sign of loyalty to the new king (1 Kgs 19:18; Ps 2:12).

10:2 Rachel's tomb. Lies somewhere between Ramah, Samuel's hometown, and Bethel to the north (Gen 35:19–20; 48:7).

10:5–6 The final sign will take place at "Gibeah of God." Saul will meet a group of prophets coming down from the high place, and they will be prophesying with musical accompaniment. The music appears to induce ecstatic prophecy. **The Spirit of the LORD will come powerfully upon you.** Empowerment to deliver Israel from the hand of their enemies (Judg 6:34; 11:29; 14:6,19; 15:14). Saul will thus be empowered as a savior of Israel in the direct sight of a Philistine outpost. **changed into a different person.** This is likely not a statement regarding Saul's salvation; rather, God has invested Saul with power to lead Israel militarily as a king.

10:8 Gilgal. One of the cities on Samuel's regular circuit of judgeship (7:16). It is located at modern Jiljulieh, some 17 miles (27 kilometers) north of Jerusalem.

10:9 God changed Saul's heart. Again, not necessarily a sign of conversion. It simply might be that God has given Saul a new heart for being king and delivering Israel from the Philistines. **that day.** Highlights the fulfillment of Samuel's word to Saul in v. 2 ("today").

10:10–12 Saul's prophetic utterances visibly signify God's presence with him. Those who know Saul and witness this event are astonished. That Saul would act this way is unexpected and shocking; they see a new man with a new heart. And so they ask in bewilderment, "Is Saul also among the prophets?" This saying becomes proverbial in Israel for people acting unexpectedly or out of character (19:24). **And who is their father?** Perhaps critically asking, "Who is the head prophet allowing Saul to prophesy with this group?" Such prophetic groups had leaders called "fathers" (2 Kgs 2:12; 6:21); Samuel himself headed up a band of prophets (1 Sam 19:20).

10:14–16 Saul's uncle asks Saul where he and his servant have been. Saul relates their fruitless search for his father's donkeys and tells of the help from the prophet Samuel regarding where to find the animals. This uncle is perhaps Ner, Abner's father (14:50), who has a vested interest in the animals because he apparently is next in line to Kish to receive Abiel's inheritance (9:1). Saul does not tell his uncle about the scene of the anointing. This sets up the next story (10:17–27), in which all Israel proclaims Saul to be king.

17 Samuel summoned the people of Israel to the LORD at Mizpah[w] 18 and said to them, "This is what
the LORD, the God of Israel, says: 'I brought Israel up out of Egypt, and I delivered you from the power
of Egypt and all the kingdoms that oppressed[x] you.' 19 But you have now rejected your God, who saves
you out of all your disasters and calamities. And you have said, 'No, appoint a king[y] over us.' So now
present[z] yourselves before the LORD by your tribes and clans."
20 When Samuel had all Israel come forward by tribes, the tribe of Benjamin was taken by lot. 21 Then
he brought forward the tribe of Benjamin, clan by clan, and Matri's clan was taken. Finally Saul son of
Kish was taken. But when they looked
for him, he was not to be found. 22 So
they inquired[a] further of the LORD,
"Has the man come here yet?"
And the LORD said, "Yes, he has hidden himself among the supplies."
23 They ran and brought him out,
and as he stood among the people
he was a head taller[b] than any of the
others. 24 Samuel said to all the people, "Do you see the man the LORD
has chosen?[c] There is no one like him
among all the people."
Then the people shouted, "Long
live[d] the king!"
25 Samuel explained to the people
the rights and duties[e] of kingship. He
wrote them down on a scroll and deposited it before the LORD. Then Samuel dismissed the people to go to their
own homes.
26 Saul also went to his home in
Gibeah,[f] accompanied by valiant men
whose hearts God had touched. 27 But
some scoundrels[g] said, "How can this
fellow save us?" They despised him
and brought him no gifts.[h] But Saul
kept silent.

Basalt slab sculpted with musicians, from Carchemish, Turkey. Hittite civilization, first millennium BC. 1 Sam 10:5–6 speaks of a similar procession of musicians.

Basalt slab sculpted with musicians, from Karkemis Palace or Carchemish, Turkey. Hittite civilization/De Agostini Picture Library/M. Seemuller/Bridgeman Images

10:17 [w] Jdg 20:1; 1Sa 7:5
10:18 [x] Jdg 6:8-9
10:19 [y] 1Sa 8:5-7; 12:12 [z] Jos 7:14; 24:1
10:22 [a] 1Sa 23:2,4,9-11
10:23 [b] 1Sa 9:2
10:24 [c] Dt 17:15; 2Sa 21:6 [d] 1Ki 1:25, 34,39
10:25 [e] Dt 17:14-20; 1Sa 8:11-18
10:26 [f] 1Sa 11:4
10:27 [g] Dt 13:13 [h] 1Ki 10:25; 2Ch 17:5

10:17–27 The Lord designates Saul to be the first king of Israel through the casting of lots. Most of Israel acclaims Saul as king, but some worthless men question Saul's ability to serve in that capacity.
10:17 This is the second assembly at Mizpah (7:5–11). At both events (1) Samuel serves as intermediary between the Lord and the people; (2) there is a foreign military threat; and (3) Israel resoundingly defeats their enemies (7:10–11; 11:11).
10:18–19 This is what the LORD . . . says. A common prophetic formula in the ancient Near East highlighting that a prophet speaks the very words of a deity. The prophet does not alter the revelation given to him in any way; he speaks the exact, precise words of the god. **I brought Israel up out of Egypt.** The Lord recites a brief history between himself and Israel (Exod 20:2; Lev 26:13; Ps 81:10). Israel is to stand before the Lord at Mizpah according to their tribes and clans. **clans.** The Hebrew word used here ("thousands") often refers to military subgroupings.
10:20–21 The Lord chooses the one on whom the lot falls (14:41–42; Josh 7:14–18). The lot proceeds to the choice of a tribe to a clan and then to an individual. **not to be found.** Saul's absence raises questions of his character: Is he shy, modest, or fearful? Or is this false humility, and does he want the people to find him and present him to the throngs?
10:22 Has the man come here yet? This translation follows the Septuagint, the pre-Christian Greek translation of the OT, which interprets the people as wondering if Saul is in Mizpah. The Lord tells the people that Saul has hidden himself among the supplies or the baggage.
10:23 When Saul is found it is his physical stature that is most impressive. In contrast, when the Lord later tells Samuel to look for a new king (David), he explicitly says not to look at his outward appearance (16:7).
10:24 Long live the king! Cf. 2 Sam 16:16; 1 Kgs 1:25,34,39; 2 Kgs 11:12.
10:25 rights and duties. The same Hebrew word appears in 8:11. Samuel is therefore repeating what he said about the ways of the king in ch. 8. These are bookends: at the beginning and the end of the episode of choosing a king, Samuel warns the people regarding the manner of the king. Samuel then writes it in a book and places the book before the Lord. Depositing a law document in the sanctuary is typical (Exod 25:16; 40:20; Deut 31:26).
10:26 Saul returns to his home in Gibeah, along with valiant soldiers whom God has compelled to follow the king.
10:27 scoundrels. A term previously used to describe the corrupt sons of Eli (see 2:12 and note). These men, in contrast to the "valiant men" (10:26),

11:1 [i]1Sa 12:12 [j]Jdg 21:8 [k]1Ki 20:34; Eze 17:13
11:2 [l]Nu 16:14 [m]1Sa 17:26
11:4 [n]1Sa 10:5,26; 15:34 [o]Jdg 2:4; 1Sa 30:4
11:6 [p]Jdg 3:10; 6:34; 13:25; 14:6; 1Sa 10:10; 16:13
11:7 [q]Jdg 19:29 [r]Jdg 21:5
11:8 [s]Jdg 20:2 [t]Jdg 1:4
11:10 [u]ver 3
11:11 [v]Jdg 7:16
11:12 [w]1Sa 10:27; Lk 19:27

Saul Rescues the City of Jabesh

11 Nahash[a][i] the Ammonite went up and besieged Jabesh Gilead.[j] And all the men of Jabesh said
to him, "Make a treaty[k] with us, and we will be subject to you."
[2]But Nahash the Ammonite replied, "I will make a treaty with you only on the condition that I gouge[l]
out the right eye of every one of you and so bring disgrace[m] on all Israel."
[3]The elders of Jabesh said to him, "Give us seven days so we can send messengers throughout Israel;
if no one comes to rescue us, we will surrender to you."
[4]When the messengers came to Gibeah[n] of Saul and reported these terms to the people, they all wept[o]
aloud. [5]Just then Saul was returning from the fields, behind his oxen, and he asked, "What is wrong
with everyone? Why are they weeping?" Then they repeated to him what the men of Jabesh had said.
[6]When Saul heard their words, the Spirit[p] of God came powerfully upon him, and he burned with anger. [7]He took a pair of oxen, cut them into pieces, and sent the pieces by messengers throughout Israel,[q]
proclaiming, "This is what will be done to the oxen of anyone[r] who does not follow Saul and Samuel."
Then the terror of the LORD fell on the people, and they came out together as one. [8]When Saul mustered[s]
them at Bezek,[t] the men of Israel numbered three hundred thousand and those of Judah thirty thousand.
[9]They told the messengers who had come, "Say to the men of Jabesh Gilead, 'By the time the sun is
hot tomorrow, you will be rescued.'" When the messengers went and reported this to the men of Jabesh,
they were elated. [10]They said to the Ammonites, "Tomorrow we will surrender[u] to you, and you can do
to us whatever you like."
[11]The next day Saul separated his men into three divisions;[v] during the last watch of the night they
broke into the camp of the Ammonites and slaughtered them until the heat of the day. Those who survived were scattered, so that no two of them were left together.

Saul Confirmed as King

[12]The people then said to Samuel, "Who[w] was it that asked, 'Shall Saul reign over us?' Turn these
men over to us so that we may put them to death."

[a] *1* Masoretic Text; Dead Sea Scrolls *gifts. Now Nahash king of the Ammonites oppressed the Gadites and Reubenites severely. He gouged out all their right eyes and struck terror and dread in Israel. Not a man remained among the Israelites beyond the Jordan whose right eye was not gouged out by Nahash king of the Ammonites, except that seven thousand men fled from the Ammonites and entered Jabesh Gilead. About a month later,* [1]*Nahash*

question God's choice of Saul and Saul's ability to deliver Israel from their enemies. **Saul kept silent.** Saul does not use his authority as king to punish those who reject him, a further sign of his humility at the start of his reign.

11:1–11 *Saul Rescues the City of Jabesh.* This opening episode of Saul's kingship portrays him well; he does his duty as king to fight against Israel's foes, just as the people hoped for in ch. 8.

11:1 The land of Ammon is located south of the Jabbok River on the east side of the Jordan River. Its capital city, Rabbah, sits next to a spring that feeds the Jabbok River. **Jabesh Gilead.** Also lies on the east side of the Jordan, but north of the Jabbok River in the tribal inheritance belonging to the half-tribe of Manasseh that settled east of the Jordan River. Nahash takes the Ammonite army and lays siege to the Israelite city. The men of Jabesh Gilead respond by asking to make a treaty.

11:2 gouge out the right eye. Ironically, the only covenant Nahash will "make" (the Hebrew uses the word "cut") with them is gouging or cutting out their right eyes. That impairment would render the soldiers of Jabesh unable to fight, so they would no longer be a threat to Ammon. It appears that the city must either submit to gouging or to full destruction.

11:3 Why the Ammonite king accedes to their request is uncertain. Perhaps it is mere hubris, or maybe he thought his army was too strong to be defeated. **rescue.** The word used here is often used of deliverers in the book of Judges (Judg 3:9,15).

11:4 While Jabesh is more than 40 miles (64 kilometers) away, there is a tight connection between it and Gibeah, Saul's hometown. In Judg 20–21, the soldiers of Jabesh Gilead refuse to participate in Israel's war against the tribe of Benjamin and its main city Gibeah. Jabesh Gilead paid a terrible price: all the people of the city were killed except 400 virgins, who were given to the Benjamites to help repopulate the ravaged tribe (Judg 21:8–15). Later, when Saul's dead body is hung on the walls of the Philistine city of Beth Shan, the men of Jabesh Gilead steal the body and bury it in their city (1 Sam 31:11–13).

11:5 Saul has been doing routine labor in the fields of Gibeah, and as he comes to the city, he wonders why all the people are weeping.

11:6 the Spirit of God came powerfully upon him. In the same way the Spirit rushed on the deliverer-judges Othniel, Gideon, Jephthah, and Samson (Judg 3:10; 6:34; 11:29; 13:25; 14:6,19; 15:14). This happened to Saul earlier when he prophesied (1 Sam 10:9–11), but now its purpose is for war.

11:7 cut them … sent the pieces. Saul's call to arms carries an implicit threat: if any group does not respond to the invitation to war, they will be cut up like the animals! The act is reminiscent of Judg 19:29–30, which relates a Levite cutting up his concubine to call Israel to arms against Benjamin and its main city Gibeah. Both episodes are centered in Gibeah.

11:8 Bezek. Located at Khirbet Ibziq, on the west side of the Jordan River about 12 miles (19 kilometers) from Jabesh Gilead. **Israel … Judah.** May reflect an early division and animosity between the two.

11:10 The men of Jabesh reply slyly and craftily to Nahash.

11:11 last watch of the night. This is between 2:00 and 6:00 a.m. Saul's sneak attack divides his forces into three pincers as a tactic of a pincer movement. **until the heat of the day.** The battle is over and won by the afternoon.

11:12–15 *Saul Confirmed as King.* Saul's kingship is now renewed at

13 But Saul said, "No one will be put to death today,[x] for this day the LORD has rescued[y] Israel."
14 Then Samuel said to the people, "Come, let us go to Gilgal[z] and there renew the kingship.[a]" 15 So
all the people went to Gilgal[b] and made Saul king in the presence of the LORD. There they sacrificed
fellowship offerings before the LORD, and Saul and all the Israelites held a great celebration.

Samuel's Farewell Speech

12 Samuel said to all Israel, "I have listened[c] to everything you said to me and have set a king[d]
over you. 2 Now you have a king as your leader.[e] As for me, I am old and gray, and my sons are
here with you. I have been your leader from my youth until this day. 3 Here I stand. Testify against me
in the presence of the LORD and his anointed.[f] Whose ox have I taken? Whose donkey[g] have I taken?
Whom have I cheated? Whom have I oppressed? From whose hand have I accepted a bribe[h] to make me
shut my eyes? If I have done[i] any of these things, I will make it right."
4 "You have not cheated or oppressed us," they replied. "You have not taken anything from anyone's hand."
5 Samuel said to them, "The LORD is witness against you, and also his anointed is witness this day,
that you have not found anything[j] in my hand.[k]"
"He is witness," they said.
6 Then Samuel said to the people, "It is the LORD who appointed Moses and Aaron and brought[l] your
ancestors up out of Egypt. 7 Now then, stand here, because I am going to confront[m] you with evidence
before the LORD as to all the righteous acts performed by the LORD for you and your ancestors.
8 "After Jacob entered Egypt, they cried[n] to the LORD for help, and the LORD sent[o] Moses and Aaron,
who brought your ancestors out of Egypt and settled them in this place.
9 "But they forgot[p] the LORD their God; so he sold them into the hand of Sisera,[q] the commander of
the army of Hazor, and into the hands of the Philistines[r] and the king of Moab,[s] who fought against
them. 10 They cried out to the LORD and said, 'We have sinned; we have forsaken[t] the LORD and served
the Baals and the Ashtoreths.[u] But now deliver us from the hands of our enemies, and we will serve
you.' 11 Then the LORD sent Jerub-Baal,[a][v] Barak,[b][w] Jephthah[x] and Samuel,[c] and he delivered you from
the hands of your enemies all around you, so that you lived in safety.
12 "But when you saw that Nahash[y] king[z] of the Ammonites was moving against you, you said to me,
'No, we want a king to rule[a] over us'—even though the LORD your God was your king. 13 Now here is
the king[b] you have chosen, the one you asked[c] for; see, the LORD has set a king over you. 14 If you fear[d]
the LORD and serve and obey him and do not rebel against his commands, and if both you and the king

11:13 [x] 2Sa 19:22 [y] Ex 14:13; 1Sa 19:5
11:14 [z] 1Sa 10:8 [a] 1Sa 10:25
11:15 [b] 1Sa 10:8,17
12:1 [c] 1Sa 8:7 [d] 1Sa 10:24; 11:15
12:2 [e] 1Sa 8:5
12:3 [f] 1Sa 10:1; 24:6; 2Sa 1:14 [g] Nu 16:15 [h] Dt 16:19 [i] Ac 20:33
12:5 [j] Ac 23:9; 24:20 [k] Ex 22:4
12:6 [l] Ex 6:26; Mic 6:4
12:7 [m] Isa 1:18; Mic 6:1-5
12:8 [n] Ex 2:23 [o] Ex 3:10; 4:16
12:9 [p] Jdg 3:7 [q] Jdg 4:2 [r] Jdg 10:7; 13:1 [s] Jdg 3:12
12:10 [t] Jdg 10:10,15 [u] Jdg 2:13
12:11 [v] Jdg 6:14,32 [w] Jdg 4:6 [x] Jdg 11:1
12:12 [y] 1Sa 11:1 [z] 1Sa 8:5 [a] Jdg 8:23; 1Sa 8:6,19
12:13 [b] 1Sa 8:5; Hos 13:11 [c] 1Sa 10:24
12:14 [d] Jos 24:14

[a] 11 Also called *Gideon* [b] 11 Some Septuagint manuscripts and Syriac; Hebrew *Bedan* [c] 11 Hebrew; some Septuagint manuscripts and Syriac *Samson*

Gilgal. Back in 10:27 certain "scoundrels" had doubted Saul's ability to lead Israel in battle. After Saul's victory, the people want revenge on these ne'er-do-wells. Saul, however, intercedes and grants amnesty to them. He exercises mercy as a king, demonstrating that at this early stage he is fit to be king.

11:14–15 renew. Saul was already proclaimed king (10:24). But this ritual is not redundant; it is a religious coronation. The previous ritual was a political enthronement (10:17–25). **fellowship offerings.** They celebrate the bond between God and his people (Lev 3). In Saul's early days as king, things appear peaceful and harmonious.

12:1–25 *Samuel's Farewell Speech.* This concludes the establishment of the monarchy in Israel. Samuel's address to the people resembles a lawsuit in a courtroom proceeding. Samuel claims his innocence before the bar (vv. 1–5) and indicts the people for being unfaithful repeatedly and rejecting God as king (vv. 6–19). Though the people are guilty, the Lord will not desert them because they are his chosen people (vv. 20–25). Although Israel now has a king, Samuel does not disappear from the story: he yet will deal with Saul extensively (ch. 15) and anoint a new king to replace Saul (ch. 16).

12:1–5 *Samuel's Plea of Innocence.* This scene follows directly after the assembly at Gilgal (11:12–15), so it likely takes place there and at that time. Samuel remains upset and offended that Israel rejected his leadership by choosing a king in his place (8:4–7). Now, in a judicial setting, Samuel declares his innocence; his plea is simply "not guilty."

12:2 Samuel contrasts himself and the new king. A literal reading of the text makes this clear: "the king is walking before you ... and I have walked before you." He mentions his sons but omits their misdeeds.

12:3 Samuel lays out his case. He is at the defense table and ready for the Lord to judge him with Israel as a witness. Samuel declares his innocence before the court. **Whose donkey have I taken?** Contrasts with the ways of the king (8:11–17).

12:4–5 The people declare Samuel's innocence, with the Lord and his king as witnesses to that declaration. The decision is in: not guilty.

12:6–19 *Samuel's Lawsuit Against the People.* Samuel brings a case of infidelity against Israel in the divine court of law.

12:6–8 The Lord has always been true to his covenant with Israel. Indeed, he delivered Israel out of Egypt.

12:9–11 Israel has repeatedly been unfaithful and idolatrous. **forgot ... sold ... cried out ... delivered.** The pattern of the period of the judges (see note 7:2b–17; Judg 2:11–16). Even though Israel continues to grip infidelity, the Lord delivers them from their enemies time and again. He is faithful; Israel is unfaithful.

12:14–15 obey ... do not rebel ... do not obey ... rebel. The people and king have a choice: (1) obey the Lord and not rebel or (2) not obey the Lord and rebel.

12:15 [e] ver 9; Jos 24:20; Isa 1:20
12:16 [f] Ex 14:13
12:17 [g] 1Sa 7:9-10 [h] Jas 5:18 [i] Pr 26:1 [j] 1Sa 8:6-7
12:18 [k] Ex 14:31
12:19 [l] ver 23; Ex 9:28; Jas 5:18; 1Jn 5:16
12:21 [m] Isa 41:24,29; Jer 16:19; Hab 2:18 [n] Dt 11:16
12:22 [o] Ps 106:8 [p] Jos 7:9 [q] 1Ki 6:13 [r] Dt 7:7; 1Pe 2:9
12:23 [s] Ro 1:9-10; Col 1:9; 2Ti 1:3 [t] 1Ki 8:36; Ps 34:11; Pr 4:11
12:24 [u] Ecc 12:13 [v] Isa 5:12 [w] Dt 10:21
12:25 [x] 1Sa 31:1-5 [y] Jos 24:20
13:2 [z] 1Sa 10:26
13:3 [a] 1Sa 10:5

who reigns over you follow the LORD your God—good! 15But if you do not obey the LORD, and if you
rebel against[e] his commands, his hand will be against you, as it was against your ancestors.
16"Now then, stand still and see[f] this great thing the LORD is about to do before your eyes! 17Is it not
wheat harvest[g] now? I will call[h] on the LORD to send thunder and rain.[i] And you will realize what an
evil[j] thing you did in the eyes of the LORD when you asked for a king."
18Then Samuel called on the LORD, and that same day the LORD sent thunder and rain. So all the
people stood in awe[k] of the LORD and of Samuel.
19The people all said to Samuel, "Pray[l] to the LORD your God for your servants so that we will not die,
for we have added to all our other sins the evil of asking for a king."
20"Do not be afraid," Samuel replied. "You have done all this evil; yet do not turn away from the
LORD, but serve the LORD with all your heart. 21Do not turn away after useless[m] idols.[n] They can do
you no good, nor can they rescue you, because they are useless. 22For the sake[o] of his great name[p] the
LORD will not reject[q] his people, because the LORD was pleased to make[r] you his own. 23As for me, far
be it from me that I should sin against the LORD by failing to pray[s] for you. And I will teach[t] you the
way that is good and right. 24But be sure to fear[u] the LORD and serve him faithfully with all your heart;
consider[v] what great[w] things he has done for you. 25Yet if you persist[x] in doing evil, both you and your
king will perish."[y]

Samuel Rebukes Saul

13 Saul was thirty[a] years old when he became king, and he reigned over Israel forty-[b] two years.
2Saul chose three thousand men from Israel; two thousand were with him at Mikmash and in
the hill country of Bethel, and a thousand were with Jonathan at Gibeah[z] in Benjamin. The rest of the
men he sent back to their homes.
3Jonathan attacked the Philistine outpost[a] at Geba, and the Philistines heard about it. Then Saul had
the trumpet blown throughout the land and said, "Let the Hebrews hear!" 4So all Israel heard the news:

a 1 A few late manuscripts of the Septuagint; Hebrew does not have *thirty.* *b 1* Probable reading of the original Hebrew text (see Acts 13:21); Masoretic Text does not have *forty-*.

12:16 stand still and see. The same command Moses gave the people at the Red Sea before God mightily divided the waters (Exod 14:13).

12:17–19 thunder and rain. During the time of the wheat harvest, rain was scarce because it was the dry season in Israel. The physical sign of rain and thunder prods Israel to confess their sin and ask Samuel to intercede for them.

12:20–25 *A Final Warning.* Samuel encourages Israel to follow the ways of the Lord and admonishes them not to pant after idols. Chief among the false gods of Canaan was Baal, god of thunder and rain; the powers of Yahweh are demonstrated in vv. 17–19.

12:21 useless idols. The Hebrew word is translated "formless" in Gen 1:2, referring to the earth's empty state at the outset of creation. In the OT it sometimes refers to false gods because of their worthless and empty nature (Isa 41:29; 44:9). Idols cannot rescue anyone, but the Lord does this for his people all the time (vv. 10–11).

12:22 Despite their sin, the Lord will not abandon his people on account of "his great name." God has chosen Israel and he will treat them with grace and mercy. This is the biblical doctrine of God's election and mercy.

12:24–25 Samuel admonishes and warns Israel with a conditional curse: the people and their king must obey the Lord and his word, and if they fail, they will perish.

13:1—15:35 *Saul's Kingship.* See map, p. 484. Saul's reign as the first king of Israel has mixed results. On the one hand, he is successful in battle against the Ammonites (11:11), against the Philistines (13:3; 14:20–23), and against others (14:47–48). So he fulfills the Israelites' hopes for a military leader (8:20). On the other hand, he disobeys the word of the Lord through the prophet Samuel (13:13; 15:19), pursues his own way and makes a rash vow (14:24–35). Because of his unfaithfulness to the word of God, God takes away Saul's kingship and kingly succession (13:13–14; 15:26). Saul's rejection as king in chs. 13–15 sets the stage for God to choose a new king who is "a man after his own heart" (13:14).

13:1–15 *Samuel Rebukes Saul.* Saul, as military leader of Israel, gathers a standing army because of the threat of the Philistines. Jonathan, Saul's son and one of his field commanders, defeats the Philistine garrison at Geba. The Philistines respond by mustering a large military force to confront Israel. Many of the Israelites flee and hide from this looming danger. Saul is driven by his immediate circumstances to offer up sacrifices to the Lord, but this action directly disobeys the word of God that the prophet Samuel spoke.

13:1 The meaning of the Hebrew text of this verse is uncertain (see NIV text note). There is a transmission problem regarding the number in the text. Literally it says that Saul was "a year old when he became king," which is nonsensical in the context of chs. 8–12. The Hebrew text also says that Saul "reigned over Israel for two years"; while that is possible, it would be hard to fit all the events of his kingship in such a tight compartment. The Latin Vulgate renders the time span as "twenty years." Most manuscripts of the Septuagint, the pre-Christian Greek translation of the OT, omit verse 1 altogether. In Acts 13:21, Paul appears to indicate that Saul was king for "forty years." We must admit that the verse has been so corrupted by transmission that it makes little sense as it stands.

13:2 Mikmash. Four miles (6.4 kilometers) northeast of Gibeah. **Gibeah.** Located at modern Tell el-Ful in the central highlands about three miles (4.8 kilometers) directly north of Jerusalem. Both sites are located in the tribal inheritance of Benjamin, Saul's tribe.

13:3 Geba. Lies in-between Israel's two armies. Because of Jonathan's minor victory, Saul summons the people of Israel to rally at Gilgal (see note on 10:8).

13:4 obnoxious. A figure of disdain in the OT (2 Sam 10:6; 16:21).

Aerial view of Mikmash area.
Todd Bolen/www.BiblePlaces.com

"Saul has attacked the Philistine outpost, and now Israel has become obnoxious[b] to the Philistines."
And the people were summoned to join Saul at Gilgal.
[5]The Philistines assembled to fight Israel, with three thousand[a] chariots, six thousand charioteers,
and soldiers as numerous as the sand[c] on the seashore. They went up and camped at Mikmash, east
of Beth Aven. [6]When the Israelites saw that their situation was critical and that their army was hard
pressed, they hid in caves and thickets, among the rocks, and in pits and cisterns.[d] [7]Some Hebrews even
crossed the Jordan to the land of Gad[e] and Gilead.

Saul remained at Gilgal, and all the troops with him were quaking with fear. [8]He waited seven[f] days,
the time set by Samuel; but Samuel did not come to Gilgal, and Saul's men began to scatter. [9]So he said,
"Bring me the burnt offering and the fellowship offerings." And Saul offered[g] up the burnt offering.
[10]Just as he finished making the offering, Samuel[h] arrived, and Saul went out to greet him.

[11]"What have you done?" asked Samuel.

Saul replied, "When I saw that the men were scattering, and that you did not come at the set time, and
that the Philistines were assembling at Mikmash,[i] [12]I thought, 'Now the Philistines will come down against
me at Gilgal, and I have not sought the LORD's favor.'[j] So I felt compelled to offer the burnt offering."

[13]"You have done a foolish thing,[k]" Samuel said. "You have not kept[l] the command the LORD your
God gave you; if you had, he would have established your kingdom over Israel for all time. [14]But now
your kingdom[m] will not endure; the LORD has sought out a man after his own heart[n] and appointed[o]
him ruler of his people, because you have not kept the LORD's command."

13:4 [b]Ge 34:30
13:5 [c]Jos 11:4
13:6 [d]Jdg 6:2
13:7 [e]Nu 32:33
13:8 [f]1Sa 10:8
13:9 [g]2Sa 24:25; 1Ki 3:4
13:10 [h]1Sa 15:13
13:11 [i]ver 2,5,16,23
13:12 [j]Jer 26:19
13:13 [k]2Ch 16:9 [l]1Sa 15:23,24
13:14 [m]1Sa 15:28 [n]Ac 7:46; 13:22 [o]2Sa 6:21

[a] 5 Some Septuagint manuscripts and Syriac; Hebrew *thirty thousand*

13:5 three thousand chariots, six thousand charioteers. The Hebrew text says that the Philistines muster an army of "thirty thousand" chariots with six thousand horsemen (see NIV text note). "Thirty thousand" appears too high, and so the Septuagint, the pre-Christian Greek translation of the OT, and the Syriac render it as "three thousand chariots." The numbering of "six thousand charioteers" fits the latter figure well because there would be two men to each chariot. **sand on the seashore.** A common metaphor for a large, intimidating force (Josh 11:4; Judg 7:12). This army marches and encamps at Mikmash, where Saul previously stationed his army (v. 2).

13:6–7 When confronted with the formidable Philistine military, many of the Israelite soldiers flee; some hide in the highlands (cf. 14:22), while others flee across the Jordan River to the east, which is in the opposite direction to the land of Philistia.

13:11 Saul attempts to justify his actions with three arguments: (1) his army is scattering from him from Gilgal; (2) Samuel arrived at Gilgal late; and (3) the Philistines were poised for battle at Mikmash. The king is simply shifting blame to others, particularly Samuel. **you did not come.** Saul employs the independent personal pronoun "you" for emphasis. In other words, it is Samuel's fault that Saul was disobedient.

13:12 Saul thinks religious ritual takes precedence over keeping God's word spoken through the prophet.

13:13–14 Saul disobeyed the Lord by usurping priestly sacrificial rights and denying Samuel's role as priest in Israel. Consequently, Saul loses his own kingdom and dynastic succession. The Lord has already sought out another king, and he is "a man after his own heart" (v. 14). This is dramatic; the successor's identity will unfold in ch. 16.

13:15 [p] 1Sa 14:2
13:17 [q] 1Sa 14:15
[r] Jos 18:23
13:18 [s] Jos 18:13-14
[t] Ne 11:34
13:19 [u] 2Ki 24:14; Jer 24:1
13:22 [v] 1Ch 9:39
[w] Jdg 5:8
13:23 [x] 1Sa 14:4
14:2 [y] 1Sa 13:15
[z] Isa 10:28
14:3 [a] 1Sa 4:21
[b] 1Sa 22:11,20
[c] 1Sa 2:28
14:4 [d] 1Sa 13:23

15 Then Samuel left Gilgal[a] and went up to Gibeah[p] in Benjamin, and Saul counted the men who
were with him. They numbered about six hundred.

Israel Without Weapons

16 Saul and his son Jonathan and the men with them were staying in Gibeah[b] in Benjamin, while
the Philistines camped at Mikmash. 17 Raiding[q] parties went out from the Philistine camp in three detachments. One turned toward Ophrah[r] in the vicinity of Shual, 18 another toward Beth Horon,[s] and the
third toward the borderland overlooking the Valley of Zeboyim[t] facing the wilderness.
19 Not a blacksmith[u] could be found in the whole land of Israel, because the Philistines had said,
"Otherwise the Hebrews will make swords or spears!" 20 So all Israel went down to the Philistines to
have their plow points, mattocks, axes and sickles[c] sharpened. 21 The price was two-thirds of a shekel[d]
for sharpening plow points and mattocks, and a third of a shekel[e] for sharpening forks and axes and
for repointing goads.
22 So on the day of the battle not a soldier with Saul and Jonathan[v] had a sword or spear[w] in his hand;
only Saul and his son Jonathan had them.

Jonathan Attacks the Philistines

14 23 Now a detachment of Philistines had gone out to the pass[x] at Mikmash. 1 One day Jonathan
son of Saul said to his young armor-bearer, "Come, let's go over to the Philistine outpost on
the other side." But he did not tell his father.
2 Saul was staying on the outskirts of Gibeah[y] under a pomegranate tree in Migron.[z] With him were
about six hundred men, 3 among whom was Ahijah, who was wearing an ephod. He was a son of Ichabod's[a] brother Ahitub[b] son of Phinehas, the son of Eli,[c] the LORD's priest in Shiloh. No one was aware
that Jonathan had left.
4 On each side of the pass[d] that Jonathan intended to cross to reach the Philistine outpost was a cliff;
one was called Bozez and the other Seneh. 5 One cliff stood to the north toward Mikmash, the other to
the south toward Geba.

[a] *15* Hebrew; Septuagint *Gilgal and went his way; the rest of the people went after Saul to meet the army, and they went out of Gilgal* [b] *16* Two Hebrew manuscripts; most Hebrew manuscripts *Geba,* a variant of *Gibeah* [c] *20* Septuagint; Hebrew *plow points* [d] *21* That is, about 1/4 ounce or about 8 grams [e] *21* That is, about 1/8 ounce or about 4 grams

13:16–22 *Israel Without Weapons.* The Israelites and the Philistines are preparing for battle. Each side has mustered its troops, and some skirmishes are taking place (vv. 17–18). Israel is at a strict disadvantage. Not only do the Philistines have a large chariot force (v. 5), but they also have a monopoly on metal weaponry.
13:16 The two armies are positioned. Gibeah and Mikmash are about one mile (1.6 kilometers) apart and separated by the Wadi es-Suwenit. Saul's force was originally at Mikmash (v. 2), but now the Philistines control that city.
13:17–18 The Philistines initiate the conflict by sending three bands of marauders throughout the central highlands in three different directions from the camp at Mikmash: Ophrah is to the north four miles (6.4 kilometers) from Bethel; Beth Horon is ten miles (16 kilometers) west of Mikmash; and the "wilderness" is to the east of the Philistine camp.
13:19–22 The Philistines have a monopoly on blacksmithing; they have not allowed Israel to have ironsmiths to make weaponry. Israel depends on the Philistine industry to sharpen and repair their agricultural tools. Iron plow points have been discovered at the site of Gibeah dating to as early as the eleventh century BC. The charges for sharpening are excessively high—another way the Philistines subject Israel. The Philistine monopoly has worked so well that in the day of battle only Saul and Jonathan are armed with metal weapons among all the Israelites. Thus, Israel's victory in the next chapter is all the more stunning.
13:19 Hebrews. Perhaps pejorative in this context.
13:23—14:46 *War Against the Philistines.* Jonathan and his armor-bearer daringly raid the Philistine camp outside the city of Mikmash (13:23—14:14). Because of its initial success, Saul and the army of Israel join in and mount a major attack (14:15–23). They are victorious and then chase the Philistines out of the highlands. But Saul vengefully makes a rash vow, quickly ending the battle (14:24–46).
13:23—14:14 *Jonathan Attacks the Philistines.* Jonathan looks to pick a fight with the Philistines.
13:23 This military move is menacing, and it sets the stage for the battle proper to begin.
14:1 armor-bearer. Not a mere slave or caddy; he has an important military posting (31:5–6). David later serves Saul in this capacity (16:21). Jonathan's aide is important to the story as evidenced by the nine times he is mentioned in vv. 1–17.
14:2–3 The story shifts away from Jonathan to view the encampment of Saul and his army.
14:2 under a pomegranate tree. Beneath a tree is a common place for a judge to sit and make decisions (22:6; Judg 4:5). **Migron.** Or "threshing floor," a place located outside the city in antiquity and where leaders sat in judgment (1 Kgs 22:10). **six hundred men.** A small force compared to the military might of the Philistines.
14:3 ephod. Appears eight times in 1 Samuel; it is always used to seek a message from God (e.g., 2:28; 23:6,9; 30:7–8).
14:4–5 The topography that Jonathan and his armor-bearer face is harsh. **Bozez ... Seneh.** There are two cliffs that are obstacles to their destination. The names of the cliffs underscore the difficulty of the terrain: Bozez means "slippery"; Seneh, "thorny."

[6]Jonathan said to his young armor-bearer, "Come, let's go over to the outpost of those uncircumcised[e] men. Perhaps the LORD will act in our behalf. Nothing[f] can hinder the LORD from saving, whether by many[g] or by few.[h]"

[7]"Do all that you have in mind," his armor-bearer said. "Go ahead; I am with you heart and soul."

[8]Jonathan said, "Come on, then; we will cross over toward them and let them see us. [9]If they say to us, 'Wait there until we come to you,' we will stay where we are and not go up to them. [10]But if they say, 'Come up to us,' we will climb up, because that will be our sign[i] that the LORD has given them into our hands."

[11]So both of them showed themselves to the Philistine outpost. "Look!" said the Philistines. "The Hebrews are crawling out of the holes they were hiding[j] in." [12]The men of the outpost shouted to Jonathan and his armor-bearer, "Come up to us and we'll teach you a lesson.[k]"

So Jonathan said to his armor-bearer, "Climb up after me; the LORD has given them into the hand[l] of Israel."

[13]Jonathan climbed up, using his hands and feet, with his armor-bearer right behind him. The Philistines fell before Jonathan, and his armor-bearer followed and killed behind him. [14]In that first attack Jonathan and his armor-bearer killed some twenty men in an area of about half an acre.

Israel Routs the Philistines

[15]Then panic[m] struck the whole army — those in the camp and field, and those in the outposts and raiding[n] parties — and the ground shook. It was a panic sent by God.[a]

[16]Saul's lookouts[o] at Gibeah in Benjamin saw the army melting away in all directions. [17]Then Saul said to the men who were with him, "Muster the forces and see who has left us." When they did, it was Jonathan and his armor-bearer who were not there.

[18]Saul said to Ahijah, "Bring[p] the ark of God." (At that time it was with the Israelites.)[b] [19]While Saul was talking to the priest, the tumult in the Philistine camp increased more and more. So Saul said to the priest,[q] "Withdraw your hand."

[20]Then Saul and all his men assembled and went to the battle. They found the Philistines in total confusion, striking[r] each other with their swords. [21]Those Hebrews who had previously been with the Philistines and had gone up with them to their camp went[s] over to the Israelites who were with Saul and Jonathan. [22]When all the Israelites who had hidden[t] in the hill country of Ephraim heard that the Philistines were on the run, they joined the battle in hot pursuit. [23]So on that day the LORD saved[u] Israel, and the battle moved on beyond Beth Aven.[v]

Jonathan Eats Honey

[24]Now the Israelites were in distress that day, because Saul had bound the people under an oath,[w] saying, "Cursed be anyone who eats food before evening comes, before I have avenged myself on my enemies!" So none of the troops tasted food.

[a] *15* Or *a terrible panic* [b] *18* Hebrew; Septuagint *"Bring the ephod." (At that time he wore the ephod before the Israelites.)*

14:6 [e] 1Sa 17:26,36; Jer 9:26 [f] Heb 11:34 [g] Jdg 7:4 [h] 1Sa 17:46-47
14:10 [i] Ge 24:14; Jdg 6:36-37
14:11 [j] 1Sa 13:6
14:12 [k] 1Sa 17:43-44 [l] 2Sa 5:24
14:15 [m] Ge 35:5; 2Ki 7:5-7 [n] 1Sa 13:17
14:16 [o] 2Sa 18:24
14:18 [p] 1Sa 30:7
14:19 [q] Nu 27:21
14:20 [r] Jdg 7:22; 2Ch 20:23
14:21 [s] 1Sa 29:4
14:22 [t] 1Sa 13:6
14:23 [u] Ex 14:30; Ps 44:6-7 [v] 1Sa 13:5
14:24 [w] Jos 6:26

14:6 uncircumcised. A derogatory term (31:4; Judg 14:3). **Nothing can hinder the LORD.** Unlike Saul (13:11), Jonathan is hopeful that God will act and is not worried that they are outnumbered.

14:9–10 The Philistines' response to Jonathan's presence is regarded as a sign of whether or not the Lord has given them into his hands. If the garrison tells the two of them to be still, then they are too suspicious and are on guard for treachery. If, however, they tell the two of them to come to the camp, then they are complacent. An attack would be the last thing on their minds.

14:11 Hebrews are crawling out of the holes. Mocking (cf. 13:6). Ironically, the Israelites who are hiding in caves end up participating in the rout of these very Philistines (v. 22).

14:14 acre. A measurement based upon what a pair of oxen can plow in a day.

14:15–23 *Israel Routs the Philistines.* Divine intervention causes panic among the Philistine force (cf. Exod 14:24). Seeing the success of Jonathan, Saul and his army mobilize and engage the Philistine army. The rout is so great that even those Israelite soldiers who had defected now participate in the conquest.

14:18–19 Saul calls for Ahijah the priest to bring forth the ark of the covenant (see NIV text note). Saul is seeking to obtain a message from God through lots cast from the ephod. He seeks a sign whether or not to join the battle. At the last minute, the noise of the panic becomes so great that Saul does not need a sign. So he stops Ahijah from performing the ritual. The time is ripe for battle.

14:21–22 The rout is on. Israelite mercenaries turn on their Philistine masters, and soldiers who earlier fled from the Philistines (13:6) join the battle.

14:23 The Lord gave victory to Israel. **Beth Aven.** Perhaps located at Khirbet at-Tall, southeast of Mikmash. The Philistines are being chased and pushed out of the highlands by the Israelite army.

14:24–46 *Jonathan Eats Honey.* The king makes the army of Israel take an oath to fast all day so that he can take personal vengeance on

14:27 [x] ver 43; 1Sa 30:12
14:29 [y] Jos 7:25; 1Ki 18:18
14:31 [z] Jos 10:12
14:32 [a] 1Sa 15:19 [b] Ge 9:4; Lev 3:17; 7:26; 17:10-14; 19:26; Dt 12:16,23-24
14:35 [c] 1Sa 7:17
14:37 [d] 1Sa 10:22; 28:6,15
14:38 [e] Jos 7:11; 1Sa 10:19
14:39 [f] 2Sa 12:5

25 The entire army entered the woods, and there was honey on the ground. 26 When they went into the woods, they saw the honey oozing out; yet no one put his hand to his mouth, because they feared the oath. 27 But Jonathan had not heard that his father had bound the people with the oath, so he reached out the end of the staff that was in his hand and dipped it into the honeycomb.[x] He raised his hand to his mouth, and his eyes brightened.[a] 28 Then one of the soldiers told him, "Your father bound the army under a strict oath, saying, 'Cursed be anyone who eats food today!' That is why the men are faint."

29 Jonathan said, "My father has made trouble[y] for the country. See how my eyes brightened when I tasted a little of this honey. 30 How much better it would have been if the men had eaten today some of the plunder they took from their enemies. Would not the slaughter of the Philistines have been even greater?"

31 That day, after the Israelites had struck down the Philistines from Mikmash to Aijalon,[z] they were exhausted. 32 They pounced on the plunder[a] and, taking sheep, cattle and calves, they butchered them on the ground and ate them, together with the blood.[b] 33 Then someone said to Saul, "Look, the men are sinning against the LORD by eating meat that has blood in it."

"You have broken faith," he said. "Roll a large stone over here at once." 34 Then he said, "Go out among the men and tell them, 'Each of you bring me your cattle and sheep, and slaughter them here and eat them. Do not sin against the LORD by eating meat with blood still in it.' "

So everyone brought his ox that night and slaughtered it there. 35 Then Saul built an altar[c] to the LORD; it was the first time he had done this.

36 Saul said, "Let us go down and pursue the Philistines by night and plunder them till dawn, and let us not leave one of them alive."

"Do whatever seems best to you," they replied.

But the priest said, "Let us inquire of God here."

37 So Saul asked God, "Shall I go down and pursue the Philistines? Will you give them into Israel's hand?" But God did not answer[d] him that day.

38 Saul therefore said, "Come here, all you who are leaders of the army, and let us find out what sin has been committed[e] today. 39 As surely as the LORD who rescues Israel lives,[f] even if the guilt lies with my son Jonathan, he must die." But not one of them said a word.

40 Saul then said to all the Israelites, "You stand over there; I and Jonathan my son will stand over here."

"Do what seems best to you," they replied.

[a] *27* Or *his strength was renewed*; similarly in verse 29

the Philistines. The irony is this saps the strength of his troops, so they struggle to fight. Jonathan rightly criticizes his father's rash vow. Saul wants to continue the battle against the Philistines. Based on priestly advice, however, he consults the Lord through a priest. God does not answer him. Saul understands it is due to some hidden sin of the people, and so lots are cast to find out who is at fault. The lot indicates Jonathan is at fault. Although Saul would have his own son killed, the army intercedes for Jonathan. In the end, the Israelites break off the attack against the Philistines.

14:24 Saul had bound the people under an oath. The Hebrew verb in the clause is related to another verb that means "to play the fool"; this is a double entendre. Saul's vow is foolish. His soldiers need sustenance throughout the day to keep up the fight.

14:25–26 As the Israelite troops enter a forest, there is honey dripping and "oozing out" all over the ground. The soldiers restrain themselves because of the vow they have taken, although the honey is enticing.

14:27 For some reason Jonathan had not gotten his father's word. Thus, he inadvertently breaks the oath. As a good soldier he does not stop to eat but merely dips his staff in the honey and eats from it as he pursues the enemy. **eyes brightened.** Renewed vigor—a strength the entire army needs.

14:29–30 After being told of his father's oath, Jonathan responds with severe criticism of Saul. **trouble.** Used of Achan's terrible sin in the battle of Jericho (Josh 7:25). If Saul had not acted so foolishly, Israel's victory would have been greater.

14:31 Aijalon. Located in the foothills 14 miles (22.5 kilometers) west of Mikmash.

14:32 The Israelites make for the Philistine encampment. They are ravenous, so they eat animals with their blood, which the Torah strictly forbids (Gen 9:4; Lev 17:10–11; Deut 12:23).

14:33 You have broken faith. Saul refuses to acknowledge his culpability in the affair; he points the finger at the Israelite troops. He sets up a large stone so they can slaughter animals and drain their blood properly (v. 34).

14:36 not leave one of them alive. Reflects the ban in which all humans are killed as a part of a holy war. Everyone agrees to his plan except a priest who says that God's permission must be sought first. Thus, Saul seeks to obtain a word from the Lord, but God is silent (v. 37).

14:38–39 sin ... guilt. Saul believes that a sin of the people is causing God not to answer his inquiry. And so he makes a vow based on the Lord's name that whoever is the guilty one shall certainly die. The king conveys the weight of the oath by saying it will be honored even if the culprit is his own son Jonathan. In his zeal, Saul makes another rash vow because, as the reader knows, Jonathan is the guilty party. The troops do not reveal it is the king's son.

14:40–42 Saul sets up a ceremony of casting lots to determine the guilty party. The lot falls on Jonathan.

41Then Saul prayed to the LORD, the God of Israel, "Why have you not answered your servant today?
If the fault is in me or my son Jonathan, respond with Urim, but if the men of Israel are at fault,[a] respond with Thummim." Jonathan and Saul were taken by lot, and the men were cleared. 42Saul said,
"Cast the lot between me and Jonathan my son." And Jonathan was taken.
43Then Saul said to Jonathan, "Tell me what you have done."[g]
So Jonathan told him, "I tasted a little honey[h] with the end of my staff. And now I must die!"
44Saul said, "May God deal with me, be it ever so severely,[i] if you do not die, Jonathan.[j]"
45But the men said to Saul, "Should Jonathan die—he who has brought about this great deliverance in Israel? Never! As surely as the LORD lives, not a hair[k] of his head will fall to the ground, for he
did this today with God's help." So the men rescued[l] Jonathan, and he was not put to death.
46Then Saul stopped pursuing the Philistines, and they withdrew to their own land.
47After Saul had assumed rule over Israel, he fought against their enemies on every side: Moab, the
Ammonites,[m] Edom, the kings[b] of Zobah,[n] and the Philistines. Wherever he turned, he inflicted punishment on them.[c] 48He fought valiantly and defeated the Amalekites,[o] delivering Israel from the hands
of those who had plundered them.

Saul's Family

49Saul's sons were Jonathan, Ishvi and Malki-Shua.[p] The name of his older daughter was Merab,
and that of the younger was Michal.[q] 50His wife's name was Ahinoam daughter of Ahimaaz. The name
of the commander of Saul's army was Abner son of Ner, and Ner was Saul's uncle. 51Saul's father Kish[r]
and Abner's father Ner were sons of Abiel.
52All the days of Saul there was bitter war with the Philistines, and whenever Saul saw a mighty or
brave man, he took[s] him into his service.

The LORD Rejects Saul as King

15 Samuel said to Saul, "I am the one the LORD sent to anoint[t] you king over his people Israel; so
listen now to the message from the LORD. 2This is what the LORD Almighty says: 'I will punish
the Amalekites[u] for what they did to Israel when they waylaid them as they came up from Egypt. 3Now
go, attack the Amalekites and totally[v] destroy[d] all that belongs to them. Do not spare them; put to death
men and women, children and infants, cattle and sheep, camels and donkeys.'"

14:43 [g] Jos 7:19 [h] ver 27
14:44 [i] Ru 1:17 [j] ver 39
14:45 [k] 1Ki 1:52; Lk 21:18; Ac 27:34 [l] 2Sa 14:11
14:47 [m] 1Sa 11:1-13 [n] ver 52; 2Sa 10:6
14:48 [o] 1Sa 15:2,7
14:49 [p] 1Sa 31:2; 1Ch 8:33 [q] 1Sa 18:17-20
14:51 [r] 1Sa 9:1
14:52 [s] 1Sa 8:11
15:1 [t] 1Sa 9:16
15:2 [u] Ex 17:8-14; Nu 24:20; Dt 25:17-19
15:3 [v] Nu 24:20; Dt 20:16-18; Jos 6:17; 1Sa 22:19

[a] *41* Septuagint; Hebrew does not have *"Why . . . at fault.* [b] *47* Masoretic Text; Dead Sea Scrolls and Septuagint *king* [c] *47* Hebrew; Septuagint *he was victorious* [d] *3* The Hebrew term refers to the irrevocable giving over of things or persons to the LORD, often by totally destroying them; also in verses 8, 9, 15, 18, 20 and 21.

14:41 Urim ... Thummim. Kept in the priest's ephod (Exod 28:30), these objects were used as a direct means of seeking God's will.
14:43–44 Jonathan, in contrast to Saul, readily admits his sin and willingly accepts his punishment.
14:45 As surely as the LORD lives. The same oath that Saul uses in v. 39. The people stand with Jonathan in this matter, not with Saul.
14:46 Just as Jonathan anticipated (v. 30), the defeat of the Philistines is not as great as it easily could have been.
14:47–52 *Summary of Saul's Kingship.* This transitional section in the story of the kingship of Saul (1) summarizes Saul's military leadership (vv. 47–48,52) and (2) briefly reviews Saul's descendants and family (vv. 49–51).
14:47–48 Saul is a successful military leader, which is exactly what Israel demanded in a king (8:19–20). David later subdues the same peoples (2 Sam 8:11–12). **delivering Israel from the hands of those who had plundered them.** Like the judges (Judg 2:16).
14:49 Ishvi. Probably Ish-Bosheth/Esh-Baal (see 1 Chr 9:39 and NIV text note). Saul later offers both of his daughters to David in marriage (18:17–27).
14:50 Abner. Saul's cousin; the only state official listed here. Including Abner here perhaps accentuates the dominating military *zeitgeist* ("spirit of the time") of Saul's reign.
14:52 The Philistines are the primary menace to Israel in Saul's time.
15:1–35 *The Lord Rejects Saul as King.* The Lord, through the prophet Samuel, commands Saul to completely destroy the Amalekites (vv. 1–3). Saul obeys by mustering a large army and attacking the Amalekites (vv. 4–7). He disobeys, however, by sparing the king and the best of the spoils (vv. 8–9). Samuel confronts Saul for not keeping the word of the Lord, and the Lord finally rejects Saul as king (vv. 10–35).
15:1 Samuel said. Samuel's speech to Saul begins in the original Hebrew with the pronoun "me." Samuel is in the position of prominence in this story as he is the conduit of God's word to the king. **message from the LORD.** The prophet urges the king to obey, literally, "the voice" of the Lord. The Hebrew word for "voice" appears seven times in the chapter, and it is an important and leading word that helps to unlock the meaning of the story.
15:3 totally destroy. This is the holy war concept of placing something under the ban, which is dedicating an enemy and his goods to a deity often by destroying them all (see NIV text note). It is an ancient Near Eastern practice found, e.g., in the text of the Moabite Stone. On it Mesha, king of Moab during the ninth century BC, devotes to the god Chemosh all the people of Israel in his land by destroying them. Bans can be total (here) or partial (Deut 20:12–15). God orders a total ban

15:6 [w]Ex 18:10,19; Nu 10:29-32; 24:22; Jdg 1:16; 4:1
15:7 [x]1Sa 14:48 [y]Ge 16:7; 25:17-18; Ex 15:22
15:8 [z]1Sa 30:1
15:9 [a]ver 3,15
15:11 [b]Ge 6:6; 2Sa 24:16 [c]Jos 22:16 [d]1Sa 13:13; 1Ki 9:6-7 [e]ver 35
15:12 [f]Jos 15:55
15:17 [g]1Sa 9:21
15:19 [h]1Sa 14:32
15:20 [i]ver 13

4So Saul summoned the men and mustered them at Telaim — two hundred thousand foot soldiers
and ten thousand from Judah. 5Saul went to the city of Amalek and set an ambush in the ravine. 6Then
he said to the Kenites,[w] "Go away, leave the Amalekites so that I do not destroy you along with them;
for you showed kindness to all the Israelites when they came up out of Egypt." So the Kenites moved
away from the Amalekites.
7Then Saul attacked the Amalekites[x] all the way from Havilah to Shur,[y] near the eastern border
of Egypt. 8He took Agag king of the Amalekites alive,[z] and all his people he totally destroyed with the
sword. 9But Saul and the army spared[a] Agag and the best of the sheep and cattle, the fat calves[a] and
lambs — everything that was good. These they were unwilling to destroy completely, but everything
that was despised and weak they totally destroyed.
10Then the word of the LORD came to Samuel: 11"I regret[b] that I have made Saul king, because he
has turned[c] away from me and has not carried out my instructions."[d] Samuel was angry,[e] and he cried
out to the LORD all that night.
12Early in the morning Samuel got up and went to meet Saul, but he was told, "Saul has gone to Carmel.[f] There he has set up a monument in his own honor and has turned and gone on down to Gilgal."
13When Samuel reached him, Saul said, "The LORD bless you! I have carried out the LORD's
instructions."
14But Samuel said, "What then is this bleating of sheep in my ears? What is this lowing of cattle
that I hear?"
15Saul answered, "The soldiers brought them from the Amalekites; they spared the best of the sheep
and cattle to sacrifice to the LORD your God, but we totally destroyed the rest."
16"Enough!" Samuel said to Saul. "Let me tell you what the LORD said to me last night."
"Tell me," Saul replied.
17Samuel said, "Although you were once small[g] in your own eyes, did you not become the head of
the tribes of Israel? The LORD anointed you king over Israel. 18And he sent you on a mission, saying,
'Go and completely destroy those wicked people, the Amalekites; wage war against them until you have
wiped them out.' 19Why did you not obey the LORD? Why did you pounce on the plunder[h] and do evil
in the eyes of the LORD?"
20"But I did obey[i] the LORD," Saul said. "I went on the mission the LORD assigned me. I completely
destroyed the Amalekites and brought back Agag their king. 21The soldiers took sheep and cattle

[a] 9 Or *the grown bulls*; the meaning of the Hebrew for this phrase is uncertain.

against the Amalekites to judge them for opposing Israel's journey to the land of Canaan (Exod 17:8–13). God thus declares war against them (Exod 17:16; Deut 25:17–19).

15:4 Telaim. A Judahite city (Josh 15:24) close to the Amalekite territory. **two hundred thousand.** Some commentators argue that this number is way too high, and they take the Hebrew word for "thousand" to signify a military unit rather than a number. Thus, Saul is mobilizing 200 units from all Israel, and Judah supports him with ten military groups. **Judah.** Singling out Judah perhaps indicates that the tribe of Judah is not fully incorporated into Saul's kingdom at this point.

15:6 Kenites. Friendly Kenites include Moses' father-in-law Jethro (Judg 1:16) and the woman Jael, who killed Sisera (Judg 4:11–22).

15:8–9 Saul directly disobeys Samuel's command (v. 3). Does Saul spare Agag to keep as a trophy or to use as a bargaining chip with the Amalekites? By keeping the best animals, is he keeping the best of royalty? The text is silent, but Saul's motive is likely self-serving: he keeps the good stuff for himself. "The army" (v. 9) also disobeys by keeping these things, but Saul is the primary instigator in the unfaithfulness: as the king, so the nation.

15:10 The scene shifts from the battle to the Lord speaking to the prophet Samuel.

15:11 I regret. God does not acknowledge a mistake; what happened grieves him (cf. Gen 6:6–7). God does not make mistakes, lie, or change his mind (v. 29). The Lord's regret closes out the chapter (v. 35), serving as an *inclusio* (i.e., brackets) for the story of Saul's rejection. **Samuel was angry.** It is not clear why. He could be angry with God, with Saul, or with the entire circumstance.

15:12 Carmel. A town in Judah about seven miles (11.3 kilometers) south of Hebron (25:2–42; Josh 15:55). **in his own honor.** Sums up the central focus of Saul's kingship (cf. 2 Sam 18:18). Although Saul was reluctant to become king, he now displays pride as king. This is linked to his downfall, which brings to mind the theme of God exalting the humble and bringing down the proud in Hannah's prayer (1 Sam 2:4–8).

15:13–14 I have carried out the LORD's instructions. This is ironic since God said that Saul "has not carried out my instructions" (v. 11). **bleating ... lowing.** Samuel immediately questions Saul regarding the sheep and oxen that he hears. Saul was supposed to obey "the message" ("voice") of the Lord (v. 1), but now Samuel hears other voices calling.

15:15 Saul senses disapproval from Samuel, so he shifts the responsibility and blames the soldiers. But "Saul and the army" (v. 9) spared the king and plunder.

15:17 you were once small in your own eyes. See 9:21; 10:22. **the head of the tribes of Israel ... king over Israel.** Saul cannot deny culpability for what the army does. Samuel confronts Saul for not taking responsibility for what has happened.

15:19 you ... you. Saul is at the center of the disobedience.

15:20 But I did obey. Saul disputes Samuel's claim. **I ... brought back Agag their king.** Saul condemns himself.

15:21 The soldiers took. Saul again shifts the blame.

from the plunder, the best of what was devoted to God, in order to sacrifice them to the LORD your God at Gilgal."

22But Samuel replied:

> "Does the LORD delight in burnt offerings and sacrifices
> as much as in obeying the LORD?
> To obey is better than sacrifice,[j]
> and to heed is better than the fat of rams.
> 23For rebellion is like the sin of divination,[k]
> and arrogance like the evil of idolatry.
> Because you have rejected[l] the word of the LORD,
> he has rejected you as king."

24Then Saul said to Samuel, "I have sinned.[m] I violated the LORD's command and your instructions. I was afraid[n] of the men and so I gave in to them. 25Now I beg you, forgive[o] my sin and come back with me, so that I may worship the LORD."

26But Samuel said to him, "I will not go back with you. You have rejected[p] the word of the LORD, and the LORD has rejected you as king over Israel!"

27As Samuel turned to leave, Saul caught hold of the hem of his robe, and it tore.[q] 28Samuel said to him, "The LORD has torn[r] the kingdom of Israel from you today and has given it to one of your neighbors—to one better than you. 29He who is the Glory of Israel does not lie[s] or change[t] his mind; for he is not a human being, that he should change his mind."

30Saul replied, "I have sinned. But please honor[u] me before the elders of my people and before Israel; come back with me, so that I may worship the LORD your God." 31So Samuel went back with Saul, and Saul worshiped the LORD.

32Then Samuel said, "Bring me Agag king of the Amalekites."

Agag came to him in chains.[a] And he thought, "Surely the bitterness of death is past."

33But Samuel said,

> "As your sword has made women childless,
> so will your mother be childless among women."[v]

And Samuel put Agag to death before the LORD at Gilgal.

34Then Samuel left for Ramah,[w] but Saul went up to his home in Gibeah[x] of Saul. 35Until the day Samuel[y] died, he did not go to see Saul again, though Samuel mourned[z] for him. And the LORD regretted that he had made Saul king over Israel.

[a] *32* The meaning of the Hebrew for this phrase is uncertain.

15:22 [j] Ps 40:6-8; 51:16; Isa 1:11-15; Jer 7:22; Hos 6:6; Mic 6:6-8; Mt 12:7; Mk 12:33; Heb 10:6-9
15:23 [k] Dt 18:10 [l] 1Sa 13:13
15:24 [m] 2Sa 12:13 [n] Pr 29:25; Isa 51:12-13
15:25 [o] Ex 10:17
15:26 [p] 1Sa 13:14
15:27 [q] 1Ki 11:11,31
15:28 [r] 1Sa 28:17; 1Ki 11:31
15:29 [s] 1Ch 29:11; Titus 1:2 [t] Nu 23:19; Eze 24:14
15:30 [u] Isa 29:13; Jn 5:44; 12:43
15:33 [v] Ge 9:6; Jdg 1:7
15:34 [w] 1Sa 7:17 [x] 1Sa 11:4
15:35 [y] 1Sa 19:24 [z] 1Sa 16:1

15:22–23 Samuel's response is devastating. He accuses Saul of performing ritual sacrifice without a true heart of obedience. Later prophets commonly indict Israel for such legalism (Hos 6:6; Amos 5:21–24).
15:22 fat. The choice part of sacrificial animals often set apart to the Lord (Lev 3:16–17; 7:22–25).
15:23 rebellion … arrogance. The main sins in Saul's actions. **idolatry.** Commonly used in divination (Gen 31:34–35; Judg 17:5; Hos 3:4). **he has rejected you as king.** The Lord's rejecting Saul as king is ironic justice because Saul rejected the word of the King.
15:24 I have sinned. Saul confesses his sin, providing a weak excuse: he was "afraid of the men," so he "listened to their voice." Samuel had commanded Saul to listen to the voice of the Lord (v. 1), but Saul disobeyed by yielding to other voices.
15:25 forgive my sin. Only God can forgive iniquity. **come back.** Saul desires Samuel's support when he returns to the people.
15:26 Samuel refuses to be party to Saul's masquerade. He tells the king a second time (v. 23) that the Lord has "rejected" him.
15:27–28 caught hold … it tore. In a final act of pleading, Saul grabs Samuel's robe and tears it. Samuel employs the incident as symbolic. **The LORD has torn the kingdom of Israel from you today.** An episode of kingships in the time of Jeroboam uses a similar symbol (1 Kgs 11:29–32).
15:29 change his mind. The same Hebrew word in vv. 11,35 is translated "regret." There is a tension here: God says, "I regret" (v. 11), but Samuel says that the Lord does not regret because "he is not a human being." The Hebrew word has breadth of meaning, and this passage uses it in two different ways: (1) the sense of "sorrow and grief" (vv. 11,35) and (2) the idea of God's immutability (v. 29).
15:30 I have sinned. Saul confesses his sin again but does not ask for forgiveness (as in v. 25). What Saul really wants is "honor" before all Israel.
15:31 went back. Inexplicably, Samuel changes his mind (unlike the Lord) and returns with Saul. Perhaps this is simply the way the prophet supports the office of king until another monarch is anointed.
15:33 This punishment is ironic justice: as Agag has killed others, he will be killed. Samuel completes the ban on the humans of the Amalekites that Saul failed to fulfill.
15:35 Samuel's anger toward Saul (v. 11) turns into mourning. The Lord's grief regarding Saul's kingship serves as the climax to Saul's entire reign.

16:1 [a] 1Sa 15:35 [b] 1Sa 15:23 [c] 2Ki 9:1 [d] Ru 4:17; 1Sa 9:16 [e] Ps 78:70; Ac 13:22
16:3 [f] Ex 4:15 [g] Dt 17:15; 1Sa 9:16
16:4 [h] Ge 48:7; Lk 2:4 [i] 1Ki 2:13; 2Ki 9:17
16:5 [j] Ex 19:10,22
16:6 [k] 1Sa 17:13
16:7 [l] Ps 147:10 [m] 1Ki 8:39; 1Ch 28:9; Isa 55:8
16:8 [n] 1Sa 17:13
16:11 [o] 1Sa 17:12
16:12 [p] 1Sa 9:17 [q] Ge 39:6; 1Sa 17:42
16:13 [r] Nu 27:18; Jdg 11:29 [s] 1Sa 10:1,6, 9-10; 11:6
16:14 [t] Jdg 16:20 [u] Jdg 9:23; 1Sa 18:10

Samuel Anoints David

16 The LORD said to Samuel, "How long will you mourn[a] for Saul, since I have rejected[b] him as king over Israel? Fill your horn with oil[c] and be on your way; I am sending you to Jesse[d] of Bethlehem. I have chosen[e] one of his sons to be king."

2 But Samuel said, "How can I go? If Saul hears about it, he will kill me."

The LORD said, "Take a heifer with you and say, 'I have come to sacrifice to the LORD.' 3 Invite Jesse to the sacrifice, and I will show[f] you what to do. You are to anoint[g] for me the one I indicate."

4 Samuel did what the LORD said. When he arrived at Bethlehem,[h] the elders of the town trembled when they met him. They asked, "Do you come in peace?[i]"

5 Samuel replied, "Yes, in peace; I have come to sacrifice to the LORD. Consecrate[j] yourselves and come to the sacrifice with me." Then he consecrated Jesse and his sons and invited them to the sacrifice.

6 When they arrived, Samuel saw Eliab[k] and thought, "Surely the LORD's anointed stands here before the LORD."

7 But the LORD said to Samuel, "Do not consider his appearance or his height, for I have rejected him. The LORD does not look at the things people look at. People look at the outward appearance,[l] but the LORD looks at the heart."[m]

8 Then Jesse called Abinadab[n] and had him pass in front of Samuel. But Samuel said, "The LORD has not chosen this one either." 9 Jesse then had Shammah pass by, but Samuel said, "Nor has the LORD chosen this one." 10 Jesse had seven of his sons pass before Samuel, but Samuel said to him, "The LORD has not chosen these." 11 So he asked Jesse, "Are these all[o] the sons you have?"

"There is still the youngest," Jesse answered. "He is tending the sheep."

Samuel said, "Send for him; we will not sit down until he arrives."

12 So he[p] sent for him and had him brought in. He was glowing with health and had a fine appearance and handsome[q] features.

Then the LORD said, "Rise and anoint him; this is the one."

13 So Samuel took the horn of oil and anointed him in the presence of his brothers, and from that day on the Spirit of the LORD[r] came powerfully upon David.[s] Samuel then went to Ramah.

David in Saul's Service

14 Now the Spirit of the LORD had departed[t] from Saul, and an evil[a] spirit[u] from the LORD tormented him.

15 Saul's attendants said to him, "See, an evil spirit from God is tormenting you. 16 Let our lord com-

[a] *14* Or *and a harmful*; similarly in verses 15, 16 and 23

16:1—31:13 *Saul's Fall and David's Rise.* The lives of Saul and David contrast but parallel each other in several ways. Both have early success followed by grievous sin. But they diverge at the point of how they deal with their sin. Saul's sins lead to bitterness, vengeance, and anger directed against David and others, but David genuinely repents. This section describes Saul's demise and David's ascent.

16:1–13 *Samuel Anoints David.* Samuel told Saul twice that his kingship and dynasty would not endure and that God had already chosen his replacement: a man after God's own heart (13:13–14) who is better than Saul (15:28). Now the identity of the new king is revealed. The drama builds as the story does not name Saul's replacement until the final verse.

16:1 Jesse. Ruth 4:18–22 lists his genealogy; he is a grandson of Ruth and Boaz, and his great-grandmother is Rahab (cf. Matt 1:5–6). **Bethlehem.** In the tribal inheritance of Judah; about ten miles (16 kilometers) south of Ramah.

16:2–3 Samuel is afraid that Saul will kill him for treason. But God tells Samuel what to do in Bethlehem. This is not subterfuge or misdirection; God is preparing to anoint the new king. **anoint for me the one I indicate.** The choice of the king is the Lord's.

16:5 Consecrate yourselves. Consists of washing their garments and abstaining from sexual relations (Exod 19:10–15).

16:6–7 Samuel as seer "sees" who he thought would be the Lord's anointed, but in reality, he did not see. Outward appearance and stature are *not* the defining features of a good king. Saul stood out this way (9:2; 10:23–24), but the true issue is the heart. God has already chosen one who is a man after his own heart (13:14).

16:10 This lists David as Jesse's eighth son (see also 17:12). But 1 Chr 2:13–15 lists him as the seventh son. Some commentators argue that possibly one of the sons died without having any children and therefore is omitted from the genealogy. Others conclude that genealogies are not exhaustive, so one brother is left out for one reason or another. Perhaps this is an example of telescoping, placing David in the seventh position as a sign of his being the climax of that genealogy. (In Hebrew culture, the number seven often indicates completion or fulfillment.)

16:12–13 God tells Samuel to anoint Jesse's youngest son, fulfilling v. 3.

16:13 from that day on. Continuously, not intermittently. **the Spirit of the LORD came powerfully upon.** Commonly used in the book of Judges when the Lord temporarily empowers a person to deliver Israel from oppression (Judg 14:6,19; 15:14). Saul also experiences this, but it is intermittent (1 Sam 10:6,10; 11:6). **David.** Means "beloved"; this is the first time 1 Samuel mentions his name.

16:14–23 *David in Saul's Service.* Whereas the Spirit of the Lord rushes on David, it now departs from Saul, and an evil or harmful spirit assails Saul. Ironically, David is the one chosen to play soothing music in Saul's court to give him relief.

16:14 departed. Not in the sense of salvation. Rather, the Spirit is no

mand his servants here to search for someone who can play the lyre.[v] He will play when the evil spirit
from God comes on you, and you will feel better."
17So Saul said to his attendants, "Find someone who plays well and bring him to me."
18One of the servants answered, "I have seen a son of Jesse of Bethlehem who knows how to play
the lyre. He is a brave man and a warrior. He speaks well and is a fine-looking man. And the LORD is
with[w] him."
19Then Saul sent messengers to Jesse and said, "Send me your son David, who is with the sheep."
20So Jesse took a donkey loaded with bread,[x] a skin of wine and a young goat and sent them with his
son David to Saul.
21David came to Saul and entered his service.[y] Saul liked him very much, and David became one of
his armor-bearers. 22Then Saul sent word to Jesse, saying, "Allow David to remain in my service,
for I am pleased with him."
23Whenever the spirit from God came on Saul, David would take up his lyre and play. Then
relief would come to Saul; he would feel better, and the evil spirit[z] would leave him.

16:16 [v] ver 23; 1Sa 18:10; 19:9; 2Ki 3:15
16:18 [w] 1Sa 3:19; 17:32-37
16:20 [x] 1Sa 10:27; Pr 18:16
16:21 [y] Ge 41:46; Pr 22:29
16:23 [z] ver 14-16
17:1 [a] 1Sa 13:5 [b] Jos 15:35; 2Ch 28:18
17:2 [c] 1Sa 21:9
17:4 [d] Jos 11:21-22; 2Sa 21:19
17:6 [e] ver 45
17:7 [f] 2Sa 21:19 [g] ver 41
17:8 [h] 1Sa 8:17

David and Goliath

17 Now the Philistines gathered their forces for war and assembled[a] at Sokoh in Judah.
They pitched camp at Ephes Dammim, between Sokoh[b] and Azekah.
2Saul and the Israelites assembled and camped in the Valley of Elah[c] and drew
up their battle line to meet the Philistines. 3The Philistines occupied one hill and
the Israelites another, with the valley between them.
4A champion named Goliath,[d] who was from Gath, came out of the Philistine
camp. His height was six cubits and a span.[a] 5He had a bronze helmet on his head
and wore a coat of scale armor of bronze weighing five thousand shekels[b]; 6on
his legs he wore bronze greaves, and a bronze javelin[e] was slung on his back. 7His
spear shaft was like a weaver's rod,[f] and its iron point weighed six hundred shekels.[c] His shield bearer[g] went ahead of him.
8Goliath stood and shouted to the ranks of Israel, "Why do you come out and
line up for battle? Am I not a Philistine, and are you not the servants of Saul?
Choose[h] a man and have him come down to me. 9If he is able to fight and kill
me, we will become your subjects; but if I overcome him and kill him, you will

[a] 4 That is, about 9 feet 9 inches or about 3 meters [b] 5 That is, about 125 pounds or about 58 kilograms [c] 7 That is, about 15 pounds or about 6.9 kilograms

Harpist on jug, eleventh century BC, Megiddo. David would play his lyre for Saul to bring him relief (1 Sam 16:23).
Kim Walton, taken at the Israel Museum, Jerusalem

longer empowering Saul to be king and lead the nation in war. **an evil spirit.** Sent by God to torment Saul because of his sin; it is judgment on him for directly disobeying the word of God. The Lord does not perform evil, but evil elements are under his command in order to bring about his purposes (Judg 9:23; 1 Kgs 22:19–22). The sovereignty of God is such that everything that happens in heaven and on earth are under his divine control.

16:18 brave man. Used for people of integrity, such as Saul's father Kish (9:1) and Boaz (Ruth 2:1). **the LORD is with him.** David's most important characteristic (18:12,14,28; 2 Sam 5:10); used of committed believers in the OT such as Joseph (Gen 39:2,21,23).

16:20 donkey. Perhaps a measurement. The Assyrians had a unit of measure with that title equal to between two and five bushels (70 and 175 liters) of grain, based on the amount of grain a donkey could carry.

16:21 armor-bearers. Close attendants and advisors to the king. See note on 14:1.

17:1–58 *David and Goliath.* David enters the scene in a most stunning way: he defeats the champion of the Philistines, although the odds of victory from a human perspective are slim. He triumphs because the Lord is with him and he fully trusts in the Lord. In this regard David serves as a foil to Saul: Saul has disobeyed the Lord and is timid in this battle episode; David is heroic and faithful—great traits for the future king to possess.

17:1–11 *The Setting of War.* The armies of the Israelites and the Philistines square off. A champion named Goliath advances between the two forces and challenges the Israelites to send forth their own champion. Goliath's imposing physical presence sends the soldiers of Israel into great despair and fear.

17:1 Sokoh. Located at Khirbet ʿAbbad, some 24 miles (38.6 kilometers) west of Bethlehem in the tribal inheritance of Judah. **Azekah.** Identified with Tell Zakariyah, approximately three miles (4.8 kilometers) northwest of Sokoh and a mere five miles (8 kilometers) east of Gath.

17:2 Valley of Elah. Located in the foothill (Shephelah) region of the land, running west to east from Gath to Bethlehem. It provides entrance to the highlands belonging to the tribe of Judah.

17:4 Goliath. An authentic Philistine name that has been found on an inscription from Gath (Tell es-Safi) from the tenth to ninth centuries BC. His physical stature is imposing and his body armor impressive (see NIV text notes on vv. 4,5,7).

17:6 greaves. Armor used to protect a soldier's shins.

17:7 shield bearer. His role is to protect a soldier by carrying a standing shield that covers the soldier's entire body. Goliath is completely well armed; no wonder the Israelites panic (v. 24).

17:9 become ... subjects. The challenge is an all-or-nothing, winner-take-all ancient duel. The Philistines later renege on this agreement (vv. 52–54).

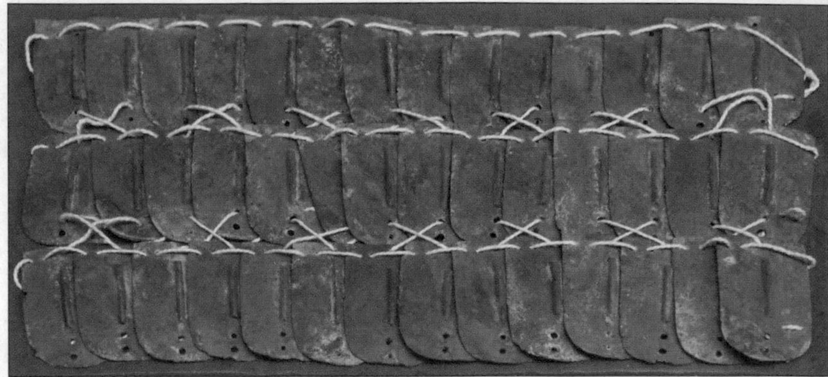

Bronze armor scales, western Iran, ninth–seventh centuries BC. Goliath had a coat of scale armor that weighed about 125 pounds (1 Sam 17:5).

Todd Bolen/www.BiblePlaces.com, taken at the British Museum

17:10 [i] ver 26, 45; 2Sa 21:21
17:12 [j] Ru 4:17; 1Ch 2:13-15 [k] Ge 35:19 [l] 1Sa 16:11
17:13 [m] 1Sa 16:6 [n] 1Sa 16:9
17:15 [o] 1Sa 16:19
17:17 [p] 1Sa 25:18
17:18 [q] Ge 37:14
17:23 [r] ver 8-10
17:25 [s] Jos 15:16; 1Sa 18:17

become our subjects and serve us.” 10Then the Philistine said, “This day I defy[i] the armies of Israel! Give
me a man and let us fight each other.” 11On hearing the Philistine’s words, Saul and all the Israelites
were dismayed and terrified.

12Now David was the son of an Ephrathite named Jesse,[j] who was from Bethlehem[k] in Judah. Jesse
had eight[l] sons, and in Saul’s time he was very old. 13Jesse’s three oldest sons had followed Saul to the
war: The firstborn was Eliab;[m] the second, Abinadab; and the third, Shammah.[n] 14David was the youngest. The three oldest followed Saul, 15but David went back and forth from Saul to tend his father’s
sheep[o] at Bethlehem.

16For forty days the Philistine came forward every morning and evening and took his stand.

17Now Jesse said to his son David, “Take this ephah[a] of roasted grain[p] and these ten loaves of bread
for your brothers and hurry to their camp. 18Take along these ten cheeses to the commander of their
unit. See how your brothers[q] are and bring back some assurance[b] from them. 19They are with Saul and
all the men of Israel in the Valley of Elah, fighting against the Philistines.”

20Early in the morning David left the flock in the care of a shepherd, loaded up and set out, as Jesse
had directed. He reached the camp as the army was going out to its battle positions, shouting the war
cry. 21Israel and the Philistines were drawing up their lines facing each other. 22David left his things
with the keeper of supplies, ran to the battle lines and asked his brothers how they were. 23As he was
talking with them, Goliath, the Philistine champion from Gath, stepped out from his lines and shouted
his usual[r] defiance, and David heard it. 24Whenever the Israelites saw the man, they all fled from him
in great fear.

25Now the Israelites had been saying, “Do you see how this man keeps coming out? He comes out to
defy Israel. The king will give great wealth to the man who kills him. He will also give him his daughter[s]
in marriage and will exempt his family from taxes in Israel.”

[a] *17* That is, probably about 36 pounds or about 16 kilograms [b] *18* Or *some token*; or *some pledge of spoils*

17:10 defy. A leading word in the episode. It occurs six times (in Hebrew) and bears the idea of taunting, jeering at, or saying sharp things against someone. Goliath is simply scorning Israel. No one from the ranks of Israel dares to accept the challenge because they are afraid.

17:12–19 *David at Home.* The scene changes from the battlefield to the region of Bethlehem.

17:15 back and forth. Apparently David is doing double duty. He is in the service of Saul (16:21–22), yet still shepherds for his father.

17:16 forty. Often signifies in Hebrew culture a time of trial, testing, and peril (Gen 7:4; Num 14:33–34; cf. Luke 4:2).

17:17–18 Jesse gives David a seemingly insignificant task, although the timing of David’s trip to the battle is the Lord’s.

17:17 ephah. 3/5 of a bushel (21 liters). See NIV text note.

17:18 assurance. Jesse requests a physical sign that his three sons are well and have received the goods.

17:20–30 *David in the Ranks of Israel.* David obeys his father and does exactly as he was ordered. After leaving the goods with the quartermaster, David runs to the battle line to determine the welfare of his brothers. While there he witnesses Goliath’s taunting of Israel and is appalled.

17:24 great fear. The exact response the Israelites had when Goliath first came out to taunt them (v. 11). Nothing has changed over this 40-day period.

17:25 Saul offers three rewards to the man who defeats Goliath: riches, his daughter in marriage, and exemption from taxes for his entire extended family.

26 David asked the men standing near him, "What will be done for the man who kills this Philistine and removes this disgrace[t] from Israel? Who is this uncircumcised[u] Philistine that he should defy[v] the armies of the living[w] God?"

27 They repeated to him what they had been saying and told him, "This is what will be done for the man who kills him."

28 When Eliab, David's oldest brother, heard him speaking with the men, he burned with anger[x] at him and asked, "Why have you come down here? And with whom did you leave those few sheep in the wilderness? I know how conceited you are and how wicked your heart is; you came down only to watch the battle."

29 "Now what have I done?" said David. "Can't I even speak?" 30 He then turned away to someone else and brought up the same matter, and the men answered him as before. 31 What David said was overheard and reported to Saul, and Saul sent for him.

32 David said to Saul, "Let no one lose heart[y] on account of this Philistine; your servant will go and fight him."

33 Saul replied,[z] "You are not able to go out against this Philistine and fight him; you are only a young man, and he has been a warrior from his youth."

34 But David said to Saul, "Your servant has been keeping his father's sheep. When a lion[a] or a bear came and carried off a sheep from the flock, 35 I went after it, struck it and rescued the sheep from its mouth. When it turned on me, I seized it by its hair, struck it and killed it. 36 Your servant has killed both the lion and the bear; this uncircumcised Philistine will be like one of them, because he has defied the armies of the living God. 37 The LORD who rescued[b] me from the paw of the lion[c] and the paw of the bear will rescue me from the hand of this Philistine."

Saul said to David, "Go, and the LORD be with[d] you."

38 Then Saul dressed David in his own tunic. He put a coat of armor on him and a bronze helmet on his head. 39 David fastened on his sword over the tunic and tried walking around, because he was not used to them.

"I cannot go in these," he said to Saul, "because I am not used to them." So he took them off. 40 Then he took his staff in his hand, chose five smooth stones from the stream, put them in the pouch of his shepherd's bag and, with his sling in his hand, approached the Philistine.

41 Meanwhile, the Philistine, with his shield bearer in front of him, kept coming closer to David. 42 He looked David over and saw that he was little more than a boy, glowing with health and handsome,[e] and he despised[f] him. 43 He said to David, "Am I a dog,[g] that you come at me with sticks?" And the Philistine cursed David by his gods. 44 "Come here," he said, "and I'll give your flesh to the birds and the wild animals![h]"

17:26 [t] 1Sa 11:2 [u] 1Sa 14:6 [v] ver 10 [w] Dt 5:26
17:28 [x] Ge 37:4,8,11; Pr 18:19; Mt 10:36
17:32 [y] Dt 20:3; 1Sa 16:18
17:33 [z] Nu 13:31
17:34 [a] Jer 49:19; Am 3:12
17:37 [b] 2Co 1:10 [c] 2Ti 4:17 [d] 1Sa 20:13; 1Ch 22:11,16
17:42 [e] 1Sa 16:12 [f] Ps 123:3-4; Pr 16:18
17:43 [g] 1Sa 24:14; 2Sa 3:8; 9:8; 2Ki 8:13
17:44 [h] 1Ki 20:10-11

17:26 David sees the battle as not a mere military conflict but as a clash between the "uncircumcised," pagan Philistines and the "armies of the living God."

17:28–29 Eliab, Jesse's firstborn, is angered by David's apparent impudence. So he questions David's motives for attending the battlefield. He falsely accuses David of neglecting their father's flock (cf. v. 20) and impugns his character by accusing him of being a mere thrill seeker. David proclaims his innocence, saying that he was only asking a simple question.

17:31–39 *David Volunteers.* When Saul hears about David's conversation with his troops, he summons David and inquires about his ability to face the Philistine. Once convinced, Saul attempts to prepare the youth for battle.

17:32 David volunteers to be the champion of Israel. **this Philistine.** By omitting Goliath's name, David indicates great disdain for Goliath.

17:33 Saul concludes that the odds are against David. Goliath is a "warrior" and greatly experienced since his "youth." David, on the other hand, is merely a "young man." What chance does a mere shepherd boy have against a seasoned warrior?

17:34–36 David makes his case. He has guarded his flock well against common predators, rescued his sheep, and killed the lion and the bear. David sees Goliath as merely another predator attempting to destroy God's sheep.

17:37 The LORD … will rescue me. This is the crux of the matter: David has great confidence because the Lord is with him and will fight for him (16:18). **the LORD be with you.** To his credit, Saul recognizes this truth and sends David to face the giant with the Lord's blessing.

17:38–39 Saul attempts to arm David in the manner of Goliath (v. 5). But David is totally inexperienced with this equipment; he is immature in these things! This contrast, again from a human perspective, highlights the improbability of David defeating Goliath.

17:40–54 *The Fight.* The one-on-one battle is really the Lord's battle, and he will not be defeated.

17:40–41 The contrast is significant: David has a shepherd's staff in one hand and a shepherd's slingshot in the other. Goliath is well protected with even a body shield in front of him (vv. 5–7).

17:43 by his gods. The Philistine taunts David, ratcheting up the rhetoric to a theological level in cursing David by his own gods. The main god of the Philistines is Dagon (see note on 5:2).

17:44 birds … wild animals. To be eaten by birds and animals is a fate worse than death because David would not receive a proper burial (Ps 79:2–3; Jer 7:33).

17:45 [i]2Sa 22:33,35; 2Ch 32:8; Ps 124:8; Heb 11:32-34 [j]ver 10
17:46 [k]Dt 28:26 [l]Jos 4:24; 1Ki 8:43; Isa 52:10 [m]1Ki 18:36; 2Ki 19:19; Isa 37:20
17:47 [n]Hos 1:7; Zec 4:6 [o]1Sa 14:6; 2Ch 14:11 [p]2Ch 20:15; Ps 44:6-7
17:50 [q]2Sa 23:21
17:51 [r]Heb 11:34 [s]1Sa 21:9
17:52 [t]Jos 15:11 [u]Jos 15:36
17:55 [v]1Sa 16:21
17:58 [w]ver 12
18:1 [x]2Sa 1:26 [y]Ge 44:30
18:3 [z]1Sa 20:8, 16,17,42

45 David said to the Philistine, "You come against me with sword and spear and javelin, but I come
against you in the name[i] of the LORD Almighty, the God of the armies of Israel, whom you have defied.[j]
46 This day the LORD will deliver you into my hands, and I'll strike you down and cut off your head. This
very day I will give the carcasses[k] of the Philistine army to the birds and the wild animals, and the whole
world[l] will know that there is a God in Israel.[m] 47 All those gathered here will know that it is not by sword[n]
or spear that the LORD saves;[o] for the battle[p] is the LORD's, and he will give all of you into our hands."
48 As the Philistine moved closer to attack him, David ran quickly toward the battle line to meet him.
49 Reaching into his bag and taking out a stone, he slung it and struck the Philistine on the forehead.
The stone sank into his forehead, and he fell facedown on the ground.
50 So David triumphed over the Philistine with a sling[q] and a stone; without a sword in his hand he
struck down the Philistine and killed him.
51 David ran and stood over him. He took hold of the Philistine's sword and drew it from the sheath.
After he killed him, he cut[r] off his head with the sword.[s]
When the Philistines saw that their hero was dead, they turned and ran. 52 Then the men of Israel
and Judah surged forward with a shout and pursued the Philistines to the entrance of Gath[a] and to
the gates of Ekron.[t] Their dead were strewn along the Shaaraim[u] road to Gath and Ekron. 53 When the
Israelites returned from chasing the Philistines, they plundered their camp.
54 David took the Philistine's head and brought it to Jerusalem; he put the Philistine's weapons in
his own tent.
55 As Saul watched David[v] going out to meet the Philistine, he said to Abner, commander of the army,
"Abner, whose son is that young man?"
Abner replied, "As surely as you live, Your Majesty, I don't know."
56 The king said, "Find out whose son this young man is."
57 As soon as David returned from killing the Philistine, Abner took him and brought him before
Saul, with David still holding the Philistine's head.
58 "Whose son are you, young man?" Saul asked him.
David said, "I am the son of your servant Jesse[w] of Bethlehem."

Saul's Growing Fear of David

18 After David had finished talking with Saul, Jonathan became one in spirit with David, and he
loved[x] him as himself.[y] 2 From that day Saul kept David with him and did not let him return
home to his family. 3 And Jonathan made a covenant[z] with David because he loved him as himself.

[a] 52 Some Septuagint manuscripts; Hebrew *of a valley*

17:46 David responds to Goliath tit for tat (cf. v. 44), but he adds that his triumph will resound through the whole earth as a demonstration that the Lord is with Israel.

17:47 the battle is the LORD's. Both the Israelite and the Philistine armies will be shown the error of placing trust in human devices for personal or national security (2:10; 14:6; 2 Chr 14:11; 20:15; Pss 33:16–22; 44:6–7; Eccl 9:11; Hos 1:7; Zech 4:6).

17:48 ran quickly. David's battle plan is to use speed. The sluggish, weighed-down Philistine cannot respond to such lightning movements.

17:49 forehead. The same Hebrew word translated "greave" in v. 6, causing some commentators to suggest that David hits Goliath in the knee or shin above the greave. **fell facedown on the ground.** The same thing previously happened to Dagon (see 5:3–4 and note).

17:51 the Philistine's sword. It is ironic that David kills Goliath and chops off his head with the Philistine's own sword (cf. 2 Sam 23:21).

17:52 The Philistines are in full flight (v. 51) and retreat before the army of Israel. **Gath ... Ekron.** Two of the capital cities of the Philistine pentapolis.

17:54 Jerusalem. The city is in the hands of the Jebusites at this time. It does not come under Israelite rule until much later (2 Sam 5:6–9). Perhaps David is taunting the Jebusites (cf. 31:9–10).

17:55–58 *David's Pedigree Revealed to Saul.* Obviously Saul knows who David is (16:14–23), but his knowledge of David's lineage is lacking.

17:55 whose son ...? Saul has already met David (vv. 32–37), but now he is interested in David's special status, background, and pedigree. David is not well-known in Israel. Saul wants this information so he can put David on his staff (18:2).

17:57 still holding the Philistine's head. This is all the pedigree and social status David needs to please the people!

18:1–30 *Saul's Growing Fear of David.* David becomes the military leader of Saul's forces. Saul's son Jonathan loves David, makes a covenant with him, and gives him his armor, which perhaps symbolizes his right of succession to the kingship. All the army and Saul's advisors are pleased with David's appointment. Verses 6–30 describe palace intrigue at its finest and most intricate. The more Saul plots and connives David's downfall, the more successful David becomes. The Lord is with David (v. 28) and not Saul.

18:1 became one in spirit ... loved him. Jonathan and David are bound by affection (2 Sam 1:26) and similarities in character (1 Sam 14).

18:2 kept. Lit. "took." Samuel declared that the king "will take your sons and make them serve with his chariots and horses" (8:11; cf. 14:52).

18:3 Their "covenant" is to the extremity of life and death: Jonathan gives up his throne for David (23:17) and risks his life for David

4 Jonathan took off the robe[a] he was wearing and gave it to David, along with his tunic, and even his
sword, his bow and his belt.
5 Whatever mission Saul sent him on, David was so successful that Saul gave him a high rank in the
army. This pleased all the troops, and Saul's officers as well.
6 When the men were returning home after David had killed the Philistine, the women came out
from all the towns of Israel to meet King Saul with singing and dancing,[b] with joyful songs and with
timbrels[c] and lyres. 7 As they danced, they sang:[d]

> "Saul has slain his thousands,
> and David his tens[e] of thousands."

8 Saul was very angry; this refrain displeased him greatly. "They have credited David with tens of
thousands," he thought, "but me with only thousands. What more can he get but the kingdom?[f]" 9 And
from that time on Saul kept a close eye on David.
10 The next day an evil[a] spirit[g] from God came forcefully on Saul. He was prophesying in his house,
while David was playing the lyre, as he usually[h] did. Saul had a spear in his hand 11 and he hurled it,
saying to himself,[i] "I'll pin David to the wall." But David eluded[j] him twice.
12 Saul was afraid[k] of David, because the LORD[l] was with[m] David but had departed from Saul. 13 So he
sent David away from him and gave him command over a thousand men, and David led[n] the troops
in their campaigns.[o] 14 In everything he did he had great success,[p] because the LORD was with[q] him.
15 When Saul saw how successful he was, he was afraid of him. 16 But all Israel and Judah loved David,
because he led them in their campaigns.[r]
17 Saul said to David, "Here is my older daughter[s] Merab. I will give her to you in marriage; only
serve me bravely and fight the battles[t] of the LORD." For Saul said to himself,[u] "I will not raise a hand
against him. Let the Philistines do that!"
18 But David said to Saul, "Who am I,[v] and what is my family or my clan in Israel, that I should
become the king's son-in-law?[w]" 19 So[b] when the time came for Merab,[x] Saul's daughter, to be given to
David, she was given in marriage to Adriel of Meholah.[y]
20 Now Saul's daughter Michal[z] was in love with David, and when they told Saul about it, he was
pleased. 21 "I will give her to him," he thought, "so that she may be a snare[a] to him and so that the hand
of the Philistines may be against him." So Saul said to David, "Now you have a second opportunity to
become my son-in-law."
22 Then Saul ordered his attendants: "Speak to David privately and say, 'Look, the king likes you, and
his attendants all love you; now become his son-in-law.' "
23 They repeated these words to David. But David said, "Do you think it is a small matter to become
the king's son-in-law? I'm only a poor man and little known."
24 When Saul's servants told him what David had said, 25 Saul replied, "Say to David, 'The king wants

a *10* Or *a harmful* *b* *19* Or *However,*

18:4 [a] Ge 41:42
18:6 [b] Ex 15:20 [c] Jdg 11:34; Ps 68:25
18:7 [d] Ex 15:21 [e] 1Sa 21:11; 29:5
18:8 [f] 1Sa 15:8
18:10 [g] 1Sa 16:14 [h] 1Sa 19:7
18:11 [i] 1Sa 20:7,33 [j] 1Sa 19:10
18:12 [k] ver 15,29 [l] 1Sa 16:13 [m] 1Sa 28:15
18:13 [n] ver 16; Nu 27:17 [o] 2Sa 5:2
18:14 [p] Ge 39:3 [q] Ge 39:2,23; Jos 6:27; 1Sa 16:18
18:16 [r] ver 5
18:17 [s] 1Sa 17:25 [t] Nu 21:14; 1Sa 25:28 [u] ver 25
18:18 [v] 1Sa 9:21; 2Sa 7:18 [w] ver 23
18:19 [x] 2Sa 21:8 [y] Jdg 7:22
18:20 [z] ver 28
18:21 [a] ver 17,26

(20:30–33), and David grants Mephibosheth, Jonathan's lame son, all of Saul's ancestral lands (2 Sam 9:1–13; 21:7).

18:4 Jonathan, as Saul's firstborn, holds the hereditary right to the throne of Israel. Giving David his robe and armor symbolizes that David is Saul's successor. Giving one's sword is a sign of submission to one who is greater.

18:6 singing and dancing. This celebration is reminiscent of the women's response to the victory at the Red Sea (Exod 15:20–21). In both episodes there is great joy from the women as they play tambourines, dance, and sing antiphonally. The support of the troops is ubiquitous because the women come out "from all the towns of Israel."

18:7–8 Saul understands the couplet that the women sing (v. 7) as an antithetical parallelism that exalts David over Saul. The text literally says that Saul struck down his "thousand" over against David's slaughter of "ten thousands." Saul interprets the ditty in the worst possible sense and fears for his throne. Seeds of suspicion begin to grow in him as he perceives that his own position is in jeopardy.

18:10–11 Saul's suspicion results in attempted murder. An "evil spirit from God" (see 16:15–16,23 and note on 16:14) rushes upon Saul so that he acts with abnormal behavior. As David tries to soothe Saul, the king tries to pin David to the wall with his spear. Ironically, Abishai later tells David that he will pin Saul to the ground with a spear (26:8).

18:12 the LORD was with David. A leading phrase during Saul's reign that contrasts Saul and David (vv. 14,28; 16:18; 17:37).

18:14–16 David's great military success breeds two responses: Saul "was afraid of him" (v. 15), but "all Israel and Judah loved David" (v. 16).

18:17 Saul begins to plot David's demise. He encourages David to fight for Israel, but he hopes to place him in great peril leading to death.

18:19 Saul takes advantage of David's humility (v. 18) and gives his eldest daughter to another man. This is double-dealing because he promised Merab to David (v. 17). Merab's marriage to Adriel is ill-fated: the Gibeonites kill all five of their sons (2 Sam 21:5–9).

18:20 David is clearly the favored one. Not only is the Lord with him, but Saul likes him (v. 22; 16:21), Jonathan loves him (v. 1), all Saul's servants love him (v. 22), all Israel and Judah love him (v. 16), and Saul's daughter Michal loves him.

18:25 [b]Ge 34:12; Ex 22:17; 1Sa 14:24 [c]ver 17
18:27 [d]ver 13; 2Sa 3:14
18:30 [e]ver 5; 2Sa 11:1
19:1 [f]1Sa 18:1 [g]1Sa 18:9
19:3 [h]1Sa 20:12
19:4 [i]1Sa 20:32; Pr 31:8, 9; Jer 18:20 [j]Ge 42:22; Pr 17:13
19:5 [k]1Sa 11:13; 17:49-50; 1Ch 11:14 [l]Dt 19:10-13; 1Sa 20:32; Mt 27:4
19:7 [m]1Sa 16:21; 18:2, 13
19:9 [n]1Sa 16:14; 18:10-11
19:10 [o]1Sa 18:11
19:11 [p]Ps 59 Title
19:12 [q]Jos 2:15; Ac 9:25
19:14 [r]Jos 2:4

no other price[b] for the bride than a hundred Philistine foreskins, to take revenge on his enemies.'" Saul's plan[c] was to have David fall by the hands of the Philistines.

26 When the attendants told David these things, he was pleased to become the king's son-in-law. So before the allotted time elapsed, 27 David took his men with him and went out and killed two hundred Philistines and brought back their foreskins. They counted out the full number to the king so that David might become the king's son-in-law. Then Saul gave him his daughter Michal[d] in marriage.

28 When Saul realized that the LORD was with David and that his daughter Michal loved David, 29 Saul became still more afraid of him, and he remained his enemy the rest of his days.

30 The Philistine commanders continued to go out to battle, and as often as they did, David met with more success[e] than the rest of Saul's officers, and his name became well known.

Saul Tries to Kill David

19 Saul told his son Jonathan[f] and all the attendants to kill[g] David. But Jonathan had taken a great liking to David 2 and warned him, "My father Saul is looking for a chance to kill you. Be on your guard tomorrow morning; go into hiding and stay there. 3 I will go out and stand with my father in the field where you are. I'll speak[h] to him about you and will tell you what I find out."

4 Jonathan spoke[i] well of David to Saul his father and said to him, "Let not the king do wrong[j] to his servant David; he has not wronged you, and what he has done has benefited you greatly. 5 He took his life in his hands when he killed the Philistine. The LORD won a great victory[k] for all Israel, and you saw it and were glad. Why then would you do wrong to an innocent[l] man like David by killing him for no reason?"

6 Saul listened to Jonathan and took this oath: "As surely as the LORD lives, David will not be put to death."

7 So Jonathan called David and told him the whole conversation. He brought him to Saul, and David was with Saul as before.[m]

8 Once more war broke out, and David went out and fought the Philistines. He struck them with such force that they fled before him.

9 But an evil[a] spirit[n] from the LORD came on Saul as he was sitting in his house with his spear in his hand. While David was playing the lyre, 10 Saul tried to pin him to the wall with his spear, but David eluded[o] him as Saul drove the spear into the wall. That night David made good his escape.

11 Saul sent men to David's house to watch[p] it and to kill him in the morning. But Michal, David's wife, warned him, "If you don't run for your life tonight, tomorrow you'll be killed." 12 So Michal let David down through a window,[q] and he fled and escaped. 13 Then Michal took an idol and laid it on the bed, covering it with a garment and putting some goats' hair at the head.

14 When Saul sent the men to capture David, Michal said,[r] "He is ill."

15 Then Saul sent the men back to see David and told them, "Bring him up to me in his bed so that I may kill him." 16 But when the men entered, there was the idol in the bed, and at the head was some goats' hair.

17 Saul said to Michal, "Why did you deceive me like this and send my enemy away so that he escaped?"

Michal told him, "He said to me, 'Let me get away. Why should I kill you?'"

[a] 9 Or *But a harmful*

18:25 price for the bride. What a groom pays to the bride's father (Exod 22:16–17; Deut 22:28–29), normally in silver. Saul appears magnanimous as he offers David a way to secure Michal as his bride through a heroic deed. The trap is sprung: Saul is deceitful as he hopes that David will die in his attempt to acquire 100 Philistine foreskins.

18:28–29 Saul is becoming more aware that David's star is on the rise. And as David's stock ascends, Saul's fear rises to an unprecedented level. From here on, Saul views David as "his enemy" (v. 29).

19:1–24 *Saul Tries to Kill David.* Saul attempted to kill David by the Philistines in ch. 18. Now he directly orders Jonathan and his staff to kill David. But Jonathan intercedes with his father on David's behalf, and Saul restores David to his previous position in the court for a short time. Saul's attempt to pin David to the wall with his spear echoes 18:10–11. Its repetition here demonstrates dramatically that Saul has not changed. He still desires to destroy David. David flees from Saul to the city of Ramah, where he comes under Samuel's protection. David is delivered from Saul's forces in a most unexpected way.

19:4–5 Jonathan makes a good case with his father.

19:7–10 Saul restores David to his work as both musician and military commander. David again successfully defeats the Philistines, renewing Saul's jealousy and anger.

19:11–13 David escapes to his house, but Saul sets a trap for him. The king's own daughter Michal springs David from Saul's trap; she is not the snare that Saul had hoped she would be (18:21). Michal further abets the fugitive by letting him down through the window of the house. She then concocts a plan to dress up an idol to look like David sleeping in the bed. Why there is an idol in David's house is uncertain.

19:17 Saul accuses Michal of betrayal. **He said to me, '... Why should**

[18]When David had fled and made his escape, he went to Samuel at Ramah[s] and told him all that Saul had done to him. Then he and Samuel went to Naioth and stayed there. [19]Word came to Saul: "David is in Naioth at Ramah"; [20]so he sent men to capture him. But when they saw a group of prophets[t] prophesying, with Samuel standing there as their leader, the Spirit of God came on[u] Saul's men, and they also prophesied.[v] [21]Saul was told about it, and he sent more men, and they prophesied too. Saul sent men a third time, and they also prophesied. [22]Finally, he himself left for Ramah and went to the great cistern at Seku. And he asked, "Where are Samuel and David?"

"Over in Naioth at Ramah," they said.

[23]So Saul went to Naioth at Ramah. But the Spirit of God came even on him, and he walked along prophesying[w] until he came to Naioth. [24]He stripped[x] off his garments, and he too prophesied in Samuel's presence. He lay naked all that day and all that night. This is why people say, "Is Saul also among the prophets?"[y]

David and Jonathan

20 Then David fled from Naioth at Ramah and went to Jonathan and asked, "What have I done? What is my crime? How have I wronged[z] your father, that he is trying to kill me?"

[2]"Never!" Jonathan replied. "You are not going to die! Look, my father doesn't do anything, great or small, without letting me know. Why would he hide this from me? It isn't so!"

[3]But David took an oath[a] and said, "Your father knows very well that I have found favor in your eyes, and he has said to himself, 'Jonathan must not know this or he will be grieved.' Yet as surely as the LORD lives and as you live, there is only a step between me and death."

[4]Jonathan said to David, "Whatever you want me to do, I'll do for you."

[5]So David said, "Look, tomorrow is the New Moon feast,[b] and I am supposed to dine with the king; but let me go and hide[c] in the field until the evening of the day after tomorrow. [6]If your father misses me at all, tell him, 'David earnestly asked my permission to hurry to Bethlehem,[d] his hometown, because an annual[e] sacrifice is being made there for his whole clan.' [7]If he says, 'Very well,' then your servant is safe. But if he loses his temper,[f] you can be sure that he is determined to harm me. [8]As for you, show kindness to your servant, for you have brought him into a covenant[g] with you before the LORD. If I am guilty, then kill[h] me yourself! Why hand me over to your father?"

[9]"Never!" Jonathan said. "If I had the least inkling that my father was determined to harm you, wouldn't I tell you?"

[10]David asked, "Who will tell me if your father answers you harshly?"

[11]"Come," Jonathan said, "let's go out into the field." So they went there together.

[12]Then Jonathan said to David, "I swear by the LORD, the God of Israel, that I will surely sound out my father by this time the day after tomorrow! If he is favorably disposed toward you, will I not send you word and let you know? [13]But if my father intends to harm you, may the LORD deal with Jonathan, be it ever so severely,[i] if I do not let you know and send you away in peace. May the

19:18 [s]1Sa 7:17
19:20 [t]ver 11,14; Jn 7:32,45 [u]Nu 11:25 [v]1Sa 10:5; Joel 2:28
19:23 [w]1Sa 10:13
19:24 [x]2Sa 6:20; Isa 20:2; Mic 1:8 [y]1Sa 10:11
20:1 [z]1Sa 24:9
20:3 [a]Dt 6:13
20:5 [b]Nu 10:10; 28:11 [c]1Sa 19:2
20:6 [d]1Sa 17:58 [e]Dt 12:5
20:7 [f]1Sa 25:17
20:8 [g]1Sa 18:3; 23:18 [h]2Sa 14:32
20:13 [i]Ru 1:17; 1Sa 3:17

I kill you?' Michal lies to save herself. The truth is that she told David to escape; he did not threaten her.

19:18 Naioth. It is unclear whether the Hebrew refers to "camps" or to a specific place. It perhaps refers to shepherding camps located outside towns and villages.

19:20–21 prophesied. Whatever the specific nature of the prophecy, its purpose is to keep the soldiers from their harmful task.

19:23–24 Saul's behavior seems to be uncontrolled and humiliating.

19:24 naked. Nakedness in the OT is often a sign of shame (2 Sam 10:4; Isa 20:4). **Is Saul also among the prophets?** First asked in 10:11–12 as a positive evaluation of Saul, confirming his changed heart and anointing to the office of king. Here it is a negative evaluation of Saul as king.

20:1–42 *David and Jonathan.* David is puzzled by the furor of Saul's actions against him, so he seeks out Jonathan's counsel (v. 1). David first must convince Jonathan that Saul is truly seeking to kill him (vv. 2–4), so David concocts a plan to find out if Saul truly wants to destroy him (vv. 5–7). David and Jonathan make a covenant (vv. 8–17), and Jonathan devises another plan to let David know Saul's intentions toward him (vv. 18–42).

20:5–7 David plans a ruse to discover Saul's true intentions toward him.

20:5 New Moon feast. A day of special sacrifices and celebration (Num 10:10; 28:11–15).

20:8 kindness. Hebrew *ḥesed*; also appears in vv. 14–15. It is best translated as "covenant loyalty." David and Jonathan are entering a covenant relationship, a blood oath that extends to the very extremes of life and death (cf. 18:3).

20:12–13 They go the field to speak privately, where no one can overhear them. Covenant formulas dominate the conversation of the two men. Jonathan appeals to "the LORD, the God of Israel" (v. 12) as a witness to the covenant with David. Oath formulas commonly include God as testifier (12:5; Gen 31:50; Mal 2:14) and self-imprecation (1 Sam 3:17; 14:44; 25:22).

20:13 as he has been with my father. The Hebrew in this context

20:13 [j] Jos 1:5; 1Sa 17:37; 18:12; 1Ch 22:11,16
20:15 [k] 2Sa 9:7
20:16 [l] 1Sa 25:22
20:17 [m] 1Sa 18:3
20:18 [n] ver 5,25
20:19 [o] 1Sa 19:2
20:22 [p] ver 37
20:23 [q] ver 14-15; Ge 31:50
20:25 [r] ver 18
20:26 [s] Lev 7:20-21; 15:5; 1Sa 16:5
20:28 [t] ver 6
20:32 [u] 1Sa 19:4; Mt 27:23 [v] Ge 31:36; Lk 23:22
20:33 [w] ver 7; 1Sa 18:11,17
20:37 [x] ver 22

LORD be with[j] you as he has been with my father. 14 But show me unfailing kindness like the LORD's kindness as long as I live, so that I may not be killed, 15 and do not ever cut off your kindness from my family[k] — not even when the LORD has cut off every one of David's enemies from the face of the earth."

16 So Jonathan made a covenant[l] with the house of David, saying, "May the LORD call David's enemies to account." 17 And Jonathan had David reaffirm his oath[m] out of love for him, because he loved him as he loved himself.

18 Then Jonathan said to David, "Tomorrow is the New Moon feast. You will be missed, because your seat will be empty.[n] 19 The day after tomorrow, toward evening, go to the place where you hid[o] when this trouble began, and wait by the stone Ezel. 20 I will shoot three arrows to the side of it, as though I were shooting at a target. 21 Then I will send a boy and say, 'Go, find the arrows.' If I say to him, 'Look, the arrows are on this side of you; bring them here,' then come, because, as surely as the LORD lives, you are safe; there is no danger. 22 But if I say to the boy, 'Look, the arrows are beyond[p] you,' then you must go, because the LORD has sent you away. 23 And about the matter you and I discussed — remember, the LORD is witness[q] between you and me forever."

24 So David hid in the field, and when the New Moon feast came, the king sat down to eat. 25 He sat in his customary place by the wall, opposite Jonathan,[a] and Abner sat next to Saul, but David's place was empty.[r] 26 Saul said nothing that day, for he thought, "Something must have happened to David to make him ceremonially unclean — surely he is unclean.[s]" 27 But the next day, the second day of the month, David's place was empty again. Then Saul said to his son Jonathan, "Why hasn't the son of Jesse come to the meal, either yesterday or today?"

28 Jonathan answered, "David earnestly asked me for permission[t] to go to Bethlehem. 29 He said, 'Let me go, because our family is observing a sacrifice in the town and my brother has ordered me to be there. If I have found favor in your eyes, let me get away to see my brothers.' That is why he has not come to the king's table."

30 Saul's anger flared up at Jonathan and he said to him, "You son of a perverse and rebellious woman! Don't I know that you have sided with the son of Jesse to your own shame and to the shame of the mother who bore you? 31 As long as the son of Jesse lives on this earth, neither you nor your kingdom will be established. Now send someone to bring him to me, for he must die!"

32 "Why[u] should he be put to death? What[v] has he done?" Jonathan asked his father. 33 But Saul hurled his spear at him to kill him. Then Jonathan knew that his father intended[w] to kill David.

34 Jonathan got up from the table in fierce anger; on that second day of the feast he did not eat, because he was grieved at his father's shameful treatment of David.

35 In the morning Jonathan went out to the field for his meeting with David. He had a small boy with him, 36 and he said to the boy, "Run and find the arrows I shoot." As the boy ran, he shot an arrow beyond him. 37 When the boy came to the place where Jonathan's arrow had fallen, Jonathan called out after him, "Isn't the arrow beyond[x] you?" 38 Then he shouted, "Hurry! Go quickly! Don't stop!"

[a] 25 Septuagint; Hebrew *wall. Jonathan arose*

means "he was" (completed action), so Jonathan acknowledges that the Lord is with David but no longer with Saul.

20:15 David is true to his word as he demonstrates "kindness" to Mephibosheth, Jonathan's son, after Jonathan dies (2 Sam 9:1–8).

20:22–23 Jonathan recognizes God's providence in the current circumstances, no matter the outcome. The covenantal link between Jonathan and David is the Lord; he is the very basis and heart of their relationship. And it is a bond that lasts "forever" (v. 23).

20:25 by the wall. Perhaps with his back to the wall, as an example of Saul's paranoia.

20:26 ceremonially unclean. One needed to be ritually pure to participate in the New Moon sacrifices (Exod 19:14–15; Lev 7:20–21; 15:16–18; Deut 23:10–11).

20:27 son of Jesse. Saul is ridiculing and disparaging David by refusing to call him by name (also vv. 30–31). Jonathan calls him "David" (v. 28).

20:30 Saul, not taken in by the ruse, explodes in anger. As he disparaged the name of David, he disparages Jonathan and his mother. He accuses Jonathan of bringing "shame" on the family because he has chosen David over Saul and indeed over his own future kingship.

20:31 must die. Saul continues to be concerned about his dynasty, although it has already been removed from him (13:13–14; 15:28). He is blind to his own end.

20:33 hurled his spear. Saul had already done the same thing to David twice (18:11; 19:10). This echo underscores that David and Jonathan are knitted together and that Saul's hatred is deep-seated.

20:34 Surprisingly, Jonathan is angry not because Saul attempted to murder him but because Saul humiliated David.

20:37 beyond you. The sign of danger (v. 22). David must flee for his life.

20:38 Hurry! Go quickly! Don't stop! Though spoken to the boy, perhaps Jonathan was subtly saying this to David as well. This staccato list of commands thus serves as an urgent warning to David to flee immediately.

Bronze arrowheads from around the time of David. The arrowheads are inscribed in proto-Canaanite script, bearing names, probably of their owners.

Z. Radovan/www.BibleLandPictures.com

The boy picked up the arrow and returned to his master. 39(The boy knew nothing about all this; only
Jonathan and David knew.) 40Then Jonathan gave his weapons to the boy and said, "Go, carry them
back to town."

41After the boy had gone, David got up from the south side of the stone and bowed down before Jonathan three times, with his face to the ground. Then they kissed each other and wept together — but David wept the most.

42Jonathan said to David, "Go in peace,[y] for we have sworn friendship[z] with each other in the name of the LORD, saying, 'The LORD is witness between you and me, and between your descendants and my descendants forever.'" Then David left, and Jonathan went back to the town.[a]

20:42 [y]ver 22; 1Sa 1:17 [z]2Sa 1:26; Pr 18:24
21:1 [a]1Sa 14:3; 22:9,19; Ne 11:32; Isa 10:32 [b]1Sa 16:4
21:4 [c]Lev 24:8-9 [d]Ex 25:30; Mt 12:4 [e]Ex 19:15
21:5 [f]1Th 4:4

David at Nob

21 [b] David went to Nob,[a] to Ahimelek the priest. Ahimelek trembled[b] when he met him, and asked, "Why are you alone? Why is no one with you?"

2David answered Ahimelek the priest, "The king sent me on a mission and said to me, 'No one is to
know anything about the mission I am sending you on.' As for my men, I have told them to meet me
at a certain place. 3Now then, what do you have on hand? Give me five loaves of bread, or whatever
you can find."

4But the priest answered David, "I don't have any ordinary bread[c] on hand; however, there is some consecrated[d] bread here — provided the men have kept[e] themselves from women."

5David replied, "Indeed women have been kept from us, as usual whenever[c] I set out. The men's
bodies are holy[f] even on missions that are not holy. How much more so today!" 6So the priest gave him

[a] *42* In Hebrew texts this sentence (20:42b) is numbered 21:1. [b] In Hebrew texts 21:1-15 is numbered 21:2-16. [c] *5* Or *from us in the past few days since*

20:41 – 42 It is an emotional parting. Indeed, as Shakespeare said, "Parting is such sweet sorrow." But their commitment to one another is not merely emotive but ultimately based on the Lord and on their covenant, which is "forever" (v. 23).

21:1 – 9 *David at Nob.* The tabernacle moved from Shiloh (1:3) to Nob after the death of Eli and his sons (4:17 – 18). David flees to Nob and asks for food and arms from the priesthood.

21:1 Nob. Probably located at the modern site of Ra's at-Tamim, about 2.5 miles (4 kilometers) southeast of Gibeah and two miles (3.2 kilometers) northeast of Jerusalem. **Ahimelek.** Brother of Ahijah, Saul's military chaplain, and great-grandson of Eli (14:2 – 3). **Why are you alone?** Ahimelek is suspicious because David, commander of a large military contingent, is alone.

21:2 David deceives Ahimelek by saying that he is on a secret mission for the king and that his soldiers are absent because they are to meet him "at a certain place." He is purposefully vague.

21:4 consecrated bread. The bread of the Presence that is placed on the table in the Holy Place of the tabernacle (Exod 25:30). Twelve fresh loaves are placed on the table each Sabbath, and only the priests may eat that bread (Lev 24:5 – 9). **kept themselves from women.** A common requirement for ritual cleanliness (Exod 19:15). David's men may eat of the bread if they are ritually clean.

21:5 men's bodies are holy. The men with David have abstained from sexual relations as an act of consecration (cf. Exod 19:14 – 15).

21:6 The priest technically breaks the law by giving the bread of the Presence to David. Jesus uses this episode to demonstrate that sometimes necessity can overrule legalism (Mark 2:25 – 26).

21:6 [g]Lev 24:8-9; Mt 12:3-4; Mk 2:25-28; Lk 6:1-5
21:7 [h]1Sa 22:9,22 [i]1Sa 14:47; Ps 52 Title
21:9 [j]1Sa 17:51 [k]1Sa 17:2
21:10 [l]1Sa 27:2
21:11 [m]1Sa 18:7; 29:5; Ps 56 Title
21:13 [n]Ps 34 Title
22:1 [o]2Sa 23:13; Ps 57 Title; 142 Title
22:2 [p]1Sa 23:13; 25:13; 2Sa 15:20
22:5 [q]2Sa 24:11; 1Ch 21:9; 29:29; 2Ch 29:25

the consecrated bread,[g] since there was no bread there except the bread of the Presence that had been removed from before the LORD and replaced by hot bread on the day it was taken away.

7 Now one of Saul's servants was there that day, detained before the LORD; he was Doeg[h] the Edomite,[i] Saul's chief shepherd.

8 David asked Ahimelek, "Don't you have a spear or a sword here? I haven't brought my sword or any other weapon, because the king's mission was urgent."

9 The priest replied, "The sword[j] of Goliath the Philistine, whom you killed in the Valley of Elah,[k] is here; it is wrapped in a cloth behind the ephod. If you want it, take it; there is no sword here but that one."

David said, "There is none like it; give it to me."

David at Gath

10 That day David fled from Saul and went[l] to Achish king of Gath. 11 But the servants of Achish said to him, "Isn't this David, the king of the land? Isn't he the one they sing about in their dances:

> " 'Saul has slain his thousands,
> and David his tens of thousands'?"[m]

12 David took these words to heart and was very much afraid of Achish king of Gath. 13 So he pretended to be insane[n] in their presence; and while he was in their hands he acted like a madman, making marks on the doors of the gate and letting saliva run down his beard.

14 Achish said to his servants, "Look at the man! He is insane! Why bring him to me? 15 Am I so short of madmen that you have to bring this fellow here to carry on like this in front of me? Must this man come into my house?"

David at Adullam and Mizpah

22 David left Gath and escaped to the cave[o] of Adullam. When his brothers and his father's household heard about it, they went down to him there. 2 All those who were in distress or in debt or discontented gathered[p] around him, and he became their commander. About four hundred men were with him.

3 From there David went to Mizpah in Moab and said to the king of Moab, "Would you let my father and mother come and stay with you until I learn what God will do for me?" 4 So he left them with the king of Moab, and they stayed with him as long as David was in the stronghold.

5 But the prophet Gad[q] said to David, "Do not stay in the stronghold. Go into the land of Judah." So David left and went to the forest of Hereth.

21:7 This parenthesis introduces Doeg, who will later play a major role in destroying the priesthood at Nob (22:6–19). **Edomite.** Being a non-Israelite raises the question of Doeg's character and adds a sinister twist to the story. **chief shepherd.** Perhaps forebodes the violence he will let loose on the priests at Nob (22:18–19). Why Doeg is "detained" at the sanctuary is uncertain, although it may be due to some particular sin on his part (Jer 36:5).

21:8–9 It is incredible that David would go on the king's official business and not be armed. He will now have Goliath's sword (17:51). It is ironic that David immediately travels to the city of Gath, Goliath's hometown, and is recognized by the Philistines (vv. 10–11).

21:10–15 *David at Gath.* David flees to Philistine territory, away from the clutches of Saul but into another great peril.

21:10 king. Normally the heads of the pentapolis cities are called "rulers" (5:8). **Gath.** One of the Philistine pentapolis cities and Goliath's hometown (17:4). It is a most unlikely and curious place for David to run to.

21:11 People immediately recognize David, so his cover is blown. **king.** Can be used of a mere local leader or chieftain (Josh 12:1,7–24). Perhaps it is anticipatory: even the Philistines are aware that God has chosen David to succeed Saul on the throne of Israel.

21:12–13 David acts as if he were crazy to get out of the dangerous fix he is in.

21:13 saliva. David purposefully foams at the mouth, a sign of derangement.

21:15 David's act of insanity fools Achish. Ironically, the Philistine king vilifies his own people by insinuating that his land is full of "madmen" already, so why should he add another one?

22:1–5 *David at Adullam and Mizpah.* David now runs to Adullam and hides in a cave. His family and a band of outcasts surround him. He travels eastward to the country of Moab, where his parents remain for safekeeping under the protection of the Moabite king. Eventually he returns to the tribal territory of Judah at the command of the prophet Gad.

22:1 Adullam. Located in the Shephelah (foothills) of Judah at Khirbet ash-Sheikh Madkur, about ten miles (16 kilometers) east of the Philistine city of Gath. David's family, who witnessed his anointing (16:13), join to support him along with a band of misfits. This motley crew includes the disadvantaged, poor, discontent, and outlaws.

22:3–4 David travels east across the Jordan River into the kingdom of Moab, where the king protects David's parents—out of Saul's reach.

22:4 stronghold. Hebrew *mĕṣûdâ*; some suggest it denotes the mesa of Masada on the western shore of the Dead Sea.

Saul Kills the Priests of Nob

[6]Now Saul heard that David and his men had been discovered. And Saul was seated,[r] spear in hand, under the tamarisk[s] tree on the hill at Gibeah, with all his officials standing at his side. [7]He said to them, "Listen, men of Benjamin! Will the son of Jesse give all of you fields and vineyards? Will he make all of you commanders[t] of thousands and commanders of hundreds? [8]Is that why you have all conspired against me? No one tells me when my son makes a covenant[u] with the son of Jesse. None of you is concerned[v] about me or tells me that my son has incited my servant to lie in wait for me, as he does today."

[9]But Doeg[w] the Edomite, who was standing with Saul's officials, said, "I saw the son of Jesse come to Ahimelek son of Ahitub at Nob.[x] [10]Ahimelek inquired[y] of the LORD for him; he also gave him provisions[z] and the sword of Goliath the Philistine."

[11]Then the king sent for the priest Ahimelek son of Ahitub and all the men of his family, who were the priests at Nob, and they all came to the king. [12]Saul said, "Listen now, son of Ahitub."

"Yes, my lord," he answered.

[13]Saul said to him, "Why have you conspired[a] against me, you and the son of Jesse, giving him bread and a sword and inquiring of God for him, so that he has rebelled against me and lies in wait for me, as he does today?"

[14]Ahimelek answered the king, "Who[b] of all your servants is as loyal as David, the king's son-in-law, captain of your bodyguard and highly respected in your household? [15]Was that day the first time I inquired of God for him? Of course not! Let not the king accuse your servant or any of his father's family, for your servant knows nothing at all about this whole affair."

[16]But the king said, "You will surely die, Ahimelek, you and your whole family."

[17]Then the king ordered the guards at his side: "Turn and kill the priests of the LORD, because they too have sided with David. They knew he was fleeing, yet they did not tell me."

But the king's officials were unwilling[c] to raise a hand to strike the priests of the LORD.

[18]The king then ordered Doeg, "You turn and strike down the priests." So Doeg the Edomite turned and struck them down. That day he killed eighty-five men who wore the linen ephod.[d] [19]He also put to the sword[e] Nob, the town of the priests, with its men and women, its children and infants, and its cattle, donkeys and sheep.

[20]But one son of Ahimelek son of Ahitub, named Abiathar,[f] escaped and fled to join David.[g] [21]He told David that Saul had killed the priests of the LORD. [22]Then David said to Abiathar, "That day, when Doeg[h] the Edomite was there, I knew he would be sure to tell Saul. I am responsible for the death of

22:6 [r]Jdg 4:5 [s]Ge 21:33
22:7 [t]1Sa 8:14
22:8 [u]1Sa 18:3; 20:16 [v]1Sa 23:21
22:9 [w]1Sa 21:7; Ps 52 Title [x]1Sa 21:1
22:10 [y]Nu 27:21; 1Sa 10:22 [z]1Sa 21:6
22:13 [a]ver 8
22:14 [b]1Sa 19:4
22:17 [c]Ex 1:17
22:18 [d]1Sa 2:18,31
22:19 [e]1Sa 15:3
22:20 [f]1Sa 23:6,9; 30:7; 1Ki 2:22,26,27 [g]1Sa 2:32
22:22 [h]1Sa 21:7

22:6–23 *Saul Kills the Priests of Nob.* In Gibeah, Doeg the Edomite relays to Saul the episode between David and the priests of Nob (21:7). Saul summons the priests to the royal court to respond to accusations of betrayal. Saul, unconvinced by Ahimelek, orders that all the priests be murdered. Doeg then performs the deed. Only one priest survives, and he runs to David for protection.

22:7 men of Benjamin. Many of Saul's close advisors are from his own tribe. Saul disparages David by saying that David, being of the tribe of Judah, would not do for them what Saul has done. Saul distributes these perquisites to his own and, thus, has become a king like that of all the nations, just as Samuel had predicted (8:12–14).

22:8 conspired. Saul accuses the men from his own tribe of conspiring against him by withholding information about David and Jonathan's conspiracy. Saul is paranoid, and he is becoming conspicuously alone.

22:9 son of Jesse. Doeg subtly proclaims his loyalty to Saul by omitting David's name (see 20:27 and note).

22:12 son of Ahitub. Saul refers to Ahimelek only by his father's name and thus perhaps demeans him in the same way he has demeaned David (see v. 9 and note).

22:13 conspired. Saul's paranoia knows no bounds. He levels the same accusation against the priests of Nob that he does of his own tribe: conspiracy (see v. 8 and note).

22:14–15 Ahimelek zealously defends both David and himself. David's credentials are impeccable: he is related to the king, a faithful subject, a commander of Saul's closest troops, and held in high esteem in Saul's own household. Ahimelek has inquired of the Lord for David at other times, so this is not unusual; he knew nothing of David's plans.

22:17 priests of the LORD. Saul recognizes their status, but he is absolutely callous to spiritual matters and to their standing in the Israelite religious hierarchy. Saul's officials refuse to be part of such an atrocious act, perhaps implicitly supporting David.

22:18–19 Doeg is called an "Edomite" three times (here; v. 9; 21:7), highlighting that a foreigner malevolently murders the Israelite priesthood. Not only does Doeg destroy 85 priests, but he places the *ḥērem* (ban) on the Levitical city of Nob. It is ironic that while Saul refused to apply the *ḥērem* to the Amalekites (ch. 15), a foreigner applies it to an Israelite priestly town in Saul's own tribe of Benjamin.

22:20 Abiathar. Only he survives the slaughter, and he brings the ephod from the sanctuary (23:6). The Israelite priesthood—or what is left of it—now follows David and no longer supports Saul. Abiathar remains a loyal priest to David throughout David's reign (30:7–8; 2 Sam 15:24–36), although Solomon later exiles him to Anathoth for supporting Adonijah to succeed David (1 Kgs 1:7; 2:26–27).

22:22 I am responsible. In contrast to Saul, David takes full responsibility for his actions. The reality is that the priests of Nob got caught in the crossfire. They died because Saul wants to kill David.

22:23 [i] 1Ki 2:26
23:1 [j] Jos 15:44
23:2 [k] ver 4,12; 1Sa 30:8; 2Sa 5:19,23
23:4 [l] Jos 8:7; Jdg 7:7
23:6 [m] 1Sa 22:20
23:9 [n] ver 6; 1Sa 22:20; 30:7
23:12 [o] ver 20
23:13 [p] 1Sa 22:2; 25:13
23:14 [q] Jos 15:24,55 [r] Ps 54:3-4 [s] Ps 32:7

your whole family. [23]Stay with me; don't be afraid. The man who wants to kill you[i] is trying to kill me
too. You will be safe with me."

David Saves Keilah

23 When David was told, "Look, the Philistines are fighting against Keilah[j] and are looting the
threshing floors," [2]he inquired[k] of the LORD, saying, "Shall I go and attack these Philistines?"
The LORD answered him, "Go, attack the Philistines and save Keilah."
[3]But David's men said to him, "Here in Judah we are afraid. How much more, then, if we go to Keilah
against the Philistine forces!"
[4]Once again David inquired of the LORD, and the LORD answered him, "Go down to Keilah, for I am
going to give the Philistines into your hand.[l]" [5]So David and his men went to Keilah, fought the Philistines and carried off their livestock. He inflicted heavy losses on the Philistines and saved the people
of Keilah. [6](Now Abiathar[m] son of Ahimelek had brought the ephod down with him when he fled to
David at Keilah.)

Saul Pursues David

[7]Saul was told that David had gone to Keilah, and he said, "God has delivered him into my hands,
for David has imprisoned himself by entering a town with gates and bars." [8]And Saul called up all his
forces for battle, to go down to Keilah to besiege David and his men.
[9]When David learned that Saul was plotting against him, he said to Abiathar[n] the priest, "Bring the
ephod." [10]David said, "LORD, God of Israel, your servant has heard definitely that Saul plans to come to
Keilah and destroy the town on account of me. [11]Will the citizens of Keilah surrender me to him? Will
Saul come down, as your servant has heard? LORD, God of Israel, tell your servant."
And the LORD said, "He will."
[12]Again David asked, "Will the citizens of Keilah surrender[o] me and my men to Saul?"
And the LORD said, "They will."
[13]So David and his men,[p] about six hundred in number, left Keilah and kept moving from place to
place. When Saul was told that David had escaped from Keilah, he did not go there.
[14]David stayed in the wilderness strongholds and in the hills of the Desert of Ziph.[q] Day after day
Saul searched[r] for him, but God did not[s] give David into his hands.

23:1–6 *David Delivers Keilah.* Although David is being hunted by Saul, he saves Keilah from the hands of the Philistines. Ironically, as king it is Saul who should have rescued the city.

23:1 Keilah. Located at Khirbet Qila in the Shephelah (foothills) of the tribe of Judah (Josh 15:44). It is close to Philistine territory (merely 11 miles [17.7 kilometers] southeast of Gath) and therefore easily subject to Philistine raiding parties. The primary reason for the incursion is plundering grain that is at the threshing floors ready to be processed.

23:2 Shall I go . . . ? David is particularly interested because Keilah is a town of his own tribe. So he seeks divine permission to jump into the fray, and he receives approval. **save.** The principal task of the judges (Judg 2:16); this portrays David as one of them.

23:3 David's men are anxious and worried, afraid of going from one dangerous situation—in Judah facing Saul—to a more dangerous one engaging the Philistines. **forces.** Or "battle lines" (17:21–23,48).

23:6 This interruption reminds us that the priesthood now supports David (22:20), and it sets up the next story, in which David seeks a word from the Lord. **the ephod.** Probably associated with the Urim and Thummim; it has a prophetic function throughout 1 Samuel (2:27–28; 14:3).

23:7–29 *Saul Pursues David.* When Saul hears that David is in Keilah, he sees an opportunity to capture him. But David escapes the snare because of divine guidance. Jonathan then comes to David in the wilderness in order to encourage him. The two of them make another covenant. The Ziphites, of the tribe of Judah, attempt to give up David to Saul. Saul is nearly successful in his attempt to capture and destroy David and his men. They are delivered at the last minute in an ironic way by a Philistine raid into Israel.

23:7–8 Keilah is a town with gates and a city wall, so its fortifications can both keep enemies out and hem enemies in (Judg 16:2). Saul still believes that God is with him, although he does not use the covenantal name "LORD." David, on the other hand, has been inquiring of the "LORD" (vv. 2,4). Instead of coming to the aid of Keilah, Saul musters his entire army to trap David and his fighting force of 600 men (v. 13).

23:9 plotting. Sometimes indicates digging up mischief (see Judg 14:18, where this verb is translated "plowed").

23:10–12 David's piety is a foil to Saul's lack of it. Although David just delivered the town of Keilah, he is afraid the inhabitants will betray him to Saul. Keilah's citizens have every right to fear Saul because he utterly destroyed the Levitical city of Nob for aiding and abetting David (22:18–19).

23:13 kept moving from place to place. A figure of speech called *idem per idem*; their movements reflect complete autonomy as an escaping force. They are on the run, and a moving target is hard to hit.

23:14 Desert of Ziph. Located in the area southeast of Hebron heading toward the Dead Sea. Ziph is also the name of a city in Judah (Josh 15:55) that is five miles (8 kilometers) southeast of Hebron. Although Saul obsessively hunts for David, God protects the future king from falling into Saul's hands.

En Gedi, where David hid from Saul.
Todd Bolen/www.BiblePlaces.com

[15]While David was at Horesh in the Desert of Ziph, he learned that[a] Saul had come out to take his
life. [16]And Saul's son Jonathan went to David at Horesh and helped him find strength[t] in God. [17]"Don't
be afraid," he said. "My father Saul will not lay a hand on you. You will be king[u] over Israel, and I will
be second to you. Even my father Saul knows this." [18]The two of them made a covenant[v] before the
LORD. Then Jonathan went home, but David remained at Horesh.

[19]The Ziphites[w] went up to Saul at Gibeah and said, "Is not David hiding among us[x] in the strongholds at Horesh, on the hill of Hakilah,[y] south of Jeshimon? [20]Now, Your Majesty, come down whenever
it pleases you to do so, and we will be responsible for giving[z] him into your hands."

[21]Saul replied, "The LORD bless you for your concern[a] for me. [22]Go and get more information. Find
out where David usually goes and who has seen him there. They tell me he is very crafty. [23]Find out
about all the hiding places he uses and come back to me with definite information. Then I will go with
you; if he is in the area, I will track him down among all the clans of Judah."

[24]So they set out and went to Ziph ahead of Saul. Now David and his men were in the Desert of
Maon,[b] in the Arabah south of Jeshimon. [25]Saul and his men began the search, and when David was
told about it, he went down to the rock and stayed in the Desert of Maon. When Saul heard this, he went
into the Desert of Maon in pursuit of David.

[26]Saul[c] was going along one side of the mountain, and David and his men were on the other
side, hurrying to get away from Saul. As Saul and his forces were closing in on David and his men

23:16 [t]1Sa 30:6
23:17 [u]1Sa 20:31; 24:20
23:18 [v]1Sa 18:3; 20:16, 42; 2Sa 9:1; 21:7
23:19 [w]1Sa 26:1 [x]Ps 54 Title [y]1Sa 26:3
23:20 [z]ver 12
23:21 [a]1Sa 22:8
23:24 [b]Jos 15:55; 1Sa 25:2
23:26 [c]Ps 17:9

[a] *15* Or *be was afraid because*

23:15 Horesh. Location uncertain; the name means "words," "grove," or "wooded height" and thus may not even be a place-name.

23:17–18 Jonathan again endorses David's kingship (18:4). **second to you.** Probably a central element of their "covenant" (v. 18; 18:3; 20:8,16–17). But Jonathan will not live long enough to hold the position under David. Jonathan's love and respect for David enable him to accept a role subordinate to David without any sign of resentment or jealousy. This is the last recorded meeting between Jonathan and David.

23:19 The reality of the Ziphites' betrayal of their own tribal members is underscored by the very specific details of the location of David and his men. David wrote Ps 54 in light of the Ziphites' treason against him.

23:21 concern for me. Saul's self-centeredness surfaces again (see 22:8). Ironically, the Benjamites would not betray David, but some Judahites have no hesitation in doing so.

23:24 Desert of Maon. Probably named after the town located at Khirbet Ma'in, about four miles (6.4 kilometers) south of Ziph on the edge of the Arabah wilderness west of the Dead Sea.

23:26–28 This is a last-second reprieve for David and his men.

23:29 [d]2Ch 20:2
24:1 [e]1Sa 23:28-29
24:2 [f]1Sa 26:2
24:3 [g]Ps 57 Title; 142 Title [h]Jdg 3:24
24:4 [i]1Sa 25:28-30 [j]1Sa 23:17; 26:8
24:5 [k]2Sa 24:10
24:6 [l]1Sa 26:11
24:8 [m]1Sa 25:23-24
24:11 [n]Ps 7:3 [o]1Sa 23:14,23; 26:20
24:12 [p]Ge 16:5; 31:53; Job 5:8 [q]Jdg 11:27; 1Sa 26:10
24:13 [r]Mt 7:20
24:14 [s]1Sa 17:43; 2Sa 9:8 [t]1Sa 26:20
24:15 [u]ver 12 [v]Ps 35:1, 23; Mic 7:9 [w]Ps 43:1 [x]Ps 119:134,154
24:16 [y]1Sa 26:17
24:17 [z]Ge 38:26; 1Sa 26:21 [a]Mt 5:44
24:18 [b]1Sa 26:23

to capture them, 27 a messenger came to Saul, saying, "Come quickly! The Philistines are raiding the
land." 28 Then Saul broke off his pursuit of David and went to meet the Philistines. That is why they
call this place Sela Hammahlekoth.[a] 29 And David went up from there and lived in the strongholds
of En Gedi.[b][d]

David Spares Saul's Life

24 [c] After Saul returned from pursuing the Philistines, he was told, "David is in the Desert of En
Gedi.[e]" 2 So Saul took three thousand able young men from all Israel and set out to look[f] for
David and his men near the Crags of the Wild Goats.

3 He came to the sheep pens along the way; a cave[g] was there, and Saul went in to relieve[h] himself.
David and his men were far back in the cave. 4 The men said, "This is the day the LORD spoke[i] of when
he said[d] to you, 'I will give your enemy into your hands for you to deal with as you wish.' "[j] Then David
crept up unnoticed and cut off a corner of Saul's robe.

5 Afterward, David was conscience-stricken[k] for having cut off a corner of his robe. 6 He said to his
men, "The LORD forbid that I should do such a thing to my master, the LORD's anointed,[l] or lay my hand
on him; for he is the anointed of the LORD." 7 With these words David sharply rebuked his men and did
not allow them to attack Saul. And Saul left the cave and went his way.

8 Then David went out of the cave and called out to Saul, "My lord the king!" When Saul looked
behind him, David bowed down and prostrated himself with his face to the ground.[m] 9 He said to
Saul, "Why do you listen when men say, 'David is bent on harming you'? 10 This day you have seen
with your own eyes how the LORD delivered you into my hands in the cave. Some urged me to kill
you, but I spared you; I said, 'I will not lay my hand on my lord, because he is the LORD's anointed.'
11 See, my father, look at this piece of your robe in my hand! I cut off the corner of your robe but
did not kill you. See that there is nothing in my hand to indicate that I am guilty[n] of wrongdoing
or rebellion. I have not wronged you, but you are hunting[o] me down to take my life. 12 May the LORD
judge[p] between you and me. And may the LORD avenge[q] the wrongs you have done to me, but my
hand will not touch you. 13 As the old saying goes, 'From evildoers come evil deeds,'[r] so my hand
will not touch you.

14 "Against whom has the king of Israel come out? Who are you pursuing? A dead dog?[s] A flea?[t] 15 May
the LORD be our judge[u] and decide between us. May he consider my cause and uphold[v] it; may he vindicate[w] me by delivering[x] me from your hand."

16 When David finished saying this, Saul asked, "Is that your voice,[y] David my son?" And he wept
aloud. 17 "You are more righteous than I,"[z] he said. "You have treated me well,[a] but I have treated you
badly. 18 You have just now told me about the good you did to me; the LORD delivered[b] me into your

[a] *28* *Sela Hammahlekoth* means *rock of parting.* [b] *29* In Hebrew texts this verse (23:29) is numbered 24:1.
[c] In Hebrew texts 24:1-22 is numbered 24:2-23. [d] *4* Or *"Today the LORD is saying*

23:28 Sela Hammahlekoth. Lit. "the rock of separations/divisions." See NIV text note.

23:29 En Gedi. An oasis located on the western shore of the Dead Sea to the east of Ziph and Maon.

24:1–22 *David Spares Saul's Life.* David is on the run from Saul. He receives a golden opportunity to kill his pursuer but refrains because he respects the Lord's anointed.

24:1 No details are given regarding the crisis with the Philistines.

24:2 able. Or "chosen"; thus, elite troops. At the outset of his reign, Saul's standing army was 3,000 soldiers (13:2); now his special forces are that large.

24:3 sheep pens. Probably a wall enclosure for animals in front of a cave. Saul enters the cave alone to relieve himself.

24:4 David's men see a wonderful opportunity for David: With Saul in David's hands, Saul can easily be killed. David, in stealth, merely cuts off a corner of Saul's robe. Saul's robe is a symbol of his kingly authority, and this act is perhaps a sign that Saul's kingdom is being "cut off" from him (cf. 15:27–28; 1 Kgs 11:29–32).

24:6 David has pangs of conscience, and he refuses to do violence against Saul. **the LORD's anointed.** Saul is still on the throne of Israel, and David is his loyal subject (26:9,11,16,23). David even calls Saul "my master." Later he orders the Amalekite killed for striking down "the LORD's anointed" (2 Sam 1:14–16).

24:10–11 David pleads his innocence before Saul. The crux of his argument is that he did not take advantage of Saul in the cave when the king was so vulnerable. David settled for a piece of Saul's robe; this proves he had no evil designs. He truly respects Saul and submits to him by calling him "my father" (v. 11).

24:13 David cites a proverbial saying that teaches that wicked acts come from wicked people. David implies that if he were truly wicked, Saul would be dead.

24:14 dead dog. A common figure signifying shame (17:43) and insignificance (2 Sam 9:8). David's self-deprecation is noteworthy.

24:16 my son. Validates their father-son relationship (cf. "my father" in v. 11). Saul's weeping reflects an emotional conviction, although this reaction is temporary.

24:17 Saul acknowledges his own sinful behavior toward David. He concedes his own guilt and David's innocence.

hands, but you did not kill me. 19 When a man finds his enemy, does he let him get away unharmed? May the LORD reward you well for the way you treated me today. 20 I know that you will surely be king[c] and that the kingdom[d] of Israel will be established in your hands. 21 Now swear[e] to me by the LORD that you will not kill off my descendants or wipe out my name from my father's family.[f]"

22 So David gave his oath to Saul. Then Saul returned home, but David and his men went up to the stronghold.[g]

David, Nabal and Abigail

25 Now Samuel died,[h] and all Israel assembled and mourned[i] for him; and they buried him at his home in Ramah.[j] Then David moved down into the Desert of Paran.[a]

2 A certain man in Maon,[k] who had property there at Carmel, was very wealthy. He had a thousand goats and three thousand sheep, which he was shearing in Carmel. 3 His name was Nabal and his wife's name was Abigail.[l] She was an intelligent and beautiful woman, but her husband was surly and mean in his dealings — he was a Calebite.[m]

4 While David was in the wilderness, he heard that Nabal was shearing sheep. 5 So he sent ten young men and said to them, "Go up to Nabal at Carmel and greet him in my name. 6 Say to him: 'Long life to you! Good health[n] to you and your household! And good health to all that is yours![o]

7 " 'Now I hear that it is sheep-shearing time. When your shepherds were with us, we did not mistreat[p] them, and the whole time they were at Carmel nothing of theirs was missing. 8 Ask your own servants and they will tell you. Therefore be favorable toward my men, since we come at a festive time. Please give your servants and your son David whatever[q] you can find for them.' "

9 When David's men arrived, they gave Nabal this message in David's name. Then they waited.

10 Nabal answered David's servants, "Who[r] is this David? Who is this son of Jesse? Many servants are breaking away from their masters these days. 11 Why should I take my bread[s] and water, and the meat I have slaughtered for my shearers, and give it to men coming from who knows where?"

12 David's men turned around and went back. When they arrived, they reported every word. 13 David said to his men, "Each of you strap on your sword!" So they did, and David strapped his on as well. About four hundred men went[t] up with David, while two hundred stayed with the supplies.[u]

14 One of the servants told Abigail, Nabal's wife, "David sent messengers from the wilderness to give our master his greetings,[v] but he hurled insults at them. 15 Yet these men were very good to us. They did not mistreat[w] us, and the whole time we were out in the fields near them nothing was missing.[x] 16 Night

[a] *1* Hebrew and some Septuagint manuscripts; other Septuagint manuscripts *Maon*

24:20 [c] 1Sa 23:17 [d] 1Sa 13:14
24:21 [e] Ge 21:23; 2Sa 21:1-9 [f] 1Sa 20:14-15
24:22 [g] 1Sa 23:29
25:1 [h] 1Sa 28:3 [i] Nu 20:29; Dt 34:8 [j] Ge 21:21; 2Ch 33:20
25:2 [k] Jos 15:55; 1Sa 23:24
25:3 [l] Pr 31:10 [m] Jos 15:13
25:6 [n] Ps 122:7; Lk 10:5 [o] 1Ch 12:18
25:7 [p] ver 15
25:8 [q] Ne 8:10
25:10 [r] Jdg 9:28
25:11 [s] Jdg 8:6
25:13 [t] 1Sa 23:13 [u] 1Sa 30:24
25:14 [v] 1Sa 13:10
25:15 [w] ver 7 [x] ver 21

24:19 Saul responds to David's proverb (v. 13) with his own traditional wisdom. But David acts contrary to Saul's proverb. **May the LORD reward you well.** Saul blesses David in the name of the Lord; it is a blessing of reciprocity: because David did a good thing to Saul (vv. 17–18), the Lord would reward David.

24:20 you will surely be king. Saul has known that David will replace him as king (23:17), but he affirms it to David. Saul's repentance and conviction are temporary; this appears to be his *modus operandi* (cf. 19:6–7).

24:22 David gave his oath. David swears to Saul that when he becomes king he will not destroy Saul's progeny (v. 21). Wiping out the line of the former king is a common act of a new monarch because the line would pose a threat to him. Saul returns to Gibeah, and David stays in the wilderness; this separation perhaps means that David does not fully trust Saul and so remains in hiding.

25:1–44 *David, Nabal, and Abigail.* After Samuel's death, David and his men remain in hiding in the wilderness areas of Paran and Maon. David seeks provisions from a man named Nabal because David's men had protected Nabal's herds from external dangers. Nabal treats David with contempt. David responds in force, but Nabal's wife, Abigail, dissuades David from acting rashly. She is a person of wisdom and prudence who serves as a foil to her foolish husband.

25:1 Samuel died. David loses perhaps his most powerful ally. **Desert of Paran.** Located way south in the northeast Sinai peninsula just to the northwest of the Gulf of Aqaba.

25:2 David and his men have returned from Paran and are near Maon again (see note on 23:24). **Carmel.** Lies about one mile (1.6 kilometers) north of Maon at Khirbet Kirmil. It is a Judahite site, but it may have some political leanings toward Saul's monarchy since Saul assembled a monument to himself there (15:12).

25:3 Nabal. Means "fool," and it fits his character. His wife, Abigail, is a contrasting figure: he is "surly and mean," but she is "intelligent and beautiful." The two contrast throughout the episode. **Calebite.** A descendant of the faithful spy in the conquest whose inheritance was the region of Hebron (Josh 14:13–14); Hebron is a mere eight miles (13 kilometers) north of Maon. Nabal is both wealthy and prominent (v. 2).

25:6 The Hebrew word *šālôm* ("peace" or "good health") appears three times in this verse. It reflects being respectful to the superlative degree.

25:10 son of Jesse. Nabal, like Saul (20:27), uses this title to belittle David. **Many servants are breaking away from their masters.** May subtly refer to David and the rabble that made up his forces (22:2).

25:12 This verse bears a staccato list of verbs that indicates that David's men left Nabal and went directly to David without getting off course.

25:13 four hundred men. Perhaps a standard militia unit (30:9–10; Gen 33:1).

25:14 A servant informs Abigail that her husband mistreated David's messengers, who had come with great respect and with a blessing. **hurled insults.** The Hebrew verb conveys the sense of "screamed."

25:16 [y] Ex 14:22; Job 1:10
25:17 [z] 1Sa 20:7
25:18 [a] 1Ch 12:40 [b] 2Sa 16:1
25:19 [c] Ge 32:20
25:21 [d] Ps 109:5
25:22 [e] 1Sa 3:17; 20:13 [f] 1Ki 14:10; 21:21; 2Ki 9:8
25:23 [g] 1Sa 20:41
25:25 [h] Pr 14:16
25:26 [i] ver 33 [j] Heb 10:30 [k] 2Sa 18:32
25:27 [l] Ge 33:11; 1Sa 30:26
25:28 [m] ver 24 [n] 2Sa 7:11,26 [o] 1Sa 18:17 [p] 1Sa 24:11
25:29 [q] Jer 10:18
25:30 [r] 1Sa 13:14
25:31 [s] Ge 40:14
25:32 [t] Ge 24:27; Ex 18:10; Lk 1:68
25:33 [u] ver 26
25:35 [v] Ge 19:21; 1Sa 20:42; 2Ki 5:19

and day they were a wall[y] around us the whole time we were herding our sheep near them. 17 Now think it over and see what you can do, because disaster is hanging over our master and his whole household. He is such a wicked[z] man that no one can talk to him."

18 Abigail acted quickly. She took two hundred loaves of bread, two skins of wine, five dressed sheep, five seahs[*a*] of roasted grain, a hundred cakes of raisins[a] and two hundred cakes of pressed figs, and loaded them on donkeys.[b] 19 Then she told her servants, "Go on ahead;[c] I'll follow you." But she did not tell her husband Nabal.

20 As she came riding her donkey into a mountain ravine, there were David and his men descending toward her, and she met them. 21 David had just said, "It's been useless—all my watching over this fellow's property in the wilderness so that nothing of his was missing. He has paid[d] me back evil for good. 22 May God deal with David,[*b*] be it ever so severely,[e] if by morning I leave alive one male[f] of all who belong to him!"

23 When Abigail saw David, she quickly got off her donkey and bowed down before David with her face to the ground.[g] 24 She fell at his feet and said: "Pardon your servant, my lord, and let me speak to you; hear what your servant has to say. 25 Please pay no attention, my lord, to that wicked man Nabal. He is just like his name—his name means Fool,[h] and folly goes with him. And as for me, your servant, I did not see the men my lord sent. 26 And now, my lord, as surely as the LORD your God lives and as you live, since the LORD has kept you from bloodshed[i] and from avenging[j] yourself with your own hands, may your enemies and all who are intent on harming my lord be like Nabal.[k] 27 And let this gift,[l] which your servant has brought to my lord, be given to the men who follow you.

28 "Please forgive[m] your servant's presumption. The LORD your God will certainly make a lasting[n] dynasty for my lord, because you fight the LORD's battles,[o] and no wrongdoing[p] will be found in you as long as you live. 29 Even though someone is pursuing you to take your life, the life of my lord will be bound securely in the bundle of the living by the LORD your God, but the lives of your enemies he will hurl[q] away as from the pocket of a sling. 30 When the LORD has fulfilled for my lord every good thing he promised concerning him and has appointed him ruler[r] over Israel, 31 my lord will not have on his conscience the staggering burden of needless bloodshed or of having avenged himself. And when the LORD your God has brought my lord success, remember[s] your servant."

32 David said to Abigail, "Praise[t] be to the LORD, the God of Israel, who has sent you today to meet me. 33 May you be blessed for your good judgment and for keeping me from bloodshed[u] this day and from avenging myself with my own hands. 34 Otherwise, as surely as the LORD, the God of Israel, lives, who has kept me from harming you, if you had not come quickly to meet me, not one male belonging to Nabal would have been left alive by daybreak."

35 Then David accepted from her hand what she had brought him and said, "Go home in peace. I have heard your words and granted[v] your request."

36 When Abigail went to Nabal, he was in the house holding a banquet like that of a king. He was in

[*a*] *18* That is, probably about 60 pounds or about 27 kilograms [*b*] *22* Some Septuagint manuscripts; Hebrew *with David's enemies*

25:17 wicked man. See notes on 1:16; 2:12.

25:22 male. This translates the Hebrew idiom "he who urinates on the wall," a vulgar and scornful expression used only to refer to killing a group of men (1 Kgs 14:10; 16:11; 21:21; 2 Kgs 9:8).

25:24 your servant ... your servant. Abigail is subservient. In contrast to her husband, she responds to David in a grateful, respectful way and takes responsibility for her husband's foolish actions.

25:25 wicked man. See note on v. 17. Abigail agrees with the servant's assessment of Nabal in v. 17. Nabal's name means "fool," illustrating the Latin proverb *Nomen est omen* ("name is omen"); his name fits his character.

25:26 As Abigail attempts to make amends for her husband's foolish acts, she now tries to direct David away from perpetuating an act of vengeance. This "bloodshed" would discredit David and call into question his fitness for kingship.

25:28 Abigail knows that David will become king because David is fighting "the LORD's battles." Abigail's assessment of David is in direct contrast with that of her husband (vv. 10–11).

25:29 Abigail draws a picture of a shepherd as a metaphor. She pleads that David be kept safe in the Lord's "bundle," or "pouch," and to the contrary that David's enemies be slung from the pouch by a slingshot (cf. 17:40), an image David would certainly appreciate!

25:32 David understands that Abigail's arrival is not happenstance; the Lord is orchestrating all these events. David, who vowed to take vengeance—perhaps rashly and foolishly (v. 22)—changes his mind. This is a good trait for a king.

25:35 granted your request. Hebrew "lifted up your face." This figure is not mere approval, but a sign of favor as well (Num 6:26).

25:36 a banquet like that of a king. Nabal acts the fool: gluttonous and drunk while the true king and his men are starving. Abigail prudently reveals nothing to him in his current state.

high[w] spirits and very drunk.[x] So she told[y] him nothing at all until daybreak. 37Then in the morning,
when Nabal was sober, his wife told him all these things, and his heart failed him and he became like
a stone. 38About ten days later, the LORD struck[z] Nabal and he died.

39When David heard that Nabal was dead, he said, "Praise be to the LORD, who has upheld my cause
against Nabal for treating me with contempt. He has kept his servant from doing wrong and has
brought Nabal's wrongdoing down on his own head."

Then David sent word to Abigail, asking her to become his wife. 40His servants went to Carmel and
said to Abigail, "David has sent us to you to take you to become his wife."

41She bowed down with her face to the ground and said, "I am your servant and am ready to serve
you and wash the feet of my lord's servants." 42Abigail[a] quickly got on a donkey and, attended by her
five female servants, went with David's messengers and became his wife. 43David had also married
Ahinoam[b] of Jezreel, and they both were his wives.[c] 44But Saul had given his daughter Michal, David's
wife, to Paltiel[a d] son of Laish, who was from Gallim.[e]

25:36 [w] 2Sa 13:23 [x] Pr 20:1; Isa 5:11,22; Hos 4:11 [y] ver 19
25:38 [z] 1Sa 26:10; 2Sa 6:7
25:42 [a] Ge 24:61-67
25:43 [b] Jos 15:56 [c] 1Sa 27:3; 30:5
25:44 [d] 2Sa 3:15 [e] Isa 10:30
26:1 [f] 1Sa 23:19 [g] Ps 54 Title
26:2 [h] 1Sa 13:2; 24:2
26:5 [i] 1Sa 14:50; 17:55
26:6 [j] Jdg 7:10-11; 1Ch 2:16
26:9 [k] 2Sa 1:14

David Again Spares Saul's Life

26 The Ziphites[f] went to Saul at Gibeah and said, "Is not David hiding[g] on the hill of Hakilah,
which faces Jeshimon?"

2So Saul went down to the Desert of Ziph, with his three thousand select Israelite troops, to search[h]
there for David. 3Saul made his camp beside the road on the hill of Hakilah facing Jeshimon, but David
stayed in the wilderness. When he saw that Saul had followed him there, 4he sent out scouts and learned
that Saul had definitely arrived.

5Then David set out and went to the place where Saul had camped. He saw where Saul and Abner[i]
son of Ner, the commander of the army, had lain down. Saul was lying inside the camp, with the army
encamped around him.

6David then asked Ahimelek the Hittite and Abishai son of Zeruiah,[j] Joab's brother, "Who will go
down into the camp with me to Saul?"

"I'll go with you," said Abishai.

7So David and Abishai went to the army by night, and there was Saul, lying asleep inside the camp
with his spear stuck in the ground near his head. Abner and the soldiers were lying around him.

8Abishai said to David, "Today God has delivered your enemy into your hands. Now let me pin him
to the ground with one thrust of the spear; I won't strike him twice."

9But David said to Abishai, "Don't destroy him! Who can lay a hand on the LORD's anointed[k] and

[a] 44 Hebrew *Palti*, a variant of *Paltiel*

25:37–38 Abigail's news devastates and undoes Nabal. Perhaps he has a stroke or heart attack; his life is clearly leaving him. **Nabal was sober.** A pun; lit. "the wine came out of Nabal" (Nabal sounds like the Hebrew word for "wineskin"). It perhaps pictures life flowing out of his body. A final blow comes ten days later as the Lord takes Nabal's life.
25:42 quickly. Used three other times (vv. 18,23,34) in this chapter regarding Abigail's activity. She is discerning and acts decisively. Nabal, on the other hand, acted rashly and impulsively.
25:43 Jezreel. Exact location uncertain, although it is in Judah somewhere near Maon, Ziph, and Carmel (Josh 15:55–56). Both Abigail and Ahinoam are from the tribe of Judah; perhaps David is attempting to solidify his political base in Judah through marriage.
25:44 The section ends on an ominous note. David has probably not seen his wife Michal, Saul's daughter, since the encounter of 19:11–17. Saul severs family ties with David by giving his daughter to another man. **Gallim.** Located about one mile (1.6 kilometers) south of Gibeah in the tribal land of Benjamin (Isa 10:28–30). Thus Saul gives his daughter to one of his own tribal members; he can act as a political animal.
26:1–25 *David Again Spares Saul's Life.* This episode echoes ch. 24. The two stories have different circumstances but essentially the same motif.
26:1–2 The Ziphites are annoyed with David's presence in their territory, so they seek to betray him again (23:19).
26:2 three thousand. The same number of soldiers he previously used to look for David (24:2).
26:5 camp. The Hebrew term has the sense of "round" or "perimeter"; Saul is lying down within this encirclement. He is well protected: the head of the army is lying next to him, and the entire army surrounds him. An intruder would have almost an impossible time trying to get to Saul.
26:6 Ahimelek the Hittite. Mentioned nowhere else in Scripture. **Abishai.** Joab's brother; he and Joab are sons of David's sister Zeruiah (1 Chr 2:13–17). Abishai is a soldier loyal to David, and he later becomes chief of the Thirty, the king's elite bodyguard (2 Sam 23:18). He is brave and violent (2 Sam 3:30; 21:16–17). It is no wonder that he volunteers for this hazardous duty to follow David into Saul's camp.
26:7–8 Saul's spear is pinned to the ground near Saul's head. Saul used this symbol of royal authority when he attempted to murder David (18:10–11; 19:10), and it provides an opportunity for David to exact ironic justice on Saul. Abishai recognizes the circumstance as a God-given opportunity (cf. 24:4). He then brags that he can kill Saul with one mere jab of the spear.
26:9 the LORD's anointed. David refuses to kill Saul based on the same grounds as 24:6 (see note there).

26:9 [l]1Sa 24:5
26:10 [m]1Sa 25:38; Ro 12:19 [n]Ge 47:29; Dt 31:14; Ps 37:13 [o]1Sa 31:6; 2Sa 1:1
26:12 [p]Ge 2:21; 15:12
26:17 [q]1Sa 24:16
26:18 [r]1Sa 24:9,11-14
26:19 [s]2Sa 16:11 [t]2Sa 14:16
26:20 [u]1Sa 24:14
26:21 [v]Ex 9:27; 1Sa 15:24 [w]1Sa 24:17
26:23 [x]Ps 62:12 [y]Ps 7:8; 18:20,24
26:24 [z]Ps 54:7
27:2 [a]1Sa 25:13 [b]1Sa 21:10 [c]1Ki 2:39

be guiltless?[l] 10 As surely as the LORD lives," he said, "the LORD himself will strike[m] him, or his time[n] will come and he will die,[o] or he will go into battle and perish. 11 But the LORD forbid that I should lay a hand on the LORD's anointed. Now get the spear and water jug that are near his head, and let's go."

12 So David took the spear and water jug near Saul's head, and they left. No one saw or knew about it, nor did anyone wake up. They were all sleeping, because the LORD had put them into a deep sleep.[p]

13 Then David crossed over to the other side and stood on top of the hill some distance away; there was a wide space between them. 14 He called out to the army and to Abner son of Ner, "Aren't you going to answer me, Abner?"

Abner replied, "Who are you who calls to the king?"

15 David said, "You're a man, aren't you? And who is like you in Israel? Why didn't you guard your lord the king? Someone came to destroy your lord the king. 16 What you have done is not good. As surely as the LORD lives, you and your men must die, because you did not guard your master, the LORD's anointed. Look around you. Where are the king's spear and water jug that were near his head?"

17 Saul recognized David's voice and said, "Is that your voice,[q] David my son?"

David replied, "Yes it is, my lord the king." 18 And he added, "Why is my lord pursuing his servant? What have I done, and what wrong[r] am I guilty of? 19 Now let my lord the king listen to his servant's words. If the LORD has incited you against me, then may he accept an offering.[s] If, however, people have done it, may they be cursed before the LORD! They have driven me today from my share in the LORD's inheritance[t] and have said, 'Go, serve other gods.' 20 Now do not let my blood fall to the ground far from the presence of the LORD. The king of Israel has come out to look for a flea[u]—as one hunts a partridge in the mountains."

21 Then Saul said, "I have sinned.[v] Come back, David my son. Because you considered my life precious[w] today, I will not try to harm you again. Surely I have acted like a fool and have been terribly wrong."

22 "Here is the king's spear," David answered. "Let one of your young men come over and get it. 23 The LORD rewards[x] everyone for their righteousness[y] and faithfulness. The LORD delivered you into my hands today, but I would not lay a hand on the LORD's anointed. 24 As surely as I valued your life today, so may the LORD value my life and deliver[z] me from all trouble."

25 Then Saul said to David, "May you be blessed, David my son; you will do great things and surely triumph."

So David went on his way, and Saul returned home.

David Among the Philistines

27 But David thought to himself, "One of these days I will be destroyed by the hand of Saul. The best thing I can do is to escape to the land of the Philistines. Then Saul will give up searching for me anywhere in Israel, and I will slip out of his hand."

2 So David and the six hundred men[a] with him left and went[b] over to Achish[c] son of Maok king of Gath. 3 David and his men settled in Gath with Achish. Each man had his family with him, and David

26:10 David will not put his hand against the king but gives Saul over to God's vengeance (cf. 24:12–13), as he had Nabal (25:38). **go into battle and perish.** Exactly what happens (ch. 31).

26:12 spear and water jug. Saul's personal equipment. David could have easily killed the king. He is bold and courageous, but he succeeds because the Lord put Saul's army into a deep stupor (cf. Gen 2:21; 15:12).

26:13 a wide space between them. Possibly not a mere physical description, but a summary of the differences in their characters and actions.

26:19 David continues to proclaim his innocence. Yet he is paying a steep price: he is being driven to give up a share in the Lord's "inheritance." **inheritance.** Refers to the land of promise (Deut 12:9; 15:4; Josh 14:9) and people of promise (1 Kgs 8:51,53). Even more dire, David is being pushed to go into other lands and to serve other gods.

26:20 David opines that Saul is making an extraordinary effort to destroy the life of one lowly citizen who is loyal to the king. **flea.** David also describes himself this way in 24:14.

26:21 I have sinned. Contra David (24:11), Saul confesses. But he has done this before (24:17), and it was a momentary pang of conscience.

26:25 The end of the matter is the same as ch. 24. Saul and David go their separate ways, and there appears to be a lingering distrust of one another (24:22).

27:1—28:2 *David Among the Philistines.* Because he fears Saul, David and his men flee into Philistine territory. They become a mercenary force for Achish, king of Gath (27:1–4), who deeds David the city of Ziklag as a base for David's military force (27:5–9). They do much damage to people living in the desert areas south of Philistia. But Achish is fooled because he believes David is attacking his own people and their allies (27:10–12). The Philistines then mobilize for war against Israel, and Achish expects David to participate (28:1–2). David is now between a rock and a hard place.

27:1–2 David is afraid and in despair, so he flees from Israel to seek protection from the Philistine enemy. He, his army, and their families go to Gath for safety under the guardianship of Achish. **Gath.** See note on 5:8. David previously acted insanely before Achish (21:10–15).

had his two wives:[d] Ahinoam of Jezreel and Abigail of Carmel, the widow of Nabal. 4When Saul was told
that David had fled to Gath, he no longer searched for him.
5Then David said to Achish, "If I have found favor in your eyes, let a place be assigned to me in one
of the country towns, that I may live there. Why should your servant live in the royal city with you?"
6So on that day Achish gave him Ziklag,[e] and it has belonged to the kings of Judah ever since. 7David
lived[f] in Philistine territory a year and four months.
8Now David and his men went up and raided the Geshurites,[g] the Girzites and the Amalekites.[h]
(From ancient times these peoples had lived in the land extending to Shur[i] and Egypt.) 9Whenever David attacked an area, he did not leave a man or woman alive,[j] but took sheep and cattle, donkeys and
camels, and clothes. Then he returned to Achish.
10When Achish asked, "Where did you go raiding today?" David would say, "Against the Negev of
Judah" or "Against the Negev of Jerahmeel[k]" or "Against the Negev of the Kenites.[l]" 11He did not leave a
man or woman alive to be brought to Gath, for he thought, "They might inform on us and say, 'This is
what David did.'" And such was his practice as long as he lived in Philistine territory. 12Achish trusted
David and said to himself, "He has become so obnoxious to his people, the Israelites, that he will be
my servant for life."

28 In those days the Philistines gathered[m] their forces to fight against Israel. Achish said to David,
"You must understand that you and your men will accompany me in the army."
2David said, "Then you will see for yourself what your servant can do."
Achish replied, "Very well, I will make you my bodyguard for life."

Saul and the Medium at Endor

3Now Samuel was dead,[n] and all Israel had mourned for him and buried him in his own town of
Ramah.[o] Saul had expelled the mediums and spiritists[p] from the land.
4The Philistines assembled and came and set up camp at Shunem,[q] while Saul gathered all Israel
and set up camp at Gilboa.[r] 5When Saul saw the Philistine army, he was afraid; terror filled his heart.
6He inquired[s] of the LORD, but the LORD did not answer him by dreams[t] or Urim[u] or prophets. 7Saul
then said to his attendants, "Find me a woman who is a medium,[v] so I may go and inquire of her."
"There is one in Endor,[w]" they said.
8So Saul disguised[x] himself, putting on other clothes, and at night he and two men went to the
woman. "Consult[y] a spirit for me," he said, "and bring up for me the one I name."
9But the woman said to him, "Surely you know what Saul has done. He has cut off[z] the mediums
and spiritists from the land. Why have you set a trap for my life to bring about my death?"

27:3 [d] 1Sa 25:43; 30:3
27:6 [e] Jos 15:31; 19:5; Ne 11:28
27:7 [f] 1Sa 29:3
27:8 [g] Jos 13:2,13 [h] Ex 17:8; 1Sa 15:7-8 [i] Ex 15:22
27:9 [j] 1Sa 15:3
27:10 [k] 1Sa 30:29; 1Ch 2:9,25 [l] Jdg 1:16
28:1 [m] 1Sa 29:1
28:3 [n] 1Sa 25:1 [o] 1Sa 7:17 [p] Ex 22:18; Lev 19:31; 20:27; Dt 18:10-11; 1Sa 15:23
28:4 [q] Jos 19:18; 2Ki 4:8 [r] 1Sa 31:1,3
28:6 [s] 1Sa 14:37; 1Ch 10:13-14; Pr 1:28 [t] Nu 12:6 [u] Ex 28:30; Nu 27:21
28:7 [v] Ac 16:16 [w] Jos 17:11
28:8 [x] 2Ch 18:29; 35:22 [y] Dt 18:10-11; 1Ch 10:13; Isa 8:19
28:9 [z] ver 3

27:5 David asks Achish, in a polite and respectful way, if he can have a base of operations. Clearly he wants to distance himself from the king and "the royal city" (Gath); he wants independence in an outlying area to perform his mercenary work as he sees fit.
27:6 Achish complies and deeds to David the town of Ziklag. **Ziklag.** The best candidate for its location is Tell Sera, which lies about 25 miles (40 kilometers) southwest of Gath in the southern part of the Shephelah (foothills) as it abuts the northern Negev. This great distance certainly gives David freedom to operate autonomously. **has belonged to the kings of Judah ever since.** Reflects authorship or editorship prior to the period of the exile (see Introduction: Date).
27:9 did not leave … alive. During David's raids on the southern tribal groups in the desert areas, he destroys all the people but takes lots of spoil. Certainly he gives part of the loot to Achish in tribute. This annihilation, which includes the Amalekites, contrasts with Saul's sparing the Amalekite king Agag (15:8).
27:10–12 David deceives Achish by saying he is raiding his own people and those friendly to Israel (cf. 30:26–29). He is doing nothing of the kind. He dupes Achish by killing all of the people he raids to prevent any refugees from telling Achish the truth.
28:1–2 David agrees to Achish's demand that he fight against Israel, but he is simply trying to buy time. The story picks up again in 29:1.
28:3–25 *Saul and the Medium at Endor.* The Philistines muster again for battle with Israel, and when Saul sees their army, he is in great fear (vv. 4–5). Saul inquires of the Lord regarding what to do, but he does not receive a response. So Saul engages a medium to tell him the future, although he had previously banned the presence of mediums in all Israel (v. 3). Samuel rises from the grave and gives Saul some sobering news.
28:3 Samuel was dead. The setting of the episode, although Samuel makes an appearance later in the account. During his reign Saul had expelled all the mediums and spiritists from the land of Israel; God prohibits those kind of practices (Lev 19:31; 20:6,27; Deut 18:9–12). **mediums.** They likely deal with the spirits of deceased ancestors.
28:4 Shunem. Located at modern Sulam in the eastern portion of the Jezreel Valley. This demonstrates the deep penetration of the Philistine army into Israel. **Gilboa.** Some eight miles (13 kilometers) southeast of Shunem.
28:6 Urim. See note on 14:41.
28:7 Because the Lord does not answer Saul's inquiries, the king resorts to seeking out a medium to divine the outcome of the military crisis. Saul's servants tell the king of a medium at Endor. **Endor.** Located four miles (6.4 kilometers) northeast of Shunem, where the Philistine army is camped. To consult with her, Saul must slip through enemy lines. By engaging a medium, Saul not only breaks his own law but God's. He is a lawmaker and a lawbreaker.
28:8 disguised … at night. Precautions to hide the king from both the Philistines and the medium.

28:14 [a]1Sa 15:27; 24:8
28:15 [b]ver 6; 1Sa 18:12
28:17 [c]1Sa 15:28
28:18 [d]1Sa 15:20 [e]1Ki 20:42
28:19 [f]1Sa 31:2
28:21 [g]Jdg 12:3; 1Sa 19:5; Job 13:14
28:23 [h]2Ki 5:13
29:1 [i]1Sa 28:1 [j]Jos 12:18; 1Sa 4:1 [k]2Ki 9:30
29:2 [l]1Sa 28:2

10 Saul swore to her by the LORD, "As surely as the LORD lives, you will not be punished for this."
11 Then the woman asked, "Whom shall I bring up for you?"
"Bring up Samuel," he said.
12 When the woman saw Samuel, she cried out at the top of her voice and said to Saul, "Why have
you deceived me? You are Saul!"
13 The king said to her, "Don't be afraid. What do you see?"
The woman said, "I see a ghostly figure[a] coming up out of the earth."
14 "What does he look like?" he asked.
"An old man wearing a robe[a] is coming up," she said.
Then Saul knew it was Samuel, and he bowed down and prostrated himself with his face to the ground.
15 Samuel said to Saul, "Why have you disturbed me by bringing me up?"
"I am in great distress," Saul said. "The Philistines are fighting against me, and God has departed[b] from
me. He no longer answers me, either by prophets or by dreams. So I have called on you to tell me what to do."
16 Samuel said, "Why do you consult me, now that the LORD has departed from you and become your
enemy? 17 The LORD has done what he predicted through me. The LORD has torn[c] the kingdom out of
your hands and given it to one of your neighbors — to David. 18 Because you did not obey[d] the LORD or
carry out his fierce wrath[e] against the Amalekites, the LORD has done this to you today. 19 The LORD will
deliver both Israel and you into the hands of the Philistines, and tomorrow you and your sons[f] will be
with me. The LORD will also give the army of Israel into the hands of the Philistines."
20 Immediately Saul fell full length on the ground, filled with fear because of Samuel's words. His
strength was gone, for he had eaten nothing all that day and all that night.
21 When the woman came to Saul and saw that he was greatly shaken, she said, "Look, your servant
has obeyed you. I took my life[g] in my hands and did what you told me to do. 22 Now please listen to
your servant and let me give you some food so you may eat and have the strength to go on your way."
23 He refused[h] and said, "I will not eat."
But his men joined the woman in urging him, and he listened to them. He got up from the ground
and sat on the couch.
24 The woman had a fattened calf at the house, which she butchered at once. She took some flour,
kneaded it and baked bread without yeast. 25 Then she set it before Saul and his men, and they ate. That
same night they got up and left.

Achish Sends David Back to Ziklag

29 The Philistines gathered[i] all their forces at Aphek,[j] and Israel camped by the spring in Jezreel.[k] 2 As
the Philistine rulers marched with their units of hundreds and thousands, David and his men were
marching at the rear[l] with Achish. 3 The commanders of the Philistines asked, "What about these Hebrews?"

[a] *13* Or *see spirits*; or *see gods*

28:12 No ritual is described; the medium apparently does not conjure up Samuel. **cried out at the top of her voice.** She is in shock when she sees Samuel, perhaps indicating that she is a false medium who really cannot speak with or raise up the dead and simply plies her trade through ventriloquism and sleight of hand. But Samuel actually comes up from the grave. There is no sense from the entire text that this is not really the great prophet.
28:13 ghostly figure. The Hebrew may refer to several ghostly figures. But Saul is interested in only one figure: Samuel.
28:14 robe. Perhaps this reminds Saul that he had ripped Samuel's robe, a sign that he would lose the kingdom (15:27–28). Saul will get the same message in this episode.
28:15 I … me … me … me … I … me. Saul is self-centered.
28:19 into the hands of the Philistines. Because Saul disobeyed the Lord in regard to the Amalekites (v. 18; see 15:19–23), God will give Israel over to the Philistines. This phrase appears twice for emphasis and certainty. **be with me.** It is not clear whether Samuel means anything more than simply the idea that Saul and his sons will join Samuel in the grave.
28:20–21 Saul collapses on the ground because of panic and fear; he has no physical or emotional strength left in him. The medium sees that Saul is "greatly shaken."
28:24 The woman believes that food will revive the terrified king, so she butchers a fattened calf and lays out a great feast. Ironically, the meal is fit for a king, and eating it is a monarch who will soon lose his kingship.
29:1–11 *Achish Sends David Back to Ziklag.* David and his men have joined the military entourage of the Philistines as they march to meet the Israelites in battle. But the commanders are suspicious of these Israelite mercenaries and prohibit them from taking part in the war. Achish trusts David and stands up for him to the commanders, but to no avail.
29:1 Aphek. Located at Ra's al-'Ain on the Great Trunk Road in the Sharon Plain. It is the northernmost town in the coastal plain of Philistia, so it is an appropriate place to muster troops to invade another country. **spring.** Perhaps the spring of Harod that sits near the foot of Mount Gilboa southeast of the city of Jezreel (Judg 7:1). **Jezreel.** The modern village of Zir'in, which lies between Megiddo and Beth Shan in the Jezreel Valley. See note on 25:43.
29:3–4 The military commanders of the Philistines vocally protest including David and his men with their army. They mistrust him, and

Achish replied, "Is this not David, who was an officer of Saul king of Israel? He has already been with
me for over a year,[m] and from the day he left Saul until now, I have found no fault in him."
4But the Philistine commanders were angry with Achish and said, "Send[n] the man back, that he
may return to the place you assigned him. He must not go with us into battle, or he will turn[o] against
us during the fighting. How better could he regain his master's favor than by taking the heads of our
own men? 5Isn't this the David they sang about in their dances:

> "'Saul has slain his thousands,
> and David his tens of thousands'?"[p]

6So Achish called David and said to him, "As surely as the LORD lives, you have been reliable, and I
would be pleased to have you serve with me in the army. From the day[q] you came to me until today, I
have found no fault in you, but the rulers[r] don't approve of you. 7Now turn back and go in peace; do
nothing to displease the Philistine rulers."
8"But what have I done?" asked David. "What have you found against your servant from the day I
came to you until now? Why can't I go and fight against the enemies of my lord the king?"
9Achish answered, "I know that you have been as pleasing in my eyes as an angel[s] of God; nevertheless, the Philistine commanders[t] have said, 'He must not go up with us into battle.' 10Now get up
early, along with your master's servants who have come with you, and leave[u] in the morning as soon
as it is light."
11So David and his men got up early in the morning to go back to the land of the Philistines, and
the Philistines went up to Jezreel.

David Destroys the Amalekites

30 David and his men reached Ziklag[v] on the third day. Now the Amalekites[w] had raided the Negev
and Ziklag. They had attacked Ziklag and burned it, 2and had taken captive the women and
everyone else in it, both young and old. They killed none of them, but carried them off as they went
on their way.
3When David and his men reached Ziklag, they found it destroyed by fire and their wives and sons
and daughters taken captive. 4So David and his men wept aloud until they had no strength left to weep.
5David's two wives[x] had been captured—Ahinoam of Jezreel and Abigail, the widow of Nabal of Carmel.
6David was greatly distressed because the men were talking of stoning[y] him; each one was bitter in spirit
because of his sons and daughters. But David found strength[z] in the LORD his God.
7Then David said to Abiathar[a] the priest, the son of Ahimelek, "Bring me the ephod.[b]" Abiathar
brought it to him, 8and David inquired[c] of the LORD, "Shall I pursue this raiding party? Will I overtake
them?"
"Pursue them," he answered. "You will certainly overtake them and succeed[d] in the rescue."
9David and the six hundred men[e] with him came to the Besor Valley, where some stayed behind.

29:3 [m] 1Sa 27:7; Da 6:5
29:4 [n] 1Ch 12:19 [o] 1Sa 14:21
29:5 [p] 1Sa 18:7; 21:11
29:6 [q] 1Sa 27:8-12 [r] ver 3
29:9 [s] 2Sa 14:17,20; 19:27 [t] ver 4
29:10 [u] 1Ch 12:19
30:1 [v] 1Sa 29:4,11 [w] 1Sa 15:7; 27:8
30:5 [x] 1Sa 25:43; 2Sa 2:2
30:6 [y] Ex 17:4; Jn 8:59 [z] Ps 27:14; 56:3-4,11; Ro 4:20
30:7 [a] 1Sa 22:20 [b] 1Sa 23:9
30:8 [c] 1Sa 23:2 [d] ver 18
30:9 [e] 1Sa 27:2

they anticipate that he will flip sides when the opportunity arises. The commanders directly disparage the Israelite mercenaries by calling them "these Hebrews" (v. 3). Achish energetically defends David to the leaders, but he is overruled and becomes the object of the commanders' anger.

29:5 This song is known not only in Israel (18:7) but also in Philistia: David is famous for killing the Philistine giant Goliath.

29:6 As surely as the LORD lives. An oath using the name of Israel's covenantal God. This is surprising, although it may simply be a special courtesy of the Philistine king to David. Achish then gives David the news that he is not allowed to accompany the Philistine army.

29:8 David protests his innocence. **my lord the king.** This may be a double entendre: Does it refer to Achish or Saul? If Achish, then David's wordplay is lost on Achish, who fully trusts him.

29:9 as an angel of God. David has not been angelic at all (27:8–11).

29:11 They go in opposite directions: David and his troops head south (ch. 30), and the Philistine army marches north (ch. 31).

30:1–31 *David Destroys the Amalekites.* After being dismissed from participating in the Philistine march against Israel, David returns to the town of Ziklag. He finds that the Amalekites have burned the city and kidnapped all the women and children. David inquires of the Lord, who tells him to pursue the Amalekites. He then wins a total victory over the Amalekites and recovers all the people and plunder. David's victory contrasts with Saul's defeat at the hands of the Philistines in ch. 31.

30:1–2 From Aphek to Ziklag is over 50 miles (80 kilometers), and it took David and his men three days to complete the trip. Ziklag is the town Achish, king of Gath, had previously deeded to David (see 27:5–6). The Amalekites knew the Philistine army had left, so they raided the southern region of Philistine land. By destroying Ziklag, the Amalekites may be retaliating for David's previous raids (27:8).

30:6 The soldiers hold David responsible for the loss of their families in spite of his own personal loss. He does not despair, but leans on the Lord for strength, fortitude, and courage.

30:9 From Ziklag to the Besor Valley is approximately 12–13 miles (19–21 kilometers).

30:10 [f] ver 9,21
30:12 [g] Jdg 15:19
30:14 [h] 2Sa 8:18; 1Ki 1:38,44; Eze 25:16; Zep 2:5 [i] ver 16; Jos 14:13; 15:13 [j] ver 1
30:16 [k] Lk 12:19 [l] ver 14
30:17 [m] 1Sa 11:11 [n] 1Sa 15:3
30:18 [o] Ge 14:16
30:21 [p] ver 10
30:24 [q] Nu 31:27; Jos 22:8
30:27 [r] Jos 7:2 [s] Jos 19:8 [t] Jos 15:48
30:28 [u] Jos 13:16 [v] Jos 15:50
30:29 [w] 1Sa 27:10 [x] Jdg 1:16; 1Sa 15:6
30:30 [y] Nu 14:45; Jdg 1:17 [z] Jos 15:42
30:31 [a] Jos 14:13; 2Sa 2:1,4

10 Two hundred of them were too exhausted[f] to cross the valley, but David and the other four hundred
continued the pursuit.
11 They found an Egyptian in a field and brought him to David. They gave him water to drink and
food to eat— 12 part of a cake of pressed figs and two cakes of raisins. He ate and was revived,[g] for he
had not eaten any food or drunk any water for three days and three nights.
13 David asked him, "Who do you belong to? Where do you come from?"
He said, "I am an Egyptian, the slave of an Amalekite. My master abandoned me when I became
ill three days ago. 14 We raided the Negev of the Kerethites,[h] some territory belonging to Judah and the
Negev of Caleb.[i] And we burned[j] Ziklag."
15 David asked him, "Can you lead me down to this raiding party?"
He answered, "Swear to me before God that you will not kill me or hand me over to my master, and
I will take you down to them."
16 He led David down, and there they were, scattered over the countryside, eating, drinking and reveling[k] because of the great amount of plunder[l] they had taken from the land of the Philistines and from
Judah. 17 David fought[m] them from dusk until the evening of the next day, and none of them got away,
except four hundred young men who rode off on camels and fled.[n] 18 David recovered[o] everything the
Amalekites had taken, including his two wives. 19 Nothing was missing: young or old, boy or girl, plunder
or anything else they had taken. David brought everything back. 20 He took all the flocks and herds, and
his men drove them ahead of the other livestock, saying, "This is David's plunder."
21 Then David came to the two hundred men who had been too exhausted[p] to follow him and who
were left behind at the Besor Valley. They came out to meet David and the men with him. As David and
his men approached, he asked them how they were. 22 But all the evil men and troublemakers among
David's followers said, "Because they did not go out with us, we will not share with them the plunder
we recovered. However, each man may take his wife and children and go."
23 David replied, "No, my brothers, you must not do that with what the LORD has given us. He has
protected us and delivered into our hands the raiding party that came against us. 24 Who will listen to
what you say? The share of the man who stayed with the supplies is to be the same as that of him who
went down to the battle. All will share alike.[q]" 25 David made this a statute and ordinance for Israel
from that day to this.
26 When David reached Ziklag, he sent some of the plunder to the elders of Judah, who were his
friends, saying, "Here is a gift for you from the plunder of the LORD's enemies."
27 David sent it to those who were in Bethel,[r] Ramoth[s] Negev and Jattir;[t] 28 to those in Aroer,[u] Siph-
moth, Eshtemoa[v] 29 and Rakal; to those in the towns of the Jerahmeelites[w] and the Kenites;[x] 30 to those
in Hormah,[y] Bor Ashan,[z] Athak 31 and Hebron;[a] and to those in all the other places where he and his
men had roamed.

30:14 Kerethites. Apparently Cretan mercenaries in the service of the Philistines at this time. They later seem to be equated with the Philistines (Ezek 25:16; Zeph 2:5). They are settled primarily in the southern regions of Philistia, as attested by pottery finds, and are therefore vulnerable to raiding parties from the desert. **Negev of Caleb.** The region just south of Hebron, where Caleb's inheritance was located (Josh 14:13).

30:16 The Amalekites are unprepared for David's retaliatory raid.

30:17 dusk. Can also mean "morning twilight" or "dawn" (Job 7:4; Ps 119:147). **evening of the next day.** The beginning of the next day. Therefore, it seems that David and his men fought the Amalekites from morning until evening of the same day. The Hebrew victory is complete, although a few hundred Amalekites escape.

30:18 recovered. Translated "succeed" in v. 8, where God said that David would certainly "succeed" in the rescue. God's message clearly comes to pass.

30:22 troublemakers. 1 Samuel often uses this Hebrew term of people who are good-for-nothings or useless, worthless people (see 1:16 ["wicked"]; 2:12 ["scoundrels"]; 10:27 ["scoundrels"]; 25:17,25 ["wicked"]). The complaint of these scoundrels is simply that if a person has not fought, then he should not share in the plunder of the Amalekites. He can recover his wife and children, but that is all.

30:23–24 David's response is twofold: (1) The victory was not by the hand of the fighting men, but by the hand of the Lord. The plunder thus belongs to the Lord, and all his people should share it. (2) The 200 men were not merely spent and lazy; they did their duty by guarding the army's equipment. David demonstrates magnanimity, a royal quality.

30:26–31 David does not keep his plunder but distributes it among his tribal people of Judah. The towns that receive a share and that we can identify are all located in the southern part of Judah to the south of Hebron: **Jattir.** Modern Khirbet 'Attir, about 13 miles (21 kilometers) southwest of Hebron. **Aroer.** Located at Khirbet 'Ar'ara, some 26 miles (42 kilometers) southwest of Hebron. **Eshtemoa.** Located at as-Samu', about 9 miles (14.5 kilometers) directly south of Hebron. **Hormah.** Located at Khirbet al-Mushash, 4 miles (6.5 kilometers) northwest of Aroer. This entire region is where David and his men lived and roamed when they were on the run from Saul. **Hebron.** See note on 2 Sam 2:1. It is listed last because this is where David will first assume his throne over Judah (2 Sam 2:1–4).

Aerial view of Beth Shan, where the Philistines fastened Saul's body to the wall (1 Sam 31:10).

Saul Takes His Life

31:1-13pp — 2Sa 1:4-12; 1Ch 10:1-12

31 Now the Philistines fought against Israel; the Israelites fled before them, and many fell dead on Mount Gilboa.[b] [2]The Philistines were in hot pursuit of Saul and his sons, and they killed his sons Jonathan, Abinadab and Malki-Shua. [3]The fighting grew fierce around Saul, and when the archers overtook him, they wounded[c] him critically.

[4]Saul said to his armor-bearer, "Draw your sword and run me through,[d] or these uncircumcised[e] fellows will come and run me through and abuse me."

But his armor-bearer was terrified and would not do it; so Saul took his own sword and fell on it. [5]When the armor-bearer saw that Saul was dead, he too fell on his sword and died with him. [6]So Saul and his three sons and his armor-bearer and all his men died together that same day.

[7]When the Israelites along the valley and those across the Jordan saw that the Israelite army had fled and that Saul and his sons had died, they abandoned their towns and fled. And the Philistines came and occupied them.

[8]The next day, when the Philistines came to strip the dead, they found Saul and his three sons fallen on Mount Gilboa. [9]They cut off his head and stripped off his armor, and they sent messengers

31:1 [b] 1Sa 28:4; 1Ch 10:1-12
31:3 [c] 2Sa 1:6
31:4 [d] Jdg 9:54; 2Sa 1:6,10 [e] 1Sa 14:6

31:1–13 *Saul Takes His Own Life.* The Philistine army completely routes the Israelites. They kill Saul's sons and leave Saul in desperate straits. He is wounded and then attempts suicide. After his death, the Philistines hang the bodies of Saul and his sons on the walls of their city (Beth Shan) as trophies. The soldiers of the Transjordanian town of Jabesh Gilead risk life and limb to rescue the bodies and bury them in their city.
31:1 The Philistine army marches about 50 miles (80 kilometers) from Aphek to Mount Gilboa, where they rout the Israelite forces under Saul.
31:2–3 After Saul's sons die, the battle presses on Saul; he is in a desperate and vulnerable situation. Some of the Philistine archers severely wound Saul.
31:4 abuse. Exod 10:2 translates this Hebrew term "dealt harshly." Saul wants to die before the Philistines capture and make sport of him; he wants to deprive them of the opportunity to ridicule him. Saul's armor-bearer refuses to kill him, perhaps because he is afraid to put his hand against the Lord's anointed (cf. 2 Sam 1:14). So Saul attempts to take his own life, although later one learns it was perhaps a failed suicide (2 Sam 1:6–10).
31:7 The Israelite forces stationed in Transjordan and lower Galilee witness the Philistines triumph over Saul. They lose heart and flee, abandoning their own cities. The Philistines then occupy their towns, controlling all the Jezreel Valley and the abutting Jordan Valley.
31:9–10 cut off his head ... put his armor in the temple of the Ashtoreths. An ironic reversal: this is what David did to the Philistine champion Goliath (17:51; 21:9).
31:9 messengers. It is likely the Philistines sent Saul's head and armor "throughout the land" as brutal, crass evidence of their victory (cf. 11:7; Judg 19:29).

31:9 [f] 2Sa 1:20 [g] Jdg 16:24
31:10 [h] Jdg 2:12-13; 1Sa 7:3 [i] Jos 17:11; 2Sa 21:12
31:11 [j] 1Sa 11:1
31:12 [k] 2Sa 2:4-7; 2Ch 16:14; Am 6:10
31:13 [l] 2Sa 21:12-14 [m] 1Sa 22:6 [n] 2Sa 1:12 [o] Ge 50:10

throughout the land of the Philistines to proclaim the news[f] in the temple of their idols and among
their people.[g] 10 They put his armor in the temple of the Ashtoreths[h] and fastened his body to the wall
of Beth Shan.[i]
11 When the people of Jabesh Gilead[j] heard what the Philistines had done to Saul, 12 all their valiant
men marched through the night to Beth Shan. They took down the bodies of Saul and his sons from
the wall of Beth Shan and went to Jabesh, where they burned[k] them. 13 Then they took their bones[l] and
buried them under a tamarisk[m] tree at Jabesh, and they fasted[n] seven days.[o]

31:10 Beth Shan. Located at modern Tell el-Husn; it sits at the confluence of the Jezreel and Jordan Valleys. The Philistines fasten Saul's corpse to the outer wall of the city as a trophy and token of their victory.

31:11 Jabesh Gilead. Located in Transjordan about 13 miles (21 kilometers) as the crow flies from Beth Shan. Saul rescued this town from the raiding Ammonites in one of his first acts as king (11:1–11), and the men of Jabesh Gilead reciprocate Saul's act on their behalf (v. 12).

31:13 After burning the flesh off the bodies of Saul and his sons (v. 12), the Jabesh Gileadites bury the bones beneath a tamarisk tree in their town. **tamarisk tree.** Perhaps symbolizes royalty. Saul held court under the same type of tree in Gibeah (22:6). **fasted.** Often accompanies the act of mourning (2 Sam 12:17–18).

INTRODUCTION TO 2 SAMUEL

See Introduction to 1 Samuel.

Below is an outline for 2 Samuel. For an outline of both 1 and 2 Samuel, see Introduction to 1 Samuel: Outline.

OUTLINE

XI. David's Early Success (2 Sam 1:1 — 10:19)
- A. David Hears of Saul's Death (1:1 – 16)
- B. David's Lament for Saul and Jonathan (1:17 – 27)
- C. David Anointed King Over Judah (2:1 – 7)
- D. War Between the Houses of David and Saul (2:8 — 3:5)
- E. Abner Goes Over to David (3:6 – 21)
- F. Joab Murders Abner (3:22 – 39)
- G. Ish-Bosheth Murdered (4:1 – 12)
- H. David Becomes King Over Israel (5:1 – 5)
- I. David Conquers Jerusalem (5:6 – 16)
- J. David Defeats the Philistines (5:17 – 25)
- K. The Ark Brought to Jerusalem (6:1 – 23)
- L. God's Promise to David (7:1 – 17)
- M. David's Prayer (7:18 – 29)
- N. David's Victories (8:1 – 14)
- O. David's Officials (8:15 – 18)
- P. David and Mephibosheth (9:1 – 13)
- Q. David Defeats the Ammonites (10:1 – 19)

XII. David's Grievous Sins (11:1 — 12:31)
- A. David and Bathsheba (11:1 – 27)
- B. Nathan Rebukes David (12:1 – 31)

XIII. Later Years of David's Rule (13:1 — 24:25)
- A. Amnon and Tamar (13:1 – 22)
- B. Absalom Kills Amnon (13:23 – 39)
- C. Absalom Returns to Jerusalem (14:1 – 33)
- D. Absalom's Conspiracy (15:1 – 12)
- E. David Flees (15:13 – 37)
- F. David and Ziba (16:1 – 4)

G. Shimei Curses David (16:5 – 14)
H. The Advice of Ahithophel and Hushai (16:15 – 23)
I. Hushai's Advice Is Accepted (17:1 – 23)
J. Absalom's Death (17:24 — 18:18)
K. David Mourns (18:19 — 19:8)
L. David Returns to Jerusalem (19:9 – 43)
M. Sheba Rebels Against David (20:1 – 22)
N. David's Officials (20:23 – 26)
O. The Gibeonites Avenged (21:1 – 14)
P. Wars Against the Philistines (21:15 – 22)
Q. David's Song of Praise (22:1 – 51)
R. David's Last Words (23:1 – 7)
S. David's Mighty Warriors (23:8 – 39)
T. David Enrolls the Fighting Men (24:1 – 17)
U. David Builds an Altar (24:18 – 25)

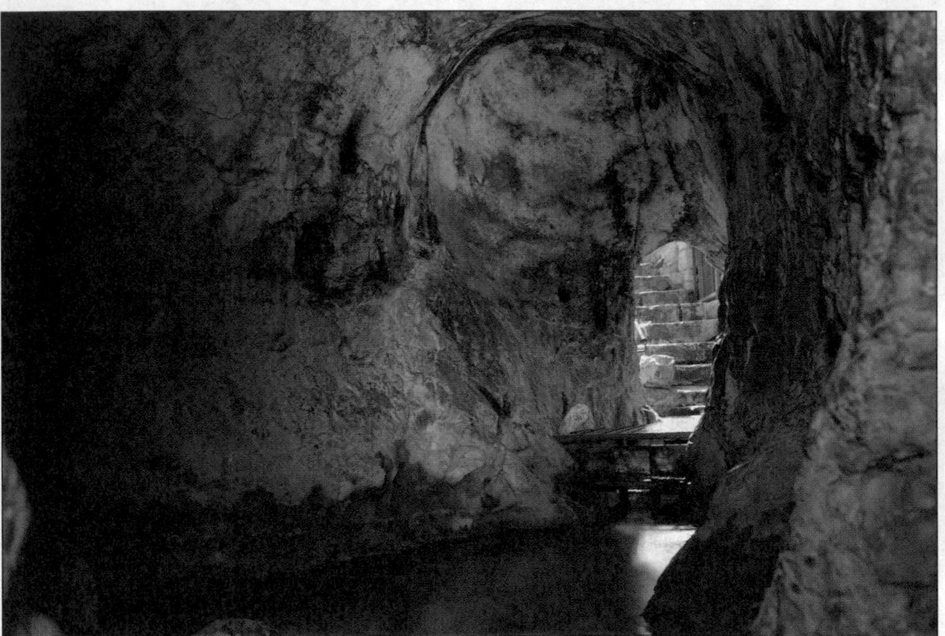

The Gihon spring (see 2 Sam 5:8) provided a natural water source for ancient Jerusalem.
Todd Bolen/www.BiblePlaces.com

2 SAMUEL

David Hears of Saul's Death

1:4-12pp — 1Sa 31:1-13; 1Ch 10:1-12

1 After the death[a] of Saul, David returned from striking down[b] the Amalekites and stayed in Ziklag
two days. 2On the third day a man[c] arrived from Saul's camp with his clothes torn and dust on his
head.[d] When he came to David, he fell to the ground to pay him honor.

3"Where have you come from?" David asked him.

He answered, "I have escaped from the Israelite camp."

4"What happened?" David asked. "Tell me."

"The men fled from the battle," he replied. "Many of them fell and died. And Saul and his son Jonathan are dead."

5Then David said to the young man who brought him the report, "How do you know that Saul and his son Jonathan are dead?"

6"I happened to be on Mount Gilboa,[e]" the young man said, "and there was Saul, leaning on his
spear, with the chariots and their drivers in hot pursuit. 7When he turned around and saw me, he called
out to me, and I said, 'What can I do?'

8"He asked me, 'Who are you?'

" 'An Amalekite,[f]' I answered.

9"Then he said to me, 'Stand here by me and kill me! I'm in the throes of death, but I'm still alive.'

10"So I stood beside him and killed him, because I knew that after he had fallen he could not survive. And I took the crown[g] that was on his head and the band on his arm and have brought them here to my lord."

1:1 [a] 1Sa 31:6 [b] 1Sa 30:17
1:2 [c] 2Sa 4:10 [d] 1Sa 4:12
1:6 [e] 1Sa 28:4; 31:2-4
1:8 [f] 1Sa 15:2; 30:13,17
1:10 [g] Jdg 9:54; 2Ki 11:12

1:1 — 10:19 *David's Early Success.* Near the beginning of 2 Samuel, the biblical author describes David's rise to the throne of Judah (2:1 – 4a) and eventually David's rule over all Israel (5:1 – 5). The early years of his rule are defined as ones of great military success because the Lord was with David and gave him victory over his foes (8:6,14).

1:1 – 16 *David Hears of Saul's Death.* The final two chapters of 1 Samuel, which recount David's victory over the Amalekites and Saul's defeat on Mount Gilboa, now come together. An Amalekite escapee from Saul's camp arrives at Ziklag to tell David that the Philistines have defeated Israel and that Saul and his sons have been killed. This man claims to have killed Saul, has evidence, and clearly expects a reward. He gets much more than he bargained for.

1:1 Chronologically, this follows David's defeat of the Amalekites in 1 Sam 30. David and his men return to Ziklag, the city that Achish, king of Gath, had deeded to David (1 Sam 27:6). **Amalekites.** A seminomadic people who roam the desert areas south of Judah and Philistia. They are a sworn enemy to Israel.

1:2 David and his men have been back in Ziklag for two days. On the third day, there is a surprising visitor to the city. The Hebrew uses a word that heightens the story's drama and the immediacy of the action. This man has escaped from Saul's camp at Mount Gilboa and fled to David at Ziklag. This is no small journey; it covers at least 50 miles (80 kilometers). **clothes torn and dust on his head.** Typical signs of sadness and mourning (13:31; 15:32; 1 Sam 4:12; Job 1:20).

1:6 I happened to be. The escapee underscores the chance encounter that he had with Saul. **leaning on his spear.** Some commentators argue that Saul is simply weak from pursuing the Philistines and supporting himself with his spear. But the circumstance appears much more dire (v. 9) because Saul's spear is actually in his body from the failed suicide attempt.

1:9 the throes of death. Saul is barely hanging on to life.

1:10 I ... killed him. Some suggest that the Amalekite tries to earn David's favor by lying. But David apparently believes his story (v. 14), and there is no reason we should not as well. **crown ... band.** Royal regalia that prove Saul is dead.

DAVID AMONG THE PHILISTINES

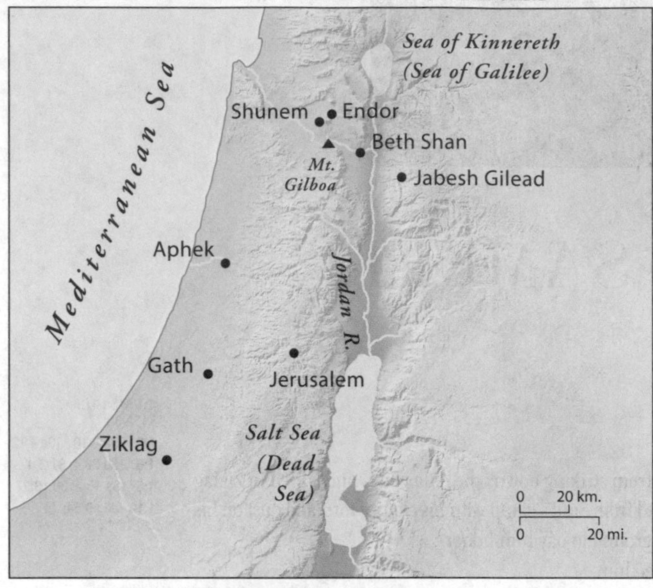

11 Then David and all the men with
him took hold of their clothes and tore[h]
them. 12 They mourned and wept and
fasted till evening for Saul and his son
Jonathan, and for the army of the LORD
and for the nation of Israel, because they
had fallen by the sword.

13 David said to the young man who
brought him the report, "Where are you
from?"

"I am the son of a foreigner, an Amalekite,[i]" he answered.

14 David asked him, "Why weren't you
afraid to lift your hand to destroy the
LORD's anointed?[j]"

15 Then David called one of his men
and said, "Go, strike him down!"[k] So he
struck him down, and he died.[l] 16 For David had said to him, "Your blood be on
your own head.[m] Your own mouth testified against you when you said, 'I killed
the LORD's anointed.'"

David's Lament for Saul and Jonathan

17 David took up this lament[n] concerning Saul and his son Jonathan, 18 and he ordered that the people of Judah be taught this lament of the bow (it is written in the Book of Jashar):[o]

19 "A gazelle[a] lies slain on your heights, Israel.
How the mighty have fallen![p]
20 "Tell it not in Gath,[q]
proclaim it not in the streets of Ashkelon,
lest the daughters of the Philistines[r] be glad,
lest the daughters of the uncircumcised rejoice.[s]

21 "Mountains of Gilboa,[t]
may you have neither dew nor rain,
may no showers fall on your terraced fields.[b][u]

1:11 [h] Ge 37:29; 2Sa 3:31; 13:31
1:13 [i] ver 8
1:14 [j] 1Sa 24:6; 26:9
1:15 [k] 2Sa 4:12 [l] 2Sa 4:10
1:16 [m] Lev 20:9; 2Sa 3:28-29; 1Ki 2:32; Mt 27:24-25; Ac 18:6
1:17 [n] 2Ch 35:25
1:18 [o] Jos 10:13; 1Sa 31:3
1:19 [p] ver 27
1:20 [q] Mic 1:10 [r] 1Sa 31:8 [s] Ex 15:20; 1Sa 18:6
1:21 [t] ver 6; 1Sa 31:1 [u] Eze 31:15

[a] *19 Gazelle* here symbolizes a human dignitary. [b] *21* Or / *nor fields that yield grain for offerings*

1:12 The people and David mourn for Saul, Jonathan, and the army and, indeed, all the people of the Lord. The wording of this last phrase is an example of hendiadys in which two names are given for one object with the purpose of emphasis. All of God's people have lost their king.
1:13 foreigner. The Hebrew term *gēr* refers to a sojourner who resides in the land of Israel and is subject to Israel's laws (Lev 19:33–34; 24:22). Thus, the Amalekite should have recognized Saul's position as king and not killed him.
1:16 The man condemned himself with his own mouth. His death reflects ironic justice: he took a life, so his life is taken (Exod 21:23; Deut 19:21). He is responsible for his own death.
1:17–27 *David's Lament for Saul and Jonathan.* David, the sweet psalmist of Israel (23:1), composes this lament as a funeral elegy for Saul and Jonathan. He is gracious to Saul although Saul's hostility toward David was infamous. David's love and loyalty to Jonathan make an endearing appearance in the lamentation.
1:17 took up. This is a funeral hymn or dirge. The elegy has the appearance of a psalm, including a superscription or heading ("lament of the bow," v. 18 and note).
1:18 the people of Judah be taught this lament of the bow. Some argue that David is encouraging the people to learn the bow as a weapon of war because the Philistines had just soundly defeated them. On the other hand, the title may simply refer to the bow of Jonathan in v. 22. **Book of Jashar.** An extrabiblical source no longer in existence; mentioned elsewhere only in Josh 10:12–13.
1:19 gazelle. The Hebrew word can also mean "glory" (they are homonyms); "gazelle" may be correct because v. 23 compares Saul and Jonathan to animals. **How the mighty have fallen!** A sorrowful sign that serves as the theme of the lament. It opens (here) and closes (v. 27) the lament.
1:20 proclaim it not. The Philistines "proclaim the news" of Saul's death throughout Philistia (1 Sam 31:9). David simply cannot stand the Philistine victory celebrations.
1:21 David curses the place where Saul and Jonathan were killed. He pleads for drought on the mountains of Gilboa as a sign of Israel's spiritual barrenness because of the loss of her leaders.

Mount Gilboa with surrounding farmland (2 Sam 1:21).

For there the shield of the mighty was despised,
the shield of Saul — no longer rubbed with oil.[v]

22 "From the blood[w] of the slain,
from the flesh of the mighty,
the bow[x] of Jonathan did not turn back,
the sword of Saul did not return unsatisfied.

23 Saul and Jonathan —
in life they were loved and admired,
and in death they were not parted.
They were swifter than eagles,[y]
they were stronger than lions.[z]

24 "Daughters of Israel,
weep for Saul,
who clothed you in scarlet and finery,
who adorned your garments with ornaments of gold.

25 "How the mighty have fallen in battle!
Jonathan lies slain on your heights.

26 I grieve for you, Jonathan my brother;[a]
you were very dear to me.
Your love for me was wonderful,[b]
more wonderful than that of women.

27 "How the mighty have fallen!
The weapons of war have perished!"[c]

1:21 [v] Isa 21:5
1:22 [w] Isa 34:3,7 [x] Dt 32:42; 1Sa 18:4
1:23 [y] Dt 28:49; Jer 4:13 [z] Jdg 14:18
1:26 [a] 1Sa 20:42 [b] 1Sa 18:1
1:27 [c] ver 19,25; 1Sa 2:4

1:24 scarlet. The color of luxury and prosperity (Prov 31:21).
1:26 David directly addresses Jonathan. There are no sexual overtones in this verse. Rather, it underscores the strong bond between the two men (1 Sam 20:17). David is in anguish over the loss of his kindred spirit.

2:1 [d] 1Sa 23:2,11-12 [e] Ge 13:18; 1Sa 30:31
2:2 [f] 1Sa 25:43; 30:5 [g] 1Sa 25:42
2:3 [h] 1Sa 27:2; 30:9
2:4 [i] 1Sa 30:31 [j] 1Sa 2:35; 2Sa 5:3-5 [k] 1Sa 31:11-13
2:5 [l] 1Sa 23:21
2:6 [m] Ex 34:6; 1Ti 1:16
2:8 [n] 1Sa 14:50 [o] Ge 32:2
2:9 [p] Nu 32:26 [q] Jdg 1:32 [r] 1Ch 12:29
2:11 [s] 2Sa 5:5
2:12 [t] Jos 18:25
2:13 [u] 2Sa 8:16; 1Ch 2:16; 11:6

David Anointed King Over Judah

2 In the course of time, David inquired[d] of the LORD. "Shall I go up to one of the towns of Judah?" he asked.

The LORD said, "Go up."

David asked, "Where shall I go?"

"To Hebron,"[e] the LORD answered.

2 So David went up there with his two wives,[f] Ahinoam of Jezreel and Abigail,[g] the widow of Nabal of Carmel. 3 David also took the men who were with him,[h] each with his family, and they settled in Hebron and its towns. 4 Then the men of Judah came to Hebron,[i] and there they anointed[j] David king over the tribe of Judah.

When David was told that it was the men from Jabesh Gilead[k] who had buried Saul, 5 he sent messengers to them to say to them, "The LORD bless[l] you for showing this kindness to Saul your master by burying him. 6 May the LORD now show you kindness and faithfulness,[m] and I too will show you the same favor because you have done this. 7 Now then, be strong and brave, for Saul your master is dead, and the people of Judah have anointed me king over them."

War Between the Houses of David and Saul

3:2-5pp — 1Ch 3:1-4

8 Meanwhile, Abner[n] son of Ner, the commander of Saul's army, had taken Ish-Bosheth son of Saul and brought him over to Mahanaim.[o] 9 He made him king over Gilead,[p] Ashuri[q] and Jezreel, and also over Ephraim, Benjamin and all Israel.[r]

10 Ish-Bosheth son of Saul was forty years old when he became king over Israel, and he reigned two years. The tribe of Judah, however, remained loyal to David. 11 The length of time David was king in Hebron over Judah was seven years and six months.[s]

12 Abner son of Ner, together with the men of Ish-Bosheth son of Saul, left Mahanaim and went to Gibeon.[t] 13 Joab[u] son of Zeruiah and David's men went out and met them at the pool of Gibeon. One group sat down on one side of the pool and one group on the other side.

14 Then Abner said to Joab, "Let's have some of the young men get up and fight hand to hand in front of us."

"All right, let them do it," Joab said.

15 So they stood up and were counted off — twelve men for Benjamin and Ish-Bosheth son of Saul, and twelve for David. 16 Then each man grabbed his opponent by the head and thrust his dagger

---

2:1–7 *David Anointed King Over Judah.* David inquires of the Lord whether he should return to his tribal region of Judah after the death of Saul. The Lord tells him to go to Hebron, and there he will rule over Judah as king for seven and a half years.

2:1 Hebron. An important city in the Judean hill country about 19 miles (30.5 kilometers) southwest of Jerusalem. It is one of the Levitical cities and a city of refuge (Josh 21:11–13). This is also the burial place of the patriarchs.

2:4 The people of Judah act independently from the other tribes of Israel.

2:7 brave. King Saul is dead, but the people of Jabesh Gilead must courageously stand against the Philistines and other enemies. David appears to offer his help now that he has been anointed king over Judah.

2:8—3:5 *War Between the Houses of David and Saul.* While David has become king over Judah, Saul's son Ish-Bosheth is anointed king over the rest of Israel. Abner, Saul's cousin, is the real power behind Israel's throne. As the commander of the northern army, he takes his troops to face the forces of Judah under the command of Joab, and Judah routs Israel. This is the first divided monarchy, and the house of David dominates the house of Saul.

2:8–9 Abner, who was Saul's army commander (1 Sam 14:50), takes Saul's son Ish-Bosheth to Mahanaim and anoints him king over "all Israel." After Saul's death, Abner attempts to fill the power vacuum by manipulating the unassertive Ish-Bosheth. Ish-Bosheth is thus a mere pawn in Abner's seething ambition. **Mahanaim.** Perhaps located at Tell ad-Dahab ash-Sharqiya, about seven miles (11.2 kilometers) east of the Jordan River on the Jabbok River in Gilead. Crowning a new king in Transjordan underscores that Abner's move is precarious.

2:10 Israel and the house of Judah are a divided Hebrew monarchy for two years before David rules all Israel. The kingship formula confirms that Ish-Bosheth is a true king (cf. 2 Kgs 8:17,26; 12:1; 14:2; etc.).

2:12 Abner and his troops cross the Jordan River into the central hill country of Israel to the town of Gibeon. **Gibeon.** Located seven miles (11.2 kilometers) northwest of Jerusalem in the tribal inheritance of Benjamin (Josh 18:25).

2:13 pool of Gibeon. Archaeologists have discovered this pool. It measures 36 feet by 36 feet (11 meters by 11 meters), and its purpose was to store water for the city. Later, in the ninth century BC, Ahab constructed a massive water system around the pool.

2:14–15 Abner proposes to Joab that they have a gladiatorial contest between the two armies: each side chooses 12 young men to engage in single combat. All 12 of Israel's men are from the tribe of Benjamin, the tribe of Saul and Ish-Bosheth. Abner attempts to use home field advantage because the contest occurs in Benjamin.

2:16 fell down together. They all died. **Helkath Hazzurim.** This name means "field of the sword edges"; it commemorates the deadly conflict at Gibeon. See NIV text note.

into his opponent's side, and they fell down together. So that place in Gibeon was called Helkath
Hazzurim.[a]
17 The battle that day was very fierce, and Abner and the Israelites were defeated[v] by David's men.
18 The three sons of Zeruiah[w] were there: Joab,[x] Abishai[y] and Asahel.[z] Now Asahel was as fleet-footed
as a wild gazelle.[a] 19 He chased Abner, turning neither to the right nor to the left as he pursued him.
20 Abner looked behind him and asked, "Is that you, Asahel?"
"It is," he answered.
21 Then Abner said to him, "Turn aside to the right or to the left; take on one of the young men and
strip him of his weapons." But Asahel would not stop chasing him.
22 Again Abner warned Asahel, "Stop chasing me! Why should I strike you down? How could I look
your brother Joab in the face?"[b]
23 But Asahel refused to give up the pursuit; so Abner thrust the butt of his spear into Asahel's stomach,[c] and the spear came out through his back. He fell there and died on the spot. And every man
stopped when he came to the place where Asahel had fallen and died.[d]
24 But Joab and Abishai pursued Abner, and as the sun was setting, they came to the hill of Ammah,
near Giah on the way to the wasteland of Gibeon. 25 Then the men of Benjamin rallied behind Abner.
They formed themselves into a group and took their stand on top of a hill.
26 Abner called out to Joab, "Must the sword devour[e] forever? Don't you realize that this will end in
bitterness? How long before you order your men to stop pursuing their fellow Israelites?"
27 Joab answered, "As surely as God lives, if you had not spoken, the men would have continued
pursuing them until morning."
28 So Joab[f] blew the trumpet,[g] and all the troops came to a halt; they no longer pursued Israel, nor
did they fight anymore.
29 All that night Abner and his men marched through the Arabah. They crossed the Jordan, continued
through the morning hours[b] and came to Mahanaim.[h]
30 Then Joab stopped pursuing Abner and assembled the whole army. Besides Asahel, nineteen of David's men were found missing. 31 But David's men had killed three hundred and sixty Benjamites who
were with Abner. 32 They took Asahel and buried him in his father's tomb[i] at Bethlehem. Then Joab and
his men marched all night and arrived at Hebron by daybreak.

3 The war between the house of Saul and the house of David lasted a long time.[j] David grew stronger
and stronger,[k] while the house of Saul grew weaker and weaker.[l]

2 Sons were born to David in Hebron:
His firstborn was Amnon the son of Ahinoam[m] of Jezreel;
3 his second, Kileab the son of Abigail[n] the widow of Nabal of Carmel;
the third, Absalom[o] the son of Maakah daughter of Talmai king of Geshur;[p]
4 the fourth, Adonijah[q] the son of Haggith;
the fifth, Shephatiah the son of Abital;

2:17 [v] 2Sa 3:1
2:18 [w] 2Sa 3:39 [x] 2Sa 3:30 [y] 1Sa 26:6 [z] 1Ch 2:16 [a] 1Ch 12:8
2:22 [b] 2Sa 3:27
2:23 [c] 2Sa 3:27; 4:6 [d] 2Sa 20:12
2:26 [e] Dt 32:42; Jer 46:10,14
2:28 [f] 2Sa 18:16 [g] Jdg 3:27
2:29 [h] ver 8
2:32 [i] Ge 49:29
3:1 [j] 1Ki 14:30 [k] 2Sa 5:10 [l] 2Sa 2:17
3:2 [m] 1Sa 25:43; 1Ch 3:1-3
3:3 [n] 1Sa 25:42 [o] 2Sa 13:1,28 [p] 1Sa 27:8; 2Sa 13:37; 14:32; 15:8
3:4 [q] 1Ki 1:5,11

[a] *16 Helkath Hazzurim* means *field of daggers* or *field of hostilities.* [b] *29* See Septuagint; the meaning of the Hebrew for this phrase is uncertain.

2:17 that day. Almost immediately the two full armies engage in warfare.
2:18–19 Asahel. David's nephew and one of the Thirty (23:24). His great attribute as a warrior is speed; he is like "a wild gazelle," a type of antelope that is swift and graceful. The Hebrew text may actually say that he is as "a gazelle in the open field," that is, one running unhindered through the country. In the heat of battle, Asahel is chasing down Abner; in his pursuit he is not distracted nor does he deviate from his task.
2:23 Abner cannot outrun Asahel, so he apparently stops suddenly, thrusts his spear backward, and impales Asahel with the butt end of the weapon. The soldiers who witness the place of Asahel's death are frozen in place, perhaps stunned by the death of one so important in Judah's army.
2:24–26 The Benjamites are on one hill supporting Abner, and Joab and the Judahites are on another hill. Abner's three rhetorical questions make one point: Must the fighting and slaughter keep going until it reaches a bitter conclusion?
2:28 blew the trumpet. To cease hostilities, a common practice (18:16; 20:22).
2:29 All that night. Abner's army travels all night to return to Mahanaim across the Jordan River. **through the morning hours.** Uncertain in Hebrew, although it appears to derive from a verb that means "to cut in two." Perhaps it refers to a ravine that cuts through the mountains.
2:32 Joab and his men travel from Bethlehem to Hebron in one night, an impressive 23-mile march after a heated battle.
3:1 The lengthy war drags on. David's forces are making headway.
3:2–5 A list of David's sons born in Hebron, all born to different women. The biblical writer makes no comment regarding the morality of polygamy here. The list demonstrates that David, in contrast to Saul, is becoming stronger in his kingdom.

3:7 [r] 2Sa 16:21-22 [s] 2Sa 21:8-11
3:8 [t] 1Sa 24:14; 2Sa 9:8; 16:9
3:9 [u] 1Sa 15:28; 1Ki 19:2
3:10 [v] Jdg 20:1; 1Sa 3:20
3:13 [w] Ge 43:5; 1Sa 18:20
3:14 [x] 1Sa 18:27
3:15 [y] Dt 24:1-4 [z] 1Sa 25:44
3:16 [a] 2Sa 16:5; 19:16
3:17 [b] Jdg 11:11
3:18 [c] 1Sa 9:16 [d] 1Sa 15:28; 2Sa 8:6
3:19 [e] 1Sa 10:20-21; 1Ch 12:2,16,29
3:21 [f] ver 10,12 [g] 1Ki 11:37

5 and the sixth, Ithream the son of David's wife Eglah.
These were born to David in Hebron.

Abner Goes Over to David

6 During the war between the house of Saul and the house of David, Abner had been strengthening
his own position in the house of Saul. 7 Now Saul had had a concubine[r] named Rizpah[s] daughter of
Aiah. And Ish-Bosheth said to Abner, "Why did you sleep with my father's concubine?"
8 Abner was very angry because of what Ish-Bosheth said. So he answered, "Am I a dog's head[t]—on
Judah's side? This very day I am loyal to the house of your father Saul and to his family and friends. I
haven't handed you over to David. Yet now you accuse me of an offense involving this woman! 9 May God
deal with Abner, be it ever so severely, if I do not do for David what the LORD promised[u] him on oath 10 and
transfer the kingdom from the house of Saul and establish David's throne over Israel and Judah from Dan
to Beersheba."[v] 11 Ish-Bosheth did not dare to say another word to Abner, because he was afraid of him.
12 Then Abner sent messengers on his behalf to say to David, "Whose land is it? Make an agreement
with me, and I will help you bring all Israel over to you."
13 "Good," said David. "I will make an agreement with you. But I demand one thing of you: Do not
come into my presence unless you bring Michal daughter of Saul when you come to see me."[w] 14 Then
David sent messengers to Ish-Bosheth son of Saul, demanding, "Give me my wife Michal,[x] whom I betrothed to myself for the price of a hundred Philistine foreskins."
15 So Ish-Bosheth gave orders and had her taken away from her husband[y] Paltiel[z] son of Laish. 16 Her
husband, however, went with her, weeping behind her all the way to Bahurim.[a] Then Abner said to him,
"Go back home!" So he went back.
17 Abner conferred with the elders[b] of Israel and said, "For some time you have wanted to make David
your king. 18 Now do it! For the LORD promised David, 'By my servant David I will rescue my people Israel
from the hand of the Philistines[c] and from the hand of all their enemies.[d]'"
19 Abner also spoke to the Benjamites in person. Then he went to Hebron to tell David everything that
Israel and the whole tribe of Benjamin[e] wanted to do. 20 When Abner, who had twenty men with him, came
to David at Hebron, David prepared a feast for him and his men. 21 Then Abner said to David, "Let me go at
once and assemble all Israel for my lord the king, so that they may make a covenant[f] with you, and that
you may rule over all that your heart desires."[g] So David sent Abner away, and he went in peace.

Joab Murders Abner

22 Just then David's men and Joab returned from a raid and brought with them a great deal of plunder. But Abner was no longer with David in Hebron, because David had sent him away, and he had gone
in peace. 23 When Joab and all the soldiers with him arrived, he was told that Abner son of Ner had come
to the king and that the king had sent him away and that he had gone in peace.

3:6–21 *Abner Goes Over to David.* Ish-Bosheth accuses Abner, the commander of the Israelite forces, of having sexual relations with one of Saul's concubines (v. 7). Abner responds with incredulity and argues that he has always been loyal to the house of Saul (v. 8). From this point on, Abner seeks to betray Ish-Bosheth and turn the Israelite kingdom over to David.

3:6 Abner appears to be the real power behind Ish-Bosheth's throne, and his influence continues to grow. **had been strengthening his own position.** Abner is self-serving and seeks this power.

3:7–8 concubine. A legitimate wife of a lower status, i.e., a second-level wife. Ish-Bosheth accuses Abner of having sexual relations with Rizpah, one of Saul's concubines (21:8). If true, Abner's action may be seen as a further grasp for power and authority (12:8; 16:21–22; 1 Kgs 2:22). Abner does not outright deny the charge, but responds with anger: **Am I a dog's head—on Judah's side?** A dog is an unclean animal of low status, so Abner asks if he is a lowly traitor serving the enemy Judahites.

3:9–10 May God deal with … if I do not. Abner makes a strong oath that is a self-curse formula (1 Sam 20:13; Ruth 1:17). He swears to help David become king over all Israel. **from Dan to Beersheba.** See note on 1 Sam 3:20.

3:13–14 bring Michal. David agrees to make a covenant with Abner based on one condition: Abner must bring Michal, David's wife and Saul's daughter, to him. Saul had taken Michal from David and given her to a Benjamite name Paltiel (1 Sam 25:44). No divorce has occurred; she is still David's wife. This move symbolizes that David is a rightful heir to Saul's throne.

3:17 For some time. This expression reflects the past (cf. 1 Sam 4:7; Gen 31:2; Exod 21:29).

3:19 Abner makes the effort to speak specifically to the tribe of Benjamin, the tribe of Saul, Ish-Bosheth, and the warriors who recently fought against Judah (2:15,25). Abner needs their support to make the transition happen.

3:21 in peace. David and Abner separate on good terms. This sets up the next episode in which Joab seeks revenge on Abner (vv. 22–39).

3:22–39 *Joab Murders Abner.* Joab kills Abner in revenge for the death of his brother Asahel.

24 So Joab went to the king and said, "What have you done? Look, Abner came to you. Why did you let him go? Now he is gone! 25 You know Abner son of Ner; he came to deceive you and observe your movements and find out everything you are doing."

26 Joab then left David and sent messengers after Abner, and they brought him back from the cistern at Sirah. But David did not know it. 27 Now when Abner[h] returned to Hebron, Joab took him aside into an inner chamber, as if to speak with him privately. And there, to avenge the blood of his brother Asahel, Joab stabbed him in the stomach, and he died.[i]

28 Later, when David heard about this, he said, "I and my kingdom are forever innocent[j] before the LORD concerning the blood of Abner son of Ner. 29 May his blood[k] fall on the head of Joab and on his whole family![l] May Joab's family never be without someone who has a running sore[m] or leprosy[a] or who leans on a crutch or who falls by the sword or who lacks food."

30 (Joab and his brother Abishai murdered Abner because he had killed their brother Asahel in the battle at Gibeon.)

31 Then David said to Joab and all the people with him, "Tear your clothes and put on sackcloth[n] and walk in mourning[o] in front of Abner." King David himself walked behind the bier. 32 They buried Abner in Hebron, and the king wept[p] aloud at Abner's tomb. All the people wept also.

33 The king sang this lament[q] for Abner:

"Should Abner have died as the lawless die?
34 Your hands were not bound,
your feet were not fettered.
You fell as one falls before the wicked."

And all the people wept over him again.

35 Then they all came and urged David to eat something while it was still day; but David took an oath, saying, "May God deal with me, be it ever so severely,[r] if I taste bread[s] or anything else before the sun sets!"

36 All the people took note and were pleased; indeed, everything the king did pleased them. 37 So on that day all the people there and all Israel knew that the king had no part[t] in the murder of Abner son of Ner.

38 Then the king said to his men, "Do you not realize that a commander and a great man has fallen[u] in Israel this day? 39 And today, though I am the anointed king, I am weak, and these sons of Zeruiah[v] are too strong for me.[w] May the LORD repay[x] the evildoer according to his evil deeds!"

Ish-Bosheth Murdered

4 When Ish-Bosheth son of Saul heard that Abner[y] had died in Hebron, he lost courage, and all Israel became alarmed. 2 Now Saul's son had two men who were leaders of raiding bands. One was named Baanah and the other Rekab; they were sons of Rimmon the Beerothite from the tribe of

3:27 [h] 2Sa 2:8 [i] 2Sa 2:22; 20:9-10; 1Ki 2:5
3:28 [j] ver 37; Dt 21:9
3:29 [k] Lev 20:9 [l] 1Ki 2:31-33 [m] Lev 15:2
3:31 [n] 2Sa 1:2,11; Ps 30:11; Isa 20:2 [o] Ge 37:34
3:32 [p] Nu 14:1; Pr 24:17
3:33 [q] 2Sa 1:17
3:35 [r] Ru 1:17; 1Sa 3:17 [s] 1Sa 31:13; 2Sa 1:12; 12:17; Jer 16:7
3:37 [t] ver 28
3:38 [u] 2Sa 1:19
3:39 [v] 2Sa 2:18 [w] 2Sa 19:5-7 [x] 1Ki 2:5-6, 33-34; Ps 41:10; 101:8
4:1 [y] 2Sa 3:27; Ezr 4:4

[a] 29 The Hebrew for *leprosy* was used for various diseases affecting the skin.

3:24–25 Joab is incredulous that David has made peace with Abner and sent him on his way. He argues that Abner is really a spy for Israel and attempting to discover David's military movements and actions. **your movements.** Lit. "your going out and your coming in"; a common *merism* (a literary figure in which two polar opposites are all-inclusive) for military maneuvers and strategies (1 Sam 18:13,16; 29:6; Josh 14:11). This is mere pretext for Joab, who has revenge in his heart because Abner killed his brother Asahel.

3:26 Sirah. According to Josephus, this site lies 2.5 miles (4 kilometers) north of Hebron. **David did not know it.** Joab acts independently of the king and calls Abner back to Hebron, so David is innocent regarding what follows.

3:27 Joab and his brother Abishai (v. 30) lure Abner into the inner chamber of the town gate. City gates at this time are elaborate structures with multiple rooms. They enter one of the secluded rooms, and Joab stabs Abner in the stomach, which is ironic justice because Abner killed Asahel by piercing him in the stomach (2:23).

3:29 When David hears of the murder, he responds with a maledictory oath against Joab and his family. He curses the house of Joab that it would always have people who are ritually unclean: **running sore.** A discharge (Lev 15). **leprosy.** A skin disease (Lev 13–14). **leans on a crutch.** Another possible understanding of the Hebrew word used here is "holds a spindle"; used of women who spin thread. Perhaps it means "May the men of Joab's house be fit only to do women's work!"

3:31 Tear your clothes and put on sackcloth. Common signs of grief and sorrow (Gen 37:34; Josh 7:6; 1 Kgs 20:31; Job 1:20). **bier.** A burial stretcher or bed.

3:33–34 This is the second lament that David composes in 2 Samuel (see 1:19–27). As he did with Jonathan (1:26), he directly addresses Abner.

3:36 David's popularity among the people of Judah is strong.

3:39 David contrasts himself with Joab and Abishai. **weak ... strong.** Antonyms that signify gentleness or tenderness in opposition to hardness or brutality. David is not weaker than Joab and Abishai, but the latter are much more violent and savage. David calls for ironic justice so that their evil and violence would turn back on their own heads.

4:1–12 *Ish-Bosheth Murdered.* Two men who are probably not native Israelites murder Saul's son Ish-Bosheth, thus removing David's rival for king over Israel.

4:1 The original text does not include the name "Ish-Bosheth," indicating

Benjamin — Beeroth[z] is considered part of Benjamin, 3 because the people of Beeroth fled to Gittaim[a]
and have resided there as foreigners to this day.
4 (Jonathan[b] son of Saul had a son who was lame in both feet. He was five years old when the news[c]
about Saul and Jonathan came from Jezreel. His nurse picked him up and fled, but as she hurried to
leave, he fell and became disabled.[d] His name was Mephibosheth.)[e]
5 Now Rekab and Baanah, the sons of Rimmon the Beerothite, set out for the house of Ish-Bosheth,[f]
and they arrived there in the heat of the day while he was taking his noonday rest. 6 They went into the
inner part of the house as if to get some wheat, and they stabbed[g] him in the stomach. Then Rekab and
his brother Baanah slipped away.
7 They had gone into the house while he was lying on the bed in his bedroom. After they stabbed
and killed him, they cut off his head. Taking it with them, they traveled all night by way of the Arabah.
8 They brought the head of Ish-Bosheth to David at Hebron and said to the king, "Here is the head of
Ish-Bosheth son of Saul,[h] your enemy, who tried to kill you. This day the LORD has avenged my lord the
king against Saul and his offspring."
9 David answered Rekab and his brother Baanah, the sons of Rimmon the Beerothite, "As surely as
the LORD lives, who has delivered[i] me out of every trouble, 10 when someone told me, 'Saul is dead,' and
thought he was bringing good news, I seized him and put him to death in Ziklag.[j] That was the reward
I gave him for his news! 11 How much more — when wicked men have killed an innocent man in his
own house and on his own bed — should I not now demand his blood[k] from your hand and rid the
earth of you!"
12 So David gave an order to his men, and they killed them.[l] They cut off their hands and feet and
hung the bodies by the pool in Hebron. But they took the head of Ish-Bosheth and buried it in Abner's
tomb at Hebron.

4:2 [z] Jos 9:17; 18:25
4:3 [a] Ne 11:33
4:4 [b] 1Sa 18:1 [c] 1Sa 31:1-4 [d] Lev 21:18 [e] 2Sa 9:3,6; 1Ch 8:34; 9:40
4:5 [f] 2Sa 2:8
4:6 [g] 2Sa 2:23
4:8 [h] 1Sa 24:4; 25:29
4:9 [i] Ge 48:16; 1Ki 1:29
4:10 [j] 2Sa 1:2-16
4:11 [k] Ge 9:5; Ps 9:12
4:12 [l] 2Sa 1:15
5:1 [m] 2Sa 19:43 [n] 1Ch 11:1
5:2 [o] 1Sa 18:5,13,16 [p] 1Sa 16:1; 2Sa 7:7 [q] 1Sa 25:30
5:3 [r] 2Sa 3:21 [s] 2Sa 2:4
5:4 [t] Lk 3:23 [u] 1Ki 2:11; 1Ch 3:4 [v] 1Ch 26:31; 29:27
5:5 [w] 2Sa 2:11; 1Ch 3:4

David Becomes King Over Israel

5:1-3pp — 1Ch 11:1-3

5 All the tribes of Israel[m] came to David at Hebron and said, "We are your own flesh and blood.[n]
2 In the past, while Saul was king over us, you were the one who led Israel on their military campaigns.[o] And the LORD said to you, 'You will shepherd[p] my people Israel, and you will become their
ruler.[q]' "
3 When all the elders of Israel had come to King David at Hebron, the king made a covenant[r] with
them at Hebron before the LORD, and they anointed[s] David king over Israel.
4 David was thirty years old[t] when he became king, and he reigned[u] forty[v] years. 5 In Hebron he
reigned over Judah seven years and six months,[w] and in Jerusalem he reigned over all Israel and Judah
thirty-three years.

---

that he has become marginalized and an irrelevant force in the palace intrigue. **lost courage.** The text uses an idiom that means Ish-Bosheth lost heart when he heard the news of Abner's death.

4:2 Beeroth. A town perhaps located at Khirbet al-Burg, about two miles (3.2 kilometers) north of Jerusalem in Benjamite territory. It was one of the Gibeonite cities that tricked Joshua into making a covenant with its pagan inhabitants (Josh 9:15–17).

4:3 Apparently the Beerothites fled to Gittaim when Saul had massacred many of the Gibeonites (21:1; see note on 21:1–14). These people, including Baanah and Rekab (v. 2), are probably not native Israelites but foreigners living within Israel.

4:4 This parenthesis interrupts the story probably to show that Mephibosheth, a direct descendant of Saul, is not made king after Ish-Bosheth is murdered because he is young and lame in his feet.

4:6–7 Rekab and Baanah pretend to be looking for wheat, perhaps to purchase it. While Ish-Bosheth is lying down for a noonday nap, the men kill him and remove his head. They then slip away and travel quickly through the Arabah, which is the Jordan River Valley. They travel about 55 miles (88.5 kilometers) as the crow flies: from Mahanaim, where Ish-Bosheth lived, to Hebron, where David resides.

4:10–11 David draws a parallel between the Amalekite's murder of Saul (1:13–16) and Baanah and Rekab's murder of Ish-Bosheth. The latter act is even more heinous: Saul allegedly asked the Amalekite to kill him, but these two murder an innocent man while he is sleeping in his bed.

4:12 The end result for Rekab and Baanah is the same as for the Amalekite (1:15). **hung the bodies.** A common manner of public display and shame (21:5–6; 1 Sam 31:10; Josh 10:26).

5:1–5 *David Becomes King Over Israel.* Samuel anointed David to be the future king over all Israel (1 Sam 16:12–13), and this promise finally comes to pass. The elders of all the tribes of Israel participate in David's formal anointing as king of all Israel.

5:1 The tribes of Israel send delegations consisting of "all the elders of Israel" (v. 3) to meet with David at Hebron. **own flesh and blood.** An idiom reflecting close physical kinship (Gen 2:23; 29:14; Judg 9:2).

5:2 you ... you ... You ... you. Emphasizes that David led Israel to victory under Saul's rule (1 Sam 18:7; 21:11; 29:5), that the Lord chose David to rule (1 Sam 16:12–13), and that David is one of their own.

5:4 This typical formula describes a king's rule; the OT uses it over 30 times. Many critical scholars maintain that the Hebrew Bible contains

David Conquers Jerusalem

5:6-10pp — 1Ch 11:4-9
5:11-16pp — 1Ch 3:5-9; 14:1-7

[6]The king and his men marched to Jerusalem[x] to attack the Jebusites,[y] who lived there. The Jebusites
said to David, "You will not get in here; even the blind and the lame can ward you off." They thought, "David cannot get in here." [7]Nevertheless, David captured the fortress of Zion — which is the City of David.[z]
[8]On that day David had said, "Anyone who conquers the Jebusites will have to use the water shaft to

5:6 [x] Jdg 1:8 [y] Jos 15:8
5:7 [z] 2Sa 6:12,16; 1Ki 2:10

very little that is historically reliable concerning David and his reign. Many believe it is fabrication along the lines of the legends of King Arthur in England. But in 1993, an inscription was discovered at Tel Dan that mentions "the house of David," and it dates to the ninth century BC. The epithet "the house of David" may also appear on the extrabiblical Moabite Stone that comes from that same time period.

5:6–16 *David Conquers Jerusalem.* David captures Jerusalem to serve as the capital of his united kingdom. This choice reflects political savvy because Jerusalem lies on the border between the tribal allotments of Judah and Benjamin. There David builds a palace with the help of Hiram king of Tyre.

5:6 Jebusites. Descendants of Canaan who first appear in the Bible in Gen 10:16. The tribe of Judah did not expel these Canaanites when they conquered the land under Joshua (Josh 15:63). At least four passages refer to Jerusalem as Jebus (Josh 15:8; 18:28; Judg 19:10; 1 Chr 11:4). The Canaanite city was located on a hill called the "Ophel," located in the southeastern part of the modern city of Jerusalem. People inhabited this area as early as the Chalcolithic period (third millennium BC), and extrabiblical texts from Egypt as far back as the twentieth century BC mention the city. At the time of David's siege, the city is so well defended that "even the blind and the lame" can keep out the Israelites.

5:7 This parenthesis summarizes what follows in vv. 8–16. **Zion.** Jerusalem. This is the first time the OT uses this term.

5:8 water shaft. The Hebrew word occurs only twice in the OT (translated "waterfalls" in Ps 42:7). In 1867, Charles Warren discovered remains of an elaborate water system in Jerusalem with a vertical shaft — called "Warren's shaft" — and connecting tunnels. The shaft dates probably to the period of the Jebusite habitation. Its purpose was to bring water from the Gihon Spring outside of the city into the walled city. Joab may have led his men through this shaft to penetrate the Jebusite city (1 Chr 11:6).

THE CITY OF THE JEBUSITES/DAVID'S JERUSALEM

Substantial historical evidence, both biblical and extrabiblical, places the temple of Solomon on the holy spot where King David built an altar to the Lord. David had purchased the land from Araunah the Jebusite, who was using the exposed bedrock as a threshing floor (2 Sam 24:18–25). Tradition claims a much older sanctity for the site, associating it with the altar of Abraham on Mount Moriah (Gen 22:1–19; see 2 Chr 3:1 and note). The writer of Genesis equates Moriah with "the mountain of the LORD" (Gen 22:14).

ca. 1000 BC

Less than 11 acres in size (4.45 hectares), Jebus, a Canaanite city, could well defend itself against attack, with walls built midway up the steep eastern slopes and a carstic spring water source (unique to the area) surrounded by magnificent fortified towers. David captured the stronghold ca. 1000 BC and made it his capital.

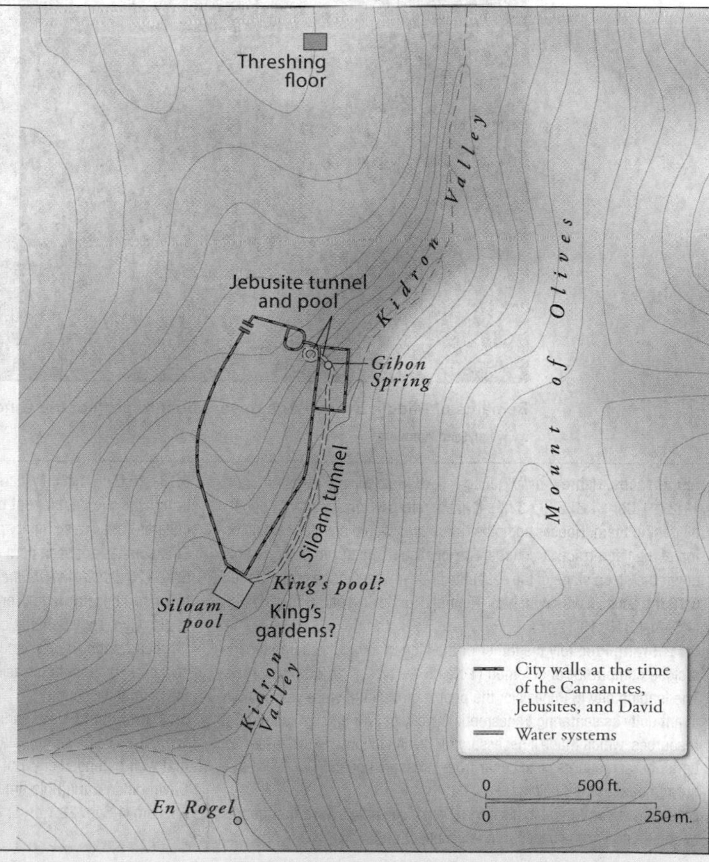

5:9 [a] ver 7; 1Ki 9:15,24
5:10 [b] 2Sa 3:1
5:11 [c] 1Ki 5:1,18; 1Ch 14:1
5:13 [d] Dt 17:17; 1Ch 3:9
5:14 [e] 1Ch 3:5
5:17 [f] 2Sa 23:14; 1Ch 11:16

reach those 'lame and blind' who are David's enemies.[a]" That is why they say, "The 'blind and lame'
will not enter the palace."
9 David then took up residence in the fortress and called it the City of David. He built up the area
around it, from the terraces[b][a] inward. 10 And he became more and more powerful,[b] because the LORD
God Almighty was with him.
11 Now Hiram[c] king of Tyre sent envoys to David, along with cedar logs and carpenters and stonemasons, and they built a palace for David. 12 Then David knew that the LORD had established him as king
over Israel and had exalted his kingdom for the sake of his people Israel.
13 After he left Hebron, David took more concubines and wives[d] in Jerusalem, and more sons and
daughters were born to him. 14 These are the names of the children born to him there:[e] Shammua,
Shobab, Nathan, Solomon, 15 Ibhar, Elishua, Nepheg, Japhia, 16 Elishama, Eliada and Eliphelet.

David Defeats the Philistines

5:17-25pp — 1Ch 14:8-17

17 When the Philistines heard that David had been anointed king over Israel, they went up in
full force to search for him, but David heard about it and went down to the stronghold.[f] 18 Now the

[a] *8* Or *are hated by David* [b] *9* Or *the Millo*

Remains of Middle Bronze Age towers built to protect the Gihon Spring water system.
www.HolyLandPhotos.org

5:9 terraces. Hebrew *millôʾ* (Judg 9:6,20 [Beth Millo]; 1 Kgs 9:15,24; 11:27; 1 Chr 11:8; 2 Chr 32:5). It likely refers to terraces that support fill behind them. Houses and other structures would have been built on top of the flat terrace structures. The location of the terraces is probably down the steep slope of the east side of the eastern ridge of the Ophel.
5:10 the LORD ... was with him. Thematic for David's early life and reign (1 Sam 16:18; 18:12,14).
5:11 Hiram. Probably the father of the king of the same name who is a close compatriot of Solomon (1 Kgs 5:1–18; 2 Chr 2:3–16). **Tyre.** The leading city in Phoenicia; the people of the land were well-known in antiquity as seafaring tradesmen. The city of Tyre had limited natural resources, which made it necessary for the inhabitants to utilize Israel's agricultural resources and cedar from Lebanon. Lebanon's cedar trees are famous for their height.
5:12 At this early point in his reign, David is keenly aware that he has become king for the benefit of the people of God.
5:13–16 David not only increases the size of his kingdom and his popularity with the people, but he also multiplies wives, concubines, and children. This is a summary passage placed early in the history because Solomon has not been born yet.
5:17–25 *David Defeats the Philistines.* When the Philistines hear that David has become king over Israel, they attack Israel to test David early in his reign. They perhaps consider his rule tenuous and vulnerable at this early stage. They invade Israel twice in the same region, and David is victorious on both occasions. He finally drives the Philistines out of the central hill country.
5:17 stronghold. Used earlier to describe Jerusalem (see "fortress" in vv. 7,9), so some commentators believe David perhaps takes shelter in that well-defended city. But the word commonly refers to refuges that David hid in during his time of flight from Saul, such as the caves at Adullam (1 Sam 22:1,4–5; 23:14,19,29; 24:22).

Philistines had come and spread out in the Valley of Rephaim;[g] 19 so David inquired[h] of the LORD, "Shall
I go and attack the Philistines? Will you deliver them into my hands?"
The LORD answered him, "Go, for I will surely deliver the Philistines into your hands."
20 So David went to Baal Perazim, and there he defeated them. He said, "As waters break out, the
LORD has broken out against my enemies before me." So that place was called Baal Perazim.[a i] 21 The
Philistines abandoned their idols there, and David and his men carried them off.[j]
22 Once more the Philistines came up and spread out in the Valley of Rephaim; 23 so David inquired
of the LORD, and he answered, "Do not go straight up, but circle around behind them and attack them
in front of the poplar trees. 24 As soon as you hear the sound[k] of marching in the tops of the poplar
trees, move quickly, because that will mean the LORD has gone out in front[l] of you to strike the Philistine army." 25 So David did as the LORD commanded him, and he struck down the Philistines all the way
from Gibeon[b m] to Gezer.[n]

The Ark Brought to Jerusalem

6:1-11pp — 1Ch 13:1-14
6:12-19pp — 1Ch 15:25–16:3

6 David again brought together all the able young men of Israel — thirty thousand. 2 He and all
his men went to Baalah[c o] in Judah to bring up from there the ark[p] of God, which is called by the
Name,[d q] the name of the LORD Almighty, who is enthroned[r] between the cherubim[s] on the ark. 3 They
set the ark of God on a new cart[t] and brought it from the house of Abinadab, which was on the hill.
Uzzah and Ahio, sons of Abinadab, were guiding the new cart 4 with the ark of God on it,[e] and Ahio was
walking in front of it. 5 David and all Israel were celebrating with all their might before the LORD, with
castanets,[f] harps, lyres, timbrels, sistrums and cymbals.[u]
6 When they came to the threshing floor of Nakon, Uzzah reached out and took hold of[v] the ark of
God, because the oxen stumbled. 7 The LORD's anger burned against Uzzah because of his irreverent act;[w]
therefore God struck him down,[x] and he died there beside the ark of God.
8 Then David was angry because the LORD's wrath[y] had broken out against Uzzah, and to this day
that place is called Perez Uzzah.[g z]
9 David was afraid of the LORD that day and said, "How[a] can the ark of the LORD ever come to me?"
10 He was not willing to take the ark of the LORD to be with him in the City of David. Instead, he took it

[a] 20 *Baal Perazim* means *the lord who breaks out.* [b] 25 Septuagint (see also 1 Chron. 14:16); Hebrew *Geba* [c] 2 That is, Kiriath Jearim (see 1 Chron. 13:6) [d] 2 Hebrew; Septuagint and Vulgate do not have *the Name.* [e] 3,4 Dead Sea Scrolls and some Septuagint manuscripts; Masoretic Text *cart* [4]*and they brought it with the ark of God from the house of Abinadab, which was on the hill* [f] 5 Masoretic Text; Dead Sea Scrolls and Septuagint (see also 1 Chron. 13:8) *songs* [g] 8 *Perez Uzzah* means *outbreak against Uzzah.*

5:18 [g] Jos 15:8; 17:15; 18:16
5:19 [h] 1Sa 23:2; 2Sa 2:1
5:20 [i] Isa 28:21
5:21 [j] Dt 7:5; 1Ch 14:12; Isa 46:2
5:24 [k] 2Ki 7:6 [l] Jdg 4:14
5:25 [m] Isa 28:21 [n] 1Ch 14:16
6:2 [o] Jos 15:9 [p] 1Sa 4:4; 7:1 [q] Lev 24:16; Isa 63:14 [r] Ps 99:1 [s] Ex 25:22; 1Ch 13:5-6
6:3 [t] Nu 7:4-9; 1Sa 6:7
6:5 [u] 1Sa 18:6-7; Ezr 3:10; Ps 150:5
6:6 [v] Nu 4:15,19-20; 1Ch 13:9
6:7 [w] 1Ch 15:13-15 [x] Ex 19:22; 1Sa 6:19
6:8 [y] Ps 7:11 [z] Ge 38:29
6:9 [a] Ps 119:120

5:18 spread out. Deployed troops throughout the valley. **Valley of Rephaim.** Leads to Jerusalem from the southwest.
5:19 As usual, David inquires of the Lord whether he should engage the Philistines in battle (Cf. 2:1; 1 Sam 23:1–2,9–12; 30:8).
5:21 idols. Ancient armies often carried sacred images into battle for divine assistance. David and the Israelite troops taunt the Philistines not only by capturing their idols but also by burning them (1 Chr 14:12).
5:23–25 The Philistines make a second military incursion into Israelite territory in the Valley of Rephaim. God gives David a different strategy from the first invasion: they are to respond not with a frontal assault but with an assault from the rear. David and his men drive out the Philistines from the central highlands. They push them approximately 22 miles (35 kilometers) from Gibeon (1 Chr 14:16) to Gezer in the west on the edge of the coastal plain of Philistia.
5:24 marching. This verb perhaps bears the idea of the rustling sound of wind in the tops of the poplar trees.
6:1–23 *The Ark Brought to Jerusalem.* As newly appointed king, David determines to bring the ark of the covenant, which indicates the very presence of God, to Jerusalem, the city of David. David, the Israelite monarch, is bringing the symbol of the true king's presence to the capital city; the ark is the very throne of Israel's God. The ark has been stored in the house of Abinadab in the town of Baalah in Judah for about 20 years (1 Sam 7:1–2).
6:2 Baalah in Judah. Also known as Kiriath Jearim (1 Sam 7:1; Josh 15:9; 1 Chr 13:6). It is located almost ten miles (1.6 kilometers) east of Beth Shemesh in the Sorek Valley and about eight miles (12.8 kilometers) from Jerusalem. **enthroned between the cherubim.** See note on 1 Sam 4:3.
6:3 new cart. A method that goes against God's instructions regarding the holy objects. Kohathites of the tribe of Levi must carry it on their shoulders (Num 7:6–9; 1 Chr 15:13–15). David and the Israelites are careless in obeying God's word, and they imitate the pagan Philistines (1 Sam 6:7–8).
6:6–7 When the oxen stumble, Uzzah grabs the ark to steady it so it won't crash to the earth. **irreverent act.** Uzzah treats the ark in an unholy way. According to the law, unauthorized people must not touch the holy objects — or even look upon them — or they will die (Num 4:15,20). In his zeal, Uzzah was guilty of breaking God's law.
6:8 Perez Uzzah. See NIV text note.
6:10–11 This incident sparks fear in David, causing him to delay transporting the ark to Jerusalem.
6:10 Obed-Edom the Gittite. Perhaps a Philistine from Gath sojourning

6:10 [b] 1Ch 13:13; 26:4-5
6:11 [c] Ge 30:27; 39:5
6:12 [d] 1Ki 8:1; 1Ch 15:25
6:13 [e] 1Ki 8:5,62
6:14 [f] Ex 19:6; 1Sa 2:18 [g] Ex 15:20
6:15 [h] Ps 47:5; 98:6
6:16 [i] 2Sa 5:7
6:17 [j] 1Ch 15:1; 2Ch 1:4 [k] Lev 1:1-17; 1Ki 8:62-64
6:18 [l] 1Ki 8:22
6:19 [m] Hos 3:1 [n] Ne 8:10
6:20 [o] ver 14,16
6:21 [p] 1Sa 13:14; 15:28
7:1 [q] 1Ch 17:1
7:2 [r] 2Sa 5:11 [s] Ex 26:1; Ac 7:45-46

to the house of Obed-Edom[b] the Gittite. 11 The ark of the LORD remained in the house of Obed-Edom the
Gittite for three months, and the LORD blessed him and his entire household.[c]
12 Now King David[d] was told, "The LORD has blessed the household of Obed-Edom and everything he
has, because of the ark of God." So David went to bring up the ark of God from the house of Obed-Edom
to the City of David with rejoicing. 13 When those who were carrying the ark of the LORD had taken six
steps, he sacrificed[e] a bull and a fattened calf. 14 Wearing a linen ephod,[f] David was dancing[g] before
the LORD with all his might, 15 while he and all Israel were bringing up the ark of the LORD with shouts
and the sound of trumpets.[h]
16 As the ark of the LORD was entering the City of David,[i] Michal daughter of Saul watched from a window. And when she saw King David leaping and dancing before the LORD, she despised him in her heart.
17 They brought the ark of the LORD and set it in its place inside the tent that David had pitched for it,[j]
and David sacrificed burnt offerings[k] and fellowship offerings before the LORD. 18 After he had finished
sacrificing[l] the burnt offerings and fellowship offerings, he blessed the people in the name of the LORD
Almighty. 19 Then he gave a loaf of bread, a cake of dates and a cake of raisins[m] to each person in the
whole crowd of Israelites, both men and women.[n] And all the people went to their homes.
20 When David returned home to bless his household, Michal daughter of Saul came out to meet him
and said, "How the king of Israel has distinguished himself today, going around half-naked[o] in full view
of the slave girls of his servants as any vulgar fellow would!"
21 David said to Michal, "It was before the LORD, who chose me rather than your father or anyone
from his house when he appointed[p] me ruler over the LORD's people Israel — I will celebrate before the
LORD. 22 I will become even more undignified than this, and I will be humiliated in my own eyes. But by
these slave girls you spoke of, I will be held in honor."
23 And Michal daughter of Saul had no children to the day of her death.

God's Promise to David

7:1-17pp — 1Ch 17:1-15

7 After the king was settled in his palace[q] and the LORD had given him rest from all his enemies
around him, 2 he said to Nathan the prophet, "Here I am, living in a house[r] of cedar, while the ark
of God remains in a tent."[s]
3 Nathan replied to the king, "Whatever you have in mind, go ahead and do it, for the LORD is with
you."

in Israel. Israelites would be hesitant to have the ark in their homes because of what just took place. There are no specifics of how the Lord "blessed" Obed-Edom (v. 11), although 1 Chr 26:4–5 says that God "blessed" him with eight sons.

6:13 The Kohathites properly carry the ark on their shoulders (1 Chr 15:12–15). After taking a mere six steps, David gives direction for the sacrifice of a bull and a fattened calf. A few commentators argue that the Israelites perform this sacrifice every six steps all the way to Jerusalem; this is unlikely, for it is simply unmanageable.

6:14 linen ephod. This often refers to a garment worn by a priest but also may refer to a waistcoat worn in worship (1 Sam 2:18). David lays aside his kingly robes and dons this garment. **dancing.** An individual act of joy.

6:16 Michal. The text identifies her not as David's wife but rather as the "daughter of Saul" (also vv. 20,23). This likely indicates that she supports her father's ways. **watched from a window.** The scene of a woman of royalty staring out of a palace window is common in Scripture (Judg 5:28; 2 Kgs 9:30). An example of an ornamental palatial window has been found at Ramet Rahel. It consists of a row of miniature palmette pillars decorated with stylized capitals abutting one another. This woman-at-the-window theme is also represented on ivories discovered in Syria, Phoenicia, and Israel. **she despised him.** Michal resented David not only because of his public display but because he was obviously not a king like her father Saul.

6:20 Michal assaults David with biting sarcasm. **half-naked.** She accuses David of indecent exposure. **as any vulgar fellow.** Like the riffraff or scoundrels of the lower classes of Israelite society (Judg 9:4; 11:3; 2 Chr 13:7).

6:22 in my own eyes. David reflects self-abasement. The king will become lowly even to himself before the Lord. David tells Michal that he will lower himself even further than what she has seen this day.

6:23 Michal unjustly reproached David for his devotion and worship, and she is put under a reproach of barrenness. The text does not say that the Lord made Michal barren. Perhaps she was barren because David never had marital relations with her again.

7:1–17 *God's Promise to David.* David seeks to build a permanent structure to house the ark of God in Jerusalem. The Lord denies David this task of building a temple. We learn later that God refuses because David is a man of war (1 Kgs 5:3; 1 Chr 22:8). To the contrary, God promises to build David a house; but this is not a mere physical structure but a dynasty — an eternal one. This oath has strong Messianic overtones. It points to the coming of a future Davidic king who will build a house, or dynasty, that is "forever" (v. 13).

7:2 David contrasts where he resides with where the ark of God resides. The contrast is clear by David's use of the same verb twice: "I am dwelling ... but the ark of God is dwelling." David's "house of cedar" is a permanent, strong, sturdy, luxurious palace; the ark's house is a temporary, flimsy "tent," a basic word for "curtains."

7:3 the LORD is with you. Thematic for David's life (5:10; 1 Sam 16:18; 17:37; 18:14,28).

4But that night the word of the LORD came to Nathan, saying:

5"Go and tell my servant David, 'This is what the LORD says: Are you[t] the one to build me a house to dwell in?[u] 6I have not dwelt in a house from the day I brought the Israelites up out of Egypt to this day. I have been moving from place to place with a tent[v] as my dwelling.[w] 7Wherever I have moved with all the Israelites,[x] did I ever say to any of their rulers whom I commanded to shepherd[y] my people Israel, "Why have you not built me a house of cedar?[z]" '

8"Now then, tell my servant David, 'This is what the LORD Almighty says: I took you from the pasture, from tending the flock,[a] and appointed you ruler[b] over my people Israel.[c] 9I have been with you wherever you have gone,[d] and I have cut off all your enemies from before you.[e] Now I will make your name great, like the names of the greatest men on earth. 10And I will provide a place for my people Israel and will plant[f] them so that they can have a home of their own and no longer be disturbed. Wicked[g] people will not oppress them anymore,[h] as they did at the beginning 11and have done ever since the time I appointed leaders*[a]*[i] over my people Israel. I will also give you rest from all your enemies.[j]

" 'The LORD declares to you that the LORD himself will establish[k] a house[l] for you: 12When your days are over and you rest[m] with your ancestors, I will raise up your offspring to succeed you, your own flesh and blood,[n] and I will establish his kingdom. 13He is the one who will build a house for my Name,[o] and I will establish the throne of his kingdom forever.[p] 14I will be his father, and he will be my son.[q] When he does wrong, I will punish him with a rod[r] wielded by men, with floggings inflicted by human hands. 15But my love will never be taken away from him, as I took it away from Saul,[s] whom I removed from before you. 16Your house and your kingdom will endure forever before me*[b]*; your throne[t] will be established forever.[u]' "

17Nathan reported to David all the words of this entire revelation.

David's Prayer

7:18-29pp — 1Ch 17:16-27

18Then King David went in and sat before the LORD, and he said:

"Who am I,[v] Sovereign LORD, and what is my family, that you have brought me this far? 19And as if this were not enough in your sight, Sovereign LORD, you have also spoken about the future of the house of your servant — and this decree,[w] Sovereign LORD, is for a mere human!*[c]*

20"What more can David say to you? For you know[x] your servant,[y] Sovereign LORD. 21For the

a 11 Traditionally *judges* *b 16* Some Hebrew manuscripts and Septuagint; most Hebrew manuscripts *you*
c 19 Or *for the human race*

7:5 [t]1Ki 8:19; 1Ch 22:8 [u]1Ki 5:3-5
7:6 [v]Ex 40:18,34 [w]1Ki 8:16
7:7 [x]Dt 23:14 [y]2Sa 5:2 [z]Lev 26:11-12
7:8 [a]1Sa 16:11 [b]2Sa 6:21 [c]Ps 78:70-72; 2Co 6:18*
7:9 [d]2Sa 5:10 [e]Ps 18:37-42
7:10 [f]Ex 15:17; Isa 5:1-7 [g]Ps 89:22-23 [h]Isa 60:18
7:11 [i]Jdg 2:16; 1Sa 12:9-11 [j]ver 1 [k]1Sa 25:28 [l]ver 27
7:12 [m]1Ki 2:1 [n]Ps 132:11-12
7:13 [o]1Ki 5:5; 8:19,29 [p]Isa 9:7
7:14 [q]Ps 89:26; Heb 1:5* [r]Ps 89:30-33
7:15 [s]1Sa 15:23,28
7:16 [t]Ps 89:36-37 [u]ver 13
7:18 [v]Ex 3:11; 1Sa 18:18
7:19 [w]Isa 55:8-9
7:20 [x]Jn 21:17 [y]1Sa 16:7

7:5 This is what the LORD says. See note on 1 Sam 2:27.
7:7 rulers. The change of one consonant in Hebrew revises the word to mean "judges," which agrees with the parallel passage (1 Chr 17:6 ["leaders"]; see NIV text note there). On the other hand, the word as it stands can also mean "scepters," which can be a figure of speech (metonymy) that reflects leaders or rulers.
7:8,9 I. The personal pronoun is emphatic. It is the Lord who called David from the pasture and elevated him to the kingship; it is the Lord who cut off David's enemies; and it is the Lord who will make his name great (cf. Gen 12:2). It is the Lord who will firmly establish his people in their own land.
7:11 establish a house. Build a royal house, or dynasty, not a building. David had wanted to build a house for God, and now it is God who promises to build a house for David.
7:12–13 This appears to be a double prophecy: (1) It predicts the birth and work of Solomon, who builds a temple for the ark of the covenant (1 Kgs 7:1 – 12). (2) The eternality of David's throne is fulfilled only in the Messiah (Acts 2:30).
7:14 I will be his father, and he will be my son. This reflects the father-son relationship between God and Solomon on one level, but the NT applies it to Jesus as the Son of God and the true, final heir to David's throne (Heb 1:5). The OT itself pictures that familial language as Messianic (Pss 2:7; 45:6; 89:27).
7:16 before me. Numerous Hebrew manuscripts and modern translations render this "before you" (see NIV text note), which underscores the point that David will live to see the throne established in the person of his son Solomon. "Before me" bears a Messianic sense that David's "throne will be established forever" in the final son of David.
7:18–29 *David's Prayer.* David responds to the Lord's message with a heartfelt prayer of thanksgiving. The king calls God by the name "Sovereign LORD" seven times, reflecting a relationship of great intimacy. He is grateful that God is building him a "house" (his future royal dynasty), a term that appears fifteen times in the Hebrew of ch. 7 and is the running theme throughout it.
7:18 David apparently enters the tent to pray. David humbly acknowledges that he is king only because of God. He thus confirms what the Lord had said to him through Nathan the prophet (vv. 8–9).
7:19 David is surprised by God's grace and mercy to him. **this decree … is for a mere human!** The Hebrew is difficult and uncertain, but it highlights that God's work in David's life is a lesson for how God works in the lives of believers. See also NIV text note.

7:22 [z]Ps 48:1; 86:10; Jer 10:6 [a]Dt 3:24 [b]Ex 15:11 [c]Ex 10:2; Ps 44:1
7:23 [d]Dt 4:32-38 [e]Dt 10:21 [f]Dt 9:26; 15:15
7:24 [g]Dt 26:18 [h]Ex 6:6-7; Ps 48:14
7:28 [i]Ex 34:6; Jn 17:17
7:29 [j]Nu 6:23-27
8:2 [k]Ge 19:37; Nu 24:17
8:3 [l]2Sa 10:16,19 [m]1Sa 14:47
8:4 [n]Jos 11:9
8:5 [o]1Ki 11:24
8:6 [p]ver 14; 2Sa 3:18; 7:9

sake of your word and according to your will, you have done this great thing and made it known
to your servant.
22“How great[z] you are,[a] Sovereign LORD! There is no one like you, and there is no God[b] but you,
as we have heard with our own ears.[c] 23And who is like your people Israel[d]—the one nation on
earth that God went out to redeem as a people for himself, and to make a name for himself, and
to perform great and awesome wonders[e] by driving out nations and their gods from before your
people, whom you redeemed[f] from Egypt?[a] 24You have established your people Israel as your very
own[g] forever, and you, LORD, have become their God.[h]
25“And now, LORD God, keep forever the promise you have made concerning your servant and his
house. Do as you promised, 26so that your name will be great forever. Then people will say, ‘The LORD
Almighty is God over Israel!’ And the house of your servant David will be established in your sight.
27“LORD Almighty, God of Israel, you have revealed this to your servant, saying, ‘I will build a
house for you.’ So your servant has found courage to pray this prayer to you. 28Sovereign LORD,
you are God! Your covenant is trustworthy,[i] and you have promised these good things to your
servant. 29Now be pleased to bless the house of your servant, that it may continue forever in your
sight; for you, Sovereign LORD, have spoken, and with your blessing[j] the house of your servant
will be blessed forever.”

David’s Victories

8:1-14pp — 1Ch 18:1-13

8 In the course of time, David defeated the Philistines and subdued them, and he took Metheg Ammah from the control of the Philistines.
2David also defeated the Moabites.[k] He made them lie down on the ground and measured them off
with a length of cord. Every two lengths of them were put to death, and the third length was allowed to
live. So the Moabites became subject to David and brought him tribute.
3Moreover, David defeated Hadadezer[l] son of Rehob, king of Zobah,[m] when he went to restore his
monument at[b] the Euphrates River. 4David captured a thousand of his chariots, seven thousand
charioteers[c] and twenty thousand foot soldiers. He hamstrung[n] all but a hundred of the chariot
horses.
5When the Arameans of Damascus[o] came to help Hadadezer king of Zobah, David struck down
twenty-two thousand of them. 6He put garrisons in the Aramean kingdom of Damascus, and the Arameans became subject to him and brought tribute. The LORD gave David victory wherever he went.[p]

[a] 23 See Septuagint and 1 Chron. 17:21; Hebrew *wonders for your land and before your people, whom you redeemed from Egypt, from the nations and their gods.* [b] 3 Or *his control along* [c] 4 Septuagint (see also Dead Sea Scrolls and 1 Chron. 18:4); Masoretic Text *captured seventeen hundred of his charioteers*

7:22 This is David’s great proclamation majestically affirming that the Lord alone is God.

7:23 Although this verse contains several textual problems, the basic sense is clear: no other people on earth are like Israel because God elected them to be his own people.

7:27 The sentence construction of God’s words to David places the emphasis on the word “house.” David wanted to build a house for the Lord (vv. 1–5), but ironically the Lord will build David a “house” (i.e., a royal dynasty).

8:1–14 *David’s Victories.* This catalogs David’s many military conflicts during his rule over Israel. It describes his wars with nations surrounding Israel on all sides: the arch-enemy Philistines to the west, the Aramean confederation to the north, the Transjordanian nations of Moab and Ammon to the east, and the Edomites to the south-southeast in the Dead Sea region. The theme is “the LORD gave David victory wherever he went” (vv. 6b,14b). The list of conflicts is not necessarily in chronological order. For example, the defeat of the Ammonites in chs. 10–12 may precede the war with the kingdom of Zobah (8:3–5,12). Thus, ch. 8 is a general summary of David’s military exploits. See map, p. 560.

8:1 Metheg Ammah. Location uncertain; it means “bridle of the mother” or “bridle of one cubit,” but that does not help in the task of identification.

8:2 This is a measured mass execution of Moabite soldiers: the captured soldiers lie down in three lines, and the men in two of the three lines are then killed. This violent deed is even more surprising because David’s great-grandmother was a Moabite (Ruth 4:21–22).

8:3 Hadadezer. Unknown outside the Bible; the name means “Hadad is (my) help.” Hadad is the storm god and the main deity of the Arameans, and his name is found as part of other Aramean royal names, such as “Ben-Hadad” (1 Kgs 15:18). **Zobah.** Located in the Beqa Valley in Syria. **monument.** Sometimes used of a physical monument but more often reflects the idea of control or power (see NIV text note). Grammatically, either David or Hadadezer could be attempting to assert control over the Euphrates River region.

8:4 seven thousand charioteers. See NIV text note. **hamstrung.** Crippled horses were of no military use.

8:6 To insure no further conflict, David puts garrisons in Aram as a long-term military presence. **gave … victory.** The verb is causative in Hebrew, and it emphasizes that the Lord is the source of all David’s conquests.

The Tel Dan Stele (ninth century BC) mentions the "house of David" (highlighted on the ninth line of text) and is the first time the name David has been found outside of the Bible.

Kim Walton, taken at the Israel Museum

7 David took the gold shields[q] that belonged to the officers
of Hadadezer and brought them to Jerusalem. 8 From Tebah[a]
and Berothai,[r] towns that belonged to Hadadezer, King David
took a great quantity of bronze.
9 When Tou[b] king of Hamath[s] heard that David had defeated the entire army of Hadadezer, 10 he sent his son Joram[c]
to King David to greet him and congratulate him on his victory in battle over Hadadezer, who had been at war with Tou.
Joram brought with him articles of silver, of gold and of bronze.
11 King David dedicated[t] these articles to the LORD, as he had done
with the silver and gold from all the nations he had subdued: 12 Edom[d]
and Moab,[u] the Ammonites[v] and the Philistines,[w] and Amalek.[x] He also
dedicated the plunder taken from Hadadezer son of Rehob, king of Zobah.
13 And David became famous[y] after he returned from striking down
eighteen thousand Edomites[e] in the Valley of Salt.[z]
14 He put garrisons throughout Edom, and all the Edomites[a] became
subject to David.[b] The LORD gave David victory wherever he went.[c]

David's Officials

8:15-18pp — 1Ch 18:14-17

15 David reigned over all Israel, doing what was just and right for all
his people. 16 Joab[d] son of Zeruiah was over the army; Jehoshaphat[e] son of Ahilud was recorder; 17 Zadok[f] son of Ahitub and Ahimelek son of Abiathar were priests; Seraiah was secretary;[g] 18 Benaiah[h] son
of Jehoiada was over the Kerethites[i] and Pelethites; and David's sons were priests.[f]

David and Mephibosheth

9 David asked, "Is there anyone still left of the house of Saul to whom I can show kindness for
Jonathan's sake?"[j]
2 Now there was a servant of Saul's household named Ziba.[k] They summoned him to appear before
David, and the king said to him, "Are you Ziba?"
"At your service," he replied.

[a] *8* See some Septuagint manuscripts (see also 1 Chron. 18:8); Hebrew *Betah.* [b] *9* Hebrew *Toi*, a variant of *Tou*; also in verse 10 [c] *10* A variant of *Hadoram* [d] *12* Some Hebrew manuscripts, Septuagint and Syriac (see also 1 Chron. 18:11); most Hebrew manuscripts *Aram* [e] *13* A few Hebrew manuscripts, Septuagint and Syriac (see also 1 Chron. 18:12); most Hebrew manuscripts *Aram* (that is, Arameans) [f] *18* Or *were chief officials* (see Septuagint and Targum; see also 1 Chron. 18:17)

8:7 [q] 1Ki 10:16
8:8 [r] Eze 47:16
8:9 [s] 1Ki 8:65; 2Ch 8:4
8:11 [t] 1Ki 7:51; 1Ch 26:26
8:12 [u] ver 2 [v] 2Sa 10:14 [w] 2Sa 5:25 [x] 1Sa 27:8
8:13 [y] 2Sa 7:9 [z] 2Ki 14:7; 1Ch 18:12
8:14 [a] Nu 24:17-18 [b] Ge 27:29,37-40 [c] ver 6
8:16 [d] 2Sa 19:13; 1Ch 11:6 [e] 2Sa 20:24; 1Ki 4:3
8:17 [f] 2Sa 15:24,29; 1Ch 16:39; 24:3 [g] 1Ki 4:3; 2Ki 12:10
8:18 [h] 2Sa 20:23; 1Ki 1:8,38; 1Ch 18:17 [i] 1Sa 30:14
9:1 [j] 1Sa 20:14-17,42
9:2 [k] 2Sa 16:1-4; 19:17, 26,29

8:7 shields. Signifies some sort of military gear, and David takes that equipment as a trophy of his victory (cf. 1 Sam 17:54; 21:9); it may refer to quivers, although it can refer to small circular shields.

8:9 Hamath. A region in Syria that lies between Zobah in the south and the Euphrates River Valley in the east.

8:13 Edomites. Many Hebrew manuscripts read "Aram," i.e., Arameans (see NIV text note), referring to Syrians. The difference between Edom and Aram in Hebrew is one consonant, and it is obvious that the author is referring to Edom (v. 14 confirms this). **Valley of Salt.** The arid territory of the Rift Valley south-southwest of the Dead Sea.

8:14 Abishai led the troops in victory over the Edomites (1 Chr 18:12). David gets credit for the triumph because he is king and oversaw the military engagement. **The LORD gave David victory wherever he went.** Duplicates v. 6b, the chapter's theme.

8:15–18 *David's Officials.* This overviews David's royal administrative officers.

8:16 recorder. Probably the royal herald, the one who reports the king's proclamations to the people.

8:17 Zadok. He is loyal to David (15:27–28; 17:15; 19:11) and later supports Solomon (1 Kgs 1:8). He anoints Solomon king over Israel (1 Kgs 1:32–40). **Abiathar.** He is also loyal to David (1 Sam 22:20; 23:6; 30:7). **secretary.** The king's scribe.

8:18 Benaiah. One of David's mighty men (23:20–22); he later becomes commander of the army under Solomon (1 Kgs 4:1–6). **David's sons were priests.** An odd statement; they certainly are not of the Levitical line. Perhaps their position is unique and impermanent. The parallel passage calls them merely "chief officials" (1 Chr 18:17). See NIV text note.

9:1–13 *David and Mephibosheth.* When David and Jonathan made a covenant with one another (1 Sam 20:12–17), David swore that he would not sever his covenant loyalty from Jonathan's posterity. David keeps that promise by seeking out and caring for Jonathan's disabled son Mephibosheth.

9:1 David promised Saul that he would not annihilate his descendants (1 Sam 24:21–22). Commonly in antiquity the new king would destroy the former king's posterity to eliminate possible rivals to the throne from that quarter. David does not do the expedient thing; he is a man of his word.

9:2 Ziba. A servant in Saul's royal household; he reappears later (16:1–4; 19:16–30). **At your service.** The Hebrew word for "servant"

DAVID'S WARS OF EXPANSION

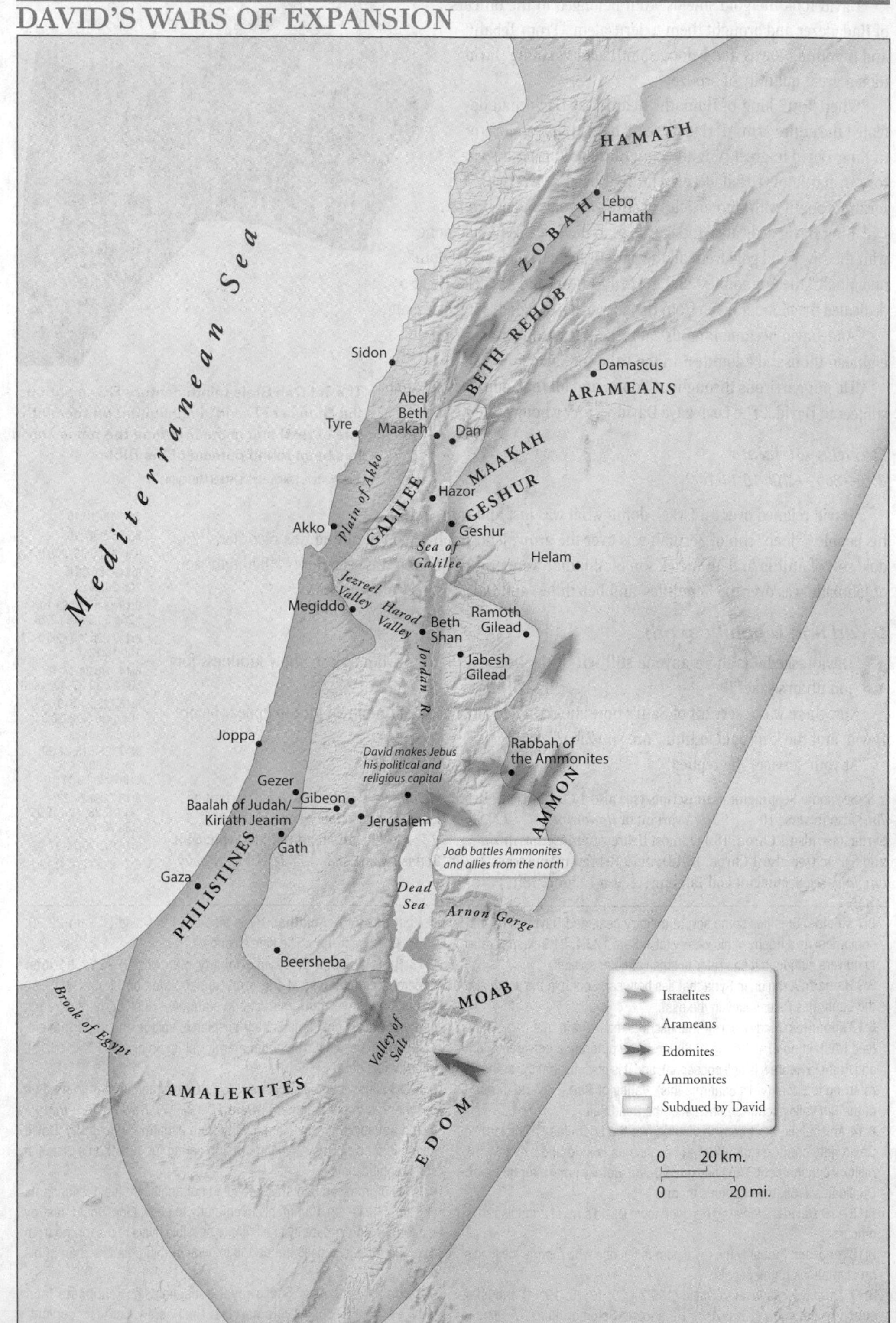
HAMATH
Lebo Hamath
ZOBAH
Mediterranean Sea
BETH REHOB
Sidon
Damascus
ARAMEANS
Abel Beth Maakah
Tyre
Dan
MAAKAH
Plain of Akko
GALILEE
Hazor
GESHUR
Akko
Geshur
Sea of Galilee
Helam
Jezreel Valley
Megiddo
Harod Valley
Ramoth Gilead
Beth Shan
Jabesh Gilead
Jordan R.
Joppa
David makes Jebus his political and religious capital
Rabbah of the Ammonites
Gezer
Gibeon
Baalah of Judah/ Kiriath Jearim
Jerusalem
AMMON
Gath
PHILISTINES
Joab battles Ammonites and allies from the north
Gaza
Dead Sea
Arnon Gorge
Beersheba
Brook of Egypt
MOAB
Valley of Salt
AMALEKITES
EDOM
Israelites
Arameans
Edomites
Ammonites
Subdued by David
0 20 km.
0 20 mi.

3The king asked, "Is there no one still alive from the house of Saul to whom I can show God's
kindness?"
Ziba answered the king, "There is still a son of Jonathan;[l] he is lame[m] in both feet."
4"Where is he?" the king asked.
Ziba answered, "He is at the house of Makir[n] son of Ammiel in Lo Debar."
5So King David had him brought from Lo Debar, from the house of Makir son of Ammiel.
6When Mephibosheth son of Jonathan, the son of Saul, came to David, he bowed down to pay him
honor.[o]
David said, "Mephibosheth!"
"At your service," he replied.
7"Don't be afraid," David said to him, "for I will surely show you kindness for the sake of your father Jonathan. I will restore to you all the land that belonged to your grandfather Saul, and you will
always eat at my table.[p]"
8Mephibosheth bowed down and said, "What is your servant, that you should notice a dead dog[q]
like me?"
9Then the king summoned Ziba, Saul's steward, and said to him, "I have given your master's grandson everything that belonged to Saul and his family. 10You and your sons and your servants are to
farm the land for him and bring in the crops, so that your master's grandson[r] may be provided for.
And Mephibosheth, grandson of your master, will always eat at my table." (Now Ziba had fifteen sons
and twenty servants.)
11Then Ziba said to the king, "Your servant will do whatever my lord the king commands his servant
to do." So Mephibosheth ate at David's[a] table like one of the king's sons.[s]
12Mephibosheth had a young son named Mika, and all the members of Ziba's household were servants of Mephibosheth.[t] 13And Mephibosheth lived in Jerusalem, because he always ate at the king's
table; he was lame in both feet.

9:3 [l] 1Sa 20:14 [m] 2Sa 4:4
9:4 [n] 2Sa 17:27-29
9:6 [o] 2Sa 16:4; 19:24-30
9:7 [p] ver 1,3; 2Sa 12:8; 19:28; 1Ki 2:7; 2Ki 25:29
9:8 [q] 2Sa 16:9
9:10 [r] ver 7,11,13; 2Sa 19:28
9:11 [s] Job 36:7; Ps 113:8
9:12 [t] 1Ch 8:34
10:2 [u] 1Sa 11:1

David Defeats the Ammonites

10:1-19pp — 1Ch 19:1-19

10 In the course of time, the king of the Ammonites died, and his son Hanun succeeded him as
king. 2David thought, "I will show kindness to Hanun son of Nahash,[u] just as his father showed
kindness to me." So David sent a delegation to express his sympathy to Hanun concerning his father.
When David's men came to the land of the Ammonites, 3the Ammonite commanders said to Hanun
their lord, "Do you think David is honoring your father by sending envoys to you to express sympathy?
Hasn't David sent them to you only to explore the city and spy it out and overthrow it?" 4So Hanun

[a] *11* Septuagint; Hebrew *my*

occurs twice in this verse for contrast: Ziba was Saul's servant but is now David's servant.

9:4 Lo Debar. Probably located at Umm ed-Debar, ten miles (16 kilometers) south of the Sea of Galilee in the Jordan Valley on the east side of the river. Mephibosheth may be hiding in Transjordan because he fears that the new king may exact revenge on the house of Saul.

9:7 David allays Mephibosheth's fears. David promises to provide abundantly for him because of David's oath to Jonathan. Mephibosheth will receive all the lands that had belonged to Saul. A regular place at David's table is quite an honor (1 Kgs 2:7; cf. 1 Kgs 18:19; 2 Kgs 25:27–30); David sat at Saul's table when he was in the king's favor (1 Sam 20:24–27).

9:8 dead dog. Used as self-deprecation (cf. 1 Sam 24:14). Mephibosheth is astonished that David is treating him in a worthy fashion.

9:9–10 Ziba appears to have been a high official in charge of all Saul's holdings after his death. David now commands Ziba to turn over all Saul's possessions to Mephibosheth, but Ziba will continue running the affairs of the estate with his 15 sons and 20 servants. He will also provide the food that Mephibosheth eats at the king's table.

9:12 Mika. He had many descendants ("Micah" in 1 Chr 8:35–40; 9:41–44), which confirms that the house of Saul and Jonathan did not come to an end, just as David promised.

10:1–19 *David Defeats the Ammonites.* Hanun succeeds his father, Nahash, as king of Ammon. David sends envoys to Hanun to extend the peace that existed between Israel and Ammon. Listening to his military advisors, Hanun mistreats and abuses David's ambassadors. This leads to a war in which the Israelites defeat the Ammonites and their Aramean mercenary troops.

10:2 Nahash. First mentioned in 1 Sam 11:1–2 as an enemy of Israel. Apparently after David came to the throne, he made a treaty with the Ammonites. Nahash now dies, and there is an orderly succession as his son Hanun assumes the throne (2 Sam 10:1). When David hears of the dynastic succession, he sends a peaceful delegation to Ammon in order to secure continued peace.

10:4 Hanun humiliates David's envoys by shaving off half of their beards and cutting off their garments so that their private parts are exposed. This immediately severs the diplomatic relations between Israel and Ammon.

10:4 [v]Lev 19:27; Isa 15:2; Jer 48:37 [w]Isa 20:4
10:6 [x]Ge 34:30 [y]2Sa 8:5 [z]Jdg 18:28 [a]Dt 3:14
10:12 [b]Dt 31:6; 1Co 16:13; Eph 6:10 [c]Jdg 10:15; 1Sa 3:18; Ne 4:14
10:19 [d]2Sa 8:6 [e]1Ki 11:25; 2Ki 5:1
11:1 [f]1Ki 20:22,26 [g]2Sa 2:18 [h]1Ch 20:1 [i]2Sa 12:26-28

seized David's envoys, shaved off half of each man's beard,[v] cut off their garments at the buttocks,[w]
and sent them away.
5 When David was told about this, he sent messengers to meet the men, for they were greatly humiliated. The king said, "Stay at Jericho till your beards have grown, and then come back."
6 When the Ammonites realized that they had become obnoxious[x] to David, they hired twenty thousand Aramean[y] foot soldiers from Beth Rehob[z] and Zobah, as well as the king of Maakah[a] with a thousand men, and also twelve thousand men from Tob.
7 On hearing this, David sent Joab out with the entire army of fighting men. 8 The Ammonites came
out and drew up in battle formation at the entrance of their city gate, while the Arameans of Zobah and
Rehob and the men of Tob and Maakah were by themselves in the open country.
9 Joab saw that there were battle lines in front of him and behind him; so he selected some of the best
troops in Israel and deployed them against the Arameans. 10 He put the rest of the men under the command of Abishai his brother and deployed them against the Ammonites. 11 Joab said, "If the Arameans
are too strong for me, then you are to come to my rescue; but if the Ammonites are too strong for you,
then I will come to rescue you. 12 Be strong,[b] and let us fight bravely for our people and the cities of our
God. The LORD will do what is good in his sight."[c]
13 Then Joab and the troops with him advanced to fight the Arameans, and they fled before him.
14 When the Ammonites realized that the Arameans were fleeing, they fled before Abishai and went inside the city. So Joab returned from fighting the Ammonites and came to Jerusalem.
15 After the Arameans saw that they had been routed by Israel, they regrouped. 16 Hadadezer had Arameans brought from beyond the Euphrates River; they went to Helam, with Shobak the commander
of Hadadezer's army leading them.
17 When David was told of this, he gathered all Israel, crossed the Jordan and went to Helam. The
Arameans formed their battle lines to meet David and fought against him. 18 But they fled before Israel,
and David killed seven hundred of their charioteers and forty thousand of their foot soldiers.[a] He also
struck down Shobak the commander of their army, and he died there. 19 When all the kings who were
vassals of Hadadezer saw that they had been routed by Israel, they made peace with the Israelites and
became subject[d] to them.
So the Arameans[e] were afraid to help the Ammonites anymore.

David and Bathsheba

11 In the spring,[f] at the time when kings go off to war, David sent Joab[g] out with the king's men
and the whole Israelite army.[h] They destroyed the Ammonites and besieged Rabbah.[i] But David
remained in Jerusalem.

[a] *18* Some Septuagint manuscripts (see also 1 Chron. 19:18); Hebrew *horsemen*

10:5 As the delegation returns from Rabbah, the capital city of Ammon (11:1), to go to Jerusalem, David sends men to meet them on the way at Jericho. Jericho is directly on the route from Rabbah to Jerusalem, and it lies in Israelite territory just west of the Jordan River. David has compassion on the men because they had been greatly humiliated, and he minimizes their shame by having them reside in Jericho until their beards grow back.

10:6 Sensing an impending conflict, the Ammonites recruit mercenaries from four Aramean cities that lie in the region to the north-northeast of Israel. **Aramean.** The word "Arameans" appears thirteen times in the Hebrew of this chapter, and this highlights that they are a powerful enemy of Israel.

10:8–10 Israel's army is trapped. Ammonite forces are lined up for battle outside the city of Rabbah on one side of Israel, and Syrian troops are on the other. Joab divides Israel's soldiers to fight a two-front battle. He chooses some special forces to face the Syrians, and he places the bulk of the army under the leadership of Abishai, his brother, to face the Ammonites.

10:12 Joab encourages his army to be courageous (cf. 1 Sam 4:9). **The LORD will do what is good in his sight.** Joab trusts the results to God's will and purpose (1 Sam 3:18), leaving the outcome to God's providence. Joab is a complicated figure. At times, like here, he demonstrates piety, but other times he is barbaric and ruthless (2 Sam 3:26–27; 18:14; 20:9–10).

10:15 regrouped. Reassembled after their defeat.

10:16 Hadadezer, king of Zobah (8:5), musters more Aramean troops to fight Israel. **Helam.** Perhaps located at the modern site of 'Alma in the Syrian Desert.

10:17–19 The danger to Israel is so great that David himself leads the army to face the Arameans at Helam. The Israelite army inflicts a devastating defeat on its enemy, forcing the vassal kings who had been subject to Hadadezer to switch allegiance and become tributary states to Israel. The text does not tell the reader the names of the kings or their nations.

11:1—12:31 *David's Grievous Sins.* In this episode David's sins are multifaceted. He covets another man's wife (11:2–3), commits adultery with her (11:4–5), attempts to cover up the affair through deceit (11:6–13), and eventually masterminds the murder of the woman's husband Uriah (11:14–17). Ultimately, the heart of David's sin is that he despised the word of the Lord and the Lord himself (12:9–10). David comes under conviction, admits his guilt, and repents (12:13,16–17).

11:1–27 *David and Bathsheba.* The Israelite-Ammonite war that began

2One evening David got up from his bed and walked around on the roof[j] of the palace. From the roof
he saw[k] a woman bathing. The woman was very beautiful, 3and David sent someone to find out about
her. The man said, "She is Bathsheba,[l] the daughter of Eliam[m] and the wife of Uriah[n] the Hittite." 4Then
David sent messengers to get her.[o] She came to him, and he slept[p] with her. (Now she was purifying
herself from her monthly uncleanness.)[q] Then she went back home. 5The woman conceived and sent
word to David, saying, "I am pregnant."

6So David sent this word to Joab: "Send me Uriah[r] the Hittite." And Joab sent him to David. 7When
Uriah came to him, David asked him how Joab was, how the soldiers were and how the war was going.
8Then David said to Uriah, "Go down to your house and wash your feet."[s] So Uriah left the palace,
and a gift from the king was sent after him. 9But Uriah slept at the entrance to the palace with all his
master's servants and did not go down to his house.

10David was told, "Uriah did not go home." So he asked Uriah, "Haven't you just come from a military campaign? Why didn't you go home?"

11Uriah said to David, "The ark[t] and Israel and Judah are staying in tents,[a] and my commander Joab and my lord's men are camped in the open country. How could I go to my house to eat and drink and make love to my wife? As surely as you live, I will not do such a thing!"

12Then David said to him, "Stay here one more day, and tomorrow I will send you back." So Uriah
remained in Jerusalem that day and the next. 13At David's invitation, he ate and drank with him, and
David made him drunk. But in the evening Uriah went out to sleep on his mat among his master's
servants; he did not go home.

14In the morning David wrote a letter[u] to Joab and sent it with Uriah. 15In it he wrote, "Put Uriah out
in front where the fighting is fiercest. Then withdraw from him so he will be struck down[v] and die.[w]"

16So while Joab had the city under siege, he put Uriah at a place where he knew the strongest defenders were. 17When the men of the city came out and fought against Joab, some of the men in David's
army fell; moreover, Uriah the Hittite died.

18Joab sent David a full account of the battle. 19He instructed the messenger: "When you have finished giving the king this account of the battle, 20the king's anger may flare up, and he may ask you,
'Why did you get so close to the city to fight? Didn't you know they would shoot arrows from the wall?
21Who killed Abimelek[x] son of Jerub-Besheth[b]? Didn't a woman drop an upper millstone on him from
the wall,[y] so that he died in Thebez? Why did you get so close to the wall?' If he asks you this, then say
to him, 'Moreover, your servant Uriah the Hittite is dead.' "

11:2 [j] Dt 22:8; Jos 2:8 [k] Mt 5:28
11:3 [l] 1Ch 3:5 [m] 2Sa 23:34 [n] 2Sa 23:39
11:4 [o] Lev 20:10; Ps 51 Title; Jas 1:14-15 [p] Dt 22:22 [q] Lev 15:25-30; 18:19
11:6 [r] 1Ch 11:41
11:8 [s] Ge 18:4; 43:24; Lk 7:44
11:11 [t] 2Sa 7:2
11:14 [u] 1Ki 21:8
11:15 [v] 2Sa 12:9 [w] 2Sa 12:12
11:21 [x] Jdg 8:31 [y] Jdg 9:50-54

[a] *11* Or *staying at Sukkoth* [b] *21* Also known as *Jerub-Baal* (that is, Gideon)

in ch. 10 is the setting for this sad episode. While Joab and the army are besieging the Ammonite capital of Rabbah, David commits adultery with the wife of one of his trusted soldiers. He attempts to cover up the affair, but in the end he plots the death of the woman's husband.

11:1 spring ... when kings go off to war. But David remains in his palace and sends Joab to lead the army against the Ammonites. Perhaps David has gotten complacent because "the Lord gave David victory wherever he went" (8:6b). He is shirking his duty. **Rabbah.** Located in modern Amman next to a spring that feeds the Jabbok River. It sits next to a main thoroughfare known as the King's Highway. The town is easily defended because of its deep valleys and easy access to water sources.

11:2 palace. A terraced structure, first built in the fourteenth to thirteenth centuries BC, has been found in Jerusalem as part of the city of King David. Over 50 feet (15 meters) in height, it may have served as the foundation for a large podium that contained the acropolis of Jerusalem. David's palace perhaps sat there overlooking the entire city. After his afternoon siesta, David goes for a walk on the roof of his palace. From there he sees a woman bathing, probably for her menstrual uncleanness (v. 4).

11:3 Eliam. May be one of David's inner ring of 30 elite loyalist warriors (23:34). **Uriah.** One of David's elite warriors (23:39).

11:4 slept with her. According to the law, both of them should be put to death. Eventually the woman discovers she is pregnant (v. 5), a secret that cannot be hidden. **purifying herself.** Based on the laws of menstruation (Lev 15:19–30).

11:6–8 David attempts to cover up his sin. David summons Uriah back from the Ammonite war hoping that Uriah will sleep with his wife and that people will view the baby as Uriah's.

11:8 wash your feet. Sometimes understood as a euphemism for sexual intercourse; "feet" can at times refer to genitalia. Perhaps it is mere innuendo or a statement of double meaning.

11:9 Uriah refuses to comply. He is a soldier on duty, and sexual intercourse is a source of impurity during a military campaign (1 Sam 21:5; cf. Exod 19:15).

11:13 David's next tactic is to order Uriah to remain in Jerusalem for another night and get him so drunk that he will go to Bathsheba. But again Uriah refuses to give in. David contrasts with Uriah: David is shirking his duty and is deceitful and manipulative; Uriah is courageous and upright, and a man of duty. And Uriah is a Hittite!

11:14–17 Ironically, Uriah carries the letter that orders his own execution. The letter is evidence that Uriah's death is premeditated murder on David's part. Joab is complicit in the murder by abetting David's crime without even knowing why David ordered it.

11:21 Joab anticipates that David may use the example of Abimelek to criticize Joab's decision to put the soldiers so close to a city wall under siege (Judg 9:50–55). Joab trumps this possible accusation by subtly

11:27 [z]2Sa 12:9; Ps 51:4-5
12:1 [a]2Sa 7:2; 1Ki 20:35-41 [b]Ps 51 Title [c]2Sa 14:4
12:5 [d]1Ki 20:40
12:6 [e]Ex 22:1; Lk 19:8
12:7 [f]1Sa 16:13 [g]1Ki 20:42
12:8 [h]2Sa 9:7
12:9 [i]Nu 15:31; 1Sa 15:19 [j]2Sa 11:15
12:10 [k]2Sa 13:28; 18:14-15; 1Ki 2:25
12:11 [l]Dt 28:30; 2Sa 16:21-22

22The messenger set out, and when he arrived he told David everything Joab had sent him to say.
23The messenger said to David, "The men overpowered us and came out against us in the open, but we
drove them back to the entrance of the city gate. 24Then the archers shot arrows at your servants from
the wall, and some of the king's men died. Moreover, your servant Uriah the Hittite is dead."
25David told the messenger, "Say this to Joab: 'Don't let this upset you; the sword devours one as well
as another. Press the attack against the city and destroy it.' Say this to encourage Joab."
26When Uriah's wife heard that her husband was dead, she mourned for him. 27After the time of
mourning was over, David had her brought to his house, and she became his wife and bore him a son.
But the thing David had done displeased[z] the LORD.

Nathan Rebukes David

11:1; 12:29-31pp — 1Ch 20:1-3

12 The LORD sent Nathan[a] to David.[b] When he came to him,[c] he said, "There were two men in a
certain town, one rich and the other poor. 2The rich man had a very large number of sheep
and cattle, 3but the poor man had nothing except one little ewe lamb he had bought. He raised it, and
it grew up with him and his children. It shared his food, drank from his cup and even slept in his arms.
It was like a daughter to him.
4"Now a traveler came to the rich man, but the rich man refrained from taking one of his own sheep
or cattle to prepare a meal for the traveler who had come to him. Instead, he took the ewe lamb that
belonged to the poor man and prepared it for the one who had come to him."
5David[d] burned with anger against the man and said to Nathan, "As surely as the LORD lives, the
man who did this must die! 6He must pay for that lamb four times over,[e] because he did such a thing
and had no pity."
7Then Nathan said to David, "You are the man! This is what the LORD, the God of Israel, says: 'I
anointed[f] you[g] king over Israel, and I delivered you from the hand of Saul. 8I gave your master's
house to you,[h] and your master's wives into your arms. I gave you all Israel and Judah. And if all
this had been too little, I would have given you even more. 9Why did you despise[i] the word of the
LORD by doing what is evil in his eyes? You struck down[j] Uriah the Hittite with the sword and took his
wife to be your own. You killed him with the sword of the Ammonites. 10Now, therefore, the sword[k]
will never depart from your house, because you despised me and took the wife of Uriah the Hittite
to be your own.'
11"This is what the LORD says: 'Out of your own household I am going to bring calamity on you.[l]
Before your very eyes I will take your wives and give them to one who is close to you, and he will sleep

informing the king that the Israelite troops were near the wall so that Uriah would be killed.

11:25 Don't let this upset you. David callously encourages Joab with the justification that people die in war as a matter of course.

11:26 mourned. The period of mourning in Hebrew culture normally lasts for seven days (1 Sam 31:13; Gen 50:10), although it can last as long as three weeks (Dan 10:2).

11:27 The drama hits a high note. **displeased the LORD.** Lit. "was evil in the eyes of the LORD" (cf. v. 25 and note). The reader gets a sense that a reckoning will soon come, and it appears in the next chapter.

12:1–31 *Nathan Rebukes David.* These events do not follow immediately on the sinful actions of David in ch. 11. The period of mourning for Uriah could last up to three weeks (see note on 11:26). David then marries Bathsheba, who bears him a son. These events thus occur perhaps as long as nine months later. At this time, Nathan presents a parable to David (vv. 1–4), who eventually comes under great conviction for his sin (see Ps 51). Even though he repents, there are still temporal consequences to his sin.

12:1–4 Nathan, a court prophet of David (7:2), confronts David with a parable. He contrasts two men in regard to their personal and material possessions. One man is described with a superlative in Hebrew of having a "very large number" of domesticated animals (12:2), and the other man is said to have "one little" animal (12:3). In Hebrew culture, wealth is often measured by owning livestock (Job 1:3; 42:12). A traveler comes to visit the rich man, and the wealthy man refuses to slaughter and prepare one of his own animals for a feast. He simply takes the lamb of the poor man for this purpose. The parable exemplifies injustice, abuse of power, and the belief that might is right.

12:5 burned with anger. In the Hebrew, David's response is given in the superlative: he is "very angry." He sees the rich man's sin with great clarity. **must die!** David's call for a death sentence is above and beyond the judicial sentence for theft (see note on v. 6)

12:6 four times over. The correct sentence is that a thief must restore fourfold what he has stolen (Exod 22:1). Some commentators point out that David himself ends up losing four children: the child born to Bathsheba (12:18), Amnon (13:33), Absalom (18:15), and Adonijah (1 Kgs 2:25).

12:7 You are the man! David is the rich man of the parable.

12:9 despise the word of the LORD. The very heart of David's sin is scorning God's word; he broke at least four of the Ten Commandments: murder, adultery, lying, and coveting. He is culpable, and he cannot shift the blame for Uriah's murder on "the sword of the Ammonites."

12:11 This predicts Absalom's rebellion when he lies with David's concubines on the rooftop of the palace for all to see (16:22).

with your wives in broad daylight. 12You did it in secret,[m] but I will do this thing in broad daylight[n]
before all Israel.' "
13Then David said to Nathan, "I have sinned[o] against the LORD."
Nathan replied, "The LORD has taken away[p] your sin.[q] You are not going to die.[r] 14But because by
doing this you have shown utter contempt for[a] the LORD,[s] the son born to you will die."
15After Nathan had gone home, the LORD struck[t] the child that Uriah's wife had borne to David, and
he became ill. 16David pleaded with God for the child. He fasted and spent the nights lying[u] in sackcloth[b] on the ground. 17The elders of his household stood beside him to get him up from the ground,
but he refused, and he would not eat any food with them.[v]
18On the seventh day the child died. David's attendants were afraid to tell him that the child was
dead, for they thought, "While the child was still living, he wouldn't listen to us when we spoke to him.
How can we now tell him the child is dead? He may do something desperate."
19David noticed that his attendants were whispering among themselves, and he realized the child
was dead. "Is the child dead?" he asked.
"Yes," they replied, "he is dead."
20Then David got up from the ground. After he had washed,[w] put on lotions and changed his
clothes,[x] he went into the house of the LORD and worshiped. Then he went to his own house, and at his
request they served him food, and he ate.
21His attendants asked him, "Why are you acting this way? While the child was alive, you fasted and
wept,[y] but now that the child is dead, you get up and eat!"
22He answered, "While the child was still alive, I fasted and wept. I thought, 'Who knows?[z] The LORD
may be gracious to me and let the child live.'[a] 23But now that he is dead, why should I go on fasting?
Can I bring him back again? I will go to him,[b] but he will not return to me."[c]
24Then David comforted his wife Bathsheba,[d] and he went to her and made love to her. She gave
birth to a son, and they named him Solomon.[e] The LORD loved him; 25and because the LORD loved him,
he sent word through Nathan the prophet to name him Jedidiah.[c][f]
26Meanwhile Joab fought against Rabbah[g] of the Ammonites and captured the royal citadel. 27Joab
then sent messengers to David, saying, "I have fought against Rabbah and taken its water supply. 28Now
muster the rest of the troops and besiege the city and capture it. Otherwise I will take the city, and it
will be named after me."
29So David mustered the entire army and went to Rabbah, and attacked and captured it. 30David took
the crown[h] from their king's[d] head, and it was placed on his own head. It weighed a talent[e] of gold,
and it was set with precious stones. David took a great quantity of plunder from the city 31and brought
out the people who were there, consigning them to labor with saws and with iron picks and axes, and
he made them work at brickmaking.[f] David did this to all the Ammonite[i] towns. Then he and his entire
army returned to Jerusalem.

[a] *14* An ancient Hebrew scribal tradition; Masoretic Text *for the enemies of* [b] *16* Dead Sea Scrolls and Septuagint; Masoretic Text does not have *in sackcloth*. [c] *25 Jedidiah* means *loved by the LORD*.
[d] *30* Or *from Milkom's* (that is, Molek's) [e] *30* That is, about 75 pounds or about 34 kilograms
[f] *31* The meaning of the Hebrew for this clause is uncertain.

12:12 [m] 2Sa 11:4-15 [n] 2Sa 16:22
12:13 [o] Ge 13:13; Nu 22:34; 1Sa 15:24; 2Sa 24:10 [p] Ps 32:1-5; 51:1,9; 103:12; Zec 3:4, 9 [q] Pr 28:13; Mic 7:18-19 [r] Lev 20:10; 24:17
12:14 [s] Isa 52:5; Ro 2:24
12:15 [t] 1Sa 25:38
12:16 [u] 2Sa 13:31; Ps 5:7
12:17 [v] 2Sa 3:35
12:20 [w] Mt 6:17 [x] Job 1:20
12:21 [y] Jdg 20:26
12:22 [z] Jnh 3:9 [a] Isa 38:1-5
12:23 [b] Ge 37:35 [c] 1Sa 31:13; 2Sa 13:39; Job 7:10; 10:21
12:24 [d] 1Ki 1:11 [e] 1Ki 1:10; 1Ch 22:9; 28:5; Mt 1:6
12:25 [f] Ne 13:26
12:26 [g] Dt 3:11; 1Ch 20:1-3
12:30 [h] 1Ch 20:2; Est 8:15; Ps 21:3; 132:18
12:31 [i] 1Sa 14:47

12:13–14 David comes under great conviction, and he confesses his sin (Ps 51). He deserves the death penalty (Deut 22:22), but the Lord is merciful to him. Though David showed no compassion on the rich man in the parable (2 Sam 12:6), the Lord is gracious to David. Yet there will be consequences to his sin. David will not die, but the son born to Bathsheba will.
12:21–23 David's servants question his activity because the normal cultural practice is to mourn for a person *after* death. David mourned *before* the child died (v. 16). David does not mourn after the child died because he has conviction that he will have a personal reunion with his son: "I will go to him."
12:24 his wife Bathsheba. By calling Bathsheba the wife of David, the text gives legitimacy to their marriage and the birth of Solomon, the fourth son of David and Bathsheba (1 Chr 3:5) and David's successor.
12:26–28 Capturing Rabbah apparently occurs in three stages: (1) Joab seizes the royal citadel. (2) Joab takes the section of the town that controls its water supply. (3) David receives the honor and credit for Rabbah's fall as he captures the remainder of the city.
12:30 their king's. This may refer to Molek, the god of the Ammonites (see NIV text note; see also 1 Kgs 11:5,33; 2 Kgs 23:13). This may help to explain why the crown weighs so much: a "talent of gold" is about 75 pounds (34 kilograms).
12:31 work at brickmaking. Lit. "pass through Malken." The Ammonites are well-known for child sacrifice, i.e., passing their children through the fire to Molek/Milkom (Lev 18:21; 2 Kgs 23:10). Some commentators argue that David, in a sense of ironic justice, is doing the same thing to the adult Ammonites. On the other hand, David may simply be putting the Ammonites to forced labor (Deut 20:11; Josh 16:10; Judg 1:28–35). See NIV text note.

13:1 [j]2Sa 3:2 [k]2Sa 14:27; 1Ch 3:9 [l]2Sa 3:3
13:3 [m]1Sa 16:9
13:9 [n]Ge 45:1
13:11 [o]Ge 39:12 [p]Ge 38:16
13:12 [q]Lev 20:17; Jdg 20:6 [r]Ge 34:7; Jdg 19:23
13:13 [s]Ge 20:12; Lev 18:9; Dt 22:21, 23-24
13:14 [t]Ge 34:2; Dt 22:25; Eze 22:11

Amnon and Tamar

13 In the course of time, Amnon[j] son of David fell in love with Tamar,[k] the beautiful sister of
Absalom[l] son of David.
2 Amnon became so obsessed with his sister Tamar that he made himself ill. She was a virgin, and it
seemed impossible for him to do anything to her.
3 Now Amnon had an adviser named Jonadab son of Shimeah,[m] David's brother. Jonadab was a very
shrewd man. 4 He asked Amnon, "Why do you, the king's son, look so haggard morning after morning?
Won't you tell me?"
Amnon said to him, "I'm in love with Tamar, my brother Absalom's sister."
5 "Go to bed and pretend to be ill," Jonadab said. "When your father comes to see you, say to him, 'I
would like my sister Tamar to come and give me something to eat. Let her prepare the food in my sight
so I may watch her and then eat it from her hand.' "
6 So Amnon lay down and pretended to be ill. When the king came to see him, Amnon said to him,
"I would like my sister Tamar to come and make some special bread in my sight, so I may eat from
her hand."
7 David sent word to Tamar at the palace: "Go to the house of your brother Amnon and prepare some
food for him." 8 So Tamar went to the house of her brother Amnon, who was lying down. She took some
dough, kneaded it, made the bread in his sight and baked it. 9 Then she took the pan and served him
the bread, but he refused to eat.
"Send everyone out of here,"[n] Amnon said. So everyone left him. 10 Then Amnon said to Tamar,
"Bring the food here into my bedroom so I may eat from your hand." And Tamar took the bread she
had prepared and brought it to her brother Amnon in his bedroom. 11 But when she took it to him to
eat, he grabbed[o] her and said, "Come to bed with me, my sister."[p]
12 "No, my brother!" she said to him. "Don't force me! Such a thing should not be done in Israel![q]
Don't do this wicked thing.[r] 13 What about me?[s] Where could I get rid of my disgrace? And what about
you? You would be like one of the wicked fools in Israel. Please speak to the king; he will not keep me
from being married to you." 14 But he refused to listen to her, and since he was stronger than she, he
raped her.[t]
15 Then Amnon hated her with intense hatred. In fact, he hated her more than he had loved her.
Amnon said to her, "Get up and get out!"
16 "No!" she said to him. "Sending me away would be a greater wrong than what you have already
done to me."
But he refused to listen to her. 17 He called his personal servant and said, "Get this woman out of
my sight and bolt the door after her." 18 So his servant put her out and bolted the door after her. She

13:1—24:25 *Later Years of David's Rule.* The last chapters of 2 Samuel are dominated by the consequences of David's sin in the matter of Bathsheba and Uriah. The Lord had promised the king that "the sword will never depart from your house" (12:10). David ends up losing four of his sons: the child of Bathsheba (12:18), Amnon (13:33), Absalom (18:15), and Adonijah (1 Kings 2:25).

13:1–22 *Amnon and Tamar.* The Lord's promise to David spoken by Nathan the prophet that "the sword will never depart from your house" (12:10) comes to pass in this explicit episode. Amnon, David's oldest son and heir to the throne of Israel, has a compulsive lust for his half sister Tamar. He attempts to seduce her, but being unsuccessful, he rapes her. Amnon then casts Tamar out of his sight to her great shame. This is the setting for Absalom's murder of Amnon in the second half of the chapter.

13:1–2 Tamar. A full sister of Absalom and a half sister of Amnon. Absalom and Tamar are children of David and Maakah (3:3); Amnon is David's oldest son, born to him by Ahinoam (3:2). **made himself ill.** Lovesick (Song 2:5; 5:8). But Amnon is kept from acting upon his love/lust because the law forbids it (Lev 18:9), and Israelite societal mores prohibit it (2 Sam 13:12).

13:3 Jonadab. One of Amnon's counselors; he is a nephew of David and a cousin of Absalom, Amnon, and Tamar. **shrewd.** Normally translated as "wise" but clearly negative in this context.

13:7 David does not suspect Amnon's trickery. There will be no oversight or constraints in Amnon's house.

13:11 grabbed. Reflects significant force in Hebrew. Amnon then demands that she "come to bed" with him by using two imperative forms. One of the imperatives was used by Potiphar's wife in her attempted seduction of Joseph (Gen 39:7,12).

13:12 Incest was outlawed in Israel, but other nations of the ancient Near East commonly practiced it (Lev 18:1–3,6).

13:13 What about me? . . . what about you? Tamar underscores the severe consequences to both of them if they have sexual relations. **he will not keep me from being married to you.** Perhaps Tamar's desperate attempt to save herself; incest is not legal in Israel.

13:16 According to the law, if a man rapes a virgin, he must marry her (Deut 22:28–29). But Amnon throws her into the street (2 Sam 13:18). Tamar pleads with him, saying that sending her out to face shame and humiliation is a "greater wrong" than having raped her.

13:17 this woman. Amnon does not refer to Tamar by name, demonstrating his utter contempt and scorn.

13:18 ornate robe. Occurs elsewhere in the OT only in Gen 37:3,23,32,

was wearing an ornate[a] robe,[u] for this was the kind of garment the virgin daughters of the king wore.
19 Tamar put ashes[v] on her head and tore the ornate robe she was wearing. She put her hands on her
head and went away, weeping aloud as she went.
20 Her brother Absalom said to her, "Has that Amnon, your brother, been with you? Be quiet for now,
my sister; he is your brother. Don't take this thing to heart." And Tamar lived in her brother Absalom's
house, a desolate woman.
21 When King David heard all this, he was furious.[w] 22 And Absalom never said a word to Amnon,
either good or bad;[x] he hated[y] Amnon because he had disgraced his sister Tamar.

Absalom Kills Amnon

23 Two years later, when Absalom's sheepshearers[z] were at Baal Hazor near the border of Ephraim, he
invited all the king's sons to come there. 24 Absalom went to the king and said, "Your servant has had
shearers come. Will the king and his attendants please join me?"
25 "No, my son," the king replied. "All of us should not go; we would only be a burden to you." Although Absalom urged him, he still refused to go but gave him his blessing.
26 Then Absalom said, "If not, please let my brother Amnon come with us."
The king asked him, "Why should he go with you?" 27 But Absalom urged him, so he sent with him
Amnon and the rest of the king's sons.

[a] *18* The meaning of the Hebrew for this word is uncertain; also in verse 19.

13:18 [u] Ge 37:23; Jdg 5:30
13:19 [v] Jos 7:6; 1Sa 4:12; 2Sa 1:2; Est 4:1; Da 9:3
13:21 [w] Ge 34:7
13:22 [x] Ge 31:24 [y] Lev 19:17-18; 1Jn 2:9-11
13:23 [z] 1Sa 25:7

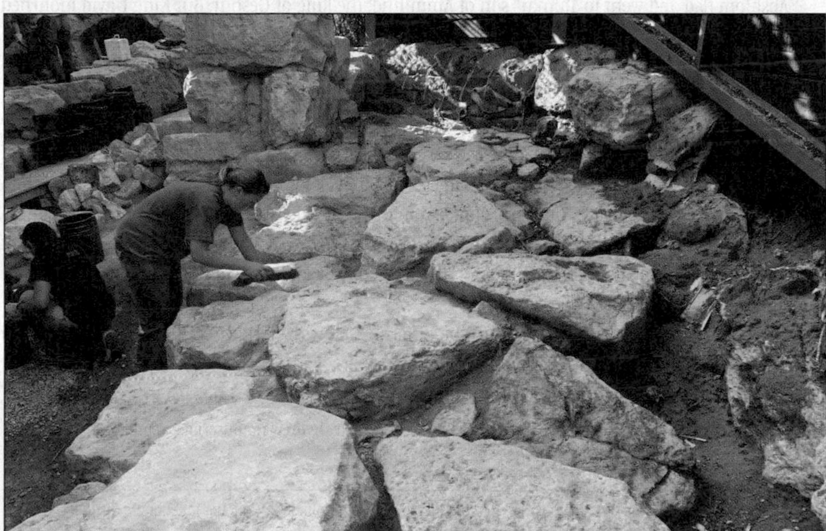

Large structure in City of David believed by some to be King David's palace.
Todd Bolen/www.BiblePlaces.com

where Joseph's brothers abuse him and throw him into a pit because of his ornate robe.

13:19 Tamar's actions are all signs of grief, sorrow, and mourning (Esth 4:3; Jonah 3:6).

13:20–22 Absalom tells his sister not to "take this thing to heart," but to keep quiet regarding the matter (v. 20). Absalom is quiet as well, not speaking to Amnon "either good or bad" (v. 22). But Absalom *has* taken it to heart and is biding his time until he finds the appropriate moment for revenge. David is "furious" (v. 21), but he takes no action. Perhaps he is protecting Amnon, who, as eldest son, is heir apparent to the throne.

13:23–39 *Absalom Kills Amnon.* Two years have passed since Amnon raped his half sister Tamar. But Absalom has a long memory and has been biding his time for retaliation. Absalom concocts a charade in order to exact revenge on Amnon. He orders the death of Amnon and then flees to the land of Geshur to be under the protection of his grandfather.

13:23 Sheepshearing is a time of joy and feasting (1 Sam 25:2–8). Absalom sees an opportunity, and he invites all of David's sons to come celebrate. This blanket invitation is part of his deception. **Baal Hazor.** Located at modern Tell 'Asur, about 15 miles (24 kilometers) north-northeast of Jerusalem, so the event is taking place away from the royal palace.

13:25–26 Absalom invites David and his close associates to the sheep-shearing event. That invitation gives an aura of royal importance to the celebration. Perhaps Absalom knows full well that David will decline, but it is part of the ruse. **Why should he go with you?** David appears to suspect Absalom because the king is aware of what happened between Amnon and Tamar (v. 21).

13:28 [a]2Sa 3:3 [b]Jdg 19:6,9,22; Ru 3:7; 1Sa 25:36 [c]2Sa 12:10
13:31 [d]Nu 14:6; 2Sa 1:11; 12:16
13:37 [e]ver 34; 2Sa 3:3; 14:23,32
13:39 [f]2Sa 14:13 [g]2Sa 12:19-23
14:1 [h]2Sa 2:18
14:2 [i]2Ch 11:6; Ne 3:5; Jer 6:1; Am 1:1 [j]2Sa 20:16 [k]Ru 3:3; 2Sa 12:20; Isa 1:6
14:3 [l]ver 19

28 Absalom[a] ordered his men, "Listen! When Amnon is in high[b] spirits from drinking wine and I say
to you, 'Strike Amnon down,' then kill him. Don't be afraid. Haven't I given you this order? Be strong
and brave.[c]" 29 So Absalom's men did to Amnon what Absalom had ordered. Then all the king's sons got
up, mounted their mules and fled.

30 While they were on their way, the report came to David: "Absalom has struck down all the king's
sons; not one of them is left." 31 The king stood up, tore[d] his clothes and lay down on the ground; and
all his attendants stood by with their clothes torn.

32 But Jonadab son of Shimeah, David's brother, said, "My lord should not think that they killed all
the princes; only Amnon is dead. This has been Absalom's express intention ever since the day Amnon
raped his sister Tamar. 33 My lord the king should not be concerned about the report that all the king's
sons are dead. Only Amnon is dead."

34 Meanwhile, Absalom had fled.

Now the man standing watch looked up and saw many people on the road west of him, coming down
the side of the hill. The watchman went and told the king, "I see men in the direction of Horonaim,
on the side of the hill."[a]

35 Jonadab said to the king, "See, the king's sons have come; it has happened just as your servant
said."

36 As he finished speaking, the king's sons came in, wailing loudly. The king, too, and all his attendants wept very bitterly.

37 Absalom fled and went to Talmai[e] son of Ammihud, the king of Geshur. But King David mourned
many days for his son.

38 After Absalom fled and went to Geshur, he stayed there three years. 39 And King David longed to go
to Absalom,[f] for he was consoled[g] concerning Amnon's death.

Absalom Returns to Jerusalem

14 Joab[h] son of Zeruiah knew that the king's heart longed for Absalom. 2 So Joab sent someone to
Tekoa[i] and had a wise woman[j] brought from there. He said to her, "Pretend you are in mourning. Dress in mourning clothes, and don't use any cosmetic lotions.[k] Act like a woman who has spent
many days grieving for the dead. 3 Then go to the king and speak these words to him." And Joab[l] put
the words in her mouth.

4 When the woman from Tekoa went[b] to the king, she fell with her face to the ground to pay him
honor, and she said, "Help me, Your Majesty!"

5 The king asked her, "What is troubling you?"

[a] *34* Septuagint; Hebrew does not have this sentence. [b] *4* Many Hebrew manuscripts, Septuagint, Vulgate and Syriac; most Hebrew manuscripts *spoke*

13:28 Absalom orders his men to kill Amnon when his guard is down due to drinking. They would naturally be afraid to kill the heir apparent of David's throne, but Absalom encourages them to do his dirty work.
13:30–31 all the king's sons. David receives a false report regarding the fate of all his sons and responds with great grief and sorrow.
13:32 Jonadab. David's nephew who earlier hatched the plan for Amnon to seduce Tamar (vv. 3–5). He is working both sides to make himself out to be a trusted advisor to the king. Absalom would certainly want revenge against this cousin if he knew of his treachery.
13:34 Meanwhile, Absalom had fled. This may be part of Jonadab's address to David in v. 33. **the road west of him.** Some commentators read this phrase as a place-name: "the Horonaim road." "Horonaim" is the dual form of Horon, and if so it may refer to the twin cities of Upper Beth Horon and Lower Beth Horon, located in the mountains of Judah (Josh 16:3,5; 2 Chr 8:5).
13:37 Absalom flees to the protection of his maternal grandfather in Geshur (3:3). **his son.** Amnon, not Absalom.
13:39 longed. The Hebrew verb has a feminine subject so it is problematic to have David as the subject. Some commentators emend "David" to the king's "spirit" (feminine in Hebrew; it occurs in a Qumran fragment) as yearning for Absalom.
14:1–33 *Absalom Returns to Jerusalem.* To convince David to return Absalom to Jerusalem, Joab sends a woman to David with a fictional story to convict the king of unreasonableness against Absalom. In a sense, she is a living parable (cf. 12:1–4). The king comes under conviction, brings Absalom back to the royal city, and eventually restores him.
14:1 longed for. Does not necessarily mean that David is positively inclined toward his son; his heart may be against his son for murdering Amnon. Perhaps the most that can be said is that David is thinking constantly about Absalom.
14:2–3 Joab hatches a plan to push David to reconcile with Absalom and cunningly enlists a "wise" or clever woman.
14:2 Tekoa. The home of the later prophet Amos (Amos 1:1); located about nine miles (14.5 kilometers) south of Jerusalem at Khirbet Tuqu' in Judah.
14:3 put the words in her mouth. Idiomatic for one telling another precisely what to say (Exod 4:15).

She said, "I am a widow; my husband is dead. 6 I your servant had two sons. They got into a fight with each other in the field, and no one was there to separate them. One struck the other and killed him. 7 Now the whole clan has risen up against your servant; they say, 'Hand over the one who struck his brother down, so that we may put him to death[m] for the life of his brother whom he killed; then we will get rid of the heir[n] as well.' They would put out the only burning coal I have left,[o] leaving my husband neither name nor descendant on the face of the earth."

8 The king said to the woman, "Go home,[p] and I will issue an order in your behalf."

9 But the woman from Tekoa said to him, "Let my lord the king pardon[q] me and my family,[r] and let the king and his throne be without guilt.[s]"

10 The king replied, "If anyone says anything to you, bring them to me, and they will not bother you again."

11 She said, "Then let the king invoke the LORD his God to prevent the avenger[t] of blood from adding to the destruction, so that my son will not be destroyed."

"As surely as the LORD lives," he said, "not one hair[u] of your son's head will fall to the ground.[v]"

12 Then the woman said, "Let your servant speak a word to my lord the king."

"Speak," he replied.

13 The woman said, "Why then have you devised a thing like this against the people of God? When the king says this, does he not convict himself,[w] for the king has not brought back his banished son?[x] 14 Like water[y] spilled on the ground, which cannot be recovered, so we must die.[z] But that is not what God desires; rather, he devises ways so that a banished person[a] does not remain banished from him.

15 "And now I have come to say this to my lord the king because the people have made me afraid. Your servant thought, 'I will speak to the king; perhaps he will grant his servant's request. 16 Perhaps the king will agree to deliver his servant from the hand of the man who is trying to cut off both me and my son from God's inheritance.'[b]

17 "And now your servant says, 'May the word of my lord the king secure my inheritance, for my lord the king is like an angel[c] of God in discerning[d] good and evil. May the LORD your God be with you.'"

18 Then the king said to the woman, "Don't keep from me the answer to what I am going to ask you."

"Let my lord the king speak," the woman said.

19 The king asked, "Isn't the hand of Joab[e] with you in all this?"

The woman answered, "As surely as you live, my lord the king, no one can turn to the right or to the left from anything my lord the king says. Yes, it was your servant Joab who instructed me to do this and who put all these words into the mouth of your servant. 20 Your servant Joab did this to change the present situation. My lord has wisdom[f] like that of an angel of God—he knows everything that happens in the land.[g]"

21 The king said to Joab, "Very well, I will do it. Go, bring back the young man Absalom."

22 Joab fell with his face to the ground to pay him honor, and he blessed the king.[h] Joab said, "Today your servant knows that he has found favor in your eyes, my lord the king, because the king has granted his servant's request."

23 Then Joab went to Geshur and brought Absalom back to Jerusalem. 24 But the king said, "He must go to his own house; he must not see my face." So Absalom went to his own house and did not see the face of the king.

14:7 [m] Nu 35:19 [n] Mt 21:38 [o] Dt 19:10-13
14:8 [p] 1Sa 25:35
14:9 [q] 1Sa 25:24 [r] Mt 27:25 [s] 1Sa 25:28; 1Ki 2:33
14:11 [t] Nu 35:12,21 [u] Mt 10:30 [v] 1Sa 14:45
14:13 [w] 2Sa 12:7; 1Ki 20:40 [x] 2Sa 13:38-39
14:14 [y] Job 14:11; Ps 58:7; Isa 19:5 [z] Job 10:8; 17:13; 30:23; Ps 22:15; Heb 9:27 [a] Nu 35:15,25-28; Job 34:15
14:16 [b] Ex 34:9; 1Sa 26:19
14:17 [c] ver 20; 1Sa 29:9; 2Sa 19:27 [d] 1Ki 3:9; Da 2:21
14:19 [e] ver 3
14:20 [f] 1Ki 3:12,28; Isa 28:6 [g] ver 17; 2Sa 18:13; 19:27
14:22 [h] Ge 47:7

14:6 The woman's story parallels the story of Cain and Abel in Gen 4:8.
14:7 the whole clan. According to Hebrew law, the family is obligated to avenge the blood of a relative (Num 35:19–21). The clan also appears to have the motivation that they will receive an inheritance when they "get rid of the heir." The woman is helpless; her only hope is her remaining son, a "burning coal" not yet extinguished.
14:9 the king and his throne. A figure called hendiadys, which expresses a single idea by two words connected by "and" for the purpose of emphasis.
14:11 The woman asks David to take a vow on the name of the Lord that he will protect her son. David immediately swears a formal oath: "as surely as the LORD lives."
14:13–14 The woman forcefully applies her story to David. The jig is up. By not returning his son to Jerusalem as heir, David is going against the interests of God's people. The reality is that God will bring back Absalom to the royal city even if David does not want that to happen.
14:18–19 David is suspicious: Is Joab behind this story? He wants complete truthfulness from the woman. She confesses, and David is on target with his suspicions.
14:21 David relents and orders Joab to bring Absalom back to Jerusalem. **young man Absalom.** This title, which appears four other times (18:5,12,29,32), stresses Absalom's youth and vigor.
14:24 David does not fully forgive nor completely relent. He refuses to see Absalom. The repetition of all the elements of the command in the second half of the verse accentuates the reality that David would not see him and did not see him.

14:26 [i] 2Sa 18:9; Eze 44:20
14:27 [j] 2Sa 18:18 [k] 2Sa 13:1
14:30 [l] Ex 9:31
14:31 [m] Jdg 15:5
14:32 [n] 2Sa 3:3 [o] 1Sa 20:8
14:33 [p] Ge 33:4; Lk 15:20
15:1 [q] 2Sa 12:11 [r] 1Sa 8:11; 1Ki 1:5
15:2 [s] Ge 23:10; 2Sa 19:8
15:3 [t] Pr 12:2
15:4 [u] Jdg 9:29
15:6 [v] Ro 16:18
15:8 [w] 2Sa 3:3; 13:37-38 [x] Ge 28:20

25 In all Israel there was not a man so highly praised for his handsome appearance as Absalom. From the top of his head to the sole of his foot there was no blemish in him. 26 Whenever he cut the hair of his head[i] — he used to cut his hair once a year because it became too heavy for him — he would weigh it, and its weight was two hundred shekels[a] by the royal standard.

27 Three sons[j] and a daughter were born to Absalom. His daughter's name was Tamar,[k] and she became a beautiful woman.

28 Absalom lived two years in Jerusalem without seeing the king's face. 29 Then Absalom sent for Joab in order to send him to the king, but Joab refused to come to him. So he sent a second time, but he refused to come. 30 Then he said to his servants, "Look, Joab's field is next to mine, and he has barley[l] there. Go and set it on fire." So Absalom's servants set the field on fire.

31 Then Joab did go to Absalom's house, and he said to him, "Why have your servants set my field on fire?[m]"

32 Absalom said to Joab, "Look, I sent word to you and said, 'Come here so I can send you to the king to ask, "Why have I come from Geshur?[n] It would be better for me if I were still there!"' Now then, I want to see the king's face, and if I am guilty of anything, let him put me to death."[o]

33 So Joab went to the king and told him this. Then the king summoned Absalom, and he came in and bowed down with his face to the ground before the king. And the king kissed[p] Absalom.

Absalom's Conspiracy

15 In the course of time,[q] Absalom provided himself with a chariot[r] and horses and with fifty men to run ahead of him. 2 He would get up early and stand by the side of the road leading to the city gate.[s] Whenever anyone came with a complaint to be placed before the king for a decision, Absalom would call out to him, "What town are you from?" He would answer, "Your servant is from one of the tribes of Israel." 3 Then Absalom would say to him, "Look, your claims are valid and proper, but there is no representative of the king to hear you."[t] 4 And Absalom would add, "If only I were appointed judge in the land![u] Then everyone who has a complaint or case could come to me and I would see that they receive justice."

5 Also, whenever anyone approached him to bow down before him, Absalom would reach out his hand, take hold of him and kiss him. 6 Absalom behaved in this way toward all the Israelites who came to the king asking for justice, and so he stole the hearts[v] of the people of Israel.

7 At the end of four[b] years, Absalom said to the king, "Let me go to Hebron and fulfill a vow I made to the LORD. 8 While your servant was living at Geshur[w] in Aram, I made this vow:[x] 'If the LORD takes me back to Jerusalem, I will worship the LORD in Hebron.[c]'"

9 The king said to him, "Go in peace." So he went to Hebron.

10 Then Absalom sent secret messengers throughout the tribes of Israel to say, "As soon as you hear

[a] *26* That is, about 5 pounds or about 2.3 kilograms [b] *7* Some Septuagint manuscripts, Syriac and Josephus; Hebrew *forty* [c] *8* Some Septuagint manuscripts; Hebrew does not have *in Hebron.*

14:25 From the top of his head to the sole of his foot. This is a *merism,* a literary figure in which two polar opposites are all-inclusive, the total person. **blemish.** Used in Lev 21:17–21 of persons who are unacceptable to be priests.

14:26 hair. This anticipates Absalom's demise: caught in a tree by his hair (18:9). **royal standard.** Different shekel systems operated in Hebrew culture simultaneously; there is a merchant standard (Gen 23:16) and also a "sanctuary shekel" (Exod 30:13,24; 38:24–26; Lev 5:15; 27:3,25).

14:27 Three sons. Perhaps they died young because Absalom later laments, "I have no son" (18:18). **Tamar.** Obviously named after his sister. **beautiful.** Like her aunt (13:1).

14:28 two years. The same amount of time it took Absalom to take revenge on Amnon (13:23).

14:29–33 Absalom feels that he is in no man's land, so he seeks an advocate with the king through Joab. Joab is unresponsive, at least until Absalom gets his attention by burning one of Joab's fields. Absalom desires resolution whether it be restoration or execution.

14:33 kissed Absalom. A sign of acceptance and return.

15:1–12 *Absalom's Conspiracy.* Absalom plots to wrestle the kingdom of Israel from his father. He presents himself in a kingly manner and steals the hearts of the people away from David. Absalom's rebellion hits its stride when he proclaims himself king over Israel at Hebron. The conspiracy is strong because many of the people side with Absalom.

15:1 chariot and horses ... fifty men to run ahead. Absalom acts like one who will soon become king (1 Sam 8:11). Later, after Absalom dies, Adonijah puts on the same show as he attempts to take David's throne (1 Kgs 1:5).

15:2–3 Absalom plants himself on a main road entering the city of Jerusalem. There is lots of traffic at this gateway, and many travelers come to seek justice from the king. Absalom intercepts them and attempts to win them over by telling them what they want to hear: that they are right but need someone to listen to their cause.

15:7 Hebron. Where David first ruled (2:4) and Absalom was born (3:2–3). See note on 2:1

15:10 secret messengers. Spies (1 Sam 26:4); Absalom's plot is clan-

the sound of the trumpets,[y] then say, 'Absalom is king in Hebron.'" 11Two hundred men from Jerusalem had accompanied Absalom. They had been invited as guests and went quite innocently, knowing nothing about the matter. 12While Absalom was offering sacrifices, he also sent for Ahithophel[z] the Gilonite, David's counselor,[a] to come from Giloh,[b] his hometown. And so the conspiracy gained strength, and Absalom's following kept on increasing.[c]

David Flees

13A messenger came and told David, "The hearts of the people of Israel are with Absalom."

14Then David said to all his officials who were with him in Jerusalem, "Come! We must flee,[d] or none of us will escape from Absalom.[e] We must leave immediately, or he will move quickly to overtake us and bring ruin on us and put the city to the sword."

15The king's officials answered him, "Your servants are ready to do whatever our lord the king chooses."

16The king set out, with his entire household following him; but he left ten concubines[f] to take care of the palace. 17So the king set out, with all the people following him, and they halted at the edge of the city. 18All his men marched past him, along with all the Kerethites[g] and Pelethites; and all the six hundred Gittites who had accompanied him from Gath marched before the king.

19The king said to Ittai[h] the Gittite, "Why should you come along with us? Go back and stay with King Absalom. You are a foreigner,[i] an exile from your homeland. 20You came only yesterday. And today shall I make you wander[j] about with us, when I do not know where I am going? Go back, and take your people with you. May the LORD show you kindness and faithfulness."[a][k]

21But Ittai replied to the king, "As surely as the LORD lives, and as my lord the king lives, wherever my lord the king may be, whether it means life or death, there will your servant be."[l]

22David said to Ittai, "Go ahead, march on." So Ittai the Gittite marched on with all his men and the families that were with him.

23The whole countryside wept aloud as all the people passed by. The king also crossed the Kidron Valley,[m] and all the people moved on toward the wilderness.

24Zadok[n] was there, too, and all the Levites who were with him were carrying the ark[o] of the covenant of God. They set down the ark of God, and Abiathar[p] offered sacrifices until all the people had finished leaving the city.

25Then the king said to Zadok, "Take the ark of God back into the city. If I find favor in the LORD's eyes, he will bring me back and let me see it and his dwelling place[q] again. 26But if he says, 'I am not pleased with you,' then I am ready; let him do to me whatever seems good to him."[r]

27The king also said to Zadok the priest, "Do you understand?[s] Go back to the city with my blessing. Take your son Ahimaaz with you, and also Abiathar's son Jonathan.[t] You and Abiathar return with your

[a] 20 Septuagint; Hebrew *May kindness and faithfulness be with you*

15:10 [y] 1Ki 1:34,39; 2Ki 9:13
15:12 [z] ver 31,34; 2Sa 16:15,23; 1Ch 27:33 [a] Job 19:14; Ps 41:9; 55:13; Jer 9:4 [b] Jos 15:51 [c] Ps 3:1
15:14 [d] 2Sa 12:11; 1Ki 2:26; Ps 3 Title; 132:1 [e] 2Sa 19:9
15:16 [f] 2Sa 16:21-22; 20:3
15:18 [g] 1Sa 30:14; 2Sa 8:18; 20:7,23; 1Ki 1:38,44; 1Ch 18:17
15:19 [h] 2Sa 18:2 [i] Ge 31:15
15:20 [j] 1Sa 23:13 [k] 2Sa 2:6
15:21 [l] Ru 1:16-17; Pr 17:17
15:23 [m] 2Ch 29:16
15:24 [n] 2Sa 8:17 [o] Nu 4:15 [p] 1Sa 22:20
15:25 [q] Ex 15:13; Ps 43:3; Jer 25:30
15:26 [r] 1Sa 3:18; 2Sa 22:20; 1Ki 10:9
15:27 [s] 1Sa 9:9 [t] 2Sa 17:17

destine. **tribes of Israel.** All the tribes including Judah. Hebron is in Judah, and it is where the rebellion begins; it is where David first ruled, so Absalom strikes at the very heart of David's strength and support.

15:12 The text can be read to say that either Absalom or Ahithophel is offering sacrifices. Absalom is more likely because the scene appears to be sacrifices at a coronation ritual (1 Sam 11:14–15). **Giloh.** A town in Judah that may be close to Hebron (Josh 15:51).

15:13–37 *David Flees.* Absalom's conspiracy continues to grow strong in numbers. David realizes that he and those loyal to him will be overrun if they remain in Jerusalem, so they flee to the wilderness. Even while in the process of escape, David sets up a spy network in Jerusalem so that he will be aware of all the moves of Absalom and his followers. Ps 3 describes David's peril at this time.

15:15–18 When the company reaches the outskirts of Jerusalem, it passes in review before the king. Three groups are in the band: (1) **servants.** David's court personnel ("the king's officials"). (2) **Kerethites and Pelethites.** David's bodyguard (8:18; 20:7). (3) **six hundred Gittites.** Philistine soldiers loyal to David.

15:16 ten concubines. Absalom later has sexual relations with them on the roof of the palace (16:21–22).

15:19 Ittai. Leader of the 600 Gittites.

15:20 yesterday. Indicates a recent action. **I do not know where I am going.** Lit. "I am going where I am going"; an example of the figure of *idem per idem*, a formula that gives total freedom to the subject in how to act. In other words, David has no idea of his destination.

15:21 As surely as the LORD lives. Ironically, Ittai, a Philistine, makes an oath of loyalty to David based upon the covenantal name of the God of Israel. Many Israelites have deserted David, but these Philistines are loyal.

15:23 Kidron Valley. Lies just east of Jerusalem between the city and the Mount of Olives (v. 30). David and his entourage are heading east toward the Judean wilderness.

15:27–28 David is explaining to Zadok that, as a seer, Zadok will be allowed back into the city of Jerusalem. **with my blessing.** There he will spy for David and update him on the rebellion.

15:28 [u] 2Sa 17:16
15:30 [v] 2Sa 19:4; Ps 126:6 [w] Est 6:12; Isa 20:2-4
15:31 [x] ver 12; 2Sa 16:23; 17:14,23
15:32 [y] Jos 16:2 [z] 2Sa 1:2
15:33 [a] 2Sa 19:35
15:34 [b] 2Sa 16:19
15:35 [c] 2Sa 17:15-16
15:36 [d] ver 27; 2Sa 17:17
15:37 [e] 2Sa 16:16-17; 1Ch 27:33 [f] 2Sa 16:15
16:1 [g] 2Sa 9:1-13 [h] 1Sa 25:18
16:2 [i] 2Sa 17:27-29
16:3 [j] 2Sa 9:9-10; 19:26-27
16:5 [k] 2Sa 3:16 [l] 2Sa 19:16-23; 1Ki 2:8-9,36,44 [m] Ex 22:28
16:8 [n] 2Sa 21:9

two sons. 28 I will wait at the fords[u] in the wilderness until word comes from you to inform me." 29 So Zadok and Abiathar took the ark of God back to Jerusalem and stayed there.

30 But David continued up the Mount of Olives, weeping[v] as he went; his head[w] was covered and he was barefoot. All the people with him covered their heads too and were weeping as they went up. 31 Now David had been told, "Ahithophel[x] is among the conspirators with Absalom." So David prayed, "LORD, turn Ahithophel's counsel into foolishness."

32 When David arrived at the summit, where people used to worship God, Hushai the Arkite[y] was there to meet him, his robe torn and dust[z] on his head. 33 David said to him, "If you go with me, you will be a burden[a] to me. 34 But if you return to the city and say to Absalom, 'Your Majesty, I will be your servant; I was your father's servant in the past, but now I will be your servant,'[b] then you can help me by frustrating Ahithophel's advice. 35 Won't the priests Zadok and Abiathar be there with you? Tell them anything you hear in the king's palace.[c] 36 Their two sons, Ahimaaz son of Zadok and Jonathan[d] son of Abiathar, are there with them. Send them to me with anything you hear."

37 So Hushai,[e] David's confidant, arrived at Jerusalem as Absalom[f] was entering the city.

David and Ziba

16 When David had gone a short distance beyond the summit, there was Ziba,[g] the steward of Mephibosheth, waiting to meet him. He had a string of donkeys saddled and loaded with two hundred loaves of bread, a hundred cakes of raisins, a hundred cakes of figs and a skin of wine.[h]

2 The king asked Ziba, "Why have you brought these?"

Ziba answered, "The donkeys are for the king's household to ride on, the bread and fruit are for the men to eat, and the wine is to refresh[i] those who become exhausted in the wilderness."

3 The king then asked, "Where is your master's grandson?"[j]

Ziba said to him, "He is staying in Jerusalem, because he thinks, 'Today the Israelites will restore to me my grandfather's kingdom.' "

4 Then the king said to Ziba, "All that belonged to Mephibosheth is now yours."

"I humbly bow," Ziba said. "May I find favor in your eyes, my lord the king."

Shimei Curses David

5 As King David approached Bahurim,[k] a man from the same clan as Saul's family came out from there. His name was Shimei[l] son of Gera, and he cursed[m] as he came out. 6 He pelted David and all the king's officials with stones, though all the troops and the special guard were on David's right and left. 7 As he cursed, Shimei said, "Get out, get out, you murderer, you scoundrel! 8 The LORD has repaid you for all the blood you shed in the household of Saul, in whose place you have reigned.[n]

15:29 back to Jerusalem. David obviously recognizes that the ark belongs in Jerusalem as a sign of God's presence with his people. It is not a mascot or a magical instrument that guarantees blessing.

15:31 Ahithophel. He was David's wise and trusted counselor (16:23; 1 Chr 27:33).

15:32 Arkite. The Arkites were a clan that inhabited territory in the land of Benjamin (Josh 16:2; 18:13). **robe torn and dust on his head.** Signs of grief and mourning; this expresses sympathy and concord with David.

15:34–45 David encourages Hushai to return to Jerusalem, pretend to be loyal to Absalom, and thwart the counsel of the traitor Ahithophel. Hushai will not be alone; Zadok, Abiathar, and their sons also constitute David's spy network.

15:37 confidant. A king's close advisor; the Israelites adopted this Egyptian court title.

16:1–4 *David and Ziba.* Ziba, a servant of Mephibosheth, supplies food and transportation for David and his fellow travelers. He attempts to ingratiate himself with David at the expense of Mephibosheth. (This story concludes in 19:24–30.)

16:1 After David and his entourage pass over the summit of the Mount of Olives (cf. 15:32), Ziba arrives with provisions for them. He was the steward of all Saul's possessions, which David ordered him to turn over to Mephibosheth (9:9–10).

16:2–3 Ziba takes credit for providing for David's troops. He betrays Mephibosheth by portraying him as attempting to depose David to restore Saul's kingship to himself.

16:4 David acts rashly by giving to Ziba all that belongs to Mephibosheth (but see 19:29). Kings certainly have the power to take land from one person and give it to another (9:7), but David should have first given a hearing to Mephibosheth.

16:5–14 *Shimei Curses David.* David and his companions cross the Mount of Olives east of Jerusalem and head northeast toward the Jordan River. They are now in Benjamite territory, Saul's tribal home. One of Saul's relatives, Shimei, approaches the entourage and begins to curse David because of what he had done to the house of Saul.

16:5 Bahurim. A Benjamite town a few miles/kilometers northeast of Jerusalem on the road to the Jordan River (3:16). Shimei continuously hurls insults at David.

16:6 special guard. The mighty men (23:8) and elite troops who protect the king.

16:7 scoundrel. See notes on 23:6–7; 1 Sam 1:16; 2:12.

16:8 all the blood you shed. Shimei holds David responsible for the demise of Saul's household. **The LORD has given.** Shimei pronounces that David's current circumstances are the Lord's means of revenge; all the blood is now coming back on David's own head as a means of divine ironic justice.

The LORD has given the kingdom into the hands of your son Absalom. You have come to ruin because
you are a murderer!"
9Then Abishai[o] son of Zeruiah said to the king, "Why should this dead dog curse my lord the king?
Let me go over and cut off his head."[p]
10But the king said, "What does this have to do with you, you sons of Zeruiah?[q] If he is cursing because the LORD said to him, 'Curse David,' who can ask, 'Why do you do this?' "[r]
11David then said to Abishai and all his officials, "My son,[s] my own flesh and blood, is trying to kill
me. How much more, then, this Benjamite! Leave him alone; let him curse, for the LORD has told him
to.[t] 12It may be that the LORD will look upon my misery[u] and restore to me his covenant blessing[v] instead of his curse today.[w]"
13So David and his men continued along the road while Shimei was going along the hillside opposite
him, cursing as he went and throwing stones at him and showering him with dirt. 14The king and all
the people with him arrived at their destination exhausted.[x] And there he refreshed himself.

16:9 [o]2Sa 9:8 [p]Ex 22:28; Lk 9:54
16:10 [q]2Sa 19:22 [r]Ro 9:20
16:11 [s]2Sa 12:11 [t]Ge 45:5
16:12 [u]Ps 4:1; 25:18 [v]Dt 23:5; Ro 8:28 [w]Ps 109:28
16:14 [x]2Sa 17:2
16:15 [y]2Sa 15:37 [z]2Sa 15:12
16:16 [a]2Sa 15:37
16:17 [b]2Sa 19:25
16:19 [c]2Sa 15:34
16:22 [d]2Sa 12:11-12; 15:16
16:23 [e]2Sa 17:14,23 [f]2Sa 15:12
17:2 [g]2Sa 16:14 [h]1Ki 22:31; Zec 13:7

The Advice of Ahithophel and Hushai

15Meanwhile, Absalom[y] and all the men of Israel came to Jerusalem, and Ahithophel[z] was with him.
16Then Hushai[a] the Arkite, David's confidant, went to Absalom and said to him, "Long live the king!
Long live the king!"
17Absalom said to Hushai, "So this is the love you show your friend? If he's your friend, why didn't
you go with him?"[b]
18Hushai said to Absalom, "No, the one chosen by the LORD, by these people, and by all the men of
Israel — his I will be, and I will remain with him. 19Furthermore, whom should I serve? Should I not
serve the son? Just as I served your father, so I will serve you."[c]
20Absalom said to Ahithophel, "Give us your advice. What should we do?"
21Ahithophel answered, "Sleep with your father's concubines whom he left to take care of the palace. Then all Israel will hear that you have made yourself obnoxious to your father, and the hands of
everyone with you will be more resolute." 22So they pitched a tent for Absalom on the roof, and he slept
with his father's concubines in the sight of all Israel.[d]
23Now in those days the advice[e] Ahithophel gave was like that of one who inquires of God. That was
how both David[f] and Absalom regarded all of Ahithophel's advice.

17 Ahithophel said to Absalom, "I would[a] choose twelve thousand men and set out tonight in
pursuit of David. 2I would attack him while he is weary and weak.[g] I would strike him with
terror, and then all the people with him will flee. I would strike down only the king[h] 3and bring all the
people back to you. The death of the man you seek will mean the return of all; all the people will be
unharmed." 4This plan seemed good to Absalom and to all the elders of Israel.

[a] *1* Or *Let me*

16:9 dead dog. A stinging insult (see notes on 9:8; 1 Sam 24:14).
16:10 sons of Zeruiah. They include Joab and Abishai; David again restrains them from violence (1 Sam 26:8–9; cf. 2 Sam 3:39).
16:11 Leave him alone. David allows that Shimei's accusations might be divinely sanctioned.
16:12 misery. This possibly reflects David's conviction for his own sin. He hopes that the Lord will relieve and restore him, and the Lord does (see Ps 3).
16:15–23 *The Advice of Ahithophel and Hushai.* The story returns to Absalom's entering Jerusalem (15:37). Hushai meets Absalom in the city and pretends to be a loyal follower (16:15–19). Ahithophel, a true loyal follower of Absalom, advises the new king on how to solidify his hold on the throne (vv. 20–23).
16:16 David's confidant. Reminds readers of Hushai's true fidelity. **Long live the king!** Hushai does not use Absalom's name; ironically, he could be referring to David rather than Absalom.
16:17–19 Absalom is rightfully suspicious of Hushai because Hushai loves his friend David. Hushai skillfully gains Absalom's confidence and convinces him of his sincerity (17:5).
16:20 Absalom seeks advice regarding his next steps to secure power over Jerusalem and the entire kingdom. **your.** Plural, probably indicating that Ahithophel is the head of a council of advisors.
16:21–22 father's concubines. These are the ten concubines David left to watch over the palace (15:16). This act is clear contempt for David and a pointed claim to the throne. It fulfills Nathan's prophecy to David that one from his own house would have sexual relations with his wives "in broad daylight" (12:11). **on the roof.** Ironically, this may be where David first saw Bathsheba (11:2).
16:23 Ahithophel is a formidable ally to Absalom and opponent against David's monarchy. Hushai has his work cut out for him.
17:1–23 *Hushai's Advice Is Accepted.* Will Absalom follow the advice of Ahithophel or Hushai regarding how to deal with David? Ahithophel advises Absalom to lead 12,000 soldiers to kill David and spare the people with him. Hushai, David's spy and confidant, thwarts Ahithophel's reasonable advice with a different plan, resulting in Ahithophel's suicide.
17:1–3 Ahithophel advises Absalom to strike swiftly while the iron is hot.

17:5 [i] 2Sa 15:32
17:8 [j] Hos 13:8 [k] 1Sa 16:18
17:9 [l] Jer 41:9
17:10 [m] 1Ch 12:8 [n] Jos 2:9,11; Eze 21:15 [o] 2Sa 23:8; 1Ch 11:11
17:11 [p] Jdg 20:1 [q] Ge 12:2; 22:17; Jos 11:4
17:13 [r] Mic 1:6
17:14 [s] 2Sa 16:23 [t] 2Sa 15:12 [u] 2Sa 15:34; Ne 4:15 [v] Ps 9:16 [w] 2Ch 10:8
17:16 [x] 2Sa 15:28 [y] 2Sa 15:35
17:17 [z] 2Sa 15:27,36 [a] Jos 15:7; 18:16
17:18 [b] 2Sa 3:16; 16:5
17:19 [c] Jos 2:6
17:20 [d] Ex 1:19; Jos 2:3-5; 1Sa 19:12-17
17:23 [e] 2Sa 15:12; 16:23

5 But Absalom said, "Summon also Hushai[i] the Arkite, so we can hear what he has to say as well." 6 When Hushai came to him, Absalom said, "Ahithophel has given this advice. Should we do what he says? If not, give us your opinion."

7 Hushai replied to Absalom, "The advice Ahithophel has given is not good this time. 8 You know your father and his men; they are fighters, and as fierce as a wild bear robbed of her cubs.[j] Besides, your father is an experienced fighter;[k] he will not spend the night with the troops. 9 Even now, he is hidden in a cave or some other place.[l] If he should attack your troops first,[a] whoever hears about it will say, 'There has been a slaughter among the troops who follow Absalom.' 10 Then even the bravest soldier, whose heart is like the heart of a lion,[m] will melt[n] with fear, for all Israel knows that your father is a fighter and that those with him are brave.[o]

11 "So I advise you: Let all Israel, from Dan to Beersheba[p]—as numerous as the sand[q] on the seashore—be gathered to you, with you yourself leading them into battle. 12 Then we will attack him wherever he may be found, and we will fall on him as dew settles on the ground. Neither he nor any of his men will be left alive. 13 If he withdraws into a city, then all Israel will bring ropes to that city, and we will drag it down to the valley[r] until not so much as a pebble is left."

14 Absalom and all the men of Israel said, "The advice[s] of Hushai the Arkite is better than that of Ahithophel."[t] For the LORD had determined to frustrate[u] the good advice of Ahithophel in order to bring disaster[v] on Absalom.[w]

15 Hushai told Zadok and Abiathar, the priests, "Ahithophel has advised Absalom and the elders of Israel to do such and such, but I have advised them to do so and so. 16 Now send a message at once and tell David, 'Do not spend the night at the fords in the wilderness;[x] cross over without fail, or the king and all the people with him will be swallowed up.[y]'"

17 Jonathan[z] and Ahimaaz were staying at En Rogel.[a] A female servant was to go and inform them, and they were to go and tell King David, for they could not risk being seen entering the city. 18 But a young man saw them and told Absalom. So the two of them left at once and went to the house of a man in Bahurim.[b] He had a well in his courtyard, and they climbed down into it. 19 His wife took a covering and spread it out over the opening of the well and scattered grain over it. No one knew anything about it.[c]

20 When Absalom's men came to the woman[d] at the house, they asked, "Where are Ahimaaz and Jonathan?"

The woman answered them, "They crossed over the brook."[b] The men searched but found no one, so they returned to Jerusalem.

21 After they had gone, the two climbed out of the well and went to inform King David. They said to him, "Set out and cross the river at once; Ahithophel has advised such and such against you." 22 So David and all the people with him set out and crossed the Jordan. By daybreak, no one was left who had not crossed the Jordan.

23 When Ahithophel saw that his advice[e] had not been followed, he saddled his donkey and set out

[a] 9 Or *When some of the men fall at the first attack* [b] 20 Or *"They passed by the sheep pen toward the water."*

17:5 Although Absalom and his leaders are sold on Ahithophel's plan, the new king seeks Hushai's counsel. **Summon also Hushai.** Indicates that Hushai was not part of Ahithophel's council.

17:7 this time. Hushai shrewdly acknowledges that Ahithophel generally gives wise and good counsel. Ahithophel has a fine reputation. Hushai, however, is merely attacking this one particular case that is before Absalom and his court.

17:8–10 Hushai counsels caution. He puts a seed of doubt in the mind of the council that perhaps David will initiate a surprise attack and send Ahithophel's forces into a panic.

17:8 wild bear robbed of her cubs. A fierce animal in a desperate situation (Prov 17:12; Hos 13:8).

17:11–13 Hushai advances his own plan, which eventually results in Absalom's defeat and death (ch. 18). He advises Absalom to gather all the troops of Israel and lead them to attack David; whereas Ahithophel called only for the death of David, Hushai argues for the total annihilation of David's army.

17:12 as dew settles on the ground. Perhaps signifies the idea of total coverage, that is, total destruction.

17:13 drag it down. Armies at this time employed grappling hooks to pull down city walls. Hushai, in contrast to Ahithophel, is making a case for all-out war against David.

17:14 The Lord's providence is ultimately why Absalom takes Hushai's advice.

17:17 Jonathan and Ahimaaz. Sons of the priests Abiathar and Zadok, respectively. As known supporters of David, they are sequestered. **En Rogel.** Located at modern Bi'r Ayyub, just southeast of Jerusalem (Josh 15:7; 1 Kgs 1:9). **A female servant.** The intermediary between Zadok, Abiathar, and Hushai in Jerusalem and the two sons in En Rogel.

17:18 David and his troops had recently come through Bahurim (16:5), so the two spies are on his trail.

17:23 his hometown. Giloh (15:12). **put his house in order.** Cf. 2 Kgs 20:1; Isa 38:1. **hanged himself.** It is not clear from the text whether

for his house in his hometown. He put his house in order[f] and then hanged himself. So he died and was buried in his father's tomb.

Absalom's Death

24 David went to Mahanaim,[g] and Absalom crossed the Jordan with all the men of Israel. 25 Absalom had appointed Amasa[h] over the army in place of Joab. Amasa was the son of Jether,[a][i] an Ishmaelite[b] who had married Abigail,[c] the daughter of Nahash and sister of Zeruiah the mother of Joab. 26 The Israelites and Absalom camped in the land of Gilead.

27 When David came to Mahanaim, Shobi son of Nahash[j] from Rabbah[k] of the Ammonites, and Makir[l] son of Ammiel from Lo Debar, and Barzillai[m] the Gileadite[n] from Rogelim 28 brought bedding and bowls and articles of pottery. They also brought wheat and barley, flour and roasted grain, beans and lentils,[d] 29 honey and curds, sheep, and cheese from cows' milk for David and his people to eat.[o] For they said, "The people have become exhausted and hungry and thirsty in the wilderness.[p]"

18 David mustered the men who were with him and appointed over them commanders of thousands and commanders of hundreds. 2 David sent out his troops,[q] a third under the command of Joab, a third under Joab's brother Abishai[r] son of Zeruiah, and a third under Ittai[s] the Gittite. The king told the troops, "I myself will surely march out with you."

3 But the men said, "You must not go out; if we are forced to flee, they won't care about us. Even if half of us die, they won't care; but you are worth ten[t] thousand of us.[e] It would be better now for you to give us support from the city."[u]

4 The king answered, "I will do whatever seems best to you."

So the king stood beside the gate while all his men marched out in units of hundreds and of thousands. 5 The king commanded Joab, Abishai and Ittai, "Be gentle with the young man Absalom for my sake." And all the troops heard the king giving orders concerning Absalom to each of the commanders.

6 David's army marched out of the city to fight Israel, and the battle took place in the forest[v] of Ephraim. 7 There Israel's troops were routed by David's men, and the casualties that day were great—twenty thousand men. 8 The battle spread out over the whole countryside, and the forest swallowed up more men that day than the sword.

9 Now Absalom happened to meet David's men. He was riding his mule, and as the mule went under the thick branches of a large oak, Absalom's hair[w] got caught in the tree. He was left hanging in midair, while the mule he was riding kept on going.

10 When one of the men saw what had happened, he told Joab, "I just saw Absalom hanging in an oak tree."

[a] *25* Hebrew *Ithra*, a variant of *Jether* [b] *25* Some Septuagint manuscripts (see also 1 Chron. 2:17); Hebrew and other Septuagint manuscripts *Israelite* [c] *25* Hebrew *Abigal*, a variant of *Abigail* [d] *28* Most Septuagint manuscripts and Syriac; Hebrew *lentils, and roasted grain* [e] *3* Two Hebrew manuscripts, some Septuagint manuscripts and Vulgate; most Hebrew manuscripts *care; for now there are ten thousand like us*

17:23 [f] 2Ki 20:1; Mt 27:5
17:24 [g] Ge 32:2; 2Sa 2:8
17:25 [h] 2Sa 19:13; 20:4, 9-12; 1Ki 2:5,32; 1Ch 12:18 [i] 1Ch 2:13-17
17:27 [j] 1Sa 11:1 [k] Dt 3:11; 2Sa 10:1-2; 12:26,29 [l] 2Sa 9:4 [m] 2Sa 19:31-39; 1Ki 2:7 [n] 2Sa 19:31; Ezr 2:61
17:29 [o] 1Ch 12:40 [p] 2Sa 16:2; Ro 12:13
18:2 [q] Jdg 7:16; 1Sa 11:11 [r] 1Sa 26:6 [s] 2Sa 15:19
18:3 [t] 1Sa 18:7 [u] 2Sa 21:17
18:6 [v] Jos 17:18
18:9 [w] 2Sa 14:26

Ahithophel does this because he realizes the rebellion is doomed or because he is ashamed that Absalom is not following his advice.

17:24—18:18 *Absalom's Death.* David's troops quash the rebellion by routing Absalom's army and killing Absalom.

17:24 Mahanaim. Located at modern Tell ad-Dahab ash-Sharqiya on the Jabbok River; Ish-Bosheth's capital city (2:8–9); approximately 30 miles (48 kilometers) from where David and his company crossed the Jordan River. Because Absalom had to muster the troops of all Israel, David could put some distance between the two armies.

17:25 Amasa. Cousin of both Absalom and Joab. **Jether, an Ishmaelite.** The Hebrew reads "Jether the Israelite," which may be a copyist's error because 1 Chr 2:17 calls him "Jether the Ishmaelite." "Ishmaelite" is probably correct based on the context. Elsewhere he is called simply "Jether" (1 Kgs 2:5,32). Absalom's force crosses the Jordan River and camps in Gilead, north of David.

17:27–29 Three wealthy foreign supporters subsidize David: **Shobi.** Brother of Hanun, king of Ammon; perhaps reigning in place of his brother (10:2). **Makir.** Gave shelter to Mephibosheth (9:4). **Barzillai.** A very wealthy man (19:32) who later accompanies David part of the way back to Jerusalem.

18:2 David divides his forces into three companies under the commands of Joab, Abishai, and Ittai the Gittite (15:19–22). **I myself will surely march out with you.** David's emphatic pronouncement includes an emphatic pronoun and an emphatic infinitive of the same verb.

18:5 Be gentle with … Absalom. David tenderly loves his son even though Absalom is resolutely antagonistic to his father (v. 33).

18:6 forest of Ephraim. East of the Jordan River in Gilead (17:24; 19:15), which was apparently famous as a forested region in antiquity (Jer 22:6).

18:8 swallowed up. It is not certain what killed the men; the dangers of a dense forest would include animals and poisonous plants. Perhaps some people died by being lost in the woods, and perhaps David's men set traps that would have killed some of them.

18:9 Absalom attempts to flee from David's men on his mule, the common transport of the king's sons (13:29). **Absalom's hair got caught.** Ironically, what he gloried in destroys him (14:26).

18:11 [x]2Sa 3:39 [y]1Sa 18:4
18:13 [z]2Sa 14:19-20
18:14 [a]2Sa 2:18; 14:30
18:15 [b]2Sa 12:10
18:16 [c]2Sa 2:28; 20:22
18:17 [d]Jos 7:26 [e]Jos 8:29
18:18 [f]Ge 14:17 [g]Ge 50:5; Nu 32:42; 1Sa 15:12 [h]2Sa 14:27
18:19 [i]2Sa 15:36 [j]ver 31; Jdg 11:36
18:24 [k]1Sa 14:16; 2Sa 19:8; 2Ki 9:17; Jer 51:12
18:26 [l]1Ki 1:42; Isa 52:7; 61:1

11 Joab said to the man who had told him this, "What! You saw him? Why didn't you strike[x] him to
the ground right there? Then I would have had to give you ten shekels[a] of silver and a warrior's belt.[y]"
12 But the man replied, "Even if a thousand shekels[b] were weighed out into my hands, I would not
lay a hand on the king's son. In our hearing the king commanded you and Abishai and Ittai, 'Protect
the young man Absalom for my sake.[c]' 13 And if I had put my life in jeopardy[d]—and nothing is hidden
from the king[z]—you would have kept your distance from me."
14 Joab[a] said, "I'm not going to wait like this for you." So he took three javelins in his hand and
plunged them into Absalom's heart while Absalom was still alive in the oak tree. 15 And ten of Joab's
armor-bearers surrounded Absalom, struck him and killed him.[b]
16 Then Joab[c] sounded the trumpet, and the troops stopped pursuing Israel, for Joab halted them.
17 They took Absalom, threw him into a big pit in the forest and piled up[d] a large heap of rocks[e] over
him. Meanwhile, all the Israelites fled to their homes.
18 During his lifetime Absalom had taken a pillar and erected it in the King's Valley[f] as a monument[g]
to himself, for he thought, "I have no son[h] to carry on the memory of my name." He named the pillar
after himself, and it is called Absalom's Monument to this day.

David Mourns

19 Now Ahimaaz[i] son of Zadok said, "Let me run and take the news to the king that the LORD has
vindicated him by delivering him from the hand of his enemies.[j]"
20 "You are not the one to take the news today," Joab told him. "You may take the news another time,
but you must not do so today, because the king's son is dead."
21 Then Joab said to a Cushite, "Go, tell the king what you have seen." The Cushite bowed down
before Joab and ran off.
22 Ahimaaz son of Zadok again said to Joab, "Come what may, please let me run behind the Cushite."
But Joab replied, "My son, why do you want to go? You don't have any news that will bring you a
reward."
23 He said, "Come what may, I want to run."
So Joab said, "Run!" Then Ahimaaz ran by way of the plain[e] and outran the Cushite.
24 While David was sitting between the inner and outer gates, the watchman[k] went up to the roof of
the gateway by the wall. As he looked out, he saw a man running alone. 25 The watchman called out to
the king and reported it.
The king said, "If he is alone, he must have good news." And the runner came closer and closer.
26 Then the watchman saw another runner, and he called down to the gatekeeper, "Look, another
man running alone!"
The king said, "He must be bringing good news,[l] too."

[a] *11* That is, about 4 ounces or about 115 grams [b] *12* That is, about 25 pounds or about 12 kilograms
[c] *12* A few Hebrew manuscripts, Septuagint, Vulgate and Syriac; most Hebrew manuscripts may be translated *Absalom, whoever you may be.* [d] *13* Or *Otherwise, if I had acted treacherously toward him*
[e] *23* That is, the plain of the Jordan

18:12–13 Even if ... I would not lay a hand on the king's son. The man who saw Absalom hanging in the tree says he would not have killed the king's son for a hundred times as much silver as Joab offered (v. 11). He has two reasons: (1) the king commanded them to protect Absalom, and (2) if he had killed Absalom and been caught, Joab would not have stood by him.

18:15 armor-bearers. These ten soldiers carry Joab's equipment and fight alongside him in battle. Here they finish what Joab began.

18:17–18 Absalom set up a glorious monument to himself near the royal city of Jerusalem, but after he dies his monument is a "large heap of rocks" piled over him somewhere in the forest of Ephraim.

18:19—19:8 *David Mourns.* David remains in Mahanaim, awaiting news of the battle. He is so devastated that Absalom is dead that he gives no thought to his victorious, loyal troops, and Joab confronts him about his thoughtless behavior.

18:19 Ahimaaz. Part of David's spy network in and outside of Jerusalem (15:36; 17:17).

18:20 you must not do so today, because the king's son is dead. Joab is apparently protecting Ahimaaz from David's inevitable anger when he hears that Absalom is dead.

18:21 a Cushite. A foreigner from Cush, located south of Egypt.

18:23 The two runners likely take different routes. Ahimaaz runs "by way of the plain" through the Jordan Valley (1 Kgs 7:46); perhaps the Cushite takes a shorter route through the mountains.

18:24 between the inner and outer gates. Ancient Israelite cities, such as Dan and Lachish, commonly had double gateways with room between them for guards. David anxiously awaits news from the battlefield.

18:25 If he is alone. In that case, the runner is a messenger, not among soldiers fleeing wildly from the battle. **good.** The runner is merely bring-

[27]The watchman said, "It seems to me that the first one runs like[m] Ahimaaz son of Zadok."
"He's a good man," the king said. "He comes with good news."
[28]Then Ahimaaz called out to the king, "All is well!" He bowed down before the king with his face to
the ground and said, "Praise be to the LORD your God! He has delivered up those who lifted their hands
against my lord the king."
[29]The king asked, "Is the young man Absalom safe?"
Ahimaaz answered, "I saw great confusion just as Joab was about to send the king's servant and me,
your servant, but I don't know what it was."
[30]The king said, "Stand aside and wait here." So he stepped aside and stood there.
[31]Then the Cushite arrived and said, "My lord the king, hear the good news! The LORD has vindicated
you today by delivering you from the hand of all who rose up against you."
[32]The king asked the Cushite, "Is the young man Absalom safe?"
The Cushite replied, "May the enemies of my lord the king and all who rise up to harm you be like
that young man."[n]
[33]The king was shaken. He went up to the room over the gateway and wept. As he went, he said:
"O my son Absalom! My son, my son Absalom! If only I had died[o] instead of you—O Absalom, my
son, my son!"[a][p]

19 [b] Joab was told, "The king is weeping and mourning for Absalom." [2]And for the whole army
the victory that day was turned into mourning, because on that day the troops heard it
said, "The king is grieving for his son." [3]The men stole into the city that day as men steal in who are
ashamed when they flee from battle. [4]The king covered his face and cried aloud, "O my son Absalom!
O Absalom, my son, my son!"
[5]Then Joab went into the house to the king and said, "Today you have humiliated all your men,
who have just saved your life and the lives of your sons and daughters and the lives of your wives and
concubines. [6]You love those who hate you and hate those who love you. You have made it clear today
that the commanders and their men mean nothing to you. I see that you would be pleased if Absalom
were alive today and all of us were dead. [7]Now go out and encourage your men. I swear by the LORD
that if you don't go out, not a man will be left with you by nightfall. This will be worse for you than all
the calamities that have come on you from your youth till now."[q]
[8]So the king got up and took his seat in the gateway. When the men were told, "The king is sitting
in the gateway,"[r] they all came before him.
Meanwhile, the Israelites had fled to their homes.

David Returns to Jerusalem

[9]Throughout the tribes of Israel, all the people were arguing among themselves, saying, "The king
delivered us from the hand of our enemies; he is the one who rescued us from the hand of the Philistines.[s] But now he has fled the country to escape from Absalom;[t] [10]and Absalom, whom we anointed to
rule over us, has died in battle. So why do you say nothing about bringing the king back?"

18:27 [m] 2Ki 9:20
18:32 [n] Jdg 5:31; 1Sa 25:26
18:33 [o] Ex 32:32 [p] Ge 43:14; 2Sa 19:4; Ro 9:3
19:7 [q] Pr 14:28
19:8 [r] 2Sa 15:2
19:9 [s] 2Sa 8:1-14 [t] 2Sa 15:14

[a] *33* In Hebrew texts this verse (18:33) is numbered 19:1. [b] In Hebrew texts 19:1-43 is numbered 19:2-44.

ing some type of news, but it is not clear at this point whether it is good or bad. David perhaps assumes it is good news because there are no refugees from the battle.

18:29 Is the young man Absalom safe? Or "Is there peace for the young man Absalom?" Ironically, Absalom's name means "father of peace," but there is nothing about him that suggests he lives up to his name. Ahimaaz's response is vague; perhaps he is trying to break the news of Absalom's death gently, or perhaps he doesn't want to tell it at all.

18:33 David uses the name "Absalom" three times, and he calls him "my son" five times. He is overcome with grief (cf. 19:4).

19:2–3 David's grief overshadows his soldiers' great victory. **stole into the city.** Victorious armies normally march into home cities with much fanfare.

19:5–6 Joab accuses David of bringing shame on his soldiers. They risked their lives to deliver David and his family, and now the king humiliates them. David would sooner have Absalom alive and his whole army dead!

19:7–8 Joab tells David what he must do so that his men do not abandon him. David must reassure them. David responds by returning to the gate and acting like a king. **seat in the gateway.** At Tel Dan, archaeologists found in the gate ornamental bases and an ashlar-built platform for a royal seat.

19:9–43 *David Returns to Jerusalem.* Although David can triumphantly return to his capital city, there is still dissension in the kingdom between the northern tribes of Israel and the tribe of Judah. David makes a great effort to reconcile them.

19:11 [u]2Sa 15:24
19:13 [v]2Sa 17:25 [w]Ge 29:14 [x]Ru 1:17; 1Ki 19:2; 8:16 [y]2Sa 2:13
19:15 [z]Jos 5:9; 1Sa 11:15
19:16 [a]2Sa 16:5-13; 1Ki 2:8
19:17 [b]2Sa 9:2; 16:1-2 [c]Ge 43:16
19:19 [d]1Sa 22:15; 2Sa 16:6-8
19:21 [e]1Sa 26:6 [f]Ex 22:28 [g]1Sa 12:3; 26:9; 2Sa 16:7-8
19:22 [h]2Sa 2:18; 16:10 [i]1Sa 11:13
19:23 [j]1Ki 2:8,42
19:24 [k]2Sa 4:4; 9:6-10
19:25 [l]2Sa 16:17
19:26 [m]Lev 21:18 [n]2Sa 9:2
19:27 [o]1Sa 29:9; 2Sa 14:17,20
19:28 [p]2Sa 16:8; 21:6-9 [q]2Sa 9:7,13
19:31 [r]2Sa 17:27-29; 1Ki 2:7

11 King David sent this message to Zadok[u] and Abiathar, the priests: "Ask the elders of Judah, 'Why should
you be the last to bring the king back to his palace, since what is being said throughout Israel has reached
the king at his quarters? 12 You are my relatives, my own flesh and blood. So why should you be the last to
bring back the king?' 13 And say to Amasa,[v] 'Are you not my own flesh and blood?[w] May God deal with me,
be it ever so severely,[x] if you are not the commander of my army for life in place of Joab.[y]' "
14 He won over the hearts of the men of Judah so that they were all of one mind. They sent word to
the king, "Return, you and all your men." 15 Then the king returned and went as far as the Jordan.
Now the men of Judah had come to Gilgal[z] to go out and meet the king and bring him across the
Jordan. 16 Shimei[a] son of Gera, the Benjamite from Bahurim, hurried down with the men of Judah
to meet King David. 17 With him were a thousand Benjamites, along with Ziba,[b] the steward of Saul's
household,[c] and his fifteen sons and twenty servants. They rushed to the Jordan, where the king was.
18 They crossed at the ford to take the king's household over and to do whatever he wished.
When Shimei son of Gera crossed the Jordan, he fell prostrate before the king 19 and said to him,
"May my lord not hold me guilty. Do not remember how your servant did wrong on the day my lord
the king left Jerusalem.[d] May the king put it out of his mind. 20 For I your servant know that I have
sinned, but today I have come here as the first from the tribes of Joseph to come down and meet my
lord the king."
21 Then Abishai[e] son of Zeruiah said, "Shouldn't Shimei be put to death for this? He cursed[f] the
LORD's anointed."[g]
22 David replied, "What does this have to do with you, you sons of Zeruiah?[h] What right do you have
to interfere? Should anyone be put to death in Israel today?[i] Don't I know that today I am king over
Israel?" 23 So the king said to Shimei, "You shall not die." And the king promised him on oath.[j]
24 Mephibosheth,[k] Saul's grandson, also went down to meet the king. He had not taken care of his
feet or trimmed his mustache or washed his clothes from the day the king left until the day he returned
safely. 25 When he came from Jerusalem to meet the king, the king asked him, "Why didn't you go with
me,[l] Mephibosheth?"
26 He said, "My lord the king, since I your servant am lame,[m] I said, 'I will have my donkey saddled
and will ride on it, so I can go with the king.' But Ziba[n] my servant betrayed me. 27 And he has slandered
your servant to my lord the king. My lord the king is like an angel[o] of God; so do whatever you wish.
28 All my grandfather's descendants deserved nothing but death[p] from my lord the king, but you gave
your servant a place among those who eat at your table.[q] So what right do I have to make any more
appeals to the king?"
29 The king said to him, "Why say more? I order you and Ziba to divide the land."
30 Mephibosheth said to the king, "Let him take everything, now that my lord the king has returned
home safely."
31 Barzillai[r] the Gileadite also came down from Rogelim to cross the Jordan with the king and to send
him on his way from there. 32 Now Barzillai was very old, eighty years of age. He had provided for the

19:11–12 David uses the support he has from the northern tribes to motivate Judah to back him as well.

19:13 Amasa. The defeated general of Absalom's army (17:25). It seems odd, therefore, that David would give him a solemn oath to lead the king's army. David rejects Joab as military leader because he directly disobeyed the king regarding Absalom (18:5). Perhaps the king is attempting to reconcile the two armies by appointing Amasa (David's nephew) to this position.

19:15 Gilgal. Probably located at modern Khirbet el-Mafjar, 1.5 miles (2.4 kilometers) northeast of Jericho in the Jordan Valley. It is the first place the Israelites encamped under Joshua in Canaan during the period of the conquest (Josh 4:19).

19:16 Shimei. Saul's relative who cursed David when David fled from Jerusalem (16:5–14). He now comes to the king to grovel, and he seeks mercy now that David is back in power.

19:17 Ziba is another groveler. He apparently lied to David and betrayed Mephibosheth (9:1–13; 16:1–4). He is part of the group who rushed to pay homage to the king.

19:20 tribes of Joseph. Often refers to the two tribes of Ephraim and Manasseh, but here probably denotes all the northern tribes.

19:21 Abishai. Joab's notoriously violent brother (16:9; 1 Sam 26:7–9).

19:23 Vengeance on Shimei is not immediate, but it does come. In David's last recorded act, he requests that his son Solomon bring justice to Shimei, and Solomon acts on the request after his father dies (1 Kgs 2:8–9,36–46).

19:27 slandered. The Hebrew comes from the root *rgl.* It is a play on words because the noun *feet,* as in Mephibosheth is "lame in both feet" (4:4; cf. "feet" in 19:24), is also from the Hebrew root *rgl.* **like an angel of God.** The king is wise "in discerning good and evil" (14:17).

19:28 Mephibosheth leaves himself completely at the king's mercy. He realizes that David could have completely destroyed Saul's house, as most new kings would have done. David did not do that, so Mephibosheth acknowledges that he has no right to ask the king for anything more.

19:29 divide the land. It is not clear whether David does not know whom to believe or is simply attempting to reconcile Mephibosheth and Ziba.

19:32–33 Barzillai supplied David with material goods when David was

king during his stay in Mahanaim, for he was a very wealthy[s] man. 33 The king said to Barzillai, "Cross
over with me and stay with me in Jerusalem, and I will provide for you."
34 But Barzillai answered the king, "How many more years will I live, that I should go up to Jerusalem
with the king? 35 I am now eighty[t] years old. Can I tell the difference between what is enjoyable and what
is not? Can your servant taste what he eats and drinks? Can I still hear the voices of male and female
singers?[u] Why should your servant be an added[v] burden to my lord the king? 36 Your servant will cross
over the Jordan with the king for a short distance, but why should the king reward me in this way? 37 Let
your servant return, that I may die in my own town near the tomb of my father[w] and mother. But here
is your servant Kimham.[x] Let him cross over with my lord the king. Do for him whatever you wish."
38 The king said, "Kimham shall cross over with me, and I will do for him whatever you wish. And
anything you desire from me I will do for you."
39 So all the people crossed the Jordan, and then the king crossed over. The king kissed Barzillai and
bid him farewell,[y] and Barzillai returned to his home.
40 When the king crossed over to Gilgal, Kimham crossed with him. All the troops of Judah and half
the troops of Israel had taken the king over.
41 Soon all the men of Israel were coming to the king and saying to him, "Why did our brothers, the
men of Judah, steal the king away and bring him and his household across the Jordan, together with
all his men?"[z]
42 All the men of Judah answered the men of Israel, "We did this because the king is closely related
to us. Why are you angry about it? Have we eaten any of the king's provisions? Have we taken anything
for ourselves?"
43 Then the men of Israel[a] answered the men of Judah, "We have ten shares in the king; so we have
a greater claim on David than you have. Why then do you treat us with contempt? Weren't we the first
to speak of bringing back our king?"
But the men of Judah pressed their claims even more forcefully than the men of Israel.

Sheba Rebels Against David

20 Now a troublemaker named Sheba son of Bikri, a Benjamite, happened to be there. He sounded
the trumpet and shouted,

"We have no share[b] in David,[c]
no part in Jesse's son![d]
Every man to his tent, Israel!"

2 So all the men of Israel deserted David to follow Sheba son of Bikri. But the men of Judah stayed by
their king all the way from the Jordan to Jerusalem.
3 When David returned to his palace in Jerusalem, he took the ten concubines[e] he had left to take
care of the palace and put them in a house under guard. He provided for them but had no sexual relations with them. They were kept in confinement till the day of their death, living as widows.
4 Then the king said to Amasa,[f] "Summon the men of Judah to come to me within three days, and

19:32 [s] 1Sa 25:2; 2Sa 17:27
19:35 [t] Ps 90:10 [u] 2Ch 35:25; Ezr 2:65; Ecc 2:8; 12:1; Isa 5:11-12 [v] 2Sa 15:33
19:37 [w] Ge 49:29; 1Ki 2:7 [x] ver 40; Jer 41:17
19:39 [y] Ge 31:55; 47:7
19:41 [z] Jdg 8:1; 12:1
19:43 [a] 2Sa 5:1
20:1 [b] Ge 31:14 [c] Ge 29:14; 1Ki 12:16 [d] 1Sa 22:7-8; 2Ch 10:16
20:3 [e] 2Sa 15:16; 16:21-22
20:4 [f] 2Sa 17:25; 19:13

on the run (17:27–29), and David wants to repay him for his kindness and loyalty.

19:37–38 Barzillai refuses David's offer because age has taken its toll (v. 35) and he wants to die in his own city.

19:37 Kimham. Some would argue that he is Barzillai's son, but the text is mute in this regard; he may be a highly valued servant. David never forgets Barzillai's loyalty to him (1 Kgs 2:7).

19:41–43 Acrimony between Israel and Judah arises over loyally supporting David as king. This conflict anticipates the later division of the kingdom after David and Solomon die. The first three pronouns in v. 42, "we" "us" and "you," and all the pronouns in v. 43 are actually singular. These singular pronouns underscore the oneness of Israel and the oneness of Judah as they stand against one another. Great dissension is apparent, but Judah wins the argument because their arguments are weightier and more forceful.

19:43 ten shares. This refers to all the tribes of Israel, excluding Judah and Simeon.

20:1–22 *Sheba Rebels Against David.* Sheba's rebellion against David comes directly on the heels of Absalom's revolt. It attempts to build on the rift that already exists between the northern tribes and Judah (19:41–43). David overestimates the strength of Sheba's popularity (20:6), and Joab and the standing army take care of the revolt fairly easily.

20:1 troublemaker. See notes on 23:6–7; 1 Sam 1:16; 2:12. When they later rebel against Rehoboam, the northern tribes repeat almost word for word Sheba's call for Israel to depart (1 Kgs 12:16).

20:3 ten concubines. David left them in Jerusalem (15:16), and Absalom defiled them (16:22). David places them under restraint, provides for them, and they become permanent widows.

20:4–6 Amasa fails to muster an army in time to pursue Sheba, so David orders Abishai to speedily engage Sheba.

20:6 [g] 2Sa 21:17
20:7 [h] 1Sa 30:14; 2Sa 8:18; 15:18; 1Ki 1:38
20:8 [i] Jos 9:3 [j] 2Sa 2:18
20:10 [k] Jdg 3:21; 2Sa 2:23; 3:27 [l] 1Ki 2:5
20:12 [m] 2Sa 2:23
20:14 [n] Nu 21:16
20:15 [o] 1Ki 15:20; 2Ki 15:29 [p] 2Ki 19:32; Isa 37:33; Jer 6:6; 32:24
20:16 [q] 2Sa 14:2
20:19 [r] Dt 2:26 [s] 1Sa 26:19; 2Sa 21:3
20:21 [t] 2Sa 4:8
20:22 [u] Ecc 9:13

be here yourself." 5 But when Amasa went to summon Judah, he took longer than the time the king
had set for him.
6 David said to Abishai,[g] "Now Sheba son of Bikri will do us more harm than Absalom did. Take your
master's men and pursue him, or he will find fortified cities and escape from us."[a] 7 So Joab's men and
the Kerethites[h] and Pelethites and all the mighty warriors went out under the command of Abishai.
They marched out from Jerusalem to pursue Sheba son of Bikri.
8 While they were at the great rock in Gibeon,[i] Amasa came to meet them. Joab[j] was wearing his
military tunic, and strapped over it at his waist was a belt with a dagger in its sheath. As he stepped
forward, it dropped out of its sheath.
9 Joab said to Amasa, "How are you, my brother?" Then Joab took Amasa by the beard with his right
hand to kiss him. 10 Amasa was not on his guard against the dagger[k] in Joab's[l] hand, and Joab plunged
it into his belly, and his intestines spilled out on the ground. Without being stabbed again, Amasa died.
Then Joab and his brother Abishai pursued Sheba son of Bikri.
11 One of Joab's men stood beside Amasa and said, "Whoever favors Joab, and whoever is for David, let
him follow Joab!" 12 Amasa lay wallowing in his blood in the middle of the road, and the man saw that
all the troops came to a halt[m] there. When he realized that everyone who came up to Amasa stopped, he
dragged him from the road into a field and threw a garment over him. 13 After Amasa had been removed
from the road, everyone went on with Joab to pursue Sheba son of Bikri.
14 Sheba passed through all the tribes of Israel to Abel Beth Maakah and through the entire region
of the Bikrites,[b][n] who gathered together and followed him. 15 All the troops with Joab came and besieged Sheba in Abel Beth Maakah.[o] They built a siege ramp[p] up to the city, and it stood against the
outer fortifications. While they were battering the wall to bring it down, 16 a wise woman[q] called from
the city, "Listen! Listen! Tell Joab to come here so I can speak to him." 17 He went toward her, and she
asked, "Are you Joab?"

"I am," he answered.

She said, "Listen to what your servant has to say."

"I'm listening," he said.

18 She continued, "Long ago they used to say, 'Get your answer at Abel,' and that settled it. 19 We are
the peaceful[r] and faithful in Israel. You are trying to destroy a city that is a mother in Israel. Why do
you want to swallow up the LORD's inheritance?"[s]
20 "Far be it from me!" Joab replied, "Far be it from me to swallow up or destroy! 21 That is not the
case. A man named Sheba son of Bikri, from the hill country of Ephraim, has lifted up his hand against
the king, against David. Hand over this one man, and I'll withdraw from the city."

The woman said to Joab, "His head[t] will be thrown to you from the wall."

22 Then the woman went to all the people with her wise advice,[u] and they cut off the head of Sheba
son of Bikri and threw it to Joab. So he sounded the trumpet, and his men dispersed from the city, each
returning to his home. And Joab went back to the king in Jerusalem.

[a] 6 Or *and do us serious injury* [b] 14 See Septuagint and Vulgate; Hebrew *Berites.*

20:8–10 Amasa finds the Judahite force in Gibeon. They have traveled about six miles (9.6 kilometers) north of Jerusalem in their quest to find Sheba. As Joab steps forward to greet his first cousin, his dagger falls to the ground. This may be deliberate on Joab's part to put Amasa at ease. But as he grasps and kisses Amasa, Joab apparently reaches to the ground, picks up the dagger, and strikes Amasa with it. This stealth murder fits Joab's character and former activity (3:27; 18:14).

20:14 Abel Beth Maakah. Located at modern Tell Abil al-Qamh, about four miles (6.4 kilometers) west of the major city of Dan (1 Kgs 15:20). Sheba traveled to the very northern parts of Israel, probably trying to drum up support for his rebellion.

20:15 The troops with Joab build a siege ramp against the city wall and attempt to knock down the city's outer wall with a battering ram or similar device. This is typical military methodology of the day. The siege ramp that Sennacherib built to attack the Judean city of Lachish at the end of the eighth century BC is still visible at the site today.

20:16 Joab earlier employed another "wise woman" when attempting to convince David to return Absalom from exile (14:2–3).

20:18–19 Get your answer at Abel. An old proverb indicating that Abel is a city of wisdom where people historically came to resolve their disputes. **peaceful and faithful.** The city is highly respected in Israel. **mother.** The important city has daughter villages around it (Judg 1:27).

20:21–22 The woman of wisdom strikes a bargain with Joab to save her city. For the head of Sheba, Joab will disperse his troops from attacking the city. Verses 1 and 22 serve as an *inclusio* (i.e., brackets) for this story: In v. 1, Sheba blows the trumpet and calls for the Israelites to leave, saying, "Every man to his tent, Israel!" In v. 22, Joab blows the trumpet and calls his men to leave the city, "each returning to his home."

David's Officials

[23]Joab[v] was over Israel's entire army; Benaiah son of Jehoiada was over the Kerethites and Pelethites; [24]Adoniram[a][w] was in charge of forced labor; Jehoshaphat[x] son of Ahilud was recorder; [25]Sheva was secretary; Zadok[y] and Abiathar were priests; [26]and Ira the Jairite[b] was David's priest.

The Gibeonites Avenged

21 During the reign of David, there was a famine[z] for three successive years; so David sought[a] the face of the LORD. The LORD said, "It is on account of Saul and his blood-stained house; it is because he put the Gibeonites to death."

[2]The king summoned the Gibeonites[b] and spoke to them. (Now the Gibeonites were not a part of Israel but were survivors of the Amorites; the Israelites had sworn to spare them, but Saul in his zeal for Israel and Judah had tried to annihilate them.) [3]David asked the Gibeonites, "What shall I do for you? How shall I make atonement so that you will bless the LORD's inheritance?"[c]

[4]The Gibeonites answered him, "We have no right to demand silver or gold from Saul or his family, nor do we have the right to put anyone in Israel to death."[d]

"What do you want me to do for you?" David asked.

[5]They answered the king, "As for the man who destroyed us and plotted against us so that we have been decimated and have no place anywhere in Israel, [6]let seven of his male descendants be given to us to be killed and their bodies exposed[e] before the LORD at Gibeah of Saul—the LORD's chosen[f] one."

So the king said, "I will give them to you."

[7]The king spared Mephibosheth[g] son of Jonathan, the son of Saul, because of the oath[h] before the LORD between David and Jonathan son of Saul. [8]But the king took Armoni and Mephibosheth, the two sons of Aiah's daughter Rizpah,[i] whom she had borne to Saul, together with the five sons of Saul's daughter Merab,[c] whom she had borne to Adriel son of Barzillai the Meholathite.[j] [9]He handed them over to the Gibeonites, who killed them and exposed their bodies on a hill before the LORD. All seven of them fell together; they were put to death[k] during the first days of the harvest, just as the barley harvest was beginning.[l]

[10]Rizpah daughter of Aiah took sackcloth and spread it out for herself on a rock. From the beginning of the harvest till the rain poured down from the heavens on the bodies, she did not let the birds touch them by day or the wild animals by night.[m] [11]When David was told what Aiah's daughter Rizpah, Saul's concubine, had done, [12]he went and took the bones of Saul[n] and his son Jonathan from the citizens of

[a] *24* Some Septuagint manuscripts (see also 1 Kings 4:6 and 5:14); Hebrew *Adoram* [b] *26* Hebrew; some Septuagint manuscripts and Syriac (see also 23:38) *Ithrite* [c] *8* Two Hebrew manuscripts, some Septuagint manuscripts and Syriac (see also 1 Samuel 18:19); most Hebrew and Septuagint manuscripts *Michal*

20:23 [v] 2Sa 2:28; 8:16-18; 24:2
20:24 [w] 1Ki 4:6; 5:14; 12:18; 2Ch 10:18 [x] 2Sa 8:16; 1Ki 4:3
20:25 [y] 1Sa 2:35; 2Sa 8:17
21:1 [z] Ge 12:10; Dt 32:24 [a] Ex 32:11
21:2 [b] Jos 9:15
21:3 [c] 1Sa 26:19; 2Sa 20:19
21:4 [d] Nu 35:33-34
21:6 [e] Nu 25:4 [f] 1Sa 10:24
21:7 [g] 2Sa 4:4 [h] 1Sa 18:3; 20:8,15; 2Sa 9:7
21:8 [i] 2Sa 3:7 [j] 1Sa 18:19
21:9 [k] 2Sa 16:8 [l] Ru 1:22
21:10 [m] ver 8; Dt 21:23; 1Sa 17:44
21:12 [n] 1Sa 31:11-13

20:23–26 *David's Officials.* This is the second list in 2 Samuel of David's court officials (8:15–18). Four of the officials are the same in each list, and this list has three replacements and one added position ("in charge of forced labor").

20:24 Adoniram. Likely mentioned in 1 Kgs 4:6; 5:14; later stoned to death when the kingdom divides (1 Kgs 12:18).

21:1–14 *The Gibeonites Avenged.* When Israel was in the process of conquering the land of Canaan under Joshua, the Gibeonites deceived the Israelites into making a covenant with them (Josh 9:1–15). Although not recorded elsewhere in Scripture, Saul sinfully broke this covenant that had been in place for a few centuries by killing many of the Gibeonites because of his "zeal for Israel and Judah" (2 Sam 21:2). This is why Israel is in a three-year famine (v. 1).

21:1 famine. Can be a sign of God's disfavor on a land (Deut 11:16–17).

21:3–4 David asks the surviving Gibeonites what he can do to make restitution for Saul's sins against them. They answer that money cannot bring resolution nor could the death of one Israelite. In addition, the Gibeonites have no right to kill an Israelite as blood vengeance. So David asks the Gibeonites to define the solution.

21:6 The Gibeonites ask that seven of Saul's "male descendants" be given to them for execution. **seven.** Probably symbolizes fullness, representing a complete satisfaction for the deeds of Saul. **Gibeah.** Some commentators adopt a reading from an old Greek text and translate this "Gibeon," but that emendation takes the sting of ironic justice out of the passage.

21:7 oath. See 1 Sam 18:1–4; 20:14–17.

21:8 Mephibosheth. Different than the Mephibosheth in v. 7. Verse 8 refers to Saul's son by the royal concubine Rizpah, whereas v. 7 refers to Saul's grandson by Jonathan. **Merab.** See NIV text note. **Barzillai.** Not to be confused with the man of the same name in 19:31–39.

21:10 Rizpah lost two sons to the Gibeonites (vv. 8–9). **sackcloth.** A material of grief and mourning that Rizpah uses as a covering or protection from the natural elements. She keeps vigil here to guard her sons' bodies from scavengers. It is uncertain how long she remains here—at least until the famine is over.

21:11–14 When David hears of Rizpah's vigilance, he is reminded to do something with the bones of Saul and Jonathan that are buried in Jabesh Gilead (1 Sam 31:11–13). It ought to be assumed that David has the bones of Saul, Jonathan, and the seven hung men all interred in Benjamin. God responds to the episode by answering the prayers of the people and stopping the famine in Israel.

21:12 [o] Jos 17:11 [p] 1Sa 31:10
21:14 [q] Jos 18:28 [r] Jos 7:26 [s] 2Sa 24:25
21:15 [t] 2Sa 5:25
21:17 [u] 2Sa 20:6 [v] 1Ki 11:36 [w] 2Sa 18:3
21:18 [x] 1Ch 11:29; 20:4; 27:11
21:19 [y] 1Sa 17:7
21:21 [z] 1Sa 16:9
22:1 [a] Ex 15:1; Jdg 5:1; Ps 18:2-50
22:2 [b] Dt 32:4; Ps 71:3 [c] Ps 31:3; 91:2 [d] Ps 144:2
22:3 [e] Dt 32:37; Jer 16:19 [f] Ge 15:1 [g] Lk 1:69

Jabesh Gilead. (They had stolen their bodies from the public square at Beth Shan,[o] where the Philistines
had hung[p] them after they struck Saul down on Gilboa.) 13 David brought the bones of Saul and his
son Jonathan from there, and the bones of those who had been killed and exposed were gathered up.
14 They buried the bones of Saul and his son Jonathan in the tomb of Saul's father Kish, at Zela[q] in Benjamin, and did everything the king commanded. After that,[r] God answered prayer[s] in behalf of the land.

Wars Against the Philistines

21:15-22pp — 1Ch 20:4-8

15 Once again there was a battle between the Philistines[t] and Israel. David went down with his men
to fight against the Philistines, and he became exhausted. 16 And Ishbi-Benob, one of the descendants
of Rapha, whose bronze spearhead weighed three hundred shekels[a] and who was armed with a new
sword, said he would kill David. 17 But Abishai[u] son of Zeruiah came to David's rescue; he struck the
Philistine down and killed him. Then David's men swore to him, saying, "Never again will you go out
with us to battle, so that the lamp[v] of Israel will not be extinguished.[w]"

18 In the course of time, there was another battle with the Philistines, at Gob. At that time Sibbekai[x]
the Hushathite killed Saph, one of the descendants of Rapha.

19 In another battle with the Philistines at Gob, Elhanan son of Jair[b] the Bethlehemite killed the
brother of[c] Goliath the Gittite, who had a spear with a shaft like a weaver's rod.[y]

20 In still another battle, which took place at Gath, there was a huge man with six fingers on each
hand and six toes on each foot — twenty-four in all. He also was descended from Rapha. 21 When he
taunted Israel, Jonathan son of Shimeah,[z] David's brother, killed him.

22 These four were descendants of Rapha in Gath, and they fell at the hands of David and his men.

David's Song of Praise

22:1-51pp — Ps 18:1-50

22 David sang[a] to the LORD the words of this song when the LORD delivered him from the hand of
all his enemies and from the hand of Saul. 2 He said:

> "The LORD is my rock,[b] my fortress[c] and my deliverer;[d]
> 3 my God is my rock, in whom I take refuge,[e]
> my shield[d][f] and the horn[e][g] of my salvation.

[a] *16* That is, about 7 1/2 pounds or about 3.5 kilograms [b] *19* See 1 Chron. 20:5; Hebrew *Jaare-Oregim*. [c] *19* See 1 Chron. 20:5; Hebrew does not have *the brother of*. [d] *3* Or *sovereign* [e] *3* *Horn* here symbolizes strength.

21:15–22 *Wars Against the Philistines.* These four episodes in which David's men battle Philistine giants (vv. 15–17,18,19,20–22) appear to come from another document such as a chronicle of the wars of David.
21:15–17 War breaks out between Israel and Philistia. David and his troops go "down" to meet the enemy in battle; the Israelites are located primarily in the highlands, so they travel down to the plain to encounter the Philistines. But David is so exhausted (cf. 1 Sam 14:28,31) that he cannot fight the Philistine warrior Ishbi-Benob one-on-one.
21:16 the descendants of Rapha. Likely refers to the Rephaim, a group of giants (Deut 2:10–11,20–21). Ishbi-Benob intends to assassinate David. Abishai, Joab's brother, steps in for the king and kills the giant.
21:17 the lamp of Israel will not be extinguished. This metaphor ("lamp") refers to the Davidic dynasty in 1 Kgs 11:36; 15:4; 2 Kgs 8:19. The soldiers are afraid that if David is killed his whole dynasty will go down with him.
21:18 Gob. Location uncertain. **Hushathite.** The Israelite warrior is from Hushah, located at modern Husan in the tribal lands of Judah about five miles (8 kilometers) directly west of Bethlehem.
21:19 The Hebrew text of this verse has two scribal difficulties: (1) It literally says that Elhanan killed "Goliath the Gittite" (see NIV text note). That is a problem because David did that (1 Sam 17). In 1 Chr 20:5 it adds that Elhanan struck down "Lahmi the brother of Goliath the Gittite." Why that detail is missing from the present account is unknown. (2) It says Elhanan's father is "Jaare-Oregim." The second part of that compound name is the same word for "weaver" at the end of the verse. This is probably an example of scribal dittography (a mistaken repetition of a letter, word, or phrase by a copyist).
21:21 taunted. A leading word in the Goliath account in 1 Sam 17 (vv. 10,25,26,36,45) that is translated there in various ways. **Shimeah.** David's third eldest brother ("Shammah" in 1 Sam 17:13).
22:1–51 *David's Song of Praise.* This is a royal psalm of the king, nearly identical to Ps 18. The differences between the two can be explained by the shift from an individual psalm of the king (1 Sam 22) to the public nature of its use in the temple by the people of God (Ps 18). David's song of praise is also reminiscent of several key themes in the song of Hannah (1 Sam 2:1–10); the two songs bracket 1–2 Samuel.
22:1 This superscription is almost identical to the heading of Ps 18, which adds some musical instructions for the song to be sung publicly in the temple ("For the director of music").
22:2–4 This hymn of praise includes a series of metaphors that describe the Lord as a source of strength, safety, and security for the believer.
22:2 rock. This metaphor also appears in vv. 32,47, and it is a core idea of Hannah's song (1 Sam 2:2).

He is my stronghold,[h] my refuge and my savior—
from violent people you save me.

4 "I called to the LORD, who is worthy[i] of praise,
and have been saved from my enemies.
5 The waves[j] of death swirled about me;
the torrents of destruction overwhelmed me.
6 The cords of the grave[k] coiled around me;
the snares of death confronted me.

7 "In my distress[l] I called[m] to the LORD;
I called out to my God.
From his temple he heard my voice;
my cry came to his ears.
8 The earth[n] trembled and quaked,[o]
the foundations[p] of the heavens[a] shook;
they trembled because he was angry.
9 Smoke rose from his nostrils;
consuming fire[q] came from his mouth,
burning coals blazed out of it.
10 He parted the heavens and came down;
dark clouds[r] were under his feet.
11 He mounted the cherubim and flew;
he soared[b] on the wings of the wind.[s]
12 He made darkness his canopy around him—
the dark[c] rain clouds of the sky.
13 Out of the brightness of his presence
bolts of lightning[t] blazed forth.
14 The LORD thundered[u] from heaven;
the voice of the Most High resounded.
15 He shot his arrows[v] and scattered the enemy,
with great bolts of lightning he routed them.
16 The valleys of the sea were exposed
and the foundations of the earth laid bare
at the rebuke[w] of the LORD,
at the blast of breath from his nostrils.

17 "He reached down from on high[x] and took hold of me;
he drew[y] me out of deep waters.
18 He rescued me from my powerful enemy,
from my foes, who were too strong for me.
19 They confronted me in the day of my disaster,
but the LORD was my support.[z]

22:3 [h] Ps 9:9
22:4 [i] Ps 48:1; 96:4
22:5 [j] Ps 69:14-15; 93:4; Jnh 2:3
22:6 [k] Ps 116:3
22:7 [l] Ps 120:1 [m] Ps 34:6, 15; 116:4
22:8 [n] Jdg 5:4; Ps 97:4 [o] Ps 77:18 [p] Job 26:11
22:9 [q] Ps 97:3; Heb 12:29
22:10 [r] 1Ki 8:12; Na 1:3
22:11 [s] Ps 104:3
22:13 [t] ver 9
22:14 [u] 1Sa 2:10
22:15 [v] Dt 32:23
22:16 [w] Na 1:4
22:17 [x] Ps 144:7 [y] Ex 2:10
22:19 [z] Ps 23:4

[a] *8* Hebrew; Vulgate and Syriac (see also Psalm 18:7) *mountains* [b] *11* Many Hebrew manuscripts (see also Psalm 18:10); most Hebrew manuscripts *appeared* [c] *12* Septuagint (see also Psalm 18:11); Hebrew *massed*

22:5–7 David looks back on his life and sees dire times of desperation before his enemies.
22:5 destruction. Hebrew "Belial," a term commonly used in 1–2 Samuel for worthless, good-for-nothing scoundrels (see notes on 23:6–7; 1 Sam 1:16; 2:12).
22:7 temple. Can refer to the tabernacle (1 Sam 1:9); may refer to the heavenly temple in which God dwells.
22:8–16 The Lord appears in great strength and with anger against the king's enemies. With his coming, the natural phenomena react.
22:8 earth … quaked. Cf. Exod 19:18; 1 Kgs 19:11. **heavens shook.** Cf. Joel 2:10.
22:9 Smoke … consuming fire … burning coals. The progression vividly intensifies along with God's anger.
22:14 thundered from heaven. Cf. 1 Sam 2:10.
22:15 great bolts of lightning. Sent against David's enemies.
22:17–20 The Lord rescues David.
22:17 drew … out. Used in Exod 2:10 for Moses being drawn out of the perilous Nile River.

22:20 [a]Ps 31:8 [b]Ps 118:5 [c]Ps 22:8 [d]2Sa 15:26
22:21 [e]1Sa 26:23 [f]Ps 24:4
22:22 [g]Ge 18:19; Ps 128:1; Pr 8:32
22:23 [h]Dt 6:4-9; Ps 119:30-32 [i]Ps 119:102
22:24 [j]Ge 6:9; Eph 1:4
22:25 [k]ver 21
22:27 [l]Mt 5:8 [m]Lev 26:23-24
22:28 [n]Ex 3:8; Ps 72:12-13 [o]Isa 2:12, 17; 5:15
22:29 [p]Ps 27:1
22:31 [q]Dt 32:4; Mt 5:48 [r]Ps 12:6; 119:140; Pr 30:5-6
22:32 [s]1Sa 2:2
22:34 [t]Hab 3:19 [u]Dt 32:13
22:35 [v]Ps 144:1
22:36 [w]Eph 6:16
22:37 [x]Pr 4:11

20 He brought me out into a spacious[a] place;
he rescued[b] me because he delighted[c] in me.[d]

21 "The LORD has dealt with me according to my righteousness;[e]
according to the cleanness of my hands[f] he has rewarded me.
22 For I have kept[g] the ways of the LORD;
I am not guilty of turning from my God.
23 All his laws are before me;[h]
I have not turned[i] away from his decrees.
24 I have been blameless[j] before him
and have kept myself from sin.
25 The LORD has rewarded me according to my
righteousness,[k]
according to my cleanness[a] in his sight.

26 "To the faithful you show yourself faithful,
to the blameless you show yourself blameless,
27 to the pure[l] you show yourself pure,
but to the devious you show yourself shrewd.[m]
28 You save the humble,[n]
but your eyes are on the haughty to bring them low.[o]
29 You, LORD, are my lamp;[p]
the LORD turns my darkness into light.
30 With your help I can advance against a troop[b];
with my God I can scale a wall.

31 "As for God, his way is perfect:[q]
The LORD's word is flawless;[r]
he shields all who take refuge in him.
32 For who is God besides the LORD?
And who is the Rock[s] except our God?
33 It is God who arms me with strength[c]
and keeps my way secure.
34 He makes my feet like the feet of a deer;[t]
he causes me to stand on the heights.[u]
35 He trains my hands[v] for battle;
my arms can bend a bow of bronze.
36 You make your saving help my shield;[w]
your help has made[d] me great.
37 You provide a broad path[x] for my feet,
so that my ankles do not give way.

38 "I pursued my enemies and crushed them;
I did not turn back till they were destroyed.

[a] *25* Hebrew; Septuagint and Vulgate (see also Psalm 18:24) *to the cleanness of my hands* [b] *30* Or *can run through a barricade* [c] *33* Dead Sea Scrolls, some Septuagint manuscripts, Vulgate and Syriac (see also Psalm 18:32); Masoretic Text *who is my strong refuge* [d] *36* Dead Sea Scrolls; Masoretic Text *shield; / you stoop down to make*

22:20 spacious place. The Lord not only delivers David but brings him into a "spacious place" over against the tight place he had been in.
22:21–28 David pleads his innocence before God.
22:24 I have been blameless. Not sinless but a person of integrity (Job 1:1).
22:28 humble … haughty. Reminiscent of Hannah's song (1 Sam 2:7–8).
22:29–35 David relates God's goodness to him. God empowers him to overcome his enemies and is the source of David's strength.
22:32 Rock. See note on v. 2.
22:34 feet of a deer. Sure-footed and secure.
22:36–46 David describes his triumph over his enemies.

39 I crushed[y] them completely, and they could not rise;
they fell beneath my feet.
40 You armed me with strength for battle;
you humbled my adversaries before me.[z]
41 You made my enemies turn their backs[a] in flight,
and I destroyed my foes.
42 They cried for help,[b] but there was no one to save them —[c]
to the LORD, but he did not answer.
43 I beat them as fine as the dust of the earth;
I pounded and trampled[d] them like mud[e] in the streets.

44 "You have delivered[f] me from the attacks of the peoples;
you have preserved[g] me as the head of nations.
People[h] I did not know now serve me,
45 foreigners cower[i] before me;
as soon as they hear of me, they obey me.
46 They all lose heart;
they come trembling[a][j] from their strongholds.

47 "The LORD lives! Praise be to my Rock!
Exalted be my God, the Rock, my Savior![k]
48 He is the God who avenges me,[l]
who puts the nations under me,
49 who sets me free from my enemies.[m]
You exalted me above my foes;
from a violent man you rescued me.
50 Therefore I will praise you, LORD, among the nations;
I will sing the praises of your name.[n]

51 "He gives his king great victories;[o]
he shows unfailing kindness to his anointed,[p]
to David[q] and his descendants forever."[r]

22:39 [y]Mal 4:3
22:40 [z]Ps 44:5
22:41 [a]Ex 23:27
22:42 [b]Isa 1:15 [c]Ps 50:22
22:43 [d]Mic 7:10 [e]Isa 10:6; Mic 7:10
22:44 [f]2Sa 3:1 [g]Dt 28:13 [h]2Sa 8:1-14; Isa 55:3-5
22:45 [i]Ps 66:3; 81:15
22:46 [j]Mic 7:17
22:47 [k]Ps 89:26
22:48 [l]Ps 94:1; 144:2; 1Sa 25:39
22:49 [m]Ps 140:1,4
22:50 [n]Ro 15:9*
22:51 [o]Ps 144:9-10 [p]Ps 89:20 [q]2Sa 7:13 [r]Ps 89:24,29
23:1 [s]2Sa 7:8-9; Ps 78:70-71; 89:27 [t]1Sa 16:12-13; Ps 89:20
23:2 [u]Mt 22:43; 2Pe 1:21
23:3 [v]Dt 32:4; 2Sa 22:2, 32 [w]Ps 72:2 [x]2Ch 19:7, 9; Isa 11:1-5

David's Last Words

23 These are the last words of David:

"The inspired utterance of David son of Jesse,
the utterance of the man exalted[s] by the Most High,
the man anointed[t] by the God of Jacob,
the hero of Israel's songs:

2 "The Spirit[u] of the LORD spoke through me;
his word was on my tongue.
3 The God of Israel spoke,
the Rock[v] of Israel said to me:
'When one rules over people in righteousness,[w]
when he rules in the fear of God,[x]

[a] *46* Some Septuagint manuscripts and Vulgate (see also Psalm 18:45); Masoretic Text *they arm themselves*

22:43 beat them as fine as the dust. Pulverize them; David's victory is total.
22:47–50 David again praises God for his victory.
22:51 The psalm concludes triumphantly (cf. the ending of Hannah's prayer in 1 Sam 2:10).
23:1–7 *David's Last Words.* David's final words proclaim that the Lord speaks through him. And at this time God tells David of the contrast between the just ruler and those who are evil, worthless people (see notes on 23:6–7; 1 Sam 1:16; 2:12). This is a common theme in wisdom literature (see, e.g., Ps 1).
23:1 Like many of the psalms, this opening verse is probably a superscription or introduction to the song. **hero of Israel's songs.** Some commentators believe "songs" means "strength" and thus refers to "the God of Jacob" from the previous line.

23:4 [y] Jdg 5:31; Ps 89:36
23:5 [z] Ps 89:29; Isa 55:3
23:6 [a] Mt 13:40-41
23:9 [b] 1Ch 27:4 [c] 1Ch 8:4
23:13 [d] 1Sa 22:1 [e] 2Sa 5:18

4 he is like the light of morning at sunrise[y]
on a cloudless morning,
like the brightness after rain
that brings grass from the earth.'

5 "If my house were not right with God,
surely he would not have made with me an everlasting covenant,[z]
arranged and secured in every part;
surely he would not bring to fruition my salvation
and grant me my every desire.
6 But evil men are all to be cast aside like thorns,[a]
which are not gathered with the hand.
7 Whoever touches thorns
uses a tool of iron or the shaft of a spear;
they are burned up where they lie."

David's Mighty Warriors

23:8-39pp — 1Ch 11:10-41

8 These are the names of David's mighty warriors:
Josheb-Basshebeth,[a] a Tahkemonite,[b] was chief of the Three; he raised his spear against eight hundred men, whom he killed[c] in one encounter.
9 Next to him was Eleazar son of Dodai[b] the Ahohite.[c] As one of the three mighty warriors, he was
with David when they taunted the Philistines gathered at Pas Dammim[d] for battle. Then the Israelites
retreated, 10 but Eleazar stood his ground and struck down the Philistines till his hand grew tired and
froze to the sword. The LORD brought about a great victory that day. The troops returned to Eleazar, but
only to strip the dead.
11 Next to him was Shammah son of Agee the Hararite. When the Philistines banded together at a
place where there was a field full of lentils, Israel's troops fled from them. 12 But Shammah took his
stand in the middle of the field. He defended it and struck the Philistines down, and the LORD brought
about a great victory.
13 During harvest time, three of the thirty chief warriors came down to David at the cave of Adullam,[d]
while a band of Philistines was encamped in the Valley of Rephaim.[e] 14 At that time David was in the

[a] 8 Hebrew; some Septuagint manuscripts suggest *Ish-Bosheth,* that is, *Esh-Baal* (see also 1 Chron. 11:11 *Jashobeam*). [b] 8 Probably a variant of *Hakmonite* (see 1 Chron. 11:11) [c] 8 Some Septuagint manuscripts (see also 1 Chron. 11:11); Hebrew and other Septuagint manuscripts *Three; it was Adino the Eznite who killed eight hundred men* [d] 9 See 1 Chron. 11:13; Hebrew *gathered there.*

23:4 light of morning at sunrise. The one who rules justly is like the early morning sun, which brings new life and vitality.

23:5 covenant. See 7:4–17.

23:6–7 But. In contrast to the righteous king who rules in the fear of God. **evil men.** Hebrew "Belial," which repeatedly occurs in 1–2 Samuel (16:7; 20:1; 22:5 [see note]; 23:6; 1 Sam 1:16; 2:12; 10:27; 25:17,25; 30:22; see notes on 1 Sam 1:16; 2:12). **thorns.** Worthless yet dangerous; a person touches them with a weapon, not their hand.

23:8–39 *David's Mighty Warriors.* This glimpse into the military tenor of the time overviews David's elite military personnel in three parts: the Three (vv. 8–17), the Two (vv. 18–23), and the Thirty (vv. 24–39). Throughout the section there is textual confusion between the numbers "three" and "thirty," so at times it is difficult to be certain in which group a particular person belongs. In addition, the list reflects the changing nature of the groups over time, so some of the Thirty died in battle—such as Asahel (v. 24; 2:18–23) and Uriah (v. 39; 11:17)—and were replaced.

23:8 These are the names of. Introduces a catalog of the inner rings of David's military establishment. **mighty warriors.** Cf. 10:7; 16:6; 17:8; 20:7. The catalog begins by describing the Three, the very top of the military chain. The chief commander of the Three is Josheb-Basshebeth, who killed 800 men in one battle.

23:9–10 Eleazar. The next in rank of the Three. He is famous for standing his ground against the Philistines when the rest of the Israelite army had retreated from the field of battle. **froze to the sword.** Perhaps some sort of paralysis that set in so that he couldn't release his weapon. The battle took place at Pas Dammim (1 Chr 11:13).

23:11–12 Shammah. The third member of the Three. Like Eleazar, he stood his ground against the Philistines when the Israelite army had fled. Apparently the Philistines had raided Israelite land to steal lentils. Shammah took his stand in the middle of the lentil fields and single-handedly defeated the Philistines through the power of the Lord.

23:13–17 No names are supplied for the three warriors of this incident, so it is likely that they are the Three from vv. 8–12, especially since the passage ends with "Such were the exploits of the three mighty warriors" (v. 17). The episode's setting is that David and his men are camped in the stronghold of the cave of Adullam (1 Sam 22:1–5) while the Philistines are in control of David's hometown of Bethlehem. David is homesick and he craves the water of his town that is by the gate of the city. The gate is normally a heavily guarded area. The Three, risking their

stronghold,[f] and the Philistine garrison was at Bethlehem.[g] 15David longed for water and said, "Oh,
that someone would get me a drink of water from the well near the gate of Bethlehem!" 16So the three
mighty warriors broke through the Philistine lines, drew water from the well near the gate of Bethlehem and carried it back to David. But he refused to drink it; instead, he poured[h] it out before the LORD.
17"Far be it from me, LORD, to do this!" he said. "Is it not the blood[i] of men who went at the risk of their
lives?" And David would not drink it.

Such were the exploits of the three mighty warriors.

18Abishai[j] the brother of Joab son of Zeruiah was chief of the Three.[a] He raised his spear against three
hundred men, whom he killed, and so he became as famous as the Three. 19Was he not held in greater
honor than the Three? He became their commander, even though he was not included among them.

20Benaiah[k] son of Jehoiada, a valiant fighter from Kabzeel,[l] performed great exploits. He struck down
Moab's two mightiest warriors. He also went down into a pit on a snowy day and killed a lion. 21And he
struck down a huge Egyptian. Although the Egyptian had a spear in his hand, Benaiah went against
him with a club. He snatched the spear from the Egyptian's hand and killed him with his own spear.
22Such were the exploits of Benaiah son of Jehoiada; he too was as famous as the three mighty warriors.
23He was held in greater honor than any of the Thirty, but he was not included among the Three. And
David put him in charge of his bodyguard.

24 Among the Thirty were:
Asahel[m] the brother of Joab,
Elhanan son of Dodo from Bethlehem,
25 Shammah the Harodite,[n]
Elika the Harodite,
26 Helez[o] the Paltite,
Ira son of Ikkesh from Tekoa,
27 Abiezer from Anathoth,[p]
Sibbekai[b] the Hushathite,
28 Zalmon the Ahohite,
Maharai[q] the Netophathite,[r]
29 Heled[c] son of Baanah the Netophathite,
Ithai son of Ribai from Gibeah[s] in Benjamin,
30 Benaiah the Pirathonite,[t]
Hiddai[d] from the ravines of Gaash,[u]
31 Abi-Albon the Arbathite,
Azmaveth the Barhumite,[v]
32 Eliahba the Shaalbonite,
the sons of Jashen,
Jonathan 33son of[e] Shammah the Hararite,
Ahiam son of Sharar[f] the Hararite,

23:14 [f] 1Sa 22:4-5 [g] Ru 1:19
23:16 [h] Ge 35:14
23:17 [i] Lev 17:10-12
23:18 [j] 2Sa 10:10,14; 1Ch 11:20
23:20 [k] 2Sa 8:18; 20:23 [l] Jos 15:21
23:24 [m] 2Sa 2:18
23:25 [n] Jdg 7:1; 1Ch 11:27
23:26 [o] 1Ch 27:10
23:27 [p] Jos 21:18
23:28 [q] 1Ch 27:13 [r] 2Ki 25:23; Ne 7:26
23:29 [s] Jos 15:57
23:30 [t] Jdg 12:13 [u] Jos 24:30
23:31 [v] 2Sa 3:16

[a] *18* Most Hebrew manuscripts (see also 1 Chron. 11:20); two Hebrew manuscripts and Syriac *Thirty* [b] *27* Some Septuagint manuscripts (see also 21:18; 1 Chron. 11:29); Hebrew *Mebunnai* [c] *29* Some Hebrew manuscripts and Vulgate (see also 1 Chron. 11:30); most Hebrew manuscripts *Heleb* [d] *30* Hebrew; some Septuagint manuscripts (see also 1 Chron. 11:32) *Hurai* [e] *33* Some Septuagint manuscripts (see also 1 Chron. 11:34); Hebrew does not have *son of.* [f] *33* Hebrew; some Septuagint manuscripts (see also 1 Chron. 11:35) *Sakar*

lives, succeed in bringing water from the well to David. The king refuses to drink it; instead, he pours it out as a drink offering to the Lord. The purpose of this act is to commemorate a special, singular, unique event before God (Gen 35:14; Lev 23:13).

23:18–23 This section describes the Two: Abishai and Benaiah are members of the Thirty but held in higher honor than the Thirty. Abishai was head over the Three, but was not a member of them. The Two do not attain to the stature and prominence of the Three (vv. 19,23).

23:18 Abishai. Joab's brother; he plays a major role in 1–2 Samuel (e.g., 2:24; 16:9–14; 1 Sam 26:6–9).

23:20 mightiest warriors. Uncertain meaning; appears to be related to "lion"; perhaps refers to two "lion-like men" from Moab.

23:21 huge. Some translations say that the Egyptian was handsome. Benaiah ironically kills the Egyptian with the man's own spear.

23:24–39 This lists the names of the Thirty. It ends with a thunderclap because the last mighty man is Uriah the Hittite, which reminds the reader of David's great sin in ch. 11. It also sets up the beginning of the next chapter, where David commits another grave sin.

23:34 [w]2Sa 11:3 [x]2Sa 15:12
23:35 [y]Jos 12:22
23:36 [z]1Sa 14:47
23:38 [a]2Sa 20:26; 1Ch 2:53
23:39 [b]2Sa 11:3
24:1 [c]Jos 9:15 [d]1Ch 27:23
24:2 [e]2Sa 20:23 [f]Jdg 20:1; 2Sa 3:10
24:3 [g]Dt 1:11
24:5 [h]Dt 2:36; Jos 13:9 [i]Nu 21:32
24:6 [j]Ge 10:19; Jos 19:28; Jdg 1:31
24:7 [k]Jos 19:29 [l]Ge 21:22-33 [m]Dt 1:7; Jos 11:3
24:9 [n]Nu 1:44-46; 1Ch 21:5
24:10 [o]1Sa 24:5

34 Eliphelet son of Ahasbai the Maakathite,
Eliam[w] son of Ahithophel[x] the Gilonite,
35 Hezro the Carmelite,[y]
Paarai the Arbite,
36 Igal son of Nathan from Zobah,[z]
the son of Hagri,[a]
37 Zelek the Ammonite,
Naharai the Beerothite, the armor-bearer of Joab son of Zeruiah,
38 Ira the Ithrite,[a]
Gareb the Ithrite
39 and Uriah[b] the Hittite.
There were thirty-seven in all.

David Enrolls the Fighting Men

24:1-17pp — 1Ch 21:1-17

24 Again[c] the anger of the LORD burned against Israel, and he incited David against them, saying,
"Go and take a census of[d] Israel and Judah."
2 So the king said to Joab[e] and the army commanders[b] with him, "Go throughout the tribes of
Israel from Dan to Beersheba[f] and enroll the fighting men, so that I may know how many there are."
3 But Joab replied to the king, "May the LORD your God multiply the troops a hundred times
over,[g] and may the eyes of my lord the king see it. But why does my lord the king want to do such
a thing?"
4 The king's word, however, overruled Joab and the army commanders; so they left the presence of
the king to enroll the fighting men of Israel.
5 After crossing the Jordan, they camped near Aroer,[h] south of the town in the gorge, and then went
through Gad and on to Jazer.[i]
6 They went to Gilead and the region of Tahtim Hodshi, and on to Dan
Jaan and around toward Sidon.[j]
7 Then they went toward the fortress of Tyre[k] and all the towns of the
Hivites and Canaanites. Finally, they went on to Beersheba[l] in the Negev[m] of Judah.
8 After they had gone through the entire land, they came back to Jerusalem at the end of nine months
and twenty days.
9 Joab reported the number of the fighting men to the king: In Israel there were eight hundred thousand able-bodied men who could handle a sword, and in Judah five hundred thousand.[n]
10 David was conscience-stricken[o] after he had counted the fighting men, and he said to the LORD, "I

[a] *36* Some Septuagint manuscripts (see also 1 Chron. 11:38); Hebrew *Haggadi* [b] *2* Septuagint (see also verse 4 and 1 Chron. 21:2); Hebrew *Joab the army commander*

24:1–17 *David Enrolls the Fighting Men.* The Lord is furious with Israel, although the text does not say why. Israel needs to be punished for its sin, so the Lord incites David to sin by taking a census of all the fighting men of Israel.

24:1 Again. God's most recent displeasure with Israel occurs at the beginning of ch. 21 when God brought a famine on Israel because Saul killed the Gibeonites (21:1). God incited David to take a military census of all Israel (cf. Num 1:1–47). The parallel passage in 1 Chr 21:1 says, "Satan … incited David to take a census." The Lord uses Satan as a secondary agent to bring about his purposes (cf. 1 Kgs 22:20–23; Job 1).

24:2 Joab and the army commanders. Or "Joab the commander of the army"; David is giving his instructions to Joab because he is the commanding general of all Israelite forces. See NIV text note. **Dan to Beersheba.** A *merism* (a literary figure in which two polar opposites are all-inclusive) that indicates the census includes all Israel from one end to the other.

24:3 Joab disapproves of the census.

24:5–8 The census takers begin in Jerusalem and then cross the Jordan River into Transjordan.

24:5 Aroer. On the northern bank of the Arnon River, which denotes the southern border of Israel in the territory of Transjordan. The census takers move north through the tribal lands of Gad to Jazer. **Jazer.** Located at modern Khirbet as-Sar about 30 miles (48 kilometers) north of the Arnon River. They continue north into Gilead and then northwest to the city of Dan. **Jaan.** Probably the city of Ijon, which lies to the north of Dan (1 Kgs 15:20). The agents then travel to the Phoenician cities of Sidon and Tyre; it is likely that Israelites are living in these towns and need to be counted. By going throughout Israel and Judah to the city of Beersheba, the counters keep David's command to include all areas from Dan to Beersheba (2 Sam 24:2). **nine months and twenty days.** The census is a vast undertaking.

24:9 Some think that the figures 800,000 and 500,000 are excessively high, so they read them as 800 and 500 military units, interpreting "thousand" as a military unit of a smaller size than a thousand men.

24:10 David's conscience strikes him with deep regret over ordering the census. The Hebrew adverb "very" is used twice in the verse: "I have sinned very" and "I have done a very foolish thing." What is his sin in taking a census? Perhaps pride in being able to count the large number of men in his army or unfaithfulness by trusting in the size of his army rather than God's power.

MAP OF LIMITS OF ISRAEL PROPER IN WHICH JOAB CONDUCTED A CENSUS FOR DAVID

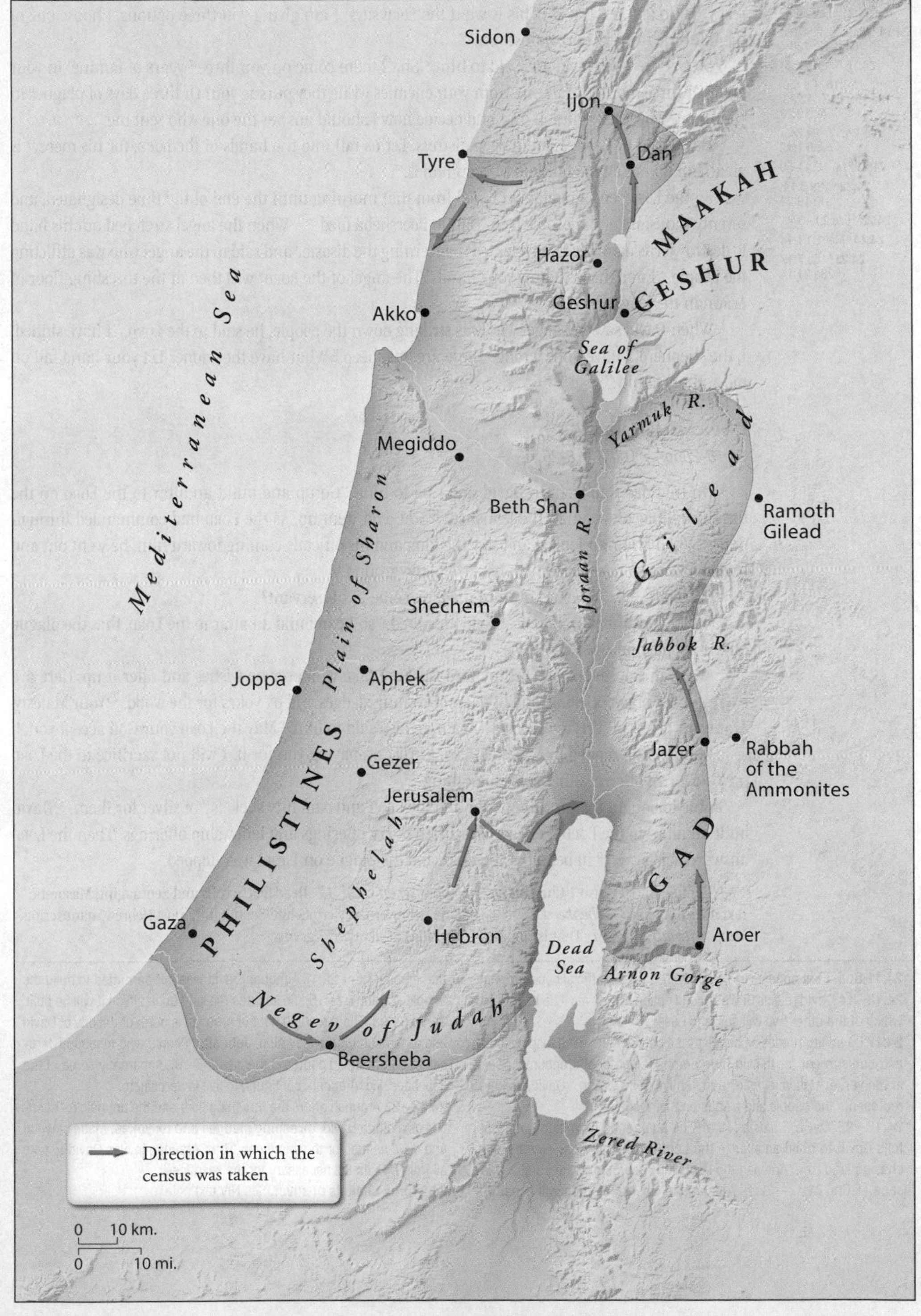

24:10 [p] 2Sa 12:13 [q] Nu 12:11; 1Sa 13:13
24:11 [r] 1Sa 22:5 [s] 1Sa 9:9; 1Ch 29:29
24:13 [t] Dt 28:38-42, 48; Eze 14:21 [u] Lev 26:25
24:14 [v] Ne 9:28; Ps 51:1; 103:8, 13; 130:4
24:15 [w] 1Ch 27:24
24:16 [x] Ge 6:6; 1Sa 15:11 [y] Ex 12:23; Ac 12:23
24:17 [z] Ps 74:1 [a] Jnh 1:12
24:21 [b] Nu 16:44-50
24:22 [c] 1Sa 6:14; 1Ki 19:21
24:23 [d] Eze 20:40-41
24:24 [e] Mal 1:13-14
24:25 [f] 1Sa 7:17 [g] 2Sa 21:14

have sinned[p] greatly in what I have done. Now, LORD, I beg you, take away the guilt of your servant. I have done a very foolish thing.[q]"

11 Before David got up the next morning, the word of the LORD had come to Gad[r] the prophet, David's seer:[s] 12 "Go and tell David, 'This is what the LORD says: I am giving you three options. Choose one of them for me to carry out against you.' "

13 So Gad went to David and said to him, "Shall there come on you three[a] years of famine[t] in your land? Or three months of fleeing from your enemies while they pursue you? Or three days of plague[u] in your land? Now then, think it over and decide how I should answer the one who sent me."

14 David said to Gad, "I am in deep distress. Let us fall into the hands of the LORD, for his mercy[v] is great; but do not let me fall into human hands."

15 So the LORD sent a plague on Israel from that morning until the end of the time designated, and seventy thousand of the people from Dan to Beersheba died.[w] 16 When the angel stretched out his hand to destroy Jerusalem, the LORD relented[x] concerning the disaster and said to the angel who was afflicting the people, "Enough! Withdraw your hand." The angel of the LORD[y] was then at the threshing floor of Araunah the Jebusite.

17 When David saw the angel who was striking down the people, he said to the LORD, "I have sinned; I, the shepherd,[b] have done wrong. These are but sheep.[z] What have they done? Let your hand fall on me and my family."[a]

David Builds an Altar

24:18-25pp — 1Ch 21:18-26

18 On that day Gad went to David and said to him, "Go up and build an altar to the LORD on the threshing floor of Araunah the Jebusite." 19 So David went up, as the LORD had commanded through Gad. 20 When Araunah looked and saw the king and his officials coming toward him, he went out and bowed down before the king with his face to the ground.

21 Araunah said, "Why has my lord the king come to his servant?"

"To buy your threshing floor," David answered, "so I can build an altar to the LORD, that the plague on the people may be stopped."[b]

22 Araunah said to David, "Let my lord the king take whatever he wishes and offer it up. Here are oxen[c] for the burnt offering, and here are threshing sledges and ox yokes for the wood. 23 Your Majesty, Araunah[c] gives[d] all this to the king." Araunah also said to him, "May the LORD your God accept you."

24 But the king replied to Araunah, "No, I insist on paying you for it. I will not sacrifice to the LORD my God burnt offerings that cost me nothing."[e]

So David bought the threshing floor and the oxen and paid fifty shekels[d] of silver for them. 25 David built an altar[f] to the LORD there and sacrificed burnt offerings and fellowship offerings. Then the LORD answered his prayer[g] in behalf of the land, and the plague on Israel was stopped.

[a] *13* Septuagint (see also 1 Chron. 21:12); Hebrew *seven* [b] *17* Dead Sea Scrolls and Septuagint; Masoretic Text does not have *the shepherd.* [c] *23* Some Hebrew manuscripts and Septuagint; most Hebrew manuscripts *King Araunah* [d] *24* That is, about 1 1/4 pounds or about 575 grams

24:11 Gad. First appears in 1 Sam 22:5. **seer.** An official court prophet.
24:13–14 David rejects God's second option but leaves it up to the Lord which of the other two will come to pass.
24:17 David intercedes on behalf of the people to take full responsibility and punishment for the sin. Two emphatic personal pronouns appear in the verse: "*I* have sinned" and "*I* have done wrong." David, as king, represents the people and pleads on their behalf.
24:18–25 *David Builds an Altar.* The book ends on a high note. Gad tells David to build an altar to the Lord, and David does so after purchasing land from Araunah the Jebusite. According to the parallel passage (1 Chr 21:1—22:1), this land is where Solomon will construct the temple (1 Chr 22:1). Although David was not permitted to build the temple (2 Sam 7:1–16), he secures the land upon which it will be built.
24:18 Go up. The threshing floor of Araunah is north of the city of David and at a much higher elevation. **Jebusite.** People who inhabited Jerusalem before David captured the city (5:6–9). Apparently some of the Jebusites, like Araunah, continued to live in Jerusalem.
24:22–23 Araunah offers the threshing floor and the animals for sacrifice as a gift to David. **threshing sledges and ox yokes.** Made of wood and used as fuel for the sacrifices. Thus, Araunah invites David to take all from him that is necessary for the sacrifices.
24:24 fifty shekels of silver. See NIV text note.

INTRODUCTION TO 1 KINGS

The history of Israel under the monarchy is the focus of 1 – 2 Kings. 1 Kings opens with the last days of David's rule and closes with the end of David's dynasty in the Babylonian exile. Together the books of Samuel and Kings recount the entire history of the monarchy from its origin during Samuel's ministry to its fall to Nebuchadnezzar and the Babylonians. Many scholars believe Joshua, Judges, 1 – 2 Samuel, and 1 – 2 Kings once comprised a major history of Israel that now forms part of our Bible (see Author, Sources, and Date). That history connects the monarchy period with events between the installation of Joshua and the birth of Samuel.

Originally written as a single book, 1 and 2 Kings were divided later at a fitting halfway point: the deaths of Ahab and Jehoshaphat. The historic reign of Ahab dominates 1 Kgs 16 – 22, and Jehoshaphat was his contemporary and ally. Elijah, Ahab's antagonist, remains active but only briefly. Elijah's main task in 2 Kings is to prepare his successor, Elisha (1 Kgs 19:15 – 21), the prophet that 2 Kgs 1 – 13 features. At the same time, several things affirm the unity of 1 and 2 Kings. Ahab dies, but the end of his dynasty that the prophets foresaw plays out in 2 Kgs 1 – 10. Elijah anoints Elisha at the end of 1 Kgs 19, but the latter's dramatic succession takes place in 2 Kgs 2. The transition between the two prophets compares to that between Moses and Joshua (Deut 34—Josh 1) and signals the dawn of a new era in 2 Kings.

AUTHOR, SOURCES, AND DATE

The author of 1 – 2 Kings is unknown. Jewish tradition deems it to be Jeremiah, but no biblical evidence supports that assumption, and what we know of Jeremiah's chronology probably rules out authorship by Jeremiah. Certainly, Jeremiah died long before the closing episode of 2 Kings, the release of Jehoiachin from prison in Babylon in 561/60 BC (2 Kgs 25:27 – 30). The prominence of prophets in the book may hint that the author was a prophet (though not Jeremiah). Internal evidence suggests that the book was finished in Babylon between 561/60 and 539 BC. The Jehoiachin episode establishes both the earliest date that the book as we know it was completed (561/60 BC) and its place of composition (Babylon). The book does not reflect events or conditions in Judah after the first return of exiles in 539 BC, so it probably was already complete by that later date. But internal evidence also suggests that 1 – 2 Kings may have originated as the final section of a long history compiled over time by several generations of authors.

It is clear that the book of Deuteronomy and its theology of history have greatly influenced 1 – 2 Kings. Deuteronomy urged Israel to worship and serve only Yahweh and to obey all his instructions. It also warned Israel that to abandon Yahweh for other gods would anger Israel's God and doom them to destruction for violating the covenant (Deut 7:4; 8:19 – 20; 11:16 – 17). That same pattern of idolatry, divine anger, and divine destruction of Israel for covenant breach also reverberates across 1 – 2 Kings (1 Kgs 11:4 – 13; 14:9 – 11; 2 Kgs 17). But links with Deuteronomy in Joshua, Judges, and 1 – 2 Samuel are also evident. The dramatic assembly of Israel between Mounts Ebal and Gerizim (Josh 8:30 – 35) fulfills the mandate of Moses (Deut 11:29; 27:1 – 8,13). Themes from Deuteronomy echo in speeches spoken at crucial historical junctures by Joshua, Samuel, David, and Solomon (Josh 23 – 24; 1 Sam 12; 1 Kgs 2:1 – 9; 8:12 – 61). The very prominence of speeches in Joshua – 2 Kings may also reflect Deuteronomy's influence because

ISRAEL UNDER DAVID AND SOLOMON

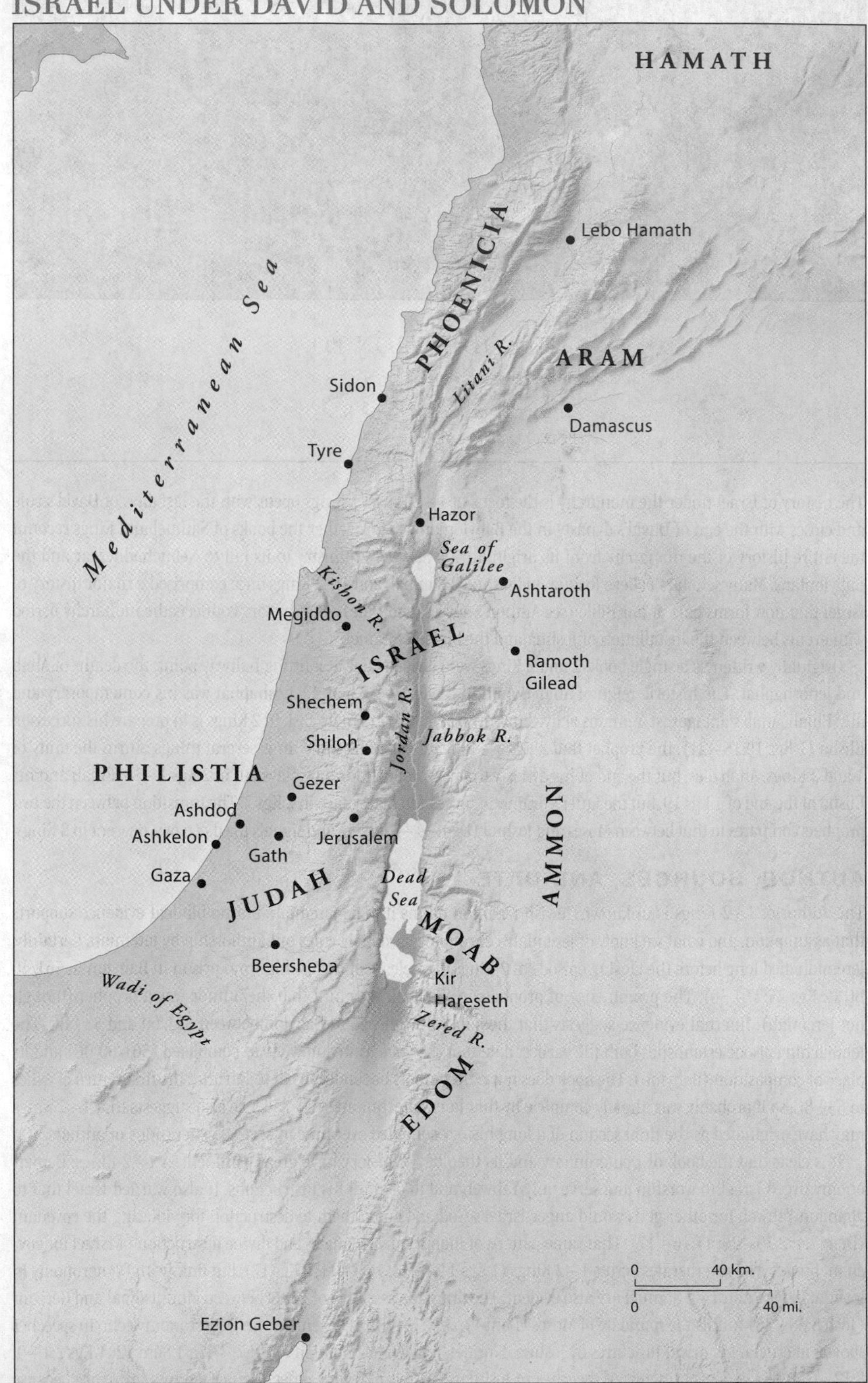
HAMATH
PHOENICIA
Lebo Hamath
Mediterranean Sea
ARAM
Litani R.
Sidon
Damascus
Tyre
Hazor
Sea of Galilee
Kisbon R.
Ashtaroth
Megiddo
ISRAEL
Ramoth Gilead
Shechem
Jordan R.
Jabbok R.
Shiloh
PHILISTIA
Gezer
Ashdod
Ashkelon
Gath
Jerusalem
AMMON
Gaza
Dead Sea
JUDAH
MOAB
Beersheba
Kir Hareseth
Wadi of Egypt
Zered R.
EDOM
0
40 km.
0
40 mi.
Ezion Geber

it features the final words of Moses. Deuteronomic theology also drives the long explanation for the destruction of the northern kingdom (2 Kgs 17). In sum, Deuteronomy's influence on Joshua to 2 Kings suggests that those books once comprised a single, long history. The accord with Deuteronomy has led some scholars to call Joshua to 2 Kings (excluding Ruth) the "Deuteronomic History" (or DH).

As for the date of the sources, two literary phenomena favor a preexilic origin for the contents of 1 Kgs 1—2 Kgs 23. The first is the recurrent retrospective phrase "to this day" to note something from the past that still continues in the time of the writer. The remark concerning the ark of the covenant's carrying poles (1 Kgs 8:8), e.g., presumes that Solomon's temple remains intact (or pre-586 BC).

Second, many scholars have observed the striking literary prominence that 1–2 Kings gives to the reign of King Josiah (1 Kgs 13:2; 2 Kgs 22:1—23:28), especially the remarkable finding of "the Book of the Law" (2 Kgs 22) and its impact on the king's religious reform. His mention by name in 1 Kgs 13:2 clearly anticipates the report of his destruction of idolatrous Bethel three centuries later in 2 Kgs 23. The two texts at least accord Josiah special importance within 1–2 Kings, as does his connection with the law book that shapes his reform efforts. The law book is usually thought to be Deuteronomy, rediscovered during temple renovations apparently after long years of disuse. The historical intersection of the reformer Josiah, the subject of an earlier prophecy, and the recently recovered words of Moses may have created the seedbed from which grew the long history (DH). Understandably, the history features Josiah's reign as its climax and comprises 1 Kgs 1—2 Kgs 23. Its purpose was to support the ongoing royal reform. The rest of the book was completed in Babylon (561/60–539 BC) to extend the history down to 561/60 BC (2 Kgs 24–25). For the purpose of the finished book, see Occasion and Purpose.

The book of 1–2 Kings clearly draws on various sources to produce the history. The importance the authors of 1–2 Kings accord Yahweh's covenant with the Davidic line shows their knowledge of parts of 1–2 Samuel (e.g., 1 Sam 16; 2 Sam 7). They repeatedly cite the royal annals of Israel and Judah (e.g., 1 Kgs 22:39,45; 2 Kgs 8:23; 10:34) and probably draw on a prophetic source for the lives of Elijah and Elisha. Palace archives may lie behind the detailed descriptions of the palace complex, the temple, and its furnishings (1 Kgs 5–7). The history reflects the perspective of someone from Judah (e.g., 1 Kgs 12:19, 2 Kgs 8:22) who apparently had access to the palace archives from Jerusalem. Presumably, some of those archives were carried into exile when Jerusalem was destroyed in 586 BC. Access to the archives in Samaria would have been more problematic given the hostile relations between the northern and southern kingdoms. The royal annals of Israel may have reached Jerusalem in the custody of refugees from the north and become available to the authors of 1–2 Kings before the Assyrians destroyed Samaria in 722 BC. The prominence of prophets, noted earlier, suggests that the authors probably also drew on the writings of prophets that were recorded throughout the monarchic period, prophets whom 1–2 Chronicles mentions (e.g., Samuel, Nathan, Gad, Ahijah, Iddo, Shemaiah, Jehu, Isaiah; see 1 Chr 29:29; 2 Chr 9:29; 12:15; 20:34; 26:22; cf. 2 Chr 24:27).

GENRE

1–2 Kings is a historical book that intends to recount accurately the people and events from a specific time and place in the past. 1–2 Kings frequently reports important royal accomplishments and failures: international alliances; royal staff appointments; the construction of palaces, temples, and fortresses; military victories and defeats; peaceful and violent conspiratorial successions, etc. As is the case with any historian, the authors' priorities and perspectives dictate what items to include or exclude and establish the standard for evaluation. But the authors clearly do not pursue the interests typical of modern historians: in-depth biography or social, economic, military, or political endeavors. Had they done so, they would have given Omri's reign more than just six verses since extrabiblical sources suggest he had political importance. The authors refer readers desiring more information to other sources that treat such subjects (e.g., 1 Kgs 11:41; 14:19,29; 16:5,14,20,27) and they instead provide God's opinion of the kings, highlighting the kings' faithfulness (or lack of it) to Yahweh and his covenant.

The repeated format in 1–2 Kings shows what the authors deem a king's most important accomplishment—whether he "did evil" or "did what was right" according to the covenant stipulations outlined in the book of Deuteronomy. If a king "did evil," he perpetuated rather than eliminated the idolatry that kept Israel from the loyal devotion to Yahweh set forth in the Mosaic covenant. If a king "did what was right," he showed loyal devotion to God and had an anti-idolatry stance. Further, the authors personify their standard of evaluation in two historic kings, each a founding father of a monarchical system. In Judah, a king was reckoned good if he followed his ancestor David in wholehearted devotion to Yahweh—and took steps to curb idolatry (e.g., 1 Kgs 15:11; 2 Kgs 22:2); he was reckoned bad if he did not (e.g., 1 Kgs 15:3,5; 2 Kgs 16:2). David's example provided the gold standard by which to measure the quality of kings of

Judah. In the northern kingdom, Israel's first king, Jeroboam I, served as the standard, and the authors of 1–2 Kings reckon all Israel's kings as bad because they all supported Jeroboam's idolatrous religious system (e.g., 1 Kgs 16:2; 2 Kgs 13:11). The authors particularly single out two other kings—Ahab of Israel (1 Kgs 16–22) and Manasseh of Judah (2 Kgs 21; 23:12,26; 24:3)—for evil reigns that proved decisive for the terrible fates of their respective realms.

In sum, the genre of 1–2 Kings is a *theological history*. It is a history of real events evaluated from the theological stance of Deuteronomy and the Davidic covenant. It asserts that the principle of cause and effect—theologically the covenant's blessings and curses (Deut 27–28)—drives the story of the monarchy. Good kings enjoy God's blessing and have successful reigns, while evil kings suffer disasters under the covenant curses.

OCCASION AND PURPOSE

The book makes no comment concerning the circumstances of its composition, but as noted above, its contents and its completion in the exile suggest a possible scenario and purpose. The exiles probably interpreted Jehoiachin's release as a positive sign, perhaps a harbinger that their captivity might soon end. Jeremiah had written to those deported in the first and second deportations (605 BC and 597 BC, respectively), advising them on how to live during the 70-year exile he prophesied (Jer 29:10; cf. Jer 25:11–12). After the exile, Zechariah still referred to that prophecy (Zech 1:12; 7:5; cf. 2 Chr 36:21–22; Dan 9:2), and Jehoiachin's release may have led the exiles to revisit its promises. They even may have begun to ponder what a return to Judah might mean. Thus, the purpose of 1–2 Kings probably was to explain the exile and to prepare the exiles for the anticipated return. To prepare, the exiles must reckon with the rebellion and idolatry (a string of covenant violations) that had angered Yahweh and led to the many decades in Babylon. The history contained in 1–2 Kings confronted them with the reasons for their tragic story and taught them what to do to avoid repeating it when the opportunity to go home came.

In short, revived hope of return from exile became the occasion for the completion of 1–2 Kings. Its purpose was to teach the exiles the God-pleasing way of life that would prevent the past from repeating itself so that they didn't ruin their future as well. Its message was, "Hold on tight to our God. Never let go. And above all, obey what he says."

CHRONOLOGY

1–2 Kings teems with chronological data. The treatment of each king typically includes a regnal introduction that dates his accession to the reign-year of his counterpart in Israel or Judah. It sometimes also reports the king's age at taking the throne and always records the length of his reign. It typically concludes with a regnal summary concerning the king's death and burial and occasionally mentions his accomplishments. To determine the historical dates of each reign, however, requires synchronization of biblical data with two well-established dates from Assyrian records. These two dates are 853 BC, the date of the battle of Qarqar in which Ahab participated and the year he died, and 841 BC, the first year of Jehu's reign and the year he paid tribute to the Assyrian king. These dates enable us to fix important dates backward and forward: the division of the united kingdom (931/30 BC), the fall of Samaria to Assyria (722 BC), the fall of Jerusalem to the Babylonians (586 BC), and the length of each king's reign.

At first glance, biblical data sometimes doesn't quite compute. For example, 1 Kgs 15 says that Abijah became Judah's king in Jeroboam's 18th year, reigned three years, and was succeeded by his son Asa in Jeroboam's 20th (not 21st) year (vv. 1–2,9). But recent study has suggested three ways to understand many of what seem like discrepancies: (1) How does a given citation count a king's first year? In Mesopotamia, a king's first year was the first full year of his rule, not the year in which he ascended the throne, whereas Egypt counted the latter as year one. Both systems figure in the chronologies of Israel and Judah. (2) What calendar system is the author using? Does New Year's Day occur in the spring or the fall? (3) The practice of coregencies (overlapping reigns of royal fathers and their sons) was common in the ancient Near East. This practice, e.g., illumines the otherwise perplexing chronology of the transition from Jotham to Uzziah as king of Judah (2 Kgs 15:1–7,32–33). In short, these three ancient factors help sort out most chronological problems in 1–2 Kings That is why royal chronological lists from different scholars noticeably vary (see "Rulers of the Divided Kingdoms of Israel and Judah," p. 635).

THEMES

The first thematic thread that weaves its way through 1–2 Kings concerns the nature of the monarchy. From the outset, the book stresses that the monarchy is not a right but a God-given task with conditions attached and articulated in the Davidic covenant. David himself instructs Solomon on what God expects of him and the risks to the dynasty of not pleasing God (1 Kgs 2:1–4). Faithfully obeying the law of Moses is the condition Israel must meet for God to remain with them and ensure the king a long and prosperous reign. God twice reiterates this point to Solomon in connection with the temple, perhaps lest the king think that the temple wins him a waiver of those demands (1 Kgs 6:11–13; 9:4–5). The book also ties the judgment on Solomon with his failure to meet those demands (1 Kgs 11:4–11, 33). The same conditions apply to God's promise of a dynasty for Jeroboam, the northern kingdom's first king (1 Kgs 11:37–38), whose reign similarly ends in judgment for disobedience (1 Kgs 14:9–11). The book later holds all Israel responsible for the same disobedience that ended in national doom (2 Kgs 17:15–17) and praises Josiah of Judah for keeping the Torah (2 Kgs 23:3).

A variant form of this theme is the frequent comparison of Judah's kings with David's kingship as the paradigm, noted above. The book stresses that exemplary kings compare to the Davidic ideal of faithfulness to God (i.e., they keep God's covenant with David) and that reprehensible kings do not (1 Kgs 15:11; 2 Kgs 14:3; 18:3; 22:2). Elsewhere, the Davidic ideal also finds expression in prophecies concerning a future, new David, the Messiah (e.g., Isa 11:1–5; Jer 23:5–6). Later, descent from David (Matt 1; Luke 1:27) and Jesus' actions lead people to recognize him as the long-awaited "son of David" (Matt 12:23; Mark 10:48). Against the Davidic ideal, 1–2 Kings highlights a notorious list of kings whose reigns decisively set God's people on an inescapable, disastrous course. Solomon heads the list (1 Kgs 11) that includes Jeroboam and Ahab in Israel (1 Kgs 14; 21:25–26) and Manasseh in Judah (2 Kgs 23:26; 24:3). In the end, 2 Kings underscores that not even Josiah's religious reform could stop the terrible judgment to which Manasseh's reign had condemned Judah. Each king's reign marks a tipping point toward inevitable judgment on both nations despite having spared Judah earlier crises out of loyalty to David (e.g., 1 Kgs 11:12–13,32; 2 Kgs 19:34; 20:6).

A second theme is the fulfillment of prophecy. The prominence of prophets in 1–2 Kings was noted above, so it is no surprise that 11 times the book highlights that something spoken by a prophet later came true (e.g., 1 Sam 2:27–36 and 1 Kgs 2:27; 2 Sam 7:13 and 1 Kgs 8:20; 1 Kgs 11:29–39 and 1 Kgs 12:15; 1 Kgs 13:2 and 2 Kgs 23:15–18). The prophets were the prime shapers of events in the history that 1–2 Kings recounts. Indeed, in one respect the prophets in 1–2 Kings differ from the prophets with books in the Bible (e.g., Isaiah, Jeremiah, Hosea). The latter speak primarily to Israel as a whole people, while the former primarily speak personally to ruling monarchs about their fates. Nathan, Ahijah, Elijah, Elisha, and Micaiah figure the most prominently, but two others also speak for Yahweh to his people (Shemaiah and Huldah). What links the historical events in 1–2 Kings is not mere happenstance or human initiatives but Israel's covenant God, who speaks through his prophets and guides his people's destiny. In 1–2 Kings the prophets are usually sent by the sovereign initiative of God rather than the king, and they function primarily as messengers. Their work marks God's corrective action in response to the nagging breakdown of royal obedience in both Israel and Judah.

A final theme is the inevitability of judgment to befall Israel and Judah and why it happened. This theme debuts in Deuteronomy (Deut 29:1–29), recurs in the Davidic covenant (2 Sam 7:14) and many times in 1–2 Kings. It appears as early as in Solomon's prayer for the temple (1 Kgs 8:46–51) and God's answer to it (1 Kgs 9:6–9), as well as in divine condemnation of Jeroboam (1 Kgs 14:15–16). Its climax is the lengthy postmortem the writer gives to detail the reasons why the northern kingdom fell (2 Kgs 17) and the detailed treatment of the southern kingdom's destruction (2 Kgs 24–25). This theme played a prominent role in the book's purpose of preparing its exilic audience for its eagerly awaited restoration to Judah. By detailing the rationale for the judgment about to end, 1–2 Kings taught them what God required for them both to go home and to avoid a replay of the past.

THEOLOGY

The sovereign good will of Israel's God, the Mosaic and Davidic covenants, and the reality of prophecy are the theological pillars on which 1–2 Kings rests. In the Davidic covenant (2 Sam 7), God promised David that he would found a royal dynasty—that God's people would always be ruled by one of David's descendants. The covenant has only two stipulations: (1) Davidic kings are to remain exclusively loyal to Yahweh alone rather than abandon Yahweh for other gods or worship and serve them alongside Yahweh. (2) They must obey the laws, statutes, teachings, and ordinances that comprise the Mosaic covenant, especially as Deuteronomy articulates them. These two considerations are inextricably bound to each other. To love God faithfully is to do what the Torah says, and to obey the Torah shows that one loves God. Both stipulations must be satisfied for Israel to enjoy the covenant's blessings. The Mosaic covenant supplies the stipulations of the Davidic covenant and so enjoys theological primacy in 1–2 Kings. Its provisions govern not only Israel's monarchs but also its people as a whole. Both king and people are to carry out what Deuteronomy stipulates, although the king is specifically responsible to lead the nation to practice covenant faithfulness. The need for a righteous king rings across 1–2 Kings.

The Torah carries with it blessings for obedience and curses for disobedience. The promised blessings for obedience (Deut 28:1–13) include abundant prosperity, protection from enemies, and the admiration of other nations. The curses promised (Deut 28:15–68) are more numerous than the blessings, and they are just as terrible as the blessings are wonderful. Disobedient Israelites can expect to suffer drought, famine, agonizing diseases, great tragedies, gruesome defeats by enemies, and violent expulsion from the promised land. The covenant framework of relationship with God underlies the summary principle that governs events in 1–2 Kings—the connection of acts and their consequences. Conduct that pleases Yahweh results in divine blessings, while reprehensible behavior yields disasters at God's hand. This cause-and-effect theological principle explains why the invasions of foreign armies enjoy such success during the reigns of disobedient kings (e.g., 1 Kgs 14:25–26; 2 Kgs 17:4–6; 23:31–35).

The prophets speak officially for Yahweh in the first person, expecting that their audiences will respond to them as they would to Yahweh himself. The primary social role of the prophets is correcting errant kings through personal messages from sovereign Yahweh. Those messages drive the book's central plot-thread, the connection of a prophetic word at one historical moment and its fulfillment at a subsequent one. 1–2 Kings makes it clear that the destruction of Israel and Judah happened because they rejected prophetic warnings to change their ways in order to escape imminent divine judgment (2 Kgs 17:13–14; 21:10–15; 24:2). Prophecy displays a fundamental theological truth: God cares so much about his people—he so passionately desires that their covenant relationship flourish and flower in blessings—that he repeatedly speaks to them in their own best interest. Rather than abandon them, he tries to get through to them through his prophets.

The sovereign good will of the Lord stands behind everything in 1–2 Kings. Echoes of God's long history with Israel appear throughout it: he is the God of Abraham, Isaac, and Jacob (1 Kgs 18:36; 2 Kgs 13:23), the God who rescued their descendants from Egyptian oppression (1 Kgs 8:16; 2 Kgs 21:15), entered into a covenant with them (1 Kgs 8:9; 2 Kgs 17:35–39), settled them in their land (1 Kgs 14:15), provided them human leadership (1 Kgs 2; 12), and defeated their enemies (1 Kgs 20:28; 2 Kgs 19:32–37). These memories attest Yahweh's unwavering commitment to his chosen people.

In 1–2 Kings God shows his sovereignty in two modes. Primarily, he shows his sovereignty by means of public acts. He twice appears to Solomon (1 Kgs 3; 9), and he sends armies to defeat Israel and defeats armies to save them. He sends fire on Mount Carmel to display his greatness (1 Kgs 18), sends Ahijah to announce Jeroboam's judgment (1 Kgs 14), and sends Isaiah to reassure Hezekiah (2 Kgs 19). He launches future events by commissioning Elijah and Elisha (1 Kgs 19; 2 Kgs 2). But occasionally God's sovereignty also adopts an indirect mode, working behind the scenes. Rehoboam's decision not to relax his policies proves to be a "turn of events ... from the LORD" (1 Kgs 12:15; cf. 1 Kgs 12:24). God ensures that the decision fulfills Ahijah's word to Jeroboam. The sovereign God of 1–2 Kings is very much in charge of his world.

Finally, the tone of the book strikes some readers as harsh and strident, but it also rings with divine grace and displays divine patience on every page. So many times God gives the Israelites much more than they deserve. Despite their idolatry, God generously preserves one tribe for Solomon and permits Jeroboam an additional generation of rule. Despite their waywardness, God gives the Israelites many victories (e.g., 2 Kgs 13:4,23) and through every judgment calls them back to himself so they may experience the full blessings of the covenant. Even evil Ahab's moment of humility wins God's grace (1 Kgs 21:29), and God is "unwilling to destroy" even idolatrous Israel (2 Kgs 13:23). Even the blustery general Naaman receives healing, a newfound faith in Yahweh, and a prophet's blessing as he returns home (2 Kgs 5). He personifies the believing foreigner who comes to know Yahweh through an anonymous Israelite: a young, captured servant girl, who gives him advice. The God of 1–2 Kings shows his sovereignty in both direct and indirect ways, in both judgment and grace, and to both Israelites and believing foreigners.

CONTENT

The first section of 1–2 Kings presents Solomon as a wise king who built an empire, brought Israel great prosperity, and left the temple as his lasting legacy (1 Kgs 3–10). But 1 Kings also sees the root of the nation's eventual doom in Solomon's worship of foreign gods (1 Kgs 11). God's punishment of Solomon launches the second focus of the book—the divided kingdom (1 Kgs 12—2 Kgs 17). The Davidic dynasty rules "Judah" (the tribes of Judah and Benjamin) and another king rules "Israel" (the northern ten tribes; ch. 12). Sadly, Israel's first king makes a fatal misstep: the "sins of Jeroboam" (1 Kgs 16:31) comprise a new, idolatrous religion (1 Kgs 12:26–33) that later kings perpetuate rather than uproot. But the book's true villains are King Ahab and Queen Jezebel, who promote the idolatry that the prophets Elijah and Elisha oppose (1 Kgs 17—2 Kgs 9). 1–2 Kings portray Elijah as a new Moses who shows

View of the Old City of Jerusalem, the capital of the united monarchy.

that Yahweh, not Baal, controls rain, fertility, and life itself (1 Kgs 17 – 19). Elijah announces that Ahab's dynasty will end (1 Kgs 20 — 2 Kgs 1). Elijah's successor, Elisha, also battles Israel's idolatry but does so through a series of striking miracles (2 Kgs 2 – 8; cf. 2 Kgs 13:1 – 21). Elisha also anoints the successor of Ahab's dynasty, Jehu (2 Kgs 9 – 10), but new rulers continue the idolatrous worship of Jeroboam (2 Kgs 11 – 15). Finally, Israel falls to Assyria (722 BC) as punishment for abandoning Yahweh with persistent idolatry (2 Kgs 17). The final chapters of 1 – 2 Kings follow the fate of the kingdom of Judah alone (2 Kgs 18 – 25). Sadly, religious reforms by Hezekiah (2 Kgs 18 – 20) and Josiah (2 Kgs 22 – 23) are insufficient to halt the judgment incurred by the idolatrous policy of King Manasseh (2 Kgs 21), Judah's counterpart to Israel's Ahab. Judah staggers through two decades of puppet-kings, finally falling to the Babylonians in 586 BC. The Babylonians destroy Jerusalem and the temple and carry thousands from Judah into exile (2 Kgs 24 – 25). Solomon's early idolatrous course and the perpetuation of Jeroboam's false worship centers condemn once-great Israel to a final disaster. Samuel's early warning about the price to be paid for idolatry proves true (1 Sam 12:25). But in the release of Jehoiachin from prison in Babylon (2 Kgs 25:27 – 30), 1 – 2 Kings hints at hope for Israel's future.

OUTLINE

I. The United Kingdom of Solomon (1 Kgs 1:1 — 11:43)

- A. Solomon's Accession (1:1 — 2:46)
  1. Adonijah Sets Himself Up as King (1:1 – 14)
  2. David's Decision Sought (1:15 – 27)
  3. David Makes Solomon King (1:28 – 53)
  4. David's Charge to Solomon (2:1 – 12)
  5. Solomon's Throne Established (2:13 – 46)
- B. Solomon's Wisdom (3:1 – 28)
  1. Solomon Asks for Wisdom (3:1 – 15)
  2. A Wise Ruling (3:16 – 28)

- C. Solomon's Kingdom (4:1–34)
  1. Solomon's Officials and Governors (4:1–19)
  2. Solomon's Realm (4:20–28)
  3. Solomon's Wisdom (4:29–34)
- D. Solomon's Temple (5:1—9:9)
  1. Preparations for Building the Temple (5:1–18)
  2. Solomon Builds the Temple (6:1–38)
  3. Solomon Builds His Palace (7:1–12)
  4. The Temple's Furnishings (7:13–51)
  5. The Temple's Dedication (8:1–66)
     - a. The Ark Brought to the Temple (8:1–21)
     - b. Solomon's Prayer of Dedication (8:22–61)
     - c. Dedicatory Sacrifices and a Festival (8:62–66)
  6. The Lord Appears to Solomon (9:1–9)
- E. Solomon's Other Activities (9:10—10:29)
  1. Solomon's Actions (9:10–28)
  2. The Queen of Sheba Visits Solomon (10:1–13)
  3. Solomon's Splendor (10:14–29)
- F. Solomon's Condemnation (11:1–43)
  1. Solomon's Wives (11:1–13)
  2. Solomon's Adversaries (11:14–25)
  3. Jeroboam Rebels Against Solomon (11:26–40)
  4. Solomon's Death (11:41–43)

II. The Kings of Israel and Judah Until Ahab (12:1—16:34)

- A. Israel Rebels Against Rehoboam (12:1–24)
- B. Golden Calves at Bethel and Dan (12:25–33)
- C. The Man of God From Judah (13:1–34)
- D. Ahijah's Prophecy Against Jeroboam (14:1–20)
- E. Rehoboam King of Judah (14:21–31)
- F. Abijah King of Judah (15:1–8)
- G. Asa King of Judah (15:9–24)
- H. Nadab King of Israel (15:25–32)
- I. Baasha King of Israel (15:33—16:7)
- J. Elah King of Israel (16:8–14)
- K. Zimri King of Israel (16:15–20)
- L. Omri King of Israel (16:21–28)
- M. Ahab Becomes King of Israel (16:29–34)

III. The Prophetic Ministries of Elijah and Elisha (1 Kgs 17:1—2 Kgs 10:36)

- A. Elijah's Confrontation With Baal (1 Kgs 17:1—18:46)
  1. Elijah Announces a Great Drought (17:1)
  2. Elijah Fed by Ravens (17:2–6)
  3. Elijah and the Widow at Zarephath (17:7–24)
  4. Elijah and Obadiah (18:1–15)
  5. Elijah on Mount Carmel (18:16–46)
- B. Elijah Flees to Horeb (19:1–9a)
- C. The Lord Appears to Elijah (19:9b–18)
- D. The Call of Elisha (19:19–21)
- E. Ahab's Conflicts With the Arameans (20:1–43)
  1. Ben-Hadad Attacks Samaria (20:1–12)
  2. Ahab Defeats Ben-Hadad (20:13–34)
  3. A Prophet Condemns Ahab (20:35–43)

- F. Naboth's Vineyard (21:1 – 29)
- G. Ahab's Death (22:1 – 40)
  1. Micaiah Prophesies Against Ahab (22:1 – 28)
  2. Ahab Killed at Ramoth Gilead (22:29 – 40)
- H. Jehoshaphat King of Judah (22:41 – 50)
- I. Ahaziah King of Israel (22:51 – 53)
- J. The Lord's Judgment on Ahaziah (2 Kgs 1:1 – 18)
- K. Elijah Taken Up to Heaven (2:1 – 18)
- L. Elisha's Ministry (2:19 — 8:15)
  1. Healing of the Water (2:19 – 22)
  2. Elisha Is Jeered (2:23 – 25)
  3. Moab Revolts (3:1 – 27)
  4. The Widow's Olive Oil (4:1 – 7)
  5. The Shunammite's Son Restored to Life (4:8 – 37)
  6. Death in the Pot (4:38 – 41)
  7. Feeding of a Hundred (4:42 – 44)
  8. Naaman Healed of Leprosy (5:1 – 27)
  9. An Axhead Floats (6:1 – 7)
  10. Elisha Traps Blinded Arameans (6:8 – 23)
  11. Famine in Besieged Samaria (6:24 — 7:2)
  12. The Siege Lifted (7:3 – 20)
  13. The Shunammite's Land Restored (8:1 – 6)
  14. Hazael Murders Ben-Hadad (8:7 – 15)
- M. Jehoram King of Judah (8:16 – 24)
- N. Ahaziah King of Judah (8:25 – 29)
- O. Jehu King of Israel (9:1 — 10:36)
  1. Jehu Anointed King of Israel (9:1 – 13)
  2. Jehu Kills Joram and Ahaziah (9:14 – 29)
  3. Jezebel Killed (9:30 – 37)
  4. Ahab's Family Killed (10:1 – 17)
  5. Servants of Baal Killed (10:18 – 36)

IV. The Kings of Israel and Judah Until Israel's Exile (11:1 — 17:41)

- A. Joash King of Israel (11:1 — 12:21)
  1. Athaliah and Joash (11:1 – 21)
  2. Joash Repairs the Temple (12:1 – 21)
- B. Jehoahaz King of Israel (13:1 – 9)
- C. Jehoash King of Israel (13:10 – 25)
- D. Amaziah King of Judah (14:1 – 22)
- E. Jeroboam II King of Israel (14:23 – 29)
- F. Azariah King of Judah (15:1 – 7)
- G. The Final Kings of Israel (15:8 – 31)
  1. Zechariah King of Israel (15:8 – 12)
  2. Shallum King of Israel (15:13 – 16)
  3. Menahem King of Israel (15:17 – 22)
  4. Pekahiah King of Israel (15:23 – 26)
  5. Pekah King of Israel (15:27 – 31)
- H. Jotham King of Judah (15:32 – 38)
- I. Ahaz King of Judah (16:1 – 20)
- J. Hoshea Last King of Israel (17:1 – 6)
- K. Israel Exiled Because of Sin (17:7 – 23)
- L. Samaria Resettled (17:24 – 41)

V. The Last Kings of Judah (18:1 — 25:30)

A. Hezekiah King of Judah (18:1 — 20:21)
1. Hezekiah's Reign (18:1 – 16)
2. Sennacherib Threatens Jerusalem (18:17 – 37)
3. Jerusalem's Deliverance Foretold (19:1 – 13)
4. Hezekiah's Prayer (19:14 – 19)
5. Isaiah Prophesies Sennacherib's Fall (19:20 – 37)
6. Hezekiah's Illness (20:1 – 11)
7. Envoys From Babylon (20:12 – 21)

B. Manasseh King of Judah (21:1 – 18)

C. Amon King of Judah (21:19 – 26)

D. Josiah King of Judah (22:1 — 23:30)
1. The Book of the Law Found (22:1 – 20)
2. Josiah Renews the Covenant (23:1 – 30)

E. The Final Four Kings of Judah (23:31 — 24:20a)
1. Jehoahaz King of Judah (23:31 – 35)
2. Jehoiakim King of Judah (23:36 — 24:7)
3. Jehoiachin King of Judah (24:8 – 17)
4. Zedekiah King of Judah (24:18 – 20a)

F. The Fall of Jerusalem (24:20b — 25:26)

G. Jehoiachin Released (25:27 – 30)

1 KINGS

Adonijah Sets Himself Up as King

1 When King David was very old, he could not keep warm even when they put covers over him. [2]So his attendants said to him, "Let us look for a young virgin to serve the king and take care of him. She can lie beside him so that our lord the king may keep warm."

[3]Then they searched throughout Israel for a beautiful young woman and found Abishag, a Shunammite,[a] and brought her to the king. [4]The woman was very beautiful; she took care of the king and waited on him, but the king had no sexual relations with her.

[5]Now Adonijah,[b] whose mother was Haggith, put himself forward and said, "I will be king." So he got chariots[c] and horses[a] ready, with fifty men to run ahead of him. [6](His father had never rebuked[d] him by asking, "Why do you behave as you do?" He was also very handsome and was born next after Absalom.)

[7]Adonijah conferred with Joab[e] son of Zeruiah and with Abiathar[f] the priest, and they gave him their support. [8]But Zadok[g] the priest, Benaiah[h] son of Jehoiada, Nathan[i] the prophet, Shimei[j] and Rei and David's special guard[k] did not join Adonijah.

[9]Adonijah then sacrificed sheep, cattle and fattened calves at the Stone of Zoheleth near En Rogel.[l] He invited all his brothers, the king's sons, and all the royal officials of Judah, [10]but he did not invite Nathan the prophet or Benaiah or the special guard or his brother Solomon.[m]

[11]Then Nathan asked Bathsheba,[n] Solomon's mother, "Have you not heard that Adonijah,[o] the son of Haggith, has become king, and our lord David knows nothing about it? [12]Now then, let me advise[p] you how you can save your own life and the life of your son Solomon. [13]Go in to King David and say to

1:3 [a] Jos 19:18
1:5 [b] 2Sa 3:4 [c] 2Sa 15:1
1:6 [d] 2Sa 3:3-4
1:7 [e] 1Ki 2:22,28; 1Ch 11:6 [f] 1Sa 22:20; 2Sa 20:25
1:8 [g] 2Sa 20:25 [h] 2Sa 8:18 [i] 2Sa 12:1 [j] 1Ki 4:18 [k] 2Sa 23:8
1:9 [l] 2Sa 17:17
1:10 [m] 2Sa 12:24
1:11 [n] 2Sa 12:24 [o] 2Sa 3:4
1:12 [p] Pr 15:22

[a] 5 Or *charioteers*

1:1—11:43 *The United Kingdom of Solomon.* The long, colorful reign of David's son Solomon opens the book's history of Israel's kings. Solomon's reign receives the longest treatment except for David's (1 Sam 16—2 Sam 24). 1 Kgs 1–11 covers Solomon's accession (chs. 1–2), wisdom (ch. 3), kingdom (ch. 4), temple (5:1—9:9), other activities (9:10—10:29), and condemnation (ch. 11).

1:1—2:46 *Solomon's Accession.* Solomon becomes king with David's blessing, and David charges him to rule properly. But Solomon's accession is not without incident: an influential faction supports his half brother, and he must deal with some threats leftover from David's era to secure his throne.

1:1–14 *Adonijah Sets Himself Up as King.* Adonijah's attempt to succeed David precipitates the crisis that quickly ends in Solomon's accession.

1:1 could not keep warm. Symptomatic of David's waning life. Heightens the need for him to publicly designate a successor.

1:2 Ancient medical practice provided warmth for the sick by having a healthy person "lie beside" them.

1:3 Shunammite. Shunem was an Issacharite town in the Jezreel Valley near the Hill of Moreh (2 Kgs 4:8; Josh 19:18). For Adonijah's later play for Abishag, see 2:17,22.

1:5 Adonijah. David's oldest surviving son; he behaves like his dead older brother, Absalom. **put himself forward.** Suggests bragging or outright campaigning, echoing Absalom's politicking (2 Sam 15:1). God rejects those who appoint themselves as kings without his approval.

1:6 handsome. A trait typical of kings (1 Sam 9:2; 16:12; 2 Sam 14:25).

1:7 Joab. The outspoken army commander with a history of violence (2 Sam 11:16–17; 18:14).

1:8 Benaiah. Joab's military rival.

1:9 sheep ... fattened calves. The expensive sacrifice reflects a joyful prince eager for the throne. **Stone of Zoheleth.** Probably a prominent landmark. **En Rogel.** "Spring of Rogel," a water source south of Jerusalem in the Kidron Valley (see note on 2:37). Traditionally, public royal accessions take place near springs (see vv. 33,38).

1:10 For obvious reasons the guest list excludes the anti-Adonijah faction (vv. 7–8) and Solomon.

1:11 knows nothing about it. Cf. v. 18; a sign that David's advancing age perhaps limits the king's involvement in daily matters of state.

1:12 save your own life and the life of your son. Life and death hang in the balance for Bathsheba and Solomon, for a usurper typically tried to liquidate all potential claimants to the throne in an attempt to secure his own position.

1:13 My lord. Shows the king the highest respect (cf. vv. 11,16–17).

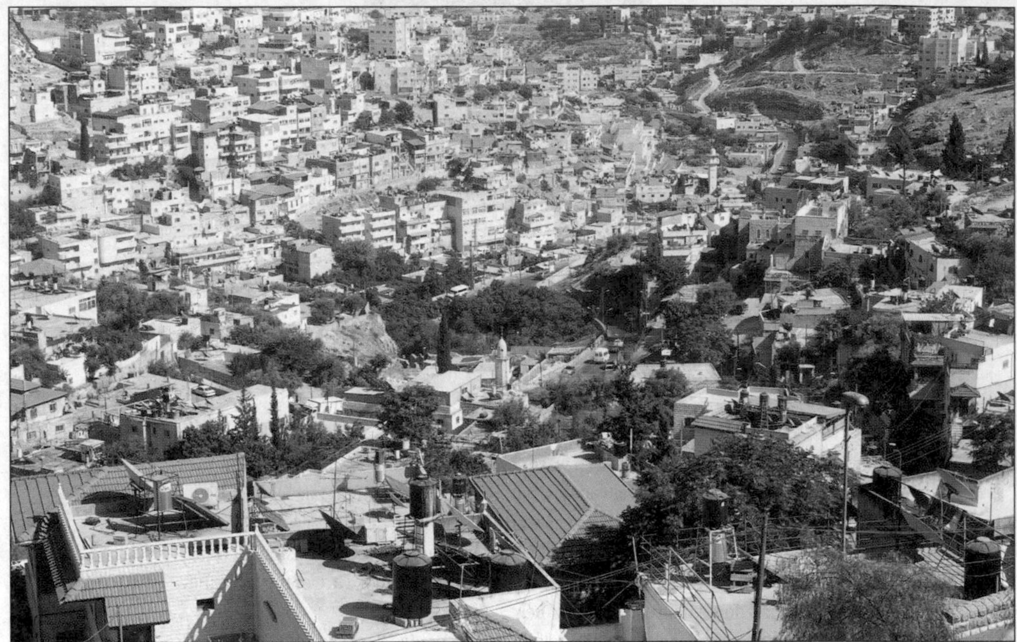

The En Rogel spring from the City of David.

A. D. Riddle/www.BiblePlaces.com

1:13 [q] ver 30; 1Ch 22:9-13
1:15 [r] ver 1
1:17 [s] ver 13,30
1:19 [t] ver 9
1:21 [u] Dt 31:16; 1Ki 2:10
1:26 [v] ver 8,10

him, 'My lord the king, did you not swear[q] to me your servant: "Surely Solomon your son shall be king
after me, and he will sit on my throne"? Why then has Adonijah become king?' 14While you are still
there talking to the king, I will come in and add my word to what you have said."

15So Bathsheba went to see the aged king in his room, where Abishag[r] the Shunammite was attending him. 16Bathsheba bowed down, prostrating herself before the king.

"What is it you want?" the king asked.

17She said to him, "My lord, you yourself swore[s] to me your servant by the LORD your God: 'Solomon
your son shall be king after me, and he will sit on my throne.' 18But now Adonijah has become king,
and you, my lord the king, do not know about it. 19He has sacrificed[t] great numbers of cattle, fattened
calves, and sheep, and has invited all the king's sons, Abiathar the priest and Joab the commander of
the army, but he has not invited Solomon your servant. 20My lord the king, the eyes of all Israel are on
you, to learn from you who will sit on the throne of my lord the king after him. 21Otherwise, as soon as
my lord the king is laid to rest[u] with his ancestors, I and my son Solomon will be treated as criminals."

22While she was still speaking with the king, Nathan the prophet arrived. 23And the king was told,
"Nathan the prophet is here." So he went before the king and bowed with his face to the ground.

24Nathan said, "Have you, my lord the king, declared that Adonijah shall be king after you, and that
he will sit on your throne? 25Today he has gone down and sacrificed great numbers of cattle, fattened
calves, and sheep. He has invited all the king's sons, the commanders of the army and Abiathar the
priest. Right now they are eating and drinking with him and saying, 'Long live King Adonijah!' 26But
me your servant, and Zadok the priest, and Benaiah son of Jehoiada, and your servant Solomon he did
not invite.[v] 27Is this something my lord the king has done without letting his servants know who should
sit on the throne of my lord the king after him?"

1:15–27 *David's Decision Sought.* The scene shifts to David's private quarters and visits in turn from Bathsheba and Nathan.
1:16 bowed down. Traditional sign of respect, especially before a king (cf. v. 23; 18:7; 2 Sam 14:4).
1:17 Quotes the king's earlier promise to name Solomon as his successor (cf. v. 30).
1:18 Cf. vv. 7–11.
1:19 not invited Solomon. Implies that Solomon and Adonijah are dangerously at odds.
1:21 treated as criminals. Terrible punishment will befall Bathsheba and Solomon if David fails to announce his choice of Solomon (cf. v. 12).
1:26 A once-united kingdom is at risk of splitting into factions.

David Makes Solomon King

1:28-53pp — 1Ch 29:21-25

28 Then King David said, "Call in Bathsheba." So she came into the king's presence and stood before
him.
29 The king then took an oath: "As surely as the LORD lives, who has delivered me out of every trouble,[w] 30 I will surely carry out this very day what I swore[x] to you by the LORD, the God of Israel: Solomon
your son shall be king after me, and he will sit on my throne in my place."
31 Then Bathsheba bowed down with her face to the ground, prostrating herself before the king, and
said, "May my lord King David live forever!"
32 King David said, "Call in Zadok the priest, Nathan the prophet and Benaiah son of Jehoiada." When
they came before the king, 33 he said to them: "Take your lord's servants with you and have Solomon my
son mount my own mule[y] and take him down to Gihon.[z] 34 There have Zadok the priest and Nathan the
prophet anoint[a] him king over Israel. Blow the trumpet[b] and shout, 'Long live King Solomon!' 35 Then
you are to go up with him, and he is to come and sit on my throne and reign in my place. I have appointed him ruler over Israel and Judah."
36 Benaiah son of Jehoiada answered the king, "Amen! May the LORD, the God of my lord the king,
so declare it. 37 As the LORD was with my lord the king, so may he be with[c] Solomon to make his throne
even greater[d] than the throne of my lord King David!"
38 So Zadok[e] the priest, Nathan the prophet, Benaiah son of Jehoiada, the Kerethites[f] and the Pelethites went down and had Solomon mount King David's mule, and they escorted him to Gihon.[g] 39 Zadok the priest took the horn of oil[h] from the sacred tent and anointed Solomon. Then they sounded the
trumpet and all the people shouted,[i] "Long live King Solomon!" 40 And all the people went up after him,
playing pipes and rejoicing greatly, so that the ground shook with the sound.
41 Adonijah and all the guests who were with him heard it as they were finishing their feast. On hearing the sound of the trumpet, Joab asked, "What's the meaning of all the noise in the city?"
42 Even as he was speaking, Jonathan[j] son of Abiathar the priest arrived. Adonijah said, "Come in. A
worthy man like you must be bringing good news."[k]
43 "Not at all!" Jonathan answered. "Our lord King David has made Solomon king. 44 The king has
sent with him Zadok the priest, Nathan the prophet, Benaiah son of Jehoiada, the Kerethites and the
Pelethites, and they have put him on the king's mule, 45 and Zadok the priest and Nathan the prophet
have anointed him king at Gihon. From there they have gone up cheering, and the city resounds[l] with
it. That's the noise you hear. 46 Moreover, Solomon has taken his seat on the royal throne. 47 Also, the
royal officials have come to congratulate our lord King David, saying, 'May your God make Solomon's
name more famous than yours and his throne greater[m] than yours!' And the king bowed in worship on
his bed 48 and said, 'Praise be to the LORD, the God of Israel, who has allowed my eyes to see a successor[n]
on my throne today.' "
49 At this, all Adonijah's guests rose in alarm and dispersed. 50 But Adonijah, in fear of Solomon, went
and took hold of the horns[o] of the altar. 51 Then Solomon was told, "Adonijah is afraid of King Solomon

1:29 [w] 2Sa 4:9
1:30 [x] ver 13,17
1:33 [y] 2Sa 20:6-7 [z] 2Ch 32:30; 33:14
1:34 [a] 1Sa 10:1; 16:3,12; 1Ki 19:16; 2Ki 9:3,13 [b] ver 25; 2Sa 5:3; 15:10
1:37 [c] Jos 1:5,17; 1Sa 20:13 [d] ver 47
1:38 [e] ver 8 [f] 2Sa 8:18 [g] ver 33
1:39 [h] Ex 30:23-32; Ps 89:20 [i] ver 34; 1Sa 10:24
1:42 [j] 2Sa 15:27,36 [k] 2Sa 18:26
1:45 [l] ver 40
1:47 [m] ver 37; Ge 47:31
1:48 [n] 2Sa 7:12; 1Ki 3:6
1:50 [o] 1Ki 2:28

1:28–53 *David Makes Solomon King.* David responds to Bathsheba and Nathan by declaring Solomon to be his successor and ordering his installation as coregent.
1:28 Call in Bathsheba. Implies that David and Nathan had talked alone. Unlike Adonijah, Solomon does nothing to promote himself as king.
1:29 As surely as the LORD lives. The traditional oath formula (cf. 2:24; 17:1; 18:10; 2 Kgs 2:2,4,6; 4:30; 5:16,20). **delivered me.** Echoes David's earlier appeal to Yahweh as deliverer (2 Sam 4:9).
1:30 Fulfills David's earlier promise (cf. v. 17).
1:33 mule. The preferred royal transportation in Israel (2 Sam 13:29; 18:9; Zech 9:9 ["donkey"]); symbolized utility and humility. **Gihon.** The underground spring south of Jerusalem at the western base of the Kidron Valley; within earshot of En Rogel to its north (cf. vv. 39–41).
1:34 anoint him. Symbolizes Solomon's divine appointment through a prophet (cf. 19:15–16; 2 Kgs 9:1–10; 1 Sam 10:1; 16:1–13).
1:35 sit on my throne. Ceremonially installs Solomon as coregent until David's death.
1:36 Amen! Enthusiastically signals that the group will execute David's orders.
1:38 the Kerethites and the Pelethites. Mercenary units in David's private army (2 Sam 8:18; 20:23).
1:39 sacred tent. The temporary structure David set up in Jerusalem to house the ark of the covenant (2 Sam 6:17; 7:2,6).
1:48 successor on my throne. Alludes to Nathan's prophecy that David would found a lasting royal dynasty (2 Sam 7:12).
1:50 horns. The four corners of Israelite altars curved upward, thus resembling horns (Exod 29:12; 30:10; Lev 4:7). See photo, p. 1147. **altar.** Ancient Near Eastern custom featured asylum shrines, while biblical practice offered sanctuary from reprisals only for unintentional crimes (2:28–35; Exod 21:14). Adonijah's treason was intentional, so only the king could extend him mercy.

and is clinging to the horns of the altar. He says, 'Let King Solomon swear to me today that he will not
put his servant to death with the sword.'"
52Solomon replied, "If he shows himself to be worthy, not a hair[p] of his head will fall to the ground;
but if evil is found in him, he will die." 53Then King Solomon sent men, and they brought him down
from the altar. And Adonijah came and bowed down to King Solomon, and Solomon said, "Go to your
home."

David's Charge to Solomon

2:10-12pp — 1Ch 29:26-28

2 When the time drew near for David to die,[q] he gave a charge to Solomon his son.
2"I am about to go the way of all the earth,"[r] he said. "So be strong,[s] act like a man, 3and observe[t]
what the LORD your God requires: Walk in obedience to him, and keep his decrees and commands, his
laws and regulations, as written in the Law of Moses. Do this so that you may prosper[u] in all you do
and wherever you go 4and that the LORD may keep his promise[v] to me: 'If your descendants watch how
they live, and if they walk faithfully[w] before me with all their heart and soul, you will never fail to have
a successor on the throne of Israel.'
5"Now you yourself know what Joab[x] son of Zeruiah did to me — what he did to the two commanders of Israel's armies, Abner[y] son of Ner and Amasa[z] son of Jether. He killed them, shedding their blood
in peacetime as if in battle, and with that blood he stained the belt around his waist and the sandals
on his feet. 6Deal with him according to your wisdom,[a] but do not let his gray head go down to the
grave in peace.
7"But show kindness to the sons of Barzillai[b] of Gilead and let them be among those who eat at your
table.[c] They stood by me when I fled from your brother Absalom.
8"And remember, you have with you Shimei[d] son of Gera, the Benjamite from Bahurim, who called
down bitter curses on me the day I went to Mahanaim. When he came down to meet me at the Jordan,
I swore[e] to him by the LORD: 'I will not put you to death by the sword.' 9But now, do not consider him
innocent. You are a man of wisdom;[f] you will know what to do to him. Bring his gray head down to
the grave in blood."
10Then David rested with his ancestors and was buried[g] in the City of David.[h] 11He had reigned[i]
forty years over Israel — seven years in Hebron and thirty-three in Jerusalem. 12So Solomon sat on the
throne[j] of his father David, and his rule was firmly established.[k]

Solomon's Throne Established

13Now Adonijah, the son of Haggith, went to Bathsheba, Solomon's mother. Bathsheba asked him,
"Do you come peacefully?"[l]
He answered, "Yes, peacefully." 14Then he added, "I have something to say to you."

1:52 [p] 1Sa 14:45; 2Sa 14:11
2:1 [q] Ge 47:29; Dt 31:14
2:2 [r] Jos 23:14 [s] Dt 31:7, 23; Jos 1:6
2:3 [t] Dt 17:14-20; Jos 1:7 [u] 1Ch 22:13
2:4 [v] 2Sa 7:13,25; 1Ki 8:25 [w] 2Ki 20:3; Ps 132:12
2:5 [x] 2Sa 2:18; 18:5,12, 14 [y] 2Sa 3:27 [z] 2Sa 20:10
2:6 [a] ver 9
2:7 [b] 2Sa 17:27; 19:31-39 [c] 2Sa 9:7
2:8 [d] 2Sa 16:5-13 [e] 2Sa 19:18-23
2:9 [f] ver 6
2:10 [g] Ac 2:29; 13:36 [h] 2Sa 5:7
2:11 [i] 2Sa 5:4,5
2:12 [j] 1Ch 29:23 [k] 2Ch 1:1
2:13 [l] 1Sa 16:4

2:1–12 *David's Charge to Solomon.* Sensing his imminent death, David prepares Solomon to reign as king of Israel. Israel's historians often feature farewell speeches by Israel's leaders to guide coming generations (Gen 47:29 — 49:33; Deut 33 – 34; Josh 23 – 24; 1 Sam 12).

2:3 David charges Solomon to live out Deuteronomy's vision of the ideal king (Deut 17:14 – 20) through faithful obedience of Moses' law (Deut 4:29,40; 6:5; 8:6; 10:12; 11:1,22; Josh 23:14 – 16). **prosper.** Royal success and continuation of the dynasty that God promised David.

2:4 David sums up God's dynastic promise in his own words (cf. 2 Sam 7:14), words that echo later in Solomon's prayer (1 Kgs 8:25) and in God's reiteration of the promise (9:4 – 5; cf. 2 Chr 7:17 – 18). Here David articulates the standard by which all later kings will be judged. The promise states that the Davidic covenant will remain in force as long as David's successors faithfully keep the Mosaic covenant.

2:5 Joab. See note on 1:7. **Abner.** Former commander of Saul's army; Joab killed him (2 Sam 3:22 – 30). **Amasa.** David's replacement for Joab as chief of staff; Joab killed him (2 Sam 17:25; 19:11 – 15; 20:4 – 10). **he stained.** Implies that leftover bloodguilt might harm Solomon's kingdom if Joab and Shimei remain unpunished (cf. Gen 9:6; Deut 21:1 – 9).

2:7 Barzillai. David's ally who supplied his entourage food during their escape from Jerusalem (2 Sam 17:27 – 29). He was deemed worthy to dine at the king's table (cf. 2 Kgs 25:29; 2 Sam 9:7).

2:8 Shimei. A Benjamite who cursed David for killing off Saul's family (2 Sam 16:5 – 13).

2:10 City of David. The small Jebusite settlement that became Jerusalem after David conquered it; implies that the city is his personal property (cf. 3:1; 2 Sam 5:6 – 9).

2:12 firmly established. Cf. vv. 45 – 46. Fulfills God's promise to David (2 Sam 7:12 – 13,16); but threats remain (see note on vv. 13 – 46).

2:13 – 46 *Solomon's Throne Established.* Solomon consolidates his hold on the kingdom by heading off threats from Adonijah, Adonijah's supporters (Abiathar the priest, Joab), and Shimei. The king's actions display a lack of true wisdom. They alienate rather than placate his opponent — they may even exceed his royal authority.

2:13 Solomon's mother. The queen mother commands great respect and influence with Solomon and Judah's royal court (cf. 1:16 – 31).

“You may say it,” she replied.
15“As you know,” he said, “the kingdom was mine. All Israel looked to me as their king. But things
changed, and the kingdom has gone to my brother; for it has come to him from the LORD. 16Now I have
one request to make of you. Do not refuse me.”
“You may make it,” she said.
17So he continued, “Please ask King Solomon — he will not refuse you — to give me Abishag[m] the
Shunammite as my wife.”
18“Very well,” Bathsheba replied, “I will speak to the king for you.”
19When Bathsheba went to King Solomon to speak to him for Adonijah, the king stood up to meet
her, bowed down to her and sat down on his throne. He had a throne brought for the king’s mother,[n]
and she sat down at his right hand.[o]
20“I have one small request to make of you,” she said. “Do not refuse me.”
The king replied, “Make it, my mother; I will not refuse you.”
21So she said, “Let Abishag[p] the Shunammite be given in marriage to your brother Adonijah.”
22King Solomon answered his mother, “Why do you request Abishag[q] the Shunammite for Adonijah?
You might as well request the kingdom for him — after all, he is my older brother[r] — yes, for him and
for Abiathar the priest and Joab son of Zeruiah!”
23Then King Solomon swore by the LORD: “May God deal with me, be it ever so severely,[s] if Adonijah does not pay with his life for this request! 24And now, as surely as the LORD lives — he who has
established me securely on the throne of my father David and has founded a dynasty for me as he
promised[t] — Adonijah shall be put to death today!” 25So King Solomon gave orders to Benaiah[u] son of
Jehoiada, and he struck down Adonijah and he died.
26To Abiathar[v] the priest the king said, “Go back to your fields in Anathoth.[w] You deserve to die, but
I will not put you to death now, because you carried the ark[x] of the Sovereign LORD before my father
David and shared all my father’s hardships.”[y] 27So Solomon removed Abiathar from the priesthood of
the LORD, fulfilling[z] the word the LORD had spoken at Shiloh about the house of Eli.
28When the news reached Joab, who had conspired with Adonijah though not with Absalom, he fled
to the tent of the LORD and took hold of the horns[a] of the altar. 29King Solomon was told that Joab had
fled to the tent of the LORD and was beside the altar. Then Solomon ordered Benaiah[b] son of Jehoiada,
“Go, strike him down!”
30So Benaiah entered the tent of the LORD and said to Joab, “The king says, ‘Come out![c]’ ”
But he answered, “No, I will die here.”
Benaiah reported to the king, “This is how Joab answered me.”
31Then the king commanded Benaiah, “Do as he says. Strike him down and bury him, and so clear
me and my whole family of the guilt of the innocent blood[d] that Joab shed. 32The LORD will repay[e] him
for the blood he shed,[f] because without my father David knowing it he attacked two men and killed
them with the sword. Both of them — Abner son of Ner, commander of Israel’s army, and Amasa[g] son
of Jether, commander of Judah’s army — were better[h] men and more upright than he. 33May the guilt
of their blood rest on the head of Joab and his descendants forever. But on David and his descendants,
his house and his throne, may there be the LORD’s peace forever.”

2:17 [m] 1Ki 1:3
2:19 [n] 1Ki 15:13 [o] Ps 45:9
2:21 [p] 1Ki 1:3
2:22 [q] 2Sa 12:8; 1Ki 1:3 [r] 1Ch 3:2
2:23 [s] Ru 1:17
2:24 [t] 2Sa 7:11; 1Ch 22:10
2:25 [u] 2Sa 8:18
2:26 [v] 1Sa 22:20 [w] Jos 21:18 [x] 2Sa 15:24 [y] 1Sa 23:6
2:27 [z] 1Sa 2:27-36
2:28 [a] 1Ki 1:7,50
2:29 [b] ver 25
2:30 [c] Ex 21:14
2:31 [d] Nu 35:33; Dt 19:13; 21:8-9
2:32 [e] Jdg 9:57; Ps 7:16 [f] Jdg 9:24 [g] 2Sa 3:27; 20:10 [h] 2Ch 21:13

2:17 Abishag. A royal concubine (cf. vv. 21–22; 1:15) and thus belonging to Solomon (2 Sam 3:6–7; 12:8; 16:21–22).

2:22 Solomon reads Adonijah’s simple request as a play for kingship and a violation of their asylum agreement (1:52). The king may merely be using the request as a pretext to get rid of Adonijah. More likely, Solomon acts in light of a popular perception that to marry Abishag, a member of the royal harem, gave Adonijah the right to claim succession to David. Abishag’s intimate association with David might have further strengthened Adonijah’s case (cf. 2 Sam 3:7; 12:8; 16:21).

2:26 Abiathar. David’s faithful servant (cf. 1:19,25) receives exile rather than death for supporting Adonijah (1:7). **Anathoth.** A village three miles (4.8 kilometers) northeast of Jerusalem; hometown of Abiathar’s descendants, including Jeremiah (Jer 1:1; 32:7–9; cf. Ezra 2:23; Neh 7:27).

2:27 fulfilling the word. Samuel’s judgment on Eli the priest (1 Sam 2:27–36; cf. 1 Kgs 4:4). **house of Eli.** Abiathar’s ancestral family.

2:28 Joab. Cf. vv. 5–6; see note on 1:7. **horns of the altar.** See note on 1:50.

2:31 innocent blood. Joab’s two innocent murder victims, Abner and Amasa (v. 32; see note on v. 5). Abner had killed Joab’s brother in battle (2 Sam 2:18–23), a justifiable act in warfare, but Joab’s killing of Abner was premeditated, vengeful murder. Jealousy over a military demotion or paranoia protective of David drove his murder of Amasa (2 Sam 19:13; 20:10). The bloodshed saddles Joab with bloodguilt (i.e., liability for punishment for the killings). But by executing Joab without a proper trial, Solomon may have gone too far.

2:33 Joab and his line pay the price for bloodguilt (see notes on vv. 31,37).

2:35 [i] 1Ki 4:4 [j] ver 27; 1Ch 29:22
2:36 [k] ver 8; 2Sa 16:5
2:37 [l] 2Sa 15:23 [m] Lev 20:9; Jos 2:19; 2Sa 1:16
2:39 [n] 1Sa 27:2
2:44 [o] 1Sa 25:39; 2Sa 16:5-13; Eze 17:19
2:45 [p] 2Sa 7:13; Pr 25:5
2:46 [q] ver 12; 2Ch 1:1
3:1 [r] 1Ki 7:8 [s] 1Ki 9:24 [t] 2Sa 5:7 [u] 1Ki 7:1; 9:15,19
3:2 [v] Lev 17:3-5; Dt 12:2, 4-5; 1Ki 22:43
3:3 [w] Dt 6:5; Ps 31:23; 1Co 8:3 [x] 1Ki 2:3; 9:4; 11:4,6,38

34 So Benaiah son of Jehoiada went up and struck down Joab and killed him, and he was buried at
his home out in the country. 35 The king put Benaiah[i] son of Jehoiada over the army in Joab's position
and replaced Abiathar with Zadok[j] the priest.
36 Then the king sent for Shimei[k] and said to him, "Build yourself a house in Jerusalem and live
there, but do not go anywhere else. 37 The day you leave and cross the Kidron Valley,[l] you can be sure
you will die; your blood will be on your own head."[m]
38 Shimei answered the king, "What you say is good. Your servant will do as my lord the king has
said." And Shimei stayed in Jerusalem for a long time.
39 But three years later, two of Shimei's slaves ran off to Achish[n] son of Maakah, king of Gath, and
Shimei was told, "Your slaves are in Gath." 40 At this, he saddled his donkey and went to Achish at Gath
in search of his slaves. So Shimei went away and brought the slaves back from Gath.
41 When Solomon was told that Shimei had gone from Jerusalem to Gath and had returned, 42 the
king summoned Shimei and said to him, "Did I not make you swear by the LORD and warn you, 'On
the day you leave to go anywhere else, you can be sure you will die'? At that time you said to me, 'What
you say is good. I will obey.' 43 Why then did you not keep your oath to the LORD and obey the command
I gave you?"
44 The king also said to Shimei, "You know in your heart all the wrong[o] you did to my father David.
Now the LORD will repay you for your wrongdoing. 45 But King Solomon will be blessed, and David's
throne will remain secure[p] before the LORD forever."
46 Then the king gave the order to Benaiah son of Jehoiada, and he went out and struck Shimei
down and he died.

The kingdom was now established[q] in Solomon's hands.

Solomon Asks for Wisdom

3:4-15pp — 2Ch 1:2-13

3 Solomon made an alliance with Pharaoh king of Egypt and married[r] his daughter.[s] He brought
her to the City of David[t] until he finished building his palace[u] and the temple of the LORD, and
the wall around Jerusalem. 2 The people, however, were still sacrificing at the high places,[v] because a
temple had not yet been built for the Name of the LORD. 3 Solomon showed his love[w] for the LORD by
walking according to the instructions[x] given him by his father David, except that he offered sacrifices
and burned incense on the high places.

2:36 As David had advised (cf. vv. 8–9,33), Solomon confines Shimei to Jerusalem rather than kill him.

2:37 Kidron Valley. The deep valley that marks Jerusalem's eastern boundary (cf. 1:9,33 and notes). **your blood will be on your own head.** Cf. vv. 32–33. Notably, under normal circumstances Shimei's route to Gath would not cross the Kidron Valley. Thus, his execution by Solomon seems as unjustified as Joab's (v. 46).

2:39 Achish. For an earlier man of the same name, see 1 Sam 21; 27–29. **Gath.** A Philistine city in the coastal plain 23 miles (37 kilometers) west of Jerusalem.

2:44 Shimei seditiously curses David (2 Sam 16:5–13).

3:1–28 *Solomon's Wisdom.* Solomon requests and receives remarkable wisdom.

3:1–15 *Solomon Asks for Wisdom.* At Gibeon, the Lord grants Solomon's request for wisdom and legitimates his rule over Israel. The scene offers an early indication of how Solomon measures up to Deuteronomy's ideal king (Deut 17:14–20).

3:1 Solomon sealed his peaceful relationship with Egypt by marrying Pharaoh's daughter (9:16). Earlier, Solomon had married Naamah, mother of Rehoboam (14:21,31), and other wives as well (cf. 11:1–3). This marriage alliance probably was with Siamun (978–959 BC), one of the last pharaohs of the Twenty-First Egyptian Dynasty, and probably took place in Solomon's third or fourth year. Construction of the temple began in his fourth year (6:1). The union suggests Egyptian recognition of Israel's emerging political and economic importance under Solomon (7:8; 9:16,24; 11:1); it served the interests of both kingdoms. However, it implies religious syncretism, clearly violates Deut 17:17, and later proves Solomon's undoing.

3:2 high places. Hilltop, open-air shrines for Israelite worship prior to the temple. Their hilltop location followed Canaanite practice, and many probably stood on existing centers of Baal worship. Their legitimacy, however, remains an open question. Clearly, the law prohibits Israelites from using high places and pagan altars to worship Yahweh (Num 33:52; Deut 7:5; 12:3). It also limited altar-building to divinely approved locales (Exod 20:24; Deut 12:5,8,13–14). Whether conformity to these conditions made the use of multiple altar-sites acceptable is uncertain (see 19:10,14; Lev 26:30–31; Deut 12; 1 Sam 9:12). What is clear, however, is that under Solomon incorporation of pagan high places into Yahweh worship was common, produced religious apostasy and syncretism, and was roundly condemned (2 Kgs 17:7–18; 21:2–9; 23:4–25). Apparently, a multiplicity of worship sites was thought normal prior to the building of the temple. Later, royal toleration of the high places became the basis for critiquing kings (11:7; 15:14; 22:43; 2 Kgs 12:3; 15:4; cf. Jer 19:5).

3:3 love for the LORD. The ideal piety in Deuteronomy and implicit in David's instructions (2:2–4). Because Solomon worshiped at local shrines, the comment may implicitly criticize Solomon. Indeed, one major flaw in Solomon's early reign was his inconsistent implementation of Mosaic requirements governing places of worship.

4 The king went to Gibeon[y] to offer sacrifices, for that was the most important high place, and Solomon offered a thousand burnt offerings on that altar. 5 At Gibeon the LORD appeared[z] to Solomon during
the night in a dream,[a] and God said, "Ask for whatever you want me to give you."
6 Solomon answered, "You have shown great kindness to your servant, my father David, because he
was faithful[b] to you and righteous and upright in heart. You have continued this great kindness to him
and have given him a son[c] to sit on his throne this very day.
7 "Now, LORD my God, you have made your servant king in place of my father David. But I am only a
little child[d] and do not know how to carry out my duties. 8 Your servant is here among the people you
have chosen,[e] a great people, too numerous to count or number.[f] 9 So give your servant a discerning[g]
heart to govern your people and to distinguish[h] between right and wrong. For who is able[i] to govern
this great people of yours?"
10 The Lord was pleased that Solomon had asked for this. 11 So God said to him, "Since you have
asked[j] for this and not for long life or wealth for yourself, nor have asked for the death of your enemies
but for discernment in administering justice, 12 I will do what you have asked.[k] I will give you a wise[l]
and discerning heart, so that there will never have been anyone like you, nor will there ever be. 13 Moreover, I will give you what you have not[m] asked for — both wealth and honor[n] — so that in your lifetime
you will have no equal[o] among kings. 14 And if you walk[p] in obedience to me and keep my decrees and
commands as David your father did, I will give you a long life."[q] 15 Then Solomon awoke[r] — and he
realized it had been a dream.

3:4 [y] 1Ch 16:39
3:5 [z] 1Ki 9:2 [a] Nu 12:6; Mt 1:20
3:6 [b] 1Ki 2:4; 9:4 [c] 1Ki 1:48
3:7 [d] Nu 27:17; 1Ch 29:1
3:8 [e] Dt 7:6 [f] Ge 15:5
3:9 [g] 2Sa 14:17; Jas 1:5 [h] Pr 2:3-9; Heb 5:14 [i] Ps 72:1-2
3:11 [j] Jas 4:3
3:12 [k] 1Jn 5:14-15 [l] 1Ki 4:29,30,31; 5:12; 10:23; Ecc 1:16
3:13 [m] Mt 6:33; Eph 3:20 [n] 1Ki 4:21-24; Pr 3:1-2, 16 [o] 1Ki 10:23
3:14 [p] ver 6; Pr 3:1-2,16 [q] Ps 61:6; 91:16
3:15 [r] Ge 41:7

3:4 Gibeon. Israel's most important high place at the time; six miles (9.7 kilometers) northwest of Jerusalem (cf. Josh 9:3–10:15; 2 Sam 2; 21:1–9). Its hosting of the tabernacle and the altar of burnt offering after the Philistines destroyed Shiloh (1 Sam 4:11–22) may account for its unique importance (1 Chr 21:29; 2 Chr 1:2–6).

3:5 appeared ... in a dream. A common way God communicated with people. Most dreams in the Bible feature a symbolic story (Gen 37:5–10; Dan 4:5–18), interaction with an angel (Gen 31:11–13; Matt 1:20; 2:13,19), or direct conversation with God (vv. 5–15; Gen 20:3–7).

3:6 great kindness. Alludes to the Davidic covenant (2 Sam 7:8–16), the sole basis for Solomon's accession.

3:7–9 Solomon sincerely desires to serve God well.

3:7 I am only a little child. May allude to Solomon's relative youth for a king (perhaps about 20 years old at his accession; see 2:11–12; cf. Jer 1:6) or simply express genuine humility in the face of the demands of wise rule.

3:9 discerning heart. The ability to distinguish between true and false testimony, key to administering justice (cf. v. 11). In making decisions, Solomon desires that his heart listen to God, not humans; only then will his rulings be truly wise (cf. vv. 16–28). He also seeks the trait that in the ancient Near East defines a "good king," i.e., to patiently hear all competing views on a matter in order to make the wisest decision (cf. Isa 11:2–5).

3:14 keep my decrees and commands. Obey Moses' law as David did. In Lev 18–20, this phrase defines the basic requirement of holiness (Lev 18:5,26; 19:37; 20:22; cf. 1 Kgs 11:38).

3:15 ark. The sacred object in Jerusalem symbolized God's ruling presence. This is where Solomon publically accepts God's promised gifts (v. 13) and the burden of lifelong obedience (v. 14).

Nebi Samwil, a possible location of Gibeon's "high place" (1 Kgs 3:4).

Todd Bolen/www.BiblePlaces.com

3:15 [s] 1Ki 8:65 [t] Mk 6:21 [u] Est 1:3,9; Da 5:1
3:26 [v] Ge 43:30; Isa 49:15; Jer 31:20; Hos 11:8
3:28 [w] ver 9,11-12; Col 2:3
4:2 [x] 1Ch 6:10
4:3 [y] 2Sa 8:16
4:4 [z] 1Ki 2:35 [a] 1Ki 2:27

He returned to Jerusalem, stood before the ark of the Lord's covenant and sacrificed burnt offerings[s] and fellowship offerings.[t] Then he gave a feast[u] for all his court.

A Wise Ruling

16 Now two prostitutes came to the king and stood before him. 17 One of them said, "Pardon me, my lord. This woman and I live in the same house, and I had a baby while she was there with me. 18 The third day after my child was born, this woman also had a baby. We were alone; there was no one in the house but the two of us.

19 "During the night this woman's son died because she lay on him. 20 So she got up in the middle of the night and took my son from my side while I your servant was asleep. She put him by her breast and put her dead son by my breast. 21 The next morning, I got up to nurse my son — and he was dead! But when I looked at him closely in the morning light, I saw that it wasn't the son I had borne."

22 The other woman said, "No! The living one is my son; the dead one is yours."

But the first one insisted, "No! The dead one is yours; the living one is mine." And so they argued before the king.

23 The king said, "This one says, 'My son is alive and your son is dead,' while that one says, 'No! Your son is dead and mine is alive.' "

24 Then the king said, "Bring me a sword." So they brought a sword for the king. 25 He then gave an order: "Cut the living child in two and give half to one and half to the other."

26 The woman whose son was alive was deeply moved[v] out of love for her son and said to the king, "Please, my lord, give her the living baby! Don't kill him!"

But the other said, "Neither I nor you shall have him. Cut him in two!"

27 Then the king gave his ruling: "Give the living baby to the first woman. Do not kill him; she is his mother."

28 When all Israel heard the verdict the king had given, they held the king in awe, because they saw that he had wisdom[w] from God to administer justice.

Solomon's Officials and Governors

4 So King Solomon ruled over all Israel. 2 And these were his chief officials:

Azariah[x] son of Zadok — the priest;
3 Elihoreph and Ahijah, sons of Shisha — secretaries;
Jehoshaphat[y] son of Ahilud — recorder;
4 Benaiah[z] son of Jehoiada — commander in chief;
Zadok[a] and Abiathar — priests;
5 Azariah son of Nathan — in charge of the district governors;

3:16–28 *A Wise Ruling.* Solomon's worldwide reputation for unrivaled wisdom debuts here (cf. 4:29–34). His famous decision confirms that God has enabled him to wisely administer justice.

3:25 The prostitutes follow an Israelite legal practice that permits Israelites and others in the land to appeal directly to the king without first consulting lower judges (Deut 16:18; cf. 2 Kgs 8:3; 2 Sam 15:2). **Cut the living child in two.** Solomon's clever ploy to find the disputed baby's true mother and thus restore a broken relationship assumes that she would rather surrender custody to her rival than witness the baby's death.

4:1–34 *Solomon's Kingdom.* This early glimpse of Solomon's new kingdom describes his royal staff appointments (vv. 1–19), the scope of his realm, and the palace's life of luxury (vv. 20–28). It closes with high praise for the king's unparalleled wisdom (vv. 29–34).

4:1–19 *Solomon's Officials and Governors.* These lists of royal officials probably derive either from royal records in Jerusalem or from "the book of the annals of Solomon" (11:41). The first concerns officials headquartered in the capital (vv. 2–6); the second lists governors who run Solomon's 12 districts (vv. 7–19). They portray Solomon as a skilled administrator and organizer, and they portray a united Israel in control of territory east and west of the Jordan River.

4:1 ruled over all Israel. Affirms the smooth, stable transition from David's rule to Solomon's. Solomon rules the same united kingdom as his father (2 Sam 8:15).

4:2 son. Azariah was the son of Ahimaaz, Zadok's son (2 Sam 15:27,36; 1 Chr 6:8–9). Zadok's grandson Azariah succeeded him probably because Ahimaaz had died. See note on v. 8. **Zadok.** See v. 4; cf. 2:27,35.

4:3 secretaries. The king's scribes. **Jehoshaphat son of Ahilud.** The same person who had held the position on David's royal staff (2 Sam 8:16; 20:24). **recorder.** See note on 2 Sam 8:16.

4:4 Benaiah. Solomon's replacement for Joab as commander of the army. See 2:35; 2 Sam 8:18. **Zadok and Abiathar.** Early in his reign Solomon banished Abiathar, a supporter of Adonijah (1:7) and replaced him with Zadok, the priest who had anointed him king (1:39; 2:27, 35). Zadok's grandson Azariah (v. 2) succeeded him.

4:5 Nathan. Either the well-known prophet (1:11) or one of David's sons (2 Sam 5:14). **district governors.** See vv. 7–19. **adviser to the king.** See v. 16 and note; see also note on 2 Sam 15:37.

Zabud son of Nathan — a priest and adviser to the king;
6 Ahishar — palace administrator;
Adoniram son of Abda — in charge of forced labor.

7 Solomon had twelve district governors over all Israel, who supplied provisions for the king and the
royal household. Each one had to provide supplies for one month in the year. 8 These are their names:

Ben-Hur — in the hill country[b] of Ephraim;
9 Ben-Deker — in Makaz, Shaalbim,[c] Beth Shemesh[d] and Elon Bethhanan;
10 Ben-Hesed — in Arubboth (Sokoh[e] and all the land of Hepher[f] were his);
11 Ben-Abinadab — in Naphoth Dor[g] (he was married to Taphath daughter of Solomon);
12 Baana son of Ahilud — in Taanach and Megiddo, and in all of Beth Shan[h] next to Zarethan[i] below Jezreel, from Beth Shan to Abel Meholah[j] across to Jokmeam;[k]
13 Ben-Geber — in Ramoth Gilead (the settlements of Jair[l] son of Manasseh in Gilead were his, as well as the region of Argob in Bashan and its sixty large walled cities[m] with bronze gate bars);
14 Ahinadab son of Iddo — in Mahanaim;[n]
15 Ahimaaz[o] — in Naphtali (he had married Basemath daughter of Solomon);
16 Baana son of Hushai[p] — in Asher and in Aloth;
17 Jehoshaphat son of Paruah — in Issachar;
18 Shimei[q] son of Ela — in Benjamin;
19 Geber son of Uri — in Gilead (the country of Sihon king of the Amorites and the country of Og[r] king of Bashan). He was the only governor over the district.

4:8 [b] Jos 24:33
4:9 [c] Jdg 1:35 [d] Jos 21:16
4:10 [e] Jos 15:35 [f] Jos 12:17
4:11 [g] Jos 11:2
4:12 [h] Jos 17:11; Jdg 5:19 [i] Jos 3:16 [j] 1Ki 19:16 [k] 1Ch 6:68
4:13 [l] Nu 32:41 [m] Dt 3:4
4:14 [n] Jos 13:26
4:15 [o] 2Sa 15:27
4:16 [p] 2Sa 15:32
4:18 [q] 1Ki 1:8
4:19 [r] Dt 3:8-10
4:20 [s] Ge 22:17; 32:12; 1Ki 3:8
4:21 [t] 2Ch 9:26; Ps 72:11 [u] Jos 1:4; Ps 72:8 [v] Ge 15:18 [w] Ps 68:29
4:24 [x] Ps 72:11 [y] 1Ch 22:9

Solomon's Daily Provisions

20 The people of Judah and Israel were as numerous as the sand[s] on the seashore; they ate, they
drank and they were happy. 21 And Solomon ruled[t] over all the kingdoms from the Euphrates River[u] to
the land of the Philistines, as far as the border of Egypt.[v] These countries brought tribute[w] and were
Solomon's subjects all his life.

22 Solomon's daily provisions were thirty cors[a] of the finest flour and sixty cors[b] of meal, 23 ten
head of stall-fed cattle, twenty of pasture-fed cattle and a hundred sheep and goats, as well as deer,
gazelles, roebucks and choice fowl. 24 For he ruled over all the kingdoms west of the Euphrates River,
from Tiphsah[x] to Gaza, and had peace[y] on all sides. 25 During Solomon's lifetime Judah and Israel,

[a] 22 That is, probably about 5 1/2 tons or about 5 metric tons [b] 22 That is, probably about 11 tons or about 10 metric tons

4:6 palace administrator. The first mention of a high-ranking royal official often noted in 1–2 Kings (16:9; 18:3; 2 Kgs 10:5; 18:18,37; 19:2). He was probably the royal chief-of-staff over palace operations and manager of royal properties. **Adoniram.** Supervisor of the compulsory labor program of David, Solomon, and Rehoboam (12:18; 2 Sam 20:24). **forced labor.** See notes on 5:13; 9:15.

4:7 twelve district governors. These districts replaced the traditional tribal boundaries with redrawn district ones. Tribal agricultural productivity varied considerably, and the new boundaries probably sought administrative efficiency attuned to those variations. Solomon's innovation, however, may have stirred up tribal jealousies and resentment that ultimately divided his unified kingdom. **provisions.** What governors provided king and palace by levying supplies from their districts (vv. 22–23,27). This echoes Samuel's warnings about having a king (1 Sam 8:11–18; cf. Deut 17:14–20).

4:8 Ben-Hur. *Ben* here means "son/grandson of" in Hebrew; cf. v. 2.

4:11 Ben-Abinadab. Probably the son of David's brother (i.e., Solomon's cousin and son-in-law).

4:12 Baana son of Ahilud. Probably a brother of the recorder Jehoshaphat (v. 3).

4:16 Baana son of Hushai. Possibly the son of David's close confidant (2 Sam 15:32,37) whose advice God used to defeat Absalom (2 Sam 17:11–14).

4:18 Shimei son of Ela. Perhaps the Shimei listed with those who did not support Adonijah (1:8).

4:20–28 *Solomon's Realm.* This section glories in the wealth, size, and peace of Solomon's empire.

4:20 Judah and Israel. Solomon's two principal constituencies; they later become two separate nations (ch. 12; cf. 1:35). **sand on the seashore.** A common metaphor for a number too huge to be counted, especially attacking enemy hordes (Josh 11:4; Judg 7:12; 1 Sam 13:5; Rev 20:8; cf. 2 Sam 17:11). Here the phrase reminds one of God's promise to the patriarchs of numerous descendants (Gen 12:2; 15:18–19; 22:17; 32:12). Israel's large population under Solomon measures one impressive moment of fulfillment, their future restoration after judgment another (Hos 1:10; cf. Heb 11:12). It will reach its maximum number at the consummation of history when believers from everywhere finally gather (Rev 7:9). Cf. v. 29.

4:21 land of the Philistines. Along the Mediterranean about where the Gaza Strip is today. **tribute.** Payments by subject nations that luxuriously supply the palace (cf. 7).

4:24 Tiphsah. A city where ancient caravans forded the Euphrates River; the northern boundary of Solomon's vast empire. **Gaza.** A Philistine city and caravan stop; the empire's southern border (cf. v. 21).

4:25 [z]Jdg 20:1 [a]Jer 23:6 [b]Mic 4:4; Zec 3:10
4:26 [c]1Ki 10:26; 2Ch 1:14
4:27 [d]ver 7
4:29 [e]1Ki 3:12
4:30 [f]Ge 25:6 [g]Ac 7:22
4:31 [h]1Ki 3:12; 1Ch 2:6; 6:33; 15:19; Ps 89 Title
4:32 [i]Pr 1:1; Ecc 12:9 [j]SS 1:1
4:34 [k]1Ki 10:1; 2Ch 9:23
5:1 [l]ver 10,18; 2Sa 5:11; 1Ch 14:1
5:3 [m]1Ch 22:8; 28:3
5:4 [n]1Ki 4:24; 1Ch 22:9

from Dan to Beersheba,[z] lived in safety,[a] everyone under their own vine and under their own fig
tree.[b]
[26]Solomon had four[a] thousand stalls for chariot horses,[c] and twelve thousand horses.[b]
[27]The district governors,[d] each in his month, supplied provisions for King Solomon and all who
came to the king's table. They saw to it that nothing was lacking. [28]They also brought to the proper
place their quotas of barley and straw for the chariot horses and the other horses.

Solomon's Wisdom

[29]God gave Solomon wisdom[e] and very great insight, and a breadth of understanding as measureless
as the sand on the seashore. [30]Solomon's wisdom was greater than the wisdom of all the people of the
East,[f] and greater than all the wisdom of Egypt.[g] [31]He was wiser[h] than anyone else, including Ethan
the Ezrahite — wiser than Heman, Kalkol and Darda, the sons of Mahol. And his fame spread to all the
surrounding nations. [32]He spoke three thousand proverbs[i] and his songs[j] numbered a thousand and
five. [33]He spoke about plant life, from the cedar of Lebanon to the hyssop that grows out of walls. He also
spoke about animals and birds, reptiles and fish. [34]From all nations people came to listen to Solomon's
wisdom, sent by all the kings[k] of the world, who had heard of his wisdom.[c]

Preparations for Building the Temple

5:1-16pp — 2Ch 2:1-18

5 [d] When Hiram[l] king of Tyre heard that Solomon had been anointed king to succeed his father
David, he sent his envoys to Solomon, because he had always been on friendly terms with David.
[2]Solomon sent back this message to Hiram:

[3]"You know that because of the wars[m] waged against my father David from all sides, he could
not build a temple for the Name of the LORD his God until the LORD put his enemies under his
feet. [4]But now the LORD my God has given me rest[n] on every side, and there is no adversary or

[a] *26* Some Septuagint manuscripts (see also 2 Chron. 9:25); Hebrew *forty* [b] *26* Or *charioteers* [c] *34* In Hebrew texts 4:21-34 is numbered 5:1-14. [d] In Hebrew texts 5:1-18 is numbered 5:15-32.

4:25 Dan to Beersheba. See note on 1 Sam 3:20; cf. Judg 20:1; 2 Sam 17:11; 24:2. **their own vine and … their own fig tree.** Symbolizes universal prosperity under Solomon.

4:26 four thousand. See NIV text note. Biblical records report that Solomon had 1,400 chariots (10:26; 2 Chr 1:14), a number that would require stalls for two horses per chariot and for about 1,200 reserve steeds. For perspective, according to an Assyrian report, a century after Solomon at the battle of Qarqar (853 BC) Damascus fielded 1,200 chariots; Hamath, 700; and Israel's northern kingdom, 2,000. The presence of numerous royal steeds attests both to Solomon's magnificent wealth and his violation of Deut 17:16.

4:27 nothing was lacking. Shows the burden that governors bore to sustain palace luxury. This explains the popular resentment that surfaces in ch. 11.

4:29–34 *Solomon's Wisdom.* This extols the superiority and international fame of Solomon's wisdom, insight, and broad understanding (see note on 7:14). These qualities attest to the greatness of the God who gifted Solomon with them.

4:29 wisdom. The primary, general term for the ability to live life with maximum success and a minimum of failure. It is the highly prized skill that Adam and Eve risked divine displeasure to acquire (Gen 3:6) and that Solomon's teaching passionately seeks to cultivate in people (Prov 2:12; 4:6). Its starting point is the fear of God (Prov 1:7), and to live wisely is to align one's conduct with the way God created the world to work (Prov 8:32–36). **insight.** The ability to perceive the heart of a matter; to "see the light" (i.e., to distill the truth lurking behind initial impressions). Often closely associated with wisdom and translated "understanding" (e.g., Exod 35:30—36:1; Prov 2:6; 3:13; 8:1), it sharpens one's grasp of wisdom as a whole. **understanding … measureless.** Vast knowledge of important information. It supplies the hard data that informs wisdom and its decisions. Wisdom, insight, and understanding are separate qualities, yet they overlap and interrelate. Paul stressed that the search for wisdom begins with Christ, the person in whom all wisdom and knowledge is hidden and awaiting discovery (Col 2:2–3).

4:31 Ethan the Ezrahite. Author of Ps 89 and among the wisest men ever known at that time. Solomon is ultimately eclipsed by Jesus Christ (see Luke 11:31). **Heman, Kalkol and Darda.** Renowned Israelite musicians. **sons of Mahol.** Probably an Israelite musical guild rather than a family.

4:32 spoke. Probably means "quoted." **three thousand proverbs.** The book of Proverbs preserves only a portion of that total. **songs.** Perhaps music both composed and sung from memory.

4:33 Solomon was a learned botanist with a vast knowledge of living things.

4:34 all the kings of the world. Evidences Solomon's regional renown as consultant of kings. In the background stands the historical emergence in the early Iron Age of mini-empires across Syro-Palestine.

5:1—9:9 *Solomon's Temple.* This details Solomon's construction projects, especially the temple, his showpiece and lasting legacy. The king's preparations (ch. 5) lead to the construction of both the temple (ch. 6) and a large palace complex (ch. 7). The lengthy temple dedication ceremony (ch. 8) elicits Yahweh's acceptance and a solemn warning about divine judgment for royal idolatry (9:1–9).

5:1–18 *Preparations for Building the Temple.* International diplomacy and the conscription of laborers supply Solomon with the materials and labor to build the temple.

5:1 Hiram. Ruler of Tyre and longtime ally of David (2 Sam 5:11). **Tyre.** An ancient, wealthy Phoenician commercial port.

disaster. 5 I intend, therefore, to build a temple[o] for the Name of the LORD my God, as the LORD told
my father David, when he said, 'Your son whom I will put on the throne in your place will build
the temple for my Name.'[p]
6 "So give orders that cedars of Lebanon be cut for me. My men will work with yours, and I will
pay you for your men whatever wages you set. You know that we have no one so skilled in felling
timber as the Sidonians."

7 When Hiram heard Solomon's message, he was greatly pleased and said, "Praise be to the LORD
today, for he has given David a wise son to rule over this great nation."
8 So Hiram sent word to Solomon:

"I have received the message you sent me and will do all you want in providing the cedar and
juniper logs. 9 My men will haul them down from Lebanon to the Mediterranean Sea[q], and I will
float them as rafts by sea to the place you specify. There I will separate them and you can take
them away. And you are to grant my wish by providing food[r] for my royal household."

10 In this way Hiram kept Solomon supplied
with all the cedar and juniper logs he wanted,
11 and Solomon gave Hiram twenty thousand
cors[a] of wheat as food for his household, in addition to twenty thousand baths[b,c] of pressed
olive oil. Solomon continued to do this for Hiram year after year. 12 The LORD gave Solomon
wisdom,[s] just as he had promised him. There
were peaceful relations between Hiram and
Solomon, and the two of them made a treaty.[t]
13 King Solomon conscripted laborers[u] from
all Israel — thirty thousand men. 14 He sent
them off to Lebanon in shifts of ten thousand
a month, so that they spent one month in Lebanon and two months at home. Adoniram[v] was
in charge of the forced labor. 15 Solomon had
seventy thousand carriers and eighty thousand
stonecutters in the hills, 16 as well as thirty-
three hundred[d] foremen[w] who supervised the
project and directed the workers. 17 At the king's
command they removed from the quarry[x] large blocks of high-grade stone[y] to provide a foundation
of dressed stone for the temple. 18 The craftsmen of Solomon and Hiram and workers from Byblos[z] cut
and prepared the timber and stone for the building of the temple.

Cedar of Lebanon.
© Sybille Yates/Shutterstock

5:5 [o] 1Ch 17:12 [p] 2Sa 7:13; 1Ch 22:10
5:9 [q] Ezr 3:7 [r] Eze 27:17; Ac 12:20
5:12 [s] 1Ki 3:12 [t] Am 1:9
5:13 [u] 1Ki 9:15
5:14 [v] 1Ki 4:6; 2Ch 10:18
5:16 [w] 1Ki 9:23
5:17 [x] 1Ki 6:7 [y] 1Ch 22:2
5:18 [z] Jos 13:5

[a] *11* That is, probably about 3,600 tons or about 3,250 metric tons [b] *11* Septuagint (see also 2 Chron. 2:10); Hebrew *twenty cors* [c] *11* That is, about 120,000 gallons or about 440,000 liters [d] *16* Hebrew; some Septuagint manuscripts (see also 2 Chron. 2:2,18) *thirty-six hundred*

5:5 Fulfills God's promise to David (cf. 2 Sam 7:13; 1 Chr 22:10; 2 Chr 6:9). **the Name of the LORD.** Yahweh's personal presence.
5:6 cedars. Source of fabled, fragrant, and durable wood for building ships and important buildings. Their height supplied long beams to erect as tall pillars and to roof over large buildings. **cut.** Hiram's skilled lumberjacks precut the lumber. **Sidonians.** Inhabitants of Sidon (in modern Lebanon), a prosperous Phoenician port 23 miles (37 kilometers) north of Tyre.
5:8 cedar and juniper. Types of logs native to Phoenicia (cf. 6:15,34).
5:9 food. The form of payment for Hiram's supplies. Implies that Hiram's palace may match Solomon's in abundant foodstuffs (cf. 4:22–23,27).
5:12 peaceful relations. Further evidence of Solomon's God-given wisdom.
5:13 conscripted laborers. See note on 9:15. After Solomon died, popular resentment over his forced labor policy spilled out in public protests and led to the division of his kingdom into two separate countries (12:1–18). Ironically, the desire for a king had originated with the people themselves (cf. 1 Sam 8:7–18), who now resented the current king.
5:14 shifts. Rotations between work in Lebanon and time at home. This posed a hardship for farmers sent abroad during planting or harvesting. **Adoniram.** The labor program's administrator (cf. 4:6; 12:18; 2 Sam 20:24).
5:15 The state's need for huge quantities of stone led to the conscription of carriers and stonecutters from non-Israelite residents conquered and incorporated into the kingdom by David (2 Chr 2:17–18).
5:17 quarry. The source of high-grade foundation stone; probably near Jerusalem; implies ingenious, labor-intensive transport to the temple site.
5:18 Byblos. An ancient coastal city 20 miles (32 kilometers) north of present-day Beirut; biblical Gebal; modern Jubayl.

6:1 [a]Ac 7:47
6:2 [b]Eze 41:1
6:4 [c]Eze 40:16; 41:16
6:5 [d]ver 16,19-21; Eze 41:5-6
6:7 [e]Ex 20:25 [f]Dt 27:5
6:9 [g]ver 14,38
6:12 [h]2Sa 7:12-16; 1Ki 2:4; 9:5
6:13 [i]Ex 25:8; Lev 26:11; Dt 31:6; Heb 13:5
6:14 [j]ver 9,38
6:15 [k]1Ki 7:7

Solomon Builds the Temple

6:1-29pp — 2Ch 3:1-14

6 In the four hundred and eightieth[a] year after the Israelites came out of Egypt, in the fourth year
of Solomon's reign over Israel, in the month of Ziv, the second month, he began to build the temple of the LORD.[a]
2 The temple[b] that King Solomon built for the LORD was sixty cubits long, twenty wide and thirty
high.[b] 3 The portico at the front of the main hall of the temple extended the width of the temple, that
is twenty cubits,[c] and projected ten cubits[d] from the front of the temple. 4 He made narrow windows[c]
high up in the temple walls. 5 Against the walls of the main hall and inner sanctuary he built a structure around the building, in which there were side rooms.[d] 6 The lowest floor was five cubits[e] wide, the
middle floor six cubits[f] and the third floor seven.[g] He made offset ledges around the outside of the
temple so that nothing would be inserted into the temple walls.
7 In building the temple, only blocks dressed[e] at the quarry were used, and no hammer, chisel or any
other iron tool[f] was heard at the temple site while it was being built.
8 The entrance to the lowest[h] floor was on the south side of the temple; a stairway led up to the middle level and from there to the third. 9 So he built the temple and completed it, roofing it with beams and
cedar[g] planks. 10 And he built the side rooms all along the temple. The height of each was five cubits,
and they were attached to the temple by beams of cedar.
11 The word of the LORD came to Solomon: 12 "As for this temple you are building, if you follow my decrees, observe my laws and keep all my commands and obey them, I will fulfill through you the promise[h]
I gave to David your father. 13 And I will live among the Israelites and will not abandon[i] my people Israel."
14 So Solomon built the temple and completed[j] it. 15 He lined its interior walls with cedar boards, paneling them from the floor of the temple to the ceiling,[k] and covered the floor of the temple with planks
of juniper. 16 He partitioned off twenty cubits at the rear of the temple with cedar boards from floor to

[a] *1* Hebrew; Septuagint *four hundred and fortieth* [b] *2* That is, about 90 feet long, 30 feet wide and 45 feet high or about 27 meters long, 9 meters wide and 14 meters high [c] *3* That is, about 30 feet or about 9 meters; also in verses 16 and 20 [d] *3* That is, about 15 feet or about 4.5 meters; also in verses 23-26 [e] *6* That is, about 7 1/2 feet or about 2.3 meters; also in verses 10 and 24 [f] *6* That is, about 9 feet or about 2.7 meters [g] *6* That is, about 11 feet or about 3.2 meters [h] *8* Septuagint; Hebrew *middle*

6:1–38 *Solomon Builds the Temple.* Construction follows the assembly of costly materials and skilled manpower. Chronological summaries bracket the report (vv. 1,37), and v. 38 dates the temple's completion. Its general layout resembles the tabernacle's (Exod 26:33–35; Lev 16:16–17). The report's rare architectural vocabulary makes the sense of some items uncertain. See illustration, pp. 614–615.

6:1 four hundred and eightieth year. The number of years between the exodus and the laying of the temple's foundation. Assyrian records and synchronizations between known extrabiblical events and events involving later Israelite kings confirm Solomon's "fourth year" as ca. 966 BC. If chronological, the 480-year figure would date the exodus to ca. 1446 BC, during the rule of Pharaoh Thutmose III of the Eighteenth Dynasty. Egyptian place-names in Exod 1:11 and other historical evidences, however, seem to preclude a date before the reign of Pharaoh Rameses II (ca. 1279 BC; cf. Gen 47:11). If so, the 480 years would be a schematic or symbolic figure (e.g., 12 generations times the traditional 40-year length of a generation [in actuality, 25 years]). It could also be an aggregate number, i.e., the sum total of a list of time periods, some partly concurrent, an ancient approach known from Egypt and Mesopotamia (cf. Deut 1:3). **Ziv.** The local Canaanite name for the second month (April–May); cf. v. 38. Ancient Near Eastern monarchs typically dated as historic events the laying of the foundations of important buildings like temples.

6:5 structure around the building. An exterior, attached, three-story structure. Each story was slightly wider than the one below it (v. 6). **side rooms.** Spaces for storage or residency (1 Chr 9:33).

6:6 offset ledges. Structures that stabilized the sanctuary's outer wall without disturbing its integrity (cf. v. 10, which describes an additional exterior structure).

6:11 The word of the LORD came to. Common preface to a prophetic message (cf. 16:1; 17:2,8; 18:1; 19:9; 21:17,28). The phrase is an important theme in 1–2 Kings. It may refer to a message given in the past that has just been fulfilled (15:29; 17:16; 2 Kgs 4:44; 10:17; 23:16; 24:2). The phrase is central to the prophecy-fulfillment theme of the book. It may also refer to a word given earlier to authorize someone to deliver a divine message (13:2,17,32; 20:35). The phrase "the word of the LORD came to" prefaces announcements by prophets of a new message (16:1,7; 18:31; 21:17), as does "Hear the word," which underscores that the urgent message demands an immediate hearing. The theme teaches that people who obey God's spoken word avoid disaster (12:24), while disaster falls on those who defy it (13:21,26). Behind it stands Israel's covenant God whose care for and commitment to his people leads him to warn them of coming destruction or to give them future hope. The Lord is a God who breaks his silence and communicates because he wants his people to know his voice and his character; he wants to tell them how to continue to enjoy his full blessings. Theologically, this is the same God whose love for humanity drove him to clothe his only Son, also called "the Word," in human flesh and send him to live, speak, die, and rise again among them (John 1:1,14; 3:16). It is the same God whose powerful spoken word called the whole universe into being (Gen 1; Ps 33:6) and still speaks powerfully today (Heb 4:12). Jesus, the Word, still urges anyone with ears to listen carefully to what he has to say, especially the good news he announced (Mark 4:9,23; Luke 8:8; 14:35). See note on 13:1.

6:15 cedar … juniper. See notes on 5:6,8. The woods would imbue the temple's interior with fragrant beauty.

6:16 Most Holy Place. See note on v. 19.

This temple in northern Syria ('Ain Dara) dates from the time of Solomon and resembles it in various details. The 'Ain Dara Temple includes side rooms (1 Kgs 6:5,10), built around the outer wall.

Rick Hess

ceiling to form within the temple an inner sanctuary, the Most Holy Place.[l] 17The main hall in front of this room was forty cubits[a] long. 18The inside of the temple was cedar,[m] carved with gourds and open flowers. Everything was cedar; no stone was to be seen.

19He prepared the inner sanctuary[n] within the temple to set the ark of the covenant[o] of the LORD there. 20The inner sanctuary[p] was twenty cubits long, twenty wide and twenty high. He overlaid the inside with pure gold, and he also overlaid the altar of cedar. 21Solomon covered the inside of the temple with pure gold, and he extended gold chains across the front of the inner sanctuary, which was overlaid with gold. 22So he overlaid the whole interior with gold. He also overlaid with gold the altar that belonged to the inner sanctuary.

23For the inner sanctuary he made a pair of cherubim[q] out of olive wood, each ten cubits high. 24One wing of the first cherub was five cubits long, and the other wing five cubits—ten cubits from wing tip to wing tip. 25The second cherub also measured ten cubits, for the two cherubim were identical in size and shape. 26The height of each cherub was ten cubits. 27He placed the cherubim[r] inside the innermost room of the temple, with their wings spread out. The wing of one cherub touched one wall, while the wing of the other touched the other wall, and their wings touched each other in the middle of the room. 28He overlaid the cherubim with gold.

29On the walls all around the temple, in both the inner and outer rooms, he carved cherubim,[s] palm trees and open flowers. 30He also covered the floors of both the inner and outer rooms of the temple with gold.

31For the entrance to the inner sanctuary he made doors out of olive wood that were one fifth of the width of the sanctuary. 32And on the two olive-wood doors he carved cherubim, palm trees and open flowers, and overlaid the cherubim and palm trees with hammered gold. 33In the same way, for the entrance to the main hall he made doorframes out of olive wood that were one fourth of the width of the hall. 34He also made two doors out of juniper wood, each having two leaves that turned in sockets. 35He carved cherubim, palm trees and open flowers on them and overlaid them with gold hammered evenly over the carvings.

[a] *17* That is, about 60 feet or about 18 meters

6:16 [l] Ex 26:33; Lev 16:2; 1Ki 8:6
6:18 [m] 1Ki 7:24; Ps 74:6
6:19 [n] 1Ki 8:6 [o] 1Sa 3:3
6:20 [p] Eze 41:3-4
6:23 [q] Ex 37:1-9
6:27 [r] Ex 25:20; 37:9; 1Ki 8:7; 2Ch 5:8
6:29 [s] ver 32,35

6:19 inner sanctuary. The Most Holy Place (v. 16). The small room at the temple's west end. **ark of the covenant.** Yahweh's portable throne (Ps 80:1) and Israel's holiest object; contained the Ten Commandments (8:9; Exod 25:16). Cf. 2 Sam 6.

6:20 pure gold. Gleaming precious metal; may symbolize the holiness and glory of God. Gold was used extensively in the construction of the tabernacle (Exod 25–26,28).

6:23 cherubim. Winged creatures symbolizing Yahweh's royal throne attendants and his flight transportation (2 Sam 22:11; Ps 18:10; Ezek 1; 10). **ten cubits high.** That is, about 15 feet (4.6 meters) high, an unusually gigantic size for cherubim. This presents the cherubim as royal guards who intimidate would-be intruders into God's sacred presence (cf. v. 32). The cherubim denying access to the tree of life in the Garden of Eden (Gen 3:24) play the same role.

6:29 palm trees. A common sight in both coastal and desert locales of the Near East. They decorate the doorjambs and walls in Ezekiel's visionary temple (Ezek 40:16,37; 41:26). **open flowers.** Cf. v. 18.

6:36 [t] 1Ki 7:12; Ezr 6:4
6:38 [u] Heb 8:5
7:1 [v] 1Ki 9:10; 2Ch 8:1
7:2 [w] 2Sa 7:2 [x] 1Ki 10:17; 2Ch 9:16

36 And he built the inner courtyard of three courses[t] of dressed stone and one course of trimmed cedar beams.

37 The foundation of the temple of the LORD was laid in the fourth year, in the month of Ziv. 38 In the eleventh year in the month of Bul, the eighth month, the temple was finished in all its details according to its specifications.[u] He had spent seven years building it.

Solomon Builds His Palace

7 It took Solomon thirteen years, however, to complete the construction of his palace.[v] 2 He built the Palace[w] of the Forest of Lebanon[x] a hundred cubits long, fifty wide and thirty high,[a] with four rows of cedar columns supporting trimmed cedar beams. 3 It was roofed with cedar above the beams that rested on the columns—forty-five beams, fifteen to a row. 4 Its windows were placed high in sets of three, facing each other. 5 All the doorways had rectangular frames; they were in the front part in sets of three, facing each other.[b]

6 He made a colonnade fifty cubits long and thirty wide.[c] In front of it was a portico, and in front of that were pillars and an overhanging roof.

[a] *2* That is, about 150 feet long, 75 feet wide and 45 feet high or about 45 meters long, 23 meters wide and 14 meters high [b] *5* The meaning of the Hebrew for this verse is uncertain. [c] *6* That is, about 75 feet long and 45 feet wide or about 23 meters long and 14 meters wide

6:36 inner courtyard. The small, walled-in, outdoor area immediately around the temple.
6:38 Bul. The local Canaanite word for the year's eighth month (October-November); see note on v. 1 ("Ziv").
7:1–12 *Solomon Builds His Palace.* A brief interlude details the construction of Solomon's palace complex before the narrative returns to the temple in vv. 13–51. The complex lies south of the sanctuary and includes three official state buildings (vv. 1–7) and two private royal residences (vv. 8–12).
7:1 thirteen years. Contrasts with the seven years it took to build the temple. The contrast, however, need not imply that Solomon was less devoted to the temple than to his own house. In fact, the king's piety and desire to honor God may account for the temple's intense, compressed completion time. On the other hand, the architectural complexity and multifaceted mission of the palace complex (i.e., both royal residence and kingdom administrative center) explain why it took longer to build.
7:2 Palace of the Forest of Lebanon. Its name probably describes its forest of cedar columns and beams.
7:4 sets of three. Implies a building of enormous size.
7:6 colonnade. A large hall with rows of stately pillars; this has royal architectural analogies at Karnak (Egypt) and Persepolis (Persia).

SOLOMON'S TEMPLE

The temple of Solomon, located near the king's palace, functioned as God's royal palace and Israel's national center of worship. The Lord said to Solomon, "I have consecrated this temple . . . by putting my Name there forever. My eyes and my heart will always be there" (1 Kgs 9:3). By its cosmological and royal symbolism, the sanctuary declared the absolute sovereignty of the Lord over the whole creation and his special headship over Israel.

The floor plan is a type that has a long history in Semitic religion, particularly among the West Semites. An early example of the tripartite division into portico, main hall and inner sanctuary has been found at Syrian Ebla (ca. 2300 BC) and, much later but more contemporaneous with Solomon, at 'Ain Dara in north Syria (tenth century BC) and at Tell Taynat in southeast Turkey (eighth century BC). Like Solomon's, the temples at 'Ain Dara and at Tell Taynat had three divisions, had two columns supporting the entrance, and were located adjacent to the royal palace.

Many archaeological parallels can be drawn to the methods of construction used in the temple, e.g., the "dressed stone and ... cedar beams" technique described in 1 Kgs 6:36. Interestingly, evidence for the largest bronze-casting industry ever found in the Holy Land comes from the same locale and period as that indicated in Scripture: Zarethan in the Jordan valley ca. 1000 BC.

960–586 BC

Temple source materials are subject to academic interpretation, and subsequent art reconstructions vary.

This model recognizes influence from the wilderness tabernacle, accepts general Near Eastern cultural diffusion, and rejects overt pagan Canaanite symbols. It uses known archaeological parallels to supplement the text and assumes interior dimensions from 1 Kgs 6:17–20.

[7]He built the throne hall, the Hall of Justice, where he was to judge,[y] and he covered it with cedar
from floor to ceiling.[a][z] [8]And the palace in which he was to live, set farther back, was similar in design.
Solomon also made a palace like this hall for Pharaoh's daughter, whom he had married.[a]
[9]All these structures, from the outside to the great courtyard and from foundation to eaves, were
made of blocks of high-grade stone cut to size and smoothed on their inner and outer faces. [10]The
foundations were laid with large stones of good quality, some measuring ten cubits[b] and some eight.[c]
[11]Above were high-grade stones, cut to size, and cedar beams. [12]The great courtyard was surrounded
by a wall of three courses[b] of dressed stone and one course of trimmed cedar beams, as was the inner
courtyard of the temple of the LORD with its portico.

7:7 [y]Ps 122:5; Pr 20:8 [z]1Ki 6:15
7:8 [a]1Ki 3:1; 2Ch 8:11
7:12 [b]1Ki 6:36
7:13 [c]2Ch 2:13
7:14 [d]Ex 31:2-5; 35:31; 36:1; 2Ch 2:14 [e]2Ch 4:11,16

The Temple's Furnishings

7:23-26pp — 2Ch 4:2-5
7:38-51pp — 2Ch 4:6,10–5:1

[13]King Solomon sent to Tyre and brought Huram,[d][c] [14]whose mother was a widow from the tribe
of Naphtali and whose father was from Tyre and a skilled craftsman in bronze. Huram was filled with
wisdom,[d] with understanding and with knowledge to do all kinds of bronze work. He came to King
Solomon and did all[e] the work assigned to him.

[a] *7* Vulgate and Syriac; Hebrew *floor* [b] *10* That is, about 15 feet or about 4.5 meters; also in verse 23
[c] *10* That is, about 12 feet or about 3.6 meters [d] *13* Hebrew *Hiram,* a variant of *Huram;* also in verses 40 and 45

7:7 Hall of Justice. Israel's Supreme Court. The king was the presiding judge.
7:8 set farther back. To ensure the privacy of the royal residences (cf. vv. 2–7). **similar in design.** Aesthetically blends with other structures. **Pharaoh's daughter.** Cf. 3:1. Ancient queens typically had their own palaces.
7:12 great courtyard. Probably the open area surrounding the palace complex. **inner courtyard.** See note on 6:36.
7:13–51 *The Temple's Furnishings.* This details the furnishings of the courtyard in front of the temple. Highly skilled craftsman from Tyre take center stage (vv. 13–45), but the king returns at the end (vv. 46–51).
7:13 Tyre. See note on 5:1.
7:14 Huram. A craftsmen of Tyrian-Israelite parentage, symptomatic of ongoing dealings between Naphtali and Phoenicia. **wisdom ... understanding ... knowledge.** Skills similar to those of Bezalel, builder of the tabernacle, but without the latter's filling by the Spirit of God (Exod 31:3; 35:31; see note on 1 Kgs 4:29). The three terms also figure prominently in the brief creation account in Prov 3:19–20.

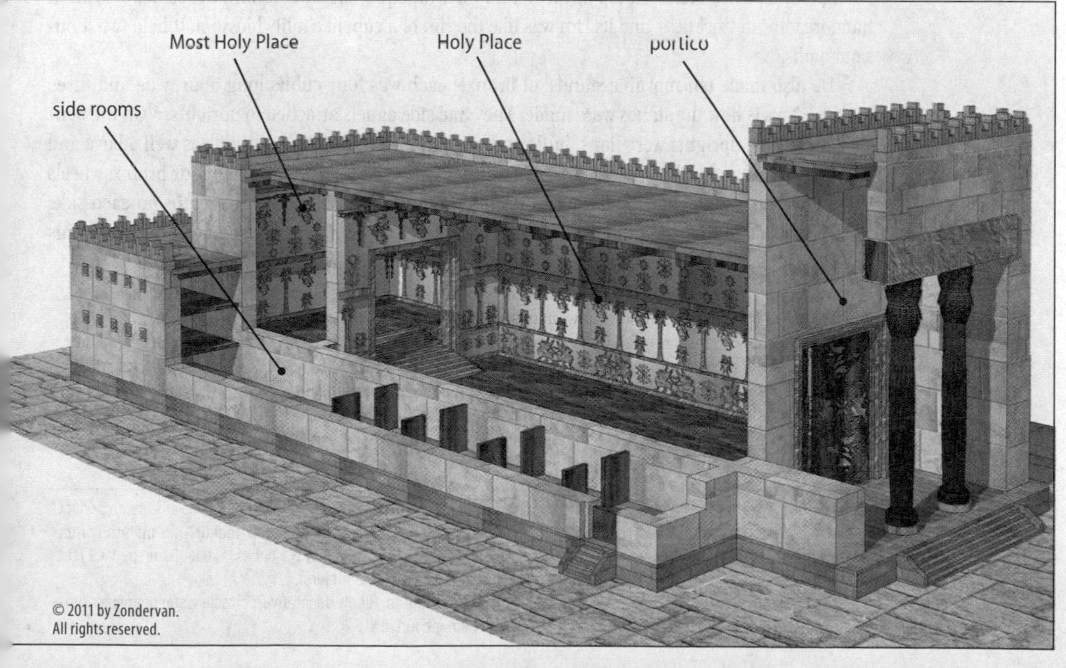

Tell Qeiyafeh inscription with the word, "judge, to judge" on it; from Judah, tenth century BC (1 Kgs 7:7).

Z. Radovan/www.BibleLandPictures.com

7:15 [f] 2Ki 25:17; 2Ch 3:15; 4:12; Jer 52:17,21
7:16 [g] 2Ki 25:17
7:20 [h] 2Ch 3:16; 4:13; Jer 52:23
7:21 [i] 1Ki 6:3; 2Ch 3:17
7:23 [j] 2Ki 25:13; 1Ch 18:8; Jer 52:17
7:25 [k] 2Ch 4:4-5; Jer 52:20
7:27 [l] ver 38; 2Ch 4:14
7:30 [m] 2Ki 16:17

15 He cast two bronze pillars,[f] each eighteen cubits high and twelve cubits in circumference.[a]
16 He also made two capitals[g] of cast bronze to set on the tops of the pillars; each capital was five
cubits[b] high. 17 A network of interwoven chains adorned the capitals on top of the pillars, seven for
each capital. 18 He made pomegranates in two rows[c] encircling each network to decorate the capitals on top of the pillars.[d] He did the same for each capital. 19 The capitals on top of the pillars in
the portico were in the shape of lilies, four cubits[e] high. 20 On the capitals of both pillars, above the
bowl-shaped part next to the network, were the two hundred pomegranates[h] in rows all around.
21 He erected the pillars at the portico of the temple. The pillar to the south he named Jakin[f] and
the one to the north Boaz.[g][i] 22 The capitals on top were in the shape of lilies. And so the work on
the pillars was completed.
23 He made the Sea[j] of cast metal, circular in shape, measuring ten cubits from rim to rim and five
cubits high. It took a line of thirty cubits[h] to measure around it. 24 Below the rim, gourds encircled
it—ten to a cubit. The gourds were cast in two rows in one piece with the Sea.
25 The Sea stood on twelve bulls,[k] three facing north, three facing west, three facing south and three
facing east. The Sea rested on top of them, and their hindquarters were toward the center. 26 It was a
handbreadth[i] in thickness, and its rim was like the rim of a cup, like a lily blossom. It held two thousand baths.[j]
27 He also made ten movable stands[l] of bronze; each was four cubits long, four wide and three
high.[k] 28 This is how the stands were made: They had side panels attached to uprights. 29 On the panels between the uprights were lions, bulls and cherubim—and on the uprights as well. Above and
below the lions and bulls were wreaths of hammered work. 30 Each stand[m] had four bronze wheels
with bronze axles, and each had a basin resting on four supports, cast with wreaths on each side.
31 On the inside of the stand there was an opening that had a circular frame one cubit[l] deep. This

[a] *15* That is, about 27 feet high and 18 feet in circumference or about 8.1 meters high and 5.4 meters in circumference [b] *16* That is, about 7 1/2 feet or about 2.3 meters; also in verse 23 [c] *18* Two Hebrew manuscripts and Septuagint; most Hebrew manuscripts *made the pillars, and there were two rows* [d] *18* Many Hebrew manuscripts and Syriac; most Hebrew manuscripts *pomegranates* [e] *19* That is, about 6 feet or about 1.8 meters; also in verse 38 [f] *21* *Jakin* probably means *he establishes.* [g] *21* *Boaz* probably means *in him is strength.* [h] *23* That is, about 45 feet or about 14 meters [i] *26* That is, about 3 inches or about 7.5 centimeters [j] *26* That is, about 12,000 gallons or about 44,000 liters; the Septuagint does not have this sentence. [k] *27* That is, about 6 feet long and wide and about 4 1/2 feet high or about 1.8 meters long and wide and 1.4 meters high [l] *31* That is, about 18 inches or about 45 centimeters

7:17–19 interwoven chains ... pomegranates ... lilies. Probably Phoenician decorative motifs. Cf. vv. 22,42.

7:21 Jakin ... Boaz. See NIV text notes. Both may comprise key words in a memorable temple motto.

7:23 Sea. Water source for priests to wash during rituals (2 Chr 4:6). Cf. the tabernacle's bronze basin (Exod 30:18–21). **thirty cubits.** Probably a round number measuring the basin's circumference as either a perfect circle (technically, 31.416 cubits [about 47 feet or 14.3 meters]) or an oval with diameters of 10 cubits by 9.1 cubits (about 15 feet by 13.7 feet or about 4.6 meters by 4.2 meters).

7:27 movable stands. Highly decorative, portable water supply for rituals in the inner courtyard.

opening was round, and with its basework it measured a cubit and a half.[a] Around its opening there
was engraving. The panels of the stands were square, not round. 32The four wheels were under the
panels, and the axles of the wheels were attached to the stand. The diameter of each wheel was a
cubit and a half. 33The wheels were made like chariot wheels; the axles, rims, spokes and hubs were
all of cast metal.
34Each stand had four handles, one on each corner, projecting from the stand. 35At the top of the
stand there was a circular band half a cubit[b] deep. The supports and panels were attached to the top
of the stand. 36He engraved cherubim, lions and palm trees on the surfaces of the supports and on the
panels, in every available space, with wreaths all around. 37This is the way he made the ten stands. They
were all cast in the same molds and were identical in size and shape.
38He then made ten bronze basins,[n] each holding forty baths[c] and measuring four cubits across, one
basin to go on each of the ten stands. 39He placed five of the stands on the south side of the temple and
five on the north. He placed the Sea on the south side, at the southeast corner of the temple. 40He also
made the pots[d] and shovels and sprinkling bowls.

So Huram finished all the work he had undertaken for King Solomon in the temple of the LORD:

41 the two pillars;
the two bowl-shaped capitals on top of the pillars;
the two sets of network decorating the two bowl-shaped capitals on top of the pillars;
42 the four hundred pomegranates for the two sets of network (two rows of pomegranates for each network decorating the bowl-shaped capitals[o] on top of the pillars);
43 the ten stands with their ten basins;
44 the Sea and the twelve bulls under it;
45 the pots, shovels and sprinkling bowls.[p]

All these objects that Huram made for King Solomon for the temple of the LORD were of burnished
bronze. 46The king had them cast in clay molds in the plain[q] of the Jordan between Sukkoth[r] and
Zarethan.[s] 47Solomon left all these things unweighed,[t] because there were so many; the weight of the
bronze was not determined.
48Solomon also made all the furnishings that were in the LORD's temple:

the golden altar;
the golden table[u] on which was the bread of the Presence;[v]
49 the lampstands[w] of pure gold (five on the right and five on the left, in front of the inner sanctuary);
the gold floral work and lamps and tongs;
50 the pure gold basins, wick trimmers, sprinkling bowls, dishes and censers;[x]
and the gold sockets for the doors of the innermost room, the Most Holy Place, and also for the doors of the main hall of the temple.

51When all the work King Solomon had done for the temple of the LORD was finished, he brought in
the things his father David had dedicated[y]—the silver and gold and the furnishings—and he placed
them in the treasuries of the LORD's temple.

[a] *31* That is, about 2 1/4 feet or about 68 centimeters; also in verse 32 [b] *35* That is, about 9 inches or about 23 centimeters [c] *38* That is, about 240 gallons or about 880 liters [d] *40* Many Hebrew manuscripts, Septuagint, Syriac and Vulgate (see also verse 45 and 2 Chron. 4:11); many other Hebrew manuscripts *basins*

7:38 [n] Ex 30:18; 2Ch 4:6
7:42 [o] ver 20
7:45 [p] Ex 27:3
7:46 [q] 2Ch 4:17 [r] Ge 33:17; Jos 13:27 [s] Jos 3:16
7:47 [t] 1Ch 22:3
7:48 [u] Ex 37:10 [v] Ex 25:30
7:49 [w] Ex 25:31-38
7:50 [x] 2Ki 25:13
7:51 [y] 2Sa 8:11

7:40 pots and shovels and sprinkling bowls. Service items for sacrificial rituals with antecedents at the tabernacle (Exod 27:3).
7:45 burnished bronze. Polished to a smooth, bright surface.
7:46 Sukkoth and Zarethan. Ancient towns just east and west, respectively, of the Jordan River and about 20 miles (32 kilometers) north of Jericho. Excavations at Sukkoth confirm the prominence of metallurgy in the area during the monarchy.
7:48 furnishings. For their tabernacle counterparts, see Exod 25:23–40; 30:1–10,17–21 and illustration, p. 165. **bread of the Presence.** Cf. Exod 25:23–30; 40:23; Lev 24:5–9; see note on Exod 25:30.
7:51 things ... David had dedicated. Cf. 2 Sam 8:9–12; 1 Chr 29:1–5. **treasuries.** Storage for the temple's metal valuables (cf. 15:18; Josh 6:19,24; 2 Chr 12:9). For palace treasuries, cf. 14:25–26; 2 Chr 36:18; Ezek 28:4. Kings of Judah often draw on both treasuries to pay for foreign military intervention in crises (15:18–20; 2 Kgs 16:8) or to end a siege (2 Kgs 12:18; 18:15). Victors also carry off the treasuries of their enemies as a prize of war (2 Kgs 14:14).

8:1 [z]Nu 7:2 [a]2Sa 6:17 [b]2Sa 5:7
8:2 [c]2Ch 7:8 [d]Lev 23:34
8:3 [e]Nu 7:9; Jos 3:3
8:4 [f]1Ki 3:4; 2Ch 1:3
8:5 [g]2Sa 6:13
8:6 [h]2Sa 6:17 [i]1Ki 6:19,27
8:8 [j]Ex 25:13-15
8:9 [k]Ex 24:7-8; 25:21; 40:20; Dt 10:2-5; Heb 9:4
8:10 [l]Ex 40:34-35; 2Ch 7:1-2
8:12 [m]Ps 18:11; 97:2
8:13 [n]Ex 15:17; 2Sa 7:13; Ps 132:13
8:14 [o]2Sa 6:18
8:15 [p]2Sa 7:12-13; 1Ch 29:10,20; Ne 9:5; Lk 1:68
8:16 [q]Dt 12:5 [r]1Sa 16:1 [s]2Sa 7:4-6,8
8:17 [t]2Sa 7:2; 1Ch 17:1
8:19 [u]2Sa 7:5 [v]2Sa 7:13; 1Ki 5:3,5
8:20 [w]1Ch 28:6

The Ark Brought to the Temple

8:1-21pp — 2Ch 5:2-6:11

8 Then King Solomon summoned into his presence at Jerusalem the elders of Israel, all the heads of the tribes and the chiefs[z] of the Israelite families, to bring up the ark[a] of the LORD's covenant from Zion, the City of David.[b] 2 All the Israelites came together to King Solomon at the time of the festival[c] in the month of Ethanim, the seventh month.[d]

3 When all the elders of Israel had arrived, the priests[e] took up the ark, 4 and they brought up the ark of the LORD and the tent of meeting[f] and all the sacred furnishings in it. The priests and Levites carried them up, 5 and King Solomon and the entire assembly of Israel that had gathered about him were before the ark, sacrificing[g] so many sheep and cattle that they could not be recorded or counted.

6 The priests then brought the ark of the LORD's covenant[h] to its place in the inner sanctuary of the temple, the Most Holy Place, and put it beneath the wings of the cherubim.[i] 7 The cherubim spread their wings over the place of the ark and overshadowed the ark and its carrying poles. 8 These poles were so long that their ends could be seen from the Holy Place in front of the inner sanctuary, but not from outside the Holy Place; and they are still there today.[j] 9 There was nothing in the ark except the two stone tablets[k] that Moses had placed in it at Horeb, where the LORD made a covenant with the Israelites after they came out of Egypt.

10 When the priests withdrew from the Holy Place, the cloud[l] filled the temple of the LORD. 11 And the priests could not perform their service because of the cloud, for the glory of the LORD filled his temple.

12 Then Solomon said, "The LORD has said that he would dwell in a dark cloud;[m] 13 I have indeed built a magnificent temple for you, a place for you to dwell[n] forever."

14 While the whole assembly of Israel was standing there, the king turned around and blessed[o] them. 15 Then he said:

"Praise be to the LORD,[p] the God of Israel, who with his own hand has fulfilled what he promised with his own mouth to my father David. For he said, 16 'Since the day I brought my people Israel out of Egypt, I have not chosen a city in any tribe of Israel to have a temple built so that my Name[q] might be there, but I have chosen[r] David[s] to rule my people Israel.'

17 "My father David had it in his heart to build a temple[t] for the Name of the LORD, the God of Israel. 18 But the LORD said to my father David, 'You did well to have it in your heart to build a temple for my Name. 19 Nevertheless, you[u] are not the one to build the temple, but your son, your own flesh and blood — he is the one who will build the temple for my Name.'[v]

20 "The LORD has kept the promise he made: I have succeeded David my father and now I sit on the throne of Israel, just as the LORD promised, and I have built[w] the temple for the Name of the LORD, the God of Israel. 21 I have provided a place there for the ark, in which is the covenant of the LORD that he made with our ancestors when he brought them out of Egypt."

8:1–66 *The Temple's Dedication.* With great ceremony, Solomon leads Israel in dedicating the temple for worshiping Israel's covenant God. The festivities include installing the ark (vv. 1–21), Solomon's dedicatory prayer (vv. 22–61), and the Festival of Tabernacles (vv. 62–66).
8:1–21 *The Ark Brought to the Temple.* Israel solemnly installs the ark of the covenant in the temple's inner sanctuary.
8:1 heads of the tribes and the chiefs of the Israelite families. The leaders of Israel's traditional kinship groups together comprise its national leadership alongside the king and priests. **ark.** See note on 6:19; cf. 2:26; 3:15. **Zion.** The Jebusite fortress-city that David conquered (2 Sam 5:7); also designates the temple hill (Ps 2:6) and Jerusalem as a whole (Ps 48:2,12). **City of David.** See note on 2:10.
8:2 festival. Probably Sukkoth, i.e., the Festival of Tabernacles (Lev 23:34; Deut 16:13–17; 31:9–13). **Ethanim.** Canaanite name for the seventh month (September-October); cf. vv. 65–66; 6:1,37–38.
8:4 tent of meeting. The tabernacle (Exod 27:21; Lev 16:7), formerly at Gibeon (3:4; 1 Sam 7:1 [see note on 1 Sam 6:21]; cf. 2 Chr 5:4–5) but now in Zion (see note on v. 1). **priests and Levites.** Custodians of the ark (Deut 31:9; 2 Sam 15:24).
8:6 inner sanctuary. See note on 6:19. **Most Holy Place.** Cf. 6:16; 7:50. **cherubim.** See note on 6:23.
8:8 still there today. Cf. 9:13; 10:12; 12:19; 2 Kgs 2:22; 8:22; 14:7; 16:6; 17:23,34,41. This indicates that the writer wrote sometime before the temple's destruction in 586 BC.
8:9 Horeb. Another name for Mount Sinai (see note on 19:8; cf. Exod 3:1; Deut 5:2).
8:10 cloud. A visible sign that the Lord currently occupies the temple (cf. v. 1; Num 12:10; Ezek 10:3). The cloud visibly verifies that God's presence has now descended to live there just as its descent upon the tabernacle below Mount Sinai did (Exod 40:34–35; Ezek 10:3–5,18–19; 43:4–5).
8:12 dark cloud. The thick darkness protects humans from the dangers of seeing God (Exod 20:21; Deut 5:22; Ps 97:2), but Solomon asserts (v. 13) that God's long-term stay in the temple (and, presumably, proper ritual protocols) offers Israel ongoing access to God's presence without such danger (cf. v. 21).
8:20 promise. To David: a dynasty and a temple built by his son (cf. vv. 24–26; 1:48; 2 Sam 7:5–16).

Solomon's Prayer of Dedication

8:22-53pp — 2Ch 6:12-40

22 Then Solomon stood before the altar of the LORD in front of the whole assembly of Israel, spread
out his hands[x] toward heaven 23 and said:
"LORD, the God of Israel, there is no God like[y] you in heaven above or on earth below — you
who keep your covenant of love[z] with your servants who continue wholeheartedly in your way.
24 You have kept your promise to your servant David my father; with your mouth you have promised and with your hand you have fulfilled it — as it is today.
25 "Now LORD, the God of Israel, keep for your servant David my father the promises[a] you made
to him when you said, 'You shall never fail to have a successor to sit before me on the throne
of Israel, if only your descendants are careful in all they do to walk before me faithfully as you
have done.' 26 And now, God of Israel, let your word that you promised[b] your servant David my
father come true.
27 "But will God really dwell[c] on earth? The heavens, even the highest heaven, cannot contain[d]
you. How much less this temple I have built! 28 Yet give attention to your servant's prayer and his
plea for mercy, LORD my God. Hear the cry and the prayer that your servant is praying in your
presence this day. 29 May your eyes be open[e] toward[f] this temple night and day, this place of which
you said, 'My Name[g] shall be there,' so that you will hear the prayer your servant prays toward this
place. 30 Hear the supplication of your servant and of your people Israel when they pray toward
this place. Hear from heaven, your dwelling place, and when you hear, forgive.[h]
31 "When anyone wrongs their neighbor and is required to take an oath and they come and
swear the oath[i] before your altar in this temple, 32 then hear from heaven and act. Judge between
your servants, condemning the guilty by bringing down on their heads what they have done, and
vindicating the innocent by treating them in accordance with their innocence.[j]
33 "When your people Israel have been defeated[k] by an enemy because they have sinned[l]
against you, and when they turn back to you and give praise to your name, praying and making
supplication to you in this temple, 34 then hear from heaven and forgive the sin of your people
Israel and bring them back to the land you gave to their ancestors.
35 "When the heavens are shut up and there is no rain[m] because your people have sinned
against you, and when they pray toward this place and give praise to your name and turn from
their sin because you have afflicted them, 36 then hear from heaven and forgive the sin of your
servants, your people Israel. Teach[n] them the right way[o] to live, and send rain on the land you
gave your people for an inheritance.
37 "When famine[p] or plague comes to the land, or blight[q] or mildew, locusts or grasshoppers,

8:22 [x] Ex 9:29; Ezr 9:5
8:23 [y] 1Sa 2:2; 2Sa 7:22 [z] Dt 7:9,12; Ne 1:5; 9:32; Da 9:4
8:25 [a] 1Ki 2:4
8:26 [b] 2Sa 7:25
8:27 [c] Ac 7:48 [d] 2Ch 2:6; Ps 139:7-16; Isa 66:1; Jer 23:24
8:29 [e] 2Ch 7:15; Ne 1:6 [f] Da 6:10 [g] Dt 12:11
8:30 [h] Ps 85:2
8:31 [i] Ex 22:11
8:32 [j] Dt 25:1
8:33 [k] Lev 26:17; Dt 28:25 [l] Lev 26:39
8:35 [m] Lev 26:19; Dt 28:24
8:36 [n] 1Sa 12:23; Ps 25:4; 94:12 [o] Ps 5:8; 27:11; Jer 6:16
8:37 [p] Lev 26:26 [q] Dt 28:22

8:22–61 *Solomon's Prayer of Dedication.* This marks the centerpiece of the text's three main events. This prayer articulates the behavioral standard of Deuteronomy by which the people and all kings will be judged. Solomon's seven petitions share a common format: "When *x* happens (condition), then, God, hear and do *y* (petition)" (vv. 30,31–32, 33–34,35–36,37–40,41–43,44–45,46–51). **8:22 altar.** Probably in the inner courtyard (cf. 6:36; 7:12), not the sanctuary proper (6:20,22). **spread out his hands toward heaven.** An action during prayers that often accompanies pleas (cf. vv. 38,54; see Exod 9:29). It symbolizes that petitioners direct their appeals to Israel's God alone and do so in a posture of humble submission. **8:23 no God like you.** God is incomparable (cf. Ps 86:8–10; Isa 40:25; 46:5; Mic 7:18). **covenant of love.** God's unwavering commitment to relationship with Israel. Solomon affirms that only Israel's God (and no others) has intervened in history through great miracles and sovereign guidance of events, all to make his long-awaited covenant promises a present reality for his people (Exod 15:11–13; Deut 4:39—7:9). See "Covenant," p. 2646. **8:24 as it is today.** The present celebration evidences God's faithfulness to David.

8:25 if only. The common proviso in 1–2 Kings that the dynasty's survival hangs on royal faithfulness (cf. 2:1–4; 9:4–9). **8:28 plea for mercy.** God answers prayer because he is merciful, not because humans deserve it (cf. v. 30). **8:30 forgive.** Implies that the petitioner's repentance and God's forgiveness precede God's answering of prayers. **8:31 swear the oath.** Oath taking is the means by which people making claims verify that they are telling the truth. They willingly accept terrible consequences for lying or not keeping their word. Through oaths, people charged with crimes prove their innocence, witnesses in court confirm they are telling the truth, and parties to agreements guarantee they will faithfully carry out their promises. **8:32 Judge between.** Settle disputes. This prayer calls on God to expose the guilty and vindicate the innocent by imposing the consequences each deserves (cf. vv. 31,39). **8:36 the right way to live.** This is the key lesson (i.e., behavior in accordance with covenant obligations) that Israel is to learn through the historical and natural disasters described (vv. 33–36). These behaviors confirm that the petitioner's repentance is genuine, and God keeps his covenant promises by granting forgiveness and sending relief.

8:39 [r] 1Sa 16:7; 1Ch 28:9; Ps 11:4; Jer 17:10; Jn 2:24; Ac 1:24
8:40 [s] Ps 130:4
8:42 [t] Dt 3:24
8:43 [u] 1Sa 17:46; 2Ki 19:19 [v] Ps 102:15
8:46 [w] Pr 20:9; Ecc 7:20; Ro 3:9; 1Jn 1:8-10 [x] Lev 26:33-39; Dt 28:64
8:47 [y] Lev 26:40; Ne 1:6 [z] Ps 106:6; Da 9:5
8:48 [a] Dt 4:29; Jer 29:12-14 [b] Da 6:10 [c] Jnh 2:4
8:50 [d] 2Ch 30:9; Ps 106:46
8:51 [e] Dt 4:20; 9:29; Ne 1:10 [f] Jer 11:4
8:53 [g] Ex 19:5; Dt 9:26-29
8:55 [h] ver 14; 2Sa 6:18
8:56 [i] Dt 12:10 [j] Jos 21:45; 23:15

or when an enemy besieges them in any of their cities, whatever disaster or disease may come, 38 and when a prayer or plea is made by anyone among your people Israel—being aware of the afflictions of their own hearts, and spreading out their hands toward this temple— 39 then hear from heaven, your dwelling place. Forgive and act; deal with everyone according to all they do, since you know[r] their hearts (for you alone know every human heart), 40 so that they will fear[s] you all the time they live in the land you gave our ancestors.

41 "As for the foreigner who does not belong to your people Israel but has come from a distant land because of your name— 42 for they will hear of your great name and your mighty hand[t] and your outstretched arm—when they come and pray toward this temple, 43 then hear from heaven, your dwelling place. Do whatever the foreigner asks of you, so that all the peoples of the earth may know[u] your name and fear[v] you, as do your own people Israel, and may know that this house I have built bears your Name.

44 "When your people go to war against their enemies, wherever you send them, and when they pray to the LORD toward the city you have chosen and the temple I have built for your Name, 45 then hear from heaven their prayer and their plea, and uphold their cause.

46 "When they sin against you—for there is no one who does not sin[w]—and you become angry with them and give them over to their enemies, who take them captive[x] to their own lands, far away or near; 47 and if they have a change of heart in the land where they are held captive, and repent and plead[y] with you in the land of their captors and say, 'We have sinned, we have done wrong, we have acted wickedly';[z] 48 and if they turn back to you with all their heart[a] and soul in the land of their enemies who took them captive, and pray[b] to you toward the land you gave their ancestors, toward the city you have chosen and the temple[c] I have built for your Name; 49 then from heaven, your dwelling place, hear their prayer and their plea, and uphold their cause. 50 And forgive your people, who have sinned against you; forgive all the offenses they have committed against you, and cause their captors to show them mercy;[d] 51 for they are your people and your inheritance,[e] whom you brought out of Egypt, out of that iron-smelting furnace.[f]

52 "May your eyes be open to your servant's plea and to the plea of your people Israel, and may you listen to them whenever they cry out to you. 53 For you singled them out from all the nations of the world to be your own inheritance,[g] just as you declared through your servant Moses when you, Sovereign LORD, brought our ancestors out of Egypt."

54 When Solomon had finished all these prayers and supplications to the LORD, he rose from before the altar of the LORD, where he had been kneeling with his hands spread out toward heaven. 55 He stood and blessed[h] the whole assembly of Israel in a loud voice, saying:

56 "Praise be to the LORD, who has given rest[i] to his people Israel just as he promised. Not one word has failed of all the good promises[j] he gave through his servant Moses. 57 May the

8:38 spreading out their hands. See note on v. 22; Exod 9:29.
8:40 fear. Revere with firm resolve. This is the ultimate goal of the disaster-plea-hear-act sequence (cf. v. 43).
8:42 they will hear. Presumes that testimonies by Israelites will spread in foreign lands. This key text bears witness to a fundamental biblical truth: God desires to bless all the nations of the earth through Israel and its worship of Yahweh (Gen 12:1–3). This truth underlies God's blessing of the non-Israelite widow of Zarephath during Elijah's residence in her home (17:8–24). It also drives the testimony the Israelite servant girl gives the enemy general Naaman and the kind treatment he receives from Elisha (2 Kgs 5). **mighty hand ... outstretched arm.** Metaphor for God's awesome power (cf. Deut 4:34; Ps 136:12; Jer 21:5; Ezek 20:33–34).
8:43 know your name and fear you. The reasons God should do whatever the foreigner asks (cf. v. 40). This signals an open door for non-Israelites to worship the Lord.
8:45 uphold their cause. Grant Israelite soldiers victory in combat only when sent by God to achieve God's (not selfish human) purposes. Theologically, the appeal is to God's nature as a warrior (Exod 15:3) and as a cosmic king (Pss 10:16; 24:7–10) who rules history to execute his plan for history (see Dan 4). As such, he promises to defend and protect his people against all enemies (Ps 44:4–7), a promise often kept in victories that Israel faithfully remembers (2 Kgs 7; 18–19; Ps 135:8–12). It is God who in Christ defeated evil and death (Rom 8:2; 1 Cor 15:22–28), who defends believers against spiritual enemies today (cf. Rom 8:31–32,37; Eph 6:10–18), and who will end history as its only king (Rev 18–20).
8:46 there is no one who does not sin. The reason Israel will likely sin and land in exile.
8:50 cause their captors to show them mercy. The clear sign that God has indeed forgiven errant Israel.
8:51 Alludes to Israel's special status and historic past with God; supports Solomon's plea for forgiveness.
8:53 singled them out. God selected Israel as his chosen nation (Exod 19:5; Lev 20:24,26; Deut 7:6). This anticipates later events (2 Kgs 17; 20; 24–25) and offers hope that Israel will return from exile.
8:56 rest. Israel's settled state in Canaan, militarily secure through God's victories, and "at home" (Deut 12:10–11; Josh 21:44). The "rest"

LORD our God be with us as he was with our ancestors; may he never leave us nor forsake[k]
us. 58May he turn our hearts[l] to him, to walk in obedience to him and keep the commands,
decrees and laws he gave our ancestors. 59And may these words of mine, which I have prayed
before the LORD, be near to the LORD our God day and night, that he may uphold the cause of
his servant and the cause of his people Israel according to each day's need, 60so that all the
peoples[m] of the earth may know that the LORD is God and that there is no other.[n] 61And may
your hearts be fully committed[o] to the LORD our God, to live by his decrees and obey his commands, as at this time."

The Dedication of the Temple

8:62-66pp — 2Ch 7:1-10

62Then the king and all Israel with him offered sacrifices before the LORD. 63Solomon offered a sacrifice of fellowship offerings to the LORD: twenty-two thousand cattle and a hundred and twenty thousand
sheep and goats. So the king and all the Israelites dedicated the temple of the LORD.
64On that same day the king consecrated the middle part of the courtyard in front of the temple of
the LORD, and there he offered burnt offerings, grain offerings and the fat of the fellowship offerings,
because the bronze altar[p] that stood before the LORD was too small to hold the burnt offerings, the grain
offerings and the fat of the fellowship offerings.
65So Solomon observed the festival[q] at that time, and all Israel with him — a vast assembly, people
from Lebo Hamath[r] to the Wadi of Egypt.[s] They celebrated it before the LORD our God for seven days
and seven days more, fourteen days in all. 66On the following day he sent the people away. They blessed
the king and then went home, joyful and glad in heart for all the good things the LORD had done for
his servant David and his people Israel.

The LORD Appears to Solomon

9:1-9pp — 2Ch 7:11-22

9 When Solomon had finished[t] building the temple of the LORD and the royal palace, and had
achieved all he had desired to do, 2the LORD appeared[u] to him a second time, as he had appeared
to him at Gibeon. 3The LORD said to him:

"I have heard[v] the prayer and plea you have made before me; I have consecrated this temple,
which you have built, by putting my Name there forever. My eyes[w] and my heart will always be
there.

4"As for you, if you walk before me faithfully with integrity of heart[x] and uprightness, as David[y]
your father did, and do all I command and observe my decrees and laws, 5I will establish[z] your
royal throne over Israel forever, as I promised David your father when I said, 'You shall never fail[a]
to have a successor on the throne of Israel.'

8:57 [k]Dt 31:6; Jos 1:5; Heb 13:5
8:58 [l]Ps 119:36
8:60 [m]Jos 4:24; 1Sa 17:46 [n]Dt 4:35; 1Ki 18:39; Jer 10:10-12
8:61 [o]1Ki 11:4; 15:3,14; 2Ki 20:3
8:64 [p]2Ch 4:1
8:65 [q]ver 2; Lev 23:34 [r]Nu 34:8; Jos 13:5; Jdg 3:3; 2Ki 14:25 [s]Ge 15:18
9:1 [t]1Ki 7:1; 2Ch 8:6
9:2 [u]1Ki 3:5
9:3 [v]2Ki 20:5; Ps 10:17 [w]Dt 11:12; 1Ki 8:29
9:4 [x]Ge 17:1 [y]1Ki 15:5
9:5 [z]1Ch 22:10 [a]2Sa 7:15; 1Ki 2:4

for believers today is "Sabbath-rest" (Heb 4:9), the full salvation that the gospel promises; both the OT and NT warn all God's people to avoid disobedience lest they, like the rebellious Israelites in the wilderness, miss its promised blessings (Ps 95:11; Heb 4:5,11).

8:60 all the peoples of the earth. Echoes the earlier international theme (cf. vv. 41–43).

8:61 hearts be fully committed. The Davidic ideal of which Solomon and many later kings, sadly, fall far short (11:4,9; 15:3).

8:62–66 *Dedicatory Sacrifices and a Festival.* Solomon presides over the formal dedication of the temple through sacrifices (vv. 62–63), and he consecrates the center of the temple's outer court so that worshipers may freely use its altar (v. 64). When the Festival of Tabernacles ends, Solomon dismisses the joyful Israelites to their hometowns (vv. 65–66).

8:63 fellowship offerings. See note on Lev 3:1; see also "Major Old Testament Offerings and Sacrifices," p. 197.

8:65 festival. See note on v. 2. **from Lebo Hamath to the Wadi of Egypt.** From all over Israel (Num 34:7–9; Josh 13:5; Ezek 47:15). Lebo Hamath, a city near the Orontes River in Aram (Syria), was one of Israel's traditional northern boundaries (Gen 15:18), and the Wadi of Egypt, probably the Wadi el-Arish in northern Sinai, was one of Israel's traditional southern boundaries (2 Kgs 24:7). **fourteen days.** Double the festival's usual duration, underscoring how joyous and monumental the occasion was.

9:1–9 *The Lord Appears to Solomon.* The Lord answers Solomon's prayer, affirming that he accepts the temple. But he also threatens to destroy it if Solomon or any successor fails to wholeheartedly obey God's laws.

9:2 A follow-up dream (probably at Jerusalem) to the one at Gibeon (see 3:5).

9:3 I have heard. Words by which God often responds to prayers in the Bible (2 Kgs 19:20; 20:5; cf. 1 Sam 25:35). God positively answers Solomon's prayer (cf. 8:16–20,41–44). **Name.** See notes on 5:5; Exod 3:15; Pss 8:1a; 74:7; cf. 1 Kgs 11:36; 14:21; 2 Kgs 21:4; 23:27.

9:4 you. Plural, addressing Solomon's descendants. **as David your father did.** The standard of faithful obedience for David's successors (2:4; 11:4; 15:3; 2 Kgs 14:3; 22:2).

9:6 [b] 2Sa 7:14
9:7 [c] 2Ki 17:23; 25:21 [d] Jer 7:14 [e] Ps 44:14 [f] Dt 28:37
9:8 [g] Dt 29:24; Jer 22:8-9
9:11 [h] 2Ch 8:2
9:13 [i] Jos 19:27
9:15 [j] Jos 16:10; 1Ki 5:13 [k] ver 24; 2Sa 5:9 [l] Jos 19:36 [m] Jos 17:11
9:17 [n] Jos 16:3; 2Ch 8:5
9:18 [o] Jos 19:44
9:19 [p] ver 1 [q] 1Ki 4:26

[6]"But if you[a] or your descendants turn away[b] from me and do not observe the commands and decrees I have given you[a] and go off to serve other gods and worship them, [7]then I will cut off Israel from the land[c] I have given them and will reject this temple I have consecrated for my Name.[d] Israel will then become a byword[e] and an object of ridicule[f] among all peoples. [8]This temple will become a heap of rubble. All[b] who pass by will be appalled and will scoff and say, 'Why has the LORD done such a thing to this land and to this temple?'[g] [9]People will answer, 'Because they have forsaken the LORD their God, who brought their ancestors out of Egypt, and have embraced other gods, worshiping and serving them — that is why the LORD brought all this disaster on them.'"

Solomon's Other Activities

9:10-28pp — 2Ch 8:1-18

[10]At the end of twenty years, during which Solomon built these two buildings — the temple of the LORD and the royal palace — [11]King Solomon gave twenty towns in Galilee to Hiram king of Tyre, because Hiram had supplied him with all the cedar and juniper and gold[h] he wanted. [12]But when Hiram went from Tyre to see the towns that Solomon had given him, he was not pleased with them. [13]"What kind of towns are these you have given me, my brother?" he asked. And he called them the Land of Kabul,[c][i] a name they have to this day. [14]Now Hiram had sent to the king 120 talents[d] of gold.

[15]Here is the account of the forced labor King Solomon conscripted[j] to build the LORD's temple, his own palace, the terraces,[e][k] the wall of Jerusalem, and Hazor,[l] Megiddo and Gezer.[m] [16](Pharaoh king of Egypt had attacked and captured Gezer. He had set it on fire. He killed its Canaanite inhabitants and then gave it as a wedding gift to his daughter, Solomon's wife. [17]And Solomon rebuilt Gezer.) He built up Lower Beth Horon,[n] [18]Baalath,[o] and Tadmor[f] in the desert, within his land, [19]as well as all his store cities[p] and the towns for his chariots[q] and for his horses[g] — whatever he desired to build in Jerusalem, in Lebanon and throughout all the territory he ruled.

[20]There were still people left from the Amorites, Hittites, Perizzites, Hivites and Jebusites (these peo-

[a] *6* The Hebrew is plural. [b] *8* See some Septuagint manuscripts, Old Latin, Syriac, Arabic and Targum; Hebrew *And though this temple is now imposing, all* [c] *13* *Kabul* sounds like the Hebrew for *good-for-nothing.* [d] *14* That is, about 4 1/2 tons or about 4 metric tons [e] *15* Or *the Millo*; also in verse 24 [f] *18* The Hebrew may also be read *Tamar.* [g] *19* Or *charioteers*

9:6 serve other gods. Idolatry, clearly violating the Torah (Deut 6:4). God's words have an ominous ring, testimony to the seriousness of the issue.

9:7 cut off Israel from the land. Exile, presumably for both king and people, as punishment for idolatry (cf. v. 9). **object of ridicule.** Public humiliation (cf. vv. 8–9).

9:8–9 The question-answer format may echo Deut 29:24–25.

9:8 heap of rubble. The temple's destruction (cf. Jer 7:14–15; Mic 3:12).

9:9 Idolatry is the cause of this disaster (cf. 2 Kgs 17:7–8; 21:11–15).

9:10—10:29 *Solomon's Other Activities.* This history portrays various aspects of Solomon's official and personal life. It reports other major projects (9:10–28) and a visit by the queen of Sheba (10:1–13). Its closing glimpse of Solomon's splendid empire (10:14–29) ominously foreshadows imminent divine judgment (ch. 11).

9:10–28 *Solomon's Actions.* Four short accounts flesh out the writer's larger portrait of Solomon: his repayment of Hiram (vv. 10–14), his compulsory labor policy (vv. 15–23), his religious life (vv. 24–25), and his new commercial fleet (vv. 26–28).

9:11 twenty towns. The balance still due Hiram for his services after Solomon's prior payments (5:6,11). It may reflect cost overruns for labor. **Galilee.** The Israelite region north of the Jezreel Valley; it extends just east of Tyre.

9:13 my brother. A royal ally in ancient diplomatic correspondence and treaties (20:32); implies that the parties are socially equal. **Kabul.** An insulting regional nickname (see NIV text note) that protests Solomon's previous payment (cf. 5:1–9).

9:14 Hiram's huge monetary advance either kept Solomon afloat financially or became gilding in the temple (cf. chs. 6–7).

9:15 Here is the account. Commonly introduces an instruction, explanation, command, or report (cf. 11:27); suggests that vv. 15–23 may derive from royal archives. **forced labor.** Solomon requires Canaanites to work on his construction projects (Josh 17:13; Judg 1:28,30). **terraces.** See NIV text note; see also note on 2 Sam 5:9. Probably an earthen platform that leveled low spots on the ridge with stones and dirt, permitting Solomon to expand Jerusalem from the City of David northward (cf. v. 24; 11:27). Archaeologists have found the enormous, stepped-stone structure that supported it. **Hazor.** See photo, p. 773.

9:16–17a This parenthesis concerning the dowry of Solomon's Egyptian wife points to the political and economic benefits that Solomon gained from that marriage. Two lucrative trade routes crossed near the Canaanite town of Gezer, the pharaoh's gift to his newlywed daughter. To the west passed a north-south road important to Egyptian commerce, and to the north was an east-west road linking Jerusalem and the Mediterranean Sea and the port of Joppa. Control of Gezer and access to Joppa provided a supply line to support the king's construction projects, including the temple.

9:17b–19 Throughout Solomon's vast realm, there were all kinds of construction projects (v. 19). Solomon desires peace (see NIV text note on 1 Chr 22:9), but his wisdom also leads him to prepare for possible wars (Deut 17:16). He strengthens his defenses by fortifying key cities close at hand (e.g., Gezer, Lower Beth Horon, Baalath; vv. 17–18) and far away (e.g., Tadmor, the ancient caravan stop in the desert of central Aram/Syria; v. 18). He builds garrisons to position his chariot corps and its horses and storage sites for grain and other goods (v. 19).

ples were not Israelites). 21 Solomon conscripted the descendants[r] of all these peoples remaining in the land — whom the Israelites could not exterminate[a][s] — to serve as slave labor,[t] as it is to this day. 22 But Solomon did not make slaves[u] of any of the Israelites; they were his fighting men, his government officials, his officers, his captains, and the commanders of his chariots and charioteers. 23 They were also the chief officials[v] in charge of Solomon's projects — 550 officials supervising those who did the work.

24 After Pharaoh's daughter[w] had come up from the City of David to the palace Solomon had built for her, he constructed the terraces.[x]

25 Three[y] times a year Solomon sacrificed burnt offerings and fellowship offerings on the altar he had built for the LORD, burning incense before the LORD along with them, and so fulfilled the temple obligations.

26 King Solomon also built ships[z] at Ezion Geber,[a] which is near Elath in Edom, on the shore of the Red Sea.[b] 27 And Hiram sent his men — sailors[b] who knew the sea — to serve in the fleet with Solomon's men. 28 They sailed to Ophir[c] and brought back 420 talents[c] of gold, which they delivered to King Solomon.

The Queen of Sheba Visits Solomon

10:1-13pp — 2Ch 9:1-12

10 When the queen of Sheba[d] heard about the fame of Solomon and his relationship to the LORD, she came to test Solomon with hard questions.[e] 2 Arriving at Jerusalem with a very great caravan — with camels carrying spices, large quantities of gold, and precious stones — she came to Solomon and talked with him about all that she had on her mind. 3 Solomon answered all her questions; nothing was too hard for the king to explain to her. 4 When the queen of Sheba saw all the wisdom of Solomon and the palace he had built, 5 the food on his table,[f] the seating of his officials, the attending servants in their robes, his cupbearers, and the burnt offerings he made at[d] the temple of the LORD, she was overwhelmed.

6 She said to the king, "The report I heard in my own country about your achievements and your wisdom is true. 7 But I did not believe these things until I came and saw with my own eyes. Indeed, not even half was told me; in wisdom and wealth[g] you have far exceeded the report I heard. 8 How happy your people must be! How happy your officials, who continually stand before you and hear[h] your wisdom! 9 Praise[i] be to the LORD your God, who has delighted in you and placed you on the throne of Israel. Because of the LORD's eternal love for Israel, he has made you king to maintain justice[j] and righteousness."

10 And she gave the king 120 talents[e] of gold,[k] large quantities of spices, and precious stones. Never again were so many spices brought in as those the queen of Sheba gave to King Solomon.

[a] *21* The Hebrew term refers to the irrevocable giving over of things or persons to the LORD, often by totally destroying them. [b] *26* Or *the Sea of Reeds* [c] *28* That is, about 16 tons or about 14 metric tons
[d] *5* Or *the ascent by which he went up to* [e] *10* That is, about 4 1/2 tons or about 4 metric tons

9:21 [r] Ge 9:25-26 [s] Jos 15:63; 17:12; Jdg 1:21,27,29 [t] Ezr 2:55,58
9:22 [u] Lev 25:39
9:23 [v] 1Ki 5:16
9:24 [w] 1Ki 3:1; 7:8 [x] 2Sa 5:9; 1Ki 11:27; 2Ch 32:5
9:25 [y] Ex 23:14; 2Ch 8:12-13,16
9:26 [z] 1Ki 22:48 [a] Nu 33:35; Dt 2:8
9:27 [b] 1Ki 10:11; Eze 27:8
9:28 [c] 1Ch 29:4
10:1 [d] Ge 10:7,28; Mt 12:42; Lk 11:31 [e] Jdg 14:12
10:5 [f] 1Ch 26:16
10:7 [g] 1Ch 29:25
10:8 [h] Pr 8:34
10:9 [i] 1Ki 5:7 [j] 2Sa 8:15; Ps 33:5; 72:2
10:10 [k] ver 2

9:22 did not make slaves. Obeys Lev 25:42,46.

9:24–25 Mentioning both Solomon's Egyptian wife and his worship life portrays ambiguous devotion.

9:24 Pharaoh's daughter. Cf. 3:1; 7:8; 11:1.

9:26 Ezion Geber. Nearby port; location uncertain. **Elath.** A town on the west coast of the modern Gulf of Aqaba. **in Edom.** Implies that Solomon either rules Edom or that Edom controls the port area. **Red Sea.** The large body of water between modern-day Sinai and Saudi Arabia.

9:28 Ophir. Perhaps somewhere along the east coast of Africa (see note on Ps 45:9). **420 talents.** See NIV text note; cf. 10:10–12,22; Job 28:16; Isa 13:12.

10:1–13 *The Queen of Sheba Visits Solomon.* The queen of Sheba personifies Solomon's international renown for wisdom, wealth, and political preeminence (cf. vv. 23–24; 4:31,34).

10:1 Sheba. Probably the kingdom of Saba (the Sabeans) in southern Arabia (modern Yemen); represents the area the new Red Sea fleet would visit. **relationship to the LORD.** This means either that the Lord's great reputation enhanced Solomon's reputation because he worshiped Yahweh or that Solomon's fine reputation in the region brought glory to the Lord.

10:3 The hallmark of a wise person without peer (Ps 49:4; Prov 1:6).

10:8 How happy your people must be! Betrays the queen's ignorance of popular resentment soon to disrupt Solomon's kingdom (12:4,16–18).

10:9 Praise be to the LORD. The queen of Sheba reads Solomon's wisdom and wealth as evidence of God's pleasure in him. Her beautiful confession shows that she fully understands Israel's covenant relationship with their God. But it should be understood in light of her polytheistic pagan background (cf. 5:7; see also 2 Chr 2:12; Dan 3:28–29). She simply recognizes that Yahweh is Israel's national God; she is not renouncing her god(s) to worship Israel's God exclusively (cf. 2 Kgs 5:15–19; Ruth 1:16–17). Hiram similarly delighted in God's choosing Solomon (5:7) without becoming a worshiper of Solomon's God.

10:10 Heads of state customarily exchanged lavish gifts when meeting (cf. vv. 13,24–25). **many spices.** Implies that spice trading was a major Sabean business. For other unparalleled items, see vv. 12,20.

10:11 [l]Ge 10:29; 1Ki 9:27-28
10:14 [m]1Ki 9:28
10:16 [n]1Ki 14:26-28
10:17 [o]1Ki 7:2
10:22 [p]1Ki 9:26
10:23 [q]1Ki 3:13 [r]1Ki 4:30
10:24 [s]1Ki 3:9,12,28
10:26 [t]Dt 17:16; 1Ki 4:26; 9:19; 2Ch 1:14; 9:25
10:27 [u]Dt 17:17
10:29 [v]2Ki 7:6-7

11 (Hiram's ships brought gold from Ophir;[l] and from there they brought great cargoes of almugwood[a] and precious stones. 12 The king used the almugwood to make supports[b] for the temple of the
LORD and for the royal palace, and to make harps and lyres for the musicians. So much almugwood has
never been imported or seen since that day.)
13 King Solomon gave the queen of Sheba all she desired and asked for, besides what he had given her
out of his royal bounty. Then she left and returned with her retinue to her own country.

Solomon's Splendor

10:14-29pp — 2Ch 1:14-17; 9:13-28

14 The weight of the gold[m] that Solomon received yearly was 666 talents,[c] 15 not including the revenues from merchants and traders and from all the Arabian kings and the governors of the territories.
16 King Solomon made two hundred large shields[n] of hammered gold; six hundred shekels[d] of gold
went into each shield. 17 He also made three hundred small shields of hammered gold, with three minas[e] of gold in each shield. The king put them in the Palace of the Forest of Lebanon.[o]
18 Then the king made a great throne covered with ivory and overlaid with fine gold. 19 The throne
had six steps, and its back had a rounded top. On both sides of the seat were armrests, with a lion standing beside each of them. 20 Twelve lions stood on the six steps, one at either end of each step. Nothing
like it had ever been made for any other kingdom. 21 All King Solomon's goblets were gold, and all the
household articles in the Palace of the Forest of Lebanon were pure gold. Nothing was made of silver,
because silver was considered of little value in Solomon's days. 22 The king had a fleet of trading ships[f][p]
at sea along with the ships of Hiram. Once every three years it returned, carrying gold, silver and ivory,
and apes and baboons.
23 King Solomon was greater in riches[q] and wisdom[r] than all the other kings of the earth. 24 The
whole world sought audience with Solomon to hear the wisdom[s] God had put in his heart. 25 Year after
year, everyone who came brought a gift — articles of silver and gold, robes, weapons and spices, and
horses and mules.
26 Solomon accumulated chariots and horses;[t] he had fourteen hundred chariots and twelve thousand horses,[g] which he kept in the chariot cities and also with him in Jerusalem. 27 The king made
silver as common[u] in Jerusalem as stones, and cedar as plentiful as sycamore-fig trees in the foothills.
28 Solomon's horses were imported from Egypt and from Kue[h] — the royal merchants purchased them
from Kue at the current price. 29 They imported a chariot from Egypt for six hundred shekels of silver,
and a horse for a hundred and fifty.[i] They also exported them to all the kings of the Hittites[v] and of
the Arameans.

[a] *11* Probably a variant of *algumwood*; also in verse 12 [b] *12* The meaning of the Hebrew for this word is uncertain. [c] *14* That is, about 25 tons or about 23 metric tons [d] *16* That is, about 15 pounds or about 6.9 kilograms; also in verse 29 [e] *17* That is, about 3 3/4 pounds or about 1.7 kilograms; or perhaps reference is to double minas, that is, about 7 1/2 pounds or about 3.5 kilograms. [f] *22* Hebrew *of ships of Tarshish* [g] *26* Or *charioteers* [h] *28* Probably *Cilicia* [i] *29* That is, about 3 3/4 pounds or about 1.7 kilograms

10:11 Cf. v. 22; 9:26–28. **almugwood.** Probably red sandalwood (see NIV text note).
10:12 never been imported or seen since. Implies that the Red Sea fleet later no longer sailed (cf. 22:48).
10:14–29 *Solomon's Splendor.* The portrait of Solomon's wealth and royal splendor reaches its climax. He is a monarch who resides in a luxurious royal quarter and presides over (and taxes) an international empire that a sizeable military protects and extends. Its closing glimpse of Solomon's splendid empire ominously foreshadows imminent divine judgment (ch. 11).
10:14 See NIV text note.
10:16 large shields. Probably full-length rectangles for full-body protection; they function here primarily as decorations (cf. 14:26–27).
10:17 small shields. Probably circle-shaped, heavier decorations. **Palace of the Forest of Lebanon.** See note on 7:2.
10:22 trading ships. These were vessels specially designed with large cargo space to facilitate long voyages.
10:26 accumulated chariots and horses. Befits a fast, highly maneuverable army (cf. 9:19,22). See note on v. 29.
10:28 Kue. An area (later called Cilicia) along the southeastern coast of Turkey.
10:29 Egypt. Source of enough horses for Solomon to sell some for profit. The reference is to the Neo-Hittites, Israel's important trading partner centered in northern Aram/Syria and southern Turkey. **Arameans.** From Aram/Syria. In Solomon's day, the Hittites and Arameans lived geographically intermingled. Bilingual inscriptions written in both Luwian (Neo-Hittite) and Aramaic have been found in the region. Ominously, however, Solomon's dealings clearly violate Deut 17:16–17, which expressly forbids kings from accumulating horses (especially not from Egypt), gold, and silver (vv. 14,25; 9:11,14,28). The hugely successful king stands liable to divine judgment for transgressing the Mosaic law, a judgment soon to unfold after he adds one more violation in ch. 11.

Solomon's Wives

11 King Solomon, however, loved many foreign women[w] besides Pharaoh's daughter — Moabites, Ammonites, Edomites, Sidonians and Hittites. 2They were from nations about which the LORD had told the Israelites, "You must not intermarry[x] with them, because they will surely turn your hearts after their gods." Nevertheless, Solomon held fast to them in love. 3He had seven hundred wives of royal birth and three hundred concubines, and his wives led him astray. 4As Solomon grew old, his wives turned his heart after other gods, and his heart was not fully devoted[y] to the LORD his God, as the heart of David his father had been. 5He followed Ashtoreth[z] the goddess of the Sidonians, and Molek[a] the detestable god of the Ammonites. 6So Solomon did evil in the eyes of the LORD; he did not follow the LORD completely, as David his father had done.

7On a hill east[b] of Jerusalem, Solomon built a high place for Chemosh[c] the detestable god of Moab, and for Molek[d] the detestable god of the Ammonites. 8He did the same for all his foreign wives, who burned incense and offered sacrifices to their gods.

9The LORD became angry with Solomon because his heart had turned away from the LORD, the God of Israel, who had appeared[e] to him twice. 10Although he had forbidden Solomon to follow other gods,[f] Solomon did not keep the LORD's command.[g] 11So the LORD said to Solomon, "Since this is your attitude and you have not kept my covenant and my decrees, which I commanded you, I will most certainly tear[h] the kingdom away from you and give it to one of your subordinates. 12Nevertheless, for the sake of David your father, I will not do it during your lifetime. I will tear it out of the hand of your son. 13Yet I will not tear the whole kingdom from him, but will give him one tribe[i] for the sake[j] of David my servant and for the sake of Jerusalem, which I have chosen."[k]

Solomon's Adversaries

14Then the LORD raised up against Solomon an adversary, Hadad the Edomite, from the royal line of Edom. 15Earlier when David was fighting with Edom, Joab the commander of the army, who had gone up to bury the dead, had struck down all the men in Edom.[l] 16Joab and all the Israelites stayed there for six months, until they had destroyed all the men in Edom. 17But Hadad, still only a boy, fled to Egypt with some Edomite officials who had served his father. 18They set out from Midian and went to Paran.[m] Then taking people from Paran with them, they went to Egypt, to Pharaoh king of Egypt, who gave Hadad a house and land and provided him with food.

11:1 [w] Dt 17:17; Ne 13:26
11:2 [x] Ex 34:16; Dt 7:3-4
11:4 [y] 1Ki 8:61; 9:4
11:5 [z] ver 33; Jdg 2:13; 2Ki 23:13 [a] ver 7
11:7 [b] 2Ki 23:13 [c] Nu 21:29; Jdg 11:24 [d] Lev 20:2-5; Ac 7:43
11:9 [e] ver 2-3; 1Ki 3:5; 9:2
11:10 [f] 1Ki 9:6 [g] 1Ki 6:12
11:11 [h] ver 31; 1Ki 12:15-16; 2Ki 17:21
11:13 [i] 1Ki 12:20 [j] 2Sa 7:15 [k] Dt 12:11
11:15 [l] Dt 20:13; 2Sa 8:14; 1Ch 18:12
11:18 [m] Nu 10:12

11:1–43 *Solomon's Condemnation.* The account of how Solomon's reign ends features his foreign wives (vv. 1–13) and adversaries (vv. 14–25), Jeroboam's rebellion (vv. 26–40), and the king's death (vv. 41–43).

11:1–13 *Solomon's Wives.* The upbeat display of Solomon's wisdom, fame, and splendor (chs. 3–10) sharply contrasts the sober, ominous indictment that his foreign wives violate the conditions attached to God's promise to David (cf. 2:4; 9:4–5).

11:1 Moabites, Ammonites, Edomites. Eastern and southern vassals of David and Solomon (2 Sam 8:2,9–14; 12:26–31). **Sidonians.** See note on 5:6. **Hittites.** See note on 10:29 ("Arameans").

11:2 You must not intermarry with them. Applies the prohibition against intermarriage with Canaanites (Deut 7:1–6; Josh 23:12–13) to non-Canaanites. **turn your hearts after their gods.** Intermarriage risks diverting devotion from Yahweh (cf. v. 3). **in love.** Genuine affection, not marriage for commerce or politics.

11:4 grew old. Increased Solomon's vulnerability to his wives' influence. Marrying Pharaoh's daughter was his first misstep (3:1; 7:8; 9:24). **after other gods.** Implies actual worship rather than mere tolerance. **not fully devoted.** Seriously departs from David's example (cf. v. 6; 15:3).

11:5 Ashtoreth. A goddess sometimes associated with Baal (cf. ch. 18) and widely popular in Phoenicia and Canaan (also known as Astarte); cf. v. 33; 14:15; 2 Kgs 23:13; see note on Judg 2:13. Compares to Mesopotamian Ishtar and Greco-Roman Aphrodite and Venus. **Molek.** Means "king, ruler" (see note on Jer 49:1) The Ammonite version of Baal; associated with child sacrifice (see 2 Kgs 23:10,13; Lev 18:21 and note). Also known as Milkom (see 2 Sam 12:30 and first NIV text note there).

11:7 hill east of Jerusalem. The Mount of Olives today. **high place.** See note on 3:2. **Chemosh.** The Moabite god mentioned in the Mesha Stele (ca. 840 BC), a stone monument with King Mesha's testimony of how Chemosh freed Moab from rule by Israel and restored its lands (cf. Num 21:29; Jer 48:7). See photo, p. 659.

11:9 twice. See 3:5–14; 9:1–9.

11:11 The disaster to follow disciplines Solomon for violating God's covenant with David. **one of your subordinates.** Cf. vv. 26–40; ch. 12.

11:12 for the sake of David. God honors David's loyal devotion by allowing his dynasty to continue (cf. v. 14; 2 Sam 7:14–15).

11:13 one tribe. Probably Benjamin (cf. 12:20–21), presuming that Solomon's successor, Rehoboam, already has authority over Judah (see note on vv. 31–32). **for the sake of Jerusalem.** Implies God's loyalty to his chosen city (cf. vv. 29–39).

11:14–25 *Solomon's Adversaries.* Rebellions on Solomon's eastern flank signal the end of his empire and bode ill for the survival of his magnificent kingdom. Hadad and Rezon, instruments of divine judgment, each pose a serious threat to Solomon and his kingdom.

11:14 Hadad. Edomite king and Pharaoh's son-in-law (v. 19); enjoyed Egypt's backing against Solomon.

11:15 Cf. 2 Sam 8:11–14.

11:18 Midian. Northeastern Arabia along the modern Gulf of Aqaba. **Paran.** Location unknown but near the Desert of Sinai (Num 10:12).

SOLOMON'S ADVERSARIES

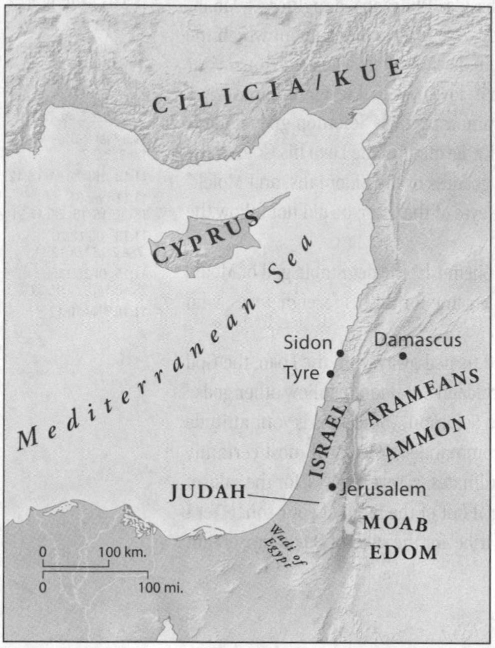

19 Pharaoh was so pleased with Hadad that he gave him a sister of his own wife, Queen Tahpenes, in marriage. 20 The sister of Tahpenes bore him a son named Genubath, whom Tahpenes brought up in the royal palace. There Genubath lived with Pharaoh's own children.

21 While he was in Egypt, Hadad heard that David rested with his ancestors and that Joab the commander of the army was also dead. Then Hadad said to Pharaoh, "Let me go, that I may return to my own country."

22 "What have you lacked here that you want to go back to your own country?" Pharaoh asked.

"Nothing," Hadad replied, "but do let me go!"

23 And God raised up against Solomon another adversary,[n] Rezon son of Eliada, who had fled from his master, Hadadezer[o] king of Zobah. 24 When David destroyed Zobah's army, Rezon gathered a band of men around him and became their leader; they went to Damascus,[p] where they settled and took control. 25 Rezon was Israel's adversary as long as Solomon lived, adding to the trouble caused by Hadad. So Rezon ruled in Aram[q] and was hostile toward Israel.

Jeroboam Rebels Against Solomon

26 Also, Jeroboam son of Nebat rebelled[r] against the king. He was one of Solomon's officials, an Ephraimite from Zeredah, and his mother was a widow named Zeruah.

27 Here is the account of how he rebelled against the king: Solomon had built the terraces[a][s] and had filled in the gap in the wall of the city of David his father. 28 Now Jeroboam was a man of standing,[t] and when Solomon saw how well[u] the young man did his work, he put him in charge of the whole labor force of the tribes of Joseph.

29 About that time Jeroboam was going out of Jerusalem, and Ahijah[v] the prophet of Shiloh met him on the way, wearing a new cloak. The two of them were alone out in the country, 30 and Ahijah took hold of the new cloak he was wearing and tore[w] it into twelve pieces. 31 Then he said to Jeroboam, "Take ten pieces for yourself, for this is what the LORD, the God of Israel, says: 'See, I am going to tear[x] the kingdom out of Solomon's hand and give you ten tribes. 32 But for the sake of my servant David and the city of Jerusalem, which I have chosen out of all the tribes of Israel, he will have one

11:23 [n] ver 14 [o] 2Sa 8:3
11:24 [p] 2Sa 8:5; 10:8,18
11:25 [q] 2Sa 10:19
11:26 [r] 2Sa 20:21; 1Ki 12:2; 2Ch 13:6
11:27 [s] 1Ki 9:24
11:28 [t] Ru 2:1 [u] Pr 22:29
11:29 [v] 1Ki 12:15; 14:2; 2Ch 9:29
11:30 [w] 1Sa 15:27
11:31 [x] ver 11

[a] 27 Or *the Millo*

11:19–20 Queen Tahpenes ... sister of Tahpenes. Two unknown Egyptian women.
11:24 destroyed Zobah's army. Cf. 2 Sam 8:3–8; 10:15–19. **Damascus.** Capital city of the Arameans; popular desert caravan stop (cf. 15:18; note at 19:15).
11:25 Rezon. Conqueror and ruler of Damascus (v. 24). **hostile toward Israel.** A persistent threatening attitude too serious to ignore.
11:26–40 *Jeroboam Rebels Against Solomon.* Jeroboam's rebellion poses the greatest threat to Solomon because Jeroboam has exemplary leadership qualities and because the prophet Ahijah authorized Jeroboam to act.
11:27 Here is the account. See note on 9:15. **terraces.** See note on 9:15.
11:28 man of standing. Designates an impressive, highly respected person (cf. Ruth 2:1; 1 Sam 9:1). **in charge of the whole labor force.** Exposed Jeroboam to grievances that Israelite workers harbored against Solomon. **tribes of Joseph.** Ephraim and Manasseh (Gen 46:20; Josh 17:17; 2 Sam 19:20).
11:29 Ahijah. For his later dealings with Jeroboam and his family, see 14:1–18; 15:29. **prophet.** Through whom Yahweh customarily authorized kings to rule (cf. 2 Kgs 9:1–6; Hos 8:4). **Shiloh.** About 20 miles (32 kilometers) north of Jerusalem; previously Israel's informal capital (Josh 18:1; 22:12); later the site of Israel's central sanctuary (1 Sam 1:3; 3:21; 4:3–4).
11:30 tore it into twelve pieces. Symbolic action in connection with a prophetic announcement is a common device among prophets (cf. Isa 20; Jer 27; Ezek 4–5). Here it visually illustrates the message that follows (vv. 31–39).
11:31–32 ten tribes ... one tribe. The eleven-tribe total either excludes Levi (it belongs to Yahweh; see Num 3:11–13) or counts Judah and Benjamin as one tribe (Judah later absorbed Benjamin as it had Simeon previously; cf. v. 13; 12:21; Josh 19:1–9). The understanding that the northern and southern tribes comprise distinct political units first emerges in Judg 5:13–18. A continuing corridor of non-Israelites from Jebusite Jerusalem west to Canaanite Gezer (see 9:16–17) may have created the north-south tribal separation. The distinction explains why David first became king of Judah (2 Sam 2:4) before the northern tribes also recognized him, thus forming a unified kingdom. David's capture of Jerusalem (2 Sam 5:6–7) and the gift of Gezer to Solomon's

tribe. 33 I will do this because they have[a] forsaken me and worshiped[y] Ashtoreth the goddess of the
Sidonians, Chemosh the god of the Moabites, and Molek the god of the Ammonites, and have not
walked in obedience to me, nor done what is right in my eyes, nor kept my decrees[z] and laws as
David, Solomon's father, did.

34 " 'But I will not take the whole kingdom out of Solomon's hand; I have made him ruler all the days
of his life for the sake of David my servant, whom I chose and who obeyed my commands and decrees.
35 I will take the kingdom from his son's hands and give you ten tribes. 36 I will give one tribe[a] to his son
so that David my servant may always have a lamp[b] before me in Jerusalem, the city where I chose to put
my Name. 37 However, as for you, I will take you, and you will rule over all that your heart desires;[c] you
will be king over Israel. 38 If you do whatever I command you and walk in obedience to me and do what
is right in my eyes by obeying my decrees[d] and commands, as David my servant did, I will be with you.
I will build you a dynasty[e] as enduring as the one I built for
David and will give Israel to you. 39 I will humble David's
descendants because of this, but not forever.' "

40 Solomon tried to kill Jeroboam, but Jeroboam fled to
Egypt, to Shishak[f] the king, and stayed there until Solomon's death.

Solomon's Death

11:41-43pp — 2Ch 9:29-31

41 As for the other events of Solomon's reign — all he did
and the wisdom he displayed — are they not written in the
book of the annals of Solomon? 42 Solomon reigned in Jerusalem over all Israel forty years. 43 Then he rested with his
ancestors and was buried in the city of David his father. And
Rehoboam[g] his son succeeded him as king.

Israel Rebels Against Rehoboam

12:1-24pp — 2Ch 10:1 – 11:4

12 Rehoboam went to Shechem, for all Israel had gone
there to make him king. 2 When Jeroboam son of Nebat heard this (he was still in Egypt, where he had fled[h] from
King Solomon), he returned from[b] Egypt. 3 So they sent for

[a] 33 Hebrew; Septuagint, Vulgate and Syriac *because he has*
[b] 2 Or *he remained in*

11:33 [y] ver 5-7 [z] 1Ki 3:3
11:36 [a] ver 13; 1Ki 12:17 [b] 1Ki 15:4; 2Ki 8:19
11:37 [c] 2Sa 3:21
11:38 [d] Dt 17:19 [e] Jos 1:5; 2Sa 7:11,27
11:40 [f] 2Ch 12:2
11:43 [g] 1Ki 14:21; Mt 1:7
12:2 [h] 1Ki 11:40

Carved ivory image of King Hadadezer of Damascus (ninth–eighth century BC).

Erich Lessing/Art Resource, NY

Egyptian wife (1 Kgs 9:16 – 17) finally unite Israel territorially, but the two political blocks separate again after Solomon's death (see ch. 12).
11:33 Repeats vv. 4 – 8 but now holds all Israel guilty of those sins.
11:36 lamp before me in Jerusalem. Symbolizes the continuation of the Davidic dynasty as God promised and in the city where the Lord's Name dwells (cf. 15:4; 2 Kgs 8:19; Ps 132:17). Elsewhere, a lamp's burning represents a life flourishing, while its snuffing out means death (2 Sam 21:17; Job 18:6; 21:17; Ps 18:28; Prov 13:9; 24:20).
11:37 Israel. The northern ten tribes.
11:38 as David ... did. The standard for Jeroboam's reign.
11:40 Shishak. Jeroboam's host in Egypt (vv. 16 – 20), Pharaoh Shoshonq I (ca. 931 – 910 BC), who will lead an invasion against Rehoboam (14:25 – 26).
11:41 – 43 *Solomon's Death.* A typical regnal summary brings the report on Solomon's reign to an end and introduces his successor, Rehoboam.
11:41 annals of Solomon. Unknown source; probably the archival records for ch. 1 – 11 (cf. 14:19,29).
11:43 city of David. See note on 2:10.
12:1 — 16:34 *The Kings of Israel and Judah Until Ahab.* This series of short sections narrates the first half century of the divided kingdom of Israel and Judah after Solomon died. Skirmishes over the location of their common border erupt and continue, while idolatry and political instability in Israel contrasts with the stable Davidic dynasty in Judah.
12:1 – 24 *Israel Rebels Against Rehoboam.* The northern tribes seek relief from Solomon's harsh labor requirements, but Rehoboam foolishly threatens an increase in demands. The tribes reject Rehoboam and appoint Jeroboam as king, and the unified kingdom that David and Solomon ruled divides.
12:1 Shechem. A major ancient city and favorite religious center for northern tribes about 40 miles (64 kilometers) north of Jerusalem (cf. v. 25; Josh 24). Occupies a small valley between Mounts Gerizim and Ebal where two major highways crisscross (see Deut 27). **all Israel.** Means representatives of the northern tribes (vv. 16,20 – 21; 2 Sam 5:5). **make him king.** The northern tribes had previously made a personal covenant with David (2 Sam 5:3), so this meeting is to renew their loyalty to the Davidic monarchy (cf. v. 4; 2 Sam 5:1 – 5). Negotiation of the terms of that renewed submission is part of the process.
12:3 Jeroboam. Respected royal official and recipient of Ahijah's prophecy against Solomon. Perhaps aware of its contents, Solomon had tried

12:4 [i] 1Sa 8:11-18; 1Ki 4:20-28
12:6 [j] 1Ki 4:2
12:7 [k] Pr 15:1
12:14 [l] Ex 1:14; 5:5-9,16-18
12:15 [m] ver 24; Dt 2:30; Jdg 14:4; 2Ch 22:7; 25:20 [n] 1Ki 11:29
12:16 [o] 2Sa 20:1
12:17 [p] 1Ki 11:13,36
12:18 [q] 2Sa 20:24; 1Ki 4:6; 5:14
12:19 [r] 2Ki 17:21
12:20 [s] 1Ki 11:13,32

Jeroboam, and he and the whole assembly of Israel went to Rehoboam and said to him: 4"Your father put a
heavy yoke[i] on us, but now lighten the harsh labor and the heavy yoke he put on us, and we will serve you."
5Rehoboam answered, "Go away for three days and then come back to me." So the people went away.
6Then King Rehoboam consulted the elders[j] who had served his father Solomon during his lifetime.
"How would you advise me to answer these people?" he asked.
7They replied, "If today you will be a servant to these people and serve them and give them a favorable answer,[k] they will always be your servants."
8But Rehoboam rejected the advice the elders gave him and consulted the young men who had
grown up with him and were serving him. 9He asked them, "What is your advice? How should we answer
these people who say to me, 'Lighten the yoke your father put on us'?"
10The young men who had grown up with him replied, "These people have said to you, 'Your father
put a heavy yoke on us, but make our yoke lighter.' Now tell them, 'My little finger is thicker than my
father's waist. 11My father laid on you a heavy yoke; I will make it even heavier. My father scourged you
with whips; I will scourge you with scorpions.' "
12Three days later Jeroboam and all the people returned to Rehoboam, as the king had said, "Come
back to me in three days." 13The king answered the people harshly. Rejecting the advice given him by
the elders, 14he followed the advice of the young men and said, "My father made your yoke heavy; I will
make it even heavier. My father scourged[l] you with whips; I will scourge you with scorpions." 15So the
king did not listen to the people, for this turn of events was from the LORD,[m] to fulfill the word the LORD
had spoken to Jeroboam son of Nebat through Ahijah[n] the Shilonite.
16When all Israel saw that the king refused to listen to them, they answered the king:

> "What share do we have in David,
> what part in Jesse's son?
> To your tents, Israel![o]
> Look after your own house, David!"

So the Israelites went home. 17But as for the Israelites who were living in the towns of Judah,[p] Rehoboam still ruled over them.
18King Rehoboam sent out Adoniram,[a][q] who was in charge of forced labor, but all Israel stoned him
to death. King Rehoboam, however, managed to get into his chariot and escape to Jerusalem. 19So Israel
has been in rebellion against the house of David[r] to this day.
20When all the Israelites heard that Jeroboam had returned, they sent and called him to the assembly and made him king over all Israel. Only the tribe of Judah remained loyal to the house of David.[s]
21When Rehoboam arrived in Jerusalem, he mustered all Judah and the tribe of Benjamin—

[a] *18* Some Septuagint manuscripts and Syriac (see also 4:6 and 5:14); Hebrew *Adoram*

to kill Jeroboam, but Jeroboam fled and took refuge with Pharaoh Shishak in Egypt until Solomon died (v. 2; 11:28,40). That the northern tribes asks him to attend the assembly attests their high regard for him.
12:4 heavy yoke … harsh labor. Voices popular resentment of Solomon's compulsory labor and heavy taxation (4:6–19; 5:13–18). In antiquity, new kings customarily granted their subjects concessions.
12:6 elders. A mature, seasoned advisory group from Solomon's cabinet.
12:7 favorable answer. Grant concessions to retain tribal loyalty.
12:8 young men. The king's inexperienced peers, compared to the advisors with years of experience serving Solomon. Rehoboam himself became king when he was 41 years of age (14:21).
12:10 My little finger is thicker than my father's waist. This may be a proverb asserting that Rehoboam's weakest demands will far surpass his father's harshest ones. "Little finger" may refer to the king's sexual organ and draw on the ancient Near Eastern association of sexual potency with power (cf. ch. 1). It claims that Rehoboam will be a more powerful king than his father, i.e., that his policy demands will far outdo Solomon's. Rather than relief, Rehoboam threatens the northern tribes with the opposite—increased demands and increased enforcement of them (see v. 11).
12:11 scorpions. Whips embedded with nails or sharp metal shards to inflict an especially painful scourge. The tribes can expect intense, painful consequences—a scorpion-like sting—for noncompliance with the king's policies.
12:15 this turn of events was from the LORD. God invisibly, sovereignly guided the sequence of events—the tribes' discontent, Jeroboam's emergence, the composition and deliberations of Rehoboam's advisors—that culminates in the king's decision (cf. v. 24; 22:20–34). **to fulfill the word the LORD had spoken.** Cf. 11:29–39; see notes on 6:11; 13:1.
12:16 What share do we have in David … ? Angrily renounces fealty to the Davidic monarchy; echoes Sheba's earlier derision of David (2 Sam 20:1); possibly a popular political slogan among the northern tribes. **tents.** Alludes to Israel's presettlement (and premonarchical) nomadic life to underscore the tribes' radical break with David's dynasty.
12:17 still ruled. Fulfills the one-tribe provision of Ahijah's prophecy (11:13,36).
12:18 Adoniram. An ill-fated royal administrator (cf. 5:14); symptomatic of pent-up popular anger. **escape to Jerusalem.** Confirms that Rehoboam no longer rules the northern ten tribes (cf. 11:31,35).
12:21 Judah and the tribe of Benjamin. Cf. v. 23; 11:31.

The high place at Dan where the golden calf was displayed (1 Kgs 12:30).

a hundred and eighty thousand able young men — to go to war[t] against Israel and to regain the
kingdom for Rehoboam son of Solomon.
22 But this word of God came to Shemaiah[u] the man of God: 23 "Say to Rehoboam son of Solomon
king of Judah, to all Judah and Benjamin, and to the rest of the people, 24 'This is what the LORD says: Do
not go up to fight against your brothers, the Israelites. Go home, every one of you, for this is my doing.' "
So they obeyed the word of the LORD and went home again, as the LORD had ordered.

Golden Calves at Bethel and Dan

25 Then Jeroboam fortified Shechem[v] in the hill country of Ephraim and lived there. From there he
went out and built up Peniel.[a][w]
26 Jeroboam thought to himself, "The kingdom will now likely revert to the house of David. 27 If
these people go up to offer sacrifices at the temple of the LORD in Jerusalem,[x] they will again give their
allegiance to their lord, Rehoboam king of Judah. They will kill me and return to King Rehoboam."
28 After seeking advice, the king made two golden calves.[y] He said to the people, "It is too much for
you to go up to Jerusalem. Here are your gods, Israel, who brought you up out of Egypt."[z] 29 One he set
up in Bethel,[a] and the other in Dan.[b] 30 And this thing became a sin;[c] the people came to worship the
one at Bethel and went as far as Dan to worship the other.[b]

12:21 [t] 2Ch 11:1
12:22 [u] 2Ch 12:5-7
12:25 [v] Jdg 9:45 [w] Jdg 8:8,17
12:27 [x] Dt 12:5-6
12:28 [y] Ex 32:4; 2Ki 10:29; 17:16 [z] Ex 32:8
12:29 [a] Ge 28:19 [b] Jdg 18:27-31
12:30 [c] 1Ki 13:34; 2Ki 17:21

[a] 25 Hebrew *Penuel,* a variant of *Peniel* [b] 30 Probable reading of the original Hebrew text; Masoretic Text *people went to the one as far as Dan*

12:22 man of God. A common way to refer to a prophet (see, e.g., 13:1; 17:18; 20:28; 2 Kgs 4:7; 13:19; Deut 33:1; 1 Sam 2:27; 9:9–10). **12:24 This is what the LORD says.** The messenger formula identifies who sent the message and alerts the recipient(s) to hear it (13:2; 20:13,14; 21:19; 22:11; 2 Kgs 3:16; 9:3; 22:16). **this is my doing.** Through a prophetic message, God informs Rehoboam that divine action, not human scheming, brought about the kingdom's division, sparing Judah a futile, disastrous war. Similarly, the Pharisee Gamaliel later counsels the Sanhedrin to release, not punish, the apostles lest the Jewish leaders find themselves "fighting against God" and powerless to stop Jesus' followers (Acts 5:34–39). **12:25–33** *Golden Calves at Bethel and Dan.* Despite his divine appointment, King Jeroboam fears that pilgrimages to the temple will drive his subjects to kill him and return to Rehoboam. He oversteps his authority and violates the Torah when he creates an alternative religious system and appoints its clergy to keep the people away from Jerusalem. **12:25 fortified Shechem.** Defensive preparations in case Rehoboam invades. Shechem (see note on v. 1) was Jeroboam's new capital. **Peniel.** A popular ford east of the Jordan River near the Jabbok River; Jacob wrestled with God there (Gen 32:30–31). **12:28 golden calves.** Probably bulls, symbolizing power and fertility (cf. 7:25; 14:9). This violates prohibitions against image-making (Exod 20:4–6; Deut 4:15–19; 5:8–10). **Here are your gods.** A partial verbatim replica of Exod 32:4,8 that compares this event to the golden calf episode in which both the people and Aaron sinned. **12:29 Bethel.** The northern kingdom's southern border; about 11 miles (17.7 kilometers) from Jerusalem. Jacob's encounter with Yahweh there (Gen 28:10–22) had already established the town as a sacred shrine (Judg 20:18–28). **Dan.** See note on 1 Sam 3:20. **12:30 became a sin.** Implies that people actually worshiped the calves. 1–2 Kings tags such worship as "the sin(s) of Jeroboam" that doomed Israel (13:34; 16:26; 22:52; 2 Kgs 17:21; 23:15).

12:31 [d] 1Ki 13:32 [e] Nu 3:10; 1Ki 13:33; 2Ki 17:32; 2Ch 11:14-15; 13:9
12:32 [f] Lev 23:33-34; Nu 29:12
12:33 [g] Nu 15:39; 1Ki 13:1; Am 7:13
13:1 [h] 2Ki 23:17 [i] 1Ki 12:32-33
13:2 [j] 2Ki 23:15-16,20
13:3 [k] Jdg 6:17; Isa 7:14; Jn 2:11; 1Co 1:22
13:6 [l] Ex 8:8; 9:28; 10:17; Lk 6:27-28; Ac 8:24; Jas 5:16
13:7 [m] 1Sa 9:7; 2Ki 5:15
13:8 [n] Nu 22:18; 24:13 [o] ver 16

31 Jeroboam built shrines[d] on high places and appointed priests[e] from all sorts of people, even
though they were not Levites. 32 He instituted a festival on the fifteenth day of the eighth[f] month, like
the festival held in Judah, and offered sacrifices on the altar. This he did in Bethel, sacrificing to the
calves he had made. And at Bethel he also installed priests at the high places he had made. 33 On the
fifteenth day of the eighth month, a month of his own choosing, he offered sacrifices on the altar he
had built at Bethel.[g] So he instituted the festival for the Israelites and went up to the altar to make
offerings.

The Man of God From Judah

13 By the word of the LORD a man of God[h] came from Judah to Bethel,[i] as Jeroboam was standing
by the altar to make an offering. 2 By the word of the LORD he cried out against the altar: "Altar,
altar! This is what the LORD says: 'A son named Josiah[j] will be born to the house of David. On you he will
sacrifice the priests of the high places who make offerings here, and human bones will be burned on
you.' " 3 That same day the man of God gave a sign:[k] "This is the sign the LORD has declared: The altar
will be split apart and the ashes on it will be poured out."

4 When King Jeroboam heard what the man of God cried out against the altar at Bethel, he stretched
out his hand from the altar and said, "Seize him!" But the hand he stretched out toward the man
shriveled up, so that he could not pull it back. 5 Also, the altar was split apart and its ashes poured out
according to the sign given by the man of God by the word of the LORD.

6 Then the king said to the man of God, "Intercede[l] with the LORD your God and pray for me that my
hand may be restored." So the man of God interceded with the LORD, and the king's hand was restored
and became as it was before.

7 The king said to the man of God, "Come home with me for a meal, and I will give you a gift."[m]

8 But the man of God answered the king, "Even if you were to give me half your possessions,[n] I would
not go with you, nor would I eat bread[o] or drink water here. 9 For I was commanded by the word of the
LORD: 'You must not eat bread or drink water or return by the way you came.' " 10 So he took another
road and did not return by the way he had come to Bethel.

11 Now there was a certain old prophet living in Bethel, whose sons came and told him all that the
man of God had done there that day. They also told their father what he had said to the king. 12 Their
father asked them, "Which way did he go?" And his sons showed him which road the man of God from
Judah had taken. 13 So he said to his sons, "Saddle the donkey for me." And when they had saddled the

12:31 high places. See note on 3:2. **not Levites.** Violates Deut 18:1–8; cf. 1 Kgs 13:33.

12:32 festival. The identity of this event is unclear. It could be the Festival of Tabernacles, but its date suggests otherwise. **fifteenth day of the eighth month.** Exactly a month later than the Tabernacles celebration that Judah would observe in Jerusalem the 15th to the 21st of the seventh month (see note on 8:2; cf. Lev 23:34; Num 29:12–38). **offered sacrifices on the altar.** Means that Jeroboam performed the duties of a priest, overstepping the boundary between priest and king (cf. 2 Chr 26:16–21).

13:1–34 *The Man of God From Judah.* Two incidents at Bethel, the northern sanctuary nearest Jerusalem, sound three themes that echo across the rest of 1–2 Kings: prophets of Yahweh condemn sinful kings (vv. 1–10; cf. Deut 18:15–22; Jer 28); God's people must distinguish between true and false prophecy (vv. 11–32); and Jeroboam's legacy is disastrous (vv. 33–34). Verses 1–32 address King Jeroboam, v. 33 reports his response, and v. 34 summarizes his negative impact on Israel. Jeroboam marks the first of a long, sordid history of evil northern monarchs who continue Jeroboam's policy and thus imperil Israel.

13:1 By the word of the LORD. The chapter's key thematic phrase. Means the spoken message God has commissioned the prophet to give King Jeroboam (vv. 2,5,9,17,18,32; cf. vv. 20,21,26). Divine initiative drives the story. **man of God.** See note on 12:22. **came from Judah to Bethel.** God's sending to the northern kingdom a prophet from the southern kingdom underscores that Yahweh remains the sovereign covenant God of all his people and warns Jeroboam that his competing religious system is illegitimate because no prophetic word authorized it. Two centuries later another prophet from the southern kingdom, Amos, visits Bethel to condemn the northern kingdom's worship and its royal patron, Jeroboam II (Amos 7:10–17; cf. 2 Kgs 23:15–20). See note on 6:11.

13:2 altar. Personifies Jeroboam's evil religious program. **This is what the LORD says.** See v. 21; see also note on 12:24. **Josiah.** King of Judah three centuries later (641/40–609 BC) who fulfills this prophecy (cf. 2 Kgs 23:15–16). **sacrifice the priests.** Defiles the altar and renders it unusable.

13:3 sign. A visible prophetic action to confirm the certainty of a prophecy's fulfillment. This short-term prediction aims to validate that the long-term prophecy is genuine (Deut 18:21–22). See v. 5 for this fulfillment.

13:6 Intercede. Prophetic mediation with God on behalf of humans (cf. Gen 20:7; 1 Sam 7:5; Jer 7:16; 14:11). **restored.** Confirms that the intercessor is a trustworthy man of God (cf. v. 1).

13:9 A meal with Jeroboam at Bethel might imply that the prophet tolerates the king's idolatry.

13:10 Acts out that the prophet disapproves of the site (cf. v. 17).

13:11 sons … father. Probably not kinship but a guild of prophet apprentices at Bethel that the old prophet led (cf. vv. 18,20,25). This was often called the "company of the prophets" (20:35; 2 Kgs 2:2–3).

donkey for him, he mounted it 14and rode after the man of God. He found him sitting under an oak tree
and asked, "Are you the man of God who came from Judah?"
"I am," he replied.
15So the prophet said to him, "Come home with me and eat."
16The man of God said, "I cannot turn back and go with you, nor can I eat bread[p] or drink water
with you in this place. 17I have been told by the word of the LORD: 'You must not eat bread or drink water
there or return by the way you came.' "
18The old prophet answered, "I too am a prophet, as you are. And an angel said to me by the word of
the LORD: 'Bring him back with you to your house so that he may eat bread and drink water.' " (But he
was lying[q] to him.) 19So the man of God returned with him and ate and drank in his house.
20While they were sitting at the table, the word of the LORD came to the old prophet who had brought
him back. 21He cried out to the man of God who had come from Judah, "This is what the LORD says: 'You
have defied[r] the word of the LORD and have not kept the command the LORD your God gave you. 22You
came back and ate bread and drank water in the place where he told you not to eat or drink. Therefore
your body will not be buried in the tomb of your ancestors.' "
23When the man of God had finished eating and drinking, the prophet who had brought him back
saddled his donkey for him. 24As he went on his way, a lion[s] met him on the road and killed him, and
his body was left lying on the road, with both the donkey and the lion standing beside it. 25Some people who passed by saw the body lying there, with the lion standing beside the body, and they went and
reported it in the city where the old prophet lived.
26When the prophet who had brought him back from his journey heard of it, he said, "It is the man
of God who defied the word of the LORD. The LORD has given him over to the lion, which has mauled
him and killed him, as the word of the LORD had warned him."
27The prophet said to his sons, "Saddle the donkey for me," and they did so. 28Then he went
out and found the body lying on the road, with the donkey and the lion standing beside it. The
lion had neither eaten the body nor mauled the donkey. 29So the prophet picked up the body of
the man of God, laid it on the donkey, and brought it back to his own city to mourn for him and
bury him. 30Then he laid the body in his own tomb, and they mourned over him and said, "Alas,
my brother!"[t]
31After burying him, he said to his sons, "When I die, bury me in the grave where the man of God is
buried; lay my bones[u] beside his bones. 32For the message he declared by the word of the LORD against
the altar in Bethel and against all the shrines on the high places[v] in the towns of Samaria[w] will certainly come true."[x]
33Even after this, Jeroboam did not change his evil ways, but once more appointed priests for the
high places from all sorts[y] of people. Anyone who wanted to become a priest he consecrated for the
high places. 34This was the sin[z] of the house of Jeroboam that led to its downfall and to its destruction[a]
from the face of the earth.

13:16 [p] ver 8
13:18 [q] Dt 13:3
13:21 [r] ver 26
13:24 [s] 1Ki 20:36
13:30 [t] Jer 22:18
13:31 [u] 2Ki 23:18
13:32 [v] ver 2; Lev 26:30 [w] 1Ki 16:24,28 [x] 2Ki 23:16
13:33 [y] 1Ki 12:31; 2Ch 11:15; 13:9
13:34 [z] 1Ki 12:30 [a] 1Ki 14:10

13:18 Bring him back. Contradicts what the man of God already knows; lacks the expected, "Thus says the LORD" (cf. v. 21; 22:27). **lying.** Implies that the man of God may have missed subtle cues to the deception.
13:21 You have defied the word of the LORD. Rejection of a prophecy already received makes the defiant recipient liable to divine judgment (vv. 22,24). See notes on v. 1; 6:11.
13:22 not be buried in the tomb of your ancestors. A painful, lonely, and humiliating fate (cf. v. 30; 2 Kgs 9:28; 2 Sam 2:32).
13:24 killed him. The fulfillment of the prophecy (vv. 21–22). It warns Jeroboam not to defy God's message lest divine judgment also destroy him.
13:25 reported it in the city. News of the miracle reached Bethel, where the prophet authenticates it as judgment by connecting it with the man of God's defiance (v. 26). For Jeroboam's response, see v. 33.
13:28 The passive lion and donkey personify silent awe before God's dramatic intervention. Normally a donkey would run and a lion would devour both it and the corpse, but here both recognize the fall of divine judgment. The man of God receives what his defiance deserves.
13:30 own tomb. Fulfills v. 22.
13:31 bury me in the grave. By seeking burial with the man of God, the old prophet signals that he sides with the former's prediction and personally authenticates it as genuine, notwithstanding the man of God's disobedience (v. 32). The prophet's concurrence may also imply that prophecy from the southern kingdom is more reliable than that coming from the northern kingdom and possibly tainted by Jeroboam's influence.
13:32 certainly come true. That the prophecy condemning the man of God was fulfilled convinces the old prophet that the man of God's prophecy against the altar in Bethel will also be fulfilled (vv. 1–3). He assumes that the hallmark of genuine prophecy is that its predictions are fulfilled (Jer 28:8–9).
13:33 Even after this. Contrasts Jeroboam's lack of repentance with the repentance of the prophet. The king's defiance earns him divine judgment (v. 34).
13:34 sin of the house of Jeroboam. The reason Jeroboam will leave neither dynasty nor survivors (cf. 12:30; 14:1–20).

14:2 [b] 1Sa 28:8; 2Sa 14:2; 1Ki 11:29
14:3 [c] 1Sa 9:7
14:7 [d] 2Sa 12:7-8; 1Ki 16:2
14:8 [e] 1Ki 11:31,33,38 [f] 1Ki 15:5
14:9 [g] Ex 34:17; 1Ki 12:28; 2Ch 11:15 [h] Ne 9:26; Ps 50:17; Eze 23:35
14:10 [i] Dt 32:36; 1Ki 21:21; 2Ki 9:8-9; 14:26 [j] 1Ki 15:29
14:11 [k] 1Ki 16:4; 21:24
14:13 [l] 2Ch 12:12; 19:3
14:15 [m] Dt 29:28; 2Ki 15:29; 17:6; Ps 52:5 [n] Jos 23:15-16 [o] Ex 34:13; Dt 12:3
14:16 [p] 1Ki 12:30; 13:34; 15:30,34; 16:2
14:17 [q] ver 12; 1Ki 15:33; 16:6-9

Ahijah's Prophecy Against Jeroboam

14 At that time Abijah son of Jeroboam became ill, [2]and Jeroboam said to his wife, "Go, disguise yourself, so you won't be recognized as the wife of Jeroboam. Then go to Shiloh. Ahijah[b] the prophet is there — the one who told me I would be king over this people. [3]Take ten loaves of bread[c] with you, some cakes and a jar of honey, and go to him. He will tell you what will happen to the boy." [4]So Jeroboam's wife did what he said and went to Ahijah's house in Shiloh.

Now Ahijah could not see; his sight was gone because of his age. [5]But the LORD had told Ahijah, "Jeroboam's wife is coming to ask you about her son, for he is ill, and you are to give her such and such an answer. When she arrives, she will pretend to be someone else."

[6]So when Ahijah heard the sound of her footsteps at the door, he said, "Come in, wife of Jeroboam. Why this pretense? I have been sent to you with bad news. [7]Go, tell Jeroboam that this is what the LORD, the God of Israel, says: 'I raised you up from among the people and appointed you ruler[d] over my people Israel. [8]I tore[e] the kingdom away from the house of David and gave it to you, but you have not been like my servant David, who kept my commands and followed me with all his heart, doing only what was right[f] in my eyes. [9]You have done more evil than all who lived before you. You have made for yourself other gods, idols[g] made of metal; you have aroused my anger and turned your back on me.[h]

[10]" 'Because of this, I am going to bring disaster on the house of Jeroboam. I will cut off from Jeroboam every last male in Israel — slave or free.[a][i] I will burn up the house of Jeroboam as one burns dung, until it is all gone.[j] [11]Dogs[k] will eat those belonging to Jeroboam who die in the city, and the birds will feed on those who die in the country. The LORD has spoken!'

[12]"As for you, go back home. When you set foot in your city, the boy will die. [13]All Israel will mourn for him and bury him. He is the only one belonging to Jeroboam who will be buried, because he is the only one in the house of Jeroboam in whom the LORD, the God of Israel, has found anything good.[l]

[14]"The LORD will raise up for himself a king over Israel who will cut off the family of Jeroboam. Even now this is beginning to happen.[b] [15]And the LORD will strike Israel, so that it will be like a reed swaying in the water. He will uproot[m] Israel from this good land that he gave to their ancestors and scatter them beyond the Euphrates River, because they aroused[n] the LORD's anger by making Asherah[o] poles.[c] [16]And he will give Israel up because of the sins[p] Jeroboam has committed and has caused Israel to commit."

[17]Then Jeroboam's wife got up and left and went to Tirzah.[q] As soon as she stepped over the threshold of the house, the boy died. [18]They buried him, and all Israel mourned for him, as the LORD had said through his servant the prophet Ahijah.

[19]The other events of Jeroboam's reign, his wars and how he ruled, are written in the book of the

[a] *10* Or *Israel — every ruler or leader* [b] *14* The meaning of the Hebrew for this sentence is uncertain. [c] *15* That is, wooden symbols of the goddess Asherah; here and elsewhere in 1 Kings

14:1 – 20 *Ahijah's Prophecy Against Jeroboam.* The prophet Ahijah announces Jeroboam's condemnation and details the disastrous fates awaiting both king and country. The king's wife and the sick prince personify the disaster about to befall Jeroboam and his family. Jeroboam instructs his wife to visit the prophet (vv. 1 – 3); God alerts Ahijah concerning it (vv. 4 – 6); Ahijah conveys a prophecy to Jeroboam through his queen (vv. 7 – 16); and its fulfillment plays out (vv. 17 – 20).
14:2 disguise yourself. The king thinks that he can fool Ahijah into giving the queen a positive prophecy concerning the sick prince. The desperate ploy betrays Jeroboam's awareness of his own guilt, genuine regard for Ahijah's prophetic power, and superstitious faith in prophecy as magic. He seems unaware, however, of God's power to inform Ahijah of the disguise (cf. v. 5; 22:30). **told me.** See 11:29 – 39.
14:3 The generous food gift probably amounts to a fee for services rendered (cf. 2 Kgs 5:15; 8:8 – 9; 1 Sam 9:7 – 8).
14:4 could not see. Implies that Ahijah is vulnerable to the deception (cf. Gen 27:1,22 – 23).
14:5 God exposes the ruse in advance.
14:6 Human disguises can never outwit God's omniscience (cf. 22:30).
14:7 what the LORD, the God of Israel, says. Cf. v. 11; 13:21; see note on 12:24. appointed you ruler. See 11:29 – 39.
14:8 my servant David. The paradigm of faithfulness for all subsequent kings (15:3 – 5,11; 2 Kgs 14:3; 16:2; 18:3; 22:2). Cf. the similar indictment of Solomon (cf. 11:4,6).
14:9 more evil than all who lived before you. Alludes to Solomon's sin (cf. vv. 22 – 24).
14:11 Not being buried was the greatest shame (cf. v. 13; 21:19,23 – 24; 2 Kgs 9:8 – 10).
14:12 Confirms the mother's worst fears.
14:15 The announcement anticipates the destruction of the northern kingdom and its exile two centuries later. **Asherah poles.** Cf. 18:19; 2 Kgs 13:6; 23:7; Isa 27:9; Mic 5:14; see note on Exod 34:13.
14:16 sins. Creation of idolatrous worship centers that imperil Israel.
14:17 Tirzah. The northern kingdom's new capital; seven miles (11.3 kilometers) northeast of Shechem (12:25; cf. 15:21; 16:8,15). **died.** Fulfills Ahijah's prophecy and ends Jeroboam's dynastic hopes.
14:19 other events. Typical introduction to a regnal summary in 1 – 2 Kings (cf. v. 29; 11:41; 15:7,31; 2 Kgs 10:34; 15:31). **annals of**

annals of the kings of Israel. [20]He reigned for twenty-two years and then rested with his ancestors. And
Nadab his son succeeded him as king.

Rehoboam King of Judah

14:21,25-31pp — 2Ch 12:9-16

[21]Rehoboam son of Solomon was king in Judah. He was forty-one years old when he became king,
and he reigned seventeen years in Jerusalem, the city the LORD had chosen out of all the tribes of Israel
in which to put his Name. His mother's name was Naamah; she was an Ammonite.[r]
[22]Judah[s] did evil in the eyes of the LORD. By the sins they committed they stirred up his jealous anger[t]
more than those who were before them had done. [23]They also set up for themselves high places, sacred
stones[u] and Asherah poles on every high hill and under every spreading tree.[v] [24]There were even male
shrine prostitutes[w] in the land; the people engaged in all the detestable practices of the nations the LORD
had driven out before the Israelites.
[25]In the fifth year of King Rehoboam, Shishak king of Egypt attacked[x] Jerusalem. [26]He carried off
the treasures of the temple[y] of the LORD and the treasures of the royal palace. He took everything, including all the gold shields[z] Solomon had made. [27]So King Rehoboam made bronze shields to replace
them and assigned these to the commanders of the guard on duty at the entrance to the royal palace.
[28]Whenever the king went to the LORD's temple, the guards bore the shields, and afterward they returned
them to the guardroom.
[29]As for the other events of Rehoboam's reign, and all he did, are they not written in the book of the
annals of the kings of Judah? [30]There was continual warfare[a] between Rehoboam and Jeroboam. [31]And
Rehoboam rested with his ancestors and was buried with them in the City of David. His mother's name
was Naamah; she was an Ammonite.[b] And Abijah[a] his son succeeded him as king.

Abijah King of Judah

15:1-2,6-8pp — 2Ch 13:1-2,22–14:1

15 In the eighteenth year of the reign of Jeroboam son of Nebat, Abijah[b] became king of Judah, [2]and he reigned in Jerusalem three years. His mother's name was Maakah[c] daughter of
Abishalom.[c]
[3]He committed all the sins his father had done before him; his heart was not fully devoted[d] to the
LORD his God, as the heart of David his forefather had been. [4]Nevertheless, for David's sake the LORD
his God gave him a lamp[e] in Jerusalem by raising up a son to succeed him and by making Jerusalem

[a] *31* Some Hebrew manuscripts and Septuagint (see also 2 Chron. 12:16); most Hebrew manuscripts *Abijam*
[b] *1* Some Hebrew manuscripts and Septuagint (see also 2 Chron. 12:16); most Hebrew manuscripts *Abijam*; also in verses 7 and 8 [c] *2* A variant of *Absalom*; also in verse 10

14:21 [r]ver 31; 1Ki 11:1; 2Ch 12:13
14:22 [s]2Ch 12:1 [t]Dt 32:21; Ps 78:58; 1Co 10:22
14:23 [u]Dt 16:22; 2Ki 17:9-10; Eze 16:24-25 [v]Dt 12:2; Isa 57:5
14:24 [w]Dt 23:17; 1Ki 15:12; 2Ki 23:7
14:25 [x]1Ki 11:40; 2Ch 12:2
14:26 [y]1Ki 15:15,18 [z]1Ki 10:17
14:30 [a]1Ki 12:21; 15:6
14:31 [b]ver 21; 2Ch 12:16
15:2 [c]2Ch 11:20; 13:2
15:3 [d]1Ki 11:4; Ps 119:80
15:4 [e]2Sa 21:17; 1Ki 11:36; 2Ch 21:7

the kings of Israel. An as yet undiscovered source of information for the reigns of northern kings.
14:20 twenty-two years. 931/30–910/9 BC.
14:21–31 *Rehoboam King of Judah.* The back-and-forth, parallel treatments of kings of Judah and Israel begin and continue until Israel's end (2 Kgs 17). In Judah, Israel-like apostasy, a disastrous Egyptian invasion, and ongoing warfare with Israel typify this period.
14:21 seventeen years. 931/30–913 BC. **the city the LORD had chosen.** Expresses Jerusalem's special status as the Lord's home. **Name.** See note on 9:3; cf. 11:12–13. **Naamah ... an Ammonite.** Mother of Rehoboam and one of Solomon's foreign wives (cf. v. 31; 11:1).
14:22 Judah's idolatry under Rehoboam eclipses that of Solomon and Jeroboam (cf. v. 24; 11:6; 14:9).
14:23 high places. See note on 3:2; cf. 12:31; 13:33–34. **sacred stones.** Stone pillars at sacred places associated with Baal. **Asherah poles.** See note on v. 15; cf. 2 Kgs 17:10; 18:4; 23:14; Exod 23:24; 34:13; Deut 7:5.
14:24 male shrine prostitutes. Perhaps a holdover from Canaanite cultic practices that Moses had forbidden Israelites to perform (Deut 23:17–18; cf. 1 Kgs 15:12; 2 Kgs 23:7; Hos 4:14).
14:25 Shishak. See note on 11:40. He attacked Jerusalem ca. 926/25 BC.
14:26 Shows Judah's military vulnerability under Rehoboam. **treasures.** Cf. 7:51. **gold shields.** See note on 10:17.
14:29 other events. See note on v. 19. **annals of the kings of Judah.** The source for royal events in Judah (cf. v. 19; 11:41; 15:7,23; 22:45; 2 Kgs 8:23; 12:19; 15:6,36; 16:19; 20:20; 21:17; 23:28).
14:30 Border skirmishes between Judah and Israel continue for a half century (cf. 15:6–7,16–23,32).
14:31 Naamah. See note on v. 21.
15:1–8 *Abijah King of Judah.* Judah's susceptibility to idolatrous influences and Yahweh's loyalty to David typify Abijah's three-year reign (913–911/10 BC).
15:2 Maakah. Abijah's mother and grandmother of his son Asa. She was perhaps a proponent of royal idolatry (cf. v. 13; 2 Chr 13:2).
15:3 all the sins his father had done. Replays Solomon's and Rehoboam's unfaithfulness (cf. 11:4).
15:4 for David's sake. Divine mercy for Abijah reciprocates David's exemplary loyalty (cf. v. 5; 2 Kgs 8:19; 19:34; 20:6). **lamp.** See note on 11:36. God continues David's dynasty.

15:5 [f] 1Ki 9:4; 14:8 [g] 2Sa 11:2-27; 12:9
15:6 [h] 1Ki 14:30
15:10 [i] ver 2
15:12 [j] 1Ki 14:24; 22:46
15:13 [k] Ex 32:20
15:14 [l] ver 3; 1Ki 8:61; 22:43
15:15 [m] 1Ki 7:51
15:16 [n] ver 32
15:17 [o] Jos 18:25; 1Ki 12:27
15:18 [p] ver 15; 1Ki 14:26 [q] 2Ki 12:18 [r] 1Ki 11:23-24
15:20 [s] Jdg 18:29; 2Sa 20:14; 2Ki 15:29
15:22 [t] Jos 18:24; 21:17

strong. [5]For David had done what was right in the eyes of the LORD and had not failed to keep[f] any of the LORD's commands all the days of his life — except in the case of Uriah[g] the Hittite.

[6]There was war[h] between Abijah[a] and Jeroboam throughout Abijah's lifetime. [7]As for the other events of Abijah's reign, and all he did, are they not written in the book of the annals of the kings of Judah? There was war between Abijah and Jeroboam. [8]And Abijah rested with his ancestors and was buried in the City of David. And Asa his son succeeded him as king.

Asa King of Judah

15:9-22pp — 2Ch 14:2-3; 15:16–16:6
15:23-24pp — 2Ch 16:11–17:1

[9]In the twentieth year of Jeroboam king of Israel, Asa became king of Judah, [10]and he reigned in Jerusalem forty-one years. His grandmother's name was Maakah[i] daughter of Abishalom.

[11]Asa did what was right in the eyes of the LORD, as his father David had done. [12]He expelled the male shrine prostitutes[j] from the land and got rid of all the idols his ancestors had made. [13]He even deposed his grandmother Maakah from her position as queen mother, because she had made a repulsive image for the worship of Asherah. Asa cut it down[k] and burned it in the Kidron Valley. [14]Although he did not remove the high places, Asa's heart was fully committed[l] to the LORD all his life. [15]He brought into the temple of the LORD the silver and gold and the articles that he and his father had dedicated.[m]

[16]There was war[n] between Asa and Baasha king of Israel throughout their reigns. [17]Baasha king of Israel went up against Judah and fortified Ramah[o] to prevent anyone from leaving or entering the territory of Asa king of Judah.

[18]Asa then took all the silver and gold that was left in the treasuries of the LORD's temple[p] and of his own palace. He entrusted it to his officials and sent[q] them to Ben-Hadad[r] son of Tabrimmon, the son of Hezion, the king of Aram, who was ruling in Damascus. [19]"Let there be a treaty between me and you," he said, "as there was between my father and your father. See, I am sending you a gift of silver and gold. Now break your treaty with Baasha king of Israel so he will withdraw from me."

[20]Ben-Hadad agreed with King Asa and sent the commanders of his forces against the towns of Israel. He conquered[s] Ijon, Dan, Abel Beth Maakah and all Kinnereth in addition to Naphtali. [21]When Baasha heard this, he stopped building Ramah and withdrew to Tirzah. [22]Then King Asa issued an order to all Judah — no one was exempt — and they carried away from Ramah the stones and timber Baasha had been using there. With them King Asa built up Geba[t] in Benjamin, and also Mizpah.

[23]As for all the other events of Asa's reign, all his achievements, all he did and the cities he built, are they not written in the book of the annals of the kings of Judah? In his old age, however, his feet became

[a] *6* Some Hebrew manuscripts and Syriac *Abijam* (that is, Abijah); most Hebrew manuscripts *Rehoboam*

15:5 Uriah the Hittite. An allusion to David's adulterous affair with Bathsheba and the subsequent murder of Uriah (2 Sam 11–12).
15:6 war between Abijah and Jeroboam. Cf. v. 7; see note on 14:30.
15:9–24 *Asa King of Judah.* Asa enjoys a long reign (911/10–870/69 BC) and ranks among the few kings of Judah whose reign approached that of David's. Asa is the first of four later Davidic kings to initiate religious reform against idolatry.
15:11 Asa's conduct satisfies the Davidic standard.
15:13 deposed his grandmother. See v. 2 and note. His action illustrates his firm commitment to religious reform. **queen mother.** A prestigious, influential position in ancient and modern monarchies. **Kidron Valley.** See note on 2:37.
15:14 high places. See note on 3:2; cf. 12:31; 13:33–34. **fully committed.** Israel's ideal of religious devotion (8:61; contrast v. 3; 11:4).
15:15 Asa's exemplary act of royal devotion confirms that his reform is sincere (cf. v. 14).
15:16 Baasha. Throughout his 24-year reign (909/8–886/85 BC) this king of the northern tribe of Israel waged war with Asa (vv. 27–30; 15:33—16:7).
15:17 Ramah. A strategic Benjamite town five miles (8 kilometers) north of Jerusalem.
15:18 treasuries. See note on 7:51; cf. 14:26–27. **Ben-Hadad.** Apparently the traditional name of Aramean kings (ch. 20; 2 Kgs 6:24; 8:9,14–15; 13:3,24–25). **Aram.** A kingdom or confederation of tribes northeast of the northern kingdom of Israel in modern Syria. **Damascus.** See 11:24; cf. 19:15.
15:19 my father and your father. Probably alludes to Aramean–Israelite relations under David and Solomon (cf. 11:23–25; 2 Sam 8:5–12; 2 Chr 8:3–4). **gift of silver and gold.** The purchase price to get Ben-Hadad to switch sides (see note on v. 21).
15:20 These towns are along Israel's northern and eastern borders — a sizeable territorial loss for Baasha.
15:21 stopped building. Confirms that Asa's diplomacy worked (v. 19). **Tirzah.** See note on 14:17; cf. 16:8,15; 2 Kgs 15:14.
15:22 Geba ... Mizpah. Fortified cities east and north of Ramah. Relocating the border three miles (4.8 kilometers) north eases the threat to Jerusalem.
15:23 other events. See note on 14:19; cf. 16:5; 2 Kgs 10:34; 13:8,12; 14:15,28; 20:20. **his feet became diseased.** The type of illness that plagues Asa is unclear; the Talmud diagnoses it as gout. Throughout his suffering Asa relies solely on his royal physicians rather than seeking God's healing (cf. 2 Chr 16:7–9,12). Later, Elijah will condemn King

diseased. [24]Then Asa rested with his ancestors and was buried with them in the city of his father David.
And Jehoshaphat[u] his son succeeded him as king.

Nadab King of Israel

[25]Nadab son of Jeroboam became king of Israel in the second year of Asa king of Judah, and he
reigned over Israel two years. [26]He did evil in the eyes of the LORD, following the ways of his father[v] and
committing the same sin his father had caused Israel to commit.
[27]Baasha son of Ahijah from the tribe of Issachar plotted against him, and he struck him down[w] at
Gibbethon,[x] a Philistine town, while Nadab and all Israel were besieging it. [28]Baasha killed Nadab in
the third year of Asa king of Judah and succeeded him as king.
[29]As soon as he began to reign, he killed Jeroboam's whole family.[y] He did not leave Jeroboam anyone that breathed, but destroyed them all, according to the word of the LORD given through his servant
Ahijah the Shilonite. [30]This happened because of the sins[z] Jeroboam had committed and had caused
Israel to commit, and because he aroused the anger of the LORD, the God of Israel.
[31]As for the other events of Nadab's reign, and all he did, are they not written in the book of the
annals of the kings of Israel? [32]There was war[a] between Asa and Baasha king of Israel throughout
their reigns.

15:24 [u]Mt 1:8
15:26 [v]1Ki 12:30; 14:16
15:27 [w]1Ki 14:14 [x]Jos 19:44; 21:23
15:29 [y]1Ki 14:10,14
15:30 [z]1Ki 14:9,16
15:32 [a]ver 16

Ahaziah of Israel for consulting Baal-Zebub of Ekron, not the Lord, concerning his recovery from an injury (2 Kgs 1:1–4).

15:25–32 *Nadab King of Israel.* During his two-year reign (910/9–909/8 BC), Nadab acts just like his father, Jeroboam.

15:26 did evil in the eyes of the LORD. The standard evaluation of bad kings from Solomon on down (cf. v. 34; 11:6; 13:33; 14:22; 16:25; 22:52; 2 Kgs 8:27; 15:24,28).

15:27 struck him down. The first of three violent coups in the northern kingdom's early history (cf. 16:10,15–16; 2 Kgs 21:23–24). Baasha removes a potential threat to his reign. **Gibbethon.** A Philistine town in the coastal plain (cf. 16:15). Nadab apparently attempted to extend Israel's southwestern border.

15:29 according to the word of the LORD. Ahijah's prophecy (14:10–11). See notes on 6:11; 13:1.

15:30 Two other causes for Jeroboam's terrible fate.

15:32 See vv. 6–7; see also note on 14:30.

RULERS OF THE DIVIDED KINGDOMS OF ISRAEL AND JUDAH

ISRAEL			JUDAH		
King	**Overlapping Reigns**	**Reign (BC)**	**King**	**Coregency**	**Reign (BC)**
Jeroboam I		931/30–910/9	Rehoboam		931/30–913
Nadab		910/9–909/8	Abijah		913–911/10
Baasha		909/8–886/85	Asa		911/10–870/69
Elah		886/85–885/84	Jehoshaphat	872/71–870/69	870/69–848
Zimri		885/84	Jehoram	853–848	848–841
Tibni		885/84–880	Ahaziah		841
Omri	885/84–880	880–874/73	Athaliah		841–835
Ahab		874/73–853	Joash		835–796
Ahaziah		853–852	Amaziah		796–767
Joram		852–841	Azariah (Uzziah)	792/91–767	767–740/39
Jehu		841–814/13	Jotham	750–740/39	740/39–732/31
Jehoahaz		814/13–798	Ahaz	735–732/31	732/31–716/15
Jehoash		798–782/81	Hezekiah	729–716/15	716/15–687/86
Jeroboam II	793/92–782/81	782/81–753	Manasseh	697/96–687/86	687/86–643/42
Zechariah		753–752	Amon		643/42–641/40
Shallum		752	Josiah		641/40–609
Menahem		752–742/41	Jehoahaz		609
Pekahiah		742/41–740/39	Jehoiakim		609–598
Pekah	752–740/39	740/39–732/31	Jehoiachin		598–597
Hoshea		732/31–723/22	Zedekiah		597–586

15:34 [b]ver 26; 1Ki 12:28-29; 13:33; 14:16
16:1 [c]ver 7; 2Ch 19:2; 20:34 [d]2Ch 16:7
16:2 [e]1Sa 2:8 [f]1Ki 14:7-9 [g]1Ki 15:34
16:3 [h]ver 11; 1Ki 14:10; 15:29; 21:22
16:4 [i]1Ki 14:11
16:5 [j]1Ki 14:19; 15:31
16:6 [k]1Ki 14:17; 15:33
16:7 [l]1Ki 15:27,29 [m]ver 1
16:9 [n]2Ki 9:30-33 [o]1Ki 18:3
16:11 [p]ver 3
16:13 [q]Dt 32:21; 1Sa 12:21; Isa 41:29
16:15 [r]Jos 19:44; 1Ki 15:27

Baasha King of Israel

33 In the third year of Asa king of Judah, Baasha son of Ahijah became king of all Israel in Tirzah,
and he reigned twenty-four years. 34 He did evil[b] in the eyes of the LORD, following the ways of Jeroboam
and committing the same sin Jeroboam had caused Israel to commit.

16 Then the word of the LORD came to Jehu[c] son of Hanani[d] concerning Baasha: 2 "I lifted you
up from the dust[e] and appointed you ruler[f] over my people Israel, but you followed the ways
of Jeroboam and caused[g] my people Israel to sin and to arouse my anger by their sins. 3 So I am about
to wipe out Baasha and his house,[h] and I will make your house like that of Jeroboam son of Nebat.
4 Dogs[i] will eat those belonging to Baasha who die in the city, and birds will feed on those who die in
the country."

5 As for the other events of Baasha's reign, what he did and his achievements, are they not written
in the book of the annals[j] of the kings of Israel? 6 Baasha rested with his ancestors and was buried in
Tirzah.[k] And Elah his son succeeded him as king.

7 Moreover, the word of the LORD came[l] through the prophet Jehu[m] son of Hanani to Baasha and his
house, because of all the evil he had done in the eyes of the LORD, arousing his anger by the things he
did, becoming like the house of Jeroboam—and also because he destroyed it.

Elah King of Israel

8 In the twenty-sixth year of Asa king of Judah, Elah son of Baasha became king of Israel, and he
reigned in Tirzah two years.

9 Zimri, one of his officials, who had command of half his chariots, plotted against him. Elah was
in Tirzah at the time, getting drunk[n] in the home of Arza, the palace administrator[o] at Tirzah. 10 Zimri
came in, struck him down and killed him in the twenty-seventh year of Asa king of Judah. Then he
succeeded him as king.

11 As soon as he began to reign and was seated on the throne, he killed off Baasha's whole family.[p] He
did not spare a single male, whether relative or friend. 12 So Zimri destroyed the whole family of Baasha,
in accordance with the word of the LORD spoken against Baasha through the prophet Jehu— 13 because
of all the sins Baasha and his son Elah had committed and had caused Israel to commit, so that they
aroused the anger of the LORD, the God of Israel, by their worthless idols.[q]

14 As for the other events of Elah's reign, and all he did, are they not written in the book of the annals
of the kings of Israel?

Zimri King of Israel

15 In the twenty-seventh year of Asa king of Judah, Zimri reigned in Tirzah seven days. The army
was encamped near Gibbethon,[r] a Philistine town. 16 When the Israelites in the camp heard that Zimri
had plotted against the king and murdered him, they proclaimed Omri, the commander of the army,
king over Israel that very day there in the camp. 17 Then Omri and all the Israelites with him withdrew

---

15:33—16:7 *Baasha King of Israel.* This reviews Baasha's 24-year reign (909/8–886/85 BC). A prophetic announcement condemns Baasha to Jeroboam's fate.

15:34 did evil. Baasha is yet another northern ruler in Jeroboam's mold who harms Israel.

16:1 Jehu. This prophet's only appearance in 1–2 Kings is in this chapter. **Hanani.** See 2 Chr 16:7–9.

16:4 Virtually quotes Ahijah's word to Jeroboam (14:11) and resembles what Elijah says to Ahab (21:24; cf. 21:23).

16:7 Summarizes vv. 2–4.

16:8–14 *Elah King of Israel.* Israel's second assassination abruptly ends Elah's two-year reign (886/85–885/84 BC). This mirrors the era's political instability (cf. vv. 9–10). The report closely follows the narrative pattern of Baasha's overthrow of Nadab (15:27–30): conspiracy leads to assassination of the current king and the killer's accession to the throne (vv. 9–10); the new king then annihilates his predecessor's whole family (v. 11) to fulfill a prophecy (v. 12) because the late king promoted idolatry (v. 13). The irony is that at Zimri's hands Elah, Baasha's son, falls victim to the same fate that his father inflicted on Nadab.

16:9 Tirzah. See note on 14:17.

16:10 killed. For the second time (see note on 15:27), judgment strikes a royal successor. Baasha killed Nadab (son of Jeroboam) in 15:27–30 and now Zimri kills Elah (son of Baasha) in 16:9–13.

16:12 word of the LORD. Again connects a king's fate with prophecy (vv. 1–4,34; cf. 14:18; 15:29; 2 Kgs 9:26; 14:25; 23:16; 24:2). See notes on 6:11; 13:1.

16:13 because of all the sins. Cf. vv. 19,26,31; 15:30,34.

16:15–20 *Zimri King of Israel.* Zimri's inglorious seven-day reign is the shortest in Israel's history. The report tracks the repercussions of his coup.

16:15 Gibbethon. See note on 15:27.

16:16 plotted against ... murdered. A royal assassination (cf. 15:27). This sparks a military countercoup.

16:17 Tirzah. See note on 14:17.

from Gibbethon and laid siege to Tirzah. 18When Zimri saw that the city was taken, he went into the
citadel of the royal palace and set the palace on fire around him. So he died, 19because of the sins he
had committed, doing evil in the eyes of the LORD and following the ways of Jeroboam and committing
the same sin Jeroboam had caused Israel to commit.
20As for the other events of Zimri's reign, and the rebellion he carried out, are they not written in the
book of the annals of the kings of Israel?

Omri King of Israel

21Then the people of Israel were split into two factions; half supported Tibni son of Ginath for king,
and the other half supported Omri. 22But Omri's followers proved stronger than those of Tibni son of
Ginath. So Tibni died and Omri became king.
23In the thirty-first year of Asa king of Judah, Omri became king of Israel, and he reigned twelve
years, six of them in Tirzah.[s] 24He bought the hill of Samaria from Shemer for two talents[a] of silver
and built a city on the hill, calling it Samaria,[t] after Shemer, the name of the former owner of the hill.
25But Omri did evil[u] in the eyes of the LORD and sinned more than all those before him. 26He followed
completely the ways of Jeroboam son of Nebat, committing the same sin Jeroboam had caused[v] Israel
to commit, so that they aroused the anger of the LORD, the God of Israel, by their worthless idols.[w]
27As for the other events of Omri's reign, what he did and the things he achieved, are they not written in the book of the annals of the kings of Israel? 28Omri rested with his ancestors and was buried in
Samaria. And Ahab his son succeeded him as king.

Ahab Becomes King of Israel

29In the thirty-eighth year of Asa king of Judah, Ahab son of Omri became king of Israel, and he
reigned in Samaria over Israel twenty-two years. 30Ahab son of Omri did more[x] evil in the eyes of the
LORD than any of those before him. 31He not only considered it trivial to commit the sins of Jeroboam
son of Nebat, but he also married[y] Jezebel daughter[z] of Ethbaal king of the Sidonians, and began
to serve Baal[a] and worship him. 32He set up an altar for Baal in the temple[b] of Baal that he built in

16:23 [s] 1Ki 15:21
16:24 [t] 1Ki 13:32; Jn 4:4
16:25 [u] Dt 4:25; Mic 6:16
16:26 [v] ver 19 [w] Dt 32:21
16:30 [x] ver 25; 1Ki 14:9
16:31 [y] Dt 7:3; 1Ki 11:2 [z] Jdg 18:7; 2Ki 9:34 [a] 2Ki 10:18; 17:16
16:32 [b] 2Ki 10:21,27; 11:18

[a] *24* That is, about 150 pounds or about 68 kilograms

16:18 citadel. Maximally fortified city space where the besieged inhabitants took their last stand.
16:19 because of the sins. Cf. v. 16; traces Zimri's fate to his week-long reign in the pattern of Jeroboam.
16:21–28 *Omri King of Israel.* After two coups and a short-lived civil war, Omri gives the northern kingdom a period of political stability and a new capital city. He also founds a dynasty that will last more than 40 years. Two of his granddaughters marry kings of Judah, for a time sealing marriage alliances between the Omride and Davidic dynasties (2 Kgs 8:16–19,26–27). One even ruled Judah as queen until she was overthrown (2 Kgs 11:1–21).
16:21 split into two factions. Evidences Israel's fragile political situation.
16:23 Omri. Ruled 885/84–874/73 BC. Remembered as Moab's oppressor in the Mesha Stele (see note on 11:7). Long after his death Assyrian annals still called Israel "the Land of Omri."
16:24 Samaria. Seven miles (11.3 kilometers) northwest of Shechem (near modern Sebastia). The northern kingdom's new capital, known as "the wreath" (see Isa 28:1–4 and note), stood on a hill above fertile valleys spread around it 300 feet (91.4 meters) below. The hill's name recalls the hill's original owner, Shemer, either to honor him or possibly as a condition of its sale to Omri (cf. Ruth 4:5). Its hilltop location gave northern kings an impregnable capital city with a royal citadel on par with the special fortification protecting kings of Judah (20:1–21; 2 Kgs 6:25; 18:9–10; 2 Sam 5:6–12). According to archaeologists, Omri and Ahab beautified the city with impressive structures comparable to those Solomon had built in Jerusalem. On occasion the royal city's name stood for the northern kingdom as a whole much as Jerusalem sometimes designated the southern kingdom (e.g., 21:1; Isa 10:10; Amos 6:1).
16:25 did evil ... more than all. The harshest criticism of any king thus far. Israel's religious life sinks to a new level (cf. v. 30).
16:26 ways of Jeroboam. Cf. vv. 2,19; 15:34. See note on 12:30.
16:27 other events. See note on 14:19.
16:28 buried in Samaria. The first burial in the new capital's royal tombs (cf. 22:37; 2 Kgs 10:35; 13:9,13; 14:16).
16:29–34 *Ahab Becomes King of Israel.* This introduces and evaluates Ahab's reign (874/73–853 BC) in severely negative terms. Yet Ahab's dynasty had a lasting impact on both Israel and Judah.
16:30 more evil ... than any of those before him. More sinful that his father (cf. vv. 25–26) and comparable to Judah's Manasseh (2 Kgs 21:9,11).
16:31 married Jezebel. Marrying a Phoenician princess forges ties with Sidon (see note on 5:6; cf. 11:1; 18:4), a center of Baal worship. This repeats Solomon's first misstep: his marriage alliances with foreign nations (3:1; 11:1–11; see note on 11:1–13). **Ethbaal.** The name implies that the family has long worshiped Baal, the Canaanite deity who debuts here (but other gods were also worshiped; see notes on 11:5,7; 12:28; 14:15,23). In the ancient Near East, parents commonly include their favorite god's name in their children's names. Jezebel's grandparents had named Ethbaal, evidence of at least three generations of Baal worship in Jezebel's family. **began to serve Baal.** Repeats Solomon's second misstep, his rejection of Yahweh by worshiping other gods, making Ahab also liable for divine judgment (11:4–13). Ahab, however, goes one step further. He introduces and promotes in Israel the worship of Baal in place of Yahweh as royal policy nationwide.
16:32 altar for Baal in the temple of Baal. Implies that Ahab sponsors Baal worship in Israel. Cf. 2 Kgs 10; 11:18.

Samaria from the north.

Todd Bolen/www.BiblePlaces.com

16:33 [c]2Ki 13:6 [d]ver 29, 30; 1Ki 14:9; 21:25
16:34 [e]Jos 6:26
17:1 [f]Mal 4:5; Jas 5:17 [g]Jdg 12:4 [h]Dt 10:8; 1Ki 18:1; 2Ki 3:14; Lk 4:25

Samaria. [33]Ahab also made an Asherah pole[c] and did more[d] to arouse the anger of the LORD, the God
of Israel, than did all the kings of Israel before him.
[34]In Ahab's time, Hiel of Bethel rebuilt Jericho. He laid its foundations at the cost of his firstborn son
Abiram, and he set up its gates at the cost of his youngest son Segub, in accordance with the word of
the LORD spoken by Joshua son of Nun.[e]

Elijah Announces a Great Drought

17 Now Elijah[f] the Tishbite, from Tishbe[a] in Gilead,[g] said to Ahab, "As the LORD, the God of Israel, lives, whom I serve, there will be neither dew nor rain[h] in the next few years except at my word."

[a] *1* Or *Tishbite, of the settlers*

16:33 Asherah pole. See note on 14:15; cf. 14:23; see photo, p. 180. **did more to arouse the anger of the LORD.** The unprecedented divine fury that Ahab's actions causes indicates how unprecedented and outrageous God regards Ahab's royal initiatives.

16:34 In Ahab's time. Signals that the following brief report illustrates something significant about the Israelite king's reign. **rebuilt Jericho.** Joshua's curse of Jericho after the city's destruction (Josh 6:26) is the background here. It said that death awaited the oldest and youngest children of anyone who rebuilds Jericho's foundations and gates. But the Jericho that Israelites safely inhabit is an unwalled town or village (e.g., 2 Kgs 2:4–5,18; Josh 18:21; Judg 1:16; 2 Sam 10:5; NT Jericho was at a separate location). The forbidden rebuilding is the restoration of Jericho as a fortified city with walls and gates (cf. 9:17, "rebuilt"). It violates God's purpose for Jericho's ruins—to remind the Israelites that God's power has defeated Canaan and God's grace gives it to them as a gift. **at the cost of.** No mention is made of how Hiel's sons die, but he may have followed a Canaanite practice by offering them as a sacrifice, or perhaps some divine judgment strikes them. **the word of the LORD spoken by Joshua.** Presents Joshua's curse as a prophetic word that finds fulfillment in Hiel's fate, and adds another example of the prophecy-fulfillment theme in 1–2 Kings (see notes on 6:11; 13:1). The incident implies that Ahab and Jezebel sanction religious rebellion in Israel and anticipates Israel's dire fate under their rule.

17:1—2 Kgs 10:36 *The Prophetic Ministries of Elijah and Elisha.* They gallantly oppose Omri's dynasty and its promotion of Baal worship. Stories probably passed down and collected by other prophets in the northern kingdom have found their way into 1–2 Kings. The conflicts between prophets and kings mirror a cosmic contest between Yahweh and Baal for Israel's worship.

17:1—18:46 *Elijah's Confrontation With Baal.* This battle turns the tide against the entrenched, state-sponsored Baal worship in Israel. It opens with a drought that Elijah announces (17:1—18:15), climaxes with Yahweh's victory over Baal on Mount Carmel (18:16–40), and ends with the dramatic return of rainfall (18:41–46).

17:1 *Elijah Announces a Great Drought.* Elijah's dramatic debut asserts that Yahweh, not the Canaanites' Baal, sovereignly controls fertility.

17:1 Tishbe. An unidentified town in Gilead. Possibly Listib, eight miles (12.9 kilometers) north of the Jabbok River. See NIV text note. **Gilead.** A mountainous region in Transjordan (today, northern Jordan). Tribal home of Gad, Reuben, and half of Manasseh. **As the LORD, the God of Israel, lives.** A traditional oath formula (see note on 1:29); invokes a condition that the Lord will enforce (cf. v. 12). **dew ... rain.** Israel's primary sources of water. Jas 5:17–18 presumes that God authorized this announcement in response to Elijah's prior prayer. Elijah's example encourages any believer to pray because Elijah was human, and God answered his prayers.

Elijah Fed by Ravens

2Then the word of the Lord came to Elijah: 3"Leave here, turn eastward and hide in the Kerith Ravine, east of the Jordan. 4You will drink from the brook, and I have directed the ravens[i] to supply you with food there."

5So he did what the Lord had told him. He went to the Kerith Ravine, east of the Jordan, and stayed there. 6The ravens brought him bread and meat in the morning[j] and bread and meat in the evening, and he drank from the brook.

Elijah and the Widow at Zarephath

7Some time later the brook dried up because there had been no rain in the land. 8Then the word of the Lord came to him: 9"Go at once to Zarephath[k] in the region of Sidon and stay there. I have directed a widow[l] there to supply you with food." 10So he went to Zarephath. When he came to the town gate, a widow was there gathering sticks. He called to her and asked, "Would you bring me a little water in a jar so I may have a drink?"[m] 11As she was going to get it, he called, "And bring me, please, a piece of bread."

12"As surely as the Lord your God lives," she replied, "I don't have any bread—only a handful of flour in a jar and a little olive oil[n] in a jug. I am gathering a few sticks to take home and make a meal for myself and my son, that we may eat it—and die."

13Elijah said to her, "Don't be afraid. Go home and do as you have said. But first make a small loaf of bread for me from what you have and bring it to me, and then make something for yourself and your son. 14For this is what the Lord, the God of Israel, says: 'The jar of flour will not be used up and the jug of oil will not run dry until the day the Lord sends rain on the land.'"

15She went away and did as Elijah had told her. So there was food every day for Elijah and for the woman and her family. 16For the jar of flour was not used up and the jug of oil did not run dry, in keeping with the word of the Lord spoken by Elijah.

17Some time later the son of the woman who owned the house became ill. He grew worse and worse, and finally stopped breathing. 18She said to Elijah, "What do you have against me, man of God? Did you come to remind me of my sin[o] and kill my son?"

19"Give me your son," Elijah replied. He took him from her arms, carried him to the upper room where he was staying, and laid him on his bed. 20Then he cried out to the Lord, "Lord my God, have you brought tragedy even on this widow I am staying with, by causing her son to die?" 21Then he

17:4 [i] Ge 8:7
17:6 [j] Ex 16:8
17:9 [k] Ob 20 [l] Lk 4:26
17:10 [m] Ge 24:17; Jn 4:7
17:12 [n] ver 1; 2Ki 4:2
17:18 [o] 2Ki 3:13; Lk 5:8

17:2–6 *Elijah Fed by Ravens.* As Israel suffers severe drought and Baal's credibility as guarantor of fertility falls, God sovereignly provides for his faithful servant Elijah. The miraculous provision keeps Elijah alive east of the Jordan River just as God sustained Israel in the wilderness in Moses' day. The contrast between a well-fed Elijah in Gilead with a hungry Israel in the promised land clearly portrays Israel's reliance on Baal for food as foolish.

17:2 the word of the Lord came to. See notes on 6:11; 13:1.

17:3 God relocates Elijah beyond Ahab's reach. **Kerith Ravine.** An unknown valley in Transjordan.

17:6 morning … evening. The quantity of Elijah's fare exceeded the amount that common people normally ate. They reserved meat only for special occasions, while the dinner tables of kings featured meat daily (4:22–23). Elijah's diet of meat twice daily was unusual and portrays him as an honored guest at King Yahweh's royal table (see Exod 29:38–41; Num 28:4–8). In 18:19, Elijah spotlights the privileged prophets who eat at Jezebel's table while the common people who follow them into apostasy go hungry.

17:7–24 *Elijah and the Widow at Zarephath.* God again relocates Elijah a long way from Ahab, though very near the king's ally in Sidon, where Jezebel grew up. This location again displays God's sovereignty over fertility and life itself in the heartland of Baal worship (cf. 2 Kgs 4:1–7,18–37).

17:7 brook. A rain-fed streambed empty in dry seasons.

17:9 Zarephath. A Phoenician coastal town eight miles (12.9 kilometers) south of Sidon and 14 miles (22.5 kilometers) north of Tyre (modern Sarafand). **Sidon.** See note on 5:6; cf. 11:1; 16:30–32.

17:10 widow … gathering sticks. Widows in Israel were often poor, surviving mainly on food distributed from local food-tithe donations (cf. Deut 14:28–29). Verse 12 confirms her poverty. For Jesus, the rejection of Elijah in Israel that leads Elijah to this non-Israelite widow compares to the rejection of Jesus and his Messianic mission in Jesus' hometown of Nazareth (Luke 4:24–26).

17:12 As surely as the Lord your God lives. An oath (see note on 1:29) to verify her claim of poverty (cf. vv. 1,14; 18:10). **eat it—and die.** She is down to her last meal.

17:13 first make a small loaf. Tests the woman's trust in Elijah as a reliable prophet (cf. v. 18) and affirms his confidence that Yahweh will provide what he promised (v. 9).

17:14 what the Lord, the God of Israel, says. See notes on 6:11; 13:1. **not be used up … not run dry.** Signifies that Israel's God, not Baal, provides food—even without any rainfall.

17:18 The distraught widow's questions imply that her hospitality toward Elijah has had an unfortunate effect. Rather than please God, she thinks that it brought her sin to God's attention. The question betrays a sense of guilt probably rooted in pagan ideas. However, it also puts into words the issue that confronts both her and Elijah: Why did the God whom Elijah promised would keep her and her son alive (vv. 13–14) send death instead? At stake for Elijah is his credibility as a reliable prophet (cf. vv. 20, 24). **man of God.** See note on 12:22.

17:21 [p]2Ki 4:34; Ac 20:10
17:24 [q]Jn 3:2; 16:30 [r]Ps 119:43; Jn 17:17
18:1 [s]1Ki 17:1; Lk 4:25; Jas 5:17 [t]Dt 28:12
18:3 [u]1Ki 16:9 [v]Ne 7:2
18:4 [w]2Ki 9:7 [x]ver 13; Isa 16:3
18:7 [y]2Ki 1:8
18:10 [z]1Ki 17:3
18:12 [a]2Ki 2:16; Eze 3:14; Ac 8:39
18:15 [b]1Ki 17:1

stretched[p] himself out on the boy three times and cried out to the LORD, "LORD my God, let this boy's
life return to him!"
22The LORD heard Elijah's cry, and the boy's life returned to him, and he lived. 23Elijah picked up
the child and carried him down from the room into the house. He gave him to his mother and said,
"Look, your son is alive!"
24Then the woman said to Elijah, "Now I know[q] that you are a man of God and that the word of the
LORD from your mouth is the truth."[r]

Elijah and Obadiah

18 After a long time, in the third[s] year, the word of the LORD came to Elijah: "Go and present
yourself to Ahab, and I will send rain[t] on the land." 2So Elijah went to present himself to Ahab.
Now the famine was severe in Samaria, 3and Ahab had summoned Obadiah, his palace administrator.[u] (Obadiah was a devout believer[v] in the LORD. 4While Jezebel[w] was killing off the LORD's prophets,
Obadiah had taken a hundred prophets and hidden[x] them in two caves, fifty in each, and had supplied
them with food and water.) 5Ahab had said to Obadiah, "Go through the land to all the springs and
valleys. Maybe we can find some grass to keep the horses and mules alive so we will not have to kill
any of our animals." 6So they divided the land they were to cover, Ahab going in one direction and
Obadiah in another.
7As Obadiah was walking along, Elijah met him. Obadiah recognized[y] him, bowed down to the
ground, and said, "Is it really you, my lord Elijah?"
8"Yes," he replied. "Go tell your master, 'Elijah is here.'"
9"What have I done wrong," asked Obadiah, "that you are handing your servant over to Ahab
to be put to death? 10As surely as the LORD your God lives, there is not a nation or kingdom where
my master has not sent someone to look[z] for you. And whenever a nation or kingdom claimed you
were not there, he made them swear they could not find you. 11But now you tell me to go to my
master and say, 'Elijah is here.' 12I don't know where the Spirit[a] of the LORD may carry you when
I leave you. If I go and tell Ahab and he doesn't find you, he will kill me. Yet I your servant have
worshiped the LORD since my youth. 13Haven't you heard, my lord, what I did while Jezebel was
killing the prophets of the LORD? I hid a hundred of the LORD's prophets in two caves, fifty in each,
and supplied them with food and water. 14And now you tell me to go to my master and say, 'Elijah
is here.' He will kill me!"
15Elijah said, "As the LORD Almighty lives, whom I serve, I will surely present[b] myself to Ahab
today."

17:21 three times. A number that commonly occurs in customary and ritual actions (18:34; 2 Kgs 13:18; Exod 23:14; Num 24:10; 1 Sam 20:41). **let this boy's life return to him.** The issue is whether Yahweh or Baal controls life and death. This incident forms part of the larger struggle between the two deities in 1–2 Kgs, the struggle that drives the confrontation between Elijah and Baal's clergy on Mount Carmel (18:19–40).

17:24 The son's resurrection confirms for the widow that Elijah is an instrument of God's power and, more important, that the prophet is a reliable spokesperson of God's word. It is ironic that a Phoenician woman confesses that God speaks through Elijah, an acknowledgment that God's own people refused to affirm. Cf. 2 Kgs 4:18–37. God's care for this needy widow also exemplifies the care of the needy that both OT and NT mandate for God's people (Exod 22:21; Deut 10:18; 27:19; Ps 68:5; Isa 1:17; Jas 1:27). For God's relation to non-Israelites, see note on 8:42.

18:1–15 *Elijah and Obadiah.* Elijah's return to Israel signals the reversal of the drought that 17:1 decreed. Through Obadiah, Elijah glimpses his homeland as a battleground between state-sponsored idolatry and the persecuted faithful of Yahweh. Their meeting marks the first step toward the climactic contest between the combatants on Mount Carmel.

18:1 Yahweh commissions Elijah to confront the king face to face. **I will send rain.** Israel's God, not Baal, controls the weather, including droughts and rainstorms, and determines whether or not Israel enjoys fertility.

18:2 famine was severe. It affected even Ahab. **Samaria.** See note on 16:24.

18:3 palace administrator. Royal chief of staff over palace operations (cf. 4:6; 16:9; 2 Kgs 10:5; 18:18; 19:2).

18:4 Jezebel. The person who most represents the official, violent oppression of God's prophets.

18:5 springs and valleys. Water sources not dependent on rainfall, perhaps unscathed by drought. **keep the horses and mules alive.** Portrays Ahab as a self-centered, calloused ruler scouring his kingdom for what little food and water remain in order to maintain his military strength rather than to ease the suffering of his subjects (cf. 10:26). The annals of the Assyrian ruler Shalmaneser III (ninth century BC) report that Ahab could bring 2,000 chariots against him.

18:7 Pictures a chance meeting. **bowed down to the ground.** See note on 1:16.

18:12 Cf. 2 Kgs 2:11; Gen 5:24; Ezek 3:14; 8:3; 40:1–3. **worshiped the LORD since my youth.** Argues that his lifelong devotion either makes him worthy of a better fate than execution or makes him more likely to be executed by Jezebel.

18:13 Another reason Obadiah feels his life is at risk (cf. vv. 3–4).

Elijah on Mount Carmel

16 So Obadiah went to meet Ahab and told him, and Ahab went to meet Elijah. 17 When he saw Elijah,
he said to him, "Is that you, you troubler[c] of Israel?"
18 "I have not made trouble for Israel," Elijah replied. "But you[d] and your father's family have. You
have abandoned[e] the LORD's commands and have followed the Baals. 19 Now summon the people from
all over Israel to meet me on Mount Carmel.[f] And bring the four hundred and fifty prophets of Baal
and the four hundred prophets of Asherah, who eat at Jezebel's table."
20 So Ahab sent word throughout all Israel and assembled the prophets on Mount Carmel. 21 Elijah
went before the people and said, "How long will you waver[g] between two opinions? If the LORD is God,
follow him; but if Baal is God, follow him."

But the people said nothing.

22 Then Elijah said to them, "I am the only one of the LORD's prophets left,[h] but Baal has four hundred and fifty prophets.[i] 23 Get two bulls for us. Let Baal's prophets choose one for themselves, and let
them cut it into pieces and put it on the wood but not set fire to it. I will prepare the other bull and
put it on the wood but not set fire to it. 24 Then you call on the name of your god, and I will call on the
name of the LORD. The god who answers by fire[j] — he is God."

Then all the people said, "What you say is good."

25 Elijah said to the prophets of Baal, "Choose one of the bulls and prepare it first, since there are
so many of you. Call on the name of your god, but do not light the fire." 26 So they took the bull given
them and prepared it.

Then they called on the name of Baal from morning till noon. "Baal, answer us!" they shouted. But
there was no response;[k] no one answered. And they danced around the altar they had made.
27 At noon Elijah began to taunt them. "Shout louder!" he said. "Surely he is a god! Perhaps he is
deep in thought, or busy, or traveling. Maybe he is sleeping and must be awakened."[l] 28 So they shouted
louder and slashed[m] themselves with swords and spears, as was their custom, until their blood flowed.
29 Midday passed, and they continued their frantic prophesying until the time for the evening sacrifice.[n]
But there was no response, no one answered, no one paid attention.[o]
30 Then Elijah said to all the people, "Come here to me." They came to him, and he repaired the
altar[p] of the LORD, which had been torn down. 31 Elijah took twelve stones, one for each of the tribes
descended from Jacob, to whom the word of the LORD had come, saying, "Your name shall be Israel."[q]
32 With the stones he built an altar in the name[r] of the LORD, and he dug a trench around it large enough

18:17 [c] Jos 7:25; 1Ki 21:20; Ac 16:20
18:18 [d] 1Ki 16:31,33; 21:25 [e] 2Ch 15:2
18:19 [f] Jos 19:26
18:21 [g] Jos 24:15; 2Ki 17:41; Mt 6:24
18:22 [h] 1Ki 19:10 [i] ver 19
18:24 [j] ver 38; 1Ch 21:26
18:26 [k] Ps 115:4-5; Jer 10:5; 1Co 8:4; 12:2
18:27 [l] Hab 2:19
18:28 [m] Lev 19:28; Dt 14:1
18:29 [n] Ex 29:41 [o] ver 26
18:30 [p] 1Ki 19:10
18:31 [q] Ge 32:28; 35:10; 2Ki 17:34
18:32 [r] Col 3:17

18:16–46 *Elijah on Mount Carmel.* The public contest between Yahweh and Baal on Mount Carmel determines who is the real God, the only one worthy of Israel's worship. Ahab convenes his religious leaders to join in the event (vv. 16–20), the contest ensues (vv. 21–40), and God sends rainfall (vv. 41–46).

18:17 you troubler of Israel. Ahab alludes to and blames Elijah for the current drought. Joshua used the same verb to describe the shaken confidence after the defeat at Ai that Achan's sin had caused Israel (cf. v. 18; Josh 7:25–26). The cause of the present disaster, however, is Ahab's rejection of Yahweh in favor of Baal, not some fault with Elijah.

18:18 Omri and Ahab are accountable for the drought.

18:19 people from all over Israel. Elijah's open invitation to all Israelites suggests the national importance of the event and the issue to be decided. **Mount Carmel.** A mountain ridge overlooking the Mediterranean near modern Haifa. **Baal ... Asherah.** See notes on Exod 34:13; Deut 12:3. Jezebel was importing Baal, the national god of Tyre, to replace the Lord as Israel's national god. Asherah was worshiped as the wife of Baal. **eat at Jezebel's table.** Suggests membership in the royal court.

18:21 waver. Elijah's question describes Israel's indecision concerning whether Baal or Yahweh is the true God. The religious ambivalence cannot continue because Yahweh demands exclusive allegiance.

18:24 The god who answers by fire. Fire commonly indicates that God is present (cf. Gen 15:17; Exod 19:18; Hos 8:14; Amos 1:4). Thunderstorms were thought to be chariots on which Yahweh and Baal rode (Ps 104:3; see note on Ps 68:4). Thunder was said to be their voice (see Ps 29:3–9 and note) and lightning ("fire") their weapons (see Ps 18:14; cf. Lev 9:24). Elijah asks the true God to prove his existence by sending a direct, visible answer.

18:27 taunt. Ridicule familiar beliefs about Baal. **deep in thought.** Pondering more important things. **busy.** Perhaps a euphemism for relieving himself. **traveling.** Out of the "office"; may allude to Baal's regular descent to the underworld in ritual death. **sleeping and must be awakened.** May refer to rituals to revive him (cf. v. 28).

18:28 slashed themselves. Self-mutilation, common in ancient mourning rites and possibly a familiar Canaanite cultic gesture; shows a last-ditch effort to rouse a lethargic Baal or persuade the death-god Mot to release him. The Mosaic law strictly forbids mutilation of the body (Lev 19:28; Deut 14:1).

18:29 evening sacrifice. At about sunset (Exod 29:39). **no response.** Silence from Baal despite his clergy's best efforts.

18:30 torn down. Possibly by Jezebel's agents, symbolizing her program to replace Yahweh with Baal (cf. vv. 4,13; 19:10,14).

18:31 one for each of the tribes. The Yahweh-Baal struggle was a national threat, not just a northern problem. **Your name shall be Israel.** Quotes Gen 35:10.

18:33 [s]Ge 22:9; Lev 1:6-8
18:36 [t]Ex 3:6; Mt 22:32 [u]1Ki 8:43; 2Ki 19:19 [v]Nu 16:28
18:38 [w]Lev 9:24; Jdg 6:21; 1Ch 21:26; 2Ch 7:1; Job 1:16
18:39 [x]ver 24
18:40 [y]Jdg 4:7 [z]Dt 13:5; 18:20; 2Ki 10:24-25
18:42 [a]ver 19-20; Jas 5:18
18:44 [b]Lk 12:54
18:46 [c]2Ki 3:15 [d]2Ki 4:29; 9:1
19:1 [e]1Ki 18:40
19:2 [f]1Ki 20:10; 2Ki 6:31; Ru 1:17
19:3 [g]Ge 31:21
19:4 [h]Nu 11:15; Jer 20:18; Jnh 4:8
19:5 [i]Ge 28:11

to hold two seahs[a] of seed. 33 He arranged[s] the wood, cut the bull into pieces and laid it on the wood.
Then he said to them, "Fill four large jars with water and pour it on the offering and on the wood."
34 "Do it again," he said, and they did it again.
"Do it a third time," he ordered, and they did it the third time. 35 The water ran down around the
altar and even filled the trench.
36 At the time of sacrifice, the prophet Elijah stepped forward and prayed: "LORD, the God of Abraham,[t]
Isaac and Israel, let it be known[u] today that you are God in Israel and that I am your servant and have
done all these things at your command.[v] 37 Answer me, LORD, answer me, so these people will know that
you, LORD, are God, and that you are turning their hearts back again."
38 Then the fire[w] of the LORD fell and burned up the sacrifice, the wood, the stones and the soil, and
also licked up the water in the trench.
39 When all the people saw this, they fell prostrate and cried, "The LORD—he is God! The LORD—he
is God!"[x]
40 Then Elijah commanded them, "Seize the prophets of Baal. Don't let anyone get away!" They
seized them, and Elijah had them brought down to the Kishon Valley[y] and slaughtered[z] there.
41 And Elijah said to Ahab, "Go, eat and drink, for there is the sound of a heavy rain." 42 So Ahab went
off to eat and drink, but Elijah climbed to the top of Carmel, bent down to the ground and put his face
between his knees.[a]
43 "Go and look toward the sea," he told his servant. And he went up and looked.
"There is nothing there," he said.
Seven times Elijah said, "Go back."
44 The seventh time the servant reported, "A cloud[b] as small as a man's hand is rising from the sea."
So Elijah said, "Go and tell Ahab, 'Hitch up your chariot and go down before the rain stops you.'"
45 Meanwhile, the sky grew black with clouds, the wind rose, a heavy rain started falling and Ahab
rode off to Jezreel. 46 The power[c] of the LORD came on Elijah and, tucking his cloak into his belt,[d] he ran
ahead of Ahab all the way to Jezreel.

Elijah Flees to Horeb

19 Now Ahab told Jezebel everything Elijah had done and how he had killed[e] all the prophets with
the sword. 2 So Jezebel sent a messenger to Elijah to say, "May the gods deal with me, be it ever
so severely,[f] if by this time tomorrow I do not make your life like that of one of them."
3 Elijah was afraid[b] and ran[g] for his life. When he came to Beersheba in Judah, he left his servant
there, 4 while he himself went a day's journey into the wilderness. He came to a broom bush, sat down
under it and prayed that he might die. "I have had enough, LORD," he said. "Take my life;[h] I am no
better than my ancestors." 5 Then he lay down under the bush and fell asleep.[i]

[a] *32* That is, probably about 24 pounds or about 11 kilograms [b] *3* Or *Elijah saw*

18:34 third time. For the significance of expressions with the number three, see note on 17:21.
18:35 The water-drenching perhaps foreshadows the coming rain and also assures the crowd that what follows is no prophetic trick by Elijah.
18:36 Elijah's simple, direct prayer contrasts with his opponents' loud, long rituals. His appeal is twofold: (1) to the Lord to act in line with his ancient covenant with Abraham, Isaac, and Israel; and (2) to the Israelites to remember everything God had done for them since those patriarchs lived.
18:38 After Baal's silence, Yahweh's answer is decisive, dramatic, and persuasive.
18:39 fell prostrate. Symbolizes renewed submission to Yahweh. **The LORD—he is God!** A double confession of faith is emphatic (cf. v. 37) and implies that only Yahweh really exists.
18:40 Kishon Valley. A small, fertile area along the northern base of Mount Carmel in the Jezreel Valley (cf. v. 42; Judg 4:7,13; 5:21; Ps 83:9). **slaughtered.** The Mosaic penalty for prophets who promote other gods (Deut 13:1–5).
18:43 look toward the sea. Typical source of rainstorms in Israel (cf. v. 44). **Seven times.** The number is common in ritual actions and is symbolic of completeness (Gen 33:3; 46:25; Lev 4:17; Josh 6:4).
18:44 cloud as small as a man's hand. Signifies an imminent, unnatural provision of rain.
18:45 Jezreel. A city 17 miles (27.4 kilometers) east of Mount Carmel; site of a second royal palace (21:1,23; 2 Kgs 8:29).
18:46 Further confirms that God empowers Elijah (17:24).
19:1–9a *Elijah Flees to Horeb.* After Elijah's triumph on Mount Carmel, Jezebel's death threat sends Elijah to again seek refuge beyond her reach (cf. 17:3,7). He flees to southern Judah and then to Horeb (see note on v. 8). Allusions to Moses' life paint Elijah as a prophet like Moses (cf. Deut 18:14–22): like Moses, Elijah escapes a royal execution and encounters God at Horeb.
19:3 Beersheba. Judah's southern frontier town (e.g., 4:25; 2 Sam 3:10); gateway to the Negev desert, Elijah's next stop.
19:4 broom bush. Probably the still-common white broom (*retama raetam*); often the only desert shade available. **Take my life.** Voices Elijah's deep despair and feelings of failure (cf. Num 11:11–15; Jonah 4:3,8).

All at once an angel touched him and said, "Get up and eat." 6He looked around, and there by his
head was some bread baked over hot coals, and a jar of water. He ate and drank and then lay down
again.
7The angel of the LORD came back a second time and touched him and said, "Get up and eat, for the
journey is too much for you." 8So he got up and ate and drank. Strengthened by that food, he traveled
forty[j] days and forty nights until he reached Horeb,[k] the mountain of God. 9There he went into a cave[l]
and spent the night.

The LORD Appears to Elijah

And the word of the LORD came to him: "What are you doing here, Elijah?"
10He replied, "I have been very zealous[m] for the LORD God Almighty. The Israelites have rejected your
covenant, torn down your altars, and put your prophets to death with the sword. I am the only one left,[n]
and now they are trying to kill me too."
11The LORD said, "Go out and stand on the mountain[o] in the presence of the LORD, for the LORD is
about to pass by."
Then a great and powerful wind[p] tore the mountains apart and shattered the rocks before the LORD,
but the LORD was not in the wind. After the wind there was an earthquake, but the LORD was not in the
earthquake. 12After the earthquake came a fire, but the LORD was not in the fire. And after the fire came
a gentle whisper.[q] 13When Elijah heard it, he pulled his cloak over his face[r] and went out and stood at
the mouth of the cave.
Then a voice said to him, "What are you doing here, Elijah?"
14He replied, "I have been very zealous for the LORD God Almighty. The Israelites have rejected your
covenant, torn down your altars, and put your prophets to death with the sword. I am the only one left,[s]
and now they are trying to kill me too."
15The LORD said to him, "Go back the way you came, and go to the Desert of Damascus. When you
get there, anoint Hazael[t] king over Aram. 16Also, anoint[u] Jehu son of Nimshi king over Israel, and
anoint Elisha[v] son of Shaphat from Abel Meholah to succeed you as prophet. 17Jehu will put to death
any who escape the sword of Hazael,[w] and Elisha will put to death any who escape the sword of Jehu.
18Yet I reserve[x] seven thousand in Israel—all whose knees have not bowed down to Baal and whose
mouths have not kissed[y] him."

19:8 [j] Ex 24:18; 34:28; Dt 9:9-11,18; Mt 4:2 [k] Ex 3:1
19:9 [l] Ex 33:22
19:10 [m] Nu 25:13 [n] 1Ki 18:4,22; Ro 11:3*
19:11 [o] Ex 24:12 [p] Eze 1:4; 37:7
19:12 [q] Job 4:16; Zec 4:6
19:13 [r] ver 9; Ex 3:6
19:14 [s] ver 10
19:15 [t] 2Ki 8:7-15
19:16 [u] 2Ki 9:1-3,6 [v] ver 21; 2Ki 2:9,15
19:17 [w] 2Ki 8:12,29; 9:14; 13:3,7,22
19:18 [x] Ro 11:4* [y] Hos 13:2

19:6 bread ... jar of water. A basic meal (cf. 17:10–11).
19:7 journey. Hints at Horeb (v. 8) as Elijah's final destination.
19:8 forty days and forty nights. God sustains Elijah for the same length of time and at the same place (Mount Sinai) as he did Moses (Exod 24:18; 34:28; cf. Exod 3:1; 19:3). Equals the time period that Jesus will spend in the wilderness (Matt 4:2,11). The question is: Like Moses, will Elijah also see God, and will that glimpse lift his spirits? **Horeb.** The larger region in which Mount Sinai is located; an alternate name for Mount Sinai (8:9; Exod 3:1; 19:1–3) where the Lord initiated a covenant with Israel (Exod 19–24). The distance from near Beersheba to Horeb was about 250 miles (400 kilometers), longer if Elijah has taken a less direct route. Rugged terrain during the journey's last leg would prolong the time it would take Elijah to arrive. **mountain of God.** Cf. Exod 3:1; 4:27; 18:5.
19:9a cave. Perhaps the cleft of the rock that protected Moses as God passed by (Exod 33:22).
19:9b–18 *The Lord Appears to Elijah.* The repetition of the same question and answer (vv. 9b–10,13–14; cf. Exod 19:19) before and after God's dramatic appearance (vv. 11–12) gives the incident the formality of a ritual. The new prophetic commission (vv. 15–18) may indicate that the story's purpose is to show that God sends Elijah back to his prophetic mission (see note on v. 12). Echoes of Moses' encounter with Yahweh abound (cf. Exod 33:12–23), including his receipt of a new commission (Exod 2:15; 3:1–4).
19:11 Israel regarded windstorms and earthquakes as among the visible signs of God's activity (Exod 19:16,18; Judg 5:4; Ps 18:11–15; Nah 1:3–5).
19:12 fire. See note on 18:24. Cf. Deut 5:22–24. **gentle whisper.** The term describes either a hushed sound or complete silence (cf. Job 4:16; Ps 107:29). It probably refers either to a soft verbal message that God gives Elijah or to some undefined, silent sign of God's nearness. Elijah receives a message through the contrast between the noisy, violent judgment that his indictment of Israel justified (wind, earthquake, fire) and the quiet, soft sound or silence he received. For the moment God's will is not to judge Israel but for Elijah and Elisha to continue God's dealings with his people from the present into the next generation (v. 16).
19:14 the only one left. Elijah believes himself to be the sole surviving worshiper of the Lord—and also to be in grave danger. The psalmists also cite imminent death as the reason God should intervene (Pss 28:1; 30:9), and Elijah's claim may be a similar but less direct appeal. For God's reply, see v. 18.
19:15 Desert of Damascus. A colorful term for the Aramean capital; highlights the city's isolation as an oasis surrounded by a vast desert but able to flourish because of its two rivers. See note on 11:24; cf. 15:18. **anoint Hazael.** See 2 Kgs 8:7–15; cf. 2 Kgs 8–10; 12:17–18; 13:1–25. **Aram.** See note on 15:18.
19:18 seven thousand. A round number connoting completeness or fullness; corrects Elijah's mistaken conclusion that he is Yahweh's only worshiper (vv. 10,14; 18:22). Despite the opposition of Ahab and Jezebel, God has preserved a godly remnant, an important biblical theme symbolized by Noah's family (Gen 6–9) and survivors of military sieges (2 Kgs 19:4,30,31) and of exile (Isa 10:20–22; 11:16; 46:3). According to Paul, Jews who believe in Christ compose a remnant that also fulfills

19:19 [z]2Ki 2:8,14
19:20 [a]Mt 8:21-22; Lk 9:61
19:21 [b]2Sa 24:22 [c]ver 16
20:1 [d]1Ki 15:18; 22:31; 2Ki 6:24
20:7 [e]2Ki 5:7
20:10 [f]2Sa 22:43; 1Ki 19:2
20:11 [g]Pr 27:1; Jer 9:23
20:12 [h]ver 16; 1Ki 16:9

The Call of Elisha

19 So Elijah went from there and found Elisha son of Shaphat. He was plowing with twelve yoke of
oxen, and he himself was driving the twelfth pair. Elijah went up to him and threw his cloak[z] around
him. 20 Elisha then left his oxen and ran after Elijah. "Let me kiss my father and mother goodbye,"[a] he
said, "and then I will come with you."
"Go back," Elijah replied. "What have I done to you?"
21 So Elisha left him and went back. He took his yoke of oxen[b] and slaughtered them. He burned the
plowing equipment to cook the meat and gave it to the people, and they ate. Then he set out to follow
Elijah and became his servant.[c]

Ben-Hadad Attacks Samaria

20 Now Ben-Hadad[d] king of Aram mustered his entire army. Accompanied by thirty-two kings
with their horses and chariots, he went up and besieged Samaria and attacked it. 2 He sent
messengers into the city to Ahab king of Israel, saying, "This is what Ben-Hadad says: 3 'Your silver and
gold are mine, and the best of your wives and children are mine.' "
4 The king of Israel answered, "Just as you say, my lord the king. I and all I have are yours."
5 The messengers came again and said, "This is what Ben-Hadad says: 'I sent to demand your silver
and gold, your wives and your children. 6 But about this time tomorrow I am going to send my officials to
search your palace and the houses of your officials. They will seize everything you value and carry it away.' "
7 The king of Israel summoned all the elders of the land and said to them, "See how this man is
looking for trouble![e] When he sent for my wives and my children, my silver and my gold, I did not
refuse him."
8 The elders and the people all answered, "Don't listen to him or agree to his demands."
9 So he replied to Ben-Hadad's messengers, "Tell my lord the king, 'Your servant will do all you
demanded the first time, but this demand I cannot meet.' " They left and took the answer back to
Ben-Hadad.
10 Then Ben-Hadad sent another message to Ahab: "May the gods deal with me, be it ever so severely,
if enough dust[f] remains in Samaria to give each of my men a handful."
11 The king of Israel answered, "Tell him: 'One who puts on his armor should not boast[g] like one
who takes it off.' "
12 Ben-Hadad heard this message while he and the kings were drinking[h] in their tents,[a] and he ordered his men: "Prepare to attack." So they prepared to attack the city.

a 12 Or *in Sukkoth*; also in verse 16

the claim of this verse (see Rom 11:2–5). **not kissed.** May allude to kissing idols during Baal worship (Hos 13:2).

19:19–21 *The Call of Elisha.* Elijah immediately completes the third item of his commission (v. 16): anointing his successor, Elisha.

19:19 threw his cloak around him. Symbolizes Elijah's transferring prophetic authority and power (cf. 2 Kgs 9:3,6–7; Exod 29:7). **cloak.** See note on 2 Kgs 2:8.

19:21 slaughtered them ... burned the plowing equipment. Though obviously from a wealthy family, Elisha decisively closes that chapter of his life. **follow Elijah ... his servant.** Implies that Elisha's new status is as an apprentice prophet.

20:1–43 *Ahab's Conflicts With the Arameans.* Ahab defends his kingdom against the territorial ambitions of the Aramean king, Ben-Hadad. His interactions with several unnamed prophets, incidents probably long remembered among them, further flesh out the portrait of Ahab in 1–2 Kings.

20:1–12 *Ben-Hadad Attacks Samaria.* Warring kings exchange messages during the siege of Samaria. The besieging king threatens violence to the city to persuade it to surrender and then prepares to attack.

20:1 Ben-Hadad ... Aram. Cf. vv. 20,33; see note on 15:18. Chronologically, the king was probably Ben-Hadad II (cf. 2 Kgs 8:7), either a son or grandson of Ben-Hadad I, whose reign began as early as 895 BC. Ch. 20 covers events over a two-year period (see vv. 22–26; cf. 22:1), after which Israel and Aram shared three years of peace before resuming warfare. In 853 BC, following that peaceful interlude, Ahab died while fighting the Arameans. This suggests ca. 857 BC as the date of the events in ch. 20. **thirty-two kings.** Rulers over cities or regions within the Aramean confederation (cf. v. 16); a sizeable force. **Samaria.** See note on 16:24.

20:6 everything you value. A sweeping demand that the Arameans be allowed to plunder the palace at will.

20:7 elders of the land. Probably a royal advisory body of tribal and or clan leaders (cf. Prov 31:23; Jer 26:17).

20:10 May the gods deal with me. An oath accepting dire consequences. By voluntarily swearing it, the king underscores that his threatened attack is imminent and that he has full confidence in its likelihood of success (cf. 19:2; Ruth 1:17). See notes on 1:29; 8:31; 17:1,12; 21:3; cf. 2 Kgs 6:31.

20:11 This proverb warns Ben-Hadad not to "count [his] chickens before they hatch." Only victorious kings, not confident ones, have the right to boast of a victory, and only after the fact. Prebattle bragging has blinded many a leader to the true dangers that await him.

Ahab Defeats Ben-Hadad

13 Meanwhile a prophet came to Ahab king of Israel and announced, "This is what the LORD says: 'Do
you see this vast army? I will give it into your hand today, and then you will know[i] that I am the LORD.'"
14 "But who will do this?" asked Ahab.
The prophet replied, "This is what the LORD says: 'The junior officers under the provincial commanders will do it.'"
"And who will start[j] the battle?" he asked.
The prophet answered, "You will."
15 So Ahab summoned the 232 junior officers under the provincial commanders. Then he assembled
the rest of the Israelites, 7,000 in all. 16 They set out at noon while Ben-Hadad and the 32 kings allied
with him were in their tents getting drunk.[k] 17 The junior officers under the provincial commanders
went out first.
Now Ben-Hadad had dispatched scouts, who reported, "Men are advancing from Samaria."
18 He said, "If they have come out for peace, take them alive; if they have come out for war, take
them alive."
19 The junior officers under the provincial commanders marched out of the city with the army
behind them 20 and each one struck down his opponent. At that, the Arameans fled, with the Israelites in pursuit. But Ben-Hadad king of Aram escaped on horseback with some of his horsemen.
21 The king of Israel advanced and overpowered the horses and chariots and inflicted heavy losses
on the Arameans.
22 Afterward, the prophet[l] came to the king of Israel and said, "Strengthen your position and see what
must be done, because next spring[m] the king of Aram will attack you again."
23 Meanwhile, the officials of the king of Aram advised him, "Their gods are gods[n] of the hills. That
is why they were too strong for us. But if we fight them on the plains, surely we will be stronger than
they. 24 Do this: Remove all the kings from their commands and replace them with other officers. 25 You
must also raise an army like the one you lost—horse for horse and chariot for chariot—so we can
fight Israel on the plains. Then surely we will be stronger than they." He agreed with them and acted
accordingly.
26 The next spring[o] Ben-Hadad mustered the Arameans and went up to Aphek[p] to fight against Israel. 27 When the Israelites were also mustered and given provisions, they marched out to meet them.
The Israelites camped opposite them like two small flocks of goats, while the Arameans covered the
countryside.[q]
28 The man of God came up and told the king of Israel, "This is what the LORD says: 'Because the
Arameans think the LORD is a god of the hills and not a god[r] of the valleys, I will deliver this vast army
into your hands, and you will know[s] that I am the LORD.'"
29 For seven days they camped opposite each other, and on the seventh day the battle was joined. The
Israelites inflicted a hundred thousand casualties on the Aramean foot soldiers in one day. 30 The rest
of them escaped to the city of Aphek,[t] where the wall collapsed on twenty-seven thousand of them. And
Ben-Hadad fled to the city and hid[u] in an inner room.

20:13 [i] ver 28; Ex 6:7
20:14 [j] Jdg 1:1
20:16 [k] ver 12; 1Ki 16:9
20:22 [l] ver 13 [m] ver 26; 2Sa 11:1
20:23 [n] 1Ki 14:23; Ro 1:21-23
20:26 [o] ver 22 [p] 2Ki 13:17
20:27 [q] Jdg 6:6; 1Sa 13:6
20:28 [r] ver 23 [s] ver 13
20:30 [t] ver 26 [u] 1Ki 22:25; 2Ch 18:24

20:13–34 *Ahab Defeats Ben-Hadad.* Ahab twice defeats Ben-Hadad after God reassures and guides him through prophets. The prophetic support of Ahab's military ventures here contrasts sharply with the negative, critical treatment of the king by prophets in chs. 16–19. The story alternates between Israelite and Aramean perspectives.
20:13 This is what the LORD says. See vv. 14,28,42; see also note on 12:24. **I will give it into your hand today.** Prophetic assurances of victory like this are a common component of ancient battle reports (cf. 22:6–8; Deut 7:24; Josh 10:8,19; 1 Sam 23:4). **you will know that I am the LORD.** Ahab had not sought divine relief from the Aramean siege of Samaria, but once again God graciously acts to reveal himself to the king and his people (see 18:36–39) by delivering the capital city. The lesson the Baal-worshiper Ahab is to learn from the victory is the same one taught on Mount Carmel (ch. 18): the Lord, not Baal, is the only true and living God (cf. v. 28).
20:14 who will do this? Request for divine tactical guidance through a prophet.
20:20 This improbable rout of superior forces fulfills God's promise (v. 13) and confirms God's presence and power.
20:22 spring. The dry, harvest season was ideal for military campaigns (cf. v. 26; 2 Sam 11:1).
20:23 The Aramean intelligence report misreads Israel as polytheistic and Yahweh's power as limited.
20:24 other officers. This is probably done because these soldiers loyal to Ben-Hadad are more likely to fight bravely than the self-centered kings unwilling to die for their Aramean ally.
20:26 Aphek. A name for several towns, here probably one about three miles (4.8 kilometers) east of the Sea of Galilee.
20:28 man of God. See note on 12:22; cf. 17:18. **you will know that I am the LORD.** See note on v. 13.

20:31 [v]Ge 37:34
20:34 [w]1Ki 15:20
[x]Jer 49:23-27 [y]Ex 23:32
20:35 [z]1Ki 13:21; 2Ki 2:3-7
20:36 [a]1Ki 13:24
20:39 [b]2Ki 10:24
20:42 [c]Jer 48:10
[d]ver 39; Jos 2:14; 1Ki 22:31-37
20:43 [e]1Ki 21:4
21:1 [f]2Ki 9:21
[g]1Ki 18:45-46
21:3 [h]Lev 25:23; Nu 36:7; Eze 46:18

31 His officials said to him, "Look, we have heard that the kings of Israel are merciful. Let us go to
the king of Israel with sackcloth[v] around our waists and ropes around our heads. Perhaps he will spare
your life."
32 Wearing sackcloth around their waists and ropes around their heads, they went to the king of
Israel and said, "Your servant Ben-Hadad says: 'Please let me live.' "
The king answered, "Is he still alive? He is my brother."
33 The men took this as a good sign and were quick to pick up his word. "Yes, your brother Ben-Hadad!" they said.
"Go and get him," the king said. When Ben-Hadad came out, Ahab had him come up into his
chariot.
34 "I will return the cities[w] my father took from your father," Ben-Hadad offered. "You may set up
your own market areas in Damascus,[x] as my father did in Samaria."
Ahab said, "On the basis of a treaty[y] I will set you free." So he made a treaty with him, and let him go.

A Prophet Condemns Ahab

35 By the word of the LORD one of the company of the prophets said to his companion, "Strike me
with your weapon," but he refused.[z]
36 So the prophet said, "Because you have not obeyed the LORD, as soon as you leave me a lion[a] will
kill you." And after the man went away, a lion found him and killed him.
37 The prophet found another man and said, "Strike me, please." So the man struck him and wounded him. 38 Then the prophet went and stood by the road waiting for the king. He disguised himself with
his headband down over his eyes. 39 As the king passed by, the prophet called out to him, "Your servant
went into the thick of the battle, and someone came to me with a captive and said, 'Guard this man. If
he is missing, it will be your life for his life,[b] or you must pay a talent[*a*] of silver.' 40 While your servant
was busy here and there, the man disappeared."
"That is your sentence," the king of Israel said. "You have pronounced it yourself."
41 Then the prophet quickly removed the headband from his eyes, and the king of Israel recognized
him as one of the prophets. 42 He said to the king, "This is what the LORD says: 'You have set free a man I
had determined should die.[*b*c] Therefore it is your life for his life,[d] your people for his people.' " 43 Sullen
and angry,[e] the king of Israel went to his palace in Samaria.

Naboth's Vineyard

21 Some time later there was an incident involving a vineyard belonging to Naboth[f] the Jezreelite.
The vineyard was in Jezreel,[g] close to the palace of Ahab king of Samaria. 2 Ahab said to Naboth,
"Let me have your vineyard to use for a vegetable garden, since it is close to my palace. In exchange I
will give you a better vineyard or, if you prefer, I will pay you whatever it is worth."
3 But Naboth replied, "The LORD forbid that I should give you the inheritance[h] of my ancestors."

a 39 That is, about 75 pounds or about 34 kilograms *b* 42 The Hebrew term refers to the irrevocable giving over of things or persons to the LORD, often by totally destroying them.

20:31 we have heard. Another Aramean intelligence brief (cf. vv. 23–25). **sackcloth.** Dark-colored, rough cloth of goat or camel hair. As clothing it symbolizes mourning or slavery (Gen 37:34; 2 Sam 3:31; Lam 2:10; cf. 21:27).
20:32 my brother. See note on 9:13.
20:33 good sign. Implies that Ahab may show mercy (v. 31).
20:35–43 *A Prophet Condemns Ahab.* An Israelite prophet condemns Ahab because he makes a treaty that spares Ben-Hadad's life.
20:35 company of the prophets. See note on 13:11. **Strike me.** Apparently to create the look of a wounded soldier (cf. vv. 37–40a).
20:36 Cf. 13:24–26.
20:38 headband. This unique headgear probably provides the prophet a disguise to avoid recognition if he wishes (cf. v. 41).
20:39–40 A parable about a legal matter; comparable to Nathan's parable confronting David with his affair with Bathsheba (cf. 2 Sam 12:1–4). In this case the story tricks Ahab into pronouncing a death sentence on himself.
20:42 your life for his. Marks the first of several prophetic condemnations of Ahab (cf. 21:1–29; 22:1–28).
20:43 Sullen and angry. See note on 21:4.
21:1–29 *Naboth's Vineyard.* This brief interlude leaves the ongoing war with Aram and the critique of Ahab's idolatrous program in order to indict him for cruel injustice. The king violates Israelite law by executing an innocent man and claiming his property as if the king had the same authority as other ancient kings (vv. 1–16). Elijah announces that God will judge Ahab and Jezebel (vv. 17–26), but God shows mercy to Ahab when he repents (vv. 27–29).
21:1 Jezreel. See note on 18:45.
21:3 The LORD forbid. An oath that forbids Naboth to consider the king's offer to buy his land (cf. 1:29; 2:24; 22:14; 2 Kgs 2:2,6; 4:30; 5:16,20).

4So Ahab went home, sullen and angry[i] because Naboth the Jezreelite had said, "I will not give you
the inheritance of my ancestors." He lay on his bed sulking and refused to eat.
5His wife Jezebel came in and asked him, "Why are you so sullen? Why won't you eat?"
6He answered her, "Because I said to Naboth the Jezreelite, 'Sell me your vineyard; or if you prefer, I
will give you another vineyard in its place.' But he said, 'I will not give you my vineyard.' "
7Jezebel his wife said, "Is this how you act as king over Israel? Get up and eat! Cheer up. I'll get you
the vineyard[j] of Naboth the Jezreelite."
8So she wrote letters in Ahab's name, placed his seal[k] on them, and sent them to the elders and nobles who lived in Naboth's city with him. 9In those letters she wrote:

"Proclaim a day of fasting and seat Naboth in a prominent place among the people. 10But seat
two scoundrels[l] opposite him and have them bring charges that he has cursed[m] both God and the
king. Then take him out and stone him to death."

11So the elders and nobles who lived in Naboth's city did as Jezebel directed in the letters she had
written to them. 12They proclaimed a fast[n] and seated Naboth in a prominent place among the people.
13Then two scoundrels came and sat opposite him and brought charges against Naboth before the people, saying, "Naboth has cursed both God and the king." So they took him outside the city and stoned
him to death.[o] 14Then they sent word to Jezebel: "Naboth has been stoned to death."
15As soon as Jezebel heard that Naboth had been stoned to death, she said to Ahab, "Get up and take possession of the vineyard[p] of Naboth the Jezreelite that he refused to sell you. He is no longer alive, but dead."
16When Ahab heard that Naboth was dead, he got up and went down to take possession of Naboth's vineyard.
17Then the word of the LORD came to Elijah the Tishbite: 18"Go down to meet Ahab king of Israel,
who rules in Samaria. He is now in Naboth's vineyard, where he has gone to take possession of it. 19Say
to him, 'This is what the LORD says: Have you not murdered a man and seized his property?' Then say
to him, 'This is what the LORD says: In the place where dogs licked up Naboth's blood,[q] dogs[r] will lick
up your blood—yes, yours!' "
20Ahab said to Elijah, "So you have found me, my enemy!"[s]
"I have found you," he answered, "because you have sold[t] yourself to do evil in the eyes of the
LORD. 21He says, 'I am going to bring disaster on you. I will wipe out your descendants and cut off
from Ahab every last male[u] in Israel—slave or free.[a] 22I will make your house[v] like that of Jeroboam son of Nebat and that of Baasha son of Ahijah, because you have aroused my anger and have
caused Israel to sin.'[w]

[a] 21 Or *Israel—every ruler or leader*

21:4 [i] 1Ki 20:43
21:7 [j] 1Sa 8:14
21:8 [k] Ge 38:18; Est 3:12; 8:8,10
21:10 [l] Ac 6:11 [m] Ex 22:28; Lev 24:15-16
21:12 [n] Isa 58:4
21:13 [o] 2Ki 9:26
21:15 [p] 1Sa 8:14
21:19 [q] 2Ki 9:26; Ps 9:12; Isa 14:20 [r] 1Ki 22:38
21:20 [s] 1Ki 18:17 [t] ver 25; 2Ki 17:17; Ro 7:14
21:21 [u] 1Ki 14:10; 2Ki 9:8
21:22 [v] 1Ki 15:29; 16:3 [w] 1Ki 12:30

inheritance. Legal term for land inherited from ancestors and owned in perpetuity; it may be sold or mortgaged but only temporarily (Lev 25:8–17,23–25; 27:16–25; Ruth 4:1–12).
21:4 sullen and angry. Like a petulant, sulking child (cf. v. 7; 20:43).
21:8 Naboth's city. Jezreel (see note on 18:45). Jezebel probably writes the letters from Samaria (cf. vv. 11,18).
21:10 two. The minimum number of witnesses for a conviction (Deut 17:6; 19:15). **scoundrels.** Lying witnesses. **has cursed both God and the king.** A crime punishable by stoning (cf. Exod 22:28; Lev 24:14–16).
21:16 take possession. Like Achan (Josh 7:24–26), both Naboth and his sons are stoned, thus eliminating the current owner and all heirs who might lay legal claim to Naboth's property. The legal basis on which Ahab assumes possession of Naboth's property, however, is unclear. Samuel argued that one downside to life under a monarchy was that kings often arbitrarily took possession of private land (1 Sam 8:14). Ahab's acquisition of Naboth's land may be one case in point. Mosaic law protected the property rights of clans and families lest inherited land pass to someone outside the extended family (Lev 25:23–28,39–42; Ruth 4:3–10; cf. Mic 2:1–5). But the injustice done Naboth by the palace may have discouraged his relatives from asserting their rights; to do so would have put their own lives at risk. Or perhaps the property rights of an executed criminal were presumed to pass from the extended family to the king as part of the legal penalty. That would explain why Jezebel engineers a legal process to remove Naboth so the land will by law fall to Ahab.
21:19 This is what the LORD says. See 22:11; see also note on 12:24. **murdered a man and seized his property.** Crimes worthy of death. **dogs will lick up your blood.** Ahab will die in the same place Naboth died and under the same shameful circumstances (cf. v. 23; 22:37–38). 2 Kings records the fulfillment of the prophecy (2 Kgs 9:25–26,36–37; 10:10–11,17), another example in 1–2 Kings of judgment brought about by the power of God's word. The incident anticipates the NT stress on the power of Christ's word (Heb 1:1–2; 4:12; Rev 19:15,21).
21:20 sold yourself. Elijah's words compare Ahab to someone who voluntarily consents to be someone's slave in exchange for payment (cf. v. 25; Deut 28:68). Ahab willingly obligates himself to do something that displeases God—the unjust execution of Naboth—and in return receives ownership of Naboth's field (cf. 2 Kgs 17:17). Such self-enslavement shows the person's desperation to achieve some outcome; however, besides the field, Ahab also earns God's anger over the legal outrage that victimized Naboth.
21:22 God denies Ahab a dynastic line (cf. v. 21; 2 Kgs 9:6–9,24–26) as he denied Jeroboam (14:10–11) and Baasha (16:3–4). **caused Israel to sin.** Promoted idolatry (cf. v. 26; 16:32–33).

21:23 [x] 2Ki 9:10,34-36
21:24 [y] 1Ki 14:11; 16:4
21:25 [z] ver 20; 1Ki 16:33
21:26 [a] Ge 15:16; Lev 18:25-30; 2Ki 21:11
21:27 [b] Ge 37:34; 2Sa 3:31; 2Ki 6:30
21:29 [c] 2Ki 9:26
22:3 [d] Dt 4:43; Jos 21:38
22:4 [e] 2Ki 3:7
22:5 [f] Ex 33:7; 2Ki 3:11
22:6 [g] 1Ki 18:19
22:7 [h] 2Ki 3:11
22:8 [i] Am 5:10 [j] Isa 5:20

23 "And also concerning Jezebel the LORD says: 'Dogs[x] will devour Jezebel by the wall of[a] Jezreel.'
24 "Dogs[y] will eat those belonging to Ahab who die in the city, and the birds will feed on those who
die in the country."
25 (There was never[z] anyone like Ahab, who sold himself to do evil in the eyes of the LORD, urged on
by Jezebel his wife. 26 He behaved in the vilest manner by going after idols, like the Amorites[a] the LORD
drove out before Israel.)
27 When Ahab heard these words, he tore his clothes, put on sackcloth[b] and fasted. He lay in sackcloth
and went around meekly.
28 Then the word of the LORD came to Elijah the Tishbite: 29 "Have you noticed how Ahab has humbled
himself before me? Because he has humbled himself, I will not bring this disaster in his day, but I will
bring it on his house in the days of his son."[c]

Micaiah Prophesies Against Ahab

22:1-28pp — 2Ch 18:1-27

22 For three years there was no war between Aram and Israel. 2 But in the third year Jehoshaphat
king of Judah went down to see the king of Israel. 3 The king of Israel had said to his officials,
"Don't you know that Ramoth Gilead[d] belongs to us and yet we are doing nothing to retake it from
the king of Aram?"
4 So he asked Jehoshaphat, "Will you go with me to fight[e] against Ramoth Gilead?"
Jehoshaphat replied to the king of Israel, "I am as you are, my people as your people, my horses
as your horses." 5 But Jehoshaphat also said to the king of Israel, "First seek the counsel[f] of the LORD."
6 So the king of Israel brought together the prophets—about four hundred men—and asked them,
"Shall I go to war against Ramoth Gilead, or shall I refrain?"
"Go,"[g] they answered, "for the Lord will give it into the king's hand."
7 But Jehoshaphat asked, "Is there no longer a prophet[h] of the LORD here whom we can inquire of?"
8 The king of Israel answered Jehoshaphat, "There is still one prophet through whom we can inquire
of the LORD, but I hate[i] him because he never prophesies anything good[j] about me, but always bad. He
is Micaiah son of Imlah."
"The king should not say such a thing," Jehoshaphat replied.
9 So the king of Israel called one of his officials and said, "Bring Micaiah son of Imlah at once."
10 Dressed in their royal robes, the king of Israel and Jehoshaphat king of Judah were sitting on their

[a] 23 Most Hebrew manuscripts; a few Hebrew manuscripts, Vulgate and Syriac (see also 2 Kings 9:26) *the plot of ground at*

21:23 Jezebel's fate will be like Ahab's (cf. vv. 19,25; 2 Kgs 9:10,22, 30–37).
21:25 never anyone like Ahab. Unparalleled idolatry, violent opposition to prophets who speak God's word, and outrageous abuse of royal power.
21:26 Amorites. Canaan's occupants before Israel; fabled for degradation (2 Kgs 21:11; Gen 15:16; Josh 10:5,12; Amos 2:9–10). **drove out.** Implies that if the Lord rid Canaan of the Amorites for their abominations, then the even more degraded Ahab deserves a worse fate.
21:27 he tore his clothes, put on sackcloth and fasted. Acts of humiliation, mourning, and repentance (see note on 20:31).
21:28 word of the LORD came to. See notes on 6:11; 13:1.
22:1–40 *Ahab's Death.* After six chapters about Ahab, this narrative returns to the Israel–Aram war and the parallel treatment of kings in both Israel and Judah. More important, it details the circumstances of Ahab's death and burial.
22:1–28 *Micaiah Prophesies Against Ahab.* Previous prophecies that condemned Ahab culminate in what the prophet Micaiah pronounces. Micaiah contradicts the prophets who serve Ahab and do not speak for Yahweh.
22:1 three years. See note on 20:1. **no war between Aram and Israel.** According to the annals of the Assyrian king Shalmaneser III (859–824 BC), in 853 BC one-time enemies Ahab and Ben-Hadad of Aram were allied with ten other rulers in fighting Assyrian forces at Qarqar on the Orontes River (in modern Syria). Assyrian sources credit Ahab with contributing 2,000 chariots and 10,000 ground troops to the coalition force. The Assyrians withdrew from the battle and over the next four or five years did not visit the west. The Assyrians' claims of victory at the Battle of Qarqar seem exaggerated and unreliable.
22:2 Jehoshaphat. The king of Judah first introduced at 15:24 who now receives full treatment in 1 Kgs 22—2 Kgs 3.
22:3 Ramoth Gilead. A Levitical city somewhere along the King's Highway in northern Transjordan (Josh 20:8; 21:38; see note on 2 Kgs 8:28; cf. 9:1–14). **belongs to us.** It is an Israelite city that Aram is occupying, which justifies the call for battle.
22:4 Jehoshaphat's reply may imply that Judah is treaty-bound to assist Ahab.
22:5 seek ... the LORD. Cf. vv. 11–12; see note on 20:14.
22:7 Jehoshaphat may doubt the authenticity of Ahab's clergy.
22:8 one. Implies that Ahab's prophets cannot inquire of the Lord. **never prophesies anything good about me.** Because he is a genuine prophet (Jer 28:8–9; Mic 3:8).
22:9 Shows that Micaiah is available but absent from the prophets (v. 6) advising the two kings on the coming battle (cf. 18:13).

thrones at the threshing floor[k] by the entrance of the gate of Samaria, with all the prophets prophesying
before them. 11Now Zedekiah son of Kenaanah had made iron horns[l] and he declared, "This is what the
LORD says: 'With these you will gore the Arameans until they are destroyed.' "
12All the other prophets were prophesying the same thing. "Attack Ramoth Gilead and be victorious,"
they said, "for the LORD will give it into the king's hand."
13The messenger who had gone to summon Micaiah said to him, "Look, the other prophets without
exception are predicting success for the king. Let your word agree with theirs, and speak favorably."
14But Micaiah said, "As surely as the LORD lives, I can tell him only what the LORD tells me."[m]
15When he arrived, the king asked him, "Micaiah, shall we go to war against Ramoth Gilead, or not?"
"Attack and be victorious," he answered, "for the LORD will give it into the king's hand."
16The king said to him, "How many times must I make you swear to tell me nothing but the truth
in the name of the LORD?"
17Then Micaiah answered, "I saw all Israel scattered on the hills like sheep without a shepherd,[n] and
the LORD said, 'These people have no master. Let each one go home in peace.' "
18The king of Israel said to Jehoshaphat, "Didn't I tell you that he never prophesies anything good
about me, but only bad?"
19Micaiah continued, "Therefore hear the word of the LORD: I saw the LORD sitting on his throne[o] with
all the multitudes[p] of heaven standing around him on his right and on his left. 20And the LORD said,
'Who will entice Ahab into attacking Ramoth Gilead and going to his death there?'
"One suggested this, and another that. 21Finally, a spirit came forward, stood before the LORD and
said, 'I will entice him.'
22" 'By what means?' the LORD asked.
" 'I will go out and be a deceiving[q] spirit in the mouths of all his prophets,' he said.
" 'You will succeed in enticing him,' said the LORD. 'Go and do it.'
23"So now the LORD has put a deceiving spirit in the mouths of all these prophets[r] of yours. The LORD
has decreed disaster for you."
24Then Zedekiah[s] son of Kenaanah went up and slapped[t] Micaiah in the face. "Which way did the
spirit from[a] the LORD go when he went from me to speak to you?" he asked.
25Micaiah replied, "You will find out on the day you go to hide[u] in an inner room."

[a] 24 Or *Spirit of*

22:10 [k] ver 6
22:11 [l] Dt 33:17; Zec 1:18-21
22:14 [m] Nu 22:18; 24:13; 1Ki 18:10,15
22:17 [n] ver 34-36; Nu 27:17; Mt 9:36
22:19 [o] Isa 6:1; Eze 1:26; Da 7:9 [p] Job 1:6; 2:1; Ps 103:20-21; Mt 18:10; Heb 1:7,14
22:22 [q] Jdg 9:23; 1Sa 16:14; 18:10; 19:9; Eze 14:9; 2Th 2:11
22:23 [r] Eze 14:9
22:24 [s] ver 11 [t] Ac 23:2
22:25 [u] 1Ki 20:30

22:11 Zedekiah. Apparently the spokesperson for the 400 prophets. **iron horns.** Symbols of power (see Deut 33:17). Ancients trusted in the power of sympathetic magic, i.e., that spoken words (e.g., blessings or curses) or symbolic actions actually set in motion the events they desired. Perhaps Zedekiah thought similarly that his words and actions produced the effect he wanted, i.e., the destruction of Aram in the coming battle. In the OT only intervention by God himself can bring about or contravene what humans declare, petition, or plan (e.g., 2 Sam 15:31; 17:14; Prov 16:9; 21:1). The theological basis of prayer is the believer's confidence that God hears, cares, and promises to reply (Matt 7:7–11; Heb 4:15–16).

22:15 Attack . . . for the LORD will give it into the king's hand. Micaiah sarcastically mimics the 400 false prophets (v. 12).

22:16 tell me nothing but the truth. Ahab immediately recognizes in Micaiah's sarcasm that the prophet's positive announcement (v. 15) is untrue. Ironically, Ahab's comment is an open invitation for Micaiah to pronounce judgment on the king.

22:17 sheep without a shepherd. A metaphor for a king and his subjects (cf. 2 Sam 5:2; 24:17; Ps 23:1; Ezek 34:5,8; John 10:2,14); suggests Ahab's imminent death.

22:19 hear the word of the LORD. A prophetic call to listen (see notes on 6:11; 13:1; cf. 2 Kgs 7:1; 20:16; Isa 1:10). **I saw the LORD sitting on his throne.** Cf. Isa 6:1–13; Zech 3:1–2. Visions are one way that God conveys the messages that his prophets are to announce to God's people. Prophets are sometimes called "seers" (e.g., 1 Sam 9:9; 2 Sam 24:11; Isa 30:10; Amos 7:12) because they "see" such visions and report them as a word from God (cf. Rev 22:8). Micaiah sees (and hears) a discussion in God's heavenly throne room about Ahab's fate (cf. v. 19; Isa 6:1), and that is why his listeners should believe him: he knows God's plans for Ahab firsthand (Jer 23:13,18–22).

22:20 entice. Influence the king to voluntarily take the actions God wants.

22:22 The prophets tell Ahab what he wants to hear: (false) assurances of victory.

22:23 the LORD has put a deceiving spirit in the mouths of all these prophets. God never does evil himself, but sometimes he carries out his purposes through evil agents. **deceiving spirit.** Some interpret this as Satan or a demon. Others view it as a spirit of God who carries out the mission of a deceiving spirit (cf. 1 Sam 15:29). Still others regard it as a symbol of the power of the lie. God handed over the 400 prophets to the power of the lie because they simply made up their messages rather than receiving them from God (Jer 14:14; 23:16; Ezek 13:2–3, 17; see note on 2 Sam 24:1; cf. 2 Thess 2:10–12 and note). Rather than listen to the truth-telling prophet, Ahab accepts the lie (it fits what he wants to hear), and the lie lures him to the execution God has ordained for him (see Ps 18:25–26; Ezek 14:9).

22:24 Which way did the spirit from the LORD go . . . ? Zedekiah's question is a sarcastic reply to Micaiah's announcement of disaster (v. 23). Zedekiah's point is that any prophet can be a liar, so his question is, "How do I know you are not lying too?"

22:25 hide in an inner room. Because of fear and disgrace at being proved wrong.

22:27 [v] 2Ch 16:10
22:28 [w] Dt 18:22
22:30 [x] 2Ch 35:32
22:31 [y] 2Sa 17:2
22:34 [z] 2Ch 35:23
22:36 [a] 2Ki 14:12
22:38 [b] 1Ki 21:19
22:39 [c] 2Ch 9:17; Am 3:15

26The king of Israel then ordered, "Take Micaiah and send him back to Amon the ruler of the city
and to Joash the king's son 27and say, 'This is what the king says: Put this fellow in prison[v] and give
him nothing but bread and water until I return safely.' "
28Micaiah declared, "If you ever return safely, the LORD has not spoken[w] through me." Then he
added, "Mark my words, all you people!"

Ahab Killed at Ramoth Gilead

22:29-36pp — 2Ch 18:28-34

29So the king of Israel and Jehoshaphat king of Judah went up to Ramoth Gilead. 30The king of Israel
said to Jehoshaphat, "I will enter the battle in disguise,[x] but you wear your royal robes." So the king of
Israel disguised himself and went into battle.
31Now the king of Aram had ordered his thirty-two chariot commanders, "Do
not fight with anyone, small or great, except the king[y] of Israel." 32When the
chariot commanders saw Jehoshaphat, they thought, "Surely this is
the king of Israel." So they turned to attack him, but when Jehoshaphat cried out, 33the chariot commanders saw that he was not the
king of Israel and stopped pursuing him.
34But someone drew his bow[z] at random and hit the king of Israel
between the sections of his armor. The king told his chariot driver,
"Wheel around and get me out of the fighting. I've been wounded."
35All day long the battle raged, and the king was propped up in his
chariot facing the Arameans. The blood from his wound ran onto
the floor of the chariot, and that evening he died. 36As the sun was
setting, a cry spread through the army: "Every man to his town.
Every man to his land!"[a]
37So the king died and was brought to Samaria, and they buried
him there. 38They washed the chariot at a pool in Samaria (where
the prostitutes bathed),[a] and the dogs[b] licked up his blood, as the
word of the LORD had declared.
39As for the other events of Ahab's reign, including all he did, the
palace he built and adorned with ivory,[c] and the cities he fortified,
are they not written in the book of the annals of the kings of Israel?
40Ahab rested with his ancestors. And Ahaziah his son succeeded him
as king.

Carved ivory depicting a woman at a window, Phoenician, ninth–eighth century BC. King Ahab was known for adorning his palace with ivory (1 Kgs 22:39).

[a] *38* Or *Samaria and cleaned the weapons*

22:27 This is what the king says. This phrase occurs infrequently in 1–2 Kings to introduce a message sent by a king (cf. 2 Kgs 1:11; 9:18–19; 18:29). It contrasts the similar phrase used frequently by prophets to introduce a message from the Lord (13:2,21; 20:13,42; 2 Kgs 1:4,16; 2:21; 20:1). **nothing but bread and water until I return safely.** The irony is that Ahab foolishly seems to think that by holding Micaiah hostage, the king can somehow prevent the fulfillment of God's word and guarantee the king's safe return from battle. He does not take God's sovereignty seriously (cf. v. 30).
22:28 Ahab's fate will validate Micaiah as an authentic prophet (cf. Deut 18:22; Jer 28:8–9).
22:29–40 *Ahab Killed at Ramoth Gilead.* This section details the circumstances of Ahab's death and burial. Ahab fails to escape what Elijah and Micaiah prophesy against him. His death in battle fulfills their words.
22:30 disguise. Ahab seeks to hide his identity and not attract attention in order to lessen the possibility that Micaiah's prophecy might be fulfilled. The king shows either arrogance or desperation. Preferring the lie to the truth, Ahab foolishly thinks that living a lie in battle is his salvation.
22:32–33 The Aramean pursuers apparently recognize both Jehoshaphat's voice and his appearance.
22:34 at random. Providence: God sovereignly guides the arrow to pick Ahab out of the crowd. **between the sections of his armor.** A miniscule gap in Ahab's protective gear; further evidence of God's intervention.
22:35 propped up in his chariot facing the Arameans. Apparently to protect Ahab by disguising his grave condition. **died.** Vindicates Micaiah's status as a true prophet.
22:36 Every man to his town. Panicked call to retreat; pictures leaderless troops scattering, as Micaiah foresaw (v. 17).
22:37 Samaria. Cf. Elijah's prophecy concerning Ahab's burial site (21:17–19).
22:38 where the prostitutes bathed. Ironically appropriate for washing Ahab's royal chariot. **dogs licked up his blood.** Graphically fulfills Elijah's prophecy (21:19); verbally connects Ahab's death with Naboth's.
22:39 other events. Cf. v. 45; see note on 14:19. **the palace he built and adorned with ivory.** Symbolizes economic prosperity, great wealth, and excess under Ahab's rule (cf. 10:18,22; Amos 3:15; 6:4). Excavations at Samaria have discovered ivory inlays in some of the ruins that date to Ahab's era. **cities he fortified.** There is archaeological evidence that Ahab improved the fortifications at Megiddo and Hazor. For example, note the large cache of Phoenician ivories found at Samaria (eighth century BC).

Jehoshaphat King of Judah

22:41-50pp — 2Ch 20:31–21:1

[41]Jehoshaphat son of Asa became king of Judah in the fourth year of Ahab king of Israel. [42]Jehosha-
phat was thirty-five years old when he became king, and he reigned in Jerusalem twenty-five years. His
mother's name was Azubah daughter of Shilhi. [43]In everything he followed the ways of his father Asa[d]
and did not stray from them; he did what was right in the eyes of the LORD. The high places,[e] however,
were not removed, and the people continued to offer sacrifices and burn incense there.[a] [44]Jehoshaphat
was also at peace with the king of Israel.

[45]As for the other events of Jehoshaphat's reign, the things he achieved and his military exploits,
are they not written in the book of the annals of the kings of Judah? [46]He rid the land of the rest of the
male shrine prostitutes[f] who remained there even after the reign of his father Asa. [47]There was then no
king[g] in Edom; a provincial governor ruled.

[48]Now Jehoshaphat built a fleet of trading ships[b][h] to go to Ophir for gold, but they never set sail—
they were wrecked at Ezion Geber. [49]At that time Ahaziah son of Ahab said to Jehoshaphat, "Let my men
sail with yours," but Jehoshaphat refused.

[50]Then Jehoshaphat rested with his ancestors and was buried with them in the city of David his father. And Jehoram his son succeeded him as king.

Ahaziah King of Israel

[51]Ahaziah son of Ahab became king of Israel in Samaria in the seventeenth year of Jehoshaphat king
of Judah, and he reigned over Israel two years. [52]He did evil[i] in the eyes of the LORD, because he followed
the ways of his father and mother and of Jeroboam son of Nebat, who caused Israel to sin. [53]He served
and worshiped Baal[j] and aroused the anger of the LORD, the God of Israel, just as his father[k] had done.

22:43 [d] 2Ch 17:3 [e] 1Ki 3:2; 15:14; 2Ki 12:3
22:46 [f] Dt 23:17; 1Ki 14:24; 15:12
22:47 [g] 2Sa 8:14; 2Ki 3:9; 8:20
22:48 [h] 1Ki 9:26; 10:22
22:52 [i] 1Ki 15:26; 21:25
22:53 [j] Jdg 2:11 [k] 1Ki 16:30-32

[a] *43* In Hebrew texts this sentence (22:43b) is numbered 22:44, and 22:44-53 is numbered 22:45-54. [b] *48* Hebrew *of ships of Tarshish*

22:41–50 *Jehoshaphat King of Judah.* This presents the account of Jehoshaphat's 25-year reign (872/71–848 BC). Except for one important shortcoming, Jehoshaphat is one of the few kings of Judah who remained faithful to Yahweh.
22:43 did what was right. Like father like son (15:11; cf. v. 53; 2 Kgs 12:2; 14:3; 15:3,34; 18:3; 22:2). **high places, however, were not removed.** Jehoshaphat's one failure; repeated by four later kings: Joash (2 Kgs 12:3), Amaziah (2 Kgs 14:4), Azariah/Uzziah (2 Kgs 15:4), and Jotham (2 Kgs 15:35). See note on 3:2.
22:44 at peace with the king of Israel. Not true of his father (15:16,32).
22:46 male shrine prostitutes. See note on 14:24; cf. 15:12; 2 Kgs 23:7.
22:48 fleet of trading ships. See 9:26,28; 10:11,22. **Ophir.** See note on 9:28. **never set sail.** Wrecked in port by some unspecified disaster: God judged the king for allying with Ahab's successor (2 Chr 20:35–37). **Ezion Geber.** See note on 9:26.
22:49 refused. Perhaps to distance Judah culturally from Israel in light of the events at Ramoth Gilead (vv. 1–40).
22:51–53 *Ahaziah King of Israel.* Ahab's son and successor (853–852 BC) continues the idolatrous policy of his parents and of Jeroboam.
22:52 did evil. See notes on 15:26,34.
22:53 served and worshiped Baal. Like father like son (16:31–33); anticipates Ahaziah's imminent condemnation and downfall (2 Kgs 1).

INTRODUCTION TO

2 KINGS

See Introduction to 1 Kings.

Below is an outline for 2 Kings. For an outline of both 1 and 2 Kings, see Introduction to 1 Kings: Outline.

OUTLINE

B. Jehoahaz King of Israel (13:1–9)
C. Jehoash King of Israel (13:10–25)
D. Amaziah King of Judah (14:1–22)
E. Jeroboam II King of Israel (14:23–29)
F. Azariah King of Judah (15:1–7)
G. The Final Kings of Israel (15:8–31)
   1. Zechariah King of Israel (15:8–12)
   2. Shallum King of Israel (15:13–16)
   3. Menahem King of Israel (15:17–22)
   4. Pekahiah King of Israel (15:23–26)
   5. Pekah King of Israel (15:27–31)
H. Jotham King of Judah (15:32–38)
I. Ahaz King of Judah (16:1–20)
J. Hoshea Last King of Israel (17:1–6)
K. Israel Exiled Because of Sin (17:7–23)
L. Samaria Resettled (17:24–41)

V. The Last Kings of Judah (18:1—25:30)
A. Hezekiah King of Judah (18:1—20:21)
   1. Hezekiah's Reign (18:1–16)
   2. Sennacherib Threatens Jerusalem (18:17–37)
   3. Jerusalem's Deliverance Foretold (19:1–13)
   4. Hezekiah's Prayer (19:14–19)
   5. Isaiah Prophesies Sennacherib's Fall (19:20–37)
   6. Hezekiah's Illness (20:1–11)
   7. Envoys From Babylon (20:12–21)
B. Manasseh King of Judah (21:1–18)
C. Amon King of Judah (21:19–26)

Tel Jezreel, aerial view from the south, where King Jehu killed Jezebel (2 Kgs 9:30–37).
Barry Beitzel/www.BiblePlaces.com

- D. Josiah King of Judah (22:1 — 23:30)
  1. The Book of the Law Found (22:1 – 20)
  2. Josiah Renews the Covenant (23:1 – 30)
- E. The Final Four Kings of Judah (23:31 — 24:20a)
  1. Jehoahaz King of Judah (23:31 – 35)
  2. Jehoiakim King of Judah (23:36 — 24:7)
  3. Jehoiachin King of Judah (24:8 – 17)
  4. Zedekiah King of Judah (24:18 – 20a)
- F. The Fall of Jerusalem (24:20b — 25:26)
- G. Jehoiachin Released (25:27 – 30)

2 KINGS

The Lord's Judgment on Ahaziah

1 After Ahab's death, Moab[a] rebelled against Israel. 2Now Ahaziah had fallen through the lattice of
his upper room in Samaria and injured himself. So he sent messengers,[b] saying to them, "Go and
consult Baal-Zebub,[c] the god of Ekron,[d] to see if I will recover[e] from this injury."
3But the angel[f] of the Lord said to Elijah[g] the Tishbite, "Go up and meet the messengers of the king
of Samaria and ask them, 'Is it because there is no God in Israel[h] that you are going off to consult
Baal-Zebub, the god of Ekron?' 4Therefore this is what the Lord says: 'You will not leave[i] the bed you
are lying on. You will certainly die!'" So Elijah went.
5When the messengers returned to the king, he asked them, "Why have you come back?"
6"A man came to meet us," they replied. "And he said to us, 'Go back to the king who sent you and
tell him, "This is what the Lord says: Is it because there is no God in Israel that you are sending messengers to consult Baal-Zebub, the god of Ekron? Therefore you will not leave the bed you are lying on.
You will certainly die!"'"
7The king asked them, "What kind of man was it who came to meet you and told you this?"
8They replied, "He had a garment of hair[a] and had a leather belt around his waist."
The king said, "That was Elijah the Tishbite."
9Then he sent[k] to Elijah a captain[l] with his company of fifty men. The captain went up to Elijah, who
was sitting on the top of a hill, and said to him, "Man of God, the king says, 'Come down!'"
10Elijah answered the captain, "If I am a man of God, may fire come down from heaven and

1:1 [a]Ge 19:37; 2Sa 8:2; 2Ki 3:5
1:2 [b]ver 16 [c]Mk 3:22 [d]1Sa 6:2; Isa 2:6; 14:29; Mt 10:25 [e]Jdg 18:5; 2Ki 8:7-10
1:3 [f]ver 15; Ge 16:7 [g]1Ki 17:1 [h]1Sa 28:8
1:4 [i]ver 6,16; Ps 41:8
1:8 [j]1Ki 18:7; Zec 13:4; Mt 3:4; Mk 1:6
1:9 [k]2Ki 6:14 [l]Ex 18:25; Isa 3:3

[a] 8 Or *He was a hairy man*

1:1–18 *The Lord's Judgment on Ahaziah.* The brief rule of Ahaziah reveals the Lord's power over false gods and their followers. Ahaziah, the son of the powerful Ahab, could not force the prophet Elijah to submit and ultimately dies from an injury he sustains at home.
1:1 After Ahab's death. See 1 Kgs 22:37. **Moab rebelled.** The loss of formerly subject territories evidences God's judgment upon Israel for covenant unfaithfulness. The record of this rebellion continues in 3:5.
1:2 The fatal injury of a king while at home is humiliating. In the context of this book, such an accident is God's judgment. **Samaria.** See note on 1 Kgs 16:24. **Baal-Zebub, the god of Ekron.** Ahaziah seeks not the God of Israel but a deity of one of the Philistine cities 40 miles (64 kilometers) southwest of Samaria. The author probably changes Baal-Zebul ("Baal the prince") to Baal-Zebub ("lord of the flies") to express scorn for this false deity (see notes on Judg 2:11,13). By NT times, the name of this god is associated with Satan (Mark 3:22).
1:3 the angel of the Lord. See notes on Gen 16:7; Exod 3:2. **Elijah the Tishbite.** As is common throughout 1–2 Kings, the Lord sends his prophet to confront the king for idolatry (17:13; 1 Kgs 11:29–39; 12:22–24; 13:1–3; 16:1–4; 17:1; 20:13; 21:17–19). The Lord shows his extraordinary grace by relentlessly pursuing idolatrous kings throughout Israel's history.
1:4 You will certainly die! Though this seems to provide no hope for the king's situation, Ahaziah has the example of his father, Ahab, who repented when Elijah condemned him and thus received a reprieve (1 Kgs 21:27–29).
1:8 garment of hair … leather belt. Elijah's distinctive dress makes him easily identifiable. Later, John the Baptist, who comes in the spirit and power of Elijah (Luke 1:17), dresses in a similar way (Matt 3:4). As with sackcloth (see note on 1 Kgs 20:31), wearing "a garment of hair" could signify distress, an appropriate symbol for prophets who call on the nation to repent (cf. 19:1–3; Zech 13:4).
1:9 sent. To counteract Elijah's message. **company of fifty men.** A unit of soldiers. **Man of God.** A common way to refer to the Lord's prophet (Deut 33:1; 1 Kgs 12:22). The use of this term five times in vv. 9–13 emphasizes that the conflict is between the king and the Lord.
1:10 may fire come down from heaven. Elijah had already called down fire from heaven in order to turn Israel away from Baal worship (1 Kgs 18:38). Since the idolatry continued, the judgment falls directly upon the king's men who sought to subject the prophet's ministry to royal authority. Jesus' disciples may have had this event in mind in Luke 9:53–54. Cf. Rev 11:5.

1:10 [m] 1Ki 18:38; Lk 9:54; Rev 11:5; 13:13
1:13 [n] 1Sa 26:21; Ps 72:14
1:15 [o] ver 3 [p] Isa 51:12; 57:11; Jer 1:17; Eze 2:6
1:16 [q] ver 2 [r] ver 4
1:17 [s] 2Ki 8:15; Jer 20:6; 28:17 [t] 2Ki 3:1; 8:16
2:1 [u] Ge 5:24; Heb 11:5 [v] ver 11; 1Ki 19:11; Isa 5:28; 66:15; Jer 4:13; Na 1:3 [w] 1Ki 19:16,21 [x] Dt 11:30; 2Ki 4:38
2:2 [y] ver 6 [z] Ru 1:16; 1Sa 1:26; 2Ki 4:30
2:3 [a] 1Sa 10:5; 2Ki 4:1,38
2:4 [b] Jos 3:16; 6:26
2:5 [c] ver 3
2:6 [d] ver 2 [e] Jos 3:15

consume you and your fifty men!" Then fire[m] fell from heaven and consumed the captain and
his men.
11 At this the king sent to Elijah another captain with his fifty men. The captain said to him, "Man
of God, this is what the king says, 'Come down at once!' "
12 "If I am a man of God," Elijah replied, "may fire come down from heaven and consume you and
your fifty men!" Then the fire of God fell from heaven and consumed him and his fifty men.
13 So the king sent a third captain with his fifty men. This third captain went up and fell on his knees
before Elijah. "Man of God," he begged, "please have respect for my life[n] and the lives of these fifty men,
your servants! 14 See, fire has fallen from heaven and consumed the first two captains and all their men.
But now have respect for my life!"
15 The angel[o] of the LORD said to Elijah, "Go down with him; do not be afraid[p] of him." So Elijah got
up and went down with him to the king.
16 He told the king, "This is what the LORD says: Is it because there is no God in Israel for you to consult that you have sent messengers[q] to consult Baal-Zebub, the god of Ekron? Because you have done
this, you will never leave[r] the bed you are lying on. You will certainly die!" 17 So he died,[s] according to
the word of the LORD that Elijah had spoken.
Because Ahaziah had no son, Joram[a][t] succeeded him as king in the second year of Jehoram son of
Jehoshaphat king of Judah. 18 As for all the other events of Ahaziah's reign, and what he did, are they
not written in the book of the annals of the kings of Israel?

Elijah Taken Up to Heaven

2 When the LORD was about to take[u] Elijah up to heaven in a whirlwind,[v] Elijah and Elisha[w] were
on their way from Gilgal.[x] 2 Elijah said to Elisha, "Stay here;[y] the LORD has sent me to Bethel."
But Elisha said, "As surely as the LORD lives and as you live, I will not leave you."[z] So they went
down to Bethel.
3 The company[a] of the prophets at Bethel came out to Elisha and asked, "Do you know that the LORD
is going to take your master from you today?"
"Yes, I know," Elisha replied, "so be quiet."
4 Then Elijah said to him, "Stay here, Elisha; the LORD has sent me to Jericho.[b]"
And he replied, "As surely as the LORD lives and as you live, I will not leave you." So they went to
Jericho.
5 The company[c] of the prophets at Jericho went up to Elisha and asked him, "Do you know that the
LORD is going to take your master from you today?"
"Yes, I know," he replied, "so be quiet."
6 Then Elijah said to him, "Stay here;[d] the LORD has sent me to the Jordan."[e]

[a] *17* Hebrew *Jehoram,* a variant of *Joram*

1:11 Ahaziah's heart is so hard that the previous judgment does not deter him from his efforts to arrest Elijah. These soldiers were not innocent bystanders but enemy combatants sent to subdue the Lord's prophet.
1:13 please have respect for my life. Though the king's heart has not changed, the third captain is spared because he shows deference to Elijah.
1:16 Elijah confirms the prophecy in person. Ahaziah forfeits his opportunity to repent and seek the Lord.
1:17 Elijah's prediction is fulfilled, showing the authority of the Lord's messenger over the king. **Ahaziah had no son.** Another mark of divine judgment. By contrast, every king of Judah had a son to carry on the line. The succession of Ahaziah's brother leaves open the possibility that the judgment prophesied upon Ahab (1 Kgs 21:29) will be fulfilled in the days of his second son. **second year of Jehoram son of Jehoshaphat.** Also the 18th year of Jehoshaphat (3:1), indicating a period of coregency in Judah. This dates Joram's accession to 852 BC.
1:18 annals of the kings of Israel. See note on 1 Kgs 14:19.
2:1–18 *Elijah Taken Up to Heaven.* Elijah's prophetic ministry ends with a divine escort from earth. Israel's real power at this time was not the unrighteous kings of Israel but the Lord working through his prophets. This story also confirms that the Lord chose Elisha to succeed Elijah.
2:1 Gilgal. Probably not the well-known town near Jericho (Josh 4:19). The name "Gilgal" means "circle" and could identify a number of sites with such an appearance. This Gilgal appears to be located north of Bethel in the hill country of Ephraim.
2:2 Stay here. Three times in this passage (also vv. 4,6) Elijah urges Elisha to remain behind, but each time Elisha refuses. Elijah may have wished to spare Elisha the pain of witnessing his departure, but Elisha may have anticipated some blessing if he persevered in following his master. Ultimately, God rewards Elisha's persistence with a double portion of his predecessor's spirit when he sees Elijah carried into heaven. **Bethel.** Where one of the golden calves set up by Jeroboam I was worshiped; about 12 miles (19 kilometers) north of Jerusalem and 13 miles (21 kilometers) northwest of Jericho. The presence of some of Elijah's disciples may have been the motivation for his visit.
2:3 company of the prophets. See note on 1 Kgs 13:11.
2:4 Jericho. Recently rebuilt (Joshua's army had destroyed it) during the reign of Ahab (1 Kgs 16:34; Josh 6:24).

And he replied, "As surely as the LORD lives and as you live, I will not leave you."[f] So the two of them
walked on.
7Fifty men from the company of the prophets went and stood at a distance, facing the place where
Elijah and Elisha had stopped at the Jordan. 8Elijah took his cloak,[g] rolled it up and struck[h] the water
with it. The water divided[i] to the right and to the left, and the two of them crossed over on dry[j] ground.
9When they had crossed, Elijah said to Elisha, "Tell me, what can I do for you before I am taken
from you?"
"Let me inherit a double[k] portion of your spirit,"[l] Elisha replied.
10"You have asked a difficult thing," Elijah said, "yet if you see me when I am taken from you, it will
be yours—otherwise, it will not."
11As they were walking along and talking together, suddenly a chariot of fire[m] and horses of fire
appeared and separated the two of them, and Elijah went up to heaven[n] in a whirlwind.[o] 12Elisha saw
this and cried out, "My father! My father! The chariots[p] and horsemen of Israel!" And Elisha saw him
no more. Then he took hold of his garment and tore[q] it in two.
13Elisha then picked up Elijah's cloak that had fallen
from him and went back and stood on the bank of the
Jordan. 14He took the cloak[r] that had fallen from Elijah
and struck[s] the water with it. "Where now is the LORD,
the God of Elijah?" he asked. When he struck the water,
it divided to the right and to the left, and he crossed over.
15The company[t] of the prophets from Jericho, who
were watching, said, "The spirit[u] of Elijah is resting on
Elisha." And they went to meet him and bowed to the
ground before him. 16"Look," they said, "we your servants
have fifty able men. Let them go and look for your master.
Perhaps the Spirit[v] of the LORD has picked him up[w]
and set him down on some mountain or in some valley."
"No," Elisha replied, "do not send them."
17But they persisted until he was too embarrassed[x] to
refuse. So he said, "Send them." And they sent fifty men,
who searched for three days but did not find him. 18When
they returned to Elisha, who was staying in Jericho, he
said to them, "Didn't I tell you not to go?"

Healing of the Water

19The people of the city said to Elisha, "Look, our lord,
this town is well situated, as you can see, but the water is
bad and the land is unproductive."

2:6 [f]Ru 1:16
2:8 [g]1Ki 19:19 [h]ver 14 [i]Ex 14:21 [j]Ex 14:22,29
2:9 [k]Dt 21:17 [l]Nu 11:17
2:11 [m]2Ki 6:17; Ps 68:17; 104:3,4; Isa 66:15; Hab 3:8; Zec 6:1 [n]Ge 5:24 [o]ver 1
2:12 [p]2Ki 6:17; 13:14 [q]Ge 37:29
2:14 [r]1Ki 19:19 [s]ver 8
2:15 [t]ver 7; 1Sa 10:5 [u]Nu 11:17
2:16 [v]1Ki 18:12 [w]Ac 8:39
2:17 [x]2Ki 8:11

ELIJAH'S MINISTRY

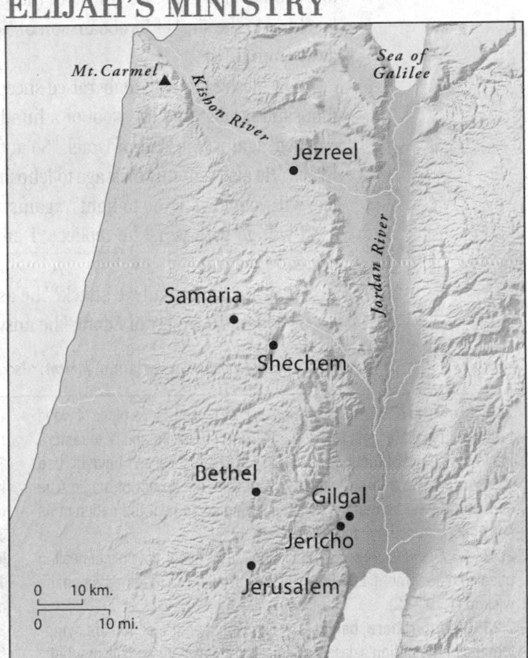

2:8 cloak. Symbolizes Elijah's power. **water divided.** Just as Moses parted the Red Sea by raising his staff (Exod 14:16). **crossed over.** To the area where Moses died (Deut 34:1–6).
2:9 double portion of your spirit. According to inheritance laws, the eldest son inherited a double portion of his father's estate (Deut 21:17). Elisha's request was not to acquire twice Elijah's miracle-working power but to be Elijah's prophetic successor.
2:11 chariot of fire and horses of fire. Reveals the might of the Lord's army (cf. 6:17; Ps 68:17). Fire often marked divine appearances (Exod 3:2; 13:21; 2 Chr 7:1; Isa 66:15). **went up to heaven.** Without dying—like Enoch (Gen 5:24).
2:12 My father! Reflects the close relationship between Elisha and his mentor. **The chariots and horsemen of Israel!** Israel's true strength was not the army of Israel's king but the Lord as represented by the prophet Elijah. **tore it in two.** Expresses Elisha's grief and signifies the beginning of a new period of ministry as Elisha assumes his master's mantle.
2:14 it divided. Shows that Elisha received his request for a double portion of Elijah's spirit (see note on v. 9), just as Joshua demonstrated that he was Moses' successor by parting the Jordan River (Josh 3:7,15–17; 4:14–18).
2:15 The prophets recognize that Elisha continues Elijah's ministry.
2:16–18 Because the prophets did not see Elijah's departure, they think that the Lord may have transported him to another area (1 Kgs 18:12) or that his body may be lying unburied. Elisha allows for a search expedition to be launched out of compassion for those requesting it.
2:19—8:15 *Elisha's Ministry.* The Lord raises up Elisha to continue Elijah's ministry to Israel. As the Lord's representative, Elisha serves the faithful (2:19–22; 4:1–44; 6:1–7), judges the guilty (2:23–25; 5:25–27), rebukes kings (3:13; 5:8), and delivers the nation (6:8—7:20).
2:19–22 *Healing of the Water.* Elisha's first miracle demonstrated that he was a true prophet. Like Moses, Elisha gives life by healing polluted water (Exod 15:25).

2:21 [y]Ex 15:25; 2Ki 4:41; 6:6
2:22 [z]Ex 15:25
2:23 [a]Ex 22:28; 2Ch 36:16; Job 19:18; Ps 31:18
2:24 [b]Ge 4:11; Ne 13:25-27 [c]Dt 18:19
2:25 [d]1Ki 18:20; 2Ki 4:25
3:1 [e]2Ki 1:17
3:2 [f]1Ki 15:26 [g]1Ki 16:30-32 [h]Ex 23:24; 2Ki 10:18, 26-28
3:3 [i]1Ki 12:28-32; 14:9,16
3:4 [j]Ge 19:37; 2Ki 1:1 [k]Ezr 7:17; Isa 16:1
3:5 [l]2Ki 1:1
3:7 [m]1Ki 22:4

20“Bring me a new bowl,” he said, “and put salt in it.” So they brought it to him.
21Then he went out to the spring and threw[y] the salt into it, saying, “This is what the LORD says: ‘I have healed this water. Never again will it cause death or make the land unproductive.’ ” 22And the water has remained pure[z] to this day, according to the word Elisha had spoken.

Elisha Is Jeered

23From there Elisha went up to Bethel. As he was walking along the road, some boys came out of the town and jeered[a] at him. “Get out of here, baldy!” they said. “Get out of here, baldy!” 24He turned around, looked at them and called down a curse[b] on them in the name[c] of the LORD. Then two bears came out of the woods and mauled forty-two of the boys. 25And he went on to Mount Carmel[d] and from there returned to Samaria.

Moab Revolts

3 Joram[a][e] son of Ahab became king of Israel in Samaria in the eighteenth year of Jehoshaphat king of Judah, and he reigned twelve years. 2He did evil[f] in the eyes of the LORD, but not as his father[g] and mother had done. He got rid of the sacred stone[h] of Baal that his father had made. 3Nevertheless he clung to the sins[i] of Jeroboam son of Nebat, which he had caused Israel to commit; he did not turn away from them.

4Now Mesha king of Moab[j] raised sheep, and he had to pay the king of Israel a tribute of a hundred thousand lambs[k] and the wool of a hundred thousand rams. 5But after Ahab died, the king of Moab rebelled[l] against the king of Israel. 6So at that time King Joram set out from Samaria and mobilized all Israel. 7He also sent this message to Jehoshaphat king of Judah: “The king of Moab has rebelled against me. Will you go with me to fight[m] against Moab?”

“I will go with you,” he replied. “I am as you are, my people as your people, my horses as your horses.”

8“By what route shall we attack?” he asked.

“Through the Desert of Edom,” he answered.

[a] *1* Hebrew *Jehoram,* a variant of *Joram*; also in verse 6

2:21 threw the salt into it. Resembles how Moses cast a piece of wood to turn bitter water into sweet (Exod 15:25). Elisha's ability to restore life to the spring authenticates him as Elijah's successor. **I have healed this water.** The miracle was a work of God, not an act of magic. The same Lord who healed the polluted spring could heal the nation of its corruption caused by idolatry.

2:23–25 *Elisha Is Jeered.* Elisha is the Lord's agent not only of healing but also of judgment. Like Elijah, he could call down judgment upon the wicked (1:10–12).

2:23 Get out of here, baldy! This disrespect and rejection are symptomatic of the nation's despising the Lord's covenant and his prophets. The presence of Bethel's idolatrous shrine (1 Kgs 12:29) may have motivated the boys' behavior and, if unanswered, their mocking could lead to greater conflict with the Lord's prophets who live in Bethel (2 Kgs 2:3).

2:24 Those who thought that Elisha was vulnerable where Elijah was not were sorely mistaken (1:10–12). The Lord warned that if his people refused to listen he would send wild animals to rob the nation of their children (Lev 26:22). Miraculous displays of the Lord's power continue through Elisha's ministry in an effort to woo the nation back from its worship of Baal.

2:25 Mount Carmel. A mountain where Elisha frequently stays (4:25) and where his master defeated the prophets of Baal (1 Kgs 18). **Samaria.** Israel's capital city, where the heart of the battle against Baal worship was.

3:1–27 *Moab Revolts.* Like his predecessor, Elisha represents the Lord as the real military power of the nation of Israel (see note on 2:12; cf. 13:14). In this case, the prophet saves the coalition forces from death in the wilderness by announcing the Lord's provision. Yet Israel ultimately has to withdraw from Moab because they cling to their idolatrous ways.

3:1 eighteenth year of Jehoshaphat. Joram comes to the throne of Israel when Jehoshaphat and Jehoram are coregents in Judah (see note on 1:17). **twelve years.** 852–841 BC.

3:2 sacred stone of Baal. Its size and design are unknown. In removing it Joram reverses some of the idolatry of his father, Ahab (1 Kgs 16:30–33). The stone is apparently put in storage because it is not destroyed until Jehu's reforms (2 Kgs 10:26–27).

3:3 sins of Jeroboam. Worshiping golden calves at Dan and Bethel (1 Kgs 12:26–33).

3:4 Since Moab was particularly good for grazing flocks, Mesha rendered his tribute in lambs and wool (cf. Isa 16:1).

3:5 A monumental inscription by Mesha confirms that he successfully overthrew Israelite domination, probably a decade after the defeat that ch. 3 describes. The Mesha Stele also describes the Moabite king's conquest of Israelite cities on the east side of the Jordan River.

3:7 Joram seeks an alliance with Judah in order to travel through its territory to attack Moab. Joram expects Judah to cooperate because his sister Athaliah had married Jehoshaphat's son. Jehoshaphat's positive response mirrors his reply to Ahab (1 Kgs 22:4) and bodes ill for the southern kingdom. But unlike the previous occasion (1 Kgs 22:5–7), Jehoshaphat does not seek the counsel of the Lord's prophet before going out to battle.

3:8 Through the Desert of Edom. The southern route takes the armies to a less protected border of Moab and allows the Edomite forces to join the coalition.

9So the king of Israel set out with the king of Judah and the king of Edom.[n] After a roundabout
march of seven days, the army had no more water for themselves or for the animals with them.
10"What!" exclaimed the king of Israel. "Has the LORD called us three kings together only to deliver
us into the hands of Moab?"
11But Jehoshaphat asked, "Is there no prophet of the LORD here, through whom we may inquire[o]
of the LORD?"
An officer of the king of Israel answered, "Elisha[p] son of Shaphat is here. He used to pour water on
the hands of Elijah.[a][q]"
12Jehoshaphat said, "The word[r] of the LORD is with him." So the king of Israel and Jehoshaphat and
the king of Edom went down to him.
13Elisha said to the king of Israel, "Why do you want to involve me? Go to the
prophets of your father and the prophets of your mother."
"No," the king of Israel answered, "because it was the LORD who called us
three kings together to deliver us into the hands of Moab."
14Elisha said, "As surely as the LORD Almighty lives, whom I serve, if I did not
have respect for the presence of Jehoshaphat king of Judah, I would not pay any
attention to you. 15But now bring me a harpist."[s]
While the harpist was playing, the hand[t] of the LORD came on Elisha 16and he
said, "This is what the LORD says: I will fill this valley with pools of water. 17For this
is what the LORD says: You will see neither wind nor rain, yet this valley will be
filled with water,[u] and you, your cattle and your other animals will drink. 18This is
an easy[v] thing in the eyes of the LORD; he will also deliver Moab into your hands.
19You will overthrow every fortified city and every major town. You will cut down
every good tree, stop up all the springs, and ruin every good field with stones."
20The next morning, about the time[w] for offering the sacrifice, there it was—
water flowing from the direction of Edom! And the land was filled with water.[x]
21Now all the Moabites had heard that the kings had come to fight against
them; so every man, young and old, who could bear arms was called up and
stationed on the border. 22When they got up early in the morning, the sun
was shining on the water. To the Moabites across the way, the water looked
red—like blood. 23"That's blood!" they said. "Those kings must have fought
and slaughtered each other. Now to the plunder, Moab!"

3:9 [n] 1Ki 22:47
3:11 [o] Ge 25:22; 1Ki 22:7 [p] Ge 20:7 [q] 1Ki 19:16
3:12 [r] Nu 11:17
3:15 [s] 1Sa 16:23 [t] Jer 15:17; Eze 1:3
3:17 [u] Ps 107:35; Isa 32:2; 35:6; 41:18
3:18 [v] Ge 18:14; 2Ki 20:10; Isa 49:6; Jer 32:17,27; Mk 10:27
3:20 [w] Ex 29:39-40 [x] Ex 17:6

Mesha Stele written by King Mesha; this stone inscription describes his wars with Israel from Moab's perspective.

Todd Bolen/www.BiblePlaces.com, taken at the Musée du Louvre

[a] *11* That is, he was Elijah's personal servant.

3:9 king of Israel. This chapter often refers to Joram by his title and not his name (vv. 4,5,9,10,11,12,13), possibly a literary device to diminish any glory for the wicked king. **king of Edom.** Jehoshaphat appointed him; the Edomites were subject to Judah (8:20; 1 Kgs 22:47). **no more water.** The dry wilderness area has few springs, and the supplies that the armies carry are exhausted after a week's journey. The armies are easy targets for an attacker.
3:10 It is not surprising that an engagement planned without the counsel of the Lord would result in disaster, and it is only at this point that the king remembers the Lord.
3:11 Is there no prophet of the LORD here . . . ? Jehoshaphat had asked the same question of Joram's father (1 Kgs 22:7). False prophets accompany Israel's kings, but Judah's kings seek the Lord's prophets. **pour water on the hands of Elijah.** See NIV text note. Elisha had served Elijah, but this apparently is the first time the kings learn about him (cf. 1 Kgs 19:21). By the end of the conflict, the Lord will firmly establish Elisha's prophetic ministry with the rulers.
3:12 The word of the LORD is with him. A prophet's most important characteristic. Any person who spoke falsely in the name of the Lord was to be put to death (Deut 18:20). Because Israel did not obey this command, false prophets were common in Israel.
3:13 the prophets of your father and the prophets of your mother. The prophets of Baal and Asherah (1 Kgs 18:19). The encounter on Mount Carmel showed that they were impotent.
3:14 respect for the presence of Jehoshaphat. Because he "did what was right in the eyes of the LORD" (1 Kgs 22:43).
3:15 bring me a harpist. Perhaps music allows Elisha to block out all distractions and hear the word of the Lord (cf. 1 Sam 10:5–11; 16:23).
3:17 A supernatural explanation is the best way to account for the divine provision of water without wind or rain. If flash floods flowing from the mountains of Edom are the explanation, then they must have occurred apart from the knowledge of the Moabites. **this valley.** Possibly the wide Arabah valley south of the Dead Sea or a wadi that drained into the Arabah.
3:19 Elisha predicts a great victory without revealing that the allied forces will ultimately withdraw (v. 27).
3:20 time for offering the sacrifice. Mid-morning, about 9:00 a.m. The writer keeps time by the temple services.
3:22–23 The Lord's provision of water not only saves the coalition from dying of thirst but also deceives the Moabites into thinking that victory is theirs.
3:22 red—like blood. The rays of the sun and the reddish color of the rock may have combined to give the water a blood-red color.
3:23 Moab's recent experience of attacking their own allies leads them

3:25 [y] ver 19; Isa 15:1; 16:7; Jer 48:31,36
3:27 [z] Dt 12:31; 2Ki 16:3; 21:6; 2Ch 28:3; Ps 106:38; Jer 19:4-5; Am 2:1; Mic 6:7
4:1 [a] 1Sa 10:5; 2Ki 2:3 [b] Ex 22:26; Lev 25:39-43; Ne 5:3-5; Job 22:6; 24:9
4:2 [c] 1Ki 17:12
4:7 [d] 1Ki 12:22
4:8 [e] Jos 19:18
4:10 [f] Mt 10:41; Ro 12:13
4:12 [g] 2Ki 8:1

24 But when the Moabites came to the camp of Israel, the Israelites rose up and fought them until
they fled. And the Israelites invaded the land and slaughtered the Moabites. 25 They destroyed the towns,
and each man threw a stone on every good field until it was covered. They stopped up all the springs
and cut down every good tree. Only Kir Hareseth[y] was left with its stones in place, but men armed with
slings surrounded it and attacked it.
26 When the king of Moab saw that the battle had gone against him, he took with him seven hundred
swordsmen to break through to the king of Edom, but they failed. 27 Then he took his firstborn[z] son,
who was to succeed him as king, and offered him as a sacrifice on the city wall. The fury against Israel
was great; they withdrew and returned to their own land.

The Widow's Olive Oil

4 The wife of a man from the company[a] of the prophets cried out to Elisha, "Your servant my husband is dead, and you know that he revered the LORD. But now his creditor[b] is coming to take my two boys as his slaves."

2 Elisha replied to her, "How can I help you? Tell me, what do you have in your house?"
"Your servant has nothing there at all," she said, "except a small jar of olive oil."[c]
3 Elisha said, "Go around and ask all your neighbors for empty jars. Don't ask for just a few. 4 Then
go inside and shut the door behind you and your sons. Pour oil into all the jars, and as each is filled,
put it to one side."
5 She left him and shut the door behind her and her sons. They brought the jars to her and she kept
pouring. 6 When all the jars were full, she said to her son, "Bring me another one."
But he replied, "There is not a jar left." Then the oil stopped flowing.
7 She went and told the man of God,[d] and he said, "Go, sell the oil and pay your debts. You and your
sons can live on what is left."

The Shunammite's Son Restored to Life

8 One day Elisha went to Shunem.[e] And a well-to-do woman was there, who urged him to stay for
a meal. So whenever he came by, he stopped there to eat. 9 She said to her husband, "I know that this
man who often comes our way is a holy man of God. 10 Let's make a small room on the roof and put
in it a bed and a table, a chair and a lamp for him. Then he can stay[f] there whenever he comes to us."
11 One day when Elisha came, he went up to his room and lay down there. 12 He said to his servant
Gehazi, "Call the Shunammite."[g] So he called her, and she stood before him. 13 Elisha said to him, "Tell

to assume that their enemies are slaughtering one another (2 Chr 20:23).

3:25 Kir Hareseth. Moab's capital located at modern Kerak, about 11 miles (18 kilometers) east of the Dead Sea. The city sat on an isolated spur and was not easily conquered.

3:27 offered him as a sacrifice. Because the king of Moab believed that his impending defeat was the result of his god Chemosh's anger. Sacrificing the crown prince was a desperate attempt to win the deity's favor. **fury.** (1) Possibly the Lord's fury, but it is unclear why he would act against Israel in response to a pagan sacrifice. (2) Probably human fury. Perhaps the Moabite forces were outraged at the sacrifice and fought with renewed vigor. Or perhaps the Israelites were so horrified by the sacrifice that they broke off the engagement and returned home.

4:1–7 *The Widow's Olive Oil.* The author records certain miracles to show the similarities between Elijah and Elisha, thus confirming the succession. In this case, Elisha saves a widow's family by multiplying oil in a way that recalls how Elijah provided for the widow in Zarephath (1 Kgs 17:7–16).

4:1 company of the prophets. See note on 1 Kgs 13:11. Apparently a group of prophets served under Elisha's leadership. **take my two boys as his slaves.** In the ancient world, financial indebtedness often led to slavery (cf. Neh 5:5; Amos 2:6). While the Mosaic covenant allowed for service to pay a debt, a time limit was set when the servant would be set free (Exod 21:2). A guardian-redeemer could pay the debt in order to free the relative (Lev 25:25), but this widow had no hope of such deliverance. By providing for the woman, Elisha showed compassion to the dependents of the deceased prophet.

4:2 Elisha uses the woman's existing resources as the basis for the miracle of multiplication. **olive oil.** A valuable commodity commonly used for cooking, cosmetics, lighting, and medicine (1 Kgs 5:11; 17:12; Exod 25:6; Ps 104:15; Isa 1:6).

4:7 The Lord graciously provides enough to eliminate all of the debt and meet future expenses. His care for the widow and fatherless was a model for the Israelites to follow (Deut 10:18; 24:19).

4:8–37 *The Shunammite's Son Restored to Life.* The prophet's miracles for faithful individuals prove that the wicked leaders of the nation did not restrain the Lord's gracious hand. The way Elisha foretells that the Lord will provide a son for the barren woman is reminiscent of Gen 18:10, and Elisha's raising the woman's son again mirrors Elijah's ministry (1 Kgs 17:17–24).

4:8 Shunem. A village (modern Solem) midway between Elisha's hometown of Abel Meholah and Mount Carmel. On the other side of the hill lay the town of Nain, where Jesus later raised a boy from the dead (Luke 7:11–17).

4:10 The king does not remunerate Elisha for his services, so he is dependent upon the kindness of the Lord's people for provision. This woman goes beyond providing meals to building a private, comfortable lodging place.

her, ‘You have gone to all this trouble for us. Now what can be done for you? Can we speak on your
behalf to the king or the commander of the army?’ ”
She replied, “I have a home among my own people.”
14 “What can be done for her?” Elisha asked.
Gehazi said, “She has no son, and her husband is old.”
15 Then Elisha said, “Call her.” So he called her, and she stood in the doorway. 16 “About this time[h]
next year,” Elisha said, “you will hold a son in your arms.”
“No, my lord!” she objected. “Please, man of God, don’t mislead your servant!”
17 But the woman became pregnant, and the next year about that same time she gave birth to a son,
just as Elisha had told her.
18 The child grew, and one day he went out to his father, who was with the reapers.[i] 19 He said to his
father, “My head! My head!”
His father told a servant, “Carry him to his mother.” 20 After the servant had lifted him up and carried
him to his mother, the boy sat on her lap until noon, and then he died. 21 She went up and laid him on
the bed[j] of the man of God, then shut the door and went out.
22 She called her husband and said, “Please send me one of the servants and a donkey so I can go to
the man of God quickly and return.”
23 “Why go to him today?” he asked. “It’s not the New Moon[k] or the Sabbath.”
“That’s all right,” she said.
24 She saddled the donkey and said to her servant, “Lead on; don’t slow down for me unless I tell you.”
25 So she set out and came to the man of God at Mount Carmel.[l]
When he saw her in the distance, the man of God said to his servant Gehazi, “Look! There’s the Shunammite! 26 Run to meet her and ask her, ‘Are you all right? Is your husband all right? Is your child all right?’ ”
“Everything is all right,” she said.
27 When she reached the man of God at the mountain, she took hold of his feet. Gehazi came over to
push her away, but the man of God said, “Leave her alone! She is in bitter distress,[m] but the LORD has
hidden it from me and has not told me why.”
28 “Did I ask you for a son, my lord?” she said. “Didn’t I tell you, ‘Don’t raise my hopes’?”
29 Elisha said to Gehazi, “Tuck your cloak into your belt,[n] take my staff[o] in your hand and run.
Don’t greet anyone you meet, and if anyone greets you, do not answer. Lay my staff on the boy’s face.”
30 But the child’s mother said, “As surely as the LORD lives and as you live, I will not leave you.” So
he got up and followed her.
31 Gehazi went on ahead and laid the staff on the boy’s face, but there was no sound or response. So
Gehazi went back to meet Elisha and told him, “The boy has not awakened.”
32 When Elisha reached the house, there was the boy lying dead on his couch.[p] 33 He went in, shut the
door on the two of them and prayed[q] to the LORD. 34 Then he got on the bed and lay on the boy, mouth
to mouth, eyes to eyes, hands to hands. As he stretched[r] himself out on him, the boy’s body grew warm.
35 Elisha turned away and walked back and forth in the room and then got on the bed and stretched
out on him once more. The boy sneezed seven times[s] and opened his eyes.[t]

4:16 [h] Ge 18:10
4:18 [i] Ru 2:3
4:21 [j] ver 32
4:23 [k] Nu 10:10; 1Ch 23:31; Ps 81:3
4:25 [l] 1Ki 18:20; 2Ki 2:25
4:27 [m] 1Sa 1:15
4:29 [n] 1Ki 18:46; 2Ki 2:8, 14; 9:1 [o] Ex 4:2; 7:19; 14:16
4:32 [p] ver 21
4:33 [q] 1Ki 17:20; Mt 6:6
4:34 [r] 1Ki 17:21; Ac 20:10
4:35 [s] Jos 6:15 [t] 2Ki 8:5

4:13 speak on your behalf to the king. Elisha’s servant Gehazi later did this to restore the woman’s house and land (8:1–6). At this point she has no such need.
4:14 no son. Not only is she barren, a social stigma, but she also faces the prospect of old age without any children to care for her or inherit the family estate.
4:16 About this time next year. Echoes Gen 18:10. Later the woman lost her child, and like Abraham, she had faith that God could raise him from the dead (cf. Heb 11:19).
4:17 just as Elisha had told her. The prophetic word is certain. This is an important theme of Kings (cf. 7:17; 1 Kgs 13:32).
4:23 Why go to him today? The woman apparently did not inform her husband that their son had died, perhaps desiring to spare him grief or fearing that he might deter her from going. Perhaps she reasoned that if Elisha’s God could bring life from a barren womb, he could bring her son back from the dead. **New Moon or the Sabbath.** Times of regular religious ceremonies (Lev 23:3; Num 28:11–15; Hos 2:11).
4:25 She traveled approximately 20 miles (32 kilometers), or one day’s journey. **Mount Carmel.** Elisha apparently had a place to stay in the vicinity of Elijah’s great miracle (2:25; 1 Kgs 18:19).
4:26 Everything is all right. The woman is willing to entrust the cause of her distress only to the prophet himself.
4:27 the LORD has hidden it from me. Elisha’s supernatural power is dependent upon the Lord’s provision.
4:29 Lay my staff on the boy’s face. To bring about the boy’s healing quickly by using a symbol of his prophetic ministry (see note on 2:8).
4:30 I will not leave you. Perhaps anticipating that Elisha’s presence would be necessary to raise her son from the dead.
4:34 In an answer to the prophet’s earnest prayers, the Lord gives life to the boy through Elisha’s body. Elisha’s ministry again parallels Elijah’s

4:36 [u]Heb 11:35
4:38 [v]2Ki 2:1 [w]Lev 26:26; 2Ki 8:1
4:41 [x]Ex 15:25; 2Ki 2:21
4:42 [y]1Sa 9:4 [z]Mt 14:17; 15:36 [a]1Sa 9:7
4:43 [b]Lk 9:13 [c]Mt 14:20; Jn 6:12
5:1 [d]Ge 10:22; 2Sa 10:19 [e]Ex 4:6; Nu 12:10; Lk 4:27
5:2 [f]2Ki 6:23; 13:20; 24:2
5:3 [g]Ge 20:7

36 Elisha summoned Gehazi and said, "Call the Shunammite." And he did. When she came, he said, "Take your son."[u] 37 She came in, fell at his feet and bowed to the ground. Then she took her son and went out.

Death in the Pot

38 Elisha returned to Gilgal[v] and there was a famine[w] in that region. While the company of the prophets was meeting with him, he said to his servant, "Put on the large pot and cook some stew for these prophets."

39 One of them went out into the fields to gather herbs and found a wild vine and picked as many of its gourds as his garment could hold. When he returned, he cut them up into the pot of stew, though no one knew what they were. 40 The stew was poured out for the men, but as they began to eat it, they cried out, "Man of God, there is death in the pot!" And they could not eat it.

41 Elisha said, "Get some flour." He put it into the pot and said, "Serve it to the people to eat." And there was nothing harmful in the pot.[x]

Feeding of a Hundred

42 A man came from Baal Shalishah,[y] bringing the man of God twenty loaves[z] of barley bread[a] baked from the first ripe grain, along with some heads of new grain. "Give it to the people to eat," Elisha said.

43 "How can I set this before a hundred men?" his servant asked.

But Elisha answered, "Give it to the people to eat.[b] For this is what the LORD says: 'They will eat and have some left over.[c]'" 44 Then he set it before them, and they ate and had some left over, according to the word of the LORD.

Naaman Healed of Leprosy

5 Now Naaman was commander of the army of the king of Aram.[d] He was a great man in the sight of his master and highly regarded, because through him the LORD had given victory to Aram. He was a valiant soldier, but he had leprosy.[a][e]

2 Now bands of raiders[f] from Aram had gone out and had taken captive a young girl from Israel, and she served Naaman's wife. 3 She said to her mistress, "If only my master would see the prophet[g] who is in Samaria! He would cure him of his leprosy."

4 Naaman went to his master and told him what the girl from Israel had said. 5 "By all means, go,"

[a] *1* The Hebrew for *leprosy* was used for various diseases affecting the skin; also in verses 3, 6, 7, 11 and 27.

(1 Kgs 17:17–24). Years later when Elisha dies, his corpse gives life to a dead man hastily thrown into Elisha's tomb (2 Kgs 13:21).

4:38–41 *Death in the Pot.* In Elijah's day, the Lord demonstrated his superiority over Baal by withholding rain from the nation but providing for his own people (1 Kgs 17; 18:3–4). Elisha continues this ministry of provision during a time of famine by healing a poisoned pot of stew (vv. 38–41) and multiplying loaves of bread (vv. 42–44).

4:38 Gilgal. The name of several OT sites; it is not clear which one is intended here (see note on 2:1).

4:40 death in the pot. In desperate times the company of prophets ate an herb with potentially fatal consequences. Elisha's curing of the stew recalls his healing of the bad water (2:19–22) and reflects the Lord's recurring provision for his prophets (cf. 1 Kgs 17:4).

4:42–44 *Feeding of a Hundred.* In the context of a book about covenant faithfulness, a famine should be understood as divine judgment, particularly in an era characterized by apostate kings (Deut 28:18). While covenant curses on the land affected the Lord's servants, the Lord brought relief through his prophet Elisha. Jesus' feeding of the 5,000 parallels Elisha's miracle in several ways, including the insufficient quantity of barley loaves, the question of the servant, and the presence of leftovers (John 6:1–13). Jesus' miracle signified that he was a prophet like Elisha.

4:42 Baal Shalishah. Location uncertain (cf. 1 Sam 9:4); named after a god that idolaters in Israel worshiped.

4:44 the word of the LORD. Once again the Lord's word through his prophet is life-giving, in contrast to the famine conditions that result when the nation pursues alleged fertility gods (4:1–7; 1 Kgs 17:1–14).

5:1–27 *Naaman Healed of Leprosy.* By making Israel his people, the Lord intended that they testify of his goodness to the world (1 Kgs 8:41–43; Gen 12:3; Ps 67:1–2). In a time when Israel's kings are worshiping the gods of other nations, a young girl in exile points her foreign master to the Lord. After Naaman's faith leads to his healing, he proclaims Israel's God to be the only true God. By contrast, the prophet's servant fails to believe God and receives the Aramean commander's disease.

5:1 king of Aram. Probably Ben-Hadad II (8:7; 1 Kgs 20:1). The Arameans were one of Israel's greatest enemies and presumably the last to receive any blessing from Israel. **through him the LORD had given victory to Aram.** The Lord was responsible for Israel's victories and defeats, and recent losses were God's punishment for the nation's idolatry (Deut 28:25). **leprosy.** See NIV text note.

5:2–3 Though the Lord intended that Israel witness to the world of its great God (1 Kgs 8:41–43), examples of such testimony are rare. In this case, a young girl tells her captors about Elisha's life-giving power. Her faithfulness in exile is a model for later Israelites who have opportunity to point Gentiles to the Lord (cf. Neh 2; Dan 1).

5:5 talents ... shekels. See NIV text notes. By contrast, Omri paid two talents of silver for the land upon which he built the capital city of

the king of Aram replied. "I will send a letter to the king of Israel." So Naaman left, taking with him
ten talents[a] of silver, six thousand shekels[b] of gold and ten sets of clothing.[h] 6 The letter that he took
to the king of Israel read: "With this letter I am sending my servant Naaman to you so that you may
cure him of his leprosy."

7 As soon as the king of Israel read the letter,[i] he tore his robes and said, "Am I God?[j] Can I kill and
bring back to life?[k] Why does this fellow send someone to me to be cured of his leprosy? See how he is
trying to pick a quarrel[l] with me!"

8 When Elisha the man of God heard that the king of Israel had torn his robes, he sent him this
message: "Why have you torn your robes? Have the man come to me and he will know that there is a
prophet[m] in Israel." 9 So Naaman went with his horses and chariots and stopped at the door of Elisha's
house. 10 Elisha sent a messenger to say to him, "Go, wash[n] yourself seven times[o] in the Jordan, and
your flesh will be restored and you will be cleansed."

11 But Naaman went away angry and said, "I thought that he would surely come out to me and stand
and call on the name of the LORD his God, wave his hand[p] over the spot and cure me of my leprosy. 12 Are
not Abana and Pharpar, the rivers of Damascus, better than all the waters[q] of Israel? Couldn't I wash
in them and be cleansed?" So he turned and went off in a rage.[r]

13 Naaman's servants went to him and said, "My father,[s] if the prophet had told you to do some great
thing, would you not have done it? How much more, then, when he tells you, 'Wash and be cleansed'!"
14 So he went down and dipped himself in the Jordan seven times,[t] as the man of God had told him, and
his flesh was restored[u] and became clean like that of a young boy.[v]

15 Then Naaman and all his attendants went back to the man of God[w]. He stood before him and
said, "Now I know[x] that there is no God in all the world except in Israel. So please accept a gift[y] from
your servant."

16 The prophet answered, "As surely as the LORD lives, whom I serve, I will not accept a thing." And
even though Naaman urged him, he refused.[z]

17 "If you will not," said Naaman, "please let me, your servant, be given as much earth[a] as a pair of
mules can carry, for your servant will never again make burnt offerings and sacrifices to any other god
but the LORD. 18 But may the LORD forgive your servant for this one thing: When my master enters the
temple of Rimmon to bow down and he is leaning[b] on my arm and I have to bow there also—when I
bow down in the temple of Rimmon, may the LORD forgive your servant for this."

19 "Go in peace,"[c] Elisha said.

[a] 5 That is, about 750 pounds or about 340 kilograms [b] 5 That is, about 150 pounds or about 69 kilograms

5:5 [h] ver 22; Ge 24:53; Jdg 14:12; 1Sa 9:7
5:7 [i] 2Ki 19:14 [j] Ge 30:2 [k] Dt 32:39; 1Sa 2:6 [l] 1Ki 20:7
5:8 [m] 1Ki 22:7
5:10 [n] Jn 9:7 [o] Ge 33:3; Lev 14:7
5:11 [p] Ex 7:19
5:12 [q] Isa 8:6 [r] Pr 14:17, 29; 19:11; 29:11
5:13 [s] 2Ki 6:21; 13:14
5:14 [t] Ge 33:3; Lev 14:7; Jos 6:15 [u] Ex 4:7 [v] Job 33:25; Lk 4:27
5:15 [w] Jos 2:11 [x] Jos 4:24; 1Sa 17:46; Da 2:47 [y] 1Sa 9:7; 25:27
5:16 [z] ver 20,26; Ge 14:23; Da 5:17
5:17 [a] Ex 20:24
5:18 [b] 2Ki 7:2
5:19 [c] 1Sa 1:17; Ac 15:33

Samaria (1 Kgs 16:24). Six thousand shekels of gold was the equivalent to the annual earnings of 600 workers. Naaman was prepared to pay a lavish amount for his restored health.

5:7 The Aramean king incorrectly assumes that Israel's king controls the Israelite prophet. Joram's estrangement from the Lord prevents him from recognizing that Elisha can work just such miracles on God's behalf.

5:8 there is a prophet in Israel. This story reveals to both Israelites and Gentiles that there is a true God who works through his faithful prophets.

5:10 sent a messenger. The commander thought that he deserved more than a servant's message delivered on the prophet's doorstep (v. 11). **wash yourself seven times in the Jordan.** Prevents Naaman from concluding that the prophet's own power or any qualities of the water healed him.

5:11 Naaman rejects Elisha's directions because they do not meet his expectations. In order to be healed, Naaman must humble himself and submit in faith to the prophetic word.

5:12 Abana. Modern Barada; it begins in a large pool high in the Anti-Lebanon mountains 23 miles (37 kilometers) northwest of Damascus. **Pharpar.** Modern Awaj; it forms on Mount Hermon and flows in a crooked channel east and northeast to Damascus. Naaman viewed his nation's rivers as superior to Israel's.

5:13 Once again servants in the story are wiser than their master (cf. v. 3).

5:14 as the man of God had told him. Obeying the prophet results in life and healing. The same blessing awaited those in Israel who would submit to the Lord and his spokesmen.

5:15 no God in all the world except in Israel. The Lord chose Israel and set her in the midst of all the nations so that such testimonies would be common as his people kept the covenant and he blessed them (Deut 4:6–8). In the context of the book of Kings, this profession of faith by a Gentile indicts the idolatrous Israelites (cf. 1 Kgs 17:24; 18:21; Luke 4:27). Naaman joins others such as Rahab, Ruth, and the sailors of Jonah's ship as Gentiles who recognized the Lord as the only true God (Josh 2:11; Ruth 1:16; Jonah 1:14–16).

5:16 Offering a gift was appropriate, but Elisha could not accept payment for what God had done.

5:17 earth. Soil from the land of Israel. Naaman believed that this was necessary perhaps to make an earthen altar for sacrificing to the God of Israel (cf. Exod 20:24).

5:18 Naaman was truly converted to worship of the God of Israel, but he asked for forbearance on the occasions when he would be forced to bow in a pagan temple while serving his master. Though his body would bow down, Naaman's heart would be committed to the Lord only. **Rimmon.** Another name for Hadad, the chief deity of the Arameans (cf. Zech 12:11). In Israel and Phoenicia, this god was known as Baal.

5:19 Go in peace. Without addressing specifics, Elisha affirms Naaman's desire to be faithful to the Lord while in service to a pagan king.

5:20 [d]Ex 20:7
5:22 [e]ver 5; Ge 45:22
5:26 [f]ver 16 [g]Jer 45:5
5:27 [h]Nu 12:10; 2Ki 15:5 [i]Col 3:5 [j]Ex 4:6
6:1 [k]1Sa 10:5; 2Ki 4:38
6:6 [l]Ex 15:25; 2Ki 2:21
6:9 [m]ver 12

After Naaman had traveled some distance, 20 Gehazi, the servant of Elisha the man of God, said to himself, "My master was too easy on Naaman, this Aramean, by not accepting from him what he brought. As surely as the LORD[d] lives, I will run after him and get something from him."

21 So Gehazi hurried after Naaman. When Naaman saw him running toward him, he got down from the chariot to meet him. "Is everything all right?" he asked.

22 "Everything is all right," Gehazi answered. "My master sent me to say, 'Two young men from the company of the prophets have just come to me from the hill country of Ephraim. Please give them a talent[a] of silver and two sets of clothing.'"[e]

23 "By all means, take two talents," said Naaman. He urged Gehazi to accept them, and then tied up the two talents of silver in two bags, with two sets of clothing. He gave them to two of his servants, and they carried them ahead of Gehazi. 24 When Gehazi came to the hill, he took the things from the servants and put them away in the house. He sent the men away and they left.

25 When he went in and stood before his master, Elisha asked him, "Where have you been, Gehazi?"

"Your servant didn't go anywhere," Gehazi answered.

26 But Elisha said to him, "Was not my spirit with you when the man got down from his chariot to meet you? Is this the time[f] to take money or to accept clothes — or olive groves and vineyards, or flocks and herds, or male and female slaves?[g] 27 Naaman's leprosy[h] will cling to you and to your descendants forever." Then Gehazi[i] went from Elisha's presence and his skin was leprous — it had become as white as snow.[j]

An Axhead Floats

6 The company[k] of the prophets said to Elisha, "Look, the place where we meet with you is too small for us. 2 Let us go to the Jordan, where each of us can get a pole; and let us build a place there for us to meet."

And he said, "Go."

3 Then one of them said, "Won't you please come with your servants?"

"I will," Elisha replied. 4 And he went with them.

They went to the Jordan and began to cut down trees. 5 As one of them was cutting down a tree, the iron axhead fell into the water. "Oh no, my lord!" he cried out. "It was borrowed!"

6 The man of God asked, "Where did it fall?" When he showed him the place, Elisha cut a stick and threw[l] it there, and made the iron float. 7 "Lift it out," he said. Then the man reached out his hand and took it.

Elisha Traps Blinded Arameans

8 Now the king of Aram was at war with Israel. After conferring with his officers, he said, "I will set up my camp in such and such a place."

9 The man of God sent word to the king[m] of Israel: "Beware of passing that place, because the

[a] *22* That is, about 75 pounds or about 34 kilograms

5:20 Gehazi recognizes the great gifts that Naaman was willing to offer for his healing and desires them for himself.
5:22 Gehazi blatantly lies.
5:24 Gehazi hides the gifts in the house.
5:25 Your servant didn't go anywhere. Gehazi lies again. Even those who serve a prophet can be blinded by their own lusts.
5:27 Naaman's leprosy will cling to you. The Lord who heals disease can also inflict disease (v. 7; Lev 26:16; Deut 7:15), and Gehazi is cursed for seeking personal profit from a divine miracle. The severity of the punishment is best understood in light of Gehazi's actions that made Elisha appear to be like the false prophets who were motivated by financial gain (cf. 2 Cor 2:17; 2 Pet 2:15). **your descendants.** The second commandment warns that idolatry leads to judgment down to the third and fourth generation (Exod 20:4–6). Unless the events are not recorded in chronological order, it appears that Gehazi repented and was restored, for he later serves in the king's presence (8:4–5).
6:1–7 *An Axhead Floats.* The compassion of the Lord extends to even apparently trivial matters, such as losing a borrowed axhead. A prophet in the Lord's service did not have the means to repay such an expensive loss, and by causing it to float, Elisha saves the man from debt and possibly servitude. As in the miracles of the oil, stew, and bread (ch. 4), Elisha provides for the people under his care. By contrast, the faithless king of Israel does not provide for his citizens (6:24–31).
6:8–23 *Elisha Traps Blinded Arameans.* This story again reveals that Israel's true military strength came from its relationship with the Lord through his prophets. Elisha could do what Israel's faithless king could not do in defending the nation and providing peace.
6:8 king of Aram. Probably Ben-Hadad II (cf. v. 24). Relations between Aram and Israel had deteriorated since Naaman's healing in ch. 5.
6:9 The man of God. Elisha (v. 10). The only character in this story whom the author names is Elisha, drawing attention to his role as the deliverer of Israel (cf. 13:14).

Arameans are going down there." 10So the king of Israel checked on the place indicated by the man of God. Time and again Elisha warned[n] the king, so that he was on his guard in such places.

11This enraged the king of Aram. He summoned his officers and demanded of them, "Tell me! Which of us is on the side of the king of Israel?"

12"None of us, my lord the king[o]," said one of his officers, "but Elisha, the prophet who is in Israel, tells the king of Israel the very words you speak in your bedroom."

13"Go, find out where he is," the king ordered, "so I can send men and capture him." The report came back: "He is in Dothan."[p] 14Then he sent[q] horses and chariots and a strong force there. They went by night and surrounded the city.

15When the servant of the man of God got up and went out early the next morning, an army with horses and chariots had surrounded the city. "Oh no, my lord! What shall we do?" the servant asked.

16"Don't be afraid,"[r] the prophet answered. "Those who are with us are more[s] than those who are with them."

17And Elisha prayed, "Open his eyes, LORD, so that he may see." Then the LORD opened the servant's eyes, and he looked and saw the hills full of horses and chariots[t] of fire all around Elisha.

18As the enemy came down toward him, Elisha prayed to the LORD, "Strike this army with blindness."[u] So he struck them with blindness, as Elisha had asked.

19Elisha told them, "This is not the road and this is not the city. Follow me, and I will lead you to the man you are looking for." And he led them to Samaria.

20After they entered the city, Elisha said, "LORD, open the eyes of these men so they can see." Then the LORD opened their eyes and they looked, and there they were, inside Samaria.

21When the king of Israel saw them, he asked Elisha, "Shall I kill them, my father?[v] Shall I kill them?"

22"Do not kill them," he answered. "Would you kill those you have captured[w] with your own sword or bow? Set food and water before them so that they may eat and drink and then go back to their master." 23So he prepared a great feast for them, and after they had finished eating and drinking, he sent them away, and they returned to their master. So the bands[x] from Aram stopped raiding Israel's territory.

Famine in Besieged Samaria

24Some time later, Ben-Hadad[y] king of Aram mobilized his entire army and marched up and laid siege[z] to Samaria. 25There was a great famine[a] in the city; the siege lasted so long that a donkey's head sold for eighty shekels[a] of silver, and a quarter of a cab[b] of seed pods[c][b] for five shekels.[d]

a 25 That is, about 2 pounds or about 920 grams *b* 25 That is, probably about 1/4 pound or about 100 grams *c* 25 Or *of doves' dung* *d* 25 That is, about 2 ounces or about 58 grams

6:10 [n]Jer 11:18
6:12 [o]ver 9
6:13 [p]Ge 37:17
6:14 [q]2Ki 1:9
6:16 [r]Ge 15:1 [s]2Ch 32:7; Ps 55:18; Ro 8:31; 1Jn 4:4
6:17 [t]2Ki 2:11,12; Ps 68:17; Zec 6:1-7
6:18 [u]Ge 19:11; Ac 13:11
6:21 [v]2Ki 5:13
6:22 [w]Dt 20:11; 2Ch 28:8-15; Ro 12:20
6:23 [x]2Ki 5:2
6:24 [y]1Ki 15:18; 20:1; 2Ki 8:7 [z]Dt 28:52
6:25 [a]Lev 26:26; Ru 1:1 [b]Isa 36:12

6:10 The Lord fought Israel's battles in many ways, this time through military intelligence from the prophet.

6:12 The Arameans had a good counterintelligence program that revealed the source of Israel's knowledge.

6:13 find out where he is. A humorous touch: Elisha knows just where the king is, but the king does not know where Elisha is. **Dothan.** An Israelite city ten miles (16 kilometers) north of the capital city of Samaria.

6:15 The Arameans were encamped in the Dothan Valley below the fortified city on the hill.

6:17 The Lord's army was present to protect Elisha, but the servant could see it only in response to the prophet's prayer. Some of these forces escorted Elijah to heaven (2:11).

6:18 Just as the Lord restores sight to the blind, so he sometimes removes the sight of his enemies (Acts 9:8; 13:11; cf. Exod 4:11). The temporary blindness in this case allows Elisha to lead them to Samaria in a dazed state.

6:19 Though the Arameans were indeed looking for Elisha, the prophet took the army to Israel's king as the one responsible for confronting the Arameans.

6:21 Shall I kill them ...? Reflects the opportunity that the king had to be rid of one of Israel's greatest enemies. **my father.** An address of respect.

6:22 Elisha denies the king's request to kill the prisoners of war because the Lord was more interested in saving the lives of the Israelites than in ending the lives of the Arameans. The king should have learned from this event that the Lord has sufficient power to protect the nation and thus is worthy of faithful obedience.

6:23 By providing the soldiers with a banquet, Elisha fosters goodwill that results in a better outcome than a military victory.

6:24—7:2 *Famine in Besieged Samaria.* This story sharply contrasts the faithless and powerless king of Israel with the Lord and his prophet Elisha. The unnamed ruler could only rend his garments, but the prophet predicted deliverance.

6:24 Some time later. The respite from Aramean attacks (v. 23) was only temporary because the Israelites continued in covenant unfaithfulness. **Ben-Hadad king of Aram.** See note on 1 Kgs 20:1. **laid siege.** By encamping the army around the city of Samaria, thus preventing the Israelites from accessing produce in their fields or goods from the trade routes.

6:25 These prices attest not only to the authentic, eyewitness nature of the account but also to the desperate conditions that led to infanticide and cannibalism. **donkey's head.** Not only undesirable for nourishment but also forbidden by the dietary laws (Lev 11:2–8). By comparison, a live horse in the time of Solomon sold for 150 shekels (1 Kgs 10:29). **seed pods.** See NIV text note. Famine conditions could be so severe that the besieged would eat what they otherwise detested. Just a half a pint (240 milliliters) sold for what it took a common laborer six months to earn.

6:29 [c]Lev 26:29; Dt 28:53-55
6:30 [d]2Ki 18:37; Isa 22:15 [e]Ge 37:34; 1Ki 21:27
6:32 [f]Eze 8:1; 14:1; 20:1 [g]1Ki 18:4 [h]ver 31
6:33 [i]Lev 24:11; Job 2:9; 14:14; Isa 40:31
7:1 [j]ver 16
7:2 [k]2Ki 5:18 [l]ver 19; Ge 7:11; Ps 78:23; Mal 3:10 [m]ver 17
7:3 [n]Lev 13:45-46; Nu 5:1-4
7:6 [o]Ex 14:24; 2Sa 5:24; Eze 1:24 [p]2Sa 10:6; Jer 46:21 [q]Nu 13:29
7:7 [r]Jdg 7:21; Ps 48:4-6; Pr 28:1; Isa 30:17

26 As the king of Israel was passing by on the wall, a woman cried to him, "Help me, my lord the
king!"
27 The king replied, "If the LORD does not help you, where can I get help for you? From the threshing
floor? From the winepress?" 28 Then he asked her, "What's the matter?"
She answered, "This woman said to me, 'Give up your son so we may eat him today, and tomorrow
we'll eat my son.' 29 So we cooked my son and ate[c] him. The next day I said to her, 'Give up your son so
we may eat him,' but she had hidden him."
30 When the king heard the woman's words, he tore[d] his robes. As he went along the wall, the people
looked, and they saw that, under his robes, he had sackcloth[e] on his body. 31 He said, "May God deal
with me, be it ever so severely, if the head of Elisha son of Shaphat remains on his shoulders today!"
32 Now Elisha was sitting in his house, and the elders[f] were sitting with him. The king sent a messenger ahead, but before he arrived, Elisha said to the elders, "Don't you see how this murderer[g] is sending
someone to cut off my head?[h] Look, when the messenger comes, shut the door and hold it shut against
him. Is not the sound of his master's footsteps behind him?" 33 While he was still talking to them, the
messenger came down to him.
The king said, "This disaster is from the LORD. Why should I wait[i] for the LORD any longer?"

7 Elisha replied, "Hear the word of the LORD. This is what the LORD says: About this time tomorrow,
a seah[a] of the finest flour will sell for a shekel[b] and two seahs[c] of barley for a shekel[j] at the gate
of Samaria."
2 The officer on whose arm the king was leaning[k] said to the man of God, "Look, even if the LORD
should open the floodgates[l] of the heavens, could this happen?"
"You will see it with your own eyes," answered Elisha, "but you will not eat[m] any of it!"

The Siege Lifted

3 Now there were four men with leprosy[d][n] at the entrance of the city gate. They said to each other,
"Why stay here until we die? 4 If we say, 'We'll go into the city'—the famine is there, and we will die.
And if we stay here, we will die. So let's go over to the camp of the Arameans and surrender. If they spare
us, we live; if they kill us, then we die."
5 At dusk they got up and went to the camp of the Arameans. When they reached the edge of the camp,
no one was there, 6 for the Lord had caused the Arameans to hear the sound[o] of chariots and horses
and a great army, so that they said to one another, "Look, the king of Israel has hired[p] the Hittite[q] and
Egyptian kings to attack us!" 7 So they got up and fled[r] in the dusk and abandoned their tents and their
horses and donkeys. They left the camp as it was and ran for their lives.

[a] *1* That is, probably about 12 pounds or about 5.5 kilograms of flour; also in verses 16 and 18 [b] *1* That is, about 2/5 ounce or about 12 grams; also in verses 16 and 18 [c] *1* That is, probably about 20 pounds or about 9 kilograms of barley; also in verses 16 and 18 [d] *3* The Hebrew for *leprosy* was used for various diseases affecting the skin; also in verse 8.

6:27 If the LORD does not help you. The king recognized his helplessness, but there is no indication that he sought the Lord for deliverance. He needed to repent by rejecting the idolatrous worship centers, a price the king considered too high.

6:28 eat him. This sickening practice fulfills what the Lord predicted in Deut 28:53–57. The story sharply contrasts with another at the beginning of the book of Kings in which a king was able to provide a wise decision in a quarrel between two women over a baby (1 Kgs 3:16–28). Years of covenant unfaithfulness led the nation to this tragic situation.

6:30 tore his robes. A sign of desperation but not repentance since he wants to execute Elisha (v. 31). **sackcloth.** See note on 1 Kgs 20:31.

6:33 This disaster is from the LORD. A correct observation, but the king stubbornly resists the Lord rather than humbly submit to his covenantal requirements. Like his father, Ahab (1 Kgs 18:17), Joram considers the prophet the cause of the problem rather than the solution.

7:1 seah … shekel. See NIV text notes. The prices of flour and barley would be greatly reduced because the siege would be lifted.

7:2 could this happen? The king's officer refuses to believe what the prophet predicted, so he would not enjoy the deliverance. His lack of faith in the Lord's ability to provide is a grievous sin that results in his death.

7:3–20 *The Siege Lifted.* Salvation comes from the Lord. Israel is delivered not by the faithless king but by the Lord's army, which puts the Aramean forces to flight.

7:3 four men with leprosy. The Lord healed the commander of the enemy's army of leprosy (5:14), but four Israelites stricken with leprosy are not healed. Later, Jesus appealed to this situation to explain why he would not do miracles for the unbelieving people of Nazareth (Luke 4:27).

7:4 Sadly, the Lord's victory was discovered not by Israelites who believed the prophet but by lepers who had nothing to lose.

7:6–7 The divine army that Elisha's servant recently saw (6:17) puts the Arameans to flight. The Lord promised to fight the battles on behalf of his people (Deut 28:7), but he did so infrequently in the northern kingdom because they refused to adhere to the covenant.

7:6 Hittite … kings. Rulers of small city-states in northern Aram/Syria that formed after the Hittite Empire collapsed (ca. 1200 BC). Throughout their history, Israel and Judah were often tempted to hire foreign powers to deliver them rather than trust the Lord (16:7; 17:4; 1 Kgs 15:19).

8 The men who had leprosy[s] reached the edge of the camp, entered one of the tents and ate and
drank. Then they took silver, gold and clothes, and went off and hid them. They returned and entered
another tent and took some things from it and hid them also.
9 Then they said to each other, "What we're doing is not right. This is a day of good news and we
are keeping it to ourselves. If we wait until daylight, punishment will overtake us. Let's go at once and
report this to the royal palace."
10 So they went and called out to the city gatekeepers and told them, "We went into the Aramean
camp and no one was there — not a sound of anyone — only tethered horses and donkeys, and the
tents left just as they were." 11 The gatekeepers shouted the news, and it was reported within the palace.
12 The king got up in the night and said to his officers, "I will tell you what the Arameans have done
to us. They know we are starving; so they have left the camp to hide[t] in the countryside, thinking, 'They
will surely come out, and then we will take them alive and get into the city.' "
13 One of his officers answered, "Have some men take five of the horses that are left in the city. Their
plight will be like that of all the Israelites left here — yes, they will only be like all these Israelites who
are doomed. So let us send them to find out what happened."
14 So they selected two chariots with their horses, and the king sent them after the Aramean army. He
commanded the drivers, "Go and find out what has happened." 15 They followed them as far as the Jordan, and they found the whole road strewn with the clothing and equipment the Arameans had thrown
away in their headlong flight. So the messengers returned and reported to the king. 16 Then the people
went out and plundered[u] the camp of the Arameans. So a seah of the finest flour sold for a shekel, and
two seahs of barley sold for a shekel,[v] as the LORD had said.
17 Now the king had put the officer on whose arm he leaned in charge of the gate, and the people
trampled him in the gateway, and he died,[w] just as the man of God had foretold when the king came
down to his house. 18 It happened as the man of God had said to the king: "About this time tomorrow, a seah of the finest flour will sell for a shekel and two seahs of barley for a shekel at the gate of
Samaria."
19 The officer had said to the man of God, "Look, even if the LORD should open the floodgates[x] of the
heavens, could this happen?" The man of God had replied, "You will see it with your own eyes, but you
will not eat any of it!" 20 And that is exactly what happened to him, for the people trampled him in the
gateway, and he died.

The Shunammite's Land Restored

8 Now Elisha had said to the woman[y] whose son he had restored to life, "Go away with your family
and stay for a while wherever you can, because the LORD has decreed a famine[z] in the land that
will last seven years."[a] 2 The woman proceeded to do as the man of God said. She and her family went
away and stayed in the land of the Philistines seven years.
3 At the end of the seven years she came back from the land of the Philistines and went to appeal to
the king for her house and land. 4 The king was talking to Gehazi, the servant of the man of God, and

7:8 [s] Isa 33:23; 35:6
7:12 [t] Jos 8:4; 2Ki 6:25-29
7:16 [u] Isa 33:4,23 [v] ver 1
7:17 [w] ver 2; 2Ki 6:32
7:19 [x] ver 2
8:1 [y] 2Ki 4:8-37 [z] Lev 26:26; Dt 28:22; Ru 1:1 [a] Ge 12:10; Ps 105:16; Hag 1:11

7:8 With the departure of the Aramean army, not only was the siege lifted, but the Israelites had immediate access to their provisions. This brought an immediate reduction in the price of food (cf. v. 16).
7:9 The men recognize that they need to share the news of the Lord's victory with all.
7:12 Not only did the king fail to lead God's people in victory by trusting the Lord, but he also refused to believe that the Lord had delivered his city even when Elisha predicted it.
7:13 They verify the good report only because one of the king's men suggests that they investigate it. The faithless king does not act.
7:16 plundered. As with the Egyptians and the Canaanites, Israel enjoys the wealth of their enemies when the Lord fights their battles for them. **as the LORD had said.** Though this phrase may seem unnecessary for the attentive reader, the failure of the Israelites to heed God's word and trust him to be faithful makes it appropriate to state explicitly the occasions when the Lord fulfills his word.
7:18 as the man of God had said. The Lord indeed threw open the floodgates of the heavens and relieved the siege of Samaria within one day.
7:20 that is exactly what happened to him. The repetition in telling of this fulfilled prophecy serves as a warning to readers who might be tempted to doubt that God can save his people.
8:1–6 *The Shunammite's Land Restored.* Elisha's ability to provide for the needy extends beyond his personal presence. In this case, the woman whose son was brought back to life (4:8–37) receives her confiscated property on account of her relationship with the prophet.
8:1 famine. A way that the Lord punished his people and sought their repentance when they forsook the covenant and followed false gods (Deut 32:24).
8:2 land of the Philistines. The southern coastal plain, west of the kingdom of Judah. The Lord had apparently spared the Philistine territory from this famine, another indication that this calamity was directly related to Israel's covenant violations.
8:3 Others claimed her property, perhaps even the king himself if he followed in the ways of his father, Ahab (1 Kgs 21).

8:5 [b]2Ki 4:35
8:7 [c]2Sa 8:5; 1Ki 11:24 [d]2Ki 6:24
8:8 [e]1Ki 19:15 [f]Ge 32:20; 1Sa 9:7; 2Ki 1:2 [g]Jdg 18:5
8:10 [h]Isa 38:1
8:11 [i]Jdg 3:25 [j]Lk 19:41
8:12 [k]1Ki 19:17; 2Ki 10:32; 12:17; 13:3,7 [l]Ps 137:9; Isa 13:16; Hos 13:16; Na 3:10; Lk 19:44 [m]Ge 34:29 [n]2Ki 15:16; Am 1:13
8:13 [o]1Sa 17:43; 2Sa 3:8 [p]1Ki 19:15
8:15 [q]2Ki 1:17
8:16 [r]2Ki 1:17; 3:1 [s]2Ch 21:1-4
8:18 [t]ver 26; 2Ki 11:1

had said, "Tell me about all the great things Elisha has done." 5 Just as Gehazi was telling the king how Elisha had restored[b] the dead to life, the woman whose son Elisha had brought back to life came to appeal to the king for her house and land.

Gehazi said, "This is the woman, my lord the king, and this is her son whom Elisha restored to life." 6 The king asked the woman about it, and she told him.

Then he assigned an official to her case and said to him, "Give back everything that belonged to her, including all the income from her land from the day she left the country until now."

Hazael Murders Ben-Hadad

7 Elisha went to Damascus,[c] and Ben-Hadad[d] king of Aram was ill. When the king was told, "The man of God has come all the way up here," 8 he said to Hazael,[e] "Take a gift[f] with you and go to meet the man of God. Consult[g] the Lord through him; ask him, 'Will I recover from this illness?' "

9 Hazael went to meet Elisha, taking with him as a gift forty camel-loads of all the finest wares of Damascus. He went in and stood before him, and said, "Your son Ben-Hadad king of Aram has sent me to ask, 'Will I recover from this illness?' "

10 Elisha answered, "Go and say to him, 'You will certainly recover.'[h] Nevertheless,[a] the Lord has revealed to me that he will in fact die." 11 He stared at him with a fixed gaze until Hazael was embarrassed.[i] Then the man of God began to weep.[j]

12 "Why is my lord weeping?" asked Hazael.

"Because I know the harm[k] you will do to the Israelites," he answered. "You will set fire to their fortified places, kill their young men with the sword, dash[l] their little children[m] to the ground, and rip open[n] their pregnant women."

13 Hazael said, "How could your servant, a mere dog,[o] accomplish such a feat?"

"The Lord has shown me that you will become king[p] of Aram," answered Elisha.

14 Then Hazael left Elisha and returned to his master. When Ben-Hadad asked, "What did Elisha say to you?" Hazael replied, "He told me that you would certainly recover." 15 But the next day he took a thick cloth, soaked it in water and spread it over the king's face, so that he died.[q] Then Hazael succeeded him as king.

Jehoram King of Judah

8:16-24pp — 2Ch 21:5-10,20

16 In the fifth year of Joram[r] son of Ahab king of Israel, when Jehoshaphat was king of Judah, Jehoram[s] son of Jehoshaphat began his reign as king of Judah. 17 He was thirty-two years old when he became king, and he reigned in Jerusalem eight years. 18 He followed the ways of the kings of Israel, as the house of Ahab had done, for he married a daughter[t] of Ahab. He did evil in the eyes of the Lord.

[a] 10 The Hebrew may also be read *Go and say, 'You will certainly not recover,' for.*

8:5 The Lord providentially brings the woman to the king at the precise moment when he will be most willing to extend grace. Either this occurred before Gehazi was struck with leprosy or after he repented and was healed (see note on 5:27).

8:7–15 *Hazael Murders Ben-Hadad.* Elisha's visit to Hazael fulfilled the Lord's commission to Elijah in which he was to anoint Hazael king over Aram to punish Israel for its Baal worship (1 Kgs 19:15). This set in motion the severe oppression that Israel will experience during the reigns of Jehu and Jehoahaz (2 Kgs 10:32–33; 13:3–7).

8:8 Will I recover from this illness? The same words as those by the injured Israelite king Ahaziah (1:2). This is a vivid contrast: while the Israelite king sought a Philistine deity in his illness, the Aramean king inquired of the God of Israel. In the decades that follow, the Lord will side with Aram against Israel in the ongoing conflict.

8:10 'You will certainly recover.' Nevertheless. See NIV text note. Elisha knows that Ben-Hadad's death is near because Hazael will usurp the throne.

8:12 Elisha is distressed because the one the Lord raised up to discipline his people (Hazael) will treat Israel brutally. This is one of the most detailed descriptions of the Aramean oppression that characterizes the reigns of Jehu and Jehoahaz (10:32–33; 13:3–7). **rip open their pregnant women.** A practice known from Assyrian literature and also in 15:16; Amos 1:13.

8:13 The Lord "deposes kings and raises up others," both in Israel and among the nations (Dan 2:21). Unlike the false gods of the ancient Near East, the Lord's sovereignty knows no bounds.

8:15 Hazael suffocates his master in his bed. Assyrian records confirm that Hazael was a usurper of the throne by applying to him the derogatory epithet "son of a nobody." Hazael ruled ca. 843–802 BC. See photo, Tel Dan Stele written by Hazael, p. 559.

8:16–24 *Jehoram King of Judah.* By marrying Ahab's daughter Athaliah, Jehoram brings the idolatrous family of the northern kingdom into Jerusalem's palace. This immediately threatens Judah's covenant obedience and ultimately brings the royal line of David into grave danger (11:1).

8:16 fifth year of Joram. 848 BC. Jehoram started ruling with his father, Jehoshaphat, in 853 BC (1:17), and he ruled alone from 848 to 841 BC.

8:18 married a daughter of Ahab. Jehoshaphat apparently arranged his son's marriage for political purposes. Just as foreign wives led Solomon astray (1 Kgs 11:1–8) and the Phoenician princess Jezebel led Ahab further astray (1 Kgs 16:31), so Athaliah was a stronger influence on Jehoram than his righteous father Jehoshaphat was.

19 Nevertheless, for the sake of his servant David, the LORD was not willing to destroy[u] Judah. He had
promised to maintain a lamp[v] for David and his descendants forever.
20 In the time of Jehoram, Edom rebelled against Judah and set up its own king.[w] 21 So Jehoram[a]
went to Zair with all his chariots. The Edomites surrounded him and his chariot commanders, but he
rose up and broke through by night; his army, however, fled back home. 22 To this day Edom has been
in rebellion[x] against Judah. Libnah[y] revolted at the same time.
23 As for the other events of Jehoram's reign, and all he did, are they not written in the book of the
annals of the kings of Judah? 24 Jehoram rested with his ancestors and was buried with them in the City
of David. And Ahaziah his son succeeded him as king.

Ahaziah King of Judah

8:25-29pp — 2Ch 22:1-6

25 In the twelfth[z] year of Joram son of Ahab king of Israel, Ahaziah son of Jehoram king of Judah
began to reign. 26 Ahaziah was twenty-two years old when he became king, and he reigned in Jerusalem
one year. His mother's name was Athaliah,[a] a granddaughter of Omri[b] king of Israel. 27 He followed the
ways of the house of Ahab[c] and did evil[d] in the eyes of the LORD, as the house of Ahab had done, for he
was related by marriage to Ahab's family.
28 Ahaziah went with Joram son of Ahab to war against Hazael king of Aram at Ramoth Gilead.[e] The
Arameans wounded Joram; 29 so King Joram returned to Jezreel[f] to recover from the wounds the Arameans had inflicted on him at Ramoth[b] in his battle with Hazael[g] king of Aram.

Then Ahaziah son of Jehoram king of Judah went down to Jezreel to see Joram son of Ahab, because he had been wounded.

Jehu Anointed King of Israel

9 The prophet Elisha summoned a man from the company[h] of the prophets and said to him, "Tuck
your cloak into your belt,[i] take this flask of olive oil[j] with you and go to Ramoth Gilead.[k] 2 When
you get there, look for Jehu son of Jehoshaphat, the son of Nimshi. Go to him, get him away from his

[a] 21 Hebrew *Joram,* a variant of *Jehoram;* also in verses 23 and 24 [b] 29 Hebrew *Ramah,* a variant of *Ramoth*

8:19 [u] Ge 6:13 [v] 2Sa 21:17; 7:13; 1Ki 11:36; Rev 21:23
8:20 [w] 1Ki 22:47
8:22 [x] Ge 27:40 [y] Nu 33:20; Jos 21:13; 2Ki 19:8
8:25 [z] 2Ki 9:29
8:26 [a] ver 18 [b] 1Ki 16:23
8:27 [c] 1Ki 16:30 [d] 1Ki 15:26
8:28 [e] Dt 4:43; 1Ki 22:3,29
8:29 [f] 2Ki 9:15 [g] 1Ki 19:15,17
9:1 [h] 1Sa 10:5 [i] 2Ki 4:29 [j] 1Sa 10:1 [k] 2Ki 8:28

8:19 for the sake of his servant David. Even gross idolatry imported from Ahab's house was not enough to keep the Lord from being faithful to his covenant to David. God promised to raise up from David's offspring a righteous king and to "establish the throne of his kingdom forever" (2 Sam 7:13). The book of Kings regularly reminds the reader that God's preservation of David's house is a guarantee of the future fulfillment of his promise (19:34; 20:6; 1 Kgs 15:4). **a lamp.** See notes on 1 Kgs 11:36; Ps 132:17.
8:20 Edom ... set up its own king. See note on 3:9. Losing subject nations signified divine displeasure. The great kingdom that David established was gradually being dismantled.
8:21 Zair. Possibly Zior near Hebron (Josh 15:54) but probably a site in Edomite territory, perhaps related to the city of Zoar south of the Dead Sea (cf. Gen 19:22).
8:22 Libnah. A Levitical city near the border of Judah and Philistia. **revolted.** That a major city defected and Jehoram was unable to regain it demonstrates that Judah was weak when they disobeyed the Lord and his prophets.
8:23 annals of the kings of Judah. See note on 1 Kgs 14:29.
8:24 The death of a 40-year-old king (v. 17) was divine judgment (cf. 2 Chr 21:18–20). The Lord promised in the Mosaic covenant long life to those who kept his decrees (Deut 6:2). Solomon's life underscored this requirement for obedience; though Solomon was given many blessings, length of life was dependent upon his obedience (cf. 1 Kgs 3:14). **City of David.** The historic portion of Jerusalem, located south of the temple complex. Most of Judah's kings were buried here in the tomb of their forefather David (1 Kgs 2:10).
8:25–29 *Ahaziah King of Judah.* The only significant event of this wicked king's brief rule is his death. His alliance with the northern kingdom results in his assassination (9:27).
8:25 twelfth year of Joram. 841 BC.
8:27 related by marriage to Ahab's family. Ahaziah was the grandson of Ahab and nephew of Israel's king Joram. He should not be confused with his uncle Ahaziah, king of Israel (853–852 BC; see 1 Kgs 22:51–53). By intermarrying with the idolatrous house of Ahab, the descendants of David put their house at risk of assimilation and extermination (cf. 2 Kgs 11:1).
8:28 This scenario is similar to a battle 12 years earlier when Ahaziah's grandfather, Jehoshaphat, joined Ahab in battle against the Arameans at Ramoth Gilead (1 Kgs 22:4). Both encounters ended poorly for the Israelite kings. **Ramoth Gilead.** A Levitical city in the hill country east of the Jordan River about 70 miles (113 kilometers) south of Damascus. See note on 1 Kgs 22:3.
8:29 Jezreel. A well-fortified city on the edge of the Valley of Jezreel; strategically located between the battlefront and the capital city of Samaria. The presence of the royal palace made it a suitable place for Joram to recover (cf. 1 Kgs 21:1).
9:1—10:36 *Jehu King of Israel.* The author virtually ignores the 27 years of Jehu's rule, focusing instead on how Jehu fulfills the Lord's words to Elijah in removing Baal worship from the land. Though Jehu is the only king of the northern kingdom whom the Lord commended, the Arameans reduced his kingdom because he perpetuated Jeroboam's idolatry.
9:1–13 *Jehu Anointed King of Israel.* The Lord brings about a dynastic change in the northern kingdom in the anointing of Jehu. This task fulfills the second of three commissions the Lord gave to Elijah on Mount Horeb (1 Kgs 19:15–17).
9:1 a man from the company of the prophets. An unknown messenger. Elisha probably sent him to anoint Jehu (vv. 2–3) to prevent raising alarm before they could accomplish the coup.

9:3 [l] 1Ki 19:16
9:6 [m] 1Ki 19:16; 2Ch 22:7
9:7 [n] Ge 4:24; Rev 6:10 [o] Dt 32:43 [p] 1Ki 18:4; 21:15
9:8 [q] 2Ki 10:17 [r] Dt 32:36; 1Sa 25:22; 1Ki 21:21; 2Ki 14:26
9:9 [s] 1Ki 14:10; 15:29; 16:3,11 [t] 1Ki 16:3
9:10 [u] ver 35-36; 1Ki 21:23
9:11 [v] Jer 29:26; Jn 10:20; Ac 26:24
9:13 [w] Mt 21:8; Lk 19:36 [x] 2Sa 15:10; 1Ki 1:34,39
9:14 [y] Dt 4:43; 2Ki 8:28
9:15 [z] 2Ki 8:29
9:16 [a] 2Ch 22:7
9:17 [b] Isa 21:6

companions and take him into an inner room. 3 Then take the flask and pour the oil[l] on his head and declare, 'This is what the LORD says: I anoint you king over Israel.' Then open the door and run; don't delay!"

4 So the young prophet went to Ramoth Gilead. 5 When he arrived, he found the army officers sitting together. "I have a message for you, commander," he said.

"For which of us?" asked Jehu.

"For you, commander," he replied.

6 Jehu got up and went into the house. Then the prophet poured the oil[m] on Jehu's head and declared, "This is what the LORD, the God of Israel, says: 'I anoint you king over the LORD's people Israel. 7 You are to destroy the house of Ahab your master, and I will avenge[n] the blood of my servants[o] the prophets and the blood of all the LORD's servants shed by Jezebel.[p] 8 The whole house[q] of Ahab will perish. I will cut off from Ahab every last male[r] in Israel—slave or free.[a] 9 I will make the house of Ahab like the house of Jeroboam[s] son of Nebat and like the house of Baasha[t] son of Ahijah. 10 As for Jezebel, dogs[u] will devour her on the plot of ground at Jezreel, and no one will bury her.'" Then he opened the door and ran.

11 When Jehu went out to his fellow officers, one of them asked him, "Is everything all right? Why did this maniac[v] come to you?"

"You know the man and the sort of things he says," Jehu replied.

12 "That's not true!" they said. "Tell us."

Jehu said, "Here is what he told me: 'This is what the LORD says: I anoint you king over Israel.'"

13 They quickly took their cloaks and spread[w] them under him on the bare steps. Then they blew the trumpet[x] and shouted, "Jehu is king!"

Jehu Kills Joram and Ahaziah

9:21-29pp — 2Ch 22:7-9

14 So Jehu son of Jehoshaphat, the son of Nimshi, conspired against Joram. (Now Joram and all Israel had been defending Ramoth Gilead[y] against Hazael king of Aram, 15 but King Joram[b] had returned to Jezreel to recover[z] from the wounds the Arameans had inflicted on him in the battle with Hazael king of Aram.) Jehu said, "If you desire to make me king, don't let anyone slip out of the city to go and tell the news in Jezreel." 16 Then he got into his chariot and rode to Jezreel, because Joram was resting there and Ahaziah[a] king of Judah had gone down to see him.

17 When the lookout[b] standing on the tower in Jezreel saw Jehu's troops approaching, he called out, "I see some troops coming."

[a] *8* Or *Israel—every ruler or leader* [b] *15* Hebrew *Jehoram,* a variant of *Joram*; also in verses 17 and 21-24

9:3 I anoint you king over Israel. Typically the biblical writers do not record the anointing of kings except when the Lord authorized a dynastic change. In this case, the Lord was removing the dynasty of Omri by anointing Jehu through the prophet Elisha.

9:6 the LORD's people Israel. Though the northern tribes had been apostate for nearly 100 years, the Lord still considered them his people and longed to return them to relationship with him through covenant obedience.

9:7 avenge. The Lord promised this vengeance when Elijah fled from Jezebel to Mount Horeb. The prophet had complained that all of the Lord's prophets had been killed, and the Lord commissioned him to anoint three leaders who would execute the guilty in Israel (1 Kgs 19:9–18; cf. 1 Kgs 18:4).

9:8 The threat to the chosen line of David in the reign of Athaliah (11:1) shows the need for eliminating all of Ahab's descendants. As Israel's history reveals, idolatrous worship quickly permeated the nation like a cancer, and its proponents were to be shown no mercy (Deut 13:6–11). See Introduction to Deuteronomy: Themes and Theology (Holy War).

9:9 house of Jeroboam ... house of Baasha. See 1 Kgs 14:7–11; 16:1–13.

9:10 dogs will devour her. To deny a proper burial was disgraceful in the ancient world (Deut 28:26). The queen's shameful end is particularly appropriate because she tried to eliminate all of the Lord's prophets (1 Kgs 18:4; 19:2). This prophecy echoes Elijah's to Ahab (1 Kgs 21:23).

9:11 maniac. Those in the company of the prophets may have had a reputation for eccentricity, but the army officers view this messenger's secretive and hasty actions as bizarre.

9:13 spread them under him. An act of respect like the modern practice of "rolling out the red carpet" for a special guest. Those who later welcomed Jesus to Jerusalem with cries that he was the long-awaited king of Israel took the same action (Matt 21:8–9).

9:14–29 *Jehu Kills Joram and Ahaziah.* Jehu fulfills the Lord's commission in killing the Israelite king Joram, but Jehu also assassinates the visiting Judahite king Ahaziah, Joram's nephew and ally.

9:15 don't let anyone slip out of the city. As the first to leave Ramoth Gilead, Jehu is able to use the element of surprise to secure the throne.

9:16 Jezreel. About 40 miles (64 kilometers) from Ramoth Gilead.

9:17 standing on the tower. The eastern side of Jezreel had a dominating view of the route coming through the Harod Valley. This provided those in Jezreel with adequate time to send out scouts to determine the identity of an incoming rider. **peace.** Hebrew *šālôm*; occurs eight times in this chapter (here; vv. 18 [twice],19 [twice],22 [twice],31) as the two parties parry on Jehu's intention. The conflict climaxes when Jehu tells Joram that it is not he who upsets the peace but Jezebel (v. 22).

"Get a horseman," Joram ordered. "Send him to meet them and ask, 'Do you come in peace?[c]' "
[18]The horseman rode off to meet Jehu and said, "This is what the king says: 'Do you come in
peace?' "

"What do you have to do with peace?" Jehu replied. "Fall in behind me."

The lookout reported, "The messenger has reached them, but he isn't coming back."

[19]So the king sent out a second horseman. When he came to them he said, "This is what the king
says: 'Do you come in peace?' "

Jehu replied, "What do you have to do with peace? Fall in behind me."

9:17 [c] 1Sa 16:4

ISRAEL AND ITS NEIGHBORS AT THE TIME OF JEHU

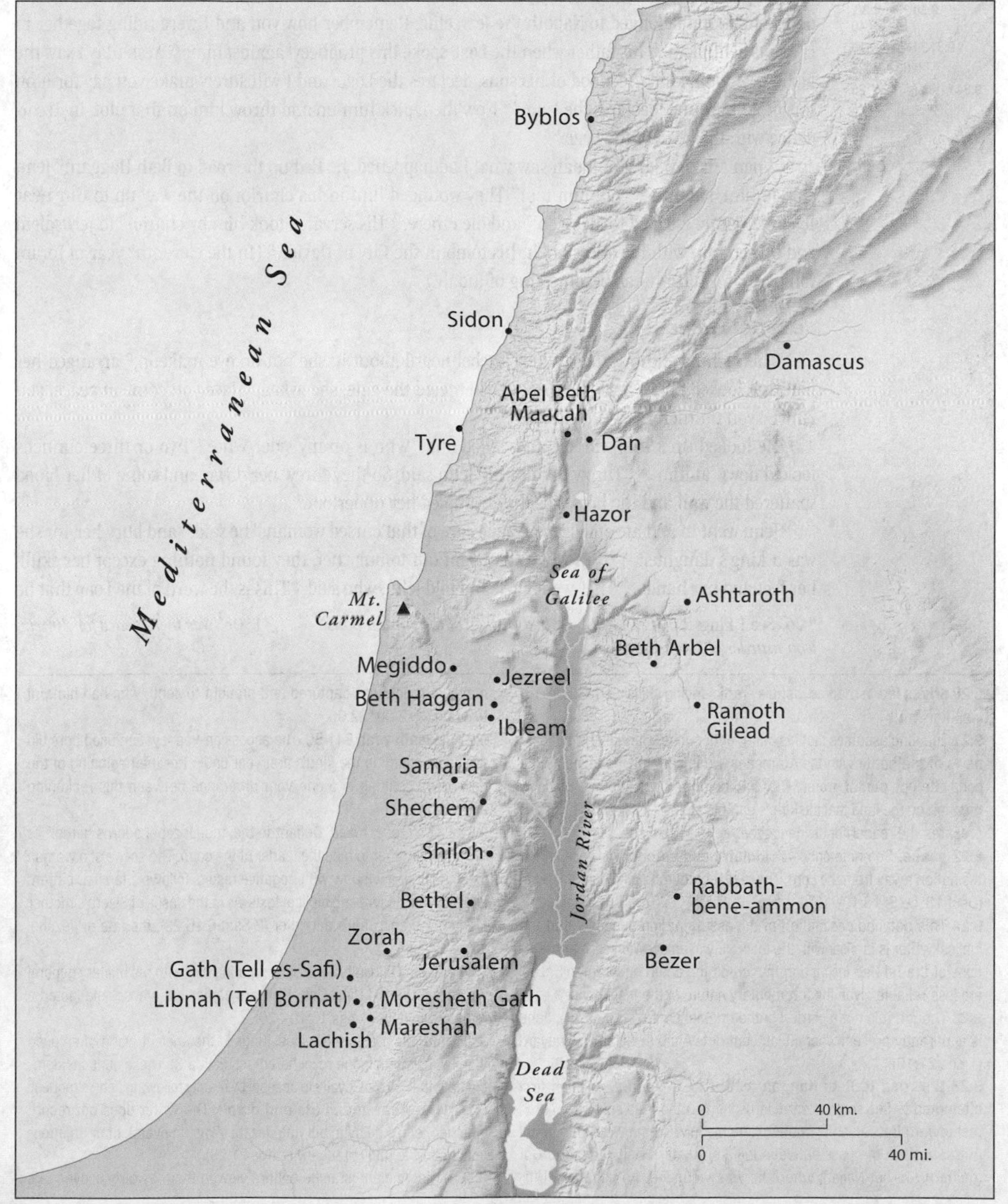

9:20 d 2Sa 18:27
9:21 e ver 26; 1Ki 21:1-7,15-19
9:22 f 1Ki 16:30-33; 18:19; 2Ch 21:13; Rev 2:20
9:23 g 2Ki 11:14
9:24 h 1Ki 22:34
9:25 i 1Ki 21:19-22, 24-29
9:26 j 1Ki 21:19 k 1Ki 21:29
9:27 l Jdg 1:27 m 2Ki 23:29
9:28 n 2Ki 14:20; 23:30
9:29 o 2Ki 8:25
9:30 p Jer 4:30; Eze 23:40
9:31 q 1Ki 16:9-10
9:33 r Ps 7:5
9:34 s 1Ki 16:31; 21:25

20 The lookout reported, "He has reached them, but he isn't coming back either. The driving is like[d]
that of Jehu son of Nimshi—he drives like a maniac."
21 "Hitch up my chariot," Joram ordered. And when it was hitched up, Joram king of Israel and
Ahaziah king of Judah rode out, each in his own chariot, to meet Jehu. They met him at the plot of
ground that had belonged to Naboth[e] the Jezreelite. 22 When Joram saw Jehu he asked, "Have you come
in peace, Jehu?"
"How can there be peace," Jehu replied, "as long as all the idolatry and witchcraft of your mother
Jezebel[f] abound?"
23 Joram turned about and fled, calling out to Ahaziah, "Treachery,[g] Ahaziah!"
24 Then Jehu drew his bow[h] and shot Joram between the shoulders. The arrow pierced his heart and
he slumped down in his chariot. 25 Jehu said to Bidkar, his chariot officer, "Pick him up and throw him
on the field that belonged to Naboth the Jezreelite. Remember how you and I were riding together in
chariots behind Ahab his father when the LORD spoke this prophecy[i] against him: 26 'Yesterday I saw the
blood of Naboth[j] and the blood of his sons, declares the LORD, and I will surely make you pay for it on
this plot of ground, declares the LORD.'[a] Now then, pick him up and throw him on that plot, in accordance with the word of the LORD."[k]
27 When Ahaziah king of Judah saw what had happened, he fled up the road to Beth Haggan.[b] Jehu
chased him, shouting, "Kill him too!" They wounded him in his chariot on the way up to Gur near
Ibleam,[l] but he escaped to Megiddo[m] and died there. 28 His servants took him by chariot[n] to Jerusalem
and buried him with his ancestors in his tomb in the City of David. 29 (In the eleventh[o] year of Joram
son of Ahab, Ahaziah had become king of Judah.)

Jezebel Killed

30 Then Jehu went to Jezreel. When Jezebel heard about it, she put on eye makeup,[p] arranged her
hair and looked out of a window. 31 As Jehu entered the gate, she asked, "Have you come in peace, you
Zimri,[q] you murderer of your master?"[c]
32 He looked up at the window and called out, "Who is on my side? Who?" Two or three eunuchs
looked down at him. 33 "Throw her down!" Jehu said. So they threw her down, and some of her blood
spattered the wall and the horses as they trampled her underfoot.[r]
34 Jehu went in and ate and drank. "Take care of that cursed woman," he said, "and bury her, for she
was a king's daughter."[s] 35 But when they went out to bury her, they found nothing except her skull,
her feet and her hands. 36 They went back and told Jehu, who said, "This is the word of the LORD that he

[a] *26* See 1 Kings 21:19. [b] *27* Or *fled by way of the garden house* [c] *31* Or *"Was there peace for Zimri, who murdered his master?"*

9:20 drives like a maniac. Jehu's erratic driving skills were apparently well-known.
9:21 The king assumes that his commander Jehu is bringing significant news of the battle with the Arameans. He is certainly not expecting a coup attempt. **plot of ground that had belonged to Naboth.** Ominously mentioning the land that the king's parents stole from Naboth (1 Kgs 21) prepares the reader for divine justice.
9:22 peace. See note on v. 17. **idolatry and witchcraft.** Jezebel led the nation away from the Lord. The punishment for such sins was death (Deut 13:1–5; 18:10–12).
9:24 This detailed description of the assassination suggests that the biblical writer is familiar with the testimony of an eyewitness. Interpretations of the Tel Dan Inscription that credit the death of Joram to Hazael are less reliable given the fragmentary nature of the inscription.
9:25 Though it is not recorded in the original context (1 Kgs 21), Jehu is apparently present when Elijah confronts Ahab in Naboth's vineyard (1 Kgs 21:19).
9:27 the road to Beth Haggan ... Gur near Ibleam. Ahaziah first attempted to flee south toward Jerusalem on the road south from Jezreel toward Beth Haggan (modern Jenin). Jehu's men were able to cut Ahaziah off at the pass between Ibleam (modern Bel'ameh) and Gur (modern Khirbet Najjar), where he was wounded. **he escaped.** Ultimately Ahaziah was captured and brought to Jehu, who had him put to death (cf. 2 Chr 22:9).
9:29 eleventh year. 841 BC. The accession-year system used here did not begin counting the king's first year until after the beginning of the new year, resulting in a one-year difference between this reckoning and that in 8:25.
9:30–37 *Jezebel Killed.* Defiant to the end, Jezebel adorns herself as the queen mother to face the leader of the coup. The scene of a woman looking out of a window with negative results follows a familiar pattern known from ancient and biblical texts. As in the cases of Sisera's mother (Judg 5:28) and Saul's daughter (2 Sam 6:16,23), the fate of Jezebel is not pleasant.
9:31 you Zimri. Insults Jehu by comparing him with the military general who assassinated King Elah 45 years earlier but whose rule lasted a mere seven days (1 Kgs 16:10–20).
9:32 eunuchs. Castrated males. Kings in the ancient world often used them as servants in the royal harem (cf. Esth 2:3). These eunuchs demonstrate their lack of loyalty to Jezebel by readily following Jehu's request.
9:34 Jehu went in and ate and drank. The writer does not record whether Jehu's delay in burying Jezebel was an oversight or an intentional effort to fulfill prophecy (1 Kgs 21:23).
9:36 dogs. Ancient Israelite culture viewed them as dirty scavengers

spoke through his servant Elijah the Tishbite: On the plot of ground at Jezreel dogs[t] will devour Jezebel's flesh.[a u] 37 Jezebel's body will be like dung[v] on the ground in the plot at Jezreel, so that no one will be able to say, 'This is Jezebel.' "

Ahab's Family Killed

10 Now there were in Samaria[w] seventy sons[x] of the house of Ahab. So Jehu wrote letters and sent them to Samaria: to the officials of Jezreel,[b y] to the elders and to the guardians[z] of Ahab's children. He said, 2 "You have your master's sons with you and you have chariots and horses, a fortified city and weapons. Now as soon as this letter reaches you, 3 choose the best and most worthy of your master's sons and set him on his father's throne. Then fight for your master's house."

4 But they were terrified and said, "If two kings could not resist him, how can we?"

5 So the palace administrator, the city governor, the elders and the guardians sent this message to Jehu: "We are your servants[a] and we will do anything you say. We will not appoint anyone as king; you do whatever you think best."

6 Then Jehu wrote them a second letter, saying, "If you are on my side and will obey me, take the heads of your master's sons and come to me in Jezreel by this time tomorrow."

Now the royal princes, seventy of them, were with the leading men of the city, who were rearing them. 7 When the letter arrived, these men took the princes and slaughtered all seventy[b] of them. They put their heads[c] in baskets and sent them to Jehu in Jezreel. 8 When the messenger arrived, he told Jehu, "They have brought the heads of the princes."

Then Jehu ordered, "Put them in two piles at the entrance of the city gate until morning."

9 The next morning Jehu went out. He stood before all the people and said, "You are innocent. It was I who conspired against my master and killed him, but who killed all these? 10 Know, then, that not a word the LORD has spoken against the house of Ahab will fail. The LORD has done what he announced[d] through his servant Elijah."[e] 11 So Jehu[f] killed everyone in Jezreel who remained of the house of Ahab, as well as all his chief men, his close friends and his priests, leaving him no survivor.[g]

12 Jehu then set out and went toward Samaria. At Beth Eked of the Shepherds, 13 he met some relatives of Ahaziah king of Judah and asked, "Who are you?"

They said, "We are relatives of Ahaziah,[h] and we have come down to greet the families of the king and of the queen mother."[i]

14 "Take them alive!" he ordered. So they took them alive and slaughtered them by the well of Beth Eked—forty-two of them. He left no survivor.

15 After he left there, he came upon Jehonadab[j] son of Rekab,[k] who was on his way to meet him. Jehu greeted him and said, "Are you in accord with me, as I am with you?"

"I am," Jehonadab answered.

9:36 [t] Ps 68:23; Jer 15:3 [u] 1Ki 21:23
9:37 [v] Ps 83:10; Isa 5:25; Jer 8:2; 9:22; 16:4; 25:33; Zep 1:17
10:1 [w] 1Ki 13:32 [x] Jdg 8:30 [y] 1Ki 21:1 [z] ver 5
10:5 [a] Jos 9:8; 1Ki 20:4,32
10:7 [b] 1Ki 21:21 [c] 2Sa 4:8
10:10 [d] 2Ki 9:7-10 [e] 1Ki 21:29
10:11 [f] Hos 1:4 [g] ver 14; Job 18:19
10:13 [h] 2Ki 8:24,29; 2Ch 22:8 [i] 1Ki 2:19
10:15 [j] Jer 35:6,14-19 [k] 1Ch 2:55; Jer 35:2

[a] *36* See 1 Kings 21:23. [b] *1* Hebrew; some Septuagint manuscripts and Vulgate *of the city*

rather than pets. It was appropriate justice that dogs licked up Ahab's blood (1 Kgs 22:38) and ate Jezebel's flesh.
9:37 The dogs prevented Jezebel's body from ever being buried, fulfilling Elijah's prophecy (v. 10; 1 Kgs 21:23).
10:1–17 *Ahab's Family Killed.* Recognizing that the survival of Ahab's descendants challenges his claim to the throne, Jehu orders them all to be killed. As a result, the word of the Lord is fulfilled.
10:1 seventy. Either a precise number or a symbolic one that represents the full number of descendants (cf. Judg 9:5). **sons.** Included grandsons as well.
10:5 The officials readily concede to Jehu, recognizing his past success and his control of the army.
10:6 take the heads of your master's sons. Could mean (1) bring the leaders of Ahab's descendants or (2) bring the sons' decapitated heads. By wording his request ambiguously, Jehu distances himself from the act of execution (v. 9). Eliminating potential heirs to the throne was standard practice in a coup attempt.
10:8 Put them ... at the entrance of the city gate. According to Assyrian records, this was an effective way of intimidating any possible opposition from the population.
10:9 The people awoke in the morning to see two grisly piles at the city gate. **who killed all these?** Jehu absolves himself of responsibility and suggests to the citizens that all opposition to him in Samaria dissolve in accordance with the decree of the Lord.
10:10 Jehu claims a divine mandate for his coup and the slaughter of Ahab's family (1 Kgs 19:15–17).
10:13–14 Jehu slaughters members of the royal family of Judah probably because Ahab's descendants and Ahaziah's family intermarried. Their visit to "the queen mother" Jezebel indicates their sympathies with the Baal-worshiping family, which puts them on the opposite side of Jehu's reforms. Nothing in this passage condemns Jehu for purging Israel of its idolatrous dynasty and Baal worshipers. Some misunderstand Hos 1:4 as contradicting 2 Kgs 9–10, but it predicts only that Jehu's dynasty would end as it began—in a bloodbath.
10:15 In contrast to those opposed to Jehu's reforms, Jehonadab, the leader of a faithful family in Israel, supports them. Two hundred years

10:15 [l]Ezr 10:19; Eze 17:18
10:16 [m]Nu 25:13; 1Ki 19:10
10:17 [n]2Ki 9:8
10:18 [o]Jdg 2:11; 1Ki 16:31-32
10:19 [p]1Ki 18:19; 22:6
10:20 [q]Ex 32:5; Joel 1:14
10:24 [r]1Ki 20:39
10:25 [s]Ex 22:20; 2Ki 11:18 [t]1Ki 18:40
10:26 [u]1Ki 14:23
10:27 [v]1Ki 16:32
10:28 [w]1Ki 19:17
10:29 [x]1Ki 12:30 [y]1Ki 12:28-29 [z]1Ki 12:32
10:30 [a]ver 35; 2Ki 15:12
10:31 [b]Pr 4:23 [c]1Ki 12:30
10:32 [d]2Ki 13:25 [e]1Ki 19:17; 2Ki 8:12
10:33 [f]Nu 32:34; Dt 2:36; Jdg 11:26; Isa 17:2

"If so," said Jehu, "give me your hand."[l] So he did, and Jehu helped him up into the chariot. [16]Jehu
said, "Come with me and see my zeal[m] for the LORD." Then he had him ride along in his chariot.
[17]When Jehu came to Samaria, he killed all who were left there of Ahab's family;[n] he destroyed them,
according to the word of the LORD spoken to Elijah.

Servants of Baal Killed

[18]Then Jehu brought all the people together and said to them, "Ahab served[o] Baal a little; Jehu will
serve him much. [19]Now summon[p] all the prophets of Baal, all his servants and all his priests. See that
no one is missing, because I am going to hold a great sacrifice for Baal. Anyone who fails to come will
no longer live." But Jehu was acting deceptively in order to destroy the servants of Baal.
[20]Jehu said, "Call an assembly[q] in honor of Baal." So they proclaimed it. [21]Then he sent word
throughout Israel, and all the servants of Baal came; not one stayed away. They crowded into the temple
of Baal until it was full from one end to the other. [22]And Jehu said to the keeper of the wardrobe, "Bring
robes for all the servants of Baal." So he brought out robes for them.
[23]Then Jehu and Jehonadab son of Rekab went into the temple of Baal. Jehu said to the servants of
Baal, "Look around and see that no one who serves the LORD is here with you — only servants of Baal."
[24]So they went in to make sacrifices and burnt offerings. Now Jehu had posted eighty men outside with
this warning: "If one of you lets any of the men I am placing in your hands escape, it will be your life
for his life."[r]
[25]As soon as Jehu had finished making the burnt offering, he ordered the guards and officers: "Go
in and kill[s] them; let no one escape."[t] So they cut them down with the sword. The guards and officers
threw the bodies out and then entered the inner shrine of the temple of Baal. [26]They brought the sacred
stone[u] out of the temple of Baal and burned it. [27]They demolished the sacred stone of Baal and tore
down the temple[v] of Baal, and people have used it for a latrine to this day.
[28]So Jehu[w] destroyed Baal worship in Israel. [29]However, he did not turn away from the sins[x] of Jeroboam son of Nebat, which he had caused Israel to commit — the worship of the golden calves[y] at
Bethel[z] and Dan.
[30]The LORD said to Jehu, "Because you have done well in accomplishing what is right in my eyes and
have done to the house of Ahab all I had in mind to do, your descendants will sit on the throne of Israel
to the fourth generation."[a] [31]Yet Jehu was not careful[b] to keep the law of the LORD, the God of Israel, with
all his heart. He did not turn away from the sins[c] of Jeroboam, which he had caused Israel to commit.
[32]In those days the LORD began to reduce[d] the size of Israel. Hazael[e] overpowered the Israelites
throughout their territory [33]east of the Jordan in all the land of Gilead (the region of Gad, Reuben and
Manasseh), from Aroer[f] by the Arnon Gorge through Gilead to Bashan.

---

later, Jeremiah praises the Rekabites for loyally obeying the commands of their forefather (Jer 35).

10:17 the word of the LORD spoken to Elijah. See 1 Kgs 21:21–22.

10:18–36 *Servants of Baal Killed.* Jehu devises a scheme to eliminate those who led Israel into idolatry. Such a slaughter may be offensive to modern sensibilities, but it was the previous failure to put to death false prophets that led to Israel's great sin before the Lord (Deut 13:5).

10:19 will no longer live. Jehu's recent massacres gives credibility to his threat.

10:22 robes. Customary in worship practices. Jehu uses them to identify those guilty of idolatry.

10:25 As soon as Jehu had finished making the burnt offering. Jehu carries on the ruse long enough that the servants of Baal let their guard down.

10:26 sacred stone. Probably installed by Ahab when he constructed the temple to Baal (1 Kgs 16:32). His son Joram removed it, so perhaps Jezebel restored it during the reign of Ahaziah (see note on 3:2).

10:27 latrine. In the contest on Mount Carmel, Elijah jested that the false prophets needed to call louder because Baal might be "busy," possibly a euphemism for relieving oneself (1 Kgs 18:27). Now Baal's chief temple in Israel is transformed into a place for the city's inhabitants to relieve themselves. The touch of humor is not muted even considering the seriousness of idolatry.

10:28–29 Jehu faithfully rid the land of Baal worship but did not eliminate the shrines at Dan and Bethel (1 Kgs 12:25–32; see note on 1 Kgs 14:23). For that reason, the writer's assessment of Jehu's rule is mixed, and Jehu receives only a limited reward.

10:30 to the fourth generation. To that time no dynasty in the northern kingdom had ruled more than two or three generations (v. 17; 1 Kgs 15:29; 16:11). Because of Jehu's obedience, the Lord gave him the longest ruling dynasty in Israel (841–752 BC).

10:31 the law of the LORD. The covenant that God had established with his people at Mount Sinai; the standard by which kings were measured. As king, Jehu was responsible to copy, carry, and obey the covenant document (Deut 17:18–20), and his failure to eliminate worship at sites where the Lord had not chosen to place his name violated the covenant (Deut 12:1–14).

10:32 Hazael overpowered the Israelites. Elijah announced (1 Kgs 19:17) and Elisha foresaw (2 Kgs 8:12) the victories of this Aramean/Syrian king. Though the Lord did not remove Jehu's dynasty because of his promise, he punished the disobedient king through military defeat.

10:33 After Hazael's depredations, Israel no longer retained sovereignty

Black Obelisk of Shalmaneser III panel with caption indicating Jehu of Israel (the one bowing).

[34]As for the other events of Jehu's reign, all he did, and all his achievements, are they not written in
the book of the annals[g] of the kings of Israel?
[35]Jehu rested with his ancestors and was buried in Samaria. And Jehoahaz his son succeeded him as
king. [36]The time that Jehu reigned over Israel in Samaria was twenty-eight years.

10:34 [g] 1Ki 15:31
11:1 [h] 2Ki 8:18
11:2 [i] ver 21; 2Ki 12:1 [j] Jdg 9:5
11:4 [k] ver 19

Athaliah and Joash

11:1-21pp — 2Ch 22:10-23:21

11 When Athaliah[h] the mother of Ahaziah saw that her son was dead, she proceeded to destroy
the whole royal family. [2]But Jehosheba, the daughter of King Jehoram[a] and sister of Ahaziah, took Joash[i] son of Ahaziah and stole him away from among the royal princes, who were about
to be murdered. She put him and his nurse in a bedroom to hide him from Athaliah; so he was not
killed.[j] [3]He remained hidden with his nurse at the temple of the LORD for six years while Athaliah
ruled the land.
[4]In the seventh year Jehoiada sent for the commanders of units of a hundred, the Carites[k] and the

[a] 2 Hebrew *Joram,* a variant of *Jehoram*

over any territory on the east side of the Jordan River. This loss of territory and access to the trade routes was the beginning of a severe oppression that continued in the reign of Jehu's son Jehoahaz (13:3–7).

10:34 other events. Such as Jehu's submission to the Assyrians in the first year of his rule. The Black Obelisk provides the only pictorial representation of an Israelite king from ancient times; it shows Jehu bowing down to Shalmaneser III. The withdrawal of the Assyrians a few years later left Jehu vulnerable to the vicious attacks of the Arameans.

10:36 twenty-eight years. 841–814/13 BC.

11:1—17:41 *The Kings of Israel and Judah Until Israel's Exile.* Jehu's revolution offered only a temporary reprieve from judgment, and the remainder of the history of the northern kingdom is a downward slide toward exile. During this period of just over 100 years, the writer moves back and forth between the two kingdoms: Judah is occasionally faithful, but Israel is consistently disobedient. The result is the exile of the ten northern tribes, a judgment so severe that the writer concludes this section with a lengthy theological explanation.

11:1—12:21 *Joash King of Israel.* Joash's 40-year reign is similar to Solomon's reign, with an initial threat to his accession (11:1–21; cf. 1 Kgs 1) followed by years focused on restoration of the temple (12:1–16; cf. 1 Kgs 5–8). Like Solomon, Joash fails to follow the Lord with all of his heart, resulting in judgment upon the nation (12:17–21; cf. 1 Kgs 11).

11:1–21 *Athaliah and Joash.* Following the assassination of Judah's king (9:27), the queen mother Athaliah attempts to eliminate the house of David and claim the throne for herself. This episode reveals the grave consequences of intermarriage with Ahab's idolatrous family; it is through the quick action of a woman that one child is spared and the Messianic line preserved. This child's restoration to the throne results in rejoicing throughout the land.

11:1 Athaliah. Daughter of Ahab (8:18). **her son was dead.** Jehu assassinated Ahaziah (9:27), so Judah's throne is empty. **destroy the whole royal family.** Jehoram had already murdered his brothers (2 Chr 21:4); the Philistines had captured Jehoram's sons (2 Chr 21:17); and Jehu had killed 42 members of the royal family (2 Kgs 10:13–14). Athaliah's grandchildren are the only remaining competition to the throne.

11:2 By saving her nephew from Athaliah's purge, Jehosheba prevents the extinction of the royal line of David. Like Haman and Herod will do later, Athaliah attacks God's people in order to thwart the fulfillment of God's promises. God's promise to David's house remains alive only through the infant Joash (2 Sam 7:16; Ps 89:34–37).

11:3 hidden ... at the temple. Because Athaliah disregards the temple, it is an ideal refuge for the infant until he can assume the throne.

11:4 seventh year. Athaliah's illegitimate rule lasted from 841 to 835 BC. **Jehoiada.** The high priest. **Carites.** Mercenary soldiers from the

11:5 [l] 1Ch 9:25 [m] 1Ki 14:27
11:10 [n] 2Sa 8:7; 1Ch 18:7
11:12 [o] Ex 25:16; 2Ki 23:3 [p] 1Sa 9:16; 1Ki 1:39 [q] Ps 47:1; 98:8; Isa 55:12 [r] 1Sa 10:24
11:14 [s] 1Ki 7:15; 2Ki 23:3; 2Ch 34:31 [t] 1Ki 1:39 [u] Ge 37:29 [v] 2Ki 9:23
11:15 [w] 1Ki 2:30
11:16 [x] Ne 3:28; Jer 31:40 [y] Ge 4:14
11:17 [z] Ex 24:8; 2Sa 5:3; 2Ch 15:12; 23:3; 29:10; 34:31; Ezr 10:3 [a] 2Ki 23:3; Jer 34:8
11:18 [b] 1Ki 16:32 [c] Dt 12:3 [d] 1Ki 18:40; 2Ki 10:25; 23:20
11:19 [e] ver 4
11:20 [f] Pr 11:10; 28:12; 29:2

guards and had them brought to him at the temple of the LORD. He made a covenant with them and put them under oath at the temple of the LORD. Then he showed them the king's son. 5 He commanded them, saying, "This is what you are to do: You who are in the three companies that are going on duty on the Sabbath[l]—a third of you guarding the royal palace,[m] 6 a third at the Sur Gate, and a third at the gate behind the guard, who take turns guarding the temple— 7 and you who are in the other two companies that normally go off Sabbath duty are all to guard the temple for the king. 8 Station yourselves around the king, each of you with weapon in hand. Anyone who approaches your ranks[a] is to be put to death. Stay close to the king wherever he goes."

9 The commanders of units of a hundred did just as Jehoiada the priest ordered. Each one took his men—those who were going on duty on the Sabbath and those who were going off duty—and came to Jehoiada the priest. 10 Then he gave the commanders the spears and shields[n] that had belonged to King David and that were in the temple of the LORD. 11 The guards, each with weapon in hand, stationed themselves around the king—near the altar and the temple, from the south side to the north side of the temple.

12 Jehoiada brought out the king's son and put the crown on him; he presented him with a copy of the covenant[o] and proclaimed him king. They anointed[p] him, and the people clapped their hands[q] and shouted, "Long live the king!"[r]

13 When Athaliah heard the noise made by the guards and the people, she went to the people at the temple of the LORD. 14 She looked and there was the king, standing by the pillar,[s] as the custom was. The officers and the trumpeters were beside the king, and all the people of the land were rejoicing and blowing trumpets.[t] Then Athaliah tore[u] her robes and called out, "Treason! Treason!"[v]

15 Jehoiada the priest ordered the commanders of units of a hundred, who were in charge of the troops: "Bring her out between the ranks[b] and put to the sword anyone who follows her." For the priest had said, "She must not be put to death in the temple[w] of the LORD." 16 So they seized her as she reached the place where the horses enter[x] the palace grounds, and there she was put to death.[y]

17 Jehoiada then made a covenant[z] between the LORD and the king and people that they would be the LORD's people. He also made a covenant between the king and the people.[a] 18 All the people of the land went to the temple[b] of Baal and tore it down. They smashed[c] the altars and idols to pieces and killed Mattan the priest[d] of Baal in front of the altars.

Then Jehoiada the priest posted guards at the temple of the LORD. 19 He took with him the commanders of hundreds, the Carites,[e] the guards and all the people of the land, and together they brought the king down from the temple of the LORD and went into the palace, entering by way of the gate of the guards. The king then took his place on the royal throne. 20 All the people of the land rejoiced,[f] and the city was calm, because Athaliah had been slain with the sword at the palace.

21 Joash[c] was seven years old when he began to reign.[d]

[a] *8* Or *approaches the precincts* [b] *15* Or *out from the precincts* [c] *21* Hebrew *Jehoash,* a variant of *Joash* [d] *21* In Hebrew texts this verse (11:21) is numbered 12:1.

Aegean, possibly descended from the Kerethites of David's time (2 Sam 20:23). **made a covenant with them.** Jehoiada's carefully planned strategy to replace Athaliah with the rightful heir requires loyal soldiers.

11:6 Sur Gate. Probably what 2 Chr 23:5 calls the Foundation Gate.

11:9 on duty ... off duty. Jehoiada chooses the time of the changing of the guard in order to have maximum protection for the new king.

11:10 The soldiers surely have their own weapons, but using King David's weapons symbolizes that Joash is restoring David's dynasty.

11:12 presented him with a copy of the covenant. Particularly appropriate since Judah's king was to lead the nation in submission to the Lord's commands (Deut 17:18–20; 1 Sam 10:25).

11:14 standing by the pillar. Probably next to one of the two pillars named Jakin and Boaz (1 Kgs 7:21). **as the custom was.** Restoring the Davidic dynasty entailed returning to the nation's traditions. **Treason! Treason!** Ironic since the queen herself had unlawfully usurped the throne: she is pronouncing her own crime, for which she deserves death.

11:15 She must not be put to death in the temple of the LORD. The queen's execution must not violate the temple's sanctity. Sadly, Joash himself later desecrates the temple by ordering the murder there of the prophet Zechariah, Jehoiada's son (cf. 2 Chr 24:21).

11:17 made a covenant. Probably similar to the covenant renewal ceremony in Josh 24:25, when the nation committed itself to keeping the Mosaic covenant. This is particularly necessary after years of covenant unfaithfulness (cf. 2 Chr 15:12).

11:18 temple of Baal. Athaliah imitated her father, Ahab, by constructing a temple to Baal in Jerusalem (cf. 1 Kgs 16:32). Such a shrine in the holy city was an abomination that showed the impact of the intermarriage of the Davidic line with Ahab's family (2 Chr 18:1). **smashed the altars and idols.** Required by the covenant that the people just made with the Lord (v. 17; cf. Deut 7:5–6). **killed Mattan the priest of Baal.** Just as Elijah had killed the prophets of Baal at the foot of Mount Carmel (1 Kgs 18:40).

11:20 Restoring peace in Jerusalem requires executing the wicked queen and destroying the idolatrous shrine.

Joash Repairs the Temple

12:1-21pp — 2Ch 24:1-14; 24:23-27

12 [a] In the seventh year of Jehu, Joash[bg] became king, and he reigned in Jerusalem forty years. His mother's name was Zibiah; she was from Beersheba. [2]Joash did what was right in the eyes of the LORD all the years Jehoiada the priest instructed him. [3]The high places,[h] however, were not removed; the people continued to offer sacrifices and burn incense there.

[4]Joash said to the priests, "Collect[i] all the money that is brought as sacred offerings[j] to the temple of the LORD — the money collected in the census,[k] the money received from personal vows and the money brought voluntarily[l] to the temple. [5]Let every priest receive the money from one of the treasurers, then use it to repair whatever damage is found in the temple."

[6]But by the twenty-third year of King Joash the priests still had not repaired the temple. [7]Therefore King Joash summoned Jehoiada the priest and the other priests and asked them, "Why aren't you repairing the damage done to the temple? Take no more money from your treasurers, but hand it over for repairing the temple." [8]The priests agreed that they would not collect any more money from the people and that they would not repair the temple themselves.

[9]Jehoiada the priest took a chest and bored a hole in its lid. He placed it beside the altar, on the right side as one enters the temple of the LORD. The priests who guarded the entrance[m] put into the chest all the money[n] that was brought to the temple of the LORD. [10]Whenever they saw that there was a large amount of money in the chest, the royal secretary[o] and the high priest came, counted the money that had been brought into the temple of the LORD and put it into bags. [11]When the amount had been determined, they gave the money to the men appointed to supervise the work on the temple. With it they paid those who worked on the temple of the LORD — the carpenters and builders, [12]the masons and stonecutters.[p] They purchased timber and blocks of dressed stone for the repair of the temple of the LORD, and met all the other expenses of restoring the temple.

[13]The money brought into the temple was not spent for making silver basins, wick trimmers, sprinkling bowls, trumpets or any other articles of gold[q] or silver for the temple of the LORD; [14]it was paid to the workers, who used it to repair the temple. [15]They did not require an accounting from those to whom they gave the money to pay the workers, because they acted with complete honesty.[r] [16]The money from the guilt offerings[s] and sin offerings[ct] was not brought into the temple of the LORD; it belonged[u] to the priests.

[17]About this time Hazael[v] king of Aram went up and attacked Gath and captured it. Then he turned to attack Jerusalem. [18]But Joash king of Judah took all the sacred objects dedicated by his predecessors — Jehoshaphat, Jehoram and Ahaziah, the kings of Judah — and the gifts he himself had

12:1 [g] 2Ki 11:2
12:3 [h] 1Ki 3:3; 2Ki 14:4; 15:35; 18:4
12:4 [i] 2Ki 22:4 [j] Ex 35:5 [k] Ex 30:12 [l] Ex 35:29; 1Ch 29:3-9
12:9 [m] Jer 35:4 [n] 2Ch 24:8; Mk 12:41; Lk 21:1
12:10 [o] 2Sa 8:17
12:12 [p] 2Ki 22:5-6
12:13 [q] 1Ki 7:48-51; 2Ch 24:14
12:15 [r] 2Ki 22:7; 1Co 4:2
12:16 [s] Lev 5:14-19; Nu 18:9 [t] Lev 4:1-35 [u] Lev 7:7
12:17 [v] 2Ki 8:12

[a] In Hebrew texts 12:1-21 is numbered 12:2-22. [b] *1* Hebrew *Jehoash,* a variant of *Joash;* also in verses 2, 4, 6, 7 and 18 [c] *16* Or *purification offerings*

12:1 – 21 *Joash Repairs the Temple.* The writer's report of Joash's 40-year reign focuses on Joash's temple restoration project. While the writer commends the king for his attention to the Lord's house, the king largely undid his accomplishment by turning over the temple treasures to a pagan king. Ultimately, Joash's own officials assassinate him, once again pointing the reader forward to a future king as David's long-awaited righteous successor.

12:1 seventh year of Jehu. 835 BC. **forty years.** 835 – 796 BC.

12:2 all the years. 2 Chr 24:17 – 25 describes Joash's apostasy after Jehoiada's death.

12:3 high places ... not removed. See note on 1 Kgs 15:14.

12:4 Revenue came from three sources: (1) a half a shekel collected from every Israelite male at 20 years of age (Exod 30:11 – 16); (2) income received from personal vows (Lev 27:1 – 25); (3) voluntary contributions such as those given for the construction of the tabernacle (Exod 35:4 – 29; cf. Lev 22:18 – 23; Deut 16:10).

12:5 The first recorded renovation of Solomon's temple, now nearly 150 years old. The temple also suffered from neglect and desecration in the time of Athaliah and her predecessors (2 Chr 24:7).

12:6 twenty-third year. 814 BC.

12:8 Since the priests had not used the money to restore the temple, Joash initiates a plan that bypasses the priests and delivers the money directly to the construction workers.

12:13 The temple's urgent need is not furnishings or utensils but structural work that stone masons and carpenters provide. Once they complete the structural work, they purchase articles for the temple (2 Chr 24:14).

12:15 The obvious integrity of the workers is readily apparent, and no audits are required to locate missing funds.

12:16 The priests continue to have sufficient income from the sacrificial offerings (Lev 5:16; 7:7 – 10; Num 5:7 – 10).

12:17 About this time. 814/13 BC. Jehu of Israel dies, and Hazael's army is able to freely pass through Israelite territory to reach the Philistine city of Gath (modern Tell es-Safi), about 25 miles (40 kilometers) west of Jerusalem. Archaeology has revealed that Gath was a large city that suffered a major siege at this time. Hazael's victory enables his army to turn east toward Jerusalem and its wealthy temple. Given differences in timing and other details, this attack is distinct from a later one that leads to Joash's death (2 Chr 24:23 – 25).

12:18 Joash faithlessly surrenders, thus undoing his sole accomplishment: temple restoration. This all-too-common practice of buying off

12:18 [w]1Ki 15:18; 2Ch 21:16-17 [x]1Ki 15:21
12:20 [y]2Ki 14:5 [z]2Ch 24:25 [a]Jdg 9:6
13:2 [b]1Ki 12:26-33
13:3 [c]Dt 31:17; Jdg 2:14 [d]1Ki 8:12; 12:17; 19:17 [e]ver 24
13:4 [f]Dt 4:29; Ps 78:34 [g]Ex 3:7; Dt 26:7 [h]2Ki 14:26
13:5 [i]ver 25; 2Ki 14:25,27
13:6 [j]1Ki 12:30 [k]1Ki 16:33
13:7 [l]2Ki 10:32-33 [m]2Sa 22:43

dedicated and all the gold found in the treasuries of the temple of the LORD and of the royal palace, and
he sent[w] them to Hazael king of Aram, who then withdrew[x] from Jerusalem.
19 As for the other events of the reign of Joash, and all he did, are they not written in the book of
the annals of the kings of Judah? 20 His officials[y] conspired against him and assassinated[z] him at Beth
Millo,[a] on the road down to Silla. 21 The officials who murdered him were Jozabad son of Shimeath and
Jehozabad son of Shomer. He died and was buried with his ancestors in the City of David. And Amaziah
his son succeeded him as king.

Jehoahaz King of Israel

13 In the twenty-third year of Joash son of Ahaziah king of Judah, Jehoahaz son of Jehu became
king of Israel in Samaria, and he reigned seventeen years. 2 He did evil[b] in the eyes of the LORD
by following the sins of Jeroboam son of Nebat, which he had caused Israel to commit, and he did not
turn away from them. 3 So the LORD's anger[c] burned against Israel, and for a long time he kept them
under the power[d] of Hazael king of Aram and Ben-Hadad[e] his son.
4 Then Jehoahaz sought[f] the LORD's favor, and the LORD listened to him, for he saw[g] how severely the
king of Aram was oppressing[h] Israel. 5 The LORD provided a deliverer[i] for Israel, and they escaped from
the power of Aram. So the Israelites lived in their own homes as they had before. 6 But they did not turn
away from the sins[j] of the house of Jeroboam, which he had caused Israel to commit; they continued
in them. Also, the Asherah pole[a][k] remained standing in Samaria.
7 Nothing had been left[l] of the army of Jehoahaz except fifty horsemen, ten chariots and ten thousand
foot soldiers, for the king of Aram had destroyed the rest and made them like the dust[m] at threshing time.
8 As for the other events of the reign of Jehoahaz, all he did and his achievements, are they not written
in the book of the annals of the kings of Israel? 9 Jehoahaz rested with his ancestors and was buried in
Samaria. And Jehoash[b] his son succeeded him as king.

Jehoash King of Israel

10 In the thirty-seventh year of Joash king of Judah, Jehoash son of Jehoahaz became king of Israel in
Samaria, and he reigned sixteen years. 11 He did evil in the eyes of the LORD and did not turn away from
any of the sins of Jeroboam son of Nebat, which he had caused Israel to commit; he continued in them.

[a] *6* That is, a wooden symbol of the goddess Asherah; here and elsewhere in 2 Kings [b] *9* Hebrew *Joash*, a variant of *Jehoash*; also in verses 12-14 and 25

the enemy with treasure from the Lord's house (16:8: 1 Kgs 15:18) dishonored the God who promised to protect his people when they trusted him (Deut 7:17–24). One day in the future, when the Lord fulfills his promise to establish a righteous Davidic ruler over Israel, the nations will bring their wealth to the temple in Jerusalem (Isa 60:6–12; Hag 2:6–8).

12:20 Joash is the first king of Judah to be killed in a conspiracy, but his assassination differs markedly from those in the northern kingdom because Joash's son is placed on the throne, so his dynasty continues.

13:1–9 *Jehoahaz King of Israel.* The Lord previously punished the covenant unfaithfulness of the northern kingdom with famine and invasion (8:1; 10:32–33), but in the reign of Jehoahaz he displays mercy in delivering Israel from severe oppression. The sad result is that whether afflicted or delivered, the nation refuses to return to its true King.

13:1 twenty-third year. 814/13 BC. **seventeen years.** 814/13–798 BC.

13:2–4 did evil ... the LORD's anger ... sought the LORD's favor. Reminiscent of the cycle of sin, suffering, and salvation in the book of Judges (Judg 2:11–19; see Introduction to Judges: The Cycles Section). The desperate condition of the nation is a direct result of their failure to keep their covenant with the Lord. In punishing his people, the Lord graciously seeks to restore them to obedience and blessing. Jehoahaz is the only ruler of the northern kingdom who seeks the Lord.

13:2 the sins of Jeroboam. See note on 1 Kgs 12:30.

13:3 Hazael. Ruled ca. 843–802 BC. **Ben-Hadad.** Ben-Hadad III ruled for several decades after Hazael. Elijah and Elisha anticipated that Hazael would oppress Israel (8:12; 1 Kgs 19:15–17).

13:5 deliverer. Possibly (1) the Assyrian king Adad-nirari III, who attacked Aram ca. 800, thus weakening Israel's persecutor, or (2) Elisha, whose final visit with Jehoash led to three Israelite victories (v. 19). **the Israelites lived in their own homes.** The severity of the oppression is made evident by this note that many Israelites had previously been forced to abandon their homes. These Israelites may have lived east of the Jordan River in Gilead (cf. 10:33).

13:6 Asherah pole. See note on Exod 34:13. The Israelites did not respond to the Lord's deliverance with repentance.

13:7 fifty horsemen, ten chariots and ten thousand foot soldiers. These military details may come from a treaty concluding Israel's defeat, and they reflect the abysmal state of the army. An Assyrian inscription reports that just 40 years earlier Ahab led 2,000 chariots at the battle of Qarqar. The totals reflect the devastation the Arameans inflicted in the decades since Hazael's accession. Elisha's weeping was not without reason (8:7–15).

13:10–25 *Jehoash King of Israel.* What is worth reporting of Jehoash's reign is the gracious work of God through the prophet Elisha. While the Israelite king is helpless before the Aramean army, Elisha predicts victory because of the Lord's compassion. Of utmost importance is the reason for this compassion: Israel's sin is not great enough to cause the Lord to forget his covenant promises to the patriarchs.

13:10 thirty-seventh year. 798 BC. **sixteen years.** 798–782/81 BC.

13:11 the sins of Jeroboam. See note on 1 Kgs 12:30.

12 As for the other events of the reign of Jehoash, all he did and his achievements, including his war
against Amaziah[n] king of Judah, are they not written in the book of the annals[o] of the kings of Israel?
13 Jehoash rested with his ancestors, and Jeroboam[p] succeeded him on the throne. Jehoash was buried
in Samaria with the kings of Israel.
14 Now Elisha had been suffering from the illness from which he died. Jehoash king of Israel went down
to see him and wept over him. "My father! My father!" he cried. "The chariots[q] and horsemen of Israel!"
15 Elisha said, "Get a bow and some arrows,"[r] and he did so. 16 "Take the bow in your hands," he said
to the king of Israel. When he had taken it, Elisha put his hands on the king's hands.
17 "Open the east window," he said, and he opened it. "Shoot!"[s] Elisha said, and he shot. "The LORD's
arrow of victory, the arrow of victory over Aram!" Elisha declared. "You will completely destroy the
Arameans at Aphek."[t]
18 Then he said, "Take the arrows," and the king took them. Elisha told him, "Strike the ground." He
struck it three times and stopped. 19 The man of God was angry with him and said, "You should have
struck the ground five or six times; then you would have defeated Aram and completely destroyed it.
But now you will defeat it only three times."[u]
20 Elisha died and was buried.
Now Moabite raiders[v] used to enter the country every spring. 21 Once while some Israelites were burying a man, suddenly they saw a band of raiders; so they threw the man's body into Elisha's tomb. When
the body touched Elisha's bones, the man came to life[w] and stood up on his feet.
22 Hazael king of Aram oppressed[x] Israel throughout the reign of Jehoahaz. 23 But the LORD was gracious
to them and had compassion and showed concern for them because of his covenant[y] with Abraham,
Isaac and Jacob. To this day he has been unwilling to destroy[z] them or banish them from his presence.[a]
24 Hazael king of Aram died, and Ben-Hadad[b] his son succeeded him as king. 25 Then Jehoash son of
Jehoahaz recaptured from Ben-Hadad son of Hazael the towns he had taken in battle from his father
Jehoahaz. Three times[c] Jehoash defeated him, and so he recovered[d] the Israelite towns.

Amaziah King of Judah

14:1-7pp — 2Ch 25:1-4,11-12
14:8-22pp — 2Ch 25:17–26:2

14 In the second year of Jehoash[*a*] son of Jehoahaz king of Israel, Amaziah son of Joash king of
Judah began to reign. 2 He was twenty-five years old when he became king, and he reigned in
Jerusalem twenty-nine years. His mother's name was Jehoaddan; she was from Jerusalem. 3 He did what
was right in the eyes of the LORD, but not as his father David had done. In everything he followed the

13:12 [n] 2Ki 14:15 [o] 1Ki 15:31
13:13 [p] 2Ki 14:23; Hos 1:1
13:14 [q] 2Ki 2:12
13:15 [r] 1Sa 20:20
13:17 [s] Jos 8:18 [t] 1Ki 20:26
13:19 [u] ver 25
13:20 [v] 2Ki 3:7; 24:2
13:21 [w] Mt 27:52
13:22 [x] 1Ki 19:17; 2Ki 8:12
13:23 [y] Ge 13:16-17; Ex 2:24 [z] Dt 29:20 [a] Ex 33:15; 2Ki 14:27; 17:18; 24:3,20
13:24 [b] ver 3
13:25 [c] ver 18,19 [d] 2Ki 10:32

a 1 Hebrew *Joash,* a variant of *Jehoash*; also in verses 13, 23 and 27

13:12 war against Amaziah. See 14:8–14; 2 Chr 25:17–24. **the annals of the kings of Israel.** See note on 1 Kgs 14:19.
13:14 suffering. Elisha's ministry began ca. 855, and he was at least 70 years old by this time. **My father! My father!** The king addresses Elisha with respect appropriate to an aged prophet of the Lord (2:12). **The chariots and horsemen of Israel!** Israel's true military strength was not its army but the Lord and his prophet (2:12; 6:8—7:20; 9:1–13).
13:17 east. The direction of Israel's enemy Aram. **Aphek.** The location of Israel's previous victory over Aram (1 Kgs 20:26); possibly on the east side of the Sea of Galilee.
13:19 only three times. Presumably reflects a hesitance coming from a lack of faith. Elisha is disappointed that the king did not obey with enthusiasm and perseverance.
13:20 Moabite raiders. Only a few decades earlier the Moabite state was subject to Israel, but the situation has so deteriorated that Israel's military is unable to protect the nation's borders.
13:21 Elisha's tomb. Probably a cave with easy access, blocked by a stone. **came to life.** Just as Elisha's corpse was able to provide life after the prophet died, so his words still hold the power of life and death for Israel as it chooses to heed or reject the prophet's message (v. 25).
13:23 gracious. Israel's salvation is the result of God's grace and nothing that they did. **his covenant.** The reason the Lord was patient with the continually rebellious nation of Israel. The people's sin was not sufficient to cause the Lord to forget what he promised to the patriarchs (Exod 2:24; Lev 26:42; Mic 7:18–20; see "Covenant," p. 2646). **To this day.** This portion was written sometime before the northern tribes began to be deported by the Assyrians beginning in 733 BC (15:29).
13:25 Three times Jehoash defeated him. The first victory for the northern kingdom in 40 years, fulfilling what Elisha prophesied to Jehoash (v. 19). **Israelite towns.** Probably the villages of Gilead that Hazael captured (10:33).
14:1–22 *Amaziah King of Judah.* The author remembers King Amaziah for his prideful attitude that leads to a great defeat when Israel routes Judah's army, attacks Jerusalem, and carries off treasures from the temple.
14:1 second year of Jehoash. 796 BC.
14:2 twenty-nine years. 796–767 BC. This includes a coregency from 792/91–767 BC with Jehoash's son Azariah, also known as Uzziah (see 15:1 and NIV text note there).
14:3 not as his father David had done. The Lord promised to raise up a son of David and establish his throne forever (2 Sam 7:13), but a

14:4 [e]2Ki 12:3; 16:4
14:5 [f]2Ki 21:24
[g]2Ki 12:20
14:6 [h]Dt 28:61
[i]Nu 26:11; Job 21:20; Jer 31:30; 44:3; Eze 18:4,20
14:7 [j]2Sa 8:13; 2Ch 25:11 [k]Jdg 1:36
14:9 [l]Jdg 9:8-15
14:10 [m]Dt 8:14; 2Ch 26:16; 32:25
14:11 [n]Jos 15:10
14:12 [o]2Sa 18:17
14:13 [p]1Ki 3:1; 2Ch 33:14; 36:19; Jer 39:2 [q]Ne 8:16; 12:39 [r]2Ch 25:23; Jer 31:38; Zec 14:10
14:15 [s]2Ki 13:12
14:19 [t]2Ki 12:20
[u]Jos 10:3; 2Ki 18:14,17

example of his father Joash. 4The high places,[e] however, were not removed; the people continued to
offer sacrifices and burn incense there.
5After the kingdom was firmly in his grasp, he executed[f] the officials[g] who had murdered his
father the king. 6Yet he did not put the children of the assassins to death, in accordance with what
is written in the Book of the Law[h] of Moses where the LORD commanded: "Parents are not to be put
to death for their children, nor children put to death for their parents; each will die for their own
sin."[a][i]
7He was the one who defeated ten thousand Edomites in the Valley of Salt[j] and captured Sela[k] in
battle, calling it Joktheel, the name it has to this day.
8Then Amaziah sent messengers to Jehoash son of Jehoahaz, the son of Jehu, king of Israel, with the
challenge: "Come, let us face each other in battle."
9But Jehoash king of Israel replied to Amaziah king of Judah: "A thistle[l] in Lebanon sent a message
to a cedar in Lebanon, 'Give your daughter to my son in marriage.' Then a wild beast in Lebanon
came along and trampled the thistle underfoot. 10You have indeed defeated Edom and now you are
arrogant.[m] Glory in your victory, but stay at home! Why ask for trouble and cause your own downfall
and that of Judah also?"
11Amaziah, however, would not listen, so Jehoash king of Israel attacked. He and Amaziah king of
Judah faced each other at Beth Shemesh[n] in Judah. 12Judah was routed by Israel, and every man fled
to his home.[o] 13Jehoash king of Israel captured Amaziah king of Judah, the son of Joash, the son of
Ahaziah, at Beth Shemesh. Then Jehoash went to Jerusalem and broke down the wall[p] of Jerusalem
from the Ephraim Gate[q] to the Corner Gate[r]—a section about four hundred cubits long.[b] 14He took
all the gold and silver and all the articles found in the temple of the LORD and in the treasuries of the
royal palace. He also took hostages and returned to Samaria.
15As for the other events of the reign of Jehoash, what he did and his achievements, including his
war[s] against Amaziah king of Judah, are they not written in the book of the annals of the kings of
Israel? 16Jehoash rested with his ancestors and was buried in Samaria with the kings of Israel. And
Jeroboam his son succeeded him as king.
17Amaziah son of Joash king of Judah lived for fifteen years after the death of Jehoash son of Jehoahaz king of Israel. 18As for the other events of Amaziah's reign, are they not written in the book of the
annals of the kings of Judah?
19They conspired[t] against him in Jerusalem, and he fled to Lachish,[u] but they sent men after him to

a *6* Deut. 24:16 *b* *13* That is, about 600 feet or about 180 meters

king less faithful than David would not be the one God promised (1 Kgs 9:4–5).
14:5 murdered. See 12:20–21.
14:6 Amaziah was familiar with the Mosaic covenant (Deut 24:16) and faithfully kept it in this situation.
14:7 defeated ten thousand Edomites. See 2 Chr 25:5–16. Amaziah's goal was to subdue the kingdom that revolted in the reign of his great-grandfather Jehoram (8:20). **Valley of Salt.** Probably in the Arabah south of the Dead Sea (2 Sam 8:13). **Sela.** Though some have identified this with the Nabatean city of Petra, a more likely location is modern Khirbet Sil, four miles (six kilometers) north of ancient Bozrah. **to this day.** Until the time when this record was written (see note on 13:23).
14:8 Pillaging by Israelite troops sent home from the battle (2 Chr 25:7–13) provokes Amaziah's challenge. He may also have been rebuffed in a proposal for a marriage alliance between the two nations (v. 9).
14:9 thistle ... cedar. Jehoash tries to dissuade Amaziah from a military confrontation by comparing the king of Judah to a lowly thistle and himself to a mighty cedar tree. Amaziah's victory deceives him into thinking that his army is a match for the more powerful north.
14:11 would not listen. The Lord's judgment upon the king for his idolatry (2 Chr 25:20). **Beth Shemesh.** A Levitical city in the western foothills of Judah 15 miles (24 kilometers) west of Jerusalem.
14:13 captured. This is the only recorded case of an Israelite king taking a Judahite king as prisoner. Because of the comment about "hostages" in v. 14 and because Amaziah's successor Uzziah likely began a coregency at this time, some speculate that Amaziah remained a prisoner in the capital city of Samaria until Jehoash's death (see note on v. 21). **Ephraim Gate.** Likely on the northern wall of the city facing the tribal territory of Ephraim (Neh 12:39). **Corner Gate.** Possibly at the northwestern corner (Jer 31:38). **four hundred cubits long.** See NIV text note. By destroying these fortifications, Jerusalem was left vulnerable on its only side without the natural protection of a valley. This suggests that Jerusalem expanded to the western hill prior to the reign of Hezekiah and his building campaign (2 Chr 32:5).
14:14 Judah's enemies plundered the temple several times, but it is particularly tragic that Israel's king did not hold the Lord's temple in special honor. The Lord had already promised four generations to Jehu (10:30), but the reader must expect that the nation of Israel will not last much beyond that.
14:15 annals of the kings of Israel. See note on 1 Kgs 14:19.
14:17 fifteen years. 782–767 BC.
14:19 conspired against him. Amaziah's rule ended like his father's did: a conspiracy that led to his assassination (12:20). **Lachish.** A major city of Judah located 30 miles (48 kilometers) southwest of Jerusalem in the western foothills.

Lachish and killed him there. [20]He was brought back by horse[v] and was buried in Jerusalem with his
ancestors, in the City of David.
[21]Then all the people of Judah took Azariah,[a][w] who was sixteen years old, and made him king in
place of his father Amaziah. [22]He was the one who rebuilt Elath[x] and restored it to Judah after Amaziah
rested with his ancestors.

14:20 [v]2Ki 9:28
14:21 [w]2Ki 15:1; 2Ch 26:23
14:22 [x]1Ki 9:26; 2Ki 16:6
14:23 [y]2Ki 13:13
14:24 [z]1Ki 15:30
14:25 [a]Nu 13:21; 1Ki 8:65 [b]Dt 3:17 [c]Jnh 1:1; Mt 12:39
14:26 [d]Dt 32:36 [e]2Ki 13:4

Jeroboam II King of Israel

[23]In the fifteenth year of Amaziah son of Joash king of Judah, Jeroboam[y] son of Jehoash king of
Israel became king in Samaria, and he reigned forty-one years. [24]He did evil in the eyes of the LORD
and did not turn away from any of the sins of Jeroboam son of Nebat, which he had caused Israel to
commit.[z] [25]He was the one who restored the boundaries of Israel from Lebo Hamath[a] to the Dead Sea,[b][b]
in accordance with the word of the LORD, the God of Israel, spoken through his servant Jonah[c] son of
Amittai, the prophet from Gath Hepher.
[26]The LORD had seen how bitterly everyone in Israel, whether slave or free,[d] was suffering;[c][e] there

[a] *21* Also called *Uzziah* [b] *25* Hebrew *the Sea of the Arabah* [c] *26* Or *Israel was suffering. They were without a ruler or leader, and*

14:20 City of David. See note on 8:24.
14:21 Azariah. Also known as Uzziah (cf. 15:13; 2 Chr 26:1); the alternate name possibly avoided confusion with Azariah the chief priest (2 Chr 26:17). **made him king.** Azariah begins his lengthy coregency with his father (see note on 15:2). **in place of his father.** Supports the theory that Amaziah is captive in Samaria at this time (see note on v. 13).
14:22 Elath. A port city on the northern tip of the Red Sea (the modern Gulf of Aqabah) where his predecessors Solomon and Jehoshaphat had constructed fleets of ships (1 Kgs 9:26; 2 Chr 20:36–37). A royal seal inscribed with the name of Azariah's son, Jotham, was discovered in excavations at Tell el-Kheleifeh near Elath. See photo, p. 685.
14:23–29 *Jeroboam II King of Israel.* Like his namesake, Jeroboam II leads the nation away from the Lord, but his rule marks a great reversal of decades of oppression and territorial loss. Jeroboam's success comes not from his own strength but from the Lord as announced through his prophet Jonah.
14:23 fifteenth year. 782/81 BC. **forty-one years.** 793/92–753 BC. This includes a coregency with his father (793/92–782/81 BC), making Jeroboam II the longest ruling king of the northern kingdom.
14:24 He did evil. From a political and military perspective, Jeroboam II is one of the greatest kings of Israel, but for the biblical writer, these accomplishments matter little because of the king's unfaithfulness to the Lord. The books of Amos and Hosea recount some of the social and religious sins of Jeroboam II.
14:25 He was the one who restored the boundaries of Israel. The Lord graciously provides relief from oppression and allows the nation to expand its territory, but sadly this kindness does not lead Jeroboam to repentance. **Lebo Hamath.** The name of the ancient city of Lebo on the southern border of the kingdom of Hamath is preserved in modern Lebweh, 50 miles (80 kilometers) north of Damascus. This is a major reversal of Israel's military position, which only a few decades earlier was quite desperate (see notes on 10:33; 12:17; 13:7). With the exception of territory that Judah holds in the south, Israel controls nearly as much territory as Solomon had once ruled (cf. 1 Kgs 4:21; 8:65). **the word of the LORD.** As in the previous chapter, the prophet instead of the king receives credit for Israel's victory (13:14–19). **Jonah son of Amittai.** The book of Jonah, while it does not record the event mentioned here, does record this prophet's mission to Nineveh. The reference here provides a date for his ministry. **Gath Hepher.** A town in Galilee two miles (3 kilometers) northeast of Nazareth. The people of Nineveh conquer Jonah's hometown a few decades after Jonah's visit (15:29). Jonah's Galilean origin is later ignored by Jewish leaders who claim that no prophet comes from Galilee (John 7:52).

14:26 The hero of the book of Kings is the Lord, whose compassion regularly extends to his covenant-breaking people.

AMAZIAH KING OF JUDAH

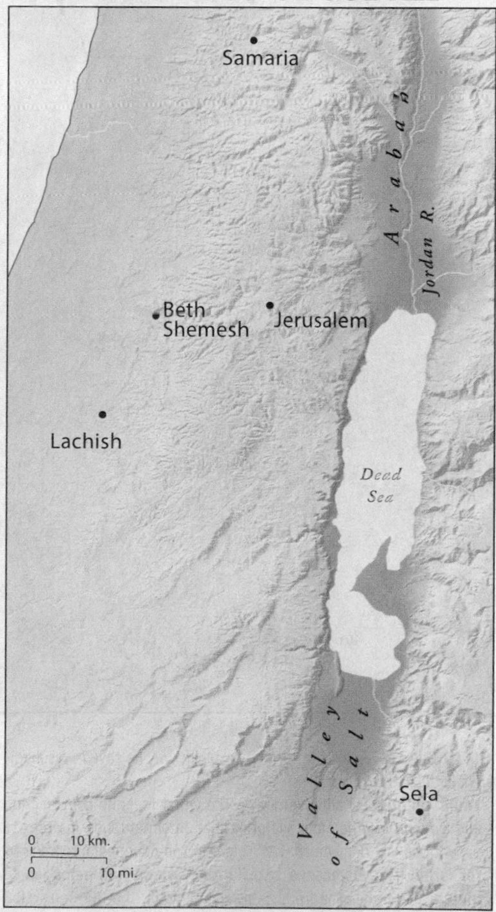

14:26 [f]Ps 18:41; 22:11; 72:12; 107:12; Isa 63:5; La 1:7
14:27 [g]2Ki 13:23 [h]Jdg 6:14
14:28 [i]2Sa 8:5; 1Ki 11:24 [j]2Ch 8:3 [k]1Ki 15:31
15:1 [l]ver 32; 2Ki 14:21
15:5 [m]Ge 12:17 [n]Lev 13:46 [o]2Ch 27:1 [p]Ge 41:40
15:7 [q]Isa 6:1; 14:28 [r]ver 5

was no one to help them.[f] [27]And since the LORD had not said he would blot out[g] the name of Israel from
under heaven, he saved[h] them by the hand of Jeroboam son of Jehoash.
[28]As for the other events of Jeroboam's reign, all he did, and his military achievements, including
how he recovered for Israel both Damascus[i] and Hamath,[j] which had belonged to Judah, are they not
written in the book of the annals[k] of the kings of Israel? [29]Jeroboam rested with his ancestors, the kings
of Israel. And Zechariah his son succeeded him as king.

Azariah King of Judah

15:1-7pp — 2Ch 26:3-4,21-23

15 In the twenty-seventh year of Jeroboam king of Israel, Azariah[a][l] son of Amaziah king of Judah
began to reign. [2]He was sixteen years old when he became king, and he reigned in Jerusalem
fifty-two years. His mother's name was Jekoliah; she was from Jerusalem. [3]He did what was right in
the eyes of the LORD, just as his father Amaziah had
done. [4]The high places, however, were not removed;
the people continued to offer sacrifices and burn
incense there.
[5]The LORD afflicted[m] the king with leprosy[b] until
the day he died, and he lived in a separate house.[c][n]
Jotham[o] the king's son had charge of the palace[p]
and governed the people of the land.
[6]As for the other events of Azariah's reign, and
all he did, are they not written in the book of the
annals of the kings of Judah? [7]Azariah rested[q] with
his ancestors and was buried near them in the City
of David. And Jotham[r] his son succeeded him as
king.

[a] *1* Also called *Uzziah*; also in verses 6, 7, 8, 17, 23 and 27 [b] *5* The Hebrew for *leprosy* was used for various diseases affecting the skin. [c] *5* Or *in a house where he was relieved of responsibilities*

JEROBOAM'S EXPANSION

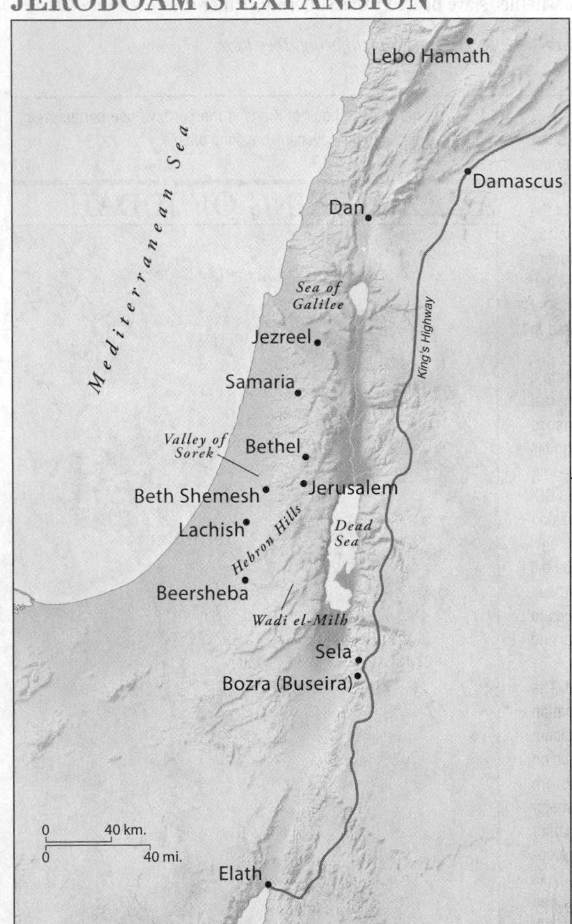

14:27 God's covenant with Abraham explains why he saves a disobedient Israel from extinction.

14:28 his military achievements. The writer feels no compunction about recording the many victories that Jeroboam won in order to expand his kingdom. Amos 6:13 refers to two conquests. **recovered for Israel both Damascus and Hamath, which had belonged to Judah.** The translation from Hebrew is difficult; the NIV translation understands this to refer to Jeroboam's recovering Aramean kingdoms that had once been subject to King David (2 Sam 8:5–10). Thus, during the contemporary reigns of Azariah and Jeroboam II, Judah recovered Elath (v. 22) and Israel recovered Damascus and Hamath, restoring to the two nations the territory once held by David and Solomon. **annals of the kings of Israel.** See note on 1 Kgs 14:19.

15:1–7 *Azariah King of Judah.* This only briefly summarizes the reign of Azariah, a long-ruling contemporary of Jeroboam II. The first half of the eighth century BC was a period of national and military strength in Israel and Judah, but the writer of Kings chooses to record little of political history that does not explain why the 12 tribes were sent into exile. With its focus upon the kings of Judah, the book of Chronicles more extensively records Azariah's accomplishments and failures (2 Chr 26).

15:1 twenty-seventh year. 767 BC. **Azariah.** Also known as Uzziah (see note on 14:21).

15:2 fifty-two years. 792/91–740/39 BC. This total includes a coregency with his father (792/91–767 BC).

15:5 leprosy. See NIV text note; 2 Chr 26:16–21. This brief summary of a 52-year reign emphasizes the king's leprosy. **lived in a separate house.** See Lev 13:46. **Jotham the king's son had charge of the palace and governed.** The clearest statement for the existence of coregencies in ancient Judah.

15:6 other events. See 2 Chr 26:1–15.

15:7 buried near them in the City of David. Azariah is the first king of

Zechariah King of Israel

[8]In the thirty-eighth year of Azariah king of Judah, Zechariah son of Jeroboam became king of Israel in Samaria, and he reigned six months. [9]He did evil[s] in the eyes of the LORD, as his predecessors had done. He did not turn away from the sins of Jeroboam son of Nebat, which he had caused Israel to commit.

[10]Shallum son of Jabesh conspired against Zechariah. He attacked him in front of the people,[a] assassinated[t] him and succeeded him as king. [11]The other events of Zechariah's reign are written in the book of the annals[u] of the kings of Israel. [12]So the word of the LORD spoken to Jehu was fulfilled:[v] "Your descendants will sit on the throne of Israel to the fourth generation."[b]

Shallum King of Israel

[13]Shallum son of Jabesh became king in the thirty-ninth year of Uzziah king of Judah, and he reigned in Samaria[w] one month. [14]Then Menahem son of Gadi went from Tirzah[x] up to Samaria. He attacked Shallum son of Jabesh in Samaria, assassinated[y] him and succeeded him as king.

[15]The other events of Shallum's reign, and the conspiracy he led, are written in the book of the annals[z] of the kings of Israel.

[16]At that time Menahem, starting out from Tirzah, attacked Tiphsah[a] and everyone in the city and its vicinity, because they refused to open[b] their gates. He sacked Tiphsah and ripped open all the pregnant women.

Menahem King of Israel

[17]In the thirty-ninth year of Azariah king of Judah, Menahem son of Gadi became king of Israel, and he reigned in Samaria ten years. [18]He did evil in the eyes of the LORD. During his entire reign he did not turn away from the sins of Jeroboam son of Nebat, which he had caused Israel to commit.

[19]Then Pul[c][c] king of Assyria invaded the land, and Menahem gave him a thousand talents[d] of silver to gain his support and strengthen his own hold on the kingdom. [20]Menahem exacted this money from Israel. Every wealthy person had to contribute fifty shekels[e] of silver to be given to the king of Assyria. So the king of Assyria withdrew[d] and stayed in the land no longer.

a *10* Hebrew; some Septuagint manuscripts *in Ibleam* *b* *12* 2 Kings 10:30 *c* *19* Also called *Tiglath-Pileser*
d *19* That is, about 38 tons or about 34 metric tons *e* *20* That is, about 1 1/4 pounds or about 575 grams

15:9 [s]1Ki 15:26
15:10 [t]2Ki 12:20
15:11 [u]1Ki 15:31
15:12 [v]2Ki 10:30
15:13 [w]ver 1,8
15:14 [x]1Ki 14:17 [y]2Ki 12:20
15:15 [z]1Ki 15:31
15:16 [a]1Ki 4:24 [b]2Ki 8:12; Hos 13:16
15:19 [c]1Ch 5:6,26
15:20 [d]2Ki 12:18

Judah not buried in the tomb of his fathers. Archaeologists confirmed this by discovering an AD first-century plaque that identified the tomb of Uzziah.

15:8–31 *The Final Kings of Israel.* This period of history consists of a quick succession of five kings, four of whom were assassinated. The total duration of their combined rule is 21 years (753–732/31 BC), about half the length of the previous ruler of Israel, Jeroboam II. The nation of Israel is clearly plunging headlong into exile with a series of weak kings and the entrance of the mighty Assyrian Empire. By the end of this period, the majority of the northern tribes are deported, and only the hill country of Samaria retains any sovereignty.

15:8–12 *Zechariah King of Israel.* "Zechariah" means "the LORD remembers," which is ironic since the Lord remembered his promise to give Jehu four generations (10:30), and once the fourth generation comes to the throne, the Lord ends the king's reign in a mere six months.

15:8 thirty-eighth year of Azariah. 753 BC.

15:10 in front of the people. See NIV text note. Jehu's dynasty ends in the same way (assassination) and in the same area (the Valley of Jezreel) as it began, fulfilling Hos 1:4 (cf. 2 Kgs 9:27).

15:13–16 *Shallum King of Israel.* Shallum's brief reign of one month may explain why he is the only northern king not said to have followed in the ways of Jeroboam.

15:13 thirty-ninth year. 752 BC. **Uzziah.** Another name for Azariah (see note on 14:21).

15:14 Menahem. Possibly the army commander stationed at Tirzah; he saw an opportunity to seize the throne from a weak usurper. **Tirzah.** The former capital of Israel (see note on 1 Kgs 14:17).

15:16 Tiphsah. The only city known by this name is on the Euphrates River, 300 miles (480 kilometers) northeast of Tirzah (cf. 1 Kgs 4:24). If this city is intended, it suggests that Menahem was trying to retain his hold on distant territory conquered by Jeroboam II. Because of the distance, some prefer the alternative name of Tappuah, listed in some Greek texts. The site of Tappuah (modern Sheikh Abu Zarad) is 13 miles (21 kilometers) southwest of Tirzah and may have been a bastion of support for Menahem's opposition. **ripped open all the pregnant women.** Such brutality is reported in an Assyrian account and in Amos 1:13 but is never elsewhere attributed to an Israelite king (cf. 2 Kgs 8:12).

15:17–22 *Menahem King of Israel.* As Menahem's reign is characterized by covenant unfaithfulness, the author highlights the king's military failure.

15:17 thirty-ninth year ... ten years. 752–742/41 BC.

15:19 Pul. Tiglath-Pileser III ruled Assyria from 745 to 727 BC and was known by the nickname Pulu in Babylonian king lists and Pul in Hebrew (cf. v. 29). **invaded the land.** Following a century of absence, Assyria's return to Israel soon results in the exile of the northern tribes. **thousand talents.** See NIV text note. **to gain his support.** Without trust in the Lord and faithfulness to his covenant, Menahem feels that he has to submit to the Assyrians to protect his position. This strategy works in the short run because Menahem is the only one of Israel's last six kings to die peacefully in office, but ultimately the nation's protector conquers it in 722 BC.

15:20 fifty shekels. See NIV text note. A calculation reveals that 60,000 people paid this tax that totaled 1,000 talents. This gives some indication of the wealth to be found in ancient Israel shortly after the prophet Amos railed against the crimes of the rich (e.g., Amos 2:6–7). **the king**

15:25 [e] 2Ch 28:6; Isa 7:1 [f] 2Ki 12:20
15:27 [g] 2Ch 28:6; Isa 7:1 [h] Isa 7:4
15:29 [i] 2Ki 16:7; 17:6; 1Ch 5:26; 2Ch 28:20; Jer 50:17 [j] 1Ki 15:20 [k] 2Ki 16:9; 17:24; 2Ch 16:4; Isa 9:1 [l] 2Ki 24:14-16; 1Ch 5:22; Isa 14:6,17; 36:17; 45:13
15:30 [m] 2Ki 17:1 [n] 2Ki 12:20
15:32 [o] 1Ch 5:17
15:34 [p] ver 3; 1Ki 14:8; 2Ch 26:4-5
15:35 [q] 2Ki 12:3

21 As for the other events of Menahem's reign, and all he did, are they not written in the book of the
annals of the kings of Israel? 22 Menahem rested with his ancestors. And Pekahiah his son succeeded
him as king.

Pekahiah King of Israel

23 In the fiftieth year of Azariah king of Judah, Pekahiah son of Menahem became king of Israel in
Samaria, and he reigned two years. 24 Pekahiah did evil in the eyes of the LORD. He did not turn away
from the sins of Jeroboam son of Nebat, which he had caused Israel to commit. 25 One of his chief officers, Pekah[e] son of Remaliah, conspired against him. Taking fifty men of Gilead with him, he assassinated[f] Pekahiah, along with Argob and Arieh, in the citadel of the royal palace at Samaria. So Pekah
killed Pekahiah and succeeded him as king.
26 The other events of Pekahiah's reign, and all he did, are written in the book of the annals of the
kings of Israel.

Pekah King of Israel

27 In the fifty-second year of Azariah king of Judah, Pekah[g] son of Remaliah[h] became king of Israel
in Samaria, and he reigned twenty years. 28 He did evil in the eyes of the LORD. He did not turn away from
the sins of Jeroboam son of Nebat, which he had caused Israel to commit.
29 In the time of Pekah king of Israel, Tiglath-Pileser[i] king of Assyria came and took Ijon,[j] Abel Beth
Maakah, Janoah, Kedesh and Hazor. He took Gilead and Galilee, including all the land of Naphtali,[k]
and deported[l] the people to Assyria. 30 Then Hoshea[m] son of Elah conspired against Pekah son of Remaliah. He attacked and assassinated[n] him, and then succeeded him as king in the twentieth year of
Jotham son of Uzziah.
31 As for the other events of Pekah's reign, and all he did, are they not written in the book of the
annals of the kings of Israel?

Jotham King of Judah

15:33-38pp — 2Ch 27:1-4,7-9

32 In the second year of Pekah son of Remaliah king of Israel, Jotham[o] son of Uzziah king of Judah
began to reign. 33 He was twenty-five years old when he became king, and he reigned in Jerusalem sixteen years. His mother's name was Jerusha daughter of Zadok. 34 He did what was right[p] in the eyes of
the LORD, just as his father Uzziah had done. 35 The high places,[q] however, were not removed; the people

---

of Assyria withdrew. Fragmentary Assyrian inscriptions confirm that Tiglath-Pileser exacted tribute from Israel in the reign of Menahem.

15:23–26 *Pekahiah King of Israel.* Because Pekahiah perpetuates the national idolatry, his record consists primarily of the conspiracy that ends his life.

15:23 fiftieth year ... two years. 742/41–740/39 BC.

15:25 assassinated Pekahiah. With the overthrow of Jehu's dynasty, the northern kingdom never again sees a dynasty last beyond the rule of the founder's son. **Argob and Arieh.** Possibly royal advisers or the king's sons.

15:27–31 *Pekah King of Israel.* Pekah's reign is characterized by wickedness and the subsequent deportation of his subjects by Assyria.

15:27 fifty-second year. 740/39 BC. **twenty years.** 752–732/31 BC. Since Pekah's rule ends with Hoshea's accession in 732/31 BC, his 20-year rule must include 12 years contemporaneous with the reigns of Menahem and Pekahiah. Pekah perhaps exercised authority over the Israelite tribes in Gilead until 740/39 BC, when he became king over all of the northern kingdom.

15:29 Tiglath-Pileser king of Assyria came. This invasion occurred in 733 BC. **Ijon, Abel Beth Maakah, Janoah, Kedesh and Hazor.** Cities in the area of the northern Jordan Valley along the route that Tiglath-Pileser traveled when he invaded Galilee from the north (cf. 1 Kgs 15:20). Archaeological excavation has uncovered evidence of a major destruction of many Israelite cities at this time. **took Gilead and Galilee.** Deportation of the ten northern tribes begins a decade before the fall of Samaria (722 BC) with the exile of the tribes of Naphtali, Issachar, Reuben, Gad, and Manasseh. Moses (Deut 29:28), Solomon (1 Kgs 8:46), and the prophet Ahijah (1 Kgs 14:15) anticipated Israel's exile. **deported the people to Assyria.** Tiglath-Pileser employs the policy of deportation to reduce the possibility of future insurrections. This is the first of many deportations of the covenant people into exile, culminating with Babylon's destruction of Jerusalem and deportation of the people of Judah in 586 BC (25:1–21).

15:30 The Assyrians, who desire a more compliant king in Israel, support the conspiracy against Pekah. **twentieth year.** 732/31 BC. Jotham begins a coregency with his father, Uzziah, in 750 BC.

15:32–38 *Jotham King of Judah.* The report of Jotham's reign consists of little more than what is given for every king. Like his predecessors, he fails to remove the high places and is buried in the City of David. He is credited for his obedience to the Lord. Some additional details are found in 2 Chr 27.

15:32 second year. Jotham began his sole reign when his father, Uzziah, died in 740/39 BC.

15:33 sixteen years. 750–735 BC. This includes the coregency (750–740/39) that began when his father, Uzziah, was struck with leprosy (v. 5) but does not include his coregency with his son Ahaz (735–732/31).

15:35 Upper Gate. Likely the entrance on the northern side of the temple complex (2 Chr 23:20).

continued to offer sacrifices and burn incense there. Jotham rebuilt the Upper Gate[r] of the temple of the LORD.

[36]As for the other events of Jotham's reign, and what he did, are they not written in the book of the annals of the kings of Judah? [37](In those days the LORD began to send Rezin[s] king of Aram and Pekah son of Remaliah against Judah.) [38]Jotham rested with his ancestors and was buried with them in the City of David, the city of his father. And Ahaz his son succeeded him as king.

Ahaz King of Judah

16:1-20pp — 2Ch 28:1-27

16 In the seventeenth year of Pekah son of Remaliah, Ahaz[t] son of Jotham king of Judah began to reign. [2]Ahaz was twenty years old when he became king, and he reigned in Jerusalem sixteen years. Unlike David his father, he did not do what was right[u] in the eyes of the LORD his God. [3]He followed the ways of the kings of Israel and even sacrificed his son[v] in the fire, engaging in the detestable[w] practices of the nations the LORD had driven out before the Israelites. [4]He offered sacrifices and burned incense at the high places, on the hilltops and under every spreading tree.[x]

[5]Then Rezin[y] king of Aram and Pekah son of Remaliah king of Israel marched up to fight against Jerusalem and besieged Ahaz, but they could not overpower him. [6]At that time, Rezin[z] king of Aram recovered Elath[a] for Aram by driving out the people of Judah. Edomites then moved into Elath and have lived there to this day.

[7]Ahaz sent messengers to say to Tiglath-Pileser[b] king of Assyria, "I am your servant and vassal. Come up and save[c] me out of the hand of the king of Aram and of the king of Israel, who are attacking me." [8]And Ahaz took the silver and gold found in the temple of the LORD and in the treasuries of the royal palace and sent it as a gift[d] to the king of Assyria. [9]The king of Assyria complied by attacking Damascus[e] and capturing it. He deported its inhabitants to Kir[f] and put Rezin to death.

[10]Then King Ahaz went to Damascus to meet Tiglath-Pileser king of Assyria. He saw an altar in Damascus and sent to Uriah[g] the priest a sketch of the altar, with detailed plans for its construction. [11]So Uriah the priest built an altar in

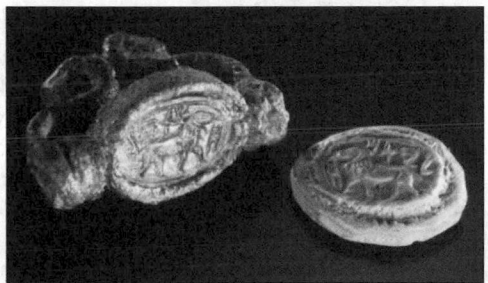

Signet ring with writing above the sphinx(?) clearly stating "*l ytm*" meaning "belonging to Jotham."

Catalogue No. A388291, Department of Anthropology, Smithsonian Institution

15:35 [r]2Ch 23:20
15:37 [s]2Ki 16:5; Isa 7:1
16:1 [t]Isa 1:1; 14:28
16:2 [u]1Ki 14:8
16:3 [v]Lev 18:21; 2Ki 21:6 [w]Lev 18:3; Dt 9:4; 12:31
16:4 [x]Dt 12:2; Eze 6:13
16:5 [y]2Ki 15:37; Isa 7:1,4
16:6 [z]Isa 9:12 [a]2Ki 14:22; 2Ch 26:2
16:7 [b]2Ki 15:29 [c]Isa 2:6; Jer 2:18; Eze 16:28; Hos 10:6
16:8 [d]2Ki 12:18
16:9 [e]2Ki 15:29 [f]Isa 22:6; Am 1:5; 9:7
16:10 [g]Isa 8:2

16:1–20 *Ahaz King of Judah.* The monarchy of Judah reaches a new low under Ahaz. He follows in the ways of Israel's evil kings, sacrifices his own son, replaces Solomon's altar, and dismantles portions of the Lord's temple furniture. The cup of the Lord's wrath soon reaches its full measure against his wayward people.

16:1 seventeenth year. In 735 BC Ahaz began his coregency with his father, Jotham. **Ahaz son of Jotham king of Judah.** In 1996 the discovery of a clay seal impression confirmed his reign: "Belonging to Ahaz (son of) Jotham, king of Judah."

16:2 sixteen years. 732/31–716/15 BC. The 16 years of Ahaz's reign are counted from the death of his father Jotham in 732/31 BC.

16:3 followed the ways of the kings of Israel. Ahaz adopts some of the syncretistic practices of Judah's northern neighbor, though this did not include worshiping the golden calves at Dan and Bethel. In light of the recent report of the beginning of Israel's exile (15:29), the author is foreshadowing a similar judgment for Judah. **sacrificed his son in the fire.** Imitates the nations around Judah and explicitly violates the Lord's command (Lev 20:1–5). The only other king of Israel or Judah who sacrifices his son is Manasseh (21:6; cf. 23:10; Jer 32:35). Imitating the practices of the Canaanites leads to the same divine judgment: God removes Judah from the land of Israel (Jer 19:1–9).

16:4 He offered sacrifices … under every spreading tree. See note on 1 Kgs 14:23.

16:5 Rezin … Pekah son of Remaliah. When Ahaz refuses to join their anti-Assyrian coalition, these two kings seek to conquer Judah and replace Ahaz with a compliant ruler (vv. 5–10; 2 Chr 28:5–23; Isa 7:1–17).

16:6 recovered Elath. Following Azariah's conquest of Elath (14:22), Judah held this Red Sea port until the reign of Ahaz. This is the last time Judah will rule this far south. **Edomites then moved into Elath.** Either Rezin gives Elath to the nearby Edomites, or the Edomites conquer the city a few years later when Assyria conquers Aram/Syria.

16:7 Ahaz chooses to seek deliverance through Assyria, despite Isaiah's specific challenge to trust the Lord (Isa 7:4–12). Ahaz's decision brings short-term deliverance from Aram and Israel, but the invitation to Assyria ultimately results in Judah's exile (Isa 7:17—8:10).

16:8 For a similar situation, see 12:18 and note. An inscription of Tiglath-Pileser mentions tribute offered by "Jehoahaz of Judah," a more complete version of Ahaz's name.

16:9 attacking Damascus. This conquest in 732 BC ends the ancient kingdom of Aram. As Isaiah had declared, Aram is nothing more than a "smoldering [stub] of firewood" (Isa 7:4). **deported its inhabitants to Kir.** This exile fulfills the prophecy of judgment in Amos 1:5. The Lord had once brought the Arameans from Kir (Amos 9:7), possibly a region in Mesopotamia (Isa 22:6).

16:10–11 Ahaz replaces the altar of Solomon's temple with the imitation of a pagan one. Israelites who recall God's judgment of Nadab and Abihu for bringing "unauthorized fire" into the sanctuary (Lev 10:1–2) should expect a similar fate for Judah.

16:12 [h]2Ch 26:16
16:13 [i]Lev 6:8-13
[j]Lev 7:11-21
16:14 [k]2Ch 4:1
16:15 [l]Ex 29:38-41
[m]1Sa 9:9
16:17 [n]1Ki 7:27
16:18 [o]Eze 16:28
17:1 [p]2Ki 15:30
17:3 [q]2Ki 18:9-12;
Hos 10:14
17:5 [r]Hos 13:16

accordance with all the plans that King Ahaz had sent from Damascus and finished it before King
Ahaz returned. 12 When the king came back from Damascus and saw the altar, he approached it and
presented offerings[a][h] on it. 13 He offered up his burnt offering[i] and grain offering, poured out his drink
offering, and splashed the blood of his fellowship offerings[j] against the altar. 14 As for the bronze altar[k]
that stood before the LORD, he brought it from the front of the temple—from between the new altar
and the temple of the LORD—and put it on the north side of the new altar.

15 King Ahaz then gave these orders to Uriah the priest: "On the large new altar, offer the morning[l]
burnt offering and the evening grain offering, the king's burnt offering and his grain offering, and the
burnt offering of all the people of the land, and their grain offering and their drink offering. Splash
against this altar the blood of all the burnt offerings and sacrifices. But I will use the bronze altar for
seeking guidance."[m] 16 And Uriah the priest did just as King Ahaz had ordered.

17 King Ahaz cut off the side panels and removed the basins from the movable stands. He removed
the Sea from the bronze bulls that supported it and set it on a stone base.[n] 18 He took away the Sabbath
canopy[b] that had been built at the temple and removed the royal entryway outside the temple of the
LORD, in deference to the king of Assyria.[o]

19 As for the other events of the reign of Ahaz, and what he did, are they not written in the book of
the annals of the kings of Judah? 20 Ahaz rested with his ancestors and was buried with them in the City
of David. And Hezekiah his son succeeded him as king.

Hoshea Last King of Israel

17:3-7pp — 2Ki 18:9-12

17 In the twelfth year of Ahaz king of Judah, Hoshea[p] son of Elah became king of Israel in Samaria, and he reigned nine years. 2 He did evil in the eyes of the LORD, but not like the kings of
Israel who preceded him.

3 Shalmaneser[q] king of Assyria came up to attack Hoshea, who had been Shalmaneser's vassal and
had paid him tribute. 4 But the king of Assyria discovered that Hoshea was a traitor, for he had sent envoys to So[c] king of Egypt, and he no longer paid tribute to the king of Assyria, as he had done year by
year. Therefore Shalmaneser seized him and put him in prison. 5 The king of Assyria invaded the entire
land, marched against Samaria and laid siege[r] to it for three years. 6 In the ninth year of Hoshea, the

[a] 12 Or *and went up* [b] 18 Or *the dais of his throne* (see Septuagint) [c] 4 *So* is probably an abbreviation for *Osorkon.*

16:13 Ahaz's offering recalls Solomon's great sacrifice at the dedication of the temple (1 Kgs 8:64) and reminds the reader just how far the nation has departed from the faithful worship that the Lord required.
16:14 Ahaz pushes aside the altar that Solomon built and no longer uses it for sacrifices.
16:15 large new altar. The Mosaic covenant did not give Ahaz the freedom to replace the Lord's altar with one of another design (Exod 31:11). Thus every sacrifice now being offered violates God's law. **seeking guidance.** Not the purpose of the Lord's altar. Ahaz is also guilty of following pagan practices of divination (17:17; Deut 18:10).
16:16 The priest chooses to obey the king instead of the Lord, unlike his predecessor (2 Chr 26:17–18).
16:17 The king of Judah usurps his authority by exercising control over tasks the Lord had explicitly assigned to the Levites. He perhaps removed the bronze objects to pay tribute to Assyria. **basins ... Sea.** See 1 Kgs 7:23–40.
16:18 Sabbath canopy ... royal entryway. Not mentioned elsewhere in Scripture; probably later additions to Solomon's temple that served the king when he visited the temple.
17:1–6 *Hoshea Last King of Israel.* The last ruler of the northern kingdom never exercises national sovereignty. Vacillating between Assyria and Egypt, Hoshea's territory is soon conquered and his people are carried off into exile. The only credit to Hoshea is the biblical writer's assessment that he is not quite as wicked as his predecessors.
17:1 twelfth year. 723 BC. **nine years.** 732/31–723/22 BC. This dating of Ahaz's 12th year counts from the first year of his coregency with his father, Jotham, in 735 BC and signals the end, not the beginning, of Hoshea's reign. This fits the description of the context, which focuses on the conquest of Israel, and translates the Hebrew as "Hoshea son of Elah had reigned over Israel in Samaria nine years." Other solutions include positing a coregency of Ahaz with his grandfather beginning in 744 BC or speculating that a copyist made an error.
17:3 Shalmaneser king of Assyria. Shalmaneser V ruled Assyria from 727 to 722 BC.
17:4 So. See NIV text note: Osorkon IV (730–715 BC) was the last pharaoh of Egypt's Twenty-Second Dynasty. Living on the strategic land bridge between Egypt and Mesopotamia, Israel's kings often vacillated between paying tribute to Egypt or the dominant northern power of the time (Hos 7:11; cf. 2 Kgs 19:9 and note; Isa 30:1–5). **put him in prison.** If this account is read sequentially, it suggests that Hoshea was captured before the city of Samaria was besieged. Yet the reference to Samaria's fall in Hoshea's ninth year (v. 6) indicates that these verses do not chronologically summarize the kingdom's final days.
17:5 three years. The siege probably began in the late spring or early summer of 724 BC and continued through the summer of 722 BC, when the city fell.
17:6 the king of Assyria captured Samaria. The Babylonian Chronicle agrees with the biblical account in crediting the conquest of Samaria to

EXILE OF THE NORTHERN KINGDOM

The mass deportation policy of the Assyrians was a companion piece to the brutal and calculated terror initiated by Ashurnasirpal and followed by all his successors. It was intended to forestall revolts, but like all draconian measures, it merely spread misery and engendered hatred. In the end, it hastened the disintegration of the Assyrian Empire.

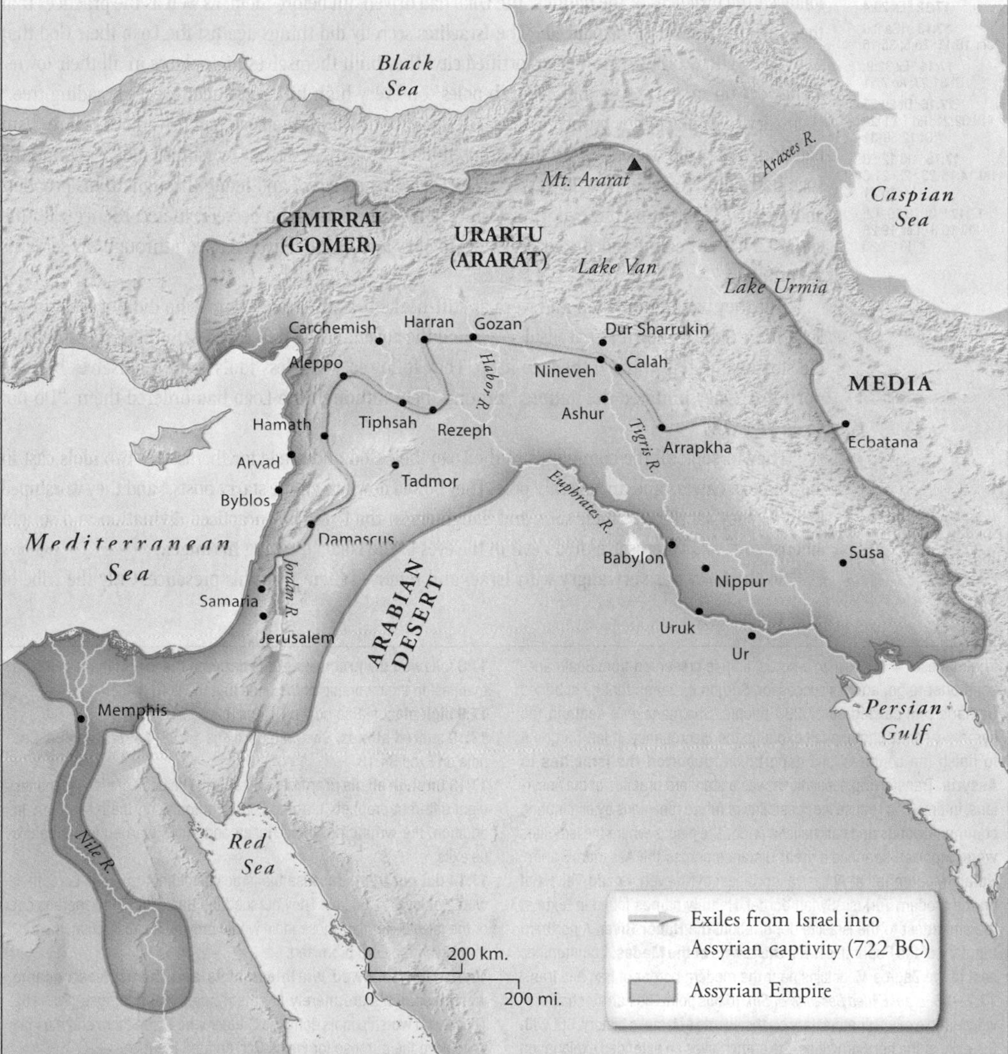

There is some evidence that Israel experienced its first deportations under Tiglath-Pileser III (745–727 BC), a cruelty repeated by Sargon II (721–705 BC) at the time of the fall of Samaria. The latter king's inscriptions boast of carrying away 27,290 inhabitants of the city "as plunder." According to 2 Kgs 17:6, they were sent to Assyria, to Halah, to Gozan on the Habor River, and apparently to the eastern frontiers of the empire (to the towns of the Medes, most probably somewhere in the vicinity of Ecbatana, the modern Hamadan).

The sequel is provided by the inscriptions of Sargon: "The Arabs who live far away in the desert, who know neither overseers nor officials, and who had not yet brought their tribute to any king, I deported ... and settled them in Samaria."

Much mythology has developed around the theme of the so-called ten lost tribes of Israel. A close examination of Assyrian records reveals that the deportations approximated only a limited percentage of the population, usually consisting of noble families. Agricultural workers, no doubt the majority, were deliberately left to care for the crops (cf. the Babylonian practice, 2 Kgs 24:14; 25:12).

17:6 [s]Hos 13:16 [t]Dt 28:36,64; 2Ki 18:10-11 [u]1Ch 5:26
17:7 [v]Jos 23:16; Jdg 6:10 [w]Ex 14:15-31
17:8 [x]Lev 18:3; Dt 18:9; 2Ki 16:3
17:9 [y]2Ki 18:8
17:10 [z]Ex 34:13; Mic 5:14 [a]1Ki 14:23
17:12 [b]Ex 20:4
17:13 [c]1Sa 9:9 [d]Jer 18:11; 25:5; 35:15
17:14 [e]Ex 32:9; Dt 31:27; Ac 7:51
17:15 [f]Dt 29:25 [g]Dt 32:21; Ro 1:21-23 [h]Dt 12:30-31
17:16 [i]1Ki 12:28 [j]1Ki 14:15,23 [k]2Ki 21:3 [l]1Ki 16:31
17:17 [m]Dt 18:10-12; 2Ki 16:3 [n]Lev 19:26 [o]1Ki 21:20

king of Assyria captured Samaria[s] and deported[t] the Israelites to Assyria. He settled them in Halah, in Gozan[u] on the Habor River and in the towns of the Medes.

Israel Exiled Because of Sin

7 All this took place because the Israelites had sinned[v] against the LORD their God, who had brought them up out of Egypt[w] from under the power of Pharaoh king of Egypt. They worshiped other gods 8 and followed the practices of the nations[x] the LORD had driven out before them, as well as the practices that the kings of Israel had introduced. 9 The Israelites secretly did things against the LORD their God that were not right. From watchtower to fortified city[y] they built themselves high places in all their towns. 10 They set up sacred stones and Asherah poles[z] on every high hill and under every spreading tree.[a] 11 At every high place they burned incense, as the nations whom the LORD had driven out before them had done. They did wicked things that aroused the LORD's anger. 12 They worshiped idols,[b] though the LORD had said, "You shall not do this."[*a*] 13 The LORD warned Israel and Judah through all his prophets and seers:[c] "Turn from your evil ways.[d] Observe my commands and decrees, in accordance with the entire Law that I commanded your ancestors to obey and that I delivered to you through my servants the prophets."

14 But they would not listen and were as stiff-necked[e] as their ancestors, who did not trust in the LORD their God. 15 They rejected his decrees and the covenant[f] he had made with their ancestors and the statutes he had warned them to keep. They followed worthless idols[g] and themselves became worthless. They imitated the nations[h] around them although the LORD had ordered them, "Do not do as they do."

16 They forsook all the commands of the LORD their God and made for themselves two idols cast in the shape of calves,[i] and an Asherah[j] pole. They bowed down to all the starry hosts,[k] and they worshiped Baal.[l] 17 They sacrificed[m] their sons and daughters in the fire. They practiced divination and sought omens[n] and sold[o] themselves to do evil in the eyes of the LORD, arousing his anger.

18 So the LORD was very angry with Israel and removed them from his presence. Only the tribe of

[*a*] *12* Exodus 20:4,5

Shalmaneser V. In Assyrian records, little is preserved from Shalmaneser's brief reign, and his successor, Sargon II, claims that he subdued Samaria and carried off 27,290 people. Shalmaneser's death in the same year that Samaria fell explains the discrepancy: it left Sargon II to finish the conquest and deportation. **deported the Israelites to Assyria.** Transferring populations was a standard practice of the Assyrians, intended to reduce the possibility of future rebellions by eliminating communal bonds and nationalistic pride. The places where the Israelites were deported spanned a great distance across the Assyrian Empire. **Halah.** Modern Tell al-Abbasiya, northeast of Nineveh. **Gozan.** Tell Halaf on the modern Turkish-Syrian border. Hebrew names found in texts at the site attest to the Israelite deportation. **the Habor River.** A northern tributary of the Euphrates River. **the towns of the Medes.** Communities east of the Zagros Mountains near the modern border of Iraq and Iran.

17:7–23 *Israel Exiled Because of Sin.* To this point the narrator has provided little explicit commentary on the events of Israel's history. But with the exile of the northern tribes, the author gives an extended explanation of God's righteousness in judging his people. All of the details show that Israel failed to honor the covenant. The nation that had pledged to keep the Lord's commands (Exod 24:7; Josh 24:24) had repeatedly disregarded their King and sought out its own way. The Israelites committed every kind of ancient iniquity to the point that they became worse than the Canaanites whom they had displaced. The Lord shows his patience by repeatedly delivering his people and sending numerous prophets to draw the nation back to the covenant. This section decisively counters any objection that the Lord was not righteous in sending Israel out of the promised land.

17:7 who had brought them up out of Egypt. The same Lord who gave them the land could remove them from it.

17:8 followed the practices of the nations. The folly of the Israelites is manifest in their worship of the gods that the Lord defeated.

17:9 high places. See note on 1 Kgs 3:2.

17:10 sacred stones. See note on 1 Kgs 14:23. **Asherah poles.** See note on Exod 34:13.

17:13 through all his prophets and seers. The book of Kings identifies eight different prophets that the Lord sent to the northern kingdom. In addition, the writing prophets Hosea and Amos warned Israel before its exile.

17:14 did not trust. Because the Israelites did not trust the Lord, they were not loyal to his law. They pursued the Baals and the Asherahs out of the false belief that those idols would provide a satisfaction superior that which the Lord promised.

17:15 They followed worthless idols and themselves became worthless. Idols are merely impotent, man-made images (Ps 115). Those who worship idols deny the Creator who made them and thus fail to achieve the purpose for which God created them.

17:16 two idols cast in the shape of calves. For 200 years without interruption, the Israelites worshiped the golden calves erected by Jeroboam (1 Kgs 12:28). **the starry hosts.** The Israelites imitated the idolatry of the nations around them by bowing down to the heavenly bodies that God created. They defied the explicit warnings of Moses (Deut 4:19) and Amos (Amos 5:26).

17:17 They sacrificed their sons and daughters in the fire. See the notes on 16:3; Jer 7:30—8:3. **practiced divination and sought omens.** Forbidden in Deut 18:10; see note on Deut 18:9–13.

17:18 Only the tribe of Judah was left. All of the other tribes belonged to the northern kingdom (1 Kgs 11:30–32) and were exiled. Yet individuals from these tribes lived in the kingdom of Judah, as is clear from

Judah was left, 19and even Judah did not keep the commands of the LORD their God. They followed the
practices Israel had introduced.[p] 20Therefore the LORD rejected all the people of Israel; he afflicted them
and gave them into the hands of plunderers,[q] until he thrust them from his presence.
21When he tore[r] Israel away from the house of David, they made Jeroboam son of Nebat their king.[s]
Jeroboam enticed Israel away from following the LORD and caused them to commit a great sin. 22The
Israelites persisted in all the sins of Jeroboam and did not turn away from them 23until the LORD removed them from his presence, as he had warned through all his servants the prophets. So the people
of Israel were taken from their homeland into exile in Assyria, and they are still there.

Samaria Resettled

24The king of Assyria[t] brought people from Babylon, Kuthah, Avva, Hamath and Sepharvaim[u] and
settled them in the towns of Samaria to replace the Israelites. They took over Samaria and lived in its
towns. 25When they first lived there, they did not worship the LORD; so he sent lions[v] among them and
they killed some of the people. 26It was reported to the king of Assyria: "The people you deported and
resettled in the towns of Samaria do not know what the god of that country requires. He has sent lions
among them, which are killing them off, because the people do not know what he requires."
27Then the king of Assyria gave this order: "Have one of the priests you took captive from Samaria
go back to live there and teach the people what the god of the land requires." 28So one of the priests
who had been exiled from Samaria came to live in Bethel and taught them how to worship the LORD.
29Nevertheless, each national group made its own gods in the several towns[w] where they settled, and
set them up in the shrines[x] the people of Samaria had made at the high places.[y] 30The people from Babylon made Sukkoth Benoth, those from Kuthah made Nergal, and those from Hamath made Ashima;
31the Avvites made Nibhaz and Tartak, and the Sepharvites burned their children in the fire as sacrifices
to Adrammelek[z] and Anammelek, the gods of Sepharvaim.[a] 32They worshiped the LORD, but they also
appointed all sorts[b] of their own people to officiate for them as priests in the shrines at the high places.
33They worshiped the LORD, but they also served their own gods in accordance with the customs of the
nations from which they had been brought.
34To this day they persist in their former practices. They neither worship the LORD nor adhere to the
decrees and regulations, the laws and commands that the LORD gave the descendants of Jacob, whom
he named Israel.[c] 35When the LORD made a covenant with the Israelites, he commanded them: "Do not
worship[d] any other gods or bow down to them, serve them or sacrifice to them. 36But the LORD, who

17:19 [p] 1Ki 14:22-23; 2Ki 16:3
17:20 [q] 2Ki 15:29
17:21 [r] 1Ki 11:11 [s] 1Ki 12:20
17:24 [t] Ezr 4:2,10 [u] 2Ki 18:34
17:25 [v] Ge 37:20
17:29 [w] Jer 2:28 [x] 1Ki 12:31 [y] Mic 4:5
17:31 [z] 2Ki 19:37 [a] ver 24
17:32 [b] 1Ki 12:31
17:34 [c] Ge 32:28; 35:10; 1Ki 18:31
17:35 [d] Ex 20:5; Jdg 6:10

later records (1 Chr 7; Ezra 1:5; Luke 2:36). Hope remains for these tribes as is clear from Ezek 37:16; 48:1–29; Rev 7:5–8.

17:19 God intended, through the exile of the northern kingdom, to warn his remaining people that he would not spare them from his curses if they continued to imitate Israel's idolatry.

17:21 he tore Israel away. The division of the kingdom was an act of the Lord in response to Solomon's sin (1 Kgs 11:31–33). **Jeroboam enticed Israel.** Jeroboam's irrational fear that he would lose the kingdom God gave him led him to construct a syncretistic religion that ultimately was responsible for the nation's demise (1 Kgs 12:26–33).

17:22–23 After patiently and actively pursuing his people for 200 years, the Lord decided to end Israel's affections for idols by sending Israel into exile.

17:23 they are still there. The author writes this record at a time near enough to the events that he knows of the deportees' present situation.

17:24–41 *Samaria Resettled.* Before resuming with the history of Judah, the author describes the Assyrian policy over the former territory of the northern kingdom in order to explain the background of the inhabitants whose descendants are later known as Samaritans. The new residents are characterized by syncretistic worship practices.

17:24 Assyria brought many people to Israel during the reign of Sargon II (722–705 BC), but the process continued through the times of Esarhaddon (681–669) and Ashurbanipal (669–627), as Ezra 4:2,9–10 reports. **Kuthah.** An important city 20 miles (32 kilometers) northeast of ancient Babylon preserved today in the mound of Tell Ibrahim. **Avva.** An unknown city in Syria or Assyria, possibly the same as Ivvah (18:34; 19:13). **Hamath.** The modern city of Hama, located 130 miles (210 kilometers) north of Damascus. **Sepharvaim.** An unknown city in Mesopotamia. Sennacherib boasted of Assyria's conquest of this city (18:34; 19:13). **settled them.** Assyria's deportation policy transferred rebellious populations throughout the empire. **Samaria.** The region of Israel's hill country.

17:25 God's judgment on these new inhabitants explains how the people of Samaria came to worship the Lord despite their pagan origins. **lions.** The Lord had previously used lions to bring judgment (1 Kgs 13:24; 20:36; cf. Lev 26:22), and here they demonstrate his continued sovereignty over the land he promised to give to Abraham.

17:29 Shows that the people of Samaria (later known as Samaritans) were not faithful to the Lord and were not to be embraced as part of the covenant nation (cf. Ezra 4:1–3).

17:30 Sukkoth Benoth. Possibly the Mesopotamian deities Banitu and Sakkut. **Nergal.** The Mesopotamian god of the underworld associated with plague, famine, and death. **Ashima.** The West Semitic god that possibly is referred to in Amos 8:14.

17:31 Nibhaz and Tartak. Possibly gods of the Elamites. **Adrammelek.** Possibly a Phoenician deity. **Anammelek.** Possibly a god of the Emarites.

17:33 Such syncretistic practice was common in the ancient world but was utterly repugnant to the only true God (Deut 6:14–15).

17:35–39 Concisely summarizes the demands of the covenant God made with Israel at Mount Sinai (Exod 19–24).

17:36 [e]Ex 3:20; 6:6; Ps 136:12
17:37 [f]Dt 5:32
17:38 [g]Dt 4:23; 6:12
17:41 [h]ver 32-33; 1Ki 18:21; Mt 6:24
18:1 [i]Isa 1:1; 2Ch 28:27
18:2 [j]Isa 38:5
18:3 [k]Isa 38:5
18:4 [l]2Ch 31:1 [m]Ex 23:24 [n]Nu 21:9
18:5 [o]2Ki 19:10; 23:25
18:6 [p]Dt 10:20; Jos 23:8
18:7 [q]Ge 39:3; 1Sa 18:14 [r]2Ki 16:7
18:8 [s]2Ki 17:9; Isa 14:29
18:9 [t]Isa 1:1

brought you up out of Egypt with mighty power and outstretched arm,[e] is the one you must worship. To
him you shall bow down and to him offer sacrifices. [37]You must always be careful[f] to keep the decrees
and regulations, the laws and commands he wrote for you. Do not worship other gods. [38]Do not forget[g]
the covenant I have made with you, and do not worship other gods. [39]Rather, worship the LORD your
God; it is he who will deliver you from the hand of all your enemies."
[40]They would not listen, however, but persisted in their former practices. [41]Even while these people
were worshiping the LORD,[h] they were serving their idols. To this day their children and grandchildren
continue to do as their ancestors did.

Hezekiah King of Judah

18:2-4pp — 2Ch 29:1-2; 31:1
18:5-7pp — 2Ch 31:20-21
18:9-12pp — 2Ki 17:3-7

18 In the third year of Hoshea son of Elah king of Israel, Hezekiah[i] son of Ahaz king of Judah began to reign. [2]He was twenty-five years old when he became king, and he reigned in Jerusalem
twenty-nine years.[j] His mother's name was Abijah[a] daughter of Zechariah. [3]He did what was right in the
eyes of the LORD, just as his father David[k] had done. [4]He removed[l] the high places, smashed the sacred
stones[m] and cut down the Asherah poles. He broke into pieces the bronze snake[n] Moses had made, for
up to that time the Israelites had been burning incense to it. (It was called Nehushtan.[b])
[5]Hezekiah trusted[o] in the LORD, the God of Israel. There was no one like him among all the kings of
Judah, either before him or after him. [6]He held fast[p] to the LORD and did not stop following him; he kept
the commands the LORD had given Moses. [7]And the LORD was with him; he was successful[q] in whatever
he undertook. He rebelled[r] against the king of Assyria and did not serve him. [8]From watchtower to fortified city,[s] he defeated the Philistines, as far as Gaza and its territory.
[9]In King Hezekiah's fourth year,[t] which was the seventh year of Hoshea son of Elah king of Israel,

[a] 2 Hebrew *Abi,* a variant of *Abijah* [b] 4 *Nehushtan* sounds like the Hebrew for both *bronze* and *snake.*

17:41 To this day. Though the following chapters turn to Judah and describe the covenant unfaithfulness that leads to the southern kingdom's exile, the writer clarifies that the people living in the area allotted to the northern tribes are not heirs of God's covenant promises.

18:1—25:30 *The Last Kings of Judah.* The final unit of the book of Kings narrates the approximately 150 years after the northern kingdom was exiled and when the Lord preserved the remnant of his people in the kingdom of Judah. Though the two greatest kings since David rule during those years, their righteous efforts cannot reverse the nation's movement toward exile. Between the faithful kings Hezekiah and Josiah, unparalleled idolatry characterizes Manasseh's rule. After Josiah's death, his sons and grandson resist the prophets until the Babylonians destroy the temple and exile the people. Yet the book concludes with a note of hope for Judah and David's royal line.

18:1—20:21 *Hezekiah King of Judah.* The record of Hezekiah's reign casts him as a second David, and for his faithfulness the Lord gives him great success. The most notable event of these years is the Assyrian invasion in 701 BC, when the conquerors of the northern kingdom threaten to eliminate Judah and deport the remnant of God's people. Hezekiah's faith never wavers as he responds to the Assyrian king's blasphemous challenge. The Lord's great deliverance of Judah is not the last word, for the prophet Isaiah declares that after Hezekiah's death Babylon will exile the nation.

18:1–16 *Hezekiah's Reign.* Hezekiah's leadership is characterized by covenant obedience, the removal of false worship, and national success. In 1998 a royal seal impression was discovered that reads "Belonging to Hezekiah (son of) Ahaz king of Judah."

18:1 third year. 729 BC. This date identifies the time when Hezekiah began a coregency with his father, Ahaz.

18:2 twenty-nine years. 716/15–687/86 BC. This calculation does not include the years of coregency with his father, Ahaz (729–716/15 BC).

18:4 Hezekiah is the first king to remove the worship sites outside Jerusalem. **bronze snake.** Though not mentioned since Num 21:9, it was preserved for 700 years and had become an object of unholy veneration. Destroying it demonstrates Hezekiah's uncompromising attitude in covenant obedience.

18:5 trusted in the LORD. Firmly believed in God and that people must obey his word. This was the basis for Hezekiah's obedience. **no one like him.** Hezekiah distinguishes himself by his unswerving loyalty to the Lord and the Lord's covenant with Israel. All of Israel's kings were required to copy, read, and follow the covenant (Deut 17:18–20), but none of Israel's kings before Hezekiah were completely faithful.

18:6 He held fast. The book of Kings begins with Solomon, who "held fast" to his foreign wives (cf. 1 Kgs 11:2). By contrast, Hezekiah's primary allegiance is to the Lord (cf. Deut 10:20). He purifies the temple and celebrates the Passover (2 Chr 29–30).

18:7 the LORD was with him. Recalls the Lord's blessing upon David (1 Sam 18:14). God promised to bless those who kept the covenant, and the king's obedience results in blessing for the nation (Deut 28:1–2). **rebelled against the king of Assyria.** Hezekiah's father made Judah a vassal of Assyria, defying the Lord's word through Isaiah (2 Chr 28:16–21; Isa 7:10–13). Hezekiah, together with many other states on the eastern Mediterranean seaboard, rebel when Sargon II dies in 705 BC; 2 Chr 32:2–8 describes his military preparations.

18:8 Gaza. The Philistine city farthest from Judah. Thus, Hezekiah subjugated all the land of the Philistines. Such territorial control had not occurred since the time of David and Solomon (1 Kgs 4:21; 2 Sam 8:1) and signifies that the Lord blessed Hezekiah's rule. Hezekiah obeyed by conquering land that the Lord had allotted to Israel (Josh 13:1–2; cf. 18:3).

18:9 fourth year. 725/24 BC. The siege of Samaria began in the fourth year of Hezekiah's coregency with Ahaz. The author provides this flashback here (17:5–7) to recall the grave danger that the Assyrians

Shalmaneser king of Assyria marched against Samaria and laid siege to it. 10 At the end of three years the Assyrians took it. So Samaria was captured in Hezekiah's sixth year, which was the ninth year of Hoshea king of Israel. 11 The king[u] of Assyria deported Israel to Assyria and settled them in Halah, in Gozan on the Habor River and in towns of the Medes. 12 This happened because they had not obeyed the LORD their God, but had violated his covenant[v]—all that Moses the servant of the LORD commanded.[w] They neither listened to the commands[x] nor carried them out.

13 In the fourteenth year of King Hezekiah's reign, Sennacherib king of Assyria attacked all the fortified cities of Judah[y] and captured them. 14 So Hezekiah king of Judah sent this message to the king of Assyria at Lachish: "I have done wrong.[z] Withdraw from me, and I will pay whatever you demand of me." The king of Assyria exacted from Hezekiah king of Judah three hundred talents[*a*] of silver and thirty talents[*b*] of gold. 15 So Hezekiah gave[a] him all the silver that was found in the temple of the LORD and in the treasuries of the royal palace.

16 At this time Hezekiah king of Judah stripped off the gold with which he had covered the doors and doorposts of the temple of the LORD, and gave it to the king of Assyria.

Sennacherib Threatens Jerusalem

18:13,17-37pp — Isa 36:1-22
18:17-35pp — 2Ch 32:9-19

17 The king of Assyria sent his supreme commander,[b] his chief officer and his field commander with a large army, from Lachish to King Hezekiah at Jerusalem. They came up to Jerusalem and stopped at the aqueduct of the Upper Pool,[c] on the road to the Washerman's Field. 18 They called for the king; and Eliakim[d] son of Hilkiah the palace administrator, Shebna[e] the secretary, and Joah son of Asaph the recorder went out to them.

19 The field commander said to them, "Tell Hezekiah:

"'This is what the great king, the king of Assyria, says: On what are you basing this confidence of yours? 20 You say you have the counsel and the might for war—but you speak only empty words. On whom are you depending, that you rebel against me? 21 Look, I know you are depending on Egypt,[f] that splintered reed of a staff,[g] which pierces the hand of anyone who leans on it! Such

18:11 [u] Isa 37:12
18:12 [v] 2Ki 17:15 [w] Da 9:6,10 [x] 1Ki 9:6
18:13 [y] 2Ch 32:1; Isa 1:7; Mic 1:9
18:14 [z] Isa 24:5
18:15 [a] 1Ki 15:18; 2Ki 16:8
18:17 [b] Isa 20:1 [c] 2Ki 20:20; 2Ch 32:4,30; Isa 7:3
18:18 [d] 2Ki 19:2; Isa 22:20 [e] Isa 22:15
18:21 [f] Isa 20:5; Eze 29:6 [g] Isa 30:5,7

[*a*] *14* That is, about 11 tons or about 10 metric tons [*b*] *14* That is, about 1 ton or about 1 metric ton

presented as well as to contrast Israel's destruction with Judah's deliverance.

18:11 See note on 17:6.

18:12 The exile is the result of covenant infidelity. In the covenant, the Lord threatened exile if his people failed to obey his commands (1 Kgs 8:46; Deut 29:28). See note on 17:7.

18:13—20:19 Very similar to Isa 36:1—39:8. This parallel reinforces the idea that the book of Kings provides a prophetic perspective on the history of Israel and Judah.

18:13 fourteenth year. 701 BC. The Assyrian invasion occurred in the 14th year of Hezekiah's sole reign, which began in 716/15 BC. **all the fortified cities of Judah.** In multiple inscriptions, Sennacherib claims to have captured 46 cities of Judah and taken captive 200,150 people of Judah. The Assyrian king never claimed to conquer Jerusalem, which agrees with the biblical account. The Assyrian invasion was not the Lord's punishment upon faithful Hezekiah but the result of the actions of faithless Ahaz (Isa 7:10—8:10).

18:14 Lachish. A major city of Judah located in the strategic western foothills 30 miles (48 kilometers) southeast of Jerusalem. Sennacherib decorated the walls of a throne room in his palace in Nineveh with panels depicting the great battle at Lachish. These scenes are fascinating for depicting the nature of warfare, the Judahite defenders, and the exile of the inhabitants of Lachish. They also indirectly confirm the biblical account, for Sennacherib surely would have chosen to depict Jerusalem's siege if it had ended favorably. **three hundred talents ... thirty talents.** See NIV text notes. Sennacherib's records detail a tribute of 800 talents of silver and 30 talents of gold. The discrepancy may be explained by an additional payment that Kings does not record or a scribal error in the Assyrian records.

18:15 It is difficult to reconcile this tribute with the continued siege that the following section describes (18:17—19:36). Some have proposed that there were two separate Assyrian campaigns, but there is no evidence for this in Sennacherib's records and the biblical text does not distinguish the two. Another possibility is that Hezekiah promised tribute before Sennacherib came to Jerusalem but that he delivered it only after the Assyrians withdrew. Perhaps best is the view that Hezekiah sent tribute but that Sennacherib was not satisfied with it and decided to continue the campaign.

18:17–37 *Sennacherib Threatens Jerusalem.* The Assyrian campaign resulted because Ahaz refused to trust the Lord (Isa 7:17). Hezekiah must decide whether he will follow his father in rejecting God's word in favor of human schemes or believe that the Lord is greater than Judah's enemies.

18:17 the aqueduct of the Upper Pool. The same place where Isaiah met Hezekiah's father, Ahaz, when Aram and Israel threatened his kingdom (Isa 7:3). **Washerman's.** Translates the same Hebrew word rendered "Launderer's" in Isa 36:2.

18:19 the great king. The issue in this conflict is who the great king is: Sennacherib or the Lord (Ps 47:2). The Assyrian king presents himself as the supreme king who is greater than Judah and its God. **basing this confidence.** Sennacherib intends to undermine Hezekiah's trust in the Lord so that he will trust in Assyria.

18:21 Egypt, that splintered reed of a staff. When attacked by one superpower, Israel and Judah were frequently tempted to seek

ASSYRIAN CAMPAIGNS AGAINST ISRAEL AND JUDAH

The Assyrian invasions of the eighth century BC were the most traumatic political events in the entire history of Israel.

The brutal Assyrian style of warfare relied on massive armies, superbly equipped with the world's first great siege machines manipulated by an efficient corps of engineers.

Psychological terror, however, was Assyria's most effective weapon. It was ruthlessly applied, with corpses impaled on stakes, severed heads stacked in heaps, and captives skinned alive.

The shock of bloody military sieges on both Israel and Judah was profound. The prophets did not fail to speak out against their horror, while at the same time pleading with the people to see God's hand in history, to recognize spiritual causes in the present punishment.

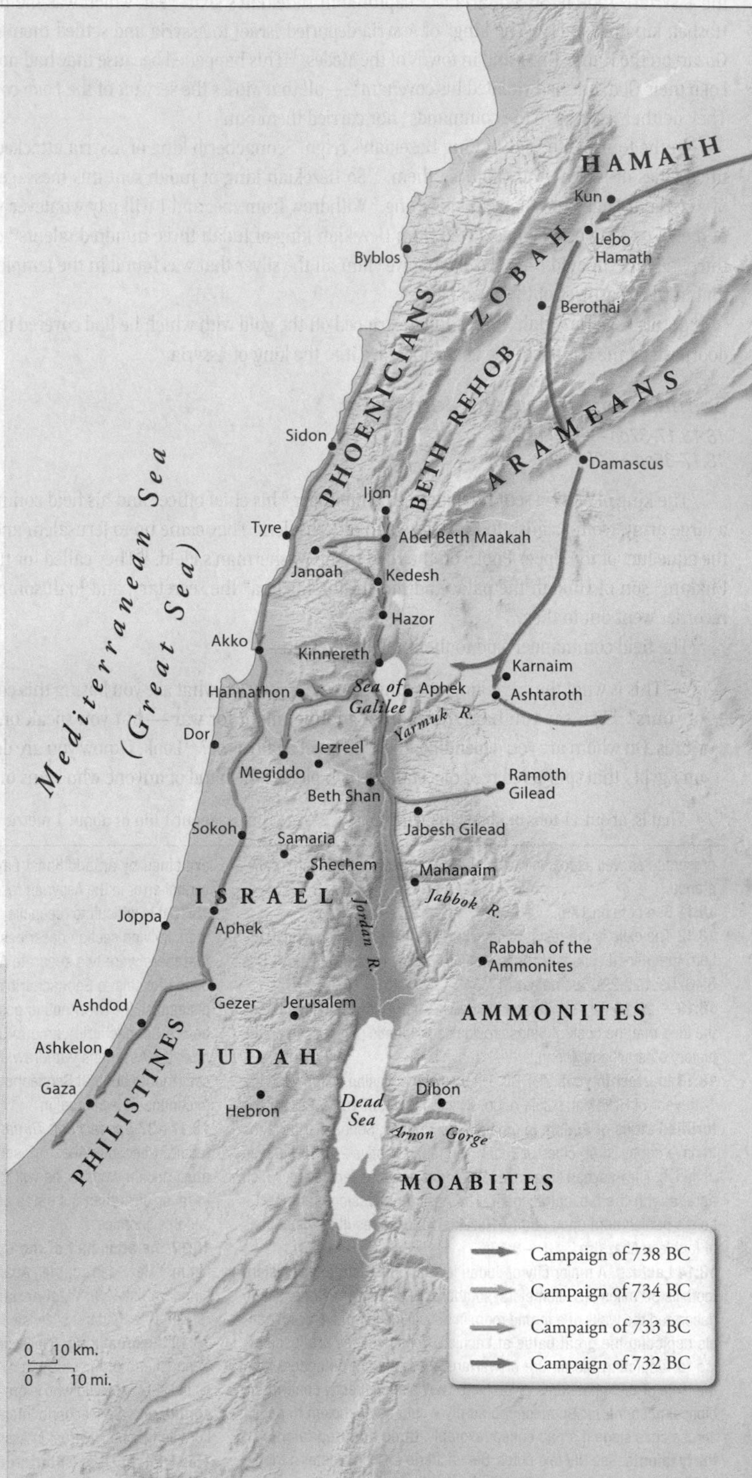

1. CAMPAIGNS OF TIGLATH-PILESER III (738–732 BC)

King Tiglath-Pileser of Assyria (745–727 BC) proved to be a vigorous campaigner, first exacting tribute from Menahem and then annexing Hamath, Philistia, Galilee, Gilead and Damascus (738–732 BC) during the reign of Pekah.

The ferocious onslaught against the northern tribes left only central Israel and the capital city of Samaria intact.

By this time Israel was a tiny nation wracked by pro- and anti-Assyrian factions, multiple assassinations, hypocrisy, arrogance, and fear.

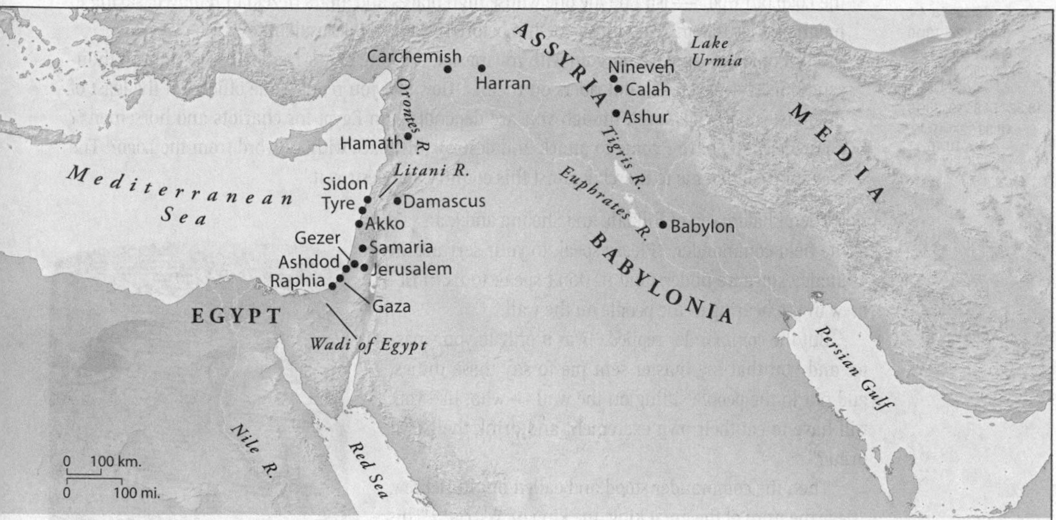

2. CAMPAIGN OF SHALMANESER V (725–722 BC)

The last king of Israel, Hoshea, conspired with Egypt and withheld the annual tribute to the Assyrians.

A protracted three-year siege conducted by Shalmaneser and concluded by Sargon II saw the end of the Israelite kingdom in 722–721 BC.

At that time, according to Assyrian annals, "I [Sargon] besieged and conquered Samaria, led away as plunder 27,290 inhabitants . . . I installed over [those remaining] an officer of mine and imposed upon them the tribute of the former king."

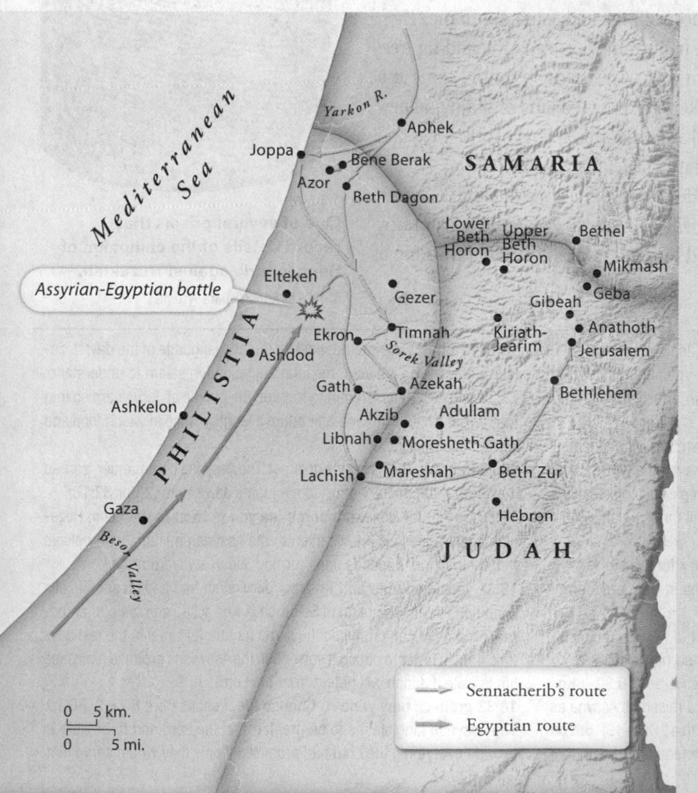

3. SENNACHERIB'S CAMPAIGN AGAINST JUDAH (701 BC)

In the fourteenth year of Hezekiah, the Assyrians finally attacked Judah. The Prism of Sennacherib calls Hezekiah "overbearing and proud," indicating that he was part of Philistia's and Egypt's effort to rebel against Assyria.

A battle in the plain of Eltekeh was won by Assyria; the Egyptian and Cushite charioteers fled. Lachish was besieged and taken. Sennacherib's annals note: "As for Hezekiah the Jew, he did not submit to my yoke. I laid siege to 46 of his strong cities, walled forts and the countless small villages in their vicinity, and conquered them by means of well-tamped earth ramps and battering-rams brought near to the walls combined with the attack by foot-soldiers, using mines, breaches and sapper work. I drove out 200,150 people, young and old, male and female, horses, mules, donkeys, camels, large and small cattle beyond counting, and considered them plunder. Himself I made a prisoner in Jerusalem, his royal residence, like a bird in a cage."

Nowhere, however, does the boastful Assyrian king record the disaster mentioned in 2 Kgs 19:35–36; 2 Chr 32:21; Isa 37:36–37.

18:24 [h]Isa 10:8
18:25 [i]2Ki 19:6,22
18:26 [j]Ezr 4:7
18:29 [k]2Ki 19:10
18:31 [l]Nu 13:23; 1Ki 4:25 [m]Jer 14:3; La 4:4
18:32 [n]Dt 8:7-9; 30:19
18:33 [o]2Ki 19:12; Isa 10:10-11

is Pharaoh king of Egypt to all who depend on him. 22 But if you say to me, "We are depending on
the LORD our God"—isn't he the one whose high places and altars Hezekiah removed, saying to
Judah and Jerusalem, "You must worship before this altar in Jerusalem"?
23 " 'Come now, make a bargain with my master, the king of Assyria: I will give you two thousand horses—if you can put riders on them! 24 How can you repulse one officer[h] of the least of
my master's officials, even though you are depending on Egypt for chariots and horsemen[a]?
25 Furthermore, have I come to attack and destroy this place without word from the LORD?[i] The
LORD himself told me to march against this country and destroy it.' "

26 Then Eliakim son of Hilkiah, and Shebna and Joah said
to the field commander, "Please speak to your servants in
Aramaic,[j] since we understand it. Don't speak to us in Hebrew in the hearing of the people on the wall."
27 But the commander replied, "Was it only to your master and you that my master sent me to say these things,
and not to the people sitting on the wall—who, like you,
will have to eat their own excrement and drink their own
urine?"
28 Then the commander stood and called out in Hebrew,
"Hear the word of the great king, the king of Assyria! 29 This
is what the king says: Do not let Hezekiah deceive[k] you. He
cannot deliver you from my hand. 30 Do not let Hezekiah
persuade you to trust in the LORD when he says, 'The LORD
will surely deliver us; this city will not be given into the hand
of the king of Assyria.'
31 "Do not listen to Hezekiah. This is what the king of Assyria says: Make peace with me and come out to me. Then
each of you will eat fruit from your own vine and fig tree[l]
and drink water from your own cistern,[m] 32 until I come and
take you to a land like your own—a land of grain and new
wine, a land of bread and vineyards, a land of olive trees and
honey. Choose life[n] and not death!
"Do not listen to Hezekiah, for he is misleading you when
he says, 'The LORD will deliver us.' 33 Has the god[o] of any
nation ever delivered his land from the hand of the king of

One of several prisms that record details of the campaign of Sennacherib against Hezekiah.

[a] 24 Or *charioteers*

the support of the opposing superpower (17:4; Isa 20:5; Hos 7:11). Isaiah strongly warns Judah against seeking Egypt's help instead of the Lord's, and Sennacherib claims that such an effort will be futile (Isa 30–31).

18:22 Sennacherib astutely appeals to the idolatrous or uneducated populace who mistakenly believe that the Lord desires the type of worship that characterizes Canaanite religion. By such psychological tactics the Assyrians hope to raise popular unrest that will force Judah's godly leadership to surrender.

18:23 Sennacherib mocks Judah's weak military forces but fails to account for the vast army of chariots and horses in the Lord's army (6:17).

18:25 Sennacherib attempts to sow doubt in order to weaken the resistance. His intelligence sources may have informed him that the Lord had previously summoned foreign armies to punish Israel (10:32; 1 Kgs 8:33; 11:14,23). Isaiah had explained that the Lord raised up Assyria as the rod of his anger in order to punish his people (Isa 10:5–19). But on this occasion Isaiah predicts that Assyria will be defeated on account of Hezekiah's faith (2 Kgs 19:7).

18:26 Aramaic. The international diplomatic language of the day. Hezekiah's officials do not want the inhabitants of Jerusalem to understand.

18:27 The Assyrians attempt to frighten the people of Jerusalem so that they will surrender rather than endure a lengthy siege in which food and water become scarce.

18:28 Hebrew. The language of Israel. The Assyrian commander learned it as part of the military effort to subjugate Jerusalem (2 Chr 32:18).

18:30 Do not let Hezekiah persuade you to trust in the LORD. Hezekiah's faithfulness is known even to the Assyrian military, who believe that their victory depends upon turning Judah away from the Lord.

18:31 your own vine and fig tree. Jerusalem had known such idyllic conditions during the reign of Solomon (1 Kgs 4:25), and the contemporary prophet Micah promised the same for faithful Israel in the last days (Mic 4:4). In order to obtain a surrender, the Assyrians promise a blessed life in exile if Judah will defect from the Lord.

18:32 grain ... new wine ... Choose life. Echoes Deut 8:7–8; 30:19. The Assyrian king claims to be greater than the Lord and to be able to provide everything the Lord had promised if only they would serve him.

Relief of Assyrian army attacking Lachish.

Assyria? [34]Where are the gods of Hamath[p] and Arpad?[q] Where are the gods of Sepharvaim, Hena and Ivvah? Have they rescued Samaria from my hand? [35]Who of all the gods of these countries has been able to save his land from me? How then can the LORD deliver Jerusalem from my hand?"[r]

[36]But the people remained silent and said nothing in reply, because the king had commanded, "Do not answer him."

[37]Then Eliakim son of Hilkiah the palace administrator, Shebna the secretary, and Joah son of Asaph the recorder went to Hezekiah, with their clothes torn,[s] and told him what the field commander had said.

Jerusalem's Deliverance Foretold

19:1-13pp — Isa 37:1-13

19 When King Hezekiah heard this, he tore[t] his clothes and put on sackcloth and went into the temple of the LORD. [2]He sent Eliakim the palace administrator, Shebna the secretary and the leading priests, all wearing sackcloth, to the prophet Isaiah[u] son of Amoz. [3]They told him, "This is what Hezekiah says: This day is a day of distress and rebuke and disgrace, as when children come to the moment of birth and there is no strength to deliver them. [4]It may be that the LORD your God will hear all the words of the field commander, whom his master, the king of Assyria, has sent to ridicule[v] the living God, and that he will rebuke[w] him for the words the LORD your God has heard. Therefore pray for the remnant that still survives."

[5]When King Hezekiah's officials came to Isaiah, [6]Isaiah said to them, "Tell your master, 'This is what

18:34 [p]2Ki 17:24; 19:13 [q]Isa 10:9
18:35 [r]Ps 2:1-2
18:37 [s]2Ki 6:30
19:1 [t]Ge 37:34; 1Ki 21:27; 2Ch 32:20-22
19:2 [u]Isa 1:1
19:4 [v]2Ki 18:35 [w]2Sa 16:12

18:34 See note on 17:24. **Arpad.** Modern Tell Rifaat, located 20 miles (32 kilometers) north of Aleppo, Syria. **Hena.** Probably in upper Mesopotamia.
18:35 The flaw in Sennacherib's propaganda is that the gods of these other nations were not gods at all. In the case of Samaria, the northern kingdom fell not because the Lord was weak but because the Israelites did not trust the Lord and keep his covenant (vv. 9–12).
18:37 their clothes torn. The officials of Judah rip their garments in sorrow (cf. 6:30). The city is in a desperate situation.
19:1–13 *Jerusalem's Deliverance Foretold.* Isaiah prophesies that Jerusalem will be spared because of Hezekiah's response of faith. This contrasts with Ahaz's failure to trust God in a similar crisis (Isa 7:4–17).
19:1 tore his clothes and put on sackcloth. Demonstrated mourning or repentance for the purpose of seeking a divine reprieve (Jer 4:8; Jonah 3:8–9).
19:2 Isaiah. The first reference to him in 2 Kings, though he was active during the reigns of Uzziah, Jotham, and Ahaz (Isa 1:1). Much of 2 Kgs 18:13—20:19 parallels Isa 36:1—39:8, suggesting that Isaiah wrote this portion of Kings.
19:3 This day is a day of distress. Such a confession of weakness is uncommon among ancient or modern leaders but characteristic of the godly kings of Judah (2 Chr 14:11; 20:12).
19:4 Hezekiah's request for Isaiah to intercede for the nation recalls this important role of Israel's prophets (Exod 32:31–32; Num 14:13–19; 1 Sam 7:8–9). **remnant.** The portion that still survives within Jerusalem's walls—Sennacherib has already conquered most of Judah (18:13).
19:6 Isaiah comforts Hezekiah by confirming that the Lord did indeed hear the Assyrian blasphemy and by predicting that the Assyrian army will withdraw.

19:6 [x]2Ki 18:25
19:7 [y]ver 37
19:8 [z]2Ki 18:14
19:10 [a]2Ki 18:5 [b]2Ki 18:29
19:12 [c]2Ki 18:33 [d]2Ki 17:6 [e]Ge 11:31
19:13 [f]2Ki 18:34
19:15 [g]Ex 25:22
19:16 [h]Ps 31:2 [i]1Ki 8:29 [j]ver 4; 2Ch 6:40
19:18 [k]Isa 44:9-11; Jer 10:3-10 [l]Ps 115:4; Ac 17:29
19:19 [m]1Ki 8:43 [n]Ps 83:18
19:20 [o]2Ki 20:5

the LORD says: Do not be afraid of what you have heard — those words with which the underlings of the
king of Assyria have blasphemed[x] me. 7 Listen! When he hears a certain report, I will make him want to
return to his own country, and there I will have him cut down with the sword.[y] ' "

8 When the field commander heard that the king of Assyria had left Lachish,[z] he withdrew and found
the king fighting against Libnah.

9 Now Sennacherib received a report that Tirhakah, the king of Cush,[a] was marching out to fight against
him. So he again sent messengers to Hezekiah with this word: 10 "Say to Hezekiah king of Judah: Do not let
the god you depend[a] on deceive[b] you when he says, 'Jerusalem will not be given into the hands of the king of
Assyria.' 11 Surely you have heard what the kings of Assyria have done to all the countries, destroying them
completely. And will you be delivered? 12 Did the gods of the nations that were destroyed by my predecessors
deliver[c] them — the gods of Gozan,[d] Harran,[e] Rezeph and the people of Eden who were in Tel Assar? 13 Where
is the king of Hamath or the king of Arpad? Where are the kings of Lair, Sepharvaim, Hena and Ivvah?"[f]

Hezekiah's Prayer

19:14-19pp — Isa 37:14-20

14 Hezekiah received the letter from the messengers and read it. Then he went up to the temple of
the LORD and spread it out before the LORD. 15 And Hezekiah prayed to the LORD: "LORD, the God of Israel,
enthroned between the cherubim,[g] you alone are God over all the kingdoms of the earth. You have
made heaven and earth. 16 Give ear,[h] LORD, and hear;[i] open your eyes,[j] LORD, and see; listen to the words
Sennacherib has sent to ridicule the living God.

17 "It is true, LORD, that the Assyrian kings have laid waste these nations and their lands. 18 They have
thrown their gods into the fire and destroyed them, for they were not gods[k] but only wood and stone,
fashioned by human hands.[l] 19 Now, LORD our God, deliver us from his hand, so that all the kingdoms[m]
of the earth may know[n] that you alone, LORD, are God."

Isaiah Prophesies Sennacherib's Fall

19:20-37pp — Isa 37:21-38
19:35-37pp — 2Ch 32:20-21

20 Then Isaiah son of Amoz sent a message to Hezekiah: "This is what the LORD, the God of Israel,
says: I have heard[o] your prayer concerning Sennacherib king of Assyria. 21 This is the word that the
LORD has spoken against him:

[a] *9* That is, the upper Nile region

19:8 Lachish. Sennacherib conquered it (cf. 18:14). **Libnah.** Another major city in Judah's western foothills, possibly at Tell Burna, five miles (8 kilometers) north of Lachish and 25 miles (40 kilometers) southwest of Jerusalem.

19:9 Tirhakah. The military leader of forces from southern Egypt. He later becomes pharaoh of Egypt's Twenty-Fifth Dynasty (690–664 BC). **marching out to fight.** Tirhakah meets the Assyrians in battle at Eltekeh, possibly modern Tell esh-Shallaf, 28 miles (45 kilometers) west of Jerusalem. It is not clear if Judah had sent tribute to Egypt in order to gain assistance or if the Egyptians saw an opportunity in attacking the Assyrian army when numerous battles had weakened it and it was far from home. Isaiah had warned Judah of the futility of trusting Egypt (Isa 31:1–5).

19:10 Concerned that the arrival of Tirhakah's army may encourage Judah, Sennacherib repeats his earlier message in order to entice Hezekiah to surrender (18:28–35).

19:12 Gozan. See note on 17:6. **Harran.** Modern Altinbalak, north of the Turkey-Syria border. Abram settled here after moving from Ur (Gen 11:31). The Assyrians destroyed the city in 763 BC. **Rezeph.** A provincial capital located on the ancient road from Harran to Palmyra. **Tel Assar.** Possibly the city of Til Barsip, modern Tell Ahmar, located on the Euphrates River in the kingdom of Bit Adini.

19:13 Lair. A city in northeastern Babylon. **Sepharvaim, Hena and Ivvah.** See notes on 17:24; 18:34.

19:14–19 *Hezekiah's Prayer.* By taking Sennacherib's blasphemous letter to the Lord, Hezekiah recognizes his role as God's vice-regent and entrusts the nation's trials to its true King. In his actions and prayer, Hezekiah models the type of kingship that the Lord intended for his people.

19:15 enthroned between the cherubim. The footstool of the throne of Israel's true King was in the temple's Most Holy Place below the cherubim, placed over the ark of the covenant (1 Kgs 8:6–7; 1 Sam 4:4). **God over all the kingdoms of the earth.** The Lord is not just a national deity like the alleged gods of the peoples around them; he is supreme over all nations as the one and only Creator. He is the true great King (Ps 47:2–9).

19:16 Hezekiah believes that the Lord will fight for Judah if he knows how Sennacherib publicly defamed him.

19:17–18 Hezekiah acknowledges the partial truth of Sennacherib's claims. The Assyrians had conquered many other nations, but their string of victories over false gods was insignificant when facing the only living God.

19:19 Hezekiah appeals to God to deliver Jerusalem so that his glory will be seen among the nations (1 Kgs 8:42; 1 Sam 17:46). Since this was the Lord's purpose in establishing Israel (2 Sam 7:23; Ps 67:1–2; cf. Isa 26:18), Hezekiah is simply praying what he knows to be God's will.

19:20–37 *Isaiah Prophesies Sennacherib's Fall.* Isaiah predicts that the Lord will defeat the Assyrian army and restore the land of Judah. The nature of a prophet as God's spokesman is particularly clear here as the Lord directly responds to Hezekiah's prayer through his prophet Isaiah.

19:21 The picture of a tender "Virgin Daughter" (Jerusalem) mock-

"'Virgin Daughter[p] Zion
despises you and mocks[q] you.
Daughter Jerusalem
tosses her head[r] as you flee.
22 Who is it you have ridiculed and blasphemed?
Against whom have you raised your voice
and lifted your eyes in pride?
Against the Holy One[s] of Israel!
23 By your messengers
you have ridiculed the Lord.
And you have said,[t]
"With my many chariots[u]
I have ascended the heights of the mountains,
the utmost heights of Lebanon.
I have cut down its tallest cedars,
the choicest of its junipers.
I have reached its remotest parts,
the finest of its forests.
24 I have dug wells in foreign lands
and drunk the water there.
With the soles of my feet
I have dried up all the streams of Egypt."

25 "'Have you not heard?[v]
Long ago I ordained it.
In days of old I planned[w] it;
now I have brought it to pass,
that you have turned fortified cities
into piles of stone.[x]
26 Their people, drained of power,
are dismayed[y] and put to shame.
They are like plants in the field,
like tender green shoots,[z]
like grass sprouting on the roof,
scorched[a] before it grows up.

27 "'But I know[b] where you are
and when you come and go
and how you rage against me.
28 Because you rage against me
and because your insolence has reached my ears,
I will put my hook[c] in your nose
and my bit[d] in your mouth,
and I will make you return[e]
by the way you came.'

19:21 [p] Jer 14:17; La 2:13 [q] Ps 22:7-8 [r] Job 16:4; Ps 109:25
19:22 [s] Ps 71:22; Isa 5:24
19:23 [t] Isa 10:18 [u] Ps 20:7
19:25 [v] Isa 40:21,28 [w] Isa 10:5; 45:7 [x] Mic 1:6
19:26 [y] Ps 6:10 [z] Isa 4:2 [a] Ps 129:6
19:27 [b] Ps 139:1-4
19:28 [c] Eze 19:9; 29:4 [d] Isa 30:28 [e] ver 33

ing the mighty Assyrian king is a striking contrast at the beginning of Isaiah's response to Sennacherib. The Assyrians fail to consider the omnipotent Father, who will protect his daughter from their attacks.
19:22 Sennacherib perhaps thought that his target was the helpless people of Judah, but unlike the previous nations he defeated, Judah's God is a living God whom Sennacherib's blasphemy offended. **the Holy One of Israel.** See notes on Isa 1:4; 41:11–14.
19:23,24 I have. Repeated five times. What Sennacherib achieved within the first three years of his reign was indeed admirable, but by failing to recognize that the Lord had ordained his victories (v. 25; Isa 10:5–19), he was deceived into thinking that he would prevail over the Lord's people.
19:27 The Lord watches over the coming and going of not only Israel (Ps 121:8) but all the peoples he has created.
19:28 hook in your nose ... bit in your mouth. Assyrian victory stelae depict the conquerors leading away the defeated with ropes attached to their lips or noses (cf. Ezek 19:4; Amos 4:2). Sennacherib will receive the same humiliating treatment he likely had meted out to so many others.

19:29 [f] 2Ki 20:8-9; Lk 2:12 [g] Lev 25:5 [h] Ps 107:37
19:30 [i] 2Ch 32:22-23
19:31 [j] Isa 9:7
19:33 [k] ver 28
19:34 [l] 2Ki 20:6 [m] 1Ki 11:12-13
19:35 [n] Ex 12:23 [o] Job 24:24
19:36 [p] Ge 10:11; Jnh 1:2
19:37 [q] ver 7 [r] Ge 8:4 [s] Ezr 4:2

29 "This will be the sign[f] for you, Hezekiah:

"This year you will eat what grows by itself,[g]
and the second year what springs from that.
But in the third year sow and reap,
plant vineyards[h] and eat their fruit.
30 Once more a remnant of the kingdom of Judah
will take root[i] below and bear fruit above.
31 For out of Jerusalem will come a remnant,
and out of Mount Zion a band of survivors.

"The zeal[j] of the LORD Almighty will accomplish this.

32 "Therefore this is what the LORD says concerning the king of Assyria:

" 'He will not enter this city
or shoot an arrow here.
He will not come before it with shield
or build a siege ramp against it.
33 By the way that he came he will return;[k]
he will not enter this city,
declares the LORD.
34 I will defend[l] this city and save it,
for my sake and for the sake of David[m] my servant.' "

35 That night the angel of the LORD[n] went out and put to death a hundred and eighty-five thousand
in the Assyrian camp. When the people got up the next morning—there were all the dead bodies![o]
36 So Sennacherib king of Assyria broke camp and withdrew. He returned to Nineveh[p] and stayed there.
37 One day, while he was worshiping in the temple of his god Nisrok, his sons Adrammelek and Sharezer killed him with the sword,[q] and they escaped to the land of Ararat.[r] And Esarhaddon[s] his son succeeded him as king.

Hezekiah's Illness

20:1-11pp — 2Ch 32:24-26; Isa 38:1-8

20 In those days Hezekiah became ill and was at the point of death. The prophet Isaiah son of Amoz went to him and said, "This is what the LORD says: Put your house in order, because you are going to die; you will not recover."

19:29 This year ... second year ... third year. The planting season for the first year had already passed, and the second year may have been a sabbatical year in which the land lay fallow. In a sign of the coming deliverance, the Lord will provide for his people until the third year, when they will again reap a bountiful harvest.
19:30 remnant. The Lord preserves them in accord with his plan to fulfill all of his promises (cf. 1 Kgs 19:18; Gen 45:7; Isa 10:20; Rom 11:5).
19:31 The zeal of the LORD Almighty will accomplish this. Israel and the nations can be certain that the Lord will not allow others to profane his name or destroy his people (Isa 26:11; 59:17). The same phrase occurs elsewhere only with the promise to establish David's son on the throne forever (Isa 9:7). God will ultimately restore his remnant when the promised Messiah rules (Isa 10:21; 11:12–16; Zech 12:10—14:9).
19:32 build a siege ramp. Assyrians did this at Lachish, which Sennacherib's Lachish reliefs depict and archaeological excavations confirm.
19:34 for my sake. The Lord often acts against foreign nations for the sake of his reputation (Exod 10:1–2; 1 Sam 5; Ps 106:8). **for the sake of David my servant.** Because the Lord promised an eternal dynasty to David (1 Kgs 9:5; 2 Sam 7:8–16), he will preserve the royal family and its capital city.
19:35 This stunning display of God's power humbles the world's superpower and forces Sennacherib to withdraw to Assyria. Assyrian records claim that they destroyed 46 cities of Judah and made Hezekiah "like a bird in a cage," but they do not boast over Jerusalem's defeat, a sure sign that God delivered the city.
19:36 Nineveh. The capital of the Assyrian Empire during Sennacherib's reign.
19:37 Nisrok. The identity of this deity is uncertain, but the irony is clear: Sennacherib mocked Hezekiah for believing that his God could save him (vv. 10–13), yet Sennacherib's god could not protect him even in his own temple. **his sons ... killed him with the sword.** See v. 7. Assyrian records confirm the name of one of Sennacherib's sons who murdered him in 681 BC. The author includes this detail to show the destiny of those who defy the Lord (cf. Dan 4:31–37). **Esarhaddon.** A younger son of Sennacherib who ruled over Assyria from 681 to 669 BC.
20:1–11 *Hezekiah's Illness.* Unlike other kings whose illnesses led to death (1:2–4; 15:5; 1 Kgs 15:23), Hezekiah is delivered and granted an additional 15 years of life.
20:1 In those days. Not a chronologically specific reference. Hezekiah's illness probably predates the Assyrian attack that chs. 18–19 describe: (1) Marduk-Baladan was seeking partners in an anti-Assyrian coalition prior to 701 BC, the date of Sennacherib's campaign against Judah

2Hezekiah turned his face to the wall and prayed to the LORD, 3"Remember,[t] LORD, how I have walked
before you faithfully[u] and with wholehearted devotion and have done what is good in your eyes." And
Hezekiah wept bitterly.
4Before Isaiah had left the middle court, the word of the LORD came to him: 5"Go back and tell Hezekiah, the ruler of my people, 'This is what the LORD, the God of your father David, says: I have heard[v]
your prayer and seen your tears;[w] I will heal you. On the third day from now you will go up to the
temple of the LORD. 6I will add fifteen years to your life. And I will deliver you and this city from the
hand of the king of Assyria. I will defend[x] this city for my sake and for the sake of my servant David.'"
7Then Isaiah said, "Prepare a poultice of figs." They did so and applied it to the boil,[y] and he recovered.
8Hezekiah had asked Isaiah, "What will be the sign that the LORD will heal me and that I will go up
to the temple of the LORD on the third day from now?"
9Isaiah answered, "This is the LORD's sign[z] to you that the LORD will do what he has promised: Shall
the shadow go forward ten steps, or shall it go back ten steps?"
10"It is a simple matter for the shadow to go forward ten steps," said Hezekiah. "Rather, have it go
back ten steps."
11Then the prophet Isaiah called on the LORD, and the LORD made the shadow go back[a] the ten steps
it had gone down on the stairway of Ahaz.

Envoys From Babylon

20:12-19pp — Isa 39:1-8
20:20-21pp — 2Ch 32:32-33

12At that time Marduk-Baladan son of Baladan king of Babylon sent Hezekiah letters and a gift, because he had heard of Hezekiah's illness. 13Hezekiah received the envoys and showed them all that was
in his storehouses — the silver, the gold, the spices and the fine olive oil — his armory and everything
found among his treasures. There was nothing in his palace or in all his kingdom that Hezekiah did
not show them.
14Then Isaiah the prophet went to King Hezekiah and asked, "What did those men say, and where
did they come from?"
"From a distant land," Hezekiah replied. "They came from Babylon."
15The prophet asked, "What did they see in your palace?"
"They saw everything in my palace," Hezekiah said. "There is nothing among my treasures that I
did not show them."
16Then Isaiah said to Hezekiah, "Hear the word of the LORD: 17The time will surely come when everything
in your palace, and all that your predecessors have stored up until this day, will be carried off to Babylon.[b]

20:3 [t]Ne 13:22 [u]2Ki 18:3-6
20:5 [v]1Sa 9:16; 1Ki 9:3; 2Ki 19:20 [w]Ps 39:12; 56:8
20:6 [x]2Ki 19:34
20:7 [y]Isa 38:21
20:9 [z]Dt 13:2; Jer 44:29
20:11 [a]Jos 10:13
20:17 [b]2Ki 24:13; 25:13; 2Ch 36:10; Jer 27:22; 52:17-23

(20:12). (2) Hezekiah probably gave some of these treasures as tribute to Sennacherib (18:15). (3) The Assyrian campaign was ongoing at the time of Hezekiah's illness (v. 6). **you are going to die.** Hezekiah began his sole rule in 716/15 BC at age 25 (18:2), so he was not quite 40 years old when he learned that he was going to die.
20:2 The king correctly believes that God will act in response to earnest prayer (cf. Ezek 33:14–15; Jas 5:16–18).
20:3 I have walked before you faithfully. Hezekiah asks the Lord to spare his life so that he can continue to rule God's people in righteousness.
20:5 your father David. Recalls the Lord's promise to preserve David's dynasty forever (1 Kgs 9:5; 2 Sam 7:8–16).
20:6 fifteen years. 701–687/86 BC. **for my sake and for the sake of my servant David.** See note on 19:34.
20:7 figs. Used in ancient times for medicinal purposes. In this case, the Lord chooses to use part of his creation to restore Hezekiah's health.
20:8 Hezekiah seeks an immediate sign as verification that in three days he will be able to leave his sickbed.
20:11 made the shadow go back the ten steps. The Lord miraculously reverses the direction of the shadow to prove to Hezekiah that his words will be fulfilled. The text does not explain how this occurred. **stairway of Ahaz.** Possibly a type of ancient sundial, examples of which are known from fifteenth-century BC Egypt and Babylon.
20:12–21 *Envoys From Babylon.* After his healing, Hezekiah's faith is tested by a visiting delegation who seek to form an alliance with Judah. Because the king fails to trust in the Lord, the prophet Isaiah predicts exile to Babylon.
20:12 Babylon had long been under the rule of Assyria, but with the rise of the young king Sennacherib, Marduk-Baladan seeks independence for Babylon with the cooperation of other vassals of Assyria, including Judah.
20:13 Hezekiah's diplomatic action reveals that he did not completely trust in the Lord. By displaying his treasures, he is boasting in his own resources and not in the Lord, and he is allying himself with an idolatrous nation (cf. 2 Chr 32:31).
20:14 Isaiah intends for his questions to reveal Hezekiah's disobedience and prompt Hezekiah to repent (cf. Gen 3:9–11). **Babylon.** Not just one among many nations but the epitome of the world's rebellion against the Lord ever since the tower was built there (Gen 11:1–9). Isaiah's book depicts Babylon as God's archenemy, whom God will destroy in the last days (Isa 13–14; 47–48; cf. Jer 50–51; Dan 2–7; Rev 18).
20:17 Isaiah's prediction comes true 100 years later (24:13; 25:13–17; cf. Ezra 1:7–11). Though God spares Hezekiah from Assyrian exile

20:18 [c]2Ki 24:15; 2Ch 33:11; Da 1:3 **20:20** [d]Ne 3:16 **21:1** [e]Isa 62:4 **21:2** [f]Jer 15:4 [g]2Ki 16:3 **21:3** [h]2Ki 18:4 [i]Jdg 6:28; 1Ki 16:32 [j]Dt 17:3; 2Ki 17:16 **21:4** [k]Jer 32:34 [l]2Sa 7:13; 1Ki 8:29 **21:5** [m]1Ki 7:12; 2Ki 23:12 **21:6** [n]Lev 18:21; Dt 18:10; 2Ki 16:3; 17:17 [o]Lev 19:31 **21:7** [p]Dt 16:21; 2Ki 23:4 [q]2Sa 7:13; 1Ki 8:29; 9:3; 2Ki 23:27; Jer 32:34 **21:8** [r]2Sa 7:10 [s]2Ki 18:12 **21:9** [t]Pr 29:12 [u]Dt 9:4 **21:11** [v]2Ki 24:3-4 [w]Ge 15:16; 1Ki 21:26

Nothing will be left, says the LORD. [18]And some of your descendants,[c] your own flesh and blood who will
be born to you, will be taken away, and they will become eunuchs in the palace of the king of Babylon."
[19]"The word of the LORD you have spoken is good," Hezekiah replied. For he thought, "Will there not
be peace and security in my lifetime?"
[20]As for the other events of Hezekiah's reign, all his achievements and how he made the pool[d] and
the tunnel by which he brought water into the city, are they not written in the book of the annals of
the kings of Judah? [21]Hezekiah rested with his ancestors. And Manasseh his son succeeded him as king.

Manasseh King of Judah

21:1-10pp — 2Ch 33:1-10
21:17-18pp — 2Ch 33:18-20

21 Manasseh was twelve years old when he became king, and he reigned in Jerusalem fifty-five
years. His mother's name was Hephzibah.[e] [2]He did evil[f] in the eyes of the LORD, following the
detestable practices[g] of the nations the LORD had driven out before the Israelites. [3]He rebuilt the high
places[h] his father Hezekiah had destroyed; he also erected altars to Baal[i] and made an Asherah pole,
as Ahab king of Israel had done. He bowed down to all the starry hosts[j] and worshiped them. [4]He built
altars[k] in the temple of the LORD, of which the LORD had said, "In Jerusalem I will put my Name."[l] [5]In
the two courts[m] of the temple of the LORD, he built altars to all the starry hosts. [6]He sacrificed his own
son[n] in the fire, practiced divination, sought omens, and consulted mediums and spiritists.[o] He did
much evil in the eyes of the LORD, arousing his anger.
[7]He took the carved Asherah pole[p] he had made and put it in the temple, of which the LORD had said
to David and to his son Solomon, "In this temple and in Jerusalem, which I have chosen out of all the
tribes of Israel, I will put my Name[q] forever. [8]I will not again[r] make the feet of the Israelites wander from
the land I gave their ancestors, if only they will be careful to do everything I commanded them and will
keep the whole Law that my servant Moses[s] gave them." [9]But the people did not listen. Manasseh led
them astray, so that they did more evil[t] than the nations[u] the LORD had destroyed before the Israelites.
[10]The LORD said through his servants the prophets: [11]"Manasseh king of Judah has committed these
detestable sins. He has done more evil[v] than the Amorites[w] who preceded him and has led Judah into
sin with his idols. [12]Therefore this is what the LORD, the God of Israel, says: I am going to bring such

because of his great faith (19:14–36), Hezekiah's lack of faith in this instance results in the prophecy of Babylonian exile.

20:18 This prophecy is fulfilled in the reigns of Jehoiachin and Zedekiah (24:15; 25:6–7). The book of 2 Kings concludes with one of Hezekiah's descendants eating at the king's table in Babylon (25:27–30).

20:19 Possibly Hezekiah's response is self-centered. Perhaps his knowledge of the prophecies of exile lead him to rejoice that the Lord has chosen to delay this judgment (Deut 28:64–66).

20:20 other events. See 2 Chr 29:1—32:33. **the pool and the tunnel.** This tunnel was carved underneath the city of Jerusalem through solid rock for a distance of 1,750 feet (533 meters); it brought water from the Gihon spring on the west side of the City of David to a reservoir inside the city's fortifications (cf. 2 Chr 32:30). This engineering feat is significant enough for the author to single it out, and visitors to Jerusalem are still impressed by it today. An ancient inscription discovered inside the tunnel describes how the builders began at both ends and met in the middle.

21:1–18 *Manasseh King of Judah.* Manasseh ruled for 55 years, the longest of any king of either the northern or southern kingdoms. Manasseh sets a new standard for wickedness, exceeding even the depravity of the Canaanites. As a result, Judah's exile becomes inevitable.

21:1 fifty-five years. 697/96–643/42 BC. Includes Manasseh's coregency with his father (697/96–687/86 BC) and his sole rule (687/86–643/42 BC).

21:2 He did evil. Manasseh puts Judah back on the path to exile by ignoring the covenant and leading the nation in idolatry worse than that which the Canaanites practiced (cf. Deut 18:9–12). He not only reestablishes ancient shrines to pagan gods but also builds new ones within the courts of the Lord's temple.

21:4 The Lord commanded the Israelites to worship him with sacrifices only at the place where he would "put his Name" and live with his people (Deut 12:5). During the reign of David, God selected Jerusalem as this place (2 Sam 7:13; 2 Chr 6:6; cf. Ezra 6:12; Ps 87:1–2).

21:5 starry hosts. See note on 17:16.

21:6 He sacrificed his own son in the fire. See note on 16:3. **divination ... omens.** See note on 17:17. **arousing his anger.** Scripture depicts the Lord not as an impassive God but as a God who is jealous for the affections of his people (Exod 20:5; Deut 32:21). From this point to its end, the book frequently mentions the Lord's anger.

21:7 carved Asherah pole. See note on Exod 34:13. No remains of a wooden Asherah pole have been preserved, but archaeologists have uncovered hundreds of small, clay, female fertility figurines that may have been used in worshiping Asherah. **I will put my Name forever.** Underscores the gravity of Manasseh's sin, reminding the reader of the temple's utter sanctity as the sole place on earth where the Lord had chosen to live with his people (1 Kgs 8:10–16; Deut 12:5).

21:8 make the feet of the Israelites wander from the land. The threat of exile looms larger as the sin of Judah increases (20:17–18).

21:9 the nations the LORD had destroyed. The Canaanites. Since Judah's sinfulness compares unfavorably to that of the Canaanites, the nation can expect that they too will be uprooted from the land (cf. Jer 3:11; Ezek 16:46–48).

21:10 the prophets. Though this does not preserve their names, it affirms that the Lord actively pursued his people even through the years of Judah's most abominable idolatry (cf. 2 Chr 33:10,18).

21:11 more evil than the Amorites. See note on 1 Kgs 21:26.

21:12 Though the Lord had positioned his people in the midst of other

disaster[x] on Jerusalem and Judah that the ears of everyone who hears of it will tingle.[y] [13]I will stretch
out over Jerusalem the measuring line used against Samaria and the plumb line[z] used against the
house of Ahab. I will wipe[a] out Jerusalem as one wipes a dish, wiping it and turning it upside down.
[14]I will forsake[b] the remnant[c] of my inheritance and give them into the hands of enemies. They will
be looted and plundered by all their enemies; [15]they have done evil[d] in my eyes and have aroused[e] my
anger from the day their ancestors came out of Egypt until this day."

[16]Moreover, Manasseh also shed so much innocent blood[f] that he filled Jerusalem from end to
end—besides the sin that he had caused Judah to commit, so that they did evil in the eyes of the LORD.

[17]As for the other events of Manasseh's reign, and all he did, including the sin he committed, are
they not written in the book of the annals of the kings of Judah? [18]Manasseh rested with his ancestors
and was buried in his palace garden,[g] the garden of Uzza. And Amon his son succeeded him as king.

Amon King of Judah

21:19-24pp — 2Ch 33:21-25

[19]Amon was twenty-two years old when he became king, and he reigned in Jerusalem two years. His
mother's name was Meshullemeth daughter of Haruz; she was from Jotbah. [20]He did evil[h] in the eyes of
the LORD, as his father Manasseh had done. [21]He followed completely the ways of his father, worshiping
the idols his father had worshiped, and bowing down to them. [22]He forsook the LORD, the God of his
ancestors, and did not walk[i] in obedience to him.

[23]Amon's officials conspired against him and assassinated[j] the king in his palace. [24]Then the people of
the land killed[k] all who had plotted against King Amon, and they made Josiah his son king in his place.

[25]As for the other events of Amon's reign, and what he did, are they not written in the book of the
annals of the kings of Judah? [26]He was buried in his tomb in the garden[l] of Uzza. And Josiah his son
succeeded him as king.

The Book of the Law Found

22:1-20pp — 2Ch 34:1-2,8-28

22 Josiah was eight years old when he became king, and he reigned in Jerusalem thirty-one years.
His mother's name was Jedidah daughter of Adaiah; she was from Bozkath.[m] [2]He did what was
right[n] in the eyes of the LORD and followed completely the ways of his father David, not turning aside
to the right[o] or to the left.

21:12 [x]2Ki 23:26; 24:3; Jer 15:4 [y]1Sa 3:11; Jer 19:3
21:13 [z]Isa 34:11; La 2:8; Am 7:7-9 [a]2Ki 23:27
21:14 [b]Ps 78:58-60 [c]2Ki 19:4; Mic 2:12
21:15 [d]Ex 32:22 [e]Jer 25:7
21:16 [f]2Ki 24:4
21:18 [g]ver 26
21:20 [h]ver 2-6
21:22 [i]1Ki 11:33
21:23 [j]2Ki 12:20; 2Ch 33:24-25
21:24 [k]2Ki 14:5
21:26 [l]ver 18
22:1 [m]Jos 15:39
22:2 [n]Dt 17:19 [o]Dt 5:32

nations so that the nations would be jealous of his blessings upon Israel (Ezek 5:5; Deut 4:6–8), the nations would also see the Lord's just nature when he punished Israel for violating his covenant (Deut 29:22–28). See also Jer 19:3 and note.

21:13 measuring line used against Samaria. Since Judah's sin is comparable to that of the northern kingdom (17:7–23), its judgment will be similar (cf. Isa 34:11; Amos 7:7–9).

21:14 I will forsake. Temporarily to induce repentance. The context of the book, the covenants with the forefathers, and the affirmations of the prophets make this clear (Gen 22:17–18; Deut 30:1–10; 2 Sam 7:12–16; Jer 31:35–37). **the remnant of my inheritance.** Judah was all that was left after the exile of the ten northern tribes (19:4).

21:15 Briefly summarizes Israel's history of sinful rebellion. The nation's survival for 700 years testifies that God is incomparably patient (cf. 2 Pet 3:9). Such a history calls for God to transform the people's hearts, a blessing that Moses and the prophets promised (Deut 30:6; Jer 31:31–34; Ezek 36:24–32).

21:16 shed so much innocent blood. Grave social injustice naturally accompanied Manasseh's religious failings. According to extrabiblical tradition, Manasseh executed the prophet Isaiah.

21:17 all he did. Though Manasseh ruled for more than half a century, the biblical author does not credit him with a single building project or military victory. Such successes are unimportant given the king's unrighteousness and the impending exile. The Chronicler records other events, including Manasseh's repentance after his exile to Babylon (2 Chr 33:10–17). The differences between the two accounts can be explained by each work's purpose: Kings stresses the guilt of the nation, while Chronicles highlights the hope of restoration.

21:18 buried in his palace garden. Not with his fathers in the dynastic tomb in the City of David—perhaps on account of his wickedness (cf. 16:20). The location of this garden is unknown today.

21:19–26 *Amon King of Judah.* Amon's brief rule is marked by his wicked acts, like those of his father. His assassination explains why Josiah ascends to the throne at a young age.

21:19 two years. 643/42–641/40 BC.

21:23 assassinated the king in his palace. Amon is the fourth king of Judah to be assassinated but the first killed in the palace in Jerusalem.

21:24 they made Josiah his son king. Unlike in the northern kingdom of Israel, in Judah the heir replaces every assassinated king in accordance with God's covenant with David (1 Kgs 9:5; 2 Sam 7:12–16).

21:26 his tomb in the garden of Uzza. The wicked Amon is buried near his unrighteous father (21:18).

22:1—23:30 *Josiah King of Judah.* Josiah is the last good king of Judah, and his reign is characterized by temple repair, covenant renewal, and the destruction of idolatrous centers. Like Hezekiah, Josiah compares favorably to David, thus evoking the promise of David's eternal dynasty (2 Sam 7:11–16).

22:1–20 *The Book of the Law Found.* Concerned with the disrepair of

22:3 [p] 2Ch 34:20; Jer 39:14
22:4 [q] 2Ki 12:4-5
22:5 [r] 2Ki 12:5,11-14
22:6 [s] 2Ki 12:11-12
22:7 [t] 2Ki 12:15
22:8 [u] Dt 31:24
22:10 [v] Jer 36:21
22:12 [w] 2Ki 25:22; Jer 26:24
22:13 [x] Dt 29:24-28; 31:17
22:16 [y] Dt 31:29; Jos 23:15 [z] Dt 29:27; Da 9:11
22:17 [a] Dt 29:25-27
22:18 [b] 2Ch 34:26; Jer 21:2
22:19 [c] Ex 10:3; 1Ki 21:29; Ps 51:17; Isa 57:15; Mic 6:8 [d] Jer 26:6 [e] Lev 26:31

[3]In the eighteenth year of his reign, King Josiah sent the secretary, Shaphan[p] son of Azaliah, the son of Meshullam, to the temple of the LORD. He said: [4]"Go up to Hilkiah the high priest and have him get ready the money that has been brought into the temple of the LORD, which the doorkeepers have collected[q] from the people. [5]Have them entrust it to the men appointed to supervise the work on the temple. And have these men pay the workers who repair[r] the temple of the LORD— [6]the carpenters, the builders and the masons. Also have them purchase timber and dressed stone to repair the temple.[s] [7]But they need not account for the money entrusted to them, because they are honest in their dealings."[t]

[8]Hilkiah the high priest said to Shaphan the secretary, "I have found the Book of the Law[u] in the temple of the LORD." He gave it to Shaphan, who read it. [9]Then Shaphan the secretary went to the king and reported to him: "Your officials have paid out the money that was in the temple of the LORD and have entrusted it to the workers and supervisors at the temple." [10]Then Shaphan the secretary informed the king, "Hilkiah the priest has given me a book." And Shaphan read from it in the presence of the king.[v]

[11]When the king heard the words of the Book of the Law, he tore his robes. [12]He gave these orders to Hilkiah the priest, Ahikam[w] son of Shaphan, Akbor son of Micaiah, Shaphan the secretary and Asaiah the king's attendant: [13]"Go and inquire of the LORD for me and for the people and for all Judah about what is written in this book that has been found. Great is the LORD's anger[x] that burns against us because those who have gone before us have not obeyed the words of this book; they have not acted in accordance with all that is written there concerning us."

[14]Hilkiah the priest, Ahikam, Akbor, Shaphan and Asaiah went to speak to the prophet Huldah, who was the wife of Shallum son of Tikvah, the son of Harhas, keeper of the wardrobe. She lived in Jerusalem, in the New Quarter.

[15]She said to them, "This is what the LORD, the God of Israel, says: Tell the man who sent you to me, [16]'This is what the LORD says: I am going to bring disaster[y] on this place and its people, according to everything written in the book[z] the king of Judah has read. [17]Because they have forsaken[a] me and burned incense to other gods and aroused my anger by all the idols their hands have made,[a] my anger will burn against this place and will not be quenched.' [18]Tell the king of Judah, who sent you to inquire[b] of the LORD, 'This is what the LORD, the God of Israel, says concerning the words you heard: [19]Because your heart was responsive and you humbled[c] yourself before the LORD when you heard what I have spoken against this place and its people—that they would become a curse[b][d] and be laid waste[e]—and

[a] *17* Or *by everything they have done*
[b] *19* That is, their names would be used in cursing (see Jer. 29:22); or, others would see that they are cursed.

the Lord's house, Josiah begins repair work that results in the rediscovery of the Book of the Law.

22:1 thirty-one years. 641/40–609 BC.

22:2 followed completely the ways of his father David. Many kings compare unfavorably with David; only Hezekiah and Josiah were obedient like David (18:3). **not turning aside to the right or to the left.** Josiah is the only king credited with following God's law unswervingly (Deut 17:20).

22:3 eighteenth year. 623/22 BC. Josiah began purifying Judah's religious practices six years earlier (2 Chr 34:3–7). In his 18th year, he initiates repairs to the temple.

22:4 Hilkiah. The Babylonians executed his grandson Seraiah when they destroyed Jerusalem (25:18–21; cf. Ezra 7:1). This is probably not the same Hilkiah who was the father of Jeremiah (Jer 1:1).

22:5–7 The description of Josiah's temple project echoes that of his ancestor Joash (12:4–16).

22:5 work on the temple. The last recorded renovation of the temple was before the long and wicked rule of Manasseh (2 Chr 29).

22:8 found the Book of the Law. The decades of idolatry under Manasseh and Amon led to the loss of the covenant document that was to guide the king and the nation to obey the Lord. The book's exact identity is difficult to determine, but because many of the reforms that Josiah enacted are based on commands in Deuteronomy, it is reasonable to conclude that the Book of the Law included at least part of Deuteronomy if not the entire Pentateuch (see note on 23:25; cf. 1 Kgs 2:3; Deut 31:26).

22:11 tore his robes. Expressed grief and repentance before God and the people of Judah. Josiah is rightly distressed that he and the people have failed to keep the covenant. The curses of Deut 28 may have provoked this response. By contrast, Josiah's son Jehoiakim later responds to the reading of God's Word by burning it in the fire (Jer 36:23).

22:12 Ahikam. An official who supported the prophet Jeremiah (Jer 26:24); he was the father of the future governor Gedaliah (2 Kgs 25:22).

22:13 Great is the LORD's anger. The nation is in grave danger of being exiled because they have violated the covenant.

22:14 Huldah. Nothing is known of Huldah outside of this passage and its parallel in 2 Chr 34:22. She is the only female prophet in the book of Kings but one of several in the OT (Exod 15:20; Judg 4:4; Neh 6:14). **New Quarter.** Possibly an expansion of the city on the Western Hill (Neh 11:9; Zeph 1:10; cf. 2 Chr 33:14).

22:15–20 Huldah's message to the king confirms that what Josiah has read will be fulfilled.

22:16 I am going to bring disaster. Judah's march toward certain exile continues. The author of Kings has anticipated exile ever since Solomon's prayer at the temple dedication (1 Kgs 8:46), but the repeated references in recent history indicate that judgment is near (2 Kgs 20:17–18; 21:13–14).

22:19 Just as Solomon prayed would happen whenever the people

because you tore your robes and wept in my presence, I also have heard you, declares the LORD. 20Therefore I will gather you to your ancestors, and you will be buried in peace.[f] Your eyes will not see all the disaster I am going to bring on this place.'"

So they took her answer back to the king.

Josiah Renews the Covenant

23:1-3pp — 2Ch 34:29-32
23:4-20Ref — 2Ch 34:3-7,33
23:21-23pp — 2Ch 35:1,18-19
23:28-30pp — 2Ch 35:20–36:1

23 Then the king called together all the elders of Judah and Jerusalem. 2He went up to the temple of the LORD with the people of Judah, the inhabitants of Jerusalem, the priests and the prophets — all the people from the least to the greatest. He read[g] in their hearing all the words of the Book of the Covenant, which had been found in the temple of the LORD. 3The king stood by the pillar and renewed the covenant[h] in the presence of the LORD — to follow[i] the LORD and keep his commands, statutes and decrees with all his heart and all his soul, thus confirming the words of the covenant written in this book. Then all the people pledged themselves to the covenant.

4The king ordered Hilkiah the high priest, the priests next in rank and the doorkeepers[j] to remove[k] from the temple of the LORD all the articles made for Baal and Asherah and all the starry hosts. He burned them outside Jerusalem in the fields of the Kidron Valley and took the ashes to Bethel. 5He did away with the idolatrous priests appointed by the kings of Judah to burn incense on the high places of the towns of Judah and on those around Jerusalem — those who burned incense to Baal, to the sun and moon, to the constellations and to all the starry hosts.[l] 6He took the Asherah pole from the temple of the LORD to the Kidron Valley outside Jerusalem and burned it there. He ground it to powder and scattered the dust over the graves of the common people.[m] 7He also tore down the quarters of the male shrine prostitutes[n] that were in the temple of the LORD, the quarters where women did weaving for Asherah.

8Josiah brought all the priests from the towns of Judah and desecrated the high places, from Geba[o] to Beersheba, where the priests had burned incense. He broke down the gateway at the entrance of the Gate of Joshua, the city governor, which was on the left of the city gate. 9Although the priests of the high places did not serve[p] at the altar of the LORD in Jerusalem, they ate unleavened bread with their fellow priests.

10He desecrated Topheth,[q] which was in the Valley of Ben Hinnom,[r] so no one could use it to sacrifice

22:20 [f] Isa 57:1
23:2 [g] Dt 31:11; 2Ki 22:8
23:3 [h] 2Ki 11:14,17 [i] Dt 13:4
23:4 [j] 2Ki 25:18 [k] 2Ki 21:7
23:5 [l] 2Ki 21:3; Jer 8:2
23:6 [m] Jer 26:23
23:7 [n] 1Ki 14:24; 15:12; Eze 16:16
23:8 [o] 1Ki 15:22
23:9 [p] Eze 44:10-14
23:10 [q] Isa 30:33; Jer 7:31,32; 19:6 [r] Jos 15:8

repented and confessed their sin (1 Kgs 8:33), the Lord gives Josiah and the people of Judah a reprieve because they return to the covenant.

22:20 you will be buried in peace. Josiah will die in battle against Egypt (23:29). Huldah's prophecy signifies that his death will occur while the nation is at peace, prior to the impending Babylonian exile. As righteous as he is, Josiah is unable to lead the people to lasting covenant faithfulness. For this, a greater king is necessary (Isa 11:1–5; 42:1–7; Jer 23:5–6).

23:1–30 *Josiah Renews the Covenant.* After being made aware of the severity of the nation's unfaithfulness by the Book of the Law, Josiah leads the nation in a covenant renewal ceremony to commit to wholehearted obedience to their King. In cleansing the land of idolatrous worship sites, Josiah fulfills a prophecy made about him 300 years earlier (1 Kgs 13:2). Though a model king in many respects, Josiah dies at a young age on the battlefield, thus ending the delay of God's judgment upon Judah.

23:2 This national covenant renewal ceremony recalls those carried out in the days of Joshua, Samuel, Joash, and Hezekiah (Josh 8:30–35; 24:1–28; 1 Sam 12; 2 Chr 23:16–21; 29:10–36). **Book of the Covenant.** See note on 22:8. Deut 31:10–13 commands the Lord's people to regularly read the law to remind them of their relationship with him.

23:3 pillar. See note on 11:14. **renewed the covenant.** The king and the people commit themselves to be faithful to the covenant that the Lord and Israel made at Mount Sinai (Exod 19:8; 24:7; cf. 1 Kgs 2:3).

23:4 articles. Manasseh's idolatrous objects (21:3). **Kidron Valley.** Borders Jerusalem on the east. **Bethel.** See 23:15.

23:6 Asherah pole. See notes on 21:7; Exod 34:13. **ground it to powder.** Imitates how Moses obliterated the golden calf (Exod 32:20). **scattered the dust over the graves.** Disposing of the remains in the place with the greatest impurities shows utter disdain for the Asherah pole.

23:7 male shrine prostitutes. Some doubt the existence of male cultic prostitution in ancient Israel and thus prefer to translate this term as a special class of male cultic priest. See also note on 1 Kgs 14:24. **weaving for Asherah.** Perhaps sewing garments for the goddess's ritual ceremonies.

23:8 desecrated the high places. Making these cultic centers ritually impure makes it more difficult to resume illicit worship. **from Geba to Beersheba.** Two cities that marked the northern and southern extremes of Judah's territory. Geba (modern Jaba) was located six miles (9.7 kilometers) north of Jerusalem, and Beersheba (modern Tell Sheba) was 45 miles (72 kilometers) southwest of Jerusalem. **Gate of Joshua.** Location uncertain, but idolatrous shrines have been excavated near Dan's city gate.

23:9 ate unleavened bread. In terminating worship at sites outside of Jerusalem, Josiah relocates the Levitical priests to Jerusalem. Though restricted from serving at the temple, they receive provisions from the offerings as if they are priests with physical defects (Lev 21:16–23).

23:10 Topheth. An important high place where people worshiped the

23:10 [s]Lev 18:21; Dt 18:10
23:11 [t]Dt 4:19
23:12 [u]Jer 19:13; Zep 1:5 [v]2Ki 21:5
23:13 [w]1Ki 11:7
23:14 [x]Ex 23:24; Dt 7:5,25
23:15 [y]1Ki 13:1-3 [z]1Ki 12:33
23:16 [a]1Ki 13:2
23:18 [b]1Ki 13:31
23:20 [c]Ex 22:20; 2Ki 10:25; 11:18 [d]1Ki 13:2
23:21 [e]Ex 12:11; Nu 9:2; Dt 16:1-8
23:24 [f]Lev 19:31; Dt 18:11; 2Ki 21:6 [g]Ge 31:19
23:25 [h]2Ki 18:5

their son[s] or daughter in the fire to Molek. 11He removed from the entrance to the temple of the LORD
the horses that the kings of Judah had dedicated to the sun. They were in the court[a] near the room of
an official named Nathan-Melek. Josiah then burned the chariots dedicated to the sun.[t]

12He pulled down the altars the kings of Judah had erected on the roof[u] near the upper room of Ahaz,
and the altars Manasseh had built in the two courts[v] of the temple of the LORD. He removed them from
there, smashed them to pieces and threw the rubble into the Kidron Valley. 13The king also desecrated
the high places that were east of Jerusalem on the south of the Hill of Corruption—the ones Solomon[w]
king of Israel had built for Ashtoreth the vile goddess of the Sidonians, for Chemosh the vile god of
Moab, and for Molek the detestable god of the people of Ammon. 14Josiah smashed[x] the sacred stones
and cut down the Asherah poles and covered the sites with human bones.

15Even the altar[y] at Bethel, the high place made by Jeroboam[z] son of Nebat, who had caused Israel
to sin—even that altar and high place he demolished. He burned the high place and ground it to
powder, and burned the Asherah pole also. 16Then Josiah[a] looked around, and when he saw the tombs
that were there on the hillside, he had the bones removed from them and burned on the altar to defile
it, in accordance with the word of the LORD proclaimed by the man of God who foretold these things.

17The king asked, "What is that tombstone I see?"

The people of the city said, "It marks the tomb of the man of God who came from Judah and pronounced against the altar of Bethel the very things you have done to it."

18"Leave it alone," he said. "Don't let anyone disturb his bones[b]." So they spared his bones and those
of the prophet who had come from Samaria.

19Just as he had done at Bethel, Josiah removed all the shrines at the high places that the kings of Israel
had built in the towns of Samaria and that had aroused the LORD's anger. 20Josiah slaughtered[c] all the priests
of those high places on the altars and burned human bones[d] on them. Then he went back to Jerusalem.

21The king gave this order to all the people: "Celebrate the Passover[e] to the LORD your God, as it is
written in this Book of the Covenant." 22Neither in the days of the judges who led Israel nor in the days
of the kings of Israel and the kings of Judah had any such Passover been observed. 23But in the eighteenth year of King Josiah, this Passover was celebrated to the LORD in Jerusalem.

24Furthermore, Josiah got rid of the mediums and spiritists,[f] the household gods,[g] the idols and all
the other detestable things seen in Judah and Jerusalem. This he did to fulfill the requirements of the
law written in the book that Hilkiah the priest had discovered in the temple of the LORD. 25Neither before
nor after Josiah was there a king like him who turned[h] to the LORD as he did—with all his heart and
with all his soul and with all his strength, in accordance with all the Law of Moses.

a *11* The meaning of the Hebrew for this word is uncertain.

Ammonite god Molek (Jer 7:31–32). **Valley of Ben Hinnom.** Borders Jerusalem on its western and southern sides. The practice of sacrificing children in the fires here may be the origin for the association of the Hinnom Valley (Hebrew *gê ben-hinnōm*) with the NT place of fiery torment known as Gehenna and translated "hell" (see note on Matt 5:22). **Molek.** See note on 1 Kgs 11:5.

23:11 horses ... chariots dedicated to the sun. Worshiping the sun was common in the ancient Near East. Manasseh even named his son Amon after the Egyptian sun-god (21:18). Deut 4:19 explicitly forbids such worship. Excavations in Jerusalem have revealed horse figurines from this period, some with solar disks on their foreheads. By destroying this valuable military hardware, Josiah imitates Joshua in trusting the Lord (Josh 11:9; Ps 20:7).

23:12 on the roof. Where they burned incense to the "starry hosts" (Jer 19:13; Zeph 1:5).

23:13 that were east of Jerusalem. Since Hezekiah destroyed the high places (18:4; 2 Chr 31:1), these high places of Solomon (1 Kgs 11:7–8) were apparently among those Manasseh restored (2 Kgs 21:3). **Hill of Corruption.** Probably the southern portion of the Mount of Olives opposite the City of David (1 Kgs 11:7).

23:14 covered the sites with human bones. Josiah's desecration reveals his utter disdain for the shrine and prevents its further use.

23:15 altar at Bethel. After Jeroboam established the centers for golden calf worship at Dan and Bethel, a man of God prophesied that a king of Judah named Josiah would desecrate the altar of Bethel by burning the bones of the sanctuary's priests on it (1 Kgs 13:2). This prophecy is fulfilled 300 years after it was given. This probably does not mention the golden calf because the Assyrians carried it off in 722 BC (17:23).

23:17 tomb. This prophet's death underscores the certainty of God's word (1 Kgs 13:26–32). This reminds the reader that what the Lord says will come to pass.

23:18 Samaria. See note on 17:24.

23:19 towns of Samaria. Formerly belonged to the northern kingdom. Josiah now had some measure of authority over this territory. With the death of king Ashurbanipal in 627 BC, the Assyrians were no longer able to retain control of their conquered lands.

23:20 priests of those high places. They led the people astray in idolatrous worship and thus are subject to the death penalty (Deut 17:2–7).

23:22 This Passover observance surpasses even Hezekiah's tremendous celebration (2 Chr 30); 2 Chr 35:1–19 gives more details.

23:24 mediums and spiritists. Deut 18:10–11 forbids consulting intermediate spiritual agents. **household gods.** Could be life-size images (1 Sam 19:13) but were usually about the size of an adult's hand (Gen 31:34). **to fulfill the requirements of the law.** King Josiah's primary obligation was to lead the nation to observe all that God decreed (Deut 17:18–20).

23:25 This superlative praise marks Josiah as unique in his law-keeping

26 Nevertheless, the LORD did not turn away from the heat of his fierce anger, which burned against Judah because of all that Manasseh[i] had done to arouse his anger. 27 So the LORD said, "I will remove[j] Judah also from my presence[k] as I removed Israel, and I will reject Jerusalem, the city I chose, and this temple, about which I said, 'My Name shall be there.'[a]"

28 As for the other events of Josiah's reign, and all he did, are they not written in the book of the annals of the kings of Judah?

29 While Josiah was king, Pharaoh Necho[l] king of Egypt went up to the Euphrates River to help the king of Assyria. King Josiah marched out to meet him in battle, but Necho faced him and killed him at Megiddo.[m] 30 Josiah's servants brought his body in a chariot[n] from Megiddo to Jerusalem and buried him in his own tomb. And the people of the land took Jehoahaz son of Josiah and anointed him and made him king in place of his father.

Jehoahaz King of Judah

23:31-34pp — 2Ch 36:2-4

31 Jehoahaz[o] was twenty-three years old when he became king, and he reigned in Jerusalem three months. His mother's name was Hamutal[p] daughter of Jeremiah; she was from Libnah. 32 He did evil in the eyes of the LORD, just as his predecessors had done. 33 Pharaoh Necho put him in chains at Riblah[q] in the land of Hamath[r] so that he might not reign in Jerusalem, and he imposed on Judah a levy of a hundred talents[b] of silver and a talent[c] of gold. 34 Pharaoh Necho made Eliakim[s] son of Josiah king in place of his father Josiah and changed Eliakim's name to Jehoiakim. But he took Jehoahaz and carried him off to Egypt, and there he died.[t] 35 Jehoiakim paid Pharaoh Necho the silver and gold he demanded. In order to do so, he taxed the land and exacted the silver and gold from the people of the land according to their assessments.[u]

Jehoiakim King of Judah

23:36–24:6pp — 2Ch 36:5-8

36 Jehoiakim[v] was twenty-five years old when he became king, and he reigned in Jerusalem eleven years. His mother's name was Zebidah daughter of Pedaiah; she was from Rumah. 37 And he did evil in the eyes of the LORD, just as his predecessors had done.

23:26 [i] 2Ki 21:12; Jer 15:4
23:27 [j] 2Ki 21:13 [k] 2Ki 18:11
23:29 [l] Jer 46:2 [m] Zec 12:11
23:30 [n] 2Ki 9:28
23:31 [o] 1Ch 3:15; Jer 22:11 [p] 2Ki 24:18
23:33 [q] 2Ki 25:6 [r] 1Ki 8:65
23:34 [s] 1Ch 3:15; 2Ch 36:5-8 [t] Jer 22:12; Eze 19:3-4
23:35 [u] ver 33
23:36 [v] Jer 26:1

[a] *27* 1 Kings 8:29 [b] *33* That is, about 3 3/4 tons or about 3.4 metric tons [c] *33* That is, about 75 pounds or about 34 kilograms

character (cf. Jer 22:15–16). **with all his heart and with all his soul and with all his strength.** Fulfills the greatest commandment (Deut 6:5; cf. Matt 22:37–38). **all the Law of Moses.** May suggest that the lost Book of the Law was not only the book of Deuteronomy but the entire Pentateuch.

23:26 Nevertheless, the LORD did not turn away. Even Josiah's obedience is not enough to remove the threat of exile. This is not an arbitrary judgment on the Lord's part; it reflects the deep-seated idolatry in the hearts of the people, which is revealed after Josiah dies. The nation not only needs a righteous king but requires a new covenant that will provide a circumcision of every person's heart (cf. Deut 30:6; Jer 31:31–34).

23:29 Necho. Ruled Egypt 610–595 BC. He mounted a campaign to Harran in 609 BC to support Assyria against the rising threat of Babylon. **King Josiah marched out.** The text does not give his motivation. He may have been trying to assert sovereignty over the former territory of the northern kingdom by meeting the Egyptian army at the strategic pass through Mount Carmel at Megiddo. It is also possible that he was siding with Babylon against the Assyrians. **killed.** See 2 Chr 35:20–25.

23:30 Jehoahaz. Jehoiakim's younger brother (vv. 31,36). Judging from Necho's hasty reaction in deposing Jehoahaz, perhaps the people of Judah chose Josiah's younger son to succeed him because Jehoahaz would likely have continued his father's anti-Egyptian policies.

23:31—24:20a *The Final Four Kings of Judah.* Three sons and a grandson succeed Josiah, none of whom follow in his ways. The way to exile is now unobstructed, and the prophecies will be fulfilled. Two of the kings rule for merely three months. Three of the kings are carried off in exile. The glorious kingdom of David and Solomon crumbles to pieces on account of the nation's treason against their great King.

23:31–35 *Jehoahaz King of Judah.* The record of Jehoahaz's brief reign highlights his arrest and deportation.

23:31 three months. In 609 BC. **Jeremiah.** Not the famous writing prophet because Jeremiah never married (Jer 16:2).

23:32 He did evil. All four of Josiah's successors fail to walk in his ways, leading to short reigns and multiple deportations.

23:33 Riblah. Modern Ribleh, eight miles (12 kilometers) south of Kadesh on the eastern bank of the Orontes River (see note on Jer 39:5). It was the headquarters for Pharaoh Necho and later the Babylonian king Nebuchadnezzar (25:6).

23:34 The Lord maintains his promise to preserve the Davidic dynasty on the throne even through a foreign power. **changed Eliakim's name.** Necho asserts his sovereignty over the nation through this action. **carried him off to Egypt.** This wicked king dies like many of his ancestors—as a slave in Egypt (cf. Jer 22:10–12).

23:36—24:7 *Jehoiakim King of Judah.* Jehoiakim's reign is characterized by rebellion against the Lord and Babylon. Additional details of this king's evil rule are given in Jer 22:13–19; 26; 36:20–31.

23:36 eleven years. 609–598 BC.

23:37 he did evil. He oppresses the people, murders the prophet Uriah, and burns Jeremiah's scroll (Jer 22:13–19; 26:20–23; 36:20–26).

24:1 [w] Jer 25:1,9; Da 1:1
24:2 [x] Jer 35:11
[y] Jer 25:9
24:3 [z] 2Ki 18:25
[a] 2Ki 21:12; 23:26
24:4 [b] 2Ki 21:16
24:6 [c] Jer 22:19
24:7 [d] Ge 15:18
[e] Jer 37:5-7; 46:2
24:8 [f] 1Ch 3:16
24:10 [g] Da 1:1
24:12 [h] 2Ki 25:27; Jer 22:24-30; 24:1; 25:1; 29:2; 52:28
24:13 [i] 2Ki 20:17
[j] 2Ki 25:15; Isa 39:6
[k] 2Ki 25:14; Jer 20:5
[l] 1Ki 7:51
24:14 [m] Jer 24:1; 52:28
[n] 2Ki 25:12; Jer 40:7; 52:16
24:15 [o] Jer 22:24-28
[p] Est 2:6; Eze 17:12-14

24 During Jehoiakim's reign, Nebuchadnezzar[w] king of Babylon invaded the land, and Jehoiakim
became his vassal for three years. But then he turned against Nebuchadnezzar and rebelled.
2The LORD sent Babylonian,[a] Aramean,[x] Moabite and Ammonite raiders against him to destroy[y] Judah,
in accordance with the word of the LORD proclaimed by his servants the prophets. 3Surely these things
happened to Judah according to the LORD's command,[z] in order to remove them from his presence because of the sins of Manasseh[a] and all he had done, 4including the shedding of innocent blood.[b] For he
had filled Jerusalem with innocent blood, and the LORD was not willing to forgive.
5As for the other events of Jehoiakim's reign, and all he did, are they not written in the book of the
annals of the kings of Judah? 6Jehoiakim rested[c] with his ancestors. And Jehoiachin his son succeeded
him as king.
7The king of Egypt[d] did not march out from his own country again, because the king of Babylon[e]
had taken all his territory, from the Wadi of Egypt to the Euphrates River.

Jehoiachin King of Judah

24:8-17pp — 2Ch 36:9-10

8Jehoiachin[f] was eighteen years old when he became king, and he reigned in Jerusalem three
months. His mother's name was Nehushta daughter of Elnathan; she was from Jerusalem. 9He did evil
in the eyes of the LORD, just as his father had done.
10At that time the officers of Nebuchadnezzar[g] king of Babylon advanced on Jerusalem and laid siege
to it, 11and Nebuchadnezzar himself came up to the city while his officers were besieging it. 12Jehoi-
achin king of Judah, his mother, his attendants, his nobles and his officials all surrendered[h] to him.
In the eighth year of the reign of the king of Babylon, he took Jehoiachin prisoner. 13As the LORD
had declared,[i] Nebuchadnezzar removed the treasures[j] from the temple of the LORD and from the royal
palace, and cut up the gold articles[k] that Solomon[l] king of Israel had made for the temple of the LORD.
14He carried all Jerusalem into exile:[m] all the officers and fighting men, and all the skilled workers and
artisans — a total of ten thousand. Only the poorest[n] people of the land were left.
15Nebuchadnezzar took Jehoiachin captive to Babylon. He also took from Jerusalem to Babylon the
king's mother,[o] his wives, his officials and the prominent people[p] of the land. 16The king of Babylon

[a] 2 Or *Chaldean*

24:1 Nebuchadnezzar ruled Babylon 605 – 562 BC and carried off exiles from Judah on three occasions. In his first campaign in 605 BC, he deported some members of the royal family, including Daniel (Dan 1:1 – 6). **turned against Nebuchadnezzar.** Jehoiakim's rebellion in ca. 602 BC was likely motivated by his hope that Egypt would protect Judah.

24:2 proclaimed by his servants. Throughout the book of Kings, the Lord sent his messengers to call the rulers back to the covenant, and since they ignored the prophets (17:13 – 14), the Lord began to fulfill his promise to exile the covenant nation (cf. 1 Kgs 8:46; Deut 29:28). The prophetic voice is unmistakable in interpreting Judah's history from a divine standpoint. Prophets not mentioned in the book of Kings who predicted exile for Judah include Jeremiah, Ezekiel, Micah, Habakkuk, and Zephaniah.

24:3 sins of Manasseh. See 21:1 – 16; see also note on 21:2.

24:6 Jehoiakim rested. This does not give the expected reference to the king's burial, suggesting that Jeremiah's prediction of Jehoiakim's disgraceful end comes to pass (Jer 22:18 – 19).

24:7 taken all his territory. In 605 BC, the Babylonians defeated the Egyptians at the battle of Carchemish (Jer 46:2). By 601 BC, Nebuchadnezzar had subdued the eastern Mediterranean seaboard as far south as the Brook of Egypt (modern Wadi el-Arish), about 50 miles (80 kilometers) southwest of the city of Gaza.

24:8 – 17 *Jehoiachin King of Judah.* The description of Jehoiachin's brief rule focuses on the Babylonian deportation of the king, the royal family, and the temple treasures.

24:8 Jehoiachin. Josiah's grandson. The other three kings who followed Josiah (Jehoahaz, Jehoiakim, and Zedekiah) were his sons. Zedekiah ruled after Jehoiachin. **three months.** The king's brief rule ended when Jerusalem surrendered on Mar. 15 or 16, 597 BC. (Cf. 2 Chr 36:9).

24:10 Nebuchadnezzar king of Babylon advanced on Jerusalem. The Babylonian Chronicle documents the capture of Jerusalem in 597 BC.

24:12 eighth year of the reign of the king of Babylon. The first time the book dates an event by the reign of a foreign ruler, signifying that Judah has lost its sovereignty.

24:13 As the LORD had declared. The author often points out both the prophecies of judgment as well as their fulfillments (e.g., 23:15 – 16; 1 Kgs 13:32; 21:19; 22:38). **removed the treasures.** Predicted in the reign of Hezekiah (20:17). King Belshazzar later profanes these sacred vessels in a banquet he gives on the night that Babylon falls (Dan 5:2 – 3).

24:14 carried all Jerusalem into exile. This is the second deportation; the first occurred in 605 BC (see note on v. 1). This second deportation includes the prophet Ezekiel (Ezek 1:2 – 3). By deporting the leaders, skilled craftsmen, and military personnel, Nebuchadnezzar strengthens his own economy and army while reducing the possibility of a future rebellion.

24:15 took Jehoiachin captive to Babylon. Fulfills Isaiah's prophecy to Hezekiah that his own descendants will be carried off to Babylon (20:18). It also fulfills Jeremiah's prophecy that Jehoiachin will be hurled out of the land of Israel (Jer 22:24 – 30).

also deported to Babylon the entire force of seven thousand fighting men, strong and fit for war, and
a thousand skilled workers and artisans.[q] 17 He made Mattaniah, Jehoiachin's uncle, king in his place
and changed his name to Zedekiah.[r]

Zedekiah King of Judah

24:18-20pp — 2Ch 36:11-16; Jer 52:1-3

18 Zedekiah[s] was twenty-one years old when he became king, and he reigned in Jerusalem eleven
years. His mother's name was Hamutal[t] daughter of Jeremiah; she was from Libnah. 19 He did evil in the
eyes of the LORD, just as Jehoiakim had done. 20 It was because of the LORD's anger that all this happened
to Jerusalem and Judah, and in the end he thrust[u] them from his presence.

The Fall of Jerusalem

25:1-12pp — Jer 39:1-10
25:1-21pp — 2Ch 36:17-20; Jer 52:4-27
25:22-26pp — Jer 40:7-9; 41:1-3,16-18

Now Zedekiah rebelled against the king of Babylon.
25 So in the ninth year of Zedekiah's reign, on the tenth day of the tenth month, Nebuchadnezzar[v] king of Babylon marched against Jerusalem with his whole army. He encamped outside
the city and built siege works[w] all around it. 2 The city was kept under siege until the eleventh year of
King Zedekiah.
3 By the ninth day of the fourth[a] month the famine[x] in the city had become so severe that there was
no food for the people to eat. 4 Then the city wall was broken through,[y] and the whole army fled at night
through the gate between the two walls near the king's garden, though the Babylonians[b] were surrounding[z] the city. They fled toward the Arabah,[c] 5 but the Babylonian[d] army pursued the king and overtook him
in the plains of Jericho. All his soldiers were separated from him and scattered,[a] 6 and he was captured.[b]
He was taken to the king of Babylon at Riblah,[c] where sentence was pronounced on him. 7 They
killed the sons of Zedekiah before his eyes. Then they put out his eyes, bound him with bronze shackles
and took him to Babylon.[d]

[a] *3* Probable reading of the original Hebrew text (see Jer. 52:6); Masoretic Text does not have *fourth.*
[b] *4* Or *Chaldeans*; also in verses 13, 25 and 26 [c] *4* Or *the Jordan Valley* [d] *5* Or *Chaldean*; also in verses 10 and 24

24:16 [q] Jer 52:28
24:17 [r] 1Ch 3:15; 2Ch 36:11; Jer 37:1
24:18 [s] Jer 52:1 [t] 2Ki 23:31
24:20 [u] Dt 4:26; 29:27
25:1 [v] Jer 34:1-7 [w] Eze 24:2
25:3 [x] Jer 14:18; La 4:9
25:4 [y] Eze 33:21 [z] Jer 4:17
25:5 [a] Eze 12:14
25:6 [b] Jer 34:21-22 [c] 2Ki 23:33
25:7 [d] Jer 21:7; 32:4-5; Eze 12:11

24:17 changed his name. See note on 23:34. **Zedekiah.** The third son of Josiah to sit on the throne (see note on v. 8). He does evil like his brothers.
24:18–20a *Zedekiah King of Judah.* Zedekiah's reign is characterized by idolatry and judgment. Additional details are given in Jer 32:1–5; 34; 37–38.
24:18 eleven years. 597–586 BC.
24:19 did evil. See 2 Chr 36:12–14.
24:20a the LORD's anger. Mentioned only three times in chs. 1–20 and nine times in chs. 21–24, the sin of the Israelites is about to result in divine judgment (13:3; 17:11,17; 21:6,15; 22:13,17; 23:19,26; 24:20). **he thrust them from his presence.** Judah's exile to Babylon is not another conquest in the history of nations but is the disciplinary action of a God faithful to fulfill his covenant promises to bless and judge.
24:20b—25:26 *The Fall of Jerusalem.* This extended treatment of the conquest of Jerusalem emphasizes the destruction and pillaging of the Lord's house. Under the curse of God for covenant disobedience, the people starve, the army scatters, and the king runs away. The poorest of the land are left behind to till the fields, but the rest are either killed or deported. The Babylonians appoint Gedaliah governor, but even this attempt at maintaining order fails when surviving rebels assassinate him. Those left alive flee back to Egypt, a sad conclusion for a people whom God had once delivered from there.
24:20b Zedekiah rebelled. Though Nebuchadnezzar placed him on the throne, Zedekiah may have grown weary of paying tribute and wrongly supposed that Babylon's campaigns elsewhere would prevent its return to Jerusalem. He may have chosen to rebel when the ambitious Hophra came to the Egyptian throne in 589 BC. Ezek 17:15–18 explains the folly of this action.
25:1 ninth year ... tenth month. Jan. 15, 588 BC. Jer 34:6–7 reports the conquest of some of the cities of Judah.
25:3 ninth day of the fourth month. July 18, 586 BC. **famine.** Predicted in Jer 38:2–9. Excavations in Jerusalem found evidence of the desperate dietary conditions in the final months of the Babylonian siege, including the presence of two human intestinal parasites associated with shortage of food.
25:4 fled. Contrasts with Joshua's valiant army that routed the Canaanites and reveals the tragic results of rebelling against the one who fought their battles for them. **gate.** Possibly the Fountain Gate at the southeastern corner of Jerusalem near the convergence of the Kidron and Hinnom Valleys (Neh 3:15). **Arabah.** The depression between the Sea of Galilee and the Dead Sea.
25:5 plains of Jericho. Judah's last king is captured near the place where the Israelites won their first great victory in Canaan (Josh 6). See note on Jer 39:5.
25:6 Riblah. See note on 23:33.
25:7 killed the sons of Zedekiah. To prevent a future uprising. **put out his eyes.** The last scene the king sees is the elimination of his family line. This fulfills the prophecies that Zedekiah would see the king of Babylon (Jer 32:4) and be carried off to Babylon but not see it (Ezek 12:13). Zedekiah disappears from the historical record at this point.

NEBUCHADNEZZAR'S CAMPAIGNS AGAINST JUDAH

605–586 BC

Events in Judah moved swiftly following the death of Josiah. Pharaoh Necho pressed his advantage by deporting Jehoahaz, the new ruler, and appointing a second son of Josiah, Jehoiakim, as king.

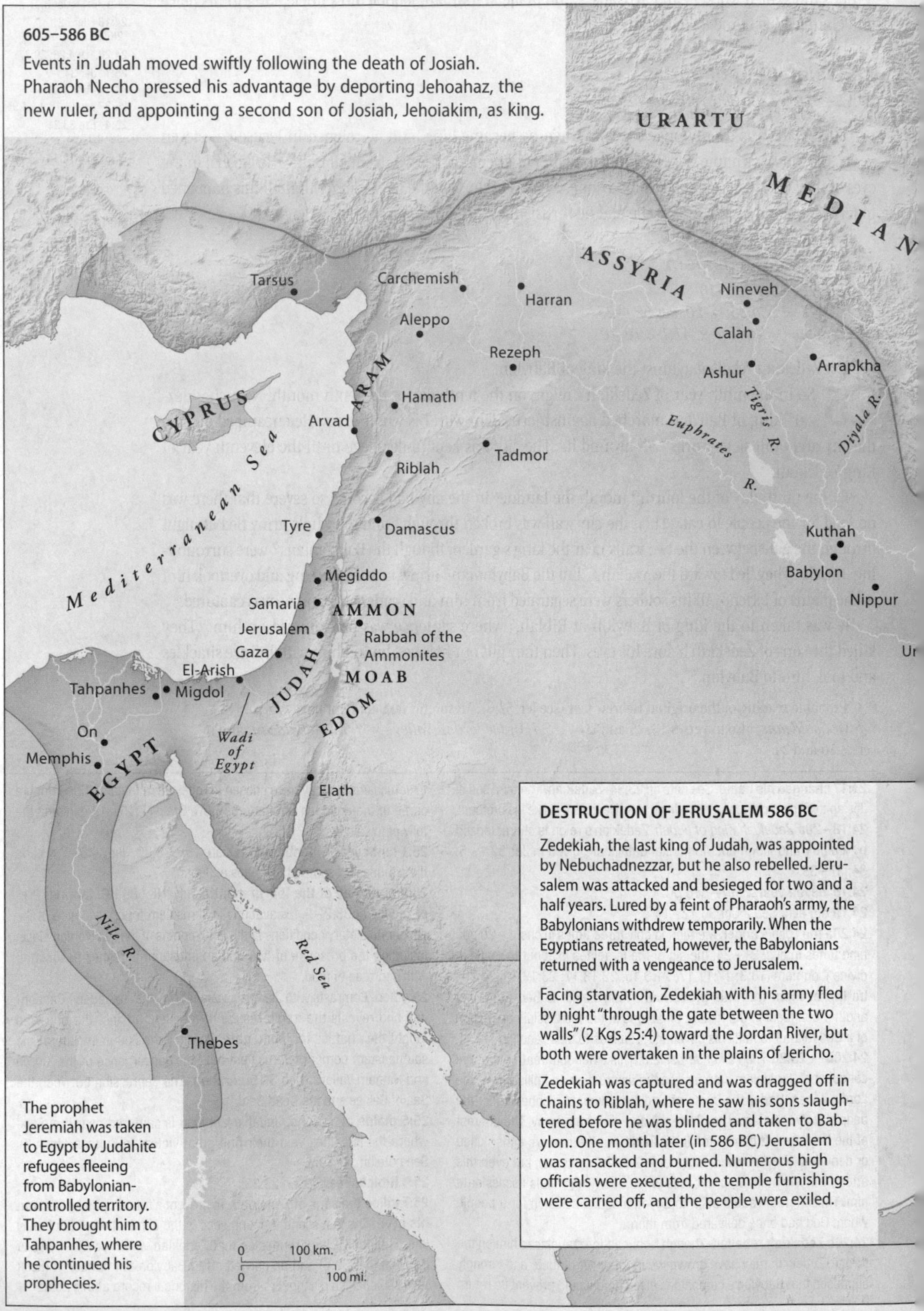

DESTRUCTION OF JERUSALEM 586 BC

Zedekiah, the last king of Judah, was appointed by Nebuchadnezzar, but he also rebelled. Jerusalem was attacked and besieged for two and a half years. Lured by a feint of Pharaoh's army, the Babylonians withdrew temporarily. When the Egyptians retreated, however, the Babylonians returned with a vengeance to Jerusalem.

Facing starvation, Zedekiah with his army fled by night "through the gate between the two walls" (2 Kgs 25:4) toward the Jordan River, but both were overtaken in the plains of Jericho.

Zedekiah was captured and was dragged off in chains to Riblah, where he saw his sons slaughtered before he was blinded and taken to Babylon. One month later (in 586 BC) Jerusalem was ransacked and burned. Numerous high officials were executed, the temple furnishings were carried off, and the people were exiled.

The prophet Jeremiah was taken to Egypt by Judahite refugees fleeing from Babylonian-controlled territory. They brought him to Tahpanhes, where he continued his prophecies.

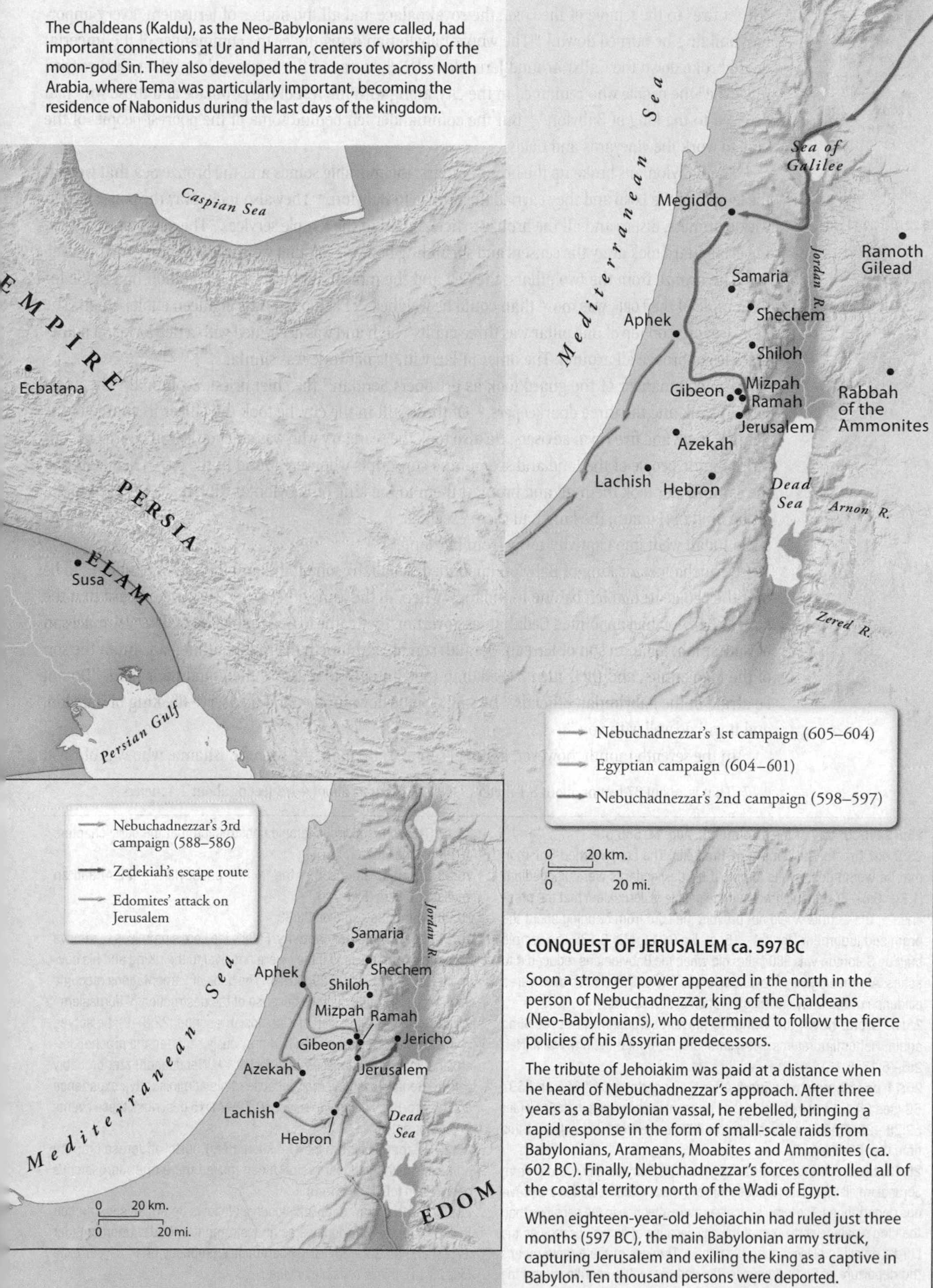

The Chaldeans (Kaldu), as the Neo-Babylonians were called, had important connections at Ur and Harran, centers of worship of the moon-god Sin. They also developed the trade routes across North Arabia, where Tema was particularly important, becoming the residence of Nabonidus during the last days of the kingdom.

CONQUEST OF JERUSALEM ca. 597 BC

Soon a stronger power appeared in the north in the person of Nebuchadnezzar, king of the Chaldeans (Neo-Babylonians), who determined to follow the fierce policies of his Assyrian predecessors.

The tribute of Jehoiakim was paid at a distance when he heard of Nebuchadnezzar's approach. After three years as a Babylonian vassal, he rebelled, bringing a rapid response in the form of small-scale raids from Babylonians, Arameans, Moabites and Ammonites (ca. 602 BC). Finally, Nebuchadnezzar's forces controlled all of the coastal territory north of the Wadi of Egypt.

When eighteen-year-old Jehoiachin had ruled just three months (597 BC), the main Babylonian army struck, capturing Jerusalem and exiling the king as a captive in Babylon. Ten thousand persons were deported.

25:9 [e]Isa 60:7 [f]Ps 74:3-8; Jer 2:15; Am 2:5; Mic 3:12
25:10 [g]Ne 1:3
25:11 [h]2Ki 24:14 [i]2Ki 24:1
25:12 [j]2Ki 24:14
25:14 [k]Ex 27:3; 1Ki 7:47-50
25:17 [l]1Ki 7:15-22
25:18 [m]1Ch 6:14; Ezr 7:1; Ne 11:11 [n]Jer 21:1; 29:25
25:21 [o]Ge 12:7; Dt 28:64; Jos 23:13; 2Ki 23:27
25:22 [p]Jer 39:14; 40:5,7

[8]On the seventh day of the fifth month, in the nineteenth year of Nebuchadnezzar king of Babylon, Nebuzaradan commander of the imperial guard, an official of the king of Babylon, came to Jerusalem. [9]He set fire[e] to the temple of the LORD, the royal palace and all the houses of Jerusalem. Every important building he burned down.[f] [10]The whole Babylonian army under the commander of the imperial guard broke down the walls[g] around Jerusalem. [11]Nebuzaradan the commander of the guard carried into exile[h] the people who remained in the city, along with the rest of the populace and those who had deserted to the king of Babylon.[i] [12]But the commander left behind some of the poorest people[j] of the land to work the vineyards and fields.

[13]The Babylonians broke up the bronze pillars, the movable stands and the bronze Sea that were at the temple of the LORD and they carried the bronze to Babylon. [14]They also took away the pots, shovels, wick trimmers, dishes and all the bronze articles[k] used in the temple service. [15]The commander of the imperial guard took away the censers and sprinkling bowls — all that were made of pure gold or silver.

[16]The bronze from the two pillars, the Sea and the movable stands, which Solomon had made for the temple of the LORD, was more than could be weighed. [17]Each pillar[l] was eighteen cubits[a] high. The bronze capital on top of one pillar was three cubits[b] high and was decorated with a network and pomegranates of bronze all around. The other pillar, with its network, was similar.

[18]The commander of the guard took as prisoners Seraiah[m] the chief priest, Zephaniah[n] the priest next in rank and the three doorkeepers. [19]Of those still in the city, he took the officer in charge of the fighting men, and five royal advisers. He also took the secretary who was chief officer in charge of conscripting the people of the land and sixty of the conscripts who were found in the city. [20]Nebuzaradan the commander took them all and brought them to the king of Babylon at Riblah. [21]There at Riblah, in the land of Hamath, the king had them executed.

So Judah went into captivity, away from her land.[o]

[22]Nebuchadnezzar king of Babylon appointed Gedaliah[p] son of Ahikam, the son of Shaphan, to be over the people he had left behind in Judah. [23]When all the army officers and their men heard that the king of Babylon had appointed Gedaliah as governor, they came to Gedaliah at Mizpah — Ishmael son of Nethaniah, Johanan son of Kareah, Seraiah son of Tanhumeth the Netophathite, Jaazaniah the son of the Maakathite, and their men. [24]Gedaliah took an oath to reassure them and their men. "Do not be afraid of the Babylonian officials," he said. "Settle down in the land and serve the king of Babylon, and it will go well with you."

[25]In the seventh month, however, Ishmael son of Nethaniah, the son of Elishama, who was of royal

[a] *17* That is, about 27 feet or about 8.1 meters [b] *17* That is, about 4 1/2 feet or about 1.4 meters

25:8 seventh day of the fifth month. Aug. 14, 586 BC.
25:9 set fire to the temple of the LORD. The Lord warned Solomon that he would destroy the temple if his descendants were disobedient (1 Kgs 9:6 – 8). Jeremiah warned the people of Jerusalem that the presence of the temple would not prevent the Lord from bringing about the promised judgment (Jer 7:4 – 15; cf. Isa 64:11; Mic 3:12). The temple built by Solomon was 380 years old when the Babylonians reduced it to ashes. Archaeological excavations in the City of David have discovered evidence of the Babylonian destruction of Jerusalem.
25:10 broke down the walls. To prevent Jerusalem from rebelling again. Nehemiah returns 140 years later to rebuild the city walls (Neh 2:5 – 6,17; 6:15).
25:11 people who remained. After the deportations of 605 and 597 BC (see 24:1,14 and notes), only a remnant is preserved in the city (Jer 52:28 – 29). The Babylonians deport 832 people from Jerusalem at this time (Jer 52:29).
25:13 carried the bronze to Babylon. The Babylonians remove from Jerusalem all the valuable pieces that they had not carried off in the previous deportations. The temple receives more attention in the narrative than the king's palace or the rest of the city because of its significance as the Lord's dwelling place among his people. The loss of the temple means the departure of God's presence, the end of atoning sacrifices, and the cessation of corporate worship. See "Temple," p. 2652.
25:17 Recalls the glorious temple construction that the early chapters of 1 Kings describe.
25:18 Seraiah. Grandson of the faithful priest Hilkiah (22:4) and an ancestor of Ezra (Ezra 7:1).
25:20 Riblah. See note on 23:33.
25:21 Judah went into captivity. Fulfills the Lord's promises to remove his people from the land if they were not loyal to their King and his covenant (Deut 4:26; 8:19 – 20; 30:18). The book of Lamentations recounts the nation's spiritual distress because of the destruction of Jerusalem.
25:22 Gedaliah. Grandson of King Josiah's scribe (22:8 – 9); he served in the royal courts as well and had previously escorted the prophet Jeremiah home from imprisonment (Jer 39:14). Nebuchadnezzar probably selects Gedaliah as governor because of his administrative experience and his pro-Babylonian views. Jer 40:7 — 41:15 describes these events in greater detail.
25:23 Mizpah. Eight miles (12 kilometers) north of Jerusalem; the administrative headquarters of Judah moved there after Jerusalem's destruction (cf. Jer 41:4 – 6).
25:24 Settle down. Gedaliah's counsel follows Jeremiah's instruction to submit to the Babylonians as an instrument of God's judgment (Jer 27:11; cf. Hab 2:2 – 20). Given Jeremiah's prophecy of a 70-year exile (Jer 25:11), this is sensible advice.
25:25 seventh month. Sept – Oct. The year is not clear. Because a

blood, came with ten men and assassinated Gedaliah and also the men of Judah and the Babylonians
who were with him at Mizpah. [26]At this, all the people from the least to the greatest, together with the
army officers, fled to Egypt[q] for fear of the Babylonians.

25:26 [q]Isa 30:2; Jer 43:7
25:27 [r]2Ki 24:12; Jer 52:31-34
25:28 [s]Ezr 5:5; Ne 2:1; Da 2:48
25:29 [t]2Sa 9:7
25:30 [u]Est 2:9; Jer 28:4

Jehoiachin Released

25:27-30pp — Jer 52:31-34

[27]In the thirty-seventh year of the exile of Jehoiachin king of Judah, in the year Awel-Marduk became
king of Babylon, he released Jehoiachin[r] king of Judah from prison. He did this on the twenty-seventh
day of the twelfth month. [28]He spoke kindly to him and gave him a seat of honor[s] higher than those
of the other kings who were with him in Babylon. [29]So Jehoiachin put aside his prison clothes and for
the rest of his life ate regularly at the king's table.[t] [30]Day by day the king gave Jehoiachin a regular
allowance as long as he lived.[u]

---

period of two months since the fall of Jerusalem seems too little time for everything to transpire (25:8), this may refer to the following year or even five years later when the Babylonians deport an additional group of Jews (Jer 52:30). Judahites who later return from the exile commemorate Gedaliah's assassination annually with a fast in the seventh month (Zech 7:5; 8:19). **Ishmael ... assassinated Gedaliah.** Ishmael's royal pedigree may have motivated his assassination of Gedaliah, but Jer 40:14 reports that the Ammonite king commissioned him.

25:26 fled to Egypt. The assassins fear reprisal from the Babylonian authorities for murdering the governor they had appointed. By returning to Egypt, they disobey the Lord's explicit command (Jer 42:18). Jer 41:16—43:13 describes these events in greater detail.

25:27–30 *Jehoiachin Released.* Though the Babylonians have destroyed Jerusalem and its temple, the house of David continues to live on, indicating that though the book has come to a close, the Lord's plans continue for the covenant nation and the Messianic line. The nation that recalls Solomon's prayer at the dedication of the temple will know that turning back to the Lord will lead to forgiveness, restoration from exile, and the fulfillment of all of God's promises (1 Kgs 8:46–51; cf. Deut 30:1–10; Jer 31:23–40).

25:27 Awel-Marduk. Nebuchadnezzar's son and successor; he ruled 562–560 BC. **released Jehoiachin.** At age 55. He was carried off at age 18 and outlived his captor, Nebuchadnezzar. Though the author does not explain that this happened "for the sake of David," the reader is expected to understand this given the repeated statements that God's grace to the evil kings of Judah was on account of his promises to David (8:19; 19:34; 20:6; 1 Kgs 11:12–13,32–39; 15:4).

25:28 a seat of honor higher than those of the other kings. Jehoiachin's prominence provides hope that God will yet fulfill his promise to establish David's house and kingdom forever (2 Sam 7:16).

25:29 ate regularly at the king's table. The former king of Judah receives food, clothing, and housing. A Babylonian administrative text that lists the rations provided for Jehoiachin and his five sons confirms the biblical account.

INTRODUCTION TO 1 CHRONICLES

The books of 1 and 2 Chronicles were originally one book that the translators of the Septuagint (the pre-Christian Greek translation of the OT) separated into two. They showcase the grace of God and the incomparable value of a God-centered life. Unfortunately, 1 – 2 Chronicles are among the most neglected books of the Bible.

AUTHOR

1 – 2 Chronicles does not indicate its author. The most common issue considered in the authorship of Chronicles is the relationship between the author(s) of Chronicles and Ezra-Nehemiah. Jewish tradition understood Ezra to be the author of 1 – 2 Chronicles, Ezra, and Nehemiah. Those who propose a common author (typically Ezra) emphasize similarity in vocabulary and Hebrew syntax, a penchant for source citations and lists, overlapping ideological and theological concerns (such as the temple and priests), and Ezra-Nehemiah picking up where 2 Chronicles ends (cf. 2 Chr 36:23 with Ezra 1:1 – 4).

There are also a number of distinctions between Chronicles and Ezra-Nehemiah, such as the level of attention directed to the Davidic monarchy (high in Chronicles, low in Ezra-Nehemiah), the Sabbath (low in Chronicles, high in Ezra-Nehemiah), and the prophetic office (high in Chronicles, low in Ezra-Nehemiah). Such points of difference have caused some to reject the view of a common author for Chronicles and Ezra-Nehemiah, although these differences may be due to the variety of sources integrated by the Chronicler and the period of history being described.

Identifying the author(s) of Chronicles remains an unsettled area of biblical scholarship. Since God determined Chronicles to be part of the Bible as an anonymous work, it seems fitting to refer to the (human) author(s) as "the Chronicler" and focus on the theological message of the book.

DATE

The setting of 1 – 2 Chronicles is the postexilic community of Judah. But the specific time of the writing of Chronicles remains open to debate. Proposals span from the Persian time frame (539 – 333 BC) to the Greek/Hellenistic time frame (333 – 166 BC) to the Maccabean/Hasmonean time frame (166 – 63 BC). The extent of Zerubbabel's family line (1 Chr 3:19 – 24), along with the Jews' resettling in Jerusalem after the exile (cf. 1 Chr 9:1 – 34 with Neh 11:1 — 12:26), indicates a date following (or toward the end of) the reforms of Ezra and Nehemiah (ca. 450 – 430 BC). The language and content of Chronicles does not reflect a Greek setting, indicating that the text was composed before 333 BC. All together, these observations suggest a range of 430 – 340 BC for the writing of Chronicles. The earlier side of this range (ca. 430 – 400 BC) might be preferable as it would place the completion of Chronicles before a time of significant unrest in the Levant in the early fourth century BC caused by Egyptian revolts against Persia.

PLACE OF COMPOSITION AND DESTINATION

The Babylonian destruction of Jerusalem in 586 BC was followed by large-scale deportations and exile in Babylon (Ps 137:1 – 6). After the Persian takeover of the Babylonian Empire in 539 BC, all of what had been Judah (and the northern kingdom) fell under an administrative unit (satrap) of the Persian Empire known by the geographic description "beyond the [Euphrates] River." Within this large region was the small province of Judah (*Yehud* in Aramaic; Ezra 5:8). The decree of Cyrus in 539 BC enabled those exiled to Babylon to return to their homeland and rebuild their communities (2 Chr 36:22 – 23; Ezra 2:1 – 35; Neh 7:5 – 73). While still under the authority of the Persian Empire, the province of Judah was granted some degree of political autonomy.

Before long, the euphoria following the decree of Cyrus gave way to the reality of the bleak situation in Judah as the returnees faced the daunting challenge of rebuilding homes, cities, social infrastructure, and the temple. Nonetheless, spurred on by the ministries of Haggai and Zechariah, work on the temple was restarted and completed in 516 or 515 BC (Ezra 6:14 – 15), resulting in another high point of optimism within the postexilic community. In time, however, the situation in Judah again became bleak (Neh 1:1 – 3), leading to the appointment of Nehemiah as governor (Neh 2:1 – 18; 5:14) and the commissioning of Ezra in the realm of religious affairs (Ezra 7:25 – 26). The leadership and rebuilding organized by Nehemiah and the spiritual revival facilitated by Ezra fostered a new era of hope and optimism. This mood of optimism was enhanced by territorial gains and the fortification and repopulation of Jerusalem. However, the end of the Ezra-Nehemiah time frame was punctuated with spiritual and societal problems (Neh 6:1 – 14; 13:4 – 28). Thus, once again, a time of hope and promise in Judah gave way to challenge and discouragement. The writing of Chronicles follows this latest downturn of hope and optimism.

Although the Chronicler's time frame may be one of disappointment, he nonetheless proclaims a message of hope and possibility. The Chronicler's review of the "whole divine history" functions to shape the theological awareness of the postexilic Judahite community — much as the book of Deuteronomy recaps "divine history" for the generation born during the "exile" in the wilderness wanderings and waiting to enter the promised land. Both Deuteronomy and Chronicles are situated in the aftermath of divine judgment that included prolonged time outside the land of promise. Both emphasize hope and possibility for a covenant community wholehearted in their commitment to the Lord. Both exhort people to remember and obey their covenantal relationship with God while recounting God's faithful acts. The recounting of the past encourages people to consider the present and pursue faithfulness in the future (Rom 15:4; Heb 11).

Beth Shan is the location of the temple of Dagon mentioned in 1 Chr 10:10. The Philistine and Israelite cities were at the top of the tell (tall mound of dirt).

PARTICULAR CHALLENGES

Challenges with Chronicles typically involve comparison with parallel (synoptic) passages from 2 Samuel and 1–2 Kings. One's approach to synoptic issues goes hand in hand with preexisting views of biblical inspiration and inerrancy.

Issues Involving Numbers

There is complete agreement in numbers between Chronicles and parallel texts in 195 out of 213 instances, but they differ in the remaining 18. In some cases, differences reflect a distinction in the basis of counting or reckoning. For example, the Chronicler has a different tabulation in 1 Chr 9:6 from that found in Neh 11:6 (690 versus 468) that may relate to a different approach to counting (Neh 11:6 counts "men of standing," whereas 1 Chr 9:6 reads "people"). Similar explanations can be posited for the difference in the number of priests in 1 Chr 9:13 and Neh 11:12–14 and census numbers in 1 Chr 21:5 and 2 Sam 24:9.

Another issue that involves numbers is the large numbers of soldiers mentioned at different points in 1–2 Chronicles (e.g., 1 Chr 21:5; 2 Chr 11:1; 14:8; 17:14–18; 26:13). The numbers mentioned in these texts (ranging from 200,000 to 1,100,000 soldiers) are considerably higher than the listings of other ancient Near Eastern armies. The Hebrew term translated "thousand" (*'elep*) may refer to military fighting units or tribal leaders rather than the quantity 1,000 (see Num 10:4; Josh 22:13–14,21,30; Zech 9:7; 12:5–6; see also Introduction to Numbers: Interpretive Issues, 3). Several passages imply that *'elep* is a unit that is smaller than a tribe (1 Sam 10:19; 23:23; Mic 5:2) and larger than a family (Judg 6:15). Using this approach, a figure such as this in 2 Chr 14:8: "three hundred thousand" (300,000) may be intended to convey "300 [military] units." Estimates for these military units range from 10–30 soldiers each, perhaps in analogy to the units of the "three" and the "thirty" used to describe David's core military leadership (1 Chr 11:10–47).

Other synoptic issues involving numbers are simply stylistic differences, such as rounding numbers, as reflected in the following summaries of David's reign: "He ruled over Israel forty years—seven in Hebron and thirty-three in Jerusalem" (1 Chr 29:27). "In Hebron he reigned over Judah seven years and six months, and in Jerusalem he reigned over all Israel and Judah thirty-three years" (2 Sam 5:5). Instances in rounding may also explain differing numbers of military figures, such as the notation of 470,000 versus 500,000 men of Judah in Joab's census (1 Chr 21:5 versus 2 Sam 24:9).

Issues Resulting From Scribal Copying

Synoptic differences may relate to the process of copying biblical books. When Christians refer to the inspiration of Scripture, they are referring to the originally crafted manuscripts of biblical books (called "autographs"), not scribal transmission of the biblical texts. By the sovereign will of God, the transmission process was not inerrant, and consequently there are variations in the manuscripts of biblical books. For example, 2 Sam 24:13 has "seven" years in the Hebrew text (Masoretic Text) rather than the "three" years recorded at 1 Chr 21:12. Nonetheless, the NIV translates "three" at 2 Sam 24:13 given the Septuagint (the pre-Christian Greek translation of the OT) at this verse as well as the parallel text here (see NIV text note on 2 Sam 24:13). While these variations are statistically miniscule, they do factor into some synoptic divergences. Careful textual criticism typically brings the correct reading to light.

Issues Involving Perspective

Synoptic differences may reflect a different point of reference or perspective that is not mutually exclusive. For example, note the following statements regarding the ascension of Solomon: "Solomon sat on the throne of his father David" (1 Kgs 2:12); "Solomon sat on the throne of the LORD" (1 Chr 29:23). These statements, while different, are both true. The statement in Kings stresses God's faithfulness to fulfill his promise with respect to the Davidic covenant, while Chronicles stresses God's kingship and the role of the Israelite king as undershepherd to God. Likewise, the inciting of David (cf. 1 Chr 21:1 and 2 Sam 24:1) reminds us that the agency of God and the actions of a supernatural adversary can operate in parallel (as seen in Job 1–2), as can the agency of God and a human adversary (1 Kgs 11:14,23).

In addition, the Chronicler emphasizes the involvement of "all Israel" in important spiritual events in line with his focus on the whole covenantal community. For example, the taking of Jerusalem in Samuel (2 Sam 5:6–10) focuses on the efforts of a small band of warriors, while the Chronicler notes the involvement of "all the Israelites" in this important event (1 Chr 11:4–8). Likewise, the Chronicler notes the involvement of the community in the relocation of the ark of the covenant to Jerusalem (1 Chr 13 versus 2 Sam 6). Lastly, the presentation of Manasseh in Kings summarizes the spiritual infidelity that characterized the vast majority of Manasseh's reign (2 Kgs 21), while the account in Chronicles showcases the forgiving and reconciling nature of God (2 Chr 33) in line with the Chronicler's message of covenantal hope for God's people.

Distinctions and differences between texts should not be held against one text or the other; differing parallel texts may simply reflect selectivity, shaping, and emphasis in line with particular authorial intent (such as thematic or theological emphasis) in a given passage.

OCCASION AND PURPOSE

The text of Chronicles extends from Adam (1 Chr 1:1) through the Persian king Cyrus (2 Chr 36:22–23). But the genealogical section at the beginning of Chronicles (1 Chr 1–9) actually extends *beyond* the time frame of 2 Chr 36 and into the postexilic setting (1 Chr 3:19–24). In a sense, the Chronicler tells the book's literary-theological message first as a genealogy and then as a story. The structure of Chronicles shows that while its *historical* time frame is postexilic, the *theological* time frame is exilic. That is to say, while the text was composed (or at least completed) in the postexilic time frame, the book of Chronicles nevertheless *ends on the eve of the postexilic time frame* (see "The Persian Empire and Postexilic Judah," this page).

GENRE

The OT books we know as 1 and 2 Chronicles have carried a variety of names over time. The Hebrew title of Chronicles is *dibrē-hayyāmîm* (translated "the book of the annals" at 1 Chr 27:24). The name of Chronicles in the Septuagint (the pre-Christian Greek translation of the OT) is *Paraleipomenōn tōn basileōn Iouda*, which means the "things omitted concerning the kings of Judah." This title influenced the relocation of Chronicles in the Christian Bible from the end of the OT to just after 1–2 Kings. This placement unfortunately suggests that the purpose of Chronicles is simply to provide supplemental information for Samuel and Kings rather than have its own literary-theological message. By comparison, the name for Chronicles in the Latin Vulgate is *Chronicon* (or *Chronikon*) *Totius Divinae Historiae*, meaning "Chronicle of the Total Divine History," suggesting a wide-ranging engagement of God's involvement in human history. This title gave rise to the name "Chronicles," used today in English translations.

Chronicles is a chronographic or annalistic text. Understanding Chronicles through the lens of an annal aids in understanding Chronicles as theological history. Annals are historical accounts written with narrative shaping and ideology. Annals feature the use of other genres such as lists, genealogies, temple records, and other archival documents. The selectivity and literary-narrative shaping of such sources is interpretively significant as compositional

THE PERSIAN EMPIRE AND POSTEXILIC JUDAH

RULER	REIGN (BC)	SIGNIFICANT EVENTS
Cyrus	559–530	Founded Persian Empire; issued the decree of Cyrus (539 BC) allowing conquered peoples to return to their native countries (*Timeframe of Daniel and Sheshbazzar; second temple's foundation laid 538 BC*)
Theological Setting of Chronicles: Eve of the Return From Exile		
Cambyses	530–522	Conquered Egypt in 525 BC
Darius I	522–486	Increased strength of Persian Empire; unsuccessful attempt at conquering Greece (*Timeframe of Haggai and Zechariah; second temple completed and dedicated during the timeframe of Zerubbabel, 516 or 515 BC*)
Xerxes I (Ahasuerus)	486–465	Destroyed Babylon in 482 BC; another unsuccessful Greek invasion; murdered in 465 BC (*Timeframe of Esther*)
Artaxerxes I	465–424	Faced six-year Egyptian rebellion; signed a peace treaty with Greece (*Timeframe of Ezra and Nehemiah*)
Likely Date of Writing/Completion of Chronicles: 430–400 BC		
Darius II	423–404	Gained control of Asia Minor after Peloponnesian War
Artaxerxes II	404–358	Egypt regained independence; significant revolts in the Levant
Artaxerxes III	358–338	Reconquered Egypt
Darius III	336–333	Decline of the Persian Empire; falls to Alexander the Great (Greek Empire) in 333 BC

strategy reveals authorial purpose and theological message. Even the genealogical survey of Chronicles (1 Chr 1–9) exhibits selectivity (note the absence of various individuals such as Seth and listings with multiples of seven) and shaping (note the presenting of family lines in such a way as to end with the person through whom God's redemptive plan unfolds). Sources cited in Chronicles include the following:

- The genealogical records during the reigns of Jotham king of Judah and Jeroboam king of Israel (1 Chr 5:17)
- The genealogies recorded in the book of the kings of Israel and Judah (1 Chr 9:1)
- The book of the annals of King David (1 Chr 27:24)
- The records of Samuel the seer (1 Chr 29:29)
- The records of Nathan the prophet (1 Chr 29:29; 2 Chr 9:29)
- The records of Gad the seer (1 Chr 29:29)
- The prophecy of Ahijah the Shilonite (2 Chr 9:29)
- The visions of Iddo the seer (2 Chr 9:29)
- The records of Shemaiah the prophet and of Iddo the seer that deal with genealogies (2 Chr 12:15)
- The annotations of the prophet Iddo (2 Chr 13:22)
- The book of the kings of Judah and Israel (2 Chr 16:11; 25:26; 28:26; 32:32)
- The annals of Jehu son of Hanani (2 Chr 20:34)
- The book of the kings of Israel (2 Chr 20:34)
- The annotations on the book of the kings (2 Chr 24:27)
- The book of the kings of Israel and Judah (2 Chr 27:7; 35:27; 36:8)
- The words of David and of Asaph the seer (2 Chr 29:30)
- The annals of the kings of Israel (2 Chr 33:18)
- The records of the seers (2 Chr 33:19)
- The instructions written by David king of Israel and by his son Solomon (2 Chr 35:4)

Many of the sources have a prophetic connection, reflecting the role of the prophet in declaring God's truth and mediating the covenant between God and Israel.

THEMES AND THEOLOGY

The central theme of Chronicles is covenant hope and possibility based in God's faithfulness.

Chronicles tells the story of all Israel through the lens of the Davidic promise and the Jerusalem temple. A theology of covenantal hope and possibility guides the selection, shaping, and structure of the Chronicler's message. With this in mind, commentators frequently stress the Chronicler's tendency to cover the history of Judah from a positive light. While this positive orientation is true to an extent, given the Chronicler's focus on covenantal hope, this perspective can be overstated as Chronicles includes significant instances of covenantal unfaithfulness (cf. 1 Chr 15:13; 21:7; 2 Chr 16; 19:1–3; 20:37). The Chronicler's emphasis on the "good days" of Judah is consistent with his intent of spurring hope and covenantal faithfulness, while his presentation of the shortcomings of people and leaders ensures that the focus of his audience is on God, not man.

The very different context of Chronicles from that of Samuel-Kings should be kept in mind. The account of the kingdoms of Israel and Judah in Samuel and Kings addresses the questions of those in exile who had experienced the destruction of Jerusalem and the temple, the removal of a Davidic ruler, and exile. Chronicles, however, addresses the postexilic community and reminds them of their heritage as God's people and the meaning of God's promises for them, notably the hope of the restoration of the Davidic monarchy as God's people seek him in prayer, humility, and obedience (e.g., 1 Chr 17:3–14; 2 Chr 7:12–22). The account of Manasseh highlights this hope of restoration.

For the Chronicler, the Levitical priesthood and the Davidic monarchy operate in tandem. The Chronicler's extended presentation of the Jerusalem temple is intertwined with the Chronicler's extended treatment of David and Solomon. As the temple had been rebuilt by the Chronicler's time, the Chronicler lays out the possibility and hope that the Davidic dynasty will be restored as well.

The Chronicler's stress on the Davidic covenant (1 Chr 17; 2 Sam 7) is reflected in the accounts of David and Solomon, which occupy 28 out of the 65 chapters of 1–2 Chronicles. The Davidic covenant focuses on David's son Solomon as ruler and temple builder (2 Chr 6:6–10) but also transcends a human king. The Aaronic priestly covenant (Num 25:10–13; Mal 2:4–7) is connected to the Mosaic covenant and focuses on the role of the priests in mediating reconciliation between God and people and teaching God's people all the decrees the Lord had given them (cf. 1 Chr 6; 16; 24–26). Idealized depictions of Judahite kings such as David, Solomon, Asa, Jehoshaphat, Hezekiah,

Mount Gilboa, where Saul died (1 Chr 10:8).
Todd Bolen/www.BiblePlaces.com

and Josiah function as a literary-theological means of hope for the coming of a promised son of David who would reign in Jerusalem. This ideal leader would embody truth and righteousness (Deut 17:14 – 20). For Christian readers of Chronicles, this hope has ultimate fulfillment in Jesus Christ, the Son of God and descendant of David, who embodied divine presence and perfect righteousness and in grace and love brought about reconciliation between God and humankind that is open to all peoples of the earth and whose authority will culminate in an everlasting kingdom.

The centrality of reconciliation and divine presence in the spiritual vibrancy and covenant fidelity of Israel is seen in the extended treatment of the Jerusalem temple. The importance of a temple relates to the notion of sacred space — a place where the human realm could intersect with the divine realm and facilitate atonement, divine presence, and blessing. The careful attention to the design of the temple and stipulations pertaining to the temple reflects the importance of properly respecting God's holiness. In short, building a temple for the Lord is a spiritual exercise as much as it is a building enterprise (1 Chr 22:11 – 13). The essence of Solomon's temple dedication prayer (2 Chr 6:12 – 42) is that God hear the prayers of the people (both Israelites and foreigners). Prayer and repentance are central to the Chronicler's message of true spirituality. Grace, forgiveness, and reconciliation are the focus of the Jerusalem temple (where the shedding of blood for sin would take place). As the episode of Manasseh shows, there is no limit to divine grace (2 Chr 33:12 – 13).

Repeated exhortations to be strong and courageous remind readers/hearers of the same words spoken to Joshua (Josh 1:5 – 9). Being strong and courageous is based on God's presence, a reality greater than any challenge an individual might face. Exhortations to devote heart and soul to seeking God are inseparably connected with obedience to God's word (1 Chr 22:17 – 19; 2 Chr 14:4; cf. the words of Christ in John 15:10,14). God's presence enables such obedience. Reminders of God's faithfulness encourage leaders and people that God will complete the good work he has begun in the covenantal life of Israel. Conversely, the fundamental issue behind covenantal unfaithfulness is lack of setting one's heart to seek God. For Israel's leaders, the distinction of whether or not a king sets his heart on seeking God establishes the trajectory of that king's reign.

Lastly, the Chronicler is careful to emphasize that deeper internal issues such as faithfulness, obedience, and personal purity must coincide with external acts of worship. The core of God's revealed will through the Sinaitic/Mosaic covenant (Exod 19 – 20; Lev 26; Deut 28) taught what was pleasing to God within the context of the Israelite covenant community and was based in loving God with all one's heart (Deut 6:5) and one's neighbor as oneself (Lev 19:18). The Chronicler repeatedly focuses on God and his covenantal faithfulness and reconciling nature. Even God's chastening has a teaching function ("teach them the right way to live," 2 Chr 6:27) as well as a sanctifying function ("so that they will fear you and walk in obedience to you," 2 Chr 6:31). This perspective makes the tone of Chronicles didactic, almost sermonic, in its literary style and presentation. The final sentence of the Chronicler's work ("you may go up," 2 Chr 36:23) leaves the audience with anticipation of what might happen next and the realization that they (the Chronicler's audience) are the ones who will finish this story. Thus, the Chronicler ends his work with a message of the hope and possibility that comes with covenantal faithfulness (Jer 29:11 – 13).

OUTLINE

I. Genealogies: From Adam to Saul (1 Chr 1:1—9:44)
- A. From Adam to the Sons of Israel (1:1—2:2)
- B. The Tribes of Israel (2:3—7:40)
  - 1. Judah (2:3—4:23)
  - 2. Simeon (4:24–43)
  - 3. The Transjordan Tribes (5:1–26)
    - a. Reuben (5:1–10)
    - b. Gad (5:11–22)
    - c. Manasseh (5:23–26)
  - 4. Levi (6:1–81)
  - 5. The Northern Tribes (7:1–40)
    - a. Issachar (7:1–5)
    - b. Benjamin (7:6–12)
    - c. Naphtali (7:13)
    - d. Manasseh (7:14–19)
    - e. Ephraim (7:20–29)
    - f. Asher (7:30–40)
- C. The Genealogy of Saul the Benjamite (8:1–40)
- D. Genealogical Summary (9:1)
- E. Postexilic Resettlement in Jerusalem (9:2–34)
- F. The Genealogy of Saul (9:35–44)

II. The Decline of Saul and the Rise of David (10:1–14)

III. The Reign of David (11:1—29:30)
- A. David's Enthronement and Consolidation of Power (11:1—12:40)
- B. Return of the Ark of the Covenant (13:1—16:43)
- C. The Davidic Covenant (17:1–27)
- D. David's Military Victories and Regional Power (18:1—20:8)
- E. David's Census and Selection of the Temple Site (21:1—22:1)
- F. David's Temple Preparations and Leadership Transfer (22:2—29:30)

IV. The Reign of Solomon and the Construction of the Temple (2 Chr 1:1—9:31)
- A. Solomon's Wisdom, Wealth, and Power (1:1–17)
- B. Construction and Dedication of the Jerusalem Temple (2:1—7:22)
- C. Solomon's Other Activities (8:1–18)
- D. The Queen of Sheba Visits Solomon (9:1–12)
- E. Solomon's Splendor (9:13–28)
- F. Solomon's Death (9:29–31)

V. The Divided Monarchy (10:1—36:19)
- A. The Reign of Rehoboam and the Division of the Kingdom (10:1—12:16)
- B. Abijah King of Judah (13:1—14:1)
- C. Asa King of Judah (14:2—16:14)
- D. Jehoshaphat King of Judah (17:1—21:3)
- E. Jehoram King of Judah (21:4–20)
- F. Ahaziah King of Judah (22:1–9)
- G. The Coup and Rule of Queen Athaliah (22:10—23:21)
- H. Joash King of Judah (24:1–27)
- I. Amaziah King of Judah (25:1–28)
- J. Uzziah King of Judah (26:1–23)
- K. Jotham King of Judah (27:1–9)
- L. Ahaz King of Judah (28:1–27)

M. The Reign of Hezekiah (29:1 — 32:33)
  1. Hezekiah Purifies the Temple (29:1 – 36)
  2. Hezekiah Celebrates the Passover (30:1 — 31:1)
  3. Contributions for Worship (31:2 – 21)
  4. Sennacherib Threatens Jerusalem (32:1 – 23)
  5. Hezekiah's Pride, Success, and Death (32:24 – 33)
N. Manasseh King of Judah (33:1 – 20)
O. Amon King of Judah (33:21 – 25)
P. The Reign of Josiah (34:1 — 36:1)
  1. Josiah's Reforms and the Discovery of the Book of the Law (34:1 – 33)
  2. Josiah Celebrates the Passover (35:1 – 19)
  3. Josiah's Confrontation With Pharaoh Necho and Death (35:20 — 36:1)
Q. Jehoahaz King of Judah (36:2 – 4)
R. Jehoiakim King of Judah (36:5 – 8)
S. Jehoiachin King of Judah (36:9 – 10)
T. The Reign of Zedekiah and the Fall of Jerusalem (36:11 – 19)

VI. The Exilic Period (36:20 – 21)

VII. The Decree of Cyrus (36:22 – 23)

1 CHRONICLES

1:1 [a] Ge 5:1-32; Lk 3:36-38
1:2 [b] Ge 5:9 [c] Ge 5:12 [d] Ge 5:15
1:3 [e] Ge 5:18; Jude 1:14 [f] Ge 5:21 [g] Ge 5:25 [h] Ge 5:29
1:4 [i] Ge 6:10; 10:1 [j] Ge 5:32

Historical Records From Adam to Abraham

To Noah's Sons

1 Adam,[a] Seth, Enosh, 2 Kenan,[b] Mahalalel,[c] Jared,[d] 3 Enoch,[e] Methuselah,[f] Lamech,[g] Noah.[h]

4 The sons of Noah:[a][i]
Shem, Ham and Japheth.[j]

The Japhethites
1:5-7pp — Ge 10:2-5

5 The sons[b] of Japheth:
Gomer, Magog, Madai, Javan, Tubal, Meshek and Tiras.
6 The sons of Gomer:
Ashkenaz, Riphath[c] and Togarmah.
7 The sons of Javan:
Elishah, Tarshish, the Kittites and the Rodanites.

The Hamites
1:8-16pp — Ge 10:6-20

8 The sons of Ham:
Cush, Egypt, Put and Canaan.

[a] *4* Septuagint; Hebrew does not have this line. [b] *5* *Sons* may mean *descendants* or *successors* or *nations;* also in verses 6-9, 17 and 23. [c] *6* Many Hebrew manuscripts and Vulgate (see also Septuagint and Gen. 10:3); most Hebrew manuscripts *Diphath*

1:1 — 9:44 *Genealogies: From Adam to Saul.* The Chronicler uses two primary types of genealogies: (1) Linear genealogies trace part of a family line, particularly those through whom God is advancing his purposes (see the Davidic kings in 3:10 – 16; see Abram in Gen 11:10 – 26). (2) Segmented genealogies provide supplementary information through a limited survey of descendants from a single ancestor (the Ishmaelites in Gen 25:12 – 18; the Edomites in 1 Chr 1:38 – 42). A significant theological element conveyed through the Chronicler's genealogical survey is the continuity of God's covenantal promises. His survey reminds his audience of their connection with Abraham, Moses, and David. The extension of the genealogy beyond the time of the exile shows that God's promises are still in effect. Mention of key tribal units from both sides of the long-divided Israelite kingdom reinforces the message of unity and covenantal hope. Thus, while the survey reviews the *past,* it also works to produce hope in God at the *present* because of the covenantal possibilities for the *future.*

1:1 — 2:2 *From Adam to the Sons of Israel.* This largely summarizes the genealogies of the book of Genesis, bringing the reader quickly from Adam to the descendants of Esau. In between, the Chronicler provides snippets of ethnic and historical information that work to ultimately place Jacob/Israel in the midst of the nations.

1:1 – 4 The Chronicler begins his account of Israel's history with the first man, Adam, connecting his account with the beginning of history as well as the beginning of the Bible (Genesis). The Chronicler's approach is similar to how Luke 3:23 – 38 presents Christ. The list of names from Adam to Noah and his sons derives from Gen 5.

1:5 – 27 This section draws from the table of nations (Gen 10:2 – 29) and summarizes the geopolitical expanse of the descendants of Noah following the flood up to Abraham. The Chronicler presents the genealogies in reverse chronological (birth) order to focus on the divinely chosen line of Shem-Abraham.

1:5 Japheth. His descendants (vv. 5 – 7) occupied the coastal regions of the Mediterranean Sea (Javan = Greece) as well as inland areas (Tubal).

1:8 Ham. His descendants (vv. 8 – 16) occupied the northern areas of Africa (Egypt and Cush) as well as the Levant (Jebus; Sidon; Hamath).

[9]The sons of Cush:
Seba, Havilah, Sabta, Raamah and Sabteka.
The sons of Raamah:
Sheba and Dedan.
[10]Cush was the father[a] of
Nimrod, who became a mighty warrior on earth.
[11]Egypt was the father of
the Ludites, Anamites, Lehabites, Naphtuhites, [12]Pathrusites, Kasluhites (from whom the Phi-
listines came) and Caphtorites.
[13]Canaan was the father of
Sidon his firstborn,[b] and of the Hittites, [14]Jebusites, Amorites, Girgashites, [15]Hivites, Arkites,
Sinites, [16]Arvadites, Zemarites and Hamathites.

The Semites

1:17-23pp — Ge 10:21-31; 11:10-27

[17]The sons of Shem:
Elam, Ashur, Arphaxad, Lud and Aram.
The sons of Aram:[c]
Uz, Hul, Gether and Meshek.
[18]Arphaxad was the father of Shelah,
and Shelah the father of Eber.
[19]Two sons were born to Eber:
One was named Peleg,[d] because in his time the earth was divided; his brother was named
Joktan.
[20]Joktan was the father of
Almodad, Sheleph, Hazarmaveth, Jerah, [21]Hadoram, Uzal, Diklah, [22]Obal,[e] Abimael, Sheba,
[23]Ophir, Havilah and Jobab. All these were sons of Joktan.

[24]Shem,[k] Arphaxad,[f] Shelah,
[25]Eber, Peleg, Reu,
[26]Serug, Nahor, Terah
[27]and Abram (that is, Abraham).

1:24 [k]Ge 10:21-25; Lk 3:34-36

The Family of Abraham

[28]The sons of Abraham:
Isaac and Ishmael.

Descendants of Hagar

1:29-31pp — Ge 25:12-16

[29]These were their descendants:
Nebaioth the firstborn of Ishmael, Kedar, Adbeel, Mibsam, [30]Mishma, Dumah, Massa, Hadad,
Tema, [31]Jetur, Naphish and Kedemah. These were the sons of Ishmael.

[a] 10 *Father* may mean *ancestor* or *predecessor* or *founder*; also in verses 11, 13, 18 and 20. [b] 13 Or *of the Sidonians, the foremost* [c] 17 One Hebrew manuscript and some Septuagint manuscripts (see also Gen. 10:23); most Hebrew manuscripts do not have this line. [d] 19 *Peleg* means *division.* [e] 22 Some Hebrew manuscripts and Syriac (see also Gen. 10:28); most Hebrew manuscripts *Ebal* [f] 24 Hebrew; some Septuagint manuscripts *Arphaxad, Cainan* (see also note at Gen. 11:10)

1:17 Shem. His descendants (vv. 17–27) occupied northeastern Canaan (Aram), Mesopotamia (Ashur = Assyria), the area east of Mesopotamia (Elam) as well as desert regions (Sheba).

1:24–27 This unit retraces and expands the Semitic line (descendants of Shem) to focus on the line of Abraham (see note on vv. 5–27).

1:28–34 The Chronicler shapes his genealogical presentation to end with an individual central to God's redemptive plan: Israel (i.e., Jacob). As the Chronicler did earlier with the sons of Noah, he first summarizes the horizontal genealogy of Ishmael before turning to that of Isaac. The summary of the family line of Hagar/Ishmael draws from Gen 25:12–18. The family of Ishmael settled in the wilderness regions south of what later became Israel (Gen 25:18), while the other sons of Abraham were sent off to "the land of the east" (Gen 25:6).

1:32 [l]Ge 22:24 [m]Ge 10:7
1:34 [n]Lk 3:34 [o]Ge 21:2-3; Mt 1:2; Ac 7:8 [p]Ge 17:5; 25:25-26
1:35 [q]Ge 36:19 [r]Ge 36:4
1:36 [s]Ex 17:14
1:37 [t]Ge 36:17
1:40 [u]Ge 36:2

Descendants of Keturah
1:32-33pp — Ge 25:1-4

32 The sons born to Keturah, Abraham's concubine:[l]
Zimran, Jokshan, Medan, Midian, Ishbak and Shuah.
The sons of Jokshan:
Sheba and Dedan.[m]
33 The sons of Midian:
Ephah, Epher, Hanok, Abida and Eldaah.
All these were descendants of Keturah.

Descendants of Sarah
1:35-37pp — Ge 36:10-14

34 Abraham[n] was the father of Isaac.[o]
The sons of Isaac:
Esau and Israel.[p]

Esau's Sons

35 The sons of Esau:[q]
Eliphaz, Reuel,[r] Jeush, Jalam and Korah.
36 The sons of Eliphaz:
Teman, Omar, Zepho,[a] Gatam and Kenaz;
by Timna: Amalek.[b][s]
37 The sons of Reuel:[t]
Nahath, Zerah, Shammah and Mizzah.

The People of Seir in Edom
1:38-42pp — Ge 36:20-28

38 The sons of Seir:
Lotan, Shobal, Zibeon, Anah, Dishon, Ezer and Dishan.
39 The sons of Lotan:
Hori and Homam. Timna was Lotan's sister.
40 The sons of Shobal:
Alvan,[c] Manahath, Ebal, Shepho and Onam.
The sons of Zibeon:
Aiah and Anah.[u]
41 The son of Anah:
Dishon.
The sons of Dishon:
Hemdan,[d] Eshban, Ithran and Keran.
42 The sons of Ezer:
Bilhan, Zaavan and Akan.[e]
The sons of Dishan[f]:
Uz and Aran.

[a] *36* Many Hebrew manuscripts, some Septuagint manuscripts and Syriac (see also Gen. 36:11); most Hebrew manuscripts *Zephi* [b] *36* Some Septuagint manuscripts (see also Gen. 36:12); Hebrew *Gatam, Kenaz, Timna and Amalek* [c] *40* Many Hebrew manuscripts and some Septuagint manuscripts (see also Gen. 36:23); most Hebrew manuscripts *Alian* [d] *41* Many Hebrew manuscripts and some Septuagint manuscripts (see also Gen. 36:26); most Hebrew manuscripts *Hamran* [e] *42* Many Hebrew and Septuagint manuscripts (see also Gen. 36:27); most Hebrew manuscripts *Zaavan, Jaakan* [f] *42* See Gen. 36:28; Hebrew *Dishon,* a variant of *Dishan*

1:35—2:2 The expanded coverage of Esau underscores the close connection historically and theologically between Israel/Jacob and Esau (Obad 21; Mal 1:2–5; Rom 9:13). The summary of Esau's lineage and the related histories of Edom and Seir (vv. 35–54) closely reflect the content of Gen 36. The account of the two sons of Isaac ends by listing the 12 sons of Israel (2:1–2), who will constitute the geographic organization of the future nation that will likewise be named Israel. Thus, the opening of ch. 2 (vv. 1–2) both concludes ch. 1 and sets up ch. 2.

The Rulers of Edom

1:43-54pp — Ge 36:31-43

43 These were the kings who reigned in Edom before any Israelite king reigned:
Bela son of Beor, whose city was named Dinhabah.
44 When Bela died, Jobab son of Zerah from Bozrah succeeded him as king.
45 When Jobab died, Husham from the land of the Temanites[v] succeeded him as king.
46 When Husham died, Hadad son of Bedad, who defeated Midian in the country of Moab, succeeded him as king. His city was named Avith.
47 When Hadad died, Samlah from Masrekah succeeded him as king.
48 When Samlah died, Shaul from Rehoboth on the river[a] succeeded him as king.
49 When Shaul died, Baal-Hanan son of Akbor succeeded him as king.
50 When Baal-Hanan died, Hadad succeeded him as king. His city was named Pau,[b] and his wife's name was Mehetabel daughter of Matred, the daughter of Me-Zahab. 51 Hadad also died.

The chiefs of Edom were:
Timna, Alvah, Jetheth, 52 Oholibamah, Elah, Pinon, 53 Kenaz, Teman, Mibzar, 54 Magdiel and Iram. These were the chiefs of Edom.

Israel's Sons

2:1-2pp — Ge 35:23-26

2 These were the sons of Israel:
Reuben, Simeon, Levi, Judah, Issachar, Zebulun, 2 Dan, Joseph, Benjamin, Naphtali, Gad and Asher.

Judah

2:5-15pp — Ru 4:18-22; Mt 1:3-6

To Hezron's Sons

3 The sons of Judah:[w]
Er, Onan and Shelah.[x] These three were born to him by a Canaanite woman, the daughter of Shua.[y] Er, Judah's firstborn, was wicked in the LORD's sight; so the LORD put him to death.[z]
4 Judah's daughter-in-law[a] Tamar[b] bore Perez[c] and Zerah to Judah. He had five sons in all.

5 The sons of Perez:[d]
Hezron[e] and Hamul.
6 The sons of Zerah:
Zimri, Ethan, Heman, Kalkol and Darda[c] — five in all.
7 The son of Karmi:
Achar,[d f] who brought trouble on Israel by violating the ban on taking devoted things.[e g]
8 The son of Ethan:
Azariah.
9 The sons born to Hezron[h] were:
Jerahmeel, Ram and Caleb.[f]

[a] *48* Possibly the Euphrates [b] *50* Many Hebrew manuscripts, some Septuagint manuscripts, Vulgate and Syriac (see also Gen. 36:39); most Hebrew manuscripts *Pai* [c] *6* Many Hebrew manuscripts, some Septuagint manuscripts and Syriac (see also 1 Kings 4:31); most Hebrew manuscripts *Dara* [d] *7* *Achar* means *trouble*; *Achar* is called *Achan* in Joshua. [e] *7* The Hebrew term refers to the irrevocable giving over of things or persons to the LORD, often by totally destroying them. [f] *9* Hebrew *Kelubai*, a variant of *Caleb*

1:45 [v] Ge 36:11
2:3 [w] Ge 29:35; 38:2-10 [x] Ge 38:5 [y] Ge 38:2 [z] Nu 26:19
2:4 [a] Ge 11:31 [b] Ge 38:11-30 [c] Ge 38:29
2:5 [d] Ge 46:12 [e] Nu 26:21
2:7 [f] Jos 7:1 [g] Jos 6:18
2:9 [h] Nu 26:21

2:3—7:40 *The Tribes of Israel.* After listing the 12 sons of Jacob/Israel (2:1–2), the Chronicler pursues the lineage of these tribes in chs. 2–8, with focus on the tribes of Judah (2:3—4:23) and Levi (ch. 6). The Chronicler also provides a detailed account of the tribe of Benjamin (in separated blocks: 7:6–12; 8:1–40; 9:35–44), partly to provide the backdrop for Saul's reign.

2:3—4:23 *Judah.* The Chronicler treats the tribe of Judah first and most extensively. This literary and theological preeminence of Judah relates to the Chronicler's attention to the Davidic monarchy that shapes his presentation of Israel's past history and future hope.

2:3–9 This section gives the genealogy for the five sons of Judah, building on the events of Gen 38 and other earlier family lists (Gen 46:12; Num 26:19–22). Although Judah was the fourth born of Jacob's less favored wife Leah, he nonetheless becomes the conduit for the Davidic dynasty. Together with the presentation of God's restorative grace is the reality of God's distaste for unfaithfulness (vv. 3,7).

2:10 [l]Lk 3:32-33 [j]Ex 6:23 [k]Nu 1:7
2:12 [l]Ru 2:1 [m]Ru 4:17
2:13 [n]Ru 4:17 [o]1Sa 16:6
2:16 [p]1Sa 26:6 [q]2Sa 2:18 [r]2Sa 2:13
2:17 [s]2Sa 17:25
2:19 [t]ver 42,50
2:20 [u]Ex 31:2
2:21 [v]Nu 27:1
2:23 [w]Nu 32:41; Dt 3:14; Jos 13:30 [x]Nu 32:42
2:24 [y]1Ch 4:5

From Ram Son of Hezron

10 Ram[i] was the father of
Amminadab[j], and Amminadab the father of Nahshon,[k] the leader of the people of Judah.
11 Nahshon was the father of Salmon,[a] Salmon the father of Boaz, 12 Boaz[l] the father of Obed
and Obed the father of Jesse.[m]

13 Jesse[n] was the father of
Eliab[o] his firstborn; the second son was Abinadab, the third Shimea, 14 the fourth Nethanel,
the fifth Raddai, 15 the sixth Ozem and the seventh David. 16 Their sisters were Zeruiah[p] and
Abigail. Zeruiah's[q] three sons were Abishai, Joab[r] and Asahel. 17 Abigail was the mother of Amasa,[s] whose father was Jether the Ishmaelite.

Caleb Son of Hezron

18 Caleb son of Hezron had children by his wife Azubah (and by Jerioth). These were her sons: Jesher,
Shobab and Ardon. 19 When Azubah died, Caleb[t] married Ephrath, who bore him Hur. 20 Hur
was the father of Uri, and Uri the father of Bezalel.[u]

21 Later, Hezron, when he was sixty years old, married the daughter of Makir the father of Gilead.[v]
He made love to her, and she bore him Segub. 22 Segub was the father of Jair, who controlled
twenty-three towns in Gilead. 23 (But Geshur and Aram captured Havvoth Jair,[b][w] as well as
Kenath[x] with its surrounding settlements — sixty towns.) All these were descendants of Makir
the father of Gilead.

24 After Hezron died in Caleb Ephrathah, Abijah the wife of Hezron bore him Ashhur[y] the father[c] of
Tekoa.

Jerahmeel Son of Hezron

25 The sons of Jerahmeel the firstborn of Hezron:
Ram his firstborn, Bunah, Oren, Ozem and[d] Ahijah. 26 Jerahmeel had another wife, whose
name was Atarah; she was the mother of Onam.

27 The sons of Ram the firstborn of Jerahmeel:
Maaz, Jamin and Eker.

28 The sons of Onam:
Shammai and Jada.
The sons of Shammai:
Nadab and Abishur.

29 Abishur's wife was named Abihail, who bore him Ahban and Molid.

30 The sons of Nadab:
Seled and Appaim. Seled died without children.

31 The son of Appaim:
Ishi, who was the father of Sheshan.
Sheshan was the father of Ahlai.

32 The sons of Jada, Shammai's brother:
Jether and Jonathan. Jether died without children.

[a] *11* Septuagint (see also Ruth 4:21); Hebrew *Salma* [b] *23* Or *captured the settlements of Jair*
[c] *24* *Father* may mean *civic leader* or *military leader*; also in verses 42, 45, 49-52 and possibly elsewhere.
[d] *25* Or *Oren and Ozem, by*

2:10–17 Verses 10–12 reflect the genealogy leading to David in Ruth 4:18–22. This genealogical summary shows that the military leaders Joab, Abishai, and Amasa (vv. 16–17) were related to each other as well as to King David.

2:15 the seventh David. 1 Sam 17:12–14 refers to David as the eighth (and youngest) son of Jesse. While the reason for this difference is not certain, the account in Samuel may be counting a half brother or even a child that died at a young age. 1 Chr 27:18 may mention another son of Jesse.

2:18–24 This genealogy has little to no parallel data in the OT.

2:20 Bezalel. He was "filled ... with the Spirit of God, with wisdom, with understanding, with knowledge and with all kinds of skills" (Exod 31:3) in the context of building the tabernacle in the wilderness.

2:21,23 father of Gilead. Being "father" of a city reflects a position of leadership within that city.

2:24 father of Tekoa. See note on vv. 21,23.

33 The sons of Jonathan:
Peleth and Zaza.
These were the descendants of Jerahmeel.
34 Sheshan had no sons — only daughters.
He had an Egyptian servant named Jarha. 35 Sheshan gave his daughter in marriage to his
servant Jarha, and she bore him Attai.
36 Attai was the father of Nathan,
Nathan the father of Zabad,[z]
37 Zabad the father of Ephlal,
Ephlal the father of Obed,
38 Obed the father of Jehu,
Jehu the father of Azariah,
39 Azariah the father of Helez,
Helez the father of Eleasah,
40 Eleasah the father of Sismai,
Sismai the father of Shallum,
41 Shallum the father of Jekamiah,
and Jekamiah the father of Elishama.

The Clans of Caleb

42 The sons of Caleb[a] the brother of Jerahmeel:
Mesha his firstborn, who was the father of Ziph, and his son Mareshah,[*a*] who was the father
of Hebron.
43 The sons of Hebron:
Korah, Tappuah, Rekem and Shema. 44 Shema was the father of Raham, and Raham the father
of Jorkeam. Rekem was the father of Shammai. 45 The son of Shammai was Maon[b], and Maon
was the father of Beth Zur.[c]
46 Caleb's concubine Ephah was the mother of Haran, Moza and Gazez. Haran was the father of
Gazez.
47 The sons of Jahdai:
Regem, Jotham, Geshan, Pelet, Ephah and Shaaph.
48 Caleb's concubine Maakah was the mother of Sheber and Tirhanah. 49 She also gave birth to
Shaaph the father of Madmannah[d] and to Sheva the father of Makbenah and Gibea. Caleb's
daughter was Aksah.[e] 50 These were the descendants of Caleb.

The sons of Hur[f] the firstborn of Ephrathah:
Shobal the father of Kiriath Jearim,[g] 51 Salma the father of Bethlehem, and Hareph the father
of Beth Gader.
52 The descendants of Shobal the father of Kiriath Jearim were:
Haroeh, half the Manahathites, 53 and the clans of Kiriath Jearim: the Ithrites,[h] Puthites, Shu-
mathites and Mishraites. From these descended the Zorathites and Eshtaolites.
54 The descendants of Salma:
Bethlehem, the Netophathites,[i] Atroth Beth Joab, half the Manahathites, the Zorites, 55 and the
clans of scribes[*b*] who lived at Jabez: the Tirathites, Shimeathites and Sucathites. These are the
Kenites[j] who came from Hammath,[k] the father of the Rekabites.[*c*][l]

[*a*] *42* The meaning of the Hebrew for this phrase is uncertain. [*b*] *55* Or *of the Sopherites* [*c*] *55* Or *father of Beth Rekab*

2:36 [z] 1Ch 11:41
2:42 [a] ver 19
2:45 [b] Jos 15:55 [c] Jos 15:58
2:49 [d] Jos 15:31 [e] Jos 15:16
2:50 [f] 1Ch 4:4 [g] ver 19
2:53 [h] 2Sa 23:38
2:54 [i] Ezr 2:22; Ne 7:26; 12:28
2:55 [j] Ge 15:19; Jdg 1:16; Jdg 4:11 [k] Jos 19:35 [l] 2Ki 10:15, 23; Jer 35:2-19

2:34 Egyptian servant named Jarha. See note on 4:18.
2:42–55 A number of these descendants of Caleb are connected with cities that play a significant role in the history of Israel (Hebron, v. 42; Kiriath Jearim, v. 53; Bethlehem, v. 54).
2:54 the Netophathites. Later associated with two of David's mighty men (11:30; 2 Sam 23:28–29). The town of Netophah served as a home to Levitical singers during the postexilic period (Neh 12:27–28).
2:55 the Kenites. Not ethnically Israelites (Gen 15:18–21) but "grafted in" to the tribe of Judah (cf. Rom 11:17), demonstrating God's trans-ethnic redemptive plan (Gen 12:1–3).

The Sons of David

3:1-4pp — 2Sa 3:2-5
3:5-8pp — 2Sa 5:14-16; 1Ch 14:4-7

3 These were the sons of David[m] born to him in Hebron:
The firstborn was Amnon the son of Ahinoam of Jezreel;[n]
the second, Daniel the son of Abigail[o] of Carmel;
2 the third, Absalom the son of Maakah daughter of Talmai king of Geshur;
the fourth, Adonijah[p] the son of Haggith;
3 the fifth, Shephatiah the son of Abital;
and the sixth, Ithream, by his wife Eglah.
4 These six were born to David in Hebron,[q] where he reigned seven years and six months.[r]
David reigned in Jerusalem thirty-three years, 5 and these were the children born to him there:
Shammua,[a] Shobab, Nathan and Solomon. These four were by Bathsheba[b][s] daughter of Ammiel.
6 There were also Ibhar, Elishua,[c] Eliphelet, 7 Nogah, Nepheg, Japhia, 8 Elishama, Eliada
and Eliphelet — nine in all. 9 All these were the sons of David, besides his sons by his concubines.
And Tamar[t] was their sister.[u]

The Kings of Judah

10 Solomon's son was Rehoboam,[v]
Abijah his son,
Asa his son,
Jehoshaphat[w] his son,
11 Jehoram[d][x] his son,
Ahaziah[y] his son,
Joash[z] his son,
12 Amaziah[a] his son,
Azariah his son,
Jotham[b] his son,
13 Ahaz[c] his son,
Hezekiah[d] his son,
Manasseh[e] his son,
14 Amon[f] his son,
Josiah[g] his son.
15 The sons of Josiah:
Johanan the firstborn,
Jehoiakim[h] the second son,
Zedekiah[i] the third,
Shallum[j] the fourth.
16 The successors of Jehoiakim:
Jehoiachin[e][k] his son,
and Zedekiah.[l]

3:1 [m] 1Ch 14:3; 28:5 [n] Jos 15:56 [o] 1Sa 25:42
3:2 [p] 1Ki 2:22
3:4 [q] 2Sa 5:4; 1Ch 29:27 [r] 2Sa 2:11; 5:5
3:5 [s] 2Sa 11:3; 12:24
3:9 [t] 2Sa 13:1 [u] 1Ch 14:4
3:10 [v] 1Ki 11:43; 14:21-31; 2Ch 12:16 [w] 2Ch 17:1-21:3
3:11 [x] 2Ki 8:16-24; 2Ch 21:1 [y] 2Ch 22:1-10 [z] 2Ki 11:1-12:21
3:12 [a] 2Ki 14:1-22; 2Ch 25:1-28 [b] Isa 1:1; Hos 1:1; Mic 1:1
3:13 [c] 2Ki 16:1-20; 2Ch 28:1; Isa 7:1 [d] 2Ki 18:1-20:21; 2Ch 29:1; Jer 26:19 [e] 2Ch 33:1
3:14 [f] 2Ki 21:19-26; 2Ch 33:21; Zep 1:1 [g] 2Ch 34:1; Jer 1:2; 3:6; 25:3
3:15 [h] 2Ki 23:34 [i] Jer 37:1 [j] 2Ki 23:31
3:16 [k] 2Ki 24:6,8; Mt 1:11 [l] 2Ki 24:18

[a] *5* Hebrew *Shimea,* a variant of *Shammua* [b] *5* One Hebrew manuscript and Vulgate (see also Septuagint and 2 Samuel 11:3); most Hebrew manuscripts *Bathshua* [c] *6* Two Hebrew manuscripts (see also 2 Samuel 5:15 and 1 Chron. 14:5); most Hebrew manuscripts *Elishama* [d] *11* Hebrew *Joram,* a variant of *Jehoram* [e] *16* Hebrew *Jeconiah,* a variant of *Jehoiachin*; also in verse 17

3:1–9 This summary lists sons of David born in Hebron (vv. 1–4a) and Jerusalem (vv. 4b–9). This genealogical information was likely gleaned from lists in 2 Samuel (e.g., 2 Sam 3:2–5; 5:13–16). The fact that each wife is associated with only one son suggests the Chronicler drew his information from a list of firstborn sons. These sons do not include those born via concubines.

3:5 Solomon. His placement last in the listing of the sons of Bathsheba is similar to the Chronicler's earlier genealogies. This arrangement places the successor in the final (emphatic) position (see note on 1:28–34).

3:9 Tamar. Mentioning only one daughter means not that David had only one daughter but that this daughter figured into the story line of the royal family (2 Sam 13).

3:10–16 This second section of the Davidic line lists Davidic kings during the divided kingdom period (931/30–722 BC) and the time after the fall of the northern kingdom (722–586 BC).

The Royal Line After the Exile

[17] The descendants of Jehoiachin the captive:
Shealtiel[m] his son, [18] Malkiram, Pedaiah, Shenazzar,[n] Jekamiah, Hoshama and Nedabiah.[o]
[19] The sons of Pedaiah:
Zerubbabel[p] and Shimei.
The sons of Zerubbabel:
Meshullam and Hananiah.
Shelomith was their sister.
[20] There were also five others:
Hashubah, Ohel, Berekiah, Hasadiah and Jushab-Hesed.
[21] The descendants of Hananiah:
Pelatiah and Jeshaiah, and the sons of Rephaiah, of Arnan, of Obadiah and of Shekaniah.
[22] The descendants of Shekaniah:
Shemaiah and his sons:
Hattush,[q] Igal, Bariah, Neariah and Shaphat — six in all.
[23] The sons of Neariah:
Elioenai, Hizkiah and Azrikam — three in all.
[24] The sons of Elioenai:
Hodaviah, Eliashib, Pelaiah, Akkub, Johanan, Delaiah and Anani — seven in all.

This sixth-century BC seal reads, "Pedaiah, son of the king" (1 Chr 3:19).
Z. Radovan/www.BibleLandPictures.com

3:17 [m] Ezr 3:2
3:18 [n] Ezr 1:8; 5:14 [o] Jer 22:30
3:19 [p] Ezr 2:2; 3:2; 5:2; Ne 7:7; 12:1; Hag 1:1; 2:2; Zec 4:6
3:22 [q] Ezr 8:2-3
4:1 [r] Ge 29:35; 46:12; 1Ch 2:3 [s] Nu 26:21
4:4 [t] 1Ch 2:50 [u] Ru 1:19
4:5 [v] 1Ch 2:24

Other Clans of Judah

4 The descendants of Judah:[r]
Perez, Hezron,[s] Karmi, Hur and Shobal.
[2] Reaiah son of Shobal was the father of Jahath, and Jahath the father of Ahumai and Lahad. These were the clans of the Zorathites.
[3] These were the sons[a] of Etam:
Jezreel, Ishma and Idbash. Their sister was named Hazzelelponi. [4] Penuel was the father of Gedor, and Ezer the father of Hushah.
These were the descendants of Hur,[t] the firstborn of Ephrathah and father[b] of Bethlehem.[u]
[5] Ashhur[v] the father of Tekoa had two wives, Helah and Naarah.
[6] Naarah bore him Ahuzzam, Hepher, Temeni and Haahashtari. These were the descendants of Naarah.
[7] The sons of Helah:
Zereth, Zohar, Ethnan, [8] and Koz, who was the father of Anub and Hazzobebah and of the clans of Aharhel son of Harum.

[9] Jabez was more honorable than his brothers. His mother had named him Jabez,[c] saying, "I gave birth to him in pain." [10] Jabez cried out to the God of Israel, "Oh, that you would bless me and enlarge

[a] *3* Some Septuagint manuscripts (see also Vulgate); Hebrew *father* *military leader*; also in verses 12, 14, 17, 18 and possibly elsewhere.
[b] *4* *Father* may mean *civic leader* or
[c] *9* *Jabez* sounds like the Hebrew for *pain.*

3:17–24 This final section of the Davidic line is a summary of the royal line during and after the exile (sixth–fifth/fourth centuries BC). The ability to trace these "descendants of Jehoiachin" (v. 17) was important for encouraging hope in God's plans for the house of David. This list extends into the postexilic period, perhaps even to the time of the Chronicler. **3:19 Pedaiah.** Zerubbabel's father here, but Shealtiel is Zerubbabel's father in Ezra 3:2 (cf. Matt 1:12). This inconsistency cannot be solved definitively but may relate to a dual understanding of the term *father* (birth father versus one who raised/discipled him) or the outworking of a Levirate marriage following the death of Shealtiel. The Septuagint (the pre-Christian Greek translation of the OT) reads "Shealtiel" here instead of "Pedaiah." **Zerubbabel.** Though his leadership corresponded with renewed prophetic hope that God was restoring the Davidic line in Judah (Zech 4; Hag 2:20–23) — a hope ultimately fulfilled in Christ (Matt 22:42; Luke 1:32; Acts 15:16) — Zerubbabel did not fill the office of king (Hag 1:1; cf. Jer 22:30). But the hope of restoration of the Davidic dynasty may be reflected in the names of Zerubbabel's sons (Meshullam [v. 19] means "restored" and Jushab-Hesed [v. 20] means "covenant loving-kindness returns").
4:9–10 This short commentary on Jabez does not connect with the surrounding genealogical material. It is the only mention of the person Jabez in the Bible (Jabez in 2:55 is a place-name). It provides a theological message through its placement within the genealogy of the Israelite tribes, perhaps in conjunction with territory and pastureland

4:13 [w] Jos 15:17
4:17 [x] Ex 15:20
4:18 [y] Jos 15:34
4:19 [z] Jos 15:44 [a] Dt 3:14
4:21 [b] Ge 38:5
4:24 [c] Ge 29:33
[d] Nu 26:12

my territory! Let your hand be with me, and keep me from harm so that I will be free from pain." And
God granted his request.

11 Kelub, Shuhah's brother, was the father of Mehir, who was the father of Eshton. 12 Eshton was the
father of Beth Rapha, Paseah and Tehinnah the father of Ir Nahash.[a] These were the men of
Rekah.

13 The sons of Kenaz:
Othniel[w] and Seraiah.
The sons of Othniel:
Hathath and Meonothai.[b] 14 Meonothai was the father of Ophrah.
Seraiah was the father of Joab,
the father of Ge Harashim.[c] It was called this because its people were skilled workers.
15 The sons of Caleb son of Jephunneh:
Iru, Elah and Naam.
The son of Elah:
Kenaz.
16 The sons of Jehallelel:
Ziph, Ziphah, Tiria and Asarel.
17 The sons of Ezrah:
Jether, Mered, Epher and Jalon. One of Mered's wives gave birth to Miriam,[x] Shammai and Ish-
bah the father of Eshtemoa. 18 (His wife from the tribe of Judah gave birth to Jered the father of
Gedor, Heber the father of Soko, and Jekuthiel the father of Zanoah.[y]) These were the children
of Pharaoh's daughter Bithiah, whom Mered had married.
19 The sons of Hodiah's wife, the sister of Naham:
the father of Keilah[z] the Garmite, and Eshtemoa the Maakathite.[a]
20 The sons of Shimon:
Amnon, Rinnah, Ben-Hanan and Tilon.
The descendants of Ishi:
Zoheth and Ben-Zoheth.
21 The sons of Shelah[b] son of Judah:
Er the father of Lekah, Laadah the father of Mareshah and the clans of the linen workers
at Beth Ashbea, 22 Jokim, the men of Kozeba, and Joash and Saraph, who ruled in Moab and
Jashubi Lehem. (These records are from ancient times.) 23 They were the potters who lived at
Netaim and Gederah; they stayed there and worked for the king.

Simeon

4:28-33pp — Jos 19:2-10

24 The descendants of Simeon:[c]
Nemuel, Jamin, Jarib,[d] Zerah and Shaul;
25 Shallum was Shaul's son, Mibsam his son and Mishma his son.

[a] *12* Or *of the city of Nahash* [b] *13* Some Septuagint manuscripts and Vulgate; Hebrew does not have *and Meonothai.* [c] *14* *Ge Harashim* means *valley of skilled workers.*

("bless me and enlarge my territory"). For possible connections, see vv. 13–16,34–43; 5:3–10.

4:9 more honorable. Perhaps because he sought God through prayer. God blessed him in a way that transcended the meaning of his name (see NIV text note). Thus, the Chronicler's message may be that in light of the pain and reduced territory of the postexilic setting, God's people should seek him in prayer and faithfulness. The prayer of Jabez is not a formulaic blueprint for achieving spiritual blessings. The motivation to pray in order to *get* reflects a focus on self that is inconsistent with the example of Christ and the teachings of the NT (Luke 9:23; 1 Cor 13:5; Phil 2:1–11).

4:13 Othniel. Israel's first judge (Judg 3:9–11). Along with Caleb, he helped expand the territory of Israel (cf. the prayer of Jabez, vv. 9–10).

4:18 Bithiah. She may have been Egyptian royalty ("Pharaoh's daughter"). As Isaiah notes, God's ultimate redemptive plan includes Israelites, Egyptians, and Assyrians serving him shoulder to shoulder (Isa 19:18–25). The chosen line of Judah includes Egyptians (Bithiah [here] and Jarha [2:34–35]), Canaanites (Tamar [Gen 38:6] and Rahab [Josh 2:1]), and a Moabite (Ruth [Ruth 1:4]). This presentation highlights God's plan to bless "all peoples on earth" (Gen 12:3).

4:24–43 *Simeon.* The history of Simeon was intertwined with that of Judah given Simeon's territory being located within that of Judah (Josh 19:1–9). Over the course of time, Simeon was subsumed into Judah

26 The descendants of Mishma:

Hammuel his son, Zakkur his son and Shimei his son.

27 Shimei had sixteen sons and six daughters, but his brothers did not have many children; so their entire clan did not become as numerous as the people of Judah. 28 They lived in Beersheba,[e] Moladah,[f] Hazar Shual, 29 Bilhah, Ezem,[g] Tolad, 30 Bethuel, Hormah,[h] Ziklag, 31 Beth Markaboth, Hazar Susim, Beth Biri and Shaaraim.[i] These were their towns until the reign of David. 32 Their surrounding villages were Etam, Ain,[j] Rimmon, Token and Ashan[k] — five towns — 33 and all the villages around these towns as far as Baalath.[a] These were their settlements. And they kept a genealogical record.

34 Meshobab, Jamlech, Joshah son of Amaziah, 35 Joel, Jehu son of Joshibiah, the son of Seraiah, the son of Asiel, 36 also Elioenai, Jaakobah, Jeshohaiah, Asaiah, Adiel, Jesimiel, Benaiah, 37 and Ziza son of Shiphi, the son of Allon, the son of Jedaiah, the son of Shimri, the son of Shemaiah.

38 The men listed above by name were leaders of their clans. Their families increased greatly, 39 and they went to the outskirts of Gedor[l] to the east of the valley in search of pasture for their flocks. 40 They found rich, good pasture, and the land was spacious, peaceful and quiet.[m] Some Hamites had lived there formerly.

41 The men whose names were listed came in the days of Hezekiah king of Judah. They attacked the Hamites in their dwellings and also the Meunites[n] who were there and completely destroyed[b] them, as is evident to this day. Then they settled in their place, because there was pasture for their flocks. 42 And five hundred of these Simeonites, led by Pelatiah, Neariah, Rephaiah and Uzziel, the sons of Ishi, invaded the hill country of Seir.[o] 43 They killed the remaining Amalekites[p] who had escaped, and they have lived there to this day.

Reuben

5 The sons of Reuben[q] the firstborn of Israel (he was the firstborn, but when he defiled his father's marriage bed,[r] his rights as firstborn were given to the sons of Joseph[s] son of Israel;[t] so he could not be listed in the genealogical record in accordance with his birthright,[u] 2 and though Judah[v] was the strongest of his brothers and a ruler[w] came from him, the rights of the firstborn[x] belonged to Joseph) — 3 the sons of Reuben[y] the firstborn of Israel:

Hanok, Pallu,[z] Hezron and Karmi.

[a] *33* Some Septuagint manuscripts (see also Joshua 19:8); Hebrew *Baal* [b] *41* The Hebrew term refers to the irrevocable giving over of things or persons to the LORD, often by totally destroying them.

4:28 [e] Ge 21:14 [f] Jos 15:26
4:29 [g] Jos 15:29
4:30 [h] Nu 14:45
4:31 [i] Jos 15:36
4:32 [j] Nu 34:11 [k] Jos 15:42
4:39 [l] Jos 15:58
4:40 [m] Jdg 18:7-10
4:41 [n] 2Ch 20:1; 26:7
4:42 [o] Ge 14:6
4:43 [p] 1Sa 15:8; 30:17; 2Sa 8:12; Est 3:1; 9:16
5:1 [q] Ge 29:32 [r] Ge 35:22; 49:4 [s] Ge 48:16,22; 49:26 [t] Ge 48:5 [u] 1Ch 26:10
5:2 [v] Ge 49:10,12 [w] 1Sa 9:16; 12:12; 2Sa 6:21; 1Ch 11:2; 2Ch 7:18; Ps 60:7; Mic 5:2; Mt 2:6 [x] Ge 25:31
5:3 [y] Ge 29:32; 46:9; Ex 6:14; Nu 26:5-11 [z] Nu 26:5

and ceased to be a distinct tribal entity (cf. Gen 49:5 – 7). The inclusion of Simeon's territorial expansion would instill hope in the Chronicler's postexilic audience that God's promises still have significance for his people (cf. vv. 9 – 10).

4:41 days of Hezekiah. Reflects his similar success in expanding Judah westward (2 Kgs 18:8). **Hamites.** The exact location of their territory is unknown, but their association with the Arabian "Meunites" might imply the western or southwestern Negev region. **Meunites.** Associated with the southern region of the Transjordan and parts of the Sinai.

4:42 Simeonites. Their expansion includes victory over areas south of the Dead Sea ("the hill country of Seir") as well as over the Amalekites (v. 43), who traversed the Negev and Sinai regions. This expansion of territory and pasturelands is reminiscent of the prayer of Jabez (vv. 9 – 10).

5:1 – 26 *The Transjordan Tribes.* As part of his survey of "all Israel" (9:1), the Chronicler now turns his attention to the Transjordan tribes of Reuben, Gad, and (half of) Manasseh. Before Israel entered Canaan, they acquired land in the Transjordan area in conjunction with the defeat of Sihon and Og (Num 21:21 – 35; Deut 2:24 — 3:10). In the time of the Chronicler, these tribes, as with the tribe of Simeon, had long ceased to exist within their tribal territory. As such, the presentation of the genealogy of these tribes continues the Chronicler's emphasis on continuity between the past and present that can foster hope within his postexilic audience. God's blessing to those who seek him in faithful prayer (vv. 20 – 22) contrasts with God's judgment of those who persist in covenantal unfaithfulness (vv. 25 – 26).

5:1 – 10 *Reuben.* The Chronicler's summary of the tribe of Reuben has an almost immediate digression that seeks to explain why the firstborn of Jacob's sons was not afforded the typical benefits of the firstborn (note the repetition of "firstborn" in vv. 1 – 3). As with the near landlessness of Simeon, the basis for this demotion is based on an event within the story line of Genesis (Gen 35:22; cf. 49:3 – 4). The demotion of Reuben is coupled with the promotion of Joseph (see note on Gen 35:22). Joseph's sons Manasseh and Ephraim are adopted by Jacob and become part of the tribes of Israel (Gen 48:1 – 20; Deut 21:15 – 17; see note on Gen 48:5). While the Chronicler places the tribe of Judah in a position of preeminence throughout his work, he likewise shows respect to the tribe of Joseph. "Judah" and "Joseph" (as well as "Ephraim," Joseph's son) would ultimately serve as monikers for the southern and northern kingdoms, respectively.

5:2 ruler. This term is used of David in 11:2; 17:7; 2 Sam 5:2; 6:21; 7:8.

5:3 – 10 While the "sons of Reuben" (v. 3) are noted elsewhere (Gen 46:9), the information on the descendants of Joel (vv. 4 – 6) is unique to Chronicles. The geographic extent of the Reubenites reflects Reuben's early territorial hub to the north of Moab and west of Ammon. The Chronicler highlights territorial expansions of the tribe of Reuben (vv. 8 – 10), which resulted in additional pastureland for the tribe (cf. 4:9 – 10).

5:6 [a] ver 26; 2Ki 15:19; 16:10; 2Ch 28:20
5:7 [b] ver 17
5:8 [c] Nu 32:34
5:9 [d] Nu 32:26; Jos 22:9
5:10 [e] ver 18-21
5:11 [f] Jos 13:24-28 [g] Dt 3:10; Jos 13:11
5:17 [h] 2Ki 15:32 [i] 2Ki 14:16,28
5:18 [j] Nu 1:3
5:19 [k] ver 10; Ge 25:15; 1Ch 1:31
5:20 [l] Ps 37:40 [m] 1Ki 8:44; 2Ch 13:14; 14:11; Ps 20:7-9; 22:5 [n] Ps 26:1; Da 6:23
5:22 [o] 2Ch 32:8 [p] 2Ki 15:29; 17:6
5:23 [q] Dt 3:8,9; SS 4:8
5:25 [r] Dt 32:15-18; 2Ki 17:7; 1Ch 9:1; 2Ch 26:16

4 The descendants of Joel:
Shemaiah his son, Gog his son,
Shimei his son, 5 Micah his son,
Reaiah his son, Baal his son,
6 and Beerah his son, whom Tiglath-Pileser[a][a] king of Assyria took into exile. Beerah was a
leader of the Reubenites.
7 Their relatives by clans,[b] listed according to their genealogical records:
Jeiel the chief, Zechariah, 8 and Bela son of Azaz, the son of Shema, the son of Joel. They settled
in the area from Aroer[c] to Nebo and Baal Meon. 9 To the east they occupied the land up to the
edge of the desert that extends to the Euphrates River, because their livestock had increased in
Gilead.[d]
10 During Saul's reign they waged war against the Hagrites[e], who were defeated at their hands;
they occupied the dwellings of the Hagrites throughout the entire region east of Gilead.

Gad

11 The Gadites[f] lived next to them in Bashan, as far as Salekah:[g]
12 Joel was the chief, Shapham the second, then Janai and Shaphat, in Bashan.
13 Their relatives, by families, were:
Michael, Meshullam, Sheba, Jorai, Jakan, Zia and Eber—seven in all.
14 These were the sons of Abihail son of Huri, the son of Jaroah, the son of Gilead, the son of
Michael, the son of Jeshishai, the son of Jahdo, the son of Buz.
15 Ahi son of Abdiel, the son of Guni, was head of their family.
16 The Gadites lived in Gilead, in Bashan and its outlying villages, and on all the pasturelands of
Sharon as far as they extended.
17 All these were entered in the genealogical records during the reigns of Jotham[h] king of Judah and
Jeroboam[i] king of Israel.

18 The Reubenites, the Gadites and the half-tribe of Manasseh had 44,760 men ready for military
service[j]—able-bodied men who could handle shield and sword, who could use a bow, and who were
trained for battle. 19 They waged war against the Hagrites, Jetur,[k] Naphish and Nodab. 20 They were
helped[l] in fighting them, and God delivered the Hagrites and all their allies into their hands, because
they cried[m] out to him during the battle. He answered their prayers, because they trusted[n] in him.
21 They seized the livestock of the Hagrites—fifty thousand camels, two hundred fifty thousand sheep
and two thousand donkeys. They also took one hundred thousand people captive, 22 and many others
fell slain, because the battle[o] was God's. And they occupied the land until the exile.[p]

The Half-Tribe of Manasseh

23 The people of the half-tribe of Manasseh were numerous; they settled in the land from Bashan to
Baal Hermon, that is, to Senir (Mount Hermon).[q]
24 These were the heads of their families: Epher, Ishi, Eliel, Azriel, Jeremiah, Hodaviah and Jahdiel.
They were brave warriors, famous men, and heads of their families. 25 But they were unfaithful[r] to the

[a] 6 Hebrew *Tilgath-Pilneser,* a variant of *Tiglath-Pileser*; also in verse 26

5:6 Tiglath-Pileser. See note on 2 Chr 28:5–25.

5:11–22 *Gad.* The close connection between the Transjordan tribes of Reuben (vv. 1–10) and Gad is underscored by the Chronicler's introduction of Gad via their geographic proximity to Reuben ("the Gadites lived next to them," v. 11). The tribe of Gad settled in the fertile pasturelands of Gilead, Bashan, and Sharon.

5:14 Gilead. Another name for the Transjordan region stretching between the Arnon River in the south (the border of Moab) and the Yarmuk River in the north (Num 32:29).

5:16 Bashan. Previously the territory of Og (Num 21:21–35; Deut 2:24—3:10).

5:18–22 Although the Chronicler has not yet given the genealogy of Manasseh, he recounts the three Transjordan tribes, intersecting with the crux of his message: God is faithful to those who seek him (vv. 20–22).

5:22 the battle was God's. When God's people seek and trust him, their battle becomes his own battle (Lev 26:6–8; Deut 20:4). The Chronicler repeatedly stresses the theme of God's faithfulness, no doubt to encourage the postexilic community (Jer 29:10–14).

5:23–26 *Manasseh.* Although Manasseh was part of the previous section, the Chronicler now provides a formal genealogical sketch of Manasseh's family line. The expansive settlement of this part of Manasseh occupied the northern and northeastern area of the Transjordan territory, at one point extending as far north as Mount Hermon (Deut 3:8).

5:25 unfaithful. Though the Transjordan tribes were successful when

God of their ancestors and prostituted[s] themselves to the gods of the peoples of the land, whom God had destroyed before them. 26 So the God of Israel stirred up the spirit of Pul[t] king of Assyria (that is, Tiglath-Pileser[u] king of Assyria), who took the Reubenites, the Gadites and the half-tribe of Manasseh into exile. He took them to Halah,[v] Habor, Hara and the river of Gozan, where they are to this day.

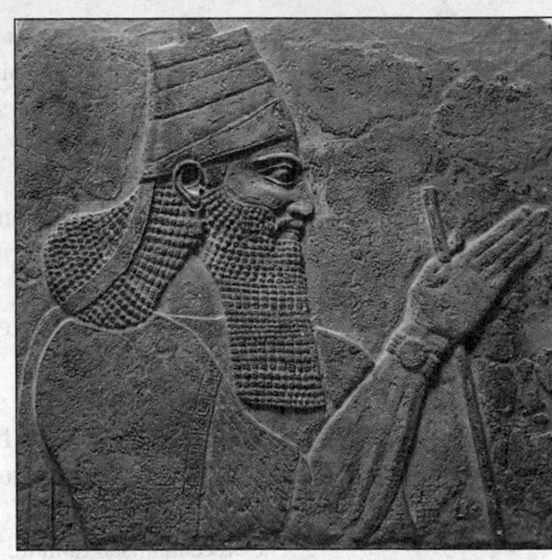

Tiglath-Pileser III.
Wikimedia Commons

Levi

6 [a] The sons of Levi:[w]
Gershon, Kohath and Merari.
2 The sons of Kohath:
Amram, Izhar, Hebron and Uzziel.
3 The children of Amram:
Aaron, Moses and Miriam.
The sons of Aaron:
Nadab, Abihu,[x] Eleazar and Ithamar.
4 Eleazar was the father of Phinehas,
Phinehas the father of Abishua,
5 Abishua the father of Bukki,
Bukki the father of Uzzi,
6 Uzzi the father of Zerahiah,
Zerahiah the father of Meraioth,
7 Meraioth the father of Amariah,
Amariah the father of Ahitub,
8 Ahitub the father of Zadok,[y]
Zadok the father of Ahimaaz,
9 Ahimaaz the father of Azariah,
Azariah the father of Johanan,
10 Johanan the father of Azariah[z] (it was he who served as priest in the temple Solomon built in Jerusalem),
11 Azariah the father of Amariah,
Amariah the father of Ahitub,
12 Ahitub the father of Zadok,
Zadok the father of Shallum,
13 Shallum the father of Hilkiah,[a]
Hilkiah the father of Azariah,
14 Azariah the father of Seraiah,[b]
and Seraiah the father of Jozadak.[b]
15 Jozadak[c] was deported when the LORD sent Judah and Jerusalem into exile by the hand of Nebuchadnezzar.

[a] In Hebrew texts 6:1-15 is numbered 5:27-41, and 6:16-81 is numbered 6:1-66. [b] *14* Hebrew *Jehozadak*, a variant of *Jozadak*; also in verse 15

5:25 [s] Ex 34:15
5:26 [t] 2Ki 15:19 [u] 2Ki 15:29 [v] 2Ki 17:6; 18:11
6:1 [w] Ge 46:11; Ex 6:16; Nu 26:57; 1Ch 23:6
6:3 [x] Lev 10:1
6:8 [y] 2Sa 8:17; 15:27; Ezr 7:2
6:10 [z] 1Ki 4:2; 6:1; 2Ch 3:1; 26:17-18
6:13 [a] 2Ki 22:1-20; 2Ch 34:9; 35:8
6:14 [b] 2Ki 25:18; Ezr 2:2; Ne 11:11
6:15 [c] 2Ki 25:18; Ne 12:1; Hag 1:1,14; 2:2,4; Zec 6:11

they sought God (vv. 1 – 23), this summary reflects the reality that ultimately these tribes were "unfaithful" to God (2 Kgs 17:7 – 17).

5:26 stirred up. God showed his sovereignty in how he used the Neo-Assyrian king Tiglath-Pileser III (745 – 727 BC; also known as "Pul"), who defeated and dispersed the Transjordan tribes (cf. Isa 10:5). See note on 2 Chr 28:5 – 25.

6:1 – 81 *Levi.* The length of Levi's genealogy is second only to Judah's. These tribes played a key role in Israel's covenant life. God chose the tribe of Levi to mediate matters of sacrifice and worship and to teach his ways to his people.

6:1 – 15 The lineage of Kohath represents the line of the Aaronic high priests (cf. Ezra 7:1 – 5). While Aaron, Moses, and Miriam were from the family of Levi, only firstborn sons from the line of Aaron could serve as high priest. The two eldest sons of Aaron, Nadab and Abihu, violated God's holy space (Lev 10:1), and Eleazar became the son through whom the high priesthood transferred. This survey of Kohath extends into the exilic period via the mention of Jozadak (v. 15). Only the lines of Judah and Levi are traced into the exilic period, further attesting to their critical role in the covenantal life of Israel.

6:13 Hilkiah. He found the Book of the Law during Josiah's temple repairs (see 2 Chr 34:14 and note).

6:16 [d]Ge 29:34; Ex 6:16; Nu 3:17-20 [e]Nu 26:57
6:19 [f]Ge 46:11; 1Ch 23:21; 24:26
6:22 [g]Ex 6:24
6:24 [h]1Ch 15:5
6:27 [i]1Sa 1:1 [j]1Sa 1:20
6:28 [k]ver 33; 1Sa 8:2
6:31 [l]1Ch 25:1; 2Ch 29:25-26; Ne 12:45 [m]1Ch 9:33; 15:19; Ezr 3:10; Ps 68:25
6:33 [n]1Ki 4:31; 1Ch 15:17; 25:1

16 The sons of Levi:[d]
Gershon,[a] Kohath and Merari.[e]
17 These are the names of the sons of Gershon:
Libni and Shimei.
18 The sons of Kohath:
Amram, Izhar, Hebron and Uzziel.
19 The sons of Merari:[f]
Mahli and Mushi.
These are the clans of the Levites listed according to their fathers:
20 Of Gershon:
Libni his son, Jahath his son,
Zimmah his son, 21 Joah his son,
Iddo his son, Zerah his son
and Jeatherai his son.
22 The descendants of Kohath:
Amminadab his son, Korah[g] his son,
Assir his son, 23 Elkanah his son,
Ebiasaph his son, Assir his son,
24 Tahath his son, Uriel[h] his son,
Uzziah his son and Shaul his son.
25 The descendants of Elkanah:
Amasai, Ahimoth,
26 Elkanah his son,[b] Zophai his son,
Nahath his son, 27 Eliab his son,
Jeroham his son, Elkanah[i] his son
and Samuel[j] his son.[c]
28 The sons of Samuel:
Joel[d][k] the firstborn
and Abijah the second son.
29 The descendants of Merari:
Mahli, Libni his son,
Shimei his son, Uzzah his son,
30 Shimea his son, Haggiah his son
and Asaiah his son.

The Temple Musicians
6:54-80pp — Jos 21:4-39

31 These are the men[l] David put in charge of the music[m] in the house of the LORD after the ark came to rest
there. 32 They ministered with music before the tabernacle, the tent of meeting, until Solomon built the temple of the LORD in Jerusalem. They performed their duties according to the regulations laid down for them.
33 Here are the men who served, together with their sons:
From the Kohathites:
Heman,[n] the musician,

[a] 16 Hebrew *Gershom,* a variant of *Gershon*; also in verses 17, 20, 43, 62 and 71 [b] 26 Some Hebrew manuscripts, Septuagint and Syriac; most Hebrew manuscripts *Ahimoth* [26]*and Elkanah. The sons of Elkanah:* [c] 27 Some Septuagint manuscripts (see also 1 Samuel 1:19,20 and 1 Chron. 6:33,34); Hebrew does not have *and Samuel his son.* [d] 28 Some Septuagint manuscripts and Syriac (see also 1 Samuel 8:2 and 1 Chron. 6:33); Hebrew does not have *Joel.*

6:16–30 The Chronicler's survey reflects Levitical lists in earlier texts (e.g., Exod 6:16–19; Num 3:17–20). While the genealogy of each son of Levi is developed by at least two generations, the lines of Gershon and Merari are enumerated for seven generations.

6:23 Elkanah. Mentioned five times in the Hebrew of vv. 16–30 (only four are recorded in the NIV for stylistic reasons: vv. 23,25,26,27).The prophet Samuel (v. 27) was a descendant of Elkanah (1 Sam 1).

6:31–47 David's organization of the musical branch of the Levites includes those appointed for music and worship. With the exception of the blowing of trumpets (15:24; 2 Chr 5:13), priests did not play a role in the musical service of ancient Israel. The presentation of this genealogy is in reverse (ascending) order (cf. vv. 22–28). As such, the subsections of this genealogy end with Kohath (v. 38), Gershon (v. 43), and Merari (v. 47), the "sons of Levi" (v. 1).

the son of Joel,[o] the son of Samuel,
34 the son of Elkanah,[p] the son of Jeroham,
the son of Eliel, the son of Toah,
35 the son of Zuph, the son of Elkanah,
the son of Mahath, the son of Amasai,
36 the son of Elkanah, the son of Joel,
the son of Azariah, the son of Zephaniah,
37 the son of Tahath, the son of Assir,
the son of Ebiasaph, the son of Korah,[q]
38 the son of Izhar,[r] the son of Kohath,
the son of Levi, the son of Israel;
39 and Heman's associate Asaph,[s] who served at his right hand:
Asaph son of Berekiah, the son of Shimea,[t]
40 the son of Michael, the son of Baaseiah,[a]
the son of Malkijah, 41 the son of Ethni,
the son of Zerah, the son of Adaiah,
42 the son of Ethan, the son of Zimmah,
the son of Shimei, 43 the son of Jahath,
the son of Gershon, the son of Levi;
44 and from their associates, the Merarites, at his left hand:
Ethan son of Kishi, the son of Abdi,
the son of Malluk, 45 the son of Hashabiah,
the son of Amaziah, the son of Hilkiah,
46 the son of Amzi, the son of Bani,
the son of Shemer, 47 the son of Mahli,
the son of Mushi, the son of Merari,
the son of Levi.

48 Their fellow Levites[u] were assigned to all the other duties of the tabernacle, the house of God. 49 But
Aaron and his descendants were the ones who presented offerings on the altar[v] of burnt offering and on
the altar of incense[w] in connection with all that was done in the Most Holy Place, making atonement
for Israel, in accordance with all that Moses the servant of God had commanded.

50 These were the descendants of Aaron:
Eleazar his son, Phinehas his son,
Abishua his son, 51 Bukki his son,
Uzzi his son, Zerahiah his son,
52 Meraioth his son, Amariah his son,
Ahitub his son, 53 Zadok[x] his son
and Ahimaaz his son.

54 These were the locations of their settlements[y] allotted as their territory (they were assigned to the
descendants of Aaron who were from the Kohathite clan, because the first lot was for them):

[a] 40 Most Hebrew manuscripts; some Hebrew manuscripts, one Septuagint manuscript and Syriac *Maaseiah*

6:33 [o] ver 28
6:34 [p] 1Sa 1:1
6:37 [q] Ex 6:24
6:38 [r] Ex 6:21
6:39 [s] 1Ch 25:1,9; 2Ch 29:13; Ne 11:17 [t] 1Ch 15:17
6:48 [u] 1Ch 23:32
6:49 [v] Ex 27:1-8 [w] Ex 30:1-7,10; 2Ch 26:18
6:53 [x] 2Sa 8:17
6:54 [y] Nu 31:10

6:48–49 The Chronicler carefully distinguishes Levites and priests from the line of Aaron. While every priest was a Levite, not every Levite was a priest (see notes on vv. 48,49).

6:48 Levites who were not priests took on other roles within the tabernacle, especially those involving music (vv. 31–48; 23:2–32; 25:1–8; 2 Chr 5:12–13). Levites also served the Aaronic priests, especially in matters of the tabernacle/temple (cf. 23:28; Num 8:19). Levites were gatekeepers, scribes, secretaries, treasurers, and temple supervisors (23:2–5,28–31; 26:20; 2 Chr 34:8–13). They were also watchful stewards over God's word (Deut 33:8–11) and entrusted with the responsibility of carrying the ark of the covenant (15:14–15; Num 4:15–33; Deut 10:8–9).

6:49 Priests were Levites of the Aaronic family line (vv. 3–15; Exod 28:1). They were responsible primarily for the matters of temple service, particularly the sacrificial system (they "presented offerings ... making atonement for Israel") and aspects of worship within the Most Holy Place (cf. 23:13). Priests were to "distinguish ... between the unclean and the clean, and ... teach the Israelites all the decrees the LORD [had] given them" (Lev 10:10–11; cf. Deut 33:8–11; Mal 2:1–9).

6:50–53 Abridges vv. 1–15 by listing the high priests.

6:54–81 The summary of Levi ends with a list of Levitical settlements. The tribe of Levi did not receive a land inheritance like the other Israelite tribes. Positively, this was because the Lord was their

6:56 [z] Jos 14:13; 15:13
6:57 [a] Nu 33:20 [b] Jos 15:48
6:58 [c] Jos 10:3
6:59 [d] Jos 15:42
6:60 [e] Jer 1:1
6:64 [f] Nu 35:1-8; Jos 21:3,41-42
6:67 [g] Jos 10:33
6:68 [h] 1Ki 4:12 [i] Jos 10:10
6:69 [j] Jos 10:12 [k] Jos 19:45
6:71 [l] 1Ch 23:7 [m] Jos 20:8
6:72 [n] Jos 19:12
6:74 [o] Jos 19:28
6:75 [p] Jos 19:34 [q] Nu 13:21
6:76 [r] Jos 19:28 [s] Nu 32:37
6:78 [t] Jos 20:8
6:79 [u] Dt 2:26
6:80 [v] Jos 20:8 [w] Ge 32:2
6:81 [x] Nu 21:32 [y] 2Ch 11:14
7:1 [z] Ge 30:18; Nu 26:23 [a] Ge 46:13

55 They were given Hebron in Judah with its surrounding pasturelands. 56 But the fields and
villages around the city were given to Caleb son of Jephunneh.[z]
57 So the descendants of Aaron were given Hebron (a city of refuge), and Libnah,[a][a] Jattir,[b]
Eshtemoa, 58 Hilen, Debir,[c] 59 Ashan,[d] Juttah[b] and Beth Shemesh, together with their pasturelands. 60 And from the tribe of Benjamin they were given Gibeon,[c] Geba, Alemeth and Anathoth,[e]
together with their pasturelands.

The total number of towns distributed among the Kohathite clans came to thirteen.

61 The rest of Kohath's descendants were allotted ten towns from the clans of half the tribe of
Manasseh.

62 The descendants of Gershon, clan by clan, were allotted thirteen towns from the tribes of Issachar,
Asher and Naphtali, and from the part of the tribe of Manasseh that is in Bashan.

63 The descendants of Merari, clan by clan, were allotted twelve towns from the tribes of Reuben,
Gad and Zebulun.

64 So the Israelites gave the Levites these towns[f] and their pasturelands. 65 From the tribes of Judah,
Simeon and Benjamin they allotted the previously named towns.

66 Some of the Kohathite clans were given as their territory towns from the tribe of Ephraim.

67 In the hill country of Ephraim they were given Shechem (a city of refuge), and Gezer,[d][g]
68 Jokmeam,[h] Beth Horon,[i] 69 Aijalon[j] and Gath Rimmon,[k] together with their pasturelands.

70 And from half the tribe of Manasseh the Israelites gave Aner and Bileam, together with their
pasturelands, to the rest of the Kohathite clans.

71 The Gershonites[l] received the following:
From the clan of the half-tribe of Manasseh
they received Golan in Bashan[m] and also Ashtaroth, together with their pasturelands;
72 from the tribe of Issachar
they received Kedesh, Daberath,[n] 73 Ramoth and Anem, together with their pasturelands;
74 from the tribe of Asher
they received Mashal, Abdon,[o] 75 Hukok[p] and Rehob,[q] together with their pasturelands;
76 and from the tribe of Naphtali
they received Kedesh in Galilee, Hammon[r] and Kiriathaim,[s] together with their pasturelands.
77 The Merarites (the rest of the Levites) received the following:
From the tribe of Zebulun
they received Jokneam, Kartah,[e] Rimmono and Tabor, together with their pasturelands;
78 from the tribe of Reuben across the Jordan east of Jericho
they received Bezer[t] in the wilderness, Jahzah, 79 Kedemoth[u] and Mephaath, together with their
pasturelands;
80 and from the tribe of Gad
they received Ramoth in Gilead,[v] Mahanaim,[w] 81 Heshbon and Jazer,[x] together with their
pasturelands.[y]

Issachar

7 The sons of Issachar:[z]
Tola, Puah,[a] Jashub and Shimron — four in all.
2 The sons of Tola:
Uzzi, Rephaiah, Jeriel, Jahmai, Ibsam and Samuel — heads of their families. During the

[a] 57 See Joshua 21:13; Hebrew *given the cities of refuge: Hebron, Libnah.* [b] 59 Syriac (see also Septuagint and Joshua 21:16); Hebrew does not have *Juttah.* [c] 60 See Joshua 21:17; Hebrew does not have *Gibeon.* [d] 67 See Joshua 21:21; Hebrew *given the cities of refuge: Shechem, Gezer.* [e] 77 See Septuagint and Joshua 21:34; Hebrew does not have *Jokneam, Kartah.*

inheritance (Num 18:20 – 24). Negatively, this lack of a land inheritance reflected the scattering of Levi and Simeon (Gen 49:5 – 7). Towns allotted to priests were located in Judah and Benjamin to provide proximity to Jerusalem. Non-priestly Levites were granted towns throughout Israel (vv. 61 – 81).

7:1 – 40 *The Northern Tribes.* The Chronicler provides genealogical

reign of David, the descendants of Tola listed as fighting men in their genealogy numbered
22,600.
3 The son of Uzzi:
Izrahiah.
The sons of Izrahiah:
Michael, Obadiah, Joel and Ishiah. All five of them were chiefs. 4 According to their family genealogy, they had 36,000 men ready for battle, for they had many wives and children.
5 The relatives who were fighting men belonging to all the clans of Issachar, as listed in their genealogy, were 87,000 in all.

Benjamin

6 Three sons of Benjamin:[b]
Bela, Beker and Jediael.
7 The sons of Bela:
Ezbon, Uzzi, Uzziel, Jerimoth and Iri, heads of families—five in all. Their genealogical record
listed 22,034 fighting men.
8 The sons of Beker:
Zemirah, Joash, Eliezer, Elioenai, Omri, Jeremoth, Abijah, Anathoth and Alemeth. All these
were the sons of Beker. 9 Their genealogical record listed the heads of families and 20,200
fighting men.
10 The son of Jediael:
Bilhan.
The sons of Bilhan:
Jeush, Benjamin, Ehud, Kenaanah, Zethan, Tarshish and Ahishahar. 11 All these sons of Jediael
were heads of families. There were 17,200 fighting men ready to go out to war.
12 The Shuppites and Huppites were the descendants of Ir, and the Hushites[a] the descendants of Aher.

Naphtali

13 The sons of Naphtali:[c]
Jahziel, Guni, Jezer and Shillem[b]—the descendants of Bilhah.

Manasseh

14 The descendants of Manasseh:[d]
Asriel was his descendant through his Aramean concubine. She gave birth to Makir the father
of Gilead.[e] 15 Makir took a wife from among the Huppites and Shuppites. His sister's name was
Maakah.
Another descendant was named Zelophehad,[f] who had only daughters.
16 Makir's wife Maakah gave birth to a son and named him Peresh. His brother was named
Sheresh, and his sons were Ulam and Rakem.

[a] 12 Or *Ir. The sons of Dan: Hushim,* (see Gen. 46:23); Hebrew does not have *The sons of Dan*. [b] 13 Some Hebrew and Septuagint manuscripts (see also Gen. 46:24 and Num. 26:49); most Hebrew manuscripts *Shallum*

7:6 [b] Ge 46:21; Nu 26:38; 1Ch 8:1-40
7:13 [c] Ge 30:8; 46:24
7:14 [d] Ge 41:51; Jos 17:1; 1Ch 5:23 [e] Nu 26:30
7:15 [f] Nu 26:33; 36:1-12

snippets on several of the tribes to the north of Judah. With the exception of Benjamin these tribes became part of the northern kingdom following the division of the kingdom in 931/30 BC. Unlike the preceding summaries, these genealogies read like a military census. This divergence suggests that the Chronicler had different sources available for the "tribes of Joseph" (i.e., Ephraim and Manasseh, Josh 17:17). This list does not include genealogical information for Dan or Zebulun. Given the variety of listings of the 12 tribes across the Bible (including the absence of one or more tribes and lists that include Joseph *and* one of his sons), these absences should not be overinterpreted. The Chronicler's genealogical coverage of the tribes of Israel totals 12 sons of Jacob, with 12 providing the important imagery of "all Israel" (9:1).

7:1–5 *Issachar.* The brief treatment of Issachar reflects a military census. The mention of David may imply a census from that time (perhaps David's ill-fated census in ch. 21).

7:6–12 *Benjamin.* The genealogy of Benjamin presented here is incomplete and does not directly include Saul's family line; however, the genealogical information in ch. 8 and 9:35–44 focuses largely on the lineage before and after Saul.

7:13 *Naphtali.* The Chronicler's summary of Naphtali is the shortest of all the Israelite tribes, a single verse that echoes Gen 46:24.

7:14–19 *Manasseh.* The Chronicler's treatment of Joseph's son Manasseh continues his earlier description (5:23–24). This genealogy incompletely summarizes earlier biblical data (Num 26:29–34; Josh 17:1–3).

7:17 [g] Nu 26:30; 1Sa 12:11
7:18 [h] Jos 17:2
7:20 [i] Ge 41:52; Nu 1:33; 26:35
7:24 [j] Jos 10:10; 16:3,5
7:28 [k] Jos 10:33; 16:7
7:29 [l] Jos 17:11
[m] Jos 11:2
7:30 [n] Ge 46:17; Nu 1:40; 26:44

17 The son of Ulam:
Bedan.
These were the sons of Gilead[g] son of Makir, the son of Manasseh. 18 His sister Hammoleketh gave
birth to Ishhod, Abiezer[h] and Mahlah.
19 The sons of Shemida were:
Ahian, Shechem, Likhi and Aniam.

Ephraim

20 The descendants of Ephraim:[i]
Shuthelah, Bered his son,
Tahath his son, Eleadah his son,
Tahath his son, 21 Zabad his son
and Shuthelah his son.
Ezer and Elead were killed by the native-born men of Gath, when they went down to seize
their livestock. 22 Their father Ephraim mourned for them many days, and his relatives
came to comfort him. 23 Then he made love to his wife again, and she became pregnant
and gave birth to a son. He named him Beriah,[a] because there had been misfortune in
his family. 24 His daughter was Sheerah, who built Lower and Upper Beth Horon[j] as well as
Uzzen Sheerah.
25 Rephah was his son, Resheph his son,[b]
Telah his son, Tahan his son,
26 Ladan his son, Ammihud his son,
Elishama his son, 27 Nun his son
and Joshua his son.
28 Their lands and settlements included Bethel and its surrounding villages, Naaran to the east,
Gezer[k] and its villages to the west, and Shechem and its villages all the way to Ayyah and its villages.
29 Along the borders of Manasseh were Beth Shan,[l] Taanach, Megiddo and Dor,[m] together with their
villages. The descendants of Joseph son of Israel lived in these towns.

Asher

30 The sons of Asher:[n]
Imnah, Ishvah, Ishvi and Beriah. Their sister was Serah.
31 The sons of Beriah:
Heber and Malkiel, who was the father of Birzaith.
32 Heber was the father of Japhlet, Shomer and Hotham and of their sister Shua.
33 The sons of Japhlet:
Pasak, Bimhal and Ashvath.
These were Japhlet's sons.
34 The sons of Shomer:
Ahi, Rohgah,[c] Hubbah and Aram.
35 The sons of his brother Helem:
Zophah, Imna, Shelesh and Amal.

[a] *23 Beriah* sounds like the Hebrew for *misfortune.* [b] *25* Some Septuagint manuscripts; Hebrew does not have *his son.* [c] *34* Or *of his brother Shomer: Rohgah*

7:20–29 *Ephraim.* Joseph's son Ephraim is presented in tandem with Joseph's son Manasseh. This summary culminates with Joshua (v. 27), whom God used to begin the process of occupying the promised land—another example in which the Chronicler uses his genealogical summaries to draw attention to covenantal hope.

7:28–29 This geographic information summarizes towns and settlements of Ephraim and the half-tribe of Manasseh west of the Jordan, both "tribes of Joseph" (Josh 17:17). These settlements partly reflect Josh 16–17, with updating to show that previously unconquered areas (Judg 1:27–29) were later under the control of these tribes. The majority of the listed towns here (e.g., Gezer, Beth Shan, Taanach, Megiddo, and Dor) were places in which the Israelites were unable to drive out the Canaanites. Including these cities fosters hope in God's faithfulness to bring about covenantal blessings as his people demonstrate obedience (Judg 3:1–4).

7:30–40 *Asher.* As seen in the other genealogies of northern tribes, the Chronicler's summary of Asher includes praiseworthy information on this northern tribe (v. 40).

[36]The sons of Zophah:
Suah, Harnepher, Shual, Beri, Imrah, [37]Bezer, Hod, Shamma, Shilshah, Ithran[a] and Beera.
[38]The sons of Jether:
Jephunneh, Pispah and Ara.
[39]The sons of Ulla:
Arah, Hanniel and Rizia.
[40]All these were descendants of Asher — heads of families, choice men, brave warriors and outstanding leaders. The number of men ready for battle, as listed in their genealogy, was 26,000.

The Genealogy of Saul the Benjamite

8:28-38pp — 1Ch 9:34-44

8 Benjamin[o] was the father of Bela his firstborn,
Ashbel the second son, Aharah the third,
[2]Nohah the fourth and Rapha the fifth.
[3]The sons of Bela were:
Addar,[p] Gera, Abihud,[b] [4]Abishua, Naaman, Ahoah,[q] [5]Gera, Shephuphan and Huram.
[6]These were the descendants of Ehud,[r] who were heads of families of those living in Geba and were
deported to Manahath:
[7]Naaman, Ahijah, and Gera, who deported them and who was the father of Uzza and Ahihud.
[8]Sons were born to Shaharaim in Moab after he had divorced his wives Hushim and Baara. [9]By
his wife Hodesh he had Jobab, Zibia, Mesha, Malkam, [10]Jeuz, Sakia and Mirmah. These were
his sons, heads of families. [11]By Hushim he had Abitub and Elpaal.
[12]The sons of Elpaal:
Eber, Misham, Shemed (who built Ono[s] and Lod with its surrounding villages), [13]and Beriah
and Shema, who were heads of families of those living in Aijalon[t] and who drove out the inhabitants of Gath.[u]
[14]Ahio, Shashak, Jeremoth, [15]Zebadiah, Arad, Eder, [16]Michael, Ishpah and Joha were the sons of
Beriah.
[17]Zebadiah, Meshullam, Hizki, Heber, [18]Ishmerai, Izliah and Jobab were the sons of Elpaal.
[19]Jakim, Zikri, Zabdi, [20]Elienai, Zillethai, Eliel, [21]Adaiah, Beraiah and Shimrath were the sons of
Shimei.
[22]Ishpan, Eber, Eliel, [23]Abdon, Zikri, Hanan, [24]Hananiah, Elam, Anthothijah, [25]Iphdeiah and Penuel
were the sons of Shashak.
[26]Shamsherai, Shehariah, Athaliah, [27]Jaareshiah, Elijah and Zikri were the sons of Jeroham.
[28]All these were heads of families, chiefs as listed in their genealogy, and they lived in Jerusalem.

[29]Jeiel[c] the father[d] of Gibeon lived in Gibeon.[v]
His wife's name was Maakah, [30]and his firstborn son was Abdon, followed by Zur, Kish, Baal,
Ner,[e] Nadab, [31]Gedor, Ahio, Zeker [32]and Mikloth, who was the father of Shimeah. They too lived
near their relatives in Jerusalem.
[33]Ner[w] was the father of Kish,[x] Kish the father of Saul[y], and Saul the father of Jonathan, Malki-
Shua, Abinadab and Esh-Baal.[f][z]

[a] *37* Possibly a variant of *Jether* [b] *3* Or *Gera the father of Ehud* [c] *29* Some Septuagint manuscripts (see also 9:35); Hebrew does not have *Jeiel.* [d] *29* *Father* may mean *civic leader* or *military leader.* [e] *30* Some Septuagint manuscripts (see also 9:36); Hebrew does not have *Ner.* [f] *33* Also known as *Ish-Bosheth*

8:1 [o]Ge 46:21; 1Ch 7:6
8:3 [p]Ge 46:21
8:4 [q]2Sa 23:9
8:6 [r]Jdg 3:12-30; 1Ch 2:52
8:12 [s]Ezr 2:33; Ne 6:2; 7:37; 11:35
8:13 [t]Jos 10:12 [u]Jos 11:22
8:29 [v]Jos 9:3
8:33 [w]1Sa 28:19 [x]1Sa 9:1 [y]1Sa 14:49 [z]2Sa 2:8

8:1 – 40 *The Genealogy of Saul the Benjamite.* The genealogical coverage of Benjamin begins in 7:6 – 12 and repeats in 9:35 – 44. Despite the Chronicler's extended coverage of Benjamin, the genealogical information is incomplete, and certain points of familial relationship are unclear. The Chronicler's survey includes several towns listed in the postexilic lists of returnees (Ezra 2:1 – 35; Neh 7:6 – 38; 11:31 – 35). The Chronicler's treatment of Benjamin ends with the family line that culminated in and proceeded from Saul (vv. 33 – 39). The majority of this genealogical survey is reiterated at the end of ch. 9 (cf. vv. 29 – 38 and 9:35 – 44) in order to set up the kingship of Saul (ch. 10). The repeated mention of Jerusalem within the genealogy of Benjamin (vv. 28,32; 9:3,38) bridges a Saulide/Benjamite kingdom with a Davidic/Judahite kingship as Jerusalem is listed among the tribal inheritance of both Benjamin and Judah (Josh 15:8; 18:28; Judg 1:21).

8:34 [a]2Sa 9:12 [b]2Sa 4:4
8:40 [c]Nu 26:38
9:1 [d]1Ch 5:25
9:2 [e]Jos 9:27; Ezr 2:70 [f]Ezr 2:43,58; 8:20; Ne 7:60
9:4 [g]Ge 38:29; 46:12
9:12 [h]Ezr 2:38; 10:22; Ne 10:3; Jer 21:1; 38:1

34 The son of Jonathan:[a]
Merib-Baal,[a][b] who was the father of Micah.
35 The sons of Micah:
Pithon, Melek, Tarea and Ahaz.
36 Ahaz was the father of Jehoaddah, Jehoaddah was the father of Alemeth, Azmaveth and Zimri,
and Zimri was the father of Moza. 37 Moza was the father of Binea; Raphah was his son, Eleasah
his son and Azel his son.
38 Azel had six sons, and these were their names:
Azrikam, Bokeru, Ishmael, Sheariah, Obadiah and Hanan. All these were the sons of Azel.
39 The sons of his brother Eshek:
Ulam his firstborn, Jeush the second son and Eliphelet the third. 40 The sons of Ulam were brave
warriors who could handle the bow. They had many sons and grandsons — 150 in all.
All these were the descendants of Benjamin.[c]

9 All Israel was listed in the genealogies recorded in the book of the kings of Israel and Judah. They
were taken captive to Babylon because of their unfaithfulness.[d]

The People in Jerusalem

9:1-17pp — Ne 11:3-19

2 Now the first to resettle on their own property in their own towns[e] were some Israelites, priests,
Levites and temple servants.[f]
3 Those from Judah, from Benjamin, and from Ephraim and Manasseh who lived in Jerusalem were:
4 Uthai son of Ammihud, the son of Omri, the son of Imri, the son of Bani, a descendant of Perez
son of Judah.[g]
5 Of the Shelanites[b]:
Asaiah the firstborn and his sons.
6 Of the Zerahites:
Jeuel.
The people from Judah numbered 690.
7 Of the Benjamites:
Sallu son of Meshullam, the son of Hodaviah, the son of Hassenuah;
8 Ibneiah son of Jeroham; Elah son of Uzzi, the son of Mikri; and Meshullam son of Shephatiah,
the son of Reuel, the son of Ibnijah.
9 The people from Benjamin, as listed in their genealogy, numbered 956. All these men were
heads of their families.
10 Of the priests:
Jedaiah; Jehoiarib; Jakin;
11 Azariah son of Hilkiah, the son of Meshullam, the son of Zadok, the son of Meraioth, the son
of Ahitub, the official in charge of the house of God;
12 Adaiah son of Jeroham, the son of Pashhur,[h] the son of Malkijah; and Maasai son of Adiel, the
son of Jahzerah, the son of Meshullam, the son of Meshillemith, the son of Immer.
13 The priests, who were heads of families, numbered 1,760. They were able men, responsible for
ministering in the house of God.
14 Of the Levites:

[a] 34 Also known as *Mephibosheth* [b] 5 See Num. 26:20; Hebrew *Shilonites*.

9:1 *Genealogical Summary.* This two-part verse summarizes the Chronicler's portrait of Israel in chs. 1–8 and the captivity and exile just prior to the Chronicler's own time. As his theological summary shows, the root cause of captivity and exile was unfaithfulness.

9:2–34 *Postexilic Resettlement in Jerusalem.* The listing of those who resettled Jerusalem after the exile reflects a connection between the Chronicler's postexilic audience and the community of ancient Israel. Such continuity provides a tangible means for covenantal hope in light of God's faithfulness. Those who returned to their own property (v. 2) in the postexilic period include Israelites from the house of Judah (Benjamin and Judah; the southern kingdom) and the house of Joseph (Ephraim and Manasseh; the northern kingdom). The mention of key tribal units from both sides of the long-divided Israelite kingdom powerfully displays the Chronicler's message of tribal unity and covenantal hope. This message of unity is striking since it had been 450–500 years since all Israel had existed as a unified nation. Cf. vv. 2–17 with Neh 11:3-20.

Shemaiah son of Hasshub, the son of Azrikam, the son of Hashabiah, a Merarite; [15]Bakbakkar,
Heresh, Galal and Mattaniah[i] son of Mika, the son of Zikri, the son of Asaph; [16]Obadiah son of
Shemaiah, the son of Galal, the son of Jeduthun; and Berekiah son of Asa, the son of Elkanah,
who lived in the villages of the Netophathites.[j]

[17]The gatekeepers:[k]
Shallum, Akkub, Talmon, Ahiman and their fellow Levites, Shallum their chief [18]being stationed at the King's Gate[l] on the east, up to the present time. These were the gatekeepers
belonging to the camp of the Levites. [19]Shallum[m] son of Kore, the son of Ebiasaph, the son
of Korah, and his fellow gatekeepers from his family (the Korahites) were responsible for
guarding the thresholds of the tent just as their ancestors had been responsible for guarding
the entrance to the dwelling of the LORD. [20]In earlier times Phinehas[n] son of Eleazar was the
official in charge of the gatekeepers, and the LORD was with him. [21]Zechariah[o] son of Meshelemiah was the gatekeeper at the entrance to the tent of meeting.

[22]Altogether, those chosen to be gatekeepers[p] at the thresholds numbered 212. They were registered
by genealogy in their villages. The gatekeepers had been assigned to their positions of trust by David and
Samuel the seer.[q] [23]They and their descendants were in charge of guarding the gates of the house of the
LORD—the house called the tent of meeting. [24]The gatekeepers were on the four sides: east, west, north
and south. [25]Their fellow Levites in their villages had to come from time to time and share their duties for
seven-day[r] periods. [26]But the four principal gatekeepers, who were Levites, were entrusted with the responsibility for the rooms and treasuries[s] in the house of God. [27]They would spend the night stationed around the
house of God,[t] because they had to guard it; and they had charge of the key[u] for opening it each morning.
[28]Some of them were in charge of the articles used in the temple service; they counted them when
they were brought in and when they were taken out. [29]Others were assigned to take care of the furnishings and all the other articles of the sanctuary,[v] as well as the special flour and wine, and the olive
oil, incense and spices. [30]But some[w] of the priests took care of mixing the spices. [31]A Levite named
Mattithiah, the firstborn son of Shallum the Korahite, was entrusted with the responsibility for baking
the offering bread. [32]Some of the Kohathites, their fellow Levites, were in charge of preparing for every
Sabbath the bread set out on the table.[x]

[33]Those who were musicians,[y] heads of Levite families, stayed in the rooms of the temple and were
exempt from other duties because they were responsible for the work day and night.[z]

[34]All these were heads of Levite families, chiefs as listed in their genealogy, and they lived in Jerusalem.

The Genealogy of Saul

9:34-44pp — 1Ch 8:28-38

[35]Jeiel[a] the father[a] of Gibeon lived in Gibeon.
His wife's name was Maakah, [36]and his firstborn son was Abdon, followed by Zur, Kish, Baal,
Ner, Nadab, [37]Gedor, Ahio, Zechariah and Mikloth. [38]Mikloth was the father of Shimeam. They
too lived near their relatives in Jerusalem.

[39]Ner[b] was the father of Kish,[c] Kish the father of Saul, and Saul the father of Jonathan,[d] Malki-
Shua, Abinadab and Esh-Baal.[b e]

[40]The son of Jonathan:
Merib-Baal,[c f] who was the father of Micah.

[41]The sons of Micah:
Pithon, Melek, Tahrea and Ahaz.[d]

[a] *35 Father* may mean *civic leader* or *military leader.* [b] *39* Also known as *Ish-Bosheth* [c] *40* Also known as *Mephibosheth* [d] *41* Vulgate and Syriac (see also Septuagint and 8:35); Hebrew does not have *and Ahaz.*

9:15 [i] 2Ch 20:14; Ne 11:22
9:16 [j] Ne 12:28
9:17 [k] ver 22; 1Ch 26:1; 2Ch 8:14; 31:14; Ezr 2:42; Ne 7:45
9:18 [l] 1Ch 26:14; Eze 43:1; 46:1
9:19 [m] Jer 35:4
9:20 [n] Nu 25:7-13
9:21 [o] 1Ch 26:2,14
9:22 [p] ver 17; 1Ch 26:1-2; 2Ch 31:15,18 [q] 1Sa 9:9
9:25 [r] 2Ki 11:5; 2Ch 23:8
9:26 [s] 1Ch 26:22
9:27 [t] Nu 3:38; 1Ch 23:30-32 [u] Isa 22:22
9:29 [v] Nu 3:28; 1Ch 23:29
9:30 [w] Ex 30:23-25
9:32 [x] Lev 24:5-8; 1Ch 23:29; 2Ch 13:11
9:33 [y] 1Ch 6:31; 25:1-31 [z] Ps 134:1
9:35 [a] 1Ch 8:29
9:39 [b] 1Ch 8:33 [c] 1Sa 9:1 [d] 1Sa 13:22 [e] 2Sa 2:8
9:40 [f] 2Sa 4:4

9:17–27 The listing of priests and Levites includes details regarding Levitical gatekeepers. The gates to the temple complex were located at the four compass points, with the eastern entrance (known as the King's Gate) being the main entrance. The emphasis on protecting God's holy space reflects the importance of guarding and watching over all that pertains to God. Such faithfulness ("positions of trust," v. 22) on the part of these gatekeepers fostered God's presence with them as God had been with Phinehas (v. 20).

9:35–44 *The Genealogy of Saul.* The reiteration of the genealogical information in 8:29–38 sets up the summary of Saul's reign (or at least

10:10 [g]Jdg 16:23
10:11 [h]Jdg 21:8
10:13 [i]2Sa 1:1 [j]1Sa 15:23; 1Ch 5:25 [k]1Sa 13:13 [l]Lev 19:31; 20:6; Dt 18:9-14; 1Sa 28:7
10:14 [m]1Ch 12:23 [n]1Sa 13:14; 15:28
11:1 [o]1Ch 9:1 [p]Ge 13:18; 23:19
11:2 [q]1Sa 18:5,16 [r]Ps 78:71; Mt 2:6 [s]1Ch 5:2

[42]Ahaz was the father of Jadah, Jadah[a] was the father of Alemeth, Azmaveth and Zimri, and Zimri was the father of Moza. [43]Moza was the father of Binea; Rephaiah was his son, Eleasah his son and Azel his son.

[44]Azel had six sons, and these were their names:

Azrikam, Bokeru, Ishmael, Sheariah, Obadiah and Hanan. These were the sons of Azel.

Saul Takes His Life

10:1-12pp — 1Sa 31:1-13; 2Sa 1:4-12

10 Now the Philistines fought against Israel; the Israelites fled before them, and many fell dead on Mount Gilboa. [2]The Philistines were in hot pursuit of Saul and his sons, and they killed his sons Jonathan, Abinadab and Malki-Shua. [3]The fighting grew fierce around Saul, and when the archers overtook him, they wounded him.

[4]Saul said to his armor-bearer, "Draw your sword and run me through, or these uncircumcised fellows will come and abuse me."

But his armor-bearer was terrified and would not do it; so Saul took his own sword and fell on it. [5]When the armor-bearer saw that Saul was dead, he too fell on his sword and died. [6]So Saul and his three sons died, and all his house died together.

[7]When all the Israelites in the valley saw that the army had fled and that Saul and his sons had died, they abandoned their towns and fled. And the Philistines came and occupied them.

[8]The next day, when the Philistines came to strip the dead, they found Saul and his sons fallen on Mount Gilboa. [9]They stripped him and took his head and his armor, and sent messengers throughout the land of the Philistines to proclaim the news among their idols and their people. [10]They put his armor in the temple of their gods and hung up his head in the temple of Dagon.[g]

[11]When all the inhabitants of Jabesh Gilead[h] heard what the Philistines had done to Saul, [12]all their valiant men went and took the bodies of Saul and his sons and brought them to Jabesh. Then they buried their bones under the great tree in Jabesh, and they fasted seven days.

[13]Saul died[i] because he was unfaithful[j] to the LORD; he did not keep[k] the word of the LORD and even consulted a medium[l] for guidance, [14]and did not inquire of the LORD. So the LORD put him to death and turned[m] the kingdom[n] over to David son of Jesse.

David Becomes King Over Israel

11:1-3pp — 2Sa 5:1-3

11 All Israel[o] came together to David at Hebron[p] and said, "We are your own flesh and blood. [2]In the past, even while Saul was king, you were the one who led Israel on their military campaigns.[q] And the LORD your God said to you, 'You will shepherd[r] my people Israel, and you will become their ruler.[s]' "

[a] *42* Some Hebrew manuscripts and Septuagint (see also 8:36); most Hebrew manuscripts *Jarah, Jarah*

its closing moments) in ch. 10. The development of Saul's lineage for 12 generations after Saul (vv. 39–44) provides enduring hope for the line of Saul and the tribe of Benjamin.

10:1–14 *The Decline of Saul and the Rise of David.* The Chronicler's interest in moving to the accounts of David and Solomon is reflected in that the account of Saul begins in the closing moments of his reign. Saul's reign shows the high cost of covenantal unfaithfulness, described as not keeping the word of the Lord (v. 13).

10:1–7 Although God used Saul to temper the Philistine threat (1 Sam 9:16; 13:3—14:23), it was not completely eradicated (1 Sam 10:3–5; 13:3–22). The Chronicler focuses on the last extended battle narrative between Saul and the Philistines, which ends in Saul's demise (see the full account in 1 Sam 28; 31). The location of this conflict is unique and may relate to control of trade routes that passed through the Jezreel and Beth Shan Valleys.

10:4–5 For more details on the final moments of Saul's life, see 1 Sam 31:4–5; 2 Sam 1:5–10. As Saul lay upon his spear, he asked an Amalekite to put him out of his misery (2 Sam 1:6–9).

10:6 While all the "house" of Saul present on the battlefield died, Saul's son Ish-Bosheth/Esh-Baal (not a participant in the battle) was anointed king by Saul's military commander (2 Sam 2:8–10).

10:8–12 The Chronicler highlights the honor of the inhabitants of Jabesh Gilead in contrast to the dishonor of the Philistines.

10:10 put his armor ... hung up his head. Displaying the spoils of war (including the bodies of enemies) was a means of thanking deities in the biblical world.

10:12 took the bodies ... brought them to Jabesh. The motivation for this may stem from the close connection between the Benjamites and the city of Jabesh Gilead (cf. Judg 21:5–12; 1 Sam 11:1–11).

10:14 the LORD put him to death and turned the kingdom over to David. Shows the high cost of being "unfaithful to the LORD" (v. 13), by not keeping God's word (1 Sam 13:14; 15:26). Worse, Saul "consulted a medium" at Endor (v. 13; 1 Sam 28:5–25), a practice the covenant vehemently prohibited (Lev 20:6). Saul's unfaithfulness caused the Lord to remove him and seek a leader "after his own heart" (1 Sam 13:14).

11:1—29:30 *The Reign of David.* After quickly dismissing the reign of

[3]When all the elders of Israel had come to King David at Hebron, he made a covenant with them at Hebron before the LORD, and they anointed[t] David king over Israel, as the LORD had promised through Samuel.

David Conquers Jerusalem

11:4-9pp — 2Sa 5:6-10

[4]David and all the Israelites marched to Jerusalem (that is, Jebus). The Jebusites[u] who lived there
[5]said to David, "You will not get in here." Nevertheless, David captured the fortress of Zion — which is the City of David.
[6]David had said, "Whoever leads the attack on the Jebusites will become commander-in-chief." Joab[v] son of Zeruiah went up first, and so he received the command.
[7]David then took up residence in the fortress, and so it was called the City of David. [8]He built up the
city around it, from the terraces[a][w] to the surrounding wall, while Joab restored the rest of the city. [9]And
David became more and more powerful,[x] because the LORD Almighty was with him.

David's Mighty Warriors

11:10-41pp — 2Sa 23:8-39

[10]These were the chiefs of David's mighty warriors — they, together with all Israel,[y] gave his kingship strong support to extend it over the whole land, as the LORD had promised[z] — [11]this is the list of David's mighty warriors:[a]

Jashobeam,[b] a Hakmonite, was chief of the officers[c]; he raised his spear against three hundred men, whom he killed in one encounter.

[12]Next to him was Eleazar son of Dodai the Ahohite, one of the three mighty warriors. [13]He was with
David at Pas Dammim when the Philistines gathered there for battle. At a place where there was a field
full of barley, the troops fled from the Philistines. [14]But they took their stand in the middle of the field.
They defended it and struck the Philistines down, and the LORD brought about a great victory.[b]
[15]Three of the thirty chiefs came down to David to the rock at the cave of Adullam, while a band of
Philistines was encamped in the Valley[c] of Rephaim. [16]At that time David was in the stronghold,[d] and
the Philistine garrison was at Bethlehem. [17]David longed for water and said, "Oh, that someone would
get me a drink of water from the well near the gate of Bethlehem!" [18]So the Three broke through the

[a] *8* Or *the Millo* [b] *11* Possibly a variant of *Jashob-Baal* [c] *11* Or *Thirty*; some Septuagint manuscripts *Three* (see also 2 Samuel 23:8)

11:3 [t]1Sa 16:1-13
11:4 [u]Ge 10:16; 15:18-21; Jos 3:10; 15:8; Jdg 1:21; 19:10
11:6 [v]2Sa 2:13; 8:16
11:8 [w]2Sa 5:9; 2Ch 32:5
11:9 [x]2Sa 3:1; Est 9:4
11:10 [y]ver 1 [z]ver 3; 1Ch 12:23
11:11 [a]2Sa 17:10
11:14 [b]Ex 14:30; 1Sa 11:13
11:15 [c]1Ch 14:9; Isa 17:5
11:16 [d]2Sa 5:17

Saul, the Chronicler begins his extended coverage of the reign of David. His account begins with David's inauguration by all Israel (11:1–3), bypassing the seven years of intrigue and drama (including a divided kingdom) caused by conflict between the house of Saul and the house of David (2 Sam 2–4). The Chronicler emphasizes the theological reality that David's military and political successes were an outworking of God's blessing upon his chosen king (11:9). God brought success to David as David did as God commanded him (14:16), an important spiritual lesson for the Chronicler's postexilic audience and God's people at all times. David led the people to seek God by returning the ark of the covenant to Jerusalem, organizing worship leaders, and diligently preparing for the Jerusalem temple. God responded to David by promising to bless his son Solomon and establish an everlasting dynasty (17:4–14).

11:1—12:40 *David's Enthronement and Consolidation of Power.* This presents an image of unity in affirming the Lord's will in David's rise to power. This section begins and ends with David's enthronement at Hebron (11:1–3; 12:38–40).

11:2 shepherd. This imagery reflects the king's role of protecting the flock (God's people) and leading them in righteousness (Deut 17:14–20; cf. Ezek 34; John 10:1–18). **my people.** Underscores that God has delegated authority to David.

11:3 Although David had been anointed king over the tribe of Judah seven and a half years earlier (2 Sam 2:11), this moment marked the beginning of David's reign over the whole nation. David's reign is usually dated 1010–970 BC. **Hebron.** A city located in the heart of the tribal territory of Judah and closely connected with the patriarchal era. The Chronicler makes God's will central to David's accession to the throne (1 Sam 16:1–13).

11:4–8 The conquest of Jerusalem and David's subsequent transfer of his capital from Hebron to Jerusalem were significant steps in deepening solidarity among the tribes as Jerusalem was geographically central to the 12 tribes and was not associated with any one tribe (it was politically neutral). These factors minimized potential tribal jealousies, promoted national unity, and demonstrated God's blessing upon David.

11:4 all the Israelites. While the conquest of Jerusalem as recorded in 2 Sam 5:6–10 focuses on the efforts of a small band of warriors, the Chronicler emphasizes the participation of the broader community.

11:5 Zion — which is the City of David. Jerusalem.

11:10 Even though the list in vv. 11–47 focuses on a group of elite military warriors, the Chronicler stresses that these military "chiefs" were aligned with "all Israel" through David's rule "over the whole land" and that God used them to bring about what "the LORD had promised."

11:14 the LORD brought about a great victory. Emphasizes that the faith of God's people should rest in their powerful God, not in powerful men.

11:18 he poured it out to the LORD. Not an act of ungratefulness but an act of selfless worship (a libation/drink offering; cf. Gen 35:14) that balanced the men's selfless courage.

11:18 [e]Dt 12:16
11:20 [f]1Sa 26:6
11:22 [g]Jos 15:21 [h]1Sa 17:36
11:23 [i]1Sa 17:7
11:26 [j]2Sa 2:18
11:27 [k]1Ch 27:8
11:28 [l]1Ch 27:12
11:29 [m]2Sa 21:18
11:31 [n]1Ch 27:14 [o]Jdg 12:13

Philistine lines, drew water from the well near the gate of Bethlehem and carried it back to David. But
he refused to drink it; instead, he poured[e] it out to the LORD. 19"God forbid that I should do this!" he
said. "Should I drink the blood of these men who went at the risk of their lives?" Because they risked
their lives to bring it back, David would not drink it.

Such were the exploits of the three mighty warriors.

20Abishai[f] the brother of Joab was chief of the Three. He raised his spear against three hundred men,
whom he killed, and so he became as famous as the Three. 21He was doubly honored above the Three
and became their commander, even though he was not included among them.

22Benaiah son of Jehoiada, a valiant fighter from Kabzeel,[g] performed great exploits. He struck down
Moab's two mightiest warriors. He also went down into a pit on a snowy day and killed a lion.[h] 23And he
struck down an Egyptian who was five cubits[a] tall. Although the Egyptian had a spear like a weaver's
rod[i] in his hand, Benaiah went against him with a club. He snatched the spear from the Egyptian's hand
and killed him with his own spear. 24Such were the exploits of Benaiah son of Jehoiada; he too was as
famous as the three mighty warriors. 25He was held in greater honor than any of the Thirty, but he was
not included among the Three. And David put him in charge of his bodyguard.

26The mighty warriors were:
Asahel[j] the brother of Joab,
Elhanan son of Dodo from Bethlehem,
27Shammoth[k] the Harorite,
Helez the Pelonite,
28Ira son of Ikkesh from Tekoa,
Abiezer[l] from Anathoth,
29Sibbekai[m] the Hushathite,
Ilai the Ahohite,
30Maharai the Netophathite,
Heled son of Baanah the Netophathite,
31Ithai son of Ribai from Gibeah in Benjamin,
Benaiah[n] the Pirathonite,[o]

[a] 23 That is, about 7 feet 6 inches or about 2.3 meters

Killing a lion in the ancient Near East was a heroic act. Here Ashurbanipal is stabbing a lion with a sword. In 1 Chr 11:22, Benaiah, one of David's mighty men, is described as a "valiant fighter," and "he also went down into a pit on a snowy day and killed a lion."

32 Hurai from the ravines of Gaash,
Abiel the Arbathite,
33 Azmaveth the Baharumite,
Eliahba the Shaalbonite,
34 the sons of Hashem the Gizonite,
Jonathan son of Shagee the Hararite,
35 Ahiam son of Sakar the Hararite,
Eliphal son of Ur,
36 Hepher the Mekerathite,
Ahijah the Pelonite,
37 Hezro the Carmelite,
Naarai son of Ezbai,
38 Joel the brother of Nathan,
Mibhar son of Hagri,
39 Zelek the Ammonite,
Naharai the Berothite, the armor-bearer of Joab son of Zeruiah,
40 Ira the Ithrite,
Gareb the Ithrite,
41 Uriah[p] the Hittite,
Zabad[q] son of Ahlai,
42 Adina son of Shiza the Reubenite, who was chief of the Reubenites, and the thirty with him,
43 Hanan son of Maakah,
Joshaphat the Mithnite,
44 Uzzia the Ashterathite,[r]
Shama and Jeiel the sons of Hotham the Aroerite,
45 Jediael son of Shimri,
his brother Joha the Tizite,
46 Eliel the Mahavite,
Jeribai and Joshaviah the sons of Elnaam,
Ithmah the Moabite,
47 Eliel, Obed and Jaasiel the Mezobaite.

Warriors Join David

12 These were the men who came to David at Ziklag,[s] while he was banished from the presence of
Saul son of Kish (they were among the warriors who helped him in battle; 2 they were armed
with bows and were able to shoot arrows or to sling stones right-handed or left-handed;[t] they were relatives of Saul[u] from the tribe of Benjamin):

3 Ahiezer their chief and Joash the sons of Shemaah the Gibeathite; Jeziel and Pelet the sons of
Azmaveth; Berakah, Jehu the Anathothite, 4 and Ishmaiah the Gibeonite, a mighty warrior among
the Thirty, who was a leader of the Thirty; Jeremiah, Jahaziel, Johanan, Jozabad the Gederathite,[a][v]
5 Eluzai, Jerimoth, Bealiah, Shemariah and Shephatiah the Haruphite; 6 Elkanah, Ishiah, Azarel,
Joezer and Jashobeam the Korahites; 7 and Joelah and Zebadiah the sons of Jeroham from Gedor.[w]

8 Some Gadites[x] defected to David at his stronghold in the wilderness. They were brave warriors, ready
for battle and able to handle the shield and spear. Their faces were the faces of lions,[y] and they were as
swift as gazelles[z] in the mountains.

[a] 4 In Hebrew texts the second half of this verse (*Jeremiah . . . Gederathite*) is numbered 12:5, and 12:5-40 is numbered 12:6-41.

11:41 [p] 2Sa 11:6 [q] 1Ch 2:36
11:44 [r] Dt 1:4
12:1 [s] Jos 15:31; 1Sa 27:2-6
12:2 [t] Jdg 3:15; 20:16 [u] 2Sa 3:19
12:4 [v] Jos 15:36
12:7 [w] Jos 15:58
12:8 [x] Ge 30:11 [y] 2Sa 17:10 [z] 2Sa 2:18

12:1–7 This unexpected loyalty of Saul's relatives underscores the theme of tribal unity. This ambidextrous group of Benjamites had particular acumen in the areas of archery and sling shooting and came to David while he was living in Philistine territory (1 Sam 27:1–7).

12:2 arrows ... sling stones. Implying warfare from a distance. **relatives of Saul.** Benjamite warriors.
12:8 shield and spear. Implying close combat. **lions.** Known for their ferocity. **gazelles.** Known for their speed.

12:14 [a]Lev 26:8 [b]Dt 32:30
12:15 [c]Jos 3:15
12:16 [d]2Sa 3:19
12:18 [e]Jdg 3:10; 6:34; 1Ch 28:12; 2Ch 15:1; 20:14; 24:20 [f]2Sa 17:25 [g]1Sa 25:5-6
12:19 [h]1Sa 29:2-11
12:20 [i]1Sa 27:6
12:23 [j]2Sa 2:3-4 [k]1Ch 10:14 [l]1Sa 16:1; 1Ch 11:10
12:28 [m]2Sa 8:17; 1Ch 6:8; 15:11; 16:39; 27:17
12:29 [n]2Sa 3:19 [o]2Sa 2:8-9
12:32 [p]Est 1:13

9 Ezer was the chief,
Obadiah the second in command, Eliab the third,
10 Mishmannah the fourth, Jeremiah the fifth,
11 Attai the sixth, Eliel the seventh,
12 Johanan the eighth, Elzabad the ninth,
13 Jeremiah the tenth and Makbannai the eleventh.

14 These Gadites were army commanders; the least was a match for a hundred,[a] and the greatest for
a thousand.[b] 15 It was they who crossed the Jordan in the first month when it was overflowing all its
banks,[c] and they put to flight everyone living in the valleys, to the east and to the west.

16 Other Benjamites[d] and some men from Judah also came to David in his stronghold. 17 David went
out to meet them and said to them, "If you have come to me in peace to help me, I am ready for you to
join me. But if you have come to betray me to my enemies when my hands are free from violence, may
the God of our ancestors see it and judge you."

18 Then the Spirit[e] came on Amasai,[f] chief of the Thirty, and he said:

"We are yours, David!
We are with you, son of Jesse!
Success,[g] success to you,
and success to those who help you,
for your God will help you."

So David received them and made them leaders of his raiding bands.

19 Some of the tribe of Manasseh defected to David when he went with the Philistines to fight against
Saul. (He and his men did not help the Philistines because, after consultation, their rulers sent him
away. They said, "It will cost us our heads if he deserts to his master Saul.")[h] 20 When David went to Ziklag,[i] these were the men of Manasseh who defected to him: Adnah, Jozabad, Jediael, Michael, Jozabad,
Elihu and Zillethai, leaders of units of a thousand in Manasseh. 21 They helped David against raiding
bands, for all of them were brave warriors, and they were commanders in his army. 22 Day after day men
came to help David, until he had a great army, like the army of God.[a]

Others Join David at Hebron

23 These are the numbers of the men armed for battle who came to David at Hebron[j] to turn[k] Saul's
kingdom over to him, as the LORD had said:[l]
24 from Judah, carrying shield and spear — 6,800 armed for battle;
25 from Simeon, warriors ready for battle — 7,100;
26 from Levi — 4,600, 27 including Jehoiada, leader of the family of Aaron, with 3,700 men, 28 and
Zadok,[m] a brave young warrior, with 22 officers from his family;
29 from Benjamin,[n] Saul's tribe — 3,000, most[o] of whom had remained loyal to Saul's house until then;
30 from Ephraim, brave warriors, famous in their own clans — 20,800;
31 from half the tribe of Manasseh, designated by name to come and make David king — 18,000;
32 from Issachar, men who understood the times and knew what Israel should do[p] — 200 chiefs,
with all their relatives under their command;

[a] 22 Or *a great and mighty army*

12:18 the Spirit. Perhaps "*a* spirit" as there is no definite article on the Hebrew word (*rûaḥ* = S/spirit) and it is not used with a proper noun (e.g., Spirit *of God*). This would be like an individual getting a surge of passion that prompts them to speak or act with conviction, as seen with Gideon in his purging of Canaanite idolatry (Judg 6:34) and with Zechariah also in the context of idolatry (2 Chr 24:20). **Success, success ... success.** The poetic words of Amasai stress that complete loyalty and service to David resulted in not only success for David (cf. Isa 26:3) but also success for those who were faithful to David. For kings and people, peace was of great concern. Again, faithfulness through obedience is central to the Chronicler's message.

12:19–21 In addition to those from Benjamin, Gad, and Judah, men from the northern tribe of Manasseh aligned themselves with David while he was at Ziklag. The Chronicler reminds his postexilic audience that David was nearly part of the Philistine coalition that led to the death of Saul and his sons (1 Sam 29). The decision by the Philistine leaders providentially prevented David from being implicated in the death of the reigning king.

12:23–40 This concludes the summary of the transition to Davidic rule. **12:23 turn Saul's kingdom over to [David].** In accordance with God's will ("as the LORD had said"; see note on 11:10).

33 from Zebulun, experienced soldiers prepared for battle with every type of weapon, to help David
with undivided loyalty—50,000;
34 from Naphtali—1,000 officers, together with 37,000 men carrying shields and spears;
35 from Dan, ready for battle—28,600;
36 from Asher, experienced soldiers prepared for battle—40,000;
37 and from east of the Jordan, from Reuben, Gad and the half-tribe of Manasseh, armed with every
type of weapon—120,000.
38 All these were fighting men who volunteered to serve in the ranks. They came to Hebron fully determined to make David king over all Israel.[q] All the rest of the Israelites were also of one mind to make
David king. 39 The men spent three days there with David, eating and drinking,[r] for their families had
supplied provisions for them. 40 Also, their neighbors from as far away as Issachar, Zebulun and Naphtali
came bringing food on donkeys, camels, mules and oxen. There were plentiful supplies[s] of flour, fig
cakes, raisin[t] cakes, wine, olive oil, cattle and sheep, for there was joy[u] in Israel.

Bringing Back the Ark

13:1-14pp — 2Sa 6:1-11

13 David conferred with each of his officers, the commanders of thousands and commanders of
hundreds. 2 He then said to the whole assembly of Israel, "If it seems good to you and if it is the
will of the LORD our God, let us send word far and wide to the rest of our people throughout the territories of Israel, and also to the priests and Levites who are with them in their towns and pasturelands, to
come and join us. 3 Let us bring the ark of our God back to us,[v] for we did not inquire[w] of[a] it[b] during
the reign of Saul." 4 The whole assembly agreed to do this, because it seemed right to all the people.
5 So David assembled all Israel,[x] from the Shihor River[y] in Egypt to Lebo Hamath,[z] to bring the ark
of God from Kiriath Jearim.[a] 6 David and all Israel went to Baalah[b] of Judah (Kiriath Jearim) to bring
up from there the ark of God the LORD, who is enthroned between the cherubim[c]—the ark that is
called by the Name.
7 They moved the ark of God from Abinadab's[d] house on a new cart, with Uzzah and Ahio guiding
it. 8 David and all the Israelites were celebrating with all their might before God, with songs and with
harps, lyres, timbrels, cymbals and trumpets.[e]
9 When they came to the threshing floor of Kidon, Uzzah reached out his hand to steady the ark, because the oxen stumbled. 10 The LORD's anger[f] burned against Uzzah, and he struck him down[g] because
he had put his hand on the ark. So he died there before God.
11 Then David was angry because the LORD's wrath had broken out against Uzzah, and to this day
that place is called Perez Uzzah.[c][h]
12 David was afraid of God that day and asked, "How can I ever bring the ark of God to me?" 13 He did

[a] *3* Or *we neglected* [b] *3* Or *him* [c] *11* *Perez Uzzah* means *outbreak against Uzzah.*

12:38 [q] 2Sa 5:1-3; 1Ch 9:1
12:39 [r] 2Sa 3:20; Isa 25:6-8
12:40 [s] 2Sa 16:1; 17:29 [t] 1Sa 25:18 [u] 1Ch 29:22
13:3 [v] 1Sa 7:1-2 [w] 2Ch 1:5
13:5 [x] 1Ch 11:1; 15:3 [y] Jos 13:3 [z] Nu 13:21 [a] 1Sa 6:21; 7:2
13:6 [b] Jos 15:9; 2Sa 6:2 [c] Ex 25:22; 2Ki 19:15
13:7 [d] Nu 4:15; 1Sa 7:1
13:8 [e] 2Sa 6:5; 1Ch 15:16,19,24; 2Ch 5:12; Ps 92:3
13:10 [f] 1Ch 15:13,15 [g] Lev 10:2
13:11 [h] 1Ch 15:13; Ps 7:11

12:38 one mind. As seen throughout chs. 11–12, the Chronicler presents a vivid picture of tribal unity and dedication toward God's chosen king. The community was unified in affirming God's choice of David as king.

13:1—16:43 *Return of the Ark of the Covenant.* Although this initial attempt to move the ark ended negatively, the Chronicler emphasizes the unity of Israel through David's leadership and closes on a note of hope. David's attention to bringing the ark to a position of physical and spiritual centrality implied that David's reign would be marked by seeking God within the framework of the covenant (the text of the covenant was housed within the ark; Deut 10:1–5). This spiritual faithfulness places David in sharp contrast to Saul.

13:1–4 While the loss of the ark was theologically connected with God's rejection of Eli's priesthood (1 Sam 2:27–34; 3:11–14; 4:12–22), the Chronicler implies that it was neglected during the time of Saul (v. 3). Such neglect is a subtle negative commentary on the spiritual priorities reflected in Saul's reign.

13:5,6 David ... all Israel. A unified commitment to seek and obey God is revealed in the priority given to this (attempted) move of the ark.

13:5 from the Shihor River in Egypt to Lebo Hamath. Reflects the anticipated geographic extent of Israel (Gen 15:18–21; Num 34:1–12). **Kiriath Jearim.** Located near the tribal boundaries of Benjamin and Judah—approximately nine miles (14.5 kilometers) from Jerusalem. The ark had been there for the 20 years following its seven-month exile in Philistine territory in the time of Samuel and Eli (1 Sam 4–6).

13:6 cherubim. See note on 2 Chr 5:7–8. **the ark that is called by the Name.** Like the temple (2 Chr 2:1; Deut 12:5), the ark is associated with the name of God. **Name.** Reflects God's character and his covenantal relationship with Israel and humankind.

13:9–10 Uzzah reached out his hand ... [the LORD] struck him down. While Uzzah's action seems well-intentioned, it was nonetheless an act of spiritual profanity that violated God's holy space (Num 4:15). This incident is reminiscent of the situation involving the two eldest sons of Aaron who likewise violated God's holiness by offering "unauthorized fire before the LORD" (Lev 10:1). In both of these situations, the individuals did what was right in their own eyes rather than what was right in God's eyes.

13:13 [i]1Ch 15:18,24; 16:38; 26:4-5,15
13:14 [j]2Sa 6:11; 1Ch 26:4-5
14:1 [k]2Ch 2:3; Ezr 3:7
14:2 [l]Nu 24:7; Dt 26:19
14:3 [m]1Ch 3:1
14:4 [n]1Ch 3:9
14:8 [o]1Ch 11:1
14:9 [p]ver 13; Jos 15:8; 1Ch 11:15
14:11 [q]Isa 28:21
14:12 [r]Ex 32:20 [s]Jos 7:15
14:13 [t]ver 9
14:16 [u]Jos 9:3 [v]Jos 10:33
14:17 [w]Jos 6:27; 2Ch 26:8 [x]Ex 15:14-16; Dt 2:25
15:1 [y]Ps 132:1-18 [z]1Ch 16:1; 17:1
15:2 [a]Nu 4:15; Dt 10:8; 2Ch 5:5 [b]Dt 31:9 [c]1Ch 23:13
15:3 [d]1Ki 8:1; 1Ch 13:5

not take the ark to be with him in the City of David. Instead, he took it to the house of Obed-Edom[i] the
Gittite. 14 The ark of God remained with the family of Obed-Edom in his house for three months, and
the LORD blessed his household[j] and everything he had.

David's House and Family

14:1-7pp — 2Sa 5:11-16; 1Ch 3:5-8

14 Now Hiram king of Tyre sent messengers to David, along with cedar logs,[k] stonemasons and
carpenters to build a palace for him. 2 And David knew that the LORD had established him as
king over Israel and that his kingdom had been highly exalted[l] for the sake of his people Israel.
3 In Jerusalem David took more wives and became the father of more sons[m] and daughters. 4 These
are the names of the children born to him there:[n] Shammua, Shobab, Nathan, Solomon, 5 Ibhar, Elishua, Elpelet, 6 Nogah, Nepheg, Japhia, 7 Elishama, Beeliada[a] and Eliphelet.

David Defeats the Philistines

14:8-17pp — 2Sa 5:17-25

8 When the Philistines heard that David had been anointed king over all Israel,[o] they went up in full
force to search for him, but David heard about it and went out to meet them. 9 Now the Philistines had
come and raided the Valley[p] of Rephaim; 10 so David inquired of God: "Shall I go and attack the Philistines? Will you deliver them into my hands?"
The LORD answered him, "Go, I will deliver them into your hands."
11 So David and his men went up to Baal Perazim,[q] and there he defeated them. He said, "As waters
break out, God has broken out against my enemies by my hand." So that place was called Baal Perazim.[b]
12 The Philistines had abandoned their gods there, and David gave orders to burn[r] them in the fire.[s]
13 Once more the Philistines raided the valley;[t] 14 so David inquired of God again, and God answered
him, "Do not go directly after them, but circle around them and attack them in front of the poplar
trees. 15 As soon as you hear the sound of marching in the tops of the poplar trees, move out to battle,
because that will mean God has gone out in front of you to strike the Philistine army." 16 So David did
as God commanded him, and they struck down the Philistine army, all the way from Gibeon[u] to Gezer.[v]
17 So David's fame[w] spread throughout every land, and the LORD made all the nations fear[x] him.

The Ark Brought to Jerusalem

15:25–16:3pp — 2Sa 6:12-19

15 After David had constructed buildings for himself in the City of David, he prepared[y] a place for the
ark of God and pitched[z] a tent for it. 2 Then David said, "No one but the Levites[a] may carry[b] the
ark of God, because the LORD chose them to carry the ark of the LORD and to minister[c] before him forever."
3 David assembled all Israel[d] in Jerusalem to bring up the ark of the LORD to the place he had prepared for it. 4 He called together the descendants of Aaron and the Levites:

5 From the descendants of Kohath,
Uriel the leader and 120 relatives;

[a] 7 A variant of *Eliada* [b] 11 *Baal Perazim* means *the lord who breaks out.*

14:1–17 This section begins and ends with statements reflecting God's blessings on David both in Israel and in the surrounding nations (vv. 2,17). In between (and not necessarily in chronological order), the Chronicler details how God enabled David to defeat the Philistines, who had been in a position of power over Israel.

14:1 Tyre. Phoenicia/Lebanon; a well-known source for quality lumber. **cedar logs.** The wood of the slow-growing cedar tree was desired for important building projects in the biblical world given its durability, size, and fragrance. **stonemasons.** Skilled in construction and specialty craftsmanship such as dressed masonry (ashlar) and carved basalt (figures shaped from stone). **to build a palace for him.** David accepted Phoenician assistance to build his palace (cf. 2 Chr 2:3–16). The Phoenicians were noted for supplying building materials and having the technical expertise to construct buildings and fabricate artistic objects with wood, metal, fabric, and stone.

14:10,14 inquired of God ... answered him. These two instances of David's success against the Philistines (vv. 8–17) highlight that David sought God, which sharply contrasts with Saul, who either did not inquire of God (10:13–14) or sought insight from ungodly sources (1 Sam 28:7–25).

14:11 Cf. 13:11.

15:1—16:43 This section recounts the successful move of the ark of the covenant to Jerusalem.

15:1–2 David's previous attempt to move the ark did not appropriately respect God's holiness (13:9–13). On this occasion, David made appropriate preparations (cf. v. 12) and consulted divine instructions (v. 13) concerning carrying the ark (Num 4:15–33; Deut 10:8–9).

6 from the descendants of Merari,
Asaiah the leader and 220 relatives;
7 from the descendants of Gershon,[a]
Joel the leader and 130 relatives;
8 from the descendants of Elizaphan,[e]
Shemaiah the leader and 200 relatives;
9 from the descendants of Hebron,[f]
Eliel the leader and 80 relatives;
10 from the descendants of Uzziel,
Amminadab the leader and 112 relatives.

11 Then David summoned Zadok[g] and Abiathar[h] the priests, and Uriel, Asaiah, Joel, Shemaiah, Eliel
and Amminadab the Levites. 12 He said to them, "You are the heads of the Levitical families; you and
your fellow Levites are to consecrate[i] yourselves and bring up the ark of the LORD, the God of Israel, to
the place I have prepared for it. 13 It was because you, the Levites,[j] did not bring it up the first time that
the LORD our God broke out in anger against us.[k] We did not inquire of him about how to do it in the
prescribed way." 14 So the priests and Levites consecrated themselves in order to bring up the ark of the
LORD, the God of Israel. 15 And the Levites carried the ark of God with the poles on their shoulders, as
Moses had commanded[l] in accordance with the word of the LORD.

16 David told the leaders of the Levites to appoint their fellow Levites as musicians[m] to make a joyful
sound with musical instruments: lyres, harps and cymbals.[n]

17 So the Levites appointed Heman[o] son of Joel; from his relatives, Asaph[p] son of Berekiah; and from
their relatives the Merarites,[q] Ethan son of Kushaiah; 18 and with them their relatives next in rank:
Zechariah,[b] Jaaziel, Shemiramoth, Jehiel, Unni, Eliab, Benaiah, Maaseiah, Mattithiah, Eliphelehu, Mikneiah, Obed-Edom[r] and Jeiel,[c] the gatekeepers.

19 The musicians Heman,[s] Asaph and Ethan were to sound the bronze cymbals; 20 Zechariah, Jaaziel,[d]
Shemiramoth, Jehiel, Unni, Eliab, Maaseiah and Benaiah were to play the lyres according to *alamoth*,[e]
21 and Mattithiah, Eliphelehu, Mikneiah, Obed-Edom, Jeiel and Azaziah were to play the harps, directing
according to *sheminith*.[e] 22 Kenaniah the head Levite was in charge of the singing; that was his responsibility because he was skillful at it.

23 Berekiah and Elkanah were to be doorkeepers for the ark. 24 Shebaniah, Joshaphat, Nethanel,
Amasai, Zechariah, Benaiah and Eliezer the priests were to blow trumpets[t] before the ark of God. Obed-
Edom and Jehiah were also to be doorkeepers for the ark.

25 So David and the elders of Israel and the commanders of units of a thousand went to bring up
the ark[u] of the covenant of the LORD from the house of Obed-Edom, with rejoicing. 26 Because God
had helped the Levites who were carrying the ark of the covenant of the LORD, seven bulls and seven
rams[v] were sacrificed. 27 Now David was clothed in a robe of fine linen, as were all the Levites who were

[a] *7* Hebrew *Gershom,* a variant of *Gershon* [b] *18* Three Hebrew manuscripts and most Septuagint manuscripts (see also verse 20 and 16:5); most Hebrew manuscripts *Zechariah son and* or *Zechariah, Ben and* [c] *18* Hebrew; Septuagint (see also verse 21) *Jeiel and Azaziah* [d] *20* See verse 18; Hebrew *Aziel,* a variant of *Jaaziel.* [e] *20,21* Probably a musical term

15:8 [e] Ex 6:22
15:9 [f] Ex 6:18
15:11 [g] 1Ch 12:28 [h] 1Sa 22:20
15:12 [i] Ex 19:14-15; Lev 11:44; 2Ch 35:6
15:13 [j] 1Ki 8:4 [k] 2Sa 6:3; 1Ch 13:7-10
15:15 [l] Ex 25:14; Nu 4:5,15
15:16 [m] Ps 68:25 [n] 1Ch 13:8; 25:1; Ne 12:27,36
15:17 [o] 1Ch 6:33 [p] 1Ch 6:39 [q] 1Ch 6:44
15:18 [r] 1Ch 26:4-5
15:19 [s] 1Ch 25:6
15:24 [t] ver 28; 1Ch 16:6; 2Ch 7:6
15:25 [u] 1Ch 13:13; 2Ch 1:4
15:26 [v] Nu 23:1-4,29

15:12 consecrate yourselves. The requirement of individuals who had responsibility in the things of God. This reflects the Chronicler's concern that deep, internal issues such as faithfulness, obedience, and personal purity must coincide with external acts of worship (2 Chr 29:11; 35:5). While the priests did not carry the ark (aside from moving the ark into the Most Holy Place [2 Chr 5:7–11]), they were part of the procession that tangibly signified the return of God's presence into the midst of the people.

15:16 make a joyful sound with musical instruments. In addition to carrying the ark (vv. 2,15), Levites had responsibilities in music that facilitated the worshipful atmosphere surrounding the movement of the ark (see 6:31–47 and note). **lyres, harps and cymbals.** See notes on 2 Chr 5:12–13.

15:17 Levites. On the distinctions between priests and Levites, see notes on 6:48–49.

15:20–21 ***alamoth … sheminith.*** Used in several psalm titles (e.g., Ps 6 title; Ps 46 title); they may be musical terms used with respect to stringed instruments (see NIV text notes on Ps 6 title; Ps 46 title; see also Introduction to Psalms: Psalm Titles).

15:23,24 doorkeepers. Worked in conjunction with the priests to insure the sanctity of sacred space and sacred objects.

15:25–28 The return of the ark tangibly marked the return of God's presence and favor (cf. Exod 25:17–22; 1 Sam 4:12–22).

15:27 linen ephod. Typically associated with the Aaronic priesthood (Exod 39:2–7,22–26). While the significance of David's linen ephod is uncertain, these linen robes may have been special regalia the king wore or they may reflect David's participation in the musical portion of the procession (v. 29). Since the Chronicler's summary of David's relocation of the ark stresses that things were done according to God's will (vv. 2,15), it is unlikely that David's attire violated covenantal boundaries.

15:28 [w] 1Ch 13:8
16:1 [x] 1Ch 15:1
16:2 [y] Ex 39:43
16:4 [z] 1Ch 15:2
16:7 [a] 2Sa 23:1
16:8 [b] ver 34; Ps 136:1
[c] 2Ki 19:19
16:9 [d] Ex 15:1
16:11 [e] 1Ch 28:9;
2Ch 7:14; Ps 24:6;
119:2,58
16:12 [f] Ps 77:11
[g] Ps 78:43

carrying the ark, and as were the musicians, and Kenaniah, who was in charge of the singing of the
choirs. David also wore a linen ephod. 28So all Israel brought up the ark of the covenant of the LORD
with shouts, with the sounding of rams' horns[w] and trumpets, and of cymbals, and the playing of lyres
and harps.

29As the ark of the covenant of the LORD was entering the City of David, Michal daughter of Saul
watched from a window. And when she saw King David dancing and celebrating, she despised him in
her heart.

Ministering Before the Ark

16:8-22pp — Ps 105:1-15
16:23-33pp — Ps 96:1-13
16:34-36pp — Ps 106:1,47-48

16 They brought the ark of God and set it inside the tent that David had pitched[x] for it, and
they presented burnt offerings and fellowship offerings before God. 2After David had finished sacrificing the burnt offerings and fellowship offerings, he blessed[y] the people in the name
of the LORD. 3Then he gave a loaf of bread, a cake of dates and a cake of raisins to each Israelite
man and woman.

4He appointed some of the Levites to minister[z] before the ark of the LORD, to extol,[a] thank, and
praise the LORD, the God of Israel: 5Asaph was the chief, and next to him in rank were Zechariah, then
Jaaziel,[b] Shemiramoth, Jehiel, Mattithiah, Eliab, Benaiah, Obed-Edom and Jeiel. They were to play the
lyres and harps, Asaph was to sound the cymbals, 6and Benaiah and Jahaziel the priests were to blow
the trumpets regularly before the ark of the covenant of God.

7That day David first appointed Asaph and his associates to give praise[a] to the LORD in this manner:

8Give praise[b] to the LORD, proclaim his name;
  make known among the nations[c] what he has done.
9Sing to him, sing praise[d] to him;
  tell of all his wonderful acts.
10Glory in his holy name;
  let the hearts of those who seek the LORD rejoice.
11Look to the LORD and his strength;
  seek[e] his face always.

12Remember[f] the wonders he has done,
  his miracles,[g] and the judgments he pronounced,
13you his servants, the descendants of Israel,
  his chosen ones, the children of Jacob.

[a] 4 Or *petition*; or *invoke* [b] 5 See 15:18,20; Hebrew *Jeiel*, possibly another name for *Jaaziel*.

16:1–3 In response to the ark's arrival in Jerusalem, worship ensued in the form of offerings. Compare the ark's move to the Solomonic temple (2 Chr 5:2–14).
16:1 tent. For the ark; it is not the same as the tabernacle constructed during the time of Moses (see note on Exod 25:22 ["I will meet with you"]). The tabernacle and the bronze altar were located at Gibeon at this time (vv. 39–42; 21:29; 2 Chr 1:2–6). **burnt offerings.** Signifying divine-human reconciliation (see Lev 1:3–17 and note; see also note on Lev 1:4). **fellowship offerings.** Signifying divine-human communion (see Lev 3 and note on Lev 3:1).
16:2 blessed. Moses (Exod 39:43), Joshua (Josh 22:6), and Solomon (2 Chr 6:3) gave similar blessings.
16:3 loaf of bread, a cake ... a cake. Gifts of food from David to each Israelite man, perhaps for the journey home.
16:8–36 This poem of thanksgiving echoes Pss 96; 105; 106: cf. vv. 8–22 with Ps 105:1–15; vv. 23–33 with Ps 96:1–13; vv. 34–36 with Ps 106:1,47–48. The three major sections begin with an invitation to thanksgiving and praise: "give praise to the LORD" (v. 8); "sing to the LORD" (v. 23); "give thanks to the LORD" (v. 34). The final section (vv. 34–36) would resonate especially with the Chronicler's postexilic audience ("gather us and deliver us from the nations," v. 35). The content of this poem spans a number of significant covenant themes including references to the patriarchs (vv. 13,16–18) and a reminder of God's protection of his people (vv. 21–22). The declaration in v. 15 that God "remembers his covenant forever"—God's covenant with Abraham probably being in view (vv. 8–22; cf. Ps 105:1–15)—provides the theological foundation for the community's songs, praise, and faith. These doxological truths are to be shared with all humankind: "make known among the nations what he has done" (v. 8); "tell of all his wonderful acts" (v. 9); "declare his glory among the nations, his marvelous deeds among all peoples" (v. 24).

[14]He is the LORD our God;
his judgments[h] are in all the earth.

[15]He remembers[a] his covenant forever,
the promise he made, for a thousand generations,
[16]the covenant[i] he made with Abraham,
the oath he swore to Isaac.
[17]He confirmed it to Jacob[j] as a decree,
to Israel as an everlasting covenant:
[18]"To you I will give the land of Canaan[k]
as the portion you will inherit."
[19]When they were but few in number,[l]
few indeed, and strangers in it,
[20]they[b] wandered from nation to nation,
from one kingdom to another.
[21]He allowed no one to oppress them;
for their sake he rebuked kings:[m]
[22]"Do not touch my anointed ones;
do my prophets[n] no harm."

[23]Sing to the LORD, all the earth;
proclaim his salvation day after day.
[24]Declare his glory among the nations,
his marvelous deeds among all peoples.

[25]For great is the LORD and most worthy of praise;[o]
he is to be feared[p] above all gods.[q]
[26]For all the gods of the nations are idols,
but the LORD made the heavens.[r]
[27]Splendor and majesty are before him;
strength and joy are in his dwelling place.
[28]Ascribe to the LORD, all you families of nations,
ascribe to the LORD glory and strength.[s]
[29]Ascribe to the LORD the glory due his name;
bring an offering and come before him.
Worship the LORD in the splendor of his[c] holiness.[t]
[30]Tremble[u] before him, all the earth!
The world is firmly established; it cannot be moved.
[31]Let the heavens rejoice, let the earth be glad;[v]
let them say among the nations, "The LORD reigns![w]"
[32]Let the sea resound, and all that is in it;[x]
let the fields be jubilant, and everything in them!
[33]Let the trees[y] of the forest sing,
let them sing for joy before the LORD,
for he comes to judge[z] the earth.

[34]Give thanks[a] to the LORD, for he is good;[b]
his love endures forever.[c]
[35]Cry out, "Save us, God our Savior;[d]
gather us and deliver us from the nations,

16:14 [h] Isa 26:9
16:16 [i] Ge 12:7; 15:18; 17:2; 22:16-18; 26:3; 28:13; 35:11
16:17 [j] Ge 35:9-12
16:18 [k] Ge 13:14-17
16:19 [l] Ge 34:30; Dt 7:7
16:21 [m] Ge 12:17; 20:3; Ex 7:15-18
16:22 [n] Ge 20:7
16:25 [o] Ps 48:1 [p] Ps 76:7; 89:7 [q] Dt 32:39
16:26 [r] Lev 19:4; Ps 102:25
16:28 [s] Ps 29:1-2
16:29 [t] Ps 29:1-2
16:30 [u] Ps 114:7
16:31 [v] Isa 44:23; 49:13 [w] Ps 93:1
16:32 [x] Ps 98:7
16:33 [y] Isa 55:12 [z] Ps 96:10; 98:9
16:34 [a] ver 8 [b] Na 1:7 [c] 2Ch 5:13; 7:3; Ezr 3:11; Ps 136:1-26; Jer 33:11
16:35 [d] Mic 7:7

[a] *15* Some Septuagint manuscripts (see also Psalm 105:8); Hebrew *Remember* [b] *18-20* One Hebrew manuscript, Septuagint and Vulgate (see also Psalm 105:12); most Hebrew manuscripts *inherit, / [19]though you are but few in number, / few indeed, and strangers in it." / [20]They* [c] *29* Or *LORD with the splendor of*

16:36 [e] Dt 27:15; 1Ki 8:15; Ps 72:18-19
16:37 [f] 2Ch 8:14
16:38 [g] 1Ch 13:13 [h] 1Ch 26:10
16:39 [i] 2Sa 8:17; 1Ch 15:11 [j] 1Ki 3:4; 2Ch 1:3
16:40 [k] Ex 29:38; Nu 28:1-8
16:41 [l] 1Ch 6:33; 25:1-6; 2Ch 5:13
16:42 [m] 2Ch 7:6
17:1 [n] 1Ch 15:1
17:2 [o] 2Ch 6:7
17:4 [p] 1Ch 28:3
17:7 [q] 2Sa 6:21

that we may give thanks to your holy name,
and glory in your praise."
36 Praise be to the LORD, the God of Israel,[e]
from everlasting to everlasting.

Then all the people said "Amen" and "Praise the LORD."

37 David left Asaph and his associates before the ark of the covenant of the LORD to minister there regularly, according to each day's requirements.[f] 38 He also left Obed-Edom[g] and his sixty-eight associates
to minister with them. Obed-Edom son of Jeduthun, and also Hosah,[h] were gatekeepers.
39 David left Zadok[i] the priest and his fellow priests before the tabernacle of the LORD at the high place
in Gibeon[j] 40 to present burnt offerings to the LORD on the altar of burnt offering regularly, morning
and evening, in accordance with everything written in the Law[k] of the LORD, which he had given Israel.
41 With them were Heman[l] and Jeduthun and the rest of those chosen and designated by name to give
thanks to the LORD, "for his love endures forever." 42 Heman and Jeduthun were responsible for the
sounding of the trumpets and cymbals and for the playing of the other instruments for sacred song.[m]
The sons of Jeduthun were stationed at the gate.
43 Then all the people left, each for their own home, and David returned home to bless his family.

God's Promise to David

17:1-15pp — 2Sa 7:1-17

17 After David was settled in his palace, he said to Nathan the prophet, "Here I am, living in a
house of cedar, while the ark of the covenant of the LORD is under a tent.[n]"
2 Nathan replied to David, "Whatever you have in mind,[o] do it, for God is with you."
3 But that night the word of God came to Nathan, saying:

4 "Go and tell my servant David, 'This is what the LORD says: You[p] are not the one to build me a
house to dwell in. 5 I have not dwelt in a house from the day I brought Israel up out of Egypt to this
day. I have moved from one tent site to another, from one dwelling place to another. 6 Wherever I
have moved with all the Israelites, did I ever say to any of their leaders[a] whom I commanded to
shepherd my people, "Why have you not built me a house of cedar?"'
7 "Now then, tell my servant David, 'This is what the LORD Almighty says: I took you from the
pasture, from tending the flock, and appointed you ruler[q] over my people Israel. 8 I have been with
you wherever you have gone, and I have cut off all your enemies from before you. Now I will make
your name like the names of the greatest men on earth. 9 And I will provide a place for my people
Israel and will plant them so that they can have a home of their own and no longer be disturbed.

[a] 6 Traditionally *judges*; also in verse 10

16:39–42 See notes on 6:31–47,48–49.

16:39 high place in Gibeon. See note on 2 Chr 1:3.

17:1–27 *The Davidic Covenant.* While the phrase "Davidic covenant" commonly describes God's promise to David, Nathan's revelation does not use the term "covenant" (vv. 4–14; cf. 2 Sam 7:5–16). The primary emphasis of the Davidic covenant articulated via the prophet Nathan focuses on a specific son of David, namely, Solomon. For example, although David would not be the one to build the temple (22:8–10, 28:2–4; 2 Chr 6:7–9), his son/descendant (singular) would build a temple for the Lord (vv. 11–12; 22:6–11; 28:5–7). David and Solomon both understood this individual to be Solomon (22:6–11; 28:5–7; 2 Chr 1:7–9). In his temple dedication prayer, Solomon repeatedly refers to the Lord fulfilling his word to David (1 Kgs 8:12–61, especially 8:15,20,24; cf. 2 Chr 6:4–10 with 1 Chr 17:7–14). Beyond this one-generation promise to David, a layer of conditionality was connected with later Davidic leaders that is reflected in God's response to Solomon's prayer (2 Chr 7:11–22; 1 Kgs 9:3–9; cf. 1 Chr 28:7). The dynamics of God's promises to David were cited by God in the midst of Solomon's later apostasy and caused the division of the kingdom to come *after* Solomon (1 Kgs 11:9–40). The Messianic (and unconditional) application of the Davidic covenant (Rom 1:3), including an eternal kingdom with everlasting peace, is gleaned from the broader setting of Nathan's prophetic word to David and subsequent biblical revelation (Pss 89:35–37; 132:11–12; Isa 9:7; Jer 33:19–22; Luke 1:32; Heb 1:5). God based this fuller promise to David on account of God's word and character rather than human effort.

17:3–6 God's initial response to David's building a temple ("house" [v. 4] for God's dwelling) was not positive. The anticipation that God would choose a place to cause his Name to dwell (Deut 12:5) is coupled with the negative reality that people tend to worship God "in their way" and "as they see fit" (Deut 12:4,8). The Lord's message to Nathan was that he is not like the gods of the nations and does not need a dwelling place ("did I ever say," v. 6).

17:7–15 Although David's idea to build a temple was not well received, God revealed that David's son would be given the honor of building a "house" (v. 12; i.e., temple) for God and that God would build a "house" (v. 10; i.e., dynasty) for David.

Wicked people will not oppress them anymore, as they did at the beginning 10and have done ever since the time I appointed leaders[r] over my people Israel. I will also subdue all your enemies.
"'I declare to you that the LORD will build a house for you: 11When your days are over and you go to be with your ancestors, I will raise up your offspring to succeed you, one of your own sons, and I will establish his kingdom. 12He is the one who will build[s] a house for me, and I will establish his throne forever.[t] 13I will be his father,[u] and he will be my son.[v] I will never take my love away from him, as I took it away from your predecessor. 14I will set him over my house and my kingdom forever; his throne[w] will be established forever.[x]'"

15Nathan reported to David all the words of this entire revelation.

David's Prayer

17:16-27pp — 2Sa 7:18-29

16Then King David went in and sat before the LORD, and he said:

"Who am I, LORD God, and what is my family, that you have brought me this far? 17And as if this were not enough in your sight, my God, you have spoken about the future of the house of your servant. You, LORD God, have looked on me as though I were the most exalted of men.

18"What more can David say to you for honoring your servant? For you know your servant, 19LORD. For the sake[y] of your servant and according to your will, you have done this great thing and made known all these great promises.[z]

20"There is no one like you, LORD, and there is no God but you,[a] as we have heard with our own ears. 21And who is like your people Israel — the one nation on earth whose God went out to redeem[b] a people for himself, and to make a name for yourself, and to perform great and awesome wonders by driving out nations from before your people, whom you redeemed from Egypt? 22You made your people Israel your very own forever,[c] and you, LORD, have become their God.

23"And now, LORD, let the promise[d] you have made concerning your servant and his house be established forever. Do as you promised, 24so that it will be established and that your name will be great forever. Then people will say, 'The LORD Almighty, the God over Israel, is Israel's God!' And the house of your servant David will be established before you.

25"You, my God, have revealed to your servant that you will build a house for him. So your servant has found courage to pray to you. 26You, LORD, are God! You have promised these good things to your servant. 27Now you have been pleased to bless the house of your servant, that it may continue forever in your sight;[e] for you, LORD, have blessed it, and it will be blessed forever."

David's Victories

18:1-13pp — 2Sa 8:1-14

18 In the course of time, David defeated the Philistines and subdued them, and he took Gath and its surrounding villages from the control of the Philistines.

2David also defeated the Moabites,[f] and they became subject to him and brought him tribute.

3Moreover, David defeated Hadadezer king of Zobah,[g] in the vicinity of Hamath, when he went to set up his monument at[a] the Euphrates River.[h] 4David captured a thousand of his chariots, seven

[a] 3 Or *to restore his control over*

17:10 [r] Jdg 2:16
17:12 [s] 1Ki 5:5 [t] 2Ch 7:18
17:13 [u] 2Co 6:18 [v] Lk 1:32; Heb 1:5*
17:14 [w] 1Ki 2:12; 1Ch 28:5 [x] Ps 132:11; Jer 33:17
17:19 [y] 2Sa 7:16-17; 2Ki 20:6; Isa 9:7; 37:35; 55:3 [z] 2Sa 7:25
17:20 [a] Ex 8:10; 9:14; 15:11; Isa 44:6; 46:9
17:21 [b] Ex 6:6
17:22 [c] Ex 19:5-6
17:23 [d] 1Ki 8:25
17:27 [e] Ps 16:11; 21:6
18:2 [f] Nu 21:29
18:3 [g] 1Ch 19:6 [h] Ge 2:14

17:16–27 David's response reflected his awe of God's promise (v. 23).
17:20–23 There is no one like you, LORD ... you redeemed from Egypt ... You made your people Israel your very own forever. David's humility and awe tie directly to God's uniqueness (cf. 2 Chr 14:11; 20:6) and his choice of Israel to be his redeemed people.
17:23 house. Dynasty.
17:24 Then people will say. David understood that God's blessing of Israel would lead to God's ways becoming known to all humankind.
18:1 — 20:8 *David's Military Victories and Regional Power.* The Chronicler summarizes various accomplishments that reflect God's hand of blessing on David.
18:1–14 This summary of David's accomplishments (cf. 2 Sam 8) overviews the political and military moves that expanded Israel's geographic extent during David's reign (cf. Pss 60:6–12; 108:7–13): in the east against the Ammonites (v. 11) and Moabites (vv. 2,11); in the west against the Philistines (vv. 1,11); in the south against Edom (vv. 11–13); in the north against the Arameans/Syrians (vv. 3–10). This summary illustrates that David controlled part of the key trade routes passing on either side of Israel: the Coastal Highway to the west and a large stretch of the Transjordan King's Highway.

18:4 [i]Ge 49:6
18:5 [j]2Ki 16:9; 1Ch 19:6
18:8 [k]1Ki 7:23; 2Ch 4:12,15-16
18:11 [l]Nu 24:18 [m]Nu 24:20
18:12 [n]1Ki 11:15
18:14 [o]1Ch 29:26 [p]1Ch 11:1
18:15 [q]2Sa 5:6-8; 1Ch 11:6
18:16 [r]2Sa 8:17; 1Ch 6:8 [s]1Ch 24:6
18:17 [t]1Sa 30:14; 2Sa 8:18; 15:18
19:1 [u]Ge 19:38; Jdg 10:17-11:33; 2Ch 20:1-2; Zep 2:8-11
19:3 [v]Nu 21:32
19:6 [w]Ge 34:30 [x]1Ch 18:3,5,9
19:7 [y]Nu 21:30; Jos 13:9,16

thousand charioteers and twenty thousand foot soldiers. He hamstrung[i] all but a hundred of the chariot horses.

[5]When the Arameans of Damascus[j] came to help Hadadezer king of Zobah, David struck down twenty-two thousand of them. [6]He put garrisons in the Aramean kingdom of Damascus, and the Arameans became subject to him and brought him tribute. The LORD gave David victory wherever he went.

[7]David took the gold shields carried by the officers of Hadadezer and brought them to Jerusalem. [8]From Tebah[a] and Kun, towns that belonged to Hadadezer, David took a great quantity of bronze, which Solomon used to make the bronze Sea,[k] the pillars and various bronze articles.

[9]When Tou king of Hamath heard that David had defeated the entire army of Hadadezer king of Zobah, [10]he sent his son Hadoram to King David to greet him and congratulate him on his victory in battle over Hadadezer, who had been at war with Tou. Hadoram brought all kinds of articles of gold, of silver and of bronze.

[11]King David dedicated these articles to the LORD, as he had done with the silver and gold he had taken from all these nations: Edom[l] and Moab, the Ammonites and the Philistines, and Amalek.[m]

[12]Abishai son of Zeruiah struck down eighteen thousand Edomites[n] in the Valley of Salt. [13]He put garrisons in Edom, and all the Edomites became subject to David. The LORD gave David victory wherever he went.

David's Officials

18:14-17pp — 2Sa 8:15-18

[14]David reigned[o] over all Israel,[p] doing what was just and right for all his people. [15]Joab[q] son of Zeruiah was over the army; Jehoshaphat son of Ahilud was recorder; [16]Zadok[r] son of Ahitub and Ahimelek[b][s] son of Abiathar were priests; Shavsha was secretary; [17]Benaiah son of Jehoiada was over the Kerethites and Pelethites;[t] and David's sons were chief officials at the king's side.

David Defeats the Ammonites

19:1-19pp — 2Sa 10:1-19

19 In the course of time, Nahash king of the Ammonites[u] died, and his son succeeded him as king. [2]David thought, "I will show kindness to Hanun son of Nahash, because his father showed kindness to me." So David sent a delegation to express his sympathy to Hanun concerning his father.

When David's envoys came to Hanun in the land of the Ammonites to express sympathy to him, [3]the Ammonite commanders said to Hanun, "Do you think David is honoring your father by sending envoys to you to express sympathy? Haven't his envoys come to you only to explore and spy out[v] the country and overthrow it?" [4]So Hanun seized David's envoys, shaved them, cut off their garments at the buttocks, and sent them away.

[5]When someone came and told David about the men, he sent messengers to meet them, for they were greatly humiliated. The king said, "Stay at Jericho till your beards have grown, and then come back."

[6]When the Ammonites realized that they had become obnoxious[w] to David, Hanun and the Ammonites sent a thousand talents[c] of silver to hire chariots and charioteers from Aram Naharaim,[d] Aram Maakah and Zobah.[x] [7]They hired thirty-two thousand chariots and charioteers, as well as the king of Maakah with his troops, who came and camped near Medeba,[y] while the Ammonites were mustered from their towns and moved out for battle.

[8]On hearing this, David sent Joab out with the entire army of fighting men. [9]The Ammonites came out and drew up in battle formation at the entrance to their city, while the kings who had come were by themselves in the open country.

[a] *8* Hebrew *Tibhath,* a variant of *Tebah* [b] *16* Some Hebrew manuscripts, Vulgate and Syriac (see also 2 Samuel 8:17); most Hebrew manuscripts *Abimelek* [c] *6* That is, about 38 tons or about 34 metric tons [d] *6* That is, Northwest Mesopotamia

18:6 The LORD gave David victory wherever he went. "David" includes the help of his military leaders, such as Abishai (see vv. 12–13). In turn, "David dedicated ... to the LORD" (v. 11) the spoils of his victories, some of which Solomon later used to construct the temple (vv. 8–11).

19:4 shaved them, cut off their garments at the buttocks. This treatment of the Israelite delegation by the Ammonites shamed David's men and by extension, David and all Israel.

[10]Joab saw that there were battle lines in front of him and behind him; so he selected some of the best
troops in Israel and deployed them against the Arameans. [11]He put the rest of the men under the command of Abishai[z] his brother, and they were deployed against the Ammonites. [12]Joab said, "If the Arameans are too strong for me, then you are to rescue me; but if the Ammonites are too strong for you,
then I will rescue you. [13]Be strong, and let us fight bravely for our people and the cities of our God. The
LORD will do what is good in his sight."

[14]Then Joab and the troops with him advanced to fight the Arameans, and they fled before him.
[15]When the Ammonites realized that the Arameans were fleeing, they too fled before his brother Abishai
and went inside the city. So Joab went back to Jerusalem.

[16]After the Arameans saw that they had been routed by Israel, they sent messengers and had Arameans brought from beyond the Euphrates River, with Shophak the commander of Hadadezer's army
leading them.

[17]When David was told of this, he gathered all Israel[a] and crossed the Jordan; he advanced against them
and formed his battle lines opposite them. David formed his lines to meet the Arameans in battle, and they
fought against him. [18]But they fled before Israel, and David killed seven thousand of their charioteers and
forty thousand of their foot soldiers. He also killed Shophak the commander of their army.

[19]When the vassals of Hadadezer saw that they had been routed by Israel, they made peace with
David and became subject to him.

So the Arameans were not willing to help the Ammonites anymore.

The Capture of Rabbah

20:1-3pp — 2Sa 11:1; 12:29-31

20 In the spring, at the time when kings go off to war, Joab led out the armed forces. He laid
waste the land of the Ammonites and went to Rabbah[b] and besieged it, but David remained
in Jerusalem. Joab attacked Rabbah and left it in ruins.[c] [2]David took the crown from the head of their
king[a] — its weight was found to be a talent[b] of gold, and it was set with precious stones — and it was
placed on David's head. He took a great quantity of plunder from the city [3]and brought out the people
who were there, consigning them to labor with saws and with iron picks and axes.[d] David did this to all
the Ammonite towns. Then David and his entire army returned to Jerusalem.

War With the Philistines

20:4-8pp — 2Sa 21:15-22

[4]In the course of time, war broke out with the Philistines, at Gezer.[e] At that time Sibbekai the Hushathite killed Sippai, one of the descendants of the Rephaites,[f] and the Philistines were subjugated.

[5]In another battle with the Philistines, Elhanan son of Jair killed Lahmi the brother of Goliath the
Gittite, who had a spear with a shaft like a weaver's rod.[g]

[6]In still another battle, which took place at Gath, there was a huge man with six fingers on each

19:11 [z] 1Sa 26:6
19:17 [a] 1Ch 9:1
20:1 [b] Dt 3:11; 2Sa 12:26 [c] Am 1:13-15
20:3 [d] Dt 29:11
20:4 [e] Jos 10:33 [f] Ge 14:5
20:5 [g] 1Sa 17:7

[a] *2* Or *of Milkom,* that is, Molek [b] *2* That is, about 75 pounds or about 34 kilograms

19:12–13 Joab's words are reminiscent of those the Lord spoke to Joshua as the Israelites prepared to enter the promised land (Josh 1:5–9; cf. Deut 31:7–8).

19:13 Be strong. Biblically speaking, this means to be immovably committed to obedience and trust in God. Joab's exhortation is rooted in the notion of God's sovereignty and goodness ("the LORD will do what is good in his sight").

20:1 In the spring, at the time when kings go off to war ... David remained in Jerusalem. While the Chronicler does not specifically mention the Bathsheba-Uriah affair that took place during this battle against the Ammonites, the opening of this chapter reminds the reader of the unfortunate backdrop to this victory (2 Sam 11:1). **spring.** The preferred time for warfare in the biblical world given the rains of the fall and winter and the stifling heat of summer.

20:2–3 At some point during Joab's impending victory over the Ammonites, David arrived at the vanquished city and assumed the position of victor (note Joab's words in 2 Sam 12:26–31).

20:2 crown. The Septuagint (the pre-Christian Greek translation of the OT) refers to this as the crown of the Ammonite god Milkom, not the crown of the Ammonite king. This may explain the sizable weight of the crown (approximately 65–75 pounds [30–34 kilograms]).

20:4–8 These summaries underscore David's dominance over the formidable champions of the Philistine city-states. Each champion was associated with the Rephaites, noted for their massive physical size. Goliath was over 9 feet (2.7 meters) tall, while the bed of Og (Deut 3:11) was about 14 feet (4 meters) long and 6 feet (1.8 meters) wide. While these short vignettes do not specifically mention God, these victories reflect the Chronicler's earlier note that the Lord gave David victory wherever he went (see 18:6 and note). To oppose David was to oppose God.

21:1 [h]2Ch 18:21; Ps 109:6 [i]2Ch 14:8; 25:5
21:2 [j]1Ch 27:23-24
21:3 [k]Dt 1:11
21:5 [l]1Ch 9:1
21:9 [m]1Sa 22:5 [n]1Sa 9:9
21:12 [o]Dt 32:24 [p]Eze 30:25 [q]Ge 19:13
21:13 [r]Ps 6:4; 86:15; 130:4,7
21:14 [s]1Ch 27:24
21:15 [t]Ge 32:1 [u]Ps 125:2 [v]Ge 6:6; Ex 32:14 [w]Ge 19:13
21:16 [x]Nu 14:5; Jos 7:6

hand and six toes on each foot — twenty-four in all. He also was descended from Rapha. 7When he taunted Israel, Jonathan son of Shimea, David's brother, killed him.

8These were descendants of Rapha in Gath, and they fell at the hands of David and his men.

David Counts the Fighting Men

21:1-26pp — 2Sa 24:1-25

21 Satan[h] rose up against Israel and incited David to take a census[i] of Israel. 2So David said to Joab and the commanders of the troops, "Go and count[j] the Israelites from Beersheba to Dan. Then report back to me so that I may know how many there are."

3But Joab replied, "May the LORD multiply his troops a hundred times over.[k] My lord the king, are they not all my lord's subjects? Why does my lord want to do this? Why should he bring guilt on Israel?"

4The king's word, however, overruled Joab; so Joab left and went throughout Israel and then came back to Jerusalem. 5Joab reported the number of the fighting men to David: In all Israel[l] there were one million one hundred thousand men who could handle a sword, including four hundred and seventy thousand in Judah.

6But Joab did not include Levi and Benjamin in the numbering, because the king's command was repulsive to him. 7This command was also evil in the sight of God; so he punished Israel.

8Then David said to God, "I have sinned greatly by doing this. Now, I beg you, take away the guilt of your servant. I have done a very foolish thing."

9The LORD said to Gad,[m] David's seer,[n] 10"Go and tell David, 'This is what the LORD says: I am giving you three options. Choose one of them for me to carry out against you.'"

11So Gad went to David and said to him, "This is what the LORD says: 'Take your choice: 12three years of famine,[o] three months of being swept away[a] before your enemies, with their swords overtaking you, or three days of the sword[p] of the LORD[q] — days of plague in the land, with the angel of the LORD ravaging every part of Israel.' Now then, decide how I should answer the one who sent me."

13David said to Gad, "I am in deep distress. Let me fall into the hands of the LORD, for his mercy[r] is very great; but do not let me fall into human hands."

14So the LORD sent a plague on Israel, and seventy thousand men of Israel fell dead.[s] 15And God sent an angel[t] to destroy Jerusalem.[u] But as the angel was doing so, the LORD saw it and relented[v] concerning the disaster and said to the angel who was destroying[w] the people, "Enough! Withdraw your hand." The angel of the LORD was then standing at the threshing floor of Araunah[b] the Jebusite.

16David looked up and saw the angel of the LORD standing between heaven and earth, with a drawn sword in his hand extended over Jerusalem. Then David and the elders, clothed in sackcloth, fell facedown.[x]

[a] 12 Hebrew; Septuagint and Vulgate (see also 2 Samuel 24:13) *of fleeing* [b] 15 Hebrew *Ornan,* a variant of *Araunah*; also in verses 18-28

21:1 — 22:1 *David's Census and Selection of the Temple Site.* Using the reality of David's sinfulness, the Chronicler presents the backdrop to the place where God later chose to dwell — a place of atonement, forgiveness, reconciliation, and prayer.

21:1 – 7 While David's motivation for ordering this census is unspecified, a military-oriented census (v. 5) implies a level of trust in troops rather than God. The Chronicler frequently highlights examples of complete trust in God (2 Chr 14:11; 20:12; 25:7 – 10) as well as breaches of complete trust in God (2 Chr 16:7 – 8; 28:16). The revulsion (v. 3) and subsequent disobedience (v. 6) of Joab toward David's command underscore the unfaithfulness reflected in David's request. Joab's admonition to David ("Why ... bring guilt on Israel?" v. 3) foreshadows the divine judgment that later struck the nation.

21:1 Satan. The personal being "Satan" is not necessarily in view here. The term S/satan transliterates the Hebrew term meaning "adversary" or "accuser," with lowercase *s* indicating a general adversary (1 Kgs 5:4) and capital *S* reflecting *the* adversary (the devil). The uses of this term wherein *the* supernatural adversary (Satan; the devil) is in view include Job 1 – 2; Zech 3:1 – 2. In these occurrences, the term "Satan" has the Hebrew definite article (underscoring the idea of "*the* adversary"). But the term here does not have the Hebrew definite article and may reflect that the Chronicler intends a human adversary. Beyond the question of the intended meaning of S/satan, the parallel account in Samuel says that "the LORD ... incited David" (2 Sam 24:1). While this at first may seem to be a perplexing difference, in biblical terms though the actions of a supernatural adversary (Job 1 – 2) or a human adversary (1 Kgs 11:14,23) may be contrary to God's revealed will, God still sovereignly directs them toward his intended ends.

21:5 On these large numbers, see Introduction: Particular Challenges (Issues Involving Numbers).

21:8 I have sinned. In the aftermath of his census, David realized his actions were "evil in the sight of God" (v. 7), and he repented.

21:9 – 13 Despite David's earnest repentance, divine judgment followed. The prophet Gad mediated this judgment (see note on vv. 18 – 27).

21:9 seer. Prophet.

21:16 clothed in sackcloth, fell facedown. In the midst of the vision of the destroying angel, David and the elders sought God's mercy (cf. "in wrath remember mercy," Hab 3:2).

[17]David said to God, "Was it not I who ordered the fighting men to be counted? I, the shepherd,[a]
have sinned and done wrong. These are but sheep.[y] What have they done? LORD my God, let your hand
fall on me and my family,[z] but do not let this plague remain on your people."

David Builds an Altar

[18]Then the angel of the LORD ordered Gad to tell David to go up and build an altar to the LORD on
the threshing floor[a] of Araunah the Jebusite. [19]So David went up in obedience to the word that Gad had
spoken in the name of the LORD.
[20]While Araunah was threshing wheat,[b] he turned and saw the angel; his four sons who were with
him hid themselves. [21]Then David approached, and when Araunah looked and saw him, he left the
threshing floor and bowed down before David with his face to the ground.
[22]David said to him, "Let me have the site of your threshing floor so I can build an altar to the LORD,
that the plague on the people may be stopped. Sell it to me at the full price."
[23]Araunah said to David, "Take it! Let my lord the king do whatever pleases him. Look, I will give the
oxen for the burnt offerings, the threshing sledges for the wood, and the wheat for the grain offering.
I will give all this."
[24]But King David replied to Araunah, "No, I insist on paying the full price. I will not take for the LORD
what is yours, or sacrifice a burnt offering that costs me nothing."
[25]So David paid Araunah six hundred shekels[b] of gold for the site. [26]David built an altar to the LORD
there and sacrificed burnt offerings and fellowship offerings. He called on the LORD, and the LORD answered him with fire[c] from heaven on the altar of burnt offering.
[27]Then the LORD spoke to the angel, and he put his sword back into its sheath. [28]At that time, when
David saw that the LORD had answered him on the threshing floor of Araunah the Jebusite, he offered
sacrifices there. [29]The tabernacle of the LORD, which Moses had made in the wilderness, and the altar
of burnt offering were at that time on the high place at Gibeon.[d] [30]But David could not go before it to
inquire of God, because he was afraid of the sword of the angel of the LORD.

22 Then David said, "The house of the LORD God[e] is to be here, and also the altar of burnt offering for Israel."

Preparations for the Temple

[2]So David gave orders to assemble the foreigners[f] residing in Israel, and from among them he
appointed stonecutters[g] to prepare dressed stone for building the house of God. [3]He provided a large
amount of iron to make nails for the doors of the gateways and for the fittings, and more bronze than

21:17 [y] 2Sa 7:8; Ps 74:1 [z] Jnh 1:12
21:18 [a] 2Ch 3:1
21:20 [b] Jdg 6:11
21:26 [c] Lev 9:24; Jdg 6:21
21:29 [d] 1Ki 3:4; 1Ch 16:39
22:1 [e] Ge 28:17; 1Ch 21:18-29; 2Ch 3:1
22:2 [f] 1Ki 9:21; Isa 56:6 [g] 1Ki 5:17-18

[a] *17* Probable reading of the original Hebrew text (see 2 Samuel 24:17 and note); Masoretic Text does not have *the shepherd.* [b] *25* That is, about 15 pounds or about 6.9 kilograms

21:17 What have they done? The outworking of God's judgment was especially difficult for David as he realized that the consequences of his sin spilled over on to his "sheep."
21:18–27 Gad also (see note on vv. 9–13) mediated the path to God's grace and reconciliation.
21:18 threshing floor of Araunah the Jebusite. God directed David (via the prophet Gad) to build an altar at the place where the Lord had already in grace held back the destroying angel (v. 15). Because God chose it as the place of sacrifice and atonement for David's sin, David's decision regarding this location for the Jerusalem temple (22:1) followed God's announced choice. The location of the temple connects with divine grace and forgiveness as well as substitutionary sacrifice and a divine encounter (cf. Gen 22:14). Thus, the Chronicler connects the temple with Abraham and David and underscores that the temple will be a place of propitiation, grace, divine presence, prayer, and forgiveness.
21:24 Even though David was the monarch of the land, David insisted on paying the "full price" for the threshing floor and the surrounding area that eventually comprised the temple complex.
21:25 six hundred shekels. 2 Sam 24:24b records the price as 50 shekels. The difference may relate to the specification of the "threshing floor" in Samuel, whereas in Chronicles "the site" (the broader parcel of land used for the temple complex) is in view.
21:26 fire from heaven. Along with God's command to the destroying angel to put away his sword (v. 27), this reflects the efficacy of David's sacrifice and God's sanctification of the altar (cf. 2 Chr 7:1).
22:1 The house of the LORD God is to be here, and also the altar of burnt offering. See note on 21:18.
22:2—29:30 *David's Temple Preparations and Leadership Transfer.* This section does not have a sustained parallel in the books of Samuel or Kings. It may correspond to the time that 1 Kgs 2:1–12 summarizes. These chapters shift from a focus on David to a focus on Solomon within the context of David's preparations for the Jerusalem temple.
22:2 David used resident aliens living within Israel for his royal workforce.
22:3–4 iron ... bronze ... cedar. The raw materials noted here reflect a combination of David's hegemony over the Philistines ("iron"), economic-political cooperation with Phoenicia ("cedar"), and military conquests ("bronze").

22:3 [h]ver 14; 1Ki 7:47; 1Ch 29:2-5
22:4 [i]1Ki 5:6
22:5 [j]1Ki 3:7; 1Ch 29:1
22:6 [k]Ac 7:47
22:7 [l]1Ch 17:2 [m]2Sa 7:2; 1Ki 8:17 [n]Dt 12:5,11
22:8 [o]1Ki 5:3 [p]1Ch 28:3
22:9 [q]1Ki 5:4 [r]2Sa 12:24 [s]1Ki 4:20
22:10 [t]1Ch 17:12 [u]2Sa 7:13 [v]2Sa 7:14; 2Ch 6:15
22:11 [w]ver 16
22:12 [x]1Ki 3:9-12; 2Ch 1:10
22:13 [y]1Ch 28:7 [z]Dt 31:6; Jos 1:6-9; 1Ch 28:20
22:14 [a]ver 3; 1Ch 29:2-5,19
22:16 [b]ver 11; 2Ch 2:7
22:17 [c]1Ch 28:1-6
22:18 [d]ver 9; 1Ch 23:25 [e]2Sa 7:1
22:19 [f]ver 7; 1Ki 8:6; 1Ch 28:9; 2Ch 5:7; 7:14
23:1 [g]1Ki 1:33-39; 1Ch 28:5 [h]1Ki 1:30; 1Ch 29:28
23:3 [i]ver 24; Nu 8:24 [j]Nu 4:3-49

could be weighed.[h] 4 He also provided more cedar logs[i] than could be counted, for the Sidonians and Tyrians had brought large numbers of them to David.

5 David said, "My son Solomon is young[j] and inexperienced, and the house to be built for the LORD should be of great magnificence and fame and splendor in the sight of all the nations. Therefore I will make preparations for it." So David made extensive preparations before his death.

6 Then he called for his son Solomon and charged him to build[k] a house for the LORD, the God of Israel. 7 David said to Solomon: "My son, I had it in my heart[l] to build[m] a house for the Name[n] of the LORD my God. 8 But this word of the LORD came to me: 'You have shed much blood and have fought many wars.[o] You are not to build a house for my Name,[p] because you have shed much blood on the earth in my sight. 9 But you will have a son who will be a man of peace[q] and rest, and I will give him rest from all his enemies on every side. His name will be Solomon,[a][r] and I will grant Israel peace and quiet[s] during his reign. 10 He is the one who will build a house for my Name.[t] He will be my son,[u] and I will be his father. And I will establish the throne of his kingdom over Israel forever.'[v]

11 "Now, my son, the LORD be with[w] you, and may you have success and build the house of the LORD your God, as he said you would. 12 May the LORD give you discretion and understanding[x] when he puts you in command over Israel, so that you may keep the law of the LORD your God. 13 Then you will have success if you are careful to observe the decrees and laws[y] that the LORD gave Moses for Israel. Be strong and courageous.[z] Do not be afraid or discouraged.

14 "I have taken great pains to provide for the temple of the LORD a hundred thousand talents[b] of gold, a million talents[c] of silver, quantities of bronze and iron too great to be weighed, and wood and stone. And you may add to them.[a] 15 You have many workers: stonecutters, masons and carpenters, as well as those skilled in every kind of work 16 in gold and silver, bronze and iron—craftsmen[b] beyond number. Now begin the work, and the LORD be with you."

17 Then David ordered[c] all the leaders of Israel to help his son Solomon. 18 He said to them, "Is not the LORD your God with you? And has he not granted you rest[d] on every side?[e] For he has given the inhabitants of the land into my hands, and the land is subject to the LORD and to his people. 19 Now devote your heart and soul to seeking the LORD your God.[f] Begin to build the sanctuary of the LORD God, so that you may bring the ark of the covenant of the LORD and the sacred articles belonging to God into the temple that will be built for the Name of the LORD."

The Levites

23 When David was old and full of years, he made his son Solomon[g] king over Israel.[h] 2 He also gathered together all the leaders of Israel, as well as the priests and Levites. 3 The Levites thirty years old or more[i] were counted, and the total number of men was thirty-eight thousand.[j]

[a] *9* *Solomon* sounds like and may be derived from the Hebrew for *peace*. [b] *14* That is, about 3,750 tons or about 3,400 metric tons [c] *14* That is, about 37,500 tons or about 34,000 metric tons

22:5 Basically repeated in 29:1. David wanted the temple to be an apex of beauty and craftsmanship that reminded God's people of the beauty of God's holiness (Ps 29:2). David's extensive preparations for the temple underscore that the Jerusalem temple was in many ways a joint project of David and Solomon. In addition, because the Jerusalem temple and the Davidic monarchy were closely linked, the restoration of the one during the postexilic period would raise expectation that the other might also be restored.

22:6–10 See note on 17:7–15.

22:11–13 the LORD be with you ... give you discretion and understanding ... to observe the decrees and laws. God's presence together with the gifts of wisdom and understanding that come from above enable obedience. **build the house of the LORD ... keep the law of the LORD ... observe the decrees and laws that the LORD gave Moses.** David's charge reflects the reality that building a temple for the Lord was a spiritual exercise as much as it was a building enterprise. What is pleasing in the eyes of the Lord has a direct correlation to obedience and covenantal faithfulness.

22:13 Be strong and courageous. Do not be afraid or discouraged. The same words spoken to Joshua by Moses (Deut 31:7–8) and by the Lord (Josh 1:5–9) as the Israelites prepared to enter the promised land. **strong and courageous.** These are inseparable from God's presence, a reality greater than any challenge Solomon would face as a leader.

22:18 David's reminder of God's faithfulness encouraged "the leaders of Israel" (v. 17) that God would complete the good work he had begun in the covenantal life of Israel (cf. Phil 1:6).

22:19 devote your heart and soul to seeking the LORD. David's charge to the leaders (vv. 18–19) was inseparably connected with their obedience to God's word (see 2 Chr 14:4; cf. John 15:10,14). As with Solomon (vv. 11,16), God's presence (v. 18) was at the center of David's admonition to the leaders of Israel, for only God's enabling power can shape human hearts to his pleasure (Phil 2:13).

23:1 When David was old and full of years. Indicates a coregency with Solomon—a paradigm for stability utilized by subsequent kings of Israel and Judah. Although most royal summaries in Chronicles and Kings do not comment on coregencies, the likelihood of coregencies is an important factor in resolving dating challenges during the divided kingdom period.

23:2–6 See notes on 6:48–49.

[4]David said, "Of these, twenty-four thousand are to be in charge[k] of the work of the temple of the LORD
and six thousand are to be officials and judges.[l] [5]Four thousand are to be gatekeepers and four thousand are to praise the LORD with the musical instruments[m] I have provided for that purpose."[n]
[6]David separated[o] the Levites into divisions corresponding to the sons of Levi: Gershon, Kohath and
Merari.

Gershonites

[7]Belonging to the Gershonites:

Ladan and Shimei.

[8]The sons of Ladan:

Jehiel the first, Zetham and Joel — three in all.

[9]The sons of Shimei:

Shelomoth, Haziel and Haran — three in all.

These were the heads of the families of Ladan.

[10]And the sons of Shimei:

Jahath, Ziza,[a] Jeush and Beriah.

These were the sons of Shimei — four in all.

[11]Jahath was the first and Ziza the second, but Jeush and Beriah did not have many sons; so they
were counted as one family with one assignment.

Kohathites

[12]The sons of Kohath:[p]

Amram, Izhar, Hebron and Uzziel — four in all.

[13]The sons of Amram:[q]

Aaron and Moses.

Aaron was set apart,[r] he and his descendants forever, to consecrate the most holy things, to offer sacrifices before the LORD, to minister before him and to pronounce blessings[s] in his name
forever. [14]The sons of Moses the man[t] of God were counted as part of the tribe of Levi.

[15]The sons of Moses:

Gershom and Eliezer.[u]

[16]The descendants of Gershom:[v]

Shubael was the first.

[17]The descendants of Eliezer:

Rehabiah was the first.

Eliezer had no other sons, but the sons of Rehabiah were very numerous.

[18]The sons of Izhar:

Shelomith was the first.

[19]The sons of Hebron:[w]

Jeriah the first, Amariah the second, Jahaziel the third and Jekameam the fourth.

[20]The sons of Uzziel:

Micah the first and Ishiah the second.

Merarites

[21]The sons of Merari:[x]

Mahli and Mushi.

The sons of Mahli:

Eleazar and Kish.

[22]Eleazar died without having sons: he had only daughters. Their cousins, the sons of Kish,
married them.

[a] *10* One Hebrew manuscript, Septuagint and Vulgate (see also verse 11); most Hebrew manuscripts *Zina*

23:4 [k]Ezr 3:8 [l]1Ch 26:29; 2Ch 19:8
23:5 [m]1Ch 15:16 [n]Ne 12:45
23:6 [o]2Ch 8:14; 29:25
23:12 [p]Ex 6:18
23:13 [q]Ex 6:20; 28:1 [r]Ex 30:7-10; Dt 21:5 [s]Nu 6:23
23:14 [t]Dt 33:1
23:15 [u]Ex 18:4
23:16 [v]1Ch 26:24-28
23:19 [w]1Ch 24:23
23:21 [x]1Ch 24:26

23:7–23 On these Levitical families, see notes on ch. 6.

23:24 [y]Nu 4:3; 10:17,21
23:25 [z]1Ch 22:9
23:26 [a]Nu 4:5,15; 7:9; Dt 10:8
23:28 [b]2Ch 29:15; Ne 13:9; Mal 3:3
23:29 [c]Ex 25:30 [d]Lev 2:4-7; 6:20-23 [e]Lev 19:35-36; 1Ch 9:29,32
23:30 [f]1Ch 9:33; Ps 134:1
23:31 [g]2Ki 4:23 [h]Lev 23:4; Nu 28:9-29:39; Isa 1:13-14; Col 2:16
23:32 [i]Nu 1:53; 1Ch 6:48 [j]Nu 3:6-8,38 [k]2Ch 23:18; 31:2; Eze 44:14
24:1 [l]1Ch 23:6; 28:13; 2Ch 5:11; 8:14; 23:8; 31:2; 35:4,5; Ezr 6:18 [m]Nu 3:2-4 [n]Ex 6:23
24:2 [o]Lev 10:1-2; Nu 3:4
24:3 [p]2Sa 8:17
24:5 [q]ver 31; 1Ch 25:8
24:6 [r]1Ch 18:16
24:7 [s]Ezr 2:36; Ne 12:6
24:8 [t]Ezr 2:39; Ne 10:5
24:10 [u]Ne 12:4,17; Lk 1:5
24:14 [v]Jer 20:1

23 The sons of Mushi:
Mahli, Eder and Jerimoth—three in all.

24 These were the descendants of Levi by their families—the heads of families as they were registered under their names and counted individually, that is, the workers twenty years old or more[y] who served in the temple of the LORD. 25 For David had said, "Since the LORD, the God of Israel, has granted rest[z] to his people and has come to dwell in Jerusalem forever, 26 the Levites no longer need to carry the tabernacle or any of the articles used in its service."[a] 27 According to the last instructions of David, the Levites were counted from those twenty years old or more.

28 The duty of the Levites was to help Aaron's descendants in the service of the temple of the LORD: to be in charge of the courtyards, the side rooms, the purification[b] of all sacred things and the performance of other duties at the house of God. 29 They were in charge of the bread set out on the table,[c] the special flour for the grain offerings,[d] the thin loaves made without yeast, the baking and the mixing, and all measurements of quantity and size.[e] 30 They were also to stand every morning to thank and praise the LORD. They were to do the same in the evening[f] 31 and whenever burnt offerings were presented to the LORD on the Sabbaths, at the New Moon[g] feasts and at the appointed festivals.[h] They were to serve before the LORD regularly in the proper number and in the way prescribed for them.

32 And so the Levites[i] carried out their responsibilities for the tent of meeting,[j] for the Holy Place and, under their relatives the descendants of Aaron, for the service of the temple of the LORD.[k]

The Divisions of Priests

24 These were the divisions[l] of the descendants of Aaron:[m]
The sons of Aaron were Nadab, Abihu, Eleazar and Ithamar.[n] 2 But Nadab and Abihu died before their father did,[o] and they had no sons; so Eleazar and Ithamar served as the priests. 3 With the help of Zadok[p] a descendant of Eleazar and Ahimelek a descendant of Ithamar, David separated them into divisions for their appointed order of ministering. 4 A larger number of leaders were found among Eleazar's descendants than among Ithamar's, and they were divided accordingly: sixteen heads of families from Eleazar's descendants and eight heads of families from Ithamar's descendants. 5 They divided them impartially by casting lots,[q] for there were officials of the sanctuary and officials of God among the descendants of both Eleazar and Ithamar.

6 The scribe Shemaiah son of Nethanel, a Levite, recorded their names in the presence of the king and of the officials: Zadok the priest, Ahimelek[r] son of Abiathar and the heads of families of the priests and of the Levites—one family being taken from Eleazar and then one from Ithamar.

7 The first lot fell to Jehoiarib,
the second to Jedaiah,[s]
8 the third to Harim,[t]
the fourth to Seorim,
9 the fifth to Malkijah,
the sixth to Mijamin,
10 the seventh to Hakkoz,
the eighth to Abijah,[u]
11 the ninth to Jeshua,
the tenth to Shekaniah,
12 the eleventh to Eliashib,
the twelfth to Jakim,
13 the thirteenth to Huppah,
the fourteenth to Jeshebeab,
14 the fifteenth to Bilgah,
the sixteenth to Immer,[v]

23:28–32 See notes on 6:48–49.

24:1–19 These priestly divisions are rooted in revelation given to Aaron (v. 19). These selections culminated in the appointment of 24 priestly divisions in the temple ("their appointed order of ministering," v. 19).

24:5 casting lots. Reflects divine involvement (Prov 16:33) in the selection of the priestly divisions.

15 the seventeenth to Hezir,[w]
the eighteenth to Happizzez,
16 the nineteenth to Pethahiah,
the twentieth to Jehezkel,
17 the twenty-first to Jakin,
the twenty-second to Gamul,
18 the twenty-third to Delaiah
and the twenty-fourth to Maaziah.

19 This was their appointed order of ministering when they entered the temple of the LORD, according to the regulations prescribed for them by their ancestor Aaron, as the LORD, the God of Israel, had commanded him.

The Rest of the Levites

20 As for the rest of the descendants of Levi:[x]
from the sons of Amram: Shubael;
from the sons of Shubael: Jehdeiah.
21 As for Rehabiah,[y] from his sons:
Ishiah was the first.
22 From the Izharites: Shelomoth;
from the sons of Shelomoth: Jahath.
23 The sons of Hebron:[z] Jeriah the first,[a] Amariah the second, Jahaziel the third and Jekameam the fourth.
24 The son of Uzziel: Micah;
from the sons of Micah: Shamir.
25 The brother of Micah: Ishiah;
from the sons of Ishiah: Zechariah.
26 The sons of Merari:[a] Mahli and Mushi.
The son of Jaaziah: Beno.
27 The sons of Merari:
from Jaaziah: Beno, Shoham, Zakkur and Ibri.
28 From Mahli: Eleazar, who had no sons.
29 From Kish: the son of Kish:
Jerahmeel.
30 And the sons of Mushi: Mahli, Eder and Jerimoth.

These were the Levites, according to their families. 31 They also cast lots,[b] just as their relatives the
descendants of Aaron did, in the presence of King David and of Zadok, Ahimelek, and the heads of families of the priests and of the Levites. The families of the oldest brother were treated the same as those of the youngest.

The Musicians

25 David, together with the commanders of the army, set apart some of the sons of Asaph,[c] Heman[d] and Jeduthun[e] for the ministry of prophesying,[f] accompanied by harps, lyres and cymbals.[g] Here is the list of the men[h] who performed this service:[i]

2 From the sons of Asaph:
Zakkur, Joseph, Nethaniah and Asarelah. The sons of Asaph were under the supervision of Asaph, who prophesied under the king's supervision.

24:15 [w] Ne 10:20
24:20 [x] 1Ch 23:6
24:21 [y] 1Ch 23:17
24:23 [z] 1Ch 23:19
24:26 [a] 1Ch 6:19; 23:21
24:31 [b] ver 5
25:1 [c] 1Ch 6:39 [d] 1Ch 6:33 [e] 1Ch 16:41, 42; Ne 11:17 [f] 1Sa 10:5; 2Ki 3:15 [g] 1Ch 15:16 [h] 1Ch 6:31 [i] 2Ch 5:12; 8:14; 34:12; 35:15; Ezr 3:10

[a] 23 Two Hebrew manuscripts and some Septuagint manuscripts (see also 23:19); most Hebrew manuscripts *The sons of Jeriah:*

25:1 the ministry of prophesying. Prophetic ministry was part of the service of select Levitical musicians. **prophesying, accompanied by harps, lyres and cymbals.** The context suggests that these acts of prophecy related to the proclamation of God's truth through music rather than other means. The Levites were responsible for teaching God's precepts and law (Deut 33:10). The singing of songs that proclaimed God's truth and exhorted people to obedience functioned in parallel to prophetic ministry, as seen in the theological content of the Psalms.

Bronze cymbals from biblical times. David set some men apart for the ministry of prophesying, accompanied by harps, lyres, and cymbals (1 Chr 25:1).

25:3 [j] 1Ch 16:41-42 [k] Ge 4:21; Ps 33:2 **25:6** [l] 1Ch 15:16 [m] 1Ch 15:19 [n] 2Ch 23:18; 29:25 **25:8** [o] 1Ch 26:13 **25:9** [p] 1Ch 6:39

3 As for Jeduthun, from his sons:[j]

Gedaliah, Zeri, Jeshaiah, Shimei,[a] Hashabiah and Mattithiah, six in all, under the supervision of their father Jeduthun, who prophesied, using the harp[k] in thanking and praising the LORD.

4 As for Heman, from his sons:

Bukkiah, Mattaniah, Uzziel, Shubael and Jerimoth; Hananiah, Hanani, Eliathah, Giddalti and Romamti-Ezer; Joshbekashah, Mallothi, Hothir and Mahazioth. 5 (All these were sons of Heman the king's seer. They were given him through the promises of God to exalt him. God gave Heman fourteen sons and three daughters.)

6 All these men were under the supervision of their father[l] for the music of the temple of the LORD, with cymbals, lyres and harps, for the ministry at the house of God.

Asaph, Jeduthun and Heman[m] were under the supervision of the king.[n] 7 Along with their relatives — all of them trained and skilled in music for the LORD — they numbered 288. 8 Young and old alike, teacher as well as student, cast lots[o] for their duties.

9 The first lot, which was for Asaph,[p] fell to Joseph,
his sons and relatives[b] 12[c]
the second to Gedaliah,
him and his relatives and sons 12
10 the third to Zakkur,
his sons and relatives 12
11 the fourth to Izri,[d]
his sons and relatives 12
12 the fifth to Nethaniah,
his sons and relatives 12

[a] *3* One Hebrew manuscript and some Septuagint manuscripts (see also verse 17); most Hebrew manuscripts do not have *Shimei.* [b] *9* See Septuagint; Hebrew does not have *his sons and relatives.* [c] *9* See the total in verse 7; Hebrew does not have *twelve.* [d] *11* A variant of *Zeri*

25:5 seer. Prophet; applied to Heman here (v. 5) but also used of Asaph (2 Chr 29:30) and Jeduthun (2 Chr 35:15).

25:6 for the music of the temple of the LORD. Following the completion of the temple, music became a primary responsibility of the Levites (23:2–32; 2 Chr 5:7–13), with numerous ("288," v. 7) Levitical ministers leading worship featuring "joyful sound with musical instruments: lyres, harps and cymbals" (15:16; see note there). The music of these Levites impacted subsequent generations, as is reflected in at least 16 psalms attributed or dedicated to three Levitical leaders (Heman: Ps 88; Asaph: Pss 50; 73–83; Jeduthun: Pss 39; 62; 77).

25:8–31 The divisions of Levitical musicians were determined by casting lots (see note on 24:5) without partiality to age or stature. The Levitical musicians appointed to music ministry at the temple were organized into 24 divisions in analogy to the 24 divisions of Aaronic priests appointed to minister at the Jerusalem temple, suggesting they ministered in tandem in temple worship, feasts, and sacrifice (23:30–31).

[13] the sixth to Bukkiah,
his sons and relatives 12
[14] the seventh to Jesarelah,[a]
his sons and relatives 12
[15] the eighth to Jeshaiah,
his sons and relatives 12
[16] the ninth to Mattaniah,
his sons and relatives 12
[17] the tenth to Shimei,
his sons and relatives 12
[18] the eleventh to Azarel,[b]
his sons and relatives 12
[19] the twelfth to Hashabiah,
his sons and relatives 12
[20] the thirteenth to Shubael,
his sons and relatives 12
[21] the fourteenth to Mattithiah,
his sons and relatives 12
[22] the fifteenth to Jerimoth,
his sons and relatives 12
[23] the sixteenth to Hananiah,
his sons and relatives 12
[24] the seventeenth to Joshbekashah,
his sons and relatives 12
[25] the eighteenth to Hanani,
his sons and relatives 12
[26] the nineteenth to Mallothi,
his sons and relatives 12
[27] the twentieth to Eliathah,
his sons and relatives 12
[28] the twenty-first to Hothir,
his sons and relatives 12
[29] the twenty-second to Giddalti,
his sons and relatives 12
[30] the twenty-third to Mahazioth,
his sons and relatives 12
[31] the twenty-fourth to Romamti-Ezer,
his sons and relatives 12.[q]

The Gatekeepers

26 The divisions of the gatekeepers:[r]

From the Korahites: Meshelemiah son of Kore, one of the sons of Asaph.
[2] Meshelemiah had sons:
Zechariah[s] the firstborn,
Jediael the second,
Zebadiah the third,
Jathniel the fourth,

[a] *14* A variant of *Asarelah* [b] *18* A variant of *Uzziel*

25:31 [q] 1Ch 9:33
26:1 [r] 1Ch 9:17
26:2 [s] 1Ch 9:21

The temple became home to a vibrant tapestry of praise and worship celebrating the splendor of God.

26:1 gatekeepers. See note on 9:17–27.

26:5 [t]2Sa 6:10; 1Ch 13:13; 16:38
26:10 [u]Dt 21:16; 1Ch 5:1
26:12 [v]1Ch 9:22
26:13 [w]1Ch 24:5, 31; 25:8
26:14 [x]1Ch 9:18 [y]1Ch 9:21
26:15 [z]1Ch 13:13; 2Ch 25:24
26:19 [a]2Ch 35:15; Ne 7:1; Eze 44:11
26:20 [b]2Ch 24:5 [c]1Ch 28:12
26:21 [d]1Ch 23:7; 29:8
26:22 [e]1Ch 9:26
26:23 [f]Nu 3:27
26:24 [g]1Ch 23:16
26:25 [h]1Ch 23:18

3 Elam the fifth,
Jehohanan the sixth
and Eliehoenai the seventh.
4 Obed-Edom also had sons:
Shemaiah the firstborn,
Jehozabad the second,
Joah the third,
Sakar the fourth,
Nethanel the fifth,
5 Ammiel the sixth,
Issachar the seventh
and Peullethai the eighth.
(For God had blessed Obed-Edom.[t])

6 Obed-Edom's son Shemaiah also had sons, who were leaders in their father's family because
they were very capable men. 7 The sons of Shemaiah: Othni, Rephael, Obed and Elzabad; his
relatives Elihu and Semakiah were also able men. 8 All these were descendants of Obed-Edom;
they and their sons and their relatives were capable men with the strength to do the work—
descendants of Obed-Edom, 62 in all.

9 Meshelemiah had sons and relatives, who were able men—18 in all.

10 Hosah the Merarite had sons: Shimri the first (although he was not the firstborn, his father had
appointed him the first),[u] 11 Hilkiah the second, Tabaliah the third and Zechariah the fourth.
The sons and relatives of Hosah were 13 in all.

12 These divisions of the gatekeepers, through their leaders, had duties for ministering[v] in the temple of the LORD, just as their relatives had. 13 Lots[w] were cast for each gate, according to their families,
young and old alike.

14 The lot for the East Gate[x] fell to Shelemiah.[a] Then lots were cast for his son Zechariah,[y] a wise
counselor, and the lot for the North Gate fell to him. 15 The lot for the South Gate fell to Obed-Edom,[z]
and the lot for the storehouse fell to his sons. 16 The lots for the West Gate and the Shalleketh Gate on
the upper road fell to Shuppim and Hosah.

Guard was alongside of guard: 17 There were six Levites a day on the east, four a day on the north,
four a day on the south and two at a time at the storehouse. 18 As for the court[b] to the west, there were
four at the road and two at the court[b] itself.

19 These were the divisions of the gatekeepers who were descendants of Korah and Merari.[a]

The Treasurers and Other Officials

20 Their fellow Levites[b] were[c] in charge of the treasuries of the house of God and the treasuries for
the dedicated things.[c]

21 The descendants of Ladan, who were Gershonites through Ladan and who were heads of families
belonging to Ladan the Gershonite,[d] were Jehieli, 22 the sons of Jehieli, Zetham and his brother Joel.
They were in charge of the treasuries[e] of the temple of the LORD.

23 From the Amramites, the Izharites, the Hebronites and the Uzzielites:[f]

24 Shubael,[g] a descendant of Gershom son of Moses, was the official in charge of the treasuries.
25 His relatives through Eliezer: Rehabiah his son, Jeshaiah his son, Joram his son, Zikri his
son and Shelomith[h] his son. 26 Shelomith and his relatives were in charge of all the trea-

[a] 14 A variant of *Meshelemiah* [b] 18 The meaning of the Hebrew for this word is uncertain.
[c] 20 Septuagint; Hebrew *As for the Levites, Ahijah was*

26:4 Obed-Edom. He was greatly blessed as he cared for the ark of the covenant for three months (13:13–14).

26:17 The eastern gate received additional protection as it faced the main entrance to the temple.

26:20–28 This section of Levitical personnel focuses on stewards of temple "treasuries" (v. 20) and other "dedicated things" (v. 20). These treasuries are connected with five individuals (David [v. 26], and Samuel, Saul, Abner, and Joab [v. 28]) and three groupings of military leaders (v. 26).

suries for the things dedicated[i] by King David, by the heads of families who were the commanders of thousands and commanders of hundreds, and by the other army commanders.
27 Some of the plunder taken in battle they dedicated for the repair of the temple of the LORD.
28 And everything dedicated by Samuel the seer[j] and by Saul son of Kish, Abner son of Ner and Joab son of Zeruiah, and all the other dedicated things were in the care of Shelomith and his relatives.

29 From the Izharites: Kenaniah and his sons were assigned duties away from the temple, as officials and judges[k] over Israel.

30 From the Hebronites: Hashabiah[l] and his relatives—seventeen hundred able men—were responsible in Israel west of the Jordan for all the work of the LORD and for the king's service.
31 As for the Hebronites,[m] Jeriah was their chief according to the genealogical records of their families. In the fortieth[n] year of David's reign a search was made in the records, and capable
men among the Hebronites were found at Jazer in Gilead. 32 Jeriah had twenty-seven hundred
relatives, who were able men and heads of families, and King David put them in charge of the Reubenites, the Gadites and the half-tribe of Manasseh for every matter pertaining to God and for the affairs of the king.

Army Divisions

27 This is the list of the Israelites—heads of families, commanders of thousands and commanders of hundreds, and their officers, who served the king in all that concerned the army divisions that were on duty month by month throughout the year. Each division consisted of 24,000 men.

2 In charge of the first division, for the first month, was Jashobeam[o] son of Zabdiel. There were 24,000
men in his division. 3 He was a descendant of Perez and chief of all the army officers for the first month.

4 In charge of the division for the second month was Dodai[p] the Ahohite; Mikloth was the leader of his division. There were 24,000 men in his division.

5 The third army commander, for the third month, was Benaiah[q] son of Jehoiada the priest. He was
chief and there were 24,000 men in his division. 6 This was the Benaiah who was a mighty warrior among the Thirty and was over the Thirty. His son Ammizabad was in charge of his division.

7 The fourth, for the fourth month, was Asahel[r] the brother of Joab; his son Zebadiah was his successor. There were 24,000 men in his division.

8 The fifth, for the fifth month, was the commander Shamhuth[s] the Izrahite. There were 24,000 men in his division.

9 The sixth, for the sixth month, was Ira[t] the son of Ikkesh the Tekoite. There were 24,000 men in his division.

10 The seventh, for the seventh month, was Helez[u] the Pelonite, an Ephraimite. There were 24,000 men in his division.

11 The eighth, for the eighth month, was Sibbekai[v] the Hushathite, a Zerahite. There were 24,000 men in his division.

12 The ninth, for the ninth month, was Abiezer[w] the Anathothite, a Benjamite. There were 24,000 men in his division.

13 The tenth, for the tenth month, was Maharai[x] the Netophathite, a Zerahite. There were 24,000 men in his division.

14 The eleventh, for the eleventh month, was Benaiah[y] the Pirathonite, an Ephraimite. There were 24,000 men in his division.

15 The twelfth, for the twelfth month, was Heldai[z] the Netophathite, from the family of Othniel.[a] There were 24,000 men in his division.

26:26 [i] 2Sa 8:11
26:28 [j] 1Sa 9:9
26:29 [k] Dt 17:8-13; 1Ch 23:4; Ne 11:16
26:30 [l] 1Ch 27:17
26:31 [m] 1Ch 23:19 [n] 2Sa 5:4
27:2 [o] 2Sa 23:8; 1Ch 11:11
27:4 [p] 2Sa 23:9
27:5 [q] 2Sa 23:20
27:7 [r] 2Sa 2:18; 1Ch 11:26
27:8 [s] 1Ch 11:27
27:9 [t] 2Sa 23:26; 1Ch 11:28
27:10 [u] 2Sa 23:26; 1Ch 11:27
27:11 [v] 2Sa 21:18
27:12 [w] 2Sa 23:27; 1Ch 11:28
27:13 [x] 2Sa 23:28; 1Ch 11:30
27:14 [y] 1Ch 11:31
27:15 [z] 2Sa 23:29 [a] Jos 15:17

26:29–32 This final section of Levitical assignments focuses on those serving "away from the temple" (v. 29) in the realm of civil service ("officials and judges," v. 29).

26:30–32 all the work of the LORD and for the king's service … every matter pertaining to God and for the affairs of the king. "Capable" Levites (v. 31; cf. "able" in v. 32) were entrusted with a two-pronged service: spiritual service and royal service.

27:17 [b] 1Ch 26:30 [c] 2Sa 8:17; 1Ch 12:28 **27:23** [d] 1Ch 21:2-5 [e] Ge 15:5 **27:24** [f] 2Sa 24:15; 1Ch 21:7 **27:28** [g] 1Ki 10:27; 2Ch 1:15 **27:31** [h] 1Ch 5:10 **27:33** [i] 2Sa 15:12 [j] 2Sa 15:37 **27:34** [k] 1Ki 1:7 [l] 1Ch 11:6

Leaders of the Tribes

16 The leaders of the tribes of Israel:

over the Reubenites: Eliezer son of Zikri;
over the Simeonites: Shephatiah son of Maakah;
17 over Levi: Hashabiah[b] son of Kemuel;
over Aaron: Zadok;[c]
18 over Judah: Elihu, a brother of David;
over Issachar: Omri son of Michael;
19 over Zebulun: Ishmaiah son of Obadiah;
over Naphtali: Jerimoth son of Azriel;
20 over the Ephraimites: Hoshea son of Azaziah;
over half the tribe of Manasseh: Joel son of Pedaiah;
21 over the half-tribe of Manasseh in Gilead: Iddo son of Zechariah;
over Benjamin: Jaasiel son of Abner;
22 over Dan: Azarel son of Jeroham.
These were the leaders of the tribes of Israel.

23 David did not take the number of the men twenty years old or less,[d] because the LORD had promised
to make Israel as numerous as the stars[e] in the sky. 24 Joab son of Zeruiah began to count the men but
did not finish. God's wrath came on Israel on account of this numbering,[f] and the number was not
entered in the book[a] of the annals of King David.

The King's Overseers

25 Azmaveth son of Adiel was in charge of the royal storehouses.

Jonathan son of Uzziah was in charge of the storehouses in the outlying districts, in the towns, the villages and the watchtowers.

26 Ezri son of Kelub was in charge of the workers who farmed the land.
27 Shimei the Ramathite was in charge of the vineyards.
Zabdi the Shiphmite was in charge of the produce of the vineyards for the wine vats.
28 Baal-Hanan the Gederite was in charge of the olive and sycamore-fig[g] trees in the western foothills.
Joash was in charge of the supplies of olive oil.
29 Shitrai the Sharonite was in charge of the herds grazing in Sharon.
Shaphat son of Adlai was in charge of the herds in the valleys.
30 Obil the Ishmaelite was in charge of the camels.
Jehdeiah the Meronothite was in charge of the donkeys.
31 Jaziz the Hagrite[h] was in charge of the flocks.
All these were the officials in charge of King David's property.

32 Jonathan, David's uncle, was a counselor, a man of insight and a scribe. Jehiel son of Hakmoni
took care of the king's sons.
33 Ahithophel[i] was the king's counselor.
Hushai[j] the Arkite was the king's confidant. 34 Ahithophel was succeeded by Jehoiada son of Benaiah
and by Abiathar.[k]
Joab[l] was the commander of the royal army.

[a] *24* Septuagint; Hebrew *number*

27:18 Elihu, a brother of David. It is intriguing that he is mentioned as the official over Judah since he is not mentioned in the Chronicler's overview of Jesse's family (2:13–15). Elihu may be another name for Eliab (as reflected in the Septuagint, the pre-Christian Greek translation of the OT) or perhaps he is the eighth son of Jesse not listed in the Chronicler's genealogy.

27:32–34 This "inner circle" of David's cabinet counseled the king. David's relationship with several of these advisors changed for the worse during the attempted coups of Absalom and Adonijah (Ahithophel: 2 Sam 16:20–23; Joab: 2 Sam 18:9–15; Abiathar: 1 Kgs 1:7). David's relationship with Hushai deepened during the Absalom crisis (2 Sam 15:32–37; 16:16–19), perhaps earning him the title "king's confidant" (v. 33).

David's Plans for the Temple

28 David summoned all the officials[m] of Israel to assemble at Jerusalem: the officers over the tribes, the commanders of the divisions in the service of the king, the commanders of thousands and commanders of hundreds, and the officials in charge of all the property and livestock belonging to the king and his sons, together with the palace officials, the warriors and all the brave fighting men.

2King David rose to his feet and said: "Listen to me, my fellow Israelites, my people. I had it in my heart[n] to build a house as a place of rest for the ark of the covenant of the LORD, for the footstool[o] of our God, and I made plans to build it. 3But God said to me,[p] 'You are not to build a house for my Name,[q] because you are a warrior and have shed blood.'[r]

4"Yet the LORD, the God of Israel, chose me[s] from my whole family[t] to be king over Israel forever. He chose Judah[u] as leader, and from the tribe of Judah he chose my family, and from my father's sons he was pleased to make me king over all Israel. 5Of all my sons — and the LORD has given me many[v] — he has chosen my son Solomon[w] to sit on the throne of the kingdom of the LORD over Israel. 6He said to me: 'Solomon your son is the one who will build my house and my courts, for I have chosen him to be my son,[x] and I will be his father. 7I will establish his kingdom forever if he is unswerving in carrying out my commands and laws,[y] as is being done at this time.'

8"So now I charge you in the sight of all Israel and of the assembly of the LORD, and in the hearing of our God: Be careful to follow all the commands[z] of the LORD your God, that you may possess this good land and pass it on as an inheritance to your descendants forever.[a]

9"And you, my son Solomon, acknowledge the God of your father, and serve him with wholehearted devotion[b] and with a willing mind, for the LORD searches every heart[c] and understands every desire and every thought. If you seek him,[d] he will be found by you; but if you forsake[e] him, he will reject[f] you forever. 10Consider now, for the LORD has chosen you to build a house as the sanctuary. Be strong and do the work."

11Then David gave his son Solomon the plans[g] for the portico of the temple, its buildings, its storerooms, its upper parts, its inner rooms and the place of atonement. 12He gave him the plans of all that the Spirit[h] had put in his mind for the courts of the temple of the LORD and all the surrounding rooms, for the treasuries of the temple of God and for the treasuries for the dedicated things.[i] 13He gave him instructions for the divisions[j] of the priests and Levites, and for all the work of serving in the temple of the LORD, as well as for all the articles to be used in its service. 14He designated the weight of gold for all the gold articles to be used in various kinds of service, and the weight of silver for all the silver articles to be used in various kinds of service: 15the weight of gold for the gold lampstands[k] and their lamps, with the weight for each lampstand and its lamps; and the weight of silver for each silver lampstand and its lamps, according to the use of each lampstand; 16the weight of gold for each table[l] for consecrated bread; the weight of silver for the silver tables; 17the weight of pure gold for the forks, sprinkling bowls[m] and pitchers; the weight of gold for each gold dish; the weight of silver for each silver dish; 18and

28:1 [m] 1Ch 11:10; 27:1-31
28:2 [n] 1Ch 17:2 [o] Ps 99:5; 132:7
28:3 [p] 2Sa 7:5 [q] 1Ch 22:8 [r] 1Ki 5:3; 1Ch 17:4
28:4 [s] 1Ch 17:23,27; 2Ch 6:6 [t] 1Sa 16:1-13 [u] Ge 49:10; 1Ch 5:2
28:5 [v] 1Ch 3:1 [w] 1Ch 22:9; 23:1
28:6 [x] 2Sa 7:13; 1Ch 22:9-10
28:7 [y] 1Ch 22:13
28:8 [z] Dt 6:1 [a] Dt 4:1
28:9 [b] 1Ch 29:19 [c] 1Sa 16:7; Ps 7:9 [d] Ps 40:16; Jer 29:13 [e] Jos 24:20; 2Ch 15:2 [f] Ps 44:23
28:11 [g] Ex 25:9
28:12 [h] 1Ch 12:18 [i] 1Ch 26:20
28:13 [j] 1Ch 24:1
28:15 [k] Ex 25:31
28:16 [l] Ex 25:23
28:17 [m] Ex 27:3

28:1–8 Following his extensive preparations (chs. 22–27), David sought to prepare the hearts of the leaders of the community. David reiterated much of what he had earlier said to Solomon regarding his desire to build a temple (22:6–10).

28:2 my fellow Israelites, my people. Stresses that David's heartfelt speech was grounded in wholehearted obedience to the covenantal framework God established.

28:4–5 chose me ... chose Judah ... chose my family ... has chosen my son Solomon. Emphasizes God's agency in shaping the path of the nation.

28:6 Solomon ... will build my house. See note on 17:7–15.

28:7 if he is unswerving in carrying out my commands and laws. David's summary of God's promise had a condition.

28:8 Be careful to follow all the commands of the LORD your God, that you may possess this good land. David connected his exhortation to obedience with Israel's continued possession of the promised land (Deut 8:1; Josh 23:6–13).

28:9–10 The essence of David's earlier private charge to Solomon (22:6–13) is repeated in the presence of all Israel.

28:9 wholehearted devotion. Stresses covenantal faithfulness. **heart ... desire ... thought.** Biblical faithfulness cannot be fabricated but must flow from pure motives, Godward thoughts, and a "willing mind" (cf. Rom 12:2; 2 Cor 10:5). **he will reject you forever.** The grave consequence of covenantal unfaithfulness.

28:11–19 David's plans and provisions for the temple were detailed and wide-ranging. David's desire was that the temple be "of great magnificence and fame and splendor in the sight of all the nations" (22:5; cf. 29:1).

28:12 all that the Spirit had put in his mind. The relationship of this verse with v. 19 (framing the details of the temple plans and provisions) supports the NIV translation of "Spirit" (i.e., God's Spirit) over translations that understand "spirit" as referring to David's mind.

28:18 [n]Ex 30:1-10 [o]Ex 25:18-22 [p]Ex 25:20
28:19 [q]1Ki 6:38 [r]Ex 25:9
28:20 [s]Dt 31:6; 1Ch 22:13; 2Ch 19:11; Hag 2:4 [t]Dt 4:31; Jos 24:20 [u]1Ki 6:14; 2Ch 7:11
28:21 [v]Ex 35:25-36:5
29:1 [w]1Ki 3:7; 1Ch 22:5; 2Ch 13:7
29:2 [x]ver 7,14,16; Ezr 1:4; 6:5; Hag 2:8 [y]Isa 54:11 [z]1Ch 22:2-5
29:3 [a]2Ch 24:10; 31:3; 35:8
29:4 [b]Ge 10:29 [c]1Ch 22:14
29:6 [d]1Ch 27:1; 28:1 [e]ver 9; Ex 25:1-8; 35:20-29; 36:2; 2Ch 24:10; Ezr 7:15
29:7 [f]Ex 25:2; Ne 7:70-71
29:8 [g]Ex 35:27 [h]1Ch 26:21
29:9 [i]1Ki 8:61; 2Co 9:7

the weight of the refined gold for the altar of incense.[n] He also gave him the plan for the chariot,[o] that
is, the cherubim of gold that spread their wings and overshadow[p] the ark of the covenant of the LORD.
19“All this,” David said, “I have in writing as a result of the LORD’s hand on me, and he enabled me
to understand all the details[q] of the plan.[r]”
20David also said to Solomon his son, “Be strong and courageous,[s] and do the work. Do not be afraid
or discouraged, for the LORD God, my God, is with you. He will not fail you or forsake[t] you until all the
work for the service of the temple of the LORD is finished.[u] 21The divisions of the priests and Levites are
ready for all the work on the temple of God, and every willing person skilled[v] in any craft will help you
in all the work. The officials and all the people will obey your every command.”

Gifts for Building the Temple

29 Then King David said to the whole assembly: “My son Solomon, the one whom God has chosen,
is young and inexperienced.[w] The task is great, because this palatial structure is not for man but
for the LORD God. 2With all my resources I have provided for the temple of my God — gold[x] for the gold
work, silver for the silver, bronze for the bronze, iron for the iron and wood for the wood, as well as onyx
for the settings, turquoise,[a][y] stones of various colors, and all kinds of fine stone and marble — all of these
in large quantities.[z] 3Besides, in my devotion to the temple of my God I now give my personal treasures of
gold and silver for the temple of my God, over and above everything I have provided[a] for this holy temple:
4three thousand talents[b] of gold (gold of Ophir)[b] and seven thousand talents[c] of refined silver,[c] for the
overlaying of the walls of the buildings, 5for the gold work and the silver work, and for all the work to be
done by the craftsmen. Now, who is willing to consecrate themselves to the LORD today?”
6Then the leaders of families, the officers of the tribes of Israel, the commanders of thousands and
commanders of hundreds, and the officials[d] in charge of the king’s work gave willingly.[e] 7They[f] gave
toward the work on the temple of God five thousand talents[d] and ten thousand darics[e] of gold, ten
thousand talents[f] of silver, eighteen thousand talents[g] of bronze and a hundred thousand talents[h] of
iron. 8Anyone who had precious stones[g] gave them to the treasury of the temple of the LORD in the custody of Jehiel the Gershonite.[h] 9The people rejoiced at the willing response of their leaders, for they had
given freely and wholeheartedly[i] to the LORD. David the king also rejoiced greatly.

David’s Prayer

10David praised the LORD in the presence of the whole assembly, saying,

“Praise be to you, LORD,
the God of our father Israel,
from everlasting to everlasting.

a 2 The meaning of the Hebrew for this word is uncertain. *b* 4 That is, about 110 tons or about 100 metric tons
c 4 That is, about 260 tons or about 235 metric tons *d* 7 That is, about 190 tons or about 170 metric tons
e 7 That is, about 185 pounds or about 84 kilograms *f* 7 That is, about 380 tons or about 340 metric tons
g 7 That is, about 675 tons or about 610 metric tons *h* 7 That is, about 3,800 tons or about 3,400 metric tons

28:19 All this. The plans for the temple. **a result of the LORD’s hand on me ... he enabled me to understand all the details of the plan.** Divine revelation. David’s portrayal of this process — along with “all that the Spirit ... put in [my] mind” (v. 12) — amounts to an insightful summary of inspiration.

28:20 Be strong and courageous ... Do not be afraid or discouraged. See note on 22:13.

29:1–5 David declared that the temple was for God and thus should have the finest of materials and craftsmanship so that it aptly reflected the beauty of God’s holiness (cf. 22:5,14; Ps 29:2). Many of these materials were also used in the construction of the tabernacle during the time of Moses.

29:3 my personal treasures. David’s gifts reflected his devotion to God (note the triple use of “the temple of my God” in vv. 2–3).

29:4 Ophir. Location uncertain; proposals range from India to coastal Africa (including Punt [modern Somalia] and ancient Nubia/Cush [modern Sudan]). As with gold from Parvaim (2 Chr 3:4–7), gold from Ophir was considered high quality in the biblical world.

29:5 who is willing to consecrate themselves to the LORD today? David challenged the congregation to follow his example.

29:6–9 In light of David’s challenge to the people, the leaders of the community gave generously “toward the work on the temple of God” (v. 7). The Chronicler emphasizes that they gave “willingly” (v. 6) and “freely and wholeheartedly to the LORD” (v. 9). The result was joy for both people and king (v. 9).

29:7 darics. See NIV text note. The Chronicler uses this Persian monetary unit to give a sense of comparison helpful to his postexilic audience.

29:10–20 David’s prayer flowed from the atmosphere of wholehearted giving and celebration on the part of the king, leaders, and community. It radiates the recognition that all glory, honor, and praise belong to God and God alone (vv. 10,11,12,13,20). David’s words repeatedly declare that every good and perfect gift comes from God (vv. 12,14,16; cf. Jas 1:17).

[11] Yours, LORD, is the greatness and the power[j]
and the glory and the majesty and the splendor,
for everything in heaven and earth is yours.[k]
Yours, LORD, is the kingdom;
you are exalted as head over all.[l]
[12] Wealth and honor[m] come from you;
you are the ruler[n] of all things.
In your hands are strength and power
to exalt and give strength to all.
[13] Now, our God, we give you thanks,
and praise your glorious name.

[14] "But who am I, and who are my people, that we should be able to give as generously as this? Everything comes from you, and we have given you only what comes from your hand. [15] We are foreigners
and strangers[o] in your sight, as were all our ancestors. Our days on earth are like a shadow,[p] without
hope. [16] LORD our God, all this abundance that we have provided for building you a temple for your Holy
Name comes from your hand, and all of it belongs to you. [17] I know, my God, that you test the heart[q] and
are pleased with integrity. All these things I have given willingly and with honest intent. And now I have
seen with joy how willingly your people who are here have given to you.[r] [18] LORD, the God of our fathers
Abraham, Isaac and Israel, keep these desires and thoughts in the hearts of your people forever, and keep
their hearts loyal to you. [19] And give my son Solomon the wholehearted devotion[s] to keep your commands,
statutes and decrees[t] and to do everything to build the palatial structure for which I have provided."[u]

[20] Then David said to the whole assembly, "Praise the LORD your God." So they all praised the LORD,
the God of their fathers; they bowed down, prostrating themselves before the LORD and the king.

Solomon Acknowledged as King

29:21-25pp — 1Ki 1:28-53

[21] The next day they made sacrifices to the LORD and presented burnt offerings to him:[v] a thousand bulls,
a thousand rams and a thousand male lambs, together with their drink offerings, and other sacrifices
in abundance for all Israel. [22] They ate and drank with great joy[w] in the presence of the LORD that day.

Then they acknowledged Solomon son of David as king a second time, anointing him before the
LORD to be ruler and Zadok[x] to be priest. [23] So Solomon sat on the throne[y] of the LORD as king in place
of his father David. He prospered and all Israel obeyed him. [24] All the officers and warriors, as well as
all of King David's sons, pledged their submission to King Solomon.

[25] The LORD highly exalted Solomon in the sight of all Israel and bestowed on him royal splendor[z]
such as no king over Israel ever had before.[a]

The Death of David

29:26-28pp — 1Ki 2:10-12

[26] David son of Jesse was king[b] over all Israel. [27] He ruled over Israel forty years — seven in Hebron
and thirty-three in Jerusalem.[c] [28] He died[d] at a good old age, having enjoyed long life, wealth and honor.
His son Solomon succeeded him as king.[e]

29:11 [j] Ps 24:8; 59:17; 62:11 [k] Ps 89:11 [l] Rev 5:12-13
29:12 [m] 2Ch 1:12 [n] 2Ch 20:6; Ro 11:36
29:15 [o] Ps 39:12; Heb 11:13 [p] Job 14:2
29:17 [q] Ps 139:23; Pr 15:11; 17:3; Jer 11:20; 17:10 [r] 1Ch 28:9; Ps 15:1-5
29:19 [s] 1Ch 28:9 [t] Ps 72:1 [u] 1Ch 22:14
29:21 [v] 1Ki 8:62
29:22 [w] 1Ch 23:1 [x] 1Ki 1:33-39
29:23 [y] 1Ki 2:12
29:25 [z] 2Ch 1:1,12 [a] 1Ki 3:13; Ecc 2:9
29:26 [b] 1Ch 18:14
29:27 [c] 2Sa 5:4-5; 1Ki 2:11; 1Ch 3:4
29:28 [d] Ge 15:15; Ac 13:36 [e] 1Ch 23:1

29:11–12 Yours, LORD, is the kingdom; you are exalted as head over all ... you are the ruler of all things. Stresses that the kingdom of Israel is ultimately God's kingdom (cf. 17:14; 28:5; 2 Chr 9:8; 13:8).
29:14 who am I, and who are my people ...? David's response to the theological realities of vv. 10–13 is one of awe and humility (cf. 17:16). These truths provide the theological foundation for hope for the rebuilding postexilic community.
29:18–19 keep their hearts loyal to you ... give my son Solomon the wholehearted devotion to keep your commands, statutes and decrees. A request that God continue the good work he began in the hearts of Solomon and the community (cf. Phil 1:6).
29:21–22a sacrifices in abundance ... great joy in the presence of the LORD. Anticipated the function of the temple.
29:22b acknowledged Solomon. The community used this occasion to publicly acknowledge Solomon as David's (and God's) chosen heir to the throne. **a second time.** This large-scale public enthronement followed David's smaller ceremony anointing Solomon as king (23:1).
29:25 The LORD highly exalted Solomon in the sight of all Israel. Underscores that Solomon's strength was a by-product of God's graciousness.
29:26–30 The Chronicler's closing remarks on the reign of David reflect God's blessings on David through "long life, wealth and honor" (v. 28; cf. v. 12).

29:29 [f]1Sa 9:9 [g]2Sa 7:2 [h]1Sa 22:5

29 As for the events of King David's reign, from beginning to end, they are written in the records of Samuel the seer,[f] the records of Nathan[g] the prophet and the records of Gad[h] the seer, 30 together with the details of his reign and power, and the circumstances that surrounded him and Israel and the kingdoms of all the other lands.

29:29 Samuel ... Nathan ... Gad. On these sources, see Introduction: Genre.

29:30 kingdoms of all the other lands. Likely a reference to David's victories over nations to the east, west, south, and north summarized in chs. 18–20 (see note on 18:1–14). Such God-given victories "make known among the nations what [God] has done" (16:8; cf. 16:24; 2 Chr 17:10; 20:29–30).

INTRODUCTION TO
2 CHRONICLES

See Introduction to 1 Chronicles.

Below is an outline of 2 Chronicles. For an outline of both 1 and 2 Chronicles, see Introduction to 1 Chronicles: Outline.

OUTLINE

IV. The Reign of Solomon and the Construction of the Temple (2 Chr 1:1 — 9:31)

- A. Solomon's Wisdom, Wealth, and Power (1:1 – 17)
- B. Construction and Dedication of the Jerusalem Temple (2:1 — 7:22)
- C. Solomon's Other Activities (8:1 – 18)
- D. The Queen of Sheba Visits Solomon (9:1 – 12)
- E. Solomon's Splendor (9:13 – 28)
- F. Solomon's Death (9:29 – 31)

V. The Divided Monarchy (10:1 — 36:19)

- A. The Reign of Rehoboam and the Division of the Kingdom (10:1 — 12:16)
- B. Abijah King of Judah (13:1 — 14:1)
- C. Asa King of Judah (14:2 — 16:14)
- D. Jehoshaphat King of Judah (17:1 — 21:3)
- E. Jehoram King of Judah (21:4 – 20)
- F. Ahaziah King of Judah (22:1 – 9)
- G. The Coup and Rule of Queen Athaliah (22:10 — 23:21)
- H. Joash King of Judah (24:1 – 27)
- I. Amaziah King of Judah (25:1 – 28)
- J. Uzziah King of Judah (26:1 – 23)
- K. Jotham King of Judah (27:1 – 9)
- L. Ahaz King of Judah (28:1 – 27)
- M. The Reign of Hezekiah (29:1 — 32:33)
  1. Hezekiah Purifies the Temple (29:1 – 36)
  2. Hezekiah Celebrates the Passover (30:1 — 31:1)
  3. Contributions for Worship (31:2 – 21)
  4. Sennacherib Threatens Jerusalem (32:1 – 23)
  5. Hezekiah's Pride, Success, and Death (32:24 – 33)
- N. Manasseh King of Judah (33:1 – 20)

O. Amon King of Judah (33:21–25)
P. The Reign of Josiah (34:1—36:1)
   1. Josiah's Reforms and the Discovery of the Book of the Law (34:1–33)
   2. Josiah Celebrates the Passover (35:1–19)
   3. Josiah's Confrontation With Pharaoh Necho and Death (35:20—36:1)
Q. Jehoahaz King of Judah (36:2–4)
R. Jehoiakim King of Judah (36:5–8)
S. Jehoiachin King of Judah (36:9–10)
T. The Reign of Zedekiah and the Fall of Jerusalem (36:11–19)

VI. The Exilic Period (36:20–21)

VII. The Decree of Cyrus (36:22–23)

Cedars of Lebanon being transported via a body of water as Solomon would have done to build the temple (2 Chr 2:16). Relief from the palace of Sargon II, ca. 713–716 BC.

Marie-Lan Nguyen/Wikimedia Commons

PROVINCE OF YEHUD (JUDAH)

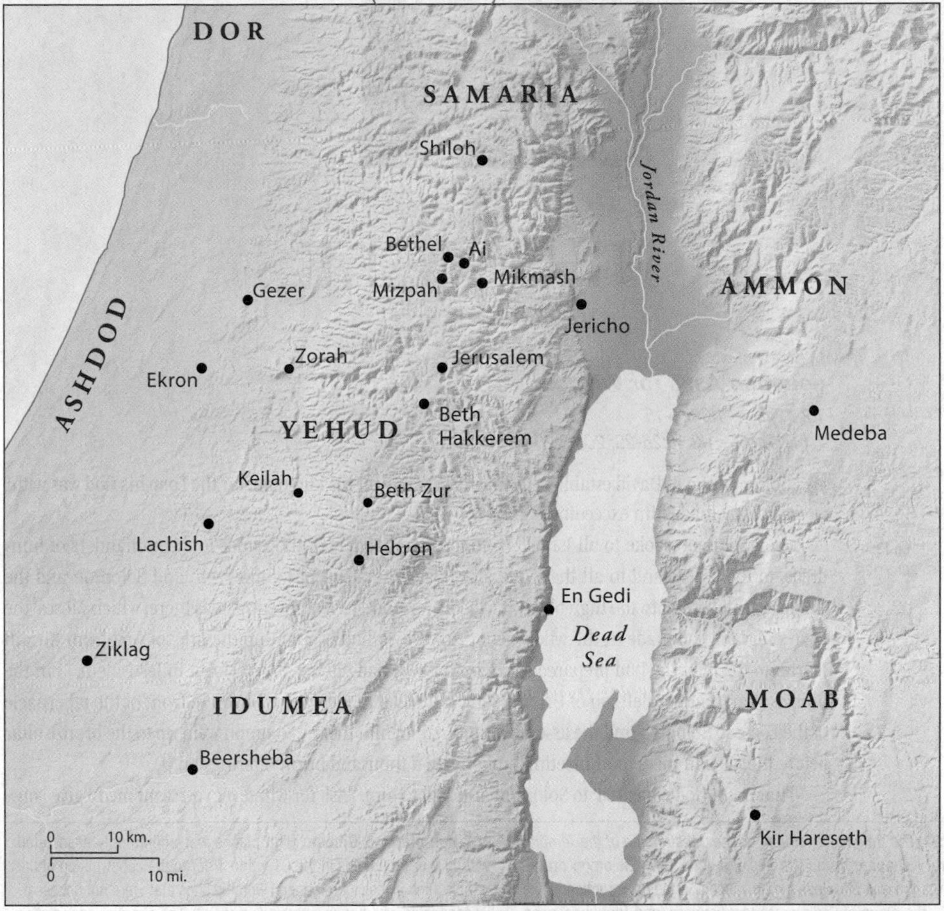

DOR
SAMARIA
Shiloh
Jordan River
Bethel
Ai
Mizpah
Mikmash
Gezer
AMMON
Jericho
ASHDOD
Zorah
Jerusalem
Ekron
Beth Hakkerem
YEHUD
Medeba
Keilah
Beth Zur
Lachish
Hebron
En Gedi
Dead Sea
Ziklag
IDUMEA
MOAB
Beersheba
Kir Hareseth
0 10 km.
0 10 mi.

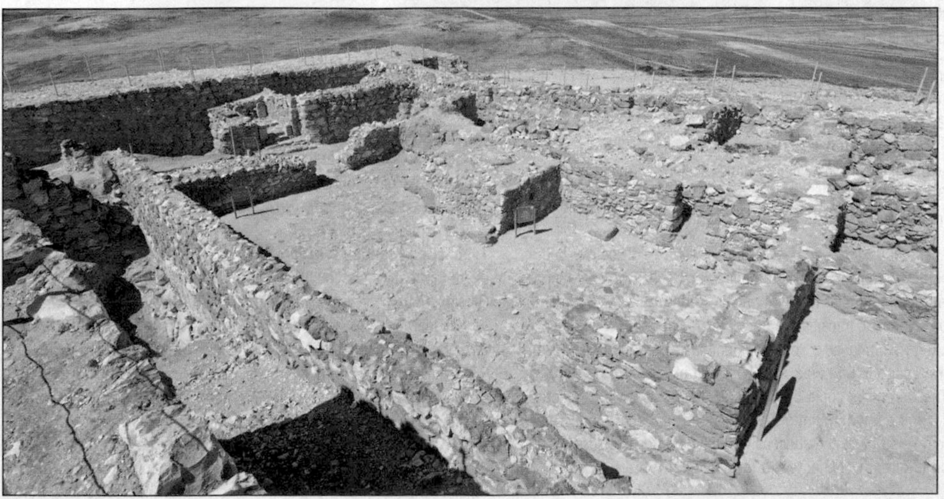

Israelite temple sanctuary at Arad. The floor plan of the Arad temple is similar to the temple Solomon builds in 2 Chr 3.

Todd Bolen/www.BiblePlaces.com

2 CHRONICLES

1:1 [a] 1Ki 2:12,26; 2Ch 12:1 [b] Ge 21:22; 39:2; Nu 14:43 [c] 1Ch 29:25
1:2 [d] 1Ch 9:1; 28:1
1:3 [e] Ex 36:8 [f] Ex 40:18
1:4 [g] 2Sa 6:2; 1Ch 15:25 [h] 2Sa 6:17; 1Ch 15:1
1:5 [i] Ex 38:2 [j] Ex 31:2 [k] 1Ch 13:3
1:7 [l] 2Ch 7:12

Solomon Asks for Wisdom

1:2-13pp — 1Ki 3:4-15
1:14-17pp — 1Ki 10:26-29; 2Ch 9:25-28

1 Solomon son of David established[a] himself firmly over his kingdom, for the LORD his God was with[b]
him and made him exceedingly great.[c]
2Then Solomon spoke to all Israel[d] — to the commanders of thousands and commanders of hundreds, to the judges and to all the leaders in Israel, the heads of families — 3and Solomon and the
whole assembly went to the high place at Gibeon, for God's tent of meeting[e] was there, which Moses[f] the
LORD's servant had made in the wilderness. 4Now David had brought up the ark[g] of God from Kiriath
Jearim to the place he had prepared for it, because he had pitched a tent[h] for it in Jerusalem. 5But the
bronze altar[i] that Bezalel[j] son of Uri, the son of Hur, had made was in Gibeon in front of the tabernacle
of the LORD; so Solomon and the assembly inquired[k] of him there. 6Solomon went up to the bronze altar
before the LORD in the tent of meeting and offered a thousand burnt offerings on it.
7That night God appeared[l] to Solomon and said to him, "Ask for whatever you want me to give you."

1:1 — 9:31 *The Reign of Solomon and the Construction of the Temple.* The literary shaping of the Chronicler's account of Solomon draws attention to the role of divinely gifted wisdom in the construction of the temple — the place of God's presence, holiness, and forgiveness, as well as the people's worship and prayer for all nations. This emphasis is reflected by points of repetition (mirroring):

- Solomon's God-given wisdom, wealth, and success (1:7 – 17)
  - Solomon's wisdom facilitates good relations with the nations (2:1 – 18)
    - Temple construction and dedication (3:1 — 7:22)
  - Solomon's wisdom facilitates good relations with the nations (8:1 — 9:22)
- Solomon's God-given wisdom, wealth, and success (9:23 – 28)

1:1 – 17 *Solomon's Wisdom, Wealth, and Power.* The Chronicler begins his account of Solomon's reign by emphasizing God's favor on Solomon. **1:1 established himself firmly over his kingdom.** Summarizes the details of Solomon's transition to power (cf. 1 Kgs 2:46, which follows two chapters summarizing Solomon's actions at the beginning of his reign). **the LORD his God was with him and made him exceedingly great.** The Chronicler notes the theological notions of God's election, presence, and empowerment of Solomon. God's presence is the basis for Solomon's strength and success. As with Solomon's wisdom, God's presence is directly connected to the building of the temple (1 Chr 28:20).
1:2 Solomon spoke to all Israel. Solomon's speech to the Israelite leadership emphasizes the breadth of unity that shapes this pilgrimage to Gibeon (cf. 1 Chr 13:5 – 6; 28:1 – 8).
1:3 high place at Gibeon. High places were commonly associated with hills or mountains in the OT world. Prior to the construction of the temple, high places were generic worship sites that were not necessarily connected with pagan worship (1 Kgs 3:2). The negative connotation of high places begins after the completion of the temple, after which high places were associated with idolatry and syncretism. Because of the possibility that the Chronicler's audience may view Solomon's trip to a high place in a negative fashion, much is done to emphasize that "the high place at Gibeon" was a legitimate place of worship. Both the tabernacle and the bronze altar (v. 5) were at Gibeon. **Gibeon.** Located in the central hill country at the intersection of roads going to the foothills and coastal plain, which facilitated its prominence from early times (cf. Josh 10:2). **tent of meeting.** The tabernacle Moses made. It underscores continuity with Moses.
1:4 pitched a tent for it in Jerusalem. Clarifies that the ark of the covenant (normally situated within the tent/tabernacle) was not located at Gibeon but had been relocated to Jerusalem (1 Chr 13). The ark was in Kiriath Jearim for 20 years following its seven-month exile in Philistine territory during the time of Samuel and Eli (1 Sam 4 – 6).
1:5 bronze altar. For burnt offerings; made by Bezalel (vv. 3 – 5; cf. Exod 38:1 – 2). It connects the site with the sacrificial system and the Aaronic priesthood (1 Chr 16:39 – 40).
1:6 a thousand burnt offerings. Solomon's extensive sacrifice at Gibeon tangibly showed his reverence for God at the outset of his reign. Similar abundant sacrifices are connected with the dedication of the temple (7:5).
1:7 God appeared. Solomon's dream (1 Kgs 3) at Gibeon included a theophany (a manifestation of God), providing the setting for Solomon's

Aerial view of the chambered gate at Hazor. Hazor has been identified as one of Solomon's chariot cities (2 Chr 1:14).
Z. Radovan/www.BibleLandPictures.com

8Solomon answered God, "You have shown great kindness to David my father and have made me[m]
king in his place. 9Now, LORD God, let your promise[n] to my father David be confirmed, for you have made
me king over a people who are as numerous as the dust of the earth.[o] 10Give me wisdom and knowledge,
that I may lead[p] this people, for who is able to govern this great people of yours?"
11God said to Solomon, "Since this is your heart's desire and you have not asked for wealth,[q] possessions or honor, nor for the death of your enemies, and since you have not asked for a long life but for
wisdom and knowledge to govern my people over whom I have made you king, 12therefore wisdom and
knowledge will be given you. And I will also give you wealth, possessions and honor,[r] such as no king
who was before you ever had and none after you will have.[s]"
13Then Solomon went to Jerusalem from the high place at Gibeon, from before the tent of meeting.
And he reigned over Israel.
14Solomon accumulated chariots[t] and horses; he had fourteen hundred chariots and twelve thousand horses,[a] which he kept in the chariot cities and also with him in Jerusalem. 15The king made

1:8 [m] 1Ch 23:1; 28:5
1:9 [n] 2Sa 7:25; 1Ki 8:25 [o] Ge 12:2
1:10 [p] Nu 27:17; 2Sa 5:2; Pr 8:15-16
1:11 [q] Dt 17:17
1:12 [r] 1Ch 29:12 [s] 1Ch 29:25; 2Ch 9:22; Ne 13:26
1:14 [t] 1Sa 8:11; 1Ki 4:26; 9:19

[a] 14 Or *charioteers*

reception of wisdom from above. Solomon's temple building project is "framed" by revelatory dreams (here and at 7:12–22, following the completion of the temple).

1:8 great kindness. Solomon's prayer begins with gratitude for God's covenantal faithfulness. **made me king in his place.** Solomon's thanksgiving draws upon the Davidic covenant (cf. 2 Sam 7:12) that leads into his petition (vv. 9–10).

1:9–10 Solomon makes two requests: (1) that God would continue to bring the fullness of the Davidic covenant to pass and (2) that God would grant him wisdom and knowledge.

1:9 promise to my father David. Stresses continuity with the Davidic covenant. **as numerous as the dust of the earth.** Stresses continuity with the Abrahamic covenant (Gen 13:16; 28:14).

1:10 Give me wisdom and knowledge. Connects with Solomon's ability to rightly govern (judge) God's people in order to facilitate an ordered, God-honoring society. **lead.** Translates a Hebrew word that is the verbal form of the noun "judge." The relationship between judgeship and kingship is stressed at the outset of the Israelite monarchy (see 1 Sam 8:1–22, especially vv. 5,6,20, where the Hebrew word for "judge" is translated "lead" [see NIV text note on 1 Sam 8:5]). The overlap between the role of judge and king implies that the office of king involved a national judgeship. Solomon's first wise act was an act of judging (1 Kgs 3:16–28). To judge wisely, Solomon needed to be able to discern and apply God's will.

1:11–13 God's response focuses on the second part of Solomon's prayer (i.e., wisdom) and illustrates God's propensity to do above and beyond what his people ask or think (Eph 3:20).

1:11 my people. The people led by the king are *God's* people; the kingdom is *God's* kingdom (13:8; 1 Chr 17:14); the king is *God's* son (1 Chr 22:10; 28:5–6); and the king sits on *God's* throne (9:8; 1 Chr 29:23). Solomon's wisdom is interwoven with his construction of *God's* temple.

1:12 wisdom and knowledge. Connects Solomon with Bezalel, who was also given wisdom and knowledge by God for the task of constructing the tabernacle in the wilderness (Exod 31:1–5; 35:30–35; 36:1).

1:14 accumulated chariots and horses. Solomon had 4,000 stalls for horses and chariots (9:25). His development of a chariot force required

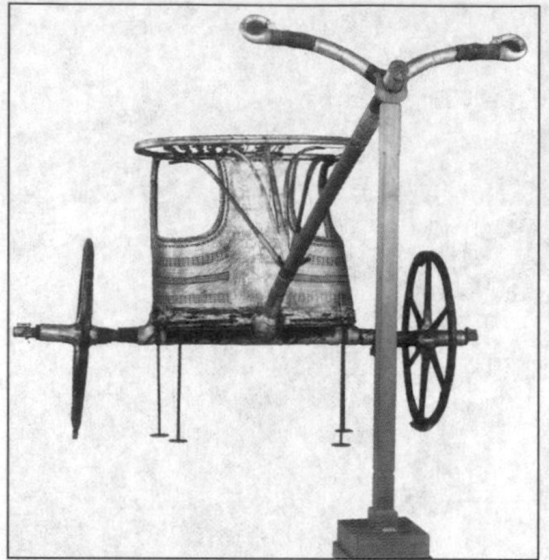

King Tut's gold chariot. King Solomon accumulated chariots, including one he imported from Egypt (2 Chr 1:17).

© CULTNAT, Dist. RMN-GP/Art Resource, NY

silver and gold[u] as common in Jerusalem as stones, and cedar as plentiful as sycamore-fig trees in the foothills. 16Solomon's horses were imported from Egypt and from Kue[a]—the royal merchants purchased
them from Kue at the current price. 17They imported a chariot[v] from
Egypt for six hundred shekels[b] of silver, and a horse for a hundred
and fifty.[c] They also exported them to all the kings of the Hittites and
of the Arameans.

Preparations for Building the Temple

2:1-18pp — 1Ki 5:1-16

2[d] Solomon gave orders to build a temple[w] for the Name of the
LORD and a royal palace for himself.[x] 2He conscripted 70,000
men as carriers and 80,000 as stonecutters in the hills and 3,600 as
foremen over them.[y]

3Solomon sent this message to Hiram[e][z] king of Tyre:

"Send me cedar logs[a] as you did for my father David when you
sent him cedar to build a palace to live in. 4Now I am about to
build a temple[b] for the Name of the LORD my God and to dedicate
it to him for burning fragrant incense[c] before him, for setting out
the consecrated bread[d] regularly, and for making burnt offerings[e] every morning and evening
and on the Sabbaths,[f] at the New Moons and at the appointed festivals of the LORD our God. This
is a lasting ordinance for Israel.

5"The temple I am going to build will be great,[g] because our God is greater than all other

1:15 [u] 1Ki 9:28; Isa 60:5
1:17 [v] SS 1:9
2:1 [w] Dt 12:5 [x] Ecc 2:4
2:2 [y] ver 18; 2Ch 10:4
2:3 [z] 2Sa 5:11 [a] 1Ch 14:1
2:4 [b] ver 1; Dt 12:5 [c] Ex 30:7 [d] Ex 25:30 [e] Ex 29:42; 2Ch 13:11 [f] Nu 28:9-10
2:5 [g] 1Ch 22:5; Ps 135:5

[a] *16* Probably Cilicia [b] *17* That is, about 15 pounds or about 6.9 kilograms [c] *17* That is, about 3 3/4 pounds or about 1.7 kilograms [d] In Hebrew texts 2:1 is numbered 1:18, and 2:2-18 is numbered 2:1-17.
[e] *3* Hebrew *Huram,* a variant of *Hiram;* also in verses 11 and 12

considerable infrastructure, as reflected in the construction of chariot cities, taxation that included provisions for horses (1 Kgs 4:28), and tribute paid in the form of horses (2 Chr 9:24). But see the prohibition on kings accumulating many horses (Deut 17:16). **chariot cities.** Identified as Hazor (in the far north), Megiddo (in the Jezreel Valley), and Gezer (in the Shephelah; i.e., the foothills). These locations were strategic and facilitated protection of trade routes and aided national security.

1:15 as common ... as stones. Israel's terrain is rocky throughout much of the country, providing an image of the abundance of "silver" and "gold" enjoyed during Solomon's reign. These raw materials will occupy a central role in the construction of the temple. The new Jerusalem is also described as adorned with various precious metals, iridescent stones, clear crystal, and pure gold (see Rev 21:9–12).

1:16–17 imported from Egypt ... Kue ... exported them to ... the Hittites ... the Arameans. Solomon was skilled in leveraging Israel's location as a land bridge connecting the continents of Africa, Asia, and Europe. Regions of northeast Africa (Egypt, Cush/Nubia [modern Sudan]) were known horse-breeding places. Ancient texts indicate that certain Egyptian horses (especially Nubian horses) were a large and prized breed of horse. Solomon's trading of horses between the northern regions (Kue and Neo-Hittite and Aramean states) implies that Solomon exerted control over these northern territories (8:3–4; 1 Chr 18:3–10).

1:16 Kue. Area of Cilicia in southeast Anatolia (southeast Turkey) known for ample pasturage and equine breeding.

1:17 six hundred shekels. This high price suggests that these were no ordinary chariots but rather richly appointed chariots for royalty.

2:1—7:22 *Construction and Dedication of the Jerusalem Temple.* The central narrative of chs. 2–7 focuses on the construction of the Jerusalem temple, which began in Solomon's fourth year (ca. 966 BC) and was completed in the eleventh year of his reign (ca. 959 BC).

2:1 temple for the Name of the LORD. Solomon's "wisdom" (1:10) is interwoven with his construction of *God's* temple. The importance of a temple relates directly to the notion of sacred space, where the human realm could intersect with the divine realm and facilitate God's presence (dwelling) and blessing. The careful attention to the design of the temple and stipulations pertaining to entering the temple reflect the importance of properly navigating sacred space—the space where God chose to disclose himself to his people and dwell with them. **the Name of the LORD.** See Deut 12:5 and note. Such "name theology" reflects God's character and his covenantal relationship with Israel. **a royal palace for himself.** Unlike the account of Solomon's building activities in 1 Kgs 7:1–12, the Chronicler mentions Solomon's palace only in passing.

2:2 conscripted. An ongoing challenge in the construction of building projects in the biblical world was the supply of workers. Workers were commonly recruited from slaves, prisoners of war, and the poor. One question that arises from this passage is whether Israelites were subject to forced labor. This verse and 8:7–9 indicate that Solomon did not impose slavery upon Israelites. Other texts (1 Kgs 5:13; 12:3–4) imply that Israelites were conscripted for royal work projects (see 1 Sam 8:10–17 and the connection of such work with the division of the kingdom; 1 Kgs 11:26–28; 12:1–18). Understood together, Solomon placed slavery-style imposed labor upon foreigners and required periods of national service of Israelites.

2:3 Solomon (like David) sought Phoenician assistance to build the temple (see note on 1 Chr 14:1).

2:4 This synopsis of temple worship reflects detailed knowledge of instructions found in the Pentateuch regarding incense (see Exod 30:1–8 and note on v. 1), the consecrated bread (see Exod 25:30 and note; Lev 24:5–9), and the offerings and festivals (see Exod 29:38–39; Num 28–29; see also note on Num 28:1—29:40). Much of the calendar year of ancient Israel was oriented around the agricultural cycle. Such calendar-based observances fostered a regular

gods.[h] 6But who is able to build a temple for him, since the heavens, even the highest heavens,
cannot contain him?[i] Who then am I[j] to build a temple for him, except as a place to burn sacrifices before him?
7"Send me, therefore, a man skilled to work in gold and silver, bronze and iron, and in purple,
crimson and blue yarn, and experienced in the art of engraving, to work in Judah and Jerusalem
with my skilled workers,[k] whom my father David provided.
8"Send me also cedar, juniper and algum[a] logs from Lebanon, for I know that your servants
are skilled in cutting timber there. My servants will work with yours 9to provide me with plenty of
lumber, because the temple I build must be large and magnificent. 10I will give your servants, the
woodsmen who cut the timber, twenty thousand cors[b] of ground wheat, twenty thousand cors[c] of
barley, twenty thousand baths[d] of wine and twenty thousand baths of olive oil.[l]"
11Hiram king of Tyre replied by letter to Solomon:

"Because the LORD loves[m] his people, he has made you their king."

12And Hiram added:

"Praise be to the LORD, the God of Israel, who made heaven and earth![n] He has given King David a wise son, endowed with intelligence and discernment, who will build a temple for the LORD and a palace for himself.
13"I am sending you Huram-Abi,[o] a man of great skill, 14whose mother was from Dan[p] and
whose father was from Tyre. He is trained[q] to work in gold and silver, bronze and iron, stone and wood, and with purple and blue[r] and crimson yarn and fine linen. He is experienced in all kinds of engraving and can execute any design given to him. He will work with your skilled workers and with those of my lord, David your father.
15"Now let my lord send his servants the wheat and barley and the olive oil[s] and wine he
promised, 16and we will cut all the logs from Lebanon that you need and will float them as rafts
by sea down to Joppa.[t] You can then take them up to Jerusalem."

2:5 [h] 1Ch 16:25
2:6 [i] 1Ki 8:27; 2Ch 6:18; Jer 23:24 [j] Ex 3:11
2:7 [k] ver 13-14; Ex 35:31; 1Ch 22:16
2:10 [l] Ezr 3:7
2:11 [m] 1Ki 10:9; 2Ch 9:8
2:12 [n] Ne 9:6; Ps 8:3; 33:6; 102:25
2:13 [o] 1Ki 7:13
2:14 [p] Ex 31:6 [q] Ex 35:31 [r] Ex 35:35
2:15 [s] ver 10; Ezr 3:7
2:16 [t] Jos 19:46; Jnh 1:3

[a] *8* Probably a variant of *almug* [b] *10* That is, probably about 3,600 tons or about 3,200 metric tons of wheat [c] *10* That is, probably about 3,000 tons or about 2,700 metric tons of barley [d] *10* That is, about 120,000 gallons or about 440,000 liters

pattern of recognizing dependence on God (see "The Lord's Appointed Festivals," p. 229).

2:6 the heavens, even the highest heavens, cannot contain him. The sum of the created order cannot house the glory of God. Instead, the temple served as a localization of God's divine glory (see note on 6:18).

2:7–8 The precious metals and fabrics used in the construction of the Jerusalem temple underscore that nothing but the best went into the construction of God's temple. Solomon also sought Phoenician assistance in the sourcing and fashioning of these precious metals and fabrics (see note on 1 Chr 14:1).

2:7 gold. The whole interior of the temple was covered in gold (3:4–9; 1 Kgs 6:20–22,30). **purple, crimson and blue yarn.** A curtain of blue, purple, and scarlet yarn was used in the tabernacle (Exod 26:36).

2:8 cedar. An especially desired wood for important building projects such as temples and palaces given its durability, size, fragrance, and ability to receive a fine finish. The area of Tyre (Phoenicia or Lebanon more broadly) was a well-known source for quality lumber such as cedar. **juniper.** Sometimes translated "cypress" or "fir"; it was also a common type of tree in Phoenicia. **algum.** A transliteration from Hebrew; its identity is uncertain.

2:10 cors ... baths. See NIV text notes.

2:11–12 The Phoenician king Hiram's declaration of God's love is striking and brings to mind comparable declarations made by other foreign leaders including the queen of Sheba (9:7–8), the Persian king Cyrus (36:22–23; Ezra 1:2–3), the Babylonian king Nebuchadnezzar (Dan 4:34–35), and the (Medo-) Persian king Darius (Dan 6:25–27).

2:12–14 wise ... great skill ... skilled workers. In the construction of the Jerusalem temple, Huram-Abi and Solomon functioned in parallel with Oholiab and Bezalel, respectively, who were appointed and equipped in the construction of the tabernacle in the wilderness. All were given some combination of wisdom, knowledge, understanding, and discernment by God for the task of constructing a place in which he would dwell (cf. 1:9–10; Exod 31:1–6; 35:30—36:1; 1 Kgs 7:14). In fact, the Hebrew words used in vv. 12–14 ("wise ... intelligence ... discernment") to describe Solomon (v. 12) and the Phoenician workers ("skill ... trained ... experienced ... skilled") sent by Hiram (vv. 13–14) are also used to describe God's creation of the cosmos: "By *wisdom* the LORD laid the earth's foundations, by *understanding* he set the heavens in place; by his *knowledge* the watery depths were divided, and the clouds let drop the dew" (Prov 3:19–20, emphasis added). In other words, these skilled workers appointed to construct God's earthly dwelling place were equipped with the same qualities that God himself used to construct the world. While the translations "great skill" and "skilled workers" in these passages are contextually accurate they do not convey the emphasis on wisdom, knowledge, and understanding.

2:16 float them. Transporting wood by floating logs was a practical option for nations that had access to seaports. The transportation of wood over sea is seen in Assyrian reliefs that show Phoenician ships towing logs. The journey from Tyre to Joppa is approximately 100 miles (160 kilometers), and the trip inland to Jerusalem is another 30 miles.

2:17 [u] 1Ch 22:2 [v] 2Sa 24:2
2:18 [w] ver 2; 1Ch 22:2; 2Ch 8:8
3:1 [x] Ac 7:47 [y] Ge 28:17 [z] 2Sa 24:18; 1Ch 21:18
3:2 [a] Ezr 5:11
3:3 [b] Eze 41:2
3:5 [c] Eze 40:16
3:7 [d] Ge 3:24; 1Ki 6:29-35; Eze 41:18
3:8 [e] Ex 26:33
3:9 [f] Ex 26:32
3:10 [g] Ex 25:18

17 Solomon took a census of all the foreigners[u] residing in Israel, after the census[v] his father David had taken; and they were found to be 153,600. 18 He assigned[w] 70,000 of them to be carriers and 80,000 to be stonecutters in the hills, with 3,600 foremen over them to keep the people working.

Solomon Builds the Temple

3:1-14pp — 1Ki 6:1-29

3 Then Solomon began to build[x] the temple of the LORD[y] in Jerusalem on Mount Moriah, where the LORD had appeared to his father David. It was on the threshing floor of Araunah[a][z] the Jebusite, the place provided by David. 2 He began building on the second day of the second month in the fourth year of his reign.[a]

3 The foundation Solomon laid for building the temple of God was sixty cubits long and twenty cubits wide[b][b] (using the cubit of the old standard). 4 The portico at the front of the temple was twenty cubits[c] long across the width of the building and twenty[d] cubits high.

He overlaid the inside with pure gold. 5 He paneled the main hall with juniper and covered it with fine gold and decorated it with palm tree[c] and chain designs. 6 He adorned the temple with precious stones. And the gold he used was gold of Parvaim. 7 He overlaid the ceiling beams, doorframes, walls and doors of the temple with gold, and he carved cherubim[d] on the walls.

8 He built the Most Holy Place,[e] its length corresponding to the width of the temple — twenty cubits long and twenty cubits wide. He overlaid the inside with six hundred talents[e] of fine gold. 9 The gold nails[f] weighed fifty shekels.[f] He also overlaid the upper parts with gold.

10 For the Most Holy Place he made a pair[g] of sculptured cherubim and overlaid them with gold. 11 The total wingspan of the cherubim was twenty cubits. One wing of the first cherub was five cubits[g] long and touched the temple wall, while its other wing, also five cubits long, touched the wing of the other cherub. 12 Similarly one wing of the second cherub was five cubits long and touched the other temple wall, and its other wing, also five cubits long, touched the wing of the first cherub.

[a] *1* Hebrew *Ornan,* a variant of *Araunah* [b] *3* That is, about 90 feet long and 30 feet wide or about 27 meters long and 9 meters wide [c] *4* That is, about 30 feet or about 9 meters; also in verses 8, 11 and 13 [d] *4* Some Septuagint and Syriac manuscripts; Hebrew *and a hundred and twenty* [e] *8* That is, about 23 tons or about 21 metric tons [f] *9* That is, about 1 1/4 pounds or about 575 grams [g] *11* That is, about 7 1/2 feet or about 2.3 meters; also in verse 15

3:1 David's idea to build a temple was initially not well received by God. God reminded David that he had not asked for a "house" (i.e., a temple) and instead promised to build David a "house" (i.e., a dynasty); this promise is called the Davidic covenant (see 1 Chr 17:1–27 and note). Nevertheless, Deut 12:5–11 anticipated the notion of a temple as an aspect of settling into the promised land. On the location of the temple, see note on 1 Chr 21:18.

3:3,4a cubits. Israel's system of linear measurement standardized commonly used measurements that were based on the length of fingers, hands, and forearms. The Chronicler's statement reveals that the length of the cubit would have had more than one option in the minds of his postexilic audience. It is difficult to unequivocally state which cubit length is in view by the Chronicler. If the longer cubit is in view (about 21 inches [53 centimeters]), the dimensions of Solomon's temple were 105 feet (32 meters) long and 35 feet (10.7 meters) wide. If the shorter (about 18 inches [46 centimeters]) cubit is in view, the dimensions of the temple were 90 feet (27 meters) long and 30 feet (9 meters) wide. By way of comparison, the playing area of a doubles tennis court is 78 feet (24 meters) long and 36 feet (11 meters) wide and an NBA basketball court is 94 feet (28.5 meters) long and 50 feet (15 meters) wide.

3:4b–6 pure gold ... fine gold ... gold of Parvaim. The description of the temple construction frequently refers to gold. In the broader context this includes beaten gold (9:15–16) and gold from Ophir (8:18; see note on 1 Chr 29:4). While the exact significance of each term (or geographic location) is not completely clear, the emphasis is clear: the temple utilized a lot of top-quality gold that was sourced from locations known for their special gold (cf. 2:7; 4:20–22). The grades of gold increased in purity as one drew closer to the Most Holy Place.

3:5 palm tree. Commonly symbolized fertility, life, and agricultural bounty in the ancient Near East, as well as God's blessings upon his people.

3:6 precious stones. Likely used in settings (1 Chr 29:2) or arranged as a mosaic. Most Israelites never saw the inside of the temple, let alone the Most Holy Place, so these descriptions of the temple provided a window into this unseen world for the Israelites then and for us today. **Parvaim.** Meaning uncertain; it most likely refers to a location, perhaps in Arabia.

3:7 cherubim. See vv. 10–13; see also note on 5:7–8.

3:8–9 The dimensions of the Most Holy Place are approximately 30 feet (9 meters) by 30 feet (9 meters), creating a cube. The new Jerusalem is likewise a cube (Rev 21:16), perhaps in analogy to the Most Holy Place since there is no temple in the city (Rev 21:22). See "Temple," p. 2652.

3:8 six hundred talents. See NIV text note. While this amount is vast, it is not without comparison. For example, the tenth-century pharaoh Osorkon I enumerates gifts totaling 383 tons (347 metric tons) of gold and silver for the gods of Egypt, while Alexander the Great claims to have taken 7,000 tons (6,350 metric tons) from the Persian Empire. Solomon accumulated gold from a variety of sources, including tribute payments (9:13–14), chariot sales (1:17), maritime ventures (8:18), profits from control of trade routes, taxation, and gifts (such as the 120 talents of gold from Hiram and the queen of Sheba).

3:10–13 See 5:7–8 and note.

13 The wings of these cherubim[h] extended twenty cubits. They stood on their feet, facing the main
hall.[a]
14 He made the curtain[i] of blue, purple and crimson yarn and fine linen, with cherubim[j] worked into it.
15 For the front of the temple he made two pillars,[k] which together were thirty-five cubits[b] long, each
with a capital[l] five cubits high. 16 He made interwoven chains[c][m] and put them on top of the pillars. He
also made a hundred pomegranates[n] and attached them to the chains. 17 He erected the pillars in the
front of the temple, one to the south and one to the north. The one to the south he named Jakin[d] and
the one to the north Boaz.[e]

The Temple's Furnishings

4:2-6,10–5:1pp — 1Ki 7:23-26,38-51

4 He made a bronze altar[o] twenty cubits long, twenty cubits wide and ten cubits high.[f] 2 He made the
Sea[p] of cast metal, circular in shape, measuring ten cubits from rim to rim and five cubits[g] high.
It took a line of thirty cubits[h] to measure around it. 3 Below the rim, figures of bulls encircled it—ten
to a cubit.[i] The bulls were cast in two rows in one piece with the Sea.
4 The Sea stood on twelve bulls, three facing north, three facing west, three facing south and three
facing east.[q] The Sea rested on top of them, and their hindquarters were toward the center. 5 It was
a handbreadth[j] in thickness, and its rim was like the rim of a cup, like a lily blossom. It held three
thousand baths.[k]
6 He then made ten basins[r] for washing and placed five on the south side and five on the north. In
them the things to be used for the burnt offerings[s] were rinsed, but the Sea was to be used by the priests
for washing.
7 He made ten gold lampstands[t] according to the specifications[u] for them and placed them in the
temple, five on the south side and five on the north.
8 He made ten tables[v] and placed them in the temple, five on the south side and five on the north. He
also made a hundred gold sprinkling bowls.[w]
9 He made the courtyard[x] of the priests, and the large court and the doors for the court, and overlaid
the doors with bronze. 10 He placed the Sea on the south side, at the southeast corner.
11 And Huram also made the pots and shovels and sprinkling bowls.
So Huram finished[y] the work he had undertaken for King Solomon in the temple of God:

12 the two pillars;
the two bowl-shaped capitals on top of the pillars;

3:13 [h] Ex 25:18
3:14 [i] Ex 26:31,33; Heb 9:3 [j] Ge 3:24
3:15 [k] 1Ki 7:15; Rev 3:12 [l] 1Ki 7:22
3:16 [m] 1Ki 7:17 [n] 1Ki 7:20
4:1 [o] Ex 20:24; 27:1-2; 40:6; 1Ki 8:64; 2Ki 16:14
4:2 [p] Rev 4:6, 15:2
4:4 [q] Nu 2:3-25; Eze 48:30-34; Rev 21:13
4:6 [r] Ex 30:18 [s] Ne 13:5, 9; Eze 40:38
4:7 [t] Ex 25:31 [u] Ex 25:40
4:8 [v] Ex 25:23 [w] Nu 4:14
4:9 [x] 1Ki 6:36; 2Ki 21:5; 2Ch 33:5
4:11 [y] 1Ki 7:14

[a] 13 Or *facing inward* [b] 15 That is, about 53 feet or about 16 meters [c] 16 Or possibly *made chains in the inner sanctuary*; the meaning of the Hebrew for this phrase is uncertain. [d] 17 *Jakin* probably means *he establishes.* [e] 17 *Boaz* probably means *in him is strength.* [f] 1 That is, about 30 feet long and wide and 15 feet high or about 9 meters long and wide and 4.5 meters high [g] 2 That is, about 7 1/2 feet or about 2.3 meters [h] 2 That is, about 45 feet or about 14 meters [i] 3 That is, about 18 inches or about 45 centimeters [j] 5 That is, about 3 inches or about 7.5 centimeters [k] 5 That is, about 18,000 gallons or about 66,000 liters

3:14 curtain. Reflects the separation between a holy God and a fallen human race. A curtain was part of the tabernacle (see Exod 26:31–35 and note) and the Herodian temple (see Matt 27:51 and note).

3:15 thirty-five cubits. See NIV text note. The two free-standing pillars were covered with polished bronze and stationed in the front of Solomon's temple. These impressive pillars included a 7–8 foot (2.0–2.5 meter) ornate top that created a stylized tree image.

3:16 pomegranates. One of the blessings of the promised land (Deut 8:7–9).

3:17 Jakin … Boaz. See NIV text notes.

4:1 bronze altar. The centerpiece of the sacrificial system. The dimensions (see NIV text note) may include the base (see 6:13), with the altar rising in a terraced fashion. The placement of the altar in the front of the temple (1:5; cf. Exod 40:6) suggests that God can be approached only once atonement has been made.

4:2 Sea of cast metal. This "bronze Sea" (1 Chr 18:8) was a massive basin (see NIV text notes) that priests used for washing. The motif of the sea in the OT includes the imagery of God sitting enthroned as eternal king over the flood (Ps 29:10) and underscores God's mastery over all creation (cf. Pss 89; 93; see note on Ps 93:3).

4:5 handbreadth … three thousand baths. See NIV text notes.

4:6 ten basins for washing. Each basin held 40 baths of water (about 240 gallons [880 liters]; see 1 Kgs 7:38 and NIV text note there). They were used for washing sacrificial utensils, emphasizing the importance of purity when approaching the presence of a holy God.

4:7 ten gold lampstands. The tabernacle of Moses' time had one gold lampstand (see Exod 25:31–40 and note). The light from these golden lampstands against a room coated in fine gold created a stunning reflection highlighting the brilliance of the Creator.

4:11–16 This list summarizes the items Huram-Abi fabricated for the temple (cf. vv. 19–22).

4:12 two pillars. See 3:15 and note.

Copper mine at ancient Punon (Feinan).
Todd Bolen/www.BiblePlaces.com

4:14 [z] 1Ki 7:27-30
4:16 [a] 1Ki 7:13
4:17 [b] Ge 33:17
4:18 [c] 1Ki 7:23
4:19 [d] Ex 25:23,30
4:20 [e] Ex 25:31
4:22 [f] Nu 7:14 [g] Lev 10:1

the two sets of network decorating the two bowl-shaped capitals on top of the pillars;
13 the four hundred pomegranates for the two sets of network (two rows of pomegranates for each network, decorating the bowl-shaped capitals on top of the pillars);
14 the stands[z] with their basins;
15 the Sea and the twelve bulls under it;
16 the pots, shovels, meat forks and all related articles.

All the objects that Huram-Abi[a] made for King Solomon for the temple of the LORD were of polished
bronze. 17 The king had them cast in clay molds in the plain of the Jordan between Sukkoth[b] and Zarethan.[a] 18 All these things that Solomon made amounted to so much that the weight of the bronze[c]
could not be calculated.

19 Solomon also made all the furnishings that were in God's temple:

the golden altar;
the tables[d] on which was the bread of the Presence;
20 the lampstands[e] of pure gold with their lamps, to burn in front of the inner sanctuary as prescribed;
21 the gold floral work and lamps and tongs (they were solid gold);
22 the pure gold wick trimmers, sprinkling bowls, dishes[f] and censers;[g] and the gold doors of the temple: the inner doors to the Most Holy Place and the doors of the main hall.

[a] 17 Hebrew *Zeredatha,* a variant of *Zarethan*

4:13 pomegranates. See 3:16 and note.
4:14 basins. See v. 6 and note.
4:15 Sea … bulls. See vv. 2–5 and note on v. 2.
4:17 cast in clay molds. The metalworking for the bronze objects of the Jerusalem temple took place on the east side of the Jordan Valley midway between the Dead Sea and the Sea of Galilee. Excavations at the Edomite Feinan mines to the southeast of the Dead Sea have revealed copper mines and production slags dating to the eleventh–ninth centuries BC.
4:19–22 Summarizes items fabricated for temple service, focusing on items made of (or coated with) gold. The gold plating noted in conjunction with the altar utensils reflects their importance in the sacrificial system and the royal status of the one inhabiting the temple.
4:19 golden altar. Most likely used to burn incense (cf. the tabernacle's altar of incense in Exod 30:1–10; see note there). For the bronze sacrificial altar, see v. 1 and note. **bread of the Presence.** Within the temple this bread was arranged on the gold-covered acacia table by the Levites and replaced each Sabbath (1 Chr 23:29). The perpetual offering of a food item possibly symbolized God's agricultural blessings (see Exod 25:30 and note; Lev 24:5–9).
4:22 censers. Used to hold and burn incense (Lev 4:7; 16:12). Burning incense was a special spiritual function limited strictly to priests (Exod 30:1–10; Num 16:40). **gold doors.** Like the curtain (3:7), they were works of art that separated the holy space from the common space.

5 When all the work Solomon had done for the temple of the LORD was finished,[h] he brought in the
things his father David had dedicated[i]—the silver and gold and all the furnishings—and he
placed them in the treasuries of God's temple.

The Ark Brought to the Temple

5:2–6:11pp — 1Ki 8:1-21

[2]Then Solomon summoned to Jerusalem the elders of Israel, all the heads of the tribes and the chiefs
of the Israelite families, to bring up the ark[j] of the LORD's covenant from Zion, the City of David. [3]And all
the Israelites[k] came together to the king at the time of the festival in the seventh month.
[4]When all the elders of Israel had arrived, the Levites took up the ark, [5]and they brought up the
ark and the tent of meeting and all the sacred furnishings in it. The Levitical priests[l] carried them up;
[6]and King Solomon and the entire assembly of Israel that had gathered about him were before the ark,
sacrificing so many sheep and cattle that they could not be recorded or counted.
[7]The priests then brought the ark[m] of the LORD's covenant to its place in the inner sanctuary of the
temple, the Most Holy Place, and put it beneath the wings of the cherubim. [8]The cherubim[n] spread
their wings over the place of the ark and covered the ark and its carrying poles. [9]These poles were so
long that their ends, extending from the ark, could be seen from in front of the inner sanctuary, but not
from outside the Holy Place; and they are still there today. [10]There was nothing in the ark except[o] the
two tablets[p] that Moses had placed in it at Horeb, where the LORD made a covenant with the Israelites
after they came out of Egypt.
[11]The priests then withdrew from the Holy Place. All the priests who were there had consecrated
themselves, regardless of their divisions.[q] [12]All the Levites who were musicians[r]—Asaph, Heman, Jeduthun and their sons and relatives—stood on the east side of the altar, dressed in fine linen and playing
cymbals, harps and lyres. They were accompanied by 120 priests sounding trumpets.[s] [13]The trumpeters
and musicians joined in unison to give praise and thanks to the LORD. Accompanied by trumpets, cymbals and other instruments, the singers raised their voices in praise to the LORD and sang:

> "He is good;
> his love endures forever."[t]

Then the temple of the LORD was filled with the cloud, [14]and the priests could not perform[u] their
service because of the cloud,[v] for the glory[w] of the LORD filled the temple of God.

5:1 [h] 1Ki 6:14 [i] 2Sa 8:11
5:2 [j] Nu 3:31; 2Sa 6:12; 1Ch 15:25
5:3 [k] 1Ch 9:1; 2Ch 7:8-10
5:5 [l] Nu 3:31; 1Ch 15:2
5:7 [m] Rev 11:19
5:8 [n] Ge 3:24
5:10 [o] Heb 9:4 [p] Ex 16:34; Dt 10:2
5:11 [q] 1Ch 24:1
5:12 [r] 1Ki 10:12; 1Ch 25:1; Ps 68:25 [s] 1Ch 13:8; 15:24
5:13 [t] 1Ch 16:34,41; 2Ch 7:3; 20:21; Ezr 3:11; Ps 100:5; 136:1; Jer 33:11
5:14 [u] Ex 40:35; Rev 15:8 [v] Ex 19:16 [w] Ex 29:43; 2Ch 7:2

5:1—7:22 After the items were crafted for the temple (4:11–22), items that David dedicated were brought into the temple (1 Chr 22:2–19; 29:2–5). Following this final step of furnishing, chs. 5–7 highlight the dedication of the temple. The account of the dedication of the temple is essentially one literary unit beginning with the assembly of the leaders of Israel in 5:2 and closing with the dismissal of this assembly in 7:10, followed by a postscript indicating God's appearance and response to Solomon's dedication prayer (7:11–22). God's response shows that covenantal blessings can be obtained and renewed through repentance and humility. This message of hope has special significance for the Chronicler's postexilic audience living in a time following God's judgment.
5:2 bring up the ark of the LORD's covenant. From the City of David to the new palace-temple complex—a short distance of about 550 yards (500 meters).
5:4–5 Levites … Levitical priests. Moved the sacred objects, including the ark and the tent of meeting (i.e., the tabernacle). See notes on 1 Chr 6:48–49.
5:7–8 wings of the cherubim … covered the ark. The ark was placed beneath and between the wings of the two golden cherubim within the Most Holy Place (cf. 3:10–13). The "wings" of these cherubim extended the full width of the Most Holy Place (20 cubits [3:11]; about 30 feet [9 meters]). This positioning of the cherubim visually portrayed the guarding of God's presence. Cherubim were also on the cover of the ark, perhaps to show God's protection over his word, as God's covenantal relationship with Israel was inscribed on the tablets within the ark (see Exod 37:7–9). Stationing the cherubim facing the main temple hall (3:13) suggests their fuller function as guardians of the sacred space (see Gen 3:24; Ps 99:1 and note; Ezek 10:18–22). The motifs of the temple interior conjure up images of the Garden of Eden (Gen 3:24) and the heavenly firmament (see Ps 18:10 and note).
5:10 nothing in the ark except the two tablets. Nothing is said about the other two items previously kept in the ark: the omer of manna (Exod 16:32–34) and Aaron's rod (Num 17:10). It is possible that these items were removed or lost during the ark's transient period (including years in Philistine possession).
5:12–13 Cf. 1 Chr 15:12—16:42. Music featuring a wide variety of instruments was an important dimension of worship in ancient Israel. Stringed instruments ranged from three to ten strings and were mounted on wooden frames of various shapes and sizes. The role of the musician or singer was closely connected with priestly and military personnel.
5:12 fine linen. A symbol of purity and religious position; worn by the priests. **cymbals.** See note on Ps 150:5. **harps and lyres.** See note on Ps 150:3. **trumpets.** Made of various metals including silver. Blowing trumpets was the only instrumental activity priests performed (1 Chr 15:24).
5:13 his love endures forever. A key theological concept that incorporates God's faithfulness and his commitment to his covenant people. See note on Ps 118:2,3,4.
5:14 the cloud … the glory of the LORD filled the temple. Reminiscent of the cloud that filled the tabernacle in the wilderness following

6:1 [x]Ex 19:9; 1Ki 8:12-50
6:2 [y]Ezr 6:12; 7:15; Ps 135:21
6:6 [z]Dt 12:5; Isa 14:1 [a]Ex 20:24; 2Ch 12:13 [b]1Ch 28:4
6:7 [c]1Sa 10:7; 1Ch 17:2; 28:2; Ac 7:46
6:11 [d]Dt 10:2; 2Ch 5:10; Ps 25:10; 50:5
6:13 [e]Ne 8:4 [f]Ps 95:6
6:14 [g]Ex 8:10; 15:11 [h]Dt 7:9
6:15 [i]1Ch 22:10
6:16 [j]2Sa 7:13,15; 1Ki 2:4; 2Ch 7:18; 23:3 [k]Ps 132:12
6:18 [l]Rev 21:3 [m]2Ch 2:6; Ps 11:4; Isa 40:22; 66:1; Ac 7:49

6 Then Solomon said, "The LORD has said that he would dwell in a dark cloud;[x] 2 I have built a magnificent temple for you, a place for you to dwell forever.[y]"
3 While the whole assembly of Israel was standing there, the king turned around and blessed them.
4 Then he said:

"Praise be to the LORD, the God of Israel, who with his hands has fulfilled what he promised
with his mouth to my father David. For he said, 5 'Since the day I brought my people out of Egypt,
I have not chosen a city in any tribe of Israel to have a temple built so that my Name might be
there, nor have I chosen anyone to be ruler over my people Israel. 6 But now I have chosen Jerusalem[z] for my Name[a] to be there, and I have chosen David[b] to rule my people Israel.'
7 "My father David had it in his heart[c] to build a temple for the Name of the LORD, the God
of Israel. 8 But the LORD said to my father David, 'You did well to have it in your heart to build a
temple for my Name. 9 Nevertheless, you are not the one to build the temple, but your son, your
own flesh and blood—he is the one who will build the temple for my Name.'
10 "The LORD has kept the promise he made. I have succeeded David my father and now I sit on
the throne of Israel, just as the LORD promised, and I have built the temple for the Name of the
LORD, the God of Israel. 11 There I have placed the ark, in which is the covenant[d] of the LORD that
he made with the people of Israel."

Solomon's Prayer of Dedication

6:12-40pp — 1Ki 8:22-53
6:41-42pp — Ps 132:8-10

12 Then Solomon stood before the altar of the LORD in front of the whole assembly of Israel and spread
out his hands. 13 Now he had made a bronze platform,[e] five cubits long, five cubits wide and three cubits
high,[a] and had placed it in the center of the outer court. He stood on the platform and then knelt down[f]
before the whole assembly of Israel and spread out his hands toward heaven. 14 He said:

"LORD, the God of Israel, there is no God like you[g] in heaven or on earth—you who keep your
covenant of love[h] with your servants who continue wholeheartedly in your way. 15 You have kept
your promise to your servant David my father; with your mouth you have promised[i] and with
your hand you have fulfilled it—as it is today.
16 "Now, LORD, the God of Israel, keep for your servant David my father the promises you made
to him when you said, 'You shall never fail[j] to have a successor to sit before me on the throne
of Israel, if only your descendants are careful in all they do to walk before me according to my
law,[k] as you have done.' 17 And now, LORD, the God of Israel, let your word that you promised your
servant David come true.
18 "But will God really dwell[l] on earth with humans? The heavens,[m] even the highest heavens,
cannot contain you. How much less this temple I have built! 19 Yet, LORD my God, give attention

[a] *13* That is, about 7 1/2 feet long and wide and 4 1/2 feet high or about 2.3 meters long and wide and 1.4 meters high

its completion (see Exod 40:34–38 and note). The cloud reminds the people of God's presence and glory.

6:4–11 Solomon's temple dedication prayer begins with expressions of praise that focus on God's faithfulness in fulfilling his promise to David (v. 4). Solomon extends his words of praise back to the exodus (v. 5), which inaugurated God's covenant relationship with Israel (Exod 19:3–6). God's choice of Jerusalem as the location of the temple (v. 6) is likewise an element of God's fulfilling his word (vv. 7–19; 1 Chr 28:4–6). Placing the ark within the temple is the capstone to the monumental day (v. 11; 1 Chr 22:19).

6:14–17 Solomon declares that God steadfastly keeps his word, particularly with respect to his covenant with Israel ("covenant of love," v. 14) and David.

6:16 You shall never fail to have a successor to sit ... on the throne of Israel. This is not explicitly found in other biblical texts associated with the Davidic covenant (e.g., 1 Chr 17:4–14; 2 Sam 7:5–16), but the idea of David never failing to have a descendant to sit on the throne of Israel is hinted at in 2 Sam 7:13,16 and reflected in subsequent biblical passages (see especially Jer 33:17). **if only your descendants are careful in all they do to walk before me.** This condition is often glossed over in discussions of the Davidic covenant. The broader context reflects the balance between God's word being fulfilled (vv. 4–10,15) and the prayerful hope that God will bring to pass the full measure of his promises (vv. 16–17). See note on 1 Chr 17:1–27.

6:18 The heavens, even the highest heavens, cannot contain you. Underscores that although God will localize his presence and glory in the temple, no man-made finite structure can house the infinite God. Yet God's accommodation to humankind in the matter of the temple and even hearing Solomon's prayer showcases God's grace and love toward his people. Solomon stresses the imagery of reconciliation and forgiveness within the setting of the temple (where the shedding of blood for sin would take place).

to your servant's prayer and his plea for mercy. Hear the cry and the prayer that your servant is
praying in your presence. 20 May your eyes[n] be open toward this temple day and night, this place
of which you said you would put your Name[o] there. May you hear[p] the prayer your servant prays
toward this place. 21 Hear the supplications of your servant and of your people Israel when they
pray toward this place. Hear from heaven, your dwelling place; and when you hear, forgive.[q]
22 "When anyone wrongs their neighbor and is required to take an oath[r] and they come and
swear the oath before your altar in this temple, 23 then hear from heaven and act. Judge between
your servants, condemning[s] the guilty and bringing down on their heads what they have done,
and vindicating the innocent by treating them in accordance with their innocence.
24 "When your people Israel have been defeated[t] by an enemy because they have sinned against
you and when they turn back and give praise to your name, praying and making supplication
before you in this temple, 25 then hear from heaven and forgive the sin of your people Israel and
bring them back to the land you gave to them and their ancestors.
26 "When the heavens are shut up and there is no rain[u] because your people have sinned
against you, and when they pray toward this place and give praise to your name and turn from
their sin because you have afflicted them, 27 then hear from heaven and forgive[v] the sin of your
servants, your people Israel. Teach them the right way to live, and send rain on the land you gave
your people for an inheritance.
28 "When famine[w] or plague comes to the land, or blight or mildew, locusts or grasshoppers, or
when enemies besiege them in any of their cities, whatever disaster or disease may come, 29 and
when a prayer or plea is made by anyone among your people Israel—being aware of their afflictions and pains, and spreading out their hands toward this temple— 30 then hear from heaven,
your dwelling place. Forgive,[x] and deal with everyone according to all they do, since you know
their hearts (for you alone know the human heart),[y] 31 so that they will fear you[z] and walk in
obedience to you all the time they live in the land you gave our ancestors.
32 "As for the foreigner who does not belong to your people Israel but has come[a] from a distant
land because of your great name and your mighty hand[b] and your outstretched arm—when
they come and pray toward this temple, 33 then hear from heaven, your dwelling place. Do whatever the foreigner[c] asks of you, so that all the peoples of the earth may know your name and fear
you, as do your own people Israel, and may know that this house I have built bears your Name.
34 "When your people go to war against their enemies,[d] wherever you send them, and when
they pray[e] to you toward this city you have chosen and the temple I have built for your Name,
35 then hear from heaven their prayer and their plea, and uphold their cause.
36 "When they sin against you—for there is no one who does not sin[f]—and you become
angry with them and give them over to the enemy, who takes them captive[g] to a land far away or
near; 37 and if they have a change of heart[h] in the land where they are held captive, and repent
and plead with you in the land of their captivity and say, 'We have sinned, we have done wrong
and acted wickedly'; 38 and if they turn back to you with all their heart and soul in the land of
their captivity where they were taken, and pray toward the land you gave their ancestors, toward
the city you have chosen and toward the temple I have built for your Name; 39 then from heaven,
your dwelling place, hear their prayer and their pleas, and uphold their cause. And forgive your
people, who have sinned against you.

6:20 [n] Ex 3:16; Ps 34:15 [o] Dt 12:11 [p] 2Ch 7:14; 30:20
6:21 [q] Ps 51:1; Isa 33:24; 40:2; 43:25; 44:22; 55:7; Mic 7:18
6:22 [r] Ex 22:11
6:23 [s] Isa 3:11; 65:6; Mt 16:27
6:24 [t] Lev 26:17
6:26 [u] Lev 26:19; Dt 11:17; 28:24; 2Sa 1:21; 1Ki 17:1
6:27 [v] ver 30,39; 2Ch 7:14
6:28 [w] 2Ch 20:9
6:30 [x] ver 27 [y] 1Sa 16:7; 1Ch 28:9; Ps 7:9; 44:21; Pr 16:2; 17:3
6:31 [z] Ps 103:11,13; Pr 8:13
6:32 [a] 2Ch 9:6; Jn 12:20; Ac 8:27 [b] Ex 3:19,20
6:33 [c] 2Ch 7:14
6:34 [d] Dt 28:7 [e] 1Ch 5:20
6:36 [f] Job 15:14; Ps 143:2; Ecc 7:20; Jer 17:9; Jas 3:1; 1Jn 1:8-10 [g] Lev 26:44
6:37 [h] 2Ch 7:14; 33:12, 19,23; Jer 29:13

6:21–39 As the temple connected the earthly realm with the divine realm, it was the ideal setting from which to seek God in prayer. The request presented in each of these scenarios is that God "hear from heaven" (vv. 21,23,25,27,30,33,35). The consequences anticipated in several of these scenarios reflect covenantal judgments of those mentioned in Deut 28 for unfaithfulness ("defeated by an enemy," v. 24; "no rain," v. 26; "famine ... plague ... blight ... enemies besiege," v. 28). Such divine chastening had a teaching function ("teach them the right way to live," v. 27) as well as a sanctifying function ("so that they will fear you and walk in obedience to you," v. 31).

Two scenarios were not related to sin: the foreigner who sought God (vv. 32–33) and the nation going out to war (vv. 34–35). Regarding foreigners who sought God (cf. Isa 56:6–7), the temple was to be "a house of prayer for all nations" (Mark 11:17). God's ultimate desire is that "all the peoples of the earth may know [his] name and fear [him]" (v. 33; cf. Mic 4:2; Zech 8:20–23).

The final section (vv. 36–39) deals with captivity and the reconciliation possible after such drastic judgment. The theological reality of sin in humankind ("there is no one who does not sin," v. 36) is balanced with the way humanity is to seek God (they are to "turn back to [God] with all their heart and soul," v. 38). When such an inner disposition of humility is shown, God is asked to "hear ... uphold ... and forgive [his] people" (v. 39). This included restoration of the Davidic monarchy.

6:40 [i]2Ch 7:15; Ne 1:6, 11; Ps 17:1,6
6:41 [j]Isa 33:10 [k]1Ch 28:2 [l]Ps 132:16 [m]Ps 116:12
6:42 [n]Ps 89:24,28; Isa 55:3
7:1 [o]Lev 9:24; 1Ki 18:38 [p]Ex 16:10 [q]Ps 26:8
7:2 [r]1Ki 8:11 [s]Ex 29:43; 40:35; 2Ch 5:14
7:3 [t]1Ch 16:34; 2Ch 5:13; 20:21
7:6 [u]1Ch 15:16 [v]2Ch 5:12
7:8 [w]2Ch 30:26 [x]Ge 15:18
7:9 [y]Lev 23:36

[40]"Now, my God, may your eyes be open and your ears attentive[i] to the prayers offered in this place.

[41]"Now arise,[j] LORD God, and come to your resting place,[k]
you and the ark of your might.
May your priests,[l] LORD God, be clothed with salvation,
may your faithful people rejoice in your goodness.[m]
[42]LORD God, do not reject your anointed one.
Remember the great love[n] promised to David your servant."

The Dedication of the Temple

7:1-10pp — 1Ki 8:62-66

7 When Solomon finished praying, fire[o] came down from heaven and consumed the burnt offering and the sacrifices, and the glory of the LORD filled[p] the temple.[q] [2]The priests could not enter[r] the temple of the LORD because the glory[s] of the LORD filled it. [3]When all the Israelites saw the fire coming down and the glory of the LORD above the temple, they knelt on the pavement with their faces to the ground, and they worshiped and gave thanks to the LORD, saying,

"He is good;
his love endures forever."[t]

[4]Then the king and all the people offered sacrifices before the LORD. [5]And King Solomon offered a sacrifice of twenty-two thousand head of cattle and a hundred and twenty thousand sheep and goats. So the king and all the people dedicated the temple of God. [6]The priests took their positions, as did the Levites[u] with the LORD's musical instruments,[v] which King David had made for praising the LORD and which were used when he gave thanks, saying, "His love endures forever." Opposite the Levites, the priests blew their trumpets, and all the Israelites were standing.

[7]Solomon consecrated the middle part of the courtyard in front of the temple of the LORD, and there he offered burnt offerings and the fat of the fellowship offerings, because the bronze altar he had made could not hold the burnt offerings, the grain offerings and the fat portions.

[8]So Solomon observed the festival[w] at that time for seven days, and all Israel with him — a vast assembly, people from Lebo Hamath to the Wadi of Egypt.[x] [9]On the eighth day they held an assembly, for they had celebrated the dedication of the altar for seven days and the festival[y] for seven days more. [10]On the twenty-third day of the seventh month he sent the people to their homes, joyful and glad in heart for the good things the LORD had done for David and Solomon and for his people Israel.

The LORD Appears to Solomon

7:11-22pp — 1Ki 9:1-9

[11]When Solomon had finished the temple of the LORD and the royal palace, and had succeeded in carrying out all he had in mind to do in the temple of the LORD and in his own palace, [12]the LORD appeared to him at night and said:

6:41 – 42 Cf. Ps 132:8 – 10. The Chronicler adds the reference to the "anointed one" (v. 42) to the account of this prayer found in 1 Kgs 8:22 – 30, underscoring his interest in the Davidic covenant and the hope that the Davidic dynasty would be restored.
7:1 fire came down from heaven. Visually showcases God's power and signifies his approval of Solomon's dedicatory prayer and offering. Fire from heaven accompanied David's sacrifice at the threshing floor of Araunah (see 1 Chr 21:26 and note) and the inauguration of priestly service at Sinai (Lev 9:23 – 24). **the burnt offering and the sacrifices.** Likely those in 5:6.
7:2 The priests could not enter the temple. Due to the intensity of God's glory (cf. Exod 40:34 – 38 and note).
7:3 the Israelites ... worshiped. Due to the dramatic exposure to God's glory.
7:6 The antiphonal arrangement of the Levites and priests is reminiscent of Joshua's covenant renewal ceremony at Mount Ebal and Mount Gerizim (Josh 8:30 – 35).
7:8 The guest list for the temple dedication festival included dignitaries from Lebo Hamath in the north to the Wadi of Egypt in the south. These place-names are significant since early patriarchal promises used them concerning the geographic extent of the promised land (Gen 15:18 – 21; Num 34:1 – 12; see map, p. 592). Solomon's festival followed the pattern of the Festival of Tabernacles, which was celebrated from the 15th to the 22nd of the seventh month (Lev 23:33 – 43; see notes on Num 29:12 – 40; Deut 16:13; see also "The Lord's Appointed Festivals," p. 229).
7:11 – 12 Solomon's second dream (see note on 1:7) took place after the completion of the temple and the palace — about 20 years after his initial revelatory dream in 1:7.

"I have heard your prayer and have chosen this place for myself[z] as a temple for sacrifices.
13"When I shut up the heavens so that there is no rain,[a] or command locusts to devour the
land or send a plague among my people, 14if my people, who are called by my name, will humble[b]
themselves and pray and seek my face[c] and turn[d] from their wicked ways, then I will hear from
heaven, and I will forgive[e] their sin and will heal[f] their land. 15Now my eyes will be open and my
ears attentive to the prayers offered in this place.[g] 16I have chosen[h] and consecrated this temple
so that my Name may be there forever. My eyes and my heart will always be there.
17"As for you, if you walk before me faithfully[i] as David your father did, and do all I command,
and observe my decrees and laws, 18I will establish your royal throne, as I covenanted with David
your father when I said, 'You shall never fail to have a successor[j] to rule over Israel.'[k]
19"But if you[a] turn away[l] and forsake[m] the decrees and commands I have given you[a] and
go off to serve other gods and worship them, 20then I will uproot[n] Israel from my land,[o] which
I have given them, and will reject this temple I have consecrated for my Name. I will make it a
byword and an object of ridicule[p] among all peoples. 21This temple will become a heap of rubble.
All[b] who pass by will be appalled and say,[q] 'Why has the LORD done such a thing to this land and
to this temple?' 22People will answer, 'Because they have forsaken the LORD, the God of their ancestors, who brought them out of Egypt, and have embraced other gods, worshiping and serving
them — that is why he brought all this disaster on them.'"

7:12 [z] Dt 12:5
7:13 [a] 2Ch 6:26-28; Am 4:7
7:14 [b] Lev 26:41; 2Ch 6:37; Jas 4:10 [c] 1Ch 16:11 [d] Isa 55:7; Zec 1:4 [e] 2Ch 6:27 [f] 2Ch 30:20; Isa 30:26; 57:18
7:15 [g] 2Ch 6:40
7:16 [h] ver 12; 2Ch 6:6
7:17 [i] 1Ki 9:4
7:18 [j] 2Ch 6:16 [k] 2Sa 7:13; 2Ch 13:5
7:19 [l] Dt 28:15 [m] Lev 26:14,33
7:20 [n] Dt 29:28 [o] 1Ki 14:15 [p] Dt 28:37
7:21 [q] Dt 29:24
8:5 [r] 1Ch 7:24; 2Ch 14:7
8:7 [s] Ge 10:16
8:8 [t] 1Ki 4:6; 9:21

Solomon's Other Activities

8:1-18pp — 1Ki 9:10-28

8 At the end of twenty years, during which Solomon built the temple of the LORD and his own palace,
2Solomon rebuilt the villages that Hiram[c] had given him, and settled Israelites in them. 3Solomon
then went to Hamath Zobah and captured it. 4He also built up Tadmor in the desert and all the store
cities he had built in Hamath. 5He rebuilt Upper Beth Horon[r] and Lower Beth Horon as fortified cities,
with walls and with gates and bars, 6as well as Baalath and all his store cities, and all the cities for his
chariots and for his horses[d] — whatever he desired to build in Jerusalem, in Lebanon and throughout
all the territory he ruled.
7There were still people left from the Hittites, Amorites, Perizzites, Hivites and Jebusites[s] (these
people were not Israelites). 8Solomon conscripted[t] the descendants of all these people remaining in
the land — whom the Israelites had not destroyed — to serve as slave labor, as it is to this day. 9But

[a] *19* The Hebrew is plural. [b] *21* See some Septuagint manuscripts, Old Latin, Syriac, Arabic and Targum; Hebrew *And though this temple is now so imposing, all* [c] *2* Hebrew *Huram,* a variant of *Hiram;* also in verse 18 [d] *6* Or *charioteers*

7:13–16 God's response to Solomon's prayer in 6:14–42 mirrors the phraseology and content of Solomon's supplications.
7:14 if my people. This statement is situated within particulars related to the God's covenant with Israel and David and the temple sacrificial system (vv. 15–16). These details regarding the hope of the restoration of the Davidic dynasty apply only to the nation of Israel within the specific geographic area of the promised land. Furthermore, the Chronicler is retelling something that had been told to Solomon about four centuries earlier. While there is a secondary line of significance to the Chronicler's time, this verse is not a promissory statement for countries around the globe. Nevertheless, God may choose to be gracious to peoples and nations according to his own sovereign will (see Jer 18:1–10).
7:16 my Name. See note on 2:1.
7:17–22 God's response to Solomon reflects a layer of conditionality for Solomon and subsequent Davidic leaders. God cited the dynamics of his promises to David in the midst of Solomon's later apostasy and the division of the kingdom (1 Kgs 11:9–40). God's response would remind the postexilic community that God fulfills his word. See note on 6:14–17; see also note on 1 Chr 17:1–27.
8:1–18 *Solomon's Other Activities.* This summarizes Solomon's various achievements (though not necessarily in chronological order) and condenses much of chs. 2–7.
8:3 The capture of Hamath Zobah and building "store cities" (v. 4) indicate a significant expansion of Israelite political-economic hegemony. Solomon's geographic control extended deep into Aram (Syria) to the north and bordered the west bank of the Euphrates River to the northeast.
8:4 Tadmor. Also known as Palmyra; an important caravan city in Syria nearly 300 miles (480 kilometers) from Jerusalem. As with Hamath Zobath (v. 3), the fortification of Tadmor reflects Solomon's control over important commercial trade routes. A textual issue creates the possibility that the city of Tamar to the south of the Dead Sea is intended here (see 1 Kgs 9:17–18 and NIV text note there).
8:5–6 The fortification of these cities is related to oversight of trade routes and protection of access routes to the heart of Israel.
8:5 Upper Beth Horon and Lower Beth Horon. Strategically located on the main east-west route linking the coastal highway and the central hill country of Judah. Upper Beth Horon was approximately 1,000 feet (300 meters) higher in altitude than Lower Beth Horon.
8:6 Baalath. Located on a secondary road leading from the coastal plain to the interior. **chariots ... horses.** See note on 1:14.
8:7–10 On the nationalized labor force, see note on 2:2.

8:11 [u] 1Ki 3:1; 7:8
8:12 [v] 1Ki 8:64; 2Ch 4:1; 15:8
8:13 [w] Ex 29:38; Nu 28:3 [x] Nu 28:9 [y] Ex 23:14; Dt 16:16 [z] Ex 23:16
8:14 [a] 1Ch 24:1 [b] 1Ch 25:1 [c] 1Ch 9:17; 26:1 [d] Ne 12:24,36 [e] 1Ch 23:6; Ne 12:45
8:18 [f] 2Ch 9:9
9:1 [g] Ge 10:7; Eze 23:42; Mt 12:42; Lk 11:31
9:3 [h] 1Ki 5:12
9:6 [i] 2Ch 6:32
9:8 [j] 1Ki 2:12; 1Ch 17:14; 28:5; 29:23; 2Ch 13:8

Solomon did not make slaves of the Israelites for his work; they were his fighting men, commanders of
his captains, and commanders of his chariots and charioteers. 10 They were also King Solomon's chief
officials — two hundred and fifty officials supervising the men.
11 Solomon brought Pharaoh's daughter[u] up from the City of David to the palace he had built for
her, for he said, "My wife must not live in the palace of David king of Israel, because the places the ark
of the LORD has entered are holy."
12 On the altar[v] of the LORD that he had built in front of the portico, Solomon sacrificed burnt offerings to the LORD, 13 according to the daily requirement[w] for offerings commanded by Moses for the
Sabbaths,[x] the New Moons and the three[y] annual festivals — the Festival of Unleavened Bread, the
Festival of Weeks[z] and the Festival of Tabernacles. 14 In keeping with the ordinance of his father David,
he appointed the divisions[a] of the priests for their duties, and the Levites[b] to lead the praise and to assist
the priests according to each day's requirement. He also appointed the gatekeepers[c] by divisions for
the various gates, because this was what David the man of God[d] had ordered.[e] 15 They did not
deviate from the king's commands to the priests or to the Levites in any matter, including
that of the treasuries.
16 All Solomon's work was carried out, from the day the foundation of the
temple of the LORD was laid until its completion. So the temple of the
LORD was finished.
17 Then Solomon went to Ezion Geber and Elath on the coast of
Edom. 18 And Hiram sent him ships commanded by his own men,
sailors who knew the sea. These, with Solomon's men, sailed to Ophir
and brought back four hundred and fifty talents[a] of gold,[f] which they
delivered to King Solomon.

Eighth-century BC ostracon that mentions the gold of Ophir (2 Chr 8:18).
Z. Radovan/www.BibleLandPictures.com

The Queen of Sheba Visits Solomon

9:1-12pp — 1Ki 10:1-13

9 When the queen of Sheba[g] heard of Solomon's fame, she came to
Jerusalem to test him with hard questions. Arriving with a very great
caravan — with camels carrying spices, large quantities of gold, and
precious stones — she came to Solomon and talked with him about all
she had on her mind. 2 Solomon answered all her questions; nothing was
too hard for him to explain to her. 3 When the queen of Sheba saw the wisdom of Solomon,[h] as well
as the palace he had built, 4 the food on his table, the seating of his officials, the attending servants in
their robes, the cupbearers in their robes and the burnt offerings he made at[b] the temple of the LORD,
she was overwhelmed.
5 She said to the king, "The report I heard in my own country about your achievements and your
wisdom is true. 6 But I did not believe what they said until I came[i] and saw with my own eyes. Indeed,
not even half the greatness of your wisdom was told me; you have far exceeded the report I heard. 7 How
happy your people must be! How happy your officials, who continually stand before you and hear your
wisdom! 8 Praise be to the LORD your God, who has delighted in you and placed you on his throne[j] as

[a] *18* That is, about 17 tons or about 15 metric tons [b] *4* Or *and the ascent by which he went up to*

8:11 Pharaoh's daughter. Solomon's marriage to her solidified his alliance with Egypt, which is first noted in 1 Kgs 3:1. **palace he had built for her.** Solomon's construction of a separate palace for the Egyptian princess reflects her high status within the royal harem.
8:14 Levites … priests. See notes on 1 Chr 6:48–49.
8:17 Ezion Geber. Port located on the northern tip of the Gulf of Aqabah.
8:18 ships … sailors. Solomon's arrangements with Phoenicia extended into maritime trade, with the Phoenicians supplying both ships and experienced sailors. The Phoenicians were noted sailors in the ancient world, and the Egyptian language included the term "Byblos Ship" to denote a high quality vessel from Phoenicia. **Ophir.** See note on 1 Chr 29:4.
9:1–12 *The Queen of Sheba Visits Solomon.* The visit of the queen of Sheba showcases God's blessings on Solomon, most notably wisdom and wealth.
9:1 Sheba. Identified with ancient Saba, a trading depot located in the vicinity of modern Yemen in the south of the Arabian peninsula 1,400–1,500 miles (2,250–2,400 kilometers) from Jerusalem. The southern provinces of Arabia were noted for species of trees and shrubs whose aromatic resin was used to produce a number of spices, gums, and balms.
9:3 wisdom of Solomon. See note on 1:10.
9:5–8 The queen of Sheba's declaration of God's delight and love for Solomon and Israel recalls the outreach element of divinely given wisdom reflected in Deut 4:6.

king to rule for the LORD your God. Because of the love of your God for Israel and his desire to uphold
them forever, he has made you king[k] over them, to maintain justice and righteousness."
9 Then she gave the king 120 talents[a] of gold,[l] large quantities of spices, and precious stones. There
had never been such spices as those the queen of Sheba gave to King Solomon.
10 (The servants of Hiram and the servants of Solomon brought gold from Ophir;[m] they also brought
algumwood[b] and precious stones. 11 The king used the algumwood to make steps for the temple of the
LORD and for the royal palace, and to make harps and lyres for the musicians. Nothing like them had
ever been seen in Judah.)
12 King Solomon gave the queen of Sheba all she desired and asked for; he gave her more than she
had brought to him. Then she left and returned with her retinue to her own country.

Solomon's Splendor

9:13-28pp — 1Ki 10:14-29; 2Ch 1:14-17

13 The weight of the gold that Solomon received yearly was 666 talents,[c] 14 not including the revenues
brought in by merchants and traders. Also all the kings of Arabia[n] and the governors of the territories
brought gold and silver to Solomon.
15 King Solomon made two hundred large shields of hammered gold; six hundred shekels[d] of hammered gold went into each shield. 16 He also made three hundred small shields[o] of hammered gold, with
three hundred shekels[e] of gold in each shield. The king put them in the Palace of the Forest of Lebanon.[p]
17 Then the king made a great throne covered with ivory[q] and overlaid with pure gold. 18 The throne had
six steps, and a footstool of gold was attached to it. On both sides of the seat were armrests, with a lion standing beside each of them. 19 Twelve lions stood on the six steps, one at either end of each step. Nothing like it
had ever been made for any other kingdom. 20 All King Solomon's goblets were gold, and all the household
articles in the Palace of the Forest of Lebanon were pure gold. Nothing was made of silver, because silver
was considered of little value in Solomon's day. 21 The king had a fleet of trading ships[f] manned by Hiram's[g]
servants. Once every three years it returned, carrying gold, silver and ivory, and apes and baboons.
22 King Solomon was greater in riches and wisdom than all the other kings of the earth.[r] 23 All the
kings[s] of the earth sought audience with Solomon to hear the wisdom God had put in his heart. 24 Year
after year, everyone who came brought a gift[t]—articles of silver and gold, and robes, weapons and
spices, and horses and mules.
25 Solomon had four thousand stalls for horses and chariots,[u] and twelve thousand horses,[b] which
he kept in the chariot cities and also with him in Jerusalem. 26 He ruled[v] over all the kings from the
Euphrates River[w] to the land of the Philistines, as far as the border of Egypt.[x] 27 The king made silver

9:8 [k]2Ch 2:11
9:9 [l]2Ch 8:18
9:10 [m]2Ch 8:18
9:14 [n]2Ch 17:11; Isa 21:13; Jer 25:24; Eze 27:21; 30:5
9:16 [o]2Ch 12:9 [p]1Ki 7:2
9:17 [q]1Ki 22:39
9:22 [r]1Ki 3:13; 2Ch 1:12
9:23 [s]1Ki 4:34
9:24 [t]2Ch 32:23; Ps 45:12; 68:29; 72:10; Isa 18:7
9:25 [u]1Sa 8:11; 1Ki 4:26
9:26 [v]1Ki 4:21 [w]Ps 72:8-9 [x]Ge 15:18-21

[a] *9* That is, about 4 1/2 tons or about 4 metric tons [b] *10* Probably a variant of *almugwood* [c] *13* That is, about 25 tons or about 23 metric tons [d] *15* That is, about 15 pounds or about 6.9 kilograms [e] *16* That is, about 7 1/2 pounds or about 3.5 kilograms [f] *21* Hebrew *of ships that could go to Tarshish* [g] *21* Hebrew *Huram,* a variant of *Hiram* [h] *25* Or *charioteers*

9:9 120 talents. See NIV text note. It is possible that this large "gift" was part of a broader commercial trading agreement between Solomon and the queen of Sheba.

9:13–28 *Solomon's Splendor.* Solomon's royal revenue reflects the economic clout ancient Israel was able to develop over neighboring countries and regions. Solomon's geographic expansion extended Israelite control over the coastal highway in the west and the Transjordan King's Highway in the east. This expansion allowed Israel to profit from the trade activity flowing between Egypt, Arabia, and Mesopotamia (vv. 13–14; 1 Kgs 9:26–27; 10:14–29).

9:13 666 talents. See NIV text note.

9:15–16 These opulent ceremonial weapons were not intended for battle but reflected a kingdom's wealth.

9:16 Palace of the Forest. Further described in 1 Kgs 7; probably derived its name from the cedar pillars inside the palace that created a tree-like appearance.

9:17–19 Solomon's throne was a magnificent work of art that brought together biblical motifs and building materials in such a way as to attain a unique level of elegance. Solomon's throne was inlaid with ivory, a material prized in the ancient world for its smoothness.

9:21 fleet of trading ships. The three-year journey implies that these ships could manage the high seas and undertake long-distance sea travel. Trading vessels ranged from 40 to 80 feet (12 to 24 meters) in length and could cover 25–40 miles (40–65 kilometers) per day.

9:22–28 Cf. 1:12–16.

9:24 God's blessing is reflected in the stream of foreign dignitaries bringing gifts and tribute payments to Israel (cf. 17:10–11).

9:25 horses and chariots. See note on 1:14.

9:26 Euphrates River ... land of the Philistines ... border of Egypt. Solomon ruled over the regions southwest of the Euphrates and over kings from Tipsah on the Euphrates in the northeast to the border of Egypt in the southwest (1 Kgs 4:24).

9:27 He received resources from his 12 taxation districts, tribute payments from vassals, trade route revenue from traveling merchants, and maritime trade.

9:29 [y]2Sa 7:2; 1Ch 29:29 [z]1Ki 11:29 [a]2Ch 10:2
9:31 [b]1Ki 2:10
10:2 [c]2Ch 9:29 [d]1Ki 11:40
10:3 [e]1Ch 9:1
10:4 [f]2Ch 2:2
10:6 [g]Job 8:8-9; 12:12; 15:10; 32:7
10:7 [h]Pr 15:1
10:8 [i]2Sa 17:14 [j]Pr 13:20

as common in Jerusalem as stones, and cedar as plentiful as sycamore-fig trees in the foothills. 28Sol-
omon's horses were imported from Egypt and from all other countries.

Solomon's Death

9:29-31pp — 1Ki 11:41-43

29As for the other events of Solomon's reign, from beginning to end, are they not written in the
records of Nathan[y] the prophet, in the prophecy of Ahijah[z] the Shilonite and in the visions of Iddo the
seer concerning Jeroboam[a] son of Nebat? 30Solomon reigned in Jerusalem over all Israel forty years.
31Then he rested with his ancestors and was buried in the city of David[b] his father. And Rehoboam his
son succeeded him as king.

Israel Rebels Against Rehoboam

10:1–11:4pp — 1Ki 12:1-24

10 Rehoboam went to Shechem, for all Israel had gone there to make him king. 2When Jeroboam[c]
son of Nebat heard this (he was in Egypt, where he had fled[d] from King Solomon), he returned
from Egypt. 3So they sent for Jeroboam, and he and all Israel[e] went to Rehoboam and said to him:
4"Your father put a heavy yoke on us,[f] but now lighten the harsh labor and the heavy yoke he put on
us, and we will serve you."

5Rehoboam answered, "Come back to me in three days." So the people went away.

6Then King Rehoboam consulted the elders[g] who had served his father Solomon during his lifetime.
"How would you advise me to answer these people?" he asked.

7They replied, "If you will be kind to these people and please them and give them a favorable answer,[h] they will always be your servants."

8But Rehoboam rejected[i] the advice the elders[j] gave him and consulted the young men who had
grown up with him and were serving him. 9He asked them, "What is your advice? How should we answer
these people who say to me, 'Lighten the yoke your father put on us'?"

9:28 horses were imported from Egypt. See note on 1:14; this directly violated the command of Deut 17:16.
9:29–31 *Solomon's Death.* This is the common literary formula for summarizing royal reigns in Kings and Chronicles. These royal summaries provide basic regnal information including the length of reign, name of successor, place of burial, and a reference to a source where more information about this king's reign can be gleaned. Oftentimes, the source is attributed to a specific prophet, as here ("the records of Nathan the prophet," v. 29), implying a close link between the prophetic office and regnal annotations in ancient Israel. These summaries set up the narratives to follow.
10:1—36:19 *The Divided Monarchy.* Chs. 10–36 constitute the final major section of the Chronicler's work: the account of Judah following the division of the kingdom in 931/30 BC. This division created two political states. The Bible typically calls the northern kingdom "Israel" and the southern kingdom "Judah," although the Chronicler occasionally uses "Israel" for the southern kingdom (12:1; 21:2; 28:19). Chronicles focuses almost exclusively on the southern kingdom of Judah in light of the Chronicler's focus on the Jerusalem temple and the Davidic dynasty.
10:1—12:16 *The Reign of Rehoboam and the Division of the Kingdom.* The division of the Israelite kingdom was part of God's judgment (10:15) and unfolded through the common human tendencies of pride, foolishness, and rebellion. Responsibility is also attached to Israel (the new designation for the northern kingdom [see 10:19]) as well as Solomon (implied in 10:4,11,14–15). The division of the Israelite kingdom entailed a variety of social, religious, and economic repercussions. These challenges were exacerbated by the frequent conflict between Israel and Judah. While the capital of the Davidic dynasty remained at Jerusalem, Israel had several capital cities at different times, including Shechem, Peniel, Tirzah, and finally Samaria, which remained the capital until the fall of the northern kingdom in 722 BC. The division of the kingdom also necessitated development of alternative religious centers in the northern kingdom: Jeroboam's infamous golden calf shrines in the north at Dan and in the south at Bethel (1 Kgs 12:26–33).
10:1 Shechem. Strategically located in the territory of Manasseh on the east side of the pass between Mount Ebal and Mount Gerizim. It is connected with important moments during the time of Abraham (Gen 12:6–7), Jacob (Gen 33:18–20), and Joshua (Josh 24:25). Rehoboam's journey to Shechem reflects the importance of securing support from the northern tribes and that such support was not automatic (cf. 1 Chr 11:1–3).
10:2–3 After falling out of favor with Solomon (1 Kgs 11:26–40), Jeroboam had fled to Egypt, but he returned after Solomon's death. The specifics of Jeroboam's time in Egypt are not detailed, but presumably the Egyptian pharaoh's hospitality toward Jeroboam had some strings attached.
10:4 heavy yoke ... harsh labor. A by-product of the significant national service and taxes Solomon had imposed to aid his building projects (see note on 2:2). Of some irony, this phraseology describes the conditions the Egyptians had imposed upon the Israelites (Exod 6:6–9). **we will serve you.** The northern tribes were not necessarily planning to revolt.
10:6–11 The two groups of counselors suggest multiple circles of political advisors. In this setting, the older counselors ("elders," v. 6) were associated with Solomon's administration (see note on v. 7), while the "young men" (v. 8) may have consisted of royal princes aligned with Rehoboam (see note on v. 8).
10:7 The elders advised Rehoboam to "be a servant to [the] people and serve them" (1 Kgs 12:7), a line of advice that resonates with the broader message of Scripture with regard to leadership (Matt 20:28; Mark 9:35; John 13:1–17).
10:8 young men. Although this brings to mind an image of youthfulness, these men were not young. Rehoboam was 41 years old (12:13;

[10]The young men who had grown up with him replied, "The people have said to you, 'Your father
put a heavy yoke on us, but make our yoke lighter.' Now tell them, 'My little finger is thicker than my
father's waist. [11]My father laid on you a heavy yoke; I will make it even heavier. My father scourged you
with whips; I will scourge you with scorpions.'"

[12]Three days later Jeroboam and all the people returned to Rehoboam, as the king had said, "Come
back to me in three days." [13]The king answered them harshly. Rejecting the advice of the elders, [14]he
followed the advice of the young men and said, "My father made your yoke heavy; I will make it even
heavier. My father scourged you with whips; I will scourge you with scorpions." [15]So the king did not
listen to the people, for this turn of events was from God,[k] to fulfill the word the LORD had spoken to
Jeroboam son of Nebat through Ahijah the Shilonite.[l]

[16]When all Israel[m] saw that the king refused to listen to them, they answered the king:

> "What share do we have in David,[n]
> what part in Jesse's son?
> To your tents, Israel!
> Look after your own house, David!"

So all the Israelites went home. [17]But as for the Israelites who were living in the towns of Judah, Rehoboam still ruled over them.

[18]King Rehoboam sent out Adoniram,[a][o] who was in charge of forced labor, but the Israelites stoned
him to death. King Rehoboam, however, managed to get into his chariot and escape to Jerusalem. [19]So
Israel has been in rebellion against the house of David to this day.

11 When Rehoboam arrived in Jerusalem,[p] he mustered Judah and Benjamin—a hundred and
eighty thousand able young men—to go to war against Israel and to regain the kingdom for
Rehoboam.

[2]But this word of the LORD came to Shemaiah[q] the man of God: [3]"Say to Rehoboam son of Solomon
king of Judah and to all Israel in Judah and Benjamin, [4]'This is what the LORD says: Do not go up to
fight against your fellow Israelites.[r] Go home, every one of you, for this is my doing.'" So they obeyed
the words of the LORD and turned back from marching against Jeroboam.

Rehoboam Fortifies Judah

[5]Rehoboam lived in Jerusalem and built up towns for defense in Judah: [6]Bethlehem, Etam, Tekoa,
[7]Beth Zur, Soko, Adullam, [8]Gath, Mareshah, Ziph, [9]Adoraim, Lachish, Azekah, [10]Zorah, Aijalon and
Hebron. These were fortified cities in Judah and Benjamin. [11]He strengthened their defenses and put
commanders in them, with supplies of food, olive oil and wine. [12]He put shields and spears in all the
cities, and made them very strong. So Judah and Benjamin were his.

[13]The priests and Levites from all their districts throughout Israel sided with him. [14]The Levites[s] even
abandoned their pasturelands and property[t] and came to Judah and Jerusalem, because Jeroboam and

10:15 [k]2Ch 11:4; 25:16-20 [l]1Ki 11:29
10:16 [m]1Ch 9:1 [n]ver 19; 2Sa 20:1
10:18 [o]1Ki 5:14
11:1 [p]1Ki 12:21
11:2 [q]2Ch 12:5-7,15
11:4 [r]2Ch 28:8-11
11:14 [s]Nu 35:2-5 [t]2Ch 13:9

[a] *18* Hebrew *Hadoram,* a variant of *Adoniram*

1 Kgs 14:21), and these individuals grew up with him (1 Kgs 12:8). Instead, "young" refers to their lack of wisdom and lack of experience in comparison to the elders who had served Solomon.

10:12–14 Rehoboam opted for the harsher approach to the northern tribes and in so doing facilitated the division of the Israelite kingdom.

10:15 this turn of events was from God. Even the actions of an unwise leader fall under the sovereign will of God.

10:16 This rallying call is reminiscent of the divisive words of Sheba in 2 Sam 20:1–2.

10:18 sent out Adoniram. This ill-fated decision may have been part of Rehoboam's mandate to make the yoke on the northern tribes even heavier since Adoniram oversaw "forced labor," which was reserved for non-Israelites rather than Israelites. Israelites provided standard, requisite national service (see note on 2:2).

11:1 The division of the kingdom was accompanied by a long civil war. On these large numbers, see Introduction to 1 Chronicles: Particular Challenges (Issues Involving Numbers).

11:4 From the perspective of God, the divided tribes were still "fellow Israelites." **this is my doing.** Although Israel was in rebellion against the "house of David" (10:19), God's sovereignty was shaping the events at hand (cf. 10:15; see note there).

11:5–12 Rehoboam's fortified cities address strategic threats to Judah from the northern kingdom and from foes to the east (Moab, Ammon), the west (Philistia), the north (Aram and Israel), and the south (Egypt).

11:6–10 The list of 15 towns focuses on three main lines of fortification that are for the most part grouped: along the eastern/southeastern edge of the hill country of Judah ("Bethlehem," v. 6), along the western edge of the foothills ("Lachish," v. 9), and along the southwestern edge of the hill country of Judah ("Hebron," v. 10). Aijalon (v. 10) would protect from threats to the north via the Beth Horon Ridge.

11:13–16 from all their districts ... from every tribe. Faithful priests, Levites, and citizens left all they had to relocate to the southern kingdom of Judah. These immigrants would have left farms, families, and tribal allotments for the greater good of being in community with God's people

11:15 [u] 1Ki 13:33 [v] 1Ki 12:31 [w] Lev 17:7 [x] 1Ki 12:28; 2Ch 13:8
11:16 [y] 2Ch 15:9
11:17 [z] 2Ch 12:1
11:20 [a] 1Ki 15:2 [b] 2Ch 13:2
11:21 [c] Dt 17:17
11:22 [d] Dt 21:15-17
12:1 [e] ver 13 [f] 2Ch 11:17
12:2 [g] 1Ki 14:22-24 [h] 1Ki 11:40
12:3 [i] 2Ch 16:8; Na 3:9
12:4 [j] 2Ch 11:10
12:5 [k] 2Ch 11:2 [l] Dt 28:15; 2Ch 15:2
12:6 [m] Ex 9:27; Da 9:14

his sons had rejected them as priests of the LORD 15when he appointed[u] his own priests[v] for the high
places and for the goat[w] and calf[x] idols he had made. 16Those from every tribe of Israel[y] who set their
hearts on seeking the LORD, the God of Israel, followed the Levites to Jerusalem to offer sacrifices to the
LORD, the God of their ancestors. 17They strengthened[z] the kingdom of Judah and supported Rehoboam
son of Solomon three years, following the ways of David and Solomon during this time.

Rehoboam's Family

18Rehoboam married Mahalath, who was the daughter of David's son Jerimoth and of Abihail, the
daughter of Jesse's son Eliab. 19She bore him sons: Jeush, Shemariah and Zaham. 20Then he married
Maakah[a] daughter of Absalom, who bore him Abijah,[b] Attai, Ziza and Shelomith. 21Rehoboam loved
Maakah daughter of Absalom more than any of his other wives and concubines. In all, he had eighteen
wives[c] and sixty concubines, twenty-eight sons and sixty daughters.

22Rehoboam appointed Abijah[d] son of Maakah as crown prince among his brothers, in order to
make him king. 23He acted wisely, dispersing some of his sons throughout the districts of Judah and
Benjamin, and to all the fortified cities. He gave them abundant provisions and took many wives for
them.

Shishak Attacks Jerusalem

12:9-16pp — 1Ki 14:21,25-31

12 After Rehoboam's position as king was established[e] and he had become strong,[f] he and all Israel[*a*] with him abandoned the law of the LORD. 2Because they had been unfaithful[g] to the LORD,
Shishak[h] king of Egypt attacked Jerusalem in the fifth year of King Rehoboam. 3With twelve hundred
chariots and sixty thousand horsemen and the innumerable troops of Libyans, Sukkites and Cushites[*b*][i]
that came with him from Egypt, 4he captured the fortified cities[j] of Judah and came as far as Jerusalem.

5Then the prophet Shemaiah[k] came to Rehoboam and to the leaders of Judah who had assembled in
Jerusalem for fear of Shishak, and he said to them, "This is what the LORD says, 'You have abandoned
me; therefore, I now abandon[l] you to Shishak.'"

6The leaders of Israel and the king humbled themselves and said, "The LORD is just."[m]

[*a*] *1* That is, Judah, as frequently in 2 Chronicles [*b*] *3* That is, people from the upper Nile region

pursuing God's will. This underscores the close connection between the Levites and the Davidic monarchy.

11:15 calf idols. Bovine were commonly associated with divinity in the ancient Near East given the bull's association with strength, potency, and fertility. Jeroboam's calves (like Aaron's golden calf of Exod 32) may reflect syncretism with prevailing notions of expressing deity in neighboring cultures. Aaron's golden calf was part of a festival to Yahweh (Exod 32:5) rather than to another god. Nonetheless, Jeroboam's idols violated the second commandment (making an image of God, Exod 20:4). Jeroboam's words in 1 Kgs 12:28, "Here are your gods, Israel, who brought you up out of Egypt," are similar to Exod 32:4, "These are your gods, Israel, who brought you up out of Egypt." This intertextuality indicates that the writer of Kings wanted his readers to understand their crisis in light of the crisis during the time of Moses. In both cases, the people rejected God's chosen leadership and opted to worship God on their own terms rather than God's terms.

11:21 eighteen wives ... sixty concubines. In the context of the biblical world, having multiple wives and concubines displayed power and wealth. Marriages were also a common component in political treaties under the notion that interweaving families increased loyalty. Such practical reasons aside, Deut 17:17 warns kings not to multiply wives. Rehoboam's multiple wives are reminiscent of his grandfather David (1 Chr 14:3) and his father Solomon (1 Kgs 11:1–3). Likewise, Rehoboam took many wives for his sons (v. 23), perpetuating the practice within the Davidic monarchy.

12:1–9 The multiethnic African coalition that Shishak king of Egypt raised likely reflects a combination of Shishak's Libyan heritage as well as Egyptian hegemony over Cush/Nubia. Because Rehoboam and Judah "abandoned" God and his word (vv. 1,5), God abandoned Judah to Shishak (v. 5). According to archaeological sources, Shishak invaded the northern kingdom. Given Jeroboam's time in Egypt, Shishak's invasion might have been a reprisal against Jeroboam for failing to follow through with some kind of agreement. The details of Shishak's invasion are celebrated in an inscription on the southwest wall of the Karnak temple in Thebes, which includes a topographical inventory of more than 150 places.

12:1 Judah began the transition into the divided kingdom on the high note of the immigration of godly spiritual leaders and citizens (see note on 11:13–16). But once Rehoboam's strength was established, Judah abandoned God. **abandoned the law of the LORD.** The opposite of the covenant responsibility of the king (see Deut 17:14–20). This covenant unfaithfulness (see v. 2) is tantamount to abandoning God (v. 5) and shows the link between obedience and genuine faith.

12:2 Shishak ... attacked Jerusalem. In ca. 925 BC. As anticipated in the framework of the covenant relationship between God and Israel and spelled out in numerous warning passages (e.g., Deut 28:25; 1 Kgs 9:6–9), God may choose to utilize the army of a foreign nation as a consequence for covenantal unfaithfulness.

12:5–8 In the aftermath of Judah's covenantal unfaithfulness and judgment, the role of the prophet is reflected in Shemaiah's proclamation of sin and resulting divine judgment (see 6:24–25; cf. Rehoboam's repentance in v. 12). While Jerusalem was not destroyed, the temple and palace treasuries were ravaged, and the southern kingdom came under the control of Egypt.

Cartouches (oblong hieroglyphs of conquered towns) along the wall of the Karnak temple describe Shishak's military campaign in Canaan. Shishak's attack on Jerusalem is recorded in 2 Chr 12:2–4.
Todd Bolen/www.BiblePlaces.com

7When the LORD saw that they humbled themselves, this word of the LORD came to Shemaiah: "Since
they have humbled themselves, I will not destroy them but will soon give them deliverance.[n] My wrath
will not be poured out on Jerusalem through Shishak. 8They will, however, become subject[o] to him, so
that they may learn the difference between serving me and serving the kings of other lands."

9When Shishak king of Egypt attacked Jerusalem, he carried off the treasures of the temple of
the LORD and the treasures of the royal palace. He took everything, including the gold shields[p] Solomon had made. 10So King Rehoboam made bronze shields to replace them and assigned these to
the commanders of the guard on duty at the entrance to the royal palace. 11Whenever the king went
to the LORD's temple, the guards went with him, bearing the shields, and afterward they returned
them to the guardroom.

12Because Rehoboam humbled himself, the LORD's anger turned from him, and he was not totally
destroyed. Indeed, there was some good[q] in Judah.

13King Rehoboam established himself firmly in Jerusalem and continued as king. He was forty-one
years old when he became king, and he reigned seventeen years in Jerusalem, the city the LORD had
chosen out of all the tribes of Israel in which to put his Name.[r] His mother's name was Naamah; she
was an Ammonite. 14He did evil because he had not set his heart on seeking the LORD.

15As for the events of Rehoboam's reign, from beginning to end, are they not written in the records
of Shemaiah[s] the prophet and of Iddo the seer that deal with genealogies? There was continual warfare

12:7 [n] 1Ki 21:29; Ps 78:38
12:8 [o] Dt 28:48
12:9 [p] 2Ch 9:16
12:12 [q] 1Ki 14:13; 2Ch 19:3
12:13 [r] Dt 12:5; 2Ch 6:6
12:15 [s] 2Ch 9:29; 11:2

12:12 the LORD's anger turned. As anticipated in Solomon's temple dedication prayer, God abounds in mercy and forgiveness when his people seek him in humility. The Chronicler stresses this theme repeatedly, no doubt to instruct and encourage the postexilic community still reeling from the sting of divine judgment.

12:13 Rehoboam ruled over the southern tribes for 17 years (931/30–913 BC), while Jeroboam ruled over the northern tribes for about 21 years (931/30–910/9 BC).

12:14 he had not set his heart on seeking the LORD. The fundamental issue behind Rehoboam's apostasy and covenantal unfaithfulness, and the opposite of the demeanor of dependence, humility, and prayerfulness that God's king and people must demonstrate. The distinction of whether a king set his heart on seeking God established the trajectory of a ruler throughout the remainder of the divided monarchy. Likewise, such a disposition determines the spiritual vibrancy of believers' lives (Ps 19:14; Prov 4:23). Believers today would do well to internalize David's charge to his son Solomon: "Devote your heart and soul to seeking the LORD your God" (1 Chr 22:19).

12:15 are they not written . . . ? A defining characteristic of Chronicles is the propensity to cite a wide range of sources. Some of the names given to the sources may be alternate names for the same document (e.g., note the variations of references to the "book of the kings"; see Introduction to 1 Chronicles: Genre).

12:16 [t]2Ch 11:20
13:2 [u]2Ch 11:20 [v]1Ki 15:6
13:4 [w]Jos 18:22 [x]1Ch 11:1
13:5 [y]2Sa 7:13 [z]Lev 2:13; Nu 18:19
13:6 [a]1Ki 11:26
13:7 [b]Jdg 9:4
13:8 [c]1Ki 12:28; 2Ch 11:15
13:9 [d]2Ch 11:14-15 [e]Ex 29:35-36 [f]Jer 2:11
13:11 [g]Ex 29:39; 2Ch 2:4 [h]Lev 24:5-9
13:12 [i]Nu 10:8-9 [j]Ac 5:39
13:13 [k]Jos 8:9
13:14 [l]2Ch 14:11
13:15 [m]2Ch 14:12
13:16 [n]2Ch 16:8
13:18 [o]1Ch 5:20; 2Ch 14:11; Ps 22:5

between Rehoboam and Jeroboam. 16Rehoboam rested with his ancestors and was buried in the City of
David. And Abijah[t] his son succeeded him as king.

Abijah King of Judah

13:1-2,22–14:1pp — 1Ki 15:1-2,6-8

13 In the eighteenth year of the reign of Jeroboam, Abijah became king of Judah, 2and he reigned
in Jerusalem three years. His mother's name was Maakah,[a] a daughter[b] of Uriel of Gibeah.
There was war between Abijah[u] and Jeroboam.[v] 3Abijah went into battle with an army of four hundred thousand able fighting men, and Jeroboam drew up a battle line against him with eight hundred
thousand able troops.
4Abijah stood on Mount Zemaraim,[w] in the hill country of Ephraim, and said, "Jeroboam and all
Israel,[x] listen to me! 5Don't you know that the LORD, the God of Israel, has given the kingship of Israel
to David and his descendants forever[y] by a covenant of salt?[z] 6Yet Jeroboam son of Nebat, an official
of Solomon son of David, rebelled[a] against his master. 7Some worthless scoundrels[b] gathered around
him and opposed Rehoboam son of Solomon when he was young and indecisive and not strong enough
to resist them.
8"And now you plan to resist the kingdom of the LORD, which is in the hands of David's descendants.
You are indeed a vast army and have with you the golden calves[c] that Jeroboam made to be your gods.
9But didn't you drive out the priests of the LORD,[d] the sons of Aaron, and the Levites, and make priests
of your own as the peoples of other lands do? Whoever comes to consecrate himself with a young bull[e]
and seven rams may become a priest of what are not gods.[f]
10"As for us, the LORD is our God, and we have not forsaken him. The priests who serve the LORD are
sons of Aaron, and the Levites assist them. 11Every morning and evening[g] they present burnt offerings
and fragrant incense to the LORD. They set out the bread on the ceremonially clean table[h] and light the
lamps on the gold lampstand every evening. We are observing the requirements of the LORD our God.
But you have forsaken him. 12God is with us; he is our leader. His priests with their trumpets will sound
the battle cry against you.[i] People of Israel, do not fight against the LORD,[j] the God of your ancestors,
for you will not succeed."
13Now Jeroboam had sent troops around to the rear, so that while he was in front of Judah the ambush[k] was behind them. 14Judah turned and saw that they were being attacked at both front and rear.
Then they cried out[l] to the LORD. The priests blew their trumpets 15and the men of Judah raised the
battle cry. At the sound of their battle cry, God routed Jeroboam and all Israel[m] before Abijah and Judah.
16The Israelites fled before Judah, and God delivered[n] them into their hands. 17Abijah and his troops
inflicted heavy losses on them, so that there were five hundred thousand casualties among Israel's able
men. 18The Israelites were subdued on that occasion, and the people of Judah were victorious because
they relied[o] on the LORD, the God of their ancestors.
19Abijah pursued Jeroboam and took from him the towns of Bethel, Jeshanah and Ephron, with their

a *2* Most Septuagint manuscripts and Syriac (see also 11:20 and 1 Kings 15:2); Hebrew *Micaiah*
b *2* Or *granddaughter*

12:16 buried in the City of David. Despite his largely negative theological assessment, Rehoboam was afforded the honor of being buried in the royal cemetery. While little is known of ancient Israel's royal burial customs, the special treatment of kings in death and burial was common in the biblical world, which is reflected in the exquisite burial chambers in the Valley of the Kings in Thebes, Egypt.

13:1 —14:1 *Abijah King of Judah.* Following Rehoboam's death, Abijah assumed the throne in Judah. Abijah reigned over the southern kingdom from 913 to 911/10 BC and may have briefly coreigned with Rehoboam. 1 Kgs 15:3 negatively summarizes Abijah's reign, but the Chronicler's account focuses on his battlefield speech and stresses that God responds to the prayers of his people and protects the Davidic kingdom.

13:4–12 Abijah's prophet-like speech from Mount Zemaraim teems with theological significance and reflects a keen understanding of the Davidic covenant (vv. 5–8) including the necessity of complete obedience to God's covenantal stipulations (vv. 9–11; cf. 10:15).

13:5 salt. An important element in the ancient world for preservation; connected with sealing treaties and covenants. Salt underscores God's commitment to preserve his covenant with the house of David (cf. Num 18:19).

13:12 God is with us. God is with his covenant people, and to fight them is to "fight against the LORD."

13:14–15 blew their trumpets ... raised the battle cry. Reminiscent of the battle at Jericho (Josh 6). Judah was victorious over the significantly larger forces of Jeroboam's army not because of their military stratagem but because they "relied on the LORD" (v. 18).

13:15–20 God routed ... God delivered ... the LORD struck [Jeroboam] down. The story emphasizes God's role in this battle.

surrounding villages. 20Jeroboam did not regain power during the time of Abijah. And the LORD struck him down and he died.

21But Abijah grew in strength. He married fourteen wives and had twenty-two sons and sixteen daughters.

22The other events of Abijah's reign, what he did and what he said, are written in the annotations of the prophet Iddo.

14 [a] And Abijah rested with his ancestors and was buried in the City of David. Asa his son succeeded him as king, and in his days the country was at peace for ten years.

Asa King of Judah

14:2-3pp — 1Ki 15:11-12

2Asa did what was good and right in the eyes of the LORD his God. 3He removed the foreign altars and the high places, smashed the sacred stones and cut down the Asherah poles.[b][p] 4He commanded Judah to seek the LORD, the God of their ancestors, and to obey his laws and commands. 5He removed the high places and incense altars[q] in every town in Judah, and the kingdom was at peace under him. 6He built up the fortified cities of Judah, since the land was at peace. No one was at war with him during those years, for the LORD gave him rest.[r]

7"Let us build up these towns," he said to Judah, "and put walls around them, with towers, gates and bars. The land is still ours, because we have sought the LORD our God; we sought him and he has given us rest on every side." So they built and prospered.

8Asa had an army of three hundred thousand men from Judah, equipped with large shields and with spears, and two hundred and eighty thousand from Benjamin, armed with small shields and with bows. All these were brave fighting men.

9Zerah the Cushite[s] marched out against them with an army of thousands upon thousands and three hundred chariots, and came as far as Mareshah.[t] 10Asa went out to meet him, and they took up battle positions in the Valley of Zephathah near Mareshah.

11Then Asa called[u] to the LORD his God and said, "LORD, there is no one like you to help the powerless

[a] In Hebrew texts 14:1 is numbered 13:23, and 14:2-15 is numbered 14:1-14. [b] *3* That is, wooden symbols of the goddess Asherah; here and elsewhere in 2 Chronicles

14:3 [p] Ex 34:13; Dt 7:5; 1Ki 15:12-14
14:5 [q] 2Ch 34:4,7
14:6 [r] 1Ch 22:9; 2Ch 15:15
14:9 [s] 2Ch 12:3; 16:8 [t] 2Ch 11:8
14:11 [u] 2Ch 13:14

14:2—16:14 *Asa King of Judah.* Asa enjoyed a long season of peace during his 41-year reign (911/10–870/69 BC), while the northern kingdom continued to face internal and external turmoil. Asa was the first of the kings of Judah described as doing what was right in God's eyes, and he was the first to inaugurate reforms designed to eradicate syncretism and revitalize covenant fidelity (15:8–18). Thus, the reign of Asa functions as a sort of precursor to that of Hezekiah and that of Josiah. Asa, like Hezekiah (30:6–11), invited those situated within the northern kingdom to assemble in Jerusalem and publicly declare their loyalty to God's ways. By contrast, the final years of Asa's reign were punctuated with compromise and ungodly behavior.

14:3 removed the foreign altars and the high places. The destruction of idolatry and syncretistic worship associated with Canaanite religious cults was a cornerstone of Asa's religious reforms (Deut 16:21–22). **sacred stones.** Rough stones or finely shaped pillars that had widespread connection to religious settings in the biblical world. **Asherah poles.** Wooden symbols of Asherah in the form of both living trees and wooden poles/pillars. The goddess Asherah was represented with tree imagery in connection to the motif of (divine) fruitfulness reflected in the tree of life. The Israelites were not immune to the allure of Asherah (Deut 16:21; Jer 17:2).

14:4 commanded Judah to seek the LORD. The portrayal of the Israelite king reading, writing, and living out the law of God was central to his role as a leader in God's covenantal framework (see Deut 17:18–20). Thus, part of the divinely intended role of the king was intimately related to the spiritual life of ancient Israel (cf. Judg 17:6; 21:25). This spiritual leadership is described in Chronicles in terms of both what is removed (e.g., smashing, cutting down, and removing articles of idolatry, as in vv. 3,5) and what is implemented (e.g., seeking and obeying God, as in this verse). **seek the LORD ... obey his laws and commands.** Inseparably connected. The notion of seeking God apart from obedience is an unknown concept in the Bible (cf. John 15:10,14).

14:5 removed the high places and incense altars. In addition to commanding the people of Judah to seek and obey God, Asa took steps to remove places associated with syncretism. **high places.** See note on 1:3. **peace.** The result of covenantal obedience.

14:6 fortified cities. Likely the same strategically located cities that Solomon and Rehoboam previously fortified (see 8:5–6; 11:5–12 and notes) but that Shishak destroyed. **rest.** Part of God's broader land promise (Deut 12:10).

14:9 Zerah the Cushite marched out. Following Asa's early reforms and rebuilding, Zerah brought a large army into the southwestern region of Judah. Although Egypt is not named within this account, the close connection between Cush/Nubia and Egypt might imply that Zerah was attacking on behalf of Egypt (cf. 12:3). **Mareshah.** One of Judah's fortified cities along the western edge of the foothills, about 30 miles (48 kilometers) southwest of Jerusalem.

14:11–15 Asa's reliance on God reflects covenant faithfulness (vv. 1–8). Asa's prayer shows Solomon's temple dedication prayer in action (6:34–35).

14:11 in your name we have come ... do not let mere mortals prevail against you. Asa understood the crisis as *God's* war (cf. note on vv. 12–14).

14:11 [v]2Ch 13:18 [w]1Sa 17:45 [x]1Sa 14:6; Ps 9:19
14:12 [y]2Ch 13:15
14:13 [z]Ge 10:19
14:14 [a]Ge 35:5; 2Ch 17:10
15:1 [b]Nu 11:25,26; 24:2; 2Ch 20:14; 24:20
15:2 [c]ver 4,15; 2Ch 20:17 [d]Jas 4:8 [e]Jer 29:13 [f]1Ch 28:9; 2Ch 24:20
15:3 [g]Lev 10:11 [h]2Ch 17:9; La 2:9
15:4 [i]Dt 4:29
15:5 [j]Jdg 5:6
15:6 [k]Mt 24:7
15:7 [l]Jos 1:7,9 [m]Ps 58:11
15:8 [n]2Ch 13:19 [o]2Ch 8:12
15:9 [p]2Ch 11:16-17
15:11 [q]2Ch 14:13
15:12 [r]2Ki 11:17; 2Ch 23:16; 34:31 [s]1Ch 16:11
15:13 [t]Ex 22:20; Dt 13:9-16
15:15 [u]Dt 4:29 [v]1Ch 22:9; 2Ch 14:7

against the mighty. Help us, LORD our God, for we rely[v] on you, and in your name[w] we have come against
this vast army. LORD, you are our God; do not let mere mortals prevail[x] against you."
12 The LORD struck down[y] the Cushites before Asa and Judah. The Cushites fled, 13 and Asa and his
army pursued them as far as Gerar.[z] Such a great number of Cushites fell that they could not recover;
they were crushed before the LORD and his forces. The men of Judah carried off a large amount of
plunder. 14 They destroyed all the villages around Gerar, for the terror[a] of the LORD had fallen on them.
They looted all these villages, since there was much plunder there. 15 They also attacked the camps of
the herders and carried off droves of sheep and goats and camels. Then they returned to Jerusalem.

Asa's Reform

15:16-19pp — 1Ki 15:13-16

15 The Spirit of God came on[b] Azariah son of Oded. 2 He went out to meet Asa and said to him,
"Listen to me, Asa and all Judah and Benjamin. The LORD is with you[c] when you are with him.[d]
If you seek[e] him, he will be found by you, but if you forsake him, he will forsake you.[f] 3 For a long time
Israel was without the true God, without a priest to teach[g] and without the law.[h] 4 But in their distress
they turned to the LORD, the God of Israel, and sought him,[i] and he was found by them. 5 In those days it
was not safe to travel about,[j] for all the inhabitants of the lands were in great turmoil. 6 One nation was
being crushed by another and one city by another,[k] because God was troubling them with every kind of
distress. 7 But as for you, be strong[l] and do not give up, for your work will be rewarded."[m]
8 When Asa heard these words and the prophecy of Azariah son of[*a*] Oded the prophet, he took courage. He removed the detestable idols from the whole land of Judah and Benjamin and from the towns
he had captured[n] in the hills of Ephraim. He repaired the altar[o] of the LORD that was in front of the
portico of the LORD's temple.
9 Then he assembled all Judah and Benjamin and the people from Ephraim, Manasseh and Simeon
who had settled among them, for large numbers[p] had come over to him from Israel when they saw
that the LORD his God was with him.
10 They assembled at Jerusalem in the third month of the fifteenth year of Asa's reign. 11 At that time
they sacrificed to the LORD seven hundred head of cattle and seven thousand sheep and goats from the
plunder[q] they had brought back. 12 They entered into a covenant[r] to seek the LORD,[s] the God of their
ancestors, with all their heart and soul. 13 All who would not seek the LORD, the God of Israel, were to
be put to death,[t] whether small or great, man or woman. 14 They took an oath to the LORD with loud
acclamation, with shouting and with trumpets and horns. 15 All Judah rejoiced about the oath because
they had sworn it wholeheartedly. They sought God[u] eagerly, and he was found by them. So the LORD
gave them rest[v] on every side.
16 King Asa also deposed his grandmother Maakah from her position as queen mother, because she

[*a*] *8* Vulgate and Syriac (see also Septuagint and verse 1); Hebrew does not have *Azariah son of.*

14:12–14 The LORD struck down ... crushed before the LORD ... terror of the LORD. The Chronicler understands the outcome as *God's* victory (cf. note on v. 11).
15:1–2 A second stage in Asa's spiritual reforms was initiated by the "Spirit of God" coming upon the otherwise unknown prophet Azariah (cf. 24:20). Asa's response and obedience significantly impacted Judah (v. 15; cf. 14:2–7) and those in the northern kingdom (vv. 9–12).
15:3 without a priest to teach. The role of priests as teachers reflects God's covenantal framework: "teach the Israelites all the decrees the LORD has given them" (Lev 10:11; cf. Deut 33:8–11). The teaching of God's will—both then and now—infuses God's people with the spiritual direction and energy needed to walk in a manner pleasing to him.
15:7–8 be strong. Spiritual (rather than physical) fortitude in times of challenge and uncertainty, reflected in Asa's response ("he took courage") as he embarked on leading the people in worship and spiritual renewal.
15:8 Asa's destruction of idols from Judah and northern tribal areas ("the hills of Ephraim") was coupled with his repairs of the altar of the Jerusalem temple. **repaired the altar.** A tangible act evidencing Asa's inward disposition of fidelity to God.
15:9–11 Following his reforms, Asa organized a significant gathering of the people from Judah as well as godly individuals who had migrated from the northern kingdom. About two centuries later the Judahite king Hezekiah likewise invited those from the northern kingdom to assemble in Jerusalem and declare their loyalty to God (30:6–11).
15:12 entered into a covenant. The highlight of Asa's gathering: the people's reaffirmation of the covenantal relationship with God based on faithfulness and obedience. **seek the LORD.** The basis of the covenant (cf. Deut 4:29–31; 10:12–21). **with all their heart and soul.** Seeking God with all of one's being is a foundational element of rightly relating to God.
15:13 put to death. While death for sin is not without precedent in the OT (Deut 13:6–11), the decree formulated by Asa and the people was more restrictive in that it was levied on those who would not seek God. This decree was not given by God.
15:16 queen mother. A significant official position in ancient societies

had made a repulsive image for the worship of Asherah.[w] Asa cut it down, broke it up and burned it in
the Kidron Valley. 17Although he did not remove the high places from Israel, Asa's heart was fully committed to the LORD all his life. 18He brought into the temple of God the silver and gold and the articles
that he and his father had dedicated.
19There was no more war until the thirty-fifth year of Asa's reign.

15:16 [w]Ex 34:13; 2Ch 14:2-5
16:1 [x]Jer 41:9
16:3 [y]2Ch 20:35
16:7 [z]1Ki 16:1
16:8 [a]2Ch 12:3; 14:9 [b]2Ch 13:16
16:9 [c]Pr 15:3; Jer 16:17; Zec 4:10 [d]1Sa 13:13

Asa's Last Years

16:1-6pp — 1Ki 15:17-22
16:11–17:1pp — 1Ki 15:23-24

16 In the thirty-sixth year of Asa's reign Baasha[x] king of Israel went up against Judah and fortified
Ramah to prevent anyone from leaving or entering the territory of Asa king of Judah.
2Asa then took the silver and gold out of the treasuries of the LORD's temple and of his own palace
and sent it to Ben-Hadad king of Aram, who was ruling in Damascus. 3"Let there be a treaty[y] between
me and you," he said, "as there was between my father and your father. See, I am sending you silver and
gold. Now break your treaty with Baasha king of Israel so he will withdraw from me."
4Ben-Hadad agreed with King Asa and sent the commanders of his forces against the towns of Israel.
They conquered Ijon, Dan, Abel Maim[a] and all the store cities of Naphtali. 5When Baasha heard this,
he stopped building Ramah and abandoned his work. 6Then King Asa brought all the men of Judah,
and they carried away from Ramah the stones and timber Baasha had been using. With them he built
up Geba and Mizpah.
7At that time Hanani[z] the seer came to Asa king of Judah and said to him: "Because you relied on the
king of Aram and not on the LORD your God, the army of the king of Aram has escaped from your hand.
8Were not the Cushites[b][a] and Libyans a mighty army with great numbers of chariots and horsemen[c]?
Yet when you relied on the LORD, he delivered[b] them into your hand. 9For the eyes[c] of the LORD range
throughout the earth to strengthen those whose hearts are fully committed to him. You have done a
foolish[d] thing, and from now on you will be at war."
10Asa was angry with the seer because of this; he was so enraged that he put him in prison. At the
same time Asa brutally oppressed some of the people.

[a] 4 Also known as *Abel Beth Maakah* [b] 8 That is, people from the upper Nile region [c] 8 Or *charioteers*

that could be exploited in various ways, as attested in the examples of Bathsheba (1 Kgs 1–2), Maacah (1 Kgs 15), Jezebel (1 Kgs 16—2 Kgs 9), and Athaliah (2 Chr 22–23). **Asherah.** See note on 14:3. **Kidron Valley.** Continues as a focal point in the destruction of unorthodoxy and idolatry in the later reforms of Hezekiah (29:15–17; 30:14) and Josiah (2 Kgs 23:1–15).

15:17 he did not remove the high places from Israel. Not at variance with 14:3–5 since that pertains to high places in Judah (the southern kingdom), while this refers to high places in Israel (the northern kingdom). **Asa's heart was fully committed to the LORD.** This summary mirrors 14:2, providing literary framing around the accounts of Asa's spiritual reforms and separating chs. 14–15 from the less flattering account of the final years of Asa's reign in ch. 16.

16:1 Following decades of peace, conflict again broke out between the northern kingdom and the southern kingdom. **thirty-sixth year of Asa's reign.** This date (cf. 15:19) is challenging since Baasha had been dead for about a decade by Asa's 36th year (cf. 1 Kgs 15:33; 16:8). It is possible that the 36th year is based on the number of years since the division of the kingdom. In this scenario, Baasha's attack took place in the 16th year of Asa's reign (895/94 BC). Another possibility is that "36" is the result of a scribal copying error for "16." **Ramah.** Located about seven miles (11 kilometers) north of Jerusalem on the important north-south route in an area known as the central Benjamin plateau.

16:2–3 Baasha's invasion prompted Asa to hire Arameans. In light of 15:8–15, this implies that something changed with respect to Asa's earlier spiritual fervor and dependency on God. Indeed, Asa's inclination to seek help from people and his plundering the temple treasury imply a weakening in his faith and character. Sadly, Asa is more inclined to pillage the temple of God than to seek God in his temple when faced with a military threat (cf. 28:16–21).

16:2 Ben-Hadad. Meaning "son of [Baal] Hadad," it was likely an Aramean royal name that implied divine selection of the ruler and thus was utilized by multiple rulers in Aram/Syria.

16:4–5 After receiving payoff from Asa, the Arameans invaded Israel and took key cities in the upper Galilee region. This attack from the north prompted Baasha to withdraw from Ramah. For the next 175 years or so (through the fall of the northern kingdom in 722 BC), the border between the north and south remained fairly stable in the area between Bethel and Mizpah.

16:7–8 The arrival of Hanani is the second recorded prophetic visit to Asa (cf. 15:1–7). While the prophet Azariah's visit to Asa was full of the possibilities and blessings of seeking God, the prophet Hanani's visit to Asa was full of rebuke in light of Asa's lack of faith ("you relied on the king of Aram and not on the LORD your God").

16:9 The prophet poetically summarizes God's omniscience and desire to bless those who seek him and rely on him (cf. 15:15). None who rely on God go unnoticed. This was a memorable exhortation to the Chronicler's postexilic audience, who faced various challenges and pressures. Conversely, trusting human beings or human institutions is a foolish thing that reaps broad consequences.

16:10 Asa's reaction to the prophet underscores that his heart had turned from seeking God. Ironically, according to the reforms Asa enacted earlier in his reign, he should have been put to death (15:12–15).

16:12 [e] Jer 17:5-6
16:14 [f] Ge 50:2; Jn 19:39-40 [g] 2Ch 21:19; Jer 34:5
17:2 [h] 2Ch 15:8
17:3 [i] 1Ki 22:43
17:4 [j] 1Ki 12:28; 2Ch 22:9
17:5 [k] 1Sa 10:27 [l] 2Ch 18:1
17:6 [m] 1Ki 8:61; 2Ch 15:17 [n] 1Ki 15:14; 2Ch 19:3; 20:33 [o] Ex 34:13 [p] 2Ch 21:12
17:7 [q] Lev 10:11; Dt 6:4-9; 2Ch 15:3; 35:3
17:8 [r] 2Ch 19:8; Ne 8:7-8
17:9 [s] Dt 6:4-9; 28:61
17:10 [t] Ge 35:5; Dt 2:25; 2Ch 14:14
17:11 [u] 2Ch 9:14; 26:8 [v] 2Ch 21:16
17:14 [w] 2Sa 24:2

11 The events of Asa's reign, from beginning to end, are written in the book of the kings of Judah and Israel. 12 In the thirty-ninth year of his reign Asa was afflicted with a disease in his feet. Though his disease was severe, even in his illness he did not seek help from the LORD,[e] but only from the physicians. 13 Then in the forty-first year of his reign Asa died and rested with his ancestors. 14 They buried him in the tomb that he had cut out for himself in the City of David. They laid him on a bier covered with spices and various blended perfumes,[f] and they made a huge fire[g] in his honor.

Jehoshaphat King of Judah

17 Jehoshaphat his son succeeded him as king and strengthened himself against Israel. 2 He stationed troops in all the fortified cities of Judah and put garrisons in Judah and in the towns of Ephraim that his father Asa had captured.[h]

3 The LORD was with Jehoshaphat because he followed the ways of his father David[i] before him. He did not consult the Baals 4 but sought[j] the God of his father and followed his commands rather than the practices of Israel. 5 The LORD established the kingdom under his control; and all Judah brought gifts[k] to Jehoshaphat, so that he had great wealth and honor.[l] 6 His heart was devoted[m] to the ways of the LORD; furthermore, he removed the high places[n] and the Asherah poles[o] from Judah.[p]

7 In the third year of his reign he sent his officials Ben-Hail, Obadiah, Zechariah, Nethanel and Micaiah to teach[q] in the towns of Judah. 8 With them were certain Levites[r]—Shemaiah, Nethaniah, Zebadiah, Asahel, Shemiramoth, Jehonathan, Adonijah, Tobijah and Tob-Adonijah—and the priests Elishama and Jehoram. 9 They taught throughout Judah, taking with them the Book of the Law[s] of the LORD; they went around to all the towns of Judah and taught the people.

10 The fear[t] of the LORD fell on all the kingdoms of the lands surrounding Judah, so that they did not go to war against Jehoshaphat. 11 Some Philistines brought Jehoshaphat gifts and silver as tribute, and the Arabs[u] brought him flocks:[v] seven thousand seven hundred rams and seven thousand seven hundred goats.

12 Jehoshaphat became more and more powerful; he built forts and store cities in Judah 13 and had large supplies in the towns of Judah. He also kept experienced fighting men in Jerusalem. 14 Their enrollment[w] by families was as follows:

16:12 Asa once again sought help from people rather than God. Asa's lack of reliance on God is at variance with his earlier faithfulness (chs. 14–15). While this was not an issue to the Chronicler, it can be a point of tension for later readers. One approach for understanding this tension is to recall that the time of Asa's reign until the events of ch. 16 (the final few years of a 41-year reign) was characterized by faithfulness to God and that ch. 16 is the unfortunate postscript to his otherwise faithful reign.

16:14 huge fire in his honor. A funerary pyre was a statement of respect and honor for those of high stature (Jer 34:4–5). A number of mounds having a similar concentric shape with evidence of burning have been discovered outside Jerusalem; perhaps they were places where fires were burned to commemorate various Judahite kings.

17:1—21:3 *Jehoshaphat King of Judah.* The time frame of Jehoram and Jehoshaphat coincides with Omri's dynasty in the northern kingdom. While Kings includes narratives on both the northern and southern kingdoms, Chronicles is largely silent on the northern kingdom. Omri's dynasty was marked by political stability, expanded relations with Phoenicia, and military strength. This peace and prosperity, however, facilitated social and religious degeneration.

17:3 The LORD was with Jehoshaphat. The Lord's presence with Jehoshaphat (cf. 20:17) enabled his success and obedience. **Baals.** The plural of Baal; may relate to the variety of deities pursued in Israel and the region of Syro-Canaan (typically localized by cities or geographic regions). The term "Baal" is an honorific title meaning "lord" and typically is used in the OT to refer to the Syro-Canaanite storm god Baal-Hadad. The pressure to honor such deities was heightened by the northern kingdom's expanded relations with Phoenicia and by peace between the north and south.

17:4 sought the God of his father and followed his commands. The Chronicler stresses the biblical connection between seeking God and obeying his commands (cf. 14:4).

17:6 high places. See note on 1:3. **Asherah.** See note on 14:3. Although Asa had previously removed Asherah poles and high places from Judah (14:3–5), in the course of time the human tendency toward idolatry resulted in their rebuilding (even Asa was unfaithful toward the end of his reign). Jehoshaphat is later critiqued for *not* removing high places (20:33; 1 Kgs 22:43), so presumably his eradication of high places was not complete or his vigilance against their rebuilding waned over time.

17:7–9 Jehoshaphat dispatched royal officials, Levites, and priests to teach God's law throughout the region of Judah. A similar commissioning of Levites is seen during the postexilic ministry of Ezra and Nehemiah (Neh 8:7–8).

17:9 the Book of the Law of the LORD. While this book is commonly identified as the book of Deuteronomy (especially Deut 4–31), points of comparison can also be drawn with Exod 20–24; Lev 26; and Num 9–10. Also see notes on 23:11 and 34:14.

17:11 gifts ... tribute. That the Philistines and Arabs brought tribute implies that Judah now controlled caravan routes across the Arabah and Negev to the coastal highway. **Arabs.** Likely seminomadic tribes in the desert regions to the south of the Negev of Judah and portions of the Sinaitic and (perhaps) Arabian peninsulas.

17:12–19 These summary statements underscore the effectiveness of Jehoshaphat's reign. But this divinely granted success did not preclude him from entering into a political treaty by marriage with the apostate Israelite king Ahab (ch. 18).

From Judah, commanders of units of 1,000:
Adnah the commander, with 300,000 fighting men;
15 next, Jehohanan the commander, with 280,000;
16 next, Amasiah son of Zikri, who volunteered[x] himself for the service of the LORD, with 200,000.
17 From Benjamin:[y]
Eliada, a valiant soldier, with 200,000 men armed with bows and shields;
18 next, Jehozabad, with 180,000 men armed for battle.

19 These were the men who served the king, besides those he stationed in the fortified cities[z] throughout Judah.[a]

Micaiah Prophesies Against Ahab

18:1-27pp — 1Ki 22:1-28

18 Now Jehoshaphat had great wealth and honor,[b] and he allied[c] himself with Ahab[d] by marriage.
2 Some years later he went down to see Ahab in Samaria. Ahab slaughtered many sheep and
cattle for him and the people with him and urged him to attack Ramoth Gilead. 3 Ahab king of Israel
asked Jehoshaphat king of Judah, "Will you go with me against Ramoth Gilead?"
Jehoshaphat replied, "I am as you are, and my people as your people; we will join you in the war."
4 But Jehoshaphat also said to the king of Israel, "First seek the counsel of the LORD."
5 So the king of Israel brought together the prophets — four hundred men — and asked them,
"Shall we go to war against Ramoth Gilead, or shall I not?"
"Go," they answered, "for God will give it into the king's hand."
6 But Jehoshaphat asked, "Is there no longer a prophet of the LORD here whom we can inquire of?"
7 The king of Israel answered Jehoshaphat, "There is still one prophet through whom we can inquire
of the LORD, but I hate him because he never prophesies anything good about me, but always bad. He
is Micaiah son of Imlah."
"The king should not say such a thing," Jehoshaphat replied.
8 So the king of Israel called one of his officials and said, "Bring Micaiah son of Imlah at once."
9 Dressed in their royal robes, the king of Israel and Jehoshaphat king of Judah were sitting on their
thrones at the threshing floor by the entrance of the gate of Samaria, with all the prophets prophesying
before them. 10 Now Zedekiah son of Kenaanah had made iron horns, and he declared, "This is what the
LORD says: 'With these you will gore the Arameans until they are destroyed.' "
11 All the other prophets were prophesying the same thing. "Attack Ramoth Gilead[e] and be victorious," they said, "for the LORD will give it into the king's hand."
12 The messenger who had gone to summon Micaiah said to him, "Look, the other prophets without
exception are predicting success for the king. Let your word agree with theirs, and speak favorably."
13 But Micaiah said, "As surely as the LORD lives, I can tell him only what my God says."[f]
14 When he arrived, the king asked him, "Micaiah, shall we go to war against Ramoth Gilead, or
shall I not?"
"Attack and be victorious," he answered, "for they will be given into your hand."
15 The king said to him, "How many times must I make you swear to tell me nothing but the truth
in the name of the LORD?"

17:16 [x] Jdg 5:9; 1Ch 29:9
17:17 [y] Nu 1:36
17:19 [z] 2Ch 11:10 [a] 2Ch 25:5
18:1 [b] 2Ch 17:5 [c] 2Ch 19:1-3; 22:3 [d] 2Ch 21:6
18:11 [e] 2Ch 22:5
18:13 [f] Nu 22:18,20,35

17:14–18 On the large number of military recruits, see Introduction to 1 Chronicles: Particular Challenges (Issues Involving Numbers).

18:1 allied himself with Ahab by marriage. Even though God established Jehoshaphat's kingdom (17:5) and gave him numerous blessings (17:5,10–11), Jehoshaphat nonetheless entered into a political alliance by marriage. The increasing strength in the north during Omri's dynasty may have motivated Jehoshaphat to seek peace with Ahab. This act of diplomacy culminated in a political marriage treaty between Jehoshaphat's son Jehoram and Ahab's daughter Athaliah (cf. 21:5–6). Such diplomatic marriage alliances were a means to facilitate mutual trust and obligation.

18:2–3 Jehoshaphat's marriage alliance led to Ahab's request for military aid from Judah against Aram at the strategically located Transjordan town of Ramoth Gilead.

18:3 I am as you are, and my people as your people. Reminiscent of Ruth's response of faithfulness to Naomi (Ruth 1:16–17).

18:4 seek the counsel of the LORD. Although Jehoshaphat committed himself to Ahab, he nonetheless requested that God be consulted prior to battle. As the account in vv. 4–27 shows, in the context of doing God's work, strength is found not in numbers (1 Kgs 18:16–39) but from faithfully proclaiming God's word.

18:9 threshing floor. A raised open flat area that could serve as a meeting place for ancient communities, similar to how a city gate functioned on a larger scale.

18:16 [g] 1Ch 9:1 [h] Nu 27:17; Eze 34:5-8
18:18 [i] Da 7:9
18:21 [j] 1Ch 21:1; Job 1:6; Zec 3:1; Jn 8:44
18:22 [k] Job 12:16; Isa 19:14; Eze 14:9
18:23 [l] Jer 20:2; Mk 14:65; Ac 23:2
18:26 [m] 2Ch 16:10; Heb 11:36
18:29 [n] 1Sa 28:8
18:31 [o] 2Ch 13:14
18:34 [p] 2Ch 22:5
19:2 [q] 1Ki 16:1 [r] 2Ch 16:2-9 [s] Ps 139:21-22 [t] 2Ch 24:18; 32:25; Ps 7:11
19:3 [u] 1Ki 14:13; 2Ch 12:12 [v] 2Ch 17:6 [w] 2Ch 18:1; 20:35; 25:7; Ezr 7:10

16 Then Micaiah answered, "I saw all Israel[g] scattered on the hills like sheep without a shepherd,[h] and the LORD said, 'These people have no master. Let each one go home in peace.'"

17 The king of Israel said to Jehoshaphat, "Didn't I tell you that he never prophesies anything good about me, but only bad?"

18 Micaiah continued, "Therefore hear the word of the LORD: I saw the LORD sitting on his throne[i] with all the multitudes of heaven standing on his right and on his left. 19 And the LORD said, 'Who will entice Ahab king of Israel into attacking Ramoth Gilead and going to his death there?'

"One suggested this, and another that. 20 Finally, a spirit came forward, stood before the LORD and said, 'I will entice him.'

"'By what means?' the LORD asked.

21 "'I will go and be a deceiving spirit[j] in the mouths of all his prophets,' he said.

"'You will succeed in enticing him,' said the LORD. 'Go and do it.'

22 "So now the LORD has put a deceiving spirit in the mouths of these prophets of yours.[k] The LORD has decreed disaster for you."

23 Then Zedekiah son of Kenaanah went up and slapped[l] Micaiah in the face. "Which way did the spirit from[a] the LORD go when he went from me to speak to you?" he asked.

24 Micaiah replied, "You will find out on the day you go to hide in an inner room."

25 The king of Israel then ordered, "Take Micaiah and send him back to Amon the ruler of the city and to Joash the king's son, 26 and say, 'This is what the king says: Put this fellow in prison[m] and give him nothing but bread and water until I return safely.'"

27 Micaiah declared, "If you ever return safely, the LORD has not spoken through me." Then he added, "Mark my words, all you people!"

Ahab Killed at Ramoth Gilead

18:28-34pp — 1Ki 22:29-36

28 So the king of Israel and Jehoshaphat king of Judah went up to Ramoth Gilead. 29 The king of Israel said to Jehoshaphat, "I will enter the battle in disguise, but you wear your royal robes." So the king of Israel disguised[n] himself and went into battle.

30 Now the king of Aram had ordered his chariot commanders, "Do not fight with anyone, small or great, except the king of Israel." 31 When the chariot commanders saw Jehoshaphat, they thought, "This is the king of Israel." So they turned to attack him, but Jehoshaphat cried out,[o] and the LORD helped him. God drew them away from him, 32 for when the chariot commanders saw that he was not the king of Israel, they stopped pursuing him.

33 But someone drew his bow at random and hit the king of Israel between the breastplate and the scale armor. The king told the chariot driver, "Wheel around and get me out of the fighting. I've been wounded." 34 All day long the battle raged, and the king of Israel propped himself up in his chariot facing the Arameans until evening. Then at sunset he died.[p]

19 When Jehoshaphat king of Judah returned safely to his palace in Jerusalem, 2 Jehu[q] the seer, the son of Hanani, went out to meet him and said to the king, "Should you help the wicked[r] and love[b] those who hate the LORD?[s] Because of this, the wrath[t] of the LORD is on you. 3 There is, however, some good[u] in you, for you have rid the land of the Asherah poles[v] and have set your heart on seeking God.[w]"

[a] 23 Or *Spirit of* [b] 2 Or *and make alliances with*

18:21,22 deceiving spirit. The supernatural realm is used by God in working out his will (cf. 1 Sam 16:14–15; Job 1:6–2:7; Ezek 14:1–11).

18:23–27 The treatment of the otherwise unknown prophet Micaiah is consistent with how ungodly individuals treat those delivering an unwanted message (cf. 16:7–10; Jer 37:16; 38:6). The veracity of the prophet's message (v. 27) is one of the criteria for determining a true prophet (Deut 18:21–22). Claims of having God's Spirit (v. 23) are irrelevant in determining true and false prophets (Jer 23:10; Mic 3:5–8).

18:23 spirit from the LORD. This translation is uncertain; it could be rendered "Spirit of the LORD" (see NIV text note). The NIV rendering is theological in the sense of avoiding connecting *the* Spirit of God with a false prophet.

18:28–34 Despite the ominous prophecy of Micaiah (vv. 16,22), Ahab and Jehoshaphat launched an attack on Ramoth Gilead that ended in defeat and the death of Ahab, fulfilling God's word. Jehoshaphat's acceptance of Ahab's plan against the word of God's prophet reflects his imperfect faith as well as his position as the weaker partner in his alliance with Ahab.

19:3 some good in you. While Jehoshaphat's lack of complete fidelity to God was serious, he did not completely abandon God (cf. vv. 5–11; 17:3–6; 20:3–12).

Jehoshaphat Appoints Judges

4Jehoshaphat lived in Jerusalem, and he went out again among the people from Beersheba to the
hill country of Ephraim and turned them back to the LORD, the God of their ancestors. 5He appointed
judges[x] in the land, in each of the fortified cities of Judah. 6He told them, "Consider carefully what you
do,[y] because you are not judging for mere mortals[z] but for the LORD, who is with you whenever you
give a verdict. 7Now let the fear of the LORD be on you. Judge carefully, for with the LORD our God there
is no injustice[a] or partiality[b] or bribery."

8In Jerusalem also, Jehoshaphat appointed some of the Levites, priests and heads of Israelite families
to administer[c] the law of the LORD and to settle disputes. And they lived in Jerusalem. 9He gave them
these orders: "You must serve faithfully and wholeheartedly in the fear of the LORD. 10In every case that
comes before you from your people who live in the cities — whether bloodshed or other concerns of the
law, commands, decrees or regulations — you are to warn them not to sin against the LORD;[d] otherwise
his wrath will come on you and your people. Do this, and you will not sin.

11"Amariah the chief priest will be over you in any matter concerning the LORD, and Zebadiah son of
Ishmael, the leader of the tribe of Judah, will be over you in any matter concerning the king, and the Levites will serve as officials before you. Act with courage,[e] and may the LORD be with those who do well."

Jehoshaphat Defeats Moab and Ammon

20 After this, the Moabites and Ammonites with some of the Meunites[a][f] came to wage war against
Jehoshaphat.

2Some people came and told Jehoshaphat, "A vast army is coming against you from Edom,[b] from
the other side of the Dead Sea. It is already in Hazezon Tamar[g]" (that is, En Gedi). 3Alarmed, Jehoshaphat resolved to inquire of the LORD, and he proclaimed a fast[h] for all Judah. 4The people of Judah
came together to seek help from the LORD; indeed, they came from every town in Judah to seek him.

5Then Jehoshaphat stood up in the assembly of Judah and Jerusalem at the temple of the LORD in
the front of the new courtyard 6and said:

"LORD, the God of our ancestors,[i] are you not the God who is in heaven?[j] You rule over all the
kingdoms[k] of the nations. Power and might are in your hand, and no one can withstand you.
7Our God, did you not drive out the inhabitants of this land before your people Israel and give it
forever to the descendants of Abraham your friend?[l] 8They have lived in it and have built in it a

[a] *1* Some Septuagint manuscripts; Hebrew *Ammonites* [b] *2* One Hebrew manuscript; most Hebrew manuscripts, Septuagint and Vulgate *Aram*

19:5 [x] Ge 47:6; Ex 18:26
19:6 [y] Lev 19:15 [z] Dt 1:17; 16:18-20; 17:8-13
19:7 [a] Ge 18:25; Dt 32:4 [b] Dt 10:17; Job 34:19; Ro 2:11; Col 3:25
19:8 [c] 2Ch 17:8-9
19:10 [d] Dt 17:8-13
19:11 [e] 1Ch 28:20
20:1 [f] 1Ch 4:41
20:2 [g] Ge 14:7
20:3 [h] 1Sa 7:6; 2Ch 19:3; Ezr 8:21; Jer 36:9; Jnh 3:5,7
20:6 [i] Mt 6:9 [j] Dt 4:39 [k] 1Ch 29:11-12
20:7 [l] Isa 41:8; Jas 2:23

19:4 Beersheba. The administrative seat of the southern region located in the Negev; it can also refer to the southern extent of Judah, as implied here.

19:5–7 Jehoshaphat's judicial appointments suggest a correlation between judicial overhaul and (lasting) spiritual renewal (Deut 16:18–20). The exhortation given to these judicial appointees is that they carry out their responsibilities in the "fear of the LORD" (v. 7) as this will facilitate decisions that are pleasing to God. Jehoshaphat's name combines God's covenant name (Yahweh) and a form of the Hebrew word meaning "judge" (Yahweh judges/will judge; Yahweh is Judge).

19:8–10 Along with the appointment of judges, Jehoshaphat appoints Levites, priests, and family heads within Jerusalem to handle appeals from throughout Judah. These appointments reflect Deut 17:8–11. Priests and Levites serve as teachers of God's ways and law (Lev 10:11; cf. Ezra 8:1–12). Jehoshaphat charges them, just as he charged the judges, to carry out their responsibilities faithfully in the "fear of the LORD." (v. 9). Not to faithfully discharge this duty is sin (v. 10). On the responsibilities of Levites and priests, see notes on 1 Chr 6:48–49.

19:11 Act with courage. Similar to exhortations given to those in watershed moments of spiritual leadership (cf. 32:6–8; Josh 1:5–9).

20:1–2 Perhaps sensing weakness following the defeat of Jehoshaphat and Ahab at Ramoth Gilead (18:2–34), an eastern coalition joins forces against Jehoshaphat.

20:1 Meunites. An Arabian tribe living in the southern region of the Transjordan and parts of the Sinai. See NIV text note.

20:2 Edom. See NIV text note. Although the manuscript support for "Edom" is minimal, the NIV rendering does make sense with regard to the geographic setting of the battle ("from the other side of the Dead Sea"). If Aram is indeed intended, the passage would indicate that these eastern nations were being supported (if not incited) by Damascus, perhaps as reprisal for Jehoshaphat's alliance with Ahab in the assault of Ramoth Gilead (ch. 18).

20:3–4 With the vast army only miles/kilometers from Jerusalem, Jehoshaphat wisely opts to seek the Lord through corporate prayer and fasting.

20:3 all Judah. Emphasizes the oneness of heart of the Judahite community in seeking God during this time of uncertainty.

20:5 the assembly ... at the temple. Evokes the imagery of Solomon's temple prayer (6:34–35).

20:6–12 Jehoshaphat's prayer draws upon God's creation power and faithfulness. It is similar to the corporate laments of Pss 44; 74. The spirit and specifics of Solomon's temple dedication permeate the prayer (cf. vv. 8–9 and 6:2–30; 7:13–15).

20:8 [m]2Ch 6:20
20:9 [n]2Ch 6:28
20:10 [o]Nu 20:14-21; Dt 2:4-6,9,18-19
20:11 [p]Ps 83:1-12
20:12 [q]Jdg 11:27 [r]Ps 25:15; 121:1-2
20:14 [s]2Ch 15:1
20:15 [t]2Ch 32:7 [u]Ex 14:13-14; 1Sa 17:47
20:17 [v]Ex 14:13; 2Ch 15:2
20:18 [w]Ex 4:31
20:20 [x]Isa 7:9 [y]Ge 39:3; Pr 16:3
20:21 [z]1Ch 16:29; Ps 29:2 [a]2Ch 5:13; Ps 136:1
20:22 [b]Jdg 7:22; 2Ch 13:13
20:23 [c]Ge 19:38 [d]2Ch 21:8 [e]Jdg 7:22; 1Sa 14:20; Eze 38:21

sanctuary[m] for your Name, saying, 9'If calamity comes upon us, whether the sword of judgment, or plague or famine,[n] we will stand in your presence before this temple that bears your Name and will cry out to you in our distress, and you will hear us and save us.'

10"But now here are men from Ammon, Moab and Mount Seir, whose territory you would not allow Israel to invade when they came from Egypt;[o] so they turned away from them and did not destroy them. 11See how they are repaying us by coming to drive us out of the possession[p] you gave us as an inheritance. 12Our God, will you not judge them?[q] For we have no power to face this vast army that is attacking us. We do not know what to do, but our eyes are on you."[r]

13All the men of Judah, with their wives and children and little ones, stood there before the LORD.

14Then the Spirit[s] of the LORD came on Jahaziel son of Zechariah, the son of Benaiah, the son of Jeiel, the son of Mattaniah, a Levite and descendant of Asaph, as he stood in the assembly.

15He said: "Listen, King Jehoshaphat and all who live in Judah and Jerusalem! This is what the LORD says to you: 'Do not be afraid or discouraged[t] because of this vast army. For the battle[u] is not yours, but God's. 16Tomorrow march down against them. They will be climbing up by the Pass of Ziz, and you will find them at the end of the gorge in the Desert of Jeruel. 17You will not have to fight this battle. Take up your positions; stand firm and see[v] the deliverance the LORD will give you, Judah and Jerusalem. Do not be afraid; do not be discouraged. Go out to face them tomorrow, and the LORD will be with you.'"

18Jehoshaphat bowed down[w] with his face to the ground, and all the people of Judah and Jerusalem fell down in worship before the LORD. 19Then some Levites from the Kohathites and Korahites stood up and praised the LORD, the God of Israel, with a very loud voice.

20Early in the morning they left for the Desert of Tekoa. As they set out, Jehoshaphat stood and said, "Listen to me, Judah and people of Jerusalem! Have faith[x] in the LORD your God and you will be upheld; have faith in his prophets and you will be successful.[y]" 21After consulting the people, Jehoshaphat appointed men to sing to the LORD and to praise him for the splendor of his*[a]* holiness[z] as they went out at the head of the army, saying:

"Give thanks to the LORD,
for his love endures forever."[a]

22As they began to sing and praise, the LORD set ambushes[b] against the men of Ammon and Moab and Mount Seir who were invading Judah, and they were defeated. 23The Ammonites[c] and Moabites rose up against the men from Mount Seir[d] to destroy and annihilate them. After they finished slaughtering the men from Seir, they helped to destroy one another.[e]

24When the men of Judah came to the place that overlooks the desert and looked toward the vast army, they saw only dead bodies lying on the ground; no one had escaped. 25So Jehoshaphat and his men went to carry off their plunder, and they found among them a great amount of equipment and clothing*[b]* and also articles of value—more than they could take away. There was so much plunder

a *21* Or *him with the splendor of* *b* *25* Some Hebrew manuscripts and Vulgate; most Hebrew manuscripts *corpses*

20:12 our eyes are on you. Jehoshaphat's waiting faith reflects his complete trust in God's strength and ability to deliver Judah (cf. 14:11).

20:15–17 Do not be afraid ... Do not be afraid. The beginning and ending words of Jahaziel's message bring to mind exhortations to Joshua (Josh 1:5–9) and Hezekiah (2 Chr 32:6–8).

20:15 the battle is not yours, but God's. These words portray God as fighting for his covenant people (Deut 20:1–4). Jahaziel's exhortation to faith brings to mind Moses' words to the Israelites at the Red Sea (Exod 14:13–14).

20:17 the LORD will be with you. The promise of divine presence will enable Jehoshaphat's obedience and success.

20:18 bowed down ... in worship. In response to Jahaziel's prophecy, the king and the people prostrated themselves in worship, accompanied by the loud sounds (perhaps singing or shouts of praise) of Levites (v. 19). Singing and music continued even as they marched into battle (vv. 21–22) and followed their return from victory (vv. 27–28).

20:20–23 Inspired by the word of God, Jehoshaphat and the people set out in faith toward the Desert of Tekoa. Jehoshaphat's exhortation to "have faith" (v. 20) reiterates Jahaziel's message (see vv. 15–17 and notes) and connects applied faith (being strong and courageous; stepping out in obedience) and divinely granted success. Going to battle in song underscores an intentional focus on God and his strength (v. 21; 13:3–20; Josh 6:1–21).

20:21 Give thanks to the LORD, for his love endures forever. Cf. Ps 136:1 (see note there); signifies God's enduring love for his people.

20:22–26 As they begin to sing words of praise, God intervenes on the battlefield. As a result, the eastern coalition armies destroy each other (cf. Judg 7:22; 1 Sam 14:20; Ezek 38:21) without any action on the part of Jehoshaphat's army.

20:25 so much plunder. The plundering of enemies is one of the ways God shows his sovereignty over the nations and his favor for his people (Exod 12:35–36; Hag 2:22).

that it took three days to collect it. [26]On the fourth day they assembled in the Valley of Berakah, where
they praised the LORD. This is why it is called the Valley of Berakah[a] to this day.
[27]Then, led by Jehoshaphat, all the men of Judah and Jerusalem returned joyfully to Jerusalem, for
the LORD had given them cause to rejoice over their enemies. [28]They entered Jerusalem and went to the
temple of the LORD with harps and lyres and trumpets.
[29]The fear[f] of God came on all the surrounding kingdoms when they heard how the LORD had
fought[g] against the enemies of Israel. [30]And the kingdom of Jehoshaphat was at peace, for his God had
given him rest[h] on every side.

20:29 [f] Ge 35:5; Dt 2:25; 2Ch 14:14; 17:10 [g] Ex 14:14
20:30 [h] 1Ch 22:9; 2Ch 14:6-7; 15:15
20:33 [i] 2Ch 17:6; 19:3
20:34 [j] 1Ki 16:1
20:35 [k] 2Ch 16:3 [l] 2Ch 19:1-3
20:37 [m] 1Ki 9:26; 2Ch 9:21
21:1 [n] 1Ch 3:11
21:3 [o] 2Ch 11:23 [p] 2Ch 11:10
21:4 [q] 1Ki 2:12 [r] Jdg 9:5
21:6 [s] 1Ki 12:28-30

The End of Jehoshaphat's Reign

20:31 – 21:1pp — 1Ki 22:41-50

[31]So Jehoshaphat reigned over Judah. He was thirty-five years old when he became king of Judah,
and he reigned in Jerusalem twenty-five years. His mother's name was Azubah daughter of Shilhi. [32]He
followed the ways of his father Asa and did not stray from them; he did what was right in the eyes of
the LORD. [33]The high places,[i] however, were not removed, and the people still had not set their hearts
on the God of their ancestors.
[34]The other events of Jehoshaphat's reign, from beginning to end, are written in the annals of Jehu[j]
son of Hanani, which are recorded in the book of the kings of Israel.
[35]Later, Jehoshaphat king of Judah made an alliance[k] with Ahaziah king of Israel, whose ways were
wicked.[l] [36]He agreed with him to construct a fleet of trading ships.[b] After these were built at Ezion Geber,
[37]Eliezer son of Dodavahu of Mareshah prophesied against Jehoshaphat, saying, "Because you have
made an alliance with Ahaziah, the LORD will destroy what you have made." The ships[m] were wrecked
and were not able to set sail to trade.[c]

21 Then Jehoshaphat rested with his ancestors and was buried with them in the City of David. And
Jehoram[n] his son succeeded him as king. [2]Jehoram's brothers, the sons of Jehoshaphat, were
Azariah, Jehiel, Zechariah, Azariahu, Michael and Shephatiah. All these were sons of Jehoshaphat king
of Israel.[d] [3]Their father had given them many gifts[o] of silver and gold and articles of value, as well as
fortified cities[p] in Judah, but he had given the kingdom to Jehoram because he was his firstborn son.

Jehoram King of Judah

21:5-10,20pp — 2Ki 8:16-24

[4]When Jehoram established[q] himself firmly over his father's kingdom, he put all his brothers[r] to the
sword along with some of the officials of Israel. [5]Jehoram was thirty-two years old when he became
king, and he reigned in Jerusalem eight years. [6]He followed the ways of the kings of Israel,[s] as the house

[a] *26 Berakah* means *praise.* [b] *36* Hebrew *of ships that could go to Tarshish* [c] *37* Hebrew *sail for Tarshish* [d] *2* That is, Judah, as frequently in 2 Chronicles

20:26 Valley of Berakah. Likely renamed in light of the victory (*bĕrākâ* means "blessing" or "praise").

20:30 peace . . . rest. Cf. Deut 12:10. See notes on Num 6:26; Deut 3:20.

20:32 – 33 While Jehoshaphat "did what was right in the eyes of the LORD," he fell short in his alliances with ungodly Israelite kings (Ahab and Ahaziah) and in the touchstone area of "high places" (see note on 1:3). The Chronicler attaches part of the responsibility for not removing the high places on the sad reality that the people "had not set their hearts" on God.

20:34 book of the kings. See Introduction to 1 Chronicles: Genre.

20:35 alliance with Ahaziah. Another ill-advised alliance with an ungodly northern kingdom king (cf. ch. 18) prompts a rebuke and punishment (v. 37).

20:36 Ezion Geber. Pushing back the Moabite-Ammonite-Meunite invasion (vv. 1 – 30) gives Jehoshaphat control of the region in the vicinity of this port city. Maritime trade from Ezion Geber during the time frame of Solomon likely prompted Jehoshaphat's attempt to restart maritime trade.

20:37 Eliezer. An otherwise unknown prophet.

21:1 – 3 The Chronicler shows the blessings of God of Jehoshaphat.

21:1 buried with [his ancestors] in the City of David. Being buried in the royal cemetery was an honor.

21:2 sons of Jehoshaphat. Having many sons, particularly seven sons, was seen as God's blessing (see notes on 1 Sam 2:4 – 5; Ruth 4:15). **king of Israel.** A title usually used of rulers of the northern kingdom, but here granted to Jehoshaphat.

21:4 – 20 *Jehoram King of Judah.* The reign of Jehoram illustrates the contrast between the unfaithfulness of human leaders and the faithfulness of God. Jehoram likely began a coregency with Jehoshaphat in 853 BC and began his sole reign in 848 BC.

21:4 put all his brothers to the sword. Eliminating potential rivals to the throne (fratricide) was common in the ancient Near East. The Hittites were famous for this.

21:6 did evil in the eyes of the LORD. Jehoram's wickedness is enhanced by his association with the apostate northern kingdom (the "house of Ahab"). Jehoram's wife, Athaliah, was the daughter of the infamous Ahab and Jezebel of the northern kingdom (22:2). Jehoram's marriage to Athaliah was part of the political marriage treaty that his father Jehoshaphat orchestrated. Such alliances show trust in humans

21:6 [t]2Ch 18:1; 22:3
21:7 [u]2Sa 7:13 [v]2Sa 7:15; 2Ch 23:3 [w]2Sa 21:17; 1Ki 11:36
21:8 [x]2Ch 20:22-23
21:10 [y]Nu 33:20
21:12 [z]2Ki 1:16-17 [a]2Ch 17:3-6 [b]2Ch 14:2
21:13 [c]ver 6,11; 1Ki 16:29-33 [d]ver 4; 1Ki 2:32
21:15 [e]ver 18-19; Nu 12:10
21:16 [f]2Ch 17:10-11; 22:1; 26:7
21:17 [g]2Ki 12:18; 2Ch 22:1; 25:23; Joel 3:5
21:19 [h]2Ch 16:14
21:20 [i]2Ch 24:25; 28:27; 33:20; Jer 22:18,28
22:1 [j]2Ch 33:25; 36:1 [k]2Ch 23:20-21; 26:1 [l]2Ch 21:16-17

of Ahab had done, for he married a daughter of Ahab.[t] He did evil in the eyes of the LORD. 7 Nevertheless, because of the covenant the LORD had made with David,[u] the LORD was not willing to destroy the house of David.[v] He had promised to maintain a lamp[w] for him and his descendants forever.

8 In the time of Jehoram, Edom[x] rebelled against Judah and set up its own king. 9 So Jehoram went there with his officers and all his chariots. The Edomites surrounded him and his chariot commanders, but he rose up and broke through by night. 10 To this day Edom has been in rebellion against Judah.

Libnah[y] revolted at the same time, because Jehoram had forsaken the LORD, the God of his ancestors. 11 He had also built high places on the hills of Judah and had caused the people of Jerusalem to prostitute themselves and had led Judah astray.

12 Jehoram received a letter from Elijah[z] the prophet, which said:

"This is what the LORD, the God of your father[a] David, says: 'You have not followed the ways of your father Jehoshaphat or of Asa[b] king of Judah. 13 But you have followed the ways of the kings of Israel, and you have led Judah and the people of Jerusalem to prostitute themselves, just as the house of Ahab did.[c] You have also murdered your own brothers, members of your own family, men who were better[d] than you. 14 So now the LORD is about to strike your people, your sons, your wives and everything that is yours, with a heavy blow. 15 You yourself will be very ill with a lingering disease[e] of the bowels, until the disease causes your bowels to come out.' "

16 The LORD aroused against Jehoram the hostility of the Philistines and of the Arabs[f] who lived near the Cushites. 17 They attacked Judah, invaded it and carried off all the goods found in the king's palace, together with his sons and wives. Not a son was left to him except Ahaziah,[a] the youngest.[g]

18 After all this, the LORD afflicted Jehoram with an incurable disease of the bowels. 19 In the course of time, at the end of the second year, his bowels came out because of the disease, and he died in great pain. His people made no funeral fire in his honor,[h] as they had for his predecessors.

20 Jehoram was thirty-two years old when he became king, and he reigned in Jerusalem eight years. He passed away, to no one's regret, and was buried[i] in the City of David, but not in the tombs of the kings.

Ahaziah King of Judah

22:1-6pp — 2Ki 8:25-29
22:7-9pp — 2Ki 9:21-29

22 The people[j] of Jerusalem[k] made Ahaziah, Jehoram's youngest son, king in his place, since the raiders,[l] who came with the Arabs into the camp, had killed all the older sons. So Ahaziah son of Jehoram king of Judah began to reign.

[a] *17* Hebrew *Jehoahaz,* a variant of *Ahaziah*

---

and political structures rather than complete trust in God. Spiritual compromise has waves of consequences, as seen in chs. 21–22.

21:7 the covenant the LORD had made. The Davidic covenant (see note on 1 Chr 17:1–27). Despite the wickedness of Jehoram (and the disastrous events that his wife later precipitated) God shows his commitment to preserve the house of David even during dark times (a "lamp" for the darkness) on account of *God's* word and *God's* character. His enduring promise to David is recalled in the poetry of Ps 89:35–37 (cf. Ps 132:11–12) and the prophetic message of Jer 33:19–22. Wickedness is temporary, and God will fulfill his word. This had particular significance in light of the uncertainties faced by the Chronicler's postexilic audience.

21:8–10 The weakness of Jehoram prompts Edom in the southeast and Libnah in the west to rebel against Judah (2 Kgs 8:20–22). Similar hostility came from the Philistines to the west and the Arabians to the south (vv. 16–17). The theological reason for this upheaval is that "Jehoram had forsaken the LORD" (v. 10).

21:11 caused the people of Jerusalem to prostitute themselves. Instead of being a spiritual leader guided by God's law (the model for the king in Deut 17:18–20), Jehoram led the people in wickedness. The imagery of prostitution is a vivid picture of unfaithfulness and spiritual wickedness.

21:12–15 Elijah's letter functions as a message of judgment that will touch every area of Jehoram's life and well-being. Elijah's ministry efforts were mostly directed against the Omri dynasty in the northern kingdom, but that did not preclude him from engaging with Judahite kings. Elijah spent at least some time in Judah, as reflected in his escape to Mount Horeb (1 Kgs 19:3–9). The dating in the context of this prophecy shows that Elijah was alive during at least some of Jehoram's reign.

21:16–17 See note on vv. 8–10.

21:16 Arabs. Located in the desert regions to the south of the Negev of Judah into portions of the Sinai peninsula. **Cushites.** Lived "near" the Arabs in the southern region of the Negev (14:9–13). The Arab raiders killed all of Jehoram's sons except Ahaziah (22:1).

21:18–20 The final words concerning the reign of Jehoram are strikingly negative: the Lord afflicts him with an "incurable disease" (v. 18); he dies in "great pain," and "no funeral fire" is made in his honor (v. 19). No one regrets his demise (v. 20). The portrayal of Jehoram is one of abject unfaithfulness, yet the Chronicler's summary of Jehoram's reign also shows God's faithfulness to bring his word to pass (vv. 14–15).

22:1–9 *Ahaziah King of Judah.* Ahaziah, also known as Jehoahaz, became king in 841 BC and was killed within a year in the midst of

2Ahaziah was twenty-two[a] years old when he became king, and he reigned in Jerusalem one year.
His mother's name was Athaliah, a granddaughter of Omri.
3He too followed[m] the ways of the house of Ahab,[n] for his mother encouraged him to act wickedly.
4He did evil in the eyes of the LORD, as the house of Ahab had done, for after his father's death they
became his advisers, to his undoing. 5He also followed their counsel when he went with Joram[b] son
of Ahab king of Israel to wage war against Hazael king of Aram at Ramoth Gilead.[o] The Arameans
wounded Joram; 6so he returned to Jezreel to recover from the wounds they had inflicted on him at
Ramoth[c] in his battle with Hazael[p] king of Aram.

Then Ahaziah[d] son of Jehoram king of Judah went down to Jezreel to see Joram son of Ahab because
he had been wounded.
7Through Ahaziah's[q] visit to Joram, God brought about Ahaziah's downfall. When Ahaziah arrived,
he went out with Joram to meet Jehu son of Nimshi, whom the LORD had anointed to destroy the house
of Ahab. 8While Jehu was executing judgment on the house of Ahab,[r] he found the officials of Judah and
the sons of Ahaziah's relatives, who had been attending Ahaziah, and he killed them. 9He then went in
search of Ahaziah, and his men captured him while he was hiding[s] in Samaria. He was brought to Jehu
and put to death. They buried him, for they said, "He was a son of Jehoshaphat, who sought[t] the LORD
with all his heart." So there was no one in the house of Ahaziah powerful enough to retain the kingdom.

22:3 [m] 2Ch 18:1 [n] 2Ch 21:6
22:5 [o] 2Ch 18:11,34
22:6 [p] 1Ki 19:15; 2Ki 8:13-15; 9:15
22:7 [q] 2Ki 9:16; 2Ch 10:15
22:8 [r] 2Ki 10:13
22:9 [s] Jdg 9:5 [t] 2Ch 17:4

Athaliah and Joash

22:10–23:21pp — 2Ki 11:1-21

10When Athaliah the mother of Ahaziah saw that her son was dead, she proceeded to destroy the
whole royal family of the house of Judah. 11But Jehosheba,[e] the daughter of King Jehoram, took Joash
son of Ahaziah and stole him away from among the royal princes who were about to be murdered and
put him and his nurse in a bedroom. Because Jehosheba,[e] the daughter of King Jehoram and wife of

[a] *2* Some Septuagint manuscripts and Syriac (see also 2 Kings 8:26); Hebrew *forty-two* [b] *5* Hebrew *Jehoram,* a variant of *Joram*; also in verses 6 and 7 [c] *6* Hebrew *Ramah,* a variant of *Ramoth* [d] *6* Some Hebrew manuscripts, Septuagint, Vulgate and Syriac (see also 2 Kings 8:29); most Hebrew manuscripts *Azariah*
[e] *11* Hebrew *Jehoshabeath,* a variant of *Jehosheba*

Jehu's revolt (vv. 7–9). Ahaziah is described as being made king by "the people of Jerusalem" (v. 1). The makeup of this group is not certain, but the expression may be another term for the sociopolitical group known as "the people of the land" that figure in several succession narratives (see note on 23:21).

22:3 followed the ways of the house of Ahab. Like Jehoram (see 21:6). This wickedness was enhanced by his close association with the apostate northern kingdom ("the house of Ahab," v. 4) as well as the direct influence of his mother Athaliah (see note on 21:6). Instead of encouraging her son in the ways of wisdom and God, Athaliah "encouraged him to act wickedly." Ahaziah also sought counsel from the northern kingdom "to his undoing" (v. 4).

22:5–6 Ahaziah's reliance on the counsel of the ungodly led to his agreement to help the northern kingdom in battle against Aram at the Transjordan city of Ramoth Gilead. The battle for Ramoth Gilead sets the scene for the outworking of divinely driven throne changes in both Aram and the northern kingdom. Elijah prophetically announced both of these throne changes (1 Kgs 19:15–18), and then Elisha reaffirmed them (2 Kgs 9:1–10). This battle also set in motion dramatic regnal change in Judah.

22:6 Jezreel. Located on the eastern side of the Jezreel Valley (opposite Megiddo) near the base of Mount Gilboa about 45 miles (72 kilometers) from Ramoth Gilead. Jehu's revolt there plays into both the condemnation and message of hope in Hosea (Hos 1:4–5,11; 2:22).

22:7 God brought about Ahaziah's downfall. The battle at Ramoth Gilead leads to upheaval, military coups, and leadership changes in Israel, Judah, and Aram (see note on v. 8).

22:8 executing judgment on the house of Ahab. In the coup in the northern kingdom (known as Jehu's revolt, ca. 841 BC), the military commander Jehu brings the Omri dynasty to an end by the assassination of Joram (2 Kgs 9:14–26) and Ahab's other sons (2 Kgs 10:1–17). In addition, Jehu kills Joram's mother Jezebel (2 Kgs 9:30–37), along with priests and prophets of Baal and Asherah (2 Kgs 10:18–27), leading the narrator of Kings to depict Jehu as a liberator. Lastly, Jehu kills Ahaziah (2 Kgs 9:27–28), which leads to the rule of Queen Athaliah in Judah.

22:10—23:21 *The Coup and Rule of Queen Athaliah.* The death of Ahaziah facilitates the rise to power of his mother, Athaliah (daughter of Ahab and Jezebel), who attempts to eliminate all male descendants of David. Jehu's murder of Jezebel had a ruinous effect on the northern kingdom's relationship with Phoenicia, while his murder of Ahaziah ended the good relations between Israel and Judah. At this time, the Aramean official Hazael assassinates Ben-Hadad and seizes control of Aram. The Tel Dan Inscription indicates that Hazael took credit for the deaths of Joram and Ahaziah, implying that Jehu may have acted in collusion with Hazael. The net effect of the nearly simultaneous murders of the kings of Israel, Judah, and Aram fosters instability in the Levant—the area between Anatolia (modern day Turkey) and Egypt that included Israel, Aram, Phoenicia, Moab, and Edom—that allows the Assyrian king Shalmaneser III to gain the upper hand in the region almost immediately.

22:10 Athaliah the mother of Ahaziah. Athaliah took the killing of Ahaziah as an opportunity to expand her power by eliminating all Davidic claimants (with the unintentional exception of Joash) to the throne of Judah. She rules for about seven years (ca. 841–835 BC). Athaliah was the only queen to rule Judah or Israel. Athaliah's ability to engineer her anti-Davidic coup and rule implies considerable preexisting power and influence.

22:11–12 The providential saving of this child (24:1) recalls God's protection of Moses (Exod 2:1–10) and Jesus (Matt 2:1–15). Hiding Joash within the temple provided both the spiritual sense of God's protection as well as the practical benefit of being the place of Jehoiada's priestly duties.

23:2 [u]Nu 35:2-5
23:3 [v]2Ki 11:17 [w]2Sa 7:12; 1Ki 2:4; 2Ch 6:16; 7:18; 21:7
23:6 [x]1Ch 23:28-29; Zec 3:7
23:8 [y]2Ki 11:9 [z]1Ch 24:1
23:11 [a]Ex 25:16; Dt 17:18; 1Sa 10:24
23:13 [b]1Ki 1:41 [c]1Ki 7:15
23:15 [d]Ne 3:28; Jer 31:40
23:16 [e]2Ch 29:10; 34:31; Ne 9:38
23:17 [f]Dt 13:6-9

the priest Jehoiada, was Ahaziah's sister, she hid the child from Athaliah so she could not kill him. 12 He
remained hidden with them at the temple of God for six years while Athaliah ruled the land.

23 In the seventh year Jehoiada showed his strength. He made a covenant with the commanders of
units of a hundred: Azariah son of Jeroham, Ishmael son of Jehohanan, Azariah son of Obed,
Maaseiah son of Adaiah, and Elishaphat son of Zikri. 2 They went throughout Judah and gathered the
Levites[u] and the heads of Israelite families from all the towns. When they came to Jerusalem, 3 the whole
assembly made a covenant[v] with the king at the temple of God.

Jehoiada said to them, "The king's son shall reign, as the LORD promised concerning the descendants of David.[w] 4 Now this is what you are to do: A third of you priests and Levites who are going on
duty on the Sabbath are to keep watch at the doors, 5 a third of you at the royal palace and a third at
the Foundation Gate, and all the others are to be in the courtyards of the temple of the LORD. 6 No one
is to enter the temple of the LORD except the priests and Levites on duty; they may enter because they
are consecrated, but all the others are to observe[x] the LORD's command not to enter.[a] 7 The Levites are
to station themselves around the king, each with weapon in hand. Anyone who enters the temple is to
be put to death. Stay close to the king wherever he goes."

8 The Levites and all the men of Judah did just as Jehoiada the priest ordered.[y] Each one took his
men—those who were going on duty on the Sabbath and those who were going off duty—for Jehoiada the priest had not released any of the divisions.[z] 9 Then he gave the commanders of units of a hundred the spears and the large and small shields that had belonged to King David and that were in the
temple of God. 10 He stationed all the men, each with his weapon in his hand, around the king—near
the altar and the temple, from the south side to the north side of the temple.

11 Jehoiada and his sons brought out the king's son and put the crown on him; they presented him
with a copy[a] of the covenant and proclaimed him king. They anointed him and shouted, "Long live
the king!"

12 When Athaliah heard the noise of the people running and cheering the king, she went to them at
the temple of the LORD. 13 She looked, and there was the king,[b] standing by his pillar[c] at the entrance.
The officers and the trumpeters were beside the king, and all the people of the land were rejoicing and
blowing trumpets, and musicians with their instruments were leading the praises. Then Athaliah tore
her robes and shouted, "Treason! Treason!"

14 Jehoiada the priest sent out the commanders of units of a hundred, who were in charge of the
troops, and said to them: "Bring her out between the ranks[b] and put to the sword anyone who follows
her." For the priest had said, "Do not put her to death at the temple of the LORD." 15 So they seized her
as she reached the entrance of the Horse Gate[d] on the palace grounds, and there they put her to death.
16 Jehoiada then made a covenant[e] that he, the people and the king[c] would be the LORD's people. 17 All
the people went to the temple of Baal and tore it down. They smashed the altars and idols and killed[f]
Mattan the priest of Baal in front of the altars.

[a] *6* Or *are to stand guard where the LORD has assigned them* [b] *14* Or *out from the precincts*
[c] *16* Or *covenant between the LORD and the people and the king that they* (see 2 Kings 11:17)

23:1 Jehoiada showed his strength. This phraseology is typically used of *kings* at the beginning of their reign. Jehoiada leverages his position to organize a pro-Davidic consortium consisting of military personnel, priests, family leaders, and Levites (vv. 1–3).

23:4–10 Jehoiada takes advantage of the double numbers and natural movement at the shift change (v. 8) to maximize protection for the young Joash.

23:5 Foundation Gate. Likely the Sur Gate mentioned in 2 Kgs 11:6.

23:11 With layers of protection in place, Jehoiada publicly anoints Joash as king. A key element of this ceremony involved presenting Joash with "a copy of the covenant," emphasizing that the enthronement of Joash was meant to be in accord with God's word. **the covenant.** Commonly considered to be some (or all) of the book of Deuteronomy. In Deut 17:18–20 (see note), the focal point is the king making his own written copy of the Torah so that God's word would be in his heart and guide him to be a righteous, humble leader.

23:13 people of the land. See note on v. 21. **Treason!** Given Athaliah's murderous coup, her shouts of treason are somewhat ironic.

23:15 Horse Gate. Associated with death and judgment (Jer 31:40).

23:16 made a covenant. The Chronicler continues his emphasis on covenant during the transition to the reign of Joash. This pivotal time in Judah's history begins with the priest Jehoiada's covenant with the military leaders (v. 1) and then his additional covenant with the military leaders, priests, Levites, and heads of families (v. 3). Afterward, Jehoiada presents Joash with a copy of the covenant (v. 11). Here the covenant involved all the people and functioned as a covenant renewal of the community.

23:17 All the people. Their destruction of objects of idolatry demonstrates the zeal of the community to purge the land from pagan worship. **temple of Baal.** This is the only reference to this temple in Jerusalem; its exact history is unknown.

18 Then Jehoiada placed the oversight of the temple of the LORD in the hands of the Levitical priests,[g] to whom David had made assignments in the temple,[h] to present the burnt offerings of the LORD as written in the Law of Moses, with rejoicing and singing, as David had ordered. 19 He also stationed gatekeepers[i] at the gates of the LORD's temple so that no one who was in any way unclean might enter.

20 He took with him the commanders of hundreds, the nobles, the rulers of the people and all the people of the land and brought the king down from the temple of the LORD. They went into the palace through the Upper Gate[j] and seated the king on the royal throne. 21 All the people of the land rejoiced, and the city was calm, because Athaliah had been slain with the sword.[k]

Joash Repairs the Temple

24:1-14pp — 2Ki 12:1-16
24:23-27pp — 2Ki 12:17-21

24 Joash was seven years old when he became king, and he reigned in Jerusalem forty years. His mother's name was Zibiah; she was from Beersheba. 2 Joash did what was right in the eyes of the LORD[l] all the years of Jehoiada the priest. 3 Jehoiada chose two wives for him, and he had sons and daughters.

4 Some time later Joash decided to restore the temple of the LORD. 5 He called together the priests and Levites and said to them, "Go to the towns of Judah and collect the money[m] due annually from all Israel,[n] to repair the temple of your God. Do it now." But the Levites[o] did not act at once.

6 Therefore the king summoned Jehoiada the chief priest and said to him, "Why haven't you required the Levites to bring in from Judah and Jerusalem the tax imposed by Moses the servant of the LORD and by the assembly of Israel for the tent of the covenant law?"[p]

7 Now the sons of that wicked woman Athaliah had broken into the temple of God and had used even its sacred objects for the Baals.

8 At the king's command, a chest was made and placed outside, at the gate of the temple of the LORD. 9 A proclamation was then issued in Judah and Jerusalem that they should bring to the LORD the tax that Moses the servant of God had required of Israel in the wilderness. 10 All the officials and all the people brought their contributions gladly,[q] dropping them into the chest until it was full. 11 Whenever the chest was brought in by the Levites to the king's officials and they saw that there was a large amount of money, the royal secretary and the officer of the chief priest would come and empty the chest and carry it back to its place. They did this regularly and collected a great amount of money. 12 The king and Jehoiada gave it to those who carried out the work required for the temple of the LORD. They hired[r] masons and carpenters to restore the LORD's temple, and also workers in iron and bronze to repair the temple.

13 The men in charge of the work were diligent, and the repairs progressed under them. They rebuilt the temple of God according to its original design and reinforced it. 14 When they had finished, they

23:18 [g] 1Ch 23:28-32; 2Ch 5:5 [h] 1Ch 23:6; 25:6
23:19 [i] 1Ch 9:22
23:20 [j] 2Ki 15:35
23:21 [k] 2Ch 22:1
24:2 [l] 2Ch 25:2; 26:5
24:5 [m] Ex 30:16; Ne 10:32-33; Mt 17:24 [n] 1Ch 11:1 [o] 1Ch 26:20
24:6 [p] Ex 30:12-16; Nu 1:50
24:10 [q] Ex 25:2; 1Ch 29:3,6,9
24:12 [r] 2Ch 34:11

23:18 As final steps toward reorienting the life of the community in line with covenantal stipulations, Jehoiada ensures that temple worship is functioning in accordance with Mosaic and Davidic regulations. **oversight of the temple ... the Levitical priests.** See notes on 1 Chr 6:48–49.

23:19 gatekeepers. Worked in conjunction with the priests to insure the purity of the temple and the protection of sacred space.

23:21 people of the land. This group factors into several regnal change narratives including Joash (here), Josiah (33:25), and Jehoahaz (36:1). Cf. Jer 1:18; 34:19; 44:21. While it is difficult to completely deduce this group's political and/or religious objectives, the narratives that include this group in conjunction with leadership changes imply that ideology was driving their participation in enthroning certain kings. The "people of the land" facilitated the coronation of Jehoahaz (36:1) following the death of Josiah at Megiddo. In putting Jehoahaz on the throne, the people of the land passed over the oldest son of Josiah (Eliakim), implying that they saw Jehoahaz as a better fit for their agenda. The "people of the land" also played a role in the political dynamics surrounding the accession of Josiah to the throne after the assassination of Amon (33:25).

24:1–27 *Joash King of Judah.* Joash's long reign (835–796 BC) overlaps primarily with Jehu and Jehoahaz in the northern kingdom and reflects a time of Aramean resurgence under Hazael and Ben-Hadad III and continued strength in Assyria. Like Rehoboam (chs. 11–12) and Asa (chs. 14–16), Joash begins his reign in an atmosphere of godliness but became unfaithful following the death of his mentor.

24:1 seven years old. Joash no doubt begins his reign under the close guidance of Jehoiada the priest and the sociopolitical group known as the "people of the land" (23:21; see note there).

24:4 Joash's repair and restoration of the temple is similar to the later efforts of Hezekiah (29:3–36) and Josiah (34:8–13). Such refurbishing is a tangible way for the ruler to show his devotion to God.

24:5–6 Despite Joash's desire to refurbish the temple, he does not receive the expected cooperation of the priests. This lack of cooperation is ironic since the priest Jehoiada raised Joash.

24:6 tax imposed by Moses. Likely the half-shekel census tax (Exod 30:11–16).

24:10–11 As a result of the proclamation made throughout Judah, the whole community begins to give generously and joyfully. The need of the temple officials to frequently empty the collection chest underscores the people's generosity as seen in earlier days (Exod 36:3–7).

24:18 [s]ver 4; Jos 24:20; 2Ch 7:19 [t]Ex 34:13; 1Ki 14:23; 2Ch 33:3; Jer 17:2 [u]Jos 22:20; 2Ch 19:2
24:19 [v]Nu 11:29; Jer 7:25; Zec 1:4
24:20 [w]Jdg 3:10; 1Ch 12:18; 2Ch 20:14 [x]Mt 23:35; Lk 11:51 [y]Nu 14:41 [z]Dt 31:17; 2Ch 15:2
24:21 [a]Jos 7:25; Ac 7:58-59 [b]Ne 9:26; Jer 26:21 [c]Jer 20:2; Mt 23:35
24:22 [d]Ge 9:5
24:23 [e]2Ki 12:17-18
24:24 [f]2Ch 14:9; 16:8; 20:2,12 [g]Lev 26:23-25; Dt 28:25
24:25 [h]2Ch 21:20
24:26 [i]2Ki 12:21 [j]Ru 1:4
25:2 [k]ver 14; 1Ki 8:61; 2Ch 24:2

brought the rest of the money to the king and Jehoiada, and with it were made articles for the LORD's temple: articles for the service and for the burnt offerings, and also dishes and other objects of gold and silver. As long as Jehoiada lived, burnt offerings were presented continually in the temple of the LORD.

15 Now Jehoiada was old and full of years, and he died at the age of a hundred and thirty. 16 He was buried with the kings in the City of David, because of the good he had done in Israel for God and his temple.

The Wickedness of Joash

17 After the death of Jehoiada, the officials of Judah came and paid homage to the king, and he listened to them. 18 They abandoned[s] the temple of the LORD, the God of their ancestors, and worshiped Asherah poles and idols.[t] Because of their guilt, God's anger[u] came on Judah and Jerusalem. 19 Although the LORD sent prophets to the people to bring them back to him, and though they testified against them, they would not listen.[v]

20 Then the Spirit[w] of God came on Zechariah[x] son of Jehoiada the priest. He stood before the people and said, "This is what God says: 'Why do you disobey the LORD's commands? You will not prosper.[y] Because you have forsaken the LORD, he has forsaken[z] you.' "

21 But they plotted against him, and by order of the king they stoned[a] him to death[b] in the courtyard of the LORD's temple.[c] 22 King Joash did not remember the kindness Zechariah's father Jehoiada had shown him but killed his son, who said as he lay dying, "May the LORD see this and call you to account."[d]

23 At the turn of the year,*[a]* the army of Aram marched against Joash; it invaded Judah and Jerusalem and killed all the leaders of the people.[e] They sent all the plunder to their king in Damascus. 24 Although the Aramean army had come with only a few men,[f] the LORD delivered into their hands a much larger army.[g] Because Judah had forsaken the LORD, the God of their ancestors, judgment was executed on Joash. 25 When the Arameans withdrew, they left Joash severely wounded. His officials conspired against him for murdering the son of Jehoiada the priest, and they killed him in his bed. So he died and was buried[h] in the City of David, but not in the tombs of the kings.

26 Those who conspired against him were Zabad,*[b]* son of Shimeath an Ammonite woman, and Jehozabad, son of Shimrith[c][i] a Moabite woman.[j] 27 The account of his sons, the many prophecies about him, and the record of the restoration of the temple of God are written in the annotations on the book of the kings. And Amaziah his son succeeded him as king.

Amaziah King of Judah

25:1-4pp — 2Ki 14:1-6
25:11-12pp — 2Ki 14:7
25:17-28pp — 2Ki 14:8-20

25 Amaziah was twenty-five years old when he became king, and he reigned in Jerusalem twenty-nine years. His mother's name was Jehoaddan; she was from Jerusalem. 2 He did what was right in the eyes of the LORD, but not wholeheartedly.[k] 3 After the kingdom was firmly in his control,

[a] *23* Probably in the spring *[b]* *26* A variant of *Jozabad* *[c]* *26* A variant of *Shomer*

24:14 As long as Jehoiada lived, burnt offerings were presented continually. Shows that Jehoiada is central to faithful temple service and anticipates the apostasy of Joash after the death of Jehoiada.
24:15 old and full of years. Old age is a blessing from God (Ps 91:16) and a by-product of wisdom (Prov 3:16).
24:16 buried with the kings. A number of details portray Jehoiada in a king-like manner: he "showed his strength" (23:1), led a covenant ratification (23:1,3), had oversight of reforms (23:18–19), and was buried in the royal cemetery (here). To an extent Jehoiada functioned as a surrogate king since Joash became king at a young age.
24:17 officials of Judah came ... and [Joash] listened to them. Jehoiada's death creates a vacuum of godly counsel for the king, who had long reigned under the watchful eye of the high priest. The advice of these officials includes compromise (see note on v. 18).
24:18–19 They abandoned ... they would not listen. The shared responsibility in the resulting apostasy ("they abandoned the temple ... and worshiped ... idols") is reflected via plural pronouns (cf. v. 24). Despite their unfaithfulness, God demonstrates his love and grace by repeatedly sending prophets to proclaim his word and urge the people to return in obedience (cf. 36:15–16).
24:21 stoned him. Sadly, the prophet Zechariah is stoned to death (the punishment for a *false* prophet, Deut 13:5; 18:20). What is striking about this low moment in Judah's history is that Zechariah would have been like a brother to Joash as Jehoiada (Zechariah's father) was like a father to Joash. **in the courtyard.** Zechariah is killed in the same place that Jehoiada arranged for the covert enthronement of Joash (23:4–13).
24:22 did not remember. A choice, not a mental lapse. **call you to account.** God's judgment is seen in the remainder of Joash's reign (vv. 23–27).
24:23–24 Cf. 2 Kgs 12:17–18. Unfaithfulness leads to defeat by enemies (Lev 26:14–17).
25:1–28 *Amaziah King of Judah.* Amaziah reigned for 29 years (796–767 BC), most of which was likely in coregency with Uzziah/Azariah (792/91–767 BC) following Amaziah's imprisonment in Samaria

he executed the officials who had murdered his father the king. 4Yet he did not put their children to death, but acted in accordance with what is written in the Law, in the Book of Moses,[l] where the LORD commanded: "Parents shall not be put to death for their children, nor children be put to death for their parents; each will die for their own sin."[a][m]

5Amaziah called the people of Judah together and assigned them according to their families to commanders of thousands and commanders of hundreds for all Judah and Benjamin. He then mustered[n] those twenty years old[o] or more and found that there were three hundred thousand men fit for military service,[p] able to handle the spear and shield. 6He also hired a hundred thousand fighting men from Israel for a hundred talents[b] of silver.

7But a man of God came to him and said, "Your Majesty, these troops from Israel[q] must not march with you, for the LORD is not with Israel—not with any of the people of Ephraim. 8Even if you go and fight courageously in battle, God will overthrow you before the enemy, for God has the power to help or to overthrow."[r]

9Amaziah asked the man of God, "But what about the hundred talents I paid for these Israelite troops?"

The man of God replied, "The LORD can give you much more than that."[s]

10So Amaziah dismissed the troops who had come to him from Ephraim and sent them home. They were furious with Judah and left for home in a great rage.[t]

11Amaziah then marshaled his strength and led his army to the Valley of Salt, where he killed ten thousand men of Seir. 12The army of Judah also captured ten thousand men alive, took them to the top of a cliff and threw them down so that all were dashed to pieces.[u]

13Meanwhile the troops that Amaziah had sent back and had not allowed to take part in the war raided towns belonging to Judah from Samaria to Beth Horon. They killed three thousand people and carried off great quantities of plunder.

14When Amaziah returned from slaughtering the Edomites, he brought back the gods of the people of Seir. He set them up as his own gods,[v] bowed down to them and burned sacrifices to them. 15The anger of the LORD burned against Amaziah, and he sent a prophet to him, who said, "Why do you consult this people's gods, which could not save[w] their own people from your hand?"

16While he was still speaking, the king said to him, "Have we appointed you an adviser to the king? Stop! Why be struck down?"

So the prophet stopped but said, "I know that God has determined to destroy you, because you have done this and have not listened to my counsel."

17After Amaziah king of Judah consulted his advisers, he sent this challenge to Jehoash[c] son of Jehoahaz, the son of Jehu, king of Israel: "Come, let us face each other in battle."

18But Jehoash king of Israel replied to Amaziah king of Judah: "A thistle[x] in Lebanon sent a message to a cedar in Lebanon, 'Give your daughter to my son in marriage.' Then a wild beast in Lebanon came along and trampled the thistle underfoot. 19You say to yourself that you have defeated Edom, and now you are arrogant and proud. But stay at home! Why ask for trouble and cause your own downfall and that of Judah also?"

[a] *4* Deut. 24:16 [b] *6* That is, about 3 3/4 tons or about 3.4 metric tons; also in verse 9 [c] *17* Hebrew *Joash,* a variant of *Jehoash;* also in verses 18, 21, 23 and 25

25:4 [l] Dt 28:61 [m] Nu 26:11; Dt 24:16
25:5 [n] 2Sa 24:2 [o] Ex 30:14 [p] Nu 1:3; 1Ch 21:1; 2Ch 17:14-19
25:7 [q] 2Ch 16:2-9; 19:1-3
25:8 [r] 2Ch 14:11; 20:6
25:9 [s] Dt 8:18; Pr 10:22
25:10 [t] ver 13
25:12 [u] Ps 141:6; Ob 3
25:14 [v] Ex 20:3; 2Ch 28:23; Isa 44:15
25:15 [w] Ps 96:5; Isa 36:20
25:18 [x] Jdg 9:8-15

(vv. 17–24). During Amaziah's reign, the Assyrian Empire began to decline, facilitating a time of peace and prosperity for Judah and Israel.

25:2 did what was right ... but. On the one hand, Amaziah makes decisions based on the law of God and responds to the admonishment of a "man of God" by reversing course and stepping out in faith (vv. 7–10). On the other hand, Amaziah adopts the gods of the Edomites as his own (v. 14), rejects the admonishment of a prophet (vv. 15–16), and acts with pride and arrogance (vv. 17–19). God's ultimate decision to destroy Judah (vv. 16,20) shows the destructive outcome of a spiritually compromised life.

25:6 hired ... fighting men. Amaziah's hiring of mercenaries shows a lack of wholehearted trust in God.

25:10 dismissed the troops ... from Ephraim. Amaziah opts for obedience; he heeds the "man of God" (v. 7) and dismisses the hired troops, despite the significant monetary loss.

25:13 raided towns belonging to Judah from Samaria to Beth Horon. No doubt the soldiers are angered by the loss of plundering opportunities. This incident illustrates the reality that consequences may follow poor decisions, even if those decisions are later reversed.

25:14–16 Honoring the gods of other peoples (even conquered peoples) was common in the biblical world. Although God gives Amaziah victory, he responds with idolatry. God again sends a prophet to confront the king's covenantal unfaithfulness. While Amaziah had responded in obedience to the earlier admonishment of the man of God (vv. 9–10; see note on v. 10), this time he rebukes the prophet and rejects the word of God.

25:20 [y] 1Ki 12:15; 2Ch 10:15; 22:7
25:23 [z] 2Ki 14:13; Ne 8:16; 12:39 [a] 2Ch 26:9; Jer 31:38
25:24 [b] 1Ch 26:15
25:27 [c] Jos 10:3
26:1 [d] 2Ch 22:1
26:5 [e] 2Ch 15:2; 24:2; Da 1:17 [f] 2Ch 27:6
26:6 [g] Isa 2:6; 11:14; 14:29; Jer 25:20 [h] Am 1:8; 3:9

20 Amaziah, however, would not listen, for God so worked that he might deliver them into the hands
of Jehoash, because they sought the gods of Edom.[y] 21 So Jehoash king of Israel attacked. He and Amaziah king of Judah faced each other at Beth Shemesh in Judah. 22 Judah was routed by Israel, and every
man fled to his home. 23 Jehoash king of Israel captured Amaziah king of Judah, the son of Joash, the
son of Ahaziah,[a] at Beth Shemesh. Then Jehoash brought him to Jerusalem and broke down the wall
of Jerusalem from the Ephraim Gate[z] to the Corner Gate[a]—a section about four hundred cubits[b] long.
24 He took all the gold and silver and all the articles found in the temple of God that had been in the
care of Obed-Edom,[b] together with the palace treasures and the hostages, and returned to Samaria.
25 Amaziah son of Joash king of Judah lived for fifteen years after the death of Jehoash son of Jehoahaz king of Israel. 26 As for the other events of Amaziah's reign, from beginning to end, are they not
written in the book of the kings of Judah and Israel? 27 From the time that Amaziah turned away from
following the LORD, they conspired against him in Jerusalem and he fled to Lachish[c], but they sent men
after him to Lachish and killed him there. 28 He was brought back by horse and was buried with his
ancestors in the City of Judah.[c]

Uzziah King of Judah

26:1-4pp — 2Ki 14:21-22; 15:1-3
26:21-23pp — 2Ki 15:5-7

26 Then all the people of Judah[d] took Uzziah,[d] who was sixteen years old, and made him king in
place of his father Amaziah. 2 He was the one who rebuilt Elath and restored it to Judah after
Amaziah rested with his ancestors.
3 Uzziah was sixteen years old when he became king, and he reigned in Jerusalem fifty-two years. His
mother's name was Jekoliah; she was from Jerusalem. 4 He did what was right in the eyes of the LORD,
just as his father Amaziah had done. 5 He sought God during the days of Zechariah, who instructed him
in the fear[e] of God.[e] As long as he sought the LORD, God gave him success.[f]
6 He went to war against the Philistines[g] and broke down the walls of Gath, Jabneh and Ashdod.[h] He
then rebuilt towns near Ashdod and elsewhere among the Philistines. 7 God helped him against the Philis-

[a] *23* Hebrew *Jehoahaz,* a variant of *Ahaziah* [b] *23* That is, about 600 feet or about 180 meters
[c] *28* Most Hebrew manuscripts; some Hebrew manuscripts, Septuagint, Vulgate and Syriac (see also 2 Kings 14:20) *David* [d] *1* Also called *Azariah* [e] *5* Many Hebrew manuscripts, Septuagint and Syriac; other Hebrew manuscripts *vision*

25:20 God so worked. God orchestrates the events in conjunction with the prophetic word delivered to Amaziah (vv. 15–16). Like Joash (24:17–19), Amaziah does not listen to the prophetic word (v. 16) but persists in unfaithfulness to God by seeking foreign gods.

25:24 As seen in prior instances of unfaithfulness, God allows military defeat (2 Chr 12:9; 16:2–3; 28:21). In addition to plundering the temple and palace, Jehoash takes hostages from Judah (including Amaziah) as a means to insure continued influence over Judah.

25:25–26 This final paragraph covers Amaziah's final 24 years, when his son Uzziah was (presumably) acting as his royal coregent during Amaziah's imprisonment (792/91–767 BC).

25:27 As with Joash (24:25), Amaziah is murdered in the midst of conspiracy. In both cases, rejecting God's word set into action events that led to their demise (vv. 16,20; 24:20,22). **Lachish.** A citadel located about 30 miles (48 kilometers) south-southwest of Jerusalem on the edge of the foothills; it guarded passes from the coastal highway leading to the central hill country.

26:1–23 *Uzziah King of Judah.* Uzziah is made king after Amaziah's imprisonment in Samaria, and he has a lengthy coregency with Amaziah (792/91–767 BC). In addition, during the final decade of his reign, Uzziah was coregent with his son Jotham (750–740/39 BC); this was due to Uzziah's skin ailment. Uzziah reigned (including coregencies) from 792/91–740/39 BC. Uzziah reigned alongside Jeroboam II of the northern kingdom (793/92–753 BC) for 40 years, a time of significant peace and prosperity for both kingdoms. During the reigns of these kings, the combined geographic extent of the northern kingdom and southern kingdom approximated that seen at the height of the united monarchy.

26:1 the people of Judah ... made [Uzziah] king. This is different from the typical regnal format used in Chronicles. The (presumed) long coregency between Uzziah and Amaziah during Amaziah's imprisonment in Samaria and the murky circumstances of Amaziah's death (25:27) may have created some type of succession uncertainty, if not crisis. **the people of Judah.** May be related to "the people of the land" (23:21; see note).

26:2 rebuilt Elath. Made possible because of Amaziah's victory over Edom. Solomon originally established this maritime port city on the Gulf of Aqabah before the area was lost during the reign of Jehoram. The port was later lost again during the time of Ahaz (2 Kgs 16:6).

26:3 fifty-two years. 792/91–740/39 BC.

26:5–7 God gave him success ... God helped him. Because of Uzziah's "fear of God" (v. 5), God gives him success in battle (vv. 6–7), wealth from foreigners (v. 8), and renown among the nations (vv. 8,15). But Uzziah later grows proud in light of his power (v. 16), and his downfall follows shortly thereafter.

26:6–8 Uzziah's dominance over areas to the east ("Ammonites," v. 8), west ("Philistines," v. 6), and south ("Gur Baal" and "Meunites," v. 7) enables Judah to leverage control over a number of trade routes and benefit from the related income. Judah's control over these regions and Uzziah's fame spreading to Egypt are reminiscent of the geopolitical hegemony attained during David and Solomon.

tines and against the Arabs[i] who lived in Gur Baal and against the Meunites.[j] 8 The Ammonites[k] brought
tribute to Uzziah, and his fame spread as far as the border of Egypt, because he had become very powerful.
9 Uzziah built towers in Jerusalem at the Corner Gate,[l] at the Valley Gate[m] and at the angle of the
wall, and he fortified them. 10 He also built towers in the wilderness and dug many cisterns, because he
had much livestock in the foothills and in the plain. He had people working his fields and vineyards in
the hills and in the fertile lands, for he loved the soil.

11 Uzziah had a well-trained army, ready to go out by divisions according to their numbers as mustered by Jeiel the secretary and Maaseiah the officer under the direction of Hananiah, one of the royal
officials. 12 The total number of family leaders over the fighting men was 2,600. 13 Under their command
was an army of 307,500 men trained for war, a powerful force to support the king against his enemies.
14 Uzziah provided shields, spears, helmets, coats of armor, bows and slingstones for the entire army.[n]
15 In Jerusalem he made devices invented for use on the towers and on the corner defenses so that soldiers could shoot arrows and hurl large stones from the walls. His fame spread far and wide, for he was
greatly helped until he became powerful.

16 But after Uzziah became powerful, his pride[o] led to his downfall.[p] He was unfaithful[q] to the LORD
his God, and entered the temple of the LORD to burn incense[r] on the altar of incense. 17 Azariah[s] the
priest with eighty other courageous priests of the LORD followed him in. 18 They confronted King Uzziah
and said, "It is not right for you, Uzziah, to burn incense to the LORD. That is for the priests,[t] the descendants[u] of Aaron,[v] who have been consecrated to burn incense.[w] Leave the sanctuary, for you have
been unfaithful; and you will not be honored by the LORD God."

19 Uzziah, who had a censer in his hand ready to burn incense, became angry. While he was raging
at the priests in their presence before the incense altar in the LORD's temple, leprosy[a][x] broke out on
his forehead. 20 When Azariah the chief priest and all the other priests looked at him, they saw that he
had leprosy on his forehead, so they hurried him out. Indeed, he himself was eager to leave, because
the LORD had afflicted him.

21 King Uzziah had leprosy until the day he died. He lived in a separate house[b][y] — leprous, and banned
from the temple of the LORD. Jotham his son had charge of the palace and governed the people of the land.

22 The other events of Uzziah's reign, from beginning to end, are recorded by the prophet Isaiah[z] son
of Amoz. 23 Uzziah[a] rested with his ancestors and was buried near them in a cemetery that belonged to
the kings, for people said, "He had leprosy." And Jotham his son succeeded him as king.[b]

Jotham King of Judah

27:1-4,7-9pp — 2Ki 15:33-38

27 Jotham[c] was twenty-five years old when he became king, and he reigned in Jerusalem sixteen
years. His mother's name was Jerusha daughter of Zadok. 2 He did what was right in the eyes
of the LORD, just as his father Uzziah had done, but unlike him he did not enter the temple of the LORD.

[a] 19 The Hebrew for *leprosy* was used for various diseases affecting the skin; also in verses 20, 21 and 23.
[b] 21 Or *in a house where he was relieved of responsibilities*

26:7 [i] 2Ch 21:16 [j] 2Ch 20:1
26:8 [k] Ge 19:38; 2Ch 17:11
26:9 [l] 2Ki 14:13; 2Ch 25:23 [m] Ne 2:13; 3:13
26:14 [n] Jer 46:4
26:16 [o] 2Ki 14:10 [p] Dt 32:15; 2Ch 25:19 [q] 1Ch 5:25 [r] 2Ki 16:12
26:17 [s] 1Ki 4:2; 1Ch 6:10
26:18 [t] Nu 16:39 [u] Nu 18:1-7 [v] Ex 30:7 [w] 1Ch 6:49
26:19 [x] Nu 12:10; 2Ki 5:25-27
26:21 [y] Ex 4:6; Lev 13:46; 14:8; Nu 5:2; 19:12
26:22 [z] 2Ki 15:1; Isa 1:1; 6:1
26:23 [a] Isa 1:1; 6:1 [b] 2Ki 14:21; 15:7; Am 1:1
27:1 [c] 2Ki 15:5,32; 1Ch 3:12

26:11 well-trained army. Reflected in the naming of Uzziah by the Assyrian king Tiglath-Pileser III as a key member of a mid-eighth-century BC coalition.

26:15 devices invented for use on the towers. While the specifics of these military machines are not clear, these devices created a formidable military advantage for a city under siege.

26:16 Burning incense was strictly limited to the Aaronic priesthood (Exod 30:1 – 10; Num 16:40), so Uzziah's actions constituted covenantal unfaithfulness. Moreover, Uzziah's entry into the temple violated God's stipulations for his holy space. Uzziah's pride in light of his God-gifted accomplishments embolden him to disregard boundaries established by God.

26:18 Uzziah's lack of a godly response to this rebuke leads to his inability to fully discharge his royal responsibilities (see note on v. 21).

26:19 leprosy. See NIV text note. Instead of acknowledging that the priests were correct and exiting the temple, Uzziah reacts as a proud fool who does not accept a rebuke (Prov 1:7; 12:15).

26:20 eager to leave. While Uzziah refuses to leave the temple when confronted by the priests, he becomes eager to leave in light of God's judgment.

26:21 had leprosy until the day he died. God's judgment lasts the remainder of Uzziah's life, a visual reminder of the consequences of covenantal unfaithfulness. Ceremonial uncleanness prohibits Uzziah from fully exercising his royal responsibilities, prompting a coregency with his son Jotham. After this, Uzziah needs to live alone and can never visit God's temple again (Lev 13:46; Num 5:1 – 3).

27:1 – 9 *Jotham King of Judah.* Uzziah's skin disease resulted in a coregency with his son Jotham from 750 to 740/39 BC. Jotham's reign extended from approximately 750 to 732/31 BC, a period when the Neo-Assyrian Empire (745 – 609 BC) was reaching new heights of power and aggression.

27:2 This summary evaluation of Jotham is very similar to that of Uzziah

27:3 [d] 2Ch 33:14; Ne 3:26
27:5 [e] Ge 19:38
27:6 [f] 2Ch 26:5
28:1 [g] 1Ch 3:13; Isa 1:1
28:2 [h] Ex 34:17; 2Ch 22:3
28:3 [i] Jos 15:8; 2Ki 23:10 [j] Lev 18:21; 2Ki 3:27; 2Ch 33:6; Eze 20:26 [k] Dt 18:9; 2Ch 33:2
28:5 [l] Isa 7:1
28:6 [m] 2Ki 15:25,27 [n] ver 8; Isa 9:21; 11:13

The people, however, continued their corrupt practices. 3Jotham rebuilt the Upper Gate of the temple
of the LORD and did extensive work on the wall at the hill of Ophel.[d] 4He built towns in the hill country
of Judah and forts and towers in the wooded areas.
5Jotham waged war against the king of the Ammonites[e] and conquered them. That year the Ammonites paid him a hundred talents[a] of silver, ten thousand cors[b] of wheat and ten thousand cors[c] of barley.
The Ammonites brought him the same amount also in the second and third years.
6Jotham grew powerful[f] because he walked steadfastly before the LORD his God.
7The other events in Jotham's reign, including all his wars and the other things he did, are written
in the book of the kings of Israel and Judah. 8He was twenty-five years old when he became king, and
he reigned in Jerusalem sixteen years. 9Jotham rested with his ancestors and was buried in the City of
David. And Ahaz his son succeeded him as king.

Ahaz King of Judah

28:1-27pp — 2Ki 16:1-20

28 Ahaz[g] was twenty years old when he became king, and he reigned in Jerusalem sixteen years.
Unlike David his father, he did not do what was right in the eyes of the LORD. 2He followed the
ways of the kings of Israel and also made idols[h] for worshiping the Baals. 3He burned sacrifices in the
Valley of Ben Hinnom[i] and sacrificed his children[j] in the fire, engaging in the detestable[k] practices of
the nations the LORD had driven out before the Israelites. 4He offered sacrifices and burned incense at
the high places, on the hilltops and under every spreading tree.
5Therefore the LORD his God delivered him into the hands of the king of Aram.[l] The Arameans defeated him and took many of his people as prisoners and brought them to Damascus.
He was also given into the hands of the king of Israel, who inflicted heavy casualties on him. 6In
one day Pekah[m] son of Remaliah killed a hundred and twenty thousand soldiers in Judah[n] — because Judah had forsaken the LORD, the God of their ancestors. 7Zikri, an Ephraimite warrior, killed

[a] 5 That is, about 3 3/4 tons or about 3.4 metric tons [b] 5 That is, probably about 1,800 tons or about 1,600 metric tons of wheat [c] 5 That is, probably about 1,500 tons or about 1,350 metric tons of barley

(26:4). As with Uzziah (see note on 26:5–7), Jotham "grew powerful" (v. 6), enjoyed success in battle (v. 5), and received tribute from foreign nations (v. 5). Unlike Uzziah, Jotham did not grow proud and challenge God's covenantal bounds but instead "walked steadfastly" before God (v. 6; see note).

27:3–4 Jotham continues the expansion and fortification efforts Uzziah undertook (26:6–10). The building projects of Uzziah and Jotham may be largely one in the same given their extensive coregency.

27:3 hill of Ophel. Located to the south of Jerusalem in the City of David.

27:5 cors. See NIV text notes.

27:6 because he walked steadfastly before the LORD his God. Might be better rendered "because he caused his ways to be [rightly] ordered before the LORD his God," suggesting an intentional effort to live in a manner pleasing to God (Rom 12:2). Jotham's success is based on his relationship with God.

28:1–27 *Ahaz King of Judah.* While the final decades of the ninth century BC were a time of decline in Assyrian dominance in the Levant — the area between Anatolia (modern day Turkey) and Egypt that included Israel, Aram, Phoenicia, Moab, and Edom — this situation changed dramatically with the ascent of Tiglath-Pileser III to the Assyrian throne in 745 BC. This period in Assyrian history is referred to as the Neo-Assyrian Empire (745–609 BC). Ahaz reigned 735–716/15 BC, including presumed coregencies with Jotham (735–732/31 BC) and Hezekiah (729–716/15 BC). In a rapid departure from his father Jotham, Ahaz became one of the most ungodly kings in the history of Judah's monarchy (cf. v. 19), underscoring how quickly one generation can abandon the values of the previous generation.

28:3 Valley of Ben Hinnom. Located on the south side of the temple mount; came to symbolize grave apostasy (Jer 32:35). This area became a dump for garbage and the bodies of executed criminals and was marked by fires and dreadful sights and smells. In light of this imagery, this valley ("Gehenna") came to symbolize hell itself (see Matt 10:28; Mark 9:43,47, where the Greek word *geenna* is translated "hell" in these examples). **sacrificed his children in the fire.** God strictly prohibited child sacrifice (Lev 20:2–3; Deut 18:10).

28:5–25 In the aftermath of Tiglath-Pileser III's campaign in ca. 734–732 BC, several western states (including Aram, Israel, Tyre, Ashkelon, and Gaza) formed an anti-Assyrian coalition reminiscent of the coalition formed in the mid-ninth century BC to stem the advance of Shalmaneser III. The formation of this coalition was impeded by Ahaz's refusal to join, which led to Aram and Israel invading Judah (vv. 5–6). Ahaz also faced pressure in the south from the Edomites and in the west from the Philistines. This crisis is the historical context of Isa 7, which notes that Israel and Aram intended to install a new king in Judah. Faced with these threats, Ahaz made the watershed decision to seek help from Tiglath-Pileser III (vv. 16,21; 2 Kgs 16:7–8). In conjunction with Ahaz's pledge of vassalage, Tiglath-Pileser III attacked Phoenicia, Philistia, Edom, Moab, and Ammon. Then the Assyrian army attacked Aram and Israel, leading to the first set of deportations imposed upon Israel (see 2 Kgs 15:29 and note). Following the fall of Damascus in 732 BC, Hoshea assassinated Pekah and succeeded him as king (2 Kgs 15:30). The death of Tiglath-Pileser III (727 BC) inspired vassals to rebel against Assyrian rule (2 Kgs 17:3–4). As a result, Shalmaneser V attacked Israel, culminating in a three-year siege of Samaria (see 2 Kgs 17:5 and note). By 722 BC (when Hoshea surrendered) Shalmaneser V defeated Samaria; his

Maaseiah the king's son, Azrikam the officer in charge of the palace, and Elkanah, second to the
king. 8 The men of Israel took captive from their fellow Israelites who were from Judah[o] two hundred
thousand wives, sons and daughters. They also took a great deal of plunder, which they carried back
to Samaria.[p]

9 But a prophet of the LORD named Oded was there, and he went out to meet the army when it returned to Samaria. He said to them, "Because the LORD, the God of your ancestors, was angry[q] with
Judah, he gave them into your hand. But you have slaughtered them in a rage that reaches to heaven.[r]
10 And now you intend to make the men and women of Judah and Jerusalem your slaves.[s] But aren't
you also guilty of sins against the LORD your God? 11 Now listen to me! Send back your fellow Israelites
you have taken as prisoners, for the LORD's fierce anger rests on you.[t]"

12 Then some of the leaders in Ephraim — Azariah son of Jehohanan, Berekiah son of Meshillemoth, Jehizkiah son of Shallum, and Amasa son of Hadlai — confronted those who were arriving
from the war. 13 "You must not bring those prisoners here," they said, "or we will be guilty before the
LORD. Do you intend to add to our sin and guilt? For our guilt is already great, and his fierce anger
rests on Israel."

14 So the soldiers gave up the prisoners and plunder in the presence of the officials and all the assembly. 15 The men designated by name took the prisoners, and from the plunder they clothed all who were
naked. They provided them with clothes and sandals, food and drink,[u] and healing balm. All those who
were weak they put on donkeys. So they took them back to their fellow Israelites at Jericho, the City of
Palms,[v] and returned to Samaria.

16 At that time King Ahaz sent to the kings[a] of Assyria[w] for help. 17 The Edomites[x] had again come and
attacked Judah and carried away prisoners,[y] 18 while the Philistines[z] had raided towns in the foothills
and in the Negev of Judah. They captured and occupied Beth Shemesh, Aijalon[a] and Gederoth, as well
as Soko, Timnah and Gimzo, with their surrounding villages. 19 The LORD had humbled Judah because
of Ahaz king of Israel,[b] for he had promoted wickedness in Judah and had been most unfaithful[b] to the
LORD. 20 Tiglath-Pileser[c][c] king of Assyria came to him, but he gave him trouble instead of help.[d] 21 Ahaz
took some of the things from the temple of the LORD and from the royal palace and from the officials
and presented them to the king of Assyria, but that did not help him.

22 In his time of trouble King Ahaz became even more unfaithful[e] to the LORD. 23 He offered sacrifices
to the gods[f] of Damascus, who had defeated him; for he thought, "Since the gods of the kings of Aram
have helped them, I will sacrifice to them so they will help me."[g] But they were his downfall and the
downfall of all Israel.

24 Ahaz gathered together the furnishings from the temple of God[h] and cut them in pieces. He shut
the doors[i] of the LORD's temple and set up altars[j] at every street corner in Jerusalem. 25 In every town
in Judah he built high places to burn sacrifices to other gods and aroused the anger of the LORD, the
God of his ancestors.

26 The other events of his reign and all his ways, from beginning to end, are written in the book
of the kings of Judah and Israel. 27 Ahaz rested[k] with his ancestors and was buried[l] in the city of Jerusalem, but he was not placed in the tombs of the kings of Israel. And Hezekiah his son succeeded
him as king.

[a] *16* Most Hebrew manuscripts; one Hebrew manuscript, Septuagint and Vulgate (see also 2 Kings 16:7) *king*
[b] *19* That is, Judah, as frequently in 2 Chronicles [c] *20* Hebrew *Tilgath-Pilneser,* a variant of *Tiglath-Pileser*

28:8 [o] Dt 28:25-41; 2Ch 11:4 [p] 2Ch 29:9
28:9 [q] 2Ch 25:15; Isa 10:6; 47:6; Zec 1:15 [r] Ezr 9:6; Rev 18:5
28:10 [s] Lev 25:39-46
28:11 [t] 2Ch 11:4; Jas 2:13
28:15 [u] 2Ki 6:22; Pr 25:21-22 [v] Dt 34:3; Jdg 1:16
28:16 [w] 2Ki 16:7
28:17 [x] Ps 137:7; Isa 34:5 [y] 2Ch 29:9
28:18 [z] Eze 16:27,57 [a] Jos 10:12
28:19 [b] 2Ch 21:2
28:20 [c] 2Ki 15:29; 1Ch 5:6 [d] 2Ki 16:7
28:22 [e] Jer 5:3
28:23 [f] 2Ch 25:14 [g] Jer 44:17-18
28:24 [h] 2Ki 16:18 [i] 2Ch 29:7 [j] 2Ch 30:14
28:27 [k] Isa 14:28-32 [l] 2Ch 21:20; 24:25

successor, Sargon II (722 – 705 BC), oversaw the massive deportation (and repopulation) that followed (see 2 Kgs 17:6,24 – 41 and notes).

28:12 – 15 Given the unfaithfulness of Ahaz, it is somewhat surprising that the military leaders of Ephraim respond to the prophet's rebuke and take steps of kindness to remedy the situation.

28:19 promoted wickedness. In direct opposition to his role as king (Deut 17:14 – 20), so the Lord "humbled Judah."

28:21 Rather than see the folly of his reliance on mankind, Ahaz attempts to further curry favor with the Assyrian king by raiding the treasures of the temple and palace.

28:22 time of trouble. The judgment of God via incursions by other nations was a direct result of the failure of Ahaz (and Judah) to fully obey and trust in the Lord (v. 19). **became even more unfaithful.** While covenantal consequences were intended to drive God's people back to him in repentance, Ahaz instead becomes even more unfaithful and pursues greater levels of wickedness. By so doing, Ahaz spurns God, who abounds in mercy and forgiveness when his people seek him in humility and contrition (6:22 – 39).

28:23 See notes on 2 Kgs 16:10 – 14.

28:24 – 25 As part of his increased unfaithfulness, Ahaz loots the sacred objects of the temple for his pagan shrines (cf. 2 Kgs 16:14 – 18) and shuts the doors of God's temple. Reopening and purifying God's temple were later the first priority in the reforms of Ahaz's son Hezekiah (29:3 – 36).

29:1 [m] 1Ch 3:13
29:2 [n] 2Ch 28:1; 34:2
29:3 [o] 2Ch 28:24
29:5 [p] 2Ch 35:6
29:6 [q] Ps 106:6-47; Jer 2:27 [r] 1Ch 5:25; Eze 8:16
29:8 [s] Dt 28:25; 2Ch 24:18 [t] Jer 18:16; 19:8; 25:9,18
29:9 [u] 2Ch 28:5-8,17
29:10 [v] 2Ch 15:12; 23:16
29:11 [w] Nu 3:6; 8:6,14 [x] 1Ch 15:2
29:12 [y] Nu 3:17-20 [z] 2Ch 31:15
29:13 [a] 1Ch 6:39
29:15 [b] ver 5; 1Ch 23:28; 2Ch 30:12
29:16 [c] 2Sa 15:23

Hezekiah Purifies the Temple

29:1-2pp — 2Ki 18:2-3

29 Hezekiah[m] was twenty-five years old when he became king, and he reigned in Jerusalem twenty-nine years. His mother's name was Abijah daughter of Zechariah. 2 He did what was right in
the eyes of the LORD, just as his father David[n] had done.
3 In the first month of the first year of his reign, he opened the doors of the temple of the LORD and
repaired[o] them. 4 He brought in the priests and the Levites, assembled them in the square on the east side
5 and said: "Listen to me, Levites! Consecrate[p] yourselves now and consecrate the temple of the LORD, the
God of your ancestors. Remove all defilement from the sanctuary. 6 Our parents[q] were unfaithful;[r] they did
evil in the eyes of the LORD our God and forsook him. They turned their faces away from the LORD's dwelling
place and turned their backs on him. 7 They also shut the doors of the portico and put out the lamps. They
did not burn incense or present any burnt offerings at the sanctuary to the God of Israel. 8 Therefore, the
anger of the LORD has fallen on Judah and Jerusalem; he has made them an object of dread and horror[s]
and scorn,[t] as you can see with your own eyes. 9 This is why our fathers have fallen by the sword and why
our sons and daughters and our wives are in captivity.[u] 10 Now I intend to make a covenant[v] with the LORD,
the God of Israel, so that his fierce anger will turn away from us. 11 My sons, do not be negligent now, for
the LORD has chosen you to stand before him and serve him,[w] to minister[x] before him and to burn incense."
12 Then these Levites[y] set to work:

from the Kohathites,
  Mahath son of Amasai and Joel son of Azariah;
from the Merarites,
  Kish son of Abdi and Azariah son of Jehallelel;
from the Gershonites,
  Joah son of Zimmah and Eden[z] son of Joah;
13 from the descendants of Elizaphan,
  Shimri and Jeiel;
from the descendants of Asaph,[a]
  Zechariah and Mattaniah;
14 from the descendants of Heman,
  Jehiel and Shimei;
from the descendants of Jeduthun,
  Shemaiah and Uzziel.

15 When they had assembled their fellow Levites and consecrated themselves, they went in to purify[b]
the temple of the LORD, as the king had ordered, following the word of the LORD. 16 The priests went into
the sanctuary of the LORD to purify it. They brought out to the courtyard of the LORD's temple everything
unclean that they found in the temple of the LORD. The Levites took it and carried it out to the Kidron
Valley.[c] 17 They began the consecration on the first day of the first month, and by the eighth day of the
month they reached the portico of the LORD. For eight more days they consecrated the temple of the
LORD itself, finishing on the sixteenth day of the first month.

29:1 — 32:33 *The Reign of Hezekiah.* Hezekiah's reign stands in juxtaposition to the reign of Ahaz (cf. 28:1–2 and 29:2; cf. 28:19,24–25 and 29:3; 30:6–9; 31:1; cf. 28:22–25 and 32:1,20). The chronology of Hezekiah's reign is difficult because of unclear synchronism across various date markers in biblical passages and records from the ancient Near East. In addition, the unclear number of coregencies that took place during the time from Amaziah to Hezekiah adds to the chronological challenges of this period.

29:1 – 36 *Hezekiah Purifies the Temple.* A highlight of the reign of Hezekiah is the reopening and purification of the temple following the defiling of the temple by his father, Ahaz (28:21–25). The consecration of the Jerusalem temple prepares the way for an emphatic return to corporate worship in Israel (vv. 20–31; 30:1–27).

29:4 – 10 In conjunction with the reopening of the temple, Hezekiah convenes an assembly of those charged with covenant duties. The emphasis of this gathering is consecration. Hezekiah's speech is a rallying call to faithfulness in light of the disastrous consequences of unfaithfulness and rises to the level of a "covenant" (v. 10).

29:15 – 16 Levites ... went into the sanctuary ... to purify it. Underscores the priority of adhering to God's covenantal stipulations reflected throughout the reign of Hezekiah. In accordance with God's instructions, only priests purified the inner part of the temple. On the responsibilities of priests and Levites, see notes on 1 Chr 6:48–49.

29:17 began the consecration. The process takes two sets of eight days. Cleansing begins from the outside and progressively works toward areas of increasing holiness. The time required for the purification of the temple complex necessitated a delay in the subsequent Passover celebration (30:2–3,15).

29:20 – 24 Once the temple is consecrated, Hezekiah convenes a temple rededication ceremony replete with the terminology of the sacrificial

[18]Then they went in to King Hezekiah and reported: "We have purified the entire temple of the LORD,
the altar of burnt offering with all its utensils, and the table for setting out the consecrated bread, with
all its articles. [19]We have prepared and consecrated all the articles[d] that King Ahaz removed in his unfaithfulness while he was king. They are now in front of the LORD's altar."

[20]Early the next morning King Hezekiah gathered the city officials together and went up to the temple of the LORD. [21]They brought seven bulls, seven rams, seven male lambs and seven male goats as a
sin offering[a][e] for the kingdom, for the sanctuary and for Judah. The king commanded the priests, the
descendants of Aaron, to offer these on the altar of the LORD. [22]So they slaughtered the bulls, and the
priests took the blood and splashed it against the altar; next they slaughtered the rams and splashed
their blood against the altar; then they slaughtered the lambs and splashed their blood[f] against the
altar. [23]The goats for the sin offering were brought before the king and the assembly, and they laid
their hands[g] on them. [24]The priests then slaughtered the goats and presented their blood on the altar
for a sin offering to atone[h] for all Israel, because the king had ordered the burnt offering and the sin
offering for all Israel.

[25]He stationed the Levites in the temple of the LORD with cymbals, harps and lyres in the way prescribed by David[i] and Gad[j] the king's seer and Nathan the prophet; this was commanded by the LORD
through his prophets. [26]So the Levites stood ready with David's instruments,[k] and the priests with their
trumpets.[l]

[27]Hezekiah gave the order to sacrifice the burnt offering on the altar. As the offering began, singing
to the LORD began also, accompanied by trumpets and the instruments[m] of David king of Israel. [28]The
whole assembly bowed in worship, while the musicians played and the trumpets sounded. All this continued until the sacrifice of the burnt offering was completed.

[29]When the offerings were finished, the king and everyone present with him
knelt down and worshiped.[n] [30]King Hezekiah and his officials ordered the
Levites to praise the LORD with the words of David and of Asaph the seer.
So they sang praises with gladness and bowed down and worshiped.

[31]Then Hezekiah said, "You have now dedicated yourselves to
the LORD. Come and bring sacrifices[o] and thank offerings to the
temple of the LORD." So the assembly brought sacrifices and
thank offerings, and all whose hearts were willing[p] brought
burnt offerings.

[32]The number of burnt offerings the assembly brought
was seventy bulls, a hundred rams and two hundred male
lambs — all of them for burnt offerings to the LORD. [33]The animals consecrated as sacrifices amounted to six hundred bulls
and three thousand sheep and goats. [34]The priests, however,
were too few to skin all the burnt offerings;[q] so their relatives
the Levites helped them until the task was finished and until other
priests had been consecrated,[r] for the Levites had been more

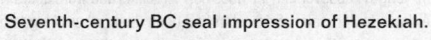

Seventh-century BC seal impression of Hezekiah.
Z. Radovan/www.BibleLandPictures.com

[a] *21* Or *purification offering*; also in verses 23 and 24

29:19 [d] 2Ch 28:24
29:21 [e] Lev 4:13-14
29:22 [f] Lev 4:18
29:23 [g] Lev 4:15
29:24 [h] Ex 29:36; Lev 4:26
29:25 [i] 1Ch 25:6; 2Ch 8:14 [j] 1Sa 22:5; 2Sa 24:11
29:26 [k] 1Ch 15:16 [l] 1Ch 15:24; 23:5; 2Ch 5:12
29:27 [m] 2Ch 23:18
29:29 [n] 2Ch 20:18
29:31 [o] Heb 13:15-16 [p] Ex 25:2; 35:22
29:34 [q] 2Ch 35:11 [r] 2Ch 30:3,15

system (see Introduction to Leviticus: Major Theological Themes [Offerings, Sacrifices, and Atonement]). Emphasis is placed on a "sin offering for the kingdom, for the sanctuary and for Judah" (v. 21) as well as for "all Israel" (v. 24). These elements of the sacrificial system portray purification, atonement, forgiveness of sin, and reconciliation.

29:22 – 23 they slaughtered the bulls ... goats for the sin offering. Reminiscent of the Day of Atonement, which (as here) has particular application to the Most Holy Place and the altar (see Lev 16:1 – 34 and notes).

29:22 splashed their blood against the altar. Underscores that the shedding of blood is necessary to atone for sin (see Lev 1:5; Heb 9:21 – 22 and notes). **slaughtered the lambs and splashed their blood against the altar.** Part of fellowship offerings (see Lev 3:1 – 17 and notes).

29:23 laid their hands on them. Implying the identification with the animal being sacrificed and substitutionary transfer of sin (see Lev 1:4 and note).

29:24 burnt offering. See Lev 1:3 – 17 and notes. **sin offering.** See Lev 4:1 — 5:13 and notes.

29:25 – 28 Stationing Levitical musicians, singers, and trumpeting priests parallels Solomon's temple dedication ceremony (5:2 – 14; 7:4 – 7). Hezekiah carefully organizes these groups "in the way prescribed by David and ... by the LORD through his prophets" (v. 25).

29:31 – 35 These additional offerings are provided by those "whose hearts were willing" (v. 31), highlighting corporate fellowship via the sharing of sacrificial meals and offerings.

29:31 thank offerings. See Lev 7:12 – 18 and notes.

29:32 burnt offerings. See Lev 1:3 – 17 and notes.

29:35 [s]Ex 29:13; Lev 3:16 [t]Lev 7:11-21 [u]Nu 15:5-10
30:1 [v]Ge 41:52 [w]Ex 12:11; Nu 28:16
30:2 [x]Nu 9:10
30:3 [y]2Ch 29:34
30:5 [z]Jdg 20:1
30:7 [a]Ps 78:8,57; 106:6; Eze 20:18 [b]2Ch 29:8
30:8 [c]Ex 32:9 [d]Nu 25:4; 2Ch 29:10
30:9 [e]Dt 30:2-5; Isa 1:16; 55:7 [f]1Ki 8:50; Ps 106:46 [g]Ex 34:6-7; Dt 4:31; Mic 7:18
30:10 [h]2Ch 36:16
30:11 [i]ver 25
30:12 [j]Jer 32:39; Eze 11:19; Php 2:13
30:13 [k]Nu 28:16
30:14 [l]2Ch 28:24 [m]2Sa 15:23

conscientious in consecrating themselves than the priests had been. 35There were burnt offerings in abundance, together with the fat[s] of the fellowship offerings[t] and the drink offerings[u] that accompanied the burnt offerings.

So the service of the temple of the LORD was reestablished. 36Hezekiah and all the people rejoiced at what God had brought about for his people, because it was done so quickly.

Hezekiah Celebrates the Passover

30 Hezekiah sent word to all Israel and Judah and also wrote letters to Ephraim and Manasseh,[v] inviting them to come to the temple of the LORD in Jerusalem and celebrate the Passover[w] to the LORD, the God of Israel. 2The king and his officials and the whole assembly in Jerusalem decided to celebrate[x] the Passover in the second month. 3They had not been able to celebrate it at the regular time because not enough priests had consecrated[y] themselves and the people had not assembled in Jerusalem. 4The plan seemed right both to the king and to the whole assembly. 5They decided to send a proclamation throughout Israel, from Beersheba to Dan,[z] calling the people to come to Jerusalem and celebrate the Passover to the LORD, the God of Israel. It had not been celebrated in large numbers according to what was written.

6At the king's command, couriers went throughout Israel and Judah with letters from the king and from his officials, which read:

> "People of Israel, return to the LORD, the God of Abraham, Isaac and Israel, that he may return to you who are left, who have escaped from the hand of the kings of Assyria. 7Do not be like your parents[a] and your fellow Israelites, who were unfaithful to the LORD, the God of their ancestors, so that he made them an object of horror,[b] as you see. 8Do not be stiff-necked,[c] as your ancestors were; submit to the LORD. Come to his sanctuary, which he has consecrated forever. Serve the LORD your God, so that his fierce anger[d] will turn away from you. 9If you return[e] to the LORD, then your fellow Israelites and your children will be shown compassion[f] by their captors and will return to this land, for the LORD your God is gracious and compassionate.[g] He will not turn his face from you if you return to him."

10The couriers went from town to town in Ephraim and Manasseh, as far as Zebulun, but people scorned and ridiculed[h] them. 11Nevertheless, some from Asher, Manasseh and Zebulun humbled themselves and went to Jerusalem.[i] 12Also in Judah the hand of God was on the people to give them unity[j] of mind to carry out what the king and his officials had ordered, following the word of the LORD.

13A very large crowd of people assembled in Jerusalem to celebrate the Festival of Unleavened Bread[k] in the second month. 14They removed the altars[l] in Jerusalem and cleared away the incense altars and threw them into the Kidron Valley.[m]

15They slaughtered the Passover lamb on the fourteenth day of the second month. The priests and

---

29:35 fellowship offerings. See Lev 3:1–17; 7:12–18 and notes. **drink offerings.** See Num 15:1–21 and note; see also "Major OT Offerings and Sacrifices," p. 197).

30:1—31:1 *Hezekiah Celebrates the Passover.* Hezekiah organizes a double-length Passover that includes non-Israelites and worshipers who come down to Jerusalem from what had been the northern kingdom.

30:1 Passover. Was celebrated in association with the Festival of Unleavened Bread (see notes on Exod 12:17–18), one of the three major pilgrimage festivals; the other two were the Festival of Tabernacles (also known as the Festival of Ingathering/Booths/*Sukkôt*) and the Festival of Weeks (also known as Harvest/Pentecost). See Exod 23:14–19; Deut 16:1–17 and notes; see also "The Lord's Appointed Festivals," p. 229.

30:2–4 Passover was normally celebrated on the 14th of the month of Aviv (Num 9:1–3; 28:16–25), but the time required for the purification of the temple necessitates a delay in the Passover celebration. Although ceremonial uncleanness is a valid reason for a delayed celebration (Num 9:9–11), the delay implies apathy on the part of some of the priests. The delay was also connected to issues in convening an assembly that included those who journeyed from the north.

30:5 The letter from Hezekiah addresses the deeper issues of spirituality that get to the core of worshiping God on his terms (cf. 29:4–11). Hezekiah's invitation includes what had been the territory of Israel ("Beersheba to Dan"; cf. v. 1). This invitation reverses a neglected element of covenant worship in accordance with God's word.

30:6–9 Hezekiah's letter calls individuals to realign themselves with God's covenant (cf. 29:4–11). Hezekiah's exhortations are articulated both in the positive ("return to the LORD," v. 6; "submit to the LORD," v. 8; "come to his sanctuary," v. 8; "serve the LORD your God," v. 8) and the negative ("do not be ... unfaithful," v. 7; "do not be stiff-necked," v. 8). The core of these exhortations is "return to the LORD" (vv. 6,9), which implies repentance and submission to God's authority. Returning to God, who is "gracious and compassionate" (v. 9), will open the way for him to return to his people. The exhortation to return to God in the aftermath of exile would have poignant significance to the Chronicler's audience.

30:10–12 Although some in the north receive Hezekiah's invitation with scorn, others begin the process of returning to God physically ("to Jerusalem," v. 11) and spiritually ("humbled themselves," v. 11). In Judah there is "unity of mind" to follow "the word of the LORD" (v. 12).

30:14 removed the altars ... cleared away the incense altars. Most of these altars Ahaz had built (28:24–25). In parallel with actions taken by priests and Levites (29:15–17), Judahites and Israelites took tangible steps in their return to God (cf. 14:3; 15:16; 23:17; 34:3–7).

30:15 slaughtered the Passover lamb. See Exod 12:6; Deut 16:5–6.

the Levites were ashamed and consecrated[n] themselves and brought burnt offerings to the temple of
the LORD. [16]Then they took up their regular positions[o] as prescribed in the Law of Moses the man of
God. The priests splashed against the altar the blood handed to them by the Levites. [17]Since many in
the crowd had not consecrated themselves, the Levites had to kill[p] the Passover lambs for all those who
were not ceremonially clean and could not consecrate their lambs[a] to the LORD. [18]Although most of the
many people who came from Ephraim, Manasseh, Issachar and Zebulun had not purified themselves,[q]
yet they ate the Passover, contrary to what was written. But Hezekiah prayed for them, saying, "May the
LORD, who is good, pardon everyone [19]who sets their heart on seeking God — the LORD, the God of their
ancestors — even if they are not clean according to the rules of the sanctuary." [20]And the LORD heard[r]
Hezekiah and healed[s] the people.[t]

[21]The Israelites who were present in Jerusalem celebrated the Festival of Unleavened Bread[u] for seven
days with great rejoicing, while the Levites and priests praised the LORD every day with resounding instruments dedicated to the LORD.[b]

[22]Hezekiah spoke encouragingly to all the Levites, who showed good understanding of the service
of the LORD. For the seven days they ate their assigned portion and offered fellowship offerings and
praised[c] the LORD, the God of their ancestors.

[23]The whole assembly then agreed to celebrate[v] the festival seven more days; so for another seven
days they celebrated joyfully. [24]Hezekiah king of Judah provided[w] a thousand bulls and seven thousand sheep and goats for the assembly, and the officials provided them with a thousand bulls and ten
thousand sheep and goats. A great number of priests consecrated themselves. [25]The entire assembly of
Judah rejoiced, along with the priests and Levites and all who had assembled from Israel[x], including
the foreigners who had come from Israel and also those who resided in Judah. [26]There was great joy in
Jerusalem, for since the days of Solomon[y] son of David king of Israel there had been nothing like this
in Jerusalem. [27]The priests and the Levites stood to bless[z] the people, and God heard them, for their
prayer reached heaven, his holy dwelling place.

31 When all this had ended, the Israelites who were there went out to the towns of Judah, smashed
the sacred stones and cut down[a] the Asherah poles. They destroyed the high places and the
altars throughout Judah and Benjamin and in Ephraim and Manasseh. After they had destroyed all of
them, the Israelites returned to their own towns and to their own property.

Contributions for Worship

31:20-21pp — 2Ki 18:5-7

[2]Hezekiah[b] assigned the priests and Levites to divisions[c] — each of them according to their duties
as priests or Levites — to offer burnt offerings and fellowship offerings, to minister,[d] to give thanks and

30:15 [n]2Ch 29:34
30:16 [o]2Ch 35:10
30:17 [p]2Ch 29:34
30:18 [q]Ex 12:43-49; Nu 9:6-10
30:20 [r]2Ch 6:20 [s]2Ch 7:14; Mal 4:2 [t]Jas 5:16
30:21 [u]Ex 12:15,17; 13:6
30:23 [v]1Ki 8:65; 2Ch 7:9
30:24 [w]1Ki 8:5; 2Ch 29:34; 35:7; Ezr 6:17; 8:35
30:25 [x]ver 11
30:26 [y]2Ch 7:8
30:27 [z]Ex 39:43; Nu 6:23; Dt 26:15; 2Ch 23:18; Ps 68:5
31:1 [a]2Ki 18:4; 2Ch 32:12; Isa 36:7
31:2 [b]2Ch 29:9 [c]1Ch 24:1 [d]1Ch 15:2

[a] *17* Or *consecrate themselves* [b] *21* Or *priests sang to the LORD every day, accompanied by the LORD's instruments of praise* [c] *22* Or *and confessed their sins to*

The Passover celebration harks back to Israel's deliverance and departure from Egypt (see Exod 12:1 – 30 and notes) en route to inaugurating a covenantal relationship with God (see Exod 19:5 – 6 and note; cf. 1 Pet 2:9 – 10 and notes). The Passover celebrated God's gracious deliverance of his people *by means of blood* (Exod 12:13,23; cf. John 1:29; 1 Cor 5:7) as well as the inauguration of a covenant confirmed *by means of blood* (Exod 24:3 – 8; cf. Matt 26:28; Heb 9:14).

30:17 had not consecrated themselves. Not surprising given the spiritually dark period in Judah during the rule of Ahaz. Levites address this issue by sacrificing the Passover lambs belonging to those who were ceremonially unclean.

30:18 had not purified themselves, yet they ate the Passover, contrary to what was written. Surprising given the frequent refrain of Hezekiah's actions being shaped through written revelation (vv. 12,16; 29:15,25; cf. 31:3,21). But the outworking of this dilemma emphasizes that God is fundamentally concerned with the *inward* disposition of a person (everyone "who sets their heart on seeking God," v. 19) as opposed to the *outward* ritual ("not clean according to the rules of the sanctuary," v. 19).

30:20 Hezekiah's prayer recalls the principle of God's *hearing* ("the LORD heard Hezekiah") and *healing* ("and healed the people"), which was underscored in Solomon's temple dedication prayer (6:12 – 42). The healing God effected was spiritual in nature (7:14; Ps 41:4).

30:23 The whole assembly then agreed to celebrate the festival seven more days. Suggests a spirit of unity in the community. The two-week length of the festival echoes the duration of Solomon's temple dedication (7:8 – 10).

30:25 entire assembly. Includes priests, Levites, pilgrims from the north, foreigners, and Judahites. **foreigners.** Non-Israelites; they are included in the Mosaic regulations for Passover (Num 9:14).

30:26 there had been nothing like this in Jerusalem. The deep unity of this diverse group along with the various anomalies of Hezekiah's Passover celebration (cf. vv. 2,17 – 18,23) are reflected in this summary statement.

31:2 – 21 *Contributions for Worship.* Hezekiah's focus on covenant fidelity and worship flow into generosity for both God's house and those dedicated to leading worship and teaching the ways of God.

31:2 Hezekiah's assignments reflect the organization established in

31:2 [e]Ps 7:17; 9:2; 47:6; 71:22 [f]1Ch 23:28-32
31:3 [g]1Ch 29:3; 2Ch 35:7; Eze 45:17 [h]Nu 28:1-29:40
31:4 [i]Nu 18:8; Dt 18:8; Ne 13:10; Mal 2:7
31:5 [j]Nu 18:12,24; Ne 13:12; Eze 44:30 [k]Dt 12:17
31:6 [l]Lev 27:30; Ne 13:10-12 [m]Dt 14:28; Ru 3:7
31:7 [n]Ex 23:16
31:8 [o]Ps 144:13-15
31:10 [p]2Sa 8:17 [q]Ex 36:5; Eze 44:30; Mal 3:10-12
31:12 [r]2Ch 35:9
31:13 [s]2Ch 35:9
31:15 [t]2Ch 29:12 [u]Jos 21:9-19
31:16 [v]1Ch 23:3; Ezr 3:4
31:19 [w]ver 12-15; Lev 25:34; Nu 35:2-5
31:20 [x]2Ki 20:3; 22:2

to sing praises[e] at the gates of the LORD's dwelling.[f] [3]The king contributed[g] from his own possessions for the morning and evening burnt offerings and for the burnt offerings on the Sabbaths, at the New Moons and at the appointed festivals as written in the Law of the LORD.[h] [4]He ordered the people living in Jerusalem to give the portion[i] due the priests and Levites so they could devote themselves to the Law of the LORD. [5]As soon as the order went out, the Israelites generously gave the firstfruits[j] of their grain, new wine,[k] olive oil and honey and all that the fields produced. They brought a great amount, a tithe of everything. [6]The people of Israel and Judah who lived in the towns of Judah also brought a tithe[l] of their herds and flocks and a tithe of the holy things dedicated to the LORD their God, and they piled them in heaps.[m] [7]They began doing this in the third month and finished in the seventh month.[n] [8]When Hezekiah and his officials came and saw the heaps, they praised the LORD and blessed[o] his people Israel.

[9]Hezekiah asked the priests and Levites about the heaps; [10]and Azariah the chief priest, from the family of Zadok,[p] answered, "Since the people began to bring their contributions to the temple of the LORD, we have had enough to eat and plenty to spare, because the LORD has blessed his people, and this great amount is left over."[q]

[11]Hezekiah gave orders to prepare storerooms in the temple of the LORD, and this was done. [12]Then they faithfully brought in the contributions, tithes and dedicated gifts. Konaniah,[r] a Levite, was the overseer in charge of these things, and his brother Shimei was next in rank. [13]Jehiel, Azaziah, Nahath, Asahel, Jerimoth, Jozabad,[s] Eliel, Ismakiah, Mahath and Benaiah were assistants of Konaniah and Shimei his brother. All these served by appointment of King Hezekiah and Azariah the official in charge of the temple of God.

[14]Kore son of Imnah the Levite, keeper of the East Gate, was in charge of the freewill offerings given to God, distributing the contributions made to the LORD and also the consecrated gifts. [15]Eden,[t] Miniamin, Jeshua, Shemaiah, Amariah and Shekaniah assisted him faithfully in the towns[u] of the priests, distributing to their fellow priests according to their divisions, old and young alike.

[16]In addition, they distributed to the males three years old or more whose names were in the genealogical records[v]—all who would enter the temple of the LORD to perform the daily duties of their various tasks, according to their responsibilities and their divisions. [17]And they distributed to the priests enrolled by their families in the genealogical records and likewise to the Levites twenty years old or more, according to their responsibilities and their divisions. [18]They included all the little ones, the wives, and the sons and daughters of the whole community listed in these genealogical records. For they were faithful in consecrating themselves.

[19]As for the priests, the descendants of Aaron, who lived on the farmlands around their towns or in any other towns,[w] men were designated by name to distribute portions to every male among them and to all who were recorded in the genealogies of the Levites.

[20]This is what Hezekiah did throughout Judah, doing what was good and right and faithful[x]

Mosaic law and further developed under David and Solomon (8:14–15; 1 Chr 23:1–32; 25:1–6; 28:13).

31:3 from his own possessions. Reflects Hezekiah's generosity toward the Lord's work (cf. 9:10–11; 1 Chr 29:2–5) as well as his continued commitment to do what was "written in the Law of the LORD" (see 29:15,25; 30:12,16; 31:21). This brief synopsis of temple worship reflects Hezekiah's knowledge of Pentateuch instructions on sacrifices (Exod 29:38–39; Num 28–29) and festivals (cf. Exod 23:14–19; 31:3; Num 10:10).

31:4–8 In conjunction with his organization of priests and Levites, Hezekiah takes steps to provide food and funds for these servants of the temple so that they may "devote themselves to the Law of the LORD" (v. 4), as reflected in the law (cf. Deut 12:5–19; 14:22–27). Faithfulness in giving tithes and offerings was mixed during the postexilic period (Neh 10:35–39; 13:10–13; Mal 3:8–10).

31:5,6 tithe. Grain, new wine, and oil are part of offerings appointed for priests (Num 18:9,12). In addition, priests received part of the offerings presented to God (Num 18:9; Lev 6:16–18,26; 7:6,28–34), firstfruits from the land (Num 18:13), and other animals and items devoted to the Lord (Num 18:18–19). All this relates to the reality that priests did not have a land inheritance and thus were limited in their ability to grow crops or raise animals (Num 18:20). Such gifts of food provide for the sustenance of the priests and their families (vv. 9–10,18; Num 18:9–11,13). Levites were granted "all the tithes in Israel as their inheritance" (Num 18:21). Like priests, the Levites did not receive a land inheritance and thus were unable to farm or pasture flocks (Num 18:23–24; Deut 10:9; 18:1–2). Thus tithes were intended to provide sustenance for Levites and their families (vv. 9–10,18; Num 18:31; Deut 14:27–29). Levites were to set apart a tithe of their received tithe ("the best part," Num 18:30; see Num 18:25,29–32), which went to the priests (Num 18:28).

31:9 heaps. This great display of generosity is reminiscent of other pivotal moments in Israel's history, including the construction of the tabernacle (Exod 36:2–7; cf. 1 Chr 29:6–9).

31:12–19 The stewardship of accumulating tithes serves as a means to God's blessing (Deut 14:29). The faithfulness of those overseeing stewardship is an aspect of spiritual service.

31:20–21 good ... right ... faithful ... obedience ... sought his God ... worked wholeheartedly ... prospered. Similar to the opening statement on Hezekiah's reign (29:2). The words frame the overwhelmingly

before the LORD his God. 21 In everything that he undertook in the service of God's temple and in
obedience to the law and the commands, he sought his God and worked wholeheartedly. And so he
prospered.[y]

Sennacherib Threatens Jerusalem

32:9-19pp — 2Ki 18:17-35; Isa 36:2-20
32:20-21pp — 2Ki 19:35-37; Isa 37:36-38

32 After all that Hezekiah had so faithfully done, Sennacherib[z] king of Assyria came and invaded Judah. He laid siege to the fortified cities, thinking to conquer them for himself.
2 When Hezekiah saw that Sennacherib had come and that he intended to wage war against Jerusalem,[a] 3 he consulted with his officials and military staff about blocking off the water from the
springs outside the city, and they helped him. 4 They gathered a large group of people who blocked all
the springs[b] and the stream that flowed through the land.
"Why should the kings[a] of Assyria come and find plenty of
water?" they said. 5 Then he worked hard repairing all the
broken sections of the wall[c] and building towers on it. He
built another wall outside that one and reinforced the terraces[b][d] of the City of David. He also made large numbers of
weapons[e] and shields.
6 He appointed military officers over the people and assembled them before him in the square at the city gate and
encouraged them with these words: 7 "Be strong and courageous.[f] Do not be afraid or discouraged[g] because of the king
of Assyria and the vast army with him, for there is a greater
power with us than with him.[h] 8 With him is only the arm of
flesh,[i] but with us[j] is the LORD our God to help us and to fight
our battles."[k] And the people gained confidence from what
Hezekiah the king of Judah said.
9 Later, when Sennacherib king of Assyria and all his forces
were laying siege to Lachish,[l] he sent his officers to Jerusalem
with this message for Hezekiah king of Judah and for all the
people of Judah who were there:

[a] 4 Hebrew; Septuagint and Syriac *king* [b] 5 Or *the Millo*

The Assyrians attack Lachish (2 Chr 32:9).

31:21 [y] Dt 29:9
32:1 [z] 2Ki 18:13-19; Isa 36:1; 37:9,17,37
32:2 [a] Isa 22:7; Jer 1:15
32:4 [b] 2Ki 18:17; 20:20; Isa 22:9,11; Na 3:14
32:5 [c] 2Ch 25:23; Isa 22:10 [d] 1Ki 9:24; 1Ch 11:8 [e] Isa 22:8
32:7 [f] Dt 31:6; 1Ch 22:13 [g] 2Ch 20:15 [h] Nu 14:9; 2Ki 6:16
32:8 [i] Job 40:9; Isa 52:10; Jer 17:5; 32:21 [j] Dt 3:22; 1Sa 17:45; 2Ch 13:12 [k] 1Ch 5:22; 2Ch 20:17; Ps 20:7; Isa 28:6
32:9 [l] Jos 10:3,31

positive events of Hezekiah's reign (chs. 29–31) and create a literary separation between these positive events and the following narrative (ch. 32), which reveals Hezekiah's imperfections.

32:1–23 *Sennacherib Threatens Jerusalem.* After Hezekiah's reforms, Judah faces a significant threat from the Assyrian Empire. Hezekiah's reforms likely contribute to his desire to throw off the Assyrian yoke he inherited from Ahaz. Following the death of Sargon II and the ascension of Sennacherib (705 BC), Hezekiah takes steps to assert Judah's independence and prepare for an Assyrian invasion (vv. 2–5; 2 Kgs 18:7). Several passages imply support from Egypt and Babylon for Hezekiah's rebellion against Assyria (v. 31; 2 Kgs 18:20–21,24; 20:12–19; Isa 36:5–6,9; 39:1–8). As seen in earlier incidents involving Asa (16:1–9), Amaziah (25:6–10), and Ahaz (28:5–25), attempts at military-political alliances theologically reflect trust in humans rather than God. Hezekiah's misdirected trust in Babylon drew the rebuke of the prophet Isaiah, ultimately foreshadowing the Babylonian captivity (Isa 39:3–7).

32:2–5 In light of the looming Assyrian invasion, Hezekiah takes impressive steps to prepare Judah for the onslaught of the Assyrian army. Sennacherib's distraction with Babylonian unrest gives Hezekiah about four years to prepare (ca. 705–701 BC).

32:3 blocking off the water. See note on v. 30.

32:5 another wall. Known as the Broad Wall (Neh 3:8; 12:38). This 20-foot-thick (6-meter-thick) wall expands Jerusalem toward the west and allows the city to accommodate the rising population as the Assyrian invasion drew near. **the terraces.** See NIV text note; see also notes on 2 Sam 5:9; 1 Kgs 9:15.

32:6–8 In additional to physical preparations, Hezekiah seeks to prepare the hearts of the men who would defend Judah. The Chronicler's summary of the Assyrian threat against Judah unfolds as a battle of words and ideologies. The people "gained confidence" through Hezekiah's exhortation (v. 8).

32:7 Be strong and courageous. Cf. 1 Chr 22:13; Deut 31:6–8; Josh 1:5–9. It means being immovably committed to obedience and trust in God. It also means being rooted in God's presence ("with us is the LORD our God," v. 8), a reality greater than any weapon an army could muster.

32:9–19 The message of the Assyrian taunt was the opposite of the exhortation Hezekiah delivered (vv. 7–8). The words of the officials are reminiscent of the taunts of Goliath, who likewise mocked "the armies of the living God" (1 Sam 17:26). The message from Sennacherib implies that the Assyrians were aware of Hezekiah's reforms (v. 12) and even Hezekiah's faith in God's deliverance (vv. 10–11).

32:9 Lachish. A well-fortified garrison city located in the western foothills about 30 miles (48 kilometers) from Jerusalem. Sennacherib's palace at Nineveh depicts this siege with over 60 feet (18.3 meters) of wall reliefs. See note on 2 Kgs 18:14.

32:10 [m] Eze 29:16
32:11 [n] Isa 37:10
32:12 [o] 2Ch 31:1
32:13 [p] ver 15
32:15 [q] Isa 37:10 [r] Da 3:15 [s] Ex 5:2
32:17 [t] Isa 37:14 [u] Ps 74:22; Isa 37:4,17 [v] 2Ki 19:12
32:19 [w] 2Ki 19:18; Ps 115:4-8; Isa 2:8; 17:8
32:21 [x] Ge 19:13 [y] 2Ki 19:7
32:23 [z] 2Ch 9:24; 17:5; Isa 45:14; Zec 14:16-17
32:25 [a] 2Ki 14:10; 2Ch 26:16 [b] 2Ch 19:2; 24:18
32:26 [c] Jer 26:18-19 [d] 2Ch 34:27,28; Isa 39:8
32:27 [e] 1Ch 29:12

10 “This is what Sennacherib king of Assyria says: On what are you basing your confidence,[m]
that you remain in Jerusalem under siege? 11 When Hezekiah says, ‘The LORD our God will save us
from the hand of the king of Assyria,’ he is misleading[n] you, to let you die of hunger and thirst.
12 Did not Hezekiah himself remove this god’s high places and altars, saying to Judah and Jerusalem, ‘You must worship before one altar[o] and burn sacrifices on it’?
13 “Do you not know what I and my predecessors have done to all the peoples of the other
lands? Were the gods of those nations ever able to deliver their land from my hand?[p] 14 Who of all
the gods of these nations that my predecessors destroyed has been able to save his people from
me? How then can your god deliver you from my hand? 15 Now do not let Hezekiah deceive[q] you
and mislead you like this. Do not believe him, for no god of any nation or kingdom has been able
to deliver[r] his people from my hand or the hand of my predecessors.[s] How much less will your
god deliver you from my hand!”

16 Sennacherib’s officers spoke further against the LORD God and against his servant Hezekiah. 17 The king
also wrote letters[t] ridiculing[u] the LORD, the God of Israel, and saying this against him: “Just as the gods[v] of
the peoples of the other lands did not rescue their people from my hand, so the god of Hezekiah will not
rescue his people from my hand.” 18 Then they called out in Hebrew to the people of Jerusalem who were
on the wall, to terrify them and make them afraid in order to capture the city. 19 They spoke about the God
of Jerusalem as they did about the gods of the other peoples of the world—the work of human hands.[w]
20 King Hezekiah and the prophet Isaiah son of Amoz cried out in prayer to heaven about this. 21 And
the LORD sent an angel,[x] who annihilated all the fighting men and the commanders and officers in
the camp of the Assyrian king. So he withdrew to his own land in disgrace. And when he went into the
temple of his god, some of his sons, his own flesh and blood, cut him down with the sword.[y]
22 So the LORD saved Hezekiah and the people of Jerusalem from the hand of Sennacherib king of
Assyria and from the hand of all others. He took care of them[a] on every side. 23 Many brought offerings
to Jerusalem for the LORD and valuable gifts[z] for Hezekiah king of Judah. From then on he was highly
regarded by all the nations.

Hezekiah’s Pride, Success and Death

32:24-33pp — 2Ki 20:1-21; Isa 37:21-38; 38:1-8

24 In those days Hezekiah became ill and was at the point of death. He prayed to the LORD, who answered him and gave him a miraculous sign. 25 But Hezekiah’s heart was proud[a] and he did not respond
to the kindness shown him; therefore the LORD’s wrath[b] was on him and on Judah and Jerusalem.
26 Then Hezekiah repented[c] of the pride of his heart, as did the people of Jerusalem; therefore the LORD’s
wrath did not come on them during the days of Hezekiah.[d]
27 Hezekiah had very great wealth and honor,[e] and he made treasuries for his silver and gold and
for his precious stones, spices, shields and all kinds of valuables. 28 He also made buildings to store the

[a] 22 Hebrew; Septuagint and Vulgate *He gave them rest*

32:20 Sharply contrasts with the sustained taunt of the Assyrian messengers and exemplifies the spirit of Chronicles, which shows that God is faithful to those who seek him (6:12—7:22).
32:21 an angel. Sent by God to decimate the Assyrian army (cf. 2 Kgs 19:35). **withdrew to his own land in disgrace.** Later, the sons of Sennacherib assassinate him.
32:22 the LORD saved ... Jerusalem. Although Jerusalem was spared as a result this divine deliverance (and a payoff from the palace and temple treasuries [see 2 Kgs 18:14–16 and notes on 2 Kgs 18:14–15]), Sennacherib’s invasion (701 BC) brought devastation and deportations to the balance of Judah.
32:24–33 *Hezekiah’s Pride, Success, and Death.* This concludes the Chronicler’s overview of Hezekiah’s reign and touches on positive and negative aspects of Hezekiah’s reign. These events are not necessarily in chronological order. Despite his imperfections, Hezekiah is buried with honor in the royal tombs.
32:24 In those days. Allows for the possibility that this illness happened earlier in Hezekiah’s reign (Isa 38:1–22). **Hezekiah became ill.** Ultimately, Hezekiah’s more serious “illness” was that of pride since “God opposes the proud but shows favor to the humble” (Jas 4:6). **sign.** The backward movement of the sun’s shadow (2 Kgs 20:8–11; Isa 38:7–8).
32:26 Hezekiah repented. Prayer and repentance are central to the Chronicler’s message of true spirituality. There is no limit to divine grace (cf. 33:12–13).
32:27–30 Hezekiah’s riches show God’s favor and have a close connection with wisdom (Prov 3:13–18; 8:15–21). Hezekiah’s blessings parallel those of David (1 Chr 29:28) and Solomon (1:11–12; 9:13–28; 1 Chr 29:25).
32:28–29 Hezekiah’s efforts at strategically storing food provisions are reflected in the discovery of more than 1,200 large storage containers (or pieces thereof) stamped with the notation “belonging to the king.”

The defeated Judahites appeal to Sennacherib for their lives.

harvest of grain, new wine and olive oil; and he made stalls for various kinds of cattle, and pens for
the flocks. 29He built villages and acquired great numbers of flocks and herds, for God had given him
very great riches.[f]

30It was Hezekiah who blocked[g] the upper outlet of the Gihon[h] spring and channeled the water down
to the west side of the City of David. He succeeded in everything he undertook. 31But when envoys were
sent by the rulers of Babylon[i] to ask him about the miraculous sign[j] that had occurred in the land, God
left him to test[k] him and to know everything that was in his heart.

32The other events of Hezekiah's reign and his acts of devotion are written in the vision of the
prophet Isaiah son of Amoz in the book of the kings of Judah and Israel. 33Hezekiah rested with his ancestors and was buried on the hill where the tombs of David's descendants are. All Judah and the people
of Jerusalem honored him when he died. And Manasseh his son succeeded him as king.

Manasseh King of Judah

33:1-10pp — 2Ki 21:1-10
33:18-20pp — 2Ki 21:17-18

33 Manasseh[l] was twelve years old when he became king, and he reigned in Jerusalem fifty-five
years. 2He did evil in the eyes of the LORD,[m] following the detestable[n] practices of the nations
the LORD had driven out before the Israelites. 3He rebuilt the high places his father Hezekiah had demolished; he also erected altars to the Baals and made Asherah poles.[o] He bowed down[p] to all the starry
hosts and worshiped them. 4He built altars in the temple of the LORD, of which the LORD had said, "My
Name[q] will remain in Jerusalem forever." 5In both courts of the temple of the LORD,[r] he built altars to

32:29 [f] 1Ch 29:12
32:30 [g] 2Ki 18:17 [h] 1Ki 1:33
32:31 [i] Isa 39:1 [j] ver 24; Isa 38:7 [k] Ge 22:1; Dt 8:16
33:1 [l] 1Ch 3:13
33:2 [m] Jer 15:4 [n] Dt 18:9; 2Ch 28:3
33:3 [o] Dt 16:21-22 [p] Dt 17:3; 2Ch 31:1
33:4 [q] 2Ch 7:16
33:5 [r] 2Ch 4:9

32:30 Gihon spring. Hezekiah's most impressive engineering achievement was tapping into the Gihon spring and channeling the water underground to the City of David. Since the only year-round source of water for Jerusalem was found outside the city walls, the lack of a safeguarded fresh water supply was an ongoing area of vulnerability for Jerusalem. To address this, Hezekiah set two teams of workmen about 1,750 feet (533 meters) apart to dig a tunnel to channel the Gihon water supply to a collection pool within the city. As a result, Jerusalem had access to fresh water that would be out of the view of the Assyrian army. The digging of this tunnel (known as Hezekiah's Tunnel and the Siloam Tunnel) was commemorated with an inscription placed within the tunnel where the two teams met.

32:31 envoys were sent. Chronologically, this visit likely preceded Sennacherib's invasion. If this is the case, the emissaries of the Babylonian leader Marduk-Baladan II likely visited Hezekiah to explore cooperation in their common goal of throwing off Assyrian rule (Babylon, like Judah, was an Assyrian vassal at this time). Placing confidence and trust outside of God is lamented in Chronicles and the prophetic literature (cf. Isa 31:1–3; 39:1–7). God's testing of Hezekiah's heart in the midst of the Assyrian crisis reveals imperfections in Hezekiah's trust and faith. The prophet Isaiah's rebuke of Hezekiah in this context foreshadow the Babylonian captivity (Isa 39:3–7).

33:1–20 *Manasseh King of Judah.* During the 55-year reign of Manasseh, Judah was a vassal to three Assyrian monarchs: Sennacherib, Esarhaddon, and Ashurbanipal. Manasseh reigned 697/96–643/42 BC, which likely included a ten-year coregency with Hezekiah (697/96–687/86 BC).

33:2–8 The breadth and depth of Manasseh's wickedness resembles his grandfather Ahaz rather than his godly father, Hezekiah. The enumeration of Manasseh's wicked practices evidences the very essence of Deuteronomic covenantal unfaithfulness (see Deut 18:9–13).

33:5 built altars to all the starry hosts. Cf. 2 Kgs 17:16; see note

33:6 [s]Lev 18:21; Dt 18:10; 2Ch 28:3 [t]Lev 19:31 [u]1Sa 28:13
33:7 [v]2Ch 7:16
33:8 [w]2Sa 7:10
33:9 [x]Jer 15:4
33:11 [y]Dt 28:36 [z]Ps 149:8
33:12 [a]2Ch 6:37; 32:26; 1Pe 5:6
33:14 [b]1Ki 1:33 [c]Ne 3:3; 12:39; Zep 1:10 [d]2Ch 27:3; Ne 3:26
33:15 [e]ver 3-7; 2Ki 23:12
33:16 [f]Lev 7:11-18
33:19 [g]2Ch 6:37 [h]2Ki 21:17
33:20 [i]2Ki 21:18; 2Ch 21:20
33:21 [j]1Ch 3:14

all the starry hosts. [6]He sacrificed his children[s] in the fire in the Valley of Ben Hinnom, practiced divination and witchcraft, sought omens, and consulted mediums[t] and spiritists.[u] He did much evil in the eyes of the LORD, arousing his anger.

[7]He took the image he had made and put it in God's temple,[v] of which God had said to David and to his son Solomon, "In this temple and in Jerusalem, which I have chosen out of all the tribes of Israel, I will put my Name forever. [8]I will not again make the feet of the Israelites leave the land[w] I assigned to your ancestors, if only they will be careful to do everything I commanded them concerning all the laws, decrees and regulations given through Moses." [9]But Manasseh led Judah and the people of Jerusalem astray, so that they did more evil than the nations the LORD had destroyed before the Israelites.[x]

[10]The LORD spoke to Manasseh and his people, but they paid no attention. [11]So the LORD brought against them the army commanders of the king of Assyria, who took Manasseh prisoner,[y] put a hook in his nose, bound him with bronze shackles[z] and took him to Babylon. [12]In his distress he sought the favor of the LORD his God and humbled[a] himself greatly before the God of his ancestors. [13]And when he prayed to him, the LORD was moved by his entreaty and listened to his plea; so he brought him back to Jerusalem and to his kingdom. Then Manasseh knew that the LORD is God.

[14]Afterward he rebuilt the outer wall of the City of David, west of the Gihon[b] spring in the valley, as far as the entrance of the Fish Gate[c] and encircling the hill of Ophel;[d] he also made it much higher. He stationed military commanders in all the fortified cities in Judah.

[15]He got rid of the foreign gods and removed[e] the image from the temple of the LORD, as well as all the altars he had built on the temple hill and in Jerusalem; and he threw them out of the city. [16]Then he restored the altar of the LORD and sacrificed fellowship offerings and thank offerings[f] on it, and told Judah to serve the LORD, the God of Israel. [17]The people, however, continued to sacrifice at the high places, but only to the LORD their God.

[18]The other events of Manasseh's reign, including his prayer to his God and the words the seers spoke to him in the name of the LORD, the God of Israel, are written in the annals of the kings of Israel.[a] [19]His prayer and how God was moved by his entreaty, as well as all his sins and unfaithfulness, and the sites where he built high places and set up Asherah poles and idols before he humbled[g] himself — all these are written in the records of the seers.[bh] [20]Manasseh rested with his ancestors and was buried[i] in his palace. And Amon his son succeeded him as king.

Amon King of Judah

33:21-25pp — 2Ki 21:19-24

[21]Amon[j] was twenty-two years old when he became king, and he reigned in Jerusalem two years. [22]He did evil in the eyes of the LORD, as his father Manasseh had done. Amon worshiped and offered

[a] *18* That is, Judah, as frequently in 2 Chronicles [b] *19* One Hebrew manuscript and Septuagint; most Hebrew manuscripts *of Hozai*

there. The worship of celestial bodies was common in the biblical world, as reflected in the number of gods named after the moon, the sun, and planets. Manasseh's actions reverse the purification of the temple that Hezekiah's reforms accomplished.

33:6 sacrificed his children. See note on 28:3.

33:10 This summary of God's efforts to bring his people back to himself is reminiscent of the closing verses of Chronicles (36:15–16).

33:11 put a hook in his nose. Implies disloyalty. **took him to Babylon.** As a consequence for unfaithfulness. Since Babylon was under the hegemony of Assyria at this time, this location may relate to the Assyrian king's attempt to diffuse recurring Babylonian uprisings. **Babylon.** Foreshadows what later happened to Judah during the exile.

33:12 sought the favor of ... God and humbled himself greatly. Unlike Ahaz (28:19,22). This short summary of Manasseh's repentance and God's response in v. 13 (absent in the Kings account, which emphasizes the role Manasseh played in the exile of Judah) is perhaps one of the most hope-inducing passages in the Bible. God can restore anyone who seeks him in true repentance, regardless of the person's ungodliness (1 Tim 1:15).

33:13 the LORD ... brought him back. The Lord brings a repentant Manasseh back from exile in Babylon and restores his kingdom (cf. Nebuchadnezzar in Dan 4). **Then Manasseh knew.** God's act of graciousness deepens Manasseh's understanding of God's strength and grace. Such restoration of a Davidic king following time in Babylon would likely give hope to the Chronicler's audience that the Davidic dynasty could likewise be restored if the people would humble themselves and seek the Lord.

33:15 got rid of the foreign gods ... removed the image from the temple ... the altars he had built. As a tangible reflection of his inner spiritual renewal.

33:16 restored the altar of the LORD. To reinstitute sacrificial worship. Although Manasseh has previously "led Judah and the people of Jerusalem astray" (v. 9), he now tells Judah to "serve the LORD."

33:17 Although temple service is reestablished, the people do not abandon their propensity for sacrificing at high places. While these high place sacrifices are "only to the LORD," this practice is nonetheless against God's established parameters.

33:21–25 *Amon King of Judah.* Amon briefly reigned 643/642–641/640 BC, a time of significant Assyrian power in the biblical world (see "Rul-

sacrifices to all the idols Manasseh had made. 23But unlike his father Manasseh, he did not humble[k] himself before the LORD; Amon increased his guilt.

24Amon's officials conspired against him and assassinated him in his palace. 25Then the people[l] of the land killed all who had plotted against King Amon, and they made Josiah his son king in his place.

Josiah's Reforms

34:1-2pp — 2Ki 22:1-2
34:3-7Ref — 2Ki 23:4-20
34:8-13pp — 2Ki 22:3-7

34 Josiah[m] was eight years old when he became king,[n] and he reigned in Jerusalem thirty-one years. 2He did what was right in the eyes of the LORD and followed the ways of his father David,[o] not turning aside to the right or to the left.

3In the eighth year of his reign, while he was still young, he began to seek the God[p] of his father David. In his twelfth year he began to purge Judah and Jerusalem of high places, Asherah poles and idols. 4Under his direction the altars of the Baals were torn down; he cut to pieces the incense altars that were above them, and smashed the Asherah poles[q] and the idols. These he broke to pieces and scattered over the graves of those who had sacrificed to them.[r] 5He burned[s] the bones of the priests on their altars, and so he purged Judah and Jerusalem. 6In the towns of Manasseh, Ephraim and Simeon, as far as Naphtali, and in the ruins around them, 7he tore down the altars and the Asherah poles and crushed the idols to powder[t] and cut to pieces all the incense altars throughout Israel. Then he went back to Jerusalem.

8In the eighteenth year of Josiah's reign, to purify the land and the temple, he sent Shaphan son of Azaliah and Maaseiah the ruler of the city, with Joah son of Joahaz, the recorder, to repair the temple of the LORD his God.

9They went to Hilkiah[u] the high priest and gave him the money that had been brought into the temple of God, which the Levites who were the gatekeepers had collected from the people of Manasseh, Ephraim and the entire remnant of Israel and from all the people of Judah and Benjamin and the inhabitants of Jerusalem. 10Then they entrusted it to the men appointed to supervise the work on the LORD's temple. These men paid the workers who repaired and restored the temple. 11They also gave money[v] to the carpenters and builders to purchase dressed stone, and timber for joists and beams for the buildings that the kings of Judah had allowed to fall into ruin.[w]

12The workers labored faithfully.[x] Over them to direct them were Jahath and Obadiah, Levites descended from Merari, and Zechariah and Meshullam, descended from Kohath. The Levites — all who were skilled in playing musical instruments —[y] 13had charge of the laborers[z] and supervised all the workers from job to job. Some of the Levites were secretaries, scribes and gatekeepers.

33:23 [k]ver 12; Ex 10:3; 2Ch 7:14; Ps 18:27; 147:6; Pr 3:34
33:25 [l]2Ch 22:1
34:1 [m]1Ch 3:14 [n]Zep 1:1
34:2 [o]2Ch 29:2
34:3 [p]1Ki 13:2; 1Ch 16:11; 2Ch 15:2; 33:17,22
34:4 [q]Ex 34:13 [r]Ex 32:20; Lev 26:30; 2Ki 23:11; Mic 1:5
34:5 [s]1Ki 13:2
34:7 [t]Ex 32:20; 2Ch 31:1
34:9 [u]1Ch 6:13; 2Ch 35:8
34:11 [v]2Ch 24:12 [w]2Ch 33:4-7
34:12 [x]2Ki 12:15 [y]1Ch 25:1
34:13 [z]1Ch 23:4

ers of the Divided Kingdoms of Israel and Judah, p. 635; and "Kings of Assyria, Judah, Israel, and Aramea," p. 1332). His reign parallels and starkly contrasts with Manasseh's. Like Manasseh, Amon's sins are legion; but unlike Manasseh, he does not humble himself and seek the Lord. Sadly, one of the consequences of Manasseh's wicked years is the poor example he set for his son. Amon was assassinated just two years into his reign, ushering in the reign of Josiah.

33:24–25 The backdrop for Amon's assassination by his palace officials is not clear, but it may have been part of a larger political objective. The "people of the land" retaliate against Amon's officials and usher in the reign of Josiah — another situation in which this sociopolitical group plays a pivotal role (see note on 23:21).

34:1 — 36:1 *The Reign of Josiah.* As with Joash (24:1) and Manasseh (33:1), Josiah is very young when he begins his reign following the assassination of Amon (33:24). Josiah's 31-year reign extended from 641/40 to 609 BC, a time of decreasing Assyrian strength. During this time, Judah began to experience what might be described as "pseudo independence." This newfound freedom likely played a role in the wide array of reforms enacted by Josiah, which take place in three periods: his 8th year (ca. 633 BC; 34:3); his 12th year (ca. 629 BC; 34:3); and his 18th year (ca. 623 BC; 34:8). The prophetic ministries of Zephaniah and Jeremiah support Josiah's reforms.

34:1–33 *Josiah's Reforms and the Discovery of the Book of the Law.* Josiah's initial period of reform (in his eighth year [v. 3]) focused on seeking God. The concept of seeking God with all of one's being is a foundational element of rightly relating to God (Deut 4:29–31; 6:5; 10:12–21). The second phase of Josiah's reforms (his 12th year [vv. 3–7]) focused on destroying idolatry (Deut 16:21–22). The final stage in Josiah's reforms (his 18th year [vv. 8–32]) focused on the restoration of the temple, which included the discovery of the Book of the Law. The Chronicler emphasizes the whole community's involvement (v. 9), the faithfulness of those involved in the refurbishment (vv. 10–13,16–17), and the oversight the high priest and Levites provided (vv. 9,12–13).

34:2 Josiah is one of the few kings of Judah noted as following the ways of David — like Jehoshaphat (17:3–4) and Hezekiah (29:2). Josiah focuses on the ways of God; he does not turn aside to the right or left. This describes a focused, disciplined, God-pleasing spiritual life (Deut 5:32–33).

34:6–7 The weakening of the Assyrian Empire greatly reduced (and eventually eliminated) Assyrian presence in what had been the northern kingdom and enabled Josiah's reforms to stretch from Judah to cities throughout Israel, "as far as Naphtali." This implies that Josiah's influence extended beyond the vicinity of the Sea of Galilee.

34:15 [a] 2Ki 22:8; Ezr 7:6; Ne 8:1
34:19 [b] Dt 28:3-68 [c] Jos 7:6; Isa 36:22; 37:1
34:20 [d] 2Ki 22:3
34:21 [e] 2Ch 29:8; La 2:4; 4:11; Eze 36:18
34:22 [f] Ex 15:20; Ne 6:14
34:24 [g] Pr 16:4; Isa 3:9; Jer 40:2; 42:10; 44:2,11 [h] 2Ch 36:14-20 [i] Dt 28:15-68
34:25 [j] 2Ch 33:3-6; Jer 22:9
34:27 [k] 2Ch 12:7; 32:26 [l] Ex 10:3; 2Ch 6:37
34:28 [m] 2Ch 35:20-25 [n] 2Ch 32:26
34:30 [o] 2Ki 23:2; Ne 8:1-3

The Book of the Law Found

34:14-28pp — 2Ki 22:8-20
34:29-32pp — 2Ki 23:1-3

[14]While they were bringing out the money that had been taken into the temple of the LORD, Hilkiah the priest found the Book of the Law of the LORD that had been given through Moses. [15]Hilkiah said to Shaphan the secretary, "I have found the Book of the Law[a] in the temple of the LORD." He gave it to Shaphan.

[16]Then Shaphan took the book to the king and reported to him: "Your officials are doing everything that has been committed to them. [17]They have paid out the money that was in the temple of the LORD and have entrusted it to the supervisors and workers." [18]Then Shaphan the secretary informed the king, "Hilkiah the priest has given me a book." And Shaphan read from it in the presence of the king.

[19]When the king heard the words of the Law,[b] he tore[c] his robes. [20]He gave these orders to Hilkiah, Ahikam son of Shaphan[d], Abdon son of Micah,[*a*] Shaphan the secretary and Asaiah the king's attendant: [21]"Go and inquire of the LORD for me and for the remnant in Israel and Judah about what is written in this book that has been found. Great is the LORD's anger that is poured out[e] on us because those who have gone before us have not kept the word of the LORD; they have not acted in accordance with all that is written in this book."

[22]Hilkiah and those the king had sent with him[*b*] went to speak to the prophet[f] Huldah, who was the wife of Shallum son of Tokhath,[*c*] the son of Hasrah,[*d*] keeper of the wardrobe. She lived in Jerusalem, in the New Quarter.

[23]She said to them, "This is what the LORD, the God of Israel, says: Tell the man who sent you to me, [24]'This is what the LORD says: I am going to bring disaster[g] on this place and its people[h] — all the curses[i] written in the book that has been read in the presence of the king of Judah. [25]Because they have forsaken me[j] and burned incense to other gods and aroused my anger by all that their hands have made,[*e*] my anger will be poured out on this place and will not be quenched.' [26]Tell the king of Judah, who sent you to inquire of the LORD, 'This is what the LORD, the God of Israel, says concerning the words you heard: [27]Because your heart was responsive[k] and you humbled[l] yourself before God when you heard what he spoke against this place and its people, and because you humbled yourself before me and tore your robes and wept in my presence, I have heard you, declares the LORD. [28]Now I will gather you to your ancestors,[m] and you will be buried in peace. Your eyes will not see all the disaster I am going to bring on this place and on those who live here.'"[n]

So they took her answer back to the king.

[29]Then the king called together all the elders of Judah and Jerusalem. [30]He went up to the temple of the LORD[o] with the people of Judah, the inhabitants of Jerusalem, the priests and the Levites — all

a 20 Also called *Akbor son of Micaiah* *b* 22 One Hebrew manuscript, Vulgate and Syriac; most Hebrew manuscripts do not have *had sent with him.* *c* 22 Also called *Tikvah* *d* 22 Also called *Harbas* *e* 25 Or *by everything they have done*

34:14 Hilkiah the priest found the Book of the Law of the LORD. This episode often comes as a surprise to readers who cannot imagine a biblical scroll being "lost" in the temple. However, the foundation and walls of temples in the biblical world were commonly used as repositories for religious texts. With this in mind, Hilkiah's discovery of the Book of the Law in conjunction with the temple repairs is not as peculiar as it may at first appear. **the Book of the Law of the LORD.** Also called the "Book of the Law" (v. 15) and the "Book of the Covenant" (v. 30). While this book is commonly identified as the book of Deuteronomy (especially Deut 4–31), points of comparison can also be drawn with Exod 20–24; Lev 26; Num 9–10. See note on 23:11.

34:21 have not acted in accordance with all that is written in this book Despite Josiah's earlier reforms, reading God's word revealed the degree to which he and his predecessors had fallen short of God's will. Josiah's words and actions reflect a recognition of the authority vested in God's word.

34:22 the prophet Huldah. Little is known about this prophetess who declares God's judgment on the nation (cf. Barak and Deborah; Judg 4–5).

34:23–28 Huldah proclaims a disaster on the land and people that would be meted out according to covenantal stipulations (Lev 26:14–43; Deut 28:15–68). She also declares that Josiah would not experience the covenantal judgments decreed for Judah.

34:27 heart was responsive ... humbled yourself. The reasons why Josiah will not see the devastation to come on Judah.

34:28 buried in peace. There is a degree of tension between this and the death of Josiah at the hand of the army of Pharaoh Necho (35:23–24). The core emphasis of Huldah's prophecy is that Josiah will be spared from the disaster to befall Judah ("your eyes will not see all the disaster"). Also it is possible that Josiah's trust in something apart from God (implicit in the support of Babylon) cause him to forfeit part of this promise (cf. 1 Sam 2:30; Jer 18:5–10).

34:30 all the people from the least to the greatest. The full spectrum of the community (elders, people of Judah, inhabitants of Jerusalem, priests, and Levites) engages in a solemn ceremony of hearing God's word and renewing their commitment to the covenant.

the people from the least to the greatest. He read in their hearing all the words of the Book of the Covenant, which had been found in the temple of the LORD. 31The king stood by his pillar[p] and renewed
the covenant[q] in the presence of the LORD — to follow[r] the LORD and keep his commands, statutes and
decrees with all his heart and all his soul, and to obey the words of the covenant written in this book.
32Then he had everyone in Jerusalem and Benjamin pledge themselves to it; the people of Jerusalem
did this in accordance with the covenant of God, the God of their ancestors.
33Josiah removed all the detestable[s] idols from all the territory belonging to the Israelites, and he
had all who were present in Israel serve the LORD their God. As long as he lived, they did not fail to follow
the LORD, the God of their ancestors.

Josiah Celebrates the Passover

35:1,18-19pp — 2Ki 23:21-23

35 Josiah celebrated the Passover[t] to the LORD in Jerusalem, and the Passover lamb was slaughtered on the fourteenth day of the first month. 2He appointed the priests to their duties and
encouraged them in the service of the LORD's temple. 3He said to the Levites, who instructed[u] all Israel
and who had been consecrated to the LORD: "Put the sacred ark in the temple that Solomon son of David
king of Israel built. It is not to be carried about on your shoulders. Now serve the LORD your God and his
people Israel. 4Prepare yourselves by families in your divisions,[v] according to the instructions written
by David king of Israel and by his son Solomon.
5"Stand in the holy place with a group of Levites for each subdivision of the families of your fellow
Israelites, the lay people. 6Slaughter the Passover lambs, consecrate yourselves[w] and prepare the lambs
for your fellow Israelites, doing what the LORD commanded through Moses."
7Josiah provided for all the lay people who were there a total of thirty thousand lambs and goats for
the Passover offerings,[x] and also three thousand cattle — all from the king's own possessions.[y]
8His officials also contributed[z] voluntarily to the people and the priests and Levites. Hilkiah,[a] Zechariah and Jehiel, the officials in charge of God's temple, gave the priests twenty-six hundred Passover
offerings and three hundred cattle. 9Also Konaniah[b] along with Shemaiah and Nethanel, his brothers,
and Hashabiah, Jeiel and Jozabad,[c] the leaders of the Levites, provided five thousand Passover offerings
and five hundred head of cattle for the Levites.
10The service was arranged and the priests stood in their places with the Levites in their divisions[d]
as the king had ordered.[e] 11The Passover lambs were slaughtered,[f] and the priests splashed against the
altar the blood handed to them, while the Levites skinned the animals. 12They set aside the burnt offerings to give them to the subdivisions of the families of the people to offer to the LORD, as it is written
in the Book of Moses. They did the same with the cattle. 13They roasted the Passover animals over the
fire as prescribed,[g] and boiled the holy offerings in pots, caldrons and pans and served them quickly
to all the people. 14After this, they made preparations for themselves and for the priests, because the
priests, the descendants of Aaron, were sacrificing the burnt offerings and the fat portions[h] until nightfall. So the Levites made preparations for themselves and for the Aaronic priests.
15The musicians,[i] the descendants of Asaph, were in the places prescribed by David, Asaph, Heman
and Jeduthun the king's seer. The gatekeepers at each gate did not need to leave their posts, because
their fellow Levites made the preparations for them.
16So at that time the entire service of the LORD was carried out for the celebration of the Passover
and the offering of burnt offerings on the altar of the LORD, as King Josiah had ordered. 17The Israelites
who were present celebrated the Passover at that time and observed the Festival of Unleavened Bread for
seven days. 18The Passover had not been observed like this in Israel since the days of the prophet Samuel; and none of the kings of Israel had ever celebrated such a Passover as did Josiah, with the priests,

34:31 [p] 1Ki 7:15; 2Ki 11:14 [q] 2Ki 11:17; 2Ch 23:16; 29:10 [r] Dt 13:4
34:33 [s] ver 3-7; Dt 18:9
35:1 [t] Ex 12:1-30; Nu 9:3; 28:16
35:3 [u] Dt 33:10; 1Ch 23:26; 2Ch 5:7; 17:7
35:4 [v] ver 10; 1Ch 9:10-13; 24:1; 2Ch 8:14; Ezr 6:18
35:6 [w] Lev 11:44; 2Ch 29:5,15
35:7 [x] 2Ch 30:24 [y] 2Ch 31:3
35:8 [z] 1Ch 29:3; 2Ch 29:31-36 [a] 1Ch 6:13
35:9 [b] 2Ch 31:12 [c] 2Ch 31:13
35:10 [d] ver 4; Ezr 6:18 [e] 2Ch 30:16
35:11 [f] 2Ch 29:22,34; 30:17
35:13 [g] Ex 12:2-11; Lev 6:25; 1Sa 2:13-15
35:14 [h] Ex 29:13
35:15 [i] 1Ch 25:1; 26:12-19; 2Ch 29:30; Ne 12:46; Ps 68:25

34:31 all his heart and all his soul. Josiah models renewal by stressing his commitment to follow God and keep his commands (cf. Deut 6:5–9; 11:13). **obey.** Loving God is inseparable from keeping God's word (Deut 11:1; Matt 22:36–40; John 15:10,14; Rom 13:8–10).
34:33 As long as he lived. Anticipates the rapid downfall that happened in Judah following Josiah's death.
35:1–19 *Josiah Celebrates the Passover.* The Passover is celebrated in the same year as Josiah's extensive temple repairs (v. 19). Various statements throughout the Passover account — e.g., "as prescribed" (v. 13) and "as it is written in the Book of Moses" (v. 12) — indicate that the Book of the Covenant was central in organizing this Passover celebration.
35:18 The assessment of the Passover celebration under Hezekiah (30:26) is similar to this. Given the differences between these celebrations (including the anomalies in the Passover celebration under

35:20 [j]Isa 10:9; Jer 46:2 [k]Ge 2:14
35:21 [l]1Ki 13:18; 2Ki 18:25
35:22 [m]Jdg 5:19; 1Sa 28:8; 2Ch 18:29
35:23 [n]1Ki 22:34
35:25 [o]Jer 22:10,15-16

the Levites and all Judah and Israel who were there with the people of Jerusalem. [19]This Passover was
celebrated in the eighteenth year of Josiah's reign.

The Death of Josiah
35:20–36:1pp — 2Ki 23:28-30

[20]After all this, when Josiah had set the temple in order, Necho king of Egypt went up to fight at
Carchemish[j] on the Euphrates,[k] and Josiah marched out to meet him in battle. [21]But Necho sent messengers to him, saying, "What quarrel is there, king of Judah, between you and me? It is not you I am
attacking at this time, but the house with which I am at war. God has told[l] me to hurry; so stop opposing
God, who is with me, or he will destroy you."
[22]Josiah, however, would not turn away from him, but disguised[m] himself to engage him in battle. He
would not listen to what Necho had said at God's command but went to fight him on the plain of Megiddo.
[23]Archers[n] shot King Josiah, and he told his officers, "Take me away; I am badly wounded." [24]So
they took him out of his chariot, put him in his other chariot and brought him to Jerusalem, where
he died. He was buried in the tombs of his ancestors, and all Judah and Jerusalem mourned for him.
[25]Jeremiah composed laments for Josiah, and to this day all the male and female singers commemorate Josiah in the laments.[o] These became a tradition in Israel and are written in the Laments.
[26]The other events of Josiah's reign and his acts of devotion in accordance with what is written in
the Law of the Lord— [27]all the events, from beginning to end, are written in the book of the kings of
36 Israel and Judah. [1]And the people of the land took Jehoahaz son of Josiah and made him king
in Jerusalem in place of his father.

Jehoahaz King of Judah
36:2-4pp — 2Ki 23:31-34

[2]Jehoahaz[a] was twenty-three years old when he became king, and he reigned in Jerusalem three
months. [3]The king of Egypt dethroned him in Jerusalem and imposed on Judah a levy of a hundred

[a] 2 Hebrew *Joahaz,* a variant of *Jehoahaz;* also in verse 4

Hezekiah), Josiah's normative celebration and Hezekiah's non-normative celebration are both in a sense unique situations in the history of Israel. For more on the Passover, see note on 30:15.

35:20—36:1 *Josiah's Confrontation With Pharaoh Necho and Death.* Josiah's encounter with Pharaoh Necho II (Neco II) took place in 609 BC, 13–14 years after the discovery of the "Book of the Law" and the Passover celebration. The Assyrian Empire entered a rapid state of decline following the death of Ashurbanipal (627 BC); the Babylonians began encroaching into the southern regions of Assyria, and the Medes invaded the northern parts of Assyrian territory. The Medes and Babylonians joined forces to attack Nineveh, which fell in 612 BC. Despite the fall of Nineveh, a portion of the Assyrian leadership retreated from Nineveh to Harran, about 100 miles (160 kilometers) to the west. A couple of years later, the Medes and Babylonians again joined forces to eradicate what was left of the Assyrian Empire. The Egyptians, under Pharaoh Psammetichus I (Psamtik I), attempted to assist the Assyrians. Following this battle at Harran, Psammetichus I died, and his son Necho II became ruler and organized another attempt to help the Assyrians at Carchemish. Josiah attacked Necho as he was en route to support Assyria.

Josiah's decision to involve Judah in this conflict was disastrous. After a long period of Assyrian vassalage, Judah began to have independence in light of the contraction of the Assyrian Empire. But in the aftermath of Judah's battle with Necho at Megiddo (609 BC), Josiah was killed, and Judah became an Egyptian vassal. Only a few years later (605 BC) Judah became a Babylonian vassal. Thus, in the span of about two decades Judah shifted from Assyrian vassalage to (pseudo) independence to Egyptian vassalage to Babylonian vassalage. Judah's subsequent rebellions against Babylonia ultimately lead to destruction and captivity (586 BC).

35:20 This sequence of events is reminiscent to Hezekiah's conflict with Assyria following his reforms and Passover celebration (cf. 32:1).

35:21–24 Egypt's support of its former enemy Assyria likely involved maintaining the balance of power in the ancient Near East and control over trade routes in the Levant, the area between Anatolia (modern day Turkey) and Egypt that included Israel, Aram, Phoenicia, Moab, and Edom. The motives for Judah's support of the Babylonian–Median coalition (implicit in Josiah's attempt to interfere with Egypt's aid of Assyria) are less clear. The message from Necho emphasizes that there were no issues between Judah and Egypt. It is likely that Josiah's actions reflect some time of alliance between Judah and Babylon. A similar alliance originated during the time of Hezekiah (see 32:1,31; cf. Isa 31:1–3; 39:1–7).

35:22 what Necho had said at God's command. In light of Josiah's misdirected faith, it is noteworthy that the message from Necho is attributed as being from God, suggesting that Josiah was given the opportunity to repent of seeking security apart from the Lord. **Megiddo.** Situated above a key pass through the Mount Carmel foothills that connected trade routes leading to Syria, Egypt, Mesopotamia, and Anatolia. Because of its strategic location, the city was frequently a place of epic battle. This is the backdrop to Armageddon (= Mount of Megiddo) in the book of Revelation as a place of epic spiritual battle (see Rev 16:16 and note).

35:25–27 Josiah's death notice underscores his special reign. Despite his imperfections, Josiah is characterized by "his acts of devotion in accordance with what is written in the Law of the Lord" (v. 26).

36:2–4 *Jehoahaz King of Judah.* Following the death of Josiah at Megiddo in 609 BC (35:23–24), his son Jehoahaz (also known as Shallum [1 Chr 3:15; Jer 22:11]) is enthroned by the "people of the land" (v. 1). Given that Jehoahaz was the younger brother of Eliakim/Jehoiakim, it is intriguing to again see the role of this group during a time of regnal crisis (see note on 23:21).

36:3 Just three months (v. 2) after "the people of the land" made Jehoahaz king (v. 1), Pharaoh Necho deposed Jehoahaz, brought him to

talents[a] of silver and a talent[b] of gold. [4]The king of Egypt made Eliakim, a brother of Jehoahaz,
king over Judah and Jerusalem and changed Eliakim's name to Jehoiakim. But Necho[p] took Eliakim's
brother Jehoahaz and carried him off to Egypt.

Jehoiakim King of Judah

36:5 8pp — 2Ki 23:36 - 24:6

[5]Jehoiakim[q] was twenty-five years old when he became king, and he reigned in Jerusalem eleven
years. He did evil in the eyes of the LORD his God. [6]Nebuchadnezzar[r] king of Babylon attacked him and
bound him with bronze shackles to take him to Babylon.[s] [7]Nebuchadnezzar also took to Babylon articles from the temple of the LORD and put them in his temple[c] there.[t]
[8]The other events of Jehoiakim's reign, the detestable things he did and all that was found against him,
are written in the book of the kings of Israel and Judah. And Jehoiachin his son succeeded him as king.

Jehoiachin King of Judah

36:9-10pp — 2Ki 24:8-17

[9]Jehoiachin[u] was eighteen[d] years old when he became king, and he reigned in Jerusalem three
months and ten days. He did evil in the eyes of the LORD. [10]In the spring, King Nebuchadnezzar sent for
him and brought him to Babylon,[v] together with articles of value from the temple of the LORD, and he
made Jehoiachin's uncle,[e] Zedekiah, king over Judah and Jerusalem.

Zedekiah King of Judah

36:11-16pp — 2Ki 24:18-20; Jer 52:1-3

[11]Zedekiah[w] was twenty-one years old when he became king, and he reigned in Jerusalem eleven
years. [12]He did evil in the eyes of the LORD[x] his God and did not humble[y] himself before Jeremiah the

36:4 [p] Jer 22:10-12
36:5 [q] Jer 22:18; 26:1; 35:1
36:6 [r] Jer 25:9; 27:6; Eze 29:18 [s] 2Ch 33:11; Eze 19:9; Da 1:1
36:7 [t] 2Ki 24:13; Ezr 1:7; Da 1:2
36:9 [u] Jer 22:24-28; 52:31
36:10 [v] ver 18; 2Ki 20:17; Ezr 1:7; Jer 22:25; 24:1; 29:1; 37:1; Eze 17:12
36:11 [w] 2Ki 24:17; Jer 27:1; 28:1
36:12 [x] Jer 37:1-39:18 [y] Dt 8:3; 2Ch 7:14; 33:23; Jer 21:3-7

[a] *3* That is, about 3 3/4 tons or about 3.4 metric tons [b] *3* That is, about 75 pounds or about 34 kilograms
[c] *7* Or *palace* [d] *9* One Hebrew manuscript, some Septuagint manuscripts and Syriac (see also 2 Kings 24:8); most Hebrew manuscripts *eight* [e] *10* Hebrew *brother,* that is, relative (see 2 Kings 24:17)

Egypt, and replaced him with Jehoahaz's older brother Eliakim, whose name he changed to Jehoiakim. **dethroned.** Possibly because Jehoahaz followed Josiah's pro-Babylonian (and thus anti-Egyptian) policies.

36:5–8 *Jehoiakim King of Judah.* Although Egypt assumed control of Syria and Canaan shortly after Josiah's death (609 BC), Nabopolassar and his son Nebuchadnezzar later defeated Necho in 605 BC. The Egyptian army retreated, and Nebuchadnezzar again routed them; they subsequently withdrew to Egypt, leaving the Levant—the area between Anatolia (modern day Turkey) and Egypt that included Israel, Aram, Phoenicia, Moab, and Edom—under the control of the Babylonians (2 Kgs 24:7). Around this time (605 BC), Nebuchadnezzar ascended the Babylonian throne, assuming control of the rapidly expanding Neo-Babylonian Empire. Jehoiakim's 11-year reign extended from 609 to 598 BC, during which time Egypt and Babylonia repeatedly battled for control of the Levant, the area between Anatolia (modern day Turkey) and Egypt that included Israel, Aram, Phoenicia, Moab, and Edom. As with Jehoahaz (2 Kgs 23:32), Jehoiakim did not walk in the God-honoring ways of Josiah but "did evil in the eyes of the LORD" (v. 5). Judah remained an Egyptian vassal until 605 BC, at which time it became a Babylonian vassal.

36:6–8 Although Egypt enthroned Jehoiakim, he had little choice but to submit to Babylonian rule. A few years later, Jehoiakim rebelled against Nebuchadnezzar (2 Kgs 24:1), perhaps with a view of restoring allegiance to Egypt. Because Nebuchadnezzar was preoccupied with rebellion elsewhere, his attack on Judah was delayed about two years. Despite Jehoiakim's rebellion, Nebuchadnezzar did not destroy Jerusalem (v. 7; Dan 1:1–2). This was likely when Jehoiakim was brought in shackles into exile in Babylon (v. 6). The prophetic ministry of Jeremiah is situated during this time (cf. Jer 25:1–11; 36:1–31; 45:1–5). Jeremiah's message to submit to God's judgment in the form of Babylonian rule is rejected, leading to the eventual destruction of Jerusalem in 586 BC.

36:9–10 *Jehoiachin King of Judah.* During the Babylonian attack on Judah, Jehoiakim died and his son Jehoiachin (also known as Jeconiah and Coniah) becomes king. Jehoiachin quickly surrenders to Nebuchadnezzar and is subsequently taken into exile to Babylon—all within three months of his enthronement. In 597 BC, Jehoiachin, royal officials, military officers, artisans, and 7,000 soldiers are taken captive to Babylon (see note on 2 Kgs 24:14). In addition, articles from the temple are taken to Babylon. Nonetheless, Jerusalem itself is spared. Jehoiachin's reign is characterized by covenantal unfaithfulness, as Jer 22:24–30 poetically captures. Although Jehoiachin was brought captive to Babylon, Judah continues to explore the possibility of throwing off Babylonian hegemony (see Jer 27–28 and notes).

36:11–19 *The Reign of Zedekiah and the Fall of Jerusalem.* Following Jehoiachin's surrender and removal to Babylon, Nebuchadnezzar appoints Jehoiachin's uncle Mattaniah (son of Josiah and brother of Jehoahaz and Eliakim/Jehoiakim) as king in Judah and changes his name to Zedekiah. His 11-year reign in Judah begins in 597 BC and ends in the downfall and destruction of Jerusalem (586 BC). As with Jehoahaz (2 Kgs 23:32), Eliakim/Jehoiakim (v. 5), and Jehoiachin (v. 9), Zedekiah's reign is characterized by covenantal unfaithfulness (vv. 12–14).

36:12–13 did evil in the eyes of the LORD ... did not humble himself ... rebelled ... stiff-necked ... hardened his heart ... would not turn to the LORD. This extended summary of Zedekiah's unfaithfulness draws on a broad theological backdrop of OT expressions used to describe persistent rebelliousness against the authority of God.

36:13 [z]Eze 17:13 [a]2Ki 17:14; 2Ch 30:8
36:14 [b]1Ch 5:25
36:15 [c]Isa 5:4; 44:26; Jer 7:25; Hag 1:13; Zec 1:4; Mal 2:7; 3:1 [d]Jer 7:13,25; 25:3-4; 35:14,15; 44:4-6
36:16 [e]2Ki 2:23; Pr 1:25; Jer 5:13 [f]Ezr 5:12; Pr 1:30-31 [g]2Ch 30:10; Pr 29:1; Zec 1:2
36:17 [h]Jer 6:11 [i]Ezr 5:12; Jer 32:28
36:18 [j]ver 7,10
36:19 [k]Jer 11:16; 17:27; 21:10,14; 22:7; 32:29; 39:8; La 4:11; Eze 20:47; Am 2:5; Zec 11:1 [l]1Ki 9:8-9 [m]2Ki 14:13 [n]La 2:6 [o]Ps 79:1-3
36:20 [p]Lev 26:44; 2Ki 24:14; Ezr 2:1; Ne 7:6 [q]Jer 27:7
36:21 [r]Lev 25:4; 26:34 [s]1Ch 22:9 [t]Jer 1:1; 25:11; 27:22; 29:10; 40:1; Da 9:2; Zec 1:12; 7:5
36:22 [u]Isa 44:28; 45:1, 13; Jer 25:12; 29:10; Da 1:21; 6:28; 10:1

prophet, who spoke the word of the LORD. 13He also rebelled against King Nebuchadnezzar, who had
made him take an oath[z] in God's name. He became stiff-necked[a] and hardened his heart and would not
turn to the LORD, the God of Israel. 14Furthermore, all the leaders of the priests and the people became
more and more unfaithful,[b] following all the detestable practices of the nations and defiling the temple
of the LORD, which he had consecrated in Jerusalem.

The Fall of Jerusalem

36:17-20pp — 2Ki 25:1-21; Jer 52:4-27
36:22-23pp — Ezr 1:1-3

15The LORD, the God of their ancestors, sent word to them through his messengers[c] again and
again,[d] because he had pity on his people and on his dwelling place. 16But they mocked God's messengers, despised his words and scoffed[e] at his prophets until the wrath[f] of the LORD was aroused
against his people and there was no remedy.[g] 17He brought up against them the king of the Babylonians,[a] who killed their young men with the sword in the sanctuary, and did not spare young men[h] or
young women, the elderly or the infirm. God gave them all into the hands of Nebuchadnezzar.[i] 18He
carried to Babylon all the articles[j] from the temple of God, both large and small, and the treasures
of the LORD's temple and the treasures of the king and his officials. 19They set fire[k] to God's temple[l]
and broke down the wall[m] of Jerusalem; they burned all the palaces and destroyed[n] everything of
value there.[o]

20He carried into exile[p] to Babylon the remnant, who escaped from the sword, and they became
servants[q] to him and his successors until the kingdom of Persia came to power. 21The land enjoyed its
sabbath rests;[r] all the time of its desolation it rested,[s] until the seventy years[t] were completed in fulfillment of the word of the LORD spoken by Jeremiah.

22In the first year of Cyrus[u] king of Persia, in order to fulfill the word of the LORD spoken by Jeremiah,

[a] *17* Or *Chaldeans*

36:13 rebelled against King Nebuchadnezzar. Proved to be a watershed moment in the history of Judah.

36:14 leaders of the priests and the people became ... unfaithful. Unfaithfulness is not limited to Zedekiah. The inclusion of priestly leaders is especially egregious since a key covenantal responsibility of priests was to teach the Israelites God's will (Lev 10:11; cf. Deut 33:8–11). This dereliction of duty on the part of priests is also an issue during the Second Temple period (Mal 2:1–9). **more and more unfaithful.** An unfortunate response of the king, priests, and people to the consequences for unfaithfulness (serving their enemies; Deut 28:48; Lev 26:14–17).

36:16 mocked ... despised ... scoffed. The response of the people to the prophets sent by God to admonish his people to return to him in righteousness (Jer 44:4–6). **no remedy.** Since the people spurned the gracious nature of God, judgment will follow.

36:17–21 all ... all ... all ... everything ... all. The fivefold use of the Hebrew word emphasizes the comprehensiveness of God's covenantal judgment on his land, his temple, and his people.

36:17–19 God brought about what he had warned would result from continued unfaithfulness (7:19–22; Deut 28:47–67; 1 Kgs 9:6–9; see note on 2 Kgs 24:20a). Nebuchadnezzar began his assault on Judah in 588 BC. After wreaking havoc in the foothills and hill country, the Babylonian army began an 18-month siege of Jerusalem. The walls of Jerusalem were breached in July 586 BC, and Nebuchadnezzar gave orders to destroy the palace, temple, and city walls (2 Kgs 25:8–10). The destruction of Jerusalem took place in Aug. 586 BC. The Babylonians seized the remaining valuables of the temple and palace and deported to Babylon many of the residents who survived. Following the destruction of Jerusalem, Nebuchadnezzar installed a non-Davidic official named Gedaliah as governor of what was left of Judah. See notes on 2 Kgs 25.

36:20–21 *The Exilic Period.* Following the destruction of Jerusalem, deportation ensues for the survivors ("the remnant," v. 20). In the aftermath of this destruction, the Chronicler offers a brief biblical-theological reflection of the exilic period. While the exilic period was one of judgment, it was also a time of restoration. The Chronicler's words echo the cost of covenantal unfaithfulness (Lev 26:33–39) as well as the possibility of restoration (Lev 26:40–45).

36:21 seventy years. While the text does not specify the beginning point and ending point of this 70-year period, there are several possibilities: (1) The destruction of the temple in 586 BC started the period and the dedication of the second temple (516 or 515 BC) ended it (Jer 25:11; 29:10). (2) The death of Josiah in 609 BC started the period and the decree of Cyrus in 539 BC ended it. (3) The Babylonian takeover of Judah in 605 BC started the period, and it extended through the start of the rebuilding of the second temple (538 BC; Jer 25:1–12). (4) The Babylonian takeover of Judah in 605 BC started the period and the fall of Babylon in 539 BC ended it. (5) The 70-year period may simply signify the completeness of God's judgment since the number seven symbolizes completion.

36:22–23 *The Decree of Cyrus.* The death of Nebuchadnezzar in 562 BC sets in motion the rapid downfall of the Babylonian Empire. Nebuchadnezzar's son is assassinated after two years, and the next two Babylonian kings reign for only about five years before Nabonidus assumes the throne. Meanwhile, the Persian Empire (539–333 BC) continues to gain strength, and the Medo-Persian ruler Cyrus takes Babylon with hardly a fight in 539 BC. Cyrus inherits the various people groups that had been exiled to Babylon, including the Jews. Within his first year he allows deported peoples to return to their homeland. The decree of Cyrus is summarized in the closing verses of 2 Chronicles and the opening verses of Ezra, and it is the outworking of prophetic messages (Ezra 6:1–12; Isa 44:28; 45:13; Jer 29:12–14).

the LORD moved the heart of Cyrus king of Persia to make a proclamation throughout his realm and
also to put it in writing:

[23] "This is what Cyrus king of Persia says:

" 'The LORD, the God of heaven, has given me all the kingdoms of the earth and he has appointed[v] me to build a temple for him at Jerusalem in Judah. Any of his people among you may
go up, and may the LORD their God be with them.' "

36:23 [v] Jdg 4:10

36:23 Any of his people . . . may go up. The final words of Chronicles leave the reader with a sense of anticipation of what will happen next and with the realization that they (the Chronicler's audience) are the ones who will finish this story. Thus Chronicles ends with a message of the hope and possibility that come with faithfulness (Jer 29:11 – 14).

INTRODUCTION TO EZRA

The book of Ezra begins a very significant part of the ongoing story of God's people as they return from exile. At first the reader may see a change of subjection from the superpower of Babylon to the superpower of Persia. The people were indeed back in the land, but no Davidic king sat on the throne, the desert was not blossoming like the rose, nor were the nations coming to Zion to worship the Lord. Yet this book and its companion, Nehemiah, deal with big issues such as how the covenant-keeping God upholds his promises and preserves the place of the temple. Ezra is a vital link between the exile and the returned remnant to whom and from whom the Messiah would come.

AUTHOR

Since the Hebrew Bible treats Ezra and Nehemiah as one, it is useful to consider the authorship of both books together. The narrative as it stands suggests that from the beginning of Ezra to the end of Nehemiah there is one continuous chronological narrative. But some scholars reverse the traditional order and assert that it was Nehemiah who came first. Those who advocate this view draw attention to Nehemiah's apparent lack of knowledge of Ezra's proceedings over divorce, a 13-year gap between Ezra's arrival and his reported reading of the Torah, and an apparent absence of much cooperation between the two reformers. This view depends on unproved and unprovable hypotheses.

The objective evidence of the manuscripts shows no order of events other than that in the Bible itself. Ezra 9:9 speaks of an existing "wall" that many assume to be Nehemiah's wall; however, the word Ezra uses does not refer to a city wall but is customarily used of a fence or hedge around a vineyard (e.g., Ps 80:12). Moreover, since this "wall" surrounds not only Jerusalem but also Judah, Ezra is likely using the word metaphorically. Ezra's Jerusalem is filled with people (10:1), while Nehemiah's city is sparsely populated (Neh 7:4). But Ezra 10:1 refers to the people who assembled to hear the Word of God, while Neh 7:4 refers to the new residents of the city. A further argument relates to the names of the high priests at the relevant times. Ezra's high priest was Jehohanan (10:6), who, it is argued, was grandson of Eliashib, Nehemiah's high priest (Neh 3:1). However, Ezra 10:6 does not say that Jehohanan was high priest but says merely that he had an office in the temple buildings, and both Ezra 10:6 and Neh 12:23 make Jehohanan Eliashib's son, not his grandson. So none of these arguments is persuasive. The view taken here flows naturally from the biblical material: Ezra arrived in Jerusalem in 458 BC and was followed by Nehemiah some 14 years later.

The book of Ezra is anonymous but includes first-person speech. Both Ezra and Nehemiah may come from the same source as 1 – 2 Chronicles, not least because 2 Chr 36:22 – 23 and Ezra 1:1 – 3a are identical. Traditionally the book is ascribed to Ezra himself.

HISTORICAL SETTING

The background of Ezra and Nehemiah is the exile and return (see "Exile and Exodus," p. 2659). Both Kings and Chronicles end with God's people in exile. But Chronicles ends with the decree of Cyrus (see photo, p. 5), which is where Ezra takes up the story. In 722 BC the northern kingdom of Israel fell to Assyria, which deported the ten tribes. However, the heartland of Judah remained: Jerusalem is "Mount Zion, the city of the Great King" (Ps 48:2;

see map, p. 771). Jerusalem's rescue from Sennacherib in 701 BC probably created a false sense of security for some Jews. This abruptly ended when the Babylonians under Nebuchadnezzar destroyed Jerusalem and burned the temple in 586 BC. Many of the people, including all their significant leaders, were taken off to Babylon and remained there until Babylon was destroyed by the Persian king Cyrus.

The story of Ezra opens with the decree of Cyrus in 539 BC. That decree allowed exiles of all religions to return and rebuild their temples and thus permitted the Jewish exiles to return and start the slow and painful process of rebuilding the temple, completed in 516 BC (chs. 1–6). Then in 458 BC Ezra himself returned (chs. 7–10), sent by Artaxerxes I (reigned 465–424 BC). In 444 BC, Nehemiah came to Jerusalem and rebuilt the walls. Thus, the books of Ezra and Nehemiah cover approximately 100 years.

GENRE

The overarching genre of Ezra is narrative. The story fits into the grand narrative from creation to new creation by recounting part of Israel's history in the postexilic period, showing how God does not give up on his people. Although he punishes them for their idolatry by banishing them in the exile, he does not abandon his promises to the patriarchs regarding the promised land: God brings his covenant people back to their homeland.

Ezra uses essentially two kinds of source material: archives and personal reminiscences.

1. The archives include the decree of Cyrus (1:2–4), the inventory of the temple vessels (1:9–11), the various letters to and from the Persian kings (chs. 4–7), and the extended lists of names (chs. 2; 10). The language is mainly Hebrew, but two sections are in Aramaic (4:8—6:18; 7:12–26), the standard language of official correspondence at the time.

2. The "Ezra memoirs" appear especially in chs. 7–10 (and perhaps Neh 8). Some are in the first person, and they add vividness and color to the narrative.

The archives and personal reminiscences demonstrate that the book of Ezra is history. But it is also theology in that the history demonstrates that what happened between the exile and the coming of the Messiah took place under the providence of God—events that include the experiences of the returned exiles, not least of which are the experiences of the two remarkable men who led them, and their interactions with the living God. The reader sees the great event

Detailed carving on Xerxes' palace at Persepolis. It is believed that Cyrus the Great chose the site of Persepolis, Darius the Great built the foundations and great palaces, and construction was completed during the reign of Xerxes. All three kings played a role in the events of the book of Ezra.

PERSIAN PROVINCES

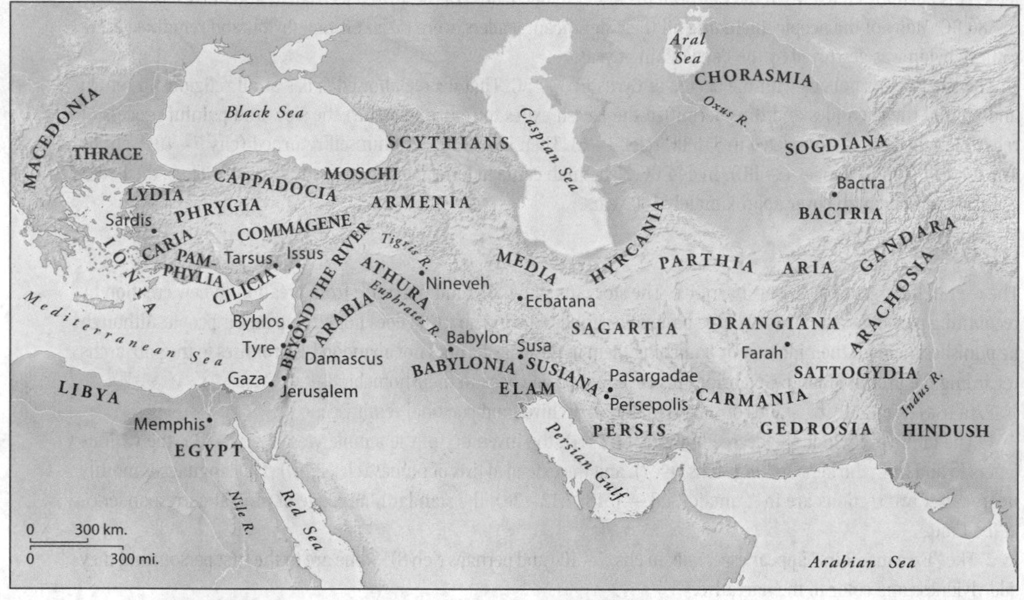

of Israel's return to the land from a number of different perspectives. The archival parts, while less immediately attractive than the personal reminiscences, offer glimpses of real people involved in great events. The reminiscences display more clearly the significance of these events, and the result is a powerful blend of the public and the personal.

THEMES

Ezra is no mere chronicle but powerfully presents a theology that has emerged from the fires of exile. The chastened group of exiles who return after the punishment of the exile need to remember that while the covenant is unbreakable, they will enjoy its blessings only when they love and obey God.

God

"The God of heaven" (1:2; 5:11; 6:9) is sovereign over both creation and history. He is the one who moves the hearts of Cyrus (1:1) and Artaxerxes (7:27). He is faithful to his covenant, and his covenant love endures forever (3:10 – 11). He both caused and reversed the exile. He is holy, which is why his people must be holy (chs. 9 – 10). The God of the past is the God of the present and future; this is central to rebuilding the community.

The Worship of God

Years before Nehemiah constructed walls and buildings for security and daily living, it was necessary to restore the regular worship of God. So the temple is the focus of this book (see "Temple," p. 2652). This is why the first action of the returned exiles is building an altar (3:2). Before anything else, they need to sacrifice offerings for the sin of the people. Then they build and dedicate the temple and celebrate the Passover. Their activities are no mere outward ritual, as the emphasis on prayer shows (especially Ezra's prayer in ch. 9).

The People of God

In many ways the situation was discouraging: only about 50,000 people returned from Babylon (2:64 – 65). Yet here was the possibility of renewal. This small community was organically related to the people who left Egypt and whom God constituted as his own people at Sinai (ch. 2 emphasizes the need to establish descent from preexilic Israel). When ch. 9 emphasizes their separation from paganism, it deliberately uses the old Canaanite names for the inhabitants of the land who were there when the people arrived from Egypt. These returned exiles are identified not simply with the kingdom of Judah but also with the undivided monarchy and those who gathered at Sinai (see "People of God," p. 2672).

The Word of God

The story frequently refers to Psalms, the Prophets, and other parts of the Bible. Ch. 7 (as well as Neh 8) underlines the fundamental importance of the law of Moses. Failing to obey God's word led to the exile, so Ezra emphasizes that God's word must be central to the life of the people. This involves more than simply studying God's law and keeping formal covenant obligations; rather, it demands wholehearted allegiance to God and all his ways (9:4).

The Ongoing Purpose of God

1. *God never abandons his purpose.* Granted, this book is low-key, unlike glowing prophecies such as Isa 2 and Mic 4 that would be fulfilled when the Messiah came. Yet this return to Jerusalem, this rebuilding of the temple, was a vital partial fulfillment that guaranteed God's ancient purposes would one day be a reality.

2. *God never gives up on his people.* The return from exile is a new exodus (see "Exile and Exodus," p. 2659). In spite of opposition from hostile officials and internal discouragement, God's people return to Zion. This great event looks back to the youth of the nation and forward to the final gathering of God's people in the new Jerusalem.

3. *God still guides his people.* The Scripture of the past is guidance for the present and future.

The book's richness and spirituality, together with its careful and orderly structure, make it a vital part of the canon. Perhaps it is especially valuable in times when the spiritual landscape is bleak, with few signs of springtime. Such days call for obedient living, faithful work, and renewed trust in God.

Ezra has two parts, and they correspond to the first and second returns (both initiated by imperial decrees). About 80 years separate the two returns.

OUTLINE

I. The First Return: Led by Zerubbabel (1:1—6:22)
- A. Cyrus Helps the Exiles to Return (1:1–11)
- B. The List of the Exiles Who Returned (2:1–70)
- C. Rebuilding the Altar (3:1–6)
- D. Rebuilding the Temple (3:7–13)
- E. Opposition to the Rebuilding (4:1–5)
- F. Later Opposition Under Xerxes and Artaxerxes (4:6–24)
- G. Tattenai's Letter to Darius (5:1–17)
- H. The Decree of Darius (6:1–12)
- I. Completion and Dedication of the Temple (6:13–18)
- J. The Passover (6:19–22)

II. The Second Return: Led by Ezra (7:1—10:44)
- A. Ezra Comes to Jerusalem (7:1–10)
- B. King Artaxerxes' Letter to Ezra (7:11–28)
- C. An Account of Those Who Returned (8:1–36)
  - 1. The List of Returning Exiles (8:1–14)
  - 2. The Return to Jerusalem (8:15–36)
- D. Ezra Prays About the Problem of Intermarriage With Pagans (9:1–15)
- E. The People's Confession of Sin (10:1–17)
- F. Those Guilty of Intermarriage (10:18–44)

EZRA

1:1 [a]Jer 25:11-12; 29:10-14 [b]2Ch 36:22,23
1:2 [c]Isa 44:28; 45:13 [d]Ezr 5:13
1:4 [e]Isa 10:20-22 [f]Nu 15:3; Ps 50:14; 54:6; 116:17 [g]Ezr 4:3; 5:13; 6:3,14
1:5 [h]Ezr 4:1; Ne 11:4 [i]ver 1; Ex 35:20-22; 2Ch 36:22; Hag 1:14; Php 2:13 [j]Ps 127:1

Cyrus Helps the Exiles to Return

1:1-3pp — 2Ch 36:22-23

1 In the first year of Cyrus king of Persia, in order to fulfill the word of the LORD spoken by Jeremiah,[a]
the LORD moved the heart[b] of Cyrus king of Persia to make a proclamation throughout his realm
and also to put it in writing:

2 "This is what Cyrus king of Persia says:

" 'The LORD, the God of heaven, has given me all the kingdoms of the earth and he has appointed[c] me to build[d] a temple for him at Jerusalem in Judah. 3 Any of his people among you may
go up to Jerusalem in Judah and build the temple of the LORD, the God of Israel, the God who is
in Jerusalem, and may their God be with them. 4 And in any locality where survivors[e] may now
be living, the people are to provide them with silver and gold, with goods and livestock, and with
freewill offerings[f] for the temple of God in Jerusalem.' "[g]

5 Then the family heads of Judah and Benjamin,[h] and the priests and Levites — everyone
whose heart God had moved[i] — prepared to go up and build the house[j] of the LORD in Jerusalem.

1:1 — 6:22 *The First Return: Led by Zerubbabel.* This first part of the book opens in 538 BC, when a party of Jewish exiles returns home as a result of the decree of Cyrus.

1:1 – 11 *Cyrus Helps the Exiles to Return.* This is the first of three returns of the people of God after the Babylonian exile: (1) here they return with Zerubbabel and Sheshbazzar in 538 BC to rebuild the temple; (2) about 80 years later (458 BC) Ezra and his party arrive; (3) then Nehemiah comes to rebuild the wall and the city (445 BC). The sequence places the people back in the land and sees the city and temple rebuilt and ready for the coming of the Lord (Mal 3:1).

1:1 – 4 Verses 1 – 3a are virtually identical with the last two verses of 2 Chronicles. Some have argued that the same person, usually referred to as the "Chronicler," wrote or at least edited 1 – 2 Chronicles and Ezra-Nehemiah. This is not impossible, but it may simply have been a linking device to dovetail the narratives. We cannot be certain.

1:1 first year. 539 BC, the year Cyrus began to reign over Babylon. Cyrus, the founder of the Persian Empire, reigned 559 – 530 BC. Isa 44:28; 45:1 speak of Cyrus as Yahweh's "shepherd" and "anointed" because of his conquest of Babylon and his policy of allowing captive peoples to return to their respective lands, which allowed God's people to return to their homeland. The Cyrus Cylinder speaks of this as Cyrus's general policy regarding conquered nations. **to fulfill the word of the LORD spoken by Jeremiah.** Jeremiah prophesied a 70-year Babylonian exile (Jer 25:11 – 12; 29:10). The exile unfolded in stages: the first deportation was in 605 BC; the second, in 597; the third, in 586. In 538, some 70 years after the first deportation, the first exiles began to return. Cyrus had his own political reasons for acting as he did, yet he was fulfilling the words spoken by the prophet Jeremiah (Dan 9:1 – 2; see note on Dan 9:2). **put it in writing.** An Aramaic copy was found 20 years later at Ecbatana, causing King Darius to rule in favor of resuming the building of the temple.

1:2 God of heaven. A Persian title for God commonly used in exilic and postexilic books. Of the 22 OT occurrences of the phrase, 17 are in Ezra-Nehemiah and Daniel.

1:4 survivors. Often translated "remnant." The expression usually refers to small groups through whom God carries out his purposes for the world. It was to and from such a group that the Messiah himself was to come; e.g., a small number of people surround Jesus at his birth: Zechariah and Elizabeth, Mary and Joseph, and Simeon and Anna represent the remnant who were "waiting for the consolation of Israel" (Luke 2:25). The Messiah came *to* them but also *from* them, especially from Mary but also from the line of David.

1:5 family heads. In the ancient world, families were extended families, more like clans than modern nuclear families. The head of the family was the patriarch (10:16; cf. 2:59; Neh 7:61; 10:34). **Judah and Benjamin.** Constituted the southern kingdom, usually called simply Judah (after the dominant tribe). **everyone whose heart God had moved.** Parallels God's moving the heart of Cyrus (v. 1). Human actions respond to God's initiatives. Cyrus speaks more wisely than he knows. The Lord has indeed given Cyrus all the kingdoms of the earth as God had earlier given them to Nebuchadnezzar (Dan 2:36 – 38). Cyrus is fulfilling God's purpose without being aware of it. However, by linking Cyrus's actions directly with the words of Jeremiah (Jer 25:11 – 12; 29:10 – 14), Ezra shows the overarching providence of God, who raises up kings and puts them down. **house of the LORD.** Links this return with the great days of temple building under Solomon, which climaxed in the king's

6 All their neighbors assisted them with articles of silver and gold, with goods and livestock, and with
valuable gifts, in addition to all the freewill offerings.
7 Moreover, King Cyrus brought out the articles belonging to the temple of the LORD, which Nebuchadnezzar had carried away from Jerusalem and had placed in the temple of his god.[a][k] 8 Cyrus king
of Persia had them brought by Mithredath the treasurer, who counted them out to Sheshbazzar[l] the
prince of Judah.
9 This was the inventory:

gold dishes	30
silver dishes	1,000
silver pans[b]	29
10 gold bowls	30
matching silver bowls	410
other articles	1,000

11 In all, there were 5,400 articles of gold and of silver. Sheshbazzar brought all these along with the
exiles when they came up from Babylon to Jerusalem.

1:7 [k] 2Ki 24:13; 2Ch 36:7,10; Ezr 5:14; 6:5
1:8 [l] Ezr 5:14

[a] 7 Or *gods* [b] 9 The meaning of the Hebrew for this word is uncertain.

great prayer of dedication (1 Kgs 8:27–30) and was followed closely by warnings of exile (1 Kgs 8:46–51). That punishment is now over and the time has come to rebuild the temple.

1:6 All their neighbors assisted them. Echoes the "spoils" of the Egyptians (Ex 12:35).

1:8 Mithredath. A common Persian name; the individual here is otherwise unknown. **Sheshbazzar.** Cyrus appointed him governor (5:14), although elsewhere Zerubbabel is governor (Hag 1:1; 2:2). It may be that the names refer to the same person, one name being a court name and the other being a personal name. Both are said to have laid the foundations of the temple (3:2–8; 5:16; Hag 1:14–15; Zech 4:6–10). Both are governors. Jews in Babylon were sometimes given "official" Babylonian names (Dan 1:7). Josephus (*Antiquities*, 11.11,14) seems to identify Sheshbazzar with Zerubbabel. On the other hand, the Apocrypha distinguishes the two men (1 Esdras 6:18). It is likely that Sheshbazzar was elderly at the time of return, while Zerubbabel was probably a younger contemporary. It may be that Sheshbazzar was the official governor, while Zerubbabel served as the popular leader, perhaps associate governor (3:8–11). Moreover, the high priest Joshua is associated with Zerubbabel, while no priest is associated with Sheshbazzar. Although Sheshbazzar presided over the foundation of the temple in 538 BC, little was accomplished, and Zerubbabel had to preside over a second foundation some 16 years later (Hag 1:14–15; Zech 4:6–10). **prince of Judah.** Possibly the same person as Shenazzar (1 Chr 3:18), fourth son of Jehoiachin, the exiled king of Judah. Some identify him with Sheshbazzar. In that case Zerubbabel would have been Sheshbazzar's nephew (cf. 3:2 with 1 Chr 3:17–19).

1:9–10 An inventory of the returned temple articles (cf. 2 Kgs 25:13–17; Dan 5:2–3).

1:11 5,400 articles. A greater number than the total of the items listed in vv. 9–10, a list that may be selective, for it does not mention the bronze artifacts that Nebuchadnezzar took. It may be that only the larger

RETURN FROM EXILE

Restoration of the Jewish exiles began under Cyrus (559–530 BC), who allowed them to return to Judah with the captured temple treasures. The temple was consecrated in 516 BC by official permission of Darius I (522–486).

Ezra won the approval of Artaxerxes I (465–424 BC) to return with additional exiles and to promote obedience to the law; Nehemiah, to rebuild the walls of Jerusalem.

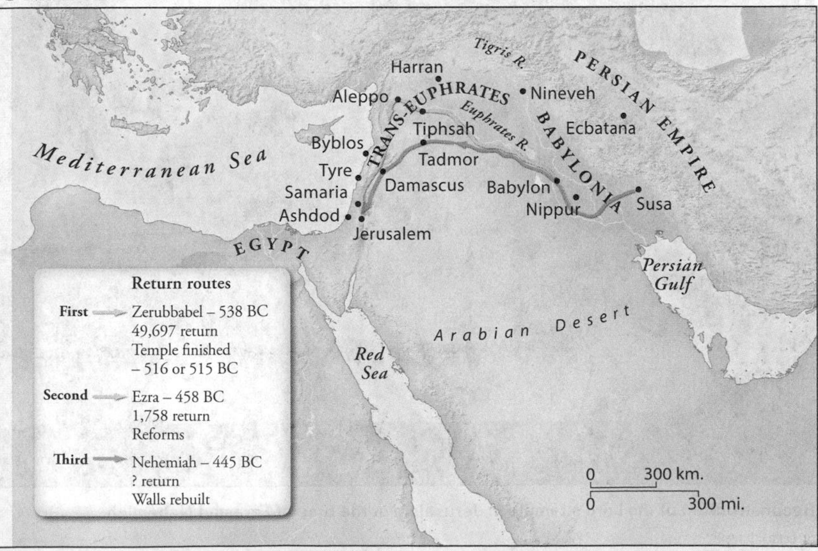

2:1 [m]2Ch 36:20; Ne 7:6 [n]2Ki 24:16; 25:12 [o]Ne 7:73
2:2 [p]1Ch 3:19 [q]Ezr 3:2 [r]Ne 10:2
2:3 [s]Ezr 8:3

The List of the Exiles Who Returned

2:1-70pp — Ne 7:6-73

2 Now these are the people of the province who came up from the captivity of the exiles,[m] whom Nebuchadnezzar king of Babylon[n] had taken captive to Babylon (they returned to Jerusalem and Judah, each to their own town,[o] [2]in company with Zerubbabel,[p] Joshua,[q] Nehemiah, Seraiah,[r] Reelaiah, Mordecai, Bilshan, Mispar, Bigvai, Rehum and Baanah):

The list of the men of the people of Israel:

[3]the descendants of Parosh[s]	2,172
[4]of Shephatiah	372
[5]of Arah	775
[6]of Pahath-Moab (through the line of Jeshua and Joab)	2,812
[7]of Elam	1,254
[8]of Zattu	945
[9]of Zakkai	760

and more valuable vessels were specified in the detailed list. Also, Cyrus may not have released all the articles at the same time. **came up from Babylon to Jerusalem.** A new exodus that reverses the exile (see "Exile and Exodus," p. 2659). The text gives no details about the journey but emphasizes the departure and arrival.

2:1–70 *The List of the Exiles Who Returned.* This list emphasizes continuity by focusing on ancestral roots. Nehemiah used it nearly a century later as a basis for organizing the community: "I found the genealogical record of those who had been the first to return" (Neh 7:5).

2:1 province. The old heartland of Judah around Jerusalem and, in terms of the Persian Empire, part of a larger unit called Trans-Euphrates (4:10). **each to their own town.** This expresses hope because at that time these places were largely ruins.

2:2 This lists 11 leaders, but Neh 7:7 adds the name Nahamani, which brings the list to 12, probably emphasizing continuity with the old tribes. **Zerubbabel.** As grandson of King Jehoiachin (1 Chr 3:17–19), he represents the Davidic line. **Joshua.** Represents the high priestly line (Zech 3:1). The Davidic and high priestly offices later unite in Jesus the Messiah. The other names in the list are otherwise unknown. Because of the date, this "Nehemiah" cannot be the well-known governor in the book of Nehemiah, nor can this "Mordecai" be Esther's cousin (Esth 2:7). **people of Israel.** The ancient people of Israel were returning to the land God promised to Abraham.

2:3–20 These family names suggest the fulfillment of God's promise to give Abraham many descendants (see "Covenant," p. 2646), though they also point to a progressive fulfillment of the promise — a promise that will have even greater fulfillment in the future.

Reconstruction of the Lord's temple in Jerusalem at the time of Ezra and Nehemiah.

Dr. Leen Ritmeyer

[10] of Bani	642
[11] of Bebai	623
[12] of Azgad	1,222
[13] of Adonikam[t]	666
[14] of Bigvai	2,056
[15] of Adin	454
[16] of Ater (through Hezekiah)	98
[17] of Bezai	323
[18] of Jorah	112
[19] of Hashum	223
[20] of Gibbar	95
[21] the men of Bethlehem[u]	123
[22] of Netophah	56
[23] of Anathoth	128
[24] of Azmaveth	42
[25] of Kiriath Jearim,[a] Kephirah and Beeroth	743
[26] of Ramah[v] and Geba	621
[27] of Mikmash	122
[28] of Bethel and Ai[w]	223
[29] of Nebo	52
[30] of Magbish	156
[31] of the other Elam	1,254
[32] of Harim	320
[33] of Lod, Hadid and Ono	725
[34] of Jericho[x]	345
[35] of Senaah	3,630

[36] The priests:

the descendants of Jedaiah[y] (through the family of Jeshua)	973
[37] of Immer[z]	1,052
[38] of Pashhur[a]	1,247
[39] of Harim[b]	1,017

[40] The Levites:[c]

the descendants of Jeshua[d] and Kadmiel (of the line of Hodaviah)	74

[41] The musicians:[e]

the descendants of Asaph	128

[42] The gatekeepers[f] of the temple:

the descendants of Shallum, Ater, Talmon, Akkub, Hatita and Shobai	139

2:13 [t] Ezr 8:13
2:21 [u] Mic 5:2
2:26 [v] Jos 18:25
2:28 [w] Ge 12:8
2:34 [x] 1Ki 16:34; 2Ch 28:15
2:36 [y] 1Ch 24:7
2:37 [z] 1Ch 24:14
2:38 [a] 1Ch 9:12
2:39 [b] 1Ch 24:8
2:40 [c] Ge 29:34; Nu 3:9; Dt 18:6-7; 1Ch 16:4; Ezr 7:7; 8:15; Ne 12:24 [d] Ezr 3:9
2:41 [e] 1Ch 15:16
2:42 [f] 1Sa 3:15; 1Ch 9:17

a 25 See Septuagint (see also Neh. 7:29); Hebrew *Kiriath Arim.*

2:21–35 These names associated with hometowns probably represent different ways of registering the returning exiles, but the reason for this is unknown. Then, as now, there were different ways of listing names in official documents (e.g., today, electoral rolls and telephone directories overlap but are by no means identical). Many ancient Near Eastern documents show the same variety of titles and structures found in this chapter.
2:36–39 The priests are essential for the temple to function and for leading the returned exiles in their role as a kingdom of priests. These verses list only 4 priestly families, far fewer than the 24 priestly families David organized (1 Chr 24:7–18). The returning priests number 4,289—about a tenth of those who returned (v. 64).
2:40 Levites. They and their descendants became prominent in honoring Yahweh in the golden-calf incident (Exod 32) and in helping make and carry the tabernacle (Exod 38:21; Num 1:47–53). Here they do not return in any great numbers, and Ezra later discovers that no Levites wish to return (8:15).
2:41 descendants of Asaph. Associated with Pss 50; 73–83.

2:43 [g] 1Ch 9:2; Ne 11:21
2:58 [h] 1Ki 9:21; 1Ch 9:2
2:59 [i] Nu 1:18
2:61 [j] 2Sa 17:27
2:62 [k] Nu 3:10; 16:39-40
2:63 [l] Lev 2:3,10 [m] Ex 28:30; Nu 27:21
2:65 [n] 2Sa 19:35
2:66 [o] Isa 66:20
2:68 [p] Ex 25:2

43 The temple servants:[g]

the descendants of
Ziha, Hasupha, Tabbaoth,
44 Keros, Siaha, Padon,
45 Lebanah, Hagabah, Akkub,
46 Hagab, Shalmai, Hanan,
47 Giddel, Gahar, Reaiah,
48 Rezin, Nekoda, Gazzam,
49 Uzza, Paseah, Besai,
50 Asnah, Meunim, Nephusim,
51 Bakbuk, Hakupha, Harhur,
52 Bazluth, Mehida, Harsha,
53 Barkos, Sisera, Temah,
54 Neziah and Hatipha

55 The descendants of the servants of Solomon:

the descendants of
Sotai, Hassophereth, Peruda,
56 Jaala, Darkon, Giddel,
57 Shephatiah, Hattil,
Pokereth-Hazzebaim and Ami

58 The temple servants[h] and the descendants of the servants of Solomon 392

59 The following came up from the towns of Tel Melah, Tel Harsha, Kerub, Addon and Immer,
but they could not show that their families were descended[i] from Israel:

60 The descendants of
Delaiah, Tobiah and Nekoda 652

61 And from among the priests:

The descendants of
Hobaiah, Hakkoz and Barzillai (a man who had married a daughter of Barzillai the
Gileadite[j] and was called by that name).
62 These searched for their family records, but they could not find them and so were excluded
from the priesthood[k] as unclean. 63 The governor ordered them not to eat any of the most sacred
food[l] until there was a priest ministering with the Urim and Thummim.[m]

64 The whole company numbered 42,360, 65 besides their 7,337 male and female slaves; and
they also had 200 male and female singers.[n] 66 They had 736 horses,[o] 245 mules, 67 435 camels
and 6,720 donkeys.

68 When they arrived at the house of the LORD in Jerusalem, some of the heads of the families[p] gave
freewill offerings toward the rebuilding of the house of God on its site. 69 According to their ability

2:43,58 temple servants. Appointed to assist the Levites (8:20). They probably carried out menial tasks, which the many foreign names may reflect.
2:59 they could not show that their families were descended from Israel. To establish continuity, there was a particular concern to verify priestly descent, possibly because of the dire example of Korah, Dathan, and Abiram, who tried to force their way into the priesthood (Num 16).
2:63 governor. Probably Zerubbabel. **most sacred food.** Reserved for the Aaronic priests (Lev 2:3). **Urim and Thummim.** Two small objects, perhaps gems, kept in the breastpiece of the high priest's ephod (see Exod 28:30 and note; Lev 8:8). They were cast as lots, and if each had a "yes" and a "no" side, then a "yes" or "no" response would be possible.
2:64–67 The totals round off the individual lists: 42,360 (v. 64) is about 12,500 higher than the sum of the preceding figures. The higher figure probably includes women. The preponderance of males may reflect a high number of young unmarried men, the group most likely to undertake such a hazardous journey. The number of male and female singers is given as 200 (v. 65), but in Neh 7:67 it is 245, but this could be a scribal error.
2:68 freewill offerings. Emphasizes that at least some of the people gave willingly.
2:69 Cf. the enthusiasm when the people prepared to build the tabernacle (Exod 25:1–7) and later for the construction of Solomon's temple (1 Chr 29:2–9).

they gave to the treasury for this work 61,000 darics[a] of gold, 5,000 minas[b] of silver and 100 priestly garments.

70The priests, the Levites, the musicians, the gatekeepers and the temple servants settled in their own towns, along with some of the other people, and the rest of the Israelites settled in their towns.[q]

Rebuilding the Altar

3 When the seventh month came and the Israelites had settled in their towns,[r] the people assembled[s] together as one in Jerusalem. 2Then Joshua[t] son of Jozadak[u] and his fellow priests and Zerubbabel son of Shealtiel[v] and his associates began to build the altar of the God of Israel to sacrifice burnt offerings on it, in accordance with what is written in the Law of Moses[w] the man of God. 3Despite their fear[x] of the peoples around them, they built the altar on its foundation and sacrificed burnt offerings on it to the LORD, both the morning and evening sacrifices.[y] 4Then in accordance with what is written, they celebrated the Festival of Tabernacles[z] with the required number of burnt offerings prescribed for each day. 5After that, they presented the regular burnt offerings, the New Moon[a] sacrifices and the sacrifices for all the appointed sacred festivals of the LORD,[b] as well as those brought as freewill offerings to the LORD. 6On the first day of the seventh month they began to offer burnt offerings to the LORD, though the foundation of the LORD's temple had not yet been laid.

Rebuilding the Temple

7Then they gave money to the masons and carpenters, and gave food and drink and olive oil to the people of Sidon and Tyre, so that they would bring cedar logs[c] by sea from Lebanon[d] to Joppa, as authorized by Cyrus[e] king of Persia.

8In the second month of the second year after their arrival at the house of God in Jerusalem, Zerubbabel[f] son of Shealtiel, Joshua son of Jozadak and the rest of the people (the priests and the Levites and all who had returned from the captivity to Jerusalem) began the work. They appointed Levites twenty[g] years old and older to supervise the building of the house of the LORD. 9Joshua[h] and his sons and brothers and Kadmiel and his sons (descendants of Hodaviah[c]) and the sons of Henadad and their sons and brothers—all Levites—joined together in supervising those working on the house of God.

10When the builders laid[i] the foundation of the temple of the LORD, the priests in their vestments

[a] *69* That is, about 1,100 pounds or about 500 kilograms [b] *69* That is, about 3 tons or about 2.8 metric tons
[c] *9* Hebrew *Yehudah,* a variant of *Hodaviah*

2:70 [q] ver 1; 1Ch 9:2; Ne 11:3-4
3:1 [r] Ne 7:73; 8:1 [s] Lev 23:24
3:2 [t] Ezr 2:2; Ne 12:1,8; Hag 2:2 [u] Hag 1:1; Zec 6:11 [v] 1Ch 3:17 [w] Ex 20:24; Dt 12:5-6
3:3 [x] Ezr 4:4; Da 9:25 [y] Ex 29:39; Nu 28:1-8
3:4 [z] Ex 23:16; Nu 29:12-38; Ne 8:14-18; Zec 14:16-19
3:5 [a] Nu 28:3,11,14; Col 2:16 [b] Lev 23:1-44; Nu 29:39
3:7 [c] 1Ch 14:1 [d] Isa 35:2 [e] Ezr 1:2-4; 6:3
3:8 [f] Zec 4:9 [g] 1Ch 23:24
3:9 [h] Ezr 2:40
3:10 [i] Ezr 5:16

2:70 Summarizes the end of an arduous journey and a complicated process.
3:1–6 *Rebuilding the Altar.* The priority is to rebuild the altar to reestablish the sacrificial worship of God.
3:1 seventh month. The culmination of Israel's year. It included important festivals: Trumpets, Day of Atonement, and Tabernacles (Lev 23:15–43; see "The Lord's Appointed Festivals," p. 229). **assembled together as one.** Shows the importance of corporate unity, whereas ch. 2 establishes the importance of individuals.
3:2 in accordance with what is written. Emphasizes continuity with Moses because no authority in the OT bypasses or supersedes his authority.
3:3 fear of the peoples around them. Becomes more specific in chs. 4–5. **burnt offerings.** The most basic sacrifice, it was completely consumed, symbolizing the offerer's total dedication to God with nothing held back (Lev 1) and God's complete acceptance of the sacrifice. This sacrifice exemplified the heart of the covenant in which God expresses his generous love, and his people respond in true worship. God provides both the animal sacrifice and the desire in the peoples' hearts to respond with an unblemished sacrifice. This sacrifice was offered both morning and evening. See "Major Old Testament Offerings and Sacrifices," p. 197.
3:4 in accordance with what is written. Disobedience led to the exile, so it is necessary for the people to return to unconditional obedience to the Torah. **Festival of Tabernacles.** Lasted eight days, from the 15th to the 22nd of the seventh month, and was also called "Booths" (Hebrew *Sukkôt*) or "Ingathering" or simply "the festival" (Num 29:12–38; John 7:37). It celebrated both the rescue from Egypt (Lev 23:42–43) and the blessings of harvest (Deut 16:13–15). Thus the returned exiles celebrated their faith in the Lord of the exodus while remembering God as the Lord of creation—themes ultimately fulfilled in the new creation flowing from a greater exodus to be accomplished at Jerusalem (Luke 9:31) and the harvest at the end of the age (Matt 13:39). See "The Lord's Appointed Festivals," p. 229; see also note on Lev 23:34.
3:5–6 The Israelites reinstate the other regular sacrifices, thus returning to patterns of worship and living established by Moses.
3:7–13 *Rebuilding the Temple.* Work on the temple begins a year after the return. This is the natural sequel to reinstating the sacrifices.
3:7 Emphasizes continuity by echoing how Solomon prepared to build the temple (2 Chr 2:10–16). The practical arrangements for transporting building materials and remuneration for the workers were important.
3:8 Zerubbabel. Initiates the work as representing the line of David and Solomon (see note on 2:2)—a further sign of continuity with the great days of the community in the past. **Joshua.** The priest. Thus, the kingly and priestly representatives unite. **twenty years old.** May seem young for a supervisor, but younger people were probably in the majority. Youths were important for this long-term project.
3:10 as prescribed by. Emphasizes continuity (see notes on vv. 2,7–8). **David king of Israel.** Not only is this a link with the great king of the past, but it points to David's greater son, Jesus Christ. 1 Chr 25 describes how David appointed temple musicians.

3:10 [j]Nu 10:2; 1Ch 16:6 [k]1Ch 25:1 [l]1Ch 6:31 [m]Zec 6:12
3:11 [n]1Ch 16:34,41; 2Ch 7:3; Ps 107:1; 118:1 [o]Ne 12:24
3:12 [p]Hag 2:3,9
3:13 [q]Job 8:21; Ps 27:6; Isa 16:9
4:2 [r]2Ki 17:24; 19:37 [s]2Ki 17:41
4:3 [t]Ezr 1:1-4; Ne 2:20
4:4 [u]Ezr 3:3
4:6 [v]Est 1:1; Da 9:1 [w]Est 3:13; 9:5
4:7 [x]Ezr 7:1; Ne 2:1 [y]2Ki 18:26; Isa 36:11; Da 2:4

and with trumpets,[j] and the Levites (the sons of Asaph) with cymbals, took their places to praise[k] the LORD, as prescribed by David[l] king of Israel.[m] 11 With praise and thanksgiving they sang to the LORD:

> "He is good;
> his love toward Israel endures forever."[n]

And all the people gave a great shout[o] of praise to the LORD, because the foundation of the house of the LORD was laid. 12 But many of the older priests and Levites and family heads, who had seen the former temple,[p] wept aloud when they saw the foundation of this temple being laid, while many others shouted for joy. 13 No one could distinguish the sound of the shouts of joy[q] from the sound of weeping, because the people made so much noise. And the sound was heard far away.

Opposition to the Rebuilding

4 When the enemies of Judah and Benjamin heard that the exiles were building a temple for the LORD, the God of Israel, 2 they came to Zerubbabel and to the heads of the families and said, "Let us help you build because, like you, we seek your God and have been sacrificing to him since the time of Esarhaddon[r] king of Assyria, who brought us here."[s]

3 But Zerubbabel, Joshua and the rest of the heads of the families of Israel answered, "You have no part with us in building a temple to our God. We alone will build it for the LORD, the God of Israel, as King Cyrus, the king of Persia, commanded us."[t]

4 Then the peoples around them set out to discourage the people of Judah and make them afraid to go on building.[a][u] 5 They bribed officials to work against them and frustrate their plans during the entire reign of Cyrus king of Persia and down to the reign of Darius king of Persia.

Later Opposition Under Xerxes and Artaxerxes

6 At the beginning of the reign of Xerxes,[b][v] they lodged an accusation against the people of Judah and Jerusalem.[w]

7 And in the days of Artaxerxes[x] king of Persia, Bishlam, Mithredath, Tabeel and the rest of his associates wrote a letter to Artaxerxes. The letter was written in Aramaic script and in the Aramaic[y] language.[c,d]

[a] 4 Or *and troubled them as they built* [b] 6 Hebrew *Ahasuerus* [c] 7 Or *written in Aramaic and translated* [d] 7 The text of 4:8–6:18 is in Aramaic.

3:11 sang. May mean they sang responsively, referring to antiphonal singing by a choir divided into two parts. **He is good; his love toward Israel endures forever.** Occurs several times in the Psalter, forming the refrain in Ps 136. **his love.** Not God's general love for humanity but his covenant love for his people to whom he makes promises that he cannot and will not break. **great shout of praise.** Signifies joy and adoration, which makes the weeping (see note on vv. 12–13) a little harder to understand.

3:12–13 wept aloud ... weeping. Praise is not the only note that sounds on this remarkable occasion. It is not altogether clear why the veterans wept. Nostalgia may have overwhelmed them, marking the beginning of the defeatism that Haggai condemned (Hag 2:3). The united community is already showing tensions. The mixture of rejoicing and sadness characterizes this event that, while a triumph, fell far short of the great hopes the people might have had (Hag 2:2–9). Thus there was joy at seeing the foundations of the temple laid but sorrow that it would not match the former temple's glory.

4:1–5 *Opposition to the Rebuilding.* This begins the account of the opposition to building the temple. This opposition to the building of the temple and city wall will continue until the end of the book of Nehemiah.

4:1 enemies. "The peoples around them" (v. 4).

4:2 Let us help. Seems like a friendly gesture. **Esarhaddon.** Son of Sennacherib (2 Kgs 19:37); reigned 681–669 BC. His resettling non-Israelite people in the former kingdom of Israel carried on the policy that the Assyrians began when they conquered the northern kingdom in 722 BC. These settlers introduced a kind of syncretism: "they worshiped the LORD, but they also served their own gods" (2 Kgs 17:33). Here, the leaders of the returned exiles fear repeating that idolatry. This is not specifically said, but it doubtless forms part of their thinking.

4:3 as King Cyrus, the king of Persia, commanded us. Shrewd politics as well as faithfulness (see ch. 1).

4:4 set out to discourage. Sets the tone for subsequent events. The opposition continued over a period of about 20 years, up to the completion of the temple in 516 or 515 BC. The discouragement apparently involved turning local officials against the project. Even though the project had the full authority of Cyrus behind it, local enemies exploited the distance of Jerusalem from the imperial center to their own advantage.

4:5 Darius king of Persia. Darius I, often called Hystaspes, who reigned 522–486 BC. Under him temple building was resumed and completed.

4:6–24 *Later Opposition Under Xerxes and Artaxerxes.* This flash-forward shows how the opposition continued and intensified during the subsequent reigns of Xerxes and Artaxerxes. Ezra jumps into the future to show that opposition was not confined to the earlier period of temple building. This parenthesis in vv. 6–23 relates to opposition at two different times in subsequent reigns. In those later periods the hostility was directed not at the temple but at the building of the walls of Jerusalem. The opposition lasted a considerable time.

4:6 Xerxes. The king at the center of the events in the book of Esther; he reigned 486–465 BC. **accusation.** The text does not give details; nothing seems to have come of it.

4:7 Artaxerxes. Opposition became more virulent in his reign (465–424

8 Rehum the commanding officer and Shimshai the secretary wrote a letter against Jerusalem to
Artaxerxes the king as follows:

9 Rehum the commanding officer and Shimshai the secretary, together with the rest of their associates[z] — the judges, officials and administrators over the people from Persia, Uruk and Babylon, the Elamites of Susa, 10 and the other people whom the great and honorable Ashurbanipal
deported and settled in the city of Samaria and elsewhere in Trans-Euphrates.[a]

11 (This is a copy of the letter they sent him.)

To King Artaxerxes,

From your servants in Trans-Euphrates:

12 The king should know that the people who came up to us from you have gone to Jerusalem
and are rebuilding that rebellious and wicked city. They are restoring the walls and repairing
the foundations.[b]
13 Furthermore, the king should know that if this city is built and its walls are restored, no more
taxes, tribute or duty[c] will be paid, and eventually the royal revenues will suffer.[a] 14 Now since we
are under obligation to the palace and it is not proper for us to see the king dishonored, we are
sending this message to inform the king, 15 so that a search may be made in the archives[d] of your
predecessors. In these records you will find that this city is a rebellious city, troublesome to kings
and provinces, a place with a long history of sedition. That is why this city was destroyed.[e] 16 We
inform the king that if this city is built and its walls are restored, you will be left with nothing
in Trans-Euphrates.

17 The king sent this reply:

To Rehum the commanding officer, Shimshai the secretary and the rest of their associates living
in Samaria and elsewhere in Trans-Euphrates:[f]

Greetings.

18 The letter you sent us has been read and translated in my presence. 19 I issued an order and
a search was made, and it was found that this city has a long history of revolt[g] against kings and
has been a place of rebellion and sedition. 20 Jerusalem has had powerful kings ruling over the
whole of Trans-Euphrates,[h] and taxes, tribute and duty were paid to them. 21 Now issue an order

4:9 [z] Ezr 5:6; 6:6,13
4:10 [a] ver 17; Ne 4:2
4:12 [b] Ezr 5:3,9
4:13 [c] Ezr 7:24; Ne 5:4
4:15 [d] Ezr 5:17; 6:1 [e] Est 3:8
4:17 [f] ver 10
4:19 [g] 2Ki 18:7
4:20 [h] Ge 15:18-21; Ex 23:31; Jos 1:4; 1Ki 4:21; 1Ch 18:3; Ps 72:8-11

[a] *13* The meaning of the Aramaic for this clause is uncertain.

BC). **Bishlam, Mithredath, Tabeel and the rest of his associates.** Probably local officials wanting to ingratiate themselves with the central government. **Aramaic.** Related to Hebrew, it was the universal language of the ancient Near East at this time. Ezra 4:18—6:18; 7:12–26 are in Aramaic.

4:8 commanding officer. Probably a civil official such as a commissioner. **Shimshai.** Probably responsible to transcribe and copy the letter. **letter.** Different from the one in v. 7.

4:9 A calculated attempt to appear significant.

4:10 the great and honorable Ashurbanipal. A shameless rewriting of history. Ashurbanipal (669–627 BC), the last significant Assyrian king, was famous for his great library, discovered in the ruins of Nineveh. He is not mentioned elsewhere in the OT but is probably the king who freed Manasseh, king of Judah, from exile (2 Chr 33:11–13). In spite of his obvious devotion to learning, he was a bloodthirsty tyrant and most certainly did not deserve the epithets "great" and "honorable."

4:11 your servants in Trans-Euphrates. Implies that the letter is a mass protest against the activities of a minority.

4:12 rebellious and wicked city. A vague and generalized accusation calculated to arouse the king's suspicion. The "Jews," or "Judahites," were repairing the walls and restoring the foundations. This had been foretold by Isaiah (Isa 58:12).

4:13 no more taxes, tribute or duty will be paid. The letter gives no supporting evidence for this accusation. The claim that the Persians would lose the whole province of Trans-Euphrates is wildly exaggerated. The Jews were a small minority in that province.

4:15 archives of your predecessors. Probably not simply the chronicles of immediate predecessors of Artaxerxes but various archives going back to Babylonian and Assyrian times (2 Chr 36; Jer 52) and including Hezekiah's defiance (2 Kgs 18–19; 2 Chr 32; Isa 36–37). **That is why this city was destroyed.** An explanation of the exile devoid of theology.

4:17–21 The king's reply repeats the earlier letter's substance, suggesting that he was only too ready to believe the allegations.

4:20 powerful kings ruling over the whole of Trans-Euphrates. Artaxerxes speaks more truth than he knows. David conquered the territory in Philistia on the Egyptian border and controlled the lands along the Euphrates (2 Sam 8:1–3), and Solomon controlled those territories (1 Kgs 4:21), thus fulfilling the promise to Abraham (Gen 15:18–19). These fulfillments were temporary and partial but were genuine glimpses of the kingdom to come; they are foretold in Ps 72, their final fulfillment is announced by Gabriel in Luke 1:32–33, and they are realized in the book of Revelation.

4:21–23 These events probably occurred before 445 BC. This setback would then be the basis of the report made to Nehemiah (Neh 1:3).

4:22 [i]Da 6:2
4:23 [j]ver 9
4:24 [k]Ne 2:1-8; Da 9:25; Hag 1:1,15; Zec 1:1
5:1 [l]Ezr 6:14; Hag 1:1,3, 12; 2:1,10,20 [m]Zec 1:1; 7:1 [n]Hag 1:14-2:9; Zec 4:9-10; 8:9
5:2 [o]1Ch 3:19; Hag 1:14; 2:21; Zec 4:6-10 [p]Ezr 2:2; 3:2 [q]ver 8; Hag 2:2-5
5:3 [r]Ezr 6:6 [s]Ezr 6:6 [t]ver 9; Ezr 1:3; 4:12
5:5 [u]2Ki 25:28; Ezr 7:6, 9,28; 8:18,22,31; Ne 2:8,18; Ps 33:18; Isa 66:14
5:8 [v]ver 2
5:9 [w]Ezr 4:12

to these men to stop work, so that this city will not be rebuilt until I so order. 22Be careful not to
neglect this matter. Why let this threat grow, to the detriment of the royal interests?[i]

23As soon as the copy of the letter of King Artaxerxes was read to Rehum and Shimshai the secretary
and their associates,[j] they went immediately to the Jews in Jerusalem and compelled them by force to stop.

24Thus the work on the house of God in Jerusalem came to a standstill until the second year of the
reign of Darius[k] king of Persia.

Tattenai's Letter to Darius

5 Now Haggai[l] the prophet and Zechariah[m] the prophet, a descendant of Iddo, prophesied[n] to the
Jews in Judah and Jerusalem in the name of the God of Israel, who was over them. 2Then Zerubbabel[o] son of Shealtiel and Joshua[p] son of Jozadak set to work[q] to rebuild the house of God in Jerusalem.
And the prophets of God were with them, supporting them.
3At that time Tattenai,[r] governor of Trans-Euphrates, and Shethar-Bozenai[s] and their associates
went to them and asked, "Who authorized you to rebuild this temple and to finish it?"[t] 4They[a] also
asked, "What are the names of those who are constructing this building?" 5But the eye of their God[u]
was watching over the elders of the Jews, and they were not stopped until a report could go to Darius
and his written reply be received.
6This is a copy of the letter that Tattenai, governor of Trans-Euphrates, and Shethar-Bozenai and
their associates, the officials of Trans-Euphrates, sent to King Darius. 7The report they sent him read
as follows:

To King Darius:

Cordial greetings.

8The king should know that we went to the district of Judah, to the temple of the great God. The
people are building it with large stones and placing the timbers in the walls. The work[v] is being
carried on with diligence and is making rapid progress under their direction.
9We questioned the elders and asked them, "Who authorized you to rebuild this temple and
to finish it?"[w] 10We also asked them their names, so that we could write down the names of their
leaders for your information.

[a] 4 See Septuagint; Aramaic *We.*

4:23–24 compelled them by force to stop ... standstill. Though a temporary setback, it must have seemed deeply depressing at the time.
4:24 The story now jumps back in time to the interrupted temple building (see note on vv. 6–24).
5:1–17 *Tattenai's Letter to Darius.* Some years have passed since they started building the temple (3:10), and they apparently reach an impasse. Chs. 5–6 show how that impasse is broken. After a period of inactivity, the leaders resume work on the temple, and provincial officials question its legitimacy.
5:1 Haggai. He begins preaching on Aug. 29, 520 BC. Temple work resumes on Sept. 21 (see notes on Hag 1:1,15a). Haggai delivers a series of four messages to stir up the people and impress on them the importance of temple building as a sign that God is present among them. **Zechariah.** Two months after Haggai's first message, Zechariah begins to prophesy (see Zech 1:1 and note). These two prophets are also known from their books, which contain prophecies made in the second year of King Darius, i.e., in 520 BC (Hag 1:1; 2:1; Zech 1:1,7). Haggai says the people are in trouble because they have lost sight of their top priority of rebuilding the temple (Hag 1:4–6). Here Ezra emphasizes the connection between this prophetic activity and the renewed action following the discouragement recorded in 4:4–5,24.
5:2 Zerubbabel ... Joshua. They again take the lead to "rebuild," which resumes the interrupted work. **supporting.** Probably by their preaching ministries (see the books of Haggai and Zechariah).
5:3 Shethar-Bozenai. Probably Tattenai's chief secretary. These officials were probably not overtly hostile but simply acting within the law as they made their inquiries. They are more neutral than the officials named in 4:8–10. They would have had no knowledge of Cyrus's decree, no doubt because the work had long stopped before they came to power. They are interested only that this project, happening on their watch, receives proper authorization. They do not actually interfere with the work's progress.
5:5 eye of their God. God's providential overruling of events (cf. "hand of God," which occurs frequently in Ezra-Nehemiah). The Persian governor gives the Jews the benefit of the doubt by not stopping the work while the inquiry is proceeding.
5:6–16 Tattenai's letter is different in tone and atmosphere from the one in ch. 4 and incorporates the Jewish leaders' reply without loaded comments such as "that rebellious and wicked city" (4:12) and "you will be left with nothing in Trans-Euphrates" (4:16).
5:8–10 A brief account with factual details.
5:8 timbers. To protect the building against earthquakes. The Hebrew word may refer to interior paneling (1Kgs 6:15–18) or to logs alternating with the brick or stone layers in the walls. **diligence.** Suggests that the governor's attitude is friendly or at least neutral.

[11]This is the answer they gave us:

"We are the servants of the God of heaven and earth, and we are rebuilding the temple[x] that was built many years ago, one that a great king of Israel built and finished. [12]But because our ancestors angered[y] the God of heaven, he gave them into the hands of Nebuchadnezzar the Chaldean, king of Babylon, who destroyed this temple and deported the people to Babylon.[z]

[13]"However, in the first year of Cyrus king of Babylon, King Cyrus issued a decree[a] to rebuild this house of God. [14]He even removed from the temple[a] of Babylon the gold and silver articles of the house of God, which Nebuchadnezzar had taken from the temple in Jerusalem and brought to the temple[a] in Babylon.[b] Then King Cyrus gave them to a man named Sheshbazzar,[c] whom he had appointed governor, [15]and he told him, 'Take these articles and go and deposit them in the temple in Jerusalem. And rebuild the house of God on its site.'

[16]"So this Sheshbazzar came and laid the foundations of the house of God[d] in Jerusalem. From that day to the present it has been under construction but is not yet finished."

[17]Now if it pleases the king, let a search be made in the royal archives[e] of Babylon to see if King Cyrus did in fact issue a decree to rebuild this house of God in Jerusalem. Then let the king send us his decision in this matter.

5:11 [x] 1Ki 6:1; 2Ch 3:1-2
5:12 [y] 2Ch 36:16 [z] Dt 21:10; 28:36; 2Ki 24:1; 25:8,9,11; Jer 1:3
5:13 [a] Ezr 1:1
5:14 [b] Ezr 1:7; 6:5; Da 5:2 [c] 1Ch 3:18
5:16 [d] Ezr 3:10; 6:15
5:17 [e] Ezr 4:15; 6:1,2
6:1 [f] Ezr 4:15; 5:17
6:3 [g] Ezr 3:10; Hag 2:3
6:4 [h] 1Ki 6:36 [i] ver 8; Ezr 7:20
6:5 [j] 1Ch 29:2 [k] Ezr 1:7; 5:14
6:6 [l] Ezr 5:3 [m] Ezr 5:3

The Decree of Darius

6 King Darius then issued an order, and they searched in the archives[f] stored in the treasury at Babylon. [2]A scroll was found in the citadel of Ecbatana in the province of Media, and this was written on it:

Memorandum:

[3]In the first year of King Cyrus, the king issued a decree concerning the temple of God in Jerusalem:

Let the temple be rebuilt as a place to present sacrifices, and let its foundations be laid.[g] It is to be sixty cubits[b] high and sixty cubits wide, [4]with three courses[h] of large stones and one of timbers. The costs are to be paid by the royal treasury.[i] [5]Also, the gold[j] and silver articles of the house of God, which Nebuchadnezzar took from the temple in Jerusalem and brought to Babylon, are to be returned to their places in the temple in Jerusalem; they are to be deposited in the house of God.[k]

[6]Now then, Tattenai,[l] governor of Trans-Euphrates, and Shethar-Bozenai[m] and you other officials of that province, stay away from there. [7]Do not interfere with the work on this temple of God. Let the governor of the Jews and the Jewish elders rebuild this house of God on its site.

[a] *14* Or *palace* [b] *3* That is, about 90 feet or about 27 meters

5:11 God of heaven and earth. The universal Lord is not confined to one place, yet he revealed himself particularly in the temple that Solomon built long ago. Solomon's great prayer encapsulates God's transcendence and immanence (1 Kgs 8:27–29).
5:12 he gave them into the hands of. The exile's theological explanation (Dan 1:2).
5:13 Cyrus issued a decree. Recorded in 1:2–4, this becomes very significant in establishing that their rebuilding is legitimate.
5:14 Sheshbazzar. See note on 1:8.
5:17 royal archives of Babylon. The natural place to begin looking, although the decree was eventually found at Ecbatana (6:2).
6:1–12 *The Decree of Darius.* The search of the royal archives leads to the discovery of the decree of Cyrus that set in motion the return of the first wave of exiles. Now the decree of Darius initiates the next phase of the action.
6:2 Ecbatana. The former capital of Media, where Cyrus spent the first summer of his reign, the year in which he issued the decree. This is another indication of the book's historical accuracy. Located at the site of the present-day Iranian city of Hamadan, it was one of the four capitals of the Persian Empire along with Babylon, Persepolis, and Susa. The word occurs nowhere else in the OT, although there are several references in the Apocrypha (Tobit 3:7; 7:1; 14:12–14; Judith 1:1–4; 2 Maccabees 9:3). The Medes were an Indo-European people in northwest Iran and were related to the Persians. Cyrus in 550 BC made them part of his empire. The name "Medes" still existed in NT times (Acts 2:9)
6:3 a place to present sacrifices. Significant because the altar symbolized atonement and the place where God's anger is set aside. **sixty cubits high and sixty cubits wide.** The precise dimensions (see NIV text note) give an air of authenticity and were doubtless the result of discussions with Jewish officials.
6:5 the gold and silver articles of the house of God. In many ways these symbolize the beginning of the exile, when Nebuchadnezzar placed them in the temple of Marduk (Dan 1:2), and the end of the exile, when they were used by Belshazzar during his drunken and blasphemous party (Dan 5:1–4). Now they are being restored to their proper use.
6:6–10 These instructions to the local authorities give the Jews the best of both worlds because King Cyrus orders the provincial government not to interfere and to supply the money and provisions the Jews need.

Late fifth-century BC papyrus from the Jewish colony of Elephantine in Egypt petitioning the Persian governor for permission to build a temple.

bpk, Berlin/Aegyptisches Museum, Staatliche Museen, Berlin, Germany/Margarete Buesing/Art Resource, NY

6:8 [n]ver 4 [o]1Sa 9:20
6:9 [p]Lev 1:3,10
6:10 [q]Ezr 7:23; 1Ti 2:1-2
6:11 [r]Dt 21:22-23; Est 2:23; 5:14; 9:14 [s]Ezr 7:26; Da 2:5; 3:29
6:12 [t]Ex 20:24; Dt 12:5; 1Ki 9:3; 2Ch 6:2 [u]ver 14
6:13 [v]Ezr 4:9
6:14 [w]Ezr 5:1

8 Moreover, I hereby decree what you are to do for these elders of the Jews in the construction
of this house of God:
Their expenses are to be fully paid out of the royal treasury,[n] from the revenues[o] of Trans-Euphrates, so that the work will not stop.
9 Whatever is needed — young bulls, rams, male lambs
for burnt offerings[p] to the God of heaven, and wheat, salt, wine and olive oil, as requested by the
priests in Jerusalem — must be given them daily without fail,
10 so that they may offer sacrifices
pleasing to the God of heaven and pray for the well-being of the king and his sons.[q]
11 Furthermore, I decree that if anyone defies this edict, a beam is to be pulled from their house
and they are to be impaled[r] on it. And for this crime their house is to be made a pile of rubble.[s]
12 May God, who has caused his Name to dwell there,[t] overthrow any king or people who lifts a
hand to change this decree or to destroy this temple in Jerusalem.
I Darius[u] have decreed it. Let it be carried out with diligence.

Completion and Dedication of the Temple

13 Then, because of the decree King Darius had sent, Tattenai, governor of Trans-Euphrates, and Shethar-Bozenai and their associates[v] carried it out with diligence.
14 So the elders of the Jews continued to
build and prosper under the preaching[w] of Haggai the prophet and Zechariah, a descendant of Iddo.

6:9 young bulls, rams, male lambs ... wheat, salt, wine and olive oil. Closely follows regulations in the Pentateuch (Exod 29:38–41; Lev 2:1; Num 28:1–15), suggesting that Darius consulted the Jewish leaders. **6:11–12** The punishment for tampering with the edict is savage. Often God judges people by allowing the law and other agencies to take their course (see Dan 6:24). According to Herodotus (3.159), Darius I impaled 3,000 Babylonians when he took the city of Babylon. **6:12 carried out with diligence.** Expressed in the next verses, especially vv. 13–15, where enthusiastic activity replaces defeatism. **6:13–18** *Completion and Dedication of the Temple.* The imperial and provincial civil powers support the work.

6:14 preaching. A major cause of the renewed effort. It was not just opposition that had delayed temple building but the people's preoccupation with their own houses. God speaks by his prophets. Haggai shows how God had sent famine as a punishment for their neglect of the Lord's house, and he inspires them to take up the work with renewed energy (Hag 1:2–13). He also speaks of the future glory of the house (Hag 2:6–9). Zechariah speaks of the coming kingdom and, especially in Zech 14, the reign of the coming king. **Artaxerxes.** Some consider mention of him out of place because he belonged to the following century, but it is under him that the Jews completed the city walls; thus, this verse views the project as a whole.

They finished building the temple according to the command of the God of Israel and the decrees of
Cyrus,[x] Darius[y] and Artaxerxes,[z] kings of Persia. 15The temple was completed on the third day of the
month Adar, in the sixth year of the reign of King Darius.[a]
16Then the people of Israel — the priests, the Levites and the rest of the exiles — celebrated the dedication[b] of the house of God with joy. 17For the dedication of this house of God they offered[c] a hundred
bulls, two hundred rams, four hundred male lambs and, as a sin offering[*a*] for all Israel, twelve male
goats, one for each of the tribes of Israel. 18And they installed the priests in their divisions[d] and the Levites
in their groups[e] for the service of God at Jerusalem, according to what is written in the Book of Moses.[f]

The Passover

19On the fourteenth day of the first month, the exiles celebrated the Passover.[g] 20The priests and
Levites had purified themselves and were all ceremonially clean. The Levites slaughtered[h] the Passover
lamb for all the exiles, for their relatives the priests and for themselves. 21So the Israelites who had returned from the exile ate it, together with all who had separated themselves[i] from the unclean practices[j]
of their Gentile neighbors in order to seek the LORD,[k] the God of Israel. 22For seven days they celebrated
with joy the Festival of Unleavened Bread,[l] because the LORD had filled them with joy by changing the attitude[m] of the king of Assyria so that he assisted them in the work on the house of God, the God of Israel.

Ezra Comes to Jerusalem

7 After these things, during the reign of Artaxerxes[n] king of Persia, Ezra son of Seraiah, the son of
Azariah, the son of Hilkiah,[o] 2the son of Shallum, the son of Zadok,[p] the son of Ahitub,[q] 3the son of
Amariah, the son of Azariah, the son of Meraioth, 4the son of Zerahiah, the son of Uzzi, the son of Bukki,

a 17 Or *purification offering*

6:14 [x]Ezr 1:1-4 [y]ver 12 [z]Ezr 7:1; Ne 2:1
6:15 [a]Zec 1:1; 4:9
6:16 [b]1Ki 8:63; 2Ch 7:5
6:17 [c]2Sa 6:13; 2Ch 29:21; 30:24; Ezr 8:35
6:18 [d]1Ch 23:6; 2Ch 35:4; Lk 1:5 [e]1Ch 24:1 [f]Nu 3:6-9; 8:9-11; 18:1-32
6:19 [g]Ex 12:11; Nu 28:16
6:20 [h]2Ch 30:15,17; 35:11
6:21 [i]Ezr 9:1; Ne 9:2 [j]Dt 18:9; Ezr 9:11; Eze 36:25 [k]1Ch 22:19; Ps 14:2
6:22 [l]Ex 12:17 [m]Ezr 1:1
7:1 [n]Ezr 4:7; 6:14; Ne 2:1 [o]2Ki 22:4
7:2 [p]1Ki 1:8; 1Ch 6:8 [q]Ne 11:11

6:15 The temple was completed. Mar. 12, 516 BC, almost 70 years after its destruction. The renewed work on the temple began on Sept. 21, 520 BC (Hag 1:15) and continued for nearly three and a half years. Hag 2:3 speaks of the older people who could remember Solomon's temple and would be disappointed at the smaller size of this one (see Ezra 3:12). Yet this temple was to have a much longer life. It was similar in plan to Solomon's temple, but the Most Holy Place was left empty because the ark of the covenant had been lost at the time of the Babylonian conquest. **Adar.** The last month of the Jewish year, in the spring and just before the Passover (vv. 19–22).

6:16–17 people of Israel ... each of the tribes. The whole people of God are involved.

6:17 The offerings are small in comparison with those Solomon offered at the dedication of the temple. On that occasion he offered 22,000 cattle and 120,000 sheep and goats (1 Kgs 8:63). What must be remembered is the wealth of resources available to Solomon at the height of his power compared to the much reduced resources of the returned exiles. In the spirit of Lev 1:14, they offered the equivalent of a dove or a pigeon rather than a bull or a lamb.

6:18 written in the Book of Moses. Some have argued that David, not Moses, established the "divisions" and "groups," but Moses established the basic distinctions between priests and Levites (Num 18:1), while David refined them (1 Chr 23–26). The authority of the Torah lies behind all that is happening here.

6:19–22 *The Passover.* This festival celebrates the release of the Israelites from slavery in Egypt, which began when the angel of death killed the firstborn in every household unless the house was secured by blood sprinkled on the doorposts and lintel, in which case the angel "passed over" the house (Exod 12:1–30).

6:19 celebrated the Passover. They resume regular patterns of worship. This stands in a direct line of continuity with the first Passover (Exod 12) and echoes the great Passovers of Hezekiah (2 Chr 30) and Josiah (2 Chr 35).

6:21 People other than Israelites were welcome if they genuinely sought the true God. We see this in Rahab (Josh 2) and especially in Ruth (Ruth 1–4).

6:22 Festival of Unleavened Bread. Essentially an extension of the Passover (Exod 12:15–20). Although it is a distinct festival, it too celebrates the deliverance of the Israelites from Egypt. For the origin and meaning of the Passover and Festival of Unleavened Bread, see notes on Exod 12:1–30. **king of Assyria.** Mention of him is rather surprising here; it probably fits the story of the exile and return into a broader perspective, beginning with the deportation of the northern kingdom of Israel to Assyria in 722 BC (2 Kgs 17). 2 Kgs 17 explains the reasons why the northern kingdom of Israel went into exile. Since no similar explanation occurs in 2 Kgs 24–25 for the exile of the southern kingdom of Judah, it is clear that the reasons for Judah's exile are the same as those for the northern kingdom's exile; this is made explicit in 2 Kgs 17:18–20. Moreover, even after the fall of Nineveh in 612 BC, the term "Assyria" continued to be used for territories formerly occupied by the Assyrians. Similarly, the Persian kings adopted a variety of titles used by their predecessors, including "king of Babylon" (Ezra 5:13; Neh 13:6). **house of God, the God of Israel.** Reflects 1:1–3 and concludes the first part of Ezra, which emphasizes reestablishing worship and rebuilding the temple (538–516/515 BC). The return from exile to rebuild the temple began when the Lord "moved the heart of Cyrus" (1:1); it now concludes with God "changing the attitude of the king."

7:1—10:44 *The Second Return: Led by Ezra.* It is now 458 BC; some 60 years have passed since the events of chs. 5–6 and some 80 years since the early pioneers returned to Jerusalem to rebuild the temple. Ezra dominates chs. 7–10 and also reappears in Neh 8.

7:1–10 *Ezra Comes to Jerusalem.* The record shows Ezra's pedigree, gifting, and dedication to the Torah (the Law of Moses).

7:1 After these things. Indicates that time elapsed (without specifying how much) between the events of the previous chapters and the beginning of ch. 7. The events of the preceding chapter concluded with the completion of the temple in 516 BC. **Artaxerxes.** Probably Artaxerxes I, which means that Ezra would have arrived in Jerusalem in 458 BC, 60

7:6 [r]Ne 12:36 [s]Ezr 5:5; Isa 41:20
7:7 [t]Ezr 8:1
7:9 [u]ver 6
7:10 [v]ver 25; Dt 33:10; Ne 8:1-8
7:12 [w]Eze 26:7; Da 2:37
7:14 [x]Est 1:14
7:15 [y]1Ch 29:6 [z]1Ch 29:6,9; 2Ch 6:2
7:16 [a]Ezr 8:25 [b]Zec 6:10
7:17 [c]2Ki 3:4 [d]Nu 15:5-12 [e]Dt 12:5-11
7:19 [f]Ezr 5:14; Jer 27:22
7:20 [g]Ezr 6:4

5 the son of Abishua, the son of Phinehas, the son of Eleazar, the son of Aaron the chief priest— 6 this Ezra[r] came up from Babylon. He was a teacher well versed in the Law of Moses, which the LORD, the God of Israel, had given. The king had granted him everything he asked, for the hand of the LORD his God was on him.[s] 7 Some of the Israelites, including priests, Levites, musicians, gatekeepers and temple servants, also came up to Jerusalem in the seventh year of King Artaxerxes.[t]

8 Ezra arrived in Jerusalem in the fifth month of the seventh year of the king. 9 He had begun his journey from Babylon on the first day of the first month, and he arrived in Jerusalem on the first day of the fifth month, for the gracious hand of his God was on him.[u] 10 For Ezra had devoted himself to the study and observance of the Law of the LORD, and to teaching[v] its decrees and laws in Israel.

King Artaxerxes' Letter to Ezra

11 This is a copy of the letter King Artaxerxes had given to Ezra the priest, a teacher of the Law, a man learned in matters concerning the commands and decrees of the LORD for Israel:

12 Artaxerxes, king of kings,[w]

To Ezra the priest, teacher of the Law of the God of heaven:

Greetings.

13 Now I decree that any of the Israelites in my kingdom, including priests and Levites, who volunteer to go to Jerusalem with you, may go. 14 You are sent by the king and his seven advisers[x] to inquire about Judah and Jerusalem with regard to the Law of your God, which is in your hand. 15 Moreover, you are to take with you the silver and gold that the king and his advisers have freely given[y] to the God of Israel, whose dwelling[z] is in Jerusalem, 16 together with all the silver and gold[a] you may obtain from the province of Babylon, as well as the freewill offerings of the people and priests for the temple of their God in Jerusalem.[b] 17 With this money be sure to buy bulls, rams and male lambs,[c] together with their grain offerings and drink offerings,[d] and sacrifice[e] them on the altar of the temple of your God in Jerusalem.

18 You and your fellow Israelites may then do whatever seems best with the rest of the silver and gold, in accordance with the will of your God. 19 Deliver[f] to the God of Jerusalem all the articles entrusted to you for worship in the temple of your God. 20 And anything else needed for the temple of your God that you are responsible to supply, you may provide from the royal treasury.[g]

21 Now I, King Artaxerxes, decree that all the treasurers of Trans-Euphrates are to provide with diligence whatever Ezra the priest, the teacher of the Law of the God of heaven, may ask of

years after the events of ch. 6. **Ezra.** The genealogy traces him back to Aaron (vv. 1–5), who was the high priest and brother of Moses (Exod 4:14; 28:1–2). The list is clearly selective; a longer list is provided in 1 Chr 6:1–15.

7:6 teacher. Or "scribe" (Neh 13:13). Earlier scribes served the kings as secretaries (e.g., Shaphan in 2 Kgs 22:3). Others recorded the words of the prophets (e.g., Baruch in Jer 36:32). After the exile they were scholars who studied and taught the Scriptures. In the NT they are sometimes referred to as "teachers of the law" (e.g., Matt 2:4; Luke 5:17) and are often addressed as "Rabbi" (e.g., Matt 23:7). Ezra is connected to the priestly line through Aaron, and he calls the people back to the words of Moses. **well versed.** Not merely well-read; Ezra understood the Torah (the Law of Moses) and could teach it. **for the hand of the LORD his God was on him.** God's providence was behind the king's decisions to grant Ezra's requests.

7:7 Ch. 8 treats this company in more detail.

7:8 fifth month of the seventh year of the king. The king is Artaxerxes I (465–424 BC), and Ezra's arrival is in 458 BC. This exacting journey of about 900 miles (1,450 kilometers) took some four months, occurring between early April and early August. Again this underlines God's providential ruling.

7:10 Outlines how Ezra was a model teacher. Not only did he study carefully, but he also practiced what he preached. Neh 8 is a glimpse of how he and others expounded the Torah in a ceremony at the Water Gate.

7:11–28 *King Artaxerxes' Letter to Ezra.* This Aramaic letter officially authorizes Ezra's teaching and administrative program. Many regard this letter as the beginning point of Daniel's first of 69 "sevens" (Dan 9:24–27). Others regard the commission of Nehemiah by the same king (Neh 1:1,11; 2:1–8) as the starting point of this prophecy.

7:12 the priest, teacher of the Law of the God of heaven. Probably Ezra's official title, which demonstrates his prestige at court.

7:13–14 Artaxerxes renews Cyrus's decree (1:1–4) granting the Israelites permission to travel to Jerusalem.

7:14 Law of your God. Perhaps the complete Pentateuch, the rule of life for the returned exiles, or more particularly the book of Deuteronomy.

7:15–24 Royal gifts, a collection from the people of Babylonia, and freewill offerings finance the project. Again this emphasizes materials for sacrifices, temple vessels (as also in 1:9–11), and the king's blanket invitation to use any necessary resources from the royal treasury. Provincial treasurers must facilitate this by providing very generous support.

you— 22up to a hundred talents[a] of silver, a hundred cors[b] of wheat, a hundred baths[c] of wine,
a hundred baths[c] of olive oil, and salt without limit. 23Whatever the God of heaven has prescribed,
let it be done with diligence for the temple of the God of heaven. Why should his wrath fall on the
realm of the king and of his sons?[h] 24You are also to know that you have no authority to impose
taxes, tribute or duty[i] on any of the priests, Levites, musicians, gatekeepers, temple servants or
other workers at this house of God.[j]

25And you, Ezra, in accordance with the wisdom of your God, which you possess, appoint[k]
magistrates and judges to administer justice to all the people of Trans-Euphrates—all who
know the laws of your God. And you are to teach[l] any who do not know them. 26Whoever does not
obey the law of your God and the law of the king must surely be punished by death, banishment,
confiscation of property, or imprisonment.[d][m]

27Praise be to the LORD, the God of our ancestors, who has put it into the king's heart[n] to bring honor[o]
to the house of the LORD in Jerusalem in this way 28and who has extended his good favor[p] to me before
the king and his advisers and all the king's powerful officials. Because the hand of the LORD my God
was on me,[q] I took courage and gathered leaders from Israel to go up with me.

7:23 [h]Ezr 6:10
7:24 [i]Ezr 4:13 [j]Ezr 8:36
7:25 [k]Ex 18:21,26; Dt 16:18 [l]ver 10; Lev 10:11
7:26 [m]Ezr 6:11
7:27 [n]Ezr 1:1; 6:22 [o]1Ch 29:12
7:28 [p]2Ki 25:28 [q]Ezr 5:5; 9:9
8:1 [r]Ezr 7:7
8:3 [s]1Ch 3:22 [t]Ezr 2:3
8:4 [u]Ezr 2:6
8:6 [v]Ezr 2:15; Ne 7:20; 10:16
8:13 [w]Ezr 2:13

List of the Family Heads Returning With Ezra

8 These are the family heads and those registered with them who came up with me from Babylon
during the reign of King Artaxerxes:[r]

2of the descendants of Phinehas, Gershom;
of the descendants of Ithamar, Daniel;
of the descendants of David, Hattush 3of the descendants of Shekaniah;[s]
of the descendants of Parosh,[t] Zechariah, and with him were registered 150 men;
4of the descendants of Pahath-Moab,[u] Eliehoenai son of Zerahiah, and with him 200 men;
5of the descendants of Zattu,[e] Shekaniah son of Jahaziel, and with him 300 men;
6of the descendants of Adin,[v] Ebed son of Jonathan, and with him 50 men;
7of the descendants of Elam, Jeshaiah son of Athaliah, and with him 70 men;
8of the descendants of Shephatiah, Zebadiah son of Michael, and with him 80 men;
9of the descendants of Joab, Obadiah son of Jehiel, and with him 218 men;
10of the descendants of Bani,[f] Shelomith son of Josiphiah, and with him 160 men;
11of the descendants of Bebai, Zechariah son of Bebai, and with him 28 men;
12of the descendants of Azgad, Johanan son of Hakkatan, and with him 110 men;
13of the descendants of Adonikam,[w] the last ones, whose names were Eliphelet, Jeuel and Shemaiah,
and with them 60 men;
14of the descendants of Bigvai, Uthai and Zakkur, and with them 70 men.

[a] *22* That is, about 3 3/4 tons or about 3.4 metric tons [b] *22* That is, probably about 18 tons or about 16 metric tons [c] *22* That is, about 600 gallons or about 2,200 liters [d] *26* The text of 7:12-26 is in Aramaic. [e] *5* Some Septuagint manuscripts (also 1 Esdras 8:32); Hebrew does not have *Zattu.* [f] *10* Some Septuagint manuscripts (also 1 Esdras 8:36); Hebrew does not have *Bani.*

7:22 a hundred talents of silver. A huge amount (see NIV text note), but the province was on the fringe of the empire, and its loyalty was important, especially since it was close to Egypt.

7:25–26 The king gives Ezra permission not only to operate in and around Jerusalem but also to establish the rule of the Torah throughout the whole province of Trans-Euphrates. Thus the Persian king recognizes the Mosaic law as part of his own law.

7:27–28 The language changes from Aramaic to Hebrew as Ezra praises the Lord in a psalm-like doxology.

7:27 the LORD, the God of our ancestors. Thanksgiving for the past because what is happening renews the promises made to the patriarchs about the land (e.g., Gen 15:17–21), the fulfillment of which the exile had interrupted.

7:28 the hand of the LORD my God was on me. Gives confidence for the present and future as Ezra steps out in faith to start this project.

8:1–36 *An Account of Those Who Returned.* This focuses not on the journey itself but on those who returned with Ezra and on their arrival.

8:1–14 *The List of Returning Exiles.* There are 12 family heads. Only about 1,500 men (probably about 5,000 people in all) returned with Ezra, a much smaller number than the 42,000 who had returned about 100 years earlier (2:64).

8:2 Phinehas ... Ithamar. Represent the priestly families. **Daniel.** Otherwise unknown; this is not the famous Daniel taken to Babylon in 605 BC, for this is now 458 (see note on 7:1—10:44). **Hattush.** A member of the royal line (1 Chr 3:22).

8:3–14 The non-priestly, or ordinary, families. The names also occur in 2:3–15.

8:15 [x]ver 21,31 [y]Ezr 2:40; 7:7
8:17 [z]Ezr 2:43
8:18 [a]Ezr 5:5
8:20 [b]1Ch 9:2; Ezr 2:43
8:21 [c]ver 15; 2Ch 20:3 [d]Ps 5:8; 107:7
8:22 [e]Ne 2:9; Ezr 7:6,9, 28 [f]Ezr 5:5 [g]Dt 31:17; 2Ch 15:2
8:23 [h]2Ch 20:3; 33:13
8:24 [i]ver 18
8:25 [j]ver 33; Ezr 7:15,16
8:28 [k]Lev 21:6; 22:2-3

The Return to Jerusalem

15 I assembled them at the canal that flows toward Ahava,[x] and we camped there three days. When
I checked among the people and the priests, I found no Levites[y] there. 16 So I summoned Eliezer, Ariel,
Shemaiah, Elnathan, Jarib, Elnathan, Nathan, Zechariah and Meshullam, who were leaders, and Joiarib and Elnathan, who were men of learning, 17 and I ordered them to go to Iddo, the leader in Kasiphia.
I told them what to say to Iddo and his fellow Levites, the temple servants[z] in Kasiphia, so that they
might bring attendants to us for the house of our God. 18 Because the gracious hand of our God was
on us,[a] they brought us Sherebiah, a capable man, from the descendants of Mahli son of Levi, the son
of Israel, and Sherebiah's sons and brothers, 18 in all; 19 and Hashabiah, together with Jeshaiah from
the descendants of Merari, and his brothers and nephews, 20 in all. 20 They also brought 220 of the
temple servants[b]—a body that David and the officials had established to assist the Levites. All were
registered by name.

21 There, by the Ahava Canal,[c] I proclaimed a fast, so that we might humble ourselves before our God
and ask him for a safe journey[d] for us and our children, with all our possessions. 22 I was ashamed to
ask the king for soldiers[e] and horsemen to protect us from enemies on the road, because we had told
the king, "The gracious hand of our God is on everyone[f] who looks to him, but his great anger is against
all who forsake him.[g]" 23 So we fasted[h] and petitioned our God about this, and he answered our prayer.

24 Then I set apart twelve of the leading priests, namely, Sherebiah,[i] Hashabiah and ten of their
brothers, 25 and I weighed out[j] to them the offering of silver and gold and the articles that the king, his
advisers, his officials and all Israel present there had donated for the house of our God. 26 I weighed out
to them 650 talents[*a*] of silver, silver articles weighing 100 talents,[*b*] 100 talents[*b*] of gold, 27 20 bowls of
gold valued at 1,000 darics,[*c*] and two fine articles of polished bronze, as precious as gold.

28 I said to them, "You as well as these articles are consecrated to the LORD.[k] The silver and gold are
a freewill offering to the LORD, the God of your ancestors. 29 Guard them carefully until you weigh them
out in the chambers of the house of the LORD in Jerusalem before the leading priests and the Levites
and the family heads of Israel." 30 Then the priests and Levites received the silver and gold and sacred
articles that had been weighed out to be taken to the house of our God in Jerusalem.

[*a*] *26* That is, about 24 tons or about 22 metric tons [*b*] *26* That is, about 3 3/4 tons or about 3.4 metric tons
[*c*] *27* That is, about 19 pounds or about 8.4 kilograms

8:15–36 *The Return to Jerusalem.* The journey begins with Ezra checking the people to see how many are Levites.

8:15 canal that flows toward Ahava. Also vv. 21,31. This may have been part of Babylon's defensive system. It probably flowed into either the Tigris or Euphrates somewhere near Babylon and was probably similar to the Kebar "River" or canal (Ezek 1:1). **no Levites.** Perhaps the Levites had not responded to the call because the chance to settle and own property in Babylon proved more attractive than a long, hazardous journey followed by the strict routines of temple service. A rabbinic comment on Ps 137 relates the tradition that the Levites were in the caravan but were not qualified to officiate because when Nebuchadnezzar had ordered them to sing for him the songs of Zion, "they refused and bit off the ends of their fingers so that they could not play on the harps." In the postexilic period their influence declined, although the Temple Scroll at Qumran (from the Dead Sea Scrolls) assigns them important roles.

8:16 To deal with the lack of Levites (v. 15), Ezra summons eleven men: nine leaders and two scholars.

8:17 Kasiphia. Otherwise unknown; possibly contained a sanctuary because of the presence of temple servants. Moreover, the Hebrew reads "Kasiphia the place," and the word rendered "place" is occasionally used for a sanctuary.

8:18–19 Only 38 Levites answered Ezra's call.

8:18 Sherebiah. The first Levite to respond (also in v. 24; Neh 8:7; 9:4–5). His family was associated with carrying the tabernacle (Num 3:33–37; 4:29–33).

8:20 temple servants. As in ch. 2, they outnumber the Levites.

8:21–23 Before starting the journey, Ezra puts the whole matter in the hands of the Lord. Fasting prepares one for action and allows for concentration on fundamental realities. Thus the fast is not an end in itself but an opportunity for the people to humble themselves before God and ask for his protection on the coming journey. Both the fasting and the humbling are in recognition of their vulnerability and total dependence on God.

8:22 ashamed to ask the king for soldiers. This is not a binding principle because Nehemiah accepted such an escort (Neh 2:9). Both Ezra and Nehemiah acted faithfully and honorably in their respective roles. This emphasizes that God protected them and answered their prayers. This holy shame is shown again in 9:6. Ezra had already proclaimed his faith in God's ability to protect the caravan and thus was embarrassed to ask for human protection.

8:24–30 Ezra arranges for the treasure to be transported safely and follows Moses by giving that responsibility to the priests and Levites (Num 3–4).

8:25–27 The list is orderly: first silver and gold, then silver and gold vessels.

8:25 I weighed out. Ezra took personal responsibility.

8:28 consecrated. See "Holiness," p. 2676.

8:29 Guard them carefully. To prevent misuse or stealing.

8:30 house of our God in Jerusalem. Links with the early pioneers who returned to build the temple (1:3). There is, however, a significant difference. In 1:3 the words are those of Cyrus, who speaks of the "God who is in Jerusalem," showing that he sees God simply as another deity; here the word "our" expresses personal relationship.

31 On the twelfth day of the first month we set out from the Ahava Canal[l] to go to Jerusalem. The hand
of our God was on us, and he protected us from enemies and bandits along the way. 32 So we arrived in
Jerusalem, where we rested three days.[m]
33 On the fourth day, in the house of our God, we weighed out the silver and gold and the sacred articles into the hands of Meremoth[n] son of Uriah, the priest. Eleazar son of Phinehas was with him, and
so were the Levites Jozabad son of Jeshua and Noadiah son of Binnui.[o] 34 Everything was accounted for
by number and weight, and the entire weight was recorded at that time.
35 Then the exiles who had returned from captivity sacrificed burnt offerings to the God of Israel: twelve
bulls for all Israel, ninety-six rams, seventy-seven male lambs and, as a sin offering,[a] twelve male goats.[p]
All this was a burnt offering to the LORD. 36 They also delivered the king's orders[q] to the royal satraps and
to the governors of Trans-Euphrates, who then gave assistance to the people and to the house of God.[r]

Ezra's Prayer About Intermarriage

9 After these things had been done, the leaders came to me and said, "The people of Israel, including the priests and the Levites, have not kept themselves separate[s] from the neighboring peoples
with their detestable practices, like those of the Canaanites, Hittites, Perizzites, Jebusites, Ammonites,[t]
Moabites, Egyptians and Amorites.[u] 2 They have taken some of their daughters[v] as wives for themselves
and their sons, and have mingled the holy race[w] with the peoples around them. And the leaders and
officials have led the way in this unfaithfulness."[x]
3 When I heard this, I tore my tunic and cloak, pulled hair from my head and beard and sat down
appalled. 4 Then everyone who trembled[y] at the words of the God of Israel gathered around me because
of this unfaithfulness of the exiles. And I sat there appalled until the evening sacrifice.
5 Then, at the evening sacrifice,[z] I rose from my self-abasement, with my tunic and cloak torn, and
fell on my knees with my hands spread out to the LORD my God 6 and prayed:

8:31 [l] ver 15
8:32 [m] Ge 40:13; Ne 2:11
8:33 [n] Ne 3:4,21 [o] Ne 3:24
8:35 [p] 2Ch 29:21; Ezr 6:17
8:36 [q] Ezr 7:21-24 [r] Est 9:3
9:1 [s] Ezr 6:21; Ne 9:2 [t] Ge 19:38 [u] Ex 13:5
9:2 [v] Ex 34:16 [w] Ex 22:31 [x] Ezr 10:2
9:4 [y] Ezr 10:3
9:5 [z] Ex 29:41

[a] 35 Or *purification offering*

8:31–36 The narration passes over the journey with little comment because what mattered was the destination.
8:31 set out. The group with Ezra "broke camp," another link with the desert journeyings of the Israelites (e.g., Exod 16:1; 19:2) and another reminder that this is a second exodus (cf. 1:6, where their neighbors assist them with money and provisions, reminiscent of Exod 12:35–36). See "Exile and Exodus," p. 2659.
8:33–34 Scrupulous attention to detail and meticulous care ensure that everything is in order.
8:35 burnt offerings. To fulfill vows they had made in Babylon and to represent total commitment (see note on Lev 1:3–17). **sin offering.** To cleanse the people of ritual defilement (see note on Lev 4:1—5:13), which they inevitably contracted during such a long journey. It is possible that some of the transported temple items were ritually cleansed as well. Observance of the sacrificial system also fulfills the terms of Artaxerxes' edict (7:17).
8:36 royal satraps ... governors. Normally a province such as Trans-Euphrates would have had only one satrap. This may use "satrap" in a less precise way that is synonymous with "governors." The double expression ("satraps ... governors") is a general way of referring to the governing officials who continued to have good relations with the community in Judah. Today, we often use the term "authorities" to refer to both local and national figures. **assistance.** Follows the stipulations of Artaxerxes' decree. Thus, "the gracious hand of ... God" (v. 18) uses the king and the local officials to carry out the work.
9:1–15 *Ezra Prays About the Problem of Intermarriage With Pagans.* Chs. 9–10, a single narrative, form the last section of the book and give the account of how Ezra responded to the problem of the Israelites' marriages to foreign wives.
9:1 After these things. This refers to the events of ch. 8, which have all the hallmarks of a promising start. We know from 7:9 that Ezra arrived in Jerusalem in the "fifth month"; now four months have passed, for 10:9 speaks of the "ninth month" as the time when Ezra begins to deal with the problem of mixed marriages (marriages between Israelites and foreigners). **leaders.** Perhaps the district governors (such as those in Neh 3:6–12). **have not kept themselves separate.** Have intermarried with non-Israelites. This was not forbidden in itself, as is evident from the cases of Moses (Num 12:1), Joseph (Gen 41:45), Ruth, and Esther. Rather this was a temptation to lapse into the worship of pagan gods and the associated lifestyles. **Canaanites, Hittites, Perizzites, Jebusites, Ammonites, Moabites, Egyptians and Amorites.** Represent the original inhabitants of Canaan before the conquest (Exod 3:8). Only the Ammonites, Moabites, and Egyptians were still living there in the postexilic period (2 Chr 8:7–8). The archaic names for the inhabitants of the land deliberately echo those in the Pentateuch, which warns Israel of the dangers they would face upon entering the land (Deut 7:1–6). The archaic references may also suggest that these women had not become Jews and thus were likely to tempt the Israelites into sin, as had happened in earlier times (e.g., Num 25).
9:2 race. Or "seed," the faithful descendants who would carry on the covenant line (see Isa 6:13, which speaks of the "holy seed"—the surviving remnant that would be brought to life again [cf. Ezek 37] after the terrible judgment of the exile). **leaders and officials.** Probably minor officials and village elders; different from those in v. 1.
9:3 tore my tunic and cloak, pulled hair. Visibly expressed sorrow and anger. Tearing one's clothes often expressed grief at someone's death (Gen 37:34; 2 Sam 1:11). When Nehemiah was confronted with the same problem of intermarriage, instead of pulling out his own hair, he pulled out the hair of the offending parties (Neh 13:25).
9:4 everyone who trembled at the words of the God of Israel. Shows the effects of Ezra's words and actions (cf. Isa 66:2). **evening sacrifice.** The ninth hour (3:00 p.m.), a regular time of prayer.
9:5 fell on my knees. Represents humility. **hands spread out.** A common posture in prayer, perhaps acknowledging need.

9:6 [a]2Ch 28:9; Job 42:6; Ps 38:4; Rev 18:5
9:7 [b]2Ch 29:6 [c]Eze 21:1-32 [d]Dt 28:64 [e]Dt 28:37
9:8 [f]Ps 25:16; Isa 33:2 [g]Ge 45:7 [h]Ecc 12:11; Isa 22:23 [i]Ps 13:3
9:9 [j]Ex 1:14; Ne 9:36 [k]Ezr 7:28 [l]Ps 69:35; Isa 43:1; Jer 32:44
9:10 [m]Dt 11:8; Isa 1:19-20
9:11 [n]Lev 18:25-28 [o]Dt 9:4
9:12 [p]Ex 34:15; Dt 7:3; 23:6
9:13 [q]Job 11:6; Ps 103:10
9:14 [r]Ne 13:27 [s]Dt 9:8 [t]Dt 9:14
9:15 [u]Ge 18:25; Ps 51:4; Jer 12:1; Da 9:7 [v]Ne 9:33; Ps 130:3; Mal 3:2 [w]1Ki 8:47
10:1 [x]2Ch 20:9; Da 9:20

"I am too ashamed and disgraced, my God, to lift up my face to you, because our sins are
higher than our heads and our guilt has reached to the heavens.[a] 7From the days of our ancestors[b] until now, our guilt has been great. Because of our sins, we and our kings and our priests
have been subjected to the sword[c] and captivity,[d] to pillage and humiliation[e] at the hand of
foreign kings, as it is today.
8"But now, for a brief moment, the LORD our God has been gracious[f] in leaving us a remnant[g]
and giving us a firm place[a][h] in his sanctuary, and so our God gives light to our eyes[i] and a little
relief in our bondage. 9Though we are slaves,[j] our God has not forsaken us in our bondage. He has
shown us kindness[k] in the sight of the kings of Persia: He has granted us new life to rebuild the house
of our God and repair its ruins,[l] and he has given us a wall of protection in Judah and Jerusalem.
10"But now, our God, what can we say after this? For we have forsaken the commands[m] 11you
gave through your servants the prophets when you said: 'The land you are entering to possess is
a land polluted[n] by the corruption of its peoples. By their detestable practices[o] they have filled it
with their impurity from one end to the other. 12Therefore, do not give your daughters in marriage to their sons or take their daughters for your sons. Do not seek a treaty of friendship with
them[p] at any time, that you may be strong and eat the good things of the land and leave it to your
children as an everlasting inheritance.'
13"What has happened to us is a result of our evil deeds and our great guilt, and yet, our God,
you have punished us less than our sins deserved[q] and have given us a remnant like this. 14Shall
we then break your commands again and intermarry[r] with the peoples who commit such detestable practices? Would you not be angry enough with us to destroy us,[s] leaving us no remnant[t]
or survivor? 15LORD, the God of Israel, you are righteous![u] We are left this day as a remnant. Here
we are before you in our guilt, though because of it not one of us can stand[v] in your presence."[w]

The People's Confession of Sin

10 While Ezra was praying and confessing,[x] weeping and throwing himself down before the house
of God, a large crowd of Israelites — men, women and children — gathered around him. They
too wept bitterly. 2Then Shekaniah son of Jehiel, one of the descendants of Elam, said to Ezra, "We have

[a] 8 Or *a foothold*

9:6–15 One of the Bible's great prayers. Its closest parallel is Daniel's prayer (Dan 9:4–19): both Daniel and Ezra identify themselves with the sins of the people and become mouthpieces for their confessions. See also the prayer in Neh 9:5–37.
9:6 ashamed and disgraced. Ezra felt both inner shame before God and outward humiliation before the people for his sins and their sins. The two Hebrew verbs used here often occur together (e.g., Ps 35:4; Isa 45:16; Jer 31:19). **higher than our heads ... reached to the heavens.** The accumulated sins of generations have so piled up that they reach to heaven itself. A similar expression is used of God's covenant love in Ps 103:11–12: God's grace is greater than our sin.
9:7 the days of our ancestors. The whole of their past history. **until now.** The sin of the people had been shown throughout their history (e.g., Moses' warning of rebelliousness [Deut 31: 27] and the numerous mentions by Jeremiah of continual disobedience [e.g., Jer 14:20; 15:6; 26:19]).
9:8 now, for a brief moment. The 80 years since Cyrus's decree that allowed the exiles to return. Though 80 years is not literally "a brief moment," it is probably being compared to the long centuries of Babylonian and Assyrian oppression. **gives light to our eyes.** Revives our spirits. In 1 Sam 14:27, this Hebrew phrase describes Jonathan when honey refreshed him after an arduous battle. Here the sense is that God's grace is still at work.
9:9 He has granted us new life to rebuild. God providentially guides the whole enterprise. This is the fundamental reason for their return. **wall of protection.** Not the physical wall around Jerusalem, which was yet to be rebuilt, but the protection that God himself provides (cf. Zech 2:5). "Wall" can also be used for a wall around a vineyard, and this would give a further nuance of Israel as a vine brought from Egypt and planted in the promised land (Ps 80:8–11). If we accept this connection, it would be a further comparison between the exodus and the return from exile (see notes on 1:6,11; 3:4; 8:31).
9:10–12 While these "commands" (v. 10) range widely throughout the prophetic canon, the allusions to Leviticus and Deuteronomy emphasize the authority of Moses, the archetypal prophet. The basic passages dealing with the polluted land are part of the Holiness Code (especially Lev 18:25–30; 20:22–24), and Deut 7:1–6 warns against corruption from the surrounding nations (cf. 2 Kgs 21:10–11; Isa 1:19–20; Jer 7:25–26).
9:12 everlasting inheritance. A reminder of God's ancient promise concerning the land (Gen 12:1) and a perspective on the future.
9:13 God punished the nation but graciously did not wipe them out completely. After all, there were many other Israelites scattered throughout the Persian Empire through whom God could fulfill his purposes. The book of Esther shows how the Lord continued to care for those who did not return to the land of promise.
9:15 righteous. Includes God's mighty acts on behalf of his people and his total integrity and just dealings with them, which includes punishing them when they are guilty (cf. Gen 18:25). **our guilt.** Corporate sin means that the whole community suffers even if they were not personally involved in the sin (here: mixed marriages). A proper sense of God's holiness makes us aware of our unworthiness (cf. Isaiah [Isa 6:1–5] and Peter [Luke 5:8]). **stand.** Be legally acquitted (Ps 130:3). Ezra does not dilute this sense of unworthiness in any way by asking for mercy; he trusts the righteous character of God, whom he praises.
10:1–17 *The People's Confession of Sin.* The people respond to Ezra's prayer and follow his lead.
10:1 weeping and throwing himself down. Adds to the powerful

been unfaithful[y] to our God by marrying foreign women from the peoples around us. But in spite of this, there is still hope for Israel.[z] 3Now let us make a covenant[a] before our God to send away[b] all these women and their children, in accordance with the counsel of my lord and of those who fear the commands of our God. Let it be done according to the Law. 4Rise up; this matter is in your hands. We will support you, so take courage and do it."

5So Ezra rose up and put the leading priests and Levites and all Israel under oath[c] to do what had been suggested. And they took the oath. 6Then Ezra withdrew from before the house of God and went to the room of Jehohanan son of Eliashib. While he was there, he ate no food and drank no water,[d] because he continued to mourn over the unfaithfulness of the exiles.

7A proclamation was then issued throughout Judah and Jerusalem for all the exiles to assemble in Jerusalem. 8Anyone who failed to appear within three days would forfeit all his property, in accordance with the decision of the officials and elders, and would himself be expelled from the assembly of the exiles.

9Within the three days, all the men of Judah and Benjamin[e] had gathered in Jerusalem. And on the twentieth day of the ninth month, all the people were sitting in the square before the house of God, greatly distressed by the occasion and because of the rain. 10Then Ezra the priest stood up and said to them, "You have been unfaithful; you have married foreign women, adding to Israel's guilt. 11Now honor[a] the LORD, the God of your ancestors, and do his will. Separate yourselves from the peoples around you and from your foreign wives."[f]

12The whole assembly responded with a loud voice:[g] "You are right! We must do as you say. 13But there are many people here and it is the rainy season; so we cannot stand outside. Besides, this matter cannot be taken care of in a day or two, because we have sinned greatly in this thing. 14Let our officials act for the whole assembly. Then let everyone in our towns who has married a foreign woman come at a set time, along with the elders and judges[h] of each town, until the fierce anger[i] of our God in this matter is turned away from us." 15Only Jonathan son of Asahel and Jahzeiah son of Tikvah, supported by Meshullam and Shabbethai[j] the Levite, opposed this.

10:2 [y] Ezr 9:2; Ne 13:27 [z] Dt 30:8-10
10:3 [a] 2Ch 34:31 [b] Ex 34:16; Dt 7:2-3; Ezr 9:4
10:5 [c] Ne 5:12; 13:25
10:6 [d] Ex 34:28; Dt 9:18
10:9 [e] Ezr 1:5
10:11 [f] ver 3; Dt 24:1; Ne 9:2; Mal 2:10-16
10:12 [g] Jos 6:5
10:14 [h] Dt 16:18 [i] Nu 25:4; 2Ch 29:10; 30:8
10:15 [j] Ne 11:16

[a] 11 Or *Now make confession to*

emotion of the scene: people realize Ezra is personally and deeply involved in this issue. **They too wept bitterly.** A genuine response by the crowd.

10:2 Shekaniah. Belonged to a family that returned to Jerusalem with the first wave of exiles (2:7) and probably welcomed and responded to Ezra's ministry. **We have been unfaithful.** Recalls Ezra's own prayer and shows a realization that they had not obeyed the words of God. **still hope.** We must not take God's forgiveness for granted; repentance in heart and action, as well as in words, can open the way back to God.

10:3 make a covenant. A covenant-renewal ceremony echoes Josiah's great reforms (2 Chr 34:29–31) and Joshua's covenant renewal (Josh 24:25). **women and their children.** Mothers were given custody of their children when a marriage was dissolved. When Hagar was sent away, Ishmael went with her (Gen 21:14). The terms here for marriage and divorce are unusual, and this may imply that these were not proper marriages. **according to the Law.** Deut 24:1–4 permits divorce in certain circumstances.

10:4 Shekaniah acknowledges Ezra's leadership and urges him to take decisive action.

10:6 withdrew. Ezra recognizes the need for continuing prayer. His continued fasting and prayer show that he is not taking God's mercy for granted. **Eliashib.** The name was common; he is almost certainly not the high priest of Neh 3:1.

10:8 within three days. Judah was small, so it was easy to reach Jerusalem from any part of Judah within three days. **forfeit.** This word occurs often in Joshua, where God sometimes commands his people to destroy cities and objects or otherwise render them unusable for ordinary purposes (Josh 6:21; 7:25).

10:9 ninth month. Kislev, which corresponds to November/December, when heavy rain (and sometimes snow) falls in Jerusalem. **square.** The location of Ezra's prayer—and possibly the reading and explaining of the law (Neh 8:1)—was either the outer court of the temple or the open space in front of the Water Gate. **greatly distressed by the occasion and because of the rain.** The vivid image of the people miserably huddling together in a downpour reinforces the occasion's solemnity. They are trembling, partly for fear of God (as in 9:4), and partly because they are cold and drenched. **rain.** A Hebrew plural of intensity is used, perhaps indicating a downpour.

10:10 unfaithful. Not only the specific failure but the age-old fickleness of the human heart. **adding to Israel's guilt.** The sins and failures of the exiles were bad enough, but they had added insult to injury by marrying pagan women.

10:11 honor. Give thanks or praise to God—which in itself is an acknowledgment of their sinfulness and God's holiness.

10:12 Their agreement was probably sincere, but their desire to get away from the wet, uncomfortable place as soon as possible doubtless also inspired it.

10:14 Let our officials act for the whole assembly. A sensible suggestion because then, as now, a large crowd is not a good forum for making important decisions. **officials.** Probably the "family heads" (v. 16) who would convene in Jerusalem and go systematically through each town and village, working with the local leaders to ensure fairness. **until the fierce anger of our God in this matter is turned away from us.** The people realize that God's anger is real; they therefore express the hope that they will have done enough to avert judgment.

10:15 Four individuals opposed the edict of v. 14. It is not clear if they thought the edict was too severe or too lax (probably the latter). **Meshullam.** Probably Ezra's companion in 8:16.

10:18 [k] Jdg 3:6 [l] Ezr 2:2 10:19 [m] 2Ki 10:15 [n] Lev 5:15; 6:6 10:20 [o] 1Ch 24:14 10:21 [p] 1Ch 24:8 10:22 [q] 1Ch 9:12 10:23 [r] Ne 8:7; 9:4 10:24 [s] Ne 3:1; 12:10; 13:7,28 10:25 [t] Ezr 2:3 10:26 [u] ver 2

16 So the exiles did as was proposed. Ezra the priest selected men who were family heads, one from
each family division, and all of them designated by name. On the first day of the tenth month they sat
down to investigate the cases, 17 and by the first day of the first month they finished dealing with all the
men who had married foreign women.

Those Guilty of Intermarriage

18 Among the descendants of the priests, the following had married foreign women:[k]

From the descendants of Joshua[l] son of Jozadak, and his brothers: Maaseiah, Eliezer, Jarib and
Gedaliah. 19 (They all gave their hands[m] in pledge to put away their wives, and for their guilt
they each presented a ram from the flock as a guilt offering.)[n]

20 From the descendants of Immer:[o]
Hanani and Zebadiah.

21 From the descendants of Harim:[p]
Maaseiah, Elijah, Shemaiah, Jehiel and Uzziah.

22 From the descendants of Pashhur:[q]
Elioenai, Maaseiah, Ishmael, Nethanel, Jozabad and Elasah.

23 Among the Levites:[r]

Jozabad, Shimei, Kelaiah (that is, Kelita), Pethahiah, Judah and Eliezer.

24 From the musicians:
Eliashib.[s]
From the gatekeepers:
Shallum, Telem and Uri.

25 And among the other Israelites:

From the descendants of Parosh:[t]
Ramiah, Izziah, Malkijah, Mijamin, Eleazar, Malkijah and Benaiah.

26 From the descendants of Elam:[u]
Mattaniah, Zechariah, Jehiel, Abdi, Jeremoth and Elijah.

27 From the descendants of Zattu:
Elioenai, Eliashib, Mattaniah, Jeremoth, Zabad and Aziza.

28 From the descendants of Bebai:
Jehohanan, Hananiah, Zabbai and Athlai.

29 From the descendants of Bani:
Meshullam, Malluk, Adaiah, Jashub, Sheal and Jeremoth.

30 From the descendants of Pahath-Moab:
Adna, Kelal, Benaiah, Maaseiah, Mattaniah, Bezalel, Binnui and Manasseh.

10:16 the priest. Shows that Ezra was acting not only on the basis of the authority the Persian king had given him but also in his role as Israel's priest and teacher (7:1–7). **first day of the tenth month.** Only ten days after the public gathering decided to set up the commission. This body completed its work in three months, discovering that about 110 men were guilty of marrying pagan wives.

10:17 first day of the first month. Exactly one year after Ezra first set out from Babylon (7:9). Here the narrative of Ezra effectively ends. What follows is a list of the names that emerged from the commission's investigation.

10:18–44 *Those Guilty of Intermarriage.* Like the other lists in Ezra, this one is carefully arranged. Unlike the other lists, this mentions the priests first: the high priest's own family is first (vv. 18–19), then all the other priests (vv. 20–22). They are followed by the Levites (vv. 23–24) and other Israelites (vv. 25–43). The list of around a hundred names is shorter than we might expect; it may be that only the most significant individuals are mentioned. In any case, Ezra's reaction shows that he recognizes the danger that even a relatively small number could pose to the whole community. The inquiry was thorough and probably considered each case separately.

10:18–19 This mentions the high priest's family first, presumably because they are most culpable for leading others into error.

10:19 all gave their hands in pledge. Probably a general statement covering all who were involved, not just the four individuals in v. 18. **guilt offering.** A sacrifice offered when someone sinned "unintentionally" (Lev 5:15; see note on Lev 5:14—6:7). Presumably, the people offered this sacrifice because at that time there was no explicit legal prohibition of marriage to people of the particular nations.

10:20–22 Priestly families also mentioned in Neh 13:28–29.

10:23–24 Levites and other temple servants. This mentions six of the 24 Levites from the census in 2:40–54 but only one of the 128 singers.

10:25–43 There are 12 family groups here. As the book ends, the term "Israelites" is probably a reminder of the unity of God's people before the divided kingdom.

[31] From the descendants of Harim:
Eliezer, Ishijah, Malkijah, Shemaiah, Shimeon, [32]Benjamin, Malluk and Shemariah.
[33] From the descendants of Hashum:
Mattenai, Mattattah, Zabad, Eliphelet, Jeremai, Manasseh and Shimei.
[34] From the descendants of Bani:
Maadai, Amram, Uel, [35]Benaiah, Bedeiah, Keluhi, [36]Vaniah, Meremoth, Eliashib, [37]Mattaniah,
Mattenai and Jaasu.
[38] From the descendants of Binnui:[a]
Shimei, [39]Shelemiah, Nathan, Adaiah, [40]Maknadebai, Shashai, Sharai, [41]Azarel, Shelemiah,
Shemariah, [42]Shallum, Amariah and Joseph.
[43] From the descendants of Nebo:
Jeiel, Mattithiah, Zabad, Zebina, Jaddai, Joel and Benaiah.

[44]All these had married foreign women, and some of them had children by these wives.[b]

[a] *37,38* See Septuagint (also 1 Esdras 9:34); Hebrew *Jaasu [38]and Bani and Binnui,* [b] *44* Or *and they sent them away with their children*

10:44 All these had married foreign women. Resumes the narrative thread from the end of the inquest. **some of them had children by these wives.** This could mean that they dismissed the children along with the wives (a parallel passage in the Apocrypha suggests this [see 1 Esdras 9:36]). That would make good sense and flow from the original decision in v. 3. Many of the women and their children could have returned to their extended families. The whole passage bristles with problems, and two major views are possible: (1) This is virtually a revival that establishes the purity of the postexilic community. (2) This action is heartless; while honoring the law that prohibits mixed marriages, it dishonors the law, which prohibits easy divorce, and doubtless caused untold grief and heartbreak. There is truth in both views, and the account illustrates the perpetual difficulty of avoiding the extremes of legalism and laxity.

The abrupt ending of the book of Ezra without a summation is probably because the book was originally joined to Nehemiah. That means that what we have here is not the conclusion of Ezra's ministry but the closing section of the first part of it. The focus now shifts to Nehemiah, another faithful servant of the Lord. Both Ezra and Nehemiah had vital parts to play in the restoring of Jerusalem. Moreover, in Neh 8 we discover how Ezra's great sermon blends with Nehemiah's work of rebuilding.

INTRODUCTION TO NEHEMIAH

The book of Nehemiah, along with its companion Ezra, comes from the time of the return from exile in Babylon and vividly narrates the obstacles and opposition the Jews encountered when they rebuilt the walls of Jerusalem and eventually made the city habitable and secure. Ezra and later Nehemiah led the restoration and rebuilding not only of the broken city but also the broken people. Their roles were different, but we should not exaggerate the difference. Ezra, although primarily a teacher, had clear ideas about the constitution of the returned community; and Nehemiah, while primarily an administrator, had a vital spiritual life. The books of Ezra and Nehemiah are both concerned with the interplay of the public and the personal and the inextricable link of the material and the spiritual.

AUTHOR AND DATE

See Introduction to Ezra: Author. The Hebrew Bible considers Ezra and Nehemiah as one book, which makes it probable that the author/editor is the same person for both. If we adopt the chronology of Ezra preceding Nehemiah, it is possible that Ezra himself composed much of both books. A date of composition during or shortly after the latter part of the reign of Darius II (423 – 404 BC) is likely.

HISTORICAL SETTING

Thirteen years have passed since Ezra's return to Jerusalem, and all is not well there. Artaxerxes I of Persia (465 – 424 BC) sends Nehemiah, his cupbearer, to Jerusalem in 445 BC as governor until 434 or 433 BC. The 13-year gap between Ezra's coming and the exposition of the Torah in Neh 8 is a problem only if we assume that Ezra did nothing during these years (see Introduction to Ezra). The later chapters of Ezra show him vigorously pressing forward with reforms, and it is reasonable to suppose that here, as elsewhere in Scripture, the history is selective and highlights theological issues. The prophet Malachi may have been active around this time, since Nehemiah addresses some of the abuses that Malachi condemns.

GENRE

Like Ezra, the book of Nehemiah has been compiled from a number of sources, public and private. Again there are letters, edicts, and lists but also the personal stories of Nehemiah (1:1 — 7:73; 8:1 — 10:39; 12:27 – 43; 13:4 – 31), which are fuller and more vivid than the stories of Ezra (Ezra 7:1 – 10,27 – 28; 8:15 — 10:17). These stories are an important part of the developing events and help establish the significance of those events. Some argue that the stories originally formed part of Nehemiah's report to the Persian king and that the book of Nehemiah adapts them for a wider audience. That may be so, but it is impossible to prove. The way that the narrative is combined with lists and accounts of the work is evidence of both historical accuracy and personal involvement. The earlier part of the book (chs. 1 – 6) is concerned mainly with rebuilding the walls; the second part (chs. 7 – 13), with reforming worship and organizing community life under the impetus of the public reading and exposition of the Torah.

LEADING THEMES

Nehemiah is a gifted storyteller. Nevertheless, his main object is more than telling stories. He wrestles with great themes that run through many parts of Scripture — themes he experiences and expounds with great intensity. Unsurprisingly, the emphases of the books of Ezra and Nehemiah overlap. Nehemiah comes to us first as a man of prayer before we see him in action as a gifted administrator and leader. All he does is driven by loyalty to the God of the covenant. He is passionate about the rebuilding of Jerusalem and the establishment of God's people in the land, including a resumption of community life and worship.

The Doctrine of God

Since the Bible is God's book *about* God and *from* God, any biblical book will focus on God even when he is peripherally mentioned in the text. As in Ezra (e.g., Ezra 1:2; 5:12; 6:9), the "God of heaven" (Neh 1:5; 2:4,20) shows his universal sovereignty. The use of this title in the book of Nehemiah implies polemic since this was the title of the Persian god Ahura-Mazda; but for Nehemiah, "You alone are the LORD" (9:6). While the distant province of *Yehud* (Judah) may seem insignificant in Susa, Judah is the city of the great God of heaven. Thus, while what Nehemiah does in Susa can seem insignificant, he sees what he is doing as continuous with the great days of Moses. In 1:8 – 9, Nehemiah refers to Lev 26:33 and Deut 30:4 about how disobedience would lead to exile, but he also echoes Jer 29:14 about how the Lord would bring the people back. Later in the book we are reminded that the Lord is the God of the covenant who keeps his promises (9:7 – 8). God is holy, and the first thing Nehemiah does in the book is confess his own sin and the people's sin (1:4 – 7). God is a forgiving God (9:16 – 19). These are some of the great truths running through Nehemiah, but Nehemiah does not hold or present them with cold detachment. Nehemiah "delight[s] in revering [God's] name" (1:11), acknowledges God's goodness (2:8,18), and confesses God's holiness (9:14). All through the book Nehemiah is passionate for the honor of God's name and the welfare of God's people.

The Supremacy of Scripture

At the heart of the book's story is the mass public gathering to hear the Torah read and expounded. Ezra leads it, but Nehemiah joins with him in encouraging the people to respond (8:9 – 11). Also, as in Ezra, the book frequently refers to earlier Scripture, including references to Abraham (9:7 – 8) and Moses (1:7; 8:1). The exodus is described in 9:9 – 25 in a way that resembles Psalms and the Prophetic Books.

Part of Nehemiah's wall in Jerusalem.

Todd Bolen/www.BiblePlaces.com

The History of Salvation

The events recorded in the books of Ezra and Nehemiah span more than a century. Both books single out events that shed light on God's ongoing purposes. The actions of the two reformers intertwine in chs. 8 – 10. The lists in 12:1 – 26 serve as a bridge between the two phases of the reform (see especially 12:26), and the expression "in the days of Zerubbabel [important in the book of Ezra] and of Nehemiah" (12:47) perceives the events of both books as part of the same stage in God's purpose. Moreover, at every stage of the return, God works through the Persian kings as his agents and assists his people against all obstacles.

The Importance of Prayer

The narrative underlines the importance of prayer. The story opens with prayer in Susa (1:4) and ends with prayer in Jerusalem (13:31). There is the great prayer of thanksgiving and adoration in 9:5 – 36, and Nehemiah frequently prays. The emphasis on God's overruling providence leads not to complacency but to fervent prayer.

The Nature of Leadership

Nehemiah emerges as a vigorous and visionary leader. He is a man of integrity and honesty and does not, e.g., conceal his own participation in money-lending when that becomes a problem. He is courageous and faces enemies boldly. He sacrifices a comfortable position at the Persian court to face unknown difficulties and dangers.

The Provisional Nature of the Work

The book ends not with a great flourish but with a renewed call for faithfulness (13:21 – 29) and a heartfelt prayer for God's help. Before the end of Nehemiah's service, initial enthusiasm is running out, leading to lapses into past ungodly practices. Until the kingdom is consummated, there will always be the need for faith, obedience, and daily dependence on the Lord's help.

THE PORTRAIT OF NEHEMIAH IN THE BOOK

Nehemiah comes across more vividly than Ezra. We should not rigidly distinguish between Ezra the spiritual leader and Nehemiah the political leader because each is prominent in both spheres. Yet Nehemiah, although a lay figure, is involved in projects of building and spiritual reformation usually associated with kings and prophets. Like Hezekiah and Josiah, he rebuilds and repairs the city and calls the people to return to the celebration of the great festivals that commemorate aspects of Israel's relationship with its covenant Lord.

King Ashurnasirpal II court scene, ninth century BC. Nehemiah was the cupbearer for Artaxerxes (Neh 1:11).

Nehemiah is not strictly a prophet, but the book opens with the phrase "The words of Nehemiah," analogous to introductions in the Prophetic Books (e.g., Jer 1:1; Amos 1:1). His words often are prophetic (e.g., 2:12,17 – 18), and false prophets harass him (6:10 – 14) as they do the great prophets. Neither is Nehemiah a priest, but he is thoroughly involved in the renewal of priests and Levites (chs. 7 – 13). He is not a perfect figure, and we are not invited to admire or imitate him in every respect — e.g., beating people and pulling out their hair (13:25)! We are not Nehemiah, but Nehemiah's God is our God; and we, like Nehemiah, are servants. Thus, we can see in the struggles he faced and the reforms he carried out a voice for our own day. Ezra and Nehemiah acted to restore Israel's covenant relationship with the Lord: they confessed their sin of turning from the Lord in disobedience; they restored the Torah at the heart of the nation's life; and they carried out the necessary restoration to allow the kind of settled life and security where progress could be made.

RELEVANCE

- It is important to be rooted in the story of God's past dealings without living in the past and pining for a mythical golden age. The hard grind of recovery and reform is calculated to bring out strong faith.
- We must emphasize the gospel's uniqueness and confront spiritual and moral compromise.
- Prayer is the link between balancing God's sovereignty with the need for action.
- In our day we will never complete the work, because God begins and finishes that for his glory.

OUTLINE

I. The Return of Nehemiah and the Rebuilding of the Walls of Jerusalem (1:1 — 7:3)

A. Nehemiah's Prayer (1:1 – 11)
B. Artaxerxes Sends Nehemiah to Jerusalem (2:1 – 10)
C. Nehemiah Inspects Jerusalem's Walls (2:11 – 20)
D. Builders of the Wall (3:1 – 32)
E. Opposition to the Rebuilding (4:1 – 23)
F. Nehemiah Helps the Poor (5:1 – 19)
G. Further Opposition to the Rebuilding (6:1 – 15)
H. Opposition to the Completed Wall (6:16 — 7:3)

II. The List of the Exiles Who Returned (7:4 – 73a)

III. Ezra Reads the Law (7:73b — 8:18)

IV. The Israelites Confess Their Sins (9:1 – 37)

V. The Agreement of the People (9:38 — 10:39)

VI. The New Residents of Jerusalem (11:1 – 36)

VII. Priests and Levites (12:1 – 26)

VIII. Dedication of the Wall of Jerusalem (12:27 – 47)

IX. Nehemiah's Final Reforms (13:1 – 31)

NEHEMIAH

1:1 [a]Ne 10:1; Zec 7:1
1:2 [b]Ne 7:2 [c]Jer 52:28
1:3 [d]2Ki 25:10; Ne 2:3,13,17
1:4 [e]Ps 137:1 [f]Ezr 9:4
1:5 [g]Dt 7:21; Ne 4:14 [h]Ex 20:6; Da 9:4
1:6 [i]1Ki 8:29 [j]Da 9:17
1:7 [k]Dt 28:14-15; Ps 106:6
1:8 [l]2Ki 20:3 [m]Lev 26:33

Nehemiah's Prayer

1 The words of Nehemiah son of Hakaliah:

In the month of Kislev[a] in the twentieth year, while I was in the citadel of Susa, 2Hanani,[b] one of my brothers, came from Judah with some other men, and I questioned them about the Jewish remnant[c] that had survived the exile, and also about Jerusalem.

3They said to me, "Those who survived the exile and are back in the province are in great trouble and disgrace. The wall of Jerusalem is broken down, and its gates have been burned with fire.[d]"

4When I heard these things, I sat down and wept.[e] For some days I mourned and fasted[f] and prayed before the God of heaven. 5Then I said:

"LORD, the God of heaven, the great and awesome God,[g] who keeps his covenant of love[h] with those who love him and keep his commandments, 6let your ear be attentive and your eyes open to hear[i] the prayer[j] your servant is praying before you day and night for your servants, the people of Israel. I confess the sins we Israelites, including myself and my father's family, have committed against you. 7We have acted very wickedly[k] toward you. We have not obeyed the commands, decrees and laws you gave your servant Moses.

8"Remember[l] the instruction you gave your servant Moses, saying, 'If you are unfaithful, I will scatter[m] you among the nations, 9but if you return to me and obey my commands, then even if

---

1:1—7:3 *The Return of Nehemiah and the Rebuilding of the Walls of Jerusalem.* Nehemiah (like Ezra) establishes the postexilic community in Jerusalem. He plays a key part in the ongoing history of Israel: ensuring that Jerusalem is rebuilt and secure. Such security would allow regularized worship at the temple, where the Lord of the covenant would come and find at least a remnant of his people waiting for him.

1:1–11 *Nehemiah's Prayer.* The bad news Nehemiah receives in v. 3 prompts this prayer.

1:1 son of Hakaliah. Distinguishes Nehemiah from other Nehemiahs (3:16; Ezra 2:2). **twentieth year.** Of the reign of Artaxerxes (465–424 BC). **citadel of Susa.** The winter residence of the Persian kings.

1:2 Hanani. Later appointed Nehemiah's deputy (7:2). In the Elephantine papyri (ca. 400 BC from a Jewish colony in South Egypt) a man called Hananiah (longer form of Hanani) is said to have been the head of Jewish affairs. Some identify him as Nehemiah's brother and suggest he may have governed between Nehemiah's first and second terms as governor. **Jewish remnant.** The true Israel through whom God carries out his purposes. In this context, the remnant refers to Jews who had returned to Jerusalem and Judah, joining up with those left behind; more broadly, the word is not always restricted to the returned exiles, for the book of Esther shows how God saved his people through Esther and Mordecai, Jews who remained in Persia.

1:3 broken down ... burned with fire. The lack of a city wall meant that the people were defenseless against attack. Excavations at Jerusalem in the 1960s revealed that the destruction of the eastern wall had also destroyed the terraces. When Nebuchadnezzar destroyed Jerusalem in 586 BC, he broke down the walls (2 Kgs 25:10). Of more immediate concern to Nehemiah is the episode recorded in Ezra 4:7–23: attempts to repair the damage had been stopped by imperial decree (see note on Ezra 4:21–23).

1:4 Nehemiah's high position in the Persian court has not diminished his love and concern for his homeland. **God of heaven.** Earthly powers cannot thwart the King of heaven's purposes.

1:5 Before turning to petition, Nehemiah reiterates the greatness of God's character and thus God's ability to answer his request in v. 11. This is coupled with an appeal to God's covenant faithfulness. Nehemiah realizes it is not, as the popular phrase puts it, that "prayer changes things" but prayer puts us in touch with the God who changes things.

1:6–7 Nehemiah confesses both corporate and personal guilt.

1:7 commands, decrees and laws you gave your servant Moses. Alludes to Deut 28:64; 30:1–4. The unique revelation to Moses forms the prayer's centerpiece. The Mosaic law is prominent in Ezra (3:2; 6:18; 7:6) and Nehemiah (v. 8; 8:1,14; 9:14; 10:29; 13:1).

1:8–9 The exile and its aftermath are evidence that God has fulfilled his promise to Moses.

1:9 The promise of restoration from "the farthest horizon" goes beyond

your exiled people are at the farthest horizon, I will gather[n] them from there and bring them to
the place I have chosen as a dwelling for my Name.'[o]
10"They are your servants and your people, whom you redeemed by your great strength and
your mighty hand.[p] 11Lord, let your ear be attentive[q] to the prayer of this your servant and to the
prayer of your servants who delight in revering your name. Give your servant success today by
granting him favor in the presence of this man."

I was cupbearer[r] to the king.

1:9 [n]Dt 30:4 [o]1Ki 8:48; Jer 29:14
1:10 [p]Ex 32:11; Dt 9:29
1:11 [q]ver 6 [r]Ge 40:1
2:1 [s]Ezr 7:1
2:3 [t]1Ki 1:31; Da 2:4; 5:10; 6:6,21 [u]Ps 137:6 [v]Ne 1:3
2:6 [w]Ne 5:14; 13:6
2:7 [x]Ezr 8:36
2:8 [y]Ne 7:2 [z]ver 18; Ezr 5:5; 7:6
2:9 [a]Ezr 8:22

Artaxerxes Sends Nehemiah to Jerusalem

2 In the month of Nisan in the twentieth year of King Artaxerxes,[s] when wine was brought for him, I
took the wine and gave it to the king. I had not been sad in his presence before, 2so the king asked
me, "Why does your face look so sad when you are not ill? This can be nothing but sadness of heart."
I was very much afraid, 3but I said to the king, "May the king live forever![t] Why should my face not
look sad when the city[u] where my ancestors are buried lies in ruins, and its gates have been destroyed
by fire?[v]"
4The king said to me, "What is it you want?"
Then I prayed to the God of heaven, 5and I answered the king, "If it pleases the king and if your servant has found favor in his sight, let him send me to the city in Judah where my ancestors are buried
so that I can rebuild it."
6Then the king[w], with the queen sitting beside him, asked me, "How long will your journey take, and
when will you get back?" It pleased the king to send me; so I set a time.
7I also said to him, "If it pleases the king, may I have letters to the governors of Trans-Euphrates,[x] so
that they will provide me safe-conduct until I arrive in Judah? 8And may I have a letter to Asaph, keeper
of the royal park, so he will give me timber to make beams for the gates of the citadel[y] by the temple and
for the city wall and for the residence I will occupy?" And because the gracious hand of my God was on
me,[z] the king granted my requests. 9So I went to the governors of Trans-Euphrates and gave them the
king's letters. The king had also sent army officers and cavalry[a] with me.

the immediate return to Jerusalem and points to the future kingdom and a time when God's people will come with singing to Zion (Isa 35:10).

1:10 redeemed by your great strength and your mighty hand. Familiar terms of God's saving power at the exodus (e.g., Deut 3:24; 4:34; 7:8; 9:26). The reversal of the exile is a new exodus (cf. Isa 51:9–11; see "Exile and Exodus," p. 2659).

1:11 name. Implies that Yahweh's presence dwells in the restored community. This echoes Solomon's prayer at the dedication of the temple: "May your eyes be open toward this temple night and day, this place of which you said, 'My Name shall be there' " (1 Kgs 8:29). **this man.** King Artaxerxes. He is a mere man and cannot thwart the purposes of the God of heaven. **cupbearer to the king.** A high position of great responsibility. He ensured that the king's wine was not poisoned and thus had regular access to and potential influence with the king. The need for such an official is evident from the intrigues that characterized the Persian court. Xerxes, the father of Artaxerxes I, was killed in his own bedroom by a courtier. God providentially placed Nehemiah in this position for such a time as this (cf. Esth 4:14).

2:1–10 *Artaxerxes Sends Nehemiah to Jerusalem.* These verses contain a crisp account of the sequence of events that bring Nehemiah to Jerusalem.

2:1 Nisan. Almost four months after Hanani came from Jerusalem, during which time Nehemiah had been praying continuously. The king may have been absent from Susa during the winter months. **sad in his presence.** Presumably court etiquette demanded that personal emotions not intrude into court business, so Nehemiah's fear in v. 2 may indicate that Nehemiah, though a brave man, is gripped with something like panic.

2:3 city. Nehemiah does not mention Jerusalem by name (see also v. 5). **where my ancestors are buried.** He emphasizes filial loyalty and respect for ancestral graves. While Nehemiah is primarily concerned for the welfare of the city, he may have felt that the king's sympathy would be more easily aroused by emphasizing first the desecration of ancestral tombs.

2:4 I prayed. Before answering the king, Nehemiah utters a brief, spontaneous prayer to God. Nehemiah's frequent prayers are one of his most striking characteristics (4:9; 5:19; 6:9,14; 13:14,22,29,31). This is the turning point in the conversation that opens the way for subsequent events.

2:6 the queen sitting beside him. May suggest that this was a private audience and that she positively influenced the king. **How long will your journey take ...?** Nehemiah probably requested a brief leave of absence that was then extended. Neh 5:14 suggests he spent at least 12 years on his first term as governor of Judah. Then he returned in the 32nd year of Artaxerxes' reign to report to the king, after which he came back to Jerusalem for a second term (13:6–7).

2:7 governors of Trans-Euphrates. The regional officials of territories that Nehemiah needed to pass through; their cooperation was essential.

2:8 Asaph. A Hebrew name; Nehemiah may have known him. **timber.** Necessary for strengthening the walls, which would need the longer beams provided by the tall cedars of Lebanon rather than shorter beams available from the shorter trees around Jerusalem. This detail suggests Nehemiah's careful planning even at this stage. **the gracious hand of my God was on me.** The same phrase (except pronouns) as in Ezra 7:9; 8:18. The ultimate success of the venture was not human resourcefulness or imperial goodwill but God's providence.

2:9 army officers and cavalry. A royal escort providing protection while traveling and impressively legitimizing Nehemiah when he arrived at the provincial courts.

2:10 [b]ver 19; Ne 4:1,7 [c]Ne 4:3; 13:4-7 [d]Est 10:3
2:11 [e]Ge 40:13
2:13 [f]2Ch 26:9 [g]Ne 3:13 [h]Ne 1:3
2:14 [i]Ne 3:15 [j]2Ki 18:17

10When Sanballat[b] the Horonite and Tobiah[c] the Ammonite official heard about this, they were very
much disturbed that someone had come to promote the welfare of the Israelites.[d]

Nehemiah Inspects Jerusalem's Walls

11I went to Jerusalem, and after staying there three days[e] 12I set out during the night with a few others. I had not told anyone what my God had put in my heart to do for Jerusalem. There were no mounts
with me except the one I was riding on.
13By night I went out through the Valley Gate[f] toward the Jackal[a] Well and the Dung Gate,[g] examining the walls[h] of Jerusalem, which had been broken down, and its gates, which had been destroyed
by fire. 14Then I moved on toward the Fountain Gate[i] and the King's Pool,[j] but there was not enough

[a] 13 Or *Serpent* or *Fig*

2:10 Sanballat. Governor of Samaria (4:1–2) and apparently the leader of the opposition against Nehemiah. **Tobiah.** Possibly governor of Ammon. Presumably he and Sanballat saw Nehemiah's coming as a threat to their own status. The authority of the Samaritan governor in particular was threatened by Nehemiah's arrival. But their underlying hostility is to the welfare of the whole people. Probably their opposition was more religious than political.

2:11–20 *Nehemiah Inspects Jerusalem's Walls.* This describes Nehemiah's nocturnal survey of the walls and the opponents' initial response. When Nehemiah arrives in Jerusalem, he does not set to work immediately but takes a rest for three days and then takes only a few trusted men with him.

2:12 Nehemiah is shrewd. Perhaps not aware of the exact nature of the opposition, he realizes that people might resent the work and attempt to stop it at this early stage.

2:13 through the Valley Gate toward the Jackal Well and the Dung Gate. Nehemiah's exact route is disputed, but the general outline is probably that he and his companions set out from the west side of the city through the ruined gate and moved south and east. The Valley Gate would give access to the Tyropoeon Valley and the Jackal Well on the south. The Dung Gate was at the extreme southern end of the City of David; refuse passed through it on its way to the Valley of Hinnom, where it was dumped.

2:14 King's Pool. Possibly the Pool of Siloam at the end of Hezekiah's

JERUSALEM OF THE RETURNING EXILES

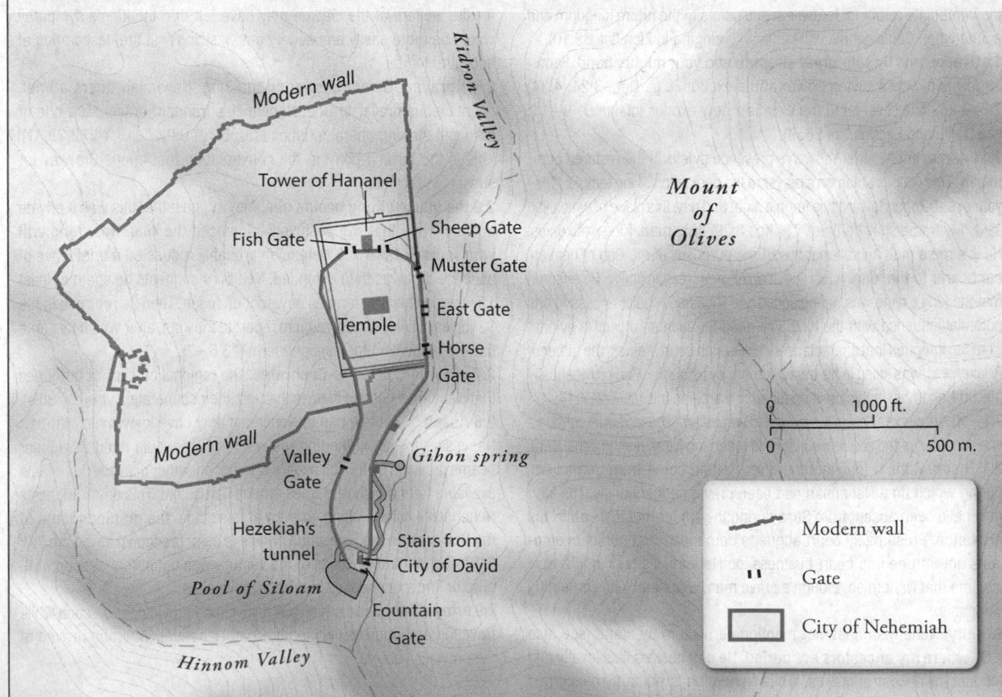

room for my mount to get through; [15]so I went up the valley by night, examining the wall. Finally, I turned back and reentered through the Valley Gate. [16]The officials did not know where I had gone or what I was doing, because as yet I had said nothing to the Jews or the priests or nobles or officials or any others who would be doing the work.

[17]Then I said to them, "You see the trouble we are in: Jerusalem lies in ruins, and its gates have been burned with fire.[k] Come, let us rebuild the wall[l] of Jerusalem, and we will no longer be in disgrace.[m]" [18]I also told them about the gracious hand of my God on me[n] and what the king had said to me.

They replied, "Let us start rebuilding." So they began this good work.

[19]But when Sanballat the Horonite, Tobiah the Ammonite official and Geshem[o] the Arab heard about it, they mocked and ridiculed us.[p] "What is this you are doing?" they asked. "Are you rebelling against the king?"

[20]I answered them by saying, "The God of heaven will give us success. We his servants will start rebuilding, but as for you, you have no share[q] in Jerusalem or any claim or historic right to it."

Builders of the Wall

3 Eliashib[r] the high priest and his fellow priests went to work and rebuilt[s] the Sheep Gate.[t] They dedicated it and set its doors in place, building as far as the Tower of the Hundred, which they dedicated, and as far as the Tower of Hananel.[u] [2]The men of Jericho[v] built the adjoining section, and Zakkur son of Imri built next to them.

[3]The Fish Gate[w] was rebuilt by the sons of Hassenaah. They laid its beams and put its doors and bolts and bars in place. [4]Meremoth son of Uriah, the son of Hakkoz, repaired the next section. Next to him Meshullam son of Berekiah, the son of Meshezabel, made repairs, and next to him Zadok son of Baana also made repairs. [5]The next section was repaired by the men of Tekoa,[x] but their nobles would not put their shoulders to the work under their supervisors.[a]

[a] 5 Or *their Lord* or *the governor*

2:17 [k] Ne 1:3 [l] Ps 102:16; Isa 30:13; 58:12 [m] Eze 5:14
2:18 [n] 2Sa 2:7
2:19 [o] Ne 6:1,2,6 [p] Ps 44:13-16
2:20 [q] Ezr 4:3
3:1 [r] Ezr 10:24 [s] Isa 58:12 [t] ver 32; Ne 12:39 [u] Ne 12:39; Jer 31:38; Zec 14:10
3:2 [v] Ne 7:36
3:3 [w] 2Ch 33:14; Ne 12:39
3:5 [x] 2Sa 14:2

tunnel. **not enough room.** Compelled Nehemiah to dismount and pick his way over the rubble on foot. This is the eastern side of the city, where the devastation caused by the Babylonians would be most obvious because of the collapse of the system of terraces that had extended the border of preexilic Jerusalem well down the slopes. Nehemiah did not make a complete circuit of the walls but only viewed the southern area. The northern walls had probably been completely demolished because that was the direction from which the Babylonians attacked. 2 Chr 26:9 says that Uzziah fortified towers in the west wall, which overlooked the central valley between the Hinnom and Kidron Valleys.

2:16 officials. Possibly refers to Persian officials, or is simply a general term for community leaders. **Jews.** Probably a blanket term for the other categories of people in v. 16.

2:17 Nehemiah does not explain how he publicized his plans for Jerusalem. He may have called an assembly like Ezra did (Ezra 10:7). **no longer be in disgrace.** Nehemiah's priority was to alleviate not his sense of insecurity or danger but rather his sense of shame that Zion, the city of the great King, lay in ruins.

2:18 the gracious hand of my God on me. Cf. Ezra 7:9,28; 8:22,31. Nehemiah, vigorous and practical as he was, emphasizes God's initiative in this enterprise. **what the king had said.** The king's approval is secondary to God's.

2:19 Geshem the Arab. Probably the king of Kedar, a vast area loosely under Persian control and occupied by Arabian tribes; it incorporated North Arabia, Edom, the Judean Negev, and extended to Egypt. This king posed a dangerous threat and, together with Sanballat and Tobiah, increased the sense of menacing forces encircling the remnant. **mocked and ridiculed.** Harassment noted in Ezra continues in Nehemiah.

2:20 The God of heaven will give us success. The power of the King of kings (not the authorization of the Persian king) is the ultimate factor. **no share.** Nehemiah insists in civic and legal terms that Sanballat and Tobiah have no past, present, or future stake in Jerusalem.

3:1–32 *Builders of the Wall.* This is a long list of those who built the wall and their allotted sections. It may be the list Nehemiah drew up as he planned the project. It moves counter-clockwise around the wall, section by section, beginning and ending at the Sheep Gate. This is a vital guide to the topography of postexilic Jerusalem. The unity of the people, led by the high priest and his associates, shows that this chapter is an account not simply of long-dead builders but of those who built the wall to outlast their own time and commemorate God's past faithfulness, his present help, and assurance of his future blessing. The point of this account is to show that the people as a whole responded to Nehemiah's challenge and believed God would give them success. The towns listed as the homes of the builders may have represented the administrative centers of the province of Judah. The account suggests that most of the rebuilding centered around the gates, where enemy assaults were always concentrated.

3:1–5 This section of the wall was near the temple, which was in the northern part of the city.

3:1 Eliashib. Related by marriage to Nehemiah's opponents (13:28), which shows something of Nehemiah's powers of persuasion. Since Eliashib was high priest, it was fitting that he set an example. The same applies to Meshullam (v. 4). **Sheep Gate.** Provided access to the temple; probably named after the animals to be sacrificed. **Tower of the Hundred.** Perhaps the headquarters of a centurion with 100 men. **Tower of Hananel.** Probably "the citadel by the temple" (2:8).

3:3 Fish Gate. Probably near a fish market; perhaps identical with the Ephraim Gate (8:16).

3:4 Some of these names occur in Ezra 2 (repeated in Neh 7), emphasizing that what is happening is part of a longer chain of events.

3:5 would not put their shoulders to the work. Their uncooperative attitude strikes a sour note.

3:6 [y] Ne 12:39
3:7 [z] Jos 9:3; Ne 2:7
3:8 [a] Ne 12:38
3:11 [b] Ne 12:38
3:13 [c] 2Ch 26:9 [d] Jos 15:34 [e] Ne 2:13
3:14 [f] Jer 6:1
3:15 [g] Isa 8:6; Jn 9:7
3:16 [h] Jos 15:58 [i] Ac 2:29
3:17 [j] Jos 15:44
3:21 [k] Ezr 8:33
3:24 [l] Ezr 8:33
3:25 [m] Jer 32:2; 37:21; 39:14 [n] Ezr 2:3
3:26 [o] Ne 7:46; 11:21 [p] 2Ch 33:14 [q] Ne 8:1,3, 16; 12:37
3:27 [r] ver 5 [s] Ps 48:12
3:28 [t] 2Ki 11:16; 2Ch 23:15; Jer 31:40

6 The Jeshanah[a] Gate[y] was repaired by Joiada son of Paseah and Meshullam son of Besodeiah. They laid its beams and put its doors with their bolts and bars in place. 7 Next to them, repairs were made by men from Gibeon[z] and Mizpah—Melatiah of Gibeon and Jadon of Meronoth—places under the authority of the governor of Trans-Euphrates. 8 Uzziel son of Harhaiah, one of the goldsmiths, repaired the next section; and Hananiah, one of the perfume-makers, made repairs next to that. They restored Jerusalem as far as the Broad Wall.[a] 9 Rephaiah son of Hur, ruler of a half-district of Jerusalem, repaired the next section. 10 Adjoining this, Jedaiah son of Harumaph made repairs opposite his house, and Hattush son of Hashabneiah made repairs next to him. 11 Malkijah son of Harim and Hasshub son of Pahath-Moab repaired another section and the Tower of the Ovens.[b] 12 Shallum son of Hallohesh, ruler of a half-district of Jerusalem, repaired the next section with the help of his daughters.

13 The Valley Gate[c] was repaired by Hanun and the residents of Zanoah.[d] They rebuilt it and put its doors with their bolts and bars in place. They also repaired a thousand cubits[b] of the wall as far as the Dung Gate.[e]

14 The Dung Gate was repaired by Malkijah son of Rekab, ruler of the district of Beth Hakkerem.[f] He rebuilt it and put its doors with their bolts and bars in place.

15 The Fountain Gate was repaired by Shallun son of Kol-Hozeh, ruler of the district of Mizpah. He rebuilt it, roofing it over and putting its doors and bolts and bars in place. He also repaired the wall of the Pool of Siloam,[c][g] by the King's Garden, as far as the steps going down from the City of David. 16 Beyond him, Nehemiah son of Azbuk, ruler of a half-district of Beth Zur,[h] made repairs up to a point opposite the tombs[d][i] of David, as far as the artificial pool and the House of the Heroes.

17 Next to him, the repairs were made by the Levites under Rehum son of Bani. Beside him, Hashabiah, ruler of half the district of Keilah,[j] carried out repairs for his district. 18 Next to him, the repairs were made by their fellow Levites under Binnui[e] son of Henadad, ruler of the other half-district of Keilah. 19 Next to him, Ezer son of Jeshua, ruler of Mizpah, repaired another section, from a point facing the ascent to the armory as far as the angle of the wall. 20 Next to him, Baruch son of Zabbai zealously repaired another section, from the angle to the entrance of the house of Eliashib the high priest. 21 Next to him, Meremoth[k] son of Uriah, the son of Hakkoz, repaired another section, from the entrance of Eliashib's house to the end of it.

22 The repairs next to him were made by the priests from the surrounding region. 23 Beyond them, Benjamin and Hasshub made repairs in front of their house; and next to them, Azariah son of Maaseiah, the son of Ananiah, made repairs beside his house. 24 Next to him, Binnui[l] son of Henadad repaired another section, from Azariah's house to the angle and the corner, 25 and Palal son of Uzai worked opposite the angle and the tower projecting from the upper palace near the court of the guard.[m] Next to him, Pedaiah son of Parosh[n] 26 and the temple servants[o] living on the hill of Ophel[p] made repairs up to a point opposite the Water Gate[q] toward the east and the projecting tower. 27 Next to them, the men of Tekoa[r] repaired another section, from the great projecting tower[s] to the wall of Ophel.

28 Above the Horse Gate,[t] the priests made repairs, each in front of his own house. 29 Next to them, Zadok son of Immer made repairs opposite his house. Next to him, Shemaiah son of Shekaniah, the guard at

[a] *6* Or *Old* [b] *13* That is, about 1,500 feet or about 450 meters [c] *15* Hebrew *Shelah,* a variant of *Shiloah,* that is, Siloam [d] *16* Hebrew; Septuagint, some Vulgate manuscripts and Syriac *tomb*
[e] *18* Two Hebrew manuscripts and Syriac (see also Septuagint and verse 24); most Hebrew manuscripts *Bavvai*

3:6–14 Describes the work on the west wall. The project continues, with many individuals undertaking tasks very different from their day jobs (v. 8).

3:12 daughters. Enlisted in this family enterprise. Shallum is the only one whose daughters helped; perhaps he had no sons (cf. Num 36).

3:15–32 Describes the work on the east wall, which apparently suffered the most extensive damage, which is why so many people worked between the Fountain Gate and the Water Gate.

3:15 The work required installing roofs, doors, bolts, and bars. **City of David.** This remnant is organically linked with the great days of the past, and the reminder of David and his connection with the city is significant in the whole sweep of the story.

3:17–18 Levites. The rebuilding is not simply a work of structural repair but a spiritual reformation. Whether the individual Levites understood it in that way is a moot point.

3:22 priests. See note on vv. 17–18.

3:25 upper palace. Solomon's palace, which was higher up the hill than David's original palace.

3:26 hill of Ophel. The beginning of the temple hill. The temple was the concern of the first returnees before the walls and city were rebuilt. See "Temple," p. 2652.

3:27 the men of Tekoa. The nobles of Tekoa shirked their duty (v. 5), but the ordinary people of Tekoa did double duty, repairing two sections of the wall (here; v. 5).

the East Gate, made repairs. 30Next to him, Hananiah son of Shelemiah, and Hanun, the sixth son of Za-
laph, repaired another section. Next to them, Meshullam son of Berekiah made repairs opposite his living
quarters. 31Next to him, Malkijah, one of the goldsmiths, made repairs as far as the house of the temple
servants and the merchants, opposite the Inspection Gate, and as far as the room above the corner; 32and
between the room above the corner and the Sheep Gate[u] the goldsmiths and merchants made repairs.

Opposition to the Rebuilding

4 [a] When Sanballat[v] heard that we were rebuilding the wall, he became angry and was greatly incensed. He ridiculed the Jews, 2and in the presence of his associates[w] and the army of Samaria, he
said, "What are those feeble Jews doing? Will they restore their wall? Will they offer sacrifices? Will they
finish in a day? Can they bring the stones back to life from those heaps of rubble[x] —burned as they are?"
3Tobiah[y] the Ammonite, who was at his side, said, "What they are building—even a fox climbing
up on it would break down their wall of stones!"[z]

4Hear us, our God, for we are despised.[a] Turn their insults back on their own heads. Give them over
as plunder in a land of captivity. 5Do not cover up their guilt[b] or blot out their sins from your sight,[c]
for they have thrown insults in the face of[b] the builders.

6So we rebuilt the wall till all of it reached half its height, for the people worked with all their heart.
7But when Sanballat, Tobiah,[d] the Arabs, the Ammonites and the people of Ashdod heard that the
repairs to Jerusalem's walls had gone ahead and that the gaps were being closed, they were very angry.
8They all plotted together[e] to come and fight against Jerusalem and stir up trouble against it. 9But we
prayed to our God and posted a guard day and night to meet this threat.
10Meanwhile, the people in Judah said, "The strength of the laborers[f] is giving out, and there is so
much rubble that we cannot rebuild the wall."
11Also our enemies said, "Before they know it or see us, we will be right there among them and will
kill them and put an end to the work."
12Then the Jews who lived near them came and told us ten times over, "Wherever you turn, they
will attack us."
13Therefore I stationed some of the people behind the lowest points of the wall at the exposed places,
posting them by families, with their swords, spears and bows. 14After I looked things over, I stood up
and said to the nobles, the officials and the rest of the people, "Don't be afraid[g] of them. Remember[h]
the Lord, who is great and awesome,[i] and fight[j] for your families, your sons and your daughters, your
wives and your homes."

a In Hebrew texts 4:1-6 is numbered 3:33-38, and 4:7-23 is numbered 4:1-17. *b* 5 Or *have aroused your anger before*

3:32 [u] ver 1; Jn 5:2
4:1 [v] Ne 2:10
4:2 [w] Ezr 4:9-10 [x] Ps 79:1; Jer 26:18
4:3 [y] Ne 2:10 [z] Job 13:12; 15:3
4:4 [a] Ps 44:13; 79:12; 123:3-4; Jer 33:24
4:5 [b] Isa 2:9; La 1:22 [c] 2Ki 14:27; Ps 51:1; 69:27-28; 109:14; Jer 18:23
4:7 [d] Ne 2:10
4:8 [e] Ps 2:2; 83:1-18
4:10 [f] 1Ch 23:4
4:14 [g] Ge 28:15; Nu 14:9; Dt 1:29 [h] Ne 1:8 [i] Ne 1:5 [j] 2Sa 10:12

4:1–23 *Opposition to the Rebuilding.* Nehemiah's first-person narrative resumes as he gives an account of how rebuilding led to renewed opposition.
4:1 angry … greatly incensed. Sanballat is less confident than he appears and thus resorts to posturing as he surrounds himself with sycophants and tries to ridicule the work.
4:2 offer sacrifices. The Jews had been doing this for over 70 years (since Ezra 3).These could refer to sacrifices given to celebrate the completion of the work.
4:3 Tobiah. He has to get his say and makes facetious remarks. Archaeology has revealed that Nehemiah's walls were nine feet (2.7 meters) thick; that would have required quite a few foxes.
4:4–5 Nehemiah's prayer gives an immediacy to the narrative and is marked by honesty and a sense of vulnerability.
4:5 Do not cover up their guilt or blot out their sins. Cf. Jer 18:23. This is not personal resentment but a plea to God to vindicate his work and honor his name. It is similar in tone to some of the prayers for deliverance from enemies in the Psalter (e.g., Pss 74; 79)
4:6 Demonstrates Nehemiah's practicality in completing the circuit of the walls even though they had reached only half the required height. The unity and commitment of the people is again emphasized.
4:7–14 Here the opposition intensifies, and the narrative returns to the time when it was reported that the actual rebuilding of the wall had started with the breaches in the structure being filled in.
4:7 The city and province are now ringed with enemies: Sanballat in the north, Arabs in the south, Ammonites in the east, and Ashdodites in the west. It is not clear how much of this was boasting, but the threat was real.
4:9 Again Nehemiah shows his spiritual stature as well as his careful planning and precautions (2:8).
4:10–11 As when they built the temple (earlier in Ezra 4:24), external opposition leads to a growing loss of morale. The weariness of unrelenting drudgery and the inevitable doubts at this midway stage compound the growing feeling of defeatism. The sense of danger is compounded by the continual enemy propaganda.
4:12–14 Nehemiah discourages an attack by mobilizing people to defend the weakest parts of the wall.
4:14 Remember the Lord, who is great and awesome. Echoes Deut 7:21. Although sensible precautions are necessary, the true defender of Jerusalem is the God who had in the past protected them.

4:15 [k]2Sa 17:14; Job 5:12
4:17 [l]Ps 149:6
4:18 [m]Nu 10:2
4:20 [n]Eze 33:3 [o]Ex 14:14; Dt 1:30; 20:4; Jos 10:14
5:3 [p]Ps 109:11 [q]Ge 47:23
5:4 [r]Ezr 4:13
5:5 [s]Ge 29:14

15 When our enemies heard that we were aware of their plot and that God had frustrated it,[k] we all
returned to the wall, each to our own work.
16 From that day on, half of my men did the work, while the other half were equipped with spears,
shields, bows and armor. The officers posted themselves behind all the people of Judah 17 who were
building the wall. Those who carried materials did their work with one hand and held a weapon[l] in the
other, 18 and each of the builders wore his sword at his side as he worked. But the man who sounded
the trumpet[m] stayed with me.
19 Then I said to the nobles, the officials and the rest of the people, "The work is extensive and spread
out, and we are widely separated from each other along the wall. 20 Wherever you hear the sound of the
trumpet,[n] join us there. Our God will fight[o] for us!"
21 So we continued the work with half the men holding spears, from the first light of dawn till the
stars came out. 22 At that time I also said to the people, "Have every man and his helper stay inside Jerusalem at night, so they can serve us as guards by night and as workers by day." 23 Neither I nor my
brothers nor my men nor the guards with me took off our
clothes; each had his weapon, even when he went for water.[a]

Nehemiah Helps the Poor

5 Now the men and their wives raised a great outcry
against their fellow Jews. 2 Some were saying, "We and
our sons and daughters are numerous; in order for us to eat
and stay alive, we must get grain."
3 Others were saying, "We are mortgaging our fields,[p] our
vineyards and our homes to get grain during the famine."[q]
4 Still others were saying, "We have had to borrow money
to pay the king's tax[r] on our fields and vineyards. 5 Although
we are of the same flesh and blood[s] as our fellow Jews and

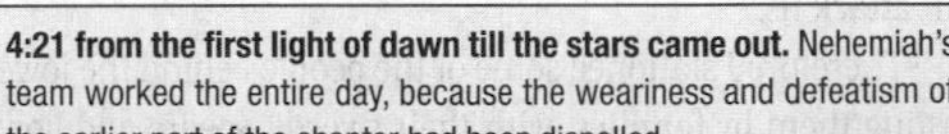

[a] 23 The meaning of the Hebrew for this clause is uncertain.

A tower—part of Nehemiah's wall—built over an earlier "stepped" structure.

4:15 God had frustrated it. Suggests that the opposition feared not only Nehemiah's careful defense but also Judah's God.

4:16–23 Nehemiah's countermeasures continue, and the work progresses.

4:16 The people maintain a more regular state of defense and divide labor between those who build and those who defend.

4:17–18 weapon … sword. Because there was probably not a large number of soldiers.

4:18 the man who sounded the trumpet stayed with me. So that he could call the people to action if necessary.

4:20 Our God will fight for us! Echoes Exod 14:14; draws attention to God the Warrior, who fights on behalf of his people. A similar phrase was used when Jehoshaphat faced a coalition of enemies (2 Chr 20:15).

4:21 from the first light of dawn till the stars came out. Nehemiah's team worked the entire day, because the weariness and defeatism of the earlier part of the chapter had been dispelled.

4:22–23 Those who commuted from the neighboring villages stayed in the city so that there would be sufficient night watchmen and so that work could begin promptly each morning. Nehemiah led by example. They were constantly alert.

5:1–19 *Nehemiah Helps the Poor.* The rest of life did not stand still while the building work proceeded, and serious problems of poverty and food shortage emerged (vv. 1–13). The 52 days of building (6:15) could not in themselves have caused these problems, but diverting manpower from the work of agriculture to concentrate on building may have seemed a step too far. Nehemiah not only eased financial burdens in Judah but also modeled generosity and social responsibility (vv. 14–19).

5:1 fellow Jews. Probably the more affluent of the returnees who were living in comfort. Nehemiah himself belonged to this stratum of society.

5:2–4 The problem here involves three groups: (1) landless people with large families who were finding it difficult to get enough to feed themselves (v. 2); (2) peasants who were having to mortgage their land and property; (3) those with mortgaged fields, vineyards, and homes who were having to pay the king's tax, which placed them in the hands of lenders, some of whom were unscrupulous. In times of economic distress, families would borrow money using family members as collateral. If a man could not repay what he owed, he and his family could be sold into forced labor. However, the debtor served his creditor as a "hired worker" (Lev 25:39–40). He was to be released in the seventh year (Deut 15:12–18) unless he volunteered to stay.

5:5 This probably does not introduce a fourth group but summarizes the complaints of all three groups (see note on vv. 2–4). **we are of the same flesh and blood.** A disastrous situation made even more

though our children are as good as theirs, yet we have to subject our sons and daughters to slavery.[t] Some of our daughters have already been enslaved, but we are powerless, because our fields and our vineyards belong to others."[u]

6When I heard their outcry and these charges, I was very angry. 7I pondered them in my mind and then accused the nobles and officials. I told them, "You are charging your own people interest!"[v] So I called together a large meeting to deal with them 8and said: "As far as possible, we have bought[w] back our fellow Jews who were sold to the Gentiles. Now you are selling your own people, only for them to be sold back to us!" They kept quiet, because they could find nothing to say.[x]

9So I continued, "What you are doing is not right. Shouldn't you walk in the fear of our God to avoid the reproach[y] of our Gentile enemies? 10I and my brothers and my men are also lending the people money and grain. But let us stop charging interest![z] 11Give back to them immediately their fields, vineyards, olive groves and houses, and also the interest[a] you are charging them—one percent of the money, grain, new wine and olive oil."

12"We will give it back," they said. "And we will not demand anything more from them. We will do as you say."

Then I summoned the priests and made the nobles and officials take an oath[b] to do what they had promised. 13I also shook[c] out the folds of my robe and said, "In this way may God shake out of their house and possessions anyone who does not keep this promise. So may such a person be shaken out and emptied!"

At this the whole assembly said, "Amen,"[d] and praised the LORD. And the people did as they had promised.

14Moreover, from the twentieth year of King Artaxerxes,[e] when I was appointed to be their governor[f] in the land of Judah, until his thirty-second year—twelve years—neither I nor my brothers ate the food allotted to the governor. 15But the earlier governors—those preceding me—placed a heavy burden on the people and took forty shekels[a] of silver from them in addition to food and wine. Their assistants also lorded it over the people. But out of reverence for God[g] I did not act like that. 16Instead,[h] I devoted myself to the work on this wall. All my men were assembled there for the work; we[b] did not acquire any land.

17Furthermore, a hundred and fifty Jews and officials ate at my table, as well as those who came to us from the surrounding nations. 18Each day one ox, six choice sheep and some poultry[i] were prepared for me, and every ten days an abundant supply of wine of all kinds. In spite of all this, I never demanded the food allotted to the governor, because the demands were heavy on these people.

19Remember[j] me with favor, my God, for all I have done for these people.

a 15 That is, about 1 pound or about 460 grams *b 16* Most Hebrew manuscripts; some Hebrew manuscripts, Septuagint, Vulgate and Syriac *I*

5:5 [t] Lev 25:39-43,47; 2Ki 4:1; Isa 50:1 [u] Dt 15:7-11; 2Ki 4:1
5:7 [v] Ex 22:25-27; Lev 25:35-37; Dt 23:19-20; 24:10-13
5:8 [w] Lev 25:47 [x] Jer 34:8
5:9 [y] Isa 52:5
5:10 [z] Ex 22:25
5:11 [a] Isa 58:6
5:12 [b] Ezr 10:5
5:13 [c] Mt 10:14; Ac 18:6 [d] Dt 27:15-26
5:14 [e] Ne 2:6; 13:6 [f] Ge 42:6; Ezr 6:7; Jer 40:7; Hag 1:1
5:15 [g] Ge 20:11
5:16 [h] 2Th 3:7-10
5:18 [i] 1Ki 4:23
5:19 [j] Ge 8:1; 2Ki 20:3; Ne 1:8; 13:14,22,31

intolerable. This is not merely a legal issue but becomes an issue of community solidarity, making action even more imperative.
5:6–7 Nehemiah first responds personally; he is angry but channels that anger into a considered course of action.
5:7 charging your own people interest. The essence of Nehemiah's case. They were acting strictly on business terms rather than treating the disadvantaged as brothers and sisters. Exod 22:22–27 emphasizes the responsibility of the community to care for widows and orphans and to treat them compassionately, as the Lord himself does. Nehemiah then summons a large public meeting to spell out the problems and propose a solution.
5:8 bought back. Following Lev 25:47–48, the Jewish community had paid ransom money for those who fell into the clutches of Gentile moneylenders. Here the absurdity is that the moneylenders are themselves Jewish.
5:9 Nehemiah does not merely desire to stay on the right side of the law. He wants to honor the Lord and glorify his name among the nations.
5:10 I … us. Nehemiah includes himself in the charge—not because he was illegally charging interest, but because poverty is so desperate that even fair loans are crippling. They need to cancel the debts in the spirit of the Jubilee (Lev 25). It was an act of kindness to lend to the poor (Pss 37:26; 112:5; Prov 19:17). Thus, Nehemiah urges creditors to forego their right to repayment with interest.
5:11 Nehemiah instructs the lenders to return land and property and cancel all interest due. **one percent.** Probably a monthly rate.
5:12 made the nobles and officials take an oath. Nehemiah is anxious that the leaders do not go back on their word.
5:13 shook out the folds of my robe. Symbolically threatens judgment for the unrepentant. **"Amen," … praised.** Shows that this is a solemn occasion.
5:14 governor. Explicitly states for the first time what has been implicit in the narrative. Nehemiah's first term of office lasted 12 years. **food allotted to the governor.** Nehemiah waived this privilege, which taxes would have financed.
5:15 reverence for God. The governing principle of Nehemiah's life. He was not unremittingly harsh like previous governors.
5:16 I devoted myself to the work on this wall. This resulted in no financial gain and probably involved considerable personal expense.
5:17–18 Nehemiah's hospitality is generous, reflecting God's own generosity. This is actually a bountiful provision, but more than that, it is a sign of the kingdom (cf. David's generosity to Mephibosheth [2 Sam 9] and the parable of the great banquet [Luke 14]).
5:19 Another of Nehemiah's brief prayers (1:4; 6:9,14; 13:14,22,31). **Remember … God.** The one who alone sees both actions and motives will give credit where credit is due.

6:1 [k]Ne 2:10 [l]Ne 2:19
6:2 [m]1Ch 8:12
6:5 [n]Ne 2:10
6:6 [o]Ne 2:19
6:10 [p]Nu 18:7
6:12 [q]Eze 13:22-23 [r]Ne 2:10
6:13 [s]Jer 20:10

Further Opposition to the Rebuilding

6 When word came to Sanballat, Tobiah,[k] Geshem[l] the Arab and the rest of our enemies that I had
rebuilt the wall and not a gap was left in it — though up to that time I had not set the doors in
the gates — [2]Sanballat and Geshem sent me this message: "Come, let us meet together in one of the
villages[a] on the plain of Ono.[m]"

But they were scheming to harm me; [3]so I sent messengers to them with this reply: "I am carrying
on a great project and cannot go down. Why should the work stop while I leave it and go down to you?"
[4]Four times they sent me the same message, and each time I gave them the same answer.

[5]Then, the fifth time, Sanballat[n] sent his aide to me with the same message, and in his hand was an
unsealed letter [6]in which was written:

> "It is reported among the nations — and Geshem[b][o] says it is true — that you and the Jews are
> plotting to revolt, and therefore you are building the wall. Moreover, according to these reports
> you are about to become their king [7]and have even appointed prophets to make this proclama-
> tion about you in Jerusalem: 'There is a king in Judah!' Now this report will get back to the king;
> so come, let us meet together."

[8]I sent him this reply: "Nothing like what you are saying is happening; you are just making it up
out of your head."

[9]They were all trying to frighten us, thinking, "Their hands will get too weak for the work, and it
will not be completed."

But I prayed, "Now strengthen my hands."

[10]One day I went to the house of Shemaiah son of Delaiah, the son of Mehetabel, who was shut in
at his home. He said, "Let us meet in the house of God, inside the temple[p], and let us close the temple
doors, because men are coming to kill you — by night they are coming to kill you."

[11]But I said, "Should a man like me run away? Or should someone like me go into the temple to save
his life? I will not go!" [12]I realized that God had not sent him, but that he had prophesied against me[q]
because Tobiah and Sanballat[r] had hired him. [13]He had been hired to intimidate me so that I would
commit a sin by doing this, and then they would give me a bad name to discredit me.[s]

[a] 2 Or *in Kephirim* [b] 6 Hebrew *Gashmu,* a variant of *Geshem*

6:1–15 *Further Opposition to the Rebuilding.* The narrative returns to wall building and recounts how the old enemies and new opponents systematically plan to intimidate the Jews. Yet the work is completed.
6:1 The work on the wall was almost complete, and the last hope for the enemies to get into the city would disappear when the gates were fitted. So Sanballat and Tobiah try to lure Nehemiah away from Jerusalem, perhaps to kidnap him.
6:2 Ono. Near Samaria, Sanballat's home territory. It was located about seven miles (11 kilometers) southeast of Joppa in the westernmost area settled by the returning Jews (7:37; 11:35) This would require Nehemiah to take a long and fruitless journey, and while it may have been proposed as neutral territory, he recognized that it was a trap.
6:3 great project. Shrewdly, Nehemiah does not directly refuse the invitation but emphasizes his priorities. While his reply may have seemed brusque, he correctly perceived the insincerity of his enemies.
6:5 unsealed letter. An open letter on papyrus with no seal; it could be read in transit. At this time a letter was usually written on papyrus or leather, which would be rolled up, tied with a string, and sealed to guarantee authenticity. Sanballat apparently wanted the contents of his letter to be public knowledge.
6:6 Geshem says it is true. Sanballat is trying to add credibility to his accusation. However, a rumor does not become true simply because a prominent individual agrees with it.
6:7 appointed prophets to make this proclamation. Sanballat may be aware that prophets were king makers before the exile (e.g., Samuel with Saul [1 Sam 9–10] and David [1 Sam 16]; Elisha with Jehu [2 Kgs 9]). He may also be referring to the Davidic role of Zerubbabel (Hag 2:20–23; Zech 3:8). But there is no evidence that Nehemiah was of Davidic descent, and like the rest of the letter, this accusation mixes lies, innuendo, and spurious plausibility.
6:8 Nehemiah bluntly and completely denies the allegations, doubtlessly thinking that meeting Sanballat and coming to a compromise would be taken as a partial admission of guilt.
6:9 all trying to frighten us. Although Sanballat wrote the letter, it was part of a wider conspiracy. **prayed.** Again Nehemiah briefly prays. He is a shrewd man but recognizes that only the Lord can truly deal with this situation.
6:10–14 The attempts to lure Nehemiah out of Jerusalem have failed, so Tobiah and Sanballat attempt to destroy Nehemiah's reputation by hiring a false prophet. Tobiah, who has close associates in Jerusalem, emerges as the main mover in this episode.
6:10 Shemaiah. An otherwise unknown prophet who presumably summoned Nehemiah on the pretext that he had a prophetic message for him. **who was shut in at his home.** An obscure phrase that may refer to some ritual defilement (e.g., Num 19:11–22). Shemaiah's subterfuge is dangerous (as a layman, Nehemiah was forbidden to enter the inner temple) and silly (as the governor, Nehemiah would have an armed guard), although this only becomes apparent in vv. 12–13.
6:11 Nehemiah sees through Shemaiah's deceit and rejects his invitation on two grounds: (1) he is the governor, a courageous and resourceful man, and (2) as a layman he is conscious of the sanctuary's holiness and has a horror of defiling it.
6:12–13 A person is not a prophet simply because he says he is. Nehemiah realizes that the invitation to defile the sanctuary could not be

14Remember[t] Tobiah and Sanballat,[u] my God, because of what they have done; remember also the
prophet[v] Noadiah and how she and the rest of the prophets[w] have been trying to intimidate me. 15So
the wall was completed on the twenty-fifth of Elul, in fifty-two days.

Opposition to the Completed Wall

16When all our enemies heard about this, all the surrounding nations were afraid and lost their self-
confidence, because they realized that this work had been done with the help of our God.
17Also, in those days the nobles of Judah were sending many letters to Tobiah, and replies from
Tobiah kept coming to them. 18For many in Judah were under oath to him, since he was son-in-law
to Shekaniah son of Arah, and his son Jehohanan had married the daughter of Meshullam son of
Berekiah. 19Moreover, they kept reporting to me his good deeds and then telling him what I said. And
Tobiah sent letters to intimidate me.

7 After the wall had been rebuilt and I had set the doors in place, the gatekeepers,[x] the musicians[y]
and the Levites[z] were appointed. 2I put in charge of Jerusalem my brother Hanani,[a] along with
Hananiah[b] the commander of the citadel,[c] because he was a man of integrity and feared[d] God more
than most people do. 3I said to them, "The gates of Jerusalem are not to be opened until the sun is hot.
While the gatekeepers are still on duty, have them shut the doors and bar them. Also appoint residents
of Jerusalem as guards, some at their posts and some near their own houses."

The List of the Exiles Who Returned

7:6-73pp — Ezr 2:1-70

4Now the city was large and spacious, but there were few people in it,[e] and the houses had not yet
been rebuilt. 5So my God put it into my heart to assemble the nobles, the officials and the common
people for registration by families. I found the genealogical record of those who had been the first to
return. This is what I found written there:

6These are the people of the province who came up from the captivity of the exiles[f] whom Nebuchadnezzar king of Babylon had taken captive (they returned to Jerusalem and Judah, each to

6:14 [t] Ne 1:8 [u] Ne 2:10 [v] Ex 15:20; Eze 13:17-23; Ac 21:9; Rev 2:20 [w] Ne 13:29; Jer 23:9-40; Zec 13:2-3
7:1 [x] 1Ch 9:27; 26:12-19; Ne 6:1,15 [y] Ps 68:25 [z] Ne 8:9
7:2 [a] Ne 1:2 [b] Ne 10:23 [c] Ne 2:8 [d] 1Ki 18:3
7:4 [e] Ne 11:1
7:6 [f] 2Ch 36:20; Ezr 2:1-70; Ne 1:2

of divine origin and that it is part of a plot to discredit him and thus nullify his work.

6:14 Nehemiah prays not for personal vengeance but for vindication. **Noadiah.** Otherwise unknown. **rest of the prophets.** Suggests that this episode was far from isolated but was rather a specific incident from a whole series of attempts to discredit Nehemiah (similar to the way false prophets dogged Jeremiah during his ministry [Jer 14; 28]).

6:15 Elul. Aug./Sept. They carry out the work mainly in high summer. **fifty-two days.** An amazingly short time: a little over seven weeks.

6:16—7:3 *Opposition to the Completed Wall.* Realizing God's help had accomplished the rapid completion of the wall, Nehemiah's enemies renewed their opposition.

6:16 afraid and lost their self-confidence. God's restraining his enemies recalls the terror that fell on the towns through which Jacob and his sons traveled (Gen 35:5). In particular, those who prominently opposed the work lost face.

6:17 in those days. A common phrase in the narrative; it does not suggest strict chronology but sees certain events happening at approximately the same time. **sending many letters ... replies.** A persistent campaign of disinformation and harassment designed to wear down Nehemiah and probably to sow disunity.

6:18 under oath. Presumably some kind of business arrangement. **Shekaniah ... Meshullam.** Tobiah's links with these individuals presumably gave him a footing in Judean society, especially with those "under oath to him." Tobiah was related to an influential family in Judah since his son Jehohanan was married to the daughter of Meshullam, who had helped to repair the wall of Jerusalem (3:4,30). There was clearly a powerful lobby in Jerusalem committed to Tobiah and opposed to Nehemiah.

6:19 good deeds. Presumably the economic benefits that came from Tobiah's network of trading interests.

7:1–73a With the wall completed, Nehemiah turns his attention to other necessary matters and deals first with Jerusalem's security and repopulation.

7:1–3 This outlines the security precautions that were even more necessary because of the continued opposition in ch. 6.

7:2 Hanani. First alerted Nehemiah to the ruined condition of Jerusalem (1:2–3). Appointing these men ensured that the next stage of the project would be carried out faithfully.

7:3 The appointed men take extra security precautions. **until the sun is hot.** Normally the city gates would be opened at dawn, but delaying their opening until the sun was high in the heavens would prevent the enemy from making a surprise attack before most people were up.

7:4–73a *The List of the Exiles Who Returned.* This (see note on 3:4) is virtually identical with Ezra 2 (see notes there about the nature of the list). Just as Nehemiah rebuilt the wall on earlier foundations, so he now rebuilds the community on the labors of earlier generations. The city of God must stand in direct continuity with the first returnees whom God rescued from Babylon in a second exodus that took them back to the land God had promised Abraham (Gen 15:18–21).

7:4 The city still had not recovered from the Babylonian devastation a century and a half earlier.

7:5 God put it into my heart. Ultimately this was God's initiative rather than Nehemiah's plan. **genealogical record.** Virtually identical with the list in Ezra 2. This would minimize the labor involved as Nehemiah had the earlier list to which he could refer.

7:7 [g] 1Ch 3:19; Ezr 2:2
7:20 [h] Ezr 8:6
7:26 [i] 2Sa 23:28; 1Ch 2:54
7:27 [j] Jos 21:18
7:29 [k] Jos 18:26
[l] Jos 18:25
7:32 [m] Ge 12:8
7:36 [n] Ne 3:2
7:37 [o] 1Ch 8:12
7:44 [p] Ne 11:23
7:45 [q] 1Ch 9:17

his own town, 7 in company with Zerubbabel,[g] Joshua, Nehemiah, Azariah, Raamiah, Nahamani,
Mordecai, Bilshan, Mispereth, Bigvai, Nehum and Baanah):

The list of the men of Israel:

8 the descendants of Parosh	2,172
9 of Shephatiah	372
10 of Arah	652
11 of Pahath-Moab (through the line of Jeshua and Joab)	2,818
12 of Elam	1,254
13 of Zattu	845
14 of Zakkai	760
15 of Binnui	648
16 of Bebai	628
17 of Azgad	2,322
18 of Adonikam	667
19 of Bigvai	2,067
20 of Adin[h]	655
21 of Ater (through Hezekiah)	98
22 of Hashum	328
23 of Bezai	324
24 of Hariph	112
25 of Gibeon	95
26 the men of Bethlehem and Netophah[i]	188
27 of Anathoth[j]	128
28 of Beth Azmaveth	42
29 of Kiriath Jearim, Kephirah[k] and Beeroth[l]	743
30 of Ramah and Geba	621
31 of Mikmash	122
32 of Bethel and Ai[m]	123
33 of the other Nebo	52
34 of the other Elam	1,254
35 of Harim	320
36 of Jericho[n]	345
37 of Lod, Hadid and Ono[o]	721
38 of Senaah	3,930

39 The priests:

the descendants of Jedaiah (through the family of Jeshua)	973
40 of Immer	1,052
41 of Pashhur	1,247
42 of Harim	1,017

43 The Levites:

the descendants of Jeshua (through Kadmiel through the line of Hodaviah)	74

44 The musicians:[p]

the descendants of Asaph	148

45 The gatekeepers:[q]

the descendants of Shallum, Ater, Talmon, Akkub, Hatita and Shobai	138

[46]The temple servants:[r]

the descendants of
Ziha, Hasupha, Tabbaoth,
[47]Keros, Sia, Padon,
[48]Lebana, Hagaba, Shalmai,
[49]Hanan, Giddel, Gahar,
[50]Reaiah, Rezin, Nekoda,
[51]Gazzam, Uzza, Paseah,
[52]Besai, Meunim, Nephusim,
[53]Bakbuk, Hakupha, Harhur,
[54]Bazluth, Mehida, Harsha,
[55]Barkos, Sisera, Temah,
[56]Neziah and Hatipha

[57]The descendants of the servants of Solomon:

the descendants of
Sotai, Sophereth, Perida,
[58]Jaala, Darkon, Giddel,
[59]Shephatiah, Hattil,
Pokereth-Hazzebaim and Amon

[60]The temple servants and the descendants of the servants of Solomon[s] 392

[61]The following came up from the towns of Tel Melah, Tel Harsha, Kerub, Addon and Immer, but they could not show that their families were descended from Israel:

[62]the descendants of
Delaiah, Tobiah and Nekoda 642

[63]And from among the priests:

the descendants of
Hobaiah, Hakkoz and Barzillai (a man who had married a daughter of Barzillai the Gileadite and was called by that name).

[64]These searched for their family records, but they could not find them and so were excluded from the priesthood as unclean. [65]The governor, therefore, ordered them not to eat any of the most sacred food until there should be a priest ministering with the Urim and Thummim.[t]

[66]The whole company numbered 42,360, [67]besides their 7,337 male and female slaves; and they also had 245 male and female singers. [68]There were 736 horses, 245 mules,[a] [69]435 camels and 6,720 donkeys.

[70]Some of the heads of the families contributed to the work. The governor gave to the treasury 1,000 darics[b] of gold, 50 bowls and 530 garments for priests. [71]Some of the heads of the families[u] gave to the treasury for the work 20,000 darics[c] of gold and 2,200 minas[d] of silver. [72]The total given by the rest of the people was 20,000 darics of gold, 2,000 minas[e] of silver and 67 garments for priests.[v]

[a] *68* Some Hebrew manuscripts (see also Ezra 2:66); most Hebrew manuscripts do not have this verse.
[b] *70* That is, about 19 pounds or about 8.4 kilograms [c] *71* That is, about 375 pounds or about 170 kilograms; also in verse 72 [d] *71* That is, about 1 1/3 tons or about 1.2 metric tons [e] *72* That is, about 1 1/4 tons or about 1.1 metric tons

7:46 [r] Ne 3:26
7:60 [s] 1Ch 9:2
7:65 [t] Ex 28:30; Ne 8:9
7:71 [u] 1Ch 29:7
7:72 [v] Ex 25:2

7:67 245 male and female singers. Ezra 2:65 records 200 male and female singers. There is no easy explanation for this discrepancy. It probably is a scribal error, with Ezra giving the correct number of singers and Nehemiah conflating that with the number of mules. Indeed, v. 68 is omitted in many Hebrew manuscripts.

7:73 [w]Ne 1:10; Ps 34:22; 103:21; 113:1; 135:1 [x]Ezr 3:1; Ne 11:1 [y]Ezr 3:1
8:1 [z]Ne 3:26 [a]Dt 28:61; 2Ch 34:15; Ezr 7:6
8:2 [b]Lev 23:23-25; Nu 29:1-6 [c]Dt 31:11
8:3 [d]Ne 3:26
8:4 [e]2Ch 6:13
8:5 [f]Jdg 3:20
8:6 [g]Ex 4:31; Ezr 9:5; 1Ti 2:8
8:7 [h]Ezr 10:23 [i]Lev 10:11; 2Ch 17:7
8:9 [j]Ne 7:1,65,70 [k]Dt 12:7,12; 16:14-15
8:10 [l]1Sa 25:8; Lk 14:12-14 [m]Lev 23:40; Dt 12:18; 16:11,14-15

[73]The priests, the Levites, the gatekeepers, the musicians and the temple servants,[w] along with certain of the people and the rest of the Israelites, settled in their own towns.[x]

Ezra Reads the Law

8 When the seventh month came and the Israelites had settled in their towns,[y] [1]all the people came together as one in the square before the Water Gate.[z] They told Ezra the teacher of the Law to bring out the Book of the Law of Moses,[a] which the LORD had commanded for Israel.

[2]So on the first day of the seventh month[b] Ezra the priest brought the Law[c] before the assembly, which was made up of men and women and all who were able to understand. [3]He read it aloud from daybreak till noon as he faced the square before the Water Gate[d] in the presence of the men, women and others who could understand. And all the people listened attentively to the Book of the Law.

[4]Ezra the teacher of the Law stood on a high wooden platform[e] built for the occasion. Beside him on his right stood Mattithiah, Shema, Anaiah, Uriah, Hilkiah and Maaseiah; and on his left were Pedaiah, Mishael, Malkijah, Hashum, Hashbaddanah, Zechariah and Meshullam.

[5]Ezra opened the book. All the people could see him because he was standing[f] above them; and as he opened it, the people all stood up. [6]Ezra praised the LORD, the great God; and all the people lifted their hands[g] and responded, "Amen! Amen!" Then they bowed down and worshiped the LORD with their faces to the ground.

[7]The Levites[h]—Jeshua, Bani, Sherebiah, Jamin, Akkub, Shabbethai, Hodiah, Maaseiah, Kelita, Azariah, Jozabad, Hanan and Pelaiah—instructed[i] the people in the Law while the people were standing there. [8]They read from the Book of the Law of God, making it clear[*a*] and giving the meaning so that the people understood what was being read.

[9]Then Nehemiah the governor, Ezra the priest and teacher of the Law, and the Levites[j] who were instructing the people said to them all, "This day is holy to the LORD your God. Do not mourn or weep."[k] For all the people had been weeping as they listened to the words of the Law.

[10]Nehemiah said, "Go and enjoy choice food and sweet drinks, and send some to those who have nothing[l] prepared. This day is holy to our Lord. Do not grieve, for the joy[m] of the LORD is your strength."

[*a*] *8* Or *God, translating it*

7:73b–12:26 Nehemiah's memoir in the first person gives way to records in the third person.

7:73b—8:18 *Ezra Reads the Law.* This is the first reference to Ezra in the almost 13 years since his arrival in 458 BC. Here he reestablishes "the Book of the Law of Moses" (8:1) at the center of national life. All the people gather for the reading and exposition of the Torah (8:1–18), and they respond (8:9–12). The reading of the law continues on the next day with a smaller audience of family heads along with priests and Levites. It focuses on the immediate occasion of the Festival of Tabernacles (8:13–18).

7:73b the seventh month. One of the most important months in the year. It started with the Festival of Trumpets, which was followed by the Day of Atonement and then the Festival of Tabernacles (Lev 23:23–44). This was Oct./Nov. 444 BC.

8:1 all the people came together as one. Suggests a certain spontaneity but doubtless there had been careful preparation behind the scenes. **Water Gate.** Possibly the same as the temple square (Ezra 10:9). **Book of the Law of Moses.** This was probably the Pentateuch as a whole but with the emphasis particularly on Deuteronomy (see note on Ezra 7:14). The people's desire to hear the Torah is underlined.

8:2 all who were able to understand. Almost certainly would include older children.

8:3 daybreak till noon. The reading lasted about six hours.

8:4 These 13 people were apparently community leaders and some might have helped in the physical task of unrolling the scroll as Ezra read. **high wooden platform.** High enough for others to see and hear Ezra and wide enough to hold his 13 associates.

8:5 opened the book ... the people all stood up. No mere formality but a declaration that from now on the words of this book were to be authoritative in the community's life. The rabbis deduced from this verse that the congregation should stand for the reading of the Torah. In Eastern Orthodox churches today, it is still customary for the congregation to stand throughout the service.

8:6 The reading and exposition was to be carried out in a spirit of worship, and the people respond not only verbally but by lifting their hands and falling on their faces before the Lord. **lifted their hands.** See Exod 9:29; Pss 28:2; 134:2; 1 Tim 2:8. **Amen! Amen!** See Deut 27:15; Rom 1:25. The repetition conveys intense feeling. **bowed down ... faces to the ground.** Private acts of worship often involved prostration to the ground, e.g., Abraham's servant (Gen 24:52), Moses (Exod 34:8), Joshua (Josh 5:14), and Job (Job 1:20). Exodus records three examples of spontaneous communal worship (Exod 4:31; 12:27; 33:10). In 2 Chr 20:18, King Jehoshaphat and the people "fell down in worship before the LORD" when they heard the promise of victory.

8:7 Levites. Most of these 13 men appear elsewhere in Nehemiah (9:4–5; 10:9–13; 11:16).

8:8 making it clear. The NIV text note suggests "translating it." What was read was Hebrew and the people spoke Aramaic. Few would have understood without translation. **giving the meaning.** Probably the articulate reading of the text as well as explaining the passage. This remains a model for all who teach and preach the Word of God.

8:9 Nehemiah. Explicitly links Nehemiah and Ezra, showing that they were contemporaries (12:26,36). Nehemiah was doubtless present during the teaching sessions and now takes the lead, associating himself with the teaching team. **Do not mourn or weep.** Repentance had been an appropriate response, but ultimately true engagement with Scripture leads to deep rejoicing.

8:10 choice food and sweet drinks. The generous provision is a fore-

[11]The Levites calmed all the people, saying, "Be still, for this is a holy day. Do not grieve."
[12]Then all the people went away to eat and drink, to send portions of food and to celebrate with great joy,[n] because they now understood the words that had been made known to them.

[13]On the second day of the month, the heads of all the families, along with the priests and the Levites, gathered around Ezra the teacher to give attention to the words of the Law. [14]They found written in the Law, which the LORD had commanded through Moses, that the Israelites were to live in temporary shelters during the festival of the seventh month [15]and that they should proclaim this word and spread it throughout their towns and in Jerusalem: "Go out into the hill country and bring back branches from olive and wild olive trees, and from myrtles, palms and shade trees, to make temporary shelters"—as it is written.[a]

[16]So the people went out and brought back branches and built themselves temporary shelters on their own roofs, in their courtyards, in the courts of the house of God and in the square by the Water Gate and the one by the Gate of Ephraim.[o] [17]The whole company that had returned from exile built temporary shelters and lived in them. From the days of Joshua son of Nun until that day, the Israelites had not celebrated[p] it like this. And their joy was very great.

[18]Day after day, from the first day to the last, Ezra read[q] from the Book of the Law of God. They celebrated the festival for seven days, and on the eighth day, in accordance with the regulation,[r] there was an assembly.

The Israelites Confess Their Sins

9 On the twenty-fourth day of the same month, the Israelites gathered together, fasting and wearing sackcloth and putting dust on their heads.[s] [2]Those of Israelite descent had separated themselves from all foreigners.[t] They stood in their places and confessed their sins and the sins of their ancestors.[u] [3]They stood where they were and read from the Book of the Law of the LORD their God for a quarter of the day, and spent another quarter in confession and in worshiping the LORD their God. [4]Standing on the stairs of the Levites[v] were Jeshua, Bani, Kadmiel, Shebaniah, Bunni, Sherebiah, Bani and Kenani. They cried out with loud voices to the LORD their God. [5]And the Levites—Jeshua, Kadmiel, Bani, Hashabneiah, Sherebiah, Hodiah, Shebaniah and Pethahiah—said: "Stand up and praise the LORD your God,[w] who is from everlasting to everlasting.[b]"

[a] *15* See Lev. 23:37-40. [b] *5* Or *God for ever and ever*

8:12 [n]Est 9:22
8:16 [o]2Ki 14:13; Ne 12:39
8:17 [p]2Ch 7:8; 8:13; 30:21
8:18 [q]Dt 31:11 [r]Lev 23:36,40; Nu 29:35
9:1 [s]Jos 7:6; 1Sa 4:12
9:2 [t]Ne 13:3,30 [u]Ezr 10:11; Ps 106:6
9:4 [v]Ezr 10:23
9:5 [w]Ps 78:4

taste of the new creation (e.g., Isa 25:6). This is not a self-indulgent party but probably includes the poor ("send some to those who have nothing prepared"). It was customary for God's people to remember the less fortunate on joyous occasions (2 Sam 6:19; Esth 9:22; contrast 1 Cor 11:20–22; Jas 2:14–16). **the joy of the LORD is your strength.** There has been little joy during the laborious weeks of building; now is the time for thanksgiving and praise to God.

8:11 The Levites are again (v. 8) involved in reinforcing the wise counsel.

8:12 because they now understood the words. Their rejoicing flows from a renewed understanding of God's gracious words and a readiness to obey them.

8:14 festival. Of Tabernacles (Exod 23:16; Lev 23:39–43), both a harvest festival and a reminder of the wilderness wanderings symbolized by people living in tents and booths (vv. 15–17). It was on the 15th of the month, which gave nearly two weeks for preparation. This was another visual link with the exodus and thus a reminder of the mighty acts of God.

8:16–17 Emphasizes mass participation.

8:17 returned from exile. Another reference to the second exodus, reinforcing the desire to be in continuity with God's people in the past. **From the days of Joshua ... until that day.** The point is not that the festival had not been celebrated since the days of Joshua but that they celebrated their return to the land just as Joshua had celebrated when the Israelites first entered the promised land.

8:18 Day after day. Deut 31:10–13 mandates that they read the law every sabbatical year but does not prescribe daily reading. But this fits well with Ezra's concern that the community should be continually under the Torah's authority.

9:1–37 *The Israelites Confess Their Sins.* This day of national mourning and confession does not contradict the previous chapter's emphasis on rejoicing but prevents that joy from being superficial. The confessional prayer (vv. 5b–37) ranges widely and richly through Israel's theology and history, starting with creation. It powerfully reinforces the fundamentals of their faith by surveying God's faithfulness and their sinfulness. The Festival of Tabernacles ended on the 22nd day of the month, and it is now the 24th. This would be Oct. 30, 444 BC.

9:2 separated. Possibly the dissolving of mixed marriages that Ezra 9–10 describes, but this cannot be proven. Though in line with the measures described in Ezra 9–10, here it refers not just to marriage but to the integrity of the community in general.

9:3 Ezra, though not mentioned, probably again led the reading and study. Some translations have "And Ezra said" at the beginning of v. 6, following the Greek text rather than the Hebrew.

9:4–5a The list of Levites differs slightly from that in 8:7. Probably there was a pool of Levites from which different people would be selected. Here the first group probably led the confession; the second group, the praise.

9:5b–6 A vigorous summons to praise is followed by an expression of the glory and majesty of the Lord in the whole created order and in the sweep of history.

9:5b from everlasting to everlasting. This puts that moment and indeed every moment in its true place as part of the great story that

9:6 [x]Dt 6:4 [y]2Ki 19:15 [z]Ge 1:1; Isa 37:16 [a]Ps 95:5 [b]Dt 10:14
9:7 [c]Ge 11:31 [d]Ge 17:5
9:8 [e]Ge 15:18-21 [f]Jos 21:45 [g]Ge 15:6; Ezr 9:15
9:9 [h]Ex 3:7 [i]Ex 14:10-30
9:10 [j]Ex 10:1 [k]Jer 32:20; Da 9:15
9:11 [l]Ex 14:21; Ps 78:13 [m]Ex 15:4-5,10; Heb 11:29
9:12 [n]Ex 15:13 [o]Ex 13:21
9:13 [p]Ex 19:11 [q]Ex 19:19 [r]Ps 119:137 [s]Ex 20:1
9:14 [t]Ge 2:3; Ex 20:8-11
9:15 [u]Ex 16:4; Jn 6:31 [v]Ex 17:6; Nu 20:7-13 [w]Dt 1:8,21
9:16 [x]Dt 1:26-33; 31:29
9:17 [y]Ps 78:42 [z]Nu 14:1-4 [a]Ex 34:6 [b]Nu 14:17-19 [c]Ps 78:11
9:18 [d]Ex 32:4
9:20 [e]Nu 11:17; Isa 63:11,14 [f]Ex 16:15 [g]Ex 17:6

"Blessed be your glorious name, and may it be exalted above all blessing and praise. [6]You
alone are the LORD.[x] You made the heavens,[y] even the highest heavens, and all their starry host,
the earth[z] and all that is on it, the seas[a] and all that is in them.[b] You give life to everything, and
the multitudes of heaven worship you.
[7]"You are the LORD God, who chose Abram and brought him out of Ur of the Chaldeans[c] and
named him Abraham.[d] [8]You found his heart faithful to you, and you made a covenant with him
to give to his descendants the land of the Canaanites, Hittites, Amorites, Perizzites, Jebusites and
Girgashites.[e] You have kept your promise[f] because you are righteous.[g]
[9]"You saw the suffering of our ancestors in Egypt;[h] you heard their cry at the Red Sea.[a][i] [10]You
sent signs[j] and wonders against Pharaoh, against all his officials and all the people of his land,
for you knew how arrogantly the Egyptians treated them. You made a name[k] for yourself, which
remains to this day. [11]You divided the sea before them,[l] so that they passed through it on dry
ground, but you hurled their pursuers into the depths, like a stone into mighty waters.[m] [12]By day
you led[n] them with a pillar of cloud,[o] and by night with a pillar of fire to give them light on the
way they were to take.
[13]"You came down on Mount Sinai;[p] you spoke[q] to them from heaven. You gave them regulations and laws that are just[r] and right, and decrees and commands that are good.[s] [14]You
made known to them your holy Sabbath[t] and gave them commands, decrees and laws through
your servant Moses. [15]In their hunger you gave them bread from heaven[u] and in their thirst you
brought them water from the rock;[v] you told them to go in and take possession of the land you
had sworn with uplifted hand to give them.[w]
[16]"But they, our ancestors, became arrogant and stiff-necked, and they did not obey your
commands.[x] [17]They refused to listen and failed to remember[y] the miracles you performed among
them. They became stiff-necked and in their rebellion appointed a leader in order to return to
their slavery.[z] But you are a forgiving God, gracious and compassionate, slow to anger[a] and
abounding in love.[b] Therefore you did not desert them,[c] [18]even when they cast for themselves
an image of a calf[d] and said, 'This is your god, who brought you up out of Egypt,' or when they
committed awful blasphemies.
[19]"Because of your great compassion you did not abandon them in the wilderness. By day the
pillar of cloud did not fail to guide them on their path, nor the pillar of fire by night to shine on
the way they were to take. [20]You gave your good Spirit[e] to instruct them. You did not withhold
your manna[f] from their mouths, and you gave them water[g] for their thirst. [21]For forty years you

[a] 9 Or *the Sea of Reeds*

alone gives the little stories their significance. Nothing in heaven or earth is outside the Lord's power.

9:5c glorious name. Yahweh, the covenant God who is committed to his people by promises that he cannot and will not break. He is the Creator of all things visible and invisible and the author of all life above and below. This evokes the basic conviction at the heart of Israel's faith (Ps 121:2). His name emphasizes his splendor and his power.

9:7–8 Briefly surveys highlights from Abraham's story to emphasize God's promise, covenant, and gift of land. God's promise to drive out other nations has particular application to this period of restoration to the land. Abraham's faithfulness challenges the present generation's fickleness, and the list of nations reminds them of the dangers of becoming absorbed into them.

9:9–12 The prayer passes quickly to the exodus story, reminding one not only of the Exodus and Deuteronomy accounts but also the poetic account of these events in Ps 78.

9:11 you hurled their pursuers into the depths. Echoes the song of Moses in Exod 15:4–5.

9:13–15 The giving of the law is the event that defined Israel as a people under God and thus must be of central importance in the life of the present community.

9:14 holy Sabbath. Shows that Israel is distinctively God's people.

9:15 bread ... water. God's gracious provision (Exod 17:1–7; Num 20:1–13). **you told them to go in and take possession of the land.** Recalls Deuteronomy (e.g., Deut 11:31).

9:16–26 In spite of God's faithfulness, his people were rebellious when they wandered in the wilderness and after they entered the land.

9:17 Reminiscent of Jer 11:10, which describes the generation immediately before the exile. This disobedience occurred repeatedly throughout the centuries. The Israelites wanted to return to the slavery of Egypt, which they painted in unrealistically positive colors. **gracious and compassionate, slow to anger and abounding in love.** Cf. Exod 34:6. Only God's covenant love prevented complete disaster.

9:18 Even the idolatry of the golden calf did not destroy the covenant, and this is shown by the continuation of the blessings described in vv. 9–12.

9:19 pillar of cloud ... pillar of fire. These daily, visible signs of the Lord's presence perpetually reminded the Israelites of his faithfulness and challenged their disobedience.

9:20 You gave your good Spirit to instruct them. Unlike the manna, the Torah was given once, but it was given to be taught throughout the centuries by those led by the Spirit, including Ezra himself in his faithful expositions.

9:21 Inward strengthening was accompanied with the outward provision of food, clothing, and physical stamina.

sustained them in the wilderness; they lacked nothing,[h] their clothes did not wear out nor did
their feet become swollen.[i]
22"You gave them kingdoms and nations, allotting to them even the remotest frontiers. They
took over the country of Sihon[a][j] king of Heshbon and the country of Og king of Bashan.[k] 23You
made their children as numerous as the stars in the sky, and you brought them into the land that
you told their parents to enter and possess. 24Their children went in and took possession of the
land.[l] You subdued before them the Canaanites, who lived in the land; you gave the Canaanites
into their hands, along with their kings and the peoples of the land, to deal with them as they
pleased. 25They captured fortified cities and fertile land; they took possession of houses filled with
all kinds of good things, wells already dug, vineyards, olive groves and fruit trees in abundance.
They ate to the full and were well-nourished;[m] they reveled in your great goodness.[n]
26"But they were disobedient and rebelled against you; they turned their backs on your law.[o]
They killed your prophets,[p] who had warned them in order to turn them back to you; they committed awful blasphemies.[q] 27So you delivered them into the hands of their enemies,[r] who oppressed them. But when they were oppressed they cried out to you. From heaven you heard them,
and in your great compassion[s] you gave them deliverers, who rescued them from the hand of
their enemies.
28"But as soon as they were at rest, they again did what was evil in your sight. Then you abandoned them to the hand of their enemies so that they ruled over them. And when they cried out to
you again, you heard from heaven, and in your compassion you delivered them[t] time after time.
29"You warned them in order to turn them back to your law, but they became arrogant[u]
and disobeyed your commands. They sinned against your ordinances, of which you said, 'The
person who obeys them will live by them.'[v] Stubbornly they turned their backs on you, became
stiff-necked and refused to listen.[w] 30For many years you were patient with them. By your Spirit
you warned them through your prophets.[x] Yet they paid no attention, so you gave them into the
hands of the neighboring peoples. 31But in your great mercy you did not put an end[y] to them or
abandon them, for you are a gracious and merciful God.
32"Now therefore, our God, the great God, mighty[z] and awesome, who keeps his covenant of
love,[a] do not let all this hardship seem trifling in your eyes — the hardship that has come on us,
on our kings and leaders, on our priests and prophets, on our ancestors and all your people, from
the days of the kings of Assyria until today. 33In all that has happened to us, you have remained
righteous;[b] you have acted faithfully, while we acted wickedly.[c] 34Our kings,[d] our leaders, our
priests and our ancestors[e] did not follow your law; they did not pay attention to your commands

9:21 [h]Dt 2:7 [i]Dt 8:4
9:22 [j]Nu 21:21 [k]Nu 21:33
9:24 [l]Jos 11:23
9:25 [m]Dt 6:10-12 [n]Nu 13:27; Dt 32:12-15
9:26 [o]1Ki 14:9 [p]Mt 21:35-36 [q]Jdg 2:12-13
9:27 [r]Jdg 2:14 [s]Ps 106:45
9:28 [t]Ps 106:43
9:29 [u]Ps 5:5; Isa 2:11; Jer 43:2 [v]Dt 30:16 [w]Zec 7:11-12
9:30 [x]2Ki 17:13-18; 2Ch 36:16
9:31 [y]Isa 48:9; Jer 4:27
9:32 [z]Ps 24:8 [a]Dt 7:9
9:33 [b]Ge 18:25 [c]Jer 44:3; Da 9:7-8,14
9:34 [d]2Ki 23:11 [e]Jer 44:17

[a] 22 One Hebrew manuscript and Septuagint; most Hebrew manuscripts *Sihon, that is, the country of the*

9:22–25 Outlines the conquest of the land and the providential overruling of every stage of the settlement.
9:22 Sihon ... Og. See Num 21:21–35; Pss 135:10–11; 136:18–20. These victories were evidence of the Lord's presence with the Israelites just before they crossed the Jordan.
9:23 numerous as the stars. Recalls God's promise to Abraham (Gen 15:5) and also goes back to God's command at creation when he hung the stars in space (Gen 1:28).
9:24 You subdued. The divine Warrior fought for his people. Their victory was not because of their military prowess.
9:25 Terms from Deuteronomy describe all the blessings of the land: "cities" (Deut 3:5); "fertile land" ("good land" in Deut 8:7–10); "houses," "wells," "vineyards," and "olive groves" (Deut 6:11).
9:26–31 This cycle of rebellion, crying to the Lord, and the Lord's deliverance echoes the book of Judges as well as later parts of Israel's history that the books of 1 and 2 Kings describe and critique. The pattern is typical of the people's history as a whole.
9:26 killed your prophets. See, e.g., 2 Chr 24:20–22; Jer 26:20–23. Doubtless there were many unknown faithful prophets who were murdered; in the case of Jeremiah, successive attempts were made on his life.
9:29 You warned. Through the prophets, who urged people to return to covenant obedience by obeying the words of Moses, which were the words of God. **The person who obeys them will live by them.** The law was life-giving, but the people opted for death (Deut 30:16).
9:30 By your Spirit you warned. Emphasizes the living nature of the prophetic word and the vital role of the prophets God raised up to confront the nation with the living Word.
9:31 This is the story of rebellious Israel and the love of God that pursues the sinner.
9:32–37 This final plea to the Lord returns to the present situation and asks him to bring the mercy he has so richly shown in the past into this moment. It is one thing to acknowledge general sin and quite another to apply that same confession to the specific sins of the present.
9:32 covenant of love. At the heart of all God's dealings in the past and the only ground of assurance now. **from the days of the kings of Assyria until today.** From Assyria's destruction of the northern kingdom through the Babylonian exile to that day (Persian times).
9:33 Mirrors Ezra's prayer in Ezra 9:5. God is consistent in both his judgment and his blessing.
9:34–35 Disobeying the covenant was not merely a failure to keep rules but was shameless ingratitude while enjoying the land's rich blessings.

9:35 [f]Isa 63:7 [g]Dt 28:45-48
9:36 [h]Dt 28:48; Ezr 9:9
9:37 [i]Dt 28:33; La 5:5
9:38 [j]2Ch 23:16 [k]Isa 44:5
10:2 [l]Ezr 2:2
10:3 [m]1Ch 9:12
10:5 [n]1Ch 24:8
10:9 [o]Ne 12:1
10:16 [p]Ezr 8:6

or the statutes you warned them to keep. 35Even while they were in their kingdom, enjoying your
great goodness[f] to them in the spacious and fertile land you gave them, they did not serve you[g]
or turn from their evil ways.
36"But see, we are slaves[h] today, slaves in the land you gave our ancestors so they could eat
its fruit and the other good things it produces. 37Because of our sins, its abundant harvest goes
to the kings you have placed over us. They rule over our bodies and our cattle as they please. We
are in great distress.[i]

The Agreement of the People

38"In view of all this, we are making a binding agreement,[j] putting it in writing,[k] and our leaders,
our Levites and our priests are affixing their seals to it."[a]

10 [b] Those who sealed it were:

Nehemiah the governor, the son of Hakaliah.
Zedekiah, 2Seraiah,[l] Azariah, Jeremiah,
3Pashhur,[m] Amariah, Malkijah,
4Hattush, Shebaniah, Malluk,
5Harim,[n] Meremoth, Obadiah,
6Daniel, Ginnethon, Baruch,
7Meshullam, Abijah, Mijamin,
8Maaziah, Bilgai and Shemaiah.
These were the priests.

9The Levites:[o]

Jeshua son of Azaniah, Binnui of the sons of Henadad, Kadmiel,
10and their associates: Shebaniah,
Hodiah, Kelita, Pelaiah, Hanan,
11Mika, Rehob, Hashabiah,
12Zakkur, Sherebiah, Shebaniah,
13Hodiah, Bani and Beninu.

14The leaders of the people:

Parosh, Pahath-Moab, Elam, Zattu, Bani,
15Bunni, Azgad, Bebai,
16Adonijah, Bigvai, Adin,[p]
17Ater, Hezekiah, Azzur,
18Hodiah, Hashum, Bezai,

[a] *38* In Hebrew texts this verse (9:38) is numbered 10:1. [b] In Hebrew texts 10:1-39 is numbered 10:2-40.

9:36 we are slaves. Recalls the Egyptian captivity but is worse because God's people are back in the promised land. They are, however, in some ways, still in exile. The nations are not flowing to Zion (Isa 2:2–5) nor is the desert bursting into bloom (Isa 35:1–3). Some promises have been fulfilled, but the ultimate fulfillment lies in the future.

9:38—10:39 *The Agreement of the People.* The people publicly and visibly respond to the reading and exposition of the law and to the prayer of confession. The leaders sign a binding agreement as an example for the rest of the community (10:1–27). The 84 names include Nehemiah, the governor (10:1); a group of priests (10:2–8); Levites (10:9–13); and leaders (10:14–27). The pledge of loyalty to the Lord includes specific promises; some reflect regular items, and others are especially pertinent to their situation (10:30–39).

9:38 This verse is a transition from ch. 9 to ch. 10. **binding agreement.** Implies a covenant.

10:1 Nehemiah. Signed first. **Zedekiah.** Signed second, perhaps as Nehemiah's chief official.

10:2 Seraiah. Probably the high priest, because his name stands at the head of other priests in vv. 2–8. Ezra is not mentioned in the list, probably because he was from the family of Seraiah or possibly because he is called Azariah, the longer form of the name Ezra.

10:9–13 This list probably contains some family and individual names as they correspond to the list of those who returned with Zerubbabel (12:8a). Some of them were Ezra's teaching associates at the reading of the law (8:7).

10:14–27 leaders of the people. Listed mainly in terms of the families they represent. The list closely follows those in ch. 7 and Ezra 2. There are, of course, new families since Zerubbabel's time, and this list, like all the others in the two books, shows a sense of continuity with past generations.

[19]Hariph, Anathoth, Nebai,
[20]Magpiash, Meshullam, Hezir,[q]
[21]Meshezabel, Zadok, Jaddua,
[22]Pelatiah, Hanan, Anaiah,
[23]Hoshea, Hananiah,[r] Hasshub,
[24]Hallohesh, Pilha, Shobek,
[25]Rehum, Hashabnah, Maaseiah,
[26]Ahiah, Hanan, Anan,
[27]Malluk, Harim and Baanah.

[28]"The rest of the people — priests, Levites, gatekeepers, musicians, temple servants[s] and all
who separated themselves from the neighboring peoples[t] for the sake of the Law of God, together
with their wives and all their sons and daughters who are able to understand — [29]all these now
join their fellow Israelites the nobles, and bind themselves with a curse and an oath[u] to follow
the Law of God given through Moses the servant of God and to obey carefully all the commands,
regulations and decrees of the LORD our Lord.

[30]"We promise not to give our daughters in marriage to the peoples around us or take their
daughters for our sons.[v]

[31]"When the neighboring peoples bring merchandise or grain to sell on the Sabbath,[w] we will
not buy from them on the Sabbath or on any holy day. Every seventh year we will forgo working
the land[x] and will cancel all debts.[y]

[32]"We assume the responsibility for carrying out the commands to give a third of a shekel[a]
each year for the service of the house of our God: [33]for the bread set out on the table;[z] for the
regular grain offerings and burnt offerings; for the offerings on the Sabbaths, at the New Moon[a]
feasts and at the appointed festivals; for the holy offerings; for sin offerings[b] to make atonement
for Israel; and for all the duties of the house of our God.[b]

[34]"We — the priests, the Levites and the people — have cast lots[c] to determine when each of
our families is to bring to the house of our God at set times each year a contribution of wood[d] to
burn on the altar of the LORD our God, as it is written in the Law.

[35]"We also assume responsibility for bringing to the house of the LORD each year the firstfruits[e]
of our crops and of every fruit tree.[f]

[36]"As it is also written in the Law, we will bring the firstborn[g] of our sons and of our cattle, of
our herds and of our flocks to the house of our God, to the priests ministering there.[h]

[37]"Moreover, we will bring to the storerooms of the house of our God, to the priests, the first
of our ground meal, of our grain offerings, of the fruit of all our trees and of our new wine and
olive oil.[i] And we will bring a tithe[j] of our crops to the Levites,[k] for it is the Levites who collect

10:20 [q] 1Ch 24:15
10:23 [r] Ne 7:2
10:28 [s] Ps 135:1 [t] 2Ch 6:26; Ne 9:2
10:29 [u] Nu 5:21; Ps 119:106
10:30 [v] Ex 34:16; Dt 7:3; Ne 13:23
10:31 [w] Ne 13:16,18; Jer 17:27; Eze 23:38; Am 8:5 [x] Ex 23:11; Lev 25:1-7 [y] Dt 15:1
10:33 [z] Lev 24:6 [a] Nu 10:10; Ps 81:3; Isa 1:14 [b] 2Ch 24:5
10:34 [c] Lev 16:8 [d] Ne 13:31
10:35 [e] Ex 22:29; 23:19; Nu 18:12 [f] Dt 26:1-11
10:36 [g] Ex 13:2; Nu 18:14-16 [h] Ne 13:31
10:37 [i] Lev 23:17; Nu 18:12 [j] Lev 27:30; Nu 18:21 [k] Dt 14:22-29

[a] *32* That is, about 1/8 ounce or about 4 grams [b] *33* Or *purification offerings*

10:28 all who separated themselves from the neighboring peoples. Perhaps those qualified to become part of the community by coming under obedience to the law.
10:29 follow … obey. A characteristic emphasis in both Ezra and Nehemiah.
10:30 The people give a high priority to the issue of mixed marriages, which Ezra 9 – 10 highlights and which arises again in Neh 13 (see also Mal 2:10 – 16).
10:31 Sabbath. Observing this day was a distinctive feature of the community's identity. Here, more specifically, it is probably related to the presence of foreign traders in Jerusalem. As a sign of the Sinaitic covenant it takes on special significance. **Every seventh year.** Allowing the land to lie fallow (Exod 23:10 – 11; Lev 25:4 – 7) led the people to trust the Lord both for fruitfulness in subsequent years and for his bountiful provision so that they would not suffer by the cancellation of debts.
10:32 for the service of the house of our God. Contributions supported the temple's regular offerings and festivals. This duplicates the spirit of Exod 30:11 – 16, which stipulates that everyone over 20 gave to the work of the tabernacle.
10:33 sin offerings to make atonement for Israel. A continual reminder of God's forgiveness and their sinfulness.
10:34 contribution of wood. Fire was to burn continually on the altar of burnt offering (Lev 6:8 – 13), and the ever-practical Nehemiah prescribes arrangements for ensuring a supply of wood. Though there is no specific reference to a wood offering in the Pentateuch, the perpetual burning of fire on the sanctuary altar would have required a continuous supply of wood.
10:35 – 39 Various regulations related to supporting the temple officials and sanctuary.
10:35 bringing … firstfruits. This honored the Creator by giving him back what he had already given them in the fruitful land.
10:36 firstborn. Related to redemption. Deut 12:5 – 6 specifically associates the firstborn with the temple that is to be "the place the LORD your God will choose … to put his Name."
10:37 the first of. Probably in the sense of prime or best, emphasizing that nothing shoddy was acceptable.

10:37 [l] Eze 44:30
10:38 [m] Nu 18:26
10:39 [n] Dt 12:6; Ne 13:11,12
11:1 [o] Ne 7:4 [p] ver 18; Isa 48:2; 52:1; 64:10; Zec 14:20-21 [q] Ne 7:73
11:3 [r] 1Ch 9:2-3; Ezr 2:1
11:4 [s] Ezr 1:5 [t] Ezr 2:70
11:11 [u] 2Ki 25:18; Ezr 2:2 [v] Ezr 7:2

the tithes in all the towns where we work.[l] [38]A priest descended from Aaron is to accompany
the Levites when they receive the tithes, and the Levites are to bring a tenth of the tithes[m] up
to the house of our God, to the storerooms of the treasury. [39]The people of Israel, including
the Levites, are to bring their contributions of grain, new wine and olive oil to the storerooms,
where the articles for the sanctuary and for the ministering priests, the gatekeepers and the
musicians are also kept.

"We will not neglect the house of our God."[n]

The New Residents of Jerusalem

11:3-19pp — 1Ch 9:1-17

11 Now the leaders of the people settled in Jerusalem. The rest of the people cast lots to bring one
out of every ten of them to live in Jerusalem,[o] the holy city,[p] while the remaining nine were to
stay in their own towns.[q] [2]The people commended all who volunteered to live in Jerusalem.

[3]These are the provincial leaders who settled in Jerusalem (now some Israelites, priests, Levites,
temple servants and descendants of Solomon's servants lived in the towns of Judah, each on their
own property in the various towns,[r] [4]while other people from both Judah and Benjamin[s] lived in
Jerusalem):[t]

From the descendants of Judah:

Athaiah son of Uzziah, the son of Zechariah, the son of Amariah, the son of Shephatiah, the son
of Mahalalel, a descendant of Perez; [5]and Maaseiah son of Baruch, the son of Kol-Hozeh, the son
of Hazaiah, the son of Adaiah, the son of Joiarib, the son of Zechariah, a descendant of Shelah.
[6]The descendants of Perez who lived in Jerusalem totaled 468 men of standing.

[7]From the descendants of Benjamin:

Sallu son of Meshullam, the son of Joed, the son of Pedaiah, the son of Kolaiah, the son of Maaseiah, the son of Ithiel, the son of Jeshaiah, [8]and his followers, Gabbai and Sallai — 928 men.
[9]Joel son of Zikri was their chief officer, and Judah son of Hassenuah was over the New Quarter
of the city.

[10]From the priests:

Jedaiah; the son of Joiarib; Jakin; [11]Seraiah[u] son of Hilkiah, the son of Meshullam, the son of Zadok, the son of Meraioth, the son of Ahitub,[v] the official in charge of the house of God, [12]and their
associates, who carried on work for the temple — 822 men; Adaiah son of Jeroham, the son of
Pelaliah, the son of Amzi, the son of Zechariah, the son of Pashhur, the son of Malkijah, [13]and his
associates, who were heads of families — 242 men; Amashsai son of Azarel, the son of Ahzai, the
son of Meshillemoth, the son of Immer, [14]and his[a] associates, who were men of standing — 128.
Their chief officer was Zabdiel son of Haggedolim.

[a] *14* Most Septuagint manuscripts; Hebrew *their*

10:38 tenth of the tithes. Levites, as recipients of the tithes, had to pass a tenth share of these to the priests, and a priest descended from Aaron, presumably the high priest, was to supervise it (Num 18:26).

10:39 We will not neglect the house of our God. Summarizes the whole chapter and underlines the concern that the temple be worthy not simply as a place for correct ritual practice but also as the place where God meets with his people.

11:1–36 *The New Residents of Jerusalem.* Nehemiah is concerned to repopulate Jerusalem and thus put both spiritual and economic life on a secure footing.

11:1–2 Community leaders were already settled in Jerusalem, but they needed large numbers of ordinary citizens to live there too, which required a costly uprooting from their native villages.

11:1 cast lots. A recognized way of discerning the Lord's will (cf. Num 26:55; 1 Sam 10:20–21). God controls all actions, however random they seem (Prov 16:33).

11:2 volunteered. Sometimes describes military service (Judg 5:2; Ps 110:3) and reflects the undertaking's hazardous nature due to the uprooting and subsequent upheaval.

11:3–19 This list of community and religious leaders is probably selective. It parallels 1 Chr 9:2–21, a list of the first residents of Jerusalem after the return from Babylon. About half the names in the two lists are the same.

11:6,14 men of standing. Can denote simply wealth or ability but also has a military nuance and again is a reminder of the need for defense.

11:9,14,22 chief officer. Has a military flavor, hardly surprising after the activities of Sanballat and Tobiah and their associates.

11:10–14 Jedaiah ... Jakin; Seraiah. Three leading priests.

[15]From the Levites:

Shemaiah son of Hasshub, the son of Azrikam, the son of Hashabiah, the son of Bunni; [16]Shab-
bethai[w] and Jozabad,[x] two of the heads of the Levites, who had charge of the outside work of the
house of God; [17]Mattaniah[y] son of Mika, the son of Zabdi, the son of Asaph,[z] the director who led
in thanksgiving and prayer; Bakbukiah, second among his associates; and Abda son of Shammua,
the son of Galal, the son of Jeduthun.[a] [18]The Levites in the holy city[b] totaled 284.

[19]The gatekeepers:

Akkub, Talmon and their associates, who kept watch at the gates—172 men.

[20]The rest of the Israelites, with the priests and Levites, were in all the towns of Judah, each on their
ancestral property.
[21]The temple servants[c] lived on the hill of Ophel, and Ziha and Gishpa were in charge of them.
[22]The chief officer of the Levites in Jerusalem was Uzzi son of Bani, the son of Hashabiah, the son of
Mattaniah,[d] the son of Mika. Uzzi was one of Asaph's descendants, who were the musicians responsible
for the service of the house of God. [23]The musicians[e] were under the king's orders, which regulated
their daily activity.
[24]Pethahiah son of Meshezabel, one of the descendants of Zerah[f] son of Judah, was the king's agent
in all affairs relating to the people.
[25]As for the villages with their fields, some of the people of Judah lived in Kiriath Arba[g] and its
surrounding settlements, in Dibon[h] and its settlements, in Jekabzeel and its villages, [26]in Jeshua, in
Moladah, in Beth Pelet,[i] [27]in Hazar Shual, in Beersheba[j] and its settlements, [28]in Ziklag,[k] in Mekonah
and its settlements, [29]in En Rimmon, in Zorah,[l] in Jarmuth,[m] [30]Zanoah, Adullam[n] and their villages,
in Lachish[o] and its fields, and in Azekah[p] and its settlements. So they were living all the way from Beersheba[q] to the Valley of Hinnom.
[31]The descendants of the Benjamites from Geba[r] lived in Mikmash,[s] Aija, Bethel and its settlements,
[32]in Anathoth,[t] Nob[u] and Ananiah, [33]in Hazor,[v] Ramah and Gittaim,[w] [34]in Hadid, Zeboim[x] and Neballat,
[35]in Lod and Ono,[y] and in Ge Harashim.
[36]Some of the divisions of the Levites of Judah settled in Benjamin.

Priests and Levites

12 These were the priests[z] and Levites who returned with Zerubbabel[a] son of Shealtiel and with
Joshua:[b]

Seraiah,[c] Jeremiah, Ezra,
[2]Amariah, Malluk, Hattush,
[3]Shekaniah, Rehum, Meremoth,
[4]Iddo,[d] Ginnethon,[a] Abijah,[e]
[5]Mijamin,[b] Moadiah, Bilgah,
[6]Shemaiah, Joiarib, Jedaiah,[f]
[7]Sallu, Amok, Hilkiah and Jedaiah.

[a] 4 Many Hebrew manuscripts and Vulgate (see also verse 16); most Hebrew manuscripts *Ginnethoi*
[b] 5 A variant of *Miniamin*

11:16 [w] Ezr 10:15 [x] Ezr 8:33
11:17 [y] 1Ch 9:15; Ne 12:8 [z] 2Ch 5:12 [a] 1Ch 25:1
11:18 [b] Rev 21:2
11:21 [c] Ezr 2:43; Ne 3:26
11:22 [d] 1Ch 9:15
11:23 [e] Ne 7:44
11:24 [f] Ge 38:30
11:25 [g] Ge 35:27; Jos 14:15 [h] Nu 21:30
11:26 [i] Jos 15:27
11:27 [j] Ge 21:14
11:28 [k] 1Sa 27:6
11:29 [l] Jos 15:33 [m] Jos 10:3
11:30 [n] Jos 15:35 [o] Jos 10:3 [p] Jos 10:10 [q] Jos 15:28
11:31 [r] Jos 21:17; Isa 10:29 [s] 1Sa 13:2
11:32 [t] Jos 21:18; Isa 10:30 [u] 1Sa 21:1
11:33 [v] Jos 11:1 [w] 2Sa 4:3
11:34 [x] 1Sa 13:18
11:35 [y] 1Ch 8:12
12:1 [z] Ne 10:1-8 [a] 1Ch 3:19 [b] Ezr 2:2 [c] Ezr 2:2
12:4 [d] Zec 1:1 [e] Lk 1:5
12:6 [f] 1Ch 24:7

11:15–24 Details the Levites and temple staff.
11:16 outside work of the house of God. Probably fabric and finance.
11:17 thanksgiving and prayer. The spiritual nature of the work.
11:19 A fuller list in 1 Chr 9:17–32 says that the gatekeepers guarded the king's gate on the east and had overall responsibility for temple security.
11:20–24 These brief notes round off the various responsibilities of the leading residents of Jerusalem.
11:21 temple servants. First mentioned in Ezra 2:43. **hill of Ophel.** At the north end of the city leading up to the temple.
11:23 under the king's orders. Possibly refers to David's ordering of the temple singers (12:24; 1 Chr 25), although it more likely refers to the Persian king.
11:25–30 This list of towns closely parallels the fuller list of the post-exodus settlement in Josh 15:20–62. Many of the places are garrison towns on the borders of Judah, and this fits in with the concern with defense.
11:31–36 Briefly recounts the Benjamite settlements and probably refers particularly to fortified towns.
12:1–26 *Priests and Levites.* Faced again with a daunting list of names, the reader needs to remember that these were real people who lived and breathed and were a part of God's people.
12:1–7 This register of the priestly houses gives 22 names. There were originally 24 priestly divisions for the sanctuary (1 Chr 24:7–19).

12:8 [g] Ne 11:17
12:10 [h] Ezr 10:24
12:16 [i] ver 4
12:24 [j] Ezr 2:40
12:27 [k] Dt 20:5

These were the leaders of the priests and their associates in the days of Joshua.
8The Levites were Jeshua, Binnui, Kadmiel, Sherebiah, Judah, and also Mattaniah,[g] who, together
with his associates, was in charge of the songs of thanksgiving. 9Bakbukiah and Unni, their associates,
stood opposite them in the services.
10Joshua was the father of Joiakim, Joiakim the father of Eliashib,[h] Eliashib the father of Joiada,
11Joiada the father of Jonathan, and Jonathan the father of Jaddua.
12In the days of Joiakim, these were the heads of the priestly families:

of Seraiah's family, Meraiah;
of Jeremiah's, Hananiah;
13 of Ezra's, Meshullam;
of Amariah's, Jehohanan;
14 of Malluk's, Jonathan;
of Shekaniah's,[a] Joseph;
15 of Harim's, Adna;
of Meremoth's,[b] Helkai;
16 of Iddo's,[i] Zechariah;
of Ginnethon's, Meshullam;
17 of Abijah's, Zikri;
of Miniamin's and of Moadiah's, Piltai;
18 of Bilgah's, Shammua;
of Shemaiah's, Jehonathan;
19 of Joiarib's, Mattenai;
of Jedaiah's, Uzzi;
20 of Sallu's, Kallai;
of Amok's, Eber;
21 of Hilkiah's, Hashabiah;
of Jedaiah's, Nethanel.

22The family heads of the Levites in the days of Eliashib, Joiada, Johanan and Jaddua, as well as
those of the priests, were recorded in the reign of Darius the Persian. 23The family heads among the
descendants of Levi up to the time of Johanan son of Eliashib were recorded in the book of the annals.
24And the leaders of the Levites[j] were Hashabiah, Sherebiah, Jeshua son of Kadmiel, and their associates, who stood opposite them to give praise and thanksgiving, one section responding to the other, as
prescribed by David the man of God.
25Mattaniah, Bakbukiah, Obadiah, Meshullam, Talmon and Akkub were gatekeepers who guarded
the storerooms at the gates. 26They served in the days of Joiakim son of Joshua, the son of Jozadak, and
in the days of Nehemiah the governor and of Ezra the priest, the teacher of the Law.

Dedication of the Wall of Jerusalem

27At the dedication[k] of the wall of Jerusalem, the Levites were sought out from where they lived and
were brought to Jerusalem to celebrate joyfully the dedication with songs of thanksgiving and with

[a] *14* Very many Hebrew manuscripts, some Septuagint manuscripts and Syriac (see also verse 3); most Hebrew manuscripts *Shebaniah's* [b] *15* Some Septuagint manuscripts (see also verse 3); Hebrew *Meraioth's*

12:8–9 A short list of the leading Levites.
12:9 opposite them. Suggests antiphonal singing (see also Ezra 3:11).
12:10–11 This high priestly genealogy bridges the gap between the time immediately after the exile (the period of vv. 1–9, when the first returnees arrived with Zerubbabel) and Nehemiah's own time.
12:12–21 The priestly families at the time of Joiakim, the son of Jeshua, who was high priest at the time of the return from Babylon. It emphasizes the community's continuity by showing that the priestly families held on to their traditional names.
12:22–24 A brief note on sources.
12:22 Darius the Persian. If the king's reign is the time when the lists were completed, then this is probably Darius II (423–404 BC).
12:23 book of the annals. A noncanonical book that preserves records in the temple archives. It may have been the official temple chronicle (cf. the annals of the Persian kings, Ezra 4:15; Esth 2:23; 6:1; 10:2).
12:24 David the man of God. Emphasizes his devotion to God, displayed not least in his organization of the corporate worship of Israel (v. 36; 2 Chr 8:14).
12:25–26 The list ends with the gatekeepers and their protective role. The historical note in v. 26 emphasizes the continuity of the family's responsibilities and closely links Ezra and Nehemiah as contemporaries.
12:27–47 *Dedication of the Wall of Jerusalem.* This reconnects with Nehemiah's personal memoir, which has been silent since 7:5. This is the culmination of Nehemiah's work on the wall. Handing over the work

the music of cymbals,[l] harps and lyres.[m] [28]The musicians also were brought together from the region
around Jerusalem — from the villages of the Netophathites,[n] [29]from Beth Gilgal, and from the area
of Geba and Azmaveth, for the musicians had built villages for themselves around Jerusalem. [30]When
the priests and Levites had purified themselves ceremonially, they purified the people,[o] the gates and
the wall.

[31]I had the leaders of Judah go up on top of[a] the wall. I also assigned two large choirs to give thanks.
One was to proceed on top of[b] the wall to the right, toward the Dung Gate.[p] [32]Hoshaiah and half the
leaders of Judah followed them, [33]along with Azariah, Ezra, Meshullam, [34]Judah, Benjamin,[q] Shemaiah, Jeremiah, [35]as well as some priests with trumpets,[r] and also Zechariah son of Jonathan, the son
of Shemaiah, the son of Mattaniah, the son of Micaiah, the son of Zakkur, the son of Asaph, [36]and his
associates — Shemaiah, Azarel, Milalai, Gilalai, Maai, Nethanel, Judah and Hanani — with musical
instruments[s] prescribed by David the man of God.[t] Ezra[u] the teacher of the Law led the procession. [37]At
the Fountain Gate[v] they continued directly up the steps of the City of David on the ascent to the wall
and passed above the site of David's palace to the Water Gate[w] on the east.

[38]The second choir proceeded in the opposite direction. I followed them on top of[c] the wall, together
with half the people — past the Tower of the Ovens[x] to the Broad Wall,[y] [39]over the Gate of Ephraim,[z]
the Jeshanah[d] Gate,[a] the Fish Gate,[b] the Tower of Hananel[c] and the Tower of the Hundred,[d] as far as
the Sheep Gate.[e] At the Gate of the Guard they stopped.

[40]The two choirs that gave thanks then took their places in the house of God; so did I, together with
half the officials, [41]as well as the priests — Eliakim, Maaseiah, Miniamin, Micaiah, Elioenai, Zechariah
and Hananiah with their trumpets — [42]and also Maaseiah, Shemaiah, Eleazar, Uzzi, Jehohanan, Malkijah, Elam and Ezer. The choirs sang under the direction of Jezrahiah. [43]And on that day they offered
great sacrifices, rejoicing because God had given them great joy. The women and children also rejoiced.
The sound of rejoicing in Jerusalem could be heard far away.

[44]At that time men were appointed to be in charge of the storerooms[f] for the contributions, firstfruits and tithes.[g] From the fields around the towns they were to bring into the storerooms the portions
required by the Law for the priests and the Levites, for Judah was pleased with the ministering priests

12:27 [l] 2Sa 6:5 [m] 1Ch 15:16,28; 25:6; Ps 92:3
12:28 [n] 1Ch 2:54; 9:16
12:30 [o] Ex 19:10; Job 1:5
12:31 [p] Ne 2:13
12:34 [q] Ezr 1:5
12:35 [r] Ezr 3:10
12:36 [s] 1Ch 15:16 [t] 2Ch 8:14 [u] Ezr 7:6
12:37 [v] Ne 2:14; 3:15 [w] Ne 3:26
12:38 [x] Ne 3:11 [y] Ne 3:8
12:39 [z] 2Ki 14:13; Ne 8:16 [a] Ne 3:6 [b] 2Ch 33:14; Ne 3:3 [c] Ne 3:1 [d] Ne 3:1 [e] Ne 3:1
12:44 [f] Ne 13:4,13 [g] Lev 27:30

[a] 31 Or *go alongside* [b] 31 Or *proceed alongside* [c] 38 Or *them alongside* [d] 39 Or *Old*

of human hands to God's ownership powerfully acts out a parable of the spiritual significance of all the hard and tedious work. It also completes the period of resettlement. The final paragraph (vv. 44–47) is a bridge to the final chapter. Nehemiah, ever practical, realizes that it is one thing to be overwhelmed with the emotion of a great occasion but quite another to channel that enthusiasm into plans for the work to continue.

12:27 The presence of singers and musicians was vital for a service of thanksgiving, so the spotlight falls first on the Levites. **sought out from where they lived.** Many had settled in country villages (3:17; 11:20) and came to Jerusalem for temple duties when necessary. **celebrate joyfully.** Cf. Ezra 3; 8.

12:28–29 These places were all within a radius of a few miles/kilometers from Jerusalem.

12:30 purified themselves ceremonially. Possibly derived from passages such as Exod 19:10–11; involved washing bodies and clothes, presenting a sin offering, fasting, and probably sexual abstinence. **purified ... the gates and the wall.** Shows an increased sense of the sanctity of Jerusalem, "the holy city" (11:1), and may also reflect the ceremony of sprinkling for cleansing private houses (Lev 14:49–53).

12:31 The procession around the walls echoes Ps 48:12–14, a psalm that may thank God for rescuing Jerusalem from Sennacherib's army (2 Kgs 18–19; 2 Chr 32:1–23; Isa 36–37). Two processions, each consisting of a group of leaders accompanied by a choir, were to set out in opposite directions; they were to complete a half circuit of the city, and meet at the temple square. Archaeological evidence suggests that the top of the wall was about nine feet (2.7 meters) wide, allowing people to walk two or three abreast. The first procession followed the route of Nehemiah's original nocturnal expedition (2:12–16.). **choirs.** Related to the word for "thanksgiving"; powerfully suggests that the singers' praise is not merely a musical performance but is part of their whole beings.

12:32–36 Describes the composition of the processions: priests, Levites, musicians, and lay leaders.

12:36 David the man of God. A link with the great days of their history, a prominent feature of both Ezra and Nehemiah. Mentioning David, the musician and "hero of Israel's songs" (2 Sam 23:1), and his organizing the singers for the future temple (1 Chr 25) is plainly of major significance. And David the warrior and king, whose city this was, is a powerful memory. **Ezra.** Associated with one procession; Nehemiah, with the other. This powerful visual aid shows that their work was fundamentally one. These two men with very different gifts consolidated and invigorated the postexilic work of restoration and rebuilding that the first returnees began over a century before.

12:37 City of David ... David's palace. In spite of exile and destruction, the link remains.

12:39 Gate of the Guard. Probably a temple gate with access to the court of the guard (3:25).

12:40–43 The choirs, Nehemiah, lay leaders, and priests join forces in the temple court for a service of praise and thanksgiving to celebrate a task well done. Walking on the walls probably led them to recall the effort they had invested in the work.

12:43 rejoicing ... great joy ... rejoiced ... rejoicing. The repetition emphasizes the magnitude of their rejoicing. This was even greater than the joy at the dedication of the temple (Ezra 6:16) or at the reading of the Torah (Neh 8:12,17). Unlike the mingled rejoicing and weeping in Ezra 3:13, here there is unrestrained gratitude.

12:44 At that time. A common phrase in narrative denoting that events

12:44 [h]Dt 18:8
12:45 [i]1Ch 25:1; 2Ch 8:14 [j]1Ch 6:31; 23:5
12:46 [k]2Ch 35:15 [l]2Ch 29:27; Ps 137:4
12:47 [m]Nu 18:21; Dt 18:8
13:1 [n]ver 23; Dt 23:3
13:2 [o]Nu 22:3-11 [p]Nu 23:7; Dt 23:3 [q]Nu 23:11; Dt 23:4-5
13:3 [r]ver 23; Ne 9:2
13:4 [s]Ne 12:44 [t]Ne 2:10
13:5 [u]Lev 27:30; Nu 18:21
13:6 [v]Ne 2:6; 5:14
13:7 [w]Ezr 10:24
13:8 [x]Mt 21:12-13; Jn 2:13-16
13:9 [y]1Ch 23:28; 2Ch 29:5
13:10 [z]Dt 12:19

and Levites.[h] 45 They performed the service of their God and the service of purification, as did also the
musicians and gatekeepers, according to the commands of David[i] and his son Solomon.[j] 46 For long
ago, in the days of David and Asaph,[k] there had been directors for the musicians and for the songs of
praise[l] and thanksgiving to God. 47 So in the days of Zerubbabel and of Nehemiah, all Israel contributed
the daily portions for the musicians and the gatekeepers. They also set aside the portion for the other
Levites, and the Levites set aside the portion for the descendants of Aaron.[m]

Nehemiah's Final Reforms

13 On that day the Book of Moses was read aloud in the hearing of the people and there it was
found written that no Ammonite or Moabite should ever be admitted into the assembly of God,[n]
2 because they had not met the Israelites with food and water but had hired Balaam[o] to call a curse
down on them.[p] (Our God, however, turned the curse into a blessing.)[q] 3 When the people heard this
law, they excluded from Israel all who were of foreign descent.[r]
4 Before this, Eliashib the priest had been put in charge of the storerooms[s] of the house of our God. He
was closely associated with Tobiah,[t] 5 and he had provided him with a large room formerly used to store
the grain offerings and incense and temple articles, and also the tithes[u] of grain, new wine and olive
oil prescribed for the Levites, musicians and gatekeepers, as well as the contributions for the priests.
6 But while all this was going on, I was not in Jerusalem, for in the thirty-second year of Artaxerxes[v]
king of Babylon I had returned to the king. Some time later I asked his permission 7 and came back to
Jerusalem. Here I learned about the evil thing Eliashib[w] had done in providing Tobiah a room in the
courts of the house of God. 8 I was greatly displeased and threw all Tobiah's household goods out of the
room.[x] 9 I gave orders to purify the rooms,[y] and then I put back into them the equipment of the house
of God, with the grain offerings and the incense.
10 I also learned that the portions assigned to the Levites had not been given to them,[z] and that all

happen at much the same time without specifying precise chronology. But there is no reason to believe that the arrangements made here were long after the celebrations. It was important not to neglect priests and Levites in the euphoria following the celebrations. **Judah was pleased with the ministering priests and Levites.** This sentence suggests that a new devotion and energy had been shown by these temple officials.

12:45 according to the commands of David and his son Solomon. The enthusiasm of the laity is matched by the zeal of the priests and Levites and other temple servants to carry out the commands of David and Solomon. David's preparations for the temple to be built are described in 1 Chr 23–26, and Solomon faithfully implemented these once the actual building had been completed (2 Chr 8:14).

12:46 Asaph. The chief musician. His name is associated with some of the psalms (Pss 50; 73–83).

12:47 the days of Zerubbabel and of Nehemiah. Covers the whole period of the books of Ezra and Nehemiah, starting with the first returnees who arrived with Zerubbabel. This is another testimony to the unity of the reform.

13:1–31 *Nehemiah's Final Reforms.* These reforms establish priorities, and then further problems emerge. This is a reminder of the need for continual reform.

13:1 On that day. Probably places this public reading at the end of the dedicatory celebrations of ch. 12. The arrangements for temple personnel in 12:44–47 would have taken some time to implement. **Book of Moses.** The Pentateuch as a whole is implied; the specific passage is Deut 23:3–6, which bans Ammonites and Moabites from the assembly of Israel. These people had now ceased to exist as distinct groups, but their spirits lived on in the various groups who opposed Nehemiah.

13:2 Two reasons are given for the exclusion of the Ammonites and Moabites from the assembly of God: (1) they had "not met the Israelites with food and water" (See Num 21, which calls the Ammonites "Amorites." "Amorites" could refer to the inhabitants of the land as a whole.); (2) the Moabites had "hired Balaam" (Num 22–24).

13:3 excluded. The extent is unclear; perhaps they were excluded from the temple rather than completely banned. Foreigners (notably Ruth) were always welcome if they were prepared to become part of the believing community.

13:4–9 An old enemy reemerges. Tobiah, taking advantage of Nehemiah's absence, arranges a temple apartment for his own use.

13:4 Before this. Tobiah was installed in the temple prior to the assembly of v. 1, during Nehemiah's absence (v. 6 explains this). **Eliashib.** Possibly the high priest (3:1; 12:10,22–23) and thus a serious opponent. Some disagree because Eliashib is "in charge of the storerooms"; but such a man would have many responsibilities, and this mentions only the relevant one. However, the name was common in the postexilic era, and in other places (v. 28; 3:1,20) he is called "high priest" and not simply "priest."

13:5 It is ironic that a room used for storing items for sacrifice and other temple worship now stores the personal possessions of God's enemy, thus giving Tobiah a place at the very heart of the holy city.

13:6 I was not in Jerusalem. The key to this situation is Nehemiah's absence. After 12 years as governor (445–433 BC), he had returned to King Artaxerxes to ask permission to return for a further period. The round trip would have taken some two months, and Nehemiah would probably have stayed at the court for an appropriate time; so it seems reasonable that he was absent from Jerusalem for at least six months. **king of Babylon.** Some question this title, but see Ezra 5:13; 6:22, where Persian kings are called "king of Babylon" and "king of Assyria," respectively. In some sense the successive empires took on the identity of their predecessors.

13:7–8 Giving Tobiah a room (probably in the temple itself, opening out on to the courts) was not merely a compromise but an affront to the temple's sanctity.

13:9 rooms. The plural seems odd because Tobiah occupied only one room, but Nehemiah probably regarded the rooms in the vicinity as polluted also.

13:10–14 Nehemiah deals with a second scandal: the people shamefully withheld the provision for the Levites. It was the Levites' only

the Levites and musicians responsible for the service had gone back to their own fields. 11So I rebuked the officials and asked them, "Why is the house of God neglected?"[a] Then I called them together and stationed them at their posts.

12All Judah brought the tithes[b] of grain, new wine and olive oil into the storerooms.[c] 13I put Shelemiah the priest, Zadok the scribe, and a Levite named Pedaiah in charge of the storerooms and made Hanan son of Zakkur, the son of Mattaniah, their assistant, because they were considered trustworthy. They were made responsible for distributing the supplies to their fellow Levites.[d]

14Remember[e] me for this, my God, and do not blot out what I have so faithfully done for the house of my God and its services.

15In those days I saw people in Judah treading winepresses on the Sabbath and bringing in grain and loading it on donkeys, together with wine, grapes, figs and all other kinds of loads. And they were bringing all this into Jerusalem on the Sabbath.[f] Therefore I warned them against selling food on that day. 16People from Tyre who lived in Jerusalem were bringing in fish and all kinds of merchandise and selling them in Jerusalem on the Sabbath[g] to the people of Judah. 17I rebuked the nobles of Judah and said to them, "What is this wicked thing you are doing—desecrating the Sabbath day? 18Didn't your ancestors do the same things, so that our God brought all this calamity on us and on this city? Now you are stirring up more wrath against Israel by desecrating the Sabbath."[h]

19When evening shadows fell on the gates of Jerusalem before the Sabbath,[i] I ordered the doors to be shut and not opened until the Sabbath was over. I stationed some of my own men at the gates so that no load could be brought in on the Sabbath day. 20Once or twice the merchants and sellers of all kinds of goods spent the night outside Jerusalem. 21But I warned them and said, "Why do you spend the night by the wall? If you do this again, I will arrest you." From that time on they no longer came on the Sabbath. 22Then I commanded the Levites to purify themselves and go and guard the gates in order to keep the Sabbath day holy.

Remember[j] me for this also, my God, and show mercy to me according to your great love.

23Moreover, in those days I saw men of Judah who had married[k] women from Ashdod, Ammon and Moab.[l] 24Half of their children spoke the language of Ashdod or the language of one of the other

13:11 [a]Ne 10:37-39; Hag 1:1-9
13:12 [b]2Ch 31:6 [c]1Ki 7:51; Ne 10:37-39; Mal 3:10
13:13 [d]Ne 12:44; Ac 6:1-5
13:14 [e]Ge 8:1
13:15 [f]Ex 20:8-11; 34:21; Dt 5:12-15; Ne 10:31
13:16 [g]Ne 10:31
13:18 [h]Ne 10:31; Jer 17:21-23
13:19 [i]Lev 23:32
13:22 [j]Ge 8:1; Ne 12:30
13:23 [k]Ezr 9:1-2; Mal 2:11 [l]ver 1; Ne 10:30

source of income as they depended on the faithful support of the people, so they deserted their posts to go back to their fields. How quickly the exuberance of the celebrations of ch. 12 vanished.

13:11 the house of God neglected. How quickly the Levites and other temple servants broke their promise (10:39).

13:12 Nehemiah reinstates the tithe.

13:13 Mattaniah. The grandson of the choir leader (11:17,22; 12:8,25). The other four men are otherwise unknown. **trustworthy.** Honest men oversaw the tithe's storage and fair distribution.

13:14 Nehemiah's brief but heartfelt prayer accompanies these actions. **do not blot out what I have so faithfully done.** Not a plea for God to recognize him for his great achievements but an expression of his deepest loyalties.

13:15–31 Nehemiah's concluding reforms include Sabbath observance (vv. 15–22) and mixed marriages (vv. 23–29). The Sabbath issue is related particularly to commercial activity, an issue that had already surfaced (10:31–32). At least 30 years had passed since Ezra dealt with mixed marriages (Ezra 9–10), and a new generation had emerged with a steady erosion of the community's identity, exemplified in the confusion of languages.

13:15 In those days. Again suggests that a general problem had emerged during Nehemiah's absence and had now come to his attention. But this was not simply a postexilic problem. Before the exile the merchant classes had become increasingly impatient with not trading on the Sabbath (Amos 8:5), and Jeremiah similarly condemned such activities (Jer 17:19–27). The time of year is fixed by the date of the grape harvest (Sept./Oct.).

13:16 People from Tyre. The trading activities of the Phoenicians are well-established (e.g., Isa 23:2–3; Ezek 27:12–25). Their role in providing timber for the temple (Ezra 3:7) echoes their role in the time of Solomon (1 Kgs 5:1–12).

13:17 rebuked the nobles. As leaders, they may not themselves have engaged in these activities, but they were responsible for good behavior in the city.

13:18 Again Nehemiah references the old prophets, especially Jer 17:19–27, which says that carrying goods into the city is the kind of behavior that would lead to exile.

13:20–21 When traders set up shop outside the walls, Nehemiah threatens to remove them forcibly.

13:21 warned. Nehemiah's recent actions in regard to Tobiah (vv. 4–8) showed that this was no idle threat.

13:22 purify themselves. Guarding of the city was a holy task that required purification, so Levites were especially appropriate. While this was an extension of the Levites' duties, it was certainly in keeping with their overall purpose of maintaining the holiness of the temple. **Remember me.** This prayer shows that Nehemiah remained acutely conscious of his own sinfulness. He was not a legalist imposing on others what he was unprepared to do himself.

13:23 Ashdod. An old Philistine city in the southwest coastal region. **Ammon and Moab.** To the east.

13:24 language of Judah. Hebrew. It was bound up with the faith and national culture, so the inability to speak it showed a weakening commitment to the faith of their ancestors. Ezra's measures (Ezra 9–10) apparently had little lasting effect. A major problem of mixed marriages is illustrated here: in losing the "language of Judah," the children of these unions were in effect losing their spiritual heritage.

13:25 [m]Ezr 10:5
13:26 [n]1Ki 3:13; 2Ch 1:12 [o]2Sa 12:25 [p]1Ki 11:3
13:27 [q]Ezr 9:14; 10:2
13:28 [r]Ezr 10:24 [s]Ne 2:10
13:29 [t]Ne 6:14
13:30 [u]Ne 10:30
13:31 [v]Ne 10:34 [w]ver 14,22; Ge 8:1

peoples, and did not know how to speak the language of Judah. 25 I rebuked them and called curses
down on them. I beat some of the men and pulled out their hair. I made them take an oath[m] in God's
name and said: "You are not to give your daughters in marriage to their sons, nor are you to take their
daughters in marriage for your sons or for yourselves. 26 Was it not because of marriages like these that
Solomon king of Israel sinned? Among the many nations there was no king like him.[n] He was loved
by his God,[o] and God made him king over all Israel, but even he was led into sin by foreign women.[p]
27 Must we hear now that you too are doing all this terrible wickedness and are being unfaithful to our
God by marrying[q] foreign women?"

28 One of the sons of Joiada son of Eliashib[r] the high priest was son-in-law to Sanballat[s] the Horonite.
And I drove him away from me.

29 Remember[t] them, my God, because they defiled the priestly office and the covenant of the priesthood and of the Levites.

30 So I purified the priests and the Levites of everything foreign,[u] and assigned them duties, each
to his own task. 31 I also made provision for contributions of wood[v] at designated times, and for the
firstfruits.

Remember[w] me with favor, my God.

13:25 I beat some of the men and pulled out their hair. Nehemiah violently reacts in his call to the people to return to the law. **made them take an oath.** Presumably helped to at least contain the problem.
13:26–27 Nehemiah links the present crisis with the people's history and specifically with the sad case of Solomon, whose pagan wives led him to sin and eventually broke up the kingdom. Solomon comprehensively disregarded covenant loyalty and allowed pagan worship to flourish in Jerusalem (see 1 Kgs 11:1–8). If Solomon, who was "loved by his God" (v. 26), came under judgment, how would the people of Nehemiah's day escape? Again the danger of further exile and punishment looms if the people do not repent.
13:28 This final issue is related to but not identical to the problem of mixed marriages, and Nehemiah sees it as an even more blatant breach of the law. Sanballat, their old enemy, had penetrated deeply into the high priest's circle by having a daughter in that family. **drove him away.** Presumably exiled this unnamed priest.
13:29 them. The whole high priestly family who approved of an alliance with Sanballat's family. **defiled the priestly office and the covenant.** Comprehensive failure: they had not only corrupted their sacred office but had been disloyal to the Lord of the covenant.
13:30–31 The book of Nehemiah ends with some final reforms and a prayer. This provides an epilogue to the whole book and indeed to the whole course of the narrative from the beginning of Ezra. Practicalities of tasks and provisions for sacrifices and festivals are his concern.
13:30 purified. Nehemiah's overriding concern from the beginning was that the people and places be fit for the holy God.
13:31 Remember me. The "remember" formula is unusual here in that it is not followed by an additional comment, which may be an indication that this was designed as the close of Nehemiah's account as a whole (cf. vv. 14,22; 1:8; 6:14). Although Nehemiah does not know the community's future or his own, the future is in higher hands. These reforms were not ends in themselves but an indispensable response to the grace of the covenant Lord, who having begun a good work, will complete it (Phil 1:6).

INTRODUCTION TO ESTHER

The story of Esther and Mordecai is a literary masterpiece with profound theology: God fulfills his redemptive promises not only through great miracles but also through divine providence working through ordinary events. Even the actions of people who do not worship him are woven into patterns and purposes determined by the sovereign Lord alone.

AUTHOR

The book of Esther makes no claim about its author, although it likely originated with a Jewish author who lived outside of the Holy Land and was familiar with Susa and the Persian palace.

DATE

The story is set in Susa (modern Iran) in the court of the Persian king Xerxes I (Ahasuerus), who ruled 486–465 BC and is remembered by ancient historians as a ruthless and powerful king. But the author writes from a perspective looking back on that time. The events occur after the decree of Cyrus (539 BC) allowed the Jews to return to their homeland, but Esther and Mordecai had remained in exile. It may have been written after 424 BC if the description of Xerxes in 1:1 as the one "who ruled over 127 provinces" was intended to distinguish him from Xerxes II, his grandson who ruled only 45 days in that year. Because the author's knowledge of Susa and the palace is consistent with archaeological evidence, and because there are many Persian loanwords in the text but few, if any, Greek words, it was probably written within 100 years of the events it records and probably before Alexander's conquest of Persia in 333 BC. It is written in Hebrew similar to that of 1 and 2 Chronicles, which are also dated to the period of 539–323 BC.

PLACE OF COMPOSITION AND DESTINATION

The story of the Jews during the reign of Xerxes explains the origin of the festival of Purim for Jews living throughout the Persian Empire. Although the first record of the events was likely written in the region of Susa, the final biblical form may have been written in another location and intended for all who celebrated Purim everywhere.

PARTICULAR CHALLENGES

The book of Esther is well known for not mentioning God, miracles, the law, the temple, or the covenant. A further challenge is the moral ambiguity of Esther and Mordecai in comparison to Daniel and his friends, who suffered similar circumstances. The story has also been implicated for inciting violence throughout Jewish history.

Five issues challenge the book's historical reliability:

1. The names of Vashti and Esther do not agree with the Greek historian Herodotus, who says that Xerxes' wife was Amestris. But perhaps only Amestris is mentioned because she was the royal wife who gave birth to Xerxes' successor, Artaxerxes. Or perhaps the name Vashti is meant to be a literary device intended to characterize the queen, for it may have sounded similar to the Old Persian word for "beautiful woman."

2. The statement in 2:6 suggests that Mordecai would have been over 100 years old. The statement, however, may mean either that Mordecai's great-grandfather Kish was the one taken into exile or that when Judah went into exile, all of God's people went into exile, even those who would be born later in Babylon.

3. The enumeration of 127 provinces in 1:1 does not agree with the much smaller number found in other historical sources. But the term translated "province" probably refers to a smaller metropolitan region that encompassed a city (cf. Ezra 2:1; Neh 7:6; Dan 2:49) and suggests that the Jews would have nowhere to hide from the decree of death against them.

4. Persian kings could add to their harem indiscriminately, but they usually married women from only seven noble families, making Xerxes' marriage to Esther very unlikely. But the ancient writer Plutarch mentions that other Persian kings did sometimes marry outside of the traditional families.

5. The practice of irrevocable decrees is unknown in any other sources from this period.

Rather than deciding whether the book of Esther is history or literature, the real question is how to understand it as both. It would be a shame to be so distracted by apparent historical "problems" that we miss what God is saying in this wonderful story.

OCCASION AND PURPOSE

The book was written to document the time when the Jews got relief from their enemies and when their sorrow was turned to joy, the occasion commemorated by the festival of Purim. It not only explains the origin of Purim but also shows how even in exile God's providential sovereignty over history fulfilled the ancient promise given at the time of the exodus to protect his covenant people (Exod 17:16).

GENRE AND STRUCTURE

The story of Esther is told with irony, satire, and humor, and because of its place in the biblical canon, it is therefore theology told with irony, satire, and humor. Like a parable, it makes its point as a whole unit. The story follows the contours of all good narrative, with the plotline rising as narrative tension is created, peaking, and then coming to closure at the end of the story. But another literary device is also in play in the story—an ancient device that

PERSIAN EMPIRE

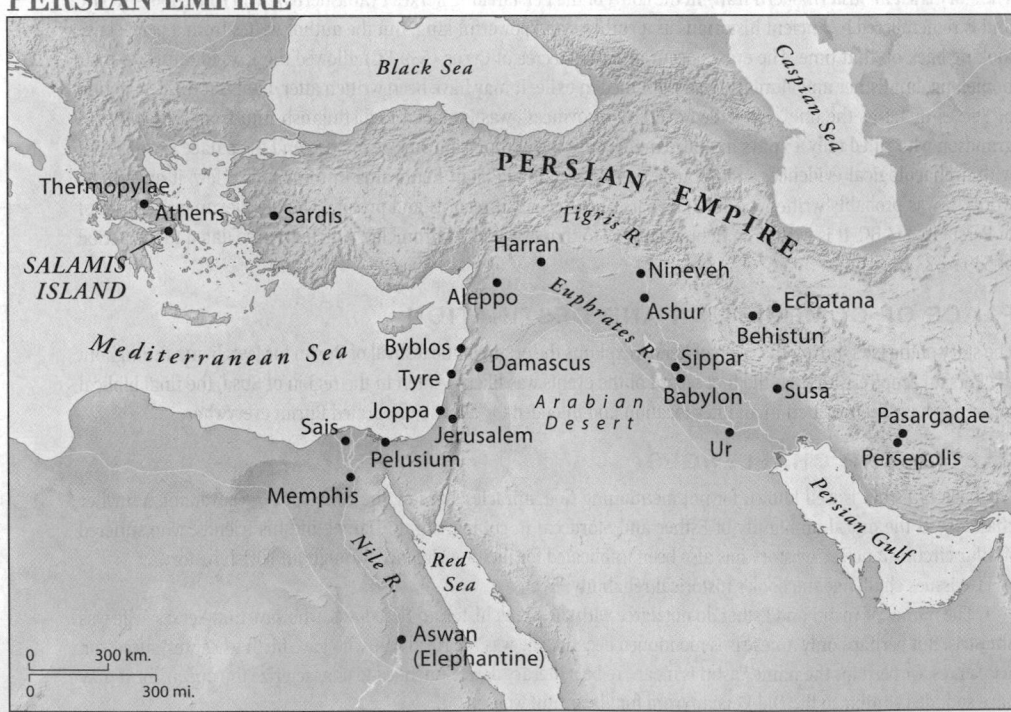

Aristotle referred to as peripety: a sudden turn of events that reverses the expected outcome of a story. The story of Esther is not simply resolved; it is resolved with a series of reversals.

This literary structure is organized around three pairs of banquets that mark the beginning, climax, and conclusion of the story (the first pair in 1:2 – 8; the second pair in 5:1 – 8 and 7:1 – 10; the third pair in 9:17 – 19), and which reinforce the theological message of the story. This motif of banqueting is especially appropriate in a story that explains the origin of the festival of Purim. The recurring banquet motif focuses the literary structure on the surprising and seemingly insignificant event of 6:1, from which the reversal of fortune proceeds.

Renaissance fresco of Queen Esther.
WikiArt

The point at which the reversals begin is between Esther's first banquet for the king and Haman and the second, when the king has a sleepless night. The narrative tension of the conflict between the Jews and Persia and their enemy, Haman, could have been resolved simply by the failure of Haman's plan and preservation of the status quo. Instead, there is a series of reversals that concludes with a great reversal of fortune for God's people (cf. 3:10 and 8:2; 3:12 and 8:9; 3:12 and 8:10; 3:13 and 8:11; 3:14 and 8:13; 3:15 and 8:14; 3:15 and 8:15; 4:1 and 8:15; 4:1 and 6:11; 5:14 and 6:13). The use of peripety in Esther is an example of how form and content mutually interact not only to produce an aesthetically pleasing story but to provide the framework in which the theological implications of the story can be understood. This literary structure of reversals found in the book of Esther and its pivot point in an ordinary and insignificant event mirrors on a small scale the structure of all redemptive history. We should expect nothing but death, but we have seen the ultimate peripety, the ultimate reversal of expected ends, in the death, resurrection, and ascension of Jesus Christ.

THEMES AND THEOLOGY

It may seem inappropriate to refer to the theology of a book that doesn't mention God at all, but the explicit absence of God is part of the genius of the book, making a major theological point that God's redemptive promises are fulfilled through his providence. The great paradox presented by the story is that God is all-powerfully present even where he is most conspicuously absent. The story explores the intriguing interplay between God's providence and human decisions and actions (1:10 – 12; 2:17,21 – 23; 4:14; 6:1 – 3). Esther and Mordecai may have been upright people who lived faithfully in exile, but the author presents their actions as morally ambiguous, and they are never evaluated by the narrator. For instance, Esther does not protest life in the king's harem, as Daniel protested life in the Babylonian court. Mordecai may have had righteous motives for refusing to bow to his superior Haman, but the narrator doesn't mention that. Despite the narrative ambiguity of their behavior, which is part of the genius of the story, God nevertheless works to fulfill his redemptive promises.

At the time Esther was written, the problem of the destruction of Jerusalem and the exile of God's people was a theological issue complicated by the problem of the return of some to rebuild Jerusalem. God's people were asking, "Are we still in covenant with the Lord? What about Jews who chose to remain outside the promised land?" The book of Esther affirms that God is still faithful to the covenant promises he made at Sinai and that those living beyond the borders of the promised land are not beyond the reach of his redemptive protection. This stage in progressive revelation anticipates the Great Commission (Matt 28:18 – 20), when the whole world would be within the gospel's embrace. The story presents a great deliverance from the threat of destruction in yet another episode of the ancient war between Israel and its many enemies, such as the Amalekites, the first nation that tried to destroy Israel in its infancy (Exod 17:8 – 16; Deut 25:17 – 19). The story also invites reflection on life issues such as the self-deceptive and destructive nature of pride (e.g., 6:4 – 14), the significance of identifying with God's people at life's defining moments (4:12 – 16), and male and female partnership in God's plan (9:29 – 32).

Being in the Christian canon of Scripture, the book of Esther is an example of the reversal of human destiny that ultimately, in the sweep of redemptive history, was accomplished by Jesus Christ. Because of our sin, we should expect nothing but death. But in the ultimate reversal of eternal destiny, because of the cross of Jesus, we have been given life.

CANONICITY

The theological message of Esther can be understood only within the larger context of the biblical canon. The canonization of Esther is closely tied to the canonization of the Writings, the third section of the Hebrew Bible in which it is found, which may have occurred as early as the second century BC. Because God and significant elements of Judaism are not mentioned in the book, its value as a canonical book has been questioned in both Jewish and Christian tradition. Despite that questioning, rabbis of the first century said that the book "made the hands unclean," a reference to its nature as authoritative Scripture. In the early centuries of the Christian church, Esther was accepted almost everywhere in the Western canon, and it attained universal canonical status by the end of the fourth century. Martin Luther famously denounced the book, wishing it were not in the Bible, but its status as a canonical text within both Judaism and Christianity remains secure.

OUTLINE

I. The Jews of Persia Are Threatened (1:1—5:14)
- A. Queen Vashti Deposed (1:1–22)
  1. Xerxes Is a Powerful and Dangerous King (1:1–8)
  2. Queen Vashti Defies Xerxes (1:9–12)
  3. The King and Nobles React to Vashti's Disobedience (1:13–22)
- B. Esther, Mordecai, and Haman (2:1—3:15)
  1. Esther Made Queen (2:1–18)
  2. Mordecai Uncovers a Conspiracy (2:19–23)
  3. Haman's Plot to Destroy the Jews (3:1–15)
- C. Mordecai Persuades Esther to Help (4:1–17)
  1. Mordecai Mourns Over Haman's Decree (4:1–5)
  2. Mordecai Begs Esther to Intercede (4:6–14)
  3. Esther Calls a Three-Day Fast (4:15–17)
- D. Esther's Request to the King (5:1–14)
  1. Esther Appears Uninvited Before the King (5:1–5a)
  2. Esther Prepares a Banquet for the King and Haman (5:5b–8)
  3. Haman's Rage Against Mordecai (5:9–14)

II. The Reversal of Outcome (6:1—9:19)
- A. Mordecai Honored (6:1–14)
  1. The King Has a Sleepless Night (6:1–3)
  2. Haman Seeks the King's Permission to Kill Mordecai Immediately (6:4–9)
  3. Mordecai Is Honored Instead (6:10–14)
- B. Haman Impaled (7:1–10)
  1. Esther Prepares a Second Banquet for the King and Haman (7:1–2)
  2. Esther Reveals Her Jewish Identity and Accuses Haman (7:3–7)
  3. The King Orders Haman Executed (7:8–10)
- C. The King's Edict in Behalf of the Jews (8:1–14)
  1. Esther Introduces Mordecai to the King (8:1)
  2. Mordecai Receives the Signet Ring Previously Worn by Haman (8:2)
  3. Esther Gives Haman's Property to Mordecai (8:3–8)
  4. Mordecai Writes the Counteredict (8:9–14)
- D. The Triumph of the Jews (8:15—9:19)
  1. A Day of Joy (8:15–17)
  2. The Jews Kill Many, Including Haman's Ten Sons (9:1–10)
  3. Esther Asks for Their Bodies to Be Displayed and for a Second Day of Killing in Susa (9:11–19)

III. Purim Established (9:20–32)
- A. Mordecai Writes to the Jews of Persia (9:20–28)
- B. Esther Writes to Confirm Mordecai's Letter (9:29–32)

IV. The Greatness of Mordecai (10:1–3)

ESTHER

Queen Vashti Deposed

1 This is what happened during the time of Xerxes,[a][a] the Xerxes who ruled over 127 provinces[b]
stretching from India to Cush[b]:[c] 2At that time King Xerxes reigned from his royal throne in
the citadel of Susa,[d] 3and in the third year of his reign he gave a banquet[e] for all his nobles and
officials. The military leaders of Persia and Media, the princes, and the nobles of the provinces
were present.

4For a full 180 days he displayed the vast wealth of his kingdom and the splendor and glory of his
majesty. 5When these days were over, the king gave a banquet, lasting seven days,[f] in the enclosed
garden[g] of the king's palace, for all the people from the least to the greatest who were in the citadel of
Susa. 6The garden had hangings of white and blue linen, fastened with cords of white linen and purple
material to silver rings on marble pillars. There were couches[h] of gold and silver on a mosaic pavement
of porphyry, marble, mother-of-pearl and other costly stones. 7Wine was served in goblets of gold, each
one different from the other, and the royal wine was abundant, in keeping with the king's liberality.[i]
8By the king's command each guest was allowed to drink with no restrictions, for the king instructed
all the wine stewards to serve each man what he wished.

9Queen Vashti also gave a banquet[j] for the women in the royal palace of King Xerxes.

10On the seventh day, when King Xerxes was in high spirits[k] from wine,[l] he commanded the

1:1 [a] Ezr 4:6; Da 9:1 [b] Est 9:30; Da 3:2; 6:1 [c] Est 8:9
1:2 [d] Ezr 4:9; Ne 1:1; Est 2:8
1:3 [e] 1Ki 3:15; Est 2:18
1:5 [f] Jdg 14:17 [g] 2Ki 21:18; Est 7:7-8
1:6 [h] Est 7:8; Eze 23:41; Am 3:12; 6:4
1:7 [i] Est 2:18; Da 5:2
1:9 [j] 1Ki 3:15
1:10 [k] Jdg 16:25; Ru 3:7 [l] Ge 14:18; Est 3:15; 5:6; 7:2; Pr 31:4-7; Da 5:1-4

[a] *1* Hebrew *Ahasuerus*; here and throughout Esther [b] *1* That is, the upper Nile region

1:1—5:14 *The Jews of Persia Are Threatened.* The book of Esther presents an episode in the history of God's ancient covenant people that threatened their annihilation by the pagan powers of ancient Persia. The first five chapters provide the background of life in Persia and how this great threat arose.

1:1–22 *Queen Vashti Deposed.* This opening incident in the book of Esther shows how treacherous life could be in the court of the Persian king, who had great wealth and power at his disposal that could be manipulated by his closest advisors. Vashti's removal as queen is the initial example of this, and it ominously sets the stage for Esther's eventual coronation into the dangerous court of the king.

1:1–8 *Xerxes Is a Powerful and Dangerous King.* The book begins with the introductory formula found in other historical books, such as Joshua, Judges, and Samuel. This suggests the author intends for readers to understand the story as events that actually happened. These opening verses locate the story during the time of Xerxes (see note on v. 1). The events of the Esther story span a period of about ten years. The wealth and opulence of his court on display would have seemed ironic to the original readers, who may have known that Xerxes had returned from a military campaign against Greece a defeated king who had depleted the royal treasury (see notes on v. 3; 2:16).

1:1 Xerxes. The king of Persia who reigned from 486 until 465 BC (cf. Ezra 4:6). Xerxes ascended the throne in 486 BC at age 32.

1:2 Susa. One of the four capital cities from which the Persian monarchs ruled during the winter. See Dan 8:2; Neh 1:1.

1:3 Xerxes holds a banquet for all his nobles, officials, and military leaders "in the third year of his reign." This corresponds well to the great war council of 483 BC, held to plan and rally support for the invasion of Greece by bridging the narrows between modern Turkey and Greece.

1:9–12 *Queen Vashti Defies Xerxes.* The events described in this section will have long-reaching consequences. Even the mighty acts of God in redemptive history are linked through long years of human history by a chain of seemingly insignificant, ordinary events. Xerxes' decision unwittingly sets in motion a series of events that will culminate in the deliverance of God's people, fulfilling the promise of the ancient covenant made ages before in a faraway place.

1:10–11 Xerxes sends seven eunuchs to fetch Vashti; seven is perhaps the number needed to carry her seated in the royal litter. Perhaps the sight of the queen attired in her royal glory was intended to inspire patriotism and loyalty to the king's cause, much as public appearances of the British queen do today.

1:10 in high spirits from wine. Unlike our modern culture, Persians deliberated matters of state under the influence of alcohol because they believed inebriation put them in closer touch with the gods, whose support they would need to go to war (cf. 3:15). It is while he is inebriated that Xerxes sends for Vashti.

1:10 [m]Est 7:9
1:11 [n]SS 2:4 [o]Ps 45:11; Eze 16:14
1:12 [p]Ge 39:19; Est 2:21; 7:7; Pr 19:12
1:13 [q]1Ch 12:32; Jer 10:7; Da 2:12
1:14 [r]2Ki 25:19; Ezr 7:14
1:18 [s]Pr 19:13; 27:15
1:19 [t]Ecc 8:4 [u]Est 8:8; Da 6:8,12
1:22 [v]Ne 13:24; Est 8:9; Eph 5:22-24; 1Ti 2:12

seven eunuchs who served him — Mehuman, Biztha, Harbona,[m] Bigtha, Abagtha, Zethar and Karkas — 11 to bring[n] before him Queen Vashti, wearing her royal crown, in order to display her beauty[o] to the people and nobles, for she was lovely to look at. 12 But when the attendants delivered the king's command, Queen Vashti refused to come. Then the king became furious and burned with anger.[p]

13 Since it was customary for the king to consult experts in matters of law and justice, he spoke with the wise men who understood the times[q] 14 and were closest to the king — Karshena, Shethar, Admatha, Tarshish, Meres, Marsena and Memukan, the seven nobles[r] of Persia and Media who had special access to the king and were highest in the kingdom.

THE ACHAEMENID DYNASTY

Cyrus (the Great)	559–530 BC
Cambyses	530–522 BC
PseudoSmerdis (illegitimate)	523–522 BC
Darius I (the Great)	522–486 BC
Xerxes I	486–465 BC
Artaxerxes I	465–424 BC
Xerxes II	425–424 BC
Darius II	423–404 BC
Artaxerxes II	404–358 BC
Artaxerxes III	358–338 BC
Arses	338–336 BC
Darius III	336–333 BC

15 "According to law, what must be done to Queen Vashti?" he asked. "She has not obeyed the command of King Xerxes that the eunuchs have taken to her."

16 Then Memukan replied in the presence of the king and the nobles, "Queen Vashti has done wrong, not only against the king but also against all the nobles and the peoples of all the provinces of King Xerxes. 17 For the queen's conduct will become known to all the women, and so they will despise their husbands and say, 'King Xerxes commanded Queen Vashti to be brought before him, but she would not come.' 18 This very day the Persian and Median women of the nobility who have heard about the queen's conduct will respond to all the king's nobles in the same way. There will be no end of disrespect and discord.[s]

19 "Therefore, if it pleases the king,[t] let him issue a royal decree and let it be written in the laws of Persia and Media, which cannot be repealed,[u] that Vashti is never again to enter the presence of King Xerxes. Also let the king give her royal position to someone else who is better than she. 20 Then when the king's edict is proclaimed throughout all his vast realm, all the women will respect their husbands, from the least to the greatest."

21 The king and his nobles were pleased with this advice, so the king did as Memukan proposed. 22 He sent dispatches to all parts of the kingdom, to each province in its own script and to each people in their own language,[v] proclaiming that every man should be ruler over his own household, using his native tongue.

1:12 Queen Vashti refused to come. This ignites the king's anger. Vashti's refusal to obey her husband's command must be extremely embarrassing when Xerxes is trying to solidify support for his command to go to war. But if Vashti and Amestris are the same woman (see Introduction: Particular Challenges, 1), she would have been in the late stage of her pregnancy with Xerxes' son. Regardless of her motives, this incident with Vashti provides a context in which to understand her successor, Queen Esther. Both women are locked in a relationship with Xerxes that is politically charged. He uses his tremendous power ostentatiously to reinforce his own glory with little or no thought for the consequences to others.

1:13–22 *The King and Nobles React to Vashti's Disobedience.* These verses show the inner workings of the Persian court and the escalation of Vashti's refusal into an empire-wide public event.

1:15 what must be done to Queen Vashti? This is decided not between a man and his wife but on the basis of a perceived insult that is more universal and includes all the nobles and the peoples of Persia. This highlights the political ramifications of Vashti's defiance, which is the defiance of a queen, not simply a wife.

1:17 the queen's conduct will become known to all the women. Memukan fears that all the women will then disrespect and despise their own husbands. By universalizing the incident, Memukan can express his personal anxiety and fears in terms of the good of the empire and thereby manipulate this powerful king to his own ends. Haman later uses the same tactic against the Jews in 3:8. Vashti's decision not to come before the king, a decision made in one moment, is to be made permanent by banishing her from the king's presence. This incident of gender politics is highlighted because in this story powerful Persian *men* are later outwitted by a Jewish *woman* to achieve God's redemptive purposes.

1:22 own script ... own language. The emphasis on the many languages of Persian society is a repeated element throughout the story. The choice of language in the home was important for maintaining the culture and religion. In Jewish homes scattered throughout the empire, the children of Jewish men were speaking the language of their pagan mothers, a situation that had to be corrected to preserve national and covenantal identity (cf. Neh 13:23–24). The use of the man's language

Esther Made Queen

2 Later when King Xerxes' fury had subsided,[w] he remembered Vashti and what she had done and what he had decreed about her. 2 Then the king's personal attendants proposed, "Let a search be made for beautiful young virgins for the king. 3 Let the king appoint commissioners in every province of his realm to bring all these beautiful young women into the harem at the citadel of Susa. Let them be placed under the care of Hegai, the king's eunuch, who is in charge of the women; and let beauty treatments be given to them. 4 Then let the young woman who pleases the king be queen instead of Vashti." This advice appealed to the king, and he followed it.

5 Now there was in the citadel of Susa a Jew of the tribe of Benjamin, named Mordecai son of Jair, the son of Shimei, the son of Kish,[x] 6 who had been carried into exile from Jerusalem by Nebuchadnezzar king of Babylon, among those taken captive with Jehoiachin[a][y] king of Judah.[z] 7 Mordecai had a cousin named Hadassah, whom he had brought up because she had neither father nor mother. This young woman, who was also known as Esther,[a] had a lovely figure[b] and was beautiful. Mordecai had taken her as his own daughter when her father and mother died.

8 When the king's order and edict had been proclaimed, many young women were brought to the citadel of Susa[c] and put under the care of Hegai. Esther also was taken to the king's palace and entrusted to Hegai, who had charge of the harem. 9 She pleased him and won his favor.[d] Immediately he provided her with her beauty treatments and special food.[e] He assigned to her seven female attendants selected from the king's palace and moved her and her attendants into the best place in the harem.

10 Esther had not revealed her nationality and family background, because Mordecai had forbidden her to do so.[f] 11 Every day he walked back and forth near the courtyard of the harem to find out how Esther was and what was happening to her.

12 Before a young woman's turn came to go in to King Xerxes, she had to complete twelve months of beauty treatments prescribed for the women, six months with oil of myrrh and six with perfumes[g] and cosmetics. 13 And this is how she would go to the king: Anything she wanted was given her to take with her from the harem to the king's palace. 14 In the evening she would go there and in the morning return to another part of the harem to the care of Shaashgaz, the king's eunuch who was in charge of the concubines.[h] She would not return to the king unless he was pleased with her and summoned her by name.[i]

15 When the turn came for Esther (the young woman Mordecai had adopted, the daughter of his uncle Abihail[j]) to go to the king,[k] she asked for nothing other than what Hegai, the king's eunuch who was in charge of the harem, suggested. And Esther won the favor[l] of everyone who saw her. 16 She was taken to King Xerxes in the royal residence in the tenth month, the month of Tebeth, in the seventh year of his reign.

[a] 6 Hebrew *Jeconiah*, a variant of *Jehoiachin*

2:1 [w] Est 1:19-20; 7:10
2:5 [x] 1Sa 9:1; Est 3:2
2:6 [y] 2Ki 24:6,15; 2Ch 36:10,20 [z] Da 1:1-5; 5:13
2:7 [a] Ge 41:45 [b] Ge 39:6
2:8 [c] ver 3,15; Ne 1:1; Est 1:2; Da 8:2
2:9 [d] Ge 39:21 [e] ver 3,12; Ge 37:3; 1Sa 9:22-24; 2Ki 25:30; Eze 16:9-13; Da 1:5
2:10 [f] ver 20
2:12 [g] Pr 27:9; SS 1:3; Isa 3:24
2:14 [h] 1Ki 11:3; SS 6:8; Da 5:2 [i] Est 4:11
2:15 [j] Est 9:29 [k] Ps 45:14 [l] Ge 18:3; 30:27; Est 5:8

in his home implied for the Jews that the wife and children were to join the covenant community of Yahweh. By issuing a decree that all parts of the kingdom in every script and language of the empire, the king ironically assures the strengthening of the Jewish community rather than the pagan conformity the advisors desired.

2:1—3:15 *Esther, Mordecai, and Haman.* The initial incident of Vashti's refusal to come when summoned by Xerxes has set the stage for the next development in the story. The complex relationships between the three main characters—Esther, Mordecai, and Haman—unfold when Esther is taken to the harem during the search for a new queen of Persia.

2:1–18 *Esther Made Queen.* The coronation of a young Jewish girl as queen of Persia begins to show God's sovereign power to oversee the protection of his people. God does this not through miracles, but through the exercise of his providence through the decisions of pagan people.

2:1–4 The gathering of virgins is an unusual way to select a new queen, though a later Persian king is said to have replenished his large harem by the same method. The author is ironically showing that the king whose word was irrevocable law actually was largely swayed by the advice of his advisors in even the most personal area of his life.

2:5–6 Mordecai ... who had been carried into exile from Jerusalem by Nebuchadnezzar. See Introduction: Particular Challenges, 2. A tablet discovered in 1904 in Persepolis, another Persian royal city, contains the name *Marduka*, who was an official during the early years of Xerxes' reign, corresponding in time to the Esther story. There is no way to know if that Marduka is the same man as Mordecai.

2:7 Mordecai raised Esther because she was an orphan. Esther is the only person in the story with two names, perhaps indicating her plight of living in two worlds—the Jewish world in which she was raised and the pagan world of the opulent and treacherous Persian court into which she was forced.

2:10 had not revealed her nationality. Cf. 2:20. Esther's reaction contrasts with that of Daniel and his friends in Babylon, who had also been carried into exile but who didn't hesitate to make their identities known and continued to hold to their religious convictions.

2:12 twelve months of beauty treatments. Archaeologists have found ancient cosmetic burners used to perfume women's skin and clothing with the scent of roses, cloves, or musk.

2:16 the seventh year of his reign. This is 479 BC, four years after the great banquet of ch. 1. During those intervening years, Xerxes was off fighting a disastrous war with Greece. His humiliating defeat depleted the treasuries of the Persian Empire, perhaps making Haman's offer in 3:9 more tempting.

2:17 [m] Est 1:11; Eze 16:9-13
2:18 [n] 1Ki 3:15; Est 1:3 [o] Ge 40:20 [p] Est 1:7
2:19 [q] ver 21; Est 3:2; 4:2; 5:13
2:20 [r] ver 10
2:21 [s] Ge 40:2; Est 6:2 [t] Est 1:12; 3:5; 5:9; 7:7
2:23 [u] Ge 40:19; Ps 7:14-16; Pr 26:27 [v] Est 6:1; 10:2
3:1 [w] ver 10; Ex 17:8-16; Nu 24:7; Dt 25:17-19; 1Sa 14:48; Est 5:11
3:3 [x] Est 5:9; Da 3:12
3:4 [y] Ge 39:10
3:5 [z] Est 2:21; 5:9
3:6 [a] Pr 16:25 [b] Ps 74:8; 83:4 [c] Est 9:24
3:7 [d] Est 9:24,26 [e] Lev 16:8; 1Sa 10:21 [f] ver 13; Ezr 6:15; Est 9:19

17 Now the king was attracted to Esther more than to any of the other women, and she won his favor
and approval more than any of the other virgins. So he set a royal crown on her head and made her
queen[m] instead of Vashti. 18 And the king gave a great banquet,[n] Esther's banquet, for all his nobles and
officials.[o] He proclaimed a holiday throughout the provinces and distributed gifts with royal liberality.[p]

Mordecai Uncovers a Conspiracy

19 When the virgins were assembled a second time, Mordecai was sitting at the king's gate.[q] 20 But
Esther had kept secret her family background and nationality just as Mordecai had told her to do, for
she continued to follow Mordecai's instructions as she had done when he was bringing her up.[r]
21 During the time Mordecai was sitting at the king's gate, Bigthana[a] and Teresh, two of the king's
officers[s] who guarded the doorway, became angry[t] and conspired to assassinate King Xerxes. 22 But
Mordecai found out about the plot and told Queen Esther, who in turn reported it to the king, giving
credit to Mordecai. 23 And when the report was investigated and found to be true, the two officials were
impaled[u] on poles. All this was recorded in the book of the annals[v] in the presence of the king.

Haman's Plot to Destroy the Jews

3 After these events, King Xerxes honored Haman son of Hammedatha, the Agagite,[w] elevating him
and giving him a seat of honor higher than that of all the other nobles. 2 All the royal officials at
the king's gate knelt down and paid honor to Haman, for the king had commanded this concerning
him. But Mordecai would not kneel down or pay him honor.
3 Then the royal officials at the king's gate asked Mordecai, "Why do you disobey the king's command?"[x] 4 Day after day they spoke to him but he refused to comply.[y] Therefore they told Haman about
it to see whether Mordecai's behavior would be tolerated, for he had told them he was a Jew.
5 When Haman saw that Mordecai would not kneel down or pay him honor, he was enraged.[z] 6 Yet
having learned who Mordecai's people were, he scorned the idea of killing only Mordecai. Instead Haman
looked for a way[a] to destroy[b] all Mordecai's people, the Jews,[c] throughout the whole kingdom of Xerxes.
7 In the twelfth year of King Xerxes, in the first month, the month of Nisan, the *pur*[d] (that is, the lot[e])
was cast in the presence of Haman to select a day and month. And the lot fell on[b] the twelfth month,
the month of Adar.[f]
8 Then Haman said to King Xerxes, "There is a certain people dispersed among the peoples in all the

[a] 21 Hebrew *Bigthan,* a variant of *Bigthana* [b] 7 Septuagint; Hebrew does not have *And the lot fell on.*

2:17 more than any of the other virgins. Despite any moral ambiguity involved in her night with the king, an uncircumcised man to whom she was not married, it is the means by which Esther becomes the queen of Persia, the role through which she later saves her whole nation, the nation from which the Messiah later comes. The author doesn't comment on Esther's night with the king and avoids the word "married," though it is implied, perhaps because at about this time intermarriage had become an issue for the exiles returning to Jerusalem (Ezra 9:12; 10:10–17).

2:19–23 *Mordecai Uncovers a Conspiracy.* In another example of God's providence, Mordecai thwarts an assassination plot that puts him in good standing with the king (see 6:1–2).

2:20 kept secret her family background and nationality. See note on v. 10. Even after becoming queen, Esther hides her identity, which puts her in even greater jeopardy when Haman proposes to annihilate the Jews without knowing he is targeting the queen herself.

3:1–15 *Haman's Plot to Destroy the Jews.* The crisis coming upon the Jewish people is defined in this chapter. Because Persia ruled such a vast area, including Judah and Jerusalem, this plot threatened to annihilate all of God's covenant people.

3:1 After Mordecai thwarts a plot against Xerxes' life, the ancient reader would expect the king to honor him. Instead, the king "honored Haman ... the Agagite." **Agagite.** Although the term means little to the modern reader, it would have identified Haman as a perennial enemy of God's people (v. 10). Agag was the king of the Amalekites at the time Saul was king of Israel (1 Sam 15). Because the Amalekites had been the first nation to try to destroy God's people as they journeyed to the promised land, God promised Moses that he would be at war with them from generation to generation (Exod 17:8–16). Once the people settled in the land, God commanded Saul to wipe out the Amalekites (Deut 25:17–19; 1 Sam 15:1–3), but Saul failed to kill Agag. The descendants of Agag were a threat to the existence of God's people ever after. By calling Haman an Agagite, the author is characterizing him as an enemy of the Jews, and his conflict with Mordecai as yet another episode in the age-old conflict between God's nation and the powers that sought to destroy it.

3:2 Mordecai would not kneel down or pay [Haman] honor. The author doesn't explain this. Whether it was personal resentment, political enmity, or religious conviction, Mordecai's personal decision set into motion life-threatening consequences for his people.

3:7 the *pur* (that is, the lot) was cast. *Pûr* (plural *pûrîm*) is the Hebrew form of an Akkadian word used to refer to cube-shaped objects similar to modern dice that were commonly used in the ancient world to inquire of deity (cf. Josh 18:6). The Jewish festival of Purim takes its name from this word in the story of Esther and celebrates that only God's sovereignty, not the roll of the dice, determines the destiny of his people. The lot was cast in the first (Jewish) month of Nisan and falls on the twelfth month of Adar, eleven months later, as the auspicious time for the plot to be carried out.

provinces of your kingdom who keep themselves separate. Their customs[g] are different from those of all
other people, and they do not obey[h] the king's laws; it is not in the king's best interest to tolerate them.[i]
9If it pleases the king, let a decree be issued to destroy them, and I will give ten thousand talents[a] of
silver to the king's administrators for the royal treasury."[j]
10So the king took his signet ring[k] from his finger and gave it to Haman son of Hammedatha, the Agagite,
the enemy of the Jews. 11"Keep the money," the king said to Haman, "and do with the people as you please."
12Then on the thirteenth day of the first month the royal secretaries were summoned. They wrote
out in the script of each province and in the language[l] of each people all Haman's orders to the king's
satraps, the governors of the various provinces and the nobles of the various peoples. These were written
in the name of King Xerxes himself and sealed[m] with his own ring. 13Dispatches were sent by couriers
to all the king's provinces with the order to destroy, kill and annihilate all the Jews[n] — young and old,
women and children — on a single day, the thirteenth day of the twelfth month, the month of Adar,[o]
and to plunder[p] their goods. 14A copy of the text of the edict was to be issued as law in every province
and made known to the people of every nationality so they would be ready for that day.[q]
15The couriers went out, spurred on by the king's command, and the edict was issued in the citadel
of Susa.[r] The king and Haman sat down to drink,[s] but the city of Susa was bewildered.[t]

3:8 [g]Ac 16:20-21 [h]Jer 29:7; Da 6:13 [i]Ezr 4:15
3:9 [j]Est 7:4
3:10 [k]Ge 41:42; Est 7:6; 8:2
3:12 [l]Ne 13:24 [m]Ge 38:18; 1Ki 21:8; Est 8:8-10
3:13 [n]1Sa 15:3; Ezr 4:6; Est 8:10-14 [o]ver 7 [p]Est 8:11; 9:10
3:14 [q]Est 8:8; 9:1
3:15 [r]Est 8:14 [s]Est 1:10 [t]Est 8:15
4:1 [u]Nu 14:6 [v]2Sa 13:19; Eze 27:30-31; Jnh 3:5-6 [w]Ex 11:6; Ps 30:11
4:2 [x]Est 2:19

Mordecai Persuades Esther to Help

4 When Mordecai learned of all that had been done, he tore his clothes,[u] put on sackcloth and
ashes,[v] and went out into the city, wailing[w] loudly and bitterly. 2But he went only as far as the
king's gate,[x] because no one clothed in sackcloth was allowed to enter it. 3In every province to which
the edict and order of the king came, there was great mourning among the Jews, with fasting, weeping
and wailing. Many lay in sackcloth and ashes.
4When Esther's eunuchs and female attendants came and told her about Mordecai, she was in great
distress. She sent clothes for him to put on instead of his sackcloth, but he would not accept them.
5Then Esther summoned Hathak, one of the king's eunuchs assigned to attend her, and ordered him to
find out what was troubling Mordecai and why.
6So Hathak went out to Mordecai in the open square of the city in front of the king's gate. 7Mor-
decai told him everything that had happened to him, including the exact amount of money Haman

[a] 9 That is, about 375 tons or about 340 metric tons

3:9 let a decree be issued to destroy them. Haman advises the king to destroy the Jews. Not satisfied with punishing Mordecai alone, Haman initiates an attempt of genocide against God's people. **ten thousand talents of silver.** Represented two-thirds of the annual income of the Persian Empire and would presumably have been confiscated from the victims of the genocide. Although Xerxes refused the money (v. 11), it would have provided enormous financial incentive to those who carried out the decree.

3:12–13 on the thirteenth day of the first month [the decree is written] ... to destroy, kill and annihilate all the Jews ... on a single day, the thirteenth ... of Adar. The genocide is to occur eleven months after the decree is written. Ironically, the decree goes out on the very eve of Passover (cf. Exod 12:18; Lev 23:5; Num 28:16), the feast that commemorates even to this day the deliverance of Israel from Egypt and the founding of God's covenant nation. The threat would have reinforced doubts at the time about the exiles' standing with God. The timing heightens the glory of the subsequent deliverance and links it to God's promises made at the time of the exodus (Exod 17:14–16).

4:1–17 *Mordecai Persuades Esther to Help.* This chapter presents the defining moment in Esther's life that makes her a good example of faithfulness to God that can be imitated by both men and women. Despite the danger to herself and her previous attempts to conceal her identity, Esther decides to identify herself with God's covenant people. This defining moment develops her identity in the story from a young Jewish girl to the powerful queen of Persia. Only after she identifies herself with God's people does she fully embrace the purpose for which God has positioned her. From this point onward, she no longer takes orders from Mordecai, but he follows her instructions (v. 17).

4:1–5 *Mordecai Mourns Over Haman's Decree.* Mordecai realizes the extent of the threat and publicly mourns in the customs of the day.

4:1 tore his clothes, put on sackcloth and ashes, and went out into the city, wailing. A sign of grief and sorrow. This gesture of tearing one's clothes is common in the stories of the OT (cf. Num 14:6; 2 Sam 1:11; 3:31; 13:31; Ezra 9:3; Isa 36:22). The Persians would have recognized the significance of Mordecai's act, for according to the historian Herodotus, they also tore their clothes in grief when defeated by the Greeks in battle at Salamis. Wearing sackcloth and ashes further indicated grief and repentance.

4:3 with fasting, weeping and wailing. Echoes traditional prophetic language (e.g., Joel 2:12–14). Even though repentance is not mentioned in Esther, those who originally heard or read the story would likely have recognized the phrase as a call to turn to God in the face of the impending calamity.

4:6–14 *Mordecai Begs Esther to Intercede.* Because Esther is isolated from the city, she is unaware of what is transpiring (v. 5) and must rely on her attendants. Mordecai's plea for Esther's intervention with the king has dark overtones. If she stays silent, he says, she and her family will still perish. Is he subtly threatening to reveal her identity if she herself does not? He reminds her of the unusual circumstances that put her into the position she holds and asks her to consider that it has been for the very reason of intervening to save the Jewish nation at this moment in history.

4:7 [y]Est 3:9; 7:4
4:11 [z]Est 2:14 [a]Da 2:9 [b]Est 5:1,2; 8:4
4:14 [c]Ecc 3:7; Isa 62:1; Am 5:13 [d]Est 9:16,22 [e]Ge 45:7; Dt 28:29 [f]Ge 50:20
4:16 [g]2Ch 20:3; Est 9:31 [h]Ge 43:14

had promised to pay into the royal treasury for the destruction of the Jews.[y] 8He also gave him a copy of the text of the edict for their annihilation, which had been published in Susa, to show to Esther and explain it to her, and he told him to instruct her to go into the king's presence to beg for mercy and plead with him for her people.

9Hathak went back and reported to Esther what Mordecai had said. 10Then she instructed him to say to Mordecai, 11"All the king's officials and the people of the royal provinces know that for any man or woman who approaches the king in the inner court without being summoned[z] the king has but one law:[a] that they be put to death unless the king extends the gold scepter[b] to them and spares their lives. But thirty days have passed since I was called to go to the king."

12When Esther's words were reported to Mordecai, 13he sent back this answer: "Do not think that because you are in the king's house you alone of all the Jews will escape. 14For if you remain silent[c] at this time, relief[d] and deliverance[e] for the Jews will arise from another place, but you and your father's family will perish. And who knows but that you have come to your royal position for such a time as this?"[f]

15Then Esther sent this reply to Mordecai: 16"Go, gather together all the Jews who are in Susa, and fast[g] for me. Do not eat or drink for three days, night or day. I and my attendants will fast as you do. When this is done, I will go to the king, even though it is against the law. And if I perish, I perish."[h]

17So Mordecai went away and carried out all of Esther's instructions.

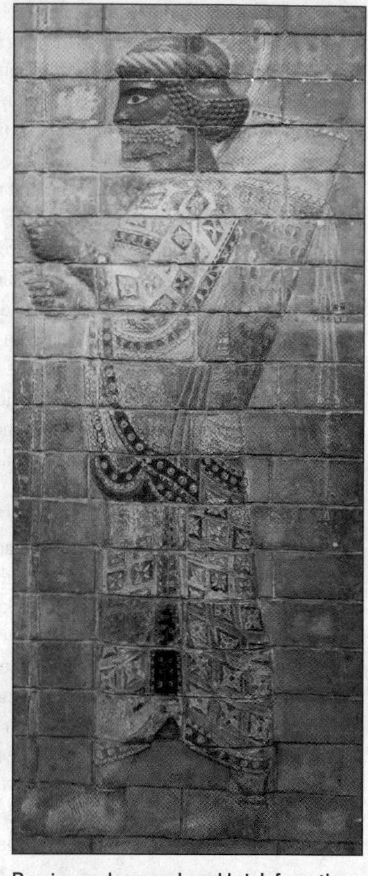

Persian archer on glazed brick from the palace in Susa (sixth century BC).

4:11 When Mordecai asks Esther to intercede for her people with the king, Esther reminds him that "any man or woman who approaches the king in the inner court without being summoned" puts their life in jeopardy. And five years into her marriage, Esther has not been summoned for 30 days. There were only seven men in the king's court, known as his "Friends," who were permitted to see the king. Haman had access to the king, but Esther seems reluctant to request an audience. Perhaps she feared being ignored or did not wish to arouse the suspicions of the court by pleading for the Jewish people. Moreover, it was likely that the ruthless king would not extend the golden scepter if the queen's death would be somehow expedient to his other interests. **4:13 Do not think ... you alone ... will escape.** Mordecai's reply seems almost a threat to reveal her identity as a Jew.
4:14 relief and deliverance for the Jews will arise from another place. Even if Esther fails to act on behalf of her people, Mordecai expresses confidence that they will be delivered. Without referring to God or the promises of his covenant, this confidence against all odds reflects a deep trust in God's ability to move circumstances to accomplish his purposes. **And who knows but that you have come to your royal position for such a time as this?** In what is probably the most famous sentence of the book, with this rhetorical question Mordecai reminds Esther of the divine providence that has guided her life. All who read this question do well to reflect on the significance of the circumstances of their own lives.

4:15–17 *Esther Calls a Three-Day Fast.* This is the first time that Esther takes the initiative, deciding that a three-day fast is called for by the dire situation she faces as she prepares for her uninvited audience with the king. Esther's call for a fast by the Jews of Susa is described in wording that strengthens the parallel with the prophetic call found, for instance, in Joel 2:15–16a. Her doubt that she will survive is not hyperbole given the intrigue in the court and Vashti's previous banishment. But this is not fatalism; it is her recognition that she is caught up in something much bigger than her own life.
4:16 And if I perish, I perish. This is the defining moment in Esther's life, when she decides to identify herself with God's people, even at the risk of her life. The author's explicit silence about God, the covenant, and Jewish practices such as prayer seems a deliberate choice that heightens and highlights the message of God's divine providence—his ability to act through the ordinary decisions of morally ambiguous and even pagan people. Esther's decision to identify herself with God's covenant people is an example to be followed in every generation. By showing all the good that came from her decision to identify with God's covenant people, the author implicitly invites his readers to consider their own relationship with God.
4:17 Up until this point in the story, Mordecai has been telling Esther what to do; from this point to the end, Queen Esther takes charge.

Esther's Request to the King

5 On the third day Esther put on her royal robes[i] and stood in the inner court of the palace, in front
of the king's[j] hall. The king was sitting on his royal throne in the hall, facing the entrance. 2When
he saw Queen Esther standing in the court, he was pleased with her and held out to her the gold scepter
that was in his hand. So Esther approached and touched the tip of the scepter.[k]

3Then the king asked, "What is it, Queen Esther? What is your request? Even up to half the kingdom,[l]
it will be given you."

4"If it pleases the king," replied Esther, "let the king, together with Haman, come today to a banquet
I have prepared for him."

5"Bring Haman at once," the king said, "so that we may do what Esther asks."

So the king and Haman went to the banquet Esther had prepared. 6As they were drinking wine,[m]
the king again asked Esther, "Now what is your petition? It will be given you. And what is your request?
Even up to half the kingdom,[n] it will be granted."[o]

7Esther replied, "My petition and my request is this: 8If the king regards me with favor[p] and if it
pleases the king to grant my petition and fulfill my request, let the king and Haman come tomorrow to
the banquet[q] I will prepare for them. Then I will answer the king's question."

Haman's Rage Against Mordecai

9Haman went out that day happy and in high spirits. But when he saw Mordecai at the king's gate
and observed that he neither rose nor showed fear in his presence, he was filled with rage[r] against
Mordecai.[s] 10Nevertheless, Haman restrained himself and went home.

Calling together his friends and Zeresh,[t] his wife, 11Haman boasted[u] to them about his vast wealth,
his many sons,[v] and all the ways the king had honored him and how he had elevated him above the
other nobles and officials. 12"And that's not all," Haman added. "I'm the only person[w] Queen Esther invited to accompany the king to the banquet she gave. And she has invited me along with the king tomorrow. 13But all this gives me no satisfaction as long as I see that Jew Mordecai sitting at the king's gate.[x]"

14His wife Zeresh and all his friends said to him, "Have a pole set up, reaching to a height of fifty
cubits,[a][y] and ask the king in the morning to have Mordecai impaled[z] on it. Then go with the king to the
banquet and enjoy yourself." This suggestion delighted Haman, and he had the pole set up.

a 14 That is, about 75 feet or about 23 meters

5:1 [i]Est 4:16; Eze 16:13 [j]Est 6:4; Pr 21:1
5:2 [k]Est 4:11; 8:4; Pr 21:1
5:3 [l]Est 7:2; Da 5:16; Mk 6:23
5:6 [m]Est 1:10 [n]Mk 6:23 [o]Est 7:2; 9:12
5:8 [p]Est 2:15; 7:3; 8:5 [q]1Ki 3:15; Est 6:14
5:9 [r]Est 2:21; Pr 14:17 [s]Est 3:3,5
5:10 [t]Est 6:13
5:11 [u]Pr 13:16 [v]Est 9:7-10,13
5:12 [w]Job 22:29; Pr 16:18; 29:23
5:13 [x]Est 2:19
5:14 [y]Est 7:9 [z]Ezr 6:11; Est 6:4

5:1–14 *Esther's Request to the King.* It is no doubt because of this scene that the book comes to be called "Esther" and not "Mordecai." Robed in her royal garments, the queen of Persia courageously goes before the king uninvited with the clever strategy of inviting the king and Haman to a banquet the next day. The suspense rises, but Haman's defenses are lowered.

5:1–5a *Esther Appears Uninvited Before the King.* Esther's uninvited audience with the king is the point of highest plot tension. It was common for the king's bodyguards to kill anyone who approached the king uninvited, and because of the nature of court intrigue, even royal wives were not beyond suspicion. Esther is putting herself at considerable risk.

5:1 Another of the story's ironies: While Vashti risked her life by refusing to appear before Xerxes when summoned (1:12), now Esther risks her life by appearing before the king unsummoned. Esther goes to the king as the queen of Persia, dressed in her royal robes, in defense of her people as she takes up the power of her position. From ch. 5 onward, Esther is portrayed as queen of the world's mightiest empire. She comes into her own only after she decides to align herself with God's people. **the third day.** In Jewish tradition, the "third day" symbolized a day of deliverance (cf. Gen 22:4; 31:22; Hos 6:2; Jonah 1:17). It is on the third day that Esther is granted life instead of death (v. 2).

5:2 gold scepter. Foreshadows the deliverance of her people. Christians and Jews alike would probably be reluctant to see in the ruthless and pagan king Xerxes a type of God himself. That was almost certainly not the author's intent. Nevertheless, this is a picture of grace as Esther approaches the king and completes the gesture by touching the tip of the extended scepter. The scene portrays the power of absolute monarchs, providing an analogy for the biblical portrayal of God as king. Had God not extended the cross of Jesus Christ to the world, all would die in his presence. On the third day, after the final judgment took place on the cross, Jesus Christ arose to imperishable life, guaranteeing safety to enter God's presence to all who reach out in faith to touch that cross-shaped scepter.

5:3 Even up to half the kingdom. An idiom commonly used by ancient royalty and not intended to be taken literally. It simply means that the king is disposed to be generous in meeting a request (cf. Mark 6:23).

5:4–8 The banqueting motif builds in this scene in which Esther uses a delay tactic to invite the king and Haman to not one, but two, banquets. Previously in the story, when Xerxes is drinking wine, Vashti ends up losing her royal position and power. Will the same thing happen to Queen Esther? Because the story tells the origin of the feast, or banquet, of Purim, the author highlights the role of banquets at decisive moments of the story.

5:5b–8 *Esther Prepares a Banquet for the King and Haman.* Esther's strategy is indirect as she simply invites the king and Haman to a banquet on the next day, where she will catch Haman with his defenses down.

5:9–14 *Haman's Rage Against Mordecai.* Esther's invitation to Haman to join her and the king for a banquet the next day increases Haman's sense of power, which ironically also heightens his anger when he sees Mordecai's refusal to bow in his presence as he leaves the palace.

5:14 fifty cubits. About 75 feet or 23 meters. It was the practice in the ancient world to display the body of a dead enemy by impaling it

6:1 [a]Da 2:1; 6:18 [b]Est 2:23; 10:2
6:3 [c]Ecc 9:13-16
6:8 [d]Ge 41:42; Isa 52:1 [e]1Ki 1:33
6:9 [f]Ge 41:43
6:11 [g]Ge 41:42
6:12 [h]2Sa 15:30; Jer 14:3,4; Mic 3:7
6:13 [i]Est 5:10 [j]Ps 57:6; Pr 26:27; 28:18
6:14 [k]1Ki 3:15; Est 5:8

Mordecai Honored

6 That night the king could not sleep;[a] so he ordered the book of the chronicles,[b] the record of his
reign, to be brought in and read to him. 2It was found recorded there that Mordecai had exposed
Bigthana and Teresh, two of the king's officers who guarded the doorway, who had conspired to assassinate King Xerxes.

3"What honor and recognition has Mordecai received for this?" the king asked.

"Nothing has been done for him,"[c] his attendants answered.

4The king said, "Who is in the court?" Now Haman had just entered the outer court of the palace to
speak to the king about impaling Mordecai on the pole he had set up for him.

5His attendants answered, "Haman is standing in the court."

"Bring him in," the king ordered.

6When Haman entered, the king asked him, "What should be done for the man the king delights
to honor?"

Now Haman thought to himself, "Who is there that the king would rather honor than me?" 7So he
answered the king, "For the man the king delights to honor, 8have them bring a royal robe[d] the king
has worn and a horse[e] the king has ridden, one with a royal crest placed on its head. 9Then let the robe
and horse be entrusted to one of the king's most noble princes. Let them robe the man the king delights
to honor, and lead him on the horse through the city streets, proclaiming before him, 'This is what is
done for the man the king delights to honor!'[f]"

10"Go at once," the king commanded Haman. "Get the robe and the horse and do just as you
have suggested for Mordecai the Jew, who sits at the king's gate. Do not neglect anything you have
recommended."

11So Haman got[g] the robe and the horse. He robed Mordecai, and led him on horseback through
the city streets, proclaiming before him, "This is what is done for the man the king delights to honor!"
12Afterward Mordecai returned to the king's gate. But Haman rushed home, with his head covered[h]
in grief, 13and told Zeresh[i] his wife and all his friends everything that had happened to him.

His advisers and his wife Zeresh said to him, "Since Mordecai, before whom your downfall[j] has
started, is of Jewish origin, you cannot stand against him—you will surely come to ruin!" 14While
they were still talking with him, the king's eunuchs arrived and hurried Haman away to the banquet[k]
Esther had prepared.

on a pole in public view. The pole Haman sets up is enormously high, making the author's point that its size is really the measure of Haman's overweening pride (cf. 6:6).

6:1—9:19 *The Reversal of Outcome.* The story of Esther documents a reversal of outcome for the Jews of Persia that is commemorated by the annual festival of Purim. Chs. 1–5 describe the background for the story, introduce the crisis, and explain the interpersonal dynamics that bring the episode to its highest point of tension. Chs. 6–9 reverse many of the events of the first half of the story and bring the denouement to the crisis that threatens to annihilate God's covenant people.

6:1–14 *Mordecai Honored.* The reversal of the Jews' outcome begins when Haman's plot to kill Mordecai backfires and he ends up honoring Mordecai instead. The relationship between Mordecai and Haman reflects the larger dynamic between God's covenant people and the pagan powers under which they live.

6:1–3 *The King Has a Sleepless Night.* During the night between Esther's first and second banquets, "the king could not sleep" (v. 1), a seemingly insignificant event. In another remarkable incident of providence, the king discovers that nothing has been done to reward Mordecai for saving the king from an assassination attempt (2:21–23), and that discovery begins the undoing of Haman.

6:4–9 *Haman Seeks the King's Permission to Kill Mordecai Immediately.* The irony of this turn of events is delightful. Becoming too impatient to wait for the edict of death against Mordecai and his people, Haman prepares to execute Mordecai immediately, just as the king prepares to honor him! And because Mordecai's honor stems from a thwarted assassination plot against the king, Haman's intense desire to kill Mordecai might raise questions in the king's mind about Haman's loyalty.

6:4 Just as the king is considering what he should do to honor Mordecai, Haman comes "to speak to the king about impaling Mordecai on the pole." Haman's and Mordecai's outcomes begin to reverse.

6:7–9 The king's robe, bed, and throne were believed to have almost magical powers to impart the benefits of royalty. For Haman, no other honor is left to him but to partake of the king's own power, prestige, and stature. Even without magical powers, a man permitted to publicly wear the king's robe would be vested with a certain dignity and prestige in the eyes of his peers and the public (cf. 1 Sam 18:1–5).

6:10–14 *Mordecai Is Honored Instead.* God's providence intervenes at just the moment Mordecai is to be condemned to death. Instead of a humiliating death, Mordecai receives prestigious honors that Haman coveted for himself.

6:10 do just as you have suggested for Mordecai the Jew. There would have been no greater humiliation for Haman than the king's words. This is arguably the most ironically comic scene in the entire Bible. An unsuspecting Haman enters the king's court and magnificently trips over his huge pride. Haman is humiliated; Mordecai is honored. The reversal of fortunes has begun.

6:13 Since Mordecai ... is of Jewish origin, you cannot stand against him. The full extent of Haman's tragic miscalculation begins to unfold, and Haman's own wife and advisors announce the victory of God's people against all odds.

Haman Impaled

7 So the king and Haman went to Queen Esther's banquet,[l] [2]and as they were drinking wine[m] on the second day, the king again asked, "Queen Esther, what is your petition? It will be given you. What is your request? Even up to half the kingdom,[n] it will be granted.[o]"

[3]Then Queen Esther answered, "If I have found favor[p] with you, Your Majesty, and if it pleases you, grant me my life—this is my petition. And spare my people—this is my request. [4]For I and my people have been sold to be destroyed, killed and annihilated.[q] If we had merely been sold as male and female slaves, I would have kept quiet, because no such distress would justify disturbing the king.[a]"

[5]King Xerxes asked Queen Esther, "Who is he? Where is he—the man who has dared to do such a thing?"

[6]Esther said, "An adversary and enemy! This vile Haman!"

Then Haman was terrified before the king and queen. [7]The king got up in a rage,[r] left his wine and went out into the palace garden.[s] But Haman, realizing that the king had already decided his fate,[t] stayed behind to beg Queen Esther for his life.

[8]Just as the king returned from the palace garden to the banquet hall, Haman was falling on the couch[u] where Esther was reclining.[v]

The king exclaimed, "Will he even molest the queen while she is with me in the house?"[w]

As soon as the word left the king's mouth, they covered Haman's face.[x] [9]Then Harbona,[y] one of the eunuchs attending the king, said, "A pole reaching to a height of fifty cubits[b][z] stands by Haman's house. He had it set up for Mordecai, who spoke up to help the king."

[a] 4 Or *quiet, but the compensation our adversary offers cannot be compared with the loss the king would suffer* [b] 9 That is, about 75 feet or about 23 meters

7:1 [l]Ge 40:20-22; Mt 22:1-14
7:2 [m]Est 1:10 [n]Est 5:3 [o]Est 9:12
7:3 [p]Est 2:15
7:4 [q]Est 3:9
7:7 [r]Ge 34:7; Est 1:12; Pr 19:12; 20:1-2 [s]2Ki 21:18 [t]Est 6:13
7:8 [u]Est 1:6 [v]Ge 39:14 [w]Ge 34:7 [x]Est 6:12
7:9 [y]Est 1:10 [z]Est 5:14

Judahites impaled by the Assyrians at the siege of Lachish. Haman was impaled for trying to annihilate the Jews (Esth 7:9).

7:1–10 *Haman Impaled.* The irony continues as Haman himself meets the humiliating death he had plotted for Mordecai.

7:1–2 *Esther Prepares a Second Banquet for the King and Haman.* Little does the king or Haman know what awaits them at Queen Esther's banquet! Esther now begins the delicate and dangerous task of accusing Haman without incriminating the king, who had, after all, sealed Haman's desired decree of death for the Jews with full knowledge and approval.

7:3–7 *Esther Reveals Her Jewish Identity and Accuses Haman.* Through a series of delay tactics, Esther has heightened the king's interest and raised the tension of the story. In a scene that brings Nathan's accusation against David to mind (2 Sam 12:1–7), Esther cleverly plays her hand as she reveals her identity to the king by inciting him to ask her a question she cannot refuse to answer. Haman is the one! And Haman cannot deny what the king already knows: that he indeed is the one who contrived the edict of death against the Jews.

7:3–5 Queen Esther finally reveals what brought her to seek the king.

7:4 I and my people. Esther's life and the life of her people are one and the same; her fate is one with that of her people. **destroyed, killed and annihilated.** By quoting the exact words of Haman's edict (cf. 3:13) but using the passive voice, Esther delays mentioning Haman's name or the fact that it was the king himself who sealed her fate (cf. 3:9,11). The tactic works for Esther, and Xerxes' anger and indignation erupt with the demand that she tell him who would dare do this (v. 5).

7:7 Esther's accusation of Haman sends Xerxes into an enraged quandary that drives him out into the garden to think. Can he punish Haman for a plot he himself approved? If his decree is irrevocable, how can he rescind it?

7:8–10 *The King Orders Haman Executed.* Did Haman know that the Persian queen was related to Mordecai when he plotted the death edict against the Jews? Perhaps not, but the king's suspicions were not working in Haman's favor. The king was enraged, and he paced in his garden as he pondered the ambiguities of the problem he faced. But Haman's final unwise act settled any doubts in the king's mind. Haman's violation of harem protocol (see v. 8 and note) was a personal betrayal!

7:8 falling on the couch where Esther was reclining. Harem protocol dictated that no one but the king could be left alone with a woman of the king's harem, much less a royal wife. Haman should have left Esther's presence when the king retreated to the garden, but his choice was either to follow the angry king or to flee the room, suggesting guilt or inviting pursuit. Even in the presence of others, a man was not to approach a woman of the king's harem within seven steps. This unfortunate moment of impropriety is Haman's last and fatal act, and it resolves the king's dilemma. It is ironic that though Mordecai refused to fall before Haman, Haman falls before a Jewish woman who has become his sovereign queen. **they covered Haman's face.** The meaning of this phrase is uncertain. In some ancient cultures, the head of those sentenced to death was covered, but it is not known if that was a practice in ancient Persia. If intended metaphorically, it may mean that this turn of events covered Haman's face with shame, much as his head had been covered in grief (6:12).

7:9 The pole Haman had set up for Mordecai ironically becomes Haman's own end. Haman turns against Mordecai at just the time the king is remembering that Mordecai had thwarted an assassination attempt on his life. This convergence of events perhaps implicates Haman with the conspirators in the king's mind, whether it was true

7:9 [a]Ps 7:14-16; 9:16; Pr 11:5-6; 26:27; Mt 7:2
7:10 [b]Pr 10:28 [c]Est 9:25 [d]Da 6:24 [e]Est 2:1
8:1 [f]Est 2:7; 7:6; Pr 22:22-23
8:2 [g]Ge 41:42; Est 3:10 [h]Pr 13:22; Da 2:48
8:4 [i]Est 4:11; 5:2
8:6 [j]Est 7:4; 9:1
8:8 [k]Est 3:12-14 [l]Ge 41:42 [m]Est 1:19; Da 6:15
8:9 [n]Est 1:1 [o]Est 1:22
8:11 [p]Est 9:10,15,16
8:12 [q]Est 3:13; 9:1
8:13 [r]Est 3:14

The king said, "Impale him on it!"[a] 10So they impaled Haman[b] on the pole[c] he had set up for Mordecai.[d] Then the king's fury subsided.[e]

The King's Edict in Behalf of the Jews

8 That same day King Xerxes gave Queen Esther the estate of Haman,[f] the enemy of the Jews. And Mordecai came into the presence of the king, for Esther had told how he was related to her. 2The king took off his signet ring,[g] which he had reclaimed from Haman, and presented it to Mordecai. And Esther appointed him over Haman's estate.[h]

3Esther again pleaded with the king, falling at his feet and weeping. She begged him to put an end to the evil plan of Haman the Agagite, which he had devised against the Jews. 4Then the king extended the gold scepter[i] to Esther and she arose and stood before him.

5"If it pleases the king," she said, "and if he regards me with favor and thinks it the right thing to do, and if he is pleased with me, let an order be written overruling the dispatches that Haman son of Hammedatha, the Agagite, devised and wrote to destroy the Jews in all the king's provinces. 6For how can I bear to see disaster fall on my people? How can I bear to see the destruction of my family?"[j]

7King Xerxes replied to Queen Esther and to Mordecai the Jew, "Because Haman attacked the Jews, I have given his estate to Esther, and they have impaled him on the pole he set up. 8Now write another decree[k] in the king's name in behalf of the Jews as seems best to you, and seal it with the king's signet ring[l]—for no document written in the king's name and sealed with his ring can be revoked."[m]

9At once the royal secretaries were summoned—on the twenty-third day of the third month, the month of Sivan. They wrote out all Mordecai's orders to the Jews, and to the satraps, governors and nobles of the 127 provinces stretching from India to Cush.[a][n] These orders were written in the script of each province and the language of each people and also to the Jews in their own script and language.[o] 10Mordecai wrote in the name of King Xerxes, sealed the dispatches with the king's signet ring, and sent them by mounted couriers, who rode fast horses especially bred for the king.

11The king's edict granted the Jews in every city the right to assemble and protect themselves; to destroy, kill and annihilate the armed men of any nationality or province who might attack them and their women and children,[b] and to plunder[p] the property of their enemies. 12The day appointed for the Jews to do this in all the provinces of King Xerxes was the thirteenth day of the twelfth month, the month of Adar.[q] 13A copy of the text of the edict was to be issued as law in every province and made known to the people of every nationality so that the Jews would be ready on that day[r] to avenge themselves on their enemies.

14The couriers, riding the royal horses, went out, spurred on by the king's command, and the edict was issued in the citadel of Susa.

[a] *9* That is, the upper Nile region [b] *11* Or *province, together with their women and children, who might attack them;*

---

or not. Although many older English Bibles describe a "gallows" here, death by asphyxiation from a noose around the neck was not a form of execution used in Persia.

8:1–14 *The King's Edict in Behalf of the Jews.* These verses record the reversals of what had happened earlier in the story against the Jews, using the same language found there. Compare the seven pairings: 8:2 and 3:10; 8:9 and 3:12; 8:10 and 3:12; 8:11 and 3:13; 8:13 and 3:14; 8:14 and 3:15; 8:15 and 4:1. Although Haman is gone, the threat against the Jews still stands in his irrevocable edict of death.

8:1 *Esther Introduces Mordecai to the King.* Although Haman planned to plunder the Jews, his own property is confiscated instead. Because Queen Esther and Mordecai are wronged by Haman's evil, "that same day King Xerxes gave Queen Esther the estate of Haman, the enemy of the Jews," as restitution.

8:2 *Mordecai Receives the Signet Ring Previously Worn by Haman.* This is the first of seven explicit reversals (see note on vv. 1–14). In 3:10 the king gave his signet ring, symbolizing his delegated authority, to Haman, expressing his approval of Haman's plot against the Jews. In this verse the king gives the same ring to Mordecai as an expression of his delegated authority.

8:3–8 *Esther Gives Haman's Property to Mordecai.* Part of Haman's scheme against the Jews was to confiscate the possessions of those killed (see 3:9 and note). Instead, the throne confiscates Haman's estate and Esther appoints Mordecai its administrator.

8:9–14 *Mordecai Writes the Counteredict.* Even though Haman himself is gone, the irrevocable edict he had issued in the king's name still stands. The reversals continue as Mordecai writes a counteredict against Haman's edict described in exactly the same terms (cf. 8:9 and 3:12; 8:10 and 3:12; 8:11 and 3:13; 8:13 and 3:14; 8:14 and 3:15; 8:15 and 4:1).

8:11 The counteredict, using exactly the same terms specified in Haman's edict in 3:13, grants the Jews the right to defend themselves when the day of death arrives. It further echoes 1 Sam 15:2–3, the Lord's words to Israel's King Saul, who failed to annihilate the Amalekites as God commanded.

The Triumph of the Jews

15When Mordecai[s] left the king's presence, he was wearing royal garments of blue and white, a large
crown of gold and a purple robe of fine linen.[t] And the city of Susa held a joyous celebration.[u] 16For the
Jews it was a time of happiness and joy,[v] gladness and honor.[w] 17In every province and in every city to
which the edict of the king came, there was joy[x] and gladness among the Jews, with feasting and celebrating. And many people of other nationalities became Jews because fear[y] of the Jews had seized them.[z]

9 On the thirteenth day of the twelfth month, the month of Adar,[a] the edict commanded by the king
was to be carried out. On this day the enemies of the Jews had hoped to overpower them, but now
the tables were turned and the Jews got the upper hand[b] over those who hated them.[c] 2The Jews assembled in their cities[d] in all the provinces of King Xerxes to attack those determined to destroy them. No
one could stand against them,[e] because the people of all the other nationalities were afraid of them.
3And all the nobles of the provinces, the satraps, the governors and the king's administrators helped
the Jews,[f] because fear of Mordecai had seized them. 4Mordecai was prominent[g] in the palace; his reputation spread throughout the provinces, and he became more and more powerful.[h]

5The Jews struck down all their enemies with the sword, killing and destroying them,[i] and they did
what they pleased to those who hated them. 6In the citadel of Susa, the Jews killed and destroyed five
hundred men. 7They also killed Parshandatha, Dalphon, Aspatha, 8Poratha, Adalia, Aridatha, 9Par-
mashta, Arisai, Aridai and Vaizatha, 10the ten sons[j] of Haman son of Hammedatha, the enemy of the
Jews. But they did not lay their hands on the plunder.[k]

11The number of those killed in the citadel of Susa was reported to the king that same day. 12The
king said to Queen Esther, "The Jews have killed and destroyed five hundred men and the ten sons of
Haman in the citadel of Susa. What have they done in the rest of the king's provinces? Now what is your
petition? It will be given you. What is your request? It will also be granted."[l]

13"If it pleases the king," Esther answered, "give the Jews in Susa permission to carry out this day's
edict tomorrow also, and let Haman's ten sons[m] be impaled[n] on poles."

14So the king commanded that this be done. An edict was issued in Susa, and they impaled[o] the ten
sons of Haman. 15The Jews in Susa came together on the fourteenth day of the month of Adar, and they
put to death in Susa three hundred men, but they did not lay their hands on the plunder.[p]

16Meanwhile, the remainder of the Jews who were in the king's provinces also assembled to protect
themselves and get relief[q] from their enemies.[r] They killed seventy-five thousand of them[s] but did not
lay their hands on the plunder. 17This happened on the thirteenth day of the month of Adar, and on the
fourteenth they rested and made it a day of feasting[t] and joy.

18The Jews in Susa, however, had assembled on the thirteenth and fourteenth, and then on the fifteenth they rested and made it a day of feasting and joy.

8:15 [s] Est 9:4 [t] Ge 41:42 [u] Est 3:15
8:16 [v] Ps 97:10-12 [w] Ps 112:4
8:17 [x] Est 9:19,27; Ps 35:27; Pr 11:10 [y] Ex 15:14,16; Dt 11:25 [z] Est 9:3
9:1 [a] Est 8:12 [b] Jer 29:4-7 [c] Est 3:12-14; Pr 22:22-23
9:2 [d] ver 15-18 [e] Est 8:11,17; Ps 71:13,24
9:3 [f] Ezr 8:36
9:4 [g] Ex 11:3 [h] 2Sa 3:1; 1Ch 11:9
9:5 [i] Ezr 4:6
9:10 [j] Est 5:11 [k] Ge 14:23; 1Sa 14:32; Est 3:13; 8:11
9:12 [l] Est 5:6; 7:2
9:13 [m] Est 5:11 [n] Dt 21:22-23
9:14 [o] Ezr 6:11
9:15 [p] Ge 14:23; Est 8:11
9:16 [q] Est 4:14 [r] Dt 25:19 [s] 1Ch 4:43
9:17 [t] 1Ki 3:15

8:15—9:19 *The Triumph of the Jews.* The day of Haman's edict finally arrives. On this day meant to annihilate the Jews, the tables are turned and the Jewish people not only survive but get "the upper hand over those who hated them" (9:1).

8:15–17 *A Day of Joy.* These verses represent the complete reversal of fortune and resolution of the risk to the Jewish people that began in 3:8–15. The joy in Susa (v. 15b) at the resolution of the conflict corresponds to the bewilderment of Susa when it first heard the decree against the Jews (3:15). Mordecai has replaced Haman as the king's closest advisor (v. 15; cf. 3:10). And rather than being the victims of a heinous plot, the Jewish race was held in esteem and even fear because of their newly gained power (v. 17b; cf. 3:13).

9:1–10 *The Jews Kill Many, Including Haman's Ten Sons.* Mordecai's counteredict gave the Jewish people the authority to defend themselves when the day of Haman's edict against them arrived. Rather than falling helplessly before powerful enemies, God's people under the leadership of Esther and Mordecai had the resources to fight back to gain victory over those who hated them. So that Haman's sons would not survive to avenge their father's death, they too fall on that tragic day that was their father's own doing (vv. 7–10).

9:1 the tables were turned. The story ends not by simply cancelling the threat but by reversing the fortunes of the Jews in Persia.

9:10,15,16 But they did not lay their hands on the plunder. Even though Haman plotted to plunder the Jews after annihilating them, the Jews do not plunder their enemies. This confirms that they perceive this episode as holy war, for when God commanded destruction of a people whose evil could be remedied in no other way, the human agents of that judgment were not to profit from it in any way. Queen Esther and Mordecai fulfill God's covenant promise (Exod 17:8,14–16; Deut 25:17–19) where King Saul had failed (1 Sam 15:18–19).

9:11–19 *Esther Asks for Their Bodies to Be Displayed and for a Second Day of Killing in Susa.* Mordecai's counteredict authorized the Jews to defend themselves throughout the empire only on Adar 13 (see v. 2 and 8:11–12), but Queen Esther asks the king to "give the Jews in Susa permission to carry out this day's edict tomorrow also" (v. 13). Interpreters have found a disquieting ambiguity in Esther's character here. Perhaps Esther's request shows that she herself had begun to feel the heady intoxication of the power she had so remarkably attained. On the other hand, Esther's reasons for a second day of killing in Susa may have been the decision of a wise and discerning leader, for Haman likely had many in the city who were loyal to him and his decree.

9:17–19 At the time the book of Esther was written, Purim was celebrated in some places on two consecutive days but in other places on only one day. Here the author explains the origin of that difference.

9:19 [u]Est 3:7 [v]ver 22; Dt 16:11,14; Ne 8:10, 12; Est 2:9; Rev 11:10
9:22 [w]Est 4:14 [x]Ne 8:12; Ps 30:11-12 [y]2Ki 25:30
9:24 [z]Ex 17:8-16 [a]Est 3:7 [b]Lev 16:8
9:25 [c]Ps 7:16 [d]Dt 21:22-23 [e]Est 7:10
9:26 [f]ver 20; Est 3:7
9:29 [g]Est 2:15
9:30 [h]Est 1:1
9:31 [i]Est 4:16 [j]Est 4:1-3
10:1 [k]Ps 72:10; 97:1; Isa 24:15
10:2 [l]Est 8:15; 9:4 [m]Ge 41:44 [n]Est 2:23
10:3 [o]Da 5:7 [p]Ge 41:43 [q]Ge 41:40 [r]Ne 2:10; Jer 29:4-7; Da 6:3

19 That is why rural Jews — those living in villages — observe the fourteenth of the month of Adar[u] as a day of joy and feasting, a day for giving presents to each other.[v]

Purim Established

20 Mordecai recorded these events, and he sent letters to all the Jews throughout the provinces of King Xerxes, near and far, 21 to have them celebrate annually the fourteenth and fifteenth days of the month of Adar 22 as the time when the Jews got relief[w] from their enemies, and as the month when their sorrow was turned into joy and their mourning into a day of celebration.[x] He wrote them to observe the days as days of feasting and joy and giving presents of food[y] to one another and gifts to the poor.

23 So the Jews agreed to continue the celebration they had begun, doing what Mordecai had written to them. 24 For Haman son of Hammedatha, the Agagite,[z] the enemy of all the Jews, had plotted against the Jews to destroy them and had cast the *pur*[a] (that is, the lot[b]) for their ruin and destruction. 25 But when the plot came to the king's attention,[*a*] he issued written orders that the evil scheme Haman had devised against the Jews should come back onto his own head,[c] and that he and his sons should be impaled[d] on poles.[e] 26 (Therefore these days were called Purim, from the word *pur*.[f]) Because of everything written in this letter and because of what they had seen and what had happened to them, 27 the Jews took it on themselves to establish the custom that they and their descendants and all who join them should without fail observe these two days every year, in the way prescribed and at the time appointed. 28 These days should be remembered and observed in every generation by every family, and in every province and in every city. And these days of Purim should never fail to be celebrated by the Jews — nor should the memory of these days die out among their descendants.

29 So Queen Esther, daughter of Abihail,[g] along with Mordecai the Jew, wrote with full authority to confirm this second letter concerning Purim. 30 And Mordecai sent letters to all the Jews in the 127 provinces[h] of Xerxes' kingdom — words of goodwill and assurance — 31 to establish these days of Purim at their designated times, as Mordecai the Jew and Queen Esther had decreed for them, and as they had established for themselves and their descendants in regard to their times of fasting[i] and lamentation.[j] 32 Esther's decree confirmed these regulations about Purim, and it was written down in the records.

The Greatness of Mordecai

10 King Xerxes imposed tribute throughout the empire, to its distant shores.[k] 2 And all his acts of power and might, together with a full account of the greatness of Mordecai,[l] whom the king had promoted,[m] are they not written in the book of the annals[n] of the kings of Media and Persia? 3 Mordecai the Jew was second[o] in rank[p] to King Xerxes,[q] preeminent among the Jews, and held in high esteem by his many fellow Jews, because he worked for the good of his people and spoke up for the welfare of all the Jews.[r]

[*a*] 25 Or *when Esther came before the king*

9:20–32 *Purim Established.* Mordecai (vv. 20–21) and Esther (v. 29) together establish the celebration of this great deliverance as an annual holiday that is still celebrated today in the Jewish religion, usually in February-March. It is fitting that the fulfillment in the Persian period of God's ancient promise to protect his people should be written down and commemorated. When God promised to wipe out the enemies of his people, he told Moses to "write [it] on a scroll as something to be remembered" (Exod 17:14). The Jewish people imprisoned in the Nazi death camps treasured the story of Esther precisely because it promised the survival of their race despite Hitler's attempts to annihilate them.

But Esther is also in the Christian canon of Scripture. Throughout history Esther has been read as symbolizing the final salvation of God's people at the end of time. It forms a link between the promises God made at the exodus and the eschatological destiny of God's people. Purim was a spontaneous celebration of the joy of finding oneself still standing the day after an irrevocable death decree was executed. The day of death had come and gone, and God's people were still alive!

9:20–28 *Mordecai Writes to the Jews of Persia.* Although there was great joy at the time of the deliverance, this event was recognized as signifying that God's faithfulness to protect his covenant people against all odds, humanly speaking, should be commemorated and celebrated annually by every generation.

9:29–32 *Esther Writes to Confirm Mordecai's Letter.* This story was canonized with the title "Esther," not "Mordecai," though it is difficult to decide which of them is the main character due to the interdependent nature of their leadership. This "daughter of Abihail" (v. 29) rose to the throne of Persia through providential circumstances to intervene and change the course of history for her people. She had full authority as queen to confirm the establishment of Purim as a holiday that could be openly and legally celebrated by the Jews throughout the Persian Empire.

10:1–3 *The Greatness of Mordecai.* This epilogue documents that, together with Esther, Mordecai rose to a high position in the Persian Empire, second only to Xerxes himself (v. 3). His work "for the good of his people" (v. 3) and his advocacy for their welfare made him a prominent leader who has long been celebrated. Later in the Hellenistic period, Purim was sometimes referred to as "Mordecai's Day" (in the Apocrypha, see 2 Maccabees 15:36).

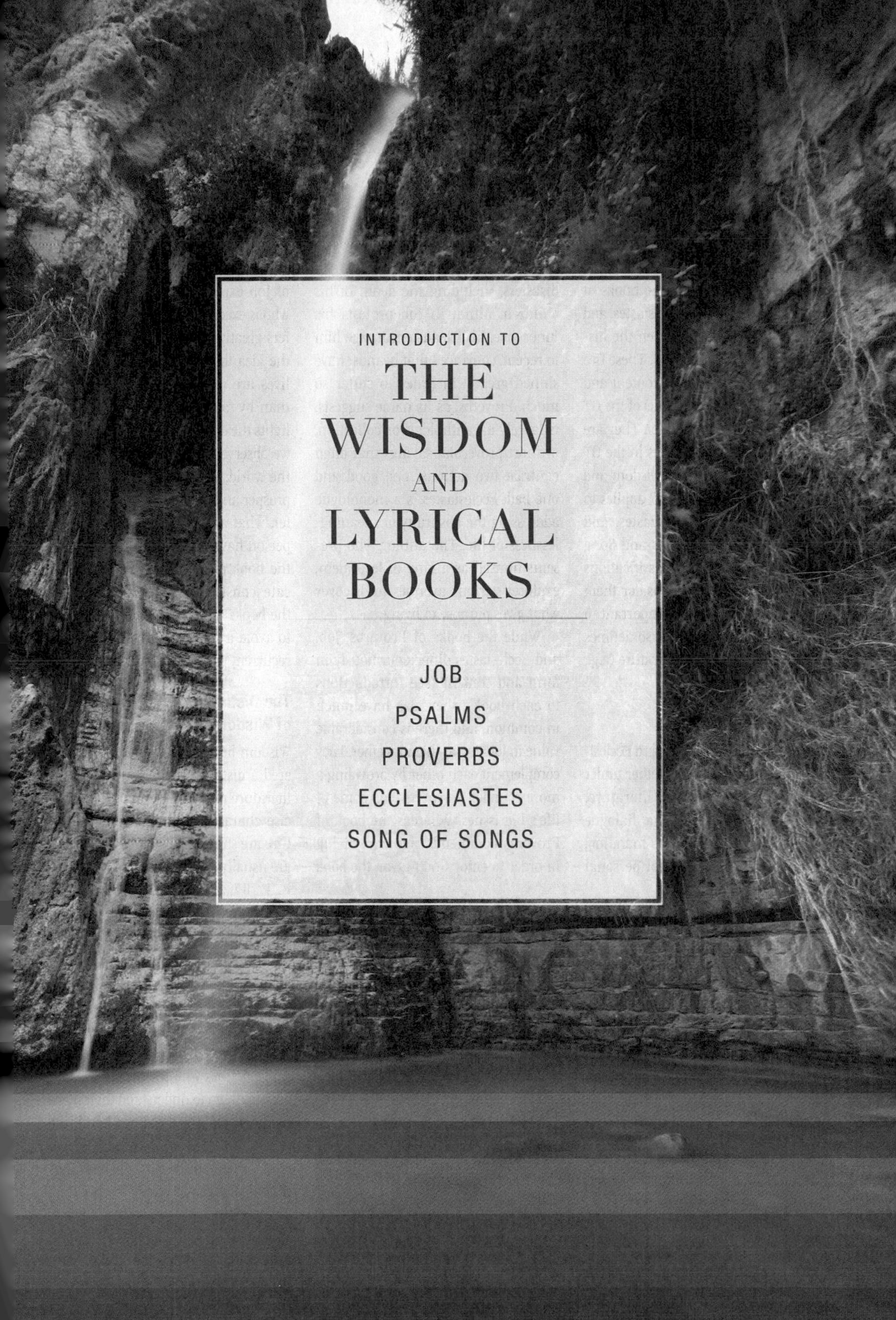

INTRODUCTION TO

THE WISDOM AND LYRICAL BOOKS

JOB

PSALMS

PROVERBS

ECCLESIASTES

SONG OF SONGS

THE WISDOM AND LYRICAL BOOKS

T. D. Alexander

In most English Bibles, the books of Job, Psalms, Proverbs, Ecclesiastes, and Song of Songs come between the historical and prophetic books. These five books differ noticeably in content and style from all the other books of the OT as well as from one another. They are the principal representatives in the OT of what is now known as wisdom and lyrical literature. "Wisdom" applies to Job, Proverbs, and Ecclesiastes, and "lyrical" relates to Psalms and Song of Songs. Since the two classifications are distinctive, we will consider them separately; however, it is important to note that a few psalms are sometimes associated with wisdom literature (e.g., Ps 49).

Wisdom Books

The books of Job, Proverbs, and Ecclesiastes are often grouped together under the heading of wisdom literature. The book of Job is mostly a dialogue that centers on a righteous man, Job, who experiences a series of personal disasters, including the death of his children. Although Job protests his innocence, his friends encourage him to repent, convinced that he must have sinned greatly in order to suffer so much. Proverbs, as its name suggests, is largely an anthology, or collection, of short proverbial sayings that often contrast two actions, one good and one bad. Ecclesiastes is a monologue addressing the absurdity or meaninglessness of life. The author, who presents himself as a king of Jerusalem, explores various avenues to discover what gives purpose to living.

While the books of Proverbs, Job, and Ecclesiastes differ enormously in form and content (see Introductions to each book), they also have much in common, and there is considerable value in looking at them together. They complement each other by providing a more rounded perspective on some of life's big issues. Whereas the book of Proverbs commends righteous living in order to enjoy God's favor, the book of Job explores the case of someone who is exceptionally righteous but suffers greatly. Whereas Proverbs conveys the idea that God blesses those whose lives are marked by integrity rather than by falsehood, Ecclesiastes highlights the disillusionment we feel when we observe the lack of moral order in the world; since the wicked appear to prosper and the righteous seem to suffer, what advantage does a righteous person have over the wicked? Whereas the book of Proverbs seeks to inculcate consistent, righteous behavior, the books of Job and Ecclesiastes look to avoid a simplistic interpretation of recurrent patterns of life.

Job and his friends.
Wikimedia Commons

The Distinctive Nature of Wisdom Literature

Wisdom literature is generally considered a distinctive category within the literature of the OT. Although the precise characteristics of wisdom literature are subject to debate, five features are usually present.

1. *Wisdom literature uniquely emphasizes the importance of human reason and understanding.* Wisdom literature contrasts with the historical books and the prophetic books. On the one hand, the historical books recount a unique story of God's dealings with the people of Israel. This grand narrative defines who the people are and enables them to understand their place in the world. On the other hand, the prophetic books record divine messages containing both threats and warnings that challenge the people to obey God. The wisdom books are neither a grand story nor divine messages. They are quite different in that they call on people to think hard about life and how they should live.

While the wisdom books do not claim to originate directly from God, unlike OT laws (such as those God gave through Moses on Mount Sinai) and divine messages of encouragement or rebuke (such as those God gave through visions to prophets), they nevertheless claim authority for what they have to say. Their advice comes in part from observing the behavior of people and thinking about creation. For example:

I went past the field of a sluggard,
past the vineyard of someone
who has no sense;
thorns had come up everywhere,
the ground was covered with
weeds,
and the stone wall was in ruins.
I applied my heart to what
I observed
and learned a lesson from what
I saw:
A little sleep, a little slumber,
a little folding of the hands to
rest—
and poverty will come on you like
a thief
and scarcity like an armed man.
(Prov 24:30–34)

Here knowledge comes through observation and reflection. This kind of understanding does not depend upon divinely given laws or prophetic visions.

2. *Wisdom originates with God.* The wisdom books view creation and life through the lens of belief in the God of Israel. We cannot find wisdom apart from him because "the fear of the LORD is the beginning of wisdom" (Prov 9:10; cf. Job 28:28; Prov 1:7; 16:6; 31:30; Eccl 5:7; 12:13). The books encourage us to use our minds and think independently within the context of trusting God:

Trust in the LORD with all your
heart
and lean not on your own
understanding;
in all your ways submit to him,
and he will make your paths
straight.

A well-tended vineyard stands in contrast to Prov 24:31, "the ground was covered with weeds, and the stone wall was in ruins."

Todd Bolen/www.BiblePlaces.com

Do not be wise in your own eyes;
fear the LORD and shun evil.
(Prov 3:5–7)

Wisdom literature encourages us to think diligently but humbly.

Basic to wisdom literature is the belief that God has created a coherent and meaningful universe:

By wisdom the LORD laid the earth's
foundations,
by understanding he set the
heavens in place. (Prov 3:19)
How many are your works, LORD!
In wisdom you made them all;
the earth is full of your
creatures. (Ps 104:24)

Based on the assumption that God designed everything in the universe, the ancient Israelites believed that "truth," in all its aspects, began and ended with God. For this reason the pursuit of "truth" brought one closer to God.

Such reasoning, however, is at odds with the beliefs of many twenty-first-century postmodern ideas. For many postmodern thinkers, it is folly to seek a rational explanation to life. There is no such thing as absolute truth, for everything is relative. Reason cannot bring us to "truth," for "truth" does not exist. From this postmodern perspective, life is meaningless not because we have yet to discover the meaning but because there is no meaning to discover. For many postmodern people, the idea that God created a meaningful universe is folly. There can be no ultimate meaning to life, for there is no God.

The wisdom writings of the OT, however, start from a very different premise, one that is alien to many people today. The authors of these books believed that God created a meaningful universe. This does not imply that they did not struggle to make sense of life in the world. On the contrary, they struggled a great deal. But through their struggle they realized that they could discover meaningful existence only by taking God into account. Wisdom itself comes through revelation. For this reason, the authors of Proverbs, Job, and Ecclesiastes unanimously affirm that "the fear of the LORD is the beginning of wisdom" (Prov 9:10; cf. Job 28:28; Eccl 12:13).

3. *Wisdom embraces all areas of life.* Since all knowledge comes from God, there was in ancient Israel no distinction between religious and secular truth. This was so because the Israelites viewed God as creator and sustainer of all life. Furthermore, they

linked wisdom with creation itself. To underline this connection, Prov 8 personifies wisdom: wisdom speaks. Wisdom was the first of God's creations (Prov 8:22–31), and she describes how she was with God and assisted him in creating the world. This has important ramifications, because it gives wisdom a unique status. By implication, if creation depends upon wisdom, then to live wisely is to live in harmony with creation. To do otherwise is to oppose God's purpose for the world.

This link between wisdom and creation undergirds the whole book of Proverbs. To live wisely is about participating positively in God's creation-purposes. It is about building a society that is in harmony with God's purposes. Aptly, the words "wisdom," "knowledge," and "understanding" together describe the creation of the cosmos, the construction of the tabernacle and temple, and the building of the family home:

> By *wisdom* the LORD laid the earth's
> foundations,
> by *understanding* he set the
> heavens in place;
> by his *knowledge* the watery depths
> were divided,
> and the clouds let drop the dew.
> (Prov 3:19–20, emphasis
> added)

The same three terms describe Bezalel and Huram, who had special responsibilities for overseeing the construction of the tabernacle and Jerusalem temple, respectively (Exod 31:3; 35:30–31; 1 Kgs 7:13–14). They construct God's earthly dwelling place with the same qualities that God used to construct the world. This parallel is all the more interesting because ancient Israelites viewed the tabernacle and temple as models of the cosmos. Extending this idea one stage further:

> By *wisdom* a house is built,
> and through *understanding* it
> is established;
> through *knowledge* its rooms are
> filled
> with rare and beautiful
> treasures. (Prov 24:3–4,
> emphasis added)

By emphasizing the role of wisdom, understanding, and knowledge in creating a family home, a significant link is made with the construction of God's dwelling place. These parallels between the cosmos, the tabernacle/temple, and the ordinary home are no coincidence, for they reflect the overall purpose of God that he should dwell on the earth, cohabiting it with humans (see "Temple," p. 2652). For people to participate in God's creation-purpose, it is essential for them to have wisdom, knowledge, and understanding. These attributes, however, are not innate. They come from God:

> For the LORD gives *wisdom*;
> from his mouth come
> *knowledge* and
> *understanding*.
> (Prov 2:6, emphasis added)

In unexpected ways the lyrical and wisdom books add to the theological richness of the OT canon by complementing the historical and prophetic books that surround them.

4. *Wisdom and ethics*. Wisdom is about much more than acquiring factual knowledge and understanding. Wisdom is not equated simply with intellectual ability. Rather, it is about "doing what is right and just and fair" (Prov 1:3).

5. *Wisdom and creation*. Unfortunately, all on earth is not as it should be, for people are drawn to folly rather than wisdom. With good reason, the father in Prov 1–9 appeals to his son to choose wisdom rather than folly. Whereas wisdom offers life, folly brings death. To highlight these contrasting ways of living, the father personifies wisdom and folly as two women. Folly is cast as a seductive adulteress who lures unsuspecting young men into her house with the promise of sexual gratification. But as the father points out, the punishment for adultery is death (Prov 7:21–27; 9:18). Wisdom also invites young men into her house, but here there is no threat of death, only life (Prov 8:35; 9:11).

Lyrical Books

The two main books of lyrical literature are Psalms and the Song of Songs. Although both books are poetry, they are very different. While the Psalter (i.e., the book of Psalms) is a collection of 150 songs devoted to the worship of God, the Song of Songs comprises a series of interconnected stanzas that express the passionate feelings of two lovers for one another. Whereas

"The clouds let drop the dew" (Prov 3:20).

the songs within the Psalter address a wide variety of human situations, the Song of Songs narrowly focuses on one important theme. Whereas the Psalter abounds in references to God, constantly putting him at the very center, the lovers in the Song of Songs have eyes only for each other; in fact, throughout the whole book God's name never appears (or appears once in 8:6, if we include the NIV text note). While the Psalter is an obvious candidate for inclusion within the canon of the OT, the Song of Songs initially appears somewhat out of place. Nevertheless, both books contribute in different ways to a deeper theological reading of the OT (see Introductions to both books).

The Psalter comprises material that ancient Israel widely used in public worship over a long period of time. The psalms, however, come from different periods of time. Some of the psalms are much older than others, with many going back to the time of King David. The present collection of 150 psalms has been created by combining shorter collections of psalms that already existed. Some of these collections probably circulated for centuries before being combined to produce the Psalter as we now know it. The final collection undoubtedly came into existence in the postexilic period, suggesting that the Psalter may well have been produced to be the hymnbook of the Jews who returned from exile to rebuild the city of Jerusalem.

As might be expected, the 150 songs within the Psalter cover a wide range of themes. In doing so, the psalms articulate a host of human emotions, from exalted praise and adoration of God to utter despondency in the face of extreme difficulties. The psalms move from distraught pleas for help to exuberant words of gratitude for God's compassion and help. The psalms acknowledge that life can be harsh and uncompromising. Nevertheless, in spite of everything negative that an individual or community may experience, there is a sovereign God who is compassionate and merciful. While the Psalter does not neglect the darker side of life, there is within it an overall movement from lament to praise.

In marked contrast to the book of Psalms, the Song of Songs centers on one theme: romantic love. From beginning to end, the entire book explores, often in vivid detail, the mutual delight that a man and woman may share. The language frequently overflows with graphic imagery as the lovers express their yearning for one another. She ardently says,

Like an apple tree among the trees
of the forest
is my beloved among the young
men.
I delight to sit in his shade,
and his fruit is sweet to my
taste.
Let him lead me to the banquet
hall,
and let his banner over me be
love.
Strengthen me with raisins,
refresh me with apples,
for I am faint with love.
His left arm is under my head,
and his right arm embraces me.
(Song 2:3 – 6)

His response is equally evocative:

Your teeth are like a flock of sheep
just shorn,
coming up from the washing.
Each has its twin;
not one of them is alone.
Your lips are like a scarlet
ribbon;
your mouth is lovely.
Your temples behind your veil
are like the halves of a
pomegranate.
Your neck is like the tower of
David,
built with courses of stone;
on it hang a thousand shields,
all of them shields of warriors.
(Song 4:2 – 4)

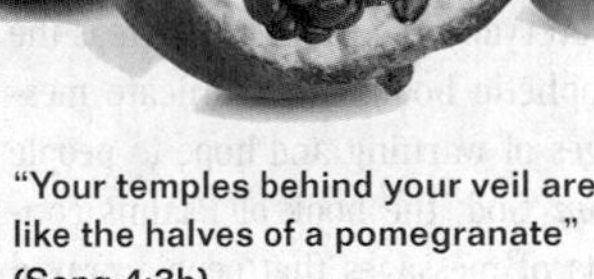

"Your temples behind your veil are like the halves of a pomegranate" (Song 4:3b).

Through nature-rich metaphors the couple share their ardent passion for each other.

Set side by side, the Psalter and the Song of Songs are vivid reminders of the significance of relationships for human existence. The Psalter emphasizes at length the importance of the divine-human relationship, recognizing that this is frequently a relationship that is, from a human perspective, difficult to sustain. By way of encouragement, the intimacy of human love illustrates indirectly something of the passion of God's love for people. The one who designed male and female for intimate union, intending that they should become one flesh, is the very one who desires to live in close and harmonious relationship with them. Human love is to be an illustration of divine love. For this reason, the apostle Paul instructs husbands to love their wives, "just as Christ loved the church and gave himself up for her" (Eph 5:25). In the same vein, the book of Revelation describes "the Holy City, the new Jerusalem,… as a bride beautifully dressed for her husband" (Rev 21:2). While the Song of Songs may not address explicitly the divine-human relationship, it uniquely contributes to the canon of Scripture.

Unity and Diversity

In unexpected ways the lyrical and wisdom books add to the theological richness of the OT canon by complementing the historical and prophetic books that surround them. Whereas the historical books describe selected actions of God at particular times and places, the wisdom books highlight the difficulty of comprehending God's role in everyday occurrences. Whereas the prophetic books communicate messages of warning and hope to people *from* God, the book of Psalms consists of messages that people prayed in private or sung in public *to* God. By reflecting on the complementary nature of these books, we may appreciate something of the rich diversity that exists within the Bible.

Unfortunately, some scholars exploit this instructive diversity by arguing that it arises out of differing and sometimes contradictory views of God. Diversity, however, is not incompatible with unity. As the human body ably illustrates, eyes and ears have little in common, yet both are vital components within a single entity. In the same way, the wisdom and lyrical books expand the variety of literary forms that comprise the Bible and significantly contribute to its theology.

King David playing his harp. Many of the psalms are attributed to David.
Westminster Abbey Psalter

While the wisdom and lyrical books are very different from one another as works of literature, they are all linked, apart from the book of Job, in some way to the Davidic monarchy: Many of the psalms are attributed to David. The book of Proverbs consists largely of collections of proverbial sayings associated with David's son Solomon. The author of Ecclesiastes introduces himself as a "son of David, king in Jerusalem" (Eccl 1:1), and the Song of Songs begins with a reference to Solomon (Song 1:1). (For the implications of these observations for authorship, see Introductions to each book.) These links to the Davidic dynasty add substantial weight to the OT expectation that the royal line of David will play a special role in the fulfillment of God's redemptive purposes. Eventually these expectations come to fulfillment in Jesus Christ, the "son of David" (Matt 1:1) and the one "greater than Solomon" (Luke 11:31). In him we see a life that reflects all that the wisdom and lyrical books have to teach. ■

INTRODUCTION TO JOB

The story of Job has left its mark on the spiritual psyches of Jews and Christians alike. Even as early as the sixth century BC, Ezekiel knew of Job's reputation for righteousness (Ezek 14:14,20), and in the first century AD, James remembered Job for his patience (Jas 5:11). Interestingly, both of these remembrances are dependent on the portrait of Job found in the prologue of the book. For some reason, at least in Christian lore, Job's argumentative personality, which is seen in the dialogue, does not receive top billing. When one reads the speeches of the dialogue with their charges and countercharges, one can understand why: the Job of the dialogue makes us feel uncomfortable because his words are often caustic and accusatory. But if we are to understand the book as a whole, then we must come to grips with this portrait.

THE MAJOR ISSUE OF JOB

The major theme of the book has traditionally been articulated as underserved suffering, an issue that strikes a chord in many human hearts. And definitely that is at the heart of the book. Yet when the Lord addresses the book's hero at the end of this literary masterpiece, he does not explain to Job why Job has suffered. While many readers may view this as a deficiency, it may be at the same time one of the earmarks of the book's literary genius. Rather than God responding to Job's demands with a simple and forthright answer, the book puts together a literary configuration that elucidates an answer. The question of why Job suffers is not an easy one. Even if the Lord were to provide a simple answer, at least from his point of view, its complexities would be so challenging that even a wise man like Job would perhaps find them incomprehensible. Eliphaz began such an explanation in his first speech (5:17), which was more fully developed by Elihu (33:14–30; 36:8–11,15–17; 37:13). Yet the idea that suffering is designed to bring one back on to the right track is only one possibility, and it is by no means entirely satisfactory. Yet Job's interaction with his friends, the reprimand he receives from Elihu, and the humbling power of God's speeches help Job come to understand that his relationship to God is ultimately the main issue and that suffering, while extremely important, is secondary. Thus, we ought to see the major issue of the book of Job more like a complex series of issues rather than a single one. It is about the suffering of the innocent, the testing of the righteous, and Job's relationship to God—all bound together in the totality of the book. The complex of issues is not theoretical but practical, which makes the book all the more relevant. Job's world is real, not a hypothetical "ivory tower" where these questions can be bandied about among the participants without anyone feeling the hurt.

Ludlul bel nemeqi**, "I Will Praise the Lord of Wisdom," is a Mesopotamian poem that features a suffering man—similar to Job in this book.**

Kim Walton, taken at the Louvre

POSSIBLE LOCATIONS OF UZ (HAURAN AND EDOM) AND REGION OF THE CHALDEANS (SABA AND BABYLON)

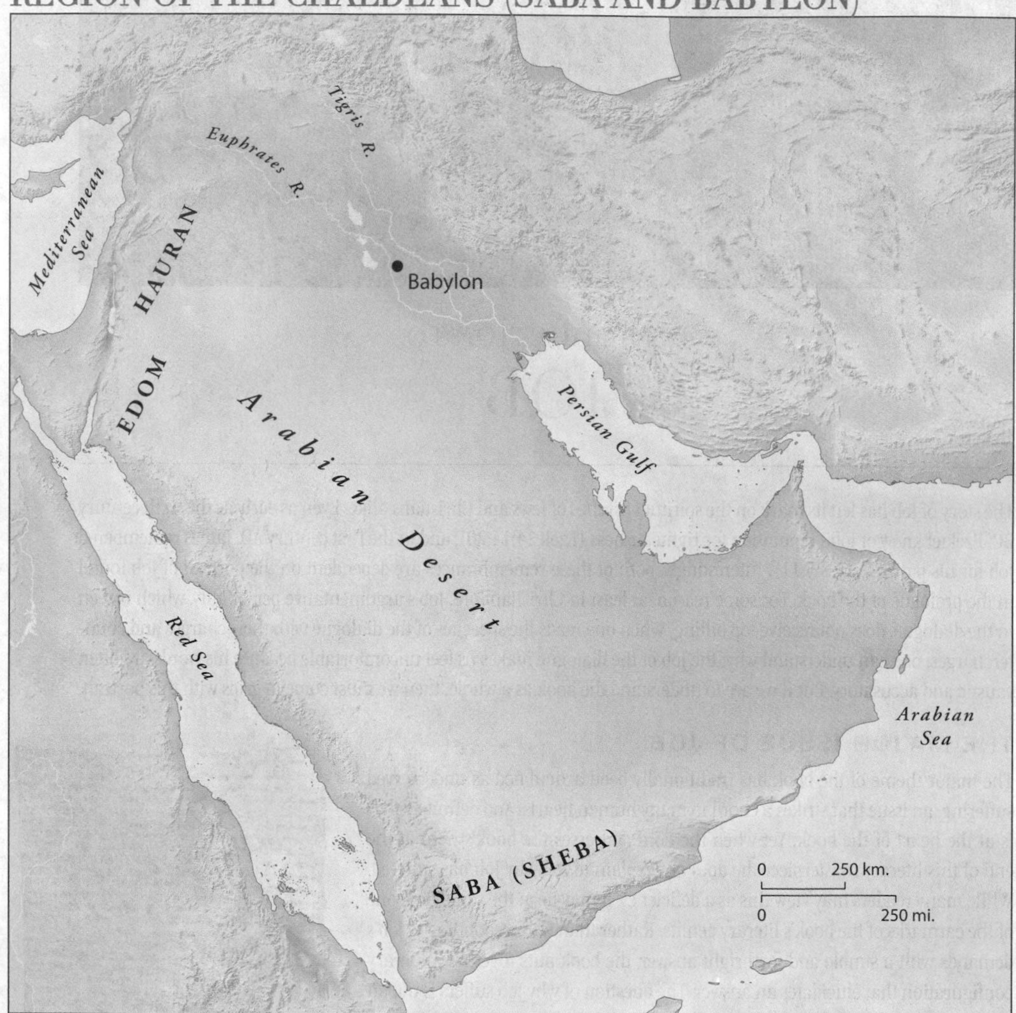

THE NATURE AND MEANING OF THE SPEECHES

There are three cycles of speeches. Each cycle is composed of three speeches, one by each of Job's three friends, followed by Job's response — except that in the third cycle, the third friend, Zophar, does not speak, even though Job gives him an opportunity to do so. The speeches do not touch like rectangles set side by side; they are more like circles, some concentric, some partially overlapping, some disjointed. From time to time the disputants seize upon each other's arguments and turn them on the anvil of their own theological platform to give them a different meaning. After Job has lamented his pitiable state of suffering, the three cycles arrange the speakers in an orderly fashion from the oldest to the youngest. Elihu comes after Job's closing words because Elihu is the youngest.

The speeches are written in poetic form, while the prologue (chs. 1 – 2) and the epilogue (42:7 – 17) are composed in prose — prose being more amenable to the biographical details than poetry. The role of Satan in the prologue is that of a catalyst, but he does not initiate the conversation with the Lord, nor does he mention Job's name until the Lord himself introduces it. Then it becomes quite obvious that Satan knew Job's situation quite well.

The friends' understanding of God and the world changes little amid a variety of topics they introduce and reintroduce, while Job remains steadfast on some issues and advances in understanding on others. On the one hand, Job remains steadfast throughout the dialogue that he is innocent (6:28 – 30; 9:15; 16:17; 23:12; 27:5 – 6), that God is acting like his enemy (6:4; 16:11–14; 19:6–12; 23:15–16; 27:2), and that God continues to elude him (9:16,33; 23:3; 31:35). On the other hand, Job's understanding of why tragedy has struck him broadside moves from complete lack of understanding to the recognition, at least momentarily, that he is suffering because God is trying to expose his true character (23:10). One of the most significant advances in Job's understanding is his belief in the afterlife. At first he is skeptical (14:7–17), but with time he comes to embrace the doctrine (19:25–27). The notion of a mediator is coupled with that belief. Job at first is skeptical (as he is regarding the afterlife), even entirely negative, about a mediator who can arbitrate between him and God (9:33), but as his confidence in the afterlife advances, so do his beliefs that there is a witness in heaven who will vouch for him (16:19) and that his hope—that he will face his redeemer—will become a reality (19:25–27). Finally, Job's beliefs in his innocence and God's justice come together when Job asserts that if he could find God the judge, God would acquit him (23:7).

AUTHOR AND DATE

We do not know who authored the book of Job, yet we are safe in saying that the author set Job's story in the patriarchal period. Job and Abraham are culturally and spiritually next of kin. Job's priestly role, his use of livestock as a measurement of wealth, and even his final repentance "in dust and ashes" (42:6) suggest the patriarchal era. While there are hints that Job knew the moral law, it is possible that the author wanted to suggest that Job, like Abraham, obeyed the law before it was ever handed down to Moses (Gen 26:5). Judging from Ezekiel's mention of our hero (Ezek 14:14,20), we may assume that the book was written in the preexilic era and long before Ezekiel's prophetic activity (ca. 593–571 BC).

Job the Man: The text hints that Job was a comparatively young man (15:10). He was wise and wealthy, and he was highly respected in his community. Though he perhaps lived in Edom, he was not likely an Edomite, for there is too much evidence that Job was a Hebrew believer. There has been much speculation about whether Job was a historical person. However, Ezekiel's reference to Job's righteousness (Ezek 14:14,20) and James's mention of Job's perseverance (Jas 5:11) suggest that Job was a real person, not merely a figure in a parable.

When we look at the following outline, it is quite obvious that the dialogue is the major section of the book, which is significant. That is where the protagonist, Job, faces his "comforters," who are at a safe distance, both emotionally and theologically. If length is any indication and if intensity is any guide, it is in the dialogue that the issues of the book are exposed, challenged, and "resolved," at least so far as the three friends are concerned. But for Job the dialogue is a platform on which to state his case and challenge God to appear in court to explain himself. That means God's speeches are central to the reader's understanding of the book, but they are presented only after the author has introduced the conceited and indicting speeches of Elihu.

OUTLINE

I. The Prologue 1:1—2:13
- A. The Main Character Introduced (1:1–5)
- B. Job's First Test Executed and Job's Response (1:6–22)
- C. Job's Second Test Executed and Job's Response (2:1–10)
- D. Job's Three Friends (2:11–13)

II. Job's Lament (3:1–26)

III. The Dialogue (4:1—27:23)
- A. The Dialogue: Cycle One (4:1—14:22)
  1. First Exchange: Eliphaz (4:1—5:27)
  2. Job's Response to Eliphaz (6:1—7:21)
  3. Second Exchange: Bildad (8:1–22)
  4. Job's Response to Bildad (9:1—10:22)
  5. Third Exchange: Zophar (11:1–20)
  6. Job's Response to Zophar (12:1—14:22)
- B. The Dialogue: Cycle Two (15:1—21:34)
  1. First Exchange: Eliphaz (15:1–35)
  2. Job's Response to Eliphaz (16:1—17:16)
  3. Second Exchange: Bildad (18:1–21)

4. Job's Response to Bildad (19:1–29)
5. Third Exchange: Zophar (20:1–29)
6. Job's Response to Zophar (21:1–34)

C. The Dialogue: Cycle Three (22:1—27:23)

1. First Exchange: Eliphaz (22:1–30)
2. Job's Response to Eliphaz (23:1—24:25)
3. Second Exchange: Bildad (25:1–6)
4. Job's Response to Bildad (26:1–14)
5. Job's Final Word to His Friends (27:1–23)

IV. Job's First Monologue: Where Wisdom Is Found (28:1–28)

V. Job's Second Monologue: Job's Final Defense (29:1—31:40)

VI. The Elihu Speeches (32:1—37:24)

A. Elihu's First Speech (32:1—33:33)
B. Elihu's Second Speech (34:1–37)
C. Elihu's Third Speech (35:1–16)
D. Elihu's Fourth Speech (36:1—37:24)

VII. God's Speeches and Job's Responses (38:1—42:6)

A. God's First Speech (38:1—40:2)
B. Job's First Response (40:3–5)
C. God's Second Speech (40:6—41:34)
D. Job's Second Response (42:1–6)

VIII. The Epilogue (42:7–17)

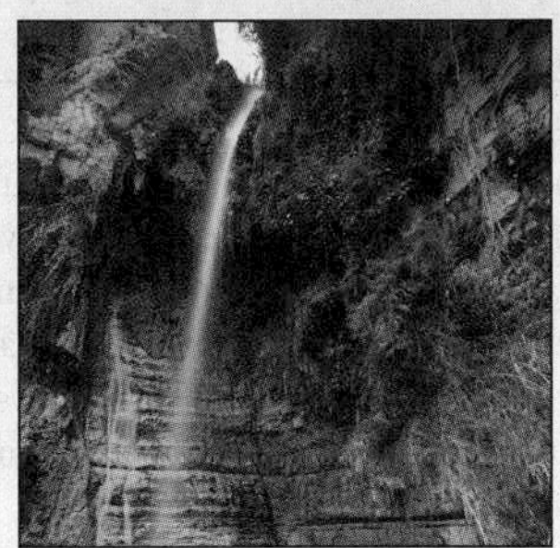

JOB

Prologue

1 In the land of Uz[a] there lived a man whose name was Job.[b] This man was blameless[c] and upright;
he feared God[d] and shunned evil. [2]He had seven sons and three daughters,[e] [3]and he owned seven
thousand sheep, three thousand camels, five hundred yoke of oxen and five hundred donkeys, and had
a large number of servants. He was the greatest man[f] among all the people of the East.
[4]His sons used to hold feasts in their homes on their birthdays, and they would invite their three
sisters to eat and drink with them. [5]When a period of feasting had run its course, Job would make arrangements for them to be purified. Early in the morning he would sacrifice a burnt offering[g] for each
of them, thinking, "Perhaps my children have sinned[h] and cursed God[i] in their hearts." This was Job's
regular custom.
[6]One day the angels[a][j] came to present themselves before the LORD, and Satan[b] also came with them.[k]
[7]The LORD said to Satan, "Where have you come from?"

[a] 6 Hebrew *the sons of God* [b] 6 Hebrew *satan* means *adversary.*

1:1 [a] Jer 25:20 [b] Eze 14:14,20; Jas 5:11 [c] Ge 6:9; 17:1 [d] Ge 22:12; Ex 18:21
1:2 [e] Job 42:13
1:3 [f] Job 29:25
1:5 [g] Ge 8:20; Job 42:8 [h] Job 8:4 [i] 1Ki 21:10,13
1:6 [j] Job 38:7 [k] Job 2:1

1:1—2:13 *The Prologue.* This prose account of Job's tragic life is composed of seven scenes: (1) Job's devotion to God (1:1–3); (2) Job's devotion to his family (1:4–5); (3) the first test of Job proposed (1:6–12); (4) the first test executed, and Job's response (1:13–22); (5) the second test of Job proposed (2:1–6); (6) the second test executed and Job's response (2:7–10); (7) introduction of Job's friends (2:11–13).
1:1–5 *The Main Character Introduced.* This brief introduction describes Job in terms of his geographic location, his devotion to God and family, and his wealth.
1:1 land of Uz. Perhaps two locations are possible: (1) Edom (Jer 25:20–21; Lam 4:21) seems preferable, or (2) in the north in Hauran (see Gen 10:23). **Job.** Cognates of the name Job appear in literature of the patriarchal period, which suggests we may believe Job was a real person, not merely a literary invention. Job, Noah, and Daniel are said to constitute the three most righteous men of all time (Ezek 14:14,20). Two pairs of virtues describe Job's religious devotion: (1) **blameless and upright.** Having personal integrity and acting justly; this does not means Job was sinless, for he admits he has sinned (7:21). (2) **feared God and shunned evil.** Having a genuine devotion toward God and avoiding evil deeds (28:28), virtues that characterize the wise individual in wisdom literature (Prov 1:7; 9:10).
1:2–3 Describes Job's family, livestock, and servants for two reasons: (1) to enhance the portrait of Job's greatness and (2) to prepare the reader for the upcoming tragedy that will destroy both Job's family and cattle. In patriarchal times people measured wealth in terms of livestock (Gen 30:43).
1:2 seven sons and three daughters. The numbers seven and three indicate the completeness of Job's blessing of children.
1:3 five hundred yoke of oxen. Equals 1,000 oxen since a "yoke" of oxen is two oxen, suggesting Job was involved in agriculture. **people of the East.** People east of the Jordan.
1:5 he would sacrifice. As spiritual leader of his family, Job acted in a priestly role (also a patriarchal practice, Gen 15:9–10) by offering "a burnt offering for each of them" after their festive occasions. These were "whole burnt offerings" (Deut 33:10), which were totally consumed by fire (see Lev 1 and note on Lev 1:9) and atoned for sin in general (see note on Lev 1:3–17), whereas sin offerings (see Lev 4 and note on Lev 4:1—5:13) atoned for individual sins. **cursed God.** Lit. "blessed God," a euphemism, since to have the words "cursed" and "God" in the same sentence seemed inappropriate (cf. v. 11; 2:5,9; 1 Kgs 21:10,13).
1:6–22 *Job's First Test Executed and Job's Response.* The Lord himself initiates the first test to show that Job serves God with no ulterior motive (v. 9). After Job loses everything of value in four successive tragedies on a single day, he blesses God for his sovereign care, not even mentioning his own losses (v. 21).
1:6 angels. See NIV text note. They came before the Lord to give an account of their activities. **the LORD.** The covenant name for God (Yahweh = LORD); occurs in the prologue and epilogue but not in the dialogue. **Satan also came with them.** Sets "Satan" (meaning "the adversary" or "the accuser") off from the others. In Hebrew the definite article is used ("the satan"), suggesting that it is a title rather than a personal name (see Zech 3:1 and note). In 1 Chr 21:1 the article is not used since "Satan" had become a proper name for the adversary by that time. **going back and forth on it.** After the Lord initiates the conversation, Satan reports that he has been searching the earth to see if there is anyone who fears God "for nothing" (v. 9), i.e., with no ulterior motive.

1:7 [l]1Pe 5:8
1:8 [m]Jos 1:7; Job 42:7-8 [n]ver 1
1:9 [o]1Ti 6:5
1:10 [p]Ps 34:7 [q]ver 3; Job 29:6; 31:25; Ps 128:1-2
1:11 [r]Job 19:21 [s]Job 2:5
1:15 [t]Ge 10:7; Job 6:19
1:16 [u]Ge 19:24 [v]Lev 10:2; Nu 11:1-3
1:17 [w]Ge 11:28,31

Satan answered the LORD, "From roaming throughout the earth, going back and forth on it."[l]
8 Then the LORD said to Satan, "Have you considered my servant Job?[m] There is no one on earth like
him; he is blameless and upright, a man who fears God and shuns evil."[n]
9 "Does Job fear God for nothing?"[o] Satan replied. 10 "Have you not put a hedge around him and his
household and everything he has?[p] You have blessed the work of his hands, so that his flocks and herds
are spread throughout the land.[q] 11 But now stretch out your hand and strike everything he has,[r] and
he will surely curse you to your face."[s]
12 The LORD said to Satan, "Very well, then, everything he has is in your power, but on the man himself do not lay a finger."
Then Satan went out from the presence of the LORD.
13 One day when Job's sons and daughters were feasting and drinking wine at the oldest brother's
house, 14 a messenger came to Job and said, "The oxen were plowing and the donkeys were grazing
nearby, 15 and the Sabeans[t] attacked and made off with them. They put the servants to the sword, and I
am the only one who has escaped to tell you!"
16 While he was still speaking, another messenger came and said, "The fire of God fell from the heavens[u] and burned up the sheep and the servants,[v] and I am the only one who has escaped to tell you!"
17 While he was still speaking, another messenger came and said, "The Chaldeans[w] formed three

1:8 There is no one on earth like him. The Lord presents Job as the exemplar of righteousness. This corroborates the portrait of Job in vv. 1–3, this time in the Lord's own words, using the same two pairs of virtues (see v. 1 and note). See also 28:28.
1:9 Satan's thorough search has not missed Job, the one challenge to Satan's assumption that no one serves God without selfish motives.
1:10 hedge. Implies a hedge of thorns to keep marauders away; Satan has observed God's protection of Job and his household.
1:11 Satan (v. 6) assumes that if God takes away Job's family and property, Job will "curse" (lit. "bless"; see note on v. 5) God. That Satan had to request permission to harm Job is testimony to God's sovereign rule of the world—here Job's personal world, elsewhere in Scripture the universe God created (Ps 2; Phil 2:9–11; Heb 1:3–4).
1:12 on the man himself. The protective "hedge" (see v. 10 and note) is removed except for Job's person.
1:13–22 Each disaster is reported by a "messenger" (v. 14), who is the only one to escape. The overlapping literary effect of the messages intensifies the emotional effect: "While he was still speaking, [yet] another messenger came" (vv. 16,17,18). Job himself receives the messenger. In keeping with the divine directive of v. 12, in this first test Job loses his livestock and servants (vv. 13–15), sheep and servants (v. 16), camels and servants (v. 17), and children (v. 18–19).
1:13 Probably a birthday celebration (see v. 4), interrupted by the bad news, making it all the more painful.
1:15 Sabeans. A distant tribe (Jer 6:20) from Sheba, probably located in present-day Yemen (see note on 1 Kgs 10:1). In the patriarchal era (the story's time frame), they might still have been a roaming tribe.
1:16 fire of God. Lightning.
1:17 Chaldeans. Early tribal marauders (like the Sabeans; v. 15). Later they took control of Babylon and built a powerful empire that eventually destroyed Judah in 586 BC.

Quneitra, Syria, (Hauran—a possible location of Uz) viewed from Mount Bental.
Todd Bolen/www.BiblePlaces.com

Flocks captured from the Arabs by the armies of Tiglath-Pileser III. Job's wealth is indicated by his many flocks (Job 1:3).
Kim Walton, taken at the British Museum

raiding parties and swept down on your camels and made off with them. They put the servants to the
sword, and I am the only one who has escaped to tell you!"
18 While he was still speaking, yet another messenger came and said, "Your sons and daughters were
feasting and drinking wine at the oldest brother's house, 19 when suddenly a mighty wind[x] swept in from
the desert and struck the four corners of the house. It collapsed on them and they are dead, and I am
the only one who has escaped to tell you!"
20 At this, Job got up and tore his robe[y] and shaved his head. Then he fell to the ground in worship[z]
21 and said:

> "Naked I came from my mother's womb,
> and naked I will depart.[a][a]
> The LORD gave and the LORD has taken away;[b]
> may the name of the LORD be praised."[c]

22 In all this, Job did not sin by charging God with wrongdoing.[d]

2 On another day the angels[b] came to present themselves before the LORD, and Satan also came
with them[e] to present himself before him. 2 And the LORD said to Satan, "Where have you come
from?"
Satan answered the LORD, "From roaming throughout the earth, going back and forth on it."

[a] 21 Or *will return there* [b] 1 Hebrew *the sons of God*

1:19 [x] Jer 4:11; 13:24
1:20 [y] Ge 37:29 [z] 1Pe 5:6
1:21 [a] Ecc 5:15; 1Ti 6:7 [b] 1Sa 2:7 [c] Job 2:10; Eph 5:20; 1Th 5:18
1:22 [d] Job 2:10
2:1 [e] Job 1:6

1:19 mighty wind. More than the east wind from the desert; a violent storm.
1:20 tore his robe and shaved his head. Signs of mourning (Isa 22:12; Jer 7:29). **fell to the ground in worship.** Prostrated himself, signifying humility in God's presence.
1:21 Job's two aphorisms acknowledge that (1) Job had nothing when he came into the world and will take nothing out of it, and (2) God is the source of all his possessions. Job acknowledges God's sovereign hand even in times of calamity.
1:22 Confirms the Lord's assessment of Job's religious devotion (v. 8) but also distinguishes this portrait of Job from the one we see of him in the coming dialogue.
2:1–10 *Job's Second Test Executed and Job's Response.* The text does not explicitly state that Satan expedites the tragedies in the first test (though we must assume it), but it does explicitly state that Satan afflicts Job with painful sores in this second test, which also includes the taunting by his wife (vv. 9–10a). Again Job passes the test. At the end of the first test, Job did not charge God with "wrongdoing" (1:22), and at the end of the second test, Job "did not sin in what he said" (v. 10b)—these are essentially two ways of saying the same thing. This is a supreme affirmation of Job's trust in God; in the dialogue Job reaffirms this faith (13:15; 16:19; 23:10). Cf. Rom 8:18.
2:1–6 The second heavenly scene is almost a duplicate of the first, with the Lord's significant commendation in v. 3b and Satan's challenge in v. 4. Now that Job has passed the first test and proven Satan wrong, the follow-up is the claim that Job will give anything to save his own life

2:3 [f] Job 1:1,8 [g] Job 27:6 [h] Job 9:17
2:5 [i] Job 19:20 [j] Job 1:11
2:6 [k] Job 1:12
2:7 [l] Dt 28:35; Job 7:5
2:8 [m] Job 42:6; Jer 6:26; Eze 27:30; Mt 11:21
2:10 [n] Job 1:21 [o] Job 1:22; Ps 39:1; Jas 1:12; 5:11
2:11 [p] Ge 36:11; Jer 49:7 [q] Ge 25:2 [r] Job 42:11; Ro 12:15
2:12 [s] Jos 7:6; Ne 9:1; La 2:10; Eze 27:30
2:13 [t] Ge 50:10; Eze 3:15
3:3 [u] Job 10:18-19; Jer 20:14-18

3Then the LORD said to Satan, "Have you considered my servant Job? There is no one on earth like him; he is blameless and upright, a man who fears God and shuns evil.[f] And he still maintains his integrity,[g] though you incited me against him to ruin him without any reason."[h]

4"Skin for skin!" Satan replied. "A man will give all he has for his own life. 5But now stretch out your hand and strike his flesh and bones,[i] and he will surely curse you to your face."[j]

6The LORD said to Satan, "Very well, then, he is in your hands; but you must spare his life."[k]

7So Satan went out from the presence of the LORD and afflicted Job with painful sores from the soles of his feet to the crown of his head.[l] 8Then Job took a piece of broken pottery and scraped himself with it as he sat among the ashes.[m]

9His wife said to him, "Are you still maintaining your integrity? Curse God and die!"

10He replied, "You are talking like a foolish[a] woman. Shall we accept good from God, and not trouble?"[n]

In all this, Job did not sin in what he said.[o]

11When Job's three friends, Eliphaz the Temanite,[p] Bildad the Shuhite[q] and Zophar the Naamathite, heard about all the troubles that had come upon him, they set out from their homes and met together by agreement to go and sympathize with him and comfort him.[r] 12When they saw him from a distance, they could hardly recognize him; they began to weep aloud, and they tore their robes and sprinkled dust on their heads.[s] 13Then they sat on the ground with him for seven days and seven nights.[t] No one said a word to him, because they saw how great his suffering was.

Job Speaks

3 After this, Job opened his mouth and cursed the day of his birth. 2He said:

3"May the day of my birth perish,
and the night that said, 'A boy is conceived!'[u]

[a] *10* The Hebrew word rendered *foolish* denotes moral deficiency.

(v. 4). In each test the Lord has a reservation: In the first test Satan must not harm Job's person; in the second test Satan must spare Job's life, though Job's person is now vulnerable.
2:1 Like 1:6 but adds that Satan comes "to present himself before [the LORD]."
2:3 he still maintains his integrity. God recognizes the result of the first test. **you incited me against him.** God impugns Satan's motives. While God cannot be incited to do things against his will, the fact that God asked Satan if he had considered his servant Job implies that the testing was part of the divine plan.
2:4 Skin for skin! A cryptic proverb perhaps equivalent to our expression "quid pro quo." **A man will give all he has for his own life.** A second proverb that probably illuminates the meaning of the first proverb. Satan may be alleging that Job would give another person's skin to save his own.
2:6 God prohibits Satan from taking Job's life; i.e., God has not fully removed the hedge he built around Job (see 1:10 and note).
2:7 painful sores. Possibilities include leprosy and boils. The term is used of skin diseases in general in Deut 28:27.
2:8 scraped himself. Either to provide some relief from the malady or to lacerate his body as a sign of grief.
2:9–10 Job's wife assumes the role of temptress and delivers to Job Satan's threat that Job would curse God (v. 5b), but Job proves himself worthy of God's faith in him.
2:11–13 *Job's Three Friends.* Upon hearing of Job's plight, his three friends plan to rendezvous and travel together to comfort him. The first two friends have connections, at least in name, to patriarchal figures.
2:11 Eliphaz. Means "my God is fine gold" or "my God is strength." In the patriarchal period, Esau's firstborn son is named Eliphaz (Gen 36:15) and comes from Teman, a region of Edom (Jer 49:7), which correlates with Job's own Edomite origin. **Bildad.** Meaning uncertain. He is a "Shuhite," which connects him by name to Shuah, the son of Abraham and Keturah (Gen 25:2). **Zophar.** Means "young bird." The name occurs only in Job. He is a "Naamathite," which indirectly connects him to the sister of Tubal-Cain (Gen 4:22). Since Job's reputation was known throughout the East (1:3), it would not be surprising for his friends to be distantly located. **met together by agreement.** May imply that the three friends came from different regions. Their purpose, however, was the same: to "comfort" Job.
2:12 could hardly recognize him. Most likely because his suffering took a heavy toll on his physical appearance (cf. Isa 52:14; 53:3). **weep aloud ... tore their robes and sprinkled dust on their heads.** Rites of mourning (Josh 7:6). Their apparent affection for their friend forms a baseline of friendship that the reader must take into account as the dialogue unfolds.
2:13 seven days. Customary period of mourning for a dead person (Gen 50:10). **No one said a word to him.** Mourners customarily did not speak until the sufferer spoke.
3:1–26 *Job's Lament.* Satan's challenge is that if God took away Job's property and health, Job would curse God to his face (1:11; 2:5). Yet when Job speaks, his lament contains (1) a curse of his birth (vv. 3a, 4,5,11–19), (2) a curse of the night of his conception (vv. 3b,6,10), and (3) expressions of mourning about life in general (vv. 20–26). This sets the tone for the dialogue. Job is disoriented due to his indescribable emotional and physical suffering.
3:1 After this. After the seven days of silence. **day of his birth.** See 1:4.
3:2 He said. A shortened form of the Hebrew formulaic introduction to all of Job's speeches: "And Job answered and said" (NIV "Job replied"; see 6:1; 9:1; 12:1; 16:1; 19:1; 21:1; 23:1; 26:1). The exceptions are 27:1 and 29:1, which read "Job continued his discourse."
3:3 night. Perhaps evokes the negative imagery of Gen 1; its variants intensify the negative implications of Job's birth (vv. 4,5,6,7,9). **A boy**

[4] That day — may it turn to darkness;
may God above not care about it;
may no light shine on it.
[5] May gloom and utter darkness[v] claim it once more;
may a cloud settle over it;
may blackness overwhelm it.
[6] That night — may thick darkness[w] seize it;
may it not be included among the days of the year
nor be entered in any of the months.
[7] May that night be barren;
may no shout of joy be heard in it.
[8] May those who curse days[a] curse that day,
those who are ready to rouse Leviathan.[x]
[9] May its morning stars become dark;
may it wait for daylight in vain
and not see the first rays of dawn,[y]
[10] for it did not shut the doors of the womb on me
to hide trouble from my eyes.

[11] "Why did I not perish at birth,
and die as I came from the womb?[z]
[12] Why were there knees to receive me[a]
and breasts that I might be nursed?
[13] For now I would be lying down[b] in peace;
I would be asleep and at rest[c]
[14] with kings and rulers of the earth,[d]
who built for themselves places now lying in ruins,[e]
[15] with princes[f] who had gold,
who filled their houses with silver.[g]
[16] Or why was I not hidden away in the ground like a stillborn
child,[h]
like an infant who never saw the light of day?
[17] There the wicked cease from turmoil,
and there the weary are at rest.[i]
[18] Captives also enjoy their ease;
they no longer hear the slave driver's shout.[j]
[19] The small and the great are there,
and the slaves are freed from their owners.

[20] "Why is light given to those in misery,
and life to the bitter of soul,[k]

3:5 [v] Job 10:21,22; Ps 23:4; Jer 2:6; 13:16
3:6 [w] Job 23:17
3:8 [x] Job 41:1,8,10,25
3:9 [y] Job 41:18
3:11 [z] Job 10:18
3:12 [a] Ge 30:3; Isa 66:12
3:13 [b] Job 17:13 [c] Job 7:8-10,21, 10:22; 14:10-12; 19:27; 21:13,23
3:14 [d] Job 12:17 [e] Job 15:28
3:15 [f] Job 12:21 [g] Job 27:17
3:16 [h] Ps 58:8; Ecc 6:3
3:17 [i] Job 17:16
3:18 [j] Job 39:7
3:20 [k] 1Sa 1:10; Jer 20:18; Eze 27:30-31

[a] 8 Or *curse the sea*

is conceived! Announcement of Job's birth is made by "the night" personified.
3:8 those who curse days. Professional magicians like Balaam (Num 22–24). **Leviathan.** See 41:1–10.
3:9 morning stars. Venus and Mercury; their appearance would have hailed the day of Job's birth.
3:12 knees. May be those of the father, who received the child after birth (Gen 50:23); in Gen 30:3 they are those of the barren woman, who welcomed a surrogate's child as her own. Job questions not only why his father was there to receive him but also why his mother survived the birth to nurse him.
3:13–15 Had Job not survived at birth, he would have joined the kings and princes of history who were lying in their graves "asleep and at rest" (v. 13).
3:16 Job asks why he was not stillborn.
3:17 There … there. Alludes to death and those who are "asleep and at rest" (v. 13). In Job's mind that would have been a great improvement to this world.
3:19 slaves are freed from their owners. Suggests the author has a negative view of slavery. See also note on 31:13–15.
3:20–26 Job moves from the thought of death at birth to question why "those in misery" (v. 20) and "the bitter of soul" (v. 20) are still living. Though he longs for death and searches for it "more than for hidden treasure" (v. 21), it escapes him. But he will rejoice when it finally comes. His intense mourning is continual (v. 24).

3:21 [l]Rev 9:6 [m]Pr 2:4
3:23 [n]Job 19:6,8,12; Ps 88:8; La 3:7
3:24 [o]Job 6:7; 33:20 [p]Ps 42:3,4
3:25 [q]Job 30:15
3:26 [r]Job 7:4,14
4:2 [s]Job 32:20
4:3 [t]Isa 35:3; Heb 12:12
4:4 [u]Isa 35:3; Heb 12:12
4:5 [v]Job 19:21 [w]Job 6:14
4:6 [x]Pr 3:26 [y]Job 1:1
4:7 [z]Job 36:7 [a]Job 8:20; Ps 37:25
4:8 [b]Job 15:35 [c]Pr 22:8; Hos 10:13; Gal 6:7-8
4:9 [d]Job 15:30; Isa 30:33; 2Th 2:8 [e]Job 40:13
4:10 [f]Job 5:15; Ps 58:6

21 to those who long for death that does not come,[l]
who search for it more than for hidden treasure,[m]
22 who are filled with gladness
and rejoice when they reach the grave?
23 Why is life given to a man
whose way is hidden,
whom God has hedged in?[n]
24 For sighing has become my daily food;[o]
my groans pour out like water.[p]
25 What I feared has come upon me;
what I dreaded[q] has happened to me.
26 I have no peace, no quietness;
I have no rest,[r] but only turmoil."

Eliphaz

4 Then Eliphaz the Temanite replied:

2 "If someone ventures a word with you, will you be impatient?
But who can keep from speaking?[s]
3 Think how you have instructed many,
how you have strengthened feeble hands.[t]
4 Your words have supported those who stumbled;
you have strengthened faltering knees.[u]
5 But now trouble comes to you, and you are discouraged;
it strikes[v] you, and you are dismayed.[w]
6 Should not your piety be your confidence[x]
and your blameless[y] ways your hope?

7 "Consider now: Who, being innocent, has ever perished?[z]
Where were the upright ever destroyed?[a]
8 As I have observed, those who plow evil[b]
and those who sow trouble reap it.[c]
9 At the breath of God[d] they perish;
at the blast of his anger they are no more.[e]
10 The lions may roar and growl,
yet the teeth of the great lions are broken.[f]

3:23 whom God has hedged in. Dramatic irony, a literary device that gives the reader information the characters of the story do not have (1:10). Job perceives that God has hedged him in for a sinister rather than a benevolent purpose. Job misinterprets God's purposes or is at least perplexed about them—a common motif in the dialogue.

4:1—27:23 *The Dialogue.* The friends speak in order of age and probably with regard to the weight of their arguments. Eliphaz's three speeches are the longest and presumably the weightiest; Bildad's three speeches are shorter and theologically lighter; Zophar speaks only twice, and his arguments are a bit more confused.

4:1—14:22 *The Dialogue: Cycle One.* A developing cycle of blame becomes evident: Eliphaz gently accuses Job of sinning; Bildad hastens to accuse Job of perverting God's justice; Zophar insensitively claims that God has exacted of Job less than Job's guilt deserves. Job, on the other hand, claims that he has done nothing wrong and is being treated unjustly by his three friends and by God, and that there is no mediator between him and God.

4:1—5:27 *First Exchange: Eliphaz.* Eliphaz articulates the basic thesis of the friends: an innocent person does not suffer (4:7–9). Then he goes on to suggest, quite positively, that the purpose of suffering is to put the offender back on the right road (5:17).

4:2 impatient. Though accusing Job of impatience, it is Eliphaz who is impatient with Job's negative perspective on life ("But who can keep from speaking?").

4:3–6 Eliphaz concedes that Job's conduct has been exemplary, but this concession is brief; otherwise his allegations of Job's impatience and lack of righteousness would not stand.

4:4–5 Eliphaz accuses Job of not taking his own advice.

4:7 While Job did not claim innocence in his lament (ch. 3), Eliphaz understands Job's lament that way and replies to it as such. In the dialogue, the friends often read between the lines of Job's speeches. The argument that the innocent do not suffer is impaired by Eliphaz's insistence that there are no exceptions. Yet, sometimes the innocent *do* suffer. **Consider now.** Or "remember," implying that Job already knew these things.

4:8 The principle of v. 7 (the innocent do not suffer) is considered from another angle: you reap what you sow (cf. Gal 6:7–8), a metaphor appropriate for Job, a farmer with 1,000 oxen (see note on 1:3).

4:9 God punishes the wicked and destroys them, a veiled threat to Job.

4:10 broken. The Hebrew for this word occurs only here in the OT; its meaning is inferred from the reference to lions' teeth, which are incapable of taking prey (v. 11).

[11]The lion perishes for lack of prey,[g]
and the cubs of the lioness are scattered.

[12]"A word was secretly brought to me,
my ears caught a whisper[h] of it.[i]
[13]Amid disquieting dreams in the night,
when deep sleep falls on people,[j]
[14]fear and trembling seized me
and made all my bones shake.[k]
[15]A spirit glided past my face,
and the hair on my body stood on end.
[16]It stopped,
but I could not tell what it was.
A form stood before my eyes,
and I heard a hushed voice:
[17]'Can a mortal be more righteous than God?[l]
Can even a strong man be more pure than his Maker?[m]
[18]If God places no trust in his servants,
if he charges his angels with error,[n]
[19]how much more those who live in houses of clay,[o]
whose foundations[p] are in the dust,[q]
who are crushed more readily than a moth!
[20]Between dawn and dusk they are broken to pieces;
unnoticed, they perish forever.[r]
[21]Are not the cords of their tent pulled up,[s]
so that they die without wisdom?'[t]

5 "Call if you will, but who will answer you?
To which of the holy ones[u] will you turn?
[2]Resentment kills a fool,
and envy slays the simple.[v]
[3]I myself have seen a fool taking root,[w]
but suddenly his house was cursed.[x]
[4]His children are far from safety,[y]
crushed in court[z] without a defender.
[5]The hungry consume his harvest,[a]
taking it even from among thorns,
and the thirsty pant after his wealth.
[6]For hardship does not spring from the soil,
nor does trouble sprout from the ground.

4:11 [g]Job 27:14; Ps 34:10
4:12 [h]Job 26:14 [i]Job 33:14
4:13 [j]Job 33:15
4:14 [k]Jer 23:9; Hab 3:16
4:17 [l]Job 9:2 [m]Job 35:10
4:18 [n]Job 15:15
4:19 [o]Job 10:9 [p]Job 22:16 [q]Ge 2:7
4:20 [r]Job 14:2,20; 20:7; Ps 90:5-6
4:21 [s]Job 8:22 [t]Job 18:21; 36:12
5:1 [u]Job 15:15
5:2 [v]Pr 12:16
5:3 [w]Ps 37:35; Jer 12:2 [x]Job 24:18
5:4 [y]Job 4:11 [z]Am 5:12
5:5 [a]Job 18:8-10

4:12–21 Eliphaz relates a terrifying dream he takes as an expression of truth. The thrust is that if God charges his angels with error, how much more so will he charge human beings (vv. 18–19).
4:17 Job did not claim to be "more righteous than God" (perhaps a bit of sarcasm), but Eliphaz infers this from Job's lament. Eliphaz, by sharing his "revelation," hopes to put the pronouncement beyond question.
4:19 crushed more readily than a moth! Moths are easy to catch and crush; humans, even easier.
4:20–21 The people who "live in houses of clay" (v. 19) are human beings (as opposed to angels, v. 18). Eliphaz stressed the weakness and moral vulnerability of mere humans; in speaking up for himself, Job casts his understanding of human beings in a broader moral vision. Here the friends make many insinuations about Job. None of the friends, however, even when speaking in the second person, use Job's name, except the young, presumptuous Elihu (chs. 32–37).
4:21 cords of their tent pulled up. A metaphor for death.
5:1 holy ones. A carryover from God's "servants"/"angels" (4:18). Eliphaz claims, as does Job also at first (9:33), that there are no heavenly beings to whom one may appeal—a thought Eliphaz repeats in 15:15. This probably alludes to the "sons of God" in chs. 1–2 (see note on 1:6), but Eliphaz knows nothing about them, only the angels of his dream.
5:2 Most likely a proverb Eliphaz uses to advise Job that overvexing himself about his troubles will get him nowhere.
5:3–5 Implies Eliphaz considers Job a "fool." Eliphaz uses the emphatic personal pronoun ("I myself") in v. 3 to shift attention to his personal experience.
5:3 his house was cursed. The loss of Job's family may be the backdrop of vv. 4–5. Eliphaz is more subtle in his references to Job's tragic loss than is Bildad (8:4).

5:7 [b] Job 14:1
5:8 [c] Ps 35:23; 50:15
5:9 [d] Job 42:3; Ps 40:5
5:10 [e] Job 36:28
5:11 [f] Ps 113:7-8
5:12 [g] Ne 4:15; Ps 33:10
5:13 [h] 1Co 3:19*
5:14 [i] Job 12:25 [j] Dt 28:29
5:15 [k] Ps 35:10 [l] Job 4:10
5:16 [m] Ps 107:42
5:17 [n] Jas 1:12 [o] Ps 94:12; Pr 3:11 [p] Heb 12:5-11
5:18 [q] Isa 30:26 [r] 1Sa 2:6
5:19 [s] Ps 34:19; 91:10
5:20 [t] Ps 33:19 [u] Ps 144:10
5:21 [v] Ps 31:20 [w] Ps 91:5
5:22 [x] Ps 91:13; Eze 34:25
5:23 [y] Ps 91:12 [z] Isa 11:6-9
5:24 [a] Job 8:6

7 Yet man is born to trouble[b]
as surely as sparks fly upward.

8 "But if I were you, I would appeal to God;
I would lay my cause before him.[c]
9 He performs wonders that cannot be fathomed,[d]
miracles that cannot be counted.
10 He provides rain for the earth;
he sends water on the countryside.[e]
11 The lowly he sets on high,[f]
and those who mourn are lifted to safety.
12 He thwarts the plans[g] of the crafty,
so that their hands achieve no success.
13 He catches the wise in their craftiness,[h]
and the schemes of the wily are swept away.
14 Darkness[i] comes upon them in the daytime;
at noon they grope as in the night.[j]
15 He saves the needy[k] from the sword in their mouth;
he saves them from the clutches of the powerful.[l]
16 So the poor have hope,
and injustice shuts its mouth.[m]

17 "Blessed is the one whom God corrects;[n]
so do not despise the discipline[o] of the Almighty.[a][p]
18 For he wounds, but he also binds up;[q]
he injures, but his hands also heal.[r]
19 From six calamities he will rescue you;
in seven no harm will touch you.[s]
20 In famine[t] he will deliver you from death,
and in battle from the stroke of the sword.[u]
21 You will be protected from the lash of the tongue,[v]
and need not fear[w] when destruction comes.
22 You will laugh at destruction and famine,
and need not fear the wild animals.[x]
23 For you will have a covenant with the stones[y] of the field,
and the wild animals will be at peace with you.[z]
24 You will know that your tent is secure;
you will take stock of your property and find nothing
missing.[a]

[a] *17* Hebrew *Shaddai*; here and throughout Job

5:7 Another proverb (cf. v. 2) that acknowledges suffering to be part of the human experience—so why be so upset about it!
5:8–27 Admitting that trouble is inevitable, Eliphaz still exhorts Job to seek God, whose work is overwhelming, providential, mysterious, avenging, impeding, and saving—all packaged together. Who can sort it out? But this much is clear: "Blessed ["happy" or "approved by God"] is the one whom God corrects" (v. 17). Eliphaz only suggests this disciplinary explanation for suffering, which God uses to turn the offender back on to the right track (cf. Prov 3:11–12), but Elihu further develops it (33:14–17; 37:13). This part of the speech contains several allusions to Job's personal tragedy: "the sword" (vv. 15,20), "destruction" (vv. 21,22), "your property" (v. 24), "your children" (v. 25).
5:13 Quoted in 1 Cor 3:19 to warn those pretending to be wise that God honors no such pretense but "catches the wise in their craftiness."
5:17 discipline. Implies preventive rather than punitive action (36:10). **Almighty.** Hebrew *šadday*; a name used for God in the patriarchal era (e.g., Gen 17:1); most of its occurrences are in Job, perhaps suggesting the age of the book or the author's retrogression of the story into the patriarchal era. Its etymology is obscure.
5:18 he wounds, but he also binds up. Admission that God does allow harm to his children, but he also heals them (cf. Hos 6:1).
5:19 From six calamities ... in seven. God is a rescuing God. The numbers are poetic and not to be taken as exact.
5:24 find ... missing. One of the basic Hebrew root words for "to sin" (*ḥṭ'*); it means "miss the mark" and is used of an old man who yet fails to reach his full quota of years (Isa 65:20) and of missing the path in haste (Prov 19:2). The metaphor is painful for Job since he has lost everything.

[25] You will know that your children will be many,[b]
and your descendants like the grass of the earth.[c]
[26] You will come to the grave in full vigor,[d]
like sheaves gathered in season.

[27] "We have examined this, and it is true.
So hear it and apply it to yourself."

Job

6 Then Job replied:

[2] "If only my anguish could be weighed
and all my misery be placed on the scales![e]
[3] It would surely outweigh the sand[f] of the seas—
no wonder my words have been impetuous.[g]
[4] The arrows[h] of the Almighty are in me,[i]
my spirit drinks[j] in their poison;
God's terrors[k] are marshaled against me.[l]
[5] Does a wild donkey bray when it has grass,
or an ox bellow when it has fodder?
[6] Is tasteless food eaten without salt,
or is there flavor in the sap of the mallow[a]?
[7] I refuse to touch it;
such food makes me ill.[m]

[8] "Oh, that I might have my request,
that God would grant what I hope for,[n]
[9] that God would be willing to crush me,
to let loose his hand and cut off my life![o]
[10] Then I would still have this consolation—
my joy in unrelenting pain—
that I had not denied the words[p] of the Holy One.[q]

[11] "What strength do I have, that I should still hope?
What prospects, that I should be patient?[r]
[12] Do I have the strength of stone?
Is my flesh bronze?
[13] Do I have any power to help myself,[s]
now that success has been driven from me?

5:25 [b] Ps 112:2 [c] Ps 72:16; Isa 44:3-4
5:26 [d] Ge 15:15
6:2 [e] Job 31:6
6:3 [f] Pr 27:3 [g] Job 23:2
6:4 [h] Ps 38:2 [i] Job 16:12, 13 [j] Job 21:20 [k] Job 30:15 [l] Ps 88:15-18
6:7 [m] Job 3:24
6:8 [n] Job 14:13
6:9 [o] Nu 11:15; 1Ki 19:4
6:10 [p] Job 22:22; 23:12 [q] Lev 19:2; Isa 57:15
6:11 [r] Job 21:4
6:13 [s] Job 26:2

[a] *6* The meaning of the Hebrew for this phrase is uncertain.

5:27 Eliphaz gives the knife in Job's heart one more twist: he demands that Job listen and apply this lesson to himself.

6:1—7:21 *Job's Response to Eliphaz.* Job retorts that his complaint is not baseless—there is a reason for it! One of Job's basic allegations: God has caused his suffering (6:4). Further, Job makes explicit what Eliphaz perceived as implicit: Job claims to be innocent (6:28–30). This speech reveals Job's emotional pain (6:2–3) as well as his physical suffering (7:5; see 19:20; 30:30). As Eliphaz began his first speech somewhat apologetically (4:2a), Job too seems reluctant to engage his friends in debate because he is afraid of what he might say (6:8–10). If God would just "cut off [his] life" (6:9), then he would have the "consolation ... that [he] had not denied the words of the Holy One" (6:10), suggesting perhaps the Lord's assessment of his righteous character in 1:8; 2:3. Job does not know what went on in the heavenly council, but the reader does. At times, as here, Job exhibits an intuitive knowledge that only God and the reader have: apart from any deviations that might follow, Job's initial affirmations of faith (1:21; 2:10) will stand, and God's character assessment of him will continue to be valid.

6:2–3 The reason Job's "words have been impetuous": if weighed, all his misery would be heavier than "the sand of the seas."

6:4 arrows of the Almighty. For God as an archer, see Deut 32:23; Pss 7:13; 38:2; 64:7; Lam 3:12–13; Ezek 5:16. Here his arrows are poisonous (doubly effective).

6:5 Does a wild donkey bray when it has grass ...? A rhetorical question that assumes the answer "yes." So too a human being will cry out when in pain.

6:6–7 tasteless food ... makes me ill. Does not seem to apply to Job's affliction, so it must refer to Eliphaz's argument.

6:8–10 Job wants to die; he hopes God will, like a weaver, "cut off" (v. 9) the thread of his life.

6:11–13 Job, physically and emotionally exhausted, has no strength to continue, which is perhaps an objection to beginning this debate in the first place.

6:15 [t]Ps 38:11; Jer 15:18
6:17 [u]Job 24:19
6:19 [v]Ge 25:15; Isa 21:14
6:20 [w]Jer 14:3
6:21 [x]Ps 38:11
6:24 [y]Ps 39:1
6:25 [z]Ecc 12:11
6:26 [a]Job 8:2; 15:3
6:27 [b]Joel 3:3; Na 3:10; 2Pe 2:3
6:28 [c]Job 27:4; 33:1,3; 36:3,4
6:29 [d]Job 23:7,10; 34:5, 36; 42:6
6:30 [e]Job 27:4 [f]Job 12:11
7:1 [g]Job 14:14; Isa 40:2 [h]Job 5:7 [i]Job 14:6
7:2 [j]Lev 19:13

14 "Anyone who withholds kindness from a friend
forsakes the fear of the Almighty.
15 But my brothers are as undependable as intermittent streams,[t]
as the streams that overflow
16 when darkened by thawing ice
and swollen with melting snow,
17 but that stop flowing in the dry season,
and in the heat[u] vanish from their channels.
18 Caravans turn aside from their routes;
they go off into the wasteland and perish.
19 The caravans of Tema[v] look for water,
the traveling merchants of Sheba look in hope.
20 They are distressed, because they had been confident;
they arrive there, only to be disappointed.[w]
21 Now you too have proved to be of no help;
you see something dreadful and are afraid.[x]
22 Have I ever said, 'Give something on my behalf,
pay a ransom for me from your wealth,
23 deliver me from the hand of the enemy,
rescue me from the clutches of the ruthless'?

24 "Teach me, and I will be quiet;[y]
show me where I have been wrong.
25 How painful are honest words![z]
But what do your arguments prove?
26 Do you mean to correct what I say,
and treat my desperate words as wind?[a]
27 You would even cast lots[b] for the fatherless
and barter away your friend.

28 "But now be so kind as to look at me.
Would I lie to your face?[c]
29 Relent, do not be unjust;
reconsider, for my integrity is at stake.[a][d]
30 Is there any wickedness on my lips?[e]
Can my mouth not discern[f] malice?

7 "Do not mortals have hard service[g] on earth?[h]
Are not their days like those of hired laborers?[i]
2 Like a slave longing for the evening shadows,
or a hired laborer waiting to be paid,[j]

[a] 29 Or *my righteousness still stands*

6:14–30 The "friendship" (see v. 14) represented here has begun to unravel, and Job equates withholding "kindness from a friend" with forsaking "the fear of the Almighty" (v. 14). Like wadis that surge during the rainy season and "stop flowing in the dry season" (v. 17), thereby proving undependable to caravans that seek water but find only dry tributaries (vv. 18–20), Job accuses the friends (using the plural "you," v. 21) of being as false to him as dry wadis are to caravans. Yet Job never asks them for favors (vv. 22–23).

6:21 see ... are afraid. A wordplay: in Hebrew these words sound alike.

6:24–27 Job challenges his friends to correct him, and he "will be quiet" (v. 24). Though Eliphaz has insinuated that Job is being punished for his sin (4:7), Job does not admit it and says, "Show me where I have been wrong" (v. 24). A friendly encounter has become an all-out debate about Job's character and his reaction to the tragic events of his life. But with friends who "would even cast lots for the fatherless" (v. 27), Job is not optimistic about the outcome.

6:28–30 Eliphaz appears to be speaking to Job without looking at him, a mark of respect in ancient Near Eastern culture. But Job demands that his friends "look at" him (v. 28), perhaps to better understand and to see his physical contortions, which are an index to his emotional trauma (7:5–6).

7:1–10 Job's emotional and physical suffering cause an erratic pattern in his speeches. Sometimes he addresses the friend who just spoke or all of the friends; at other times, without warning, he addresses God directly; at still other times, he moves quite unnotice-

[3] so I have been allotted months of futility,
and nights of misery have been assigned to me.[k]
[4] When I lie down I think, 'How long before I get up?'[l]
The night drags on, and I toss and turn until
dawn.
[5] My body is clothed with worms[m] and scabs,
my skin is broken and festering.

[6] "My days are swifter than a weaver's shuttle,[n]
and they come to an end without hope.[o]
[7] Remember, O God, that my life is but a breath;[p]
my eyes will never see happiness again.[q]
[8] The eye that now sees me will see me no longer;
you will look for me, but I will be no more.[r]
[9] As a cloud vanishes and is gone,
so one who goes down to the grave[s] does not
return.[t]
[10] He will never come to his house again;
his place[u] will know him no more.[v]

[11] "Therefore I will not keep silent;[w]
I will speak out in the anguish of my spirit,
I will complain in the bitterness of my soul.[x]
[12] Am I the sea, or the monster of the deep,[y]
that you put me under guard?
[13] When I think my bed will comfort me
and my couch will ease my complaint,[z]
[14] even then you frighten me with dreams
and terrify[a] me with visions,
[15] so that I prefer strangling and death,[b]
rather than this body of mine.
[16] I despise my life;[c] I would not live forever.
Let me alone; my days have no meaning.

[17] "What is mankind that you make so much of them,
that you give them so much attention,[d]
[18] that you examine them every morning
and test them every moment?[e]
[19] Will you never look away from me,
or let me alone even for an instant?[f]
[20] If I have sinned, what have I done to you,[g]
you who see everything we do?

7:3 [k] Job 16:7; Ps 6:6
7:4 [l] Dt 28:67
7:5 [m] Job 17:14; Isa 14:11
7:6 [n] Job 9:25 [o] Job 13:15; 17:11,15
7:7 [p] Ps 78:39; Jas 4:14 [q] Job 9:25
7:8 [r] Job 20:7,9,21
7:9 [s] Job 11:8 [t] 2Sa 12:23; Job 30:15
7:10 [u] Job 27:21,23 [v] Job 8:18
7:11 [w] Ps 40:9 [x] 1Sa 1:10
7:12 [y] Eze 32:2-3
7:13 [z] Job 9:27
7:14 [a] Job 9:34
7:15 [b] 1Ki 19:4
7:16 [c] Job 9:21; 10:1
7:17 [d] Ps 8:4; 144:3; Heb 2:6
7:18 [e] Job 14:3
7:19 [f] Job 9:18
7:20 [g] Job 35:6

ably into a monologue. Here he addresses God (v. 7) and describes his life with metaphors: the hard life of a day laborer (vv. 1b,2b), a slave longing for evening to come (v. 2), the swiftness of a weaver's shuttle (v. 6), a breath (v. 7a), and a vanishing cloud (v. 9). He believes his death is imminent, yet he turns his attention momentarily to the general plight of humankind. Putting his personal tragedy in the larger context of others' suffering shows that Job has begun the arduous journey to healing.

7:2 hired laborer. See Deut 24:15.

7:3 months. A hint of either how long Job's ordeal has been going on or his anticipation of the long ordeal ahead.

7:8 God will look for Job, but Job will not be there for God to use him as a target (v. 20b; 6:4).

7:11–16 Despite his trouble, Job is determined to speak and not keep silent. Why would God frighten him with dreams rather than let sleep provide him with relief from his suffering?

7:17–21 Again, attention is given to the plight of humanity (cf. v. 1). Why are human beings so important to God that he makes such sport of them? Job intuitively recognizes that God is testing him. He again reminds God that he is about to die, so why does God not just pardon his sins and let bygones be bygones (v. 21)?

7:17 A similar question to Ps 8:4 but with a different intent. Ps 8 questions human worth in light of God's marvelous creation; Job asks why man is so important that God would, as it were, use him for target practice—man's not worth it.

7:19 even for an instant. Also can be worded, "till I swallow my spittle." God does not give him time even to swallow before he starts his target practice again.

7:20 [h] Job 16:12
7:21 [i] Job 10:14
[j] Job 10:9; Ps 104:29
8:2 [k] Job 6:26
8:3 [l] Dt 32:4; 2Ch 19:7; Ro 3:5 [m] Ge 18:25
8:4 [n] Job 1:19
8:5 [o] Job 11:13
8:6 [p] Ps 7:6 [q] Job 5:24
8:7 [r] Job 42:12
8:8 [s] Dt 4:32; 32:7; Job 15:18
8:9 [t] Ge 47:9 [u] 1Ch 29:15; Job 7:6
8:12 [v] Ps 129:6; Jer 17:6
8:13 [w] Ps 9:17
[x] Job 11:20; 13:16; 15:34; Pr 10:28
8:14 [y] Isa 59:5

Why have you made me your target?[h]
Have I become a burden to you?[a]
21 Why do you not pardon my offenses
and forgive my sins?[i]
For I will soon lie down in the dust;[j]
you will search for me, but I will be no more."

Bildad

8 Then Bildad the Shuhite replied:

2 "How long will you say such things?
Your words are a blustering wind.[k]
3 Does God pervert justice?[l]
Does the Almighty pervert what is right?[m]
4 When your children sinned against him,
he gave them over to the penalty of their sin.[n]
5 But if you will seek God earnestly
and plead[o] with the Almighty,
6 if you are pure and upright,
even now he will rouse himself on your behalf[p]
and restore you to your prosperous state.[q]
7 Your beginnings will seem humble,
so prosperous[r] will your future be.

8 "Ask the former generation[s]
and find out what their ancestors learned,
9 for we were born only yesterday and know nothing,[t]
and our days on earth are but a shadow.[u]
10 Will they not instruct you and tell you?
Will they not bring forth words from their understanding?
11 Can papyrus grow tall where there is no marsh?
Can reeds thrive without water?
12 While still growing and uncut,
they wither more quickly than grass.[v]
13 Such is the destiny of all who forget God;[w]
so perishes the hope of the godless.[x]
14 What they trust in is fragile[b];
what they rely on is a spider's web.[y]

[a] *20* A few manuscripts of the Masoretic Text, an ancient Hebrew scribal tradition and Septuagint; most manuscripts of the Masoretic Text *I have become a burden to myself.* [b] *14* The meaning of the Hebrew for this word is uncertain.

8:1–22 *Second Exchange: Bildad.* Bildad's speech is much shorter than Eliphaz's, perhaps suggesting declining importance of the arguments as well as his younger age (see note on 4:1—27:23). He confines himself to the third part of Job's speech, the bitter lot of humanity. Bildad, seemingly provoked by Job's accusation of God, defends the Almighty (v. 3) This topic dominates Bildad's whole speech, and he affirms Eliphaz's contention that God does not reject an innocent person (v. 20; 4:7).
8:2 How long will you say such things? Already Bildad is impatient. **blustering wind.** Suggests Job's words are noisy but empty.
8:3 pervert justice. This is not what Job said, but Bildad understands Job's words that way. Job said that God treated him harshly (6:4), thus unjustly.
8:4 Brash and insensitive, Bildad says Job's children got what they deserved.
8:5 seek God earnestly. Cf. Eliphaz's call to repentance (5:8). If Job is "pure and upright" (v. 6), God will take action and restore Job's prosperity.
8:8–10 Bildad insists that reviewing the past will provide answers his generation is unable to give since each generation passes as quickly as a "shadow" (v. 9). The accumulative wisdom of past generations will "instruct" Job (v. 10).
8:11–19 Three illustrations from nature: (1) The papyrus plant, useful for baskets and writing materials, grows in marshy areas, but when the marsh dries up, it withers and is useless; thus is the lot of those who forget God (vv. 11–13). (2) The spider's web gives flimsy support when leaned on; such is the wicked person's hope (vv. 14–15). (3) A plant sends its roots down around stones and secures its place, but when it is pulled up, the garden disowns it and it withers; such is the fate of the wicked (vv. 16–19). These metaphors allude to Job; the last one articulates Job's sense of alienation, which he puts into words in 19:13–19.

[15]They lean on the web,[z] but it gives way;
they cling to it, but it does not hold.[a]
[16]They are like a well-watered plant in the sunshine,
spreading its shoots[b] over the garden;[c]
[17]it entwines its roots around a pile of rocks
and looks for a place among the stones.
[18]But when it is torn from its spot,
that place disowns it and says, 'I never saw you.'[d]
[19]Surely its life withers[e] away,
and[a] from the soil other plants grow.[f]

[20]"Surely God does not reject one who is blameless[g]
or strengthen the hands of evildoers.[h]
[21]He will yet fill your mouth with laughter[i]
and your lips with shouts of joy.[j]
[22]Your enemies will be clothed in shame,[k]
and the tents of the wicked will be no more."[l]

8:15 [z]Job 27:18 [a]Ps 49:11
8:16 [b]Ps 80:11 [c]Ps 37:35; Jer 11:16
8:18 [d]Job 7:8; Ps 37:36
8:19 [e]Job 20:5 [f]Ecc 1:4
8:20 [g]Job 1:1 [h]Job 21:30
8:21 [i]Job 5:22 [j]Ps 126:2; 132:16
8:22 [k]Ps 35:26; 109:29; 132:18 [l]Job 18:6,14,21
9:2 [m]Job 4:17; Ps 143:2; Ro 3:20
9:3 [n]Job 10:2; 40:2
9:4 [o]Job 11:6 [p]Job 36:5 [q]2Ch 13:12
9:5 [r]Mic 1:4
9:6 [s]Isa 2:21; Hag 2:6; Heb 12:26 [t]Job 26:11
9:7 [u]Isa 13:10; Eze 32:8
9:8 [v]Ge 1:6; Ps 104:2-3 [w]Job 38:16; Ps 77:19
9:9 [x]Ge 1:16; Job 38:31; Am 5:8
9:10 [y]Ps 71:15 [z]Job 5:9

Job

9 Then Job replied:

[2]"Indeed, I know that this is true.
But how can mere mortals prove their innocence
before God?[m]
[3]Though they wished to dispute with him,
they could not answer him one time out of a
thousand.[n]
[4]His wisdom[o] is profound, his power is vast.[p]
Who has resisted him and come out unscathed?[q]
[5]He moves mountains without their knowing it
and overturns them in his anger.[r]
[6]He shakes the earth[s] from its place
and makes its pillars tremble.[t]
[7]He speaks to the sun and it does not shine;
he seals off the light of the stars.[u]
[8]He alone stretches out the heavens[v]
and treads on the waves of the sea.[w]
[9]He is the Maker of the Bear[b] and Orion,
the Pleiades and the constellations of the south.[x]
[10]He performs wonders[y] that cannot be fathomed,
miracles that cannot be counted.[z]

Seventh-century BC relief depicting Ashur standing on a composite creature that displays divine symbols: winged disc, star, crescent, and Pleiades (Job 9:9) — the seven small circles.
Kim Walton, taken at the Pergamon Museum, Berlin

[a] 19 Or *Surely all the joy it has / is that* [b] 9 Or *of Leo*

8:20 God does not reject one who is blameless. Based on his earlier admonition (vv. 6–7), Bildad holds out hope that Job will be restored to his former happy condition (vv. 21–22).

9:1—10:22 *Job's Response to Bildad.* Job's second speech responds to both Eliphaz and Bildad, quite characteristic of Job's style. Eliphaz spoke of God's grandeur (5:9), and Job repeats those words (9:10) but says God is elusive to him (9:11). To his credit, Job does not retort—at least not yet—with the same kind of personal impudence as Bildad. At this point Job is more focused on God than his friends, and he raises the objection that a mere human being cannot meet God on his own terms (9:3,32). Moreover, God is all-powerful (9:3–12) but incomprehensible at times (9:22)—at least that is Job's opinion at this stage of the argument. In the absence of a fair hearing before God, Job refutes the idea that there is a mediator who can stand between him and God (9:33). God's problem (mark Job's insolence!) may be that he does not understand how it feels to be human (10:4–7). Job again declares his innocence (10:7).

9:2 I know that this is true. Job acknowledges Bildad's assertion that God is just (8:20–22).

9:9 Job acknowledges God as Creator of the constellations, here identified as the "Bear," "Orion," and "Pleiades." **constellations of the south.** Suggests the chambers of the south wind (Ps 78:26).

9:11 [a] Job 23:8-9; 35:14
9:12 [b] Job 11:10 [c] Isa 45:9; Ro 9:20
9:13 [d] Job 26:12; Ps 89:10; Isa 30:7; 51:9
9:15 [e] Job 10:15 [f] Job 8:5
9:17 [g] Job 16:12 [h] Job 30:22 [i] Job 16:14 [j] Job 2:3
9:18 [k] Job 7:19; 27:2
9:21 [l] Job 1:1 [m] Job 7:16
9:22 [n] Job 10:8; Ecc 9:2, 3; Eze 21:3
9:23 [o] Heb 11:36 [p] Job 24:1,12
9:24 [q] Job 10:3; 16:11 [r] Job 12:6
9:25 [s] Job 7:6
9:26 [t] Isa 18:2 [u] Hab 1:8
9:27 [v] Job 7:11
9:28 [w] Job 3:25; Ps 119:120 [x] Job 7:21

11 When he passes me, I cannot see him;
when he goes by, I cannot perceive him.[a]
12 If he snatches away, who can stop him?[b]
Who can say to him, 'What are you doing?'[c]
13 God does not restrain his anger;
even the cohorts of Rahab[d] cowered at his feet.

14 "How then can I dispute with him?
How can I find words to argue with him?
15 Though I were innocent, I could not answer him;[e]
I could only plead[f] with my Judge for mercy.
16 Even if I summoned him and he responded,
I do not believe he would give me a hearing.
17 He would crush me[g] with a storm[h]
and multiply[i] my wounds for no reason.[j]
18 He would not let me catch my breath
but would overwhelm me with misery.[k]
19 If it is a matter of strength, he is mighty!
And if it is a matter of justice, who can challenge him*[a]*?
20 Even if I were innocent, my mouth would condemn me;
if I were blameless, it would pronounce me guilty.

21 "Although I am blameless,[l]
I have no concern for myself;
I despise my own life.[m]
22 It is all the same; that is why I say,
'He destroys both the blameless and the wicked.'[n]
23 When a scourge[o] brings sudden death,
he mocks the despair of the innocent.[p]
24 When a land falls into the hands of the wicked,[q]
he blindfolds its judges.[r]
If it is not he, then who is it?

25 "My days are swifter than a runner;[s]
they fly away without a glimpse of joy.
26 They skim past like boats of papyrus,[t]
like eagles swooping down on their prey.[u]
27 If I say, 'I will forget my complaint,[v]
I will change my expression, and smile,'
28 I still dread[w] all my sufferings,
for I know you will not hold me innocent.[x]

a 19 See Septuagint; Hebrew *me.*

9:11–12 Job says that for a God whose creation is so wonderful, God certainly keeps himself out of reach of his human creatures, particularly out of his (Job's) reach.
9:13 Rahab. Figurative name for Egypt (Ps 87:4; Isa 30:7). Thus, "the cohorts of Rahab" might be the armies of Egypt that were defeated at the Red Sea. Some, however, take Rahab to be a mythological creature of the sea, along with Leviathan (3:8; 41:1–34). Even so, there is no evidence that Job espouses a full-fledged mythology of the ancient world, because his God has no competitors.
9:14–15 Job returns to the topic of God's elusiveness in the conduct of an argument (v. 11). If God does not want to be found and is determined to win the argument, there's not much a mortal can do about it.
9:16–18 The setting is the law court, and Job sees God as both judge and executioner.
9:20 Even if Job were innocent (he is sure that he is), God would be so overpowering in the courtroom and Job so weak and confused that Job's own mouth would pronounce him guilty. There is no way to win a case against this Prosecutor.
9:21–24 Job claims innocence (also in 10:7) and declares God incomprehensible (v. 22). Job even perceives that God mocks those who are victims of calamity and blindfolds the faces of their judges, but Job holds open the possibility that he could be mistaken ("If it is not he, then who is it?" [v. 24]).
9:25–31 Job returns to lamenting his own life, using three metaphors to describe his hasty demise: "swifter than a runner" (v. 25), "skim past like boats of papyrus" (v. 26), and "like eagles swooping down on their prey" (v. 26). He feels doomed by his affliction and by God's preemptive verdict of "guilty" (v. 29).

[29] Since I am already found guilty,
why should I struggle in vain?[y]
[30] Even if I washed myself with soap
and my hands[z] with cleansing powder,[a]
[31] you would plunge me into a slime pit
so that even my clothes would detest me.

[32] "He is not a mere mortal like me that I might answer him,[b]
that we might confront each other in court.[c]
[33] If only there were someone to mediate between us,[d]
someone to bring us together,
[34] someone to remove God's rod from me,[e]
so that his terror would frighten me no more.
[35] Then I would speak up without fear of him,
but as it now stands with me, I cannot.[f]

10 "I loathe my very life;[g]
therefore I will give free rein to my complaint
and speak out in the bitterness of my soul.[h]
[2] I say to God: Do not declare me guilty,
but tell me what charges[i] you have against me.
[3] Does it please you to oppress me,[j]
to spurn the work of your hands,[k]
while you smile on the plans of the wicked?[l]
[4] Do you have eyes of flesh?
Do you see as a mortal sees?[m]
[5] Are your days like those of a mortal
or your years like those of a strong man,[n]
[6] that you must search out my faults
and probe after my sin[o]—
[7] though you know that I am not guilty
and that no one can rescue me from your hand?

[8] "Your hands shaped[p] me and made me.
Will you now turn and destroy me?
[9] Remember that you molded me like clay.[q]
Will you now turn me to dust again?[r]
[10] Did you not pour me out like milk
and curdle me like cheese,
[11] clothe me with skin and flesh
and knit me together[s] with bones and sinews?
[12] You gave me life[t] and showed me kindness,
and in your providence watched over my spirit.

9:29 [y] Ps 37:33
9:30 [z] Job 31:7 [a] Jer 2:22
9:32 [b] Ro 9:20 [c] Ps 143:2; Ecc 6:10
9:33 [d] 1Sa 2:25
9:34 [e] Job 13:21; Ps 39:10
9:35 [f] Job 13:21
10:1 [g] 1Ki 19:4 [h] Job 7:11
10:2 [i] Job 9:29
10:3 [j] Job 9:22 [k] Job 14:15; Ps 138:8; Isa 64:8 [l] Job 21:16; 22:18
10:4 [m] 1Sa 16:7
10:5 [n] Ps 90:2,4; 2Pe 3:8
10:6 [o] Job 14:16
10:8 [p] Ps 119:73
10:9 [q] Isa 64:8 [r] Ge 2:7
10:11 [s] Ps 139:13,15
10:12 [t] Job 33:4

9:32–35 When it comes to the deity, Job's humanity is a liability (v. 32), so Job longs for a mediator (v. 33). While this mediator might not have divine status, he would have to be in a position to arbitrate between God and Job. **9:33 someone to mediate between us.** While Job longs for a mediator between him and God, he is not at all confident that such a mediator exists. But he eventually becomes more confident that his "advocate is on high" (16:19). In 19:25 he affirms that he *does* have an advocate. **someone to bring us together.** I.e., someone to arbitrate in such a way that both agree to the terms of the decision.
10:1 See 9:21.
10:2 Job's address turns from the friends to God.
10:3 In 9:22 Job accused God of caring for neither right nor wrong. Here Job charges God with favoring the schemes of the wicked.
10:4–7 Four rhetorical questions focus on Job's thoughts regarding God's inability to understand what it is like to be human (vv. 4–5). Their implied answer is "no." God cannot understand what it feels like to be hemmed in on one side by birth and on the other side by death. The idea is that if God could understand Job's humanness, God would not "search out [Job's] faults and probe after [his] sin" (v. 6)—even though God knows that Job is not guilty. Yet Job is helpless: "no one can rescue me from [God's] hand" (v. 7).
10:8–12 Using the figure of God as a potter and Job as clay (vv. 8–9), Job wonders how he is to understand the enigma of the Creator treating his creation so badly. Job sees God as his enemy, and Job is helpless to do anything about it except to plead as strongly as he can.

10:13 [u]Job 23:13
10:14 [v]Job 7:21
10:15 [w]Job 9:13; Isa 3:11 [x]Job 9:15
10:16 [y]Isa 38:13; La 3:10 [z]Job 5:9
10:17 [a]Job 16:8 [b]Ru 1:21
10:18 [c]Job 3:11
10:20 [d]Job 14:1 [e]Job 7:19 [f]Job 7:16
10:21 [g]2Sa 12:23; Job 3:13; 16:22 [h]Ps 23:4; 88:12
11:2 [i]Job 8:2
11:3 [j]Job 17:2; 21:3
11:4 [k]Job 6:10 [l]Job 10:7
11:6 [m]Job 9:4 [n]Ezr 9:13; Job 15:5
11:7 [o]Ecc 3:11; Ro 11:33

13 "But this is what you concealed in your heart,
and I know that this was in your mind:[u]
14 If I sinned, you would be watching me
and would not let my offense go unpunished.[v]
15 If I am guilty—woe to me![w]
Even if I am innocent, I cannot lift my head,[x]
for I am full of shame
and drowned in[a] my affliction.
16 If I hold my head high, you stalk me like a lion[y]
and again display your awesome power against me.[z]
17 You bring new witnesses against me[a]
and increase your anger toward me;[b]
your forces come against me wave upon wave.

18 "Why then did you bring me out of the womb?[c]
I wish I had died before any eye saw me.
19 If only I had never come into being,
or had been carried straight from the womb to the grave!
20 Are not my few days[d] almost over?[e]
Turn away from me[f] so I can have a moment's joy
21 before I go to the place of no return,[g]
to the land of gloom and utter darkness,[h]
22 to the land of deepest night,
of utter darkness and disorder,
where even the light is like darkness."

Zophar

11 Then Zophar the Naamathite replied:

2 "Are all these words to go unanswered?[i]
Is this talker to be vindicated?
3 Will your idle talk reduce others to silence?
Will no one rebuke you when you mock?[j]
4 You say to God, 'My beliefs are flawless[k]
and I am pure[l] in your sight.'
5 Oh, how I wish that God would speak,
that he would open his lips against you
6 and disclose to you the secrets of wisdom,[m]
for true wisdom has two sides.
Know this: God has even forgotten some of your sin.[n]

7 "Can you fathom[o] the mysteries of God?
Can you probe the limits of the Almighty?

[a] 15 Or *and aware of*

10:13–17 Job thinks that God has concealed a miserable plan for him and that God has always been watching for any sin, stalking Job like a lion.
10:18–22 Job returns to lamenting why he was not stillborn (cf. ch. 3). He pitifully pleads for God to give him a moment's joy before he dies (v. 20).
11:1–20 *Third Exchange: Zophar.* Zophar minces no words with Job and even intimates that the first two speakers have not sufficiently answered Job (v. 3). He contends that God has exacted of Job less than Job's guilt warrants (v. 6), and like the other two friends (5:8; 8:5–7), he challenges Job to acknowledge his sin and seek God. If Job will do so, God will have mercy (vv. 13–19). But if Job will not do so, he is lost (v. 20)!
11:1 Zophar the Naamathite. Cf. 2:11.
11:2 Like Bildad (8:2), Zophar refers to Job's words to justify his response, calling Job a "talker."
11:3 idle talk. Zophar hears contempt in Job's words ("when you mock"; cf. Prov 30:17), and he wonders why neither of the friends has properly rebuked Job for his insolent babble.
11:4 This is Zophar's version of Job's claim to innocence.
11:5–6 If God would speak, he would reveal the other side of "wisdom": that Job's sins are so numerous that God cannot even remember them all.
11:7–9 Skeptically, Zophar indicts Job for assuming that he can comprehend God, who is without "limits" (v. 7). Theologically, Zophar is right, but

[8] They are higher than the heavens[p] above — what can you do?
They are deeper than the depths below — what can you know?
[9] Their measure is longer than the earth
and wider than the sea.

[10] "If he comes along and confines you in prison
and convenes a court, who can oppose him?[q]
[11] Surely he recognizes deceivers;
and when he sees evil, does he not take note?[r]
[12] But the witless can no more become wise
than a wild donkey's colt can be born human.[a]

[13] "Yet if you devote your heart[s] to him
and stretch out your hands to him,[t]
[14] if you put away the sin that is in your hand
and allow no evil[u] to dwell in your tent,[v]
[15] then, free of fault, you will lift up your face;[w]
you will stand firm and without fear.
[16] You will surely forget your trouble,[x]
recalling it only as waters gone by.[y]
[17] Life will be brighter than noonday,[z]
and darkness will become like morning.
[18] You will be secure, because there is hope;
you will look about you and take your rest[a] in safety.[b]
[19] You will lie down, with no one to make you afraid,[c]
and many will court your favor.[d]
[20] But the eyes of the wicked will fail,[e]
and escape will elude them;[f]
their hope will become a dying gasp."[g]

Job

12

Then Job replied:

[2] "Doubtless you are the only people who matter,
and wisdom will die with you![h]
[3] But I have a mind as well as you;
I am not inferior to you.
Who does not know all these things?[i]

[4] "I have become a laughingstock[j] to my friends,
though I called on God and he answered[k] —
a mere laughingstock, though righteous and blameless![l]

11:8 [p] Job 22:12
11:10 [q] Job 9:12; Rev 3:7
11:11 [r] Job 34:21-25; Ps 10:14
11:13 [s] 1Sa 7:3; Ps 78:8 [t] Ps 88:9
11:14 [u] Ps 101:4 [v] Job 22:23
11:15 [w] Job 22:26; 1Jn 3:21
11:16 [x] Isa 65:16 [y] Job 22:11
11:17 [z] Job 22:28; Ps 37:6; Isa 58:8,10
11:18 [a] Ps 3:5 [b] Lev 26:6; Pr 3:24
11:19 [c] Lev 26:6 [d] Isa 45:14
11:20 [e] Dt 28:65; Job 17:5 [f] Job 27:22; 34:22 [g] Job 8:13
12:2 [h] Job 17:10
12:3 [i] Job 13:2
12:4 [j] Job 21:3 [k] Ps 91:15 [l] Job 6:29

[a] 12 Or *wild donkey can be born tame*

practically, Job — who is shut up in his world with God and his indescribable suffering and who has no cause to explain it — must try to explore the limits of a world where justice and God meet, if there is such an overlap.

11:10 confines ... in prison. Translates a verb used of a leper who is quarantined (e.g., "isolate" in Lev 13:5,11,21,26,31); here Job's afflictions metaphorically confine him. **convenes a court.** Suggests a court of law where God is a perceptive judge who recognizes evil.

11:12 This is probably a proverb, but its meaning is difficult (see NIV text note). If this alludes to Job, it is caustic, which would not be surprising on the lips of Zophar.

11:13–20 Like Eliphaz and Bildad (5:8; 8:5), Zophar calls Job to repentance, which Zophar says would result in a happy, secure, and socially productive life (cf. note on 8:5). But for Job to confess sin in order to have God's blessings would undermine Job's integrity and prove correct Satan's claim that Job fears God for selfish motives (cf. 1:9; 2:4).

12:1 — 14:22 *Job's Response to Zophar.* Job sarcastically indicts his friends because of their petty claim to wisdom (12:2–3). His attention turns more and more toward God. Job wants to make his case before the Almighty, hoping that his friends will keep silent now that the dialogue has run its course (13:3–5). Job's only hope is that God is just (13:16).

12:2 Job sarcastically indicts the friends (plural "you") for assuming they have a monopoly on wisdom.

12:3 This could be motivated by Zophar's reference to a "wild donkey's colt" (11:12).

12:4 laughingstock. There is no evidence that the friends have laughed at him, but they have certainly been derisive.

12:6 [m] Job 22:18 [n] Job 9:24; 21:9
12:9 [o] Isa 41:20
12:10 [p] Job 27:3; 33:4; Ac 17:28
12:11 [q] Job 34:3
12:12 [r] Job 15:10 [s] Job 32:7,9
12:13 [t] Job 11:6 [u] Job 9:4 [v] Job 32:8; 38:36
12:14 [w] Job 19:10 [x] Job 37:7; Isa 25:2
12:15 [y] 1Ki 8:35 [z] 1Ki 17:1 [a] Ge 7:11
12:16 [b] Job 13:7,9
12:17 [c] Job 19:9 [d] Job 3:14
12:18 [e] Ps 116:16
12:19 [f] Job 24:12,22; 34:20,28; 35:9
12:20 [g] Job 32:9
12:22 [h] 1Co 4:5 [i] Job 3:5 [j] Da 2:22

5 Those who are at ease have contempt for misfortune
as the fate of those whose feet are slipping.
6 The tents of marauders are undisturbed,[m]
and those who provoke God are secure[n]—
those God has in his hand.[a]

7 "But ask the animals, and they will teach you,
or the birds in the sky, and they will tell you;
8 or speak to the earth, and it will teach you,
or let the fish in the sea inform you.
9 Which of all these does not know
that the hand of the LORD has done this?[o]
10 In his hand is the life of every creature
and the breath of all mankind.[p]
11 Does not the ear test words
as the tongue tastes food?[q]
12 Is not wisdom found among the aged?[r]
Does not long life bring understanding?[s]

13 "To God belong wisdom[t] and power;[u]
counsel and understanding are his.[v]
14 What he tears down[w] cannot be rebuilt;[x]
those he imprisons cannot be released.
15 If he holds back the waters,[y] there is drought;[z]
if he lets them loose, they devastate the land.[a]
16 To him belong strength and insight;
both deceived and deceiver are his.[b]
17 He leads rulers away stripped[c]
and makes fools of judges.[d]
18 He takes off the shackles[e] put on by kings
and ties a loincloth[b] around their waist.
19 He leads priests away stripped
and overthrows officials long established.[f]
20 He silences the lips of trusted advisers
and takes away the discernment of elders.[g]
21 He pours contempt on nobles
and disarms the mighty.
22 He reveals the deep things of darkness[h]
and brings utter darkness[i] into the light.[j]

[a] 6 Or *those whose god is in their own hand* [b] 18 Or *shackles of kings / and ties a belt*

12:5–6 Job explains their derision: they have not experienced his affliction.

12:6 those God has in his hand. The meaning of this clause is uncertain. The NIV interprets it to mean that the "marauders" are undisturbed in God's hand (while Job is terribly troubled). Others view it to mean that the marauders have made a god out of their own power ("hand"; see NIV text note). However, since there is virtually no reference to idolatry in the dialogue, the NIV interpretation is preferable.

12:7–12 Job responds sarcastically to Zophar's disparaging words in 11:7–12, where Zophar contends that the universe is too mysterious for humans to understand and that so far as wisdom is concerned, man is comparable to a "wild donkey's colt" (11:12)—he's not very wise! Job turns the argument on Zophar and asserts that even the animals are wiser than humans. Metaphorically speaking, Job takes the enemy's sword in his own hand and fights with it.

12:9 that the hand of the LORD has done this. Echoes Isa 41:20.

12:11 This is probably a proverb; Elihu quotes it in 34:3 to justify his appraisal of the friends' speeches.

12:12 Is not wisdom found among the aged? Sarcasm, which fits the mood of Job's speeches.

12:13–25 Job insists that God is the only viable possessor of wisdom, yet as the Sovereign over all things, both good and evil, his wisdom is neither so deep as to be unfathomable nor so contradictory as to be beyond understanding. Yet we are still too early in the dialogue to accept this position as the author's view of God. If we perceive the author's theology to follow the lines of Job's arguments, then we must understand his method to involve false theses and false antitheses.

12:15 God is in complete control of nature.

12:16 both deceived and deceiver are his. All of nature is under God's control (cf., e.g., Jer 4:10; 20:7; Ezek 14:9).

[23]He makes nations great, and destroys them;[k]
he enlarges nations,[l] and disperses them.
[24]He deprives the leaders of the earth of their reason;
he makes them wander in a trackless waste.[m]
[25]They grope in darkness with no light;[n]
he makes them stagger like drunkards.[o]

13 "My eyes have seen all this,
my ears have heard and understood it.
[2]What you know, I also know;
I am not inferior to you.[p]
[3]But I desire to speak to the Almighty
and to argue my case with God.[q]
[4]You, however, smear me with lies;[r]
you are worthless physicians, all of you!
[5]If only you would be altogether silent!
For you, that would be wisdom.[s]
[6]Hear now my argument;
listen to the pleas of my lips.
[7]Will you speak wickedly on God's behalf?
Will you speak deceitfully for him?[t]
[8]Will you show him partiality?[u]
Will you argue the case for God?
[9]Would it turn out well if he examined you?
Could you deceive him as you might deceive
a mortal?[v]
[10]He would surely call you to account
if you secretly showed partiality.
[11]Would not his splendor[w] terrify you?
Would not the dread of him fall on you?
[12]Your maxims are proverbs of ashes;
your defenses are defenses of clay.

[13]"Keep silent and let me speak;
then let come to me what may.
[14]Why do I put myself in jeopardy
and take my life in my hands?
[15]Though he slay me, yet will I hope[x] in him;[y]
I will surely[a] defend my ways to his face.[z]
[16]Indeed, this will turn out for my deliverance,[a]
for no godless person would dare come
before him!

12:23 [k]Jer 25:9 [l]Ps 107:38; Isa 9:3; 26:15
12:24 [m]Ps 107:40
12:25 [n]Job 5:14 [o]Ps 107:27; Isa 24:20
13:2 [p]Job 12:3
13:3 [q]Job 23:3-4
13:4 [r]Ps 119:69; Jer 23:32
13:5 [s]Pr 17:28
13:7 [t]Job 36:4
13:8 [u]Lev 19:15
13:9 [v]Job 12:16; Gal 6:7
13:11 [w]Job 31:23
13:15 [x]Job 7:6 [y]Ps 23:4; Pr 14:32 [z]Job 27:5
13:16 [a]Isa 12:1

[a] *15* Or *He will surely slay me; I have no hope — / yet I will*

13:1–2 Job defends his own knowledge and asserts that he is not inferior to his friends, which they have implied.

13:3 Here at the end of Cycle One (see note on 4:1—14:22), after all three friends have spoken, Job insists that he wants to argue his case before God, not before his friends. Indeed, if they will be silent, that will be wisdom (cf. Prov 17:28). Job seems to hope that this is the end of the discussion (v. 5).

13:7–12 Job faults the friends for arguing "the case for God" (v. 8). Later, God himself also indicts Job, saying, "You condemn me to justify yourself" (40:8).

13:11 Zophar said that if God should speak, he would rebuke Job (11:5–6). Job counters that if God did speak, it would "terrify" Zophar and his two companions ("you" is plural).

13:13–19 This is a change in Job's tone and is, in fact, a significant turn in the argument, at least from Job's perspective, for Job is quite confident that he will be vindicated (v. 18). While Job's wife and friends have deserted him and he is shut up in his world with God, sure of his innocence (v. 16b), Job is slowly turning from his adversarial position to one of trust (v. 15). From now on Job's speeches are characterized by a tone of trust—but not entirely, for he is still a troubled man.

13:15 Though he slay me, yet will I hope in him. Note Job's shift of confidence in God's favor (see vv. 16,18).

13:17 [b] Job 21:2
13:18 [c] Job 23:4
13:19 [d] Job 40:4; Isa 50:8 [e] Job 10:8
13:21 [f] Ps 39:10
13:22 [g] Job 14:15 [h] Job 9:16
13:23 [i] 1Sa 26:18
13:24 [j] Dt 32:20; Ps 13:1; Isa 8:17 [k] Job 19:11; La 2:5
13:25 [l] Lev 26:36 [m] Job 21:18; Isa 42:3
13:26 [n] Ps 25:7
13:27 [o] Job 33:11
13:28 [p] Isa 50:9; Jas 5:2

17 Listen carefully to what I say;[b]
let my words ring in your ears.
18 Now that I have prepared my case,[c]
I know I will be vindicated.
19 Can anyone bring charges against me?[d]
If so, I will be silent and die.[e]

20 "Only grant me these two things, God,
and then I will not hide from you:
21 Withdraw your hand[f] far from me,
and stop frightening me with your terrors.
22 Then summon me and I will answer,[g]
or let me speak, and you reply to me.[h]
23 How many wrongs and sins have I committed?[i]
Show me my offense and my sin.
24 Why do you hide your face[j]
and consider me your enemy?[k]
25 Will you torment a windblown leaf?[l]
Will you chase after dry chaff?[m]
26 For you write down bitter things against me
and make me reap the sins of my youth.[n]
27 You fasten my feet in shackles;[o]
you keep close watch on all my paths
by putting marks on the soles of my feet.

28 "So man wastes away like something rotten,
like a garment eaten by moths.[p]

13:18 In Job's mind, and also in the substance of his arguments in his three speeches of Cycle One (see notes on 6:1—7:21; 9:1—10:22; 12:1—14:22), he has "prepared" his case. **prepared.** The Hebrew verb is usually used of military preparations. Applied to an argument, it is peculiar to Job (23:4; 32:14; 33:5; 37:19).
13:19 Can anyone bring charges against me? Some suggest that this is the opening formula of a plaintiff in a court of law. Cf. Isa 50:8.
13:20–28 Characteristic of Job's shift in emotions and language, he turns from the friends to God.
13:20–22 Job makes two requests of God: (1) "Withdraw your hand far from me" (i.e., stop frightening me with your terrors), and (2) "Let me speak, and you reply to me."
13:23 In 10:4–7 (see note there) Job accuses God of stalking him for his sins; here he asks God to make an accounting of his sins if he has any (i.e., bring a bill of indictment against him).
13:24 hide your face. An idiom that here means "to be hostile" (cf. Num 6:25 for the opposite idiom).
13:25 windblown leaf … dry chaff. Metaphors of helplessness and fragility in the presence of God's overwhelming power.
13:26 sins of my youth. When Job claims innocence, he seems not to include these, probably because he considers them forgiven.
13:27 shackles. Job's description of God's ill-treatment of him. **marks on the soles of my feet.** Probably marks from the shackles.

Relief from Abu Simbel, temple in Egypt, showing prisoners of war bound hand and foot. "You fasten my feet in shackles" (Job 13:27).

14

"Mortals, born of woman,
are of few days and full of trouble.[q]
[2] They spring up like flowers[r] and wither away;[s]
like fleeting shadows,[t] they do not endure.
[3] Do you fix your eye on them?[u]
Will you bring them[a] before you for judgment?[v]
[4] Who can bring what is pure[w] from the impure?[x]
No one![y]
[5] A person's days are determined;
you have decreed the number of his months[z]
and have set limits he cannot exceed.
[6] So look away from him and let him alone,[a]
till he has put in his time like a hired laborer.[b]

[7] "At least there is hope for a tree:
If it is cut down, it will sprout again,
and its new shoots will not fail.
[8] Its roots may grow old in the ground
and its stump die in the soil,
[9] yet at the scent of water it will bud
and put forth shoots like a plant.
[10] But a man dies and is laid low;
he breathes his last and is no more.[c]
[11] As the water of a lake dries up
or a riverbed becomes parched and dry,[d]
[12] so he lies down and does not rise;
till the heavens are no more,[e] people will not awake
or be roused from their sleep.[f]

[13] "If only you would hide me in the grave
and conceal me till your anger has passed![g]
If only you would set me a time
and then remember me!
[14] If someone dies, will they live again?
All the days of my hard service
I will wait for my renewal[b] to come.
[15] You will call and I will answer you;[h]
you will long for the creature your hands have made.
[16] Surely then you will count my steps[i]
but not keep track of my sin.[j]

14:1 [q] Job 5:7; Ecc 2:23 **14:2** [r] Jas 1:10 [s] Ps 90:5-6 [t] Job 8:9 **14:3** [u] Ps 8:4; 144:3 [v] Ps 143:2 **14:4** [w] Ps 51:10 [x] Eph 2:1-3 [y] Jn 3:6; Ro 5:12 **14:5** [z] Job 21:21 **14:6** [a] Job 7:19 [b] Job 7:1,2; Ps 39:13 **14:10** [c] Job 13:19 **14:11** [d] Isa 19:5 **14:12** [e] Rev 20:11; 21:1 [f] Ac 3:21 **14:13** [g] Isa 26:20 **14:15** [h] Job 13:22 **14:16** [i] Ps 139:1-3; Pr 5:21; Jer 32:19 [j] Job 10:6

[a] *3* Septuagint, Vulgate and Syriac; Hebrew *me* [b] *14* Or *release*

14:1–22 Job returns to the brevity of human life and its misery (cf. 7:1–10,17–21) and sets his personal situation in that context (vv. 13–17).
14:2 Job compares human life to "flowers" that "wither away" and to "fleeting shadows." Neither lasts very long.
14:3 In view of the ephemeral nature of humanity, it seems to Job unworthy of God to pursue such a defenseless creature.
14:5 Stresses the limitations of human life (cf. 10:1–7).
14:6 hired laborer. His days are miserable enough without God introducing complications.
14:7–17 A dying tree may sprout again if it is cut off close to the ground. In comparison, "man dies … and is no more" (v. 10). Job hints that he does not accept the concept of life after death. Verses 13–17 put the object lesson of the dying tree in personal terms: "If someone dies, will they live again?" (v. 14). It is essentially a rhetorical question whose answer is "no," at least so far as Job is concerned at this point. It is not clear whether Job has the same conception of resurrection described more fully in the NT (in 19:26 there is such a possibility). Some take "my renewal" (v. 14) to imply this, but he is definitely speaking of the continuation of life after death.
14:14 If someone dies, will they live again? His tentative answer to the question is that if he were assured of a positive answer to the question, he would wait through his miserable life until that moment came (v. 14b). But he is not yet confident of that hope (cf. 19:25–27). **hard service.** Reveals how Job views his life.
14:15–17 If life after death were a reality (suggesting a continuing relationship between God and man), then that relationship in this life would be far more cordial (v. 15), and God would "count [Job's] steps" (implying thoughtful care) and "not keep track of my sin" (v. 16).

14:17 [k]Dt 32:34 [l]Hos 13:12
14:19 [m]Job 7:6
14:21 [n]Ecc 9:5; Isa 63:16
15:2 [o]Job 6:26
15:5 [p]Job 5:13
15:6 [q]Lk 19:22
15:7 [r]Job 38:21 [s]Ps 90:2; Pr 8:25
15:8 [t]Ro 11:34; 1Co 2:11
15:9 [u]Job 13:2

17 My offenses will be sealed up in a bag;[k]
you will cover over my sin.[l]

18 "But as a mountain erodes and crumbles
and as a rock is moved from its place,
19 as water wears away stones
and torrents wash away the soil,
so you destroy a person's hope.[m]
20 You overpower them once for all, and they are gone;
you change their countenance and send them away.
21 If their children are honored, they do not know it;
if their offspring are brought low, they do not see it.[n]
22 They feel but the pain of their own bodies
and mourn only for themselves."

Eliphaz

15 Then Eliphaz the Temanite replied:

2 "Would a wise person answer with empty notions
or fill their belly with the hot east wind?[o]
3 Would they argue with useless words,
with speeches that have no value?
4 But you even undermine piety
and hinder devotion to God.
5 Your sin prompts your mouth;
you adopt the tongue of the crafty.[p]
6 Your own mouth condemns you, not mine;
your own lips testify against you.[q]

7 "Are you the first man ever born?[r]
Were you brought forth before the hills?[s]
8 Do you listen in on God's council?[t]
Do you have a monopoly on wisdom?
9 What do you know that we do not know?
What insights do you have that we do not have?[u]

14:18–19 Under God's direction, humanity's hope erodes like the mountains under nature's power.

14:21 children. Of the dead; alludes to Job's terrible pain when remembering his children's fate. This is one of the few hints about his children. Perhaps their death was too painful to discuss, so he mentions it only indirectly.

15:1—21:34 *The Dialogue: Cycle Two.* Eliphaz insists that Job's own words have condemned him, a theme shared by his colleagues. Job turns less toward his three friends, who are more and more caustic, and turns more toward God, insisting that there is someone in heaven who vouches for his innocence.

15:1–35 *First Exchange: Eliphaz.* Eliphaz's second speech is not as conciliatory as his first was. He begins by questioning Job's wisdom (v. 2a). Eliphaz previously phrased the issue of Job's innocence in a rhetorical question (4:7). But here he is more direct (v. 6a). Moreover, in his first speech (4:6), Eliphaz held that Job's "piety" (i.e., "fear" of God) was his confidence, but here Eliphaz accuses Job of undermining "piety" (see v. 4 and note). Sometimes Job and the friends seize each other's words and, metaphorically speaking, fight with each other's sword, illustrated here by Eliphaz's use of Job's arguments. For example, Job claimed that he has as much understanding as the friends have and that he is not inferior to them (12:3). Put on the defensive, Eliphaz makes the same claim (v. 9). Eliphaz sounds offended that Job did not respond to the gentleness of his first speech (v. 11). Eliphaz raises an argument that he used in the first speech (4:17–19)—that humans cannot be righteous before God—and he uses it to indict Job. This is probably the most direct indictment of Job anywhere in Eliphaz's first two speeches.

15:2–3 According to Eliphaz, "a wise person" (which Job claims to be [12:3; 13:2]) would have better arguments than Job's. Job is filled with "the hot east wind" (what is known today as the *hamsin*, which brings heat and sand).

15:4 piety. Hebrew "fear"; a shortened form of "the fear of God/the LORD." Job uses an altered longer phrase in 6:14 ("the fear of the Almighty [Hebrew *šadday*])" and 28:28 ("the fear of the Lord" [Hebrew *'ădōnāy*]). The longer phrase occurs frequently in Proverbs (e.g., Prov 1:7) and elsewhere (e.g., 2 Chr 19:9; Ps 19:9).

15:6 Compared to his gentle approach in ch. 4, this is as gentle as Eliphaz gets in this speech. Rather than Eliphaz's condemnation, Job's own mouth condemns him.

15:8 By dramatic irony the reader knows that God has held a council (1:6; 2:1) that Job is not privy to (cf. 3:23 and note).

[10] The gray-haired and the aged[v] are on our side,
men even older than your father.
[11] Are God's consolations[w] not enough for you,
words[x] spoken gently to you?[y]
[12] Why has your heart[z] carried you away,
and why do your eyes flash,
[13] so that you vent your rage against God
and pour out such words from your mouth?

[14] "What are mortals, that they could be pure,
or those born of woman,[a] that they could be righteous?[b]
[15] If God places no trust in his holy ones,
if even the heavens are not pure in his eyes,[c]
[16] how much less mortals, who are vile and corrupt,[d]
who drink up evil like water![e]

[17] "Listen to me and I will explain to you;
let me tell you what I have seen,
[18] what the wise have declared,
hiding nothing received from their ancestors[f]
[19] (to whom alone the land was given
when no foreigners moved among them):
[20] All his days the wicked man suffers torment,
the ruthless man through all the years stored up for him.[g]
[21] Terrifying sounds fill his ears;[h]
when all seems well, marauders attack him.[i]
[22] He despairs of escaping the realm of darkness;
he is marked for the sword.[j]
[23] He wanders about[k] for food like a vulture;
he knows the day of darkness is at hand.[l]
[24] Distress and anguish fill him with terror;
troubles overwhelm him, like a king poised to attack,
[25] because he shakes his fist at God
and vaunts himself against the Almighty,[m]
[26] defiantly charging against him
with a thick, strong shield.

[27] "Though his face is covered with fat
and his waist bulges with flesh,[n]
[28] he will inhabit ruined towns
and houses where no one lives,[o]
houses crumbling to rubble.[p]
[29] He will no longer be rich and his wealth will not endure,[q]
nor will his possessions spread over the land.

15:10 [v] Job 32:6-7
15:11 [w] 2Co 1:3-4 [x] Zec 1:13 [y] Job 36:16
15:12 [z] Job 11:13
15:14 [a] Job 14:4; 25:4 [b] Pr 20:9; Ecc 7:20
15:15 [c] Job 4:18; 25:5
15:16 [d] Ps 14:1 [e] Job 34:7; Pr 19:28
15:18 [f] Job 8:8
15:20 [g] Job 24:1; 27:13-23
15:21 [h] Job 18:11; 20:25 [i] Job 27:20; 1Th 5:3
15:22 [j] Job 19:29; 27:14
15:23 [k] Ps 59:15; 109:10 [l] Job 18:12
15:25 [m] Job 36:9
15:27 [n] Ps 17:10
15:28 [o] Isa 5:9 [p] Job 3:14
15:29 [q] Job 27:16-17

15:10 In Cycle One (12:12), in a tone of refutation, Job quotes the friends' positive view of the relationship of age and wisdom, but Eliphaz is perturbed about Job's view, noting that their age is a positive factor.

15:11 Eliphaz identifies his gentle and comforting words of 4:7–11 as "God's consolations."

15:14–16 If God does not trust "his holy ones" (v. 15), why would he trust human beings? This reference to some heavenly rebellion (cf. Isa 14:12–20; 2 Pet 2:4) virtually duplicates Eliphaz's argument in 4:18–19.

15:20–35 Describing the wicked man is a feature of wisdom literature, and the book of Job is no exception. Here it is likely a veiled reference to Job. Eliphaz in effect asks, "Do the wicked really suffer for their sins?" Job answers differently than his friends. Eliphaz offers the first explanation of the wicked person's fate: he spends his life in pain and in constant fear that he will suddenly lose his wealth (vv. 20–21).

15:21 In 12:6 Job contended that "marauders" prosper. Eliphaz may be answering him, but with more subtlety; he has Job in mind.

15:24–26 Tacitly describes Job.

15:25 shakes his fist at God. Metaphorically describes Job's defiant attitude as Eliphaz perceives it.

15:30 [r] Job 5:14 [s] Job 22:20 [t] Job 4:9 **15:31** [u] Isa 59:4 **15:32** [v] Ecc 7:17 [w] Job 22:16; Ps 55:23 [x] Job 18:16 **15:33** [y] Hab 3:17 **15:34** [z] Job 8:22 **15:35** [a] Ps 7:14; Isa 59:4; Hos 10:13 **16:2** [b] Job 13:4 **16:3** [c] Job 6:26 **16:4** [d] Ps 22:7; 109:25; La 2:15; Zep 2:15; Mt 27:39 **16:7** [e] Job 7:3 **16:8** [f] Job 19:20 [g] Job 10:17 **16:9** [h] Hos 6:1 [i] Ps 35:16; La 2:16; Ac 7:54 [j] Job 13:24

30 He will not escape the darkness;[r]
a flame[s] will wither his shoots,
and the breath of God's mouth[t] will carry him away.
31 Let him not deceive himself by trusting what is worthless,[u]
for he will get nothing in return.
32 Before his time[v] he will wither,[w]
and his branches will not flourish.[x]
33 He will be like a vine stripped of its unripe grapes,[y]
like an olive tree shedding its blossoms.
34 For the company of the godless will be barren,
and fire will consume the tents of those who love bribes.[z]
35 They conceive trouble and give birth to evil;[a]
their womb fashions deceit."

Job

16

Then Job replied:

2 "I have heard many things like these;
you are miserable comforters, all of you![b]
3 Will your long-winded speeches never end?
What ails you that you keep on arguing?[c]
4 I also could speak like you,
if you were in my place;
I could make fine speeches against you
and shake my head[d] at you.
5 But my mouth would encourage you;
comfort from my lips would bring you relief.

6 "Yet if I speak, my pain is not relieved;
and if I refrain, it does not go away.
7 Surely, God, you have worn me out;[e]
you have devastated my entire household.
8 You have shriveled me up — and it has become a witness;
my gauntness[f] rises up and testifies against me.[g]
9 God assails me and tears[h] me in his anger
and gnashes his teeth at me;[i]
my opponent fastens on me his piercing eyes.[j]

15:32–33 Eliphaz compares the wicked to a tree that withers, a vine that bears no fruit, and an "olive tree shedding its blossoms" (v. 33). The olive tree has numerous blooms, only a few of which become fruit, suggesting a loss of hope. Job submitted his question about the afterlife (14:7–17), which was at the same time a veiled hope, and Eliphaz discourages his speculation.

16:1—17:16 *Job's Response to Eliphaz.* This speech, like Job's others, directly addresses the friends only in part (e.g., 16:2–5 and possibly 17:10), with another part addressed to God (16:7–8; 17:3–4). Job apostrophizes the earth (16:18), while much of the speech is a monologue (16:6–17,20–22; 17:1–2,5–9,11–16). Job begins this speech by addressing *all* of the friends, not just Eliphaz, saying, "You are miserable comforters, all of you!" (16:2). Job evidently hopes that the friends will leave him alone (13:5), but now that Eliphaz has shattered that hope by starting a second round of speeches, Job turns to him ("you ... you" in 16:3 are singular). Job continues to maintain his innocence (16:17). Just as Job shifted in a positive direction in his final speech of Cycle One, here his view significantly changes regarding a mediator between him and God. Although he had disavowed such a mediator (9:33), he is confident, at least for the moment, that his "witness" represents him "in heaven" (16:19). With sharpening spiritual insight, Job thinks of a way for God to show him that he is concerned about him and will vindicate him: God could himself become a "pledge" for Job (17:3). Much like 10:4–7 represents his spiritual depth (perhaps pointing in the direction of the incarnation), Job points in the same direction — when Christ became a "pledge" for us (see "guarantor" in Heb 7:22). See note on 10:4–7.

16:2 miserable comforters. The friends' arguments have become repetitive and their ideas specious.

16:4 Job hypothesizes that if the roles were switched, he could also talk like the friends.

16:7 Job addresses God, and most of the remainder of the speech is about God, though not addressed directly to him.

16:8 gauntness. Evidence that God has assaulted Job.

16:9 my opponent. Some see this as a reference to Satan, but it likely refers to Job's human opponents (v. 10).

[10]People open their mouths[k] to jeer at me;
they strike my cheek[l] in scorn
and unite together against me.[m]
[11]God has turned me over to the ungodly
and thrown me into the clutches of the wicked.[n]
[12]All was well with me, but he shattered me;
he seized me by the neck and crushed me.[o]
He has made me his target;[p]
13 his archers surround me.
Without pity, he pierces[q] my kidneys
and spills my gall on the ground.
[14]Again and again[r] he bursts upon me;
he rushes at me like a warrior.[s]

[15]"I have sewed sackcloth[t] over my skin
and buried my brow in the dust.
[16]My face is red with weeping,
dark shadows ring my eyes;
[17]yet my hands have been free of violence[u]
and my prayer is pure.

[18]"Earth, do not cover my blood;[v]
may my cry never be laid to rest![w]
[19]Even now my witness[x] is in heaven;
my advocate is on high.
[20]My intercessor is my friend[a]
as my eyes pour out[y] tears to God;
[21]on behalf of a man he pleads[z] with God
as one pleads for a friend.

[22]"Only a few years will pass
before I take the path of no return.[a]

17

[1]My spirit is broken,
my days are cut short,
the grave awaits me.[b]
[2]Surely mockers[c] surround me;
my eyes must dwell on their hostility.

[3]"Give me, O God, the pledge you demand.[d]
Who else will put up security[e] for me?[f]
[4]You have closed their minds to understanding;
therefore you will not let them triumph.
[5]If anyone denounces their friends for reward,
the eyes of their children will fail.[g]

[a] 20 Or *My friends treat me with scorn*

16:10 [k]Ps 22:13 [l]Isa 50:6; La 3:30; Mic 5:1; Ac 23:2 [m]Ps 35:15
16:11 [n]Job 1:15,17
16:12 [o]Job 9:17 [p]La 3:12
16:13 [q]Job 20:24
16:14 [r]Job 9:17 [s]Joel 2:7
16:15 [t]Ge 37:34
16:17 [u]Isa 59:6; Jnh 3:8
16:18 [v]Isa 26:21 [w]Ps 66:18-19
16:19 [x]Ge 31:50; Ro 1:9; 1Th 2:5
16:20 [y]La 2:19
16:21 [z]Ps 9:4
16:22 [a]Ecc 12:5
17:1 [b]Ps 88:3-4
17:2 [c]1Sa 1:6-7
17:3 [d]Ps 119:122 [e]Pr 6:1 [f]Isa 38:14
17:5 [g]Job 11:20

16:11 The friends made allusive references to Job; here Job refers to them as "the ungodly" and "the wicked."
16:16 Involuntary weeping is sometimes connected with leprosy, a disease some think Job had. However, Job's troubles are enough to cause this condition without attributing it to leprosy.
16:17 Job still insists that he is innocent.
16:18 Unavenged "blood" spilled on the ground cries out for vengeance (Gen 4:10), so Job commands the earth not to cover his unavenged blood in the hope that vengeance will eventually come.
16:19–21 Job now believes he has a "witness [who] is in heaven" who serves as his "advocate" (v. 19). Cf. 9:33. Job addresses the friends and informs them that his appeal is to God, not to them.
17:2 Job acknowledges that he must endure "their hostility."
17:3 See note on 16:1—17:16.
17:4 In this brief appeal to God, Job prays that his friends' arguments will not prevail (see Pss 30:1; 41:11).
17:5 This may be a proverb.

17:6 [h] Job 30:9
17:7 [i] Job 16:8
17:8 [j] Job 22:19
17:9 [k] Pr 4:18 [l] Job 22:30
17:10 [m] Job 12:2
17:11 [n] Job 7:6
17:13 [o] Job 3:13
17:14 [p] Job 13:28; 30:28, 30; Ps 16:10 [q] Job 21:26
17:15 [r] Job 7:6
17:16 [s] Job 3:17-19; Jnh 2:6
18:3 [t] Ps 73:22
18:4 [u] Job 13:14
18:5 [v] Job 21:17; Pr 13:9; 20:20; 24:20
18:7 [w] Pr 4:12 [x] Job 5:13 [y] Job 15:6
18:8 [z] Job 22:10; Ps 9:15; 35:7

6 "God has made me a byword[h] to everyone,
a man in whose face people spit.
7 My eyes have grown dim with grief;[i]
my whole frame is but a shadow.
8 The upright are appalled at this;
the innocent are aroused[j] against the ungodly.
9 Nevertheless, the righteous[k] will hold to their ways,
and those with clean hands[l] will grow stronger.

10 "But come on, all of you, try again!
I will not find a wise man among you.[m]
11 My days have passed, my plans are shattered.
Yet the desires of my heart[n]
12 turn night into day;
in the face of the darkness light is near.
13 If the only home I hope for is the grave,[o]
if I spread out my bed in the realm of darkness,
14 if I say to corruption,[p] 'You are my father,'
and to the worm,[q] 'My mother' or 'My sister,'
15 where then is my hope —[r]
who can see any hope for me?
16 Will it go down to the gates of death?[s]
Will we descend together into the dust?"

Bildad

18 Then Bildad the Shuhite replied:

2 "When will you end these speeches?
Be sensible, and then we can talk.
3 Why are we regarded as cattle
and considered stupid in your sight?[t]
4 You who tear yourself[u] to pieces in your anger,
is the earth to be abandoned for your sake?
Or must the rocks be moved from their place?

5 "The lamp of a wicked man is snuffed out;[v]
the flame of his fire stops burning.
6 The light in his tent becomes dark;
the lamp beside him goes out.
7 The vigor of his step is weakened;[w]
his own schemes[x] throw him down.[y]
8 His feet thrust him into a net;[z]
he wanders into its mesh.

17:6 Cf. Deut 25:9.
17:7 Physically, Job is a mere shadow of his former self.
17:8 the upright are appalled. May be a satirical jibe at his friends (as v. 10 clearly is). **this.** Job's condition. But even though the friends are not appalled, Job, the righteous man, will cling to his way (v. 9).
17:11–16 Job contemplates the end of his life.
18:1–21 *Second Exchange: Bildad.* As in Eliphaz's second speech, the social courtesies are over. Bildad begins by claiming that Job looks on the friends as no more than stupid cattle (v. 3). Following Eliphaz's example, Bildad offers a long description of the wicked man (vv. 5–21), perhaps an oblique reference to Job, adding that the wicked know nothing but terror and suffering (vv. 11–13). The hints that Bildad is describing Job are references to Job's skin disease (v. 13; see 2:7–8), the "burning sulfur ... scattered over his dwelling" (v. 15; cf. "the fire of God" in 1:16), and the loss of family (v. 19; cf. Bildad's reference to Job's children in 8:4). Again we have a word picture of Job's suffering as he scrapes himself with potsherds (v. 4).
18:2–4 Bildad addresses Job in the plural since Job indicated that others hold his opinion (17:8–9).
18:5–21 The friends embrace the doctrine of retribution (see also Prov 13:9; 20:20; 24:20), which Job has questioned. The undergirding principle of Bildad's speech is that the wicked man's "own schemes throw him down" (v. 7). The final judgment is that Job "does not know God" (v. 21).

[9] A trap seizes him by the heel;
a snare holds him fast.
[10] A noose is hidden for him on the ground;
a trap lies in his path.
[11] Terrors startle him on every side[a]
and dog[b] his every step.
[12] Calamity is hungry[c] for him;
disaster is ready for him when he falls.
[13] It eats away parts of his skin;
death's firstborn devours his limbs.[d]
[14] He is torn from the security of his tent[e]
and marched off to the king of terrors.
[15] Fire resides[a] in his tent;
burning sulfur[f] is scattered over his dwelling.
[16] His roots dry up below[g]
and his branches wither above.[h]
[17] The memory of him perishes from the earth;
he has no name in the land.[i]
[18] He is driven from light into the realm of darkness[j]
and is banished from the world.
[19] He has no offspring[k] or descendants[l] among his people,
no survivor where once he lived.[m]
[20] People of the west are appalled at his fate;[n]
those of the east are seized with horror.
[21] Surely such is the dwelling[o] of an evil man;
such is the place of one who does not know God."[p]

Job

19 Then Job replied:

[2] "How long will you torment me
and crush me with words?
[3] Ten times now you have reproached me;
shamelessly you attack me.
[4] If it is true that I have gone astray,
my error[q] remains my concern alone.
[5] If indeed you would exalt yourselves above me[r]
and use my humiliation against me,

[a] 15 Or *Nothing he had remains*

18:11 [a] Job 15:21; Jer 6:25; 20:3 [b] Job 20:8
18:12 [c] Isa 8:21
18:13 [d] Zec 14:12
18:14 [e] Job 8:22
18:15 [f] Ps 11:6
18:16 [g] Isa 5:24; Hos 9:1-16; Am 2:9 [h] Job 15:30; Mal 4:1
18:17 [i] Ps 34:16; Pr 2:22; 10:7
18:18 [j] Job 5:14
18:19 [k] Jer 22:30 [l] Isa 14:22 [m] Job 27:14-15
18:20 [n] Ps 37:13; Jer 50:27,31
18:21 [o] Job 21:28 [p] Jer 9:3; 1Th 4:5
19:4 [q] Job 6:24
19:5 [r] Ps 35:26; 38:16; 55:12

18:13 This pictures Job's skin-eating disease.
18:17 Alludes to Job's loss of reputation and perhaps also the loss of his children, to whom v. 19 explicitly refers.
19:1–29 *Job's Response to Bildad.* Job again addresses all of the friends rather than the one who has just finished speaking: "How long will you [plural] torment me and crush me with words?" (v. 2). Job returns to the idea of God as his enemy, leading his troops against Job (vv. 6–12). In a pitiful description of his social position, Job laments the breakdown of all his social relationships—even young children despise and talk about him (vv. 13–19). Then, in a moment of desperation, he pleads with his friends to have pity on him (vv. 21–22). Once more the text describes Job's physical condition: emaciated by his disease, he looks like skin stretched over a skeleton (v. 20). Then comes a climax of spiritual insight as Job contemplates what it would mean if his words were permanently recorded in a book as a record preserved for the day of vindication. As in 16:19 (where he expresses the confidence that his "witness is in heaven"), Job declares in a confidence not attained up to now, "I know that my redeemer lives, and that in the end he will stand on the earth" (v. 25). For the first time, he expresses the belief that he will be vindicated after death.
19:3 Ten times. There have not been ten speeches by the friends so far, so this must be figurative (cf. Gen 31:7; Num 14:22).
19:4 Not admitting guilt, this is a conditional statement: "even *if* I erred, my error would remain with *me*, not with *you*."
19:5–22 This honestly, if not caustically, indicts God, whom Job believes has caused all his woes, which include the social and familial breakdown of his relationships (vv. 13–19). So reversed are they that he must even supplicate his slave rather than give him orders (v. 16).

19:6 [s] Job 27:2 [t] Job 18:8
19:7 [u] Job 30:20 [v] Job 9:24; Hab 1:2-4
19:8 [w] Job 3:23; La 3:7 [x] Job 30:26
19:9 [y] Job 12:17 [z] Ps 89:39,44; La 5:16
19:10 [a] Job 12:14 [b] Job 7:6 [c] Job 24:20
19:11 [d] Job 16:9 [e] Job 13:24
19:12 [f] Job 16:13 [g] Job 30:12
19:13 [h] Ps 69:8 [i] Job 16:7; Ps 88:8
19:18 [j] 2Ki 2:23
19:19 [k] Ps 55:12-13 [l] Ps 38:11
19:20 [m] Job 33:21; Ps 102:5
19:22 [n] Job 13:25; 16:11 [o] Ps 69:26
19:23 [p] Isa 30:8
19:25 [q] Ps 78:35; Pr 23:11; Isa 43:14; Jer 50:34 [r] Job 16:19

6 then know that God has wronged me[s]
and drawn his net[t] around me.

7 "Though I cry, 'Violence!' I get no response;[u]
though I call for help, there is no justice.[v]
8 He has blocked my way so I cannot pass;[w]
he has shrouded my paths in darkness.[x]
9 He has stripped[y] me of my honor
and removed the crown from my head.[z]
10 He tears me down[a] on every side till I am gone;
he uproots my hope[b] like a tree.[c]
11 His anger[d] burns against me;
he counts me among his enemies.[e]
12 His troops advance in force;[f]
they build a siege ramp[g] against me
and encamp around my tent.

13 "He has alienated my family[h] from me;
my acquaintances are completely estranged from me.[i]
14 My relatives have gone away;
my closest friends have forgotten me.
15 My guests and my female servants count me a foreigner;
they look on me as on a stranger.
16 I summon my servant, but he does not answer,
though I beg him with my own mouth.
17 My breath is offensive to my wife;
I am loathsome to my own family.
18 Even the little boys[j] scorn me;
when I appear, they ridicule me.
19 All my intimate friends[k] detest me;[l]
those I love have turned against me.
20 I am nothing but skin and bones;[m]
I have escaped only by the skin of my teeth.[a]

21 "Have pity on me, my friends, have pity,
for the hand of God has struck me.
22 Why do you pursue[n] me as God does?
Will you never get enough of my flesh?[o]

23 "Oh, that my words were recorded,
that they were written on a scroll,[p]
24 that they were inscribed with an iron tool on[b] lead,
or engraved in rock forever!
25 I know that my redeemer[c][q] lives,[r]
and that in the end he will stand on the earth.[d]

[a] 20 Or *only by my gums* [b] 24 Or *and* [c] 25 Or *vindicator* [d] 25 Or *on my grave*

19:23–24 Resignation is sometimes mistaken for hopelessness, and Job, resigned to his pitiable lot, is still indomitable in his desire to present his case to God. But since God will not confront him personally, Job prefaces his hope for a redeemer by desiring that his words be recorded "on a scroll" (v. 23) or "engraved in rock forever" (v. 24), anticipating the day of vindication.

19:25 This is one of the most beloved verses in Job. Many Christians through the centuries have appropriated this verse as a precious hope in the afterlife. The "redeemer" in Israel could ransom those sold into slavery (Lev 25:47–55), redeem property (Lev 25:23–24), avenge the blood of a kinsman (Num 35:19), and preserve the line of a deceased relative (Deut 25:5–10). While the term usually refers to a human being, sometimes God is called a redeemer (Exod 6:6; 15:13; Ps 103:4). Job had wished for "someone to mediate between us" (9:33), and he has come to believe that he has a "witness … in heaven" (16:19). Now he is confident that God is his redeemer. **will stand.** Comes from the law court, where one appears as a witness, in this case, for the defendant.

Behistun monument where Persian King Darius recorded his deeds on a rock cliff. Job also speaks of recording his words in rock (Job 19:24).

Wikimedia Commons

26 And after my skin has been destroyed,
yet[a] in[b] my flesh I will see God;[s]
27 I myself will see him
with my own eyes—I, and not another.
How my heart yearns[t] within me!

28 "If you say, 'How we will hound him,
since the root of the trouble lies in him,[c]'
29 you should fear the sword yourselves;
for wrath will bring punishment by the sword,[u]
and then you will know that there is judgment.[d]"[v]

19:26 [s] Ps 17:15; Mt 5:8; 1Co 13:12; 1Jn 3:2
19:27 [t] Ps 73:26
19:29 [u] Job 15:22 [v] Job 22:4; Ps 1:5; 9:7
20:3 [w] Job 19:3
20:5 [x] Job 8:12; Ps 37:35-36; 73:19

Zophar

20 Then Zophar the Naamathite replied:

2 "My troubled thoughts prompt me to answer
because I am greatly disturbed.
3 I hear a rebuke[w] that dishonors me,
and my understanding inspires me to reply.

4 "Surely you know how it has been from of old,
ever since mankind[e] was placed on the earth,
5 that the mirth of the wicked is brief,
the joy of the godless lasts but a moment.[x]

[a] *26* Or *And after I awake, / though this body has been destroyed, / then* [b] *26* Or *destroyed, / apart from* [c] *28* Many Hebrew manuscripts, Septuagint and Vulgate; most Hebrew manuscripts *me* [d] *29* Or *sword, / that you may come to know the Almighty* [e] *4* Or *Adam*

19:26–27 Another reference to Job's deteriorating flesh. Yet when this has happened, Job "will see God." What he had hoped for, even demanded, is now within faith's grasp. The baseline is that he now believes in life after death, although "in my flesh" (implying a bodily resurrection) can also be rendered "apart from my flesh" (see second NIV text note on v. 26) and imply consciousness after death but not the bodily resurrection. But there are two clear references in the OT to the bodily resurrection: Isa 26:19; Dan 12:2.

20:1–29 *Third Exchange: Zophar.* Given how blunt Zophar is, we should not be surprised that he makes his second speech and then does not speak again in the third cycle—he had already said everything! His forthright manner of speaking leaves no doubt that he believes Job is guilty of gross sins and is a wicked man. Like the other friends, he never mentions Job by name (he talks only about the wicked man in general), but he obviously has Job in mind. Eliphaz introduced the idea of the prosperity of the wicked (15:20–35); Bildad had picked up on it; and Zophar follows suit. His explanation for the prosperity of the wicked is that it is brief and that judgment will catch up with him (v. 5). Humankind and the universe are so structured that wickedness cannot be tolerated (vv. 16,27).

20:3 a rebuke that dishonors me. Job's words personally offended Zophar.

20:6 [y] Isa 14:13-14; Ob 3-4
20:7 [z] Job 4:20 [a] Job 7:10; 8:18
20:8 [b] Ps 73:20 [c] Job 27:21-23 [d] Job 18:18 [e] Ps 90:5
20:9 [f] Job 7:8
20:10 [g] Job 5:4 [h] Job 27:16-17
20:11 [i] Job 13:26 [j] Job 21:26
20:13 [k] Nu 11:18-20
20:16 [l] Dt 32:32 [m] Dt 32:24
20:17 [n] Dt 32:13 [o] Job 29:6
20:19 [p] Job 24:4,14; 35:9
20:20 [q] Ecc 5:12-14
20:21 [r] Job 15:29
20:23 [s] Ps 78:30-31
20:24 [t] Isa 24:18; Am 5:19
20:25 [u] Job 18:11 [v] Job 16:13
20:26 [w] Job 18:18 [x] Ps 21:9
20:27 [y] Dt 31:28

6 Though the pride of the godless person reaches to
the heavens
and his head touches the clouds,[y]
7 he will perish forever,[z] like his own dung;
those who have seen him will say, 'Where is he?'[a]
8 Like a dream[b] he flies away,[c] no more to be found,
banished[d] like a vision of the night.[e]
9 The eye that saw him will not see him again;
his place will look on him no more.[f]
10 His children[g] must make amends to the poor;
his own hands must give back his wealth.[h]
11 The youthful vigor[i] that fills his bones
will lie with him in the dust.[j]

12 "Though evil is sweet in his mouth
and he hides it under his tongue,
13 though he cannot bear to let it go
and lets it linger in his mouth,[k]
14 yet his food will turn sour in his stomach;
it will become the venom of serpents within him.
15 He will spit out the riches he swallowed;
God will make his stomach vomit them up.
16 He will suck the poison[l] of serpents;
the fangs of an adder will kill him.[m]
17 He will not enjoy the streams,
the rivers flowing with honey[n] and cream.[o]
18 What he toiled for he must give back uneaten;
he will not enjoy the profit from his trading.
19 For he has oppressed the poor and left them destitute;[p]
he has seized houses he did not build.

20 "Surely he will have no respite from his craving;[q]
he cannot save himself by his treasure.
21 Nothing is left for him to devour;
his prosperity will not endure.[r]
22 In the midst of his plenty, distress will overtake him;
the full force of misery will come upon him.
23 When he has filled his belly,
God will vent his burning anger against him
and rain down his blows on him.[s]
24 Though he flees[t] from an iron weapon,
a bronze-tipped arrow pierces him.
25 He pulls it out of his back,
the gleaming point out of his liver.
Terrors[u] will come over him;[v]
26 total darkness[w] lies in wait for his treasures.
A fire unfanned will consume him[x]
and devour what is left in his tent.
27 The heavens will expose his guilt;
the earth will rise up against him.[y]

20:12–14 Evil is like a tidbit that, when taken upon one's tongue, turns to poison.
20:15 God causes the wicked person to disgorge their ill-gotten gain.
20:19 Zophar, anticipating Eliphaz's third speech (ch. 22), spells out Job's sins: "he has oppressed the poor ... seized houses he did not build."
20:24 bronze-tipped arrow. A more deadly weapon than other types.

[28] A flood will carry off his house,[z]
rushing waters[a] on the day of God's wrath.[a]
[29] Such is the fate God allots the wicked,
the heritage appointed for them by God."[b]

Job

21

Then Job replied:

[2] "Listen carefully to my words;
let this be the consolation you give me.
[3] Bear with me while I speak,
and after I have spoken, mock on.[c]

[4] "Is my complaint directed to a human being?
Why should I not be impatient?[d]
[5] Look at me and be appalled;
clap your hand over your mouth.[e]
[6] When I think about this, I am terrified;
trembling seizes my body.
[7] Why do the wicked live on,
growing old and increasing in power?[f]
[8] They see their children established around them,
their offspring before their eyes.[g]
[9] Their homes are safe and free from fear;[h]
the rod of God is not on them.
[10] Their bulls never fail to breed;
their cows calve and do not miscarry.[i]
[11] They send forth their children as a flock;
their little ones dance about.
[12] They sing to the music of timbrel and lyre;
they make merry to the sound of the pipe.[j]
[13] They spend their years in prosperity[k]
and go down to the grave in peace.[b]
[14] Yet they say to God, 'Leave us alone![l]
We have no desire to know your ways.[m]
[15] Who is the Almighty, that we should serve him?
What would we gain by praying to him?'[n]
[16] But their prosperity is not in their own hands,
so I stand aloof from the plans of the wicked.

[17] "Yet how often is the lamp of the wicked snuffed out?[o]
How often does calamity come upon them,
the fate God allots in his anger?

20:28 [z] Dt 28:31 [a] Job 21:17,20,30
20:29 [b] Job 27:13
21:3 [c] Job 16:10
21:4 [d] Job 6:11
21:5 [e] Jdg 18:19; Job 29:9; 40:4
21:7 [f] Job 12:6; Ps 73:3; Jer 12:1; Hab 1:13
21:8 [g] Ps 17:14
21:9 [h] Ps 73:5
21:10 [i] Ex 23:26
21:12 [j] Ps 81:2
21:13 [k] Job 36:11
21:14 [l] Job 22:17 [m] Pr 1:29
21:15 [n] Ex 5:2; Job 34:9; Mal 3:14
21:17 [o] Job 18:5

[a] *28* Or *The possessions in his house will be carried off, / washed away* [b] *13* Or *in an instant*

21:1–34 *Job's Response to Zophar.* Job countercharges the allegations of his friends—the wicked do not really prosper, their prosperity is only apparent, and their prosperity is temporary: "the wicked live on, growing old and increasing in power" (v. 7). Job is preoccupied with this thought throughout the speech. It is his strongest and clearest statement on the matter. He closes with a direct indictment that anything else the friends could say would be only falsehood (v. 34). That should be a strong hint that he would like to end the conversation right there, but, alas, Eliphaz has still more to say.
21:5 clap your hand over your mouth. A gesture of awe.
21:7–16 Job's description of the prosperity of the wicked, i.e., the wicked prosper, their children prosper (vv. 7–8), and they live a happy life and die in peace. The full description is essentially the reverse of Job's own situation.
21:17–34 Job continues to lay out the case for the prosperity of the wicked. His experience is that they get away with their wicked schemes without repercussion. One explanation is that the next generation suffers for them (v. 19a), when the present generation are the ones who deserve to be punished (vv. 19b–20). Exod 20:5 expresses the principle of retribution upon the children, but Deut 24:16; Jer 31:29–30; Ezek 18 reverses that principle.

21:18 [p] Job 13:25; Ps 1:4
21:19 [q] Ex 20:5; Jer 31:29; Eze 18:2
21:20 [r] Ps 75:8; Isa 51:17 [s] Jer 25:15; Rev 14:10
21:21 [t] Job 14:5
21:22 [u] Job 35:11; 36:22; Isa 40:13-14; Ro 11:34 [v] Ps 82:1
21:24 [w] Pr 3:8
21:26 [x] Job 24:20; Ecc 9:2-3; Isa 14:11
21:28 [y] Job 1:3; 12:21; 31:37 [z] Job 8:22
21:30 [a] Pr 16:4 [b] Job 20:22,28; 2Pe 2:9
21:33 [c] Job 3:22; 17:16; 24:24 [d] Job 3:19
21:34 [e] Job 16:2
22:2 [f] Lk 17:10

18 How often are they like straw before the wind,
like chaff[p] swept away by a gale?
19 It is said, 'God stores up the punishment of the wicked for their children.'[q]
Let him repay the wicked, so that they themselves will experience it!
20 Let their own eyes see their destruction;
let them drink[r] the cup of the wrath of the Almighty.[s]
21 For what do they care about the families they leave behind
when their allotted months[t] come to an end?

22 "Can anyone teach knowledge to God,[u]
since he judges even the highest?[v]
23 One person dies in full vigor,
completely secure and at ease,
24 well nourished in body,[a]
bones rich with marrow.[w]
25 Another dies in bitterness of soul,
never having enjoyed anything good.
26 Side by side they lie in the dust,
and worms cover them both.[x]

27 "I know full well what you are thinking,
the schemes by which you would wrong me.
28 You say, 'Where now is the house of the great,[y]
the tents where the wicked lived?'[z]
29 Have you never questioned those who travel?
Have you paid no regard to their accounts—
30 that the wicked are spared from the day of calamity,[a]
that they are delivered from[b] the day of wrath?[b]
31 Who denounces their conduct to their face?
Who repays them for what they have done?
32 They are carried to the grave,
and watch is kept over their tombs.
33 The soil in the valley is sweet to them;[c]
everyone follows after them,
and a countless throng goes[c] before them.[d]
34 "So how can you console me[e] with your nonsense?
Nothing is left of your answers but falsehood!"

Eliphaz

22

Then Eliphaz the Temanite replied:

2 "Can a man be of benefit to God?[f]
Can even a wise person benefit him?

[a] 24 The meaning of the Hebrew for this word is uncertain. [b] 30 Or *wicked are reserved for the day of calamity, / that they are brought forth to* [c] 33 Or *them, / as a countless throng went*

22:1—27:23 *The Dialogue: Cycle Three.* The friends have either turned their accusations into real indictments of immoral conduct (Eliphaz), reduced Job as a person to something less than human (Bildad), or altogether given up on him (Zophar). Job, on the other hand, contends that if he could only find God, God would listen and acquit him, and Job would "come forth as gold" (23:10).

22:1–30 *First Exchange: Eliphaz.* Eliphaz makes a complete turnaround. In this speech he even details the sins of Job, although in the first speech he merely derided Job for being impatient when the adversities he had seen in other people's lives had come to him (4:4–5). Now, however, he accuses him of exacting pledges, taking the clothing of the poor, refusing to feed the hungry, and showing no compassion for widows and orphans (vv. 6–9).

22:2–3 Job accused God of having an ulterior motive in his dealings with him. Eliphaz insists that Job can bring no benefit to God, so why should God have an ulterior motive? Elihu says the same thing in 34:9,

[3]What pleasure would it give the Almighty if you were righteous?
What would he gain if your ways were blameless?

[4]"Is it for your piety that he rebukes you
and brings charges against you?[g]
[5]Is not your wickedness great?
Are not your sins[h] endless?
[6]You demanded security[i] from your relatives for no reason;
you stripped people of their clothing, leaving them naked.
[7]You gave no water to the weary
and you withheld food from the hungry,[j]
[8]though you were a powerful man, owning land—
an honored man,[k] living on it.
[9]And you sent widows away empty-handed[l]
and broke the strength of the fatherless.
[10]That is why snares are all around you,
why sudden peril terrifies you,
[11]why it is so dark[m] you cannot see,
and why a flood of water covers you.[n]

[12]"Is not God in the heights of heaven?[o]
And see how lofty are the highest stars!
[13]Yet you say, 'What does God know?[p]
Does he judge through such darkness?[q]
[14]Thick clouds[r] veil him, so he does not see us
as he goes about in the vaulted heavens.'
[15]Will you keep to the old path
that the wicked have trod?
[16]They were carried off before their time,[s]
their foundations washed away by a flood.[t]
[17]They said to God, 'Leave us alone!
What can the Almighty do to us?'[u]
[18]Yet it was he who filled their houses with good things,[v]
so I stand aloof from the plans of the wicked.[w]

22:4 [g]Job 14:3; 19:29; Ps 143:2
22:5 [h]Job 11:6; 15:5
22:6 [i]Ex 22:26; Dt 24:6, 17; Eze 18:12,16
22:7 [j]Job 31:17,21,31
22:8 [k]Isa 3:3; 9:15
22:9 [l]Job 24:3,21
22:11 [m]Job 5:14 [n]Ps 69:1-2; 124:4-5; La 3:54
22:12 [o]Job 11:8
22:13 [p]Ps 10:11; Isa 29:15 [q]Eze 8:12
22:14 [r]Job 26:9
22:16 [s]Job 15:32 [t]Job 14:19; Mt 7:26-27
22:17 [u]Job 21:15
22:18 [v]Job 12:6 [w]Job 21:16

The Mesad Hashavyahu ostracon, a Hebrew inscription in which a man pleads that his garment be returned. Eliphaz claims that, despite all his wealth, Job took the poor man's garment as a pledge of loan repayment and left him naked (Job 22:6).

Kim Walton, taken at the Israel Museum, Jerusalem

and Job said it with another meaning in 7:20. God gets no benefit if we sin or if we are righteous, so he is the only one who has no ulterior motive. In one sense, Eliphaz is right, because God does not receive any benefit personally; but in another sense, he is wrong, because God initiated this entire process of suffering so that he could prove to Satan that there is at least one man in the world who serves God with absolutely no ulterior motive.

22:4 piety. The Hebrew word is sometimes translated "fear" (of God). Sometimes the friends sarcastically stumble upon the truth, which, of course, they do not recognize, and this is such an instance. Yes, it is for Job's fear of God that he is suffering (1:1), although Eliphaz frames it in negative terms: God "rebukes … and brings charges against" Job. Yet with dramatic irony the reader knows the truth from having listened in on the heavenly council in the prologue.

22:5 In Cycle One Eliphaz essentially insisted that all human beings sin; in Cycle Two he became a bit more personal and accused Job of showing himself to be a sinner by his own bitter words; in Cycle Three he takes the next step and catalogs Job's specific sins (vv. 6–9).

22:6–9 The verbs here occur frequently, indicating that this was Job's ongoing practice. Eliphaz claims that despite all his wealth Job (1) took the poor man's garment as a pledge of loan repayment ("security," v. 6) and left him naked, whereas the law stipulated that he should return it before sundown (Exod 22:26; Deut 24:10–13); (2) refused food and water to the hungry (Isa 58:7,10); (3) confiscated land that did not belong to him (Isa 5:8); and (4) oppressed the widows and orphans in violation of the law that instructed compassionate care for them (e.g., Deut 24:19–21).

22:11 Still in his personal-indictment mode, Eliphaz applies the lesson of Bildad's speech (18:8–10) to Job directly.

22:12–14 God's transcendence can mean that either (1) he is so distant that he cannot know what is going on in the world, or (2) he is so high that he has a perfect perspective on all that goes on in the world. Eliphaz suggests that Job assumes the former.

22:15 old path. In Jer 6:16 it is the good way, but here it is the path of the wicked.

22:17 Using the same words ("Leave us alone!") but from the other end of the process, Job argued that those who dismiss God from their lives prosper (21:13–14). Eliphaz argues from the outcome of the process that those who dismiss God from their lives come to ruin. Job is his object lesson.

22:19 [x] Ps 58:10; 107:42 [y] Ps 52:6
22:20 [z] Job 15:30
22:21 [a] Ps 34:8-10
22:23 [b] Job 8:5; Isa 31:6; Zec 1:3 [c] Isa 19:22; Ac 20:32 [d] Job 11:14
22:24 [e] Job 31:25
22:25 [f] Isa 33:6
22:26 [g] Job 27:10; Isa 58:14
22:27 [h] Job 33:26; 34:28; Isa 58:9
22:29 [i] Mt 23:12; 1Pe 5:5
22:30 [j] Job 42:7-8
23:2 [k] Job 7:11 [l] Job 6:3
23:4 [m] Job 13:18
23:6 [n] Job 9:4

19 The righteous see their ruin and rejoice;[x]
the innocent mock[y] them, saying,
20 'Surely our foes are destroyed,
and fire[z] devours their wealth.'
21 "Submit to God and be at peace with him;
in this way prosperity will come to you.[a]
22 Accept instruction from his mouth
and lay up his words in your heart.
23 If you return[b] to the Almighty, you will be restored:[c]
If you remove wickedness far from your tent[d]
24 and assign your nuggets to the dust,
your gold of Ophir to the rocks in the ravines,[e]
25 then the Almighty will be your gold,
the choicest silver for you.[f]
26 Surely then you will find delight in the Almighty[g]
and will lift up your face to God.
27 You will pray to him,[h] and he will hear you,
and you will fulfill your vows.
28 What you decide on will be done,
and light will shine on your ways.
29 When people are brought low and you say, 'Lift them up!'
then he will save the downcast.[i]
30 He will deliver even one who is not innocent,
who will be delivered through the cleanness of your hands."[j]

Job 23

Then Job replied:

2 "Even today my complaint[k] is bitter;[l]
his hand[a] is heavy in spite of[b] my groaning.
3 If only I knew where to find him;
if only I could go to his dwelling!
4 I would state my case[m] before him
and fill my mouth with arguments.
5 I would find out what he would answer me,
and consider what he would say to me.
6 Would he vigorously oppose me?[n]
No, he would not press charges against me.

[a] 2 Septuagint and Syriac; Hebrew / *the hand on me* [b] 2 Or *heavy on me in*

22:21 Eliphaz admonishes Job to "submit to God" (cf. 5:8).
22:22–30 Similar to the dream that became the instrument of divine instruction in 4:12–21, Eliphaz offers God's instructions without stipulating the instrument by which he received them, whether a dream, a prophecy, or some other means.
22:24 Ophir. Location unknown; a source of fine gold (1 Kgs 9:28).
22:25 the Almighty will be your gold. Perhaps a pun on Eliphaz's name, which means "God is my fine gold."
22:28–30 A righteous man has great influence with God: the stories of Moses (Num 14:13–25) and Abraham (Gen 18:21–33) bear this out, and Ezek 14:14,20 (which names Job) affirms it.
23:1 — 24:25 *Job's Response to Eliphaz.* Job still wishes he knew where to find God, and he believes that if he could confront him, God would listen to him and acquit him (23:6–7). Nevertheless, God "knows the way that I take; when he has tested me, I will come forth as gold" (23:10). Job expresses his intuitive insight so far into what is going on between him and God: God is trying him in order to show the purity of his character. And indeed that is precisely the case! (1:8). This explanation for Job's suffering may be called the probationary explanation: God is trying Job to reveal his genuine religious faith. The metaphor "I will come forth as gold" builds off Eliphaz's assurance that if Job submits to God, God will become his gold (22:25). Slowly Job is moving away from his friends and their speeches and counter-speeches and moving closer to losing himself in his own thoughts about God and his personal dilemma; his position becomes virtually two monologues (chs. 28; 29–31) that form a capstone to the dialogue.
23:3 Eliphaz instructed Job to "return to the Almighty" (22:23); Job replies, "If only I knew where to find him."
23:6–7 Job's confidence in a benevolent God has been growing since he declared in ch. 9 that even if he could approach God, God would

7 There the upright can establish their innocence before him,[o]
and there I would be delivered forever from my judge.

8 "But if I go to the east, he is not there;
if I go to the west, I do not find him.
9 When he is at work in the north, I do not see him;
when he turns to the south, I catch no glimpse of him.[p]
10 But he knows the way that I take;
when he has tested me,[q] I will come forth as gold.[r]
11 My feet have closely followed his steps;[s]
I have kept to his way without turning aside.[t]
12 I have not departed from the commands of his lips;[u]
I have treasured the words of his mouth more than my daily bread.[v]

13 "But he stands alone, and who can oppose him?
He does whatever he pleases.[w]
14 He carries out his decree against me,
and many such plans he still has in store.[x]
15 That is why I am terrified before him;
when I think of all this, I fear him.
16 God has made my heart faint;[y]
the Almighty[z] has terrified me.
17 Yet I am not silenced by the darkness,[a]
by the thick darkness that covers my face.

24 "Why does the Almighty not set times for judgment?[b]
Why must those who know him look in vain for such days?[c]
2 There are those who move boundary stones;[d]
they pasture flocks they have stolen.
3 They drive away the orphan's donkey
and take the widow's ox in pledge.[e]
4 They thrust the needy from the path
and force all the poor[f] of the land into hiding.[g]
5 Like wild donkeys in the desert,
the poor go about their labor[h] of foraging food;
the wasteland provides food for their children.
6 They gather fodder in the fields
and glean in the vineyards of the wicked.
7 Lacking clothes, they spend the night naked;
they have nothing to cover themselves in the cold.[i]

23:7 [o] Job 13:3
23:9 [p] Job 9:11
23:10 [q] Ps 66:10; 139:1-3 [r] 1Pe 1:7
23:11 [s] Ps 17:5 [t] Ps 44:18
23:12 [u] Job 6:10 [v] Jn 4:32,34
23:13 [w] Ps 115:3
23:14 [x] 1Th 3:3
23:16 [y] Dt 20:3; Ps 22:14; Jer 51:46 [z] Job 27:2
23:17 [a] Job 19:8
24:1 [b] Jer 46:10 [c] Ac 1:7
24:2 [d] Dt 19:14; 27:17; Pr 23:10
24:3 [e] Dt 24:6,10,12,17; Job 22:6
24:4 [f] Job 29:12; 30:25; Ps 41:1 [g] Pr 28:28
24:5 [h] Ps 104:23
24:7 [i] Ex 22:27; Job 22:6

Kassite period *kudurru* known as the Michaux stone, a boundary stone (Job 24:2).

Wikimedia Commons

prevail against him because of his power. Job insists, "No godless person would dare come before him!" (13:16), thus anticipating this moment. Now Job is sure that if he could find God, God "would not press charges" against him. On the contrary, God could establish Job's innocence.

23:8–12 Reminiscent of Ps 139:7–12, Job depicts his desperate search for God, in contrast to the psalmist's desperate flight from God. Yet as in Ps 139, God always knows where Job is, and when he has tested him, Job "will come forth as gold" (v. 10), just as Eliphaz suggested (22:25). In another moment of faith, Job seems to get a glimpse into the heavenly council and God's motive for testing him. Even though that chapter is not open to him, he has read between the lines and intuited this conclusion by the give-and-take of the dialogue, by insisting on his innocence, and by his growing spiritual insight.

23:10–11 With uncanny insight, Job momentarily expresses that God knows his way, that he is being tested for his faith, and that in the end he "will come forth as gold." It is ironic that if Job had at any point succumbed to the friends' insistence that he plead guilty, he would have, by that sentiment alone, proved God wrong.

24:1 times for judgment. Job wonders why God does not have such times, and the reader, by dramatic irony, knows that he does (1:6; 2:1).

24:2–12 Job again "seizes the enemy's sword" and cites violations of social ethics that Eliphaz had accused him of (22:6–9), insisting that God has not charged the wrongdoers (v. 12c).

24:3 widow's ox. The means of her livelihood (see 22:6,9).

24:6 Perhaps suggests that the owner of the field had not left the unharvested grain for the poor as the law required (Deut 24:19–22) but instead required them to glean in the fields of strangers.

24:7 Perhaps alludes to taking the widow's garment in pledge (Deut 24:17).

24:8 [j] La 4:5
24:9 [k] Dt 24:17
24:12 [l] Eze 26:15 [m] Job 9:23
24:13 [n] Jn 3:19-20 [o] Isa 5:20
24:14 [p] Ps 10:9
24:15 [q] Pr 7:8-9 [r] Ps 10:11
24:16 [s] Ex 22:2; Mt 6:19 [t] Jn 3:20
24:18 [u] Job 9:26 [v] Job 22:16
24:19 [w] Job 6:17 [x] Job 21:13
24:20 [y] Job 18:17; Pr 10:7 [z] Ps 31:12; Da 4:14
24:21 [a] Job 22:9
24:22 [b] Dt 28:66
24:23 [c] Job 12:6 [d] Job 11:11
24:24 [e] Job 14:21; Ps 37:10 [f] Isa 17:5
24:25 [g] Job 6:28; 27:4

8 They are drenched by mountain rains
and hug[j] the rocks for lack of shelter.
9 The fatherless[k] child is snatched from the breast;
the infant of the poor is seized for a debt.
10 Lacking clothes, they go about naked;
they carry the sheaves, but still go hungry.
11 They crush olives among the terraces[a];
they tread the winepresses, yet suffer thirst.
12 The groans of the dying rise from the city,
and the souls of the wounded cry out for help.[l]
But God charges no one with wrongdoing.[m]

13 "There are those who rebel against the light,[n]
who do not know its ways
or stay in its paths.[o]
14 When daylight is gone, the murderer rises up,
kills the poor and needy,
and in the night steals forth like a thief.[p]
15 The eye of the adulterer watches for dusk;[q]
he thinks, 'No eye will see me,'[r]
and he keeps his face concealed.
16 In the dark, thieves break into houses,[s]
but by day they shut themselves in;
they want nothing to do with the light.[t]
17 For all of them, midnight is their morning;
they make friends with the terrors of darkness.

18 "Yet they are foam[u] on the surface of the water;[v]
their portion of the land is cursed,
so that no one goes to the vineyards.
19 As heat and drought snatch away the melted snow,[w]
so the grave[x] snatches away those who have sinned.
20 The womb forgets them,
the worm feasts on them;
the wicked are no longer remembered[y]
but are broken like a tree.[z]
21 They prey on the barren and childless woman,
and to the widow they show no kindness.[a]
22 But God drags away the mighty by his power;
though they become established, they have no assurance of life.[b]
23 He may let them rest in a feeling of security,[c]
but his eyes are on their ways.[d]
24 For a little while they are exalted, and then they are gone;[e]
they are brought low and gathered up like all others;
they are cut off like heads of grain.[f]
25 "If this is not so, who can prove me false
and reduce my words to nothing?"[g]

[a] *11* The meaning of the Hebrew for this word is uncertain.

24:12 wrongdoing. Cf. 1:22.
24:13–17 Job indicts those who violate the sixth, seventh, and eighth commandments (Exod 20:13–15), preferring to do their deeds in darkness.
24:18–20,22–24 It sounds like Job is rehearsing the position of his friends, although he admitted in ch. 21 that the wicked sometimes meet an unhappy end. To clarify, however, some translations prefix "But you say" to each statement.
24:25 Job challenges the friends to prove him wrong!

Bildad

25 Then Bildad the Shuhite replied:

[2] "Dominion and awe belong to God;[h]
he establishes order in the heights of heaven.
[3] Can his forces be numbered?
On whom does his light not rise?[i]
[4] How then can a mortal be righteous before God?
How can one born of woman be pure?[j]
[5] If even the moon[k] is not bright
and the stars are not pure in his eyes,[l]
[6] how much less a mortal, who is but a maggot —
a human being,[m] who is only a worm!"[n]

Job

26 Then Job replied:

[2] "How you have helped the powerless![o]
How you have saved the arm that is feeble![p]
[3] What advice you have offered to one without wisdom!
And what great insight you have displayed!
[4] Who has helped you utter these words?
And whose spirit spoke from your mouth?

[5] "The dead are in deep anguish,[q]
those beneath the waters and all that live in them.
[6] The realm of the dead[r] is naked before God;
Destruction[a] lies uncovered.[s]
[7] He spreads out the northern skies[t] over empty space;
he suspends the earth over nothing.
[8] He wraps up the waters[u] in his clouds,[v]
yet the clouds do not burst under their weight.
[9] He covers the face of the full moon,
spreading his clouds[w] over it.
[10] He marks out the horizon on the face of the waters[x]
for a boundary between light and darkness.[y]
[11] The pillars of the heavens quake,
aghast at his rebuke.
[12] By his power he churned up the sea;[z]
by his wisdom[a] he cut Rahab to pieces.

25:2 [h] Job 9:4; Rev 1:6
25:3 [i] Jas 1:17
25:4 [j] Job 4:17; 14:4
25:5 [k] Job 31:26 [l] Job 15:15
25:6 [m] Job 7:17 [n] Ps 22:6
26:2 [o] Job 6:12 [p] Ps 71:9
26:5 [q] Ps 88:10
26:6 [r] Ps 139:8 [s] Job 41:11; Pr 15:11; Heb 4:13
26:7 [t] Job 9:8
26:8 [u] Pr 30:4 [v] Job 37:11
26:9 [w] Job 22:14; Ps 97:2
26:10 [x] Pr 8:27,29 [y] Job 38:8-11
26:12 [z] Ex 14:21; Isa 51:15; Jer 31:35 [a] Job 12:13

[a] 6 Hebrew *Abaddon*

25:1 – 6 *Second Exchange: Bildad.* Only this speech (v. 2) and Zophar's second speech (20:2) begin with a declarative sentence rather than a question containing some allusion to Job. The friends' speeches, thankfully for Job, are getting shorter, and in this cycle Zophar does not speak at all. Bildad raises an argument that Eliphaz made (4:17 – 19; 15:14 – 16) and that Job seems to agree with (9:2): man cannot be righteous before God. Bildad insinuates that Job is about as low as a man can get (v. 6). This is complimentary of neither Job nor the human race!
25:4 – 6 A variation of Eliphaz's words in 15:14 – 16.
26:1 – 14 *Job's Response to Bildad.* This speech drips with sarcasm (vv. 2 – 4). Job describes the Creator (vv. 7 – 13) and his creative power much like the friends have, but Job's conclusion is different from theirs (v. 14). When one knows God as Creator, as awesome as the Creator is, one has still only explored the "outer fringe of his works" and heard only "the whisper" of his voice (v. 14). There is yet "the thunder of his power" (v. 14) that brings real understanding. The friends have certainly not heard that, and Job himself has yet to hear it.

Regarding Zophar's missing speech, we can assume that Zophar exhausted his arsenal of words and has nothing more he wants to say to Job. Some believe that Zophar's speech is lost among the other speeches, perhaps 26:1 – 4; but taken as irony, those words fit Job's mood and tone perfectly. The author gives us a hint of Job's awareness that Zophar was expected to speak and did not by introducing Job's following orations with a different formula than he has used to introduce his other speeches: "Job continued his discourse" (27:1; 29:1). The implication is that Job twice paused for Zophar to speak, and he did not, so Job continued.

26:13 [b] Isa 27:1
26:14 [c] Job 36:29
27:1 [d] Job 29:1
27:2 [e] Job 34:5 [f] Job 9:18
27:3 [g] Job 32:8; 33:4
27:4 [h] Job 6:28
27:5 [i] Job 2:9; 13:15
27:6 [j] Job 2:3
27:8 [k] Job 8:13 [l] Job 11:20; Lk 12:20
27:9 [m] Job 35:12; Pr 1:28; Isa 1:15; Jer 14:12; Mic 3:4
27:10 [n] Job 22:26
27:13 [o] Job 15:20; 20:29
27:14 [p] Dt 28:41; Job 15:22; Hos 9:13 [q] Job 20:10
27:15 [r] Ps 78:64
27:16 [s] Zec 9:3
27:17 [t] Pr 28:8; Ecc 2:26
27:18 [u] Job 8:14 [v] Isa 1:8
27:19 [w] Job 7:8
27:20 [x] Job 15:21 [y] Job 20:8

13 By his breath the skies became fair;
his hand pierced the gliding serpent.[b]
14 And these are but the outer fringe of his works;
how faint the whisper we hear of him!
Who then can understand the thunder of his power?"[c]

Job's Final Word to His Friends

27 And Job continued his discourse:[d]

2 "As surely as God lives, who has denied me justice,[e]
the Almighty, who has made my life bitter,[f]
3 as long as I have life within me,
the breath of God[g] in my nostrils,
4 my lips will not say anything wicked,
and my tongue will not utter lies.[h]
5 I will never admit you are in the right;
till I die, I will not deny my integrity.[i]
6 I will maintain my innocence and never let go of it;
my conscience will not reproach me as long as I live.[j]

7 "May my enemy be like the wicked,
my adversary like the unjust!
8 For what hope have the godless[k] when they are cut off,
when God takes away their life?[l]
9 Does God listen to their cry
when distress comes upon them?[m]
10 Will they find delight in the Almighty?[n]
Will they call on God at all times?

11 "I will teach you about the power of God;
the ways of the Almighty I will not conceal.
12 You have all seen this yourselves.
Why then this meaningless talk?

13 "Here is the fate God allots to the wicked,
the heritage a ruthless man receives from the Almighty:[o]
14 However many his children, their fate is the sword;[p]
his offspring will never have enough to eat.[q]
15 The plague will bury those who survive him,
and their widows will not weep for them.[r]
16 Though he heaps up silver like dust
and clothes like piles of clay,[s]
17 what he lays up the righteous will wear,[t]
and the innocent will divide his silver.
18 The house he builds is like a moth's cocoon,[u]
like a hut[v] made by a watchman.
19 He lies down wealthy, but will do so no more;[w]
when he opens his eyes, all is gone.
20 Terrors overtake him like a flood;[x]
a tempest snatches him away in the night.[y]

27:1–23 *Job's Final Word to His Friends.* Because vv. 7–23 seem more consistent with the friends' speeches, some have suggested that they are out of place and ought to be considered part of Bildad's short speech in ch. 25. Yet in this final speech to his friends, Job still maintains his integrity (v. 5), correlating the thesis that God has deprived him of justice (vv. 2,5–6), and rehearses the friends' flawed theology (vv. 13–19).

27:2 As surely as God lives. Introduces an oath, the first in the book.

27:7–10 Perhaps Job hopes that God will declare his friends ("my enemy ... my adversary," v. 7) wicked because of their slanderous words.

[21] The east wind carries him off, and he is gone;
it sweeps him out of his place.[z]
[22] It hurls itself against him without mercy[a]
as he flees headlong from its power.[b]
[23] It claps its hands in derision
and hisses him out of his place."[c]

27:21 [z] Job 7:10; 21:18
27:22 [a] Jer 13:14; Eze 5:11; 24:14 [b] Job 11:20
27:23 [c] Job 18:18
28:2 [d] Dt 8:9
28:3 [e] Ecc 1:13
28:5 [f] Ps 104:14
28:12 [g] Ecc 7:24
28:13 [h] Pr 3:15; Mt 13:44-46
28:15 [i] Pr 3:13-14; 8:10-11; 16:16

Interlude: Where Wisdom Is Found

28 There is a mine for silver
and a place where gold is refined.
[2] Iron is taken from the earth,
and copper is smelted from ore.[d]
[3] Mortals put an end to the darkness;[e]
they search out the farthest recesses
for ore in the blackest darkness.
[4] Far from human dwellings they cut a shaft,
in places untouched by human feet;
far from other people they dangle and sway.
[5] The earth, from which food comes,[f]
is transformed below as by fire;
[6] lapis lazuli comes from its rocks,
and its dust contains nuggets of gold.
[7] No bird of prey knows that hidden path,
no falcon's eye has seen it.
[8] Proud beasts do not set foot on it,
and no lion prowls there.
[9] People assault the flinty rock with their hands
and lay bare the roots of the mountains.
[10] They tunnel through the rock;
their eyes see all its treasures.
[11] They search[a] the sources of the rivers
and bring hidden things to light.

[12] But where can wisdom be found?[g]
Where does understanding dwell?
[13] No mortal comprehends its worth;[h]
it cannot be found in the land of the living.
[14] The deep says, "It is not in me";
the sea says, "It is not with me."
[15] It cannot be bought with the finest gold,
nor can its price be weighed out in silver.[i]
[16] It cannot be bought with the gold of Ophir,
with precious onyx or lapis lazuli.

[a] *11* Septuagint, Aquila and Vulgate; Hebrew *They dam up*

28:1–28 *Job's First Monologue: Where Wisdom Is Found.* This speech is self-contained, like chs. 29–31, but it does not interrupt the flow of the poetry. Up to this point, none of the friends has comprehended wisdom. This poem is constructed around the question that constitutes the refrain: "Where can wisdom be found?" (vv. 12,20). It divides the poem into three strophes: (1) the human search has not discovered wisdom (vv. 1–11); (2) human wealth cannot buy wisdom (vv. 13–19); (3) only God knows the way to wisdom (vv. 21–28). When the poet finally provides the classical definition of wisdom (v. 28), it comes as no surprise that Job is its representative (1:1). Yet something of the mystery of wisdom is still hidden from Job. In this way the poem points away from itself to God's speeches.

28:1–9 This description of mining is unique in the OT (cf. Deut 8:9). Silver and gold were not found in the Holy Land but were imported. There is, however, evidence of copper mining in the Negev at Timnah.

28:12,20 This refrain asks the question the poem seeks to answer, and Job begins the answer in v. 13 with a series of denials (vv. 14–19); the question is again introduced in v. 20 to present the positive answer (vv. 23–28): only God knows the way to wisdom.

Cylinder seal (left) and impression (right) depicting Utu, the sun god (standing on the lion), emerging from a depression between mountains and Enki (seated), the Sumerian god from the waters. Job 28:11 describes how wisdom is sought at the source of the rivers.

Scala/Art Resource, NY

28:17 [j] Pr 16:16
28:18 [k] Pr 3:15
28:19 [l] Pr 8:19
28:20 [m] ver 23,28
28:22 [n] Job 26:6
28:23 [o] Pr 8:22-31
28:24 [p] Ps 33:13-14 [q] Pr 15:3
28:25 [r] Job 12:15; Ps 135:7
28:26 [s] Job 37:3,8,11; 38:25,27
28:28 [t] Dt 4:6; Ps 111:10; Pr 1:7; 9:10
29:1 [u] Job 13:12; 27:1
29:2 [v] Jer 31:28

17 Neither gold nor crystal can compare with it,
nor can it be had for jewels of gold.[j]
18 Coral and jasper are not worthy of mention;
the price of wisdom is beyond rubies.[k]
19 The topaz of Cush cannot compare with it;
it cannot be bought with pure gold.[l]

20 Where then does wisdom come from?
Where does understanding dwell?[m]
21 It is hidden from the eyes of every living thing,
concealed even from the birds in the sky.
22 Destruction[a][n] and Death say,
"Only a rumor of it has reached our ears."
23 God understands the way to it
and he alone knows where it dwells,[o]
24 for he views the ends of the earth[p]
and sees everything under the heavens.[q]
25 When he established the force of the wind
and measured out the waters,[r]
26 when he made a decree for the rain
and a path for the thunderstorm,[s]
27 then he looked at wisdom and appraised it;
he confirmed it and tested it.
28 And he said to the human race,
"The fear of the Lord—that is wisdom,
and to shun evil is understanding."[t]

Job's Final Defense

29 Job continued his discourse:[u]

2 "How I long for the months gone by,
for the days when God watched over me,[v]

[a] 22 Hebrew *Abaddon*

28:22 Destruction and Death. Hebrew "Abaddon and Death." In 26:6 "Destruction" (Abaddon) is associated with the "realm of the dead"; here it is associated with death. It is probably a synonym for the netherworld.

28:28 he said. This is the only time we hear God's voice in the dialogue. Yet it is particularly significant because it is the voice of God identifying Job, by association (1:1,8; 2:3), as the truly wise man. Having heard this brief but essential character confirmation, Job must wait a while longer before he again hears the divine word in God's speeches (chs. 38–41).

29:1—31:40 *Job's Second Monologue: Job's Final Defense.* God still has not appeared to or answered Job as Job had challenged God to do. At this stage, Job sums up his defense, never once addressing his

[3]when his lamp shone on my head
and by his light I walked through darkness![w]
[4]Oh, for the days when I was in my prime,
when God's intimate friendship blessed my house,[x]
[5]when the Almighty was still with me
and my children were around me,
[6]when my path was drenched with cream[y]
and the rock[z] poured out for me streams of olive oil.[a]

[7]"When I went to the gate[b] of the city
and took my seat in the public square,
[8]the young men saw me and stepped aside
and the old men rose to their feet;
[9]the chief men refrained from speaking
and covered their mouths with their hands;[c]
[10]the voices of the nobles were hushed,
and their tongues stuck to the roof of their mouths.[d]
[11]Whoever heard me spoke well of me,
and those who saw me commended me,
[12]because I rescued the poor[e] who cried for help,
and the fatherless[f] who had none to assist them.[g]
[13]The one who was dying blessed me;[h]
I made the widow's[i] heart sing.
[14]I put on righteousness[j] as my clothing;
justice was my robe and my turban.
[15]I was eyes[k] to the blind
and feet to the lame.
[16]I was a father to the needy;[l]
I took up the case of the stranger.
[17]I broke the fangs of the wicked
and snatched the victims from their teeth.[m]

[18]"I thought, 'I will die in my own house,
my days as numerous as the grains of sand.[n]
[19]My roots will reach to the water,[o]
and the dew will lie all night on my branches.
[20]My glory will not fade;
the bow[p] will be ever new in my hand.'[q]

[21]"People listened to me expectantly,
waiting in silence for my counsel.

29:3 [w]Job 11:17
29:4 [x]Ps 25:14; Pr 3:32
29:6 [y]Job 20:17 [z]Ps 81:16 [a]Dt 32:13
29:7 [b]Job 31:21
29:9 [c]Job 21:5
29:10 [d]Ps 137:6
29:12 [e]Job 24:4 [f]Job 31:17,21 [g]Ps 72:12; Pr 21:13
29:13 [h]Job 31:20 [i]Job 22:9
29:14 [j]Job 27:6; Ps 132:9; Isa 59:17; 61:10; Eph 6:14
29:15 [k]Nu 10:31
29:16 [l]Job 24:4; Pr 29:7
29:17 [m]Ps 3:7
29:18 [n]Ps 30:6
29:19 [o]Job 18:16; Jer 17:8
29:20 [p]Ps 18:34 [q]Ge 49:24

friends. First, he reflects on the past, when he was a respected member of the community (ch. 29); second, he laments his present plight (ch. 30), which includes a loss of his wealth and honor; third, he climaxes the speech with a series of oaths to establish his innocence (ch. 31). One oath would have been enough, but the series reinforces Job's belief in his innocence. He closes this speech with the challenge that God write out his indictment against him (31:35–37) and concludes with the last oath, intimating that he is not guilty of violating the created order (31:38–40). One of the important issues in the book is God's silence. He cannot intervene because this would prove Satan's claim. Job must receive no support from God. It is important that Elihu's speeches separate Job's speech from that of God, suggesting that God does not respond directly to Job's plea.

29:2–6 Job longs for the good life when God "watched over" him (v. 2). Only the reader knows by dramatic irony how carefully God is still watching over him. Job reflects that his children and wealth were tangible tokens of God's favor.

29:7–11 Job's community greatly esteemed him.

29:7 gate of the city. The gathering place for friends and the place where the court convened to decide legal matters (see Ruth 4).

29:12 the poor ... the fatherless. In keeping with the law and the Hebrew faith, Job defended the weak and helpless (vv. 12–17).

29:14 I put on righteousness as my clothing. A way to express his intimate relationship with God. This is, in different words, very close to God's description of Job in the prologue (1:1,8; 2:3). For similar imagery, see Ps 132:9,16; Isa 59:17; 61:10; Rom 13:14; Eph 4:24; 6:14–17.

29:18–20 Job thought his life would turn out totally different.

29:21–25 Repeats the thought of vv. 7–10 (his compatriots' esteem for him) and transitions to words about his friends' contempt for him in ch. 30.

29:22 [r] Dt 32:2
29:25 [s] Job 1:3; 31:37 [t] Job 4:4
30:1 [u] Job 12:4
30:9 [v] Ps 69:11 [w] Job 12:4; La 3:14,63 [x] Job 17:6
30:10 [y] Nu 12:14; Dt 25:9; Isa 50:6; Mt 26:67
30:11 [z] Ru 1:21 [a] Ps 32:9
30:12 [b] Ps 140:4-5 [c] Job 19:12
30:13 [d] Isa 3:12
30:15 [e] Job 31:23; Ps 55:4-5 [f] Job 3:25; Hos 13:3

22 After I had spoken, they spoke no more;
my words fell gently on their ears.[r]
23 They waited for me as for showers
and drank in my words as the spring rain.
24 When I smiled at them, they scarcely believed it;
the light of my face was precious to them.[a]
25 I chose the way for them and sat as their chief;
I dwelt as a king[s] among his troops;
I was like one who comforts mourners.[t]

30

"But now they mock me,[u]
men younger than I,
whose fathers I would have disdained
to put with my sheep dogs.
2 Of what use was the strength of their hands to me,
since their vigor had gone from them?
3 Haggard from want and hunger,
they roamed[b] the parched land
in desolate wastelands at night.
4 In the brush they gathered salt herbs,
and their food[c] was the root of the broom bush.
5 They were banished from human society,
shouted at as if they were thieves.
6 They were forced to live in the dry stream beds,
among the rocks and in holes in the ground.
7 They brayed among the bushes
and huddled in the undergrowth.
8 A base and nameless brood,
they were driven out of the land.

9 "And now those young men mock me[v] in song;[w]
I have become a byword[x] among them.
10 They detest me and keep their distance;
they do not hesitate to spit in my face.[y]
11 Now that God has unstrung my bow and afflicted me,[z]
they throw off restraint[a] in my presence.
12 On my right the tribe[d] attacks;
they lay snares for my feet,[b]
they build their siege ramps against me.[c]
13 They break up my road;[d]
they succeed in destroying me.
'No one can help him,' they say.
14 They advance as through a gaping breach;
amid the ruins they come rolling in.
15 Terrors overwhelm me;[e]
my dignity is driven away as by the wind,
my safety vanishes like a cloud.[f]

[a] *24* The meaning of the Hebrew for this clause is uncertain. [b] *3* Or *gnawed* [c] *4* Or *fuel*
[d] *12* The meaning of the Hebrew for this word is uncertain.

30:1–15 In sharp contrast to the respect he once enjoyed in the community, Job informs the reader that a group of scavengers, human in form but animal in behavior (vv. 6–7) and "younger" (v. 1) than he, mock him in word and song. They make a sport of it, and their fathers are no better than they are. Perhaps they are motivated by the three friends and their disrespect for Job, which is generally known in the community (the debate is most likely public).

30:1 In the ancient Near East, dogs were wild scavengers. Sheep dogs were more domesticated but not much more socially respectable.

[16] "And now my life ebbs away;[g]
days of suffering grip me.
[17] Night pierces my bones;
my gnawing pains never rest.
[18] In his great power God becomes like clothing to me[a];
he binds me like the neck of my garment.
[19] He throws me into the mud,[h]
and I am reduced to dust and ashes.

[20] "I cry out to you, God, but you do not answer;[i]
I stand up, but you merely look at me.
[21] You turn on me ruthlessly;[j]
with the might of your hand[k] you attack me.[l]
[22] You snatch me up and drive me before the wind;[m]
you toss me about in the storm.[n]
[23] I know you will bring me down to death,[o]
to the place appointed for all the living.[p]

[24] "Surely no one lays a hand on a broken man
when he cries for help in his distress.[q]
[25] Have I not wept for those in trouble?
Has not my soul grieved for the poor?[r]
[26] Yet when I hoped for good, evil came;
when I looked for light, then came darkness.[s]
[27] The churning inside me never stops;[t]
days of suffering confront me.
[28] I go about blackened,[u] but not by the sun;
I stand up in the assembly and cry for help.[v]
[29] I have become a brother of jackals,[w]
a companion of owls.[x]
[30] My skin grows black and peels;[y]
my body burns with fever.[z]
[31] My lyre is tuned to mourning,[a]
and my pipe to the sound of wailing.

31 "I made a covenant with my eyes
not to look lustfully at a young woman.[b]
[2] For what is our lot from God above,
our heritage from the Almighty on high?[c]
[3] Is it not ruin[d] for the wicked,
disaster for those who do wrong?[e]
[4] Does he not see my ways[f]
and count my every step?[g]

[5] "If I have walked with falsehood
or my foot has hurried after deceit[h] —
[6] let God weigh me in honest scales[i]
and he will know that I am blameless —

[a] 18 Hebrew; Septuagint *power he grasps my clothing*

30:16 [g] Job 3:24; Ps 22:14; 42:4
30:19 [h] Ps 69:2,14
30:20 [i] Job 19:7
30:21 [j] Job 19:6,22 [k] Job 16:9,14 [l] Job 10:3
30:22 [m] Job 27:21 [n] Job 9:17
30:23 [o] Job 9:22; 10:8 [p] Job 3:19
30:24 [q] Job 19:7
30:25 [r] Job 24:4; Ps 35:13-14; Ro 12:15
30:26 [s] Job 3:25-26; 19:8; Jer 8:15
30:27 [t] La 2:11
30:28 [u] Ps 38:6; 42:9; 43:2 [v] Job 19:7
30:29 [w] Ps 44:19 [x] Ps 102:6; Mic 1:8
30:30 [y] La 4:8 [z] Ps 102:3
30:31 [a] Isa 24:8
31:1 [b] Mt 5:28
31:2 [c] Job 20:29
31:3 [d] Job 21:30 [e] Job 34:22
31:4 [f] 2Ch 16:9 [g] Pr 5:21
31:5 [h] Mic 2:11
31:6 [i] Job 6:2; 27:5-6

Relief from Saqqara showing starving Egyptians. Job 30 describes how Job's body is wasting away.

Werner Forman Archive/Heritage Images/Glow Images

30:16 – 23 Job laments his present suffering.
30:24 – 31 Job again reviews how he compassionately treated the poor (29:12 – 17), quite the opposite of how these human scavengers treat him (vv. 1 – 15).
30:30 Another description of his deteriorating physical condition (vv. 17, 27,28; 7:5; 16:16; 18:4; 33:19 – 22).
31:1 – 4 Because Job believes that God punishes wrong, he has lived by a moral code, knowing that God is aware of his actions.
31:1 Like the tenth commandment (Exod 20:17), this moral principle regulates Job's thought life.
31:5 – 40 This series of oaths is a capstone to the dialogue, sealing Job's belief in his innocence.

31:7 [j] Job 23:11 [k] Job 9:30
31:8 [l] Lev 26:16; Job 20:18 [m] Mic 6:15
31:9 [n] Job 24:15
31:10 [o] Dt 28:30; Jer 8:10
31:11 [p] Ge 38:24; Lev 20:10; Dt 22:22-24
31:12 [q] Job 15:30 [r] Job 26:6 [s] Job 20:28
31:13 [t] Dt 24:14-15
31:15 [u] Job 10:3
31:16 [v] Job 5:16; 20:19 [w] Job 22:9
31:17 [x] Job 22:7; 29:12
31:19 [y] Job 22:6 [z] Job 24:4
31:21 [a] Job 22:9
31:22 [b] Job 38:15
31:23 [c] Job 13:11
31:24 [d] Job 22:25 [e] Mt 6:24; Mk 10:24
31:25 [f] Ps 62:10
31:26 [g] Eze 8:16

7 if my steps have turned from the path,[j]
if my heart has been led by my eyes,
or if my hands[k] have been defiled,
8 then may others eat what I have sown,[l]
and may my crops be uprooted.[m]

9 "If my heart has been enticed[n] by a woman,
or if I have lurked at my neighbor's door,
10 then may my wife grind another man's grain,
and may other men sleep with her.[o]
11 For that would have been wicked,
a sin to be judged.[p]
12 It is a fire[q] that burns to Destruction[a];[r]
it would have uprooted my harvest.[s]

13 "If I have denied justice to any of my servants,
whether male or female,
when they had a grievance against me,[t]
14 what will I do when God confronts me?
What will I answer when called to account?
15 Did not he who made me in the womb make them?
Did not the same one form us both within our mothers?[u]

16 "If I have denied the desires of the poor[v]
or let the eyes of the widow[w] grow weary,
17 if I have kept my bread to myself,
not sharing it with the fatherless[x]—
18 but from my youth I reared them as a father would,
and from my birth I guided the widow—
19 if I have seen anyone perishing for lack of clothing,[y]
or the needy[z] without garments,
20 and their hearts did not bless me
for warming them with the fleece from my sheep,
21 if I have raised my hand against the fatherless,[a]
knowing that I had influence in court,
22 then let my arm fall from the shoulder,
let it be broken off at the joint.[b]
23 For I dreaded destruction from God,
and for fear of his splendor[c] I could not do such things.

24 "If I have put my trust in gold[d]
or said to pure gold, 'You are my security,'[e]
25 if I have rejoiced over my great wealth,[f]
the fortune my hands had gained,
26 if I have regarded the sun[g] in its radiance
or the moon moving in splendor,
27 so that my heart was secretly enticed
and my hand offered them a kiss of homage,

[a] 12 Hebrew *Abaddon*

31:9–12 Job takes an oath that he has not committed adultery (Exod 20:14).
31:13–15 Job swears that he has not mistreated his servants, whom he considers like himself: God's creations.
31:16–23 Job takes an oath that he has cared for the widow, orphan, and needy.
31:24–28 Job takes an oath that he has not worshiped any other gods, including the god of wealth (Exod 20:3–6).

[28]then these also would be sins to be judged,[h]
for I would have been unfaithful to God on high.

[29]"If I have rejoiced at my enemy's misfortune[i]
or gloated over the trouble that came to him[j]—
[30]I have not allowed my mouth to sin
by invoking a curse against their life—
[31]if those of my household have never said,
'Who has not been filled with Job's meat?'[k]—
[32]but no stranger had to spend the night in the street,
for my door was always open to the traveler[l]—
[33]if I have concealed[m] my sin as people do,[a]
by hiding[n] my guilt in my heart
[34]because I so feared the crowd[o]
and so dreaded the contempt of the clans
that I kept silent and would not go outside—

[35]("Oh, that I had someone to hear me![p]
I sign now my defense—let the Almighty answer me;
let my accuser[q] put his indictment in writing.
[36]Surely I would wear it on my shoulder,
I would put it on like a crown.
[37]I would give him an account of my every step;
I would present it to him as to a ruler.[r])—

[38]"if my land cries out against me[s]
and all its furrows are wet with tears,
[39]if I have devoured its yield without payment[t]
or broken the spirit of its tenants,[u]
[40]then let briers[v] come up instead of wheat
and stinkweed instead of barley."

The words of Job are ended.

Elihu

32 So these three men stopped answering Job, because he was righteous in his own eyes.[w] [2]But
Elihu son of Barakel the Buzite,[x] of the family of Ram, became very angry with Job for justifying himself rather than God.[y] [3]He was also angry with the three friends, because they had found

[a] 33 Or *as Adam did*

31:28 [h]Dt 17:2-7
31:29 [i]Ob 12 [j]Pr 17:5; 24:17-18
31:31 [k]Job 22:7
31:32 [l]Ge 19:2-3; Ro 12:13
31:33 [m]Pr 28:13 [n]Ge 3:8
31:34 [o]Ex 23:2
31:35 [p]Job 19:7; 30:28 [q]Job 27:7; 35:14
31:37 [r]Job 1:3; 29:25
31:38 [s]Ge 4:10
31:39 [t]1Ki 21:19 [u]Lev 19:13; Jas 5:4
31:40 [v]Ge 3:18
32:1 [w]Job 10:7; 33:9
32:2 [x]Ge 22:21 [y]Job 27:5; 30:21

31:29–32 Job takes an oath that he has not "gloated over" (v. 29) his enemies' downfall or failed to offer hospitality to strangers.
31:33–34 Job takes an oath that he has not been hypocritical.
31:35–37 Job breaks into his string of oaths (note the parentheses) with a wish that there was "someone to hear" him (v. 35) and that he could make his case before such a person (16:19; 23:3–7,10). This is Job's signature as he submits his indictment to God.
31:38–40a Job takes a final oath: he has not abused the soil or those who cultivate it—perhaps an allusion to the basic curse on the soil (Gen 3:18; 4:12)—and has not violated the created order.
31:40b A formula indicating the end of the dialogue. Cf. Ps 72:20.
32:1—37:24 *The Elihu Speeches.* Only here is the reader informed that Elihu was present during the dialogue. After his four speeches (cf. three for each of the friends except Zophar), we do not hear about him again, not even in the epilogue, which mentions all three men as the object of Job's prayer (42:7–9). The tone of Elihu's speeches is set by multiple references that he was angry (32:1–5). On a more logical note, he explains that he is younger than the three friends, and in deference to their age, he did not speak (32:6). But now that the dialogue is obviously ended, Elihu feels the compulsion to speak because Job "was righteous in his own eyes" (32:1) and justified himself rather than God and because the three friends "found no way to refute Job" (32:3; see 32:1–5). He claims to understand Job's arguments, and several times he repeats or summarizes Job's words (33:8–11,13; 34:5–6; 35:2–3). Twice he challenges Job to answer his arguments (33:32; 34:33), but Job never dignifies Elihu's speeches with a reply. Some view the Elihu speeches as comic relief; i.e., Job was ready for God to speak (31:35), but Elihu steps in to claim he has the answer, only to rehash the friends' arguments and add little new to the debate. He is the only one of the participants to use Job's name, perhaps suggesting his youthful, yet artless, demeanor. Though his claims fall short, he believes he has contributed to the argument of the dialogue. Indeed, his contribution that suffering is sometimes *disciplinary* is of significance to the larger discussion regarding suffering: God uses suffering to discipline and correct a wayward individual (33:14–30; 36:8–11,15–17; 37:13); but Eliphaz had already suggested this argument in his first speech (5:17–18). Yet

32:6 [z] Job 15:10
32:8 [a] Job 27:3; 33:4 [b] Pr 2:6
32:9 [c] 1Co 1:26
32:13 [d] Jer 9:23

no way to refute Job, and yet had condemned him.[a] 4 Now Elihu had waited before speaking to Job
because they were older than he. 5 But when he saw that the three men had nothing more to say, his
anger was aroused.

6 So Elihu son of Barakel the Buzite said:

"I am young in years,
  and you are old;[z]
that is why I was fearful,
  not daring to tell you what I know.
7 I thought, 'Age should speak;
  advanced years should teach wisdom.'
8 But it is the spirit[b] in a person,
  the breath of the Almighty,[a] that gives them understanding.[b]
9 It is not only the old[c] who are wise,[c]
  not only the aged who understand what is right.

10 "Therefore I say: Listen to me;
  I too will tell you what I know.
11 I waited while you spoke,
  I listened to your reasoning;
while you were searching for words,
12 I gave you my full attention.
But not one of you has proved Job wrong;
  none of you has answered his arguments.
13 Do not say, 'We have found wisdom;[d]
  let God, not a man, refute him.'
14 But Job has not marshaled his words against me,
  and I will not answer him with your arguments.

15 "They are dismayed and have no more to say;
  words have failed them.
16 Must I wait, now that they are silent,
  now that they stand there with no reply?
17 I too will have my say;
  I too will tell what I know.
18 For I am full of words,
  and the spirit within me compels me;
19 inside I am like bottled-up wine,
  like new wineskins ready to burst.
20 I must speak and find relief;
  I must open my lips and reply.

[a] *3* Masoretic Text; an ancient Hebrew scribal tradition *Job, and so had condemned God* [b] *8* Or *Spirit*; also in verse 18 [c] *9* Or *many*; or *great*

Elihu, unlike the reader, had no notion of the reason for Job's suffering. The prologue spells out that Job's suffering was to show what an exemplary man Job was, that he served God with no ulterior motives, phrased in Satan's famous question, "Does Job fear God for nothing?" (1:9).

32:1—33:33 *Elihu's First Speech.* Elihu explains to the friends (32:6–22) and to Job (33:1–7) how he is going to intervene. He recalls the three friends' failed efforts (32:12,14–16) and Job's arguments (33:9–11), and further describes Job's physical distress and emaciated body (33:19–33).

32:2 Elihu. Means "he is my God." He is given a full patronymic of father, tribe, and clan, thus reinforcing his pretentious claim of importance. His ethnic origin is uncertain.

32:3 Job ... condemned him. See NIV text note.

32:6 Elihu is speaking to the three friends.

32:8 Elihu insists (see v. 18 and note) that the "breath of the Almighty," not age, gives wisdom ("understanding"). For him, true wisdom is an understanding of Job's suffering and what lies behind it. More practically, wisdom is to provide a solution to Job's problem.

32:14 I will not answer him with your arguments. A jab at the three friends.

32:15 words have failed them. Along with v. 14, this gives the reader a window into Elihu's uncomplimentary estimate of the three friends.

32:16 they stand there with no reply. Implies that the friends have miserably failed to answer Job, augmenting his negative view of their efforts.

32:18 the spirit within me compels me. Elihu claims that God is the inspiration of his compulsion to speak (v. 8).

[21] I will show no partiality,[e]
nor will I flatter anyone;
[22] for if I were skilled in flattery,
my Maker would soon take me away.

33

"But now, Job, listen to my words;
pay attention to everything I say.[f]
[2] I am about to open my mouth;
my words are on the tip of my tongue.
[3] My words come from an upright heart;
my lips sincerely speak what I know.[g]
[4] The Spirit of God has made me;[h]
the breath of the Almighty[i] gives me life.
[5] Answer me[j] then, if you can;
stand up[k] and argue your case before me.
[6] I am the same as you in God's sight;
I too am a piece of clay.[l]
[7] No fear of me should alarm you,
nor should my hand be heavy on you.[m]

[8] "But you have said in my hearing—
I heard the very words—
[9] 'I am pure,[n] I have done no wrong;[o]
I am clean and free from sin.
[10] Yet God has found fault with me;
he considers me his enemy.[p]
[11] He fastens my feet in shackles;[q]
he keeps close watch on all my paths.'[r]

[12] "But I tell you, in this you are not right,
for God is greater than any mortal.[s]
[13] Why do you complain to him[t]
that he responds to no one's words[a]?
[14] For God does speak[u]—now one way, now another—
though no one perceives it.
[15] In a dream,[v] in a vision of the night,
when deep sleep falls on people
as they slumber in their beds,
[16] he may speak[w] in their ears
and terrify them with warnings,
[17] to turn them from wrongdoing
and keep them from pride,
[18] to preserve them from the pit,[x]
their lives from perishing by the sword.[b][y]

[19] "Or someone may be chastened on a bed of pain
with constant distress in their bones,[z]

32:21 [e] Lev 19:15; Job 13:10; Mt 22:16
33:1 [f] Job 13:6
33:3 [g] Job 6:28; 27:4; 36:4
33:4 [h] Ge 2:7; Job 10:3 [i] Job 27:3
33:5 [j] ver 32 [k] Job 13:18
33:6 [l] Job 4:19
33:7 [m] Job 9:34; 13:21; 2Co 2:4
33:9 [n] Job 10:7 [o] Job 13:23; 16:17
33:10 [p] Job 13:24
33:11 [q] Job 13:27 [r] Job 14:16
33:12 [s] Ecc 7:20
33:13 [t] Job 40:2; Isa 45:9
33:14 [u] Ps 62:11
33:15 [v] Job 4:13
33:16 [w] Job 36:10,15
33:18 [x] ver 22,24,28,30 [y] Job 15:22
33:19 [z] Job 30:17

[a] *13* Or *that he does not answer for any of his actions* [b] *18* Or *from crossing the river*

33:1 Elihu addresses Job using his personal name, unlike the friends in the dialogue, which may imply an inappropriate familiarity edging on disrespect.
33:5 Answer me then, if you can. Job had concluded the dialogue by expressing his desire for someone to answer him (31:35–37)—but Job had God in mind, not Elihu.
33:9–11 Elihu quotes Job's words (13:24,27).
33:15 Like Eliphaz (4:12–21), Elihu claims that God speaks in dreams and visions.
33:19–27 The person described in vv. 19–22 is most likely Job. Elihu holds out hope of deliverance for Job if Job will admit his sin (v. 27; cf. the friends' view in 4:6–8; 10:6).

33:20 [a] Ps 107:18 [b] Job 3:24; 6:6
33:21 [c] Job 16:8; 19:20
33:22 [d] Ps 88:3
33:23 [e] Mic 6:8
33:24 [f] Isa 38:17
33:25 [g] 2Ki 5:14
33:26 [h] Job 34:28 [i] Job 22:26 [j] Ps 50:15; 51:12
33:27 [k] 2Sa 12:13 [l] Lk 15:21 [m] Ro 6:21
33:28 [n] Job 22:28
33:29 [o] 1Co 12:6; Eph 1:11; Php 2:13
33:30 [p] Ps 56:13
33:33 [q] Ps 34:11
34:3 [r] Job 12:11
34:4 [s] 1Th 5:21
34:5 [t] Job 33:9 [u] Job 27:2

20 so that their body finds food[a] repulsive
and their soul loathes the choicest meal.[b]
21 Their flesh wastes away to nothing,
and their bones, once hidden, now stick out.[c]
22 They draw near to the pit,
and their life to the messengers of death.[a][d]
23 Yet if there is an angel at their side,
a messenger, one out of a thousand,
sent to tell them how to be upright,[e]
24 and he is gracious to that person and says to God,
'Spare them from going down to the pit;[f]
I have found a ransom for them—
25 let their flesh be renewed like a child's;
let them be restored as in the days of their youth'[g]—
26 then that person can pray to God and find favor with him,[h]
they will see God's face and shout for joy;[i]
he will restore them to full well-being.[j]
27 And they will go to others and say,
'I have sinned,[k] I have perverted what is right,[l]
but I did not get what I deserved.[m]
28 God has delivered me from going down to the pit,
and I shall live to enjoy the light of life.'[n]

29 "God does all these things to a person[o]—
twice, even three times—
30 to turn them back from the pit,
that the light of life[p] may shine on them.

31 "Pay attention, Job, and listen to me;
be silent, and I will speak.
32 If you have anything to say, answer me;
speak up, for I want to vindicate you.
33 But if not, then listen to me;
be silent, and I will teach you wisdom.[q]"

34 Then Elihu said:

2 "Hear my words, you wise men;
listen to me, you men of learning.
3 For the ear tests words
as the tongue tastes food.[r]
4 Let us discern for ourselves what is right;
let us learn together what is good.[s]

5 "Job says, 'I am innocent,[t]
but God denies me justice.[u]

[a] 22 Or *to the place of the dead*

33:23 messenger. Comparable to "someone to mediate between us" (9:33), but in this case it is someone to explain how Job can be upright. **33:31** Elihu again addresses Job by his personal name (see v. 1 and note). **33:33** Elihu has a bloated sense of his own wisdom and a blighted sense of Job's. **34:1–37** *Elihu's Second Speech.* Elihu addresses the friends and refutes Job's claim to innocence (vv. 1–15); he then addresses Job, insisting that divine governance and divine justice are inseparable (vv. 16–30), and calls Job to repentance (vv. 31–33). **34:2** Address to the friends, perhaps sarcastically. **34:3** Evidently a proverb (cf. 12:11). In view of other quotations of Job's words (33:9–11), Elihu had listened well. **34:5** Cites Job's claim of innocence in 27:2a.

[6]Although I am right,
I am considered a liar;
although I am guiltless,
his arrow inflicts an incurable wound.'[v]
[7]Is there anyone like Job,
who drinks scorn like water?[w]
[8]He keeps company with evildoers;
he associates with the wicked.[x]
[9]For he says, 'There is no profit
in trying to please God.'[y]

[10]"So listen to me, you men of understanding.
Far be it from God to do evil,[z]
from the Almighty to do wrong.[a]
[11]He repays everyone for what they have done;[b]
he brings on them what their conduct deserves.[c]
[12]It is unthinkable that God would do wrong,
that the Almighty would pervert justice.[d]
[13]Who appointed him over the earth?
Who put him in charge of the whole world?[e]
[14]If it were his intention
and he withdrew his spirit[a] and breath,[f]
[15]all humanity would perish together
and mankind would return to the dust.[g]

[16]"If you have understanding, hear this;
listen to what I say.
[17]Can someone who hates justice govern?[h]
Will you condemn the just and mighty One?[i]
[18]Is he not the One who says to kings, 'You are worthless,'
and to nobles, 'You are wicked,'[j]
[19]who shows no partiality[k] to princes
and does not favor the rich over the poor,[l]
for they are all the work of his hands?[m]
[20]They die in an instant, in the middle of the night;[n]
the people are shaken and they pass away;
the mighty are removed without human hand.[o]

[21]"His eyes are on the ways of mortals;
he sees their every step.[p]
[22]There is no deep shadow,[q] no utter darkness,[r]
where evildoers can hide.

34:6 [v]Job 6:4
34:7 [w]Job 15:16
34:8 [x]Job 22:15; Ps 50:18
34:9 [y]Job 21:15; 35:3
34:10 [z]Ge 18:25 [a]Dt 32:4; Job 8:3; Ro 9:14
34:11 [b]Ps 62:12; Mt 16:27; Ro 2:6; 2Co 5:10 [c]Jer 32:19; Eze 33:20
34:12 [d]Job 8:3
34:13 [e]Job 38:4,6
34:14 [f]Ps 104:29
34:15 [g]Ge 3:19; Job 9:22
34:17 [h]2Sa 23:3-4 [i]Job 40:8
34:18 [j]Ex 22:28
34:19 [k]Dt 10:17; Ac 10:34 [l]Lev 19:15 [m]Job 10:3
34:20 [n]Ex 12:29 [o]Job 12:19
34:21 [p]Job 31:4; Pr 15:3
34:22 [q]Am 9:2-3 [r]Ps 139:12

[a] *14* Or *Spirit*

34:7–9 Another description of Job (cf. Eliphaz's description of Job in 22:5–9). It is totally the opposite of who Job is, according to the prologue. Although Elihu boasted that he would not answer Job with the friends' arguments (32:14), he is already violating his pledge.
34:10–12 Addressing the friends rather than Job, Elihu's defense of God's justice implies he thought that the friends had misrepresented divine justice or that they had let Job get away with such a misrepresentation: "Far be it from God to do evil" (v. 10). The principle is retributive justice: "He repays everyone for what they have done" (v. 11). Verse 12 echoes Bildad's question in 8:3.
34:13 Who appointed him over the earth? God rules the earth and is answerable to no one since he is self-appointed. As a counter argument, Job has argued that God rules the earth and is therefore responsible for what happens to human beings (9:12,24).
34:16 Elihu turns from the friends to address Job.
34:17 God must be just in order to govern; therefore, since he governs the world, no one can accuse him of injustice.
34:21–25 Job asked in 24:1 why the Almighty does not keep times of judgment when his subjects can present their claims to him. Elihu argues that God does not need to do so because he sees everything. The reader knows that God does judge.

34:23 [s] Job 11:11
34:24 [t] Job 12:19 [u] Da 2:21
34:27 [v] Ps 28:5; Isa 5:12 [w] 1Sa 15:11
34:28 [x] Ex 22:23; Job 35:9; Jas 5:4
34:30 [y] Pr 29:2-12
34:32 [z] Job 35:11; Ps 25:4 [a] Job 33:27
34:33 [b] Job 41:11
34:35 [c] Job 35:16; 38:2
34:36 [d] Job 22:15
34:37 [e] Job 27:23 [f] Job 23:2
35:3 [g] Job 9:29-31; 34:9

23 God has no need to examine people further,
that they should come before him for judgment.[s]
24 Without inquiry he shatters the mighty[t]
and sets up others in their place.[u]
25 Because he takes note of their deeds,
he overthrows them in the night and they are crushed.
26 He punishes them for their wickedness
where everyone can see them,
27 because they turned from following him[v]
and had no regard for any of his ways.[w]
28 They caused the cry of the poor to come before him,
so that he heard the cry of the needy.[x]
29 But if he remains silent, who can condemn him?
If he hides his face, who can see him?
Yet he is over individual and nation alike,
30 to keep the godless from ruling,
from laying snares for the people.[y]

31 "Suppose someone says to God,
'I am guilty but will offend no more.
32 Teach me what I cannot see;[z]
if I have done wrong, I will not do so again.'[a]
33 Should God then reward you on your terms,
when you refuse to repent?[b]
You must decide, not I;
so tell me what you know.

34 "Men of understanding declare,
wise men who hear me say to me,
35 'Job speaks without knowledge;[c]
his words lack insight.'
36 Oh, that Job might be tested to the utmost
for answering like a wicked man![d]
37 To his sin he adds rebellion;
scornfully he claps his hands[e] among us
and multiplies his words against God."[f]

35 Then Elihu said:

2 "Do you think this is just?
You say, 'I am in the right, not God.'
3 Yet you ask him, 'What profit is it to me,[a]
and what do I gain by not sinning?'[g]

4 "I would like to reply to you
and to your friends with you.

[a] 3 Or *you*

34:31–32 Elihu, as in 33:27, indirectly proposes that Job confess his sin, which would be a confession of guilt. However, the dialogue is built in part upon Job's claim of innocence—a claim the prologue supports. To confess his sin would be a falsehood on Job's part.
34:33 Elihu accuses Job of setting his own terms for dealing with God. **You must decide, not I.** An abbreviated way of saying, "Do you believe God will say, 'You must decide, not I'?"
34:36 See 35:16.
35:1–16 *Elihu's Third Speech.* Elihu addresses Job and maintains that God pays no attention to the empty cries of people who have no consciousness of their sin.
35:2 The concern is Job's claim to be innocent (e.g., 6:30; 9:20).

[5]Look up at the heavens[h] and see;
gaze at the clouds so high above you.[i]
[6]If you sin, how does that affect him?
If your sins are many, what does that do to him?[j]
[7]If you are righteous, what do you give to him,[k]
or what does he receive[l] from your hand?[m]
[8]Your wickedness only affects humans like yourself,
and your righteousness only other people.

[9]"People cry out[n] under a load of oppression;
they plead for relief from the arm of the powerful.[o]
[10]But no one says, 'Where is God my Maker,[p]
who gives songs in the night,[q]
[11]who teaches[r] us more than he teaches[a] the beasts of the earth
and makes us wiser than[b] the birds in the sky?'
[12]He does not answer[s] when people cry out
because of the arrogance of the wicked.
[13]Indeed, God does not listen to their empty plea;
the Almighty pays no attention to it.[t]
[14]How much less, then, will he listen
when you say that you do not see him,[u]
that your case[v] is before him
and you must wait for him,
[15]and further, that his anger never punishes
and he does not take the least notice of wickedness.[c]
[16]So Job opens his mouth with empty talk;
without knowledge he multiplies words."[w]

36 Elihu continued:

[2]"Bear with me a little longer and I will show you
that there is more to be said in God's behalf.
[3]I get my knowledge from afar;
I will ascribe justice to my Maker.[x]
[4]Be assured that my words are not false;[y]
one who has perfect knowledge[z] is with you.

[5]"God is mighty, but despises no one;[a]
he is mighty, and firm in his purpose.[b]
[6]He does not keep the wicked alive[c]
but gives the afflicted their rights.[d]

[a] *10,11* Or *night, / [11]who teaches us by* [b] *11* Or *us wise by* [c] *15* Symmachus, Theodotion and Vulgate; the meaning of the Hebrew for this word is uncertain.

35:5 [h]Ge 15:5 [i]Job 22:12
35:6 [j]Pr 8:36
35:7 [k]Ro 11:35 [l]Pr 9:12 [m]Job 22:2-3; Lk 17:10
35:9 [n]Ex 2:23 [o]Job 12:19
35:10 [p]Job 27:10; Isa 51:13 [q]Ps 42:8; 149:5; Ac 16:25
35:11 [r]Ps 94:12
35:12 [s]Pr 1:28
35:13 [t]Job 27:9; Pr 15:29; Isa 1:15; Jer 11:11
35:14 [u]Job 9:11 [v]Ps 37:6
35:16 [w]Job 34:35,37
36:3 [x]Job 8:3; 37:23
36:4 [y]Job 33:3 [z]Job 37:5,16,23
36:5 [a]Ps 22:24 [b]Job 12:13
36:6 [c]Job 8:22 [d]Job 5:15

35:6 Job's question in 7:20.
35:7–8 Neither Job's sin nor his righteousness does anything for God; it affects only other people.
35:9–16 The question: Why doesn't God answer prayer, in this case, Job's prayer? Elihu's answer: Job's prayers are "empty" (v. 13), prayed out of a spirit of "arrogance" (v. 12). Elihu's wish that Job might be "tested to the utmost" (34:36) is based on his assumption that "without knowledge he multiplies words" (v. 16; see 34:35). God's lack of response to Job is linked to the test, but Elihu is utterly unaware of this.
36:1—37:24 *Elihu's Fourth Speech.* Elihu addresses Job exclusively and sounds his theme that God sends suffering to bring about moral correction (36:8–11,16–17). He ends by asserting that God does not oppress (37:23), thus countering one of Job's favorite arguments in the dialogue.
36:1 Elihu continued. This introductory formula only occurs here in the Elihu speeches, evidently to signal the fact that he knew he was going beyond the three speeches of the friends.
36:2 Bear with me a little longer. Elihu is conscious of his long and wearying speeches, but he justifies them by saying that he is speaking "in God's behalf."
36:4 one who has perfect knowledge. Elihu's bloated self-conceit underlies all that he has to say.

36:7 [e]Ps 33:18 [f]Ps 113:8
36:8 [g]Ps 107:10,14
36:9 [h]Job 15:25
36:10 [i]Job 33:16 [j]2Ki 17:13
36:11 [k]Isa 1:19
36:12 [l]Job 15:22 [m]Job 4:21
36:13 [n]Ro 2:5
36:14 [o]Dt 23:17
36:16 [p]Hos 2:14 [q]Ps 23:5
36:17 [r]Job 22:11
36:18 [s]Job 34:33
36:20 [t]Job 34:20,25
36:21 [u]Ps 66:18 [v]Heb 11:25
36:22 [w]Isa 40:13; 1Co 2:16
36:23 [x]Job 34:13 [y]Job 8:3
36:24 [z]Ps 92:5; 138:5 [a]Ps 59:16; Rev 15:3

7 He does not take his eyes off the righteous;[e]
he enthrones them with kings[f]
and exalts them forever.
8 But if people are bound in chains,[g]
held fast by cords of affliction,
9 he tells them what they have done—
that they have sinned arrogantly.[h]
10 He makes them listen[i] to correction
and commands them to repent of their evil.[j]
11 If they obey and serve him,[k]
they will spend the rest of their days in prosperity
and their years in contentment.
12 But if they do not listen,
they will perish by the sword[a][l]
and die without knowledge.[m]

13 "The godless in heart[n] harbor resentment;
even when he fetters them, they do not cry for help.
14 They die in their youth,
among male prostitutes of the shrines.[o]
15 But those who suffer he delivers in their suffering;
he speaks to them in their affliction.

16 "He is wooing[p] you from the jaws of distress
to a spacious place free from restriction,
to the comfort of your table[q] laden with choice food.
17 But now you are laden with the judgment due the wicked;
judgment and justice have taken hold of you.[r]
18 Be careful that no one entices you by riches;
do not let a large bribe turn you aside.[s]
19 Would your wealth or even all your mighty efforts
sustain you so you would not be in distress?
20 Do not long for the night,[t]
to drag people away from their homes.[b]
21 Beware of turning to evil,[u]
which you seem to prefer to affliction.[v]

22 "God is exalted in his power.
Who is a teacher like him?[w]
23 Who has prescribed his ways for him,[x]
or said to him, 'You have done wrong'?[y]
24 Remember to extol his work,[z]
which people have praised in song.[a]
25 All humanity has seen it;
mortals gaze on it from afar.

[a] 12 Or *will cross the river* [b] 20 The meaning of the Hebrew for verses 18-20 is uncertain.

36:8–11 This explanation that suffering is *disciplinary* is Elihu's main contribution to the argument.
36:14 male prostitutes. Male and female prostitutes were employed in the Canaanite cult (e.g., Deut 23:17–18; 1 Kgs 14:24).
36:15 The argument summarizes Elihu's doctrine in 33:16–30.
36:16 He is wooing you. A call for Job to submit to God's disciplinary ways that will, according to Elihu, lead Job to a new life.
36:21 evil, which you seem to prefer to affliction. Elihu, like Eliphaz (22:7–9), has turned Job's moral profile upside down, now accusing him of preferring evil (34:7–9).
36:22 God is exalted in his power. Job certainly does not disagree with this thought, but he has maintained that although God is powerful and wise, he has acted unjustly.

[26]How great is God — beyond our understanding![b]
The number of his years is past finding out.[c]

[27]"He draws up the drops of water,
which distill as rain to the streams[a];[d]
[28]the clouds pour down their moisture
and abundant showers fall on mankind.[e]
[29]Who can understand how he spreads out the clouds,
how he thunders from his pavilion?[f]
[30]See how he scatters his lightning about him,
bathing the depths of the sea.
[31]This is the way he governs[b] the nations[g]
and provides food in abundance.[h]
[32]He fills his hands with lightning
and commands it to strike its mark.[i]
[33]His thunder announces the coming storm;
even the cattle make known its approach.[c]

37 "At this my heart pounds
and leaps from its place.
[2]Listen! Listen to the roar of his voice,
to the rumbling that comes from his mouth.[j]
[3]He unleashes his lightning beneath the whole heaven
and sends it to the ends of the earth.
[4]After that comes the sound of his roar;
he thunders with his majestic voice.
When his voice resounds,
he holds nothing back.
[5]God's voice thunders in marvelous ways;
he does great things beyond our understanding.[k]
[6]He says to the snow,[l] 'Fall on the earth,'
and to the rain shower, 'Be a mighty downpour.'[m]
[7]So that everyone he has made may know his work,
he stops all people from their labor.[d][n]
[8]The animals take cover;
they remain in their dens.[o]
[9]The tempest comes out from its chamber,
the cold from the driving winds.
[10]The breath of God produces ice,
and the broad waters become frozen.[p]
[11]He loads the clouds with moisture;
he scatters his lightning through them.[q]
[12]At his direction they swirl around
over the face of the whole earth
to do whatever he commands them.[r]
[13]He brings the clouds to punish people,[s]
or to water his earth and show his love.[t]

36:26 [b] 1Co 13:12 [c] Job 10:5; Ps 90:2; 102:24; Heb 1:12
36:27 [d] Job 38:28; Ps 147:8
36:28 [e] Job 5:10
36:29 [f] Job 26:14; 37:16
36:31 [g] Job 37:13 [h] Ps 136:25; Ac 14:17
36:32 [i] Job 37:12,15
37:2 [j] Ps 29:3-9
37:5 [k] Job 5:9
37:6 [l] Job 38:22 [m] Job 36:27
37:7 [n] Job 12:14
37:8 [o] Job 38:40; Ps 104:22
37:10 [p] Job 38:29-30; Ps 147:17
37:11 [q] Job 36:27,29
37:12 [r] Ps 148:8
37:13 [s] 1Sa 12:17 [t] Ex 9:18; 1Ki 18:45; Job 38:27

[a] 27 Or *distill from the mist as rain* [b] 31 Or *nourishes* [c] 33 Or *announces his coming — / the One zealous against evil* [d] 7 Or *work, / he fills all people with fear by his power*

37:5 beyond our understanding. That God's ways and thoughts are higher than ours is a theme in chs. 38 – 41 (see Isa 55:8 – 9; Rom 11:33 – 36).

37:16 [u] Job 36:4
37:18 [v] Job 9:8; Ps 104:2; Isa 44:24
37:23 [w] Job 9:4; 36:4; 1Ti 6:16 [x] Job 8:3 [y] Isa 63:9; Eze 18:23,32
37:24 [z] Mt 10:28 [a] Mt 11:25
38:1 [b] Job 40:6
38:2 [c] Job 35:16; 42:3; 1Ti 1:7

14 "Listen to this, Job;
stop and consider God's wonders.
15 Do you know how God controls the clouds
and makes his lightning flash?
16 Do you know how the clouds hang poised,
those wonders of him who has perfect knowledge?[u]
17 You who swelter in your clothes
when the land lies hushed under the south wind,
18 can you join him in spreading out the skies,[v]
hard as a mirror of cast bronze?

19 "Tell us what we should say to him;
we cannot draw up our case because of our darkness.
20 Should he be told that I want to speak?
Would anyone ask to be swallowed up?
21 Now no one can look at the sun,
bright as it is in the skies
after the wind has swept them clean.
22 Out of the north he comes in golden splendor;
God comes in awesome majesty.
23 The Almighty is beyond our reach and exalted in power;[w]
in his justice[x] and great righteousness, he does not oppress.[y]
24 Therefore, people revere him,[z]
for does he not have regard for all the wise[a] in heart?[a]"

The Lord Speaks

38 Then the LORD spoke to Job out of the storm.[b] He said:

2 "Who is this that obscures my plans
with words without knowledge?[c]

[a] 24 Or *for he does not have regard for any who think they are wise.*

37:18 spreading out the skies. Reference to God's creative work; cf. the opening words of God's speeches (ch. 38).

37:24 revere. The NIV turns the final clause into a question, but given Elihu's conceited attitude, it could be declarative: "he does not have regard for all the wise in heart." It is tinged with sarcasm.

38:1 — 42:6 *God's Speeches and Job's Responses.* God's speeches divide into two parts, each followed by Job's response: God's first speech (38:1 — 40:2); Job's response (40:3 – 5); God's second speech (40:6 — 41:34); Job's response (42:1 – 6).

If the meaning of the book of Job is framed as *suffering and divine justice*, then God's speeches (38:1 — 40:2; 40:6 — 41:34) do not provide an answer. The Lord nowhere explains generally why the innocent suffer or specifically why Job suffers. Rather, the Lord challenges Job to stand up and answer some compelling questions about Job's human status as opposed to God's divine power and glory. The Lord's questions are not rhetorical — the Lord demands an answer of Job. But if the meaning of the book is framed as *relationship with God*, which is precisely the way the prologue lays it out (1:8; 2:3), then God's speeches certainly provide an answer. We should ask, however, why God's speeches do not describe Job in the affirming words of the prologue. To the contrary, Job is the object of the Lord's challenge (38:4). But Job's two responses to God's speeches (40:3 – 5; 42:1 – 6) hint at an answer. First (40:3 – 5), Job confesses his unworthiness and inability to answer God's challenge — he is human, not divine. Second (42:1 – 6), Job confesses that he has spoken out of insufficient knowledge of God, and his former experience (dialogue) compared with his latter experience (God's speaking) is the difference between "hearing" and "seeing" (42:5), thus suggesting the progress he has made in his relationship with God. His repentance, therefore, is not repentance of sins as demanded by his friends, but repentance of insufficient knowledge of God. That is precisely the challenge the Lord poses to Job in 38:2: "Who is this that obscures my plans *with words without knowledge*?" (emphasis added).

Yet while his humanness manifests itself in the diatribes of the dialogue, Job never curses God, as Satan claimed he would (1:11; 2:5) and as his wife advised him to do (2:9). Again he has passed the test of faith as administered by Satan. In God's speeches, however, Job is exposed to the overwhelming power and glory of the Creator and Sustainer of the universe, and Job's demand for answers and his caricature of God come under the scrutiny of the Lord who also makes demands (38:3).

Since God presented his servant Job to Satan's scrutiny and pleasure, why should he object when his servant Job, in the dialogue, presented *him* to the readers' scrutiny and pleasure? In a sense, Job turned the tables on God, yet God affirms Job again in the epilogue, giving balance to the book. So the book is about Job's relationship with God. It is the book about God and humanity.

38:1 — 40:2 *God's First Speech.* By a series of questions and challenges, prefaced by a challenge of Job's knowledge (38:2), the Lord draws a series of tightening circles around Job: (1) "Where were you when I laid the earth's foundation?" (38:4), followed by a series of collateral questions (38:5 – 11) that challenge Job's knowledge of the created world; (2) "Have you ever given orders to the morning, or shown

[3]Brace yourself like a man;
I will question you,
and you shall answer me.[d]

[4]"Where were you when I laid the earth's foundation?[e]
Tell me, if you understand.
[5]Who marked off its dimensions?[f] Surely you know!
Who stretched a measuring line across it?
[6]On what were its footings set,
or who laid its cornerstone[g] —
[7]while the morning stars sang together
and all the angels[a] shouted for joy?

[8]"Who shut up the sea behind doors[h]
when it burst forth from the womb,[i]
[9]when I made the clouds its garment
and wrapped it in thick darkness,
[10]when I fixed limits for it[j]
and set its doors and bars in place,[k]
[11]when I said, 'This far you may come and no farther;
here is where your proud waves halt'?[l]

[12]"Have you ever given orders to the morning,
or shown the dawn its place,
[13]that it might take the earth by the edges
and shake the wicked[m] out of it?
[14]The earth takes shape like clay under a seal;
its features stand out like those of a garment.
[15]The wicked are denied their light,[n]
and their upraised arm is broken.[o]

[16]"Have you journeyed to the springs of the sea
or walked in the recesses of the deep?[p]
[17]Have the gates of death[q] been shown to you?
Have you seen the gates of the deepest darkness?

38:3 [d]Job 40:7
38:4 [e]Ps 104:5; Pr 8:29
38:5 [f]Pr 8:29; Isa 40:12
38:6 [g]Job 26:7
38:8 [h]Jer 5:22 [i]Ge 1:9-10
38:10 [j]Ps 33:7; 104:9 [k]Job 26:10
38:11 [l]Ps 89:9
38:13 [m]Ps 104:35
38:15 [n]Job 18:5 [o]Ps 10:15
38:16 [p]Ps 77:19
38:17 [q]Ps 9:13

[a] 7 Hebrew *the sons of God*

the dawn its place ...?" (38:12), followed by questions that challenge Job's personal involvement with the created order (38:13–38); (3) "Do you hunt the prey for the lioness and satisfy the hunger of the lions when they crouch in their dens or lie in wait in a thicket?" (38:39–40), followed by collateral questions and challenges that test Job's ability to manage and control the animal kingdom (38:41—39:30).

38:1 the LORD. God's speeches use the covenant name of Israel's God, *yhwh* (Yahweh, rendered "the LORD"), as do the prologue (e.g., 1:6) and the epilogue (e.g., 42:7). In comparison, references to the deity in the dialogue employ the generic names *ʾĕlōhîm, ēl,* and *ĕlōah* (also *šadday* = Almighty). This is no literary accident but part of the theological design. The author would not use the covenant name of the deity in a context of words that puts the deity in a negative light. Thus, the generic names are more appropriate to the dialogue. **spoke.** Can also be translated "answered" (this applies also to 40:1) because this is what Job challenged the Lord to do throughout the dialogue: to answer him. **out of the storm.** This is the "theophany" that Job had hoped for, even though technically a "theophany" is the *appearance* of God, not merely the voice of God.

38:2 obscures my plans. Job concealed ("darkened") God's divine plan for the world. This is the essence of God's indictment of Job (see also 42:3a). Job simply does not understand the divine plan that lies behind the universe.

38:3 you shall answer me. The Lord turns the tables on Job and challenges him to answer.

38:4 Where were you ...? The implication is that Job did not exist when God created the world, so how could he understand it? God uses the metaphor of building a house to describe his work of creation. He poetically describes his creative activity very differently from that described in Gen 1–2. **the earth's foundations.** Laying the foundations or the capstone of a building was an occasion for joyful celebration. This is not a rhetorical question; an answer is expected, but Job is unable to answer (40:5).

38:7 shouted for joy. A poetic description of God's joy in creating the world.

38:8 the sea ... when it burst forth from the womb. The language of birth describes the creation of the seas (cf. Gen 1:9–10).

38:12 Have you ever ... The questions in the following verses depict Job in a role of manager of creation, a role that only God can occupy, thus exposing Job's humanness.

38:13 and shake the wicked out of it. The idea is that the dawn illuminates the dark places where the wicked hide (v. 15; 24:13–17).

38:18 [r]Job 28:24
38:20 [s]Job 26:10
38:21 [t]Job 15:7
38:22 [u]Job 37:6
38:23 [v]Isa 30:30; Eze 13:11 [w]Ex 9:18; Jos 10:11; Rev 16:21
38:25 [x]Job 28:26
38:26 [y]Job 36:27
38:27 [z]Ps 104:14; 107:35
38:28 [a]Ps 147:8; Jer 14:22
38:29 [b]Ps 147:16-17
38:30 [c]Job 37:10
38:31 [d]Job 9:9; Am 5:8
38:33 [e]Ps 148:6; Jer 31:36
38:34 [f]Job 22:11; 36:27-28
38:35 [g]Job 36:32; 37:3
38:36 [h]Job 9:4 [i]Job 32:8; Ps 51:6; Ecc 2:26

18 Have you comprehended the vast expanses of the earth?[r]
Tell me, if you know all this.

19 "What is the way to the abode of light?
And where does darkness reside?
20 Can you take them to their places?
Do you know the paths[s] to their dwellings?
21 Surely you know, for you were already born![t]
You have lived so many years!

22 "Have you entered the storehouses of the snow[u]
or seen the storehouses of the hail,
23 which I reserve for times of trouble,[v]
for days of war and battle?[w]
24 What is the way to the place where the lightning is dispersed,
or the place where the east winds are scattered over the earth?
25 Who cuts a channel for the torrents of rain,
and a path for the thunderstorm,[x]
26 to water[y] a land where no one lives,
an uninhabited desert,
27 to satisfy a desolate wasteland
and make it sprout with grass?[z]
28 Does the rain have a father?[a]
Who fathers the drops of dew?
29 From whose womb comes the ice?
Who gives birth to the frost from the heavens[b]
30 when the waters become hard as stone,
when the surface of the deep is frozen?[c]

31 "Can you bind the chains[a] of the Pleiades?
Can you loosen Orion's belt?[d]
32 Can you bring forth the constellations in their seasons[b]
or lead out the Bear[c] with its cubs?
33 Do you know the laws[e] of the heavens?
Can you set up God's[d] dominion over the earth?

34 "Can you raise your voice to the clouds
and cover yourself with a flood of water?[f]
35 Do you send the lightning bolts on their way?[g]
Do they report to you, 'Here we are'?
36 Who gives the ibis wisdom[e][h]
or gives the rooster understanding?[f][i]
37 Who has the wisdom to count the clouds?
Who can tip over the water jars of the heavens

[a] *31* Septuagint; Hebrew *beauty* [b] *32* Or *the morning star in its season* [c] *32* Or *out Leo* [d] *33* Or *their* [e] *36* That is, wisdom about the flooding of the Nile [f] *36* That is, understanding of when to crow; the meaning of the Hebrew for this verse is uncertain.

38:18 Tell me, if you know all this. A continuing demand that Job reveal his knowledge of the created world, a knowledge that he obviously does not possess (40:5).
38:19 the abode of light. God separated light and darkness on the first day of creation (Gen 1:4), and here the Lord poetically describes them as having different abodes.
38:20 to their places. With biting irony the Lord asks Job if he can direct light and darkness to their respective homes.
38:21 Surely you know. Again with irony, the Lord taunts Job with this challenge because Job's speeches in the dialogue made him appear to know so much about the world, as if he is Wisdom personified (Prov 8:22–31). God indicts Job because Job assumes greater knowledge than he actually possesses, as Job confesses in his second response (42:3).
38:26 a land where no one lives. God is so concerned about and knowledgeable of his creation that he waters those places where no human being lives—a witness to God's goodness.

[38]when the dust becomes hard
and the clods of earth stick together?

[39]"Do you hunt the prey for the lioness
and satisfy the hunger of the lions[j]
[40]when they crouch in their dens[k]
or lie in wait in a thicket?
[41]Who provides food for the raven[l]
when its young cry out to God
and wander about for lack of food?[m]

39 "Do you know when the mountain goats[n] give birth?
Do you watch when the doe bears her fawn?
[2]Do you count the months till they bear?
Do you know the time they give birth?
[3]They crouch down and bring forth their young;
their labor pains are ended.
[4]Their young thrive and grow strong in the wilds;
they leave and do not return.

[5]"Who let the wild donkey[o] go free?
Who untied its ropes?
[6]I gave it the wasteland[p] as its home,
the salt flats as its habitat.[q]
[7]It laughs at the commotion in the town;
it does not hear a driver's shout.[r]
[8]It ranges the hills for its pasture
and searches for any green thing.

[9]"Will the wild ox[s] consent to serve you?
Will it stay by your manger at night?
[10]Can you hold it to the furrow with a harness?
Will it till the valleys behind you?
[11]Will you rely on it for its great strength?
Will you leave your heavy work to it?
[12]Can you trust it to haul in your grain
and bring it to your threshing floor?

[13]"The wings of the ostrich flap joyfully,
though they cannot compare
with the wings and feathers of the stork.
[14]She lays her eggs on the ground
and lets them warm in the sand,
[15]unmindful that a foot may crush them,
that some wild animal may trample them.
[16]She treats her young harshly,[t] as if they were not hers;
she cares not that her labor was in vain,
[17]for God did not endow her with wisdom
or give her a share of good sense.[u]

38:39 [j]Ps 104:21
38:40 [k]Job 37:8
38:41 [l]Lk 12:24 [m]Ps 147:9; Mt 6:26
39:1 [n]Dt 14:5
39:5 [o]Job 6:5; 11:12; 24:5
39:6 [p]Job 24:5; Ps 107:34; Jer 2:24 [q]Hos 8:9
39:7 [r]Job 3:18
39:9 [s]Nu 23:22; Dt 33:17
39:16 [t]La 4:3
39:17 [u]Job 35:11

39:1 Do you know ...? God continues to press Job's knowledge of the universe, which obviously is inadequate. **know.** Its verbal and noun derivatives occur in God's speeches and Job's responses 14 times, revealing how central this theme is in showing Job's inadequate knowledge of the universe. Cf. Zophar's questions concerning Job's knowledge of God (11:7–12).

39:13–18 The "ostrich" (v. 13) certainly does not fit the category of what we would call a sensible animal, but God has provided it with strength and speed so that it "laughs at horse and rider" (v. 18).

39:20 [v] Joel 2:4-5 [w] Jer 8:16
39:21 [x] Jer 8:6
39:24 [y] Jer 4:5,19; Eze 7:14; Am 3:6
39:25 [z] Jos 6:5 [a] Am 1:14; 2:2
39:27 [b] Jer 49:16; Ob 4
39:29 [c] Job 9:26
39:30 [d] Mt 24:28; Lk 17:37

18 Yet when she spreads her feathers to run,
she laughs at horse and rider.

19 "Do you give the horse its strength
or clothe its neck with a flowing mane?
20 Do you make it leap like a locust,[v]
striking terror with its proud snorting?[w]
21 It paws fiercely, rejoicing in its strength,
and charges into the fray.[x]
22 It laughs at fear, afraid of nothing;
it does not shy away from the sword.
23 The quiver rattles against its side,
along with the flashing spear and lance.
24 In frenzied excitement it eats up the ground;
it cannot stand still when the trumpet sounds.[y]
25 At the blast of the trumpet[z] it snorts, 'Aha!'
It catches the scent of battle from afar,
the shout of commanders and the battle cry.[a]

26 "Does the hawk take flight by your wisdom
and spread its wings toward the south?
27 Does the eagle soar at your command
and build its nest on high?[b]
28 It dwells on a cliff and stays there at night;
a rocky crag is its stronghold.
29 From there it looks for food;[c]
its eyes detect it from afar.
30 Its young ones feast on blood,
and where the slain are, there it is."[d]

39:19–25 This describes the use of horses as cavalry. Israel did not begin using horses and chariots extensively until the time of Solomon. This could intimate that the book of Job originates in another culture than Israel or that it is from the time of the Israelite monarchy after David.

39:26–30 The Lord ends this speech by describing the hawk and eagle, whose majestic flight Job cannot command; when they look for food, there are the carcasses.

A man grasps two ostriches by the throat, Assyrian, ca. 1000–539 BC. Job 39:13–18 describes the speed and behavior of ostriches.

Werner Forman Archive/British Museum/Glow Images

40 The LORD said to Job:[e]

[2] "Will the one who contends with the Almighty correct him?
Let him who accuses God answer him!"

[3]Then Job answered the LORD:

[4] "I am unworthy[f] — how can I reply to you?
I put my hand over my mouth.[g]
[5] I spoke once, but I have no answer[h] —
twice, but I will say no more."[i]

[6]Then the LORD spoke to Job out of the storm:[j]

[7] "Brace yourself like a man;
I will question you,
and you shall answer me.[k]
[8] "Would you discredit my justice?[l]
Would you condemn me to justify yourself?
[9] Do you have an arm like God's,[m]
and can your voice thunder like his?[n]
[10] Then adorn yourself with glory and splendor,
and clothe yourself in honor and majesty.[o]
[11] Unleash the fury of your wrath,[p]
look at all who are proud and bring them low,[q]
[12] look at all who are proud and humble them,[r]
crush[s] the wicked where they stand.
[13] Bury them all in the dust together;
shroud their faces in the grave.
[14] Then I myself will admit to you
that your own right hand can save you.[t]
[15] "Look at Behemoth,
which I made along with you
and which feeds on grass like an ox.

40:1 [e] Job 10:2; 13:3; 23:4; 31:35; 33:13
40:4 [f] Job 42:6 [g] Job 29:9
40:5 [h] Job 9:3 [i] Job 9:15
40:6 [j] Job 38:1
40:7 [k] Job 38:3; 42:4
40:8 [l] Job 27:2; Ro 3:3
40:9 [m] 2Ch 32:8 [n] Job 37:5; Ps 29:3-4
40:10 [o] Ps 93:1; 104:1
40:11 [p] Isa 42:25; Na 1:6 [q] Isa 2:11,12,17; Da 4:37
40:12 [r] 1Sa 2:7 [s] Isa 13:11; 63:2-3,6
40:14 [t] Ps 20:6; 60:5; 108:6

40:2 Let him who accuses God answer him! Job said he would present his case to the Almighty if he had the opportunity, and now the Lord presents him with the challenge. In the absence of "someone to mediate" (9:33), Job has come to play that role himself. The table is turned: Job challenged God to answer his accusations, and now God demands that Job answer him. But Job plays the role of the *mediator/accuser* in the dialogue, which God seems to recognize in the epilogue when he says to Eliphaz, "You have not spoken the truth about me, as my servant Job has" (42:7). While we need not take this statement to include every detail of Job's descriptions of God in the dialogue, especially his overstatements, we should recognize that his theology was tempered by his emotional and physical pain, sometimes resulting in hyperbole and exaggeration.

40:3–5 *Job's First Response.* Job's response is not the kind of defense he said he would give; it is virtually an apology that now he has "no answer" (v. 5).

40:6—41:34 *God's Second Speech.* The beginning of God's second speech repeats almost verbatim the beginning of the first speech, with the exception of 38:2, which is missing here, and may be in response to Job's refusal to answer (40:5).

40:8 Would you condemn me to justify yourself? The Lord gets rather personal with Job and sounds a lot like the friends in the dialogue (cf. 8:3; 15:4) and also Elihu, who was "angry with Job for justifying himself rather than God" (32:2).

40:9 can your voice thunder like his? Elihu had said that since humans do not have God's power, they have no right to question his justice (33:12; 36:22–23). Job himself said that the friends could not understand the thunder of God's power (26:14).

40:10–14 Job is invited to assume divine attributes and, since he claimed to know so much about God's operation, do God's work of bringing justice: "look at all who are proud and humble them" (v. 12). This follows logically on the question of v. 8.

40:15 Behemoth. The identities of Behemoth and Leviathan (41:1) have been much discussed. (1) Traditionally Behemoth (Hebrew plural for "beast") has been identified as the hippopotamus; Leviathan, the crocodile. Some of the descriptive terms fit these two animals: e.g., the hippopotamus is an amphibious beast and eats grass (vv. 15,21–22), and the crocodile is strong and has a double coat of armor, fearsome teeth, and a strong neck (41:12–14,22). According to this interpretation, Behemoth is the fiercest land animal; Leviathan, the most awesome water creature. (2) Some interpret these two beasts as mythological, drawing upon comparable creatures in Ugaritic mythology. However, though there are some references in Job that may be taken as mythological, the book seems otherwise to have no underlying mythological substructure. The Lord is the only deity Job knows. (3) Behemoth and Leviathan are the author's literary creations. He takes, perhaps, the images of the hippopotamus and crocodile and augments their features to develop images of creatures that resemble terrestrial animals but in

40:19 [u] Job 41:33
40:20 [v] Ps 104:14 [w] Ps 104:26
40:22 [x] Isa 44:4
40:24 [y] Job 41:2,7,26
41:1 [z] Job 3:8; Ps 104:26; Isa 27:1
41:2 [a] Isa 37:29
41:4 [b] Ex 21:6
41:10 [c] Job 3:8 [d] Jer 50:44
41:11 [e] Ro 11:35 [f] Ex 19:5; Dt 10:14; Ps 24:1; 50:12; 1Co 10:26

16 What strength it has in its loins,
what power in the muscles of its belly!
17 Its tail sways like a cedar;
the sinews of its thighs are close-knit.
18 Its bones are tubes of bronze,
its limbs like rods of iron.
19 It ranks first among the works of God,[u]
yet its Maker can approach it with his sword.
20 The hills bring it their produce,[v]
and all the wild animals play[w] nearby.
21 Under the lotus plants it lies,
hidden among the reeds in the marsh.
22 The lotuses conceal it in their shadow;
the poplars by the stream[x] surround it.
23 A raging river does not alarm it;
it is secure, though the Jordan should surge against
its mouth.
24 Can anyone capture it by the eyes,
or trap it and pierce its nose?[y]

41[a]

"Can you pull in Leviathan[z] with a fishhook
or tie down its tongue with a rope?
2 Can you put a cord through its nose
or pierce its jaw with a hook?[a]
3 Will it keep begging you for mercy?
Will it speak to you with gentle words?
4 Will it make an agreement with you
for you to take it as your slave for life?[b]
5 Can you make a pet of it like a bird
or put it on a leash for the young women in your house?
6 Will traders barter for it?
Will they divide it up among the merchants?
7 Can you fill its hide with harpoons
or its head with fishing spears?
8 If you lay a hand on it,
you will remember the struggle and never do it again!
9 Any hope of subduing it is false;
the mere sight of it is overpowering.
10 No one is fierce enough to rouse it.[c]
Who then is able to stand against me?[d]
11 Who has a claim against me that I must pay?[e]
Everything under heaven belongs to me.[f]

[a] In Hebrew texts 41:1-8 is numbered 40:25-32, and 41:9-34 is numbered 41:1-26.

a literary sense, are far fiercer and more awesome. The point is that in the world Job knows, the world God has created, Job cannot handle the most awesome land and sea animals. They are representative of the creation, which Job has no ability to direct, manage, or control. (4) Some hold that whatever Behemoth and Leviathan are, they point beyond themselves to the power of Satan. Even if that were true, the point would be the same: Job has no power to control or subdue such creatures.

40:19 first among the works of God. First not in time but in strength and awe. God is the only one who can control this creature.

41:1–9 Though similar to a description of the capture of a crocodile in the works of the Greek historian Herodotus, the author is probably not dependent upon Herodotus. The point is that "any hope of subduing it is false" (v. 9).

41:1 Leviathan. See note on 40:15.

41:10 Who then is able to stand against me? If no human being can subdue this creature, then how could a person think they can stand against God?

41:11 This indicts Job, who implies from time to time in the dialogue that God owes him something. But "everything under heaven" belongs to God, so no one can tell God how to conduct himself in his own world. Paul makes this point in his doxology in Rom 11:33–36, where he cel-

12 "I will not fail to speak of Leviathan's limbs,
its strength and its graceful form.
13 Who can strip off its outer coat?
Who can penetrate its double coat of armor[a]?
14 Who dares open the doors of its mouth,
ringed about with fearsome teeth?
15 Its back has[b] rows of shields
tightly sealed together;
16 each is so close to the next
that no air can pass between.
17 They are joined fast to one another;
they cling together and cannot be parted.
18 Its snorting throws out flashes of light;
its eyes are like the rays of dawn.[g]
19 Flames stream from its mouth;
sparks of fire shoot out.
20 Smoke pours from its nostrils
as from a boiling pot over burning reeds.
21 Its breath[h] sets coals ablaze,
and flames dart from its mouth.[i]
22 Strength resides in its neck;
dismay goes before it.
23 The folds of its flesh are tightly joined;
they are firm and immovable.
24 Its chest is hard as rock,
hard as a lower millstone.
25 When it rises up, the mighty are terrified;
they retreat before its thrashing.
26 The sword that reaches it has no effect,
nor does the spear or the dart or the javelin.
27 Iron it treats like straw
and bronze like rotten wood.
28 Arrows do not make it flee;
slingstones are like chaff to it.
29 A club seems to it but a piece of straw;
it laughs at the rattling of the lance.
30 Its undersides are jagged potsherds,
leaving a trail in the mud like a threshing sledge.[j]
31 It makes the depths churn like a boiling caldron
and stirs up the sea like a pot of ointment.
32 It leaves a glistening wake behind it;
one would think the deep had white hair.
33 Nothing on earth is its equal[k] —
a creature without fear.
34 It looks down on all that are haughty;
it is king over all that are proud.[l]"

41:18 [g] Job 3:9
41:21 [h] Isa 40:7 [i] Ps 18:8
41:30 [j] Isa 41:15
41:33 [k] Job 40:19
41:34 [l] Job 28:8

[a] *13* Septuagint; Hebrew *double bridle* [b] *15* Or *Its pride is its*

ebrates "the depth of the riches of the wisdom and knowledge of God!" (Rom 11:33). God's point here is essentially the same.

41:12–34 An enhanced description of the crocodile, a literary creation to show Job that no mortal can bring this creature under subjection. It is an argument from the lesser to the greater: if no human being can conquer this beast, the fiercest water animal in God's creation, then how could a person think they can bring God under subjection (v. 10)?

42:2 [m] Ge 18:14; Mt 19:26 [n] 2Ch 20:6
42:3 [o] Job 38:2 [p] Ps 40:5; 131:1; 139:6
42:4 [q] Job 38:3; 40:7
42:5 [r] Job 26:14; Ro 10:17 [s] Jdg 13:22; Isa 6:5; Eph 1:17-18
42:6 [t] Job 40:4 [u] Ezr 9:6
42:7 [v] Job 32:3
42:8 [w] Nu 23:1,29 [x] Job 1:5 [y] Ge 20:17; Jas 5:15-16; 1Jn 5:16 [z] Job 22:30
42:10 [a] Dt 30:3; Ps 14:7

Job

42 Then Job replied to the LORD:

2 "I know that you can do all things;[m]
no purpose of yours can be thwarted.[n]
3 You asked, 'Who is this that obscures my plans without
knowledge?'[o]
Surely I spoke of things I did not understand,
things too wonderful for me to know.[p]

4 "You said, 'Listen now, and I will speak;
I will question you,
and you shall answer me.'[q]
5 My ears had heard of you[r]
but now my eyes have seen you.[s]
6 Therefore I despise myself[t]
and repent in dust and ashes."[u]

Epilogue

7 After the LORD had said these things to Job, he said to Eliphaz the Temanite, "I am angry with you
and your two friends,[v] because you have not spoken the truth about me, as my servant Job has. 8 So
now take seven bulls and seven rams[w] and go to my servant Job and sacrifice a burnt offering[x] for
yourselves. My servant Job will pray for you, and I will accept his prayer[y] and not deal with you according to your folly.[z] You have not spoken the truth about me, as my servant Job has." 9 So Eliphaz the
Temanite, Bildad the Shuhite and Zophar the Naamathite did what the LORD told them; and the LORD
accepted Job's prayer.
10 After Job had prayed for his friends, the LORD restored his fortunes[a] and gave him twice as much as

42:1–6 *Job's Second Response.* These are words of submission and concession to the overwhelming power of God. Among Job's words, these perhaps most affirm how God assesses Job's character in the prologue (1:8; 2:3). Any person who humbly submits to the Creator's majesty and power stands out in the universe as unique. God has revealed himself to Job as the all-powerful Creator of the universe, and Job submits to the omnipotent God. Job's words of submission employ the verb "to know" that is so prominent in God's speeches (see note on 39:1). Now Job's knowledge is adequate; he does not possess a knowledge of the universe as such, but he knows the Lord of the universe who "can do all things" (v. 2).

42:3 Job is quoting God. The indictment of 38:2—"Who is this that obscures my plans ... without knowledge?"—was omitted in God's second speech (see note on 40:6—41:34), but here Job appeals to it himself. He confesses that God's revelation of himself and the marvels of his universe are too "wonderful" for him to understand. (The Hebrew for "wonderful" is translated "marvelous deeds" [e.g., 1 Chr 16:24; Pss 72:18; 86:10] to refer to God's marvelous works in creation and in history.) God's revelation of himself, as Job anticipated, made all the difference in how he understood God. He sees himself in relationship to God as he has never been able to do before. The last words we hear from Job are words of repentance: "I ... repent in dust and ashes" (v. 6). But Job does not repent for the reason that the friends insisted; he repents for his lack of understanding God, not for moral infractions. His understanding is the difference between "hearing" about God and "seeing" God (v. 5). It is a measurement of the colossal gain he has made in understanding his relationship to God.

42:7–17 *The Epilogue.* In God's second speech, he indicted Job with the question, "Would you discredit my justice?" (40:8). God does not make an issue of justice in the speech itself; however, in the larger context of the book, it certainly is not laid to the side. Implicitly the epilogue deals with the question. Strictly speaking, God could do Job justice by simply restoring his property, but instead he restores it in double measure, which moves beyond justice to grace (v. 12). God concludes the story in four ways: (1) He rebukes Job's friends and commands them to ask Job to intercede on their behalf (vv. 7–9). (2) He twice affirms Job as "my servant Job" (vv. 7,8), which he did in the prologue (1:8; 2:3). (3) He restores Job's property twofold and gives him seven sons and three daughters, reconstituting the original number of his children (1:2). (4) He gives Job a long life (vv. 16–17).

42:7 these things. God's speeches. **to Eliphaz.** Because he is the oldest and thus the leader of the group. The rebuke justifies Job, thus humiliating the friends. **truth.** What is correct/right. (1) Some take this to confirm the portrait of Job presented in the prologue. (2) If this refers to what Job says in the dialogue, then we have to assume that God is not speaking so much about Job's words (he rebukes Job for them [40:8]) as about Job's disposition (Job insisted on his innocence and demanded that God answer his claim that he has been treated unfairly). (3) The word "truth" may apply to Job's admitting deficient knowledge and repenting for speaking out of a lack of understanding. This explanation preserves the integrity of the book and the characters.

42:8 seven bulls and seven rams. Implies that the friends' sin was very serious because nowhere in the Pentateuch do we find this magnitude of individual sacrifices. Balak offered "seven bulls and seven rams" hoping to placate God (Num 23:29–30). **My servant.** The term God used for Job in the prologue (1:8; 2:3); it is a relational term, suggesting Job's submissive attitude toward God. **pray for you.** Job, like Abraham, acts in a priestly role (1:5; Gen 12:8; 13:4). **I will accept his prayer.** Another affirmation of Job. **truth.** See note on v. 7.

42:10 This may imply that Job's insistence on God's justice in the dialogue may have neglected another important attribute: God's grace.

he had before.[b] [11]All his brothers and sisters and everyone who had known him before[c] came and ate
with him in his house. They comforted and consoled him over all the trouble the LORD had brought on
him, and each one gave him a piece of silver[a] and a gold ring.
[12]The LORD blessed the latter part of Job's life more than the former part. He had fourteen thousand
sheep, six thousand camels, a thousand yoke of oxen and a thousand donkeys. [13]And he also had seven
sons and three daughters. [14]The first daughter he named Jemimah, the second Keziah and the third
Keren-Happuch. [15]Nowhere in all the land were there found women as beautiful as Job's daughters, and
their father granted them an inheritance along with their brothers.
[16]After this, Job lived a hundred and forty years; he saw his children and their children to the fourth
generation. [17]And so Job died, an old man and full of years.[d]

42:10 [b]Job 1:3; Ps 85:1-3; 126:5-6
42:11 [c]Job 19:13
42:17 [d]Ge 15:15; 25:8

[a] *11* Hebrew *him a kesitah*; a kesitah was a unit of money of unknown weight and value.

Job's prayer for those who had abused him is a touching OT illustration of the high Christian virtue Jesus taught in Matt 5:44.
42:11 all the trouble the LORD had brought on him. We know that God initiated the cycle that brought about Job's suffering; we also know that God, and God alone, is the ruler of the universe and human life. Moreover, Job's social life is an important part of his restoration (29:7–13). **each one gave him a piece of silver and a gold ring.** It was customary to bring a gift when invited into the house of a neighbor or friend. **piece of silver.** This unit of money (Hebrew *qĕśîṭâ*) is mentioned in Gen 33:19 and is another connection to the patriarchal period.
42:12 Personal wealth was measured by livestock as well as gold and silver (Gen 13:2). Job's personal wealth is doubled (1:3).
42:13–14 Job's greatest blessing is his children (1:5; 29:5). The fact that the daughters' names are given seems to be significant, added to the fact that Job "granted them an inheritance along with their brothers" (v. 15; cf. Num 36:1–12 for the stipulation that a woman who has an inheritance must marry within her own tribe so the inheritance is not transferred to another tribe, a stipulation not mentioned here).
42:16 a hundred and forty years. An indicator of God's blessings on Job.

INTRODUCTION TO PSALMS

The book of Psalms (or the Psalter) has been the hymnbook and prayer book for countless generations of Jews and Christians over the centuries. It contains the entire range of human emotion, from the highest points of joy and thanksgiving to the lowest points of depression and loss and everything in between. The psalms are timeless — hence their popularity among believers in all times and all places. Their presence in the Bible instructs the faithful in the best ways to praise and thank God, and they model legitimate ways to grieve and to address God boldly and directly in the midst of pain and sorrow. The psalms are transparent, passionate, emotive, personal, and genuine, and they provide believers with language with which to express their own deepest emotions and passions.

The Psalter expresses almost every major OT theme, adding to our understanding of them. The single, overarching theme of the book of Psalms is God's kingship, his status as the divine King who rules over all peoples, nations, gods, even elements of nature. So its message inextricably follows some important threads of biblical theology, including the Abrahamic, Mosaic, and Davidic covenants, and it anticipates the new covenant in significant ways.

TITLE

The English title "Psalms" comes from the Greek title, *psalmoi*, which was already established by the time of the NT (Luke 20:42; Acts 1:20). *Psalmos* translates the Hebrew word *mizmôr* ("a psalm"), both having to do with songs sung to the accompaniment of stringed instruments, giving us an initial insight into the nature of this book: it is a collection of songs, most (if not all) of which informed part of the life of worship for God's people, even in NT times (Eph 5:19; Col 3:16).

The Hebrew title is *tĕhillîm* ("praises"), which gives us a further insight into the book's nature. Despite the many psalms of lament and disorientation, the Psalter's overall message is that praising God is the desired mode in which people should strive to live.

AUTHOR

Like all other books in the Bible, the book of Psalms is a divine-human effort: humans wrote in their own words and styles, inspired by the Holy Spirit (2 Tim 3:16 – 17; 2 Pet 1:20 – 21). But unlike the other books in the Bible, the book of Psalms consists primarily of humans' words to and about God, not God's words to humans, such as those in the books of Leviticus or Isaiah or the Gospel of John (but see Introduction: The Psalms as God's Word). In addition, Psalms is a collection of individual compositions that many authors wrote, not a unified narrative or systematic treatise that one person wrote. Here too the Holy Spirit guided the individual authors in their writing (2 Sam 23:1 – 3; Matt 22:43 – 44; Acts 1:16; 4:25).

The psalm titles (or "superscripts") provide clues to the authorship of individual psalms. Of the 150 psalms, 100 have titles of authorship. The Hebrew preposition *lĕ* — which, depending on the context, can mean "by," "of," "belonging to," "for," "concerning," or "dedicated to" — usually indicates authorship. In the psalm titles, the NIV most often renders *lĕ* as "of," as in "Of David" (e.g., Ps 25 title). This is best understood as a title of authorship (i.e., "By David"); indeed, the NT assumes that David was the author of psalms attributed to him (Matt 22:43–44; Acts 2:25; 4:25; Rom 4:6; 11:9). But sometimes *lĕ* does not indicate authorship, as in "For [*lĕ*] the director of music" (e.g., Pss 4–6; 8) or "For [*lĕ*] giving grateful praise" (Ps 100). (For subscripts appearing in certain psalms, see Introduction: Psalm Titles.)

In the Hebrew text, 73 psalms have "Of David" in the title, and the NT adds two additional references to David as author: Ps 2 (Acts 4:25–26) and Ps 95 (Heb 4:7). Beyond these, others are attributed to "the Sons of Korah" (Pss 42–49; 84–85; 87–88), Asaph (Pss 50; 73–83), Solomon (Pss 72; 127), Heman (Ps 88), Ethan (Ps 89), and Moses (Ps 90). Ps 88 is doubly attributed to "the Sons of Korah" and "Heman the Ezrahite" (see note on Ps 39 title).

Many scholars discount the reliability of the titles—both the titles of authorship and the "historical" titles (see Introduction: Psalm Titles)—citing supposed discrepancies between information in the titles and circumstances within the psalms themselves (e.g., Pss 30; 51); however, even in such cases, one can legitimately explain the supposed discrepancies (see notes on Ps 30 title; 51:18). In the case of Ps 72, "Of Solomon" might be a prayer on behalf of Solomon, as many scholars suggest, but it is equally plausible that Solomon composed the prayer himself with full knowledge of the awesome responsibility that was his and his successors' as God's representatives (see 1 Kgs 8; 1 Chr 28:5; 29:23; 2 Chr 9:8; 13:8; see also introduction to Ps 72).

Unless otherwise indicated (e.g., see note on 74 title), the study notes assume that titles like "Of David" indicate direct authorship.

THE PSALMS AS GOD'S WORD

As noted above, the psalms consist (on the surface) of human words to and about God. But the psalmists were not writing simply for themselves as private individuals. In almost all cases, they wrote with a view to others preserving and singing their words. In other words, even though many psalms are intensely personal (e.g., Pss 17; 51), their authors wrote not only to express their own private sentiments but also for the benefit of others. For example, many psalms attributed to an individual (like David) nevertheless are psalms of the community: they use "we," not "I" (e.g., Pss 65; 80). Further support is that the psalms, for the most part, lack specific historical references; they often appear to be intentionally vague so that any person in any time and any place can relate to the joys or sorrows, enemies, sins, or circumstances and sing or pray right along with the psalmists. In the case of David, his traditional image as a shepherd boy (1 Sam 16:11; 17:34–35) may form the backdrop to some psalms (e.g., Ps 23), but more commonly David wrote with an acute consciousness that he was God's anointed king, God's representative on earth,

Fifteenth-century BC wall painting from Thebes of musicians at a banquet.
Z. Radovan/www.BibleLandPictures.com

and that his joys and sorrows were usually those of the nation as well (see, e.g., notes on 4:2; 13:3–4; 22:22–24; see also introduction to Ps 28).

While the psalmists each wrote in their own words, employing their own style, they were not doing so on their own authority; they were doing so under the guidance of the Holy Spirit (as noted above). As such, we can understand them to be prophets (2 Pet 1:20–21). Prophets were God's mouthpieces, speaking God's words to their own generation and often to later generations as well. When God revealed his words to the prophets, their task was to speak them to the people (Amos 3:1–8). Sometimes God directly revealed to his prophets things that were otherwise unknowable (e.g., 2 Kgs 6:12). And the apostle Peter specifically speaks of David as a prophet when quoting from David's words in Ps 16:8–11 (Acts 2:29–31).

Several times the OT connects prophecy with music (e.g., 1 Sam 10:5; 2 Chr 29:25–26). In 2 Kgs 3:15–16, Elisha prophesies with music as "background" accompaniment. And in 1 Chr 25:1, the sons of Asaph, Heman, and Jeduthun — all associated with psalm writing in one way or another — are set aside for "the ministry of prophesying, accompanied by harps, lyres, and cymbals." David's skill with the lyre is also associated with the Lord's presence with him (1 Sam 16:18). All of this warrants seeing the psalmists as prophets, conveying God's words — not in the same sense that the classical writing prophets like Isaiah, Jeremiah, or Amos did but nevertheless bringing words from God inspired by the Holy Spirit to the world, in their case, with musical accompaniment.

Furthermore, the psalmists did not write in a vacuum, unaware of God's previous revelation through history and Scripture. So, e.g., Pss 78; 105–106; 136 all reflect on God's actions in history in order to instruct later generations of God's people in how to live (or how not to live). And the psalms often allude to previous Scriptures, showing the high regard that the psalmists had for God's Word (e.g., see 4:6; 9:5; 16:5; 27:8,9; 67:1–2 and notes).

As they composed their songs and poems, the psalmists were doing so not simply as private individuals, composing words to and about God. They were also God's mouthpieces: they passed along great truths via the praises, thanksgivings, laments (and more) that they composed; they revered God's revelation in event and word; and they modeled proper ways to express our joys, sorrows, and much more. Their words *to God* are also God's words *to us*.

STRUCTURE

The Psalter as we have it is divided into five "books":

- Book I: Pss 1–41
- Book II: Pss 42–72
- Book III: Pss 73–89
- Book IV: Pss 90–106
- Book V: Pss 107–150

The final psalm in each of the first four books ends with a similar-sounding doxology, including a command to praise the Lord forever and a double "Amen" (except for 106:48, which has only one "Amen"). The final psalm (Ps 150) does not have such a doxology, but the entire psalm itself may function as the concluding doxology to the whole book of Psalms (see introduction to Ps 150).

This division into five "books" occurred early since these doxologies already appear in the Septuagint (the pre-Christian Greek translation of the OT), dating to the third century BC. Indeed, the rabbis noted parallels between Moses and David: the tenth-century AD *Midrash* (a rabbinical commentary) on the Psalms states, "Just as Moses gave five books of laws to Israel, so David gave five books of Psalms to Israel." In this way, their human words to and about God are also God's words to us.

A more nuanced perspective recognizes a modified doxology at the end of Ps 145 (v. 21) and sees Pss 146–150 collectively functioning as a final burst of praise to end the entire Psalter. Pss 146–150 begin and end with *hallĕlû-yāh* ("Praise the LORD"), and they build in a great, rising crescendo to the climactic Ps 150, instructing readers that praising God is how we are to live.

A further nuance recognizes that Pss 1–2 introduce the entire Psalter, not just Book I; the themes in these two psalms signal most of the great themes that follow in the rest of the book of Psalms (see Introduction: Theology of the Psalms). So "The First Collection of David's Prayers" begins with Ps 3 (see introduction to Pss 3–41).

We can represent this more nuanced structure as follows:

- Introduction to the Psalter (Pss 1–2): The Righteous and the Wicked, the Lord and His King
- Book I (Pss 3–41): The First Collection of David's Prayers

- Book II (Pss 42–72): The Second Collection of David's Prayers
- Book III (Pss 73–89): The Book of Crisis
- Book IV (Pss 90–106): The Lord Reigns
- Book V (Pss 107–150): The Return of the King
- Conclusion (Pss 146–150): Praise the Lord!

But the doxology at the end of Ps 72 is not the final word in that psalm. An additional verse (v. 20) states, "This concludes the prayers of David son of Jesse." Since the title of Ps 72 states that it is "Of Solomon," it appears that v. 20 refers to a smaller collection that ends there, not something concerning Ps 72 itself. (This is especially true given that there are 18 additional psalms of David after Ps 72, i.e., 72:20 marks off a collection of [mostly] Davidic psalms, but there are more Davidic psalms to come.) Most scholars believe that this note in 72:20 refers to Books I and II having been joined together as an independent collection prior to the final collection of the psalms into the book of Psalms.

Beyond this, other smaller collections occur within the Psalter that probably existed independently before being incorporated into the book. These include the following:

- Psalms of David (Pss 3–41)
- Psalms of the Sons of Korah (Pss 42–49)
- Psalms of David (Pss 51–65)
- Psalms of Asaph (Pss 73–83)
- Kingship of Yahweh Psalms (Pss 93–99)
- Songs of Ascents (Pss 120–134)
- Psalms of David (Pss 138–145)
- hallĕlû-yāh Psalms (Pss 146–150)

In addition, a varying pattern in the use of God's name is visible in the five books: *yhwh* ("the LORD"), God's personal name (see note on 8:1), predominates in Pss 1–41; 84–150, whereas *'ĕlōhîm* ("God") predominates in Pss 42–83 (i.e., Book II and the Asaph psalms of Book III). This is especially striking when we note that Ps 14 and Ps 53 are practically identical psalms, but where "the LORD" is found in Ps 14, "God" is found in Ps 53.

The presence of the same psalm in two different "books" of the Psalter (Pss 14; 53) suggests that Books I and II at one time existed independently of each other, coming together later as "The Prayers of David," as noted (see introductions to Pss 3–41; Pss 42–72). Further evidence of the independent existence of Books I and II is suggested by Ps 70 (in Book II), which is taken from 40:13–17 (in Book I), and Ps 108 (in Book V), which is composed almost entirely of sections from two earlier psalms (in Book II): 57:7–11; 60:5–12.

Oil lamp. "Your word is a lamp for my feet, a light on my path" (Ps 119:105).

Kim Walton, taken at The Oriental Institute Museum, University of Chicago

So we now have a picture of individual psalms coming together into small collections that over time were joined with other collections until the final book of Psalms as we know it coalesced, all under the guidance of the Holy Spirit. This would have happened sometime at the end of the OT period, i.e., in the postexilic period (though exact dating is impossible). Many scholars have despaired of finding any unity in the Psalter as a whole, but an apt analogy is sometimes made to a medieval European cathedral, whose construction stretched out over many decades, even centuries, during which time architectural styles may have changed, resulting in a great, multifaceted building. In the end, such a cathedral was one building with many components, each reflecting its own time. Similarly, the Psalter is composed of many individual psalms and smaller collections, each reflecting its own time, that ultimately came together into one great book. And despite the despair of many scholars, it is indeed possible to discern some overarching themes in that book (see Introduction: Theology of the Psalms).

THE PSALMS IN THE SEPTUAGINT AND AT QUMRAN

The Septuagint, the pre-Christian Greek translation of the OT, adds one psalm of David (Ps 151), but it notes that this psalm is "outside the number," i.e., that it is not one of the "standard" 150 psalms. In addition, the Septuagint numbers the psalms differently than do our English (and Hebrew) Bibles.

English (and Hebrew) Bibles	Septuagint
1–8	1–8
9–10	9
11–113	10–112
114–115	113
116	114–115
117–146	116–145
147	146–147
148–150	148–150
	151

The so-called Dead Sea Scrolls discovered at Qumran in the 1940s and 1950s include at least 39 psalms manuscripts among them. Most are fragmentary, but for the most part they follow the same structure and order as the Hebrew Bible. One important scroll differs significantly: it includes 39 psalms, many in a different order than we find in our Bibles, and it includes 8 psalms not found among the standard 150 psalms. But this scroll may have been a prayer book that intentionally reordered the psalms and interspersed them with new compositions for devotional or worship purposes.

PSALM TITLES

Most psalms (116 of 150) carry short titles, or superscripts, at the beginning of the psalm. The titles appear very early: they are included in the Septuagint, the pre-Christian Greek translation of the OT, which adds titles for all the psalms except for Pss 1–2, and the NT seems to be aware of these (Acts 4:25; Heb 4:7). The titles are an integral part of the Hebrew text as well, appearing as v. 1 of the psalms (or vv. 1–2).

The following are the main types of psalm titles:

- Authorship (see Introduction: Author).
- Name of a collection, e.g., "Of the Sons of Korah" (Pss 42–49) or "A song of ascents" (Pss 120–134).
- Type of psalm, e.g., *mizmôr* ("psalm"), *šir* ("song"), *maśkîl*, or *miktām*. Many of these ancient classifications are not fully understood today, and the NIV simply includes notes such as "Title: Probably a literary or musical term" (see NIV text note on the title of Ps 7).
- Musical notations such as a tune title (e.g., Pss 9; 22; 45; 56), a musical instruction—such as "For the director of music" (e.g., Pss 4–6) or "With stringed instruments" (e.g., Pss 4; 6; 54–55)—or other designation (e.g., Pss 6–8; 12).
- Notes on the use of a psalm (e.g., Pss 30; 100; 102).
- Historical notes about an occasion in David's life (Pss 3; 7; 18; 30; 34; 51–52; 54; 56–57; 59–60; 63; 142).

These categories are not mutually exclusive; several appear together in the title of some psalms, e.g., Pss 4–7; 45; 52; 60.

The psalm in Hab 3 has a title (superscript) characteristic of those in the Psalter—"A prayer of Habakkuk the prophet. On *shigionoth*" (Hab 3:1)—but it also has a postscript—"For the director of music. On my stringed instruments" (Hab 3:19). This (and other evidence) has led some scholars to propose that whenever "For the director of music" appears followed by an "optional" prepositional phrase (as in Hab 3:19b: "On my stringed instruments"), this part of the superscript should actually be considered a postscript to the previous psalm.

The psalm titles are not numbered in English Bibles, but they appear as v. 1—or occasionally as vv. 1–2 (Pss 51–52; 54; 60)—in the Hebrew Bible. Accordingly, verse numberings in the Hebrew Bible differ slightly from those in English Bibles. In the NIV, the original psalm titles appear in italics before v. 1 of a psalm.

PSALM TYPES

The ancient psalmists had their own classifications for psalms (e.g., *mizmôr*, *šiggāyôn*, *miktām*, etc.), many of which are not understood today. Most scholars today pay little attention to these terms. The NIV usually includes a text note such as "Title: Probably a literary or musical term" in these cases (see, e.g., the NIV text note on the title for Ps 7).

In the past century, scholars have created their own categories of psalms that are sometimes, though not always, helpful in understanding the psalms. In broadest terms, psalms are classified as individual or communal compositions, though individuals sometimes wrote on behalf of the community (e.g., Pss 65; 80) or vice versa (e.g., Pss 42–43; 88). Psalms are also classified as (1) praise (e.g., Pss 8; 33; 100; 103; 113; 117; 150) or thanksgiving (e.g.,

Pss 9; 107; 118; 136) psalms or (2) lament (e.g., Pss 5–6; 42–43; 86; 88) psalms. Within these broad categories, many scholars find subcategories such as psalms of trust or confidence, petition, penitence, imprecation (cursing), and more; but many of these overlap and, in the end, such exercises often reveal more about the ingenuity of the scholar than about the truths of the psalm. Because of this, minimal attention is paid to modern-day subcategories in the study notes of this Bible.

Man playing a lyre, from the Standard of Ur. Musical instruments are frequently mentioned throughout the psalms.

A. D. Riddle/www.BiblePlaces.com, taken at the British Museum

Praise is often understood as exalting God for his character (i.e., for who he is), whereas thanksgiving is understood as responding to God for things he has done for the psalmist, especially after a difficult time. However, the two actually overlap, because God's character can only be known through the things he does. So even when the psalmists are thanking God for things he has done, they are praising him, in keeping with the Hebrew title of the book (*tĕhillîm*, "praises"). The psalms of praise typically follow a pattern: (1) a call to praise, (2) reasons for praise, and sometimes (3) a renewed call to praise. Thanksgiving psalms also typically follow a pattern: (1) a call to praise, sometimes (2) reasons for praise, then (3) a focus on the psalmists' needs and what God has done in answering their prayers, and (4) further praise.

Lament psalms tend to follow a more complex pattern: (1) address to God and introductory petition, (2) the lament proper, (3) confession of trust or assurance of being heard, (4) petition, and (5) praise or vow to praise. Though these are psalms of deep pain and emotion, it is instructive to note that in almost all lament psalms, praise is a component, confirming that praising God is the desired mode in which people should strive to live. (Ps 88 is a notable exception; see introduction to Ps 88.) It is instructive to note that more than half of the psalms are laments of some type; their inclusion in the Psalter provides a rich (though sadly underused) resource for instruction on legitimate ways to express grief, pain, discontent, and even anger — all within the framework of a relationship with God.

Sometimes psalms are grouped according to content, and some of these are identified as such in the study notes. These include the following: Kingship of Yahweh psalms (Pss 47; 93–99; 145); royal or Messianic psalms (Pss 2; 18; 20–21; 45; 72; 89; 101; 110; 132; 144); wisdom psalms (Pss 1; 19; 32; 34; 37; 49; 73; 112; 119; 128), a subcategory of which is Torah psalms (dealing with God's instruction or law: Pss 1; 19; 119); and historical psalms (Pss 78; 105–106; 136). Some scholars would include more or less psalms in each of these individual categories, which shows the fluidity of such modern classifications.

THE PSALMS AS POETRY

The NIV lays out the psalms in poetic form with short lines paralleling other short lines. Most are balanced two-line pairs, though there are occasional three-line groupings. The two most fundamental aspects of Hebrew poetry are *terseness* (short lines typically consisting of 3–4 words in Hebrew) and *parallelism* (lines that echo each other in some way).

Synonymous Parallelism

"Synonymous" parallelism typically consists of two lines, with the second playing off the first in some way. An example is 1:5:

Therefore	the wicked	will not stand	in the judgment,	
nor	sinners		in the assembly	of the righteous.

In this example, the parallelism is "synonymous" but "incomplete," because the verb phrase "will not stand" is missing in the second line, even though its force carries over to that line. To maintain the balance between the two lines, the poet has added the additional phrase "of the righteous" as "compensation."

The often-stated idea that the second poetic line "says the same thing as the first" is misleading, as it tends to downplay the contribution of the second line in explaining the first, adding to it, narrowing its focus, or any number of other ways in which it might play off of the first line. A better way of understanding the relationship between two poetic lines is to think of them in this way: The first line makes a statement; the second line then expands upon that statement, limits it, clarifies it, or in some other way plays off of the thought in the first line. This idea can be expressed as follows: "Line A is so and, what's more, Line B is so." This elevates the second line to the status of being equally as important as the first line, as it adds its own distinctive contributions, rather than unimaginatively restating the thought of the first line. In our example from 1:5, the second line, then, shows that the general category of "the wicked" is more specifically "sinners" and that the righteous will stand in the judgment but that the wicked will not survive that judgment nor stand with the righteous.

Antithetical Parallelism

"Antithetical" parallelism involves contrasts; an example is 37:9:

For those who	are evil		will be destroyed,	
but those who	hope	in the LORD	will inherit	the land.

In this case, the second line contrasts with the first, both in terms of the overall message of each line as well as in the contrasts between each element of the two lines.

Acrostic Poems

Acrostic poems were built using successive letters of the 22-letter Hebrew alphabet, typically one verse (though sometimes more than one) per letter. The acrostic poems in the OT are Pss 9–10 (which together constitute an acrostic poem); 25; 34; 37; 111; 112; 119; 145; Prov 31:10–31; Lam 1; 2; 3; 4. The acrostic pattern would have served as a mnemonic device for remembering the poems.

Selah

Selah (*selâ*) occurs 71 times in 39 different psalms. It does not occur with any regularity, and its meaning is unclear. It likely was a musical or liturgical notation. Because of this uncertainty, the NIV does not include this word in the text of the psalms but refers to it only in NIV text notes (see, e.g., NIV text note on 3:2).

Other Characteristics of Hebrew Poetry

Hebrew poetry frequently employs literary devices—alliteration, assonance, onomatopoeia, paronomasia, chiasms, and more—to accentuate its message and impact on readers and hearers. But most of these are not accessible without knowledge of Hebrew.

A shepherd leading his sheep.

Beyond the formal characteristics of terseness and parallelism, Hebrew poetry contrasts with prose in several ways:

- *Selectivity.* Poetry tends to be more selective than prose due to the limits the poetic structure itself imposes as well as the terseness of the individual lines. For example, compare the prose (narrative) account of the Israelites' crossing the Red Sea in Exod 14 with the poetic (hymnic) reflection on that event in Exod 15:1–18; the prose text is much more detailed.
- *Figurative and Emotive Language.* Poetry tends to use more figurative language than prose, and it tends to be more emotive. For example, David uses highly figurative and emotive language to describe his desperate plight in 69:1–4, which contrasts sharply with the unembellished, straightforward narrative account of his grief in another situation in 2 Sam 12:16.
- *The Stage.* Poetry tends to reach into the heavenly realms more than prose does. For example, compare (a) the straightforward narrative summary of the battle against the Canaanites in Judg 4:23–24, where the stage upon which the events unfold is confined to a specific battlefield, with (b) the poetic description of that same battle in Judg 5:4–5,20, where the stage includes the cosmos.
- *Time Frame.* Prose tends to be confined to past-time events, as narrative texts mostly tell us about events that have already taken place, while poetry is not so time-bound. The past, the present, and even the future all figure prominently in the poetry of the psalms.

Poetry Outside the Book of Psalms

The book of Psalms is not the only repository for poems. Many occur elsewhere in the OT, usually in narrative contexts (see Gen 49:1–28; Exod 15:1–18; Deut 32:1–43; 33; Judg 5; 1 Sam 2:1–10; 2 Sam 1:17–27; 22; 23:1–7; 1 Chr 16:7–36; Isa 38:9–20; the book of Lamentations; Jonah 2:1–9; Hab 3). And most of the wisdom and prophetic books are written in poetic form, though not as individual, self-contained compositions as in the Psalter.

THEOLOGY OF THE PSALMS

As human words to and about God, the psalms instruct us in myriad ways about how to worship God. They teach us how to sing, dance, rejoice, give thanks, confess sin, grieve, express anger, make requests of God, proclaim God's name far and wide, and much more. They are a rich resource both for individual and corporate use.

As God's Word to us (see Introduction: The Psalms as God's Word), the book of Psalms engages almost all of the great themes of the Bible. Beginning with the introductory Pss 1–2, the Psalter lays out the two ways (that of the righteous versus that of the wicked), the importance of relying on God and his Word, God's sovereignty and rule over all people and nations (and his attendant concern for them), the interplay between divine and human kingship, and God as a place of refuge for all.

The Psalter's overarching theme celebrates God's sovereign rule as the great King over all things. The climactic declaration is that "the LORD reigns" (see note on 93:1). God rules over creation itself and over all nations and people groups—including his own chosen people Israel—down to each individual person. He is a good God: holy, loving, merciful, protective of his people, faithful, a keeper of promises, a giver of good gifts. He is a just God: vindicating his people, punishing evil, caring for the marginalized. He is a great and powerful God: the Creator and Sustainer of all things, mightier than any god humans can conjure up, more powerful than all the nations and armies of the world.

As the sovereign King, God asserts his control over the most powerful forces in nature (see notes on 24:1; 93:3; 96:5,12; 135:5–7). He proclaims his authority over all the false gods of the nations, gods that were such a temptation for his own people time and time again (see notes on 82:1; 95:3; 96:4,5; 97:7). He opposes the wicked, whether individuals (e.g., 1:4–6) or nations (e.g., Ps 2), and will mete out justice for their wickedness (see notes on 1:4–6; 11:6; 62:12; 75:7; 91:8; 149:6,7–9; see also introduction to Ps 2). He protects the vulnerable in society—the widow, the fatherless, the outsider, and the poor—and expects his representatives on earth to carry out this mission (see note on 82:3–4).

God's plan for the nations is that his people Israel be a testimony to them, causing them to turn to God; it is an inclusive vision that shows God's desire for all peoples to know him (see notes on 83:16,18; see also introductions to Pss 67; 117). God chose Jerusalem (i.e., Mount Zion) to be the earthly "capital" of God's kingdom (see notes on 2:6; 9:11; see also introduction to Ps 132); this was the site of the temple, which was God's dwelling place on the earth (see notes on 5:7; 26:8; 28:2; see also introduction to Ps 24). He anointed David and his descendants to be his royal representatives on earth—his vice-regents—and so the Davidic kings had great responsibility for leading the nation in following the Lord and defending the cause of justice in society (see notes on 2:6,7; 40:6–10; 89:3; see also introductions to Pss 45; 101; 132). In all of this, God himself is the source of ultimate refuge for those who are troubled (see notes on 2:12; 18:1 – 2; 144:2).

The Abrahamic, Mosaic, and Davidic covenants all play a prominent role in the psalms, the first and third of these also pointing ahead to the new covenant promised in the prophetic books (especially Jer 31:31 – 34) and fulfilled in the person and work of Jesus Christ. On the Abrahamic covenant, see notes on 72:17b; 105:9 – 11; see also introductions to Pss 37; 67; 105. On the Mosaic covenant, see note on 25:10. On the Davidic covenant, see notes on 2:6,7; 40:6 – 10; 89:3; see also introductions to Pss 45; 132). On the new covenant, see notes on Jer 31:32 – 33. See "Covenant," p. 2646.

The structure of the book of Psalms — with its many individual psalms coming together into collections of like-minded psalms that ultimately were joined into the five "books" of psalms — is not a random structure. Rather, an unfolding story line reflects the great, overarching theme of God's sovereign rule as the great King.

In the introductory Pss 1 – 2, God the King installs his chosen, anointed king on Mount Zion as his royal representative (Ps 2) and the exemplar of the righteous man (Ps 1). David is the OT symbol of the righteous king, and his psalms dominate Book I (Pss 3 – 41), where the prevailing note is one of lament, arising out of David's distresses.

In Book II (Pss 42 – 72), other voices join David's (the sons of Korah, Asaph), and it occasionally notes national concerns alongside individual ones. The book ends on a high note, speaking of the ideal human king as one with a universal reign (Ps 72).

Book III (Pss 73 – 89) is one of crisis, both personal and national. It begins with doubts about God's justice (Ps 73) and ends with two despairing psalms (Pss 88 – 89), the final one questioning God's commitment to the Davidic covenant.

Book IV (Pss 90 – 106) marks a major turning point in the Psalter. The focus turns to a time when there was no human king: the time of Moses (Ps 90). It celebrates God's role as the great King (Pss 93 – 99). Book IV answers the despair at the end of Book III. It says, in effect, that if people were tempted to look for their security in the Davidic king, then they would end up disappointed; they needed to look to the Lord as their refuge and strength and as their great King.

Book V (Pss 107 – 150) shows that God's commitment to his promises to David remained unwavering, and David therefore returns to prominence in this book, especially at the beginning and end (Pss 108 – 110; 138 – 145) and in the important Ps 132. The book ends by extolling David, the Lord's anointed king (Ps 144), and the Lord himself, the divine King (Ps 145), echoing the beginning of the Psalter (Pss 1 – 2), which also features the Lord and his anointed king. And in the final climax of praise (Pss 146 – 150), Ps 149 anticipates God's victory over the rebellious nations and rulers introduced in Ps 2.

Jesus, the Son of God and son of David, embodies and fulfills the promises of the psalms, which are rooted in the promises God gave to Abraham and David concerning the blessings he would give their descendants, and through them, all peoples. God promised Abraham that kings would come from his line (Gen 17:6,16; 35:11), later revealed as being through the line of Judah (Gen 49:10). In 2 Sam 7:11 – 16, God promised David — who was from the line of Judah — that he would always have a descendant on the throne (see also 89:3 – 4,28 – 37; 132). He was God's chosen, anointed king, sitting on "the throne of the LORD" (1 Chr 29:23), with God's kingdom entrusted into the care of his descendants (2 Chr 13:5,8). David was the symbol of the ideal, godly king, the standard by which later kings were judged (e.g., 1 Kgs 15:3,11; 2 Kgs 14:3; 16:2; 18:3; 22:2). In the Psalter, the royal psalms celebrate this ideal, which David embodies (see introductions to Pss 2; 18; 20; 21; 45; 72; 89; 101; 132; 144).

But even the godliest OT kings — David, Hezekiah, Josiah — fell short of the true, ideal King, and so the ultimate fulfillment of the promises to Abraham and David had to await the coming of their great descendant, Jesus Christ, i.e., Jesus the Messiah (see Matt 1:1). The Davidic psalms, then, ultimately point ahead to Jesus, the anointed King and the greatest of the sons of David.

Jesus was the ultimate example of the righteous person in Ps 1 and of God's anointed son, the King Messiah, in Ps 2. Jesus also experienced most of the same travails that David and other psalmists did, so their laments and prayers anticipated his own (e.g., Pss 16; 22; 69). The NT repeatedly shows the psalms being fulfilled in the life and ministry of Jesus (e.g., Matt 13:34 – 35; 21:16,42; John 2:17; 15:25; 19:24,28,36; Acts 2:25 – 35; 13:32 – 37; Rom 15:3; 1 Cor 15:25 – 27; 1 Pet 2:7).

The psalms thus represent a priceless treasure trove of resources for relating to God in all circumstances. They instruct us in how to live, and they teach us great truths about God the great King, his sovereign rule over all things, and his plan for reconciling the world to himself through his Son Jesus, the Christ.

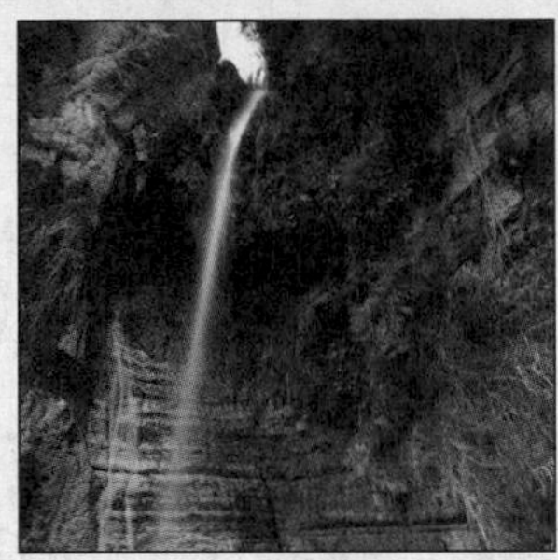

PSALMS

BOOK I

Psalms 1–41

Psalm 1

[1]Blessed is the one
who does not walk[a] in step with the wicked
or stand in the way that sinners take
or sit[b] in the company of mockers,
[2]but whose delight[c] is in the law of the LORD,[d]
and who meditates[e] on his law day and night.
[3]That person is like a tree[f] planted by streams of water,[g]
which yields its fruit[h] in season

1:1 [a]Pr 4:14 [b]Ps 26:4; Jer 15:17
1:2 [c]Ps 119:16,35 [d]Ps 119:1 [e]Jos 1:8
1:3 [f]Ps 128:3 [g]Jer 17:8 [h]Eze 47:12

Pss 1–2 *Introduction to the Psalter: The Righteous and the Wicked, The Lord and His King.* The first two psalms of Book I introduce most of the great themes of the book of Psalms. These include the contrast between the two ways (that of the righteous versus that of the wicked), the importance of relying on God and his instructions, God's sovereignty and rule over all people and nations (and his attendant concern for them), the interplay between divine and human kingship, and God as a place of refuge for all.

Although composed separately, the two psalms complement each other well:

- Ps 1 presents the two "ways" on the level of the individual, while Ps 2 does so on the level of the nations.
- Ps 1 presents the ideal righteous individual, rooted in God's Word, while Ps 2 highlights God's chosen king, whose primary kingly duty was also to be rooted in God's Word (Deut 17:18–20).
- Ps 1 begins with the blessedness (1:1) of the righteous individual rooted in God's Word, while Ps 2 ends with the blessedness (2:12c) of all persons who take refuge in the Lord.
- Ps 1 speaks of the righteous one who "meditates" (*hāgâ*) on God's Word (1:2), while Ps 2 speaks of God's enemies who "meditate" (*hāgâ*, which the NIV translates as "plot") on rebellion (2:1). The difference in their focus (God's Word versus rebellion) reveals the contrasts between the two types of people.

Ps 1 *The Key to Success: Stay Rooted in God's Word.* This psalm succinctly contrasts the way of the righteous (vv. 1–3) and the way of the wicked (vv. 4–5), ending by concisely summarizing the two ways (v. 6). The righteous are "like a tree" (v. 3) and the wicked "like chaff" (v. 4); God's word (the focal point of vv. 1–3) is missing in the life of the wicked (vv. 4–5 do not mention it). Because Ps 1 focuses on God's word (or law or instruction: *tōrâ*), some classify it as a "wisdom" psalm (see introduction to Ps 34). As such, it signals that rootedness in God's instruction is the key to success in life.

1:1 Blessed. Hebrew *ʾašrê*; often translated "happy" or "fortunate." It refers to how true happiness comes to those who refuse to identify with the way of the wicked but who instead are rooted in God's word. (For the other main Hebrew word for blessing, see note on 3:8.) **walk in step ... stand ... sit.** These verbs of bodily motion are metaphors for the progressive internal attitudes and external behaviors of God's enemies. The progression moves from casual identification ("walk in step") to complete association ("sit"). The single righteous individual of vv. 1–3 contrasts with the many wicked ones in v. 1; that is, the righteous person is to stand out and away from the crowd.

1:2 The key to the psalm: success in life depends on saturation in God's word. **delight.** The righteous person takes joy or pleasure in God's word because of the inherently valuable qualities in it; this word elsewhere speaks of a person's delight in other valuable objects, such as gold, a secure dwelling place, or even a man's delight in a woman. **law of the LORD.** Some take this to refer to the law of Moses given in Deuteronomy, others to the larger body of Mosaic laws in Exodus to Deuteronomy, and still others to the entire Pentateuch. **meditates.** Here, one who delights in God's law "meditates" on it day and night. Such an attitude is also at the heart of what the ideal Israelite king should display (Deut 17:18–20) as well as the key to Joshua's leadership (Josh 1:7–8). The underlying idea is something audible. In the ancient world, reading was done aloud, so to "meditate" meant to read aloud and ponder.

1:3 tree planted by streams of water. The results of saturation in God's word are found in a delightful horticultural image: a tree firmly rooted in well-watered soil (cf. Jer 17:5–8). **they.** A singular "they," since its antecedent is singular, and it continues the image of the righteous individual

Wall painting in the tomb of Sennedjem (Sinjin), Deir el-Medina, Thebes, shows a tree planted by water (Ps 1:3).

Richard Ashworth/Robert Harding/Glow Images

1:3 [i] Ge 39:3
1:4 [j] Job 21:18; Isa 17:13
1:5 [k] Ps 5:5 [l] Ps 9:7-8,16
1:6 [m] Ps 37:18; 2Ti 2:19 [n] Ps 9:6
2:1 [o] Ps 21:11

and whose leaf does not wither—
whatever they do prospers.[i]

4 Not so the wicked!
They are like chaff[j]
that the wind blows away.
5 Therefore the wicked will not stand[k] in the judgment,[l]
nor sinners in the assembly of the righteous.
6 For the LORD watches over[m] the way of the righteous,
but the way of the wicked leads to destruction.[n]

Psalm 2

1 Why do the nations conspire[a]
and the peoples plot[o] in vain?

[a] *1* Hebrew; Septuagint *rage*

standing out against the crowd that v. 1 introduces. **prospers.** Not financial well-being, but ultimate success in life when properly oriented to God and one's relationship with him. It echoes God's promise to Joshua in Josh 1:8 and also resembles Jesus' words in Matt 6:33. Sometimes the blessing of the righteous is near in time (Gen 24:35; 1 Kgs 3:11–13); other times God's people must wait for his timing (Hab 2:2–3; 3:16).

1:4 Not so the wicked! Contrasts with the final statement of v. 3: "whatever they do prospers." **chaff.** Useless husks of grains such as wheat; blows away in the winnowing process; even the lightest wind will carry it away. This contrasts powerfully with the firmly rooted tree in v. 3.

1:5 the judgment ... the assembly of the righteous. Represent the institutions of the community in Israel (for "judgment," cf. Prov 2:22; for "assembly," cf. Josh 20:9), although certainly the statements in v. 4 hold true for the final judgment as well (Eccl 12:14; Matt 5:5). See note on 40:9,10. Significantly, there is no trace of God's word in the lives of the wicked (cf. v. 2).

1:6 A final, succinct contrast wraps up the psalm's message. **watches over.** Or "knows," a relational word used even for sexual union (e.g., "made love to" in Gen 4:1). The Lord has intimate knowledge and experience of the way of all "righteous" persons (the word is now plural); the flip side is that the way of the wicked leads to destruction (see note on 2:12).

Ps 2 *The Key to Success: Serve the Lord and Kiss His Son.* The focus now shifts to the national and international levels, and the key to success here is defined in terms of submission to God, the great King, and his anointed son. This psalm looks back at the promises God made to David (2 Sam 7) and ahead to the Son of God, Jesus, the Christ (i.e., the Anointed One), who is also the great "son of David" (Matt 1:1). This psalm unfolds in four parts: the nations rebel against the Lord and his anointed king (vv. 1–3); the Lord responds with derision, affirming his anointed one (vv. 4–6); the Lord's anointed repeats God's promises to him (vv. 7–9); and the psalmist warns rebellious kings and nations (vv. 10–12). It is one of several "royal" or "Messianic" psalms in the Psalter (see introduction to Ps 18).

[2]The kings[p] of the earth rise up
and the rulers band together
against the LORD and against his anointed,[q] saying,
[3]"Let us break their chains
and throw off their shackles."[r]

[4]The One enthroned in heaven laughs;[s]
the Lord scoffs at them.
[5]He rebukes them in his anger
and terrifies them in his wrath,[t] saying,
[6]"I have installed my king
on Zion, my holy mountain."

[7]I will proclaim the LORD's decree:

He said to me, "You are my son;
today I have become your father.[u]
[8]Ask me,
and I will make the nations your inheritance,
the ends of the earth[v] your possession.
[9]You will break them with a rod of iron[a];[w]
you will dash them to pieces[x] like pottery.[y]"

[10]Therefore, you kings, be wise;
be warned, you rulers of the earth.
[11]Serve the LORD with fear
and celebrate his rule[z] with trembling.[a]
[12]Kiss his son,[b] or he will be angry
and your way will lead to your destruction,
for his wrath[c] can flare up in a moment.
Blessed are all who take refuge[d] in him.

2:2 [p]Ps 48:4 [q]Ps 74:18, 23; Jn 1:41; Ac 4:25-26*
2:3 [r]Jer 5:5
2:4 [s]Ps 37:13; 59:8; Pr 1:26
2:5 [t]Ps 21:9; 78:49-50
2:7 [u]Ac 13:33*; Heb 1:5*
2:8 [v]Ps 22:27
2:9 [w]Rev 12:5 [x]Ps 89:23 [y]Rev 2:27*
2:11 [z]Heb 12:28 [a]Ps 119:119-120
2:12 [b]Jn 5:23 [c]Rev 6:16 [d]Ps 34:8; Ro 9:33

[a] 9 Or *will rule them with an iron scepter* (see Septuagint and Syriac)

2:1 plot. The Hebrew is translated "meditates" in 1:2 (see note there). In Ps 1, the righteous one "meditates" on God's word; in Ps 2, the nations "plot" rebellion.
2:2 rise up … against. God promised Joshua, "No one will be able to stand against you" (Josh 1:5). Therefore, even if the nations stand "against" the Lord and his anointed one, their efforts are doomed from the start. **anointed.** Israel's kings, beginning with Saul and David, were anointed with oil when they assumed office. The reference here to the Lord's anointed is more specialized, referring to any royal descendant of David. This recalls the promises God made to David about always having a descendant on the throne (2 Sam 7:11b–16), and it looks ahead to the fulfillment of these promises in Jesus Christ (see Matt 1:1; 21:9; 22:42). The Greek word derived from *māšîaḥ* is *Messias* (see John 4:25); more commonly it is translated *christos.* These terms are rendered in English as "Messiah" and "Christ," respectively. See notes on vv. 7–9.
2:4 laughs. God, who is "enthroned in heaven," responds to the kings' rebellion (v. 2) with derision. Laughter often expresses mockery or derision (37:13; 59:8; Gen 38:23). God's derisive laughter here expresses his wrath (v. 5), and he responds to the kings' pitiful conspiracies by reminding them that he has installed his own king on Mount Zion (v. 6).
2:6 my king. David was Israel's first great king, anointed three different times (1 Sam 16:13; 2 Sam 2:4; 5:3), the final time over all Israel immediately prior to his taking Jerusalem (Zion) from the Jebusites and making it his own "City of David" (2 Sam 5:7). Following this, God promised David a perpetual dynasty on the throne in Jerusalem in what is called the "Davidic covenant" (see 2 Sam 7). See "Covenant," p. 2646. **Zion, my holy mountain.** See note on 9:11. Mount Zion was the earthly "capital" of God's kingdom, and from there God would extend his reign over all the earth (48:2; 132:13; 133:3; Isa 24:23; 60:14; Zech 8:3; 9:9; Matt 21:5; Rev 14:1). It was also the site of God's house, the temple (see note on 5:7).
2:7 You are my son. Recalls God's promise to David regarding his son Solomon: "I will be his father, and he will be my son" (2 Sam 7:14). The Davidic kings would henceforth be "sons" of God, reflecting the close bond between the divine King and human kings. David's descendants were expected to be vice-regents in God's stead on earth in a kingdom whose "capital" was Zion (see v. 6 and note). Scripture later reflects this many times (e.g., 1 Chr 28:5; 2 Chr 13:8). See "Sonship," p. 2664. These words are repeated at Jesus' baptism (Mark 1:11) and are also applied to his resurrection (Act 13:33). They also proclaim his superiority to the angels (Heb 1:5) and his appointment as the new high priest (Heb 5:5).
2:8 ends of the earth. Historically, the Davidic kingdom reached its zenith under Solomon, extending its influence from the Euphrates River in the northeast all the way to the border of Egypt in the southwest (1 Kgs 4:21). This obviously was not the literal "ends of the earth." But the OT repeatedly speaks of David's great descendant, the Messiah, and his future rule extending to the ends of the earth (e.g., 72:8; Mic 5:4; Zech 9:10).
2:9 You will break them with a rod of iron. Again, David's rule never lived up to this ideal, though he did conquer the smaller nations around Israel (e.g., 2 Sam 5:6–10,17–25; 8:1–14; 10:1–19). The NT shows that this will be fulfilled by Christ's reign at the end of time (Rev 12:5; 19:15–16) and that those who remain faithful to him will share in this rule (Rev 2:26–27).
2:12 Kiss his son. A sign of homage (see 1 Sam 10:1; 1 Kgs 19:18). Jesus presented a similar idea about people honoring the Son (cf. John

3:Title [e]2Sa 15:14
3:2 [f]Ps 71:11
3:3 [g]Ge 15:1; Ps 28:7 [h]Ps 27:6
3:4 [i]Ps 2:6
3:5 [j]Lev 26:6; Pr 3:24
3:6 [k]Ps 27:3
3:7 [l]Ps 7:6 [m]Ps 6:4 [n]Job 16:10 [o]Ps 58:6
3:8 [p]Isa 43:3,11

Psalm 3[a]

A psalm of David. When he fled from his son Absalom.[e]

1 LORD, how many are my foes!
How many rise up against me!
2 Many are saying of me,
"God will not deliver him."[f][b]

3 But you, LORD, are a shield[g] around me,
my glory, the One who lifts my head high.[h]
4 I call out to the LORD,
and he answers me from his holy mountain.[i]

5 I lie down and sleep;[j]
I wake again, because the LORD sustains me.
6 I will not fear[k] though tens of thousands
assail me on every side.

7 Arise,[l] LORD!
Deliver me,[m] my God!
Strike[n] all my enemies on the jaw;
break the teeth[o] of the wicked.

8 From the LORD comes deliverance.[p]
May your blessing be on your people.

[a] In Hebrew texts 3:1-8 is numbered 3:2-9. [b] 2 The Hebrew has *Selah* (a word of uncertain meaning) here and at the end of verses 4 and 8.

5:23). **destruction.** The nations' rebellion will lead to their ruin, just as "the way of the wicked leads to destruction" (1:6). **refuge.** The book of Psalms develops this theme at length, using a rich vocabulary of related words: "rock," "fortress," "stronghold," "deliverer," "shield," "dwelling place," and more. See notes on 18:1 – 2; 144:2; cf. also 31:1 – 3; 46:1 – 3; 71:1 – 3.

Pss 3 – 41 *Book I: The First Collection of David's Prayers.* After the introductory Pss 1 – 2, Book I gives an extended grouping of Davidic psalms. Every psalm in this section is attributed to David except for Pss 10 and 33 (see introductions to Pss 9; 10; 33). For more on Book I, see Introduction: Structure.

Ps 3 *The Lord Is My Shield.* This psalm is about trust: David begins on a note that becomes familiar (occurring countless times in the following psalms) by lamenting the oppressive opposition of his enemies (vv. 1 – 2). But he quickly expresses his trust in God (vv. 3 – 6), petitions God to deliver him (v. 7), again expresses confidence in God, and prays for blessing (v. 8).

3 title This is the first psalm with a title in the Psalter, and it heads the string of Davidic psalms that comprise the main body of Book I. This is the first of 14 psalms with "historical" titles that tie these psalms to some event in David's life (7; 18; 30; 34; 51; 52; 54; 56; 57; 59; 60; 63; 142). This title refers to David's flight from Absalom, his rebellious son (2 Sam 15 – 17). The words are somewhat generic, even hyperbolic, applying to any number of situations in David's life, including the crisis with Absalom. Ironically, not only did the nations rebel against David, the Lord's anointed (2:2), but even his own son did so.

3:1 rise up. The wicked will not "rise up" in the judgment (1:5 ["stand"]), so God will ultimately vindicate the righteous; but David's present experience is a far cry from that. Absalom and his allies certainly presented a challenge to David, but here he seems to be referring to enemies arrayed against him who reflect any and all who would rebel against the Lord and his anointed king (2:1 – 3). Indeed, opposition to God's rule on earth is to be found everywhere.

3:2 Many are saying of me. See note on 10:6. Hebrew has the word "Selah," see NIV text note; see also Introduction: The Psalms as Poetry (Selah).

3:3 But you, LORD. David begins by focusing on God, not himself; God is the foundation of his trust, not his own might. **shield.** Vivid imagery of protection rooted in the language of refuge in 2:12. God's shield surrounds David, in contrast to ordinary shields, which protect only in one direction. The most common type of shield in David's day was a small circular shield made of oiled animal hide stretched on a wooden frame. **lifts my head high.** Refers to exalting kings. David uses the same imagery in 27:6, and he applies it to God's exalting the Messiah (110:7). Here David is expressing confidence in God's favor in the face of his enemies, echoing the idea in 2:6.

3:4 his holy mountain. Mount Zion (see note on 2:6). David affirms his trust that God, who has installed him on Mount Zion, also answers him from there.

3:7 Arise. Just as David's foes were "rising up" against him (see v. 1), he now calls on God to "rise up" against them. (On prayers for vengeance, see notes on 5:9 – 10; 69:22 – 28.) The Psalms commonly use this language to ask God to take action (e.g., 7:6; 9:19; 10:12; 35:2; 59:4). On occasion, this may have been a formalized cry as part of a processional ritual (e.g., 68:1; 132:8). Some psalms combine this request with one for God to awaken (e.g., 7:6; 35:23; 78:65; cf. 44:23). When God does arise, he vanquishes his foes as if they were nothing (73:18 – 20).

3:8 David ends with a final note of confidence and then prays for "blessing" (*bĕrākâ*), which denotes the blessing of a recipient whom God favors or empowers; it complements the different word for blessing in 1:1 and 2:12 (*ʾašrê*), which denotes more of a state of happiness (see note on 1:1). David, conscious of his responsibilities as king, asks God's blessing on the people under his rule.

Psalm 4[a]

For the director of music. With stringed instruments.
A psalm of David.

1 Answer me when I call to you,
my righteous God.
Give me relief from my distress;
have mercy[q] on me and hear my prayer.[r]

2 How long will you people turn my glory into shame?
How long will you love delusions and seek false
gods[b]?[c][s]
3 Know that the LORD has set apart his faithful servant[t]
for himself;
the LORD hears[u] when I call to him.

4 Tremble and[d] do not sin;[v]
when you are on your beds,[w]
search your hearts and be silent.
5 Offer the sacrifices of the righteous
and trust in the LORD.[x]

6 Many, LORD, are asking, "Who will bring us prosperity?"
Let the light of your face shine on us.[y]
7 Fill my heart[z] with joy[a]
when their grain and new wine abound.

8 In peace I will lie down and sleep,[b]
for you alone, LORD,
make me dwell in safety.[c]

4:1 [q]Ps 25:16 [r]Ps 17:6
4:2 [s]Ps 31:6
4:3 [t]Ps 31:23 [u]Ps 6:8
4:4 [v]Eph 4:26* [w]Ps 77:6
4:5 [x]Dt 33:19; Ps 37:3
4:6 [y]Nu 6:25
4:7 [z]Ac 14:17 [a]Isa 9:3
4:8 [b]Ps 3:5 [c]Lev 25:18

[a] In Hebrew texts 4:1-8 is numbered 4:2-9. [b] *2* Or *seek lies* [c] *2* The Hebrew has *Selah* (a word of uncertain meaning) here and at the end of verse 4. [d] *4* Or *In your anger* (see Septuagint)

Ps 4 *Let the Light of Your Face Shine on Us.* In another psalm of trust or confidence, David now speaks more in his capacity as king (see note on v. 2) than he does in Ps 3. The occasion seems to be a drought or famine (vv. 6–7 refer to God's restoring grain and new wine). David begins in classic lament style, asking for relief from distress (v. 1), but then he rebukes the highborn in society (see note on v. 2), urging them to stop sinning and to trust in the Lord (vv. 2–5). He concludes with his petition on behalf of his people (vv. 6–7) and expresses his trust in God (v. 8).

4 title Many psalms have titles with musical notations. This possibly tells "the director of music" (or choirmaster) that stringed instruments should accompany this psalm.

4:1 Answer me ... Give me relief ... have mercy ... hear. Four petitions piled one upon the other express the urgency of David's situation.

4:2 you people. Or "sons of man." In the Psalms, this phrase possibly refers to the highborn of society (49:2; 62:9). Here David rebukes people of social status, influence, and wealth who are opposing him. In vv. 2–5, he writes with a self-conscious eye to his role as king, for the king was to be an exemplary spiritual leader (72:1–7,12–14; Deut 17:18–20). His concern is not as personal as it is in Ps 3, but he rebukes the highborn; his interest is that the people as a whole, especially the highborn, would turn to God. **my glory.** Elsewhere this phrase refers always to God and his glory, and it possibly does here too (i.e., this verse possibly represents a short word from God inserted among David's words). But the context of vv. 2–5 makes it more likely that David is referring to his own inherited glory and that he is consciously speaking on God's behalf as Israel's anointed king. David has already acknowledged that God himself is his glory (3:3), so here he is speaking out of that well of confidence as God's representative. **delusions.** Translated "in vain" in 2:1; David picks up on the vanity of the peoples in 2:1 as he condemns the highborn. **false gods.** Or "lies" (see NIV text note). The Hebrew word is the normal one for "lying" and fits well here: these people are chasing after lies. The highborn and "a lie" are also connected in 62:9.

4:3 David justifies his own position and explains why he is entitled to rebuke sinners: he is God's set apart, faithful servant. This echoes 2:4–9 and 2 Sam 7:11b–16.

4:4 Tremble. With fear. This injunction is part of a string of seven commands that David addresses to the highborn in vv. 3–5, rebuking them and urging them to trust in God. In Eph 4:26 ("In your anger do not sin" [or 'be angry and do not sin']), Paul uses the wording in the Greek version of this verse to make a point about harmonious relations among Christians.

4:6 Many ... are asking. Reminiscent of the skeptics David cites in 3:1 (see note on 10:6), though it may refer to God's people who have lacked trust but whom God blesses nevertheless (v. 7). **light of your face shine.** David asks for God's favor in terms reminiscent of the blessing that Aaron was to pronounce upon the people (Num 6:24–26).

4:8 Despite the turmoil and skepticism of the highborn (vv. 2,6), David does not let these things bring him down. The Lord alone is his source of security, and he can lie down and sleep, just as he does in 3:5. Ultimately, the two psalms make the same point: the Lord is David's shield, security, and safety.

5:2 [d]Ps 3:4 [e]Ps 84:3
5:3 [f]Ps 88:13
5:4 [g]Ps 11:5; 92:15
5:5 [h]Ps 73:3 [i]Ps 1:5
[j]Ps 11:5
5:6 [k]Ps 55:23; Rev 21:8
5:7 [l]Ps 138:2
5:8 [m]Ps 31:1 [n]Ps 27:11

Psalm 5[a]

For the director of music. For pipes. A psalm of David.

1 Listen to my words, LORD,
consider my lament.
2 Hear my cry for help,[d]
my King and my God,[e]
for to you I pray.

3 In the morning,[f] LORD, you hear my voice;
in the morning I lay my requests before you
and wait expectantly.
4 For you are not a God who is pleased with
wickedness;
with you, evil people[g] are not welcome.
5 The arrogant[h] cannot stand[i]
in your presence.
You hate[j] all who do wrong;
6 you destroy those who tell lies.[k]
The bloodthirsty and deceitful
you, LORD, detest.
7 But I, by your great love,
can come into your house;
in reverence I bow down[l]
toward your holy temple.

8 Lead me, LORD, in your righteousness[m]
because of my enemies—
make your way straight[n] before me.

[a] In Hebrew texts 5:1-12 is numbered 5:2-13.

Ps 5 *You Are Not a God Who Is Pleased With Wickedness.* David moves on in this psalm to focus more on wickedness, those who practice it, and how it is an affront to God. After an introductory petition for God to hear him (vv. 1–2), he affirms his trust that God *will* hear him because God does not tolerate evil (vv. 3–7). He then asks God to lead and protect him and all who trust in God and to punish the wicked (vv. 8–11), and he ends with a declaration of confidence that God does favor the righteous (v. 12).
5 title pipes. The wind instruments for accompanying this psalm were probably flutes of some type.
5:1 lament. Or "groaning" or "meditation"; the word is related to "meditates" in 1:2. This is an anguished lament based on thoughtful reflection or meditation. See also 39:3.
5:2 Hear my cry. Mirrors David's cry in 4:1. **my King and my God.** Makes explicit the idea of the Lord as King that is implicit in Ps 2. It emphasizes the close relationship between God and his anointed king ("my son"; 2:7). David acknowledges the Lord as his King and his God (see note on 10:16).
5:3 In the morning. David begins his day in prayer and expectant waiting.
5:5 The arrogant cannot stand. The "arrogant" here are boastful persons opposed to God (cf. 10:3; 73:3; 75:4), similar to the mockers of 1:1. But even though kings and rulers "rise up" (or "take their stand") against the Lord and his anointed (2:1), in the end, they "cannot stand in [God's] presence."
5:7 by your great love. It is only by God's grace that David can come into God's presence. See note on 6:4. **your house.** The tabernacle in David's day (1 Chr 6:31,48). The temple had not yet been built; that was for David's son Solomon to accomplish (2 Sam 7:12–13; 1 Kgs 5–8). There were regular religious observances at the tabernacle at Gibeon (1 Chr 16:39–40) as well as at the tent that David built for the ark in Jerusalem (1 Chr 15:1; 16:1,4). **your holy temple.** Sometimes this expression refers to God's heavenly sanctuary (11:4; Mic 1:2; Hab 2:20) and sometimes to the temple in Jerusalem (65:4; 79:1; 138:2). If David here intended the latter, he was anticipating the temple that his son would build because he helped in many ways with the preparations for it: he gave Solomon the plans for it (1 Chr 28:11–12,18–19); he made elaborate arrangements for building and staffing it (1 Chr 22–27); and he gave of his own personal treasure for it (1 Chr 29:2–5). The Lord's house (temple) was the earthly place where he could be found—even though, at the same time, the highest heaven could not contain him (1 Kgs 8:27)—where true worshipers longed and delighted to be (Pss 26:8; 27:4; 65:4; 122:1). The temple contained the ark of the covenant, which was God's footstool (1 Chr 28:2); indeed, the temple itself was also seen as God's footstool (Pss 99:5; 132:7), so the heavenly and earthly sanctuaries were inextricably linked. Ezekiel had a vision of a great, restored temple in the future (Ezek 40–43), but there will be no need for a temple in the new Jerusalem because "the Lord God Almighty and the Lamb are its temple" (Rev 21:22). See "Temple," p. 2652.
5:8 Lead me, LORD. David waits on the Lord for help rather than trying to make his own way. **because of my enemies.** David acknowledges that he needs God to lead him and to make the way straight because his enemies threaten to make him lose his way. See also v. 12.

[9] Not a word from their mouth can be trusted;
their heart is filled with malice.
Their throat is an open grave;[o]
with their tongues they tell lies.[p]
[10] Declare them guilty, O God!
Let their intrigues be their downfall.
Banish them for their many sins,[q]
for they have rebelled[r] against you.
[11] But let all who take refuge in you be glad;
let them ever sing for joy.[s]
Spread your protection over them,
that those who love your name[t] may rejoice in you.[u]

[12] Surely, LORD, you bless the righteous;
you surround them[v] with your favor as with a shield.

5:9 [o]Lk 11:44 [p]Ro 3:13* **5:10** [q]Ps 9:16 [r]Ps 107:11 **5:11** [s]Ps 2:12 [t]Ps 69:36 [u]Isa 65:13 **5:12** [v]Ps 32:7 **6:1** [w]Ps 38:1 **6:2** [x]Hos 6:1 [y]Ps 22:14; 31:10 **6:3** [z]Jn 12:27 [a]Ps 90:13 **6:4** [b]Ps 17:13 **6:5** [c]Ps 30:9; 88:10-12; Ecc 9:10; Isa 38:18

Psalm 6[a]

For the director of music. With stringed instruments. According to *sheminith.*[b] A psalm of David.

[1] LORD, do not rebuke me in your anger[w]
or discipline me in your wrath.
[2] Have mercy on me, LORD, for I am faint;
heal me,[x] LORD, for my bones are in agony.[y]
[3] My soul is in deep anguish.[z]
How long,[a] LORD, how long?

[4] Turn, LORD, and deliver me;
save me because of your unfailing love.[b]
[5] Among the dead no one proclaims your name.
Who praises you from the grave?[c]

[a] In Hebrew texts 6:1-10 is numbered 6:2-11. [b] Title: Probably a musical term

5:9–10 David speaks harsh words about his enemies because of their rebellion against God. But David never indicates that he is going to exact private vengeance for himself; he always asks God to do this or vows to take vengeance in his capacity as king. In doing so, he is simply asking God to be true to his own promises: God promised Abraham, "Whoever curses you I will curse" (Gen 12:3), and God reminded the Israelites, "It is mine to avenge; I will repay" (Deut 32:35). See notes on 7:6; 9:5; 17:2; 31:18; 41:10; 69:22–28; see also introduction to Ps 35.
5:9 Their throat is an open grave. Paul cites this verse in making the point that all have sinned (Rom 3:13). **tongues ... tell lies.** On the evil and harm that can come from the wicked's mouth and tongue (see note on 10:7).
5:11 This expresses two of the Psalter's great themes: (1) God is a refuge and protection for the righteous, and (2) joy in the Lord results in finding refuge in God ("be glad ... sing for joy ... rejoice").
5:12 If the righteous allow God to lead them along his own straight way (see v. 8), then he will certainly bless them. **shield.** See note on 3:3.
Ps 6 *Have Mercy on Me, Lord, for I Am Faint.* The ancient church identified this psalm as one of seven penitential psalms (the others: 32; 38; 51; 102; 130; 143). It takes us into David's inner life more than any previous psalm. While David mentions his enemies (vv. 7–8,10), he focuses much more on his weak condition: he is faint, in agony and anguish (vv. 1–3), fearful of death (vv. 4–5), exhausted from his weeping (vv. 6–7), and his cries for mercy and deliverance (vv. 1–2,4) sound feeble. References to God's anger and discipline in v. 1 point indirectly to David's sin, even though this psalm specifies no sin. In the end, David has confidence that God has heard him (vv. 8–10).
6:1 rebuke ... anger ... discipline ... wrath. David is not crying out as the innocent sufferer (as he does in Pss 3; 4; 5). He is conscious of his (unspecified) sins, and they are taking their toll on him as he feels God's displeasure.
6:2 David's sins result in physical ailments: he feels faint and his bones are in agony. **bones.** As the inner skeleton, they represent David's whole being. Cf. 32:3–4.
6:3 soul. Represents the essence of one's being; parallel to "bones" in v. 2. The two are not contrasted as a spiritual-physical dichotomy; both represent the core self. See 35:9–10, where the two are also juxtaposed and the NIV translates the Hebrew for "bones" as "whole being." **How long, LORD, how long?** This plaintive cry reflects David's weariness; it occurs in many of the lament psalms (e.g., 35:17; 62:3; 89:46; 94:3; see note on 13:1,2).
6:4 unfailing love. David appeals to God's unfailing covenant love as the basis for his hope. This term (Hebrew *ḥesed*) is one of the richest in the Bible, often denoting God's steadfast, loyal love for his covenant people Israel. It had special meaning for God's people coming out of Egypt (Exod 15:13; 20:6; 34:6–7), and God promised this love to many generations of Israelites, including David (89:24,28,33; 2 Sam 7:15; Isa 55:3). More than half of the Bible's references to this covenantal love are found in Psalms, about half of those in psalms of David.
6:5 David affirms that the purpose of life is to praise God, but he does so by a negative formulation: the dead cannot praise God. This affirmation is from a "this life" perspective, one found in several psalms (30:9; 88:10–12; 115:17). The Psalter does reflect on the afterlife (see notes on 16:9–11), but it is more commonly focused on this life. Implicit is

6:6 [d]Ps 69:3 [e]Ps 42:3
6:7 [f]Ps 31:9
6:8 [g]Ps 119:115 [h]Mt 7:23; Lk 13:27
6:9 [i]Ps 116:1
6:10 [j]Ps 71:24; 73:19
7:1 [k]Ps 31:15
7:2 [l]Isa 38:13 [m]Ps 50:22
7:3 [n]1Sa 24:11; Isa 59:3

6 I am worn out[d] from my groaning.

All night long I flood my bed with weeping
and drench my couch with tears.[e]
7 My eyes grow weak[f] with sorrow;
they fail because of all my foes.

8 Away from me,[g] all you who do evil,[h]
for the LORD has heard my weeping.
9 The LORD has heard my cry for mercy;[i]
the LORD accepts my prayer.
10 All my enemies will be overwhelmed with shame
and anguish;
they will turn back and suddenly be put to shame.[j]

Psalm 7[a]

A *shiggaion*[b] of David, which he sang to the LORD concerning Cush, a Benjamite.

1 LORD my God, I take refuge in you;
save and deliver me from all who pursue me,[k]
2 or they will tear me apart like a lion[l]
and rip me to pieces with no one to rescue[m] me.

3 LORD my God, if I have done this
and there is guilt on my hands[n]—
4 if I have repaid my ally with evil
or without cause have robbed my foe—
5 then let my enemy pursue and overtake me;
let him trample my life to the ground
and make me sleep in the dust.[c]

[a] In Hebrew texts 7:1-17 is numbered 7:2-18. [b] Title: Probably a literary or musical term [c] 5 The Hebrew has *Selah* (a word of uncertain meaning) here.

David's vow to praise God if God should spare him. **name.** Or "memory" (see 30:4; 97:12). God's character and reputation are inextricably bound up with his name, "Yahweh" (rendered in the OT as "LORD"), the significance of which God revealed to Moses at the burning bush (Exod 3:12–15). See note on 8:1. The idea here is that God's name is blotted out among the dead. **grave.** This is the realm of the dead. Sometimes it denotes a place of punishment (16:10; 55:15; Job 24:19; Isa 14:9–10,15), while other times it refers simply to the grave (88:5; Gen 37:35; Job 7:9). See note on 88:4.

6:6 Structurally, this stands at the very center of the psalm (see note on 100:3), highlighting David's despair.

6:7 my foes. For the first time, David mentions his enemies, who have overwhelmed him. David is very much a victim here.

6:8–10 A dramatic mood shift now finds David experiencing God's hearing his petitions. God has heard his weeping (v. 8), his cry for mercy (v. 9), and his prayer (v. 9), echoing his pleas in vv. 1–2,4. The psalm ends, therefore, with David confidently ordering his enemies away from him (v. 8)—a far cry from the victim of v. 7. Because of God's response to his prayers, his entire situation has been turned around.

Ps 7 *My Shield Is God Most High.* David expresses his trust in the Lord to deliver him when he is faced with his enemies. The feeble David of Ps 6 now boldly claims his innocence and his confidence that God should—and will—deliver him. In this way, the psalm provides a model for prayer in the midst of troubles.

7 title Cush, a Benjamite. Not known elsewhere in the Bible, although King Saul, one of David's tormentors, was from the tribe of Benjamin, and Cush perhaps was allied with Saul. Some scholars link this psalm with the "Cushite" of 2 Sam 18:20–32, who delivered news to David of his son Absalom's death. "Cush" was a land south of Egypt in what today is Sudan (Gen 2:13; 2 Kgs 19:9; Isa 11:11). But the term here clearly refers to a person from the tribe of Benjamin, not a foreigner or a foreign land. It is likely that this title refers to an event that has been lost to history. This is the second of 14 psalms with a "historical" title linked to an event in David's life (see note on Ps 3 title).

7:1 David begins by expressing confidence in the Lord and requesting deliverance from all his pursuers. This certainly could fit his situation when he was fleeing from Saul, the Benjamite, and his allies (see note on title).

7:2 like a lion. From his shepherding days David knew of attacks by lions (1 Sam 17:34–35), which were fierce and ravenous animals (Num 23:24; Judg 14:18). Such imagery occurs elsewhere in the Psalms to depict the ferocity of the psalmists' enemies, almost always in the psalms of David (e.g., 10:9; 17:12; 22:13; 35:17; 57:4).

7:3–5 In contrast to the weak, frail, sinful David of Ps 6, David now protests his innocence in strong terms.

[6] Arise,[o] LORD, in your anger;
rise up against the rage of my enemies.[p]
Awake,[q] my God; decree justice.
[7] Let the assembled peoples gather around you,
while you sit enthroned over them on high.
[8] Let the LORD judge the peoples.
Vindicate me, LORD, according to my righteousness,[r]
according to my integrity, O Most High.
[9] Bring to an end the violence of the wicked
and make the righteous secure —[s]
you, the righteous God[t]
who probes minds and hearts.[u]

[10] My shield[a] is God Most High,
who saves the upright in heart.[v]
[11] God is a righteous judge,[w]
a God who displays his wrath every day.
[12] If he does not relent,
he[b] will sharpen his sword;[x]
he will bend and string his bow.
[13] He has prepared his deadly weapons;
he makes ready his flaming arrows.

[14] Whoever is pregnant with evil
conceives trouble and gives birth[y] to
disillusionment.
[15] Whoever digs a hole and scoops it out
falls into the pit they have made.[z]
[16] The trouble they cause recoils on them;
their violence comes down on their own heads.

[17] I will give thanks to the LORD because of his
righteousness;[a]
I will sing the praises[b] of the name of the LORD
Most High.

7:6 [o] Ps 94:2 [p] Ps 138:7 [q] Ps 44:23
7:8 [r] Ps 18:20; 96:13
7:9 [s] Ps 37:23 [t] Jer 11:20 [u] 1Ch 28:9; Ps 26:2; Rev 2:23
7:10 [v] Ps 125:4
7:11 [w] Ps 50:6
7:12 [x] Dt 32:41
7:14 [y] Job 15:35; Isa 59:4; Jas 1:15
7:15 [z] Job 4:8
7:17 [a] Ps 71:15-16 [b] Ps 9:2

[a] *10* Or *sovereign* [b] *12* Or *If anyone does not repent, / God*

7:6 Arise. See note on 3:7. **in your anger.** David, who had experienced God's anger against him (6:1), now asks God to direct that anger against his enemies. Here and throughout this psalm — indeed, throughout the entire Psalter — David never declares an intention to take his own personal, private vengeance; he always asks God to do this. See note on 69:22–28.
7:7 sit enthroned. Picks up the keynote of the Lord's kingship sounded in 2:4. It is a recurring thread throughout the Psalter (9:4,11; 22:3; 29:10; 55:19; 80:1; 99:1; 102:12; 113:5; 123:1; 132:14).
7:8 judge. Has legal overtones, referring to the proceedings in a courtroom. David is asking God to indict the wicked among the nations. See also 96:10. **Vindicate.** Or "judge." This also has legal connotations, but it also refers to deliverance or salvation. David is asking God not only for legal vindication but that it be manifested as deliverance from his enemies. See also v. 6. **my integrity.** David was not reluctant to admit his sin (Pss 32; 51), but he also stoutly defended his integrity when he knew he had done no wrong (25:21; 41:12; see 15:2; 78:72). In this respect, he was like Job (Job 1:1,8,22; 2:10). **Most High.** An honorific title, first spoken by Melchizedek, a priest of "God Most High," in Abraham's time (Gen 14:18,19,20; cf. Heb 7:1). It emphasizes God's sovereignty over all of humanity (83:18; 97:9; Deut 32:8; 1 Sam 2:10; Dan 4:17) as well as God's role as Israel's protector (21:7; 57:2; 78:35). A variant form of this title occurs in vv. 10,17.
7:9 hearts. Denotes the innermost being of a person, the seat of one's moral character (26:2; Jer 11:20; 17:10; 20:12). David is characteristically transparent as he asks God to examine him (see 139:23–24).
7:10 shield. See note on 3:3. **Most High.** See note on v. 8.
7:11 his wrath every day. God's judgments are not all kept in store for the final judgment day.
7:12–13 David has confidence that God will destroy his enemies, referring to God's arsenal: sword, bow, deadly weapons, flaming arrows. Similar imagery occurs elsewhere as God always stood ready to be his people's warrior when they trusted in him (e.g., 18:14; 21:12; 64:7; 144:6; Deut 32:41–42; Josh 10:14).
7:14 pregnant … conceives … gives birth. David uses vivid imagery here to show how wickedness comes from the innermost being of the wicked. See somewhat similar imagery in Job 15:35; Isa 59:4; Jas 1:15.
7:17 The psalm ends, as most laments and psalms of confidence or trust do, with a vow to praise. Such a pattern models for us that life is to be lived thanking and praising God, even when present situations do not seem to warrant this.

8:1 [c]Ps 57:5; 113:4; 148:13
8:2 [d]Mt 21:16* [e]Ps 44:16; 1Co 1:27
8:3 [f]Ps 89:11 [g]Ps 136:9
8:4 [h]Job 7:17; Ps 144:3; Heb 2:6
8:5 [i]Ps 21:5; 103:4
8:6 [j]Ge 1:28 [k]1Co 15:25, 27*; Eph 1:22; Heb 2:6-8*
8:9 [l]ver 1

Psalm 8[a]

For the director of music. According to *gittith.*[b] A psalm of David.

1 Lord, our Lord,
how majestic is your name in all the earth!

You have set your glory
in the heavens.[c]
2 Through the praise of children and infants
you have established a stronghold[d] against your enemies,
to silence the foe[e] and the avenger.
3 When I consider your heavens,[f]
the work of your fingers,
the moon and the stars,[g]
which you have set in place,
4 what is mankind that you are mindful of them,
human beings that you care for them?[c][h]

5 You have made them[d] a little lower than the angels[e]
and crowned them[d] with glory and honor.[i]
6 You made them rulers[j] over the works of your hands;
you put everything under their[f] feet:[k]
7 all flocks and herds,
and the animals of the wild,
8 the birds in the sky,
and the fish in the sea,
all that swim the paths of the seas.

9 Lord, our Lord,
how majestic is your name in all the earth![l]

[a] In Hebrew texts 8:1-9 is numbered 8:2-10. [b] Title: Probably a musical term [c] 4 Or *what is a human being that you are mindful of him, / a son of man that you care for him?* [d] 5 Or *him* [e] 5 Or *than God* [f] 6 Or *made him ruler . . . ; / . . . his*

Ps 8 *How Majestic Is Your Name in All the Earth!* David now breaks into robust, full-throated, unrestrained praise of God. He powerfully affirms God's majesty, which centers in his name (vv. 1a,9). He first leads down to a seeming dead end at the midpoint of the psalm, where he compares God and mankind (vv. 1b–4). The comparison is obvious: mankind is nothing! Yet immediately the mood shifts, and David magnificently asserts that God has crowned mankind as the capstone of his creation (vv. 5–8).

8:1 Lord. Though this English rendering sounds like a title, it is actually the personal name of Israel's God: *yhwh* ("Yahweh," rendered "Jehovah" in the ASV and "Lord" in most modern translations). See Exod 3:13–15 and notes. This is the God who made a covenant with his people. The use of this personal, covenantal name of God reminded faithful Israelites that this was *their* God, just as Baal was the Canaanites' god or Marduk was the Babylonians' god. **Lord.** The form is *ʾādôn*, and it *is* a title, meaning "one who is sovereign over his realm; master." When referring to humans, it characteristically referred to the king in Israel (e.g., 1 Kgs 1:11,43,47). **name.** Bound up with Yahweh's reputation (see note on 23:3). The entire psalm reflects on the majesty of God, focusing on his absolute grandeur and sovereignty over all things (vv. 1b–4) and his elevation of mankind to a high position as his vice-regents over creation (vv. 5–8).

8:2 praise. It is certainly strange imagery to say that children's words build a stronghold that deters God's enemies. Yet that is precisely what the passage says: God takes these babblings and turns them into a stronghold that silences his enemies in their rebellion against him. It shows that God takes the weakest of all things and makes something great and strong from it (cf. 1 Cor 1:27).

8:4–6 Heb 2:6–8 (see notes) applies these verses to Jesus. Paul does the same with v. 6 in 1 Cor 15:27 (see Eph 1:22 and note).

8:4 mankind. Here refers to humanity in its weak and frail existence (e.g., 9:20; 10:18; 90:3; 103:15). **human beings.** See NIV text note; "son of man" is a literal translation of a Hebrew phrase commonly used to refer to a human being, especially in contrast to God (80:17; 144:3; see note on Ezek 2:1 and NIV text note there). This phrase marks the exact center of the psalm (see note on 100:3), highlighting the importance of humanity in God's eyes. It sets the stage for the soaring language about humanity's place in creation in vv. 5–8.

8:5 angels. See NIV text note. The Hebrew term here, *ʾĕlōhîm*, can refer to "gods" (e.g., 96:4,5) or "angels" (e.g., Job 1:6; 2:1; cf. Isa 6:2 ["seraphim"]; Heb 2:7) or to God himself (Gen 1:1). In any case, the point now is that God has placed humans far above the rest of creation, an echo of Gen 1:26,28. The Septuagint (the pre-Christian Greek translation of the OT) renders the term as "angels," which the author of Hebrews has followed in Heb 2:7. See also note on 82:1.

8:6 rulers. Denotes royalty and dominion ("rules" in 22:28; 59:13; 66:7; 103:19). It is closely related to "rule over" in Gen 1:26,28. Thus, humans in a very real sense are God's vice-regents over creation. This status was marred due to the sin of Adam and Eve and was restored by Jesus Christ, the "second Adam" (Rom 5:12–21).

Psalm 9[a,b]

For the director of music. To the tune of "The Death of the Son." A psalm of David.

[1] I will give thanks to you, LORD, with all my heart;[m]
I will tell of all your wonderful deeds.[n]
[2] I will be glad and rejoice[o] in you;
I will sing the praises of your name,[p] O Most High.

[3] My enemies turn back;
they stumble and perish before you.
[4] For you have upheld my right and my cause,[q]
sitting enthroned as the righteous judge.[r]
[5] You have rebuked the nations and destroyed the wicked;
you have blotted out their name[s] for ever and ever.
[6] Endless ruin has overtaken my enemies,
you have uprooted their cities;
even the memory of them[t] has perished.

[7] The LORD reigns forever;
he has established his throne[u] for judgment.
[8] He rules the world in righteousness[v]
and judges the peoples with equity.
[9] The LORD is a refuge for the oppressed,
a stronghold in times of trouble.[w]
[10] Those who know your name[x] trust in you,
for you, LORD, have never forsaken[y] those who seek you.

[11] Sing the praises of the LORD, enthroned in Zion;[z]
proclaim among the nations[a] what he has done.[b]
[12] For he who avenges blood[c] remembers;
he does not ignore the cries of the afflicted.

9:1 [m] Ps 86:12 [n] Ps 26:7
9:2 [o] Ps 5:11 [p] Ps 92:1; 83:18
9:4 [q] Ps 140:12 [r] 1Pe 2:23
9:5 [s] Pr 10:7
9:6 [t] Ps 34:16
9:7 [u] Ps 89:14
9:8 [v] Ps 96:13
9:9 [w] Ps 32:7
9:10 [x] Ps 91:14 [y] Ps 37:28
9:11 [z] Ps 76:2 [a] Ps 107:22 [b] Ps 105:1
9:12 [c] Ge 9:5

[a] Psalms 9 and 10 may originally have been a single acrostic poem in which alternating lines began with the successive letters of the Hebrew alphabet. In the Septuagint they constitute one psalm. [b] In Hebrew texts 9:1-20 is numbered 9:2-21.

Ps 9 *He Rules the World in Righteousness.* This psalm of thanksgiving and praise builds upon the language of preceding psalms. David previously asked God to deliver him from his enemies and other hardships. Now he thanks God for hearing his prayers and pushing back his enemies, and for the first time in the Psalter, David shows a concern for others who are oppressed and afflicted (vv. 9,12,18). This psalm begins with full-throated praise for God (vv. 1–2), then focuses on the defeat of David's enemies, which comes from the Lord's hand (vv. 3–6). David then affirms God's everlasting kingship (vv. 7–10), which naturally leads to the imperative to proclaim this among the nations (vv. 11–12). David asks for God's mercy and deliverance (vv. 13–14) and reflects on the fate of the wicked (vv. 15–17) and the poor and needy (v. 18), ending with another prayer that God would assert himself against those who would oppose him (vv. 19–20).

Many scholars believe that Ps 9 and Ps 10 were originally one psalm because they together constitute an acrostic poem of sorts and because Ps 10 has no title (see NIV text note). But the perspective in the two psalms is different: the enemies in Ps 9 are mostly David's foreign adversaries, whereas the focus in Ps 10 is more the individual "wicked man" (10:2).

9:1–2 These verses pick up on the full-throated praise of God in Ps 8.

9:2 I will sing the praises. Replicates the end of Ps 7 (v. 17) almost word for word. **your name.** See note on 8:1. **Most High.** See note on 7:8.

9:4 sitting enthroned. This verse and vv. 7,11 reiterate Ps 2, which first expresses the idea of God as king, enthroned on high, sovereign over all nations, and a refuge for the oppressed. God is the great king as well as the righteous judge (v. 8), a refuge for the oppressed (v. 9), and a reliable source of security for those who seek him (v. 10).

9:5 you have blotted out their name. This language is harsh, but it shows God's absolute righteous nature. It also shows him doing what he promised to do as far back as in Abraham's time ("whoever curses you I will curse" [Gen 12:3]). Other examples of blotting out the name of the wicked include Num 5:23; Deut 9:14; 25:19; 29:20. The language anticipates what David asks God to do in several "imprecatory" psalms (35:4–10,26; 69:28; 109:13–15). See notes on 5:9–10; 69:22–28.

9:7 reigns. A common motif in the Psalter (see especially 93:1; 96:10; 97:1; 99:1; see also notes on 10:16; 93:1).

9:9 oppressed. Victims of a violent, crushing oppression (see 10:10).

9:11 Zion. Jerusalem, the "capital" of God's kingdom; it was the one place on earth most closely associated with God's presence, and it was the capital of the Davidic kingdom (2:6; 132:13–18; 2 Sam 5:6–10). Ezekiel spoke of God's presence in the new Jerusalem when he said it would henceforth be called "THE LORD IS THERE" (Ezek 48:35), and the apostle John saw the city as the central focus of the new heavens and the new earth (Rev 21–22). See note on 2:6.

9:13 [d] Ps 38:19
9:14 [e] Ps 106:2 [f] Ps 13:5; 51:12
9:15 [g] Ps 7:15-16 [h] Ps 35:8; 57:6
9:17 [i] Ps 49:14 [j] Job 8:13; Ps 50:22
9:18 [k] Ps 71:5; Pr 23:18 [l] Ps 12:5
9:20 [m] Ps 62:9; Isa 31:3
10:1 [n] Ps 22:1,11 [o] Ps 13:1
10:3 [p] Ps 94:4
10:4 [q] Ps 14:1; 36:1
10:6 [r] Rev 18:7

13 LORD, see how my enemies[d] persecute me!
Have mercy and lift me up from the gates of death,
14 that I may declare your praises[e]
in the gates of Daughter Zion,
and there rejoice in your salvation.[f]

15 The nations have fallen into the pit they have dug;[g]
their feet are caught in the net they have hidden.[h]
16 The LORD is known by his acts of justice;
the wicked are ensnared by the work of their hands.[a]
17 The wicked go down to the realm of the dead,[i]
all the nations that forget God.[j]
18 But God will never forget the needy;
the hope[k] of the afflicted[l] will never perish.

19 Arise, LORD, do not let mortals triumph;
let the nations be judged in your presence.
20 Strike them with terror, LORD;
let the nations know they are only mortal.[m]

Psalm 10[b]

1 Why, LORD, do you stand far off?[n]
Why do you hide yourself[o] in times of trouble?

2 In his arrogance the wicked man hunts down the weak,
who are caught in the schemes he devises.
3 He boasts[p] about the cravings of his heart;
he blesses the greedy and reviles the LORD.
4 In his pride the wicked man does not seek him;
in all his thoughts there is no room for God.[q]
5 His ways are always prosperous;
your laws are rejected by[c] him;
he sneers at all his enemies.
6 He says to himself, "Nothing will ever shake me."
He swears, "No one will ever do me harm."[r]

[a] *16* The Hebrew has *Higgaion* and *Selah* (words of uncertain meaning) here; *Selah* occurs also at the end of verse 20. [b] Psalms 9 and 10 may originally have been a single acrostic poem in which alternating lines began with the successive letters of the Hebrew alphabet. In the Septuagint they constitute one psalm. [c] *5* See Septuagint; Hebrew / *they are haughty, and your laws are far from*

9:17 realm of the dead. See note on 6:5.

9:18 needy ... afflicted. Ties Ps 9 and Ps 10 together (here, v. 12; 10:14,17). God instructed his people to show special favor to such people (see note on 82:3–4).

9:19 David ends with another prayer that God would assert himself against those who oppose him. **mortals.** In 8:4 David reflected on the low position of "mankind," referring to humanity in its weak and frail existence. Here he uses the same Hebrew word in vv. 19–20 (translated "mortal[s]"), asking God to remind the rebellious nations that they are all fleeting and mortal. David, speaking as the Lord's anointed, looks to God to bring to fulfillment that which is mentioned in Ps 2 regarding the subjugation of those nations that rebel against God.

Ps 10 *Arise, Lord! Do Not Forget the Helpless.* This psalm of lament turns the focus away from David's national enemies (Ps 9) to the individual "wicked man" (v. 2) who literally seems to get away with murder (v. 8). Like the prophet Habakkuk (Hab 1:2–4), the psalmist is dismayed to see evil prevailing all around him. Like Ps 9, this psalm expresses concern for the oppressed and the afflicted (vv. 14,17–18; 9:9,12,18). The psalmist begins by questioning God as to why he stands aloof while the wicked man seems to prosper (vv. 1–6), causing great harm (vv. 7–11). He asks God to arise on behalf of the wicked man's victims (vv. 12–15) and concludes by reaffirming God's place as King and his ongoing concern for the helpless (vv. 16–18). The ending of an incomplete acrostic poem begun in Ps 9 can be seen in the Hebrew in the psalm's final verses (see introduction to Ps 9).

10:1 Why, LORD ...? The psalmists often very directly address God, confident enough in their relationship with him that they can bring their hard questions to him. "Why?" and "How long?" are questions that the lament psalms repeatedly ask God. See note on 13:1,2.

10:5 His ways are always prosperous. It sometimes seems as though the wicked get away with their evil schemes and prosper at the expense of the righteous (73:3; Prov 29:16), but their sinful self-reliance ensures that in the end their way will not stand (1:5; 11:6; 37:13,17,20; Prov 2:22; 3:33; 10:3,28).

10:6 He says to himself ... He swears. The psalmists sometimes quote the words of God's enemies in order to reveal their clear intent.

[7]His mouth is full[s] of lies and threats;[t]
trouble and evil are under his tongue.[u]
[8]He lies in wait near the villages;
from ambush he murders the innocent.[v]
His eyes watch in secret for his victims;
[9] like a lion in cover he lies in wait.
He lies in wait to catch the helpless;[w]
he catches the helpless and drags them off in his net.
[10]His victims are crushed, they collapse;
they fall under his strength.
[11]He says to himself, "God will never notice;[x]
he covers his face and never sees."

[12]Arise, LORD! Lift up your hand,[y] O God.
Do not forget the helpless.[z]
[13]Why does the wicked man revile God?
Why does he say to himself,
"He won't call me to account"?
[14]But you, God, see the trouble[a] of the afflicted;
you consider their grief and take it in hand.
The victims commit themselves to you;[b]
you are the helper[c] of the fatherless.
[15]Break the arm of the wicked man;[d]
call the evildoer to account for his wickedness
that would not otherwise be found out.

[16]The LORD is King for ever and ever;[e]
the nations[f] will perish from his land.
[17]You, LORD, hear the desire of the afflicted;[g]
you encourage them, and you listen to their cry,
[18]defending the fatherless[h] and the oppressed,[i]
so that mere earthly mortals
will never again strike terror.

10:7 [s]Ro 3:14* [t]Ps 73:8 [u]Ps 140:3
10:8 [v]Ps 94:6
10:9 [w]Ps 17:12; 59:3; 140:5
10:11 [x]Job 22:13
10:12 [y]Ps 17:7; Mic 5:9 [z]Ps 9:12
10:14 [a]Ps 22:11 [b]Ps 37:5 [c]Ps 68:5
10:15 [d]Ps 37:17
10:16 [e]Ps 29:10 [f]Dt 8:20
10:17 [g]1Ch 29:18; Ps 34:15
10:18 [h]Ps 82:3 [i]Ps 9:9
11:1 [j]Ps 56:11

Psalm 11

For the director of music. Of David.

[1]In the LORD I take refuge.[j]
How then can you say to me:
"Flee like a bird to your mountain.

Cf. vv. 11,13; 3:2; 13:4; 14:1; 22:8; 35:21,25; 41:5,7–8; 42:3,10; 64:5–6; 71:11; 73:11; 83:4; 94:7; 115:2.
10:7 tongue. A source of great "trouble and evil" (12:3–4; 50:19; 52:2–4; 57:4; 64:3–4; 120:3; Jer 9:8; Jas 3:5–6,8). The wicked man's mouth "is full of lies and threats" (see 5:9). Paul cites the Greek version of this verse to make the point that all have sinned (Rom 3:14).
10:10 crushed. Translated "oppressed" in v. 18 and 9:9; the wicked man violently oppresses his victims, crushing them under the weight of his assault.
10:14 fatherless. See notes on 82:3–4.
10:15 call the evildoer to account. This is precisely what the wicked man has declared to himself that God would *not* do (v. 13). He is unaware that God does remember the needy and the afflicted (v. 14; 9:12,19).
10:16 The LORD is King for ever and ever. One of the great motifs in the Psalms: God is King! As such, all nations will be subject to him (24:7–10; 29:10; 44:4; 47:2,6–7; 66:7; 68:24; 74:12; 84:3; 95:3; 98:6; 145:1; 149:2), and he remembers the afflicted in society (see 5:2; 99:4). Exod 15:18 is the first explicit expression of God's kingship. It is also a motif that ties this psalm to Ps 9 (see 9:7,11). See notes on 22:27–28; 93:1.
10:18 mere earthly mortals. The Hebrew word emphasizes humanity in its weak, frail state (see note on 8:4). It ties this psalm to Ps 9 (9:19–20): in both places, referring to God's enemies in this way defines their true status.
Ps 11 *In the Lord I Take Refuge.* David expresses confidence in the Lord as his refuge (v. 1a), echoing Pss 3; 4; 7. He rejects the counsel of despair of those fearful of the wicked (vv. 1b–3). From God's dual vantage points of his holy temple and his heavenly throne (see note on 5:7), his eyes survey the world, examining and judging both the righteous and the wicked (vv. 4–6) and vindicating the upright (v. 7).
11:1 refuge. This psalm begins like Ps 7, affirming the Lord as David's refuge (7:1; see notes on 2:12; 18:1–2). After this ringing expression of trust (v. 1a), David cites the defeatist counsel that his fearful friends were advising, so that he can rebut them (v. 1b).

11:2 [k]Ps 7:13 [l]Ps 64:3-4 **11:3** [m]Ps 82:5 **11:4** [n]Ps 18:6 [o]Ps 103:19 [p]Ps 33:13 [q]Ps 34:15-16 **11:5** [r]Ge 22:1; Jas 1:12 [s]Ps 5:5 **11:6** [t]Eze 38:22 [u]Jer 4:11-12 **11:7** [v]Ps 7:9,11; 45:7 [w]Ps 33:5 [x]Ps 17:15 **12:1** [y]Isa 57:1 **12:2** [z]Ps 10:7; 41:6; 55:21; Ro 16:18 **12:3** [a]Da 7:8; Rev 13:5 **12:5** [b]Ps 10:18; 34:6

2 For look, the wicked bend their bows;
they set their arrows[k] against the strings
to shoot from the shadows
at the upright in heart.[l]
3 When the foundations[m] are being destroyed,
what can the righteous do?"

4 The LORD is in his holy temple;[n]
the LORD is on his heavenly throne.[o]
He observes everyone on earth;[p]
his eyes examine[q] them.
5 The LORD examines the righteous,[r]
but the wicked, those who love violence,
he hates with a passion.[s]
6 On the wicked he will rain
fiery coals and burning sulfur;[t]
a scorching wind[u] will be their lot.

7 For the LORD is righteous,[v]
he loves justice;[w]
the upright will see his face.[x]

Psalm 12[a]

For the director of music. According to *sheminith*.[b] A psalm of David.

1 Help, LORD, for no one is faithful anymore;[y]
those who are loyal have vanished from the human race.
2 Everyone lies to their neighbor;
they flatter with their lips
but harbor deception in their hearts.[z]

3 May the LORD silence all flattering lips
and every boastful tongue—[a]
4 those who say,
"By our tongues we will prevail;
our own lips will defend us—who is lord over us?"

5 "Because the poor are plundered and the needy groan,
I will now arise," says the LORD.
"I will protect them[b] from those who malign them."

[a] In Hebrew texts 12:1-8 is numbered 12:2-9. [b] Title: Probably a musical term

11:2 bend their bows. The ominous sight of the wicked doing this against God's people also occurs in 37:14.
11:3 what can the righteous do? In their defeatist mode, the fearful do not know where to turn.
11:4 holy temple ... heavenly throne. The temple and the ark within it were the earthly manifestations of God's heavenly throne. Cf. 150:1; see note on 5:7. **his eyes.** See note on 33:18.
11:6 burning sulfur. This recalls not only the same punishment that befell Sodom and Gomorrah (Gen 19:24) but also the fiery lake of Rev 14:10; 20:10; 21:8.
11:7 David affirms that the Lord, the righteous judge, will show his face to the upright, in effect rebutting the words of the wicked who assert that "he covers his face and never sees" (10:11). **see his face.** Used of humans, this expression denotes one's having access to the king or his representative (Gen 43:3,5; 44:23,26; 2 Sam 14:24,28,32). Here David speaks of special freedom of access before the heavenly king for the upright. See also note on 27:8.

Ps 12 *Help, Lord, for No One Is Faithful Anymore.* David's prayer addresses a time when people have sacrificed loyalty, faithfulness, and truth on the altar of selfishness and ego (cf. Mic 7:1–7). The mood has shifted dramatically from Ps 11, in which David expresses great confidence in God. Here he focuses more on the damage in society that disloyalty, lies, and deception cause. He begins by asking for God's help amidst the breakdown of societal standards (vv. 1–2). A cult of personality seems to be the norm, with flattery, boasting, and self-sufficiency the currency of the day (vv. 3–4). In contrast, God promises to arise to help the poor and needy (v. 5). David praises God's words, which are like refined silver and gold (v. 6), and trusts in him to help (vv. 7–8).
12:2 harbor deception in their hearts. They speak with insincere speech, not meaning what they say.
12:4 who is lord over us? Those who say this are clearly rejecting God's authority over them. See note on 10:6.
12:5 poor ... needy. See note on 82:3–4. **I will now arise.** This prom-

[6]And the words of the LORD are flawless,[c]
like silver purified in a crucible,
like gold[a] refined seven times.

[7]You, LORD, will keep the needy safe
and will protect us forever from the wicked,[d]
[8]who freely strut[e] about
when what is vile is honored by the human race.

Psalm 13[b]

For the director of music. A psalm of David.

[1]How long, LORD? Will you forget me forever?
How long will you hide your face[f] from me?
[2]How long must I wrestle with my thoughts[g]
and day after day have sorrow in my heart?
How long will my enemy triumph over me?[h]

[3]Look on me and answer,[i] LORD my God.
Give light to my eyes,[j] or I will sleep in death,[k]
[4]and my enemy will say, "I have overcome him,[l]"
and my foes will rejoice when I fall.

[5]But I trust in your unfailing love;[m]
my heart rejoices in your salvation.[n]
[6]I will sing[o] the LORD's praise,
for he has been good to me.

Psalm 14

14:1-7pp — Ps 53:1-6

For the director of music. Of David.

[1]The fool[c] says in his heart,
"There is no God."[p]

12:6 [c]2Sa 22:31; Ps 18:30; Pr 30:5
12:7 [d]Ps 37:28
12:8 [e]Ps 55:10-11
13:1 [f]Job 13:24; Ps 44:24
13:2 [g]Ps 42:4 [h]Ps 42:9
13:3 [i]Ps 5:1 [j]Ezr 9:8 [k]Jer 51:39
13:4 [l]Ps 25:2
13:5 [m]Ps 52:8 [n]Ps 9:14
13:6 [o]Ps 116:7
14:1 [p]Ps 10:4

[a] *6* Probable reading of the original Hebrew text; Masoretic Text *earth* [b] In Hebrew texts 13:1-6 is numbered 13:2-6. [c] *1* The Hebrew words rendered *fool* in Psalms denote one who is morally deficient.

ise answers the prayer of v. 1, and it also provides an answer of sorts to the similar prayer of 10:12–15 on behalf of the helpless, afflicted, and fatherless.

12:6 purified … refined. These images from metalworking speak of the process of removing all imperfections from precious metals; God's words do not need to go through that process, but they are like the finished product: flawless and priceless. On the other hand, Christians may experience such refining and testing, which they will undergo to the honor and glory of God (1 Pet 1:7). See note on 66:10.

12:8 strut about. The wicked have no purpose but to honor themselves.

Ps 13 *I Trust in Your Unfailing Love.* The note of lament struck in Ps 12 continues here, but both psalms also express strong confidence in God (vv. 5–6; 12:6–7). This psalm is somewhat introspective, focusing on David's inner thoughts and his experience of his enemies' taunts and oppression (vv. 2–4) as well as God's perceived distance (v. 1). But in the end he is confident in God's unfailing love and salvation because of his past experiences of God's goodness (vv. 5–6).

13:1,2 How long …? David begins with an urgent question. These words occur 22 times in the Psalter as a standard feature of lament psalms, indicating the psalmists' sense that God is distant, that God has forgotten his people, and that God does not seem to intervene to punish evil (e.g., 4:2; 6:3; 35:17; 62:3; 74:9–10; 89:46; 94:3). Nowhere else in the OT is this question posed with such urgency as in these verses (i.e., four times in quick succession).

13:1 hide your face. See note on 27:9.

13:3–4 David fears death (v. 3) and his enemies' taunts (v. 4). As with almost all of David's psalms, he is speaking not simply as a private individual but also with a consciousness that he is God's anointed, the representative of all God's people. So an attack on him was also an attack on the nation. We do not know when this psalm was written, but even if it was written before David became king, during the days when Saul was seeking his life, he was still conscious that he was God's anointed successor to Saul (1 Sam 16:8–13), and indeed he respected the office of king so much that twice he refused to kill King Saul precisely because Saul was God's anointed king (1 Sam 24:6; 26:9–11).

13:5–6 David concludes with an expression of full confidence in God's protection, rooted in God's unfailing love (v. 5; see note on 6:4). He vows to praise God because of his past experience that God has been good to him (v. 6); that is, his confidence in the future is rooted in his experience of God in the past.

Ps 14 *The Fool Says in His Heart, "There Is No God."* David turns his thoughts outward to consider what the fool says about God and the

14:2 [q]Ps 33:13 [r]Ps 92:6
14:3 [s]Ps 58:3 [t]Ps 143:2 [u]Ro 3:10-12*
14:4 [v]Ps 82:5 [w]Ps 27:2 [x]Ps 79:6; Isa 64:7
14:6 [y]Ps 9:9; 40:17
14:7 [z]Ps 53:6
15:1 [a]Ps 27:5-6 [b]Ps 24:3-5
15:2 [c]Ps 24:4; Zec 8:3, 16; Eph 4:25
15:3 [d]Ex 23:1

They are corrupt, their deeds are vile;
there is no one who does good.

2 The LORD looks down from heaven[q]
on all mankind
to see if there are any who understand,[r]
any who seek God.
3 All have turned away, all have become corrupt;[s]
there is no one who does good,[t]
not even one.[u]

4 Do all these evildoers know nothing?[v]

They devour my people[w] as though eating bread;
they never call on the LORD.[x]
5 But there they are, overwhelmed with dread,
for God is present in the company of the righteous.
6 You evildoers frustrate the plans of the poor,
but the LORD is their refuge.[y]
7 Oh, that salvation for Israel would come out of Zion!
When the LORD restores[z] his people,
let Jacob rejoice and Israel be glad!

Psalm 15

A psalm of David.

1 LORD, who may dwell in your sacred tent?[a]
Who may live on your holy mountain?[b]

2 The one whose walk is blameless,
who does what is righteous,
who speaks the truth[c] from their heart;
3 whose tongue utters no slander,[d]
who does no wrong to a neighbor,
and casts no slur on others;

effects of his words on God's people. There is little of David's personal involvement that we have seen in Ps 13 and earlier psalms (only the reference to "my people" in v. 4). What he sees is a complete denial of God, total corruption (vv. 1–3), and the oppression of God's people (v. 4). But he also sees God's presence among the righteous and his defense of the poor (vv. 5–6), and David concludes with a wish for blessing and an expression of confidence that God *would* restore his people (v. 7). This psalm is almost identical to Ps 53 (see notes there).

14:1 The breathtaking arrogance of the fool's assertion in v. 1a is reinforced by David's assertions about their character and their deeds in v. 1b. **fool.** See NIV text note. Cf. 39:8; 74:18,22; Prov 17:7,21; 30:22,32.

14:2–3 In an echo of 11:4–5, the Lord surveys the earth, and all he sees is corruption. Paul quotes v. 3 in Rom 3:12; see also Rom 3:23: "all have sinned and fall short of the glory of God."

14:4 The functional atheism displayed earlier (v. 1; 10:6,11; 12:4) is fully expressed here: these evildoers live as though God does not exist.

14:6 refuge. See notes on 2:12; 18:1–2.

14:7 David concludes with a final prayer for his people, expressing his joyful confidence that the Lord would indeed restore them. **Zion.** A synonym for Jerusalem, the place from which God reigned on earth. See notes on 2:6; 9:11. **Jacob ... Israel.** These alternate names for Isaac's son are synonyms for the nation (Gen 32:28; 35:10).

Ps 15 *Lord, Who May Dwell in Your Sacred Tent?* In contrast to the fool's functional atheism and ungodly life (Ps 14), this psalm focuses on the qualities of a God-honoring life. It displays many of the qualities of wisdom literature, especially as found in Proverbs. Similar passages also occur in 24:3–6; Isa 33:14–16. And in Ps 101, David reflects on the royal ideals he should live up to in ways that also imitate this psalm. David begins in v. 1 with two rhetorical questions that he then proceeds to answer in vv. 2–5.

15:1 sacred tent. This was the tabernacle, constructed by Israel in the Sinai wilderness (Exod 26); it was the place where God "dwelt" until Solomon built the temple (2 Sam 7:6; 1 Chr 6:32). **holy mountain.** Mount Zion, where Solomon built the temple (1 Kgs 8:1). This motif is also found in 14:7; indeed, the location of God's earthly presence is an important motif throughout the Psalter (see notes on 2:6; 9:11).

15:2–5 David lists 12 requirements that would qualify a person to dwell with God at his holy mountain. While some of these have counterparts in the Mosaic law (e.g., lending money without interest [v. 5; cf. Deut 23:19–20]), most go beyond specific dos and don'ts and reflect deeper matters of character. The list focuses especially on proper relationships with others, honoring them and not speaking ill of them or doing them wrong. Many OT passages similarly speak of the overall intent of the law, which goes far beyond obeying one specific commandment or another, to focus on right relationships with God and others (e.g., Lev 19:18; Deut 6:5; 10:12–13; 1 Sam 15:22; Hos 6:6; Amos 5:21–24; Mic 6:8).

[4] who despises a vile person
but honors[e] those who fear the LORD;
who keeps an oath[f] even when it hurts,
and does not change their mind;
[5] who lends money to the poor without interest;[g]
who does not accept a bribe[h] against the innocent.

Whoever does these things
will never be shaken.[i]

Psalm 16

A *miktam*[a] of David.

[1] Keep me safe,[j] my God,
for in you I take refuge.[k]

[2] I say to the LORD, "You are my Lord;
apart from you I have no good thing."[l]
[3] I say of the holy people who are in the land,[m]
"They are the noble ones in whom is all my delight."
[4] Those who run after other gods[n] will suffer[o] more and more.
I will not pour out libations of blood to such gods
or take up their names[p] on my lips.

[5] LORD, you alone are my portion[q] and my cup;[r]
you make my lot secure.
[6] The boundary lines have fallen for me in pleasant places;
surely I have a delightful inheritance.[s]
[7] I will praise the LORD, who counsels me;[t]
even at night[u] my heart instructs me.
[8] I keep my eyes always on the LORD.
With him at my right hand,[v] I will not be shaken.

15:4 [e] Ac 28:10 [f] Jdg 11:35
15:5 [g] Ex 22:25 [h] Ex 23:8; Dt 16:19 [i] 2Pe 1:10
16:1 [j] Ps 17:8 [k] Ps 7:1
16:2 [l] Ps 73:25
16:3 [m] Ps 101:6
16:4 [n] Ps 106:37-38 [o] Ps 32:10 [p] Ex 23:13
16:5 [q] Ps 73:26 [r] Ps 23:5
16:6 [s] Ps 78:55; Jer 3:19
16:7 [t] Ps 73:24 [u] Ps 77:6
16:8 [v] Ps 73:23

[a] Title: Probably a literary or musical term

15:4 fear the LORD. See note on 19:9.
15:5 without interest. Lending was to be an act of mercy, not a commercial investment (Exod 22:25–27; Lev 25:35–38; see also note on Ps 37:21. **not accept a bribe.** This injunction is rooted in God's very nature (Deut 10:17–18) and is also featured in the Mosaic law (Deut 16:19; cf. Deut 27:25).
Ps 16 *Lord, You Alone Are My Portion and My Cup.* In this psalm of trust, David reflects on his relationship with God, giving thanks for the blessings that God has afforded him. These have come because of David's God-oriented life, making him worthy to live on God's holy mountain (15:1; cf. 2:6). David begins with a brief petition, affirming his close relationship with God and his delight in God's holy people, in contrast to those who follow after other gods (vv. 1–4). Life seems to be going well because he is praising the Lord and keeping his eyes on him (vv. 5–8). David ends with a strong affirmation of security in the Lord that extends even beyond death (vv. 9–11).
16:2 LORD ... Lord. See note on 8:1.
16:3 holy people. God's people, set apart from sinful practices and the worship of other gods (see 34:9; 89:5,7). The Lord had instructed his people to be holy because he is holy (Lev 19:2), and the apostle Peter echoes this in his instructions to the church (1 Pet 1:15–16). In the NT era, God's "holy people" constitute the church (Acts 9:13; Rom 1:7; 1 Cor 1:2; 2 Cor 1:1; Eph 1:1,18; 3:18; 5:3; Phil 1:1; Col 1:2,12; 2 Thess 1:10; Phlm 5; Jude 3).
16:4 libations. Or "drink offerings." Israelites were to offer God drink offerings made of wine along with other sacrifices at the tabernacle (Exod 29:40; Lev 23:13; Num 28:7–10), but the prophets denounced God's people when they offered these to other gods (Isa 57:6; Jer 7:18; 19:13; 32:29), including the Queen of Heaven (Jer 44:17–19,25). A drink offering "of blood" is not mentioned elsewhere in the OT, but it clearly was a perversion of true worship.
16:5 portion. This can refer to portions of food (Gen 43:34), the choicest part of a sacrifice to be offered to God (Lev 2:2,9,16; 5:12; 6:15; Num 18:29), or a tract of land (Josh 15:13; 17:14; 19:9). Sometimes it refers metaphorically to a blessing (1 Sam 1:5; 2 Kgs 2:9; Isa 61:7). In the Psalms and other poetic texts, it usually refers to God as the psalmist's blessing (73:26; 119:57; 142:5; Jer 10:16; 51:19; Lam 3:24), although in two instances, God's people are *his* portion (Deut 32:9; Zech 2:12). **cup.** The metaphor here indicates God's blessing (cf. 23:5; 116:13); elsewhere it can refer to God's punishment (75:8; Isa 51:22; Jer 25:15–17; Ezek 23:33; Hab 2:16).
16:6 boundary lines. Demarcated tribal or national borders. Measuring lines or ropes sometimes marked off such borders. David rejoices that the "boundary lines" of God's blessings have been nothing but favorable for him.
16:8 my right hand. The seat at one's right hand was the position of honor (v. 11; 45:9; 110:1; 1 Chr 6:39). In v. 11, David looks forward to eternal pleasures at God's right hand, but here the Lord is at *David's* right hand, suggesting that David is writing in his capacity as king and that he sees God as his helper and defender (see note on 13:3–4). God's right hand in other contexts symbolizes power (see note on 20:6).

16:9 [w]Ps 4:7; 30:11 [x]Ps 4:8
16:10 [y]Ac 13:35*
16:11 [z]Mt 7:14 [a]Ac 2:25-28* [b]Ps 36:7-8
17:1 [c]Ps 61:1 [d]Isa 29:13
17:3 [e]Ps 26:2; 66:10 [f]Job 23:10; Jer 50:20 [g]Ps 39:1
17:5 [h]Ps 44:18; 119:133 [i]Ps 18:36
17:6 [j]Ps 86:7 [k]Ps 116:2 [l]Ps 88:2
17:7 [m]Ps 31:21 [n]Ps 20:6
17:8 [o]Dt 32:10
17:9 [p]Ps 31:20; 109:3
17:10 [q]Ps 73:7 [r]1Sa 2:3

9 Therefore my heart is glad[w] and my tongue rejoices;
my body also will rest secure,[x]
10 because you will not abandon me to the realm of the dead,
nor will you let your faithful[a] one see decay.[y]
11 You make known to me the path of life;[z]
you will fill me with joy in your presence,[a]
with eternal pleasures[b] at your right hand.

Psalm 17

A prayer of David.

1 Hear me, LORD, my plea is just;
listen to my cry.[c]
Hear my prayer—
it does not rise from deceitful lips.[d]
2 Let my vindication come from you;
may your eyes see what is right.

3 Though you probe my heart,
though you examine me at night and test me,[e]
you will find that I have planned no evil;[f]
my mouth has not transgressed.[g]
4 Though people tried to bribe me,
I have kept myself from the ways of the violent
through what your lips have commanded.
5 My steps have held to your paths;[h]
my feet have not stumbled.[i]

6 I call on you, my God, for you will answer me;[j]
turn your ear to me[k] and hear my prayer.[l]
7 Show me the wonders of your great love,[m]
you who save by your right hand[n]
those who take refuge in you from their foes.
8 Keep me as the apple of your eye;[o]
hide me in the shadow of your wings
9 from the wicked who are out to destroy me,
from my mortal enemies who surround me.[p]

10 They close up their callous hearts,[q]
and their mouths speak with arrogance.[r]

[a] *10* Or *holy*

16:9–11 David ends by strongly affirming his security in the Lord, which extends even beyond death. The Psalms usually focus on this life, but not exclusively. Other references in the Psalms to life beyond the grave include 17:15; 49:15,19; 73:24–26. Texts elsewhere in the OT that point to life after death include 1 Sam 2:6; 2 Sam 12:22–23; Job 14:13–17; 19:25–27; Isa 26:19; Ezek 37; Dan 12:1–2; Hos 6:2; 13:14. Peter quoted vv. 8–11 of this psalm in his sermon on the day of Pentecost, applying it to Jesus' resurrection from the dead (Acts 2:25–28), and Paul did the same with v. 10 in his speech at Pisidian Antioch (Acts 13:35).
16:9 rest. See note on 62:1.
16:10 realm of the dead. See note on 6:5. **decay.** Or "the pit." The term "pit" is sometimes a synonym for the realm of the dead.
16:11 path of life. This concerns the mode of living in accordance with God's instructions, which leads to an abundant life, even after death. Cf. Ps 1; Deut 30:19; Prov 5:6; 12:28; 15:24; Matt 7:14.
Ps 17 *Let My Vindication Come From You.* In this psalm of petition, David again boldly calls on God to vindicate him. He affirms his own righteousness (vv. 1–5) and calls on God to shelter him from his enemies (vv. 6–9). These are fierce adversaries (vv. 10–12) and David calls on God to save him and to repay them what they deserve (vv. 13–14). He concludes with words of assurance that he will indeed be vindicated and see God's face (v. 15), echoing his confidence in 16:9–11. This psalm continues in the mode of Pss 15–16, which affirm the virtues of a God-oriented life (Ps 15) and David's living such a life (Ps 16).
17:2 Let my vindication come from you. David never asserts that he will take personal revenge; he always relies on the Lord to take proper vengeance (see note on 5:9–10; cf. Deut 32:35). At the end of the psalm, David affirms that he will indeed be vindicated (v. 15). For the quasi-legal setting of this request, see note on 43:1.
17:3 probe. David affirms that his life is an open book; God can examine it and no guile will be found. See 7:9; 11:4–5; 139:23–24.
17:8 apple. Or "pupil," a part of the body that one would protect at all costs (Deut 32:10; Prov 7:2; Zech 2:8). See note on 33:18. **shadow of your wings.** This too is a place of refuge and security. See note on 36:7.

[11]They have tracked me down, they now surround me,[s]
with eyes alert, to throw me to the ground.
[12]They are like a lion[t] hungry for prey,
like a fierce lion crouching in cover.

[13]Rise up, LORD, confront them, bring them down;[u]
with your sword rescue me from the wicked.
[14]By your hand save me from such people, LORD,
from those of this world[v] whose reward is in this life.
May what you have stored up for the wicked fill their bellies;
may their children gorge themselves on it,
and may there be leftovers[w] for their little ones.

[15]As for me, I will be vindicated and will see your face;
when I awake, I will be satisfied with seeing your likeness.[x]

17:11 [s]Ps 37:14; 88:17
17:12 [t]Ps 7:2; 10:9
17:13 [u]Ps 7:12; 22:20; 73:18
17:14 [v]Lk 16:8 [w]Ps 73:3-7
17:15 [x]Nu 12:8; Ps 4:6-7; 16:11; 1Jn 3:2
18:2 [y]Ps 19:14 [z]Ps 59:11 [a]Ps 75:10

Psalm 18[a]

18:Title–50pp — 2Sa 22:1-51

For the director of music. Of David the servant of the LORD. He sang to the LORD the words of this song when the LORD delivered him from the hand of all his enemies and from the hand of Saul. He said:

[1]I love you, LORD, my strength.

[2]The LORD is my rock,[y] my fortress and my deliverer;
my God is my rock, in whom I take refuge,
my shield[b][z] and the horn[c] of my salvation,[a] my stronghold.

[a] In Hebrew texts 18:1-50 is numbered 18:2-51. [b] 2 Or *sovereign* [c] 2 *Horn* here symbolizes strength.

17:12 like a lion. See note on 7:2.

17:14 whose reward is in this life. God's enemies would have to content themselves with whatever rewards this life could offer: their bellies should be filled with God's bitter vengeance, which will have continuing effects down through the generations. In contrast, David could look forward to being with God forever (v. 15).

17:15 Like 16:9–11, this psalm also affirms a future hope for David in the next life, fully vindicated and enjoying God's presence. **I will be vindicated.** David's initial request for vindication in v. 2 (see note) comes full circle here. **see your face.** The beautiful imagery of the upright seeing God's face (see 11:7 and note) is now personalized: David himself looks forward to experiencing this joy. See note on 27:8. **awake.** Arise from the "sleep" of death.

Ps 18 *My God Is My Rock, in Whom I Take Refuge.* This is a long royal psalm of thanksgiving, an almost exact duplicate of David's song of thanksgiving in 2 Sam 22. Its title ties it in with David's deliverance from his enemies, including Saul. This psalm fits the narrative context well: David was finally rid of the threats from the house of Saul (2 Sam 21:1–14), and he thanked God for deliverance. The Psalter's emphasis on David, the ideal, righteous king, fits the context developed from the very beginning: David is God's chosen, anointed king.

The royal psalms focus on Israel's King, usually David, showing him in his position as the wise, godly leader of the nation. Scholars do not agree on which psalms are royal psalms, but a list should include: Pss 2; 18; 20–21; 45; 72; 89; 101; 110; 132; 144. Many of these may also be called "Messianic" psalms because David (and any of his royal descendants) was a forerunner of the great Messiah (see "anointed," 2:2).

This psalm begins and ends with powerful images of the Lord as David's rock and refuge (vv. 1–2,46–50). After this come images of the death that threatened David (vv. 3–5), followed by a majestic theophany, i.e., an appearance of God (vv. 6–15). The Lord did deliver David (vv. 16–19), which shows God's faithfulness to those who are faithful (vv. 20–29). God—whose way and word are perfect (v. 30) and who is incomparable (v. 31)—equips, trains, and protects David for any and all battles (vv. 32–36). God's hand was clearly with David in his victories, but David was the one who had to actually fight the battles against the enemy, which are described in vivid terms (vv. 37–45). The psalm comes full circle, praising God, David's Rock (vv. 2,46), who subdued the nations and saved David from his enemies (vv. 47–50).

18 title This is the third of 14 psalms with a "historical" title linked to an event in David's life (see note on Ps 3 title), and it is the longest of those titles. It ties the psalm in with David's life of conflict with Saul and other enemies. It could apply to any number of situations in David's life, although the near-death experiences of vv. 4–5,16–18 would neatly fit Saul's ongoing pursuits of David in 1 Samuel. The deliverance "from the hand of Saul" could refer to Saul's death (1 Sam 31) or to the killing of seven descendants of Saul (2 Sam 21:1–14), effectively eliminating the stain of Saul's reign on the land. The latter is the context of this same psalm in 2 Sam 22. **servant of the LORD.** This phrase most commonly designates Moses in the OT (e.g., Deut 34:5), especially in the book of Joshua (Josh 1:1; see note on Josh 1:1). It refers to Joshua twice (Josh 24:29; Judg 2:8) and David twice (here; Ps 36 title). In all these cases, it designates a strong leader of the nation, one who had a special relationship with God.

18:1–2 An impressive list describes David's relationship with his God: the Lord is his strength, rock, fortress, deliverer, refuge, shield, horn, salvation, and stronghold. Most of these terms refer to places of natural security, not fortresses that humans have built. So the message is clear: David sees that whatever success he might have as king comes directly from the Lord; he does not rely on his own strength (see 144:1–2). This continues a theme of the Lord as a refuge that begins in 2:12 (cf. 3:3–6; 4:8; 5:11; 7:1; 9:9; 11:1; 14:6; 16:1,5; 17:7).

18:2 rock ... rock. Translates two different Hebrew words. The first is a

18:3 [b]Ps 48:1
18:4 [c]Ps 116:3 [d]Ps 124:4
18:5 [e]Ps 116:3
18:6 [f]Ps 34:15
18:7 [g]Jdg 5:4 [h]Ps 68:7-8
18:8 [i]Ps 50:3
18:9 [j]Ps 144:5
18:10 [k]Ps 80:1 [l]Ps 104:3
18:11 [m]Dt 4:11; Ps 97:2
18:12 [n]Ps 104:2 [o]Ps 97:3
18:13 [p]Ps 29:3; 104:7
18:14 [q]Ps 144:6
18:15 [r]Ps 76:6; 106:9
18:16 [s]Ps 144:7
18:17 [t]Ps 35:10

3 I called to the LORD, who is worthy of praise,[b]
and I have been saved from my enemies.
4 The cords of death[c] entangled me;
the torrents[d] of destruction overwhelmed me.
5 The cords of the grave coiled around me;
the snares of death[e] confronted me.

6 In my distress I called to the LORD;
I cried to my God for help.
From his temple he heard my voice;[f]
my cry came before him, into his ears.
7 The earth trembled and quaked,[g]
and the foundations of the mountains shook;
they trembled because he was angry.[h]
8 Smoke rose from his nostrils;
consuming fire[i] came from his mouth,
burning coals blazed out of it.
9 He parted the heavens and came down;[j]
dark clouds were under his feet.
10 He mounted the cherubim[k] and flew;
he soared on the wings of the wind.[l]
11 He made darkness his covering,[m] his canopy around him —
the dark rain clouds of the sky.
12 Out of the brightness of his presence[n] clouds advanced,
with hailstones and bolts of lightning.[o]
13 The LORD thundered[p] from heaven;
the voice of the Most High resounded.[a]
14 He shot his arrows and scattered the enemy,
with great bolts of lightning he routed them.[q]
15 The valleys of the sea were exposed
and the foundations of the earth laid bare
at your rebuke,[r] LORD,
at the blast of breath from your nostrils.

16 He reached down from on high and took hold of me;
he drew me out of deep waters.[s]
17 He rescued me from my powerful enemy,
from my foes, who were too strong for me.[t]

[a] *13* Some Hebrew manuscripts and Septuagint (see also 2 Samuel 22:14); most Hebrew manuscripts *resounded, / amid hailstones and bolts of lightning*

rocky crag (78:16; 104:18) or cliff (141:6; 2 Chr 25:12; Job 39:28); the second is a large boulder or a rocky hill or mountain in which a cave could be found (Exod 33:22; Isa 2:10,19). Metaphorically, the psalmists depict God as a rock, i.e., a place of refuge (vv. 31,46; 19:14; 28:1; 31:3; cf. Deut 32:4,18). **shield.** See note on 3:3. **horn.** Though the "horns of the altar" could signify a place of refuge (1 Kgs 1:50–51; 2:28), it is more likely that the singular form here is a symbol of power and strength (see NIV text note; see also 1 Sam 2:10; Jer 48:25; Lam 2:3; cf. Luke 1:69).

18:6–15 In this section, David relates a theophany, i.e., an encounter with God, in which God reveals himself as the divine Warrior, terrifying nations and nature alike. Here God comes down against David's enemies, responding to David's cry for help (v. 6).

18:6 temple. See note on 5:7.

18:10 cherubim. Winged celestial beings, first encountered as guardians of the Garden of Eden (Gen 3:24). Two golden cherubim were mounted on the ark of the covenant in the tabernacle, their wings stretched out over the mercy seat, "guarding" it (Exod 25:18–22; Heb 9:5). They formed a pedestal of sorts for God's throne on earth (80:1; 99:1; 1 Sam 4:4; 2 Sam 6:2). In Solomon's temple, two additional cherubim, 15 feet (4.5 meters) high, stood in the Most Holy Place, wings outstretched over the ark (1 Kgs 6:26–27). In the ancient Near East, winged creatures of different kinds are known from various cultures, some with human faces and four legs, others appearing as winged bulls or lions, symbols of strength. In the theophany here, the cherubim carried the Lord on "the wings of the wind." See note on 68:4.

18:13 thundered. The image of God's voice represented as thunder is a powerful one. See 29:3–9; Job 37:2–5; cf. Exod 19:16–19. **Most High.** See note on 7:8.

18:16–19 In a breathtaking transition, the terrifying God of vv. 6–15, who caused the earth to tremble and the mountains to shake, has condescended to rescue David from his enemies. What foe could harm David when his God is the one who terrifies all nature and nations?

18 They confronted me in the day of my disaster,
but the LORD was my support.[u]
19 He brought me out into a spacious place;[v]
he rescued me because he delighted in me.[w]

20 The LORD has dealt with me according to my righteousness;
according to the cleanness of my hands[x] he has rewarded me.
21 For I have kept the ways of the LORD;[y]
I am not guilty of turning[z] from my God.
22 All his laws are before me;[a]
I have not turned away from his decrees.
23 I have been blameless before him
and have kept myself from sin.
24 The LORD has rewarded me according to my righteousness,[b]
according to the cleanness of my hands in his sight.

25 To the faithful[c] you show yourself faithful,
to the blameless you show yourself blameless,
26 to the pure you show yourself pure,
but to the devious you show yourself shrewd.[d]
27 You save the humble
but bring low those whose eyes are haughty.[e]
28 You, LORD, keep my lamp burning;
my God turns my darkness into light.[f]
29 With your help[g] I can advance against a troop[a];
with my God I can scale a wall.

30 As for God, his way is perfect:[h]
The LORD's word is flawless;[i]
he shields all who take refuge[j] in him.
31 For who is God besides the LORD?[k]
And who is the Rock[l] except our God?
32 It is God who arms me with strength[m]
and keeps my way secure.
33 He makes my feet like the feet of a deer;[n]
he causes me to stand on the heights.[o]
34 He trains my hands for battle;[p]
my arms can bend a bow of bronze.
35 You make your saving help my shield,
and your right hand sustains[q] me;
your help has made me great.
36 You provide a broad path for my feet,
so that my ankles do not give way.

18:18 [u]Ps 59:16
18:19 [v]Ps 31:8 [w]Ps 118:5
18:20 [x]Ps 24:4
18:21 [y]2Ch 34:33 [z]Ps 119:102
18:22 [a]Ps 119:30
18:24 [b]1Sa 26:23
18:25 [c]1Ki 8:32; Ps 62:12; Mt 5:7
18:26 [d]Pr 3:34
18:27 [e]Pr 6:17
18:28 [f]Job 18:6; 29:3
18:29 [g]Heb 11:34
18:30 [h]Dt 32:4; Rev 15:3 [i]Ps 12:6 [j]Ps 17:7
18:31 [k]Dt 32:39; 86:8; Isa 45:5,6,14,18,21 [l]Dt 32:31; 1Sa 2:2
18:32 [m]Isa 45:5
18:33 [n]Hab 3:19 [o]Dt 32:13
18:34 [p]Ps 144:1
18:35 [q]Ps 119:116

[a] 29 Or *can run through a barricade*

18:19 spacious place. See note on 31:8.

18:20–24 David now asserts his upright life, totally dedicated to walking in God's ways, keeping his laws, and avoiding sin (vv. 21–23). This transparency echoes the thoughts he expressed in 17:3–5, inviting God to examine him. The paragraph begins and ends with almost identical affirmations that God has rewarded David because of his righteousness (vv. 20,24). David was certainly conscious of his own sinfulness (see Pss 32; 51; cf. 2 Sam 12:13), so he is not claiming absolute perfection (see 14:3). But he claims that his life has been one of integrity, oriented faithfully to God and to pleasing him; as a result, God has favored him over his enemies.

18:30–36 The idea of God as refuge, introduced in v. 2, surfaces again in v. 30. Because God shields all who take refuge in him (including David), David can walk safely and securely (v. 36). David gives the credit to the Lord for all his successes (vv. 32–35) and affirms via two rhetorical questions that his God is without peer (v. 31).

18:34 bow of bronze. Most bows were made of wood; bending a bronze bow would demonstrate David's strength. The final royal psalm (Ps 144) also depicts God as David's refuge and the one who trained David's hands for battle in language very similar to this verse (see also v. 2).

18:37 [r]Ps 37:20; 44:5
18:38 [s]Ps 36:12 [t]Ps 47:3
18:40 [u]Ps 21:12 [v]Ps 94:23
18:41 [w]Ps 50:22 [x]Job 27:9; Pr 1:28
18:43 [y]2Sa 8:1-14 [z]Isa 52:15; 55:5
18:44 [a]Ps 66:3
18:45 [b]Mic 7:17
18:46 [c]Ps 51:14
18:47 [d]Ps 47:3
18:48 [e]Ps 59:1
18:49 [f]Ps 108:1 [g]Ro 15:9*
18:50 [h]Ps 144:10 [i]Ps 89:4
19:1 [j]Isa 40:22 [k]Ps 50:6; Ro 1:19

37 I pursued my enemies[r] and overtook them;
I did not turn back till they were destroyed.
38 I crushed them so that they could not rise;[s]
they fell beneath my feet.[t]
39 You armed me with strength for battle;
you humbled my adversaries before me.
40 You made my enemies turn their backs[u] in flight,
and I destroyed[v] my foes.
41 They cried for help, but there was no one to save them[w] —
to the LORD, but he did not answer.[x]
42 I beat them as fine as windblown dust;
I trampled them[a] like mud in the streets.
43 You have delivered me from the attacks of the people;
you have made me the head of nations.[y]
People I did not know[z] now serve me,
44 foreigners[a] cower before me;
as soon as they hear of me, they obey me.
45 They all lose heart;
they come trembling from their strongholds.[b]

46 The LORD lives! Praise be to my Rock!
Exalted be God my Savior![c]
47 He is the God who avenges me,
who subdues nations[d] under me,
48 who saves[e] me from my enemies.
You exalted me above my foes;
from a violent man you rescued me.
49 Therefore I will praise you, LORD, among the nations;
I will sing[f] the praises of your name.[g]

50 He gives his king great victories;
he shows unfailing love to his anointed,
to David[h] and to his descendants forever.[i]

Psalm 19[b]

For the director of music. A psalm of David.

1 The heavens[j] declare[k] the glory of God;
the skies proclaim the work of his hands.

[a] *42* Many Hebrew manuscripts, Septuagint, Syriac and Targum (see also 2 Samuel 22:43); Masoretic Text *I poured them out* [b] In Hebrew texts 19:1-14 is numbered 19:2-15.

18:43 nations. David's vanquished foes included Edomites, Moabites, Ammonites, Philistines, Amalekites, and Arameans (2 Sam 8; 10). See also v. 47.

18:46–49 David sums up his thoughts, praising the Lord, who has subdued nations under him and saved him from his enemies, including a "violent man" (v. 48, perhaps Saul). David vows to praise God "among the nations" (v. 49), in keeping with the universal vision of the OT, in which God's blessing was to be for all nations (67; Gen 12:3), marking a rebuke to the nations' rebelling against God in Ps 2.

18:50 Summarizes the essence of the Davidic covenant, in which God promised David a descendant on the throne in perpetuity (2 Sam 7:11b–16). **unfailing love.** See note on 6:4. **his anointed.** See notes on 2:2,7–9; 13:3–4.

Ps 19 *The Heavens Declare the Glory of God. The Law of the Lord Is Perfect.* This psalm is a majestic meditation on how God has revealed himself; indeed, it is a celebration of two different modes of revelation: God reveals himself in creation (vv. 1–6) and in his word (vv. 7–14), corresponding to what theologians call "general" and "special" revelation, respectively. Each section has two parts: vv. 1–4a celebrate the cosmos and how it praises God, vv. 4b–6 celebrate the sun, vv. 7–9 celebrate the law of the Lord, and vv. 10–14 focus on proper responses to the treasures of the word of the Lord. Links with Ps 18: characterizations of God's ways and his law as "perfect" (v. 7; 18:30), praise for God's law (vv. 7–9; 18:22), and God as David's Rock (v. 14; 18:2,46). Because of the focus on God's law (*tôrâ*), some classify Ps 19 as a "wisdom" psalm (see introduction to Ps 34).

19:1 heavens ... skies. Directs our attention back to Gen 1, which introduces these two words. The heavens are the place of God's dwelling

[2] Day after day they pour forth speech;
night after night they reveal knowledge.[l]
[3] They have no speech, they use no words;
no sound is heard from them.
[4] Yet their voice[a] goes out into all the earth,
their words to the ends of the world.[m]
In the heavens God has pitched a tent[n] for the sun.
[5] It is like a bridegroom coming out of his chamber,
like a champion rejoicing to run his course.
[6] It rises at one end of the heavens
and makes its circuit to the other;[o]
nothing is deprived of its warmth.

[7] The law of the LORD is perfect,
refreshing the soul.[p]
The statutes of the LORD are trustworthy,[q]
making wise the simple.[r]
[8] The precepts of the LORD are right,[s]
giving joy to the heart.
The commands of the LORD are radiant,
giving light to the eyes.
[9] The fear of the LORD is pure,
enduring forever.
The decrees of the LORD are firm,
and all of them are righteous.[t]

[10] They are more precious than gold,[u]
than much pure gold;
they are sweeter than honey,
than honey from the honeycomb.
[11] By them your servant is warned;
in keeping them there is great reward.
[12] But who can discern their own errors?
Forgive my hidden faults.[v]
[13] Keep your servant also from willful sins;
may they not rule over me.
Then I will be blameless,
innocent of great transgression.

19:2 [l] Ps 74:16
19:4 [m] Ro 10:18* [n] Ps 104:2
19:6 [o] Ps 113:3; Ecc 1:5
19:7 [p] Ps 23:3 [q] Ps 93:5; 111:7 [r] Ps 119:98-100
19:8 [s] Ps 12:6; 119:128
19:9 [t] Ps 119:138,142
19:10 [u] Pr 8:10
19:12 [v] Ps 51:2; 90:8; 139:6

[a] 4 Septuagint, Jerome and Syriac; Hebrew *measuring line*

(2:4; 8:1; 115:3), but in this context, which links them with the "skies" (translated "vault" in Gen 1:6–8), the focus is on these great expanses testifying to the glory of the God who made them. **glory of God ... work of his hands.** The parallelism shows that everything that God made testifies to his glory (see 8:3,6).

19:2–4a The heavens and the skies, by their very existence and majesty, testify unceasingly to God's glory. The apostle Paul similarly argues that God has revealed himself through creation (Rom 1:19–20).

19:4b tent. See note on 104:2.

19:7–9 David abruptly transitions to "special" revelation: the law of the Lord. Six parallel statements affirm the great value of God's law. The first part of each one differently describes the Lord's law, characterizing it in very appealing terms: it is perfect, trustworthy, right, radiant, pure, firm. The second part of each one does likewise: the Lord's law is refreshing, makes one wise, gives joy and light, endures forever, and is righteous.

19:9 fear of the LORD. This rarely refers to actual fright or terror; Ps 76:7,8,11,12; 2 Chr 17:10 are instances of that meaning. Usually, the fear of the Lord refers to holding God in proper reverence and awe. It is the beginning of wisdom and knowledge (111:10; Job 28:28; Prov 1:7; 9:10) and a source of life for God's people (Prov 10:27; 14:27; 19:23). It is to be treasured (Prov 15:16; Isa 33:6), something to delight in (Isa 11:3), and a source of rejoicing (Ps 40:3). Humility is at its core (Prov 22:4). See note on 130:4.

19:12 Forgive. See note on 32:1–2. **hidden faults.** These are sins committed unawares (cf. Lev 5:2–4).

19:13 willful sins. Sins of open rebellion against God that lead to being cut off from God (Num 15:30–31). For other words for sin, see note on 32:5. **rule over.** David prays that such willful sins will not take control of his life; common experience shows that repeated deliberate sins can and do end up controlling people. God warned Cain to "rule over" sin after Cain killed Abel (Gen 4:7).

Chariot and horses coming before a Canaanite king on a second-millennium BC ivory from Meggido. "Some trust in chariots and some in horses, but we trust in the name of the LORD our God" (Ps 20:7).

Kim Walton, taken at the Israel Museum, Jerusalem

19:14 [w]Ps 104:34 [x]Ps 18:2 [y]Isa 47:4
20:1 [z]Ps 46:7,11 [a]Ps 91:14
20:2 [b]Ps 3:4
20:3 [c]Ac 10:4 [d]Ps 51:19
20:4 [e]Ps 21:2; 145:16,19
20:5 [f]Ps 9:14; 60:4 [g]1Sa 1:17
20:6 [h]Ps 28:8; 41:11; Isa 58:9

[14] May these words of my mouth and this meditation of
my heart
be pleasing[w] in your sight,
LORD, my Rock[x] and my Redeemer.[y]

Psalm 20[a]

For the director of music. A psalm of David.

[1] May the LORD answer you when you are in distress;
may the name of the God of Jacob[z] protect you.[a]
[2] May he send you help from the sanctuary[b]
and grant you support from Zion.
[3] May he remember[c] all your sacrifices
and accept your burnt offerings.[b][d]
[4] May he give you the desire of your heart[e]
and make all your plans succeed.
[5] May we shout for joy over your victory
and lift up our banners[f] in the name of our God.

May the LORD grant all your requests.[g]

[6] Now this I know:
The LORD gives victory to his anointed.[h]
He answers him from his heavenly sanctuary
with the victorious power of his right hand.

[a] In Hebrew texts 20:1-9 is numbered 20:2-10. [b] *3* The Hebrew has *Selah* (a word of uncertain meaning) here.

19:14 meditation. See note on 1:2. **pleasing.** Proper sacrifices offered to God were to be pleasing to him (Lev 22:20–21; 23:18). **Rock.** See note on 18:2. **Redeemer.** Used in legal contexts dealing with family law and redemption of property or relatives in distress (e.g., Lev 25); it is also prominent in the story of Ruth (Ruth 4). The Psalms use the term primarily of God's rescuing his people from distress (78:35; 119:134,154), as we also see in Exod 15:13.

Ps 20 *Lord, Give Victory to the King!* This is a prayer on behalf of the king. It is paired with Ps 21, another royal psalm, which gives thanks for answered prayer on behalf of the king; both psalms pick up on motifs from Ps 18, another royal psalm: see vv. 6,9; 18:50; 21:1,5. (On royal psalms, see introduction to Ps 18.) The people pray for the king's victory in battle (vv. 1–5), express trust that the Lord will give the victory (vv. 6–8), and conclude with a final petition for victory (v. 9).

20:2 Zion. Jerusalem was the earthly "capital" of God's kingdom. See notes on 2:6; 9:11.

20:4 desire of your heart. This is not a prayer for God to grant anything one desires. The blessing follows one bringing proper sacrifices and burnt offerings (v. 3), implying that the petitioner wishes to be in full communion with God, echoing Pss 15; 16:2–8; 17:3–9; 19:10–14. Jesus made a similar point when he told his followers to "ask ... anything in my name" (John 14:14); the key is that prayer be "in [his] name," which naturally implies that such a prayer will be in tune with God's will.

20:5 banners. Rallying flags for troops going into battle (Song 6:4; Jer 50:2; 51:12,27).

20:6–9 The identity of the speaker in vv. 6–8 is not clear; it could be the king himself, but in this context it more likely represents the congregation speaking as one voice.

20:6 Now this I know. Stands at the exact structural center of the psalm (see note on 100:3), highlighting the assurances to follow. **his anointed.** See notes on 2:2,7–9; 13:3–4. **right hand.** See note on 16:8. God's right hand was a source of power that would guarantee victory for his king and his people (see 21:8; 44:3; 45:4; 78:54; 89:13; 91:7; 98:1; 118:15–16).

[7]Some trust in chariots and some in horses,[i]
but we trust in the name of the LORD our God.[j]
[8]They are brought to their knees and fall,
but we rise up[k] and stand firm.[l]
[9]LORD, give victory to the king!
Answer us[m] when we call!

Psalm 21[a]

For the director of music. A psalm of David.

[1]The king rejoices in your strength, LORD.
How great is his joy in the victories you give![n]

[2]You have granted him his heart's desire[o]
and have not withheld the request of his lips.[b]
[3]You came to greet him with rich blessings
and placed a crown of pure gold[p] on his head.
[4]He asked you for life, and you gave it to him—
length of days, for ever and ever.[q]
[5]Through the victories[r] you gave, his glory is great;
you have bestowed on him splendor and majesty.
[6]Surely you have granted him unending blessings
and made him glad with the joy[s] of your presence.[t]
[7]For the king trusts in the LORD;
through the unfailing love of the Most High
he will not be shaken.

[8]Your hand will lay hold[u] on all your enemies;
your right hand will seize your foes.
[9]When you appear for battle,
you will burn them up as in a blazing furnace.

20:7 [i]Ps 33:17; Isa 31:1 [j]2Ch 32:8
20:8 [k]Mic 7:8 [l]Ps 37:23
20:9 [m]Ps 3:7; 17:6
21:1 [n]Ps 59:16-17
21:2 [o]Ps 37:4
21:3 [p]2Sa 12:30
21:4 [q]Ps 61:5-6; 91:16; 133:3
21:5 [r]Ps 18:50
21:6 [s]Ps 43:4 [t]1Ch 17:27
21:8 [u]Isa 10:10

[a] In Hebrew texts 21:1-13 is numbered 21:2-14. [b] *2* The Hebrew has *Selah* (a word of uncertain meaning) here.

20:7 chariots ... horses. Horses and chariots were the backbone of armies in antiquity; chariots were the ancient equivalent of tanks. Israel was not to put its trust in such things (see Deut 17:16). **name.** See note on 8:1.
20:9 victory to the king! This idea is first found in the promise of royal authority granted to Judah, whose descendants the nations would obey (Gen 49:10), and it also finds expression in the Psalter (e.g., 2:6–9; 144:1–2). The king will bring blessing through the defeat of evil.
Ps 21 *How Great Is the King's Joy.* This psalm expresses thanksgiving to God for granting King David victory over his enemies (vv. 1,5) and answering his prayers (vv. 2,4); it exudes a sense of joy (vv. 1–6,13). As a royal psalm following another royal psalm (Ps 20), it stands as the answer to the prayers for victory offered in that psalm. Ps 20 addresses David as the people pray a blessing over him, whereas Ps 21 addresses God in thanksgiving for what he has granted the king.
21:1 Immediately the psalm reveals its nature as a royal psalm and shows the king in proper perspective: dependent on God for whatever victories will come his way. When presenting David as king, the Bible almost always presents him as relying on God as the divine Warrior (cf. v. 7; 18:39–40). This verse recalls the affirmations of 20:6,9, where God gives victory to his king (cf. 18:50).
21:2–7 Because of the close relationship David had with God (v. 7; cf. 20:7), God granted David his every request (v. 2), recalling the peoples' prayer for David in 20:4. This includes rich and unending blessings (vv. 3,6), a gold crown (v. 3), long life (v. 4), great victories (v. 5), splendor and majesty (v. 5), and, best of all, joy in experiencing God's presence and unfailing love (vv. 6–7).
21:4 life ... length of days. David asked God to spare his life numerous times (e.g., 17:8–9; 18:3,6) and expressed confidence that he would see God after death (16:9–11; 17:15). This confirms that God did spare him and granted him a long life "for ever and ever." On one level, this statement recalls the standard expression "Long live the king!" (1 Sam 10:24; see 1 Kgs 1:25,31,34,39; Dan 2:4; 3:9). David died a physical death, but he lived a long and rich life (1 Kgs 2:10–11). On another level, David's name was to live on forever through the dynasty that God promised him (2 Sam 7:11b–16) and through the greatest Son that his dynasty would give birth to (Matt 1:1,18–25; Luke 1:32–33; 2:11).
21:7 trusts in the LORD. The key to the king's success (cf. 2 Kgs 18:5), reinforced by these words standing at the exact midpoint of the psalm (see note on 100:3). **unfailing love.** See note on 6:4. **Most High.** See note on 7:8.
21:8–12 David affirms that God is the powerful divine Warrior, vanquishing his enemies. The ferocity and decisiveness of God's victories recalls the vivid language of the theophany in 18:6–15. Some scholars see these words addressing David, the king, rather than the Lord. If so, the language quickly outstrips any real victories of David's life; v. 9b points explicitly to Yahweh's actions. In either case, the psalm clearly shows that God's intervention was critical in any of David's successes.
21:8 right hand. See note on 20:6.

21:9 [v] Ps 50:3; La 2:2; Mal 4:1
21:10 [w] Dt 28:18; Ps 37:28
21:11 [x] Ps 2:1 [y] Ps 10:2
21:12 [z] Ps 7:12-13; 18:40
22:1 [a] Mt 27:46*; Mk 15:34* [b] Ps 10:1
22:2 [c] Ps 42:3
22:3 [d] Ps 99:9 [e] Dt 10:21
22:5 [f] Isa 49:23
22:6 [g] Job 25:6; Isa 41:14 [h] Ps 31:11 [i] Isa 49:7; 53:3
22:7 [j] Mt 27:39,44 [k] Mk 15:29
22:8 [l] Ps 91:14

The LORD will swallow them up in his wrath,
and his fire will consume them.[v]
10 You will destroy their descendants from the earth,
their posterity from mankind.[w]
11 Though they plot evil[x] against you
and devise wicked schemes,[y] they cannot succeed.
12 You will make them turn their backs[z]
when you aim at them with drawn bow.

13 Be exalted in your strength, LORD;
we will sing and praise your might.

Psalm 22[a]

For the director of music. To the tune of "The Doe of the Morning." A psalm of David.

1 My God, my God, why have you forsaken me?[a]
Why are you so far[b] from saving me,
so far from my cries of anguish?
2 My God, I cry out by day, but you do not answer,
by night,[c] but I find no rest.[b]

3 Yet you are enthroned as the Holy One;[d]
you are the one Israel praises.[c][e]
4 In you our ancestors put their trust;
they trusted and you delivered them.
5 To you they cried out and were saved;
in you they trusted and were not put to shame.[f]

6 But I am a worm[g] and not a man,
scorned by everyone,[h] despised[i] by the people.
7 All who see me mock me;
they hurl insults,[j] shaking their heads.[k]
8 "He trusts in the LORD," they say,
"let the LORD rescue him.[l]

[a] In Hebrew texts 22:1-31 is numbered 22:2-32. [b] *2* Or *night, and am not silent* [c] *3* Or *Yet you are holy, / enthroned on the praises of Israel*

Ps 22 *My God, My God, Why Have You Forsaken Me?* This psalm expresses an almost unparalleled depth of passion and pain in its first section (vv. 1–21) and then takes a very abrupt turn to praising God in the second section (vv. 22–31). The first part focuses on David as an individual experiencing unmatched suffering in his person. In the second part, David returns to his accustomed role as king, thanking God before the people and extending his vision to the nations. This psalm sharply contrasts with the immediately preceding psalms, which celebrate David the godly king (Pss 18; 20–21); here he seems helpless and alone.

The language of suffering in the first part might fit some of David's travails when he was fleeing from Saul (1 Sam 19–30) or Absalom (2 Sam 15–17), but the intensity and the specific details, especially in vv. 12–18, outstrip anything that David is recorded to have experienced. As in many psalms, he resorts to figurative language to express the depth of his distress. In the second part, his vision extends beyond any reality of his own day as he affirms that "all the families of the nations will bow down before" the Lord (v. 27).

No Christian can read Ps 22 without hearing resonances of this psalm as applied to the sufferings of Jesus (see especially Matt 27:34–35,43,46; Mark 15:24,29,34; Luke 23:34; John 15:24; 19:28; Heb 2:12). What were figurative expressions of David's suffering became literal sufferings of Jesus. David prefigured Jesus in many ways as the great heir to the throne that God promised him (2 Sam 7:11b–16): he suffered great hardships before he was hailed as Israel's undisputed king. So too did Jesus undergo great suffering before he is exalted as the world's undisputed King. The apostle Paul affirms that all Christ-followers must also share in Christ's sufferings if they are to share in his glory (Rom 8:17–18).

22:1–2 David's words reflect a deep sense of anguish and abandonment by God; they are echoed by Jesus on the cross (Matt 27:46; Mark 15:34).

22:2 rest. See note on 62:1.

22:3–5 Despite the anguish of vv. 1–2, David affirms God as the "Holy One" (v. 3), who is "enthroned on the praises of Israel" (see NIV text note on v. 3), reminding God of his past deliverances when Israel trusted in him (vv. 4–5).

22:6–8 David's acute pain from everyone's rejection leads him to call himself a "worm" (v. 6). The taunters' words in v. 8 are ironic, because David previously gloried in God's rescue (18:17,19,48); at this point in Ps 22, he experiences none of that. The enemies' words almost exactly prefigure the words of Jesus' mockers at the cross (Matt 27:41–43).

Let him deliver him,
since he delights[m] in him."
9 Yet you brought me out of the womb;[n]
you made me trust in you, even at my mother's breast.
10 From birth[o] I was cast on you;
from my mother's womb you have been my God.

11 Do not be far from me,
for trouble is near
and there is no one to help.[p]

12 Many bulls[q] surround me;
strong bulls of Bashan[r] encircle me.
13 Roaring lions[s] that tear their prey
open their mouths wide[t] against me.
14 I am poured out like water,
and all my bones are out of joint.[u]
My heart has turned to wax;
it has melted[v] within me.
15 My mouth[a] is dried up like a potsherd,
and my tongue sticks to the roof of my mouth;[w]
you lay me in the dust[x] of death.

16 Dogs[y] surround me,
a pack of villains encircles me;
they pierce[b][z] my hands and my feet.
17 All my bones are on display;
people stare[a] and gloat over me.[b]
18 They divide my clothes among them
and cast lots[c] for my garment.

19 But you, LORD, do not be far from me.
You are my strength; come quickly[d] to help me.
20 Deliver me from the sword,
my precious life[e] from the power of the dogs.
21 Rescue me from the mouth of the lions;
save me from the horns of the wild oxen.

22 I will declare your name to my people;
in the assembly I will praise you.[f]

22:8 [m] Mt 27:43
22:9 [n] Ps 71:6
22:10 [o] Isa 46:3
22:11 [p] Ps 72:12
22:12 [q] Ps 68:30 [r] Dt 32:14
22:13 [s] Ps 17:12 [t] Ps 35:21
22:14 [u] Ps 31:10 [v] Job 30:16; Da 5:6
22:15 [w] Ps 38:10; Jn 19:28 [x] Ps 104:29
22:16 [y] Ps 59:6 [z] Isa 53:5; Zec 12:10; Jn 19:34
22:17 [a] Lk 23:35 [b] Lk 23:27
22:18 [c] Mt 27:35*; Lk 23:34; Jn 19:24*
22:19 [d] Ps 70:5
22:20 [e] Ps 35:17
22:22 [f] Heb 2:12*

[a] *15* Probable reading of the original Hebrew text; Masoretic Text *strength* [b] *16* Dead Sea Scrolls and some manuscripts of the Masoretic Text, Septuagint and Syriac; most manuscripts of the Masoretic Text *me, / like a lion*

22:12 bulls. Symbols of strength (see note on 18:10). **Bashan.** An especially fertile area lying northeast of the Sea of Galilee; it produced the finest, strongest animals (Deut 32:14; Ezek 39:18), which intensifies the imagery here.
22:13 lions. Fierce and terrifying beasts (see note on 7:2). Peter uses the imagery of a roaring lion to describe the work of the devil seeking someone to devour (1 Pet 5:8).
22:15 My mouth is dried up like a potsherd. Jesus' words on the cross, "I am thirsty" (John 19:28), echo David's words here.
22:16 Dogs. Despised animals in the ancient Near East, commonly known as scavengers that would eat the flesh of the dead (1 Kgs 14:11; 16:4; 21:23–24) and lick their blood (1 Kgs 21:19; 22:38). A common insult was to compare someone to a dog (e.g., 1 Sam 17:43; 2 Sam 3:8; 16:9). In the Psalms, they usually represent bitter enemies (here; v. 20; 59:6,14). **they pierce my hands and my feet.** Continuing the imagery of fierce beasts opposing him, this would suggest the dogs attacking and biting David, which follows the readings in the Dead Sea Scrolls and the Septuagint (the pre-Christian Greek translation of the OT; see NIV text note). The image becomes prophetic of the wounds the suffering servant would suffer (Isa 53:5) and was literally fulfilled in Jesus' wounds on the cross (John 19:34; Acts 2:23).
22:18 Shows the depth of David's despair and his feelings of utter helplessness. These words were fulfilled literally at the death of the great Son of David (Matt 27:35; John 19:23–24).
22:22–24 In an abrupt shift, David returns to his usual role as royal representative of the people, and he remains in that role for the rest of the psalm. He now speaks as one whose prayers have been answered, affirming that the Lord has listened to the cry of the afflicted (v. 24).

22:23 [g]Ps 86:12; 135:19 [h]Ps 33:8
22:24 [i]Ps 69:17 [j]Heb 5:7
22:25 [k]Ps 35:18 [l]Ecc 5:4
22:26 [m]Ps 107:9 [n]Ps 40:16
22:27 [o]Ps 2:8 [p]Ps 86:9
22:28 [q]Ps 47:7-8
22:29 [r]Ps 45:12 [s]Isa 26:19
22:30 [t]Ps 102:28
22:31 [u]Ps 78:6
23:1 [v]Isa 40:11; Jn 10:11; 1Pe 2:25 [w]Php 4:19
23:2 [x]Eze 34:14; Rev 7:17
23:3 [y]Ps 19:7 [z]Ps 5:8; 85:13

23 You who fear the LORD, praise him![g]
All you descendants of Jacob, honor him!
Revere him,[h] all you descendants of Israel!
24 For he has not despised or scorned
the suffering of the afflicted one;
he has not hidden his face[i] from him
but has listened to his cry for help.[j]

25 From you comes the theme of my praise in the great assembly;[k]
before those who fear you[a] I will fulfill my vows.[l]
26 The poor will eat[m] and be satisfied;
those who seek the LORD will praise him—[n]
may your hearts live forever!

27 All the ends of the earth[o]
will remember and turn to the LORD,
and all the families of the nations
will bow down before him,[p]
28 for dominion belongs to the LORD[q]
and he rules over the nations.

29 All the rich[r] of the earth will feast and worship;
all who go down to the dust[s] will kneel before him—
those who cannot keep themselves alive.
30 Posterity[t] will serve him;
future generations will be told about the Lord.
31 They will proclaim his righteousness,
declaring to a people yet unborn:[u]
He has done it!

Psalm 23

A psalm of David.

1 The LORD is my shepherd,[v] I lack nothing.[w]
2 He makes me lie down in green pastures,
he leads me beside quiet waters,[x]
3 he refreshes my soul.[y]
He guides me along the right paths[z]
for his name's sake.

[a] *25* Hebrew *him*

Because of this, he vows to lead the people in praise to God (v. 22), urging all of the faithful to do so (v. 23). Heb 2:12 quotes v. 22 as the words of Jesus, making the point that Jesus' work brings all of the redeemed into relationship with him as brothers and sisters ("my people" in v. 22 is "my brothers and sisters" in Heb 2:12).

22:26 God meets the needs of the poor (see note on 82:3–4).

22:27–28 Yahweh (see note on 8:1) was not only Israel's God but God over all nations (45:17; 67:1–7; 96:3–10; 98:2–3; Isa 42:6; 49:6; 51:4). The idea of the Lord as King (v. 28) is developed especially in Pss 24; 29; 47; 93; 95–99; 145; see also notes on 10:16; 93:1. His rule will cause people to turn from their idols and embrace the true God (cf. 1 Thess 1:9).

Ps 23 *The Lord Is My Shepherd, I Lack Nothing.* One of the most beautiful expressions of trust in God in the Psalter, this psalm uses the soothing imagery of a pastoral scene, with the Lord as the shepherd (vv. 1–4) and the host (vv. 5–6). The central affirmation is "you are with me" (v. 4).

23:1 my shepherd. This beautiful metaphor of a divine Shepherd who cares for his people, individually and corporately, occurs numerous places in the OT (e.g., 80:1; 95:7; 100:3; Gen 48:15; 49:24). The NT also portrays Jesus as our great and good shepherd (e.g., John 10:11,14; Heb 13:20; 1 Pet 5:4; Rev 7:17).

23:2 lie down in green pastures. The shepherd provides security for his sheep. See Isa 14:30; 17:2; Jer 33:12; Ezek 34:14–16; Zeph 2:7; cf. John 10:9.

23:3 for his name's sake. Yahweh's reputation is bound up with his holy name (see note on 8:1; see also 79:9; 106:8; 109:21; 143:11; Isa 48:9; Ezek 20:44; cf. Rom 1:5). He promised to care for his people, including David, his anointed king, so he did so for the sake of his own glory.

[4] Even though I walk
through the darkest valley,[a][a]
I will fear no evil,[b]
for you are with me;[c]
your rod and your staff,
they comfort me.

[5] You prepare a table before me
in the presence of my enemies.
You anoint my head with oil;[d]
my cup[e] overflows.
[6] Surely your goodness and love will follow me
all the days of my life,
and I will dwell in the house of the LORD
forever.

Psalm 24

Of David. A psalm.

[1] The earth is the LORD's,[f] and everything in it,
the world, and all who live in it;[g]

23:4 [a] Job 10:21-22 [b] Ps 3:6; 27:1 [c] Isa 43:2
23:5 [d] Ps 92:10 [e] Ps 16:5
24:1 [f] Ex 9:29; Job 41:11; Ps 89:11 [g] 1Co 10:26*

[a] 4 Or *the valley of the shadow of death*

23:4 darkest valley. The peaceful and luxuriant picture of security in vv. 2–3 ("green pastures," "quiet waters") gives way to a terrifying image; the Hebrew evokes "the shadow of death" (see NIV text note). The type of valley in view here is the deep, rocky wadi, a dry streambed carved by rushing waters in the spring but dark and forbidding most of the year. Dangers included flash floods and attacks from animals or outlaws. Yet even here, Yahweh leads David so that he fears no evil. **you are with me.** These words—affirming God's presence and relationship—stand out by virtue of their being at the exact structural center of the psalm (see note on 100:3). God promised his presence to David (118:6–7) and to his people throughout the ages (Gen 26:3; 31:3; Exod 3:12; Josh 1:5; Judg 6:16; 1 Kgs 11:38; Isa 43:2).

23:5 anoint my head with oil. This was done to the honored guest at a banquet (Eccl 9:8; Luke 7:46; cf. also 92:10; 133:2; 2 Sam 12:20; Dan 10:3).

23:6 love. This is a covenantal term rooted in God's very nature. See note on 6:4. **house of the LORD.** See note on 5:7. **forever.** Or "for length of days." This echoes God's granting life to David in 21:4 (see note there); the expression often refers simply to long life (e.g., 91:16; Prov 3:2,16).

Ps 24 *He Is the King of Glory.* Ps 23:6 speaks of David dwelling in the Lord's house forever. This psalm tells of the Lord himself entering Jerusalem to take his rightful place on "the mountain of the LORD" (v. 3), where "his holy place" (v. 3) stands. This psalm was likely composed for a processional into the city where Yahweh's kingship was celebrated, the details on which the Bible does not elaborate. A plausible occasion

A shepherd (bottom left) playing a musical instrument leads a herd of sheep and goats from a pen.

Werner Forman Archive/Heritage Images/Glow Images

24:3 [h]Ps 2:6 [i]Ps 15:1; 65:4
24:4 [j]Job 17:9 [k]Mt 5:8
24:6 [l]Ps 27:8
24:7 [m]Isa 26:2 [n]Ps 97:6; 1Co 2:8
24:8 [o]Ps 76:3-6
25:1 [p]Ps 86:4

2 for he founded it on the seas
and established it on the waters.

3 Who may ascend the mountain[h] of the LORD?
Who may stand in his holy place?[i]
4 The one who has clean hands[j] and a pure heart,[k]
who does not trust in an idol
or swear by a false god.[a]

5 They will receive blessing from the LORD
and vindication from God their Savior.
6 Such is the generation of those who seek him,
who seek your face,[l] God of Jacob.[b,c]

7 Lift up your heads, you gates;[m]
be lifted up, you ancient doors,
that the King of glory[n] may come in.
8 Who is this King of glory?
The LORD strong and mighty,
the LORD mighty in battle.[o]
9 Lift up your heads, you gates;
lift them up, you ancient doors,
that the King of glory may come in.
10 Who is he, this King of glory?
The LORD Almighty—
he is the King of glory.

Psalm 25[d]

Of David.

1 In you, LORD my God,
I put my trust.[p]

[a] 4 Or *swear falsely* [b] 6 Two Hebrew manuscripts and Syriac (see also Septuagint); most Hebrew manuscripts *face, Jacob* [c] 6 The Hebrew has *Selah* (a word of uncertain meaning) here and at the end of verse 10. [d] This psalm is an acrostic poem, the verses of which begin with the successive letters of the Hebrew alphabet.

is when David had the ark of the covenant brought into Jerusalem and then danced before the Lord (2 Sam 6). The temple was not yet built, but the tabernacle still served as God's house (see note on 5:7); in later years, entering the temple precincts would have been in view. This psalm begins by affirming Yahweh's claim of ownership of all the earth based on his having established it on firm foundations (vv. 1–2). It then reviews (in terms that echo Ps 15) who is worthy to ascend the mountain of the Lord (vv. 3–6). It ends with words that may have been shouted in the processional, affirming Yahweh as the King of glory, worthy to enter the city and his own house (vv. 7–10).

24:1 the LORD's. God's name is the first word of the psalm in Hebrew, placing the emphasis on him: he is the one—not anyone else (like another god)—who owns the earth and everything in it. **everything in it.** Everything that exists in the created world, living and non-living (50:12; 89:11). Paul quotes this verse in 1 Cor 10:26 to explain that since God owns everything, all foods may be enjoyed without qualms.

24:2 The Bible affirms that God established the earth on firm foundations (93:1; 104:5; Job 38:4–6). Here the point is not that the earth is bobbing along on top of unstable, moving waters; rather, the imagery is from day three of creation, when God made the dry land to "appear" from out of the seas (Gen 1:9–10). It is the place where life flourishes: rich vegetation, land animals, humans (Gen 1:11–12,24–30).

24:3–6 David now returns to a question he had asked in 15:1: who is worthy to dwell where God himself dwells? The answers in Ps 15 and this psalm are similar, though with different emphases: the person who has "clean hands and a pure heart" (v. 4), who is "blameless" (15:2). Going beyond Ps 15, this psalm includes those who reject idolatry (v. 4). God will bless and vindicate his faithful ones (vv. 5–6).

24:3 the mountain of the LORD ... his holy place. Mount Zion, where God established his dwelling place on earth. See notes on 2:6; 5:7; 9:11; see also "The City of God," p. 2666.

24:5 vindication. For the first time in the Psalter, David speaks of God's vindication of all the faithful, not just David. Cf. 7:8; 17:2,15; see note on 43:1.

24:6 seek your face. Captures the desire of the faithful to find and commune with God (see note on 27:8; cf. 105:4; 1 Chr 16:11; 2 Chr 7:14).

24:10 Almighty. Traditional translation "of hosts." The Lord is strong and mighty in battle (v. 8), the head of both heavenly armies (68:17; Deut 33:2; Josh 5:14; Hab 3:8) and Israel's armies (1 Sam 17:45). The hosts here probably include both, showing God's sovereignty over any and all powers of the universe (thus the NIV's rendering "the LORD Almighty"). See note on 68:14 for a different Hebrew title also translated "Almighty."

Ps 25 *For the Sake of Your Name, Lord, Forgive.* This psalm is another alphabetic acrostic poem (see NIV text note; see also introduction to Ps 9). The message of Ps 25 is not as straightforward as that of

[2] I trust in you;[q]
do not let me be put to shame,
nor let my enemies triumph over me.
[3] No one who hopes in you
will ever be put to shame,[r]
but shame will come on those
who are treacherous without cause.

[4] Show me your ways, LORD,
teach me your paths.[s]
[5] Guide me in your truth and teach me,
for you are God my Savior,
and my hope is in you all day long.
[6] Remember, LORD, your great mercy and love,[t]
for they are from of old.
[7] Do not remember the sins of my youth[u]
and my rebellious ways;
according to your love[v] remember me,
for you, LORD, are good.

[8] Good and upright[w] is the LORD;
therefore he instructs[x] sinners in his ways.
[9] He guides[y] the humble in what is right
and teaches them[z] his way.
[10] All the ways of the LORD are loving and faithful[a]
toward those who keep the demands of his covenant.[b]
[11] For the sake of your name,[c] LORD,
forgive my iniquity, though it is great.

25:2 [q] Ps 41:11
25:3 [r] Isa 49:23
25:4 [s] Ex 33:13
25:6 [t] Ps 103:17; Isa 63:7,15
25:7 [u] Job 13:26; Jer 3:25 [v] Ps 51:1
25:8 [w] Ps 92:15 [x] Ps 32:8
25:9 [y] Ps 23:3 [z] Ps 27:11
25:10 [a] Ps 40:11 [b] Ps 103:18
25:11 [c] Ps 31:3; 79:9

other psalms, but it touches on a number of themes, including trust and hope (vv. 1–3,5,20–21), honor and shame (vv. 2–3,20), guidance (vv. 4–5,8–9,12–14), deliverance (vv. 2,15–22), forgiveness (vv. 6–7,11,18), and the Lord's covenant (vv. 4–6,8–10,14). The psalm's central affirmation focuses on the Lord's reputation: "for the sake of your name, LORD" (v. 11).

25:1 In you . . . I put my trust. This contrasts with those who trust in an idol in 24:4. Trust in God is one of the core theological concepts in the OT, showing the rich, deep relationship available to people when they abandon all reliance on self, other people, or other gods. Trust is often connected with confidence in God's deliverance or vindication (vv. 1–2; cf. 22:5; 28:7; 31:14–15; 86:2).

25:2 put to shame. In ancient Near Eastern societies, including Israel, honor and shame were integral parts of the culture. The Bible usually portrays shame in the context of public exposure, when someone violates societal or religious norms and people ridicule or ostracize the violator (e.g., 1 Sam 20:30; 2 Sam 19:3; Prov 3:35; 19:26; Ezek 16:52,54,61,63). The Psalms speak of shame more than any other book. Often trusting in the Lord is the key to avoiding being shamed (vv. 2–3,20; see 22:5; 31:1; 69:6; 71:1; 119:31). Other Scriptures also affirm this: being in right relationship with God allows the believer to have no shame (e.g., Gen 2:25; Rom 5:5; 9:33; 10:11; 1 Pet 2:6).

25:5 Guide me. Recalls 23:2–4. **my hope is in you.** The psalmist's hope is grounded in faith that God will answer. He waits, not in anger or despair, but in hope.

25:6–7 Remember . . . Do not remember . . . remember. A logical sequence characterizes these requests: (1) David asks God to remember aspects of his own character (mercy and love). (2) That remembrance forms the basis for his request that God *not* remember David's sins (i.e., that God would forgive David's sins). (3) Now forgiven, David asks God to remember him according to God's faithful, covenant love. **mercy . . . love . . . sins . . . rebellious ways.** Resembles terms used in God's promises in Exod 34:6–7: God shows his graciousness to his people and his wrath upon the unrepentant. **love . . . love.** Or "faithful love" (see note on 6:4; see also v. 10).

25:10 covenant. Its first explicit reference in the Psalter (see also v. 14). Here and elsewhere in the Psalter (e.g., 50:5; 78:10,37; 103:18) it refers to the great Mosaic covenant God gave to Israel, first at Mount Sinai (Exod 20) and then renewed on the plains of Moab (Deut 5); it consists of God's promises of his unfailing love for his people, along with his guidelines for how to live in relationship with him (Exod 19:4–6; 24:7–8; 34:10,28; Deut 5:2–3; 29:14–15). The central core of the Mosaic covenant is the Ten Commandments (Exod 20:1–17; Deut 5:6–21; see the direct references to these in Exod 34:28; Deut 4:13; 10:4), but it also includes the entire vast repertoire of laws in Exodus–Deuteronomy, governing everything from the proper sacrifices to how to deal with law-breakers, and much more. In essence, the Mosaic covenant provided instruction for how God's people were to live under the umbrella of the covenant that God made with Abraham. On other uses of "covenant" in the Psalms, see notes on 105:8–11 (regarding the Abrahamic covenant); 89:3 (regarding the Davidic covenant). See also "Covenant," p. 2646.

25:11 For the sake of your name, LORD. God's reputation is at stake, so David asks for forgiveness for Yahweh's name's sake. God had long ago promised to forgive sin (Exod 34:6–7); if he would now refuse to forgive David's sins when David asked for forgiveness, this would damage the very name—the reputation—of Israel's God. David's concern extended beyond his own personal situation to a concern for God's reputation. See note on 31:3. The importance of this idea is reinforced by the

25:12 [d] Ps 37:23
25:13 [e] Pr 19:23
[f] Ps 37:11
25:14 [g] Pr 3:32 [h] Jn 7:17
25:15 [i] Ps 141:8
25:16 [j] Ps 69:16
25:17 [k] Ps 107:6
25:18 [l] 2Sa 16:12
25:19 [m] Ps 3:1
25:20 [n] Ps 86:2
25:21 [o] Ps 41:12
25:22 [p] Ps 130:8
26:1 [q] Ps 7:8; Pr 20:7
[r] Ps 28:7 [s] 2Ki 20:3; Heb 10:23
26:2 [t] Ps 17:3 [u] Ps 7:9
26:3 [v] 2Ki 20:3

[12] Who, then, are those who fear the LORD?
He will instruct them in the ways[d] they should choose.[a]
[13] They will spend their days in prosperity,[e]
and their descendants will inherit the land.[f]
[14] The LORD confides[g] in those who fear him;
he makes his covenant known[h] to them.
[15] My eyes are ever on the LORD,[i]
for only he will release my feet from the snare.

[16] Turn to me[j] and be gracious to me,
for I am lonely and afflicted.
[17] Relieve the troubles of my heart
and free me from my anguish.[k]
[18] Look on my affliction and my distress[l]
and take away all my sins.
[19] See how numerous are my enemies[m]
and how fiercely they hate me!

[20] Guard my life[n] and rescue me;
do not let me be put to shame,
for I take refuge in you.
[21] May integrity[o] and uprightness protect me,
because my hope, LORD,[b] is in you.

[22] Deliver Israel,[p] O God,
from all their troubles!

Psalm 26

Of David.

[1] Vindicate me, LORD,
for I have led a blameless life;[q]
I have trusted[r] in the LORD
and have not faltered.[s]
[2] Test me,[t] LORD, and try me,
examine my heart and my mind;[u]
[3] for I have always been mindful of your unfailing love
and have lived[v] in reliance on your faithfulness.

[a] 12 Or *ways he chooses* [b] 21 Septuagint; Hebrew does not have *LORD*.

statement's position at the structural center of the psalm (see note on 100:3). **forgive.** See note on 32:1–2.

25:12–15 Those whose lives are oriented to God will live in prosperity and sweet relationship with God. The godly king Jehoshaphat exhibited this truth when he prayed, in the face of grave national threats, "We do not know what to do, but our eyes are on you" (2 Chr 20:12).

25:12 fear the LORD. See note on 19:9.

25:20 put to shame. See note on v. 2. **refuge.** See notes on 2:12; 18:1–2.

25:22 This verse stands outside the alphabetic acrostic extending through v. 21. It also shows David for the first time stepping away from his own individual concerns to show concern for the nation over which he is king. Just as he petitions God for deliverance from his own afflictions, he does so too for the nation.

Ps 26 *I Lead a Blameless Life; Vindicate Me.* Leading a blameless life was important to David. He proclaimed his own virtue (18:23; see note on 18:20–24), prayed for it (19:13), affirmed it in principle (15:2), and vowed to dedicate himself to it (101:2). Here he asserts his integrity more directly and at more length than in any other psalm. He does not claim sinlessness; indeed, in the previous psalm, he confessed his sin (25:7,18). But his confidence is in God's forgiveness and in God's ability to wipe the slate clean so that he can proclaim his own integrity (25:21) and blamelessness (vv. 1–7,11). He begins by asserting his guiltlessness, asking God to test him (vv. 1–3). He continues by showing how he stays clear of sinners and proclaims God's glory (vv. 4–7). He concludes by affirming his place in God's house and in the congregation of the righteous (vv. 8–12).

26:1 Vindicate me. See note on 43:1.

26:2 Test … try … examine. The first and third of these three closely related words refer to refining precious metals; they often (as here) refer metaphorically to refining and purifying the human heart so that it becomes more godly. See notes on 12:6; 66:10.

26:3 unfailing love. See note on 6:4.

[4] I do not sit[w] with the deceitful,
nor do I associate with hypocrites.
[5] I abhor[x] the assembly of evildoers
and refuse to sit with the wicked.
[6] I wash my hands in innocence,[y]
and go about your altar, LORD,
[7] proclaiming aloud your praise
and telling of all your wonderful deeds.[z]

[8] LORD, I love[a] the house where you live,
the place where your glory dwells.
[9] Do not take away my soul along with sinners,
my life with those who are bloodthirsty,[b]
[10] in whose hands are wicked schemes,
whose right hands are full of bribes.[c]
[11] I lead a blameless life;
deliver me[d] and be merciful to me.

[12] My feet stand on level ground;[e]
in the great congregation[f] I will praise the LORD.

Psalm 27

Of David.

[1] The LORD is my light[g] and my salvation[h]—
whom shall I fear?
The LORD is the stronghold of my life—
of whom shall I be afraid?[i]

[2] When the wicked advance against me
to devour[a] me,
it is my enemies and my foes
who will stumble and fall.[j]
[3] Though an army besiege me,
my heart will not fear;[k]
though war break out against me,
even then I will be confident.[l]

26:4 [w] Ps 1:1
26:5 [x] Ps 31:6; 139:21
26:6 [y] Ps 73:13
26:7 [z] Ps 9:1
26:8 [a] Ps 27:4
26:9 [b] Ps 28:3
26:10 [c] 1Sa 8:3
26:11 [d] Ps 69:18
26:12 [e] Ps 27:11; 40:2 [f] Ps 22:22
27:1 [g] Isa 60:19 [h] Ex 15:2 [i] Ps 118:6
27:2 [j] Ps 9:3; 14:4
27:3 [k] Ps 3:6 [l] Job 4:6

[a] 2 Or *slander*

26:6 go about your altar. This may indicate David's love for God's house (v. 8) and his regular presence there, or it may be part of the ritual processional described in 24:7–10.
26:7 wonderful deeds. Translates a Hebrew word that sometimes refers specifically to God's victory over the Egyptians and their gods through the ten plagues (78:4,11–12; 106:7–8; Exod 3:20; Judg 6:13; Mic 7:15), sometimes refers to his mighty deeds in providing for his people in the wilderness (78:13–16; Neh 9:17), and sometimes refers even to driving out the Canaanites from before Israel (Exod 34:10) or stopping up the waters of the Jordan River (Josh 3:5). Most often, it is a more general term referring to all of God's mighty deeds (e.g., 86:10; 88:10,12; 89:5; 96:3; Isa 29:14; Jer 21:2) or simply wonders too deep to fathom (e.g., Job 5:9; 9:10; 37:5,14). Sometimes this Hebrew word is translated "miracles" (e.g., 77:11,14; 78:12; 105:5; Neh 9:17; Job 5:9; 9:10). In all cases, these "wonderful deeds" were so out of the ordinary as to be explainable only as mighty acts of God. In Ps 26, David is speaking in general of all of God's mighty deeds.
26:8 house where you live. In David's day, this would have been the tabernacle (see note on 5:7). David's expression of love for God's house echoes his words in 23:6 and 24:3, and it anticipates the references to God's house in 27:4–6; 28:2. **where your glory dwells.** The emphasis on the Lord as the King of glory in 24:7–10 is renewed here. God's glory was associated especially with the tabernacle (Exod 29:42–46; 40:34–35) and then later with the temple (1 Kgs 8:11; 2 Chr 5:14; 7:1–3). These were his dwelling places on earth. The apostle John developed this imagery when he declared that Jesus Christ now represents that glory and that dwelling place in the new Jerusalem (Rev 21:22–23; cf. John 1:14).
Ps 27 *The Lord Is My Light and My Salvation.* David expresses his confidence in the Lord's protection in the face of his enemies (vv. 1–6), and he asks God not to turn him over to such enemies (vv. 7–12). He concludes by reiterating his confidence in the Lord, vowing to wait expectantly for him (vv. 13–14). This psalm evokes previous ones: God's dwelling place is important (vv. 4–6; cf. 23:6; 24:3; 26:8), David prays for protection (v. 12; cf. 26:1,9–10), and David expresses confidence (vv. 13–14; cf. 26:12).
27:1 The LORD is my light. God's light was a source of guidance and protection for the psalmists (43:3; 44:3) and a symbol of well-being (4:6; 97:11; 112:4).

27:4 [m] Ps 90:17 [n] Ps 23:6; 26:8
27:5 [o] Ps 17:8; 31:20 [p] Ps 40:2
27:6 [q] Ps 3:3 [r] Ps 107:22
27:7 [s] Ps 13:3
27:9 [t] Ps 69:17
27:11 [u] Ps 5:8; 25:4; 86:11
27:12 [v] Mt 26:60; Ac 9:1
27:13 [w] Ps 31:19 [x] Jer 11:19; Eze 26:20
27:14 [y] Ps 40:1

4 One thing[m] I ask from the LORD,
this only do I seek:
that I may dwell in the house of the LORD
all the days of my life,[n]
to gaze on the beauty of the LORD
and to seek him in his temple.
5 For in the day of trouble
he will keep me safe in his dwelling;
he will hide me[o] in the shelter of his sacred tent
and set me high upon a rock.[p]

6 Then my head will be exalted[q]
above the enemies who surround me;
at his sacred tent I will sacrifice[r] with shouts of joy;
I will sing and make music to the LORD.

7 Hear my voice when I call, LORD;
be merciful to me and answer me.[s]
8 My heart says of you, "Seek his face!"
Your face, LORD, I will seek.
9 Do not hide your face[t] from me,
do not turn your servant away in anger;
you have been my helper.
Do not reject me or forsake me,
God my Savior.
10 Though my father and mother forsake me,
the LORD will receive me.
11 Teach me your way, LORD;
lead me in a straight path[u]
because of my oppressors.
12 Do not turn me over to the desire of my foes,
for false witnesses[v] rise up against me,
spouting malicious accusations.

13 I remain confident of this:
I will see the goodness of the LORD[w]
in the land of the living.[x]
14 Wait[y] for the LORD;
be strong and take heart
and wait for the LORD.

27:4–6 The passion of David's life was to dwell in God's presence. He uses four different words—"house" (see note on 5:7), "temple," "dwelling," and "sacred tent"—to affirm that wherever God chooses to reveal himself, that is where he wants to be. David feels so safe and secure in the Lord's dwelling, in the shelter of his tent, or high on a secure rock (v. 5) that he vows to worship the Lord joyfully and publicly (v. 6).

27:8 Seek his face! Desire the utmost intimacy with God (cf. 24:6; 105:4; 1 Chr 16:11; 2 Chr 7:14; Hos 5:15). Two individuals saw God "face to face": Jacob (Gen 32:30) and Moses (Exod 33:11; Deut 34:10). Gideon saw the angel of the Lord face to face (Judg 6:22), and God revealed himself "face to face" to the entire nation of Israel at Mount Sinai through the fire on the mountain (Deut 5:4), as well as through the pillars of cloud and fire in the wilderness (Num14:14). But to encounter God directly (i.e., to see the fullness of his glory) was not granted to anyone, lest they die (Exod 33:18–23; cf. John 1:18; 6:46; 1 John 4:12). See note on 11:7.

27:9 hide your face. Indicates God's anger with his people (Deut 31:17–18; 32:20; Jer 33:5). Job and the psalmists experienced God's hiding his face from them as rejection, a terrifying experience; it was the polar opposite of seeing God's face (e.g., 13:1; 44:24; 69:17; 88:14; 102:2; 143:7; Job 13:24). See note on 11:7.

27:11 Teach me your way. This request, along with the others in this section, shows that David's desire is not simply deliverance from enemies; he also sincerely desires to know God and see his face (v. 8). This is a clear duplication of his requests in 25:4–5, and it is a request repeated many times throughout the Psalter (e.g., 86:11; 119:12,26, 29,33,64,66,68,108,124,135,171; 143:10).

27:14 Wait. Or "hope" (see note on 25:5; cf. Isa 40:31). The verb is singular, so David may be addressing himself.

Psalm 28

Of David.

[1] To you, LORD, I call;
you are my Rock,
do not turn a deaf ear to me.
For if you remain silent,[z]
I will be like those who go down to the pit.[a]
[2] Hear my cry for mercy[b]
as I call to you for help,
as I lift up my hands
toward your Most Holy Place.[c]

[3] Do not drag me away with the wicked,
with those who do evil,
who speak cordially with their neighbors
but harbor malice in their hearts.[d]
[4] Repay them for their deeds
and for their evil work;
repay them for what their hands have done[e]
and bring back on them what they deserve.[f]

[5] Because they have no regard for the deeds of the LORD
and what his hands have done,[g]
he will tear them down
and never build them up again.
[6] Praise be to the LORD,
for he has heard my cry for mercy.
[7] The LORD is my strength[h] and my shield;
my heart trusts[i] in him, and he helps me.
My heart leaps for joy,
and with my song I praise him.[j]

[8] The LORD is the strength of his people,
a fortress of salvation for his anointed one.[k]
[9] Save your people and bless your inheritance;[l]
be their shepherd[m] and carry them[n] forever.

28:1 [z] Ps 83:1 [a] Ps 88:4
28:2 [b] Ps 138:2; 140:6 [c] Ps 5:7
28:3 [d] Ps 12:2; Ps 26:9; Jer 9:8
28:4 [e] 2Ti 4:14; Rev 22:12 [f] Rev 18:6
28:5 [g] Isa 5:12
28:7 [h] Ps 18:1 [i] Ps 13:5 [j] Ps 40:3; 69:30
28:8 [k] Ps 20:6
28:9 [l] Dt 9:29; Ezr 1:4 [m] Isa 40:11 [n] Dt 1:31; 32:11

Ps 28 *He Has Heard My Cry for Mercy.* David speaks as an individual threatened by the wicked and by evildoers (vv. 1–7). But he concludes with prayers for the nation (vv. 8–9), which suggests that he is conscious in vv. 1–7 of his role as representative of the nation, just as he is in other psalms (e.g., 18; 20–21; 22:22–31). David's confidence in the Lord in vv. 6–9 mirrors the confidence he expressed in Ps 27. Other connections between this psalm and Ps 27 include David's calling on the Lord (v. 1; 27:7), the rock as David's place of security (v. 1; 27:5), David's pleas that God not turn a deaf ear (v. 1) or hide his face (27:9), David's cry for mercy (vv. 2,6; 27:7), God's house as the place David wants to be (v. 2; 27:4–6), the Lord as David's helper (v. 7; 27:9) and strong fortress (vv. 7–8; 27:1), and David's joy and songs of praise (v. 7; 27:6). Yet unlike Ps 27, this psalm includes imprecations against David's enemies (vv. 4–5; see notes on 5:9–10; 69:22–28).

28:1 pit. A metaphor for death, usually also denoting God's judgment and punishment. Sometimes "pit" is an alternative name for the realm of the dead. See notes on 6:5; 88:4.

28:2 I lift up my hands. An easily recognizable act of worship. Sometimes, as here, it represents petition (cf. 141:2; Lam 2:19); other times it represents praise (63:4; 134:2; Neh 8:6). See 1 Tim 2:8. **Most Holy Place.** The inner sanctuary of the tabernacle and later the temple; it housed the ark of the covenant and (in the temple) two large, winged cherubim (Exod 26:33–34; 1 Kgs 6:16,19,23; 8:6). This continues the emphasis on God's house found in 23:6; 24:3; 26:8; 27:4–6.

28:4 Repay them. David utters some harsh imprecations (i.e., curses) against those who have done evil and opposed the Lord (also v. 5). Though harsh, these words simply echo what God had promised to do, as far back as Abraham's day, to those who oppose him and his people (Gen 12:3). See notes on 5:9–10; 69:22–28.

28:7 shield. See note on 3:3. On the Lord as a refuge, see notes on 2:12; 18:1–2.

28:8 anointed one. David respected the office of God's anointed king, having refused to kill Saul, whom God had anointed king (1 Sam 24:6,10; 26:9–11; 2 Sam 1:14). In David's psalms, he almost always writes with the consciousness that he is now the anointed king, and he is grateful for the Lord's protection and guidance. See notes on 2:2,7–9; 13:3–4; see also "The Kingdom of God," p. 2662.

28:9 shepherd. Recalls 23:1–4,6.

29:1 [o] 1Ch 16:28 [p] Ps 96:7-9
29:2 [q] 2Ch 20:21
29:3 [r] Job 37:5 [s] Ps 18:13
29:4 [t] Ps 68:33
29:5 [u] Jdg 9:15
29:6 [v] Ps 114:4 [w] Dt 3:9

Psalm 29

A psalm of David.

1 Ascribe to the LORD,[o] you heavenly beings,
ascribe to the LORD glory[p] and strength.
2 Ascribe to the LORD the glory due his name;
worship the LORD in the splendor of his[a] holiness.[q]

3 The voice[r] of the LORD is over the waters;
the God of glory thunders,[s]
the LORD thunders over the mighty waters.
4 The voice of the LORD is powerful;[t]
the voice of the LORD is majestic.
5 The voice of the LORD breaks the cedars;
the LORD breaks in pieces the cedars of Lebanon.[u]
6 He makes Lebanon leap[v] like a calf,
Sirion[b][w] like a young wild ox.
7 The voice of the LORD strikes
with flashes of lightning.

[a] 2 Or *LORD with the splendor of* [b] 6 That is, Mount Hermon

Ps 29 *The God of Glory Thunders.* This psalm celebrates the Lord's power over creation, manifested in mighty waters, majestic cedars, even the vast desert. In particular, the Lord's name and his thunderous voice are exalted: his name "Yahweh" ("LORD," see note on 8:1) occurs 18 times, and his "voice" occurs 7 times. This psalm answers David's prayer in 28:1—that God not remain silent. The geographic scope of the psalm encompasses almost all of Canaan, from Mount Hermon ("Sirion") in the north (v. 6) to the "Desert of Kadesh" in the south (v. 8).
29:1 heavenly beings. The term can refer to angels (e.g., 89:6; 148:2; Job 1:6; 2:1), but sometimes also to pagan deities that existed only in people's imaginations and in the elaborate religious establishments created to serve them in most ancient Near Eastern cultures. See notes on 82:1; 97:7.
29:2 splendor of his holiness. On full display in God's sanctuary (see note on 96:9; see also Exod 40:34–35; 1 Kgs 8:10–11; Isa 6:1–4).
29:3–9 These verses celebrate the Lord's name and his powerful voice thundering over creation. The imagery is a theophany, a manifestation of God. His voice is the mighty sound of the storm sweeping eastward over the waters of the Mediterranean (v. 3) to landfall in northern Canaan, breaking the mightiest cedars (vv. 5,9; cf. Isa 2:13) and causing the mountains of Lebanon in the north to quake (v. 6) and even the Desert of Kadesh in the south to shake (v. 8).
29:3 mighty waters. See note on 93:3.
29:6 leap. God's voice is cause for fearful leaping or skipping away in retreat, not happy frolicking. See also 114:4,6.

Clouds gather before a storm on Mount Zaphon.
Todd Bolen/www.BiblePlaces.com

[8] The voice of the LORD shakes the desert;
the LORD shakes the Desert of Kadesh.[x]
[9] The voice of the LORD twists the oaks[a]
and strips the forests bare.
And in his temple all cry, "Glory!"[y]
[10] The LORD sits enthroned over the flood;[z]
the LORD is enthroned as King forever.[a]
[11] The LORD gives strength to his people;[b]
the LORD blesses his people with peace.[c]

Psalm 30[b]

A psalm. A song. For the dedication of the temple.[c] Of David.

[1] I will exalt you, LORD,
for you lifted me out of the depths
and did not let my enemies gloat over me.[d]
[2] LORD my God, I called to you for help,[e]
and you healed me.[f]
[3] You, LORD, brought me up from the realm of the dead;
you spared me from going down to the pit.[g]
[4] Sing the praises of the LORD, you his faithful people;[h]
praise his holy name.[i]
[5] For his anger[j] lasts only a moment,
but his favor lasts a lifetime;
weeping may stay for the night,
but rejoicing comes in the morning.[k]
[6] When I felt secure, I said,
"I will never be shaken."
[7] LORD, when you favored me,
you made my royal mountain[d] stand firm;

29:8 [x] Nu 13:26
29:9 [y] Ps 26:8
29:10 [z] Ge 6:17 [a] Ps 10:16
29:11 [b] Ps 28:8 [c] Ps 37:11
30:1 [d] Ps 25:2; 28:9
30:2 [e] Ps 88:13 [f] Ps 6:2
30:3 [g] Ps 28:1; 86:13
30:4 [h] Ps 149:1 [i] Ps 97:12
30:5 [j] Ps 103:9 [k] 2Co 4:17

[a] 9 Or *LORD makes the deer give birth* [b] In Hebrew texts 30:1-12 is numbered 30:2-13. [c] Title: Or *palace*
[d] 7 That is, Mount Zion

29:9 his temple. The theophany comes full circle to the Lord's temple, where his glory is proclaimed (cf. v. 2). This psalm thus continues the sequence of psalms that speak of the Lord's house (23:6; 24:7–10; 26:8; 27:4–6; 28:2).

29:10 enthroned as King. See notes on 10:16; 22:27–28.

Ps 30 *I Called to You for Help, and You Healed Me.* This is a psalm of thanksgiving in which David thanks the Lord for healing and deliverance from near death. The specifics are unknown, though there are any number of incidents in David's life to which this psalm could apply. This psalm echoes Ps 28 in several places: David's call for help (v. 2; 28:2), going "down to the pit" (v. 3; 28:1), and David's cry for mercy (v. 8; 28:6). Ps 30 continues the remarkable string of psalms referring to the Lord's house (23:6; 24:7–10; 26:8; 27:4–6; 28:2; 29:9). In most of these, the Lord's majesty and glory are praised, his kingship affirmed, and his role as protector declared. In this psalm, we see a more intimate picture of God: his anger at David's sin causes him to bring David close to death, but his mercy leads to David's healing, redemption, and renewed praise. David begins with thanks to God for deliverance (vv. 1–3), followed by instruction to the congregation to praise the Lord (vv. 4–5). David then reflects on his own arrogance (vv. 6–7) and his desire to be spared so that he might praise God (vv. 8–10). He ends with joyful thanks and praise (vv. 11–12).

30 title This is the fourth of 14 psalms with a "historical" title linked to an event in David's life (see note on Ps 3 title). This title, which speaks of "the dedication of the temple," is difficult at first glance to link with the content of this psalm, which relates the affliction that brought David close to death. Furthermore, David did not dedicate the temple; his son Solomon did (1 Kgs 8). But David was heavily invested in the temple that Solomon built and dedicated. David went to great lengths to provide the plans, workers, and materials for it (1 Chr 22; 28–29), even going so far as to contribute from his personal treasure (1 Chr 29:2–5). Thus, it is easy to imagine him also writing this psalm for its dedication.

30:2 you healed me. There is no record elsewhere of any illness that David suffered. This could be an unknown illness, or David could be speaking metaphorically of God's deliverance from dire circumstances. Elsewhere in the Psalter, healing refers sometimes to real sickness or disease (41:4; 103:3; 107:20) and sometimes to metaphoric distresses (6:2; 147:3; cf. 2 Chr 7:14; Prov 12:18; 13:17).

30:3 realm of the dead. See note on 6:5. **pit.** See note on 88:4.

30:4 his holy name. God's holy name (Yahweh) is like no other and is eminently worthy of praise. See notes on 8:1; 23:3.

30:5 anger … favor. The Lord's anger ceases when people repent. He delights to extend favor for a lifetime, even to a thousand generations (Deut 7:9).

30:7 royal mountain. Some scholars understand this simply as a metaphor for unshakable security, and it surely is that. But in context,

30:7 [l] Dt 31:17; Ps 104:29
30:9 [m] Ps 6:5
30:11 [n] Ps 4:7; Jer 31:4,13
30:12 [o] Ps 16:9 [p] Ps 44:8
31:2 [q] Ps 18:2
31:3 [r] Ps 18:2 [s] Ps 23:3
31:4 [t] Ps 25:15
31:5 [u] Lk 23:46; Ac 7:59

but when you hid your face,[l]
I was dismayed.

8 To you, LORD, I called;
to the Lord I cried for mercy:
9 "What is gained if I am silenced,
if I go down to the pit?
Will the dust praise you?
Will it proclaim your faithfulness?[m]
10 Hear, LORD, and be merciful to me;
LORD, be my help."

11 You turned my wailing into dancing;
you removed my sackcloth and clothed me with joy,[n]
12 that my heart may sing your praises and not be silent.
LORD my God, I will praise[o] you forever.[p]

Psalm 31[a]

31:1-4pp — Ps 71:1-3

For the director of music. A psalm of David.

1 In you, LORD, I have taken refuge;
let me never be put to shame;
deliver me in your righteousness.
2 Turn your ear to me,
come quickly to my rescue;
be my rock of refuge,[q]
a strong fortress to save me.
3 Since you are my rock and my fortress,[r]
for the sake of your name[s] lead and guide me.
4 Keep me free from the trap that is set for me,
for you are my refuge.[t]
5 Into your hands I commit my spirit;[u]
deliver me, LORD, my faithful God.

[a] In Hebrew texts 31:1-24 is numbered 31:2-25.

with David speaking, this certainly is more than a metaphor; it refers to Mount Zion (see NIV text note), which David captured (2 Sam 5:6–10; see note on 2:6). In the Psalter, this is the place of security for David and all godly kings (2:6–7; 3:4). **hid your face.** See note on 27:9.

30:8–10 David reveals that the true purpose of life is to praise God. He desires to live not simply out of a self-centered survival instinct but out of a deeply rooted desire to praise God, who has done so much for him. The questions in v. 9 reflect the view of death as the end of life on this earth and thus the end of praising God (cf. 88:10–12; 115:17). It does not consider the possibility of life after death, as some other psalms do (see note on 16:9–11).

Ps 31 *I Am Forgotten as Though I Were Dead ... Yet You Heard My Cry for Mercy.* This is an especially passionate prayer for deliverance from overwhelming foes. It communicates utter despair as well as intense confidence in God's ability and intent to deliver. Fittingly, Jesus used words from this psalm as he hung on the cross in far deeper despair than David (v. 5; cf. Luke 23:46). This psalm begins with David's pleas for deliverance and affirmations of God as a place of refuge (vv. 1–8); then it descends to the depths of despair, for even David's closest friends have abandoned him, and he is as forgotten as if he were dead (vv. 9–13). David reaffirms his trust in the Lord, asking God to deal with the wicked (vv. 14–18). It concludes with praise to the God whom David trusts to answer all his prayers (vv. 19–24).

31:1 put to shame. See note on 25:2. The interplay between David's pleas not to be put to shame (vv. 1,17) and his prayer that his enemies be put to shame (v. 17) shows the tension running throughout the Psalter between the way of the righteous and the way of the wicked that is first proclaimed in Ps 1 (see introduction to Ps 1).

31:2 rock ... refuge ... fortress. The concentrated images of refuge here recall other such images in 18:1–2; 144:1–2.

31:3 for the sake of your name. David understands that his own plight is not merely personal; God's reputation is at stake as well. This is because God had promised him his presence and protection (2 Sam 7:8–11), and for David to fall to his enemies would be to undermine God's very promises and damage his name (i.e., his reputation). See note on 25:11. **lead and guide.** Imagery of the shepherd (see also 23:1–2).

31:5 Into your hands I commit my spirit. David displays his trust in the Lord (see vv. 6,14–15), confident that God will spare his life in order that he can praise him (vv. 7,21; cf. 30:9). When Jesus uttered these words from the cross (Luke 23:46), he was literally at death's door and committed his spirit to his Father for safekeeping after his death.

[6]I hate those who cling to worthless idols;
as for me, I trust in the LORD.[v]
[7]I will be glad and rejoice in your love,
for you saw my affliction[w]
and knew the anguish[x] of my soul.
[8]You have not given me into the hands[y] of the enemy
but have set my feet in a spacious place.

[9]Be merciful to me, LORD, for I am in distress;
my eyes grow weak with sorrow,[z]
my soul and body with grief.
[10]My life is consumed by anguish
and my years by groaning;[a]
my strength fails because of my affliction,[a]
and my bones grow weak.[b]
[11]Because of all my enemies,
I am the utter contempt of my neighbors[c]
and an object of dread to my closest friends —
those who see me on the street flee from me.
[12]I am forgotten as though I were dead;[d]
I have become like broken pottery.
[13]For I hear many whispering,
"Terror on every side!"[e]
They conspire against me
and plot to take my life.[f]

[14]But I trust[g] in you, LORD;
I say, "You are my God."
[15]My times[h] are in your hands;
deliver me from the hands of my enemies,
from those who pursue me.
[16]Let your face shine[i] on your servant;
save me in your unfailing love.
[17]Let me not be put to shame,[j] LORD,
for I have cried out to you;
but let the wicked be put to shame
and be silent[k] in the realm of the dead.

31:6 [v]Jnh 2:8
31:7 [w]Ps 90:14 [x]Ps 10:14; Jn 10:27
31:8 [y]Dt 32:30
31:9 [z]Ps 6:7
31:10 [a]Ps 13:2 [b]Ps 38:3; 39:11
31:11 [c]Job 19:13; Ps 38:11; 64:8; Isa 53:4
31:12 [d]Ps 88:4
31:13 [e]Jer 20:3,10; La 2:22 [f]Mt 27:1
31:14 [g]Ps 140:6
31:15 [h]Job 24:1; Ps 143:9
31:16 [i]Nu 6:25; Ps 4:6
31:17 [j]Ps 25:2-3 [k]Ps 115:17

[a] *10* Or *guilt*

31:6 hate. To hate evil is to have the heart of God: God hates evil and commands his people to do so also (5:5; 97:10; Prov 8:13; Isa 61:8; Amos 5:15; Zech 8:17; Rom 12:9). Evil deeds or attitudes are difficult to separate from those who commit such deeds or hold such attitudes, so the Scriptures occasionally speak of hating the persons, as here (see 119:113; 139:21–22). Yet the Scriptures also affirm that believers are not to hate their neighbors, but to love them (e.g., Lev 19:17–18; Matt 5:43–44; 22:39; Mark 12:33). **worthless idols.** Or "vain emptiness." This pejorative reference to idols emphasizes their worthlessness or emptiness, connoting things that do not really exist. See notes on 96:5.
31:7,16,21 love. See note on 6:4.
31:8 spacious place. The psalmists use different images to portray places of security, such as green pastures and quiet waters (23:2), a royal mountain (30:7), a strong fortress (v. 2), or a wide-open space (here; 4:1 ["give me relief"]; 18:19; 118:5).
31:9 soul and body. Represents not two separate entities, but rather two ways David refers to himself. Cf. 63:1; see note on 6:3.
31:11 neighbors … friends. See note on 38:11.
31:14 You are my God. David recognizes that the Lord is a personal God, one he can trust in and call upon, not a distant, disinterested one, like so many of the gods of surrounding cultures (1 Kgs 18:27–29). See note on 59:5.
31:15 My times are in your hands. This is more than a statement about the passage of time. It reveals a deep dependence on God for each new moment, each new critical time in David's life. Each one has the potential for decisive turns for good or ill. Chronicles speaks of the events of David's life and "the circumstances [or 'times'] that surrounded him" (1 Chr 29:30). This also recalls statements elsewhere about wise people who "understood the times" (1 Chr 12:32; Esth 1:13).
31:16 Let your face shine. God's light shining on his people is a beautiful expression of his favor. See 4:6; 67:1; 80:1,3,7,19; 97:11; 118:27; 119:135; Num 6:25. See note on 27:8.
31:17 the realm of the dead. See note on 6:5.

31:18 [l] Ps 120:2 [m] Ps 94:4
31:19 [n] Ro 11:22 [o] Isa 64:4
31:20 [p] Ps 27:5 [q] Job 5:21
31:21 [r] Ps 17:7 [s] 1Sa 23:7
31:22 [t] Ps 116:11 [u] La 3:54
31:23 [v] Ps 34:9 [w] Ps 145:20 [x] Ps 94:2
31:24 [y] Ps 27:14
32:1 [z] Ps 85:2
32:2 [a] Ro 4:7-8*; 2Co 5:19 [b] Jn 1:47

18 Let their lying lips[l] be silenced,
for with pride and contempt
they speak arrogantly[m] against the righteous.
19 How abundant are the good things[n]
that you have stored up for those who fear you,
that you bestow in the sight of all,[o]
on those who take refuge in you.
20 In the shelter of your presence you hide[p] them
from all human intrigues;[q]
you keep them safe in your dwelling
from accusing tongues.

21 Praise be to the LORD,
for he showed me the wonders of his love[r]
when I was in a city under siege.[s]
22 In my alarm[t] I said,
"I am cut off from your sight!"
Yet you heard my cry[u] for mercy
when I called to you for help.
23 Love the LORD, all his faithful people![v]
The LORD preserves those who are true to him,[w]
but the proud he pays back[x] in full.
24 Be strong and take heart,[y]
all you who hope in the LORD.

Psalm 32

Of David. A *maskil*.[a]

1 Blessed is the one
whose transgressions are forgiven,
whose sins are covered.[z]
2 Blessed is the one
whose sin the LORD does not count against them[a]
and in whose spirit is no deceit.[b]

[a] Title: Probably a literary or musical term

31:18 Let their lying lips be silenced. David never vows to take vengeance against his enemies; he asks God to do this since God said, "It is mine to avenge; I will repay" (Deut 32:35; cf. Deut 32:41). David hates evil so much (v. 6) that he asks God to blot out those who openly defy God with their pride, contempt, and arrogant opposition to the righteous. On seeking vengeance, see notes on 5:9–10; 69:22–28.
31:19 those who fear you. Proper reverence and awe of the Lord are the hallmarks of believers. See note on 19:9.
31:20 dwelling. Refers most often to a temporary hut or booth. The Festival of Tabernacles (or "Booths") celebrated God's protection of Israel when they came out of Egypt and lived in temporary shelters (Lev 23:33–43). Here God's protection in his "booth" represents ultimate security.
Ps 32 *You Forgave the Guilt of My Sin.* The ancient church identified this psalm as one of seven penitential psalms (the others: 6; 38; 51; 102; 130; 143). This psalm presents a unique perspective, an after-the-fact view focusing on the release that David felt after he finally confessed his sins and was forgiven. The other penitential psalms are all from the perspective of the psalmist still awaiting God's forgiveness. David begins by celebrating the happy state enjoyed by all who have been forgiven (vv. 1–2). He recounts his wasted condition when he did not confess his sins and then tells of God's forgiveness when he confessed his sins (vv. 3–5). In the remainder of the psalm, David is the wise teacher exhorting the faithful to pray and trust in the Lord (vv. 6–10), concluding with an upbeat exhortation that all should praise the Lord (v. 11).
32:1–2 David's joy and relief at being forgiven are clear. **Blessed.** Or "happy" or "fortunate" (see note on 1:1). David comes at the idea of forgiveness from four different perspectives: (1) **forgiven.** Conceptually, this primary word for forgiveness denotes sin being "lifted up" off a person; the sin that has burdened them weighs on them no more. (2) **covered.** Another way to consider forgiveness is that the sinner's sins are covered over, never to be seen again. (3) **does not count against them.** Just as God "credited" Abraham's faith to him as righteousness (Gen 15:6), God does not "count" the sins against the one who confesses; the Hebrew words here and in Gen 15:6 are the same. (4) **no deceit.** The result of confession is a clean slate: one's life is an open book. God declared to Moses at Mount Sinai his all-encompassing forgiveness for those who repent (Exod 34:9–10). See note on 52:2. The apostle Paul quotes this text in dealing with justification by faith alone (Rom 4:6–8).

3 When I kept silent,
my bones wasted away[c]
through my groaning all day long.
4 For day and night
your hand was heavy[d] on me;
my strength was sapped
as in the heat of summer.[a]

5 Then I acknowledged my sin to you
and did not cover up my iniquity.
I said, "I will confess[e]
my transgressions[f] to the LORD."
And you forgave
the guilt of my sin.[g]

6 Therefore let all the faithful pray to you
while you may be found;[h]
surely the rising of the mighty waters
will not reach them.[i]
7 You are my hiding place;
you will protect me from trouble[j]
and surround me with songs of deliverance.[k]

8 I will instruct[l] you and teach you in the way you
should go;
I will counsel you with my loving eye on[m] you.
9 Do not be like the horse or the mule,
which have no understanding
but must be controlled by bit and bridle[n]
or they will not come to you.
10 Many are the woes of the wicked,[o]
but the LORD's unfailing love
surrounds the one who trusts[p] in him.

11 Rejoice in the LORD[q] and be glad, you righteous;
sing, all you who are upright in heart!

32:3 [c]Ps 31:10
32:4 [d]Job 33:7
32:5 [e]Pr 28:13 [f]Ps 103:12 [g]Lev 26:40
32:6 [h]Ps 69:13; Isa 55:6 [i]Isa 43:2
32:7 [j]Ps 9:9 [k]Ex 15:1
32:8 [l]Ps 25:8 [m]Ps 33:18
32:9 [n]Pr 26:3
32:10 [o]Ro 2:9 [p]Pr 16:20
32:11 [q]Ps 64:10

[a] 4 The Hebrew has *Selah* (a word of uncertain meaning) here and at the end of verses 5 and 7.

32:5 David mentions sin five times using three different Hebrew words: **sin ... sin.** The common word that can refer to the sin itself (Gen 4:7; 18:20) or to the sin offering (Exod 29:14; Lev 4:8,20). Its basic meaning has to do with missing a mark (cf. Judg 20:16), i.e., sin is off the "target" of right living. It is a direct offense against God himself (51:4; Gen 39:9; 2 Sam 12:13) and results in alienation from God (Gen 4:14). But it also can be a sin against others (Gen 31:36; Num 5:6). **iniquity.** A close synonym to "sin" (38:18; 51:2; 85:2). It can also refer to guilt emanating from that sin (Jer 14:20; Hos 13:12). Its basic meaning denotes something that is bent, twisted, or bowed down (38:6; Lam 3:9), i.e., iniquity twists the course of life away from God's standards. **transgressions.** Or "rebellions, crimes." It is closely related to "sin" and "iniquity," but its nuance refers more to crime generally or specific crimes committed against God (Lev 16:16; Isa 53:8; Ezek 21:24) or neighbor (Gen 31:36; 1 Sam 24:11), which thereby break relationships. **guilt.** The same Hebrew word is translated "iniquity" earlier in this verse. This emphasizes the guilt sin causes and the freedom achieved when that guilt is wiped away. For other words for sin, see notes on 19:12–13.

32:6 while you may be found. God's long-suffering and forbearance are not unlimited. Sometimes he withdrew his favor from his people and turned his face away from them because their sin reached a critical point, as when he allowed Jerusalem to be destroyed (2 Kgs 24:3–4). David urges the faithful not to test God to that point (cf. Isa 55:6). **mighty waters.** See notes on 24:2; 33:7; 93:3.

32:8–10 The psalm no longer addresses God. David could be speaking to the faithful (v. 6), instructing them in how to live wisely, in a similar way to the vow he makes in 51:13. Slightly more probable is that God is speaking to David, instructing him (and, by extension, the faithful) not to be foolish. The phrase "with my loving eye on you" (v. 8) is more appropriately something that God says (cf. 33:18).

32:8 loving eye. God's eye is a figure of speech for his loving counsel and protection (see notes on 17:8; 33:18)

32:9 horse ... mule. Isaiah proclaimed that dumb animals—ox and donkey—knew more than wayward Israel knew (Isa 1:3). Here the instruction for God's people is that they should be wiser than similar animals.

33:1 [r]Ps 147:1 [s]Ps 32:11
33:2 [t]Ps 92:3
33:3 [u]Ps 96:1
33:4 [v]Ps 19:8
33:5 [w]Ps 11:7 [x]Ps 119:64
33:6 [y]Heb 11:3
33:8 [z]Ps 67:7; 96:9
33:9 [a]Ge 1:3; Ps 148:5
33:10 [b]Isa 8:10
33:11 [c]Job 23:13
33:12 [d]Ps 144:15 [e]Ex 19:5; Dt 7:6
33:13 [f]Job 28:24; Ps 11:4
33:14 [g]1Ki 8:39

Psalm 33

1 Sing joyfully to the LORD, you righteous;
it is fitting[r] for the upright[s] to praise him.
2 Praise the LORD with the harp;
make music to him on the ten-stringed lyre.[t]
3 Sing to him a new song;[u]
play skillfully, and shout for joy.

4 For the word of the LORD is right[v] and true;
he is faithful in all he does.
5 The LORD loves righteousness and justice;[w]
the earth is full of his unfailing love.[x]

6 By the word[y] of the LORD the heavens were made,
their starry host by the breath of his mouth.
7 He gathers the waters of the sea into jars[a];
he puts the deep into storehouses.
8 Let all the earth fear the LORD;
let all the people of the world revere him.[z]
9 For he spoke, and it came to be;
he commanded,[a] and it stood firm.

10 The LORD foils the plans of the nations;[b]
he thwarts the purposes of the peoples.
11 But the plans of the LORD stand firm forever,
the purposes[c] of his heart through all generations.

12 Blessed is the nation whose God is the LORD,[d]
the people he chose[e] for his inheritance.
13 From heaven the LORD looks down
and sees all mankind;[f]
14 from his dwelling place[g] he watches
all who live on earth—

[a] 7 Or *sea as into a heap*

Ps 33 *Blessed Is the Nation Whose God Is the Lord.* This great psalm begins with a joyful call to praise (vv. 1–3) that strongly parallels 32:11. Next is an extended reflection on the reasons for praise (vv. 4–19), anchored in God's unfailing love and word (vv. 4–5), the word by which he made the universe (vv. 6–9). He is a great God who thwarts the plans of nations (vv. 10–11), yet he desires that nations and people respond to him (vv. 12–15). His eyes are on those who fear him, the only guarantor of their lives (vv. 16–19). The psalm concludes with a reflection on the hope in God that the righteous have (vv. 20–22). This psalm can be seen as a response to the Lord's counsel in 32:8–10 about heeding his instruction and waiting on his unfailing love; the psalm affirms the Lord's word (vv. 4–11), and it ends with God's people waiting and hoping in the Lord (vv. 20–22). This psalm and Ps 10 are the only untitled psalms (see the introductions to Pss 9; 10) in Book I (Pss 3–41). Several Hebrew manuscripts, along with the Greek translation, attribute this psalm to David, which is understandable given the predominance of "David" elsewhere in Book I as well as the ties just noted with Ps 32.

33:1–3 This joyful call to praise restates 32:11, especially the twin addressees: the righteous and the upright. Seven words of praise add to the urgency: "Sing joyfully ... praise ... Praise [or 'Give thanks to'] ... make music ... Sing ... play skillfully ... shout for joy."

33:2 harp ... lyre. The first references to musical instruments in the Psalter (see note on 150:3).

33:3 new song. Praising God should not be confined to "old wineskins" of familiar songs, great as they may be. Growing, joyful faith requires new outlets for praising God, and the psalmists affirm this repeatedly (here; 40:3; 96:1; 98:1; 144:9; 149:1; cf. also Isa 42:10). The end of the age also finds thousands upon thousands of angels and others singing a "new song" before the throne of the Lamb of God (Rev 5:9; 14:3).

33:7 waters of the sea into jars. Left unchecked and untamed, water can be a mighty force for devastation. Therefore, the OT repeatedly asserts Yahweh's sovereignty over these parts of creation, specifically (as here) that he controls them, marks off their boundaries, puts them into "jars" and "storehouses," i.e., they are thus tamed. Cf. 104:8–10; Gen 1:9–10; Job 38:8–11; Prov 8:29; Jer 5:22.

33:8 fear the LORD. See note on 19:9.

33:12 Blessed. See note on 1:1. **the people he chose.** Of all the nations and peoples of the earth, God chose Israel as his special, treasured possession (Exod 19:5; Acts 13:17). This was not by any merit of their own, but because he loved them (Deut 4:37; 7:6–8; 10:15). Yet vv. 13–15 show that God loves all of humanity too, not just Israel. See introduction to Ps 67; see also notes on Ps 67.

[15]he who forms[h] the hearts of all,
who considers everything they do.[i]
[16]No king is saved by the size of his army;[j]
no warrior escapes by his great strength.
[17]A horse[k] is a vain hope for deliverance;
despite all its great strength it cannot save.
[18]But the eyes[l] of the LORD are on those who fear him,
on those whose hope is in his unfailing love,[m]
[19]to deliver them from death
and keep them alive in famine.[n]

[20]We wait[o] in hope for the LORD;
he is our help and our shield.
[21]In him our hearts rejoice,[p]
for we trust in his holy name.
[22]May your unfailing love be with us, LORD,
even as we put our hope in you.

Psalm 34[a,b]

Of David. When he pretended to be insane before Abimelek, who drove him away, and he left.

[1]I will extol the LORD at all times;[q]
his praise will always be on my lips.
[2]I will glory[r] in the LORD;
let the afflicted hear and rejoice.[s]
[3]Glorify the LORD with me;
let us exalt[t] his name together.

[4]I sought the LORD,[u] and he answered me;
he delivered me from all my fears.
[5]Those who look to him are radiant;[v]
their faces are never covered with shame.[w]
[6]This poor man called, and the LORD heard him;
he saved him out of all his troubles.

33:15 [h]Job 10:8 [i]Jer 32:19
33:16 [j]Ps 44:6
33:17 [k]Ps 20:7; Pr 21:31
33:18 [l]Job 36:7; Ps 34:15 [m]Ps 147:11
33:19 [n]Job 5:20
33:20 [o]Ps 130:6
33:21 [p]Zec 10:7; Jn 16:22
34:1 [q]Ps 71:6; Eph 5:20
34:2 [r]Jer 9:24; 1Co 1:31 [s]Ps 119:74
34:3 [t]Lk 1:46
34:4 [u]Mt 7:7
34:5 [v]Ps 36:9 [w]Ps 25:3

[a] This psalm is an acrostic poem, the verses of which begin with the successive letters of the Hebrew alphabet.
[b] In Hebrew texts 34:1-22 is numbered 34:2-23.

33:17 horse. Despite their strength, horses could not save kings or warriors; only the Lord could (vv. 18–19). God explicitly prohibited Israelite kings from trusting in horses for deliverance (Deut 17:16) because God himself would be Israel's warrior (Exod 14:14; 15:3; Deut 1:30; 3:22; 20:4; Josh 10:42; 23:3; 2 Chr 20:29; 32:8; cf. Neh 4:14).
33:18 eyes of the LORD. God's watchful eyes signify protection for his people (32:8; 34:15; see 11:4; 66:7; 139:16; see also 17:8 and note).
33:20 shield. See note on 3:3.
Ps 34 *The Lord Will Rescue His Servants.* Continuing the note of praise struck in Ps 33, David praises God for deliverance from his troubles (vv. 1–7) and then turns to instruct his people to learn the proper fear (i.e., reverence) of the Lord (vv. 8–14). He affirms that the Lord is a tender, watchful caretaker of those who take refuge in him (vv. 15–22). Because of the instruction that David offers in vv. 9–14, this psalm is usually understood to be a wisdom psalm. Such psalms reflect wisdom motifs found especially in the book of Proverbs, such as the contrast between the ways of the righteous and the wicked, or between the wise person and the fool. Wisdom texts also emphasize practical advice and instruction, the fear of the Lord, retribution, and a focus on God's word (*tôrâ*). The other wisdom psalms include Pss 1; 19; 32; 37; 49; 73; 112; 119; 128. Ps 34 is also an alphabetic acrostic (see NIV text note), as are several of the wisdom psalms (see Introduction: The Psalms as Poetry [Acrostic Poems]).
34 title This is the fifth of 14 psalms with a "historical" title linked to an event in David's life (see note on Ps 3 title). It links this psalm with an episode in David's life when he fled from Saul to the Philistine city of Gath; while there, David pretended to be insane because he feared the Philistines (1 Sam 21:10–15). "Achish" (1 Sam 21:10) was another name for Abimelek.
34:1–3 David begins with a standard vow to praise (vv. 1–2a), but he expands it to a call for others to join him in this (vv. 2b–3). The idea of always praising God (v. 1) is similar to the apostle Paul's exhortation to rejoice and pray without ceasing (1 Thess 5:16–17). Glorifying God is not just for the fortunate; the afflicted should also hear David's testimony and rejoice (v. 2b).
34:4–7 David emphasizes his own situation, testifying that the Lord did hear his call and answer him (vv. 4,6) and generalizing that the same is true for all who look to God (vv. 5,7).

34:7 [x]2Ki 6:17; Da 6:22
34:8 [y]1Pe 2:3 [z]Ps 2:12
34:9 [a]Ps 23:1
34:10 [b]Ps 84:11
34:11 [c]Ps 32:8
34:12 [d]1Pe 3:10
34:13 [e]1Pe 2:22
34:14 [f]Ps 37:27 [g]Heb 12:14
34:15 [h]Ps 33:18 [i]Job 36:7
34:16 [j]Lev 17:10; Jer 44:11 [k]1Pe 3:10-12* [l]Pr 10:7
34:17 [m]Ps 145:19
34:18 [n]Ps 145:18 [o]Isa 57:15
34:19 [p]ver 17 [q]ver 4,6; Pr 24:16
34:20 [r]Jn 19:36*

7 The angel of the LORD[x] encamps around those who
fear him,
and he delivers them.

8 Taste and see that the LORD is good;[y]
blessed is the one who takes refuge[z] in him.
9 Fear the LORD, you his holy people,
for those who fear him lack nothing.[a]
10 The lions may grow weak and hungry,
but those who seek the LORD lack no good thing.[b]
11 Come, my children, listen to me;
I will teach you[c] the fear of the LORD.
12 Whoever of you loves life[d]
and desires to see many good days,
13 keep your tongue from evil
and your lips from telling lies.[e]
14 Turn from evil and do good;[f]
seek peace[g] and pursue it.

15 The eyes of the LORD[h] are on the righteous,[i]
and his ears are attentive to their cry;
16 but the face of the LORD is against[j] those who do evil,[k]
to blot out their name[l] from the earth.

17 The righteous cry out, and the LORD hears[m] them;
he delivers them from all their troubles.
18 The LORD is close[n] to the brokenhearted[o]
and saves those who are crushed in spirit.

19 The righteous person may have many troubles,[p]
but the LORD delivers him from them all;[q]
20 he protects all his bones,
not one of them will be broken.[r]

34:7 angel of the LORD. God's representative or messenger, appearing to individuals such as Hagar (Gen 16:7–12), Abraham (Gen 22:11–18), Jacob (Gen 31:11–13), Moses (Exod 3:2), Balaam (Num 22:22–35), Gideon (Judg 6:11–22), Samson's parents (Judg 13:2–22), Elijah (1 Kgs 19:5–9; 2 Kgs 1:3–4,15), and Daniel (Dan 6:22). In all of these cases, the angel spoke authoritatively with words of instruction or encouragement. In this psalm, the angel is the protector of all who fear the Lord. In the next psalm, the angel is David's fierce protector against his enemies (35:5–6). These are the only references to the angel of the Lord in the book of Psalms. See note on Gen 16:7.

34:8–14 David assumes the role of teacher of his people (see 51:13), instructing them in the fear of the Lord out of his own personal experience. Being a spiritual leader for the nation was part of God's expectations for a godly king (see notes on 4:2; 16:8). Such instruction is characteristic of wisdom literature as represented in the book of Proverbs (e.g., Prov 1:8; 4:1,11; 8:10,33; 9:9).

34:8 Taste and see. David urges the use of many senses to experience God as fully as possible (he also urges people to "listen" in v. 11). **Taste.** Used figuratively here and in 119:103 (the only other reference in the Psalms) for experiencing God; it usually occurs in its literal sense in the OT. The NT uses "taste" figuratively more often: to taste death (Matt 16:28; John 8:52; Heb 2:9) or to taste the goodness of God (Heb 6:4–5; 1 Pet 2:3). **blessed.** See note on 1:1. **the one.** Although the Hebrew word can refer to a man generically, it most commonly means "warrior" or "strong man." So it would be especially striking to see such a man taking refuge in the Lord. This statement closely resembles 2:12d.

34:11 I will teach you. See note on 51:13. **fear of the LORD.** See note on 19:9.

34:12–16 The apostle Peter quotes these verses in 1 Pet 3:10–12 to make his point about peaceable living among Christians.

34:15 eyes of the LORD. This is the third psalm in a row that speaks of God's eyes watching over his people (see 32:8; 33:18 and notes).

34:16 face of the LORD. In contrast to the beauty of the Lord's face for those who trust in him (11:7; 17:15; see note on 27:8), his face is set against those who oppose him by doing evil (see note on 27:9). **blot out their name.** See note on 9:5.

34:18 brokenhearted ... crushed in spirit. A broken and contrite heart indicates the humility of one who has truly repented of sin (51:17). However, in this context brokenness (parallel to "crushed in spirit") is the result of external, hostile forces (cf. 31:12; 69:20; 109:16; 147:3). The Lord compassionately saves those who have been beaten down in this way.

34:20 he protects all his bones. The "bones" represent David's whole being (see note on 6:2). John 19:31–36 notes that Jesus' legs were not broken on the cross, in fulfillment of the Scriptures: "Not one of his bones will be broken" (John 19:36). John may be quoting this psalm or perhaps Exod 12:46 (see NIV text note on John 19:36), which speaks of not breaking any of the bones of the Passover lamb when it is killed and eaten, making the link with Jesus as the Lamb of God (John 1:29,36; cf. 1 Cor 5:7; 1 Pet 1:19).

[21] Evil will slay the wicked;[s]
the foes of the righteous will be condemned.
[22] The LORD will rescue[t] his servants;
no one who takes refuge in him will be condemned.

Psalm 35

Of David.

[1] Contend, LORD, with those who contend with me;
fight[u] against those who fight against me.
[2] Take up shield and armor;
arise[v] and come to my aid.
[3] Brandish spear and javelin[a]
against those who pursue me.
Say to me,
"I am your salvation."

[4] May those who seek my life
be disgraced[w] and put to shame;
may those who plot my ruin
be turned back in dismay.
[5] May they be like chaff[x] before the wind,
with the angel of the LORD driving them away;
[6] may their path be dark and slippery,
with the angel of the LORD pursuing them.

[7] Since they hid their net for me without cause
and without cause dug a pit for me,
[8] may ruin overtake them by surprise—[y]
may the net they hid entangle them,
may they fall into the pit,[z] to their ruin.
[9] Then my soul will rejoice[a] in the LORD
and delight in his salvation.[b]
[10] My whole being will exclaim,
"Who is like you,[c] LORD?
You rescue the poor from those too strong[d] for them,
the poor and needy[e] from those who rob them."

[11] Ruthless witnesses[f] come forward;
they question me on things I know nothing about.
[12] They repay me evil for good[g]
and leave me like one bereaved.

[a] 3 Or *and block the way*

34:21 [s] Ps 94:23
34:22 [t] 1Ki 1:29; Ps 71:23
35:1 [u] Ps 43:1
35:2 [v] Ps 62:2
35:4 [w] Ps 70:2
35:5 [x] Job 21:18; Ps 1:4; Isa 29:5
35:8 [y] 1Th 5:3 [z] Ps 9:15
35:9 [a] Lk 1:47 [b] Isa 61:10
35:10 [c] Ex 15:11 [d] Ps 18:17 [e] Ps 37:14
35:11 [f] Ps 27:12
35:12 [g] Jn 10:32

Ps 35 *Contend, Lord, With Those Who Contend With Me.* David pleads with God to fight for him, to vindicate him against vicious attacks by those who return evil for good. This is the most intense psalm yet encountered in the Psalter in which David rails against his enemies. (On such "imprecatory" psalms, see notes on 5:9–10; 69:22–28.) David encountered more than his share of enemies as he was fleeing Saul; in Ps 34, he praises God for delivering him from Philistine opposition, but in Ps 35 he unleashes passionate prayers for God to take vengeance against such enemies, reiterating his assertions in 34:16. After an initial call to God to arise as the divine Warrior on David's behalf (vv. 1–3), David launches into an extended series of wishes for his enemies to be utterly defeated (vv. 4–8), culminating with a vow to praise God when this has been accomplished (vv. 9–10). David recounts the viciousness of his enemies' attacks (vv. 11–16) and again calls on God to intervene (vv. 17–25). He ends with a final imprecation (v. 26) and a final voice of praise (vv. 27–28).

35:1–3 We do not know the precise occasion for this psalm, but David appeals in a more extended way than in any previous psalm for God to arise and fight on his behalf (see notes on 7:12–13; 18:6–15), mentioning several implements of war: shield, armor, spear, and javelin.

35:4 put to shame. See note on 25:2.

35:5 chaff before the wind. From the very first psalm, the wicked are seen as chaff: insignificant, unsubstantial, blown by the wind (see 1:4 and note). **angel of the LORD.** See note on 34:7.

35:10 poor ... needy. Cf. 12:5; see note on 82:3–4.

Model of a regiment of Nubian infantry. Spears and javelins (Ps 35:3) were common battle weapons throughout biblical history.

35:13 [h] Job 30:25; Ps 69:10
35:15 [i] Job 30:1,8
35:16 [j] Job 16:9; La 2:16
35:17 [k] Hab 1:13 [l] Ps 22:20
35:18 [m] Ps 22:25 [n] Ps 22:22
35:19 [o] Ps 38:19; 69:4; Jn 15:25* [p] Ps 13:4; Pr 6:13

13 Yet when they were ill, I put on sackcloth
and humbled myself with fasting.[h]
When my prayers returned to me unanswered,
14 I went about mourning
as though for my friend or brother.
I bowed my head in grief
as though weeping for my mother.
15 But when I stumbled, they gathered in glee;
assailants gathered against me without my knowledge.
They slandered[i] me without ceasing.
16 Like the ungodly they maliciously mocked;[a]
they gnashed their teeth[j] at me.

17 How long,[k] Lord, will you look on?
Rescue me from their ravages,
my precious life[l] from these lions.
18 I will give you thanks in the great assembly;[m]
among the throngs I will praise you.[n]
19 Do not let those gloat over me
who are my enemies without cause;
do not let those who hate me without reason[o]
maliciously wink the eye.[p]
20 They do not speak peaceably,
but devise false accusations
against those who live quietly in the land.

[a] *16* Septuagint; Hebrew may mean *Like an ungodly circle of mockers,*

35:16 gnashed their teeth. In the OT, gnashing one's teeth is a sign of malice against another (37:12; 112:10; Job 16:9; Lam 2:16; cf. Acts 7:54). In the NT, it most often refers to the hopelessness of those who have been cast into outer darkness and the blazing furnace at the end of the age (Matt 8:12; 13:42,50; 22:13; 24:51; 25:30; Luke 13:28).
35:17 How long . . . ? See note on 13:1,2.
35:18 among the throngs. David desires to join with the celebratory throngs that would gather at God's house to offer praise and thanksgiving. This is similar to the desire of the isolated psalmist of 42:4, who wanted to return to such throngs, which he remembered from happier days.
35:19 those who hate me without reason. Reflects vv. 11 – 16. This was not an uncommon experience for the psalmists (38:19; 69:4; 109:3; 119:78,86,161; cf. Lam 3:52). Jesus spoke of the world hating his followers, just as it hated him and his Father (John 15:18 – 25), and he possibly quoted from this psalm (or perhaps 69:4) as being fulfilled in him (John 15:25).

[21] They sneer[q] at me and say, "Aha! Aha![r]
With our own eyes we have seen it."

[22] LORD, you have seen[s] this; do not be silent.
Do not be far[t] from me, Lord.
[23] Awake,[u] and rise to my defense!
Contend for me, my God and Lord.
[24] Vindicate me in your righteousness, LORD my God;
do not let them gloat over me.
[25] Do not let them think, "Aha, just what we wanted!"
or say, "We have swallowed him up."[v]

[26] May all who gloat over my distress
be put to shame[w] and confusion;
may all who exalt themselves over me[x]
be clothed with shame and disgrace.
[27] May those who delight in my vindication[y]
shout for joy[z] and gladness;
may they always say, "The LORD be exalted,
who delights[a] in the well-being of his servant."
[28] My tongue will proclaim your righteousness,[b]
your praises all day long.

35:21 [q]Ps 22:13 [r]Ps 40:15
35:22 [s]Ex 3:7 [t]Ps 10:1; 28:1
35:23 [u]Ps 44:23
35:25 [v]La 2:16
35:26 [w]Ps 40:14; 109:29 [x]Ps 38:16
35:27 [y]Ps 9:4 [z]Ps 32:11 [a]Ps 40:16; 147:11
35:28 [b]Ps 51:14
36:1 [c]Ro 3:18*
36:3 [d]Ps 10:7 [e]Ps 94:8 [f]Jer 4:22

Psalm 36[a]

For the director of music. Of David the servant of the LORD.

[1] I have a message from God in my heart
concerning the sinfulness of the wicked:[b]
There is no fear of God
before their eyes.[c]

[2] In their own eyes they flatter themselves
too much to detect or hate their sin.
[3] The words of their mouths[d] are wicked and deceitful;
they fail to act wisely[e] or do good.[f]

[a] In Hebrew texts 36:1-12 is numbered 36:2-13. [b] *1* Or *A message from God: The transgression of the wicked / resides in their hearts.*

35:22–23 LORD ... Lord ... God ... Lord. See note on 8:1.
35:23 Awake. See note on 3:7.
35:24 Vindicate me. See also v. 27 and note on 43:1.
35:27 his servant. David was conscious of his position as God's anointed one (see note on 28:8) and God's chosen servant (see notes on 4:3; Ps 18 title). So the welfare of David, the Lord's chosen servant, reflected on God himself, and David often prayed for God to act for the sake of the Lord's name (see note on 31:3).
35:28 My tongue will proclaim your righteousness. David, confident in the Lord's answers to his prayers, vows to praise God "all day long."
Ps 36 *See How the Evildoers Lie Fallen.* This is the third of three psalms in which David speaks as an individual opposed by his enemies. Ps 34 is primarily a thanksgiving for deliverance from such enemies in which David also instructs the nation out of his experience, whereas Ps 35 is an intense, extended prayer for God to exact vengeance on those enemies. In Ps 36 the mood is more reflective, focusing on the nature of the wicked and on God's love. David begins by affirming a fundamental truth about the wicked: they do not fear God (v. 1). He then reflects again about the nature of the wicked (vv. 2–4). The rest of the psalm is more positive in orientation, reflecting on God's love (vv. 5–10) and concluding with one last reference to the wicked and their fate (vv. 11–12).
36 title servant of the LORD. Links this psalm with the previous one (see 35:27 and note).
36:1 David's message from God is clear: the wicked make no room for "fear of God" (see note on 19:9). The apostle Paul quotes this verse (Rom 3:18), along with a string of other OT passages, in making the point that all have sinned (Rom 3:9–20). **message.** Translates a Hebrew term that occurs most frequently in the Prophets, where it refers to a solemn oracle from God that the prophet is passing down to the people, sometimes translated "declares" (e.g., Isa 1:24; 55:8; Jer 1:8,15; Ezek 11:8,21). The term also occurs elsewhere with essentially the same meaning, even though not delivered through a formally recognized prophet (e.g., Gen 22:16; Num 14:28; 1 Sam 2:30; 2 Kgs 9:26; 22:19).

36:4 [g]Pr 4:16; Mic 2:1 [h]Isa 65:2 [i]Ps 52:3; Ro 12:9
36:6 [j]Job 11:8; Ps 77:19; Ro 11:33
36:7 [k]Ru 2:12; Ps 17:8
36:8 [l]Ps 65:4 [m]Job 20:17; Rev 22:1
36:9 [n]Jer 2:13 [o]1Pe 2:9
36:12 [p]Ps 140:10
37:1 [q]Pr 23:17-18 [r]Ps 73:3
37:2 [s]Ps 90:6

4 Even on their beds they plot evil;[g]
they commit themselves to a sinful course[h]
and do not reject what is wrong.[i]
5 Your love, LORD, reaches to the heavens,
your faithfulness to the skies.
6 Your righteousness is like the highest mountains,
your justice like the great deep.[j]
You, LORD, preserve both people and animals.
7 How priceless is your unfailing love, O God!
People take refuge in the shadow of your wings.[k]
8 They feast on the abundance of your house;[l]
you give them drink from your river[m] of delights.
9 For with you is the fountain of life;[n]
in your light[o] we see light.

10 Continue your love to those who know you,
your righteousness to the upright in heart.
11 May the foot of the proud not come against me,
nor the hand of the wicked drive me away.
12 See how the evildoers lie fallen—
thrown down, not able to rise![p]

Psalm 37[a]

Of David.

1 Do not fret because of those who are evil
or be envious[q] of those who do wrong;[r]
2 for like the grass they will soon wither,
like green plants they will soon die away.[s]

[a] This psalm is an acrostic poem, the stanzas of which begin with the successive letters of the Hebrew alphabet.

36:5–9 The Lord's love, faithfulness, and righteousness extend to all of creation ("the heavens ... the skies ... the highest mountains ... the great deep"), including both man and beast. This concern even for animals recalls God's concerns for Nineveh and its animals (Jonah 4:11).
36:5,7,10 love. Or "unfailing love" (Hebrew *ḥesed*). This refers to God's steadfast, loyal covenant love for his people. See note on 6:4.
36:7 shadow of your wings. This beautiful image of security under the Lord's protection similarly occurs in 17:8; 57:1; 61:4; 63:7; 91:1; 121:5.
36:8 feast ... drink. These sensory images of abundance echo 34:8,10: "Taste ... see ... listen" (see note on 34:8). **your house.** See note on 5:7.
36:9 fountain of life. A fountain or spring is a source of fresh, clean, and sustaining water. The imagery of fresh, sustaining life under God's protection (v. 7) also occurs in Prov 10:11; 13:14; 14:27; 16:22; cf. 18:4. Cf. also "river of delights" in v. 8. **see light.** Equivalent to experiencing life, not death (see 49:19; 56:13; Job 3:20; 33:28; cf. Isa 9:2; 53:11).
36:10–12 David concludes with a prayer that God would continue to be faithful to those who know God, i.e., "the upright in heart" (v. 10), and that God's opponents would be thwarted from doing him harm (v. 11).
36:12 evildoers lie fallen. This is a warning to those who do evil.
Ps 37 *Do Not Fret Because of Those Who Are Evil ... Take Delight in the Lord.* This is an extended reflection on how the righteous should respond when they see the wicked prospering. Pss 34–37 contrast the righteous and the wicked, and they wrestle with the issue as a righteous individual persecuted by the wicked; Ps 37 addresses it from a "wisdom" perspective. David juxtaposes the lives, actions, attitudes, and "rewards" of the wicked against those of the righteous, intermixed with repeated exhortations to the righteous to seek their satisfaction in the Lord, who is the ultimate source of blessing and security. The very beginning of the Psalter signals this contrast between the "two ways" (see Ps 1; see also introduction to Pss 1–2).

A keynote in this psalm questions who will inherit or dwell in "the land." The answer is that the righteous will (vv. 3,27,29); they are characterized as those who hope in the Lord (vv. 9,34), those who are meek (v. 11), and those whom the Lord blesses (v. 22). Dwelling in the land God promised to Abraham and his descendants (Gen 12:7; Deut 1:8) represented God's blessing on the nation when it remained true to him (Deut 4:40; 5:33), but God repeatedly threatened to uproot his people from the land if they turned away from him (Deut 4:25–26; 6:14–15; 11:16–17; 28:33,52,63). David uses this imagery to refer to the blessings that all righteous individuals will enjoy if they remain faithful to the Lord.

This psalm is an alphabetic acrostic poem (see NIV text note and introduction to Ps 9). As such, the psalm's argument does not proceed in as linear a fashion as most psalms; it circles back around again and again on certain topics in a somewhat random pattern, akin to portions of the book of Proverbs.
37:1–11 David lays out the main thrust of his argument: the righteous need not worry about the wicked (vv. 1,7) because they will wither away and die (vv. 2,9). He urges the righteous to live blameless lives, trusting and delighting in the Lord, hoping and waiting patiently for him, doing good, refraining from anger (in terms similar to those in Pss 15; 112).

[3]Trust in the LORD and do good;
dwell in the land[t] and enjoy safe pasture.[u]
[4]Take delight[v] in the LORD,
and he will give you the desires of your heart.

[5]Commit your way to the LORD;
trust in him[w] and he will do this:
[6]He will make your righteous reward[x] shine like the dawn,[y]
your vindication like the noonday sun.

[7]Be still[z] before the LORD
and wait patiently[a] for him;
do not fret when people succeed in their ways,
when they carry out their wicked schemes.

[8]Refrain from anger[b] and turn from wrath;
do not fret — it leads only to evil.
[9]For those who are evil will be destroyed,
but those who hope in the LORD will inherit the land.[c]

[10]A little while, and the wicked will be no more;[d]
though you look for them, they will not be found.
[11]But the meek will inherit the land[e]
and enjoy peace and prosperity.

[12]The wicked plot against the righteous
and gnash their teeth[f] at them;
[13]but the Lord laughs at the wicked,
for he knows their day is coming.[g]

[14]The wicked draw the sword
and bend the bow[h]
to bring down the poor and needy,[i]
to slay those whose ways are upright.
[15]But their swords will pierce their own hearts,[j]
and their bows will be broken.

[16]Better the little that the righteous have
than the wealth[k] of many wicked;

37:3 [t]Dt 30:20 [u]Isa 40:11; Jn 10:9
37:4 [v]Isa 58:14
37:5 [w]Ps 4:5; Ps 55:22; Pr 16:3; 1Pe 5:7
37:6 [x]Mic 7:9 [y]Job 11:17
37:7 [z]Ps 62:5; La 3:26 [a]Ps 40:1
37:8 [b]Eph 4:31; Col 3:8
37:9 [c]Isa 57:13; 60:21
37:10 [d]Job 7:10; 24:24
37:11 [e]Mt 5:5
37:12 [f]Ps 35:16
37:13 [g]1Sa 26:10; Ps 2:4
37:14 [h]Ps 11:2 [i]Ps 35:10
37:15 [j]Ps 9:16
37:16 [k]Pr 15:16

If they do this, the Lord will give them the desires of their hearts (v. 4), and vindicate them (v. 6), and they will inherit the land, enjoying peace and prosperity (vv. 9,11).
37:4 desires of your heart. This does not mean that God will grant anything a person desires, however whimsical or irresponsible. A godly person's desires are in line with what God wants for them (vv. 23,31).
37:6 vindication. See note on 43:1.
37:11 the meek. Or "humble, lowly." Jesus' reference to the meek inheriting the earth in the Sermon on the Mount (Matt 5:5) probably quotes from this psalm.
37:12–13 plot ... laughs. God laughs in derision at the feeble attempts of the wicked to plot against the righteous. Cf. 2:1,4.
37:12 gnash their teeth. See note on 35:16.
37:13 Lord. This psalm uses God's personal name, Yahweh (translated "the LORD"), 17 times, but this translates *ʾădōnāy,* which is a title, not a personal name (see note on 8:1). **their day.** A day of reckoning for the wicked. The prophets develop this idea in much more detail, calling it "the day of the LORD" (e.g., Ezek 13:5; Joel 1:15; Amos 5:18). It is a day of judgment for the Lord's enemies and one of vindication for all who turn to him. It can refer variously to nations in general (Isa 13:6,9; Ezek 30:3; Obad 15) or to different days of judgment for different nations (e.g., Edom: Obad 8; Egypt: Isa 19:16–25) or to the great final judgment at the end of the age (Isa 24:21–23; Zeph 1:14–18; Zech 12–14). God's people were not spared: Amos promised that Israel had a "day of the LORD" coming to it (Amos 5:18–20), and Judah experienced its own "day" of reckoning with the destruction of Jerusalem (Isa 22:5–8; Lam 2:22; Ezek 13:5; Obad 11–14; Zeph 1:7–13). The day of the Lord was not simply punitive; it had a restorative function for those peoples and nations who learned from its lessons and turned to the Lord (e.g., Isa 19:16–25, especially vv. 24–25). It would be a great and glorious day for God's people (e.g., Isa 25:9; 26–27). In all cases, the Lord's "day" symbolizes God settling all accounts and making all things right.
37:16 Better the little that the righteous have. The quality of life is not measured by one's wealth. Many such "better than" statements occur in Proverbs; they show that God's values are worth more than societal norms and values (e.g., Prov 12:9; 15:16; 16:8,16,19,32; 17:1,12; 19:1,22; 21:9).

37:17 [l] Job 38:15; Ps 10:15
37:18 [m] Ps 1:6
37:20 [n] Ps 102:3
37:21 [o] Ps 112:5
37:22 [p] Job 5:3; Pr 3:33
37:23 [q] 1Sa 2:9 [r] Ps 147:11
37:24 [s] Pr 24:16 [t] Ps 145:14; 147:6
37:25 [u] Heb 13:5
37:26 [v] Ps 147:13
37:27 [w] Ps 34:14
37:28 [x] Ps 21:10; Isa 14:20
37:29 [y] ver 9; Pr 2:21
37:31 [z] Dt 6:6; Ps 40:8; Isa 51:7 [a] ver 23
37:32 [b] Ps 10:8
37:33 [c] Ps 109:31; 2Pe 2:9

17 for the power of the wicked will be broken,[l]
but the LORD upholds the righteous.

18 The blameless spend their days under the LORD's care,[m]
and their inheritance will endure forever.
19 In times of disaster they will not wither;
in days of famine they will enjoy plenty.

20 But the wicked will perish:
Though the LORD's enemies are like the flowers of the field,
they will be consumed, they will go up in smoke.[n]

21 The wicked borrow and do not repay,
but the righteous give generously;[o]
22 those the LORD blesses will inherit the land,
but those he curses[p] will be destroyed.

23 The LORD makes firm the steps[q]
of the one who delights[r] in him;
24 though he may stumble, he will not fall,[s]
for the LORD upholds[t] him with his hand.

25 I was young and now I am old,
yet I have never seen the righteous forsaken[u]
or their children begging bread.
26 They are always generous and lend freely;
their children will be a blessing.[a][v]

27 Turn from evil and do good;[w]
then you will dwell in the land forever.
28 For the LORD loves the just
and will not forsake his faithful ones.

Wrongdoers will be completely destroyed[b];
the offspring of the wicked will perish.[x]
29 The righteous will inherit the land[y]
and dwell in it forever.

30 The mouths of the righteous utter wisdom,
and their tongues speak what is just.
31 The law of their God is in their hearts;[z]
their feet do not slip.[a]

32 The wicked lie in wait[b] for the righteous,
intent on putting them to death;
33 but the LORD will not leave them in the power of the wicked
or let them be condemned when brought to trial.[c]

[a] 26 Or *freely; / the names of their children will be used in blessings* (see Gen. 48:20); or *freely; / others will see that their children are blessed* [b] 28 See Septuagint; Hebrew *They will be protected forever*

37:17 wicked … righteous. Displays the contrast between the "two ways" of Ps 1 (see especially 1:6; see also introduction to Pss 1–2).

37:21 the righteous give generously. God had promised centuries earlier that his blessings on the faithful would include such bounty that they would be able to lend to many and never have to borrow (Deut 15:6; 28:12). In contrast, the wicked would be forced to borrow, and they could not (or would not) repay.

37:25 I was young and now I am old. David speaks from his own experience and observations. He takes the long view in what he affirms about the righteous never suffering or being in want; he certainly has expressed concerns about the righteous suffering in many of his psalms. But in the end, God does reward the righteous and punish the wicked. See vv. 32–33; see also notes on 1:3,6.

37:31 The law of their God is in their hearts. Contrary to what many Christians believe, OT faith was not simply a matter of externals (sacrifice, circumcision, good works). True faith was and is a matter of the heart (40:8; 119:11; Gen 15:6; Deut 6:6; 10:16; Jer 4:4). Externals were outward signs of the believer's internal faith, just as James affirmed about the relationship between faith and works (Jas 2:14–26). Being rooted in God's instruction is the key to a godly life according to Ps 1:2–3.

[34]Hope in the LORD[d]
and keep his way.
He will exalt you to inherit the land;
when the wicked are destroyed, you will see[e] it.

[35]I have seen a wicked and ruthless man
flourishing[f] like a luxuriant native tree,
[36]but he soon passed away and was no more;
though I looked for him, he could not be found.[g]

[37]Consider the blameless, observe the upright;
a future awaits those who seek peace.[a][h]
[38]But all sinners will be destroyed;
there will be no future[b] for the wicked.[i]

[39]The salvation[j] of the righteous comes from the LORD;
he is their stronghold in time of trouble.[k]
[40]The LORD helps[l] them and delivers[m] them;
he delivers them from the wicked and saves them,
because they take refuge in him.

Psalm 38[c]

A psalm of David. A petition.

[1]LORD, do not rebuke me in your anger
or discipline me in your wrath.[n]
[2]Your arrows[o] have pierced me,
and your hand has come down on me.
[3]Because of your wrath there is no health in my body;
there is no soundness in my bones[p] because of my sin.
[4]My guilt has overwhelmed me
like a burden too heavy to bear.[q]

[5]My wounds fester and are loathsome
because of my sinful folly.[r]

[a] *37* Or *upright; / those who seek peace will have posterity* [b] *38* Or *posterity* [c] In Hebrew texts 38:1-22 is numbered 38:2-23.

37:34 [d] Ps 27:14 [e] Ps 52:6
37:35 [f] Job 5:3
37:36 [g] Job 20:5
37:37 [h] Isa 57:1-2
37:38 [i] Ps 1:4
37:39 [j] Ps 3:8 [k] Ps 9:9
37:40 [l] 1Ch 5:20 [m] Isa 31:5
38:1 [n] Ps 6:1
38:2 [o] Job 6:4; Ps 32:4
38:3 [p] Ps 6:2; Isa 1:6
38:4 [q] Ezr 9:6
38:5 [r] Ps 69:5

37:35 I have seen a wicked and ruthless man. David again speaks out of personal experience (see note on v. 25), affirming that in the end the wicked pass away (v. 36).

37:39 stronghold. The image of God as the believer's refuge is a strong and vivid one found many times in the Psalter (see notes on 2:12; 18:1–2).

Ps 38 *I Am Troubled by My Sin.* David shifts gears from philosophical reflections on how to deal with the wicked prospering in Ps 37 to an intensely personal plea for forgiveness. Connections with Ps 37 include the wicked lying in wait for the righteous (v. 12; 37:32), the righteous waiting on the Lord (v. 15; 37:7), and the imagery of feet slipping (v. 16; 37:31). The ancient church identified Ps 38 as one of seven penitential psalms (the others: 6; 32; 51; 102; 130; 143). David acknowledges that he has sinned (vv. 3,5) and confesses his sin (v. 18). He emphasizes the heavy toll that his sin is taking on him physically, emotionally, and socially. In this respect, this psalm resembles Pss 6; 32 (see notes on 6:2; 32:5). David begins with a litany of ills that he is suffering because of his sin (vv. 1–4), expressed in more explicit terms in vv. 5–8; a keynote in both sections is "there is no health in my body" (vv. 3,7). He lays out his appeal to God (v. 9), because he has been abandoned by those closest to him (v. 11). He is at the end of his rope, unable to speak, able only to wait for the Lord (vv. 13–16). Finally, in the depths of his despair, he confesses his sin (vv. 17–20), and urgently petitions God to help him (vv. 21–22).

38 title A petition. The root here (*zkr,* "to remember") also occurs in the title of Ps 70. It is related to the Hebrew word used in Leviticus for the "memorial portion" associated with the grain and sin offerings (Lev 2:2,9,16; 5:12; 6:15). To ask God to remember was to ask him to act (see note on 25:6–7). David's request in v. 1 that God not rebuke him in his anger is analogous to his request in 25:7 that God not "remember" his sin.

38:3 my sin. See note on 32:5. David does not appeal as an innocent sufferer, as he does in many psalms; he openly acknowledges that he has sinned.

38:4 My guilt. See note on 32:5.

38:5–8 The physical toll of his sins on David is even more marked here than in vv. 1–4. Not all human suffering is due to sin (e.g., Pss 7; 17; 26; the book of Job), but in this psalm there is a clear connection, which David himself acknowledges; he is suffering because of his sin. See note on 41:4.

38:5 sinful folly. This denotes the way of the foolish person, who is opposed to God; the word "folly" occurs many times in Proverbs in

38:6 [s] Job 30:28; Ps 35:14; 42:9
38:7 [t] Ps 102:3
38:8 [u] Ps 22:1
38:9 [v] Job 3:24; Ps 6:6; 10:17
38:10 [w] Ps 31:10 [x] Ps 6:7
38:11 [y] Ps 31:11
38:12 [z] Ps 140:5 [a] Ps 35:4; 54:3 [b] Ps 35:20
38:15 [c] Ps 39:7 [d] Ps 17:6
38:16 [e] Ps 35:26 [f] Ps 13:4
38:18 [g] Ps 32:5
38:19 [h] Ps 18:17 [i] Ps 35:19
38:20 [j] Ps 35:12; 1Jn 3:12
38:21 [k] Ps 35:22
38:22 [l] Ps 40:13 [m] Ps 27:1

6 I am bowed down and brought very low;
all day long I go about mourning.[s]
7 My back is filled with searing pain;[t]
there is no health in my body.
8 I am feeble and utterly crushed;
I groan[u] in anguish of heart.

9 All my longings lie open before you, Lord;
my sighing[v] is not hidden from you.
10 My heart pounds, my strength fails[w] me;
even the light has gone from my eyes.[x]
11 My friends and companions avoid me because of my
wounds;[y]
my neighbors stay far away.
12 Those who want to kill me set their traps,[z]
those who would harm me talk of my ruin;[a]
all day long they scheme and lie.[b]

13 I am like the deaf, who cannot hear,
like the mute, who cannot speak;
14 I have become like one who does not hear,
whose mouth can offer no reply.
15 LORD, I wait[c] for you;
you will answer,[d] Lord my God.
16 For I said, "Do not let them gloat[e]
or exalt themselves over me when my feet slip."[f]

17 For I am about to fall,
and my pain is ever with me.
18 I confess my iniquity;[g]
I am troubled by my sin.
19 Many have become my enemies[h] without cause[a];
those who hate me without reason[i] are numerous.
20 Those who repay my good with evil[j]
lodge accusations against me,
though I seek only to do what is good.

21 LORD, do not forsake me;
do not be far[k] from me, my God.
22 Come quickly to help me,[l]
my Lord and my Savior.[m]

a 19 One Dead Sea Scrolls manuscript; Masoretic Text *my vigorous enemies*

contrast to the wise or the prudent person (e.g., Prov 12:23; 13:16; 14:8,18,24,29; 15:2,14).

38:8 crushed. Denotes an oppressive, violent destruction of one's victim. See note on 10:10.

38:11 friends and companions ... neighbors. David's agonies are not just physical; he suffers the emotional and social pain of being abandoned by those closest to him. See also 31:11; 41:9; 88:8,18.

38:13–16 David stands mute, unable to offer any defense (vv. 13–14), because he knows he has sinned. His only option is to wait on the Lord (vv. 15–16), who will answer his pleas for forgiveness.

38:18 iniquity. Translated "guilt" in v. 4; see note on 32:5. **troubled.** To his credit, David's anxiety relates not only to the consequences of his sin but also to the sin itself. In Jer 42:16, the same Hebrew word is translated "dread." It is a sign of spiritual maturity to see beyond the ill effects of sin and to be troubled by the sin itself. David's anxiety here recalls his words in 2 Sam 12:13 ("I have sinned against the LORD") and in Ps 51:4 ("Against you, you only, have I sinned"), where he realized that, ultimately, sin is an offense against God; even if there seem to be no consequences, it is still sin, and it should still trouble the believer (51:3).

38:19 enemies without cause ... who hate me without reason. Closely echoes David's words in 35:19; see 69:4; 109:3; 119:86,161. The assertion here reverts back to other psalms in which David protests his innocence. He has just confessed his sin (v. 18), but here he maintains his innocence with regard to his enemies.

38:20 repay my good with evil. Cf. 35:12.

Psalm 39[a]

For the director of music. For Jeduthun. A psalm of David.

1 I said, "I will watch my ways[n]
and keep my tongue from sin;[o]
I will put a muzzle on my mouth
while in the presence of the wicked."
2 So I remained utterly silent,[p]
not even saying anything good.
But my anguish increased;
3 my heart grew hot within me.
While I meditated, the fire burned;
then I spoke with my tongue:

4 "Show me, LORD, my life's end
and the number of my days;[q]
let me know how fleeting my life is.[r]
5 You have made my days[s] a mere handbreadth;
the span of my years is as nothing before you.
Everyone is but a breath,[t]
even those who seem secure.[b]

6 "Surely everyone goes around like a mere phantom;[u]
in vain they rush about,[v] heaping up wealth
without knowing whose it will finally be.[w]

7 "But now, Lord, what do I look for?
My hope is in you.[x]
8 Save me[y] from all my transgressions;[z]
do not make me the scorn of fools.

39:1 [n] 1Ki 2:4 [o] Job 2:10; Jas 3:2
39:2 [p] Ps 38:13
39:4 [q] Ps 90:12 [r] Ps 103:14
39:5 [s] Ps 89:45 [t] Ps 62:9
39:6 [u] 1Pe 1:24 [v] Ps 127:2 [w] Lk 12:20
39:7 [x] Ps 38:15
39:8 [y] Ps 51:9 [z] Ps 44:13

[a] In Hebrew texts 39:1-13 is numbered 39:2-14. [b] 5 The Hebrew has *Selah* (a word of uncertain meaning) here and at the end of verse 11.

Ps 39 *Everyone Is but a Breath.* David's suffering leads him to reflect on life's fleeting nature. Whereas in Ps 38 he was speechless before his enemies (38:13–14), here he is speechless before God as he contemplates the fragility of life (vv. 1–3,9). In both psalms, David suffers because of his sins (vv. 8,11; 38:17–18). As in several preceding psalms, David asserts that his ultimate hope is in the Lord (v. 7; 31:24; 33:17–18,20,22; 37:9,34). He begins with a vow of silence but finds that he cannot hold his tongue (vv. 1–3), so he speaks, asking God to show him how fleeting life is (vv. 4–6). He looks to God, the source of his sufferings, asking him to relent (vv. 7–11). He concludes with pleas that God hear his prayer and pull back from treating David harshly (vv. 12–13).

39 title Jeduthun. A court musician from the tribe of Levi whom David appointed (along with Asaph and Heman) to oversee worship at the tabernacle when it was at Gibeon. Responsibilities included sounding the trumpets, cymbals, and other instruments such as the harp and lyre (1 Chr 16:41–42; 25:1,6). His ministry also included prophesying (1 Chr 25:1), though it was more of the musical variety (cf. 1 Sam 10:5; 2 Kgs 3:15) than the traditional variety of prophets such as Isaiah, Jeremiah, and Amos. Jeduthun is also called "the king's seer" (2 Chr 35:15). He appears to have been called "Ethan" as well, perhaps a shortened form of the same name or family name before David appointed him to his official duties (1 Chr 6:44; 15:17,19). Jeduthun's descendants carried on his ministry in the days of Hezekiah, Josiah, and Nehemiah (2 Chr 29:14; 35:15; Neh 11:17). His name also appears in the titles of Pss 62; 77. The titles "For Jeduthun" may indicate that David gave Jeduthun special responsibility for using this psalm in worship, or it might indicate that Jeduthun had lent his name to a certain tune that this psalm was to be sung to.

39:1 muzzle. David wanted to be sure not to let sinful words slip from his mouth, so he forced himself to keep quiet, as if he were wearing a muzzle.

39:3 meditated. See notes on 1:2; 5:1. As David silently reflected on his questions, his anguish only increased, the fire within him burned, and he finally had to speak (cf. Jer 20:9).

39:4 number of my days. In 90:12, Moses asks God, "Teach us to number our days, that we may gain a heart of wisdom." Here David is speaking more from a position of despair, asking God to show him how transient his life is.

39:5 span of my years. David worries that his short life is as nothing to a God who is timeless (90:4). **Everyone is but a breath.** Summarizes David's feelings of futility in vv. 4–6. See also v. 11; cf. 144:4; Job 14:2; Eccl 6:12.

39:6 heaping up wealth. David shows the futility of trying to heap up wealth (see v. 11) in a manner similar to Jesus' parable about the rich man who was obsessed with building bigger and better barns for his crops (Luke 12:16–21).

39:7–11 David now confesses his sins, which are unspecified (vv. 8,11), asking God to remove his scourge from him (v. 10). This reveals that David's suffering has been because of his sins, just as in Ps 38. He had been silent before God (v. 9; cf. vv. 2–3), but now he cries out to be spared.

39:9 [a] Job 2:10
39:10 [b] Job 9:34; Ps 32:4
39:11 [c] 2Pe 2:16 [d] Job 13:28
39:12 [e] 1Pe 2:11 [f] Heb 11:13
39:13 [g] Job 10:21; 14:10
40:1 [h] Ps 27:14 [i] Ps 34:15
40:2 [j] Ps 69:14 [k] Ps 27:5
40:3 [l] Ps 33:3
40:4 [m] Ps 34:8 [n] Ps 84:12

9 I was silent; I would not open my mouth,[a]
for you are the one who has done this.
10 Remove your scourge from me;
I am overcome by the blow of your hand.[b]
11 When you rebuke[c] and discipline anyone for their sin,
you consume their wealth like a moth[d]—
surely everyone is but a breath.

12 "Hear my prayer, LORD,
listen to my cry for help;
do not be deaf to my weeping.
I dwell with you as a foreigner,[e]
a stranger,[f] as all my ancestors were.
13 Look away from me, that I may enjoy life again
before I depart and am no more."[g]

Psalm 40[a]

40:13-17pp — Ps 70:1-5

For the director of music. Of David. A psalm.

1 I waited patiently[h] for the LORD;
he turned to me and heard my cry.[i]
2 He lifted me out of the slimy pit,
out of the mud and mire;[j]
he set my feet on a rock[k]
and gave me a firm place to stand.
3 He put a new song[l] in my mouth,
a hymn of praise to our God.
Many will see and fear the LORD
and put their trust in him.

4 Blessed is the one[m]
who trusts in the LORD,[n]
who does not look to the proud,
to those who turn aside to false gods.[b]

[a] In Hebrew texts 40:1-17 is numbered 40:2-18. [b] 4 Or *to lies*

39:11 you consume their wealth. See note on v. 6. **everyone is but a breath.** See note on v. 5.

39:12 I dwell with you as a foreigner, a stranger. David's sense of alienation is clear. He expressed a similar thought in his prayer near the end of his life (1 Chr 29:15). **foreigner.** Someone who had left home and country to live in a new place (Ruth 1:1; 2 Sam 4:3; Isa 16:4 ["fugitives"]; see note on 82:3–4). **stranger.** A "temporary resident" in a place not originally his own (Exod 12:45; Lev 25:40,45). When Abraham's wife Sarah died, he told the local Hittites that he was "a foreigner and stranger" among them (Gen 23:4). Years later, Moses reminded the Israelites that their ancestor Jacob was "a wandering Aramean" who went down to Egypt (Deut 26:5). The NT uses the imagery of foreigners and strangers to speak of a Christian's true home being not here on earth but elsewhere (Heb 11:13; 1 Pet 2:11).

39:13 Look away from me. Ironically, David, who has just urgently asked God to listen to him (v. 12), now asks God to look away from him. He feels stifled by God's attention, for he sees God as the source of his troubles (vv. 9–11). His feelings here are like Job's (Job 7:17–19; 10:20–21).

Ps 40 *He Put a New Song in My Mouth ... You Are My God, Do Not Delay.* This psalm is a mixed one in that it carries a twofold message of what a believer's experience may be like: (1) David praises God for deliverance, affirming the wonders that God performs, using the language common to many praise or thanksgiving psalms (vv. 1–10). (2) David cries out for God to save him from his enemies, using the language of standard lament psalms (vv. 11–17). In the ebb and flow of the Psalter, we find many psalms of one type or the other, but only rarely do we find what could be a standalone psalm knitted together like this one (see Pss 44; 89). The message is that even when God answers prayer and provides relief (vv. 1–10), there will usually come a new crisis that forces a return to God as one's refuge and deliverer (vv. 11–17). Ps 70 slightly revises vv. 13–17.

40:3 new song. This signifies a new start, with renewed joy. See note on 33:3. **Many will see and fear the LORD.** Most of God's mighty works are not only to help his people but also to demonstrate to unbelievers that he is the one and only God, which causes them to tremble before him (e.g., Exod 12:29,33; Josh 2:9–11; 4:23–24; 5:1). So too here: David writes that not only will many see what God has done for him and fear the Lord but they will also put their trust in the Lord. See 18:49; 22:22–31; 64:9; see also introduction to Ps 67 and notes on Ps 67).

40:4 Blessed. See note on 1:1.

5 Many, LORD my God,
are the wonders[o] you have done,
the things you planned for us.
None can compare[p] with you;
were I to speak and tell of your deeds,
they would be too many to declare.

6 Sacrifice and offering you did not desire —[q]
but my ears you have opened[a] —
burnt offerings[r] and sin offerings[b] you did not require.
7 Then I said, "Here I am, I have come —
it is written about me in the scroll.[c]
8 I desire to do your will,[s] my God;
your law is within my heart."[t]
9 I proclaim your saving acts in the great assembly;[u]
I do not seal my lips, LORD,
as you know.[v]
10 I do not hide your righteousness in my heart;
I speak of your faithfulness[w] and your saving help.
I do not conceal your love and your faithfulness
from the great assembly.[x]

11 Do not withhold your mercy from me, LORD;
may your love[y] and faithfulness[z] always protect me.
12 For troubles[a] without number surround me;
my sins have overtaken me, and I cannot see.[b]
They are more than the hairs of my head,[c]
and my heart fails[d] within me.
13 Be pleased to save me, LORD;
come quickly, LORD, to help me.[e]

40:5 [o] Ps 136:4 [p] Ps 139:18; Isa 55:8
40:6 [q] 1Sa 15:22; Am 5:22 [r] Isa 1:11
40:8 [s] Jn 4:34 [t] Ps 37:31
40:9 [u] Ps 22:25 [v] Jos 22:22; Ps 119:13
40:10 [w] Ps 89:1 [x] Ac 20:20
40:11 [y] Pr 20:28 [z] Ps 43:3
40:12 [a] Ps 116:3 [b] Ps 38:4 [c] Ps 69:4 [d] Ps 73:26
40:13 [e] Ps 70:1

[a] 6 Hebrew; some Septuagint manuscripts *but a body you have prepared for me* [b] 6 Or *purification offerings* [c] 7 Or *come / with the scroll written for me*

40:5 wonders. God's mighty deeds and miracles (see note on 26:7). **things you planned for us.** God's plans stand firm forever (33:11; cf. Isa 46:10–11), and they are good (Isa 25:1; Jer 29:11), though his people often resist them (106:13; 107:11). **None can compare with you.** See note on 86:8.

40:6–10 David speaks of his responsibilities as king, referring back to the scroll that was to be the king's (v. 7; cf. Deut 17:18–19). As king, he was to copy the words of God on a scroll, internalizing its teachings and leading his people in following the Lord. David proclaims God's goodness publicly (vv. 9–10). Because he knew God's law, which was written within his heart (v. 8), he understood that the key to a right relationship with God was not through sacrifices and offerings (see v. 6 and note). Heb 10:5–7 quotes the Septuagint version (the pre-Christian Greek translation of the OT) of vv. 6–8 as Jesus' words, showing that Jesus is the ultimate fulfillment of the Davidic covenant. Jesus is the great Son of David—not only physically (genetically) but also spiritually—the heir to the Davidic promises (see notes on 2:7–9).

40:6 Sacrifice and offering you did not desire. This is the same point David makes in his great confessional psalm (51:16–17): God values a right heart attitude and obedience over external rituals. This echoes many similar affirmations elsewhere in the OT (e.g., Deut 6:6; 10:16; 30:6; 1 Sam 15:22; Jer 4:4; Hos 6:6; Amos 5:21–24; Mic 6:8). This is not to say that sacrifices and offerings were as nothing to God; after all, it was he who instituted them in the first place, instructing his people in how to observe them (see the book of Leviticus). Rather, sacrifices offered without a right heart attitude are worthless. Jesus talked about the "more important matters of the law—justice, mercy and faithfulness" (Matt 23:23).

40:7 Here I am, I have come. David is willing to undertake his kingly responsibilities (2 Sam 7, especially vv. 18–29). Isaiah displayed the same servant attitude when God called him (Isa 6:8). **scroll.** The scroll that the godly king was to copy God's words on and keep by his side (Deut 17:18–19; cf. Josh 24:26; 2 Kgs 11:12).

40:8 your law is within my heart. See note on v. 6; cf. 37:31; 119:11.

40:9,10 great assembly. The gathering of the worshiping community at God's sanctuary. David is conscious of his leadership responsibility in the nation to testify to what God has done for him, so he proclaims what God has done in this assembly. See 22:25; 26:12 ("great congregation"); 35:18; 111:1; see also note on 1:5.

40:11–13 David is experienced enough to know that even when God has answered his prayers (vv. 1–10), new challenges certainly await. So he petitions God again for delivery from mounting troubles (vv. 11–17). He cites his troubles (v. 12) and pleads with God to save him (vv. 11,13).

40:12 troubles without number ... more than the hairs of my head. David's hyperbole here vividly reveals the depth of his distress. See also 69:4.

40:14 [f]Ps 35:4
40:16 [g]Ps 35:27
40:17 [h]Ps 70:5
41:1 [i]Ps 82:3-4; Pr 14:21
41:2 [j]Ps 37:22 [k]Ps 27:12
41:4 [l]Ps 6:2 [m]Ps 51:4
41:5 [n]Ps 38:12
41:6 [o]Ps 12:2 [p]Pr 26:24

14 May all who want to take my life
be put to shame and confusion;
may all who desire my ruin[f]
be turned back in disgrace.
15 May those who say to me, "Aha! Aha!"
be appalled at their own shame.
16 But may all who seek you
rejoice and be glad in you;
may those who long for your saving help always say,
"The LORD is great!"[g]

17 But as for me, I am poor and needy;
may the Lord think of me.
You are my help and my deliverer;
you are my God, do not delay.[h]

Psalm 41[a]

For the director of music. A psalm of David.

1 Blessed are those who have regard for the weak;
the LORD delivers them in times of trouble.
2 The LORD protects and preserves them —
they are counted among the blessed in the land —[j]
he does not give them over to the desire of their
foes.[k]
3 The LORD sustains them on their sickbed
and restores them from their bed of illness.

4 I said, "Have mercy[l] on me, LORD;
heal me, for I have sinned[m] against you."
5 My enemies say of me in malice,
"When will he die and his name perish?[n]"
6 When one of them comes to see me,
he speaks falsely,[o] while his heart gathers slander;[p]
then he goes out and spreads it around.

[a] In Hebrew texts 41:1-13 is numbered 41:2-14.

40:14–16 David again asks God to turn his enemies' threats back on them (vv. 14–15) and to reward all who seek God (v. 16).
40:15 Aha! Aha! See note on 10:6.
40:16 seek you. See note on 27:8.
40:17 David casts himself on God's mercy, affirming what he has stated numerous times before: God is his help and deliverer. **poor and needy.** David has referred to the poor and needy previously (12:5; 35:10; 37:14), but here for the first time he identifies himself as such (see 70:5; 86:1; 109:22). See notes on 82:3–4; 86:1.
Ps 41 *Praise Be to the Lord, the God of Israel, From Everlasting to Everlasting.* This is a psalm of David on his sickbed. It is also the last in the "Davidic Psalter" (Pss 3–41), a remarkable string of psalms chronicling the ups and downs of life. David writes while conscious of the role of the king to help the weak and the needy (vv. 1–3; see also Solomon's awareness in 72:4,12–14) and to live with integrity (v. 12; see 15:2; 24:4; 101:2–7). This psalm echoes Ps 2, which speaks of the nations rebelling against the Lord and his anointed king (2:1–3): David's enemies who speak and plot against him (vv. 5–9) are a reminder that such rebellions always seem to be at hand. And this psalm completes a series of four consecutive psalms in which David confesses his sin (v. 4; cf. 38:3–5; 39:8,11; 40:12). David begins by affirming that those who help the weak are blessed (vv. 1–3). He cries out for mercy and healing from God, since he has sinned (v. 4), and he then directs his attention to his enemies and tormentors who have turned against him (vv. 5–9). But he is confident that the Lord will restore him to health and cause him to prevail over his enemies (vv. 10–12), and he concludes with a great note of praise (v. 13).
41:1 Blessed. See note on 1:1. **weak.** How a society treats its marginalized members is a measure of that society's moral compass. David praises all who have regard for the weak. The king had special responsibility for them (72:4,12–13; Prov 29:14; 31:8–9), but all people were also to help the weak (82:3–4).
41:4 Have mercy. David twice asks God for mercy (see also v. 10), restating the same plea from 40:11. **heal me, for I have sinned.** David understands that God sent his sickness to punish him for his sins. This cause-and-effect relationship between sin and its consequences has its roots in God's own nature and promises (e.g., Deut 28). But this direct link does not hold 100 percent of the time; God deals with his people in different ways (see note on 38:5–8).
41:5 My enemies say. Cf. vv. 7–8. See note on 10:6.

[7]All my enemies whisper together[q] against me;
they imagine the worst for me, saying,
[8]"A vile disease has afflicted him;
he will never get up from the place where he lies."
[9]Even my close friend,[r]
someone I trusted,
one who shared my bread,
has turned[a] against me.[s]
[10]But may you have mercy on me, LORD;
raise me up,[t] that I may repay them.
[11]I know that you are pleased with me,[u]
for my enemy does not triumph over me.[v]
[12]Because of my integrity you uphold me[w]
and set me in your presence forever.[x]

[13]Praise be to the LORD, the God of Israel,[y]
from everlasting to everlasting.
Amen and Amen.[z]

BOOK II

Psalms 42–72

Psalm 42[b,c]

For the director of music. A *maskil*[d] of the Sons of Korah.

[1]As the deer pants for streams of water,
so my soul pants[a] for you, my God.

41:7 [q]Ps 56:5; 71:10-11
41:9 [r]2Sa 15:12; Ps 55:12 [s]Job 19:19; Ps 55:20; Mt 26:23; Jn 13:18*
41:10 [t]Ps 3:3
41:11 [u]Ps 147:11 [v]Ps 25:2
41:12 [w]Ps 37:17 [x]Job 36:7
41:13 [y]Ps 72:18 [z]Ps 89:52; 106:48
42:1 [a]Ps 119:131

[a] 9 Hebrew *has lifted up his heel* [b] In many Hebrew manuscripts Psalms 42 and 43 constitute one psalm. [c] In Hebrew texts 42:1-11 is numbered 42:2-12. [d] Title: Probably a literary or musical term

41:9 my close friend. See note on 38:11. Jesus refers to this verse in John 13:18.
41:10 that I may repay them. At first glance, it looks as if David is vowing to take private vengeance against his enemies. But the psalm makes it clear that David is conscious of his role as king, as the godly leader of the nation; thus an attack on the king is, in effect, an attack on God himself, and David vows to stop God's enemies. See notes on 5:9–10; 69:22–28.
41:12 integrity. The psalmists repeatedly affirm their integrity before God (15:2; 18:23,25; 26:1,11; 37:18,37; 84:11; 101:2,6; 119:1). **set me in your presence forever.** Recalls David's thankful affirmations in 23:5–6.
41:13 This doxology is a fitting end to Book I of the Psalter (Pss 3–41). The doxologies that wrap up the other Books are at 72:18–19; 89:52; 106:48; 145:21. Pss 146–150 serve as the great concluding climax to the entire Psalter (see Introduction: Structure).
Pss 42–72 *Book II: The Second Collection of David's Prayers.* Unlike Book I (see introduction to Pss 3–41), in which all the psalms are Davidic except for Ps 10 and Ps 33, only a little more than half are Davidic in Book II: 18 of 31 psalms (Pss 51–65; 68–70). The first eight psalms are from the sons of Korah (Pss 42–49). Book II thus focuses less on David's personal successes and struggles and turns its eye outward a bit more, emphasizing God's concern for the nations (especially Pss 65–67; see also Ps 68).

The single most common psalm type in Book II continues to be the psalm of lament, petition, or confession (Pss 42–44; 51–64; 69–70). Psalms of praise are rare (Pss 65–68); these also happen to be the psalms in which God's concern for the nations is the focus. Book II uses God's personal name Yahweh ("LORD") far less than Book I; more common is the designation "God" (Hebrew *ʾĕlōhîm*). (On God's names, see note on 8:1.) Whereas most psalms in Book I are individually oriented, a greater number in Book II are from the community (Pss 44–48; 60; 65–68; 72).
Pss 42–43 *My Soul Thirsts for God.* These two psalms were almost certainly one psalm originally. They begin a sequence of psalms belonging to the sons of Korah (Pss 42–49); Ps 43 is the only one with no title, suggesting that it belongs with Ps 42. The joint psalm's structure consists of three short stanzas (42:1–5,6–11; 43:1–5), each concluding with the identical refrain (42:5,11; 43:5). The first two stanzas are a passionate lament about the psalmist's condition; he does not cry out for help until the third stanza (43:1).
42 title Sons of Korah. They were from a Levitical family with musical and other responsibilities at the tabernacle and temple. Their ancestor Korah rebelled against the authority of Moses and Aaron, and he and his family were put to death because of it (Exod 6:24; Num 16), though the clan did not completely die out (Num 26:11). In the days of David and Solomon, they served as musicians and gatekeepers at the tabernacle and temple (1 Chr 6:22–38; 9:19–34), and they were still ministering at the temple in the days of Jehoshaphat, more than a century after David (2 Chr 20:19). Pss 42; 44–49; 84–85; 87–88 are all attributed to the sons of Korah.
42:1 soul. The psalmist's core being; the essence of who he is (see note on 6:3). The repeated references to the psalmist's core being is a key concept in Pss 42–43, originally one psalm (42:1–2,4–6,11; 43:5).

42:2 [b]Ps 63:1 [c]Jer 10:10 [d]Ps 43:4
42:3 [e]Ps 80:5 [f]Ps 79:10
42:4 [g]Isa 30:29 [h]Ps 100:4
42:5 [i]Ps 38:6; 77:3 [j]La 3:24 [k]Ps 44:3
42:7 [l]Ps 88:7; Jnh 2:3
42:8 [m]Ps 57:3 [n]Job 35:10 [o]Ps 63:6; 149:5

2 My soul thirsts[b] for God, for the living God.[c]
When can I go[d] and meet with God?
3 My tears[e] have been my food
day and night,
while people say to me all day long,
"Where is your God?"[f]
4 These things I remember
as I pour out my soul:
how I used to go to the house of God[g]
under the protection of the Mighty One[a]
with shouts of joy and praise[h]
among the festive throng.

5 Why, my soul, are you downcast?[i]
Why so disturbed within me?
Put your hope in God,[j]
for I will yet praise him,
my Savior[k] and my God.

6 My soul is downcast within me;
therefore I will remember you
from the land of the Jordan,
the heights of Hermon—from Mount Mizar.
7 Deep calls to deep
in the roar of your waterfalls;
all your waves and breakers
have swept over me.[l]

8 By day the LORD directs his love,[m]
at night[n] his song[o] is with me—
a prayer to the God of my life.

[a] 4 See Septuagint and Syriac; the meaning of the Hebrew for this line is uncertain.

He is very transparent in speaking of his inner thoughts. **my God.** The psalmist clearly identifies with a personal God, calling on him repeatedly: "God" occurs 21 times in 16 verses, along with other labels: "my Savior" (42:5,11; 43:5), "the Mighty One" (42:4), "the LORD" (42:8). In most of these instances, the psalmist's personal relationship with his God is plain to see. Even a believer with a close relationship to God will sometimes feel far away from him and long to be restored to fellowship with him.

Ivory stag, Phoenician, 900–800 BC. "As the deer pants for streams of water, so my soul pants for you, my God" (Ps 42:1).

Cleveland Museum of Art, OH, USA/Purchase from the J. H. Wade Fund/Bridgeman Images

42:2 meet with God. Commune with God at the sanctuary (Exod 19:17; 29:42–43; 30:6,36), a place where the psalmist previously had worshiped God (v. 4).

42:3 Where is your God? See also v. 10; 79:10; 115:2.

42:5 In this first refrain, the psalmist engages in an internal dialogue in which he encourages himself to hope in God. Other than this refrain also in v. 11 (and the pivotal v. 8), the first two stanzas are unrelentingly bleak.

42:6 therefore I will remember you. It is precisely because the psalmist is downcast that he will remember his God. His tribulations drive him toward God, not away from him. **heights of Hermon.** Mount Hermon is north of the Sea of Galilee, outside the usual boundaries of Israel. The psalmist is thus far from where he wants to be (v. 4; 43:3). The Hebrew term is plural (i.e., "Hermons"), suggesting the mountain range, not a specific peak. **Mount Mizar.** This peak is unknown but was probably part of the Mount Hermon range. "Mount Mizar" means "little hill" in Hebrew, perhaps suggesting a contrast between Hermon and Zion since Zion will be established as the "highest" of the mountains (Isa 2:2; cf. Ps 48:2). The psalmist appears to be in exile, dwelling in the mountains where the headwaters of the Jordan River begin, far north of Jerusalem.

42:7 waves and breakers. The images of powerful, cascading water effectively captures the psalmist's tenuous position: God's own waves and breakers overwhelm him. Ironically, the psalmist opens with the imagery of no water and his desperate panting and thirsting for God (vv. 1–2), but here he is overwhelmed with too much water. See note on 93:3.

42:8 the LORD directs his love ... his song is with me. This verse

[9]I say to God my Rock,
"Why have you forgotten me?
Why must I go about mourning,[p]
oppressed by the enemy?"
[10]My bones suffer mortal agony
as my foes taunt me,
saying to me all day long,
"Where is your God?"

[11]Why, my soul, are you downcast?
Why so disturbed within me?
Put your hope in God,
for I will yet praise him,
my Savior and my God.[q]

Psalm 43[a]

[1]Vindicate me, my God,
and plead my cause[r]
against an unfaithful nation.
Rescue me from those who are
deceitful and wicked.[s]
[2]You are God my stronghold.
Why have you rejected[t] me?
Why must I go about mourning,
oppressed by the enemy?[u]
[3]Send me your light[v] and your faithful care,
let them lead me;
let them bring me to your holy mountain,[w]
to the place where you dwell.[x]
[4]Then I will go to the altar[y] of God,
to God, my joy and my delight.
I will praise you with the lyre,[z]
O God, my God.

[5]Why, my soul, are you downcast?
Why so disturbed within me?
Put your hope in God,
for I will yet praise him,
my Savior and my God.[a]

[a] In many Hebrew manuscripts Psalms 42 and 43 constitute one psalm.

42:9 [p] Ps 38:6
42:11 [q] Ps 43:5
43:1 [r] 1Sa 24:15; Ps 26:1; 35:1 [s] Ps 5:6
43:2 [t] Ps 44:9 [u] Ps 42:9
43:3 [v] Ps 36:9 [w] Ps 42:4 [x] Ps 84:1
43:4 [y] Ps 26:6 [z] Ps 33:2
43:5 [a] Ps 42:6

breaks up the pattern of the three stanzas (vv. 1–5,6–11; 43:1–5), the first and third of which have five verses apiece. It stands at the center of the second stanza—indeed, at the exact structural center of the psalm (see note on 100:3 ["his people"])—and it expresses confidence in the Lord, the only place outside of the refrains where there is any such expression and the only place in the psalm where God's personal name Yahweh ("the LORD") occurs (see note on 8:1). **with me.** The central words, accentuating the relationship the psalmist has with his God.
42:9 Why have you forgotten me? Echoes David's words in 22:1.
42:10 My bones. The psalmist's core being, parallel to "soul" (v. 1; see note there). **Where is your God?** See note on v. 3.
42:11 See note on v. 5.
Ps 43 *Vindicate Me, O God.* Probably a continuation of Ps 42 (see introduction to Pss 42–43). The psalmist now turns from past memories to focus on God in prayer, appealing directly to him and dialoguing with him, ending with a vow to worship God joyfully again (v. 4).
43:1 Vindicate me. The psalmist pleads with God as though this were a court proceeding, asking God to justify his case against an unnamed nation. It is the prayer of an innocent sufferer who wants God to act as his advocate, to argue his case against his oppressors. Similar prayers for vindication include 17:2,15; 24:5; 26:1; 35:24,27; 37:6; 54:1; 57:2; 135:14; 138:8.
43:2 This verse repeats 42:9 almost verbatim.
43:3 your holy mountain ... the place where you dwell. Mount Zion, the place God chose as his dwelling place (see notes on 2:6; 9:11). Rather than dwelling in exile on a faraway mountain, the psalmist wants to return home to the earthly "capital" of God's kingdom. See 42:6 and note. **place.** See note on 84:1.
43:4 my joy and my delight. The psalmist fairly bursts with joy at the thought of returning to worship God again at his holy altar (42:4).
43:5 See note on 42:5.

44:1 [b]Ex 12:26; Ps 78:3
44:2 [c]Ps 78:55 [d]Ex 15:17 [e]Ps 80:9
44:3 [f]Dt 8:17; Jos 24:12 [g]Ps 77:15 [h]Dt 4:37; 7:7-8
44:4 [i]Ps 74:12
44:5 [j]Ps 108:13
44:6 [k]Ps 33:16
44:7 [l]Ps 136:24 [m]Ps 53:5
44:8 [n]Ps 34:2 [o]Ps 30:12
44:9 [p]Ps 74:1 [q]Ps 60:1,10
44:10 [r]Lev 26:17; Jos 7:8; Ps 89:41
44:11 [s]Ro 8:36 [t]Dt 4:27; 28:64; Ps 106:27
44:12 [u]Isa 52:3; Jer 15:13
44:13 [v]Ps 79:4; 80:6 [w]Dt 28:37
44:14 [x]Ps 109:25; Jer 24:9

Psalm 44[a]

For the director of music. Of the Sons of Korah.
A *maskil.*[b]

1 We have heard it with our ears, O God;
our ancestors have told us[b]
what you did in their days,
in days long ago.
2 With your hand you drove out[c] the nations
and planted[d] our ancestors;
you crushed the peoples
and made our ancestors flourish.[e]
3 It was not by their sword[f] that they won the land,
nor did their arm bring them victory;
it was your right hand, your arm,[g]
and the light of your face, for you loved[h] them.

4 You are my King[i] and my God,
who decrees[c] victories for Jacob.
5 Through you we push back our enemies;
through your name we trample[j] our foes.
6 I put no trust in my bow,[k]
my sword does not bring me victory;
7 but you give us victory[l] over our enemies,
you put our adversaries to shame.[m]
8 In God we make our boast[n] all day long,
and we will praise your name forever.[d][o]

9 But now you have rejected[p] and humbled us;
you no longer go out with our armies.[q]
10 You made us retreat[r] before the enemy,
and our adversaries have plundered us.
11 You gave us up to be devoured like sheep[s]
and have scattered us among the nations.[t]
12 You sold your people for a pittance,[u]
gaining nothing from their sale.

13 You have made us a reproach to our neighbors,[v]
the scorn[w] and derision of those around us.
14 You have made us a byword among the nations;
the peoples shake their heads[x] at us.

[a] In Hebrew texts 44:1-26 is numbered 44:2-27. [b] Title: Probably a literary or musical term [c] 4 Septuagint, Aquila and Syriac; Hebrew *King, O God; / command* [d] 8 The Hebrew has *Selah* (a word of uncertain meaning) here.

Ps 44 *You Drove Out the Nations and Planted Our Ancestors. Awake, Lord! Do Not Reject Us Forever.* A psalm of national mourning on the occasion of an unknown crisis at the hands of the nation's enemies. The psalm begins by praising God for fighting Israel's battles in days of old (vv. 1–8). But now, the nation faces a dire crisis: it feels like God has rejected his people, leaving them to be devoured like sheep (vv. 9–16). The pain is made worse because the people are innocent of any sin; they have remained faithful to God, yet he still has allowed this crisis (vv. 17–22). The psalm concludes with urgent pleas that God rise up and help his people (vv. 23–26).

44:1 our ancestors have told us. Israel was to tell its stories over and over again, reminding every new generation what God had done for them. See 78:3; Deut 6:20–25; Josh 4:21–24.

44:4 my King and my God. See notes on 5:2; 10:16.

44:8 your name. See note on 8:1.

44:9 you have rejected and humbled us. See 89:38–39, which voices similar concerns after initially praising God for what he had done for his people (89:1–37). See 107:39; Deut 8:3; 31:17; Isa 5:15.

44:12 You sold your people. Even though God promised to protect his people, he did not give them a blank check to do anything they wanted. He would "sell" them into the clutches of their enemies if they turned

15 I live in disgrace all day long,
and my face is covered with shame
16 at the taunts of those who reproach and revile[y] me,
because of the enemy, who is bent on revenge.

17 All this came upon us,
though we had not forgotten[z] you;
we had not been false to your covenant.
18 Our hearts had not turned[a] back;
our feet had not strayed from your path.
19 But you crushed[b] us and made us a haunt for jackals;
you covered us over with deep darkness.[c]

20 If we had forgotten[d] the name of our God
or spread out our hands to a foreign god,[e]
21 would not God have discovered it,
since he knows the secrets of the heart?[f]
22 Yet for your sake we face death all day long;
we are considered as sheep to be slaughtered.[g]

23 Awake,[h] Lord! Why do you sleep?[i]
Rouse yourself! Do not reject us forever.[j]
24 Why do you hide your face[k]
and forget our misery and oppression?[l]

25 We are brought down to the dust;[m]
our bodies cling to the ground.
26 Rise up[n] and help us;
rescue[o] us because of your unfailing love.

44:16 [y] Ps 74:10
44:17 [z] Ps 78:7,57; Da 9:13
44:18 [a] Job 23:11
44:19 [b] Ps 51:8 [c] Job 3:5
44:20 [d] Ps 78:11 [e] Dt 6:14; Ps 81:9
44:21 [f] Ps 139:1-2; Jer 17:10
44:22 [g] Isa 53:7; Ro 8:36*
44:23 [h] Ps 7:6 [i] Ps 78:65 [j] Ps 77:7
44:24 [k] Job 13:24 [l] Ps 42:9
44:25 [m] Ps 119:25
44:26 [n] Ps 35:2 [o] Ps 25:22

Psalm 45[a]

For the director of music. To the tune of "Lilies." Of the Sons of Korah. A *maskil.*[b] A wedding song.

1 My heart is stirred by a noble theme
as I recite my verses for the king;
my tongue is the pen of a skillful writer.

[a] In Hebrew texts 45:1-17 is numbered 45:2-18. [b] Title: Probably a literary or musical term

away from him (cf. Deut 32:30; Judg 2:14; 2 Kgs 17:7–23; 24:3–4). In vv. 17–22, the nation protests its innocence, however.
44:17 your covenant. See note on 25:10.
44:19 jackals. A variety of scavenging wolf. In the Bible it usually symbolizes desolation and destruction: the prophets spoke of cities like Babylon and Jerusalem being left desolate, fit only as haunts for hyenas, jackals, and owls (e.g., Isa 13:21–22; Jer 9:11; 51:37; Lam 5:18; cf. Isa 34:13; Jer 10:22; 49:33). The reference to jackals here fits this imagery: the nation feels completely crushed and abandoned by God.
44:20 name of our God. See note on 8:1.
44:22 Israel faced hostility from the very beginning, from its infancy as a nation coming out of Egypt to the hostility of the Canaanites in Joshua's day to the threat from the Philistines in David's day to the many threats from its immediate neighbors during the monarchies to the existential threats from the great powers of Assyria and Babylon and more. The apostle Paul quoted this verse (Rom 8:36), applying it to the church: even though many oppose believers, nothing can separate us from the love of God because the risen Christ is now interceding for us (Rom 8:31–39).
44:23 Awake. See note on 3:7.
44:24 hide your face. See note on 27:9.
44:26 unfailing love. See note on 6:4.
Ps 45 *A Wedding Song.* This psalm praises the king on his wedding day. Its imagery and praise are lavish; no other psalm praises a human being in such extravagant terms. The psalmist inserts himself in a dramatic way in vv. 1,17, forming a frame around the psalm. Verses 2,16 form a secondary frame praising the king. The psalmist praises the king (vv. 3–9) and addresses the bride (vv. 10–15). Even in vv. 10–15 the king is the true subject since the psalm portrays the bride mainly in relation to the bridegroom. One can hear echoes of this psalm in Ps 72, which is also a prayer on behalf of the king; both psalms are "royal psalms" (see introduction to Ps 18).

The psalm does not identity any specific king; it was probably written for use by any of the descendants of David. The bride appears to be a foreigner (see vv. 9–10,12), reflecting the international stature of this king. As a psalm of the sons of Korah (see note on Ps 42 title), the psalm reflects approval of the honored king in Levitical circles, bestowing God's blessing on the marital union. The psalm very much reflects the divine approval of Israel's king affirmed in the Davidic covenant (2 Sam 7:11–16; 1 Chr 28:5; 2 Chr 13:8). As such, David and his descendants

45:2 [p] Lk 4:22
45:3 [q] Heb 4:12; Rev 1:16 [r] Isa 9:6
45:4 [s] Rev 6:2
45:6 [t] Ps 93:2; 98:9
45:7 [u] Ps 33:5 [v] Isa 61:1 [w] Ps 21:6; Heb 1:8-9*
45:8 [x] SS 1:3
45:9 [y] SS 6:8 [z] 1Ki 2:19
45:10 [a] Dt 21:13
45:11 [b] Ps 95:6 [c] Isa 54:5
45:12 [d] Ps 22:29; Isa 49:23
45:13 [e] Isa 61:10

2 You are the most excellent of men
and your lips have been anointed with grace,[p]
since God has blessed you forever.

3 Gird your sword[q] on your side, you mighty one;[r]
clothe yourself with splendor and majesty.
4 In your majesty ride forth victoriously[s]
in the cause of truth, humility and justice;
let your right hand achieve awesome deeds.
5 Let your sharp arrows pierce the hearts of the king's enemies;
let the nations fall beneath your feet.
6 Your throne, O God,[a] will last for ever and ever;[t]
a scepter of justice will be the scepter of your kingdom.
7 You love righteousness[u] and hate wickedness;
therefore God, your God, has set you above your
companions
by anointing[v] you with the oil of joy.[w]
8 All your robes are fragrant[x] with myrrh and aloes and cassia;
from palaces adorned with ivory
the music of the strings makes you glad.
9 Daughters of kings[y] are among your honored women;
at your right hand[z] is the royal bride in gold of Ophir.

10 Listen, daughter, and pay careful attention:
Forget your people[a] and your father's house.
11 Let the king be enthralled by your beauty;
honor[b] him, for he is your lord.[c]
12 The city of Tyre will come with a gift,[b][d]
people of wealth will seek your favor.
13 All glorious[e] is the princess within her chamber;
her gown is interwoven with gold.

[a] 6 Here the king is addressed as God's representative. [b] 12 Or *A Tyrian robe is among the gifts*

are types (i.e., prefigurements or foreshadowings) of Christ, a point that the author of Hebrews makes (Heb 1:8–9).

45 title "Lilies." This tune title also occurs in the title of Ps 69, and a variant of it, "The Lily/Lilies of the Covenant," occurs in the titles of Pss 60; 80. It is an especially appropriate title for this wedding psalm, given the prominence of lilies in the greatest of love songs in the Bible, the Song of Songs (Song 2:16; 4:5; 5:13; 6:2,3; 7:2). **wedding song.** Can also be read as a "song of love."

45:1 The psalm begins in grandiose fashion: the psalmist claims to be "a skillful writer" writing about a "noble theme."

45:2 most excellent of men. None of the historical kings who occupied the royal throne in Jerusalem ever lived up to the lavish praise in this psalm during their reigns, not even David. The psalm is about God's establishing a royal dynasty that would, in effect, rule over his kingdom on earth (1 Chr 28:5; 2 Chr 13:8). As such, and because of God's blessing "forever," the psalmist can praise the king in this way. It was because of God's favor that the kings merited such praise, not because of anything they individually could do.

45:3 splendor and majesty. The king's appearance reflected that of God himself (see note on 29:2).

45:6 Your throne, O God. The king, as God's representative, is addressed as God himself (see NIV text note), certainly a startling use of language at first glance. Yet it reflects the close relationship between any godly king and his God. God himself declared that any royal descendant of David would be his "son" (2 Sam 7:14). Thus, in this psalm, where the language is lavish throughout, to see the king—the "son" of God—being addressed simply as "God" should not be surprising. The king occupied God's throne (1 Chr 28:5), and a close relationship existed between God and king. There is no hint here or elsewhere, however, that the kings in Israel or Judah were actually considered divine (in the way that the Egyptians thought of their pharaohs); indeed, the very next verse refers to God as "your" God (i.e., the king's God). The king is not truly God; only God is. **scepter of justice.** A symbol of royal power and authority (110:2; Esth 4:11; 5:2; 8:4; Isa 14:5; Jer 48:17). The patriarch Jacob blessed the tribe of Judah with the promise of a scepter (Gen 49:10), and since David was from this tribe, this blessing was played out in the Davidic covenant (see note on 89:3). But the godly king was to wield his scepter in service of justice and righteousness (vv. 6–7; see 72:1–4,12–14).

45:7 God, your God. There was to be a close relationship between the king and his God (2 Sam 7:14,16). The godly king ruled as God's vice-regent, under his authority. **anointing.** See notes on 2:2; 89:20.

45:9 Daughters of kings. The great occasion of the king's wedding would attract international recognition. **gold of Ophir.** The location of Ophir is unknown, but it was a place from which gold, fine wood, and precious stones were shipped to Israel (1 Kgs 9:28; 10:11). Its gold was of such high quality that it was the standard for comparison (Job 22:24; Isa 13:12).

45:10–12 your people ... Tyre. May suggest that the bride is a foreigner.

[14] In embroidered garments she is led to the king;[f]
her virgin companions follow her—
those brought to be with her.
[15] Led in with joy and gladness,
they enter the palace of the king.

[16] Your sons will take the place of your fathers;
you will make them princes throughout the land.

[17] I will perpetuate your memory through all generations;[g]
therefore the nations will praise you[h] for ever and ever.

Psalm 46[a]

For the director of music. Of the Sons of Korah. According to *alamoth.*[b] A song.

[1] God is our refuge[i] and strength,
an ever-present[j] help in trouble.
[2] Therefore we will not fear,[k] though the earth give way[l]
and the mountains fall[m] into the heart of the sea,
[3] though its waters roar[n] and foam
and the mountains quake with their surging.[c]

[4] There is a river whose streams make glad the city of God,[o]
the holy place where the Most High dwells.
[5] God is within her,[p] she will not fall;
God will help[q] her at break of day.
[6] Nations[r] are in uproar, kingdoms[s] fall;
he lifts his voice, the earth melts.[t]

[7] The LORD Almighty is with us;[u]
the God of Jacob is our fortress.[v]

[8] Come and see what the LORD has done,[w]
the desolations[x] he has brought on the earth.
[9] He makes wars[y] cease
to the ends of the earth.

45:14 [f] SS 1:4
45:17 [g] Mal 1:11 [h] Ps 138:4
46:1 [i] Ps 9:9; 14:6 [j] Dt 4:7
46:2 [k] Ps 23:4 [l] Ps 82:5 [m] Ps 18:7
46:3 [n] Ps 93:3
46:4 [o] Ps 48:1,8; Isa 60:14
46:5 [p] Isa 12:6; Eze 43:7 [q] Ps 37:40
46:6 [r] Ps 2:1 [s] Ps 68:32 [t] Mic 1:4
46:7 [u] 2Ch 13:12 [v] Ps 9:9
46:8 [w] Ps 66:5 [x] Isa 61:4
46:9 [y] Isa 2:4

[a] In Hebrew texts 46:1-11 is numbered 46:2-12. [b] Title: Probably a musical term [c] *3* The Hebrew has *Selah* (a word of uncertain meaning) here and at the end of verses 7 and 11.

45:16 Your sons ... princes. With his bride, the king will possibly have sons to carry on his legacy, and they will represent him as princes throughout the land.

45:17 your memory. The psalmist, who has claimed special skills as a writer (v. 1), comes full circle to assure the king that he will help to guarantee his memory in perpetuity. **nations.** The nations who rebelled against the Lord and his anointed (Ps 2) would now praise the king forever. The worldwide vision of Ps 67 is also reflected here.

Ps 46 *God Is Our Refuge and Strength.* This psalm responds to the laments of Pss 42–44 by affirming that God is Israel's refuge, strength, and fortress, sovereign over nature and nations. It also responds to Ps 45 by refocusing attention on God rather than the king. It inspired Martin Luther's hymn "A Mighty Fortress Is Our God." It is the first of what are sometimes called the "psalms of Zion" (Pss 48; 76; 84; 87; 122; 132). Four of the seven are psalms of the sons of Korah (Pss 46; 48; 84; 87). On the importance of Zion, see notes on 2:6; 9:11.

The psalm begins by affirming God as his people's refuge and strength over all of creation (vv. 1–3) and then highlights the importance of Zion, the "city of God (v. 4), as the so-called capital of God's earthly kingdom (vv. 4–6). The refrain (vv. 7,11) brackets the final affirmations that God is also over all the nations (vv. 8–10).

46:1 refuge. The theme of refuge sounded at the beginning of the Psalter (see note on 2:12) is prominent in this psalm (vv. 1,7,11).

46:3 waters roar and foam. See note on 93:3.

46:4 a river. There is no river in Jerusalem, so the reference here is symbolic: such a river would sustain Jerusalem (in contrast to the raging waters of v. 3). Ezek 47:1–12 and Rev 22:1–2 also speak of a river of life flowing from Jerusalem. **city of God.** Mount Zion (Jerusalem), the place God chose to place his name (Deut 12:5–7), the earthly "capital" of God's kingdom (see notes on 2:6; 9:11). **holy place.** See note on 84:1. **Most High.** See note on 7:8.

46:6 God's power is on display: with even a simple raised voice, nations are rebuked, the earth melts. This is reminiscent of the power of God's word in creation in Gen 1 ("And God said").

46:7 The LORD. Only the second time that Book II of the Psalter (Pss 42–72) uses God's personal name (the first is in 42:8). See note on 8:1 for the significance of this name. **Almighty.** See note on 24:10, referring to all of the heavenly forces, whether simply to the sun, moon, and stars or to angelic forces. The term highlights the Lord's omnipotence over all things. **the God of Jacob is our fortress.** The refrain, repeated in v. 11, affirms the theme of refuge as well as the Lord's presence with his people (see note on 18:1–2). **Jacob.** See note on 135:4.

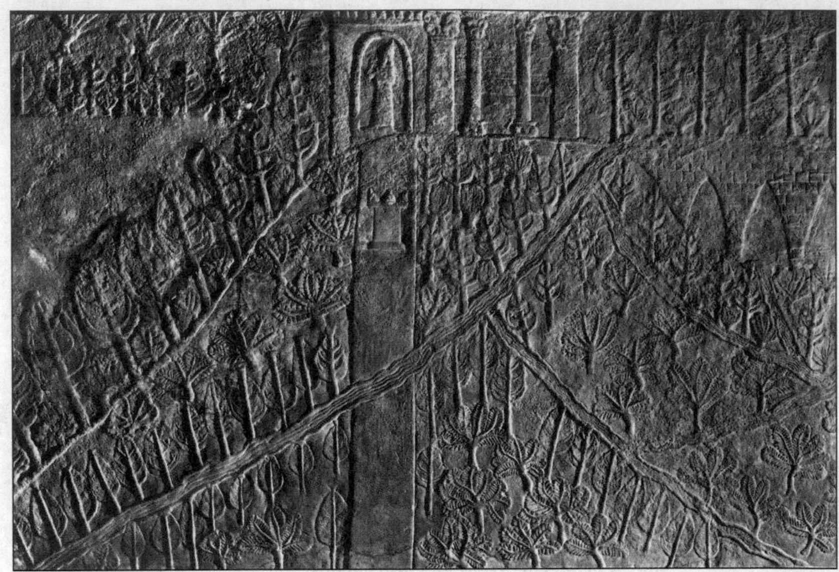

Seventh-century BC relief of an aqueduct bringing water to the city of Nineveh. "There is a river whose streams make glad the city of God" (Ps 46:4).

Werner Forman Archive/British Museum, London/Glow Images

46:9 [z]Ps 76:3 [a]Eze 39:9 **46:10** [b]Ps 100:3 [c]Isa 2:11 **47:1** [d]Ps 98:8; Isa 55:12 [e]Ps 106:47 **47:2** [f]Dt 7:21 [g]Mal 1:14

He breaks the bow[z] and shatters the spear;
he burns the shields[a] with fire.[a]
10 He says, "Be still, and know that I am God;[b]
I will be exalted[c] among the nations,
I will be exalted in the earth."

11 The LORD Almighty is with us;
the God of Jacob is our fortress.

Psalm 47[b]

For the director of music. Of the Sons of Korah. A psalm.

1 Clap your hands,[d] all you nations;
shout to God with cries of joy.[e]
2 For the LORD Most High is awesome,[f]
the great King[g] over all the earth.

[a] *9* Or *chariots* [b] In Hebrew texts 47:1-9 is numbered 47:2-10.

46:10 Be still, and know that I am God. The primary addressees are the nations (vv. 6,8–9,10b), but the secondary addressees seem to be God's people (cf. in the Hebrew the plural command in v. 8: "Come"). So the psalm ends (before the final refrain) by reassuring God's people that the Lord indeed is their fortress and that he is in their midst, in the very "city of God" (v. 4). Moreover, the nations should stop striving against God's people.

46:11 See note on v. 7.

Ps 47 *God Reigns Over the Nations.* This psalm is the exclamation point to Ps 46. The two psalms together emphatically assert that the Lord is mighty over all of creation and all nations and that the pessimism of Pss 42–44 must give way to praising the Almighty God. Pss 46–47 also make clear that as exalted as the king is (see Ps 45), the Lord is the true King over all kings and nations. This is the first of what are often called the "Kingship of Yahweh" hymns. While the idea of God's kingship is present in many more psalms than this, the core group of the Kingship of Yahweh psalms also includes Pss 93–99; 145 (see note on 93:1). The psalm issues a call to praise and the reasons for praise (vv. 1–4), followed by a second call to praise and reasons centered around the Lord's kingship (vv. 5–7), and ends with all the nations' kings giving homage to the God who reigns (vv. 8–9). Thus, Ps 47 affirms that entire nations, under their leaders, will respond to Yahweh. This triumph of God's kingdom anticipates the NT triumph under Christ (e.g., Rev 11:15; 12:10).

47:1 Clap your hands. The nations are called to joyfully praise God. Previously, they have been the nemeses of God's people (44:11,14; 46:6), but now the nations are invited to rejoice in the Lord, as 45:5,17; 46:10 affirm.

47:2 the LORD. Book II (Pss 42–72) uses God's personal name, Yahweh

[3]He subdued[h] nations under us,
peoples under our feet.
[4]He chose our inheritance[i] for us,
the pride of Jacob, whom he loved.[a]

[5]God has ascended amid shouts of joy,
the LORD amid the sounding of trumpets.[j]
[6]Sing praises[k] to God, sing praises;
sing praises to our King, sing praises.
[7]For God is the King of all the earth;[l]
sing to him a psalm[m] of praise.

[8]God reigns[n] over the nations;
God is seated on his holy throne.
[9]The nobles of the nations assemble
as the people of the God of Abraham,
for the kings[b] of the earth belong to God;[o]
he is greatly exalted.[p]

Psalm 48[c]

A song. A psalm of the Sons of Korah.

[1]Great is the LORD,[q] and most worthy of praise,
in the city of our God,[r] his holy mountain.[s]

[2]Beautiful[t] in its loftiness,
the joy of the whole earth,
like the heights of Zaphon[d] is Mount Zion,
the city of the Great King.[u]

47:3 [h]Ps 18:39,47
47:4 [i]1Pe 1:4
47:5 [j]Ps 68:33; 98:6
47:6 [k]Ps 68:4; 89:18
47:7 [l]Zec 14:9 [m]Col 3:16
47:8 [n]1Ch 16:31
47:9 [o]Ps 72:11; 89:18 [p]Ps 97:9
48:1 [q]Ps 96:4 [r]Ps 46:4 [s]Isa 2:2-3; Mic 4:1; Zec 8:3
48:2 [t]Ps 50:2; La 2:15 [u]Mt 5:35

[a] *4* The Hebrew has *Selah* (a word of uncertain meaning) here. [b] *9* Or *shields* [c] In Hebrew texts 48:1-14 is numbered 48:2-15. [d] *2* *Zaphon* was the most sacred mountain of the Canaanites.

(see note on 8:1), sparingly, but it occurs in all the Kingship of Yahweh psalms (see introduction to Ps 47; see also note on 93:1). **Most High.** See note on 7:8. **great King over all the earth.** Yahweh, not Baal, Marduk, or any other pagan god.

47:4 our inheritance. The land of Canaan, a point the Psalms reiterate many times (37:9,11,22,29,34; 105:11; 135:12; 136:21–22). **pride of Jacob.** See note on 135:4.

47:5–7 Just as Ps 24 likely was part of a processional ritual in which the Lord "entered" Jerusalem to take his place on his holy mountain (see introduction to Ps 24), Ps 47 seems to be part of a joyful ritual in which the Lord "ascended" (v. 5) to his rightful throne (v. 8). The Bible does not give the details of these rituals except those which we can discern from psalms such as these. Images of God as King are predominant in this section.

47:5 trumpets. They were made of ram's horns. See note on 98:6.

47:8 God reigns. See note on 93:1. **his holy throne.** The book of Psalms affirms many times the Lord's enthronement on high (e.g., 2:4; 7:7; 9:4,7,11; 11:4; 22:3; 29:10; 93:2; 97:2; 99:1; 102:12). The reference here could be to the heavenly throne, with the "footstool"—the ark of the covenant (1 Chr 28:2)—being in the Most Holy Place (Exod 26:34). God's "throne" is mentioned repeatedly in Revelation (Rev 4:9,10; 5:1,7,13; 6:16; 7:10,11,15; 19:4).

47:9 as the people of the God of Abraham. Thus, the promises to Abraham will be fulfilled (see Gen 12:2–3 and notes; Gen 17:4–6; 22:17–18). **kings.** The Hebrew word here is usually translated "shields" (see NIV text note). Since the prime function of a king in the ancient Near East was as the nations' warrior-protector, "shields" is a way of referring to the king. This verse emphasizes that Israel's God is sovereign over all kings and nations as they acknowledge him to be the Great King: those that raged against him and his anointed one (2:1–3) now assemble to honor him as he sits on his holy throne.

Ps 48 *Beautiful in Its Loftiness Is Mount Zion, the City of the Great King.* This psalm in praise of God's holy mountain is the quintessential "psalm of Zion" (see introduction to Ps 46). Almost every psalm of the sons of Korah thus far has focused on Zion, either directly or indirectly (42:4; 43:3; 46:4–5; 47:5,8), and now full-throated praise breaks forth of the place where God chose to establish himself. "Zion" is another name for Jerusalem (see note on 9:11). Praise of God brackets the psalm (vv. 1,14). The first section then introduces the beauty and uniqueness of Mount Zion (vv. 2–3), followed by an account of how its appearance routed hostile kings because of God's presence there (vv. 4–8). The focus then shifts to God himself; even Mount Zion praises his judgments (vv. 9–11). And finally, Zion's memory is to be passed down to the generations (vv. 12–13).

48:1 Great is the LORD. The opening praise to God (which also occurs in 96:4; 99:2; 145:3) is rooted in his holy city. While God created all things (Gen 1) and is himself above and beyond the farthest reaches of the cosmos (139:7–8), the OT affirms that on earth the one place he most identified with was Mount Zion, the place where he dwelt "enthroned between the cherubim" of the ark of the covenant (1 Sam 4:4), which was housed in the Most Holy Place of the tabernacle and temple.

48:2 This celebrates the beauty and great height of Mount Zion. Its strength comes from God, who dwells there (v. 3). Mount Zion is not the

48:3 [v] Ps 46:7
48:4 [w] 2Sa 10:1-19
48:5 [x] Ex 15:16
48:7 [y] Jer 18:17; Eze 27:26
48:8 [z] Ps 87:5
48:9 [a] Ps 26:3
48:10 [b] Dt 28:58; Jos 7:9 [c] Isa 41:10
48:11 [d] Ps 97:8
48:13 [e] ver 3; Ps 122:7 [f] Ps 78:6
48:14 [g] Ps 23:4

3 God is in her citadels;
he has shown himself to be her fortress.[v]

4 When the kings joined forces,
when they advanced together,[w]
5 they saw her and were astounded;
they fled in terror.[x]
6 Trembling seized them there,
pain like that of a woman in labor.
7 You destroyed them like ships of Tarshish
shattered by an east wind.[y]

8 As we have heard,
so we have seen
in the city of the LORD Almighty,
in the city of our God:
God makes her secure
forever.[a][z]

9 Within your temple, O God,
we meditate on your unfailing love.[a]
10 Like your name,[b] O God,
your praise reaches to the ends of the earth;[c]
your right hand is filled with righteousness.
11 Mount Zion rejoices,
the villages of Judah are glad
because of your judgments.[d]

12 Walk about Zion, go around her,
count her towers,
13 consider well her ramparts,
view her citadels,[e]
that you may tell of them
to the next generation.[f]
14 For this God is our God for ever and ever;
he will be our guide[g] even to the end.

[a] *8* The Hebrew has *Selah* (a word of uncertain meaning) here.

highest mountain in its region, but the psalmist uses lavish overstatement to glorify it as God's dwelling place, just as he does in praising the king in Ps 45. And in the last days, Zion will indeed be the highest of the mountains, and nations will stream to it (Isa 2:2; Rev 21:24,26). In the apostle John's vision of the new Jerusalem, the city is 1,400 miles (2,250 kilometers) in height, breadth, and width (Rev 21:9–27, especially v. 16). **Zaphon.** Hebrew for "north"; the term is also the name of a mountain marking the boundary between the Holy Land and Syria. The Canaanites believed that Baal resided there (see NIV text note). Canaanite texts refer to this mountain as Baal's "beautiful hill," his "inheritance," his "holy mountain," and a "lovely, mighty mountain." So by affirming these things about Mount Zion, Ps 48 deliberately argues that Yahweh is greater than Baal and that his dwelling place is greater than Baal's.

48:4–7 The nations mounted futile attacks and then fled in terror at the sight of Zion. Historical events may be in view: e.g., the defeat of the Moabites and Ammonites in Jehoshaphat's day (2 Chr 20:1–30) when some of the Korahites praised God (2 Chr 20:19) or the defeat of the Assyrians in Hezekiah's day (2 Kgs 19:35–36). But the language in the psalm looks beyond those events and evokes the "ideal" Zion of the last days (see note on v. 2).

48:7 ships of Tarshish. Translated "trading ships" in 1 Kgs 10:22; 22:48; 2 Chr 9:21 (see NIV text note); Isa 2:16 (see NIV text note). Tarshish was a faraway land or city somewhere in the central or western Mediterranean (see Jonah 1:3), and "ships of Tarshish" were sturdy vessels capable of traveling that far.

48:8 The presence of "the LORD Almighty" (see note on 46:7) there underscores and guarantees Zion's claim as the place of security.

48:9–11 Mount Zion has no merit on its own. It is the great mountain celebrated in this psalm only because God chose to place his name there, to locate his temple there, to dwell there. His righteous judgments emanate from there (v. 11). Because of this, God's people meditate within the temple there (v. 9), and his praise extends to the "ends of the earth" from there (v. 10).

48:9 meditate. Or "ponder, think about," different from the Hebrew word in 1:2 (see note there). **unfailing love.** God's covenant love for his people (see note on 6:4).

48:13 tell of them. The memory of this great city's strength is to be kept alive for following generations (see note on 44:1).

Ashtaroth (in northern Jordan) with its towers as portrayed by the eighth-century BC Assyrian king who captured it. The psalmist encourages readers to "Walk about Zion ... count her towers" (Ps 48:12).

Kim Walton, taken at the British Museum

Psalm 49[a]

For the director of music. Of the Sons of Korah. A psalm.

[1] Hear this, all you peoples;[h]
listen, all who live in this world,[i]
[2] both low and high,
rich and poor alike:
[3] My mouth will speak words of wisdom;[j]
the meditation of my heart will give you understanding.[k]
[4] I will turn my ear to a proverb;[l]
with the harp I will expound my riddle:[m]

[5] Why should I fear[n] when evil days come,
when wicked deceivers surround me—
[6] those who trust in their wealth[o]
and boast of their great riches?
[7] No one can redeem the life of another
or give to God a ransom for them—
[8] the ransom for a life is costly,
no payment is ever enough—[p]

49:1 [h] Ps 78:1 [i] Ps 33:8
49:3 [j] Ps 37:30 [k] Ps 119:130
49:4 [l] Ps 78:2 [m] Nu 12:8
49:5 [n] Ps 23:4
49:6 [o] Job 31:24
49:8 [p] Mt 16:26

[a] In Hebrew texts 49:1-20 is numbered 49:2-21.

Ps 49 *The Wise Die, the Foolish and the Senseless Also Perish.* This last psalm of the sons of Korah in Book II is a wisdom psalm that reflects on the fate of the wicked, like Pss 37; 39. It is more focused than Pss 37; 39: it affirms that the godly should not envy the prosperity of the wicked because all people die and cannot take their wealth with them, and because God redeems the faithful to himself. It also does not echo the pessimism of Ps 39. It is a word of instruction that would have emanated from Zion and the temple, so it continues the string of psalms that focus on these themes (see introduction to Ps 48). On wisdom psalms, see introduction to Ps 34.

The psalm begins with the psalmist's announcement that he has important things to say (vv. 1–4), followed by his assertions that no one should envy the wicked, because they die, as all people do, and cannot take their wealth with them (vv. 5–11). He makes the point again in vv. 13–19, this time adding that God does redeem the righteous (v. 15). Two pithy refrains, in proverbial form, summarize the psalm's main points (vv. 12,20).

49:3 My mouth will speak. The psalmist announces that he has important things to say, as did David in Ps 36, the psalmist of Ps 45, and Asaph in Ps 78.

49:4 proverb. A short, compact saying that is the basic building block of wisdom literature (see Introduction to Proverbs: Literary Features, 3). Solomon uttered 3,000 proverbs (1 Kgs 4:32), hundreds of which are recorded in the book of Proverbs (Prov 1:1,6). Other examples include Eccl 12:9; Ezek 12:22–23; 16:44; 18:2–3.

49:7 redeem ... ransom. No one can buy their way into immortality, no matter how wealthy they are (cf. v. 6); all persons will die—the rich and the poor (v. 2), the wise and the foolish (v. 10). Not even the laws of redemption (Exod 21:30; Lev 25:45–47) were enough to ransom the wicked; only God could do this (v. 15). Jesus' parable about the rich fool makes essentially the same point (Luke 12:16–21).

49:9 [q]Ps 22:29; 89:48
49:10 [r]Ecc 2:16 [s]Ecc 2:18,21
49:11 [t]Ge 4:17; Dt 3:14
49:13 [u]Lk 12:20
49:14 [v]Job 24:19; Ps 9:17 [w]Da 7:18; Mal 4:3; 1Co 6:2; Rev 2:26
49:15 [x]Ps 56:13; Hos 13:14 [y]Ps 73:24
49:17 [z]Ps 17:14; 1Ti 6:7
49:18 [a]Dt 29:19; Lk 12:19
49:19 [b]Ge 15:15 [c]Job 33:30
49:20 [d]Ecc 3:19
50:1 [e]Jos 22:22 [f]Ps 113:3

9 so that they should live on[q] forever
and not see decay.
10 For all can see that the wise die,[r]
that the foolish and the senseless also perish,
leaving their wealth to others.[s]
11 Their tombs will remain their houses[a] forever,
their dwellings for endless generations,
though they had[b] named[t] lands after themselves.

12 People, despite their wealth, do not endure;
they are like the beasts that perish.

13 This is the fate of those who trust in themselves,[u]
and of their followers, who approve their sayings.[c]
14 They are like sheep and are destined to die;[v]
death will be their shepherd
(but the upright will prevail[w] over them in the morning).
Their forms will decay in the grave,
far from their princely mansions.
15 But God will redeem me from the realm of the dead;[x]
he will surely take me to himself.[y]
16 Do not be overawed when others grow rich,
when the splendor of their houses increases;
17 for they will take nothing with them when they die,
their splendor will not descend with them.[z]
18 Though while they live they count themselves blessed—[a]
and people praise you when you prosper—
19 they will join those who have gone before them,[b]
who will never again see the light[c] of life.

20 People who have wealth but lack understanding
are like the beasts that perish.[d]

Psalm 50

A psalm of Asaph.

1 The Mighty One, God, the LORD,[e]
speaks and summons the earth
from the rising of the sun to where it sets.[f]

[a] *11* Septuagint and Syriac; Hebrew *In their thoughts their houses will remain* [b] *11* Or *generations, / for they have* [c] *13* The Hebrew has *Selah* (a word of uncertain meaning) here and at the end of verse 15.

49:10 all can see. The practical nature of wisdom is evident: these truths are available for all to see, i.e., it doesn't take any special genius to know them. **leaving their wealth to others.** Eccl 2:18,21 affirms this common-sense truth.

49:12 they are like the beasts that perish. This short, proverbial saying captures the obvious point the psalm makes elsewhere: wealth does nothing for a person when life is over (v. 20).

49:14 death will be their shepherd. Similar imagery occurs in Canaanite mythology: the god Mot, whose name means "Death," boasted of devouring and consuming his adversaries. One Canaanite text even warns, "Do not approach divine Mot, lest he put you like a lamb into his mouth." This starkly contrasts with the Lord, who is the Shepherd for all who trust in him (see Ps 23 and note on 23:1).

49:15 God will redeem me. The psalmist is confident that God will rescue him from death (see note on 6:5 ["grave"]) and cause him to live; this likely refers to life after death (see note on 16:9–11; cf. 56:13; Hos 13:14). **take me to himself.** Ps 73:24 also makes this point; it is reminiscent of how God took Enoch and Elijah to be with him (Gen 5:24; 2 Kgs 2:1,11–12).

49:19 light of life. See also 56:13; Job 33:28,30; Isa 53:11; John 8:12.

49:20 like the beasts that perish. See note on v. 12.

Ps 50 *Sacrifice Thank Offerings to God, Fulfill Your Vows.* This is a rare psalm because it features God speaking directly to humans (it is more common for psalmists to speak to God or to others about God). It might be called a "prophetic exhortation." Its subject matter is properly understanding sacrifice: sacrifices are not favors that people bestow upon God or rituals that he needs in order to survive, which is what some people seem to have thought. Rather, sacrifices should be responses of gratitude to God for who he is and what he has done for his people. God desires attitudes of thanksgiving, not mere ritual. With its reference

[2]From Zion, perfect in beauty,[g]
God shines forth.[h]
[3]Our God comes[i]
and will not be silent;
a fire devours before him,[j]
and around him a tempest rages.
[4]He summons the heavens above,
and the earth,[k] that he may judge his people:
[5]"Gather to me this consecrated people,[l]
who made a covenant[m] with me by sacrifice."
[6]And the heavens proclaim[n] his righteousness,
for he is a God of justice.[a,b][o]

[7]"Listen, my people, and I will speak;
I will testify[p] against you, Israel:
I am God, your God.[q]
[8]I bring no charges against you concerning your sacrifices
or concerning your burnt offerings,[r] which are ever before me.
[9]I have no need of a bull[s] from your stall
or of goats from your pens,
[10]for every animal of the forest is mine,
and the cattle on a thousand hills.[t]
[11]I know every bird in the mountains,
and the insects in the fields are mine.
[12]If I were hungry I would not tell you,
for the world[u] is mine, and all that is in it.
[13]Do I eat the flesh of bulls
or drink the blood of goats?

[14]"Sacrifice thank offerings[v] to God,
fulfill your vows[w] to the Most High,
[15]and call[x] on me in the day of trouble;
I will deliver you, and you will honor[y] me."

50:2 [g]Ps 48:2 [h]Dt 33:2; Ps 80:1
50:3 [i]Ps 96:13 [j]Ps 97:3; Da 7:10
50:4 [k]Dt 4:26; Isa 1:2
50:5 [l]Ps 30:4 [m]Ex 24:7
50:6 [n]Ps 89:5 [o]Ps 75:7
50:7 [p]Ps 81:8 [q]Ex 20:2
50:8 [r]Ps 40:6; Hos 6:6
50:9 [s]Ps 69:31
50:10 [t]Ps 104:24
50:12 [u]Ex 19:5
50:14 [v]Heb 13:15 [w]Dt 23:21
50:15 [x]Ps 81:7 [y]Ps 22:23

[a] *6* With a different word division of the Hebrew; Masoretic Text *for God himself is judge* [b] *6* The Hebrew has *Selah* (a word of uncertain meaning) here.

to Zion in v. 2 as the place from which God speaks, the psalm fits well here, following a string of psalms of Zion (see introduction to Ps 48). And with its references to sacrifices of thanksgiving (vv. 14,23), it anticipates David's reflection on proper sacrifice in 51:16–17.

The psalm begins with God summoning heaven and earth and his covenant people to listen to his words (vv. 1–6). He then indicts the people for failing to understand the proper meaning of sacrifice and urges gratitude (vv. 7–15). He concludes by indicting the wicked (vv. 16–21) and once again upholding the importance of giving thanks (vv. 22–23).

50 title Asaph. Pss 73–83 are also psalms of Asaph (see note on Ps 73 title). This psalm is likely separated out from the others because of its ties with its immediate neighboring psalms (see introduction to Ps 50).

50:2 Zion. See introduction to Ps 48.

50:4 heavens ... earth. God calls them as witnesses to the charge that he is bringing, as Moses did in his day (Deut 30:19; 31:28). This evokes images of court proceedings (vv. 7,21).

50:6 the heavens proclaim his righteousness. See the similar affirmations in 19:1; 97:6.

50:7–15 God delivers his indictment: his people do not understand sacrifice or the essence of relationship with him. He rejects the notion that sacrifices somehow make God indebted to those that bring them. In reality, God does not need sacrifices (vv. 9–13). What he desires far more are offerings from a thankful heart, vows offered voluntarily and joyfully to him, genuine prayers of petition (vv. 14–15). Similar passages include 1 Sam 15:22; Hos 6:6; Amos 5:21–24. See notes on vv. 8,14; 40:6.

50:8 sacrifices. A broad term covering any of the various types of sacrifices offered up to God (see "Major Old Testament Offerings and Sacrifices," p. 197). **burnt offerings.** One of the five major offerings (Lev 1:1—6:7): burnt (see note on Lev 1:3–17); grain (see note on Lev 2:1); fellowship (see note on Lev 3:1); sin (see note on Lev 4:1—5:13); and guilt (see note on Lev 5:14—6:7).

50:14 Of the five major offerings (see note on v. 8), the fellowship offering was the only one that allowed the worshiper to partake of the communal meal associated with it (Lev 7:11–38). There were three types of fellowship offerings (all voluntary): thank offerings—brought in thanksgiving to God for any reason; votive offerings—brought to fulfill a vow; or freewill offerings—brought to express love and worship of the Lord. Fellowship offerings symbolized communion or peace with God. For this reason, God is saying here that he prefers expressions of thanksgiving and fellowship rather than rituals that focus on the worshiper's sins.

50:16 [z] Isa 29:13
50:17 [a] Ne 9:26; Ro 2:21-22
50:18 [b] Ro 1:32; 1Ti 5:22
50:19 [c] Ps 10:7; 52:2
50:20 [d] Mt 10:21
50:21 [e] Ecc 8:11; Isa 42:14 [f] Ps 90:8
50:22 [g] Job 8:13; Ps 9:17 [h] Ps 7:2
50:23 [i] Ps 91:16
51:1 [j] Ac 3:19 [k] Isa 43:25; Col 2:14
51:2 [l] 1Jn 1:9 [m] Heb 9:14
51:3 [n] Isa 59:12
51:4 [o] Ge 20:6; Lk 15:21

16 But to the wicked person, God says:

"What right have you to recite my laws
or take my covenant on your lips?[z]
17 You hate my instruction
and cast my words behind[a] you.
18 When you see a thief, you join[b] with him;
you throw in your lot with adulterers.
19 You use your mouth for evil
and harness your tongue to deceit.[c]
20 You sit and testify against your brother[d]
and slander your own mother's son.
21 When you did these things and I kept silent,[e]
you thought I was exactly[a] like you.
But I now arraign you
and set my accusations[f] before you.

22 "Consider this, you who forget God,[g]
or I will tear you to pieces, with no one to rescue you:[h]
23 Those who sacrifice thank offerings honor me,
and to the blameless[b] I will show my salvation.[i]"

Psalm 51[c]

For the director of music. A psalm of David. When the prophet Nathan came to him after David had committed adultery with Bathsheba.

1 Have mercy on me, O God,
according to your unfailing love;
according to your great compassion
blot out[j] my transgressions.[k]
2 Wash away[l] all my iniquity
and cleanse[m] me from my sin.

3 For I know my transgressions,
and my sin is always before me.[n]
4 Against you, you only, have I sinned
and done what is evil in your sight;[o]

[a] *21* Or *thought the 'I AM' was* [b] *23* Probable reading of the original Hebrew text; the meaning of the Masoretic Text for this phrase is uncertain. [c] In Hebrew texts 51:1-19 is numbered 51:3-21.

50:19 deceit. See note on 52:2.
50:21 arraign ... accusations. See note on v. 4.
50:22 Consider. Or "understand." This key word links Ps 50 to Ps 49, which ends with a Hebrew word of the same three Hebrew letters (49:20, "understanding"). In Ps 49, people who pursue wealth lack understanding; in Ps 50, God calls those who forget him to "understand" that thankfulness and relationship are more important than meaningless sacrifices.
Ps 51 *Cleanse Me From My Sin, O God.* In what may be the most deeply passionate and transparent psalm of confession in the Psalter, David pours out his heart to God, asking for forgiveness after Nathan the prophet had exposed his sins against Bathsheba and Uriah. It is written from David's perspective before he had experienced forgiveness. This contrasts with another great confession, Ps 32, which speaks of the delight and sense of release after sin is confessed and forgiven. The ancient church identified Ps 50 as one of seven penitential psalms (the others: Pss 6; 32; 38; 102; 130; 143). This psalm is the first of a string of Davidic psalms in Book II: Pss 51–65; 68–70. It logically follows a psalm that deals with proper sacrifices (50:8–15,23; 51:16–19).
51 title The title refers to the events recounted in 2 Sam 11–12. It is the sixth psalm with a "historical" title connecting it with events in David's life (see note on Ps 3 title) and the first in a sequence of eight in Book II: Pss 51; 52; 54; 56; 57; 59; 60; 63.
51:1–2 David is completely transparent; he casts himself on God's mercy from the outset and names his sins, not hiding them or making excuses for them. **transgressions ... iniquity ... sin.** See note on 32:5.
51:1 unfailing love. See note on 6:4. David knows that God's unfailing, covenantal love is the basis for God's mercy. **compassion.** A plural noun in Hebrew; the singular refers to the womb, usually connoting the tender care one gives to an infant in its most vulnerable state. It is a very rich word, rooted in tenderness and mercy, and David knows that God is compassionate to the truly repentant. **blot out.** A beautiful image of forgiveness (v. 9; cf. Isa 43:25).
51:4 Against you, you only, have I sinned. David's declaration that his sin is against God alone is startling in light of its terrible effects: his abuse of Bathsheba, the death of Uriah, and the death of his own child. The Bible does not deny that sin has dreadful consequences and can

so you are right in your verdict
and justified when you judge.[p]
[5] Surely I was sinful[q] at birth,
sinful from the time my mother conceived me.
[6] Yet you desired faithfulness even in the womb;
you taught me wisdom[r] in that secret place.[s]
[7] Cleanse me with hyssop,[t] and I will be clean;
wash me, and I will be whiter than snow.[u]
[8] Let me hear joy and gladness;[v]
let the bones you have crushed rejoice.
[9] Hide your face from my sins[w]
and blot out all my iniquity.

[10] Create in me a pure heart,[x] O God,
and renew a steadfast spirit within me.[y]
[11] Do not cast me from your presence
or take your Holy Spirit[z] from me.
[12] Restore to me the joy of your salvation[a]
and grant me a willing spirit, to sustain me.

[13] Then I will teach transgressors your ways,[b]
so that sinners will turn back to you.[c]
[14] Deliver me from the guilt of bloodshed,[d] O God,
you who are God my Savior,[e]
and my tongue will sing of your righteousness.[f]
[15] Open my lips, Lord,[g]
and my mouth will declare your praise.
[16] You do not delight in sacrifice,[h] or I would bring it;
you do not take pleasure in burnt offerings.

51:4 [p] Ro 3:4*
51:5 [q] Job 14:4
51:6 [r] Pr 2:6 [s] Ps 15:2
51:7 [t] Lev 14:4; Heb 9:19 [u] Isa 1:18
51:8 [v] Isa 35:10
51:9 [w] Jer 16:17
51:10 [x] Ps 78:37; Ac 15:9 [y] Eze 18:31
51:11 [z] Eph 4:30
51:12 [a] Ps 13:5
51:13 [b] Ac 9:21-22 [c] Ps 22:27
51:14 [d] 2Sa 12:9 [e] Ps 25:5 [f] Ps 35:28
51:15 [g] Ps 9:14
51:16 [h] 1Sa 15:22; Ps 40:6

cause untold suffering. But David's perspective here is the same that he articulated when Nathan confronted him with his sin: "I have sinned against the LORD" (2 Sam 12:13). In both cases, David recognized the deeper truth that, ultimately, all sin is a grievous offense against God. Indeed, when considering the admittedly terrible effects of sin on the human level, these are insignificant when compared to the rupture that sin causes in the divine-human relationship. Because of this, David can assert that his sin is against God alone (cf. Gen 39:6–9). **so you are right ... when you judge.** Paul quotes this from the Septuagint (the pre-Christian Greek translation of the OT) in making a point about God's righteousness (Rom 3:4).

51:5 David could not have committed sinful acts at birth, let alone at conception. Thus, his assertions here show that the sinful nature of humans, inherited from Adam's sin, is passed down generation to generation and that all humans do act upon this and sin (Rom 3:23). **sinful from the time my mother conceived me.** David, like all human beings, had a sinful nature at his conception; the act of conception is not sinful. See also 58:3; Gen 8:21; John 9:34; Eph 2:3.

51:6 womb. This is not the normal word for "womb" (see note on v. 1). It is parallel with "secret place." David is making the point that even from conception, God desires faithfulness and wisdom; obviously, these are not worked out in life until later. The words "secret place" can also refer to a person's own inner self, where faithfulness and wisdom are nurtured.

51:7 hyssop. A plant (also known as "marjoram") with hairy leaves that can hold liquids. It was used to cleanse those who were ceremonially unclean by dipping the leaves in water and sprinkling the water over those who were unclean (Lev 14:4; Num 19:18). Such cleansing in the OT points ahead to Christ's greater work of cleansing from all sin (Heb 9:19–28).

51:8 bones you have crushed. The psalmists often speak of torments penetrating to their very bones (e.g., 6:2; 22:14,17; 31:10; 32:3; 34:20; 38:3; 42:10).

51:10 Create. Only God can do this (Gen 1:1; Isa 65:17; Jer 31:22). The word usually connotes God's creating something entirely new. David's point here is that his sin so tainted his heart that he needed a completely new one that only God could give him.

51:11 Holy Spirit. He was clearly active in OT times, including filling the lives of believers (Num 27:18; Isa 63:10–11,14; Mic 3:8; Hag 2:5; Zech 7:12). David did not want God's Spirit to leave him the way the Spirit had left Saul (1 Sam 16:14).

51:13–17 David desires to teach others the lessons he has learned and to praise God (vv. 13–15), and he realizes that God wants true repentance from the inside out rather than simply external observances (vv. 16–17).

51:13 teach. As king, David had spiritual responsibilities for the nation (72:1–7,12–14; Deut 17:18–20); he was to be the model of a faithful follower of the Lord. And in this capacity, he was also aware of his status as a teacher (34:11; 72:1; cf. 37). In this case, he was prepared to teach his people out of his own experience as a sinner, having learned from his sins.

51:16 David refers to insincere sacrifice without a proper heart attitude. No sacrifice, on its own, was sufficient for forgiveness. Sacrifice had to be accompanied by a repentant heart. Verse 19 shows that God does delight in proper sacrifices, those offered with a broken and contrite heart (see note on 40:6).

51:17 [i]Ps 34:18
51:18 [j]Ps 102:16; Isa 51:3
51:19 [k]Ps 4:5 [l]Ps 66:13 [m]Ps 66:15
52:Title [n]1Sa 22:9
52:1 [o]Ps 94:4
52:2 [p]Ps 50:19 [q]Ps 57:4
52:3 [r]Jer 9:5
52:4 [s]Ps 120:2,3
52:5 [t]Isa 22:19 [u]Pr 2:22 [v]Ps 27:13

17 My sacrifice, O God, is[a] a broken spirit;
a broken and contrite heart[i]
you, God, will not despise.

18 May it please you to prosper Zion,[j]
to build up the walls of Jerusalem.
19 Then you will delight in the sacrifices of the righteous,[k]
in burnt offerings[l] offered whole;
then bulls[m] will be offered on your altar.

Psalm 52[b]

For the director of music. A *maskil*[c] of David. When Doeg the Edomite[n] had gone to Saul and told him: "David has gone to the house of Ahimelek."

1 Why do you boast of evil, you mighty hero?
Why do you boast[o] all day long,
you who are a disgrace in the eyes of God?
2 You who practice deceit,[p]
your tongue plots destruction;
it is like a sharpened razor.[q]
3 You love evil rather than good,
falsehood[r] rather than speaking the truth.[d]
4 You love every harmful word,
you deceitful tongue![s]

5 Surely God will bring you down to everlasting ruin:
He will snatch you up and pluck[t] you from your tent;
he will uproot[u] you from the land of the living.[v]

[a] *17* Or *The sacrifices of God are* [b] In Hebrew texts 52:1-9 is numbered 52:3-11. [c] Title: Probably a literary or musical term [d] *3* The Hebrew has *Selah* (a word of uncertain meaning) here and at the end of verse 5.

51:17 broken and contrite. Renewed from within, purged of any self-righteousness.
51:18–19 David concludes by asking God for blessing on Zion and vowing to offer proper sacrifices in due time.
51:18 Zion. This continues the interest in this place found in the preceding psalms (see introduction to Ps 50; see also notes on 2:6; 9:11). **build up the walls.** Many commentators take this to refer to rebuilding the walls of Jerusalem after the Babylonians had razed the city and exiled the people (hundreds of years after David). But one could understand David to be speaking metaphorically here: as king, he was acutely aware of God's protection of him and the people (e.g., 5:11; 12:5,7; 41:2). He knew that his sins affected not just him, but also the nation (2 Sam 24:17; 1 Chr 21:17). Ezra speaks metaphorically of a "wall of protection" in Judah and Jerusalem (Ezra 9:9), and David could be thinking in the same mode: his sin "broke down" the protection that God offered Jerusalem—protection that was much more than a mere physical wall (e.g., 2 Kgs 19:35–36)—and he could be asking God to restore the damage that his sin had caused.
51:19 sacrifices of the righteous. God delights in sacrifices that his people offer with proper motives and repentant hearts. See notes on v. 16; 50:7–15.
Ps 52 *Why Do You Boast of Evil?* David confronts an arrogant and cruel enemy, Doeg the Edomite, who had killed many innocent people (see note on Ps 52 title). He aims his words at a single person, echoing God's words in 50:18–22. "Trusted in his great wealth" (v. 7) duplicates how Ps 49 emphasizes the false hopes that people place in wealth. This is the first in a sequence of psalms in which David's enemies feature prominently and in which he finds himself crying out for help (Pss 52–64). Several of these psalms are from his days before he became king, as Saul was pursuing him, seeking his life (Pss 52; 54; 56; 57; 59).

The first two sections of the psalm address Doeg directly, the first condemning him for loving evil and not good (vv. 1–4) and the second calling for his ruin (vv. 5–7). David concludes by introducing his own faithfulness to God, in sharp contrast to Doeg (vv. 8–9).
52 title This is the seventh psalm with a "historical" title connecting it with events in David's life (see note on Ps 3 title). It is the second in a sequence of eight psalms with historical titles in Book II (see note on Ps 51 title). **Doeg the Edomite.** One of King Saul's shepherds; he cruelly massacred 85 priests at Nob at Saul's order, along with the rest of the town, because their leader Ahimelek aided David (1 Sam 21:7; 22:6–23).
52:2 deceit. Far more than slightly shading the truth now and then; this identifies a fraudulent, scheming person who plots all manner of evil. Doeg's deceit led to the slaughter of the 85 priests (see note on Ps 52 title; see also 32:2; 50:19; 101:7).
52:5 God will bring you down to everlasting ruin. Doeg's fate is in the hands of God. As one who trusts in his wealth (see notes on 39:6; 49:7; see also introduction to Ps 49), Doeg will suffer the same dire fate as the wealthy in Ps 49.

[6]The righteous will see and fear;
they will laugh[w] at you, saying,
[7]"Here now is the man
who did not make God his stronghold
but trusted in his great wealth[x]
and grew strong by destroying others!"

[8]But I am like an olive tree[y]
flourishing in the house of God;
I trust[z] in God's unfailing love
for ever and ever.
[9]For what you have done I will always praise you[a]
in the presence of your faithful people.
And I will hope in your name,
for your name is good.[b]

Psalm 53[a]

53:1-6pp — Ps 14:1-7

For the director of music. According to *mahalath*.[b] A *maskil*[c] of David.

[1]The fool[c] says in his heart,
"There is no God."[d]
They are corrupt, and their ways are vile;
there is no one who does good.

[2]God looks down from heaven[e]
on all mankind
to see if there are any who understand,
any who seek God.[f]
[3]Everyone has turned away, all have become corrupt;
there is no one who does good,
not even one.[g]

[4]Do all these evildoers know nothing?

They devour my people as though eating bread;
they never call on God.
[5]But there they are, overwhelmed with dread,
where there was nothing to dread.[h]
God scattered the bones[i] of those who attacked you;
you put them to shame, for God despised them.

[6]Oh, that salvation for Israel would come out of Zion!
When God restores his people,
let Jacob rejoice and Israel be glad!

52:6 [w]Job 22:19; Ps 37:34; 40:3
52:7 [x]Ps 49:6
52:8 [y]Jer 11:16 [z]Ps 13:5
52:9 [a]Ps 30:12 [b]Ps 54:6
53:1 [c]Ps 14:1-7; Ro 3:10 [d]Ps 10:4
53:2 [e]Ps 33:13 [f]2Ch 15:2
53:3 [g]Ro 3:10-12*
53:5 [h]Lev 26:17 [i]Eze 6:5

[a] In Hebrew texts 53:1-6 is numbered 53:2-7. [b] Title: Probably a musical term [c] Title: Probably a literary or musical term

52:8 olive tree. Has an average lifespan of 500 years. **house of God.** See note on 5:7. **I trust in God's unfailing love.** David affirms his trust in God's love and vows to praise him. **unfailing love.** See note on 6:4.

Ps 53 *The Fool Says in His Heart, "There Is No God."* This psalm is almost identical to Ps 14, but it fits its present context well, dealing as it does with an arrogant fool very much like Doeg the Edomite (see Ps 52 and notes; see also introduction to Ps 14).

53:1–5a See notes on 14:1–4.

53:5b–d Here, instead of speaking of God's presence among the righteous and his defense of the poor (as in 14:5b–6), David declares God's overwhelming victory over any fool who would oppose him. This reflects 52:5–7; the juxtaposition of the two psalms shows Doeg, the arrogant and cruel mass murderer, to be the type of fool whom God promised to crush.

53:6 See note on 14:7.

54:1 [j]Ps 20:1 [k]2Ch 20:6
54:2 [l]Ps 5:1; 55:1
54:3 [m]Ps 86:14 [n]Ps 40:14 [o]Ps 36:1
54:4 [p]Ps 118:7 [q]Ps 41:12
54:5 [r]Ps 94:23 [s]Ps 89:49; 143:12
54:6 [t]Ps 50:14 [u]Ps 52:9
54:7 [v]Ps 34:6 [w]Ps 59:10
55:1 [x]Ps 27:9; 61:1
55:2 [y]Ps 66:19 [z]Ps 77:3; Isa 38:14
55:3 [a]2Sa 16:6-8; Ps 17:9 [b]Ps 71:11

Psalm 54[a]

For the director of music. With stringed instruments. A *maskil*[b] of David. When the Ziphites had gone to Saul and said, "Is not David hiding among us?"

1 Save me, O God, by your name;[j]
vindicate me by your might.[k]
2 Hear my prayer, O God;[l]
listen to the words of my mouth.

3 Arrogant foes are attacking me;[m]
ruthless people are trying to kill me[n]—
people without regard for God.[c][o]

4 Surely God is my help;[p]
the Lord is the one who sustains me.[q]

5 Let evil recoil[r] on those who slander me;
in your faithfulness[s] destroy them.

6 I will sacrifice a freewill offering[t] to you;
I will praise your name, LORD, for it is good.[u]
7 You have delivered me[v] from all my troubles,
and my eyes have looked in triumph on my foes.[w]

Psalm 55[d]

For the director of music. With stringed instruments. A *maskil*[b] of David.

1 Listen to my prayer, O God,
do not ignore my plea;[x]
2 hear me and answer me.[y]
My thoughts trouble me and I am distraught[z]
3 because of what my enemy is saying,
because of the threats of the wicked;
for they bring down suffering on me[a]
and assail me in their anger.[b]

[a] In Hebrew texts 54:1-7 is numbered 54:3-9. [b] Title: Probably a literary or musical term [c] *3* The Hebrew has *Selah* (a word of uncertain meaning) here. [d] In Hebrew texts 55:1-23 is numbered 55:2-24.

Ps 54 *Surely God Is My Help.* In the previous two psalms, David deals with enemies, named (Doeg, Ps 52 title) and unnamed (the fool and the evildoer: 53:1,4). He has another set of enemies in view in this psalm: the Ziphites, who betrayed David to Saul (1 Sam 23:19; 26:1). He begins with typical petitions (vv. 1–2) and then turns his attention to arrogant enemies (vv. 3,5). The psalm's central affirmation is that God is David's "help" (v. 4; see note there), followed by a concluding vow to praise and sacrifice (vv. 6–7). It is part of the continuing sequence of psalms dealing with David's enemies (see introduction to Ps 52).

54 title This is the eighth psalm with a "historical" title connecting it with events in David's life (see note on Ps 3 title). It is also the third in a sequence of eight psalms with historical titles in Book II (see note on Ps 51 title). **Ziphites.** Ziph was a town southeast of Hebron in Judah (Josh 15:55); the Desert of Ziph was a desolate area to the east, and it is the region where David fled with 600 men when Saul was seeking to kill him (1 Sam 23:14–16). On two occasions, the Ziphites attempted to betray David by revealing his location to Saul (1 Sam 23:19; 26:1). The psalm title refers to the first of these betrayals.

54:1 by your name. God's name here represents his power (see the parallel "your might" in the next line). **vindicate me.** See note on 43:1.

54:4 help. Stands at the exact structural midpoint (see note on 100:3 ["his people"]). This emphasizes the core truth that God is David's reliable source of help and sustenance in the face of whatever hostile enemies he might face. **the Lord.** See note on 8:1.

54:6 David concludes with a vow to praise and sacrifice (50:23; see notes on 50:14; 51:19) to God because God has delivered him. As in many psalms, such a vow is written from the perspective that God already has answered the prayer, even if in actual time and space the answer is yet to come. **freewill offering.** A type of fellowship offering (Lev 7:16; see note on Ps 50:14). It was completely voluntary and required no special occasion for being offered. David pledges to offer it in thanksgiving for God's deliverance. **your name, LORD.** See note on v. 1.

Ps 55 *My Companion Violates His Covenant.* A psalm of lament in which David finds himself in danger from a former trusted friend. The friend and the circumstances are unknown, but the shock of the betrayal that David expresses is real. It continues the string of psalms preoccupied with David's enemies (see introduction to Ps 52). The psalm does not unfold in an orderly fashion but veers from one topic to another, perhaps reflecting the turmoil in which David finds himself. He is not so upset, however, that he does not to affirm that God is ultimately in control (vv. 16–19,22–23).

[4] My heart is in anguish within me;
the terrors[c] of death have fallen on me.
[5] Fear and trembling[d] have beset me;
horror has overwhelmed me.
[6] I said, "Oh, that I had the wings of a dove!
I would fly away and be at rest.
[7] I would flee far away
and stay in the desert;[a]
[8] I would hurry to my place of shelter,
far from the tempest and storm.[e]"

[9] Lord, confuse the wicked, confound their words,
for I see violence and strife[f] in the city.
[10] Day and night they prowl about on its walls;
malice and abuse are within it.
[11] Destructive forces[g] are at work in the city;
threats and lies[h] never leave its streets.

[12] If an enemy were insulting me,
I could endure it;
if a foe were rising against me,
I could hide.
[13] But it is you, a man like myself,
my companion, my close friend,[i]
[14] with whom I once enjoyed sweet fellowship
at the house of God,[j]
as we walked about
among the worshipers.

[15] Let death take my enemies by surprise;[k]
let them go down alive to the realm of the dead,[l]
for evil finds lodging among them.

[16] As for me, I call to God,
and the LORD saves me.
[17] Evening,[m] morning[n] and noon
I cry out in distress,
and he hears my voice.
[18] He rescues me unharmed
from the battle waged against me,
even though many oppose me.
[19] God, who is enthroned from of old,[o]
who does not change—

55:4 [c] Ps 116:3
55:5 [d] Job 21:6; Ps 119:120
55:8 [e] Isa 4:6
55:9 [f] Jer 6:7
55:11 [g] Ps 5:9 [h] Ps 10:7
55:13 [i] 2Sa 15:12; Ps 41:9
55:14 [j] Ps 42:4
55:15 [k] Ps 64:7 [l] Nu 16:30,33
55:17 [m] Ps 141:2; Ac 3:1 [n] Ps 5:3
55:19 [o] Dt 33:27

[a] 7 The Hebrew has *Selah* (a word of uncertain meaning) here and in the middle of verse 19.

55:4–8 The depths of despair in which David finds himself are clear in vv. 4–5, and he longs passionately to escape far from his troubles, even to the desert (v. 7). See also Jer 9:2–6.
55:6 rest. See note on 62:1.
55:9–11 The wicked seem to have free rein, wreaking havoc everywhere they go (31:13), so David asks the "Lord" (v. 9; see note on 8:1) to oppose them. Habakkuk too questioned God about how and why evil could go unchecked in front of his very eyes (Hab 1:3–4).
55:12–14 As if David's sufferings were not enough by themselves—which he "could endure" (v. 12)—they are made that much worse because they come from a once-trusted "companion" (v. 13), a "close friend" (v. 13; see 31:11; 38:11; 41:9; 88:8,18) with whom he used to enjoy fellowship at "the house of God" (v. 14; see note on 5:7).
55:14 as we walked about. Echoes the nostalgia for God's house that 42:4 expresses.
55:15 In a burst of fury, David asks God to consign all of his enemies to "the realm of the dead" (see note on 6:5 ["grave"]). On such imprecatory prayers, see note on 69:22–28.
55:19 enthroned from of old. See the similar statement in 93:1–2. **who does not change.** Or "those who never change their ways." The Hebrew is ambiguous here: the NIV understands it to mean that God never changes (Jas 1:17), but the phrase could also refer to stubborn

55:19 [p]Ps 78:59
55:20 [q]Ps 7:4 [r]Ps 89:34
55:21 [s]Pr 5:3 [t]Ps 28:3; 57:4; 59:7
55:22 [u]Ps 37:5; Mt 6:25-34; 1Pe 5:7 [v]Ps 37:24
55:23 [w]Ps 73:18 [x]Ps 5:6 [y]Job 15:32; Pr 10:27 [z]Ps 25:2
56:1 [a]Ps 57:1-3
56:2 [b]Ps 57:3 [c]Ps 35:1
56:3 [d]Ps 55:4-5
56:4 [e]Ps 118:6; Heb 13:6
56:5 [f]Ps 41:7

he will hear[p] them and humble them,
because they have no fear of God.

20 My companion attacks his friends;[q]
he violates his covenant.[r]
21 His talk is smooth as butter,
yet war is in his heart;
his words are more soothing than oil,[s]
yet they are drawn swords.[t]

22 Cast your cares on the LORD
and he will sustain you;[u]
he will never let
the righteous be shaken.[v]
23 But you, God, will bring down the wicked
into the pit[w] of decay;
the bloodthirsty and deceitful[x]
will not live out half their days.[y]

But as for me, I trust in you.[z]

Psalm 56[a]

For the director of music. To the tune of "A Dove on Distant Oaks." Of David. A *miktam*.[b] When the Philistines had seized him in Gath.

1 Be merciful to me, my God,
for my enemies are in hot pursuit;[a]
all day long they press their attack.
2 My adversaries pursue me all day long;[b]
in their pride many are attacking me.[c]

3 When I am afraid,[d] I put my trust in you.
4 In God, whose word I praise—
in God I trust and am not afraid.
What can mere mortals do to me?[e]

5 All day long they twist my words;[f]
all their schemes are for my ruin.

[a] In Hebrew texts 56:1-13 is numbered 56:2-14. [b] Title: Probably a literary or musical term

evildoers who do not fear the Lord. **they have no fear of God.** A functional atheism is at work here: for these wicked people, God does not matter; they do not fear him (36:1). In the immediately preceding psalms, David also deals with denying God in the actual atheism of the fool (53:1) and the functional atheism of the arrogant (54:3).

55:20–21 David returns his focus to his betrayer (cf. vv. 12–14).

55:20 violates. Or "profanes." There is an element of the sacred in any covenant, and this betrayal was more than a social breach; rather, it represented profaning a sacred oath. **his covenant.** Not specified; it probably refers to a person-to-person oath like the one between David and Jonathan (1 Sam 18:3) rather than one of the great covenants that God established (e.g., Abrahamic or Mosaic covenants). "His" covenant (as opposed to "God's" covenant) supports this. The betrayer remains anonymous.

55:22–23 David steps back from his own troubles and assumes the mantle of teacher again (see note on 51:13), urging his listeners to rely completely on the Lord (v. 22) and then urging God one more time to judge the wicked (v. 23; see v. 15 and note there).

Ps 56 *When I Am Afraid, I Put My Trust in You.* The key to this psalm revolves around trusting in God, a repeated refrain (vv. 3–4,10–11) that picks up from where Ps 55 leaves off (55:23b). The opening appeal to God (vv. 1–2) is balanced by the concluding vow to praise him (vv. 12–13). The refrains bracket David's actual petitions that God turn back his enemies (vv. 5–9).

56 title This is the ninth psalm with a "historical" title connecting it to events in David's life (see note on Ps 3 title). It is also the fourth in a sequence of eight psalms with historical titles in Book II (see note on Ps 51 title)—and part of the ongoing sequence of psalms dealing with David's enemies (see introduction to Ps 52). The historical backdrop is the episode in 1 Sam 21:10–15.

56:1 enemies. Or "mortals." The word normally refers to humanity in its weak, frail condition (see note on 8:4 ["mankind"]). Its use here may indicate that David feels so defeated that even frail enemies are overwhelming him. But his mood changes shortly (see note on v. 4).

56:4 mere mortals. Or "flesh." The answer to the question in this verse is that such mortals can do nothing to David; compared to God they are powerless. See note on v. 1.

[6] They conspire,[g] they lurk,
they watch my steps,
hoping to take my life.[h]
[7] Because of their wickedness do not[a] let them escape;
in your anger, God, bring the nations down.[i]

[8] Record my misery;
list my tears on your scroll[b] —
are they not in your record?[j]
[9] Then my enemies will turn back[k]
when I call for help.[l]
By this I will know that God is for me.[m]

[10] In God, whose word I praise,
in the LORD, whose word I praise—
[11] in God I trust and am not afraid.
What can man do to me?

[12] I am under vows[n] to you, my God;
I will present my thank offerings to you.
[13] For you have delivered me from death[o]
and my feet from stumbling,
that I may walk before God
in the light of life.[p]

56:6 [g] Ps 59:3 [h] Ps 71:10
56:7 [i] Ps 36:12; 55:23
56:8 [j] Mal 3:16
56:9 [k] Ps 9:3 [l] Ps 102:2 [m] Ro 8:31
56:12 [n] Ps 50:14
56:13 [o] Ps 116:8 [p] Job 33:30
57:1 [q] Ps 2:12 [r] Ps 17:8 [s] Isa 26:20

Psalm 57[c]

57:7-11pp — Ps 108:1-5

For the director of music. To the tune of "Do Not Destroy." Of David. A *miktam*.[d]
When he had fled from Saul into the cave.

[1] Have mercy on me, my God, have mercy on me,
for in you I take refuge.[q]
I will take refuge in the shadow of your wings[r]
until the disaster has passed.[s]

[a] 7 Probable reading of the original Hebrew text; Masoretic Text does not have *do not.* [b] 8 Or *misery; / put my tears in your wineskin* [c] In Hebrew texts 57:1-11 is numbered 57:2-12. [d] Title: Probably a literary or musical term

56:7 bring the nations down. Echoes 55:23. God is not against any and all nations, but only those opposing him (2:1–3). David vows to praise God "among the nations" in the very next psalm (57:9), and Ps 67 has a welcoming perspective that the nations should respond to God.
56:8 Record my misery. The Bible often says that God keeps records (e.g., 87:6; 139:16; Exod 32:32–33; Neh 13:14; Dan 7:10; Mal 3:16). Such references accommodate human language to make vivid word pictures. **list my tears on your scroll.** See NIV text note; either translation presents a vivid word picture. The imagery thus suggests that David's abundant tears would constantly be with God as a reminder of his misery, just as the written record of his misery was.
56:11 man. All of humanity generically. The emphasis changes slightly from v. 4, where "mere mortals" cannot harm David, to a broader assertion (in the form of a rhetorical question) that no one can do him damage.
56:12 vows … thank offerings. See note on 50:14.
56:13 light of life. Ps 49:19 uses this beautiful metaphor—as does Elihu, one of Job's questioners (Job 33:28,30)—to contrast with the pit or the grave (49:14). Isaiah speaks of the servant of the Lord, i.e., the Messiah, seeing the light of life after his suffering (Isa 53:11).
Ps 57 *Be Exalted, O God, Above the Heavens.* A psalm of petition that begins as a lament (vv. 1–4,6) and concludes with praise (vv. 5,7–11). It begins a sequence of seven psalms (excluding Ps 58) emphasizing the theme of God as a refuge (see notes on 2:12; 18:1–2). It is also part of the continuing sequence of psalms dealing with David's enemies (see introduction to Ps 52). The psalm shares similarities with Ps 56, which should not be surprising since the historical settings are similar. It begins with David's prayer for deliverance, rooted in his confidence in God (vv. 1–3). His description of the dire straits in which he finds himself (vv. 4,6) is interrupted by a refrain praising God (v. 5). The psalm builds to a crescendo of praise in vv. 7–10 and concludes with the repeated refrain (v. 11).
57 title This is the tenth psalm with a "historical" title connecting it with events in David's life (see note on Ps 3 title). It is also the fifth in a sequence of eight psalms with historical titles in Book II (see note on Ps 51 title). The historical backdrop is most likely the episode in 1 Sam 22:1–2, though it could conceivably be the events in 1 Sam 24.
57:1 shadow of your wings. See note on 36:7.

57:2 [t]Ps 138:8
57:3 [u]Ps 18:9,16 [v]Ps 56:1 [w]Ps 40:11
57:4 [x]Ps 35:17 [y]Ps 55:21; Pr 30:14
57:5 [z]Ps 108:5
57:6 [a]Ps 145:14 [b]Ps 35:7 [c]Ps 7:15; Pr 28:10
57:7 [d]Ps 108:1
57:8 [e]Ps 16:9; 30:12; 150:3
57:10 [f]Ps 36:5; 103:11
57:11 [g]ver 5
58:1 [h]Ps 82:2

2 I cry out to God Most High,
to God, who vindicates me.[t]
3 He sends from heaven and saves me,[u]
rebuking those who hotly pursue me —[a][v]
God sends forth his love and his faithfulness.[w]

4 I am in the midst of lions;[x]
I am forced to dwell among ravenous beasts —
men whose teeth are spears and arrows,
whose tongues are sharp swords.[y]

5 Be exalted, O God, above the heavens;
let your glory be over all the earth.[z]

6 They spread a net for my feet —
I was bowed down[a] in distress.
They dug a pit[b] in my path —
but they have fallen into it themselves.[c]

7 My heart, O God, is steadfast,
my heart is steadfast;[d]
I will sing and make music.
8 Awake, my soul!
Awake, harp and lyre![e]
I will awaken the dawn.

9 I will praise you, Lord, among the nations;
I will sing of you among the peoples.
10 For great is your love, reaching to the heavens;
your faithfulness reaches to the skies.[f]

11 Be exalted, O God, above the heavens;
let your glory be over all the earth.[g]

Psalm 58[b]

For the director of music. To the tune of "Do Not Destroy." Of David. A *miktam*.[c]

1 Do you rulers indeed speak justly?[h]
Do you judge people with equity?

[a] 3 The Hebrew has *Selah* (a word of uncertain meaning) here and at the end of verse 6. [b] In Hebrew texts 58:1-11 is numbered 58:2-12. [c] Title: Probably a literary or musical term

57:2 God Most High. See note on 7:8. **God, who vindicates me.** See note on 43:1.
57:4 lions. See note on 7:2.
57:6 David returns to the subject of his enemies (v. 4), who lay in wait for him. But happily, they are stymied, falling into their own pit (whether figuratively or literally). David speaks in several psalms of his enemies' pits and their nets (here; 9:15; 10:9; 35:7–8; 140:5).
57:7–11 Ps 108 combines these verses of praise with the battle hymn from 60:5–12.
57:8 Awake ... Awake ... awaken. Expresses David's excitement as he anticipates the dawn of his deliverance (Isa 51:9,17; 52:1). **harp and lyre.** See note on 150:3.
57:9 nations. God's love extends to all nations and peoples, not just his own chosen people (Ps 67; Gen 12:3). See note on 56:7.
Ps 58 *Surely There Is a God Who Judges the Earth.* An impassioned cry that God, the righteous Judge, should put right the injustices that wicked and unjust judges perpetrate. It continues assurances in preceding psalms that God is in control, even when it seems the wicked are prevailing (vv. 10–11; cf. 55:23; 56:10–11; 57:2–3), and it is similar to David's vivid language in Ps 57 about his enemies being lions with sharp teeth and arrows (57:4; 58:6–7). It is also part of the ongoing sequence of psalms dealing with David's enemies (see introduction to Ps 52).

David begins by directly addressing the dishonest judges who are perverting justice and meting out violence (vv. 1–2). He then characterizes their wickedness, likening them to venomous snakes (vv. 3–5) and lions (v. 6), and he asks God to mete out proper punishment on them (vv. 6–8). He concludes with confident statements that God will indeed exact vengeance on them, so that people will know that the God of justice is still in control (vv. 9–11).
58:1 rulers. The Hebrew term (*ʾēlîm*) is an infrequent alternate form of the normal Hebrew term for gods (*ʾĕlōhîm*) and usually refers to heavenly beings (89:6; Dan 11:36; see note on Ps 29:1). Here it refers to human "rulers" who have perverted justice and caused evil to spread

[2]No, in your heart you devise injustice,
and your hands mete out violence on the earth.[i]

[3]Even from birth the wicked go astray;
from the womb they are wayward, spreading lies.
[4]Their venom is like the venom of a snake,[j]
like that of a cobra that has stopped its ears,
[5]that will not heed the tune of the charmer,
however skillful the enchanter may be.

[6]Break the teeth in their mouths, O God;[k]
LORD, tear out the fangs of those lions![l]
[7]Let them vanish like water that flows away;[m]
when they draw the bow, let their arrows fall short.[n]
[8]May they be like a slug that melts away as it moves along,
like a stillborn child[o] that never sees the sun.

[9]Before your pots can feel the heat of the thorns[p]—
whether they be green or dry—the wicked will be swept away.[a][q]
[10]The righteous will be glad when they are avenged,[r]
when they dip their feet in the blood of the wicked.[s]
[11]Then people will say,
"Surely the righteous still are rewarded;
surely there is a God who judges the earth."[t]

58:2 [i]Ps 94:20; Mal 3:15
58:4 [j]Ps 140:3; Ecc 10:11
58:6 [k]Ps 3:7 [l]Job 4:10
58:7 [m]Jos 7:5; Ps 112:10 [n]Ps 64:3
58:8 [o]Job 3:16
58:9 [p]Ps 118:12 [q]Pr 10:25
58:10 [r]Ps 64:10; 91:8 [s]Ps 68:23
58:11 [t]Ps 9:8; 18:20
59:1 [u]Ps 143:9
59:2 [v]Ps 139:19
59:3 [w]Ps 56:6

Psalm 59[b]

For the director of music. To the tune of "Do Not Destroy." Of David. A *miktam*.[c] When Saul had sent men to watch David's house in order to kill him.

[1]Deliver me from my enemies, O God;[u]
be my fortress against those who are attacking me.
[2]Deliver me from evildoers
and save me from those who are after my blood.[v]
[3]See how they lie in wait for me!
Fierce men conspire[w] against me
for no offense or sin of mine, LORD.

[a] *9* The meaning of the Hebrew for this verse is uncertain. [b] In Hebrew texts 59:1-17 is numbered 59:2-18.
[c] Title: Probably a literary or musical term

throughout the earth; the references to their birth and the womb in v. 3 confirm that this refers to humans, not gods. Occasionally the term *ʾĕlōhîm* (usually rendered "God" or "gods") also refers to human judges (e.g., Exod 21:6; 22:8–9; see note on Ps 82:1).

58:3 from birth ... from the womb. David, who declared that God desires faithfulness "even in the womb" (51:6), declares that the wicked are not like that: they are "sinful" from birth, like David (51:5). The difference is that David yielded his sinful nature to God and turned away from his sins, while the wicked actively and continually pursue their wicked ways.

58:9 heat of the thorns. The fire of thornbushes used as fuel for cooking (118:12; Eccl 7:6).

58:10 dip their feet in the blood. In a psalm that uses vivid imagery throughout to describe the wicked, this final image is especially vivid, if not disturbing. But it reveals the depth of David's passion against injustice, his desire to see it overturned. The verse—indeed, the entire psalm—instructs us that we should be outraged at evil around us. See the similar language in 68:23; see also notes on 5:9–10; 69:22–28.

Ps 59 *You, God, Are My Fortress.* This is another prayer for deliverance in the face of cruel attacks from David's enemies. It is part of a lengthy sequence of psalms dealing with David's enemies (see introduction to Ps 52) and part of a series of psalms emphasizing God as David's place of refuge (see introduction to Ps 57; see also notes on 2:12; 18:1–2). The title links it with the events of 1 Sam 19:11–18, but it also would be appropriate for any number of crises that David faced. It is divided into two major parts by a repeated refrain in vv. 9–10a and v. 17: David pleads for God to deliver him in the face of fierce enemies (vv. 1–10a), and he confidently asserts that God *will* deliver him. David vows to praise God when he answers (vv. 10b–17).

59 title The title refers to the events of 1 Sam 19:11–18. It is the 11th psalm with a "historical" title connecting it with events in David's life (see note on Ps 3 title), and the sixth in a sequence of eight in Book II (see note on Ps 51 title).

59:1 fortress. David's opening cry for deliverance from his enemies also affirms that he knows that God is his source of security (see note on 18:1–2).

59:3–4 offense ... sin ... wrong. The three major words for sin (see note on 32:5). David protests his innocence in the strongest possible terms.

59:4 [x]Ps 35:19,23
59:5 [y]Jer 18:23
59:6 [z]ver 14
59:7 [a]Ps 57:4 [b]Ps 10:11
59:8 [c]Ps 37:13; Pr 1:26 [d]Ps 2:4
59:9 [e]Ps 9:9; 62:2
59:11 [f]Ps 84:9 [g]Dt 4:9 [h]Ps 106:27
59:12 [i]Ps 10:7 [j]Pr 12:13 [k]Zep 3:11
59:13 [l]Ps 104:35 [m]Ps 83:18
59:15 [n]Job 15:23

4 I have done no wrong, yet they are ready to attack me.[x]
Arise to help me; look on my plight!
5 You, LORD God Almighty,
you who are the God of Israel,
rouse yourself to punish all the nations;
show no mercy to wicked traitors.[a][y]

6 They return at evening,
snarling like dogs,[z]
and prowl about the city.
7 See what they spew from their mouths—
the words from their lips are sharp as swords,[a]
and they think, "Who can hear us?"[b]
8 But you laugh at them, LORD;[c]
you scoff at all those nations.[d]

9 You are my strength, I watch for you;
you, God, are my fortress,[e]
10 my God on whom I can rely.

God will go before me
and will let me gloat over those who slander me.
11 But do not kill them, Lord our shield,[b][f]
or my people will forget.[g]
In your might uproot them
and bring them down.[h]
12 For the sins of their mouths,[i]
for the words of their lips,[j]
let them be caught in their pride.[k]
For the curses and lies they utter,
13 consume them in your wrath,
consume them till they are no more.[l]
Then it will be known to the ends of the earth
that God rules over Jacob.[m]

14 They return at evening,
snarling like dogs,
and prowl about the city.
15 They wander about for food[n]
and howl if not satisfied.

[a] 5 The Hebrew has *Selah* (a word of uncertain meaning) here and at the end of verse 13. [b] 11 Or *sovereign*

59:5 LORD God Almighty. See notes on 8:1; 24:10. **God of Israel.** Just as Baal was the god of the Canaanites and Marduk was the god of the Babylonians. God promised Abraham a special relationship with him and his descendants (Gen 17:7) and reiterated this many times to the people in Moses' day (e.g., Exod 6:7; 19:5–6; Lev 18:2; Deut 1:31; 4:31; 7:6,9,12). He promised Joshua and David this special relationship (Josh 1:5,9; 2 Sam 7:9), and the prophets reiterated it many times (e.g., Isa 40:1; 51:16; 52:6; Jer 7:23; 11:4; 30:22; 31:1; 32:28; Ezek 36:28). This special covenantal relationship between God and his chosen people is the rich backdrop to such terms as "the God of Israel" (here), "your God" and "my people" (50:7). **punish all the nations.** David's concern extends beyond the one-time situation he faced in 1 Sam 19:11–18 (see note on Ps 59 title); he also is aware of his larger role as God's anointed king over Israel and his interactions with other nations (cf. Ps 2).

59:6 dogs. See note on 22:16.

59:7 spew ... sharp as swords. The enemies' words are toxic (cf. 57:4).

59:8 laugh ... scoff. Derisive, scornful laughter (see note on 2:4).

59:9–10 The first refrain wraps up this section of the psalm, affirming God as David's reliable and strong source of refuge.

59:9 watch. See 25:5; 27:14, where David hopes or waits for the Lord; the words are different, but the ideas are related (see notes on 25:5; 27:14).

59:11 shield. See note on 3:3.

59:13 it will be known. The idea of God's deeds being known far and wide parallels the conclusion of the previous psalm (58:11). Scripture affirms this many times (e.g., Exod 8:10; 10:2; Deut 4:35; 29:6; Josh 2:9–11; 4:24). **God rules.** God's position as Jacob's (i.e., Israel's) king is an important motif in the Psalter (see note on 10:16).

59:14 An exact copy of v. 6.

16 But I will sing of your strength,[o]
in the morning[p] I will sing of your love;[q]
for you are my fortress,
my refuge in times of trouble.[r]

17 You are my strength, I sing praise to you;
you, God, are my fortress,
my God on whom I can rely.

Psalm 60[a]

60:5-12pp — Ps 108:6-13

For the director of music. To the tune of "The Lily of the Covenant." A *miktam*[b] of David. For teaching. When he fought Aram Naharaim[c] and Aram Zobah,[d] and when Joab returned and struck down twelve thousand Edomites in the Valley of Salt.

1 You have rejected us,[s] God, and burst upon us;
you have been angry[t] — now restore us![u]
2 You have shaken the land[v] and torn it open;
mend its fractures,[w] for it is quaking.
3 You have shown your people desperate times;[x]
you have given us wine that makes us stagger.[y]
4 But for those who fear you, you have raised a banner
to be unfurled against the bow.[e]
5 Save us and help us with your right hand,[z]
that those you love[a] may be delivered.
6 God has spoken from his sanctuary:
"In triumph I will parcel out Shechem[b]
and measure off the Valley of Sukkoth.

59:16 [o] Ps 21:13 [p] Ps 88:13 [q] Ps 101:1 [r] Ps 46:1
60:1 [s] 2Sa 5:20; Ps 44:9 [t] Ps 79:5 [u] Ps 80:3
60:2 [v] Ps 18:7 [w] 2Ch 7:14
60:3 [x] Ps 71:20 [y] Isa 51:17; Jer 25:16
60:5 [z] Ps 17:7; 108:6 [a] Ps 127:2
60:6 [b] Ge 12:6

[a] In Hebrew texts 60:1-12 is numbered 60:3-14. [b] Title: Probably a literary or musical term [c] Title: That is, Arameans of Northwest Mesopotamia [d] Title: That is, Arameans of central Syria [e] 4 The Hebrew has *Selah* (a word of uncertain meaning) here.

59:17 The second refrain shows David singing God's praises (instead of watching for God, as in v. 9), a fitting conclusion to a prayer for God's help.

Ps 60 *Judah Is My Scepter. Moab Is My Washbasin.* The centerpiece of this psalm, composed for a time of national crisis, is a message from God in which he affirms his sovereignty over all nations and his special relationship with his own people (vv. 6–8). Its historical backdrop is likely the events of 2 Sam 8:1–14 (see note on Ps 60 title). It is part of the continuing sequence of psalms dealing with David's enemies (see introduction to Ps 52) and part of another sequence emphasizing the theme of God as a refuge (see introduction to Ps 57; see also notes on 2:12; 18:1–2). The encouraging words of vv. 5–12 occur again in Ps 108:6–13 (see introduction to Ps 108).

60 title This refers to the events of 2 Sam 8:1–14, when David battled enemies that included Philistines, Moabites, and Edomites, though the number of Edomites slain there is "eighteen thousand" (2 Sam 8:13) and here it is "twelve thousand." The difference may reflect different tallies at different stages of the battle, or it may be simply a mistake in the copying process. This is the 12th psalm with a "historical" title connecting it with events in David's life (see note on Ps 3 title) and the seventh in a sequence of eight in Book II (see note on Ps 51 title). **For teaching.** This expression occurs only here in the psalm titles; it recalls David's decree that people be taught his lament at the deaths of Saul and Jonathan (2 Sam 1:17–18). It may indicate that people should use this psalm as an example of how to pray at any time of national crisis, in the same way that Jesus intended the Lord's Prayer (Matt 6:9–13) to model how Christians should pray.

60:3 wine. God in his anger has made his people drink wine that overwhelms their senses. This may foreshadow the "wine of God's fury" spoken of in Revelation (Rev 14:10; cf. Rev 16:19).

60:4 those who fear you. See note on 19:9. David is speaking on behalf of God's faithful people; he protests their innocence and does not confess sin. **banner.** Served as a rallying point (Isa 5:26; 11:10,12; 13:2; 18:3; 30:17; 49:22; 62:10; Jer 50:2; 51:12,27; cf. Exod 17:15).

60:6 has spoken. Indicates past tense, suggesting that the following message from God is not a response to David's pleas in the psalm but is something God spoke previously. If so, the affirmations in vv. 6–8 hark back to God's giving of the land of Canaan to the Israelites under Joshua, though they also anticipate God's ongoing conflicts with his enemies. **from his sanctuary.** The place where God uttered the message of hope (vv. 6–8) reinforces its impact (see 150:1). This was the tabernacle in David's day and later the temple (see note on 5:7). Within these was the Most Holy Place, in which resided the ark of the covenant, where God was enthroned on the mercy seat (see notes on 18:10; 28:2 ["Most Holy Place"]). With God in his sanctuary, where he belonged, all was well, and the pronouncement from this place was assured. Alternatively, "from his sanctuary" could be rendered "by his holiness," as in Amos 4:2 (cf. Ps 89:35: "by my holiness"). This rendering focuses more on the solemnity of the divine message than on the place from which it emanates. Both renderings emphasize the importance of the divine

60:7 [c] Jos 13:31 [d] Dt 33:17 [e] Ge 49:10
60:8 [f] 2Sa 8:1
60:10 [g] Jos 7:12; Ps 44:9; 108:11
60:11 [h] Ps 146:3
60:12 [i] Nu 24:18; Ps 44:5
61:1 [j] Ps 64:1 [k] Ps 86:6

7 Gilead[c] is mine, and Manasseh is mine;
Ephraim is my helmet,
Judah[d] is my scepter.[e]
8 Moab is my washbasin,
on Edom I toss my sandal;
over Philistia I shout in triumph.[f]"

9 Who will bring me to the fortified city?
Who will lead me to Edom?
10 Is it not you, God, you who have now rejected us
and no longer go out with our armies?[g]
11 Give us aid against the enemy,
for human help is worthless.[h]
12 With God we will gain the victory,
and he will trample down our enemies.[i]

Psalm 61[a]

For the director of music. With stringed instruments. Of David.

1 Hear my cry, O God;[j]
listen to my prayer.[k]

[a] In Hebrew texts 61:1-8 is numbered 61:2-9.

message. **Shechem.** A city west of the Jordan River in the territory of Manasseh near the hill country of Ephraim (Josh 17:7; 20:7); it was where Joshua led the people in a solemn covenant-renewal ceremony, and it symbolized the completion of God's giving the land of Canaan to his people (Josh 24:1,25). **Sukkoth.** A city east of the Jordan River in the territory of Gad (Josh 13:27).
60:7 Gilead. A region east of the Jordan River; the territory of Gad and the Valley of Sukkoth were located there (Josh 22:9,13,15). **Manasseh.** One of the largest tribes in Israel, with territories both east and west of the Jordan River (Josh 13:29–31; 17:1–13). **Ephraim.** One of the two largest tribes in Israel. It was west of the Jordan River (Josh 16:5–10). Both Ephraim and Manasseh were named for Joseph's two sons, so they were sometimes called "the tribes of Joseph" (Josh 17:17). Sometimes "Ephraim" is used to refer to the entire northern kingdom of Israel, as here (e.g., 2 Chr 25:7,10; 28:7; Isa 7:9; Jer 31:18,20; Hos 4:17). **helmet.** Ephraim, representing Israel, would be an important part of the Lord's armor (his helmet) as he marched against his enemies, as Judah would be. **Judah.** The most important tribe of all (along with Levi) since it was the tribe of David and since God promised it royal authority (Gen 49:10; 2 Sam 7:11b–16). Here it represents the southern kingdom. **scepter.** Symbolizes royal authority. See note on 45:6.
60:8 Moab. The Moabites were descended from Lot, Abraham's nephew (Gen 19:37), and were thus distantly related to the Israelites. Their territory was east of the Dead Sea. **Edom.** The Edomites were descended from Esau, Jacob's brother, and thus were also related to the Israelites; their territory was southeast of the Dead Sea (Gen 36:1,8). **toss my sandal.** A gesture of contempt. **Philistia.** The Philistine territory was southwest of Judah along the Mediterranean coast. All three neighbors of Israel were hostile to Israel; for the present context of hostilities, see 2 Sam 8:1–14.
Ps 61 *I Long to Dwell in Your Tent Forever.* David writes as one who is weak and faltering, far from Jerusalem, longing to return to God's sanctuary there. It is similar to the psalmist's plight in Pss 42–43. No

Shechem (Ps 60:6).

[2]From the ends of the earth I call to you,
I call as my heart grows faint;[l]
lead me to the rock[m] that is higher than I.
[3]For you have been my refuge,[n]
a strong tower against the foe.[o]

[4]I long to dwell[p] in your tent forever
and take refuge in the shelter of your wings.[a][q]
[5]For you, God, have heard my vows;[r]
you have given me the heritage of those who fear your name.[s]

[6]Increase the days of the king's life,
his years for many generations.[t]
[7]May he be enthroned in God's presence forever;[u]
appoint your love and faithfulness to protect him.[v]

[8]Then I will ever sing in praise of your name[w]
and fulfill my vows day after day.

Psalm 62[b]

For the director of music. For Jeduthun. A psalm of David.

[1]Truly my soul finds rest[x] in God;
my salvation comes from him.
[2]Truly he is my rock[y] and my salvation;
he is my fortress, I will never be shaken.

[3]How long will you assault me?
Would all of you throw me down—
this leaning wall,[z] this tottering fence?

61:2 [l]Ps 77:3 [m]Ps 18:2
61:3 [n]Ps 62:7 [o]Pr 18:10
61:4 [p]Ps 23:6 [q]Ps 91:4
61:5 [r]Ps 56:12 [s]Ps 86:11
61:6 [t]Ps 21:4
61:7 [u]Ps 41:12 [v]Ps 40:11
61:8 [w]Ps 65:1; 71:22
62:1 [x]Ps 33:20
62:2 [y]Ps 89:26
62:3 [z]Isa 30:13

[a] *4* The Hebrew has *Selah* (a word of uncertain meaning) here. [b] In Hebrew texts 62:1-12 is numbered 62:2-13.

historical setting is specified, but it fits David's time in exile from Jerusalem when his son Absalom usurped his throne (2 Sam 15–17; see Ps 3 and note on Ps 3 title). David begins by calling on God from afar (vv. 1–3). He longs to dwell in God's tent forever because of the rich heritage God has given him (vv. 4–5). He includes a short prayer on behalf of the king (vv. 6–7) and concludes with his vow to praise God in perpetuity (v. 8).

Ps 61 is in the midst of several psalms that emphasize the theme of God as a refuge (see introduction to Ps 57; see also notes on 2:12; 18:1–2). And its location immediately following Ps 60, which affirms Israel's place in God's plan, lends a backdrop to the security David is praying for in this psalm. In Ps 60, he asks God to lead him to victory over Edom (60:9); here he asks God to lead him to the solid rock (v. 2). It is part of the ongoing sequence of psalms dealing with David's enemies (see introduction to Ps 52).

61:2 rock that is higher than I. Possibly Jerusalem, built atop a mountain ridge (cf. Jer 21:13), but v. 3 suggests that it is God himself (see note on 18:2). Ps 48 brings both images together.

61:4 your tent. See notes on 5:7; 15:1. **shelter of your wings.** See note on 36:7.

61:5 vows. See note on 50:14. **heritage.** The heritage (or inheritance) that God gave Israel was the land of Canaan (Deut 1:21; Josh 1:2–3), and those who feared the Lord would remain in the land (Deut 4:40; 11:9). But a special component of those promises was that the king who feared the Lord would reign a long time in Israel (Deut 17:18–20). David's words undoubtedly reflect his consciousness that he was God's chosen king who received this rich heritage.

61:6 Increase the days of the king's life. This prayer for longevity recalls God's promise to David and David's prayer of response (2 Sam 7:16,29), as well as Solomon's prayer for the king (Ps 72:15,17). **generations.** David's concern extends beyond himself; his prayer in v. 7 that the king be enthroned "forever" reinforces this. The Davidic lineage continued unbroken in Judah, leading all the way to the greatest Son of David, Jesus the Messiah (Matt 1:1).

61:7 May he be enthroned. This harks back to God's establishing David as king on Zion, God's holy mountain (2:6). The throne of David and his descendants was, in a very real sense, God's throne, as 1 Chr 28:5 ("the throne of the kingdom of the LORD") and 1 Chr 29:23 ("the throne of the LORD") affirm. That is, David and his descendants were God's "vice-regents," representing God's kingdom on earth.

61:8 vows. See note on 50:14.

Ps 62 *Truly My Soul Finds Rest in God.* In this psalm of trust or confidence, David feels the weight of his enemies' attacks and affirms his trust in God, who is the ultimate source of refuge and rest. It continues the sequence of psalms dealing with David's enemies (see introduction to Ps 52), and it is part of a different string that emphasizes the theme of God as a refuge (see introduction to Ps 57; see also notes on 2:12; 18:1–2). David twice, in a refrain of sorts (vv. 1–2,5–8), affirms God as his source of rest and refuge, which provides the psalm's central theme: the believer can find secure rest in God. This brackets a direct question David poses to his enemies about how long they will persecute him (vv. 3–4). He concludes with a reflection on the fleeting nature of life (vv. 9–10) and an affirmation that God is the ultimate source of power, faithful love, and justice (vv. 11–12).

62 title Jeduthun. See note on Ps 39 title.

62:1 finds rest. Or "waits in silence." The idea here is the security to be found in waiting on the Lord, as in 37:7.

62:2 rock … fortress. See notes on 2:12; 18:1–2.

62:3 How long … ? See note on 13:1,2. **tottering fence.** An indication of David's vulnerability.

62:4 [a]Ps 28:3
62:7 [b]Ps 46:1; 85:9; Jer 3:23
62:8 [c]1Sa 1:15; Ps 42:4; La 2:19
62:9 [d]Ps 39:5,11 [e]Isa 40:15
62:10 [f]Isa 61:8 [g]Job 31:25; 1Ti 6:6-10
62:12 [h]Job 34:11; Mt 16:27

4 Surely they intend to topple me
from my lofty place;
they take delight in lies.
With their mouths they bless,
but in their hearts they curse.[a][a]

5 Yes, my soul, find rest in God;
my hope comes from him.
6 Truly he is my rock and my salvation;
he is my fortress, I will not be shaken.
7 My salvation and my honor depend on God[b];
he is my mighty rock, my refuge.[b]
8 Trust in him at all times, you people;
pour out your hearts to him,[c]
for God is our refuge.

9 Surely the lowborn are but a breath,[d]
the highborn are but a lie.
If weighed on a balance,[e] they are nothing;
together they are only a breath.
10 Do not trust in extortion
or put vain hope in stolen goods;[f]
though your riches increase,
do not set your heart on them.[g]

11 One thing God has spoken,
two things I have heard:
"Power belongs to you, God,
12 and with you, Lord, is unfailing love";
and, "You reward everyone
according to what they have done."[h]

Psalm 63[c]

A psalm of David. When he was in the Desert of Judah.

1 You, God, are my God,
earnestly I seek you;

[a] 4 The Hebrew has *Selah* (a word of uncertain meaning) here and at the end of verse 8. [b] 7 Or / *God Most High is my salvation and my honor* [c] In Hebrew texts 63:1-11 is numbered 63:2-12.

62:5 find rest. See note on v. 1.
62:6 rock ... fortress. See notes on 2:12; 18:1–2.
62:9–10 David takes comfort in the fleeting nature of life and the attendant futility of attempting to rely on ill-gotten gain. Cf. Pss 39; 91; see 37:1; 78:39; 103:14–16; 144:4. This is equally true for the most exalted and the lowest in society.
62:10 riches. See notes on 39:6; 49:7.
62:11 One thing ... two things. Such a "stair step" progression emphasizes the declaration that follows. See Prov 30:15,18,21,29; Amos 1:3,6,9,11,13; 2:1,4,6.
62:12 unfailing love. See note on 6:4. **You reward everyone.** As a just God, the Lord metes out reward and punishment in keeping with people's deeds (Deut 28; Jer 17:10; 32:19; Ezek 18:20). The NT reiterates the principle (1 Cor 3:8; Eph 6:8; cf. Matt 25:31–46).
Ps 63 / *Earnestly Seek You.* As in Ps 62, David expresses his trust in the Lord, but from a different perspective: he speaks to God from the desert, far removed from the sanctuary where he would rather be (vv. 1–2), and afflicted by enemies (v. 9). His ongoing reflections on what God has done for him sustain him (vv. 3–8) such that he is confident that his enemies will receive from God what they deserve (vv. 9–10). He ends on a confident note, affirming that the king and all the faithful will be able to again "rejoice in God" (v. 11). The two psalms are linked by references to God's power and unfailing love (62:11–12; 63:2–3), as well as the point that justice will prevail: everyone will get what they deserve (62:12; 63:9–10).

Ps 63 continues the sequence of psalms dealing with David's enemies (see introduction to Ps 52) and is part of a different string that emphasizes the theme of God as a refuge (see introduction to Ps 57; see also notes on 2:12; 18:1–2).
63 title David spent time in the wilderness of Judah fleeing Saul (1 Sam 19–31), but the reference to "the king" in v. 11 suggests that his flight from Jerusalem after his son Absalom's coup is in view here (2 Sam 15–17; see especially 15:23–28). The trauma of his physical state is clearly visible in 2 Sam 16:13–14. This is the 13th psalm with a "historical" title connecting it with events in David's life (see note on Ps 3 title) and the final psalm in a sequence of eight such psalms in Book II (see note on Ps 51 title).

I thirst for you,[i]
my whole being longs for you,
in a dry and parched land
where there is no water.

2 I have seen you in the sanctuary[j]
and beheld your power and your glory.
3 Because your love is better than life,[k]
my lips will glorify you.
4 I will praise you as long as I live,[l]
and in your name I will lift up my hands.[m]
5 I will be fully satisfied as with the richest of foods;[n]
with singing lips my mouth will praise you.

6 On my bed I remember you;
I think of you through the watches of the night.[o]
7 Because you are my help,[p]
I sing in the shadow of your wings.
8 I cling to you;
your right hand upholds me.[q]

9 Those who want to kill me will be destroyed;[r]
they will go down to the depths of the earth.[s]
10 They will be given over to the sword
and become food for jackals.

11 But the king will rejoice in God;
all who swear by God will glory in him,[t]
while the mouths of liars will be silenced.

Psalm 64[a]

For the director of music. A psalm of David.

1 Hear me, my God, as I voice my complaint;[u]
protect my life from the threat of the enemy.[v]

2 Hide me from the conspiracy of the wicked,[w]
from the plots of evildoers.

[a] In Hebrew texts 64:1-10 is numbered 64:2-11.

63:1 [i] Ps 42:2; 84:2
63:2 [j] Ps 27:4
63:3 [k] Ps 69:16
63:4 [l] Ps 104:33 [m] Ps 28:2
63:5 [n] Ps 36:8
63:6 [o] Ps 42:8
63:7 [p] Ps 27:9
63:8 [q] Ps 18:35
63:9 [r] Ps 40:14 [s] Ps 55:15
63:11 [t] Dt 6:13; Ps 21:1; Isa 45:23
64:1 [u] Ps 55:2 [v] Ps 140:1
64:2 [w] Ps 56:6; 59:2

63:1 David's vivid imagery of thirsting in the parched desert, far from God, recalls 42:1–4.
63:2 sanctuary. See notes on 5:7; 60:6.
63:3 love. God's unfailing, covenantal love, as in 62:12. See note on 6:4.
63:4 lift up my hands. This signifies praise, as it does in 134:2. Elsewhere, this action more commonly signifies prayer (e.g., 28:2; 44:20; 77:2; 88:9; 141:2; 143:6).
63:6 watches of the night. David, in wakefulness, remembered God throughout the night. The Hebrews divided the night into three watches: sunset to 10:00 p.m.; 10:00 p.m. to 2:00 a.m.; and 2:00 a.m. to sunrise (Judg 7:19; 1 Sam 11:11). Other references to the psalmists' deep reflection at night include 4:4; 16:7; 90:4; 119:55,148.
63:7 shadow of your wings. See note on 36:7.
63:8 cling. The verb connotes a tight bonding. It first occurs in the Bible to speak of the marriage bond ("is united," Gen 2:24); God's people were to cling or "hold fast" to God (Deut 10:20; 11:22; 13:4; 30:20; Josh 22:5; 23:8). King Hezekiah clung to the Lord and was judged to be one of Judah's greatest kings as a result (2 Kgs 18:5–6). Here David's relationship with God involves two aspects: (1) he clings to God, and (2) God's right hand upholds him. Both are essential.
63:10 jackals. See note on 44:19.
63:11 the king … all who swear. Both king and people will rejoice and glory in God. David's concern for the office of king here echoes his thoughts in 61:6–7. Indeed, as God's representative, the king is also to be the source of blessing for the people (e.g., 72:12–14,17). See also note on 3:8.
Ps 64 *Hide Me From the Conspiracy of the Wicked.* David faces a threat from enemies who conspire against him. He focuses on the damage that their cruel and unbridled tongues cause (vv. 1–6) and then shifts his focus to God, who will turn his enemies' evil back upon them (vv. 7–8), which leads to all people's glorifying God (vv. 9–10).

This is the final psalm in the sequence of psalms dealing with David's enemies (see introduction to Ps 52); David returns to full-blown praise again in Ps 65. Ps 64 is also part of a string of psalms emphasizing the theme of God as a refuge (see introduction to Ps 57; see also notes on 2:12; 18:1–2). The reference in v. 9 to "all people" points the way to the next cluster of psalms, which deal with God's concern for the nations (Pss 65–67).

64:3 [x] Ps 58:7
64:4 [y] Ps 11:2 [z] Ps 55:19
64:5 [a] Ps 10:11
64:8 [b] Ps 9:3; Pr 18:7 [c] Ps 22:7
64:9 [d] Jer 51:10
64:10 [e] Ps 25:20 [f] Ps 32:11
65:1 [g] Ps 116:18
65:2 [h] Isa 66:23
65:3 [i] Ps 38:4 [j] Heb 9:14
65:4 [k] Ps 4:3; 33:12 [l] Ps 36:8
65:5 [m] Ps 85:4

3 They sharpen their tongues like swords
and aim cruel words like deadly arrows.[x]
4 They shoot from ambush at the innocent;[y]
they shoot suddenly, without fear.[z]

5 They encourage each other in evil plans,
they talk about hiding their snares;
they say, "Who will see it*[a]*?"[a]
6 They plot injustice and say,
"We have devised a perfect plan!"
Surely the human mind and heart are cunning.

7 But God will shoot them with his arrows;
they will suddenly be struck down.
8 He will turn their own tongues against them[b]
and bring them to ruin;
all who see them will shake their heads[c] in scorn.
9 All people will fear;
they will proclaim the works of God
and ponder what he has done.[d]

10 The righteous will rejoice in the LORD
and take refuge in him;[e]
all the upright in heart will glory in him![f]

Psalm 65*[b]*

For the director of music. A psalm of David. A song.

1 Praise awaits*[c]* you, our God, in Zion;
to you our vows will be fulfilled.[g]
2 You who answer prayer,
to you all people will come.[h]
3 When we were overwhelmed by sins,[i]
you forgave*[d]* our transgressions.[j]
4 Blessed are those you choose[k]
and bring near to live in your courts!
We are filled with the good things of your house,[l]
of your holy temple.

5 You answer us with awesome and righteous deeds,
God our Savior,[m]

a *5* Or *us* *b* In Hebrew texts 65:1-13 is numbered 65:2-14. *c* *1* Or *befits*; the meaning of the Hebrew for this word is uncertain. *d* *3* Or *made atonement for*

64:3 swords. Their tongues can do great damage (see note on 10:7); they are sharp and dangerous (see note on 59:7). Cf. Jas 3:1–12.
64:6 cunning. The word has the sense of "deep, deceptive, mysterious." In Prov 18:4, the words of the mouth are "deep waters" (the same Hebrew term), contrasted to the more positive image of a fountain of wisdom as a rushing stream. See also Prov 20:5.
64:9 All people. This anticipates the concern for all people and nations expressed in Pss 65–66 and especially the glorious prayer for them in Ps 67. **fear.** See note on 19:9. **works of God.** See notes on 26:7; 40:3.
64:10 all the upright in heart will glory in him! Cf. 63:11.
Ps 65 *To You All People Will Come.* Pss 65–67 focus on God's concern for all nations and all people. Ps 65 is a psalm of praise on behalf of the community. It begins with praise centered in Zion, at the temple, where all people would come (vv. 1–4), continues with praise for God's wondrous deeds and power over creation itself so that the entire world is filled with his awe (vv. 5–8), and concludes with a reflection on God's ongoing care for the land and its bounty (vv. 9–13). Its tone is joyous and admiring of the awesome God who blesses and cares for the entire world and its people.
65 title See note on Ps 68 title.
65:1 Zion. See notes on 2:6; 9:11. **vows.** See note on 50:14.
65:2 all people. This sounds the keynote for Pss 65–67, repeating the reference to "all people" in 64:9, where God's concern for all is now in view, not just David or Israel. See introduction to Ps 67.
65:3 sins … transgressions. See note on 32:5. The Hebrew word translated "sins" here is translated "iniquity" in 32:5.
65:4 Blessed. See note on 1:1. **courts … house … temple.** See note on 5:7.
65:5 awesome … deeds. See note on 26:7.

the hope of all the ends of the earth
and of the farthest seas,[n]
6 who formed the mountains by your power,
having armed yourself with strength,[o]
7 who stilled the roaring of the seas,[p]
the roaring of their waves,
and the turmoil of the nations.[q]
8 The whole earth is filled with awe at your wonders;
where morning dawns, where evening fades,
you call forth songs of joy.

9 You care for the land and water it;[r]
you enrich it abundantly.
The streams of God are filled with water
to provide the people with grain,[s]
for so you have ordained it.[a]
10 You drench its furrows and level its ridges;
you soften it with showers and bless its crops.
11 You crown the year with your bounty,
and your carts overflow with
abundance.
12 The grasslands of the wilderness overflow;[t]
the hills are clothed with gladness.
13 The meadows are covered with flocks[u]
and the valleys are mantled with grain;[v]
they shout for joy and sing.[w]

Psalm 66

For the director of music. A song. A psalm.

1 Shout for joy to God, all the earth![x]
2 Sing the glory of his name;[y]
make his praise glorious.
3 Say to God, "How awesome are your deeds![z]
So great is your power
that your enemies cringe[a] before you.
4 All the earth bows down[b] to you;
they sing praise[c] to you,
they sing the praises of your name."[b]

Shell plaque depicting a god contesting with a seven-headed monster.

Z. Radovan/www.BibleLandPictures.com

65:5 [n]Ps 107:23
65:6 [o]Ps 93:1
65:7 [p]Mt 8:26 [q]Isa 17:12-13
65:9 [r]Ps 68:9-10 [s]Ps 46:4; 104:14
65:12 [t]Job 28:26
65:13 [u]Ps 144:13 [v]Ps 72:16 [w]Ps 98:8; Isa 55:12
66:1 [x]Ps 100:1
66:2 [y]Ps 79:9
66:3 [z]Ps 65:5 [a]Ps 18:44
66:4 [b]Ps 22:27 [c]Ps 67:3

[a] 9 Or *for that is how you prepare the land* [b] 4 The Hebrew has *Selah* (a word of uncertain meaning) here and at the end of verses 7 and 15.

65:7 roaring of the seas. See notes on 33:7; 93:3.

65:8 wonders. See note on 26:7.

65:9 streams of God. God controls the waters (v. 7), and his "streams" are the abundant waters coming from storehouses, or jugs, in the heavens. See 33:7 and note; Job 38:8–11,22,37; Jer 10:13.

Ps 66 *Praise Our God, All Peoples.* This joyous praise psalm unfolds in two separate stages. (1) It is a praise psalm of the community, celebrating God's deliverances in a general way (vv. 1–12). Verse 6 harkens back to God's delivering Israel at the Red Sea (Exod 14), but the rest is general enough that it could readily apply to any number of instances when God delivered his people. (2) It is the thanksgiving of an individual for prayers answered (vv. 13–20). It would appear that the psalmist's thanks for God's response to his personal plea leads him to think more broadly about God's deliverance on a national scale. Indeed, he highlights this by opening the psalm with communal praise and only then does he express his personal praise.

This is the first psalm in Book II that is not attributed to any author (but see introduction to Pss 42–43). Like Ps 50, it affirms the importance of proper sacrifices (vv. 13–16; 50:5,7–15,23), and the two bracket a series of 15 psalms of David, most of which focus on David's struggles against his enemies (see introduction to Ps 52). It is the middle psalm in a short sequence (Pss 65–67) that focuses on God's concern for all the earth and its peoples and nations.

66 title See note on Ps 68 title.

66:1–4 The psalm opens with a burst of unfettered joy, a joyful call for all the earth to praise God and testify to his awesome deeds. It affirms God's sovereignty throughout all the earth; indeed, all the earth bows down and sings praises to him (v. 4).

66:5 [d]Ps 106:22
66:6 [e]Ex 14:22
66:7 [f]Ps 145:13 [g]Ps 11:4 [h]Ps 140:8
66:8 [i]Ps 98:4
66:9 [j]Ps 121:3
66:10 [k]Ps 17:3; Isa 48:10; Zec 13:9; 1Pe 1:6-7
66:11 [l]La 1:13
66:12 [m]Isa 51:23 [n]Isa 43:2
66:13 [o]Ecc 5:4
66:15 [p]Nu 6:14; Ps 51:19
66:16 [q]Ps 34:11 [r]Ps 71:15,24
66:18 [s]Job 36:21; Isa 1:15; Jas 4:3
66:19 [t]Ps 116:1-2

5 Come and see what God has done,
his awesome deeds[d] for mankind!
6 He turned the sea into dry land,[e]
they passed through the waters on foot—
come, let us rejoice in him.
7 He rules forever[f] by his power,
his eyes watch[g] the nations—
let not the rebellious[h] rise up against him.

8 Praise[i] our God, all peoples,
let the sound of his praise be heard;
9 he has preserved our lives
and kept our feet from slipping.[j]
10 For you, God, tested us;
you refined us like silver.[k]
11 You brought us into prison
and laid burdens[l] on our backs.
12 You let people ride over our heads;[m]
we went through fire and water,
but you brought us to a place of abundance.[n]

13 I will come to your temple with burnt offerings
and fulfill my vows[o] to you—
14 vows my lips promised and my mouth spoke
when I was in trouble.
15 I will sacrifice fat animals to you
and an offering of rams;
I will offer bulls and goats.[p]

16 Come and hear,[q] all you who fear God;
let me tell[r] you what he has done for me.
17 I cried out to him with my mouth;
his praise was on my tongue.
18 If I had cherished sin in my heart,
the Lord would not have listened;[s]
19 but God has surely listened
and has heard[t] my prayer.

66:5 what God has done. God has done awesome deeds by turning the sea and the river "into dry land" (v. 6), reminding the faithful what he did in the great events of the exodus from Egypt (Exod 14) and crossing the Jordan River (Josh 3).
66:6 waters. The Hebrew word here is normally translated "river," so the psalmist may be referring to the crossing of the Jordan River, not the Red Sea, in the second line of v. 6; this emphasizes both miraculous partings of water: the Red Sea (v. 6a) and the Jordan River (v. 6b).
66:7 He rules forever. See notes on 10:16; 93:1. God is the powerful, eternal ruler who keeps the rebellious in their place (cf. v. 3b).
66:8 all peoples. Just as in the preceding and following psalms, the vision is that God is sovereign over all the earth (vv. 1,4) and all people, not just his own chosen people. Thus, the psalmist calls all people to praise God for what he has done for Israel. By implication, he will do the same for any and all people and nations who respond to him. See note on 47:9; see also introduction to Ps 67. Today, Gentile Christians are also the heirs of this inclusive vision.
66:10 tested. Examining a person to see if they meet God's standards. The word sometimes refers to refining gold (Zech 13:9), but more commonly to refining and testing people and their hearts (e.g., Pss 17:3; 26:2; 81:7; 139:23; 1 Chr 29:17; Prov 17:3; Jer 9:7; 20:12). It commonly occurs in tandem with words for refining and purifying. **refined.** God's testing, while hard for the moment, produces a more pure, godly people. See note on 12:6.
66:13–15 burnt offerings ... vows ... sacrifice ... offering. See notes on 50:8,14.
66:13 temple. The place of God's earthly residence (see note on 5:7).
66:16 what he has done for me. The foundation for why the psalmist wants all the earth and all its peoples to praise God lies in his own personal experience of God's answer to his prayer. His is not a purely private experience; he longs for all people to hear and see what God has done (vv. 5,16). He treasures God as one who answers prayer (vv. 19–20), just as David does in the previous psalm (65:2). In both cases, the psalmist desires all people to know this and rejoice. God's ability to answer prayer is to be shared with others, not kept to oneself.
66:18 sin in my heart. Sin harbored in the heart will be cause for prayers to go unanswered. This echoes David's sentiment in 32:3–4, where he wastes away as long as he refuses to acknowledge and confess his sin.

[20] Praise be to God,
who has not rejected[u] my prayer
or withheld his love from me!

Psalm 67[a]

For the director of music. With stringed instruments. A psalm. A song.

[1] May God be gracious to us and bless us
and make his face shine on us—[b][v]
[2] so that your ways may be known on earth,
your salvation[w] among all nations.[x]
[3] May the peoples praise you, God;
may all the peoples praise you.
[4] May the nations be glad and sing for joy,
for you rule the peoples with equity[y]
and guide the nations of the earth.
[5] May the peoples praise you, God;
may all the peoples praise you.

[6] The land yields its harvest;[z]
God, our God, blesses us.
[7] May God bless us still,
so that all the ends of the earth will fear him.[a]

Psalm 68[c]

For the director of music. Of David. A psalm. A song.

[1] May God arise, may his enemies be scattered;
may his foes flee[b] before him.

[a] In Hebrew texts 67:1-7 is numbered 67:2-8. [b] *1* The Hebrew has *Selah* (a word of uncertain meaning) here and at the end of verse 4. [c] In Hebrew texts 68:1-35 is numbered 68:2-36.

66:20 [u] Ps 22:24; 68:35
67:1 [v] Nu 6:24-26; Ps 4:6
67:2 [w] Isa 52:10 [x] Titus 2:11
67:4 [y] Ps 96:10-13
67:6 [z] Lev 26:4; Ps 85:12; Eze 34:27
67:7 [a] Ps 33:8
68:1 [b] Nu 10:35; Isa 33:3

Ps 67 *Be Gracious, O God, So That Your Ways May Be Known on Earth.* No other psalm captures more clearly and simply the grand vision that God is the God of *all* people and nations, that he wants all of them to embrace him, and that he wants his own people to mediate that blessing to the nations. The psalm is rooted in God's promise to Abraham that he would bless him and his descendants so that they would be a blessing to others (Gen 12:2–3). God promised the Israelites at Sinai that he could make them a "kingdom of priests" (Exod 19:6), i.e., the nation as a whole would function as intermediaries between God and the nations. Pss 65–66 also celebrate God's concern for all people and nations, as do 22:27–31 and the psalms that celebrate the Lord's kingship (e.g., Pss 47; 96–99; 145). But Ps 67 stands out above all others, reiterating these themes clearly and repeatedly. The apostle Paul echoes the sentiment that God invites all Gentiles to respond to his call (Rom 1:5).

67 title See note on Ps 68 title.

67:1–2 The psalm begins with a prayer asking God to bless his people. It is almost a word-for-word repetition of the first part of the Aaronic Blessing in Num 6:24–26, with the important difference that here the people are asking for the blessing themselves instead of the priests pronouncing it upon them. And here a critical word change in the Hebrew highlights the people's role in bringing God's blessing to the nations: "on us" may denote "among us." The people are asking God to shine among them, radiating his light and truth outward as a testimony to the nations, precisely so that his ways and his salvation would be known everywhere (v. 2).

67:3–5 Five of the seven poetic lines in this section are prayers that the nations would respond to God and praise him. The sentiment here is the polar opposite of Jonah's myopic worldview: Jonah resented God's blessing on a foreign nation (Jonah 4). The other two poetic lines (v. 4b–c) give the reasons the people should praise God: he is a good and just God. Verse 5 repeats v. 3, adding urgency and emphasis to the prayer that all peoples will praise God.

67:6–7 The evidence that God does bless his people is the abundant harvest (v. 6), after which the psalmist reiterates the prayer of vv. 1–2 in v. 7. See note on 40:3.

67:7 fear. See note on 19:9.

Ps 68 *Sing to God, You Kingdoms of the Earth.* David celebrates God as the King (v. 24) who rode majestically before the Israelites as they made their way from slavery in Egypt through the wilderness into the promised land of Canaan and who later triumphantly took his place in his sanctuary on Mount Zion. No specific occasion for the psalm can be pinpointed with certainty, but David's bringing the ark into Jerusalem (2 Sam 6) is a possibility. The psalm was likely used as a part of a ritual procession into Jerusalem and up to God's house (see introduction to Ps 24). On its connections with Pss 65–67, see note on Ps 68 title.

David praises God in general, triumphant terms at the outset (vv. 1–6) and celebrates the journey from Egypt to Canaan (vv. 7–14). The rest of the psalm focuses on God's triumphant establishment in his sanctuary on Mount Zion (vv. 15–35), which did not happen until David's time (2 Sam 6; 1 Chr 16).

68 title A psalm. A song. This is the fourth psalm in a row with these words in its title. All deal with the nations. The first three do this with joyful praise and an inclusive spirit, highlighting God's concern for the

68:2 [c]Hos 13:3 [d]Isa 9:18; Mic 1:4
68:3 [e]Ps 32:11
68:4 [f]Ps 66:2 [g]Dt 33:26 [h]Ex 6:3; Ps 83:18
68:5 [i]Ps 10:14 [j]Dt 10:18 [k]Dt 26:15
68:6 [l]Ps 113:9 [m]Ac 12:6 [n]Ps 107:34
68:7 [o]Ex 13:21; Jdg 4:14
68:8 [p]Jdg 5:4 [q]Ex 19:16,18
68:9 [r]Dt 11:11
68:10 [s]Ps 74:19
68:12 [t]Jos 10:16
68:13 [u]Ge 49:14

2 May you blow them away like smoke —[c]
as wax melts[d] before the fire,
may the wicked perish before God.
3 But may the righteous be glad
and rejoice[e] before God;
may they be happy and joyful.

4 Sing to God, sing in praise of his name,[f]
extol him who rides on the clouds[a][g];
rejoice before him — his name is the LORD.[h]
5 A father to the fatherless,[i] a defender of widows,[j]
is God in his holy dwelling.[k]
6 God sets the lonely in families,[b][l]
he leads out the prisoners[m] with singing;
but the rebellious live in a sun-scorched land.[n]

7 When you, God, went out[o] before your people,
when you marched through the wilderness,[c]
8 the earth shook, the heavens poured down rain,[p]
before God, the One of Sinai,[q]
before God, the God of Israel.
9 You gave abundant showers,[r] O God;
you refreshed your weary inheritance.
10 Your people settled in it,
and from your bounty, God, you provided[s] for the poor.

11 The Lord announces the word,
and the women who proclaim it are a mighty throng:
12 "Kings and armies flee[t] in haste;
the women at home divide the plunder.
13 Even while you sleep among the sheep pens,[d][u]
the wings of my dove are sheathed with silver,
its feathers with shining gold."

[a] 4 Or *name, / prepare the way for him who rides through the deserts* [b] 6 Or *the desolate in a homeland*
[c] 7 The Hebrew has *Selah* (a word of uncertain meaning) here and at the end of verses 19 and 32.
[d] 13 Or *the campfires;* or *the saddlebags*

nations. Ps 68 treats the nations as enemies and affirms God's triumph over them. But in the end, this is for the purpose of including them in the great throng that bows the knee to him, so it too affirms many of the same themes as do Pss 65–67. Pss 65; 68 are from David, while the other two are anonymous.

68:1 arise. Perhaps the opening cry of the processional ritual (see note on 3:7).

68:4 who rides on the clouds. Echoes other passages where God rides on the clouds or the wind (18:10; 104:3; Deut 33:26; Isa 19:1). In Canaanite mythology, the god Baal was the "Rider on the Clouds," so the biblical writers may be asserting that the Lord, not Baal, is the true "Cloud Rider." An alternative reading portrays God as the one riding through the wilderness (see NIV text note), referring to God's caring for his people as they traveled through the desert on the way to the land of Canaan. See also note on 18:10.

68:5 holy dwelling. God's heavenly dwelling, from which he cares for the disadvantaged (Deut 26:15; 2 Chr 30:27; Jer 25:30; cf. Ps 90:1). A variant of the expression can refer to God's earthly dwelling place (26:8; 1 Sam 2:29,32).

68:7 when you marched. David paints the journey from Egypt to Sinai to Canaan in the broad brushstrokes of poetry.

68:8–9 rain ... abundant showers. Another manifestation of God's power (cf. Judg 5:4), and a subtle reminder that he was greater than Baal, the Canaanite god of the storm clouds (see note on v. 4). Presumably this was one way God provided for his people in the wilderness (though the Pentateuch does not mention such).

68:8 earth shook. In Exod 19:18, Mount Sinai quaked amid smoke and fire.

68:10 your bounty. God provided bounty for his people when they entered the land of Canaan (Josh 5:11–12), and this extended to the poor, who are added to the list in vv. 5–6 of the disadvantaged for whom God provides. See note on 82:3–4.

68:11 women who proclaim it. Other examples of groups of women announcing victories in public include Exod 15:20–21; 1 Sam 18:6–7 (for women publicly mourning, see Jer 9:17–20).

68:12 women at home divide the plunder. Probably the plunder the armies brought home (Judg 5:29–30).

68:13 The Hebrew of this verse and its images are very difficult to interpret. The basic thrust of the verse emphasizes God's victory over his enemies. **my dove.** Probably a bird released to fly away and thus proclaim the victory, a common ancient Egyptian custom (Eccl 10:20). For slightly different imagery, see Gen 8:6–12.

[14]When the Almighty[a] scattered[v] the kings in the land,
it was like snow fallen on Mount Zalmon.

[15]Mount Bashan, majestic mountain,
Mount Bashan, rugged mountain,
[16]why gaze in envy, you rugged mountain,
at the mountain where God chooses[w] to reign,
where the LORD himself will dwell forever?
[17]The chariots of God are tens of thousands
and thousands of thousands;[x]
the Lord has come from Sinai into his sanctuary.[b]
[18]When you ascended on high,
you took many captives;[y]
you received gifts from people,[z]
even from[c] the rebellious—
that you,[d] LORD God, might dwell there.

[19]Praise be to the Lord, to God our Savior,[a]
who daily bears our burdens.[b]
[20]Our God is a God who saves;
from the Sovereign LORD comes escape from death.[c]
[21]Surely God will crush the heads[d] of his enemies,
the hairy crowns of those who go on in their sins.
[22]The Lord says, "I will bring them from Bashan;
I will bring them from the depths of the sea,[e]
[23]that your feet may wade in the blood of your foes,[f]
while the tongues of your dogs[g] have their share."
[24]Your procession, God, has come into view,
the procession of my God and King into the sanctuary.[h]

68:14 [v]Jos 10:10
68:16 [w]Dt 12:5
68:17 [x]Dt 33:2; Da 7:10
68:18 [y]Jdg 5:12 [z]Eph 4:8*
68:19 [a]Ps 65:5 [b]Ps 55:22
68:20 [c]Ps 56:13
68:21 [d]Ps 110:5; Hab 3:13
68:22 [e]Nu 21:33
68:23 [f]Ps 58:10 [g]1Ki 21:19
68:24 [h]Ps 63:2

Winged god Ashur shooting his bow among rain clouds, ninth century BC. Ps 68:4 describes God as "[he] who rides on the clouds."

[a] *14* Hebrew *Shaddai* [b] *17* Probable reading of the original Hebrew text; Masoretic Text *Lord is among them at Sinai in holiness* [c] *18* Or *gifts for people, / even* [d] *18* Or *they*

68:14 Almighty. See NIV text note. This epithet for God occurs again in Psalms only in 91:1 but frequently elsewhere in Scripture, especially in Job (e.g., Job 5:17; 6:4,14; 8:3,5). God revealed himself to the patriarchs as "God Almighty" (Hebrew *ēl šadday*: Gen 17:1; 28:3; 35:11; see note on Exod 6:3). The word for God, *ʾēl*, is a generic term for deity, used even in Canaanite texts; in the Bible, it refers to the true God and appears as a shortened form of *ʾĕlōhîm* ("God"). The exact meaning of *šadday* is unclear, but the early Greek and Latin translations rendered it as "Almighty." See notes on 8:1; 24:10. **Mount Zalmon.** There was a mountain with this name near Shechem (Judg 9:48), but the location of this one appears to be northeast of the Sea of Galilee in the area of Bashan (v. 15).
68:15 Mount Bashan. Bashan is the fertile region northeast of the Sea of Galilee (see note on 22:12). The highest peak there is Mount Hermon; therefore, Mount Bashan may refer to Mount Hermon. The point here is that even this mighty mountain cannot begin to compare with Mount Zion (i.e., Jerusalem), "the mountain where God chooses to reign" for his eternal abode (v. 16; see notes on 2:6; 9:11; see also vv. 24,29,35).
68:17 chariots. The ancient equivalent of tanks, the backbone of any army. The poetic language emphasizes the devastating power of God's heavenly armies.
68:18 ascended on high. A reference to God's establishing his throne on Mount Zion, having come from Sinai (v. 17). See introduction to Ps 24; see also note on 47:5–7. The apostle Paul applies this to the resurrected and triumphant Christ (Eph 4:8–13). This shows the continuity between God's triumphs in the OT, establishing his earthly kingdom in Zion, and Christ's ultimate victory over death and all opposition, leading eventually to the triumphal images in the book of Revelation, with Zion as the "capital" of the new heavens and new earth (see especially Rev 21–22).
68:22 God will retrieve his enemies from everywhere: from the highest mountain heights (Bashan; see note on v. 15) to the lowest ocean depths, and from east (Bashan) to west (the Mediterranean Sea).
68:23 blood of your foes. See note on 58:10. **dogs.** See note on 22:16.
68:24 procession. See introduction to Ps 24; see also note on 47:5–7. **sanctuary.** See notes on 5:7; 60:6.

68:25 [i] Jdg 11:34; 1Ch 13:8
68:26 [j] Ps 26:12; Isa 48:1
68:27 [k] 1Sa 9:21
68:29 [l] Ps 72:10
68:30 [m] Ps 22:12 [n] Ps 89:10
68:31 [o] Isa 19:19; 45:14
68:33 [p] Ps 18:10 [q] Ps 29:4
68:34 [r] Ps 29:1
68:35 [s] Ps 29:11 [t] Ps 66:20
69:1 [u] Jnh 2:5
69:2 [v] Ps 40:2

25 In front are the singers, after them the musicians;
with them are the young women playing the timbrels.[i]
26 Praise God in the great congregation;
praise the LORD in the assembly of Israel.[j]
27 There is the little tribe[k] of Benjamin, leading them,
there the great throng of Judah's princes,
and there the princes of Zebulun and of Naphtali.

28 Summon your power, God[a];
show us your strength, our God, as you have done before.
29 Because of your temple at Jerusalem
kings will bring you gifts.[l]
30 Rebuke the beast among the reeds,
the herd of bulls[m] among the calves of the nations.
Humbled, may the beast bring bars of silver.
Scatter the nations[n] who delight in war.
31 Envoys will come from Egypt;[o]
Cush[b] will submit herself to God.

32 Sing to God, you kingdoms of the earth,
sing praise to the Lord,
33 to him who rides[p] across the highest heavens, the ancient heavens,
who thunders with mighty voice.[q]
34 Proclaim the power[r] of God,
whose majesty is over Israel,
whose power is in the heavens.
35 You, God, are awesome in your sanctuary;
the God of Israel gives power and strength to his people.[s]

Praise be to God![t]

Psalm 69[c]

For the director of music. To the tune of "Lilies." Of David.

1 Save me, O God,
for the waters have come up to my neck.[u]
2 I sink in the miry depths,[v]
where there is no foothold.
I have come into the deep waters;
the floods engulf me.

[a] *28* Many Hebrew manuscripts, Septuagint and Syriac; most Hebrew manuscripts *Your God has summoned power for you* [b] *31* That is, the upper Nile region [c] In Hebrew texts 69:1-36 is numbered 69:2-37.

68:25 timbrels. See note on 150:4.
68:27 Benjamin and Judah were the smallest and largest tribes, respectively. They were located in the far south of the land; Zebulun and Naphtali were in the far north. The point is all-inclusive: all tribes—from least to greatest, from south to north—would participate in praising God.
68:29 your temple. See notes on 5:7; 60:6 ("from his sanctuary"). God's presence would draw kings and nations to the temple (1 Kgs 8:41–43). This anticipates the great procession to Mount Zion in the last days (Isa 2:2–5).
68:30 beast among the reeds. The pharaoh of Egypt (Ezek 29:3).
68:31 Egypt. Symbolizes all nations that opposed the Lord; Israel had a long history of involvement with that great power, and in David's day Egypt was still the one great power that could threaten Israel. But David also prayed that this beast (see note on v. 30) would submit to God.
68:33 who rides. See note on v. 4.
68:35 sanctuary. See notes on 5:7; 60:6 ("from his sanctuary").
Ps 69 *As for Me, Afflicted and in Pain—May Your Salvation, God, Protect Me.* David laments during an unknown crisis when he was being persecuted severely and unjustly for sins he had committed (vv. 5,26). His emotions are raw, and the imagery is vivid. The NT applies many of the psalm's sentiments to Jesus, who also suffered like David, only more so. The psalm begins with four alternating sections focusing on deep waters as metaphors for David's troubles (vv. 1–4,13–18) and on the vicious scorn heaped upon him by his enemies (vv. 5–12,19–21). David unleashes a series of bitter imprecations (i.e., curses) against his enemies (vv. 22–28) and concludes by acknowledging God in praise and thanksgiving for his anticipated deliverance (vv. 29–36).

[3]I am worn out calling for help;[w]
my throat is parched.
My eyes fail,[x]
looking for my God.
[4]Those who hate me without reason[y]
outnumber the hairs of my head;
many are my enemies without cause,[z]
those who seek to destroy me.
I am forced to restore
what I did not steal.

[5]You, God, know my folly;[a]
my guilt is not hidden from you.[b]

[6]Lord, the LORD Almighty,
may those who hope in you
not be disgraced because of me;
God of Israel,
may those who seek you
not be put to shame because of me.
[7]For I endure scorn for your sake,[c]
and shame covers my face.[d]
[8]I am a foreigner to my own family,
a stranger to my own mother's children;[e]
[9]for zeal for your house consumes me,[f]
and the insults of those who insult you fall on me.[g]
[10]When I weep and fast,[h]
I must endure scorn;
[11]when I put on sackcloth,[i]
people make sport of me.
[12]Those who sit at the gate mock me,
and I am the song of the drunkards.[j]
[13]But I pray to you, LORD,
in the time of your favor;[k]
in your great love,[l] O God,
answer me with your sure salvation.
[14]Rescue me from the mire,
do not let me sink;
deliver me from those who hate me,
from the deep waters.[m]
[15]Do not let the floodwaters[n] engulf me
or the depths swallow me up[o]
or the pit close its mouth over me.

[16]Answer me, LORD, out of the goodness of your love;[p]
in your great mercy turn to me.

69:3 [w]Ps 6:6 [x]Ps 119:82; Isa 38:14
69:4 [y]Jn 15:25* [z]Ps 35:19; 38:19
69:5 [a]Ps 38:5 [b]Ps 44:21
69:7 [c]Jer 15:15 [d]Ps 44:15
69:8 [e]Ps 31:11; Isa 53:3
69:9 [f]Jn 2:17* [g]Ps 89:50-51; Ro 15:3*
69:10 [h]Ps 35:13
69:11 [i]Ps 35:13
69:12 [j]Job 30:9
69:13 [k]Isa 49:8; 2Co 6:2 [l]Ps 51:1
69:14 [m]ver 2; Ps 144:7
69:15 [n]Ps 124:4-5 [o]Nu 16:33
69:16 [p]Ps 63:3

69:4 my enemies without cause. David had many enemies throughout his life. He also was the great royal ancestor of Jesus (Matt 1:1), and his words often apply to Jesus, who made the explicit connection by quoting this verse in John 15:25. See note on 35:19.
69:9 zeal for your house. David's zeal for God's house prefigures Jesus' even greater zeal, seen in his cleansing of the temple (John 2:14–17). On God's house and David's zeal for it, see 55:14; 122:1; see also note on 5:7. **insults ... fall on me.** Insults directed at God also fall on his servants (74:18,22; 2 Kgs 18:31–35). Paul quotes this verse, affirming that even Jesus himself experienced such insults (Rom 15:3).
69:13 time of your favor. When God is still near and responds to people's prayers. See Isa 49:8; 61:2; 2 Cor 6:2; see also note on 32:6. **your great love.** See note on 6:4.
69:15 pit. See note on 28:1.
69:16 love. See note on 6:4.

69:17 [q]Ps 27:9 [r]Ps 66:14
69:18 [s]Ps 49:15
69:19 [t]Ps 22:6
69:20 [u]Job 16:2 [v]Isa 63:5
69:21 [w]Mt 27:34; Mk 15:23; Jn 19:28-30
69:23 [x]Isa 6:9-10; Ro 11:9-10*
69:24 [y]Ps 79:6

17 Do not hide your face[q] from your servant;
answer me quickly, for I am in trouble.[r]
18 Come near and rescue me;
deliver[s] me because of my foes.

19 You know how I am scorned,[t] disgraced and shamed;
all my enemies are before you.
20 Scorn has broken my heart
and has left me helpless;
I looked for sympathy, but there was none,
for comforters,[u] but I found none.[v]
21 They put gall in my food
and gave me vinegar for my thirst.[w]

22 May the table set before them become a snare;
may it become retribution and[a] a trap.
23 May their eyes be darkened so they cannot see,
and their backs be bent forever.[x]
24 Pour out your wrath[y] on them;
let your fierce anger overtake them.

[a] 22 Or *snare / and their fellowship become*

69:17 hide your face. See note on 27:9.

69:21 gall … vinegar. Bitter food and drink are vivid metaphors of the deep-seated scorn of David's enemies; David feels disgraced and ashamed, without friend or comforter (v. 20). Jesus found himself in a similar state on the cross, abandoned by all, including his Father, and he was given sour wine to drink (Matt 27:34,48; John 19:28–29).

69:22–28 David utters a series of imprecations (i.e., curses) against his enemies. They are so fierce that they have caused many Christians to recoil from them and to disavow their language as inappropriate for any believer. It is argued that the "law of love" supersedes or corrects such imprecations—"Love your neighbor as yourself" (Lev 19:18; Matt 22:39; Mark 12:31; Gal 5:14)—and that no NT believer should countenance such fierce imprecations. Indeed, some argue that David himself was wrong to express such thoughts. (Similar imprecations occur in 41:10; 109:6–20; 137:8–9; 139:19–22; see note on 5:9–10.)

These Christians are correct that believers should not take it upon themselves to exact vengeance. The OT makes this clear: God says, "It is mine to avenge; I will repay" (Deut 32:35, which is quoted in Rom 12:19; cf. Prov 20:22). But there are several reasons why they are mistaken to say that David's imprecations were wrong or that they are inappropriate for Christians even to consider.

1. These imprecations show a proper outrage at sin, even if it is sin directed at David himself. Sin is sin, and David was justified in showing his outrage at people violating God's standards.

2. David was God's kingly representative on earth, his vice-regent (see note on 2:7), and any attack on him was, by extension, an attack on God himself.

3. In asking God to punish evil, he was appealing to God's very nature as a righteous judge (Jer 11:20). And as a descendant of Abraham, he was asking only that God be faithful to his own warnings: "whoever curses you I will curse" (Gen 12:3).

4. David never vowed to take personal vengeance. The imprecations are prayers asking God to rouse himself and act against the wicked. David showed great personal restraint against Saul, for example, and refused to take vengeance against him even when he had the opportunity (1 Sam 24; 26). He left Saul's fate in God's hands, not his own, even though he lamented Saul's persecution many times (e.g., Pss 7; 18; 34; 52; 54; 57; 59).

5. David was acutely sensitive to the possibility of wrong motives in asking God to act in such ways. For example, in Ps 139, after especially harsh thoughts about his enemies (139:19–22), he prays, "Search me, God, and know my heart; test me and know my anxious thoughts. See if there is any offensive way in me, and lead me in the way everlasting" (139:23–24).

6. In keeping with the nature of poetry, which paints in broad brushstrokes and often uses highly figurative language that we intuitively know is not literal (see introduction to Ps 69), the language of imprecation in many cases can be seen in the same way: it expresses outrage at sin and injustice, but it is not to be taken literally in every detail.

7. Christians who recoil at the harsh language of the OT tend to forget that the NT also has similarly harsh, even judgmental, language. Examples include Jesus' words in Matt 10:14; 11:21–24; 23:33–39; Paul's words in 1 Tim 1:19–20; 2 Tim 4:14; and the voice of the saints in Rev 6:9–10.

8. Sometimes, if not always, the imprecations are not absolute. Rather, they must be seen as prayers to bring people to repentance, not to punish for the sake of punishment. The words of 83:16 are instructive: "Cover their faces with shame, LORD, so that they will seek your name." So too is the example of Nineveh, against whom Jonah uttered what appeared to be an absolute judgment: "Forty more days and Nineveh will be overthrown" (Jonah 3:4). God reversed that judgment when Nineveh repented.

David's cursings show a man greatly afflicted yet acutely in tune with God's heart and so confident in God's justice as to ask him to punish evil wherever it manifested itself. He is aware of representing both God and the nation, such that attacks on him are, in the end, attacks against God himself and his chosen people. Christians should not harbor thoughts of personal vengeance, but they should, with David, be outraged at evil and pray that God would restrain evil and restore justice.

69:22–23 The apostle Paul quotes these verses to show why the Jews' hearts were hardened (Rom 11:9–10). This hardening was for the purpose of including the Gentiles and was only temporary for those who would repent and believe in Jesus (Rom 11:11–12,23–25).

25 May their place be deserted;[z]
let there be no one to dwell in their tents.[a]
26 For they persecute those you wound
and talk about the pain of those you hurt.[b]
27 Charge them with crime upon crime;[c]
do not let them share in your salvation.[d]
28 May they be blotted out of the book of life[e]
and not be listed with the righteous.[f]

29 But as for me, afflicted and in pain —
may your salvation, God, protect me.[g]

30 I will praise God's name in song[h]
and glorify him[i] with thanksgiving.
31 This will please the LORD more than an ox,
more than a bull with its horns and hooves.[j]
32 The poor will see and be glad[k] —
you who seek God, may your hearts live![l]
33 The LORD hears the needy[m]
and does not despise his captive people.

34 Let heaven and earth praise him,
the seas and all that move in them,[n]
35 for God will save Zion[o]
and rebuild the cities of Judah.[p]
Then people will settle there and possess it;
36 the children of his servants will inherit it,
and those who love his name will dwell there.[q]

Psalm 70[a]

70:1-5pp — Ps 40:13-17

For the director of music. Of David. A petition.

1 Hasten, O God, to save me;
come quickly, LORD, to help me.[r]

[a] In Hebrew texts 70:1-5 is numbered 70:2-6.

69:25 [z] Mt 23:38 [a] Ac 1:20* **69:26** [b] Isa 53:4; Zec 1:15 **69:27** [c] Ne 4:5 [d] Ps 109:14; Isa 26:10 **69:28** [e] Ex 32:32-33; Lk 10:20; Php 4:3 [f] Eze 13:9 **69:29** [g] Ps 59:1; 70:5 **69:30** [h] Ps 28:7 [i] Ps 34:3 **69:31** [j] Ps 50:9-13 **69:32** [k] Ps 34:2 [l] Ps 22:26 **69:33** [m] Ps 12:5; 68:6 **69:34** [n] Ps 96:11; 148:1; Isa 44:23; 49:13; 55:12 **69:35** [o] Ob 17 [p] Ps 51:18; Isa 44:26 **69:36** [q] Ps 37:29; 102:28 **70:1** [r] Ps 40:13

69:25 The apostle Peter applies this verse to Judas (Acts 1:20).
69:26 David acknowledges that God has wounded him, so just as in v. 5, he does not claim to be without guilt. But his enemies have greatly overstepped the bounds and have persecuted him unjustly.
69:28 blotted out of the book of life. The OT gives many indications of a book in which God records the deeds of both the righteous and the wicked (e.g., 56:8; 87:6; 130:3; 139:16; Dan 7:10) and from which sinners could be blotted out if they persisted in their sin (Exod 32:32–33; Neh 13:14; see note on 9:5). The NT speaks of the book of life as recording the names of those destined for eternal life (Phil 4:3; Rev 3:5; 13:8; 17:8; 20:12,15; 21:27). Here David is asking for God to exact the ultimate punishment for the unrepentant.
69:31 ox ... bull. Praise and thanksgiving will please the Lord more than animal sacrifices. David's sentiment suggests his thoughts in 51:16–17 about a broken and contrite heart, as well as the thoughts of Asaph in 50:9–15,23 about thank offerings.
69:32 poor. See note on 82:3–4.
69:34 heaven and earth. The focus on all of creation repeats the perspective in Ps 65. See note on 50:4.
69:35 God will save Zion. David's affirmation that God will save Zion and the cities of Judah anticipates the great, final restoration of that city as the "new Jerusalem" (Rev 21; see note on 2:6).
Ps 70 *Lord, Do Not Delay.* This is the second of three psalms dealing with the psalmist's enemies (see introductions to Pss 69; 71). It is an urgent prayer for help. Its roots are in Ps 40, as it is a slightly revised version of 40:13–17, now made into a free-standing psalm. Its references to the psalmist's enemies in vv. 2–3 and especially to the poor and needy in v. 5 tie it in with Ps 69 (69:32–33). There are also similarities between vv. 2–3 and 71:10–13. Indeed, many scholars believe that Ps 70 was included in its present location as an introduction of sorts to Ps 71; the latter's lack of title would bind it more closely with Ps 70 (see introduction to Pss 42–43).

David begins by appealing for God to save him (v. 1). He prays against the wicked (vv. 2–3; cf. Ps 69), and he prays for those who seek the Lord (v. 4). He concludes with a final appeal to God (v. 5).
70 title A petition. See note on Ps 38 title.
70:1–5 See 40:13–17 and notes.

70:2 [s]Ps 35:4 [t]Ps 35:26
70:5 [u]Ps 40:17 [v]Ps 141:1
71:1 [w]Ps 25:2-3; 31:1
71:2 [x]Ps 17:6
71:3 [y]Ps 18:2; 31:2-3; 44:4
71:4 [z]Ps 140:4
71:5 [a]Job 4:6; Jer 17:7
71:6 [b]Ps 22:10 [c]Ps 22:9; Isa 46:3 [d]Ps 9:1; 34:1; 52:9; 119:164; 145:2
71:7 [e]Isa 8:18; 1Co 4:9 [f]2Sa 22:3; Ps 61:3

2 May those who want to take my life[s]
be put to shame and confusion;
may all who desire my ruin
be turned back in disgrace.[t]
3 May those who say to me, "Aha! Aha!"
turn back because of their shame.
4 But may all who seek you
rejoice and be glad in you;
may those who long for your saving help always say,
"The LORD is great!"

5 But as for me, I am poor and needy;[u]
come quickly to me,[v] O God.
You are my help and my deliverer;
LORD, do not delay.

Psalm 71

71:1-3pp — Ps 31:1-4

1 In you, LORD, I have taken refuge;
let me never be put to shame.[w]
2 In your righteousness, rescue me and deliver me;
turn your ear[x] to me and save me.
3 Be my rock of refuge,
to which I can always go;
give the command to save me,
for you are my rock and my fortress.[y]
4 Deliver me, my God, from the hand of the wicked,[z]
from the grasp of those who are evil and cruel.

5 For you have been my hope, Sovereign LORD,
my confidence[a] since my youth.
6 From birth[b] I have relied on you;
you brought me forth from my mother's womb.[c]
I will ever praise[d] you.
7 I have become a sign[e] to many;
you are my strong refuge.[f]

Ps 71 *Do Not Cast Me Away When I Am Old. I Will Always Have Hope.* This psalm is a prayer for deliverance from enemies, and it easily continues the thoughts in Ps 70. But there is much more confidence and hope in this psalm than in Ps 70. Ps 71 builds around three sections of petition (vv. 1–4,9–13,18), following each by expressing trust and praise (vv. 5–8,14–17,19–24). Indeed, the structural midpoint, v. 14, emphasizes hope and praise. Though the psalm does not attribute authorship, it sounds very much like that which a king, possibly David, would say. As such, then, it fits with the short series of Davidic psalms immediately preceding (Pss 68–70), and it anticipates Ps 72, which is attributed to Solomon and is a prayer for the king.

Ps 71 continues the theme of concern for the nations expressed in Pss 65–67 by referring to God's mighty deeds (cf. vv. 15–18; 65:5; 66:3,5). The focus on enemies in vv. 10–13 also echoes the overall emphasis and tone of Ps 69, including (1) the imprecation (i.e., curse) in v. 13, which uses similar language as 69:22–28, and (2) the scorn motif (cf. vv. 10–11,13; 69:5–12,19–21). The psalm's links with Ps 70 revolve around the psalmists' enemies, including the appeal for God to come quickly to help him (v. 12; 70:1,5), the request that the psalmist's enemies be put to shame and be disgraced (v. 13; 70:2), and the plea for deliverance (v. 2; 70:1).

The psalmist has used portions of other psalms to compose his own, stitching them together in such a way as to create a completely new psalm with its own internal logic and integrity. Ties with Ps 31 are the most prominent, especially vv. 1–3, which essentially duplicate 31:1–3. For other ties, see the cross references. Interestingly, Ps 71 follows immediately upon Ps 70, which is also taken mostly from another psalm (cf. 70:1–5 with 40:13–17). On Ps 71's lack of a title, see the introduction to Ps 70.

71:1 refuge. God as the psalmist's refuge is a prominent motif early in the psalm (vv. 1–3,7). It is also one of the most important themes running through the Psalter (see notes on 2:12; 18:1–2). In Book II (Pss 42–72), this theme is especially prominent (see introductions to Pss 46; 57).

71:3 rock. See note on 18:2.

71:5 For you have been my hope, Sovereign LORD. The psalmist follows his first petitions with expressions of trust and praise.

8 My mouth[g] is filled with your praise,
declaring your splendor[h] all day long.

9 Do not cast[i] me away when I am old;[j]
do not forsake me when my strength is gone.
10 For my enemies speak against me;
those who wait to kill[k] me conspire[l] together.
11 They say, "God has forsaken him;
pursue him and seize him,
for no one will rescue[m] him."
12 Do not be far[n] from me, my God;
come quickly, God, to help[o] me.
13 May my accusers perish in shame;
may those who want to harm me
be covered with scorn and disgrace.[p]

14 As for me, I will always have hope;[q]
I will praise you more and more.
15 My mouth will tell[r] of your righteous deeds,
of your saving acts all day long —
though I know not how to relate them all.
16 I will come and proclaim your mighty acts,[s] Sovereign
LORD;
I will proclaim your righteous deeds, yours alone.
17 Since my youth, God, you have taught[t] me,
and to this day I declare your marvelous deeds.[u]
18 Even when I am old and gray,[v]
do not forsake me, my God,
till I declare your power to the next generation,
your mighty acts to all who are to come.[w]

19 Your righteousness, God, reaches to the heavens,[x]
you who have done great things.[y]
Who is like you, God?[z]
20 Though you have made me see troubles,[a]
many and bitter,
you will restore[b] my life again;
from the depths of the earth
you will again bring me up.
21 You will increase my honor[c]
and comfort[d] me once more.

71:8 [g] Ps 51:15; 63:5 [h] Ps 35:28; 96:6; 104:1
71:9 [i] Ps 51:11 [j] ver 18; Ps 92:14; Isa 46:4
71:10 [k] Ps 10:8; 59:3; Pr 1:18 [l] Ps 31:13; 56:6; Mt 12:14
71:11 [m] Ps 7:2
71:12 [n] Ps 35:22; 38:21 [o] Ps 38:22; 70:1
71:13 [p] ver 24
71:14 [q] Ps 130:7
71:15 [r] Ps 35:28; 40:5
71:16 [s] Ps 106:2
71:17 [t] Dt 4:5 [u] Ps 26:7
71:18 [v] ver 9 [w] Ps 22:30, 31; 78:4
71:19 [x] Ps 36:5; 57:10 [y] Ps 126:2; Lk 1:49 [z] Ps 35:10
71:20 [a] Ps 60:3 [b] Hos 6:2
71:21 [c] Ps 18:35 [d] Ps 23:4; 86:17; Isa 12:1; 49:13

71:8 your splendor. See note on 29:2.
71:9 when I am old. The psalmist writes from a perspective late in life; see also vv. 5,17 ("since my youth") and v. 18 ("when I am old and gray"). This likely accounts for the recurring notes of hope and trust in the psalm, as the psalmist has experienced God as his refuge (vv. 1–3,7) and witnessed God's mighty deeds throughout his life (vv. 15–19,24). These form the basis of his hope in the midst of his current troubles.
71:11 They say. Many times the psalmists quote their enemies' words directly. See note on 10:6.
71:13 On the psalmist's imprecations (i.e., curses), see note on 69:22–28.
71:14 This stands at the structural midpoint of the psalm (see note on 100:3 ["his people"]) and expresses the heart of the psalm's message: hope.
71:15–17 righteous deeds ... saving acts ... righteous deeds ... marvelous deeds. These refer to great things that God has done on his people's behalf. See note on 26:7.
71:18 the next generation. The psalmist knows that it was critical that the faith be passed down through the generations. God told the Israelites to teach their children of him at any time of day or night (Deut 6:7), and he stressed that each generation needed to enter into the covenant anew (Deut 5:2–3; 29:14–15; Josh 24:25–27). It was not enough to be born an Israelite; each generation had to appropriate the faith for themselves, and it was the responsibility of the entire community to proclaim the faith boldly and to pass it down: parents, priests, and even the king (as here).
71:19 Who is like you, God? See note on 89:6.

71:22 [e]Ps 33:2 [f]Ps 92:3; 144:9 [g]2Ki 19:22
71:23 [h]Ps 103:4
71:24 [i]Ps 35:28 [j]ver 13
72:2 [k]Isa 9:7; 11:4-5; 32:1
72:4 [l]Isa 11:4
72:6 [m]Dt 32:2; Hos 6:3
72:7 [n]Ps 92:12; Isa 2:4
72:8 [o]Ex 23:31 [p]Zec 9:10

22 I will praise you with the harp[e]
for your faithfulness, my God;
I will sing praise to you with the lyre,[f]
Holy One of Israel.[g]
23 My lips will shout for joy
when I sing praise to you—
I whom you have delivered.[h]
24 My tongue will tell of your righteous acts
all day long,[i]
for those who wanted to harm me[j]
have been put to shame and confusion.

Psalm 72

Of Solomon.

1 Endow the king with your justice, O God,
the royal son with your righteousness.
2 May he judge your people in righteousness,[k]
your afflicted ones with justice.

3 May the mountains bring prosperity to the people,
the hills the fruit of righteousness.
4 May he defend the afflicted among the people
and save the children of the needy;[l]
may he crush the oppressor.
5 May he endure[a] as long as the sun,
as long as the moon, through all generations.
6 May he be like rain[m] falling on a mown field,
like showers watering the earth.
7 In his days may the righteous flourish[n]
and prosperity abound till the moon is no more.

8 May he rule from sea to sea
and from the River[b][o] to the ends of the earth.[p]
9 May the desert tribes bow before him
and his enemies lick the dust.

[a] 5 Septuagint; Hebrew *You will be feared* [b] 8 That is, the Euphrates

71:22 harp ... lyre. See note on 150:3. **Holy One of Israel.** This label for God emphasizes not only God's holiness but also his relationship with his people: he is *Israel's* Holy One. It occurs most frequently in the book of Isaiah (25 times) but also in 78:41; 89:18 (cf. 22:3).

Ps 72 *Endow the King With Your Justice, O God.* A prayer on behalf of the king, attributed to Solomon, the great and wise son of David. It uses extravagant language asking God that the king will endure like the sun (vv. 5,15,17), that kings of the earth will come to offer him tribute (v. 10), and that his rule will extend to the "ends of the earth" (v. 8). Yet the psalm shows that the king was not simply to receive acclamation; he was to judge God's people in righteousness (v. 2) and defend the helpless of society: the afflicted, weak, and needy (vv. 4,12–14). This is one of the so-called royal psalms (see introduction to Ps 18), and it is unique among them in emphasizing the king's role in defending and protecting the weakest in society. It also stands at an important "seam" in the Psalter: between Books II and III (see Introduction: Structure). Ultimately, this psalm points to the greatest descendant of David and Solomon: Jesus the Messiah, who perfectly fulfills the image of the king in this psalm, including modeling for us a concern for the helpless of society.

72 title Only two psalms are ascribed to Solomon: Pss 72 and 127. Solomon was the anointed son of David and heir to the promises made to David; God said that he would be Solomon's father and that Solomon would be his son (2 Sam 7:14). Known for his great wisdom, Solomon composed many proverbs and songs (1 Kgs 4:29–34).

72:1–2 The opening prayer unfolds in mirror-image fashion: the psalmist asks God to endow the king with his righteousness and justice (v. 1) and then prays that the king would exercise these wisely (v. 2).

72:3–7 The prayer for the king continues by asking God to bring prosperity and abundance (vv. 3,7) and by asking for the king's rule to extend as long as the sun and the moon (vv. 5,7). A key component of the king's benevolent rule is that he should champion the cause of the powerless in society (v. 4).

72:8–11 The grandiosity of the language increases as the psalmist sees the king's rule extending from "sea to sea," even "to the ends of the earth" (v. 8); tribes and kings come from near and far to pay him tribute (vv. 9–11).

[10]May the kings of Tarshish and of distant shores
bring tribute to him.
May the kings of Sheba[q] and Seba
present him gifts.[r]
[11]May all kings bow down to him
and all nations serve him.

[12]For he will deliver the needy who cry out,
the afflicted who have no one to help.
[13]He will take pity on the weak and the needy
and save the needy from death.
[14]He will rescue[s] them from oppression and
violence,
for precious[t] is their blood in his sight.

[15]Long may he live!
May gold from Sheba[u] be given him.
May people ever pray for him
and bless him all day long.
[16]May grain abound throughout the land;
on the tops of the hills may it sway.
May the crops flourish like Lebanon[v]
and thrive[a] like the grass of the field.
[17]May his name endure forever;[w]
may it continue as long as the sun.[x]

Then all nations will be blessed through him,[b]
and they will call him blessed.[y]

[18]Praise be to the LORD God, the God of Israel,[z]
who alone does marvelous deeds.[a]
[19]Praise be to his glorious name forever;
may the whole earth be filled with his glory.[b]
Amen and Amen.[c]

[20]This concludes the prayers of David son of Jesse.

a 16 Probable reading of the original Hebrew text; Masoretic Text *Lebanon, / from the city* *b 17* Or *will use his name in blessings* (see Gen. 48:20)

72:10 [q]Ge 10:7 [r]2Ch 9:24
72:14 [s]Ps 69:18 [t]1Sa 26:21; Ps 116:15
72:15 [u]Isa 60:6
72:16 [v]Ps 104:16
72:17 [w]Ex 3:15 [x]Ps 89:36 [y]Ge 12:3; Lk 1:48
72:18 [z]1Ch 29:10; Ps 41:13; 106:48 [a]Job 5:9
72:19 [b]Nu 14:21; Ne 9:5 [c]Ps 41:13

A divine gift of justice (Ps 72:1) to eighteenth-century BC King Hammurabi, from the top of the Hammurabi law code.

72:10 Tarshish. A faraway land or city (see note on 48:7). **Sheba.** Land in the southwestern Arabian peninsula whose queen came to Solomon when she heard of his fame (1 Kgs 10:1–13). It was a rich source of gold (1 Kgs 10:2; Isa 60:6), frankincense (Isa 60:6; Jer 6:20), and spices and precious stones (1 Kgs 10:2; Ezek 27:22). **Seba.** Land near Sheba. Many scholars consider these to be simply two versions of the same place-name. The point of all three place-names is that kings from faraway places and different points of the compass were to come and pay tribute to Israel's king.
72:12–13 needy ... afflicted ... weak. See note on 82:3–4.
72:15–17a The acclaim rendered to the king reaches a climax in this final section of prayers, jumping from topic to topic in quick succession, and beginning and ending with prayer for the king's long life.
72:17b This brief allusion to the Abrahamic covenant (Gen 22:18: "through your offspring all nations on earth will be blessed") is a powerful reminder that God's people, especially their king, were to mediate God's covenant to the nations. See introduction to Ps 67.
72:18–19 This second doxology in the Psalter (see note on 41:13) ends Book II. This is the longest of the five doxologies of the Psalter (each one coming at the end of a "book"), and it highlights some themes covered in the latter parts of Book II. It includes the relational phrase "the God of Israel" (v. 18), which echoes the reference to the "Holy One of Israel" in 71:22 (see note there); the Lord's "marvelous deeds" (v. 18), echoing Ps 71:15–17 (see note there); and the declaration that "the whole earth be filled with [God's] glory" (v. 19), recalling the worldwide perspectives in Pss 65–67.
72:20 the prayers of David son of Jesse. This appears to be a later editorial addition to the psalm. It is somewhat strange to see this attribution of psalms to David at the end of a psalm attributed to Solomon. It suggests a collection of David's prayers that concludes here, but this does not end the Davidic psalms: there are 18 more in Books III–V. So the most likely scenario is that a smaller collection of psalms ended here, perhaps Pss 3–72, which circulated as an independent collection for some time, which was identified as such by the comment in v. 20, and which eventually was incorporated into the larger Psalter.

73:1 [d]Mt 5:8
73:3 [e]Ps 37:1; Pr 23:17 [f]Job 21:7; Jer 12:1
73:5 [g]Job 21:9
73:6 [h]Ge 41:42 [i]Ps 109:18
73:7 [j]Ps 17:10
73:8 [k]Ps 17:10; Jude 16

BOOK III

Psalms 73–89

Psalm 73

A psalm of Asaph.

1 Surely God is good to Israel,
to those who are pure in heart.[d]

2 But as for me, my feet had almost slipped;
I had nearly lost my foothold.
3 For I envied[e] the arrogant
when I saw the prosperity of the wicked.[f]

4 They have no struggles;
their bodies are healthy and strong.[a]
5 They are free[g] from common human burdens;
they are not plagued by human ills.
6 Therefore pride is their necklace;[h]
they clothe themselves with violence.[i]
7 From their callous hearts[j] comes iniquity[b];
their evil imaginations have no limits.
8 They scoff, and speak with malice;
with arrogance[k] they threaten oppression.
9 Their mouths lay claim to heaven,
and their tongues take possession of the earth.
10 Therefore their people turn to them
and drink up waters in abundance.[c]

[a] 4 With a different word division of the Hebrew; Masoretic Text *struggles at their death; / their bodies are healthy* [b] 7 Syriac (see also Septuagint); Hebrew *Their eyes bulge with fat* [c] 10 The meaning of the Hebrew for this verse is uncertain.

Pss 73–89 *Book III: The Book of Crisis.* Most of the psalms in Book III deal with crises, present or past: Pss 73–74; 78–80; 83; 85–86; 88–89. The historical situation behind most psalms is impossible to specify with any certainty, but at least three deal with the Babylonian exile (Pss 74; 79; 80) and one may be postexilic (Ps 85). The absence of Davidic psalms (except Ps 86) fits this tendency (since David lived centuries before the exile). The grouping of psalms of Asaph at the beginning (Pss 73–83) dominates the book; a small collection of psalms by the sons of Korah follows (Pss 84–85; 87–88). In contrast to the highly individualistic nature of much of Books I and II—which deal with David's or others' personal struggles or thanksgivings—most of the psalms in Book III deal with communal or national issues (Pss 74–76; 78–83; 85; 87; 89); only Pss 73; 77; 84; 86; 88 focus on the individual. The book ends with two very downbeat psalms: the darkest psalm in the Psalter (Ps 88) precedes a psalm that questions God severely about the "broken" covenant that he made with David (Ps 89). The answer to the questions about the destruction of Jerusalem and the temple and the exile are not fully answered until Books IV and V.

Ps 73 *It Is Good to Be Near God.* This psalm eloquently expresses total abandonment to the God of the universe. It reflects on the seemingly carefree life of the wicked who prosper (vv. 3–12), echoing sentiments expressed in Ps 49. Concern for the downtrodden in the previous psalm (72:4) contrasts with the grim present reality—the pride of the wicked (v. 6). Ps 73 picks up on Solomon's prayer in 72:7 that the righteous would flourish and prosper (as 1:3 also asserts), but Ps 73 turns that prayer around, asserting that the wicked seem to prosper without any consequences (contrary to what 1:4 asserts). But Ps 73 ends by expressing profound truth about the meaning of life, which is revealed only in God's presence (vv. 15–28, especially vv. 17,28) and only in one's total abandonment to him (vv. 25–26). This is one of the so-called wisdom psalms (see introduction to Ps 34), which reflect on many of life's deepest issues.

73 title Asaph. A descendant of Levi (1 Chr 6:39–43); served as chief musician at the sanctuary; appointed by David (1 Chr 16:5,7). He led in sounding the cymbals along with Heman and Ethan/Jeduthun (1 Chr 15:19; see notes on Ps 39 title; Ps 88 title; Ps 89 title), and he led in the dedication of Solomon's temple along with Heman, Ethan/Jeduthun, and their families (2 Chr 5:12). He also was a seer (1 Chr 25:2; 2 Chr 29:30), or prophet (1 Sam 9:9), and composed songs of praise that the people used in worship long after his own time (2 Chr 29:30). His descendants continued as chief musicians into the postexilic period, many centuries after Asaph (1 Chr 25:1–2, 6–9; 2 Chr 20:14; 35:15; Ezra 3:10; Neh 11:17,22; 12:35). A series of 11 psalms of Asaph (73–83) introduces Book III. This groups together all of the Asaphic psalms except for Ps 50, which owes its place to its connections with Ps 51 (see introduction to Ps 50).

73:1 pure in heart. Blameless in attitudes and motives. See also v. 13, where "pure" translates a related Hebrew word denoting a cleansed heart (cf. 24:4).

73:4 They have no struggles. The lives of the wicked often seem to be carefree. This theme carries through all of vv. 4–12, and it resembles thoughts from 10:2–11 (cf. Job 21:7–33; Hab 1:13–17).

[11]They say, "How would God know?
Does the Most High know anything?"

[12]This is what the wicked are like —
always free of care, they go on amassing wealth.[l]

[13]Surely in vain[m] I have kept my heart pure
and have washed my hands in innocence.[n]

[14]All day long I have been afflicted,
and every morning brings new punishments.

[15]If I had spoken out like that,
I would have betrayed your children.

[16]When I tried to understand[o] all this,
it troubled me deeply

[17]till I entered the sanctuary[p] of God;
then I understood their final destiny.[q]

[18]Surely you place them on slippery ground;[r]
you cast them down to ruin.

[19]How suddenly[s] are they destroyed,
completely swept away by terrors!

[20]They are like a dream[t] when one awakes;[u]
when you arise, Lord,
you will despise them as fantasies.

[21]When my heart was grieved
and my spirit embittered,

[22]I was senseless[v] and ignorant;
I was a brute beast[w] before you.

[23]Yet I am always with you;
you hold me by my right hand.

[24]You guide[x] me with your counsel,[y]
and afterward you will take me into glory.

[25]Whom have I in heaven but you?
And earth has nothing I desire besides you.[z]

[26]My flesh and my heart[a] may fail,[b]
but God is the strength of my heart
and my portion forever.

[27]Those who are far from you will perish;[c]
you destroy all who are unfaithful to you.

[28]But as for me, it is good to be near God.[d]
I have made the Sovereign LORD my refuge;
I will tell of all your deeds.[e]

73:12 [l]Ps 49:6
73:13 [m]Job 21:15; 34:9 [n]Ps 26:6
73:16 [o]Ecc 8:17
73:17 [p]Ps 77:13 [q]Ps 37:38
73:18 [r]Ps 35:6
73:19 [s]Isa 47:11
73:20 [t]Job 20:8 [u]Ps 78:65
73:22 [v]Ps 49:10; 92:6 [w]Ecc 3:18
73:24 [x]Ps 48:14 [y]Ps 32:8
73:25 [z]Php 3:8
73:26 [a]Ps 84:2 [b]Ps 40:12
73:27 [c]Ps 119:155
73:28 [d]Heb 10:22; Jas 4:8 [e]Ps 40:5

73:11 Most High. See note on 7:8.

73:13 pure. See note on v. 1.

73:14 Asaph's sufferings seem endless, and each day is worse than the previous one. This contrasts with Lam 3:22–23: God's faithfulness and compassions are "new every morning."

73:15 The structural center of the psalm (see note on 100:3) highlights Asaph's pivot away from pessimistic envy of the wicked (vv. 2–14) toward his embrace of God at the sanctuary (v. 17). **that.** What Asaph now realizes were his ill-advised words in vv. 2–14.

73:17 sanctuary. See note on 5:7. God's presence makes all the difference. **their final destiny.** Contrasts with the glorious future awaiting the righteous (v. 24).

73:20 arise. See note on 3:7.

73:23 I am always with you. Asaph's outlook changed dramatically when he entered God's sanctuary (v. 17). He takes comfort knowing that God always cares for and protects him, leading him to recognize that being near to God is his highest good (v. 28).

73:24 Asaph expects to be with God after death. This contrasts with the "final destiny" of the wicked (v. 17). See note on 16:9–11.

73:25 Asaph's abandonment to God contrasts with the rich young ruler in Matt 19:16–22, who clung to his possessions and missed out on the greatest gift in life: God's presence.

73:28 refuge. See notes on 2:12; 18:1–2.

74:1 [f]Dt 29:20; Ps 44:23 [g]Ps 79:13; 95:7; 100:3
74:2 [h]Ex 15:16 [i]Dt 32:7 [j]Ex 15:13 [k]Ps 68:16
74:4 [l]La 2:7 [m]Nu 2:2
74:5 [n]Jer 46:22
74:6 [o]1Ki 6:18
74:8 [p]Ps 83:4
74:9 [q]1Sa 3:1
74:10 [r]Ps 44:16
74:11 [s]La 2:3

Psalm 74

A *maskil*[a] of Asaph.

[1] O God, why have you rejected us forever?[f]
Why does your anger smolder against the sheep of your pasture?[g]
[2] Remember the nation you purchased[h] long ago,[i]
the people of your inheritance, whom you redeemed[j]—
Mount Zion, where you dwelt.[k]
[3] Turn your steps toward these everlasting ruins,
all this destruction the enemy has brought on the sanctuary.

[4] Your foes roared[l] in the place where you met with us;
they set up their standards[m] as signs.
[5] They behaved like men wielding axes
to cut through a thicket of trees.[n]
[6] They smashed all the carved[o] paneling
with their axes and hatchets.
[7] They burned your sanctuary to the ground;
they defiled the dwelling place of your Name.
[8] They said in their hearts, "We will crush[p] them completely!"
They burned every place where God was worshiped in the land.

[9] We are given no signs from God;
no prophets[q] are left,
and none of us knows how long this will be.
[10] How long will the enemy mock you, God?
Will the foe revile[r] your name forever?
[11] Why do you hold back your hand, your right hand?[s]
Take it from the folds of your garment and destroy them!

[a] Title: Probably a literary or musical term

Ps 74 *Remember Mount Zion, Where You Dwelt.* Immediately following Ps 73, in which the psalmist finds meaning in God's presence at the sanctuary, Ps 74 deals with the crisis of that sanctuary's destruction and God's seeming abandonment of his people to their enemies. The setting is the time of the exile in Babylon, after the destruction of Jerusalem (see Ps 79; Jer 52; Lam 2). The psalmist calls on God to remember his people and Mount Zion, the place of his dwelling (vv. 1–3), because God's enemies have overwhelmed that place (vv. 4–8). The psalmist feels abandoned and alone (vv. 9–11), but in the central declaration of the psalm, he affirms God as his King (v. 12). This God is the one whose power over the waters and all of creation (vv. 13–17) gives the psalmist the confidence to call upon God to remember his people, have regard for his covenant, and defend his cause (vv. 18–23).
74 title Asaph. Not the individual from David's day (1 Chr 16:5,7) but a descendant of the family of Asaph (see note on Ps 73 title) since the psalm is written from the perspective of the destruction of Jerusalem, hundreds of years after the original Asaph lived.
74:1 Why ...? See note on 10:1. See also "How long ...?" in v. 10. **sheep.** See note on 23:1.
74:2 purchased. Long ago in Egypt (Exod 15:16) at considerable cost. **inheritance.** From the people's beginnings in Egypt (Exod 34:9; Deut 9:29; 32:9), God highly valued them even if at times he was angry with them (here; 28:9; 33:12; 78:62; 94:5,14; 106:40; 1 Sam 10:1). **redeemed.** Out of Egyptian bondage (Exod 15:13). This language of purchase and redemption is a reminder of Ruth 4:1–10, suggesting that God was Israel's "guardian-redeemer" who was willing to pay a costly price for his people. **Mount Zion.** See notes on 2:6; 9:11.
74:3 sanctuary. See notes on 5:7.
74:4 standards. Probably banners, often used in battle as rallying points (20:5; Isa 31:9; Jer 4:21; cf. Num 1:52).
74:6 carved paneling. Solomon's temple was richly overlaid with cedar (1 Kgs 6:15).
74:7 burned your sanctuary. See 2 Kgs 25:9; Jer 52:13. **Name.** See note on 8:1. The NIV capitalizes "Name" when it is bound up with God's presence (also in 75:1; cf. 1 Kgs 3:2; see Deut 12:5 and note). Here and 75:1 are the only two references in Psalms where the NIV capitalizes "Name"; it does so to emphasize God's presence. In Ps 74, the sanctuary—the place of God's Name—is destroyed; in Ps 75, God's Name is "near" to his people (75:1), which mirrors 73:28.
74:8 every place where God was worshiped. The temple in Jerusalem was the main place God's people should worship him, but before the temple was built, there were other such places, such as Shiloh (Josh 18:1; 1 Sam 1:3; 3:21; see note on 78:60), Mizpah (1 Sam 7:5–12), and certain high places (1 Kgs 3:2), as well as places of false worship (2 Kgs 18:4; 23:5). Apparently, some of the places where worship took place—including Mizpah—still existed when the Babylonians devastated the land and those places continued to exist afterward (see 2 Kgs 25:23; Jer 40:10).
74:9 no signs ... no prophets. God had done many signs and wonders for Israel throughout its history (78:43; see note on 26:7), but now these and God's prophets were absent, echoing the time centuries earlier when the "the word of the LORD was rare" (1 Sam 3:1).
74:10 How long ...? Hints at the "Why?" question in v. 1 (see notes on v. 1; 13:1,2).

[12] But God is my King[t] from long ago;
he brings salvation on the earth.

[13] It was you who split open the sea[u] by your power;
you broke the heads of the monster[v] in the waters.
[14] It was you who crushed the heads of Leviathan
and gave it as food to the creatures of the desert.
[15] It was you who opened up springs[w] and streams;
you dried up[x] the ever-flowing rivers.
[16] The day is yours, and yours also the night;
you established the sun and moon.[y]
[17] It was you who set all the boundaries[z] of the earth;
you made both summer and winter.[a]

[18] Remember how the enemy has mocked you, LORD,
how foolish people[b] have reviled your name.
[19] Do not hand over the life of your dove to wild beasts;
do not forget the lives of your afflicted[c] people forever.
[20] Have regard for your covenant,[d]
because haunts of violence fill the dark places of the land.
[21] Do not let the oppressed[e] retreat in disgrace;
may the poor and needy[f] praise your name.
[22] Rise up, O God, and defend your cause;
remember how fools[g] mock you all day long.
[23] Do not ignore the clamor of your adversaries,[h]
the uproar of your enemies, which rises continually.

74:12 [t] Ps 44:4
74:13 [u] Ex 14:21 [v] Isa 51:9; Eze 29:3
74:15 [w] Ex 17:6; Nu 20:11 [x] Jos 2:10; 3:13
74:16 [y] Ge 1:16; Ps 136:7-9
74:17 [z] Dt 32:8; Ac 17:26 [a] Ge 8:22
74:18 [b] Dt 32:6; Ps 39:8
74:19 [c] Ps 9:18
74:20 [d] Ge 17:7; Ps 106:45
74:21 [e] Ps 103:6 [f] Ps 35:10
74:22 [g] Ps 53:1
74:23 [h] Ps 65:7
75:1 [i] Ps 145:18 [j] Ps 44:1; 71:16

Psalm 75[a]

For the director of music. To the tune of "Do Not Destroy." A psalm of Asaph. A song.

[1] We praise you, God,
we praise you, for your Name is near;[i]
people tell of your wonderful deeds.[j]

[a] In Hebrew texts 75:1-10 is numbered 75:2-11.

74:12 Structurally, the central verse of the psalm (see note on 100:3). Its message is the basis for the psalmist's confidence that God could and would respond to his prayers. As the Sovereign King, he showed his power over all of nature (vv. 13–17). The Lord's kingship is one of the great themes of the Psalter (see notes on 10:16; 93:1; cf. 1 Tim 6:15; Rev 17:14).
74:13–17 The imagery in vv. 13–14 possibly echoes ancient Near Eastern creation myths that speak of great conflicts with monsters of the sea; God the King is sovereign over all of these (Gen 1:2,6–10; Job 41; Isa 27:1; see notes on Pss 93:3; 104:26; Gen 1:2 ["deep"]; Job 40:15 ["Behemoth"]). The imagery in v. 15 evokes the stories of the exodus from Egypt (Exod 17:1–7) and entry into Canaan (Josh 3:17), but vv. 16–17 go beyond specific historical incidents to affirm God's sovereignty over all of creation, echoing Gen 1.
74:14 Leviathan. See notes on 104:26; Job 40:15.
74:18 Remember. The urgent questioning of God in vv. 1,10 gives way to urgent petitioning: "remember" (vv. 18,22), "do not" (vv. 19,21,23), "have regard" (v. 20), "rise up" (v. 22), "defend" (v. 22). This language conveys the sense of urgency and desperation as well as the psalmist's security in his God, whom he approaches with boldness (see v. 1 and note on 10:1). **foolish people.** See note on 14:1.
74:19 your dove. Sometimes a term of endearment (Song 2:14; 5:2; 6:9). Here it also appears to symbolize helplessness, referring to Israel (cf. note on 68:13).
74:20 your covenant. See note on 25:10.
74:21 poor and needy. See notes on 82:3,4.
74:22 Rise up. See note on 3:7.
Ps 75 *The Horns of the Righteous Will Be Lifted Up.* In its present location in the Psalter, Ps 75 answers the crises that Ps 74 addresses, though it is difficult to date historically. God directly rebukes his enemies (v. 4), foes who dared to speak arrogant words against God's people (74:8). They destroyed the place of God's Name (see 74:7 and note), but now God's Name is near (v. 1). Verses 3,6 resound with what 74:16–17 affirms about God's sovereignty over the earth and all of nature. God will judge his enemies harshly and vindicate the righteous, and the psalmist celebrates this with praise. He opens by expressing corporate praise (v. 1) and closes with his own individual praise (vv. 9–10). In between, he quotes God himself, who declares his own justice and power and rebukes the arrogant (vv. 2–4), and the psalmist affirms this (vv. 5–8).
75:1 Name. See note on 74:7. **wonderful deeds.** God's mighty acts and miracles on behalf of his people (see note on 26:7).

75:3 [k]Isa 24:19 [l]1Sa 2:8
75:4 [m]Zec 1:21
75:7 [n]Ps 50:6 [o]1Sa 2:7; Ps 147:6; Da 2:21
75:8 [p]Pr 23:30 [q]Job 21:20; Jer 25:15
75:9 [r]Ps 40:10
75:10 [s]Ps 89:17; 92:10; 148:14
76:2 [t]Ge 14:18
76:3 [u]Ps 46:9

2 You say, "I choose the appointed time;
it is I who judge with equity.
3 When the earth and all its people quake,[k]
it is I who hold its pillars[l] firm.[a]
4 To the arrogant I say, 'Boast no more,'
and to the wicked, 'Do not lift up your horns.[b][m]
5 Do not lift your horns against heaven;
do not speak so defiantly.' "

6 No one from the east or the west
or from the desert can exalt themselves.
7 It is God who judges:[n]
He brings one down, he exalts another.[o]
8 In the hand of the LORD is a cup
full of foaming wine mixed[p] with spices;
he pours it out, and all the wicked of the earth
drink it down to its very dregs.[q]

9 As for me, I will declare[r] this forever;
I will sing praise to the God of Jacob,
10 who says, "I will cut off the horns of all the wicked,
but the horns of the righteous will be lifted up."[s]

Psalm 76[c]

For the director of music. With stringed instruments. A psalm of Asaph. A song.

1 God is renowned in Judah;
in Israel his name is great.
2 His tent is in Salem,[t]
his dwelling place in Zion.
3 There he broke the flashing arrows,
the shields and the swords, the weapons of war.[d][u]

4 You are radiant with light,
more majestic than mountains rich with game.

[a] *3* The Hebrew has *Selah* (a word of uncertain meaning) here. [b] *4* *Horns* here symbolize strength; also in verses 5 and 10. [c] In Hebrew texts 76:1-12 is numbered 76:2-13. [d] *3* The Hebrew has *Selah* (a word of uncertain meaning) here and at the end of verse 9.

75:2 judge with equity. God, in his capacity as King (74:12), will always ensure that justice is done on the earth for both the righteous and the wicked (9:4–5; 82:8; 94:2; 96:10; see notes on 96:13; 99:8).
75:3 God, who sets the earth's boundaries (74:17), can shake the earth and its pillars (Job 9:6) and support it on a firm foundation (18:15; 82:5; 1 Sam 2:8; Prov 8:29; Isa 24:18; see also note on Ps 24:2).
75:4 horns. See NIV text note. An animal lifting its horns expresses its will and power; in vv. 4–5 it expresses human rebellion against God. But it is good when God lifts the horn of the righteous (v. 10; 89:17,24).
75:7 brings one down ... exalts. God distributes punishment and reward according to his own righteous justice (vv. 2,7), a point that Hannah also affirms in 1 Sam 2:7. See also 113:7–9 and note.
75:8 cup. Of judgment (see note on 16:5). **foaming wine.** Still fermenting (cf. Deut 32:14). **mixed with spices.** See Prov 9:2; Song 8:2. It is God's special concoction by which to judge the wicked. He compels the wicked to drink every drop.
75:10 wicked ... righteous. A contrast, as in 1:6.
Ps 76 *It Is You Alone Who Are to Be Feared.* Ps 76 continues the note of praise in Ps 75 to the God who vanquishes his enemies; in their present location in the Psalter, both psalms respond to the crisis in Ps 74. The psalm celebrates God's power: he is to be feared (vv. 7–8,11–12), and he overwhelms his opponents (vv. 3,5–7,10,12). Mount Zion, God's dwelling place that the Babylonians destroyed (74:2–3,7), is now where God securely dwells (v. 2). The psalm is one of several "psalms of Zion" (see introduction to Ps 46). The psalmist begins by affirming God's renown in the nation and his secure place in Zion (vv. 1–2) and by emphasizing his power over his enemies, none of whom can withstand him (vv. 3–6). God is the wrathful but righteous judge (vv. 7–10), and all nations should submit to and fear him (vv. 11–12).
76:2 Salem. Another name for Jerusalem (Gen 14:18). **Zion.** God's holy mountain, the place of his earthly dwelling (74:2; see notes on 2:6; 9:11). The heavens are also his dwelling place (v. 8; 1 Kgs 8:30; Isa 66:1), but nothing—not the earthly temple, not Mount Zion, not heaven itself—can contain God (1 Kgs 8:27).
76:3 Possibly describes God's specific victory over the Assyrians in Hezekiah's day (2 Kgs 19:32–36), but the language applies generally to any occasion when God triumphs.
76:4 more majestic than mountains. Or "majestic from the mountains," which would emphasize God's lion-like fierceness and remoteness (see note on v. 2).

5 The valiant lie plundered,
they sleep their last sleep;[v]
not one of the warriors
can lift his hands.
6 At your rebuke, God of Jacob,
both horse and chariot[w] lie still.

7 It is you alone who are to be feared.[x]
Who can stand[y] before you when you are angry?[z]
8 From heaven you pronounced judgment,
and the land feared[a] and was quiet—
9 when you, God, rose up to judge,[b]
to save all the afflicted of the land.
10 Surely your wrath against mankind brings you praise,[c]
and the survivors of your wrath are restrained.[a]

11 Make vows to the LORD your God and fulfill them;[d]
let all the neighboring lands
bring gifts[e] to the One to be feared.
12 He breaks the spirit of rulers;
he is feared by the kings of the earth.

Psalm 77[b]

For the director of music. For Jeduthun. Of Asaph. A psalm.

1 I cried out to God[f] for help;
I cried out to God to hear me.
2 When I was in distress,[g] I sought the Lord;
at night I stretched out untiring hands,[h]
and I would not be comforted.[i]

3 I remembered you, God, and I groaned;
I meditated, and my spirit grew faint.[c][j]

76:5 [v] Ps 13:3
76:6 [w] Ex 15:1
76:7 [x] 1Ch 16:25 [y] Ezr 9:15; Rev 6:17 [z] Ps 2:5; Na 1:6
76:8 [a] 1Ch 16:30; 2Ch 20:29-30
76:9 [b] Ps 9:8
76:10 [c] Ex 9:16; Ro 9:17
76:11 [d] Ps 50:14; Ecc 5:4-5 [e] 2Ch 32:23; Ps 68:29
77:1 [f] Ps 3:4
77:2 [g] Ps 50:15; Isa 26:9, 16 [h] Job 11:13 [i] Ge 37:35
77:3 [j] Ps 143:4

[a] *10* Or *Surely the wrath of mankind brings you praise, / and with the remainder of wrath you arm yourself*
[b] In Hebrew texts 77:1-20 is numbered 77:2-21. [c] *3* The Hebrew has *Selah* (a word of uncertain meaning) here and at the end of verses 9 and 15.

76:6 horse and chariot. Backbones of any ancient army. See note on 20:7.
76:9 rose up. Answers 74:22. **afflicted.** Echoes 74:21. See note on 82:3–4.
76:10 God's wrath against his enemies results in people praising him because of his great power (in keeping with vv. 1–4); those who survive his wrath are restrained out of fear of him (see v. 7). The first line of the NIV text note assumes that it is human wrath directed against God, which God then crushes (v. 3); this in turn results in people's praising him. The second line of the NIV text note then indicates that God has "unused" wrath left over, which he will direct against other enemies. In the end, both understandings exalt God as the victor over his enemies.
76:11 Make vows. See note on 50:14. **bring gifts.** When the Lord delivered Hezekiah from the Assyrians, many did precisely that (2 Chr 32:23). This is the spirit of praise in v. 10: the Lord's victory would result in people praising him.
76:12 Vindicates God's scorn for the rebellious kings of the earth in Ps 2 since these kings now fear him.
Ps 77 *You Are the God Who Performs Miracles.* This intensely personal psalm of an individual returns to the lament mode of Ps 74, following two communal hymns praising God for his victories over his enemies (Pss 75; 76). In their present location in the Psalter, each of the three responds in its own way to the existential crisis that Ps 74 describes. In the present psalm, the psalmist finds himself in a reflective mode, meditating on God's mighty deeds and his triumphs over his enemies, which gives the psalmist confidence that God will answer him in the present crisis. Asaph begins with a cry for help (vv. 1–2), followed by introspection about the former days, leading him to question whether God has now forgotten his people (vv. 3–9). Then he remembers to reflect on God's mighty deeds from the past, when God delivered his people (vv. 10–15). The psalmist envisions God's triumphs over mighty waters and the elements of nature (vv. 16–19) and recalls God's deliverance through his servants Moses and Aaron (v. 20). The emphasis on God's mighty works in vv. 10–20 lays the foundation for the extensive review of these in Ps 78.
77:2 The psalmist's distress keeps him up at night (6:6; 22:2; 42:3; see 63:6 and note; 88:1; 119:148).
77:3–6 The psalmist has had a close relationship with God in the past, and he longs for it to be renewed; but his present distress consumes him. During times past (v. 5), he had felt God's presence close by at night (v. 6; contrast v. 2; cf. 42:8). His feelings recollect 42:3–4,8.
77:3 meditated. Also in v. 6. See note on 1:2.

77:5 [k] Dt 32:7; Ps 44:1; 143:5; Isa 51:9
77:7 [l] Ps 85:1
77:8 [m] 2Pe 3:9
77:9 [n] Ps 25:6; 40:11; 51:1 [o] Isa 49:15
77:10 [p] Ps 31:22
77:11 [q] Ps 143:5
77:13 [r] Ex 15:11; Ps 71:19; 86:8
77:15 [s] Ex 6:6; Dt 9:29
77:16 [t] Ex 14:21,28; Hab 3:8 [u] Ps 114:4; Hab 3:10
77:17 [v] Jdg 5:4

4 You kept my eyes from closing;
I was too troubled to speak.
5 I thought about the former days,[k]
the years of long ago;
6 I remembered my songs in the night.
My heart meditated and my spirit asked:

7 "Will the Lord reject forever?
Will he never show his favor[l] again?
8 Has his unfailing love vanished forever?
Has his promise[m] failed for all time?
9 Has God forgotten to be merciful?[n]
Has he in anger withheld his compassion?[o]"

10 Then I thought, "To this I will appeal:
the years when the Most High stretched out his right hand.[p]
11 I will remember the deeds of the LORD;
yes, I will remember your miracles[q] of long ago.
12 I will consider all your works
and meditate on all your mighty deeds."

13 Your ways, God, are holy.
What god is as great as our God?[r]
14 You are the God who performs miracles;
you display your power among the peoples.
15 With your mighty arm you redeemed your people,[s]
the descendants of Jacob and Joseph.

16 The waters[t] saw you, God,
the waters saw you and writhed;[u]
the very depths were convulsed.
17 The clouds poured down water,[v]
the heavens resounded with thunder;
your arrows flashed back and forth.

77:6 heart. See note on 7:9.
77:7 reject forever? Mimics Asaph's cries in 74:1; 80:3–4; 83:1. But this psalm moves on to hope, based on remembering God's great deeds in the past (vv. 10–20).
77:8 unfailing love. God's covenantal love for his people. See note on 6:4.
77:10–12 The psalmist turns his thoughts to God's mighty works on behalf of Israel, and his perspective completely changes from his previous despair. Verses 11–12 contain four different words for God's mighty works (see notes on vv. 11–12); no matter from which perspective one views them, God's actions are mighty, awe-inspiring, and confidence building.
77:10 Most High. See note on 7:8. **right hand.** Symbolizes God's power (see note on 20:6).
77:11 deeds. An infrequent Hebrew word denoting any deeds, good or bad. Used of God only here; 78:7; Mic 2:7a ("do"). **miracles.** Also in v. 14; refers to God's most extraordinary deeds (see note on 26:7).
77:12 works. This Hebrew word is used mostly in poetry for actions or accomplishments of humans or God. **mighty deeds.** The Hebrew is used of God's deeds relatively infrequently (9:11 ["what ... done"]; 66:5 ["deeds"]; 78:11 ["what ... done"]; 103:7 ["deeds"]; 105:1 ["what ... done"]).
77:13–20 Reviews God's mighty acts. This most immediately applies to the exodus from Egypt, but the poetic language (especially in vv. 17–19) outstrips the descriptions in Exodus. The cosmic upheavals show God in his most awe-inspiring power, recalling manifestations of God (18:6–15; Exod 19:16–19; Hab 3:6–16; cf. Ps 114:3–5).
77:13 Echoes the poetic reflection on the exodus miracle in Exod 15:11. The answer to the rhetorical question is an emphatic "No one!"
77:14 peoples. God's power was greatly feared by the nations who heard of the exodus from Egypt (Exod 15:14–15; Josh 2:9–11).
77:15 redeemed. Reiterates 74:2 (see note there). **Joseph.** Jacob's favorite son; he received a special gift and generous blessing from his father (Gen 37:3–4; 49:22–26); he was the father of Ephraim and Manasseh, whose descendants formed the most prominent tribes of the northern kingdom of Israel after Solomon's time. The southern kingdom was Judah, descended from Jacob's fourth son, who also received a prominent blessing (Gen 49:8–12). Sometimes "Joseph" is a synonym for this northern kingdom (e.g., 78:67; 2 Sam 19:20; 1 Kgs 11:28), but here it stands for the entire nation of the 12 tribes (e.g., 80:1; 81:5; Obad 18).
77:16 God's power tamed even the most violent seas. In the exodus story, it was the Red Sea (Exod 14:21–28; 15:8,10). See notes on 74:13–17; 93:3.
77:17 thunder. See note on 18:13. **your arrows.** God's lightning bolts (see the parallel "your lightning" in v. 18). See also 7:13; Hab 3:11; Zech 9:14.

Temple at 'Ain Dara' where the giant footprints of the false god were made visible. The psalmist describes God's mighty acts, even though his footprints were unseen (Ps 77:19).

Mark Connally

[18]Your thunder was heard in the whirlwind,
your lightning lit up the world;
the earth trembled and quaked.[w]
[19]Your path led through the sea,[x]
your way through the mighty waters,
though your footprints were not seen.

[20]You led your people[y] like a flock[z]
by the hand of Moses and Aaron.

Psalm 78

A *maskil*[a] of Asaph.

[1]My people, hear my teaching;[a]
listen to the words of my mouth.
[2]I will open my mouth with a parable;[b]
I will utter hidden things, things from of old—

77:18 [w]Jdg 5:4
77:19 [x]Hab 3:15
77:20 [y]Ex 13:21
[z]Ps 78:52; Isa 63:11
78:1 [a]Isa 51:4; 55:3
78:2 [b]Ps 49:4; Mt 13:35*

[a] Title: Probably a literary or musical term

77:20 flock. This shepherd imagery (see note on 23:1) in the psalms of Asaph usually refers to God's leading Israel out of Egypt (here; 78:52; 80:1; cf. 79:13).

Ps 78 *Tell the Next Generation the Praiseworthy Deeds of the Lord.* This is one of the "historical psalms," which reviews aspects of Israel's history (see also Pss 105; 106; 136), doing so to instruct present and future generations so they would learn lessons from the past. Some scholars classify this psalm as a "wisdom" psalm (see introduction to Ps 34) because of this intent to instruct, as Ps 73 also does in a different way. Ps 78 builds on the review of God's mighty deeds in 77:10–20, and both psalms end with God's chosen servants shepherding his people: in 77:20, they are Moses and Aaron; in 78:70–72, it is David.

The psalmist signals his intent to instruct in a general purpose statement (vv. 1–8). God performed mighty acts in the exodus and the early wilderness wanderings (vv. 9–16). He provided food for his people, yet they complained (vv. 17–31). Israel recklessly vacillated between turning to God and turning away (vv. 32–39), and God acted on their behalf in the wonders in Egypt (the plagues and exodus) and the entry into the promised land (vv. 40–55). Yet Israel did not learn its lessons and repeatedly tested God in the time of the judges (vv. 56–64). God chose David as his servant to carry out his mission on earth (vv. 65–72).

78:1–8 Affirms the importance of keeping alive the memory of God's great deeds and his instructions for his people over the generations (cf. Exod 10:2; 12:26–27; 13:8,14; Deut 4:9; 6:6–9,20–21; 29:14–15; Josh 4:6–7,21–23). Both remembering God's acts and keeping his commandments are important (vv. 4–5).

78:1 my teaching. See note on 51:13.

78:2 parable. A specific mode of teaching common in the OT wisdom

78:3 [c]Ps 44:1
78:4 [d]Dt 11:19 [e]Ps 26:7; 71:17
78:5 [f]Ps 19:7; 81:5 [g]Ps 147:19
78:6 [h]Ps 22:31; 102:18
78:7 [i]Dt 6:12 [j]Dt 5:29
78:8 [k]2Ch 30:7 [l]Ex 32:9 [m]ver 37; Isa 30:9
78:9 [n]ver 57; 1Ch 12:2 [o]Jdg 20:39
78:10 [p]2Ki 17:15
78:11 [q]Ps 106:13
78:12 [r]Ps 106:22 [s]Ex 7-12 [t]Nu 13:22
78:13 [u]Ex 14:21; Ps 136:13 [v]Ex 15:8
78:14 [w]Ex 13:21; Ps 105:39
78:15 [x]Nu 20:11; 1Co 10:4
78:17 [y]Dt 9:22; Isa 63:10; Heb 3:16

3 things we have heard and known,
things our ancestors have told us.[c]
4 We will not hide them from their descendants;[d]
we will tell the next generation
the praiseworthy deeds[e] of the LORD,
his power, and the wonders he has done.
5 He decreed statutes[f] for Jacob[g]
and established the law in Israel,
which he commanded our ancestors
to teach their children,
6 so the next generation would know them,
even the children yet to be born,[h]
and they in turn would tell their children.
7 Then they would put their trust in God
and would not forget[i] his deeds
but would keep his commands.[j]
8 They would not be like their ancestors[k]—
a stubborn[l] and rebellious[m] generation,
whose hearts were not loyal to God,
whose spirits were not faithful to him.

9 The men of Ephraim, though armed with bows,[n]
turned back on the day of battle;[o]
10 they did not keep God's covenant[p]
and refused to live by his law.
11 They forgot what he had done,[q]
the wonders he had shown them.
12 He did miracles[r] in the sight of their ancestors
in the land of Egypt,[s] in the region of Zoan.[t]
13 He divided the sea[u] and led them through;
he made the water stand up like a wall.[v]
14 He guided them with the cloud by day
and with light from the fire all night.[w]
15 He split the rocks[x] in the wilderness
and gave them water as abundant as the seas;
16 he brought streams out of a rocky crag
and made water flow down like rivers.

17 But they continued to sin[y] against him,
rebelling in the wilderness against the Most High.

and prophetic traditions and in Jesus' teaching (Prov 1:6; Ezek 17:2; 20:49; 24:3; Hos 12:10; see Introduction to Proverbs: Literary Features; see also note on Matt 13:1–52). Matthew quotes this verse as predicting Jesus' teaching in parables (Matt 13:35), though the parable in this psalm is more like a historical review with an instructional purpose (see introduction to Ps 78), akin to Stephen's speech in Acts 7. **things from of old.** For example, God is King (74:12; 93:2).

78:4 wonders. God's miracles (v. 12; 77:11,14; see note on 26:7).

78:5 statutes ... law. See introduction to Ps 119. **teach their children.** See note on vv. 1–8.

78:8 rebellious generation. See 95:7d–11 and note; Deut 9:6–7; 10:16; 31:27.

78:9 men of Ephraim ... turned back. Either the tribe of Ephraim or the entire nation of Israel. If the tribe, then several historical events could form the backdrop to the condemnation in vv. 9–11: they did not drive out the Canaanites from their land (Judg 1:29); they did not help Jephthah the judge in battle (Judg 12:2); Philistines "of Gath" killed some Ephraimites (1 Chr 7:21). If the entire nation of Israel (see note on 60:7), then the account in vv. 56–67 speaks of the nation's defeat at Shiloh (1 Sam 4:10), which was in Ephraim's territory (see Judg 21:19 and map, p. 380), and also at Mount Gilboa where the Philistines defeated Israel and killed King Saul (1 Sam 31:1,7).

78:12–16 Summarizes the events of God's miracles on Israel's behalf in Egypt, at the Red Sea, and in the wilderness (vv. 17–31,40–55).

78:12 Zoan. An important city in the northeastern Nile Delta, near where the Israelites lived when they were in Egypt (v. 43; Num 13:22; Ezek 30:14).

78:13 Parting the waters of the Red Sea (Exod 14:21–22).

78:14 God's cloud and pillar of fire guided Israel in the wilderness (Exod 13:21–22).

78:15–16 God provided water in the wilderness (Exod 17:1–7).

78:17–31 Reviews Israel's rebelliousness in the wilderness.

78:17 Most High. Also in vv. 35,56; see note on 7:8.

[18] They willfully put God to the test[z]
by demanding the food they craved.[a]
[19] They spoke against God;[b]
they said, "Can God really
spread a table in the wilderness?
[20] True, he struck the rock,
and water gushed out,[c]
streams flowed abundantly,
but can he also give us bread?
Can he supply meat[d] for his people?"
[21] When the LORD heard them, he was furious;
his fire broke out[e] against Jacob,
and his wrath rose against Israel,
[22] for they did not believe in God
or trust[f] in his deliverance.
[23] Yet he gave a command to the skies above
and opened the doors of the heavens;[g]
[24] he rained down manna[h] for the people to eat,
he gave them the grain of heaven.
[25] Human beings ate the bread of angels;
he sent them all the food they could eat.
[26] He let loose the east wind[i] from the heavens
and by his power made the south wind blow.
[27] He rained meat down on them like dust,
birds like sand on the seashore.
[28] He made them come down inside their camp,
all around their tents.
[29] They ate till they were gorged —[j]
he had given them what they craved.
[30] But before they turned from what they craved,
even while the food was still in their mouths,[k]
[31] God's anger rose against them;
he put to death the sturdiest[l] among them,
cutting down the young men of Israel.
[32] In spite of all this, they kept on sinning;
in spite of his wonders,[m] they did not believe.[n]
[33] So he ended their days in futility[o]
and their years in terror.
[34] Whenever God slew them, they would seek[p] him;
they eagerly turned to him again.
[35] They remembered that God was their Rock,[q]
that God Most High was their Redeemer.[r]

78:18 [z] 1Co 10:9 [a] Ex 16:2; Nu 11:4
78:19 [b] Nu 21:5
78:20 [c] Nu 20:11 [d] Nu 11:18
78:21 [e] Nu 11:1
78:22 [f] Dt 1:32; Heb 3:19
78:23 [g] Ge 7:11; Mal 3:10
78:24 [h] Ex 16:4; Jn 6:31*
78:26 [i] Nu 11:31
78:29 [j] Nu 11:20
78:30 [k] Nu 11:33
78:31 [l] Isa 10:16
78:32 [m] ver 11 [n] ver 22
78:33 [o] Nu 14:29,35
78:34 [p] Hos 5:15
78:35 [q] Dt 32:4 [r] Dt 9:26

78:18 The people grumbled in the wilderness (Exod 16:2–3; 17:2–3).
78:20 God provided water in the wilderness (Exod 17:1–7), as well as manna (vv. 24–25; Exod 16:13–16) and quail (vv. 26–30; Exod 16:13; Num 11:31–32).
78:21 his fire broke out. When the people complained in the wilderness (Num 11:1) and when two of Aaron's sons offered unauthorized sacrifices (Lev 10:1–2).
78:23–30 Reflects on God's providing manna and quail (see note on v. 20).
78:23 doors of the heavens. Source of God's abundant provision (cf. 2 Kgs 7:2; Mal 3:10).
78:25 bread of angels. The manna came from heaven, where the angels dwelled. **angels.** Translated "mighty ones" elsewhere (e.g., 103:20, where the word is parallel to a more common word for "angels"), illustrating that the two words are closely connected.
78:26–28 God sent great clouds of quail in on strong winds for the people to gather and eat (Num 11:31–32).
78:30–31 God punished the people for their rebellion (Num 11:33–34).
78:32–39 Israel persisted in its sin, causing God to punish them (vv. 32–33). They would turn to him (vv. 34–35), but their devotion was short-lived and insincere (vv. 36–37). Despite this, God was merciful (vv. 38–39). This cycle of vacillations also characterized the period of the judges (Judg 2:6—3:6).

78:36 [s]Eze 33:31
78:37 [t]ver 8; Ac 8:21
78:38 [u]Ex 34:6 [v]Isa 48:10 [w]Nu 14:18,20
78:39 [x]Ge 6:3; Ps 103:14 [y]Job 7:7; Jas 4:14
78:40 [z]Heb 3:16 [a]Ps 95:8; 106:14 [b]Eph 4:30
78:41 [c]Nu 14:22 [d]2Ki 19:22; Ps 89:18
78:44 [e]Ex 7:20-21; Ps 105:29
78:45 [f]Ex 8:24; Ps 105:31 [g]Ex 8:2,6
78:46 [h]Ex 10:13
78:47 [i]Ex 9:23; Ps 105:32
78:48 [j]Ex 9:25
78:49 [k]Ex 15:7
78:51 [l]Ex 12:29; Ps 135:8 [m]Ps 105:23; 106:22
78:52 [n]Ps 77:20
78:53 [o]Ex 14:28 [p]Ps 106:10
78:54 [q]Ex 15:17; Ps 44:3

36 But then they would flatter him with their mouths,[s]
lying to him with their tongues;
37 their hearts were not loyal[t] to him,
they were not faithful to his covenant.
38 Yet he was merciful;[u]
he forgave[v] their iniquities[w]
and did not destroy them.
Time after time he restrained his anger
and did not stir up his full wrath.
39 He remembered that they were but flesh,[x]
a passing breeze[y] that does not return.

40 How often they rebelled[z] against him in the wilderness[a]
and grieved him[b] in the wasteland!
41 Again and again they put God to the test;[c]
they vexed the Holy One of Israel.[d]
42 They did not remember his power—
the day he redeemed them from the oppressor,
43 the day he displayed his signs in Egypt,
his wonders in the region of Zoan.
44 He turned their river into blood;[e]
they could not drink from their streams.
45 He sent swarms of flies[f] that devoured them,
and frogs[g] that devastated them.
46 He gave their crops to the grasshopper,
their produce to the locust.[h]
47 He destroyed their vines with hail[i]
and their sycamore-figs with sleet.
48 He gave over their cattle to the hail,
their livestock[j] to bolts of lightning.
49 He unleashed against them his hot anger,[k]
his wrath, indignation and hostility—
a band of destroying angels.
50 He prepared a path for his anger;
he did not spare them from death
but gave them over to the plague.
51 He struck down all the firstborn of Egypt,
the firstfruits of manhood in the tents of Ham.[m]
52 But he brought his people out like a flock;[n]
he led them like sheep through the wilderness.
53 He guided them safely, so they were unafraid;
but the sea engulfed[o] their enemies.[p]
54 And so he brought them to the border of his holy land,
to the hill country his right hand[q] had taken.

78:37 covenant. The Sinai covenant. See note on 25:10; see also "Covenant," p. 2646.
78:38 forgave. God was merciful beyond that which Israel deserved (Exod 32:14; Num 14:20). See note on 32:1–2.
78:40–55 Another review of Israel's rebellion in Egypt and the wilderness, putting God to the test, and God's mighty acts on their behalf.
78:41 Holy One of Israel. See note on 71:22.
78:44–51 Mentions six of the signs and wonders in Egypt (see Exod 7–12): water to blood (v. 44), flies (v. 45), frogs (v. 45), locusts (v. 46), hail (vv. 47–48), and death of the firstborn (v. 51).
78:51 Ham. One of Noah's sons (Gen 5:32); his descendants became associated with Egypt (Gen 10:6; see Pss 105:23,27; 106:22).
78:52–55 God's mighty acts on Israel's behalf in Egypt (vv. 52–53), the wilderness (v. 54), and the promised land (v. 55).
78:52 like a flock. See note on 77:20.
78:54 holy land. The promised land of Canaan (cf. Zech 2:12). **his right hand.** Symbolizes power (see note on 20:6).

[55] He drove out nations[r] before them
and allotted their lands to them as an inheritance;[s]
he settled the tribes of Israel in their homes.

[56] But they put God to the test
and rebelled against the Most High;
they did not keep his statutes.
[57] Like their ancestors[t] they were disloyal and faithless,
as unreliable as a faulty bow.[u]
[58] They angered him[v] with their high places;[w]
they aroused his jealousy with their idols.[x]
[59] When God heard them, he was furious;
he rejected Israel[y] completely.
[60] He abandoned the tabernacle of Shiloh,[z]
the tent he had set up among humans.
[61] He sent the ark of his might[a] into captivity,[b]
his splendor into the hands of the enemy.
[62] He gave his people over to the sword;
he was furious with his inheritance.
[63] Fire consumed[c] their young men,
and their young women had no wedding songs;[d]
[64] their priests were put to the sword,[e]
and their widows could not weep.

[65] Then the Lord awoke as from sleep,[f]
as a warrior wakes from the stupor of wine.
[66] He beat back his enemies;
he put them to everlasting shame.[g]
[67] Then he rejected the tents of Joseph,
he did not choose the tribe of Ephraim;
[68] but he chose the tribe of Judah,
Mount Zion,[h] which he loved.
[69] He built his sanctuary like the heights,
like the earth that he established forever.

78:55 [r] Ps 44:2 [s] Jos 13:7
78:57 [t] Eze 20:27 [u] Hos 7:16
78:58 [v] Jdg 2:12 [w] Lev 26:30 [x] Ex 20:4; Dt 32:21
78:59 [y] Dt 32:19
78:60 [z] Jos 18:1
78:61 [a] Ps 132:8 [b] 1Sa 4:17
78:63 [c] Nu 11:1 [d] Jer 7:34; 16:9
78:64 [e] 1Sa 4:17; 22:18
78:65 [f] Ps 44:23
78:66 [g] 1Sa 5:6
78:68 [h] Ps 87:2

78:55 drove out nations. God fought for Israel when he gave them the land of Canaan (Josh 10:14,42), driving out the nations before them (Exod 34:11,24; Deut 7:22; 11:23; Josh 3:10; 24:18).
78:56–64 Israel sank to new lows in their apostasy during the period of the judges.
78:56 put God to the test. This specific wording refers elsewhere to the rebellion at Massah (Exod 17:2,7; see Ps 106:14; see also vv. 18,41). In this psalm, however, the period of the judges is in view, especially Judg 2:6—3:6; see also 1 Sam 2:12—7:2, a dark period during which God's glory departed (1 Sam 4:21). **Most High.** See note on 7:8.
78:58 high places. Places of worship throughout Canaan; often located on a hill but sometimes at a city gate (2 Kgs 23:8) or valley (Jer 7:31). Occasionally they were sites of true worship (1 Sam 9:12–14,19; 1 Kgs 3:4; 2 Chr 1:3), but most were dedicated to false worship (e.g., Lev 26:30; Num 33:52; 1 Kgs 11:7; 12:31–32; 14:23). Even most of the godly kings neglected to remove the high places when they carried out reforms of worship in the land: Asa (1 Kgs 15:14), Jehoshaphat (1 Kgs 22:43), Joash (2 Kgs 12:3), Amaziah (2 Kgs 14:4), Azariah (2 Kgs 15:4), and Jotham (2 Kgs 15:35). Hezekiah and Josiah did remove them (2 Kgs 18:4; 23:8,13,15,19–20). **his jealousy.** God demanded complete allegiance from his people; he did not tolerate worship of other gods. See 79:5; Exod 20:5 and note.
78:60 Shiloh. A center of worship since the days of Joshua (Josh 18:1; 19:51; 21:1–2; Judg 18:31; 1 Sam 1:3,24; 3:21); destroyed before the temple was built in Jerusalem, possibly by the Philistines when they captured the ark (v. 61; 1 Sam 4:10–11); located in the territory of Ephraim (Judg 21:19). Jeremiah used its ruins as an object lesson to warn people against apostasy (Jer 7:12; 26:6,9).
78:61 The Philistines captured the ark (1 Sam 4:1–11), which symbolized God's presence, where his power and glory were powerfully displayed (Pss 26:8; 63:2; 1 Sam 4:3,21–22).
78:62 inheritance. See note on 74:2.
78:64 widows could not weep. Silenced with no tears to shed because the calamity was so great. One widow even named her son "Ichabod," which means "[there is] no Glory" (1 Sam 4:19–22; cf. Job 27:15).
78:65–72 God finally defeated his enemies on behalf of his people, but he rejected the northern tribes (v. 67) and chose Judah instead; he chose David to shepherd his people.
78:65 awoke. See note on 3:7.
78:67 Joseph … Ephraim. Here these terms stand for the entirety of the northern kingdom of Israel, showing what became of it (see notes on v. 9; 60:7; 77:15).
78:68 God chose Judah in the time of Jacob (Gen 49:8–12). **Mount Zion.** See 74:2; notes on 2:6; 9:11.
78:69 his sanctuary. See note on 5:7.

78:70 [i] 1Sa 16:1
78:71 [j] 2Sa 5:2; Ps 28:9
78:72 [k] 1Ki 9:4
79:1 [l] Ps 74:2 [m] 2Ki 25:9
79:2 [n] Dt 28:26; Jer 7:33
79:3 [o] Jer 16:4
79:4 [p] Ps 44:13; 80:6
79:5 [q] Ps 74:10 [r] Ps 74:1; 85:5 [s] Dt 29:20; Ps 89:46; Zep 3:8
79:6 [t] Ps 69:24; Rev 16:1 [u] Jer 10:25; 2Th 1:8 [v] Ps 14:4
79:8 [w] Isa 64:9 [x] Ps 116:6; 142:6
79:9 [y] 2Ch 14:11 [z] Ps 25:11; 31:3; Jer 14:7

70 He chose David[i] his servant
and took him from the sheep pens;
71 from tending the sheep he brought him
to be the shepherd[j] of his people Jacob,
of Israel his inheritance.
72 And David shepherded them with integrity of heart;[k]
with skillful hands he led them.

Psalm 79

A psalm of Asaph.

1 O God, the nations have invaded your inheritance;[l]
they have defiled your holy temple,
they have reduced Jerusalem to rubble.[m]
2 They have left the dead bodies of your servants
as food for the birds of the sky,
the flesh of your own people for the animals of the wild.[n]
3 They have poured out blood like water
all around Jerusalem,
and there is no one to bury the dead.[o]
4 We are objects of contempt to our neighbors,
of scorn and derision to those around us.[p]

5 How long,[q] LORD? Will you be angry[r] forever?
How long will your jealousy burn like fire?[s]
6 Pour out your wrath[t] on the nations
that do not acknowledge[u] you,
on the kingdoms
that do not call on your name;[v]
7 for they have devoured Jacob
and devastated his homeland.

8 Do not hold against us the sins of past generations;[w]
may your mercy come quickly to meet us,
for we are in desperate need.[x]
9 Help us,[y] God our Savior,
for the glory of your name;
deliver us and forgive our sins
for your name's sake.[z]

78:70–72 The shepherd imagery and God's choice of David hark back to David's days as a shepherd (1 Sam 16:11–13; 17:15,34–37). Ps 132 links David and Mount Zion; David captured the city and renamed it the "City of David" (2 Sam 5:6–10).
78:70 his servant. See notes on 4:3; Ps 18 title.
78:72 Ps 101 speaks of David's godly leadership of the nation in more depth.
Ps 79 *Pour Out Your Wrath on the Nations.* Whereas Ps 78 ends by reciting how God punished his people because they continued to apostatize (78:56–64), Ps 79 asks God to turn his attention back to the enemies who persecute his people while it also acknowledges that past generations had indeed sinned (v. 8). The psalm appears to be set against the backdrop of the Babylonian exile. It begins with anguish by describing how the nation's enemies destroyed Jerusalem (vv. 1–4). Then follows a cry of distress and a request that God would punish the enemies and help his people (vv. 5–10a). Another request for vindication follows (vv. 10b–13), ending with a vow to praise God when he delivers them (v. 13), which contrasts with the choice of David and Zion at the end of Ps 78.
79:1 Links with themes at the end of the previous psalm (78:62,69,71). **inheritance.** See note on 74:2. **holy temple.** See note on 5:7. **rubble.** Refers to the destruction of Jerusalem by the Babylonians in 586 BC (2 Kgs 25; Jer 52).
79:2–3 Devastation that recollects 78:63–64.
79:5 How long ...? See note on 13:1,2. **jealousy.** See note on 78:58.
79:6–7 Repeats almost verbatim Jer 10:25. This recalls the godless Babylonians in Habakkuk and God's guarantee to judge them (Hab 1:5–12; 2:4–19).
79:7 Jacob. Israel (Gen 32:28; see note on Ps 135:4).
79:8 Ps 79 asks God to pour out mercy on his people instead of judgment. **sins of past generations.** See Introduction to Ps 78 (cf. 2 Kgs 17:7–23; 23:26–27; 24:3–4).
79:9 for the glory of your name. See note on 23:3.

[10] Why should the nations say,
"Where is their God?"[a]

Before our eyes, make known among the nations
that you avenge[b] the outpoured blood of your servants.
[11] May the groans of the prisoners come before you;
with your strong arm preserve those condemned to die.
[12] Pay back into the laps[c] of our neighbors seven times[d]
the contempt they have hurled at you, Lord.
[13] Then we your people, the sheep of your pasture,[e]
will praise you forever;[f]
from generation to generation
we will proclaim your praise.

Psalm 80[a]

For the director of music. To the tune of "The Lilies of the Covenant."
Of Asaph. A psalm.

[1] Hear us, Shepherd of Israel,
you who lead Joseph like a flock.[g]
You who sit enthroned between the cherubim,[h]
shine forth [2] before Ephraim, Benjamin and Manasseh.[i]
Awaken[j] your might;
come and save us.

[3] Restore[k] us,[l] O God;
make your face shine on us,
that we may be saved.

[4] How long, LORD God Almighty,
will your anger smolder
against the prayers of your people?
[5] You have fed them with the bread of tears;
you have made them drink tears by the bowlful.[m]
[6] You have made us an object of derision[b] to our neighbors,
and our enemies mock us.[n]

a In Hebrew texts 80:1-19 is numbered 80:2-20. *b* *6* Probable reading of the original Hebrew text; Masoretic Text *contention*

79:10 [a] Ps 42:10 [b] Ps 94:1
79:12 [c] Isa 65:6; Jer 32:18 [d] Ge 4:15
79:13 [e] Ps 74:1; 95:7 [f] Ps 44:8
80:1 [g] Ps 77:20 [h] Ex 25:22
80:2 [i] Nu 2:18-24 [j] Ps 35:23
80:3 [k] Ps 85:4; La 5:21 [l] Nu 6:25
80:5 [m] Ps 42:3; Isa 30:20
80:6 [n] Ps 79:4

79:10a the nations say. See note on 10:6. **"Where is their God?"** A taunt from the enemies (also in 42:3,10; 115:2).
79:10b–12 Cries for God to exact vengeance against his people's enemies. They leave this in God's hands (Deut 32:35,43).
79:11 prisoners … condemned to die. The conditions of the exile were extreme for devastated Jerusalem and exiles in Babylon (cf. 102:20). But the Bible does not record Babylon's pronouncing death sentences upon the exiles; indeed, they treated their prisoners somewhat humanely, allowing them a measure of freedom (2 Kgs 25:27–30; Jer 29:4–7). Nevertheless, far more preferable than dying in Babylon would be a return to the promised land.
79:13 sheep of your pasture. See notes on 23:1; 95:7a–c.
Ps 80 *Restore Us, Lord God Almighty.* Like Ps 79, this psalm urgently petitions God to deliver and restore his people out of their distressing exile. A recurring refrain asking God for this frames the psalm (vv. 3,7,19). The psalm begins with urgent pleas for God to awaken and save his people (vv. 1–2). Then follows the first refrain (v. 3), a classic lament (vv. 4–6), and the second refrain (v. 7). The psalm reviews what God did for Israel in Egypt and Canaan, using the imagery of a vine that God planted (vv. 8–11), describes its present desolation (vv. 12–13,16), and asks God to revive his people (vv. 14–15,17–18), ending with the third refrain (v. 19).
80:1 Shepherd … flock. This echoes the shepherd imagery at the end of the previous psalm (79:13; see notes on 23:1; 95:7a–c). **enthroned between the cherubim.** See note on 99:1.
80:2 Ephraim, Benjamin and Manasseh. Tribes of the northern kingdom of Israel, in the center of the land (see notes on 60:7; 77:15; 78:9). All three are associated with Rachel, Jacob's favorite wife: she was the mother of Joseph—whose two sons were Ephraim and Manasseh—and Benjamin. **Awaken.** See note on 3:7.
80:3 The first of three refrains (also vv. 7,19). The second and third refrains use more terms for God: "God Almighty" (v. 7) and "LORD God Almighty" (v. 19). **your face shine.** Similar to 67:1 (see note on 67:1–2).
80:4 How long …? See note on 13:1,2. This restates the lament in 79:5. **Almighty.** See note on 24:10.
80:5 bread of tears. A bitter diet; contrasts with God's feeding his people "the bread of angels" (78:25) and water from a rock in the wilderness (78:20).

80:8 [o]Isa 5:1-2; Jer 2:21 [p]Jos 13:6; Ac 7:45
80:11 [q]Ps 72:8
80:12 [r]Ps 89:40; Isa 5:5
80:13 [s]Jer 5:6
80:14 [t]Isa 63:15
80:16 [u]Ps 39:11; 76:6
81:1 [v]Ps 66:1

7 Restore us, God Almighty;
make your face shine on us,
that we may be saved.

8 You transplanted a vine[o] from Egypt;
you drove out[p] the nations and planted it.
9 You cleared the ground for it,
and it took root and filled the land.
10 The mountains were covered with its shade,
the mighty cedars with its branches.
11 Its branches reached as far as the Sea,[a]
its shoots as far as the River.[bq]

12 Why have you broken down its walls[r]
so that all who pass by pick its grapes?
13 Boars from the forest ravage[s] it,
and insects from the fields feed on it.
14 Return to us, God Almighty!
Look down from heaven and see![t]
Watch over this vine,
15 the root your right hand has planted,
the son[c] you have raised up for yourself.

16 Your vine is cut down, it is burned with fire;
at your rebuke[u] your people perish.
17 Let your hand rest on the man at your right hand,
the son of man you have raised up for yourself.
18 Then we will not turn away from you;
revive us, and we will call on your name.

19 Restore us, LORD God Almighty;
make your face shine on us,
that we may be saved.

Psalm 81[d]

For the director of music. According to *gittith*.[e] Of Asaph.

1 Sing for joy to God our strength;
shout aloud to the God of Jacob![v]

[a] *11* Probably the Mediterranean [b] *11* That is, the Euphrates [c] *15* Or *branch* [d] In Hebrew texts 81:1-16 is numbered 81:2-17. [e] Title: Probably a musical term

80:7 The second refrain (see note on v. 3).
80:8–11 By bringing his people out from Egypt into Canaan (cf. 78:52), God transplanted a vine that took root and flourished (Isa 3:14; 5:1–7; Jer 2:21; 12:10; Ezek 15:1–8; 17:6–8; 19:10–14; Hos 10:1; 14:7; cf. Matt 20:1–16; Mark 12:1–9; Luke 20:9–16; John 15:1–5).
80:11 Sea … River. See NIV text notes; see also notes on Exod 23:31; Josh 1:4.
80:12–13 The psalmist, in anguish, asks God about Israel's present desolation (see v. 16). He sees it as coming from God's hand, using common language found in the laments (see note on 10:1).
80:14 Return to us. The first of a series of urgent requests that God should act on his people's behalf and restore them (vv. 17–18).
80:15 son. Refers to Israel in Exod 4:22–23; Hos 11:1. Pairing "root" and "son" in poetic parallel is somewhat unnatural, but it prepares the way for the pairing in v. 17 (see note there). This may also echo the common pairing of "root[s]" and "branch[es]" (e.g., Job 18:16; 29:19; Ezek 17:7; Mal 4:1; Rom 11:16; cf. also Isa 5:24; 27:6; 37:31; Ezek 17:9; 31:7; Hos 9:16; Amos 2:9). See "Sonship," p. 2664.
80:16 your rebuke. The phrase powerfully displays God's control of elements of creation, such as the seas or the heavens (18:15; 104:7; 106:9; Job 26:11; Isa 50:2; Nah 1:4), or a rebuff of his enemies (9:5; 68:30; 76:6; Isa 17:13). Here it powerfully expresses wrath against his own people (Isa 51:20; Mal 2:3).
80:17 the man at your right hand. Probably the king who represents the nation. To be at God's right hand is a position of honor (see note on 16:8). **son of man.** Parallel with "the man at your right hand" as well as "son" in v. 15, where "son" refers to the nation. Verse 15 focuses on the nation, while v. 17 narrows the focus to the nation's representative, the king. See also 110:1, where the future Davidic King is installed at God's right hand.
80:19 The third refrain (see note on v. 3).
Ps 81 *In Your Distress You Called and I Rescued You.* This psalm responds to the pleas for God's help that his people uttered in Pss

[2] Begin the music, strike the timbrel,[w]
play the melodious harp[x] and lyre.
[3] Sound the ram's horn at the New Moon,
and when the moon is full, on the day of our festival;
[4] this is a decree for Israel,
an ordinance of the God of Jacob.
[5] When God went out against Egypt,[y]
he established it as a statute for Joseph.

I heard an unknown voice say:[z]

[6] "I removed the burden from their shoulders;[a]
their hands were set free from the basket.
[7] In your distress you called[b] and I rescued you,
I answered[c] you out of a thundercloud;
I tested you at the waters of Meribah.[a][d]
[8] Hear me, my people,[e] and I will warn you —
if you would only listen to me, Israel!
[9] You shall have no foreign god[f] among you;
you shall not worship any god other than me.
[10] I am the LORD your God,
who brought you up out of Egypt.[g]
Open wide your mouth and I will fill[h] it.

[11] "But my people would not listen to me;
Israel would not submit to me.[i]
[12] So I gave them over[j] to their stubborn hearts
to follow their own devices.

[13] "If my people would only listen to me,[k]
if Israel would only follow my ways,

81:2 [w] Ex 15:20 [x] Ps 92:3
81:5 [y] Ex 11:4 [z] Ps 114:1
81:6 [a] Isa 9:4
81:7 [b] Ex 2:23; Ps 50:15 [c] Ex 19:19 [d] Ex 17:7
81:8 [e] Ps 50:7
81:9 [f] Ex 20:3; Dt 32:12; Isa 43:12
81:10 [g] Ex 20:2 [h] Ps 107:9
81:11 [i] Ex 32:1-6
81:12 [j] Ac 7:42; Ro 1:24
81:13 [k] Dt 5:29; Isa 48:18

[a] 7 The Hebrew has *Selah* (a word of uncertain meaning) here.

79–80. It addresses the people (not God) throughout and, like Ps 80 (80:8), mentions that God delivered them from Egypt (81:5). Ps 81 begins on a joyful note (vv. 1–2) because God has decreed that his people should rejoice (vv. 3–5b). The reason for rejoicing is God's words (v. 5c), which occupy the rest of the psalm (vv. 6–16). God reviews his actions on behalf of his people (vv. 6–7) and calls them to listen and turn to him (vv. 8–10). They had *not* listened, so he had turned them over to their own devices (vv. 11–12). But blessings could be theirs if only they would listen to and follow him (vv. 13–16).

81:1–2 The psalm begins on an extraordinarily joyful note, with five imperative verbs: sing, shout, begin, strike, and play.

81:1 Jacob. Israel (also in v. 4; 79:6–7; see notes on 135:4; Gen 32:28).

81:2 timbrel ... harp ... lyre. See notes on 150:3,5.

81:3 ram's horn. A trumpet for musical worship contexts (150:3) and for sounding the alarm for a city in danger (Amos 3:6). Here it announces God's decree regarding the festival. **New Moon ... moon is full.** The psalmist apparently composed the psalm for two annual observances, the Festival of Trumpets (later called Rosh Hashanah: New Year's Day) and the Festival of Tabernacles (see "The Lord's Appointed Festivals," p. 229; see also notes on Lev 23:24,34). **our festival.** Probably the Festival of Tabernacles, sometimes called simply "the festival" (1 Kgs 8:2,65).

81:4–5 decree ... ordinance ... statute. Joyfully worshiping God at the festivals for what he had done for Israel (vv. 1–3) was not optional.

81:5 God decisively defeated the Egyptians in Moses' day, allowing the Israelites to escape after long years under Egyptian subjugation (80:8; Exod 7–12; 14–15). **Joseph.** See note on 77:15. **an unknown voice say.** Or "a language you do not know" (cf. Deut 28:49; Jer 5:15). In either case, it is clear that this God was speaking (vv. 6–16) and that the psalmist somehow understood the words.

81:6 The Egyptians treated the Israelites harshly (Exod 1:11–14,22).

81:7 you called and I rescued. God saw the Israelites' plight and heard their pleas (Exod 3:7–10). **tested.** See note on 66:10. **waters of Meribah.** A place near Kadesh Barnea where the Israelites quarreled with God when they found no water (Num 20:1–13,24; cf. Ps 106:32; Deut 32:51; 33:8). "Meribah" means "quarreling" or "contention," an apt name for such a place. Another site, this one near Sinai, is also named "Meribah" (or "Massah and Meribah"; Exod 17:7); the Israelites also found no water there and rebelled (Exod 17:1–7; cf. Ps 95:8). In both incidents, the Israelites "tested" God (95:9), whereas here God is "testing" the Israelites because of their quarreling.

81:8 if you would only listen. Cf. 95:7d, which similarly introduces a message from (or about) God (95:8–11).

81:9–10 Sounds like the opening words of the Ten Commandments (Exod 20:2–5; Deut 5:6–9).

81:10 God abundantly and generously provides for his people if they turn to him.

81:11 Israel persisted in their stubbornness (cf. 78:10,17,32,40,56; see Deut 9:7,24; Jer 7:24–26; 23:17).

81:12 Cf. Rom 1:24,26,28.

81:13–16 Israel would have prospered if they had only listened to the Lord.

81:14 [l]Ps 47:3 [m]Am 1:8
81:16 [n]Dt 32:14
82:1 [o]Ps 58:11; Isa 3:13
82:2 [p]Dt 1:17
[q]Ps 58:1-2; Pr 18:5
82:3 [r]Dt 24:17
[s]Jer 22:16
82:5 [t]Ps 14:4; Mic 3:1
[u]Isa 59:9 [v]Ps 11:3

14 how quickly I would subdue[l] their enemies
and turn my hand against[m] their foes!
15 Those who hate the LORD would cringe before him,
and their punishment would last forever.
16 But you would be fed with the finest of wheat;[n]
with honey from the rock I would satisfy you."

Psalm 82

A psalm of Asaph.

1 God presides in the great assembly;
he renders judgment[o] among the "gods":

2 "How long will you[a] defend the unjust
and show partiality[p] to the wicked?[b][q]
3 Defend the weak and the fatherless;[r]
uphold the cause of the poor[s] and the oppressed.
4 Rescue the weak and the needy;
deliver them from the hand of the wicked.

5 "The 'gods' know nothing, they understand nothing.[t]
They walk about in darkness;[u]
all the foundations[v] of the earth are shaken.

[a] *2* The Hebrew is plural. [b] *2* The Hebrew has *Selah* (a word of uncertain meaning) here.

81:16 God would feed his people abundantly with the best food available, resounding with the imagery of Deut 32:13–14. **honey from the rock.** Possibly honey from beehives built in rocky crevices or crags (Isa 7:18–19) but more likely this parallels the idea of water from a rock (Exod 17:6; Num 20:8–11). Normally, neither water nor honey would come from a rock, but these show that God extraordinarily provides for his people.

Ps 82 *How Long Will You Defend the Unjust?* God indicts unjust leaders and judges in this psalm, condemning the abuses he sees. He also utters a message in the previous psalm (81:6–16), but those words address the community at large and mostly encourage them; the words here condemn. This psalm focuses on the poor, the outcast, and the marginalized (vv. 3–4). It begins and ends (vv. 1,8) with the psalmist's words framing the message from God (vv. 2–7).

82:1 great assembly. Or "assembly of God"; the divine assembly, where God presides over all the heavenly beings (89:5; 103:19–21; 1 Kgs 22:19; Job 1:6; 2:1; Isa 6:1–4). **"gods."** Hebrew *'ĕlōhîm*; most commonly refers to God (e.g., Gen 1:1) but can also refer to angels (8:5; cf. Job 1:6; 2:1), pagan deities (Pss 96:4,5; 97:7,9; 135:5), or even humans such as the king (45:6), judges (Exod 21:6; 22:8–9), or a leader like Moses (Exod 4:16; 7:1). In this context they are most likely human leaders because they "will die like mere mortals" (Ps 82:7) and because Jesus argued that God himself called such people "gods" (see v. 6; John 10:34–36). See notes on 8:5; 29:1; 58:1; 97:7.

82:2 How long ...? Usually people in distress ask this of God, wondering how long he will remain distant (see note on 13:1,2). But here God utters these words to indict unjust leaders. For other places where God speaks, see Pss 60:6 and note; 108:7; introduction to Ps 81.

82:3–4 Psalms consistently portrays God as the defender of the weak, the poor, the outcast, the marginalized (e.g., 10:12–18; 12:5; 14:6; 22:26; 35:10; 40:17; 68:5,10; 69:32; 70:5; 72:12–13; 102:17; 113:7–9; 132:15; 140:12; 146:7–9). And the king, as God's royal representative, or vice-regent, on earth (see notes on 2:6–7) protected these marginalized groups (72:12–14; cf. Prov 31:1–9). All Israelites shared responsibility for those who were relatively helpless in society: the marginalized (including widows, the fatherless, and foreigners) and the poor and needy (e.g., Exod 22:22; Lev 19:10; 23:22; Deut 10:18; 14:29; 15:11; 24:14,17,19–21; 26:12–13; 27:19; Prov 14:31; 17:5; 19:17; 21:13; 22:9,22; Isa 1:17,23; 3:15; 10:2; Jer 5:28; 7:6; 22:3; Ezek 22:29; Amos 2:7; 5:11–12; 8:4–6; Zech 7:10; cf. Jas 1:27). In this psalm, God holds all of Israel's leaders responsible for taking care of such people.

82:3 weak. Hebrew *dal*; the needy and afflicted but with a special nuance of being vulnerable to those who would prey on them (e.g., 41:1; 72:13; Gen 41:19 ["scrawny"]; Judg 6:15). **fatherless.** Hebrew *yātôm*. God is the defender of the fatherless (see 10:14; 68:5; 146:9). **poor.** Hebrew *'ānî*; the poor without land, dependent on others, and often persecuted. The three Hebrew terms translated "weak," "fatherless," and "poor" can also have the sense of "meek, humble, oppressed, helpless," referring to marginalized people living on the edge and whom others despise and oppress. God is their special advocate (e.g., 9:12,18; 18:27; 37:14; 76:9; 107:41; 147:6; see note on vv. 3–4). **oppressed.** Hebrew *rāš*; "poor," "weak," and "needy" people who are usually in poverty because others oppress them (72:13; Prov 13:23; 14:20; 18:23; 19:7; 22:7; Eccl 5:8)—although occasionally they are poor through their own laziness (Prov 10:4).

82:4 needy. Hebrew *'ebyôn*; the poor who are completely dependent on others' generosity. God instructed the Israelites to generously care for them (Exod 23:6,11; Deut 15:7,9,11; 24:14). God is their special advocate (Pss 9:18; 12:5; 35:10; 69:33; 107:41; 113:7; 140:12), and the king is expected to fulfill this role (72:4,12–14; cf. Prov 31:8–9). In Ps 82, any of Israel's leaders—kings, judges, or otherwise—are in view.

82:5 Condemns the corrupt and impotent leaders; falls at the structural center of the psalm, highlighting its importance (see note on 100:3 ["his people"]). Their injustices seem to shake the very foundations of the created order; by contrast, when the Lord reigns, the world is established, firm, and secure (93:1). Prophetic denunciations of the impotent gods that people so often worshiped are mirror images of this (Isa 44:9,18; 46:1–2,6–7; Jer 10:3–5).

[6] "I said, 'You are "gods";[w]
you are all sons of the Most High.'
[7] But you will die[x] like mere mortals;
you will fall like every other ruler."

[8] Rise up,[y] O God, judge the earth,
for all the nations are your inheritance.[z]

Psalm 83[a]

A song. A psalm of Asaph.

[1] O God, do not remain silent;[a]
do not turn a deaf ear,
do not stand aloof, O God.
[2] See how your enemies growl,[b]
how your foes rear their heads.[c]
[3] With cunning they conspire[d] against your people;
they plot against those you cherish.
[4] "Come," they say, "let us destroy[e] them as a nation,
so that Israel's name is remembered[f] no more."

[5] With one mind they plot together;[g]
they form an alliance against you—
[6] the tents of Edom[h] and the Ishmaelites,
of Moab[i] and the Hagrites,[j]
[7] Byblos,[k] Ammon and Amalek,
Philistia, with the people of Tyre.[l]
[8] Even Assyria has joined them
to reinforce Lot's descendants.[b][m]

[9] Do to them as you did to Midian,[n]
as you did to Sisera and Jabin at the river Kishon,[o]

82:6 [w] Jn 10:34*
82:7 [x] Ps 49:12; Eze 31:14
82:8 [y] Ps 12:5 [z] Ps 2:8; Rev 11:15
83:1 [a] Ps 28:1; 35:22
83:2 [b] Ps 2:1; Isa 17:12 [c] Jdg 8:28; Ps 81:15
83:3 [d] Ps 31:13
83:4 [e] Est 3:6 [f] Jer 11:19
83:5 [g] Ps 2:2
83:6 [h] Ps 137:7 [i] 2Ch 20:1 [j] Ge 25:16
83:7 [k] Jos 13:5 [l] Eze 27:3
83:8 [m] Dt 2:9
83:9 [n] Jdg 7:1-23 [o] Jdg 4:23-24

[a] In Hebrew texts 83:1-18 is numbered 83:2-19. [b] *8* The Hebrew has *Selah* (a word of uncertain meaning) here.

82:6 "gods" ... sons of the Most High. Human leaders who will die (v. 7; see note on v. 1). **Most High.** See note on 7:8.
82:8 The psalmist, who last spoke in v. 1, concludes with his appeal for God's justice to prevail. **Rise up.** Translates the same word as 3:7 (see note there). **inheritance.** See note on 74:2.
Ps 83 *Cover Their Faces With Shame, Lord, So That They Will Seek Your Name.* This psalm reverts to a theme that Ps 79 strikes: the nations are crushing God's people, so the psalmist cries out for God to punish them. This is not blind retribution for its own sake but retribution so that the nations would turn to God, seeking his name (v. 16). The psalm begins by calling upon God to act in the face of the threats against his people (vv. 1–4), detailing their enemies (vv. 5–8). The psalm requests that God do to these nations what he previously did to others (vv. 9–16) so that, ultimately, they will acknowledge God themselves (v. 16). The conclusion again requests divine punishment that would reveal the true God in all his glory (vv. 17–18).
83:4 they say. See note on 10:6.
83:5–8 An impressive array of enemies who opposed God's people.
83:6 Edom. Esau (Gen 25:30; 36:1,8,19), who fathered the nation of the Edomites, who settled south and southeast of the Dead Sea. Despite their close genetic relationship, the Edomites had prickly relations with the Israelites (e.g., 137:7; Num 20:14–21; 1 Sam 14:47; 2 Sam 8:13–14; 2 Kgs 8:20–22; 14:7; 2 Chr 28:17). **Ishmaelites.** Descendants of Ishmael, son of Abraham and Hagar (Gen 16); settled in the desert areas east and southeast of the Jordan River; identified with the Midianites (Gen 37:28,36; Judg 7; 8:24), whom Gideon defeated (Judg 7–8). **Moab.** Descendants of Lot (Gen 19:36–37); lived east of the Dead Sea and opposed Israel through much of Israel's history (e.g., Num 25:1–3; Judg 3:12–30; 1 Sam 14:47; 2 Sam 8:2,11–12; 2 Kgs 1:1; 13:20; 24:2). **Hagrites.** A prosperous people living east of Gilead, whom Saul defeated in battle (1 Chr 5:10,18–22).
83:7 Byblos. An important Phoenician coastal city, home to skilled craftsmen (1 Kgs 5:18; Ezek 27:9). **Ammon.** Ammonites, descendants of Lot (Gen 19:36,38); lived east of the Jordan River and opposed Israel through much of Israel's history (e.g., Judg 3:13; 10:7–9; 1 Sam 11:1–11; 2 Sam 10; 12:26–31; 2 Kgs 24:2; 2 Chr 20:1; 27:5). **Amalek.** Amalekites, descendants of Esau (Gen 36:12); they lived nomadic lives in the Negev and Sinai deserts and opposed Israel throughout its history (e.g., Exod 17:8–13; Num 14:45; Judg 3:13; 6:3–5,33; 7:12; 1 Sam 15:7–9; 30:1–2). **Philistia.** Philistines lived in southwest Canaan, along the Mediterranean coast, and perennially opposed Israel (e.g., Judg 3:2–3,31; 13:1—16:31; 1 Sam 4; 14; 17–18; 2 Sam 5:25; Isa 9:12). **Tyre.** The most important Phoenician seaport. It had good relations with Israel in the days of David and Solomon (2 Sam 5:11; 1 Kgs 5:1; 7:13–14; 9:10–14), but prophets later denounced it for opposing God's people (e.g., Jer 27:1–11; Ezek 26:1—28:19; Joel 3:4–6; Zech 9:2–4).
83:8 Assyria. The great empire to the east that destroyed the northern kingdom of Israel in 722 BC (2 Kgs 17). **Lot's descendants.** Moab and Ammon (see vv. 6–7 and notes).
83:9–16 The psalmist asks God to judge these enemies as he did others, but he places the request in a redemptive context (v. 16).
83:9 Midian. Midianites, descendants of Midian, son of Abraham and

83:10 [p] Zep 1:17
83:11 [q] Jdg 7:25 [r] Jdg 8:12,21
83:12 [s] 2Ch 20:11
83:13 [t] Ps 35:5; Isa 17:13
83:14 [u] Dt 32:22; Isa 9:18
83:15 [v] Job 9:17
83:16 [w] Ps 109:29; 132:18
83:17 [x] Ps 35:4
83:18 [y] Ps 59:13
84:1 [z] Ps 27:4; 43:3; 132:5
84:2 [a] Ps 42:1-2

10 who perished at Endor
and became like dung[p] on the ground.
11 Make their nobles like Oreb and Zeeb,[q]
all their princes like Zebah and Zalmunna,[r]
12 who said, "Let us take possession[s]
of the pasturelands of God."

13 Make them like tumbleweed, my God,
like chaff[t] before the wind.
14 As fire consumes the forest
or a flame sets the mountains ablaze,[u]
15 so pursue them with your tempest
and terrify them with your storm.[v]
16 Cover their faces with shame,[w] LORD,
so that they will seek your name.

17 May they ever be ashamed and dismayed;
may they perish in disgrace.[x]
18 Let them know that you, whose name is the LORD —
that you alone are the Most High over all the
earth.[y]

Psalm 84[a]

For the director of music. According to *gittith*.[b]
Of the Sons of Korah. A psalm.

1 How lovely is your dwelling place,[z]
LORD Almighty!
2 My soul yearns,[a] even faints,
for the courts of the LORD;
my heart and my flesh cry out
for the living God.

[a] In Hebrew texts 84:1-12 is numbered 84:2-13. [b] Title: Probably a musical term

Keturah (Gen 25:1 – 2); lived in desert areas east and southeast of the Jordan River and in the northwest portion of the Arabian peninsula. Associated with the Ishmaelites (see note on v. 6), they often opposed Israel (e.g., Num 22; 25; Josh 13:21). This recalls when the Israelites defeated them under Gideon (Judg 7 – 8). **Sisera.** Commanded the Canaanite army, which Deborah and Barak defeated near Hazor (Judg 4 – 5). **Jabin.** The "king of Canaan" defeated in the same battle as Sisera.

83:10 Endor. A town within the territory allotted to Manasseh (Josh 17:11); near the Kishon River where the Israelites defeated Sisera and Jabin (v. 9).

83:11 Oreb and Zeeb. Leaders or "princes" of Midian whom Gideon defeated (Judg 7:25). **Zebah and Zalmunna.** Kings of Midian whom Gideon defeated (Judg 8).

83:15 God vanquishes his enemies out of the storm (cf. 18:7 – 15; 68:33; 77:17 – 18; Josh 10:11; Judg 5:4,20 – 21; 1 Sam 2:10; 7:10; Hab 3:3 – 15) as he rides on the clouds (see 68:4 and note).

83:16 The ultimate goal is reconciling even Israel's (and God's) worst enemies to God (v. 18). This fits well with the message of Ps 67 (see notes there).

83:18 The psalm concludes on the note that v. 16 sounds: all should acknowledge that the Lord alone is over all things. God's desire is not to punish for punishment's sake but to redeem. **Let them know.** See note on 59:13. **Most High.** See note on 7:8.

Ps 84 *How Lovely Is Your Dwelling Place, Lord Almighty!* The first of the non-Asaph psalms in Book III — a psalm of the Sons of Korah — harks back to a theme found in the earlier collection of Korahite psalms (Pss 42 – 49): a delight in God's dwelling place, the temple established on Mount Zion (see introduction to Ps 48). As such, Psalm 84 is one of several "psalms of Zion" (see introduction to Ps 46), and it also echoes Ps 76, another "Zion psalm." Its dominant note is a yearning for God's house and the blessing there, a theme also in Pss 42 – 43 (see notes there). The psalm is structured around a threefold reference to blessing (vv. 4,5,12): an opening section reveals the psalmist's longing for God's house (vv. 1 – 4), while a final section petitions God for his favor, again revealing a longing for God's house (vv. 8 – 11), capped by affirming God's blessing (v. 12). The central section affirms that God will bless all who make the pilgrimage to Zion and meet him there (vv. 5 – 7).

84 title Sons of Korah. See note on Ps 42 title.

84:1 dwelling place. Though the Hebrew noun is plural, the psalm clearly refers to the temple in Jerusalem. The plural noun refers to the various imposing parts of the temple complex (see the references to God's "courts" in vv. 2,10; cf. 43:3; 46:4; 132:5, where the same Hebrew plural form occurs). On the temple itself, see note on 5:7. **Almighty.** See vv. 3,8,12; see also note on 24:10.

84:2 Reminiscent of the first Korahite psalm (42:1 – 2). **My ... my.** Affirms the close relationship of such worshipers. **courts.** See note on v. 1.

[3] Even the sparrow has found a home,
and the swallow a nest for herself,
where she may have her young —
a place near your altar,[b]
LORD Almighty, my King and my God.[c]
[4] Blessed are those who dwell in your house;
they are ever praising you.[a]

[5] Blessed are those whose strength[d] is in you,
whose hearts are set on pilgrimage.[e]
[6] As they pass through the Valley of Baka,
they make it a place of springs;
the autumn[f] rains also cover it with pools.[b]
[7] They go from strength to strength,[g]
till each appears[h] before God in Zion.

[8] Hear my prayer, LORD God Almighty;
listen to me, God of Jacob.
[9] Look on our shield,[c][i] O God;
look with favor on your anointed one.[j]

[10] Better is one day in your courts
than a thousand elsewhere;
I would rather be a doorkeeper[k] in the house
of my God
than dwell in the tents of the wicked.
[11] For the LORD God is a sun[l] and shield;[m]
the LORD bestows favor and honor;
no good thing does he withhold[n]
from those whose walk is blameless.

[12] LORD Almighty,
blessed[o] is the one who trusts in you.

84:3 [b] Ps 43:4 [c] Ps 5:2
84:5 [d] Ps 81:1 [e] Jer 31:6
84:6 [f] Joel 2:23
84:7 [g] Pr 4:18 [h] Dt 16:16
84:9 [i] Ps 59:11 [j] 1Sa 16:6; Ps 2:2; 132:17
84:10 [k] 1Ch 23:5
84:11 [l] Isa 60:19; Rev 21:23 [m] Ge 15:1 [n] Ps 34:10
84:12 [o] Ps 2:12

[a] *4* The Hebrew has *Selah* (a word of uncertain meaning) here and at the end of verse 8. [b] *6* Or *blessings*
[c] *9* Or *sovereign*

84:3 If even the smallest of birds can find rest and security at the Lord's altar, how much more his faithful worshipers. **King.** See notes on 10:16; 93:1.
84:4,5,12 Blessed. See note on 1:1.
84:4 house. The temple (v. 1; see note on 5:7).
84:5–7 The psalm's central section focuses on the blessedness of the pilgrimage up to Jerusalem, with the ultimate goal of appearing before God himself in Zion.
84:5 Faithful worshipers find their strength in God; indeed, they increase in strength (see v. 7, where a different Hebrew word for "strength" is used). **hearts.** See note on 7:9. **pilgrimage.** See note on Ps 120 title.
84:6 Valley of Baka. An unknown location, but apparently a dry place that turns into "a place of springs" that "autumn rains" water because of the faithful pilgrims' presence. **Baka.** Refers to the poplar or balsam tree (2 Sam 5:23–24), which is known to grow in arid places. "Baka" also sounds like the Hebrew word for "weeping," leading to the expression "Valley (or Vale) of Tears." But this is a less likely understanding since the verse contrasts arid and well-watered land.
84:7 strength to strength. Success upon success that the faithful experience on the pilgrimage, which culminates in meeting God in Zion. The construction indicates progression; cf. 144:13 ("by thousands, by tens of thousands"); Jer 9:3 ("one sin to another").
84:8–9 A brief prayer on behalf of the king, akin to that in Ps 72. As the king prospers in Jerusalem, the faithful will more easily be able to go from "strength to strength" (v. 7) and come to this place.
84:8 Jacob. Israel (79:7; 81:1,4; cf. Gen 32:28; see note on 135:4).
84:9 shield. The king, who protects the people (cf. 89:18). See note on 3:3. Usually psalms depict God as the king's or the people's shield (e.g., v. 11; 3:3; 7:10; 18:2; 28:7; 33:20; 59:11; 115:9,10,11; 119:114; 144:2; cf. Gen 15:1). **anointed one.** The divinely appointed Davidic king. See notes on 2:2,7.
84:10–11 Faithful worshipers who come to Zion experience the joy of being in God's house, receiving God's favor, protection, and bounty.
84:10 doorkeeper. A low-level attendant in the temple (2 Kgs 22:4; 23:4; 25:18; Jer 35:4). **tents.** The normal abode and place of security for people (see, e.g., 52:5; 69:25; 78:28,51), even the righteous (118:15); but "tents of the wicked," of those who do not honor God, are not desired (e.g., 83:6–7).
84:11 sun and shield. A source of light (i.e., guidance) and protection (see notes on v. 9; 3:3; 27:1). Most ancient societies falsely worshiped the sun as a supreme deity.
84:12 Reflects one of the main themes of the Psalter: trusting in the Lord and taking refuge in him (see note on 2:12).

85:1 [p]Ps 14:7; Jer 30:18; Eze 39:25
85:2 [q]Nu 14:19 [r]Ps 78:38
85:3 [s]Ps 106:23 [t]Ex 32:12; Dt 13:17; Ps 78:38; Jnh 3:9
85:4 [u]Ps 80:3,7
85:5 [v]Ps 79:5
85:6 [w]Ps 80:18; Hab 3:2
85:8 [x]Zec 9:10
85:9 [y]Isa 46:13 [z]Zec 2:5
85:10 [a]Ps 89:14; Pr 3:3 [b]Ps 72:2-3; Isa 32:17
85:11 [c]Isa 45:8
85:12 [d]Ps 84:11; Jas 1:17 [e]Lev 26:4; Ps 67:6; Zec 8:12

Psalm 85[a]

For the director of music. Of the Sons of Korah. A psalm.

1 You, LORD, showed favor to your land;
you restored the fortunes[p] of Jacob.
2 You forgave[q] the iniquity[r] of your people
and covered all their sins.[b]
3 You set aside all your wrath[s]
and turned from your fierce anger.[t]

4 Restore[u] us again, God our Savior,
and put away your displeasure toward us.
5 Will you be angry with us forever?[v]
Will you prolong your anger through all generations?
6 Will you not revive[w] us again,
that your people may rejoice in you?
7 Show us your unfailing love, LORD,
and grant us your salvation.

8 I will listen to what God the LORD says;
he promises peace[x] to his people, his faithful
servants—
but let them not turn to folly.
9 Surely his salvation[y] is near those who fear him,
that his glory[z] may dwell in our land.

10 Love and faithfulness[a] meet together;
righteousness[b] and peace kiss each other.
11 Faithfulness springs forth from the earth,
and righteousness[c] looks down from heaven.
12 The LORD will indeed give what is good,[d]
and our land will yield[e] its harvest.
13 Righteousness goes before him
and prepares the way for his steps.

[a] In Hebrew texts 85:1-13 is numbered 85:2-14. [b] 2 The Hebrew has *Selah* (a word of uncertain meaning) here.

Ps 85 *Restore Us Again, God Our Savior.* This psalm is a communal prayer for restoration out of a time of crisis (cf. Ps 126). It reviews a past occasion when God restored his people's fortunes (vv. 1–3), but the people now face another crisis so they again cry out for God's help (vv. 4–7). God responds with a promise of restoration and exhorts them not to return to their foolish ways (vv. 8–9). The psalm vividly portrays a restored world (vv. 10–13). Many churches use the psalm at Christmastime, a time like no other, when God promised peace and blessing to the world. It is an example of a bold prayer for restoration and God's generous response of blessing, appropriate in any era.

85:1–3 God poured out his special favor and forgiveness upon his people. This fits the time after the Babylonian exile (e.g., see the joy at this time in Ezra 3:12–13; 6:16,22), but any number of occasions in the nation's history could be in view here. The hint of a drought in v. 12, for example, would fit the postexilic situation that Hag 1:5–11 describes: people were suffering a drought because of their sin.

85:1 Jacob. Israel (see 135:4; Gen 32:28 and notes).

85:2–3 forgave ... covered ... set aside ... turned. Four verbs of forgiveness in succession picture God wiping the slate completely clean. Ps 32:1–5 uses many of these verbs to capture the joy attending such forgiveness.

85:4–7 The anguished request for God to restore his people confirms that they had experienced his favor in the past but that they were now in a crisis again.

85:7 unfailing love. God's covenant love (the same Hebrew word is used in v. 10 ["love"]). See note on 6:4.

85:8–9 The psalmist speaks as an attentive individual now, learning the lesson of God's promises in answer to the prayers of vv. 4–7. The shift from the communal first part of the psalm ("us") to this individual part of the psalm ("I") focuses on God's promises as though each individual should appropriate the message for themselves.

85:9 glory. See notes on 4:2; 26:8.

85:10–13 One of the most beautiful pictures of restoration in Scripture. The expressions of God's favor for his people in v. 10 take on personal qualities of harmonious existence arising from creation itself in v. 11. Verse 12 implies that there has been a famine and points to an abundant harvest. But God's righteousness and blessing entail far more than simply physical abundance; the psalm ends with another picture of God's righteousness on the march—a messenger heralding God's approach as he brings blessing (v. 13).

Psalm 86

A prayer of David.

[1] Hear me, LORD, and answer[f] me,
for I am poor and needy.
[2] Guard my life, for I am faithful to you;
save your servant who trusts in you.[g]
You are my God; [3] have mercy[h] on me, Lord,
for I call[i] to you all day long.
[4] Bring joy to your servant, Lord,
for I put my trust[j] in you.

[5] You, Lord, are forgiving and good,
abounding in love[k] to all who call to you.
[6] Hear my prayer, LORD;
listen to my cry for mercy.
[7] When I am in distress,[l] I call to you,
because you answer me.

[8] Among the gods there is none like you,[m] Lord;
no deeds can compare with yours.
[9] All the nations you have made
will come and worship[n] before you, Lord;
they will bring glory[o] to your name.
[10] For you are great and do marvelous deeds;[p]
you alone[q] are God.

[11] Teach me your way,[r] LORD,
that I may rely on your faithfulness;

86:1 [f] Ps 17:6
86:2 [g] Ps 25:2; 31:14
86:3 [h] Ps 4:1; 57:1 [i] Ps 88:9
86:4 [j] Ps 25:1; 143:8
86:5 [k] Ex 34:6; Ne 9:17; Ps 103:8; 145:8; Joel 2:13; Jnh 4:2
86:7 [l] Ps 50:15
86:8 [m] Ex 15:11; Dt 3:24; Ps 89:6
86:9 [n] Ps 66:4; Rev 15:4 [o] Isa 43:7
86:10 [p] Ps 72:18 [q] Dt 6:4; Mk 12:29; 1Co 8:4
86:11 [r] Ps 25:5

Ps 86 *All the Nations Will Come and Worship Before You, Lord.* This is an intensely personal psalm of David—the only Davidic psalm in Book III—in which David urgently asks God for his help and affirms both God's gracious attributes and his uniqueness among all the gods. It prepares the way for the darkly negative note at the end of Book III in Pss 88–89, including what is called the "darkest corner of the Psalter" (Ps 88).

David emphasizes his special relationship with God: seven times he calls God *ʾădōnay* ("Lord": vv. 3,4,5,8,9,12,15); three times he calls himself "your servant" (vv. 2,4,16), affirming that he is loyally dependent on God; four times he uses God's personal, covenantal name (Yahweh or "the LORD": vv. 1,6,11,17). (On the names of God, see note on 8:1.) A series of imperative verbs at the beginning and ending of the psalm highlight the sense of urgency: hear, answer (v. 1); guard, save (v. 2); have mercy (v. 3); bring joy (v. 4); hear, listen (v. 6); turn, have mercy, show, save (v. 16); give (v. 17). And two are in the middle: teach, give (v. 11).

The psalm opens with David's repeated requests for God's help (vv. 1–4), followed by a refrain (v. 5) and more requests (vv. 6–7). The central focal point of the psalm is God's uniqueness among all the gods (vv. 8–10). Further requests occur in v. 11, this time for God to transform David, followed by a vow to praise God because of his love toward David (vv. 12–13). The psalm ends with another lament (v. 14), another refrain (v. 15), and more requests for help (vv. 16–17a).

86:1 I am poor and needy. See note on 82:3–4. David elsewhere uses this exact language (see 40:17 and note; 70:5; 109:22) and similar language (e.g., 6:2,6; 25:16; 38:6,8; 69:17,19).

86:2 your servant. See vv. 4,16; see also notes on 4:3; 35:27.

86:5 David models a faithful believer's prayer by pausing to affirm God's attributes in this first refrain: God forgives, he is good, and he overflows love to all who call upon him. This anticipates the second refrain (v. 15), which catalogs more of God's attributes.

86:6 Hear my prayer. Reiterates v. 1 (and links to 84:8). See also 4:1; 17:1,6; 39:12; 54:2; 102:1; 143:1; cf. 88:2.

86:7 David has the confidence to call on God now because God has answered him in the past. The same confidence—using the same Hebrew terms—occurs in 3:4; 17:6; 118:5; 138:3 (cf. Jonah 2:2). God himself assures those who call on him that he does indeed answer (81:7; 91:15; 99:6; cf. Zech 13:9).

86:8–10 The psalm's central point: Yahweh is the only true God; he is incomparable, does great things, and all nations will acknowledge him as Lord. Fittingly, the exact structural center of the psalm (see note on 100:3 ["his people"]) is the word "worship" (v. 9).

86:8 none like you. See also v. 10 ("you alone"). Yahweh is incomparable; he performs mighty deeds, causes the nations to bow to him, and is greater than all other gods (16:5; 71:16; 72:18; 76:7; 83:18; 95:3; 96:4; 97:7,9; 136:4; 148:13; cf. Exod 15:11; Deut 4:35; 2 Sam 7:22; 1 Kgs 8:23; Isa 46:9; Mic 7:18). None can compare with him (see 89:6 and note).

86:9 See Pss 67; 87; 117. The great song of praise in Rev 15:3–4 draws from this.

86:10 marvelous deeds. See note on 26:7. **you alone.** See note on v. 8.

86:11 Teach me. Even in his distress, David is eager for God to teach him (see note on 27:11). **undivided heart.** Wholehearted commitment to God. God wants this from his people. When God promised to bring his people back to the land after the exile in Babylon, he promised to give them an undivided heart and put a new spirit within them (Ezek 11:19). Such an undivided heart is the ideal behind Jesus' contrast between serving God or money (Matt 6:24; Luke 16:13).

86:11 [s] Jer 32:39
86:14 [t] Ps 54:3
86:15 [u] Ps 103:8
[v] Ex 34:6; Ne 9:17; Joel 2:13
86:16 [w] Ps 116:16
87:2 [x] Ps 78:68
87:3 [y] Ps 46:4; Isa 60:1
87:4 [z] Job 9:13

give me an undivided[s] heart,
that I may fear your name.
12 I will praise you, Lord my God, with all my heart;
I will glorify your name forever.
13 For great is your love toward me;
you have delivered me from the depths,
from the realm of the dead.

14 Arrogant foes are attacking me, O God;
ruthless people are trying to kill me—
they have no regard for you.[t]
15 But you, Lord, are a compassionate and gracious[u] God,
slow to anger, abounding in love and faithfulness.[v]
16 Turn to me and have mercy on me;
show your strength in behalf of your servant;
save me, because I serve you
just as my mother did.[w]
17 Give me a sign of your goodness,
that my enemies may see it and be put to shame,
for you, LORD, have helped me and comforted me.

Psalm 87

Of the Sons of Korah. A psalm. A song.

1 He has founded his city on the holy mountain.
2 The LORD loves the gates of Zion[x]
more than all the other dwellings of Jacob.

3 Glorious things are said of you,
city of God:[a][y]
4 "I will record Rahab[b][z] and Babylon
among those who acknowledge me—

[a] 3 The Hebrew has *Selah* (a word of uncertain meaning) here and at the end of verse 6. [b] 4 A poetic name for Egypt

86:12 all my heart. Reflects David's prayer for "an undivided heart" in v. 11 (see note on v. 11).
86:13 me. Or "my soul," see note on 6:3. **from the depths, from the realm of the dead.** Or "from the lowest grave." The same construction is found in Deut 32:22, where the NIV has "to the realm of the dead below"; similarly, see Ps 88:6, where the NIV has "in the lowest pit." See note on 6:5 ["grave"]; on "pit," see note on 88:4.
86:15 David does not simply complain (v. 14); he affirms more of God's good attributes, repeating the perspective of v. 5. He uses the words of Exod 34:6.
86:16 save me ... as my mother did. Or "save the son of your handmaid." David's mother is unknown. The reference to David as the son of God's handmaid emphasizes (as in 116:16) his servant-like submission to God (vv. 2,4,16; see note on 35:27). This may also emphasize that he was born into a faithful household and was God's servant by choice; he was not a slave.
86:17 Give me a sign. David knows of God's goodness (vv. 5,10,15), but he desires a tangible sign of it so that his enemies would also see God's goodness.
Ps 87 *This One Was Born in Zion.* This is another "psalm of Zion" (see introduction to Ps 46), following two previously in Book III (Pss 76; 84). Like the other Zion psalms, it extols the virtues of God's chosen city (see notes on 2:6; 9:11), but it goes well beyond the others by affirming that the nations—and not just Israel—will be counted as citizens of Zion, after the fashion of many prophetic affirmations, especially by Isaiah (e.g., Isa 2:2–4; 19:19–25; 25:6; 45:14,22–24; 56:6–8; 60:3; 66:23; Mic 4:1–3; Zech 8:23; 14:16). This accords well with the inclusive vision of the previous psalm (86:8–10), as well as that of Pss 67; 117. In its present location, it provides an encouraging counterpoint to the pessimism in Pss 85–86; 88–89. The psalm opens by extolling Zion (vv. 1–2) and then mentions many of the nations that will be considered as citizens by the Lord himself (vv. 3–6), concluding with a chorus of the nations in praise of the Lord (v. 7).
87:1 his city. Zion was the "capital" of God's earthly kingdom (see notes on 2:6; 9:11), and God established it (Isa 14:32) with a firm foundation (Isa 28:16).
87:2 Jacob. Israel (see notes on 135:4; Gen 32:28).
87:4 God speaks words of endearment and welcome about nations that usually have appeared as his enemies in the OT. **Rahab.** A mythical sea monster that here represents Egypt (see NIV text note; cf. Isa 30:7; 51:9) and elsewhere represents chaos (Ps 89:10; Job 9:13; 26:12). (The name of Rahab the Canaanite prostitute is spelled differently in Hebrew.) **born in Zion.** Enjoys God's favor, including the nations (cf. vv. 5–6).

Philistia too, and Tyre[a], along with Cush[a]—
and will say, 'This one was born in Zion.'"[b][b]
[5] Indeed, of Zion it will be said,
"This one and that one were born in her,
and the Most High himself will establish her."
[6] The LORD will write in the register[c] of the peoples:
"This one was born in Zion."

[7] As they make music[d] they will sing,
"All my fountains[e] are in you."

87:4 [a] Ps 45:12 [b] Isa 19:25
87:6 [c] Ps 69:28; Isa 4:3; Eze 13:9
87:7 [d] Ps 149:3 [e] Ps 36:9
88:1 [f] Ps 51:14 [g] Ps 22:2; 27:9; Lk 18:7
88:3 [h] Ps 107:18,26
88:4 [i] Ps 28:1
88:5 [j] Ps 31:22; Isa 53:8
88:6 [k] Ps 69:15; La 3:55

Psalm 88[c]

A song. A psalm of the Sons of Korah. For the director of music. According to *mahalath leannoth.*[d] A *maskil*[e] of Heman the Ezrahite.

[1] LORD, you are the God who saves me;[f]
day and night I cry out[g] to you.
[2] May my prayer come before you;
turn your ear to my cry.

[3] I am overwhelmed with troubles
and my life draws near to death.[h]
[4] I am counted among those who go down to the pit;[i]
I am like one without strength.
[5] I am set apart with the dead,
like the slain who lie in the grave,
whom you remember no more,
who are cut off[j] from your care.

[6] You have put me in the lowest pit,
in the darkest depths.[k]

[a] 4 That is, the upper Nile region [b] 4 Or *"I will record concerning those who acknowledge me: / 'This one was born in Zion.' / Hear this, Rahab and Babylon, / and you too, Philistia, Tyre and Cush."* [c] In Hebrew texts 88:1-18 is numbered 88:2-19. [d] Title: Possibly a tune, "The Suffering of Affliction" [e] Title: Probably a literary or musical term

87:5 Most High. See note on 7:8.
87:6 The LORD will write. See also v. 4: "I will record." This is God's guarantee of his favor: he records and remembers the names of those "born in Zion." See notes on 9:5; 69:28.
87:7 A glorious climax of praise in song by peoples of all the nations, whom God now welcomes. **fountains.** A beautiful image of life-giving waters flowing from Zion (46:4; Ezek 47:1–12; Rev 22:1–2; cf. God's "river of delights" in 36:8).
Ps 88 *Darkness Is My Closest Friend.* This is the darkest psalm in the Psalter. Whereas the psalms of lament typically contain some statement of intent to praise God when he answers the psalmists' prayers (or they simply break out into praise), Ps 88 does not do this. Its presence in the Psalter shows that a believer can feel depressed and even have nothing good to say to God at the moment. The psalmist can barely gasp a few hints about his positive feelings toward God. For example, he affirms his relationship with God, calling him "the God who saves me" (v. 1), and he prays to this God (vv. 2,9,13); he also assumes that praise is the normal mode of life, and he wants to return to that mode (vv. 10–12). But his feelings are overwhelmingly negative. The psalm thus exemplifies a believer's proper response in the depths of despair, when sometimes all one can do is pour out one's heart to God and simply wait.

The psalmist opens with an anguished cry of distress (vv. 1–2) and then recites his troubles, permeated with images of death (vv. 3–5). He points to God as the source of his problems (vv. 6–9). As a result of this, he turns to the only one he can: God. He poses a series of six questions for God, all of which are variations on one theme: the dead do not praise God (vv. 10–12). He gives another desperate litany of his troubles, crying out to God, describing in more detail the ways in which God is afflicting him (vv. 13–18), and ending on a bleak, dark note (v. 18).
88 title Heman. A court musician from the tribe of Levi along with Asaph and Jeduthun (see notes on Ps 39 title; Ps 73 title). **Ezrahite.** The exact meaning of the term is uncertain. Two individuals named "Heman" and "Ethan the Ezrahite" (see Ps 89 title) are wise men (1 Kgs 4:31), and an "Ethan" and a "Heman" are descendants of Judah (1 Chr 2:6); they may be different individuals from the musicians with these names from the tribe of Levi (1 Chr 15:17,19).
88:3 death. See note on 6:5 ("grave").
88:4 pit. Grave; symbolizes death (see v. 3 and note). See 30:3; Prov 1:12; Isa 14:15; 38:18; Ezek 31:16. Sufferers may fear going down to the pit (i.e., dying) and ask God to deliver them, which God may do (vv. 4,6; 28:1; 30:3,9; 69:15; 103:4; 143:7; Job 33:28,30; Jonah 2:6). Going down to the pit may symbolize God's judgment (v. 6; 35:8; 55:23; 94:13; Job 33:18,22,24; Prov 28:18; Isa 14:15,19; 24:17; Jer 48:43; Ezek 26:20; 28:8; 32:23–25,29–30).
88:6 See note on 86:13.

88:7 [l]Ps 42:7
88:8 [m]Job 19:13; Ps 31:11 [n]Jer 32:2
88:9 [o]Ps 38:10 [p]Ps 86:3 [q]Job 11:13; Ps 143:6
88:10 [r]Ps 6:5
88:11 [s]Ps 30:9
88:13 [t]Ps 30:2 [u]Ps 5:3 [v]Ps 119:147
88:14 [w]Ps 43:2 [x]Job 13:24; Ps 13:1
88:15 [y]Job 6:4
88:17 [z]Ps 22:16; 124:4
88:18 [a]ver 8; Job 19:13; Ps 38:11
89:1 [b]Ps 59:16; Ps 101:1 [c]Ps 36:5; 40:10

7 Your wrath lies heavily on me;
you have overwhelmed me with all your waves.[a][l]
8 You have taken from me my closest friends[m]
and have made me repulsive to them.
I am confined[n] and cannot escape;
9 my eyes[o] are dim with grief.

I call[p] to you, LORD, every day;
I spread out my hands[q] to you.
10 Do you show your wonders to the dead?
Do their spirits rise up and praise you?[r]
11 Is your love declared in the grave,
your faithfulness[s] in Destruction[b]?
12 Are your wonders known in the place of darkness,
or your righteous deeds in the land of oblivion?

13 But I cry to you for help,[t] LORD;
in the morning[u] my prayer comes before you.[v]
14 Why, LORD, do you reject[w] me
and hide your face[x] from me?

15 From my youth I have suffered and been close to death;
I have borne your terrors[y] and am in despair.
16 Your wrath has swept over me;
your terrors have destroyed me.
17 All day long they surround me like a flood;[z]
they have completely engulfed me.
18 You have taken from me friend[a] and neighbor—
darkness is my closest friend.

Psalm 89[c]

A *maskil*[d] of Ethan the Ezrahite.

1 I will sing[b] of the LORD's great love forever;
with my mouth I will make your faithfulness known[c]
through all generations.

[a] *7* The Hebrew has *Selah* (a word of uncertain meaning) here and at the end of verse 10. [b] *11* Hebrew *Abaddon* [c] In Hebrew texts 89:1-52 is numbered 89:2-53. [d] Title: Probably a literary or musical term

88:7 your waves. The OT sometimes portrays bodies of water as God's unruly opponents (see note on 93:3), but these are *God's* waves.
88:8 my closest friends. See note on 38:11.
88:10–12 These six questions all presume that the dead do not praise God. The psalmist wants to live so that he might again engage in such praise. For him, the relationship between praising and not praising was the same as that between living and not living. If you were alive, you were praising God (cf. 6:5; 30:9; 115:17; Isa 38:18). See notes on 6:5; 30:8–10.
88:18 darkness is my closest friend. Or "those who know me. Oh, Darkness!" The Hebrew poetry of this verse is fractured, likely intending to show the shattered state in which the psalmist finds himself. The word "friend" is plural in Hebrew ("those who know me") and likely refers to the "friend and neighbor" in the first half of the verse, leaving the word "darkness" to serve as a final, despairing cry. The psalmist ends on a bleak, dark note because he has no praise to offer God. He stops, awaiting "the God who saves me" to deliver him (v. 1). Sometimes it is enough simply to wait on God (5:3; 27:14; 37:7; 38:15; 119:166; 130:5–6). We don't need to mouth platitudes that we don't really mean in the moment; words of praise will come in due time.
Ps 89 *Lord, Where Is Your Former Great Love, Which You Swore to David?* Like Book II, Book III ends with a so-called royal psalm (see introduction to Ps 72). Ps 89 focuses on God's promises to David (vv. 3–4,19–37; see note on v. 3). It does so from the perspective that God gave those promises long ago (see v. 19 and note) but that now it seems as though God has broken those promises (vv. 38–45), so it ends on a note of lament, questioning why God seems to have abandoned his king (vv. 46–51). The historical setting of the psalm is unknown; it could fit almost any time of crisis, but the Babylonian exile is certainly a fitting setting for it. Along with the dark and brooding Ps 88—and the many laments in Book III (see introduction to Pss 73–89)—Ps 89 contributes to a sense of pessimism at the end of Book III, perhaps the lowest point in the Psalter. Things get better in Books IV and V, but for now God seems very distant.
89 title Ethan the Ezrahite. A court musician from the tribe of Levi (1 Kgs 4:31; 1 Chr 15:17,19; see notes on Ps 39 title; Ps 88 title).
89:1–4 The psalm opens with a burst of enthusiastic praise (vv. 1–2), based on God's promises to David (vv. 3–4).
89:1 great love. See note on 6:4. The Hebrew word is plural here: "great

[2] I will declare that your love stands firm forever,
that you have established your faithfulness in heaven
itself.[d]
[3] You said, "I have made a covenant with my chosen one,
I have sworn to David my servant,
[4] 'I will establish your line forever
and make your throne firm through all generations.' "[ae]

[5] The heavens[f] praise your wonders, LORD,
your faithfulness too, in the assembly of the holy ones.
[6] For who in the skies above can compare with the LORD?
Who is like the LORD among the heavenly beings?[g]
[7] In the council of the holy ones God is greatly feared;
he is more awesome than all who surround him.[h]
[8] Who is like you,[i] LORD God Almighty?
You, LORD, are mighty, and your faithfulness surrounds you.

[9] You rule over the surging sea;
when its waves mount up, you still them.[j]
[10] You crushed Rahab[k] like one of the slain;
with your strong arm you scattered[l] your enemies.
[11] The heavens are yours, and yours also the earth;[m]
you founded the world and all that is in it.[n]
[12] You created the north and the south;
Tabor[o] and Hermon[p] sing for joy[q] at your name.
[13] Your arm is endowed with power;
your hand is strong, your right hand exalted.

[14] Righteousness and justice are the foundation of your throne;[r]
love and faithfulness go before you.
[15] Blessed are those who have learned to acclaim you,
who walk in the light[s] of your presence, LORD.
[16] They rejoice in your name[t] all day long;
they celebrate your righteousness.

89:2 [d] Ps 36:5
89:4 [e] 2Sa 7:12-16; 1Ki 8:16; Ps 132:11-12; Isa 9:7; Lk 1:33
89:5 [f] Ps 19:1
89:6 [g] Ps 113:5
89:7 [h] Ps 47:2
89:8 [i] Ps 71:19
89:9 [j] Ps 65:7
89:10 [k] Ps 87:4 [l] Ps 68:1
89:11 [m] 1Ch 29:11; Ps 24:1 [n] Ge 1:1
89:12 [o] Jos 19:22 [p] Dt 3:8; Jos 12:1 [q] Ps 98:8
89:14 [r] Ps 97:2
89:15 [s] Ps 44:3
89:16 [t] Ps 105:3

[a] 4 The Hebrew has *Selah* (a word of uncertain meaning) here and at the end of verses 37, 45 and 48.

loves," probably to reflect on God's many wonderful deeds (v. 5) that demonstrate that love. The same Hebrew word is singular in v. 2. In light of the harsh questioning of God's commitment to his covenant promises in vv. 38–45, this affirmation of God's faithfulness at the outset is important.

89:3 covenant. The Davidic covenant (2 Sam 7:11b–16): God promised David a perpetual dynasty; David would always have an heir on the throne of Israel (2 Sam 7:13,16; 22:51; 1 Kgs 2:45; 9:5; 2 Kgs 8:19; 1 Chr 16:15; 17:12,14; 22:10; 28:4,7,8; 2 Chr 13:5; 21:7). When David's son Solomon sinned and God withdrew his favor from him, God nevertheless left one tribe in his line for the sake of the promises he had made to David (1 Kgs 11:12–13,32,34,36; 15:4–5; 2 Kgs 8:19; 19:34; 20:6). Ultimately, the great Son of David, Jesus, fulfilled these promises (Isa 11; Amos 9:11–15; Matt 1:1; 21:9,15; Mark 11:10; Luke 1:32,69; Acts 13:34; Rev 5:5; 22:16). See "Covenant," p. 2646.

89:5–8 The praise continues. God is incomparable; there is no one like him, even among the heavenly beings.

89:5 wonders. See note on 26:7. **holy ones.** Angels (Deut 33:2,3; Job 15:15; Dan 4:13,17; 8:13; Zech 14:5; Mark 8:38; Acts 10:22; 1 Thess 3:13; Jude 14; Rev 14:10) who comprise the heavenly assembly (v. 5), or divine council (v. 7). Verse 6 calls them "heavenly beings" (see note on v. 6). These exalted beings all praise and fear the Lord, and they are as nothing compared to him (vv. 5–8).

89:6 Who is like the LORD ... ? See also v. 8 (cf. 35:10; 71:19; 113:5). The answer is "no one." None can compare with the Lord God (40:5; see note on 86:8). **heavenly beings.** See note on 29:1.

89:7 council. The heavenly circle of God's confidants, whose plans are secret. See note on v. 5; see also 82:1 and note; Job 15:8; Jer 23:18,22; Ezek 13:9.

89:9–13 Praises God's power as sovereign over all of creation.

89:9 sea ... waves. See v. 25 and note.

89:10 Rahab. A mythological sea monster symbolizing chaos (see note on 87:4).

89:12 Tabor. A mountain in the plain of Jezreel, in the north of the land, where Barak mustered the Israelite forces against the Canaanites (Judg 4:6). **Hermon.** See note on 42:6. **your name.** God's nature and reputation are bound up with his name, and even the mountains will rejoice in it; see also v. 16, where the faithful do likewise. See note on 8:1.

89:14–18 Praises God's attributes (v. 14) and extols those who follow him (vv. 15–16), especially the king (vv. 17–18).

89:15 Blessed. See note on 1:1.

89:16 your name. See note on v. 12.

89:17 [u]Ps 75:10; 92:10; 148:14
89:18 [v]Ps 47:9
89:20 [w]Ac 13:22 [x]Ps 78:70 [y]1Sa 16:1,12
89:21 [z]Ps 18:35
89:22 [a]2Sa 7:10
89:23 [b]Ps 18:40 [c]2Sa 7:9
89:24 [d]2Sa 7:15
89:25 [e]Ps 72:8
89:26 [f]2Sa 7:14 [g]2Sa 22:47
89:27 [h]Col 1:18 [i]Nu 24:7 [j]Rev 1:5; 19:16
89:28 [k]ver 33-34; Isa 55:3
89:29 [l]ver 4,36; Dt 11:21; Jer 33:17
89:32 [m]2Sa 7:14
89:33 [n]2Sa 7:15

17 For you are their glory and strength,
and by your favor you exalt our horn.[a][u]
18 Indeed, our shield[b] belongs to the LORD,
our king[v] to the Holy One of Israel.

19 Once you spoke in a vision,
to your faithful people you said:
"I have bestowed strength on a warrior;
I have raised up a young man from among the people.
20 I have found David[w] my servant;[x]
with my sacred oil I have anointed[y] him.
21 My hand will sustain him;
surely my arm will strengthen him.[z]
22 The enemy will not get the better of him;
the wicked will not oppress[a] him.
23 I will crush his foes before him[b]
and strike down his adversaries.[c]
24 My faithful love will be with him,[d]
and through my name his horn[c] will be exalted.
25 I will set his hand over the sea,
his right hand over the rivers.[e]
26 He will call out to me, 'You are my Father,[f]
my God, the Rock my Savior.'[g]
27 And I will appoint him to be my firstborn,[h]
the most exalted[i] of the kings[j] of the earth.
28 I will maintain my love to him forever,
and my covenant with him will never fail.[k]
29 I will establish his line forever,
his throne as long as the heavens endure.[l]

30 "If his sons forsake my law
and do not follow my statutes,
31 if they violate my decrees
and fail to keep my commands,
32 I will punish their sin with the rod,
their iniquity with flogging;[m]
33 but I will not take my love from him,[n]
nor will I ever betray my faithfulness.

[a] *17 Horn* here symbolizes strong one. [b] *18* Or *sovereign* [c] *24 Horn* here symbolizes strength.

89:18 shield. The Davidic king (see note on 84:9). **Holy One of Israel.** See note on 71:22.
89:19–37 Reviews the Davidic covenant (see note on v. 3) in great detail, including God's promises that it would stand forever (vv. 28–29, 33–37). But that was in the distant past; things seem a lot different in the present (vv. 38–51).
89:19 Once. A long time ago (cf. "long ago" in 93:2). See note on 89:19–37.
89:20 anointed. See note on 2:2. David was anointed as king three times: in private at his father's home (1 Sam 16:13), in public over the tribe of Judah (2 Sam 2:4), and in public over all Israel (2 Sam 5:1–5).
89:25 the sea. God, who is over the sea and waves (v. 9), has given sovereignty over the waters to his anointed king. See note on 93:3.
89:26 my Father. The Davidic king would be the "son" of God (see 2:7 and note; 2 Sam 7:14). **my God, the Rock my Savior.** David depended completely on God (cf. 144:1–2).
89:27 firstborn. The highest position in the family. Israel as a nation was God's firstborn (Exod 4:22); the reference here designates David as God's "firstborn" king, exalted above all kings of the earth. The NT designates Jesus as the "firstborn over all creation" (Col 1:15), the "firstborn among many brothers and sisters" (Rom 8:29), God's "firstborn" (Heb 1:6), and the "firstborn from among the dead" (Col 1:18; cf. Rev 1:5). **most exalted of the kings.** David never literally achieved this status in his lifetime, but he represented the promised lineage that culminated in Jesus, the Christ, whom the NT proclaims as the "King of kings" and "Lord of lords" (Rev 17:14; 19:16).
89:28 love. See vv. 1,2,24; see also note on 6:4.
89:29 establish ... forever. See note on v. 3.
89:30–34 God did not anticipate that the Davidic kings would be without sin; he would punish them, but his covenant would remain unbroken nonetheless (2 Sam 7:14–15).

[34]I will not violate my covenant
or alter what my lips have uttered.[o]
[35]Once for all, I have sworn by my holiness —
and I will not lie to David —
[36]that his line will continue forever
and his throne endure before me like the sun;
[37]it will be established forever like the moon,
the faithful witness in the sky."

[38]But you have rejected,[p] you have spurned,
you have been very angry with your anointed one.
[39]You have renounced the covenant with your servant
and have defiled his crown in the dust.[q]
[40]You have broken through all his walls[r]
and reduced his strongholds[s] to ruins.
[41]All who pass by have plundered him;
he has become the scorn of his neighbors.[t]
[42]You have exalted the right hand of his foes;
you have made all his enemies rejoice.[u]
[43]Indeed, you have turned back the edge of his sword
and have not supported him in battle.[v]
[44]You have put an end to his splendor
and cast his throne to the ground.
[45]You have cut short the days of his youth;
you have covered him with a mantle of shame.[w]

[46]How long, LORD? Will you hide yourself forever?
How long will your wrath burn like fire?[x]
[47]Remember how fleeting is my life.[y]
For what futility you have created all humanity!
[48]Who can live and not see death,
or who can escape the power of the grave?[z]
[49]Lord, where is your former great love,
which in your faithfulness you swore to David?
[50]Remember, Lord, how your servant has[a] been mocked,[a]
how I bear in my heart the taunts of all the nations,
[51]the taunts with which your enemies, LORD, have mocked,
with which they have mocked every step of your anointed one.[b]

[52]Praise be to the LORD forever!
Amen and Amen.[c]

[a] 50 Or *your servants have*

89:34 [o] Nu 23:19
89:38 [p] Dt 32:19; 1Ch 28:9; Ps 44:9
89:39 [q] La 5:16
89:40 [r] Ps 80:12 [s] La 2:2
89:41 [t] Ps 44:13
89:42 [u] Ps 13:2; 80:6
89:43 [v] Ps 44:10
89:45 [w] Ps 44:15; 109:29
89:46 [x] Ps 79:5
89:47 [y] Job 7:7; Ps 39:5
89:48 [z] Ps 22:29; 49:9
89:50 [a] Ps 69:19
89:51 [b] Ps 74:10
89:52 [c] Ps 41:13; 72:19

89:35–37 God's commitment to his covenant with David could not be clearer (see note on v. 3). This sets the stage for a jarring discord in vv. 38–45.

89:38–45 Harshly and vividly asserts that God had broken his promises, that he had renounced the covenant with David and had left the king vulnerable to his enemies. This dramatically reverses the laudatory tone concerning the Davidic covenant in vv. 19–37. The psalmist here ignores the many instances of Israel's and Judah's unfaithfulness to God recorded throughout the books of 1–2 Kings and the reasons for his abandoning them to their enemies (see especially 2 Kgs 17:7–23; 24:3–4), focusing instead on the psalmist's present plight.

89:39 covenant. See note on v. 3.

89:41 Cf. 88:8,18.

89:46–51 Continues the sense of God's abandonment (begun in vv. 38–45), couched in typical language of laments ("How long ...?"). This urges God not to hide himself but to remember his "former great love" (v. 49) for David and how the nations now mock the Davidic king.

89:46 How long ...? See note on 13:1,2.

89:47 fleeting is my life. Anticipates 90:4–5,9–10.

89:48 grave. See notes on 6:5; 88:4.

89:51 anointed one. The end of Book III comes full circle, suggesting the introduction to the Psalter (see introductions to Pss 1–2; Ps 2): in both places, the Lord's enemies bitterly oppose him and his anointed king (see 2:2 and note).

89:52 Concluding doxology to Book III (Pss 73–89). See note on 41:13.

90:1 [d]Dt 33:27; Eze 11:16
90:2 [e]Job 15:7; Pr 8:25 [f]Ps 102:24-27
90:3 [g]Ge 3:19; Job 34:15
90:4 [h]2Pe 3:8
90:5 [i]Ps 73:20; Isa 40:6
90:6 [j]Mt 6:30; Jas 1:10
90:8 [k]Ps 19:12

BOOK IV

Psalms 90–106

Psalm 90

A prayer of Moses the man of God.

1 Lord, you have been our dwelling place[d]
throughout all generations.
2 Before the mountains were born[e]
or you brought forth the whole world,
from everlasting to everlasting you are God.[f]

3 You turn people back to dust,
saying, "Return to dust, you mortals."[g]
4 A thousand years in your sight
are like a day that has just gone by,
or like a watch in the night.[h]
5 Yet you sweep people away[i] in the sleep of death—
they are like the new grass of the morning:
6 In the morning it springs up new,
but by evening it is dry and withered.[j]

7 We are consumed by your anger
and terrified by your indignation.
8 You have set our iniquities before you,
our secret sins[k] in the light of your presence.

Pss 90–106 *Book IV: The Lord Reigns.* The placement of Book IV is significant, especially in the light of the downbeat ending of Book III. But, with the opening psalm in Book IV attributed to Moses and the many allusions to the time of Moses in following psalms, the book also recalls a time when there was no king in Israel, when the Lord reigned over his people (Exod 15:18; cf. Pss 93–99) and was faithful to his promises even in the bleakest of circumstances (Exod 2:23–25). Three themes weave throughout Book IV: (1) The Lord reigns as King (see especially Pss 93–99). (2) God's people have an eternal hope grounded in an eternal God (90:1–2,4; 92:8,14–15; 93:2,5; 102:23–28; 103:17–18; 106:48). (3) The figure of David begins to slowly reemerge, as evidenced by the two Davidic psalms in the book (Pss 101; 103) and the repeated pronouncement that the Lord's covenant faithfulness is eternal (100:5; 103:17–18; 106:1,45; cf. 89:38–45 and note). This paves the way toward the "return of the (Davidic) king" in Book V.

Ps 90 *Satisfy Us in the Morning With Your Unfailing Love.* Ps 90 is a prayer for long life that is satisfied in the Lord. It juxtaposes the Lord's eternal nature (vv. 1–2) with the temporal nature of humanity (vv. 3–6), focusing on human sin as the reason for the brevity of the human lifespan (vv. 7–12) and concluding with a prayer that humans could enjoy a long life satisfied in the Lord's unfailing love (vv. 13–17). These four sections follow a pattern: eternality (vv. 1–2), temporality (vv. 3–6), temporality (vv. 7–12), long life (vv. 13–17).

The key features of Ps 90 respond to the challenges that Ps 89 raises. The theme of time figures prominently in Ps 90. Only vv. 7–8,11,17 do not address time or the passing of time in some way. This picks up on the dissonance in Ps 89 between the Lord's eternal promises and his apparent rejection of the covenant with David. Whereas Ps 89 questions the Lord's eternal faithfulness, Ps 90 portrays the Lord's eternal nature as a source of refuge (vv. 1–2) in which mankind longs to partake (vv. 3–17).

90 title man of God. A title of respect. It appears 76 times in the OT, most often referring to Moses (Deut 33:1; Josh 14:6; 1 Chr 23:14; 2 Chr 30:16; Ezra 3:2) and other prophets, including Elijah and Elisha (2 Kgs 1:9; 4:16). Moses is the only person the Pentateuch refers to as a "man of God."

90:1 dwelling place. A place of refuge (91:9; see notes on 2:12; 18:1–2); the Hebrew is translated "refuge" in 71:3, where it is parallel to "fortress."

90:2 born … brought forth. Poetically portrays the world as the Lord's "baby." **from … to.** When the Hebrew construction here refers to time, it suggests an interval (Gen 46:34; Exod 10:6; 1 Sam 30:17). The sense is "from eternity past to eternity future." **everlasting.** Eternality is a key theme of the psalm (vv. 1,4); mankind, in contrast, is ephemeral (vv. 3,5–6,9–10,12).

90:3 turn … Return. Translate the same Hebrew word, which also appears twice in Gen 3:19, where it pronounces the curse of death against humanity. **dust.** Also appears in Gen 3:19 and thus connotes death. Humankind's humble demise contrasts with the Lord's eternal nature in vv. 1–2.

90:4 Highlights the difference between the Lord's and humankind's existence in time; 2 Pet 3:8, a call to patience, cites this to affirm that the Lord does not account for time in the same way that humans do.

90:5 sweep people away. The Hebrew root usually refers to a violent rain shower and signifies God's judgment or his presence (77:17; Isa 4:6; 25:4; 28:2). **sleep.** The Hebrew words for "sleep" (*šēnâ*) and "year" (*šānâ*, see v. 4) are almost identical. They serve to contrast the Lord with humankind.

90:6 morning … evening. Emphasizes the brevity of human life (Job 4:20), a common theme in Scripture (37:2,20,36; 39:5,11; 62:9; 78:39; 102:3,11; 103:15–16; 144:4; Isa 40:6–8; Jas 1:10–11).

90:7–9 anger … indignation … wrath. Toward sin and rebellion; this is the reason human life is short (2:5; Gen 3:14–19).

90:8 light of your presence. Illumines the entire world so that nothing is done in "secret" beyond God's awareness (33:13–15; 139:7–12; 2 Chr 16:9; Job 34:21–22; Heb 4:13).

[9] All our days pass away under your wrath;
we finish our years with a moan.[l]
[10] Our days may come to seventy years,
or eighty, if our strength endures;
yet the best of them are but trouble and sorrow,
for they quickly pass, and we fly away.[m]
[11] If only we knew the power of your anger!
Your wrath is as great as the fear that is your due.[n]
[12] Teach us to number our days,[o]
that we may gain a heart of wisdom.[p]

[13] Relent, LORD! How long[q] will it be?
Have compassion on your servants.[r]
[14] Satisfy[s] us in the morning with your unfailing love,
that we may sing for joy[t] and be glad all our days.[u]
[15] Make us glad for as many days as you have afflicted us,
for as many years as we have seen trouble.
[16] May your deeds be shown to your servants,
your splendor to their children.[v]

[17] May the favor[a] of the Lord our God rest on us;
establish the work of our hands for us—
yes, establish the work of our hands.[w]

Psalm 91

[1] Whoever dwells in the shelter[x] of the Most High
will rest in the shadow[y] of the Almighty.[b]
[2] I will say of the LORD, "He is my refuge[z] and my fortress,
my God, in whom I trust."

90:9 [l] Ps 78:33
90:10 [m] Job 20:8
90:11 [n] Ps 76:7
90:12 [o] Ps 39:4 [p] Dt 32:29
90:13 [q] Ps 6:3 [r] Dt 32:36; Ps 135:14
90:14 [s] Ps 103:5 [t] Ps 85:6 [u] Ps 31:7
90:16 [v] Ps 44:1; Hab 3:2
90:17 [w] Isa 26:12
91:1 [x] Ps 31:20 [y] Ps 17:8
91:2 [z] Ps 142:5

[a] *17* Or *beauty* [b] *1* Hebrew *Shaddai*

90:10 seventy … eighty. A typical lifespan; pales in comparison to the Lord's existence (vv. 1–2). **sorrow.** The brevity of human life is ultimately the result of sin.
90:12 number our days. See notes on 31:15; 39:4. **wisdom.** Making the most of whatever days remain to a person; a by-product of a healthy fear of the Lord (v. 11; see note on 111:10). See introduction to Ps 34.
90:13 Relent. Translated "turn" and "return" in v. 3 (see note there). Prays that the Lord would reverse the curse, which, according to v. 3, is death. **How long … ?** A rhetorical question characteristic of lament psalms (see 6:3; 13:1,2 and note; 89:46; 119:84); presupposes that there will eventually be an answer, so there is a muted sense of hope that God will reverse the curse of death. **Have compassion.** This request is answered by an affirmation at the end of Book IV that the Lord "relented" when his people cried out to him (106:45). One emphasis in Book IV is that the Lord is compassionate toward his people and remembers their low estate.
90:14 morning. Symbolizes brevity in v. 6 (see note there); here it represents the new life that comes after the "evening." The ultimate fulfillment of this prayer comes at the end of time with the resurrection (49:14; Rom 8:18; 2 Cor 4:16–18). **unfailing love.** The Lord's covenant faithfulness (see note on 6:4).
90:15 Prays that the Lord would somehow make up for all the days in which his people have experienced affliction and evil. This is an oblique request for eternal life, because v. 10 states that a human's earthly life is characterized by trouble and iniquity. So the only way that joy can match the affliction is if there is another life.
90:16 to their children. Just as previous generations passed down stories of the Lord's faithfulness (v. 1), Moses prays that there would continue to be an inheritance of faith (see also 78:3–8; 103:17; 145:4).
90:17 favor. See NIV text note; as opposed to anger, indignation, and wrath (vv. 7–9). **establish.** Prays that even as the lives of God's people are transitory, their work would endure and thus more closely match their God's nature (7:9; 9:7; 48:8). **work of our hands.** The product of one's labor, which the Lord must bless for it to be effective (127:1–2; 128:2; see 138:8 and note; Deut 14:29; 16:15; 24:19; Isa 26:12).
Ps 91 *He Is My Refuge and My Fortress, My God, in Whom I Trust.* Ps 91 continues the themes of Ps 90, presenting them in clear, affirmative statements: the Lord is a refuge (vv. 1–2,4,9,14; cf. 90:1), and human life can endure (vv. 14–16; cf. 90:13–17). The psalmist's chief theme is that the Lord is his refuge (vv. 1–2). This has three benefits: the Lord protects from danger (vv. 3–8), guards against calamity by providing supernatural assistance (vv. 9–13), rescues from trouble (vv. 14–15), and grants eternal life (v. 16).
91:1 shelter. A secure covering, which the Lord provides for the godly (32:7; 61:4; 119:114). At times, this refers more specifically to the temple (27:5; 31:20; cf. 23:6; 27:4). **Most High.** See note on 7:8. **rest.** Connotes dwelling or abiding (Job 39:28; see notes on 62:1; 116:7). **shadow.** Denotes security (see note on 36:7). **Almighty.** See note on 68:14.
91:2 refuge. A key theme in Psalms (see notes on 2:12; 18:1–2). **fortress.** A source of security from attack (see note on 18:1–2). **trust.** Engendered from a position of security (see notes on 25:1; 115:9–11).

Fifteenth-century wall painting from Thebes shows Egyptians in the marshes hunting birds with a net. "Surely he will save you from the fowler's snare" (Ps 91:3).

Z. Radovan/www.BibleLandPictures.com

91:3 [a]Ps 124:7; Pr 6:5 [b]1Ki 8:37
91:4 [c]Ps 17:8 [d]Ps 35:2
91:5 [e]Job 5:21
91:8 [f]Ps 37:34; 58:10; Mal 1:5
91:10 [g]Pr 12:21

3 Surely he will save you
from the fowler's snare[a]
and from the deadly pestilence.[b]
4 He will cover you with his feathers,
and under his wings you will find refuge;[c]
his faithfulness will be your shield[d] and rampart.
5 You will not fear[e] the terror of night,
nor the arrow that flies by day,
6 nor the pestilence that stalks in the darkness,
nor the plague that destroys at midday.
7 A thousand may fall at your side,
ten thousand at your right hand,
but it will not come near you.
8 You will only observe with your eyes
and see the punishment of the wicked.[f]

9 If you say, "The LORD is my refuge,"
and you make the Most High your dwelling,
10 no harm[g] will overtake you,
no disaster will come near your tent.

91:3 fowler's snare. A hidden danger (119:110; 140:5; 141:9; 142:3); a common metaphor for distress. **pestilence.** As opposed to the hidden danger of a fowler's snare, this is an evident danger. It is also one of the covenant curses (Deut 28:21; see 1 Kgs 8:37).
91:4 cover. For protection (5:11; cf. 91:1). **feathers ... wings.** Depicts the Lord as a protective bird (cf. 17:8; 36:7; 57:1; 63:7; Deut 32:10–12; Matt 23:37; Luke 13:34). **refuge.** See note on 2:12; 18:1–2. **shield.** A large one that covers the whole body. See note on 3:3. **rampart.** A defensive wall.
91:5 Corresponds to the protection the Lord provides in v. 4. The rampart protects against "the terror of night," and the large shield provides refuge from "the arrow."
91:6 darkness. Translates a Hebrew word that can refer to the deep darkness of the underworld (Job 10:22; 28:3) and to spiritual darkness (Job 30:26; Isa 29:18).
91:7–8 These verses teach that the Lord will shield believers from the judgment against the wicked, but they do not promise absolute protection from every harmful circumstance (v. 7).
91:7 thousand ... ten thousand. Pictures the carnage that results from battle, plague, or natural disaster (see note on v. 8). **ten thousand.** The largest numeral in the Hebrew language.
91:8 punishment. Clarifies that the horrific scene in v. 7 is the recompense for evil, so those who take shelter in the Lord are safe from that kind of judgment.
91:9 refuge. See v. 2 and note. **Most High.** See note on 7:8. **dwelling.** The same Hebrew word used in 90:1 (see note there); it occurs only four times (68:5; 71:3; 90:1; 91:9) with the meaning "dwelling as a refuge," and two of them are here in adjacent psalms.

[11] For he will command his angels[h] concerning you
to guard you in all your ways;[i]
[12] they will lift you up in their hands,
so that you will not strike your foot against a stone.[j]
[13] You will tread on the lion and the cobra;
you will trample the great lion and the serpent.[k]

[14] "Because he[a] loves me," says the LORD, "I will rescue him;
I will protect him, for he acknowledges my name.
[15] He will call on me, and I will answer him;
I will be with him in trouble,
I will deliver him and honor him.[l]
[16] With long life[m] I will satisfy him
and show him my salvation.[n]"

Psalm 92[b]

A psalm. A song. For the Sabbath day.

[1] It is good to praise the LORD
and make music to your name,[o] O Most High,[p]
[2] proclaiming your love in the morning[q]
and your faithfulness at night,
[3] to the music of the ten-stringed lyre
and the melody of the harp.[r]

[4] For you make me glad by your deeds, LORD;
I sing for joy at what your hands have done.[s]

91:11 [h] Heb 1:14 [i] Ps 34:7
91:12 [j] Mt 4:6*; Lk 4:10-11*
91:13 [k] Da 6:22; Lk 10:19
91:15 [l] 1Sa 2:30; Ps 50:15; Jn 12:26
91:16 [m] Dt 6:2; Ps 21:4 [n] Ps 50:23
92:1 [o] Ps 147:1 [p] Ps 135:3
92:2 [q] Ps 89:1
92:3 [r] 1Sa 10:5; Ne 12:27; Ps 33:2
92:4 [s] Ps 8:6; 143:5

[a] *14* That is, probably the king [b] In Hebrew texts 92:1-15 is numbered 92:2-16.

91:11–12 Satan quotes this in order to tempt Jesus to ostentatiously display his power and authority (Matt 4:6; Luke 4:10–11). Not only was Satan's demand contrary to the Father's plan of redemption through his Son's humbling himself and suffering, but it also misused this Scripture. This does not promise that the Lord will rescue a believer from all danger, especially when a believer presumptuously manufactures a perilous situation (as Satan was tempting Jesus to do). Rather, this reveals how the Lord will supply supernatural help to aid the believer when it is most necessary, as the Father did in Jesus' life (Matt 4:11; Luke 22:43).
91:13 Snakes and lions (as wild beasts) represent the cursed aspects of creation (Gen 3:14–15; Num 21:6; 2 Kgs 17:25). While the Bible does speak of instances when the Lord protects believers from lions and snakes (e.g., Dan 6:22; Acts 28:6; Heb 11:33; cf. 2 Tim 4:17), this does not mean that these creatures will never harm believers in any way, in any circumstance, or that believers can approach or treat these creatures lightly.
91:14 he loves me ... he acknowledges my name. Further clarifies what it means to take refuge in the Lord and to trust him (vv. 1–2). **name.** See note on 8:1.
91:15 I will answer. Answered prayer manifests God's love and evidences vindication (see 118:5; 138:3,8 and notes; John 11:41–42).
91:16 long life. The Hebrew phrase typically refers to a long (and blessed) physical life (e.g., Exod 20:12; Deut 30:20; Prov 3:2; cf. Exod 23:26), but it sometimes means "forever," indicating life beyond this earthly life (e.g., 21:4; 23:6; 93:5). In combination with the Lord's "salvation," the emphasis in this verse may be on both, in the same way that Paul assures Timothy that godliness holds promise for both this life and the next (1 Tim 4:8–9). The request for long life in 90:13–17 is certainly answered here.
Ps 92 *But You, Lord, Are Forever Exalted.* This celebrates the Lord's love and faithfulness as he cares for the righteous and judges the wicked. It relates closely to Pss 90–91, joyfully praising God in light of the theme of long life in those psalms. The psalm flows nicely from the assurance of salvation in 91:16, to an emphasis on eternal life. It has three main sections, and the main point occurs at the center, v. 8. First, there are two motivations for praise: it is good (vv. 1–3), and God's works inspire joy (vv. 4–5). Second, the state of the wicked is deplorable, contrasting with the exalted position of the Lord and his leader (vv. 6–11). Third, the righteous are like healthy, fruitful trees planted in the temple that bear witness to the goodness of God (vv. 12–15).
92 title The Sabbath was a day of rest celebrated on the seventh day of the week; it was instituted at creation (Gen 2:3) and codified at Sinai (Exod 20:8–11). The rest that God's people enjoyed on the Sabbath was more than simply the cessation of labor; it also signified a spiritual and final rest that was to come (95:11; Deut 12:8–11; Heb 3:7—4:11). As the title indicates, God's people used this psalm for the weekly Sabbath worship, so it also expressed a longing for ultimate rest. Thus, it fits well with the emphasis on eternal life in Pss 90–91.
92:1 praise. Or "give thanks" (see note on 107:1). **Most High.** See note on 7:8; cf. 91:1,9.
92:2 Seems to answer the request in 90:14. **love.** The Lord's covenant faithfulness (see notes on 6:4; 107:1). **morning ... night.** Describes man's temporality in 90:6; here it depicts Sabbath worship.
92:3 lyre. A small, mobile version of the harp. It could be played like a guitar. **harp.** An instrument played like a modern harp (see note on 150:3).
92:4 you make me glad. Answers the request in 90:15 (see also 90:14); the point is that the Lord makes his people glad on the Sabbath (see Ps 92 title).

92:5 [t]Rev 15:3 [u]Ps 40:5; 139:17; Isa 28:29; Ro 11:33
92:6 [v]Ps 73:22
92:9 [w]Ps 68:1; 89:10
92:10 [x]Ps 89:17 [y]Ps 23:5
92:11 [z]Ps 54:7; 91:8
92:12 [a]Ps 1:3; 52:8; Jer 17:8; Hos 14:6
92:13 [b]Ps 100:4
92:14 [c]Jn 15:2
92:15 [d]Job 34:10
93:1 [e]Ps 97:1 [f]Ps 104:1 [g]Ps 65:6 [h]Ps 96:10
93:2 [i]Ps 45:6

5 How great are your works,[t] LORD,
how profound your thoughts![u]
6 Senseless people[v] do not know,
fools do not understand,
7 that though the wicked spring up like grass
and all evildoers flourish,
they will be destroyed forever.

8 But you, LORD, are forever exalted.

9 For surely your enemies, LORD,
surely your enemies will perish;
all evildoers will be scattered.[w]
10 You have exalted my horn[a][x] like that of a wild ox;
fine oils[y] have been poured on me.
11 My eyes have seen the defeat of my adversaries;
my ears have heard the rout of my wicked foes.[z]

12 The righteous will flourish like a palm tree,
they will grow like a cedar of Lebanon;[a]
13 planted in the house of the LORD,
they will flourish in the courts of our God.[b]
14 They will still bear fruit[c] in old age,
they will stay fresh and green,
15 proclaiming, "The LORD is upright;
he is my Rock, and there is no wickedness in him.[d]"

Psalm 93

1 The LORD reigns,[e] he is robed in majesty;[f]
the LORD is robed in majesty and armed with strength;[g]
indeed, the world is established, firm and secure.[h]
2 Your throne was established long ago;
you are from all eternity.[i]

[a] *10 Horn* here symbolizes strength.

92:6 fools. Contrast with the "wise" (94:8; Prov 3:35; 10:1; 14:8). The wise worship the Lord (vv. 1–5) and recognize that their life is fleeting (v. 7; 90:12).
92:7 Encapsulates the message of Ps 73 (see especially 73:15–28; see also introduction to Ps 73). **flourish.** Humankind's period of flourishing is brief (90:6).
92:8 The psalm's midpoint (see note on 100:3 ["his people"]) articulates its central theme (cf. 90:1,2,4). The Lord's eternal exaltation contrasts with the eternal destruction of the wicked (v. 7).
92:9 perish. Corresponds to "destroyed" in v. 7. The Psalter begins by affirming that the way of the wicked will perish (1:6; see 9:6; 73:27–28; 145:20). **scattered.** A manifestation of God's judgment. The image here is of a routed army scattering in defeat (68:1).
92:10 The exalted Lord (v. 8) is the one who exalts. **fine oils.** Used for anointing (see note on 133:2) or hospitality (see note on 23:5).
92:13 house of the LORD. The temple (see note on 5:7). Trees growing in the temple creates a vision of the end-time temple (Ezek 47:1–12; Rev 22:1–2). See "Temple," p. 2652.
92:14–15 Pictures eternal life: perpetual youth and worship.
92:14 bear fruit. Signifies the Lord's blessing (1:3; Gen 1:11–12; 2:9; Jer 17:8; Ezek 47:12; John 15:2–5).
Ps 93 *The Lord Reigns.* This is the first of a series of psalms (Pss 93–99) that stress the Lord's status and authority as King. These psalms positively answer to the problem presented in Ps 89 concerning the diminished state of the Davidic dynasty. The people of God continue to have a King: the Lord, even if there is not an earthly king ruling over the nation. Like Pss 90–92, Ps 93 emphasizes the theme of the Lord's eternality (vv. 2,5). It begins by grounding the world's stability in the Lord's kingship (vv. 1–2). Then it describes how the Lord is higher and greater than even the most dangerous of threats such as raging floodwater (vv. 3–4). It ends by praising the Lord's royal decrees and acknowledging his eternality (v. 5).
93:1 The LORD reigns. The Lord's kingship is a prominent theme in Pss 93–99 (93:1; 95:3; 96:10; 97:1; 98:6; 99:1–4), establishing this section of Book IV as a high point in the Psalter, a sure antidote to the pessimism at the end of Book III. The only other psalms that refer directly to the Lord as King are 47:2,6–8; 145:1; 149:2 (cf. Exod 15:18; Zech 14:9). But God's position as King is also announced indirectly at the very beginning of the Psalter, in Ps 2. The Lord's reign is given as a reason for rejoicing in 97:1; 1 Chr 16:31. Pss 93–99 also focus on the justice established by God, the King (see 94; 96:10,13; 97:2,8; 98:9; 99:4,8). See notes on 10:16; 22:27–28.
93:2 Your throne ... long ago. See 55:19. **eternity.** A chief theme in Book IV so far (90:1–2,4; 91:16; 92:8).

[3] The seas[j] have lifted up, LORD,
the seas have lifted up their voice;
the seas have lifted up their pounding waves.
[4] Mightier than the thunder[k] of the great waters,
mightier than the breakers of the sea —
the LORD on high is mighty.

[5] Your statutes, LORD, stand firm;
holiness[l] adorns your house
for endless days.

Psalm 94

[1] The LORD is a God who avenges.[m]
O God who avenges, shine forth.[n]
[2] Rise up, Judge[o] of the earth;
pay back[p] to the proud what they deserve.
[3] How long, LORD, will the wicked,
how long will the wicked be jubilant?

[4] They pour out arrogant[q] words;
all the evildoers are full of boasting.[r]
[5] They crush your people,[s] LORD;
they oppress your inheritance.
[6] They slay the widow and the foreigner;
they murder the fatherless.
[7] They say, "The LORD does not see;[t]
the God of Jacob takes no notice."

93:3 [j] Ps 96:11
93:4 [k] Ps 65:7
93:5 [l] Ps 29:2
94:1 [m] Na 1:2; Ro 12:19 [n] Ps 80:1
94:2 [o] Ge 18:25 [p] Ps 31:23
94:4 [q] Ps 31:18 [r] Ps 52:1
94:5 [s] Isa 3:15
94:7 [t] Job 22:14; Ps 10:11

93:3–4 An example of step parallelism, a poetic technique that builds to a climax. The technique complements the content perfectly as the poetry mimics the way a large wave builds height and then crashes. **93:3 seas.** Scripture often portrays the seas or mighty waters as unruly forces of devastation (e.g., 32:6; 42:7; 46:3; 65:7; 69:2,14–15; 89:9; 124:4–5; Isa 51:10; Jonah 2:2–3), sometimes directly opposing the Lord (29:3; 65:7; Isa 17:13; Hab 3:15). For Jonah, the sea was a grave, a place of exile (Jonah 2:2–6). John's vision of the end views it as a source of chaos and evil, done away with in the new earth (Rev 13:1; 21:1). **pounding waves.** The Hebrew term here means "crush, oppress," so the seas are seen in opposition to God (just as God's enemies oppose him in 94:5, which uses the same term). In the literatures of ancient Egypt, Canaan, and Babylon, the forces of the seas were powerful deities opposing the gods that these cultures worshiped, and the Bible's treatment of such forces parallels this. God is sovereign over all such forces of nature (and the imaginary gods associated with them) because he created and tamed them (24:1–2; 33:7; 65:7; 89:9; 104:8–10; Gen 1:9–10; Job 38:8–11; Prov 8:29; Isa 40:12; Jer 5:22; Jonah 1:14–16; Luke 8:22–25).
93:4 high. Translated "exalted" in 92:8; the Lord is higher (more exalted) than the frightening seas.
93:5 statutes. The word of the Lord: his testimony about himself and his world (see introduction to Ps 119). **holiness.** To be holy means to be set apart for a specific purpose (Exod 28:36; Jer 2:3; Zech 14:10). Typically, that means to be set apart from sin for the purpose of serving and/or bringing glory to God. See "Holiness," p. 2676. **endless days.** Translated "long life" in Ps 91:16; contributes to the theme of eternality in Pss 90–93.
Ps 94 *Rise Up, Judge of the Earth.* Ps 94 emphasizes one of the primary roles of God the King: to establish justice (96:10,13; 97:8,10–12; 98:9; 99:4). After an introductory appeal to the Lord to act as judge (vv. 1–3), there are five sections of four verses each: the psalmist charges the oppressors (vv. 4–7); the Lord knows the situation (vv. 8–11); the Lord will not abandon his people, and oppression is a form of discipline (vv. 12–15); only the Lord provides help against evil (vv. 16–19); and the Lord himself stands against unjust rulers (vv. 20–23).
94:1 God who avenges. Repeated twice; portrays God in a royal light, which fits the context of the surrounding psalms (Pss 93; 95–99). The vengeance of God is a just recompense for evil (18:47; 79:10; 149:7; Deut 32:35,43; Jer 51:6,11,36).
94:2 pay back ... what they deserve. The Lord's vengeance (v. 1) is not capricious or unrestrained; rather, it expresses retributive justice: wrongdoers get what they deserve (see notes on 69:22–28; 109:6–20; 137:8 ["repays you ... done to us"]).
94:3 How long ...? Repeated twice; the classic question of lament (see note on 13:1,2). The question inherently recognizes that there will be an end to the suffering. **wicked be jubilant.** The wicked apparently triumph (cf. 13:2; 37:1,7; 73:1–14; 92:7a), but in time they will receive their just reward (37:2,8–9; 73:16–28; 92:7).
94:4 pour out. Arrogance flows from the mouth of the wicked like a constant water stream (see Prov 18:4 ["rushing"], which uses the same Hebrew word).
94:5 crush. The word often occurs in contexts of oppression (143:3; Prov 22:22; Isa 3:15; Lam 3:34). **inheritance.** The Lord's people (v. 14; 28:9; 33:12; 74:2; 106:40; Deut 32:9; 1 Sam 10:1): God owns and stewards them (see note on 74:2).
94:6 widow ... foreigner ... fatherless. Vulnerable groups among God's people. See note on 82:3–4.
94:7 They say. See also v. 4 and note on 10:6. The arrogant foolishly surmise that the Judge of the earth does not notice their deeds (10:11; 59:7; 73:11; Isa 29:15; Ezek 8:12; 9:9).

94:8 [u]Ps 92:6
94:9 [v]Ex 4:11; Pr 20:12
94:10 [w]Job 35:11; Isa 28:26
94:11 [x]1Co 3:20*
94:12 [y]Job 5:17; Heb 12:5 [z]Dt 8:3
94:13 [a]Ps 55:23
94:14 [b]1Sa 12:22; Ps 37:28; Ro 11:2
94:15 [c]Ps 97:2
94:16 [d]Nu 10:35; Ps 17:13 [e]Ps 59:2
94:17 [f]Ps 124:2
94:18 [g]Ps 38:16
94:20 [h]Ps 58:2
94:21 [i]Ps 56:6 [j]Ps 106:38; Pr 17:15,26
94:22 [k]Ps 18:2; 59:9

8 Take notice, you senseless ones[u] among the people;
you fools, when will you become wise?
9 Does he who fashioned the ear not hear?
Does he who formed the eye not see?[v]
10 Does he who disciplines nations not punish?
Does he who teaches[w] mankind lack knowledge?
11 The LORD knows all human plans;
he knows that they are futile.[x]

12 Blessed is the one you discipline,[y] LORD,
the one you teach[z] from your law;
13 you grant them relief from days of trouble,
till a pit[a] is dug for the wicked.
14 For the LORD will not reject his people;[b]
he will never forsake his inheritance.
15 Judgment will again be founded on righteousness,[c]
and all the upright in heart will follow it.

16 Who will rise up[d] for me against the wicked?
Who will take a stand for me against evildoers?[e]
17 Unless the LORD had given me help,[f]
I would soon have dwelt in the silence of death.
18 When I said, "My foot is slipping,[g]"
your unfailing love, LORD, supported me.
19 When anxiety was great within me,
your consolation brought me joy.

20 Can a corrupt throne be allied with you—
a throne that brings on misery by its decrees?[h]
21 The wicked band together[i] against the righteous
and condemn the innocent[j] to death.
22 But the LORD has become my fortress,
and my God the rock in whom I take refuge.[k]

94:8–11 The response to the conceited taunt of v. 7. **94:8 Take notice.** Repeats the same Hebrew verb in v. 7, where the fool thinks that the Lord "takes no notice" of evil. This calls upon the fool to "take notice." **94:9 formed.** As a potter. The human body is the Lord's work of art. **94:11** Paul quotes this in 1 Cor 3:20 to encourage the church not to boast in human leaders: even the best and wisest leaders are fallible. **plans.** Or "thoughts." The senseless ones assume that the Lord does not see what takes place on the earth (v. 7), but the Lord's knowledge extends beyond human speech and action to an individual's inner thoughts and plans (139:2; Matt 9:4). **futile.** The same word translated "meaningless" throughout Ecclesiastes (e.g., Eccl 1:2,14; 2:1,11,15; 3:19; 8:14) and elsewhere as "breath" (e.g., Pss 39:5,11; 62:9; 144:4; Isa 57:13). Human plans lack substance; they are short-lived and passing. **94:12 Blessed.** See note on 1:1. The Lord's disciplining his people signifies his fatherly love (Deut 8:5; Prov 3:11–12; 1 Cor 11:32; Heb 12:5–11). **teach.** The Lord disciplines by teaching from his word (see v. 10). **94:14** This verse may stand behind Paul's statement in Rom 11:1–2. **inheritance.** See v. 5; see also note on 74:2. **94:15 upright.** Or "straight," as opposed to "crooked" and "treacherous" (Prov 3:32; 11:3,6). This is an attribute of God (25:8; 92:15) and his word (19:8; 33:4), and it is often related to righteousness (11:7; 32:11; 33:1; 64:10; 92:15; 97:11).

94:16 evildoers. The chief perpetrators in this psalm, who are boastful (v. 4) and may be bloodthirsty (59:2). Though they flourish for a short time, they will eventually receive their due (92:7–9). **94:17 the LORD.** The answer to the two questions in v. 16. He upholds the righteous and upright in their battle against evil (vv. 14–15). **silence.** Associated with death (see 115:17 and note). **94:18 slipping.** Removed from a position of security (17:5; 38:16). **unfailing love.** Faithful covenant love (see notes on 6:4; 107:1). **supported.** Strengthened—the effect of bread on a hungry man (104:15; Gen 18:5; Judg 19:5,8). **94:20 misery by its decrees.** Just because something is lawful does not make it just. The Lord can provide refuge from institutionalized injustice because he is the ultimate lawgiver and judge (vv. 1–2; 93:5; 99:7). **94:21 band together.** Alliances are prominent in vv. 20–21. The Lord does not ally himself with wicked rulers, but they "band together" against the righteous, who reflect his character (2:2; 83:3–5; Neh 4:8). **94:22 fortress ... rock ... refuge.** A continuing theme so far in Book IV (see note on 90:1; cf. 91:1–2,9; 92:15). It fits within the overall trajectory of the Psalter (see 2:12 and note; 18:1–2 and note). Here the Lord is a refuge from all kinds of injustice, especially political injustice (see note on v. 20).

[23] He will repay[l] them for their sins
and destroy them for their wickedness;
the LORD our God will destroy them.

Psalm 95

[1] Come, let us sing for joy to the LORD;
let us shout aloud[m] to the Rock[n] of our salvation.
[2] Let us come before him[o] with thanksgiving
and extol him with music[p] and song.

[3] For the LORD is the great God,[q]
the great King above all gods.[r]
[4] In his hand are the depths of the earth,
and the mountain peaks belong to him.
[5] The sea is his, for he made it,
and his hands formed the dry land.[s]

[6] Come, let us bow down[t] in worship,
let us kneel[u] before the LORD our Maker;[v]
[7] for he is our God
and we are the people of his pasture,[w]
the flock under his care.

Today, if only you would hear his voice,
[8] "Do not harden your hearts as you did at Meribah,[a][x]
as you did that day at Massah[b] in the wilderness,

94:23 [l] Ps 7:16
95:1 [m] Ps 81:1 [n] 2Sa 22:47
95:2 [o] Mic 6:6 [p] Ps 81:2; Eph 5:19
95:3 [q] Ps 48:1; 145:3 [r] Ps 96:4; 97:9
95:5 [s] Ge 1:9; Ps 146:6
95:6 [t] Php 2:10 [u] 2Ch 6:13 [v] Ps 100:3; 149:2; Isa 17:7; Da 6:10-11; Hos 8:14
95:7 [w] Ps 74:1; 79:13
95:8 [x] Ex 17:7

[a] 8 *Meribah* means *quarreling.* [b] 8 *Massah* means *testing.*

94:23 The double repetition at the end of the psalm is reminiscent of 90:17. **repay.** A request for retribution. God's judgments are just, never exceeding what people deserve (see notes on 109:6–20; 137:8 ["repays you ... done to us"]). **destroy.** The judgment of the wicked is a hopeful expectation throughout the Psalter (1:6; 2:9; 73:18–20; 92:9; 145:20).

Ps 95 *For the Lord Is the Great God, the Great King Above All Gods.* According to the structure of Ps 95, right living flows from right worship. The first section (vv. 1–7c) speaks of right worship, highlighting the ways and means of worship (vv. 1–2,6) and the grounds for it (vv. 3–5,7a–c). The second section is an encouragement to enter God's rest by obeying him (vv. 7d–11). The first section engenders an attitude of joyful and humble confidence in the Lord, which the second section calls for. As a part of the series of psalms that emphasizes the Lord's reign (Pss 93–99), this psalm teaches that people should worship and obey the Lord as King, and it concludes with an example from Israel's history in which they did neither, thus warning future generations of believers.

95:1 Rock. Repeats the end of the previous psalm (see note on 94:22).

95:3 God. Translates the short form for God (*'ēl* instead of the usual *'ĕlōhîm*). One of the high Canaanite gods was named El, and this may be intentionally making a pejorative jab at this deity, along with all the other "gods" (v. 3b), asserting that the Lord occupies the position that others thought El held. See also Pss 29; 82; 115:4–8; 135:15–18.

95:4–5 hand ... hands. Binds together this summary of the Lord's sovereignty over all of creation.

95:4 depths ... peaks. All of creation from bottom to top and everything in between.

95:5 sea. See note on 93:3.

95:6 bow down ... kneel. A position of humility and submission (72:9). Right worship is humble worship (2 Chr 6:13; Isa 45:23). **our Maker.** A reference not to God's creating humanity but to God's constituting his people Israel. See note on 100:3.

95:7a–c he is our God. Affirms the covenant (118:28; Gen 17:8; Exod 6:7; 29:45–46; Lev 26:12; Deut 29:13; Rev 21:7). **people of his pasture, the flock under his care.** A mixed metaphor: one expects "sheep of his pasture, the people under his care" (cf. 74:1; 79:13; Jer 23:1; Ezek 34:31). But the switch heightens the poetic imagery because the two notions are interchangeable. As his flock, God's people receive pasture, which means that they are under his care (23:1–6; 100:3).

95:7d–11 Combines the story about the Israelites' lack of faith at Massah and Meribah in Exod 17:1–7 with the pronouncement of judgment on the Israelites' lack of faith in Num 14:21–35. The two events are related; these were the very same people who experienced God's deliverance from Egypt (Num 14:22). The psalmist correlates the experience of God's people in the wilderness with the experience of God's people in the present by adding, "Today, if only you would hear his voice" (v. 7d). Thus, Ps 95 applies to all generations of believers because the message is for "today." And like the wilderness generation who witnessed the glory of God (Num 14:21–22), the current generation experiences the glory of God when it hears his voice (v. 7d). The NT quotes and exposits this passage in Heb 3:7—4:13, which (like the psalmist) applies the message to the current audience. From the perspective of the writer of the book of Hebrews, Jesus' followers, like the ancient Israelites, need to exercise faith so that they might inherit all that God has promised them.

95:7d Today. The psalmist applies the message of Exod 17:1–7; Num 14:21–35 to each reader's generation.

95:8 harden your hearts. The same obstinate attitude that the pharaoh in Moses' day displayed (Exod 7:3; 13:15; cf. Exod 7:14; 8:15). **Meribah ... Massah.** See note on 81:7.

95:9 [y] Nu 14:22; Ps 78:18; 1Co 10:9
95:10 [z] Ac 7:36; Heb 3:17
95:11 [a] Nu 14:23 [b] Dt 1:35; Heb 4:3*
96:1 [c] 1Ch 16:23
96:2 [d] Ps 71:15
96:4 [e] Ps 18:3; 145:3 [f] Ps 89:7 [g] Ps 95:3
96:5 [h] Ps 115:15
96:6 [i] Ps 29:1
96:7 [j] Ps 29:1 [k] Ps 22:27
96:8 [l] Ps 45:12; 72:10

9 where your ancestors tested[y] me;
they tried me, though they had seen what I did.
10 For forty years[z] I was angry with that generation;
I said, 'They are a people whose hearts go astray,
and they have not known my ways.'
11 So I declared on oath[a] in my anger,
'They shall never enter my rest.'"[b]

Psalm 96

96:1-13pp — 1Ch 16:23-33

1 Sing to the LORD[c] a new song;
sing to the LORD, all the earth.
2 Sing to the LORD, praise his name;
proclaim his salvation[d] day after day.
3 Declare his glory among the nations,
his marvelous deeds among all peoples.

4 For great is the LORD and most worthy of praise;[e]
he is to be feared[f] above all gods.[g]
5 For all the gods of the nations are idols,
but the LORD made the heavens.[h]
6 Splendor and majesty are before him;
strength and glory[i] are in his sanctuary.

7 Ascribe to the LORD,[j] all you families of nations,[k]
ascribe to the LORD glory and strength.
8 Ascribe to the LORD the glory due his name;
bring an offering[l] and come into his courts.

95:9 what I did. The wilderness generation was privileged to witness the Lord's work, e.g., in the signs and wonders in Egypt (Exod 7–12) or in the triumph over Pharaoh's army at the Red Sea (Exod 14–15).
95:11 my rest. For the wilderness generation, the promised land (Deut 12:9). For subsequent generations, God's "rest" was what the promised land prefigured: an ultimate and final destination of Sabbath rest (cf. Heb 4:3–11). This allusion to eternal life fits well in the context of Book IV up to this point (see notes on 90:13–15; 91:16; 92:13–15).
Ps 96 *He Will Judge the World in Righteousness and the Peoples in His Faithfulness.* Ps 96 is a universal call to recognize that the Lord reigns. It corresponds closely in theme with the psalms that surround it (Pss 93–95; 97–99). Ps 96 has two sections: (1) a universal call to worship the Lord because of his beauty and glory (vv. 1–6), and (2) a universal call to worship the Lord because of his just judgment (vv. 7–13). Both sections are related to the Lord's reign as king: his beauty and glory are fit for a king (vv. 1–6), and his just judgment is the prerogative of a king (vv. 7–13). The psalm is part of a larger hymn of praise that David sang on the occasion of bringing the ark of the covenant up to Jerusalem in 1 Chr 16:8–36 (especially vv. 23–33). See introductions to Pss 105; 106.
96:1 new song. A response to a fresh experience of God's grace (see note on 33:3). **all the earth.** Emphasizes the Lord's universal reign. Whereas the previous two psalms focus on the covenant people of God (94:5,8,14; 95:7–11), Ps 96 expands the focus to incorporate all of creation. See also Ps 67 and note.
96:2 day after day. A figure of speech that encompasses all of time (cf. 113:2): the Lord's praise should fill "all the earth" (v. 1) all the time.
96:3 among the nations ... among all peoples. The Psalter invites the nations to join the worshiping community (see Ps 67 and introduction; 117:1 and note; see also "Mission," p. 2691, and "The Glory of God," p. 2640).
96:4 above all gods. One of the ways that the Lord displays his authority over the nations is by demonstrating his superiority over their gods (see 97:7; see also notes on 95:3; 115:4–8; 135:15–18; 1 Sam 5:1–5; Isa 44:9–20). Even the ten plagues in Exodus can be read as a contest between the Lord and the gods of Egypt, with the Lord emerging as victor (Exod 12:12; see notes on Exod 1:10; 12:12; 15:11).
96:5 idols. Not the common Hebrew word for idols but a pejorative term: "worthless things." On such rhetorical polemics, see notes on 31:6; 95:3. On the ineffectual nature of such gods, see 115:4–8 and note; 135:15–18 and note; Isa 44:9–20; Jer 10:3–5. **made the heavens.** The Lord is Creator, making him sovereign over all he has created (95:4–7). The Lord's role as Creator contrasts with the folly of idolatry (cf. 115:4–8 with 115:15; cf. Isa 44:9–20 with Isa 44:24; cf. Jer 10:3–5 with Jer 10:11–12).
96:6 Splendor. Such splendor elsewhere is associated with the human king (see 21:5; 45:3–4), and this reference ascribes it to God, the heavenly King (see also v. 9 and note). **glory.** The Hebrew word is often associated with the temple (Exod 28:2,40 ["honor"]; Isa 60:7 ["glorious"]) and the king (Isa 4:2 ["glory"]; 28:5 ["glorious"]; Jer 13:18 ["glorious"]).
96:7–8 Ascribe ... ascribe ... Ascribe. The same wording occurs in 29:1–2, which enjoins heavenly beings to praise the Lord. This calls the "families of nations" (v. 7) to do so (see note on v. 7).
96:7 families. Translated "peoples" in Gen 12:3. The Lord's plan from the beginning was to bring all the families of the nations into the worshiping community (Gen 12:3; see Pss 22:27; 67; 117:1 and note; Matt 28:18–20; Rom 15:8–21).
96:8 courts. Of the temple (65:4; 84:10; 92:13; 100:4; 2 Kgs 21:5; Isa 62:9; see note on 100:4).

[9]Worship the LORD in the splendor of his[a] holiness;[m]
tremble[n] before him, all the earth.[o]
[10]Say among the nations, "The LORD reigns.[p]"
The world is firmly established, it cannot be moved;[q]
he will judge the peoples with equity.[r]
[11]Let the heavens rejoice, let the earth be glad;[s]
let the sea resound, and all that is in it.
[12]Let the fields be jubilant, and everything in them;
let all the trees of the forest[t] sing for joy.[u]
[13]Let all creation rejoice before the LORD, for he comes,
he comes to judge[v] the earth.
He will judge the world in righteousness
and the peoples in his faithfulness.

Psalm 97

[1]The LORD reigns,[w] let the earth be glad;[x]
let the distant shores rejoice.
[2]Clouds and thick darkness[y] surround him;
righteousness and justice are the foundation of his
throne.[z]
[3]Fire[a] goes before[b] him
and consumes[c] his foes on every side.
[4]His lightning lights up the world;
the earth sees and trembles.[d]
[5]The mountains melt[e] like wax before the LORD,
before the Lord of all the earth.[f]
[6]The heavens proclaim his righteousness,[g]
and all peoples see his glory.[h]

96:9 [m]Ps 29:2 [n]Ps 114:7 [o]Ps 33:8
96:10 [p]Ps 97:1 [q]Ps 93:1 [r]Ps 67:4
96:11 [s]Ps 97:1; 98:7; Isa 49:13
96:12 [t]Isa 44:23 [u]Ps 65:13
96:13 [v]Rev 19:11
97:1 [w]Ps 96:10 [x]Ps 96:11
97:2 [y]Ex 19:9; Ps 18:11 [z]Ps 89:14
97:3 [a]Da 7:10 [b]Hab 3:5 [c]Ps 18:8
97:4 [d]Ps 104:32
97:5 [e]Ps 46:2,6; Mic 1:4 [f]Jos 3:11
97:6 [g]Ps 50:6 [h]Ps 19:1

[a] 9 Or *LORD with the splendor of*

96:9 Worship ... in the splendor of his holiness. Some interpreters understand the command here as one for worshipers to be arrayed in holiness ("worship the LORD in holy array"; see NIV text note), but the NIV, by adding "his," is correct in seeing God's splendor in view here: God's holiness manifests his grandeur (see note on v. 6; see also 29:2; 145:5). **96:10 The LORD reigns.** The most prominent feature of Pss 93–99 (see note on 93:1). **established.** An indication of the Lord's reign (see 93:1–2; 99:4). **judge ... with equity.** Another indication of his reign (v. 13; 94; 97:2,8; 98:9; 99:4,8). For God's final judgment, see Rev 20:11–15. See also note on 75:2.
96:11–12 The Psalter often depicts the inanimate parts of creation as praising the Lord (65:13; 89:12; 98:7–9; 103:22; 145:10; 148:3–4).
96:12 all the trees ... sing for joy. Pictures creation untainted by the curse (Isa 55:12). All creation longs for its release from corruption (Rom 8:19–25).
96:13 judge ... judge. The reason for the praise in vv. 11–13. **righteousness ... faithfulness.** Qualifies God's judgment: the true King brings real and lasting justice (vv. 10,13; 94; 97:2,8; 98:9; 99:4,8; Rev 19:1–2).
Ps 97 *The Lord Reigns, Let the Earth Be Glad.* This psalm reiterates the prevailing motif of the Lord's royal authority (Pss 93–99; see introduction to Ps 93), announcing at the outset the most conspicuous phrase of this section of psalms: "The LORD reigns" (v. 1; 93:1; 96:10; 99:1). This psalm emphasizes righteousness, one feature of the Lord's reign (vv. 2,6,11–12), which the last verse of the previous psalm also references (96:13). Ps 97 expounds ways in which the Lord's reign exhibits righteousness: his throne is founded in it (v. 2); his handiwork proclaims it (v. 6); and his people reflect it (vv. 11–12).

Ps 97 has three sections: vv. 1–5 describe the dread associated with the presence of the Lord; vv. 6–9 declare that the Lord is exalted over the idols; and vv. 10–12 entreat the righteous to reflect God's character. All three sections relate back to the pronouncement that opens the psalm: "the LORD reigns."
97:1 The LORD reigns. The ground for rejoicing that follows (see note on 93:1). **let the earth be glad.** Repeats 96:11; the reason for the earth's gladness is the same in both instances: "the LORD reigns" (96:10), which has cosmic consequences (see notes on 96:11–12). **distant shores.** This is the Hebrew way of referring to the most distant places (Isa 11:11; 41:5; 42:4; 66:19; Jer 31:10), what the NT would call "the ends of the earth" (Matt 12:42; Acts 1:8).
97:2–5 Manifests the Lord's royal splendor (96:6–9) and resembles what took place when the Lord revealed himself from Sinai (Exod 19:16–20; Deut 4:11; 5:22). Cf. Ps 68:2,8; 77:18; Judg 5:4–5; 1 Kgs 8:10–12; Amos 9:5; Mic 1:4; Nah 1:5.
97:2 righteousness. A common theme in this group of psalms that emphasizes how justice characterizes the Lord's reign (96:13; 98:9; 99:4).
97:4 trembles. See 96:9; see also notes on 99:1; 119:120.
97:6 Because the knowledge of the Lord has been broadcast across the earth (19:1; 50:6; 98:2; Rom 1:19–20), the nations have no excuse for their idolatry (vv. 7–9; Rom 1:20–25). **all peoples see his glory.** Envisioned in 96:3,7–8.

97:7 [i]Lev 26:1 [j]Jer 10:14 [k]Heb 1:6
97:8 [l]Ps 48:11
97:9 [m]Ps 83:18; 95:3 [n]Ex 18:11
97:10 [o]Ps 34:14; Am 5:15; Ro 12:9 [p]Pr 2:8 [q]Da 3:28 [r]Ps 37:40; Jer 15:21
97:11 [s]Job 22:28
97:12 [t]Ps 30:4
98:1 [u]Ps 96:1 [v]Ps 96:3 [w]Ex 15:6 [x]Isa 52:10
98:2 [y]Isa 52:10
98:3 [z]Lk 1:54

7 All who worship images[i] are put to shame,[j]
those who boast in idols—
worship him,[k] all you gods!

8 Zion hears and rejoices
and the villages of Judah are glad
because of your judgments,[l] LORD.
9 For you, LORD, are the Most High over all the earth;[m]
you are exalted[n] far above all gods.
10 Let those who love the LORD hate evil,[o]
for he guards the lives of his faithful ones[p]
and delivers[q] them from the hand of the wicked.[r]
11 Light shines[a][s] on the righteous
and joy on the upright in heart.
12 Rejoice in the LORD, you who are righteous,
and praise his holy name.[t]

Psalm 98

A psalm.

1 Sing to the LORD a new song,[u]
for he has done marvelous things;[v]
his right hand[w] and his holy arm[x]
have worked salvation for him.
2 The LORD has made his salvation known[y]
and revealed his righteousness to the nations.
3 He has remembered[z] his love
and his faithfulness to Israel;

[a] *11* One Hebrew manuscript and ancient versions (see also 112:4); most Hebrew manuscripts *Light is sown*

97:7 The structural midpoint of the psalm (v. 7) is also its rhetorical climax: the psalmist condemns idolaltors here, because the gods who are the object of people's worship in turn must worship the Lord themselves (29:1). (On the structural center of psalms, see note on 100:3 ["his people"].) **idols.** Or "worthless things" (see note on 96:5). **gods.** False gods worshiped as idols. These gods exist in the minds of their worshipers, but they are simply crafted pieces of wood, stone, or metal (e.g., Deut 4:35; 1 Cor 8:4–6). It is possible that demons were behind some or all of the OT's false gods (1 Cor 10:20). The Bible never places these imagined false gods in a position equal to or greater than the Lord; they are always subordinate (86:8; 95:3; 96:4–5; Exod 12:12; 2 Chr 2:5). See note on 82:1.
97:8 your judgments. Another reason for rejoicing (see note on v. 1). The Lord's judgments manifest his reign (see note on 93:1).
97:9 Most High. See note on 7:8. **over … far above.** Emphasizes the Lord's exalted position as King.
97:10–12 Gives God's people three commands ("hate evil" [v. 10]; "rejoice" [v. 12]; "praise" [v. 12]) and four promises (God "guards" [v. 10]; God "delivers" [v. 10]; "light shines" [v. 11]; "joy" shines [v. 11]). The first two promises are consistent with the refuge motif prominent in Book IV up to this point (90:1; 91:1–2,9; 92:15; 95:1).
97:11 Light. A source of guidance and a symbol of well-being (see 27:1 and note). It also manifests the Lord's presence (v. 4; 77:18; John 1:5,9).
Ps 98 *Shout for Joy Before the Lord, the King.* Ps 98 joyfully celebrates the Lord's righteousness (vv. 2,9) as he reveals it in salvation (v. 2) and judgment (v. 9). It closely parallels Ps 96 in both its introduction (cf. 96:1–3; 98:1–2) and conclusion (cf. 96:10–13; 98:7–9), and it maintains the general thrust of the wider group of psalms in the surrounding context (Pss 93–97; 99): the Lord is King (v. 6) and as such will judge the earth (v. 9). Ps 98 has three sections: it expands its focus of praise from the worshiping community (vv. 1–3) to all the earth (vv. 4–6) and then finally to the realm of nature (vv. 7–9). In each case the Lord is praiseworthy because of a different manifestation of his sovereign rule: his righteous salvation (vv. 1–3), his status as King (vv. 4–6), and his righteous judgment (vv. 7–9). Ps 98 was the inspiration for Isaac Watts's hymn "Joy to the World."
98:1 new song. A response to a fresh experience of God's grace (see note on 33:3). **marvelous things.** Or "wonderful deeds" (see note on 26:7); most often refers to acts of salvation (vv. 1–3; 78:11,32; Exod 3:20). **salvation.** Also in vv. 2,3; the act of rescuing or providing aid in a time of distress (33:16–19; 62:1–2; 140:7; Exod 14:13,30; 15:2). Here it is the reason for singing "a new song" and is evidence of the Lord's love and faithfulness to Israel (v. 3).
98:2 revealed. The Lord is a revealer (111:6; Rom 1:18–32; see notes on 19:2–4a; Rom 1:19–23). **nations.** The Lord's sovereign rule over all people, not just his own people, is a hallmark of Pss 93–99 (see 94:2,10; 96:2–3; 97:9; 99:1–2). Here God makes known his acts of salvation to the nations, intimating that his plan of salvation includes them (see 117:1 and note; Isa 12:4–6 and note; see also Isa 52:10). This verse may stand behind Paul's announcement in Rom 1:16–17 that salvation has come for all nations.
98:3 remembered. A covenantal term when the Lord is the subject (see note on 115:12). **love.** Or "faithfulness to his covenant" (see notes on 6:4; 107:1; cf. 103:17–18). **ends of the earth.** The distant parts of the earth, where the nations dwell (v. 2; 22:27; 48:10; Isa 52:10; see note on 97:1 ["distant shores"]). **salvation.** The product

all the ends of the earth have seen
the salvation of our God.

4 Shout for joy[a] to the LORD, all the earth,
burst into jubilant song with music;
5 make music to the LORD with the harp,[b]
with the harp and the sound of singing,[c]
6 with trumpets[d] and the blast of the ram's horn—
shout for joy before the LORD, the King.[e]

7 Let the sea resound, and everything in it,
the world, and all who live in it.[f]
8 Let the rivers clap their hands,
let the mountains[g] sing together for joy;
9 let them sing before the LORD,
for he comes to judge the earth.
He will judge the world in righteousness
and the peoples with equity.[h]

Psalm 99

1 The LORD reigns,[i]
let the nations tremble;
he sits enthroned between the cherubim,[j]
let the earth shake.
2 Great is the LORD[k] in Zion;
he is exalted[l] over all the nations.
3 Let them praise your great and awesome name[m]—
he is holy.

4 The King is mighty, he loves justice[n]—
you have established equity;[o]

98:4 [a] Isa 44:23
98:5 [b] Ps 92:3 [c] Isa 51:3
98:6 [d] Nu 10:10 [e] Ps 47:7
98:7 [f] Ps 24:1
98:8 [g] Isa 55:12
98:9 [h] Ps 96:10
99:1 [i] Ps 97:1 [j] Ex 25:22
99:2 [k] Ps 48:1 [l] Ps 97:9; 113:4
99:3 [m] Ps 76:1
99:4 [n] Ps 11:7 [o] Ps 98:9

of the Lord's faithfulness to his covenant according to this verse (see v. 1 and note).
98:4 Shout for joy. A natural reaction to victory (60:8; Isa 42:13; Jer 51:14). It appears throughout this section (v. 6; 95:1–2; 100:1).
98:5 harp. See note on 150:3.
98:6 trumpets. The only time this Hebrew word occurs in the Psalter; priests used them (Num 10:2–10; 2 Chr 13:14; Ezra 3:10; Neh 12:35,41), including for celebration (1 Chr 13:8; 15:28; 2 Chr 5:13). **ram's horn.** Created a trumpet-like sound; also used in worship (see note on 150:3).
98:7 sea. Often symbolizes an unruly force of devastation (see note on 93:3); here part of the worshiping chorus. **world.** This incorporates the whole by referring to the parts: everything that is in the sea and on the land should praise God.
98:8 rivers ... mountains. Creation joins the praise chorus, a common theme in the Psalter (65:13; 89:12; 96:11–13; 103:22; 145:10; 148:3). **clap their hands.** Expresses jubilation (47:1; Isa 55:12).
98:9 judge ... in righteousness and ... equity. Cf. 96:13; 99:4. According to Isa 11:3–4, the branch from the stump of Jesse, the Messiah, will represent the Lord in doing this.
Ps 99 *The Lord Reigns, Let the Nations Tremble.* Like the preceding psalms in this section (Pss 93–99), Ps 99 exalts the Lord as King (vv. 1,4) and extols his just judgment (v. 4). But Ps 99 especially emphasizes the Lord's holiness (vv. 3,5,9), notably as it relates to his relationship with his people (vv. 6–8). It addresses one of the fundamental questions arising from the Bible's storyline: how can a holy God be in relationship with sinful people? The answer is in v. 8: although God has been just in his judgment, he is also a forgiving God, which is why his people experience his grace (vv. 6–8). Ps 99 has three sections, each concluding with a reference to the Lord's holiness (vv. 3,5,9): the Lord reigns over all peoples (vv. 1–3); as King, the Lord has established justice (vv. 4–5); and this holy King shows grace toward his people (vv. 6–9).
99:1 The LORD reigns. The most conspicuous feature of this section of psalms (Pss 93–99; see note on 93:1). **tremble.** A response of fear (77:16–18; Exod 15:14–16; Deut 2:25). The fear of the Lord means more than simply respect or reverence (see 119:120 and note). **enthroned between the cherubim.** Cherubim sat atop the ark of the covenant, which was considered to be the footstool to the Lord's throne (v. 5; 132:7–8; 1 Chr 28:2; see 1 Sam 4:4). **cherubim.** Angelic beings who guard the presence of the Lord. When God expelled Adam and Eve from the garden, cherubim stood guard at the entrance (Gen 3:24). Two golden cherubim were hammered out of gold on the lid of the ark of the covenant, standing guard in the Most Holy Place (Exod 25:17–22). When the glory of the Lord departs the temple in Ezek 8–10, the cherubim lead the way (Ezek 9:3; 10:2–22). See photo, p. 1145, depicting a Canaanite king on a throne decorated with cherubim.
99:2 Zion. The "capital" of the kingdom of God (see notes on 2:6; 9:11). **nations.** A prominent theme in Pss 93–99 (see 98:2 and note).
99:3 holy. The dominant theme of the psalm (vv. 5,9). See "Holiness," p. 2676.
99:4 King ... loves justice. The Lord's reputation for justice (see 94; 96:10,13; 97:2,8; 98:9) is the model for the ideal human king as well

99:5 [p]Ps 132:7
99:6 [q]Ex 24:6 [r]Jer 15:1 [s]1Sa 7:9
99:7 [t]Ex 33:9
99:8 [u]Nu 14:20
100:1 [v]Ps 98:4
100:2 [w]Ps 95:2
100:3 [x]Ps 46:10 [y]Job 10:3 [z]Ps 74:1; Eze 34:31

in Jacob you have done
 what is just and right.
5 Exalt[p] the LORD our God
 and worship at his footstool;
 he is holy.

6 Moses[q] and Aaron were among his priests,
 Samuel[r] was among those who called on his name;
they called on the LORD
 and he answered[s] them.
7 He spoke to them from the pillar of cloud;[t]
 they kept his statutes and the decrees he gave them.

8 LORD our God,
 you answered them;
you were to Israel a forgiving God,[u]
 though you punished their misdeeds.[a]
9 Exalt the LORD our God
 and worship at his holy mountain,
 for the LORD our God is holy.

Psalm 100

A psalm. For giving grateful praise.

1 Shout for joy[v] to the LORD, all the earth.
2 Worship the LORD with gladness;
 come before him[w] with joyful songs.
3 Know that the LORD is God.[x]
 It is he who made us,[y] and we are his[b];
 we are his people, the sheep of his pasture.[z]

[a] 8 Or *God, / an avenger of the wrongs done to them* [b] 3 Or *and not we ourselves*

(45:6–7; 72:1–4,12–14). **mighty ... right.** A picture of perfect justice. The Lord is right, and he has the might to establish what is right.

99:5 footstool. This reference to the ark of the covenant (132:7–8; 1 Chr 28:2)—which is a poetic way of referring to the temple (see note on 5:7)—emphasizes God's position as the exalted King.

99:6 Moses ... Aaron ... Samuel. Examples of those who were in relationship with the Lord (Exod 19:24; 24:9–11; 34:29; Num 12:8; 1 Sam 3:19–21; Jer 15:1). **called on the LORD.** Prayer is one of the ways (see note on v. 7) these men lived in relationship with the Lord (Exod 32:30–34; Num 12:13; 16:47–48; 1 Sam 7:5,9; 12:18).

99:7 kept his statutes and ... decrees. Obedience is another way (see note on v. 6) that the men mentioned in v. 6 lived in relationship with the Lord (Exod 7:6; 40:16; Num 8:1–3; 1 Sam 16:4).

99:8 forgiving God. One of the fundamental components of the Lord's character (103:3; 130:4; Exod 34:7; Neh 9:17). Their relationship with God was dependent upon his gracious forgiveness. **punished their misdeeds.** Qualifies God's forgiveness. God both punishes and forgives (Exod 32:35; 34:6–7).

99:9 holy mountain. The sanctuary (see notes on 2:6; 9:11). This is the third reference to the sanctuary in this psalm (see vv. 1,5). **holy.** See note on v. 3.

Ps 100 *For the Lord Is Good; His Steadfast Love Endures Forever.* Ps 100 is a joyful call to thanks and praise. It has two sections (vv. 1–3; 4–5), each giving a call to praise and then a reason for praise. The psalm celebrates the Lord's creation of his people (see v. 3 and note) and his care for his people (v. 5). Ps 100 transitions from the first part of Book IV (Pss 90–99) to the final part of Book IV (Pss 101–106). In addition, Pss 95 and 100 form a bracket around the sustained praise of the Lord as King (Pss 96–99).

100 title The psalm was specifically for "grateful praise" or "thanksgiving" (v. 4). Some think this refers to the thank offering (Lev 7:11–21; 22:29–30; see note on Ps 50:14).

100:1–2 The psalm opens with a threefold call to praise. Its exuberance is based on the Lord's intimate presence (v. 3) and his goodness and faithfulness (v. 5).

100:1 Shout for joy. See note on 98:4. **all the earth.** The call to praise begins broadly here and narrows to focus on the people of God in vv. 3–5.

100:3 us. This most likely refers to God's "people" and "sheep" (see the rest of the verse). The emphasis is not on God's creation of all humankind but on the fact that the Lord is the one who brought forth the nation of Israel (95:6; 149:2; Deut 32:6,15,18). **we are his.** The corollary logical outcome to God's having brought Israel into being as a nation is that Israel belonged to him. **his people.** Translates a Hebrew word that structurally is at the very center of the psalm. Everything preceding this leads up to this fundamental affirmation of God's relationship with his people, and everything following it springs from it. This phenomenon of locating a poem's main point at its structural center—whether it be a word, a phrase, or an entire verse—occurs many times in Psalms (6:6; 8:4; 20:6; 21:7; 23:4; 25:11; 42:8; 54:4; 71:14; 73:15; 74:12; 82:5; 92:8; 97:7; 142:4 and notes). **sheep of his pasture.** God's people (74:1; 79:13; 95:7; Jer 23:1; Ezek 34:31); connotes the Lord's tender care and careful provision (see 95:7a–c and note).

4 Enter his gates with thanksgiving
and his courts with praise;
give thanks to him and praise his name.[a]
5 For the LORD is good[b] and his love endures forever;[c]
his faithfulness[d] continues through all generations.

Psalm 101

Of David. A psalm.

1 I will sing of your love[e] and justice;
to you, LORD, I will sing praise.
2 I will be careful to lead a blameless life—
when will you come to me?

I will conduct the affairs of my house
with a blameless heart.
3 I will not look with approval
on anything that is vile.[f]

I hate what faithless people do;[g]
I will have no part in it.
4 The perverse of heart[h] shall be far from me;
I will have nothing to do with what is evil.

5 Whoever slanders their neighbor[i] in secret,
I will put to silence;
whoever has haughty eyes[j] and a proud heart,
I will not tolerate.

6 My eyes will be on the faithful in the land,
that they may dwell with me;
the one whose walk is blameless[k]
will minister to me.

100:4 [a] Ps 116:17
100:5 [b] 1Ch 16:34; Ps 25:8 [c] Ezr 3:11; Ps 106:1 [d] Ps 119:90
101:1 [e] Ps 51:14; 89:1; 145:7
101:3 [f] Dt 15:9 [g] Ps 40:4
101:4 [h] Pr 11:20
101:5 [i] Ps 50:20 [j] Ps 10:5; Pr 6:17
101:6 [k] Ps 119:1

100:4 A fourfold call to praise echoes the threefold call in vv. 1–2. **gates … courts.** Refers to the sanctuary temple by mentioning its component parts (84:10; Exod 27:16; 40:33; 2 Kgs 21:5; see note on 84:1). **give thanks.** See note on 107:1.
100:5 Cf. 106:1; 118:1,29. **love … faithfulness.** Combined in 36:5; 40:10; 88:11; 89:1,2,24,33,49; 92:2; 98:3. The Lord's love is a faithful love (see note on 107:1), and his faithfulness demonstrates his love.
Ps 101 *I Will Sing of Your Love and Justice.* David expresses his commitment to uphold all the standards of justice outlined in Pss 93–99. As the earthly king, his rule will resemble that of the Lord's ideal reign. The first verse announces the theme of the psalm, picking up key emphases of previous psalms: love (cf. 90:14; 92:2; 94:18; 98:3; 100:5) and justice (cf. 94:15; 97:2,8; 99:4). David commits to living justly himself (vv. 2–4) and resolves to oversee a just kingdom (vv. 5–8). In both his personal life and his leadership of social life, David embodies the ideal king who ensures justice (45:6–7; 72:1–4,12–14). David sinned in some spectacular ways (2 Sam 11), but he confessed his sins and God forgave (2 Sam 12; Ps 51); overall, the Bible judges David as a model of a man after God's own heart (1 Sam 13:14; Acts 13:22). In the light of the surrounding psalms, which highlight the Lord's eternal covenant with the Davidic line (89:1–4,19–37; see note on 89:3) and the Lord's reign as ideal king (93:1; 94; 96:10; 97:1–2; 98:6; 99:1), this psalm is a reminder that the Lord's ideal king would come from the Davidic line; this was ultimately fulfilled in Jesus the Messiah.
101 title The first psalm "of David" since Ps 86; the only other in Book IV is Ps 103. Although David's presence is muted in Book IV, he is not absent. These superscriptions (or "titles") witness to the Davidic hope that still existed even though his lineage had been greatly humbled (89:38–45).
101:1 love and justice. Key themes in the previous psalms (see introduction to Ps 101); they embody the piety the prophets promoted (Hos 12:6; Mic 6:8; Zech 7:9). "Love" appears in the final verse of the previous psalm (100:5).
101:2 blameless. Used to describe Job's character (Job 1:1,8; 2:3; cf. Ps 15:2). **when will you come to me?** A plea for the Lord's presence to aid in David's commitment to right living. **heart.** See note on 7:9.
101:3–4 Five negative statements of piety resemble how the Psalter begins, contrasting the ways of the godly with the ungodly (see 1:1). The ideal king in Ps 101 resembles the ideal person of Ps 1.
101:3 I will have no part in it. Or "it will not cling to me." The Hebrew verb connotes holding fast to someone or something (44:25 ["cling"]; 137:6 ["cling"]; Gen 2:24 ["united"]; Deut 10:20 ["hold fast"]; 2 Kgs 18:6 ["held fast"]).
101:5 slanders. Especially menacing because one's reputation—both legally and socially—was so important (see 120:2 and note). David prays in 140:11 that God would wipe out all slanderers from the land.
101:6 blameless. See note on v. 2.

101:8 [l] Jer 21:12 [m] Ps 75:10 [n] Ps 118:10-12 [o] Ps 46:4
102:1 [p] Ex 2:23
102:2 [q] Ps 69:17
102:3 [r] Jas 4:14
102:4 [s] Ps 37:2
102:6 [t] Job 30:29; Isa 34:11
102:7 [u] Ps 77:4 [v] Ps 38:11

[7] No one who practices deceit
will dwell in my house;
no one who speaks falsely
will stand in my presence.

[8] Every morning[l] I will put to silence
all the wicked[m] in the land;
I will cut off every evildoer[n]
from the city of the LORD.[o]

Psalm 102[a]

A prayer of an afflicted person who has grown weak and pours out a lament before the LORD.

[1] Hear my prayer, LORD;
let my cry for help[p] come to you.
[2] Do not hide your face[q] from me
when I am in distress.
Turn your ear to me;
when I call, answer me quickly.

[3] For my days vanish like smoke;[r]
my bones burn like glowing embers.
[4] My heart is blighted and withered like grass;[s]
I forget to eat my food.
[5] In my distress I groan aloud
and am reduced to skin and bones.
[6] I am like a desert owl,[t]
like an owl among the ruins.
[7] I lie awake;[u] I have become
like a bird alone[v] on a roof.
[8] All day long my enemies taunt me;
those who rail against me use my name as a curse.

[a] In Hebrew texts 102:1-28 is numbered 102:2-29.

101:7 deceit. See note on 52:2.
101:8 morning. Speaks to the psalmist's readiness and willingness to execute justice (Jer 21:12).
Ps 102 *For the Lord Will Rebuild Zion and Appear in His Glory.* As the title states, Ps 102 is the lament of an "afflicted person." The psalmist opens by crying out for help (vv. 1–2). Then he complains in familiar terms found in other lament psalms (vv. 3–11). The tenor of the psalm shifts at v. 12 with a hopeful statement of Zion's future that is grounded in the Lord's eternal reign (vv. 12–17; cf. Pss 93–99; see introduction to Ps 93; see also note on 93:1). Zion continues to be a prominent theme (vv. 18–22) even as the focus shifts to a future generation who will recognize that the Lord has fulfilled his salvational purposes for Zion that vv. 16–17 outline. The psalm concludes with a return to lament language, this time tempered by the hope that the Lord can provide exactly what the psalmist lacks: an enduring legacy (vv. 23–28).

The ancient church identified this as one of seven penitential psalms (the others: Pss 6; 32; 38; 51; 130; 143). Sandwiched between two Davidic psalms (Pss 101; 103), we can read this psalm as a lament over Zion's decline as manifested in the diminished state of the Davidic dynasty that 89:38–45 describes; Pss 89 and 102 are related by their anguished plea for the restoration of God's kingdom purposes, represented by the Davidic covenant in Ps 89 (see note on 89:3) and represented by Zion here. Along with Pss 101 and 103, Ps 102 transitions the Psalter from the downbeat ending of Book III (especially Pss 88–89) to the positive affirmations of the Lord's covenant faithfulness to David and Zion in Book V.
102 title A specific description of the psalm's intended use. The title does not ascribe the psalm to any author, nor does it give any liturgical or historical details about the psalm (unique in the Psalter).
102:2 hide your face. Remove his special presence to bless (see note on 27:9; see also 13:1; 22:24; 30:7; 44:24; 69:17; 88:14; 143:7; cf. Num 6:24–26).
102:3 days vanish. A key theme in Ps 90 (90:5–6,9–10; see 37:20; 68:2); contemplating this makes one wise (90:12).
102:4 forget to eat my food. A response of mourning and sorrow (1 Sam 1:7; 2 Sam 12:17; 1 Kgs 21:4; Job 33:20).
102:5 groan. Expresses deep distress (6:6; 31:10; 38:8; Job 3:24; Lam 1:22).
102:6 desert owl … owl. Unclean animals that symbolize loneliness in desolate places (Lev 11:13–18; Deut 14:11–17; Isa 34:10–11; Zeph 2:13–14).
102:7 lie awake. Peaceful sleep is a gift from the Lord (3:5–6; 4:8; 127:2), so the psalmist's sleeplessness adds to his distress.
102:8 use my name as a curse. Associated with shame so that one's name stands for it (Isa 65:15; Jer 29:22), such as "Judas" referring to a traitor.

[9] For I eat ashes as my food
and mingle my drink with tears[w]
[10] because of your great wrath,[x]
for you have taken me up and thrown me aside.
[11] My days are like the evening shadow;[y]
I wither away like grass.

[12] But you, LORD, sit enthroned forever;[z]
your renown endures[a] through all generations.
[13] You will arise and have compassion[b] on Zion,
for it is time to show favor to her;
the appointed time has come.
[14] For her stones are dear to your servants;
her very dust moves them to pity.
[15] The nations will fear[c] the name of the LORD,
all the kings[d] of the earth will revere your glory.
[16] For the LORD will rebuild Zion
and appear in his glory.[e]
[17] He will respond to the prayer[f] of the destitute;
he will not despise their plea.

[18] Let this be written[g] for a future generation,
that a people not yet created[h] may praise the LORD:
[19] "The LORD looked down[i] from his sanctuary on high,
from heaven he viewed the earth,
[20] to hear the groans of the prisoners[j]
and release those condemned to death."
[21] So the name of the LORD will be declared[k] in Zion
and his praise in Jerusalem
[22] when the peoples and the kingdoms
assemble to worship the LORD.

[23] In the course of my life[a] he broke my strength;
he cut short my days.

102:9 [w] Ps 42:3
102:10 [x] Ps 38:3
102:11 [y] Job 14:2
102:12 [z] Ps 9:7 [a] Ps 135:13
102:13 [b] Isa 60:10
102:15 [c] 1Ki 8:43 [d] Ps 138:4
102:16 [e] Isa 60:1-2
102:17 [f] Ne 1:6
102:18 [g] Ro 15:4 [h] Ps 22:31
102:19 [i] Dt 26:15
102:20 [j] Ps 79:11
102:21 [k] Ps 22:22

[a] *23* Or *By his power*

102:10 your great wrath. Manifest in the expressions of grief and distress in vv. 4–9 (see note on 90:7–9). **thrown me aside.** Like God's wrath, this is his righteous response to sin (51:11; 2 Kgs 17:20; 24:20; cf. 2 Kgs 13:23).
102:11 evening shadow. An image of gradually fading away (109:23; 144:4). **wither.** The opposite of what happens to the righteous in 92:12–15, who are vibrant and virile.
102:12 sit enthroned. The Lord reigns as king (the chief theme of Pss 93–99; see note on 93:1). See also 113:5. **forever.** Contrasts with the psalmist's fleeting existence in vv. 3–11.
102:13 Presupposes distress in "Zion" (see note on v. 16), like that which 89:38–45 describe. It expresses a confident hope that the Lord will reverse the fortunes of his people.
102:14 stones ... very dust. Even the smallest and most insignificant parts of the city are meaningful to God's people (1 Kgs 20:10; Neh 4:2; Lam 4:1).
102:15 nations. God plans to include them in his worshiping people (see introduction to Ps 67; see also note on 117:1; cf. 96:3,7–10; 108:3; 148:11–13). **kings of the earth.** Rebels (2:2) who must ultimately submit to the Lord in praise (see note on 138:4–5).
102:16 The Lord's commitment to Zion draws the nations. **Zion.** Originally the city of David in Jerusalem (2 Sam 5:7; 1 Kgs 8:1; 1 Chr 11:5; 2 Chr 5:2); it came to symbolize the center of God's kingdom (see notes on 2:6; 9:11). Here it refers to God's kingdom, envisioning that the Lord will build up his kingdom (see introduction to Ps 132). God does this by appearing in his glory and responding to the prayers of the destitute (v. 17; see 91:15 and note; Isa 4:5; 60:1–3).
102:18 Let this be written. As a perpetual testimony to the Lord's faithfulness to his promises. Elsewhere this verifies the potency of the Lord's word (Deut 31:19; Isa 8:1–4; 30:8; Hab 2:2). **people not yet created.** The beneficiaries of the Lord's word, both written and proclaimed (22:30–31; 145:4; cf. Deut 29:14–15).
102:19 sanctuary on high. The heavenly sanctuary (see also 150:1). The earthly sanctuary (tabernacle and temple) was patterned after the heavenly one (Exod 25:9,40; 26:30; 27:8; Num 8:4; Acts 7:44). See note on 5:7; see also "Temple," p. 2652.
102:20 groans. The Lord is attentive to cries from his people (12:5; 79:11), a sign of his covenant faithfulness (107:6–8,13–15,19–21, 28–31; Exod 2:23–25; 3:6–9).
102:21–22 Peoples and kingdoms will gather in Jerusalem to worship (22:27; 87; Isa 2:2–4; Mic 4:1–3; Zech 8:20–23).
102:23–24 The psalmist's fleeting life contrasts with the Lord's eternal nature (see introduction to Ps 90).

102:24 [l]Ps 90:2; Isa 38:10
102:25 [m]Ge 1:1; Heb 1:10-12*
102:26 [n]Isa 34:4; Mt 24:35; 2Pe 3:7-10; Rev 20:11
102:27 [o]Mal 3:6; Heb 13:8; Jas 1:17
102:28 [p]Ps 69:36 [q]Ps 89:4
103:1 [r]Ps 104:1
103:3 [s]Ps 130:8 [t]Ex 15:26
103:5 [u]Isa 40:31

24 So I said:
"Do not take me away, my God, in the midst of my days;
your years go on[l] through all generations.
25 In the beginning[m] you laid the foundations of the earth,
and the heavens are the work of your hands.
26 They will perish,[n] but you remain;
they will all wear out like a garment.
Like clothing you will change them
and they will be discarded.
27 But you remain the same,[o]
and your years will never end.
28 The children of your servants[p] will live in your presence;
their descendants[q] will be established before you."

Psalm 103

Of David.

1 Praise the LORD, my soul;[r]
all my inmost being, praise his holy name.
2 Praise the LORD, my soul,
and forget not all his benefits—
3 who forgives all your sins[s]
and heals[t] all your diseases,
4 who redeems your life from the pit
and crowns you with love and compassion,
5 who satisfies your desires with good things
so that your youth is renewed like the eagle's.[u]

6 The LORD works righteousness
and justice for all the oppressed.

102:25–27 Heb 1:10–12 draws upon this distinction between the Lord's eternal nature and creation's temporal nature (see vv. 23–24 and note). Hebrews applies this passage to Jesus to demonstrate that Jesus is better than angels. This passage points ahead to Jesus, the incarnate Son of God and Creator of the universe (John 1:1–3; Col 1:16; Heb 1:2)
102:28 their descendants will be established before you. Even though the psalmist is afflicted (see title; vv. 1–11) and recognizes that life is transient (vv. 3,11,23–24a), there is also hope grounded in God's eternal nature (vv. 12,24b–27; Mal 3:6).
Ps 103 *From Everlasting to Everlasting the Lord's Love Is With Those Who Fear Him.* This psalm of praise begins with the individual (vv. 1–5), extends to every part of creation (vv. 20–22a), and concludes with the individual (v. 22b). In between the bookends of praise, the psalm highlights the Lord's character, especially as it relates to human frailty and sinfulness. As with the other Davidic psalm in this section (Ps 101), its keynote is the Lord's love and justice (vv. 6,8,11,17; cf. 101:1). God manifests his love and justice by forgiving sin and showing compassion toward feeble humanity.

Ps 103 has four sections: the introduction calls to praise and outlines the Lord's benefits (vv. 1–5); the Lord forgives (vv. 6–12); the Lord shows compassion toward his people (vv. 13–19); and the conclusion's call to praise (vv. 20–22) corresponds to the introduction. Although a psalm "of David," there are reflections of Moses here: v. 7 mentions Moses; vv. 6–19 echo significant junctures in the Pentateuch (see notes on vv. 3,8,11–12,13,14,18); and the themes hark back to the only Mosaic psalm in the Psalter: Ps 90. Both Ps 90 and Ps 103 contrast the eternal God (v. 17; 90:1–2) with sinful and temporal humanity (vv. 7–12,14–16; 90:5–11). The Mosaic presence in this psalm is consistent with the tenor of Book IV (see introduction to Pss 90–106; see also introduction to Ps 90).
103 title See introduction to Ps 101; Ps 101 title.
103:1 soul. In Psalms, "soul" most often refers to the nonphysical aspects of a person or to the totality of the human essence (see note on 6:3).
103:3 forgives. See Exod 34:7,9. Verses 7–8 also allude to Exod 33–34, and vv. 6–12 could be a meditation on that passage. **diseases.** A judgment for disobeying the covenant (Deut 29:22; Jer 14:18 ["ravages"]; 16:4). This portrays the Lord as reversing the punishments for unfaithfulness to the covenant.
103:4 pit. The abodes of prisoners and dead people (see notes on 88:4; 143:7). **crowns.** To be crowned with something is to be characterized by it, in this case, love and compassion (8:5; 65:11; Song 3:11). **love and compassion.** Characterizes God's people (vv. 8,11,13,17). Love is God's covenantal faithfulness (see notes on 6:4; 107:1).
103:5 youth is renewed like the eagle's. In Isa 40:30–31, the eagle symbolizes youthful vigor and stamina. In the NT, endurance and perseverance are evidence that the Lord is at work in a believer's life (Rom 5:3–5; 2 Cor 4:16–17; Jas 1:2–12).
103:6 righteousness and justice. Two related themes that mutually inform each other (see 97:2 and note). **oppressed.** Are singled out for special privilege by the Lord (see 146:7 and note).

[7] He made known[v] his ways[w] to Moses,
his deeds[x] to the people of Israel:
[8] The LORD is compassionate and gracious,[y]
slow to anger, abounding in love.
[9] He will not always accuse,
nor will he harbor his anger forever;[z]
[10] he does not treat us as our sins deserve[a]
or repay us according to our iniquities.
[11] For as high as the heavens are above the earth,
so great is his love[b] for those who fear him;
[12] as far as the east is from the west,
so far has he removed our transgressions[c] from us.
[13] As a father has compassion[d] on his children,
so the LORD has compassion on those who fear him;
[14] for he knows how we are formed,[e]
he remembers that we are dust.
[15] The life of mortals is like grass,[f]
they flourish like a flower[g] of the field;
[16] the wind blows[h] over it and it is gone,
and its place[i] remembers it no more.
[17] But from everlasting to everlasting
the LORD's love is with those who fear him,
and his righteousness with their children's children—
[18] with those who keep his covenant
and remember to obey his precepts.[j]
[19] The LORD has established his throne in heaven,
and his kingdom rules[k] over all.

[20] Praise the LORD, you his angels,[l]
you mighty ones[m] who do his bidding,
who obey his word.
[21] Praise the LORD, all his heavenly hosts,[n]
you his servants who do his will.
[22] Praise the LORD, all his works[o]
everywhere in his dominion.
Praise the LORD, my soul.

103:7 [v] Ps 99:7; 147:19 [w] Ex 33:13 [x] Ps 106:22
103:8 [y] Ex 34:6; Ps 86:15; Jas 5:11
103:9 [z] Ps 30:5; Isa 57:16; Jer 3:5,12; Mic 7:18
103:10 [a] Ezr 9:13
103:11 [b] Ps 57:10
103:12 [c] 2Sa 12:13
103:13 [d] Mal 3:17
103:14 [e] Isa 29:16
103:15 [f] Ps 90:5 [g] Job 14:2; Jas 1:10; 1Pe 1:24
103:16 [h] Isa 40:7 [i] Job 7:10
103:18 [j] Dt 7:9
103:19 [k] Ps 47:2
103:20 [l] Ps 148:2; Heb 1:14 [m] Ps 29:1
103:21 [n] 1Ki 22:19
103:22 [o] Ps 145:10

103:7 ways. God's revealed principles for living (see introduction to Ps 119; see also 25:4,9–10; 27:11; 143:8; Exod 33:13).
103:8 This is based on the foundational statement of God's character in Exod 34:6 (see note on Ps 103:3 ["forgives"]; cf. 86:15; 111:4; 145:8; Neh 9:17; Joel 2:13). **compassionate … love.** See v. 4 and note.
103:10 The Lord's mercy in judgment reveals his grace (Ezra 9:13; Rom 6:23).
103:11–12 high … far. The breadth of God's forgiveness reveals the greatness of his love (Exod 34:6–7; Mic 7:18–20).
103:13 father. How the Lord relates to his people (see Exod 4:22–23; Deut 8:5; Prov 3:12; Mal 2:10). By word and deed, Jesus taught his disciples to approach God in this way (Matt 6:1,9; Mark 14:36). God reveals his fatherly care in both compassion (Exod 4:22–23) and discipline (Deut 8:5; Heb 12:5–11).
103:14 An allusion to Gen 2:7. As the Creator, God is intimately aware of humanity's frailty. **dust.** Connotes death; obliquely refers to the original curse against sin (see 90:3 and note; Gen 3:19).
103:15 grass. A common metaphor in Book IV for the brevity of life (90:5–6; 92:7; 102:4,11; cf. Isa 40:6–8). **flourish.** See note on 92:7.
103:16 wind blows. Highlights the frailty of human life: even the wind can blow it over so that there is no memory of it.
103:17 everlasting to everlasting. Appears three other times in the Psalter (41:13; 90:2; 106:48). In both 90:2 and here, it contrasts the Lord's nature and character with humanity's transience. **love.** Related to covenant keeping (see notes on 6:4; 107:1). **fear.** Properly recognize the Lord's nature and character (vv. 11,13; see note on 19:9).
103:18 keep his covenant … obey his precepts. Parallel to "fear him" (v. 17): those who fear the Lord keep his covenant and obey his precepts (Exod 19:5; Deut 7:9).
103:19 throne in heaven. See 104:1–4 and notes.
103:20–21 angels … mighty ones … heavenly hosts … servants. Angelic beings who obey the Lord's bidding (78:25; 104:4 [see NIV text note]; 148:2; Gen 32:1–2; Josh 5:13–15; 1 Kgs 22:19).
103:22 all his works everywhere … my soul. From the universal to the individual: this calls all aspects of creation to praise the Lord because his dominion extends over all (v. 19; see 146:1 and note).

104:1 [p]Ps 103:22
104:2 [q]Da 7:9 [r]Isa 40:22
104:3 [s]Am 9:6 [t]Isa 19:1 [u]Ps 18:10
104:4 [v]Ps 148:8; Heb 1:7* [w]2Ki 2:11
104:5 [x]Job 26:7; Ps 24:1-2
104:6 [y]Ge 7:19 [z]Ge 1:2
104:7 [a]Ps 18:15
104:8 [b]Ps 33:7
104:10 [c]Ps 107:33; Isa 41:18

Psalm 104

1 Praise the LORD, my soul.[p]

LORD my God, you are very great;
you are clothed with splendor and majesty.

2 The LORD wraps[q] himself in light as with a garment;
he stretches out the heavens[r] like a tent
3 and lays the beams[s] of his upper chambers on their waters.
He makes the clouds[t] his chariot
and rides on the wings of the wind.[u]
4 He makes winds his messengers,[a][v]
flames of fire[w] his servants.

5 He set the earth[x] on its foundations;
it can never be moved.
6 You covered it[y] with the watery depths[z] as with a garment;
the waters stood above the mountains.
7 But at your rebuke[a] the waters fled,
at the sound of your thunder they took to flight;
8 they flowed over the mountains,
they went down into the valleys,
to the place you assigned[b] for them.
9 You set a boundary they cannot cross;
never again will they cover the earth.

10 He makes springs[c] pour water into the ravines;
it flows between the mountains.
11 They give water to all the beasts of the field;
the wild donkeys quench their thirst.

[a] 4 Or *angels*

Ps 104 *He Set the Earth on Its Foundations.* The first of three consecutive psalms that trace salvation history from creation to exile, Ps 104 celebrates the Lord's work at creation. It views God's work of creation as both a past event and a present reality. Verb tenses shift between past and present throughout, highlighting how the Lord, who brought all things into existence, continues to maintain the order of that creation. Both acts involving creation are praiseworthy.

Ps 104 opens by describing the Lord's heavenly dwelling place (vv. 1–4). From his lofty perch he oversees the establishment of the land and sea (vv. 5–9), disperses water (vv. 10–13), and provides for his creation (vv. 14–18); he maintains the chronological cycles of night and day (vv. 19–23), and he enjoys watching the great sea creatures play in the oceans (vv. 24–26). God's act of creation continues into the present (vv. 27–30). The psalm concludes with joyful praise (vv. 31–35).

104:1 The first line repeats verbatim the last line of the previous psalm (103:22; see also 103:1,2) and frames this psalm (v. 35). **soul.** The whole person (see note on 6:3). **splendor and majesty.** In the Psalter these words appear together only in royal contexts (21:5; 45:3; 96:6), depicting the Lord as King robed in these (see also 29:2).

104:2 light. Envelops the heavenly abode, acting as the Lord's covering (cf. 1 Tim 6:16). At other times he may use darkness as his cover (18:11). **heavens like a tent.** Creation is the Lord's tent (19:4; Isa 40:22).

104:3 beams of his upper chambers. The Lord's abode is in the highest heavens. The highest point of creation is only the beginning of the Lord's abode (115:15–16; 1 Kgs 8:27; Amos 9:6). **clouds his chariot.** See note on 68:4.

104:4 Heb 1:7 quotes this to demonstrate that the Son of God is superior to angels. Jesus, as the divine Son of God, is of the same essence as the Lord in the OT. **messengers.** See NIV text note. **flames of fire.** Associated with the Lord's presence (Exod 3:2; 1 Kgs 18:24,38; 2 Kgs 1:10; Isa 66:15).

104:5 foundations. See note on 24:2. **never be moved.** From a position of security (see 15:5; 16:8; 93:1; 112:6). This is not saying that the earth does not actually move or that this earth will remain forever without any kind of transformation; rather, it means simply that because the Lord established the earth, he will uphold its position of security.

104:6 watery depths. Tamed and brought into order at creation (Gen 1:2,9–10). The Lord sovereignly controls what people of the time understood to be an unruleable part of creation (see notes on 93:3; 107:24).

104:7 rebuke ... thunder. The Lord exercises authority over the waters (18:15; 77:16–19; 106:9). So it is significant that Jesus "rebuked" the wind and commanded the waters (Mark 4:39). This helps answer the disciples' question in Mark 4:41: "Who is this?"

104:9 boundary they cannot cross. The Lord maintains order on the earth by setting a limit for the sea (Job 38:8–11; cf. Pss 33:7; 65:7; 89:9; Prov 8:29). **never again ... cover the earth.** Either the primordial waters of Gen 1:2 or the floodwaters of Noah's time (Gen 9:11–15).

104:10–13 The Lord not only holds the waters at bay (vv. 6–9) but also directs them for beneficial purposes.

104:11 beasts of the field; the wild donkeys. Not domesticated animals but wild animals (Gen 2:19–20; 3:1; 16:12; Isa 32:14; Jer 2:24). They are completely under the Lord's care, and he ensures that they are watered.

[12] The birds of the sky[d] nest by the waters;
they sing among the branches.
[13] He waters the mountains[e] from his upper chambers;
the land is satisfied by the fruit of his work.
[14] He makes grass grow[f] for the cattle,
and plants for people to cultivate—
bringing forth food[g] from the earth:
[15] wine[h] that gladdens human hearts,
oil[i] to make their faces shine,
and bread that sustains their hearts.
[16] The trees of the LORD are well watered,
the cedars of Lebanon that he planted.
[17] There the birds[j] make their nests;
the stork has its home in the junipers.
[18] The high mountains belong to the wild goats;
the crags are a refuge for the hyrax.[k]

[19] He made the moon to mark the seasons,[l]
and the sun[m] knows when to go down.
[20] You bring darkness,[n] it becomes night,[o]
and all the beasts of the forest[p] prowl.
[21] The lions roar for their prey
and seek their food from God.[q]
[22] The sun rises, and they steal away;
they return and lie down in their dens.[r]
[23] Then people go out to their work,[s]
to their labor until evening.

[24] How many are your works,[t] LORD!
In wisdom you made[u] them all;
the earth is full of your creatures.
[25] There is the sea,[v] vast and spacious,
teeming with creatures beyond number—
living things both large and small.
[26] There the ships[w] go to and fro,
and Leviathan,[x] which you formed to frolic there.

[27] All creatures look to you
to give them their food[y] at the proper time.

104:12 [d] Mt 8:20
104:13 [e] Ps 147:8; Jer 10:13
104:14 [f] Job 38:27; Ps 147:8 [g] Ge 1:30; Job 28:5
104:15 [h] Jdg 9:13 [i] Ps 23:5; 92:10; Lk 7:46
104:17 [j] ver 12
104:18 [k] Pr 30:26
104:19 [l] Ge 1:14 [m] Ps 19:6
104:20 [n] Isa 45:7 [o] Ps 74:16 [p] Ps 50:10
104:21 [q] Job 38:39; Ps 145:15; Joel 1:20
104:22 [r] Job 37:8
104:23 [s] Ge 3:19
104:24 [t] Ps 40:5 [u] Pr 3:19
104:25 [v] Ps 69:34
104:26 [w] Ps 107:23; Eze 27:9 [x] Job 41:1
104:27 [y] Job 36:31; Ps 136:25; 145:15; 147:9

104:13 upper chambers. See v. 3 and note.
104:17–18 The Lord provides for countless animals without human assistance (see vv. 10–13 and note). **stork ... hyrax.** Unclean animals (Lev 11:5,19; Deut 14:7,18) benefit from the Lord's care.
104:18 wild goats. Their habitation is far removed from mankind (Job 39:1).
104:19 mark the seasons. One of the five purposes Gen 1:14–15 mentions for creating the great lights.
104:20 The Lord is sovereign over both darkness and light, both night and day (see v. 2 and note; Isa 45:7; Amos 5:8).
104:21 seek their food from God. As a domesticated animal looks to its master to feed it, so the wild animals look to God. This portrays wild animals as the Lord's livestock; he is the overseer of the entire earth, and he provides for them (vv. 27–28; 145:15; 147:9; Matt 6:25–33).
104:22–23 The Lord provides for lions by night (vv. 20–21) and humans by day, following the cycle that the great lights establish.
104:23 labor. Cultivating the earth; translates a Hebrew word that occurs only twice in the Psalter, both times in this psalm (translated "cultivate" in v. 14).
104:24 wisdom. See introduction to Ps 34; the Hebrew word sometimes refers to skill in craftsmanship, as here (Exod 31:3–4; 35:31; 1 Kgs 7:14). Creation reflects the Lord's wisdom (Prov 3:19; 8:22–31; Jer 10:12; 51:15).
104:25 sea ... teeming with creatures. Resembles the fifth day of creation (Gen 1:20–23). The sea continues to be a repository of life.
104:26 Leviathan. A sea creature prominent in Canaanite mythology, in the Bible it represents what was chaotic and frightening (74:14; Job 3:8; 41:1–34; Isa 27:1). Here, God clearly controls it.
104:27–28 you ... you ... you. The animals are dependent on the Lord for their food, so they look to him (see v. 21 and note). Jesus teaches his disciples to have the same attitude as the animals (Matt 6:11,25–33).

104:28 [z] Ps 145:16
104:29 [a] Dt 31:17 [b] Job 34:14; Ecc 12:7
104:31 [c] Ge 1:31
104:32 [d] Ps 97:4 [e] Ex 19:18 [f] Ps 144:5
104:33 [g] Ps 63:4
104:34 [h] Ps 9:2
104:35 [i] Ps 37:38 [j] Ps 105:45; 106:48
105:1 [k] 1Ch 16:34 [l] Ps 99:6

28 When you give it to them,
they gather it up;
when you open your hand,
they are satisfied[z] with good things.
29 When you hide your face,[a]
they are terrified;
when you take away their breath,
they die and return to the dust.[b]
30 When you send your Spirit,
they are created,
and you renew the face of the ground.

31 May the glory of the LORD endure forever;
may the LORD rejoice in his works[c]—
32 he who looks at the earth, and it trembles,[d]
who touches the mountains,[e] and they smoke.[f]

33 I will sing[g] to the LORD all my life;
I will sing praise to my God as long as I live.
34 May my meditation be pleasing to him,
as I rejoice[h] in the LORD.
35 But may sinners vanish[i] from the earth
and the wicked be no more.

Praise the LORD, my soul.

Praise the LORD.[a][j]

Psalm 105

105:1-15pp — 1Ch 16:8-22

1 Give praise to the LORD,[k] proclaim his name;[l]
make known among the nations what he has done.

[a] 35 Hebrew *Hallelu Yah*; in the Septuagint this line stands at the beginning of Psalm 105.

104:29 hide your face. Remove his blessing (see 102:2 and note). **return to the dust.** Almost an exact quotation of Gen 3:19. Death characterizes creation life after the fall (see 90:3; 103:14 and notes).
104:31 rejoice. The Lord takes great delight in what he has done (see v. 26; Gen 1:31; Prov 8:30–31).
104:32 trembles ... smoke. The Creator God (vv. 5–30) is the same awe-inspiring God who appeared at Sinai (Exod 19:18; cf. 144:5).
104:34 meditation. Often translated "complaint"; it can also refer to troubled thoughts or a lament (55:2 ["thoughts"]; 64:1; 102 title ["lament"]; 142:2; Job 7:13; 9:27). The "meditation" looks ahead to the brief reflection on life's difficulties in v. 35. The psalmist prays that the Lord would take delight even in those thoughts, as the psalmist of Ps 102 also prays (see 102 title). **be pleasing.** Translates a Hebrew word that sometimes describes peaceful and refreshing sleep (Prov 3:24 ["sweet"]) or the feeling that comes from a fulfilled desire (Prov 13:19 ["sweet"]). The Lord's delight in creation is again at the forefront (see v. 31 and note).
104:35 A plea that sin and wickedness would not spoil God's wonderful creation. In that way, it is a prayer for the new creation (Isa 35:8; 52:1; Joel 3:17; Zech 14:21; Rev 21:27; 22:14–15). **soul.** See v. 1 and note.
Ps 105 *He Remembers His Covenant Forever.* This continues the story of salvation history that the previous psalm began. It recounts the experience surrounding the exodus, complete with episodes from before and after the release from Egypt. It tells these stories to highlight the Lord's faithfulness to his covenant (vv. 8–11,42–45), and it views the exodus from a covenantal perspective: the Lord made promises to the patriarchs (vv. 8–11), and the exodus was necessary to accomplish those promises (vv. 42–45). This psalm explains how the Lord was faithful in keeping his covenant regarding the land, particularly emphasizing how this led him to overcome the most powerful nation on earth at the time and the challenges that the harsh desert sojourn posed both before and after the exodus. The Lord will not allow anything—no matter how daunting—to nullify his commitment to the covenant promises he has made.

Ps 105 fits well with Book IV's conclusion by extolling the Lord's *ḥesed,* his eternal love for his covenant people and his faithfulness to his covenant (100:5; 103:17; 106:1,45; see note on 6:4). In the light of Ps 89, which questions the Lord's faithfulness to the Davidic covenant, these psalms encourage God's people to continue to trust his promises to David in spite of the seemingly insurmountable obstacles to fulfilling those promises.

The psalm opens with an invocation to praise (vv. 1–7). Then it outlines the substance of praise and the theme of the psalm: the Lord remembers his covenant (vv. 8–11). Everything that follows in the psalm evidences that the Lord remembered his covenant with the patriarchs. He protected his people when they were a vulnerable minority (vv. 12–15). He sovereignly orchestrated Joseph's arrival in Egypt, bringing fruitfulness from famine (vv. 16–25). He appointed Moses to lead his people out of Egyptian oppression (vv. 26–38). He then provided for his people in the inhospitable desert (vv. 39–41). The psalm

[2] Sing to him,[m] sing praise to him;
tell of all his wonderful acts.
[3] Glory in his holy name;
let the hearts of those who seek the LORD rejoice.
[4] Look to the LORD and his strength;
seek his face[n] always.

[5] Remember the wonders[o] he has done,
his miracles, and the judgments he pronounced,[p]
[6] you his servants, the descendants of Abraham,[q]
his chosen[r] ones, the children of Jacob.
[7] He is the LORD our God;
his judgments are in all the earth.

[8] He remembers his covenant[s] forever,
the promise he made, for a thousand generations,
[9] the covenant he made with Abraham,[t]
the oath he swore to Isaac.
[10] He confirmed it[u] to Jacob as a decree,
to Israel as an everlasting covenant:
[11] "To you I will give the land of Canaan[v]
as the portion you will inherit."

[12] When they were but few in number,[w]
few indeed, and strangers in it,[x]
[13] they wandered from nation to nation,
from one kingdom to another.
[14] He allowed no one to oppress[y] them;
for their sake he rebuked kings:[z]
[15] "Do not touch[a] my anointed ones;
do my prophets no harm."

[16] He called down famine[b] on the land
and destroyed all their supplies of food;

105:2 [m] Ps 96:1
105:4 [n] Ps 27:8
105:5 [o] Ps 40:5 [p] Ps 77:11
105:6 [q] ver 42 [r] Ps 106:5
105:8 [s] Ps 106:45; Lk 1:72
105:9 [t] Ge 12:7; 17:2; 22:16-18; Gal 3:15-18
105:10 [u] Ge 28:13-15
105:11 [v] Ge 13:15; 15:18
105:12 [w] Ge 34:30; Dt 7:7 [x] Ge 23:4; Heb 11:9
105:14 [y] Ge 35:5 [z] Ge 12:17-20
105:15 [a] Ge 26:11
105:16 [b] Ge 41:54; Lev 26:26; Isa 3:1; Eze 4:16

concludes by summarizing the body of the psalm (vv. 12–41): all of this had to happen for the Lord to keep his promises to the patriarchs, whom Abraham represents (vv. 42–45).
105:1 praise. Or "thanks." Appears in the opening verse of four consecutive psalms (see 106:1; 107:1 and note). Verses 1–15 are part of a larger hymn that David sang on the occasion of bringing the ark of the covenant up to Jerusalem in 1 Chr 16:8–36 (vv. 1–15 parallel 1 Chr 16:8–22). **nations.** The audience in the theater of praise (9:11; 18:49; 57:9; 96:3,10; 108:3; 117:1 and note; 126:2).
105:2 wonderful acts. The Lord's miraculous, salvational deeds (see note on 26:7).
105:3–4 seek the LORD … seek his face. Expresses passionate worship (27:8; 34:10; 119:2,10; Deut 4:29; 1 Chr 22:19; 2 Chr 11:16; 14:4; Ezra 6:21).
105:5 Remember. Occurs in vv. 5,8,42; 106:4,7,45, each with covenantal overtones (see note on 115:12). **miracles.** See 106:7,22; see also note on 26:7.
105:6 servants … chosen ones. God's people (vv. 26,42–43).
105:8 remembers. See v. 5 and note. **covenant.** An oath-bound agreement that secures a relationship between two parties (see 89:3 and note; Gen 15:18; 17:2–21; 26:28; 1 Sam 18:3). See "Covenant," p. 2646. **forever.** The Lord's faithfulness to his covenant promises does not expire (see notes on 89:3; 107:1). Much of Books IV and V of the Psalter responds to 89:39, which questions the Lord's faithfulness to the Davidic covenant. The final two books of the Psalter highlight the enduring nature of the Lord's faithfulness to his covenant (100:5; 103:17; 106:1,45; 107:1 and note; 111:5; 118:1,29; 136).
105:9–10 Abraham … Isaac … Jacob … Israel. The covenant promise of land (see v. 11 and note) passed down through the generations (Gen 17:7–9; Exod 6:8; Num 14:23,30; Deut 34:4; Josh 21:43). **covenant … everlasting covenant.** See notes on v. 8; 89:3; Gen 12:1–3. In order to encourage God's people to trust the Lord's covenant promises, the psalmist will demonstrate how the Lord went to great lengths to fulfill this covenant.
105:11 give the land. Alludes to God's promise of land to Abraham and his descendants (Gen 17:2–21; Exod 6:8; Num 14:23,30; Deut 34:4; Josh 21:43).
105:12–15 Recalls the years of sojourning during the lives of Abraham, Isaac, and Jacob.
105:12 few in number. Thus, vulnerable (Gen 14:14; 34:30; Deut 7:7). **strangers.** Thus, vulnerable (Gen 23:4; Exod 22:21; Deut 10:19; 26:5; Heb 11:9).
105:14 rebuked kings. The Lord protected his people when Abraham's wife Sarah (Sarai) ended up in a foreign king's harem (Gen 12:17; 20:3,6–7; cf. Gen 26:6–16).
105:15 prophets. The Lord called Abraham a prophet in Gen 20:7.
105:16–17 The famine during Jacob's life was not random (Gen 41:57; 42:5). The Lord prepared for it when he "sent a man [Joseph] before them" (v. 17). Thus, the Lord worked out all the circumstances for good (Gen 50:20; Rom 8:28).

105:17 [c] Ge 37:28; 45:5; Ac 7:9
105:18 [d] Ge 40:15
105:19 [e] Ge 40:20-22
105:20 [f] Ge 41:14
105:22 [g] Ge 41:43-44
105:23 [h] Ge 46:6; Ac 13:17
105:24 [i] Ex 1:7,9
105:25 [j] Ex 4:21 [k] Ex 1:6-10; Ac 7:19
105:26 [l] Ex 3:10 [m] Nu 16:5; 17:5-8
105:27 [n] Ex 7:8-12:51
105:28 [o] Ex 10:22
105:29 [p] Ps 78:44 [q] Ex 7:21
105:30 [r] Ex 8:2,6
105:31 [s] Ex 8:21-24 [t] Ex 8:16-18
105:32 [u] Ex 9:22-25
105:33 [v] Ps 78:47
105:34 [w] Ex 10:4,12-15
105:36 [x] Ex 12:29
105:37 [y] Ex 12:35

17 and he sent a man before them—
Joseph, sold as a slave.[c]
18 They bruised his feet with shackles,[d]
his neck was put in irons,
19 till what he foretold[e] came to pass,
till the word of the LORD proved him true.
20 The king sent and released him,
the ruler of peoples set him free.[f]
21 He made him master of his household,
ruler over all he possessed,
22 to instruct his princes[g] as he pleased
and teach his elders wisdom.

23 Then Israel entered Egypt;[h]
Jacob resided as a foreigner in the land of Ham.
24 The LORD made his people very fruitful;
he made them too numerous[i] for their foes,
25 whose hearts he turned[j] to hate his people,
to conspire[k] against his servants.
26 He sent Moses[l] his servant,
and Aaron, whom he had chosen.[m]
27 They performed[n] his signs among them,
his wonders in the land of Ham.
28 He sent darkness[o] and made the land dark—
for had they not rebelled against his words?
29 He turned their waters into blood,[p]
causing their fish to die.[q]
30 Their land teemed with frogs,[r]
which went up into the bedrooms of their rulers.
31 He spoke, and there came swarms of flies,[s]
and gnats[t] throughout their country.
32 He turned their rain into hail,[u]
with lightning throughout their land;
33 he struck down their vines[v] and fig trees
and shattered the trees of their country.
34 He spoke, and the locusts came,[w]
grasshoppers without number;
35 they ate up every green thing in their land,
ate up the produce of their soil.
36 Then he struck down all the firstborn[x] in their land,
the firstfruits of all their manhood.
37 He brought out Israel, laden with silver and gold,[y]
and from among their tribes no one faltered.

105:21 ruler over all he possessed. The Lord went to the extreme of taking a prisoner (Joseph) and making him a ruler of the most powerful nation on earth (Gen 41), thereby showing his faithfulness to the covenant he had made with the patriarchs.
105:23 land of Ham. The Table of Nations in Gen 10:6 reckoned the Egyptians as descendants of Ham (see also v. 27; 78:51 and note).
105:24 fruitful. Another way that the Lord displayed faithfulness to his covenant promises (Gen 15:5; 22:17; 26:4; Exod 1:7–11).
105:25–38 Recounts events in Exod 1:8—12:51.
105:25 conspire. Translates a rare Hebrew word that also appears in Gen 37:18 ("plotted"), where Joseph's brothers conspire against him. The conspiracy against the Israelites in Egypt included their harsh enslavement (Exod 1:9–14) and the policy of male infanticide (Exod 1:15–22).
105:27–36 Recounts eight of the ten plagues (Exod 7–12). Only the fifth and sixth plagues (livestock and boils, respectively) are lacking. The plagues here do not appear in the same order as the plagues in Exodus. "Darkness," the ninth plague, occurs first (v. 28), but the tenth plague remains in the final and climactic position (v. 36).
105:27 signs ... wonders. A reference to the plagues in Egypt (78:43; 135:9; Exod 7:3; Jer 32:20–21).
105:37 silver and gold. The Lord promised that the Israelites would

[38]Egypt was glad when they left,
because dread of Israel[z] had fallen on them.

[39]He spread out a cloud[a] as a covering,
and a fire to give light at night.[b]
[40]They asked,[c] and he brought them quail;[d]
he fed them well with the bread of heaven.[e]
[41]He opened the rock,[f] and water gushed out;
it flowed like a river in the desert.

[42]For he remembered his holy promise[g]
given to his servant Abraham.
[43]He brought out his people with rejoicing,[h]
his chosen ones with shouts of joy;
[44]he gave them the lands of the nations,[i]
and they fell heir to what others had toiled for—
[45]that they might keep his precepts
and observe his laws.[j]

Praise the LORD.[a]

Psalm 106

106:1,47-48pp — 1Ch 16:34-36

[1]Praise the LORD.[b]

Give thanks to the LORD, for he is good;[k]
his love endures forever.

105:38 [z]Ex 12:33; 15:16
105:39 [a]Ex 13:21 [b]Ne 9:12; Ps 78:14
105:40 [c]Ps 78:18,24 [d]Ex 16:13 [e]Jn 6:31
105:41 [f]Ex 17:6; Nu 20:11; Ps 78:15-16; 1Co 10:4
105:42 [g]Ge 15:13-16
105:43 [h]Ex 15:1-18; Ps 106:12
105:44 [i]Jos 13:6-7
105:45 [j]Dt 4:40; 6:21-24
106:1 [k]Ps 100:5; 105:1

a 45 Hebrew *Hallelu Yah* *b 1* Hebrew *Hallelu Yah*; also in verse 48

despoil their Egyptian oppressors in Exod 3:22, and they did so in Exod 12:35–36.
105:39–41 Summarizes key events after the Israelites fled into the wilderness (Exod 13:17—17:7); reminds God's people that he provided for them in difficult circumstances and that they themselves are the evidence of God's faithfulness to his promises.
105:40 bread of heaven. Manna (Exod 16:4). In John 6, Jesus teaches that he is this bread of heaven (v. 35). Just as God sent the bread of heaven to save his people from (physical) death and to sustain them in the wilderness, so he sent Jesus to save his people from (final) death and to sustain them on their journey to the new heavens and new earth.
105:42 he remembered his holy promise. Explains all that the Lord did in vv. 12–41. **given to ... Abraham.** See vv. 9–11 and notes.
105:44 gave them the lands. Refers to v. 11, where the promise is about land. **others had toiled for.** The inheritance of the promised land was not the result of the people's efforts; it was a gift from the Lord (Deut 6:10–12; Josh 24:13).
105:45 that. Introduces the purpose of the gift of land. **precepts.** This is the plural form of the Hebrew word translated in v. 10 as "decree." The Lord was faithful to his "decree" so that Israel would keep his "decrees." The Lord's desire to create a people who reflect his character drives the Bible's storyline (Gen 1:26–28; Exod 19:6; Lev 19:2; Deut 6:21–25; Isa 5:1–7; Rom 8:29; 1 Pet 2:5,9).
Ps 106 *They Did Not Remember Your Many Kindnesses.* After a psalm about the Lord's faithfulness to his covenant with the patriarchs, comes a psalm that highlights the people's unfaithfulness to the Sinai (i.e., Mosaic) covenant. Ps 106 does not ignore the Lord's love and faithfulness (vv. 1,7–8,44–46), but its dominant theme is the waywardness of the people (vv. 6–46). Couched as a confession, Ps 106 tracks the rebelliousness of the people from Egypt to the period of the judges (and possibly the exile). So what causes the psalmist to rejoice in hope at the beginning and end of the psalm in the face of such stubborn recalcitrance? The Lord's great love (vv. 1,45b), which his covenant faithfulness reveals (v. 45a).

The psalm begins with a joyous call to praise and a pronouncement of blessing (vv. 1–3). The perspective of the psalm then shifts to an individual supplication as the psalmist asks God to save him (vv. 4–5). A community confession follows, sprinkled with references to God's redemptive mercy (vv. 6–46). The confession traces the people's rebelliousness across the Bible's storyline without necessarily maintaining Scripture's order of events. The psalm begins with the exodus (vv. 6–12) and then mentions the people's faithless craving for food in the wilderness (vv. 13–15; cf. Num 11:1–15,31–34), the rebellion that Dathan and Abiram led (vv. 16–18; cf. Num 16:1–40), the golden calf debacle (vv. 19–23; cf. Exod 32:1–14), the defeatist report that the ten spies gave (vv. 24–27; cf. Num 13:32—14:38), the idolatrous worship of Baal of Peor (vv. 28–31; cf. Num 25:1–15), and Moses' sin at Meribah (vv. 32–33; Num 20:2–13). The final historical reference in vv. 34–46 picks up the story in the promised land and could refer to either the period of the judges or the entire preexilic history of the people. It is not explicit in the text, but the lack of any mention of the monarchical era indicates that this refers to the period of the judges. The psalm concludes with a prayer and a doxology (vv. 47–48). Verses 1,46–47 conclude the hymn of praise that David sang on the occasion of bringing the ark of the covenant up to Jerusalem in 1 Chr 16:8–36 (vv. 1,47–48 parallel 1 Chr 16:34–36). See introductions to Pss 96; 105.
106:1 Book V (Pss 107–150) repeats the last sentence of this verse four times (see 107:1 and note; 118:1,29; 136:1). Shortened versions appear in 100:5; 105:1; 136:2–26.

106:2 [l]Ps 145:4,12
106:3 [m]Ps 15:2
106:4 [n]Ps 119:132
106:5 [o]Ps 1:3 [p]Ps 118:15
106:6 [q]Da 9:5
106:7 [r]Ps 78:11,42 [s]Ex 14:11-12
106:8 [t]Ex 9:16
106:9 [u]Ps 18:15 [v]Ex 14:21; Na 1:4 [w]Isa 63:11-14
106:10 [x]Ex 14:30 [y]Ps 107:2
106:11 [z]Ex 14:28; 15:5
106:12 [a]Ex 15:1-21
106:13 [b]Ex 15:24
106:14 [c]1Co 10:9
106:15 [d]Nu 11:31 [e]Isa 10:16

2 Who can proclaim the mighty acts[l] of the LORD
or fully declare his praise?
3 Blessed are those who act justly,
who always do what is right.[m]

4 Remember me,[n] LORD, when you show favor to your people,
come to my aid when you save them,
5 that I may enjoy the prosperity[o] of your chosen ones,
that I may share in the joy[p] of your nation
and join your inheritance in giving praise.

6 We have sinned,[q] even as our ancestors did;
we have done wrong and acted wickedly.
7 When our ancestors were in Egypt,
they gave no thought to your miracles;
they did not remember[r] your many kindnesses,
and they rebelled by the sea,[s] the Red Sea.[a]
8 Yet he saved them for his name's sake,[t]
to make his mighty power known.
9 He rebuked[u] the Red Sea, and it dried up;[v]
he led them through[w] the depths as through a desert.
10 He saved them[x] from the hand of the foe;
from the hand of the enemy he redeemed them.[y]
11 The waters covered[z] their adversaries;
not one of them survived.
12 Then they believed his promises
and sang his praise.[a]

13 But they soon forgot[b] what he had done
and did not wait for his plan to unfold.
14 In the desert they gave in to their craving;
in the wilderness they put God to the test.[c]
15 So he gave them[d] what they asked for,
but sent a wasting disease[e] among them.

[a] 7 Or *the Sea of Reeds*; also in verses 9 and 22

106:2 This rhetorical question heightens the pitch of praise (cf. 18:31; 71:19; 76:7; 77:13; 89:6–8; 113:5–6; 147:17).
106:3 Blessed. Reveals the path to true happiness (see note on 1:1). **act justly.** Characterizes the Lord's reign in Pss 93–99 (see note on 93:1). The Lord's people must reflect his character (see 105:45 and note).
106:4–5 The psalmist prays for a radical association with God's people. Salvation is not simply individualistic; it also has communal aspects (Exod 19:3–6; Eph 2:11–22; 5:25–27; 1 Pet 2:4–5).
106:4 Remember. Significant in the latter part of Book IV (vv. 7,45; 103:18; 105:5,8,42). When the Lord is the subject of it, it has covenantal implications (see 115:12 and note).
106:6 Opens a prayer of confession (cf. Ezra 9:6–15; Neh 9:5–37; Dan 9:4–19). **We.** After praying to be associated with the people of God in salvation (vv. 4–5), the psalmist associates with the people of God in their sin. **sinned ... done wrong ... acted wickedly.** These same verbs occur in 1 Kgs 8:47, where Solomon explains how the people should confess if they find themselves in exile.
106:7 miracles. The Lord's miraculous, saving acts (also in v. 22; 105:5; see note on 26:7). **remember.** The Lord remembers his covenant promises (v. 45; 105:42; see note on 115:12), but the people do not reciprocate. **kindnesses.** Or "acts of covenant faithfulness"; derives from the same Hebrew word translated "love" (*hesed*), which connotes the Lord's faithfulness to his promises (see note on 6:4).
106:8 for his name's sake. See notes on 8:1; 23:3.
106:9 Compares the Lord's provision in crossing the Red Sea (see note on Exod 10:19) to the experience in the desert. Having crossed the Red Sea, God's people should have trusted him when they actually made it to the desert (Exod 16:2–3; 17:1–3).
106:12 believed. What the Lord desires in response to his great acts of revelation (Gen 15:6; Exod 14:31). Unbelief was ultimately the people's—as well as Moses'—undoing (Num 14:11; 20:12; Deut 1:32; 9:23).
106:13 forgot. See v. 7 and note ["remember"]. **his plan.** See 107:11; see also note on 40:5.
106:14 gave in to their craving. This exact Hebrew phrase occurs in Num 11:4 to describe the people's desire for meat. In that passage, the Lord supplies the meat that they desire, but it is accompanied by a great plague (v. 15; Num 11:33). Therefore, the name of that place was "Kibroth Hattaavah" or the "graves of craving" (Num 11:34). **put God to the test.** Doubted God's faithfulness (78:18,41,56; 95:8–9; Exod 17:7; Num 14:22); the opposite of faith and obedience (Deut 6:16–17).
106:15 gave them what they asked for. The Lord sent quail to satisfy the people's desire for meat (see v. 14 and note). The Lord's

[16] In the camp they grew envious[f] of Moses
and of Aaron, who was consecrated to the LORD.
[17] The earth opened[g] up and swallowed Dathan;
it buried the company of Abiram.
[18] Fire blazed[h] among their followers;
a flame consumed the wicked.
[19] At Horeb they made a calf[i]
and worshiped an idol cast from metal.
[20] They exchanged their glorious God[j]
for an image of a bull, which eats grass.
[21] They forgot the God[k] who saved them,
who had done great things[l] in Egypt,
[22] miracles in the land of Ham[m]
and awesome deeds by the Red Sea.
[23] So he said he would destroy[n] them—
had not Moses, his chosen one,
stood in the breach[o] before him
to keep his wrath from destroying them.

[24] Then they despised the pleasant land;[p]
they did not believe[q] his promise.
[25] They grumbled[r] in their tents
and did not obey the LORD.
[26] So he swore[s] to them with uplifted hand
that he would make them fall in the wilderness,[t]
[27] make their descendants fall among the nations
and scatter[u] them throughout the lands.

[28] They yoked themselves to the Baal of Peor[v]
and ate sacrifices offered to lifeless gods;
[29] they aroused the LORD's anger by their wicked deeds,
and a plague broke out among them.
[30] But Phinehas stood up and intervened,
and the plague was checked.[w]
[31] This was credited to him[x] as righteousness
for endless generations to come.

106:16 [f] Nu 16:1-3
106:17 [g] Dt 11:6
106:18 [h] Nu 16:35
106:19 [i] Ex 32:4
106:20 [j] Jer 2:11; Ro 1:23
106:21 [k] Ps 78:11 [l] Dt 10:21
106:22 [m] Ps 105:27
106:23 [n] Ex 32:10 [o] Ex 32:11-14
106:24 [p] Dt 8:7; Eze 20:6 [q] Heb 3:18-19
106:25 [r] Nu 14:2
106:26 [s] Eze 20:15; Heb 3:11 [t] Nu 14:28-35
106:27 [u] Lev 26:33; Ps 44:11
106:28 [v] Nu 25:2-3; Hos 9:10
106:30 [w] Nu 25:8
106:31 [x] Nu 25:11-13

acquiescence to sinful desires manifests his wrath (see Rom 1:18–32, especially vv. 24,26,28).
106:16 grew envious. The cause of Dathan and Abiram's rebellion against the Lord's appointed leadership (Num 16:1–40).
106:19 See Exod 32:1–14.
106:20 exchanged their glorious God. The essence of idolatry (Jer 2:11). Paul affirms this understanding of idolatry in Rom 1:23, where he writes that idolaters "exchanged the glory of the immortal God for images made to look like a mortal human being and birds and animals and reptiles."
106:21 forgot. See vv. 7,13 and note on v. 7 ["remember"]; in contrast to the Lord, who remembers (v. 45; 98:3; 105:8; 115:12–13; see note on 115:12). The people do not respond to the Lord's mighty acts in faith. They are not faithful to the covenant.
106:22 miracles. See v. 7; 105:5; and note on 26:7.
106:23 chosen one. This term refers to an individual four times in the OT: Moses (here), David (89:3), the servant of the Lord (Isa 42:1), and Saul (2 Sam 21:6). The idea is that the Lord has set this person apart for a task. **breach.** Can symbolize God's judgment (80:12; 89:40; Judg 21:15; Isa 5:5; cf. Ezek 22:30). Moses stood in the place of judgment as a mediator between God and people (Exod 32:11–14; Num 11:2; Deut 9:19), prefiguring the work of Jesus (2 Cor 5:21; 1 Tim 2:5; Heb 12:24).
106:24 despised the pleasant land. Responded faithlessly when they heard the discouraging report from 10 of the 12 spies (Num 13:32—14:38). **did not believe.** Whereas Abraham believed God (Gen 15:6), the exodus generation ultimately did not (Num 14:11; Deut 1:32; 9:23), including Moses (Num 20:12).
106:27 scatter. Manifests God's judgment (92:9; Lev 26:33; Jer 23:1–2; 31:10).
106:28 Baal of Peor. An idolatrous episode in Israel's history (Num 25:1–15).
106:30 Phinehas. A devout priest whose zeal appeased the Lord's wrath against his people over the illicit worship of Baal of Peor (Num 25:7–15).
106:31 credited to him as righteousness. The same outcome as Abraham's faith in Gen 15:6. Phinehas's faithfulness to the Lord was manifest in his zeal and, like Abraham, he was credited with righteousness. The NT presents faith and works as two sides of the same coin: saving faith is a faith that works (Matt 12:33–37; Eph 2:8–10; Jas 2:14–26; see note on Jas 2:24).

106:32 [y] Nu 20:2-13; Ps 81:7 **106:33** [z] Nu 20:8-12 **106:34** [a] Jdg 1:21 [b] Dt 7:16 **106:35** [c] Jdg 3:5-6 **106:36** [d] Jdg 2:12 **106:37** [e] 2Ki 16:3; 17:17 **106:38** [f] Nu 35:33 **106:39** [g] Eze 20:18 [h] Lev 17:7; Nu 15:39 **106:40** [i] Jdg 2:14; Ps 78:59 [j] Dt 9:29 **106:41** [k] Jdg 2:14; Ne 9:27 **106:43** [l] Jdg 2:16-19 **106:44** [m] Jdg 3:9; 10:10 **106:45** [n] Lev 26:42; Ps 105:8 [o] Jdg 2:18 **106:46** [p] Ezr 9:9; Jer 42:12 **106:47** [q] Ps 147:2

32 By the waters of Meribah[y] they angered the LORD,
and trouble came to Moses because of them;
33 for they rebelled against the Spirit of God,
and rash words came from Moses' lips.[a][z]

34 They did not destroy[a] the peoples
as the LORD had commanded[b] them,
35 but they mingled[c] with the nations
and adopted their customs.
36 They worshiped their idols,[d]
which became a snare to them.
37 They sacrificed their sons[e]
and their daughters to false gods.
38 They shed innocent blood,
the blood of their sons[f] and daughters,
whom they sacrificed to the idols of Canaan,
and the land was desecrated by their blood.
39 They defiled themselves[g] by what they did;
by their deeds they prostituted[h] themselves.

40 Therefore the LORD was angry[i] with his people
and abhorred his inheritance.[j]
41 He gave them into the hands[k] of the nations,
and their foes ruled over them.
42 Their enemies oppressed them
and subjected them to their power.
43 Many times he delivered them,
but they were bent on rebellion[l]
and they wasted away in their sin.
44 Yet he took note of their distress
when he heard their cry;[m]
45 for their sake he remembered his covenant[n]
and out of his great love[o] he relented.
46 He caused all who held them captive
to show them mercy.[p]

47 Save us, LORD our God,
and gather us[q] from the nations,
that we may give thanks to your holy name
and glory in your praise.

[a] *33* Or *against his spirit, / and rash words came from his lips*

106:32 Meribah. See note on 81:7. **trouble came to Moses.** Moses was not allowed to enter the promised land because he faithlessly responded to the people's grumbling (Num 20:10–13).
106:35 The inherent danger of disobeying the Lord's directives about destroying the nations (v. 34) was that those nations would ultimately influence God's people (Deut 7:1–4; Judg 3:5–6; Ezra 9:1–2). **their customs.** Idolatry and child sacrifice (see vv. 36–39).
106:38 Shedding blood pollutes the land (Num 35:33).
106:39 prostituted themselves. The OT often compares idolatry to prostitution because prostitution is an act of unfaithfulness (Exod 34:15; Num 15:39; 25:1–3; Judg 2:17; 8:33; Jer 3:1–9; Ezek 6:9; Hos 1:2; 4:10–18).
106:40 inheritance. God's people (see 94:5 and note).
106:41 He gave. When foreign powers judged God's people, it was not merely because they were mighty but because the Lord decreed it (Judg 2:14; 2 Kgs 17:20; Hab 1:5–11).
106:44 In Judges, the Lord's deliverance (v. 43) follows the cry of his people (Judg 3:9; 4:3,23; 6:7–8; 10:10,16).
106:45 remembered his covenant. In contrast to the people's forgetfulness (vv. 7,13,21). "Remember" is a covenantal term when the Lord is the subject of the verb (see 115:12 and note). The Lord graciously responded to his people when they rebelled, because he is faithful to his covenant promises. **love.** Or "covenant faithfulness" (see notes on 6:4; 107:1). **relented.** The first psalm of Book IV (Ps 90) pleads with the Lord to relent and show pity toward his people (see 90:13 and note). Here, the people of God experience that pity. It is based on the Lord's great love and faithfulness to his covenant.
106:47 gather us. The opposite of scattered (see v. 27 and note). The very beginning of Book V (Pss 107–150) provides an answer to this prayer (see 107:3 and note). **give thanks.** This is one of the keynote

[48] Praise be to the LORD, the God of Israel,
from everlasting to everlasting.
Let all the people say, "Amen!"[r]
Praise the LORD.

BOOK V

Psalms 107–150

Psalm 107

[1] Give thanks to the LORD,[s] for he is good;
his love endures forever.

[2] Let the redeemed[t] of the LORD tell their story—
those he redeemed from the hand of the foe,
[3] those he gathered[u] from the lands,
from east and west, from north and south.[a]

[4] Some wandered in desert[v] wastelands,
finding no way to a city where they could settle.
[5] They were hungry and thirsty,
and their lives ebbed away.
[6] Then they cried out[w] to the LORD in their trouble,
and he delivered them from their distress.

106:48 [r] Ps 41:13
107:1 [s] Ps 106:1
107:2 [t] Ps 106:10
107:3 [u] Ps 106:47; Isa 43:5-6
107:4 [v] Nu 14:33; 32:13
107:6 [w] Ps 50:15

[a] 3 Hebrew *north and the sea*

themes in Book V (107:1,8,15,21,31; 108:3 ["praise"]; 109:30 ["extol"]; 111:1 ["extol"]; 118:1,29; 136:1–3; 138:1–4 ["praise"]).

106:48 A doxology concludes Book IV (see note on 41:13). **from everlasting to everlasting.** The eternal nature of all that is associated with the Lord is one of the prominent themes of Book IV (see notes on 90:2; 103:17).

Pss 107–150 *Book V: The Return of the King.* Book V signals a renewed hope in God's covenantal promises to King David (89:1–4,20–37; 2 Sam 7:11b–16). David is the primary figure of Books I–II, but he fades into near obscurity in Books III–IV. He reemerges in Book V as a symbol of God's chosen one, pointing ahead to the Messiah. Two collections of Davidic psalms (108–110; 138–145) and royal themes throughout Book V highlight this. This Davidic emphasis coincides well with the hope that existed in the OT that a Davidic heir would save God's people from all that threatened them (e.g., Isa 11:1–10; Jer 23:5–6; Ezek 34:23–24; Hos 3:5; Amos 9:11). Thus, the message of Psalms is consistent with the message of these other books: God will not abandon his covenant with David (see note on 89:3; see also "Covenant," p. 2646). This promise is still part of God's plan of salvation.

Ps 107 *Let Them Give Thanks to the Lord for His Unfailing Love.* Ps 107 portrays how God rescues people in various states of trouble and distress (vv. 2,6,13,19,28). God's rescuing activity is grounded in his unfailing love. The psalm begins with a call to praise (vv. 1–3), followed by four crises: wilderness wanderings (vv. 4–9), prison bondage (vv. 10–16), suffering from sin (vv. 17–22), and distress at sea (vv. 23–32). These four crises have a similar structure: a description of the problem, a prayer for deliverance, and a call to praise for the deliverance. The psalm ends by highlighting how the Lord can reverse fortunes, both in salvation and judgment (vv. 33–43). God's love ensures that a great reversal will occur one day, and indications of this reversal are already evident (vv. 4–32). God will save those who humbly cry out to him, but he will judge the proud and the arrogant. This great reversal prefigures a prevalent theme in Jesus' preaching (e.g., Matt 5:3–6,10; 19:30; 20:26–28).

107:1 Give thanks. Or "praise" (see 99:3; 105:1). This act of worship entails an active response, whether with musical instruments (33:2) or with a vocal confession (35:18; 109:30). **for.** Introduces two reasons for giving thanks (cf. 52:9; 54:6; 118:21). **good.** One of the most fundamental aspects of God's nature (cf. 135:3; 136:1); thus, it should be a fundamental part of a believer's praise. Adam and Eve doubted God's goodness in the garden because they thought he was withholding something "good" from them (Gen 3:6). **love.** Covenant faithfulness (see note on 6:4). This further clarifies the Lord's goodness, which is tied to his love (see 118:1,29; 136:1). **endures forever.** His faithfulness to his covenant promises does not have an expiration date; it will endure into eternity. These words are a recurring refrain in Ps 136.

107:2 the redeemed. Those gathered from exile (see v. 3 and note), an answer to the prayer in 106:47. **foe.** Translated "trouble" in vv. 6,13,19,28. "Foes" and "trouble" are linked with exile. The rescue from "foes" and "trouble" recalls 106:44, which translates this word as "distress": "he took note of their distress."

107:3 gathered. Delivered from exile (Isa 56:8; Ezek 11:17; 20:34,41). **from east and west, from north and south.** From every corner of the globe (Neh 1:9; Isa 43:5–6).

107:4 wandered in desert wastelands. Recalls Israel's wilderness wanderings (Num 21:20; 23:28) and the place from which God rescued them (Deut 32:10). **city where they could settle.** A hospitable home; the ultimate hope of all exiles (see Heb 11:13–16).

107:5 hungry and thirsty. As in Israel's wilderness wanderings (Exod 15:22; 16:3). **lives ebbed away.** Lamentable circumstances (Jonah 2:7).

107:6 cried out to the LORD. The proper response to trouble (Exod 2:23; Num 20:16; Judg 3:9,15; 6:6–8; 1 Sam 9:16; Neh 9:27–28). **trouble.** Translated "foe" in v. 2 (see note there), but here it is impersonal.

107:7 [x] Ezr 8:21
107:9 [y] Ps 22:26; Lk 1:53 [z] Ps 34:10
107:10 [a] Lk 1:79 [b] Job 36:8
107:11 [c] Ps 106:7; La 3:42 [d] 2Ch 36:16
107:12 [e] Ps 22:11
107:14 [f] Ps 116:16; Lk 13:16; Ac 12:7
107:17 [g] Isa 65:6-7; La 3:39
107:18 [h] Job 33:20 [i] Job 33:22; Ps 9:13; 88:3
107:20 [j] Mt 8:8 [k] Ps 103:3 [l] Job 33:28 [m] Ps 30:3; 49:15
107:22 [n] Lev 7:12; Ps 50:14; 116:17 [o] Ps 9:11; 73:28; 118:17

7 He led them by a straight way[x]
to a city where they could settle.
8 Let them give thanks to the LORD for his unfailing love
and his wonderful deeds for mankind,
9 for he satisfies[y] the thirsty
and fills the hungry with good things.[z]

10 Some sat in darkness,[a] in utter darkness,
prisoners suffering in iron chains,[b]
11 because they rebelled[c] against God's commands
and despised the plans[d] of the Most High.
12 So he subjected them to bitter labor;
they stumbled, and there was no one to help.[e]
13 Then they cried to the LORD in their trouble,
and he saved them from their distress.
14 He brought them out of darkness, the utter darkness,
and broke away their chains.[f]
15 Let them give thanks to the LORD for his unfailing love
and his wonderful deeds for mankind,
16 for he breaks down gates of bronze
and cuts through bars of iron.

17 Some became fools through their rebellious ways
and suffered affliction[g] because of their iniquities.
18 They loathed all food[h]
and drew near the gates of death.[i]
19 Then they cried to the LORD in their trouble,
and he saved them from their distress.
20 He sent out his word[j] and healed them;[k]
he rescued[l] them from the grave.[m]
21 Let them give thanks to the LORD for his unfailing love
and his wonderful deeds for mankind.
22 Let them sacrifice thank offerings[n]
and tell of his works[o] with songs of joy.

23 Some went out on the sea in ships;
they were merchants on the mighty waters.

107:7 straight way. Free from obstacles. The prophets portray Israel's return from exile as a second exodus (e.g., Isa 40:3; see also Isa 11:16). **city.** See note on v. 4.
107:8 unfailing love. Demonstrated by the Lord's delivering Israel from the exile of wandering in the wilderness. The Lord demonstrates his love by guiding those who are lost to a secure home. See note on 6:4. **wonderful deeds.** The Lord's miraculous, saving acts (vv. 15,21,24,31; 78:11,32; Exod 3:20). See note on 26:7. Salvation from distress is a type of miracle.
107:9 Completely reverses vv. 4–5. Recalls how the Lord provided for his people in the wilderness (Exod 15:25; 16:13–35).
107:10 In the ancient world, prisons were often pits below the ground (Exod 12:29; Jer 37:16), where there was little light. **darkness.** Often symbolizes evil and alienation from the Lord (35:6; 1 Sam 2:9; Isa 5:30; 59:9).
107:11 rebelled. The reason they suffered. Sometimes there is a correspondence between suffering and sin in one's life (32:3–5; 51:8–9; Hag 1:3–8; John 5:14; Rom 1:18–32; 1 Cor 11:29–30), although not always (Job 1:1; John 9:3; 2 Cor 12:7).
107:12 bitter labor. Reminiscent of God's sentence against Adam for his sin (Gen 3:17–19). **no one to help.** Lonely and helpless—a mark of alienation and vulnerability (22:11; 72:12; 2 Kgs 14:26; Job 29:12; 30:13; Lam 1:7).
107:13–16 God reverses vv. 10–12. His salvation ushers in a new and better way of living, and all of this flows from his unfailing love (see notes on v. 1; 6:4).
107:17 fools. Always associated with sin in Psalms (see 38:5 and note; 69:5; see also note on Prov 1:7; see further Introduction to Proverbs: Character Types). **suffered affliction because of their iniquities.** See note on v. 11.
107:18 loathed all food. Food sustains life and provides pleasure (104:21,27; 145:15; Eccl 2:24–25; 3:12–13; 5:18–20). God's judgment is manifest here in that the fool was able to enjoy neither. **gates of death.** The entrance to the realm of the dead (9:13; Job 38:17). The fool lives at death's door.
107:20 his word. An agent of healing and salvation (Ezek 37:4; see also John 1:1,14) and an antidote for foolishness (Ps 119:11,105).
107:21 unfailing love. See note on 6:4. God's grace toward rebellious fools reveals his unfailing covenantal love.
107:23 sea. Often portrayed as an unruly force of devastation (see notes

[24]They saw the works of the LORD,
his wonderful deeds in the deep.
[25]For he spoke[p] and stirred up a tempest[q]
that lifted high the waves.[r]
[26]They mounted up to the heavens and went down to the depths;
in their peril their courage melted[s] away.
[27]They reeled and staggered like drunkards;
they were at their wits' end.
[28]Then they cried out to the LORD in their trouble,
and he brought them out of their distress.
[29]He stilled the storm[t] to a whisper;
the waves[u] of the sea[a] were hushed.
[30]They were glad when it grew calm,
and he guided them to their desired haven.
[31]Let them give thanks to the LORD for his unfailing love
and his wonderful deeds for mankind.
[32]Let them exalt him in the assembly[v] of the people
and praise him in the council of the elders.

[33]He turned rivers into a desert,[w]
flowing springs into thirsty ground,
[34]and fruitful land into a salt waste,[x]
because of the wickedness of those who lived there.
[35]He turned the desert into pools of water[y]
and the parched ground into flowing springs;
[36]there he brought the hungry to live,
and they founded a city where they could settle.
[37]They sowed fields and planted vineyards[z]
that yielded a fruitful harvest;
[38]he blessed them, and their numbers greatly increased,[a]
and he did not let their herds diminish.

[39]Then their numbers decreased,[b] and they were humbled
by oppression, calamity and sorrow;
[40]he who pours contempt on nobles[c]
made them wander in a trackless waste.[d]

107:25 [p] Ps 105:31 [q] Jnh 1:4 [r] Ps 93:3
107:26 [s] Ps 22:14
107:29 [t] Mt 8:26 [u] Ps 89:9
107:32 [v] Ps 22:22,25; 35:18
107:33 [w] 1Ki 17:1; Ps 74:15
107:34 [x] Ge 13:10; 14:3; 19:25
107:35 [y] Ps 114:8; Isa 41:18
107:37 [z] Isa 65:21
107:38 [a] Ge 12:2; 17:16, 20; Ex 1:7
107:39 [b] 2Ki 10:32; Eze 5:12
107:40 [c] Job 12:21 [d] Job 12:24

[a] *29* Dead Sea Scrolls; Masoretic Text / *their waves*

on 33:7; 93:3). For Jonah it was a grave and a place of exile (Jonah 2:2–4). Those around the eastern Mediterranean viewed it as a source of chaos and evil (Rev 13:1; 21:1). Here it is both a source of wonder and terror.
107:24 The Lord displays his power by taming the mighty deep (Exod 15:4–6; Job 38:8–11; Luke 8:22–25).
107:25–29 God is sovereign over natural events (see 148:8; Job 37:11–12), whether he stirs up devastating weather events (v. 25) or stills the storm (v. 29).
107:30 desired haven. Much like a city where they could settle (vv. 4,7,36). The Lord guides frightened and disoriented exiles to a safe place when they cry out to him in their trouble.
107:31 unfailing love. See note on 6:4. Salvation from the storm at sea is another testament to God's love.
107:32 assembly. The gathering of the worshiping community (see note on 40:9,10). Praise is not a purely private matter. Each testimony of the Lord's faithfulness and love encourages his people. **elders.** The leaders in a family or clan. Elders convened councils to act as judges in legal cases (Deut 22:13–19) and to make decisions for the community (Exod 3:16). They also led military expeditions (Josh 8:10 ["leaders of Israel"]).
107:33–34 The Lord enacts a great reversal because of the wickedness of those who turned away from him. Sin leads to curse and blight (Gen 3:14–19; Isa 42:15).
107:35–36 The reversal benefits the godly. This encourages God's people to walk by faith and not by sight (2 Cor 5:7). God will accomplish a great reversal that favors the humble who have called out to him for salvation (Matt 5:3–6; 19:30; 20:26–28).
107:37 sowed ... planted. A sign of stability in the land (Isa 37:30; Jer 32:1–15). **fruitful harvest.** Represents a thriving economy in an agricultural society; a sign of the Lord's favor and blessing (see Deut 28:11).
107:38 Recalls Gen 1:28; 9:1, which represents God's ideal world. The Lord is leading the exiles into a new Eden. **blessed.** See note on 3:8.
107:39–41 Even though oppression brought the needy low (v. 39), God punished their oppressors (v. 40) and restored them (v. 41).
107:40 waste. An uninhabitable land, in contrast to "a city where they could settle" (v. 36). The Hebrew is translated "formless" in Gen 1:2 and "barren" in Deut 32:10. It resembles the "desert wastelands" of v. 4. Thus,

107:41 [e] 1Sa 2:8; Ps 113:7-9
107:42 [f] Job 22:19 [g] Job 5:16; Ps 63:11; Ro 3:19
107:43 [h] Jer 9:12; Hos 14:9 [i] Ps 64:9
108:5 [j] Ps 57:5

41 But he lifted the needy[e] out of their affliction
and increased their families like flocks.
42 The upright see and rejoice,[f]
but all the wicked shut their mouths.[g]
43 Let the one who is wise[h] heed these things
and ponder the loving deeds[i] of the LORD.

Psalm 108[a]

108:1-5pp — Ps 57:7-11
108:6-13pp — Ps 60:5-12

A song. A psalm of David.

1 My heart, O God, is steadfast;
I will sing and make music with all my soul.
2 Awake, harp and lyre!
I will awaken the dawn.
3 I will praise you, LORD, among the nations;
I will sing of you among the peoples.
4 For great is your love, higher than the heavens;
your faithfulness reaches to the skies.
5 Be exalted, O God, above the heavens;
let your glory be over all the earth.[j]

6 Save us and help us with your right hand,
that those you love may be delivered.
7 God has spoken from his sanctuary:
"In triumph I will parcel out Shechem
and measure off the Valley of Sukkoth.

[a] In Hebrew texts 108:1-13 is numbered 108:2-14.

the Lord has led the exiles who called out to him into a fruitful dwelling, and he has led the proud into a place where life cannot be supported.

107:42 upright ... wicked. The contrast permeates the Psalter, and it is especially prominent as an opening keynote in Ps 1 (see introduction to Ps 1).

107:43 Let the one who is wise. Cf. Deut 32:29; Hos 14:9. **heed these things and ponder.** Contemplate this psalm's message like a proverb (92:6; Prov 1:2,5–6). **loving deeds.** The psalm's dominant theme. The wise understand that the Lord will enact a great reversal, so even if the wicked prosper for a time and the godly suffer, their faith and hope remain in the Lord (73:17). The wise build their lives on that teaching (Matt 7:24–25).

Ps 108 *Great Is Your Love, Higher Than the Heavens.* This highlights the Lord's love (v. 4), as does Ps 107 (cf. 107:1,8,15,21,31,43). God displays his love on the world stage (vv. 3,7–10) as he delivers his people from their enemies. David trusts that the Lord will deliver his people on account of his love, faithfulness, and glory (vv. 4–5); the defeat of enemies is an integral aspect of salvation (vv. 6,12). As the Lord's anointed leader, David is dedicated to seeing this accomplished, so he turns to the Lord to grant victory (vv. 12–13). Moreover, the Lord's reign extends beyond the borders of Israel. He is more than a parochial deity; he is the God of all creation.

Ps 108 combines 57:7–11 and 60:5–12, but these sections have different purposes in Ps 108. The first section (vv. 1–5) functions as the psalm's praise introduction with the "nations" and "peoples" as the primary audience (v. 3). Then vv. 6–13 relate the reason for praise: the Lord will "save" and deliver his people (v. 6), granting them "victory" (v. 13) over the enemy nations (vv. 12–13). The main difference between Ps 108 and Pss 57; 60 is that Pss 57; 60 begin with danger and peril, while Ps 108 uses only the more positive final portions of these earlier psalms. So while Ps 108 acknowledges that real challenges exist (v. 11), it has a more hopeful and triumphant tone throughout than Pss 57; 60.

108 title This is only the fourth Davidic psalm since Ps 70 (the others: Pss 86; 101; 103). See introduction to Pss 107–150. The first small collection of Davidic psalms (Pss 108–110) complement one another: Pss 108 and 109 look to the Lord for deliverance from enemies as a sign of his love; Ps 110 reveals a warrior king-priest who will lead a conquest against God's enemies.

108:1 The psalm begins with a note of confidence. **soul.** Or "glory," which refers to David's whole being (see note on 6:3). To be created in God's image gives people glory (see 8:5), a subordinate glory that reflects the greater glory of the Creator.

108:2 Awake. See note on 57:8. David begins the day in praise, rising even before dawn.

108:3 The Lord is God of all nations and peoples, so his praise should echo everywhere (see note on 57:9).

108:4 For. Introduces the ground of David's praise, even in the midst of threats. **love.** Extolled in 107:1,8,15,21,31,43.

108:5 glory. Creates a frame with "soul," or "glory," in v. 1 (see note there). David uses his glory to magnify God's glory, which he prays would be over all the earth. The glory of the image-maker far surpasses the glory of the image-bearer.

108:6 us ... us. The words in Hebrew are singular. David recognizes that as the anointed leader of God's people, what happens to him affects the entire nation. He is their covenant representative. As he goes, so go the people.

108:7–9 Possibly a prophetic message (see note on 60:6 ["from his

[8]Gilead is mine, Manasseh is mine;
Ephraim is my helmet,
Judah[k] is my scepter.
[9]Moab is my washbasin,
on Edom I toss my sandal;
over Philistia I shout in triumph."

[10]Who will bring me to the fortified city?
Who will lead me to Edom?
[11]Is it not you, God, you who have rejected us
and no longer go out with our armies?[l]
[12]Give us aid against the enemy,
for human help is worthless.
[13]With God we will gain the victory,
and he will trample down our enemies.

Psalm 109

For the director of music. Of David. A psalm.

[1]My God, whom I praise,
do not remain silent,[m]
[2]for people who are wicked and deceitful
have opened their mouths against me;
they have spoken against me with lying tongues.[n]
[3]With words of hatred[o] they surround me;
they attack me without cause.[p]
[4]In return for my friendship they accuse me,
but I am a man of prayer.[q]
[5]They repay me evil for good,[r]
and hatred for my friendship.

[6]Appoint someone evil to oppose my enemy;
let an accuser[s] stand at his right hand.

108:8 [k]Ge 49:10
108:11 [l]Ps 44:9
109:1 [m]Ps 83:1
109:2 [n]Ps 52:4; 120:2
109:3 [o]Ps 69:4 [p]Ps 35:7; Jn 15:25
109:4 [q]Ps 69:13
109:5 [r]Ps 35:12; 38:20
109:6 [s]Zec 3:1

sanctuary"]). It was common for kings to inquire of the Lord and to receive an oracle from him (see 1 Sam 30:7–8; 1 Kgs 20:13–14; 22:5–28; 2 Kgs 14:25).
108:7 Shechem ... Valley of Sukkoth. See note on 60:6.
108:8 All of these places fall within the boundaries of the nation under David's leadership. **helmet.** The Lord wages battle through his people (see note on 60:7). **scepter.** Symbolizes royal authority (see note on 45:6).
108:9 Moab ... Edom ... Philistia. See note on 60:8. **washbasin.** The residual filth from washing household items and the body would have made a washbasin, much like a sandal, a term of derision.
108:10 Edom. According to the title of Ps 60, that psalm was written in response to the great victory that David and his army won against Edom (2 Sam 8:13–14). Verses 6–13 here duplicate 60:5–12.
Ps 109 *Out of the Goodness of Your Love, Deliver Me.* This psalm continues the theme of deliverance from enemies that Ps 108 begins. But in this psalm, the enemies are individuals, not nations, and one enemy in particular appears to lead the attack (vv. 6–19). As the Lord's anointed, David is not just threatened by the unruly nations at Israel's borders but must also contend with accusations of an enemy who incites a rebellion against his leadership (vv. 4,6,20,25,29). But David trusts that he will be saved from his accuser(s) because of the Lord's unfailing love (vv. 21,26). The psalm summarizes the contest between David and his opponents (vv. 1–5), and then David singles out the leader and prays that the Lord would justly condemn him as the representative of his band of accusers (vv. 6–20). The psalm then turns from focusing on the hatred of the enemies to focusing on the Lord's faithful love: although his enemies oppose and revile him, David knows that the Lord's faithful love is greater than their hatred (vv. 21–31). The key hinge verse of this psalm is v. 21, which fits well with the theme that 107:1 announces: God's goodness. The NT interprets this psalm Christologically, with Jesus as the Lord's anointed and Judas as the accuser (see Acts 1:16–20).
109 title The second consecutive psalm ascribed to David in a mini-collection of Davidic psalms (see note on Ps 108 title).
109:1 David is waiting for the word of the Lord that will bring healing and rescue him from distress (107:20). God's word brings life and salvation, so his apparent silence can be mysterious to a believer.
109:2 God is silent (v. 1), but David's enemies are speaking.
109:3 without cause. David proclaims his innocence. Sometimes enemy attacks are the result of the psalmist's folly (e.g., 69:5), but sometimes they are unwarranted (e.g., 7:3–5; 35:7; 38:19; 59:3,4; 119:161).
109:4,5 friendship. Or "love." The enemies return accusation for friendship and evil for good. This contrasts David and his accusers.
109:6–20 A prayer of imprecation (i.e., a curse). See note on 69:22–28. Christians sometimes recoil at the harsh language these prayers use. Some interpreters read an implied "they said" at the beginning of v. 6 so that these verses quote the curses that David's enemies hurled at him. But the early church did not read this section as a quotation of David's enemies (see Acts 1:16–20). They knew what David knew: God is just, and an attack on his anointed ruler is an attack against God and

109:7 [t] Pr 28:9
109:8 [u] Ac 1:20*
109:9 [v] Ex 22:24
109:11 [w] Job 5:5
109:12 [x] Isa 9:17
109:13 [y] Job 18:19; Ps 37:28 [z] Pr 10:7
109:14 [a] Ex 20:5; Ne 4:5; Jer 18:23
109:15 [b] Job 18:17; Ps 34:16
109:16 [c] Ps 37:14,32 [d] Ps 34:18
109:17 [e] Pr 14:14; Eze 35:6
109:18 [f] Ps 73:6 [g] Nu 5:22
109:20 [h] Ps 94:23; 2Ti 4:14 [i] Ps 71:10
109:21 [j] Ps 79:9 [k] Ps 69:16

7 When he is tried, let him be found guilty,
  and may his prayers condemn[t] him.
8 May his days be few;
  may another take his place[u] of leadership.
9 May his children be fatherless
  and his wife a widow.[v]
10 May his children be wandering beggars;
  may they be driven[a] from their ruined homes.
11 May a creditor seize all he has;
  may strangers plunder the fruits of his labor.[w]
12 May no one extend kindness to him
  or take pity[x] on his fatherless children.
13 May his descendants be cut off,[y]
  their names blotted out[z] from the next generation.
14 May the iniquity of his fathers[a] be remembered before the LORD;
  may the sin of his mother never be blotted out.
15 May their sins always remain before the LORD,
  that he may blot out their name[b] from the earth.

16 For he never thought of doing a kindness,
  but hounded to death the poor
  and the needy[c] and the brokenhearted.[d]
17 He loved to pronounce a curse —
  may it come back on him.[e]
He found no pleasure in blessing —
  may it be far from him.
18 He wore cursing[f] as his garment;
  it entered into his body like water,[g]
  into his bones like oil.
19 May it be like a cloak wrapped about him,
  like a belt tied forever around him.
20 May this be the LORD's payment[h] to my accusers,
  to those who speak evil[i] of me.

21 But you, Sovereign LORD,
  help me for your name's sake;[j]
  out of the goodness of your love,[k] deliver me.

[a] *10* Septuagint; Hebrew *sought*

his kingdom (2:1 – 3). This specific prayer appears to request retributive justice: that God would do to David's accuser what David's accuser wanted to do to David (cf. v. 6 with vv. 2,4; see vv. 17 – 20).

109:6 David addresses his request to God. This is not the rant of a vigilante; it is a prayer of faith that entrusts retribution and justice to God (see Deut 32:35). Whereas in vv. 1 – 5 the enemies are plural, here David directs his prayer against the leader of the group.

109:7 When he is tried. Either in an earthly court (Lev 19:15; Deut 25:1) or in the court of God's judgment (Pss 7:8,11; 9:5,9; 96:13; 98:9). **his prayers condemn him.** The evidence used against him will be his prayers. The words a person speaks will be an integral part of God's judgment (Matt 5:21 – 22; 12:36 – 37).

109:8 May his days be few. A short life is the opposite of God's ideal (Gen 15:15; 25:7 – 8; Exod 20:12; Deut 6:2; 34:7).

109:9 David asks God to display his wrath (Exod 22:22 – 24). Jeremiah prayed a similar prayer when others accused him (Jer 18:18 – 22).

109:10 wandering beggars. A judgment that resembles Cain's exile (Gen 4:12 – 14).

109:11 plunder the fruits of his labor. Plundered property is a curse for covenant unfaithfulness (Deut 28:15,33; Jer 20:5; Ezek 23:29).

109:12 Retribution for not showing kindness (v. 16).

109:13 names blotted out. See note on 9:5.

109:14 sin ... never be blotted out. Contrasts with "names blotted out" in v. 13.

109:15 name. This Hebrew word is related to the Hebrew word for "be remembered" in v. 14a. Thus, David prays that their sin would be remembered but nothing else.

109:16 the poor. Whom the Lord defends (12:5; Lev 19:10; 23:22) and the ideal king delivers (72:2,4,12). So this enemy is at odds with the Lord and his anointed (see note on 82:3 – 4). "Poor" does not necessarily refer to economic status; it can also refer to spiritual status, much like "poor in spirit" in Matt 5:3 (cf. Isa 11:4; 29:19).

109:20 the LORD's payment. Not David's payment. David looks to the Lord for justice. He does not take it into his own hands.

109:21 But you, Sovereign LORD. The turning point in the psalm. The focus shifts from the enemy to the Lord. **for your name's sake.** The

[22] For I am poor and needy,
and my heart is wounded within me.
[23] I fade away like an evening shadow;[l]
I am shaken off like a locust.
[24] My knees give[m] way from fasting;
my body is thin and gaunt.
[25] I am an object of scorn[n] to my accusers;
when they see me, they shake their heads.[o]

[26] Help me,[p] LORD my God;
save me according to your unfailing love.
[27] Let them know[q] that it is your hand,
that you, LORD, have done it.
[28] While they curse,[r] may you bless;
may those who attack me be put to shame,
but may your servant rejoice.[s]
[29] May my accusers be clothed with disgrace
and wrapped in shame[t] as in a cloak.

[30] With my mouth I will greatly extol the LORD;
in the great throng[u] of worshipers I will praise him.
[31] For he stands at the right hand[v] of the needy,
to save their lives from those who would condemn them.

109:23 [l] Ps 102:11
109:24 [m] Heb 12:12
109:25 [n] Ps 22:6 [o] Mt 27:39; Mk 15:29
109:26 [p] Ps 119:86
109:27 [q] Job 37:7
109:28 [r] 2Sa 16:12 [s] Isa 65:14
109:29 [t] Ps 35:26; 132:18
109:30 [u] Ps 35:18; 111:1
109:31 [v] Ps 16:8; 73:23; 121:5
110:1 [w] Mt 22:44*; Mk 12:36*; Lk 20:42*; Ac 2:34* [x] 1Co 15:25

Psalm 110

Of David. A psalm.

[1] The LORD says[w] to my lord:[a]

"Sit at my right hand
until I make your enemies
a footstool for your feet."[x]

[a] *1* Or *Lord*

reason for David's unselfish plea for justice: he wants to preserve and defend the Lord's reputation, something that the Lord himself is committed to (see 23:3 and note; 25:11; 31:3; Exod 9:16; Isa 48:9; Ezek 20:9,14,22,44; 36:22–23).

109:22 I am poor and needy. David associates himself with the poor (see v. 16 and note).

109:23 evening shadow. Gradually fades away (102:11; 144:4). **locust.** Easily blown away on the wind (see Exod 10:19).

109:26–29 Concluding prayer grounded in the Lord's unfailing love.

109:27 David desires that God's help (v. 26) would glorify God because David's adversaries "know" that it has come from God (v. 21).

109:30 With my mouth. Worship is active and vocal. **in the great throng of worshipers.** Worship is more than a private experience; it is a public and corporate expression of devotion (42:4; 107:32; 111:1).

109:31 stands at the right hand of the needy. Contrast v. 6. This foreshadows the reference in 110:1, where David refers to his "lord," i.e., the Messiah (see note on 110:1), sitting at the right hand of God himself. Jesus is clearly able to save the needy and save all of humanity from death (e.g., John 11:25; Heb 2:14–15; Rev 1:18). **those who would condemn them.** Anyone who would stand in the place of God as judge.

Ps 110 *You Are a Priest Forever.* Ps 110 depicts a Messianic King-Priest who will ultimately and finally accomplish the deliverance that Pss 107–109 long for. It has two main sections, each headed by a statement from the Lord (vv. 1,4). After each statement, images of victory and triumph abound (vv. 2–3,5–7). Ps 110 has enjoyed a long history of Messianic interpretation for three primary reasons: (1) David has a vision of a figure whom he refers to as "my lord," and this figure accomplishes an ultimate victory over God's enemies that none of David's purely human offspring approached; (2) there is an affinity between Ps 110 and other Messianic psalms, such as Pss 2; 45; 72; 132; 144 (see introduction to Ps 2); and (3) the NT references Ps 110 more than any other psalm (see Acts 2:34–35; 1 Cor 15:25; Eph 1:20; Col 3:1; Heb 1:13; 7:17,21; 1 Pet 3:22). It applies Ps 110 to Jesus as evidence of his Messianic nature (Matt 22:44; Heb 5:6). Ps 110 provides hope that the Lord has not abandoned his covenant with David: an heir of David will reign forever (89:4,36; 2 Sam 7:16).

110 title See note on Ps 108 title. Jesus affirms that David is the author of this psalm (Matt 22:43–45).

110:1 lord. Sovereign or superior (Hebrew *ʾādôn*; see note on 8:1). In the OT, this word most often refers to human masters (see Gen 24:9; 1 Kgs 22:17; 2 Kgs 2:3) and is thus not capitalized. It can, however, refer to God (Josh 3:11,13; see NIV text note on Ps 110:1). Jesus interprets it as a reference to himself, and so it is capitalized in the NT quotations of this passage (Matt 22:44; Mark 12:36; Luke 20:42). Jesus presses his adversaries about this observation by pointing out that David saw this "lord" as his superior, making the point that he himself was David's "lord" (Matt 22:43–45). This is affirmed elsewhere in the NT (Acts 2:34–35). **Sit.** The Levitical high priest always stood, but Jesus sat

King Tut's footstool, which portrays his enemies (300 years before David).

Detail from the ceremonial footstool of Tutankhamun (ca. 1370 – 52 BC) New Kingdom, Egyptian 18th Dynasty/Egyptian National Museum, Cairo, Egypt/Bridgeman Images

110:2 [y]Ps 45:6
110:3 [z]Jdg 5:2; Ps 96:9
110:4 [a]Nu 23:19
[b]Heb 5:6*; 7:21*
[c]Heb 7:15-17*

2 The LORD will extend your mighty scepter[y] from Zion,
saying,
"Rule in the midst of your enemies!"
3 Your troops will be willing
on your day of battle.
Arrayed in holy splendor,[z]
your young men will come to you
like dew from the morning's womb.[a]

4 The LORD has sworn
and will not change his mind:[a]
"You are a priest forever,[b]
in the order of Melchizedek.[c]"

[a] 3 The meaning of the Hebrew for this sentence is uncertain.

down after offering a perfect sacrifice (Heb 10:11 – 12). **right hand.** Cf. v. 5. The position of honor (45:9; 1 Kgs 2:19; see notes on 16:8; 109:31). Jesus assumed this position after his resurrection (Matt 26:64; Acts 2:33; Eph 1:20; Col 3:1; Heb 1:3,13; 8:1; 10:12; 12:2; 1 Pet 3:22). **your enemies.** Enemies of God's anointed, the backdrop of Pss 108; 109. **footstool for your feet.** A metaphor for submission (1 Kgs 5:3). When an enemy is underfoot, it is vanquished; Gen 3:15 depicts the same image with different language. Jesus' enemies will submit as vanquished foes (1 Cor 15:25; Eph 1:22; Heb 1:13).

110:2 extend your mighty scepter. Spread your royal power and authority (see note on 45:6). **Zion.** The "capital" of God's kingdom where his anointed king reigned and the place from which God's kingdom would expand (see notes on 2:6; 9:11). **Rule.** The mandate God gave Adam and Eve in Gen 1:28. **in the midst of your enemies.** The Lord and his anointed face opposition (2:1 – 3), and yet the psalm affirms that the anointed one will rule at the very heart of where they are. Verse 2 contains echoes of Gen 49:8 – 12, which conveys Jacob's promise to Judah of royal authority in his line.

110:3 Your troops. These belong to the leader of an army, thus a warrior king. **willing.** Freely, by one's own choice. This is the same Hebrew word used to denote "freewill offerings." Here the troops will freely offer themselves in service of the king (Judg 5:2; Rom 12:1). **battle.** Spiritual war between God and the forces of evil (Dan 10:13; 12:1; Rev 12:7 – 9). **Arrayed in holy splendor.** Cf. 29:2; 45:3; 96:9 (see note there); 104:1. Here the king's army fights not with technologically advanced weaponry but with the power of holiness (Eph 6:10 – 18). **your young men will come to you like dew from the morning's womb.** See NIV text note. The meaning here is obscure, but this phrase seems to be poetically comparing the emergence of dew in the morning with the appearance of the king's army. They miraculously appear from a mysterious womb — possibly a veiled reference to the mystery of regeneration (Ezek 36:25 – 27; John 3:3 – 8).

110:4 The warrior king is also a priest (Zech 6:13). **has sworn.** An oath guaranteeing an eternal priesthood. This parallels the promise to David that his lineage would have an eternal kingship (89:35 – 37; 2 Sam 7:11b – 16). The writer of Hebrews explains the importance of this oath in Heb 6:16 – 18; 7:20 – 22. **forever.** Permanently. This quite possibly informed the crowd's question to Jesus in John 12:34. His priesthood will never cease. The Lord's covenant love will endure "forever" (107:1; 111:3,5,9; 117:2; 118:1,2,3,4,29; see note on 89:3). **order of Melchizedek.** Differs from the order of Levitical priests. The Davidic heir could not be a Levitical priest because David and his offspring descended from Judah, not Levi (Heb 7:14). Melchizedek appears in Gen 14:18 – 20, a context similar to Ps 110: Melchizedek is both a priest and king against the backdrop of a great battle in which God's people triumph (Gen 14:1 – 16). Melchizedek even reigns in the same place as the lord of that text: Salem (Gen 14:18), an earlier name for Jerusalem, or Mount Zion (v. 2). Based on the interaction between Melchizedek and Abraham, Heb 7:4 – 10 argues that Melchizedek's priesthood is greater than the Levitical priesthood for two reasons: (1) Melchizedek blessed Abraham (and by extension, Levi, who was metaphorically present in Abraham), and the blessing always comes from the greater party to the lesser; (2) Abraham gave tithes to Melchizedek after the battle, so Abraham (and by extension, Levi) would have acknowledged the superiority of Melchizedek's priesthood.

[5]The Lord is at your right hand[a];[d]
he will crush kings[e] on the day of his wrath.[f]
[6]He will judge the nations,[g] heaping up the dead[h]
and crushing the rulers[i] of the whole earth.
[7]He will drink from a brook along the way,[b]
and so he will lift his head high.[j]

Psalm 111[c]

[1]Praise the LORD.[d]

I will extol the LORD with all my heart
in the council of the upright and in the assembly.

[2]Great are the works[k] of the LORD;
they are pondered by all who delight in them.
[3]Glorious and majestic are his deeds,
and his righteousness endures forever.
[4]He has caused his wonders to be remembered;
the LORD is gracious and compassionate.[l]
[5]He provides food[m] for those who fear him;
he remembers his covenant forever.

[6]He has shown his people the power of his works,
giving them the lands of other nations.
[7]The works of his hands are faithful and just;
all his precepts are trustworthy.[n]
[8]They are established for ever[o] and ever,
enacted in faithfulness and uprightness.

110:5 [d]Ps 16:8 [e]Ps 2:12 [f]Ps 2:5; Ro 2:5
110:6 [g]Isa 2:4 [h]Isa 66:24 [i]Ps 68:21
110:7 [j]Ps 27:6
111:2 [k]Ps 92:5; 143:5
111:4 [l]Ps 103:8
111:5 [m]Mt 6:26,31-33
111:7 [n]Ps 19:7; Rev 15:3
111:8 [o]Isa 40:8; Mt 5:18

[a] *5* Or *My lord is at your right hand, LORD* [b] *7* The meaning of the Hebrew for this clause is uncertain. [c] This psalm is an acrostic poem, the lines of which begin with the successive letters of the Hebrew alphabet. [d] *1* Hebrew *Hallelu Yah*

110:5 at your right hand. Near to assist you (see note on v. 1). Cf. v. 1. **crush kings.** The warrior king triumphs over the rebellious "kings of the earth" (2:2). **day of his wrath.** Ps 2:10–12 warns kings to repent and submit to the Lord and his anointed lest they experience the fury of his wrath.
110:6 judge the nations. Judgment, especially universal judgment, is ascribed to the Lord (9:8; 1 Sam 2:10), so there may be an indication here that the king-priest assumes divine roles. **heaping up the dead.** Punitive judgment flows from the Lord's wrath (see Isa 5:25; Rev 19:17–18). **crushing the rulers.** See v. 5; 68:21.
110:7 drink from a brook along the way. See NIV text note. Two possibilities are most plausible: (1) to drink water, especially in a foreign land, could be seen as an act of aggression and superiority in the ancient world, so this may signify the king-priest's superiority over his enemies; (2) as Gideon's army was comprised of warriors who did not kneel by the water source and thus demonstrated their readiness for battle (Judg 7:4–6), so the king-priest quenches his thirst quickly to continue on with the battle. **lift his head high.** The Lord will exalt his king-priest (see note on 3:3).
Ps 111 *He Remembers His Covenant Forever.* This is an acrostic psalm (see NIV text note; see also Introduction: The Psalms as Poetry [Acrostic Poems]). The dominant theme is the eternal (vv. 3,5,8–10), which, in the immediate literary context, picks up on the reference to the eternal priesthood in 110:4. The Lord (and all that is associated with him) is eternal, including his faithfulness to his covenant (vv. 5,9). Ps 111 begins with an invitation to praise the Lord (v. 1). The rest of the psalm is organized around the main theme of eternality: the Lord's righteousness abides forever (vv. 2–4), he remembers his covenant forever (v. 5), all his precepts are steadfast forever (vv. 6–8), he establishes his covenant forever (v. 9), and his praise abides forever (v. 10).
111:1 extol. Translated "give thanks" in 107:1 (see note there). **heart.** Innermost being (see note on 7:9). This praise is not timid or passive. **assembly.** A general congregation; a crowd. Worship is more than a private matter (see note on 109:30).
111:2 See notes on 26:7; 40:3. **works.** Any of God's acts, whether in creation or salvation. **delight in them.** God's works are a source of joy for all who see his reflection in them.
111:3 righteousness. Discernible in what God has done. **endures forever.** Never exhausted (see note on 107:1).
111:4 wonders. The Lord's acts of salvation (see notes on 26:7; 107:8). **remembered.** A significant component of right worship: God's people must remember what he has done (42:6; 45:17; 71:16–18; Exod 17:14; Josh 4:7; see note on v. 5). **gracious and compassionate.** One of the most fundamental expressions of the Lord's character (Exod 34:6), displayed by his saving acts.
111:5 remembers his covenant forever. Another fundamental expression of the Lord's character (98:3; 105:8; 106:45; Gen 9:15–16; Exod 2:24; 6:5). The Lord's faithfulness to his covenant promises will endure for all time (see 107:1 and note). God's remembering mirrors v. 4: God's people must remember because they serve a God who remembers.
111:6 shown. The Lord is a revealer (19:1–4). **lands of other nations.** Part of the Lord's covenant promises, to which he will be faithful forever (78:55; Gen 12:7; 15:18).
111:7–8 The Lord's work in the world and his revealed instruction together display that he is trustworthy and faithful (Ps 19).
111:7 works. In creation (8:3,6). **precepts.** Revealed instruction (19:8; 119:4).

111:9 [p] Lk 1:68 [q] Ps 99:3; Lk 1:49
111:10 [r] Pr 9:10 [s] Ecc 12:13 [t] Ps 145:2
112:1 [u] Ps 128:1 [v] Ps 119:14,16,47,92
112:4 [w] Job 11:17 [x] Ps 97:11
112:5 [y] Ps 37:21,26
112:6 [z] Pr 10:7
112:7 [a] Ps 57:7; Pr 1:33
112:8 [b] Ps 59:10

9 He provided redemption[p] for his people;
he ordained his covenant forever —
holy and awesome[q] is his name.

10 The fear of the LORD is the beginning of wisdom;[r]
all who follow his precepts have good
understanding.[s]
To him belongs eternal praise.[t]

Psalm 112[a]

1 Praise the LORD.[b]

Blessed are those who fear the LORD,[u]
who find great delight[v] in his commands.

2 Their children will be mighty in the land;
the generation of the upright will be blessed.
3 Wealth and riches are in their houses,
and their righteousness endures forever.
4 Even in darkness light dawns[w] for the upright,
for those who are gracious and compassionate and
righteous.[x]
5 Good will come to those who are generous and lend
freely,[y]
who conduct their affairs with justice.

6 Surely the righteous will never be shaken;
they will be remembered[z] forever.
7 They will have no fear of bad news;
their hearts are steadfast,[a] trusting in the LORD.
8 Their hearts are secure, they will have no fear;
in the end they will look in triumph on their foes.[b]

[a] This psalm is an acrostic poem, the lines of which begin with the successive letters of the Hebrew alphabet.
[b] *1* Hebrew *Hallelu Yah*

111:9 redemption. As an act of God, it most often refers to the exodus (see Deut 9:26; 13:5; 15:15; 21:8; 24:18). **ordained his covenant forever.** The exodus is historical evidence that the Lord is a faithful covenant keeper (Deut 7:8).
111:10 fear of the LORD. Properly recognizing his nature and character (see note on 19:9). **beginning of wisdom.** See Job 28:28; Prov 1:7; 9:10. True wisdom is living in the light of the Lord's nature and character (cf. 112:1). **precepts.** See note on v. 7 **belongs eternal praise.** Because he is an eternal God (vv. 3,5,8–9).
Ps 112 *Blessed Are Those Who Fear the Lord.* Ps 112 mirrors Ps 111. Both are acrostic poems (see NIV text note; see also Introduction: The Psalms as Poetry [Acrostic Poems]). They are nearly identical in length and share vocabulary and themes. The main difference is that Ps 111 is about the Lord, and Ps 112 is about the one who fears the Lord. The one who fears the Lord in Ps 112 resembles the Lord's nature and character in Ps 111, echoing the close dynamic that exists between the Lord and his king-priest in Ps 110. Ps 112 begins with an invitation to praise the Lord (v. 1a). It describes the character of the one who fears the Lord (vv. 1b–5), emphasizing the eternality of their righteousness (v. 3b). Then it renews its focus on the righteous and their reward (vv. 6–9) and concludes by briefly describing the wicked (v. 10). This is one of the so-called wisdom psalms, in which the psalmists reflect on many of life's deep issues (see introduction to Ps 34).
112:1 Blessed. See note on 1:1. **fear the LORD.** See 111:10 and note. Demonstrates a close link between Ps 111 and Ps 112. **great delight in his commands.** See 111:2.
112:2 be blessed. God blesses the children of the "blessed" (v. 1; cf. Gen 12:1–3).
112:3 righteousness endures forever. This psalm's dominant theme (vv. 6,9). In 111:3, it is the righteousness of the Lord that endures forever; here it is the righteousness of those who fear the Lord. The godly reflect God's character (Lev 19:2; Eph 4:24; Heb 12:10; 1 John 3:2).
112:4 in darkness light dawns. The Lord provides light for his people, even in the darkest of places (97:11; Exod 13:21; 14:20). **gracious and compassionate.** See 111:4 and note. **righteous.** See note on v. 3.
112:5 justice. God is just, and those who fear him are just.
112:6 shaken. Removed from a position of security (15:5; 16:8). **remembered forever.** See 111:4–5. This is only for the righteous.
112:7–8 Those who fear the Lord (v. 1) will not fear what can happen on earth (cf. Matt 10:28; Luke 12:4–5).
112:7 steadfast. Not unsettled by fear (cf. 108:1). **trusting in the LORD.** The antidote to fear (Isa 12:2; 26:3). To fear the Lord is to trust the Lord.
112:8 look in triumph on their foes. Cf. 108:13; 110:1–2,5–7.

9 They have freely scattered their gifts to the poor,[c]
their righteousness endures forever;
their horn[a] will be lifted[d] high in honor.

10 The wicked will see[e] and be vexed,
they will gnash their teeth[f] and waste away;[g]
the longings of the wicked will come to nothing.[h]

Psalm 113

1 Praise the LORD.[b]

Praise the LORD, you his servants;[i]
praise the name of the LORD.
2 Let the name of the LORD be praised,
both now and forevermore.[j]
3 From the rising of the sun[k] to the place where it sets,
the name of the LORD is to be praised.

4 The LORD is exalted[l] over all the nations,
his glory above the heavens.[m]
5 Who is like the LORD our God,[n]
the One who sits enthroned[o] on high,
6 who stoops down to look[p]
on the heavens and the earth?

7 He raises the poor[q] from the dust
and lifts the needy[r] from the ash heap;
8 he seats them[s] with princes,
with the princes of his people.
9 He settles the childless[t] woman in her home
as a happy mother of children.

Praise the LORD.

112:9 [c] 2Co 9:9* [d] Ps 75:10
112:10 [e] Ps 86:17 [f] Ps 37:12 [g] Ps 58:7-8 [h] Pr 11:7
113:1 [i] Ps 135:1
113:2 [j] Da 2:20
113:3 [k] Isa 59:19; Mal 1:11
113:4 [l] Ps 99:2 [m] Ps 8:1; 97:9
113:5 [n] Ps 89:6 [o] Ps 103:19
113:6 [p] Ps 11:4; 138:6; Isa 57:15
113:7 [q] 1Sa 2:8 [r] Ps 107:41
113:8 [s] Job 36:7
113:9 [t] 1Sa 2:5; Ps 68:6; Isa 54:1

[a] *9* *Horn* here symbolizes dignity. [b] *1* Hebrew *Hallelu Yah*; also in verse 9

112:9 freely scattered their gifts to the poor. Those who fear the Lord are generous, and they can be so because the Lord provides for them (111:5; see note on 82:3–4). Paul quotes this when he encourages the Corinthians to give to the Judean poor (2 Cor 9:8–11) because God will bless them with all that they need and because it will manifest their righteousness as they "abound in every good work" (2 Cor 9:8).
112:10 wicked. Contrasts with the righteous (cf. 1:6). **gnash their teeth.** An act of despair (Matt 8:12; 13:42,50; 24:51; 25:30). Elsewhere in the OT, gnashing of teeth is an act of aggression or opposition (see 35:16 and note; 37:12; Job 16:9; Lam 2:16).
Pss 113–118 *Give Thanks to the Lord, for He Is Good; His Love Endures Forever.* Called the "Egyptian Hallel" because the command to praise (Hebrew *hll*) occurs throughout and because these psalms became a part of the Jewish Passover liturgy, celebrating their escape from Egypt. The hymn that Jesus and the disciples sang after the Lord's Supper (Matt 26:30) could have been one of these psalms.
Ps 113 *Who Is Like the Lord Our God?* This psalm highlights the Lord's character and nature, especially his ability to accomplish great reversals (see introduction to Ps 107). The psalm calls for praise (vv. 1–3) and gives reasons for praise: the Lord is both high above his creation (vv. 4–6) and near it (vv. 7–9). Like Ps 111, this emphasizes the Lord's deeds.
113:1 Praise … Praise … praise. Sets the psalm within a context of worship. Since the psalm focuses primarily on the Lord's nature and character (vv. 4–9), the call to praise at the beginning of the psalm (vv. 1–3) reveals that the knowledge of God (1) should inform praise, (2) should be sought in an attitude of worship, not simply out of intellectual curiosity, and (3) inspires praise.
113:2–3 God is to be praised at all times (v. 2) and in all places (v. 3).
113:2 now and forevermore. The Lord's praise should be never ending because his faithfulness is never ending (107:1; 111:5,9).
113:3 the rising of the sun to the place where it sets. A phrase used in ancient literature to denote universal dominion. In the Amarna Letter 288, 'Abdu-Heba, king of Jerusalem, writes to Pharaoh Akhenaten, describing him as having "set his name at the rising of the sun and at the setting of the sun!"
113:4–6 The Lord is transcendent, i.e., he is high above all of creation. He is separate and distinct from his creation because he is so much greater than it.
113:5 Who is like the LORD …? See note on 89:6.
113:7–9 The Lord is immanent, i.e., he is near to his creation. Although he is also transcendent (see note on vv. 4–6), he intervenes in creation to accomplish a great reversal in the life of the lowliest and most humble. This closely resembles Hannah's song in 1 Sam 2:5–8, in which she praises God for accomplishing a great reversal in her life by giving her a son.
113:7 poor … needy. See note on 82:3–4.

114:1 [u]Ex 13:3
114:3 [v]Ex 14:21; Ps 77:16 [w]Jos 3:16
114:7 [x]Ps 96:9
114:8 [y]Ex 17:6; Nu 20:11; Ps 107:35
115:1 [z]Ps 96:8; Isa 48:11; Eze 36:32
115:2 [a]Ps 42:3; 79:10
115:3 [b]Ps 103:19 [c]Ps 135:6; Da 4:35
115:4 [d]Dt 4:28; Jer 10:3-5

Psalm 114

1 When Israel came out of Egypt,[u]
Jacob from a people of foreign tongue,
2 Judah became God's sanctuary,
Israel his dominion.

3 The sea looked and fled,[v]
the Jordan turned back;[w]
4 the mountains leaped like rams,
the hills like lambs.

5 Why was it, sea, that you fled?
Why, Jordan, did you turn back?
6 Why, mountains, did you leap like rams,
you hills, like lambs?

7 Tremble, earth,[x] at the presence of the Lord,
at the presence of the God of Jacob,
8 who turned the rock into a pool,
the hard rock into springs of water.[y]

Psalm 115

115:4-11pp — Ps 135:15-20

1 Not to us, LORD, not to us
but to your name be the glory,[z]
because of your love and faithfulness.

2 Why do the nations say,
"Where is their God?"[a]
3 Our God is in heaven;[b]
he does whatever pleases him.[c]
4 But their idols are silver and gold,
made by human hands.[d]

Ps 114 *Tremble, Earth, at the Presence of the Lord.* Building on Ps 113, this psalm extols the Lord for his control over creation. The earth obeys his command: the sea, the Jordan River, the mountains, the hills, and the rocks (vv. 3–8). And the Lord does all this for his people, displaying his faithfulness (vv. 1–2).
114:1–2 God's dominion included his people, his treasured possession (Exod 19:5–6). In ancient Canaanite accounts, Baal builds his sanctuary after gaining victory over his enemies. Here the true God delivers his people and then his sanctuary is built to give praise to him.
114:3–6 Personification vividly portrays the earth's obedience to the Lord.
114:3 sea looked and fled. See Exod 14–15; depicts the sea as a defeated and frightened foe (see notes on 93:3; 107:23). **Jordan turned back.** See Josh 3 (especially vv. 15–17).
114:5–6 Restates vv. 3–4 with questions.
114:7 Tremble. Summons the earth as an awestruck worshiper (77:16; 96:9; 1 Chr 16:30). Throughout the psalm, the earth is personified as a model worshiper, obeying the bidding of the Lord.
114:8 hard rock into springs of water. The Lord provided water in the wilderness (Exod 17:6; Num 20:11).
Ps 115 *Not to Us But to Your Name Be the Glory.* Ps 115 elaborates on a theme that Ps 114 presents—the majesty of the Lord—by exposing the folly of idolatry in vv. 1–8. Then vv. 9–18 encourage the people to praise the only God worthy of their worship.
115:1–2 The Lord's faithfulness to his people is a testimony to the nations.
115:1 Connects the Lord's glory to his love, which is one of the dominant themes of Pss 107–118. **name.** See note on 23:3. **be the glory.** Receive all the honor. God's people find fulfillment when they live to make the Lord famous and bring honor to him. **love and faithfulness.** The Lord is made famous by his enduring faithfulness to his promises of love.
115:2 Where is their God? A taunt (cf. 42:3,10; 79:10). The nations mock Israel with this question when it experiences calamity (see Joel 2:17; Mic 7:10).
115:3 does whatever pleases him. When Israel experiences calamity (see note on v. 2), God is actively accomplishing his will. The calamity is not the result of God's absence or inactivity, nor can it be traced to the superiority of the idols. The true God is at work in all circumstances. Gentile nations confess this in Dan 4:35; Jonah 1:14.
115:4–8 A satirical polemic against the idolatry of the nations (see 135:15–18 and note; Isa 44:9–20). The psalmist has turned the tables and is asking essentially, "Where are your gods?" (see v. 2). This lampoons the idolatry of the nations for three primary reasons: (1) human hands made their idols (vv. 4,8) in the likeness of humans (vv. 5–7); (2) their idols do not even function like a human, let alone like a deity (vv. 5–7); and (3) the tragedy of idolatry is that those who participate in it begin to resemble their subhuman deities (v. 8).

[5] They have mouths, but cannot speak,[e]
eyes, but cannot see.
[6] They have ears, but cannot hear,
noses, but cannot smell.
[7] They have hands, but cannot feel,
feet, but cannot walk,
nor can they utter a sound with their throats.
[8] Those who make them will be like them,
and so will all who trust in them.

[9] All you Israelites, trust in the LORD—
he is their help and shield.
[10] House of Aaron,[f] trust in the LORD—
he is their help and shield.
[11] You who fear him, trust in the LORD—
he is their help and shield.

[12] The LORD remembers us and will bless us:
He will bless his people Israel,
he will bless the house of Aaron,
[13] he will bless those who fear[g] the LORD—
small and great alike.

[14] May the LORD cause you to flourish,[h]
both you and your children.
[15] May you be blessed by the LORD,
the Maker of heaven[i] and earth.

[16] The highest heavens belong to the LORD,[j]
but the earth he has given[k] to mankind.
[17] It is not the dead[l] who praise the LORD,
those who go down to the place of silence;
[18] it is we who extol the LORD,
both now and forevermore.[m]

Praise the LORD.[a]

Psalm 116

[1] I love the LORD,[n] for he heard my voice;
he heard my cry[o] for mercy.

[a] *18* Hebrew *Hallelu Yah*

115:5 [e] Jer 10:5
115:10 [f] Ps 118:3
115:13 [g] Ps 128:1,4
115:14 [h] Dt 1:11
115:15 [i] Ge 1:1; 14:19; Ps 96:5
115:16 [j] Ps 89:11 [k] Ps 8:6-8
115:17 [l] Ps 6:5; 88:10-12; Isa 38:18
115:18 [m] Ps 113:2; Da 2:20
116:1 [n] Ps 18:1 [o] Ps 66:19

115:9,10,11 Although the nations tragically trust their idols (v. 8), the people of God must "trust in the LORD."
115:11 fear him. Involves trusting God. **help and shield.** Symbolizes protection (28:7; 33:20; see note on 3:3).
115:12 remembers. A covenantal term when the Lord is the subject (Gen 9:15–16; Exod 6:5; Jer 14:21; Ezek 16:60): the Lord is already acting faithfully toward his covenant (see v. 1 and note). **bless.** Another covenantal term (Gen 12:1–3; Deut 28:1–14).
115:14–15 A priestly blessing (Deut 28:1–14; contrast Ps 109:13).
115:16 highest heavens. Where God dwells (v. 3). **given to mankind.** To rule over and subdue it (8:6–8; Gen 1:26–28).
115:17 silence. The dead cannot give glory to God in the presence of the nations (vv. 1–3) in this life because they exist in a place of silence (30:9; 88:10–12; 94:17).
115:18 now and forevermore. See 113:2 and note.

Ps 116 *Precious in the Sight of the Lord Is the Death of His Faithful Servants.* This psalm of praise celebrates deliverance from death (vv. 3,8). As the ultimate form of exile, death separates the worshiper from praising God among the congregation (115:17). In keeping with the theme of exile prominent in Pss 107–118, this psalm describes how the Lord has rescued the psalmist from the exile of death (see introduction to Ps 107). Ps 116 has two main sections (vv. 1–9,10–19). Each section closely mirrors the other, but vv. 1–9 focus on the nature and character of the Lord, whereas vv. 10–19 emphasize the response of the psalmist.
116:1–2 Encapsulates the drama of worship: the Lord acts, and his people respond in worship. The psalmist prays, and God delivers him, which inspires more prayer.
116:1 love the LORD. The proper response of a worshiper (31:23; Deut 6:5; 11:1).

116:2 [p] Ps 40:1
116:3 [q] Ps 18:4-5
116:4 [r] Ps 118:5
[s] Ps 22:20
116:5 [t] Ezr 9:15; Ne 9:8; Ps 103:8; 145:17
116:6 [u] Ps 19:7; 79:8
116:7 [v] Jer 6:16; Mt 11:29 [w] Ps 13:6
116:8 [x] Ps 56:13
116:9 [y] Ps 27:13
116:10 [z] 2Co 4:13*
116:11 [a] Ro 3:4
116:13 [b] Ps 16:5; 80:18
116:14 [c] Ps 22:25; Jnh 2:9
116:15 [d] Ps 72:14

2 Because he turned his ear[p] to me,
I will call on him as long as I live.

3 The cords of death[q] entangled me,
the anguish of the grave came over me;
I was overcome by distress and sorrow.
4 Then I called on the name[r] of the LORD:
"LORD, save me![s]"

5 The LORD is gracious and righteous;[t]
our God is full of compassion.
6 The LORD protects the unwary;
when I was brought low,[u] he saved me.

7 Return to your rest,[v] my soul,
for the LORD has been good[w] to you.

8 For you, LORD, have delivered me[x] from death,
my eyes from tears,
my feet from stumbling,
9 that I may walk before the LORD
in the land of the living.[y]

10 I trusted[z] in the LORD when I said,
"I am greatly afflicted";
11 in my alarm I said,
"Everyone is a liar."[a]

12 What shall I return to the LORD
for all his goodness to me?

13 I will lift up the cup of salvation
and call on the name[b] of the LORD.
14 I will fulfill my vows[c] to the LORD
in the presence of all his people.

15 Precious in the sight[d] of the LORD
is the death of his faithful servants.

116:3 cords of death entangled me. As if the psalmist is being pulled into the realm of the dead (cf. 18:4–5). Jonah prayed similarly in the belly of the great fish (Jonah 2:5). **anguish of the grave.** See 18:5; see also note on 6:5.
116:4 Paul also teaches that those who call out to the Lord will be saved (Rom 10:13; cf. Ps 18:3; Joel 2:32).
116:5 These expressions of the Lord's character are reflected in those who fear him (see notes on 86:5,15; 111:4; see also 112:4; Exod 34:6). This statement of the Lord's character in Exod 34:6 appears in the context of the golden calf debacle (Exod 32–34), when the Lord threatens to abandon the covenant with the Israelites because they broke it; Exod 34:6 affirms that the Lord is a faithful God. Here the Lord's character affirms that he is faithful toward even the most vulnerable members of the community (v. 6).
116:6 unwary. A description of someone with childlike trust in the Lord (19:7; cf. Matt 18:3–4).
116:7 rest. A place of blessing. Rest for the land was a sign of God's blessing his people (e.g., Judg 3:11,30; 5:31; 8:28). God denied rest to his people in his anger when they rebelled in the wilderness (95:11). Salvation is a Sabbath-rest that the people of God must enter (Heb 4:1–11; cf. Rev 14:13). See also note on 62:1.
116:8 The psalmist is delivered from: (1) **death.** See Isa 25:8; John 3:16,36. (2) **tears.** See Isa 25:8; Rev 7:17; 21:4. (3) **stumbling.** A way of referring to death (see 56:13).
116:9 walk before the LORD. Because the psalmist has been saved from death (56:13).
116:10 Paul quotes this from the Septuagint (the pre-Christian Greek translation of the OT) in 2 Cor 4:13. The basic premise is the same in the Hebrew OT, Greek OT, and Greek NT: faith is what compels the believer to speak *to* the Lord and *about* the Lord.
116:11 Everyone is a liar. Therefore, we must trust the Lord. Paul alludes to this verse in Rom 3:4 to highlight the Lord's faithfulness.
116:12 Reveals a heart of worship (see note on vv. 1–2).
116:13–14 The first answer to the question in v. 12. The second answer comes in vv. 17–19.
116:13 cup of salvation. Symbolizes God's blessing (16:5; 23:5). A drink offering often accompanied other offerings and sacrifices that celebrated the Lord's deliverance (Num 15:1–12). The "cup of salvation" may be a reference to a drink offering accompanying a thanksgiving offering (Lev 7:11–21). **call on the name of the LORD.** Appears three other times in the psalm in this exact form (vv. 4 ["called"],13,17) and once in a different form (v. 2).
116:14 vows. An agreement between a worshiper and God that the worshiper typically initiates in a time of crisis (Gen 28:20–22; Num 30:1–15; Deut 23:21–23; 1 Sam 1:11; Acts 18:18; 21:23–24).
116:15 As part of the Egyptian Hallel (see introduction to Pss 113–118), which was a part of the Passover liturgy, this verse takes on added

[16] Truly I am your servant, LORD;[e]
I serve you just as my mother did;[f]
you have freed me from my chains.

[17] I will sacrifice a thank offering[g] to you
and call on the name of the LORD.
[18] I will fulfill my vows to the LORD
in the presence of all his people,
[19] in the courts[h] of the house of the LORD—
in your midst, Jerusalem.

Praise the LORD.[a]

Psalm 117

[1] Praise the LORD, all you nations;[i]
extol him, all you peoples.
[2] For great is his love toward us,
and the faithfulness of the LORD[j] endures forever.

Praise the LORD.[a]

Psalm 118

[1] Give thanks to the LORD,[k] for he is good;
his love endures forever.[l]

[2] Let Israel say:[m]
"His love endures forever."
[3] Let the house of Aaron say:
"His love endures forever."
[4] Let those who fear the LORD say:
"His love endures forever."

[a] *19,2* Hebrew *Hallelu Yah*

116:16 [e] Ps 119:125; 143:12 [f] Ps 86:16
116:17 [g] Lev 7:12; Ps 50:14
116:19 [h] Ps 96:8; 135:2
117:1 [i] Ro 15:11*
117:2 [j] Ps 100:5
118:1 [k] 1Ch 16:8 [l] Ps 106:1; 136:1
118:2 [m] Ps 115:9

Canaanite king on Megiddo ivory celebrating victory and his own success with a cup raised to his lips. "I will lift up the cup of salvation" (Ps 116:13).

Kim Walton, taken at the Israel Museum, Jerusalem

significance when read in the context of the Last Supper and Jesus' impending death (Matt 26:30; Mark 14:26). **Precious.** Costly or weighty; thus, not a light matter (see also 72:14; Isa 43:4). **death.** See introduction to Ps 116. **faithful servants.** Related to the Hebrew word translated "love" and "unfailing love" throughout Pss 107–118 (see 107:1 and note). The Lord is faithful to his faithful ones (2 Sam 22:26), who reciprocate the Lord's love.

116:16 as my mother did. See note on 86:16.

116:17–18 Repeats vv. 13–14 almost verbatim (see note there).

116:18 in the presence of all his people. Public praise. The people of God worship together, sharing each other's joys and sorrows (see 111:1 and note; Rom 12:15; 1 Cor 12:26).

116:19 courts ... house. See note on 5:7. **Jerusalem.** See note on 9:11.

Ps 117 *For Great Is His Love Toward Us.* This psalm captures the essence of praise in miniature—it is the shortest psalm in the Psalter and the shortest chapter in the Bible. The psalm opens with a call for the nations to praise the Lord (v. 1) and then gives the reason for praise: the Lord's great love and eternal faithfulness toward his people (v. 2). Ps 67 develops more fully this same motif of God's concern for all peoples and nations (see introduction to Ps 67).

117:1 The Lord is more than a parochial or tribal deity; he is Lord of all the earth (114:3–8; 115:15–16). Consequently, all nations must praise him. Psalms pictures a great contest between the rebellious nations and their Creator (see 2:1–6 and notes). The nations submit to their Creator by praising him (see 2:10–12; 108:3 and note). The NT attests that the nations have submitted to God because they praise the Son (see 2:10–12). Paul quotes this verse in Rom 15:11 to show that the salvation of the nations (Gentiles) has always been God's plan. Thus, they should be welcomed into the worshiping family of God.

117:2 love. The Lord's faithful covenant love (see notes on 6:4; 107:1). **endures forever.** Never wears out (see note on 107:1).

Ps 118 *Give Thanks to the Lord, for He Is Good; His Love Endures Forever.* The psalm begins and ends by affirming God's goodness and everlasting love (vv. 1,29), the dominant theme of Pss 107–118. The enduring nature of the Lord's love dominates vv. 1–4, and vv. 5–18 celebrate the Lord as deliverer. Finally, vv. 19–29 depict the worshiper entering the temple precincts as an individual (vv. 19–21) and then joining with the festive throng (vv. 23–27; see 42:4). Like Ps 117, this psalm picks up on many of the themes that appear in this section of Book V (Pss 107–118).

118:1 Repeats 107:1 verbatim (see note there).

118:2–4 Israel ... house of Aaron ... those who fear the LORD. The people of God: Jews, priests, and Gentile converts (115:9–11).

118:2,3,4 love. See notes on 6:4; 107:1. **endures forever.** Never ends (see note on 107:1). This calls the people of God to celebrate that the Lord's faithfulness to his loving covenant promises will never end. This includes all of his covenant promises, most specifically his covenant promises to David (see introduction to Pss 107–150).

118:5 [n] Ps 120:1 [o] Ps 18:19
118:6 [p] Heb 13:6* [q] Ps 27:1; 56:4
118:7 [r] Ps 54:4 [s] Ps 59:10
118:8 [t] Ps 40:4 [u] Jer 17:5
118:9 [v] Ps 146:3
118:10 [w] Ps 18:40
118:11 [x] Ps 88:17 [y] Ps 3:6
118:12 [z] Dt 1:44 [a] Ps 58:9
118:13 [b] Ps 86:17; 140:4
118:14 [c] Ex 15:2 [d] Isa 12:2
118:15 [e] Ps 68:3 [f] Ps 89:13
118:17 [g] Ps 6:5; Hab 1:12 [h] Ex 15:6; Ps 73:28
118:18 [i] 2Co 6:9
118:19 [j] Isa 26:2
118:20 [k] Ps 24:7; Isa 35:8; Rev 22:14

5 When hard pressed,[n] I cried to the LORD;
he brought me into a spacious place.[o]
6 The LORD is with me;[p] I will not be afraid.
What can mere mortals do to me?[q]
7 The LORD is with me; he is my helper.[r]
I look in triumph on my enemies.[s]

8 It is better to take refuge in the LORD[t]
than to trust in humans.[u]
9 It is better to take refuge in the LORD
than to trust in princes.[v]
10 All the nations surrounded me,
but in the name of the LORD I cut them down.[w]
11 They surrounded me[x] on every side,[y]
but in the name of the LORD I cut them down.
12 They swarmed around me like bees,[z]
but they were consumed as quickly as burning thorns;[a]
in the name of the LORD I cut them down.
13 I was pushed back and about to fall,
but the LORD helped me.[b]
14 The LORD is my strength[c] and my defense[a];
he has become my salvation.[d]

15 Shouts of joy[e] and victory
resound in the tents of the righteous:
"The LORD's right hand[f] has done mighty things!
16 The LORD's right hand is lifted high;
the LORD's right hand has done mighty things!"
17 I will not die[g] but live,
and will proclaim[h] what the LORD has done.
18 The LORD has chastened me severely,
but he has not given me over to death.[i]
19 Open for me the gates[j] of the righteous;
I will enter and give thanks to the LORD.
20 This is the gate of the LORD
through which the righteous may enter.[k]

[a] 14 Or *song*

118:5 spacious place. Salvation (see 18:19; 31:8 and note; 2 Sam 22:20).
118:6 The Lord's presence casts out fear (Deut 20:3–4; 31:6). Heb 13:6 quotes this to encourage God's people to be content with their economic position, especially believers who experience economic pressure because of their faith.
118:7 triumph on my enemies. A recurring theme in Pss 107–118 (see 108:7–13; 109:28–29; 110:1–3,5–7; 114:1–2 and note; 115:2–8).
118:8–9 Only the Lord can provide true security (see 2:12 and note; 3:3–6; 4:8; 5:11; 7:1; 9:9; 11:1; 14:6; 16:1,5; 17:7; 18:1–2 and note; 144:2). **trust ... trust.** Cf. 115:8–11.
118:10–12 The drama of the Psalter unfolds in the theater of the nations (see 2:1–6 and notes; 67:2–7; 108:3; 117:1 and note). **surrounded me ... surrounded me ... swarmed around me.** Connote siege, pressure, and distress.
118:10,11,12 in the name of the LORD I cut them down. The Lord delivers from seemingly insurmountable obstacles.
118:13 In the battle against the nations (vv. 10–12), the psalmist is on the verge of death (vv. 17–18), but the Lord delivers him (see 116:8 and note).
118:14 A common confession of praise (Exod 15:2; Isa 12:2).
118:15–16 The scene in the battle camp after the victory.
118:16 right hand. A source of power that guarantees victory (see note on 20:6).
118:17 I will not die. See v. 13 and note. Death is a common theme in Pss 115–118 (115:17; 116:3,8,15) because the ability to proclaim what the Lord has done is at stake (see 115:17 and note).
118:18 chastened me severely. Difficulties are not evidence that the Lord has abandoned his people (vv. 5,10–12; 107) but evidence that he is disciplining them (Prov 3:11–12; Heb 12:5–11).
118:19–20 Recalls the images of a processional entering into Jerusalem in Ps 24 (see introduction to Ps 24).
118:19 Open for me. Suggests that the psalmist is leading a procession into the temple (vv. 26–27). **gates.** Entering into the temple precincts. **of the righteous.** Not the name of an actual gate in Jerusalem; symbolizes how the righteous may enter into fellowship with God (v. 20; see Isa 26:2).

[21] I will give you thanks, for you answered me;[l]
you have become my salvation.

[22] The stone the builders rejected
has become the cornerstone;[m]
[23] the LORD has done this,
and it is marvelous in our eyes.
[24] The LORD has done it this very day;
let us rejoice today and be glad.

[25] LORD, save us!
LORD, grant us success!
[26] Blessed is he who comes[n] in the name of the LORD.
From the house of the LORD we bless you.[a]
[27] The LORD is God,
and he has made his light shine[o] on us.
With boughs in hand, join in the festal procession
up[b] to the horns of the altar.
[28] You are my God, and I will praise you;
you are my God,[p] and I will exalt[q] you.
[29] Give thanks to the LORD, for he is good;
his love endures forever.

118:21 [l] Ps 116:1
118:22 [m] Mt 21:42; Mk 12:10; Lk 20:17*; Ac 4:11*; 1Pe 2:7*
118:26 [n] Mt 21:9*; Mk 11:9*; Lk 13:35*; 19:38*; Jn 12:13*
118:27 [o] 1Pe 2:9
118:28 [p] Isa 25:1 [q] Ex 15:2
119:1 [r] Ps 128:1

Horned altar (facsimile) from Beersheba. Ps 118:27 mentions "the horns of the altar."

Psalm 119[c]

א Aleph

[1] Blessed are those whose ways are blameless,
who walk[r] according to the law of the LORD.

[a] *26* The Hebrew is plural. [b] *27* Or *Bind the festal sacrifice with ropes / and take it* [c] This psalm is an acrostic poem, the stanzas of which begin with successive letters of the Hebrew alphabet; moreover, the verses of each stanza begin with the same letter of the Hebrew alphabet.

118:22 cornerstone. The first stone set in a building project. It is the most important stone because it determines the direction of the walls (length and width) and establishes plumb for the walls (height). The concept became a rich theological metaphor in the OT and NT. In the OT (including here) it symbolizes the Lord's replacing arrogant, selfish leaders with his appointed leader, who would be the starting point of a new work of God (Isa 28:14–17; Zech 10:3–5): the Lord uses the stone that the builders rejected to begin a new work. Paul interprets the new work to be a new temple (Eph 2:19–22; cf. 1 Pet 2:4–8), which is quite plausible considering that the temple is so prominent in Ps 118 (vv. 19–20,26–27). Jesus' parable of the tenants depicts how the Lord is beginning a new work by entrusting his kingdom to new "tenants" (Matt 21:42–43). The builders are the Jewish leaders, and the cornerstone is Jesus (Acts 4:11).
118:24 has done it. Refers to the work of establishing "the stone the builders rejected ... the cornerstone" (v. 22). **this very day.** The specific time when the work of v. 22 is accomplished, possibly celebrated at one of the festivals.
118:25 save us! The word "Hosanna" transliterates this Hebrew command (Matt 21:9–15; Mark 11:9–10; John 12:13). This depicts laying the cornerstone as an act of salvation.
118:26 Blessed is he who comes in the name of the LORD. Because the Lord is the cornerstone (v. 22) who saves (v. 25). The crowds shouted these words during Jesus' Triumphal Entry ("Lord" in NT: Matt 21:9; Mark 11:9; Luke 19:38; John 12:13).
118:27 made his light shine on us. The cornerstone God sent to save his people fulfills the Aaronic blessing (Num 6:24–26). **boughs in hand.** To celebrate the Lord's salvation and provision (Lev 23:40; Matt 21:8; John 12:13; Rev 7:9–10).
118:28 You are my God. The chief covenantal confession ("I will be their/your God" in Gen 17:8; Exod 6:7; 29:45–46; Lev 26:12; Rev 21:7; "that he may be your God" in Deut 29:13).
118:29 Concludes Ps 118 and also the first part of Book V (Pss 107–118) in the way that they both begin (107:1; 118:1), thus highlighting its importance as an overarching theme in this section.
Ps 119 *Oh, How I Love Your Law! I Meditate on It All Day Long.* The Lord's instruction permeates Ps 119. Almost every verse of this massive psalm—the longest chapter in the Bible—mentions it or one of its synonyms. The uniform theme has dismayed some, leading them to think that the psalm is too long and repetitive. A better way to think about it, however, is that the uniformity sharpens the focus on the psalm's theme: the word of the Lord. Line after line provides a slightly different perspective on this rich and multifaceted topic. As one admires a diamond from every angle in order to truly appreciate its beauty, Ps 119 sets the word of the Lord before the reader and rotates it by degrees so that we can truly appreciate its beauty.

Ps 119 is an acrostic poem (see Introduction: The Psalms as Poetry [Acrostic Psalms]). It is a complex acrostic poem because it devotes eight lines to each letter, so each letter forms its own stanza (see NIV text note). It is also one of the so-called wisdom psalms, in which the psalmists reflect on many of life's deep issues (see introduction to Ps 34).

119:2 [s]Dt 6:5
119:3 [t]1Jn 3:9; 5:18
119:9 [u]2Ch 6:16
119:10 [v]2Ch 15:15 [w]ver 21,118
119:11 [x]Ps 37:31; Lk 2:19,51
119:12 [y]ver 26
119:13 [z]Ps 40:9

2 Blessed are those who keep his statutes
and seek him with all their heart —[s]
3 they do no wrong[t]
but follow his ways.
4 You have laid down precepts
that are to be fully obeyed.
5 Oh, that my ways were steadfast
in obeying your decrees!
6 Then I would not be put to shame
when I consider all your commands.
7 I will praise you with an upright heart
as I learn your righteous laws.
8 I will obey your decrees;
do not utterly forsake me.

ב Beth

9 How can a young person stay on the path
of purity?
By living according to your word.[u]
10 I seek you with all my heart;[v]
do not let me stray from your commands.[w]
11 I have hidden your word in my heart[x]
that I might not sin against you.
12 Praise be to you, LORD;
teach me your decrees.[y]
13 With my lips I recount
all the laws that come from your mouth.[z]
14 I rejoice in following your statutes
as one rejoices in great riches.

Terms for the word of the Lord in Psalm 119

Ps 119 uses ten different Hebrew terms for the word of the Lord. Each of these synonyms refers to God's word in its own way, emphasizing different aspects of that word.

1. "Law" (Hebrew *tôrâ*) occurs first (v. 1) and most often (25 times). It refers to the instruction the Lord reveals to his people (1:2; 19:7; Deut 4:8,44; Josh 1:8; Matt 5:17–20), not just the specific laws found in that instruction.

2. "Laws" (Hebrew *mišpāṭ*) highlights what the legal authority deems to be right (v. 7; Lev 19:15 ["justice"]; Mic 6:8 ["justly"]).

3. "Statutes" (Hebrew *ʿēdût*), occurring first in v. 2, is related to the Hebrew word "to give testimony," highlighting that the word of the Lord is his testimony about himself and his world. The same word describes the tablets Moses brought down from the mountain (Exod 31:18; 32:15; 34:29).

4. "Ways" (Hebrew *derek*) emphasizes that the word of the Lord reveals the "way" to live (v. 1; Isa 2:3; 58:2).

5. "Precepts" (Hebrew *piqqûd*) outlines what we should do (v. 4; 19:8; 103:18; 111:7).

6. "Decrees" (Hebrew *ḥōq*) are what the King announces (v. 5; Exod 12:24 ["ordinance"]; 15:25 ["ruling"]; 18:16).

7. "Word" (Hebrew *dābār*) is what the Lord has spoken (v. 9; Isa 2:3; Hag 1:1).

8. "Promise" (Hebrew *ʾimrâ*) emphasizes how the word of the Lord is often communicated through speech (v. 38; Gen 4:23 ["words"]; Deut 33:9 ["word"]).

9. "Commands" (Hebrew *miṣwâ*) are what the chief lawgiver has stipulated (v. 6; Deut 6:1; Dan 9:4b ["commandments"]).

10. "Faithfulness" (Hebrew *ʾemûnâ*) highlights how the Lord's promises have been written down and thus act as a witness to his faithfulness (v. 75; Deut 32:4 ["faithful"]; Isa 25:1).

Ps 119 by itself is an entire section of Book V. And with its unmistakable emphasis on the word of the Lord, and especially on the study of that word, it recollects the ideal (royal) figure of Ps 1, a devoted student of God's word (see 1:2 and note). There are also many similarities between Ps 119 and Deut 17:14–20, which commands the king to copy and study the word of the Lord. Thus, it is best to see the "I" of Ps 119 as a royal figure who is a committed student of God's word. So Ps 119 contributes to Book V's unfolding narrative by presenting a picture of the ideal king; this is what any godly king (and those under him) should aspire to be, and it points ahead to what the greatest of them, the Messiah, will look like when he arrives.

119:1 Blessed. The same opening word as the Psalter (see 1:1 and note). The word of the Lord is the path to blessing.

119:2 seek him with all their heart. An act of worship that incorporates one's entire being (v. 10; Deut 4:29).

119:7 praise you with an upright heart. Pure worship — one of the goals of Ps 119 (vv. 9,11,29,34,145,174–175).

119:9 The word of the Lord can direct those who have little to no life experience.

119:11 Carefully studying and memorizing the Lord's instruction are ways to battle sin.

119:12 teach me. See vv. 26,29,33,64,66,68,108,124,135,171; see also note on 27:11.

[15] I meditate on your precepts[a]
and consider your ways.
[16] I delight[b] in your decrees;
I will not neglect your word.

ג Gimel

[17] Be good to your servant[c] while I live,
that I may obey your word.
[18] Open my eyes that I may see
wonderful things in your law.
[19] I am a stranger on earth;[d]
do not hide your commands from me.
[20] My soul is consumed[e] with longing
for your laws[f] at all times.
[21] You rebuke the arrogant, who are accursed,
those who stray[g] from your commands.
[22] Remove from me their scorn[h] and contempt,
for I keep your statutes.
[23] Though rulers sit together and slander me,
your servant will meditate on your decrees.
[24] Your statutes are my delight;
they are my counselors.

ד Daleth

[25] I am laid low in the dust;[i]
preserve my life[j] according to your word.
[26] I gave an account of my ways and you answered me;
teach me your decrees.[k]
[27] Cause me to understand the way of your precepts,
that I may meditate on your wonderful deeds.[l]
[28] My soul is weary with sorrow;[m]
strengthen me[n] according to your word.
[29] Keep me from deceitful ways;
be gracious to me and teach me your law.
[30] I have chosen the way of faithfulness;
I have set my heart on your laws.
[31] I hold fast[o] to your statutes, LORD;
do not let me be put to shame.
[32] I run in the path of your commands,
for you have broadened my understanding.

ה He

[33] Teach me,[p] LORD, the way of your decrees,
that I may follow it to the end.[a]
[34] Give me understanding, so that I may keep your law
and obey it with all my heart.

119:15 [a] Ps 1:2
119:16 [b] Ps 1:2
119:17 [c] Ps 13:6; 116:7
119:19 [d] 1Ch 29:15; Ps 39:12; 2Co 5:6; Heb 11:13
119:20 [e] Ps 42:2; 84:2 [f] Ps 63:1
119:21 [g] ver 10
119:22 [h] Ps 39:8
119:25 [i] Ps 44:25 [j] Ps 143:11
119:26 [k] Ps 25:4; 27:11; 86:11
119:27 [l] Ps 145:5
119:28 [m] Ps 107:26 [n] Ps 20:2; 1Pe 5:10
119:31 [o] Dt 11:22
119:33 [p] ver 12

[a] 33 Or *follow it for its reward*

119:18 Open. Without the Lord's intervention, we will miss the wonderful treasures in the word.
119:19 stranger. Temporary resident (see note on 39:12).
119:25 The word of the Lord produces life (vv. 37,40; 33:6,9; Ezek 37:4–5; John 1:1,14; 10:10).
119:27 meditate. Remember or ponder (77:12; 143:5). This verb appears six times in Ps 119 (vv. 15,23,27,48,78,148). See note on 1:2.

119:36 [q] 1Ki 8:58 [r] Eze 33:31; Mk 7:21-22; Lk 12:15; Heb 13:5
119:37 [s] Ps 71:20; Isa 33:15
119:38 [t] 2Sa 7:25
119:40 [u] ver 20
119:42 [v] Pr 27:11
119:46 [w] Mt 10:18; Ac 26:1-2
119:50 [x] Ro 15:4
119:51 [y] Jer 20:7 [z] ver 157; Job 23:11; Ps 44:18
119:52 [a] Ps 103:18
119:53 [b] Ezr 9:3 [c] Ps 89:30

35 Direct me in the path of your commands,
for there I find delight.
36 Turn my heart[q] toward your statutes
and not toward selfish gain.[r]
37 Turn my eyes away from worthless things;
preserve my life[s] according to your word.[a]
38 Fulfill your promise[t] to your servant,
so that you may be feared.
39 Take away the disgrace I dread,
for your laws are good.
40 How I long[u] for your precepts!
In your righteousness preserve my life.

ו Waw

41 May your unfailing love come to me, LORD,
your salvation, according to your promise;
42 then I can answer[v] anyone who taunts me,
for I trust in your word.
43 Never take your word of truth from my mouth,
for I have put my hope in your laws.
44 I will always obey your law,
for ever and ever.
45 I will walk about in freedom,
for I have sought out your precepts.
46 I will speak of your statutes before kings[w]
and will not be put to shame,
47 for I delight in your commands
because I love them.
48 I reach out for your commands, which I love,
that I may meditate on your decrees.

ז Zayin

49 Remember your word to your servant,
for you have given me hope.
50 My comfort in my suffering is this:
Your promise preserves my life.[x]
51 The arrogant mock me[y] unmercifully,
but I do not turn[z] from your law.
52 I remember,[a] LORD, your ancient laws,
and I find comfort in them.
53 Indignation grips me[b] because of the wicked,
who have forsaken your law.[c]

[a] *37* Two manuscripts of the Masoretic Text and Dead Sea Scrolls; most manuscripts of the Masoretic Text *life in your way*

119:35 delight. Joy derived from what is valuable (see 1:2 and note)—the proper response to the word of the Lord.
119:36 Turn my heart. God must bend one's heart toward obedience and away from disobedience. Salvation is a work that affects the heart, transforming it and redirecting it (Jer 31:33; Ezek 11:19–20; 36:26–27; Heb 8:10).
119:41 unfailing love. The Lord's covenant love (see note on 6:4). This has been a prominent theme so far in Book V (see 107:1; 118:29 and notes) and will continue to be in Ps 119 (vv. 64,76,88,124,149,159).
119:44 More than an exuberant but unrealistic vow, this prefigures the ultimate, ideal King (the Messiah), who will be a perfect covenant keeper (2 Cor 5:21; Heb 4:15; 1 Pet 2:22; 1 John 3:5).
119:50 The word of the Lord provides comfort because it preserves life, even in the most challenging of circumstances.
119:53 Indignation grips me. The Lord's instruction shapes emotions and, at times, elicits a godly anger (vv. 113,115,139,158; 69:9; John 2:13–17).

54 Your decrees are the theme of my song
wherever I lodge.
55 In the night, LORD, I remember[d] your name,
that I may keep your law.
56 This has been my practice:
I obey your precepts.

ח Heth

57 You are my portion,[e] LORD;
I have promised to obey your words.
58 I have sought your face with all my heart;
be gracious to me[f] according to your promise.[g]
59 I have considered my ways[h]
and have turned my steps to your statutes.
60 I will hasten and not delay
to obey your commands.
61 Though the wicked bind me with ropes,
I will not forget[i] your law.
62 At midnight[j] I rise to give you thanks
for your righteous laws.
63 I am a friend to all who fear you,[k]
to all who follow your precepts.
64 The earth is filled with your love,[l] LORD;
teach me your decrees.

ט Teth

65 Do good to your servant
according to your word, LORD.
66 Teach me knowledge and good judgment,
for I trust your commands.
67 Before I was afflicted I went astray,[m]
but now I obey your word.
68 You are good,[n] and what you do is good;
teach me your decrees.[o]
69 Though the arrogant have smeared me with lies,[p]
I keep your precepts with all my heart.
70 Their hearts are callous[q] and unfeeling,
but I delight in your law.
71 It was good for me to be afflicted
so that I might learn your decrees.
72 The law from your mouth is more precious to me
than thousands of pieces of silver and gold.[r]

י Yodh

73 Your hands made me[s] and formed me;
give me understanding to learn your commands.

119:55 [d] Ps 63:6
119:57 [e] Ps 16:5; La 3:24
119:58 [f] 1Ki 13:6 [g] ver 41
119:59 [h] Lk 15:17-18
119:61 [i] Ps 140:5
119:62 [j] Ac 16:25
119:63 [k] Ps 101:6-7
119:64 [l] Ps 33:5
119:67 [m] Jer 31:18-19; Heb 12:11
119:68 [n] Ps 106:1; 107:1; Mt 19:17 [o] ver 12
119:69 [p] Job 13:4; Ps 109:2
119:70 [q] Ps 17:10; Isa 6:10; Ac 28:27
119:72 [r] Ps 19:10; Pr 8:10-11,19
119:73 [s] Job 10:8; Ps 100:3; 138:8; 139:13-16

119:60 True obedience does not look for more opportune circumstances to obey. The best time to obey is right now.
119:62 midnight. The psalmist praises the Lord throughout the day and night (vv. 55,147–148,164; 108:2).
119:66 There is a close connection between knowledge and trusting the Lord (Prov 1:7; 9:10; John 8:31–32).
119:71 For a believer, suffering is redemptive (Gen 50:20; Rom 8:28; Heb 12:5–11; Jas 1:2–4; 1 Pet 1:6–7). It is a sign of the Lord's faithfulness (v. 75).

119:74 [t]Ps 34:2
119:75 [u]Heb 12:5-11
119:77 [v]ver 41
119:78 [w]Jer 50:32 [x]ver 86,161
119:81 [y]Ps 84:2
119:82 [z]Ps 69:3; La 2:11
119:84 [a]Ps 39:4; Rev 6:10
119:85 [b]Ps 35:7; Jer 18:20,22
119:86 [c]Ps 35:19 [d]Ps 109:26 [e]ver 78
119:87 [f]Isa 58:2
119:89 [g]Mt 24:34-35; 1Pe 1:25
119:90 [h]Ps 36:5 [i]Ps 148:6; Ecc 1:4
119:91 [j]Jer 33:25

74 May those who fear you rejoice[t] when they see me,
for I have put my hope in your word.
75 I know, LORD, that your laws are righteous,
and that in faithfulness[u] you have afflicted me.
76 May your unfailing love be my comfort,
according to your promise to your servant.
77 Let your compassion[v] come to me that I may live,
for your law is my delight.
78 May the arrogant[w] be put to shame for wronging me
without cause;[x]
but I will meditate on your precepts.
79 May those who fear you turn to me,
those who understand your statutes.
80 May I wholeheartedly follow your decrees,
that I may not be put to shame.

כ Kaph

81 My soul faints[y] with longing for your salvation,
but I have put my hope in your word.
82 My eyes fail,[z] looking for your promise;
I say, "When will you comfort me?"
83 Though I am like a wineskin in the smoke,
I do not forget your decrees.
84 How long[a] must your servant wait?
When will you punish my persecutors?
85 The arrogant dig pits[b] to trap me,
contrary to your law.
86 All your commands are trustworthy;[c]
help me,[d] for I am being persecuted without
cause.[e]
87 They almost wiped me from the earth,
but I have not forsaken[f] your precepts.
88 In your unfailing love preserve my life,
that I may obey the statutes of your mouth.

ל Lamedh

89 Your word, LORD, is eternal;[g]
it stands firm in the heavens.
90 Your faithfulness[h] continues through all generations;
you established the earth, and it endures.[i]
91 Your laws endure[j] to this day,
for all things serve you.
92 If your law had not been my delight,
I would have perished in my affliction.
93 I will never forget your precepts,
for by them you have preserved my life.

119:74 A prayer that the Lord's instruction would so influence the psalmist's life that it would encourage the godly.
119:79 A prayer that the psalmist would lead God's people. One's authority to lead derives from the word, not from charisma.
119:83 like a wineskin in the smoke. Describes someone who has been cut off from what they were made for and whose inward life is shriveling up. A wineskin is made for moisture; the smoke dries it out and shrivels it (Josh 9:4,13; Job 32:19; Matt 9:17).
119:84 The first question is a rhetorical question of lament (e.g., 6:3; 13:1–2; 79:5; 89:46; Rev 6:10).
119:89 Your word, LORD, is eternal. Book V emphasizes that which lasts (107:1; 110:4; 111:3,5,8–10; 112:3,6,9; 113:2; 117:2; 118:1,29).

[94]Save me, for I am yours;
I have sought out your precepts.
[95]The wicked are waiting to destroy me,
but I will ponder your statutes.
[96]To all perfection I see a limit,
but your commands are boundless.

מ Mem

[97]Oh, how I love your law!
I meditate[k] on it all day long.
[98]Your commands are always with me
and make me wiser[l] than my enemies.
[99]I have more insight than all my teachers,
for I meditate on your statutes.
[100]I have more understanding than the elders,
for I obey your precepts.[m]
[101]I have kept my feet[n] from every evil path
so that I might obey your word.
[102]I have not departed from your laws,
for you yourself have taught me.
[103]How sweet are your words to my taste,
sweeter than honey[o] to my mouth![p]
[104]I gain understanding from your precepts;
therefore I hate every wrong path.[q]

נ Nun

[105]Your word is a lamp for my feet,
a light[r] on my path.
[106]I have taken an oath[s] and confirmed it,
that I will follow your righteous laws.
[107]I have suffered much;
preserve my life, LORD, according to your word.
[108]Accept, LORD, the willing praise of my mouth,[t]
and teach me your laws.
[109]Though I constantly take my life in my hands,[u]
I will not forget your law.
[110]The wicked have set a snare[v] for me,
but I have not strayed[w] from your precepts.
[111]Your statutes are my heritage forever;
they are the joy of my heart.
[112]My heart is set on keeping your decrees
to the very end.[a][x]

119:97 [k] Ps 1:2
119:98 [l] Dt 4:6
119:100 [m] Job 32:7-9
119:101 [n] Pr 1:15
119:103 [o] Ps 19:10; Pr 8:11 [p] Pr 24:13-14
119:104 [q] ver 128
119:105 [r] Pr 6:23
119:106 [s] Ne 10:29
119:108 [t] Hos 14:2; Heb 13:15
119:109 [u] Jdg 12:3; Job 13:14
119:110 [v] Ps 140:5; 141:9 [w] ver 10
119:112 [x] ver 33

[a] *112* Or *decrees / for their enduring reward*

119:96 God's instruction exceeds the limits of perfection.
119:97 The psalmist is drawn to the word of the Lord; there is no coercion or compulsion in it.
119:99–100 more insight than all my teachers ... more understanding than the elders. God's word grants knowledge that cannot simply be acquired by schooling or by life experience. Students of God's word should not expect to outsmart their teachers in all cases. In context, those teachers and elders who oppose the righteous psalmist are in view (v. 98).
119:103 The word of the Lord is more than simple spiritual nourishment, such as a feeding tube would provide. It is a treat that provides enjoyment as well as nourishment (19:10).
119:105 lamp ... light. The word of the Lord is like the pillar of fire that led the Israelites in the desert at night and protected them from the Egyptians (see Exod 13:21; 14:24); it is a source of security in a dark place, and it guides the believer's steps.
119:111 The word of the Lord is a secure storehouse of joy because it is eternal (v. 89).

119:113 [y] Jas 1:8
119:114 [z] Ps 32:7; 91:1 [a] ver 74
119:115 [b] Ps 6:8; 139:19; Mt 7:23
119:116 [c] Ps 54:4 [d] Ps 25:2; Ro 5:5; 9:33
119:119 [e] Eze 22:18,19
119:120 [f] Hab 3:16
119:122 [g] Job 17:3
119:123 [h] ver 82
119:124 [i] ver 12
119:125 [j] Ps 116:16
119:127 [k] Ps 19:10
119:128 [l] ver 104,163
119:130 [m] Pr 6:23 [n] Ps 19:7
119:131 [o] Ps 42:1 [p] ver 20

ס Samekh

113 I hate double-minded people,[y]
but I love your law.
114 You are my refuge and my shield;[z]
I have put my hope[a] in your word.
115 Away from me,[b] you evildoers,
that I may keep the commands of my God!
116 Sustain me,[c] my God, according to your promise,
and I will live;
do not let my hopes be dashed.[d]
117 Uphold me, and I will be delivered;
I will always have regard for your decrees.
118 You reject all who stray from your decrees,
for their delusions come to nothing.
119 All the wicked of the earth you discard like dross;[e]
therefore I love your statutes.
120 My flesh trembles[f] in fear of you;
I stand in awe of your laws.

ע Ayin

121 I have done what is righteous and just;
do not leave me to my oppressors.
122 Ensure your servant's well-being;[g]
do not let the arrogant oppress me.
123 My eyes fail, looking for your salvation,
looking for your righteous promise.[h]
124 Deal with your servant according to your love
and teach me your decrees.[i]
125 I am your servant;[j] give me discernment
that I may understand your statutes.
126 It is time for you to act, LORD;
your law is being broken.
127 Because I love your commands
more than gold,[k] more than pure gold,
128 and because I consider all your precepts right,
I hate every wrong path.[l]

פ Pe

129 Your statutes are wonderful;
therefore I obey them.
130 The unfolding of your words gives light;[m]
it gives understanding to the simple.[n]
131 I open my mouth and pant,[o]
longing for your commands.[p]

119:118 delusions. Or misconceptions about the truth (Jer 8:5; 14:14; 23:26). The word of the Lord is truth (vv. 142,160,172; John 17:17).
119:120 My flesh trembles in fear of you. Job 4:15 uses a similar phrase ("the hair on my body stood on end") and the same Hebrew verb (translated "stood on end"). The "fear" of the Lord is more than simply respect; it includes an element of holy fright at the Lord's grandeur (see note on 19:9).
119:126 The psalmist desires that the Lord vindicate his name. God's apparent passivity in the face of injustice could be interpreted as meaning (1) there is no God or (2) God is not concerned about justice. The Lord's actions prove that he is a just God.
119:127 more than gold, more than pure gold. The value of the Lord's word is great—more precious than money (19:10).
119:131 pant. The way a woman in labor breathes (Isa 42:14); sometimes it is a metaphor for strong desire (Ps 42:1; Job 5:5; 7:2).

132 Turn to me and have mercy[q] on me,
as you always do to those who love your name.
133 Direct my footsteps according to your word;[r]
let no sin rule[s] over me.
134 Redeem me from human oppression,[t]
that I may obey your precepts.
135 Make your face shine[u] on your servant
and teach me your decrees.
136 Streams of tears[v] flow from my eyes,
for your law is not obeyed.[w]

צ Tsadhe

137 You are righteous,[x] LORD,
and your laws are right.[y]
138 The statutes you have laid down are righteous;[z]
they are fully trustworthy.
139 My zeal wears me out,[a]
for my enemies ignore your words.
140 Your promises have been thoroughly tested,[b]
and your servant loves them.
141 Though I am lowly and despised,[c]
I do not forget your precepts.
142 Your righteousness is everlasting
and your law is true.[d]
143 Trouble and distress have come upon me,
but your commands give me delight.
144 Your statutes are always righteous;
give me understanding[e] that I may live.

ק Qoph

145 I call with all my heart; answer me, LORD,
and I will obey your decrees.
146 I call out to you; save me
and I will keep your statutes.
147 I rise before dawn[f] and cry for help;
I have put my hope in your word.
148 My eyes stay open through the watches of the
night,[g]
that I may meditate on your promises.
149 Hear my voice in accordance with your love;
preserve my life, LORD, according to your laws.
150 Those who devise wicked schemes are near,
but they are far from your law.
151 Yet you are near,[h] LORD,
and all your commands are true.[i]
152 Long ago I learned from your statutes
that you established them to last forever.[j]

119:132 [q] Ps 25:16; 106:4
119:133 [r] Ps 17:5 [s] Ps 19:13; Ro 6:12
119:134 [t] Ps 142:6; Lk 1:74
119:135 [u] Nu 6:25; Ps 4:6
119:136 [v] Jer 9:1,18 [w] Eze 9:4
119:137 [x] Ezr 9:15; Jer 12:1 [y] Ne 9:13
119:138 [z] Ps 19:7
119:139 [a] Ps 69:9; Jn 2:17
119:140 [b] Ps 12:6
119:141 [c] Ps 22:6
119:142 [d] Ps 19:7
119:144 [e] Ps 19:9
119:147 [f] Ps 5:3; 57:8; 108:2
119:148 [g] Ps 63:6
119:151 [h] Ps 34:18; 145:18 [i] ver 142
119:152 [j] Lk 21:33

119:136 Jesus pronounces a blessing on those who mourn (Matt 5:4).
119:140 Faith is not irrational; it is built on the proven faithfulness of the Lord. **tested.** See note on 66:10.
119:144 that I may live. The psalmist's life is dependent on the word of the Lord (vv. 25,37,40,50,77,93,107; Deut 8:3; Matt 4:4).
119:150–151 The Lord walks with his people in the midst of suffering and oppression (Deut 31:6; Matt 28:20).

119:153 [k]La 5:1 [l]Pr 3:1
119:154 [m]Mic 7:9 [n]1Sa 24:15
119:155 [o]Job 5:4
119:156 [p]2Sa 24:14
119:157 [q]Ps 7:1
119:158 [r]Ps 139:21
119:161 [s]1Sa 24:11
119:162 [t]1Sa 30:16
119:165 [u]Pr 3:2; Isa 26:3,12; 32:17
119:166 [v]Ge 49:18
119:168 [w]Pr 5:21
119:169 [x]Ps 18:6
119:170 [y]Ps 28:2 [z]Ps 31:2
119:171 [a]Ps 51:15 [b]Ps 94:12

ר Resh

153 Look on my suffering[k] and deliver me,
for I have not forgotten[l] your law.
154 Defend my cause[m] and redeem me;[n]
preserve my life according to your promise.
155 Salvation is far from the wicked,
for they do not seek out[o] your decrees.
156 Your compassion, LORD, is great;
preserve my life[p] according to your laws.
157 Many are the foes who persecute me,[q]
but I have not turned from your statutes.
158 I look on the faithless with loathing,[r]
for they do not obey your word.
159 See how I love your precepts;
preserve my life, LORD, in accordance with
your love.
160 All your words are true;
all your righteous laws are eternal.

ש Sin and Shin

161 Rulers persecute me[s] without cause,
but my heart trembles at your word.
162 I rejoice in your promise
like one who finds great spoil.[t]
163 I hate and detest falsehood
but I love your law.
164 Seven times a day I praise you
for your righteous laws.
165 Great peace[u] have those who love your law,
and nothing can make them stumble.
166 I wait for your salvation,[v] LORD,
and I follow your commands.
167 I obey your statutes,
for I love them greatly.
168 I obey your precepts and your statutes,
for all my ways are known[w] to you.

ת Taw

169 May my cry come[x] before you, LORD;
give me understanding according to
your word.
170 May my supplication come[y] before you;
deliver me[z] according to your promise.
171 May my lips overflow with praise,[a]
for you teach me[b] your decrees.

119:155 Salvation is far from the wicked. Not because the Lord is unable to reach them, but because of their own rebellious choice (Matt 9:12–13; John 9:39–41).

119:160 all your righteous laws are eternal. See Matt 5:17–20.

119:162 See Matt 13:44–46: when one finds a treasure, they must sell everything in order to gain it.

119:165 Great peace. A settled wellness of the whole person (37:11).

119:171–172 lips overflow with praise ... tongue sing of your word. God's word is both the source and object of praise. True worship flows from God's word.

[172]May my tongue sing of your word,
for all your commands are righteous.
[173]May your hand be ready to help[c] me,
for I have chosen[d] your precepts.
[174]I long for your salvation,[e] LORD,
and your law gives me delight.
[175]Let me live[f] that I may praise you,
and may your laws sustain me.
[176]I have strayed like a lost sheep.[g]
Seek your servant,
for I have not forgotten your commands.

119:173 [c]Ps 37:24 [d]Jos 24:22
119:174 [e]ver 166
119:175 [f]Isa 55:3
119:176 [g]Isa 53:6
120:1 [h]Ps 102:2; Jnh 2:2
120:2 [i]Pr 12:22 [j]Ps 52:4
120:4 [k]Ps 45:5
120:5 [l]Ge 25:13; Jer 49:28

Psalm 120

A song of ascents.

[1]I call on the LORD in my distress,[h]
and he answers me.
[2]Save me, LORD,
from lying lips[i]
and from deceitful tongues.[j]
[3]What will he do to you,
and what more besides,
you deceitful tongue?
[4]He will punish you with a warrior's sharp arrows,[k]
with burning coals of the broom bush.
[5]Woe to me that I dwell in Meshek,
that I live among the tents of Kedar![l]
[6]Too long have I lived
among those who hate peace.
[7]I am for peace;
but when I speak, they are for war.

119:176 strayed like a lost sheep. The psalmist is lost, so the Lord needs to seek his servant. The Bible pictures the Lord as a shepherd (23:1) who seeks out his lost sheep (Luke 15:4–5; see John 10:11–18). The way the Lord will rescue his lost sheep is by transferring their iniquity to his suffering servant (Isa 53:6).

Ps 120 *Woe to Me That I Dwell in Meshek.* Ps 120 depicts a believer who is exiled from their home. Verses 1–2 begin with a prayer for deliverance from those who attack with their words; vv. 3–4 describe the judgment for those who act in such a manner; and vv. 5–7 conclude with a lament that the psalmist is in a foreign land, cut off from the place of the Lord's blessing. When read in the context of the other psalms in this section (120–137), that place of the Lord's blessing is Zion, the "capital" of the kingdom of God (see 132; 134).

120 title A song of ascents. Pss 120–134 are commonly called the "songs of ascents." The title denotes songs that pilgrims sang on their way *up* to Jerusalem for one of the major festivals (84:5–7; Exod 23:14–17; Deut 16:16; Mic 4:2; see Zech 14:16 and note). According to the OT spatial perspective, Jerusalem is always "up," regardless of the actual elevation of the starting point (2 Sam 6:12; Jer 31:6; Mic 4:2). One cannot discern a geographic progression in the songs (i.e., following a certain path or moving through the city along a certain route); rather, the songs focus on the pilgrimage's destination: Zion/Jerusalem.

120:2 lying lips ... deceitful tongues. The most common weapon in Psalms is the tongue, and the most common form of attack is verbal (5:9; 10:7; 12:2–4; 55:21; 57:4; 59:7; 109:2–3). The tongue is the source of great evil (Jas 3:5–12). Bearing false witness against someone in the ancient world was especially sinister because there were few means of vindicating one's claims and reputation, such as with a contract or other written documentation. Consequently, the Bible addresses this topic frequently (Exod 20:16; 23:1–3; Lev 19:16; Deut 19:16–18; 22:13–19; Prov 6:16–19; 12:17–19; 25:18).

120:3 what more besides. Pronounces a curse that highlights the certainty of judgment, usually translated "be it ever so severely" (Ruth 1:17; 1 Sam 3:17; 14:44; 20:13; 25:22; 2 Sam 3:9,35; 1 Kgs 2:23; 2 Kgs 6:31).

120:4 broom bush. The wood of this desert shrub created quality charcoal, which made hot and lasting fires. It was a convenient source of fuel in the desert. Elijah slept under a broom bush in the desert and ate a meal likely prepared over the coals from a broom bush (1 Kgs 19:4–6).

120:5 Meshek. In Asia Minor (modern-day Turkey; see Gen 10:2; Ezek 27:13). **Kedar.** In Arabia (Song 1:5; Isa 21:16–17). The psalmist cannot be in both places at the same time, so poetically mentioning these faraway places in opposite directions refers to the sense of alienation from God's worshiping people, centered in Zion.

120:6–7 peace ... peace. Hebrew *šālôm*, a part of the word "Jerusalem" in Hebrew; thus, this may be a veiled way of referring to the city (122:6–9). The prophets see Jerusalem as the home of peace (Isa 2:2–4; Mic 4:1–3). When exiled from the city of God, the psalmist is cut off from "peace" but eventually wants to find "peace."

121:2 [m]Ps 115:15; 124:8
121:5 [n]Isa 25:4
121:6 [o]Ps 91:5; Isa 49:10; Rev 7:16
121:7 [p]Ps 41:2; 91:10-12
121:8 [q]Dt 28:6

Psalm 121

A song of ascents.

[1] I lift up my eyes to the mountains —
where does my help come from?
[2] My help comes from the LORD,
the Maker of heaven and earth.[m]

[3] He will not let your foot slip —
he who watches over you will not slumber;
[4] indeed, he who watches over Israel
will neither slumber nor sleep.

[5] The LORD watches over[n] you —
the LORD is your shade at your right hand;
[6] the sun[o] will not harm you by day,
nor the moon by night.

[7] The LORD will keep you from all harm[p] —
he will watch over your life;
[8] the LORD will watch over your coming and going
both now and forevermore.[q]

Psalm 122

A song of ascents. Of David.

[1] I rejoiced with those who said to me,
"Let us go to the house of the LORD."

Ps 121 *I Lift Up My Eyes to the Mountains.* As the people of God made their pilgrimage to Zion to celebrate the festivals (see note on Ps 120 title), this psalm would remind them that the Lord was with them every step of the way. Regardless of the challenges they faced on the journey, the Lord would be their helper. There are four scenarios of danger that the psalmist asks the Lord to resolve: (1) General danger introduces the main theme of the psalm: the Lord provides help (vv. 1 – 2). (2) The pilgrim's foot could slip on the journey, but the Lord watches over his people (vv. 3 – 4). (3) The elements are unpredictable, symbolized by the sun and moon, but the Lord counteracts them (vv. 5 – 6). (4) Travelers were susceptible to robbers and bandits on their journeys because the roads and trails were unevenly policed, but the Lord provides cover from the evil people who might seek to do harm (vv. 7 – 8).

121 title See note on Ps 120 title.

121:1 mountains. Some think this refers to the "mountains" around Jerusalem (125:2) or else Mount Zion itself (48:2; 68:15 – 16; 133:3; Isa 2:2 – 4). In this case, the mountains symbolize God's protecting presence (125:2), and v. 2 affirms this; just as Daniel prayed toward Jerusalem and asked God for help (Dan 6:10 – 11), so the psalmist looks to the Lord's chosen dwelling place for help.

121:2 My help comes from the LORD. The mountains, in and of themselves, are not the source of salvation (see v. 1 and note); salvation comes from the Lord, who dwells on the most important mountain: Zion (48:2; 68:16). **Maker of heaven and earth.** The Lord is more than a tribal deity who exists on only one mountain in the midst of his people. He is the Lord of all the earth (Deut 10:14; 1 Kgs 8:27; Neh 9:6), the one who has made all things (115:15; 124:8; 134:3; Gen 1:1).

121:3 foot slip. Ruts, rocks, and roots threatened a traveler's journey in an era before paved roads and walkways. Injuries could occur simply by falling to the ground or by damaging the foot or ankle, but what is most likely in view here is the danger of slipping and then falling down a steep slope. It came to symbolize falling into danger or chaos (38:16; 66:9; 94:18).

121:4 The reason the traveler's foot will not slip is that the Lord is watching over his people. The Lord's care for his people extends to the most minute details, even where they step (Matt 6:25 – 34). **neither slumber nor sleep.** He is ever vigilant in keeping watch (cf. 1 Kgs 18:27).

121:5 shade at your right hand. A metaphor for protection (91:1; Isa 49:2; 51:16).

121:6 sun ... moon. Represent the heavenly bodies and thus all the elements of the heavens: heat, cold, rain, snow, lightning, and wind. Because the "shade" of v. 5 acts as a shelter (91:1), the Lord is a refuge for his people. Scorching heat is a plague and a curse (Rev 7:16; 16:9).

121:7 harm. Or "evil," typically the product of personal intent (140:1 – 2; 141:4; Job 1:1,8; 2:3; Prov 1:16; 3:7; 6:14). Thus, the Lord will protect the pilgrim from the evil intent of the wicked (10:8 – 11; Gen 19:5,9; Judg 19:1 – 30; Prov 1:10 – 19).

121:8 coming and going. The entire journey. The Hebrew phrase often occurs in military contexts (e.g., 1 Sam 29:6; 2 Sam 3:25) and can refer to the duties of a leader (Deut 31:2; 1 Kgs 3:7), including leading the army. This promises that God will protect his people not merely during life's mundane routine but also when evildoers actively seek to take the pilgrim's life (see v. 7 and note).

Ps 122 *Let Us Go to the House of the Lord.* This psalm celebrates arriving in Jerusalem and highlights the importance of the city for worshipers. Three sections divide the psalm, each with a reference to "house" (vv. 1,5,9) — Jerusalem is the home of the Lord and David, his anointed servant. Worshipers rejoice that they are in Jerusalem on their way to the house of the Lord (vv. 1 – 2). Jerusalem is important for worship and for the house of David (vv. 3 – 5). The psalmist exhorts others to seek the peace of Jerusalem (vv. 6 – 9).

[2]Our feet are standing
in your gates, Jerusalem.

[3]Jerusalem is built like a city
that is closely compacted together.
[4]That is where the tribes go up—
the tribes of the LORD—
to praise the name of the LORD
according to the statute given to Israel.
[5]There stand the thrones for judgment,
the thrones of the house of David.

[6]Pray for the peace of Jerusalem:
"May those who love[r] you be secure.
[7]May there be peace within your walls
and security within your citadels."
[8]For the sake of my family and friends,
I will say, "Peace be within you."
[9]For the sake of the house of the LORD our God,
I will seek your prosperity.[s]

Psalm 123

A song of ascents.

[1]I lift up my eyes to you,
to you who sit enthroned[t] in heaven.
[2]As the eyes of slaves look to the hand of their master,
as the eyes of a female slave look to the hand of her mistress,
so our eyes look to the LORD[u] our God,
till he shows us his mercy.

[3]Have mercy on us, LORD, have mercy on us,
for we have endured no end of contempt.

122:6 [r]Ps 51:18
122:9 [s]Ne 2:10
123:1 [t]Ps 11:4; 121:1; 141:8
123:2 [u]Ps 25:15

122 title See note on Ps 120 title. **Of David.** David's name appears in four of the superscriptions for the songs of ascents (Pss 122; 124; 131; 133), and he figures prominently in Ps 132, even though his name does not appear in the superscription. His reappearance in these psalms that focus on Zion is fitting because David and his anointed heir are closely connected to Zion (see 2:6 and note; 110:2; 132:13–18; 2 Sam 5:6–10). On the "psalms of Zion," see introduction to Ps 46.
122:1–2 Encapsulates the entire pilgrimage process from start to finish.
122:4 go up. Pilgrims always "ascend" to Jerusalem because it is "above" every other location (see note on Ps 120 title; see also Isa 2:2; Mic 4:1). **according to the statute.** Three major festivals drew pilgrims to Jerusalem: the Festival of Unleavened Bread (includes Passover), the Festival of Harvest (Weeks or Pentecost), and the Festival of Ingathering (Booths or Tabernacles) (Exod 23:14–19; Deut 16:1–17); see "The Lord's Appointed Festivals," p. 229.
122:5 thrones of the house of David. Jerusalem is not simply the home of the Lord; the house of David is there also. There is a close relationship between the Lord's presence in Jerusalem/Zion and the installation of his anointed leader there (2:6; 48:1,8; 68:16; 84:1–5; 110:2; 132:13–18; see also "The City of God," p. 2666). The reign of the Lord and the reign of his anointed do not compete against one another; rather, they are complementary.
122:6–7 peace … Jerusalem … secure … security. These words sound alike in Hebrew (see 120:6–7 and note). Jerusalem is the peaceful and secure city (Isa 2:2–4; Mic 4:1–3).
122:8–9 The prayer for peace in v. 6 has two beneficiaries: (1) "my family and friends" and (2) "the house of the LORD." The people of God thrive when the center of God's kingdom is secure, because they can fully participate in the worship the Lord stipulated.
Ps 123 *Our Eyes Look to the Lord Our God.* This psalm pleads for deliverance from contempt and ridicule. The people of God, whom the psalmist represents in v. 1, confess that they are looking to the Lord to show mercy to them (vv. 1–2). Specifically, they are appealing for mercy because they experience contempt and ridicule from the arrogant and proud (vv. 3–4). In the context of the songs of ascents (Pss 120–134), the contempt and ridicule may be due to the piety of God's people, manifest in their strong desire to worship in Jerusalem (122:1). Their journey to worship in the holy city was beset by detractors.
123 title See note on Ps 120 title.
123:1 I lift up my eyes to you. Nearly identical wording with 121:1, only "you" replaces "the mountains"; expresses hopeful longing (25:15; 121:1; 141:8). **sit enthroned in heaven.** Highlights the Lord's majesty. He exists above the fray of daily life (2:4).
123:2 slaves. God's people recognize their state of dependence on the Lord: they are like slaves, or servants, a common designation for a believer (Gen 18:3; 32:10; Exod 32:13; Judg 15:18; 1 Kgs 14:18; Luke 1:38; Rom 1:1).
123:3 mercy. "Unmerited favor"; this is a plea for grace. The Lord is not in the psalmist's debt, so he is not obligated to answer favorably.

124:1 [v] Ps 129:1
124:7 [w] Ps 91:3; Pr 6:5
124:8 [x] Ge 1:1; Ps 121:2; 134:3
125:1 [y] Ps 46:5

4 We have endured no end
of ridicule from the arrogant,
of contempt from the proud.

Psalm 124

A song of ascents. Of David.

1 If the LORD had not been on our side—
let Israel say[v]—
2 if the LORD had not been on our side
when people attacked us,
3 they would have swallowed us alive
when their anger flared against us;
4 the flood would have engulfed us,
the torrent would have swept over us,
5 the raging waters
would have swept us away.
6 Praise be to the LORD,
who has not let us be torn by their teeth.
7 We have escaped like a bird
from the fowler's snare;[w]
the snare has been broken,
and we have escaped.
8 Our help is in the name of the LORD,
the Maker of heaven[x] and earth.

Psalm 125

A song of ascents.

1 Those who trust in the LORD are like Mount Zion,
which cannot be shaken[y] but endures forever.

123:4 The psalmist asks God to deliver his people from ridicule and contempt. **arrogant.** Complacent, "at ease," thus not spiritually vigilant (Isa 32:9,11,18 ["undisturbed"]; Amos 6:1).

Ps 124 *Our Help Is in the Name of the Lord.* This psalm celebrates the Lord's delivering his people from an enemy that could have destroyed them. It corresponds well with the previous psalm because it recounts the deliverance Ps 123 seeks. Verses 1–5 relate the possible outcomes if the Lord had not defended his people, and vv. 6–8 extol the Lord's work in delivering them.

124 title See note on Ps 120 title. **Of David.** See note on Ps 122 title.

124:1 on our side. For us, working for our advantage (see also v. 2). **let Israel say.** David expects a communal response. It is good for the people of God to testify together (see 107:32 and note).

124:3 swallowed us alive. See 106:17; Num 16:30–33; 26:10; Deut 11:6. The enemy in this psalm threatens to extinguish in an instant the people of God.

124:4–5 flood ... torrent ... raging waters. Water can be an unruly force of devastation (see notes on 93:3; 107:23). **engulfed us ... swept over us ... swept us away.** How a dangerous flash flood progressively overtakes an unsuspecting victim.

124:6 torn by their teeth. Compares the enemy to a wild animal. Israel viewed being ravaged by a wild animal as a curse (Deut 32:23–24; 2 Kgs 17:25; Ezek 5:17; 14:15; 33:27).

124:7 fowler's snare. A common metaphor for distress (91:3; 119:110; 140:5; 141:9; 142:3; see Amos 3:5).

Fowler's snare (Ps 124:7).
Kim Walton, taken at the Art Institute of Chicago

124:8 Ultimately, salvation and deliverance come from the Lord (3:8; 62:1; 2 Sam 23:12). **Maker of heaven and earth.** See 121:2 and note.

Ps 125 *Those Who Trust in the Lord Are Like Mount Zion.* This psalm compares the faithful to Mount Zion. Just as other mountains surround the holy mount, so the Lord protects the faithful (vv. 1–2). Evil lurks on the fringes (v. 3), but the Lord will banish the wicked from the land so that the influence of the righteous will eventually hold sway (vv. 4–5).

125 title See note on Ps 120 title.

125:1 Those who trust. See 112:7; 115:9,10,11 and notes. **Mount Zion.** The "capital" of the kingdom of God (see 2:6; 9:11 and notes;

[2]As the mountains surround Jerusalem,
so the LORD surrounds[z] his people
both now and forevermore.

[3]The scepter of the wicked will not remain[a]
over the land allotted to the righteous,
for then the righteous might use
their hands to do evil.[b]

[4]LORD, do good[c] to those who are good,
to those who are upright in heart.[d]
[5]But those who turn[e] to crooked ways[f]
the LORD will banish with the evildoers.

Peace be on Israel.[g]

Psalm 126

A song of ascents.

[1]When the LORD restored[h] the fortunes of[a] Zion,
we were like those who dreamed.[b]
[2]Our mouths were filled with laughter,
our tongues with songs of joy.[i]
Then it was said among the nations,
"The LORD has done great things[j] for them."
[3]The LORD has done great things for us,
and we are filled with joy.[k]

[4]Restore our fortunes,[c] LORD,
like streams in the Negev.[l]

125:2 [z]Ps 121:8; Zec 2:4-5
125:3 [a]Ps 89:22; Pr 22:8; Isa 14:5 [b]1Sa 24:10; Ps 55:20
125:4 [c]Ps 119:68 [d]Ps 7:10; 36:10; 94:15
125:5 [e]Job 23:11 [f]Pr 2:15; Isa 59:8 [g]Ps 120:6
126:1 [h]Ps 85:1; Hos 6:11
126:2 [i]Job 8:21; Ps 51:14 [j]Ps 71:19
126:3 [k]Isa 25:9
126:4 [l]Isa 35:6; 43:19

[a] *1* Or *LORD brought back the captives to* [b] *1* Or *those restored to health* [c] *4* Or *Bring back our captives*

see also "The City of God," p. 2666). **cannot be shaken.** Zion's security is sure because it is so closely connected to the kingdom of God (46:4–5; 48:2–5). For Zion to fall would mean that God's kingdom and purposes have failed. It is important to note, however, that this promise was not a guarantee that Jerusalem and the temple would never experience calamity (126:1; Jer 7:1—8:3, especially 7:4). It relates more to Zion's standing as the "capital" of the kingdom of God than to the physical location of Zion in the kingdom of Israel/ Judah.

125:2 As the mountains surround Jerusalem. As a protective barrier against threats from outside, so the Lord encircles his people to protect them from the evil that presses against them (v. 3). **now and forevermore.** The promise does not have an expiration date (see 113:2 and note).

125:3 scepter. Symbolizes royal power and authority (see note on 45:6). **wicked will not remain.** The influence of evil that wicked rulers model will not always press against God's people. The Lord removes the old, wicked leaders of his people and replaces them with a new "cornerstone" (see 118:22 and note). Jesus, as that "cornerstone," is leading his people in righteousness until he banishes the influence of evil from creation (Rev 20:14–15; 21:1,27; 22:3).

125:4–5 The comparison of the righteous and the wicked recalls 1:6. God will finally vindicate the upright in the judgment.

125:5 Peace. A common theme of the songs of ascents (see 120:6–7 and note; 122:6–8; 128:6). When God's kingdom is fully established, there will be true and lasting peace (Isa 2:2–4; Mic 4:1–3) that the Prince of Peace administers (Isa 9:6–7; 32:1–20, especially vv. 17–18). See "Shalom," p. 2693.

Ps 126 *The Lord Restored the Fortunes of Zion.* Ps 126 relates how Zion is the central place for the Lord's praise and the centerpiece of his plan. The restored fortunes of Zion (vv. 1–3) act as a foil for the current, lamentable state of the people (vv. 4–6). If the Lord can restore Zion after a period of decline, he can do the same among God's people. This psalm highlights the importance of remembering the past deeds of the Lord; they can encourage God's people along the same line of reasoning as this psalm: if the Lord was able to do it in the past, he can do it again.

126 title See note on Ps 120 title.

126:1 restored the fortunes of Zion. See NIV text note, which would provide a specific context for the calamity the people experienced. But in other instances, the phrase relates a general restoration of fortune (14:7; 85:1; Job 42:10), not a specific release from exile.

126:2–3 There were two effects of the restoration: (1) the people were filled with joy, and (2) the testimony of the restoration reached the nations. The Lord's dealings with his people in the presence of the nations is a common theme in Scripture (see 96:10; 115:2 and note; 117:1 and note; Deut 29:24–28; Josh 4:24; Ezek 36:23).

126:4 Restore our fortunes. Nearly identical language as that found in v. 1, only here it is in a prayer. **Negev.** The arid region in the south of the country. Dry stream beds, caused by periods of drought, would become flowing streams again after a substantial rain shower. The psalmist desires to be like the streambed: dry for a season but restored to its original purpose after the Lord's intervention.

126:5 [m] Isa 35:10
127:1 [n] Ps 78:69
[o] Ps 121:4
127:2 [p] Ge 3:17
[q] Job 11:18
127:3 [r] Ge 33:5
127:5 [s] Pr 27:11
128:1 [t] Ps 112:1
[u] Ps 119:1-3

5 Those who sow with tears
will reap with songs of joy.[m]
6 Those who go out weeping,
carrying seed to sow,
will return with songs of joy,
carrying sheaves with them.

Psalm 127

A song of ascents. Of Solomon.

1 Unless the LORD builds[n] the house,
the builders labor in vain.
Unless the LORD watches[o] over the city,
the guards stand watch in vain.
2 In vain you rise early
and stay up late,
toiling for food[p] to eat—
for he grants sleep[q] to[a] those he loves.

3 Children are a heritage from the LORD,
offspring a reward[r] from him.
4 Like arrows in the hands of a warrior
are children born in one's youth.
5 Blessed is the man
whose quiver is full of them.
They will not be put to shame
when they contend with their opponents[s] in court.

Psalm 128

A song of ascents.

1 Blessed are all who fear the LORD,[t]
who walk in obedience to him.[u]

[a] 2 Or *eat— / for while they sleep he provides for*

126:5 sow ... reap. An agricultural metaphor describing a great reversal (see introduction to Ps 107). The Lord's character grounds this reversal; he has accomplished these kinds of restorations before (v. 1).
126:6 weeping. God responds to the tears of his people (2 Kgs 20:5; Rev 7:17; 21:4). **carrying seed to sow.** God's people must still sow seeds for the harvest in a world of tribulation and sorrow (Matt 13:1–23). Ultimately, the Lord will cause his people to return with songs of joy, carrying sheaves with them because God is "the Lord of the harvest" (Matt 9:38; cf. 1 Cor 3:5–9).
Ps 127 *Unless the Lord Builds the House, the Builders Labor in Vain.* Ps 127 touches upon the mysterious interaction between God's sovereignty and human responsibility, focusing on the home and family. It reminds pilgrims that the security of both is dependent on the Lord. Although there is an obvious, and assumed, part that humanity plays in building a house, guarding a city, and having children, the emphasis here lies with the Lord's role in all three. Pss 127 and 128 are closely related: both speak of ways the Lord blesses (127:5; 128:1–2,4–5), and this blessing is found in Zion (128:5). Thus, pilgrims on their way to Zion would be heading in the right direction for blessing on family life. The psalm has two parts: any kind of labor without the Lord's help is in vain (vv. 1–2), and children are a blessing (vv. 3–5).
127 title See note on Ps 120 title. **Of Solomon.** The only other psalm ascribed to Solomon is Ps 72 (see note on Ps 72 title).
127:1 house. Both a physical dwelling place and a family: the psalm begins by referring to physical labor (guarding a city and toiling for food, vv. 1–2), which certainly includes building a physical dwelling place, but then in vv. 3–5 the focus shifts to children, that is, building a family. This same interplay between images exists in 2 Sam 7:1–17, where in response to David's desire to build the Lord a house, i.e., a temple (2 Sam 7:4–7), the Lord promises to build David a house, i.e., a family heritage or dynasty (2 Sam 7:11b). See photo, p. 351.
127:2 toiling for food to eat. Quotes almost verbatim the curse against the man in Gen 3:17.
127:3 Children are a blessing from the Lord (113:9; Gen 1:26–28; Deut 7:14; 28:2–4; Prov 17:6).
127:5 quiver. A container for arrows (Gen 27:3; Lam 3:13). **not be put to shame.** Many children are a blessing from God (v. 3), and in court, they provide multiple character witnesses. **in court.** Or "in the gate." The city gate was the place where judgments were rendered and punishment was sometimes meted out (Deut 17:5; 21:19; 22:15,24; 25:7; Ruth 4:1; Isa 29:21 ["court"]; Amos 5:12 ["courts"]).
Ps 128 *The Lord Bless You From Zion.* This psalm continues the theme of blessing that concludes Ps 127. After an introduction (v. 1), it speaks

[2]You will eat the fruit of your labor;[v]
blessings and prosperity[w] will be yours.
[3]Your wife will be like a fruitful vine[x]
within your house;
your children will be like olive shoots[y]
around your table.
[4]Yes, this will be the blessing
for the man who fears the LORD.

[5]May the LORD bless you from Zion;[z]
may you see the prosperity of Jerusalem
all the days of your life.
[6]May you live to see your children's children —[a]
peace be on Israel.[b]

128:2 [v]Isa 3:10 [w]Ecc 8:12
128:3 [x]Eze 19:10 [y]Ps 52:8; 144:12
128:5 [z]Ps 20:2; 134:3
128:6 [a]Ge 50:23; Job 42:16 [b]Ps 125:5
129:1 [c]Ps 88:15; Hos 2:15 [d]Ps 124:1
129:2 [e]Mt 16:18
129:4 [f]Ps 119:137
129:5 [g]Mic 4:11 [h]Ps 71:13

Psalm 129

A song of ascents.

[1]"They have greatly oppressed me from my youth,"[c]
let Israel say;[d]
[2]"they have greatly oppressed me from my youth,
but they have not gained the victory[e] over me.
[3]Plowmen have plowed my back
and made their furrows long.
[4]But the LORD is righteous;[f]
he has cut me free from the cords of the wicked."

[5]May all who hate Zion[g]
be turned back in shame.[h]

of blessing on the table (v. 2), around the table (vv. 3–4), and among the people of God (vv. 5–6). All three are related not only because they are blessings from the Lord but because the people of God (vv. 5–6) consist of strong families (vv. 3–4) who must have enough to eat (v. 2). This blessing, then, is crucial for the strength of God's kingdom, and the blessing comes from the Lord at Zion. Thus, all those who want to experience this blessing must sojourn in Zion. This is one of the so-called wisdom psalms, in which the psalmists reflect on many of life's deep issues (see introduction to Ps 34).
128 title See note on Ps 120 title.
128:1 Blessed. See 1:1 and note. **fear the LORD.** See note on 19:9. **walk in obedience to him.** True happiness is found in living according to God's word (119:1–3).
128:2 A blessing on what they eat counteracts the curse that came because of what Adam and Eve ate (Gen 3:6,17). **You will eat the fruit of your labor.** A covenant blessing (see Deut 28:1–6); the opposite is a covenant curse (see 109:11 and note; Deut 28:33; Ezek 23:29).
128:3 fruitful vine. Symbolizes bearing children and can symbolize sexual availability and enjoyment (Song 7:8–12). **olive shoots.** Provide three vital necessities: wood, food, and oil. Just as with arrows in the hands of the warrior (127:3–4), children are a boon to the family.
128:5 bless. Translates a different Hebrew word than that in vv. 1,2; emphasizes blessing that comes from the Lord's intervention (see 3:8 and note). **Zion.** The "capital" of and central place for God's kingdom. Because Zion and the kingdom of God were so closely associated, to journey to Zion was to seek the kingdom of God. See notes on 2:6; 9:11; see also "The City of God," p. 2666.
128:6 peace. More than the absence of conflict or turmoil; this associates peace with grandchildren (see Prov 17:6), thus revealing that it incorporates notions such as fruitfulness, fullness, life, and vitality (see 119:165 and note; see also "Shalom," p. 2693).
Ps 129 *May All Who Hate Zion Be Turned Back in Shame.* Ps 129 is the antithesis of Ps 128. Blessing proceeds from Zion in Ps 128, but Ps 129 pronounces curses on those who hate Zion. Like Ps 123, this psalm would have reminded pilgrims that the road to Zion, which is the path to blessing (128:5), is not free from obstacles and detractors. There are two sections: vv. 1–4 speak of the psalmist's oppression, and vv. 5–8 focus on the enemies of the people of God. Both address how the wicked oppose God's people on their way to Zion.
129 title See note on Ps 120 title.
129:1 youth. Also in 127:4; 144:12. People of all ages should be committed to God's kingdom.
129:2 Although oppressed, believers can rest assured that they will ultimately not be defeated (cf. Jer 1:19; 15:20; 20:11; Rom 8:31–39).
129:3 plowed my back. A metaphor for harsh treatment. It literally describes what the back looks like after a whipping or scourging (cf. Matt 20:19; 27:26; Mark 15:15; John 19:1). This is plausible because v. 4 mentions "cords," which were used to subdue and restrain someone (cf. Judg 15:13–14; 16:11–12; Ezek 3:25), possibly for a whipping.
129:5 hate. In Psalms, enemies are opposed to Zion and all that it represents (18:17,40; 21:8; 25:19; 38:19; 118:7; 120:6). They oppose God and his kingdom (cf. 2:1–3). Thus, the curses that appear in this psalm are not retaliation for a personal slight but rather a desire for judgment against God's enemies.

129:6 [i] Ps 37:2
129:8 [j] Ru 2:4; Ps 118:26
130:1 [k] Ps 42:7; 69:2; La 3:55
130:2 [l] Ps 28:2 [m] 2Ch 6:40; Ps 64:1
130:3 [n] Ps 76:7; 143:2
130:4 [o] Ex 34:7; Isa 55:7; Jer 33:8 [p] 1Ki 8:40
130:5 [q] Ps 27:14; 33:20; Isa 8:17 [r] Ps 119:81
130:6 [s] Ps 63:6 [t] Ps 119:147
130:7 [u] Ps 131:3
130:8 [v] Lk 1:68

6 May they be like grass on the roof,
which withers[i] before it can grow;
7 a reaper cannot fill his hands with it,
nor one who gathers fill his arms.
8 May those who pass by not say to them,
"The blessing of the LORD be on you;
we bless you[j] in the name of the LORD."

Psalm 130

A song of ascents.

1 Out of the depths[k] I cry to you, LORD;
2 Lord, hear my voice.[l]
Let your ears be attentive[m]
to my cry for mercy.

3 If you, LORD, kept a record of sins,
Lord, who could stand?[n]
4 But with you there is forgiveness,[o]
so that we can, with reverence, serve you.[p]

5 I wait for the LORD,[q] my whole being waits,
and in his word[r] I put my hope.
6 I wait for the Lord
more than watchmen[s] wait for the
morning,
more than watchmen wait for the
morning.[t]

7 Israel, put your hope[u] in the LORD,
for with the LORD is unfailing love
and with him is full redemption.
8 He himself will redeem[v] Israel
from all their sins.

129:6 grass. Symbolizes brevity (37:2; 90:5–6; 103:15), especially because it is on the roof and thus exposed to full sun.
129:8 Those who hate the kingdom of God (v. 5) will not ultimately be blessed; they will not receive blessing in the name of the Lord.
Ps 130 *Out of the Depths I Cry to You, Lord.* The ancient church identified this psalm as one of seven penitential psalms (the others: Pss 6; 32; 38; 51; 102; 143). Ps 130 expresses hope that the Lord will one day remove the chief barrier to serving him: sin. As pilgrims made their way to Zion, they remembered that the greatest obstacle to true worship was not their enemies (Pss 123; 129), who simply made their journey more difficult; the greatest obstacle was their sin, which actually hindered them from serving God (v. 4). Ps 130 has four sections, two verses each (vv. 1–2,3–4,5–6,7–8). It both pleads for mercy and encourages God's people to wait on that mercy.
130 title See note on Ps 120 title.
130:1–2 Taking the rest of the psalm into account with its emphasis on sin, this describes the psalmist as dead in sin (Eph 2:1,5). Accordingly, the psalmist can only cry for mercy (cf. Luke 18:13; Eph 2:4,7).
130:1 Out of the depths. Of the sea (69:2,14; Isa 51:10; Ezek 27:34); represents death and exile (see notes on 93:3; 107:23).
130:3 who could stand? All have sinned and therefore will receive judgment (1 Kgs 8:46; Nah 1:6; Rom 3:9,23; Rev 6:17).
130:4 forgiveness. This is at the heart of God's nature (32; Exod 34:6–7). The psalmist holds in tension God's just judgment of sin with his mercy and grace (Neh 9:17; Dan 9:9). This tension ultimately leads to the cross of Christ (Rom 3:21–26; 5:8).
130:5–6 After crying for mercy in v. 2 and acknowledging that forgiveness is with the Lord in v. 4, the psalmist waits for the Lord. This reveals that the plea for mercy in v. 2 is more than a manipulative demand that obligates the Lord to forgive. Rather, the psalmist prays and acknowledges God's character and then waits in confident expectation that the Lord will respond.
130:6 more than watchmen wait for the morning. Watchmen know that the morning will come and provide relief from their burdensome task, but they still must wait for that relief. Likewise, the sinner can be confident that the Lord's forgiveness will eventually come, but in God's own timing.
130:7 unfailing love. See 6:4 and note. **full redemption.** A complete redemption from sin, which the psalmist awaits (Rom 6:10; Heb 9:28; 1 Pet 3:18).
130:8 See 111:9; 2 Sam 7:23–24; Isa 43:1–4. Such passages ultimately point to the cross, where God in the flesh redeemed the people of God from their sin (Titus 2:14; Heb 9:12; 1 Pet 1:18–19).

Psalm 131

A song of ascents. Of David.

[1]My heart is not proud,[w] LORD,
my eyes are not haughty;
I do not concern myself with great matters
or things too wonderful for me.
[2]But I have calmed and quieted myself,
I am like a weaned child with its mother;
like a weaned child I am content.[x]

[3]Israel, put your hope[y] in the LORD
both now and forevermore.

Psalm 132

132:8-10pp — 2Ch 6:41-42

A song of ascents.

[1]LORD, remember David
and all his self-denial.

[2]He swore an oath to the LORD,
he made a vow to the Mighty One of Jacob:[z]
[3]"I will not enter my house
or go to my bed,
[4]I will allow no sleep to my eyes
or slumber to my eyelids,
[5]till I find a place[a] for the LORD,
a dwelling for the Mighty One of Jacob."

[6]We heard it in Ephrathah,[b]
we came upon it in the fields of Jaar:[ac]

131:1 [w]Ps 101:5; Ro 12:16
131:2 [x]Mt 18:3; 1Co 14:20
131:3 [y]Ps 130:7
132:2 [z]Ge 49:24
132:5 [a]Ac 7:46
132:6 [b]1Sa 17:12 [c]1Sa 7:2

[a] 6 Or *heard of it in Ephrathah, / we found it in the fields of Jearim.* (See 1 Chron. 13:5,6) (And no quotation marks around verses 7-9)

Ps 131 *Israel, Put Your Hope in the Lord.* Ps 131 maintains the theme that concludes Ps 130 by repeating verbatim "Israel, put your hope in the LORD" (v. 3; 130:7). Ps 131 expands on what it means to hope in the Lord—negatively (v. 1) and positively (v. 2).
131 title See note on Ps 120 title. **Of David.** See note on Ps 122 title.
131:1 Believers who hope in the Lord submit to him. They are willing to leave certain questions unanswered because they have full confidence that the Lord knows the answers (Deut 29:29).
131:2 Like a weaned child with its mother. A young child anywhere from three to five years old. Just as a child of this age finds confidence in the presence of its mother, regardless of the circumstance, so the believer needs only the presence of their God to console them. Even though believers may not understand all that is happening or why it is happening (see v. 1 and note), they still confidently trust the Lord.
131:3 now and forevermore. See 113:2 and note; 115:18; 125:2.
Ps 132 *Here I Will Make a Horn Grow for David.* Ps 132 combines two themes: (1) the promises made to David and (2) Zion as the center of God's kingdom. It has two sections: David swore that he would secure a dwelling place for the Lord (vv. 1–10), and the Lord swore that he would secure David's dynasty, most closely associated with his throne (vv. 11–18). The thrones (i.e., dwelling places) of the Lord, the heavenly ruler, and of David, the earthly ruler, are in the same place: they both reign from Zion (vv. 11–14). This is one of the so-called psalms of Zion (see introduction to Ps 46); it may also be considered a "royal" psalm (see introducction to Ps 18).

Ps 132 strongly affirms David's place in God's redemption plan. God reaffirms his promises to David regarding the perpetuity of his line (vv. 11–12,17–18; 2 Sam 7:11–16; see note on 89:3). These promises are closely bound with the Lord's commitment to Zion (v. 13). The connection between Zion and the Davidic throne is implicit (v. 13) and explicit (vv. 17–18). A variety of blessings flow from God's decision in v. 13, including installing a Davidic king *at Zion* (78:68–72). By linking Zion with the king, Ps 132 demonstrates that the program that Ps 2 outlines still stands: an earthly king whose throne is at Zion will represent the Lord's reign as vice-regent, assuming the original role intended for Adam in creation (Gen 1:26–28).
132 title See note on Ps 120 title.
132:1 remember. Does not assume that the Lord has forgotten David; it is a covenantal term when the Lord is the subject (see 115:12 and note).
132:2 swore an oath. David committed to build a temple for the Lord (2 Sam 7:1–2,5–7; 1 Chr 22:2–19).
132:3 Begins a series of statements that progressively refer to taking a rest. David's commitment to his oath will be untiring.
132:5 David desired to construct a secure dwelling for the ark of the covenant, which represented the Lord's presence (2 Sam 6–7; 1 Chr 22:2–19). **place.** See note on 84:1.
132:6 Ephrathah. The region around, and including, Bethlehem (1 Sam 17:12). **fields of Jaar.** Most likely Kiriath-Jearim, where the ark was for 20 years (1 Sam 7:1–2) until David moved it to Jerusalem (2 Sam 6:1–19).

132:7 [d]Ps 5:7 [e]Ps 99:5
132:8 [f]Nu 10:35; Ps 78:61
132:9 [g]Job 29:14; Isa 61:3,10
132:11 [h]Ps 89:3-4,35 [i]2Sa 7:12
132:12 [j]Lk 1:32; Ac 2:30
132:13 [k]Ps 48:1-2
132:14 [l]Ps 68:16
132:15 [m]Ps 107:9; 147:14
132:16 [n]2Ch 6:41
132:17 [o]Eze 29:21; Lk 1:69 [p]1Ki 11:36; 2Ch 21:7
132:18 [q]Ps 35:26; 109:29

7 "Let us go to his dwelling place,[d]
let us worship at his footstool,[e] saying,
8 'Arise, LORD,[f] and come to your resting place,
you and the ark of your might.
9 May your priests be clothed with your righteousness;[g]
may your faithful people sing for joy.' "

10 For the sake of your servant David,
do not reject your anointed one.

11 The LORD swore an oath to David,[h]
a sure oath he will not revoke:
"One of your own descendants[i]
I will place on your throne.
12 If your sons keep my covenant
and the statutes I teach them,
then their sons will sit
on your throne[j] for ever and ever."

13 For the LORD has chosen Zion,[k]
he has desired it for his dwelling, saying,
14 "This is my resting place for ever and ever;[l]
here I will sit enthroned, for I have desired it.
15 I will bless her with abundant provisions;
her poor I will satisfy with food.[m]
16 I will clothe her priests[n] with salvation,
and her faithful people will ever sing for joy.

17 "Here I will make a horn[a] grow[o] for David
and set up a lamp[p] for my anointed one.
18 I will clothe his enemies with shame,[q]
but his head will be adorned with a radiant crown."

[a] *17 Horn* here symbolizes strong one, that is, king.

132:7 his footstool. The ark (1 Chr 28:2), which implicitly symbolized a greater throne that was invisible.
132:8 Arise. See note on 3:7. **come to your resting place.** The ark and its movement could not manipulate the Lord. It symbolized his presence but did not guarantee it (1 Sam 4:3–11,17). Solomon recognized this when he dedicated the temple (1 Kgs 8:27–30; 2 Chr 6:18–21).
132:9 priests be clothed with your righteousness. Represent the Lord's character to the people (Hos 4:4–9; Zech 3:1–5; Mal 2:1–9). This is spiritual clothing. Cf. God's detailed instructions for the priests' physical clothing in Exod 28; 39:1–31.
132:10 do not reject. Be faithful to his covenant promises to David. **anointed one.** The Hebrew is *māšîaḥ*. The "anointed one" includes any of David's children, but it ultimately looks to the great Messiah, who would come from David's line (see 2:2 and note).
132:11–12 Faithfully represents the promises God made to David in 2 Sam 7:12–16 (see 89:3–4,29–37 and note on 89:3), culminating in Jesus the Messiah, the great son of David (Matt 1:1; see "Covenant," p. 2646). Jesus outstrips any Davidic descendant, as he is also a priest in the order of Melchizedek (Heb 7:11–28), serving at the right hand of God himself (Heb 8:1–2). The passage here emphasizes the promise's eternality; thus, not to have a Davidic heir on the throne would have created a crisis of faith for God's people. But as the rest of the psalm and Book V (Pss 107–150) more broadly demonstrate, the people still had faith in God's promises.
132:11 The LORD swore. Corresponds to "[David] swore" in v. 2. When the Lord established the covenant with David, he responded to David's desire to build a house for him by promising instead to build a house (i.e., a dynasty) for David (2 Sam 7:1–17). This psalm follows the same pattern: the Lord's oath responds to David's oath.
132:12 Jesus fulfills this promise because he comes from the Davidic line (Matt 1:1–16) and is a king whose reign will never end (Luke 1:32–33; Rev 5:13).
132:13 has chosen Zion ... desired it for his dwelling. The Lord chose to dwell in Zion (vv. 5,7–8; 2 Sam 5:6–10; 6:1–19). See notes on 2:6; 9:11; see also "The City of God," p. 2666.
132:14–16 The Lord is answering the prayer in vv. 8–9.
132:14 for ever and ever. The Lord's commitment to Zion is eternal. His eternal commitments are one of the main emphases of Book V (see introduction to Pss 107–150).
132:15 poor I will satisfy with food. As the center of God's kingdom, justice reigns in Zion. How people treat the poor marks true social justice (72:12–14; 82:3–4; 146:7–9; Exod 23:6; Lev 19:10; 23:22; Deut 15:7,11; Prov 14:31; 28:27; 31:20; Isa 58:6–12; Matt 25:34–46; Jas 2:14–24). See note on 82:3–4.
132:16 clothe her priests with salvation. Cf. v. 9. Salvation and righteousness are linked.
132:17 horn. Symbolizes strength and power (Lam 2:3; Ezek 29:21); here it refers to the king (see NIV text note; Dan 7:24; Rev 17:12). **for David.** One of David's heirs will also reign from Zion (1 Sam 2:10; Jer 33:15). **set up a lamp.** As a remembrance (1 Kgs 11:36; 2 Kgs 8:19; 2 Chr 21:7). **anointed one.** See note on v. 10.
132:18 clothe ... with shame. The opposite of vv. 9,16.

Psalm 133

A song of ascents. Of David.

[1] How good and pleasant it is
when God's people live together[r] in unity!
[2] It is like precious oil poured on the head,[s]
running down on the beard,
running down on Aaron's beard,
down on the collar of his robe.
[3] It is as if the dew of Hermon[t]
were falling on Mount Zion.
For there the LORD bestows his blessing,[u]
even life forevermore.[v]

Psalm 134

A song of ascents.

[1] Praise the LORD, all you servants[w] of the LORD
who minister by night[x] in the house of the LORD.
[2] Lift up your hands[y] in the sanctuary
and praise the LORD.
[3] May the LORD bless you from Zion,[z]
he who is the Maker of heaven[a] and earth.

Psalm 135

135:15-20pp — Ps 115:4-11

[1] Praise the LORD.[a]

Praise the name of the LORD;
praise him, you servants[b] of the LORD,

133:1 [r] Ge 13:8; Heb 13:1
133:2 [s] Ex 30:25
133:3 [t] Dt 4:48 [u] Lev 25:21; Dt 28:8 [v] Ps 42:8
134:1 [w] Ps 135:1-2 [x] 1Ch 9:33
134:2 [y] Ps 28:2; 1Ti 2:8
134:3 [z] Ps 128:5 [a] Ps 124:8
135:1 [b] Ps 113:1; 134:1

[a] *1* Hebrew *Hallelu Yah*; also in verses 3 and 21

Ps 133 *How Good and Pleasant It Is When God's People Live Together in Unity.* Ps 133 extols the virtues of unity among God's people with two similes: the oil used to anoint the high priest (v. 2) and the dew that appears on Mount Hermon (v. 3).
133 title See note on Ps 120 title. **Of David.** See note on Ps 122 title.
133:1 As God's people fill Jerusalem to celebrate the great festivals, this reminds them that unity is good and pleasant. Their pilgrimage is not simply an individualistic act of piety but expresses solidarity with the larger body of God's people.
133:2 precious oil. For anointing, not just regular olive oil (Exod 30:22–33). **poured on the head.** To set apart Aaron (and priests in general) for service (Exod 29:7). Pictures complete consecration for service. So unity sets apart God's people to serve him and witnesses to those outside the community (John 17:20–23).
133:3 dew. Represents life because it provided moisture for crops in a region where it typically did not rain for much of the year (cf. Gen 27:28,39). **Hermon.** A snow-capped mountain peak in the far northeast of Israel (see note on 42:6); its dew is particularly dense because of the air's moisture. The air around Jerusalem is often too dry to produce dew. **falling on Mount Zion.** Hermon's dense dew transfers to arid Mount Zion, thus enriching the life there. **there the LORD bestows his blessing.** A dominant theme in Pss 120–137 (128:5; 132:13–16; 134:3). **life forevermore.** The blessing is eternal life.
Ps 134 *May the Lord Bless You From Zion.* The final psalm in the songs of ascents (Pss 120–134) fittingly concludes the section by encouraging those who are serving in the temple (possibly after the final worship services of the evening) to praise the Lord through the night (vv. 1–2). Although the gathered people of God must disperse from the temple, the Lord's praise continues there. The psalm concludes with an important theme in the songs of ascents: blessing comes from Zion (see v. 3; 128:5 and notes).
134 title See note on Ps 120 title.
134:1 servants. Priests and Levites who ministered in the temple (1 Kgs 8:11; 1 Chr 9:33; 23:28–32). **by night.** See 1 Chr 23:30; possibly after the worshipers had departed.
134:2 Lift up your hands. Expresses praise (see 28:2 and note; 63:4; 141:2; 1 Tim 2:8).
134:3 bless. Translates a Hebrew word with the same root as "praise" in vv. 1,2. The psalm depicts reciprocity in that the Lord's people "bless" him on Zion (vv. 1–2) and then he blesses from Zion (v. 3). Zion stands at the center of the reciprocal movement. **Maker of heaven and earth.** Appears two other times in the songs of ascents (121:2; 124:8), which focus on Zion specifically to underscore that the Lord's authority extends beyond one hill or one city (see note on 121:2).
Ps 135 *Praise Be to the Lord From Zion.* Pss 135–137 are an addendum to the collection of psalms in the songs of ascents (Pss 120–134). Ps 135 affirms many of the same themes: vv. 1–2 repeat almost verbatim 134:1, and v. 21 is a slight variation of 134:3.

Ps 135 begins and ends with the command to "praise the LORD"

135:2 [c] Lk 2:37 [d] Ps 116:19
135:3 [e] Ps 119:68 [f] Ps 147:1
135:4 [g] Dt 10:15; 1Pe 2:9 [h] Ex 19:5; Dt 7:6
135:5 [i] Ps 48:1 [j] Ps 97:9
135:6 [k] Ps 115:3
135:7 [l] Jer 10:13; Zec 10:1 [m] Job 28:25 [n] Job 38:22
135:8 [o] Ex 12:12; Ps 78:51
135:9 [p] Dt 6:22 [q] Ps 136:10-15
135:10 [r] Nu 21:21-25; Ps 136:17-21
135:11 [s] Nu 21:21 [t] Jos 12:7-24
135:12 [u] Ps 78:55
135:13 [v] Ex 3:15 [w] Ps 102:12
135:14 [x] Dt 32:36

2 you who minister in the house[c] of the LORD,
in the courts[d] of the house of our God.

3 Praise the LORD, for the LORD is good;[e]
sing praise to his name, for that is pleasant.[f]
4 For the LORD has chosen Jacob[g] to be his own,
Israel to be his treasured possession.[h]

5 I know that the LORD is great,[i]
that our Lord is greater than all gods.[j]
6 The LORD does whatever pleases him,[k]
in the heavens and on the earth,
in the seas and all their depths.
7 He makes clouds rise from the ends of the earth;
he sends lightning with the rain[l]
and brings out the wind[m] from his storehouses.[n]

8 He struck down the firstborn[o] of Egypt,
the firstborn of people and animals.
9 He sent his signs[p] and wonders into your midst,
Egypt,
against Pharaoh and all his servants.[q]
10 He struck down many[r] nations
and killed mighty kings—
11 Sihon[s] king of the Amorites,
Og king of Bashan,
and all the kings of Canaan[t]—
12 and he gave their land as an inheritance,[u]
an inheritance to his people Israel.

13 Your name, LORD, endures forever,[v]
your renown,[w] LORD, through all generations.
14 For the LORD will vindicate his people
and have compassion on his servants.[x]

(vv. 1,21). It has six sections: the outer two sections frame the psalm in praise (vv. 1–4,19–21), while the four sections in the middle magnify the Lord's greatness (vv. 5–7,8–12,13–14,15–18). Especially prominent are the Lord's power over the nations (vv. 8–12) and his superiority over idols (vv. 5–7,15–18).

135:1 Copies 113:1 almost verbatim. **Praise the LORD.** The dominant command in the psalm (vv. 3,19,20,21). **name of the LORD.** See 5:11; 7:17; 8:1,9; 33:21; 92:1; 96:2; see also note on 8:1. It can also refer to his presence in the tabernacle or temple (see 74:7 and note; Deut 12:5,11). **servants.** See note on 134:1.

135:3 good ... pleasant. Used here to describe praise; these terms are also found together in 133:1 to describe unity. There is a link between praise and unity.

135:4 Jacob ... Israel. God's people; harks back to the patriarch Jacob, whose 12 sons were the progenitors of the 12 tribes. God changed Jacob's name to "Israel" after he wrestled with God (see Gen 32:28 and note). **treasured possession.** A highly prized, valuable item (1 Chr 29:3; Eccl 2:8). God's people have a special place above all other peoples (Exod 19:5; Deut 7:6; 14:2; 26:18; Mal 3:17). God's choice of Israel and its special position should elicit praise to God (as here), not be a source of pride (Deut 7:6–11).

135:5–7 Further reasons to praise the Lord.

135:6 does whatever pleases him. See 115:3 and note; Dan 4:35; Jonah 1:14. Acknowledges God's sovereignty, especially over other deities and powers. **in the seas and all their depths.** God's sovereignty extends to all parts of creation, even to the unruly and chaotic seas (see notes on 33:7; 93:3; 107:23; see also Jonah 1:14–16; Luke 8:22–25).

135:7 The Lord is sovereign over the weather. This is a polemic against ancient Near Eastern cultures that believed that deities controlled the weather.

135:8–12 The Lord is sovereign over the nations.

135:9 signs and wonders. Demonstrated the Lord's power over the most powerful nation on earth and its false gods (see note on 26:7).

135:10–11 The Lord has demonstrated his power against more nations than Egypt.

135:11 Amorites. See Num 21:21–30; Deut 2:26–37. **Bashan.** See Num 21:31–35; Deut 3:1–11. **Canaan.** See Josh 6; 10–12.

135:12 gave their land. An implication of God's election of Israel (v. 4; Deut 7:1–8).

135:13 name. See v. 1 and note. **endures forever.** The worship of the Lord is more than a passing fad; it is to continue through all generations (see 107:1 and note).

135:14 vindicate his people. The reason the Lord's worship endures. The Lord does not abandon his people; he proves that their faith convictions are well-founded over time (54:1; see note on 43:1).

15 The idols of the nations are silver and gold,
made by human hands.
16 They have mouths, but cannot speak,
eyes, but cannot see.
17 They have ears, but cannot hear,
nor is there breath in their mouths.
18 Those who make them will be like them,
and so will all who trust in them.

19 All you Israelites, praise the LORD;
house of Aaron, praise the LORD;
20 house of Levi, praise the LORD;
you who fear him, praise the LORD.
21 Praise be to the LORD from Zion,[y]
to him who dwells in Jerusalem.

Praise the LORD.

Psalm 136

1 Give thanks to the LORD, for he is good.[z]
His love endures forever.[a]
2 Give thanks to the God of gods.[b]
His love endures forever.
3 Give thanks to the Lord of lords:
His love endures forever.
4 to him who alone does great wonders,[c]
His love endures forever.
5 who by his understanding[d] made the heavens,[e]
His love endures forever.

135:21 [y] Ps 134:3
136:1 [z] Ps 106:1 [a] 1Ch 16:34; 2Ch 20:21
136:2 [b] Dt 10:17
136:4 [c] Ps 72:18
136:5 [d] Pr 3:19; Jer 51:15 [e] Ge 1:1

135:15–18 A polemic against the idols of the nations; closely related to 115:4–8 (see note there). Idolatry is folly because a human exercises sovereignty over the god by making it out of silver and gold (Isa 44:9–20). The mute, blind, deaf, and idols with no breath measure up poorly when compared to the Lord, who is sovereign over all creation (see vv. 5–7 and notes).
135:19–20 Representative groups among God's people (see 118:2–4 and note).
135:21 The psalm begins and ends in praise (v. 1). **Zion.** See note on 134:3 ("bless"). The Lord is both the subject and the object of blessing from Zion.
Ps 136 *His Love Endures Forever.* Ps 136 celebrates the enduring nature of the Lord's love; each verse ends with a refrain, the only psalm that does so. Possibly, in public worship, a priest or a group of Levitical singers led in singing the first part of each verse, with the congregation or the Levitical singers responding with the refrain (1 Chr 16:41; 2 Chr 5:13; 7:3,6; Ezra 3:11). The refrain repeats the psalm's main theme, which can be overlooked because of its repetition, but it has deep significance for the psalm: the love of the Lord is a love that lasts. After a call to praise (vv. 1–3), the psalm outlines the Lord's wonderful works (vv. 4–25) and concludes in v. 26 by reaffirming the call to praise in vv. 1–3.

The psalm's body (vv. 4–22) restates highlights from the Pentateuch. Other OT passages do this (Pss 78; 105–106; 135; Neh 9), but only this psalm exactly follows the order of events in the Pentateuch.

Creation	Gen 1–2	Ps 136:4–9
Exodus	Exod 1:1—13:16	Ps 136:10–12
Red Sea	Exod 14–15	Ps 136:13–15
Wilderness	Num 1–20	Ps 136:16
Sihon/Og	Num 21	Ps 136:17–20
Land Grant	Num 34–35	Ps 136:21–22

Even within the smaller units, the order follows the Pentateuch. For instance, the order of the creation events in vv. 4–9 follows the order in Gen 1. The Scripture—as well as present experience (vv. 23–25)—testifies to the Lord's enduring love.
136:1 Repeats verbatim 107:1 (see note there); 118:1,29. **love.** The Lord's covenant faithfulness (see note on 6:4), which he demonstrates in his great acts for his people (vv. 4–22; John 3:16; Rom 5:8). This psalm, then, is an illustrative definition of the Lord's love: more than a feeling, his love is a faithful commitment to fulfill the promises he has made to his people. **endures forever.** God has not demonstrated his love to only one generation or in only one epoch of history; his love endures into the current generation and will even extend beyond it (see note on 107:1).
136:3 Lord of lords. The one true God (Deut 10:17). This title strongly affirms deity, and the NT ascribes it to Jesus (1 Tim 6:15; Rev 17:14; 19:16).
136:4 An implied "Give thanks" occurs before each "to him" in this psalm (here; vv. 10,13,16,17). **alone.** Uniquely, especially compared to the lifeless idols of the nations (see 135:15–18 and note). **wonders.** The Lord's great acts of creation and salvation (see note on 26:7).
136:5 understanding. Closely related to wisdom (1 Kgs 4:29 ["insight"]; 7:14; Prov 2:2,6; 3:13). It can refer to skill in craftsmanship (Exod 31:3; 35:31; 36:1; 1 Kgs 7:14), and it portrays the Lord as a master craftsman in creation (Prov 3:19; Jer 10:12; 51:15).

136:6 [f]Ge 1:9; Jer 10:12 [g]Ps 24:2
136:7 [h]Ge 1:14,16
136:8 [i]Ge 1:16
136:10 [j]Ex 12:29; Ps 135:8
136:11 [k]Ex 6:6; 12:51
136:12 [l]Dt 4:34; Ps 44:3
136:13 [m]Ex 14:21; Ps 78:13
136:14 [n]Ex 14:22
136:15 [o]Ex 14:27; Ps 135:9
136:16 [p]Ex 13:18
136:17 [q]Ps 135:9-12
136:18 [r]Dt 29:7
136:19 [s]Nu 21:21-25
136:21 [t]Jos 12:1
136:23 [u]Ps 113:7

6 who spread out the earth[f] upon the waters,[g]
His love endures forever.

7 who made the great lights[h] —
His love endures forever.

8 the sun to govern[i] the day,
His love endures forever.

9 the moon and stars to govern the night;
His love endures forever.

10 to him who struck down the firstborn[j] of Egypt
His love endures forever.

11 and brought Israel out[k] from among them
His love endures forever.

12 with a mighty hand and outstretched arm;[l]
His love endures forever.

13 to him who divided the Red Sea[a][m] asunder
His love endures forever.

14 and brought Israel through[n] the midst of it,
His love endures forever.

15 but swept Pharaoh and his army into the Red Sea;[o]
His love endures forever.

16 to him who led his people through the wilderness;[p]
His love endures forever.

17 to him who struck down great kings,[q]
His love endures forever.

18 and killed mighty kings[r] —
His love endures forever.

19 Sihon king of the Amorites[s]
His love endures forever.

20 and Og king of Bashan —
His love endures forever.

21 and gave their land[t] as an inheritance,
His love endures forever.

22 an inheritance to his servant Israel.
His love endures forever.

23 He remembered us[u] in our low estate
His love endures forever.

[a] *13* Or *the Sea of Reeds*; also in verse 15

136:6–9 The same language occurs in the account of creation in Gen 1:6–8,14–16.
136:10–16 The Creator of the universe (vv. 4–9) is the same God who saves his people (vv. 10–16). There is a strong connection in the OT between creation and salvation (104–106; Isa 43:1–3,10–16; 44:24) because the OT depicts salvation as a new creation (Isa 43:1; 65:17–25; 66:22).
136:10 See Exod 12:12,29.
136:11 See Exod 12:31–39.
136:13 See Exod 14:21.
136:14 See Exod 14:22.
136:15 See Exod 14:23–28.
136:17–22 The conquest of other nations testifies to the Lord's love for his people.
136:17 The Lord is a mighty warrior who fights on behalf of his people (24:8; Exod 15:3). Both Sihon and Og attacked the Israelites in spite of the Israelites' promise to go peacefully through their territory (Num 21:21–35).
136:19–21 See 135:10–11 and notes.
136:23–24 God's people now include themselves, not just their ancestors, as recipients of God's enduring love — evidenced by the first-person plural "us" instead of third person "his people" (v. 16) and "Israel" (vv. 11,14,22). Because of the enduring nature of the Lord's love, the current generation benefits from it as well.
136:23 remembered. A covenantal term that denotes God's action in faithfulness to his promises (see note on 115:12).

[24] and freed us from our enemies.[v]
His love endures forever.

[25] He gives food[w] to every creature.
His love endures forever.

[26] Give thanks to the God of heaven.
His love endures forever.

Psalm 137

[1] By the rivers of Babylon[x] we sat and wept[y]
when we remembered Zion.
[2] There on the poplars
we hung our harps,
[3] for there our captors asked us for songs,
our tormentors demanded[z] songs of joy;
they said, "Sing us one of the songs of Zion!"

[4] How can we sing the songs of the LORD
while in a foreign land?
[5] If I forget you, Jerusalem,
may my right hand forget its skill.
[6] May my tongue cling to the roof[a] of my mouth
if I do not remember you,
if I do not consider Jerusalem
my highest joy.

[7] Remember, LORD, what the Edomites[b] did
on the day Jerusalem fell.[c]
"Tear it down," they cried,
"tear it down to its foundations!"
[8] Daughter Babylon, doomed to destruction,[d]
happy is the one who repays you
according to what you have done to us.

136:24 [v] Ps 107:2
136:25 [w] Ps 104:27; 145:15
137:1 [x] Eze 1:1,3 [y] Ne 1:4
137:3 [z] Ps 80:6
137:6 [a] Eze 3:26
137:7 [b] Jer 49:7; La 4:21-22; Eze 25:12 [c] Ob 11
137:8 [d] Isa 13:1,19; Jer 25:12,26; Jer 50:15; Rev 18:6

136:24 freed us. Has violent connotations. This same Hebrew word describes breaking the yoke off of a neck (Gen 27:40 ["throw ... off"]) and what a lion does to its prey (Ps 7:2 ["rip ... to pieces"]). God's salvation demonstrates his love.
136:25 God's constant care of creation (see 104:27; 145:15) demonstrates his love.
136:26 God of heaven. Refers to the Lord in a way that would have resonated with the nations (Ezra 5:12; Neh 1:4; Dan 2:18,19,28,37,44).
Ps 137 *By the Rivers of Babylon We Sat and Wept When We Remembered Zion.* Ps 137 concludes the grouping of psalms that begins at Ps 120. Like Ps 120, this psalm assumes an exilic setting (vv. 1–3), but the orientation toward Zion is much stronger. Famous for its vivid and striking imagery, Ps 137 masterfully expresses the raw emotions of exile with poetic artistry. It has three sections: the first is characterized by "we/our/us" language (vv. 1–4); the second switches to an "I/my" orientation (vv. 5–6); the third focuses on the nations using "they/you/your" pronouns (vv. 7–9). But the point of the psalm is consistent throughout: the psalmist longs for Zion/Jerusalem's exaltation as well as the destruction of hostile nations. It is a psalm of imprecation (see notes on 69:22–28; 109:6–20) in which the psalmist prays that the enemies of God's people would receive justice for what they have done.
137:1 rivers of Babylon. The Euphrates River ran through the ancient city of Babylon, and the region was filled with river branches and canals that flowed from it (Jer 51:13; Ezek 1:1,3). **sat and wept.** Expresses mourning (Judg 20:26; 2 Sam 12:21; Jonah 3:6). **when we remembered Zion.** Because the Babylonians had ravished it (Jer 39:1–10; 52:4–16; Lam 1:1,4,7,10). God's people are in exile, but their hearts are still in Zion.
137:2 poplars. Trees that flourish near streams of water (Job 40:22; Isa 44:4). **hung our harps.** Expresses grief. Harps are associated with joyful praise (92:3; 98:5; 108:2; 147:7; 149:3; 150:3), so this means to cease praising joyfully, presumably because of the status of Zion.
137:3 Their request was a reproach, not a good-natured desire for cultural exchange. **songs of Zion.** Joyfully extolled its inviolability (see introduction to Ps 46; 48:12–14; 76:2–3; 87:1–7), so this magnified the irony of the situation now facing the exiles.
137:4 in a foreign land. Contrasts to the songs of ascents, which God's people sang on the way to Zion (but see Ps 120 and introduction to Ps 120). God's people are exiled from Zion and cannot travel to Jerusalem in order to celebrate the festivals (Lam 1:4).
137:5–6 A bitter prayer that the psalmist should lose the very ability to praise if he were to forget Zion.
137:5 Jerusalem. Represents God's kingdom, not just the city's geographic area (see "The City of God," p. 2666). **forget.** A covenantal term (see 115:12 and note). The concern is not that the psalmist would forget that Jerusalem exists but that the psalmist's chief loyalties would no longer be with the city, that the psalmist would not consider Jerusalem his highest joy.
137:7 The Edomites mocked and despoiled the Judahites when the Babylonians overran them (Ezek 35:15; Obad 10–14).
137:8 Daughter Babylon. The nation as a whole (Isa 47:1; Jer 50:42;

137:9 [e] 2Ki 8:12; Isa 13:16
138:1 [f] Ps 95:3; 96:4
138:2 [g] 1Ki 8:29; Ps 5:7; 28:2 [h] Isa 42:21
138:4 [i] Ps 102:15
138:6 [j] Ps 113:6; Isa 57:15 [k] Pr 3:34; Jas 4:6
138:7 [l] Ps 23:4 [m] Jer 51:25 [n] Ps 20:6 [o] Ps 71:20

9 Happy is the one who seizes your infants
and dashes them[e] against the rocks.

Psalm 138

Of David.

1 I will praise you, LORD, with all my heart;
before the "gods"[f] I will sing your praise.
2 I will bow down toward your holy temple[g]
and will praise your name
for your unfailing love and your faithfulness,
for you have so exalted your solemn decree
that it surpasses your fame.[h]
3 When I called, you answered me;
you greatly emboldened me.

4 May all the kings of the earth[i] praise you, LORD,
when they hear what you have decreed.
5 May they sing of the ways of the LORD,
for the glory of the LORD is great.

6 Though the LORD is exalted, he looks kindly on the lowly;[j]
though lofty, he sees them[k] from afar.
7 Though I walk[l] in the midst of trouble,
you preserve my life.
You stretch out your hand against the anger of my foes;[m]
with your right hand[n] you save me.[o]

51:33; Zech 2:7). **doomed to destruction.** Isaiah and Jeremiah contain prophecies of judgment against Babylon (Isa 13:1—14:23; 21:1–9; 46:1–2; 47:1–15; Jer 50:1—51:64). **happy.** See 1:1 and note. This pronounces a blessing on those who execute judgment against Babylon. **repays you according to what you have done to us.** Retributive justice: the punishment fits the crime. This is a way of *limiting* judgment in the Torah (Exod 21:22–25; Lev 24:19–20). As a part of imprecation (i.e., curse), it is simply a request for justice, which should inform how one interprets v. 9.

137:9 A Christian's instinct is often to dismiss this prayer as an overzealous desire for vengeance, but together with v. 8 (see note there) it may be one specific form of retribution that the psalmist desires. It is not unreasonable to think that the psalmist may have had a child seized and slaughtered upon the rocks, because it commonly occurred when one nation conquered another (2 Kgs 8:12; Hos 10:14; 13:16; Nah 3:10; cf. 141:6). Although Christians desire mercy for their enemies (Matt 5:44; Luke 6:27–28)—a mercy that leads to repentance—whenever they pray for justice, their prayer assumes the same kind of retributive justice against evil that this reveals, even if Christians' prayers are not as specific as this one (Rev 6:9–10; 16:4–11; 18:20–24; 19:2–3). On imprecations in general, see note on 69:22–28.

Ps 138 *The Lord Will Vindicate Me; Your Love, Lord, Endures Forever.* Ps 138 begins a new section (Pss 138–145), as evidenced by the titles of Pss 138–145 (all are Davidic psalms). But Ps 138 also resonates with some of the themes that concluded the previous section (Pss 120–137). Verse 8 mentions the eternality of the Lord's love, which forms the refrain of Ps 136. And Ps 138 picks up on the foreign context of Ps 137 by referring to the "gods" (138:1) and by calling on all the kings of the earth to praise the Lord (138:4). Ps 138 pictures the people of God and their king as being in a position of power, in contrast to the exilic setting of Ps 137. Ps 138 has three sections: David approaches the Lord (vv. 1–3); David invites the kings of the earth to approach the Lord in the same way he does (vv. 4–5); the Lord treats David compassionately (vv. 6–8).

138 title A group of eight psalms of David (Pss 138–145) moves Book V (Pss 107–150) to a close, just prior to the concluding crescendo of praise psalms (Pss 146–150). David's stamp permeates the Psalter, appearing at both the beginning and the end. He is the most prominent human figure in the book.

138:1 "gods." The so-called gods of the nations, objects of Israel's idolatrous worship. David metaphorically desires an audience with the very deities themselves who dare to act as rivals of the one true God.

138:2 holy temple. See note on 5:7. **unfailing love.** See note on 6:4. This is often a source of praise (107:1; 118:1,29; 136:1–3,26). **your solemn decree.** God's promise that a Davidic heir would reign forever (89:3–4; 2 Sam 7:11–16; see v. 4 and note).

138:3 Both lines demonstrate the Lord's unfailing love toward David.

138:4–5 The program set forth at the beginning of the Psalter envisions that the Lord and his anointed leader (2:10–12) would subdue the rebellious kings of the earth (2:1–3). This thread is woven through the Psalter (72:11; 102:15).

138:4 what you have decreed. Presumably the promises made to David and his line (see v. 2 and note). The rebellious kings will be drawn to worship by this decree and by the glory of the Lord. Ps 138 reveals that the plan at the beginning of the Psalter remains the plan at its end.

138:6 Emphasized in 113:4–9; see also 1 Sam 2:7–8.

138:7–8 David sees two more indications of the Lord's unfailing love toward him: (1) the Lord preserves his life in the "midst of trouble," and (2) the Lord saves him from the anger of his foes. The Lord does not direct his favor toward David because David is better than everyone else; to the contrary, David confesses that he is "lowly" (v. 6). The reason for the Lord's unfailing love toward him is that the Lord's love "endures forever."

[8]The LORD will vindicate[p] me;
your love, LORD, endures forever—
do not abandon the works of your hands.[q]

Psalm 139

For the director of music. Of David. A psalm.

[1]You have searched me,[r] LORD,
and you know[s] me.
[2]You know when I sit and when I rise;[t]
you perceive my thoughts[u] from afar.
[3]You discern my going out and my lying down;
you are familiar with all my ways.[v]
[4]Before a word is on my tongue
you, LORD, know it completely.[w]
[5]You hem me in[x] behind and before,
and you lay your hand upon me.
[6]Such knowledge is too wonderful for me,
too lofty[y] for me to attain.

[7]Where can I go from your Spirit?
Where can I flee[z] from your presence?
[8]If I go up to the heavens,[a] you are there;
if I make my bed[b] in the depths, you are there.
[9]If I rise on the wings of the dawn,
if I settle on the far side of the sea,
[10]even there your hand will guide me,[c]
your right hand will hold me fast.

138:8 [p]Ps 57:2; Php 1:6 [q]Job 10:3,8; 14:15
139:1 [r]Ps 17:3 [s]Jer 12:3
139:2 [t]2Ki 19:27 [u]Mt 9:4; Jn 2:24
139:3 [v]Job 31:4
139:4 [w]Heb 4:13
139:5 [x]Ps 34:7
139:6 [y]Job 42:3; Ro 11:33
139:7 [z]Jer 23:24; Jnh 1:3
139:8 [a]Am 9:2-3 [b]Pr 15:11
139:10 [c]Ps 23:3

138:8 vindicate. Fulfill the promises made to David (see note on 43:1). The psalm concludes with a prayer that the Lord would not abandon the works of his hands, which can refer to elements in nature (8:3,6) or to a house for David (see note on 127:1; 2 Sam 7:1–17) or even to David himself (139:13–16).

Ps 139 *Search Me, God, and Know My Heart.* David finds himself in a world of ruthless enemies (vv. 19–24) and vv. 1–18 reveal how he deals with it. Ps 139 has four sections, six verses each: (1) David meditates on the Lord's omniscience (vv. 1–6). (2) David reflects upon the Lord's omnipresence (vv. 7–12). (3) David's knowledge of the Lord as Creator derives from his awareness of the Lord's omniscience and omnipresence (vv. 13–18). (4) What is at issue is those who oppose the Lord (vv. 19–24). The enemies in this psalm are the Lord's enemies, not David's enemies. They become David's enemies only because they hate the Lord (vv. 21–22). The psalm concludes with a request (vv. 23–24) that resembles the opening verse: David desires that God know him so that David will walk with God.

139 title Of David. See note on Ps 138 title.

139:1 searched. Made a diligent study (Deut 13:14; Judg 18:2; 1 Sam 20:12; 2 Sam 10:3). **know.** A key word in this psalm: David can live in a hostile world because he knows (v. 14) that the Lord knows him and his situation completely (vv. 1–2,4), and he finds security in being known (v. 23).

139:2–4 David professes that the Lord has complete knowledge of him—his movements, his thoughts, and his words. In each case a modifier enhances the description: "from afar" (v. 2), "all my ways" (v. 3), and "completely" (v. 4). David is meditating on the Lord's omniscience (comprehensive knowledge), especially as it relates to him.

139:2 when I sit and when I rise. Implies a knowledge that goes deeper than just knowledge of movement (2 Kgs 19:27).

139:4 The Lord knows of events before they occur (Jer 1:5; John 21:17; 1 John 3:20). Isaiah emphasizes how the Lord demonstrates his superiority over false gods by foretelling the future (Isa 41:26; 42:9; 43:9,12; 44:7–8; 46:10). God knew before the foundation of the world that his Son would provide salvation through the Son's death and resurrection (Acts 2:23; 1 Pet 1:19–20). He also knew that certain people would enjoy the benefits of that salvation (Rom 8:29; Eph 1:5; 1 Pet 1:2).

139:5 hem … in. Elsewhere the Hebrew describes besieged cities (1 Chr 20:1; Jer 21:4,9; 32:2; Dan 1:1). David sees the Lord's knowledge as a blanket of security: it surrounds and guards him (cf. Song 8:9 ["enclose"]). **lay your hand upon me.** Accompanies blessing (Gen 48:14,17).

139:7 The focus shifts to the Lord's omnipresence: God is present in all places. The answer to David's rhetorical questions is "Nowhere." Jonah learned this by experience (Jonah 1:3,10). **your Spirit.** Parallel to "your presence": the Lord's Spirit manifests his presence. Although a robust doctrine of the Trinity cannot be derived from this verse alone, the reference to the Lord's Spirit indicates a plurality within the Godhead. **flee.** A play on being besieged in v. 5, because fleeing is often the response to siege (Jer 39:4; 52:7). The Lord's knowledge hems David in: he cannot flee from the Lord.

139:8–9 The Lord is present from one end of the world to the other. David first contrasts the height of the heavens with the depths: the Lord is present in both places. Then he mentions the east, where the dawn appears, and the west; according to an Israelite geographic orientation, the sea is always to the west (e.g., 113:3). The Lord is present in the farthest extremes of the world, thus implying that he is present in all places in between.

139:8 the depths. See note on 6:5 ("grave").

139:10 Even if David fled to the farthest end of the world, he could not escape the Lord's beneficent hand upon him (see v. 5 and note).

139:12 [d]Job 34:22; Da 2:22
139:13 [e]Ps 119:73 [f]Job 10:11
139:14 [g]Ps 40:5
139:15 [h]Job 10:11 [i]Ps 63:9
139:17 [j]Ps 40:5
139:19 [k]Isa 11:4 [l]Ps 119:115
139:20 [m]Jude 15
139:21 [n]2Ch 19:2; Ps 31:6; 119:113; 119:158
139:23 [o]Job 31:6; Ps 26:2 [p]Jer 11:20

11 If I say, "Surely the darkness will hide me
and the light become night around me,"
12 even the darkness will not be dark[d] to you;
the night will shine like the day,
for darkness is as light to you.

13 For you created my inmost being;[e]
you knit me together[f] in my mother's womb.
14 I praise you because I am fearfully and wonderfully made;
your works are wonderful,[g]
I know that full well.
15 My frame was not hidden from you
when I was made in the secret place,
when I was woven together[h] in the depths of the earth.[i]
16 Your eyes saw my unformed body;
all the days ordained for me were written in your book
before one of them came to be.
17 How precious to me are your thoughts,[a] God![j]
How vast is the sum of them!
18 Were I to count them,
they would outnumber the grains of sand—
when I awake, I am still with you.

19 If only you, God, would slay the wicked![k]
Away from me,[l] you who are bloodthirsty!
20 They speak of you with evil intent;
your adversaries misuse your name.[m]
21 Do I not hate those[n] who hate you, LORD,
and abhor those who are in rebellion against you?
22 I have nothing but hatred for them;
I count them my enemies.
23 Search me,[o] God, and know my heart;[p]
test me and know my anxious thoughts.

[a] 17 Or *How amazing are your thoughts concerning me*

139:11–12 Darkness, whether physical or moral, does not hide anything from God. As the Creator, he is sovereign over both darkness and light, for he names them and uses them for his purpose (Gen 1:3–5).
139:13 David's knowledge of the Lord's omniscience and omnipresence is derived from creation. As David meditates on creation, specifically his own creation, he discerns the nature of the Creator. **inmost being.** Not just the human's visible parts. **knit me together.** This Hebrew verb refers only to the creation of a human (Job 10:11). The Lord carefully and skillfully created each person.
139:15 secret place. The womb; the Lord intimately knows each person there (Isa 44:2,24; 49:5; Jer 1:5). This should inform how we view preborn children: they are persons whom God knows. **depths of the earth.** A dark and mysterious place; a poetic way of referring to the womb.
139:16 all the days ordained for me were written in your book. The Lord is sovereign over the span and content of every human life. **before.** The Lord is sovereign over each person even before that person actually appears (Eph 1:4,11; 2 Tim 1:9).
139:17–18 Concludes this section on creation by tying it to the previous two sections. The Lord's "thoughts" (knowledge) are precious and unsearchable. Even if David attempted to number every one of God's thoughts, when he finished, he knows he would still be present with the Lord.
139:19 David desires to be rid of the wicked among whom he finds himself, a common feature of imprecations (see notes on 69:22–28; 109:6–20).
139:20 adversaries. Typically, the psalmist's enemies are in view (3:1; 23:5; 27:2; 59:1), but these are the Lord's enemies. **misuse your name.** Directly violates the third commandment (Exod 20:7). People must treat the Lord's name with reverence, not as a form of manipulation to get their way or as a talisman to gain good luck. See note on 8:1.
139:21–22 David identifies completely with the Lord. The Lord's enemies are David's enemies. This echoes the very close relationship between the Lord and his anointed ruler in Ps 2: to rebel against the anointed is to rebel against the Lord (2:10–12), and the kings of the earth sought to rebel against both the Lord and his anointed (2:1–3). Throughout the Psalter, David acts as a type of the anointed ruler in Ps 2. Ultimately, however, Jesus fulfills this type (see note on 2:2).
139:23–24 Restates v. 1. **test.** See notes on 12:6; 66:10. David wants to lead a life that is the exact opposite of the life his enemies lead: whereas they are bloodthirsty and covenant breakers, David wants God to expose any offensive way in him and lead him "in the way everlasting." This desire provides a proper context for the imprecations David utters in vv. 19–22.

[24] See if there is any offensive way in me,
and lead me[q] in the way everlasting.

Psalm 140[a]

For the director of music. A psalm of David.

[1] Rescue me,[r] LORD, from evildoers;
protect me from the violent,[s]
[2] who devise evil plans[t] in their hearts
and stir up war every day.
[3] They make their tongues as sharp as[u] a serpent's;
the poison of vipers[v] is on their lips.[b]

[4] Keep me safe,[w] LORD, from the hands of the wicked;[x]
protect me from the violent,
who devise ways to trip my feet.
[5] The arrogant have hidden a snare for me;
they have spread out the cords of their net
and have set traps[y] for me along my path.

[6] I say to the LORD, "You are my God."[z]
Hear, LORD, my cry for mercy.[a]
[7] Sovereign LORD,[b] my strong deliverer,
you shield my head in the day of battle.
[8] Do not grant the wicked[c] their desires, LORD;
do not let their plans succeed.

[9] Those who surround me proudly rear their heads;
may the mischief of their lips engulf them.[d]
[10] May burning coals fall on them;
may they be thrown into the fire,[e]
into miry pits, never to rise.
[11] May slanderers not be established in the land;
may disaster hunt down the violent.[f]

[12] I know that the LORD secures justice for the poor
and upholds the cause[g] of the needy.[h]

139:24 [q] Ps 5:8; 143:10; Pr 15:9
140:1 [r] Ps 17:13 [s] Ps 18:48
140:2 [t] Ps 36:4; 56:6
140:3 [u] Ps 57:4 [v] Ps 58:4; Jas 3:8
140:4 [w] Ps 141:9 [x] Ps 71:4
140:5 [y] Ps 31:4; 35:7
140:6 [z] Ps 16:2 [a] Ps 116:1; 143:1
140:7 [b] Ps 28:8
140:8 [c] Ps 10:2-3
140:9 [d] Ps 7:16
140:10 [e] Ps 11:6; 21:9
140:11 [f] Ps 34:21
140:12 [g] Ps 9:4 [h] Ps 35:10

a In Hebrew texts 140:1-13 is numbered 140:2-14. *b* *3* The Hebrew has *Selah* (a word of uncertain meaning) here and at the end of verses 5 and 8.

Ps 140 *Rescue Me, Lord, From Evildoers.* David prays for deliverance from his enemies, entrusting himself to a just God. The psalm begins with a prayer for deliverance and a confession of trust (vv. 1–8), followed by a prayer for the enemies' downfall (vv. 9–11) and a commitment to the Lord's justice (vv. 12–13).
140 title of David. See note on Ps 138 title.
140:1 violent. Characterizes David's enemies in this psalm (vv. 4,11). As king, David was susceptible to violent enemies and therefore needed God to deliver him from them (18:48; 2 Sam 22:3,49).
140:2 devise evil plans. The activity of the wicked (36:4; 52:2). **stir up war.** Resort to violence without justification or provocation (56:6; 59:3).
140:3 tongues ... serpent's. David compares the speech of his enemies to deadly snakes. Paul references the second half of this verse in Rom 3:12–13 as evidence that all stand before God as sinners—Jews and Gentiles alike.
140:4 Repeats vv. 1–2a almost exactly.
140:5 Deception by David's enemies (9:15; 31:4; 35:7–8; 64:5; 69:22; 142:3; Jer 18:22). Three hunting metaphors reveal that David feels pursued like an animal.
140:6 You are my God. A confession of loyalty to the Lord (see note on 118:28). **Hear, LORD, my cry.** Similar Hebrew phrasing as in 141:1; 142:1; 143:1.
140:8 David prays that the Lord would remove his favor from David's enemies (contrasts Prov 8:35; 12:2; 18:22).
140:9 A prayer for retributive justice (see notes on 109:6–20; 137:8).
140:11 Because sin defiles the land (106:38; Num 35:33–34; Jer 3:1; Ezek 36:17–18), David prays that slanderers would not permanently dwell in the land and thus defile the rest of God's people. **hunt down.** A form of retributive justice in the light of v. 5 (see note there).
140:12 David entrusts himself to a just God. He knows that injustice will not ultimately triumph. **poor ... needy.** See note on 82:3–4. **upholds the cause.** God, as King of his people, acts as the advocate of the vulnerable and disenfranchised (9:18; 12:5; 35:10; 69:33).

140:13 [i]Ps 97:12 [j]Ps 11:7
141:1 [k]Ps 22:19; 70:5 [l]Ps 143:1
141:2 [m]Rev 5:8; 8:3 [n]1Ti 2:8 [o]Ex 29:39,41
141:4 [p]Pr 23:6
141:5 [q]Pr 9:8 [r]Ps 23:5
141:7 [s]Ps 53:5
141:8 [t]Ps 25:15 [u]Ps 2:12

13 Surely the righteous will praise your name,[i]
and the upright will live[j] in your presence.

Psalm 141

A psalm of David.

1 I call to you, LORD, come quickly[k] to me;
hear me[l] when I call to you.
2 May my prayer be set before you like incense;[m]
may the lifting up of my hands[n] be like the evening sacrifice.[o]

3 Set a guard over my mouth, LORD;
keep watch over the door of my lips.
4 Do not let my heart be drawn to what is evil
so that I take part in wicked deeds
along with those who are evildoers;
do not let me eat their delicacies.[p]

5 Let a righteous man strike me — that is a kindness;
let him rebuke me[q] — that is oil on my head.[r]
My head will not refuse it,
for my prayer will still be against the deeds of evildoers.

6 Their rulers will be thrown down from the cliffs,
and the wicked will learn that my words were well spoken.
7 They will say, "As one plows and breaks up the earth,
so our bones have been scattered at the mouth[s] of the grave."

8 But my eyes are fixed[t] on you, Sovereign LORD;
in you I take refuge[u] — do not give me over to death.

140:13 Links the poor and needy of v. 12 with the righteous and upright. "Poor" and "needy" do not necessarily refer to economic status; they can also refer to spiritual status (see 109:16,22 and notes).

Ps 141 *In You I Take Refuge.* Ps 141 shares many similarities with Ps 140: both are individual laments; body-part imagery occurs throughout both (140:3–4,7,9; 141:2–5,7–8); both are concerned with justice; and they use the same hunting imagery (140:5; 141:9–10). But unlike Ps 140, in Ps 141 David prays that he would remain righteous and faithful in the midst of his ungodly enemies. David pleads with the Lord to hear his prayer (vv. 1–2), asking God to keep him from reflecting the nature and character of his enemies (vv. 3–5); indeed, he prays that the Lord would do to these enemies what they have planned to do to him (vv. 6–7). He entrusts their retribution to the Lord; he does not have to respond to them in kind. The key to David's living a godly life in the midst of ungodly enemies is focusing on the Lord, not on those who oppose him (vv. 8–10).

141 title See note on Ps 138 title.

141:1 hear me. See note on 140:6.

141:2 incense. A part of Israel's sacrificial system: it created a cloud that obscured God's presence in order to protect the priests (Lev 16:12–13), and it provided a sweet, pleasing aroma (Exod 35:15,28; 2 Chr 2:4; 13:11; Prov 27:9). David asks that his prayers, like incense, would usher him into the holy presence of God and please God. The prayers of God's people are like incense in Rev 5:8; 8:3–4. **lifting up of my hands.** Expresses prayer and praise (see note on 28:2). **evening sacrifice.** Noted for its pleasing aroma (Exod 29:38–41; Num 28:3–8).

141:3 The wicked and violent use their mouths as weapons (140:3,9), but David asks God to restrain his tongue (34:13; cf. Prov 10:19; 17:28; 21:23; Jas 1:26; 3:1–12).

141:4 David does not want to resemble the character of his violent enemies. **heart.** Where evildoers devise evil (140:2). **their delicacies.** Most likely refers to luxuriant foods that the wicked obtain by unjust means. They can be a temptation toward evil, but they come at a price (Prov 23:3,6).

141:5 A prayer for discipline, which a good, righteous friend can provide (Prov 27:6; 28:23). **for my prayer will still be against the deeds of evildoers.** There is a link between David's request for discipline and his prayers against evil: his desire for personal integrity matches his prayers for justice.

141:6 When God finally accomplishes justice against all those who oppose the message of his people, he will vindicate that message.

141:7 mouth. Near Eastern literature pictured death as the devouring god Mot, whose giant mouth swallowed people (see Prov 1:12 and note). Recollects the judgment against Korah and his sons in Num 16:30–33. **the grave.** See note on 6:5.

141:8 fixed on you. David focuses on the Lord, not on the evildoers and their judgment (cf. 2 Chr 20:12). Heb 12:1–2 encourages believers to focus on Jesus, which implies that their focus is not on this world. **take refuge.** One of the dominant themes of the Psalter (see notes on 2:12; 18:1–2). It is a confession of faith and trust (9:9–10; 62:8; 118:8–9).

9 Keep me safe[v] from the traps set by evildoers,
from the snares[w] they have laid for me.
10 Let the wicked fall[x] into their own nets,
while I pass by in safety.

Psalm 142[a]

A *maskil*[b] of David. When he was in the cave. A prayer.

1 I cry aloud to the LORD;
I lift up my voice to the LORD for mercy.[y]
2 I pour out before him my complaint;[z]
before him I tell my trouble.

3 When my spirit grows faint[a] within me,
it is you who watch over my way.
In the path where I walk
people have hidden a snare for me.
4 Look and see, there is no one at my right hand;
no one is concerned for me.
I have no refuge;
no one cares[b] for my life.

5 I cry to you, LORD;
I say, "You are my refuge,[c]
my portion[d] in the land of the living."[e]

6 Listen to my cry,[f]
for I am in desperate need;[g]
rescue me from those who pursue me,
for they are too strong for me.
7 Set me free from my prison,[h]
that I may praise your name.
Then the righteous will gather about me
because of your goodness to me.[i]

141:9 [v] Ps 140:4 [w] Ps 38:12
141:10 [x] Ps 35:8
142:1 [y] Ps 30:8
142:2 [z] Isa 26:16
142:3 [a] Ps 140:5; 143:4,7
142:4 [b] Ps 31:11; Jer 30:17
142:5 [c] Ps 46:1 [d] Ps 16:5 [e] Ps 27:13
142:6 [f] Ps 17:1 [g] Ps 79:8; 116:6
142:7 [h] Ps 146:7 [i] Ps 13:6

[a] In Hebrew texts 142:1-7 is numbered 142:2-8. [b] Title: Probably a literary or musical term

141:9–10 traps ... snares ... nets. See 140:5 and note.
141:10 A prayer for retributive justice (7:15; 35:8; 57:6; see also note on 137:8).
Ps 142 *You Are My Refuge.* Ps 142, the third of four consecutive individual laments, is a prayer for God's mercy in the midst of a trial. Although it is similar to Pss 140–141, it more closely resembles Ps 143 because David does not pray for retributive justice against his enemies. He prays (vv. 1–2) that the Lord would notice his vulnerability (vv. 3–4) and rescue him from his enemies (vv. 5–7). Set in the context of a cave, which can be a place of safety (Josh 10:16–27; Judg 6:2; 1 Sam 13:6; 1 Kgs 18:4), the issue of refuge is at the forefront of the psalm. David confesses that he has no refuge in creation (v. 4); the Lord alone is his refuge (v. 5).
142 title of David. See note on Ps 138 title. **When he was in the cave.** An unspecified incident in David's life. It could be the same event in the title of Ps 57 (see note on Ps 57 title). The Bible mentions two incidents in which David was in a cave (1 Sam 22:1; 24:3–10). This is the final psalm with a "historical" title linked to an event in David's life (see note on Ps 3 title).
142:1 See note on 140:6.
142:2 complaint. Denotes deep vexation and anxiety; describes Hannah's plight (1 Sam 1:16 ["anguish"]) and Job's great trial (Job 7:13; 9:27; 10:1; 21:4; 23:2). **trouble.** The Lord cares about the difficulties his people face (31:7; 34:6,17; 46:1; 50:15; 81:7).
142:3 faint. Completely spent without any more resources from which to draw (77:3; Isa 57:16; Lam 2:12; Jonah 2:7). **watch over my way.** The Lord meets David in his weakness and leads him when he has reached the end of his strength (Ps 121). **hidden a snare.** See 140:5; 141:9–10. The Lord watches over the path upon which enemies are setting a trap.
142:4 The low point of the psalm stands at its exact structural center (see note on 100:3 ["his people"]). After this, David looks expectantly to God for deliverance. **right hand.** A position of honor (see notes on 16:8; 110:1). **refuge.** Assistance from another human. The Lord is David's refuge (v. 5).
142:5 You are my refuge. A confession of faith and trust (see notes on 2:12; 18:1–2; 141:8). **my portion.** God is David's blessing (see note on 16:5).
142:6–7 David calls out to the Lord because his situation is desperate. His deliverance will lead to praise, first by David himself and then by the community. The king's deliverance leads to the praise of the people.

143:1 [j]Ps 140:6 [k]Ps 89:1-2 [l]Ps 71:2
143:2 [m]Ps 14:3; Ecc 7:20; Ro 3:20
143:4 [n]Ps 142:3
143:5 [o]Ps 77:6
143:6 [p]Ps 63:1; 88:9
143:7 [q]Ps 69:17 [r]Ps 27:9; 28:1
143:8 [s]Ps 46:5; 90:14 [t]Ps 27:11 [u]Ps 25:1-2
143:9 [v]Ps 31:15

Psalm 143

A psalm of David.

[1] LORD, hear my prayer,
listen to my cry for mercy;[j]
in your faithfulness[k] and righteousness[l]
come to my relief.
[2] Do not bring your servant into judgment,
for no one living is righteous[m] before you.
[3] The enemy pursues me,
he crushes me to the ground;
he makes me dwell in the darkness
like those long dead.
[4] So my spirit grows faint within me;
my heart within me is dismayed.[n]
[5] I remember[o] the days of long ago;
I meditate on all your works
and consider what your hands have done.
[6] I spread out my hands[p] to you;
I thirst for you like a parched land.[a]

[7] Answer me quickly,[q] LORD;
my spirit fails.
Do not hide your face[r] from me
or I will be like those who go down to the pit.
[8] Let the morning bring me word of your unfailing love,[s]
for I have put my trust in you.
Show me the way[t] I should go,
for to you I entrust my life.[u]
[9] Rescue me from my enemies,[v] LORD,
for I hide myself in you.
[10] Teach me to do your will,
for you are my God;

[a] *6* The Hebrew has *Selah* (a word of uncertain meaning) here.

Ps 143 *Let the Morning Bring Me Word of Your Unfailing Love.* Ps 143 is the final individual lament in a series of four. It is also the last of the seven penitential psalms that the ancient church identified (see Pss 6; 32; 38; 51; 102; 130). Enemies pursue David as in Pss 140–142, but here he is acutely aware of his own sin (vv. 1–2). He prays for deliverance as well as forgiveness (vv. 3–10). His deliverance will not be because of his own righteousness but rather because of the Lord's righteousness, unfailing love, and commitment to the honor of his name (vv. 11–12).
143 title See note on Ps 138 title.
143:1 listen to my cry for mercy. See note on 140:6. **faithfulness.** The reason God will answer David's prayer: God is faithful to the promises he made to David, not because of any merit David earned. **righteousness.** David's hope is found in the Lord's moral perfection.
143:2 David would be found wanting in the courtroom of God's justice. God's judgment should inspire dread and fear (Isa 19:16; 33:14; Heb 10:26–31). **no one living is righteous before you.** "All have sinned" (Rom 3:23; cf. 14:1–3; 36:1; 53:1–3; 140:3).
143:3 pursues. To persecute (7:1,5; 31:15; 69:26; 71:11; 109:16; 142:6). **long dead.** Abandoned and forgotten in the darkness (88:6,18; Lam 3:6).
143:4 my spirit grows faint. See 142:3 and note.
143:5–6 David draws strength from remembering what the Lord has done and from praying.
143:5 meditate … consider Ponder what the Lord has said and done (77:11–15). The purpose is to recall the Lord's might and power (119:27).
143:6 spread out my hands. A posture of prayer (44:20; Isa 1:15). David expresses his spiritual thirst in prayer (42:1–4; 63:1–4).
143:7 hide your face. Deprive of the benefits of the Lord's presence (see 13:1; 22:24; 27:9 and note; 30:7). **go down to the pit.** Like prisoners and dead people (28:1; 30:3; Isa 14:15,19; 24:22; 38:18; Jer 37:16; 38:6–13). See notes on 88:4; Jer 37:16.
143:8 unfailing love. See Ps 6:4 and note; deliverance from enemies indicates this. **I have put my trust in you.** David has faith that the Lord will graciously, based on no merit of David's own (v. 2), deliver him from his enemies.
143:9 I hide myself in you. The Lord is David's protection. This fits with the refuge motif in Pss 140–143 (140:7; 141:8; 142:5).
143:10 David prays for the Lord's guidance so that he can walk in a way that pleases the Lord. **Teach me.** See 119:12,26,64,66,68,108,124,135; see also note on 27:11. **you are my God.** A confession of loyalty to God (see 118:28 and note; 140:6).

may your good Spirit
lead[w] me on level ground.

[11] For your name's sake, LORD, preserve my life;[x]
in your righteousness,[y] bring me out of trouble.
[12] In your unfailing love, silence my enemies;
destroy all my foes,[z]
for I am your servant.[a]

Psalm 144

Of David.

[1] Praise be to the LORD my Rock,[b]
who trains my hands for war,
my fingers for battle.
[2] He is my loving God and my fortress,[c]
my stronghold and my deliverer,
my shield,[d] in whom I take refuge,
who subdues peoples[a] under me.

[3] LORD, what are human beings[e] that you care for them,
mere mortals that you think of them?
[4] They are like a breath;
their days are like a fleeting shadow.[f]

[5] Part your heavens,[g] LORD, and come down;
touch the mountains, so that they smoke.[h]
[6] Send forth lightning and scatter the enemy;
shoot your arrows[i] and rout them.
[7] Reach down your hand from on high;
deliver me and rescue me

143:10 [w] Ne 9:20; Ps 23:3; 25:4-5
143:11 [x] Ps 119:25 [y] Ps 31:1
143:12 [z] Ps 52:5; 54:5 [a] Ps 116:16
144:1 [b] Ps 18:2,34
144:2 [c] Ps 59:9; 91:2 [d] Ps 84:9
144:3 [e] Ps 8:4; Heb 2:6
144:4 [f] Ps 39:11; 102:11
144:5 [g] Ps 18:9; Isa 64:1 [h] Ps 104:32
144:6 [i] Ps 7:12-13; 18:14

[a] *2* Many manuscripts of the Masoretic Text, Dead Sea Scrolls, Aquila, Jerome and Syriac; most manuscripts of the Masoretic Text *subdues my people*

143:11 For your name's sake. David appeals to the Lord's reputation (see 23:3 and note). **in your righteousness.** The Lord's moral perfection, not David's own, is the basis for David's confidence (vv. 1,2).
143:12 unfailing love. Corresponds to "faithfulness" in v. 1 because both terms are introduced by "in your" and both are the grounds for the prayers in vv. 1,12. God's "unfailing love" is a faithful love (see note on 6:4).
Ps 144 *Sing to the One Who Gives Victory to Kings, Who Delivers His Servant David.* David, the Lord's anointed ruler, pleads that God would defeat his foreign foes. David recognizes his dependence on the Lord and cries out to him to gain victory (vv. 1–11), and he recounts blessings that would flow from that victory (vv. 12–15). Many of the dominant themes throughout the Psalter appear here: the Lord as refuge, request for divine intervention, rescue from enemies, and the centrality of David. These themes closely parallel Ps 2, where the Lord grants victory to his anointed ruler over the ruler's enemies and his own. In both Ps 2 and Ps 144, the Lord is a refuge, a blessing formula concludes the psalm, and the Lord and his anointed enjoy an extremely close relationship as they oppose outsiders. The chief difference is that the king in Ps 2 is unnamed, while Ps 144 explicitly names the victorious king as David.
144 title See note on Ps 138 title.
144:1 Rock. A rocky hill or mountain, symbolizing a place of refuge (see note on 18:1–2; see also 18:31,46; 19:14; 28:1; 31:3). **trains.** The Hebrew is translated "teach" in 143:10. After requesting that God teach him to do his will in Ps 143, David acknowledges that the Lord's teaching extends to the art of war. God's anointed ruler in Ps 2 would wage war against rebellious kings (2:7–12).
144:2 my loving God. Though the Hebrew has "my faithful love," the NIV translation clarifies that God is the referent. This word is translated elsewhere as "love" or "unfailing love" (see 6:4 and note; 107:1; 118:1,29; 136:1–26; Exod 34:6–7). **fortress ... stronghold ... deliverer ... shield.** See notes on 2:12; 18:1–2. **in whom I take refuge.** A dominant theme throughout the Psalter (see 2:12; 18:1–2 and notes), it has appeared twice since Ps 141 (141:8; 142:5). **subdues.** One of the commands God gave humanity in Gen 1:28. When it refers to enemies, it signifies the Lord's favor on his own people (18:47; 47:3; 81:14; Isa 45:1).
144:3–4 David marvels at the Lord's involvement in his life (8:4).
144:5–8 This language suggests a theophany, a divine appearance (see note on 18:6–15).
144:5 Part your heavens ... come down. The heavens create a barrier between the realm of the divine above and the earth below. For the Lord to appear on earth, he must break through the heavens and come down (18:9; Isa 64:1; cf. Matt 3:16). **mountains.** Symbolize majesty and stability; evidence the Lord's presence (18:7; Judg 5:5; Isa 64:1,3; Mic 1:4).
144:6 lightning. Evidences the Lord's presence (18:14; Exod 19:16; Zech 9:14). **arrows.** Lightning is like an arrow the Lord shoots (7:13; 18:14; 77:17; Hab 3:11). The Lord defeats his enemies by shooting his arrows (7:13; 18:14; 64:7; 77:17; Deut 32:23,42).
144:7 rescue. David requests the theophany (appearance of God) so that God will deliver him. **mighty waters.** Symbolizes foreigners. Water

144:7 [j]Ps 69:2 [k]Ps 18:44
144:8 [l]Ps 12:2
144:9 [m]Ps 33:2-3
144:10 [n]Ps 18:50
144:11 [o]Ps 12:2; Isa 44:20
144:12 [p]Ps 128:3
144:15 [q]Ps 33:12
145:1 [r]Ps 30:1; 34:1 [s]Ps 5:2

from the mighty waters,[j]
from the hands of foreigners[k]
8 whose mouths are full of lies,[l]
whose right hands are deceitful.

9 I will sing a new song to you, my God;
on the ten-stringed lyre[m] I will make music to you,
10 to the One who gives victory to kings,
who delivers his servant David.[n]

From the deadly sword 11 deliver me;
rescue me from the hands of foreigners
whose mouths are full of lies,
whose right hands are deceitful.[o]

12 Then our sons in their youth
will be like well-nurtured plants,[p]
and our daughters will be like pillars
carved to adorn a palace.
13 Our barns will be filled
with every kind of provision.
Our sheep will increase by thousands,
by tens of thousands in our fields;
14 our oxen will draw heavy loads.[a]
There will be no breaching of walls,
no going into captivity,
no cry of distress in our streets.
15 Blessed is the people[q] of whom this is true;
blessed is the people whose God is the LORD.

Psalm 145[b]

A psalm of praise. Of David.

1 I will exalt you,[r] my God the King;[s]
I will praise your name for ever and ever.

[a] 14 Or *our chieftains will be firmly established* [b] This psalm is an acrostic poem, the verses of which (including verse 13b) begin with the successive letters of the Hebrew alphabet.

could symbolize deadly chaos in the ancient Near East (see notes on 93:3; 107:23).
144:9 new song. A response to a fresh experience of God's grace (see note on 33:3). **ten-stringed lyre.** A small harp that one could carry easily (33:2).
144:10 victory. Or salvation. Victory over enemies and salvation are closely linked (20:5). Jesus, as David's greater Son, saves God's people by gaining victory over their enemies (Col 2:15; Heb 2:14–15; 1 John 3:8). **David.** The king above all others in the OT (18:50; 78:70; 89:20–29,35) because of the covenant God made with him (see 89:3 and note; 132:11–12; 2 Sam 7:12–16). His name could symbolize his lineage, which would ultimately include the Messiah (18:50; 132:11–12; Isa 9:6–7; 11:1–10; Hos 3:5).
144:11 foreigners. People outside the community of faith who oppose the Lord's rule (18:44–45; Exod 12:43; Neh 9:2; Ezek 44:9).
144:12–14 Describes God's blessing that depicts an ideal, Edenic world (see 128:2–3 and note on v. 2; Deut 28:1–14; Joel 2:23–24).
144:15 Blessed. The path of true happiness (see note on 1:1).
Ps 145 *I Will Exalt You, My God the King.* Ps 145 extols the Lord as king, enumerating his praiseworthy character in an acrostic form (see introduction to Ps 9). Praise permeates the psalm from beginning to end. The Lord's majesty is transcendent (vv. 1–10), his kingdom endures (vv. 11–13a), and he beneficently cares for his people (vv. 13b–21). The psalm concludes the section of Davidic psalms that began at Ps 138, and it acts as a gateway to the concluding praise psalms that close the Psalter (Pss 146–150). Pss 144–145 mirror the program that Pss 1–2 set forth: God is king (Ps 145), and he has an earthly vice-regent from the line of David (Ps 144).
145 title praise. Dominates Pss 146–150, so Ps 145 connects this Davidic collection and all of Book V with the concluding section of praise psalms. **Of David.** See note on Ps 138 title.
145:1 exalt. Raise up in priority and esteem (18:46; 21:13; 30:1; 34:3; 46:10; 112:9; 118:28). **King.** Even as Psalms emphasizes the role of the earthly ruler of God's people (see notes on 2:2,6–7), his reign never overshadows the Lord's kingship (5:2; 47:2,6–8; 93:1–2; 95:3; 96:10; 97:1; 98:6; 99:1; see note on 93:1). The royal authority of the Lord's anointed ruler reflects and depends on the Lord's reign (see Pss 2; 110 and introductions). **for ever and ever.** The enduring nature of the Lord's

2 Every day I will praise[t] you
and extol your name for ever and ever.

3 Great is the LORD and most worthy of praise;
his greatness no one can fathom.[u]
4 One generation[v] commends your works to another;
they tell of your mighty acts.
5 They speak of the glorious splendor of your majesty —
and I will meditate on your wonderful works.[a][w]
6 They tell of the power of your awesome works —[x]
and I will proclaim[y] your great deeds.
7 They celebrate your abundant goodness[z]
and joyfully sing of your righteousness.[a]

8 The LORD is gracious and compassionate,[b]
slow to anger and rich in love.[c]

9 The LORD is good[d] to all;
he has compassion on all he has made.
10 All your works praise you,[e] LORD;
your faithful people extol you.[f]
11 They tell of the glory of your kingdom
and speak of your might,
12 so that all people may know of your mighty acts[g]
and the glorious splendor of your kingdom.
13 Your kingdom is an everlasting kingdom,[h]
and your dominion endures through all generations.

The LORD is trustworthy in all he promises
and faithful in all he does.[b]

145:2 [t] Ps 71:6
145:3 [u] Job 5:9; Ps 147:5; Ro 11:33
145:4 [v] Isa 38:19
145:5 [w] Ps 119:27
145:6 [x] Ps 66:3 [y] Dt 32:3
145:7 [z] Isa 63:7 [a] Ps 51:14
145:8 [b] Ps 86:15 [c] Ex 34:6; Nu 14:18
145:9 [d] Ps 100:5
145:10 [e] Ps 19:1 [f] Ps 68:26
145:12 [g] Ps 105:1
145:13 [h] 1Ti 1:17; 2Pe 1:11

[a] *5* Dead Sea Scrolls and Syriac (see also Septuagint); Masoretic Text *On the glorious splendor of your majesty / and on your wonderful works I will meditate* [b] *13* One manuscript of the Masoretic Text, Dead Sea Scrolls and Syriac (see also Septuagint); most manuscripts of the Masoretic Text do not have the last two lines of verse 13.

praise and his kingdom is a prevailing theme throughout the psalm (vv. 2,4,13,21).
145:2 Every. The Lord's reign extends to all people and through all time.
145:3 Great … praise. The nearly identical phrase in 96:4 emphasizes the Lord's uniqueness as opposed to worthless idols; here it more generally affirms his unfathomable greatness. **no one can fathom.** The Lord's greatness is unsearchable (Job 9:10; Prov 25:3; Isa 40:28); it complements this psalm's emphasis on the vast extent of everything associated with the Lord (see notes on vv. 1–2).
145:4 The Lord's praise endures through all generations (v. 21) because it is passed on from one generation to the next (see 78:2–4; Gen 18:19; Deut 6:1–7). **commends.** Entails more than simply retelling events or restating doctrine (117:1 ["extol"]; Eccl 8:10 ["receive praise"]); parallel to "speak" (v. 5), "tell" (v. 6), "celebrate" (v. 7), and "joyfully sing" (v. 7). One generation bears testimony to the benefits of trusting the Lord, urging the next generation to trust him too.
145:5 splendor. The grandeur, honor, and majesty associated with a king (8:5: 21:5; 45:3–4; see note on 96:6). **meditate.** See note on 143:5. **wonderful works.** See note on 26:7; parallel to "mighty acts" (v. 4), "awesome works" (v. 6), and "great deeds" (v. 6).
145:8 Restates Exod 34:6, a foundational statement of the Lord's character (86:15; 103:8; 111:4; Neh 9:17; Joel 2:13). **slow to anger.** The Lord provides opportunities for repentance before he fully displays his wrath (103:8–14; Gen 15:13–16; 19:15–16; 2 Chr 30:9; Neh 9:16–21). **love.** The Lord's faithful covenant love (see note on 6:4). It is often connected to the Lord's mercy, compassion, and slowness to anger. His grace toward sinners exhibits his commitment to his covenant promises.
145:9 all. God's common grace — his general benevolence toward all of his creation — extends to all people without exception (vv. 15–16; 136:25; Matt 5:45; Acts 14:17). This grace, however, does not save the rebellious from judgment (v. 20). Only God's special grace, which he extends to those who believe (John 1:12; Rom 3:22), can do that (Matt 24:31; Rom 11:5).
145:10 your works praise you. All of creation is part of the Lord's praise choir (89:12; 98:8; 103:22; Isa 44:23; 55:12).
145:11 kingdom. The realm over which the Lord reigns; the preeminent theme of vv. 11–13. As Creator, the Lord's kingdom includes all of creation (47:2; 103:19; Dan 4:17; 5:21), but there are parts of creation that still have not submitted to his royal authority (2:1–3,10–12; Matt 19:24; 1 Cor 6:9; Gal 5:21b), so the Lord's kingdom is fully realized when all submit to his reign (Matt 12:28; Phil 2:9–11; Rev 11:15–17).
145:12 so that all people may know. Israel's status as the people of God entailed a responsibility to witness to the rest of the world (9:11; 105:1; Deut 4:6–8; 1 Kgs 8:41–43), but their witness too often profaned the name of the Lord (e.g., Ezek 36:20–23; Mal 1:11–12).
145:13 everlasting kingdom. The Lord will reign as king over his creation forever (10:16; 29:10; 45:6; 146:10; Exod 15:18). The Son of Man receives an eternal kingdom that will surpass all other kingdoms (Dan 7:13–14), and his people will share in the reign of that eternal kingdom (Dan 7:18,27). Jesus is the Son of Man who rules over an

145:14 [i] Ps 37:24 [j] Ps 146:8
145:15 [k] Ps 104:27; 136:25
145:16 [l] Ps 104:28
145:18 [m] Dt 4:7 [n] Jn 4:24
145:19 [o] Ps 37:4 [p] Pr 15:29
145:20 [q] Ps 31:23; 97:10 [r] Ps 9:5
145:21 [s] Ps 71:8 [t] Ps 65:2
146:1 [u] Ps 103:1
146:2 [v] Ps 104:33
146:3 [w] Ps 118:9 [x] Isa 2:22

14 The LORD upholds[i] all who fall
and lifts up all[j] who are bowed down.
15 The eyes of all look to you,
and you give them their food[k] at the
proper time.
16 You open your hand
and satisfy the desires[l] of every living thing.

17 The LORD is righteous in all his ways
and faithful in all he does.
18 The LORD is near[m] to all who call on him,[n]
to all who call on him in truth.
19 He fulfills the desires[o] of those who fear him;
he hears their cry[p] and saves them.
20 The LORD watches over all who love him,[q]
but all the wicked he will destroy.[r]

21 My mouth will speak[s] in praise of the LORD.
Let every creature[t] praise his holy name
for ever and ever.

Psalm 146

1 Praise the LORD.[a]

Praise the LORD,[u] my soul.

2 I will praise the LORD all my life;[v]
I will sing praise to my God as long as I live.
3 Do not put your trust in princes,[w]
in human beings,[x] who cannot save.

[a] *1* Hebrew *Hallelu Yah*; also in verse 10

eternal kingdom, and his church is comprised of the people who share in its rule (Mark 14:62; Acts 7:55–56; 2 Tim 2:12; 2 Pet 1:11; Rev 11:15; 20:4).

145:14 lifts up … bowed down. The irony of God's kingdom: God exalts the humble and supports those in need (37:24; 113:7–9; 146:8; 1 Sam 2:4–8; Matt 20:16).

145:15–16 Part of a king's responsibility was to ensure that the people had basic provisions (72:3,16; Isa 36:13–17). God, as king, supplies the needs of all creation (see v. 9 and note; 104:27–28; 147:9; Matt 6:25–33).

145:17 faithful. One who displays unfailing love; the adjectival form of the important noun typically translated "unfailing love" (see note on 6:4). All that the Lord does reveals his faithful covenant love.

145:18 call on him. One of the basic acts of worship in Psalms (4:3; 18:3; 102:2; 105:1; 116:2,4,13,17; 118:5; 138:3; 141:1). All who call on the Lord will be saved (Rom 10:13). **in truth.** A sincere and orthodox confession (contrast Matt 7:21–23).

145:19 fear him. Properly recognize his nature and character. See note on 19:9.

145:20 Almost identical to 1:6, except "the righteous" of Ps 1 have become those who love the Lord here. Even though the Lord shows grace to all creation, including the wicked (see v. 9 and note; vv. 15–16), those whose lives do not bear the fruit of repentance will ultimately bear his judgment (73:18–22; Dan 12:2; Matt 25:41–46).

145:21 A concluding doxology to Book V, before the great crescendo of praise that concludes the entire Psalter (Pss 146–150), echoes (in modified form) the previous doxologies at the ends of Books I–IV (see note on 41:13). **praise.** The same word in the psalm's title (see note on Ps 145 title). Thus, this verse fittingly concludes this psalm and is an appropriate gateway to the next.

Ps 146 *Praise the Lord, My Soul.* After a personal vow of praise (vv. 1–2) the psalm exhorts the people of God to trust the true ruler, the God of Zion (vv. 5–10), as opposed to earthly rulers (vv. 3–4). The Lord is the one who can truly care for the marginalized and oppressed (vv. 7–9). This psalm—along with all the psalms in this section (Pss 146–150), each of which begins and ends with "Praise the LORD" (*hallĕlû-yāh*)—reiterates themes from the rest of the Psalter.

146:1 Praise the LORD. See NIV text note. **Praise.** Extol the virtues of; commend. Most often the Lord is the object of praise (vv. 1,10; 145:2; 147:1,20; 148:1,14; 149:1,9; 150:1,6). Praise is associated with singing (v. 2), making music (Ps 150), dancing (149:3), and bearing testimony (22:22). **soul.** Represents the person's essence (see note on 6:3). Pss 146–150 move from the private praise of an individual (146:1) to the all-inclusive "everything that has breath" (150:6). The same type of movement occurs in the concluding verse of the previous psalm: from "my mouth" to "every creature" (145:21).

146:2 all my life. Only the living can testify among the community to the Lord's goodness (30:9; 115:17; see notes on 6:5 ["grave"]; 88:10–12). The psalmist takes the opportunity to do what only the living can do.

146:3 princes. Symbolizes the noblest of humanity. This Hebrew term does not necessarily denote royalty; it can refer to those who are generous and magnanimous (Exod 35:5,22 ["willing"]; Isa 32:8 ["noble"]). Even such good people cannot save us. We should not trust humans; only the Lord can ultimately save (118:8–9,14).

[4]When their spirit departs, they return to the ground;[y]
on that very day their plans come to nothing.[z]
[5]Blessed are those[a] whose help[b] is the God of Jacob,
whose hope is in the LORD their God.

[6]He is the Maker of heaven[c] and earth,
the sea, and everything in them —
he remains faithful[d] forever.
[7]He upholds the cause of the oppressed[e]
and gives food to the hungry.[f]
The LORD sets prisoners free,[g]
8 the LORD gives sight to the blind,[h]
the LORD lifts up those who are bowed down,
the LORD loves the righteous.
[9]The LORD watches over the foreigner
and sustains the fatherless and the widow,[i]
but he frustrates the ways of the wicked.

[10]The LORD reigns[j] forever,
your God, O Zion, for all generations.

Praise the LORD.

Psalm 147

[1]Praise the LORD.[a]

How good it is to sing praises to our God,
how pleasant[k] and fitting to praise him![l]

[2]The LORD builds up Jerusalem;[m]
he gathers the exiles[n] of Israel.
[3]He heals the brokenhearted
and binds up their wounds.

146:4 [y]Ps 104:29; Ecc 12:7 [z]Ps 33:10; 1Co 2:6
146:5 [a]Ps 144:15; Jer 17:7 [b]Ps 71:5
146:6 [c]Ps 115:15; Ac 14:15; Rev 14:7 [d]Ps 117:2
146:7 [e]Ps 103:6 [f]Ps 107:9 [g]Ps 68:6
146:8 [h]Mt 9:30
146:9 [i]Ex 22:22; Dt 10:18; Ps 68:5
146:10 [j]Ex 15:18; Ps 10:16
147:1 [k]Ps 135:3 [l]Ps 33:1
147:2 [m]Ps 102:16 [n]Dt 30:3

[a] *1* Hebrew *Hallelu Yah*; also in verse 20

146:4 return to the ground. God created humans from the dust of the earth (Gen 2:7), and to the dust each human will return (103:14; Gen 3:19; Eccl 12:7). **come to nothing.** Only God's purposes will stand forever (v. 10; 90:2; 107:1; Isa 40:28).
146:5 Blessed. The path to true happiness (see note on 1:1). **help.** By sustaining and saving (vv. 7–9; see 3:8; 54:4 and note; 62:1; 124:8 and note).
146:6 Maker of heaven and earth. And thus sovereign over all creation (Gen 1). This phrase appears in 115:15; 121:2; 124:8; 134:3. **forever.** As opposed to humanity's transitory nature (vv. 3–4).
146:7 cause of the oppressed. As a righteous king, the Lord defends those who are helpless (72:4; 103:6; 105:14; Lev 19:13–14; Deut 24:14–15). **food to the hungry.** Everyone has enough in God's kingdom (see 107:9; 145:15–16 and note; Matt 6:25–27).
146:8 sight to the blind. One evidence of God's kingdom. In Isaiah, the servant is instrumental in mediating this blessing (Isa 42:7; cf. Isa 29:18; 35:5), and Jesus draws attention to his healing of the blind as a sign that he is the servant representing God's kingdom (Matt 11:5). **bowed down.** See note on 145:14. **the LORD loves the righteous.** Reiterates one of the themes that opens the Psalter (1:6; see 11:7; 33:5).
146:9 foreigner ... fatherless ... widow. See notes on 39:12; 82:3,4; 94:6. **sustains.** Gives support and relief (147:6). **the ways of the wicked.** Repeats 1:6 almost verbatim. The ways of the wicked contrast with those of the righteous (v. 8) as in 1:6. The end of the Psalter thus echoes the beginning.
146:10 reigns. The Lord is the true ruler, not the princes of v. 3 (93:1; 97:1; 1 Chr 16:31). **forever.** As opposed to the transitory rule of the princes (vv. 3–4). **Zion.** The capital city of the Lord's reign (see note on 9:11).
Ps 147 *How Good It Is to Sing Praises to Our God.* Like Ps 146, this psalm is a call to praise. Like Ps 19, the reason for praise is the Lord's universal care of all creation and his particular devotion and revelation to his people. After an opening command to praise (v. 1), Ps 147 alternates between celebrating the Lord's particular care for his people (vv. 2–3,10–14,19–20) and his general benevolence toward all creation (vv. 4–9,15–18). And the two are related: the God of all the earth is the same God who acts on behalf of his people, the Creator God is Israel's God.
147:1 This gives two reasons for praise: (1) it is good, and (2) it is pleasant and fitting (see 135:3 and note). **Praise.** See note on 146:1. **pleasant.** Enjoyable, pleasing, charming (16:6,11; 133:1; 135:3; Prov 22:18; 24:4 ["beautiful"]; Song 1:16). **fitting.** Proper and right (33:1; Prov 19:10).
147:2 Jerusalem. The actual city and/or the people (51:18; 69:35; 102:21). **gathers.** Restores (Ezek 39:27–28). **exiles.** Banished from the land by foreign enemies (Jer 40:12; 43:5; 49:5). Gathering exiles is an act of salvation (106:43; Isa 11:12; 27:13; 56:8).
147:3 brokenhearted. Crushed in spirit by outside forces (see 34:18 and note; 69:20; 109:16). **binds up.** Part of the healing process; it

147:4 [o] Isa 40:26
147:5 [p] Ps 48:1 [q] Isa 40:28
147:6 [r] Ps 146:8-9
147:7 [s] Ps 33:3
147:8 [t] Job 38:26 [u] Ps 104:14
147:9 [v] Ps 104:27-28; Mt 6:26 [w] Job 38:41
147:10 [x] 1Sa 16:7 [y] Ps 33:16-17
147:14 [z] Isa 60:17-18 [a] Ps 132:15
147:15 [b] Job 37:12
147:16 [c] Job 37:6 [d] Job 38:29
147:18 [e] Ps 33:9
147:19 [f] Dt 33:4; Mal 4:4

4 He determines the number of the stars[o]
and calls them each by name.
5 Great is our Lord[p] and mighty in power;
his understanding has no limit.[q]
6 The LORD sustains the humble[r]
but casts the wicked to the ground.

7 Sing to the LORD[s] with grateful praise;
make music to our God on the harp.

8 He covers the sky with clouds;
he supplies the earth with rain[t]
and makes grass grow[u] on the hills.
9 He provides food[v] for the cattle
and for the young ravens[w] when they call.

10 His pleasure is not in the strength[x] of the horse,[y]
nor his delight in the legs of the warrior;
11 the LORD delights in those who fear him,
who put their hope in his unfailing love.

12 Extol the LORD, Jerusalem;
praise your God, Zion.

13 He strengthens the bars of your gates
and blesses your people within you.
14 He grants peace[z] to your borders
and satisfies you[a] with the finest of wheat.
15 He sends his command[b] to the earth;
his word runs swiftly.
16 He spreads the snow[c] like wool
and scatters the frost[d] like ashes.
17 He hurls down his hail like pebbles.
Who can withstand his icy blast?
18 He sends his word[e] and melts them;
he stirs up his breezes, and the waters flow.

19 He has revealed his word to Jacob,
his laws and decrees[f] to Israel.

involves closing an open wound (Job 5:18; Isa 1:6 ["bandaged"]; 30:26; Ezek 30:21; Hos 6:1).
147:4 Reminiscent of Isa 40:25–28, where the Lord's intimate care of the stars is assurance that he will care for his people, especially those who are weak and disenfranchised (cf. v. 6; Isa 40:29–31).
147:5 limit. This Hebrew word is the same as the one translated as "number" in v. 4. The Lord determines the number or limit of the stars, but his understanding cannot be fathomed.
147:6 A contrast between the humble and the wicked. Ps 1:6 is similar, contrasting the righteous and the wicked (see note on 146:9). **sustains.** See 146:9 and note. **humble.** See note on 82:3. **ground.** The destination of every human in 146:4; it is a place of death.
147:7 Sing. Exultant and celebratory; associated with victory songs (Exod 15:21; 1 Sam 18:7; 21:11; 29:5) and other celebrations (Num 21:17; Jer 51:14).
147:8–9 The Lord's general benevolence toward creation.
147:9 ravens. Jesus echoes this passage when he refers generally to "the birds of the air" (Matt 6:26). The Lord's care of creation should encourage God's people to trust him: if he takes care of the animals and plants, then he will certainly take care of his people.
147:10 pleasure. When the Lord is the subject, it means to look upon favorably (37:23; 40:6; 41:11; 51:6,16,19). **strength of the horse.** Represents the power of the created realm (33:16–17).
147:11 fear him. Properly recognize the Lord's nature and character (see 19:9 and note; 111:10 and note; 112:1). This links fearing the Lord to hoping in his unfailing love (33:18; 103:11). **unfailing love.** The Lord's faithful covenant love (see note on 6:4).
147:12 Jerusalem and Zion both represent the center of God's kingdom (see note on 9:11). In this verse, they poetically refer to God's faithful people (97:8; 2 Kgs 19:21,31; Isa 1:27).
147:13–14 Blessing is closely associated with Zion in 128:5; 134:3.
147:14 satisfies. All people have enough to eat—a blessing that displays the Lord's reign from Zion (132:15).
147:15 his word. Refers to God's "command," which upholds and governs the forces of nature (see v. 18). This contrasts with God's written word in v. 19 (see note there).
147:16–17 snow ... hail. God's control of these powerfully display his sovereignty (Job 38:22).
147:19 word. God's special revelation revealed in written form (119:9,16,17,42,74). Contrast God's word ("command") in vv. 15–18.

[20]He has done this for no other nation;[g]
they do not know his laws.[a]

Praise the LORD.

Psalm 148

[1]Praise the LORD.[b]

Praise the LORD from the heavens;
praise him in the heights above.
[2]Praise him, all his angels;[h]
praise him, all his heavenly hosts.
[3]Praise him, sun and moon;
praise him, all you shining stars.
[4]Praise him, you highest heavens
and you waters above the skies.[i]

[5]Let them praise the name of the LORD,
for at his command[j] they were created,
[6]and he established them for ever and ever—
he issued a decree[k] that will never pass away.

[7]Praise the LORD from the earth,
you great sea creatures[l] and all ocean depths,
[8]lightning and hail, snow and clouds,
stormy winds that do his bidding,[m]
[9]you mountains and all hills,[n]
fruit trees and all cedars,
[10]wild animals and all cattle,
small creatures and flying birds,
[11]kings of the earth and all nations,
you princes and all rulers on earth,

147:20 [g]Dt 4:7-8,32-34
148:2 [h]Ps 103:20
148:4 [i]Ge 1:7; 1Ki 8:27
148:5 [j]Ge 1:1,6; Ps 33:6,9
148:6 [k]Job 38:33; Ps 89:37; Jer 33:25
148:7 [l]Ps 74:13-14
148:8 [m]Ps 147:15-18
148:9 [n]Isa 44:23; 49:13; 55:12

[a] *20* Masoretic Text; Dead Sea Scrolls and Septuagint *nation; / he has not made his laws known to them*
[b] *1* Hebrew *Hallelu Yah*; also in verse 14

Jacob. God entrusted his people with his unique revelation (v. 20; Deut 4:7–8,32–34; Rom 9:4).
147:20 know. True knowledge derives from God's revelation (cf. v. 19; see 119:66,98–100; Prov 9:10).
Ps 148 *His Splendor Is Above the Earth and the Heavens.* Ps 148 is the midpoint of praise in the five psalms that conclude the Psalter. The scope of praise continues to expand from 146:1 (see 148:1,7), but it has not yet reached the zenith of 150:6. This psalm has two sections: part 1 begins with a call for heaven to praise the Lord (v. 1) and part 2 for the earth to praise the Lord (v. 7a). Each section then lists different entities within those realms of creation that should praise the Lord (vv. 2–4,7b–12), and each then concludes with a two-verse summary (vv. 5–6,13–14). The psalm pictures creation as a two-part choir, with the praise resounding from the heavens matched by what arises from the earth and sea.
148:1 Praise. See note on 146:1. **heights above.** There is a strong directional perspective in this psalm, especially contrasting high and low ("highest heavens" in v. 4; "above" in vv. 4,13; "ocean depths" in v. 7; "exalted" in v. 13; "raised up" in v. 14).
148:2 angels. Heavenly beings who obediently serve the Lord (34:7; 91:11; 103:20; Exod 23:20). **heavenly hosts.** The Lord's angelic army (103:21; Josh 5:13–15; 1 Kgs 22:19), of which he is the leader (24:10; Isa 31:4). Ps 103:20–21 associates the two.
148:3 sun ... moon ... stars. The Psalter often depicts inanimate creation praising the Lord (65:13; 89:12; 96:11–13; 98:7–9; 103:22; 145:10).
148:4 waters above the skies. The source of rain (104:3; cf. Gen 7:11: "the floodgates of the heavens"). According to Gen 1:6–8, on the second day of creation God separated the waters above from the waters below (oceans, lakes, rivers).
148:5 The Lord created by the power of his word (33:9; Gen 1:3,6,9, 11,14,20,24; John 1:1–3).
148:6 The Lord's word sustains and upholds creation (see 147:15 and note).
148:7 great sea creatures ... ocean depths. Parts of the created order (Gen 1:10,21) that seem unruly and chaotic (74:13; Job 7:12; Isa 27:1; Jer 51:34; Ezek 29:3; 32:2). See notes on 87:4; 93:3; 107:23.
148:8–10 Summons meteorological (v. 8), geological (v. 9a), botanical (v. 9b), and zoological (v. 10) elements in creation to praise the Lord (see note on v. 3).
148:11 The kings of the earth, the nations, and the rulers of the earth all prominently oppose the Lord in 2:1–2,10. Here they are a part of the terrestrial praise choir. **kings of the earth.** See 138:4–5 and note. **all nations.** See 117:1 and note. **princes.** Or human nobility (see 146:3 and note).

148:13 [o] Isa 12:4 [p] Ps 8:1; 113:4
148:14 [q] Ps 75:10
149:1 [r] Ps 33:2 [s] Ps 35:18
149:2 [t] Ps 95:6 [u] Ps 47:6; Zec 9:9
149:3 [v] Ps 81:2; 150:4
149:4 [w] Ps 35:27 [x] Ps 132:16
149:5 [y] Ps 132:16 [z] Job 35:10
149:6 [a] Ps 66:17 [b] Heb 4:12; Rev 1:16

12 young men and women,
old men and children.

13 Let them praise the name of the LORD,[o]
for his name alone is exalted;
his splendor is above the earth and the heavens.[p]
14 And he has raised up for his people a horn,[a][q]
the praise of all his faithful servants,
of Israel, the people close to his heart.

Praise the LORD.

Psalm 149

1 Praise the LORD.[b][r]

Sing to the LORD a new song,
his praise in the assembly[s] of his faithful people.

2 Let Israel rejoice in their Maker;[t]
let the people of Zion be glad in their King.[u]
3 Let them praise his name with dancing
and make music to him with timbrel and harp.[v]
4 For the LORD takes delight[w] in his people;
he crowns the humble with victory.[x]
5 Let his faithful people rejoice[y] in this honor
and sing for joy on their beds.[z]

6 May the praise of God be in their mouths[a]
and a double-edged[b] sword in their hands,
7 to inflict vengeance on the nations
and punishment on the peoples,

[a] *14* *Horn* here symbolizes strength. [b] *1* Hebrew *Hallelu Yah*; also in verse 9

148:12 young ... old. Two contrasting pairs symbolize all of humanity. **148:13 name.** See note on 8:1. **exalted.** High above all the elements of creation in vv. 1–4,7–12 (inanimate and animate, creaturely and human alike). See 107:41; 139:6; Deut 2:36 ("strong"); Isa 33:5. **splendor.** See 145:5 and note. **above the earth and the heavens.** God is greater than all the aspects of creation that this psalm calls upon to praise him (vv. 1,7).

148:14 horn. Symbolizes a king (Dan 7:24; 8:20; Rev 17:12; see note on 18:2). The Lord's response to the unruly nations, kings of the earth, and rulers of the earth in Ps 2 (see 148:11 and note) is to install his king on Zion (2:4–6,10–12). **praise.** The dominant theme of Pss 146–150; specifically refers here to the horn. The king that the Lord raises up will be the people's reason to obey the recurring command to praise in Pss 146–150.

Ps 149 *Let the People of Zion Be Glad in Their King.* As it calls God's people to praise him, this psalm also celebrates the honor (vv. 4–5) and glory (v. 9) that God's people receive from praising their King. It begins with a call to praise (v. 1) and then moves to the honor that the faithful receive: their victory shows that the Lord delights in them (vv. 2–5). The psalm concludes with the glory they receive: they will share in the governance of God's kingdom, especially in judgment (vv. 6–9).

Ps 149, especially vv. 6–9, parallels Ps 2 in several ways. The main difference between the two psalms is that in Ps 149 God's people accomplish the tasks of God's anointed king in Ps 2. When read together, these two psalms reveal the close connection between the anointed king and his people: God's anointed king represents his people, and the people reflect the godly anointed king. See notes on 2:2,6–7.

149:1 Praise. See note on 146:1. **new song.** See note on 33:3. **assembly.** See note on 40:9,10. **faithful.** Also in vv. 5,9; 148:14; related to the important Hebrew word translated "love" and "unfailing love" throughout the Psalter (see notes on 6:4; 107:1); describes people who show this unfailing love.

149:2 their Maker. A reference to God's making his people Israel as a nation (see note on 100:3; see also 95:6; Deut 32:18; Isa 27:11; 43:1,15). **Zion.** Represents the center of God's kingdom (see note on 9:11). **King.** The Lord reigns from Zion (9:11; 48:2; see note on 145:1).

149:3 dancing ... timbrel ... harp. See notes on 150:3–4.

149:4 takes delight. Looks favorably upon (see note on 147:10 ["pleasure"]). Those who "fear" the Lord receive his delight (147:11), so God's people are those who fear him (see 19:9 and note; 111:10 and note; 112:1). **crowns.** Beautifies, glorifies (Isa 55:5; 60:7,9,13). **victory.** Or salvation (see note on 144:10).

149:5 faithful people. See note on v. 1. **on their beds.** When they are alone and in the house; contrasts with "the assembly" in v. 1.

149:6 God enlists his people into his army to punish the nations. Ps 2:1–3 foreshadows a conflict: the Lord and his anointed are on one side, and the rebellious kings of the earth are on the other (see 110:3 and note). When God's faithful people praise him, they enter the battle on the Lord's side, so they must be properly armed for their task (cf. Eph 6:10–18).

149:7–9 inflict ... bind ... carry out. Tasks accomplished with the sword ("inflict" and "carry out" translate the same Hebrew word). They closely resemble what is outlined in 2:8–9. According to the NT, followers of Jesus the Messiah will participate as agents in the judgment

[8]to bind their kings with fetters,
their nobles with shackles of iron,
[9]to carry out the sentence written against them —[c]
this is the glory of all his faithful people.[d]

Praise the LORD.

149:9 [c]Dt 7:1; Eze 28:26 [d]Ps 148:14
150:1 [e]Ps 102:19 [f]Ps 19:1
150:2 [g]Dt 3:24 [h]Ps 145:5-6
150:3 [i]Ps 149:3
150:4 [j]Ex 15:20 [k]Isa 38:20
150:5 [l]1Ch 13:8; 15:16
150:6 [m]Ps 145:21

Psalm 150

[1]Praise the LORD.[a]

Praise God in his sanctuary;[e]
praise him in his mighty heavens.[f]
[2]Praise him for his acts of power;[g]
praise him for his surpassing greatness.[h]
[3]Praise him with the sounding of the trumpet,
praise him with the harp and lyre,[i]
[4]praise him with timbrel and dancing,[j]
praise him with the strings[k] and pipe,
[5]praise him with the clash of cymbals,[l]
praise him with resounding cymbals.

[6]Let everything[m] that has breath praise the LORD.

Praise the LORD.

[a] *1* Hebrew *Hallelu Yah*; also in verse 6

Musician in the court of the Assyrian king Ashurbanipal, 645 BC. The psalms encourage God's people to praise him with all types of instruments (Ps 150:3).

Z. Radovan/www.BibleLandPictures.com

(Matt 19:28; 1 Cor 6:2–3; Jude 14–15; Rev 20:4), which this and Dan 7:22 foreshadow.

149:9 glory. See 145:5 and note. **faithful people.** See note on v. 1.

Ps 150 *Let Everything That Has Breath Praise the Lord.* The final psalm in the Psalter fittingly completes the book with a resounding call to praise God. It is the most purely praise-oriented psalm in the Psalter, every poetic line beginning with a command to praise God (with only one variation: v. 6a); it gives no reasons for praise. In effect, this psalm's placement here announces that all is now said and done in this massive book of Psalms; all that is left is simply to praise God — nothing else matters. This is to be done wherever God may be found (v. 1), for both his deeds and his character (v. 2), and with any and all means available (vv. 3–5). It then concludes with a universal call to praise ("everything that has breath," v. 6) that complements the individual call to praise at the beginning of this final section ("my soul," 146:1); the words for "soul" in 146:1 and "has breath" in 150:6 are related to each other.

150:1 Praise. See note on 146:1. **sanctuary.** Or "holy place"; where God's people gathered for worship (134:2; 138:2). **heavens.** Represents creation (19:1; Gen 1:6–17). Creation is an important component of the cosmic praise choir (see 148:3–4 and notes).

150:2 Two reasons for worship: (1) **acts of power.** Or mighty deeds; display God's authority over creation (65:6; 66:7; 106:2; 145:4,11–12; Deut 3:24). (2) **surpassing greatness.** Demonstrated in God's power over death (79:11), his deliverance from oppression (Deut 9:26), and his revelation (Deut 5:24).

150:3 trumpet. Fashioned from a ram's horn (Josh 6:4–20); associated with authority (Exod 19:16,19; 20:18; Judg 3:27); used as both a signal (1 Sam 13:3; 2 Sam 2:28; 15:10; 18:16; Isa 18:3; Jer 4:19) and an instrument of war (Josh 6:4–20; Judg 7:8–22); incorporated into worship (47:5; 98:6; 2 Sam 6:15). **harp.** A stringed instrument (33:2; 147:7) made of wood (1 Kgs 10:12; 2 Chr 9:11); very similar to the lyre except that the harp was larger and thus not as mobile. **lyre.** A stringed instrument made of wood (1 Kgs 10:12; 2 Chr 9:11); a smaller version of the harp and much more common; played like a guitar. When mentioned in the psalms, it is often coupled with the harp (33:2; 57:8; 71:22; 81:2; 92:3; 108:2).

150:4 timbrel. Or tambourine; a shallow drum played with the hands, often by women, and associated with dancing (149:3; Exod 15:20; Judg 11:34; 1 Sam 18:6; Jer 31:4). **dancing.** Performed by a group in a circle; associated with revelry and joy (30:11; 149:3; Exod 15:20; Judg 11:34; 21:21; Jer 31:13). **strings.** Generally refers to all stringed instruments. **pipe.** A wind instrument, probably most like a flute but may generally refer to all wind instruments.

150:5 cymbals. Made of copper or bronze (1 Chr 15:19). Clashing cymbals were hit together; the resounding cymbal was struck by another implement, either the hand or some kind of stick.

150:6 The Psalter concludes with a universal call to praise, an ideal woven throughout the book (2:10–12; 22:27; 33:8; 48:10; 67:3,5,7; 97:1; 98:4–9; 99:1–3; 100:1; 103:20–22; 113:3; 117:1; 145:21; 148:1–14).

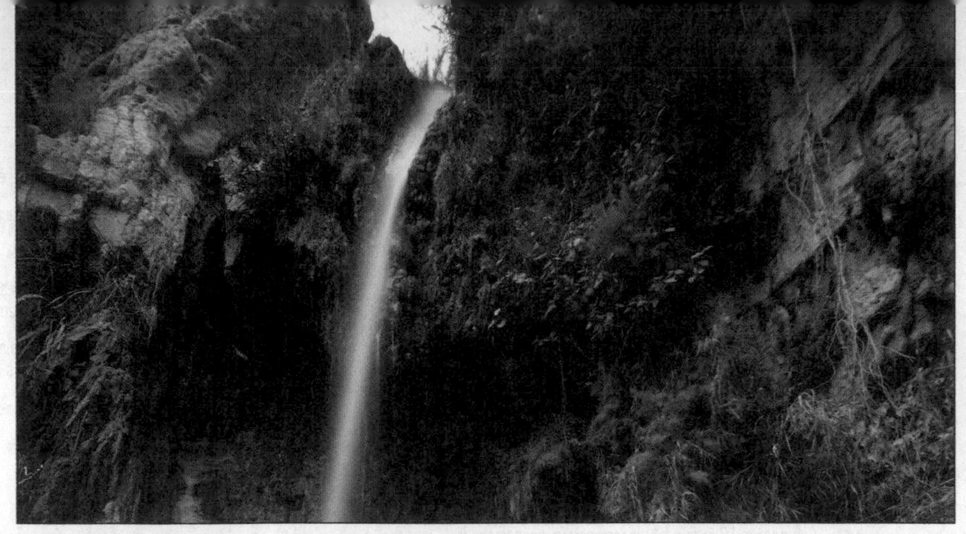

INTRODUCTION TO PROVERBS

The book of Proverbs is an anthology of seven collections attributed to Solomon and other wise individuals (see Outline). The number seven symbolizes divine perfection. The initial collection plays a significant role in the book, for it illuminates the value of wisdom and identifies the prerequisite for acquiring the wisdom presented within the remainder of the book.

AUTHORS

As is true of all Scripture, the book of Proverbs was authored by human authors and the divine author (2 Tim 3:16). Regarding its human authors, the superscript (1:1) identifies Solomon (970 – 931 BC) as the book's principal author. The internal evidence of the book supports this identification. Collection I (1:8 — 9:18) is associated with Solomon, as is Collection II (10:1 — 22:16), and Hezekiah's scribes attribute Collection V (25:1 — 29:27) to Solomon as well (25:1). Probably Solomon was responsible for adapting the sayings of other sages in Collections III (22:17 — 24:22) and IV (24:23 – 34). Collection VI is attributed to Agur (30:1 – 33); Collection VII, to King Lemuel (31:1 – 31). The titles within the book indicate that several authors produced the material over an extended period of time, and they imply that an anonymous sage edited the whole collection.

There are good reasons to accept these biblical ascriptions of authorship at face value. Biblical references to Solomon's wisdom are numerous (1 Kgs 3:5 – 14; 4:29 – 34; 5:7,12; 10:1 – 9,23 – 24; 11:41; 2 Chr 1:7 – 12; 9:1 – 8,22 – 23). Moreover, there are striking similarities in structure and content to comparable wisdom literature from Egypt, Mesopotamia, and the Levant, straddling the biblical world from the third millennium BC to Greco-Roman times. The forms and motifs of Collection I are similar to Egyptian "instructions" that date as early as 2500 BC; the titles of Collections I (1:1) and II (10:1) resemble the titles of Egyptian collections at the time of Solomon. The first ten sayings of Collection III, called "Thirty Sayings of the Wise," share similarities with the Egyptian "Thirty Sayings of Amenemope." Also, the collections attributed to Solomon teem with linguistic characteristics of his time. By contrast, the Aramaisms in Collection VII give scholars reason to think that the material was composed in the postexilic period, i.e., during the period of the book's final editing. While the ascriptions to Solomon do not demand that he wrote every proverb within the collections that bear his name, they suggest that he played an important role in the composition and collection of the materials in the book. If one asks how Solomon could be so

Fragment of Instruction of Shuruppak, Sumerian proverbs from the third millenium BC.

Kim Walton, taken at the Oriental Institute Museum, University of Chicago

wise and die a fool, his own proverb provides the answer: "Stop listening to instruction, my son, and you will stray from the words of knowledge" (19:27). Being wise one day is no guarantee of being wise the next.

Regarding the divine author, Israel's canonical historian informs us that God gave Solomon wisdom "greater than the wisdom of all the people of the East, and greater than all the wisdom of Egypt" (1 Kgs 4:30). In addition, the parental voice within Prov 1–9 asserts that the Lord gave the wisdom (i.e., the "words" [2:1]) found in the book: "For the LORD gives wisdom; from his mouth come knowledge and understanding" (2:6). Even the sayings of Agur son of Jakeh and of King Lemuel are identified as "inspired utterance[s]" (30:1; 31:1). When Solomon's proverbs and the sayings of the wise are internalized into the heart by memory and faith, the wisdom of God himself enters hearts of flesh (2:10).

AUDIENCE

In light of the preamble (1:1–7), the original audience consisted of two groups of people: (1) youths (1:4) and (2) the wise (1:5). The youths are characterized as simple, uncommitted (see note on 1:4), and gullible individuals on the brink of adulthood. The sage, in the guise of Lady Wisdom, challenges them to repent and choose wisdom, for they are headed for eternal death. She addresses them at the gate of the city, pleading with them to repent and embrace wisdom before they meet the temptations within the city. The book seeks to illuminate the value of wisdom and persuade these youths to choose the path of life. The second group addressed are those characterized as wise, i.e., individuals who cherish and choose wisdom but recognize that the search for wisdom is a lifelong process. In this respect, they are teachable, and the book seeks to develop their wisdom by sharpening the mind, softening the heart, and shaping the character of these wise and righteous people.

While the courtly setting of the parallel ancient Near Eastern texts and the royal texture of the collections (cf. 8:15; 16:12; 23:1; 27:23–24; 31:4) suggest the book was originally written for budding royal officials, the material has been democratized for all of Israel's youth, especially young men of marriageable age (1:1–4). This explains the male-centered nature of much of the material in chs. 1–9, which focuses on illicit sexual relations with females. Nonetheless, this male-centered focus does not mean that the book's instruction excludes women. To the contrary, virtues and vices presented in the material are relevant to both males and females. In this case, the "son" within chs. 1–9 may be taken as a child, a youth preparing to exit the household and enter the community as an independent adult.

The domestic, or familial, setting of the materials within Proverbs is intimated by the father-son discourses in chs. 1–9 as well as by the inclusion of the mother in the instructions (1:8; 6:20; 31:1). While the father-son idiom could refer to a teacher-pupil relationship, the inclusion of the mother, as well as the absence of any reference to schools in Israel during biblical times, makes this suggestion less than convincing.

Even though the material in the book is cast in a specific social and dialogical context (i.e., parents to a child within the home), as part of holy Scripture, the book of Proverbs now addresses the church. Christ's apostles cite the book in various ways about 60 times. Peter uses 26:11 as a proverb with reference to false teachers (2 Pet 2:22). Paul uses 25:21–22 to teach about feeding your enemies (Rom 12:20). And the writer of Hebrews uses 3:11–12 to convince the audience that hardships are a manifestation of God's correction, care, and commitment rather than a sign of his indifference (Heb 12:5–6). Beyond these explicit quotations within the NT, the book of Proverbs plays a significant role in the church's understanding of ethics. On the whole, the book distills and reapplies the ethical principles presented in Israel's covenant tradition (e.g., Exod 20–23; Lev 17–25; Deut 5–26) and provides the foundation for Jesus' and the NT writers' conception of kingdom ethics. In this sense, the book describes not only how people might live in accordance with the wise life but also how people might embody the virtues that mark the kingdom.

CHARACTER TYPES

Within the book's domestic setting, the reader encounters a variety of different characters, each of which plays a significant rhetorical and educational role within the book. As noted above, the preamble identifies two prominent characters within the anthology: the *wise* (1:5) and the *simple* (or *youth*, 1:4). While "the wise in heart accept commands" and "store up knowledge" (10:8,14; cf. 15:31), the simple remain open, committed to nothing. The simple person loves being uncommitted and is gullible and easily misled (14:15). This disposition explains the father's and Lady Wisdom's interest in the simple (1:20–26; 7:6–27; 8:4–5). The simple encounter various voices and characters vying for their allegiance within chs. 1–9 (sinful people, the wicked, evildoers, and the adulterous woman, who is presented in the guise of the woman Folly). The father and Lady Wisdom attempt to expose these bad character types—the futility of their promises and the consequences associated with following their path—and illuminate the value of wisdom. The father instructs his son about the danger of being simple (7:1–23), and Lady Wisdom, who represents the book's wisdom, motivates the simple to commit their lives to the path of wisdom (1:33).

While the simple love being open to any opinion and committed to none (1:22), fools are fixed in the correctness of their own opinions — opinions that fly in the face of the values that restore humanity to the moral order that God ordained and Proverbs reveals (12:15; 15:5,20). Their morally deficient character prompts their irrational behavior. They are simpletons because they are deaf to wisdom. From their distorted moral vision, of which they are certain, they delight in twisting values that benefit the community.

Worse than fools are *mockers*, those who are hardened apostates. They hate the wise and mock their wisdom (9:7–8); they are beyond Wisdom's call. Their spiritual problem is rooted in their boundless pride (21:24).

Also worse than fools are *sluggards* (26:13–16; cf. 6:6–11; 10:26; 13:4; 15:19; 19:24; 20:4; 21:25; 22:13; 24:30–34). Their unreliable and procrastinating natures make them constant sources of irritation to all those who need to do business with them (10:26), and they lose their families' heritage (24:30–34).

Nonetheless, despite these gradations of character types, it is important to recognize that Proverbs employs a variety of terms to describe the multifaceted character of the wise ("upright" [2:6–7], "righteous" [9:9], "generous" [11:25], "diligent" [12:24]) and the fool ("wicked" [10:23], "lazy" [26:15], "stingy" [28:22]). These descriptive terms do not denote different groups of people. Rather they illuminate the social, moral, and intellectual traits of the same type of person. In this respect, not only are the wise marked by an intellectual and practical ability to live in accordance with God's design, but they also embody righteousness, integrity, diligence, and generosity. In the same way, fools are not simply senseless dolts; they are also wicked, brash, and greedy. While Proverbs employs a variety of terms to describe diverse character types, on the whole, the book divides humanity into three basic categories: the wise/righteous, the simple, and the fool/wicked. Through these categories and the book's graphic portrayal of various character types, Proverbs attempts to shape the character and worldview of its readers by providing them with a vision of life rooted in the fear of the Lord and characterized by wisdom, which is inseparable from virtue. In this respect, the portrayals of these character types are not merely descriptive; they are also transformative. They form our feelings, sharpen our thinking, pinpoint our vices, cultivate virtue, and offer us a wise perspective on life.

LITERARY FEATURES

As an anthology of wisdom, Proverbs contains a variety of different materials, ranging from extended parental instructions (1:8–19) to autobiographical reflections (24:30–34) to alphabetic acrostics (31:10–31) to short, pithy sayings (22:17 — 24:22). While the literary frame of the book contains longer didactic discourses (1:1 — 9:18; 30:1–33; 31:1–9,10–31), scholarly opinion differs regarding whether the central collections are a random smorgasbord of individual proverbs or whether they are connected with one another in various ways. Despite the literary or generic variety within the book, however, four literary features characterize the diverse materials in Proverbs.

1. *Hebrew Poetry.* Like all poetry, Hebrew poetry is marked by terseness, vivid imagery, and figures of speech. Unlike English poetry, it is characterized by parallel lines in which the second line either (1) emphatically restates the first line (e.g., "Let someone else praise you, and not your own mouth; an outsider, and not your own lips" [27:2]), (2) expands the first line (e.g., "Honor the LORD with your wealth, with the firstfruits of all your crops" [3:9]), or (3) presents a contrast to the first line (e.g., "A wise son brings joy to his father, but a foolish son brings grief to his mother" [10:1]).

2. *Wisdom Literature.* The various materials within the book are an integral component of the international tradition of wisdom literature. In contrast to the materials in the Pentateuch and the Prophets, Israel's wisdom literature is characterized by a remarkable secularity; it focuses on the world of nature (30:18–19) as well as human behavior (24:30–34) and experience (4:1–9). This focus does not mean that Israel's wisdom literature is a brand of natural theology, for Proverbs refers to God by his covenantal, personal name ("LORD") and observes the creation through the lens of Israel's covenant values. Indeed, all of the observations on nature, as well as human experience and behavior within the book, are passed through the filter of faith (i.e., "the fear of the LORD" [1:7; 2:5; 9:10; etc.]). From this theological perspective, Israel's wisdom literature teaches covenant values but makes no mention of Israel's historic covenants. That is, it complements Israel's covenant tradition by reflecting upon and recontextualizing its ethical and theological worldview from a distinct frame of reference (see Introduction: Theme).

3. *Wise Sayings.* The sayings within the central collections of the book are quite distinct. As proverbs, they represent short, pithy sayings that communicate a traditional or popular truth, such as "A stitch in time saves nine." But unlike this English proverb, the sayings of Proverbs have currency among *the people of God*, not the world in

general, because they are based on faith in Israel's covenant-keeping God. "Do not be wise in your own eyes; fear the LORD and shun evil" (3:7) runs counter to the popular sayings of unbelievers such as "Believe in yourself" and "The Lord helps those who help themselves." The book's sound bites function as exemplars by which the people of God are to compare their own behavior or thinking.

4. *Contextual Truth.* It is important to note that proverbs express a truth, but only a limited truth that other proverbs must nuance or qualify. For example, "The LORD does not let the righteous go hungry, but he thwarts the craving of the wicked" (10:3) seems to contradict the experiences of many believers and of the Lord Jesus Christ, who hungered for 40 days in the wilderness (Matt 4:1 – 2). The preceding proverb, however, safeguards that saying from misunderstanding: "Ill-gotten treasures have no lasting value, but righteousness delivers from death" (10:2). In other words, the wicked have treasures for a while, but in the end they will lose all, whereas the righteous in the end will be delivered even from death. This proverb pair also shows that Proverbs looks at the end of a matter. The proverb "Though the righteous fall seven times, they rise again, but the wicked stumble when calamity strikes" (24:16) grants that the righteous may be completely knocked down, presumably even by death, but they will rise, unlike the final catastrophic end of the wicked. In addition, one should not read "Start children off on the way they should go, and even when they are old they will not turn from it" (22:6) to mean that a child is a programmed robot. This proverb teaches that parental training has its effect throughout a person's life, but the proverb must be nuanced by other proverbs and sayings such as "The eye that mocks a father, that scorns an aged mother, will be pecked out by the ravens of the valley, will be eaten by the vultures" (30:17). Each proverb presents a truth, but this truth must be discovered within the context of the entire collection of sayings and contextualized or applied to appropriate circumstances (see 16:10 – 15; 26:4 – 5; 28:15). The same is true of English proverbs. The sayings "Don't cry over spilled milk," "Many hands make light work," and "Too many cooks spoil the broth" are true. But one has to discern which proverb is appropriate within a particular situation. In this case, a proverb should not be read only as an independent, isolated saying that communicates a truth; it should also be read in its immediate and broad literary context as well as in conversation with other proverbs that reflect on the truth or topic treated by the saying.

THEME

In essence, Proverbs seeks to teach wisdom (1:1 – 2). By definition, *wisdom* means "masterful understanding, skill." While the term elsewhere describes those with physical, moral, technical, or intellectual skills, in Proverbs it refers to the skill of godly living with respect to God and people.

In this respect, wisdom is distinct from knowledge but cannot be had apart from it. The Wright brothers flew the first airplane because they had first figured out the fundamental laws of aerodynamics; a mechanic's skill depends

A scribe registering quantities of harvested wheat, possibly for taxing purposes. Thebes, fifteenth century BC. Proverbs were collected and written down by trained scribes.

Z. Radovan/www.BibleLandPictures.com

on his knowledge of the motor. The wise have social skill because they know *personally*, not merely *about*, the proverbs and sayings of this book. This knowledge is gained in the fear of the Lord, which entails humbly accepting the book's instruction; disciples embrace the inspired sages' knowledge and wisdom because they trust and fear the Lord, who inspired these sayings and upholds them (1:7). As cement without water cannot produce mortar, so the proverb without faith that submits to the Lord's Word cannot produce wisdom. The wise have faith not in the proverbs per se but in the Lord who upholds the truth in the proverbs. "Trust in the LORD with all your heart" (3:5) means to trust the one who has inspired this book.

Out of his grace, God gave the Mosaic law and the Prophets to his people in order to reveal his will after the fall into original sin in Adam. But the book of Proverbs takes up those matters that are too fine to be caught in the mesh of the law and too small to be hit by the broadsides of the Prophets. The proverbs concern themselves with qualities such as honesty, integrity, diligence, kindness, generosity, readiness to forgive, truthfulness, patience, humility, cheerfulness, loyalty, temperance, and self-control. Anger is to be held in check, violence and quarrelsomeness shunned, gossip avoided, arrogance repudiated. Drunkenness, gluttony, envy, and greed are also to be renounced. The poor are not to be exploited, the courts are not to be unjustly manipulated, legitimate authorities are to be honored. Parents are responsible to care for the proper instruction and discipline of their children, and children are to duly honor their parents and bring no disgrace on them. To embrace these values brings God's rule to earth; they are the way of life; to defy them is the way of death.

The dominant metaphor for the moral life in Proverbs is the "way." The metaphor portrays life as a journey (cf. Paul's use of *peripateō*, the Greek word for "walk," in Rom 6:4 ["live"]; 8:4 ["live]; 13:13 ["behave"]; 2 Cor 12:18 ["walk"]; Eph 2:2 ["live"]; 2:10 ["do"]; 5:2 ["walk"]; 5:15 ["live"]). By virtue of its use with the lifestyles of the wise and the fool, as well as those of the righteous and the wicked, the metaphor refers to a person's character, social context, conduct, and, above all, the consequences of these characteristics. The wise always keep in mind the consequences of their actions: either life or death; there is no third way.

LADY WISDOM

The wisdom that this book gives (see 1:1–2) is personified as a woman in chs. 1–9 (1:20–33; 8:1–36; 9:1–6). This literary device is significant in at least three respects: (1) Personification creates a framework through which to understand Wisdom's multifaceted character. It provides a means by which we may understand the diverse images of prophet, teacher, counselor, lover, daughter, mother, and host. (2) Personification transforms abstract knowledge into an attractive form. (3) Personification allows wisdom (as Lady Wisdom) to represent the antithesis of both the adulterous woman (5:1–6; 6:20–35; 7:1–27) and the woman Folly (9:13–18). Lady Wisdom is the object of desire, the one who understands the fundamental patterns within the universe (see 8:22–31 and notes), and the one who can align her devotees' lives in step with those patterns to live in harmony with God's creative activity. Wisdom's female persona also plays an important role in the book as a whole, serving as the metaphoric counterpart to the woman that 31:10–31 describes.

While Lady Wisdom is a distinct figure within the prologue, it is important to recognize that she makes her appeals to the simple youths (see note on 1:4), who are represented as not living in their parents' home, to accept the book's wisdom (1:20–33; 8:1–36; 9:1–6); the parents, presumably in the home, exhort the covenant child to accept its wisdom. Striking parallels link Lady Wisdom's addresses with those of the parents. Her admonitions and her motivations in 8:32–36 match those of the parents elsewhere (e.g., 3:3–4; 4:20–22). And in light of the introductions to Lady Wisdom's formal speeches, it appears that the father serves as Lady Wisdom's voice. Together with the parents, Lady Wisdom provides readers with an antidote for seductive speech. That is, she interprets the sly rhetoric and deceptive promises of the other characters in the prologue to move readers to embrace her and the way of life.

THE WISDOM OF PROVERBS AND JESUS CHRIST

The poetic description of Lady Wisdom in 8:22–31 contributes to an understanding of Jesus' nature and identity. Similar to the way John 1:1–5 describes Jesus, Prov 8:22–29 affirms that Wisdom existed before the creation of any element within the cosmos. In Wisdom's address to the simple in 1:20–33, she humbles herself, calls sinners to repentance, and serves as a mediator between the Lord and humanity in much the same way that Jesus humbled himself, called sinners to himself, and serves as the only Mediator between God and humanity (1 Tim 2:5; Heb 9:11–28). As the truly wise king, one greater than Solomon, Jesus exemplifies God's wisdom. But unlike Jesus Christ, Lady Wisdom is represented as being born (8:24), and so she is not eternal. She is also represented as an instrument of creation

(3:18–19) and as present at the creation (8:30), but she is never represented as the Creator. The NT never identifies Lady Wisdom with Jesus Christ, who is the Creator (John 1:1–5; Col 1:16–20). Rather the NT uses wisdom as a theological category to describe Jesus' identity, deity, and redemptive work.

Accordingly, the trajectory of Proverbs' words of wisdom terminates in Jesus Christ and in his church. Jesus is the eternal Word made flesh (John 1:1–18); in him "are hidden all the treasures of wisdom and knowledge" (Col 2:3). His church participates in this more-than-fulfillment by abiding in him (John 15:1–6). The church is being conformed to his likeness by faith in him (1 Cor 1:24,30; Col 2:2–3).

The culmination of Proverbs' wisdom being in Jesus is apparent through the various ways in which the book's ethical advice and description of the Lord's actions are displayed in Christ. This is not surprising because Jesus is God and his wisdom is superior to the wisdom of Solomon (Matt 12:42). Whereas Proverbs teaches its disciples to wait for God to repay the wrongdoer (24:12), Jesus declares that he will repay them (Matt 25:41–46). Whereas Proverbs depends on God to discipline those he loves (3:11–12), Jesus affirms that he disciplines those he loves (Rev 3:19). Whereas Proverbs teaches that God will reward those who share with the poor (14:21), Jesus identifies himself with the poor and as the one who rewards those who sacrifice for the poor (Matt 25:31–46). While no human has ascended into heaven (Prov 30:4), Christ both descended from heaven and ascended into it (John 3:13). While Proverbs calls on its disciples to write its teachings on their hearts (3:3), Christ sends his Spirit to write God's word on believers' hearts (2 Cor 3:3). And whereas Proverbs calls on its disciples to feed their enemies (25:21), Christ died for his enemies (Rom 5:8).

The NT manifests the ethical and theological significance of the instructions within Proverbs through the teaching of Jesus. And the activities of God within Proverbs are connected with Jesus in the NT. No wonder Paul describes Jesus as "the wisdom of God" (1 Cor 1:24), the one through whom the believer receives wisdom (Eph 1:7–10).

OUTLINE

I. Preamble and Prologue (1:1—9:18)
- A. Preamble: Purpose and Theme (1:1–7)
- B. Prologue: Exhortations to Embrace Wisdom (1:8—9:18)
  1. Warning Against the Invitation of Sinful Men (1:8–19)
  2. Wisdom's Rebuke (1:20–33)
  3. Moral Benefits of Wisdom (2:1–22)
  4. Wisdom Bestows Well-Being (3:1–35)
     - a. The Lord's Promises and the Son's Obligations (3:1–12)
     - b. The Value of Wisdom (3:13–35)
  5. Get the Family Heritage (4:1–9)
  6. Stay Off the Wrong Way (4:10–19)
  7. Don't Swerve From the Right Way (4:20–27)
  8. Warning Against Adultery (5:1–23)
  9. Warnings Against Folly (6:1–19)
  10. Warning Against Adultery (6:20–35)
  11. Warning Against the Adulterous Woman (7:1–27)
  12. Wisdom's Call (8:1–36)
  13. Invitations of Wisdom and Folly (9:1–18)

II. Proverbs of Solomon (10:1—22:16)

III. Thirty Sayings of the Wise (22:17—24:22)

IV. Further Sayings of the Wise (24:23–34)

V. More Proverbs of Solomon (25:1—29:27)

VI. Sayings of Agur (30:1–33)

VII. Sayings of King Lemuel's Mother (31:1–31)
- A. Sayings of King Lemuel (31:1–9)
- B. Epilogue: The Wife of Noble Character (31:10–31)

PROVERBS

1:1 [a]1Ki 4:29-34 [b]Pr 10:1; 25:1; Ecc 1:1
1:4 [c]Pr 8:5 [d]Pr 2:10-11; 8:12
1:5 [e]Pr 9:9

Purpose and Theme

1 The proverbs of Solomon[a] son of David, king of Israel:[b]

[2] for gaining wisdom and instruction;
for understanding words of insight;
[3] for receiving instruction in prudent behavior,
doing what is right and just and fair;
[4] for giving prudence to those who are simple,[a][c]
knowledge and discretion[d] to the young—
[5] let the wise listen and add to their learning,[e]
and let the discerning get guidance—

[a] *4* The Hebrew word rendered *simple* in Proverbs denotes a person who is gullible, without moral direction and inclined to evil.

1:1—9:18 *Preamble and Prologue.* The initial collection consists of two parts. The preamble (1:1–7) identifies the book's author, nature, purpose, principal audiences, and fundamental assumption, while the prologue (1:8—9:18) contains introductory lectures that shape the collections of proverbs and prepare readers to acquire the wisdom presented in these proverbs.

1:1–7 *Preamble: Purpose and Theme.* The preamble presents the book's title (v. 1), purpose (vv. 2–6), and fundamental underlying assumption (v. 7). In so doing, it provides a lens through which to understand the materials in the remainder of the book.

1:1 proverbs. The genre, or nature, of the materials in the book (see Introduction: Literary Features). **Solomon son of David, king of Israel.** The author of many of the proverbs. As known from Egyptian instructional literature, the long heading of v. 1 and the short heading of 10:1 mark off two sections of one original work (see Introduction: Authors).

1:2–6 for ... for ... for ... for ... for. The series of purpose clauses captures the goal of the book. This goal is described through the intellectual (vv. 2,6), instrumental (vv. 3a,4–5), and moral or communal (v. 3b) virtues that pervade the preamble. The absence of the preposition "for" in v. 3b is significant, because it identifies these moral and communal virtues as the center of the preamble's structural design as well as the fundamental values the book seeks to instill in its readers.

1:2 gaining. Implies knowing something personally rather than simply knowing about something (2:1–4). **wisdom.** The book's theme; refers to the skill of godly living with respect to God and people (see Introduction: Theme). **instruction.** While the term means "discipline" in the context of corporal correction, here it carries the sense of intellectual training; it assumes that innate human waywardness must be shed. **understanding.** The ability to discern and grasp the wisdom presented in the book. **words.** The book's materials, i.e., the forms through which wisdom is communicated. **insight.** The skill to apply sound reason, which characterizes these inspired materials.

1:3 receiving. Accepting with approval, as with a gift. **prudent behavior.** Grasping the meaning of the book's wisdom and applying it to concrete situations in order to make a beneficial decision. **what is right and just.** Moral and communal virtues, frequently occurring together in the OT to denote one who lives, judges, and governs rightly (Gen 18:19; Ps 106:3). **fair.** The Hebrew word derives from the geometric notion of being straight, vertically or horizontally; when behavior does not stray from God's "straight" order, there is peace and prosperity.

1:4 prudence. An intellectual virtue that involves shrewdness: the ability to devise adroit practices in order to achieve a godly outcome. **simple.** As one of the book's principal addressees, the "simple" are open (i.e., committed to neither wisdom nor folly [see Introduction: Audience; Character Types]). **knowledge.** The book's teaching. **discretion.** Private, unrevealed planning informed by Proverbs. **young.** Parallel with "simple"; reveals their lack of experience (2 Sam 14:21; 18:5; Jer 1:6) and their age. Though the Hebrew word can range from infancy to any time before becoming an elder (Gen 37:2; 41:12; cf. Exod 2:6; 1 Sam 1:22), in this book it refers to youths at the point of adulthood.

1:5 wise. Extends the book's reach beyond the simple youth. Instead of being self-assured (26:5,11–12,16), the wise are teachable (2:1–5; 10:8; 12:1; 13:1; 15:31)—even loving reproof (9:8)—and store up (i.e., memorize with affection) knowledge (2:1; 10:14). **listen.** The primary means of education and the channel for receiving instruction. This exhortation subtly includes the son (cf. v. 8). **add to.** Implies a lifelong process of moral improvement through God's Word (4:18–19) in the fear of the Lord (1:7). **discerning.** Or "insightful"; i.e., a person of understanding. **guidance.** With its parallels, includes plans accompanied with advice (20:18; cf. 11:14; 12:5).

6 for understanding proverbs and parables,[f]
the sayings and riddles[g] of the wise.[a]

7 The fear of the LORD[h] is the beginning of knowledge,
but fools[b] despise wisdom and instruction.

1:6 [f]Ps 49:4; 78:2 [g]Nu 12:8
1:7 [h]Job 28:28; Ps 111:10; Pr 9:10; 15:33; Ecc 12:13
1:8 [i]Pr 4:1 [j]Pr 6:20
1:9 [k]Pr 4:1-9
1:10 [l]Ge 39:7 [m]Dt 13:8 [n]Pr 16:29; Eph 5:11
1:11 [o]Ps 10:8

Prologue: Exhortations to Embrace Wisdom

Warning Against the Invitation of Sinful Men

8 Listen, my son,[i] to your father's instruction
and do not forsake your mother's teaching.[j]
9 They are a garland to grace your head
and a chain to adorn your neck.[k]

10 My son, if sinful men entice[l] you,
do not give in[m] to them.[n]
11 If they say, "Come along with us;
let's lie in wait[o] for innocent blood,
let's ambush some harmless soul;

[a] 6 Or *understanding a proverb, namely, a parable, / and the sayings of the wise, their riddles*
[b] 7 The Hebrew words rendered *fool* in Proverbs, and often elsewhere in the Old Testament, denote a person who is morally deficient.

1:6 proverbs and parables ... riddles of the wise. Refers to the whole book of Proverbs, not to different kinds of literary forms in the book. The clustering of these terms suggests that the book demands diligent study (2.4, see Introduction: Literary Features).
1:7 The fear of the LORD. The book's basic presupposition as well as the prerequisite for acquiring wisdom. It is a disposition cultivated in relationship with God. It entails the humility to accept the book's teaching out of the conviction that God upholds it, rewarding the faithful with life and punishing the unfaithful with death. It also is an attitude that shapes one's worldview and serves as the seedbed in which wisdom might be cultivated. This presupposition frames Collection I (i.e., 1:8—9:18; cf. 9:10) and the book as a whole (cf. 31:30), suggesting that it provides the reader with a theological perspective on life as well as a means to discover truth about God in the world. **the LORD.** The name of Israel's covenant-keeping God (see notes on Exod 3:14–15), indicating that the book addresses his chosen people. **beginning.** That is, the first step or fundamental requirement to achieve the goal of the book. **fools.** A fool is a simpleton who is morally deficient and characterized by irrational behavior (see Introduction: Character Types). Fools and their way of life represent one of the two major alternatives offered in the book: the way of wisdom and life on the one hand and the way of folly and death on the other. **wisdom and instruction.** Frames the book's purpose and fundamental assumption to attain that end (v. 2).
1:8—9:18 *Prologue: Exhortations to Embrace Wisdom.* The exhortations and instructions within the prologue are arranged in a concentric pattern:

- *a* Rival invitations to the son from the parents and the gang (1:8–19)
  - *b* Interlude: Wisdom's rebuke of the simple (1:20–33)
    - *c* Hinge: Parents' lecture to heed teaching to safeguard against evil men and adulteress (2:1–22)
      - *d* Parents' four lectures to heed teaching (3:1—4:27)
      - *d´* Parents' three lectures to safeguard against evil men and adulteress (5:1—6:35)
    - *c´* Hinge: Parents' lecture against adulteress by the foil of the simple (7:1–27)
  - *b´* Interlude: Wisdom's invitation to the simple (8:1–36)
- *a´* Rival invitations of Wisdom and Folly to the simple (9:1–18)

This structural pattern indicates that ch. 7 marks a transition within the prologue, for it not only looks back to the adulteress in chs. 5–6 but also looks ahead to the simple in chs. 8–9. The parents' instructions (1:8–19; 2:1–22; 3:1–12,13–35; 4:1–9,10–19,20–27; 5:1–6,7–23; 6:1–19,20–35) address the son in the home, whereas Lady Wisdom's exhortations address the simple at the city gate (see Introduction: Lady Wisdom). The parents and Wisdom use all their rhetorical skill to expose the seductive rhetoric of evil men and women, to illuminate the value of wisdom, and to win the allegiance of the simple youth to the wisdom presented in the collections that follow.
1:8–19 *Warning Against the Invitation of Sinful Men.* The instructions to the son are cast in the home, where a father (perhaps Solomon) or mother exhorts their tender child to seek the wisdom of this book. To safeguard the son from accepting the crafty invitation of sinful men, the parents expose those empty promises as well as the self-destructive nature of their claims. The parents' introduction summarizes the sinner's seduction (v. 10a) and warns their son (v. 10b). The body elaborates upon the seduction (vv. 11–14) and warning (vv. 15–18). The instruction then concludes with a lesson (v. 19).
1:8 Listen. See note on v. 5. **son.** The primary addressee of the book—and one in need of instruction. In light of the inclusion of the mother and the absence of formal schools in ancient Israel, it appears the son is both the biological and spiritual heir of the father (see 4:3). **father's ... mother's.** Establishes the setting of the instructions in the home. Both parents are set in parallel at the introductions of Collections I and II (i.e., 1:8—9:18 and 10:1—22:16, respectively; see 10:1), suggesting that the mother's presence is assumed in the father's other lectures (cf. 6:20; 23:22). Together, they are responsible for the son's social, moral, and theological education.
1:9 garland ... a chain. Ornamental metaphors that highlight the attractiveness, value, and distinction of the parents' teaching.
1:11 they say. "Come along with us." The deceptive invitation of the sinful men. Similar to the voice of Lady Wisdom (vv. 20–21; 8:1–3), the father warns against the sinful men who prey upon the innocent. In light of their plot, their intention is to claim the lives of the harmless, violating the sixth commandment: "You shall not murder" (Exod 20:13).

1:12 [p]Ps 28:1
1:15 [q]Ps 119:101 [r]Ps 1:1; Pr 4:14
1:16 [s]Pr 6:18; Isa 59:7
1:19 [t]Pr 15:27
1:20 [u]Pr 8:1; 9:1-3,13-15
1:22 [v]Pr 8:5; 9:4,16
1:24 [w]Isa 65:12; 66:4; Jer 7:13; Zec 7:11
1:26 [x]Ps 2:4 [y]Pr 6:15; 10:24

12 let's swallow them alive, like the grave,
and whole, like those who go down to the pit;[p]
13 we will get all sorts of valuable things
and fill our houses with plunder;
14 cast lots with us;
we will all share the loot" —
15 my son, do not go along with them,
do not set foot[q] on their paths;[r]
16 for their feet rush into evil,
they are swift to shed blood.[s]
17 How useless to spread a net
where every bird can see it!
18 These men lie in wait for their own blood;
they ambush only themselves!
19 Such are the paths of all who go after ill-gotten gain;
it takes away the life of those who get it.[t]

Wisdom's Rebuke

20 Out in the open wisdom calls aloud,[u]
she raises her voice in the public square;
21 on top of the wall[a] she cries out,
at the city gate she makes her speech:

22 "How long will you who are simple[v] love your simple ways?
How long will mockers delight in mockery
and fools hate knowledge?
23 Repent at my rebuke!
Then I will pour out my thoughts to you,
I will make known to you my teachings.
24 But since you refuse to listen when I call[w]
and no one pays attention when I stretch out my hand,
25 since you disregard all my advice
and do not accept my rebuke,
26 I in turn will laugh[x] when disaster strikes you;
I will mock when calamity overtakes you[y] —

[a] *21* Septuagint; Hebrew */ at noisy street corners*

1:12 swallow them alive, like the grave. Depicts the sinful men in alliance with *šĕʾôl* (Hebrew for "grave") and death. Similar to the description of Death in Isaiah 5:14, these men are depicted as a giant mouth, the entryway to the pit.

1:13 valuable things ... plunder. The goal of the sinners' plot: money. By exploiting the innocent, they seek to fatten their pockets through their get-rich-quick schemes. This desire for wealth and the inevitable destruction that follows in its wake is captured in the following verses as well as in 1 Tim 6:9.

1:16 blood. Refers to both the innocent (vv. 11–14) and sinners (vv. 17–18). For a partial quotation of the verse, see Isa 59:7 (cf. Rom 3:15).

1:17 a net. A hunter's trap. Setting the trap in sight of the bird defeats its purpose. The sinners' unbelief in ultimate justice makes them more senseless than birds, for they set their own trap.

1:19 Such. Signifies a general, universal lesson that applies to analogous situations in which sinful people pursue wealth through wicked means. The lesson is based on the conviction that God governs the world with justice. Since the innocent died prematurely, ultimate justice lies beyond the grave. While the OT does not discuss the afterlife in much detail, it is amplified throughout the NT. And when the claim that sin yields death (Rom 6:23) is understood through the work of Jesus, one may find both forgiveness and life through faith in him (1 John 2:1–2; 5:12).

1:20–33 *Wisdom's Rebuke.* Just as the father serves as the voice of the sinful men, so he now represents the voice of Lady Wisdom in her address to the youths who are at the city gate, not in their homes. Here wisdom appears as a teacher or prophet. Her rebuke has three parts: (1) an introduction that identifies the location of her address (vv. 20–21); (2) a main body in which Wisdom rebukes the unresponsive simpletons (vv. 22–27); and (3) a reflection on the consequences of their rejection (vv. 28–33; cf. 8:32–36).

1:20–21 calls aloud ... cries out. Wisdom delivers her rebuke above the din and bustle of the city.

1:20 public square. Perhaps at the city gate, the public forum for counsel and judgment (Deut 22:15; 25:7; Ruth 4:1,11; 2 Sam 19:8).

1:22 simple ... mockers ... fools. See Introduction: Audience; Character Types; cf. 8:1–5; 9:7–8.

[27] when calamity overtakes you like a storm,
when disaster sweeps over you like a whirlwind,
when distress and trouble overwhelm you.

[28] "Then they will call to me but I will not answer;[z]
they will look for me but will not find me.[a]
[29] since they hated knowledge
and did not choose to fear the LORD.[b]
[30] Since they would not accept my advice
and spurned my rebuke,[c]
[31] they will eat the fruit of their ways
and be filled with the fruit of their schemes.[d]
[32] For the waywardness of the simple will kill them,
and the complacency of fools will destroy them;[e]
[33] but whoever listens to me will live in safety[f]
and be at ease, without fear of harm."[g]

1:28 [z] 1Sa 8:18; Isa 1:15; Jer 11:11; Mic 3:4 [a] Job 27:9; Pr 8:17; Eze 8:18; Zec 7:13
1:29 [b] Job 21:14
1:30 [c] ver 25; Ps 81:11
1:31 [d] Job 4:8; Pr 14:14; Isa 3:11; Jer 6:19
1:32 [e] Jer 2:19
1:33 [f] Ps 25:12; Pr 3:23 [g] Ps 112:8
2:2 [h] Pr 22:17
2:4 [i] Job 3:21; Pr 3:14; Mt 13:44
2:5 [j] Pr 1:7
2:6 [k] 1Ki 3:9,12; Jas 1:5
2:7 [l] Pr 30:5-6 [m] Ps 84:11
2:8 [n] 1Sa 2:9; Ps 66:9

Moral Benefits of Wisdom

2 My son, if you accept my words
and store up my commands within you,
[2] turning your ear to wisdom
and applying your heart to understanding[h]—
[3] indeed, if you call out for insight
and cry aloud for understanding,
[4] and if you look for it as for silver
and search for it as for hidden treasure,[i]
[5] then you will understand the fear of the LORD
and find the knowledge of God.[j]
[6] For the LORD gives wisdom;[k]
from his mouth come knowledge and understanding.
[7] He holds success in store for the upright,
he is a shield[l] to those whose walk is blameless,[m]
[8] for he guards the course of the just
and protects the way of his faithful ones.[n]

1:28 not answer. Wisdom will not provide those who reject her with the skills to get out of trouble when it inevitably comes. When they search for wisdom to wiggle out of a tight spot, she will be absent.
1:31 eat the fruit. Experience fully the inevitable consequence of their rejection (cf. Gal 6:7).
1:32 For. Introduces the sweeping conclusion. **waywardness**. An ironic pun on "repent" (v. 23). The Hebrew word for "repent" and "turning" (NIV "waywardness") is the same.
2:1–22 *Moral Benefits of Wisdom.* The second parental instruction aims to safeguard the son against wicked men and women by describing the transformative and protective powers of wisdom. The instruction consists of two equal halves: the development of his character (vv. 1–11) and his deliverance from the wicked (vv. 12–22). Meeting the conditions of vv. 1–4 will result in a religious (vv. 5–8) and an ethical (vv. 9–11) education. The son's ethical education is dependent on his religious education; both educations will offer protection (vv. 7–8,11).
2:1–4 if ... if ... if. Introduces the conditions and functions rhetorically to induce the search for wisdom. **accept ... store up ... turning your ear ... applying your heart ... call out ... cry aloud ... look for ... search.** Portrays the search for wisdom as a quest in which one not only launches a hunt for wisdom but also receives, memorizes, and internalizes the teaching of the wise.
2:1–3 words ... wisdom ... understanding ... insight. Repeats the book's aim (1:2).
2:5–11 The consequences of religious and ethical education are set in an alternating structure (italics added):

a *Understand* the fear of the LORD (v. 5; see 1:7)
b For the LORD gives *wisdom* (v. 6; see 1:2)
c He *guards* ... and *protects* the way (v. 8; see Introduction: Theme)
a´ *Understand* what is right and just and fair (v. 9; see 1:3)
b´ For *wisdom* will enter your heart (v. 10; see 1:2)
c´ Discretion will *protect* ... *guard* you (v. 11; see 1:4)

Understanding the fear of the Lord is foundational to knowing what is right. Wisdom in the father's mouth originates in the heart of God and is mediated to the son's heart through the conditions of vv. 1–4. While the son searches for wisdom, it is God who graciously bestows wisdom on those who diligently seek her. And the acquisition of wisdom yields reward: an understanding of what is right, just, and fair (v. 9; see 1:3b), as well as protection (vv. 7–8,11,12–17). The move from *guards-protects* to *protect-guard* brings closure to the lecture's first half.

2:10 [o]Pr 14:33
2:11 [p]Pr 4:6; 6:22
2:13 [q]Pr 4:19; Jn 3:19
2:14 [r]Pr 10:23; Jer 11:15
2:15 [s]Ps 125:5 [t]Pr 21:8
2:16 [u]Pr 5:1-6; 6:20-29; 7:5-27
2:17 [v]Mal 2:14
2:18 [w]Pr 7:27
2:19 [x]Ecc 7:26
2:21 [y]Ps 37:29
2:22 [z]Job 18:17; Ps 37:38 [a]Dt 28:63; Pr 10:30
3:1 [b]Pr 4:5
3:2 [c]Pr 4:10

9 Then you will understand what is right and just
and fair — every good path.
10 For wisdom will enter your heart,[o]
and knowledge will be pleasant to your soul.
11 Discretion will protect you,
and understanding will guard you.[p]

12 Wisdom will save you from the ways of wicked men,
from men whose words are perverse,
13 who have left the straight paths
to walk in dark ways,[q]
14 who delight in doing wrong
and rejoice in the perverseness of evil,[r]
15 whose paths are crooked[s]
and who are devious in their ways.[t]

16 Wisdom will save you also from the adulterous
woman,[u]
from the wayward woman with her seductive words,
17 who has left the partner of her youth
and ignored the covenant she made before God.[a][v]
18 Surely her house leads down to death
and her paths to the spirits of the dead.[w]
19 None who go to her return
or attain the paths of life.[x]

20 Thus you will walk in the ways of the good
and keep to the paths of the righteous.
21 For the upright will live in the land,[y]
and the blameless will remain in it;
22 but the wicked will be cut off from the land,[z]
and the unfaithful will be torn from it.[a]

Wisdom Bestows Well-Being

3 My son, do not forget my teaching,[b]
but keep my commands in your heart,
2 for they will prolong your life many years[c]
and bring you peace and prosperity.

[a] *17* Or *covenant of her God*

2:10 heart. The heart is the essence of the self and the spring from which a person's life proceeds (cf. Matt 12:34; Mark 7:14 – 23; Luke 6:45; see note on Ps 7:9).
2:12 words are perverse. Words have dynamic spiritual power for good and evil (cf. 1:11 – 14; 2:16).
2:13 have left the straight paths. In contrast to the good paths of the wise and righteous (vv. 9,20), the path, or lifestyle, of the wicked is dark and crooked (v. 15).
2:14 delight in doing wrong. See Rom 1:32.
2:16 adulterous woman. An unfaithful wife. This woman is mentioned in 65 verses, more than any other figure in the book (5:1 – 23; 6:20 – 35; 7:1 – 27; 22:14; 23:27). She is depicted as an unfaithful wife who seeks to undermine the social and moral foundations of the family and community. **seductive words.** Speech rather than external beauty is the primary mechanism of seduction. Wisdom enables the son to interpret the adulterous woman's enticing rhetoric and understand the consequences of his actions.
2:17 left the partner of her youth. Betrays her husband. **the covenant she made before God.** Her marriage covenant.
2:18 leads down to death. See Lev 20:10; Deut 22:22. **spirits of the dead.** Refers to corpses in the underworld or realm of the dead (1:12; 9:18).
2:20 ways. See Introduction: Theme.
2:21 – 22 land ... land. Possibly the Holy Land, God's gift to Israel (cf. Ps 37:11). Whereas the upright will enjoy the fruits of this glorious inheritance, the wicked will be expelled from the land.
3:1 – 35 *Wisdom Bestows Well-Being.* The chapter contains two distinct units: (1) the nature of genuine piety (vv. 1 – 12) and (2) an instruction that describes the value of wisdom (vv. 13 – 35).
3:1 – 12 *The Lord's Promises and the Son's Obligations.* The third parental lecture consists of five sections in which the son's religious and ethical obligations are stated in the odd-numbered verses and the Lord's reciprocal, beneficial promises, are stated in the even-numbered verses. The son's obligations shift from those to his parents (v. 1), to others (vv. 3 – 4),

3 Let love and faithfulness never leave you;
bind them around your neck,
write them on the tablet of your heart.[d]
4 Then you will win favor and a good name
in the sight of God and man.[e]

5 Trust in the LORD[f] with all your heart
and lean not on your own understanding;
6 in all your ways submit to him,
and he will make your paths[g] straight.[a][h]

7 Do not be wise in your own eyes;[i]
fear the LORD and shun evil.[j]
8 This will bring health to your body[k]
and nourishment to your bones.[l]

9 Honor the LORD with your wealth,
with the firstfruits[m] of all your crops;
10 then your barns will be filled[n] to overflowing,
and your vats will brim over with new wine.[o]

11 My son, do not despise the LORD's discipline,[p]
and do not resent his rebuke,
12 because the LORD disciplines those he loves,[q]
as a father the son he delights in.[b][r]

13 Blessed are those who find wisdom,
those who gain understanding,

3:3 [d]Ex 13:9; Pr 6:21; 7:3; 2Co 3:3
3:4 [e]1Sa 2:26; Lk 2:52
3:5 [f]Ps 37:3,5
3:6 [g]1Ch 28:9 [h]Pr 16:3; Isa 45:13
3:7 [i]Ro 12:16 [j]Job 1:1; Pr 16:6
3:8 [k]Pr 4:22 [l]Job 21:24
3:9 [m]Ex 22:29; 23:19; Dt 26:1-15
3:10 [n]Dt 28:8 [o]Joel 2:24
3:11 [p]Job 5:17
3:12 [q]Pr 13:24; Rev 3:19 [r]Dt 8:5; Heb 12:5-6*

[a] *6* Or *will direct your paths* [b] *12* Hebrew; Septuagint *loves, / and he chastens everyone he accepts as his child*

and to the Lord (vv. 5,7,9); the Lord's promises shift from inner piety to its outward manifestation. Only the Lord can promise to bestow long life (v. 2), his favor (v. 4; see 15:25), and abundant health and prosperity (vv. 6,8,10; see 10:22). These sections present an important, yet partial, truth (see Introduction: Literary Features, 4). While the Lord grants these benefits, other proverbs show that the Lord does not fulfill his promises immediately (20:22; 22:22–23); if he did, there would be no need for the son to trust him (v. 5). The concluding section (vv. 11–12) teaches that the Lord disciplines the son so that he may experience the Lord's benefits.

3:2 prolong your life. Used elsewhere to describe the suffering servant after he pours out his life as a sin offering (Isa 53:10). The Bible never envisions death as the end of the godly. **peace and prosperity.** God's gifts of contentment, delight, joy, and pleasure; without them, endless years are wretched. This condition of mental and physical wholeness is the certain reward of the wise, who by faith keep the end in view (15:16; cf. 16:8,19,32; 17:1; 19:1,22; 21:9,19; 22:1; 25:24; 28:6).

3:3 love. Denotes a strong, intimate commitment to another. **faithfulness.** Denotes reliability (cf. 20:28; Exod 34:6). **bind them around your neck, write them on the tablet of your heart.** Exhortations to embody love and faithfulness to the extent that they become external ornaments for all to see and internal qualities that shape one's character. **heart.** See note on 2:10.

3:4 favor and a good name. Approval and a virtuous reputation. The Lord Jesus in his youth won favor and a good name (Luke 2:52), but later, men crucified him because they feared humankind rather than God. Today Jesus' name is exalted above all names (Phil 2:9–10).

3:5 Trust in. Depend upon and believe. Together with fearing the Lord, this call is fundamental to the wise life. The son is called not to trust in a code of ethics but to trust in the Lord, who revealed this wisdom (cf. 2:6; 16:3,20; 22:19; 28:25; 29:25). **with all your heart.** Highlights the comprehensive nature of one's trust. **heart.** See note on 2:10. **lean not on your own understanding.** The exclusive nature of one's trust.

3:6 in all your ways. The exhaustive nature of one's trust. **submit.** A response of dependence upon God that flows from fully relying upon him (cf. 2:6,10). **make your paths straight.** Does not necessarily mean that trusting in the Lord will ensure one's life is easy and free of obstacles. Those who trust in the Lord will progress morally and intellectually as they journey toward the appointed goal.

3:7 wise in your own eyes. Inflated and incorrect self-evaluation; a state worse than being a fool (26:12; Rom 12:16).

3:9 Honor the LORD with your wealth. By giving the best of one's income to God, a person manifests their inward trust in and fear of the Lord (vv. 5–8) and their gratitude for his provision (cf. Num 18:12).

3:10 your barns will be filled to overflowing. A general reward. This reward for honoring the Lord highlights God's delight in those who worship him; it does not indicate that God governs the world according to a rigid, hard-and-fast system of reward, nor does it entail that God is a cosmic vending machine who is forced to dole out rewards in some sort of mechanical fashion.

3:11–12 Quoted in Heb 12:5–6.

3:11 do not despise. Instruction cannot succeed when the recipient rejects it. **discipline.** Proof of God's love (see note on 1:2). God disciplines those he loves to make them fit for his rewards (vv. 2,4,6,8,10).

3:13–35 *The Value of Wisdom.* After praising the value of wisdom to humankind (vv. 13–18) and to the Lord as Creator (vv. 19–20), this fourth parental instruction shows the value of wisdom to the son (vv. 21–26) and then gives a sample of that wisdom (vv. 27–35).

3:13 Blessed. A laudatory exclamation reserved for people who experience life optimally, as God intended. This word frames the value of wisdom to humankind (v. 18).

3:14 [s] Job 28:15; Pr 8:19; 16:16
3:15 [t] Job 28:18 [u] Pr 8:11
3:16 [v] Pr 8:18
3:17 [w] Pr 16:7; Mt 11:28-30
3:18 [x] Ge 2:9; Pr 11:30; Rev 2:7
3:19 [y] Ps 104:24 [z] Pr 8:27-29
3:21 [a] Pr 4:20-22
3:22 [b] Pr 1:8-9
3:23 [c] Ps 37:24; Pr 4:12
3:24 [d] Lev 26:6; Ps 3:5 [e] Job 11:18
3:26 [f] 1Sa 2:9
3:28 [g] Lev 19:13; Dt 24:15
3:31 [h] Ps 37:1; Pr 24:1-2
3:32 [i] Pr 11:20 [j] Job 29:4; Ps 25:14

14 for she is more profitable than silver
and yields better returns than gold.[s]
15 She is more precious than rubies;[t]
nothing you desire can compare with her.[u]
16 Long life is in her right hand;
in her left hand are riches and honor.[v]
17 Her ways are pleasant ways,
and all her paths are peace.[w]
18 She is a tree of life[x] to those who take hold of her;
those who hold her fast will be blessed.

19 By wisdom the LORD laid the earth's foundations,[y]
by understanding he set the heavens[z] in place;
20 by his knowledge the watery depths were divided,
and the clouds let drop the dew.

21 My son, do not let wisdom and understanding out of your sight,[a]
preserve sound judgment and discretion;
22 they will be life for you,
an ornament to grace your neck.[b]
23 Then you will go on your way in safety,
and your foot will not stumble.[c]
24 When you lie down,[d] you will not be afraid;
when you lie down, your sleep[e] will be sweet.
25 Have no fear of sudden disaster
or of the ruin that overtakes the wicked,
26 for the LORD will be at your side
and will keep your foot[f] from being snared.

27 Do not withhold good from those to whom it is due,
when it is in your power to act.
28 Do not say to your neighbor,
"Come back tomorrow and I'll give it to you"—
when you already have it with you.[g]
29 Do not plot harm against your neighbor,
who lives trustfully near you.
30 Do not accuse anyone for no reason—
when they have done you no harm.

31 Do not envy[h] the violent
or choose any of their ways.
32 For the LORD detests the perverse[i]
but takes the upright into his confidence.[j]

3:14–16 silver ... gold ... rubies ... riches and honor. Terms of economic and social prosperity that are used rhetorically to highlight the great value of wisdom.
3:18 a tree of life. A metaphor of delight and refreshment that ensures eternal life (cf. 11:30; 13:12; 15:4; Gen 2:9; 3:24; Rev 22:1–2,19). See photo of tree, p. 978.
3:19–20 wisdom ... understanding ... knowledge. These attributes serve not only as the principles by which the Lord separated and ordered the cosmos but also as the principles built into the very fabric of the cosmos, i.e., the principles by which the cosmos continues to function. In the same way, through the divine gifts of wisdom, understanding, and knowledge, Bezalel crafted designs for the tabernacle, a portable shrine that served as an earthly replica of the heavenly reality (Exod 31:2–3). The same wisdom, understanding, and knowledge that the Lord employed to order creation he employs to order redemption. This redemption finds fulfillment in Christ, who created and upholds all things (Col 1:16–17).
3:21 wisdom and understanding. See 1:2 and note. **discretion.** See 1:4 and note.
3:22 ornament. See 1:9 and note.
3:27 good. Material benefits (Acts 9:36; Gal 6:10; 1 John 3:17–18). **to whom it is due.** To those who have the right to it (cf. Exod 23:11; Deut 24:19). **when it is in your power to act.** The faithful do not give what they do not possess (cf. 6:1–5; 2 Cor 8:12).

[33]The LORD's curse[k] is on the house of the wicked,[l]
but he blesses the home of the righteous.[m]
[34]He mocks proud mockers
but shows favor to the humble[n] and oppressed.
[35]The wise inherit honor,
but fools get only shame.

Get Wisdom at Any Cost

4 Listen, my sons,[o] to a father's instruction;
pay attention and gain understanding.
[2]I give you sound learning,
so do not forsake my teaching.
[3]For I too was a son to my father,
still tender, and cherished by my mother.
[4]Then he taught me, and he said to me,
"Take hold of my words with all your heart;
keep my commands, and you will live.[p]
[5]Get wisdom,[q] get understanding;
do not forget my words or turn away from them.
[6]Do not forsake wisdom, and she will protect you;[r]
love her, and she will watch over you.
[7]The beginning of wisdom is this: Get[a] wisdom.
Though it cost all[s] you have,[b] get understanding.[t]
[8]Cherish her, and she will exalt you;
embrace her, and she will honor you.[u]
[9]She will give you a garland to grace your head
and present you with a glorious crown.[v]"

[10]Listen, my son, accept what I say,
and the years of your life will be many.[w]
[11]I instruct[x] you in the way of wisdom
and lead you along straight paths.
[12]When you walk, your steps will not be hampered;
when you run, you will not stumble.[y]
[13]Hold on to instruction, do not let it go;
guard it well, for it is your life.[z]
[14]Do not set foot on the path of the wicked
or walk in the way of evildoers.[a]

3:33 [k]Dt 11:28; Mal 2:2 [l]Zec 5:4 [m]Ps 1:3
3:34 [n]Jas 4:6*; 1Pe 5:5*
4:1 [o]Pr 1:8
4:4 [p]Pr 7:2
4:5 [q]Pr 16:16
4:6 [r]2Th 2:10
4:7 [s]Mt 13:44-46 [t]Pr 23:23
4:8 [u]1Sa 2:30; Pr 3:18
4:9 [v]Pr 1:8-9
4:10 [w]Pr 3:2
4:11 [x]1Sa 12:23
4:12 [y]Job 18:7; Pr 3:23
4:13 [z]Pr 3:22
4:14 [a]Ps 1:1; Pr 1:15

[a] 7 Or *Wisdom is supreme; therefore get* [b] 7 Or *wisdom. / Whatever else you get*

3:34 the humble and oppressed. It appears that these do not represent different groups of people; rather, the humble are those who are poor because the wicked have exploited or oppressed them (22:22; 30:14; 31:5,9). This verse is quoted in Jas 4:6 and 1 Pet 5:5 to encourage humility.

4:1–9 *Get the Family Heritage.* The fifth parental instruction consists of the typical introduction (vv. 1–3) and lesson (vv. 4–9), which is the grandfather's lecture to the father. By quoting his father and by setting himself as an example, the father gives credibility to his teaching, implying its antiquity and place within the tradition. Children rely on their parents' knowledge to learn facts and on their parents' authority for matters of opinion.

4:1 my sons. The plural is unique among the parental instructions; the expression may refer to a group of children or emphasize the transgenerational nature of the instruction (i.e., from grandfather to father to son); cf. v. 3.

4:4 heart. See note on 2:10.

4:5,7 Get ... get. Buy or acquire.

4:6 protect ... watch over. See 2:7–11.

4:7 beginning of wisdom. See 1:7 and note. What is needed to get wisdom is a decision; those who seek her diligently find her (8:17; see note on 2:1–4). **Though it cost all.** Cf. Matt 13:44–46.

4:10–19 *Stay Off the Wrong Way.* The sixth parental instruction consists of three sections (vv. 10–13,14–17,18–19) contrasting the way of life and the way of death (see note on 1:19). For the significance of the metaphor "way," see Introduction: Theme. Each section presents this contrast by images of walking.

4:11–12 the way of wisdom ... you will not stumble. By embracing wisdom, a person is led down a path of life that is straight and clear.

4:16 [b] Ps 36:4; Mic 2:1
4:18 [c] Isa 26:7 [d] 2Sa 23:4; Da 12:3; Mt 5:14; Php 2:15
4:19 [e] Job 18:5; Pr 2:13; Isa 59:9-10; Jn 12:35
4:20 [f] Pr 5:1
4:21 [g] Pr 3:21; 7:1-2
4:22 [h] Pr 3:8; 12:18
4:23 [i] Mt 12:34; Lk 6:45
4:26 [j] Heb 12:13*
4:27 [k] Dt 5:32; 28:14
5:1 [l] Pr 4:20; 22:17
5:3 [m] Ps 55:21; Pr 2:16; 7:5

15 Avoid it, do not travel on it;
turn from it and go on your way.
16 For they cannot rest until they do evil;[b]
they are robbed of sleep till they make someone stumble.
17 They eat the bread of wickedness
and drink the wine of violence.

18 The path of the righteous[c] is like the morning sun,
shining ever brighter till the full light of day.[d]
19 But the way of the wicked is like deep darkness;[e]
they do not know what makes them stumble.

20 My son, pay attention to what I say;
turn your ear to my words.[f]
21 Do not let them out of your sight,[g]
keep them within your heart;
22 for they are life to those who find them
and health to one's whole body.[h]
23 Above all else, guard your heart,
for everything you do flows from it.[i]
24 Keep your mouth free of perversity;
keep corrupt talk far from your lips.
25 Let your eyes look straight ahead;
fix your gaze directly before you.
26 Give careful thought to the[a] paths for your feet[j]
and be steadfast in all your ways.
27 Do not turn to the right or the left;[k]
keep your foot from evil.

Warning Against Adultery

5 My son, pay attention to my wisdom,
turn your ear to my words[l] of insight,
2 that you may maintain discretion
and your lips may preserve knowledge.
3 For the lips of the adulterous woman drip honey,
and her speech is smoother than oil;[m]

[a] 26 Or *Make level*

4:16–17 they cannot rest until they do evil … They eat the bread of wickedness and drink the wine of violence. The path, or lifestyle, of the wicked is sustained and nourished by evil; it fills their stomach, quenches their thirst, and allows them to sleep at night.
4:19 they do not know what makes them stumble. Without the light of wisdom to guide their way in life, the wicked do not see the consequences of their actions, and they fall.
4:20–27 *Don't Swerve From the Right Way.* The seventh parental instruction focuses on the anatomy of discipleship: ear (v. 20), sight (vv. 21a), heart (vv. 21b, 23), body (v. 22b), mouth (v. 24a), lips (v. 24b), eyes (v. 25a), feet (v. 26), foot (v. 27b). The whole body must be oriented constantly toward the parents' teaching (i.e., the collection of adages that follow the prologue).
4:23 your heart, for everything you do flows from it. The reference to the heart (see note on 2:10) stands at the center of the poem. The body parts mentioned before the heart in v. 23 function as receptive organs: ear (v. 20), eye (v. 21a); those mentioned after the heart are controlled by it: the mouth for speaking (v. 24); eyes for keeping direction, for preventing one from stumbling, and for remaining on the right path (v. 25); and feet for traveling on the way of wisdom (vv. 26–27).
4:26 Quoted in Heb 12:13.
5:1–23 *Warning Against Adultery.* The eighth instruction is the first of three warnings against the adulteress (5:1–23; 6:20–35; 7:1–27). The instruction has three parts: (1) an introduction (vv. 1–2) with motivation (vv. 3–6); (2) a description of the folly of adultery (vv. 7–14) and an allegory on the delight of lovemaking within marriage (vv. 15–20); (3) a conclusion (vv. 21–23). The theme of accepting the parent's teaching punctuates the whole lecture (vv. 1,7,20). The adulteress provides the father with a literary persona through which to highlight the dangers of illicit sexual activity.
5:1 son. Of marriageable age (see Introduction: Audience).
5:3 lips … drip honey … speech is smoother than oil. The appealing, sweet, slippery words of the woman serve as the instrument of seduction (see 2:16 and note).

[4]but in the end she is bitter as gall,[n]
sharp as a double-edged sword.
[5]Her feet go down to death;
her steps lead straight to the grave.[o]
[6]She gives no thought to the way of life;
her paths wander aimlessly, but she does not know it.[p]

[7]Now then, my sons, listen[q] to me;
do not turn aside from what I say.
[8]Keep to a path far from her,[r]
do not go near the door of her house,
[9]lest you lose your honor to others
and your dignity[a] to one who is cruel,
[10]lest strangers feast on your wealth
and your toil enrich the house of another.
[11]At the end of your life you will groan,
when your flesh and body are spent.
[12]You will say, "How I hated discipline!
How my heart spurned correction![s]
[13]I would not obey my teachers
or turn my ear to my instructors.
[14]And I was soon in serious trouble
in the assembly of God's people."

[15]Drink water from your own cistern,
running water from your own well.
[16]Should your springs overflow in the streets,
your streams of water in the public squares?
[17]Let them be yours alone,
never to be shared with strangers.
[18]May your fountain[t] be blessed,
and may you rejoice in the wife of your youth.[u]
[19]A loving doe, a graceful deer[v] —
may her breasts satisfy you always,
may you ever be intoxicated with her love.
[20]Why, my son, be intoxicated with another man's wife?
Why embrace the bosom of a wayward woman?

[21]For your ways are in full view[w] of the LORD,
and he examines all your paths.[x]

5:4 [n]Ecc 7:26
5:5 [o]Pr 7:26-27
5:6 [p]Pr 30:20
5:7 [q]Pr 7:24
5:8 [r]Pr 7:1-27
5:12 [s]Pr 1:29; 12:1
5:18 [t]SS 4:12-15 [u]Ecc 9:9; Mal 2:14
5:19 [v]SS 2:9; 4:5
5:21 [w]Ps 119:168; Hos 7:2 [x]Job 14:16; Job 31:4; 34:21; Pr 15:3; Jer 16:17; 32:19; Heb 4:13

[a]9 Or *years*

5:4 in the end she is bitter … sharp. Pain and affliction are the consequences associated with accepting this woman's way of life.
5:5 grave. See 1:12 and note.
5:9–10 others … strangers. Those not part of the son's community (vv. 12–14). This may explain the loss of wealth: it is handed over to compensate the adulterous woman's husband for the illicit sexual activity (6:34–35; see note on 6:35).
5:9 honor. Here, one's zeal, passion, and vitality.
5:14 assembly of God's people. The legal assembly at a public court hearing (26:26; cf. Jer 26:9–10). Adultery is a public, not merely private, concern.
5:15 Drink water. A metaphor for being refreshed in lovemaking. **own cistern … own well.** Likens the wife to a prized possession for storing rainwater in arid and stony Canaan.
5:16 springs overflow in the streets … streams of water in the public squares. In contrast to cisterns and wells, which were private property (i.e., marriage), these public places describe sexual relations with others, i.e., sexual activities that violate the privacy of marriage (cf. 30:20).
5:18–20 A prayer that the son will find delight and experience enjoyment with his wife (cf. Mal 2:14).
5:19 breasts satisfy you. See Song 7:7–8. **intoxicated.** In the context of marriage, lovemaking is better than wine (cf. Song 1:2; 4:10; 7:9).
5:20 Why … ? Why … ? The questions function rhetorically. In light of the sheer joy found within the marital relationship and the serious troubles associated with sexual activity outside it, it is unthinkable that anyone would commit adultery.
5:21–22 in full view of the LORD … evil deeds of the wicked ensnare them. Grounds the teaching in the Lord's omniscience and his justice to consign sinners to death.

5:22 [y] Ps 9:16 [z] Nu 32:23; Ps 7:15-16; Pr 1:31-32
5:23 [a] Job 4:21; 36:12
6:1 [b] Pr 17:18 [c] Pr 11:15; 22:26-27
6:4 [d] Ps 132:4
6:5 [e] Ps 91:3
6:6 [f] Pr 20:4
6:8 [g] Pr 10:4
6:9 [h] Pr 24:30-34
6:10 [i] Pr 24:33
6:11 [j] Pr 24:30-34

22 The evil deeds of the wicked ensnare them;[y]
the cords of their sins hold them fast.[z]
23 For lack of discipline they will die,[a]
led astray by their own great folly.

Warnings Against Folly

6 My son, if you have put up security for your neighbor,[b]
if you have shaken hands in pledge[c] for a stranger,
2 you have been trapped by what you said,
ensnared by the words of your mouth.
3 So do this, my son, to free yourself,
since you have fallen into your neighbor's hands:
Go — to the point of exhaustion —[a]
and give your neighbor no rest!
4 Allow no sleep to your eyes,
no slumber to your eyelids.[d]
5 Free yourself, like a gazelle from the hand of the hunter,
like a bird from the snare of the fowler.[e]

6 Go to the ant, you sluggard;[f]
consider its ways and be wise!
7 It has no commander,
no overseer or ruler,
8 yet it stores its provisions in summer
and gathers its food at harvest.[g]

9 How long will you lie there, you sluggard?[h]
When will you get up from your sleep?
10 A little sleep, a little slumber,
a little folding of the hands to rest[i] —
11 and poverty[j] will come on you like a thief
and scarcity like an armed man.

12 A troublemaker and a villain,
who goes about with a corrupt mouth,

[a] 3 Or *Go and humble yourself,*

5:23 led astray. Translates the same Hebrew word rendered "intoxicated" in v. 19, suggesting a pun on the right and wrong ways to be led astray: one into delight, the other into destruction.
6:1–19 *Warnings Against Folly.* This parental instruction provides counsel in dealing with morally inferior types of people in specific situations. These people include the surety (vv. 1–5), the sluggard (vv. 6–11), and the troublemaker (vv. 12–19). The unit includes: (1) a warning against serving as the financial guarantor for another, (2) an exhortation to the sluggard to follow the industrious example of the ant, and (3) a description of the character of the troublemaker and the types of things the Lord hates.
6:1 My son. The other two inferior types are not addressed as a "son." **put up security ... shaken hands in pledge for a stranger.** Taking legal responsibility for satisfying someone else's debt. Since this person may default, they control the surety's life (v. 3), for failure to satisfy his obligation can end in abject poverty or even slavery (11:15; 17:18; 20:16; 22:26–27; cf. Job 17:3).
6:2 words. Imprudent speech can be a trap just as ruinous as a fowler's snare is to a bird or as a trap is to a gazelle (v. 5).
6:3–4 Four admonitions explain how to get out of the foolish situation: (1) **Go.** Stimulates immediate action. (2) **to the point of exhaustion.** Exhaust all of your energy. (3) **give your neighbor no rest!** Badger him. (4) **Allow [yourself] no sleep.** Do it immediately, before nightfall; be as persistent and as shamelessly audacious as the friend in Luke 11:5–8 and the widow in Luke 18:1–5.
6:6 ant. Occurs elsewhere only in 30:25, where it is marked by prudence and diligence. **sluggard.** See Introduction: Character Types.
6:7 has no commander. God gave the ant its innate initiative to work and accomplish a goal in a wise and timely manner.
6:10 A little sleep, a little slumber. This captures the distorted thinking of the sluggard: *just a little more.* **hands.** The Hebrew word includes arms; the gesture of folding his arms across his breast epitomizes his refusal to budge.
6:11 a thief ... an armed man. The sluggard's poverty is personified as a covert and unforgiving force. It is reiterated in 24:33–34.
6:12 troublemaker. The Hebrew denotes a nefarious revolutionary who agitates against all that is right. This name for the devilish human in later Jewish literature and in the NT became identified with Belial, a name for the devil (2 Cor 6:15). **villain.** A malevolent person who misuses their power to inflict others.

13 who winks maliciously with his eye,[k]
signals with his feet
and motions with his fingers,
14 who plots evil[l] with deceit in his heart—
he always stirs up conflict.[m]
15 Therefore disaster will overtake him in an instant;
he will suddenly be destroyed—without remedy.[n]

16 There are six things the LORD hates,
seven that are detestable to him:
17 haughty eyes,
a lying tongue,[o]
hands that shed innocent blood,[p]
18 a heart that devises wicked schemes,
feet that are quick to rush into evil,[q]
19 a false witness[r] who pours out lies
and a person who stirs up conflict in the
community.[s]

6:13 [k]Ps 35:19
6:14 [l]Mic 2:1 [m]ver 16-19
6:15 [n]2Ch 36:16
6:17 [o]Ps 120:2; Pr 12:22 [p]Dt 19:10; Isa 1:15; 59:7
6:18 [q]Ge 6:5
6:19 [r]Ps 27:12 [s]ver 12-15
6:20 [t]Pr 1:8
6:21 [u]Pr 3:3; 7:1-3
6:23 [v]Ps 19:8; 119:105
6:24 [w]Pr 2:16; 7:5
6:26 [x]Pr 7:22-23; 29:3

Warning Against Adultery

20 My son, keep your father's command
and do not forsake your mother's teaching.[t]
21 Bind them always on your heart;
fasten them around your neck.[u]
22 When you walk, they will guide you;
when you sleep, they will watch over you;
when you awake, they will speak to you.
23 For this command is a lamp,
this teaching is a light,[v]
and correction and instruction
are the way to life,
24 keeping you from your neighbor's wife,
from the smooth talk of a wayward woman.[w]

25 Do not lust in your heart after her beauty
or let her captivate you with her eyes.

26 For a prostitute can be had for a loaf of bread,
but another man's wife preys on your very life.[x]

6:13 winks … signals … motions. Malicious, deceptive signals by which the troublemaker exploits people and situations for personal gain.
6:15 Therefore. This conclusion is rooted in the notion of divine justice and retribution and is explained by the catalog of characteristics the Lord hates in vv. 16–19 (see 1:19; 2:20–22; 4:18–19; 5:21–23).
6:16–19 This sevenfold catalog of what the Lord hates revolves around the inner heart (see 2:10; 4:23 and notes).
6:16 six … seven. Similar to other numerical sayings (cf. 30:15–31), the final element (v. 19b) is the focus of attention.
6:17 haughty eyes. A perspective or attitude characterized by pride and arrogance; the Lord humbles those with this perspective (Ps 18:27).
6:19 stirs up conflict. As the climactic element, the desire for disruption, fighting, and hostility summarizes the vices listed in vv. 16–19, defines the troublemaker and explains God's judgment of this person.
6:20–35 *Warning Against Adultery.* The tenth instruction, the second warning against adultery (ch. 5), begins with a typical introduction (vv. 20–22) and a motivation (vv. 23–24). The lesson (vv. 25–35) consists of an admonition not to desire your neighbor's wife (v. 25), which is supported by two matters, each of which focuses on the destructive nature of adultery (marked off by "For" in vv. 26,34): (1) The price of adultery is severe, inevitable, unending, and totally destructive (vv. 26–33). (2) The husband will never accept any compensation less than the total destruction of the adulterer (vv. 34–35).
6:20 mother's. See note on 1:8.
6:25 Do not lust in your heart. Jesus also connected lust and adultery (Matt 5:28).
6:26 a prostitute can be had for a loaf of bread. Contrasts the price of a prostitute (a cheap meal) with the price of the adulterous wife (one's life). This does not condone prostitution (cf. 1 Cor 6:13–20; Gal 5:19–21; Eph 5:5; 1 Thess 4:3–8). Engaging in adultery is worse than engaging in prostitution because it involves breaking the marriage vow (2:17), wronging a spouse, destroying a home, and incurring an immeasurable debt. Adultery is comparable to playing with fire (vv. 27–29).

6:29 [y] Ex 20:14 [z] Pr 2:16-19; 5:8
6:31 [a] Ex 22:1-14
6:32 [b] Ex 20:14 [c] Pr 7:7; 9:4,16
6:33 [d] Pr 5:9-14
6:34 [e] Nu 5:14 [f] Ge 34:7
6:35 [g] Job 31:9-11; SS 8:7
7:1 [h] Pr 1:8; 2:1
7:2 [i] Pr 4:4
7:3 [j] Dt 6:8; Pr 3:3
7:5 [k] ver 21; Job 31:9; Pr 2:16; 6:24
7:7 [l] Pr 1:22; 6:32

27 Can a man scoop fire into his lap
without his clothes being burned?
28 Can a man walk on hot coals
without his feet being scorched?
29 So is he who sleeps[y] with another man's wife;[z]
no one who touches her will go unpunished.

30 People do not despise a thief if he steals
to satisfy his hunger when he is starving.
31 Yet if he is caught, he must pay sevenfold,[a]
though it costs him all the wealth of his house.
32 But a man who commits adultery[b] has no sense;[c]
whoever does so destroys himself.
33 Blows and disgrace are his lot,
and his shame will never[d] be wiped away.

34 For jealousy[e] arouses a husband's fury,[f]
and he will show no mercy when he takes revenge.
35 He will not accept any compensation;
he will refuse a bribe, however great it is.[g]

Warning Against the Adulterous Woman

7

My son,[h] keep my words
and store up my commands within you.
2 Keep my commands and you will live;[i]
guard my teachings as the apple of your eye.
3 Bind them on your fingers;
write them on the tablet of your heart.[j]
4 Say to wisdom, "You are my sister,"
and to insight, "You are my relative."
5 They will keep you from the adulterous woman,
from the wayward woman with her seductive words.[k]

6 At the window of my house
I looked down through the lattice.
7 I saw among the simple,
I noticed among the young men,
a youth who had no sense.[l]

6:29 no one who touches her will go unpunished. God ultimately upholds the moral order (5:21–23), though he may uphold it immediately through the husband of the adulteress (see vv. 34–35).
6:31 sevenfold. A figure of speech for full compensation (see Gen 4:15; Lev 26:28; Matt 18:21–22). According to the law, the maximum fine for theft was fourfold or fivefold (Exod 22:1; Luke 19:8).
6:35 not accept any compensation. The husband of the woman will not be bought off by a material gift that establishes a settlement between an injured party and an offending party. Whereas a thief can compensate for his wrongdoing, the adulterer cannot escape the blows, social scorn, and unending reproach of a healthy society (vv. 32–35).
7:1–27 *Warning Against the Adulterous Woman.* This instruction, the third full discourse on the adulteress (5:1–23; 6:20–35; cf. 2:16–19), focuses on the adulterous woman's tactics. The instruction moves from an introduction (vv. 1–5), which emphasizes the protective power of the father's words, to an extended autobiographical account that describes the adulterous woman's seduction of a simpleton (vv. 6–23). The lesson then culminates in the father associating the way of the adulterous woman with death (vv. 24–27). While the noble wife embodies wisdom by staying at home and diligently engaging in her entrepreneurial work (see 31:10–31, the book's final poem), the adulteress embodies folly by roaming the city streets looking for sensual pleasure as darkness falls.
7:3 Bind them on your fingers. Either literal (cf. Matt 23:5; Josephus, *Antiquities*, 4:213) or a figure of speech for keeping them always in mind (cf. 6:21; Deut 6:8). **write them on the tablet of your heart.** Connotes their indelible impression upon one's character (see note on 3:3). Internalizing the father's teaching changes and develops a person's character (2:2; 4:23; cf. Jer 31:31–34).
7:4 my sister. The metaphor invites the reader to accept wisdom as a dear family member, or more probably, as an intimate bride (Song 4:9,10,12; 5:1,2) for whom the groom abandons even father and mother (Gen 2:23–24). **my relative.** A metaphoric foil to protect the son against the adulterous woman (see note on 2:16) who is hostile to the covenant community.
7:5 adulterous … wayward. Cf. 2:16.
7:6 window of my house. Symbolizes the father's distance and captures his unique perspective.
7:7 simple. See Introduction: Audience; Character Types. Whereas the

[8]He was going down the street near her corner,
walking along in the direction of her house
[9]at twilight,[m] as the day was fading,
as the dark of night set in.

[10]Then out came a woman to meet him,
dressed like a prostitute and with crafty intent.
[11](She is unruly[n] and defiant,
her feet never stay at home;
[12]now in the street, now in the squares,
at every corner she lurks.)[o]
[13]She took hold of him[p] and kissed him
and with a brazen face she said:[q]

[14]"Today I fulfilled my vows,
and I have food from my fellowship offering[r]
at home.
[15]So I came out to meet you;
I looked for you and have found you!
[16]I have covered my bed
with colored linens from Egypt.
[17]I have perfumed my bed[s]
with myrrh,[t] aloes and cinnamon.
[18]Come, let's drink deeply of love till morning;
let's enjoy ourselves with love![u]
[19]My husband is not at home;
he has gone on a long journey.
[20]He took his purse filled with money
and will not be home till full moon."

[21]With persuasive words she led him astray;
she seduced him with her smooth talk.[v]
[22]All at once he followed her
like an ox going to the slaughter,
like a deer[a] stepping into a noose[b][w]
[23]till an arrow pierces[x] his liver,
like a bird darting into a snare,
little knowing it will cost him his life.[y]

7:9 [m]Job 24:15
7:11 [n]Pr 9:13; 1Ti 5:13
7:12 [o]Pr 8:1-36; 23:26-28
7:13 [p]Ge 39:12 [q]Pr 1:20
7:14 [r]Lev 7:11-18
7:17 [s]Est 1:6; Isa 57:7; Eze 23:41; Am 6:4 [t]Ge 37:25
7:18 [u]Ge 39:7
7:21 [v]Pr 5:3
7:22 [w]Job 18:10
7:23 [x]Job 15:22; 16:13 [y]Pr 6:26; Ecc 7:26; 9:12

[a] *22* Syriac (see also Septuagint); Hebrew *fool* [b] *22* The meaning of the Hebrew for this line is uncertain.

other instructions concerning the adulterous woman emphasize the consequences of adultery, this instruction focuses on how the simple are caught in adultery (vv. 21–23; cf. 5:8).

7:10 dressed like a prostitute. Perhaps in a provocative or obvious manner (Ezek 16:16). To the insightful, the woman's shameless outfit betrays her hidden intentions.

7:13 with a brazen face. Symbolizes the adulterous woman's shameless behavior and may indicate she tells a bold-faced lie.

7:14 fellowship offering. A specific kind of sacrifice aimed to bind together the deity and worshiper by a shared meal (Lev 7:11–21; 1 Sam 9:11–13; Jer 7:21). Ironic, for this woman knows nothing of fellowship; she feigns fidelity to her husband and dupes the simple by her "smooth" speech, knowing full well she will destroy him if he is caught in the act of adultery (6:20–35). The meal that fulfilled the vow had to be eaten on the same or following day (Lev 7:16–18; 19:5–7). If she practices the Canaanite religion, her invitation to have sex with him also could be an invitation to participate in that religion's fertility rites.

7:16 colored linens from Egypt. Expensive, embroidered bedcovers.

7:17 myrrh, aloes and cinnamon. Perfumes purchased from great distances and prized by kings (cf. "spices" in 2 Kgs 20:13). The adulterous woman's implicit argument is that her victim should not miss out on such an opportunity.

7:18 love. A sexual relationship. The adulterous woman promises sexual love without restraint but denies committing herself, the fundamental requirement of true love.

7:19 My husband is not at home. The adulterous woman's self-confessed infidelity to her husband should have warned the simple that she is untrustworthy. To judge from the dire consequences (vv. 26–27), she is lying.

7:21 she led him astray. As in the other instructions, the adulterous woman seduces the youth by deceitful speech (2:16; 5:3; 6:24).

7:22–23 like an ox ... like a deer ... like a bird. Just as these animals are unaware of the tragic fate that awaits them, so also the simple is oblivious to his fate: death.

7:24 [z]Pr 1:8-9; 5:7; 8:32
7:25 [a]Pr 5:7-8
7:27 [b]Pr 2:18; 5:5; 9:18; Rev 22:15
8:1 [c]Pr 1:20; 9:3
8:3 [d]Job 29:7
8:5 [e]Pr 1:22 [f]Pr 1:4
8:7 [g]Ps 37:30; Jn 8:14
8:10 [h]Pr 3:14-15
8:11 [i]Job 28:17-19 [j]Pr 3:13-15
8:12 [k]Pr 1:4
8:13 [l]Pr 16:6 [m]Jer 44:4

24 Now then, my sons, listen[z] to me;
pay attention to what I say.
25 Do not let your heart turn to her ways
or stray into her paths.[a]
26 Many are the victims she has brought down;
her slain are a mighty throng.
27 Her house is a highway to the grave,
leading down to the chambers of death.[b]

Wisdom's Call

8 Does not wisdom call out?[c]
Does not understanding raise her voice?
2 At the highest point along the way,
where the paths meet, she takes her stand;
3 beside the gate leading into the city,
at the entrance, she cries aloud:[d]
4 "To you, O people, I call out;
I raise my voice to all mankind.
5 You who are simple,[e] gain prudence;[f]
you who are foolish, set your hearts on it.[a]
6 Listen, for I have trustworthy things to say;
I open my lips to speak what is right.
7 My mouth speaks what is true,[g]
for my lips detest wickedness.
8 All the words of my mouth are just;
none of them is crooked or perverse.
9 To the discerning all of them are right;
they are upright to those who have found knowledge.
10 Choose my instruction instead of silver,
knowledge rather than choice gold,[h]
11 for wisdom is more precious[i] than rubies,
and nothing you desire can compare with her.[j]

12 "I, wisdom, dwell together with prudence;
I possess knowledge and discretion.[k]
13 To fear the LORD is to hate evil;[l]
I hate[m] pride and arrogance,
evil behavior and perverse speech.

[a] 5 Septuagint; Hebrew *foolish, instruct your minds*

7:26 her slain are a mighty throng. The conclusion is an admonition to avoid the adulterous woman with this motivation: her bedroom is not a place of pleasure but a battlefield with corpses lying about it.

8:1–36 *Wisdom's Call.* Against the backdrop of the warnings about the adulterous wife (5:1–23; 6:20–35; 7:1–27), Lady Wisdom emerges as an antithetical figure who offers an alternative way of life. She is deliberately contrasted with the adulterous wife, who will become a personification of folly in ch. 9. Whereas Wisdom's first address denounced simpletons for rejecting her (1:20–33), this address offers them salvation. The speech consists of three main sections: (1) an extended introduction (vv. 1–11); (2) a main body, which moves from Wisdom's activity in historical time (vv. 12–21) to her birth in primordial time (vv. 22–31); (3) a conclusion (vv. 32–36). The speech illuminates Wisdom's immense value, intimate relationship with the Lord, and knowledge of the order within the cosmos in order to convince the son to embrace her and, by implication, receive the ability to live in accordance with the order the Lord has woven into the fabric of the world.

8:1 wisdom. See Introduction: Lady Wisdom. For the setting of the speech, see 1:20–21.

8:5 simple … foolish. For the character of the addressees, see Introduction: Character Types.

8:6 right. Straight.

8:8 just. Spoken in righteousness. **crooked or perverse.** Twisted, tricky, or a distortion of the ethical norm. Wisdom's speech stands in sharp contrast to the speech of the adulterous wife (2:16; 5:3; 6:24; 7:21).

8:9 the discerning. Those who are wise and able to recognize the trustworthiness of Wisdom's speech.

8:12–14 prudence … sound judgment. These attributes are inseparable from one another. The first is described as Wisdom's roommate, while the rest are depicted as her personal belongings.

8:13 To fear the LORD. See note on 1:7. **I hate pride … evil behavior.** An attitude that determines whether a person fears the Lord.

[14] Counsel and sound judgment are mine;
I have insight, I have power.[n]
[15] By me kings reign
and rulers[o] issue decrees that are just;
[16] by me princes govern,
and nobles — all who rule on earth.[a]
[17] I love those who love me,[p]
and those who seek me find me.[q]
[18] With me are riches and honor,[r]
enduring wealth and prosperity.[s]
[19] My fruit is better than fine gold;
what I yield surpasses choice silver.[t]
[20] I walk in the way of righteousness,
along the paths of justice,
[21] bestowing a rich inheritance on those who love me
and making their treasuries full.[u]

[22] "The LORD brought me forth as the first of his works,[b,c]
before his deeds of old;
[23] I was formed long ages ago,
at the very beginning, when the world came to be.
[24] When there were no watery depths, I was given birth,
when there were no springs overflowing with water;[v]
[25] before the mountains were settled in place,
before the hills, I was given birth,[w]
[26] before he made the world or its fields
or any of the dust of the earth.[x]
[27] I was there when he set the heavens in place,[y]
when he marked out the horizon on the face of the deep,
[28] when he established the clouds above
and fixed securely the fountains of the deep,
[29] when he gave the sea its boundary[z]
so the waters would not overstep his command,[a]
and when he marked out the foundations of the earth.[b]
[30] Then I was constantly[d] at his side.[c]
I was filled with delight day after day,
rejoicing always in his presence,

8:14 [n] Pr 21:22; Ecc 7:19
8:15 [o] Da 2:21; Ro 13:1
8:17 [p] 1Sa 2:30; Ps 91:14; Jn 14:21-24 [q] Pr 1:28; Jas 1:5
8:18 [r] Pr 3:16 [s] Dt 8:18; Mt 6:33
8:19 [t] Pr 3:13-14; 10:20
8:21 [u] Pr 24:4
8:24 [v] Ge 7:11
8:25 [w] Job 15:7
8:26 [x] Ps 90:2
8:27 [y] Pr 3:19
8:29 [z] Ge 1:9; Job 38:10; Ps 16:6 [a] Ps 104:9 [b] Job 38:5
8:30 [c] Jn 1:1-3

[a] 16 Some Hebrew manuscripts and Septuagint; other Hebrew manuscripts *all righteous rulers*
[b] 22 Or *way*; or *dominion* [c] 22 Or *The LORD possessed me at the beginning of his work*; or *The LORD brought me forth at the beginning of his work* [d] 30 Or *was the artisan*; or *was a little child*

8:14 power. The strength of character necessary to carry out prudent planning in the face of opposition.
8:17 I love those who love me. The heart of the wise is aligned with Wisdom's in the same way that the heart of the believer is aligned with Christ's (Rom 8:1–11; Eph 3:16–19). **those who seek me find me.** Just as God grants wisdom to those who seek or ask (2:1–11; Matt 7:7; Jas 1:5), so also Wisdom reveals herself to those who search for her.
8:18 enduring wealth. A description of Wisdom's value and the reward for her character rather than the goal or aim of her life. A person loves either Wisdom or wealth (vv. 17–21; see 3:14–15); there is no third way (Matt 6:24).
8:19 better than fine gold. See 3:13–18.
8:22–24 brought ... forth ... I was given birth. Together, these expressions depict Wisdom's delivery in primordial time as the Lord's daughter. In this case, wisdom issues from the very character of God; it is not something created apart from him. And as an attribute of God, wisdom is a characteristic he employed to create the cosmos (see Introduction: Lady Wisdom; see also Col 1:15–20). Consequently, Lady Wisdom has certain knowledge about God's ways (cf. 30:3–4).
8:30 constantly. Expresses Wisdom's reliability; translates a Hebrew word that with slight textual changes can mean "the artisan" or "little child" (see NIV text note). The reading "constantly" is supported by the parallel expressions "day after day" and "always." Wisdom is portrayed as a faithful devotee, celebrating before the Lord and delighting in his creation. Unlike Job, who was not present at the creation and so did not understand God's ways (Job 38:4), Wisdom was present at the creation and so has certain knowledge about the creation order.

8:31 [d]Ps 16:3; 104:1-30
8:32 [e]Lk 11:28 [f]Ps 119:1-2
8:34 [g]Pr 3:13,18
8:35 [h]Pr 3:13-18 [i]Pr 12:2
8:36 [j]Pr 15:32
9:1 [k]Eph 2:20-22; 1Pe 2:5
9:2 [l]Lk 14:16-23
9:3 [m]Pr 8:1-3 [n]ver 14
9:4 [o]Pr 6:32
9:5 [p]Isa 55:1
9:6 [q]Pr 8:35
9:7 [r]Pr 23:9
9:8 [s]Pr 15:12 [t]Ps 141:5
9:9 [u]Pr 1:5,7

31 rejoicing in his whole world
and delighting in mankind.[d]

32 "Now then, my children, listen to me;
blessed are[e] those who keep my ways.[f]
33 Listen to my instruction and be wise;
do not disregard it.
34 Blessed are those who listen[g] to me,
watching daily at my doors,
waiting at my doorway.
35 For those who find me[h] find life
and receive favor from the LORD.[i]
36 But those who fail to find me harm themselves;[j]
all who hate me love death."

Invitations of Wisdom and Folly

9 Wisdom has built[k] her house;
she has set up[a] its seven pillars.
2 She has prepared her meat and mixed her wine;
she has also set her table.[l]
3 She has sent out her servants, and she calls[m]
from the highest point of the city,[n]
4 "Let all who are simple come to my house!"
To those who have no sense[o] she says,
5 "Come, eat my food
and drink the wine I have mixed.[p]
6 Leave your simple ways and you will live;[q]
walk in the way of insight."

7 Whoever corrects a mocker invites insults;
whoever rebukes the wicked incurs abuse.[r]
8 Do not rebuke mockers[s] or they will hate you;
rebuke the wise and they will love you.[t]
9 Instruct the wise and they will be wiser still;
teach the righteous and they will add to their learning.[u]

[a] *1* Septuagint, Syriac and Targum; Hebrew *has hewn out*

8:32 children. See note on 4:1. **blessed.** See 3:13 and note. As in Wisdom's first address (1:20–27), she shifts her focus from simpletons to the generations of children who are willing to listen (cf. vv. 32–36; 1:28–33).

8:36 death. As stated in the conclusions to Wisdom's other addresses, listening to her is a matter of life and death (1:19,32; 2:22; 3:33; 5:22–23; 7:27; 9:18).

9:1–18 *Invitations of Wisdom and Folly.* Here the prologue's juxtaposition of the wise versus the foolish reaches a climax. Both Wisdom and Folly invite the simple to their houses for a feast. The invitations are identical, but the consequences are distinct: those who accept Wisdom's invitation live; those who accept Folly's invitation die. The rival invitations move from a description of the preparation for the banquet (vv. 1–3,13–15) to the invitation (vv. 4–5,16–17) to the conclusion (vv. 6,18). The sayings in vv. 7–12 supplement the invitations, for they illustrate the different responses to the requests of Wisdom and Folly. On the whole, the text demands that the son choose a woman, a house, and a banquet, and in so doing choose a way of life. Only those who choose Wisdom may proceed through the remainder of the book and enjoy her sumptuous feast.

9:1 Wisdom. See Introduction: Lady Wisdom. **built.** Creatively brought into existence (cf. 14:1); this contrasts with Folly, who "sits at the door of her house" (v. 14). **seven pillars.** Represents a large and perfect house with ample room for all (cf. John 14:2).

9:4–6 simple … simple ways. Frames Wisdom's invitation, which encourages the simple to abandon their uncommitted state, commit to the way of wisdom, and receive the promise of eternal life. See Introduction: Audience; Character Types.

9:6 live. Finds fuller expression in John 6 (e.g., John 6:27,35,47–51), where Jesus describes the nature of eternal life and the satisfaction he offers to those who commit to him. **walk in the way.** See Introduction: Theme.

9:7–9 mocker … wicked … wise … righteous. See Introduction: Character Types. These characters respond to Wisdom's invitation in different ways: rejection and criticism versus acceptance and love (cf. 1 Pet 4:3–5). The "righteous" are synonymous with the "wise," just as "wise" and "righteous" refer to the same type of person; so also the "mocker" and the "wicked" refer to the same type of person (vv. 7–8; see Ps 1:1).

9:8 love you. The wise are teachable (1:5; 12:1; 13:1; 14:6; 15:31; 18:15; 19:25; 21:11; Matt 13:12).

One of the temples at Luxor with two sets of seven pillars (Prov 9:1).

© Dima Fadeev/Shutterstock

10 The fear of the LORD[v] is the beginning of wisdom,
and knowledge of the Holy One is understanding.
11 For through wisdom[a] your days will be many,
and years will be added to your life.[w]
12 If you are wise, your wisdom will reward you;
if you are a mocker, you alone will suffer.

13 Folly is an unruly woman;[x]
she is simple and knows nothing.[y]
14 She sits at the door of her house,
on a seat at the highest point of the city,[z]
15 calling out to those who pass by,
who go straight on their way,
16 "Let all who are simple come to my house!"
To those who have no sense she says,
17 "Stolen water is sweet;
food eaten in secret is delicious!"[a]
18 But little do they know that the dead are there,
that her guests are deep in the realm of the dead.[b]

9:10 [v] Job 28:28; Pr 1:7
9:11 [w] Pr 3:16; 10:27
9:13 [x] Pr 7:11 [y] Pr 5:6
9:14 [z] ver 3
9:17 [a] Pr 20:17
9:18 [b] Pr 2:18; 7:26-27

[a] *11* Septuagint, Syriac and Targum; Hebrew *me*

9:10 The fear of the LORD. See note on 1:7. It forms a frame with the preamble.
9:11 your days will be many. See 3:2. The end for the righteous is life not death (see Introduction: Theme).
9:12 alone. The individual is the ultimate gainer or loser (cf. 15:32; Ezek 18:20; Gal 6:4–5).
9:13 Folly. As a personification, this woman serves as the metaphoric counterpart to the adulterous wife (5:1–23; 6:20–35; 7:1–27) and the antithesis of Lady Wisdom. **knows nothing.** About morals; she knows a lot about seduction.
9:14 sits. Having prepared no meat, mixed and decanted no wine, set no table, and sent no messengers. She needs no discipline, industry, or investment to attract the senseless, because her lifestyle titillates and demands no moral rectitude. **on a seat.** Represents the imposter's pretentious rule of the masses (Matt 7:13–14).
9:15 calling out. Like the malevolent serpent, she has no advantage until she gets a person's attention (Gen 3:1–3). The wise keep their eyes fixed on the right path (4:25–27). **go straight on their way.** The simple do not set out to do wrong; they stray through their lack of commitment to the right way (see Introduction: Audience; Character Types).
9:17 Stolen water. Possibly a metaphor for the sexual pleasure of adultery (5:15; cf. 2:17; 6:30–35; 7:18–19). **sweet.** Sin gives pleasure for a season (cf. Heb 11:25).
9:18 realm of the dead. See notes on 1:12; 2:18.

10:1 [c]Pr 1:1 [d]Pr 15:20; 29:3
10:2 [e]Pr 21:6 [f]Pr 11:4,19
10:3 [g]Mt 6:25-34
10:4 [h]Pr 19:15 [i]Pr 12:24; 13:4; 21:5
10:6 [j]ver 8,11,14
10:7 [k]Ps 112:6 [l]Ps 109:13 [m]Ps 9:6
10:8 [n]Mt 7:24-27
10:9 [o]Isa 33:15 [p]Ps 23:4 [q]Pr 28:18
10:10 [r]Ps 35:19
10:11 [s]Ps 37:30; Pr 13:12,14,19 [t]ver 6
10:12 [u]Pr 17:9; 1Co 13:4-7; 1Pe 4:8

Proverbs of Solomon

10 The proverbs of Solomon:[c]

A wise son brings joy to his father,[d]
but a foolish son brings grief to his mother.

2 Ill-gotten treasures have no lasting value,[e]
but righteousness delivers from death.[f]

3 The LORD does not let the righteous go hungry,[g]
but he thwarts the craving of the wicked.

4 Lazy hands make for poverty,[h]
but diligent hands bring wealth.[i]

5 He who gathers crops in summer is a prudent son,
but he who sleeps during harvest is a disgraceful son.

6 Blessings crown the head of the righteous,
but violence overwhelms the mouth of the wicked.[a][j]

7 The name of the righteous[k] is used in blessings,[b]
but the name of the wicked[l] will rot.[m]

8 The wise in heart accept commands,
but a chattering fool comes to ruin.[n]

9 Whoever walks in integrity[o] walks securely,[p]
but whoever takes crooked paths will be found out.[q]

10 Whoever winks maliciously[r] causes grief,
and a chattering fool comes to ruin.

11 The mouth of the righteous is a fountain of life,[s]
but the mouth of the wicked conceals violence.[t]

12 Hatred stirs up conflict,
but love covers over all wrongs.[u]

[a] 6 Or *righteous, / but the mouth of the wicked conceals violence* [b] 7 See Gen. 48:20.

10:1—22:16 *Proverbs of Solomon.* This collection contains a variety of individual proverbs and coherent proverbial units. It falls into two parts: (1) antithetical sayings in which the wise/righteous sharply contrast with the fool/wicked dominating 10:1—15:29, and (2) diverse literary forms dominating 15:30—22:16. The second half of the collection contains only a few antithetical sayings. The materials show what wisdom looks like in everyday life and offer the son a worldview based on the fear of the Lord (see 1:7 and note).
10:1 The proverbs of Solomon. See Introduction: Authors. **father … mother.** See note on 1:8.
10:2 Ill-gotten treasures have no lasting value. Riches gained by wickedness may be valuable for the moment, but they have no value in light of death (see v. 16). **righteousness delivers from death.** Righteous behavior is depicted as a rescuer; the expression may be a pun for delivering oneself and others.
10:3 The LORD. The agent who upholds the moral order of v. 2. **righteous … wicked.** See Introduction: Character Types. **go hungry.** While the righteous tend to experience a secure lifestyle, this saying does not serve as a universal promise of God's provision. For the nature of proverbs, see Introduction: Literary Features.
10:4–5 wealth … gathers crops in summer. A good harvest. In contrast to modern conceptions, wealth here does not entail a healthy bank account. Rather, in the agrarian society of ancient Israel, wealth consisted of a good harvest, a healthy family, and a stable household and inheritance. Wealth is a gift from God. But, as many proverbs declare, virtue is better than wealth (e.g., 16:19; 19:1,22; 22:1).
10:6 Blessings. The gifts of fruitfulness and victory. Jesus Christ had no physical offspring, but he blessed his disciples, making them spiritually fruitful and victorious. All blessings come from God, but they are mediated by others, including the prayers of God's sacred congregation (see 11:26).
10:10 Whoever winks maliciously. Probably refers to those who conceal the true intentions of their actions or passively approve ungodly behavior.
10:11 fountain of life. Life depends on water. The open, benevolent speech of the righteous is just as necessary for a community as a fountain of water, offering all abundant life. The right word spoken at the right time (15:23) and in the right way (15:1; 17:27) supports or corrects a community in a way that promotes its life.
10:12 Hatred. An attitude that misperceives innocent intentions as bad motives. **stirs up conflict.** The disagreement and discord provoked by hatred; among the things the Lord hates (6:16–19). **love.** An attitude that cherishes the wrongdoer as a friend to be won, not as an enemy with whom to get even. **covers over.** To protect the wrongdoer, the one

[13] Wisdom is found on the lips of the discerning,[v]
but a rod is for the back of one who has no sense.[w]

[14] The wise store up knowledge,
but the mouth of a fool invites ruin.[x]

[15] The wealth of the rich is their fortified city,[y]
but poverty is the ruin of the poor.[z]

[16] The wages of the righteous is life,
but the earnings of the wicked are sin and death.[a]

[17] Whoever heeds discipline shows the way to life,[b]
but whoever ignores correction leads others astray.

[18] Whoever conceals hatred with lying lips
and spreads slander is a fool.

[19] Sin is not ended by multiplying words,
but the prudent hold their tongues.[c]

[20] The tongue of the righteous is choice silver,
but the heart of the wicked is of little value.

[21] The lips of the righteous nourish many,
but fools die for lack of sense.[d]

[22] The blessing of the LORD brings wealth,[e]
without painful toil for it.

[23] A fool finds pleasure in wicked schemes,[f]
but a person of understanding delights in wisdom.

[24] What the wicked dread[g] will overtake them;
what the righteous desire will be granted.[h]

[25] When the storm has swept by, the wicked are gone,
but the righteous stand firm[i] forever.[j]

[26] As vinegar to the teeth and smoke to the eyes,
so are sluggards to those who send them.[k]

[27] The fear of the LORD adds length to life,[l]
but the years of the wicked are cut short.[m]

[28] The prospect of the righteous is joy,
but the hopes of the wicked come to nothing.[n]

[29] The way of the LORD is a refuge for the blameless,
but it is the ruin of those who do evil.[o]

10:13 [v] ver 31 [w] Pr 26:3
10:14 [x] Pr 18:6,7
10:15 [y] Pr 18:11 [z] Pr 19:7
10:16 [a] Pr 11:18-19
10:17 [b] Pr 6:23
10:19 [c] Pr 17:28; Ecc 5:3; Jas 1:19; 3:2-12
10:21 [d] Pr 5:22-23; Hos 4:1,6,14
10:22 [e] Ge 24:35; Ps 37:22
10:23 [f] Pr 2:14; 15:21
10:24 [g] Isa 66:4 [h] Ps 145:17-19; Mt 5:6; 1Jn 5:14-15
10:25 [i] Ps 15:5 [j] Pr 12:3, 7; Mt 7:24-27
10:26 [k] Pr 26:6
10:27 [l] Pr 9:10-11 [m] Job 15:32
10:28 [n] Job 8:13; Pr 11:7
10:29 [o] Pr 21:15

who loves draws a veil over all wrongs, however many and however bad (cf. Jas 5:20; 1 Pet 4:8). Nevertheless, a good friend corrects another (cf. 27:5–6; Lev 19:17; Gal 6:1), and public discipline may be necessary (cf. 5:14; Matt 18:15–20; 1 Cor 5:2).

10:15 wealth. Crops as well as revenue in general. This commodity may serve as a source of security and comfort, but it should never usurp God as the source of one's trust and confidence (3:9). **rich.** In Proverbs, the rich have wealth but tragically are wise in their own eyes (28:11; cf. 3:7; 30:8–9) and harshly lord it over the poor (18:23; 22:7). For a moment their wealth is their fortified city against imminent disaster, but their folly finally ruins them, unlike the righteous (11:28; 18:10–11). **ruin.** Constant suspense, fear, and worry due to imminent disaster. This word links the folly of poor speech with the folly of being a rich person (vv. 13–14,15–16). **poor.** They are destitute, like the homeless.

10:16 the earnings of the wicked are sin and death. See Rom 6:23.

10:18 conceals hatred. By pretending friendliness (26:24,26,28). **spreads slander.** And so dissension (cf. v. 13).

10:19–20 prudent … righteous. Those marked by these virtues are able to interpret people and situations to determine when it is appropriate to speak.

10:22 painful toil. Strenuous work; comes from self-ambition and stands under God's judgment (cf. 20:21; 28:22; Ps 127:1; see also Gal 6:9–10; Jas 3:13–16).

10:30 [p] Ps 37:9,28-29; Pr 2:20-22
10:31 [q] Ps 37:30
10:32 [r] Ecc 10:12
11:1 [s] Lev 19:36; Dt 25:13-16; Pr 20:10, 23 [t] Pr 16:11
11:2 [u] Pr 16:18 [v] Pr 18:12; 29:23
11:3 [w] Pr 13:6
11:4 [x] Eze 7:19; Zep 1:18 [y] Ge 7:1; Pr 10:2
11:5 [z] Pr 5:21-23
11:7 [a] Pr 10:28
11:8 [b] Pr 21:18
11:10 [c] Pr 28:12
11:11 [d] Pr 29:8

30 The righteous will never be uprooted,
but the wicked will not remain in the land.[p]

31 From the mouth of the righteous comes the fruit of wisdom,[q]
but a perverse tongue will be silenced.

32 The lips of the righteous know what finds favor,[r]
but the mouth of the wicked only what is perverse.

11

The LORD detests dishonest scales,[s]
but accurate weights find favor with him.[t]

2 When pride comes, then comes disgrace,[u]
but with humility comes wisdom.[v]

3 The integrity of the upright guides them,
but the unfaithful are destroyed by their duplicity.[w]

4 Wealth is worthless in the day of wrath,[x]
but righteousness delivers from death.[y]

5 The righteousness of the blameless makes their paths straight,
but the wicked are brought down by their own wickedness.[z]

6 The righteousness of the upright delivers them,
but the unfaithful are trapped by evil desires.

7 Hopes placed in mortals die with them;
all the promise of[a] their power comes to nothing.[a]

8 The righteous person is rescued from trouble,
and it falls on the wicked instead.[b]

9 With their mouths the godless destroy their neighbors,
but through knowledge the righteous escape.

10 When the righteous prosper, the city rejoices;[c]
when the wicked perish, there are shouts of joy.

11 Through the blessing of the upright a city is exalted,
but by the mouth of the wicked it is destroyed.[d]

[a] 7 Two Hebrew manuscripts; most Hebrew manuscripts, Vulgate, Syriac and Targum *When the wicked die, their hope perishes; / all they expected from*

10:30 land. The source of one's income and security in the ancient world. Similar to the exile of disobedient Israel, the wicked will lose their source of security and the manifestation of God's favor.
11:1 The LORD. The one who upholds the moral order (3:34). Dishonest merchants defraud their neighbors and deny God. **detests.** An emotive term of disgust and revulsion; implies that God is no passive spectator of the marketplace. **weights.** Stones carved into shapes to make them easy to recognize; but they had a margin of error of up to 6 percent.
11:2 pride. Denotes a psychological state of an exaggerated opinion of oneself that does not correspond to social reality; the proud usurp the place of God.
11:3 guides. Leads through adversity.
11:4 Wealth. Tarnished, not righteous wealth (cf. 3:9; 8:18; 10:22). The double of this verse (10:2) substitutes "wealth" with "ill-gotten treasures" (see note on 10:2).
11:5 righteousness ... makes their paths straight. Makes their way in life clear and unencumbered. But along that way the righteous must be delivered from death and "rescued from trouble" (v. 8).
11:7 Hopes placed in mortals. The expectation of something good dependent on the continued existence of humans. See NIV text note. The NIV follows the reading of two Hebrew manuscripts that omit the word "wicked." Since v. 7a includes the word "mortals," it appears the term "wicked" was added by other versions in order to clarify that only the hope of the wicked will perish, not the hope of the righteous. **power.** Bodily strength. While the term may denote wealth, its relationship to misplaced trust in mortals suggests that the fleeting strength and promise of humans is in view.
11:9 knowledge. Possibly of the details of the godless person's attempt to destroy their neighbor (v. 9a). But elsewhere in the book, this term refers to knowledge of God and his will, which allows the righteous to respond appropriately to the speech of the godless. **the righteous escape.** See v. 8.
11:11 blessing of the upright. A pun: God's blessing on them (cf. v. 10) and their blessing on a city (cf. v. 11b).

[12] Whoever derides their neighbor has no sense,[e]
but the one who has understanding holds their tongue.

[13] A gossip betrays a confidence,[f]
but a trustworthy person keeps a secret.

[14] For lack of guidance a nation falls,[g]
but victory is won through many advisers.[h]

[15] Whoever puts up security[i] for a stranger will surely suffer,
but whoever refuses to shake hands in pledge is safe.

[16] A kindhearted woman gains honor,[j]
but ruthless men gain only wealth.

[17] Those who are kind benefit themselves,
but the cruel bring ruin on themselves.

[18] A wicked person earns deceptive wages,
but the one who sows righteousness reaps a sure reward.[k]

[19] Truly the righteous attain life,
but whoever pursues evil finds death.

[20] The LORD detests those whose hearts are perverse,
but he delights in those whose ways are blameless.[l]

[21] Be sure of this: The wicked will not go unpunished,
but those who are righteous will go free.[m]

[22] Like a gold ring in a pig's snout
is a beautiful woman who shows no discretion.

[23] The desire of the righteous ends only in good,
but the hope of the wicked only in wrath.

[24] One person gives freely, yet gains even more;
another withholds unduly, but comes to poverty.

[25] A generous person will prosper;
whoever refreshes others will be refreshed.[n]

[26] People curse the one who hoards grain,
but they pray God's blessing on the one who is willing to sell.

11:12 [e] Pr 14:21
11:13 [f] Lev 19:16; Pr 20:19; 1Ti 5:13
11:14 [g] Pr 20:18 [h] Pr 15:22; 24:6
11:15 [i] Pr 6:1
11:16 [j] Pr 31:31
11:18 [k] Hos 10:12-13
11:20 [l] 1Ch 29:17; Ps 119:1; Pr 12:2,22
11:21 [m] Pr 16:5
11:25 [n] Mt 5:7; 2Co 9:6-9

11:12 holds their tongue. Does not blurt out thoughts or feelings. The wise hold their tongues in check, even when belittled, and do not respond in kind because they love their neighbors and do not harbor hatred in their hearts (10:12,18). They speak at the right time in the right place (12:23; 15:2,28). Prudent silence (cf. v. 13) matches prudent speech (cf. 10:11).
11:13 a trustworthy person. One who is loyal and true to the interests of others. **keeps a secret.** Does not divulge sensitive information, even in court (25:9).
11:14 many advisers. Guarantees an issue will be looked at from every side. Proverbs never speaks of a single counselor.
11:15 See note on 6:1.
11:16 kindhearted woman. Or a gracious woman. While this quality may refer to the woman's physical beauty, the internal beauty of her character appears to be in view. **honor.** Social esteem, which is of greater value than the temporary wealth of ruthless men. The proverb signals the superiority of grace over brute force.
11:18 deceptive wages. A reward for work whose appearance differs from its reality. The work is performed out of self-interest in the hope of securing life, peace, and prosperity (see 10:16).
11:22 a gold ring ... a beautiful woman. Compares inner grace (v. 16) with outward beauty (31:30): a precious ornament and an attractive woman may be pleasing, but these outward trappings are repulsive when accompanied by indiscretion and a distorted character.
11:23 desire. Denotes aspirations rooted in one's nature. **ends only in good.** To others and to the righteous themselves. **hope of the wicked.** Advantaging themselves by disadvantaging others. **wrath.** The wicked experience what they intended for others.
11:24 gives freely. Distributes widely, loosely, and freely. **gains even more.** Increases in size or number on top of what was given away. This paradox regarding payments is qualified in the following verses. The liberality in v. 25 elaborates on the generosity in v. 24a, and the hoarding in v. 26a complements the stinginess in v. 24b.
11:25 refreshes. The term evokes the activities of watering and food distribution that characterize the generous.
11:26 one who hoards grain. Presumably to sell it during a time of

11:27 [o]Est 7:10; Ps 7:15-16
11:28 [p]Job 31:24-28; Ps 49:6; 52:7; Mk 10:25; 1Ti 6:17 [q]Ps 1:3; 92:12-14; Jer 17:8
11:29 [r]Pr 14:19
11:30 [s]Jas 5:20
11:31 [t]Pr 13:21; Jer 25:29; 1Pe 4:18
12:1 [u]Pr 9:7-9; 15:5,10,12,32
12:3 [v]Pr 10:25
12:4 [w]Pr 14:30
12:6 [x]Pr 14:3
12:7 [y]Ps 37:36 [z]Pr 10:25
12:11 [a]Pr 28:19

27 Whoever seeks good finds favor,
but evil comes to one who searches for it.[o]

28 Those who trust in their riches will fall,[p]
but the righteous will thrive like a green leaf.[q]

29 Whoever brings ruin on their family will inherit only wind,
and the fool will be servant to the wise.[r]

30 The fruit of the righteous is a tree of life,[s]
and the one who is wise saves lives.

31 If the righteous receive their due[t] on earth,
how much more the ungodly and the sinner!

12

Whoever loves discipline loves knowledge,
but whoever hates correction is stupid.[u]

2 Good people obtain favor from the LORD,
but he condemns those who devise wicked schemes.

3 No one can be established through wickedness,
but the righteous cannot be uprooted.[v]

4 A wife of noble character is her husband's crown,
but a disgraceful wife is like decay in his bones.[w]

5 The plans of the righteous are just,
but the advice of the wicked is deceitful.

6 The words of the wicked lie in wait for blood,
but the speech of the upright rescues them.[x]

7 The wicked are overthrown and are no more,[y]
but the house of the righteous stands firm.[z]

8 A person is praised according to their prudence,
and one with a warped mind is despised.

9 Better to be a nobody and yet have a servant
than pretend to be somebody and have no food.

10 The righteous care for the needs of their animals,
but the kindest acts of the wicked are cruel.

11 Those who work their land will have abundant food,
but those who chase fantasies have no sense.[a]

need for greater profit. **one who is willing to sell.** A generous person who cares more for the well-being of the community than for the balance of his bank account.
11:28 fall. The image may imply a house built on a faulty foundation.
11:29 servant. Indentured slave. Having lost their property, the fool loses their freedom. Consequently, a competent person uses the fool's energy positively, while the fool uses it only to their own and others' detriment.
11:31 due. Rightful treatment or just deserts. The righteous person's due is remedial punishment while on earth (e.g., Num 20:11–12; 2 Sam 12:10); the ungodly person's due is penal punishment in an indefinite future (cf. 1 Pet 4:18).
12:1 discipline. See note on 1:2. **loves ... hates.** Strikes at the heart of one's motivation. **knowledge.** The means by which one's character, affections, and behavior may be conformed to the way of wisdom (1:2). **stupid.** Brutish (cf. Ps 73:22; see also 15:10).
12:4 noble. Strong or powerful with reference to the wife's character and physical capacity (see 31:10). **crown.** She is valued and prized highly (cf. 31:28–29). **disgraceful.** See 10:5. **bones.** His skeletal frame. His crown is highly visible; his hurt is deep and invisible.
12:6 lie in wait for blood. Captures the deadly and murderous content and style of the wicked person's speech, which seeks to entrap and kill unsuspecting people (cf. 1:11).
12:8 one with a warped mind. One who lacks the ability to see reality; they compromise themselves without knowing it.
12:9–10 have a servant ... care for the needs of their animals. Both are needed to do the hard work the land requires.
12:11 those who chase fantasies. Pursuers of get-rich-quick schemes to avoid hard work. Such people "have no food" (v. 9) because they lack "sense" (v. 11).

[12]The wicked desire the stronghold of evildoers,
but the root of the righteous endures.

[13]Evildoers are trapped by their sinful talk,[b]
and so the innocent escape trouble.[c]

[14]From the fruit of their lips people are filled with good things,[d]
and the work of their hands brings them reward.[e]

[15]The way of fools seems right to them,[f]
but the wise listen to advice.

[16]Fools show their annoyance at once,
but the prudent overlook an insult.[g]

[17]An honest witness tells the truth,
but a false witness tells lies.[h]

[18]The words of the reckless pierce like swords,[i]
but the tongue of the wise brings healing.[j]

[19]Truthful lips endure forever,
but a lying tongue lasts only a moment.

[20]Deceit is in the hearts of those who plot evil,
but those who promote peace have joy.

[21]No harm overtakes the righteous,[k]
but the wicked have their fill of trouble.

[22]The LORD detests lying lips,[l]
but he delights in people who are trustworthy.[m]

[23]The prudent keep their knowledge to
themselves,[n]
but a fool's heart blurts out folly.

[24]Diligent hands will rule,
but laziness ends in forced labor.[o]

[25]Anxiety weighs down the heart,[p]
but a kind word cheers it up.

[26]The righteous choose their friends
carefully,
but the way of the wicked leads them
astray.

[27]The lazy do not roast[a] any game,
but the diligent feed on the riches of
the hunt.

[28]In the way of righteousness there is life;[q]
along that path is immortality.

[a] 27 The meaning of the Hebrew for this word is uncertain.

12:13 [b]Pr 18:7 [c]Pr 21:23; 2Pe 2:9
12:14 [d]Pr 13:2; 15:23; 18:20 [e]Isa 3:10-11
12:15 [f]Pr 14:12; 16:2, 25; Lk 18:11
12:16 [g]Pr 29:11
12:17 [h]Pr 14:5,25
12:18 [i]Ps 57:4 [j]Pr 15:4
12:21 [k]Ps 91:10
12:22 [l]Pr 6:17; Rev 22:15 [m]Pr 11:20
12:23 [n]Pr 10:14; 13:16
12:24 [o]Pr 10:4
12:25 [p]Pr 15:13; Isa 50:4
12:28 [q]Dt 30:15

Assyrians grooming and feeding their horses (Prov 12:10).

Kim Walton, taken at the British Museum

12:18 words of the reckless. Rash, thoughtless, hasty, careless words. They hurt others, piercing the heart like a sharp sword. In contrast, the thoughtful words of the wise restore others (10:11; cf. Eph 4:29).
12:23 blurts out folly. Cries out loud and clear. As Jesus declared, the words that come out of a person's mouth stem from their heart, and "these defile them" (Matt 15:18).
12:24 rule. Govern and retain independence.
12:26 choose their friends carefully. Denotes a careful, diligent, and penetrating investigation to find what is concealed.
12:27 do not roast any game. Do not secure the most available food (i.e., wild animals) to sustain life, either by catching or preparing it.

13:1 [r] Pr 10:1
13:2 [s] Pr 12:14
13:3 [t] Jas 3:2 [u] Pr 21:23 [v] Pr 18:7,20-21
13:6 [w] Pr 11:3,5
13:7 [x] 2Co 6:10
13:9 [y] Job 18:5; Pr 4:18-19; 24:20
13:11 [z] Pr 10:2
13:13 [a] Nu 15:31; 2Ch 36:16
13:14 [b] Pr 10:11 [c] Pr 14:27

13

A wise son heeds his father's instruction,
but a mocker does not respond to rebukes.[r]

2 From the fruit of their lips people enjoy good things,[s]
but the unfaithful have an appetite for violence.

3 Those who guard their lips[t] preserve their lives,[u]
but those who speak rashly will come to ruin.[v]

4 A sluggard's appetite is never filled,
but the desires of the diligent are fully satisfied.

5 The righteous hate what is false,
but the wicked make themselves a stench
and bring shame on themselves.

6 Righteousness guards the person of integrity,
but wickedness overthrows the sinner.[w]

7 One person pretends to be rich, yet has nothing;
another pretends to be poor, yet has great wealth.[x]

8 A person's riches may ransom their life,
but the poor cannot respond to threatening rebukes.

9 The light of the righteous shines brightly,
but the lamp of the wicked is snuffed out.[y]

10 Where there is strife, there is pride,
but wisdom is found in those who take advice.

11 Dishonest money dwindles away,[z]
but whoever gathers money little by little makes it grow.

12 Hope deferred makes the heart sick,
but a longing fulfilled is a tree of life.

13 Whoever scorns instruction will pay for it,[a]
but whoever respects a command is rewarded.

14 The teaching of the wise is a fountain of life,[b]
turning a person from the snares of death.[c]

15 Good judgment wins favor,
but the way of the unfaithful leads to their destruction.[a]

[a] *15* Septuagint and Syriac; the meaning of the Hebrew for this phrase is uncertain.

13:2 fruit of their lips. An idiom for one's words or speech (12:14; 18:20); proper speech produces edible fruit that nourishes both the speaker and others. **appetite.** An inner craving or desire.
13:3 those who speak rashly. Chatty, incautious, without self-control.
13:4 the desires of the diligent are fully satisfied. These unqualified desires may include everything the diligent aspire to, such as eating, drinking, and the opposite sex (Deut 14:26; 2 Sam 23:15; Ps 45:11; cf. Mic 7:1). The proverb assumes that the diligent experience satisfaction through God's provision of the basic needs of life.
13:5 shame. Public humiliation and personal embarrassment.
13:7 pretends to be rich. To give the appearance of success in order to command social respect (12:9). Appearances cannot always be trusted, for things are not always as they seem. **pretends to be poor.** Perhaps out of humility.
13:8 A person's riches may ransom their life. The rich are able to pay off enemies or extortioners. The poor, however, have little and are unconcerned about or unable to meet such financial demands.
13:9 light. Enduring joy, delight, and success. **lamp.** Carries the same sense as "light." **snuffed out.** Extinguished; may refer to the ultimate end, or death, of the wicked.
13:10 pride. The colossal ego that cannot accept advice and responds with bickering and disagreement. **those who take advice.** The teachable. The wise life is marked by a teachable spirit as well as openness to the counsel of others (12:15).
13:11 Dishonest. Wealth gained quickly through unjust dealings is not earned, and its value is not recognized. As a result, it tends to be mismanaged and squandered. **little by little.** With patience; enduring wealth grows by gathering it gradually.
13:12 Hope deferred. An expectation or aspiration whose realization is postponed or delayed. **a tree of life.** See note on 3:18.
13:14 teaching of the wise. This refers to instruction that is found in or corresponds with the teaching of Proverbs. **fountain of life.** An image of

16 All who are prudent act with[a] knowledge,
but fools expose their folly.[d]

17 A wicked messenger falls into trouble,
but a trustworthy envoy brings healing.[e]

18 Whoever disregards discipline comes to poverty and shame,
but whoever heeds correction is honored.[f]

19 A longing fulfilled is sweet to the soul,
but fools detest turning from evil.

20 Walk with the wise and become wise,
for a companion of fools suffers harm.[g]

21 Trouble pursues the sinner,
but the righteous[h] are rewarded with good things.

22 A good person leaves an inheritance for their children's children,
but a sinner's wealth is stored up for the righteous.[i]

23 An unplowed field produces food for the poor,
but injustice sweeps it away.

24 Whoever spares the rod hates their children,
but the one who loves their children is careful to discipline them.[j]

25 The righteous eat to their hearts' content,
but the stomach of the wicked goes hungry.[k]

14

The wise woman builds her house,[l]
but with her own hands the foolish one tears hers down.

2 Whoever fears the LORD walks uprightly,
but those who despise him are devious in their ways.

3 A fool's mouth lashes out with pride,
but the lips of the wise protect them.[m]

4 Where there are no oxen, the manger is empty,
but from the strength of an ox come abundant harvests.

5 An honest witness does not deceive,
but a false witness pours out lies.[n]

6 The mocker seeks wisdom and finds none,
but knowledge comes easily to the discerning.

13:16 [d] Pr 12:23
13:17 [e] Pr 25:13
13:18 [f] Pr 15:5,31-32
13:20 [g] Pr 15:31
13:21 [h] Ps 32:10
13:22 [i] Job 27:17; Ecc 2:26
13:24 [j] Pr 19:18; 22:15; 23:13-14; 29:15,17; Heb 12:7
13:25 [k] Ps 34:10; Pr 10:3
14:1 [l] Pr 24:3
14:3 [m] Pr 12:6
14:5 [n] Pr 6:19; 12:17

[a] 16 Or *prudent protect themselves through*

refreshment and vitality that describes the excellence and truthfulness of wise teaching.
13:17 brings healing. Therapeutically refreshes a client and provides a remedy for the havoc wrought on a sick community.
13:20 Walk with the wise. One's company plays an important role in shaping one's character.
13:23 An unplowed field. Either the marginal fields of the poor or the land that an owner left unplowed and unused so that the poor could get food from it (cf. Exod 23:10–11; Lev 25:1–7; see also Hos 10:12).
13:24 hates. In the context of parental discipline, this attitude allows children to continue in their folly. **loves.** The motivation for the discipline commended in the proverb (3:11–12; Heb 12:5–11). Love inspires and tempers the form of the physical punishment. **discipline.** A common educational technique in Proverbs (10:13; 22:15; 23:13–14). While discipline tends to be physical (but is not always—see 17:10; 19:18), its intention is to correct, train, and cultivate godly character by driving out folly and wrong behavior.
14:1 builds her house. Similar to Wisdom (see 9:1 and note), the wise woman embodies moral strength and diligence (31:10–31), working for the benefit of her household and the community.
14:2 devious in their ways. Twisted and perverse in beliefs, commitments, and manner of life.
14:3 lashes out. Beats the fool or others. **pride.** See note on 13:10. This attitude makes fools lash out to their destruction; humility produces thoughtful speech that protects the wise.
14:4 strength of an ox. The ox plows the ground to plant seed and ensure a fruitful harvest. A vacant manger spells trouble: a meager harvest.
14:6 mocker. See Introduction: Character Types. This person is not

14:8 [o]ver 24
14:11 [p]Pr 3:33; 12:7
14:12 [q]Pr 12:15
[r]Pr 16:25
14:13 [s]Ecc 2:2
14:14 [t]Pr 1:31 [u]Pr 12:14
14:16 [v]Pr 22:3
14:17 [w]ver 29
14:19 [x]Pr 11:29
14:20 [y]Pr 19:4,7

7 Stay away from a fool,
for you will not find knowledge on their lips.

8 The wisdom of the prudent is to give thought to their ways,
but the folly of fools is deception.[o]

9 Fools mock at making amends for sin,
but goodwill is found among the upright.

10 Each heart knows its own bitterness,
and no one else can share its joy.

11 The house of the wicked will be destroyed,
but the tent of the upright will flourish.[p]

12 There is a way that appears to be right,[q]
but in the end it leads to death.[r]

13 Even in laughter[s] the heart may ache,
and rejoicing may end in grief.

14 The faithless will be fully repaid for their ways,[t]
and the good rewarded for theirs.[u]

15 The simple believe anything,
but the prudent give thought to their steps.

16 The wise fear the LORD and shun evil,[v]
but a fool is hotheaded and yet feels secure.

17 A quick-tempered person does foolish things,[w]
and the one who devises evil schemes is hated.

18 The simple inherit folly,
but the prudent are crowned with knowledge.

19 Evildoers will bow down in the presence of the good,
and the wicked at the gates of the righteous.[x]

20 The poor are shunned even by their neighbors,
but the rich have many friends.[y]

discerning and cannot seize wisdom. **knowledge comes easily to the discerning.** Because they are humble (see Introduction: Theme; see also 8:9 and note).
14:7 you will not find knowledge. See note on 13:20.
14:8 give thought to their ways. The prudent manifest their wisdom by considering the nature of and the consequences associated with their actions.
14:9 Fools mock at making amends for sin. Fools delight in ridicule and discord; they scoff at opportunities to make appropriate reparations for wrongdoing and restore relations with God and others.
14:10 Each heart knows its own bitterness. No one can completely understand the emotional state of another. The proverb acknowledges the dignity of emotions—from bitterness to joy—and cautions against evaluating others by outward appearances.
14:11 house ... tent. Contrary to appearances, the more solidly built house of the wicked is less secure than the portable tent of the righteous. The proverb instructs the son to live by faith, not by sight.
14:13 laughter ... rejoicing. These outward expressions of joy may mask the heartache of the deceptive fool, but in the end, when they are fully repaid for being "faithless" (v. 14), their grief will manifest itself.
14:15 The simple believe anything. Because they lack perception and discernment, the simple trust deceptive appearances and human opinion. They do not consider the outcome of sin.
14:16 shun evil. Persistently avoid wrongdoing, which demonstrates the fear of the Lord (see 1:7; 3:7). **hotheaded ... feels secure.** Fools carelessly jump into things because they have an inadequate view of and trust in self rather than God.
14:18 inherit. Signifies a permanent possession. Ironically, it is intended to sustain life, but the inheritance of "the simple" destroys their lives.
14:19 gates of the righteous. A place of justice; the submission of the wicked at this place implies that the righteous will distribute the justice that punishes evildoers.
14:20 rich. Within Proverbs, the rich are self-autonomous and never defined as good (see 10:15 and note). **many friends.** Despite their number, it appears these friendships are rooted in the friend's wealth rather than in their character. The poor have a material deficit but in this book are never said to have a moral deficit. The proverb lays bare the hard truth about human nature, which often bases friendship on a person's economic status. People desire the company of the rich and shun the poor. The proverb functions as a biting observation on human nature and does not approve of this attitude toward the poor.

21 It is a sin to despise one's neighbor,[z]
but blessed is the one who is kind to the needy.[a]

22 Do not those who plot evil go astray?
But those who plan what is good find[a] love and
faithfulness.

23 All hard work brings a profit,
but mere talk leads only to poverty.

24 The wealth of the wise is their crown,
but the folly of fools yields folly.

25 A truthful witness saves lives,
but a false witness is deceitful.[b]

26 Whoever fears the LORD has a secure fortress,[c]
and for their children it will be a refuge.

27 The fear of the LORD is a fountain of life,
turning a person from the snares of death.[d]

28 A large population is a king's glory,
but without subjects a prince is ruined.

29 Whoever is patient has great understanding,
but one who is quick-tempered displays folly.[e]

30 A heart at peace gives life to the body,
but envy rots the bones.[f]

31 Whoever oppresses the poor shows contempt for their
Maker,[g]
but whoever is kind to the needy honors God.

32 When calamity comes, the wicked are brought down,[h]
but even in death the righteous seek refuge in God.[i]

33 Wisdom reposes in the heart of the discerning[j]
and even among fools she lets herself be known.[b]

34 Righteousness exalts a nation,[k]
but sin condemns any people.

35 A king delights in a wise servant,
but a shameful servant arouses his fury.[l]

14:21 [z] Pr 11:12 [a] Ps 41:1; Pr 19:17
14:25 [b] ver 5
14:26 [c] Pr 18:10; 19:23; Isa 33:6
14:27 [d] Pr 13:14
14:29 [e] Ecc 7:8-9; Jas 1:19
14:30 [f] Pr 12:4
14:31 [g] Pr 17:5
14:32 [h] Pr 6:15 [i] Job 13:15; 2Ti 4:18
14:33 [j] Pr 2:6-10
14:34 [k] Pr 11:11
14:35 [l] Mt 24:45-51; 25:14-30

[a] 22 Or *show* [b] 33 Hebrew; Septuagint and Syriac *discerning / but in the heart of fools she is not known*

14:21 the needy. The poor and afflicted. This saying protects misinterpreting v. 20 as a rationalization for shunning a poor person. The saying teaches that the greedy, dark side of human nature can be redeemed into the happy state of being pronounced blessed (3:13) as one shows kindness to the poor (22:9).
14:22 go astray. Leave the ethical path, where one should extend and receive kindness, and so be on the way to death.
14:26 a secure fortress ... a refuge. Images of protection and security that God provides to those who fear him. This security should inspire confidence.
14:27 a fountain of life. An energizing and sustaining source that issues from the fear of the Lord and guides the individual on the path of wisdom.
14:28 king's glory. Locates the fame and honor of the king in his service to the community. Here leadership is a call to service and responsibility rather than a call to power and self-interest (31:1–9).
14:31 shows contempt for their Maker. Since God is the Creator of the poor and the needy, they possess an inherent dignity as those created in the image of God (Gen 1:26–28). To oppress, exploit, or treat them as subhuman is to insult God's character and design.
14:32 seek refuge. See v. 26. Just as those who fear the Lord find security and confidence in life through their relationship with God (v. 27; 10:27), so also the righteous find security and confidence in God when faced with death.
14:34 Righteousness exalts a nation. The status of a nation is determined by the piety of its people rather than by the scope of its territory, the size of its treasury, or the extent of its military.

15:1 [m] Pr 25:15
15:2 [n] Pr 12:23
15:3 [o] 2Ch 16:9 [p] Job 31:4; Heb 4:13 [q] Job 34:21; Jer 16:17
15:5 [r] Pr 13:1
15:6 [s] Pr 8:21
15:8 [t] Pr 21:27; Isa 1:11; Jer 6:20 [u] ver 29
15:9 [v] Pr 21:21; 1Ti 6:11
15:10 [w] Pr 1:31-32; 5:12
15:11 [x] Job 26:6; Ps 139:8 [y] 2Ch 6:30; Ps 44:21
15:12 [z] Am 5:10
15:13 [a] Pr 12:25; 17:22; 18:14
15:14 [b] Pr 18:15
15:15 [c] ver 13
15:16 [d] Ps 37:16-17; Pr 16:8; 1Ti 6:6

15

A gentle answer turns away wrath,[m]
  but a harsh word stirs up anger.

2 The tongue of the wise adorns knowledge,
  but the mouth of the fool gushes folly.[n]

3 The eyes[o] of the LORD are everywhere,[p]
  keeping watch on the wicked and the good.[q]

4 The soothing tongue is a tree of life,
  but a perverse tongue crushes the spirit.

5 A fool spurns a parent's discipline,
  but whoever heeds correction shows prudence.[r]

6 The house of the righteous contains great treasure,[s]
  but the income of the wicked brings ruin.

7 The lips of the wise spread knowledge,
  but the hearts of fools are not upright.

8 The LORD detests the sacrifice of the wicked,[t]
  but the prayer of the upright pleases him.[u]

9 The LORD detests the way of the wicked,
  but he loves those who pursue righteousness.[v]

10 Stern discipline awaits anyone who leaves the path;
  the one who hates correction will die.[w]

11 Death and Destruction[a] lie open before the LORD[x]—
  how much more do human hearts![y]

12 Mockers resent correction,[z]
  so they avoid the wise.

13 A happy heart makes the face cheerful,
  but heartache crushes the spirit.[a]

14 The discerning heart seeks knowledge,[b]
  but the mouth of a fool feeds on folly.

15 All the days of the oppressed are wretched,
  but the cheerful heart has a continual feast.[c]

16 Better a little with the fear of the LORD
  than great wealth with turmoil.[d]

[a] *11* Hebrew *Abaddon*

15:1 A gentle answer turns away wrath. A tender and considerate response pacifies a situation and quells anger.
15:2 The tongue of the wise adorns knowledge. Speech controlled by loving emotions and sound thought beautifies the internal knowledge of the wise.
15:3 The eyes of the LORD. Highlights God's omniscience. He is no passive bystander of human behavior.
15:4 The soothing tongue is a tree of life. A gentle word in an appropriate situation brings nourishment, healing, and life.
15:6 the income of the wicked. The yield, profit, and benefits accrued through sinful activity.
15:8,9 detests. See note on 11:1.
15:8 sacrifice of the wicked. External, superficial acts of homage that do not flow from a right heart or character. **prayer of the upright.** A genuine act of worship that flows from an honest heart and the pursuit of righteousness.
15:10 the path. See Introduction: Theme.
15:11 how much more. Focuses attention on the Lord's omniscience and justice.
15:13 makes the face cheerful. When the inner self is well, it brightens one's appearance and attitude continually (v. 15).
15:14 discerning heart. An insightful disposition. To cultivate a wise and cheerful heart, one must seek knowledge.
15:16,17 Better … than. A common comparative in Proverbs. Comparative proverbs illuminate the importance of contentment through a value system that pits internal satisfaction against posh external products. This internal satisfaction is rooted in the "fear of the LORD" and "love" (see note on 1:7). And this disposition is preferable to "great

[17] Better a small serving of vegetables with love
than a fattened calf with hatred.[e]

[18] A hot-tempered person stirs up conflict,[f]
but the one who is patient calms a quarrel.[g]

[19] The way of the sluggard is blocked with thorns,[h]
but the path of the upright is a highway.

[20] A wise son brings joy to his father,[i]
but a foolish man despises his mother.

15:17 [e] Pr 17:1
15:18 [f] Pr 26:21 [g] Ge 13:8
15:19 [h] Pr 22:5
15:20 [i] Pr 10:1

wealth" and a "fattened calf" (i.e., a lavish meal) accompanied by "turmoil" and "hatred."

15:20,21,23 joy. A state of delight. This state frames this group of proverbs, which moves from the parent's joy (v. 20) to the misplaced joy of folly (v. 21) to the joy found in a response delivered in an appropriate manner and at the appropriate time (v. 23).

CHARACTER TRAITS IN PROVERBS

TRAITS TO BE PROMOTED	
avoidance of strife	20:3
compassion for animals	12:10
contentment	13:25; 14:30; 15:27
diligence	6:6–13; 12:24,27; 13:4
faithful love	20:6
faithfulness	3:5–6; 5:15–17; 25:13; 28:20
generosity	21:26; 22:9
honesty	16:11; 24:26
humility	11:2; 16:19; 25:6–7; 29:23
integrity	11:3; 25:26; 28:18
kindness to others	11:16–17
kindness to enemies	25:21–22
leadership	30:19–31
loyalty	19:22
nobility	12:4; 31:10,29
patience	15:18; 16:32
peacefulness	16:7
praiseworthiness	27:21
righteousness	4:26–27; 11:5–6,30; 12:28; 13:6; 29:2
self-control	17:27; 25:28; 29:11
strength and honor	20:29
strength in adversity	24:10
teachableness	15:31
truthfulness	12:19,22; 23:23

TRAITS TO BE AVOIDED	
anger	29:22
antisocial behavior	18:1
beauty without discretion	11:22
blaming God	19:3
dishonesty	24:28
greed	28:25
hatred	29:27
hot temper	19:19; 29:22
immorality	6:20–35
inappropriate desire	27:7
injustice	22:16
jealousy	27:4
lack of mercy	21:13
laziness	6:6–11; 18:9; 19:15; 20:4; 24:30–34; 26:13–15
maliciousness	6:27
meddling	26:17; 30:10
pride	15:5; 16:18; 21:4,24; 29:23; 30:13
quarrelsomeness	26:21
self-conceit	26:12,16
self-deceit	28:11
self-glory	25:27
self-righteousness	30:12
social disruption	19:10
stubbornness	29:1
unfaithfulness	25:19
unneighborliness	3:27–30
vengeance	24:28–29
wickedness	21:10
wicked scheming	16:30

15:21 [j] Pr 10:23
15:22 [k] Pr 11:14
15:23 [l] Pr 12:14 [m] Pr 25:11
15:25 [n] Pr 12:7 [o] Dt 19:14; Ps 68:5-6; Pr 23:10-11
15:26 [p] Pr 6:16
15:27 [q] Ex 23:8; Isa 33:15
15:28 [r] 1Pe 3:15
15:29 [s] Ps 145:18-19
15:31 [t] ver 5
15:32 [u] Pr 1:7
15:33 [v] Pr 1:7 [w] Pr 18:12
16:1 [x] Pr 19:21
16:2 [y] Pr 21:2
16:3 [z] Ps 37:5-6; Pr 3:5-6

21 Folly brings joy to one who has no sense,[j]
but whoever has understanding keeps a straight course.

22 Plans fail for lack of counsel,
but with many advisers they succeed.[k]

23 A person finds joy in giving an apt reply[l]—
and how good is a timely word![m]

24 The path of life leads upward for the prudent
to keep them from going down to the realm of the dead.

25 The LORD tears down the house of the proud,[n]
but he sets the widow's boundary stones in place.[o]

26 The LORD detests the thoughts of the wicked,[p]
but gracious words are pure in his sight.

27 The greedy bring ruin to their households,
but the one who hates bribes will live.[q]

28 The heart of the righteous weighs its answers,[r]
but the mouth of the wicked gushes evil.

29 The LORD is far from the wicked,
but he hears the prayer of the righteous.[s]

30 Light in a messenger's eyes brings joy to the heart,
and good news gives health to the bones.

31 Whoever heeds life-giving correction
will be at home among the wise.[t]

32 Those who disregard discipline despise themselves,[u]
but the one who heeds correction gains understanding.

33 Wisdom's instruction is to fear the LORD,[v]
and humility comes before honor.[w]

16

To humans belong the plans of the heart,
but from the LORD comes the proper answer of the tongue.[x]

2 All a person's ways seem pure to them,
but motives are weighed by the LORD.[y]

3 Commit to the LORD whatever you do,
and he will establish your plans.[z]

15:22 counsel. The open, loving guidance or advice of others. The wise joyfully accept and give ethical counsel (vv. 22–23).
15:24 path. See Introduction: Theme. **upward.** This proverb projects the wise ascending on the journey of life rather than descending to the grave. **the realm of the dead.** Hebrew *šěʾôl* (see note on 1:12).
15:25 he sets the widow's boundary stones in place. The Lord oversees the property boundaries of the weak, ensuring that the widow's land remains intact and safe from exploitation or injustice.
15:27 hates bribes. Abhors corruption and injustice.
15:28 weighs its answers. Considers, ponders, or meditates on words before speaking. The wise are prudent and discerning; they carefully contemplate their words, as well as the context of the conversation, before they speak.
15:29 the prayer of the righteous. See note on v. 8.
15:30 Light in a messenger's eyes. When a messenger has good news, one can see it in their lives, and everyone rejoices. Proverbs associates light and life exclusively with the wise (cf. v. 13a).
15:31 heeds. Adheres to, follows, and obeys correction. Receptivity to wisdom and a teachable spirit distinguish the wise from the fool.
15:33 fear the LORD. The essence of wisdom and the prerequisite for acquitting the book's instruction (see 1:7 and note). **humility.** A lack of pride as well as an attitude that is cultivated through the fear of the Lord. This attitude is required in order to gain wisdom and favor.
16:1 the LORD. Occurs in every verse of vv. 1–9 except v. 8. **answer of the tongue.** Good and effective speech that is dependent upon careful planning, weighing and arranging arguments, and God's direction.
16:2 a person's ways seem pure ... motives are weighed by the LORD. Humans are unable to understand truly the intentions behind their plans, for they are finite and limited (Job 28:12–13,20–28).
16:3 he will establish your plans. The wise submit their plans to God's

[4]The LORD works out everything to its proper end[a]—
even the wicked for a day of disaster.[b]

[5]The LORD detests all the proud of heart.[c]
Be sure of this: They will not go unpunished.[d]

[6]Through love and faithfulness sin is atoned for;
through the fear of the LORD evil is avoided.[e]

[7]When the LORD takes pleasure in anyone's way,
he causes their enemies to make peace with them.

[8]Better a little with righteousness
than much gain[f] with injustice.

[9]In their hearts humans plan their course,
but the LORD establishes their steps.[g]

[10]The lips of a king speak as an oracle,
and his mouth does not betray justice.

[11]Honest scales and balances belong to the LORD;
all the weights in the bag are of his making.[h]

[12]Kings detest wrongdoing,
for a throne is established through righteousness.[i]

[13]Kings take pleasure in honest lips;
they value the one who speaks what is right.[j]

[14]A king's wrath is a messenger of death,[k]
but the wise will appease it.

[15]When a king's face brightens, it means life;[l]
his favor is like a rain cloud in spring.

[16]How much better to get wisdom than gold,
to get insight rather than silver![m]

[17]The highway of the upright avoids evil;
those who guard their ways preserve their lives.

16:4 [a]Isa 43:7 [b]Ro 9:22
16:5 [c]Pr 6:16 [d]Pr 11:20-21
16:6 [e]Pr 14:16
16:8 [f]Ps 37:16
16:9 [g]Jer 10:23
16:11 [h]Pr 11:1
16:12 [i]Pr 25:5
16:13 [j]Pr 14:35
16:14 [k]Pr 19:12
16:15 [l]Job 29:24
16:16 [m]Pr 8:10,19

providential care, trusting that he will accomplish their goals in accordance with his sovereign purposes (3:5–6).
16:4 works out everything to its proper end. As the one who governs every facet of life and history, the Lord oversees and guides all things to their proper goal in accordance with his purposes (Acts 3:17–26; Rom 8:28). **the wicked for a day of disaster.** The manifestation of God's glory, holiness, and power through his justice and the eradication of evil are included in the divine plan and God's guidance of all things toward their proper goal (Rom 2:5–11).
16:6 Through love and faithfulness sin is atoned for. Divine attributes describe the nature of the sacrificial system, which manifests God's commitment to and forgiveness of sin (Exod 34:6; Joel 2:13; Jonah 4:2). In the same way, the sacrificial work of Christ embodies God's love and fidelity to his people. **the fear of the LORD.** The proper response to this display of God's love and faithfulness (see 1:7 and note).
16:8 Better a little with righteousness. Even when the tangible rewards of righteousness are not experienced, this moral state is better than abundant riches secured through injustice.
16:10 king. Occurs in every verse of vv. 10–15 except v. 11. **oracle.** The inspired verdicts of the king. Since God endows his representative with wisdom to establish justice, the king's judgments are authoritative and indisputable.
16:11 Honest scales and balances. A concrete illustration of justice. Since just economic practices are the creation and concern of the Lord, the wise king executes economic equity by enforcing standard weights and measures.
16:12–13 Kings detest wrongdoing ... take pleasure in honest lips. The moral ideal of kings. The revulsion of kings against wickedness and their delight in truthful speech reveal their moral sensibilities and identify them with the moral tastes of Lady Wisdom (8:7) and the Lord (6:16–19; 15:9).
16:14 messenger of death. A metaphor for the legitimate wrath of the king, a sign of impending death. In context, this anger is against those things kings should detest (v. 12). While the Lord ultimately inflicts death on the wicked in an unspecified future, the king serves as his immediate agent (Eccl 8:4). **the wise will appease it.** The wise may pacify or quell the king's anger through humility (15:33), repentance (28:13), and patience with a gentle answer (15:1; 25:15).
16:15 king's face brightens ... like a rain cloud in spring. The light of a king's face and the meteorological images of natural renewal symbolize the ruler's favor. As the author of life, God mediates life and renewal through his just king (Ps 72:15–17).
16:16 See 3:13–18 and note on 3:14–16.

16:18 [n]Pr 11:2; 18:12
16:20 [o]Ps 2:12; 34:8; Pr 19:8; Jer 17:7
16:21 [p]ver 23
16:22 [q]Pr 13:14
16:24 [r]Pr 24:13-14
16:25 [s]Pr 12:15 [t]Pr 14:12
16:27 [u]Jas 3:6
16:28 [v]Pr 15:18 [w]Pr 17:9
16:29 [x]Pr 1:10; 12:26
16:31 [y]Pr 20:29
16:33 [z]Pr 18:18; 29:26

18 Pride goes before destruction,
a haughty spirit before a fall.[n]

19 Better to be lowly in spirit along with the oppressed
than to share plunder with the proud.

20 Whoever gives heed to instruction prospers,[a]
and blessed is the one who trusts in the LORD.[o]

21 The wise in heart are called discerning,
and gracious words promote instruction.[bp]

22 Prudence is a fountain of life to the prudent,[q]
but folly brings punishment to fools.

23 The hearts of the wise make their mouths prudent,
and their lips promote instruction.[c]

24 Gracious words are a honeycomb,
sweet to the soul and healing to the bones.[r]

25 There is a way that appears to be right,[s]
but in the end it leads to death.[t]

26 The appetite of laborers works for them;
their hunger drives them on.

27 A scoundrel plots evil,
and on their lips it is like a scorching fire.[u]

28 A perverse person stirs up conflict,[v]
and a gossip separates close friends.[w]

29 A violent person entices their neighbor
and leads them down a path that is not good.[x]

30 Whoever winks with their eye is plotting perversity;
whoever purses their lips is bent on evil.

31 Gray hair is a crown of splendor;[y]
it is attained in the way of righteousness.

32 Better a patient person than a warrior,
one with self-control than one who takes a city.

33 The lot is cast into the lap,
but its every decision is from the LORD.[z]

[a] 20 Or *whoever speaks prudently finds what is good* [b] 21 Or *words make a person persuasive* [c] 23 Or *prudent / and make their lips persuasive*

16:18 fall. Stumbling; probably connected to the metaphor of "ways" in v. 17.
16:20 See 3:1–6.
16:21 gracious words promote instruction. The prudent, careful, and judicious (see NIV text note on v. 20) speech of the wise is attractive, persuasive, and accepted by others (see NIV text notes on vv. 21,23).
16:22 fountain of life. See note on 10:11.
16:24 Gracious words are a honeycomb. This metaphor captures the pleasant and medicinal value of prudent speech.
16:25 See note on v. 2.
16:30 winks with their eye. See notes on 6:13; 10:10. **purses their lips.** Puckers or presses together their lips as a gesture or sign, perhaps to a partner in crime.
16:31 Gray hair ... crown of splendor. The external marks of old age that serve as a sign of glory (20:29). **in the way of righteousness.** Since long life is the reward of the wise, this crown is acquired by walking in accordance with the way of wisdom (see Introduction: Theme).
16:32 a patient person. A person who is able to control their appetites and emotions is stronger than the most powerful warrior who sacks a city.
16:33 The lot. A small marked stone (or stones) used to reveal God's selection of someone or something out of several possibilities in cases in which a clear choice was not otherwise evident.

17 Better a dry crust with peace and quiet
than a house full of feasting, with strife.[a]

2 A prudent servant will rule over a disgraceful son
and will share the inheritance as one of the family.

3 The crucible for silver and the furnace for gold,[b]
but the LORD tests the heart.[c]

4 A wicked person listens to deceitful lips;
a liar pays attention to a destructive tongue.

5 Whoever mocks the poor shows contempt for their Maker;[d]
whoever gloats over disaster[e] will not go unpunished.[f]

6 Children's children[g] are a crown to the aged,
and parents are the pride of their children.

7 Eloquent lips are unsuited to a godless fool —
how much worse lying lips to a ruler!

8 A bribe is seen as a charm by the one who gives it;
they think success will come at every turn.

9 Whoever would foster love covers over an offense,[h]
but whoever repeats the matter separates close friends.[i]

10 A rebuke impresses a discerning person
more than a hundred lashes a fool.

11 Evildoers foster rebellion against God;
the messenger of death will be sent against them.

12 Better to meet a bear robbed of her cubs
than a fool bent on folly.

13 Evil will never leave the house
of one who pays back evil[j] for good.

14 Starting a quarrel is like breaching a dam;
so drop the matter before a dispute breaks out.[k]

15 Acquitting the guilty and condemning the innocent[l] —
the LORD detests them both.[m]

16 Why should fools have money in hand to buy wisdom,
when they are not able to understand it?[n]

17 A friend loves at all times,
and a brother is born for a time of adversity.

17:1 [a] Pr 15:16,17
17:3 [b] Pr 27:21 [c] 1Ch 29:17; Ps 26:2; Jer 17:10
17:5 [d] Pr 14:31 [e] Job 31:29 [f] Ob 12
17:6 [g] Pr 13:22
17:9 [h] Pr 10:12 [i] Pr 16:28
17:13 [j] Ps 109:4-5; Jer 18:20
17:14 [k] Pr 20:3
17:15 [l] Pr 18:5 [m] Ex 23:6-7; Isa 5:23
17:16 [n] Pr 23:23

17:1 Better … than. See 15:17; see also note on 15:16,17.
17:2 A prudent servant will rule over a disgraceful son. Wisdom and industriousness can elevate one's social and economic status.
17:3 crucible … furnace. The image of precious metals subjected to high temperatures to separate the dross and produce a purified form of the mineral. **the LORD tests the heart.** Through trials and diverse circumstances, the Lord identifies the dross within the human heart and the degree to which that heart trusts in the Lord.
17:5 contempt for their Maker. See note on 14:31.
17:8 bribe. A gift that adversely affects the administration of justice (6:35). It is akin to robbery (1 Sam 8:3; Isa 33:15), is used by the rich to exploit the poor (Ps 15:5; cf. Isa 5:23), and will come under God's judgment (Job 15:34; Ps 26:9–10; Mic 3:11–12).
17:9 love covers over. See 10:12 and note.
17:11 messenger of death. Probably personifies death (cf. 16:14).
17:12 a bear robbed of her cubs. Illuminates the physical danger involved in encountering a fool.
17:14 Starting a quarrel is like breaching a dam. Advocates restraint, prudence, and discretion through the vivid image of bursting through a dam. It is better to drop the matter (walk away from a situation of strife) than to push the issue and unleash the waters of dispute.
17:15 detests. See notes on 11:1; 15:8,9.
17:16 buy wisdom. Wisdom cannot be bought (see Job 28 and note on Job 28:1–28). **not able to understand it.** If wisdom could be acquired by economic means, fools could not comprehend it, because they are intractable, lost souls who despise wisdom (see Introduction: Character Types).

17:18 [o]Pr 6:1-5; 11:15; 22:26-27
17:21 [p]Pr 10:1
17:22 [q]Ps 22:15; Pr 15:13
17:23 [r]Ex 23:8
17:24 [s]Ecc 2:14
17:25 [t]Pr 10:1
17:26 [u]Pr 18:5
17:27 [v]Pr 14:29; Jas 1:19
17:28 [w]Job 13:5
18:2 [x]Pr 12:23
18:5 [y]Lev 19:15; Pr 24:23-25; 28:21 [z]Ps 82:2; Pr 17:15
18:7 [a]Ps 140:9 [b]Ps 64:8; Pr 10:14; 12:13; 13:3; Ecc 10:12

18 One who has no sense shakes hands in pledge
and puts up security for a neighbor.[o]

19 Whoever loves a quarrel loves sin;
whoever builds a high gate invites destruction.

20 One whose heart is corrupt does not prosper;
one whose tongue is perverse falls into trouble.

21 To have a fool for a child brings grief;
there is no joy for the parent of a godless fool.[p]

22 A cheerful heart is good medicine,
but a crushed spirit dries up the bones.[q]

23 The wicked accept bribes[r] in secret
to pervert the course of justice.

24 A discerning person keeps wisdom in view,
but a fool's eyes[s] wander to the ends of the earth.

25 A foolish son brings grief to his father
and bitterness to the mother who bore him.[t]

26 If imposing a fine on the innocent is not good,[u]
surely to flog honest officials is not right.

27 The one who has knowledge uses words with restraint,
and whoever has understanding is even-tempered.[v]

28 Even fools are thought wise if they keep silent,
and discerning if they hold their tongues.[w]

18

An unfriendly person pursues selfish ends
and against all sound judgment starts quarrels.

2 Fools find no pleasure in understanding
but delight in airing their own opinions.[x]

3 When wickedness comes, so does contempt,
and with shame comes reproach.

4 The words of the mouth are deep waters,
but the fountain of wisdom is a rushing stream.

5 It is not good to be partial to the wicked[y]
and so deprive the innocent of justice.[z]

6 The lips of fools bring them strife,
and their mouths invite a beating.

7 The mouths of fools are their undoing,
and their lips are a snare[a] to their very lives.[b]

17:18 See 6:1–5; 20:16; see also note on 6:1.
17:19 whoever builds a high gate invites destruction. This image from the realm of architecture describes the pride of the one who loves arguments and disputes (v. 14). They seek to destroy others and arrogantly believe that they will remain secure. Their attitude and actions, however, provoke God's judgment.
17:21 See v. 25 and note.
17:24 A discerning person. A perceptive person incorporates wisdom in the shaping of their lives and goals. Fools are scatterbrained and look anywhere but to wisdom.
17:25 the mother who bore him. Highlights the intimacy of the relationship and the corresponding trauma that follows from the child's character. This verse and v. 21 illuminate the value of both parents and children seeking wisdom.
18:4 deep waters. Connotes that a person's words and plans may be unfathomable, inaccessible, not beneficial, and potentially dangerous. **the fountain … a rushing stream.** The words of the wise constantly and inexhaustibly supply living water with ready accessibility.
18:5 See 17:15.
18:6 their mouths invite a beating. The fool's misuse of speech provokes the flogging of either fools (by order of the court) or the innocent.
18:7 a snare to their very lives. The fool's speech is a fatal trap.

8 The words of a gossip are like choice morsels;
they go down to the inmost parts.[c]

9 One who is slack in his work
is brother to one who destroys.[d]

10 The name of the LORD is a fortified tower;[e]
the righteous run to it and are safe.

11 The wealth of the rich is their fortified city;[f]
they imagine it a wall too high to scale.

12 Before a downfall the heart is haughty,
but humility comes before honor.[g]

13 To answer before listening—
that is folly and shame.[h]

14 The human spirit can endure in sickness,
but a crushed spirit who can bear?[i]

15 The heart of the discerning acquires knowledge,[j]
for the ears of the wise seek it out.

16 A gift[k] opens the way
and ushers the giver into the presence of the great.

17 In a lawsuit the first to speak seems right,
until someone comes forward and cross-examines.

18 Casting the lot settles disputes[l]
and keeps strong opponents apart.

19 A brother wronged is more unyielding than a fortified
city;
disputes are like the barred gates of a citadel.

20 From the fruit of their mouth a person's stomach is
filled;
with the harvest of their lips they are satisfied.[m]

21 The tongue has the power of life and death,
and those who love it will eat its fruit.[n]

22 He who finds a wife finds what is good[o]
and receives favor from the LORD.[p]

18:8 [c] Pr 26:22
18:9 [d] Pr 28:24
18:10 [e] 2Sa 22:3; Ps 61:3
18:11 [f] Pr 10:15
18:12 [g] Pr 11:2; 15:33; 16:18
18:13 [h] Pr 20:25; Jn 7:51
18:14 [i] Pr 15:13; 17:22
18:15 [j] Pr 15:14
18:16 [k] Ge 32:20
18:18 [l] Pr 16:33
18:20 [m] Pr 12:14
18:21 [n] Pr 13:2-3; Mt 12:37
18:22 [o] Pr 12:4 [p] Pr 19:14; 31:10

Together with v. 6, these two proverbs move from the fool's punishment (v. 6) to the fool's death (v. 7).
18:8 choice morsels. Food imagery that illustrates the attractive, tasty nature of gossip and innuendo. Just as one savors and digests a good meal, so also the words of a gossip are eaten, savored, and digested by others. The image explains why people love to hear and share gossip (26:22).
18:10 The name of the LORD. God's name entails his person, character, and attributes, which serve as the righteous person's fortification against destructive forces.
18:11 fortified city. The rich believe that their wealth is like a city with an unscalable wall, a source of defense and security (versus a "tower," v. 10). This false sense of security does not provide the assurance offered to the righteous who trust in the Lord and are safe.
18:12 a downfall. The external destruction that is triggered by the internal attitude of the heart (16:18). **haughty.** Arrogant, proud, refusing to accept instruction.
18:13–15 See 15:12–14.
18:16 gift. Translates the same Hebrew word translated "bribes" in 15:27 (cf. Eccl 7:7), and that is its meaning here. In this case, it is a present that greases the palm of another so that the giver may be granted an audience with a superior. **the great.** Probably influential people closely associated with the king (cf. 2 Kgs 10:6).
18:17 the first to speak seems right. In the context of the court or everyday life, it is important to hear and weigh both sides of the case or alternative perspectives before rushing to judgment.
18:18 the lot. See note on 16:33; used to reveal God's resolution in an irreconcilable dispute. **strong opponents.** Disputants, perhaps in a court case.
18:21 the power of life and death. Words may be used to bring satisfaction, healing, and restoration or to destroy others.

18:24 [q] Pr 17:17; Jn 15:13-15
19:1 [r] Pr 28:6
19:2 [s] Pr 29:20
19:4 [t] Pr 14:20
19:5 [u] Ex 23:1 [v] Dt 19:19; Pr 21:28
19:6 [w] Pr 29:26 [x] Pr 17:8; 18:16
19:7 [y] ver 4; Ps 38:11
19:8 [z] Pr 16:20
19:9 [a] ver 5
19:10 [b] Pr 26:1 [c] Pr 30:21-23; Ecc 10:5-7
19:11 [d] Pr 16:32
19:12 [e] Ps 133:3 [f] Pr 16:14-15

23 The poor plead for mercy,
but the rich answer harshly.

24 One who has unreliable friends soon comes to ruin,
but there is a friend who sticks closer than a brother.[q]

19

Better the poor whose walk is blameless
than a fool whose lips are perverse.[r]

2 Desire without knowledge is not good—
how much more will hasty feet miss the way![s]

3 A person's own folly leads to their ruin,
yet their heart rages against the LORD.

4 Wealth attracts many friends,
but even the closest friend of the poor person deserts them.[t]

5 A false witness[u] will not go unpunished,
and whoever pours out lies will not go free.[v]

6 Many curry favor with a ruler,[w]
and everyone is the friend of one who gives gifts.[x]

7 The poor are shunned by all their relatives—
how much more do their friends avoid them!
Though the poor pursue them with pleading,
they are nowhere to be found.[a][y]

8 The one who gets wisdom loves life;
the one who cherishes understanding will soon prosper.[z]

9 A false witness will not go unpunished,
and whoever pours out lies will perish.[a]

10 It is not fitting for a fool[b] to live in luxury—
how much worse for a slave to rule over princes![c]

11 A person's wisdom yields patience;[d]
it is to one's glory to overlook an offense.

12 A king's rage is like the roar of a lion,
but his favor is like dew[e] on the grass.[f]

[a] 7 The meaning of the Hebrew for this sentence is uncertain.

18:24 closer than a brother. True friendship is a valuable asset. While a relative is born into familial solidarity, a friend enters into this fraternity and manifests loyalty through commitment in times of trouble (17:17).
19:1 a fool whose lips are perverse. One who despises wisdom through lies and twisted speech, presumably to gain riches or success. Virtue, even when accompanied by poverty, is more valuable than wealth.
19:2 Desire without knowledge. Describes a greedy or impulsive person whose decisions or actions follow their reckless desires.
19:3 A person's own folly ... their heart rages against the LORD. Humans are personally responsible for their destruction, yet they elevate themselves as rulers over the universe and become angry with God when he punishes them for their folly.
19:4 many friends. Wealth attracts pseudo-friends, i.e., those interested in what the wealthy can provide.
19:5 See 6:19; 12:17; 14:5,25.
19:6–7 a ruler ... one who gives gifts ... The poor are shunned. Power and wealth attract so-called friends, while poverty yields abandonment, even by family members (see v. 4 and note).
19:8 See 1:5 and note; 4:5,7; 15:32; 16:16; 17:16 and note; 18:15.
19:10 not fitting ... for a slave to rule over princes! Neither prohibits elevating a slave nor seeks to lock individuals into particular social classes. Rather, this proverb operates under the assumption that an indentured slave does not possess the capabilities to rule well, in the same way that a fool does not possess the capability to appreciate wealth and luxury.
19:12 the roar of a lion. Conveys the way in which the king expresses rage to inspire awe and rein in insubordinate subjects (20:2). **like dew on the grass.** The king's refreshing and life-giving favor.
19:13 A foolish child ... a quarrelsome wife. Both destroy the fabric

[13] A foolish child is a father's ruin,[g]
and a quarrelsome wife is like
the constant dripping of a leaky roof.[h]

[14] Houses and wealth are inherited from parents,[i]
but a prudent wife is from the LORD.[j]

[15] Laziness brings on deep sleep,
and the shiftless go hungry.[k]

[16] Whoever keeps commandments keeps their life,
but whoever shows contempt for their ways will die.[l]

[17] Whoever is kind to the poor lends to the LORD,
and he will reward them for what they have done.[m]

[18] Discipline your children, for in that there is hope;
do not be a willing party to their death.[n]

[19] A hot-tempered person must pay the penalty;
rescue them, and you will have to do it again.

[20] Listen to advice and accept discipline,[o]
and at the end you will be counted among the wise.[p]

[21] Many are the plans in a person's heart,
but it is the LORD's purpose that prevails.[q]

[22] What a person desires is unfailing love[a];
better to be poor than a liar.

[23] The fear of the LORD leads to life;
then one rests content, untouched by trouble.[r]

[24] A sluggard buries his hand in the dish;
he will not even bring it back to his mouth![s]

[25] Flog a mocker, and the simple will learn prudence;
rebuke the discerning, and they will gain knowledge.[t]

[26] Whoever robs their father and drives out their mother[u]
is a child who brings shame and disgrace.

[27] Stop listening to instruction, my son,
and you will stray from the words of knowledge.

[28] A corrupt witness mocks at justice,
and the mouth of the wicked gulps down evil.[v]

19:13 [g]Pr 10:1 [h]Pr 21:9
19:14 [i]2Co 12:14 [j]Pr 18:22
19:15 [k]Pr 6:9; 10:4
19:16 [l]Pr 16:17; Lk 10:28
19:17 [m]Mt 10:42; 2Co 9:6-8
19:18 [n]Pr 13:24; 23:13-14
19:20 [o]Pr 4:1 [p]Pr 12:15
19:21 [q]Ps 33:11; Pr 16:9; Isa 14:24,27
19:23 [r]Ps 25:13; Pr 12:21; 1Ti 4:8
19:24 [s]Pr 26:15
19:25 [t]Pr 9:9; 21:11
19:26 [u]Pr 28:24
19:28 [v]Job 15:16

[a] 22 Or *Greed is a person's shame*

of the family (10:1–5). **the constant dripping of a leaky roof.** As water destroys the physical structure of a home, so this type of wife ruins the very structure of the family.
19:14 a prudent wife. She reinforces the fabric and structure of the home. As a gift from God, she is better than the vast wealth inherited from parents.
19:17 the poor. See notes on 14:21,31.
19:18 Discipline your children. See notes on 1:2; 3:11; 13:24. Most proverbs that deal with raising children are addressed to the child and assume parental instruction. By contrast, this saying is a command addressed to parents.
19:19 rescue them, and you will have to do it again. Getting involved in the dysfunctional life of an angry person only forestalls the inevitable consequences of that person's actions, and it gets the "rescuer" caught in the web of the angry person's lifestyle.
19:21 See 16:1,9,33.
19:24 A sluggard. The sluggard is so lazy that he cannot feed himself.
19:25 See note on 9:7–9.
19:26 robs their father and drives out their mother. Rejects one's basic responsibility to one's parents. In the ancient world, children were responsible for the care and well-being of their elderly parents. Children were their parents' source of security since governmental programs and retirement communities were not yet created. To spurn this responsibility and discard one's parents would be the ultimate in shame and disgrace.

19:29 [w] Pr 26:3
20:1 [x] Pr 31:4
20:2 [y] Pr 19:12 [z] Pr 8:36
20:3 [a] Pr 17:14
20:6 [b] Ps 12:1
20:7 [c] Ps 37:25-26; 112:2
20:8 [d] ver 26; Pr 25:4-5
20:9 [e] 1Ki 8:46; Ecc 7:20; 1Jn 1:8
20:10 [f] ver 23; Pr 11:1
20:11 [g] Mt 7:16
20:12 [h] Ps 94:9
20:13 [i] Pr 6:11; 19:15

29 Penalties are prepared for mockers,
and beatings for the backs of fools.[w]

20

Wine is a mocker and beer a brawler;
whoever is led astray by them is not wise.[x]

2 A king's wrath strikes terror like the roar of a lion;[y]
those who anger him forfeit their lives.[z]

3 It is to one's honor to avoid strife,
but every fool is quick to quarrel.[a]

4 Sluggards do not plow in season;
so at harvest time they look but find nothing.

5 The purposes of a person's heart are deep waters,
but one who has insight draws them out.

6 Many claim to have unfailing love,
but a faithful person who can find?[b]

7 The righteous lead blameless lives;
blessed are their children after them.[c]

8 When a king sits on his throne to judge,
he winnows out all evil with his eyes.[d]

9 Who can say, "I have kept my heart pure;
I am clean and without sin"?[e]

10 Differing weights and differing measures—
the LORD detests them both.[f]

11 Even small children are known by their actions,
so is their conduct really pure[g] and upright?

12 Ears that hear and eyes that see—
the LORD has made them both.[h]

13 Do not love sleep or you will grow poor;[i]
stay awake and you will have food to spare.

14 "It's no good, it's no good!" says the buyer—
then goes off and boasts about the purchase.

20:1 Wine ... beer. These intoxicants are personified as villains and bullies that transform people into those who ridicule virtue.
20:2 roar of a lion. See note on 19:12. **those who anger him.** Presumably those who are wicked and distort justice. The saying does not commend the king's wrath; it simply describes it.
20:4 plow in season. Preparing a field for sowing seed.
20:5 deep waters. Captures the unfathomable and inaccessible nature of another's intentions (18:4).
20:8 winnows out all evil. To distinguish evil from good and then remove the evil (cf. Matt 25:31–46). The metaphor is taken from one of the processes used in the harvest; to winnow was to separate the wheat from the chaff and remove the latter (Matt 3:12; Luke 3:17).
20:9 Who can say, "I have kept my heart pure; I am ... without sin"? All are sinful. The rhetorical question demands a negative response: no one. This illuminates the sinful state of all people (Rom 3:10–18) as well as the universal need for the redemption accomplished through Jesus Christ (Rom 5:12–21).
20:10 Differing weights and ... measures. Cf. 16:11; see note there. **detests.** See note on 11:1.
20:11 known by their actions. People manifest their character or internal state through their external actions. This is true even of children. **is their conduct really pure and upright?** The rhetorical question demands a negative answer (cf. v. 9; see note there).
20:12 Ears that hear ... eyes that see. May be a double entendre referring both to the ears and eyes of all people and to only those of the wise. In Proverbs, the ear is the organ through which wisdom enters into the heart (2:2; see note on 15:31). Among the many uses of eyes, sight in Proverbs refers to moral discernment or discretion (see 3:7; 7:7). To correct humanity's moral disability (vv. 9,11), the Lord created these receptive organs to inform the wise heart for good (2:2; 4:21; 24:32).
20:14 "It's no good ...!" The buyer minimizes the value of the product in order to acquire it at a lower cost and sell it for a greater profit. Wisdom enables a person to interpret the deceptive speech and character of others.

15 Gold there is, and rubies in abundance,
but lips that speak knowledge are a rare jewel.

16 Take the garment of one who puts up security for a stranger;
hold it in pledge[j] if it is done for an outsider.[k]

17 Food gained by fraud tastes sweet,[l]
but one ends up with a mouth full of gravel.

18 Plans are established by seeking advice;
so if you wage war, obtain guidance.[m]

19 A gossip betrays a confidence;[n]
so avoid anyone who talks too much.

20 If someone curses their father or mother,[o]
their lamp will be snuffed out in pitch darkness.[p]

21 An inheritance claimed too soon
will not be blessed at the end.

22 Do not say, "I'll pay you back for this wrong!"[q]
Wait for the LORD, and he will avenge you.[r]

23 The LORD detests differing weights,
and dishonest scales do not please him.[s]

24 A person's steps are directed by the LORD.
How then can anyone understand their own way?[t]

25 It is a trap to dedicate something rashly
and only later to consider one's vows.[u]

26 A wise king winnows out the wicked;
he drives the threshing wheel over them.[v]

27 The human spirit is[a] the lamp of the LORD
that sheds light on one's inmost being.

28 Love and faithfulness keep a king safe;
through love his throne is made secure.[w]

29 The glory of young men is their strength,
gray hair the splendor of the old.[x]

20:16 [j] Ex 22:26 [k] Pr 27:13
20:17 [l] Pr 9:17
20:18 [m] Pr 11:14; 24:6
20:19 [n] Pr 11:13
20:20 [o] Pr 30:11 [p] Ex 21:17; Job 18:5
20:22 [q] Pr 24:29 [r] Ro 12:19
20:23 [s] ver 10
20:24 [t] Jer 10:23
20:25 [u] Ecc 5:2,4-5
20:26 [v] ver 8
20:28 [w] Pr 29:14
20:29 [x] Pr 16:31

[a] 27 Or *A person's words are*

20:16 See 6:1–5; 11:15; 17:18; see also note on 6:1.
20:18 wage war. An extreme example of the need for counsel, so the principle pertains to lesser issues as well (cf. 11:14).
20:20 lamp will be snuffed out in pitch darkness. An image that depicts the foolish child's untimely and unfortunate death as tragic and hopeless.
20:21 inheritance. The family's land and holdings that are handed down as a parental legacy. **claimed too soon.** Rashly and with haste, without wisdom; depicts one laying hands on the family fortune prematurely (cf. Luke 15:11–16). **will not be blessed.** God will not grant the anticipated blessings of the inheritance: long life, descendants, prosperity, success, and power.
20:22 Wait for the LORD, and he will avenge you. Vengeance is not the business of humans; it is God's business (Deut 32:35; Rom 12:17–21). He engages in vengeance in order to establish justice and maintain order within the world. Through the example of Jesus (1 Pet 2:21–23), one discovers that it is a profound act of faith to trust in God's justice and wait for his vindication.
20:23 See note on 16:11.
20:24 How then can anyone understand their own way? See 16:9. In view of God's providential guidance, this rhetorical question describes the limited vision of humans. People may understand aspects of their course in life, but only God understands the full scope of its trajectory (Eccl 3:9–14).
20:25 dedicate something rashly. Careless vows or promises, whether to God or others (Deut 23:21; Judg 11:30–39; Eccl 5:4–7).
20:26 winnows out. See note on v. 8. **threshing wheel.** Highlights the pulverizing nature of the wise king's judgment upon the wicked.
20:28 Love and faithfulness. Attributes that characterize God (Exod 34:6); they describe the nature of God's character and rule through his loyalty, fidelity, and covenant commitment. As the earthly representative of God, the king is to embody these attributes, which will secure his throne and contribute to the flourishing of the kingdom.
20:29 gray hair. See 16:31 and note.

20:30 [y] Pr 22:15
21:2 [z] Pr 16:2; 24:12; Lk 16:15
21:3 [a] 1Sa 15:22; Pr 15:8; Isa 1:11; Hos 6:6; Mic 6:6-8
21:4 [b] Pr 6:17
21:5 [c] Pr 10:4; 28:22
21:6 [d] 2Pe 2:3
21:8 [e] Pr 2:15
21:9 [f] Pr 25:24
21:11 [g] Pr 19:25
21:12 [h] Pr 14:11
21:13 [i] Mt 18:30-34; Jas 2:13
21:14 [j] Pr 18:16; 19:6

30 Blows and wounds scrub[y] away evil,
and beatings purge the inmost being.

21

In the LORD's hand the king's heart is a stream of water
that he channels toward all who please him.

2 A person may think their own ways are right,
but the LORD weighs the heart.[z]

3 To do what is right and just
is more acceptable to the LORD than sacrifice.[a]

4 Haughty eyes[b] and a proud heart—
the unplowed field of the wicked—produce sin.

5 The plans of the diligent lead to profit[c]
as surely as haste leads to poverty.

6 A fortune made by a lying tongue
is a fleeting vapor and a deadly snare.[a][d]

7 The violence of the wicked will drag them away,
for they refuse to do what is right.

8 The way of the guilty is devious,[e]
but the conduct of the innocent is upright.

9 Better to live on a corner of the roof
than share a house with a quarrelsome wife.[f]

10 The wicked crave evil;
their neighbors get no mercy from them.

11 When a mocker is punished, the simple gain wisdom;
by paying attention to the wise they get knowledge.[g]

12 The Righteous One[b] takes note of the house of the wicked
and brings the wicked to ruin.[h]

13 Whoever shuts their ears to the cry of the poor
will also cry out and not be answered.[i]

14 A gift given in secret soothes anger,
and a bribe concealed in the cloak pacifies great wrath.[j]

[a] 6 Some Hebrew manuscripts, Septuagint and Vulgate; most Hebrew manuscripts *vapor for those who seek death*
[b] 12 Or *The righteous person*

20:30 Blows ... beatings. Bodily wounds that are inflicted by an adversary or by a friend for one's good (see Gen 4:23; Exod 21:23–25). **scrub away.** Remove dirt or the film formed on certain metals by oxidation. The metaphor compares moral evil to tarnish that must be removed through hard rubbing.
21:1 a stream of water. A trench to irrigate crops. Just as a farmer directs water to crops, so also the Lord directs the decisions of the ruler and channels his blessings through his king (16:1–4,9; Isa 45:1–7; Dan 4:31–35; Rom 13:1–7).
21:2 weighs the heart. Ancient Egyptian paintings have been found that depict a deity weighing a human heart on scales to determine whether the weight of its sins is heavier than a feather (i.e., the standard of truth, justice, and righteousness).
21:3 do what is right and just. See 1:3 and note. This saying promotes a traditional OT ideal: God demands that our sacrifices be accompanied by ethical conduct. God prefers a life that embodies what is right and just over empty worship practices or external actions in which people merely go through the motions (1 Sam 15:22; Isa 1:10–17; Hos 6:6; Mic 6:6–8).
21:4 unplowed field. Denotes being without discipline. By failing to tend to the soil and vegetation of their hearts, the wicked produce sin.
21:9 A husband is better off living exposed to the natural elements on an ancient Near Eastern roof, which was solid and flat, than inside with an argumentative wife (cf. 13:10).
21:11 the simple gain wisdom. The gullible person learns through a twofold process: by observing the punishment of a mocker and by heeding the instruction of the wise. The former teaches the simple the connection between crime and punishment; the latter teaches the simple the connection between virtues and rewards.
21:12 The Righteous One. The Lord, the King of humanity, the ultimate Judge of the wicked.
21:14 gift ... bribe. A present delivered at the appropriate time may placate anger and defuse a hostile situation. **given in secret ... con-**

Drawing of ancient Egyptian Weighing of the Heart ceremony (Prov 21:2).

[15] When justice is done, it brings joy to the righteous
but terror to evildoers.[k]

[16] Whoever strays from the path of prudence
comes to rest in the company of the dead.[l]

[17] Whoever loves pleasure will become poor;
whoever loves wine and olive oil will never be rich.[m]

[18] The wicked become a ransom[n] for the righteous,
and the unfaithful for the upright.

[19] Better to live in a desert
than with a quarrelsome and nagging wife.[o]

[20] The wise store up choice food and olive oil,
but fools gulp theirs down.

[21] Whoever pursues righteousness and love
finds life, prosperity[a] and honor.[p]

[22] One who is wise can go up against the city of the mighty[q]
and pull down the stronghold in which they trust.

[23] Those who guard their mouths[r] and their tongues
keep themselves from calamity.[s]

21:15 [k] Pr 10:29
21:16 [l] Ps 49:14
21:17 [m] Pr 23:20-21, 29-35
21:18 [n] Pr 11:8; Isa 43:3
21:19 [o] ver 9
21:21 [p] Mt 5:6
21:22 [q] Ecc 9:15-16
21:23 [r] Jas 3:2 [s] Pr 12:13; 13:3

[a] 21 Or *righteousness*

cealed. A present hidden from public scrutiny distorts justice. **pacifies great wrath.** Turning away wrath may be a virtue (15:1; 29:8) but not when a bribe turns away righteous indignation (cf. 24:17–18). The bribe may save the wicked for a moment but not forever.

21:16 in the company of the dead. Vividly depicts the unpleasant and perhaps untimely end of all who stray from the path of wisdom and understanding and follow the path of folly. See 7:22–23; 9:18.

21:17 loves pleasure … wine and olive oil. This does not condemn pleasure or consuming these products. Rather, this illuminates the consequences of an excessive lifestyle and advocates the virtues of moderation over indulgence (23:20–21). Ecclesiastes calls people to enjoy these pleasures as God's gifts (Eccl 2:24–26; 3:12–14; 5:18–20; 9:7–10).

21:18 ransom. Does not mean that the wicked serve as the payment for the righteous or upright. Rather, the wicked will experience the miseries they intended for others and ultimately receive punishment. In the case of Jesus, the sinless one became a ransom for sinners so that they might be set free from sin and made alive to righteousness (Mark 10:45; 1 Tim 2:5–6).

21:19 See v. 9. **a desert.** An uncivilized land where one can barely eke out an existence (Job 24:5–8); this place is a better environment than a home with a grumbling wife. Pride, the source of most quarrels (13:10), destroys a home and a community. The Bible never instructs the husband to control his wife; it is his responsibility to love and care for her, and her responsibility to honor him.

21:22 stronghold. See 14:26; see also Eccl 9:13–16.

21:24 [t]Ps 1:1; Pr 1:22; Isa 16:6; Jer 48:29
21:25 [u]Pr 13:4
21:26 [v]Ps 37:26; Mt 5:42; Eph 4:28
21:27 [w]Isa 66:3; Jer 6:20; Am 5:22 [x]Pr 15:8
21:28 [y]Pr 19:5
21:30 [z]Jer 9:23 [a]Isa 8:10; Ac 5:39
21:31 [b]Ps 3:8; 33:12-19; Isa 31:1
22:1 [c]Ecc 7:1
22:2 [d]Job 31:15
22:3 [e]Pr 14:16 [f]Pr 27:12
22:5 [g]Pr 15:19
22:6 [h]Eph 6:4

24 The proud and arrogant person[t]—"Mocker" is his
name—
behaves with insolent fury.

25 The craving of a sluggard will be the death of him,[u]
because his hands refuse to work.
26 All day long he craves for more,
but the righteous give without sparing.[v]

27 The sacrifice of the wicked is detestable[w]—
how much more so when brought with evil intent![x]

28 A false witness will perish,[y]
but a careful listener will testify successfully.

29 The wicked put up a bold front,
but the upright give thought to their ways.

30 There is no wisdom,[z] no insight, no plan
that can succeed against the LORD.[a]

31 The horse is made ready for the day of battle,
but victory rests with the LORD.[b]

22

A good name is more desirable than great riches;
to be esteemed is better than silver or gold.[c]

2 Rich and poor have this in common:
The LORD is the Maker of them all.[d]

3 The prudent see danger and take refuge,[e]
but the simple keep going and pay the penalty.[f]

4 Humility is the fear of the LORD;
its wages are riches and honor and life.

5 In the paths of the wicked are snares and pitfalls,[g]
but those who would preserve their life stay far from them.

6 Start children off on the way they should go,[h]
and even when they are old they will not turn from it.

7 The rich rule over the poor,
and the borrower is slave to the lender.

21:27 The sacrifice of the wicked. Artificial, fraudulent worship; an external display divorced from the internal reality of the heart. **with evil intent!** God views worship through the lens of a person's motives and intentions.
21:29 bold front. Imprudent and shameless in one's behavior; comparable to the arrogant, unashamed behavior of the adulterous woman in 7:13, whose unabashed invitation seeks to disguise the horrific consequences associated with following her path.
21:30 Emphasizes human limitations and the Lord's sovereignty over human planning and power. This does not negate the necessity of prudent planning for national, military, or personal success (11:14; 15:22; 20:18); rather, it places this planning into perspective by highlighting the Lord's freedom and ability to enforce his will independent of human cooperation or action.
22:1 good name. Represents a person's character (10:7; 18:10; 21:24); it depends on wisdom (3:1–4). A good reputation is better than wealth.
22:2 The LORD is the Maker of them all. See note on 14:31.
22:4 See 1:7 and note; 3:16; 15:33 and note; 18:12.
22:5 snares and pitfalls. Traps made of nets that were used by fowlers (7:23).
22:6 Start children off on the way they should go [i.e., the way of wisdom]. The initial verb could also be translated "train" but probably here has the sense "dedicate children to a course of action or training." For children to be steered away from the deadly "way" of the wicked, they must be directed away from their innate folly (cf. v. 15; 1:4; 7:7; 20:11; 23:13). The saying must be nuanced by others (see Introduction: Literary Features, 4). It indicates that early, moral training has an effect on a person for good and conveys the truth that those directed or steered down the path of wisdom will be influenced by it through their life. But it does not assure that the child will embrace wisdom, because children make their own choices; they are not programmed robots. If it were otherwise, the parents' and Lady Wisdom's exhortations to accept wisdom would be pointless.
22:7 The rich rule over the poor. Warns against poverty by describing the loss of freedom to creditors.

[8]Whoever sows injustice reaps calamity,[i]
and the rod they wield in fury will be broken.[j]

[9]The generous will themselves be blessed,[k]
for they share their food with the poor.[l]

[10]Drive out the mocker, and out goes strife;
quarrels and insults are ended.[m]

[11]One who loves a pure heart and who speaks with grace
will have the king for a friend.[n]

[12]The eyes of the LORD keep watch over knowledge,
but he frustrates the words of the unfaithful.

[13]The sluggard says, "There's a lion outside![o]
I'll be killed in the public square!"

[14]The mouth of an adulterous woman is a deep pit;[p]
a man who is under the LORD's wrath falls into it.[q]

[15]Folly is bound up in the heart of a child,
but the rod of discipline will drive it far away.[r]

[16]One who oppresses the poor to increase his wealth
and one who gives gifts to the rich—both come to poverty.

22:8 [i] Job 4:8 [j] Ps 125:3
22:9 [k] 2Co 9:6 [l] Pr 19:17
22:10 [m] Pr 18:6; 26:20
22:11 [n] Pr 16:13; Mt 5:8
22:13 [o] Pr 26:13
22:14 [p] Pr 2:16; 5:3-5; 7:5; 23:27 [q] Ecc 7:26
22:15 [r] Pr 13:24; 23:14
22:17 [s] Pr 5:1

Thirty Sayings of the Wise

Saying 1

[17]Pay attention and turn your ear to the sayings of the wise;[s]
apply your heart to what I teach,
[18]for it is pleasing when you keep them in your heart
and have all of them ready on your lips.
[19]So that your trust may be in the LORD,
I teach you today, even you.

22:8–9 See 11:25–26; 14:21; 19:17; 2 Cor 9:6–10; Gal. 6:7–10.
22:10 mocker. One who causes arguments and cannot learn (See Introduction: Character Types; cf. 9:7–8).
22:11 speaks with grace. Attractive speech that flows from a pure heart. **friend.** Perhaps a technical term for the king's confidant.
22:13 There's a lion outside! A ridiculous excuse to avoid work or involvement in communal affairs; ironically, the lazy person's indolence and resultant poverty will destroy them, rather than the imaginary lion roaming the city streets.
22:14 mouth. Marked by deceptive speech (2:16; 5:3; 6:24; 7:5). **a deep pit.** A way of life from which one is unable to escape on their own. One who refuses to walk in the way of wisdom and follows the way of folly may receive God's judgment and fall into this trap.
22:15 the rod of discipline. The instrument that will keep the child on the right path (see v. 6 and note). Children will stray from the path of wisdom; it is the parents' responsibility to correct them and steer them back toward that path. In 4:3 the son is regarded as tender and cherished by his parents.
22:16 See v. 2; 14:31; 17:5,8; 18:16 and note; 19:6.
22:17—24:22 *Thirty Sayings of the Wise.* Though not headed by a formal superscription, this section, Collection III, is demarcated as a distinct collection in several ways. As Collection I (1:8—9:18) functions as a prologue to the proverbs of Collection II (10:1—22:16), so 22:17–21 functions as a prologue to the sayings of 22:22—24:22. This prologue identifies these sayings as the "sayings of the wise" (22:17), and it numbers the sayings as "thirty sayings" (22:20). These "thirty sayings" share several similarities with the first ten sayings of the Egyptian "Sayings of Amenemope," which consists of 30 chapters. The NIV considers the prologue as the first saying, for it corresponds with the first chapter of Amenemope. The sayings are demarcated into four sections by their rhetoric and substance (22:17; 23:12,26; 24:13). The teachings to "trust ... in the LORD" (22:19) and to "fear the LORD" (24:21) frame the collection. In view of the similarities to Amenemope, it appears Solomon ("what I teach," 22:17; see Introduction: Authors) creatively adopted and adapted "the sayings of the wise" to Israel's covenant teachings, especially by calling for devotion to the Lord, the God of Israel (Introduction: Literary Features, 2).
22:17–21 Saying 1.
22:17–18 ear ... heart ... lips. As in Egyptian instruction (see note on 22:17—24:22), the learning process progresses from the outward ear that acquires the sayings (v. 17a) to the interior heart that is set on their acquisition (vv. 17b–18a) to the outward lips that represent them to oneself and to others (v. 18b; cf. 4:20–27).
22:19 trust ... in the LORD. The fundamental purpose of the collection. The realization of the saying's truth depends on the Lord. **today.** Each day of the son's life, for the sayings are to be fixed on his lips. The sayings demand a constant commitment to the Lord and his words.

22:21 [t]Lk 1:3-4; 1Pe 3:15
22:22 [u]Zec 7:10 [v]Ex 23:6; Mal 3:5
22:23 [w]Ps 12:5 [x]1Sa 25:39; Pr 23:10-11
22:25 [y]1Co 15:33
22:26 [z]Pr 11:15
22:27 [a]Pr 17:18
22:28 [b]Dt 19:14; Pr 23:10
22:29 [c]Ge 41:46

20 Have I not written thirty sayings for you,
sayings of counsel and knowledge,
21 teaching you to be honest and to speak the truth,[t]
so that you bring back truthful reports
to those you serve?

Saying 2

22 Do not exploit the poor[u] because they are poor
and do not crush the needy in court,[v]
23 for the LORD will take up their case[w]
and will exact life for life.[x]

Saying 3

24 Do not make friends with a hot-tempered person,
do not associate with one easily angered,
25 or you may learn their ways
and get yourself ensnared.[y]

Saying 4

26 Do not be one who shakes hands in pledge[z]
or puts up security for debts;
27 if you lack the means to pay,
your very bed will be snatched from under you.[a]

Saying 5

28 Do not move an ancient boundary stone[b]
set up by your ancestors.

Saying 6

29 Do you see someone skilled in their work?
They will serve[c] before kings;
they will not serve before officials of low rank.

Saying 7

23 When you sit to dine with a ruler,
note well what[a] is before you,
2 and put a knife to your throat
if you are given to gluttony.

[a] *1* Or *who*

22:21 honest ... speak the truth. Has the sense of right, justice, and rectitude. Together with v. 19, this verse describes the purpose or goal of the sayings in the collection; it seeks to transform the character and speech of the addressee. **bring back truthful reports.** Those to whom the son reports can make good decisions because they can count on him not to distort or misrepresent a situation or to be involved in a conspiracy.

22:22–23 Saying 2.

22:22 because they are poor. The economic vulnerability of the marginalized serves as the motive or temptation for their exploitation. **do not crush.** An image that depicts the extinction of the poor or needy as free citizens; these people are unable to pay and are pressed into a state of dependence.

22:23 the LORD ... will exact life for life. When Israel's judicial system fails, the Maker of the poor (14:21; 17:5) will take the case of the marginalized and avenge them in an indefinite future (15:25; Deut 10:17–18; Isa 11:4; cf. Isa 1:23; 10:1–2; Amos 5:12).

22:24–25 Saying 3. See note on 13:20; cf. 14:16–17; 15:18; 29:22.

22:26–27 Saying 4. See note on 6:1; cf. 11:15; 17:18; 20:16; 27:13.

22:28 Saying 5. **ancient boundary stone.** Marked the age of the family's property and its boundaries. Land served as the fundamental source of their livelihood and security and was transferred to subsequent generations (15:25; 23:10–11).

22:29 Saying 6. **see someone skilled in their work?** Indirectly an exhortation to excellence. Those who attend to their work and produce excellent materials will receive notice.

23:1–3 Saying 7.

23:2 put a knife to your throat. The hyperbole is similar to Jesus' teaching: "If your right eye causes you to stumble, gouge it out and throw it away" (Matt 5:29).

[3] Do not crave his delicacies,[d]
for that food is deceptive.

Saying 8

[4] Do not wear yourself out to get rich;
do not trust your own cleverness.
[5] Cast but a glance at riches, and they are gone,
for they will surely sprout wings
and fly off to the sky like an eagle.[e]

Saying 9

[6] Do not eat the food of a begrudging host,
do not crave his delicacies;[f]
[7] for he is the kind of person
who is always thinking about the cost.[a]
"Eat and drink," he says to you,
but his heart is not with you.
[8] You will vomit up the little you have eaten
and will have wasted your compliments.

Saying 10

[9] Do not speak to fools,
for they will scorn your prudent words.[g]

Saying 11

[10] Do not move an ancient boundary stone[h]
or encroach on the fields of the fatherless,
[11] for their Defender[i] is strong;
he will take up their case against you.[j]

Saying 12

[12] Apply your heart to instruction
and your ears to words of knowledge.

23:3 [d] ver 6-8
23:5 [e] Pr 27:24
23:6 [f] Ps 141:4
23:9 [g] Pr 1:7; 9:7; Mt 7:6
23:10 [h] Dt 19:14; Pr 22:28
23:11 [i] Job 19:25 [j] Pr 22:22-23

[a] 7 Or *for as he thinks within himself, / so he is*; or *for as he puts on a feast, / so he is*

23:3 that food is deceptive. The food aims not to feed him but to either test the guest's character or entrap the guest to do the host's bidding. If the first, the ruler will detest the guest as a glutton and wreck his career. If the second, the guest will feel obliged to do the ruler's bidding.
23:4–5 Saying 8. This saying is similar to ch. 7 of the "Sayings of Amenemope": "Ill-gotten riches made for themselves wings like geese and flew away to the sky." Jesus echoes this counsel concerning one's desire for riches (Luke 16:10–13; cf. Luke 12:22–34; 1 Tim 6:7–10).
23:4 Do not wear yourself out. Prohibits the quest for riches by depicting the intelligent workaholic. The prohibition is rooted in the false security riches provide.
23:5 will surely sprout wings and fly off. Wealth is depicted as a departing bird, because it is fleeting.
23:6–8 Saying 9.
23:6–7 begrudging host … "Eat and drink." Outwardly, the bitter host conforms to his social obligation according to ancient Near Eastern rules of hospitality, but inwardly he is revolted by his guest and resents the cost.
23:8 You will vomit up the little you have eaten. The reaction of an unwanted guest when they realize what a fool they have been.
23:9 Saying 10. **Do not speak to fools.** Because the obstinacy of fools precludes them from accepting advice. Similar to 26:5, this implies that one must discern the spiritual measure of a person before responding in order to estimate beforehand the effect of one's words on them.
23:10–11 Saying 11. See 22:28 and note there.
23:11 Defender. The family guardian-redeemer, a needy person's nearest relative, who is responsible to stand up for them and redeem their property (Lev 25:25–35; see notes on Lev 25:25; Ruth 2:20) and/or their body from slavery to a foreigner (Lev 25:47–55; see note on Lev 25:44), or to avenge the murder of a relative (Num 35:12,19–27; Deut 19:6,12; Josh 20:2–3,5,9; see notes on Num 35:12; Deut 19:6; Josh 20:3,5,9). Here the Lord assumes the role and responsibilities of this figure to protect the rights of the marginalized. See Ps 68:5; cf. Ps 119:154.
23:12–14 Saying 12 and Saying 13.
23:12–13 instruction … discipline. Both words translate the Hebrew *mûsār* (see "instruction" in 1:2; see also note there) that links the two sayings together: Saying 13 advances the admonition of Saying 12. Not only does Saying 12 command the acquisition and embodiment of wisdom, but in relation to Saying 13 it also indicates that one must practice and manifest wisdom before becoming a disciplinarian (cf. Deut 6:5–9).

23:16 [k]ver 24; Pr 27:11
23:17 [l]Ps 37:1; Pr 28:14
23:18 [m]Ps 9:18; Pr 24:14,19-20
23:20 [n]Isa 5:11,22; Ro 13:13; Eph 5:18
23:21 [o]Pr 21:17
23:22 [p]Lev 19:32; Pr 1:8; 30:17; Eph 6:1-2
23:23 [q]Pr 4:7
23:24 [r]ver 15-16; Pr 10:1; 15:20
23:26 [s]Pr 3:1; 5:1-6 [t]Ps 18:21; Pr 4:4
23:27 [u]Pr 22:14

Saying 13

13 Do not withhold discipline from a child;
if you punish them with the rod, they will not die.
14 Punish them with the rod
and save them from death.

Saying 14

15 My son, if your heart is wise,
then my heart will be glad indeed;
16 my inmost being will rejoice
when your lips speak what is right.[k]

Saying 15

17 Do not let your heart envy[l] sinners,
but always be zealous for the fear of the LORD.
18 There is surely a future hope for you,
and your hope will not be cut off.[m]

Saying 16

19 Listen, my son, and be wise,
and set your heart on the right path:
20 Do not join those who drink too much wine[n]
or gorge themselves on meat,
21 for drunkards and gluttons become poor,[o]
and drowsiness clothes them in rags.

Saying 17

22 Listen to your father, who gave you life,
and do not despise your mother when she is old.[p]
23 Buy the truth and do not sell it—
wisdom, instruction and insight as well.[q]
24 The father of a righteous child has great joy;
a man who fathers a wise son rejoices in him.[r]
25 May your father and mother rejoice;
may she who gave you birth be joyful!

Saying 18

26 My son,[s] give me your heart
and let your eyes delight in my ways,[t]
27 for an adulterous woman is a deep pit,[u]
and a wayward wife is a narrow well.

23:13–14 they will not die … save them from death. Flogging will save them from the fate of the fool. Appropriate punishment in child rearing is commended here. Nonetheless, the motivation for this discipline is the formation of the child's character, not anger.
23:17–18 Saying 15.
23:17 Do not let your heart envy sinners. Do not fret over the life and passing rewards of the wicked; instead, focus on and possess a passion for glorifying God (see Ps 37).
23:18 future hope. That in the future God will reverse the present situation by punishing the wicked with the loss of everything and rewarding those who fear the Lord with eternal life. **will not be cut off.** This reinforces that this hope will be realized (Jer 29:11; Jas 5:11; cf. Prov 24:20; Ps 73:17–28; Rev 13:10).
23:19–21 Saying 16.
23:21 drunkards and gluttons. People who are incorrigible, delinquent, and self-indulgent. They progress from revelry to rags.
23:22–25 Saying 17.
23:22 Listen to your father … do not despise your mother. Reminiscent of the instructions in Collection I (1:8—9:18), for it advocates the acceptance of parental instruction and the pursuit of wisdom (e.g., 1:8–9; 2:1–22; 4:1–10). The one who acquires wisdom and heeds parental advice brings great delight and honor to their father and mother.
23:26–28 Saying 18. See 5:1–23; 6:20–35; 7:1–27; 9:13–18.
23:27 a deep pit … a narrow well. Shows that there is no escape once one enters the adulterous woman's clutches and commits to her way of life (see note on 22:14).

[28]Like a bandit she lies in wait[v]
and multiplies the unfaithful among men.

Saying 19

[29]Who has woe? Who has sorrow?
Who has strife? Who has complaints?
Who has needless bruises? Who has bloodshot
eyes?
[30]Those who linger over wine,[w]
who go to sample bowls of mixed wine.
[31]Do not gaze at wine when it is red,
when it sparkles in the cup,
when it goes down smoothly!
[32]In the end it bites like a snake
and poisons like a viper.
[33]Your eyes will see strange sights,
and your mind will imagine confusing things.
[34]You will be like one sleeping on the high seas,
lying on top of the rigging.
[35]"They hit me," you will say, "but I'm not hurt!
They beat me, but I don't feel it!
When will I wake up
so I can find another drink?"

Saying 20

24

Do not envy[x] the wicked,
do not desire their company;
[2]for their hearts plot violence,
and their lips talk about making trouble.[y]

Saying 21

[3]By wisdom a house is built,[z]
and through understanding it is established;
[4]through knowledge its rooms are filled
with rare and beautiful treasures.[a]

Saying 22

[5]The wise prevail through great power,
and those who have knowledge muster their strength.
[6]Surely you need guidance to wage war,
and victory is won through many advisers.[b]

23:28 [v]Pr 7:11-12; Ecc 7:26
23:30 [w]Ps 75:8; Isa 5:11; Eph 5:18
24:1 [x]Ps 37:1; 73:3; Pr 3:31-32; 23:17-18
24:2 [y]Ps 10:7
24:3 [z]Pr 14:1
24:4 [a]Pr 8:21
24:6 [b]Pr 11:14; 20:18; Lk 14:31

23:28 Like a bandit she lies in wait. The adulterous woman's motives and methods: she conspires to plunder her victims in a cold, calculating, and ruthless way. **multiplies the unfaithful among men.** She seduces men to abandon their loyalty to God and the covenant community.
23:29–35 Saying 19.
23:29 Six riveting questions vividly lampoon the drunkard (vv. 19–21). Similar to the adulterous woman (vv. 26–28), wine is a seductive, hidden, deadly trap.
23:30 mixed wine. With spices (9:2).
23:32 bites like a snake. Deadly (cf. Num 21:6).
23:34 lying on top of the rigging. Pictures the drunkard's unsteady gait and/or uncontrollable nausea as in seasickness. After listing a series of horrible and humiliating experiences, the passage ends with the drunkard starting the whole cycle over again (cf. 26:11).
24:1–2 Saying 20. See note on 23:17.
24:3–4 Saying 21.
24:3 By wisdom a house is built. Intimately related to 9:1–6 (see notes there); incorporates vivid images to illuminate the benefits associated with wisdom. These benefits include a stable household and family as well as material provision and tangible wealth.
24:5–6 Saying 22.
24:5 The wise prevail through great power. Wisdom is essential to strength, especially in producing strategies for warfare.
24:6 victory is won through many advisers. See 11:14; 20:18 and notes.

24:10 [c] Job 4:5; Jer 51:46; Heb 12:3
24:11 [d] Ps 82:4; Isa 58:6-7
24:12 [e] Pr 21:2 [f] Job 34:11; Ps 62:12; Ro 2:6*
24:14 [g] Ps 119:103; Pr 16:24; 23:18
24:16 [h] Job 5:19; Ps 34:19; Mic 7:8
24:17 [i] Ob 12 [j] Job 31:29

Saying 23

7 Wisdom is too high for fools;
in the assembly at the gate they must not open
their mouths.

Saying 24

8 Whoever plots evil
will be known as a schemer.
9 The schemes of folly are sin,
and people detest a mocker.

Saying 25

10 If you falter in a time of trouble,
how small is your strength![c]
11 Rescue those being led away to death;
hold back those staggering toward slaughter.[d]
12 If you say, "But we knew nothing about this,"
does not he who weighs[e] the heart perceive it?
Does not he who guards your life know it?
Will he not repay everyone according to what they
have done?[f]

Saying 26

13 Eat honey, my son, for it is good;
honey from the comb is sweet to your taste.
14 Know also that wisdom is like honey for you:
If you find it, there is a future hope for you,
and your hope will not be cut off.[g]

Saying 27

15 Do not lurk like a thief near the house of the righteous,
do not plunder their dwelling place;
16 for though the righteous fall seven times, they rise again,
but the wicked stumble when calamity strikes.[h]

Saying 28

17 Do not gloat[i] when your enemy falls;
when they stumble, do not let your heart rejoice,[j]
18 or the LORD will see and disapprove
and turn his wrath away from them.

24:7 Saying 23. **at the gate.** The place where public affairs are settled (see 1:21; 8:2–3; 31:23). If fools had any prudence (and they do not), they would keep silent (cf. 17:28).
24:8–9 Saying 24.
24:10–12 Saying 25.
24:11 those being led away to death ... staggering toward slaughter. Perhaps those treading down the path of folly or those weak members of the community exploited by the wicked (1:15–19; 9:13–18).
24:12 But we knew nothing about this. An attempt to cloak a lack of moral fiber and fortitude in ignorance and excuse the failure to establish justice for or secure the well-being of other members of the community. **Does not he who guards your life ...? Will he not repay everyone ...?** The rhetorical questions demand a positive response; they illuminate God's omniscience, omnipotence, and justice (Ps 62:12; Matt 16:27; Rom 2:6; 2 Tim 4:14; Rev 18:6).
24:13–14 Saying 26. **honey ... wisdom.** Wisdom must be internalized. It is good, providing a hope that will last for eternity; and it is pleasant, bringing joy and contentment.
24:15–16 Saying 27.
24:15 like a thief. With cunning and deceit. **house of the righteous.** Built with wisdom (vv. 3–4). The prohibition of v. 15a rests on the conviction that the righteous have "a future hope" (v. 14).
24:16 they rise again. Because the Lord protects and sustains them (3:33; 10:3; 18:10).
24:17–18 Saying 28.
24:17 Do not gloat. God disapproves of cruelty, cold-heartedness, smug arrogance, and callously despising his image. He has no pleasure in the death of the wicked (Ezek 33:11) and will not promote evil by gratifying depraved gloating.

Saying 29

[19]Do not fret[k] because of evildoers
or be envious of the wicked,
[20]for the evildoer has no future hope,
and the lamp of the wicked will be snuffed out.[l]

Saying 30

[21]Fear the LORD and the king,[m] my son,
and do not join with rebellious officials,
[22]for those two will send sudden destruction on them,
and who knows what calamities they can bring?

Further Sayings of the Wise

[23]These also are sayings of the wise:[n]

To show partiality[o] in judging is not good:[p]
[24]Whoever says to the guilty, "You are innocent,"[q]
will be cursed by peoples and denounced by nations.
[25]But it will go well with those who convict the guilty,
and rich blessing will come on them.

[26]An honest answer
is like a kiss on the lips.

[27]Put your outdoor work in order
and get your fields ready;
after that, build your house.

[28]Do not testify against your neighbor without
cause[r]—
would you use your lips to mislead?
[29]Do not say, "I'll do to them as they have done to me;
I'll pay them back for what they did."[s]

[30]I went past the field of a sluggard,[t]
past the vineyard of someone who has no sense;
[31]thorns had come up everywhere,
the ground was covered with weeds,
and the stone wall was in ruins.

24:19 [k]Ps 37:1
24:20 [l]Job 18:5; Pr 13:9; 23:17-18
24:21 [m]Ro 13:1-5; 1Pe 2:17
24:23 [n]Pr 1:6 [o]Lev 19:15 [p]Pr 28:21
24:24 [q]Pr 17:15
24:28 [r]Ps 7:4; Pr 25:18; Eph 4:25
24:29 [s]Pr 20:22; Mt 5:38-41; Ro 12:17
24:30 [t]Pr 6:6-11; 26:13-16

24:19–20 Saying 29.
24:19 Do not fret. Do not become distressed by the temporary successes of the wicked.
24:20 evildoer has no future hope. Unlike the righteous (v. 14). **the lamp of the wicked will be snuffed out.** See note on 20:20.
24:21–22 Saying 30.
24:21 Fear the LORD. See Introduction: Theme; see also note on 1:7. **king.** See Eccl 8:2–5; Rom 13:1–7; 1 Pet 2:17. God and the king are the agents through whom this punishment is levied against the rebellious. The king represents God and his rule on earth (see note on 16:10). This rule is being reestablished through the work of Jesus Christ, and it awaits its consummation in the new heavens and the new earth (cf. John 5:27–30; Rev 21–22). **rebellious officials.** Seek to grab power and advance themselves through intrigue. The way to advancement is to revere legitimate authority and avoid becoming involved in plots to undermine God and legitimate authority.
24:23–34 *Further Sayings of the Wise.* This small collection supplements Collection III (22:17—24:22) with five sayings that are cast in an alternating structure:

a Honest justice in the court (vv. 23–26)
b Wise economy in the field (v. 27)
a′ Honest justice in the court (vv. 28–29)
b′ Wise economy in the field (vv. 30–34)

24:24 "You are innocent." Quotes an unjust judge to illustrate v. 23b.
24:26 kiss on the lips. Implies affection and trust, as does an honest answer.
24:27 Put your outdoor work in order. Prepare or cultivate the arable fields, for they sustain life and serve as the primary source of a family's income. **after that.** After your source of income is established. **build your house.** See vv. 3–4.
24:29 I'll do to them … I'll pay them back. See 20:22 and note. Vengeance is God's business, not the business of humans (Deut 32:35; Rom 12:17–21). Jesus calls us to love our enemies rather than retaliate against others with improper speech (Matt 5:43–48; cf. Lev 19:15–18).
24:30–34 See 6:9–11.

24:33 [u] Pr 6:10
24:34 [v] Pr 10:4; Ecc 10:18
25:1 [w] 1Ki 4:32 [x] Pr 1:1
25:2 [y] Pr 16:10-15
25:5 [z] Pr 20:8 [a] 2Sa 7:13 [b] Pr 16:12; 29:14
25:7 [c] Lk 14:7-10
25:8 [d] Mt 5:25-26

32 I applied my heart to what I observed
and learned a lesson from what I saw:
33 A little sleep, a little slumber,
a little folding of the hands to rest[u] —
34 and poverty will come on you like a thief
and scarcity like an armed man.[v]

More Proverbs of Solomon

25 These are more proverbs[w] of Solomon, compiled by the men of Hezekiah king of Judah:[x]

2 It is the glory of God to conceal a matter;
to search out a matter is the glory of kings.[y]
3 As the heavens are high and the earth is deep,
so the hearts of kings are unsearchable.

4 Remove the dross from the silver,
and a silversmith can produce a vessel;
5 remove wicked officials from the king's presence,[z]
and his throne will be established[a] through righteousness.[b]

6 Do not exalt yourself in the king's presence,
and do not claim a place among his great men;
7 it is better for him to say to you, "Come up here,"[c]
than for him to humiliate you before his nobles.

What you have seen with your eyes
8 do not bring[a] hastily to court,
for what will you do in the end
if your neighbor puts you to shame?[d]

9 If you take your neighbor to court,
do not betray another's confidence,
10 or the one who hears it may shame you
and the charge against you will stand.

[a] 7,8 Or *nobles / on whom you had set your eyes. / 8Do not go*

24:34 thief ... armed man. Personifies the poverty that the sluggard's indolence causes. The vineyard of the sleeping sluggard is an analogy for an inheritance lost through negligence.

25:1—29:27 *More Proverbs of Solomon.* This collection is comparable to the first Solomonic collection (10:1—22:16) but distinct in that it contains larger, transparently more coherent collections of sayings (e.g., 26:1–12). This collection has five main sections: (1) God and the king, and the righteous and the wicked (25:2–27); (2) seven moral inferiors (25:28—26:28); (3) friendship (27:1–22); (4) sustaining blessings for the future (27:23–27); (5) God and kings, instruction and righteousness (28:1—29:27).

25:1 compiled. To copy and arrange, presumably a select number of the 3,000 proverbs by Solomon (1 Kgs 4:32). These proverbs reflect their court background. As God's earthly representative (cf. 8:15–16; 16:10–15; 21:1), the king had the task of maintaining order and justice in all areas of his kingdom; these proverbs provide prudent advice for many situations. **men of Hezekiah.** Perhaps scribes in the royal court. See Introduction: Authors.

25:2 to search out a matter. To investigate an issue that God has concealed in creation and/or in social behavior—but not matters too deep (v. 27; cf. Deut 29:29).

25:3 the hearts of kings. Like God's heart, the heart of kings is inscrutable. The proverb thus establishes the hierarchy of God-king-subjects.

25:4–5 Remove the dross ... remove wicked officials. As a silversmith can produce a beautiful and lasting vessel only with purified silver, so a king can produce an enduring kingdom only when wicked officials have been removed from his presence (cf. 16:12; 20:8,26; see Isa 1:21–26; Ezek 22:6,18–22; Zech 13:7–9; Mal 3:2–4).

24:5 throne. A symbol of royal glory.

25:6 Do not exalt yourself. Commends humility. The courtier on his own initiative must not transgress into the higher social rank and dignity of the king and his nobles.

25:7a Come up here. It is better for a courtier to be elevated by the king because the courtier's aptitude warrants it, than for a courtier to overreach the limits and risk the king's reprimand and a loss of face that damages his career prospects (cf. Isa 22:15–19; Luke 14:7–11).

25:7b What you have seen with your eyes. A partial, incomplete picture of the situation.

25:8 what will you do in the end ...? This question assumes that you failed to prove your case solely on the basis of what your eyes have seen. **puts you to shame.** Perhaps ruins your career. Implicitly, instead of going hastily to court, one should prepare assiduously the credibility of one's eyewitness account.

25:9 do not betray another's confidence. Gives priority to confidentiality over winning a case, for the judge may heap permanent shame on what may not be substantiated.

25:10 the one who hears it. The mediator or arbiter in the court who discerns the divulged confidence.

[11] Like apples[a] of gold in settings of silver[e]
is a ruling rightly given.
[12] Like an earring of gold or an ornament of fine gold
is the rebuke of a wise judge to a listening ear.[f]
[13] Like a snow-cooled drink at harvest time
is a trustworthy messenger to the one who sends him;
he refreshes the spirit of his master.[g]
[14] Like clouds and wind without rain
is one who boasts of gifts never given.
[15] Through patience a ruler can be persuaded,[h]
and a gentle tongue can break a bone.[i]
[16] If you find honey, eat just enough—
too much of it, and you will vomit.[j]
[17] Seldom set foot in your neighbor's house—
too much of you, and they will hate you.
[18] Like a club or a sword or a sharp arrow
is one who gives false testimony against a neighbor.[k]
[19] Like a broken tooth or a lame foot
is reliance on the unfaithful in a time of trouble.
[20] Like one who takes away a garment on a cold day,
or like vinegar poured on a wound,
is one who sings songs to a heavy heart.
[21] If your enemy is hungry, give him food to eat;
if he is thirsty, give him water to drink.
[22] In doing this, you will heap burning coals[l] on his head,
and the LORD will reward you.[m]
[23] Like a north wind that brings unexpected rain
is a sly tongue—which provokes a horrified look.
[24] Better to live on a corner of the roof
than share a house with a quarrelsome wife.[n]
[25] Like cold water to a weary soul
is good news from a distant land.[o]

25:11 [e] ver 12; Pr 15:23
25:12 [f] ver 11; Ps 141:5; Pr 13:18; 15:31
25:13 [g] Pr 10:26; 13:17
25:15 [h] Ecc 10:4 [i] Pr 15:1
25:16 [j] ver 27
25:18 [k] Ps 57:4; Pr 12:18
25:22 [l] Ps 18:8 [m] 2Sa 16:12; 2Ch 28:15; Mt 5:44; Ro 12:20*
25:24 [n] Pr 21:9
25:25 [o] Pr 15:30

Tablet records Mari king Zimri-Lim building an ice house in Terqa to store ice brought down from the mountains (Prov 25:13).

Wikimedia Commons

[a] *11* Or possibly *apricots*

25:11 apples of gold in settings of silver. The beauty and value of a carefully crafted court decision.
25:12 an earring of gold or an ornament of fine gold. The beauty and value of a reproving decision that is accepted.
25:13 Like a snow-cooled drink at harvest time. A simile for a reliable envoy; it revives and refreshes the weary harvester. Laborers stored snow in snow houses or snow caves.
25:14 Like clouds and wind without rain. A simile for an unreliable windbag who boasts about a gift only to defraud the expected beneficiary.
25:15 a gentle tongue can break a bone. A paradox that describes the power of words; through sensitive and tactful speech a person can persuade others and break down the deepest resistance to an idea.
25:16,17 too much. An excessive amount that breaks proper boundaries. Just as an excessive amount of something sweet makes a person sick, so also excessive time at a neighbor's house transgresses proper social boundaries and wears out one's welcome.
25:19 a broken tooth or a lame foot. Metaphors that describe the impotence, ineffectiveness, and pain associated with dependence on an unreliable person.
25:21–22 Quoted in Rom 12:20.
25:22 heap burning coals on his head. An expression that may reflect an Egyptian expiation ritual in which a guilty person, as a sign of repentance, carried a basin of glowing coals on the head. In other words, by being kind to your enemy, you cause them to become red in the face (i.e., embarrassed or humiliated) and move them to repent.
25:23 north. May connote the hidden, dark regions of the world. **wind that brings unexpected rain.** Because, in Israel, rain comes from the west, not the north. The sly tongue is like the north wind because it is hidden, dark, and unexpected. The advantage or disadvantage of rain depends on the season. Here the icy blast from the north takes the farmer by surprise and ruins his crop (cf. 26:1; 28:3). So the unaware victim of the sly tongue, when he hears the slander, realizes that the benefits he expected to reap from his work are suddenly ruined.
25:24 See 19:13; 21:9,19.
25:25 cold water to a weary soul. An image that highlights the life-giving value of a good word.

25:27 [p]ver 16 [q]Pr 27:2; Mt 23:12
26:1 [r]1Sa 12:17 [s]ver 8; Pr 19:10
26:2 [t]Nu 23:8; Dt 23:5
26:3 [u]Ps 32:9 [v]Pr 10:13
26:4 [w]ver 5; Isa 36:21
26:5 [x]ver 4; Pr 3:7
26:6 [y]Pr 10:26
26:7 [z]ver 9
26:8 [a]ver 1
26:9 [b]ver 7
26:11 [c]2Pe 2:22* [d]Ex 8:15; Ps 85:8

26 Like a muddied spring or a polluted well
are the righteous who give way to the wicked.

27 It is not good to eat too much honey,[p]
nor is it honorable to search out matters that
are too deep.[q]

28 Like a city whose walls are broken through
is a person who lacks self-control.

26

Like snow in summer or rain[r] in harvest,
honor is not fitting for a fool.[s]
2 Like a fluttering sparrow or a darting swallow,
an undeserved curse does not come to rest.[t]
3 A whip for the horse, a bridle for the donkey,[u]
and a rod for the backs of fools![v]
4 Do not answer a fool according to his folly,
or you yourself will be just like him.[w]
5 Answer a fool according to his folly,
or he will be wise in his own eyes.[x]
6 Sending a message by the hands of a fool[y]
is like cutting off one's feet or drinking
poison.
7 Like the useless legs of one who is lame
is a proverb in the mouth of a fool.[z]
8 Like tying a stone in a sling
is the giving of honor to a fool.[a]
9 Like a thornbush in a drunkard's hand
is a proverb in the mouth of a fool.[b]
10 Like an archer who wounds at random
is one who hires a fool or any passer-by.
11 As a dog returns to its vomit,[c]
so fools repeat their folly.[d]

25:26 muddied spring. Describes the communal devastation caused when the righteous compromise their commitment and yield to the wicked: they contaminate the waters of justice and pollute the resources necessary for well-being.
25:27 too much ... too deep. Highlights the reality of human limitations. See v. 2 and note.
25:28 a city whose walls are broken through. Defenseless and disgraced. **lacks self-control.** Has uncontrollable passions and appetites that prompt impulsive, irrational behavior (cf. 12:16).
26:1 honor is not fitting for a fool. To bestow social respect on a fool is as inappropriate and catastrophic to a society as anomalous weather patterns that destroy the resources of the community. **fool.** See Introduction: Character Types. In vv. 1–12, the term occurs in every verse except v. 2. On the whole, vv. 1–12 identify the nature of the fool and indicate that it is unfitting to honor a foolish person by educating them with proverbs and entrusting them with responsible service.
26:2 As a flying bird does not "come to rest" in the air, so a curse will not rest on an innocent person.
26:3 A whip for the horse, a bridle for the donkey. Simple beasts that describe the nature of a fool. **a rod for the backs of fools!** For prodding to do right and restraining from doing wrong.
26:4 Do not answer a fool according to his folly. It is unfitting to counter a fool's folly with corresponding folly (cf. 1 Pet 3:9). Should someone reply vindictively, harshly, and/or with lies (the way fools talk), they too would come under the fool's condemnation (see Introduction: Character Types). **or you yourself will be just like him.** Because you have spoken as a fool.
26:5 Answer a fool according to his folly. It is fitting to show the fool their folly for what it is and for their own good—but do so not by lowering oneself to the fool's level but by overcoming evil with good (25:21). **or he will be wise in his own eyes.** By not correcting the fool, you silently affirm their thinking. The wise do not silently accept and tolerate folly and thereby confirm fools in it. The apparent contradiction between the proverbs of vv. 4–5 is resolved by noting the reasons given in vv. 4b and 5b.
26:6 Sending a message by the hands of a fool. Fools are not cut out for important business. Whereas faithful messengers bring refreshment to their patrons (see 25:13 and note), foolish emissaries inflict trouble, crippling their masters and instigating violence.
26:8 tying a stone in a sling. An action that renders the weapon ineffectual and endangers the life of the warrior. In the same way, granting social honor or status to a fool endangers one's reputation.
26:9 a thornbush in a drunkard's hand. Has the potential to wound or lacerate others because the person does not know what they are doing (cf. 20:1). In the fool's mouth a proverb is dangerous because the fool will detrimentally misapply its wisdom.
26:10 an archer who wounds at random. An armed madman who launches attacks on his employer as well as the community (cf. v. 6).
26:11 As a dog returns to its vomit. The fool is incapable of saving himself; quoted in 2 Pet 2:22 with reference to false teachers.

12 Do you see a person wise in their own eyes?[e]
There is more hope for a fool than for them.[f]

13 A sluggard says,[g] "There's a lion in the road,
a fierce lion roaming the streets!"[h]
14 As a door turns on its hinges,
so a sluggard turns on his bed.[i]
15 A sluggard buries his hand in the dish;
he is too lazy to bring it back to his mouth.[j]
16 A sluggard is wiser in his own eyes
than seven people who answer discreetly.

17 Like one who grabs a stray dog by the ears
is someone who rushes into a quarrel not their own.

18 Like a maniac shooting
flaming arrows of death
19 is one who deceives their neighbor
and says, "I was only joking!"

20 Without wood a fire goes out;
without a gossip a quarrel dies down.[k]
21 As charcoal to embers and as wood to fire,
so is a quarrelsome person for kindling strife.[l]
22 The words of a gossip are like choice morsels;
they go down to the inmost parts.[m]

23 Like a coating of silver dross on earthenware
are fervent[a] lips with an evil heart.
24 Enemies disguise themselves with their lips,[n]
but in their hearts they harbor deceit.[o]
25 Though their speech is charming,[p] do not believe them,
for seven abominations fill their hearts.[q]
26 Their malice may be concealed by deception,
but their wickedness will be exposed in the assembly.
27 Whoever digs a pit[r] will fall into it;[s]
if someone rolls a stone, it will roll back on them.[t]
28 A lying tongue hates those it hurts,
and a flattering mouth[u] works ruin.

26:12 [e] Pr 3:7 [f] Pr 29:20
26:13 [g] Pr 6:6-11; 24:30-34 [h] Pr 22:13
26:14 [i] Pr 6:9
26:15 [j] Pr 19:24
26:20 [k] Pr 22:10
26:21 [l] Pr 14:17; 15:18
26:22 [m] Pr 18:8
26:24 [n] Ps 31:18 [o] Ps 41:6; Pr 10:18; 12:20
26:25 [p] Ps 28:3 [q] Jer 9:4-8
26:27 [r] Ps 7:15 [s] Est 6:13 [t] Est 2:23; 7:9; Ps 35:8; 141:10; Pr 28:10; 29:6; Isa 50:11
26:28 [u] Ps 12:3; Pr 29:5

[a] *23* Hebrew; Septuagint *smooth*

26:12 wise in their own eyes. A perspective of inflated, self-valuation that prevents one from growing in wisdom. This delusional condition is worse than that of the fool. As the climax of vv. 1–12, this seeks to instill humility and forms a transition to the collection of proverbs on the sluggard, who is wise in his own eyes (v. 16).
26:13–16 See notes on 6:6–11; 24:34.
26:16 wiser in his own eyes. See note on v. 12.
26:17 grabs a stray dog by the ears. Captures the confrontational and outspoken character of the busybody, who cannot resist getting embroiled in the conflicts of others and who gets badly hurt.
26:18–19 a maniac shooting flaming arrows of death ... one who deceives their neighbor. The activity of the mischief maker, who uses deception to inflict horrible tragedy on a community and then passes it off as a practical joke.
26:20–21 fire ... charcoal to embers ... wood to fire. Incendiary images that illuminate the communal destruction of malicious gossip; it burns down a community. These images are similar to those James uses to describes the devastation caused by the tongue (Jas 3:5–6).
26:22 like choice morsels. See note on 18:8. Others swallow gossip greedily, and it makes a deep impact on their lives.
26:23 a coating of silver dross on earthenware. Compares the enemy's speech to an attractive but cheap glaze of dross over a potsherd. What appears as precious or attractive is corrupt or counterfeit because it disguises something impure.
26:25 do not believe them. The climactic admonition of vv. 23–25: do not trust enemies or anything they have to say, no matter how seemingly attractive.
26:28 ruin. Of the enemy; this meaning best fits the parallels in vv. 26b,27b, and Proverbs teaches that the righteous may fall but only the wicked are ruined (cf. 1:19; see Introduction: Literary Features, 4).

27:1 [v] 1Ki 20:11 [w] Mt 6:34; Lk 12:19-20; Jas 4:13-16
27:2 [x] Pr 25:27
27:3 [y] Job 6:3
27:4 [z] Nu 5:14
27:6 [a] Ps 141:5; Pr 28:23
27:8 [b] Isa 16:2
27:9 [c] Est 2:12; Ps 45:8
27:10 [d] Pr 17:17; 18:24
27:11 [e] Pr 10:1; 23:15-16 [f] Ge 24:60
27:12 [g] Pr 22:3
27:13 [h] Pr 20:16

27

Do not boast[v] about tomorrow,
for you do not know what a day may bring.[w]

2 Let someone else praise you, and not your own mouth;
an outsider, and not your own lips.[x]

3 Stone is heavy and sand[y] a burden,
but a fool's provocation is heavier than both.

4 Anger is cruel and fury overwhelming,
but who can stand before jealousy?[z]

5 Better is open rebuke
than hidden love.

6 Wounds from a friend can be trusted,
but an enemy multiplies kisses.[a]

7 One who is full loathes honey from the comb,
but to the hungry even what is bitter tastes sweet.

8 Like a bird that flees its nest[b]
is anyone who flees from home.

9 Perfume[c] and incense bring joy to the heart,
and the pleasantness of a friend
springs from their heartfelt advice.

10 Do not forsake your friend or a friend of your family,
and do not go to your relative's house when disaster[d]
strikes you—
better a neighbor nearby than a relative far away.

11 Be wise, my son, and bring joy to my heart;[e]
then I can answer anyone who treats me with contempt.[f]

12 The prudent see danger and take refuge,
but the simple keep going and pay the penalty.[g]

13 Take the garment of one who puts up security for a
stranger;
hold it in pledge if it is done for an outsider.[h]

27:1 you do not know what a day may bring. Illuminates human limitations and calls for humility before God, who alone knows and controls the future (cf. Eccl 3:1 – 15).
27:2 Let someone else praise you ... an outsider. The judgment of a stranger is not likely to be biased; it is better than self-praise (cf. 2 Cor 10:12,18).
27:3 Stone ... sand. These natural images capture the heavy, unbearable nature of the fool's insults.
27:4 who can stand before jealousy? The rhetorical question heightens the insurmountable character of this emotion, which poisons one's thinking and clouds one's reason.
27:5 – 6 open rebuke ... Wounds from a friend. Genuine friendship provides correction. It is a relationship that manifests its love and devotion through candid, even cutting, correction and concern for the good of the other.
27:5 hidden love. Fails to provide the open correction necessary.
27:6 multiplies kisses. Covers the intention to harm; this artificial, external expression of love is deceptive and designed to satisfy the heart rather than nurture the relationship.
27:7 One who is full. Stuffed or satisfied. This person cannot enjoy the sweetness of honey, i.e., they cannot accept wise counsel or correction, because they are stuffed with errors. **the hungry.** These people also have sick appetites, for they crave bad food. **what is bitter tastes sweet.** Or, "every bitter thing is sweet." The undiscriminating appetite of the hungry cannot detect error.
27:8 flees its nest. Leaves the basis of its security and forfeits its future.
27:9 Perfume and incense. Substances that please the senses and represent the delight of the sincere counsel of a friend.
27:10 a neighbor nearby. A close friend who can provide comfort and support in times of need.
27:11 Be wise, my son, and bring joy to my heart. Reflects an intense sense of family solidarity and of mutual pride of the generations in one another (cf. 17:6). **anyone who treats me with contempt.** Through the tangible reality of a wise son, the father can prove his worth to those who make an accusation against him (10:1; cf. Ps 127:4 – 5; see also 2 Cor 3:1 – 3; 1 Thess 2:19 – 20; 3:8 – 9).
27:12 See 22:3.
27:13 Repeats 20:16 (see note there).

[14]If anyone loudly blesses their neighbor early in the morning,
it will be taken as a curse.

[15]A quarrelsome wife is like the dripping[i]
of a leaky roof in a rainstorm;
[16]restraining her is like restraining the wind
or grasping oil with the hand.

[17]As iron sharpens iron,
so one person sharpens another.

[18]The one who guards a fig tree will eat its fruit,[j]
and whoever protects their master will
be honored.[k]

[19]As water reflects the face,
so one's life reflects the heart.[a]

[20]Death and Destruction[b] are never
satisfied,[l]
and neither are human eyes.[m]

[21]The crucible for silver and the furnace for
gold,[n]
but people are tested by their praise.

[22]Though you grind a fool in a mortar,
grinding them like grain with a pestle,
you will not remove their folly from
them.

[23]Be sure you know the condition of your
flocks,[o]
give careful attention to your herds;
[24]for riches do not endure forever,[p]
and a crown is not secure for all generations.

27:15 [i]Est 1:18; Pr 19:13
27:18 [j]1Co 9:7 [k]Lk 19:12-27
27:20 [l]Pr 30:15-16; Hab 2:5 [m]Ecc 1:8; 6:7
27:21 [n]Pr 17:3
27:23 [o]Pr 12:10
27:24 [p]Pr 23:5

Egyptian model of a woman grinding grain. Prov 27:22 uses to "grind a fool" as a metaphor.
Wikimedia Commons

[a] *19* Or *so others reflect your heart back to you* [b] *20* Hebrew *Abaddon*

27:14 loudly blesses their neighbor early in the morning. A greeting or word delivered in an inappropriate manner and at an inappropriate time; it may be interpreted as hypocritical or insincere.
27:15 quarrelsome wife. See notes on 19:13; 21:9,19.
27:16 restraining the wind ... grasping oil with the hand. Cannot be concealed or controlled. This proverb develops previous sayings by describing the quarrelsome wife's irrepressible nature (25:24). When viewed together with other proverbs concerning marriage or marriage preparation, the saying serves as a warning. Not only should a man look for these character traits before committing to a marriage, but he should also consider whether his attitudes or actions have fostered this disposition in the home.
27:17 iron sharpens iron. Sharpening an iron sword or tool by a whetting iron is like a person or friend forming, honing, and shaping the character and deportment of another.
27:18 one who guards a fig tree ... whoever protects their master. Faithful servants or employees will reap the reward of their labors.
27:19 one's life reflects the heart. One can gain insight into a person's heart or character by observing their conduct. Or, following the NIV text note, one can evaluate one's character by looking to a friend's objective compliments (v. 2), sincere criticisms (vv. 6,17), and earnest counsel (v. 9).
27:20 Death and Destruction. The realm of death is ruthless, destructive, and never satisfied. **eyes.** These organs awaken the lust to own and possess whatever desirable thing they see (Eccl 1:8; 2:10; 4:8; 1 John 2:16).
27:21 The crucible ... the furnace. See note on 17:3. In 17:3, the Lord tests the hearts of people, but here a person's character is assessed according to the praise they receive. This serves as a reliable touchstone of one's character and guards against inflated self-valuation (v. 2; 26:12,16). **people are tested by their praise.** An intentional pun. Their true mettle is tested both by what they praise and/or by the praise given to them, i.e., by their reputation (3:4; 12:8; Luke 2:52; Acts 2:47; Rom 14:18; 1 Tim 3:2–4,7).
27:22 grind a fool in a mortar. An image of pulverizing or crushing a product within a bowl; signifies inflicting severe punishment in order to correct another. **you will not remove their folly from them.** The fool is intractable. See Introduction: Character Types. Divine grace that regenerates the fool is the fool's only hope of being converted into a useful person (cf. 26:11).
27:23 flocks ... herds. A metaphor for the king's servants or those entrusted to his care.
27:24 riches do not endure forever. Money and status are depreciating, not self-renewing, resources. **crown.** An image of royal glory,

28:1 [q]2Ki 7:7 [r]Lev 26:17; Ps 53:5 [s]Ps 138:3
28:6 [t]Pr 19:1
28:7 [u]Pr 23:19-21
28:8 [v]Ex 18:21 [w]Job 27:17; Pr 13:22 [x]Ps 112:9; Pr 14:31; Lk 14:12-14
28:9 [y]Ps 66:18; 109:7; Pr 15:8; Isa 1:13
28:10 [z]Pr 26:27
28:12 [a]2Ki 11:20 [b]Pr 11:10; 29:2

25 When the hay is removed and new growth appears
and the grass from the hills is gathered in,
26 the lambs will provide you with clothing,
and the goats with the price of a field.
27 You will have plenty of goats' milk to feed your family
and to nourish your female servants.

28

The wicked flee[q] though no one pursues,[r]
but the righteous are as bold as a lion.[s]

2 When a country is rebellious, it has many rulers,
but a ruler with discernment and knowledge maintains order.

3 A ruler[a] who oppresses the poor
is like a driving rain that leaves no crops.

4 Those who forsake instruction praise the wicked,
but those who heed it resist them.

5 Evildoers do not understand what is right,
but those who seek the LORD understand it fully.

6 Better the poor whose walk is blameless
than the rich whose ways are perverse.[t]

7 A discerning son heeds instruction,
but a companion of gluttons disgraces his father.[u]

8 Whoever increases wealth by taking interest[v] or profit from the poor
amasses it for another,[w] who will be kind to the poor.[x]

9 If anyone turns a deaf ear to my instruction,
even their prayers are detestable.[y]

10 Whoever leads the upright along an evil path
will fall into their own trap,[z]
but the blameless will receive a good inheritance.

11 The rich are wise in their own eyes;
one who is poor and discerning sees how deluded they are.
12 When the righteous triumph, there is great elation;[a]
but when the wicked rise to power, people go into hiding.[b]

[a] *3* Or *A poor person*

indicating that the poem (vv. 23–27) is a metaphor for the king's wisely caring for his subjects; by promoting their well-being, he establishes his crown.
27:25–27 new growth ... grass from the hills ... lambs will provide you with clothing ... goats with the price of a field ... goats' milk to feed your family. Animals are self-renewing and an increasing source of wealth. As a metaphor for the king's servants or people, care for these creatures creates a kingdom and society that will likely flourish.
28:1 bold as a lion. The inward security of the righteous, which mauls its attackers and has no reason to fear. Paradoxically, because the wicked do not fear God, they fear people, but because the righteous fear God, they do not fear people.
28:2 many rulers. Government officials. Whether this refers to the frequent turnover in leadership or to the necessity of a large bureaucracy to keep an eye on other arms of the government, the message is clear: many rulers contribute to the discontinuity and disorder of society, whereas a ruler armed with discernment establishes order and stability throughout the land (see 16:10–15).
28:3 a driving rain that leaves no crops. A torrential rainstorm that sweeps away the soil.
28:6 See 19:1 and note.
28:8 amasses it for another. By God's secret providence through which he protects the vulnerable poor and gives back to them the wealth unjustly taken from them (13:22; Ps 140:12).
28:9 prayers. See note on 15:8. External acts of worship accompanied by disobedience are abominable in God's sight. This saying suggests that God loathes the prayers of the apostate when they are in need.
28:11 wise in their own eyes. See note on 26:12. This deluded, terminal brand of wisdom is mentioned with the fool and the sluggard. There is more hope for a fool than for the rich (cf. Matt 19:24; 1 Tim 6:10).
28:12 great elation ... people go into hiding. Illustrates how one's leadership affects the character and well-being of the community.

13 Whoever conceals their sins[c] does not prosper,
but the one who confesses and renounces them finds mercy.[d]

14 Blessed is the one who always trembles before God,
but whoever hardens their heart falls into trouble.

15 Like a roaring lion or a charging bear
is a wicked ruler over a helpless people.

16 A tyrannical ruler practices extortion,
but one who hates ill-gotten gain will enjoy a long reign.

17 Anyone tormented by the guilt of murder
will seek refuge[e] in the grave;
let no one hold them back.

18 The one whose walk is blameless is kept safe,
but the one whose ways are perverse will fall[f] into the pit.[a]

19 Those who work their land will have abundant food,
but those who chase fantasies will have their fill of poverty.[g]

20 A faithful person will be richly blessed,
but one eager to get rich will not go unpunished.[h]

21 To show partiality is not good[i] —
yet a person will do wrong for a piece of bread.[j]

22 The stingy are eager to get rich
and are unaware that poverty awaits them.[k]

23 Whoever rebukes a person will in the end gain favor
rather than one who has a flattering tongue.[l]

24 Whoever robs their father or mother[m]
and says, "It's not wrong,"
is partner to one who destroys.[n]

25 The greedy stir up conflict,
but those who trust in the LORD[o] will prosper.

26 Those who trust in themselves are fools,[p]
but those who walk in wisdom are kept safe.

27 Those who give to the poor will lack nothing,[q]
but those who close their eyes to them receive many curses.

28:13 [c] Job 31:33 [d] Ps 32:1-5; 1Jn 1:9
28:17 [e] Ge 9:6
28:18 [f] Pr 10:9
28:19 [g] Pr 12:11
28:20 [h] ver 22; Pr 10:6; 1Ti 6:9
28:21 [i] Pr 18:5 [j] Eze 13:19
28:22 [k] ver 20; Pr 23:6
28:23 [l] Pr 27:5-6
28:24 [m] Pr 19:26 [n] Pr 18:9
28:25 [o] Pr 29:25
28:26 [p] Ps 4:5; Pr 3:5
28:27 [q] Dt 15:7; 24:19; Pr 19:17; 22:9

[a] 18 Syriac (see Septuagint); Hebrew *into one*

Leadership is a call to service, and a person's character defines the nature of their service on behalf of others.

28:13 one who confesses and renounces. Genuine piety is marked by confession, a tender heart, and a proper attitude before God.

28:14 trembles before God. Equivalent to fearing the Lord (see 1:7 and note).

28:15 Like a roaring lion or a charging bear. The two most savage beasts on the prowl for prey. Like these ravenous animals, a wicked ruler feeds on and exploits his people. No principle of justice regulates his conduct.

28:16 tyrannical. The Hebrew term implies being devoid of competence.

28:17 seek refuge in the grave. May imply that the murderer is so haunted by a guilty conscience that he attempts to commit suicide. Alternatively, it may prohibit assisting or delivering a fugitive from justice (see Gen 9:5–6).

28:19 Those who work their land. Honest work comes from a person's inner stability, and their reward of abundant food is escalated to being richly blessed by the Lord (v. 20a). **those who chase fantasies.** A person pursuing an empty dream to get rich quick, apart from hard work and without character.

28:21 do wrong for a piece of bread. An exaggeration designed to show how even the smallest gift or bribe can move a person to sin.

28:25 trust in the LORD. Uphold God's divinely established moral boundaries: honest work, contentment, and benevolence (v. 5; 3:5; 16:20; 18:10).

28:27 See 11:24; 21:13; 22:16.

28:28 [r] ver 12
29:1 [s] 2Ch 36:16; Pr 6:15
29:2 [t] Est 8:15 [u] Pr 28:12
29:3 [v] Pr 10:1
[w] Pr 5:8-10; Lk 15:11-32
29:4 [x] Pr 8:15-16
29:6 [y] Ecc 9:12
29:7 [z] Job 29:16; Ps 41:1; Pr 31:8-9
29:8 [a] Pr 11:11; 16:14
29:10 [b] 1Jn 3:12
29:11 [c] Pr 12:16; 19:11
29:13 [d] Pr 22:2; Mt 5:45
29:14 [e] Ps 72:1-5; Pr 16:12
29:15 [f] Pr 10:1; 13:24; 17:21,25

28 When the wicked rise to power, people go into hiding;[r]
but when the wicked perish, the righteous thrive.

29

Whoever remains stiff-necked after many rebukes
will suddenly be destroyed—without remedy.[s]

2 When the righteous thrive, the people rejoice;[t]
when the wicked rule, the people groan.[u]

3 A man who loves wisdom brings joy to his father,[v]
but a companion of prostitutes squanders his wealth.[w]

4 By justice a king gives a country stability,[x]
but those who are greedy for[a] bribes tear it down.

5 Those who flatter their neighbors
are spreading nets for their feet.

6 Evildoers are snared by their own sin,[y]
but the righteous shout for joy and are glad.

7 The righteous care about justice for the poor,[z]
but the wicked have no such concern.

8 Mockers stir up a city,
but the wise turn away anger.[a]

9 If a wise person goes to court with a fool,
the fool rages and scoffs, and there is no peace.

10 The bloodthirsty hate a person of integrity
and seek to kill the upright.[b]

11 Fools give full vent to their rage,
but the wise bring calm in the end.[c]

12 If a ruler listens to lies,
all his officials become wicked.

13 The poor and the oppressor have this in common:
The LORD gives sight to the eyes of both.[d]

14 If a king judges the poor with fairness,
his throne will be established forever.[e]

15 A rod and a reprimand impart wisdom,
but a child left undisciplined disgraces its mother.[f]

[a] 4 Or *who give*

28:28 go into hiding … the righteous thrive. See note on v. 12.
29:1 stiff-necked. Those who defy authority and are characterized as stubborn or recalcitrant (see Deut 10:16). **many rebukes.** Includes this collection of proverbs that condemn the wicked. When the door of opportunity to side with the righteous finally shuts at death, the incorrigible fool is beyond all hope of a cure.
29:2 the righteous. In light of the corporate nature of the saying, it appears these individuals represent righteous rulers. **people rejoice.** See note on 28:12.
29:4 greedy for bribes. Depicts the wicked king as one who accepts kickbacks from lobbyists.
29:5–6 spreading nets … snared by. Trapping images that suggest that those who seek to trap others will themselves be trapped (cf. 1:10–19).
29:7 care about justice for the poor. A defining feature of moral righteousness (Job 29:11–17; Ps 140:12; Isa 10:1–2; Zech 7:9–10; cf. Jas 1:27); reflects God's concern for the rights of the weak and exploited members of society.
29:8 the wise turn away anger. See notes on 15:1,2.
29:9 rages and scoffs. Refuses to listen to reason (13:20; 14:7; 26:4–5).
29:12 listens to lies. Assumes that the king may breed corruption in his officials through his indifference to truth and his adherence to deceptive testimony.
29:13 have this in common. All humans, irrespective of their character or social standing, have a dignity that derives from their common Creator (14:31).
29:14 throne will be established forever. See 16:12; 25:5.
29:15 A rod and a reprimand. See 22:15; 23:12–14 and notes.

[16] When the wicked thrive, so does sin,
but the righteous will see their downfall.[g]

[17] Discipline your children, and they will give you peace;
they will bring you the delights you desire.[h]

[18] Where there is no revelation, people cast off restraint;
but blessed is the one who heeds wisdom's instruction.[i]

[19] Servants cannot be corrected by mere words;
though they understand, they will not respond.

[20] Do you see someone who speaks in haste?
There is more hope for a fool than for them.[j]

[21] A servant pampered from youth
will turn out to be insolent.

[22] An angry person stirs up conflict,
and a hot-tempered person commits many sins.[k]

[23] Pride brings a person low,
but the lowly in spirit gain honor.[l]

[24] The accomplices of thieves are their own enemies;
they are put under oath and dare not testify.[m]

[25] Fear of man will prove to be a snare,
but whoever trusts in the LORD[n] is kept safe.

[26] Many seek an audience with a ruler,[o]
but it is from the LORD that one gets justice.

[27] The righteous detest the dishonest;
the wicked detest the upright.[p]

29:16 [g] Ps 37:35-36; 58:10; 91:8; 92:11
29:17 [h] ver 15; Pr 10:1
29:18 [i] Ps 1:1-2; 119:1-2; Jn 13:17
29:20 [j] Pr 26:12; Jas 1:19
29:22 [k] Pr 14:17; 15:18; 26:21
29:23 [l] Pr 11:2; 15:33; 16:18; Isa 66:2; Mt 23:12
29:24 [m] Lev 5:1
29:25 [n] Pr 28:25
29:26 [o] Pr 19:6
29:27 [p] ver 10

Sayings of Agur

30 The sayings of Agur son of Jakeh—an inspired utterance.

This man's utterance to Ithiel:

"I am weary, God,
but I can prevail.[a]

[a] *1* With a different word division of the Hebrew; Masoretic Text *utterance to Ithiel, / to Ithiel and Ukal:*

29:17 Discipline your children. See v. 15; 13:24; 19:18 and notes. **29:18 revelation.** Occurs only here in Proverbs. Elsewhere in the OT, it refers to the vision of a prophet. When it is read in conjunction with "wisdom's instruction" (28:4–5,7a), it represents the community's authoritative means of divine guidance (Lam 2:9; Ezek 7:26). **29:19 cannot be corrected by mere words.** Implicitly, as with children (v. 17), servants may require discipline to free them from the slavery of their rebellious hearts. An Egyptian instruction, *Papyrus Insinger* (14:11), teaches, "If the rod is far from his master, the servant will not obey him." The Bible conceives as parallel hierarchical structures the relations between family members, between servant and master, and in the body politic; this is evident in the NT's domestic codes (Rom 13:1–7; Eph 5:21—6:9; Col 3:18—4:1; Titus 2:2,9–10; cf. 1 Pet 3:13–22). **29:20 someone who speaks in haste.** This person chooses words without regard for their moral effectiveness to get what they want when they want it. **There is more hope for a fool.** Intractable fools are ruled by their passions, but the hasty, without quibbling about ethics, choose to be ruled by greed. They are fools of the worst kind. **29:21 pampered.** Allowed to lead a pleasant, easy, and prosperous life. **29:23 Pride ... lowly in spirit.** See 11:2 and note; 15:33 and note; 16:18; 18:12. **29:24 put under oath.** A judicial obligation requiring those who witnessed a crime to offer truthful testimony; failing to fulfill the requirement was considered a sin of omission (see Lev 5:1,5,6 and notes). **dare not testify.** The accomplices lie by their silence and place themselves under the power of God's curse (cf. 12:17; 14:25; 19:28). **29:25 Fear of man.** The wise are not cowardly; they do not shrink in the face of public opinion or run at the threat of persecution. **30:1–33** *Sayings of Agur.* Though Agur is otherwise unknown, his superscript introduces his sayings as an "inspired utterance" (see Introduction: Authors). He addresses a son or disciple, Ithiel. His prophetic burden falls into three parts: (1) introduction: an autobiographical confession (vv. 1–9); (2) body: six numerical sayings (vv. 10–31; see 6:16

30:3 [q] Pr 9:10
30:4 [r] Ps 24:1-2; Jn 3:13; Eph 4:7-10 [s] Ps 104:3; Isa 40:12 [t] Job 26:8; 38:8-9 [u] Ge 1:2 [v] Rev 19:12
30:5 [w] Ps 12:6; 18:30 [x] Ge 15:1; Ps 84:11
30:6 [y] Dt 4:2; 12:32; Rev 22:18
30:8 [z] Mt 6:11
30:9 [a] Jos 24:27; Isa 1:4; 59:13 [b] Dt 6:12; 8:10-14; Hos 13:6 [c] Dt 8:12
30:11 [d] Pr 20:20
30:12 [e] Pr 16:2; Lk 18:11 [f] Jer 2:23,35
30:13 [g] 2Sa 22:28; Job 41:34; Ps 131:1; Pr 6:17

2 Surely I am only a brute, not a man;
I do not have human understanding.
3 I have not learned wisdom,
nor have I attained to the knowledge of the
Holy One.[q]
4 Who has gone up[r] to heaven and come down?
Whose hands[s] have gathered up the wind?
Who has wrapped up the waters[t] in a cloak?[u]
Who has established all the ends of the earth?
What is his name,[v] and what is the name of his son?
Surely you know!

5 "Every word of God is flawless;[w]
he is a shield[x] to those who take refuge in him.
6 Do not add[y] to his words,
or he will rebuke you and prove you a liar.

7 "Two things I ask of you, LORD;
do not refuse me before I die:
8 Keep falsehood and lies far from me;
give me neither poverty nor riches,
but give me only my daily bread.[z]
9 Otherwise, I may have too much and disown[a] you
and say, 'Who is the LORD?'[b]
Or I may become poor and steal,
and so dishonor the name of my God.[c]

10 "Do not slander a servant to their master,
or they will curse you, and you will pay for it.

11 "There are those who curse their fathers
and do not bless their mothers;[d]
12 those who are pure in their own eyes[e]
and yet are not cleansed of their filth;[f]
13 those whose eyes are ever so haughty,[g]
whose glances are so disdainful;

and note); (3) conclusion: a warning to Ithiel not to rebel (vv. 32–33). This collection functions to provide a theological perspective on the pursuit of wisdom. For Agur, wisdom is found not only in the world but also in the Lord's revelation to Israel (vv. 1–6).

30:1 an inspired utterance. A prophetic formula that suggests Agur's sayings originated from God and are invested with divine authority (31:1; 2 Sam 23:1; see Num 24:4,15). **I am weary, God.** Captures the intellectual and psychological exhaustion associated with efforts to attain knowledge of God and wisdom by mere human ability.

30:2–3 understanding ... wisdom ... knowledge of the Holy One. See 1:2; 9:10. While the book has attempted to instill these virtues, Agur has failed to grasp them through mere human ingenuity (see note on v. 2).

30:2 only a brute, not a man. An expression of self-loathing and subhuman status that stems from Agur's inability to acquire knowledge of God and wisdom.

30:4 Rhetorical questions heighten the gulf that separates humanity from God; they highlight the intellectual limits and restricted faculties of humans (Deut 30:12; Job 28:12–28; Isa 40:12–14). They illuminate the extent of God's wisdom and power, for he is able to accomplish all of these awesome feats. By contrast, Lady Wisdom was with God at the creation and therefore has the knowledge that Agur lacks (see Introduction: Lady Wisdom; see also note on 8:1–36).

30:5–6 Every word of God is flawless ... Do not add to his words. Divine revelation is the authentic and sufficient source of wisdom. Here Agur reorients the quest for wisdom by acknowledging the necessity of divine revelation for the acquisition of true wisdom. This divine revelation is seen most clearly in Jesus (John 1:18). Verse 5 adapts 2 Sam 22:31 (see Ps 18:30); v. 6 adapts Prov 13:1 (Deut 4:2).

30:7–9 The only prayer in the book. Agur expresses his dependence upon God through an appeal for truth and modesty.

30:8 Keep falsehood and lies far from me. Implies that his following sayings are true. His sayings condemn pride and greed, so he depends upon God for salvation from them. **give me neither poverty nor riches.** A plea for moderation and contentment. This request provides a unique perspective on wealth and poverty. Whereas other sayings within the book reflect on the two extremes, Agur desires a middle way: a life of moderation.

30:9 dishonor the name of my God. Misrepresent and ruin God's reputation.

30:11 those who curse their fathers. See v. 17; 20:20; cf. 10:1.

30:12 pure in their own eyes. See 16:2; 20:9; 26:12 and notes.

[14] those whose teeth[h] are swords
and whose jaws are set with knives[i]
to devour[j] the poor[k] from the earth
and the needy from among mankind.[l]

[15] "The leech has two daughters.
'Give! Give!' they cry.

"There are three things that are never satisfied,[m]
four that never say, 'Enough!':
[16] the grave,[n] the barren womb,
land, which is never satisfied with water,
and fire, which never says, 'Enough!'

[17] "The eye that mocks[o] a father,
that scorns an aged mother,
will be pecked out by the ravens of the valley,
will be eaten by the vultures.[p]

[18] "There are three things that are too amazing for me,
four that I do not understand:
[19] the way of an eagle in the sky,
the way of a snake on a rock,
the way of a ship on the high seas,
and the way of a man with a young woman.

[20] "This is the way of an adulterous woman:
She eats and wipes her mouth
and says, 'I've done nothing wrong.'[q]

[21] "Under three things the earth trembles,
under four it cannot bear up:
[22] a servant who becomes king,[r]
a godless fool who gets plenty to eat,
[23] a contemptible woman who gets married,
and a servant who displaces her mistress.

[24] "Four things on earth are small,
yet they are extremely wise:

30:14 [h] Job 4:11; 29:17; Ps 3:7 [i] Ps 57:4 [j] Job 24:9; Ps 14:4 [k] Am 8:4; Mic 2:2 [l] Job 19:22
30:15 [m] Pr 27:20
30:16 [n] Pr 27:20; Isa 5:14; 14:9,11; Hab 2:5
30:17 [o] Dt 21:18-21; Pr 23:22 [p] Job 15:23
30:20 [q] Pr 5:6
30:22 [r] Pr 19:10; 29:2

30:14 those whose teeth are swords ... to devour the poor from the earth. The dominant vice of this perverse generation is greed; its members exploit the weak and abuse power for personal gain. **30:15 The leech has two daughters.** These girls are the suckers with which this parasite draws blood from its victims; they symbolize the unquenchable appetite of parasitic people. **never say, 'Enough!'** Never satisfied. **30:16 the grave.** Ever yearns to end life. **the barren womb.** Ever yearns to produce life (cf. Gen 30:1; 1 Sam 1:11; Luke 1:5–25). As long as the earth endures, the wise recognize that life and death are engaged in an unending battle. Since Christ by his resurrection swallowed up death (1 Cor 15:50–57), believers may look forward to the final day when God terminates death. **30:17** See vv. 11–13. **pecked out by the ravens ... eaten by the vultures.** An unburied carcass symbolizes a tragic and dishonorable end. The thoroughness of destruction is symbolized by the carnivorous birds acting in concert and the desolate nature of the valley (cf. 1 Kgs 17:4,6). Similar to v. 10, this saying reflects on actions that undermine the hierarchical order of the world in order to promote social and moral stability. **30:19 way.** The mysterious movement of four things within the created order. The amazement is not necessarily directed toward the path of these creatures but is directed toward their irrecoverable courses. This amazement culminates in the final element: **a man with a young woman.** The saying captures the mystery of love. Just as one cannot trace the precise course of an eagle, a serpent, or a ship, so one cannot explain the magnetic attraction of love—what brings together a man and a woman in true love. **30:20 the way of.** See Introduction: Theme. **adulterous woman.** See note on 2:16. In contrast to the "ways" in v. 19, the path or lifestyle of this woman evokes horror. **eats and wipes her mouth.** She gratifies her sexual palate as one appeases one's appetite (cf. 9:16–17). **30:21–23** This unit presents an upside-down, inverted world that collapses under the weight of four individuals. **30:22–23 a servant ... a godless fool ... a contemptible woman ... a servant.** These individuals violate traditional social boundaries and upset the divine order; they do not possess the wisdom to manage their new social position. Rewarding vice destroys society. **30:24–28** The four creatures mentioned compensate for their small stature by their wisdom: ants, by timely industry (v. 25); hyraxes, by

30:25 [s] Pr 6:6-8
30:26 [t] Ps 104:18
30:27 [u] Ex 10:4
30:32 [v] Job 21:5; 29:9
31:1 [w] Pr 22:17
31:2 [x] Jdg 11:30; Isa 49:15
31:3 [y] Dt 17:17; 1Ki 11:3; Ne 13:26; Pr 5:1-14
31:4 [z] Pr 20:1; Ecc 10:16-17; Isa 5:22
31:5 [a] 1Ki 16:9 [b] Pr 16:12; Hos 4:11

25 Ants are creatures of little strength,
yet they store up their food in the summer;[s]
26 hyraxes[t] are creatures of little power,
yet they make their home in the crags;
27 locusts[u] have no king,
yet they advance together in ranks;
28 a lizard can be caught with the hand,
yet it is found in kings' palaces.

29 "There are three things that are stately in their stride,
four that move with stately bearing:
30 a lion, mighty among beasts,
who retreats before nothing;
31 a strutting rooster, a he-goat,
and a king secure against revolt.[a]

32 "If you play the fool and exalt yourself,
or if you plan evil,
clap your hand over your mouth![v]
33 For as churning cream produces butter,
and as twisting the nose produces blood,
so stirring up anger produces strife."

Sayings of King Lemuel

31 The sayings[w] of King Lemuel—an inspired utterance his mother taught him.

2 Listen, my son! Listen, son of my womb!
Listen, my son, the answer to my prayers![x]
3 Do not spend your strength[b] on women,
your vigor on those who ruin kings.[y]

4 It is not for kings, Lemuel—
it is not for kings to drink wine,[z]
not for rulers to crave beer,
5 lest they drink[a] and forget what has been decreed,[b]
and deprive all the oppressed of their rights.

[a] *31* The meaning of the Hebrew for this phrase is uncertain. [b] *3* Or *wealth*

seeking shelter (v. 26); locusts, by working in unity with strict discipline (v. 27; cf. Joel 2:2); a lizard, by accessing places barred to others (v. 28).
30:30–31 lion ... strutting rooster ... he-goat. These creatures stride with regal dignity over their respective communities. **king.** Like the creatures, a king, whose wisdom is shown by being secure against revolt, maintains divinely ordained social boundaries.
30:32 play the fool and exalt yourself. Censures pride expressed in self-exultation and devious schemes that subvert the social order.
30:33 churning cream ... twisting the nose ... stirring up anger. Activities that involve the application of pressure. The sequence demonstrates that anger produces provocation when pressed beyond proper limits. As the conclusion to the collection, the saying promotes humility, respect, and social order in the place of hubris and self-exaltation.
31:1–31 *Sayings of King Lemuel's Mother.* The superscript introduces two poems by King Lemuel, which his mother taught him: the noble king (vv. 1–9) and the noble wife (vv. 10–31).
31:1–9 *Sayings of King Lemuel.* This unit is a royal instruction that focuses on the nature of responsible leadership.
31:1 King Lemuel. An unknown ruler (see Introduction: Authors). **inspired utterance.** See note on 30:1. **his mother taught him.** The mother was often an influential figure in the ancient Near East (cf. 1 Kgs 1:11–13), but the sayings of a mother are unique in the biblical world.
31:2 my son! ... son of my womb! ... my son ...! Endearing epithets that trace the close relations between mother and son. The terms move backward from the present to Lemuel's gestation in his mother's womb to the answer to her prayers before pregnancy (cf. 1 Sam 1:11).
31:3 Do not spend your strength on women. Unrestrained sexual gratification distracts the king's attention from serving the people, blunts his wit, undermines his good judgment, exposes him to palace intrigues, and squanders the national wealth (see NIV text note) better spent to promote the national good.
31:4–5 not for kings ... lest they drink and forget. Debauchery undermines just decrees already enacted to protect the poor. Other texts warn that unrestrained drinking befuddles the king's mind, weakens his will, and drives him to plunder his subjects to pay for his expensive addiction (1 Kgs 16:9; 20:16; Esth 1:10–11; Eccl 10:16; Hos 7:5; Mark 6:21–28; cf. Isa 5:22–23; 28:7; 56:12; Mic 2:11; 1 Tim 3:3; Titus 1:7).

[6] Let beer be for those who are perishing,
wine[c] for those who are in anguish!
[7] Let them drink[d] and forget their poverty
and remember their misery no more.

[8] Speak[e] up for those who cannot speak for themselves,
for the rights of all who are destitute.
[9] Speak up and judge fairly;
defend the rights of the poor and needy.[f]

Epilogue: The Wife of Noble Character

[10] [a]A wife of noble character[g] who can find?[h]
She is worth far more than rubies.
[11] Her husband[i] has full confidence in her
and lacks nothing of value.[j]
[12] She brings him good, not harm,
all the days of her life.
[13] She selects wool and flax
and works with eager hands.[k]
[14] She is like the merchant ships,
bringing her food from afar.
[15] She gets up while it is still night;
she provides food for her family
and portions for her female servants.
[16] She considers a field and buys it;
out of her earnings she plants a vineyard.
[17] She sets about her work vigorously;
her arms are strong for her tasks.
[18] She sees that her trading is profitable,
and her lamp does not go out at night.

31:6 [c] Ge 14:18
31:7 [d] Est 1:10
31:8 [e] 1Sa 19:4; Job 29:12-17
31:9 [f] Lev 19:15; Dt 1:16; Pr 24:23; 29:7; Isa 1:17; Jer 22:16
31:10 [g] Ru 3:11; Pr 12:4; 18:22 [h] Pr 8:35; 19:14
31:11 [i] Ge 2:18 [j] Pr 12:4
31:13 [k] 1Ti 2:9-10

[a] *10* Verses 10-31 are an acrostic poem, the verses of which begin with the successive letters of the Hebrew alphabet.

31:6–7 Let beer be for those who are perishing ... Let them drink and forget their poverty. These sayings may be interpreted in three basic ways: (1) as a call to provide the poor with strong drink so that they might anesthetize themselves from their suffering; (2) as rhetorical commands that indicate the king has no need to resort to drink, unlike those who may need it to dull pain; or (3) as sarcastic commands that reinforce the negative appeals within vv. 4–5 and underscore the ineffectual nature of intoxicants. Intoxicants may serve a positive purpose for the destitute (i.e., for medicine or merriment), but they do not solve their plight (20:1; 23:29–30). The commands encourage the king to acknowledge his principal responsibility: the establishment of justice for the poor (vv. 8–9).

31:10–31 *Epilogue: The Wife of Noble Character.* The poem is structured as an acrostic (see NIV text note on v. 10), which serves as a rhetorical device that seeks to provide a comprehensive treatment of the subject (i.e., from A to Z). In general, the poem is divided into three parts: (1) the introduction reflects on the wife's value (vv. 10–12); (2) the body describes her activities (vv. 13–27); and (3) the conclusion praises her (vv. 28–31). This describes the wife with terms and expressions used elsewhere only for Lady Wisdom. She is the incarnation of wisdom in everyday life, the embodiment of the book's virtues, and a concrete example of what it means to fear the Lord. Ruth in the book of Ruth, which in many Hebrew Bibles follows Prov 31, is this kind of wife.

31:10 noble. The wife's physical and socioeconomic power, as well as her moral and spiritual nobility. Elsewhere in the OT, this term describes the physical strength and military exploits of men. **She is worth far more than rubies.** Because she uses her strength and wisdom totally and unselfishly for others. She is a gift from God (19:14).

31:13 wool and flax. The former is taken from the flock, whereas the latter is a fiber taken from the stalk of a plant to make linen garments. This not only assumes her weaving skill but also intimates that she is a perceptive purveyor who procures these raw materials (v. 14). A good woolen garment cost over two months' average wage; an inexpensive linen garment cost a half-month's wage.

31:15 gets up. An incomplete metaphor for a lioness that seeks its prey. **while it is still night.** She does not lie in bed and wait for servants to attend to her; rather, by providing for them, she multiplies her effectiveness.

31:16 considers a field and buys it. Demonstrates wisdom and foresight by acquiring property suitable for returns. **earnings.** From her cottage industry (v. 13).

31:18 her lamp does not go out at night. Signifies her wealth, not that she works all night, which is folly (cf. Ps 127:2). In a Middle Eastern proverb, "he sleeps in the dark" is equated with "he has not another penny in the house." In well-ordered houses, the lamp burned all night as a sign of life; its extinction marked calamity (cf. 13:9; 20:20; 24:20; Job 18:5–6; Jer 25:10).

31:20 [l] Dt 15:11; Eph 4:28; Heb 13:16
31:23 [m] Ex 3:16; Ru 4:1,11; Pr 12:4
31:26 [n] Pr 10:31
31:31 [o] Pr 11:16

19 In her hand she holds the distaff
and grasps the spindle with her fingers.
20 She opens her arms to the poor
and extends her hands to the needy.[l]
21 When it snows, she has no fear for her household;
for all of them are clothed in scarlet.
22 She makes coverings for her bed;
she is clothed in fine linen and purple.
23 Her husband is respected at the city gate,
where he takes his seat among the elders[m] of the land.
24 She makes linen garments and sells them,
and supplies the merchants with sashes.
25 She is clothed with strength and dignity;
she can laugh at the days to come.
26 She speaks with wisdom,
and faithful instruction is on her tongue.[n]
27 She watches over the affairs of her household
and does not eat the bread of idleness.
28 Her children arise and call her blessed;
her husband also, and he praises her:
29 "Many women do noble things,
but you surpass them all."
30 Charm is deceptive, and beauty is fleeting;
but a woman who fears the LORD is to be praised.
31 Honor her for all that her hands have done,
and let her works bring her praise[o] at the city gate.

31:19 distaff. A stick onto which wool or flax (v. 13) is placed for spinning and from which thread is drawn on a spinning wheel. **spindle.** A rod used to wind thread from the wool and flax on the distaff. This activity highlights the wife's remarkable skills and gracious contributions to the community (v. 20).
31:21 When it snows. This woman does not fear the onslaught of bad weather, for she prepares her household's wardrobe in advance. **scarlet.** A palatial, dyed fabric that represents wealth and royalty (cf. 2 Sam 1:24; Jer 4:30).
31:22 fine linen and purple. Refers to imported Egyptian fabric and purple-dyed wool, which symbolized royalty.
31:23 city gate. The center for civic and commercial activity. The wife's management of the household mirrors her husband's management of the community. Her prominence in the home and activity within the community forms the foundation for her husband's respected position among the elders at the city gate.
31:24 linen garments. See v. 16, which also describes the wife's entrepreneurial prowess.
31:25 clothed with strength and dignity. The wife embodies these virtues to such an extent that they appear as her clothing, visible to all (cf. Job 29:14). **laugh at the days to come.** She is neither worried nor anxious about what the future might bring.
31:27 does not eat the bread of idleness. She is not marked by laziness or indolence.
31:28 arise. Presumably in her presence; shows the family's respect for her (cf. Job 29:8; Isa 49:7).
31:29 noble things. See note on v. 10.
31:30 fears the LORD. The theme of the book (see note on 1:7). The book begins by declaring the prerequisite for acquiring wisdom (1:7), and it ends by concretely describing a woman who embodies what the theme of the book looks like in everyday life. True wisdom and the fear of the Lord are not mere intellectual qualities; they are a way of life.
31:31 city gate. See note on v. 23.

INTRODUCTION TO ECCLESIASTES

TITLE AND PURPOSE

Ecclesiastes is named after its central character, Qohelet (1:1,2,12; 7:27; 12:8 – 10), which the NIV translates as "the Teacher." The Septuagint (the pre-Christian Greek translation of the OT) word for "Teacher" is *ekklēsiastēs*, from which most English titles of the book are taken. Ecclesiastes is one of three OT books that clearly belong to the category of wisdom, the other two being Proverbs and Job (see "Introduction to the Wisdom and Lyrical Books," p. 895). Proverbs sets out the main contours of OT wisdom and is the essential background to reading Job and Ecclesiastes. The OT wisdom books wrestle with how to live wisely amid the many challenges of life. Ecclesiastes brings us into the journey of "the Teacher" as he works through his struggle as to whether life is meaningful. Ecclesiastes ultimately affirms life and joy but only as the end result of a struggle with the brokenness of life in a fallen world.

AUTHOR

The narrator presents the Teacher as Solomon (1:1,12), but many scholars now think that the Teacher was not actually Solomon but one whom we are to imagine as like Solomon with his wisdom and power. We know from 12:9 – 10 that the Teacher was a wisdom teacher who carefully gathered and arranged his material as he taught the people. We do not know the identity of the narrator who presents the Teacher's sayings, and so overall the author of Ecclesiastes is unknown. To understand Ecclesiastes, however, it is important to note that the narrator, whose voice is heard in 1:1; 7:27 and in the epilogue (12:9 – 14), presents the Teacher's journey and teachings in the context of his introduction, conclusion, and note in 7:27.

DATE

A variety of dates have been proposed for Ecclesiastes. Some argue that its type of Hebrew and the presence of Persian loanwords confirm that it was not written in Solomon's time, but this could just mean that a much earlier book was updated at a later time. Ecclesiastes' skepticism could show awareness of Greek philosophical influence, but evidence for such skepticism is also found much earlier. If the Persian loanwords and Greek influence do indicate the date of writing, then Ecclesiastes was most likely written in the postexilic period, probably in the fourth century BC. At that time it would have appeared to many, in what was left of Israel, as if God's purposes with them had run aground, thereby giving rise to the sort of questions the teacher struggles with. However, we cannot be sure of the date when Ecclesiastes was written.

PARTICULAR CHALLENGES

Ecclesiastes never mentions the OT covenant name for God, "LORD," but it clearly has this God in mind and is fully aware of many of the OT teachings, including creation, law, and wisdom.

In terms of the OT context, it is particularly important to read Ecclesiastes against the background of Proverbs, which sets out the characteristic *character-consequence* wisdom teaching rooted in creation. This approach assumes the rich meaningfulness of life and teaches that the fear of the Lord and wisdom flowing from it will in general lead to blessing and prosperity. A wise character will lead to good consequences!

Whenever the author lived, clearly many of his fellow believers were experiencing a crisis of faith. The Teacher sums up his many questions in the opening question of 1:3: "What do people gain from all their labors at which they toil under the sun?"

Skepticism was in the air and the Teacher draws from an autonomous, human-centered way of exploring such questions dependent on human reason, observation, and experience alone, using them to examine the question of whether life is meaningful or meaningless. A result is that in the course of his explorations the Teacher expresses some unorthodox views that a reader may find disturbing. It is important to remember that the crisis the Teacher is undergoing is finally resolved and that his unorthodox sayings must be seen in the light of the book as a whole.

Ecclesiastes *is* a carefully crafted whole, but as befits the Teacher's search for meaning, the book tracks back and forth as he explores area after area of life. His autonomous way of knowing, starting not with the fear of the Lord but depending on his experience and reason, leads him repeatedly to the conclusion that life is "meaningless" no matter what area of life he examines.

A challenge in Ecclesiastes is how to translate and understand the Hebrew word *hĕbēl*, which is translated "meaningless" (e.g., 1:2,14; 2:1,11,15,17,19,21,23,26). *Hĕbēl* certainly indicates the Teacher's despair in his quest for meaning in life, but it should not be understood as a *final* conclusion. A parallel expression in Ecclesiastes is "a chasing after the wind" (e.g., 1:14,17; 2:11,17,26), which helps us grasp what the Teacher means by "meaningless." It is not that there is no meaning in life; rather, if there is meaning in life, the Teacher simply cannot grasp it—just like he cannot grasp the wind. Life is utterly enigmatic.

This would seem to indicate that for the Teacher, Proverbs' character-consequence teaching is quite wrong! Surprisingly, however, throughout the book, next to his dark conclusions we find joy passages that affirm the meaningfulness of life (2:24–26; 3:12–14,22; 5:18–20; 8:15; 9:7–10; 11:7—12:7). A major challenge of reading Ecclesiastes is determining how to read the joy passages in relation to the conclusions of meaninglessness. Commentators take a variety of views on this issue: some read them as advocating seeking pleasure amidst the meaninglessness of life, others read them as the answer to the Teacher's problems, and still others read them as expressing a different view of life that the Teacher cannot reconcile with his findings.

The joy passages are probably not answers to the conclusions of meaninglessness but are set deliberately next to them to show us the extent of the Teacher's struggle. As a believer, he knows that life is meaningful (as expressed in

Wall painting of a feast for Nebamun, depicting people wearing fine clothes, with oil and incense on their heads (Eccl 9:8).

the joy passages), but his examination of area after area of life leads him to the opposite conclusion (the conclusions of meaninglessness). The resulting tension between these two approaches to life is at the heart of Ecclesiastes. The book poses this question for the believer: How do you resolve this tension when your faith teaches you that life is meaningful but everything you observe and experience seems to point in the opposite direction? Thus the big question Ecclesiastes poses is not just about the meaningfulness of work (1:3) but about *how* you know if life is meaningful amid circumstances in which nothing seems to make sense. This is a challenge that people have faced through the ages and that can be traced back to Gen 3, where the tree of the knowledge of good and evil stands for the temptation to make ourselves, not God, the center of life and knowledge.

Silver ingot hoard from En Gedi, ca. eighth–seventh centuries BC. The writer of Ecclesiastes "amassed silver and gold," but felt he had gained nothing (2:8,11).

Todd Bolen/www.BiblePlaces.com, taken at the Israel Museum

DIRECTION OF THE BOOK

In order to see how resolution comes for the Teacher, we have to follow him on his journey. The path to resolution comes from two directions:

First, as his journey progresses, it becomes increasingly apparent that his autonomous method of knowing, based on his experience, reason, and observation alone is not that of wisdom but that of folly. There are two key passages in this respect: (1) Eccl 5:1–7, which some scholars regard as the center of Ecclesiastes, urges the reader to approach the temple cautiously in order to *listen to God's instruction*, and it concludes with the similar exhortation to *fear God*. The teaching of this section is comparable to Proverbs' insistence that "the fear of the LORD is the beginning of wisdom" (Prov 9:10). (2) Eccl 7:23–29 reveals in dramatic fashion that the Teacher's autonomous way of knowing has led him right into the arms of Lady Folly! Thus one way in which resolution comes is in the growing recognition that an autonomous way of knowing will get one only into deeper and deeper despair when one is faced with the enigmas of life.

Second, resolution comes through the indication of a better way of knowing in 11:7—12:7. The proverb of 11:7 shines out like a beacon or lighthouse indicating that hope and resolution are possibilities. The two dominating exhortations of this section are to rejoice and to remember. "Remember your Creator" (12:1) is the second major clue to resolving the Teacher's struggle. Remembrance is far more than a casual reminder; it means letting your whole perspective on life be informed by the view that God created everything. This is precisely what has been missing in the Teacher's autonomous method; it has all been rooted in *himself*—indeed one of the great characteristics of Ecclesiastes is the endless use of the first person "I." The answer to the perplexities of life is to find a way back to the starting point of God as the Creator of everything. This does not take one away from the struggles of life (12:2–7), but it puts one in a position to affirm life and its meaningfulness amid the very real struggles of life in a fallen world.

Like the struggle of the Teacher to fit the pieces of life together, Ecclesiastes is not an easy book to grasp. Some scholars read parts of Ecclesiastes differently than others, as the reader will see in the notes. One must read this book patiently and, as with suffering, wait to see how resolution comes.

OCCASION AND PURPOSE

Ecclesiastes is an extraordinary book. We might think the Teacher less than a good example as he goes through his experience and speaks about it so honestly. But 12:9 is clear that the Teacher was wise and taught wisdom! Eccl 12:9 is comparable to Job 42:7, which commends Job for speaking the truth about God, unlike the friends.

Ecclesiastes thus validates the struggle of believers to find the meaning of life when such an experience overtakes them. In the postexilic period or in other times when Israel's future seemed threatened, many Israelites probably experienced such a struggle, and Ecclesiastes probably was a great comfort to many in such situations.

Ecclesiastes also provides insight into how resolution can emerge from such a struggle. In particular, it shows us the folly of trying to understand "life under the sun" based on our experience, reason, and observation alone. It is only as we start remembering our Creator that we can find a way through such a dilemma.

GENRE AND STRUCTURE

Ecclesiastes is a wisdom book; however, unlike Proverbs but like Job, it also has a story or an autobiographical dimension to it. The narrator introduces the Teacher to us (1:1), sums up his struggle (1:2–3), and provides a poem that evokes the depths of the teacher's struggles (1:4–11). In 1:12 the Teacher himself comes on the stage, and in 1:12–18 he explains his quest for wisdom. Apart from 7:27, which is the only place in the main body of Ecclesiastes where the narrator's voice intrudes, we only hear the Teacher speak in 1:12—12:7. In 12:8–14 the narrator concludes the book with the epilogue. Eccl 1:2 and its repetition in 12:8 form a frame for the book, alerting the reader to the theme that Ecclesiastes explores.

Its structure is organic rather than strictly logical. The tension between the Teacher's analysis of life based on his experience, reason, and observation alone and the positive affirmation of life exemplified in the joy passages, combined with the growing sense that, ironically, his method of knowing is not wisdom but folly, drive the book forward to its denouement in 11:7—12:14.

THEMES AND THEOLOGY

The central theme of Ecclesiastes is the question of whether or not life is meaningful. Proverbs affirms life as full of meaning, but Ecclesiastes looks at life through the eyes of the Teacher, who finds life an enigma no matter what area of life he explores. The Teacher's examination of life is comprehensive, as captured in the recurring phrase "under the sun" (e.g., 1:3,9,14; 2:11,17,18,19,20,22). He explores all of life: pleasure, great building projects, wealth, music, work, time, justice and oppression, the problem of death, companionship, government and leadership, etc., but no matter what area of life he explores, he concludes that all is meaningless. At the same time, the joy passages affirm the rich texture of ordinary life: marriage, work, and eating and drinking.

In a fallen world, the meaning of life is often perplexing. Indeed, the same Greek word translated "meaningless" in Ecclesiastes is the one Paul uses for "frustration" in Rom 8:20. The Teacher ruthlessly exposes the many ways in which life does not match up to the character-consequence theme of Proverbs. But he does resolve the tension in his journey by going to the starting point of remembering his Creator (12:1,6), which is Ecclesiastes' equivalent of Proverbs' "the fear of the LORD" (e.g., Prov 1:7; 2:5; 9:10). From this perspective, even amid the brokenness, life is meaningful in *all* of its many created dimensions. Indirectly, Ecclesiastes thus affirms creation as good, just as God did (Gen 1). Thus, Ecclesiastes opens up a whole range of topics for exploration: pleasure, music, time, work, companionship, justice and oppression, politics, death, etc.

A major theme of Ecclesiastes is determining how to go about ***knowing and finding truth*** in a world that is often perplexing. Ecclesiastes rigorously exposes the results of a human-centered quest for truth (cf. Gen 3). If, like the Teacher, we make ourselves the center of truth, then truth will continually evade us, and we will find ourselves in despair.

Ecclesiastes also deals with the theme of ***suffering***. The Teacher's suffering is less obvious than Job's. Nevertheless, the intellectual struggle the Teacher goes through has its own agony, and pastorally it is important to note that Ecclesiastes affirms the Teacher's struggle. Believers are not alien to the sort of existential and intellectual crisis the Teacher finds himself in.

As noted earlier in this section, there is a connection between Ecclesiastes and Rom 8. It is also possible that Paul quotes Eccl 7:20 in Rom 3:10. Both contexts in Romans connect Ecclesiastes and its meaninglessness with the fall and sin. Clearly God's redemption in Christ shows the meaningfulness of life with much greater clarity than was possible in the Teacher's day. Nevertheless, prior to the consummation of the kingdom of God, mystery and suffering remain, and we will continue to need Ecclesiastes to help us on our journeys.

CANON

In the Hebrew Bible, Ecclesiastes is part of the Writings (the third section of the Hebrew Bible), and its acceptance as Scripture may have occurred as early as the second century BC. Because of some of the radical statements in Ecclesiastes, it is not surprising that some rabbis in the first century AD doubted its canonicity. Despite that questioning, the view of Ecclesiastes as authoritative Scripture won the day among the rabbis. In the early centuries of the Christian church, Ecclesiastes appears to have been universally accepted as canonical.

OUTLINE

I. Everything Is Meaningless (1:1–11)
- A. Title (1:1)
- B. Statement of the Theme of the Book (1:2)
- C. The Programmatic Question (1:3)
- D. A Poem About the Enigma of Life (1:4–11)

II. Wisdom Is Meaningless (1:12–18)

III. Pleasures Are Meaningless (2:1–11)

IV. Wisdom and Folly Are Meaningless (2:12–16)

V. Toil Is Meaningless (2:17–26)

VI. A Time for Everything (3:1–22)

VII. Oppression, Toil, Friendlessness (4:1–12)

VIII. Advancement Is Meaningless (4:13–16)

IX. Stand in Awe of God (5:1–7)

X. Riches Are Meaningless (5:8—6:12)

XI. Wisdom (7:1—8:1)

XII. Obey the King (8:2–17)

XIII. A Common Destiny for All (9:1–12)

XIV. Wisdom Better Than Folly (9:13—10:20)

XV. Invest in Many Ventures (11:1–6)

XVI. Remember Your Creator While Young (11:7—12:8)

XVII. The Conclusion of the Matter (12:9–14)

ECCLESIASTES

1:1 [a]ver 12; Ecc 7:27; 12:10 [b]Pr 1:1
1:2 [c]Ps 39:5-6; 62:9; 144:4; Ecc 12:8; Ro 8:20-21
1:3 [d]Ecc 2:11,22; 3:9; 5:15-16
1:4 [e]Ps 104:5; 119:90
1:5 [f]Ps 19:5-6

Everything Is Meaningless

1 The words of the Teacher,[a][a] son of David, king in Jerusalem:[b]

2 "Meaningless! Meaningless!"
says the Teacher.
"Utterly meaningless!
Everything is meaningless."[c]

3 What do people gain from all their labors
at which they toil under the sun?[d]
4 Generations come and generations go,
but the earth remains forever.[e]
5 The sun rises and the sun sets,
and hurries back to where it rises.[f]
6 The wind blows to the south
and turns to the north;

[a] *1* Or *the leader of the assembly*; also in verses 2 and 12

1:1–11 *Everything Is Meaningless.* The narrator introduces the Teacher, summarizes his teaching, and shares a poem that evokes his struggle.
1:1 *Title.* The narrator introduces the Teacher (see Introduction: Title and Purpose).
1:1 the Teacher. The main character in the book. The Hebrew term (*qōhelet*) is related to that for "assembly" (see NIV text note; Exod 16:3; Num 16:3). The Teacher taught wisdom to the people (12:9–10), presumably in their assembly or once he assembled them to be taught. **son of David, king in Jerusalem.** Only Solomon fits this description, but it is not clear whether Solomon himself is being described or whether the famous king is being used as a literary device to refer to someone else (see Introduction: Author). We are to imagine the Teacher as exceptionally wise and wealthy, like Solomon (1 Kgs 1–11).
1:2 *Statement of the Theme of the Book.* This succinctly states the book's theme, which 12:8 repeats, thus forming a frame for the book.
1:2 Meaningless! Hebrew *hěbēl*; occurs 36 times in the book. *Hěbēl* literally means "breath" (Pss 39:5,11; 62:9; 144:4), but its precise meaning in Ecclesiastes is much debated. The parallel expression "a chasing after the wind" (e.g., vv. 14,17; 2:11,17,26) indicates that "meaningless" is not a final conclusion but an utterance of despair; just as one cannot catch the wind, so the meaning of life seems utterly elusive to the Teacher. *Hěbēl* is also the name given to Abel in Gen 4, and the murder of Abel is an example of the kind of unjust slaying that has raised questions for the Teacher about the meaningfulness of life. In light of v. 1, which associates the Teacher with Solomon, nothing prepares the reader for this despairing statement. One wonders how someone as wise as Solomon could come to this conclusion. But a close reading of 1 Kgs 1–11 reveals that Solomon was a more complex and sinful character than people often realize. The *gift* of wisdom does not automatically make one wise in practice or in all areas of one's life.
1:3 *The Programmatic Question.* If v. 2 summarizes a conclusion the Teacher keeps coming to in the book, v. 3 provides the question that frames his entire quest: People work hard in life, but what is really the point of it all? The implied answer to the rhetorical question is, "Nothing!"
1:3 under the sun. Repeated 29 times in the book. Parallel expressions, though used less frequently, are "under the heavens" (e.g., v. 13; 2:3) and "on earth" (e.g., 7:20; 8:14). These expressions refer to created life in all its dimensions. Some think that "under the sun" refers to human life apart from God. This is unlikely because the Teacher includes God in his reflections on life "under the sun."
1:4–11 *A Poem About the Enigma of Life.* The poem draws from the circularities observable in nature (vv. 5–7) and history (vv. 4,9–11) to argue that there is never real progress; life just endlessly repeats itself. Human generations come and go and are not even remembered (vv. 4,11). The center and climax to the poem is in v. 8, which anticipates the sort of conclusion the Teacher comes to repeatedly.
1:4 earth remains forever. In contrast to the transience of human generations, the earth appears to remain forever.

round and round it goes,
ever returning on its course.
7 All streams flow into the sea,
yet the sea is never full.
To the place the streams come from,
there they return again.[g]
8 All things are wearisome,
more than one can say.
The eye never has enough of seeing,[h]
nor the ear its fill of hearing.
9 What has been will be again,
what has been done will be done again;[i]
there is nothing new under the sun.
10 Is there anything of which one can say,
"Look! This is something new"?
It was here already, long ago;
it was here before our time.
11 No one remembers the former generations,
and even those yet to come
will not be remembered
by those who follow them.[j]

Wisdom Is Meaningless

12 I, the Teacher,[k] was king over Israel in Jerusalem. 13 I applied my mind to study and to explore by
wisdom all that is done under the heavens. What a heavy burden God has laid on mankind![l] 14 I have
seen all the things that are done under the sun; all of them are meaningless, a chasing after the wind.[m]

15 What is crooked cannot be straightened;[n]
what is lacking cannot be counted.

16 I said to myself, "Look, I have increased in wisdom more than anyone who has ruled over Jerusalem before me;[o] I have experienced much of wisdom and knowledge." 17 Then I applied myself to the
understanding of wisdom,[p] and also of madness and folly,[q] but I learned that this, too, is a chasing
after the wind.

18 For with much wisdom comes much sorrow;
the more knowledge, the more grief.[r]

1:7 [g]Job 36:28
1:8 [h]Pr 27:20
1:9 [i]Ecc 2:12; 3:15
1:11 [j]Ecc 2:16
1:12 [k]ver 1
1:13 [l]Ge 3:17; Ecc 3:10
1:14 [m]Ecc 2:11,17
1:15 [n]Ecc 7:13
1:16 [o]1Ki 3:12; 4:30; Ecc 2:9
1:17 [p]Ecc 7:23 [q]Ecc 2:3,12; 7:25
1:18 [r]Ecc 2:23; 12:12

1:11 No one remembers. Remembrance is an important motif in the book. It is also a major theme in the Bible. God himself is described as remembering (e.g., Gen 8:1; 9:15–16), and God's people are repeatedly encouraged to "remember" (Exod 20:8; Deut 7:18; 8:18; 9:7). Here it functions negatively: what people think is new is simply what they have forgotten. In 12:9 it provides a way to resolve the Teacher's crisis.
1:12—12:7 The main body of Ecclesiastes deals with the Teacher's search for meaning in life. In 1:12 the Teacher comes on the stage and from this point on speaks in the first person.
1:12–18 *Wisdom Is Meaningless.* The Teacher describes his journey of exploration. The range of his search for meaning is comprehensive; he aims to explore "all that is done under the heavens" (v. 13). He conducts his search "by wisdom" (v. 13; cf. 2:3,9), the same word that is central to Proverbs (e.g., 1:2,7; 2:2,6,10); the use of this word suggests that the Teacher conducts his quest in the fear of the Lord. As becomes apparent in the book, his method is very different from the wisdom of Proverbs, already suggested by the constant repetition of "I" in this section and by his consistently negative conclusions. See Introduction: Particular Challenges.
1:13 God. The only name the Teacher uses for God is *ʾĕlōhîm* (used 40 times in the book), which emphasizes God's sovereignty. He does not use the covenant name Yahweh (translated "Lord"; see notes on Gen 2:4; Exod 3:14,15).
1:14 chasing after the wind. An evocative metaphor for the elusive nature of meaning. There may be meaning in life, but trying to grasp it is like trying to grasp the wind. The first half of Ecclesiastes uses this expression nine times (here; v. 17; 2:11,17,26; 4:4,6,16; 6:9).
1:15 The Teacher quotes two proverbs in this section (here; v. 18). The proverb here expresses that reality is broken (cf. 7:13) and incomplete.
1:16 increased in wisdom. Cf. 1 Kgs 3:12; 4:29–34. **more than anyone who has ruled over Jerusalem before me.** If "before me" is temporal, then the reference is not to Solomon, since only David ruled over Jerusalem before Solomon among the Israelite kings. It could, however, refer to kings who ruled over Jerusalem before David established it as his capital. If "before me" is a spatial rather than a temporal reference, then it could refer to those around the Teacher.
1:18 This proverb argues that the quest for "wisdom" brings sorrow and grief. Prov 1:1–7, in contrast, states that wisdom is derived from "fear of the Lord" (Prov 1:7).

2:1 [s]Ecc 7:4; 8:15; Lk 12:19
2:2 [t]Pr 14:13; Ecc 7:6
2:3 [u]ver 24-25; Ecc 3:12-13 [v]Ecc 1:17
2:4 [w]1Ki 7:1-12 [x]SS 8:11
2:8 [y]1Ki 9:28; 10:10,14, 21 [z]2Sa 19:35
2:9 [a]1Ch 29:25; Ecc 1:16
2:11 [b]Ecc 1:14 [c]Ecc 1:3
2:12 [d]Ecc 1:17 [e]Ecc 1:9; 7:25
2:13 [f]Ecc 7:19; 9:18 [g]Ecc 7:11-12
2:14 [h]Ps 49:10; Pr 17:24; Ecc 3:19; 6:6; 7:2; 9:3,11-12
2:15 [i]Ecc 6:8

Pleasures Are Meaningless

2 I said to myself, “Come now, I will test you with pleasure[s] to find out what is good.” But that also
proved to be meaningless. 2“Laughter,”[t] I said, “is madness. And what does pleasure accomplish?”
3I tried cheering myself with wine,[u] and embracing folly[v]—my mind still guiding me with wisdom.
I wanted to see what was good for people to do under the heavens during the few days of their lives.
4I undertook great projects: I built houses for myself[w] and planted vineyards.[x] 5I made gardens and
parks and planted all kinds of fruit trees in them. 6I made reservoirs to water groves of flourishing trees. 7I
bought male and female slaves and had other slaves who were born in my house. I also owned more herds
and flocks than anyone in Jerusalem before me. 8I amassed silver and gold[y] for myself, and the treasure of
kings and provinces. I acquired male and female singers,[z] and a harem[a] as well—the delights of a man's
heart. 9I became greater by far than anyone in Jerusalem before me.[a] In all this my wisdom stayed with me.

10 I denied myself nothing my eyes desired;
  I refused my heart no pleasure.
My heart took delight in all my labor,
  and this was the reward for all my toil.
11 Yet when I surveyed all that my hands had done
  and what I had toiled to achieve,
everything was meaningless, a chasing after the wind;[b]
  nothing was gained under the sun.[c]

Wisdom and Folly Are Meaningless

12 Then I turned my thoughts to consider wisdom,
  and also madness and folly.[d]
What more can the king's successor do
  than what has already been done?[e]
13 I saw that wisdom[f] is better than folly,[g]
  just as light is better than darkness.
14 The wise have eyes in their heads,
  while the fool walks in the darkness;
but I came to realize
  that the same fate overtakes them both.[h]

15Then I said to myself,

“The fate of the fool will overtake me also.
  What then do I gain by being wise?”[i]

[a] *8* The meaning of the Hebrew for this phrase is uncertain.

2:1–11 *Pleasures Are Meaningless.* The Teacher gives himself to pleasure and great building projects. In the process he achieves greatness, but his quest for the meaning of life fails: “everything [is] meaningless” (v. 11).
2:1 pleasure. The Teacher gives himself over to hedonism, including laughter, wine, and sex (“a harem,” v. 8). **good.** A key word in the book; “good” and “better” occur about 40 times. Cf. Gen 1, where God repeatedly declares his work of creation “good.” The Teacher is after the right goal, but his method for getting there is skewed.
2:3 embracing folly. In Proverbs, folly is the opposite of wisdom. The Teacher does not hold back in giving himself over to folly (cf. v. 10). **wisdom.** See note on 1:12–18.
2:4–9 Great kings in the ancient Near East typically “undertook great projects” (v. 4; cf. 1 Kgs 4–11). The Teacher amassed treasures and the best singers of the day.
2:4–6 Many of the words here also occur in Gen 1–2: “planted” (vv. 4,5; cf. Gen 2:8); “gardens” (v. 5; cf. Gen 2:8,9,10,15,16); “all kinds of fruit trees” (v. 5; cf. Gen 1:11,12,29; 2:9,16,17); “to water” (v. 6; cf. Gen 2:6,10; “flourishing” (v. 6; cf. Gen 1:22,28); “made” (vv. 5,6; cf. Gen 1:7,16,25,26–27,31; 2:3,4). It is as though the Teacher is trying to recreate Eden—but without God! This is a God-less Eden project. The Teacher poses not only as a king but also as God!
2:8 provinces. Probably the new districts Solomon created to sustain the state (cf. 1 Kgs 4:7–19). **harem.** This Hebrew word occurs only here in the OT (see NIV text note). An early Egyptian letter uses a similar Canaanite term for concubines. The picture fits with what we know of Solomon, who had 300 concubines in addition to 700 wives (1 Kgs 11:3).
2:9 greater … than anyone. See 1:16. **wisdom.** See note on 1:12–18.
2:10–11 Work (labor and toil) is a central theme in the book. It was a major way in which the Teacher sought to find meaning in his life. See 1:3.
2:12–16 *Wisdom and Folly Are Meaningless.* The Teacher follows Proverbs in affirming that wisdom is better than folly (vv. 13–14), but then he subverts this view by arguing that both the wise and the fool will die and neither will be remembered (vv. 15–16).
2:12 king's successor. Probably the Teacher himself.
2:14 same fate. Death renders wisdom meaningless in the eyes of the Teacher.

I said to myself,
"This too is meaningless."
16 For the wise, like the fool, will not be long remembered;
the days have already come when both have been forgotten.[j]
Like the fool, the wise too must die!

Toil Is Meaningless

17 So I hated life, because the work that is done under the sun was grievous to me. All of it is
meaningless, a chasing after the wind.[k] 18 I hated all the things I had toiled for under the sun, because I must leave them to the one who comes after me.[l] 19 And who knows whether that person will
be wise or foolish? Yet they will have control over all the fruit of my toil into which I have poured
my effort and skill under the sun. This too is meaningless. 20 So my heart began to despair over all
my toilsome labor under the sun. 21 For a person may labor with wisdom, knowledge and skill, and
then they must leave all they own to another who has not toiled for it. This too is meaningless and
a great misfortune. 22 What do people get for all the toil and anxious striving with which they labor
under the sun?[m] 23 All their days their work is grief and pain;[n] even at night their minds do not rest.
This too is meaningless.

24 A person can do nothing better than to eat and drink[o] and find satisfaction in their own toil.[p] This
too, I see, is from the hand of God,[q] 25 for without him, who can eat or find enjoyment? 26 To the person
who pleases him, God gives wisdom, knowledge and happiness, but to the sinner he gives the task of
gathering and storing up wealth[r] to hand it over to the one who pleases God.[s] This too is meaningless,
a chasing after the wind.

A Time for Everything

3 There is a time[t] for everything,
and a season for every activity under the heavens:

2 a time to be born and a time to die,
a time to plant and a time to uproot,
3 a time to kill and a time to heal,
a time to tear down and a time to build,
4 a time to weep and a time to laugh,
a time to mourn and a time to dance,

2:16 [j] Ecc 1:11; 9:5
2:17 [k] Ecc 4:2
2:18 [l] Ps 39:6; 49:10
2:22 [m] Ecc 1:3; 3:9
2:23 [n] Job 5:7; 14:1; Ecc 1:18
2:24 [o] Ecc 8:15; 1Co 15:32 [p] Ecc 3:22 [q] Ecc 3:12-13; 5:17-19; 9:7-10
2:26 [r] Job 27:17 [s] Pr 13:22
3:1 [t] ver 11,17; Ecc 8:6

2:16 remembered. Remembrance is a central motif in the book (see note on 1:11).

2:17–26 *Toil Is Meaningless.* No matter how hard a person works, they have no control over their legacy (vv. 17–23). The Teacher reaches his conclusion that toil is "meaningless" and sets it next to his belief in joy (see Introduction: Particular Challenges).

2:18 hated. The problem with seeking to locate the meaning of life in work is that when a person dies they have no control over their legacy. This frustrates the Teacher in his quest—so much so that he hates life (v. 17) and the things he has toiled for. **under the sun.** See note on 1:3.

2:19 who knows . . . ? Cf. 3:21. The Teacher's lack of knowledge in these areas drives him to despair.

2:24–26 Eating, drinking, and enjoying one's labor is the first joy passage in the book (see Introduction: Particular Challenges); the others are 3:12–14,22; 5:18–20; 8:15; 9:7–10; 11:7—12:7). It starkly contrasts with the preceding verses. God is central to this section, whereas vv. 1–23 do not mention him once. The joy passages do not express a despairing hedonism but affirm the positive view of creation found in Genesis and Proverbs regarding the activities of eating, drinking, and enjoying one's work (cf. Gen 1:29; 2:9; Deut 7:13). Here we hear the voice of the Teacher as a believer. Life is a gift from God that should be fully enjoyed. Indeed, the motif of God giving gifts is a central one in Ecclesiastes.

2:26 The character-consequence theme: "the person who pleases [God]" receives many blessings, but the "sinner" has the fruits of his labor given to another. **This too is meaningless.** The Teacher cannot see how the two different perspectives can be brought together. The tension between despair and affirming life is at the heart of his struggle.

3:1–22 *A Time for Everything.* The Teacher sets out in a poem the typical wisdom teaching about time (vv. 1–8). Every activity has its right time in accordance with God's ordering of the creation. Apart from birth and death (v. 2), every activity is one that humans have some control over. The problem for the Teacher is that God has set eternity in the human heart (v. 11), i.e., every person has a desire to know the big story of which they are a part. However, humans are limited and lack the necessary knowledge of the beginning and the end in order to know the time for everything.

3:1–8 A poem about time. Each line refers to a list of opposite activities covering the range of human life. All of life is subject to God's order for creation. As is often the case with poetry, it is not always possible to be sure what activity is being referred to.

3:1 The theme of the poem. **under the heavens.** See note on 1:3.

3:2 plant . . . uproot. Refers literally to the practice of agriculture but, as is typical in poetry, may have a wider reference (cf. Jer 1:10).

3:3 kill. Probably refers to legitimate forms of killing in the OT such as capital punishment and holy war.

3:7 [u]Am 5:13
3:9 [v]Ecc 1:3
3:10 [w]Ecc 1:13
3:11 [x]ver 1 [y]Job 11:7; Ecc 8:17 [z]Job 28:23; Ro 11:33
3:13 [a]Ecc 2:3 [b]Ps 34:12 [c]Dt 12:7,18; Ecc 2:24; 5:19
3:14 [d]Job 23:15; Ecc 5:7; 7:18; 8:12-13; Jas 1:17
3:15 [e]Ecc 6:10 [f]Ecc 1:9
3:17 [g]Job 19:29; Ecc 11:9; Mt 16:27; Ro 2:6-8; 2Th 1:6-7 [h]ver 1
3:18 [i]Ps 73:22
3:19 [j]Ecc 2:14
3:20 [k]Ge 2:7; 3:19; Job 34:15
3:21 [l]Ecc 12:7

5 a time to scatter stones and a time to gather them,
a time to embrace and a time to refrain from embracing,
6 a time to search and a time to give up,
a time to keep and a time to throw away,
7 a time to tear and a time to mend,
a time to be silent[u] and a time to speak,
8 a time to love and a time to hate,
a time for war and a time for peace.

9 What do workers gain from their toil?[v] 10 I have seen the burden God has laid on the human race.[w] 11 He has made everything beautiful in its time.[x] He has also set eternity in the human heart; yet[a] no one can fathom[y] what God has done from beginning to end.[z] 12 I know that there is nothing better for people than to be happy and to do good while they live. 13 That each of them may eat and drink,[a] and find satisfaction[b] in all their toil—this is the gift of God.[c] 14 I know that everything God does will endure forever; nothing can be added to it and nothing taken from it. God does it so that people will fear him.[d]

15 Whatever is has already been,[e]
and what will be has been before;[f]
and God will call the past to account.[b]

16 And I saw something else under the sun:

In the place of judgment—wickedness was there,
in the place of justice—wickedness was there.

17 I said to myself,

"God will bring into judgment[g]
both the righteous and the wicked,
for there will be a time for every activity,
a time to judge every deed."[h]

18 I also said to myself, "As for humans, God tests them so that they may see that they are like the animals.[i] 19 Surely the fate of human beings[j] is like that of the animals; the same fate awaits them both: As one dies, so dies the other. All have the same breath[c]; humans have no advantage over animals. Everything is meaningless. 20 All go to the same place; all come from dust, and to dust all return.[k] 21 Who knows if the human spirit rises upward[l] and if the spirit of the animal goes down into the earth?"

[a] *11* Or *also placed ignorance in the human heart, so that* [b] *15* Or *God calls back the past*
[c] *19* Or *spirit*

3:5 scatter stones … gather them. The precise reference is unclear; possibly refers to clearing a field of stone and gathering stones to build.
3:7 The wise person knows when to be silent and when to speak. Job's friends illustrate well the difficulty of knowing when "to be silent" and when "to speak."
3:9 See note on 1:3.
3:10–11 The Teacher responds to the order of creation with despair and frustration.
3:11 eternity. The same Hebrew word refers to God's activity in v. 14 ("forever"). Humans need a God's-eye view of the world in order to discern his order in the creation, but we lack this perspective because we are limited.
3:12–14 The Teacher responds to the order of creation with belief, again starkly contrasting his despairing response. This is the second joy passage in the book (see note on 2:24–26).
3:13 eat and drink … the gift of God. See note on 2:24–26.
3:14 fear him. Cf. 5:7; 12:13; Prov 1:7. The Teacher struggles to bridge the gap between these two responses (belief and despair).
3:16 place of judgment … place of justice. Where legal issues were decided, normally by the city elders in the city gates.
3:17 As a believer, the Teacher affirms that God will judge everyone. **a time.** See 3:1–8 and note.
3:18–21 The Teacher subverts his affirmation of God's justice in v. 17. There is no apparent difference between humans and animals: both end up in the grave. Thus the Teacher concludes again: "Everything is meaningless" (v. 19). To some Christians these verses are worrying because they appear to deny hope for life after death. It is important to remember that the Teacher is here arguing on the basis of his own insights *apart from* God's revelation.
3:21 Who knows … ? See 2:19. In vv. 19–20, the Teacher sees the fate of animals and humans as identical; here he despairingly raises the question of whether the destinations of their spirits might be different. See 12:7, where the spirit returns to God (cf. Job 34:14–15; Ps 104:29–30).

[22]So I saw that there is nothing better for a person than to enjoy their work,[m] because that is their lot.[n] For who can bring them to see what will happen after them?

3:22 [m]Ecc 2:24; 5:18 [n]Job 31:2
4:1 [o]Ps 12:5; Ecc 3:16 [p]La 1:16
4:2 [q]Jer 20:17-18; 22:10 [r]Job 3:17; 10:18
4:3 [s]Job 3:16; Ecc 6:3 [t]Job 3:22
4:4 [u]Ecc 1:14
4:5 [v]Pr 6:10
4:6 [w]Pr 15:16-17; 16:8
4:8 [x]Pr 27:20

Oppression, Toil, Friendlessness

4 Again I looked and saw all the oppression[o] that was taking place under the sun:

I saw the tears of the oppressed —
 and they have no comforter;
power was on the side of their oppressors —
 and they have no comforter.[p]
[2] And I declared that the dead,[q]
 who had already died,
are happier than the living,
 who are still alive.[r]
[3] But better than both
 is the one who has never been born,[s]
who has not seen the evil
 that is done under the sun.[t]

[4]And I saw that all toil and all achievement spring from one person's envy of another. This too is meaningless, a chasing after the wind.[u]

[5] Fools fold their hands[v]
 and ruin themselves.
[6] Better one handful with tranquillity
 than two handfuls with toil[w]
 and chasing after the wind.

[7]Again I saw something meaningless under the sun:

[8] There was a man all alone;
 he had neither son nor brother.
There was no end to his toil,
 yet his eyes were not content[x] with his wealth.
"For whom am I toiling," he asked,
 "and why am I depriving myself of enjoyment?"
This too is meaningless —
 a miserable business!

[9] Two are better than one,
 because they have a good return for their labor:
[10] If either of them falls down,
 one can help the other up.
But pity anyone who falls
 and has no one to help them up.
[11] Also, if two lie down together, they will keep warm.
 But how can one keep warm alone?

3:22 This is the third joy passage in the book (see note on 2:24–26) and represents a quite different response to injustice than that in vv. 19–21. **For who ...?** The Teacher either despairs at reconciling his two approaches or affirms God's control in line with his affirmation of joy.

4:1–12 *Oppression, Toil, Friendlessness.* Observation of oppression, work done from the wrong motivation, and human isolation make the Teacher question the meaning of life.

4:1–3 The Teacher observes the pain and powerlessness of the oppressed. He concludes that the dead are better off than the living but that it is even better never to be born.

4:1 oppression. A theme already mentioned in 3:16.

4:4–6 The Teacher reflects on the motivation for work and observes that it springs from "one person's envy of another" (v. 4). Work is a major theme in the book (see note on 1:3).

4:5 fold their hands. Cease from work. **ruin themselves.** Cf. 10:18; Prov 6:6–11; 24:30–34.

4:7–12 The Teacher observes a hardworking man who is all alone and whose work seems to have no purpose amid his isolation (vv. 8–10), and the Teacher reflects on the advantages of community (vv. 9–12).

5:2 [y] Jdg 11:35 [z] Job 6:24; Pr 10:19; 20:25
5:3 [a] Job 20:8 [b] Ecc 10:14
5:4 [c] Dt 23:21; Jdg 11:35; Ps 119:60 [d] Nu 30:2; Ps 66:13-14; 76:11
5:5 [e] Nu 30:2-4; Pr 20:25; Jnh 2:9; Ac 5:4
5:7 [f] Ecc 3:14; 12:13
5:8 [g] Ps 12:5; Ecc 4:1

12 Though one may be overpowered,
  two can defend themselves.
A cord of three strands is not quickly broken.

Advancement Is Meaningless

13 Better a poor but wise youth than an old but foolish king who no longer knows how to heed a warning. 14 The youth may have come from prison to the kingship, or he may have been born in poverty within his kingdom. 15 I saw that all who lived and walked under the sun followed the youth, the king's successor. 16 There was no end to all the people who were before them. But those who came later were not pleased with the successor. This too is meaningless, a chasing after the wind.

Fulfill Your Vow to God

5 [a] Guard your steps when you go to the house of God. Go near to listen rather than to offer the sacrifice of fools, who do not know that they do wrong.

2 Do not be quick with your mouth,
  do not be hasty in your heart
  to utter anything before God.[y]
God is in heaven
  and you are on earth,
  so let your words be few.[z]
3 A dream[a] comes when there are many cares,
  and many words mark the speech of a fool.[b]

4 When you make a vow to God, do not delay to fulfill it.[c] He has no pleasure in fools; fulfill your vow.[d] 5 It is better not to make a vow than to make one and not fulfill it.[e] 6 Do not let your mouth lead you into sin. And do not protest to the temple messenger, "My vow was a mistake." Why should God be angry at what you say and destroy the work of your hands? 7 Much dreaming and many words are meaningless. Therefore fear God.[f]

Riches Are Meaningless

8 If you see the poor oppressed[g] in a district, and justice and rights denied, do not be surprised at such things; for one official is eyed by a higher one, and over them both are others higher still. 9 The increase from the land is taken by all; the king himself profits from the fields.

10 Whoever loves money never has enough;
  whoever loves wealth is never satisfied with their income.
  This too is meaningless.

[a] In Hebrew texts 5:1 is numbered 4:17, and 5:2-20 is numbered 5:1-19.

4:12 two ... three. A climactic construction: if two are good, three are even better.
4:13–16 *Advancement Is Meaningless.* The Teacher recognizes the vital importance of wise government, but people do not always recognize it—in his story a later generation rejects the better ruler (v. 16).
4:13 who no longer knows how to heed a warning. Listening is essential to good government (Prov 20:18). Solomon, e.g., wisely asked for a listening heart (1 Kgs 3:9).
5:1–7 *Stand in Awe of God.* This passage is a milestone on the path to the resolution of the Teacher's dilemma (see Introduction: Particular Challenges). In his exhortation the Teacher speaks as a believer and provides an important clue as to the source of his problem.
5:1 Guard your steps. Approach God's presence reverently and carefully. **house of God.** Probably a reference to Solomon's temple (cf. v. 6). **listen.** A central theme of OT wisdom. The Teacher speaks many words, but here he counsels listening to God's address through the priests' instruction (cf. v. 2). **sacrifice of fools.** Thoughtless worship.
5:2 quick with your mouth. As in a rash vow (cf. Judg 11:30). **before God.** God is truly present in the temple. **God ... heaven ... you ... earth.** God is transcendent, and humans are earthly creatures.
5:3 Disturbing dreams, overwork ("many cares"), and too many words are negative, and v. 7 links them to the experience of meaninglessness. This is a clue to why the Teacher struggles with the meaning of life.
5:4–5 Quotes Deut 23:21 almost verbatim.
5:7 fear God. Cf. 12:13 (see note there).
5:8—6:12 *Riches Are Meaningless.* A joy passage (5:18–20) is sandwiched between despairing reflections on the problem of wealth (see note on 2:24–26; see also Introduction: Particular Challenges).
5:8–17 The Teacher returns to the subject of oppression (vv. 8–9; 4:1–3) and then explores how the love of money destroys people (vv. 10–17).
5:8 one official ... higher still. Pictures systemic economic corruption.
5:9 the king himself profits from the fields. Could also be translated "a king for a plowed field." If the latter translation is correct, then the proverb may indicate that the king should ensure economic justice for all.
5:10 Cf. 1 Tim 6:10, where Paul points out that the love of money can

11 As goods increase,
so do those who consume them.
And what benefit are they to the owners
except to feast their eyes on them?

12 The sleep of a laborer is sweet,
whether they eat little or much,
but as for the rich, their abundance
permits them no sleep.[h]

13 I have seen a grievous evil under the sun:[i]

wealth hoarded to the harm of its owners,
14 or wealth lost through some misfortune,
so that when they have children
there is nothing left for them to inherit.
15 Everyone comes naked from their mother's womb,
and as everyone comes, so they depart.[j]
They take nothing from their toil[k]
that they can carry in their hands.[l]

16 This too is a grievous evil:

As everyone comes, so they depart,
and what do they gain,
since they toil for the wind?[m]
17 All their days they eat in darkness,
with great frustration, affliction and anger.

18 This is what I have observed to be good: that it is appropriate for a person to eat, to drink[n] and
to find satisfaction in their toilsome labor[o] under the sun during the few days of life God has given
them — for this is their lot. 19 Moreover, when God gives someone wealth and possessions,[p] and the ability to enjoy them,[q] to accept their lot[r] and be happy in their toil — this is a gift of God.[s] 20 They seldom
reflect on the days of their life, because God keeps them occupied with gladness of heart.[t]

6 I have seen another evil under the sun, and it weighs heavily on mankind: 2 God gives some people
wealth, possessions and honor, so that they lack nothing their hearts desire, but God does not grant
them the ability to enjoy them,[u] and strangers enjoy them instead. This is meaningless, a grievous evil.[v]
3 A man may have a hundred children and live many years; yet no matter how long he lives, if he
cannot enjoy his prosperity and does not receive proper burial, I say that a stillborn[w] child is better off
than he.[x] 4 It comes without meaning, it departs in darkness, and in darkness its name is shrouded.
5 Though it never saw the sun or knew anything, it has more rest than does that man — 6 even if he lives
a thousand years twice over but fails to enjoy his prosperity. Do not all go to the same place?

7 Everyone's toil is for their mouth,
yet their appetite is never satisfied.[y]

5:12 [h] Job 20:20
5:13 [i] Ecc 6:1-2
5:15 [j] Job 1:21 [k] Ps 49:17; 1Ti 6:7 [l] Ecc 1:3
5:16 [m] Pr 11:29; Ecc 1:3
5:18 [n] Ecc 2:3 [o] Ecc 2:10,24
5:19 [p] 1Ch 29:12; 2Ch 1:12 [q] Ecc 6:2 [r] Job 31:2 [s] Ecc 2:24; 3:13
5:20 [t] Dt 12:7,18
6:2 [u] Ps 17:14; Ecc 5:19 [v] Ecc 5:13
6:3 [w] Job 3:16; Ecc 4:3 [x] Job 3:3
6:7 [y] Pr 16:26; 27:20

lead to all sorts of evil. Here the Teacher's point is that wealth is inadequate as a basis for finding meaning in life.
5:12 Excessive concern with amassing wealth causes anxiety.
5:15 Birth and death teach us that wealth cannot be the meaning of life. See Luke 12:13–21; 1 Tim 6:7.
5:18–20 This is the fourth joy passage (see note on 2:24–26). The contrast with vv. 16–17 is remarkable: in v. 17, "they eat in darkness, with great frustration, affliction and anger," but in v. 18 what is good is "to eat, to drink and to find satisfaction." Wealth and possessions, a source of such trouble in the previous section, are a gift to enjoy. The reference to God's giving, a central motif in Ecclesiastes, occurs three times in this section. The tension with the previous section is palpable, and the Teacher deliberately sets these different perspectives against each other.
6:1–12 After the joy passage in 5:18–20, the Teacher plunges back into despair. As throughout Ecclesiastes, the challenge is to know how to relate the passages expressing despair to those expressing hope and joy. Whereas labor and wealth are a gift in 5:18–20, here God gives some people wealth but does not give them the ability to enjoy it (vv. 1–2). The mood darkens as the Teacher asserts that if a person can't enjoy his wealth, it is better for him to have been stillborn (vv. 3–6).
6:3 does not receive proper burial. Dies unlamented or dishonored, like King Jehoiakim (Jer 22:18–19). **stillborn child.** If life is meaningless and "all go to the same place" at death (v. 6; 3:20), then the shortest route to such extinction is being stillborn (cf. Job 3:16; Ps 58:8). The Teacher poses the destiny of everyone as a question, a question based on observation.
6:7 Cf. 1:7.

6:8 [z] Ecc 2:15
6:9 [a] Ecc 1:14
6:12 [b] Job 10:20 [c] Job 14:2; Ps 39:6; Jas 4:14
7:1 [d] Pr 22:1; SS 1:3
7:2 [e] Pr 11:19 [f] Ps 90:12
7:3 [g] Pr 14:13
7:4 [h] Ecc 2:1; Jer 16:8
7:5 [i] Ps 141:5; Pr 13:18; 15:31-32
7:6 [j] Ps 58:9; 118:12 [k] Ecc 2:2
7:7 [l] Ex 18:21; 23:8; Dt 16:19
7:8 [m] Pr 14:29; Gal 5:22; Eph 4:2
7:9 [n] Mt 5:22; Pr 14:17; Jas 1:19

8 What advantage have the wise over fools?[z]
What do the poor gain
by knowing how to conduct themselves before others?
9 Better what the eye sees
than the roving of the appetite.
This too is meaningless,
a chasing after the wind.[a]
10 Whatever exists has already been named,
and what humanity is has been known;
no one can contend
with someone who is stronger.
11 The more the words,
the less the meaning,
and how does that profit anyone?

12 For who knows what is good for a person in life, during the few and meaningless days[b] they pass
through like a shadow?[c] Who can tell them what will happen under the sun after they are gone?

Wisdom

7 A good name is better than fine perfume,[d]
and the day of death better than the day of birth.
2 It is better to go to a house of mourning
than to go to a house of feasting,
for death[e] is the destiny[f] of everyone;
the living should take this to heart.
3 Frustration is better than laughter,[g]
because a sad face is good for the heart.
4 The heart of the wise is in the house of mourning,
but the heart of fools is in the house of pleasure.[h]
5 It is better to heed the rebuke[i] of a wise person
than to listen to the song of fools.
6 Like the crackling of thorns[j] under the pot,
so is the laughter[k] of fools.
This too is meaningless.

7 Extortion turns a wise person into a fool,
and a bribe[l] corrupts the heart.
8 The end of a matter is better than its beginning,
and patience[m] is better than pride.
9 Do not be quickly provoked[n] in your spirit,
for anger resides in the lap of fools.

6:8 From this perspective wisdom has no advantage over folly. Cf. Prov 1:1–6.
6:10 The Teacher revisits the theme that there is nothing new in life (1:9–10).
6:11 Ironically, the Teacher speaks many words in the quest for wisdom, but the more he says, the more elusive wisdom becomes. Cf. 5:7.
6:12 Central motifs in the book are "who knows?" and "what is good" (contrast 5:18).
7:1—8:1 *Wisdom.* The Teacher explores traditional wisdom and then reflects (7:23–29) on where he has come in his quest for meaning in life (see Introduction: Particular Challenges).
7:1–13 This section contains a list of proverbs as the Teacher attempts to answer the question in 6:12: "who knows what is good for a person in life . . . ?" This quest also leads to meaninglessness (vv. 6b,13).
7:1 The first half of this verse sounds like Prov 22:1, but the second half is a statement of despair that parallels death with a good name and birth with perfume (cf. 6:3–6).
7:2 better . . . than. This form is common in Proverbs (see note on 9:16), but here a funeral is better than a feast because it is important to remember that all die.
7:3 Frustration. In 5:17, frustration is a bad thing, but here, ironically, it is better than laughter.
7:5–6 See Prov 17:10 for a similar view. But lest we think the Teacher is affirming proverbial type wisdom, note the last line of v. 6.
7:7 Even the wise are corruptible. And if a wise person is corruptible, then their rebuke might be worthless (v. 5).
7:8–9 This advice sounds like Prov 14:29, but the same Hebrew word translated "anger" in v. 9 is translated "frustration" in v. 3.

[10]Do not say, "Why were the old days better than these?"
For it is not wise to ask such questions.

[11]Wisdom, like an inheritance, is a good thing[o]
and benefits those who see the sun.[p]
[12]Wisdom is a shelter
as money is a shelter,
but the advantage of knowledge is this:
Wisdom preserves those who have it.

[13]Consider what God has done:[q]

Who can straighten
what he has made crooked?[r]
[14]When times are good, be happy;
but when times are bad, consider this:
God has made the one
as well as the other.
Therefore, no one can discover
anything about their future.

[15]In this meaningless life[s] of mine I have seen both of these:

the righteous perishing in their righteousness,
and the wicked living long in their wickedness.[t]
[16]Do not be overrighteous,
neither be overwise —
why destroy yourself?
[17]Do not be overwicked,
and do not be a fool —
why die before your time?[u]
[18]It is good to grasp the one
and not let go of the other.
Whoever fears God[v] will avoid all extremes.[a]

[19]Wisdom[w] makes one wise person more powerful[x]
than ten rulers in a city.

7:11 [o]Pr 8:10-11; Ecc 2:13 [p]Ecc 11:7
7:13 [q]Ecc 2:24 [r]Ecc 1:15
7:15 [s]Job 7:7 [t]Ecc 8:12-14; Jer 12:1
7:17 [u]Job 15:32; Ps 55:23
7:18 [v]Ecc 3:14
7:19 [w]Ecc 2:13 [x]Ecc 9:13-18

[a] *18* Or *will follow them both*

7:10 Why were the old days better ...? The Teacher does not explain why this is an unwise question, but it makes sense in the light of the view that history endlessly repeats itself (cf. 1:4–11; 6:10).
7:11 like an inheritance. Could be translated "with an inheritance." If the latter translation is correct, then the point is that wisdom is beneficial only if it provides wealth. Such a reading might fit better with v. 12. **see the sun.** Are alive.
7:13 Cf. 1:15. This verse can be read in more than one way. It could imply that the Teacher holds God responsible for the world's brokenness. Nothing can be done about it. Alternatively, the focus could be on the fact that the world is broken and no matter how hard we try, we cannot fix it.
7:14–22 The Teacher articulates a determinist view of life: good times and bad times come from God, and since we cannot control them, the only response is to be neither overly wise nor overly wicked!
7:14 God ... other. The Teacher holds God responsible for difficult times in the world. **their future.** People cannot know whether it will be good or bad.
7:15 have seen. Cf. v. 27. The Teacher's argument is based on what he has observed. In the OT, "righteous" and "wicked" can refer to opposing lifestyles but can also refer to being in the right legally and in the wrong legally. As in 8:14, the Teacher may have legal injustice in mind here. Observation is a core element in his method, and this verse alerts us to its inadequacy in dealing with the great issues he is exploring. Attempts to gain wisdom that ignore God's revelation always lead to confusion (see Introduction: Particular Challenges; Occasion and Purpose). Proverbs is well aware of such paradoxes (e.g., Prov 11:24 and note), but for the Teacher, in the grip of his autonomous approach to knowing, they mean that it is folly to seek to be wise.
7:16–18 If the righteous perish in their righteousness (v. 15), then it is hard to *see* the advantage in pursuing righteousness. Verse 16 is interpreted in different ways. Some see it as a positive answer to the problem of vv. 14–15, recommending moderation. Alternatively, the Teacher is pursuing his logic based on observation alone. If so, this is a view contrary to Proverbs and the rest of the Bible, which encourages us to hunger and thirst after righteousness (Matt 5:6) and to avoid wickedness. As so often in Ecclesiastes, we see what happens if we depend entirely on our own insights apart from God and his revelation.
7:18 fears God. The Teacher, perhaps ironically, declares that such moderation is a sign of fearing God. If he is being ironic, this is a different view than that found in 5:7; 12:13.
7:19–20 Verse 19 sounds just like Proverbs, but see v. 16: "neither be overwise." Verse 20 is the one verse of the book that the NT may quote

7:20 [y] Ps 14:3 [z] 1Ki 8:46; 2Ch 6:36; Pr 20:9; Ro 3:23
7:21 [a] Pr 30:10
7:23 [b] Ecc 1:17; Ro 1:22
7:24 [c] Job 28:12
7:25 [d] Job 28:3 [e] Ecc 1:17
7:26 [f] Ex 10:7; Jdg 14:15 [g] Pr 2:16-19; 5:3-5; 7:23; 22:14
7:27 [h] Ecc 1:1
7:28 [i] 1Ki 11:3

20 Indeed, there is no one on earth who is righteous,[y]
no one who does what is right and never sins.[z]
21 Do not pay attention to every word people say,
or you[a] may hear your servant cursing you —
22 for you know in your heart
that many times you yourself have cursed others.

23 All this I tested by wisdom and I said,

"I am determined to be wise"[b] —
but this was beyond me.
24 Whatever exists is far off and most profound —
who can discover it?[c]
25 So I turned my mind to understand,
to investigate and to search out wisdom and the scheme of things[d]
and to understand the stupidity of wickedness
and the madness of folly.[e]

26 I find more bitter than death
the woman who is a snare,[f]
whose heart is a trap
and whose hands are chains.
The man who pleases God will escape her,
but the sinner she will ensnare.[g]

27 "Look," says the Teacher,[a][h] "this is what I have discovered:

"Adding one thing to another to discover the scheme of things —
28 while I was still searching
but not finding —
I found one upright man among a thousand,
but not one upright woman[i] among them all.
29 This only have I found:
God created mankind upright,
but they have gone in search of many schemes."

8

Who is like the wise?
Who knows the explanation of things?
A person's wisdom brightens their face
and changes its hard appearance.

[a] *27* Or *the leader of the assembly*

(Rom 3:10). It expresses a profound insight, but in context it subverts v. 19. If wisdom and righteousness go together, as they do in Proverbs (e.g., Prov 10:31), then no matter how powerful wisdom is (v. 19), it is never fully achieved because no one is righteous.

7:21–22 The Teacher cautions against listening because one may hear destructive content.

7:23–29 The Teacher reflects on his journey and the inaccessibility of wisdom. Like 5:1–7, this passage is a milestone on the Teacher's journey. As in 1:13; 2:3,9, he presents his quest as one conducted by "wisdom." But his quest has led him instead to folly, and this raises profound questions about the wisdom of his method. The reader is compelled to ask how the Teacher's "wisdom" got him into this position.

7:23 wisdom. The previous section shows the potential dangers in the Teacher's quest. He continues to refer to his method of investigation as "wisdom," but it is becoming apparent that this "wisdom" is very different from that which Proverbs calls wisdom. **beyond me.** He has been unable to find what he has been looking for: wisdom and meaning in life.

7:25 A summary description of the Teacher's quest.

7:26 This verse appears to presuppose Prov 1–9 with its evocative images of Lady Folly and Lady Wisdom. **bitter.** Used for Lady Folly in Prov 5:4. Ironically, rather than leading the Teacher to Lady Wisdom, his quest has led him into the arms of Lady Folly! **the sinner.** By implication the Teacher here recognizes himself as a sinner. His sin has led him into the arms of Lady Folly.

7:28 The verse is hard to understand. But if the Teacher has Prov 1–9 in mind, it is possible that the one upright woman he cannot find is Lady Wisdom.

7:29 A profound insight: the problem is not that God has made the world crooked (cf. 1:15; 7:13) but that humans have sinned.

8:1 This expresses the typical OT wisdom perspective that the wise person knows how to interpret a word, thing, or event. **brightens their face.** The infusion of God's grace. In the OT, God causes his face to shine on his people and wisdom, as a gift from God, has this effect (cf. Num 6:25; Ps 31:16).

Obey the King

[2]Obey the king's command, I say, because you took an oath before God. [3]Do not be in a hurry to leave the king's presence.[j] Do not stand up for a bad cause, for he will do whatever he pleases. [4]Since a king's word is supreme, who can say to him, "What are you doing?[k]"

[5]Whoever obeys his command will come to no harm,
and the wise heart will know the proper time and procedure.
[6]For there is a proper time and procedure for every matter,[l]
though a person may be weighed down by misery.

[7]Since no one knows the future,
who can tell someone else what is to come?
[8]As no one has power over the wind to contain it,
so[a] no one has power over the time of their death.
As no one is discharged in time of war,
so wickedness will not release those who practice it.

[9]All this I saw, as I applied my mind to everything done under the sun. There is a time when a man lords it over others to his own[b] hurt. [10]Then too, I saw the wicked buried[m] — those who used to come and go from the holy place and receive praise[c] in the city where they did this. This too is meaningless.

[11]When the sentence for a crime is not quickly carried out, people's hearts are filled with schemes to do wrong. [12]Although a wicked person who commits a hundred crimes may live a long time, I know that it will go better[n] with those who fear God,[o] who are reverent before him.[p] [13]Yet because the wicked do not fear God,[q] it will not go well with them, and their days[r] will not lengthen like a shadow.

[14]There is something else meaningless that occurs on earth: the righteous who get what the wicked deserve, and the wicked who get what the righteous deserve.[s] This too, I say, is meaningless.[t] [15]So I commend the enjoyment of life[u], because there is nothing better for a person under the sun than to eat and drink[v] and be glad.[w] Then joy will accompany them in their toil all the days of the life God has given them under the sun.

[16]When I applied my mind to know wisdom[x] and to observe the labor that is done on earth[y] — people getting no sleep day or night — [17]then I saw all that God has done.[z] No one can comprehend what goes on under the sun. Despite all their efforts to search it out, no one can discover its meaning. Even if the wise claim they know, they cannot really comprehend it.[a]

[a] 8 Or *over the human spirit to retain it, / and so* [b] 9 Or *to their* [c] 10 Some Hebrew manuscripts and Septuagint (Aquila); most Hebrew manuscripts *and are forgotten*

8:3 [j] Ecc 10:4
8:4 [k] Job 9:12; Est 1:19; Da 4:35
8:6 [l] Ecc 3:1
8:10 [m] Ecc 1:11
8:12 [n] Dt 12:28; Ps 37:11,18-19; Pr 1:32-33; Isa 3:10-11 [o] Ex 1:20 [p] Ecc 3:14
8:13 [q] Ecc 3:14; Isa 3:11 [r] Dt 4:40; Job 5:26; Ps 34:12; Isa 65:20
8:14 [s] Job 21:7; Ps 73:14; Mal 3:15 [t] Ecc 7:15
8:15 [u] Ps 42:8 [v] Ex 32:6; Ecc 2:3 [w] Ecc 2:24; 3:12-13; 5:18; 9:7
8:16 [x] Ecc 1:17 [y] Ecc 1:13
8:17 [z] Job 28:3 [a] Job 5:9; 28:23; Ecc 3:11; Ro 11:33

8:2–17 *Obey the King.* Kings in the ancient world exercised near absolute power, and in this section the Teacher wrestles with how to behave in the service of a king. Some see 8:2–8 as advice on how to cope with such absolute authority in a fallen world. Alternatively, one can see here a recurrence of the Teacher's despair. One might expect after the Teacher's penetrating insights into his quest in the previous section that he would now move forward. Alas, in this section he lapses back into his despairing mode (see his conclusion in 8:10) as he reflects upon government once again. Such lapses are characteristic of this sort of existential journey in which so much is at stake.
8:2 because you took an oath before God. Could be translated "as in the manner of an oath to God." The authority of the king in the ancient world was such that it was hard to contradict him. The temptation was thus to practice absolute obedience to the king. What is missing is a sense that the king too was subject to wisdom and God's rule (cf. Prov 8:15–16).
8:3 a bad cause. Probably a bad idea, a plan that the king dislikes.
8:5,6 proper time. See 3:1–8.
8:7–8 The Teacher reverts to his earlier themes of (1) an unknown and uncontrollable future, (2) death, and (3) the impossibility of escaping from wickedness.
8:8 war. May be literal or a metaphor for the sort of struggle the Teacher is engaged in. **wickedness.** Cf. 7:20.
8:10–17 The Teacher, who previously reflected on injustice and oppression, contemplates the problem of delayed judgment: it encourages evil.
8:10 People praise the wicked and give them a proper burial despite their hypocritical religion.
8:12–13 Here the Teacher expresses the typical wisdom character-consequence view. He does not give evidence contrary to his observation, but he confesses that it is better to fear God.
8:14 This is a problem that Job struggled with repeatedly (e.g., Job 21; cf. Ps 73). The NT provides a final explanation with the end of history, the resurrection of the dead, and the final judgment at the second coming of Christ. In this verse the Teacher finds the injustice he observes meaningless. He lapses again into despair (see 3:16).
8:15 The fifth joy passage (see note on 2:24–26) starkly juxtaposes with the Teacher's conclusion in v. 14.
8:16–17 In this section the Teacher returns to the theme of the limits of human knowledge (cf. 3:11). Some see this as a positive admission of humility and of humankind's creatureliness. Certainly we cannot figure out the meaning of life without God's help. Alternatively, the Teacher here despairs again because of the limits of being human. Whereas toil is joyful in v. 15, here it is a burden. Whereas in v. 15 the Teacher knows what is good, here he argues that life is incomprehensible.

9:1 [b]Dt 33:3; Job 12:10; Ecc 10:14
9:2 [c]Job 9:22; Ecc 2:14; 6:6; 7:2
9:3 [d]Job 9:22; Ecc 2:14 [e]Jer 11:8; 13:10; 16:12; 17:9 [f]Job 21:26
9:5 [g]Job 14:21 [h]Ps 9:6 [i]Ecc 1:11; 2:16; Isa 26:14
9:6 [j]Job 21:21
9:7 [k]Nu 6:20 [l]Ecc 2:24; 8:15
9:8 [m]Ps 23:5; Rev 3:4
9:9 [n]Pr 5:18 [o]Job 31:2
9:10 [p]1Sa 10:7 [q]Ecc 11:6; Ro 12:11; Col 3:23 [r]Nu 16:33 [s]Ecc 2:24

A Common Destiny for All

9 So I reflected on all this and concluded that the righteous and the wise and what they do are in
God's hands, but no one knows whether love or hate awaits them.[b] 2All share a common destiny — the righteous and the wicked, the good and the bad,[a] the clean and the unclean, those who
offer sacrifices and those who do not.

As it is with the good,
so with the sinful;
as it is with those who take oaths,
so with those who are afraid to take them.[c]

3This is the evil in everything that happens under the sun: The same destiny overtakes all.[d] The
hearts of people, moreover, are full of evil and there is madness in their hearts while they live,[e] and
afterward they join the dead.[f] 4Anyone who is among the living has hope[b] — even a live dog is better
off than a dead lion!

5For the living know that they will die,
but the dead know nothing;[g]
they have no further reward,
and even their name[h] is forgotten.[i]
6Their love, their hate
and their jealousy have long since vanished;
never again will they have a part
in anything that happens under the sun.[j]

7Go, eat your food with gladness, and drink your wine[k] with a joyful heart,[l] for God has already
approved what you do. 8Always be clothed in white,[m] and always anoint your head with oil. 9Enjoy life
with your wife,[n] whom you love, all the days of this meaningless life that God has given you under the
sun — all your meaningless days. For this is your lot[o] in life and in your toilsome labor under the sun.
10Whatever[p] your hand finds to do, do it with all your might,[q] for in the realm of the dead,[r] where you
are going, there is neither working nor planning nor knowledge nor wisdom.[s]

[a] 2 Septuagint (Aquila), Vulgate and Syriac; Hebrew does not have *and the bad.* [b] 4 Or *What then is to be chosen? With all who live, there is hope*

9:1–12 *A Common Destiny for All.* This section is an anguished reflection on death as the destiny of all (vv. 1–6) that contains another joy passage (vv. 7–10). The joy passage can either be seen as an answer to the certainty of death or be set next to it to contrast the Teacher's faith; what he believes in contrast with what he observes. This section concludes with a despairing reflection on time and chance (vv. 11–12).

9:1 all this. Includes both his past reflections and this present one. **in God's hands ... whether love or hate.** The Teacher recognizes God's sovereignty but despairs of knowing whether this will guarantee pain or pleasure in this life. He lacks any assurance that goodness and justice will ultimately triumph.

9:2 common destiny. Death (cf. v. 3; 3:20). Some suggest that the Teacher here refers only to physical death, but vv. 5–6 suggest that he means more than that. As far as he can observe, death is the end. The Teacher repeatedly returns to the theme of death (see 2:14; 3:2; 5:16; 9:10; 12:7). **the righteous and the wicked, the good and the bad, the clean and the unclean, those who offer sacrifices and those who do not.** Fundamental distinctions in Proverbs and OT law (on "the clean and the unclean" and offering sacrifices, see Introduction to Leviticus: Major Theological Themes [Holiness and Purity; Offerings, Sacrifices, and Atonement]). For the Teacher, death obliterates the importance of these distinctions. **take oaths.** Here, whether one takes an oath or not, death is one's destiny. Cf. 5:1–7, where the Teacher urges care in oath taking.

9:3 hearts of people ... full of evil. Cf. Gen 6:5.

9:4–5 live dog ... dead lion ... know that they will die ... know nothing. Dogs were not highly prized in Israelite culture, so v. 4 appears to say that being alive is better than being dead, but v. 5 questions this because the living know they will die. Thus, the "hope" of being alive is dashed. Alternatively, v. 4 could indicate that the advantage of being alive is that one has "hope" and can change before one dies.

9:7–10 This is the sixth joy passage in the book (see note on 2:24–26).

9:8 clothed in white ... anoint your head with oil. Expressions of celebration and gladness (cf. Ps 45:7). Wearing white and anointing the head with oil was like dressing up for a party.

9:9 meaningless life ... meaningless days. Some see the meaningless passages as always in the background of the joy passages because they provide the Teacher's response to his despair. Alternatively, if the joy passages are set in contrast to the despair conclusions, not as an answer but as an alternative perspective, then here we see the tension between the two perspectives heading toward a climax. For the first time the Teacher's language of despair enters into the joy passage, indicating that the tension of holding the two perspectives (despair and joy) is becoming unsustainable.

9:10 Cf. Col 3:23, but note the element of despair creeping in here. **realm of the dead.** The Teacher sees it here as a decidedly negative place to which all go. It is not his final word on the matter (12:7).

11 I have seen something else under the sun:

The race is not to the swift
or the battle to the strong,[t]
nor does food come to the wise[u]
or wealth to the brilliant
or favor to the learned;
but time and chance[v] happen to them all.[w]

12 Moreover, no one knows when their hour will come:

As fish are caught in a cruel net,
or birds are taken in a snare,
so people are trapped by evil times[x]
that fall unexpectedly upon them.[y]

Wisdom Better Than Folly

13 I also saw under the sun this example of wisdom[z] that greatly impressed me: 14 There was once
a small city with only a few people in it. And a powerful king came against it, surrounded it and built
huge siege works against it. 15 Now there lived in that city a man poor but wise, and he saved the city
by his wisdom. But nobody remembered that poor man.[a] 16 So I said, "Wisdom is better than strength."
But the poor man's wisdom is despised, and his words are no longer heeded.[b]

17 The quiet words of the wise are more to be heeded
than the shouts of a ruler of fools.
18 Wisdom[c] is better than weapons of war,
but one sinner destroys much good.

10 As dead flies give perfume a bad smell,
so a little folly[d] outweighs wisdom and honor.
2 The heart of the wise inclines to the right,
but the heart of the fool to the left.
3 Even as fools walk along the road,
they lack sense
and show everyone[e] how stupid they are.
4 If a ruler's anger rises against you,
do not leave your post;[f]
calmness can lay great offenses to rest.[g]

5 There is an evil I have seen under the sun,
the sort of error that arises from a ruler:
6 Fools are put in many high positions,[h]
while the rich occupy the low ones.

9:11 [t] Am 2:14-15 [u] Job 32:13; Isa 47:10; Jer 9:23 [v] Ecc 2:14 [w] Dt 8:18
9:12 [x] Pr 29:6 [y] Ps 73:22; Ecc 2:14; 8:7
9:13 [z] 2Sa 20:22
9:15 [a] Ge 40:14; Ecc 1:11; 2:16; 4:13
9:16 [b] Pr 21:22; Ecc 7:19
9:18 [c] ver 16
10:1 [d] Pr 13:16; 18:2
10:3 [e] Pr 13:16; 18:2
10:4 [f] Ecc 8:3 [g] Pr 16:14; 25:15
10:6 [h] Pr 29:2

9:11 Using five images (athletics, war, food, wealth, favor), the Teacher denies the character-consequence theme: "time and chance happen to ... all."
9:12 hour. A time of evil and disaster. Cf. Eph 6:13.
9:13—10:20 *Wisdom Better Than Folly.* Through various examples and proverbs, the Teacher explores whether or not wisdom is better than folly.
9:13–18 As so often with the Teacher, he tells a story that seems to support wisdom and then subverts it. The poor wise man saves the city by his wisdom, but then no one remembers him or his teachings.
9:15 remembered. Remembrance is an important theme in the book (see note on 1:11).
9:16 better than. A common proverbial form (e.g., 4:6,13; Prov 8:19; 12:9; 15:16,17; 16:16,19,32; 17:1,12; 19:1; 21:9; 25:24; 27:10).
9:17–18 Wisdom appears very valuable, but the end of v. 18 undermines this: one sinner can destroy the good arising from wisdom.
10:1–20 Verses 4–5,16–20 deal with the king and government. The Teacher begins with traditional wisdom but then problematizes it, as he so often has done before.
10:1 dead. Could mean poisonous. **a little folly outweighs.** The "perfume" example illustrates that folly is more powerful than wisdom.
10:2–3 These verses express traditional wisdom, but v. 1 observes that a small amount of folly outweighs wisdom. No matter how valuable wisdom is, a little folly can destroy it. It takes only one fly!
10:2 The directions of people's hearts are antithetical. **right.** May signify here what is good. **left.** May signify what is bad (cf. Matt 25:31–46).
10:6–7 Cf. Prov 30:21–23. The world is turned upside down.
10:6 Fools ... the rich. The Teacher sets fools not against the wise but

10:7 [i] Pr 19:10
10:8 [j] Ps 7:15; 57:6; Pr 26:27 [k] Est 2:23; Ps 9:16; Am 5:19
10:9 [l] Pr 26:27
10:11 [m] Ps 58:5; Isa 3:3
10:12 [n] Pr 10:32 [o] Pr 10:14; 14:3; 15:2; 18:7
10:14 [p] Pr 15:2; Ecc 5:3; 6:12; 8:7 [q] Ecc 9:1
10:16 [r] Isa 3:4-5,12
10:17 [s] Dt 14:26; 1Sa 25:36; Pr 31:4
10:18 [t] Pr 20:4; 24:30-34
10:19 [u] Ge 14:18; Jdg 9:13
10:20 [v] Ex 22:28

7 I have seen slaves on horseback,
while princes go on foot like slaves.[i]

8 Whoever digs a pit may fall into it;[j]
whoever breaks through a wall may be bitten by a snake.[k]
9 Whoever quarries stones may be injured by them;
whoever splits logs may be endangered by them.[l]

10 If the ax is dull
and its edge unsharpened,
more strength is needed,
but skill will bring success.

11 If a snake bites before it is charmed,
the charmer receives no fee.[m]

12 Words from the mouth of the wise are gracious,[n]
but fools are consumed by their own lips.[o]
13 At the beginning their words are folly;
at the end they are wicked madness—
14 and fools multiply words.[p]

No one knows what is coming—
who can tell someone else what will happen after them?[q]

15 The toil of fools wearies them;
they do not know the way to town.

16 Woe to the land whose king was a servant[a][r]
and whose princes feast in the morning.
17 Blessed is the land whose king is of noble birth
and whose princes eat at a proper time—
for strength and not for drunkenness.[s]

18 Through laziness, the rafters sag;
because of idle hands, the house leaks.[t]

19 A feast is made for laughter,
wine[u] makes life merry,
and money is the answer for everything.

20 Do not revile the king[v] even in your thoughts,
or curse the rich in your bedroom,

[a] *16* Or *king is a child*

against the rich. See v. 19: "money is the answer for everything." The Teacher is expressing a view that values wealth above all else (cf. 7:11).
10:7 I have seen. What the Teacher has observed appears to render life absurd.
10:8 digs a pit ... breaks through a wall. These could refer to accidental events and thus the randomness of life. Alternatively, they could be metaphors for evildoing. If "will" is the correct translation rather than "may" (as in Prov 26:27), then this expresses the character-consequence theme of traditional wisdom: evildoing will have bad consequences. From this perspective, fools destroy themselves by their own folly.
10:9 This refers to accidental negative consequences, either extending the thought of v. 8 or problematizing it, since not only fools suffer bad consequences.
10:10–11 Verse 10 appears to express the advantage of wisdom: persistence brings success. But the accidental dangers attending log splitting (v. 9) and the snake biting the snake charmer (v. 11) raise questions about traditional wisdom.
10:13–14 This portrays folly negatively (but see v. 1). **the end ... what is coming.** The end of folly may be "wicked madness," but no one knows what the final end will be.
10:16–17 Woe ... Blessed. The contrast expresses what is at stake in good leadership. These verses approximate traditional wisdom, but the Teacher's insistence that the king should be a "noble" harks back to the Teacher's false opposition between folly and wealth in v. 6. Cf. 9:13–15, where the good leader is poor but wise.
10:18 Sloth has bad consequences, which expresses traditional wisdom (cf. Prov 6:6–11; 10:26; 13:4; 15:19).
10:19 money is the answer for everything. If v. 18 sounds like Proverbs, then v. 19 gives the game away. The answer is not wisdom but wealth!
10:20 If money answers everything (v. 19), then at all costs one must

because a bird in the sky may carry your words,
and a bird on the wing may report what you say.

Invest in Many Ventures

11 Ship[w] your grain across the sea;
after many days you may receive a return.[x]
2 Invest in seven ventures, yes, in eight;
you do not know what disaster may come upon the land.

3 If clouds are full of water,
they pour rain on the earth.
Whether a tree falls to the south or to the north,
in the place where it falls, there it will lie.
4 Whoever watches the wind will not plant;
whoever looks at the clouds will not reap.

5 As you do not know the path of the wind,[y]
or how the body is formed[a] in a mother's womb,[z]
so you cannot understand the work of God,
the Maker of all things.

6 Sow your seed in the morning,
and at evening let your hands not be idle,[a]
for you do not know which will succeed,
whether this or that,
or whether both will do equally well.

Remember Your Creator While Young

7 Light is sweet,
and it pleases the eyes to see the sun.[b]
8 However many years anyone may live,
let them enjoy them all.
But let them remember[c] the days of darkness,
for there will be many.
Everything to come is meaningless.

9 You who are young, be happy while you are young,
and let your heart give you joy in the days of your youth.

11:1 [w]ver 6; Isa 32:20; Hos 10:12 [x]Dt 24:19; Pr 19:17; Mt 10:42
11:5 [y]Jn 3:8-10 [z]Ps 139:14-16
11:6 [a]Ecc 9:10
11:7 [b]Ecc 7:11
11:8 [c]Ecc 12:1

[a] 5 Or *know how life* (or *the spirit*) / *enters the body being formed*

remain in favor with the elite. Nothing must be allowed to upset being in favor with the king.

11:1–6 *Invest in Many Ventures.* In the face of the challenges of life, the Teacher explores the advantage of proactive behavior.

11:1 Ship your grain across the sea. Or "Release your bread upon the waters." There is no agreement about how to read this instruction. Three interpretations of it have been suggested: (1) in older Jewish and Christian interpretation, it is thought to express generosity, in which case finding it again means receiving generosity in return; (2) it refers to maritime trade and encourages one to be adventurous in this respect (cf. Prov 11:24), perhaps spreading one's investments in multiple directions; (3) it refers to a senseless act since the bread dissolves and no one know what happens after that.

11:2 Invest in seven ventures, yes, in eight. Investment or generosity may be in view here, but the motivation is the uncertainty of the future (cf. 9:12).

11:5 The wonderful mysteries of life evoke in the Teacher a sense that one cannot understand God's ways.

11:6 In the context of the unknown, the Teacher recommends hard and diverse work since one does not know which venture will succeed.

11:7—12:8 *Remember Your Creator While Young.* In this section the teacher moves toward resolution of his struggle. The key is found in rejoicing and remembering.

11:7—12:7 This is the seventh and last joy passage in the book (see note on 2:24–26).

11:7 A sign that resolution of his struggle is at hand. Up until now, life "under the sun" has been largely negative, but now the sun is a source of joy.

11:8 An exhortation to rejoice. Cf. Phil 4:4. **remember.** A major theme of the book (see 1:11). The resolution of the Teacher's struggle does not deny the brokenness in the world he has observed, but it places the problem in a larger context. **meaningless.** This does not mean that there is no meaning but that humans cannot grasp it by themselves (see Introduction: Particular Challenges).

11:9 for all these things God will bring you into judgment. Cf. 12:14. This verse can refer to the fact either that God will hold young people

11:9 [d] Job 19:29; Ecc 2:24; 3:17; 12:14; Ro 14:10
11:10 [e] Ps 94:19 [f] Ecc 2:24
12:1 [g] Ecc 11:8 [h] 2Sa 19:35
12:4 [i] Jer 25:10

Follow the ways of your heart
and whatever your eyes see,
but know that for all these things
God will bring you into judgment.[d]
10 So then, banish anxiety[e] from your heart
and cast off the troubles of your body,
for youth and vigor are meaningless.[f]

12

Remember[g] your Creator
in the days of your youth,
before the days of trouble[h] come
and the years approach when you will say,
"I find no pleasure in them"—
2 before the sun and the light
and the moon and the stars grow dark,
and the clouds return after the rain;
3 when the keepers of the house tremble,
and the strong men stoop,
when the grinders cease because they are few,
and those looking through the windows grow dim;
4 when the doors to the street are closed
and the sound of grinding fades;
when people rise up at the sound of birds,
but all their songs grow faint;[i]
5 when people are afraid of heights
and of dangers in the streets;
when the almond tree blossoms
and the grasshopper drags itself along
and desire no longer is stirred.

accountable for doing what they like or that God will hold them accountable for living life joyfully and to the full. Either way God will judge people for how they live. Real enjoyment of life is found only within the bounds God sets.

11:10 meaningless. See note on v. 8.

12:1–7 Resolution of the Teacher's struggles does not come by avoiding the challenges of life in a fallen world; however, by remembering one's Creator one can live with the contradictions without having to solve all of them. Three main ways of reading 12:1–7 have been suggested: (1) The allegorical approach takes the Teacher to be describing a house or village, while the objects and activities represent the challenges of old age. "Before" would then relate back to youth in v. 1, i.e., before one grows old. (2) A literal reading finds here a description of death and dying, albeit with many metaphors. (3) A symbolic reading sees something larger being described through a portrayal of death. This third view sees the images as similar to the language the prophets use of the "day of the LORD" (Isa 13:6; cf. Isa 5:30; 13:10; Jer 25:10–11; Amos 8:9; see note on Amos 2:16). From this perspective, God's final judgment is coming, and one must prepare for it.

12:1 Remember your Creator. The Teacher's method of investigation, which has gotten him into such trouble, has been based on his reason, experience, and observation—the reverse of Proverb's recommendation to begin with the "fear of the LORD" (Prov 1:7). Resolution to his struggle comes not by starting with himself but by remembering his Creator. **Remember.** Far more than simply not forgetting; it is letting the fact that God is the Creator and you are a creature shape your whole view of life (cf. 1:11). **your youth.** As in Proverbs, which often addresses the reader as "my son" (e.g., Prov 1:8,10,15; 2:1; 3:1), this reference is to the formative stages of one's life before the struggles come.

12:2 the sun and the light. The distinction between them appears in Gen 1, and if this section is read symbolically (see note on vv. 1–7), a cosmic catastrophe may be in view. **grow dark.** If this section is read allegorically or literally (see note on vv. 1–7), this refers to the problems of aging and heading toward death. **clouds return after the rain.** Even more rain follows rain, perhaps symbolizing judgment (cf. Gen 6–9).

12:3 If read allegorically (see note on vv. 1–7), these could be references to parts of the body as they decay. **keepers of the house.** Servants of the house. **tremble.** A strong verb implying they are terrified. Allegorically this could refer to the hands trembling. **strong men.** Often used of soldiers in the OT. **stoop.** In old age the muscles start to decline. **grinders.** Those who work in the mill to produce grain for bread. Alternatively, this could be an allegorical reference to an inability to eat. **the windows.** Allegorically, this would refer to the eyes.

12:4 doors to the street. The doors to the business and public areas. Normal life is closing down. **sound of birds.** Probably the sounds of birds of prey, symbolically this could be an image of judgment. As an allegory of old age, "rise up at the sound of birds" would refer to an inability to sleep. **all their songs grow faint.** Symbolically, it could indicate that even lament ceases. As an allegory of old age, it would indicate the decline of speech and the capacity to sing and enjoy life.

12:5 heights. In old age people become fearful of heights; symbolically, it refers to the places from which attacks can emerge. **almond tree blossoms.** The pale blossoms of the almond tree could evoke the white hair of old age. **grasshopper drags itself along.** The slowness of movement in old age. Symbolically, nature itself is in travail (cf. Rom 8:19–22). **eternal home.** See note on v. 7 for what this might mean for the Teacher. It certainly includes death, which has invaded this creation.

Then people go to their eternal home[j]
and mourners[k] go about the streets.

6 Remember him — before the silver cord
is severed,
and the golden bowl is broken;
before the pitcher is shattered at the
spring,
and the wheel broken at the well,
7 and the dust returns[l] to the ground it
came from,
and the spirit returns to God[m] who
gave it.[n]

8 "Meaningless! Meaningless!" says the
Teacher.[a]
"Everything is meaningless![o]"

Blossoming almond tree (Eccl 12:5).

The Conclusion of the Matter

9 Not only was the Teacher wise, but he also imparted knowledge to the people. He pondered and
searched out and set in order many proverbs.[p] 10 The Teacher searched to find just the right words, and
what he wrote was upright and true.[q]
11 The words of the wise are like goads, their collected sayings like firmly embedded nails[r] — given
by one shepherd.[b] 12 Be warned, my son, of anything in addition to them.
Of making many books there is no end, and much study wearies the body.[s]

13 Now all has been heard;
here is the conclusion of the matter:
Fear God and keep his commandments,[t]
for this is the duty of all mankind.[u]
14 For God will bring every deed into judgment,[v]
including every hidden thing,[w]
whether it is good or evil.

12:5 [j] Job 17:13; 10:21 [k] Jer 9:17; Am 5:16
12:7 [l] Ge 3:19; Job 34:15; Ps 146:4 [m] Ecc 3:21 [n] Job 20:8; Zec 12:1
12:8 [o] Ecc 1:2
12:9 [p] 1Ki 4:32
12:10 [q] Pr 22:20-21
12:11 [r] Ezr 9:8
12:12 [s] Ecc 1:18
12:13 [t] Dt 4:2; 10:12 [u] Mic 6:8
12:14 [v] Ecc 3:17 [w] Mt 10:26; 1Co 4:5

[a] *8* Or *the leader of the assembly*; also in verses 9 and 10 [b] *11* Or *Shepherd*

12:6 silver cord ... golden bowl. A strand of twisted silver holding a hanging golden bowl. **severed.** If one link breaks, the whole falls, perhaps indicating the fragility of life. The bowl, pitcher, and wheel are all basic utilities of daily life, now shattered. Possible they were also all used to hold water, and since water symbolizes life (2 Sam 14:14; John 4:14; Rev 21:6), their destruction could refer to death.
12:7 Cf. Gen 3:19. **the spirit returns to God who gave it.** See 3:21. In comparison to the Teacher's uncertainty about what happens at death in earlier parts of the book, here he is clear that the spirit of a person returns to God.
12:8 Restatement of the theme. See note on 1:2; see also Introduction: Themes and Theology.
12:9–14 *The Conclusion of the Matter.* The Teacher moves offstage, and the narrator returns to conclude the book.
12:9–12 The Teacher has taken us on an extraordinary journey, and the reader is keen to see what the narrator makes of it. The narrator affirms the struggle of the Teacher toward resolution of his dilemma.
12:9–10 Having seen the depths of despair to which the Teacher plummeted, affirming him as "wise" (v. 9) is akin to God's remarkable declaration in Job 42:7 that Job, unlike his friends, spoke what is true about God.
12:10 what he wrote was upright and true. Wisdom involves not just right knowledge but transformation through deep, existential struggle.
12:11 The Teacher is one of the wise men in Israel. **goads.** They prod into action. **embedded nails.** Provide strength and firmness. One can hang one's life on them. **one shepherd.** Possibly refers to God as the shepherd of his people (see Ps 23 and note on v. 1 there) and the source of their wisdom. Alternatively, it could simply be comparing the words of the wise to the faithful work of a shepherd caring for his flock.
12:12 We have seen what trouble the teacher got into by depending on a type of investigating alien to OT wisdom. The reader is warned against such autonomous investigation that is not built on the fear of the Lord.
12:13–14 The narrator sums up the message of the book.
12:13 Fear God. The foundational principle of traditional wisdom (cf. Prov 1:7; Job 28:28). **duty of all mankind.** Humans are made for God, and we become fully human in living according to his instruction.
12:14 every deed into judgment. We catch glimpses of this truth throughout this book (see 3:17; 8:12–13; 11:9). In the NT, this is crystal clear. See Matt 12:36; 1 Cor 3:12–15 and notes; 2 Cor 5:9–10; Heb 4:12–13. **every hidden thing.** See Rom 2:16.

INTRODUCTION TO SONG OF SONGS

TITLE

The "Song of Songs" (1:1) is traditionally named the "Song of Solomon" based on the connection with Solomon (1:1). Like the "Most Holy Place" (the "Holy of Holies" in Hebrew) in the tabernacle (Exod 26:33 – 34) describes the holiest of holy places, so "Song of Songs" describes the best of all songs. The book consists of 117 verses of love poetry. Most of the verses are dialog between a woman and a man who deeply love one another.

AUTHOR AND DATE

The Song nowhere clearly identifies its author or the date of composition. The mention of Solomon in 1:1 may suggest that Solomon is the author or that someone wrote the book for Solomon. Mention of Tirzah (6:4; cf. 1 Kgs 16:23) may imply a time when Tirzah was the capital of the northern kingdom of Israel (ca. 925 – 879 BC), or it may simply suggest Tirzah as an example of a city renowned for its beauty. A few individual words may suggest a later date (fifth – fourth centuries BC), but since linguistic updating could have occurred, later vocabulary is not conclusive for dating the Song's primary composition. Many word pictures in the Song imply the period of the monarchy.

"My beloved is like a gazelle" (Song 2:9).

INTERPRETATION

Perhaps more interpretations have been proposed for the Song than for any other biblical book. An early popular approach was to interpret this book as an allegory. In Judaism, one interpretation is that the man represents God, and the woman symbolizes Israel. In Christianity, the man represents Christ, and the woman symbolizes the church. The absence of any indication of allegory or identification of these symbols and the problematic nature of consistent application argue against this approach. For example, the woman rouses the man (8:5); in what way does the church rouse Christ?

Another popular approach sees the book as a drama. Interpretations adopting this approach suggest that there are three main characters: the poor but noble shepherd, the scheming King Solomon, and the virtuous shepherdess. Several difficulties arise with this interpretation. King Solomon plays no active role; he never speaks. Given the attribution to Solomon in 1:1, why would the Song portray him in such a negative light? Further, there is no agreement on an overall plot for this drama. While some mini-dramas occur (e.g., 3:1 – 5; 5:2 – 8), the man and woman start each main section apart and then reunite.

It is preferable to interpret the Song as romantic love poetry. Love poetry does not tell a story but is descriptive. The Song is the most richly metaphoric book in the Bible. Some see the work as an anthology of separate love poems. That seems unlikely given the complex interplay of word pictures, phrases, and themes through every part of the Song. Although Egyptian and other contemporary love poetry tend toward shorter poems than the Song, its 117 verses do not make it too long to form a unified and beautiful romantic poem.

PURPOSE AND THEOLOGY

Why is this romantic love poem found in the Bible? The Bible is full of references to sexuality. God created man and woman for one another in the exclusive committed relationship of marriage (Gen 2 – 3). However, Adam and Eve's rebellion against God broke apart this harmonious, loving union. The laws of the Pentateuch contain many commands against deviant forms of sex. The historical and prophetic books indict Israel for sexual sins and compare idolatry to adultery. Proverbs warns young men of sexual temptation (Prov 7). Jesus observes that some have made themselves eunuchs for the sake of the kingdom of heaven (Matt 19:12), and Paul suggests value in remaining unmarried if possible (1 Cor 7:8). The Song reminds us that romantic love within marriage is one of the good things created by God. It assumes marriage and proceeds to extol the joys of romantic love. The Song places a garden of delights within the fences that the other books of the Bible erect to protect the powerful gift of sexuality.

The key to the Song's major theological theme appears in 8:5 – 7: the lovers' union is as strong as death, fire, and water. The final words of 8:6 provide the Song's sole mention of God's name in its "mighty flame" (see NIV text note). This romantic love is a gift from God that he intends us to receive with thanksgiving.

The book is rich in metaphors, chiefly of sexual love. The Greek translators of the Septuagint (the pre-Christian Greek translation of the OT) understood this. They translated the Hebrew word for love that occurs some 18 times in the book with a Greek term (*agapē*) that, although it can refer to loving the wrong sorts of thing (2 Tim 4:10), is the same word Paul, John, and the other NT writers use to refer to Christ's love for us and our love for one another (e.g., John 13:35; Rom 8:35; Eph 3:18; 1 Pet 4:8; 1 John 3:16). The Song becomes a metaphor, or signpost, wherein romantic love is not an end in itself. Instead, it provides one of the greatest examples on earth of the love that God had for us in sending his Son to die for us (John 3:16).

PLACES MENTIONED IN SONG OF SONGS

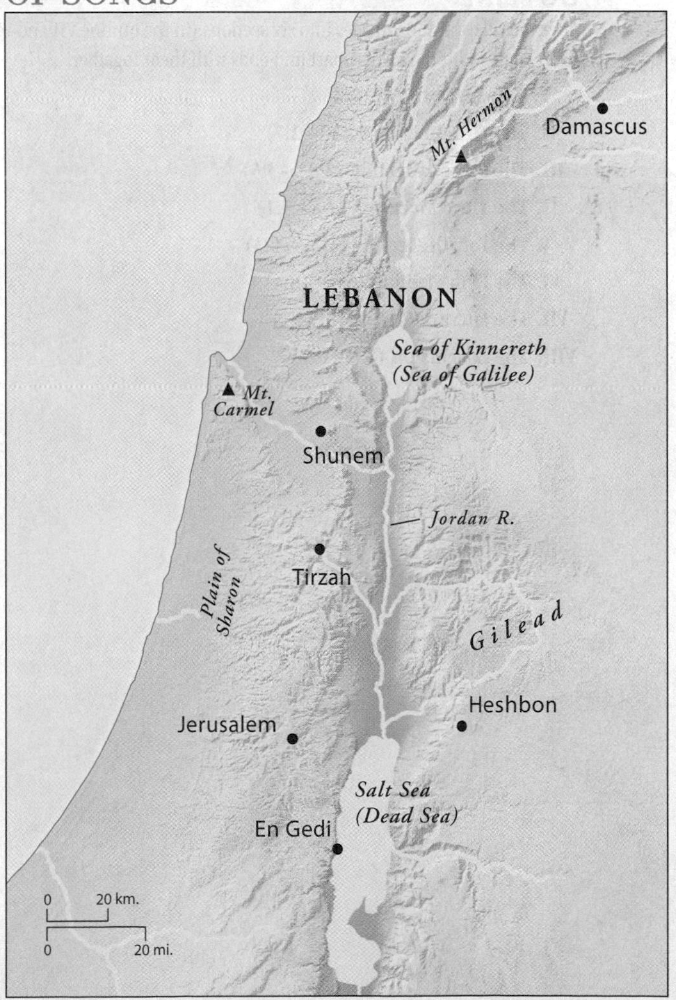

Human sexual love at its best points toward the much greater love of God that he now gives to us as Christ's love for the church.

Although much could be said regarding the theme of love in the Song, one of the most important points is the exclusive commitment of the lovers. Again and again they focus on the eyes, as the man and woman have eyes only for each other (1:15; 4:1,9; 5:12; 6:5; 7:4; 8:10). Neither the daughters of Jerusalem, the woman's brothers, nor Solomon himself can interfere with this love. Though 1:1 and 8:12 may refer to King Solomon as the author and the owner of vineyards, other references to him (1:5; 3:7,9,11; 8:11,12) describe how the woman sees her beloved. He is everything she could want; he is her Solomon. The same is true of the woman's name in 6:13: "Shulammite" is a feminine form of "Solomon," so the woman is the man's "Solomon," providing all that he could want in their loving relationship.

Because of its many metaphors, the Song cannot be taken as a series of literal events. It is instead a collection of pictures, imaginings, and flights of fantasy. In the poem, the man and woman are real, as is their love. However, as is true in love poetry, there is no clear division between fantasy and reality. The same is true of their marriage relationship. Six times in the middle of the Song the man calls the woman his "bride" (4:8,9,10,11,12; 5:1). However, it is not possible to determine if the couple is already married or if their marriage is a hope and dream that will shortly take place. The many romantic descriptions should not then be taken as a license for premarital sex, which the Bible considers sin (1 Cor 7:1 – 2). Instead, the Song describes the joys of a sexual relationship within marriage without indicating whether that relationship is reality or fantasy.

OUTLINE

After the title, the Song divides into six sections (in the outline VII and VIII can be considered one single section). Each begins with the lovers apart and ends with them together.

I. Title (1:1)

II. The First Meeting (1:2 — 2:7)

III. The Second Meeting (2:8 — 3:5)

IV. The Third Meeting (3:6 — 5:1)

V. The Fourth Meeting (5:2 — 6:3)

VI. The Fifth Meeting (6:4 — 8:4)

VII. The Literary Climax (8:5 – 7)

VIII. The Conclusion (8:8 – 14)

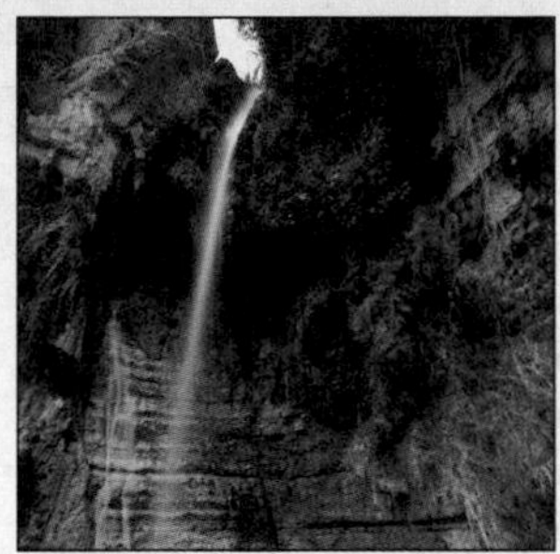

SONG OF SONGS

1 Solomon's Song of Songs.[a]

She[a]

[2] Let him kiss me with the kisses of his mouth —
for your love[b] is more delightful than wine.
[3] Pleasing is the fragrance of your perfumes;[c]
your name[d] is like perfume poured out.
No wonder the young women[e] love you!
[4] Take me away with you — let us hurry!
Let the king bring me into his chambers.[f]

Friends

We rejoice and delight in you[b];
we will praise your love more than wine.

She

How right they are to adore you!

[5] Dark am I, yet lovely,[g]
daughters of Jerusalem,[h]

1:1 [a] 1Ki 4:32
1:2 [b] SS 4:10
1:3 [c] SS 4:10 [d] Ecc 7:1 [e] Ps 45:14
1:4 [f] Ps 45:15
1:5 [g] SS 2:14; 4:3 [h] SS 2:7; 5:8; 5:16

[a] The main male and female speakers (identified primarily on the basis of the gender of the relevant Hebrew forms) are indicated by the captions *He* and *She* respectively. The words of others are marked *Friends*. In some instances the divisions and their captions are debatable. [b] *4* The Hebrew is masculine singular.

1:1 *Title.* The title connects the Song with Solomon, the leading purveyor of Israelite wisdom (1 Kgs 4:32).
1:1 Solomon's. Solomon could be the author or the one to whom the Song is dedicated (see Introduction: Author and Date). **Song of Songs.** Most likely a superlative (see Introduction: Title).
1:2—2:7 *The First Meeting.* The female speaks first and apart from the male (1:2). The two interact (1:3—2:2) with the friends speaking (1:4b,8), and then the couple comes together in an embrace (2:3–7). In the midst of this, they encourage one another in love. For the caption "She" in 1:2, as well as the other captions in the book, see NIV text note.
1:2–3 The senses are inundated: touch ("kiss"), taste ("wine"), smell ("perfumes"), and hearing (the "name" of her lover). The poem begins with multiple images of intense delight and intoxication to emphasize the joy of love.
1:2 kiss. In the OT, friends and family exchanged kisses (Gen 27:26–27; 1 Sam 10:1; 20:41), but only 8:1 and Prov 7:13 suggest romantic kissing a private, rather than public, act. For kissing as false worship, see 1 Kgs 19:18. **love.** Hebrew *dōdîm*; emphasizes passion and desire in lovemaking (4:10; Prov 7:18; cf. Ezek 16:8; 23:17). **wine.** An image of the joys of love; it refers to the sense of taste, further heightening the powerful images of the beloved.
1:3 perfumes. Aromatics infused in olive oil; worn at parties and festivals. **love.** Hebrew *ʾāhab*; translated in the Septuagint (the pre-Christian Greek translation of the OT) as *agapaō* wherever it occurs in the Song (1:4,7; 3:1,2,3,4,5,10; 5:8; 7:6; 8:4,6,7). Here it is used in the sense of the love of which God approves. The romantic love of the Song points to the greater love that God has for his people and that God's people should have for God and each other (see Introduction: Purpose and Theology).
1:4a king. The woman sees her lover as a king, like Solomon (3:9,11; 8:12).
1:4b We rejoice and delight. Cf. Isa 25:9 for the same Hebrew phrase characterizing the people's response to God's salvation. **wine.** See note on v. 2.
1:5 Dark. Or "black" (5:11; Lev 13:31,37; Job 30:30; Zech 6:2,6); deeply tanned by the sun (v. 6). It introduces the fifth sense, sight (see note on vv. 2–3). **yet lovely.** Among the fair women of Jerusalem the speaker fears she will appear less beautiful because of her deeply tanned skin. **daughters of Jerusalem.** A group addressed seven times

1:6 [i]Ps 69:8; SS 8:12
1:7 [j]SS 3:1-4; Isa 13:20
1:8 [k]SS 5:9; 6:1
1:9 [l]2Ch 1:17
1:10 [m]SS 5:13
[n]Isa 61:10
1:12 [o]SS 4:11-14

dark like the tents of Kedar,
like the tent curtains of Solomon.[a]
6 Do not stare at me because I am dark,
because I am darkened by the sun.
My mother's sons were angry with me
and made me take care of the vineyards;[i]
my own vineyard I had to neglect.
7 Tell me, you whom I love,
where you graze your flock
and where you rest your sheep[j] at midday.
Why should I be like a veiled woman
beside the flocks of your friends?

Friends

8 If you do not know, most beautiful of women,[k]
follow the tracks of the sheep
and graze your young goats
by the tents of the shepherds.

He

9 I liken you, my darling, to a mare
among Pharaoh's chariot horses.[l]
10 Your cheeks[m] are beautiful with earrings,
your neck with strings of jewels.[n]
11 We will make you earrings of gold,
studded with silver.

She

12 While the king was at his table,
my perfume spread its fragrance.[o]
13 My beloved is to me a sachet of myrrh
resting between my breasts.

[a] 5 Or *Salma*

(vv. 5–6; 2:7; 3:5,10; 5:8,16; 8:4). **Kedar.** Ishmael's son; lived to the east in the Arabian deserts on the edge of the civilized world (Gen 25:13; Jer 2:10; 49:28). His tents were made from the hides of black-haired goats. The woman's darkness suggests an exotic beauty and wildness about her. **tent curtains of Solomon.** As King Solomon would have the best, so the woman claims that her "tent" (appearance) is most beautiful compared to others.
1:6 Do not stare at me. She doesn't want the women of Jerusalem or anyone else to gaze at her deeply tanned skin. **dark.** An intensive form of the Hebrew word in v. 5, implying that she self-consciously feels that she is too dark. **mother's sons.** This designation instead of "brothers" may suggest a close bond among the females of the woman's family while it separates her from her brothers. Like Ruth, this woman may have no close male relative to protect her (see Ruth 1–2). The woman knows only her mother (3:4; 6:9; 8:1–2); the Song does not mention her father. **were angry.** The anger of her brothers sent her into the vineyards to work. **my own vineyard.** A metaphor for the female's physical appearance. Darkness indicates her insecurity, her fear that she is not beautiful enough, but it is also a badge of devotion to her family.
1:7 love. See v. 3 and note. **veiled woman.** Or "cloaked" (used of a man in 1 Sam 28:14). As seen in reliefs of the siege of Lachish (701 BC), a Judahite woman wore an outer garment as a cloak with a mantle that could cover her head. See photo, p. 1308. This was the customary dress of a shepherdess.
1:8 These words follow v. 7a in answering each of the woman's questions. **most beautiful of women.** Emphasizing the woman's beauty begins a paean of praise (vv. 8–10) that serves to reassure any insecurity.
1:9 my darling. Used nine times in the Song (here; v. 15; 2:2,10,13; 4:1,7; 5:2; 6:4) and only by the man for the woman; this favorite expression of endearment sounds like the word for "graze" (v. 7). **a mare among Pharaoh's chariot horses.** Reflects a known Egyptian military strategy in which a mare placed before stallions pulling the chariots caused chaos in the battle formation.
1:10 cheeks ... neck. The man's praise modestly focuses on the woman's face and neck. **earrings ... jewels.** Enhance the beauty; appropriate for one so lovely.
1:11 We. Could be a plural indicating the man is carried away by his love. It could also indicate the daughters of Jerusalem are agreeing with the man's words. The emphasis, however, is on the woman's beauty, not on the speaker(s).
1:12 king. See v. 4a and note. **perfume.** The Hebrew word refers to nard. Native to the Himalayas, this is the most exotic fragrance in the Song. It identifies an exclusive and special love.
1:13 My beloved. Hebrew *dôdî*; used 27 times in the Song (here;

[14]My beloved is to me a cluster of henna[p] blossoms
from the vineyards of En Gedi.[q]

He

[15]How beautiful[r] you are, my darling!
Oh, how beautiful!
Your eyes are doves.[s]

She

[16]How handsome you are, my beloved!
Oh, how charming!
And our bed is verdant.

He

[17]The beams of our house are cedars;[t]
our rafters are firs.

She[a]

2 I am a rose[b][u] of Sharon,[v]
a lily[w] of the valleys.

He

[2]Like a lily among thorns
is my darling among the young women.

She

[3]Like an apple[c] tree among the trees of the forest
is my beloved[x] among the young men.
I delight[y] to sit in his shade,
and his fruit is sweet to my taste.[z]
[4]Let him lead me to the banquet hall,[a]
and let his banner[b] over me be love.

[a] Or *He* here and elsewhere in Song of Songs [b] *1* Probably a member of the crocus family [c] *3* Or possibly *apricot;*

1:14 [p]SS 4:13 [q]1Sa 23:29
1:15 [r]SS 4:7 [s]SS 2:14; 4:1; 5:2,12; 6:9
1:17 [t]1Ki 6:9
2:1 [u]Isa 35:1 [v]S 1Ch 27:29 [w]SS 5:13; Hos 14:5
2:3 [x]SS 1:14 [y]SS 1:4 [z]SS 4:16
2:4 [a]Est 1:11 [b]Nu 1:52

Bust of Nefertiti, wife of Akhenaten, an Egyptian pharaoh, eighteenth dynasty. "Your cheeks are beautiful with earrings, your neck with strings of jewels" (Song 1:10).

A. D. Riddle/www.BiblePlaces.com, taken at the Berlin Egyptian Museum

vv. 14,16; 2:3,8,9,10,16,17; 4:16; 5:2,4,5,6,8,9,10,16; 6:1,2,3; 7:9,10,11,13; 8:5,14), it is the woman's favorite expression of love for the man. **sachet of myrrh.** An exotic spice from southern Arabia and the horn of Africa; used in the temple incense (Exod 30:23). One could wear a sachet "between [the] breasts" for its perfume. Here it describes the depth of intimacy experienced.

1:14 henna blossoms. A yellow-flowered plant native to Israel producing a reddish dye that is applied directly to the body as perfume or deodorant. **vineyards of En Gedi.** An isolated site on the west shore of the Dead Sea that evokes (1) the place David hid from Saul (1 Sam 23:29; 24:1)—the Hebrew consonants of "David" match those of "beloved" (v. 13); (2) a romantic retreat; and (3) the location of a center for producing perfume from the time of the monarchy. **vineyards.** The vineyard is a metaphor for the body (see v. 6 and note). The plural suggests intimacy between the two lovers.

1:15 How beautiful you are, my darling! Cf. vv. 8,9 and notes. **eyes are doves.** Doves represent love (Matt 3:16–17; Mark 1:10–11; Luke 3:22), and eyes can determine one's plainness (Gen 29:17) or beauty (1 Sam 16:12 in the Hebrew text). The lovers gaze into one another's eyes, admiring each other's beauty.

1:16 handsome. The same Hebrew word translated "beautiful" in v. 15. **bed is verdant.** Pictures the spreading foliage of a tree (v. 17) and anticipates the natural outdoor setting (ch. 2) and fruitfulness and life. For the lovers, the fruitfulness of their love gives their lives joy, meaning, and purpose.

1:17 beams of our house are cedars. The tall trees provided planks that could roof over large areas.

2:1 rose of Sharon. Likely a hyacinth, crocus, or asphodel. The fertile Sharon plain lay near the Mediterranean. Cf. Isa 35:1, where the flower blooms and brings beauty and life to the desert. **lily.** The lotus, or water lily, appearing on Egyptian and Israelite art (1 Kgs 7:26). Both the rose and the lily here symbolize the beauty and life with which the woman is identified.

2:2 thorns. Not only unattractive but also insignificant (2 Kgs 14:9). The man has eyes only for his lover. His commitment is exclusive. **my darling.** See note on 1:9.

2:3 apple tree. The apple was a refreshment (rather than a nutritional source) that stimulated the sense of taste. Some suggest that the Hebrew term refers to an apricot instead of an apple (see NIV text note), but the apple was known in the world of early Israel. **among the trees of the forest.** The woman has eyes only for her lover. Her commitment is exclusive (cf. v. 2).

2:4 banquet hall. Or "house of wine"; symbolizes a place of sensual pleasure. **his banner.** The military context of a banner (Num 2; Ps 20:5) may identify the king's dignity. But some suggest that the possible meaning "his intent (for me)" is more appropriate to vv. 4–6.

2:5 [c]SS 7:8 [d]SS 5:8
2:6 [e]SS 8:3
2:7 [f]SS 5:8 [g]SS 3:5; 8:4
2:8 [h]ver 17; SS 8:14
2:9 [i]2Sa 2:18 [j]ver 17; SS 8:14
2:13 [k]Isa 28:4; Jer 24:2; Hos 9:10; Mic 7:1; Na 3:12 [l]SS 7:12
2:14 [m]Ge 8:8; SS 1:15 [n]SS 1:5; 8:13
2:15 [o]Jdg 15:4

5 Strengthen me with raisins,
refresh me with apples,[c]
for I am faint with love.[d]
6 His left arm is under my head,
and his right arm embraces me.[e]
7 Daughters of Jerusalem, I charge you[f]
by the gazelles and by the does of the field:
Do not arouse or awaken love
until it so desires.[g]

8 Listen! My beloved!
Look! Here he comes,
leaping across the mountains,
bounding over the hills.[h]
9 My beloved is like a gazelle[i] or a young stag.[j]
Look! There he stands behind our wall,
gazing through the windows,
peering through the lattice.
10 My beloved spoke and said to me,
"Arise, my darling,
my beautiful one, come with me.
11 See! The winter is past;
the rains are over and gone.
12 Flowers appear on the earth;
the season of singing has come,
the cooing of doves
is heard in our land.
13 The fig tree forms its early fruit;[k]
the blossoming[l] vines spread their fragrance.
Arise, come, my darling;
my beautiful one, come with me."

He

14 My dove[m] in the clefts of the rock,
in the hiding places on the mountainside,
show me your face,
let me hear your voice;
for your voice is sweet,
and your face is lovely.[n]
15 Catch for us the foxes,[o]
the little foxes

2:5 raisins. A delicacy tasted at celebrations (2 Sam 6:19; Hos 3:1). **apples.** See note on v. 3. Both raisins and apples refresh and revive.
2:6 embraces me. The climax of "The First Meeting" (see note on 1:2—2:7): the lovers come together and melt into one another's arms.
2:7 Daughters of Jerusalem. See note on 1:5. **gazelles ... does.** Rather than using God's name in an oath, the woman uses these pictures of nature that symbolize her physical attributes (4:5; 7:3; see Prov 5:19). **Do not arouse or awaken love until it so desires.** Cf. 3:5; 8:4. Though there are many proposed interpretations, most likely this either warns others not to disturb the lovers or encourages lovers to wait for love until the proper context of marriage.
2:8—3:5 *The Second Meeting.* This section depicts love as an invitation (2:8–14), as joy (2:15–17), and as a longing search (3:1–5).
2:8 leaping. The woman finds skill and beauty in her lover's movements.
2:9 gazelle ... young stag. Male counterparts to the animals of v. 7.
2:10–13 This invitation begins and ends the finest picture of springtime (the transition from the rainy season to the dry season) in the Bible.
2:12–13 Flowers ... singing ... doves ... fig tree ... vines. The spring arouses the senses of smell, hearing, sight, and taste.
2:14 clefts of the rock. Two groups of clefts northwest of the Dead Sea and the Sea of Galilee are homes for thousands of doves. Here the man longs to see and hear the woman, but she remains hidden like a dove.
2:15 foxes. Represent those who threaten the couple's loving union ("vineyards"). With an appetite for grapes, foxes climb over walls (Neh 4:3) and dig out vines.

that ruin the vineyards,[p]
our vineyards that are in bloom.[q]

She

16 My beloved is mine and I am his;[r]
he browses among the lilies.[s]
17 Until the day breaks
and the shadows flee,[t]
turn, my beloved,[u]
and be like a gazelle
or like a young stag[v]
on the rugged hills.[a][w]

3 All night long on my bed
I looked[x] for the one my heart loves;
I looked for him but did not find him.
2 I will get up now and go about the city,
through its streets and squares;
I will search for the one my heart loves.
So I looked for him but did not find him.
3 The watchmen found me
as they made their rounds in the city.[y]
"Have you seen the one my heart loves?"
4 Scarcely had I passed them
when I found the one my heart loves.
I held him and would not let him go
till I had brought him to my mother's house,[z]
to the room of the one who conceived me.[a]
5 Daughters of Jerusalem, I charge you[b]
by the gazelles and by the does of the field:
Do not arouse or awaken love
until it so desires.[c]

6 Who is this coming up from the wilderness[d]
like a column of smoke,
perfumed with myrrh[e] and incense
made from all the spices[f] of the merchant?

a 17 Or *the hills of Bether*

2:15 [p]SS 1:6 [q]SS 7:12
2:16 [r]SS 7:10 [s]SS 4:5; 6:3
2:17 [t]SS 4:6 [u]SS 1:14 [v]ver 9 [w]ver 8
3:1 [x]SS 5:6; Isa 26:9
3:3 [y]SS 5:7
3:4 [z]SS 8:2 [a]SS 6:9
3:5 [b]SS 2:7 [c]SS 8:4
3:6 [d]SS 8:5 [e]SS 1:13; 4:6,14 [f]Ex 30:34

2:16 browses among the lilies. A gazelle or young stag (v. 9) eating lotuses (see "lily" in vv. 1–2 and note on v. 1) represents the man's physical union with the woman. Perhaps this is a dream not yet realized (cf. v. 17).
2:17 turn. The woman releases the man (see note on v. 9) to his world.
3:1 All night long. The woman's desire is not abated. She goes out to find her lover but without success. The night is a time for dreaming. This, like other parts of the Song (5:2–8), may be a dream (see note on 2:16).
3:2 heart. The source of life's vitality (cf. Prov 16:26, where the word is translated "appetite"). The woman's love is equal in intensity to her desire to live.
3:4 mother's house. The most personal part of her home; a refuge where only family would come (Gen 24:28,67; Ruth 1:8). See note on 1:6.
3:5 Do not arouse ... desires. See note on 2:7. The woman interrupts the romantic picture with a note of caution.
3:6—5:1 *The Third Meeting.* If the woman's dream (3:1–5) was searching for, finding, and bringing her lover to her home, the man's love fantasy is protecting his lover and consummating that security in marriage (3:6–11). The man's praise of the woman's body (4:1–7) recovers the value of the essential physical nature of being human. This leads to the permanent and exclusive commitment of marriage (4:8–15), just as God calls us to an exclusive commitment in discipleship (Rom 12:1–2; 2 Cor 6:15–18). Although there is the call to relieve suffering in the world, there is also the need to recognize the good world as created by God, to rejoice when the Bridegroom is present (Matt 9:15), and to look forward to the great wedding banquet to come (Matt 8:11; Rev 19:7,9; 22:17). See note on 2:8—3:5.
3:6 Who is this ...? "This" is feminine. **myrrh.** See 1:13 and note. **incense.** Frankincense, like myrrh, is imported from Arabia (hence "the merchant"). The value of these spices signals a wealthy and powerful person.

3:7 [g] 1Sa 8:11
3:8 [h] Job 15:22; Ps 91:5
3:11 [i] Isa 4:4 [j] Isa 62:5
4:1 [k] SS 1:15; 5:12 [l] SS 6:5; Mic 7:14
4:2 [m] SS 6:6
4:3 [n] SS 5:16 [o] SS 6:7
4:4 [p] SS 7:4 [q] Eze 27:10

[7] Look! It is Solomon's carriage,
escorted by sixty warriors,[g]
the noblest of Israel,
[8] all of them wearing the sword,
all experienced in battle,
each with his sword at his side,
prepared for the terrors of the night.[h]
[9] King Solomon made for himself the carriage;
he made it of wood from Lebanon.
[10] Its posts he made of silver,
its base of gold.
Its seat was upholstered with purple,
its interior inlaid with love.
Daughters of Jerusalem, [11] come out,
and look, you daughters of Zion.[i]
Look[a] on King Solomon wearing a crown,
the crown with which his mother crowned him
on the day of his wedding,
the day his heart rejoiced.[j]

He

4

How beautiful you are, my darling!
Oh, how beautiful!
Your eyes behind your veil are doves.[k]
Your hair is like a flock of goats
descending from the hills of Gilead.[l]
[2] Your teeth are like a flock of sheep just shorn,
coming up from the washing.
Each has its twin;
not one of them is alone.[m]
[3] Your lips are like a scarlet ribbon;
your mouth[n] is lovely.
Your temples behind your veil
are like the halves of a pomegranate.[o]
[4] Your neck is like the tower[p] of David,
built with courses of stone[b];
on it hang a thousand shields,[q]
all of them shields of warriors.

[a] *10,11* Or *interior lovingly inlaid / by the daughters of Jerusalem. / [11] Come out, you daughters of Zion, / and look* [b] *4* The meaning of the Hebrew for this phrase is uncertain.

3:7 Solomon's carriage. A sedan-chair of Solomon-like opulence. The object of the speaker's affection lies upon the bed. **sixty warriors.** Emphasizes security for the traveler. The number is associated with Solomonic activities (1 Kgs 4:13,22; 6:2).

3:9–10 wood from Lebanon … silver … gold … purple. The finest materials; appropriate to the occupant riding in the carriage to his wedding.

3:10 Daughters of Jerusalem. See note on 1:5. They are invited to participate for the first time in the Song.

3:11 wearing a crown. As in Jewish weddings, where the bride and groom wear crowns, the groom here becomes the bride's King Solomon. Her eyes are only for him, unsurpassed in glory and beauty.

4:1–7 This is the first of three songs praising the female's physical attributes (6:4–9; 7:1–9a).

4:1 Your eyes. The man begins by describing his lover's eyes as he gazes at her. **veil.** A symbol of modesty (Isa 47:2); did not conceal the eyes or cheeks. **doves.** See note on 1:15. **goats.** See note on 1:5 ("Kedar"). **hills of Gilead.** Whether west (Judg 7:3) or east (Josh 20:8; 21:38) of the Jordan River, a steep descent evokes a picture of a dark, shimmering waterfall.

4:2 teeth … sheep … washing … twin. Portrays teeth that are white (reflecting youthfulness), clean, whole, and straight; a beautiful smile.

4:3 scarlet ribbon. Red, full lips are desirable. **halves of a pomegranate.** The translucent veil reveals the ripe, reddish hues of the fruit that suggest fertility, life, and beauty.

4:4 neck … a thousand shields. The small, round shields that could be represented in the stone of a tower symbolized strength and security. This may picture layers of jewelry that adorn the woman's neck and describe her personal security. Love, not neediness, draws the lovers together.

5 Your breasts[r] are like two fawns,
like twin fawns of a gazelle[s]
that browse among the lilies.[t]
6 Until the day breaks
and the shadows flee,[u]
I will go to the mountain of myrrh[v]
and to the hill of incense.
7 You are altogether beautiful,[w] my darling;
there is no flaw in you.

8 Come with me from Lebanon, my bride,[x]
come with me from Lebanon.
Descend from the crest of Amana,
from the top of Senir,[y] the summit of Hermon,[z]
from the lions' dens
and the mountain haunts of leopards.
9 You have stolen my heart, my sister, my bride;
you have stolen my heart
with one glance of your eyes,
with one jewel of your necklace.[a]
10 How delightful[b] is your love[c], my sister, my bride!
How much more pleasing is your love than wine,
and the fragrance of your perfume
more than any spice!
11 Your lips drop sweetness as the honeycomb, my bride;
milk and honey are under your tongue.[d]
The fragrance of your garments
is like the fragrance of Lebanon.[e]
12 You are a garden locked up, my sister, my bride;
you are a spring enclosed, a sealed fountain.[f]
13 Your plants are an orchard of pomegranates[g]
with choice fruits,
with henna[h] and nard,
14 nard and saffron,
calamus and cinnamon,[i]

4:5 [r] SS 7:3 [s] Pr 5:19 [t] SS 2:16; 6:2-3
4:6 [u] SS 2:17 [v] ver 14
4:7 [w] SS 1:15
4:8 [x] SS 5:1 [y] Dt 3:9 [z] 1Ch 5:23
4:9 [a] Ge 41:42
4:10 [b] SS 7:6 [c] SS 1:2
4:11 [d] Ps 19:10; SS 5:1 [e] Hos 14:6
4:12 [f] Pr 5:15-18
4:13 [g] SS 6:11; 7:12 [h] SS 1:14
4:14 [i] Ex 30:23

4:5 Cf. 2:16; 7:3. **breasts.** Represent beauty ("lilies"; see note on 2:1), youth ("fawns"), and grace ("gazelle").
4:6 mountain of myrrh ... hill of incense. For the connection with the woman's breasts, see 1:13; 3:6 and notes. The aromatics symbolize the intoxication of love that the man experiences.
4:8 my bride. The woman is or soon will be married to the man. Occurring only in the center of the Song (vv. 9,10,11,12; 5:1), "bride" describes a legal relationship of marriage that is otherwise not mentioned in the Song. The Song assumes legal matters, but its poetry soars beyond them. **Lebanon ... Amana ... Senir ... Hermon.** The highest mountains in Israel, comprising the south end of the Lebanon and anti-Lebanon ranges. The Hebrew name of Lebanon resembles the Hebrew word for frankincense (*lĕbônâ*; see 3:6 and note; 4:6,14) and contributes to the pictures of the woman's inaccessibility (cf. "lions' dens" and "mountain haunts of leopards") and the man's desire for her.
4:9 heart. See note on 3:2. **my sister.** For a man to address his love as "sister" (vv. 10,12; 5:1,2) is known in Egyptian love poetry. **one glance of your eyes.** Although "glance" is not in the original text, its intended meaning is likely. As in v. 1, her eyes captivate the man. **one jewel of your necklace.** Perhaps the bottom strand because it was the most beautiful and radiant, enhancing the woman's beauty (see note on v. 4).
4:10 wine ... spice. See notes on 1:2–3.
4:11 lips drop sweetness. Indicates honey from bees and honey from dates; it provided the sweetest taste known in ancient Israel. **milk and honey ... tongue.** Describes the woman's romantic delights (5:1) and pictures fruitfulness in the promised land (see Josh 5:6 and note). Here these words describe kissing. More generally, they portray longing, energy, and fruitfulness. **fragrance of your garments.** Cf. Ps 45:8. **Lebanon.** For the wordplay with frankincense, see note on v. 8. Touch and taste combine to stimulate desire.
4:12 garden locked up ... spring enclosed ... sealed fountain. Pictures the woman's body and her sexuality (vv. 15–16; 5:1; 6:2; 8:13). Inaccessible except to her lover, the woman provides him with refreshment (Prov 5:15–19).
4:13 pomegranates. See note on v. 3. **henna.** See note on 1:14. **nard.** See note on 1:12.
4:14 saffron. Or turmeric; a yellow spice from exotic lands. **calamus.** See Jer 6:20 and note; used with cinnamon in the anointing oil (Exod 30:23,25). **myrrh and aloes.** For associations with sexual desire, see Ps 45:8 (a wedding song); Prov 7:17. **myrrh.** See note on 1:13.

4:14 [j]SS 3:6 [k]SS 1:12
4:16 [l]SS 2:3; 5:1
5:1 [m]SS 4:8 [n]SS 4:11; Isa 55:1
5:2 [o]SS 4:7 [p]SS 6:9

with every kind of incense tree,
with myrrh[j] and aloes
and all the finest spices.[k]
15 You are[a] a garden fountain,
a well of flowing water
streaming down from Lebanon.

She

16 Awake, north wind,
and come, south wind!
Blow on my garden,
that its fragrance may spread everywhere.
Let my beloved come into his garden
and taste its choice fruits.[l]

He

5 I have come into my garden, my sister, my bride;[m]
I have gathered my myrrh with my spice.
I have eaten my honeycomb and my honey;
I have drunk my wine and my milk.[n]

Friends

Eat, friends, and drink;
drink your fill of love.

She

2 I slept but my heart was awake.
Listen! My beloved is knocking:
"Open to me, my sister, my darling,
my dove, my flawless[o] one.[p]
My head is drenched with dew,
my hair with the dampness of the night."
3 I have taken off my robe—
must I put it on again?
I have washed my feet—
must I soil them again?
4 My beloved thrust his hand through the latch-opening;
my heart began to pound for him.

[a] 15 Or *I am* (spoken by *She*)

4:15 flowing water … from Lebanon. The freshest, most invigorating of waters are available to the man; pictures sexual delight and refreshment.

4:16 Each line contains a verb: "Awake … come … Blow … spread … come … taste." The woman seeks to arouse the man ("awake"; see note on 2:7) with cold ("north") and warm ("south") winds and invites him to her love.

5:1a honeycomb … honey. Describes either sweetness from the same source (see note on 4:11) or, in light of the following comparison of wine and milk, perhaps honey from bees (honeycomb) and from dates (honey). **wine … milk.** These conclude the sensual images begun in 4:10.

5:1b Eat … drink; drink your fill. The group encourages the couple in lovemaking. The first two verbs here repeat the verbs in v. 1a; the last command often refers to intoxication (Gen 9:21; 1 Sam 1:14; 2 Sam 11:13; Isa 29:9).

5:2—6:3 *The Fourth Meeting.* A frustrated meeting (contrast 3:1–5) leads to the woman's search for her lover. Here it ends in suffering (5:2–8). While love is freely given, the cost can be everything one has. The woman's loving description of the man emphasizes protection and security (5:10–16), and it concludes with union (6:2–3). The elements of risk, suffering, and protection characterize love here. The security of both lovers anticipates a family in which children feel secure. The love of the man and woman creates a commitment and unity that describes an eternal love.

5:2 I slept but my heart was awake. Cf. 3:1 and note. **Open.** Pictures physical intimacy as the woman opens herself to the one she loves (also in vv. 5,6). **drenched with dew.** Cf. Judg 6:38.

5:3 taken off. Some see the woman's response as still half asleep. Perhaps this is a coy response intended to elicit further interest.

5:4 latch-opening. However, he is unable to open the door.

[5]I arose to open for my beloved,
and my hands dripped with myrrh,[q]
my fingers with flowing myrrh,
on the handles of the bolt.
[6]I opened for my beloved,[r]
but my beloved had left; he was gone.[s]
My heart sank at his departure.[a]
I looked[t] for him but did not find him.
I called him but he did not answer.
[7]The watchmen found me
as they made their rounds in the city.[u]
They beat me, they bruised me;
they took away my cloak,
those watchmen of the walls!
[8]Daughters of Jerusalem, I charge you[v]—
if you find my beloved,
what will you tell him?
Tell him I am faint with love.[w]

Friends

[9]How is your beloved better than others,
most beautiful of women?[x]
How is your beloved better than others,
that you so charge us?

She

[10]My beloved is radiant and ruddy,
outstanding among ten thousand.[y]
[11]His head is purest gold;
his hair is wavy
and black as a raven.
[12]His eyes are like doves[z]
by the water streams,
washed in milk,[a]
mounted like jewels.
[13]His cheeks[b] are like beds of spice[c]
yielding perfume.
His lips are like lilies[d]
dripping with myrrh.
[14]His arms are rods of gold
set with topaz.

5:5 [q]ver 13
5:6 [r]SS 6:1 [s]SS 6:2 [t]SS 3:1
5:7 [u]SS 3:3
5:8 [v]SS 2:7; 3:5 [w]SS 2:5
5:9 [x]SS 1:8; 6:1
5:10 [y]Ps 45:2
5:12 [z]SS 1:15; 4:1 [a]Ge 49:12
5:13 [b]SS 1:10 [c]SS 6:2 [d]SS 2:1

[a] 6 Or *heart had gone out to him when he spoke*

5:5 flowing myrrh. Sought in 4:14; represents desire—all the delights of the woman's body as it flows toward the man (see note on 1:13).
5:6 I opened. After 40 Hebrew words, this answers the command in v. 2. **he was gone.** This single Hebrew word (*ʿābar*) is the turning point in the story of vv. 2–7. **My heart sank.** The woman is devastated.
5:7 The first two lines parallel 3:3. **They beat me.** Rough treatment at this second encounter with the watchmen. **cloak.** Not the robe of v. 3 (that she was wearing) but a shawl or veil, perhaps to aid in her identification.
5:9 The group invites the woman to describe the man and thus introduces the one song praising his physical attributes (vv. 10–16; for the woman, see 4:1–7; 6:4–9; 7:1–9a).
5:10 radiant and ruddy. Connotes health and well-being.
5:11 head ... purest gold ... hair ... black as a raven. The head marks one's identity (Ezek 9:4–6). Its brightness contrasts with the sensual hair, black like a raven against the sky.
5:12 eyes ... doves. Like the man (4:1), the woman focuses on the eyes of her lover more than on any other part of him.
5:13 beds of spice. The woman's place of jewelry (1:10) becomes the man's source of fragrance.
5:14–15 gold ... topaz ... ivory ... lapis lazuli ... marble ... pure gold ... cedars. The woman finds great value, beauty, and strength in her lover.

5:14 [e] Job 28:6
5:15 [f] 1Ki 4:33; SS 7:4
5:16 [g] SS 4:3 [h] SS 7:9 [i] SS 1:5
6:1 [j] SS 5:6 [k] SS 1:8
6:2 [l] SS 5:6 [m] SS 4:12 [n] SS 5:13
6:3 [o] SS 7:10 [p] SS 2:16
6:4 [q] Jos 12:24 [r] Ps 48:2; 50:2 [s] ver 10
6:5 [t] SS 4:1
6:6 [u] SS 4:2
6:7 [v] Ge 24:65 [w] SS 4:3
6:8 [x] Ps 45:9 [y] Ge 22:24

His body is like polished ivory
decorated with lapis lazuli.[e]
15 His legs are pillars of marble
set on bases of pure gold.
His appearance is like Lebanon,[f]
choice as its cedars.
16 His mouth[g] is sweetness itself;
he is altogether lovely.
This is my beloved,[h] this is my friend,
daughters of Jerusalem.[i]

Friends

6

Where has your beloved[j] gone,
most beautiful of women?[k]
Which way did your beloved turn,
that we may look for him with you?

She

2 My beloved has gone[l] down to his garden,[m]
to the beds of spices,[n]
to browse in the gardens
and to gather lilies.
3 I am my beloved's and my beloved is mine;[o]
he browses among the lilies.[p]

He

4 You are as beautiful as Tirzah,[q] my darling,
as lovely as Jerusalem,[r]
as majestic as troops with banners.[s]
5 Turn your eyes from me;
they overwhelm me.
Your hair is like a flock of goats
descending from Gilead.[t]
6 Your teeth are like a flock of sheep
coming up from the washing.
Each has its twin,
not one of them is missing.[u]
7 Your temples behind your veil[v]
are like the halves of a pomegranate.[w]
8 Sixty queens[x] there may be,
and eighty concubines,[y]
and virgins beyond number;

5:16 sweetness. See 4:11 and note. **my beloved ... my friend.** Terms of endearment that also tell the other women of the couple's exclusive relationship.
6:1 Where has your beloved gone ...? Recalling the woman's search (5:6) and anticipates the woman's answer (v. 2).
6:2 gone down ... browse ... gather. Depicts the man's exclusive interest in the woman. **garden ... beds of spices ... lilies.** Alludes to the romantic joys that the woman shares with her lover (see 1:13; 2:1; 4:11 and notes).
6:3 I am my beloved's and my beloved is mine. The lovers are in complete unity.
6:4—8:4 *The Fifth Meeting.* Following the woman's loving description of the man (5:10–16), he reciprocates with two descriptive songs about her (6:4–9; 7:1–9a). The first focuses on the power of her beauty and its effects. The second provides the strongest of romantic images. The couple journey to the countryside; the woman longs for her lover's kiss, and this leads to an embrace. Beauty, desire, and love all find their origin in the work of a divine Artist at the center of this section (7:1; cf. Ps 19:1).
6:4 Tirzah. Both a stronghold and beautiful with wildflowers, it was the capital of the northern kingdom of Israel before Samaria became the capital; it corresponds to Jerusalem, capital of the southern kingdom of Judah. **majestic as troops.** With the sense "fearful, terrible," it describes the woman as beautiful and a force in her own right.
6:5 eyes. Cf. 4:1; 5:12; focus on eyes introduces songs of praise. **Gilead.** Cf. 4:1.
6:8 Sixty. This may be a number associated with royalty (see 3:7 and note). **queens ... concubines ... virgins.** The social rank descends as

[9]but my dove,[z] my perfect one,[a] is unique,
the only daughter of her mother,
the favorite of the one who bore her.[b]
The young women saw her and called her blessed;
the queens and concubines praised her.

Friends

[10]Who is this that appears like the dawn,
fair as the moon, bright as the sun,
majestic as the stars in procession?

He

[11]I went down to the grove of nut trees
to look at the new growth in the valley,
to see if the vines had budded
or the pomegranates were in bloom.[c]
[12]Before I realized it,
my desire set me among the royal chariots of my people.[a]

Friends

[13]Come back, come back, O Shulammite;
come back, come back, that we may gaze on you!

He

Why would you gaze on the Shulammite
as on the dance[d] of Mahanaim?[b]

7[c] How beautiful your sandaled feet,
O prince's[e] daughter!
Your graceful legs are like jewels,
the work of an artist's hands.
[2]Your navel is a rounded goblet
that never lacks blended wine.
Your waist is a mound of wheat
encircled by lilies.
[3]Your breasts[f] are like two fawns,
like twin fawns of a gazelle.
[4]Your neck is like an ivory tower.[g]
Your eyes are the pools of Heshbon[h]
by the gate of Bath Rabbim.

6:9 [z]SS 1:15 [a]SS 5:2 [b]SS 3:4
6:11 [c]SS 7:12
6:13 [d]Ex 15:20
7:1 [e]Ps 45:13
7:3 [f]SS 4:5
7:4 [g]Ps 144:12; SS 4:4 [h]Nu 21:26

[a] *12* Or *among the chariots of Amminadab*; or *among the chariots of the people of the prince* [b] *13* In Hebrew texts this verse (6:13) is numbered 7:1. [c] In Hebrew texts 7:1-13 is numbered 7:2-14.

the number increases. Their reappearance in v. 9 positions the woman in their center and above them all.
6:9 one … unique. Contrast v. 8, which includes large numbers. **praised her.** Cf. 5:9; 6:1; Prov 31:28.
6:10 dawn … moon … sun … stars. The woman (clearly mortal, v. 9) is like the sky in awesome beauty.
6:11 nut trees. Perhaps this is the Kidron Valley northeast of Jerusalem, referred to in Arabic as "walnut tree valley." **new growth … budded … in bloom.** The fruitful springtime. **vines.** See 1:14 and note; 2:13; 7:8,12. **pomegranates.** See 4:3 and note; 4:13; 6:7; 7:12; 8:2. Vines and pomegranates depict the woman's physical attributes, which the man explores.
6:12 This obscure verse has several possible translations (see NIV text note). Perhaps the woman speaks, imagining love as the excitement and danger of war with the elite chariotry.
6:13a Shulammite. A feminine form of "Solomon" (see Introduction: Purpose and Theology); it less likely indicates that her hometown is Shulem/Shunem (in ancient Semitic languages the letters *l* and *n* were sometimes interchanged; see Josh 19:18; 1 Kgs 1:3).
6:13b dance of Mahanaim. Matches a dance performed by women at victories (Exod 15:20; Judg 11:34; 1 Sam 18:6; 21:11; 29:5). Mahanaim is a war camp east of the Jordan River (Gen 32:2; 2 Sam 2:8; 17:24).
7:1 beautiful. For this word at the beginning of such songs, cf. 4:1; 6:4. **feet.** Unlike the other songs, this one begins with the feet and progresses to the head (cf. 4:1–17; 6:4–9). **artist's.** Cf. 6:4—8:4 and note.
7:2 navel … wine … wheat. The navel represents beauty; the wine and wheat provide a feast for the woman's lover. **lilies.** See note on 2:16.
7:3 breasts. See note on 4:5.
7:4 neck … ivory tower. Cf. 1:10; 4:4. Ivory adorns a strong fortress,

7:4 [i]SS 5:15
7:5 [j]Isa 35:2
7:6 [k]SS 1:15 [l]SS 4:10
7:7 [m]SS 4:5
7:8 [n]SS 2:5
7:9 [o]SS 5:16
7:10 [p]Ps 45:11 [q]SS 2:16; 6:3
7:12 [r]SS 1:6 [s]SS 2:15 [t]SS 2:13 [u]SS 4:13 [v]SS 6:11
7:13 [w]Ge 30:14 [x]SS 4:16

Your nose is like the tower of Lebanon[i]
looking toward Damascus.
5 Your head crowns you like Mount Carmel.[j]
Your hair is like royal tapestry;
the king is held captive by its tresses.
6 How beautiful[k] you are and how pleasing,
my love, with your delights![l]
7 Your stature is like that of the palm,
and your breasts[m] like clusters of fruit.
8 I said, "I will climb the palm tree;
I will take hold of its fruit."
May your breasts be like clusters of grapes
on the vine,
the fragrance of your breath like apples,[n]
9 and your mouth like the best wine.

She

May the wine go straight to my beloved,[o]
flowing gently over lips and teeth.[a]
10 I belong to my beloved,
and his desire[p] is for me.[q]
11 Come, my beloved, let us go to the countryside,
let us spend the night in the villages.[b]
12 Let us go early to the vineyards[r]
to see if the vines have budded,[s]
if their blossoms[t] have opened,
and if the pomegranates[u] are in bloom[v]—
there I will give you my love.
13 The mandrakes[w] send out their fragrance,
and at our door is every delicacy,
both new and old,
that I have stored up for you, my beloved.[x]

8

If only you were to me like a brother,
who was nursed at my mother's breasts!
Then, if I found you outside,
I would kiss you,
and no one would despise me.

[a] *9* Septuagint, Aquila, Vulgate and Syriac; Hebrew *lips of sleepers* [b] *11* Or *the henna bushes*

representing beauty and strength. **pools of Heshbon.** Archaeologists have discovered cisterns at Tell Hesban, east of the Dead Sea. **Bath Rabbim.** The name means "daughter of many"; identifies how popular the pools are that represent the woman's eyes. **nose ... tower of Lebanon.** May be an Israelite lookout on Mount Hermon for watching for threats from Damascus. It represents the woman's personal security.
7:5 head ... Mount Carmel. This promontory faces the Mediterranean and provides a commanding view of the Sharon, Akko, and Jezreel plains. **hair.** See 5:11 and note. **king.** King Solomon; for this "Solomon," see Introduction: Purpose and Theology.
7:7–8 The man indulges four senses (see 1:2–3; 2:12–13 and notes): sight ("palm"), touch ("take hold"), taste ("grapes"; cf. 1:2), and smell ("breath like apples").
7:8 palm tree. The stately date palm with its sweet fruit (see 4:11 and note).
7:9a your mouth. The palate, the sensuous inner mouth. **best wine.** Of many references to wine (see note on 1:2), only this connection with the palate makes a special appeal to the sense of taste.
7:9b May the wine. The woman echoes the man's desire for this kissing, represented as wine (see 1:2 and note).
7:10 I belong. Cf. 2:16; 6:3. **desire.** Elsewhere this Hebrew word occurs only in Gen 3:16; 4:7. This reverses the picture of Gen 3:16, where the prepositions are different and where perhaps there is something improper about the desire. Here the man desires the woman, the woman equally desires the man, and the lovers are united.
7:11 Come. Cf. 2:10,13.
7:13 mandrakes. The same Hebrew root as "beloved" (*dwd*); they exude an intoxicating aroma. **new and old.** Like new and aged wine, the woman promises many delights of love.
8:1 I would kiss you. While kissing between family members in public was acceptable in ancient Israel, romantic kissing was not.

[2] I would lead you
and bring you to my mother's house[y] —
she who has taught me.
I would give you spiced wine to drink,
the nectar of my pomegranates.
[3] His left arm is under my head
and his right arm embraces me.[z]
[4] Daughters of Jerusalem, I charge you:
Do not arouse or awaken love
until it so desires.[a]

Friends

[5] Who is this coming up from the wilderness[b]
leaning on her beloved?

She

Under the apple tree I roused you;
there your mother conceived[c] you,
there she who was in labor gave you birth.
[6] Place me like a seal over your heart,
like a seal on your arm;
for love[d] is as strong as death,
its jealousy[a][e] unyielding as the grave.
It burns like blazing fire,
like a mighty flame.[b]
[7] Many waters cannot quench love;
rivers cannot sweep it away.
If one were to give
all the wealth of one's house for love,
it[c] would be utterly scorned.[f]

Friends

[8] We have a little sister,
and her breasts are not yet grown.
What shall we do for our sister
on the day she is spoken for?
[9] If she is a wall,
we will build towers of silver on her.

8:2 [y] SS 3:4
8:3 [z] SS 2:6
8:4 [a] SS 2:7; 3:5
8:5 [b] SS 3:6 [c] SS 3:4
8:6 [d] SS 1:2 [e] Nu 5:14
8:7 [f] Pr 6:35

[a] 6 Or *ardor* [b] 6 Or *fire, / like the very flame of the* LORD [c] 7 Or *he*

8:2 wine … pomegranates. See notes on 1:2; 4:3.
8:4 Do not arouse or awaken love … desires. Cf. 2:7; 3:5.
8:5–7 *The Literary Climax.* If v. 5b connects sexuality with procreation, vv. 6–7 produce a love whose unity is stronger than anything in this world.
8:5 roused. Possibly "awoke" but probably "aroused in desire." **conceived … was in labor.** The same verb's repetition (meaning "be/become pregnant"; Gen 4:1) moves the sexuality beyond personal pleasure to the realm of family and procreation. The Song does not envision any sexuality outside of marriage.
8:6 seal over your heart. A seal contained the name of the bearer. Thus the woman shares her identity with the man. The heart was the source of love (Deut 6:5) as well as a picture of the seal hung around the neck (Gen 38:18,25). **seal on your arm.** The arm could include the fingers, where one wore a seal as a ring (Jer 22:24). **love is as strong as death.** Nothing on earth is stronger (1 Cor 13). **fire.** Love can be destructive but can also inflame passions (see note on 8:7). **mighty flame.** See second NIV text note. The alternative reading is possible: the final syllable, *yāh*, is a shortened form of "LORD" (*Yahweh*) and the only occurrence of God's name in the Song. This signals its key message: romantic love is a powerful gift from God.
8:7 Many waters cannot quench love. Waters follow fire as one of the most powerful natural forces. The two forces of nature appear in Isa 43:2, where God guards Israel just as here love guards the lovers.
8:8–14 *The Conclusion.* The friends are brothers who care for their sister's purity (8:8–9), but the sister now assumes responsibility for her life and love (vv. 10,12). The book concludes with an open-ended view of the lovers as they continue to grow in intimacy.
8:9 In many cultures such as Israel the brothers protected their sisters' virginity (Gen 34; 2 Sam 13:22–33). **we will build towers.** The woman's brothers promise to preserve her purity (4:4; 7:4; and notes). **cedar.** See notes on 1:17; 5:15.

8:11 [g]Ecc 2:4 [h]Isa 7:23
8:12 [i]SS 1:6
8:14 [j]Pr 5:19 [k]SS 2:9
[l]SS 2:8,17

If she is a door,
we will enclose her with panels of cedar.

She

10 I am a wall,
and my breasts are like towers.
Thus I have become in his eyes
like one bringing contentment.
11 Solomon had a vineyard[g] in Baal Hamon;
he let out his vineyard to tenants.
Each was to bring for its fruit
a thousand shekels[a][h] of silver.
12 But my own vineyard[i] is mine to give;
the thousand shekels are for you, Solomon,
and two hundred[b] are for those who tend its fruit.

He

13 You who dwell in the gardens
with friends in attendance,
let me hear your voice!

She

14 Come away, my beloved,
and be like a gazelle[j]
or like a young stag[k]
on the spice-laden mountains.[l]

[a] *11* That is, about 25 pounds or about 12 kilograms; also in verse 12 [b] *12* That is, about 5 pounds or about 2.3 kilograms

8:10 I am a wall. The woman claims a mature independence.
8:11–12 vineyard ... vineyard ... vineyard. See notes on 1:6,14; 2:15.
8:11 Baal Hamon. Place name meaning "lord/owner of multitudes"; connotes wealth and power.
8:12 my own vineyard is mine. Contrasting 1:6, the woman now maintains independence from her brothers and others, however influential. **two hundred ... tend.** The profits of Solomon's vineyard must be shared with others, whereas the woman shares her vineyard with no one except her beloved.
8:13 dwell in the gardens. The couple permanently share love. **friends.** The same word refers to the shepherds in 1:7. **voice.** Cf. 2:14.
8:14 Come away. The woman wants her lover to leave his friends (v. 13) and be with her. **gazelle ... young stag.** Cf. 2:9,17. **spice-laden mountains.** Spice occurs in the woman's fragrance (4:10) and in her garden, or physical attributes (4:12–16; 5:1; 6:2). The man's cheeks are spice-laden (5:13). The couple comes away from their companions to enjoy each other's romantic love.

INTRODUCTION TO

THE PROPHETIC BOOKS

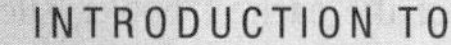

ISAIAH

JEREMIAH

LAMENTATIONS

EZEKIEL

DANIEL

HOSEA

JOEL

AMOS

OBADIAH

JONAH

MICAH

NAHUM

HABAKKUK

ZEPHANIAH

HAGGAI

ZECHARIAH

MALACHI

THE PROPHETIC BOOKS

Richard S. Hess

The Prophetic Books include four Major Prophets (Isaiah, Jeremiah, Ezekiel, and Daniel) and 12 Minor Prophets (Hosea, Joel, Amos, Obadiah, Jonah, Micah, Nahum, Habakkuk, Zephaniah, Haggai, Zechariah, and Malachi). The distinction is based on the length of the books. As the authors first wrote their words on scrolls, the Major Prophets would each fit on a separate scroll, whereas all the Minor Prophets eventually filled a single scroll. The Major Prophets follow a chronological arrangement: Isaiah ca. 735–681 BC, Jeremiah ca. 622–586 BC, Ezekiel ca. 593–571 BC, Daniel ca. 605–536 BC. The Minor Prophets also begin with some of the earliest books, such as Hosea and Amos, from the mid-eighth century BC. They conclude with the latest books, Haggai and Zechariah, in the latter part of the sixth century BC, and Malachi from the middle or late fifth century BC.

Prophets

A prophecy is a God-given message that speaks to people about their condition, urges change, and may describe future events as a means to motivate the people to faithfulness. Prophets, as intermediaries who brought God's word to people, were present before some of their number began to write their prophecies. One title of a prophet, Hebrew *ro'eh* (1 Sam 9:9), describes a "seer," one whose ability to see goes beyond normal human abilities — either beyond the ability of the eyes (e.g., to find Saul's donkeys in 1 Sam 9:3–10,20) or into the court of God (e.g., to recognize God's choice for Israel's king in 1 Sam 9:15–17; cf. Isa 6:1–8). Another frequent title, Hebrew *nabi'* (Gen 20:7), identifies someone who named or summoned God or who decreed or proclaimed the word of God.

Non-Israelite prophets served royal courts outside of Israel. Such prophets in the eighteenth century BC wrote some of the earliest prophetic texts that we have. Along with magical rites to determine the will of their gods, these pagan prophets reported to their kings regarding the best time to go to war and to undertake other matters for their kingdoms. This type of prophecy continued for more than a thousand years, often including predictions of success for the prophet's own country and of divine judgment and failure for other countries.

Prophecies against other nations and endorsements of present leaders occur in the biblical prophetic books. However, prophets also indict their own nation and leaders for failing to follow God's covenant. They often criticize the people as a whole for their immorality, injustice, and lack of faith. Above all, they frequently predict judgment for Israel and Judah, God's people. Therefore, destruction of these nations comes because of the sin of the people, not due to any weakness on God's part. Yet God's mercy and grace extend beyond the punishment to an age of restoration, hope, and blessing, which the prophets often proclaim will

TIMELINE OF PROPHETS

9TH CENTURY BC PROPHETS
Elijah
Elisha
8TH CENTURY BC PROPHETS
Jonah
Amos
Hosea
Micah
Isaiah
PROPHETS FROM BEFORE AND DURING THE TIME OF THE BABYLONIAN DESTRUCTION OF JERUSALEM (586 BC)
Nahum
Zephaniah
Joel(?)
Habakkuk
Jeremiah
Obadiah
Ezekiel
Daniel
LATE 6TH CENTURY BC PROPHETS
Haggai
Zechariah
Joel(?)
5TH CENTURY BC PROPHET
Malachi

come in the future. As fearless critics of their own rulers and society, the biblical prophets may be contrasted with prophets in other nations who served the interests of the royal court.

Deuteronomy describes the requirements of a prophet of God. Even if a prophet predicts signs and wonders that come to pass, Deut 13:1–5 warns God's people to reject such a prophet if they counsel following other gods. Deut 18:18–22 identifies the tests to determine a true prophet: they must speak in God's name, and what they proclaim must occur just as they have said it. Otherwise, their message is not trustworthy.

The Bible describes Abraham, Moses, Deborah, and Samuel as prophets, as well as Nathan, Elijah, Elisha, and others. All of these served in a time before the prophets who wrote the named prophetic books. The earliest prophetic books include Hosea, Amos, and Jonah. These three prophets addressed their messages to the northern kingdom of Israel. They prophesied in the mid-eighth century BC at the time of King Jeroboam II's expansion of the northern kingdom when Israel enjoyed prosperity. Hosea deplored the prosperity that brought idolatry, immorality, and the loss of faithfulness, love, and awareness of God (Hos 4:1). Amos warned against the injustices of the age, both in international acts between nations (Amos 1:3—2:5) and in the acts of Israel, where the wealthy abused the poor (Amos 2:7; 4:1; 5:11–12; 8:4–6). God called Jonah to warn Nineveh, Israel's enemy, of judgment and thus afford them opportunity for repentance (2 Kgs 14:25; Jonah 1–3).

Isaiah and Micah prophesied later in the eighth century BC and into the seventh century BC. Micah's message focused on God's people, whom God chose and to whom he gave his land as an inheritance for all, not just the rich (Mic 2:1–11; 6:1–5). Many prophets address the need for justice, humility, and love for God that Mic 6:6–8 so aptly summarizes. Indeed, Jeremiah later drew upon many texts in Micah to describe a similar situation (Jer 26:18).

Isaiah in many ways exemplifies the prophetic books. It includes all the major prophetic themes and traces the history of the people of God from their early confrontation with Damascus and the northern kingdom of Israel (734–732 BC) through the challenge for survival against the Assyrian attack upon Judah (701 BC) down to the destruction of Jerusalem by the Babylonians (586 BC) and the exile of God's people. The book predicts the coming of Cyrus, the Persian king who allowed the exiles to return to Jerusalem (Isa 44:28—45:1). It looks forward to the rebuilding of Jerusalem (Isa 54:1–2) and its exaltation in the last days, when God will rule over all peoples of the earth (Isa 66). Thus Isaiah touches upon the various periods of

Jonah preaching in Nineveh.
Providence Collection/Goodsalt

Michelangelo's painting of the prophet Isaiah in the Sistine Chapel.
Planet Art

time that the prophetic books address. The other writing prophets expand upon aspects of this proclamation.

Key Themes in the Prophets' Messages

The prophets delivered God's word to God's people, Israel, and also to other people (e.g., the people of Nineveh in the book of Jonah). They spoke to the general public and to leaders as well as to false prophets. Because prophets spoke words from God, their messages reflect the concerns of God for his people. These include:

1. *The holiness and power of God, who speaks through the prophet.* Isa 40–45 acknowledges the limitless power of God the Creator, who has brought the world into being. Jer 18–20 declares that God raises up some nations and destroys others according to his will and according to their decisions to either follow him or refuse his grace. God speaks through his prophets, calling them to their roles from his throne (Isa 6) in his splendor (Ezek 1), in spite of their occasional reluctance (Jer 1). The holiness of God was visible to Isaiah in his vision of God when the seraphim called, "Holy, holy, holy is the LORD Almighty" (Isa 6:3). The prophetic books apply "holy" to God an additional 40 times. Carried along by the Holy Spirit (2 Pet 1:21), the prophets repeatedly proclaimed their messages as the very word of God. "This is what the LORD says" occurs 236 times in the prophetic books.

2. *Israel's past relationship with God, especially the covenant they have with him.* Israel encountered God when he redeemed them from Egypt (Jer 2:6; 7:22; 11:4; 16:14; 23:7; 32:21) and made a covenant with them (Jer 31:32; 34:13). God remembers the wilderness wanderings of Israel (Jer 2:2) as a time when Israel loved and followed him. God gave Israel their land (Amos 2:10). Although the prophetic writings do not often mention Saul (Isa 10:29) and Solomon (Jer 52:20), David's name appears 39 times. God's covenant with David becomes the standard for a future covenant with redeemed Israel (Isa 55:3) and guarantees that God will fulfill his promises (Jer 33:20–22). Nevertheless, it is God's covenants with Abraham and with Israel at Sinai that form the basis for the understanding of God's ongoing relationship with his people. This covenantal concern appears in references to lawsuits and charges that God brings against his people (Jer 2:9,29; Hos 4:1; 12:2; Mic 6:2). Isa 3:13 is one of the clearest references: "The LORD takes his place in court; he rises to judge the people."

3. *The sin of Israel and the nations.* God challenges his people to justify their sins in Isa 41:21: "'Present your case,' says the LORD. 'Set forth your arguments,' says Jacob's King." The prophets use various images to portray Israel's sin. Jer 13:1–11 describes Jeremiah's ruined belt as a picture of how God bound Israel to himself but they would not obey. Perhaps most dramatic of all is Gomer's unfaithfulness toward her husband, the prophet Hosea. Hos 2:2 describes Israel's broken commitment with the words of divorce: "She is not my wife, and I am not her husband." Israel has sinned against God. Isa 1 summarizes the indictment, a theme also presented in many of the remaining prophets. Only Jonah, Nahum, and Obadiah do not deal directly with the sin and consequent judgment of God's people. The sin extends through all of Israel and reaches into each Israelite (Isa 1:4–6). It extends into the depths of their hearts and reaches into the courts of the temple in Jerusalem (Ezek 8:1–18; 11:19; 36:26). Even after the punishment of the exile, sin remains so that the prophet Malachi later provides a catalog of Israel's offenses (Mal 1:1—3:18).

The prophetic books also address the sins of the nations. Amos 1:3—2:3 indicts many of the surrounding peoples for their sins. These are not violations of God's law to Moses but failures against the basic understanding of human decency in the treatment of conquered nations. Isa 13:1—23:18 lists many more nations and presents their offenses in greater detail (cf. Jer 46:1—51:64; Ezek 25:1—32:32). Isa 66:16 declares fiery judgment on "all people." The prophet Jonah cries against the sins of Assyrian Nineveh (Jonah 1:1–2; 3:1–4). This leads to repentance (Jonah 3:5,10), but the sins of Assyria appear again in Nahum.

Isaiah's vision of God (Isa 6).
Mary Evans Picture Library

Obadiah describes the sins of Edom, while Habakkuk (Hab 1:12—2:1) focuses on Babylon. Joel 3:1–16 and Zeph 2:1—3:8 mingle the sins of the nations with God's judgment against them.

4. *The judgment and punishment that God brings as a result of disobedience.* Just as the sin and judgment of foreign nations are interwoven, so many texts that describe the sins of God's people also pronounce the judgment and punishment of God for those sins. Isaiah focuses on the leaders of Israel (Isa 3:14; cf. Jer 21–24; Hos 5:1). Despite their protests of innocence, God will pass judgment on his people (Jer 2:35). Flight is not possible (Ezek 11:10–11). Dan 9:11 looks back to judgments that have already occurred and sees them as already described in the law of Moses (Deut 28:15–68). Amos 7:4 describes fiery judgment against God's own people. Hab 1:6,12 identifies the Babylonians as the instrument through which God will judge his people.

For the northern kingdom of Israel, the punishment came when the Assyrian army destroyed the kingdom and deported its inhabitants in 722 BC (2 Kgs 17; Hos 10:6; 11:5). Amos uses a series of dramatic visions to describe this deportation (Amos 5:27; 6:7,14; 7:9,17; 8:9—9:10). Twenty years later, in 701 BC, another Assyrian king came against King Hezekiah of Jerusalem and Judah. Because of Assyria's blasphemy and Hezekiah's faith, God spared Jerusalem and his temple (Isa 36–38). Nevertheless, Isaiah records Hezekiah's pride in his own defenses and the consequent prophetic warning that another people, the Babylonians, would come against Judah (Isa 39). Much of Jeremiah's prophecy deals with the events leading up to the Babylonian destruction of Jerusalem in 586 BC and the consequent executions, deportations, and desperate events within the land—whether as a prophecy foretold (Jer 25–29) or as a historical narrative (Jer 39–45; 52). The unbelieving King Jehoiakim cuts up and burns Jeremiah's prophecies of Jerusalem's doom, leading Jeremiah to prepare a second scroll with the same words and more besides (Jer 36). King Zedekiah imprisons Jeremiah (Jer 37–38). Considered a traitor by his fellow Israelites, Jeremiah pens a collection of "confessions" that describe how this message was not one he wished to proclaim (Jer 11–20). God overpowered him, however, and the divine word became a fire shut up in his bones that he could not refrain from speaking (Jer 20:7–9). The reader gains insight into a prophet's burden in a manner not found elsewhere in the Bible.

The prophets acknowledged God as Creator.

The Creation, from the Luther Bible, ca. 1530, German School/Bible Society, London, UK/Bridgeman Images

Ezekiel had been deported to Babylonia a few years before its army's final destruction of Jerusalem. With other exiles, he viewed the Babylonian destruction of the temple. Jeremiah had to deal with citizens who looked back upon God's miraculous deliverance in 701 BC and were therefore convinced that God would never allow his city and temple to be destroyed; Ezekiel, on the other hand, faced those who saw

Much of Jeremiah's prophecy deals with the events leading up to the Babylonian destruction of Jerusalem.

The destruction of Jerusalem by Nebuzar-adan, Hole, William Brassey/Private Collection/© Look and Learn/ Bridgeman Images

it happen and were tempted to believe that the Lord was too weak to resist the Babylonians and their god Marduk. To explain what actually occurred, God transported the prophet Ezekiel back to Jerusalem, where he witnessed every kind of idolatrous worship in the temple (Ezek 8). God had no choice but to punish these idolaters (Ezek 9).

In a dramatic series of scenes, Ezekiel watches the divine Spirit leave the temple, depart from the city, and pass eastward beyond the Mount of Olives (Ezek 10:1 — 11:25). Jerusalem did not fall because God was weak. Jerusalem fell because Judah continued to sin to such an extent that the Spirit of the Lord could no longer remain among them. God abandoned the temple and the city; then the Babylonians came and destroyed it.

Habakkuk asked why God would allow so evil a people as the Babylonians to destroy his people (Hab 1:2 – 17). In a dramatic response, God commanded the prophet to record his revelation that would come to pass (Hab 2:2 – 3), but God asserted that "the righteous person will live by his faithfulness" (Hab 2:4). Among later Jews and Christians (Rom 1:17; Gal 3:11; Heb 10:38), this text became an important summary of the appropriate human response to God's grace.

5. *God's redemption and the promise of the world to come.* This constitutes a promise found in every prophetic book. Even the generally negative prophecies of Amos conclude with a promise of the restoration of the fallen shelter of David (Amos 9:11 – 15). The people would return from exile and experience restoration. Thus Isaiah devotes Isa 40 – 66 to this theme, which the twofold command to comfort those suffering God's punishment summarizes (Isa 40:1). Jeremiah (Jer 30 – 33) promises a new covenant that will bring faithfulness to God because it will be written on the human heart (31:31 – 34) rather than on tablets of stone. Ezekiel envisions a heart transplant (Ezek 11:19; 36:26), allowing the hearts of Israel to become responsive to God's will. Ezekiel also anticipates a resurrection of the nation, pictured by dry bones taking on flesh and returning to life (Ezek 37). Ezekiel sees a restored Israel with a rebuilt temple from which a miraculous flow of water brings life to the desert and the Dead Sea (Ezek 40 – 48). Daniel provides a more detailed account of future kingdoms and events (Dan 2; 5; 7 – 12). Habakkuk concludes with a psalm praising the power of God (Hab 3). Zephaniah declares God's promises to gather the exiles and bless them (Zeph 3:9 – 20). Haggai promises blessings for the people of God and for their temple (Hag 2:1 – 19). Zechariah concludes more in the style of Daniel and Habakkuk, promising a future and terrible war in which God will fight for

Ezekiel anticipates a resurrection of the nation, pictured by dry bones taking on flesh and returning to life (Ezek 37).

Wikimedia Commons

Zechariah prophesied that Israel's ruler would come to Jerusalem riding on a donkey (Zech 9:9).

Wikimedia Commons

his people and against all the nations, bringing into being the Lord's universal reign (Zech 14:2 – 21).

The theme of a believing remnant from among Israel occurs in Isaiah, where Isaiah's testimony is bound up for his disciples, who will accept it while others will not (Isa 8:16). This remnant will return from the deportations and exile caused by Assyria (Isa 10:20 – 22; 11:11,16; 37:4; Amos 5:15; Mic 2:12) and by Babylonia (Isa 37:31 – 32; 46:3; Jer 23:3; 50:20; Zeph 2:7,9). Malachi develops the theme of the surviving faithful, who will be God's treasured possession (Mal 3:16 – 18).

6. The One to Come. Malachi also promises that God will send Elijah, who will bring reconciliation (Mal 4:5 – 6). Earlier God spoke through the prophet Haggai and identified the governor Zerubbabel as his chosen servant through whom he would bring victory over Israel's enemies (Hag 2:20 – 23). God appointed Zechariah to identify in the high priest Joshua one who would rebuild the temple (Zech 6:9 – 15). These applications draw from an older and more profound divine vision of an anointed king and priest who would come to rule Israel and all the peoples, restoring them to what God intended them to be. Zechariah saw the people mourning for this ruler as one whom they pierced (Zech 12:10 – 14); he would serve as a shepherd but would be struck down, and his people would be scattered (Zech 13:7 – 9). He would come to Jerusalem riding on a donkey (Zech 9:9). Micah spoke of him as born in Bethlehem from the line of David (Mic 5:2). Daniel saw him in the divinely appointed son of man to whom God gave authority over everything (Dan 7:8 – 14,26 – 27).

Isaiah identifies this future leader in more detail than any other prophet. He appears in the sign of Immanuel ("God with us") in Isa 7:14. He comes from the line of David with wisdom (Isa 11:1 – 3), divine authority, and universal kingship (Isa 9:1 – 6). In Isa 41:8 – 16, God redeems his servant, who is the nation of Israel empowered to overcome all nations. Yet in Isa 42:1 – 4 this servant of the Lord appears to be a single individual endowed with God's Spirit and bringing justice on earth without making a great noise. Israel as God's servant recurs in Isa 42:18 – 20, where it is blind and unresponsive to God. Nevertheless, God has redeemed Israel and brought the people back from captivity (Isa 43:1 – 7). Israel is God's chosen servant, and as such the people will receive his Spirit and his blessing (Isa 44:1 – 5). In Isa 49:1 – 7, the servant of the Lord is called to redeem Israel. However, the servant also becomes a light to the nations. The "servant of the Lord" texts reach a climax in Isa 52:13 — 53:12, where the text follows one who comes proclaiming the advent of God's reign (Isa 52:7 – 10). The suffering servant of Isa 53 willingly suffers and dies for the sins of his people before seeing life and receiving "a portion among the great" from God. The role of the servant of the Lord continues in Isa 61:1 – 3, where the Spirit anoints him to proclaim good news and bring healing and salvation to those who recognize their need.

At the transfiguration, Jesus' face shone like that of the prophet Moses.

PhotoNonStop/Glow Images

In Deut 18:15 God promised a prophet to come who would be like Moses. Jesus Christ fulfilled this expectation in a way that the earlier prophets did not. At the transfiguration, Jesus' face shone like that of the prophet Moses (Exod 34:29 – 35; Matt 17:2; 2 Cor 3:7 – 18). The command to listen to God's Son (Matt 17:5; Mark 9:7; Luke 9:35) recalls the same command in Deut 18:15. Peter also argued that Jesus fulfilled the prophecy of a prophet like Moses (Acts 3:22). Stephen made the same point (Acts 7:37). Many of the people of Israel, however, did not welcome this prophet. They rejected him just as they had the prophets of the OT (Matt 13:10 – 17,57; 23:37; Mark 6:4). God spoke through the prophets of the OT, but he has now spoken once for all through Jesus (Heb 1:1 – 2). As the true image of God (Col 1:15 – 17), Jesus brings the message of God's judgment, grace, and salvation more clearly and powerfully than any who preceded him. ■

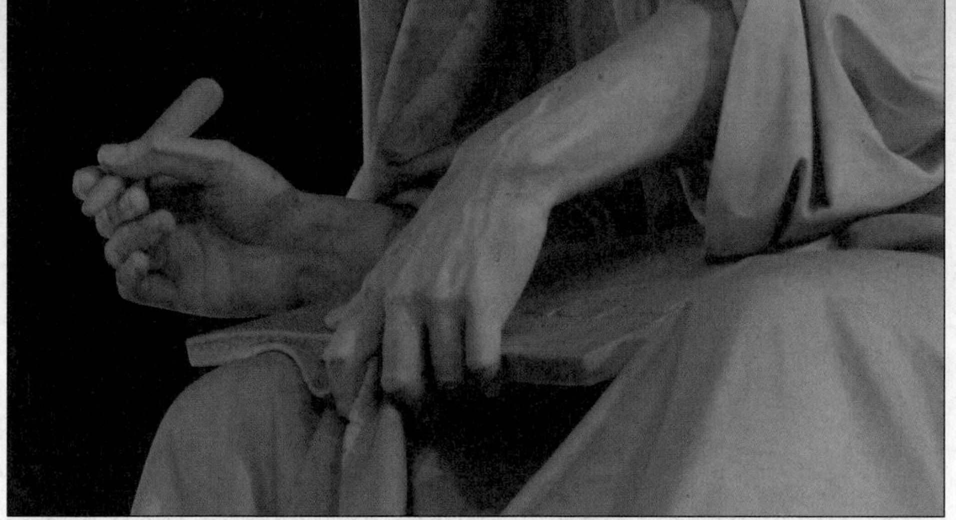

INTRODUCTION TO

ISAIAH

The book of Isaiah is a great masterpiece from at least two perspectives. (1) It is a literary masterpiece in its stirring poetic cadences and its gripping imagery. (2) It is a theological masterpiece, managing to contain in its 66 chapters virtually the whole of biblical theology, from God's transcendence through creation and redemption to the final destiny of the cosmos.

AUTHOR AND DATE

Isaiah ("Yahweh saves") is said to be the son of Amoz, but we do not have any information about Amoz or any other of Isaiah's family. Information about the book's date and location is by implication. All of Isaiah's activity seems to have been in and around Jerusalem, and his messages were apparently delivered between the dates of King Uzziah's death (739 BC) and Sennacherib's attack on Judah (701 BC). The book itself mentions only one author: "Isaiah son of Amoz" (1:1; 2:1; 13:1). On this basis, the traditional view is that Isaiah authored the entire book. However, certain factors (noted even in ancient times) cause some to question this conclusion. Among these are differences in vocabulary and style in chs. 40 – 66. Furthermore, chs. 40 – 66 seem to address two different historical situations, both far beyond the prophet's own lifetime.

As a result of these and other factors, it has become common for Isaiah scholars to posit a number of authors for the book. But there are strong reasons to maintain the traditional view:

1. The text does not identify any writers other than Isaiah. Why would later authors go to such great lengths to hide their own identities and try to make it appear that Isaiah was the sole author?

2. Chs. 40 – 48 proclaim that God's ability to predict the future through his prophets is the primary evidence of his Godhood. But critical scholars have argued that Isaiah of Jerusalem could not have made such predictions and therefore could not have written chs. 40 – 66. That would mean that the author of chs. 40 – 55 was making an argument he knew to be fallacious.

3. Chs. 40 – 66 do not refer to any historical persons or events except for one glaring exception: Cyrus, the Persian emperor. One explanation for this fact is that such details were originally present in the work of "Second Isaiah" (chs. 40 – 55) and "Third Isaiah" (chs. 56 – 66) but that the writers themselves or later editors removed them to promote the illusion that Isaiah son of Amoz wrote the whole book. A better solution is that the historical details are not there simply because Isaiah, writing long before the fact, did not know them except for the one fact he learned by inspiration: Cyrus.

4. One further argument for the unity of the book is a linguistic one. Although there are linguistic differences between chs. 1 – 39 and chs. 40 – 66 (and especially chs. 40 – 55), there are also some important connections between the two parts. One such connection is the occurrence of the phrase "the Holy One of Israel." Of the 31 occurrences of this phrase in the OT, 25 are found in Isaiah, with 12 occurrences in chs. 1 – 39 and 13 in chs. 40 – 66. When the Bible's single occurrence of "the Holy One of Jacob" (29:23) is added, the distribution is 13 and 13. There are also many examples of terms occurring in both parts of the book that hardly occur elsewhere in the Bible.

A Judahite family being deported from Lachish after the town was taken over by Assyrians.

For these reasons and others, it seems less problematic to assert that the materials in the book come from Isaiah than to assert that the materials come from a number of authors. There are two possible explanations for the differences in vocabulary and style between chs. 1 – 39 and chs. 40 – 55: (1) Perhaps Isaiah's moving from talking about his own time to talking about an only broadly perceived distant future causes the differences. This would be especially possible if a number of years elapsed between his writing chs. 1 – 39 and chs. 40 – 66. (2) Perhaps a disciple is responsible for actually writing the later chapters. If so, the ideas come from Isaiah himself, but the vocabulary and sentence structure are those of the disciple.

COMPOSITION

The book may be divided into three main units: chs. 1 – 39; 40 – 55; 56 – 66. But within these units, with the possible exception of chs. 40 – 55, there are no clear organizing principles. It seems probable that either Isaiah himself or his disciples transcribed his oral declarations during his lifetime and combined them to form the book.

Chs. 1 – 39 have recognized groupings of materials, but there is not much agreement as to how they relate to each other or function together. The subunits are chs. 1 – 5; 6 – 12; 13 – 23; 24 – 27; 28 – 35; 36 – 39. A strong possibility for their interrelationship is as follows: Chs. 1 – 5 introduce the book, starkly contrasting the Israel of the prophet's own time and the Israel of the future. Ch. 6 bridges chs. 1 – 5 and chs. 7 – 12. On the one hand, ch. 6 presents the prophet's own experience as the model for what needs to happen in the nation of Israel to move the actual Israel of the present to the ideal Israel of the future. On the other hand, chs. 7 – 12 further develop ch. 6's prediction that the prophet's words would only harden the hearts of the present generation.

In ch. 7 Isaiah issues King Ahaz a challenge to trust Yahweh, not Assyria's power. Ahaz refuses the challenge, and much of Judah's history between that point (734 BC) and the destruction of Sennacherib's army in 701 BC revolves around the results of Ahaz's refusal. A burning question unites chs. 7 – 39: Will Israel trust Yahweh or the surrounding nations? Chs. 7 – 12 not only give the answer (no) but also give the answer's implications. Chs. 13 – 35 are lessons in trust: in a variety of ways they contrast Yahweh's infinite trustworthiness with the folly of trusting the nations.

The issue of trust surfaces again in chs. 36 – 39: Will Ahaz's son Hezekiah trust Yahweh in the face of the Assyrian threat? The answer is a qualified yes. The qualification is how Hezekiah responds to the Babylonian envoys (ch. 39). That qualification provides Isaiah with the basis for transitioning to the future Babylonian exile in the following chapters. But in any case, this conclusively answers the question of Yahweh's trustworthiness as the sovereign of history: Hezekiah trusts Yahweh in the face of overwhelming Assyrian power, and Yahweh delivers him.

Chs. 40 – 55 seem to fall into three subunits: chs. 40; 41 – 48; 49 – 55. Ch. 40 introduces the entire unit, asserting Yahweh's desire, ability, and intention to deliver his people.

Chs. 41 – 48 focus on Yahweh's deliverance of his people from Babylon and their gods. Far from casting Israel away on account of their sins, Yahweh intends to use the nation as his servant to demonstrate his sole Godhood. But that raises an issue: What about the sin that separates Israel from their God? Can God simply ignore it?

The answer to that question is found in chs. 49 – 55, which present Yahweh's desire, ability, and intention to deliver his people from the sin that alienates them from him. The key to that deliverance is the servant of the Lord, first introduced in ch. 42. The servant, famously explained in 52:13 — 53:12, unexpectedly manifests Yahweh's mighty arm of deliverance, making possible the ringing invitations to reconciliation in chs. 54 – 55.

From the perspective of gracious deliverance, chs. 56 – 66 seem somewhat anticlimactic. But viewed in the larger context of the book and its concerns, their message is an integral part of the whole. Chs. 1 – 5 declare that somehow sinful Israel will become holy Israel and that all the nations of the earth will come to the holy mountain to learn the instructions (*tôrâ* or "law") of God. Ch. 6 suggests that just encountering the holy God's fire purifies the prophet Isaiah to declare the message to his people; the same may be true for the nation, making them the promised light to the nations. Chs. 56 – 66 show how it will be possible for that promise to become a reality. These chapters seem to be arranged in pyramid fashion, culminating in the Anointed One in ch. 61; they address the character of the nation that must bear the light of God. So the prophet Isaiah declares that righteous, covenant-keeping foreigners are more pleasing to Yahweh than unrighteous purebred returnees. But the people of Israel declare themselves unable to be righteous. In response, Yahweh reveals his righteous Warrior (59:15b – 21; 63:1 – 6), who will defeat sin and graciously empower Israel to live righteously and thus become the promised light to the nations.

PLACE OF COMPOSITION AND DESTINATION

Isaiah addresses chs. 1 – 39 to the people of his own day. These people are not only from Judah (1:1) but also from the northern kingdom of Israel prior to that kingdom's final fall to Assyria in 722 BC (28:1 – 4). Jerusalem is the only location Isaiah identifies as a place where he delivers his messages (7:3; 22:15; 37:5; 38:1; 39:3).

The audience of chs. 40 – 55 and 56 – 66 is much less certain. There are elements in these chapters that would be appropriate to an eighth-century BC audience, but there are others that seem less appropriate. The earlier part of the book addresses people who are concerned about impending national calamity and inclined to trust the nations, whether Assyria or Egypt, to avert that calamity. But chs. 40 – 55 address a captive people who doubt that their God wants to, is able to, or intends to deliver them. Whereas God calls the earlier people to trust him and not the nations, he calls these people to believe his promises of deliverance.

Chs. 56 – 66 seem to address yet another situation. Deliverance from captivity is not the issue; rather, the people cannot live righteously and consequently fail their national mission to bring light to the nations. Again, there would be a message here for corrupt Jerusalem during Isaiah's lifetime, yet it seems more likely to be describing the situation after the return of the exiles, as represented in the books of Ezra, Nehemiah, and Malachi.

It seems likely that if it is correct that Isaiah addressed not only persons in his own time but also persons in the distant future, his message was prompted by the fall of Samaria in 722 BC. That event was the beginning of the exilic period, with all the great questions the exile would raise. Thus God gave Isaiah a single divine revelation putting all of Israel's experience of defeat, exile, and return (722 – 500 BC) into one encompassing theological treatment. It is also possible that the book of Isaiah's canonical position as first of the Prophetic Books means that he is given a panoramic vision of all that the OT prophets would address.

OCCASION AND PURPOSE

The overarching occasion of the book's writing was the ongoing political-theological crisis produced by the dominance of the great Mesopotamian powers. Judah and Israel were taught to believe that Yahweh, their God, was the sole creator of the universe and the sovereign Lord of history. They were also taught that they were God's uniquely chosen people, partners with him in an eternal covenant. From these truths they extrapolated some erroneous conclusions: as long as they faithfully perform the prescribed rituals, their royal city of Jerusalem and their holy temple of Yahweh would be inviolable; furthermore, they were destined to rule the world through the endless line of David. The successes of the Solomonic kingdom seemed to give credence to these ideas.

However, some events shocked their understanding: Assyria and then Babylon dominated the ancient Near East from about 900 BC until about 540 BC. Assyria destroyed and exiled the northern kingdom of Israel in 722 BC, and Babylon delivered the crowning blow by destroying and exiling Judah in 586 BC. How could Yahweh be the sole Lord of the cosmos if oppressors were forcing his people to bow down to them? While all of the Prophetic Books deal with these issues to some extent, Isaiah responds to and reflects on the issues most comprehensively.

NATIONS AND CITIES MENTIONED IN ISAIAH

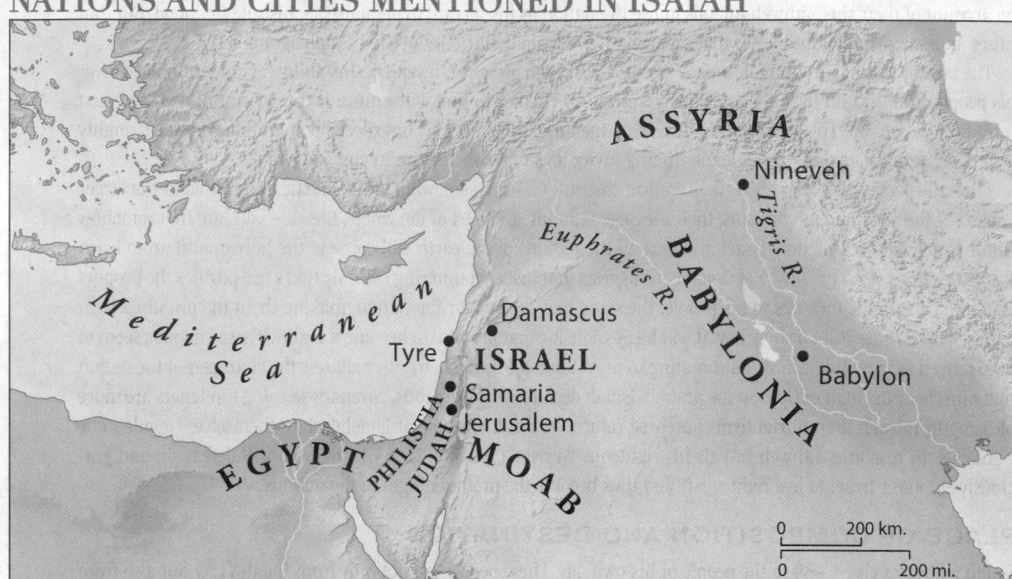

The occasion of chs. 7 – 39 is the complex of events stretching from about 734 to 701 BC. During these years, the Assyrians were pressing southward through what is modern Syria and Israel toward their ultimate goal: Egypt. The small nations that stood in their way tried a number of tactics to avoid or at least blunt the oppressor's terrifying power. In all of the crises provoked by the Assyrian activities, Isaiah calls the Judahites to trust Yahweh rather than human power and glory. They certainly should not make an alliance with Assyria, as Ahaz did, for Assyria will turn on them and all but drown them (chs. 7 – 12). Neither should they rely on Egypt, as Hezekiah and his officers are tempted to do, for Egypt will fail them in the end (chs. 28 – 33).

The predictions Isaiah includes in his prophecies came true with a vengeance. In 701 BC Assyria flooded into Judah, and Egypt failed Judah. When a high Assyrian officer calls on Hezekiah to surrender (ch. 36), Hezekiah instead trusts Yahweh for deliverance, and Yahweh vindicates that trust by killing 185,000 Assyrian soldiers in one night (37:36).

Chs. 40 – 55 primarily address the theological questions that the exile would pose rather than the historical setting itself. (To see what a prophecy given in the historical setting of exile looks like, cf. the book of Ezekiel.) Chs. 40 – 55 address and boldly answer questions that the exile would raise: Have the Babylonian gods defeated God? Have our sins defeated God? Put another way, does God *want* to deliver us from exile? *Can* he deliver us from exile? *Will* he deliver us from exile? Furthermore, how could Israel be restored to a relationship with God in the light of the sins that would result in exile?

Similarly, chs. 56 – 66 address the theological issues that arose most clearly in Israel's return from exile. But again, it is not the historical experiences specific to that setting that shape what Isaiah says here (see the books of Haggai and Zechariah for prophecies so shaped). Rather, like chs. 40 – 55, theological issues provide the occasion. Those issues focus on what it would mean to be the people of God in a new historical setting: without king, army, or state. Reflecting on the causes of the return evidently heighten this question. Chs. 40 – 55 do not make repentance or promises to do better a condition for restoration. Rather, it appears that Israel would have to do nothing but continue to believe God's gracious promises that he would deliver. That might lead to the conclusion that the character of the returnees' lives after the return would be of little importance; it would be only birthright that was really important.

Chs. 56 – 66 sharply dispel such notions. God will still require righteous behavior, as demonstrated in covenant-keeping. The people cry that they cannot do this, but God promises that the divine Warrior (59:16 – 17; 63:1) will come to defeat their enemy, namely, sin. As a result, the righteous nation will be a bright lamp through which the light of God can shine out to all the world (chs. 60 – 62).

GENRE

The book of Isaiah includes a wide variety of genres, ranging from narrative to messages of judgment. These genres are mixed together in often bewildering ways. This variety supports the conclusion that Isaiah may have originally delivered many of the individual units independently from each other and later combined them in their present form. The reader would benefit from examining the present form of the book and seeking the rationale for its arrangement. While some scholars believe that the arrangement is either accidental or arbitrary, there is a growing appreciation among scholars for the care with which Isaiah constructed the final form of the text.

Except for a few portions in prose, most of the book is composed of poetry. Properly interpreting poetry requires appreciating its particular character (see "Introduction to the Wisdom and Lyrical Books," p. 896).

THEMES AND THEOLOGY

In a book as large and profound as Isaiah, there are many important theological themes. Some of the most important ones are: (1) the nature and character of God, (2) the nature of sin, (3) the nature of salvation, (4) servanthood, and (5) the Messiah.

The Nature and Character of God

The view of God in the book of Isaiah is more complete and profound than in any other single book in the Bible. God is absolutely transcendent: there is no other being in the universe like him; he is utterly without comparison; he is the Holy One. But at the same time he intimately cares for his creatures and is personally involved with them. On the one hand, he is a God of implacable cause and effect; his creation plan *will* be fulfilled, and those who defy it *will* suffer the consequences. But on the other hand, God is so creative that he can find a way to satisfy his justice and deliver the sinner at the same time. God is true; he is absolutely dependable and trustworthy. God will do what is right, whatever the cost to himself. Was it right to send sinful Israel into exile? Of course. But would it be right for him to leave them there? Never. For him, his righteous ways are both the motive and the cause of deliverance.

The Nature of Sin

In Isaiah sin is seen especially as rebellion (1:2; 66:24; see 36:5; 63:10). It is a refusal to recognize the character and nature of God — not only as transcendent creator but also as loving Father, which should result in loving obedience. Sin is also seen as self-exaltation, or pride (2:9 – 11; 14:13 – 14). Here again, this is folly in view of the absolute holiness of God. The only appropriate response to God's holiness is the humility demonstrated by Isaiah himself in his experience in the temple (6:5). Furthermore, sin expresses itself in the worship of creation, demonstrated in idolatry. To make God into an image of humanity out of created matter is the height of folly (44:9 – 20). It is to reduce oneself to nothing.

The Nature of Salvation

Fundamental to all divine deliverance in the book of Isaiah is trust in God. This theme is central to chs. 7 – 39. It is highlighted by the Assyrian crisis that provides the backdrop for those chapters. The Judahites are tempted to trust the exalted nations of the earth to deliver them. Isaiah goes to great pains to show them that only Yahweh is exalted and that anything they trust in place of him will necessarily fail them. If they "wait" for him (26:8; 30:18), he will deliver them (26:3 – 6; 30:15 – 18). Eventually, Yahweh demonstrates his full trustworthiness when Hezekiah trusts him in defiance of the Assyrians' mockery of that trust (36:15; 37:36 – 37).

The book also makes it very clear that divine grace is the only means of salvation. Clearly, the Judahites are absolutely helpless to deliver themselves from Babylon (42:18 – 22). Furthermore, they are clearly unable in themselves to turn back to God. He alone is able to defeat the gods of Babylon, and in so doing he will even use Jacob/Israel as the witnesses to his grace (43:8 – 13). But not only will he restore the people of Judah from captivity to their homeland, he will also restore them from their sin to himself. He will do this through the self-giving death of the servant, who will be for Jacob what Jacob could never be in himself (52:13 — 53:12).

The expression of salvation is a life of righteousness. This is made particularly clear in chs. 56 – 66. Here a strong contrast is painted between foreigners and eunuchs who keep God's covenants (56:3 – 8) and people of Judah/Israel who do not. The latter grope in darkness (59:1 – 15a) when they are supposed to be a light to the nations (60:1 – 3). Once again, it is through divine intervention that such a change is possible.

Servanthood

In chs. 40–66 the theme of servanthood is especially prominent. Servanthood stands in direct contrast to the sins of rebellion and distrust. The true servant is the one who willingly submits to the master because of trust in the master. It is possible for Yahweh to take Israel as his servant, in spite of the sins of the past, because of the work of the servant. There is a striking contrast between the blind, rebellious servants whose deliverance is a witness to the nations (43:20–28) and the perceptive, obedient servant who lays down his life so that Jacob may be restored and justice may be brought to the nations (49:1–12). The goal of this servanthood is not merely that the nations might know that Yahweh alone is God but that they should join in his worship and obedience (2:1–4; 56:6–7; 66:19–24).

The Messiah

In many ways the theme that draws all of the above together is the Messiah. From the outset of the book, the coming King is a key figure. He is the child Immanuel in chs. 7–9. He is "the Root of Jesse" and the "banner" (11:10) for the nations in ch. 11. He sits on the throne of David displaying divine qualities in 16:5. He is the noble king and lawgiver of chs. 32–33. He is the one who brings "justice to the nations" (42:1) in chs. 42; 49. He is the one who continues to trust God in spite of misunderstanding and abuse in chs. 49–50. And he is the one who lays down his life for his people in ch. 53. He is the one who comes in power to enable his people to live righteous lives (59:15b–21; 63:1–6), the means by which God's light can shine on the nations. All of this is done through the power of the Spirit (chs. 11; 61) so that he can rule over a kingdom of light, peace, and deliverance.

These themes are often presented in polarities. For instance, the Messiah is both king and servant. These two pictures complement each other throughout the book. The king of ch. 11 is one who rules not through brutality but through gentleness. So also the servant of 52:13—53:12 will put kings to shame and divide the spoils with the strong.

Another polarity is the one between hope and judgment that is especially displayed in chs. 1–5. Whereas the Judahites look for a hope that will allow them to *escape* judgment, Isaiah tells them that the only hope for those in their state of corruption is ***through*** the fires of judgment. Contrary to their expectation, God does not intend that judgment will destroy them. Rather, he intends that it will be the means of their purification, just as the coal from the altar was the means of Isaiah's purification (6:6–7).

OUTLINE

I. Introduction: The Problem of Servanthood (1:1—5:30)
- A. Charges Against Rebellious Israel (1:1–31)
  - 1. Isaiah's Vision Concerning Judah and Jerusalem Introduced (1:1)
  - 2. Israel's Condition (1:2–9)
  - 3. Two Possible Solutions (1:10–20)
  - 4. The Perverse Character of the People (1:21–23)
  - 5. The Results of Sin (1:24–31)
- B. The Nations Will Come to Jerusalem (2:1–5)
- C. Israel's Pride Brought Low (2:6—4:1)
  - 1. The Lord Alone Will Be Exalted (2:6–22)
  - 2. Judgment on Jerusalem and Judah (3:1–15)
  - 3. The Humiliation of the Haughty Daughters of Jerusalem (3:16—4:1)
- D. The Branch of the Lord (4:2–6)
- E. The Song of the Vineyard (5:1–30)
  - 1. Israel's Condition (5:1–24)
    - a. The Vineyard (5:1–7)
    - b. Israel's Bitter Grapes (5:8–24)
      - (1) Greed (5:8–10)
      - (2) Self-Indulgence (5:11–17)
      - (3) Intentional Sin (5:18–19)
      - (4) Perversity (5:20)
      - (5) Self-Determination of Good and Evil (5:21)
      - (6) Link Between Self-Indulgence and Social Injustice (5:22–24)
  - 2. The Destruction of the Vineyard (5:25–30)

II. Isaiah's Commission (6:1–13)

III. Trust: The Basis of Servanthood (7:1—39:8)

- A. Ahaz's Refusal to Trust (7:1—12:6)
  - 1. Signs of the Promise (7:1—9:7)
    - a. The Sign and the Consequences of Its Rejection (7:1–25)
      - (1) Judah Pressured to Join Coalition Against Assyria (7:1–2)
      - (2) A Challenge to Trust Yahweh (7:3–9)
      - (3) The Rejection of the Sign (7:10–25)
        - (a) The Sign of Immanuel (7:10–17)
        - (b) The Coming Assyrian Attack (7:18–25)
    - b. Isaiah and His Children as Signs (8:1–22)
      - (1) The Sign of Maher-Shalal-Hash-Baz (8:1–10)
      - (2) Yahweh: Sanctuary or Stumbling Block (8:11–15)
      - (3) God's Word or the Occult (8:16–22)
    - c. Light Through the Child (9:1–7)
  - 2. The Lord's Anger Against Israel (9:8—10:4)
    - a. Pride (9:8–12)
    - b. Wicked Leaders (9:13–17)
    - c. Tribal Jealousy (9:18–21)
    - d. Social Injustice (10:1–4)
  - 3. Redemption Through the Branch (10:5—11:16)
    - a. Assyria, the Tool in Yahweh's Hand (10:5–34)
      - (1) Assyria's Judgment (10:5–19)
      - (2) A Remnant Will Survive (10:20–23)
      - (3) God to Strike Down Assyria (10:24–34)
    - b. The Branch, Deliverer of His People (11:1–16)
  - 4. Hymns of Deliverance (12:1–6)
- B. Lessons in Trust (13:1—35:10)
  - 1. Prophecies Against the Nations (13:1—23:18)
    - a. Babylon and Briefly Assyria (13:1—14:27)
      - (1) A Prophecy Against Babylon (13:1—14:2)
      - (2) A Prophecy Against the King of Babylon (14:3–23)
      - (3) A Prophecy Against Assyria (14:24–27)
    - b. Judgments on the Nearer Neighbors (14:28—17:11)
      - (1) A Prophecy Against Philistia (14:28–32)
      - (2) A Prophecy Against Moab (15:1—16:14)
      - (3) A Prophecy Against Damascus (17:1–11)
    - c. A Prophecy Against Cush (17:12—18:7)
    - d. A Prophecy Against Egypt (19:1—20:6)
    - e. A Prophecy Against Babylon (21:1–10)
    - f. A Prophecy Against Edom (21:11–12)
    - g. A Prophecy Against Arabia (21:13–17)
    - h. A Prophecy About Judah (22:1–25)
      - (1) A Prophecy About Jerusalem (22:1–14)
      - (2) Judgment on Shebna (22:15–25)
    - i. A Prophecy Against Tyre (23:1–18)
  - 2. The Lord: Sovereign Actor in History (24:1—27:13)
    - a. The Lord's Devastation of the Earth (24:1—25:12)
    - b. The Lord's Day (26:1—27:13)
  - 3. Woe to Those Who Will Not Wait (28:1—33:24)
    - a. Woe to False Leaders (28:1–29)

b. Woe to David's City (29:1–14)
c. Woe to Those Who Try to Hide Their Plans From Yahweh (29:15–24)
d. Woe to the Obstinate Nation (30:1–33)
e. Woe to Those Who Rely on Egypt (31:1—32:20)
(1) A Message of Judgment (31:1–3)
(2) A Message of Salvation (31:4—32:20)
f. Woe to the Destroyer (33:1–24)
4. Conclusion: The Desert or the Garden (34:1—35:10)
C. Hezekiah's Willingness to Trust (36:1—39:8)
1. The Lord Delivers From Assyria (36:1—37:38)
2. Hezekiah's Mortality and Fallibility (38:1—39:8)

IV. Grace: The Motive and Means of Servanthood (40:1—55:13)
A. Gracious Deliverance (40:1–31)
1. Yahweh Desires to Deliver His People (40:1–11)
2. Yahweh Is Able to Deliver His People (40:12–26)
3. Yahweh Intends to Deliver His People (40:27–31)
B. Israel Graciously Chosen to Be God's Servant (41:1—48:22)
1. The Lord's Court Case Against Idols (41:1—46:13)
a. The Two Servants (41:1—42:9)
(1) The Fearful Servant: Israel (41:1–20)
** The First Presentation of the Case Against Idols (41:21–29)
(2) The First Revelation of the Ministering Servant (42:1–9)
b. The Basis of Deliverance (42:10—44:22)
(1) The Song of Salvation (42:10–17)
(2) Israel, the Deaf and Blind Witness (42:18—43:13)
(a) Israel's Condition Is Desperate (42:18–25)
(b) The Lord's Promise to Deliver Israel (43:1–7)
** The Second Presentation of the Case Against Idols (43:8–13)
(3) The Lord's New Thing (43:14—44:5)
** The Third Presentation of the Case Against Idols (44:6–20)
(4) The Announcement of Salvation (44:21–22)
c. The Restoration of Jerusalem Through Cyrus (44:23—46:13)
(1) Call to Praise (44:23)
(2) Cyrus Announced (44:24–28)
(3) Cyrus Affirmed as Yahweh's "Anointed" (45:1–8)
(4) Yahweh's Right to Use Cyrus (45:9–19)
** The Final Presentation of the Case Against Idols (45:20—46:7)
(5) Conclusion: Yahweh's Absolute Uniqueness (46:8–13)
2. Implications of the Case Against Idols (47:1—48:22)
a. The Sentence Upon Babylon (47:1–15)
(1) Babylon's Humiliation (47:1–4)
(2) Babylon's False Pride (47:5–11)
(3) Babylon's Helplessness (47:12–15)
b. Israel Called Upon to Believe God's Promises (48:1–22)
(1) Everything Has Been Predicted (48:1–11)
(2) Israel Freed (48:12–22)
C. The Servant: Gracious Means of Israel's Servanthood (49:1—55:13)
1. Anticipation of Deliverance (49:1—52:12)
a. The Second Revelation of the Ministering Servant (49:1–12)
b. Zion Is Not Forgotten (49:13—50:3)
c. The Third Revelation of the Ministering Servant (50:4–9)

d. Obey the Voice of the Ministering Servant (50:10—51:8)
e. Awake and Be Delivered (51:9—52:12)
2. The Final Revelation of the Ministering Servant (52:13—53:12)
a. The Triumph and the Shock of the Servant's Work (52:13–15)
b. The Rejection of the Servant (53:1–3)
c. The Substitutionary Suffering of the Servant (53:4–6)
d. The Apparent Outcome of the Servant's Suffering (53:7–9)
e. The Real Outcome of the Servant's Suffering (53:10–12)
3. Invitation to Deliverance (54:1—55:13)
a. The Heritage of the Lord's Servants (54:1–17)
(1) Restoration of Marriage With Yahweh (54:1–8)
(2) Protection From Enemies (54:9–17)
b. Seek the Lord (55:1–13)

V. Righteousness: The Character of Servanthood (56:1—66:24)
A. Righteous Foreigners and Eunuchs (56:1–8)
B. Israel's Inability to Do Righteousness (56:9—59:21)
1. God's Accusation Against the Wicked (56:9—57:13)
a. Blind Watchmen (56:9–12)
b. A Righteous Generation Quietly Disappears (57:1–2)
c. A Diatribe Against Worshipers of Idols (57:3–13)
2. Comfort for the Contrite (57:14–21)
3. Declare Their Rebellion (58:1—59:15a)
a. The Sin of Hypocrisy (58:1–2)
b. False Versus True Fasting (58:3–12)
c. Sabbath-Keeping (58:13–14)
d. Failure to Do Righteousness (59:1–15a)
4. The Divine Warrior, Solution to the Problem (59:15b–21)
C. Light to the Nations (60:1—62:12)
1. The Lord's Light Shines on the Nations (60:1–22)
2. The Messiah Announces Good News of Deliverance (61:1–3)
3. The Lord's Righteousness Is Displayed to the Nations (61:4—62:12)
a. The People Whom the Lord Has Blessed (61:4–11)
b. Zion's New Name (62:1–12)
D. Israel's Inability to Do Righteousness (63:1—66:17)
1. The Divine Warrior (63:1–6)
2. A History of Redemption and Rebellion (63:7—65:16)
a. A Résumé of Redemption and Rebellion (63:7–14)
b. A Cry for Yahweh to Intervene (63:15—64:12)
c. Yahweh's Response (65:1–16)
3. New Heavens and a New Earth (65:17–25)
4. Unrighteousness and Redemption (66:1–17)
E. Righteous Gentiles (66:18–24)

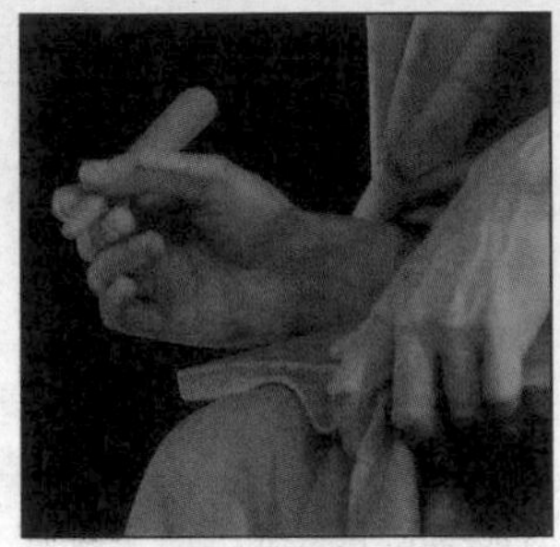

ISAIAH

1:1 [a]Nu 12:6 [b]Isa 40:9 [c]Isa 2:1 [d]2Ch 26:22 [e]2Ki 16:1
1:2 [f]Mic 1:2 [g]Isa 30:1,9; 65:2
1:3 [h]Jer 8:7; 9:3,6
1:4 [i]Isa 14:20 [j]Isa 5:19,24

1 The vision[a] concerning Judah and Jerusalem[b] that Isaiah son of Amoz saw[c] during the reigns of
Uzziah,[d] Jotham, Ahaz[e] and Hezekiah, kings of Judah.

A Rebellious Nation

2 Hear me, you heavens! Listen, earth!
For the LORD has spoken:[f]
"I reared children and brought them up,
but they have rebelled[g] against me.
3 The ox knows its master,
the donkey its owner's manger,
but Israel does not know,[h]
my people do not understand."

4 Woe to the sinful nation,
a people whose guilt is great,
a brood of evildoers,[i]
children given to corruption!
They have forsaken the LORD;
they have spurned the Holy One[j] of Israel
and turned their backs on him.

1:1—5:30 *Introduction: The Problem of Servanthood.* These chapters sharply contrast the rebellious, hypocritical, unjust Israel of the present (1:2–31; 2:6—4:1; 5:1–30) and the holy, purified remnant of the future (4:2–6) that will somehow draw the nations of the world to come to the holy mountain to learn the *tôrâ* (instructions) of God (2:1–5). These chapters do not spell out how God will effect this change. Strictly speaking, Isaiah speaks to Judah, but he seems to have in mind all of Israel—the nation as a whole.

1:1–31 *Charges Against Rebellious Israel.* These verses supply the basics of the introduction: the author is "Isaiah son of Amoz" (v. 1); the nation's present condition is tragic (vv. 2–15,21–25,29–31); and the nation may experience cleansing and restoration in the future (vv. 16–20,25–28).

1:1 *Isaiah's Vision Concerning Judah and Jerusalem Introduced.* What follows is what Isaiah received from God; it is not merely Isaiah's intellectual or artistic creation.

1:1 Uzziah, Jotham, Ahaz and Hezekiah, kings of Judah. Isaiah is defining when he received from God the materials recorded in the book. It was during the reigns of these four kings. However, his ministry only began in the final year of Uzziah's reign (740/39 BC) and did not necessarily extend entirely through Hezekiah's reign.

1:2–9 *Israel's Condition.* Here the prophet vividly describes Israel's condition and explains the reasons for it. He compares them to someone who has been beaten and has untreated wounds (vv. 5–6) and to an abandoned shack in a field (vv. 7–9). The reason for this devastation is that they have rebelliously turned away from the Lord (vv. 2–4).

1:2–4 God's charges against his people.

1:2 Hear me, you heavens! The call of a prosecutor for witnesses to hear charges. Isaiah calls upon nature, which obeys God's commands, to witness how humans, the highest of God's creatures, astonishingly refuse to obey him (see vv. 20,23,28; Deut 30:19; 32:1). **the LORD.** This name expresses God's eternal self-existence; he is the "I AM" (see notes on Exod 3:13,14,15). **rebelled.** They are like "children" who have "rebelled against" their father. Rebellion is the most serious of all sins because it intentionally defies God's revealed will (43:27; 46:8; 48:8; 57:4; 63:10; 66:24).

1:3 Another illustration from nature. Farm animals are intelligent enough to recognize their "master" who provides for them, but Israel is not that intelligent.

1:4 Woe. Transliterates a Hebrew word that expresses grief and consternation more than condemnation. It is associated with death and mourning. **forsaken.** The same Hebrew word used for divorce. **the Holy One of Israel.** A favorite title for the Lord in the book of Isaiah. It occurs 26 times in the book (counting one occurrence of "the Holy One of Jacob" [29:23]) and only 6 other places in the OT. Its frequency in Isaiah may reflect the impact of Isaiah's call, in which the holiness of God is a central feature (ch. 6).

[5]Why should you be beaten anymore?
Why do you persist in rebellion?[k]
Your whole head is injured,
your whole heart afflicted.[l]
[6]From the sole of your foot to the top of your head
there is no soundness[m] —
only wounds and welts
and open sores,
not cleansed or bandaged[n]
or soothed with olive oil.[o]
[7]Your country is desolate,[p]
your cities burned with fire;
your fields are being stripped by foreigners
right before you,
laid waste as when overthrown by strangers.
[8]Daughter Zion is left
like a shelter in a vineyard,
like a hut[q] in a cucumber field,
like a city under siege.
[9]Unless the LORD Almighty
had left us some survivors,[r]
we would have become like Sodom,
we would have been like Gomorrah.[s]

1:5 [k]Isa 31:6 [l]Isa 33:6,24
1:6 [m]Ps 38:3 [n]Isa 30:26; Jer 8:22 [o]Lk 10:34
1:7 [p]Lev 26:34
1:8 [q]Job 27:18
1:9 [r]Isa 10:20-22; 37:4, 31-32 [s]Ge 19:24; Ro 9:29*

1:5–9 As a result of their rebellion, the people are in terrible condition. By this time, Assyria has already made devastating inroads into the northern kingdom of Israel. The nation is broken and bleeding. But they have rejected the only one who can heal them: the Lord.
1:8 Daughter Zion. Expresses the tender feeling that God has for his people. Zion is like a precious daughter to a loving father. **Zion.** Often refers to the city of Jerusalem but also may extend (as here) to the people as a whole. **shelter … hut.** Abandoned, deteriorating structures. Because the people normally lived in villages that were some distance from their fields, they often built temporary shelters in the harvest field to avoid walking back and forth during that busy time. After the harvest, these shacks were abandoned.
1:9 the LORD Almighty. That is, "the Lord of armies." These armies are the angelic hosts of heaven. This title, which stresses Yahweh's power, occurs 62 times in the book, 56 of them in chs. 1–39. **survivors.** A remnant (see "Exile and Exodus," p. 2659). **Sodom … Gomorrah.** Cities completely destroyed (Gen 19:24–25). Only the undeserved grace of God (Rom 9:29) has prevented the nation of Israel from being destroyed.

KINGS OF JUDAH, ISRAEL, AND ASSYRIA

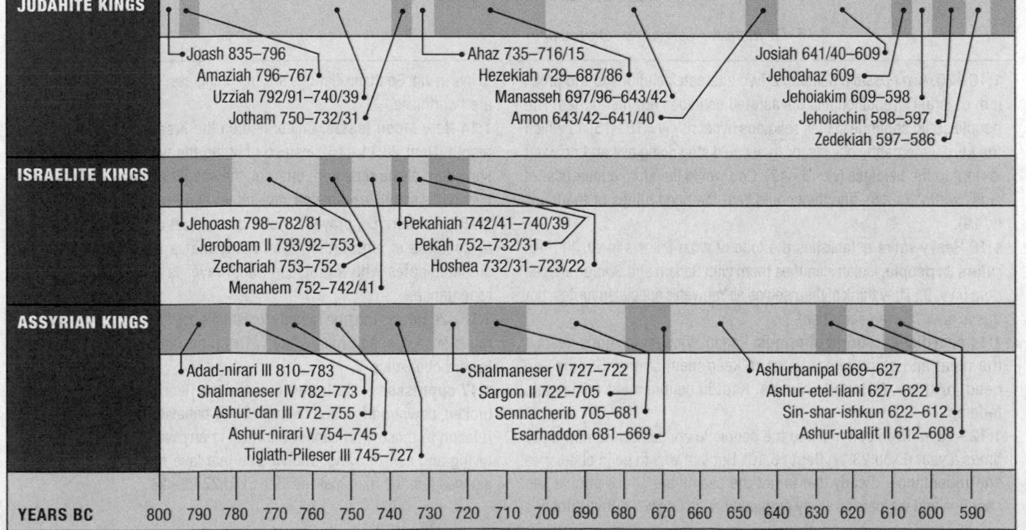

1:10 [t]Isa 28:14 [u]Isa 3:9; Eze 16:49; Ro 9:29; Rev 11:8 [v]Isa 8:20
1:11 [w]Ps 50:8 [x]Jer 6:20 [y]1Sa 15:22; Mal 1:10
1:12 [z]Ex 23:17
1:13 [a]Isa 66:3 [b]Jer 7:9 [c]1Ch 23:31
1:14 [d]Lev 23:1-44; Nu 28:11-29:39; Isa 29:1 [e]Isa 7:13; 43:22,24
1:15 [f]Isa 8:17; 59:2; Mic 3:4 [g]Isa 59:3
1:16 [h]Isa 52:11 [i]Isa 55:7; Jer 25:5
1:17 [j]Zep 2:3 [k]Ps 82:3

10 Hear the word of the LORD,[t]
you rulers of Sodom;[u]
listen to the instruction[v] of our God,
you people of Gomorrah!
11 "The multitude of your sacrifices —
what are they to me?" says the LORD.
"I have more than enough of burnt offerings,
of rams and the fat of fattened animals;[w]
I have no pleasure
in the blood of bulls[x] and lambs and goats.[y]
12 When you come to appear before me,
who has asked this of you,[z]
this trampling of my courts?
13 Stop bringing meaningless offerings![a]
Your incense[b] is detestable to me.
New Moons, Sabbaths and convocations[c] —
I cannot bear your worthless assemblies.
14 Your New Moon feasts and your appointed festivals[d]
I hate with all my being.
They have become a burden to me;
I am weary[e] of bearing them.
15 When you spread out your hands in prayer,
I hide[f] my eyes from you;
even when you offer many prayers,
I am not listening.

Your hands are full of blood![g]

16 Wash and make yourselves clean.
Take your evil deeds out of my sight;[h]
stop doing wrong.[i]
17 Learn to do right; seek justice.[j]
Defend the oppressed.[a]
Take up the cause of the fatherless;[k]
plead the case of the widow.

[a] 17 Or *justice. / Correct the oppressor*

1:10–20 *Two Possible Solutions.* Two alternate solutions to the problem of Israel's rebellion and devastated condition are mentioned. The people could continue in their religious hypocrisy (vv. 10–15), to which the Lord vehemently objects, or they could stop doing evil and do what is right to the helpless (vv. 16–17). God would then make their scarlet sins "white" (v. 18), and they could "eat the good things of the land" (v. 19).
1:10 Heavy satire establishes the tone of what follows in vv. 11–15. **rulers ... people.** Isaiah identifies them with Sodom and Gomorrah (see note on v. 9). They think of themselves as Yahweh's special favorites, but this is how Yahweh sees them.
1:11 sacrifices ... burnt offerings. Pagans thought the gods needed the meat and blood of sacrifices to keep them strong. God has no need for them. **fattened animals.** Kept in confinement for special feeding.
1:12–13 Yahweh commanded the people to appear before him three times a year (Exod 23:17; Deut 16:16). But that was to be in obedience and repentance. Clearly that is not the case here. These people see sacrifice and worship as a way of manipulating God while they continue to live in sin. So their offerings are "meaningless," and their assemblies are "worthless."
1:14 New Moon feasts. Celebrated on the first day of each Hebrew month (Num 28:11–15). Instead of lifting the weight of sin from the shoulders of the repentant offerers, the sacrifices and worship of the hypocrites simply became an intolerable "burden" to God.
1:15 Like sacrifice, prayer is not a device that allows sinful persons to continue in sin. Rather, it is a way that a repentant worshiper communicates with a gracious God. Prayer is useless without true repentance.
1:16–20 Here is the true remedy for Israel's battered condition: genuine repentance ("repent" means "turn away [from sinful behavior] and turn toward obedience").
1:17 oppressed ... fatherless ... widow. Represent the vulnerable, broken, downtrodden, and outcast. Godly behavior is most manifest in relation to those who cannot repay us in any way. God's love is self-giving and self-denying, and we see that love most clearly when he extends it to the marginalized. See Exod 22:22–24.

[18] "Come now, let us settle the matter,"[l]
says the LORD.
"Though your sins are like scarlet,
they shall be as white as snow;[m]
though they are red as crimson,
they shall be like wool.
[19] If you are willing and obedient,
you will eat the good things of the land;[n]
[20] but if you resist and rebel,
you will be devoured by the sword."[o]
For the mouth of the LORD has spoken.[p]

[21] See how the faithful city
has become a prostitute![q]
She once was full of justice;
righteousness used to dwell in her—
but now murderers!
[22] Your silver has become dross,
your choice wine is diluted with water.
[23] Your rulers are rebels,
partners with thieves;
they all love bribes[r]
and chase after gifts.
They do not defend the cause of the fatherless;
the widow's case does not come before them.[s]

[24] Therefore the Lord, the LORD Almighty,
the Mighty One of Israel, declares:
"Ah! I will vent my wrath on my foes
and avenge[t] myself on my enemies.
[25] I will turn my hand against you;[a]
I will thoroughly purge away your dross
and remove all your impurities.[u]
[26] I will restore your leaders as in days of old,[v]
your rulers as at the beginning.
Afterward you will be called
the City of Righteousness,[w]
the Faithful City."[x]
[27] Zion will be delivered with justice,
her penitent ones with righteousness.[y]

1:18 [l] Isa 41:1; 43:9,26 [m] Ps 51:7; Rev 7:14
1:19 [n] Dt 30:15-16; Isa 55:2
1:20 [o] Isa 3:25; 65:12 [p] Isa 34:16; 40:5; 58:14; Mic 4:4
1:21 [q] Isa 57:3-9; Jer 2:20
1:23 [r] Ex 23:8 [s] Isa 10:2; Jer 5:28; Eze 22:6-7; Zec 7:10
1:24 [t] Isa 35:4; 59:17; 61:2; 63:4
1:25 [u] Eze 22:22; Mal 3:3
1:26 [v] Jer 33:7,11 [w] Isa 33:5; 62:1; Zec 8:3 [x] Isa 60:14; 62:2
1:27 [y] Isa 35:10; 62:12; 63:4

[a] *25* That is, against Jerusalem

1:18 This verse does not say that changed behavior (v. 17) causes forgiveness and restoration. Rather, such behavior shows the sincerity of intention (repentance) and the complete dependence on God (faith) that make these possible. Ultimately, cleansing is dependent on Christ's sacrifice (Heb 10:1–10).
1:19–20 These are the results of the two ways of responding to vv. 16–17. **eat ... devoured.** A wordplay on the Hebrew word: the obedient will "eat" the produce of the land, but those who rebel will be "devoured ['eaten'] by the sword."
1:21–23 *The Perverse Character of the People.* Their behavior is the opposite of what their covenant with God required of them.
1:23 rulers are rebels. Instead of promoting righteous living, they are promoting lawlessness.
1:24–31 *The Results of Sin.* Because of the people's sinfulness, judgment is coming. But the purpose of the judgment is not destruction but purification. This is one of the main themes of the book.
1:24 the Lord, the LORD Almighty, the Mighty One of Israel. Isaiah frequently piles up epithets to convey to the people how serious their situation is (see 41:11–14; 43:14–15; 44:6–8; 49:26 and notes). The one they have offended, whose covenant they have broken, is the mightiest power in the universe. **my foes ... my enemies.** The people of Israel, particularly those of Judah and Jerusalem.
1:25–26 The effect of Yahweh's judgment will be to restore the people, the leaders, and "the City of Righteousness" to their former pristine condition.
1:27–28 While the intent of the judgment is not destruction, that will be the result for those "rebels and sinners ... who forsake the LORD."

1:28 [z] Ps 9:5; Isa 24:20; 66:24; 2Th 1:8-9
1:29 [a] Isa 57:5 [b] Isa 65:3; 66:17
1:31 [c] Isa 5:24; 9:18-19; 26:11; 33:14; 66:15-16,24
2:1 [d] Isa 1:1
2:2 [e] Isa 27:13; 56:7; 66:20; Mic 4:7
2:3 [f] Isa 51:4,7 [g] Lk 24:47

28 But rebels and sinners will both be broken,
and those who forsake the LORD will perish.[z]
29 "You will be ashamed because of the sacred oaks[a]
in which you have delighted;
you will be disgraced because of the gardens[b]
that you have chosen.
30 You will be like an oak with fading leaves,
like a garden without water.
31 The mighty man will become tinder
and his work a spark;
both will burn together,
with no one to quench the fire.[c]"

The Mountain of the LORD

2:1-4pp — Mic 4:1-3

2 This is what Isaiah son of Amoz saw concerning Judah and Jerusalem:[d]

2 In the last days

the mountain[e] of the LORD's temple will be established
as the highest of the mountains;
it will be exalted above the hills,
and all nations will stream to it.

3 Many peoples will come and say,

"Come, let us go up to the mountain of the LORD,
to the temple of the God of Jacob.
He will teach us his ways,
so that we may walk in his paths."
The law[f] will go out from Zion,
the word of the LORD from Jerusalem.[g]
4 He will judge between the nations
and will settle disputes for many peoples.

1:29–31 The imagery of wilting trees and parched gardens describes the condition of those who persist in glorifying themselves while defying God. Isaiah elsewhere uses the images of trees and gardens to describe (1) pride in one's own attainments, and (2) the rich results of depending on God (5:1–5; 10:33–34; 16:8; 19:5–7; 27:2–6; 30:23–26; 33:9; 35:1–2; 40:24; 41:19; 42:15; 44:4,23; 51:3; 55:12–13; 58:11; 60:13; 61:3,11; 65:3,22; 66:17).

1:29 sacred oaks ... **gardens.** Places of pagan worship (cf. 65:3 and note; 66:17). But these places have no power to give life, and those who look for life there will be "ashamed" and "disgraced" because what they trusted in will fail them (cf. 65:3). See photo, p. 180.

1:30–31 Although a "mighty man" might seem to be self-created and self-perpetuating, it is not so. He is "like a garden without water," unable to survive apart from God, who alone gives life.

2:1–5 *The Nations Will Come to Jerusalem.* In spite of Israel's condition in Isaiah's own time, Isaiah predicts that the nations of the earth would come to "the LORD's temple" (v. 2) to learn God's instructions, his *tôrâ*, for life. This mission to the nations is a recurring theme in the book (cf. 11:10; 19:23–25; 26:18; 42:1; 49:6; 56:6–8; 60:3; 62:10; 66:18–24). If those Gentiles would someday seek to "walk in his paths" (v. 3), should not Israel now "walk in the light of the LORD" (v. 5)?

2:2–4 Nearly identical to Mic 4:1–3. Scholars are divided over which is original or whether both use a common source. But whatever the intermediate source, "what Isaiah ... saw" (v. 1) makes it plain that the Lord inspired Isaiah's words; Isaiah did not merely copy them from someone else.

2:2 the last days. May be interpreted in one of three ways: the vague distant future (Gen 49:1), the Christian era (Hos 3:5; Acts 2:17; 2 Pet 3:3), or the end of the age (Jas 5:3). In one sense this prediction has been fulfilled since the coming of Christ, but there will be yet a greater fulfillment at the end of the age. See note on Amos 2:16. **mountains.** Thought to be the homes of the gods. By calling Mount Zion "the highest of the mountains," Isaiah is saying that the nations will one day realize that Yahweh is the one true God.

2:3 walk. How the Bible describes our relationship with God; it is not a static position but a dynamic companionship that moves from its beginning to its appointed destination (see, e.g., Gen 5:22,24; 17:1; 48:15; Deut 28:9; 1 Kgs 3:6 ["faithful"]; Ps 15:2; Jer 32:23 ["follow"]; Mal 2:6; John 8:12; Rom 6:4 ["live"]; Gal 5:16; Col 1:10 ["live a life"]). **law.** God's instructions for life (not the negative sense: what condemns us when we try to use it as a means of justification). **Zion.** Jerusalem. The name expresses its theological significance. It represents the people of God, whether they are in a sinful present state, rebelling against their Lord (1:8; 3:16), or, more frequently, in their final redeemed state, living in fellowship with him (4:3–5).

2:4 Pictures a world in which genuine peace exists on the earth as the Holy Spirit enables people to live out God's holy character. Some

They will beat their swords into plowshares
and their spears into pruning hooks.[h]
Nation will not take up sword against nation,[i]
nor will they train for war anymore.

5 Come, descendants of Jacob,[j]
let us walk in the light[k] of the LORD.

The Day of the LORD

6 You, LORD, have abandoned[l] your people,
the descendants of Jacob.
They are full of superstitions from the East;
they practice divination like the Philistines[m]
and embrace[n] pagan customs.[o]
7 Their land is full of silver and gold;
there is no end to their treasures.
Their land is full of horses;[p]
there is no end to their chariots.[q]
8 Their land is full of idols;[r]
they bow down to the work of their hands,
to what their fingers[s] have made.
9 So people will be brought low[t]
and everyone humbled[u] —
do not forgive them.[av]

10 Go into the rocks, hide in the ground
from the fearful presence of the LORD
and the splendor of his majesty![w]
11 The eyes of the arrogant will be humbled
and human pride[x] brought low;
the LORD alone will be exalted in that day.

12 The LORD Almighty has a day in store
for all the proud and lofty,
for all that is exalted[y]
(and they will be humbled),[z]
13 for all the cedars of Lebanon, tall and lofty,
and all the oaks of Bashan,[a]

2:4 [h] Joel 3:10 [i] Ps 46:9; Isa 9:5; 11:6-9; 32:18; Hos 2:18; Zec 9:10
2:5 [j] Isa 58:1 [k] Isa 60:1, 19-20; 1Jn 1:5,7
2:6 [l] Dt 31:17 [m] 2Ki 1:2 [n] Pr 6:1 [o] 2Ki 16:7
2:7 [p] Dt 17:16 [q] Isa 31:1; Mic 5:10
2:8 [r] Isa 10:9-11 [s] Isa 17:8
2:9 [t] Ps 62:9 [u] Isa 5:15 [v] Ne 4:5
2:10 [w] 2Th 1:9; Rev 6:15-16
2:11 [x] Isa 5:15; 37:23
2:12 [y] Isa 24:4,21; Mal 4:1 [z] Job 40:11
2:13 [a] Zec 11:2

[a] 9 Or *not raise them up*

interpreters understand the reference to be to Christ's millennial reign. See 11:1–10 for many of the same themes.

2:6—4:1 *Israel's Pride Brought Low.* Isaiah, unwilling to let his hearers use a prophecy of a glorious future to escape from grim realities in the present, defines the present condition and the inevitable result of that condition. He shows how the people are enamored with human and earthly greatness (2:6–8,12–16; 3:1–3,16–23) and how that must necessarily result in desolation and humiliation (2:9–11,17–22; 3:4–15; 3:24—4:1). As the textual unit progresses, there are more and more graphic illustrations of both (1) self-exaltation, and (2) desolation and humiliation. The people flee into "caves in the rocks" (2:19; see 2:21). Mere "youths" (3:4,12) replace the falsely revered leaders "who have ruined [God's] vineyard" (3:14). Finally, Isaiah compares Jerusalem to a haughty, exquisitely dressed woman who is stripped and brought down into the dust (3:16—4:1).

2:6–22 *The Lord Alone Will Be Exalted.* The people are "full" of things this world calls great (vv. 6–8). As a result, they will be "brought low" (v. 9). All the lofty things of creation (vv. 12–16) will be "brought low" (v. 17), and the people who trusted in them, making "idols" of them (v. 20), "will flee to caverns in the rocks" (v. 21).

2:6 The "descendants of Jacob" are "full" of pagan superstitions, magical customs that seem to make the powers of creation subject to human manipulation.

2:7 Their land is "full" of wealth and military armaments.

2:8 idols. Human hands made these gods in human form—the ultimate exaltation of humanity.

2:9–11 All human attempts to exalt themselves are doomed to failure because everything in creation is subordinate to Yahweh, the only one who is "exalted" (v. 11; see v. 17). He alone is self-existent, the only one who can say, "I AM" (see 1:2 and note). When humans try to make themselves ultimate in the universe, they render themselves meaningless.

2:12–17 God will humble (v. 12) every great thing on the earth in which humans tend to glory—whether natural (vv. 13–14) or man-made (vv. 15–16).

2:14 [b]Isa 30:25; 40:4
2:15 [c]Isa 25:2,12
2:16 [d]1Ki 10:22
2:17 [e]ver 11
2:18 [f]Isa 21:9
2:19 [g]Heb 12:26
2:20 [h]Lev 11:19
2:21 [i]ver 19
2:22 [j]Ps 146:3; Jer 17:5 [k]Ps 8:4; 144:3; Isa 40:15; Jas 4:14
3:1 [l]Lev 26:26 [m]Isa 5:13; Eze 4:16
3:2 [n]Eze 17:13 [o]2Ki 24:14; Isa 9:14-15

14 for all the towering mountains
and all the high hills,[b]
15 for every lofty tower
and every fortified wall,[c]
16 for every trading ship[a][d]
and every stately vessel.
17 The arrogance of man will be brought low
and human pride humbled;
the LORD alone will be exalted in that day,[e]
18 and the idols will totally disappear.[f]

19 People will flee to caves in the rocks
and to holes in the ground
from the fearful presence of the LORD
and the splendor of his majesty,
when he rises to shake the earth.[g]
20 In that day people will throw away
to the moles and bats[h]
their idols of silver and idols of gold,
which they made to worship.
21 They will flee to caverns in the rocks
and to the overhanging crags
from the fearful presence of the LORD
and the splendor of his majesty,
when he rises to shake the earth.[i]

22 Stop trusting in mere humans,[j]
who have but a breath in their nostrils.
Why hold them in esteem?[k]

Judgment on Jerusalem and Judah

3 See now, the Lord,
the LORD Almighty,
is about to take from Jerusalem and Judah
both supply and support:
all supplies of food[l] and all supplies of water,[m]
2 the hero and the warrior,[n]
the judge and the prophet,
the diviner and the elder,[o]
3 the captain of fifty and the man of rank,
the counselor, skilled craftsman and clever
enchanter.

[a] 16 Hebrew *every ship of Tarshish*

2:17 Almost identical to v. 11.
2:18–22 The idolatry by which humans attempt to make themselves equal to God can only humiliate them. In the day of judgment it will utterly fail them, and they will throw away all their idols—their human-made attempts to manipulate the universe—as they try to hide from God's all-seeing eye (cf. Rev 6:15–17).
2:20 moles and bats. They were considered unclean. The people will consider their supposedly holy idols, made of precious metals, both worthless and unclean.
2:22 A powerful concluding statement. Humans are utterly dependent creatures who are only one breath away from death. Why put any trust in them?
3:1–15 *Judgment on Jerusalem and Judah.* Isaiah speaks of a day when Israel's leaders, who exalt themselves while actually encouraging wickedness (cf. 1:23), will be taken away and replaced by weak, unworthy people.
3:1 the LORD Almighty. See note on 1:9. **take from.** God will take away all those who might have been expected to undergird the stability and moral order of the nation. **supply and support.** Both physical supplies and leadership. May be understood both metaphorically and literally. The prophet is probably envisioning the end of Judah, when the enemy armies are besieging the city.

[4] "I will make mere youths their officials;
children will rule over them."[p]

[5] People will oppress each other—
man against man, neighbor against neighbor.[q]
The young will rise up against the old,
the nobody against the honored.

[6] A man will seize one of his brothers
in his father's house, and say,
"You have a cloak, you be our leader;
take charge of this heap of ruins!"
[7] But in that day he will cry out,
"I have no remedy.[r]
I have no food or clothing in my house;
do not make me the leader of the people."

[8] Jerusalem staggers,
Judah is falling;[s]
their words[t] and deeds are against the LORD,
defying[u] his glorious presence.
[9] The look on their faces testifies against them;
they parade their sin like Sodom;[v]
they do not hide it.
Woe to them!
They have brought disaster[w] upon themselves.

[10] Tell the righteous it will be well[x] with them,
for they will enjoy the fruit of their deeds.[y]
[11] Woe to the wicked!
Disaster[z] is upon them!
They will be paid back
for what their hands have done.

[12] Youths[a] oppress my people,
women rule over them.
My people, your guides lead you astray;[b]
they turn you from the path.

[13] The LORD takes his place in court;
he rises to judge[c] the people.

3:4 [p] Ecc 10:16 *fn*
3:5 [q] Isa 9:19; Jer 9:8; Mic 7:2,6
3:7 [r] Eze 34:4; Hos 5:13
3:8 [s] Isa 1:7 [t] Isa 9:15,17 [u] Ps 73:9,11
3:9 [v] Ge 13:13 [w] Pr 8:36; Ro 6:23
3:10 [x] Dt 28:1-14 [y] Ps 128:2
3:11 [z] Dt 28:15-68
3:12 [a] ver 4 [b] Isa 9:16
3:13 [c] Mic 6:2

3:4–12 Deprived of true leadership the nation will spiral into moral chaos. People who might undertake leadership refuse it, and those who do take it are unworthy of it.
3:4 youths ... children. Probably metaphors: incompetents will replace the great men to whom the people of Judah give too much honor (cf. v. 12).
3:5 As a result of incompetent leadership, all social order breaks down.
3:6–7 Probably anticipates a scene during the exile when Jerusalem, the proud city, is only a "heap of ruins." Things fall so far that merely possessing a cloak qualifies one for leadership. This graphically illustrates the point of this section: exalting humans must lead to humiliation (see note on 2:6—4:1).
3:8–15 The conditions in Jerusalem and Judah could not be laid solely at the feet of the rulers. It was ultimately the result of the people's defying God. As a result, "disaster" (vv. 9,11) lay ahead for them. But that should not discourage "the righteous" (v. 10). They could look forward to another result: enjoying the "fruit of their deeds" (v. 10) if they persevere in spite of the deteriorating conditions around them. As Christians know, this might be in eternity, but it will come.
3:9 Once again Isaiah compares Judah to Sodom (cf. 1:10). This must have been galling to many who considered themselves morally superior to those sinners of the past (cf. Ezek 16:49). **Woe.** See note on 1:4.
3:10 The promise of this verse seems to point to eternal life since "the righteous" suffered along with the wicked in the decline and eventual destruction of Judah and Jerusalem.
3:12 women rule. History (e.g., Athaliah and Jezebel) did not provide a good precedent.
3:13–15 Israel's true ruler ("the LORD," v. 13) judges the evil rulers ("elders and leaders," v. 14), taking them to task in particular for mistreating the poor. Judah's rulers succumbed to the great temptation of leaders everywhere: using their position as one of privilege instead of responsibility. They naturally preyed upon the weakest segment of society. But God's instructions for leaders were the very opposite: give

Jewelry found at a tomb near Jerusalem, 700 BC. Isa 3:16 describes women "with ornaments jingling on their ankles."
Jewelry, Israelite Period/Israel Museum, Jerusalem, Israel/Bridgeman Images

3:14 [d] Job 22:4 [e] Job 24:9; Jas 2:6
3:15 [f] Ps 94:5
3:16 [g] SS 3:11

14 The LORD enters into judgment[d]
against the elders and leaders of his people:
"It is you who have ruined my vineyard;
the plunder[e] from the poor is in your houses.
15 What do you mean by crushing my people[f]
and grinding the faces of the poor?"
declares the Lord, the LORD Almighty.

16 The LORD says,
"The women of Zion[g] are haughty,
walking along with outstretched necks,
flirting with their eyes,
strutting along with swaying hips,
with ornaments jingling on their ankles.

special care to the poor precisely to prevent others from abusing them (Deut 15:7–11; 16:18–20; 17:14–20).
3:14 vineyard. A metaphor for Israel (see chs. 5; 27; Luke 20:9–16). It was particularly meaningful to Judahite listeners, for whom one major agricultural crop was grapes.
3:15 crushing ... grinding. Words of the grape and grain harvests. The rulers were treating the poor like the produce of the soil: to be used for the rulers' own benefit. **the Lord, the LORD Almighty.** See notes on 1:9,24.
3:16—4:1 *The Humiliation of the Haughty Daughters of Jerusalem.* Isaiah graphically illustrates that self-exaltation results in humiliation.
3:16–17 A summary statement of the cause and its effect: because these women are "haughty," flaunting their dainty beauty as if it is their own to use as they wish, Yahweh will make them bald and scabbed. As in vv. 6–7 and 3:24—4:1, these conditions are a result of the enemy conquering them. No human greatness could defend Zion; only Yahweh could do that. If they insist upon glorifying that greatness, not only will Yahweh not *defend* them from the enemy, he will *become* their enemy (cf. 1:24).
3:16 women of Zion. Perhaps specifically directed against them; however, the Hebrew (which refers to "daughters of Zion") is used metaphorically elsewhere, so the entire nation of Judah may be in view (cf. v. 26, which depicts Zion as a woman).

17 Therefore the Lord will bring sores on the heads of the women of Zion;
the LORD will make their scalps bald."

18 In that day the Lord will snatch away their finery: the bangles and headbands and crescent necklaces,[h] 19 the earrings and bracelets and veils, 20 the headdresses[i] and anklets and sashes, the perfume
bottles and charms, 21 the signet rings and nose rings, 22 the fine robes and the capes and cloaks, the
purses 23 and mirrors, and the linen garments and tiaras and shawls.

24 Instead of fragrance[j] there will be a stench;
instead of a sash,[k] a rope;
instead of well-dressed hair, baldness;[l]
instead of fine clothing, sackcloth;[m]
instead of beauty,[n] branding.
25 Your men will fall by the sword,[o]
your warriors in battle.
26 The gates of Zion will lament and mourn;[p]
destitute, she will sit on the ground.[q]

4 1 In that day seven women
will take hold of one man[r]
and say, "We will eat our own food[s]
and provide our own clothes;
only let us be called by your name.
Take away our disgrace!"[t]

The Branch of the LORD

2 In that day the Branch of the LORD[u] will be beautiful and glorious, and the fruit[v] of the land will be
the pride and glory of the survivors in Israel. 3 Those who are left in Zion, who remain[w] in Jerusalem,
will be called holy,[x] all who are recorded[y] among the living in Jerusalem. 4 The Lord will wash away the
filth[z] of the women of Zion; he will cleanse the bloodstains[a] from Jerusalem by a spirit[a] of judgment[b]
and a spirit[a] of fire.[c] 5 Then the LORD will create over all of Mount Zion and over those who assemble
there a cloud of smoke by day and a glow of flaming fire by night;[d] over everything the glory[b][e] will
be a canopy. 6 It will be a shelter[f] and shade from the heat of the day, and a refuge[g] and hiding place
from the storm and rain.

[a] 4 Or *the Spirit*   [b] 5 Or *over all the glory there*

3:18 [h] Jdg 8:21
3:20 [i] Ex 39:28
3:24 [j] Est 2:12 [k] Pr 31:24 [l] Isa 22:12 [m] La 2:10; Eze 27:30-31 [n] 1Pe 3:3
3:25 [o] Isa 1:20
3:26 [p] Jer 14:2 [q] La 2:10
4:1 [r] Isa 13:12 [s] 2Th 3:12 [t] Ge 30:23
4:2 [u] Isa 11:1-5; 53:2; Jer 23:5-6; Zec 3:8; 6:12 [v] Ps 72:16
4:3 [w] Ro 11:5 [x] Isa 52:1; 60:21 [y] Lk 10:20
4:4 [z] Isa 3:24 [a] Isa 1:15 [b] Isa 28:6 [c] Isa 1:31; Mt 3:11
4:5 [d] Ex 13:21 [e] Isa 60:1
4:6 [f] Ps 27:5 [g] Isa 25:4

3:18—4:1 A more detailed statement of the cause (3:18–23) and effect (3:24—4:1), making the same point as 3:16–17 (see note there).
3:18–23 This lengthy list of finery drives the point home with ironic force: all these exterior accoutrements are worthless without inner integrity.
3:24 This sentence's abruptness and structure (parallel clauses) reinforce the contrast.
3:25—4:1 The men of Zion will be killed by their enemies in battle so that the city and its women will be desolate (3:26—4:1). There will be so few men available that there will be "seven women" for every "one man" (4:1). In that society, a woman had to be attached to a man, either her father or her husband. For her to be detached from a man was a "disgrace" (4:1).
4:2–6 *The Branch of the Lord.* Much like ch. 1 abruptly transitions to ch. 2, so ch. 4 abruptly presents a note of hope. Both v. 1 and v. 2 begin with "in that day" but speak of two very different futures. The hope of vv. 2–6 is not that Israel will somehow escape judgment but that the judgment will result in purification instead of destruction.
4:2 Branch. This reference is uncertain. By capitalizing "Branch," the NIV prefers a Messianic reference (see Jer 23:5; 33:15; Zech 3:8; 6:12, where "Branch" clearly refers to the Messiah). But this verse is somewhat ambiguous. The fact that "Branch" is paralleled with "the fruit of the land" suggests to some interpreters that the reference is to the remnant (see "Exile and Exodus," p. 2659). In this case the verse is saying that after the desolation brought about by sin, God will cause his land to be spiritually fruitful again, something that would be impossible without him.
4:3–4 The prophet predicts that a day will come when the people who have just been described as arrogantly sinful will be called "holy" (see "Holiness," p. 2676). Beyond that, the city's "filth" and "bloodstains" will be washed away. The means of this surprising effect is "a spirit of judgment and a spirit of fire" (see note on v. 4).
4:4 women of Zion. See note on 3:16. **spirit ... spirit.** The Hebrew word has a wide range of meanings, including "wind," "breath," "spirit," and "Spirit." Perhaps the sense here is a metaphoric one of a fiery wind. The exile certainly was that for the Israelite people. Only a remnant would emerge from the exile, but it would purify them.
4:5–6 Language reminiscent of the exodus with its pillar of "cloud" and "fire" that both directed and protected God's people (Exod 13:21–22; 14:19–20). In a similar way, Ezekiel saw the return from exile as a new exodus (cf. Ezekiel's use of the exodus motif "they will be my people, and I will be their God," Ezek 11:20). Now the "glory" (v. 5) of God that the people once defied will be a much-appreciated "canopy" over them, affording both "shade" and "refuge."

5:1 [h]Ps 80:8-9
5:2 [i]Jer 2:21 [j]Mt 21:19; Mk 11:13; Lk 13:6
5:3 [k]Mt 21:40
5:4 [l]2Ch 36:15; Jer 2:5-7; Mic 6:3-4; Mt 23:37

The Song of the Vineyard

5 I will sing for the one I love
a song about his vineyard:[h]
My loved one had a vineyard
on a fertile hillside.
2 He dug it up and cleared it of stones
and planted it with the choicest vines.[i]
He built a watchtower in it
and cut out a winepress as well.
Then he looked for a crop of good grapes,
but it yielded only bad fruit.[j]

3 "Now you dwellers in Jerusalem and people of Judah,
judge between me and my vineyard.[k]
4 What more could have been done for my vineyard
than I have done for it?[l]
When I looked for good grapes,
why did it yield only bad?

5:1–30 *The Song of the Vineyard.* As judgment (2:6—4:1) immediately follows hope (2:1–5) in 2:1—4:1, so here Isaiah is unwilling to let the people use future hope to blind themselves to the present reality. He calls them to face their present condition (vv. 1–24) and the necessary results of that condition should it continue unchanged (vv. 25–30).

5:1–24 *Israel's Condition.* As in 3:14, Isaiah describes Israel as the Lord's vineyard, but he does so in a greatly extended metaphor (vv. 1–7). The vineyard has produced "bad fruit" (v. 2; see v. 4), and vv. 8–24 detail what that bad fruit is in a series of woe messages (vv. 8–10,11–17,18–19,20,21,22–24).

5:1–7 *The Vineyard.* Comparing Israel to a vineyard would be very compelling to Isaiah's Judahite hearers because work in vineyards was their livelihood. He describes in detail the three-year effort to produce the first crop of grapes (vv. 1–2; see note on v. 2), rhetorically asks what should be done with a worthless vineyard (vv. 3–4), announces what will be done to it (vv. 5–6), and clarifies that he is talking about Israel and Judah (v. 7).

5:1 My loved one. Yahweh; expresses something of Isaiah's deep feeling for the Lord.

5:2 Clearing the land of stones and using them to build walls and a watchtower would involve an entire season of labor. Planting "the choicest vines" would take a second season, during which a winepress would be hewn out of rock. Finally, in the third season the firstfruits of all that labor would be expected.

5:3–6 The response to the rhetorical question (v. 4) was probably a rousing one in which the hearers counseled Isaiah to destroy the vineyard. Whatever their response, Isaiah makes it clear that God will destroy it.

Vineyard and wine-making scene from an Egyptian tomb. Isa 5:1–7 describes a vineyard and the wine-making process.

Wikimedia Commons

5 Now I will tell you
what I am going to do to my vineyard:
I will take away its hedge,
and it will be destroyed;
I will break down its wall,[m]
and it will be trampled.[n]
6 I will make it a wasteland,
neither pruned nor cultivated,
and briers and thorns[o] will grow there.
I will command the clouds
not to rain on it."

7 The vineyard[p] of the LORD Almighty
is the nation of Israel,
and the people of Judah
are the vines he delighted in.
And he looked for justice,[q] but saw bloodshed;
for righteousness, but heard cries of distress.

Woes and Judgments

8 Woe[r] to you who add house to house
and join field to field[s]
till no space is left
and you live alone in the land.

9 The LORD Almighty has declared in my hearing:[t]

"Surely the great houses will become desolate,[u]
the fine mansions left without occupants.
10 A ten-acre vineyard will produce only a bath[a] of wine;
a homer[b] of seed will yield only an ephah[c] of grain."[v]

11 Woe to those who rise early in the morning
to run after their drinks,
who stay up late at night
till they are inflamed with wine.[w]
12 They have harps and lyres at their banquets,
pipes and timbrels and wine,
but they have no regard[x] for the deeds of the LORD,
no respect for the work of his hands.[y]
13 Therefore my people will go into exile[z]
for lack of understanding;[a]

[a] *10* That is, about 6 gallons or about 22 liters [b] *10* That is, probably about 360 pounds or about 160 kilograms [c] *10* That is, probably about 36 pounds or about 16 kilograms

5:5 [m] Ps 80:12 [n] Isa 28:3, 18; La 1:15; Lk 21:24
5:6 [o] Isa 7:23,24; Heb 6:8
5:7 [p] Ps 80:8 [q] Isa 59:15
5:8 [r] Jer 22:13 [s] Mic 2:2; Hab 2:9-12
5:9 [t] Isa 22:14 [u] Isa 6:11-12; Mt 23:38
5:10 [v] Lev 26:26
5:11 [w] Pr 23:29-30
5:12 [x] Job 34:27 [y] Ps 28:5; Am 6:5-6
5:13 [z] Hos 4:6 [a] Isa 1:3; Hos 4:6

5:7 Isaiah explains the metaphor, which involves a Hebrew wordplay. **bloodshed.** The Hebrew (*miśpah*) sounds like the Hebrew for "justice" (*mišpaṭ*). **cries of distress.** The Hebrew (*ṣĕʿāqâ*) sounds like the Hebrew for "righteousness" (*ṣĕʿdāqâ*).

5:8–24 *Israel's Bitter Grapes.* There is perhaps an intentional progression from greed (vv. 8–10) to perversion of moral law (vv. 20–21).

5:8–10 *Greed.* The land in Israel was a gift from God to be held in trust by each family. But the rich had ways of skirting this requirement and dispossessing people, especially the poor, from their land. Isaiah says that the result will be that the land will produce only about a tenth of what might be expected (see NIV text notes for the amounts).

5:11–17 *Self-Indulgence.* Those who pay attention only to their own desires for wealth, pleasure, and entertainment (vv. 11–12) and have no time for the Creator and his work will be deprived of those very things as "exile" and "Death" come upon them (vv. 13–14). Verses 15–16 refer to arrogance and humiliation, reminiscent of ch. 2. The "lack of understanding" (v. 13) refers to these misplaced priorities. When people forget the place of God in the world in the rush to fulfill their own desires, they doom themselves because God's "righteous acts" in the world will demonstrate his true holiness (v. 16).

5:14 [b]Pr 30:16 [c]Nu 16:30
5:15 [d]Isa 10:33 [e]Isa 2:9 [f]Isa 2:11
5:16 [g]Isa 28:17; 30:18; 33:5; 61:8 [h]Isa 29:23
5:17 [i]Isa 7:25; Zep 2:6,14
5:18 [j]Isa 59:4-8; Jer 23:14
5:19 [k]Jer 17:15; Eze 12:22; 2Pe 3:4
5:20 [l]Mt 6:22-23; Lk 11:34-35 [m]Am 5:7
5:21 [n]Pr 3:7; Ro 12:16; 1Co 3:18-20
5:22 [o]Pr 23:20
5:23 [p]Ex 23:8 [q]Isa 10:2 [r]Ps 94:21; Jas 5:6
5:24 [s]Job 18:16 [t]Isa 8:6; 30:9,12
5:25 [u]2Ki 22:13

those of high rank will die of hunger
and the common people will be parched with thirst.
14 Therefore Death[b] expands its jaws,
opening wide its mouth;[c]
into it will descend their nobles and masses
with all their brawlers and revelers.
15 So people will be brought low[d]
and everyone humbled,[e]
the eyes of the arrogant[f] humbled.
16 But the LORD Almighty will be exalted by his justice,[g]
and the holy God will be proved holy[h] by his righteous acts.
17 Then sheep will graze as in their own pasture;[i]
lambs will feed[a] among the ruins of the rich.

18 Woe to those who draw sin along with cords of deceit,
and wickedness[j] as with cart ropes,
19 to those who say, "Let God hurry;
let him hasten his work
so we may see it.
The plan of the Holy One of Israel—
let it approach, let it come into view,
so we may know it."[k]

20 Woe to those who call evil good
and good evil,
who put darkness for light
and light for darkness,[l]
who put bitter for sweet
and sweet for bitter.[m]

21 Woe to those who are wise in their own eyes[n]
and clever in their own sight.

22 Woe to those who are heroes at drinking wine[o]
and champions at mixing drinks,
23 who acquit the guilty for a bribe,[p]
but deny justice[q] to the innocent.[r]
24 Therefore, as tongues of fire lick up straw
and as dry grass sinks down in the flames,
so their roots will decay[s]
and their flowers blow away like dust;
for they have rejected the law of the LORD Almighty
and spurned the word[t] of the Holy One of Israel.
25 Therefore the LORD's anger[u] burns against his people;
his hand is raised and he strikes them down.

[a] *17* Septuagint; Hebrew / *strangers will eat*

5:18–19 *Intentional Sin.* The "cords of deceit" and "cart ropes" suggest that sinning is something they are consciously working at. Verse 19 confirms this: the sinners dare "the Holy One of Israel" to do something against them that they can see.
5:20 *Perversity.* The apparent progression reaches its climax: they turn moral reality on its head by reversing good and evil.
5:21 *Self-Determination of Good and Evil.* Instead of looking to the Creator of the universe to determine what moral reality is, these persons "are wise in their own eyes." This is what Gen 3:5 refers to: the desire to determine good and evil for oneself. This seems to explain v. 20.
5:22–24 *Link Between Self-Indulgence and Social Injustice.* This final woe summarizes the previous ones. Self-indulgence and social injustice are linked (vv. 22–23), and they are the result of rejecting the revelation ("law … word") of the universe's transcendent ("Holy One") powerful One ("LORD Almighty"). The only result can be the loss of the very permanence that self-exaltation pretends to give.
5:25–30 *The Destruction of the Vineyard.* Just as walls were torn down and wild animals were permitted to trample the vines, so God calls the enemy nations to punish Israel. The great powers of the day were only tools to accomplish Yahweh's purposes.

The mountains shake,
and the dead bodies are like refuse[v] in
the streets.

Yet for all this, his anger is not turned away,[w]
his hand is still upraised.[x]

26 He lifts up a banner for the distant nations,
he whistles[y] for those at the ends of the earth.[z]
Here they come,
swiftly and speedily!
27 Not one of them grows tired or stumbles,
not one slumbers or sleeps;
not a belt is loosened at the waist,[a]
not a sandal strap is broken.[b]
28 Their arrows are sharp,[c]
all their bows[d] are strung;
their horses' hooves seem like flint,
their chariot wheels like a whirlwind.
29 Their roar is like that of the lion,[e]
they roar like young lions;
they growl as they seize[f] their prey
and carry it off with no one to rescue.[g]
30 In that day they will roar over it
like the roaring of the sea.[h]
And if one looks at the land,
there is only darkness and distress;[i]
even the sun will be darkened[j] by clouds.

5:25 [v] 2Ki 9:37 [w] Jer 4:8; Da 9:16 [x] Isa 9:12, 17,21; 10:4
5:26 [y] Isa 7:18; Zec 10:8 [z] Dt 28:49; Isa 13:5; 18:3
5:27 [a] Job 12:18 [b] Joel 2:7-8
5:28 [c] Ps 45:5 [d] Ps 7:12
5:29 [e] Jer 51:38; Zep 3:3; Zec 11:3 [f] Isa 10:6; 49:24-25 [g] Isa 42:22; Mic 5:8
5:30 [h] Lk 21:25 [i] Isa 8:22; Jer 4:23-28 [j] Joel 2:10
6:1 [k] 2Ch 26:22,23 [l] 2Ki 15:7 [m] Jn 12:41 [n] Rev 4:2
6:2 [o] Rev 4:8 [p] Eze 1:11
6:3 [q] Ps 72:19; Rev 4:8

Isaiah's Commission

6 In the year that King Uzziah[k] died,[l] I saw the Lord,[m] high and exalted,
seated on a throne;[n] and the train of his robe filled the temple. 2 Above
him were seraphim,[o] each with six wings: With two wings they covered their
faces, with two they covered their feet,[p] and with two they were flying. 3 And
they were calling to one another:

"Holy, holy, holy is the LORD Almighty;
the whole earth is full of his glory."[q]

Relief from Tell Halaf depicting six-winged creature similar to a seraph.

Slab with Six-Winged Goddess, Tell Halaf, Syrian /© Walters Art Museum, Baltimore, USA/Bridgeman Images

5:25 Israel must come to terms with Yahweh, not the nations. **Yet for all this ... upraised.** This refrain appears four more times: 9:12,17,21; 10:4. **5:26 banner.** A characteristic term in the book, appearing nine more times: three, as here, calling destroyers (13:2; 18:3; 31:9 ["battle standard"]), four calling God's people home (11:10,12; 49:22; 62:10), and twice in more casual settings (30:17; 33:23 [translated "sail" in the latter case]).

6:1–13 *Isaiah's Commission.* Chs. 1–5, the introduction of the book, raises a question: How can the arrogant, defiant, perverse people of Israel ever become the pure, undefiled people through whom the nations can learn God's ways? The prophet seems to offer his own call experience as a model for this. This probably explains why he defers the call narrative to this point in the book. Isaiah sees God in all his glory (vv. 1–4), sees himself in all his uncleanness (v. 5), experiences cleansing (vv. 6–7), hears God's concern and offers himself (v. 8), receives the commission (vv. 9–10), questions the commission (v. 11a), and hears God's response to his question (vv. 11b–13).

6:1 the year that King Uzziah died. 740/39 BC. Probably included to show that Isaiah received the vision during a time of crisis. Though a strong and effective king, Uzziah had been struck with leprosy when he tried to play the part of a priest in the temple (2 Chr 26:16–21). His immediate successors were not strong and effective. **high and exalted.** Description occurs twice more in the book: 57:15 (referring to God again); 52:13 (referring to the servant). **throne ... temple.** Conveys divine kingship. **the train ... filled the temple.** Gives a sense of the immensity of God in Isaiah's vision. It may also be a way of making visual the following statement that God's glory filled the earth (v. 3). Note that no mention is made of the appearance of God himself (cf. Exod 33:20–23).

6:2 seraphim. The origin of the Hebrew word suggests that these beings had the appearance of flames. The word does not appear elsewhere in the Bible, but the "living creatures" of Rev 4:6–9 are also described as having six wings. **six wings.** Suggest supernatural power. **covered their faces.** Seems to say that even though they were supernatural beings, they could not look on the holy God. **covered their feet.** Implies their createdness.

6:3 Holy, holy, holy. In Hebrew, triple repetition expresses the superlative: absolutely holy. **glory.** Connotes significance and weightiness (cf. 2 Cor 4:17). All glory in the earth belongs ultimately to Yahweh, not to humans.

6:5 [r]Jer 9:3-8 [s]Jer 51:57
6:7 [t]Jer 1:9 [u]1Jn 1:7
6:8 [v]Ac 9:4
6:9 [w]Eze 3:11
[x]Mt 13:15*; Lk 8:10*
6:10 [y]Dt 32:15;
Ps 119:70 [z]Jer 5:21
[a]Mt 13:13-15; Mk 4:12*;
Ac 28:26-27*
6:11 [b]Ps 79:5
[c]Lev 26:31
6:12 [d]Dt 28:64 [e]Jer 4:29
6:13 [f]Isa 1:9

4 At the sound of their voices the doorposts and thresholds
shook and the temple was filled with smoke.
5 "Woe to me!" I cried. "I am ruined! For I am a man of
unclean lips, and I live among a people of unclean lips,[r]
and my eyes have seen the King,[s] the LORD Almighty."
6 Then one of the seraphim flew to me with a live
coal in his hand, which he had taken with tongs
from the altar. 7 With it he touched my mouth and
said, "See, this has touched your lips;[t] your guilt is
taken away and your sin atoned for.[u]"
8 Then I heard the voice[v] of the Lord saying,
"Whom shall I send? And who will go for us?"
And I said, "Here am I. Send me!"
9 He said, "Go[w] and tell this people:

"'Be ever hearing, but never
understanding;
be ever seeing, but never perceiving.'[x]
10 Make the heart of this people calloused;[y]
make their ears dull
and close their eyes.[a]
Otherwise they might see with their eyes,
hear with their ears,[z]
understand with their hearts,
and turn and be healed."[a]

11 Then I said, "For how long, Lord?"[b]
And he answered:

"Until the cities lie ruined[c]
and without inhabitant,
until the houses are left deserted
and the fields ruined and ravaged,
12 until the LORD has sent everyone far away[d]
and the land is utterly forsaken.[e]
13 And though a tenth remains[f] in the land,
it will again be laid waste.

Clay bulla is decorated with two winged serpents (cf. with seraphim in Isa 6:2). The inscription reads, "Belonging to Amos, servant of Hezekiah."
Z. Radovan/www.BibleLandPictures.com

[a] 9,10 Hebrew; Septuagint *'You will be ever hearing, but never understanding; / you will be ever seeing, but never perceiving.' / 10 This people's heart has become calloused; / they hardly hear with their ears, / and they have closed their eyes*

6:4 May suggest that everything in God's creation joins in praise of him, even the inanimate objects (Luke 19:40).
6:5 unclean lips. A figure of speech for Isaiah's life. Whatever he might claim about the nature of his inner life, his outer life refuted that when compared to God's holy character. **among a people of unclean lips.** Reinforces Isaiah's point about himself (cf. Judg 6:15; 1 Sam 9:21). **seen the King.** The earthly king has died, and Isaiah has seen the one who is truly King.
6:6 live coal. Probably came from the bronze altar just outside the temple. Live coals were brought into the Most Holy Place to ignite the incense on the Day of Atonement (Lev 16:12).
6:7 guilt is taken away and your sin atoned for. God has provided a way whereby the guilt and sin of humanity can be removed. The sacrifice on the altar symbolized the perfect sacrifice of God himself in Jesus Christ (John 1:29).
6:8 us. Also refers to God in two other important places that speak of his activity: Gen 1:26; 11:7. While the plural of majesty is possible, or a reference to the seraphim comprising his court, we cannot rule out a latent expression of the Trinity.
6:9–10 Given the spiritual condition of Isaiah's own generation, the truth would only harden them in their sin. So Isaiah, having faithfully preached God's message, sealed it up (8:16–18) to wait for another generation that would hear and respond. This passage is frequently quoted or alluded to in the NT (Matt 13:14–15; Mark 4:12; Luke 8:10; John 12:40; Acts 28:26–27; cf. Rom 11:8).
6:11 For how long, Lord? The answer is not encouraging. The only hope for Isaiah's land was through destruction. Mere superficial deliverance would not cure the wounds (1:5–6); they required cauterization (see note on v. 13).
6:13 laid waste. Destruction is never Yahweh's intended last word. From one of the burned-out "stumps" would spring up a "holy seed," a remnant of faithful believers who, cleansed and purified (see 4:3–4), would continue to bear God's word to the nations through the Messiah who would come through their line.

But as the terebinth and oak
leave stumps when they are cut down,
so the holy seed will be the stump in the land."[g]

The Sign of Immanuel

7 When Ahaz son of Jotham, the son of Uzziah, was king of Judah, King Rezin[h] of Aram[i] and Pekah[j]
son of Remaliah king of Israel marched up to fight against Jerusalem, but they could not overpower it.
2 Now the house of David[k] was told, "Aram has allied itself with[a] Ephraim[l]"; so the hearts of Ahaz
and his people were shaken, as the trees of the forest are shaken by the wind.
3 Then the LORD said to Isaiah, "Go out, you and your son Shear-Jashub,[b] to meet Ahaz at the end
of the aqueduct of the Upper Pool, on the road to the Launderer's Field.[m] 4 Say to him, 'Be careful,
keep calm[n] and don't be afraid.[o] Do not lose heart[p] because of these two smoldering stubs[q] of firewood—because of the fierce anger[r] of Rezin and Aram and of the son of Remaliah. 5 Aram, Ephraim
and Remaliah's son have plotted your ruin, saying, 6 "Let us invade Judah; let us tear it apart and divide
it among ourselves, and make the son of Tabeel king over it." 7 Yet this is what the Sovereign LORD says:

"'It will not take place,
it will not happen,[s]
8 for the head of Aram is Damascus,[t]
and the head of Damascus is only Rezin.
Within sixty-five years
Ephraim will be too shattered[u] to be a people.
9 The head of Ephraim is Samaria,
and the head of Samaria is only Remaliah's son.
If you do not stand firm in your faith,[v]
you will not stand at all.'"[w]

[a] 2 Or *has set up camp in* [b] 3 *Shear-Jashub* means *a remnant will return.*

6:13 [g] Job 14:7
7:1 [h] 2Ki 15:37 [i] 2Ch 28:5 [j] 2Ki 15:25
7:2 [k] ver 13; Isa 22:22 [l] Isa 9:9
7:3 [m] 2Ki 18:17; Isa 36:2
7:4 [n] Isa 30:15 [o] Isa 35:4 [p] Dt 20:3 [q] Zec 3:2 [r] Isa 10:24
7:7 [s] Isa 8:10; Ac 4:25
7:8 [t] Ge 14:15 [u] Isa 17:1-3
7:9 [v] 2Ch 20:20 [w] Isa 8:6-8; 30:12-14

7:1—39:8 *Trust: The Basis of Servanthood.* If the nation of unclean lips could have the same experience as the man of unclean lips, then they could bear Yahweh's message to the nations just as Isaiah did to them. Like Isaiah, they need to truly perceive Yahweh's holiness, power, and reliability, bringing them to a place where they will trust him rather than humanity's illusory power and glory. So this major division of the book is united around the question of divine versus human trustworthiness. Chs. 7–12 and 36–39 provide contrasting "bookends": King Ahaz of Judah refuses to trust Yahweh, but his son, King Hezekiah, does trust Yahweh in a far more serious situation than his father had faced. Chs. 13–35 show why Ahaz's decision was wrong and provide a basis for Hezekiah's right decision.
7:1—12:6 *Ahaz's Refusal to Trust.* This section has four parts: 7:1—9:7 deals with Ahaz's bad decision and its immediate implications; the remaining three parts (9:8—10:4; 10:5—11:16; 12:1–6) explore the deeper causes of what was happening and the ultimate solution to the problem. Through it all is an underlying issue: Who is the real king and the nation's ultimate hope?
7:1—9:7 *Signs of the Promise.* Yahweh declares his faithfulness to King Ahaz through Isaiah. He demonstrates this with a series of signs. The ultimate sign and proof is the child Immanuel.
7:1–25 *The Sign and the Consequences of Its Rejection.* Yahweh gave Isaiah a message for Ahaz: Ahaz could trust Yahweh to protect him from his enemies (vv. 1–9). God offered a sign to confirm the promise, but Ahaz, having already determined to trust Assyria (2 Kgs 16:7–9), rejected the sign (Isa 7:10–12). Isaiah gave the sign anyway, indicating that its immediate significance would be that the nation would shortly be all but destroyed (vv. 13–25).
7:1–2 *Judah Pressured to Join Coalition Against Assyria.* The Assyrian Empire, after about 50 years of relative quiescence, was pushing aggressively southward toward Egypt. The two smaller nations north of Judah—Aram and Israel (see note on v. 1)—were trying to compel Judah to join them in a coalition against Assyria. They threatened to depose Ahaz if he refused (see v. 6).
7:1 Aram. Syria. **Israel.** The northern kingdom of Israel, also identified as "Ephraim" (see note on v. 2).
7:2 house of David. Probably refers not only to Ahaz, a member of the Davidic dynasty, but also to the entire royal family of that time. **Ephraim.** The main northern tribe and thus another name for the northern kingdom of Israel.
7:3–9 *A Challenge to Trust Yahweh.* Ahaz had already made arrangements to send a large sum of money to the Assyrian emperor to attack Aram (i.e., Syria) and Israel, something the emperor was planning to do anyway (2 Kgs 16:7–9).
7:3 Shear-Jashub. See NIV text note. A judgment on Ahaz's foolish plan (see note on vv. 1–25).
7:4 smoldering stubs of firewood. The two enemy kings have no real power to do anything. **son of Remaliah.** Contemptuously refers to Pekah, king of Israel (also in vv. 5,9). He was a usurper, and his father was a nobody.
7:5–9 It does not matter what the two kings might be saying; it is what the Sovereign Lord says that counts. If he says that the threats will come to nothing, that is how it will be.
7:8 sixty-five years. It is not clear what this event refers to. It is probable that the encounter between Isaiah and Ahaz took place in 734 BC. The fall of Samaria (the capital of the northern kingdom of Israel) occurred in 722 BC. Possibly this reference is to the settlement in Israel of the foreign colonists who were, through intermarriage with the remaining Israelites, to become the later Samaritans.
7:9 stand firm ... stand. Another wordplay; the same word is used for what Ahaz must do and what God would do. Ahaz must be firm in his faith if God would make him firm in the face of the enemy.

7:13 [x] Isa 25:1

10 Again the LORD spoke to Ahaz, 11 "Ask the LORD your God for a sign, whether in the deepest depths
or in the highest heights."
12 But Ahaz said, "I will not ask; I will not put the LORD to the test."
13 Then Isaiah said, "Hear now, you house of David! Is it not enough to try the patience of humans?
Will you try the patience of my God[x] also? 14 Therefore the Lord himself will give you[a] a sign: The virgin[b]

[a] *14* The Hebrew is plural. [b] *14* Or *young woman*

7:10–25 *The Rejection of the Sign.* Since Ahaz already decided to rely on Assyria, he did not welcome any confirmation that such reliance was not only unnecessary but wrong. Although Ahaz tries to cover his unbelief with hypocritical piety, Isaiah sees through it and gives the sign anyway. The sign's significance is twofold: (1) Its immediate portent is quite negative: the Assyria Ahaz trusted would turn on him and threaten his nation far more seriously than Pekah and Rezin ever could. (2) But there is a positive sense as well, which 9:1–7 (see note) and 11:1–16 (see note) further expand upon.

7:10–17 *The Sign of Immanuel.* Isaiah offers Ahaz a sign of immense significance ("deepest depths [hell] … highest heights [heaven]," v. 11) that will prove God's saving presence with his people. Ahaz attempts to refuse it, but Isaiah gives it anyway. It is a sign full of mystery, with the portents of near-term judgment and long-term salvation caught up in it. **7:12 put the LORD to the test.** Disbelieve his promises (cf. Exod 17:2,7). **7:14 virgin.** Hebrew *ʿalmâ*, which means "young woman of marriageable age." In Israelite society a young woman of marriageable age would have been a virgin (as the Septuagint, the pre-Christian Greek

KINGS OF ASSYRIA, JUDAH, ISRAEL, AND ARAMEA

YEAR	ASSYRIAN KINGS	JUDAHITE KINGS	ISRAELITE KINGS	ARAMEAN KINGS OF DAMASCUS
999				Hadadezer first quarter of the tenth century
950				Rezon third quarter of the tenth century
925				Hezion fourth quarter of the tenth century Tabrimmon end of the tenth century
900				Ben-Hadad I ca. 900–880
880				Ben-Hadad II ca. 880–844/843
850				Hazael ca. 844/843–803
825				Ben-Hadad III ca. 803–775
800		Uzziah 792/91–740/39		
775	Ashur-nirari V 754–745		Menahem 752–742/41	Hezion II (not mentioned in the Bible) ca. 775–750
750	Tiglath-Pileser III 745–727 Shalmaneser V 727–722	Jotham 750–732/31 Ahaz 735–716/15 Hezekiah 729–687/86	Pekahiah 742/41–740/39 Pekah 752–732/31 Hoshea 732/31–723/22	Rezin ca. 750–732
725	Sargon II 722–705 Sennacherib 705–681			
700		Manasseh 697/96–643/42		

Aramean information from *A Political History of the Arameans: From Their Origins to the End of Their Polities* by K. Lawson Younger Jr. (Atlanta: SBL, in press). Used by permission.

Carved relief of King Tiglath-Pileser III receiving homage from a vanquished warrior, 745–737 BC. Tiglath-Pileser III of Assyria conquered Damascus and much of the Israelite kingdom.

Carved relief of Tiglath-Pileser III, south-west palace, Nimrud (Kalah) Mesopotamian/Detroit Institute of Arts, USA/Founders Society purchase, Ralph Harman Booth Bequest fund/Bridgeman Images

will conceive and give birth to a son,[y] and[a] will call him Immanuel.[bz] 15He will be eating curds and
honey[a] when he knows enough to reject the wrong and choose the right, 16for before the boy knows[b]
enough to reject the wrong and choose the right, the land of the two kings you dread will be laid waste.[c]
17The LORD will bring on you and on your people and on the house of your father a time unlike any
since Ephraim broke away[d] from Judah—he will bring the king of Assyria.[e]"

Assyria, the LORD's Instrument

18In that day the LORD will whistle[f] for flies from the Nile delta in Egypt and for bees from the land of
Assyria.[g] 19They will all come and settle in the steep ravines and in the crevices[h] in the rocks, on all the
thornbushes and at all the water holes. 20In that day the Lord will use[i] a razor hired from beyond the
Euphrates River—the king of Assyria[j]—to shave your head and private parts, and to cut off your beard
also. 21In that day, a person will keep alive a young cow and two goats. 22And because of the abundance of
the milk they give, there will be curds to eat. All who remain in the land will eat curds and honey. 23In that
day, in every place where there were a thousand vines worth a thousand silver shekels,[c] there will be only
briers and thorns.[k] 24Hunters will go there with bow and arrow, for the land will be covered with briers and
thorns. 25As for all the hills once cultivated by the hoe, you will no longer go there for fear of the briers and
thorns; they will become places where cattle are turned loose and where sheep run.[l]

7:14 [y]Lk 1:31 [z]Isa 8:8, 10; Mt 1:23*
7:15 [a]ver 22
7:16 [b]Isa 8:4 [c]Isa 17:3; Hos 5:9,13; Am 1:3-5
7:17 [d]1Ki 12:16 [e]2Ch 28:20
7:18 [f]Isa 5:26 [g]Isa 13:5
7:19 [h]Isa 2:19
7:20 [i]Isa 10:15 [j]Isa 8:7; 10:5
7:23 [k]Isa 5:6
7:25 [l]Isa 5:17

[a] *14* Masoretic Text; Dead Sea Scrolls *son, and he* or *son, and they* [b] *14* *Immanuel* means *God with us.*
[c] *23* That is, about 25 pounds or about 12 kilograms

translation of the OT, makes plain). Otherwise, she would have been a prostitute. But the Hebrew word is not the technical term meaning "virgin." Isaiah uses this more ambiguous term because of the double reference of this sign. In its immediate reference the virginity of the mother is not the most significant point. Rather, God is saying that before a child conceived at that time would reach age 12 or 13 (v. 16), the two nations of which Ahaz was so terrified would cease to exist. But in the long term, this sign, higher than heaven and deeper than hell (see note on vv. 10–17), referred to the coming of Jesus Christ, the true Immanuel (Matt 1:23), and the virginity of his mother was vitally important. This is why Isaiah did not use a simple word meaning "woman" or "young woman." **Immanuel.** Means "God with us." The Bible emphasizes the importance of God being "with" his people (e.g., 41:10; Gen 39:2,23). God would be with his people to defend them from their enemies if they would stand with him in faith. But this is more than a figure of speech. In Jesus it has become a fact: God has become a human being and is with us in every respect except one: he has not committed sin (Heb 4:15).

7:15–17 Before the child conceived by the young woman would become 12 or 13 years old ("reject the wrong," vv. 15,16), both Syria and Israel would be "laid waste" by Assyria. But because of Ahaz's faithlessness, Judah would feel the lash as well (v. 17).

7:15 curds and honey. A figure of speech for rich food. The land would be so depopulated that those who remained would have an abundance of food to eat (see v. 22).

7:18–25 *The Coming Assyrian Attack.* In his typical fashion (e.g., 5:26–30), Isaiah emphasizes his point with a graphic illustration. He pictures the enemies in their multitudes as "flies" and "bees" (vv. 18–19). He pictures Assyria as a "razor" disgracing the men of Israel by shaving off all their body hair (v. 20). He depicts the depopulation of the land as providing the few who remain with the amounts and kinds of food the nobility would eat (vv. 21–22). But at the same time, with only a handful of people left, the arable land would grow only briers and thorns (vv. 23–25), perhaps a reference to the situation in 701 BC when Sennacherib ravaged the land (36:1).

8:1 [m]Isa 30:8; Hab 2:2 [n]ver 3; Hab 2:2
8:2 [o]2Ki 16:10
8:4 [p]Isa 7:16 [q]Isa 7:8
8:6 [r]Isa 5:24 [s]Jn 9:7 [t]Isa 7:1
8:7 [u]Isa 17:12-13 [v]Isa 7:20
8:8 [w]Isa 7:14
8:9 [x]Isa 17:12-13 [y]Joel 3:9
8:10 [z]Job 5:12 [a]Isa 7:7 [b]Isa 7:14; Ro 8:31
8:11 [c]Eze 3:14 [d]Eze 2:8
8:12 [e]Isa 7:2; 30:1

Isaiah and His Children as Signs

8 The LORD said to me, "Take a large scroll[m] and write on it with an ordinary pen: Maher-Shalal-Hash-
Baz."[a][n] 2 So I called in Uriah[o] the priest and Zechariah son of Jeberekiah as reliable witnesses for me.
3 Then I made love to the prophetess, and she conceived and gave birth to a son. And the LORD said to me,
"Name him Maher-Shalal-Hash-Baz. 4 For before the boy knows[p] how to say 'My father' or 'My mother,' the
wealth of Damascus and the plunder of Samaria will be carried off by the king of Assyria.[q]"

5 The LORD spoke to me again:

6 "Because this people has rejected[r]
the gently flowing waters of Shiloah[s]
and rejoices over Rezin
the son of Remaliah,[t]
7 therefore the Lord is about to bring against them
the mighty floodwaters[u] of the Euphrates —
the king of Assyria[v] with all his pomp.
It will overflow all its channels,
run over all its banks
8 and sweep on into Judah, swirling over it,
passing through it and reaching up to the neck.
Its outspread wings will cover the breadth of your land,
Immanuel[b]!"[w]

9 Raise the war cry,[c][x] you nations, and be shattered!
Listen, all you distant lands.
Prepare[y] for battle, and be shattered!
Prepare for battle, and be shattered!
10 Devise your strategy, but it will be thwarted;[z]
propose your plan, but it will not stand,[a]
for God is with us.[d][b]

11 This is what the LORD says to me with his strong hand upon me,[c] warning me not to follow[d] the
way of this people:

12 "Do not call conspiracy[e]
everything this people calls a conspiracy;

[a] *1 Maher-Shalal-Hash-Baz* means *quick to the plunder, swift to the spoil*; also in verse 3. [b] *8 Immanuel* means *God with us.* [c] *9* Or *Do your worst* [d] *10* Hebrew *Immanuel*

8:1–22 *Isaiah and His Children as Signs.* This segment of the larger section (7:1—9:7) continues to focus on the immediate portent of the sign in 7:14. God being with us is not a positive thing if we refuse to trust him. In that case, his presence will become a stumbling block rather than a sanctuary (vv. 14–15).

8:1–10 *The Sign of Maher-Shalal-Hash-Baz.* On the meaning of the name, see NIV text note. Clearly confirms the negative aspect of the Immanuel sign (see note on 7:10–25). The similarity in language between v. 3 and 7:14 has suggested to some that this child was the immediate fulfillment of that promise. In this case, it is before the child can speak clearly (three years of age?) that Damascus (the capital of Syria) and Samaria (the capital of Israel) would be plundered by the king of Assyria. Damascus fell to Assyria in 732 BC. Verses 5–8 explain this negative aspect further by predicting the attack of the Assyrians on Judah under the leadership of Sennacherib (see 36:1). However, as is common in the book of Isaiah, judgment is not Yahweh's intended last word, and the passage ends (8:9–10) with the announcement that Assyria herself will be judged (see also 10:5–19).

8:5–8 Because Judah rejected Yahweh's seemingly gentle promises and instead rejoiced over what the Assyrians were going to do to Syria and Israel, God was going to bring the great Assyrian Empire against them.

8:6 gently flowing waters of Shiloah. A metaphor for God's promises. **Shiloah.** The meaning of the name is unclear.

8:7 mighty ... Euphrates. A metaphor for the king of Assyria.

8:8 reaching up to the neck. Probably refers to Sennacherib's future attack, which captured the rest of Judah except Jerusalem (chs. 36–37). **your land, Immanuel!** Suggests that, at the least, this is not ultimately an ordinary child, but one of royal lineage.

8:9–10 God's presence with his people would prevent the nations from carrying out the total destruction they planned.

8:11–15 *Yahweh: Sanctuary or Stumbling Block.* These verses continue the thought of the section: if Yahweh is not made the central focus of one's life, then he becomes an obstruction over which one must constantly fall.

8:11–13 Two different understandings of history: (1) Give God the central place that only the Holy One must have, or (2) explain historical events as the result of human conspiracy, with the constant dread of the unknown that this view engenders. Yahweh counsels Isaiah that if he is going to dread something, it ought to be the Lord Almighty (cf. Matt 10:28). But in the end, the fear of the Lord is not something defiling and demeaning; it is pure (Ps 19:9). It means ordering one's life around the Holy One's power, goodness, and reliability.

do not fear what they fear,
and do not dread it.[f]
13 The LORD Almighty is the one you are to regard as holy,[g]
he is the one you are to fear,
he is the one you are to dread.[h]
14 He will be a holy place;[i]
for both Israel and Judah he will be
a stone that causes people to stumble
and a rock that makes them fall.[j]
And for the people of Jerusalem he will be
a trap and a snare.[k]
15 Many of them will stumble;[l]
they will fall and be broken,
they will be snared and captured."

16 Bind up this testimony of warning
and seal[m] up God's instruction among my disciples.
17 I will wait[n] for the LORD,
who is hiding[o] his face from the descendants of Jacob.
I will put my trust in him.

18 Here am I, and the children the LORD has given me.[p] We are signs[q] and symbols in Israel from the
LORD Almighty, who dwells on Mount Zion.[r]

The Darkness Turns to Light

19 When someone tells you to consult[s] mediums and spiritists, who whisper and mutter,[t] should
not a people inquire of their God? Why consult the dead on behalf of the living? 20 Consult God's instruction[u] and the testimony of warning. If anyone does not speak according to this word, they have
no light[v] of dawn. 21 Distressed and hungry, they will roam through the land; when they are famished,
they will become enraged and, looking upward, will curse[w] their king and their God. 22 Then they will
look toward the earth and see only distress and darkness and fearful gloom, and they will be thrust
into utter darkness.[x]

9 [a] Nevertheless, there will be no more gloom for those who were in distress. In the past he humbled
the land of Zebulun and the land of Naphtali,[y] but in the future he will honor Galilee of the
nations, by the Way of the Sea, beyond the Jordan—

[a] In Hebrew texts 9:1 is numbered 8:23, and 9:2-21 is numbered 9:1-20.

8:12 [f] 1Pe 3:14*
8:13 [g] Nu 20:12 [h] Isa 29:23
8:14 [i] Isa 4:6; Eze 11:16 [j] Lk 2:34; Ro 9:33*; 1Pe 2:8* [k] Isa 24:17-18
8:15 [l] Isa 28:13; 59:10; Lk 20:18; Ro 9:32
8:16 [m] Isa 29:11-12
8:17 [n] Hab 2:3 [o] Dt 31:17; Isa 54:8
8:18 [p] Heb 2:13* [q] Lk 2:34 [r] Ps 9:11
8:19 [s] 1Sa 28:8 [t] Isa 29:4
8:20 [u] Isa 1:10; Lk 16:29 [v] Mic 3:6
8:21 [w] Rev 16:11
8:22 [x] ver 20; Isa 5:30
9:1 [y] 2Ki 15:29

8:14–15 The same God will be either a sanctuary ("a holy place") or "a snare," depending on the place God's people give him in their lives. For a similar thought, see Ps 18:24–26.

8:14 a stone ... stumble ... a rock ... fall. See Rom 9:32,33 and notes; 1 Pet 2:7,8 and notes.

8:16–22 *God's Word or the Occult.* Instead of seeking God's revelation ("testimony" and "instruction," v. 16) as given to Isaiah and his "disciples" (v. 16), the people turn to "mediums and spiritists" (v. 19), in whom there is "no light" (v. 20). As a result, they "curse their king" and, ironically, "their God" (v. 21). In so doing, they plunge themselves into "utter darkness" (v. 22).

8:17 wait. Hebrew *ḥākâ* (cf. 30:18; 64:4). **put my trust in.** Hebrew *qāwâ*, which the NIV translates in a variety of ways, depending on context: (cf. 25:9 ["trusted in"]; 26:8 ["wait for"]; 33:2 ["long for"]; 40:31 ["hope in"]; 49:23 ["hope in"]; 51:5 ["look to"]; 59:9,11 ["look for"]; 60:9 ["look to"]; 64:3 ["expect"]). Trusting God involves not rushing ahead of him to solve our problems in our own time, in our own way, and with our own resources, but waiting for him to reveal how he plans to act.

8:18 signs and symbols. Isaiah and his children (which perhaps includes Isaiah's disciples as well as his physical children Shear-Jashub and Maher-Shalal-Hash-Baz) were the evidence of the truth of all that Yahweh had said. They represented faithfulness to God, and when the exile of the northern tribes and the devastation of Judah by the Assyrians occurred, Isaiah's words would be fully vindicated.

9:1–7 *Light Through the Child.* If a child born in Isaiah's own time immediately fulfilled the sign to Ahaz, this child ultimately fulfills that sign: God promises to be with his people. Children (Shear-Jashub, Maher-Shalal-Hash-Baz, and Immanuel) are important in this entire segment (7:1—9:7) as a way of underlining that a child in God's hands is more powerful than the powerful nations of this world.

9:1–2 This is another of Isaiah's powerfully abrupt transitions. Although the people's refusal to trust God plunged them into darkness (8:22), God is unwilling to leave them there but graciously brings light to them.

9:1 Zebulun ... Naphtali ... Galilee. The region in the far north of Israel's territory, where the Assyrian depredations started. The people there will see the "great light" (v. 2). This is the place where much of the ministry of Jesus, Immanuel, the light of the world, took place (Matt 4:12–17). **Way of the Sea.** The great highway that ran from the Euphrates River to Egypt, the route of the conquerors.

9:2 [z]Eph 5:8 [a]Lk 1:79 [b]Mt 4:15-16*
9:4 [c]Jdg 7:25 [d]Isa 14:25 [e]Isa 10:27 [f]Isa 14:4; 49:26; 51:13; 54:14
9:5 [g]Isa 2:4
9:6 [h]Isa 53:2; Lk 2:11 [i]Jn 3:16 [j]Mt 28:18 [k]Isa 28:29 [l]Isa 10:21; 11:2 [m]Isa 26:3,12; 66:12
9:7 [n]Da 2:44; Lk 1:33 [o]Isa 11:4; 16:5; 32:1,16 [p]Isa 37:32; 59:17

2 The people walking in darkness
have seen a great light;[z]
on those living in the land of deep darkness[a]
a light has dawned.[b]
3 You have enlarged the nation
and increased their joy;
they rejoice before you
as people rejoice at the harvest,
as warriors rejoice
when dividing the plunder.
4 For as in the day of Midian's defeat,[c]
you have shattered
the yoke[d] that burdens them,
the bar across their shoulders,[e]
the rod of their oppressor.[f]
5 Every warrior's boot used in battle
and every garment rolled in blood
will be destined for burning,[g]
will be fuel for the fire.
6 For to us a child is born,[h]
to us a son is given,[i]
and the government[j] will be on his shoulders.
And he will be called
Wonderful Counselor,[k] Mighty God,[l]
Everlasting Father, Prince of Peace.[m]
7 Of the greatness of his government and peace
there will be no end.[n]
He will reign on David's throne
and over his kingdom,
establishing and upholding it
with justice[o] and righteousness
from that time on and forever.
The zeal[p] of the LORD Almighty
will accomplish this.

The LORD's Anger Against Israel

8 The Lord has sent a message against Jacob;
it will fall on Israel.

9:3–5 This describes the results of the light's coming in terms of deliverance from military oppression. The people "rejoice" (v. 3) because the slavery ("the yoke ... the bar ... the rod," v. 4) that the various oppressors had imposed upon them has been removed and all the military accoutrements of oppression have been destroyed (v. 5).
9:4 Midian's defeat. Gideon's victory over a great horde with only a tiny army (10:26; Judg 7:22–25).
9:6 child. Surprisingly, the deliverer is a child. Some believe he is Hezekiah. But apart from dating problems, it is clear that no ordinary human is intended. The child's names ("Wonderful Counselor, Mighty God, Everlasting Father, Prince of Peace") were not for any Israelite king, no matter how arrogant. At the same time, this child is somehow a descendant of the human David (v. 7). Yet unlike many of the Davidic kings (especially Ahaz), he would rule "with justice and righteousness" (v. 7; see 16:5). All of these factors present conundrums that are finally satisfactorily resolved only in Jesus Christ, the true Immanuel. **Wonderful Counselor, Mighty God, Everlasting Father, Prince of Peace.** The combination of these four titles, or throne names, in one person represents the totality of this child's royal power. **Counselor.** Just as God needed no other counselor when he created the world (40:12–14) nor any other to give him plans for the nations (14:26–27), so this child is his own counselor. **Mighty God.** This title, which belongs to Yahweh (10:20–21), also belongs to this child. **Everlasting Father.** The ideal king who provides for his people and protects them, in this case forever (63:16). **Prince of Peace.** Unlike the princes in the pagan pantheon who were always the source of trouble and upheaval, this child will be the source of "peace," a biblical concept that includes much more than mere absence of conflict; it speaks of wholeness and integration with no issues left unresolved (26:3; 32:17; 52:7; 66:12).
9:8—10:4 *The Lord's Anger Against Israel.* In four symmetrically constructed stanzas (9:8–12,13–17,18–21; 10:1–4), each of which ends with the same refrain, this poem focuses on the real issues that the inhabitants of Israel and Judah should be attending to: not the threat of Assyria but their relation to God and what he expected of them as his

[9]All the people will know it—
Ephraim and the inhabitants of Samaria[q]—
who say with pride
and arrogance[r] of heart,
[10]"The bricks have fallen down,
but we will rebuild with dressed stone;
the fig trees have been felled,
but we will replace them with cedars."
[11]But the LORD has strengthened Rezin's[s] foes against them
and has spurred their enemies on.
[12]Arameans[t] from the east and Philistines[u] from the west
have devoured[v] Israel with open mouth.

Yet for all this, his anger is not turned away,
his hand is still upraised.[w]

[13]But the people have not returned to him who struck[x] them,
nor have they sought[y] the LORD Almighty.
[14]So the LORD will cut off from Israel both head and tail,
both palm branch and reed[z] in a single day;[a]
[15]the elders[b] and dignitaries are the head,
the prophets who teach lies are the tail.
[16]Those who guide[c] this people mislead them,
and those who are guided are led astray.[d]
[17]Therefore the Lord will take no pleasure in the young men,[e]
nor will he pity[f] the fatherless and widows,
for everyone is ungodly[g] and wicked,[h]
every mouth speaks folly.[i]

Yet for all this, his anger is not turned away,
his hand is still upraised.[j]

[18]Surely wickedness burns like a fire;[k]
it consumes briers and thorns,
it sets the forest thickets ablaze,[l]
so that it rolls upward in a column of smoke.
[19]By the wrath[m] of the LORD Almighty
the land will be scorched
and the people will be fuel for the fire;[n]
they will not spare one another.[o]
[20]On the right they will devour,
but still be hungry;[p]

9:9 [q]Isa 7:9 [r]Isa 46:12
9:11 [s]Isa 7:8
9:12 [t]2Ki 16:6 [u]2Ch 28:18 [v]Ps 79:7 [w]Isa 5:25
9:13 [x]Jer 5:3 [y]Isa 31:1; Hos 7:7,10
9:14 [z]Isa 19:15 [a]Rev 18:8
9:15 [b]Isa 3:2-3
9:16 [c]Mt 15:14; 23:16, 24 [d]Isa 3:12
9:17 [e]Jer 18:21 [f]Isa 27:11 [g]Isa 10:6 [h]Isa 1:4 [i]Mt 12:34 [j]Isa 5:25
9:18 [k]Mal 4:1 [l]Ps 83:14
9:19 [m]Isa 13:9,13 [n]Isa 1:31 [o]Mic 7:2,6
9:20 [p]Lev 26:26

covenant partners. They were in mortal danger because they refused a trusting and obedient relationship with God. While the poem addresses specifically the northern kingdom, the issues are perennial ones facing both Judah and Israel.

9:8–12 *Pride.* As in chs. 2–3 and elsewhere in the book, the most basic human problem is our attempt to usurp God's place and exalt ourselves over him. Perhaps by this time Damascus and its king, Rezin, have already fallen. Nevertheless, the people of Ephraim and Samaria arrogantly insist that they can survive and prosper in spite of what their enemies might do to them. Israel must come to terms with the anger of Yahweh, not of Assyria. They should be concerned about his threatening fist ("hand … upraised," v. 12). This point is underlined four times in the repeated refrain (vv. 12,17,21; 10:4; see 5:25). Although Yahweh's unfailing love is central to his nature, as Exod 34:6–7 makes clear, (echoed by John in 1 John 4:7–8), he is also righteous, and to presume on that righteousness by living wicked lives is ultimately disastrous (see Exod 34:7; 1 John 5:16; see "Wrath," p. 2681).

9:13–17 *Wicked Leaders.* The leaders of the people have not led them to repent or seek the Lord after previous calamities (cf. Amos 4:6–11). Instead, they have "led [them] astray" (v. 16). So God will deprive them of any leaders at all (cf. 3:1–15; Hos 10:3).

9:18–21 *Tribal Jealousy.* Throughout the history of Israel, there had been a tendency among its leaders to subordinate the concerns of the people of God as a whole to those of the leader's own tribe (e.g., Judg 8:1; 12:1–6; 20:12–16). That tendency only intensified after the division of Solomon's kingdom. Under the pressure of Assyrian conquest, it was exacerbated still further. So Ephraim and Manasseh fought each other, and together they fought against Judah instead of uniting to combat the common wickedness facing them.

9:20 [q]Isa 49:26
9:21 [r]2Ch 28:6 [s]Isa 5:25
10:1 [t]Ps 58:2
10:2 [u]Isa 3:14 [v]Isa 5:23
10:3 [w]Job 31:14; Hos 9:7 [x]Lk 19:44 [y]Isa 20:6
10:4 [z]Isa 24:22 [a]Isa 22:2; 34:3; 66:16 [b]Isa 5:25
10:5 [c]Isa 14:25; Zep 2:13 [d]Jer 51:20 [e]Isa 13:3,5,13; 30:30; 66:14
10:6 [f]Isa 9:17 [g]Isa 9:19 [h]Isa 5:29
10:7 [i]Ge 50:20; Ac 4:23-28

on the left they will eat,[q]
but not be satisfied.
Each will feed on the flesh of their own offspring[a]:
21 Manasseh will feed on Ephraim, and Ephraim on Manasseh;
together they will turn against Judah.[r]

Yet for all this, his anger is not turned away,
his hand is still upraised.[s]

10

Woe to those who make unjust laws,
to those who issue oppressive decrees,[t]
2 to deprive[u] the poor of their rights
and withhold justice from the oppressed of my people,[v]
making widows their prey
and robbing the fatherless.
3 What will you do on the day of reckoning,[w]
when disaster[x] comes from afar?
To whom will you run for help?[y]
Where will you leave your riches?
4 Nothing will remain but to cringe among the captives[z]
or fall among the slain.[a]

Yet for all this, his anger is not turned away,[b]
his hand is still upraised.

God's Judgment on Assyria

5 "Woe to the Assyrian,[c] the rod of my anger,
in whose hand is the club[d] of my wrath![e]
6 I send him against a godless[f] nation,
I dispatch him against a people who anger me,[g]
to seize loot and snatch plunder,[h]
and to trample them down like mud in the streets.
7 But this is not what he intends,[i]
this is not what he has in mind;
his purpose is to destroy,
to put an end to many nations.

[a] 20 Or *arm*

10:1–4 *Social Injustice.* In a sense this condition is the culmination of the previous three: because of pride, leaders mislead, civil strife prevails, and justice is perverted. So in many ways this latter element of justice to the poor is the touchstone of covenant faithfulness. If people give God his proper place, leaders will lead rightly, the common good will be more important than one's own group, and all people will be treated fairly, especially the weak and vulnerable.

10:5—11:16 *Redemption Through the Branch.* This unit develops the thought of the previous two: the promise of Immanuel (7:1—9:7) and the sovereignty of Yahweh (9:8—10:4). It addresses these in reverse order: Assyria is only a tool in Yahweh's hand (see 10:5–34 and note), and the Messiah is the ultimate fulfillment of the Immanuel promise (see 11:1–16 and note).

10:5–34 *Assyria, the Tool in Yahweh's Hand.* If Israel and Judah would genuinely trust and obey Yahweh, they would have no reason to fear Assyria. This is a radical concept, assuming that the God of the small nation of Judah is actually Lord of the entire earth and that all nations, whether they know it or not, are simply instruments for accomplishing his will. The same point is made with the prediction of Cyrus, the Persian emperor who would free Judah from Babylon (44:28). The God of Judah controls the destinies of Babylon and Persia. The unit contains three segments: vv. 5–19,20–23,24–34. The first and third speak of God's judgment upon his arrogant tool, Assyria, and the second predicts the return of a remnant from the impending exile.

10:5–19 *Assyria's Judgment.* Since Assyria is no more than an "ax" or a "saw" in a craftsman's hand (v. 15), its arrogance is completely unjustified. As in chs. 1 and 6, "trees" symbolize haughtiness and pride (v. 19). But even the mighty "forests" (vv. 18,19) cannot withstand the "flame" that is Israel's "Holy One" (v. 17). Another occurrence of "child" (v. 19; 9:6; 11:6–8; cf. 7:3,14,16; 8:4,18) in this part of the book contrasts with pride and power.

10:6 godless nation. Israel is in no place to claim special favors from Yahweh (cf. 1:24; 58:1–2).

10:7–14 Assyria did not consider itself to be Yahweh's tool; it believed itself to be carrying out its own "purpose" (v. 7), namely, to spoil the nations out of their own lust for power and domination. Looking at what it did to other nations and cities (up to and including Samaria), it expected to do the same things to Jerusalem.

8 'Are not my commanders[j] all kings?' he says.
9 'Has not Kalno[k] fared like Carchemish?[l]
Is not Hamath like Arpad,
and Samaria[m] like Damascus?[n]
10 As my hand seized the kingdoms of the idols,[o]
kingdoms whose images excelled those of Jerusalem and Samaria—
11 shall I not deal with Jerusalem and her images
as I dealt with Samaria and her idols?' "

12When the Lord has finished all his work[p] against Mount Zion[q] and Jerusalem, he will say, "I will
punish the king of Assyria[r] for the willful pride of his heart and the haughty look in his eyes. 13For he says:

" 'By the strength of my hand I have done this,[s]
and by my wisdom, because I have understanding.
I removed the boundaries of nations,
I plundered their treasures;[t]
like a mighty one I subdued[a] their kings.
14 As one reaches into a nest,[u]
so my hand reached for the wealth[v] of the nations;
as people gather abandoned eggs,
so I gathered all the countries;
not one flapped a wing,
or opened its mouth to chirp.' "

15 Does the ax raise itself above the person who swings it,
or the saw boast against the one who uses it?[w]
As if a rod were to wield the person who lifts it up,
or a club[x] brandish the one who is not wood!
16 Therefore, the Lord, the LORD Almighty,
will send a wasting disease[y] upon his sturdy warriors;
under his pomp[z] a fire will be kindled
like a blazing flame.
17 The Light of Israel will become a fire,[a]
their Holy One[b] a flame;
in a single day it will burn and consume
his thorns[c] and his briers.[d]
18 The splendor of his forests[e] and fertile fields
it will completely destroy,
as when a sick person wastes away.
19 And the remaining trees of his forests will be so few[f]
that a child could write them down.

10:8 [j] 2Ki 18:24
10:9 [k] Ge 10:10 [l] 2Ch 35:20 [m] 2Ki 17:6 [n] 2Ki 16:9
10:10 [o] 2Ki 19:18
10:12 [p] Isa 28:21-22; 65:7 [q] 2Ki 19:31 [r] Jer 50:18
10:13 [s] Isa 37:24; Da 4:30 [t] Eze 28:4
10:14 [u] Jer 49:16; Ob 4 [v] Job 31:25
10:15 [w] Isa 45:9; Ro 9:20-21 [x] ver 5
10:16 [y] ver 18; Isa 17:4 [z] Isa 8:7
10:17 [a] Isa 31:9 [b] Isa 37:23 [c] Nu 11:1-3 [d] Isa 9:18
10:18 [e] 2Ki 19:23
10:19 [f] Isa 21:17
10:20 [g] Isa 11:10,11

The Remnant of Israel

20 In that day[g] the remnant of Israel,
the survivors of Jacob,

[a] 13 Or *treasures; / I subdued the mighty,*

10:10–11 The Assyrians do not understand the fundamental difference between Jerusalem and all the other cities they conquered, including Samaria. Given the ubiquity of "images" and "idols" everywhere else in the ancient world, they assume that Jerusalem has the same things. But that is the irony. The Judahites who remain faithful to God are not worshiping things they made; they worship the one who made both them and the Assyrians, and he will call Assyria to account.

10:12 his work against ... Jerusalem. Speaks of the judgment that Yahweh was going to bring upon the nation and city through Assyria because of Ahaz's refusal to lead them to trust Yahweh. **pride.** The most basic human sin: taking for oneself the place of God.

10:13–14 This poetically expresses the attitude of Assyria and all those who think they are self-sufficient. The world is simply a bird's nest for the strong to plunder.

10:20–23 *A Remnant Will Survive.* Since Yahweh (not Assyria) is sending Israel into exile, Yahweh is completely capable of restoring them again

10:20 [h]2Ki 16:7 [i]2Ch 28:20 [j]Isa 17:7
10:21 [k]Isa 6:13 [l]Isa 9:6
10:22 [m]Ro 9:27-28 [n]Isa 28:22; Da 9:27
10:23 [o]Isa 28:22; Ro 9:27-28*
10:24 [p]Ps 87:5-6 [q]Ex 5:14
10:25 [r]Isa 17:14 [s]ver 5; Da 11:36
10:26 [t]Isa 37:36-38 [u]Isa 9:4 [v]Ex 14:16
10:27 [w]Isa 9:4 [x]Isa 14:25
10:28 [y]1Sa 14:2 [z]1Sa 13:2
10:29 [a]Jos 18:25
10:30 [b]1Sa 25:44 [c]Ne 11:32

will no longer rely[h] on him
who struck them down[i]
but will truly rely[j] on the LORD,
the Holy One of Israel.
21 A remnant[k] will return,[a] a remnant of Jacob
will return to the Mighty God.[l]
22 Though your people be like the sand by the sea, Israel,
only a remnant will return.[m]
Destruction has been decreed,[n]
overwhelming and righteous.
23 The Lord, the LORD Almighty, will carry out
the destruction decreed upon the whole land.[o]

24 Therefore this is what the Lord, the LORD Almighty, says:

"My people who live in Zion,[p]
do not be afraid of the Assyrians,
who beat[q] you with a rod
and lift up a club against you, as Egypt did.
25 Very soon[r] my anger against you will end
and my wrath[s] will be directed to their destruction."
26 The LORD Almighty will lash[t] them with a whip,
as when he struck down Midian[u] at the rock of Oreb;
and he will raise his staff over the waters,[v]
as he did in Egypt.
27 In that day their burden will be lifted from your shoulders,
their yoke[w] from your neck;[x]
the yoke will be broken
because you have grown so fat.[b]
28 They enter Aiath;
they pass through Migron;[y]
they store supplies at Mikmash.[z]
29 They go over the pass, and say,
"We will camp overnight at Geba."
Ramah[a] trembles;
Gibeah of Saul flees.
30 Cry out, Daughter Gallim![b]
Listen, Laishah!
Poor Anathoth![c]

[a] 21 Hebrew *shear-jashub* (see 7:3 and note); also in verse 22 [b] 27 Hebrew; Septuagint *broken / from your shoulders*

if they will only turn back to trust ("rely on," v. 20) him. The coming "destruction" (v. 23) is his work, and while "only a remnant" (v. 22) will survive (cf. 7:3 and the name of Isaiah's son, "a remnant will return"), still there will be such a remnant, regardless of Assyria. Ahaz's reliance on Assyria would result in only defeat and desolation, but reliance on Yahweh would mean that long-term hope would follow near-term judgment.

10:24–34 *God to Strike Down Assyria.* Given a correct perspective upon the relationship of Yahweh and Assyria, Judah should "not be afraid" (v. 24) even though the northern kingdom fell. If they would trust Yahweh, then Assyria's depredations of them would be limited (vv. 24–25,27). Yahweh would not allow Assyria to completely destroy the land but would strike down the Assyrians. This prediction was fulfilled when the Assyrian emperor, Sennacherib, was forced to withdraw from the final siege of Jerusalem because most of his army died in one night (37:36–37).

10:26 rock of Oreb. Recalls Gideon's victory over the Midianites (9:4; Judg 7:25). Oreb was the enemy leader who was killed at that spot. Gideon did not prevail over Midian any more than Moses parted "the waters … in Egypt." In both cases, it was really the work of God through his agents.

10:28–34 Isaiah again brings his point to a climax with a graphic illustration. He pictures the relentless march of an army moving southward along the central ridge toward Jerusalem. The poet depicts one village after another falling amidst increasing panic. Finally the army reaches Nob, the hill overlooking Jerusalem from the north. Surely there is nothing to prevent the fall of the city. But it is not to be. The Sovereign, Yahweh of Heaven's Armies ("the Lord, the LORD Almighty," v. 33; see vv. 16,23; see also notes on 1:9,24) will suddenly "cut down" Assyria's mighty "forest thickets with an ax" (v. 34). The irony is heavy: Yahweh's arrogant ax, Assyria (v. 15), will itself be cut down with an ax.

[31] Madmenah is in flight;
the people of Gebim take cover.
[32] This day they will halt at Nob;[d]
they will shake their fist
at the mount of Daughter Zion,[e]
at the hill of Jerusalem.

[33] See, the Lord, the LORD Almighty,
will lop off the boughs with great power.
The lofty trees will be felled,
the tall[f] ones will be brought low.
[34] He will cut down the forest thickets with an ax;
Lebanon will fall before the Mighty One.

The Branch From Jesse

11 A shoot will come up from the stump of Jesse;[g]
from his roots a Branch[h] will bear fruit.
[2] The Spirit[i] of the LORD will rest on him—
the Spirit of wisdom[j] and of understanding,
the Spirit of counsel and of might,[k]
the Spirit of the knowledge and fear of the LORD—
[3] and he will delight in the fear of the LORD.

He will not judge by what he sees with his eyes,[l]
or decide by what he hears with his ears;[m]
[4] but with righteousness[n] he will judge the needy,
with justice[o] he will give decisions for the poor[p] of the earth.
He will strike[q] the earth with the rod of his mouth;
with the breath[r] of his lips he will slay the wicked.
[5] Righteousness will be his belt
and faithfulness[s] the sash around his waist.[t]

[6] The wolf will live with the lamb,[u]
the leopard will lie down with the goat,
the calf and the lion and the yearling[a] together;
and a little child will lead them.

[a] 6 Hebrew; Septuagint *lion will feed*

10:32 [d] 1Sa 21:1 [e] Jer 6:23
10:33 [f] Am 2:9
11:1 [g] ver 10; Isa 9:7; Rev 5:5 [h] Isa 4:2
11:2 [i] Isa 42:1; 48:16; 61:1; Mt 3:16; Jn 1:32-33 [j] Eph 1:17 [k] 2Ti 1:7
11:3 [l] Jn 7:24 [m] Jn 2:25
11:4 [n] Ps 72:2 [o] Isa 9:7 [p] Isa 3:14 [q] Mal 4:6 [r] Job 4:9; 2Th 2:8
11:5 [s] Isa 25:1 [t] Eph 6:14
11:6 [u] Isa 65:25

11:1–16 *The Branch, Deliverer of His People.* This unit seems to have two main parts: vv. 1–9 describe the Messiah's nature (vv. 1–5) and kingdom (vv. 6–9), and vv. 10–16 describe his deliverance of his people.

11:1 A shoot … from the stump. The forest of arrogant human evil has been cut down, and here in contrast is a "Branch" coming out of a stump one would think lifeless. Yet this seemingly weak thing is clearly the king of a universal kingdom. Probably this Messianic use of "Branch" accounts for its similar use in Jeremiah (Jer 23:5; 33:15) and Zechariah (Zech 3:8; 6:12). **stump.** A different Hebrew word than that used in 6:13, but the sense is clearly the same: out of judgment comes hope, and the weakness of God is greater than the strength of humans (cf. 53:2). **Jesse.** Also in v. 10, may be used in place of David in order to push the promise back further than merely the house of David, which was at that moment corrupt. It implies a future "new David."

11:2 Isaiah makes a special point of the relationship between the Messiah and the Spirit (see 42:1; 61:1). **The Spirit of the LORD.** The dynamic presence of God within creation (Gen 1:2), the empowerer (Judg 6:34), and the revealer (Mic 3:8). The Messiah's qualities (wisdom, understanding, etc.) are divine both in their origins and in their outworking in his life (cf. Luke 2:47). **fear of the LORD.** Connotes an appropriate understanding of God and of one's own relationship to him (cf. 8:13; John 4:24).

11:3–5 Verse 3a closes the previous thought and also introduces the following thought (vv. 3b–5), explaining how a ruler who fears God acts. Such a person will not be influenced by appearances (v. 3b) but will treat all persons with dignity and equity. He will not merely make pronouncements as human kings are inclined to do. As the divine Word of God, his speech will have the very weight of eternity behind it (v. 4; cf. Mark 1:27; John 1:1; Rev 19:15). "Righteousness" and "faithfulness" will be as intimate to him as a "sash around his waist" (v. 5; see note on vv. 6–9).

11:6–9 A description of the Messianic kingdom. Some interpreters take these conditions to be literal, describing those that will actually exist in the new heaven and the new earth (65:17–25). This would involve a radical change in the natures of the animals involved. But perhaps this is what Paul envisions when he speaks of the redemption of nature (Rom 8:19–22). Others see the descriptions as more poetic. The point is that of v. 9: where the Messiah rules, where "the knowledge of the LORD" prevails, there will be no place for violence or destruction. Precisely how that is to be realized must be left to the

11:9 [v]Job 5:23 [w]Ps 98:2-3; Isa 52:10 [x]Isa 45:6,14; Hab 2:14
11:10 [y]Jn 12:32 [z]Isa 49:23; Lk 2:32 [a]Ro 15:12* [b]Isa 14:3; 28:12; 32:17-18
11:11 [c]Isa 10:20 [d]Isa 19:24; Hos 11:11; Mic 7:12; Zec 10:10 [e]Ge 10:22 [f]Isa 42:4,10, 12; 66:19
11:12 [g]Zep 3:10
11:13 [h]Jer 3:18; Eze 37:16-17,22; Hos 1:11
11:14 [i]Da 11:41; Joel 3:19 [j]Isa 16:14; 25:10
11:15 [k]Isa 19:16 [l]Isa 7:20
11:16 [m]Isa 19:23; 62:10 [n]Ex 14:26-31

7 The cow will feed with the bear,
their young will lie down together,
and the lion will eat straw like the ox.
8 The infant will play near the cobra's den,
and the young child will put its hand into the viper's nest.
9 They will neither harm nor destroy[v]
on all my holy mountain,
for the earth[w] will be filled with the knowledge[x] of the LORD
as the waters cover the sea.

10 In that day the Root of Jesse will stand as a banner[y] for the peoples; the nations[z] will rally to him,[a]
and his resting place[b] will be glorious. 11 In that day[c] the Lord will reach out his hand a second time
to reclaim the surviving remnant of his people from Assyria,[d] from Lower Egypt, from Upper Egypt,
from Cush,[a] from Elam,[e] from Babylonia,[b] from Hamath and from the islands[f] of the Mediterranean.

12 He will raise a banner for the nations
and gather the exiles of Israel;
he will assemble the scattered people[g] of Judah
from the four quarters of the earth.
13 Ephraim's jealousy will vanish,
and Judah's enemies[c] will be destroyed;
Ephraim will not be jealous of Judah,
nor Judah hostile toward Ephraim.[h]
14 They will swoop down on the slopes of Philistia to the west;
together they will plunder the people to the east.
They will subdue Edom[i] and Moab,[j]
and the Ammonites will be subject to them.
15 The LORD will dry up
the gulf of the Egyptian sea;
with a scorching wind he will sweep his hand[k]
over the Euphrates River.[l]
He will break it up into seven streams
so that anyone can cross over in sandals.
16 There will be a highway[m] for the remnant of his people
that is left from Assyria,
as there was for Israel
when they came up from Egypt.[n]

[a] *11* That is, the upper Nile region [b] *11* Hebrew *Shinar* [c] *13* Or *hostility*

imagination; it will be utterly different from anything citizens of the present fallen creation know. It may now be realized person by person, but one day it will be universal.

11:10–16 The Messiah will make possible the final ingathering of Yahweh's people. He will be the "banner" (vv. 10,12; see note on 5:26; see also 49:22) to call them home. They will come from all corners of the earth (vv. 11–12), specifically from Mesopotamia (vv. 15–16). The tribalism of the past (see note on 9:18–21) will be forgotten as they are united against enemies on the west ("Philistia") and east ("Edom," "Moab," and "the Ammonites," v. 14). As with vv. 8–9, it is a mistake to make the only acceptable interpretation of such a poetic passage as this a literal one. *That* these predictions will be fulfilled is certain, but *how* they will be fulfilled will become plain only after the fact. Paul quotes the Septuagint (the pre-Christian Greek translation of the OT) of v. 10 to support his ministry to the Gentiles (Rom 15:12).

11:11 second time. The reference is unclear. Possibly it refers to the return from exile between 539 and ca. 450 BC, with the first being the exodus. But the mention of the Messiah in connection with this return has led some to think that it refers to a return after the incarnation, with the return from Babylonian exile being the first. **remnant.** An important biblical concept. Although the people as a whole fall into sin and disappear, yet God has a righteous remnant who will keep the faith and who will be purified, not destroyed, by the fires of adversity (v. 16; 10:20–22; 37:31–32; cf. Jer 23:3; Ezek 6:8; Mic 2:12; Zeph 3:12; Zech 8:12; Rom 9:27; 11:5).

11:15 gulf of the Egyptian sea. The specific referent of this phrase is unclear. **Euphrates River.** The context suggests the Euphrates, but the Greek translation takes the entire verse to refer to Egypt. Whatever the correct reading, the passage says that just as the sea was no barrier to Israel's deliverance in the past, so no watery barrier can prevent deliverance in the future.

11:16 highway. Like "banner" (see note on 5:26) and "trees" (see notes on 1:29–31; 10:5–19), this is another characteristic term in Isaiah (7:3 ["road"]; 19:23; 33:8; 35:8; 36:2 ["road"]; 40:3; 49:11; 62:10). It speaks of the idea of easy access: God to us (40:3), and us to him and his blessedness (35:8).

Songs of Praise

12 In that day you will say:

"I will praise[o] you, LORD.
Although you were angry with me,
your anger has turned away
and you have comforted me.
2 Surely God is my salvation;
I will trust[p] and not be afraid.
The LORD, the LORD himself, is my strength and my defense[a];
he has become my salvation.[q]"
3 With joy you will draw water[r]
from the wells of salvation.

4 In that day you will say:

"Give praise to the LORD, proclaim his name;[s]
make known among the nations what he has done,
and proclaim that his name is exalted.
5 Sing[t] to the LORD, for he has done glorious things;[u]
let this be known to all the world.
6 Shout aloud and sing for joy, people of Zion,
for great is the Holy One of Israel[v] among you.[w]"

A Prophecy Against Babylon

13 A prophecy against Babylon that Isaiah son of Amoz saw:

2 Raise a banner[x] on a bare hilltop,
shout to them;
beckon to them
to enter the gates of the nobles.

[a] 2 Or *song*

12:1 [o] Isa 25:1
12:2 [p] Isa 26:3 [q] Ex 15:2; Ps 118:14
12:3 [r] Jn 4:10,14
12:4 [s] Ps 105:1; Isa 24:15
12:5 [t] Ex 15:1 [u] Ps 98:1
12:6 [v] Isa 49:26 [w] Zep 3:14-17
13:2 [x] Jer 50:2; 51:27

12:1–6 *Hymns of Deliverance.* "In that day" (v. 1; i.e., the time of salvation) introduces both of these two songs of praise (vv. 1–3,4–6). The appropriate response to God's saving work is always song (26:1–6; 42:10–12; 49:13; cf. Exod 15:1–21; Rev 5:9–14).
12:1–3 This song includes one of the key themes of chs. 40–55: God's unmerited grace motivates people to trust him. He satisfies his own anger, and instead of berating his suffering people, he encourages ("comforted") them (v. 1; see 40:1; 49:13; 52:9). Instead of being the one who condemns, he becomes a "strength" and "defense" (v. 2). Chs. 7–12 begin with a refusal to trust and end with a declaration of trust.
12:1 I will praise you. The prophet speaks for the nation, praising God for his deliverance.
12:4–6 The second song includes one of the key themes of chs. 56–66: to "make known among the nations what [God] has done" (v. 4). God's saving "name" (v. 4) must be declared "to all the world" (v. 5; see 2:1–5; 27:6; 37:20; 41:17–20; 49:5–6; 52:10; 62:2; 66:18–24).
13:1—35:10 *Lessons in Trust.* Ahaz, representative of his people, trusted humanity's glory rather than Yahweh's faithfulness. So this section shows that Yahweh *can* be trusted and that trusting humanity is folly. It begins with prophecies against the nations (chs. 13–23), continues with a more general statement of God's sovereignty in the world (chs. 24–27), moves to a series of woes against those who trust Egypt rather than Yahweh (chs. 28–33), and graphically pictures the contrasting results of the two trusts: a desert or a garden (chs. 34–35).
13:1—23:18 *Prophecies Against the Nations.* Collections of such prophecies also appear in Jeremiah and Ezekiel, and their placement in each book reflects the particular thought structure of that book. Here they demonstrate the folly of trusting such nations since they are all under judgment from Israel's God. It is difficult to determine any intentional organization of the prophecies except that they begin and conclude with the great political and military power on the east (Babylon, chs. 13–14) and the commercial power on the west (Tyre, ch. 23). Possibly this inclusio, representing the two gods of human security, suggests that all the nations of the earth are intended. Judah's inclusion in the collection (22:1–25) shows that even though they were the people of God, he would treat them no differently if they acted like the other nations.
13:1—14:27 *Babylon and Briefly Assyria.* Although Assyria was the great power of Isaiah's day, Babylon was always the center of glory and sophistication. That great city was always restive under Assyria's control and always seeking allies in its effort to shake off that control (39:1). Finally, of course, it would be Babylon, not Assyria, that would bring Judah down. For all of these reasons, it is appropriate that Isaiah should begin his discussion of the folly of trusting all human glory with a treatment of Babylon. That treatment takes three parts: a prophecy against Babylon itself (13:1—14:2), a prophecy against the king of Babylon (14:3–23), and a prophecy against Assyria (14:24–27).
13:1—14:2 *A Prophecy Against Babylon.* While this prophecy explicitly addresses Babylon, much of the language is universal (especially 13:2–16), suggesting that Babylon represents the world. This is likely since a later prophecy (21:1–10) is more specific concerning historical Babylon.
13:1 Isaiah understands that Babylon, not Assyria, is the ultimate threat to Judah. God inspires him to predict the future.
13:2 banner. See note on 5:26.

13:3 [y]Joel 3:11 [z]Ps 149:2
13:4 [a]Joel 3:14
13:5 [b]Isa 5:26 [c]Isa 24:1
13:6 [d]Eze 30:2 [e]Isa 2:12; Joel 1:15
13:7 [f]Eze 21:7
13:8 [g]Isa 21:4 [h]Na 2:10
13:10 [i]Isa 24:23 [j]Isa 5:30; Rev 8:12 [k]Eze 32:7; Mt 24:29*; Mk 13:24*
13:11 [l]Isa 3:11; 11:4; 26:21
13:12 [m]Isa 4:1
13:13 [n]Isa 34:4; 51:6; Hag 2:6
13:14 [o]1Ki 22:17

3 I have commanded those I prepared for battle;
I have summoned my warriors[y] to carry out my wrath—
those who rejoice[z] in my triumph.

4 Listen, a noise on the mountains,
like that of a great multitude![a]
Listen, an uproar among the kingdoms,
like nations massing together!
The LORD Almighty is mustering
an army for war.
5 They come from faraway lands,
from the ends of the heavens[b]—
the LORD and the weapons of his wrath—
to destroy[c] the whole country.

6 Wail,[d] for the day[e] of the LORD is near;
it will come like destruction from the Almighty.[a]
7 Because of this, all hands will go limp,
every heart will melt with fear.[f]
8 Terror[g] will seize them,
pain and anguish will grip them;
they will writhe like a woman in labor.
They will look aghast at each other,
their faces aflame.[h]

9 See, the day of the LORD is coming
—a cruel day, with wrath and fierce anger—
to make the land desolate
and destroy the sinners within it.
10 The stars of heaven and their constellations
will not show their light.
The rising sun[i] will be darkened[j]
and the moon will not give its light.[k]
11 I will punish[l] the world for its evil,
the wicked for their sins.
I will put an end to the arrogance of the haughty
and will humble the pride of the ruthless.
12 I will make people[m] scarcer than pure gold,
more rare than the gold of Ophir.
13 Therefore I will make the heavens tremble;[n]
and the earth will shake from its place
at the wrath of the LORD Almighty,
in the day of his burning anger.

14 Like a hunted gazelle,
like sheep without a shepherd,[o]

[a] 6 Hebrew *Shaddai*

13:3 those I prepared for battle. Or "my consecrated ones," perhaps a reference to the Medes and Persians who would bring Babylon down (see 41:2).

13:4–5 kingdoms ... nations ... faraway lands ... ends of the heavens ... the whole country. Universal language for the whole earth (see vv. 10–13).

13:6 day of the LORD. Not a 24-hour day but a period of time when God would take direct action (v. 9; cf. Joel 1:15; Amos 5:20; Zeph 1:7; see note on Amos 2:16). Many of the Israelites believed that since they were God's chosen people, that time would necessarily be one of blessing. The prophets declared that it could just as well be a time of judgment, as here, if a people, including God's people, were living in disobedience.

13:11 arrogance ... pride. One of the recurring issues of this part of the book (cf. 2:11): the earth is full of the glory of Yahweh (6:3), not the glory of humanity.

they will all return to their own people,
they will flee to their native land.[p]
15 Whoever is captured will be thrust through;
all who are caught will fall[q] by the sword.[r]
16 Their infants[s] will be dashed to pieces before their eyes;
their houses will be looted and their wives violated.

17 See, I will stir up[t] against them the Medes,
who do not care for silver
and have no delight in gold.[u]
18 Their bows will strike down the young men;
they will have no mercy on infants,
nor will they look with compassion on children.
19 Babylon, the jewel of kingdoms,
the pride and glory[v] of the Babylonians,[a]
will be overthrown[w] by God
like Sodom and Gomorrah.[x]
20 She will never be inhabited[y]
or lived in through all generations;
there no nomads[z] will pitch their tents,
there no shepherds will rest their flocks.
21 But desert creatures[a] will lie there,
jackals will fill her houses;
there the owls will dwell,
and there the wild goats will leap about.
22 Hyenas will inhabit her strongholds,[b]
jackals[c] her luxurious palaces.
Her time is at hand,[d]
and her days will not be prolonged.

14 The LORD will have compassion[e] on Jacob;
once again he will choose[f] Israel
and will settle them in their own land.
Foreigners[g] will join them
and unite with the descendants of Jacob.
2 Nations will take them
and bring[h] them to their own place.
And Israel will take possession of the nations[i]
and make them male and female servants in the LORD's land.
They will make captives of their captors
and rule over their oppressors.[j]

[a] 19 Or *Chaldeans*

13:14 [p] Jer 50:16
13:15 [q] Jer 51:4 [r] Isa 14:19; Jer 50:25
13:16 [s] Ps 137:9
13:17 [t] Jer 51:1 [u] Pr 6:34-35
13:19 [v] Da 4:30 [w] Rev 14:8 [x] Ge 19:24
13:20 [y] Isa 14:23; 34:10-15 [z] 2Ch 17:11
13:21 [a] Rev 18:2
13:22 [b] Isa 25:2 [c] Isa 34:13 [d] Jer 51:33
14:1 [e] Ps 102:13; Isa 49:10,13; 54:7-8,10 [f] Isa 41:8; 44:1; 49:7; Zec 1:17; 2:12 [g] Eph 2:12-19
14:2 [h] Isa 60:9 [i] Isa 49:7, 23 [j] Isa 60:14; 61:5

13:16 A picture of total war, as practiced in the ancient world (see Ps 137:8–9; Hos 10:14; Nah 3:10).
13:17—14:2 This seems to speak more specifically of the fall of the city of Babylon and the consequent return of the Jews from exile.
13:17 Medes. A warlike people from the Zagros Mountains east of Babylon. Initially, they teamed up with Babylon to destroy Assyria. But then they turned against Babylon and helped Persia wipe out the Babylonian Empire (note "Darius the Mede," Dan 5:31). Nevertheless, although the Medes were the instrument, God brought Babylon down.
13:20 She will never be inhabited. A shocking statement about one of the greatest cities of the ancient world. But that is exactly what happened. By the end of the Roman Empire, the city of Babylon was almost forgotten, and by the time of the Muslim conquest, even its location was lost.
13:21–22 jackals ... owls ... Hyenas. Unclean animals living in wastelands (cf. 2:20; 34:11–15). In Rev 18:2 impure spirits and unclean birds and animals inhabit fallen Babylon (cf. Zech 5:5–11).
14:1–2 When the Persians conquered Babylon, the Persian emperor Cyrus decreed that any captive people could return home. The Jews accepted the offer and returned to their homeland (Ezra 1:1–5). The language of these two verses is reminiscent of chs. 60–62. This is the first expression of a theme that appears several times in these prophecies: Why trust in these nations when Yahweh will be not only Judah's hope but ultimately the hope of these nations as well? On the other hand, any of these former oppressor nations that will not join in worship of Yahweh will be ruled over by Israel (v. 2; cf. 60:10–12).

14:3 [k]Isa 11:10
14:4 [l]Hab 2:6 [m]Isa 9:4
14:5 [n]Ps 125:3
14:6 [o]Isa 10:14 [p]Isa 47:6
14:7 [q]Ps 98:1; 126:1-3
14:8 [r]Eze 31:16
14:9 [s]Eze 32:21
14:10 [t]Eze 32:21
14:11 [u]Isa 51:8
14:12 [v]Isa 34:4; Lk 10:18 [w]2Pe 1:19; Rev 2:28; 8:10; 9:1
14:13 [x]Da 5:23; 8:10; Mt 11:23

[3]On the day the LORD gives you relief[k] from your suffering and turmoil and from the harsh labor
forced on you, [4]you will take up this taunt[l] against the king of Babylon:

How the oppressor[m] has come to an end!
How his fury[a] has ended!
[5]The LORD has broken the rod of the wicked,[n]
the scepter of the rulers,
[6]which in anger struck down peoples[o]
with unceasing blows,
and in fury subdued nations
with relentless aggression.[p]
[7]All the lands are at rest and at peace;
they break into singing.[q]
[8]Even the junipers[r] and the cedars of Lebanon
gloat over you and say,
"Now that you have been laid low,
no one comes to cut us down."

[9]The realm of the dead[s] below is all astir
to meet you at your coming;
it rouses the spirits of the departed to greet you—
all those who were leaders in the world;
it makes them rise from their thrones—
all those who were kings over the nations.
[10]They will all respond,
they will say to you,
"You also have become weak, as we are;
you have become like us."[t]
[11]All your pomp has been brought down to the grave,
along with the noise of your harps;
maggots are spread out beneath you
and worms[u] cover you.

[12]How you have fallen[v] from heaven,
morning star,[w] son of the dawn!
You have been cast down to the earth,
you who once laid low the nations!
[13]You said in your heart,
"I will ascend[x] to the heavens;

[a] 4 Dead Sea Scrolls, Septuagint and Syriac; the meaning of the word in the Masoretic Text is uncertain.

14:3–23 *A Prophecy Against the King of Babylon.* The passage poetically describes creaturely pride and its inevitable humiliation. It is artfully developed in four stanzas, each from a different perspective: the earth (vv. 3b–8), the underworld (vv. 9–11), heaven (vv. 12–15), and a battlefield (vv. 16–21). Since the Assyrian emperor Sargon, who carried out the exile of the Israelites from Samaria, died on the battlefield, there is some reason to think that he might have been the model for this poetic figure of fallen pride.

14:4–8 relentless aggression ... break into singing. Earth rejoices over the death of the "oppressor" (vv. 4–7). Even the trees rejoice (v. 8). The Mesopotamian emperors often boasted about all the trees they cut down.

14:9–11 The residents of the underworld sarcastically welcome the dead conqueror. All his accomplishments and "pomp" (v. 11) have come to nothing. All that is left to him is "maggots" and "worms" (v. 11).

14:12–15 Although it has been common in Christian literature to see this passage as a description of the fall of Satan (cf. Luke 10:18; Rev 12:9), the passage itself argues for a continued reference to creaturely pride. However, Satan is a creature, and application of these descriptions to him is not inappropriate.

14:12 fallen from heaven. A Canaanite myth that speaks of one of the lesser gods attempting to sit on Baal's throne may be the background for this stanza. **morning star.** The Hebrew is translated "Lucifer" in the Latin Vulgate, which was carried over into many early English translations. Jesus is the true Morning Star (Rev 22:16; cf. Num 24:17; 2 Pet 1:19).

14:13 mount of assembly ... Mount Zaphon. Canaanite terms for the place of the gods (see NIV text note). But this is not a god. It is a man who, because he "laid low the nations" (v. 12), thinks he can take the place of God (cf. 36:18–20; 37:11–12) in "the heavens." Instead, like every other human, he will go down to the "realm of the dead" (v. 15; Ps 49:15 suggests that the righteous can be redeemed from this realm).

Mount Zaphon (Casius) on the border of modern Syria and Turkey (Isa 14:13).
A.D. Riddle/www.BiblePlaces.com

I will raise my throne[y]
above the stars of God;
I will sit enthroned on the mount of assembly,
on the utmost heights of Mount Zaphon.[a]
14 I will ascend above the tops of the clouds;
I will make myself like the Most High."[z]
15 But you are brought down to the realm of the dead,
to the depths[a] of the pit.

16 Those who see you stare at you,
they ponder your fate:[b]
"Is this the man who shook the earth
and made kingdoms tremble,
17 the man who made the world a wilderness,[c]
who overthrew its cities
and would not let his captives go home?"

18 All the kings of the nations lie in state,
each in his own tomb.
19 But you are cast out[d] of your tomb
like a rejected branch;
you are covered with the slain,
with those pierced by the sword,
those who descend to the stones of the pit.[e]
Like a corpse trampled underfoot,
20 you will not join them in burial,
for you have destroyed your land
and killed your people.

14:13 [y] Eze 28:2; 2Th 2:4
14:14 [z] Isa 47:8; 2Th 2:4
14:15 [a] Mt 11:23; Lk 10:15
14:16 [b] Jer 50:23
14:17 [c] Joel 2:3
14:19 [d] Isa 22:16-18 [e] Jer 41:7-9

[a] *13* Or *of the north*; Zaphon was the most sacred mountain of the Canaanites.

14:16–21 This arrogant man suffers the ultimate humiliation: he is left unburied ("cast out of [his] tomb") among the "slain," abandoned on the battlefield (v. 19). This seems to have happened to the Assyrian monarch Sargon (see note on vv. 3–23).

14:19 rejected branch. A miscarried child. In many ancient cultures, the miscarried fetus did not receive a respectful burial.

14:20–21 The Mesopotamian emperors in their pride imagined that their family line would rule forever. However, it was common for a

14:20 [f]Job 18:19 [g]Isa 1:4 [h]Ps 21:10
14:21 [i]Ex 20:5; Lev 26:39
14:22 [j]1Ki 14:10; Job 18:19
14:23 [k]Isa 34:11-15; Zep 2:14
14:24 [l]Isa 45:23 [m]Ac 4:28
14:25 [n]Isa 10:5,12 [o]Isa 9:4 [p]Isa 10:27
14:26 [q]Isa 23:9 [r]Ex 15:12
14:27 [s]2Ch 20:6; Isa 43:13; Da 4:35
14:28 [t]Isa 13:1 [u]2Ki 16:20
14:29 [v]2Ch 26:6 [w]Isa 11:8
14:30 [x]Isa 3:15 [y]Isa 7:21-22 [z]Isa 8:21; 9:20; 51:19 [a]Jer 25:16
14:31 [b]Isa 3:26

Let the offspring[f] of the wicked[g]
never be mentioned[h] again.
21 Prepare a place to slaughter his children
for the sins of their ancestors;[i]
they are not to rise to inherit the land
and cover the earth with their cities.

22 "I will rise up against them,"
declares the LORD Almighty.
"I will wipe out Babylon's name and survivors,
her offspring and descendants,[j]"
declares the LORD.

23 "I will turn her into a place for owls[k]
and into swampland;
I will sweep her with the broom of destruction,"
declares the LORD Almighty.

24 The LORD Almighty has sworn,[l]

"Surely, as I have planned, so it will be,
and as I have purposed, so it will happen.[m]
25 I will crush the Assyrian[n] in my land;
on my mountains I will trample him down.
His yoke[o] will be taken from my people,
and his burden removed from their shoulders.[p]"

26 This is the plan[q] determined for the whole world;
this is the hand[r] stretched out over all nations.
27 For the LORD Almighty has purposed, and who can thwart him?
His hand is stretched out, and who can turn it back?[s]

A Prophecy Against the Philistines

28 This prophecy[t] came in the year King Ahaz[u] died:

29 Do not rejoice, all you Philistines,[v]
that the rod that struck you is broken;
from the root of that snake will spring up a viper,[w]
its fruit will be a darting, venomous serpent.
30 The poorest of the poor will find pasture,
and the needy[x] will lie down in safety.[y]
But your root I will destroy by famine;[z]
it will slay[a] your survivors.

31 Wail, you gate![b] Howl, you city!
Melt away, all you Philistines!

---

dynasty to last only two or three generations before some other arrogant ruler wiped it out and took over the throne.

14:22–23 Babylon might exalt itself to the skies, but Yahweh would "sweep her with the broom of destruction" (v. 23; cf. 13:20–22). No human or human institution can stand in defiance of him.

14:24–27 *A Prophecy Against Assyria.* Having utilized Babylon as a figure for the human pride typified by the various Mesopotamian powers, Isaiah now turns to talk about Assyria, the specific Mesopotamian power that was threatening Judah in Isaiah's own day, the power that Ahaz trusted to deliver him from Syria and the northern kingdom of Israel. It is not what Assyria may have "planned" or "purposed" (v. 24; see vv. 26–27) but what God has planned and purposed that matters (cf. 19:12; 23:9; 46:11). Assyria might plan to exterminate Judah, but God planned to break Assyrian power in his "land" (v. 25; see 10:26–27; 37:36–37; cf. Ps 2:8–9).

14:28—17:11 *Judgments on the Nearer Neighbors.* This section includes judgments against Philistia (14:28–32), Moab (15:1—16:14), and Syria and Israel (17:1–11).

14:28–32 *A Prophecy Against Philistia.* The Philistine cities on the coastal plain west of Judah will be destroyed, but Jerusalem ("Zion," v. 32) will survive (see note on vv. 1–2).

14:28 year King Ahaz died. 716 or 715 BC.

14:29 rod. Apparently Ahaz, although the Bible does not report him as having achieved any victories over the Philistines. **viper.** Probably Hezekiah, who achieved such victories (2 Kgs 18:8).

14:31 cloud of smoke ... from the north. The Assyrian armies. All

A cloud of smoke comes from the north,[c]
and there is not a straggler in its ranks.
32 What answer shall be given
to the envoys[d] of that nation?
"The LORD has established Zion,[e]
and in her his afflicted people will find refuge.[f]"

A Prophecy Against Moab

16:6-12pp — Jer 48:29-36

15 A prophecy against Moab:[g]

Ar in Moab is ruined,[h]
destroyed in a night!
Kir in Moab is ruined,
destroyed in a night!
2 Dibon goes up to its temple,
to its high places[i] to weep;
Moab wails over Nebo and Medeba.
Every head is shaved[j]
and every beard cut off.
3 In the streets they wear sackcloth;
on the roofs and in the public squares[k]
they all wail,
prostrate with weeping.[l]
4 Heshbon and Elealeh[m] cry out,
their voices are heard all the way to Jahaz.
Therefore the armed men of Moab cry out,
and their hearts are faint.

5 My heart cries out over Moab;[n]
her fugitives flee as far as Zoar,
as far as Eglath Shelishiyah.
They go up the hill to Luhith,
weeping as they go;
on the road to Horonaim[o]
they lament their destruction.[p]
6 The waters of Nimrim are dried up[q]
and the grass is withered;[r]
the vegetation is gone
and nothing green is left.
7 So the wealth they have acquired[s] and stored up
they carry away over the Ravine of the Poplars.

14:31 [c] Jer 1:14
14:32 [d] Isa 37:9 [e] Ps 87:2,5; Isa 44:28; 54:11 [f] Isa 4:6; Jas 2:5
15:1 [g] Isa 11:14 [h] Jer 48:24,41
15:2 [i] Jer 48:35 [j] Lev 21:5
15:3 [k] Jer 48:38 [l] Isa 22:4
15:4 [m] Nu 32:3
15:5 [n] Jer 48:31 [o] Jer 48:3,34 [p] Jer 4:20; 48:5
15:6 [q] Isa 19:5-7; Jer 48:34 [r] Joel 1:12
15:7 [s] Isa 30:6; Jer 48:36

the Mesopotamian forces came into Canaan from the north, because the desert prevented them from taking a straight route from east to west. Cf. 41:25.

14:32 envoys of that nation. Most likely the Philistines, but the circumstances of the visit are unknown. Perhaps the Assyrians.

15:1—16:14 *A Prophecy Against Moab.* The Moabites lived east of Judah across the Dead Sea. They were understood to be relatives of Israel through Lot (cf. Gen 19:36–37). The people of Judah apparently had a closer relationship with Moab than did the northern kingdom of Israel (cf. Ruth 1:1). That may be reflected in the prophet's weeping over Moab's fate (15:5; 16:9,11). Here, as with Babylon, a central issue is Moab's "pride" (16:6) with its associated "wealth" (15:7) and "splendor" (16:14).

15:1–9 Isaiah poetically describes Moab's fate. He pictures refugees fleeing from the northern cities of Moab (e.g., Ar, Kir, Dibon, Nebo, Medeba, vv. 1–2), dragging their wealth southward away from the invading armies that would be coming south on the highway from Damascus. So they pass through Zoar and Nimrim (vv. 5–6) on their way to the "Ravine of the Poplars" (see v. 7 and note). But the sound of their weeping reaches all the way to the northern cities of Eglaim and Beer Elim (v. 8).

15:7 Ravine of the Poplars. May be the Zered River at the southern end of the Dead Sea; it formed the border between Moab and Edom.

15:9 [t]2Ki 17:25
16:1 [u]2Ki 3:4 [v]2Ki 14:7 [w]Isa 10:32
16:2 [x]Pr 27:8 [y]Nu 21:13-14; Jer 48:20
16:3 [z]1Ki 18:4
16:4 [a]Isa 9:4
16:5 [b]Da 7:14; Mic 4:7 [c]Lk 1:32 [d]Isa 9:7
16:6 [e]Am 2:1; Zep 2:8 [f]Ob 3; Zep 2:10
16:7 [g]Jer 48:20

[8]Their outcry echoes along the border of Moab;
their wailing reaches as far as Eglaim,
their lamentation as far as Beer Elim.
[9]The waters of Dimon[a] are full of blood,
but I will bring still more upon Dimon[a]—
a lion[t] upon the fugitives of Moab
and upon those who remain in the land.

16 Send lambs[u] as tribute
to the ruler of the land,
from Sela,[v] across the desert,
to the mount of Daughter Zion.[w]
[2]Like fluttering birds
pushed from the nest,[x]
so are the women of Moab
at the fords of the Arnon.[y]

[3]"Make up your mind," Moab says.
"Render a decision.
Make your shadow like night—
at high noon.
Hide the fugitives,[z]
do not betray the refugees.
[4]Let the Moabite fugitives stay with you;
be their shelter from the destroyer."

The oppressor[a] will come to an end,
and destruction will cease;
the aggressor will vanish from the land.
[5]In love a throne[b] will be established;
in faithfulness a man will sit on it—
one from the house[b] of David[c]—
one who in judging seeks justice[d]
and speeds the cause of righteousness.

[6]We have heard of Moab's[e] pride[f]—
how great is her arrogance!—
of her conceit, her pride and her insolence;
but her boasts are empty.
[7]Therefore the Moabites wail,[g]
they wail together for Moab.

[a] *9 Dimon*, a wordplay on *Dibon* (see verse 2), sounds like the Hebrew for *blood*. [b] *5* Hebrew *tent*

15:9 Dimon. Location unknown; possibly it is a copying error for Dibon or a wordplay (see NIV text note).

16:1–14 This seems to have three segments: (1) vv. 1–5 apparently appeal to Judah for refuge; (2) vv. 6–12 lament over Moab's pride and its destruction; and (3) vv. 13–14 predict the time of Moab's destruction.

16:1 Sela. A place in Edom; perhaps the fugitives are seen as having reached that far and are sending gifts to Judah ("Daughter Zion") with a request for help.

16:2 the Arnon. This river, which feeds into the Dead Sea, historically formed the northern border of Moab. It may have been a route for people to get to Judah.

16:3–4a Moab requests Judah to give them refuge.

16:4b–5 This seems almost like a parenthesis. Perhaps Isaiah intends it to be understood as coming from the mouths of the Moabite envoys. This would be in keeping with other parts of these prophecies, which predict that the other nations will end up worshiping the God of Judah and Israel (18:7; 19:18–25; 23:17–18). The oppression that has driven Moab to call to Judah for help will be brought to an end by someone "from the house of David" who will embody the four qualities most characteristic of Yahweh himself: "love," "faithfulness," "justice," and "righteousness" (cf. 9:6).

16:6–12 A lament (v. 7) over the downfall of Moab caused by their pride.

16:7 Much of the imagery in this passage has to do with vines and grapes. **raisin cakes of Kir Hareseth.** While the exact significance is unknown, it does fit in with the general imagery.

Lament and grieve
for the raisin cakes[h] of Kir Hareseth.[i]
8 The fields of Heshbon wither,
the vines of Sibmah also.
The rulers of the nations
have trampled down the choicest vines,
which once reached Jazer
and spread toward the desert.
Their shoots spread out
and went as far as the sea.[a]
9 So I weep,[j] as Jazer weeps,
for the vines of Sibmah.
Heshbon and Elealeh,
I drench you with tears!
The shouts of joy over your ripened fruit
and over your harvests[k] have been stilled.
10 Joy and gladness are taken away from the orchards;[l]
no one sings or shouts in the vineyards;
no one treads[m] out wine at the presses,[n]
for I have put an end to the shouting.
11 My heart laments for Moab[o] like a harp,
my inmost being[p] for Kir Hareseth.
12 When Moab appears at her high place,
she only wears herself out;
when she goes to her shrine[q] to pray,
it is to no avail.[r]

13 This is the word the LORD has already spoken concerning Moab. 14 But now the LORD says: "Within
three years, as a servant bound by contract would count them, Moab's splendor and all her many people
will be despised,[s] and her survivors will be very few and feeble."[t]

A Prophecy Against Damascus

17 A prophecy against Damascus:[u]

"See, Damascus will no longer be a city
but will become a heap of ruins.[v]
2 The cities of Aroer will be deserted
and left to flocks,[w] which will lie down,
with no one to make them afraid.[x]
3 The fortified city will disappear from Ephraim,
and royal power from Damascus;

[a] 8 Probably the Dead Sea

16:7 [h] 1Ch 16:3 [i] 2Ki 3:25
16:9 [j] Isa 15:3 [k] Jer 40:12
16:10 [l] Isa 24:7-8 [m] Jdg 9:27 [n] Job 24:11
16:11 [o] Isa 15:5 [p] Isa 63:15; Hos 11:8; Php 2:1
16:12 [q] Isa 15:2 [r] 1Ki 18:29
16:14 [s] Isa 25:10; Jer 48:42 [t] Isa 21:17
17:1 [u] Ge 14:15; Jer 49:23; Ac 9:2 [v] Isa 25:2; Am 1:3; Zec 9:1
17:2 [w] Isa 7:21; Eze 25:5 [x] Jer 7:33; Mic 4:4

16:8–10 This extended metaphor pictures Moab as a vine creeping northward to Jazer, located in the territory of Reuben that both Israel and Moab contested. It also reached eastward "toward the desert" (v. 8) and westward to the "sea" (v. 8; i.e., the Dead Sea). But "the rulers of the nations have trampled [it] down" (v. 8) so that there is no "ripened fruit" (v. 9) and no one treading out "wine" in the winepresses (v. 10). The weeping of desolation replaces the "joy" (v. 9) of a good harvest (cf. 5:1–7; 27:3–4).
16:12 high place. The "shrine" of the gods. Moab's idolatrous religion was "to no avail." It produced only weariness. Isaiah has an unspoken question: Why place any confidence in a nation doomed to destruction and whose gods cannot help it?
16:13–14 The prophet puts himself on record: "within three years"—as carefully reckoned as an indentured servant counting the days until his release—Moab will no longer be a force to be reckoned with. Their glory ("splendor") will be of no significance at all. The precise date of Moab's fall is unknown.
17:1–11 *A Prophecy Against Damascus.* Although this segment is labeled as a prophecy against Damascus (v. 1), by v. 3 it is also speaking of Ephraim (the northern kingdom of Israel), and vv. 4–11 seem to address the northern kingdom exclusively. Perhaps Syria and Israel receive dual treatment because they were so closely allied in their attempt to depose Ahaz (7:1–2,5).
17:2 Aroer. In Moab but located on the Kings Highway, which ran from the Gulf of Elath to Damascus, and therefore perhaps was considered a colony of Damascus.
17:3–4 The "glory" of Syria (Aram) and Israel cannot survive.

17:3 [y] ver 4; Hos 9:11 [z] Isa 7:8,16; 8:4
17:4 [a] Isa 10:16
17:5 [b] ver 11; Jer 51:33; Joel 3:13; Mt 13:30
17:6 [c] Dt 4:27; Isa 24:13 [d] Isa 27:12
17:7 [e] Isa 10:20 [f] Mic 7:7
17:8 [g] Isa 2:18,20; 30:22
17:10 [h] Isa 51:13 [i] Ps 68:19; Isa 12:2
17:11 [j] Ps 90:6 [k] Hos 8:7 [l] Job 4:8
17:12 [m] Ps 18:4; Jer 6:23; Lk 21:25

the remnant of Aram will be
like the glory[y] of the Israelites,"[z]
declares the LORD Almighty.

4 "In that day the glory of Jacob will fade;
the fat of his body will waste[a] away.
5 It will be as when reapers harvest the standing grain,
gathering[b] the grain in their arms—
as when someone gleans heads of grain
in the Valley of Rephaim.
6 Yet some gleanings will remain,[c]
as when an olive tree is beaten,[d]
leaving two or three olives on the topmost branches,
four or five on the fruitful boughs,"
declares the LORD, the God of Israel.

7 In that day people will look[e] to their Maker
and turn their eyes to the Holy One[f] of Israel.
8 They will not look to the altars,
the work of their hands,[g]
and they will have no regard for the Asherah poles[a]
and the incense altars their fingers have made.

9 In that day their strong cities, which they left because of the Israelites, will be like places abandoned
to thickets and undergrowth. And all will be desolation.

10 You have forgotten[h] God your Savior;[i]
you have not remembered the Rock, your fortress.
Therefore, though you set out the finest plants
and plant imported vines,
11 though on the day you set them out, you make them grow,
and on the morning[j] when you plant them, you bring them to bud,
yet the harvest will be as nothing[k]
in the day of disease and incurable pain.[l]

12 "Woe to the many nations that rage—
they rage like the raging sea![m]
Woe to the peoples who roar—
they roar like the roaring of great waters!

[a] *8* That is, wooden symbols of the goddess Asherah

17:5–6 After the invading armies have had their way, Israel will look like a harvested grain field with only a few heads of grain left on the ground or like a beaten olive tree with only a few olives left on the boughs (cf. 24:13).
17:7–8 A result of the destruction is that some will turn away from idolatry and back to "their Maker ... the Holy One of Israel."
17:8 Asherah poles. The Canaanite fertility goddess Asherah seems to have been worshiped in poplar groves (Hos 4:13). See photo, p. 180. **poles.** May be a contemptuous reference to these trees, or perhaps poles could be substituted for trees (cf. Deut 16:21).
17:9 The Hebrew is obscure. An alternative rendering, based on the Septuagint (the pre-Christian Greek translation of the OT), reads, "In that day their strong cities will be deserted like the cities of the Hivites and the Amorites were deserted before the Israelites. They will be desolate."
17:10–11 All of the efforts of Syria (Aram) and Israel to make themselves secure and prosperous will fail because they have "forgotten God" (cf. Hag 1:5–11).
17:12—18:7 *A Prophecy Against Cush.* The NIV includes 17:12–14 with the preceding verses, and 18:1, mentioning Cush, introduces a new section. However, 18:1 lacks the standard rubric "a prophecy against" (Hebrew *maśśāʾ*), which is found with all the other prophecies against nations in chs. 13–23. Instead, 18:1 uses "woe," as does 17:12, which addresses "many nations." Furthermore, there are some similarities between the language and thought of 17:12–14 and 18:1–7. Therefore, while the NIV follows one text indicator in its division, it is also useful to see that the material in 17:12–14 and 18:1–7 has a number of parallels. The point is that though the nations surge about "like the raging sea" (17:12), though they send "envoys" (18:2) from one end of the earth to the other (Cush-Ethiopia), "the LORD" (18:4) will bring all of that to nothing (7:14; 18:5–6). In fact, those envoys will come to "Mount Zion" with gifts for "the LORD Almighty" (18:7). Thus, this unit may summarize the main points of the larger section (chs. 13–23): Why trust hapless nations that will one day bring tribute to your God?
17:12–14 Cf. Ps 2:2–4. The "nations" may "rage" (v. 12), but at the rebuke of God, they fly away like "chaff" (v. 13).

13 Although the peoples roar like the roar of surging waters,
when he rebukes[n] them they flee[o] far away,
driven before the wind like chaff[p] on the hills,
like tumbleweed before a gale.[q]
14 In the evening, sudden terror!
Before the morning, they are gone![r]
This is the portion of those who loot us,
the lot of those who plunder us.

A Prophecy Against Cush

18 Woe to the land of whirring wings[a]
along the rivers of Cush,[b][s]
2 which sends envoys by sea
in papyrus[t] boats over the water.

Go, swift messengers,
to a people tall and smooth-skinned,
to a people feared far and wide,
an aggressive[u] nation of strange speech,
whose land is divided by rivers.[v]

3 All you people of the world,
you who live on the earth,
when a banner[w] is raised on the mountains,
you will see it,
and when a trumpet sounds,
you will hear it.
4 This is what the LORD says to me:
"I will remain quiet and will look on from my dwelling place,[x]
like shimmering heat in the sunshine,
like a cloud of dew[y] in the heat of harvest."
5 For, before the harvest, when the blossom is gone
and the flower becomes a ripening grape,
he will cut off the shoots with pruning knives,
and cut down and take away the spreading branches.[z]
6 They will all be left to the mountain birds of prey
and to the wild animals;[a]
the birds will feed on them all summer,
the wild animals all winter.

7 At that time gifts will be brought to the LORD Almighty
from a people tall and smooth-skinned,
from a people feared far and wide,

a *1* Or *of locusts* *b* *1* That is, the upper Nile region

17:13 [n]Ps 9:5 [o]Isa 13:14 [p]Isa 41:2,15-16 [q]Job 21:18
17:14 [r]2Ki 19:35
18:1 [s]Isa 20:3-5; Eze 30:4-5,9; Zep 2:12; 3:10
18:2 [t]Ex 2:3 [u]Ge 10:8-9; 2Ch 12:3 [v]ver 7
18:3 [w]Isa 5:26
18:4 [x]Isa 26:21; Hos 5:15 [y]Isa 26:19; Hos 14:5
18:5 [z]Isa 17:10-11; Eze 17:6
18:6 [a]Isa 56:9; Jer 7:33; Eze 32:4; 39:17

17:14 evening ... morning. Reminiscent of the deliverance from Sennacherib (37:36–37).
18:1 whirring wings. See NIV text note. It also may refer to the sails on the "papyrus boats" (v. 2) skimming up and down the Nile.
18:2 people. May be the Ethiopians themselves, but more likely some other people to whom the Ethiopian "envoys" are sent. (Ancient Ethiopia was located in modern Sudan.) They are possibly not a specific people but a composite of all the mighty, warlike people of the earth (v. 3).
18:3 The "people of the world" (cf. 17:12) must prepare for a signal, a "banner" (see note on 5:26). The signal will be a call to destruction (18:5–6).
18:4 God is not troubled by the raging of the nations but will "remain quiet" until the moment of "harvest"; he is an irresistible force, like "heat" and "dew." Cf. Matt 13:24–30; see also Ps 2:1–4.
18:5–6 The tendrils of the vines will be cut off with the bunches of grapes still on them, and they will be left for the birds and animals to feed on. So it will be for the riches that the nations have accumulated.
18:7 The nations that Israel alternatively feared and trusted will come to serve Israel's God (cf. Ps 68:31). If the nations will do that, why should Israel not do it? Cf. Isa 2:4–5.

18:7 [b]Ps 68:31
19:1 [c]Isa 13:1; Jer 43:12 [d]Ex 12:12; Joel 3:19 [e]Ps 18:10; 104:3; Rev 1:7 [f]Jos 2:11
19:2 [g]Jdg 7:22; Mt 10:21,36 [h]2Ch 20:23
19:3 [i]Isa 8:19; 47:13; Da 2:2,10
19:4 [j]Isa 20:4; Jer 46:26; Eze 29:19
19:5 [k]Jer 51:36
19:6 [l]Ex 7:18 [m]Isa 37:25; Eze 30:12 [n]Isa 15:6
19:7 [o]Isa 23:3
19:8 [p]Eze 47:10 [q]Hab 1:15
19:9 [r]Pr 7:16; Eze 27:7

an aggressive nation of strange speech,
whose land is divided by rivers—
the gifts will be brought to Mount Zion, the place of the Name of the LORD Almighty.[b]

A Prophecy Against Egypt

19 A prophecy[c] against Egypt:[d]

See, the LORD rides on a swift cloud[e]
and is coming to Egypt.
The idols of Egypt tremble before him,
and the hearts of the Egyptians melt[f] with fear.

2 "I will stir up Egyptian against Egyptian—
brother will fight against brother,[g]
neighbor against neighbor,
city against city,
kingdom against kingdom.[h]
3 The Egyptians will lose heart,
and I will bring their plans to nothing;
they will consult the idols and the spirits of the dead,
the mediums and the spiritists.[i]
4 I will hand the Egyptians over
to the power of a cruel master,
and a fierce king[j] will rule over them,"
declares the Lord, the LORD Almighty.

5 The waters of the river will dry up,[k]
and the riverbed will be parched and dry.
6 The canals will stink;[l]
the streams of Egypt will dwindle and dry up.[m]
The reeds and rushes will wither,[n]
7 also the plants along the Nile,
at the mouth of the river.
Every sown field[o] along the Nile
will become parched, will blow away and be no more.
8 The fishermen[p] will groan and lament,
all who cast hooks[q] into the Nile;
those who throw nets on the water
will pine away.
9 Those who work with combed flax will despair,
the weavers of fine linen[r] will lose hope.

19:1—20:6 *A Prophecy Against Egypt.* This prophecy has two parts: the message itself (ch. 19) and a specific prediction regarding an Egyptian defeat at the hands of the Assyrians (ch. 20; cf. 16:13–14).

19:1–25 The message to Egypt has both: words of judgment (vv. 1–17) and redemption (vv. 18–25).

19:1–17 The word of judgment focuses on three areas, all of which are reasons for Egyptian pride: Egypt's religion (vv. 1–4), Egypt's river (vv. 5–10), and Egypt's wisdom (vv. 11–15).

19:1–4 Egypt, famous for its sophisticated and complex religion, had a god or a goddess for every conceivable force or function. But when Yahweh would come to them, all their idols would be useless, and as was typical of Egypt, their fragile political system would come apart in civil warfare, with each locality rejecting the national gods and turning back to the ancestral gods and practices of the past.

19:1 rides on a swift cloud. Probably boldly appropriates the language of myth (see Pss 68:4; 104:3; cf. Isa 27:1; 51:9–10). Baal was said to be the Rider on the Clouds, and in Egypt the storm-god Seth was often pictured in the same terms. Isaiah is saying that those two gods were only impostors.

19:4 The Assyrians achieved their goal of conquering Egypt for a brief time in the middle of the seventh century BC. After them, the Persians and then the Greeks ruled Egypt.

19:5–10 The Nile was the glory and lifeline of Egypt. The annual floods were quite predictable, washing away the debris of the previous year and depositing a fresh layer of fertile soil for the coming year. The Nile also provided fish for food and resources for various industries. But it is under the complete control of Israel's God, who can dry it up at will.

10 The workers in cloth will be dejected,
and all the wage earners will be sick at heart.

11 The officials of Zoan[s] are nothing but fools;
the wise counselors of Pharaoh give senseless advice.
How can you say to Pharaoh,
"I am one of the wise men,[t]
a disciple of the ancient kings"?
12 Where are your wise men[u] now?
Let them show you and make known
what the LORD Almighty
has planned[v] against Egypt.
13 The officials of Zoan have become fools,
the leaders of Memphis[w] are deceived;
the cornerstones of her peoples
have led Egypt astray.
14 The LORD has poured into them
a spirit of dizziness;[x]
they make Egypt stagger in all that she does,
as a drunkard staggers around in his vomit.
15 There is nothing Egypt can do—
head or tail, palm branch or reed.[y]

16 In that day the Egyptians will become weaklings.[z] They will shudder with fear[a] at the uplifted
hand[b] that the LORD Almighty raises against them. 17 And the land of Judah will bring terror to the
Egyptians; everyone to whom Judah is mentioned will be terrified, because of what the LORD Almighty
is planning[c] against them.
18 In that day five cities in Egypt will speak the language of Canaan and swear allegiance[d] to the LORD
Almighty. One of them will be called the City of the Sun.[a]
19 In that day there will be an altar[e] to the LORD in the heart of Egypt, and a monument[f] to the LORD
at its border. 20 It will be a sign and witness to the LORD Almighty in the land of Egypt. When they cry out
to the LORD because of their oppressors, he will send them a savior and defender, and he will rescue[g]
them. 21 So the LORD will make himself known to the Egyptians, and in that day they will acknowledge[h]
the LORD. They will worship[i] with sacrifices and grain offerings; they will make vows to the LORD and
keep them. 22 The LORD will strike[j] Egypt with a plague; he will strike them and heal them. They will
turn[k] to the LORD, and he will respond to their pleas and heal[l] them.
23 In that day there will be a highway[m] from Egypt to Assyria. The Assyrians will go to Egypt and the

a 18 Some manuscripts of the Masoretic Text, Dead Sea Scrolls, Symmachus and Vulgate; most manuscripts of the Masoretic Text *City of Destruction*

19:11 [s] Nu 13:22 [t] 1Ki 4:30; Ac 7:22 **19:12** [u] 1Co 1:20 [v] Isa 14:24; Ro 9:17 **19:13** [w] Jer 2:16; Eze 30:13,16 **19:14** [x] Mt 17:17 **19:15** [y] Isa 9:14 **19:16** [z] Jer 51:30; Na 3:13 [a] Heb 10:31 [b] Isa 11:15 **19:17** [c] Isa 14:24 **19:18** [d] Zep 3:9 **19:19** [e] Jos 22:10 [f] Ge 28:18 **19:20** [g] Isa 49:24-26 **19:21** [h] Isa 11:9 [i] Isa 56:7; Mal 1:11 **19:22** [j] Heb 12:11 [k] Isa 45:14; Hos 14:1 [l] Dt 32:39 **19:23** [m] Isa 11:16

19:11–15 Whereas the Mesopotamians were known for their law codes, the Egyptians were known for their wisdom. Their collections of proverbs extend back almost to the invention of writing. But none of those wise men will be able to divine what "the LORD Almighty [Yahweh of Hosts] has planned against Egypt" (v. 12). Their wisdom has its origins only on earth.
19:11 Zoan. Located in the Nile delta, it was the capital of Egypt during Isaiah's time.
19:14 Cf. 44:25–26.
19:15 head … reed. Terminology for leadership (see 9:14–15).
19:16–17 This is transitional: it points back to judgment but forward to Egypt's looking to Judah and their God. The language is metaphoric. The Egyptians do not dread Judah as much as they dread Judah's God.
19:18–25 Egypt's hope is in Judah's God. Judah certainly should not look to Egypt for help (cf. chs. 28–33) when Egypt will one day be worshiping Yahweh. As with all people, God does not bring judgment with the intent that it is irreversible. Rather, he intends that the look of dread will be replaced with the look of adoration. It is a matter of conjecture as to how many of these predictions will be fulfilled in a literal sense. In one sense they have already been fulfilled in that for the first six centuries after Christ, Egypt was one of the main centers of Christendom. The main point, however, is to remind the Israelites that their God is God of all the world.
19:18 City of the Sun. Heliopolis, the center of worship of the sun-god, Re.
19:19–22 The Egyptians will fully integrate into the worship of Yahweh, experiencing him just as faithful Judahites did.
19:22 plague. The Egyptians would have the same opportunity as the Hebrews did: if Yahweh struck them with a natural disaster, they could turn to him and pray for deliverance This was one of the purposes to which Solomon dedicated the temple (1 Kgs 8:35–40).
19:23–25 This picture of a "highway" (see note on 11:16) extending "from Egypt to Assyria" (v. 23) is a striking statement of Yahweh's

19:23 [n]Isa 27:13
19:25 [o]Ps 100:3 [p]Isa 29:23; 45:11; 60:21; 64:8; Eph 2:10 [q]Hos 2:23
20:1 [r]2Ki 18:17
20:2 [s]Isa 13:1 [t]Zec 13:4; Mt 3:4 [u]Eze 24:17,23 [v]1Sa 19:24 [w]Mic 1:8
20:3 [x]Isa 8:18 [y]Isa 37:9; 43:3
20:4 [z]Isa 19:4 [a]Isa 47:3; Jer 13:22,26
20:5 [b]2Ki 18:21; Isa 30:5
20:6 [c]Isa 10:3 [d]Jer 30:15-17; Mt 23:33; 1Th 5:3; Heb 2:3
21:1 [e]Isa 13:21; Jer 51:43 [f]Zec 9:14
21:2 [g]Ps 60:3 [h]Isa 33:1 [i]Isa 22:6; Jer 49:34
21:3 [j]Ps 48:6; Isa 26:17

Egyptians to Assyria. The Egyptians and Assyrians will worship[n] together. 24 In that day Israel will be
the third, along with Egypt and Assyria, a blessing[a] on the earth. 25 The LORD Almighty will bless them,
saying, "Blessed be Egypt my people,[o] Assyria my handiwork,[p] and Israel my inheritance.[q]"

A Prophecy Against Egypt and Cush

20 In the year that the supreme commander,[r] sent by Sargon king of Assyria, came to Ashdod and
attacked and captured it— 2 at that time the LORD spoke through Isaiah son of Amoz.[s] He said
to him, "Take off the sackcloth[t] from your body and the sandals[u] from your feet." And he did so, going
around stripped[v] and barefoot.[w]

3 Then the LORD said, "Just as my servant Isaiah has gone stripped and barefoot for three years, as a
sign[x] and portent against Egypt and Cush,[b][y] 4 so the king[z] of Assyria will lead away stripped and barefoot the Egyptian captives and Cushite exiles, young and old, with buttocks bared—to Egypt's shame.[a]
5 Those who trusted in Cush and boasted in Egypt[b] will be dismayed and put to shame. 6 In that day the
people who live on this coast will say, 'See what has happened to those we relied on, those we fled to for
help[c] and deliverance from the king of Assyria! How then can we escape?[d]'"

A Prophecy Against Babylon

21 A prophecy against the Desert[e] by the Sea:

Like whirlwinds sweeping through the southland,[f]
  an invader comes from the desert,
  from a land of terror.

2 A dire[g] vision has been shown to me:
  The traitor betrays,[h] the looter takes loot.
Elam,[i] attack! Media, lay siege!
  I will bring to an end all the groaning she caused.

3 At this my body is racked with pain,
  pangs seize me, like those of a woman in labor;[j]
I am staggered by what I hear,
  I am bewildered by what I see.
4 My heart falters,
  fear makes me tremble;

[a] 24 Or *Assyria, whose names will be used in blessings* (see Gen. 48:20); or *Assyria, who will be seen by others as blessed* [b] 3 That is, the upper Nile region; also in verse 5

universal lordship. Assyria was the great threat, and after the northern kingdom of Israel fell, Egypt seemed to be the only hope for Judah's survival, humanly speaking. But Isaiah says that all of that is wrong. The oppressor and the ally will both be partners with the supposed victim in worshiping Israel's God. Israel's election was for the salvation of the world (see note on 2:1–5).

20:1–6 God calls Isaiah to symbolize by his own behavior what was going to happen to the Egyptians and all who trusted in them and in the Cushite (Nubian) dynasty ruling them. He was to go "stripped and barefoot" (v. 2) like those whom the "king of Assyria" (v. 4) would take into exile (cf. 2 Chr 28:14–15). At times God required his prophets to act out their messages in order to make the messages more striking (cf. 1 Kgs 18; Jer 13; 19; 27–28; 43; Ezek 3:22—5:17; 12:1–20; 24:15–27).

20:1 The particular incident reflected here is the Assyrian conquest of the Philistine city of Ashdod in 711 BC and the flight of its ruler, Yamani, to Egypt for refuge. As the dash at the end of the verse in the NIV indicates, it seems that God directed Isaiah to perform his action "three years" (v. 3) before the incident took place. When it did, Yahweh gave Isaiah the message recorded in vv. 3–5. It was an entirely appropriate message because when the Assyrian emperor Sargon demanded that Egypt give up Yamani, they did so, sending him all the way to Assyria. Clearly, it was folly to put any trust in Egypt. As throughout chs. 7–39, the challenge is not to put one's trust in the nations, which will surely fail you and put you to shame, but to trust the Lord.

21:1–17 The three prophecies in this chapter seem to be grouped around the theme of travelers and watchers. Perhaps the thread is the trade route stretching across the desert from Babylon (vv. 1–10) to Edom (i.e., Seir, vv. 11–12) through Arabia (vv. 13–17). The mention of lookouts (vv. 6,8), watchmen (v. 11), and fugitives (v. 14) suggest that the remnants of the population of Babylon are fleeing west along the trade route after the fall of the city.

21:1–10 *A Prophecy Against Babylon.* Although this passage does not name Babylon until v. 9, it is still clear that "the Desert by the Sea" (v. 1) refers to Babylon. This prophecy may be more specific than that in ch. 13, where Babylon seems to represent the glory of the world (see note on 13:1—14:2).

21:2 Elam. Persia, which united with Media to bring Babylon down (see note on 13:17).

21:3–4 The thought of Babylon's fall would have been as shocking to citizens of the ancient Near East as was the fall of Rome to citizens of that empire.

the twilight I longed for
has become a horror to me.

[5] They set the tables,
they spread the rugs,
they eat, they drink![k]
Get up, you officers,
oil the shields!

[6] This is what the Lord says to me:

"Go, post a lookout
and have him report what he sees.
[7] When he sees chariots[l]
with teams of horses,
riders on donkeys
or riders on camels,
let him be alert,
fully alert."

[8] And the lookout[a][m] shouted,

"Day after day, my lord, I stand on the
watchtower;
every night I stay at my post.
[9] Look, here comes a man in a chariot
with a team of horses.
And he gives back the answer:
'Babylon[n] has fallen,[o] has fallen!
All the images of its gods[p]
lie shattered on the ground!' "

[10] My people who are crushed on the threshing floor,[q]
I tell you what I have heard
from the LORD Almighty,
from the God of Israel.

A Prophecy Against Edom

[11] A prophecy against Dumah[b]:[r]

Someone calls to me from Seir,[s]
"Watchman, what is left of the night?
Watchman, what is left of the night?"
[12] The watchman replies,
"Morning is coming, but also the night.
If you would ask, then ask;
and come back yet again."

21:5 [k] Jer 51:39,57; Da 5:2
21:7 [l] ver 9
21:8 [m] Hab 2:1
21:9 [n] Rev 14:8 [o] Jer 51:8; Rev 18:2 [p] Isa 46:1; Jer 50:2; 51:44
21:10 [q] Jer 51:33
21:11 [r] Ge 25:14 [s] Ge 32:3

[a] *8* Dead Sea Scrolls and Syriac; Masoretic Text *A lion* [b] *11 Dumah*, a wordplay on *Edom*, means *silence* or *stillness.*

21:5 This might speak of Belshazzar's feast and the sudden fall of the city.
21:6–9 The shocking news spreads.
21:9 Babylon has fallen. These words are adapted in Rev 14:8; 18:2 to refer to the fall of the evil powers revolting against God at the end of time.
21:10 crushed on the threshing floor. How oppressed peoples sometimes thought of themselves: like grain being crushed under a heavy drag pulled by oxen. To them the news of an evil empire's fall was good news.
21:11–12 *A Prophecy Against Edom.* This enigmatic prophecy perhaps relates to the foregoing verses.
21:11 Dumah. May be a wordplay on Edom (see NIV text note); it was also a very important oasis on the route between southern Mesopotamia and Edom.

21:13 [t]Isa 13:1
21:14 [u]Ge 25:15
21:15 [v]Isa 13:14
21:16 [w]Isa 16:14 [x]Isa 17:3 [y]Ps 120:5; Isa 60:7
21:17 [z]Isa 10:19
22:1 [a]Isa 13:1 [b]Ps 125:2; Jer 21:13; Joel 3:2,12,14
22:2 [c]Isa 32:13
22:4 [d]Isa 15:3; Lk 19:41 [e]Jer 9:1
22:5 [f]La 1:5

A Prophecy Against Arabia

13 A prophecy[t] against Arabia:

You caravans of Dedanites,
  who camp in the thickets of Arabia,
14 bring water for the thirsty;
you who live in Tema,[u]
  bring food for the fugitives.
15 They flee[v] from the sword,
  from the drawn sword,
from the bent bow
  and from the heat of battle.

16 This is what the Lord says to me: "Within one year, as a servant bound by contract[w] would count
it, all the splendor[x] of Kedar[y] will come to an end. 17 The survivors of the archers, the warriors of Kedar,
will be few.[z]" The LORD, the God of Israel, has spoken.

A Prophecy About Jerusalem

22 A prophecy[a] against the Valley[b] of Vision:

What troubles you now,
  that you have all gone up on the roofs,
2 you town so full of commotion,
  you city of tumult and revelry?[c]
Your slain were not killed by the sword,
  nor did they die in battle.
3 All your leaders have fled together;
  they have been captured without using the bow.
All you who were caught were taken prisoner
    together,
  having fled while the enemy was still far away.
4 Therefore I said, "Turn away from me;
  let me weep[d] bitterly.
Do not try to console me
  over the destruction of my people."[e]

5 The Lord, the LORD Almighty, has a day
  of tumult and trampling and terror[f]
  in the Valley of Vision,

21:13–17 *A Prophecy Against Arabia.* This is evidently a plea for help for fugitives, perhaps from Babylon, although that is not specified.
21:13–14 Tema and Dedan were two other important oases (see note on v. 11) in the northwest part of the Arabian desert known as Kedar (see v. 16). The last Babylonian king, Nabonidus, moved his capital to Tema, leaving Belshazzar in charge.
21:16–17 This specifically announces the end of the "splendor" of Kedar (northwestern Arabia) (cf. 16:13–14). This particular devastation occurred under the Assyrians Sargon (722–705 BC) and Sennacherib (705–681 BC) a century and a half before the fall of Babylon.
22:1–25 *A Prophecy About Judah.* Although the passage does not mention Judah until v. 9, it clearly addresses Judah throughout. This suggests that "the Valley of Vision" (v. 1) is ironic. One does not see anything from a valley, yet the people of Judah claim to see eternal reality clearly. The message has two parts: (1) Judah fails to repent (vv. 1–14), and (2) "Shebna the palace administrator" (v. 15) fails in his office (vv. 16–19), so Eliakim replaces Shebna (vv. 20–25). It is surprising that this series of prophecies against the nations includes Judah. Isaiah seems to be saying that they have all but forfeited their special relationship to Yahweh and are becoming just one more of the world nations.
22:1–14 *A Prophecy About Jerusalem.* It is not clear what specific events this refers to. Building a "reservoir" (v. 11) seems to point to the time of Hezekiah and Isaiah (2 Kgs 20:20). However, vv. 2–3 might be a predictive reference to the futile flight of Zedekiah and his troops from the Babylonians in 586 BC (2 Kgs 25:4–7). Perhaps a historical event such as the Assyrian attack on Philistia in 711 BC and its subsequent withdrawal provides the basis for the message that Isaiah then supplements with additional images. The point is that the nation experienced a deliverance (after many of the leaders fled), but instead of prompting repentance and renewed trust in God, it resulted in fatalistic partying and "revelry" (vv. 2,13).
22:2–4 The leaders failed their people in the moment of crisis, fleeing to escape the enemy that was "still far away" (v. 3). But the leaders were captured anyway and without a fight. For Isaiah, this cowardly flight signals the rot that is at the core of the nation, which will lead to its eventual "destruction" (v. 4).
22:5–7 A vision of Jerusalem's coming destruction.

a day of battering down walls
and of crying out to the mountains.
[6] Elam[g] takes up the quiver,[h]
with her charioteers and horses;
Kir[i] uncovers the shield.
[7] Your choicest valleys are full of chariots,
and horsemen are posted at the city gates.[j]

[8] The Lord stripped away the defenses of Judah,
and you looked in that day
to the weapons[k] in the Palace of the Forest.[l]
[9] You saw that the walls of the City of David
were broken through in many places;
you stored up water
in the Lower Pool.[m]
[10] You counted the buildings in Jerusalem
and tore down houses to strengthen the wall.
[11] You built a reservoir between the two walls[n]
for the water of the Old Pool,[o]
but you did not look to the One who made it,
or have regard for the One who planned it long ago.

[12] The Lord, the LORD Almighty,
called you on that day
to weep[p] and to wail,
to tear out your hair[q] and put on sackcloth.[r]
[13] But see, there is joy and revelry,
slaughtering of cattle and killing of sheep,
eating of meat and drinking of wine![s]
"Let us eat and drink," you say,
"for tomorrow we die!"[t]

[14] The LORD Almighty has revealed this in my hearing:[u] "Till your dying day this sin will not be atoned[v] for," says the Lord, the LORD Almighty.

[15] This is what the Lord, the LORD Almighty, says:

"Go, say to this steward,
to Shebna[w] the palace administrator:
[16] What are you doing here and who gave you permission
to cut out a grave[x] for yourself here,
hewing your grave on the height
and chiseling your resting place in the rock?

22:6 [g] Isa 21:2 [h] Jer 49:35 [i] 2Ki 16:9
22:7 [j] 2Ch 32:1-2
22:8 [k] 2Ch 32:5 [l] 1Ki 7:2
22:9 [m] 2Ch 32:4
22:11 [n] 2Ki 25:4; Jer 39:4 [o] 2Ch 32:4
22:12 [p] Joel 2:17 [q] Mic 1:16 [r] Joel 1:13
22:13 [s] Isa 5:22; 28:7-8; 56:12; Lk 17:26-29 [t] 1Co 15:32*
22:14 [u] Isa 5:9 [v] Isa 13:11; 26:21; 30:13-14; Eze 24:13
22:15 [w] 2Ki 18:18; Isa 36:3
22:16 [x] Mt 27:60

22:6 Elam ... Kir. The historical homeland of Persia; probably represents warlike peoples since there is no record of any Persian attack on Jerusalem.
22:8–11 looked ... to the weapons. This condemns leaders who depended on physical defenses instead of Yahweh, "the One who planned [all these events] long ago" (v. 11). The book of Isaiah is ambivalent toward Hezekiah. It never criticizes him directly, and it holds up his eventual trust as a model in chs. 36–37; but here it criticizes some of the policies that he was heavily involved with that seem to reveal his trust in something other than the Lord (cf. 39:1–8).
22:8 Palace of the Forest. Part of the temple complex Solomon built (1 Kgs 7:2–6).
22:10 Houses abutting the city wall were torn down to provide both access to the wall for the defenders and materials to repair the walls both before and during an attack.
22:13 joy and revelry. Only a temporary cover-up for ultimate despair. The city and nation might have escaped immediately, but these people could not envision any final escape from Assyria's seemingly irresistible strength. **tomorrow we die!** Reveals a fatalism that is the opposite of hope and trust. Sorrow over sin and a genuine turning to God could bring renewed hope in his universal power.
22:15–25 *Judgment on Shebna.* Isaiah graphically illustrates the folly of Judah's leadership and the destruction it will lead to. Shebna's main interest was constructing a fine rock-cut tomb for himself.
22:15 palace administrator. Apparently equivalent to prime minister (1 Kgs 4:6; 16:9; 18:3; cf. 2 Kgs 15:5).

22:18 [y] Isa 17:13
22:20 [z] 2Ki 18:18; Isa 36:3
22:22 [a] Rev 3:7 [b] Isa 7:2 [c] Job 12:14
22:23 [d] Zec 10:4 [e] Ezr 9:8 [f] 1Sa 2:7-8; Job 36:7
22:25 [g] ver 23 [h] Isa 46:11; Mic 4:4
23:1 [i] Jos 19:29; 1Ki 5:1; Jer 47:4; Eze 26,27,28; Joel 3:4-8; Am 1:9-10; Zec 9:2-4 [j] 1Ki 10:22 [k] Ge 10:4; Isa 2:16 *fn*
23:3 [l] Isa 19:7 [m] Eze 27:3
23:4 [n] Ge 10:15,19

17 "Beware, the LORD is about to take firm hold of you
and hurl you away, you mighty man.
18 He will roll you up tightly like a ball
and throw[y] you into a large country.
There you will die
and there the chariots you were so proud of
will become a disgrace to your master's house.
19 I will depose you from your office,
and you will be ousted from your position.

20 "In that day I will summon my servant, Eliakim[z] son of Hilkiah. 21 I will clothe him with your robe
and fasten your sash around him and hand your authority over to him. He will be a father to those who
live in Jerusalem and to the people of Judah. 22 I will place on his shoulder the key[a] to the house of David;[b] what he opens no one can shut, and what he shuts no one can open.[c] 23 I will drive him like a peg[d]
into a firm place;[e] he will become a seat[*a*] of honor[f] for the house of his father. 24 All the glory of his family will hang on him: its offspring and offshoots—all its lesser vessels, from the bowls to all the jars.

25 "In that day," declares the LORD Almighty, "the peg[g] driven into the firm place will give way; it
will be sheared off and will fall, and the load hanging on it will be cut down." The LORD has spoken.[h]

A Prophecy Against Tyre

23 A prophecy against Tyre:[i]

Wail, you ships[j] of Tarshish![k]
For Tyre is destroyed
and left without house or harbor.
From the land of Cyprus
word has come to them.

2 Be silent, you people of the island
and you merchants of Sidon,
whom the seafarers have enriched.
3 On the great waters
came the grain of the Shihor;
the harvest of the Nile[*b*][l] was the revenue of Tyre,[m]
and she became the marketplace of the nations.

4 Be ashamed, Sidon,[n] and you fortress of the sea,
for the sea has spoken:

[*a*] *23* Or *throne* [*b*] *2,3* Masoretic Text; Dead Sea Scrolls *Sidon, / who cross over the sea; / your envoys* [3] *are on the great waters. / The grain of the Shihor, / the harvest of the Nile,*

22:17–18 While nothing is known of the circumstances of Shebna's death, Isaiah says that Shebna will not be buried in that tomb, nor even in Judah. Instead of bringing honor to his king, he will bring "disgrace" upon the king through his misplaced priorities.

22:19–25 Eliakim will replace Shebna (see 36:3). Unlike Shebna, Eliakim will be trustworthy, "a father" to the people (v. 21), an "honor" to his family (v. 23), and a "peg" upon which people can depend (v. 23).

22:22 the key to the house of David. May indicate that Eliakim would function as prime minister. The "key" may have been the symbol of his authority. Cf. the expression of Christ's authority in Rev 3:7 and his conferring authority upon his disciples in Matt 16:19.

22:25 the peg ... will give way. Eliakim will eventually fail.

23:1–18 *A Prophecy Against Tyre.* Tyre and Sidon (25 miles [40 kilometers] north of Tyre) were for much of ancient history the principal seaports on the central east coast of the Mediterranean Sea. They were able to control trade up and down that coast and were the primary outlet to the West for Syria and the various peoples of Canaan and Transjordan. In this capacity both cities became wealthy. They tended to trade dominance, with Tyre prevailing more frequently than Sidon. By coming at the end of the sequence of nations in chs. 13–23, Tyre on the west may function as a bookend with Babylon on the east; together they express the heights of human glory (see note on 13:1—23:18).

23:1 Tarshish. See also vv. 6,10,14. It was probably located on the Mediterranean coast of Spain. As such it represents the farthest point west that the trade of Tyre might reach (see Jonah 1:3). Its ships, laden with merchandise from the West, land on the island of Cyprus (v. 12) and receive the news that their ultimate port of Tyre is destroyed (cf. v. 14).

23:2–5 The "merchants of Sidon" are "silent" (v. 2) because the lucrative grain trade from Egypt has come to an end. Like a person who is infertile, the sea can produce no "sons" or "daughters" (i.e., trade goods, v. 4). The Egyptians too "will be in anguish" (v. 5), having no outlet for their grain.

23:2 island. As part of the Tyre's larger port complex, this island off the coast of Tyre formed a citadel to which the people could flee when Tyre's

"I have neither been in labor nor given birth;
 I have neither reared sons nor brought up daughters."
[5] When word comes to Egypt,
 they will be in anguish at the report from Tyre.

[6] Cross over to Tarshish;
 wail, you people of the island.
[7] Is this your city of revelry,[o]
 the old, old city,
whose feet have taken her
 to settle in far-off lands?
[8] Who planned this against Tyre,
 the bestower of crowns,
whose merchants are princes,
 whose traders are renowned in the earth?
[9] The LORD Almighty planned it,
 to bring down[p] her pride in all her splendor
 and to humble[q] all who are renowned[r] on the earth.

[10] Till[a] your land as they do along the Nile,
 Daughter Tarshish,
 for you no longer have a harbor.
[11] The LORD has stretched out his hand[s] over the sea
 and made its kingdoms tremble.
He has given an order concerning Phoenicia
 that her fortresses be destroyed.[t]
[12] He said, "No more of your reveling,[u]
 Virgin Daughter[v] Sidon, now crushed!

"Up, cross over to Cyprus;
 even there you will find no rest."
[13] Look at the land of the Babylonians,[b]
 this people that is now of no account!
The Assyrians[w] have made it
 a place for desert creatures;
they raised up their siege towers,
 they stripped its fortresses bare
 and turned it into a ruin.[x]
[14] Wail, you ships of Tarshish;[y]
 your fortress is destroyed!

[15] At that time Tyre[z] will be forgotten for seventy years, the span of a king's life. But at the end of these seventy years, it will happen to Tyre as in the song of the prostitute:

23:7 [o] Isa 22:2; 32:13 **23:9** [p] Job 40:11 [q] Isa 13:11 [r] Isa 5:13; 9:15 **23:11** [s] Ex 14:21 [t] Isa 25:2; Zec 9:3-4 **23:12** [u] Rev 18:22 [v] Isa 47:1 **23:13** [w] Isa 10:5 [x] Isa 10:7 **23:14** [y] Isa 2:16 *fn* **23:15** [z] Jer 25:22

[a] *10* Dead Sea Scrolls and some Septuagint manuscripts; Masoretic Text *Go through* [b] *13* Or *Chaldeans*

city proper was attacked (also v. 6). This island resisted all attacks until it finally fell to Alexander the Great in 332 BC.

23:6–9 From Tarshish to the island of Tyre itself, the collapse of such a great commercial power would seem incomprehensible. Who could have planned such a thing (v. 8)? To Isaiah the answer is obvious: it is the Lord, the one who planned the downfall of Assyria (14:24) and Egypt (19:12). The nations of the earth might believe they are the masters of their own destiny, but it is not so. The one who made the earth is the one who determines the destiny of the nations of the earth (cf. 22:11; 40:15,23–24).

23:9 Yahweh's plans are directed against every expression, whether individual or national, of "pride" that would elevate its own glory ("splendor") over that of its Maker.

23:10–14 Isaiah counsels Tarshish to give up its dreams as a seaport and to give itself to agriculture ("till your land," v. 10) because its trading partner Phoenicia is destroyed (v. 11). For an alternate reading of v. 10, see NIV text note.

23:13 In 710 and 689 BC, the Assyrians devastated Babylon. Although Babylon would recover and go on to repay Assyria in kind, Isaiah's point is that if even mighty Babylon could not escape destruction, the Phoenicians, with much less military potential, certainly could not do so.

23:15–18 It is difficult to pinpoint when this prediction was fulfilled.

23:15 forgotten for seventy years. No precise period of 70 years is known for Tyre's being "forgotten." Possibly the number simply conveys completion. There are several periods from the sixth to the second

23:17 [a] Eze 16:26; Na 3:4; Rev 17:1
23:18 [b] Ex 28:36; Ps 72:10 [c] Isa 60:5-9; Mic 4:13
24:1 [d] ver 20; Isa 2:19-21; 33:9
24:2 [e] Hos 4:9 [f] Eze 7:12 [g] Lev 25:35-37; Dt 23:19-20
24:3 [h] Isa 6:11-12
24:4 [i] Isa 2:12
24:5 [j] Ge 3:17; Nu 35:33 [k] Isa 10:6; 59:12

16 "Take up a harp, walk through the city,
you forgotten prostitute;
play the harp well, sing many a song,
so that you will be remembered."

17 At the end of seventy years, the LORD will deal with Tyre. She will return to her lucrative prostitution[a] and will ply her trade with all the kingdoms on the face of the earth. 18 Yet her profit and her
earnings will be set apart for the LORD;[b] they will not be stored up or hoarded. Her profits will go to those
who live before the LORD,[c] for abundant food and fine clothes.

The LORD's Devastation of the Earth

24 See, the LORD is going to lay waste the earth[d]
and devastate it;
he will ruin its face
and scatter its inhabitants—
2 it will be the same
for priest as for people,[e]
for the master as for his servant,
for the mistress as for her servant,
for seller as for buyer,[f]
for borrower as for lender,
for debtor as for creditor.[g]
3 The earth will be completely laid waste
and totally plundered.[h]
The LORD has spoken this word.

4 The earth dries up and withers,
the world languishes and withers,
the heavens[i] languish with the earth.
5 The earth is defiled[j] by its people;
they have disobeyed[k] the laws,
violated the statutes
and broken the everlasting covenant.

centuries BC when Tyre was in eclipse. The point is that, as elsewhere in this unit, Judah should not trust Tyre when in the end Tyre will serve Judah's God.

23:16 Probably a stanza from a well-known song.

24:1—27:13 *The Lord: Sovereign Actor in History.* Chs. 13–23 might give the impression that the nations are the primary actors on the stage of history and that Yahweh merely reacts to them. These chapters clarify that this is a wrong impression. Yahweh is the sovereign actor on the world's stage. He is the one in whose hand history unfolds. Chs. 24–27 are sometimes called "The Little Apocalypse" because, like the apocalyptic literature of the second and first centuries BC, they see God as dictating events behind the scenes so as to engineer his triumph at the end of time. But many of the usual characteristic features of apocalyptic literature are missing—including colors, numbers, and fantastic imagery, all of which have coded significance. Furthermore, apocalyptic literature tends to be pessimistic about history, seeing God as having to intervene at the end to redeem it. These chapters do not betray such pessimism; God is at work among his people now. Two themes dominate: city and song. And each develops by means of contrast: (1) the city of earth versus the city of God, and (2) the songs of the ruthless versus the song of salvation. The unit divides into two parts: (1) chs. 24–25 emphasize the destruction of the Earth City and the consequent deliverance of God's people, and (2) chs. 26–27 focus on the City of God and the impact of that reality on the world's destiny.

24:1—25:12 *The Lord's Devastation of the Earth.* God will judge the earth and will produce a great feast on Mount Zion for all peoples who will recognize his lordship.

24:1–23 The book of Isaiah is notable for its transitions between sections. In some cases it is difficult to decide whether these transitional elements go more closely with the preceding or the following segments. This chapter is one of those. In one way its pronouncements of judgment on the earth as a whole may summarize the preceding series of judgments on particular nations. On the other hand, the recurrence of "song" and "city" and the reference to Mount Zion at the end unite ch. 24 more closely with ch. 25 (and chs. 26–27). In any case this chapter links chs. 13–23 closely to chs. 25–27.

24:1–6 This segment effectively repeats the word "earth." There is no question of the Lord's position in relation to the world: he alone is the one who has a right to call it to account. In the midst of this universal language, v. 2 is equally powerful in its particularity. Not only the whole earth but every single human on the earth is liable for judgment.

24:5 It is not only Israel but all people who are in a "covenant" relationship with Yahweh, who has "laws" and "statutes" that are to be obeyed. Isaiah holds that nature reveals enough about God and his plan for human behavior to bring all of us who violate that plan under condemnation (cf. Rom 1:18–32). **everlasting covenant.** May be that of Noah, with its prohibition of human bloodshed (Gen 9:4–6).

[6] Therefore a curse consumes the earth;
its people must bear their guilt.
Therefore earth's inhabitants are burned up,[l]
and very few are left.
[7] The new wine dries up and the vine withers;[m]
all the merrymakers groan.[n]
[8] The joyful timbrels[o] are stilled,
the noise[p] of the revelers has stopped,
the joyful harp[q] is silent.[r]
[9] No longer do they drink wine[s] with a song;
the beer is bitter[t] to its drinkers.
[10] The ruined city lies desolate;
the entrance to every house is barred.
[11] In the streets they cry out for wine;
all joy turns to gloom,[u]
all joyful sounds are banished from the earth.
[12] The city is left in ruins,
its gate is battered to pieces.
[13] So will it be on the earth
and among the nations,
as when an olive tree is beaten,[v]
or as when gleanings are left after the grape harvest.

[14] They raise their voices, they shout for joy;[w]
from the west they acclaim the LORD's majesty.
[15] Therefore in the east give glory[x] to the LORD;
exalt[y] the name of the LORD, the God of Israel,
in the islands of the sea.
[16] From the ends of the earth we hear singing:
"Glory[z] to the Righteous One."

But I said, "I waste away, I waste away!
Woe to me!
The treacherous betray!
With treachery the treacherous betray![a]"
[17] Terror and pit and snare[b] await you,
people of the earth.
[18] Whoever flees at the sound of terror
will fall into a pit;

24:6 [l] Isa 1:31
24:7 [m] Joel 1:10-12 [n] Isa 16:8-10
24:8 [o] Isa 5:12 [p] Jer 7:34; 16:9; 25:10; Hos 2:11 [q] Rev 18:22 [r] Eze 26:13
24:9 [s] Isa 5:11,22 [t] Isa 5:20
24:11 [u] Isa 16:10; 32:13; Jer 14:3
24:13 [v] Isa 17:6
24:14 [w] Isa 12:6
24:15 [x] Isa 66:19 [y] Isa 25:3; Mal 1:11
24:16 [z] Isa 28:5 [a] Isa 21:2; Jer 5:11
24:17 [b] Jer 48:43

24:7–13 Earth is pictured as a "ruined city" (v. 10). Its "gate" (v. 12) is broken down, and the surrounding fields have been stripped bare (vv. 7–9; cf. 16:9–10). Where once there were drunken songs, now there is only "gloom" (v. 11). The vintage is dried up (v. 7), and all songs are "banished" (v. 11). Earth looks like a picked-over vineyard or olive orchard after harvest is complete (cf. 17:5–6).
24:14–16 Differing reactions to the Lord's judgment. Verses 14–16a seem to be the song of the righteous in response to the earth's judgment. The praise is universal: from "west" (v. 14) to "east" (v. 15) and reaching to the "ends of the earth" (v. 16). The God of Israel receives the glory due him (v. 15). But v. 16b gives a contrasting reaction that seems to come from the prophet ("I . . . I . . . I . . . me"). Perhaps this is Isaiah's typical inability to allow a glorious promise to obscure the dark reality of the present (see notes on 2:6—4:1; 5:1–30). He cannot overlook the "treachery" that characterizes so much of human relations (v. 16).
24:15 islands of the sea. Represent the "ends of the earth" (v. 16).
24:17–23 This poem about the earth's judgment and Yahweh's reign perhaps comes the closest to having an apocalyptic flavor (see note on 24:1—27:13). The earth suffers a climactic judgment that is depicted in two ways: (1) vv. 17–18b picture human beings running from "terror" to "pit" to "snare," with each escape leading to a worse disaster, and (2) vv. 18c–20 picture the earth as a mound of soil upon which a flood is let loose: it is "broken" and "shaken," falling, "never to rise again." The final stanza (vv. 21–23) highlights well the theme of chs. 24–27. It is Yahweh who brings this terrific punishment about. As is especially prevalent in chs. 7–39, the people who presume to stand on the same plane as God are brought down. So "the powers in the heavens above and the kings on the earth below" (v. 21) are brought down into "a dungeon" (v. 22).

24:18 [c] Ge 7:11 [d] Ps 18:7
24:19 [e] Dt 11:6
24:20 [f] Isa 19:14 [g] Isa 1:2,28; 43:27
24:21 [h] Isa 10:12
24:22 [i] Isa 10:4 [j] Isa 42:7, 22 [k] Eze 38:8
24:23 [l] Isa 13:10 [m] Rev 22:5 [n] Heb 12:22 [o] Isa 60:19
25:1 [p] Ps 98:1 [q] Nu 23:19
25:2 [r] Isa 17:1 [s] Isa 17:3 [t] Isa 13:22
25:3 [u] Isa 13:11
25:4 [v] Isa 4:6; 17:10; 27:5; 33:16

whoever climbs out of the pit
will be caught in a snare.

The floodgates of the heavens[c] are opened,
the foundations of the earth shake.[d]
19 The earth is broken up,
the earth is split asunder,[e]
the earth is violently shaken.
20 The earth reels like a drunkard,[f]
it sways like a hut in the wind;
so heavy upon it is the guilt of its rebellion[g]
that it falls — never to rise again.

21 In that day the LORD will punish[h]
the powers in the heavens above
and the kings on the earth below.
22 They will be herded together
like prisoners[i] bound in a dungeon;[j]
they will be shut up in prison
and be punished[a] after many days.[k]
23 The moon will be dismayed,
the sun[l] ashamed;
for the LORD Almighty will reign[m]
on Mount Zion[n] and in Jerusalem,
and before its elders — with great glory.[o]

Praise to the LORD

25

LORD, you are my God;
I will exalt you and praise your name,
for in perfect faithfulness
you have done wonderful things,[p]
things planned[q] long ago.
2 You have made the city a heap of rubble,[r]
the fortified[s] town a ruin,
the foreigners' stronghold[t] a city no more;
it will never be rebuilt.
3 Therefore strong peoples will honor you;
cities of ruthless[u] nations will revere you.
4 You have been a refuge[v] for the poor,
a refuge for the needy in their distress,

[a] 22 Or *released*

24:23 The moon … the sun. Illustrate the heavenly powers (cf. Jer 4:28; Joel 2:30 – 31; 3:14 – 16; Zech 14:6 – 7; Rev 6:12 – 16; 8:12). It is not clear whether these images should be taken literally. Perhaps they should be. On the other hand, they may simply be an attempt to represent visually God's sovereignty over things we think of as permanent. **the LORD Almighty.** See note on 1:9. The culmination of all things is that he alone will be glorified, reigning over his creation in Jerusalem without a rival (cf. Rev 19:4,6).

25:1 – 12 The fortified city and the mountain of God. God is praised not only for his faithfulness and trustworthiness in redemption but also for his judgment. Verses 1 – 5 are a song of praise for deliverance; vv. 6 – 9 depict a divine feast prepared for all the world; but vv. 10 – 12 contain a reminder that God's blessings are not for those who persist in their pride.

25:1 – 5 Yahweh is praised for destroying the cities of the ruthless and the strong, silencing their "song" (v. 5). Instead, he has made himself 'a refuge for the poor [and] … the needy" (v. 4).

25:1 faithfulness. Complete reliability, one of the defining characteristics of Yahweh throughout the OT (Pss 36:5; 89:5; 119:90; Lam 3:23; Hos 2:20). The praise given him here because of this characteristic underlines the theme of this entire division of the book (7:1 — 39:8): divine trustworthiness (see note on 7:1 — 39:8). See also v. 9.

25:4 – 5 Compared to the roar of the "storm" and the intensity of the "heat," some shelters, such as a great rock or a "cloud" may seem unimpressive. But the storm breaks on the rock, and the shadow of a cloud dissipates the heat. So God's help may not call attention to itself, but it is more effective than whatever opposes it (see 18:4).

a shelter from the storm
and a shade from the heat.
For the breath of the ruthless[w]
is like a storm driving against a wall
5 and like the heat of the desert.
You silence[x] the uproar of foreigners;
as heat is reduced by the shadow of a cloud,
so the song of the ruthless is stilled.

6 On this mountain[y] the LORD Almighty will prepare
a feast[z] of rich food for all peoples,
a banquet of aged wine —
the best of meats and the finest of wines.[a]
7 On this mountain he will destroy
the shroud[b] that enfolds all peoples,
the sheet that covers all nations;
8 he will swallow up death[c] forever.
The Sovereign LORD will wipe away the tears[d]
from all faces;
he will remove his people's disgrace[e]
from all the earth.
The LORD has spoken.

9 In that day they will say,

"Surely this is our God;[f]
we trusted in him, and he saved[g] us.
This is the LORD, we trusted in him;
let us rejoice[h] and be glad in his salvation."

10 The hand of the LORD will rest on this mountain;
but Moab[i] will be trampled in their land
as straw is trampled down in the manure.
11 They will stretch out their hands in it,
as swimmers stretch out their hands to swim.
God will bring down[j] their pride[k]
despite the cleverness[a] of their hands.
12 He will bring down your high fortified walls
and lay them low;[l]
he will bring them down to the ground,
to the very dust.

a 11 The meaning of the Hebrew for this word is uncertain.

25:4 [w] Isa 29:5; 49:25
25:5 [x] Jer 51:55
25:6 [y] Isa 2:2 [z] Isa 1:19; Mt 8:11; 22:4 [a] Pr 9:2
25:7 [b] 2Co 3:15-16; Eph 4:18
25:8 [c] Hos 13:14; 1Co 15:54-55* [d] Isa 30:19; 35:10; 51:11; 65:19; Rev 7:17; 21:4 [e] Mt 5:11; 1Pe 4:14
25:9 [f] Isa 40:9 [g] Ps 20:5; Isa 33:22; 35:4; 49:25-26; 60:16 [h] Isa 35:2,10
25:10 [i] Am 2:1-3
25:11 [j] Isa 5:25; 14:26; 16:14 [k] Job 40:12
25:12 [l] Isa 15:1

25:6–9 A description of God's great Messianic banquet at the end of time (Matt 8:11; Luke 14:15; 22:16; cf. 1 Chr 12:38–40). It is remarkable for two reasons: (1) It unequivocally promises that Yahweh "will swallow up death forever" (v. 8; cf. Rev 7:17; 21:4). (2) Even more remarkably, he will do this for "all peoples" (vv. 6,7; see note on vv. 10–12), not just the chosen people of Israel. This is especially poignant in that the ruthless peoples are twice identified as "foreigners" (vv. 2,5), but clearly God intends to include those persons as well in his great "feast" (v. 6). Cf. 56:1–8; 66:18–24 and notes. This points to the work of Christ, whose resurrection is the crowning evidence that he is the Son of God and can give new life to all who come to him in repentance and faith (Rom 6:1–10).

25:8 his people's disgrace. The shame that results from a failed trust (cf. Ps 25:2–3). When the Assyrians and then the Babylonians captured first Israel and then Judah, it seemed as though Yahweh had failed his people and that their vaunted trust in him had been worthless; they were shamed (cf. Ezek 36:20). But in the end, God's people will be able to hold up their heads joyfully, their trust vindicated in every particular (v. 9; cf. 54:4; Ps 27:5–6).

25:10–12 In typical fashion, Isaiah does not allow a promise to be misinterpreted. "All peoples" (mentioned in vv. 6,7) does not include everyone indiscriminately. Those who continue to defy God in their "pride" and "cleverness" (v. 11) will not feel his hand of deliverance. Instead, he will "bring them down to the ground" (v. 12).

25:11 it. Unclear; perhaps a manure pit (see v. 10).

26:1 [m]Isa 14:32 [n]Isa 60:18
26:2 [o]Isa 54:14; 58:8; 62:2
26:4 [p]Isa 12:2; 50:10
26:5 [q]Isa 25:12
26:6 [r]Isa 3:15
26:7 [s]Isa 42:16
26:8 [t]Isa 56:1 [u]Isa 12:4
26:9 [v]Ps 63:1; 78:34; Isa 55:6 [w]Mt 6:33
26:10 [x]Isa 32:6 [y]Isa 22:12-13; Hos 11:7; Jn 5:37-38; Ro 2:4

A Song of Praise

26 In that day this song will be sung in the land of Judah:

We have a strong city;[m]
God makes salvation
its walls[n] and ramparts.
[2] Open the gates
that the righteous[o] nation may enter,
the nation that keeps faith.
[3] You will keep in perfect peace
those whose minds are steadfast,
because they trust in you.
[4] Trust[p] in the LORD forever,
for the LORD, the LORD himself, is the Rock eternal.
[5] He humbles those who dwell on high,
he lays the lofty city low;
he levels it to the ground[q]
and casts it down to the dust.
[6] Feet trample it down—
the feet of the oppressed,
the footsteps of the poor.[r]

[7] The path of the righteous is level;
you, the Upright One, make the way of the righteous smooth.[s]
[8] Yes, LORD, walking in the way of your laws,[a][t]
we wait for you;
your name[u] and renown
are the desire of our hearts.
[9] My soul yearns for you in the night;
in the morning my spirit longs[v] for you.
When your judgments come upon the earth,
the people of the world learn righteousness.[w]
[10] But when grace is shown to the wicked,
they do not learn righteousness;
even in a land of uprightness they go on doing evil[x]
and do not regard[y] the majesty of the LORD.

[a] 8 Or *judgments*

26:1—27:13 *The Lord's Day.* This section reflects on the meaning of the victory portrayed in the previous chapters. "In that day" appears four times (26:1; 27:1,2,12). The twin themes continue: "city" (26:1,5; 27:10) and "song" (26:1; cf. 27:2). The section has five stanzas: a song of thanksgiving (26:1–6), longing for God's judgments in the world (26:7–15), a lament over the people's helplessness (26:16–18), Yahweh's power (26:19—27:1), and God's passion for his vineyard (27:2–13).

26:1–6 In contrast to the "song of the ruthless" (25:5), this is a "song" about "salvation" (v. 1). God has brought "the lofty city low" (v. 5), and in its place he has erected "a strong city ... that the righteous ... may enter" (vv. 1–2; see 54:11–12). As in 25:9, the response to this unmerited favor is a renewed declaration of trust (vv. 3–4). Why trust the arrogant human nations? God has brought them down and the feet of the oppressed walk on them (v. 6). Trust instead in Yahweh, "the Rock eternal" (v. 4).

26:3 perfect peace. Complete wholeness that God can bring into a nation or a person who will trust completely in him. It is not merely absence of conflict, but an integration of all the separate parts. See "Shalom," p. 2693. **minds.** Cf. Gen 6:5; 1 Chr 28:9; 29:18.

26:7–15 The righteous person not only praises God for a smooth path to walk on (v. 7) but also prays that God will soon vindicate his people by punishing the wicked (v. 11). As long as God's grace (v. 10) allows his enemies (v. 11) to continue their oppressive, evil ways, they will not turn from those ways. Isaiah then reflects on what God has done for his people in the past (vv. 12–15). Rulers who oppressed them in the past are "now dead" (v. 14), and Yahweh has gained glory for himself by extending "all the borders of the land" (v. 15). This might reflect the days of the judges (oppressive rulers) and the subsequent kingdom period (extended borders). Yahweh replaced the foreign rulers with the Davidic dynasty. That memory fortifies the righteous person to trust that it can happen again.

26:7–9 A description of the righteous life. Righteousness involves a walk, a pattern of behavior that is shaped by God's regulations ("laws," v. 8) for human life. It is behavior that is shaped by continual trust ("wait," v. 8) in God and a passion for his reputation ("name and renown," v. 8) in the world. It is characterized by a longing to know God personally ("my soul yearns for you," v. 9).

[11] LORD, your hand is lifted high,
but they do not see[z] it.
Let them see your zeal for your people and be put to shame;
let the fire[a] reserved for your enemies consume them.

[12] LORD, you establish peace for us;
all that we have accomplished you have done for us.
[13] LORD our God, other lords[b] besides you have ruled over us,
but your name alone do we honor.[c]
[14] They are now dead,[d] they live no more;
their spirits do not rise.
You punished them and brought them to ruin;[e]
you wiped out all memory of them.
[15] You have enlarged the nation, LORD;
you have enlarged the nation.
You have gained glory for yourself;
you have extended all the borders[f] of the land.

[16] LORD, they came to you in their distress;[g]
when you disciplined them,
they could barely whisper a prayer.[a]
[17] As a pregnant woman about to give birth[h]
writhes and cries out in her pain,
so were we in your presence, LORD.
[18] We were with child, we writhed in labor,
but we gave birth[i] to wind.
We have not brought salvation[j] to the earth,
and the people of the world have not come to life.

[19] But your dead[k] will live, LORD;
their bodies will rise—
let those who dwell in the dust
wake up and shout for joy—
your dew is like the dew of the morning;
the earth will give birth to her dead.[l]

[20] Go, my people, enter your rooms
and shut the doors[m] behind you;
hide[n] yourselves for a little while
until his wrath has passed by.[o]
[21] See, the LORD is coming[p] out of his dwelling[q]
to punish[r] the people of the earth for their sins.

[a] *16* The meaning of the Hebrew for this clause is uncertain.

26:11 [z] Isa 44:9,18 [a] Heb 10:27
26:13 [b] Isa 2:8; 10:5,11 [c] Isa 63:7
26:14 [d] Dt 4:28 [e] Isa 10:3
26:15 [f] Isa 33:17
26:16 [g] Hos 5:15
26:17 [h] Jn 16:21
26:18 [i] Isa 33:11; 59:4 [j] Ps 17:14
26:19 [k] Isa 25:8; Eph 5:14 [l] Eze 37:1-14; Da 12:2
26:20 [m] Ex 12:23 [n] Ps 91:1,4 [o] Ps 30:5; Isa 54:7-8
26:21 [p] Jude 1:14 [q] Mic 1:3 [r] Isa 13:9,11; 30:12-14

26:11 put to shame. See note on 25:8.
26:12–15 Repeatedly referring to God as "you" underlines the point: "all that we have accomplished you have done for us" (v. 12). Neither the people of Israel nor anyone else can save themselves.
26:13 Israel did not always give "honor" to God's "name alone," which is made clear by the various prophets' diatribes against the worship of idols. But there were those who did give God honor in every age, even when many others did not (e.g., Judg 6:25–28; 1 Kgs 19:18; Jer 26:24).
26:16–18 Underlines the thought of vv. 12–15: The people of Israel were helpless to bring "salvation to the earth" (v. 18) or even to themselves. They were like a "pregnant woman" (v. 17) unable to give birth. Cf. 37:3.
26:19—27:1 Three related statements assert God's grace and power in spite of the helplessness in 26:16–18.
26:19 their bodies. This verse, like 25:7–8, asserts the reality of the resurrection. Yahweh can defeat every enemy, including the final one: death. Although some would say this refers only to the restoration of the people to the land, it is more likely that it refers to personal, bodily resurrection, particularly in light of 25:8 (see note there; cf. Dan 12:2; see "Death and Resurrection," p. 2670).
26:20–21 Seems to answer the plea in vv. 9–11. Israel should continue waiting (cf. v. 8) in quiet faith ("enter your rooms"), confident in the assurance that God will act to vindicate their faith by bringing about the punishment of "the earth" (as ch. 24 predicted).

26:21 [s] Job 16:18; Lk 11:50-51
27:1 [t] Isa 34:6; 66:16 [u] Job 3:8 [v] Ps 74:13
27:2 [w] Jer 2:21
27:3 [x] Isa 58:11
27:4 [y] Isa 10:17; Mt 3:12; Heb 6:8
27:5 [z] Isa 25:4 [a] Job 22:21; Ro 5:1; 2Co 5:20
27:6 [b] Hos 14:5-6 [c] Isa 37:31
27:7 [d] Isa 37:36-38
27:8 [e] Isa 50:1; 54:7

The earth will disclose the blood[s] shed on it;
the earth will conceal its slain no longer.

Deliverance of Israel

27 In that day,

the LORD will punish with his sword[t]—
his fierce, great and powerful sword—
Leviathan[u] the gliding serpent,
Leviathan the coiling serpent;
he will slay the monster[v] of the sea.

2 In that day—

"Sing about a fruitful vineyard:[w]
3 I, the LORD, watch over it;
I water[x] it continually.
I guard it day and night
so that no one may harm it.
4 I am not angry.
If only there were briers and thorns confronting me!
I would march against them in battle;
I would set them all on fire.[y]
5 Or else let them come to me for refuge;[z]
let them make peace[a] with me,
yes, let them make peace with me."

6 In days to come Jacob will take root,
Israel will bud and blossom[b]
and fill all the world with fruit.[c]

7 Has the LORD struck her
as he struck[d] down those who struck her?
Has she been killed
as those were killed who killed her?
8 By warfare[a] and exile[e] you contend with her—
with his fierce blast he drives her out,
as on a day the east wind blows.

[a] 8 See Septuagint; the meaning of the Hebrew for this word is uncertain.

27:1 Graphically illustrates the point in 26:19–21 by utilizing the language of the Canaanite myth of origins. **Leviathan.** A "monster" (Ps 74:13) representing the chaotic watery matter from which people of the ancient Near East thought all things emerged and that threatened to plunge the natural order back into chaos (cf. Job 41; Ps 74:13–17). They believed that one of the gods (usually Baal) defeated Leviathan in primordial time, and they thought that performance of the myth would ensure the continuing effect of that victory in time and space. Scripture nowhere indicates that such a myth was ever normative for Israelite faith. The point here is that Yahweh has all power in the universe and can defeat the moral wickedness that constitutes the true threat to life. (See "Rahab" in 30:7; 51:9–10.)

27:2–13 This song of the Lord's "vineyard" (v. 2), i.e., Israel, is reminiscent of ch. 5, but it depicts Israel positively rather than negatively. Like the earlier example, this passage begins with a metaphor (vv. 2–6) and then interprets it (vv. 7–13). It concludes chs. 24–27 by asserting that Yahweh is indeed sovereign over history.

27:2–6 Yahweh loves Israel and is determined to protect her. He wishes that there were "briers and thorns" (v. 4; see 5:6; 7:23–25; 9:18; 10:17; 32:13; cf. 33:12) that he might chop them out with his hoe and "set them all on fire" (v. 4). This contrasts with ch. 5, where Yahweh refuses to cultivate the vineyard because of its bitter grapes. Here Yahweh asserts again that the judgments are intended not to be final but to result in purification and new hope.

27:5 Continuing the theme from ch. 25, God's anger against the oppressors of Israel is not implacable. He is not determined to destroy them. If they will "make peace" with him, they too can find "refuge" in him.

27:6 fill all the world with fruit. Israel's election is not merely for itself but for the sake of the world (see note on 2:1–5; cf. Eph 3:6; Col 1:26–27).

27:7–13 This explains God's work with his vineyard. If the people of Israel have suffered, it is not because God wishes to destroy them; in fact, they should not compare themselves to the enemy nations that will be removed from the earth. Rather, God intends to discipline (not destroy) them, to purify (not extinguish) them (vv. 7–9). The enemy nations ("the fortified city," v. 10) are "desolate" (v. 10); denying their Maker, they receive "no compassion" from him (v. 11). The people of Israel, on the other hand, like kernels of grain that have endured the

9 By this, then, will Jacob's guilt be atoned for,
and this will be the full fruit of the removal of his sin:[f]
When he makes all the altar stones
to be like limestone crushed to pieces,
no Asherah poles[a][g] or incense altars
will be left standing.
10 The fortified city stands desolate,[h]
an abandoned settlement, forsaken like the wilderness;
there the calves graze,
there they lie down;[i]
they strip its branches bare.
11 When its twigs are dry, they are broken off
and women come and make fires with them.
For this is a people without understanding;[j]
so their Maker has no compassion on them,
and their Creator[k] shows them no favor.[l]

12 In that day the LORD will thresh from the flowing Euphrates to the Wadi of Egypt,[m] and you, Israel, will be gathered[n] up one by one. 13 And in that day a great trumpet[o] will sound. Those who were
perishing in Assyria and those who were exiled in Egypt[p] will come and worship the LORD on the holy
mountain in Jerusalem.

Woe to the Leaders of Ephraim and Judah

28 Woe to that wreath, the pride of Ephraim's[q] drunkards,
to the fading flower, his glorious beauty,
set on the head of a fertile valley[r] —
to that city, the pride of those laid low by wine![s]
2 See, the Lord has one who is powerful[t] and strong.
Like a hailstorm[u] and a destructive wind,[v]
like a driving rain and a flooding[w] downpour,
he will throw it forcefully to the ground.
3 That wreath, the pride of Ephraim's[x] drunkards,
will be trampled underfoot.

27:9 [f]Ro 11:27* [g]Ex 34:13
27:10 [h]Isa 32:14; Jer 26:6 [i]Isa 17:2
27:11 [j]Dt 32:28; Isa 1:3; Jer 8:7 [k]Dt 32:18; Isa 43:1,7,15; 44:1-2, 21,24 [l]Isa 9:17
27:12 [m]Ge 15:18 [n]Dt 30:4; Isa 11:12; 17:6
27:13 [o]Lev 25:9; Mt 24:31 [p]Isa 19:21,25
28:1 [q]ver 3; Isa 9:9 [r]ver 4 [s]Hos 7:5
28:2 [t]Isa 40:10 [u]Isa 30:30; Eze 13:11 [v]Isa 29:6 [w]Isa 8:7
28:3 [x]ver 1

[a] *9* That is, wooden symbols of the goddess Asherah

harsh experience of threshing, will be gathered up from the threshing floors of Assyria and Egypt and brought back to "the holy mountain in Jerusalem" (v. 13; see 24:23; 25:6,7,10; cf. 11:9; 65:25).

27:9 This suggests that either the punishment of "exile" (v. 8) or the work of removing "altar stones" and "Asherah poles" (see note on 17:8) will somehow atone for Israel's sins. Exile is the result of sin, and removing idolatry is the appropriate response to the atonement, indicating that it has truly been received. But atonement is the work of God's grace, as 52:13—53:12 makes clear (cf. 6:7; Rom 3:25; Heb 2:17).

27:11 a people without understanding. Applies to Israel in 1:3; here the context (the "fortified city," v. 10) suggests that it applies to the nations. The prophet's bold assertion is that Yahweh is the "Maker" and "Creator" of the whole world, including all the enemy peoples.

28:1—33:24 *Woe to Those Who Will Not Wait.* Chs. 13–23 present the particulars of Yahweh's lordship over the nations; chs. 24–27 express this theme in a more generalized way; and chs. 28–33 return to a particular treatment, looking at the refusal of Ephraim (the northern kingdom of Israel) and Judah to trust God in the face of the Assyrian threat. They look to their human leaders to protect them, accepting their policy of Egyptian alliance instead of looking to their true leader, the divine King. The judgments on this failure to trust are expressed in a series of woe messages (28:1–29; 29:1–14,15–24; 30:1–33; 31:1—32:20; 33:1–24).

28:1–29 *Woe to False Leaders.* Beginning to address "Ephraim's drunkards" (v. 1), the message changes at v. 14 to speak to the "scoffers who rule this people in Jerusalem." Given that the remainder of the section (chs. 29–33) seems to address Judah and Jerusalem, it is possible that vv. 1–13 are a message spoken to the people of Israel before the fall of Samaria in 722 BC; Isaiah reuses it here to try to make the point with the leaders of Jerusalem after that date: If Samaria could not escape its doom, what makes you think you can escape unless you turn back to trust in Yahweh?

28:1–13 The leaders of Ephraim are "drunkards" (v. 1). Incapable of pointing their people to their true hope in Yahweh (vv. 5–6), they rely on rote commands (v. 10). Consequently, God will have to teach them the truth through people who speak in "strange tongues" (v. 11) and who will also give commands.

28:1–4 "Wreath" (vv. 1,3) is probably used with a double meaning: it can refer to party attire on the head of a drunken reveler, but the particular language of vv. 1,4 suggests that it also describes the "city" (v. 1) of Samaria, whose crenellated walls around the top of the hill set in a "fertile valley" (v. 4) looked like a wreath on someone's head. But the Lord will hurl that wreath "to the ground" (v. 2).

28:4 [y]ver 1 [z]Hos 9:10; Na 3:12
28:5 [a]Isa 62:3
28:6 [b]Isa 11:2-4; 32:1, 16 [c]Jn 5:30 [d]2Ch 32:8
28:7 [e]Isa 22:13 [f]Isa 56:10-12 [g]Isa 24:2 [h]Isa 9:15 [i]Isa 29:11; Hos 4:11
28:8 [j]Jer 48:26
28:9 [k]ver 26; Isa 30:20; 48:17; 50:4; 54:13 [l]Ps 131:2 [m]Heb 5:12-13
28:11 [n]Isa 33:19 [o]1Co 14:21*
28:12 [p]Isa 11:10; Mt 11:28-29

4 That fading flower, his glorious beauty,
set on the head of a fertile valley,[y]
will be like figs[z] ripe before harvest —
as soon as people see them and take them in hand,
they swallow them.

5 In that day the LORD Almighty
will be a glorious crown,[a]
a beautiful wreath
for the remnant of his people.
6 He will be a spirit of justice[b]
to the one who sits in judgment,[c]
a source of strength
to those who turn back the battle[d] at the gate.

7 And these also stagger from wine[e]
and reel[f] from beer:
Priests[g] and prophets[h] stagger from beer
and are befuddled with wine;
they reel from beer,
they stagger when seeing visions,[i]
they stumble when rendering decisions.
8 All the tables are covered with vomit[j]
and there is not a spot without filth.

9 "Who is it he is trying to teach?[k]
To whom is he explaining his message?
To children weaned[l] from their milk,[m]
to those just taken from the breast?
10 For it is:
Do this, do that,
a rule for this, a rule for that[a];
a little here, a little there."

11 Very well then, with foreign lips and strange
tongues[n]
God will speak to this people,[o]
12 to whom he said,
"This is the resting place, let the weary rest";[p]
and, "This is the place of repose" —
but they would not listen.
13 So then, the word of the LORD to them will become:
Do this, do that,
a rule for this, a rule for that;
a little here, a little there —

[a] *10* Hebrew / *sav lasav sav lasav / kav lakav kav lakav* (probably meaningless sounds mimicking the prophet's words); also in verse 13

28:5 – 6 Chs. 28 – 33 alternate between representing the false leadership of humans and the true leadership of God. It begins here briefly and continues with larger and larger segments. Ephraim's (and Judah's) true "wreath" is "the LORD Almighty" (see notes on 1:9,24). He can inspire both civil and military leaders.
28:5 remnant. See note on 11:11.
28:7 – 8 The drunkenness described here is probably both metaphoric and literal. Because these leaders are selfishly motivated, they are blind to the truth of God's revelation (29:9), but they are also prone to the kind of self-indulgence that results in the abuse of alcohol.
28:9 – 10 Having no real experience or understanding of God, all the leaders can offer the people are prescriptions from the law to be learned by rote. The Hebrew of v. 10 may well be a mockery of the rote repetitions the leaders offer (see NIV text note on v. 10).
28:11 – 13 Since the people "would not listen" (v. 12) to the words of their true leaders, God would turn them over to the Assyrians, who spoke

so that as they go they will fall backward;
they will be injured[q] and snared and captured.[r]

14 Therefore hear the word of the LORD,[s] you scoffers
who rule this people in Jerusalem.
15 You boast, "We have entered into a covenant with death,
with the realm of the dead we have made an agreement.
When an overwhelming scourge sweeps by,[t]
it cannot touch us,
for we have made a lie[u] our refuge
and falsehood[a] our hiding place.[v]"

16 So this is what the Sovereign LORD says:

"See, I lay a stone in Zion, a tested stone,[w]
a precious cornerstone for a sure foundation;
the one who relies on it
will never be stricken with panic.[x]
17 I will make justice[y] the measuring line
and righteousness the plumb line;[z]
hail will sweep away your refuge, the lie,
and water will overflow your hiding place.
18 Your covenant with death will be annulled;
your agreement with the realm of the dead will
not stand.[a]
When the overwhelming scourge sweeps by,[b]
you will be beaten down[c] by it.
19 As often as it comes it will carry you away;[d]
morning after morning, by day and by night,
it will sweep through."

The understanding of this message
will bring sheer terror.[e]
20 The bed is too short to stretch out on,
the blanket too narrow to wrap around you.[f]
21 The LORD will rise up as he did at Mount Perazim,[g]
he will rouse himself as in the Valley of Gibeon[h] —
to do his work,[i] his strange work,
and perform his task, his alien task.
22 Now stop your mocking,
or your chains will become heavier;
the Lord, the LORD Almighty, has told me
of the destruction decreed[j] against the whole land.[k]

[a] 15 Or *false gods*

28:13 [q] Mt 21:44 [r] Isa 8:15
28:14 [s] Isa 1:10
28:15 [t] ver 2, 18; Isa 8:7-8; 30:28; Da 11:22 [u] Isa 9:15 [v] Isa 29:15
28:16 [w] Ps 118:22; Isa 8:14-15; Mt 21:42; Ac 4:11; Eph 2:20 [x] Ro 9:33*; 10:11*; 1Pe 2:6*
28:17 [y] Isa 5:16 [z] 2Ki 21:13
28:18 [a] Isa 7:7 [b] ver 15 [c] Da 8:13
28:19 [d] 2Ki 24:2 [e] Job 18:11
28:20 [f] Isa 59:6
28:21 [g] 1Ch 14:11 [h] Jos 10:10, 12; 1Ch 14:16 [i] Isa 10:12; Lk 19:41-44
28:22 [j] Isa 10:22 [k] Isa 10:23

with "foreign lips" (v. 11). Their rote commands would lead to fall and capture.
28:14–29 Isaiah addresses the leaders of Jerusalem.
28:14 scoffers. One of the strongest words of condemnation in the OT. It speaks of one who knows the right but mocks it (v. 22; see also 5:18–20 and notes; cf. Ps 1:1; Prov 3:34; 21:24).
28:15 covenant with death. Perhaps mockingly refers to an alliance with Egypt (cf. 29:15 and note on 29:15–16; 30:1–2; 31:1). But whatever it is, it will do no good (v. 18). Yahweh will defeat death; Israel can do nothing to defeat it.
28:16–17 The "Sovereign LORD" (see note on 7:5–9) has established fixed standards of measurements that will show the falsity of all human pretenses. His Messiah ("cornerstone"; see Eph 2:20; 1 Pet 2:6) will reveal true "justice" and "righteousness" (cf. 16:5). In contrast to the injustice and oppression of the world, he will show the world how it was intended to be ruled. So "Zion" will be the true city of God, as opposed to the Jerusalem of human construction.
28:20 All human attempts to ensure one's own security will fail.
28:21 Mount Perazim. Where Yahweh attacked the Philistines (2 Sam 5:20). **Gibeon.** Where Yahweh used hail against the Amorites (Josh 10:10–12). **strange work.** Now Israel has become God's enemy (see 1:24).

28:25 [l] Mt 23:23 [m] Ex 9:32
28:29 [n] Isa 9:6 [o] Ro 11:33
29:1 [p] Isa 22:12-13 [q] 2Sa 5:9 [r] Isa 1:14
29:2 [s] Isa 3:26; La 2:5
29:3 [t] Lk 19:43-44
29:4 [u] Isa 8:19

23 Listen and hear my voice;
pay attention and hear what I say.
24 When a farmer plows for planting, does he plow
continually?
Does he keep on breaking up and working the soil?
25 When he has leveled the surface,
does he not sow caraway and scatter cumin?[l]
Does he not plant wheat in its place,[a]
barley in its plot,[a]
and spelt[m] in its field?
26 His God instructs him
and teaches him the right way.

27 Caraway is not threshed with a sledge,
nor is the wheel of a cart rolled over cumin;
caraway is beaten out with a rod,
and cumin with a stick.
28 Grain must be ground to make bread;
so one does not go on threshing it forever.
The wheels of a threshing cart may be rolled over it,
but one does not use horses to grind grain.
29 All this also comes from the LORD Almighty,
whose plan is wonderful,[n]
whose wisdom is magnificent.[o]

Woe to David's City

29 Woe[p] to you, Ariel, Ariel,[q]
the city where David settled!
Add year to year
and let your cycle of festivals[r] go on.
2 Yet I will besiege Ariel;
she will mourn and lament,[s]
she will be to me like an altar hearth.[b]
3 I will encamp against you on all sides;
I will encircle[t] you with towers
and set up my siege works against you.
4 Brought low, you will speak from the ground;
your speech will mumble[u] out of the dust.

[a] *25* The meaning of the Hebrew for this word is uncertain. [b] *2* The Hebrew for *altar hearth* sounds like the Hebrew for *Ariel*.

28:23–29 A graphic illustration: an uneducated farmer understands the ways of nature according to the "plan" and "wisdom" of the Lord Almighty (v. 29), but Ephraim and Judah, led by drunkards and scoffers, do not understand that they should trust God, not human nations.

28:27 Caraway ... cumin. Very small seeds that cannot be separated from their husks (as wheat and barley can) by threshing the stalks with a sledge or running over them with "the wheels of a threshing cart" (v. 28). They must be "beaten" with a "rod" or "stick."

29:1–14 *Woe to David's City.* This message is composed of two parts: vv. 1–8 promise judgment and redemption, and vv. 9–14 recall the theme of 28:1–13: an inability to understand what God is saying and the harsh consequences resulting from that failure.

29:1–8 On the one hand, Ariel (see note on v. 1) is going to be "brought low" (v. 4) by God ("I will besiege," v. 2). On the other hand, all those "nations that fight against Ariel" (v. 7) will be defeated, becoming "like fine dust" (v. 5). Their dreams of conquest will be frustrated (v. 8). This could refer to (1) the attack of Sennacherib when his plan to conquer Jerusalem was frustrated or (2) the larger theme that God, using the nations, brings Israel down and for that very reason can finally defeat those nations and take his people out of their hands (cf. 49:24–26 and note).

29:1 Ariel. Jerusalem, as indicated by the reference to David and its description as the place where the festivals occurred. The exact significance of the name is unknown, though the two most likely are "city of God" and "lion of God." It sounds like the word translated "altar hearth" (see NIV text note on v. 2).

29:3 towers. Used by besieging forces to fire missiles down into the besieged city.

29:4–5 Yahweh may bring his city down into the "dust," but he will also make Jerusalem's enemies "like fine dust."

Your voice will come ghostlike from the earth;
out of the dust your speech will whisper.

5 But your many enemies will become like fine dust,
the ruthless hordes like blown chaff.[v]
Suddenly,[w] in an instant,
6 the LORD Almighty will come
with thunder and earthquake[x] and great noise,
with windstorm and tempest and flames of a devouring fire.
7 Then the hordes of all the nations[y] that fight against Ariel,
that attack her and her fortress and besiege her,
will be as it is with a dream,[z]
with a vision in the night—
8 as when a hungry person dreams of eating,
but awakens[a] hungry still;
as when a thirsty person dreams of drinking,
but awakens faint and thirsty still.
So will it be with the hordes of all the nations
that fight against Mount Zion.

9 Be stunned and amazed,
blind yourselves and be sightless;
be drunk,[b] but not from wine,[c]
stagger, but not from beer.
10 The LORD has brought over you a deep sleep:
He has sealed your eyes[d] (the prophets);[e]
he has covered your heads (the seers).[f]

11 For you this whole vision is nothing but words sealed[g] in a scroll. And if you give the scroll to
someone who can read, and say, "Read this, please," they will answer, "I can't; it is sealed." 12 Or if you
give the scroll to someone who cannot read, and say, "Read this, please," they will answer, "I don't
know how to read."

13 The Lord says:

"These people come near to me with their mouth
and honor me with their lips,
but their hearts are far from me.[h]
Their worship of me
is based on merely human rules they have been taught.[a][i]
14 Therefore once more I will astound these people
with wonder upon wonder;[j]
the wisdom of the wise[k] will perish,
the intelligence of the intelligent will vanish.[l]"
15 Woe to those who go to great depths
to hide their plans from the LORD,

29:5 [v] Isa 17:13 [w] Isa 17:14; 1Th 5:3
29:6 [x] Mt 24:7; Mk 13:8; Lk 21:11; Rev 11:19
29:7 [y] Mic 4:11-12; Zec 12:9 [z] Job 20:8
29:8 [a] Ps 73:20
29:9 [b] Isa 51:17 [c] Isa 51:21-22
29:10 [d] Ps 69:23; Isa 6:9-10; Ro 11:8* [e] Mic 3:6 [f] 1Sa 9:9
29:11 [g] Isa 8:16; Mt 13:11; Rev 5:1-2
29:13 [h] Eze 33:31 [i] Mt 15:8-9*; Mk 7:6-7*; Col 2:22
29:14 [j] Hab 1:5 [k] Jer 8:9; 49:7 [l] Isa 6:9-10; 1Co 1:19*

[a] *13* Hebrew; Septuagint *They worship me in vain; / their teachings are merely human rules*

29:7–8 The "dreams" belong to both the attackers and the attacked. The attackers' dreams of destroying the city will be just that: dreams. It will not actually happen. For the attacked, the siege will be like a bad dream that disappears at dawn.
29:9–14 God's promises of deliverance to those who will trust him are perfectly clear, but the prophets of Judah are just as "drunk" and "blind" (v. 9) as their counterparts in the northern kingdom of Israel (cf. 28:7–8). God's words are unintelligible to them; they are like children who "cannot read" (v. 12) or even open a scroll (v. 11). Their religion has no personal reality ("their hearts are far from me," v. 13); it is merely a matter of carrying out human rules (cf. 28:9–10).
29:14 Quoted in part in 1 Cor 1:19.
29:15–24 *Woe to Those Who Try to Hide Their Plans From Yahweh.* The message has two parts: (1) Isaiah condemns refusing to trust Yahweh and planning to make an alliance with Egypt (vv. 15–16; see 30:1–2; 31:1). (2) But God promises that he will defend his people and that this alliance with Egypt is both unnecessary and futile (vv. 17–24).
29:15–16 Probably those who are urging an alliance with Egypt are

29:15 [m] Ps 10:11-13; 94:7; Isa 57:12 [n] Job 22:13
29:16 [o] Isa 45:9; 64:8; Ro 9:20-21*
29:17 [p] Ps 84:6 [q] Isa 32:15
29:18 [r] Mk 7:37 [s] Isa 32:3; 35:5; Mt 11:5
29:19 [t] Isa 61:1; Mt 5:5; 11:29 [u] Isa 14:30; Mt 11:5; Jas 1:9; 2:5
29:20 [v] Isa 28:22 [w] Isa 59:4; Mic 2:1
29:21 [x] Am 5:10,15 [y] Isa 5:23; 32:7
29:22 [z] Isa 41:8; 63:16 [a] Isa 49:23
29:23 [b] Isa 49:20-26 [c] Isa 19:25
29:24 [d] Isa 28:7; Heb 5:2 [e] Isa 41:20; 60:16 [f] Isa 30:21
30:1 [g] Isa 29:15 [h] Isa 1:2 [i] Isa 8:12

who do their work in darkness and think,
"Who sees us?[m] Who will know?"[n]
16 You turn things upside down,
as if the potter were thought to be like the clay!
Shall what is formed say to the one who formed it,
"You did not make me"?
Can the pot say to the potter,[o]
"You know nothing"?

17 In a very short time, will not Lebanon be turned into a fertile field[p]
and the fertile field seem like a forest?[q]
18 In that day the deaf[r] will hear the words of the scroll,
and out of gloom and darkness
the eyes of the blind will see.[s]
19 Once more the humble[t] will rejoice in the LORD;
the needy[u] will rejoice in the Holy One of Israel.
20 The ruthless will vanish,
the mockers[v] will disappear,
and all who have an eye for evil[w] will be cut down—
21 those who with a word make someone out to be guilty,
who ensnare the defender in court[x]
and with false testimony deprive the innocent of justice.[y]

22 Therefore this is what the LORD, who redeemed Abraham,[z] says to the descendants of Jacob:

"No longer will Jacob be ashamed;[a]
no longer will their faces grow pale.
23 When they see among them their children,[b]
the work of my hands,[c]
they will keep my name holy;
they will acknowledge the holiness of the Holy One of Jacob,
and will stand in awe of the God of Israel.
24 Those who are wayward[d] in spirit will gain understanding;[e]
those who complain will accept instruction."[f]

Woe to the Obstinate Nation

30 "Woe[g] to the obstinate children,"[h]
declares the LORD,
"to those who carry out plans that are not mine,
forming an alliance,[i] but not by my Spirit,
heaping sin upon sin;

trying to keep Isaiah from hearing about these "plans," knowing he will disapprove. But trying to keep anything from the Lord and his man is like a "pot" telling the "potter" that he does not know what he is doing.
29:17–24 All the elaborate secret plans are unnecessary because God already determined that the Assyrians will not be victorious (cf. 30:31). The "deaf" and "blind" (v. 18) and the "humble" and "needy" (v. 19) will survive to worship "the Holy One of Israel" (v. 19; see note on 1:4), but the powerful and unjust ("ruthless" and "mockers," v. 20) will be swept away.
29:17 This probably illustrates the reversal between humble and proud that the rest of the segment (vv. 18–24) is forecasting. The lush forest of Lebanon will be reduced to a plowed field, while the former lowly field will become a lush forest.
29:18 hear ... see. Ordinary people, formerly "deaf" and "blind," will perceive the truth that the intelligentsia cannot make out (cf. vv. 14,24).
29:21 See 5:23.
29:22 ashamed. See note on 25:8.
29:23 children. Exiled Israel pictures herself as a widow whose children all died. But God promises that she will have more children than she can imagine (49:17–21; 54:1–8; cf. 47:8–9; 48:18–19).
30:1–33 *Woe to the Obstinate Nation.* Like the previous message, this divides into one of judgment (vv. 1–18) and salvation (vv. 19–33). The judgment falls because the people trust Egypt (v. 2), not Yahweh (v. 15). The salvation comes because Yahweh is "gracious ... when you cry for help!" (v. 19). The proportion of the promises of salvation increases through the section (see note on 28:1—33:24).
30:1–18 This message of judgment has two parts: it is futile to trust in Egypt (vv. 1–7) and foolish not to trust the Lord (vv. 8–18).
30:1–2 carry out plans ... without consulting me. Doing so is dangerous (cf. Gen 16; Josh 9:14; 1 Kgs 22:1–38; Prov 16:1; Jer 10:23; 42:19–22).

2 who go down to Egypt[j]
without consulting[k] me;
who look for help to Pharaoh's protection,[l]
to Egypt's shade for refuge.
3 But Pharaoh's protection will be to your shame,
Egypt's shade will bring you disgrace.[m]
4 Though they have officials in Zoan[n]
and their envoys have arrived in Hanes,
5 everyone will be put to shame
because of a people[o] useless to them,
who bring neither help nor advantage,
but only shame and disgrace."

6 A prophecy concerning the animals of the Negev:

Through a land of hardship and distress,[p]
of lions and lionesses,
of adders and darting snakes,[q]
the envoys carry their riches on donkeys' backs,
their treasures[r] on the humps of camels,
to that unprofitable nation,
7 to Egypt, whose help is utterly useless.
Therefore I call her
Rahab the Do-Nothing.

8 Go now, write it on a tablet for them,
inscribe it on a scroll,[s]
that for the days to come
it may be an everlasting witness.
9 For these are rebellious people, deceitful[t] children,
children unwilling to listen to the LORD's instruction.[u]
10 They say to the seers,
"See no more visions[v]!"
and to the prophets,
"Give us no more visions of what is right!
Tell us pleasant things,[w]
prophesy illusions.[x]
11 Leave this way,
get off this path,
and stop confronting[y] us
with the Holy One of Israel!"

12 Therefore this is what the Holy One of Israel says:

30:2 [j] Isa 31:1 [k] Nu 27:21 [l] Isa 36:9
30:3 [m] Isa 20:4-5; 36:6
30:4 [n] Isa 19:11
30:5 [o] ver 7
30:6 [p] Ex 5:10,21; Isa 8:22; Jer 11:4 [q] Dt 8:15 [r] Isa 15:7
30:8 [s] Isa 8:1; Hab 2:2
30:9 [t] Isa 28:15; 59:3-4 [u] Isa 1:10
30:10 [v] Jer 11:21; Am 7:13 [w] 1Ki 22:8 [x] Eze 13:7; Ro 16:18
30:11 [y] Job 21:14

30:3 Pharaoh's protection. Results only in "shame" and "disgrace" (see note on 25:8).
30:6–7 Isaiah graphically pictures a caravan laden with "riches" struggling through the Sinai desert ("Negev") toward Egypt. Presumably the Assyrian armies closed the direct coast road. But even if the caravan survives all the difficulty, it will be for nothing.
30:7 Rahab the Do-Nothing. In 51:9–10 Rahab is the name given to a dragon (Hebrew *tannîn*), which Ezekiel particularly associated with Egypt (Ezek 29:3; 32:2). (The name of Rahab the Canaanite prostitute is spelled differently in Hebrew.) This seems to be another version of the tale of the chaos monster (see note on 27:1), but Isaiah says that this monster, Egypt, is really toothless.
30:8–18 The people refuse to trust Yahweh. The "rebellious people" (v. 9) tell the prophets to stop prophesying "what is right" (v. 10), and Isaiah tells them what will happen to them as a result (vv. 8–14). Verses 15–18 contrast what the Lord would like to do for them with what is actually going to happen to them.
30:8 Cf. 8:1; Hab 2:2.
30:9 rebellious people, deceitful children. Cf. 1:2; 65:2.
30:10–11 The people have become scoffers, people who know what is right but reject it (see note on 28:14).
30:11–12 The people demand to hear no more from "the Holy One of Israel" (see note on 1:4), but for that very reason they are going to hear what the Holy One of Israel has to say. Because they preferred coercion to fairness and deceit to truth, they constructed a fragile edifice that cannot stand.

30:12 [z]Isa 5:24 [a]Isa 5:7
30:13 [b]Ps 62:3 [c]1Ki 20:30 [d]Isa 29:5
30:14 [e]Ps 2:9; Jer 19:10-11
30:15 [f]Isa 32:17
30:16 [g]Isa 31:1,3
30:17 [h]Lev 26:8; Jos 23:10 [i]Lev 26:36; Dt 28:25
30:18 [j]Isa 42:14; 2Pe 3:9,15 [k]Isa 5:16 [l]Isa 25:9
30:19 [m]Isa 60:20; 61:3 [n]Ps 50:15; Isa 58:9; 65:24; Mt 7:7-11
30:20 [o]1Ki 22:27 [p]Ps 74:9; Am 8:11
30:21 [q]Isa 29:24
30:22 [r]Ex 32:4

"Because you have rejected this message,[z]
relied on oppression[a]
and depended on deceit,
13 this sin will become for you
like a high wall,[b] cracked and bulging,
that collapses[c] suddenly,[d] in an instant.
14 It will break in pieces like pottery,[e]
shattered so mercilessly
that among its pieces not a fragment will be found
for taking coals from a hearth
or scooping water out of a cistern."

15 This is what the Sovereign LORD, the Holy One of Israel, says:

"In repentance and rest is your salvation,
in quietness and trust[f] is your strength,
but you would have none of it.
16 You said, 'No, we will flee on horses.'[g]
Therefore you will flee!
You said, 'We will ride off on swift horses.'
Therefore your pursuers will be swift!
17 A thousand will flee
at the threat of one;
at the threat of five[h]
you will all flee[i] away,
till you are left
like a flagstaff on a mountaintop,
like a banner on a hill."

18 Yet the LORD longs[j] to be gracious to you;
therefore he will rise up to show you compassion.
For the LORD is a God of justice.[k]
Blessed are all who wait for him![l]

19 People of Zion, who live in Jerusalem, you will weep no more.[m] How gracious he will be when
you cry for help! As soon as he hears, he will answer[n] you. 20 Although the Lord gives you the bread[o]
of adversity and the water of affliction, your teachers will be hidden[p] no more; with your own eyes
you will see them. 21 Whether you turn to the right or to the left, your ears will hear a voice[q] behind
you, saying, "This is the way; walk in it." 22 Then you will desecrate your idols[r] overlaid with silver
and your images covered with gold; you will throw them away like a menstrual cloth and say to
them, "Away with you!"

30:13–14 Israel is like a high city wall with an inadequate foundation. Left unrepaired the wall develops cracks into which rainwater flows. The cracks weaken the wall, so that over time bulges appear, and suddenly, with no further warning, the whole wall collapses into pieces no bigger than a potsherd (pottery fragment) that is too small even to be used as a scoop.

30:15–18 Because the people refuse to trust God, preferring to put their trust in horses instead, they will be helpless in the face of the enemy. Since they will not "wait for him" (v. 18), he will have to wait for them to come to their senses.

30:16 horses. The most valuable military instrument of that time. They first pulled light chariots and were devastating in that role. But by this time, people began riding them, and the resulting cavalry detachments were even more fearsome. The Assyrian officer mockingly offers to give Judah horses if they only had people trained to ride them (36:8). Here the horses' speed would not be used for fighting, but for flight.

30:18 longs. The same Hebrew verb is also translated "wait." If the people will not wait trustingly for Yahweh to act on their behalf, then he will wait patiently for them to be brought down to the place (cf. v. 19) where they are willing to receive the grace and compassion that he continually extends to them.

30:19–33 Though the coming day may be one of "adversity" (v. 20), it will nevertheless be a day when people clearly hear God's word (vv. 21–22). As a result, they will throw away old idols (cf. 17:8; 27:9). Furthermore, nature will respond to Israel's salvation with great abundance (vv. 23–26). In the end, Yahweh will turn on the enemies of his people "like a rushing torrent" (v. 28) and hurl them into the "fire pit" (v. 33) that was prepared for them (v. 27–33).

30:19–22 This sounds like the time between the OT and NT, when teachers similar to Ezra proclaimed the Word (Neh 9:1–3) and idolatry ultimately became a thing of the past.

[23]He will also send you rain[s] for the seed you sow in the ground, and the food that comes from the
land will be rich and plentiful. In that day your cattle will graze in broad meadows.[t] [24]The oxen and
donkeys that work the soil will eat fodder and mash, spread out with fork[u] and shovel. [25]In the day of
great slaughter, when the towers[v] fall, streams of water will flow[w] on every high mountain and every
lofty hill. [26]The moon will shine like the sun,[x] and the sunlight will be seven times brighter, like the
light of seven full days, when the LORD binds up the bruises of his people and heals[y] the wounds he
inflicted.

[27] See, the Name[z] of the LORD comes from afar,
with burning anger[a] and dense clouds of smoke;
his lips are full of wrath,[b]
and his tongue is a consuming fire.
[28] His breath[c] is like a rushing torrent,
rising up to the neck.[d]
He shakes the nations in the sieve[e] of destruction;
he places in the jaws of the peoples
a bit[f] that leads them astray.
[29] And you will sing
as on the night you celebrate a holy festival;
your hearts will rejoice
as when people playing pipes go up
to the mountain[g] of the LORD,
to the Rock of Israel.
[30] The LORD will cause people to hear his majestic voice
and will make them see his arm coming down
with raging anger and consuming fire,
with cloudburst, thunderstorm and hail.
[31] The voice of the LORD will shatter Assyria;[h]
with his rod he will strike[i] them down.
[32] Every stroke the LORD lays on them
with his punishing club
will be to the music of timbrels and harps,
as he fights them in battle with the blows of his arm.[j]
[33] Topheth[k] has long been prepared;
it has been made ready for the king.
Its fire pit has been made deep and wide,
with an abundance of fire and wood;
the breath of the LORD,
like a stream of burning sulfur,[l]
sets it ablaze.

30:23 [s]Isa 65:21-22 [t]Ps 65:13
30:24 [u]Mt 3:12; Lk 3:17
30:25 [v]Isa 2:15 [w]Isa 41:18
30:26 [x]Isa 24:23; 60:19-20; Rev 21:23; 22:5 [y]Dt 32:39; Isa 1:5
30:27 [z]Isa 59:19 [a]Isa 66:14 [b]Isa 10:5
30:28 [c]Isa 11:4 [d]Isa 8:8 [e]Am 9:9 [f]2Ki 19:28; Isa 37:29
30:29 [g]Ps 42:4
30:31 [h]Isa 10:5,12 [i]Isa 11:4
30:32 [j]Isa 11:15; Eze 32:10
30:33 [k]2Ki 23:10 [l]Ge 19:24

30:23–33 This uses language typically associated with the end of time; it is more apocalyptic than chs. 24–27 (see note on 24:1—27:13). Verses 23–26 seem to envision when God ultimately redeems nature as a result of finally redeeming humanity (cf. Rom 8:19–21). Destroying the enemy nations is similar to Ezek 38–39; Zech 12:1–9; 14:1–5 (cf. Rev 20:7–10).
30:23–24 In the Prophets, natural disasters were one of the chief judgments God delivered on his sinful people (cf. 5:10; Jer 9:10; Joel 1:11–12; Amos 4:6–9; Hag 2:16–17). So here the abundance of nature is a sign of his renewed blessing.
30:25 streams ... will flow on every high mountain and ... hill. Expresses God's ability to do the impossible (cf. 35:6; see also Ezek 47:1), even redeem a sinful world (cf. John 7:37–39).
30:26 sunlight ... seven times brighter. Since this would burn up the earth, we should understand this passage figuratively, not literally. God will finally and totally disperse the darkness of sin.
30:27–33 The destruction of the enemies that have threatened God's plan of salvation for the world, as represented by Assyria, is a cause for worship (vv. 29,32).
30:27–30 lips ... tongue ... voice. Cf. 11:4; Ps 29:1–9; Heb 4:12; Rev 19:15. God's word accomplishes this destruction. Just as God's word brought the world into existence (Gen 1), so it will be the instrument of the world's final judgment.
30:33 Yahweh's enemies are consigned to the fire (cf. Zech 12:6; Rev 20:9–10; see also Isa 31:9). **Topheth.** Mentioned frequently in Jeremiah (Jer 7:31–32; 19:6–14). It refers to the place in the Hinnom Valley at the south edge of Jerusalem where children were sacrificed in fire to the god Molek. It may have also been the place where refuse was burned. Here Isaiah uses the term figuratively to describe the total destruction of the Assyrian king and his army.

31:1 [m] Dt 17:16; Isa 30:2,5 [n] Isa 2:7 [o] Ps 20:7; Da 9:13
31:2 [p] Ro 16:27 [q] Isa 45:7 [r] Nu 23:19 [s] Isa 32:6
31:3 [t] Isa 36:9 [u] Eze 28:9; 2Th 2:4 [v] Isa 9:17,21 [w] Isa 30:5-7
31:4 [x] Nu 24:9; Hos 11:10; Am 3:8 [y] Isa 42:13
31:5 [z] Ps 91:4 [a] Isa 37:35; 38:6
31:7 [b] Isa 2:20; 30:22
31:8 [c] Isa 10:12 [d] Isa 14:25; 37:7 [e] Ge 49:15
31:9 [f] Dt 32:31,37

Woe to Those Who Rely on Egypt

31 Woe to those who go down to Egypt[m] for help,
who rely on horses,
who trust in the multitude of their chariots[n]
and in the great strength of their horsemen,
but do not look to the Holy One of Israel,
or seek help from the LORD.[o]
2 Yet he too is wise[p] and can bring disaster;[q]
he does not take back his words.[r]
He will rise up against that wicked nation,[s]
against those who help evildoers.
3 But the Egyptians[t] are mere mortals and not God;[u]
their horses are flesh and not spirit.
When the LORD stretches out his hand,[v]
those who help will stumble,
those who are helped[w] will fall;
all will perish together.

4 This is what the LORD says to me:

"As a lion[x] growls,
a great lion over its prey—
and though a whole band of shepherds
is called together against it,
it is not frightened by their shouts
or disturbed by their clamor—
so the LORD Almighty will come down[y]
to do battle on Mount Zion and on its heights.
5 Like birds hovering overhead,
the LORD Almighty will shield[z] Jerusalem;
he will shield it and deliver[a] it,
he will 'pass over' it and will rescue it."

6 Return, you Israelites, to the One you have so greatly revolted against. 7 For in that day every one of
you will reject the idols of silver and gold[b] your sinful hands have made.

8 "Assyria[c] will fall by no human sword;
a sword, not of mortals, will devour[d] them.
They will flee before the sword
and their young men will be put to forced labor.[e]
9 Their stronghold[f] will fall because of terror;
at the sight of the battle standard their commanders will panic,"

31:1—32:20 *Woe to Those Who Rely on Egypt.* Like the previous messages, this contains an opening prophecy of judgment (31:1–3) followed by a prophecy of salvation (31:4—32:20). As is characteristic in this section, the disproportion between the two is further increased over the previous oracles (see note on 28:1—33:24).
31:1–3 *A Message of Judgment.* This section increasingly brings to life the policy of trust in the "chariots" and "horsemen" of Egypt (v. 1) and explicitly attacks it. Israel has foolishly chosen humanity instead of deity, "flesh" instead of "spirit" (v. 3), and they will perish with their helper.
31:1 seek help from. Yahweh, the transcendent Creator of the universe, has graciously given himself to Israel. Yet Israel would rather rush into an alliance with their former captors than ask what Yahweh, their Savior, would like to do with them and for them (cf. the judgment on King Asa, 2 Chr 16:1–9).
31:4—32:20 *A Message of Salvation.* The alliance with Egypt is foolish not only because it will fail but also because Yahweh has glorious plans for his people. This message of salvation has four parts: Assyria will fall (31:4–9), the revelation of the true King (32:1–8), a warning against complacency (32:9–15), and the coming of the Spirit (32:16–20).
31:4–9 Much as Isaiah told Ahaz that his attempt to get Assyria to defend him from Israel and Aram (i.e., Syria) was unnecessary because God already had plans to do that for him (7:1–17), so here he tells the people of Judah some 30 years later that they need not depend on Egypt because Yahweh had already decreed Assyria's defeat.
31:4,5 LORD Almighty. See notes on 1:9,24.
31:7 See 17:8; 30:19–33 and notes.
31:8–9 This predicts the decimation of the Assyrian army through a divine "sword," not human military defeat (37:36; see also 14:25).

declares the LORD,
whose fire[g] is in Zion,
whose furnace is in Jerusalem.

The Kingdom of Righteousness

32 See, a king[h] will reign in righteousness
and rulers will rule with justice.[i]
2 Each one will be like a shelter[j] from the wind
and a refuge from the storm,
like streams of water in the desert
and the shadow of a great rock in a thirsty land.

3 Then the eyes of those who see will no longer be closed,[k]
and the ears of those who hear will listen.
4 The fearful heart will know and understand,[l]
and the stammering tongue will be fluent and clear.
5 No longer will the fool[m] be called noble
nor the scoundrel be highly respected.
6 For fools speak folly,[n]
their hearts are bent on evil:
They practice ungodliness[o]
and spread error[p] concerning the LORD;
the hungry they leave empty[q]
and from the thirsty they withhold water.
7 Scoundrels use wicked methods,[r]
they make up evil schemes[s]
to destroy the poor with lies,
even when the plea of the needy[t] is just.
8 But the noble make noble plans,
and by noble deeds[u] they stand.

The Women of Jerusalem

9 You women who are so complacent,
rise up and listen[v] to me;
you daughters who feel secure,[w]
hear what I have to say!
10 In little more than a year
you who feel secure will tremble;

31:9 [g]Isa 10:17
32:1 [h]Eze 37:24 [i]Ps 72:1-4; Isa 9:7
32:2 [j]Isa 4:6
32:3 [k]Isa 29:18
32:4 [l]Isa 29:24
32:5 [m]1Sa 25:25
32:6 [n]Pr 19:3 [o]Isa 9:17 [p]Isa 9:16 [q]Isa 3:15
32:7 [r]Jer 5:26-28 [s]Mic 7:3 [t]Isa 61:1
32:8 [u]Pr 11:25
32:9 [v]Isa 28:23 [w]Isa 47:8; Am 6:1; Zep 2:15

32:1–8 This reveals the true king. By implication it severely criticizes Judah's leadership. Although it does not specifically name Hezekiah (see note on 22:8–11), it implies that judgment extends to the very top of the nation. Judah's hope is not in any human leader, even if he personally might be a good man (see 38:1—39:8 and note). Judah's ultimate hope lies in an ideal king and in the human transformation he will bring about.
32:1 righteousness ... justice. See 11:4; 16:5; 42:1.
32:2 In this kingdom the leaders will see their relationship to their followers as one of responsibility, not privilege.
32:3–4 These leaders will themselves be able to discern truth ("see") and receive guidance ("hear") and will thus be able to lead even "the fearful" and "the stammering" into knowing and declaring the truth. This contrasts with the situation that 28:7–13 and 29:9–14 describe.
32:5 fool ... noble. There is a wordplay between Hebrew *nābāl* ("senseless, disgraceful") and *nādīb* ("generous, willing, volunteering"). This contrasts foolish and noble leaders. The noble will make "plans" (v. 8) and perform "deeds" (v. 8) that seek the best for others, not for themselves; whereas fools and scoundrels, having exalted "evil" by speaking "error concerning the LORD" (v. 6), do not merely fail in their duties to the needy but actively mistreat them.
32:9–14 This is something of a parenthesis between revealing the king and announcing the Spirit's coming. These verses represent a typical Isaianic feature: not allowing a promise of the glorious future to obscure present realities (e.g., 5:1–30; 9:8—10:4). Even if a king is promised, that does not relieve the people of the need to confront the terrible situation facing them in the present (cf. Amos 6:6). Repentance and deeds of righteousness should be the order of the day in the face of the desolation before them. Physical desolation was a part of what the Assyrian invasion would bring upon them, but the physical language was also a metaphor for the spiritual desolation that affected the nation (cf. 1:1–9).
32:9–11 The women could say that the condition of the nation was the men's business while they pressed their husbands to provide them with more and more of the luxury goods that abundant harvests could make available (cf. Amos 4:1; 6:1–6). The prophet says that they cannot avoid their responsibility.
32:10 In little more than a year. Suggests that this judgment was

32:10 [x]Isa 5:5-6; 24:7
32:11 [y]Isa 47:2
32:12 [z]Na 2:7
32:13 [a]Isa 5:6 [b]Isa 22:2
32:14 [c]Isa 13:22 [d]Isa 6:11; 27:10 [e]Isa 34:13 [f]Ps 104:11
32:15 [g]Isa 11:2; Joel 2:28 [h]Ps 107:35; Isa 35:1-2 [i]Isa 29:17
32:17 [j]Ps 119:165; Ro 14:17; Jas 3:18 [k]Isa 30:15
32:18 [l]Hos 2:18-23
32:19 [m]Isa 28:17; 30:30 [n]Isa 10:19; Zec 11:2 [o]Isa 24:10; 27:10
32:20 [p]Ecc 11:1 [q]Isa 30:24
33:1 [r]Hab 2:8; Mt 7:2 [s]Isa 21:2

the grape harvest will fail,[x]
and the harvest of fruit will not come.
11 Tremble, you complacent women;
shudder, you daughters who feel secure!
Strip off your fine clothes[y]
and wrap yourselves in rags.
12 Beat your breasts[z] for the pleasant fields,
for the fruitful vines
13 and for the land of my people,
a land overgrown with thorns and briers[a]—
yes, mourn for all houses of merriment
and for this city of revelry.[b]
14 The fortress[c] will be abandoned,
the noisy city deserted;[d]
citadel and watchtower[e] will become a wasteland forever,
the delight of donkeys,[f] a pasture for flocks,
15 till the Spirit[g] is poured on us from on high,
and the desert becomes a fertile field,[h]
and the fertile field seems like a forest.[i]
16 The LORD's justice will dwell in the desert,
his righteousness live in the fertile field.
17 The fruit of that righteousness will be peace;[j]
its effect will be quietness and confidence[k] forever.
18 My people will live in peaceful dwelling places,
in secure homes,
in undisturbed places of rest.[l]
19 Though hail[m] flattens the forest[n]
and the city is leveled[o] completely,
20 how blessed you will be,
sowing[p] your seed by every stream,
and letting your cattle and donkeys range free.[q]

Distress and Help

33 Woe to you, destroyer,
you who have not been destroyed!
Woe to you, betrayer,
you who have not been betrayed!
When you stop destroying,
you will be destroyed;[r]
when you stop betraying,
you will be betrayed.[s]

pronounced in 702 BC, before the arrival of Sennacherib's army the following year.

32:13 thorns and briers. See 7:23–24; see also note on 27:2–6.

32:15–20 The Spirit is poured out (v. 15). The Spirit's particular fruit is "justice" and "righteousness" (v. 16) The repetition of these terms from v. 1 suggests that this passage connects with the revelation of the king in vv. 1–9 and thus continues the characteristics of the promised kingdom.

32:15 the Spirit. See note on 11:2. He brings fertility and abundance.

32:16–17 The Spirit's fruits (see note on vv. 15–20) are qualities that the Israelites confess themselves unable to produce on their own (see 59:9–15). But when the Spirit makes them available (cf. Ezek 36:27–28; see also Jer 31:33; John 16:8–11), they will experience a "peace" (Hebrew *šālôm*) that the world cannot give (John 14:27; see note on Isa 9:6). This mention of the Spirit's producing fruit seems to point to the same figure of speech used in the NT (Gal 5:22).

32:18–20 As vv. 12–14 describe the sinful condition metaphorically, so this describes the condition of Spirit-given righteousness. In spite of outward adversity ("hail ... the city is leveled," v. 19), there will still be blessing (v. 20; cf. John 16:33).

33:1–24 *Woe to the Destroyer.* Verses 1–6 are a summarizing introduction: God arises, destroys the destroyer, and transforms Zion. Verses 7–24 are the message's body and develop the themes. It has two parts: a lament and response (vv. 7–16) and a description of God's kingly rule (vv. 17–24).

33:1 destroyer. Probably Assyria. Having disposed of the plan to rely on Egypt, Isaiah reveals where Judah's real hope lies.

[2] LORD, be gracious to us;
we long for you.
Be our strength[t] every morning,
our salvation[u] in time of distress.
[3] At the uproar of your army, the peoples flee;
when you rise up,[v] the nations scatter.
[4] Your plunder, O nations, is harvested as by young locusts;
like a swarm of locusts people pounce on it.

[5] The LORD is exalted,[w] for he dwells on high;
he will fill Zion with his justice[x] and righteousness.[y]
[6] He will be the sure foundation for your times,
a rich store of salvation[z] and wisdom and knowledge;
the fear[a] of the LORD is the key to this treasure.[a]

[7] Look, their brave men cry aloud in the streets;
the envoys[b] of peace weep bitterly.
[8] The highways are deserted,
no travelers are on the roads.[c]
The treaty is broken,
its witnesses[b] are despised,
no one is respected.
[9] The land dries up[d] and wastes away,
Lebanon[e] is ashamed and withers;[f]
Sharon is like the Arabah,
and Bashan and Carmel drop their leaves.

[10] "Now will I arise,[g]" says the LORD.
"Now will I be exalted;
now will I be lifted up.
[11] You conceive[h] chaff,
you give birth[i] to straw;
your breath is a fire[j] that consumes you.
[12] The peoples will be burned to ashes;
like cut thornbushes they will be set ablaze.[k]"

[13] You who are far away,[l] hear[m] what I have done;
you who are near, acknowledge my power!
[14] The sinners in Zion are terrified;
trembling[n] grips the godless:

33:2 [t] Isa 40:10; 51:9; 59:16 [u] Isa 25:9
33:3 [v] Isa 59:16-18
33:5 [w] Ps 97:9 [x] Isa 28:6 [y] Isa 1:26
33:6 [z] Isa 51:6 [a] Isa 11:2-3; Mt 6:33
33:7 [b] 2Ki 18:37
33:8 [c] Jdg 5:6; Isa 35:8
33:9 [d] Isa 3:26 [e] Isa 2:13; 35:2 [f] Isa 24:4
33:10 [g] Ps 12:5; Isa 2:21
33:11 [h] Ps 7:14; Isa 59:4; Jas 1:15 [i] Isa 26:18 [j] Isa 1:31
33:12 [k] Isa 10:17
33:13 [l] Ps 48:10; 49:1 [m] Isa 49:1
33:14 [n] Isa 32:11

[a] 6 Or *is a treasure from him* [b] 8 Dead Sea Scrolls; Masoretic Text / *the cities*

33:2 Isaiah speaks on behalf of those among the people who realize where their real help lies (cf. 30:18). **we long.** Expresses trust (also in 40:31, which translates the word as "hope").
33:5–6 The other side of Yahweh's rising up ("is exalted") is to transform the nation. When he receives his proper place ("the fear of the LORD," v. 6; see note on 11:2), then all the benefits of his character can be reproduced among his people (see note on 11:3–5). They no longer will be merely Jerusalem but will become Zion, the city of God.
33:7–16 The nation is terrified, perhaps at the onslaught of the Assyrian emperor Sennacherib and his progressive decimation of the land (cf. 2 Kgs 18:13). But Yahweh responds that he will "arise" (v. 10) and will in turn decimate the enemy (vv. 11–13). While this revelation of God's power will not be good news for "the sinners in Zion" (v. 14), it will be great good news for "those who walk righteously" (v. 15), because it will vindicate their faith, which their obedient life demonstrates (vv. 15–16).
33:7 envoys of peace weep. Perhaps those who spoke with the Assyrian officer (36:22).
33:8 The treaty is broken. Perhaps Sennacherib's accepting Hezekiah's money but still refusing to withdraw (2 Kgs 18:14–16), or it may refer to the failed alliance with Egypt. Egypt proved helpless against Sennacherib; the Egyptian army sallied northward on two occasions, and the Assyrians sent them reeling back homeward each time.
33:9 Lebanon. Noted for its great cedar forests. **Sharon.** A fruitful plain on the shore of the Mediterranean Sea. **Arabah.** The barren valley south of the Dead Sea. **Bashan.** The grasslands on the heights northeast of the Sea of Galilee (today's "Golan Heights"). **Carmel.** Grazing land southeast of Hebron in Judah (cf. 1 Sam 25:2).
33:11–12 chaff ... straw ... cut thornbushes. Exceedingly flammable.
33:14 The sinners see God not as a source of protection but as a threat,

Arid Arabah, south of the Dead Sea (Isa 33:9).

A. D. Riddle/www.BiblePlaces.com

"Who of us can dwell with the consuming fire?[o]
Who of us can dwell with everlasting burning?"
15 Those who walk righteously[p]
and speak what is right,[q]
who reject gain from extortion
and keep their hands from accepting bribes,
who stop their ears against plots of murder
and shut their eyes[r] against contemplating evil—
16 they are the ones who will dwell on the heights,
whose refuge[s] will be the mountain fortress.[t]
Their bread will be supplied,
and water will not fail[u] them.

17 Your eyes will see the king[v] in his beauty
and view a land that stretches afar.[w]
18 In your thoughts you will ponder the former terror:[x]
"Where is that chief officer?
Where is the one who took the revenue?
Where is the officer in charge of the towers?"
19 You will see those arrogant people no more,
people whose speech is obscure,
whose language is strange and incomprehensible.[y]

20 Look on Zion, the city of our festivals;
your eyes will see Jerusalem,
a peaceful abode,[z] a tent that will not be moved;[a]

33:14 [o] Isa 30:30; Heb 12:29
33:15 [p] Isa 58:8 [q] Ps 15:2; 24:4 [r] Ps 119:37
33:16 [s] Isa 25:4 [t] Isa 26:1 [u] Isa 49:10
33:17 [v] Isa 6:5 [w] Isa 26:15
33:18 [x] Isa 17:14
33:19 [y] Isa 28:11; Jer 5:15
33:20 [z] Isa 32:18 [a] Ps 46:5; 125:1-2

because their lives are no different from those of the enemies (cf. vv. 11–12).
33:15 An excellent, brief summary of the righteous life.
33:16 heights ... mountain fortress. Symbols of security.
33:17–24 Describes God's kingly rule.
33:17–19 God promises protection from enemies. The Assyrian officers who were with the field commander (36:2) calculating what it would cost to conduct a siege and how much tribute they might get from the captured city would be gone. The Assyrian language was related to Hebrew but distant enough to be "incomprehensible" (v. 19) to ordinary Hebrew speakers (cf. 28:11).
33:20–24 This collection of metaphors expresses the peace and security in the place where God is King.
33:20 city of our festivals. Contrast 29:1. The value of ritual is dependent on a right relationship with God (cf. 1:10–15; 30:29–32). Jerusalem is like a "tent that will not be moved" (cf. Amos 9:11, which refers to the "shelter" [tent] of David being restored).

its stakes will never be pulled up,
nor any of its ropes broken.
21 There the LORD will be our Mighty One.
It will be like a place of broad rivers and streams.[b]
No galley with oars will ride them,
no mighty ship will sail them.
22 For the LORD is our judge,[c]
the LORD is our lawgiver,[d]
the LORD is our king;[e]
it is he who will save[f] us.

23 Your rigging hangs loose:
The mast is not held secure,
the sail is not spread.
Then an abundance of spoils will be divided
and even the lame[g] will carry off plunder.[h]
24 No one living in Zion will say, "I am ill";[i]
and the sins of those who dwell there will be forgiven.[j]

33:21 [b] Isa 41:18; 48:18; 66:12
33:22 [c] Isa 11:4 [d] Isa 2:3; Jas 4:12 [e] Ps 89:18 [f] Isa 25:9
33:23 [g] 2Ki 7:8 [h] 2Ki 7:16
33:24 [i] Isa 30:26 [j] Jer 50:20; 1Jn 1:7-9
34:1 [k] Isa 41:1; 43:9 [l] Ps 49:1 [m] Dt 32:1
34:2 [n] Isa 13:5 [o] Isa 30:25
34:3 [p] Joel 2:20; Am 4:10 [q] ver 7; Eze 14:19; 35:6; 38:22
34:4 [r] Isa 13:13; 2Pe 3:10 [s] Eze 32:7-8 [t] Joel 2:31; Mt 24:29*; Rev 6:13

Judgment Against the Nations

34 Come near, you nations, and listen;
pay attention, you peoples![k]
Let the earth[l] hear, and all that is in it,
the world, and all that comes out of it![m]
2 The LORD is angry with all nations;
his wrath is on all their armies.
He will totally destroy[a][n] them,
he will give them over to slaughter.[o]
3 Their slain will be thrown out,
their dead bodies will stink;[p]
the mountains will be soaked with their blood.[q]
4 All the stars in the sky will be dissolved[r]
and the heavens rolled up[s] like a scroll;
all the starry host will fall[t]
like withered leaves from the vine,
like shriveled figs from the fig tree.

[a] *2* The Hebrew term refers to the irrevocable giving over of things or persons to the LORD, often by totally destroying them; also in verse 5.

33:21 A mighty river where no warships ("galley with oars") are found will nourish the land where Yahweh is King. This may contrast with the restless sea (cf. Ps 46:1–4).
33:22 There is security and abundance because Yahweh is "judge," "lawgiver," "king," and savior. All of these are synonyms for the supreme ruler of a people. **judge.** Not primarily a legal figure in the Semitic languages. "Champion" or "defender" expresses the sense of the term more closely (see Introduction to Judges: Title of the Book and Role of the Judges). The king was also the one who promulgated the laws of his nation.
33:23 This refers to an obscure figure perhaps related to v. 21. This seems to depict the enemy as a great ocean-going ship that has run aground where anyone can plunder its cargo.
33:24 Not only will there be peace and security in Yahweh's kingdom, but there will also be healing, both physical and spiritual.
34:1—35:10 *Conclusion: The Desert or the Garden.* This concludes chs. 13–35 by dramatically contrasting the opposite results of trusting human nations (ch. 34) or Yahweh (ch. 35). Those who trust the nations will become a desert, but trusting Yahweh will transform one's desert into a garden.
34:1–17 Most of ch. 34 is a message of judgment against Edom (vv. 5–15), but Edom symbolizes the judgment that falls on the entire cosmos (vv. 1–4). To trust the nations and their gods ("the starry host," v. 4) is to share in their fate.
34:1 nations ... peoples ... earth ... world. The judgment is universal. Verse 2 confirms this impression. Verses 2–3 reveal the destruction's intensity.
34:2–3 He will totally destroy them ... the mountains will be soaked with their blood. Isaiah uses hyperbole to indicate just how devastating the wrath of God against the nations will be.
34:4 This may be hyperbole to convey that the destruction is total. But it may also express that Yahweh alone rules the universe. **starry host.** Pagans considered them gods; God will destroy not only the military power of the nations but also what they call gods (cf. 40:25–26). It is also possible that the language may speak literally of the end of the world.

34:5 [u]Dt 32:41-42; Jer 46:10; Eze 21:5 [v]Am 1:11-12 [w]Isa 24:6; Mal 1:4
34:7 [x]Ps 68:30
34:8 [y]Isa 63:4
34:10 [z]Rev 14:10-11; 19:3 [a]Isa 13:20; 24:1; Eze 29:12; Mal 1:3
34:11 [b]Zep 2:14; Rev 18:2 [c]2Ki 21:13; La 2:8
34:12 [d]Jer 27:20; 39:6 [e]Isa 41:11-12
34:13 [f]Isa 13:22; 32:13 [g]Ps 44:19; Jer 9:11; 10:22
34:14 [h]Isa 13:22

5 My sword[u] has drunk its fill in the heavens;
see, it descends in judgment on Edom,[v]
the people I have totally destroyed.[w]
6 The sword of the LORD is bathed in blood,
it is covered with fat—
the blood of lambs and goats,
fat from the kidneys of rams.
For the LORD has a sacrifice in Bozrah
and a great slaughter in the land of Edom.
7 And the wild oxen will fall with them,
the bull calves and the great bulls.[x]
Their land will be drenched with blood,
and the dust will be soaked with fat.

8 For the LORD has a day of vengeance,[y]
a year of retribution, to uphold Zion's cause.
9 Edom's streams will be turned into pitch,
her dust into burning sulfur;
her land will become blazing pitch!
10 It will not be quenched night or day;
its smoke will rise forever.[z]
From generation to generation it will lie desolate;[a]
no one will ever pass through it again.
11 The desert owl[a][b] and screech owl[a] will possess it;
the great owl[a] and the raven will nest there.
God will stretch out over Edom
the measuring line of chaos
and the plumb line[c] of desolation.
12 Her nobles will have nothing there to be called a kingdom,
all her princes[d] will vanish[e] away.
13 Thorns will overrun her citadels,
nettles and brambles her strongholds.[f]
She will become a haunt for jackals,[g]
a home for owls.
14 Desert creatures will meet with hyenas,[h]
and wild goats will bleat to each other;

[a] *11* The precise identification of these birds is uncertain.

34:5 Edom. Located south and east of Judah, around the lower end of the Dead Sea. The long history of hostility between Judah and Edom climaxed when the Edomites helped the Babylonians sack Jerusalem (see Obad 13). As a result, Edom came to represent the evil of the world opposed to God (63:1–6; see Mal 1:3–5).
34:6 Bozrah. Edom's capital city, located in the mountains on the east side of the Arabah (see note on 33:9).
34:7 wild oxen ... bull calves ... great bulls. Possibly represent the leaders of the nation who fall with the common people.
34:8 day of vengeance. A positive concept both here and in 61:2, where it refers to a time when God will right the wrongs done to his people (cf. Rev 6:9–11). **day.** Parallel with "year," showing that a general period of time is intended (cf. 63:4 for the same parallelism).
34:9–15 The land turned into a desert. This section does not actually name Edom (see note on v. 5), which lends force to its representative nature (see note on vv. 1–17).
34:9–10 The tar pits and deposits of sulfur south of the Dead Sea probably gave rise to this imagery. Sodom and Gomorrah were located in this area, and the language is reminiscent of what is said of them (Gen 19:24–28; Deut 29:23; Ps 11:6; Jer 49:18).
34:11 See NIV text note. The birds are probably ritually unclean, contributing to the overall sense of separation from God (see 2:20 and note). **measuring line ... desolation.** Ironic: the tools of construction (cf. 28:17) become the tools of destruction (cf. 2 Kgs 21:13). **chaos ... desolation.** Translate the same Hebrew words that describe the "formless" and "empty" world of Gen 1:2.
34:12 The Hebrew is obscure, but the general sense is clear: the "nobles" and "princes" will amount to nothing.
34:13–15 These animals, most of them unclean, express an untamed wilderness.
34:13 Thorns ... brambles. See 7:23–24; see also note on 27:2–6. **jackals ... owls.** Associated with mourning in Job 30:29; Mic 1:8.
34:14 wild goats ... night creatures. Perhaps demonic figures but more likely rare terms for ordinary animals that heighten the sense of the bizarre in this poem.

there the night creatures will also lie down
and find for themselves places of rest.
15 The owl will nest there and lay eggs,
she will hatch them, and care for her young
under the shadow of her wings;
there also the falcons[i] will gather,
each with its mate.
16 Look in the scroll[j] of the LORD and read:

None of these will be missing,
not one will lack her mate.
For it is his mouth[k] that has given the order,
and his Spirit will gather them together.
17 He allots their portions;[l]
his hand distributes them by measure.
They will possess it forever
and dwell there from generation to generation.[m]

Joy of the Redeemed

35

The desert[n] and the parched land will be glad;
the wilderness will rejoice and blossom.[o]
Like the crocus, 2 it will burst into bloom;
it will rejoice greatly and shout for joy.[p]
The glory of Lebanon[q] will be given to it,
the splendor of Carmel[r] and Sharon;
they will see the glory of the LORD,
the splendor of our God.[s]

3 Strengthen the feeble hands,
steady the knees[t] that give way;
4 say to those with fearful hearts,
"Be strong, do not fear;
your God will come,
he will come with vengeance;[u]
with divine retribution
he will come to save you."
5 Then will the eyes of the blind be opened[v]
and the ears of the deaf[w] unstopped.
6 Then will the lame[x] leap like a deer,
and the mute tongue[y] shout for joy.
Water will gush forth in the wilderness
and streams[z] in the desert.

34:15 [i] Dt 14:13
34:16 [j] Isa 30:8 [k] Isa 1:20; 58:14
34:17 [l] Isa 17:14; Jer 13:25 [m] ver 10
35:1 [n] Isa 27:10; 41:18-19 [o] Isa 51:3
35:2 [p] Isa 25:9; 55:12 [q] Isa 32:15 [r] SS 7:5 [s] Isa 25:9
35:3 [t] Job 4:4; Heb 12:12
35:4 [u] Isa 1:24; 34:8
35:5 [v] Mt 11:5; Jn 9:6-7 [w] Isa 29:18; 50:4
35:6 [x] Mt 15:30; Jn 5:8-9; Ac 3:8 [y] Isa 32:4; Mt 9:32-33; 12:22; Lk 11:14 [z] Isa 41:18; Jn 7:38

34:16–17 The destruction is certain: it is written in a scroll, spoken by God, and fulfilled through his Spirit. This is anti-creation (cf. Gen 1:2, see note on Isa 34:11). God gives ownership of the earth to the wild animals of the desert.
35:1–10 Those who trust in the Lord find themselves on a highway leading home through a transformed desert, a garden. This poem expresses spiritual truth that should not be pressed too literally in any one direction. It might describe the return from exile, the millennial kingdom, the new heaven and earth, or all of them, but that is not the poem's main purpose. Its purpose is to highlight the blessed results of trust.
35:1–2 All humans have chosen to trust humanity instead of God (Rom 1:18–23; 3:23) and have therefore plunged themselves into a "desert." But God has no desire to leave us in that "parched land." Instead, he means to transform the desert into a land of great fertility (32:15), a place of gladness and rejoicing; "like the crocus, it will burst into bloom." It will be a place where the "glory of the LORD" is once more seen in the earth (cf. 6:3). If ch. 34 speaks of anti-creation (see notes on 34:11,16–17), ch. 35 speaks of re-creation.
35:2 Lebanon. See note on 33:9.
35:3–6 feeble … fearful … blind … deaf … lame … mute. Those whom arrogant, self-serving leaders have marginalized (5:20–23; 29:18–21; 30:12; 32:7). They are less likely to trust in themselves, and Yahweh encourages them and promises them "retribution" (v. 4) for all the wrongs done to them. The inauguration of God's kingdom is clearly seen in Christ's healing of these kinds of persons.
35:6 streams in the desert. See note on 30:25.

35:7 [a]Isa 49:10 [b]Isa 13:22
35:8 [c]Isa 11:16; 33:8; Mt 7:13-14 [d]Isa 4:3; 1Pe 1:15 [e]Isa 52:1
35:9 [f]Isa 30:6 [g]Isa 34:14 [h]Isa 51:11; 62:12; 63:4
35:10 [i]Isa 25:9 [j]Isa 30:19; 51:11; Rev 7:17; 21:4
36:1 [k]2Ch 32:1
36:2 [l]Isa 7:3
36:3 [m]Isa 22:20-21

7 The burning sand will become a pool,
the thirsty ground bubbling springs.[a]
In the haunts where jackals[b] once lay,
grass and reeds and papyrus will grow.

8 And a highway[c] will be there;
it will be called the Way of Holiness;[d]
it will be for those who walk on that Way.
The unclean[e] will not journey on it;
wicked fools will not go about on it.
9 No lion[f] will be there,
nor any ravenous beast;[g]
they will not be found there.
But only the redeemed[h] will walk there,
10 and those the LORD has rescued will return.
They will enter Zion with singing;
everlasting joy[i] will crown their heads.
Gladness and joy will overtake them,
and sorrow and sighing will flee away.[j]

Sennacherib Threatens Jerusalem

36:1-22pp — 2Ki 18:13,17-37; 2Ch 32:9-19

36 In the fourteenth year of King Hezekiah's reign, Sennacherib[k] king of Assyria attacked
all the fortified cities of Judah and captured them. 2 Then the king of Assyria sent his field
commander with a large army from Lachish to King Hezekiah at Jerusalem. When the commander
stopped at the aqueduct of the Upper Pool, on the road to the Launderer's Field,[l] 3 Eliakim[m] son of

35:7 haunts ... jackals. See 34:13. Clearly there is an intentional contrast between the two statements.

35:8–10 A "highway" (v. 8; see notes on 11:16; 40:3–5) runs though the garden. It is a way home to "Zion" (v. 10), the city of God, for the "redeemed" (v. 9; cf. Heb 13:14; Rev 21–22).

35:8 Way of Holiness. Speaks of (1) ownership: this way belongs to the Holy One; and (2) the character of those who "walk" there: they have been made clean (Acts 11:9; Rev 7:14) and are not "wicked fools" (see 32:5–7 and note on 32:5).

35:10 Redemption and homecoming are causes for singing and joy (see 26:1–2; 55:12–13; 61:3,11; Ps 68:6; Acts 16:25; Rev 5:13). Israel's return from captivity anticipates the final ingathering of God's people to the new Jerusalem (Heb 12:22–24; Rev 21:3–4).

36:1—39:8 *Hezekiah's Willingness to Trust.* Chs. 36–39 contrast with chs. 7–12, the first subdivision of chs. 7–39 ("Trust: the Basis of Servanthood"; see Introduction: Outline). Chs. 7–12 show a son of David, a king of Judah, who is more ready to trust Assyria than Yahweh in a time of national crisis. As a result, Isaiah predicted Assyria would one day flood Judah up to the neck (8:6–8). Chs. 36–39 depict the situation, some 35 years later, when Isaiah's prediction comes true. Of all Jerusalem's fortifications, only Jerusalem and Lachish (about 25 miles [40 kilometers] southwest of Jerusalem) remain, and Lachish is about to fall. In the face of this ultimate threat, Hezekiah shows he has learned the kinds of lessons in trust that chs. 13–35 present. But the answer is qualified. In chs. 36–37, Hezekiah trusts God in spite of the threats of the Assyrian emperor Sennacherib, and Yahweh miraculously delivers Jerusalem. But chs. 38–39 present a somewhat different picture. Ch. 38 shows a very mortal Hezekiah, while ch. 39 depicts a very fallible Hezekiah. These seem to show that while Yahweh has been proven trustworthy, the ultimate hope of Israel is not in any human son of David, even the best one. Clearly we wait for a more-than-human Son of David. Thus, chs. 36–39 prepare the way for chs. 40–66.

The material in these chapters is repeated in very similar, often identical, form in 2 Kgs 18:13—20:19. One of the passages seems to be dependent on the other. Although some scholars consider the passage here to be dependent on the one in Kings, the organization of the material makes more sense in the context of Isaiah (see the notes on 38:1; 39:1). For that reason, it seems likely that Kings is dependent on Isaiah.

36:1—37:38 *The Lord Delivers From Assyria.* Chs. 36–37 have largely two elements: the Assyrians demand that Jerusalem surrender (36:1–20; 37:9–13), and Yahweh promises to deliver (37:5–7,21–35). Two other important components are Hezekiah's prayer of trust (37:14–20) and the report of the deliverance (37:36–38).

36:1—37:8 The field commander visits. Following the fall of Samaria in 722 BC, the Assyrians continued to push aggressively southward along the coast road toward Egypt. They began to campaign against the Philistine cities as early as 720 and returned several times in the succeeding years to press the attack. But in 705 the Assyrian emperor Sargon was killed in battle. The succession was contentious, and by the time Sennacherib gained the throne, revolt had broken out in several parts of the empire, including the West, where Hezekiah, king of Judah, was a leader. In 701 BC Sennacherib came to punish the rebels. He seems to have had little difficulty in doing so (36:1; see 2 Kgs 18:13), and as Lachish was about to fall, he sent his field commander to demand that Jerusalem surrender.

36:1 fourteenth year. Of Hezekiah's sole reign; 701 BC. There is some uncertainty about Hezekiah's dates, but it appears that he became coregent with his father, Ahaz, perhaps as early as 729 BC. At any rate he was in that role when Samaria fell in 722 (2 Kgs 18:10).

36:2 aqueduct. The very spot outside the city walls where Isaiah met Ahaz 35 years earlier and challenged him to trust Yahweh, predicting what would happen if he did not (7:3). The repetition confirms the intentional structure of this division around the theme of Yahweh's trustworthiness and that chs. 36–39 contrast with chs. 7–12.

36:3 Eliakim ... Shebna ... Joah. These three persons would have

Hilkiah the palace administrator, Shebna[n] the secretary, and Joah son of Asaph the recorder went
out to him.
4The field commander said to them, "Tell Hezekiah:

" 'This is what the great king, the king of Assyria, says: On what are you basing this confidence of yours? 5You say you have counsel and might for war — but you speak only empty words.
On whom are you depending, that you rebel[o] against me? 6Look, I know you are depending on
Egypt,[p] that splintered reed[q] of a staff, which pierces the hand of anyone who leans on it! Such
is Pharaoh king of Egypt to all who depend on him. 7But if you say to me, "We are depending on
the LORD our God" — isn't he the one whose high places and altars Hezekiah removed,[r] saying to
Judah and Jerusalem, "You must worship before this altar"?[s]
8" 'Come now, make a bargain with my master, the king of Assyria: I will give you two thousand
horses — if you can put riders on them! 9How then can you repulse one officer of the least of my
master's officials, even though you are depending on Egypt[t]
for chariots and horsemen[a]?[u] 10Furthermore, have I come to
attack and destroy this land without the LORD? The LORD himself
told[v] me to march against this country and destroy it.' "
11Then Eliakim, Shebna and Joah said to the field commander,
"Please speak to your servants in Aramaic,[w] since we understand it.
Don't speak to us in Hebrew in the hearing of the people on the wall."
12But the commander replied, "Was it only to your master and
you that my master sent me to say these things, and not to the people
sitting on the wall — who, like you, will have to eat their own excrement and drink their own urine?"
13Then the commander stood and called out in Hebrew,[x] "Hear the
words of the great king, the king of Assyria! 14This is what the king
says: Do not let Hezekiah deceive you. He cannot deliver you! 15Do
not let Hezekiah persuade you to trust in the LORD when he says, 'The
LORD will surely deliver us; this city will not be given into the hand
of the king of Assyria.'[y]
16"Do not listen to Hezekiah. This is what the king of Assyria says:
Make peace with me and come out to me. Then each of you will eat
fruit from your own vine and fig tree[z] and drink water from your own
cistern,[a] 17until I come and take you to a land like your own — a
land of grain and new wine, a land of bread and vineyards.

36:3 [n] 2Ki 18:18
36:5 [o] 2Ki 18:7
36:6 [p] Isa 30:2,5 [q] Eze 29:6-7
36:7 [r] 2Ki 18:4 [s] Dt 12:2-5
36:9 [t] Isa 31:3 [u] Isa 30:2-5
36:10 [v] 1Ki 13:18
36:11 [w] Ezr 4:7
36:13 [x] 2Ch 32:18
36:15 [y] Isa 37:10
36:16 [z] 1Ki 4:25; Zec 3:10 [a] Pr 5:15

Sennacherib as crown prince.
Kim Walton, taken at the Oriental Institute Museum, University of Chicago

[a] 9 Or *charioteers*

been members of Hezekiah's "cabinet." **Eliakim.** See 22:19–25 and notes.

36:4–20 This masterful psychological appeal is not logically consistent but piles up several points that together have a powerful effect. The central issue is trust (the Hebrew word appears six times in vv. 4–7). The officer asserts that neither Hezekiah, Egypt, nor Yahweh is trustworthy but that the Assyrian emperor is.

36:4–6 Egypt is not trustworthy (see vv. 8–10).

36:4 The field commander expresses calculated contempt: he refuses to call Hezekiah king while calling Sennacherib "the great king, the king of Assyria."

36:6 splintered reed of a staff. Already cracked, Egypt will break the moment a person puts weight on it.

36:7 The field commander says that the Lord will not help Judah because he is offended that Hezekiah removed the "high places" (2 Kgs 18:3–5; 2 Chr 31:1; see note on 16:12). The Assyrian, a polytheist, cannot understand that Yahweh, being one, demands to be worshiped in one place (Num 33:52; Deut 12:11–14). Thus, Yahweh is pleased at Hezekiah's actions, not offended.

36:8–9 This mocks Judah's alliance with Egypt. If they need horses (cf. 30:16; 31:1), they should have asked Sennacherib for them. But Judah has no trained cavalrymen, so what good would horses do them? They are unable to hold off "the least" one of Assyria's soldiers (cf. 30:17; see also Deut 28:25).

36:10 The LORD himself told me. The commander, who carefully prepared for this encounter (e.g., he learned the Hebrew dialect, v. 11), may be aware of what Isaiah was saying about Yahweh's using the nations as disciplinary tools. He does not believe this (vv. 18–20).

36:11 Aramaic. The Semitic language of Syria. It had become the common language used for trade and diplomacy in the various parts of the Assyrian Empire. The common people did not understand it, but the Assyrian boldly replies that he wants them to understand his message. If the city does not surrender and instead is besieged, they will suffer terribly.

36:13–17 The commander exhorts the inhabitants of Jerusalem to trust not Hezekiah but the king of Assyria: if they trust Hezekiah, then the city will be captured, but if they trust the king of Assyria and surrender to him, he will take them to a lush and fertile land where they will have their own property and food sources (a rather rosy view of captivity).

36:20 [b] 1Ki 20:23
36:21 [c] Pr 9:7-8; 26:4
37:2 [d] Isa 1:1
37:3 [e] Isa 26:18; 66:9; Hos 13:13
37:4 [f] Isa 36:13,18-20
[g] Isa 1:9
37:6 [h] Isa 7:4
37:7 [i] ver 9
37:8 [j] Nu 33:20
37:9 [k] ver 7
37:10 [l] Isa 36:15
37:11 [m] Isa 36:18-20
37:12 [n] 2Ki 18:11
[o] Ge 11:31; 12:1-4; Ac 7:2

18“Do not let Hezekiah mislead you when he says, ‘The LORD will deliver us.’ Have the gods of any
nations ever delivered their lands from the hand of the king of Assyria? 19Where are the gods of Hamath
and Arpad? Where are the gods of Sepharvaim? Have they rescued Samaria from my hand? 20Who of all
the gods[b] of these countries have been able to save their lands from me? How then can the LORD deliver
Jerusalem from my hand?”
21But the people remained silent and said nothing in reply, because the king had commanded, “Do
not answer him.”[c]
22Then Eliakim son of Hilkiah the palace administrator, Shebna the secretary and Joah son of Asaph
the recorder went to Hezekiah, with their clothes torn, and told him what the field commander had said.

Jerusalem’s Deliverance Foretold

37:1-13pp — 2Ki 19:1-13

37 When King Hezekiah heard this, he tore his clothes and put on sackcloth and went into the
temple of the LORD. 2He sent Eliakim the palace administrator, Shebna the secretary, and the
leading priests, all wearing sackcloth, to the prophet Isaiah son of Amoz.[d] 3They told him, “This is
what Hezekiah says: This day is a day of distress and rebuke and disgrace, as when children come to
the moment of birth[e] and there is no strength to deliver them. 4It may be that the LORD your God will
hear the words of the field commander, whom his master, the king of Assyria, has sent to ridicule the
living God, and that he will rebuke him for the words the LORD your God has heard.[f] Therefore pray for
the remnant[g] that still survives.”
5When King Hezekiah’s officials came to Isaiah, 6Isaiah said to them, “Tell your master, ‘This is what
the LORD says: Do not be afraid[h] of what you have heard — those words with which the underlings of the
king of Assyria have blasphemed me. 7Listen! When he hears a certain report,[i] I will make him want to
return to his own country, and there I will have him cut down with the sword.’ ”
8When the field commander heard that the king of Assyria had left Lachish, he withdrew and found
the king fighting against Libnah.[j]
9Now Sennacherib received a report[k] that Tirhakah, the king of Cush,[a] was marching out to fight
against him. When he heard it, he sent messengers to Hezekiah with this word: 10“Say to Hezekiah king
of Judah: Do not let the god you depend on deceive you when he says, ‘Jerusalem will not be given into
the hands of the king of Assyria.’[l] 11Surely you have heard what the kings of Assyria have done to all
the countries, destroying them completely. And will you be delivered?[m] 12Did the gods of the nations
that were destroyed by my predecessors[n] deliver them — the gods of Gozan, Harran,[o] Rezeph and the
people of Eden who were in Tel Assar? 13Where is the king of Hamath or the king of Arpad? Where are
the kings of Lair, Sepharvaim, Hena and Ivvah?”

[a] *9* That is, the upper Nile region

36:18 – 20 The commander blatantly contradicts v. 10, stating his case bluntly: Yahweh cannot prevent the king of Assyria from taking Jerusalem. He is no different from the gods of all the other countries that have fallen. This is not a contest between gods but between a man and God, and the man counts himself superior.
36:19 Hamath and Arpad. Major Syrian cities located northwest of Damascus. **Sepharvaim.** Location unknown.
36:22 clothes torn. A sign of grief and mourning. The men carried bad news to Hezekiah: his attempt to buy off Sennacherib failed (see 2 Kgs 18:14 – 16).
37:3 distress ... disgrace. Judah and their God have been publicly mocked, and it has been said that trusting Yahweh is futile, a mere man being able to do with him as he pleases. **no strength to deliver.** The great trial of faith has come, and humanly speaking, it is impossible for anything to be done. Unless Yahweh intervenes, Judah will be like a pregnant woman who dies in childbirth, too weak to deliver the child (cf. 26:18; contrast 66:7).
37:4 Hezekiah correctly identifies the issue: Assyria has ridiculed not Hezekiah or Judah but “the living God” (see v. 17). **remnant.** Jerusalem is all that remains of the nation.
37:6 underlings. If the field commander spoke contemptuously of Hezekiah (see note on 36:4), Yahweh has similar contempt for the field commander. **blasphemed.** An even stronger word than “ridicule” (v. 4).
37:7 An enigmatic promise but dramatically fulfilled (vv. 37 – 38).
37:8 left Lachish. Probably because of the Egyptian action in v. 9. The Assyrians quickly defeated the Egyptians and captured Lachish. The withdrawal of the field commander may have given rise to false hopes (cf. 22:1 – 4).
37:9 – 35 Sennacherib’s letter and the response to it.
37:9 Tirhakah, the king of Cush. See note on 18:2.
37:10 – 13 Recaps the central point of the field commander’s remarks: “the gods of the nations” (v. 12) could not deliver their people from the kings of Assyria, and neither can Yahweh.
37:12 Gozan ... Tel Assar. All cities lying between the Tigris and Euphrates Rivers. **Gozan.** The farthest east. **Tel Assar.** The farthest west. They all fell earlier.
37:13 king ... king ... kings. Their mention aims directly at Hezekiah. Those kings were all dead. **Hamath ... Ivvah.** All cities lying west of the Euphrates River in Syria (cf. 36:19); they fell more recently than those mentioned in v. 12.

Hezekiah's Prayer

37:14-20pp — 2Ki 19:14-19

14 Hezekiah received the letter from the messengers and read it. Then he went up to the temple of the
Lord and spread it out before the Lord. 15 And Hezekiah prayed to the Lord: 16 "Lord Almighty, the God
of Israel, enthroned between the cherubim, you alone are God[p] over all the kingdoms of the earth. You
have made heaven and earth. 17 Give ear, Lord, and hear;[q] open your eyes, Lord, and see;[r] listen to all
the words Sennacherib has sent to ridicule the living God.
18 "It is true, Lord, that the Assyrian kings have laid waste all these peoples and their lands.[s] 19 They
have thrown their gods into the fire and destroyed them,[t] for they were not gods[u] but only wood and
stone, fashioned by human hands. 20 Now, Lord our God, deliver us from his hand, so that all the kingdoms of the earth may know that you, Lord, are the only God.[a][v]"

Sennacherib's Fall

37:21-38pp — 2Ki 19:20-37; 2Ch 32:20-21

21 Then Isaiah son of Amoz[w] sent a message to Hezekiah: "This is what the Lord, the God of Israel,
says: Because you have prayed to me concerning Sennacherib king of Assyria, 22 this is the word the
Lord has spoken against him:

"Virgin Daughter Zion
despises and mocks you.
Daughter Jerusalem
tosses her head[x] as you flee.
23 Who is it you have ridiculed and blasphemed?[y]
Against whom have you raised your voice
and lifted your eyes in pride?[z]
Against the Holy One of Israel!
24 By your messengers
you have ridiculed the Lord.
And you have said,
'With my many chariots
I have ascended the heights of the mountains,
the utmost heights of Lebanon.[a]
I have cut down its tallest cedars,
the choicest of its junipers.
I have reached its remotest heights,
the finest of its forests.

a 20 Dead Sea Scrolls (see also 2 Kings 19:19); Masoretic Text *you alone are the Lord*

37:16 [p] Dt 10:17; Ps 86:10; 136:2-3
37:17 [q] 2Ch 6:40 [r] Da 9:18
37:18 [s] 2Ki 15:29; Na 2:11-12
37:19 [t] Isa 26:14 [u] Isa 41:24,29
37:20 [v] Ps 46:10
37:21 [w] ver 2
37:22 [x] Job 16:4
37:23 [y] ver 4 [z] Isa 2:11
37:24 [a] Isa 14:8

37:14–20 Hezekiah prays. He approaches Yahweh directly, spreading out the letter before him in the temple. He asks God to deliver him and his people—not for their own sakes but for God's reputation in the world.
37:16 Lord Almighty, the God of Israel. See notes on 1:9,24. **enthroned between the cherubim.** On the ark of the covenant; God promised to be particularly available to his people from that location (Exod 25:22). Because Yahweh "made heaven and earth," he is the one "God over all the kingdoms of the earth."
37:17 living God. Cf. Deut 5:26; Josh 3:10; 1 Sam 17:26; Ps 42:2; Jer 10:10; Matt 16:16; Acts 14:15; 2 Cor 6:16; Heb 9:14; 12:22; Rev 7:2. Unlike idols, God has no eyes or ears, but he can see and hear, which they cannot (cf. 2 Chr 6:40; Pss 115:5–9; 135:15–18; Dan 5:23; Rev 9:20).
37:18–19 The gods the Assyrians destroyed were only the works of human hands. Cf. 44:9–20.
37:20 Hezekiah did not ask that God deliver them because they deserved it or because they were his chosen people but "so that all the kingdoms of the earth may know." Cf. 2:2–4; 12:4–6; 42:1–4; 49:6–7; 56:6–8; 60:3; 66:18–23. He was concerned for Yahweh's reputation in the world.
37:21–35 Yahweh judges Assyria. The poem has four stanzas: Assyria's pride (vv. 22–25); Assyria, Yahweh's tool (vv. 26–29); a sign for Hezekiah (vv. 30–32); Assyria's destruction (vv. 33–35).
37:22 God compares Jerusalem to an apparently helpless young woman who yet mocks the mighty man as he flees.
37:23 The Assyrians have exalted themselves in "pride" (see 2:6–22 and applicable notes) over not just anyone but the one transcendent God of the universe, "the Holy One of Israel" (see note on 1:4), who has given himself to his people.
37:24–25 Assyria boasts. As the field commander did his "homework" on Israel (see note on 36:10), so Isaiah did his on Assyria. This reflects the language of the Royal Annals of Assyria.

37:25 [b] Dt 11:10
37:26 [c] Ac 2:23; 4:27-28; 1Pe 2:8 [d] Isa 10:6; 25:1 [e] Isa 25:2
37:27 [f] Ps 129:6
37:28 [g] Ps 139:1-3 [h] Ps 2:1
37:29 [i] Isa 10:12 [j] Isa 30:28; Eze 38:4 [k] ver 34
37:31 [l] Isa 27:6
37:32 [m] Isa 9:7

25 I have dug wells in foreign lands[a]
and drunk the water there.
With the soles of my feet
I have dried up all the streams of Egypt.[b]'
26 "Have you not heard?
Long ago I ordained[c] it.
In days of old I planned[d] it;
now I have brought it to pass,
that you have turned fortified cities
into piles of stone.[e]
27 Their people, drained of power,
are dismayed and put to shame.
They are like plants in the field,
like tender green shoots,
like grass sprouting on the roof,[f]
scorched[b] before it grows up.
28 "But I know where you are
and when you come and go[g]
and how you rage[h] against me.
29 Because you rage against me
and because your insolence[i] has reached my ears,
I will put my hook in your nose[j]
and my bit in your mouth,
and I will make you return
by the way you came.[k]

30 "This will be the sign for you, Hezekiah:

"This year you will eat what grows by itself,
and the second year what springs from that.
But in the third year sow and reap,
plant vineyards and eat their fruit.
31 Once more a remnant of the kingdom of Judah
will take root below and bear fruit[l] above.
32 For out of Jerusalem will come a remnant,
and out of Mount Zion a band of survivors.
The zeal[m] of the LORD Almighty
will accomplish this.

33 "Therefore this is what the LORD says concerning the king of Assyria:

"He will not enter this city
or shoot an arrow here.

[a] *25* Dead Sea Scrolls (see also 2 Kings 19:24); Masoretic Text does not have *in foreign lands.* [b] *27* Some manuscripts of the Masoretic Text, Dead Sea Scrolls and some Septuagint manuscripts (see also 2 Kings 19:26); most manuscripts of the Masoretic Text *roof / and terraced fields*

37:26–27 Assyria could do what they did to the cities and peoples of the world only because they were a tool in Yahweh's plans (cf. 14:24,26; 23:9; 46:11).
37:28–29 God will call the raging and insolent tool to account. Assyria, like a captive on a hook or a horse with a bit, will be dragged back the way it came, the same direction it planned to drag the captives from Judah.
37:30 Within three years (see 16:14; 20:3), all evidence of the Assyrian depredations will be gone from the land. Apparently they were not able to harvest the crops that year or plant anything for the coming year. But by the fall of the coming year, they would be able to plant for the harvest in the following spring and summer.
37:31–32 Like the crops, the remnant that Hezekiah is concerned about (v. 4) will also flourish again. This will be so because of the Lord's zeal for his people. He is jealous for them, and even if he allows them to be punished, he will not allow them to be exterminated (cf. Hos 11:8–11).
37:33–35 In spite of all Sennacherib's boasting, he will be unable to carry out his plans because Yahweh has other plans for him. Those

He will not come before it with shield
or build a siege ramp against it.
34 By the way that he came he will return;[n]
he will not enter this city,"
declares the LORD.
35 "I will defend[o] this city and save it,
for my sake[p] and for the sake of David[q] my servant!"

36 Then the angel of the LORD went out and put to death a hundred and eighty-five thousand in the
Assyrian[r] camp. When the people got up the next morning—there were all the dead bodies! 37 So Sennacherib king of Assyria broke camp and withdrew. He returned to Nineveh[s] and stayed there.
38 One day, while he was worshiping in the temple of his god Nisrok, his sons Adrammelek and
Sharezer killed him with the sword, and they escaped to the land of Ararat.[t] And Esarhaddon his son
succeeded him as king.

Hezekiah's Illness

38:1-8pp — 2Ki 20:1-11; 2Ch 32:24-26

38 In those days Hezekiah became ill and was at the point of death. The prophet Isaiah son of
Amoz[u] went to him and said, "This is what the LORD says: Put your house in order,[v] because
you are going to die; you will not recover."
2 Hezekiah turned his face to the wall and prayed to the LORD, 3 "Remember, LORD, how I have walked[w]
before you faithfully and with wholehearted devotion[x] and have done what is good in your eyes.[y]" And
Hezekiah wept[z] bitterly.
4 Then the word of the LORD came to Isaiah: 5 "Go and tell Hezekiah, 'This is what the LORD, the God
of your father David, says: I have heard your prayer and seen your tears; I will add fifteen years[a] to your
life. 6 And I will deliver you and this city from the hand of the king of Assyria. I will defend[b] this city.
7 " 'This is the LORD's sign[c] to you that the LORD will do what he has promised: 8 I will make the shadow
cast by the sun go back the ten steps it has gone down on the stairway of Ahaz.' " So the sunlight went
back the ten steps it had gone down.[d]

9 A writing of Hezekiah king of Judah after his illness and recovery:

10 I said, "In the prime of my life[e]
must I go through the gates of death[f]
and be robbed of the rest of my years?[g]"

37:34 [n]ver 29
37:35 [o]Isa 31:5; 38:6 [p]Isa 43:25; 48:9,11 [q]2Ki 20:6
37:36 [r]Isa 10:12
37:37 [s]Ge 10:11
37:38 [t]Ge 8:4; Jer 51:27
38:1 [u]Isa 37:2 [v]2Sa 17:23
38:3 [w]Ne 13:14; Ps 26:3 [x]1Ch 29:19 [y]Dt 6:18 [z]Ps 6:8
38:5 [a]2Ki 18:2
38:6 [b]Isa 31:5; 37:35
38:7 [c]Isa 7:11,14
38:8 [d]Jos 10:13
38:10 [e]Ps 102:24 [f]Ps 107:18; 2Co 1:9 [g]Job 17:11

plans occurred just as Isaiah predicted. There was no Assyrian siege of Jerusalem.

37:36–37 The report's brevity underlines its shocking nature. All of Sennacherib's boasts ended in one short night. Having lost the bulk, if not all, of his army, he fled back to Nineveh; he never campaigned in the west again.

37:38 Assyrian reports confirm that two of Sennacherib's sons killed him in 681 BC while he was in the temple of one of the Assyrian gods, just as Isaiah said (v. 7). Since this report occurs after the fact, either Isaiah lived that long or a later editor added it to confirm what Isaiah said.

38:1—39:8 *Hezekiah's Mortality and Fallibility.* Chs. 7–12 end on a positive note (in spite of Ahaz's faithlessness, God's Messiah will come to earth with salvation for Israel and all people), but chs. 36–39, which begin so positively by vindicating Hezekiah's trust, end on a much more somber note. They make it plain that Hezekiah is not the promised Messiah: he is both mortal (ch. 38) and fallible (ch. 39).

38:1–8 Hezekiah becomes ill, and Isaiah announces that he will recover.

38:1 In those days. Hezekiah's recovery and the envoys' visit may have taken place in 710 BC (see note on 39:1), whereas chs. 36–37 are dated to 701 BC. If so, Isaiah reports it out of chronological order to make the point that Hezekiah is not the promised Messiah (see the note on 38:1—39:8).

38:3 walked before you. Cf. Gen 17:1. **faithfully.** Cf. 1 Kgs 2:4. Hezekiah has fulfilled God's command to David and his successors. Depending on when Hezekiah and Manasseh lived, it is possible that Hezekiah has no heir at this point and that if he died, the Davidic dynasty would end. **wholehearted devotion.** As opposed to devotion that is divided by worship of self or of other gods (cf. 1 Kgs 11:4; 15:14; 2 Chr 25:2; Rom 1:9; Phil 3:7–15; 1 Thess 5:23). But cf. v. 17 and note.

38:5 God of your father David. Hezekiah fulfilled the commands to David and merited special consideration.

38:6 deliver ... city. While this could date the passage to the attack of Sennacherib (chs. 36–37), the Assyrian threat was very real from Samaria's fall (722 BC) onward.

38:7–8 According to 2 Kgs 20:8, Hezekiah requested a sign, but Ahaz refused one (Isa 7:12).

38:8 go back the ten steps. This "stairway" was used as a sort of sun dial. This is a miraculous event.

38:9–20 In these circumstances one might expect an individual song of thanksgiving, but this poem does not conform to the pattern of such songs. While Hezekiah does recognize that God has delivered him from death (v. 17), he does not thank God for it. Instead, after reflecting on the terror brought on by impending death (vv. 10–14), he determines to "walk humbly" (v. 15) during his extended life and to praise God, something the dead cannot do (vv. 15–20). The reader recognizes that the added 15 years are only a reprieve.

38:11 [h]Ps 27:13; 116:9
38:12 [i]2Co 5:1,4; 2Pe 1:13-14 [j]Job 4:21 [k]Heb 1:12 [l]Job 7:6 [m]Ps 73:14
38:13 [n]Ps 51:8 [o]Job 10:16; Da 6:24
38:14 [p]Isa 59:11 [q]Job 17:3
38:15 [r]Ps 39:9 [s]1Ki 21:27 [t]Job 7:11
38:16 [u]Ps 119:25
38:17 [v]Ps 30:3 [w]Jer 31:34 [x]Isa 43:25; Mic 7:19
38:18 [y]Ecc 9:10 [z]Ps 6:5; 88:10-11; 115:17 [a]Ps 30:9
38:19 [b]Dt 6:7; Ps 118:17; 119:175 [c]Dt 11:19
38:20 [d]Ps 68:25 [e]Ps 33:2 [f]Ps 116:2 [g]Ps 116:17-19

11 I said, "I will not again see the LORD himself
in the land of the living;[h]
no longer will I look on my fellow man,
or be with those who now dwell in this world.
12 Like a shepherd's tent[i] my house
has been pulled down[j] and taken from me.
Like a weaver I have rolled[k] up my life,
and he has cut me off from the loom;[l]
day and night[m] you made an end of me.
13 I waited patiently till dawn,
but like a lion he broke[n] all my bones;[o]
day and night you made an end of me.
14 I cried like a swift or thrush,
I moaned like a mourning dove.[p]
My eyes grew weak as I looked to the heavens.
I am being threatened; Lord, come to my aid!"[q]

15 But what can I say?
He has spoken to me, and he himself has
done this.[r]
I will walk humbly[s] all my years
because of this anguish of my soul.[t]
16 Lord, by such things people live;
and my spirit finds life in them too.
You restored me to health
and let me live.[u]
17 Surely it was for my benefit
that I suffered such anguish.
In your love you kept me
from the pit[v] of destruction;
you have put all my sins[w]
behind your back.[x]
18 For the grave[y] cannot praise you,
death cannot sing your praise;[z]
those who go down to the pit[a]
cannot hope for your faithfulness.
19 The living, the living — they praise[b] you,
as I am doing today;
parents tell their children[c]
about your faithfulness.

20 The LORD will save me,
and we will sing[d] with stringed instruments[e]
all the days of our lives[f]
in the temple[g] of the LORD.

38:11 not again see the LORD. Expresses the frequent OT view that the underworld is a dim, dusty place (Hebrew *šĕʾôl*; vv. 10,18) lacking in joy or praise (see also v. 18; cf. Pss 6:5; 30:9; 88:11; 115:17). That view was not universally held, as 26:19; Dan 12:2 show (see also such statements as "I will praise you forever" [Ps 30:12]), but it was common. By intertestamental times a significant number of Jews believed in resurrection to new life, but Jesus' death and resurrection gave that hope genuine theological basis (John 14:1–4; 1 Cor 15:12–22). See "Death and Resurrection," p. 2670.

38:12 Hezekiah compares life to a piece of cloth on a "loom": it grows progressively longer until it is suddenly "cut … off."

38:13–14 If Yahweh has broken Hezekiah's bones, then Yahweh has the power to come to his aid. Yahweh is the first cause of all things; nothing can defy his good purposes.

38:15–16 In his additional years, Hezekiah will remember that every day is a gift. He will not forget his anguish when he thought he would die.

38:17 Hezekiah recognizes that his good behavior is not the cause of the

[21]Isaiah had said, "Prepare a poultice of figs and apply it to the boil, and he will recover."
[22]Hezekiah had asked, "What will be the sign that I will go up to the temple of the LORD?"

Envoys From Babylon

39:1-8pp — 2Ki 20:12-19

39 At that time Marduk-Baladan son of Baladan king of Babylon[h] sent Hezekiah letters and a gift, because he had heard of his illness and recovery. [2]Hezekiah received the envoys[i] gladly and showed them what was in his storehouses — the silver, the gold,[j] the spices, the fine olive oil — his entire armory and everything found among his treasures. There was nothing in his palace or in all his kingdom that Hezekiah did not show them.

[3]Then Isaiah the prophet went to King Hezekiah and asked, "What did those men say, and where did they come from?"

"From a distant land,[k]" Hezekiah replied. "They came to me from Babylon."

[4]The prophet asked, "What did they see in your palace?"

"They saw everything in my palace," Hezekiah said. "There is nothing among my treasures that I did not show them."

[5]Then Isaiah said to Hezekiah, "Hear the word of the LORD Almighty: [6]The time will surely come when everything in your palace, and all that your predecessors have stored up until this day, will be carried off to Babylon.[l] Nothing will be left, says the LORD. [7]And some of your descendants, your own flesh and blood who will be born to you, will be taken away, and they will become eunuchs in the palace of the king of Babylon.[m]"

[8]"The word of the LORD you have spoken is good," Hezekiah replied. For he thought, "There will be peace and security in my lifetime.[n]"

Comfort for God's People

40 Comfort, comfort[o] my people,
says your God.
[2]Speak tenderly[p] to Jerusalem,
and proclaim to her

39:1 [h]2Ch 32:31
39:2 [i]2Ch 32:31 [j]2Ki 18:15
39:3 [k]Dt 28:49
39:6 [l]2Ki 24:13; Jer 20:5
39:7 [m]2Ki 24:15; Da 1:1-7
39:8 [n]2Ch 32:26
40:1 [o]Isa 12:1; 49:13; 51:3,12; 52:9; 61:2; 66:13; Jer 31:13; Zep 3:14-17; 2Co 1:3
40:2 [p]Isa 35:4

gift of lengthened life. Grace is never earned. God puts our "sins behind [his] back" (cf. Rom 5:15).

38:21–22 Additional material perhaps added from a different source (cf. 2 Kgs 20:7–8).

39:1 Marduk-Baladan. A Babylonian leader who periodically led rebellions against Assyria. He would be in power for a year or two and then in eclipse. He seems to have been in power in 710 BC, but he had been deposed and was probably dead before 701. This is an opportunity for Hezekiah to give glory to God before a foreign nation (cf. 12:4–6).

39:2 A tragic mistake. The Babylonians had come because of Hezekiah's miraculous recovery. Instead of telling them about Yahweh, Hezekiah showed them his "treasures," which the Babylonians had much more of than Judah had. What Babylon did not have was the miracle-working Yahweh.

39:4 Hezekiah shows no awareness of his failure.

39:6 carried off to Babylon. This will happen not because Hezekiah failed but because like him the people of Judah will fail to make trust in Yahweh a settled pattern of behavior. Isaiah sees the future and understands that Assyria is not Judah's major problem. Thus ch. 39 sets the stage for what will follow in chs. 40–66.

39:7–8 Some of the house of David would be reduced to being "eunuchs" in the Babylonian court. But instead of being concerned over what he might do to carry out his responsibility for the continuance of the Davidic line, Hezekiah comforts himself that these circumstances will not occur in his "lifetime." This came to typify how Judah responded to prophetic warnings over the next century and a quarter.

40:1 — 55:13 *Grace: The Motive and Means of Servanthood.* Chs. 7–39 establish that Yahweh is trustworthy and will deliver his servants when they trust him. They also demonstrate Yahweh's absolute holiness, which provides the foundation of the vision in ch. 6: he *is* the Holy One of Israel. But what will move Israel, the nation of unclean lips, to actually trust him and become the messengers of his unique saviorhood to a lost world? Furthermore, assuming that they do trust him and are willing to become his servants, what will make it possible for sinful Israel to become holy Israel? The answer to both questions is divine grace. Grace will motivate Israel to trust God, and then grace will make it possible for them to actually serve him. Ch. 40 introduces these ideas. Chs. 41–48 present the grace of God in its motivating light: Yahweh has not cast Israel off but has chosen Israel as his servant. Chs. 49–55 show how God's grace is the means whereby he cleanses sinful Israel to serve him. In order to make these points that are essential to the total theological vision that the exile (beginning with Samaria's exile in Isaiah's own day) will make necessary, the Holy Spirit gives Isaiah a vision of the distant future that encompasses Judah's exile and return.

Chs. 40–55 represent a high point, both in Hebrew poetic expression and in theological revelation. The language has a lyrical beauty unmatched elsewhere in the OT, and the concepts of transcendent monotheism and creation as something completely new are developed here as nowhere else in the Bible.

40:1–31 *Gracious Deliverance.* Ch. 40 introduces the concerns of chs. 41–55 by addressing three questions the Jewish exiles will be asking: (1) Does Yahweh *want* to deliver us (vv. 1–11)? (2) *Can* Yahweh deliver us (vv. 12–26)? (3) *Will* Yahweh deliver us (vv. 27–31)? By answering all of these questions affirmatively, Isaiah successfully establishes the foundation of divine grace for chs. 41–55.

40:1–11 *Yahweh Desires to Deliver His People.* These verses make it

40:2 [q]Isa 41:11-13; 49:25 [r]Isa 61:7; Jer 16:18; Zec 9:12; Rev 18:6
40:3 [s]Mal 3:1 [t]Mt 3:3*; Mk 1:3*; Jn 1:23*
40:4 [u]Isa 45:2,13
40:5 [v]Isa 52:10; Lk 3:4-6* [w]Isa 1:20; 58:14
40:6 [x]Job 14:2
40:7 [y]Job 41:21
40:8 [z]Isa 55:11; 59:21 [a]Mt 5:18; 1Pe 1:24-25*
40:9 [b]Isa 52:7-10; 61:1; Ro 10:15 [c]Isa 25:9
40:10 [d]Rev 22:7 [e]Isa 9:6-7 [f]Isa 59:16

that her hard service has been completed,[q]
that her sin has been paid for,
that she has received from the LORD's hand
double[r] for all her sins.

3 A voice of one calling:
"In the wilderness prepare
the way[s] for the LORD[a];
make straight in the desert
a highway for our God.[b][t]
4 Every valley shall be raised up,
every mountain and hill made low;
the rough ground shall become level,[u]
the rugged places a plain.
5 And the glory of the LORD will be revealed,
and all people will see it together.[v]
For the mouth of the LORD has spoken."[w]

6 A voice says, "Cry out."
And I said, "What shall I cry?"

"All people are like grass,[x]
and all their faithfulness is like the flowers of the field.
7 The grass withers and the flowers fall,
because the breath[y] of the LORD blows on them.
Surely the people are grass.
8 The grass withers and the flowers fall,
but the word[z] of our God endures forever.[a]"

9 You who bring good news[b] to Zion,
go up on a high mountain.
You who bring good news to Jerusalem,[c]
lift up your voice with a shout,
lift it up, do not be afraid;
say to the towns of Judah,
"Here is your God!"[c]
10 See, the Sovereign LORD comes[d] with power,
and he rules[e] with a mighty arm.[f]

[a] 3 Or *A voice of one calling in the wilderness: / "Prepare the way for the LORD* [b] 3 Hebrew; Septuagint *make straight the paths of our God* [c] 9 Or *Zion, bringer of good news, / go up on a high mountain. / Jerusalem, bringer of good news*

unmistakably clear that the destruction of Jerusalem in 586 BC will not be a sign that Yahweh's ancient promises have failed or that Yahweh is impotent in the face of the people's sin. His goal is not to condemn them but to encourage them ("comfort," v. 1; cf. 51:12). Four stanzas announce (1) Yahweh's intention (vv. 1–2), (2) Yahweh's coming (vv. 3–5), (3) humanity's weakness (vv. 6–8), and (4) Yahweh's rule (vv. 9–11). Commands to speak are prominent; the good news must be proclaimed. Three different voices are mentioned (vv. 3,6,9). The NT associates the first with John the Baptist (Matt 3:3; Mark 1:2–3; Luke 3:4–6).

40:1 Comfort. The sense here is to encourage or strengthen. It is said twice here for emphasis.

40:2 Speak tenderly to. Or "speak to the heart of." Cf. Joseph (Gen 50:21), Boaz (Ruth 2:13), and Hezekiah (2 Chr 30:22; Hos 2:14)—each of whom reassures and encourages someone who is fearful. **her sin.** Jerusalem's sins will not be held against her because they have been paid for (cf. 53:10). **received ... double for all her sins.** Full retribution for Israel's sin has been paid out, and no more punishment will be forthcoming.

40:3–5 No obstacle can prevent Yahweh from delivering his people (cf. 57:14; 62:10).

40:3 voice. Reflects the herald who preceded the king in his procession (cf. 52: 7). **highway.** Cf. 35:8; see note on 11:16.

40:5 glory. See 6:3 and note.

40:6–8 Humans will present no barrier to God's grace on behalf of his people. Humans are like grass and wild flowers: they wither and fall to the ground (v. 24); they are completely unreliable. In contrast, "the word of our God endures forever" (v. 8; cf. 1 Pet 1:23–25, which uses this passage to affirm the infallibility of God's word, especially in its life-giving power).

40:8 word of our God. God's promise to deliver.

40:10–11 There are two aspects of God's "mighty arm." (1) His arm is the manifestation of the power of the "Sovereign LORD" to accom-

See, his reward[g] is with him,
and his recompense accompanies him.
11 He tends his flock like a shepherd:[h]
He gathers the lambs in his arms
and carries them close to his heart;
he gently leads those that have young.

12 Who has measured the waters[i] in the hollow of his hand,[j]
or with the breadth of his hand marked off the heavens?[k]
Who has held the dust of the earth in a basket,
or weighed the mountains on the scales
and the hills in a balance?
13 Who can fathom the Spirit[a] of the LORD,
or instruct the LORD as his counselor?[l]
14 Whom did the LORD consult to enlighten him,
and who taught him the right way?
Who was it that taught him knowledge,[m]
or showed him the path of understanding?

15 Surely the nations are like a drop in a bucket;
they are regarded as dust on the scales;
he weighs the islands as though they were fine dust.
16 Lebanon is not sufficient for altar fires,
nor its animals[n] enough for burnt offerings.
17 Before him all the nations[o] are as nothing;[p]
they are regarded by him as worthless
and less than nothing.[q]

18 With whom, then, will you compare God?[r]
To what image[s] will you liken him?
19 As for an idol,[t] a metalworker casts it,
and a goldsmith[u] overlays it with gold[v]
and fashions silver chains for it.
20 A person too poor to present such an offering
selects wood that will not rot;
they look for a skilled worker
to set up an idol that will not topple.[w]

40:10 [g] Isa 62:11; Rev 22:12
40:11 [h] Eze 34:23; Mic 5:4; Jn 10:11
40:12 [i] Job 38:10 [j] Pr 30:4 [k] Heb 1:10-12
40:13 [l] Ro 11:34*; 1Co 2:16*
40:14 [m] Job 21:22; Col 2:3
40:16 [n] Ps 50:9-11; Mic 6:7; Heb 10:5-9
40:17 [o] Isa 30:28 [p] Isa 29:7 [q] Da 4:35
40:18 [r] Ex 8:10; 1Sa 2:2; Isa 46:5 [s] Ac 17:29
40:19 [t] Ps 115:4 [u] Isa 41:7; Jer 10:3 [v] Isa 2:20
40:20 [w] 1Sa 5:3

[a] *13* Or *mind*

plish his redeeming purpose (v. 10; see also 50:2; 51:5,9; 52:10; 53:1). (2) His arms gather the lambs (v. 11).

40:10 recompense. See note on 34:8.

40:12–26 *Yahweh Is Able to Deliver His People.* He is incomparable; nothing—particularly not the gods of Babylon (vv. 18–20,25–26; cf. chs. 41–46)—can prevent him from fulfilling his desire to deliver. He is the sole Creator (vv. 12–14,21–22) before whom the great empires "are as nothing" (v. 17; see vv. 15–17,23–24).

40:12–14 The formidable series of rhetorical questions in vv. 12–14 can be distilled into three basic questions: Who created the universe; Who counseled him in the process; and Who in creation can be compared to him? The implied answer to the first is: none but God, and the implied answers to the second and third are: no one at all. Yahweh is another order of magnitude over the creation (v. 12). He does *not* personify the forces of nature. He was alone in creation (vv. 13–14). Unlike the pagan stories of origins, which speak of the gods taking counsel with one another, Yahweh did not consult anyone.

40:13 Spirit of the LORD. Underlines the role of the Spirit in Gen 1:1. Paul quotes v. 13 in Rom 11:34; 1 Cor 2:16.

40:15–17 If Yahweh alone is Creator, then the nations can hardly claim equality with him, much less superiority (see 36:18–20; 37:10–13). Yahweh permits them to do what they do, and he will reverse it whenever he chooses.

40:15 islands. The ends of the earth.

40:16 Lebanon. Had the greatest forests on earth. They could not provide enough wood to give God the kinds of "altar fires" he deserves.

40:18–20 Can a humanly conceived and fabricated idol possibly compare to the Creator of the universe, the one who made the wood, gold, and silver being used? Of course not! Isaiah would have understood that the gods were not confined to the images. But the gods, being only humanly conceived representations of cosmic forces, were no more able to save than the physical images were. Cf. 41:5–7; 42:17; 44:6–20; 46:1–2,5–7.

40:21 [x]Ps 19:1; 50:6; Ac 14:17 [y]Ro 1:19 [z]Isa 48:13; 51:13
40:22 [a]Nu 13:33; Ps 104:2; Isa 42:5 [b]Job 22:14 [c]Job 36:29
40:23 [d]Isa 34:12 [e]Job 12:21; Ps 107:40
40:24 [f]Isa 41:16
40:25 [g]ver 18
40:26 [h]Isa 51:6 [i]Ps 89:11-13; Isa 42:5 [j]Ps 147:4 [k]Isa 34:16
40:27 [l]Job 27:2; Lk 18:7-8
40:28 [m]ver 21 [n]Ps 90:2 [o]Ps 147:5; Ro 11:33
40:29 [p]Isa 50:4; Jer 31:25
40:30 [q]Isa 9:17; Jer 6:11; 9:21

21 Do you not know?
Have you not heard?
Has it not been told[x] you from the beginning?
Have you not understood[y] since the earth was founded?[z]
22 He sits enthroned above the circle of the earth,
and its people are like grasshoppers.[a]
He stretches out the heavens like a canopy,[b]
and spreads them out like a tent[c] to live in.
23 He brings princes[d] to naught
and reduces the rulers of this world to nothing.[e]
24 No sooner are they planted,
no sooner are they sown,
no sooner do they take root in the ground,
than he blows[f] on them and they wither,
and a whirlwind sweeps them away like chaff.

25 "To whom will you compare me?[g]
Or who is my equal?" says the Holy One.
26 Lift up your eyes and look to the heavens:[h]
Who created[i] all these?
He who brings out the starry host[j] one by one
and calls forth each of them by name.
Because of his great power and mighty strength,
not one of them is missing.[k]

27 Why do you complain, Jacob?
Why do you say, Israel,
"My way is hidden from the LORD;
my cause is disregarded by my God"?[l]
28 Do you not know?
Have you not heard?[m]
The LORD is the everlasting[n] God,
the Creator of the ends of the earth.
He will not grow tired or weary,
and his understanding no one can fathom.[o]
29 He gives strength to the weary[p]
and increases the power of the weak.
30 Even youths grow tired and weary,
and young men[q] stumble and fall;

40:21–26 This recaps the answers to the three basic questions in vv. 12–14 (see note): Yahweh is the Creator (vv. 21–22); as such, he is superior to "the rulers of this world" (v. 23) and to the "starry host" of heaven (v. 26).

40:21 Do you not know? If it were not for our fallen natures, the message of the natural realm would be unmistakable. Thus, we are left without excuse (cf. Rom 1:18).

40:22 tent. May reflect the idea that the tabernacle was a model of the cosmos.

40:24 See vv. 6–7.

40:25–26 While this argument includes Yahweh's lordship of the actual stars, numbering now in multiplied billions, the context (especially vv. 18–20) suggests that here the "starry host" also refers to the visible representation of the gods as the pagans understood them. Is Yahweh one of the gods? Can he be compared to them? No, the so-called gods do his bidding.

40:27–31 *Yahweh Intends to Deliver His People.* It is one thing for Yahweh to *want* to save and another for him to be *able* to save, but those assertions do not mean much unless he actually *intends* to save. These verses establish that he does.

40:27–28 Although some of the Israelites in exile might say that God does not really care about his people's plight ("my cause is disregarded," v. 27; cf. 49:14), perhaps because deliverance does not occur at once, God asserts that as Creator neither his strength nor understanding can be equated with anything in the cosmos.

40:29–31 The source of strength is in the realm not of the physical but of the spiritual. The argument is exactly the same as that in ch. 30 (see note on 30:1–18). Those who rush to rely on the strength resident in creation ("youths," v. 30) will inevitably fail, but those who "hope in" (v. 31) the Lord, the Creator, will discover reservoirs of strength and endurance of which the world knows nothing.

31 but those who hope[r] in the LORD
will renew their strength.[s]
They will soar on wings like eagles;[t]
they will run and not grow weary,
they will walk and not be faint.[u]

The Helper of Israel

41 "Be silent[v] before me, you islands![w]
Let the nations renew their strength!
Let them come forward[x] and speak;
let us meet together[y] at the place of judgment.

2 "Who has stirred[z] up one from the east,[a]
calling him in righteousness to his service[a]?
He hands nations over to him
and subdues kings before him.
He turns them to dust[b] with his sword,
to windblown chaff[c] with his bow.
3 He pursues them and moves on unscathed,
by a path his feet have not traveled before.
4 Who has done this and carried it through,
calling forth the generations from the beginning?[d]
I, the LORD — with the first of them
and with the last[e] — I am he."

5 The islands[f] have seen it and fear;
the ends of the earth tremble.
They approach and come forward;
6 they help each other
and say to their companions, "Be strong!"

40:31 [r]Lk 18:1 [s]2Co 4:16 [t]Ex 19:4; Ps 103:5 [u]2Co 4:1; Heb 12:1-3
41:1 [v]Hab 2:20; Zec 2:13 [w]Isa 11:11 [x]Isa 48:16 [y]Isa 1:18; 34:1; 50:8
41:2 [z]Ezr 1:2 [a]ver 25; Isa 45:1,13 [b]2Sa 22:43 [c]Isa 40:24
41:4 [d]ver 26; Isa 46:10 [e]Isa 44:6; 48:12; Rev 1:8,17; 22:13
41:5 [f]Eze 26:17-18

[a] 2 Or *east, / whom victory meets at every step*

41:1 — 48:22 *Israel Graciously Chosen to Be God's Servant.* The exiles from Judah could well feel that all is now lost: if the Babylonian gods did not defeat Yahweh, then the sins of his people did; in any case, the ancient promises are now null and void. But chs. 41 – 48 say that this is not the case at all. Yahweh is *not* defeated. In fact, he has chosen Israel as his servant (41:8; 43:10; 44:1,21; 45:4) to demonstrate that idols are nothing and that he alone can save the world because he alone created it. This election based on grace should motivate them to trust him and enter his service. Chs. 41 – 46 assert Yahweh's superiority over the idols, particularly through repeated legal cases in which Israel's testimony is critical. Idols do not know the future, but Yahweh does. The unit closes with two addresses in the light of the foregoing: judgment on Babylon (ch. 47) and a challenge to Israel (ch. 48).

41:1 — 46:13 *The Lord's Court Case Against Idols.* There is no clear development of thought in this unit. Rather, several themes recur: idolatry is foolish; idols cannot explain the future; Yahweh's predictions (to which Israel is witness) are valid; Israel is Yahweh's servant; Yahweh is the sole Creator; Yahweh is the only one capable of redemption; and redemption results from his unmerited grace. The section may have three groupings: 41:1 — 42:9; 42:10 — 44:22; 44:23 — 46:13.

41:1 — 42:9 *The Two Servants.* This introduces two rather different servants: a fearful one, Israel, (41:1 – 20) and a ministering one, who is not yet clearly identified (42:1 – 9). They are not the same (see note on 42:1 – 9). But God makes gracious promises to both of them. In 41:21 – 29 the Lord presents his first case against idols (see note on 41:21 – 29).

41:1 – 20 *The Fearful Servant: Israel.* God has aroused a mighty conqueror "from the east" (v. 2). As a result the nations are terrified (vv. 5 – 7). But God counsels fearful "Israel" (v. 8) "not [to] be afraid" (v. 14) because "the Holy One of Israel" (vv. 14,16,20) will protect them as evidence of his lordship.

41:1 – 4 The nations are summoned to judgment (v. 1). They must answer to Yahweh — "the first … the last" (v. 4; cf. 48:12; see also Rev 1:8,17; 2:8; 21:6; 22:13, where Jesus identifies himself as the First and the Last) — who has brought forth a great new conqueror "from the east" (v. 2; cf. 44:24 — 45:5; 45:13; 46:11).

41:2 in righteousness. Yahweh's calling forth Cyrus was the right thing to do (see note on 45:9 – 19). **hands nations over.** Cyrus leads a coalition of Medes (see note on 13:17) and Persians who defeated the Babylonian armies during the 540s BC, culminating in the conquest of Babylon in 539. Within 40 years the Persian Empire was the largest empire the world had ever known, stretching from the Indus River in the east to Macedonia in the west and from southern Egypt to the Caucasus Mountains in the north.

41:4 I am he. Bluntly asserts self-existence growing out of the divine name (43:10,13,25; 46:4; 48:12; see note on 1:2). None of the gods can say such a thing. Jesus boldly appropriates this phrase for himself (John 8:24; 18:5,6,8; cf. Mark 14:62; John 6:35; 8:12; 9:5; 10:7,9,11,14; 11:25; 13:19; 14:6; 15:1,5).

41:5 – 7 People from "the ends of the earth" (v. 5), terrified at the news of Cyrus's approach, ask craftsmen to make idols for them.

41:7 [g] Isa 40:19
41:8 [h] Isa 29:22; 51:2; 63:16 [i] 2Ch 20:7; Jas 2:23
41:9 [j] Isa 11:12 [k] Dt 7:6
41:10 [l] Jos 1:9; Isa 43:2, 5; Ro 8:31 [m] ver 13-14; Isa 44:2; 49:8
41:11 [n] Isa 17:12 [o] Isa 45:24 [p] Ex 23:22 [q] Isa 29:8
41:12 [r] Ps 37:35-36 [s] Isa 17:14
41:13 [t] Isa 42:6; 45:1 [u] ver 10
41:15 [v] Mic 4:13

7 The metalworker encourages the goldsmith,[g]
and the one who smooths with the hammer
spurs on the one who strikes the anvil.
One says of the welding, "It is good."
The other nails down the idol so it will not topple.

8 "But you, Israel, my servant,
Jacob, whom I have chosen,
you descendants of Abraham[h] my friend,[i]
9 I took you from the ends of the earth,[j]
from its farthest corners I called you.
I said, 'You are my servant';
I have chosen[k] you and have not rejected you.
10 So do not fear, for I am with you;[l]
do not be dismayed, for I am your God.
I will strengthen you and help[m] you;
I will uphold you with my righteous right hand.

11 "All who rage[n] against you
will surely be ashamed and disgraced;[o]
those who oppose[p] you
will be as nothing and perish.[q]
12 Though you search for your enemies,
you will not find them.[r]
Those who wage war against you
will be as nothing[s] at all.
13 For I am the LORD your God
who takes hold of your right hand[t]
and says to you, Do not fear;
I will help[u] you.
14 Do not be afraid, you worm Jacob,
little Israel, do not fear,
for I myself will help you," declares the LORD,
your Redeemer, the Holy One of Israel.
15 "See, I will make you into a threshing sledge,[v]
new and sharp, with many teeth.
You will thresh the mountains and crush them,
and reduce the hills to chaff.

41:7 so it will not topple. Sarcastic; the idols are helpless (see note on 40:18–20).

41:8–20 But Israel does not need to fear, because their God is not one of the useless idols. His covenant with them is still in force: they are his "chosen" ones (vv. 8,9), "descendants of Abraham" (v. 8). He will use them in his judgment of the world (vv. 11–16), and he will provide for them, turning the desert into a place of water and vegetation (vv. 17–20; cf. 35:1–7; 43:19–21).

41:8 my servant. Yahweh declares that far from being cast off, Israel is being given a special position in his kingdom similar to that of Moses (Mal 4:4), David (1 Kgs 11:13), and the prophets (2 Kgs 17:13). In particular, their service will consist of bearing witness to who Yahweh is, what he has said, and what he has done (43:8–13).

41:10 I am with you. God's presence with his people in the world is the ultimate antidote to fear (cf. 43:5; Gen 26:24; Josh 1:9; see note on 7:14, "Immanuel"). **righteous right hand.** The hand that can be trusted to do the right thing in every circumstance. God will not do wrong; so he acted righteously when he sent the people into exile. And it will also be an act of righteousness for him to deliver them (42:21; 45:21).

41:11–14 Their enemies will disappear (cf. 29:5–8; 30:27–33) because their "Redeemer, the Holy One of Israel" (v. 14) will help them. The three occurrences of "Holy One of Israel" (vv. 14,16,20) seem to draw on the occurrences of the phrase in chs. 1–39, where it typically is associated with transcendent power (10:17; 12:6; 17:7; 30:11,12). In this latter part of the book, that power is associated particularly with redemption (43:14; 47:4; 48:17; 49:7; 54:5).

41:14 you worm Jacob. Not a derogatory comment but simply a recognition that in comparison to the great power that held the nation in captivity, the nation seemed very small indeed. But that smallness ("little Israel") was no problem for holy Yahweh.

41:15–16 In the end God will use Israel as a tool in his judgment of the world (cf. Mic 4:13: Zech 12:1–6). For Israel to become God's instruments to "thresh" the nations was to say that nothing could stand in Israel's way if they were wholly yielded to him as his servants.

41:15 mountains and ... hills. Symbolize unchanging power as seen in the natural universe.

[16] You will winnow[w] them, the wind will pick them up,
and a gale will blow them away.
But you will rejoice in the LORD
and glory[x] in the Holy One of Israel.

[17] "The poor and needy search for water,[y]
but there is none;
their tongues are parched with thirst.
But I the LORD will answer[z] them;
I, the God of Israel, will not forsake them.
[18] I will make rivers flow[a] on barren heights,
and springs within the valleys.
I will turn the desert[b] into pools of water,
and the parched ground into springs.[c]
[19] I will put in the desert
the cedar and the acacia, the myrtle and the olive.
I will set junipers in the wasteland,
the fir and the cypress together,[d]
[20] so that people may see and know,
may consider and understand,
that the hand of the LORD has done this,
that the Holy One of Israel has created[e] it.

[21] "Present your case," says the LORD.
"Set forth your arguments," says Jacob's King.[f]
[22] "Tell us, you idols,
what is going to happen.[g]
Tell us what the former things were,
so that we may consider them
and know their final outcome.
Or declare to us the things to come,[h]
[23] tell us what the future holds,
so we may know[i] that you are gods.
Do something, whether good or bad,[j]
so that we will be dismayed and filled with fear.
[24] But you are less than nothing[k]
and your works are utterly worthless;
whoever chooses you is detestable.[l]

[25] "I have stirred up one from the north,[m] and he comes—
one from the rising sun who calls on my name.
He treads[n] on rulers as if they were mortar,
as if he were a potter treading the clay.
[26] Who told of this from the beginning, so we could know,
or beforehand, so we could say, 'He was right'?

41:16 [w] Jer 51:2 [x] Isa 45:25
41:17 [y] Isa 43:20 [z] Isa 30:19
41:18 [a] Isa 30:25 [b] Isa 43:19 [c] Isa 35:7
41:19 [d] Isa 60:13
41:20 [e] Job 12:9
41:21 [f] Isa 43:15
41:22 [g] Isa 43:9; 45:21 [h] Isa 46:10
41:23 [i] Isa 42:9; 44:7-8; 45:3 [j] Jer 10:5
41:24 [k] Isa 37:19; 44:9; 1Co 8:4 [l] Ps 115:8
41:25 [m] ver 2 [n] 2Sa 22:43

41:17–20 Although the mighty of the earth have oppressed the "poor and needy" (v. 17), Yahweh will provide for them (cf. 11:4; 14:30; 32:7). He does all this "so that people may ... know" (v. 20) what sort of redemption he can create (cf. 2:1–5; 12:4–6 and notes).

41:21–29 *The First Presentation of the Case Against Idols.* Far from having defeated Yahweh, the so-called gods of the Babylonians do not even merit the title "gods" (vv. 24,29). That is because they can neither explain where the world came from ("the former things," v. 22) nor tell "what the future holds" (v. 23). They merely personify natural forces and thus cannot explain either the past or the future. Yahweh, on the other hand, stands outside the circle of time and space (40:22) and sees everything from that perspective. He can predict something far in advance, and it will come to pass. Cyrus is a premier example of this (vv. 25–27). See the notes on 43:8–13; 44:6–20; 45:20—46:7.

41:25 north ... rising sun. Although Cyrus came from Persia in the east (cf. v. 2), he first bypassed the city of Babylon and defeated the Babylonian armies in the north. Only then did he turn south to take the city itself.

41:26 He was right. Predictions from the idols were notoriously vague and ambiguous. They were never so specific that they could be proven right or wrong.

41:26 [o] Hab 2:18-19
41:27 [p] Isa 48:3,16 [q] Isa 40:9
41:28 [r] Isa 50:2; 59:16; 63:5 [s] Isa 40:13-14
41:29 [t] ver 24 [u] Jer 5:13
42:1 [v] Isa 43:10; Lk 9:35; 1Pe 2:4,6 [w] Isa 11:2; Mt 3:16-17; Jn 3:34
42:3 [x] Ps 72:2
42:4 [y] Ge 49:10; Mt 12:18-21*
42:5 [z] Ps 24:2 [a] Ac 17:25
42:6 [b] Isa 43:1 [c] Jer 23:6

No one told of this,
no one foretold it,
no one heard any words[o] from you.
27 I was the first to tell[p] Zion, 'Look, here they are!'
I gave to Jerusalem a messenger of good news.[q]
28 I look but there is no one[r] —
no one among the gods to give counsel,[s]
no one to give answer when I ask them.
29 See, they are all false!
Their deeds amount to nothing;[t]
their images are but wind[u] and confusion.

The Servant of the Lord

42 "Here is my servant, whom I uphold,
my chosen one[v] in whom I delight;
I will put my Spirit[w] on him,
and he will bring justice to the nations.
2 He will not shout or cry out,
or raise his voice in the streets.
3 A bruised reed he will not break,
and a smoldering wick he will not snuff out.
In faithfulness he will bring forth justice;[x]
4 he will not falter or be discouraged
till he establishes justice on earth.
In his teaching the islands will put their hope."[y]

5 This is what God the Lord says —
the Creator of the heavens, who stretches them out,
who spreads out the earth with all that springs from it,[z]
who gives breath[a] to its people,
and life to those who walk on it:
6 "I, the Lord, have called[b] you in righteousness;[c]
I will take hold of your hand.

42:1 – 9 *The First Revelation of the Ministering Servant.* Chs. 41 – 55 describe two different servants. The first servant (Israel) is blind, rebellious, and fearful, but God chooses to use this servant as his witness, promising to redeem him. The second servant (first described here) is obedient, sensitive, and suffers unjustly, and God promises to uphold him and use him to bring Israel and the nations back to God, restoring God's divine order ("justice," vv. 1,3,4) to the world. All except one of the references in chs. 41 – 48 refer to the first servant (Israel), and all except one of the references in chs. 49 – 55 refer to the second servant, the ministering servant. The one occurrence of the ministering servant in chs. 41 – 48 occurs in 42:1 – 9, a preliminary treatment of what appears in greater detail in chs. 49 – 55. It answers the question that ch. 41 raises: How can God use Israel as his servant when the Israelites have sinned so terribly? The answer to the question is the ministry of the second servant, the ministering servant. The other three discussions of this servant appear in 49:1 – 12; 50:4 – 9; 52:13 — 53:12. All four of these passages have been pointed to by the NT as predictions of Christ (for specific references, see the notes on these passages). The increasing emphasis upon the atoning nature of the servant's ministry throughout the four passages demonstrates that this is the correct understanding of Isaiah's intent. In his ministry, Jesus fulfilled the divine promises to David (11:1; 55:3 – 5). In Jesus' sufferings he made it possible for Israel to return to God and for the nations to come to him (v. 6; 49:6). In his kingdom he brings God's justice, his divine order, to the world (v. 4).

42:1 put my Spirit on him. See 11:1 – 5. **justice.** Hebrew *mišpaṭ* (cf. 51:5). Its connotations are considerably more extensive than the English word "justice." One connotation is legal equity, but the larger complex of God's divine order for life contains that. That divine order has been deeply disarranged since sin entered the world. As a part of the problem, the nation of Israel could never restore the divine order. Bringing "justice" to the earth would have to be the task of someone other than the fearful servant Israel.

42:5 – 9 Yahweh further defines the ministry of the servant (vv. 6 – 7). But he does this between enveloping statements (vv. 5,8 – 9) concerning his right and ability to do "new things" (v. 9). These sweeping statements show that what he intends to do through the servant has cosmic significance. He is the Creator of the cosmos and the one who gives life to humanity (v. 5). He is the Lord, whose glory is incomparable, especially with regard to idols (vv. 8 – 9). All this means that he can enable his servant to somehow satisfy the old covenant with his people (cf. 49:5,8) and at the same time be "a light for the Gentiles" (v. 6), or "nations" (cf. 49:6; Luke 2:32; Acts 13:47; Gal 3:14). This results in bringing sight to a blind world and release to an imprisoned world (v. 7; cf. 61:1 – 3). It envisions not renovation but transformation. Jesus' ministry to the blind, lame, and oppressed demonstrated that he had power to heal the spiritually blind and release the spiritually imprisoned (Mark 2:1 – 12). He is Lord of both the physical world and the spiritual world.

I will keep[d] you and will make you
to be a covenant[e] for the people
and a light for the Gentiles,[f]
7 to open eyes that are blind,[g]
to free[h] captives from prison[i]
and to release from the dungeon those who sit in darkness.

8 "I am the LORD; that is my name![j]
I will not yield my glory to another[k]
or my praise to idols.
9 See, the former things have taken place,
and new things I declare;
before they spring into being
I announce them to you."

42:6 [d] Isa 26:3 [e] Isa 49:8 [f] Lk 2:32; Ac 13:47
42:7 [g] Isa 35:5 [h] Isa 49:9; 61:1 [i] Lk 4:19; 2Ti 2:26; Heb 2:14-15
42:8 [j] Ex 3:15 [k] Isa 48:11
42:10 [l] Ps 33:3; 40:3; 98:1 [m] Isa 49:6 [n] 1Ch 16:32; Ps 96:11
42:11 [o] Isa 32:16 [p] Isa 60:7 [q] Isa 52:7; Na 1:15
42:12 [r] Isa 24:15
42:13 [s] Isa 9:6 [t] Isa 26:11 [u] Hos 11:10 [v] Isa 66:14
42:15 [w] Eze 38:20 [x] Isa 50:2; Na 1:4-6
42:16 [y] Lk 1:78-79 [z] Isa 32:3 [a] Lk 3:5 [b] Heb 13:5

Song of Praise to the LORD

10 Sing to the LORD a new song,[l]
his praise from the ends of the earth,[m]
you who go down to the sea, and all that is in it,[n]
you islands, and all who live in them.
11 Let the wilderness[o] and its towns raise their voices;
let the settlements where Kedar[p] lives rejoice.
Let the people of Sela sing for joy;
let them shout from the mountaintops.[q]
12 Let them give glory[r] to the LORD
and proclaim his praise in the islands.
13 The LORD will march out like a champion,[s]
like a warrior he will stir up his zeal;[t]
with a shout[u] he will raise the battle cry
and will triumph over his enemies.[v]

14 "For a long time I have kept silent,
I have been quiet and held myself back.
But now, like a woman in childbirth,
I cry out, I gasp and pant.
15 I will lay waste[w] the mountains and hills
and dry up all their vegetation;
I will turn rivers into islands
and dry up[x] the pools.
16 I will lead[y] the blind[z] by ways they have not known,
along unfamiliar paths I will guide them;
I will turn the darkness into light before them
and make the rough places smooth.[a]
These are the things I will do;
I will not forsake[b] them.

42:10—44:22 *The Basis of Deliverance.* This unit, as well as the following one (44:23—46:13), begins with a call to praise in light of God's saving work in the world. Yahweh will triumph over those forces that would hold his people in subjection.

42:10–17 *The Song of Salvation.* This song testifies to the significance of what immediately precedes it. It is because of the work of the servant that "the ends of the earth" (v. 10) and every place in it (vv. 11–12) are called upon to break into a song of praise. This is not merely a reference to the restoration of Israel; the salvation of the whole world is in view. Here it is the Lord himself who will "lead the blind" and give "light" (v. 16), something attributed to the servant a few verses previously. This makes it clear that Yahweh is at work through the servant to deliver both servant Israel and the world. This ministering servant is not the nation of Israel.

42:11 Kedar. See notes on 21:13–14,16–17.

42:13 champion. See 63:1–6 and note.

42:15 lay waste the mountains. This devastation of nature associated with deliverance reminds the reader of chs. 34–35. God can reduce the rich world of the mighty to a desert and can turn the desert of the helpless into a garden, through which runs a "smooth" highway (v. 16).

42:17 [c]Ps 97:7; Isa 1:29; 44:11; 45:16
42:18 [d]Isa 35:5
42:19 [e]Isa 43:8; Eze 12:2 [f]Isa 41:8-9 [g]Isa 44:26 [h]Isa 26:3
42:20 [i]Jer 6:10
42:21 [j]ver 4
42:22 [k]Isa 24:18 [l]Isa 24:22
42:23 [m]Isa 48:18
42:24 [n]Isa 30:15
42:25 [o]2Ki 25:9 [p]Isa 29:13; 47:7; 57:1, 11; Hos 7:9
43:1 [q]ver 7 [r]Ge 32:28; Isa 44:21 [s]Isa 44:2,6 [t]Isa 42:6; 45:3-4

17 But those who trust in idols,
who say to images, 'You are our gods,'
will be turned back in utter shame.[c]

Israel Blind and Deaf

18 "Hear, you deaf;[d]
look, you blind, and see!
19 Who is blind[e] but my servant,[f]
and deaf like the messenger[g] I send?
Who is blind like the one in covenant[h] with me,
blind like the servant of the LORD?
20 You have seen many things, but you pay no attention;
your ears are open, but you do not listen."[i]
21 It pleased the LORD
for the sake of his righteousness
to make his law[j] great and glorious.
22 But this is a people plundered and looted,
all of them trapped in pits[k]
or hidden away in prisons.[l]
They have become plunder,
with no one to rescue them;
they have been made loot,
with no one to say, "Send them back."

23 Which of you will listen to this
or pay close attention[m] in time to come?
24 Who handed Jacob over to become loot,
and Israel to the plunderers?
Was it not the LORD,
against whom we have sinned?
For they would not follow[n] his ways;
they did not obey his law.
25 So he poured out on them his burning anger,
the violence of war.
It enveloped them in flames,[o] yet they did not understand;
it consumed them, but they did not take it to heart.[p]

Israel's Only Savior

43

But now, this is what the LORD says—
he who created you, Jacob,
he who formed[q] you, Israel:[r]
"Do not fear, for I have redeemed[s] you;
I have summoned you by name;[t] you are mine.

42:17 These promises of deliverance are all predicated upon not falling into the worship of nature as represented by the idols (see note on 40:18–20).

42:18—43:13 *Israel, the Deaf and Blind Witness.* This identifies Israel as a deaf and blind servant whom Yahweh has allowed others to plunder (42:18–25). Yet he promises to deliver Israel (43:1–7), and he is going to use Israel's testimony to prove that the Babylonian idols are not gods at all (43:8–13).

42:18–25 *Israel's Condition Is Desperate.* Like the idols, they have eyes but cannot see, ears but cannot hear (cf. 1:2–3; 28:7–8; 29:9–10; 43:8; Ezek 12:2). This proves the prediction God gave Isaiah in his call (6:9–10). God graciously gave Israel his "law" (Hebrew *tôrâ*, "instructions") as a revelation of his "righteousness" (v. 21), but it was a closed book to them. As a result of their blindness, the nation has been easily trapped and has fallen into "pits" and "prisons" (v. 22). But the crucial theological point is that Babylon did not cause this to happen. Israel became "plunder" and "loot" (v. 22) because they "sinned" against Yahweh (v. 24). The Babylonians were only the instruments of his "anger," even if the people of Judah could not understand that (v. 25; cf. Jer 25:9; 27:6).

43:1–7 *The Lord's Promise to Deliver Israel.* Because Yahweh (not Babylon) took the people into captivity, Yahweh can get them out, and that is what he promises to do. They are "precious" to him (v. 4).

43:1 Yahweh "created" the nation of Israel (see v. 7; cf. 41:8; Gen 12:1–3), calling it "by name" (Gen 32:28). **I have redeemed you.**

2 When you pass through the waters,[u]
I will be with you;[v]
and when you pass through the rivers,
they will not sweep over you.
When you walk through the fire,[w]
you will not be burned;
the flames will not set you ablaze.[x]
3 For I am the LORD your God,[y]
the Holy One of Israel, your Savior;
I give Egypt for your ransom,
Cush[a][z] and Seba in your stead.[a]
4 Since you are precious and honored in my sight,
and because I love[b] you,
I will give people in exchange for you,
nations in exchange for your life.
5 Do not be afraid,[c] for I am with you;[d]
I will bring your children[e] from the east
and gather you from the west.
6 I will say to the north, 'Give them up!'
and to the south,[f] 'Do not hold them back.'
Bring my sons from afar
and my daughters[g] from the ends of the earth—
7 everyone who is called by my name,[h]
whom I created for my glory,
whom I formed and made.[i]"

8 Lead out those who have eyes but are blind,[j]
who have ears but are deaf.[k]
9 All the nations gather together[l]
and the peoples assemble.
Which of their gods foretold[m] this
and proclaimed to us the former things?
Let them bring in their witnesses to prove they were right,
so that others may hear and say, "It is true."
10 "You are my witnesses," declares the LORD,
"and my servant[n] whom I have chosen,
so that you may know and believe me
and understand that I am he.
Before me no god[o] was formed,
nor will there be one after me.

43:2 [u] Isa 8:7 [v] Dt 31:6,8 [w] Isa 29:6; 30:27 [x] Ps 66:12; Da 3:25-27
43:3 [y] Ex 20:2 [z] Isa 20:3 [a] Pr 21:18
43:4 [b] Isa 63:9
43:5 [c] Isa 44:2 [d] Jer 30:10-11 [e] Isa 41:8
43:6 [f] Ps 107:3 [g] 2Co 6:18
43:7 [h] Isa 56:5; 63:19; Jas 2:7 [i] ver 1,21; Ps 100:3; Eph 2:10
43:8 [j] Isa 6:9-10 [k] Isa 42:20; Eze 12:2
43:9 [l] Isa 41:1 [m] Isa 41:26
43:10 [n] Isa 41:8-9 [o] Isa 44:6,8

[a] *3* That is, the upper Nile region

Another reason not to "fear" (cf. 41:10,13). Redemption is an important theme in chs. 40–66. Words having to do with this theme occur 23 times in this part of the book.

43:2 I will be with you. See v. 5; see also note on 41:10.

43:3 The Holy One of Israel. See notes on 1:4; 41:11–14. **Egypt ... Cush.** The Persians were the first Mesopotamian power that was able to gain complete control of Egypt. The statement that Yahweh will give Cush (Nubia) in exchange for setting his people free and rebuilding his city seems to refer to this (vv. 3–4; cf. 44:28—45:6).

43:5–7 One of the reasons exile is so devastating is that it means a people's children would be assimilated into the culture of the conquerors and their culture would disappear. That will not happen here. Yahweh will bring Israel's children back to their homeland from "east ... west ... north ... south" (vv. 5–6; cf. 29:22–23; 49:12; 60:4).

43:8–13 *The Second Presentation of the Case Against Idols.* Israel, though "blind" and "deaf" (v. 8), is called to bear witness (vv. 10,12) that Yahweh is the only God; he predicted the future and the prediction came to pass ("proclaimed to us the former things," v. 9). See note on 41:21–29.

43:10 God predicted the exile and the return from exile so that the people of Israel would "know and believe me and understand that I am he" (see note on 41:4). His ability to predict the future specifically is evidence that he is self-existent and does not personify nature. He is unique, the only God, with none "before" and none "after."

43:11 [p]Isa 45:21
43:12 [q]Dt 32:12; Ps 81:9 [r]Isa 44:8
43:13 [s]Ps 90:2 [t]Job 9:12; Isa 14:27
43:14 [u]Isa 13:14-15 [v]Isa 23:13
43:16 [w]Ps 77:19; Isa 11:15; 51:10
43:17 [x]Ps 118:12; Isa 1:31 [y]Ex 14:9
43:19 [z]2Co 5:17; Rev 21:5 [a]Ex 17:6; Nu 20:11
43:20 [b]Isa 13:22 [c]Isa 48:21
43:21 [d]Ps 102:18; 1Pe 2:9

11 I, even I, am the LORD,
and apart from me there is no savior.[p]
12 I have revealed and saved and proclaimed—
I, and not some foreign god[q] among you.
You are my witnesses,[r]" declares the LORD, "that I am God.
13 Yes, and from ancient days[s] I am he.
No one can deliver out of my hand.
When I act, who can reverse it?"[t]

God's Mercy and Israel's Unfaithfulness

14 This is what the LORD says—
your Redeemer, the Holy One of Israel:
"For your sake I will send to Babylon
and bring down as fugitives[u] all the Babylonians,[a][v]
in the ships in which they took pride.
15 I am the LORD, your Holy One,
Israel's Creator, your King."

16 This is what the LORD says—
he who made a way through the sea,
a path through the mighty waters,[w]
17 who drew out[x] the chariots and horses,
the army and reinforcements together,[y]
and they lay there, never to rise again,
extinguished, snuffed out like a wick:
18 "Forget the former things;
do not dwell on the past.
19 See, I am doing a new thing![z]
Now it springs up; do you not perceive it?
I am making a way in the wilderness[a]
and streams in the wasteland.
20 The wild animals honor me,
the jackals[b] and the owls,
because I provide water[c] in the wilderness
and streams in the wasteland,
to give drink to my people, my chosen,
21 the people I formed for myself
that they may proclaim my praise.[d]

[a] 14 Or *Chaldeans*

43:11–13 Given Yahweh's uniqueness, "apart from [him] there is no savior" (v. 11). The gods cannot take anyone "out of [his] hand" (v. 13). He can deliver anyone he chooses, and no one "can reverse it" (v. 13).

43:14—44:5 *The Lord's New Thing.* There is no record of any captive people going home from forced exile before the decree of Cyrus. One of the purposes of exile was to break down the cultural and ethnic distinctions that would make it difficult to govern an empire. Thus, for the prophets to predict a return from exile was to predict something unheard of. The gods, representing natural forces, were incapable of doing something completely new. But Yahweh, the I AM, standing outside the cosmos, and creating it as a completely new thing, could certainly do so. He can deliver from the Babylonians (who will become "fugitives," 43:14) in a new way (43:16–21) in spite of Israel's ancient attempts to manipulate him (43:22–28); as a result, Israel will have a renewed physical and spiritual identity (44:1–5).

43:14–15 Yahweh can defeat Babylon. Isaiah characteristically piles up titles (e.g., "Redeemer, the Holy One of Israel") to convey Yahweh's lordship (see notes on 1:24; 41:11–14; 44:6–8; 49:26).

43:16–17 Alludes to the exodus from Egypt (Exod 13:17—14:31).

43:18 Forget the former things. Because God is going to do a "new thing" (v. 19): returning them from exile. Although the people should remember the lessons they learned about themselves and God through the exodus event, they should forget the way he did it. Fixating on what God did in the past, confines him to certain ways of doing things. But he is too creative for such confinement. He will indeed deliver his people from Babylon, but in an altogether new way. Note how the NT utilizes this language in reference to the "new creation" (2 Cor 5:17; see "Exile and Exodus," p. 2659).

43:19,20 streams in the wasteland. Metaphorically expresses the return from exile (cf. 35:6; see note on 30:25).

43:21 people I formed for myself. Expresses something of the relationship God desires with his people (v. 1). He does not deliver from bondage

22 "Yet you have not called on me, Jacob,
you have not wearied yourselves for[a] me, Israel.[e]
23 You have not brought me sheep for burnt offerings,
nor honored[f] me with your sacrifices.[g]
I have not burdened you with grain offerings
nor wearied you with demands[h] for incense.[i]
24 You have not bought any fragrant calamus[j] for me,
or lavished on me the fat of your sacrifices.
But you have burdened me with your sins
and wearied[k] me with your offenses.[l]

25 "I, even I, am he who blots out
your transgressions,[m] for my own sake,[n]
and remembers your sins no more.[o]
26 Review the past for me,
let us argue the matter together;[p]
state the case[q] for your innocence.
27 Your first father sinned;
those I sent to teach[r] you rebelled against me.
28 So I disgraced the dignitaries of your temple;
I consigned Jacob to destruction[b]
and Israel to scorn.[s]

Israel the Chosen

44 "But now listen, Jacob, my servant,[t]
Israel, whom I have chosen.
2 This is what the LORD says—
he who made you, who formed you in the womb,
and who will help[u] you:
Do not be afraid, Jacob, my servant,
Jeshurun,[c][v] whom I have chosen.
3 For I will pour water[w] on the thirsty land,
and streams on the dry ground;
I will pour out my Spirit[x] on your offspring,
and my blessing on your descendants.[y]
4 They will spring up like grass in a meadow,
like poplar trees[z] by flowing streams.[a]
5 Some will say, 'I belong to the LORD';
others will call themselves by the name of Jacob;

43:22 [e] Isa 30:11
43:23 [f] Zec 7:5-6; Mal 1:6-8 [g] Am 5:25 [h] Jer 7:22 [i] Ex 30:35; Lev 2:1
43:24 [j] Ex 30:23 [k] Isa 1:14; 7:13 [l] Mal 2:17
43:25 [m] Ac 3:19 [n] Isa 37:35; Eze 36:22 [o] Isa 38:17; Jer 31:34
43:26 [p] Isa 1:18 [q] Isa 41:1; 50:8
43:27 [r] Isa 9:15; 28:7; Jer 5:31
43:28 [s] Jer 24:9; Eze 5:15
44:1 [t] ver 21; Jer 30:10; 46:27-28
44:2 [u] Isa 41:10 [v] Dt 32:15
44:3 [w] Joel 3:18 [x] Joel 2:28; Ac 2:17 [y] Isa 61:9; 65:23
44:4 [z] Lev 23:40 [a] Job 40:22

[a] *22* Or *Jacob; / surely you have grown weary of* [b] *28* The Hebrew term refers to the irrevocable giving over of things or persons to the LORD, often by totally destroying them. [c] *2* *Jeshurun* means *the upright one,* that is, Israel.

merely to perform a judicial function. Rather, as Father (9:6; 45:10; 63:16; 64:8) and Bridegroom (62:5), he seeks a mutually satisfying relationship.
43:22–28 God intends to save, but Israel has never really sought a relationship with him.
43:22–24 This seems to say that Israel's sacrifices never really expressed sorrow for sin but merely attempted to manipulate God's favor. Clearly Israel *had* been giving all these offerings, but it was as though they had not done so. Instead of giving gifts of love, all they were doing was burdening God with their unrepentant sins (cf. 1:10–15). The repetition of "wearied" with different subjects and objects underlines the theme of the stanza (cf. Mal 1:12–13; 2:17).
43:25–28 Israel's only hope is God's undeserved grace. He must forgive them for his "own sake" (v. 25), because there is no "case for [their] innocence" or, "that you may be justified," v. 26). The nation has been sinful from their "first father" (v. 27)—perhaps Adam (Gen 5:3) or Abraham (Isa 51:2) or, perhaps most likely, Jacob (vv. 22,28)—onward, even including the priests, "the dignitaries of [their] temple" (v. 28; cf. 1 Sam 2:12–17; Ezek 8:9–12; Mal 2:1–9).
44:1–5 God will restore his "chosen" (v. 1). God wishes a personal relationship with his people (see note on 43:21), thus the special name "Jeshurun" (v. 2; see NIV text note). He will restore this relationship by pouring out his "Spirit" (v. 3; cf. 32:15–17) on their "offspring" (v. 3). This outpouring will have two results: abundance (v. 4; see note on 43:5–7) and a renewed willingness to identify themselves with God and his people (v. 5). Any fears that the exile would mean the extinction of Israel and the disappearance of the worship of Yahweh were groundless.

44:5 [b]Ex 13:9 [c]Zec 8:20-22
44:6 [d]Isa 41:21 [e]Isa 43:1 [f]Isa 41:4; Rev 1:8,17; 22:13
44:7 [g]Isa 41:22,26
44:8 [h]Isa 43:10 [i]Dt 4:35; 1Sa 2:2
44:9 [j]Isa 41:24
44:10 [k]Isa 41:29; Jer 10:5; Ac 19:26
44:11 [l]Isa 1:29 [m]Isa 42:17
44:12 [n]Isa 40:19; 41:6-7 [o]Jer 10:3-5; Ac 17:29
44:13 [p]Isa 41:7 [q]Ps 115:4-7 [r]Jdg 17:4-5

still others will write on their hand,[b] ‘The LORD’s,’[c]
and will take the name Israel.

The LORD, Not Idols

6 “This is what the LORD says—
Israel’s King[d] and Redeemer,[e] the LORD Almighty:
I am the first and I am the last;[f]
apart from me there is no God.
7 Who then is like me? Let him proclaim it.
Let him declare and lay out before me
what has happened since I established my ancient people,
and what is yet to come—
yes, let them foretell[g] what will come.
8 Do not tremble, do not be afraid.
Did I not proclaim this and foretell it long ago?
You are my witnesses. Is there any God[h] besides me?
No, there is no other Rock;[i] I know not one.”

9 All who make idols are nothing,
and the things they treasure are worthless.[j]
Those who would speak up for them are blind;
they are ignorant, to their own shame.
10 Who shapes a god and casts an idol,
which can profit nothing?[k]
11 People who do that will be put to shame;[l]
such craftsmen are only human beings.
Let them all come together and take their stand;
they will be brought down to terror and shame.[m]

12 The blacksmith[n] takes a tool
and works with it in the coals;
he shapes an idol with hammers,
he forges it with the might of his arm.[o]
He gets hungry and loses his strength;
he drinks no water and grows faint.
13 The carpenter[p] measures with a line
and makes an outline with a marker;
he roughs it out with chisels
and marks it with compasses.
He shapes it in human form,[q]
human form in all its glory,
that it may dwell in a shrine.[r]

44:6–20 *The Third Presentation of the Case Against Idols.* This describes the process of making an idol to show how foolish idolatry really is (vv. 9–20; see notes on 40:18–20; 41:21–29).

44:6–8 On piling up divine epithets, see notes on 1:24; 41:11–14; 43:14–15; 49:26; see also 41:4 and note. The people of Israel are “witnesses” (v. 8) that Yahweh did indeed “foretell what will come” (v. 7), something the idols cannot do. The Lord’s conclusion: “apart from me there is no God” (v. 6).

44:9–20 Idol making is foolish. Idolaters make themselves nothing (vv. 9–11). They are confused (vv. 12–17) and know nothing (vv. 18–20). Cf. 46:1–7; Ps 115:3–7; Jer 10:1–5.

44:9–11 When human beings attempt to make a god for themselves, in effect making the divine in their own image, they render themselves meaningless (“nothing” and “worthless,” v. 9). For if there is no reality greater than humans, then human life has neither purpose nor meaning. The humanly created idols cannot satisfy the deepest human needs.

44:12–17 In vv. 12–14, the prophet moves backward through the process of idol making, from metal plating (v. 12) through carpentry (v. 13) to the choice of the wood (v. 14). It appears that he chooses this direction in order to conclude with the ultimate folly that the god is made from one end of the same log that the idolater uses for his fire (vv. 15–17).

44:12 He gets hungry. The task is arduous and urgent (41:5–7), which is ironic since the whole undertaking is futile.

44:13 human form in all its glory. Ironic since human glory is nothing compared to the glory of the Creator (6:3; 40:5–6; 43:7; 48:11).

14 He cut down cedars,
or perhaps took a cypress or oak.
He let it grow among the trees of the forest,
or planted a pine, and the rain made it grow.
15 It is used as fuel[s] for burning;
some of it he takes and warms himself,
he kindles a fire and bakes bread.
But he also fashions a god and worships it;
he makes an idol and bows[t] down to it.
16 Half of the wood he burns in the fire;
over it he prepares his meal,
he roasts his meat and eats his fill.
He also warms himself and says,
"Ah! I am warm; I see the fire."
17 From the rest he makes a god, his idol;
he bows down to it and worships.
He prays[u] to it and says,
"Save[v] me! You are my god!"
18 They know nothing, they understand[w] nothing;
their eyes[x] are plastered over so they cannot see,
and their minds closed so they cannot understand.
19 No one stops to think,
no one has the knowledge or understanding[y] to say,
"Half of it I used for fuel;
I even baked bread over its coals,
I roasted meat and I ate.
Shall I make a detestable[z] thing from what is left?
Shall I bow down to a block of wood?"
20 Such a person feeds on ashes;[a] a deluded[b] heart misleads him;
he cannot save himself, or say,
"Is not this thing in my right hand a lie?[c]"

21 "Remember[d] these things, Jacob,
for you, Israel, are my servant.
I have made you, you are my servant;[e]
Israel, I will not forget you.[f]
22 I have swept away[g] your offenses like a cloud,
your sins like the morning mist.
Return[h] to me,
for I have redeemed[i] you."
23 Sing for joy,[j] you heavens, for the LORD has done this;
shout aloud, you earth[k] beneath.

44:15 [s] ver 19 [t] 2Ch 25:14
44:17 [u] 1Ki 18:26 [v] Isa 45:20
44:18 [w] Isa 1:3 [x] Isa 6:9-10
44:19 [y] Isa 5:13; 27:11; 45:20 [z] Dt 27:15
44:20 [a] Ps 102:9 [b] Job 15:31; Ro 1:21-23, 28; 2Th 2:11; 2Ti 3:13 [c] Isa 59:3, 4, 13; Ro 1:25
44:21 [d] Isa 46:8; Zec 10:9 [e] ver 1-2 [f] Isa 49:15
44:22 [g] Isa 43:25; Ac 3:19 [h] Isa 55:7 [i] 1Co 6:20
44:23 [j] Isa 42:10 [k] Ps 148:7

44:14 The idolater may have even planted the tree in the first place; the entire process originates with humans.

44:16–17 The idolater bows down to the same log that made him warm as it burned, and he calls on it to save him.

44:18–20 Making idols is not merely humorously foolish; it denies the world as God has made it. Not only does it refuse to give the Creator his due, but it also adds insult to injury when created people worship what they made in place of the Creator. It is thus an abomination ("a detestable thing," v. 19; cf. Deut 7:25; 18:9–13), it violates the creation order, and it is fundamentally a "lie" (v. 20). It is as though one chose to eat ashes rather than food. Cf. Acts 15:29; Rom 1:18–32; Col 3:5; 1 John 5:21.

44:21–22 *The Announcement of Salvation.* This may conclude vv. 6–20, in which case "these things" that Jacob must "remember" are the teachings that idols cannot save. But it may conclude 42:10—44:20, in which case "these things" refers to what 42:10—44:20 say about Yahweh's sole lordship, his unique ability to save, his choosing of Israel as his servant, and his unmerited grace. The content of these verses, which seems to summarize much of this teaching, lends some support to this latter option.

44:23—46:13 *The Restoration of Jerusalem Through Cyrus.* Although many of the themes in 42:10—44:22 recur, this section is slightly more specific regarding how God uses Cyrus to deliver his people from exile. The unit begins (as the previous one does) with a call to praise (44:23),

44:23 [l]Ps 98:8 [m]Isa 61:3
44:24 [n]Isa 43:14 [o]Isa 42:5
44:25 [p]Ps 33:10 [q]Isa 47:13 [r]1Co 1:27 [s]2Sa 15:31; 1Co 1:19-20
44:26 [t]Zec 1:6 [u]Isa 55:11; Mt 5:18 [v]Isa 49:8-21
44:28 [w]2Ch 36:22 [x]Isa 14:32 [y]Ezr 1:2-4
45:1 [z]Ps 73:23; Isa 41:13; 42:6 [a]Jer 50:35

Burst into song, you mountains,[l]
you forests and all your trees,
for the LORD has redeemed Jacob,
he displays his glory[m] in Israel.

Jerusalem to Be Inhabited

24 "This is what the LORD says—
your Redeemer,[n] who formed you in the womb:

I am the LORD,
the Maker of all things,
who stretches out the heavens,[o]
who spreads out the earth by myself,
25 who foils[p] the signs of false prophets
and makes fools of diviners,[q]
who overthrows the learning of the wise[r]
and turns it into nonsense,[s]
26 who carries out the words[t] of his servants
and fulfills[u] the predictions of his messengers,

who says of Jerusalem, 'It shall be inhabited,'
of the towns of Judah, 'They shall be rebuilt,'
and of their ruins, 'I will restore them,'[v]
27 who says to the watery deep, 'Be dry,
and I will dry up your streams,'
28 who says of Cyrus,[w] 'He is my shepherd
and will accomplish all that I please;
he will say of Jerusalem,[x] "Let it be rebuilt,"
and of the temple,[y] "Let its foundations be laid."'

45 "This is what the LORD says to his anointed,
to Cyrus, whose right hand I take hold[z] of
to subdue nations[a] before him
and to strip kings of their armor,
to open doors before him
so that gates will not be shut:

announces Cyrus (44:24–28), affirms Cyrus (45:1–8), declares Yahweh's right to use Cyrus (45:9–19), presents the final case against idols (45:20—46:7), and concludes (46:8–13). Cyrus ruled Persia (in modern Iran) from 559 BC until his death in 530 BC. Initially subject to Babylon, he allied himself with the Medes (lived in modern northwest Iran), and at the end of a series of battles, gained control of Babylon in 539, inaugurating the Persian Empire.

44:23 *Call to Praise.* This transitional verse may be the concluding response to the announcement of salvation in vv. 21–22 (as translated here). However, on the pattern of 42:10–17, it may introduce the next section consequent on the announcement just made. Like that segment, this salvation has cosmic implications: the natural world that was called upon to witness to Israel's rebellion (1:2) is called upon to rejoice over Israel's redemption (see 55:12–13).

44:23 glory. See note on v. 13.

44:24–28 *Cyrus Announced.* God delegates to Cyrus the rebuilding of Jerusalem.

44:24–26 Yahweh—as "Maker of all things" (v. 24), who "formed" Israel (v. 24), who confounds "prophets" who claim to know the future but do not (v. 25), who confirms the predictions of his own "messengers" (v. 26)—is fully able to be his people's "Redeemer" (v. 24).

44:26–28 This specifically predicts the future: "Jerusalem '… shall be inhabited' " (v. 26), and the Persian emperor Cyrus will be the one to accomplish this feat (v. 28). See photo of Cyrus Cylinder, p. 5.

44:27 watery deep. This probably alludes to the pagan creation myth, asserting that the power to conquer chaos is truly seen in Yahweh's power to redeem (see 27:1; 30:7; 51:9–10 and notes).

45:1–8 *Cyrus Affirmed as Yahweh's "Anointed."* God gives Cyrus the right to conquer "nations" and "kings" (v. 1). Yahweh promises to "break down" every obstacle (v. 2) and give him "hidden treasures" (v. 3). Although Cyrus does not know who Yahweh is (vv. 4–5), Yahweh knows who Cyrus is and has called him "by name" (vv. 3,4); the specific prediction of Cyrus's name is one example of Yahweh's unique capacity to predict the future, something the idols could not do (see the note on 41:21–29). Yahweh has done this as a way of demonstrating that he, "the God of Israel" (v. 3), is the only "I am" (vv. 3,5,6) in the universe ("I AM" is the divine name reflected in "the LORD"). He alone is self-existent; "there is no other" (v. 5; cf. v. 6).

45:1 anointed. One specifically appointed to a task; here it is the task of delivering God's people (see 61:1). Later the term would become specifically applied to the promised one, the Messiah, who would bring salvation (Dan 9:25–26).

[2]I will go before you
and will level[b] the mountains[a];
I will break down gates of bronze
and cut through bars of iron.[c]
[3]I will give you hidden treasures,[d]
riches stored in secret places,[e]
so that you may know[f] that I am the LORD,
the God of Israel, who summons you by name.[g]
[4]For the sake of Jacob my servant,[h]
of Israel my chosen,
I summon you by name
and bestow on you a title of honor,
though you do not acknowledge[i] me.
[5]I am the LORD, and there is no other;[j]
apart from me there is no God.[k]
I will strengthen you,[l]
though you have not acknowledged me,
[6]so that from the rising of the sun
to the place of its setting[m]
people may know there is none besides me.[n]
I am the LORD, and there is no other.
[7]I form the light and create darkness,
I bring prosperity and create disaster;[o]
I, the LORD, do all these things.

[8]"You heavens above, rain[p] down my righteousness;[q]
let the clouds shower it down.
Let the earth open wide,
let salvation[r] spring up,
let righteousness flourish with it;
I, the LORD, have created it.

[9]"Woe to those who quarrel[s] with their Maker,
those who are nothing but potsherds
among the potsherds on the ground.
Does the clay say to the potter,[t]
'What are you making?'
Does your work say,
'The potter has no hands'?
[10]Woe to the one who says to a father,
'What have you begotten?'

45:2 [b]Isa 40:4 [c]Ps 107:16; Jer 51:30
45:3 [d]Jer 50:37 [e]Jer 41:8 [f]Isa 41:23 [g]Ex 33:12; Isa 43:1
45:4 [h]Isa 41:8-9 [i]Ac 17:23
45:5 [j]Isa 44:8 [k]Ps 18:31 [l]Ps 18:39
45:6 [m]Isa 43:5; Mal 1:11 [n]ver 5,18
45:7 [o]Isa 31:2; Am 3:6
45:8 [p]Ps 72:6; Joel 3:18 [q]Ps 85:11; Isa 60:21; 61:10,11; Hos 10:12 [r]Isa 12:3
45:9 [s]Job 15:25 [t]Isa 29:16; Ro 9:20-21*

[a] *2* Dead Sea Scrolls and Septuagint; the meaning of the word in the Masoretic Text is uncertain.

45:7 disaster. What is contrary to human well-being, elsewhere rendered "evil." Dualism explains its existence in the world by positing two eternal entities: the author of good and the author of bad. But this means that the good entity is limited. The Bible will have none of this. There is one God who is thoroughly good and does good. He may bring about disaster, as he would do to Babylon through Cyrus, or he may deliver from disaster, as he was about to do to the people of Judah through Cyrus. But in either case the events of history are completely under his control.

45:8 righteousness. Often parallels "salvation" in this part of the book. When God expresses his righteousness on behalf of this people, salvation is always the result. See notes on 46:12–13; 56:1.

45:9–19 *Yahweh's Right to Use Cyrus.* It is Yahweh's right to use Cyrus, a pagan emperor who does not acknowledge him, to deliver his people. Yahweh insists that as the Creator he has a perfect right to do so (vv. 9–13). Verses 14–19 seem to record a dialogue between Yahweh and Jerusalem in which Yahweh makes a promise (v. 14), Jerusalem speaks of God's hiddenness (v. 15), Yahweh responds (vv. 16–18a), and Isaiah speaks for Yahweh, directly quoting him in vv.18b–19.

45:9–13 The choice of Cyrus prompts the tart words of vv. 9–12 (see v. 13). Yahweh is the "Maker" of Israel (v. 11) and the whole world (vv. 8–9,12). By what right does what is made question its maker (vv. 9,11) or does a child question its parent (vv. 10–11)? Here is another example of Yahweh's ability as the one transcendent God (the Holy One) to do something new (see note on 43:18). Humans would expect to see a repeat of Moses, but the Creator chooses another way.

45:11 [u]Isa 19:25
45:12 [v]Ge 2:1; Isa 42:5 [w]Ne 9:6
45:13 [x]2Ch 36:22; Isa 41:2 [y]Isa 52:3
45:14 [z]Isa 14:1-2 [a]Jer 16:19; Zec 8:20-23 [b]1Co 14:25
45:15 [c]Ps 44:24
45:16 [d]Isa 44:9,11
45:17 [e]Ro 11:26 [f]Isa 26:4

or to a mother,
'What have you brought to birth?'

11 "This is what the LORD says—
the Holy One of Israel, and its Maker:
Concerning things to come,
do you question me about my children,
or give me orders about the work of my hands?[u]
12 It is I who made the earth
and created mankind on it.
My own hands stretched out the heavens;[v]
I marshaled their starry hosts.[w]
13 I will raise up Cyrus[a][x] in my righteousness:
I will make all his ways straight.
He will rebuild my city
and set my exiles free,
but not for a price or reward,[y]
says the LORD Almighty."

14 This is what the LORD says:

"The products of Egypt and the merchandise of Cush,[b]
and those tall Sabeans—
they will come over to you
and will be yours;
they will trudge behind you,
coming over to you in chains.[z]
They will bow down before you
and plead[a] with you, saying,
'Surely God is with you,[b] and there is no other;
there is no other god.'"

15 Truly you are a God who has been hiding[c] himself,
the God and Savior of Israel.
16 All the makers of idols will be put to shame and disgraced;[d]
they will go off into disgrace together.
17 But Israel will be saved[e] by the LORD
with an everlasting salvation;[f]
you will never be put to shame or disgraced,
to ages everlasting.

18 For this is what the LORD says—
he who created the heavens,
he is God;

[a] *13* Hebrew *him* [b] *14* That is, the upper Nile region

45:13 righteousness. Capacity for doing what is right. Raising up Cyrus was the right thing for Yahweh to do as an expression of his own holy character. **not for a price or reward.** The right to conquer Egypt that Yahweh gave to Cyrus and his successors (43:3–4) is not a payment.

45:14–19 Yahweh is not a hidden God. Merely because he chose to do a new thing in salvation does not mean that his plans or his nature are somehow shrouded in mystery. When he has called his people to seek him, his revelation has been plain.

45:14 you. Israel. God promises that after Cyrus restores the people of Judah to their homeland, the nations—represented by Egypt, Cush (see 18:1), and the Sabeans (cruel people from the desert; see Job 1:15; Joel 3:8)—would come to Jerusalem as captives ("in chains") or as fellow worshipers ("no other god"). See 60:14; 62:5–6. Alternatively, "you" could refer to Cyrus (see 43:3 and note on 43:1–7).

45:15 If God is going to use a pagan emperor, it seems that the ways of the "Savior" are a mystery.

45:16–17 The idols will not deliver their makers, with the result that the idol makers will be "disgraced" (see note on 25:8). But Israel will not be disgraced, because Yahweh will save his people "with an everlasting salvation."

45:18–19 God is absolutely trustworthy, in contrast to the idols (v. 16). That trustworthiness has been revealed through speech ("says ... says ... spoken ... said ... speak"). The transcendent God can be known only if he discloses himself and what he has done through communication in lan-

he who fashioned and made the earth,
he founded it;
he did not create it to be empty,[g]
but formed it to be inhabited[h] —
he says:
"I am the LORD,
and there is no other.[i]
19 I have not spoken in secret,[j]
from somewhere in a land of darkness;
I have not said to Jacob's descendants,[k]
'Seek me in vain.'
I, the LORD, speak the truth;
I declare what is right.[l]

20 "Gather together[m] and come;
assemble, you fugitives from the nations.
Ignorant[n] are those who carry[o] about idols of wood,
who pray to gods that cannot save.[p]
21 Declare what is to be, present it —
let them take counsel together.
Who foretold[q] this long ago,
who declared it from the distant past?
Was it not I, the LORD?
And there is no God apart from me,[r]
a righteous God and a Savior;
there is none but me.

22 "Turn[s] to me and be saved,[t]
all you ends of the earth;[u]
for I am God, and there is no other.
23 By myself I have sworn,[v]
my mouth has uttered in all integrity[w]
a word that will not be revoked:[x]
Before me every knee will bow;
by me every tongue will swear.[y]
24 They will say of me, 'In the LORD alone
are deliverance[z] and strength.' "
All who have raged against him
will come to him and be put to shame.[a]
25 But all the descendants of Israel
will find deliverance in the LORD
and will make their boast in him.[b]

45:18 [g] Ge 1:2 [h] Ge 1:26; Isa 42:5 [i] ver 5
45:19 [j] Isa 48:16 [k] Isa 41:8 [l] Dt 30:11
45:20 [m] Isa 43:9 [n] Isa 44:19 [o] Isa 46:1; Jer 10:5 [p] Isa 44:17; 46:6-7
45:21 [q] Isa 41:22 [r] ver 5
45:22 [s] Zec 12:10 [t] Nu 21:8-9; 2Ch 20:12 [u] Isa 49:6,12
45:23 [v] Ge 22:16 [w] Heb 6:13 [x] Isa 55:11 [y] Ps 63:11; Isa 19:18; Ro 14:11*; Php 2:10-11
45:24 [z] Jer 33:16 [a] Isa 41:11
45:25 [b] Isa 41:16

guage, and he has. He did not create the world to be a chaos ("empty") with humans as an afterthought, which is how the ancient Near Eastern myths saw the origins of the world. He created it "to be inhabited" by persons to whom he could reveal himself. The gods might revel in their inexplicable ways, but not the Lord, who speaks "the truth" and "what is right."

45:20—46:7 *The Final Presentation of the Case Against Idols.* The central theme is that idols "cannot save" (45:20) their worshipers. People must carry the idols instead of the idols carrying the people (45:20; 46:1–2). Yahweh is not like that; he will carry his people, even down to their old age, when they can do nothing for him (46:3–4). Isa 45:20—46:1 repeats earlier themes: Yahweh alone is God, and he predicts the future (45:21); he uniquely can save not only Israel but the whole world as well (45:22–25). It is foolish to worship something that humans made (46:5–7).

45:20 Idolatry is not only the result but also the cause of ignorance (see note on 44:9–11).

45:21 Deliverance from exile at the hand of Cyrus had been predicted long in advance (in the time of the prophet Isaiah of Jerusalem), something the gods could not have done. This is presented as conclusive evidence that the Babylonians' gods are not gods at all.

45:22–25 God intends that the whole earth acknowledge him as God and come to him to be saved. No one will be exempt (v. 23; cf. Rom 14:11; Phil 2:10–11). There is no other savior (v. 24; cf. Acts 4:12). Those "who have raged against him" (v. 24) and remain unrepentant must still come before him; there the falseness of all the things they have trusted in will be revealed.

45:25 make their boast. They trusted God, who does not fail them.

46:1 [c]Isa 21:9; Jer 50:2; 51:44 [d]Isa 45:20
46:2 [e]Jdg 18:17-18; 2Sa 5:21
46:3 [f]ver 12
46:4 [g]Ps 71:18 [h]Isa 43:13
46:5 [i]Isa 40:18,25
46:6 [j]Isa 40:19 [k]Isa 44:17
46:7 [l]ver 1 [m]Isa 44:17; Isa 45:20
46:8 [n]Isa 44:21
46:9 [o]Dt 32:7 [p]Isa 45:5,21
46:10 [q]Isa 45:21 [r]Pr 19:21; Ac 5:39

Gods of Babylon

46 Bel[c] bows down, Nebo stoops low;
their idols are borne by beasts of burden.[a]
The images that are carried[d] about are burdensome,
a burden for the weary.
2 They stoop and bow down together;
unable to rescue the burden,
they themselves go off into captivity.[e]

3 "Listen[f] to me, you descendants of Jacob,
all the remnant of the people of Israel,
you whom I have upheld since your birth,
and have carried since you were born.
4 Even to your old age and gray hairs[g]
I am he,[h] I am he who will sustain you.
I have made you and I will carry you;
I will sustain you and I will rescue you.

5 "With whom will you compare me or count me equal?
To whom will you liken me that we may be compared?[i]
6 Some pour out gold from their bags
and weigh out silver on the scales;
they hire a goldsmith[j] to make it into a god,
and they bow down and worship it.[k]
7 They lift it to their shoulders and carry[l] it;
they set it up in its place, and there it stands.
From that spot it cannot move.
Even though someone cries out to it, it cannot answer;
it cannot save[m] them from their troubles.

8 "Remember[n] this, keep it in mind,
take it to heart, you rebels.
9 Remember the former things, those of long ago;[o]
I am God, and there is no other;
I am God, and there is none like me.[p]
10 I make known the end from the beginning,
from ancient times,[q] what is still to come.
I say, 'My purpose will stand,[r]
and I will do all that I please.'
11 From the east I summon a bird of prey;
from a far-off land, a man to fulfill my purpose.

[a] *1* Or *are but beasts and cattle*

46:1–2 The Babylonians carry their idols ("Bel" and "Nebo") into captivity. The idea of these gods bowing and stooping is ironic. They should be bowed to. Instead they are only a heavy "burden"; they are "unable to rescue the burden" (i.e., their people).
46:3–4 This language differs strikingly from vv. 1–2. These verses are much more full and developed, whereas vv. 1–2 are terse. This speaks to the richer personal aspect of the relationship between Yahweh and his people. From "birth" to "old age" Yahweh carries them; he not only "made" them in the beginning but will also "sustain" them all along the way.
46:3 remnant. See note on 11:11.
46:4 I am he. See note on 41:4.
46:5–7 The Creator of heaven and earth cannot be compared to a thing of "silver" or "gold" made by a craftsman (v. 6), carried on human "shoulders" (v. 7), and needing to be fixed "in its place" (v. 7) when it is put down (see note on 40:18–20).
46:8–13 *Conclusion: Yahweh's Absolute Uniqueness.* He alone *can* foretell the future with specificity, and he alone *has* done so (see note on 41:21–29). He did this all in keeping with his overarching purposes for the human race and his particular plans for accomplishing those purposes (14:24–27; 19:12; 23:9). The idols, like the thunder storm, have neither purposes nor plans. God said there would be an exile (39:6–7), and the exiles will know that it has happened. He also said there would be restoration from exile (11:10–16), and there surely would be.
46:8 rebels. See note on 1:2. Restoration will not be the result of the exiles correcting their character and behavior by their own ability (v. 11; cf. Ezek 36:22).
46:11 bird of prey. Cyrus (see 41:2).

What I have said, that I will bring about;
what I have planned, that I will do.
12 Listen[s] to me, you stubborn-hearted,
you who are now far from my righteousness.[t]
13 I am bringing my righteousness near,
it is not far away;
and my salvation will not be delayed.
I will grant salvation to Zion,
my splendor[u] to Israel.

46:12 [s]ver 3 [t]Ps 119:150; Isa 48:1; Jer 2:5
46:13 [u]Isa 44:23
47:1 [v]Isa 23:12 [w]Ps 137:8; Jer 50:42; 51:33; Zec 2:7 [x]Dt 28:56
47:2 [y]Ex 11:5; Mt 24:41 [z]Jdg 16:21 [a]Ge 24:65 [b]Isa 32:11
47:3 [c]Eze 16:37; Na 3:5 [d]Isa 20:4 [e]Isa 34:8
47:4 [f]Jer 50:34
47:5 [g]Isa 13:10 [h]Isa 13:19
47:6 [i]2Ch 28:9 [j]Isa 10:13

The Fall of Babylon

47 "Go down, sit in the dust,
Virgin Daughter[v] Babylon;
sit on the ground without a throne,
queen city of the Babylonians.[a][w]
No more will you be called
tender or delicate.[x]
2 Take millstones[y] and grind[z] flour;
take off your veil.[a]
Lift up your skirts,[b] bare your legs,
and wade through the streams.
3 Your nakedness[c] will be exposed
and your shame[d] uncovered.
I will take vengeance;[e]
I will spare no one."

4 Our Redeemer—the LORD Almighty is his
name[f]—
is the Holy One of Israel.

5 "Sit in silence, go into darkness,[g]
queen city of the Babylonians;
no more will you be called
queen of kingdoms.[h]
6 I was angry[i] with my people
and desecrated my inheritance;
I gave them into your hand,[j]
and you showed them no mercy.

Image of god carried off as plunder by soldiers of Tiglath-Pileser III. Isa 46:6–7 describes idols being created and carried around.

Caryn Reeder, taken at the British Museum

[a] *1* Or *Chaldeans*; also in verse 5

46:12–13 righteousness ... righteousness. Used in two different ways. The first refers to the character of God that the people have not manifested. The second refers to God's righteous act of salvation. It would not be right for him, given his nature and character, to leave his people in captivity, even if they deserved it (cf. Exod 32:11–13).

47:1—48:22 *Implications of the Case Against Idols.* God sentences Babylon (47:1–15) and calls upon Israel to believe his promises (48:1–22).

47:1–15 *The Sentence Upon Babylon.* Despite Babylon's power and arcane wisdom, God will reduce her to nothing. The poem has three stanzas: Babylon's humiliation (vv. 1–4), false pride (vv. 5–11), and helplessness (vv. 12–15).

47:1–4 *Babylon's Humiliation.* Babylon is like a proud "queen" forced to come off her "throne" and "sit on the ground" (v. 1), where she will perform menial labor (v. 2). She will no longer wear beautiful robes but will wear rags that will not even cover her "nakedness" (v. 3). She has entered into a contest with "the Holy One of Israel" (v. 4; see note on 41:11–14), and it is no contest.

47:1 Virgin Daughter Babylon. A figure of speech expressing pristine beauty (cf. 37:22).

47:3 vengeance. See note on 34:8.

47:4 On the multiplication of divine titles, see note on 43:14–15.

47:5–11 *Babylon's False Pride.* The Babylonians felt they were "eternal" (v. 7), arrogating the very place of Yahweh (vv. 8,10). They trusted in their "security" (v. 8), "sorceries" (v. 9), "wickedness," and "wisdom" (v. 10) to make their proof against the fears they forced upon others: "loss of children and widowhood" (v. 9; see note on 29:23). But they did not foresee that in spite of all their conjuring, "disaster" would sweep all these things away (v. 11; see note on 21:5; see also Dan 5:22–31).

47:6 Babylon was God's tool to discipline his people (cf. Jer 25:6–11; Hab 1:6–7), but that did not give the Babylonians license to do so with brutality nor did it give them immunity from God's judgment (cf. Jer 25:12; Ezek 36:5–7; Hab 2:4–20).

47:7 [k]ver 5; Rev 18:7 [l]Isa 42:23,25 [m]Dt 32:29
47:8 [n]Isa 32:9 [o]Isa 45:6; Zep 2:15 [p]Rev 18:7
47:9 [q]Ps 73:19; 1Th 5:3; Rev 18:8-10 [r]Isa 13:18 [s]Na 3:4 [t]Rev 18:23
47:10 [u]Ps 52:7; 62:10 [v]Isa 29:15 [w]Isa 5:21 [x]Isa 44:20
47:11 [y]1Th 5:3
47:12 [z]ver 9
47:13 [a]Isa 57:10; Jer 51:58 [b]Isa 44:25 [c]ver 15
47:14 [d]Isa 5:24; Na 1:10 [e]Isa 10:17; Jer 51:30,32,58

Even on the aged
you laid a very heavy yoke.
7 You said, 'I am forever—
the eternal queen!'[k]
But you did not consider these things
or reflect[l] on what might happen.[m]

8 "Now then, listen, you lover of pleasure,
lounging in your security[n]
and saying to yourself,
'I am, and there is none besides me.[o]
I will never be a widow[p]
or suffer the loss of children.'
9 Both of these will overtake you
in a moment,[q] on a single day:
loss of children[r] and widowhood.
They will come upon you in full measure,
in spite of your many sorceries[s]
and all your potent spells.[t]
10 You have trusted[u] in your wickedness
and have said, 'No one sees me.'[v]
Your wisdom[w] and knowledge mislead[x] you
when you say to yourself,
'I am, and there is none besides me.'
11 Disaster will come upon you,
and you will not know how to conjure it away.
A calamity will fall upon you
that you cannot ward off with a ransom;
a catastrophe you cannot foresee
will suddenly[y] come upon you.

12 "Keep on, then, with your magic spells
and with your many sorceries,[z]
which you have labored at since childhood.
Perhaps you will succeed,
perhaps you will cause terror.
13 All the counsel you have received has only worn you out![a]
Let your astrologers[b] come forward,
those stargazers who make predictions month by month,
let them save[c] you from what is coming upon you.
14 Surely they are like stubble;[d]
the fire will burn them up.
They cannot even save themselves
from the power of the flame.[e]
These are not coals for warmth;
this is not a fire to sit by.

47:8,10 I am, and there is none besides me. Only Yahweh can say this (cf. 41:4; 45:5,21; 46:9). For any created thing to say this is the rankest arrogance.

47:9 sorceries … spells. The libraries of Babylon were filled with manuals of magical spells.

47:10 Your wisdom and knowledge mislead you. The Babylonians gave great attention to cataloging all the possible omens that might occur and what they would mean when they did; it was a great but vain intellectual effort. When disaster came, their magical wisdom was useless to either foretell it or prevent it (v. 11).

47:12–15 *Babylon's Helplessness.* The prophet sarcastically invites the magicians and astrologers to utilize their skills to do something, whether good or ill (cf. 41:23). They will be helpless, unable to "even save themselves" (v. 14), let alone "save" Babylon (v. 15). All the attention lavished on paganism (v. 15) accomplished nothing.

[15]That is all they are to you—
these you have dealt with
and labored[f] with since childhood.
All of them go on in their error;
there is not one that can save you.

Stubborn Israel

48 "Listen to this, you descendants of Jacob,
you who are called by the name of Israel
and come from the line of Judah,
you who take oaths in the name of the LORD
and invoke[g] the God of Israel—
but not in truth[h] or righteousness—
[2]you who call yourselves citizens of the holy city[i]
and claim to rely[j] on the God of Israel—
the LORD Almighty is his name:
[3]I foretold the former things[k] long ago,
my mouth announced[l] them and I made them known;
then suddenly I acted, and they came to pass.
[4]For I knew how stubborn[m] you were;
your neck muscles[n] were iron,
your forehead[o] was bronze.
[5]Therefore I told you these things long ago;
before they happened I announced them to you
so that you could not say,
'My images brought them about;[p]
my wooden image and metal god ordained them.'
[6]You have heard these things; look at them all.
Will you not admit them?

"From now on I will tell you of new things,
of hidden things unknown to you.
[7]They are created now, and not long ago;
you have not heard of them before today.
So you cannot say,
'Yes, I knew of them.'
[8]You have neither heard nor understood;
from of old your ears have not been open.

47:15 [f]Rev 18:11
48:1 [g]Isa 58:2 [h]Jer 4:2
48:2 [i]Isa 52:1 [j]Isa 10:20; Mic 3:11; Ro 2:17
48:3 [k]Isa 41:22 [l]Isa 45:21
48:4 [m]Dt 31:27 [n]Ex 32:9; Ac 7:51 [o]Eze 3:9
48:5 [p]Jer 44:15-18

48:1–22 *Israel Called Upon to Believe God's Promises.* In the light of Yahweh's desire, ability, and intent to save his people from exile (see notes on 40:1–11,12–26,27–31), he calls upon them not to lose heart or become absorbed into Babylon's culture. Instead, they must maintain their faith and be ready for the release when it comes. God has demonstrated his trustworthiness and revealed his grace. Will that grace motivate the Israelites to trust God for deliverance? The poem has two parts: God has predicted everything (vv. 1–11), and Israel must listen to the Lord (vv. 12–22).

48:1–11 *Everything Has Been Predicted.* The argument recapitulates the central argument in the case against idols. In view of Yahweh's predictions and their fulfillments, Israel should obey God in ways they previously did not. They can begin by believing his promises of redemption. Verses 1–6 speak of the former things, the prediction of the exile, while vv. 7–11 speak of new things, the return from exile.

48:1 Listen. Words having to do with hearing occur seven times in ch. 48, and words having to do with divine speaking occur 12 times. In Hebrew "hearing" is inseparable from taking appropriate action (cf. v. 18). Not to take action is not to have heard. **take oaths ... but not in truth.** The prophet argues that the people are not sincere in their professed faith (cf. 1:10–15; 57:3–13; 58:1–2; 65:1–5).

48:3–6a Fulfilled predictions make Yahweh's superiority over the idols unmistakable. The "stubborn" (v. 4) say that those events occurred because they ritually manipulated their "images" (v. 5). This offers the illusion of controlling events. But now they are forced to "admit" that God freely brought to pass just what he said he would (v. 6a).

48:6b new things. Cf. 43:18–19. Yahweh is now foretelling something unheard of, something that had not happened before: a nation might survive exile with its culture and religion intact and then return to its own homeland. But beyond these, there is the promise of the worldwide ministry to come through the Messiah (chs. 60–62), and the new heavens and the new earth (65:17–25).

48:8 neither heard nor understood. Cf. 1:2; 42:18–23. God promised their return from exile before, but blind, deaf Israel, "a rebel from birth,"

48:8 [q]Dt 9:7,24; Ps 58:3
48:9 [r]Ps 78:38; Isa 30:18 [s]Ne 9:31
48:10 [t]1Ki 8:51
48:11 [u]1Sa 12:22; Isa 37:35 [v]Dt 32:27; Jer 14:7,21; Eze 20:9, 14,22,44 [w]Isa 42:8
48:12 [x]Isa 46:3 [y]Isa 41:4; Rev 1:17; 22:13
48:13 [z]Heb 1:10-12 [a]Ex 20:11 [b]Isa 40:26
48:14 [c]Isa 43:9 [d]Isa 46:10-11
48:15 [e]Isa 45:1
48:16 [f]Isa 41:1 [g]Isa 45:19 [h]Zec 2:9,11
48:17 [i]Isa 49:7 [j]Isa 43:14 [k]Isa 49:10 [l]Ps 32:8

Well do I know how treacherous you are;
you were called a rebel[q] from birth.
9 For my own name's sake I delay my wrath;[r]
for the sake of my praise I hold it back from you,
so as not to destroy you completely.[s]
10 See, I have refined you, though not as silver;
I have tested you in the furnace[t] of affliction.
11 For my own sake,[u] for my own sake, I do this.
How can I let myself be defamed?[v]
I will not yield my glory to another.[w]

Israel Freed

12 "Listen[x] to me, Jacob,
Israel, whom I have called:
I am he;
I am the first and I am the last.[y]
13 My own hand laid the foundations of the earth,[z]
and my right hand spread out the heavens;[a]
when I summon them,
they all stand up together.[b]

14 "Come together,[c] all of you, and listen:
Which of the idols has foretold these things?
The LORD's chosen ally
will carry out his purpose[d] against Babylon;
his arm will be against the Babylonians.[a]
15 I, even I, have spoken;
yes, I have called[e] him.
I will bring him,
and he will succeed in his mission.

16 "Come near[f] me and listen to this:

"From the first announcement I have not spoken in secret;[g]
at the time it happens, I am there."

And now the Sovereign LORD has sent[h] me,
endowed with his Spirit.

17 This is what the LORD says—
your Redeemer,[i] the Holy One[j] of Israel:
"I am the LORD your God,
who teaches you what is best for you,
who directs[k] you in the way[l] you should go.

[a] 14 Or *Chaldeans*; also in verse 20

could not hear it. They thought they could not go into exile because their covenant with Yahweh made them immune. So return from exile was completely unimaginable.

48:9–11 Why would God restore them from exile? It was not for their sake; they in no way deserved it. It was for his "own [name's] sake" (vv. 9,11), which expresses his grace (see note on 43:25–28; cf. Ezek 36:22). Furthermore, he never intended that the exile would "destroy [them] completely" (v. 9); he intended that it would refine them (v. 10; see 4:4).

48:12–22 *Israel Freed.* Israel should listen to the Lord because he is unique in the world (vv. 12–16), his commandments are a source of blessing (vv. 17–19), and he will keep his promises (vv. 20–22).

48:12–16 This concisely summarizes the previous arguments for Yahweh's superiority over the idols. He is the only God ("I am the first and I am the last," v. 12), the sole Creator (v. 13). Therefore he can carry out his announced plan (v. 16) to use his "ally" (Cyrus, v. 14; see 41:2; 44:28; 45:1) to bring down "Babylon" (v. 14).

48:16 me. The speaker might be the servant (cf. 42:1; 61:1) or the prophet (cf. Mic 3:8).

48:17–19 Had Israel truly listened (see note on v. 1), none of this would have happened. They would have experienced "peace" (v. 18) and would not now be worried about "descendants" (v. 19; see note on 29:23).

18 If only you had paid attention[m] to my commands,
your peace[n] would have been like a river,
your well-being[o] like the waves of the sea.
19 Your descendants would have been like the sand,
your children like its numberless grains;[p]
their name would never be blotted out[q]
nor destroyed from before me."

20 Leave Babylon,
flee[r] from the Babylonians!
Announce this with shouts of joy[s]
and proclaim it.
Send it out to the ends of the earth;
say, "The LORD has redeemed[t] his servant Jacob."
21 They did not thirst[u] when he led them through the deserts;
he made water flow[v] for them from the rock;
he split the rock
and water gushed out.[w]

22 "There is no peace," says the LORD, "for the wicked."[x]

48:18 [m] Dt 32:29 [n] Ps 119:165; Isa 66:12 [o] Isa 45:8
48:19 [p] Ge 22:17 [q] Isa 56:5; 66:22
48:20 [r] Jer 50:8; 51:6, 45; Zec 2:6-7; Rev 18:4 [s] Isa 49:13 [t] Isa 52:9; 63:9
48:21 [u] Isa 41:17 [v] Isa 30:25 [w] Ex 17:6; Nu 20:11; Ps 105:41; Isa 35:6
48:22 [x] Isa 57:21
49:1 [y] Isa 44:24; 46:3; Mt 1:20 [z] Isa 7:14; 9:6; 44:2; Jer 1:5; Gal 1:15
49:2 [a] Isa 11:4; Rev 1:16
49:3 [b] Zec 3:8 [c] Isa 44:23

The Servant of the LORD

49 Listen to me, you islands;
hear this, you distant nations:
Before I was born[y] the LORD called[z] me;
from my mother's womb he has spoken my name.
2 He made my mouth like a sharpened sword,[a]
in the shadow of his hand he hid me;
he made me into a polished arrow
and concealed me in his quiver.
3 He said to me, "You are my servant,[b]
Israel, in whom I will display my splendor."[c]

48:20 Leave Babylon. This command underlines the certainty of the release that is coming. **ends of the earth.** Israel's redemption has implications for the entire world.
48:21 did not thirst. God's provision during the exodus (Exod 17:6; Num 20:11). If God cared for his people in the past, his people can trust him to do so again, even if in new ways (cf. 43:18–19).
48:22 Repeated in 57:21 (see note there). It may appear here as a mechanical way of dividing chs. 40–66 into three nine-chapter groupings.
49:1—55:13 *The Servant: Gracious Means of Israel's Servanthood.* The theme of deliverance continues, but there are no more explicit references to Babylon. All the references to "servant," with one exception in 54:17, are to the ministering servant, not the blind, fearful servant (see note on 42:1–9). This section seems to address these questions: How can sinful Israel actually become the servants of the Holy God? If God delivers them from Babylon and restores them to their land, what is to be done about the sin that alienates them from God in the first place? Will the undeserved grace (43:25; 44:21–22; 48:9,11) consist simply in Yahweh's overlooking their sin? The answer is that God will "bare his holy arm" (52:10; cf. 50:2; 51:5,9) and deliver them from the sin that separates them from him. That arm is the ministering servant (49:1–12; 50:4–9; 52:13—53:12). The structure of the subdivision confirms that this understanding is the correct one: 49:1—52:12 promises salvation, one that grows in excitement to 52:12; then 54:1—55:13 invites them to participate in a salvation that has been realized. What stands between these two is the revelation of the ministering servant in 52:13—53:12. God delivers his people by means of his servant's self-sacrifice.
49:1—52:12 *Anticipation of Deliverance.* This looks forward with increasing excitement to a salvation that restores Israel's relationship with Yahweh.
49:1–12 *The Second Revelation of the Ministering Servant.* This uses language very similar to the first revelation in 42:1–9. The servant is the means by which God restores his order ("justice," 42:1) to the world. Not only will he restore Jacob; he will be "a light for the Gentiles" (49:6; 42:6). A new feature is a sense of frustration (49:4). This increases and includes actual rejection in the third and final revelations (50:4–9; 52:13—53:12). The servant speaks (49:1–6), and two messages from Yahweh address the servant (vv. 7–12).
49:1–6 The servant reports his calling (vv. 1–3), his confidence in God in spite of a sense of frustration (v. 4), and the nature of the ministry given to him (vv. 5–6).
49:1 islands ... distant nations. The servant's ministry has worldwide implications. **called me ... womb.** The servant was destined for this ministry even before his birth. It is not just a facet of his life; it is the central meaning of it (see John 12:27).
49:2 sharpened sword. The servant's ministry is one of speech, as is the Messiah's (11:4). He will pronounce God's judgment on the wicked and speak peace to the contrite (57:15; Ps 98:7–9; John 5:21–22; Rev 5:1–10; 19:15).
49:3 Israel. This is clearly not the sinful nation that 42:18–25 and 59:1–15a describe. This is the ideal Israel, an individual who will make it possible for actual Israel to survive in the presence of the Holy One (see 49:5–6,8). **splendor.** Glory (cf. 55:5; 60:9,21; John 1:14; 17:1,22,24).

49:4 [d]Isa 65:23 [e]Isa 35:4
49:5 [f]Isa 11:12 [g]Isa 43:4
49:6 [h]Lk 2:32 [i]Ac 13:47*
49:7 [j]Isa 48:17 [k]Ps 22:6; 69:7-9 [l]Isa 52:15
49:8 [m]Ps 69:13 [n]2Co 6:2* [o]Isa 26:3 [p]Isa 42:6 [q]Isa 44:26
49:9 [r]Isa 42:7; 61:1; Lk 4:19 [s]Isa 41:18
49:10 [t]Isa 33:16 [u]Ps 121:6; Rev 7:16 [v]Isa 14:1 [w]Isa 35:7

4 But I said, "I have labored in vain;[d]
I have spent my strength for nothing at all.
Yet what is due me is in the LORD's hand,
and my reward[e] is with my God."

5 And now the LORD says—
he who formed me in the womb to be his servant
to bring Jacob back to him
and gather Israel[f] to himself,
for I am[a] honored[g] in the eyes of the LORD
and my God has been my strength—
6 he says:
"It is too small a thing for you to be my servant
to restore the tribes of Jacob
and bring back those of Israel I have kept.
I will also make you a light for the Gentiles,[h]
that my salvation may reach to the ends of the earth."[i]

7 This is what the LORD says—
the Redeemer and Holy One of Israel[j]—
to him who was despised[k] and abhorred by the nation,
to the servant of rulers:
"Kings[l] will see you and stand up,
princes will see and bow down,
because of the LORD, who is faithful,
the Holy One of Israel, who has chosen you."

Restoration of Israel

8 This is what the LORD says:

"In the time of my favor[m] I will answer you,
and in the day of salvation I will help you;[n]
I will keep[o] you and will make you
to be a covenant for the people,[p]
to restore the land[q]
and to reassign its desolate inheritances,
9 to say to the captives,[r] 'Come out,'
and to those in darkness, 'Be free!'
"They will feed beside the roads
and find pasture on every barren hill.[s]
10 They will neither hunger nor thirst,[t]
nor will the desert heat or the sun beat down on
them.[u]
He who has compassion[v] on them will guide them
and lead them beside springs[w] of water.

[a] 5 Or *him, / but Israel would not be gathered; / yet I will be*

49:4 If his labor seems to have been "in vain," this servant will submissively leave the outcome "in the LORD's hand." He does not obey for short-term "reward."
49:5–6 The servant's ministry is not only to "bring Jacob back" to Yahweh but also to cause "salvation ... [to] reach to the ends of the earth" (cf. Acts 1:8; 13:47).
49:7–12 Two messages from Yahweh to the servant: vv. 7,8–12.
49:7 A similar message to that of 52:13–15. People will initially reject the servant, but one day the great ones of the earth will honor him because of what the Lord, "who is faithful," will accomplish through him.
49:8–12 God will restore his people through the servant. The immediate reference here is to the people physically returning to the land; in the larger context, that physical return is inseparable from a spiritual return.
49:9–11 See 35:1–7; 41:18–19; 42:15–16; 43:19–20; 48:21; 55:12–13.

[11] I will turn all my mountains into roads,
and my highways[x] will be raised up.[y]
[12] See, they will come from afar[z] —
some from the north, some from the west,
some from the region of Aswan.[a]"
[13] Shout for joy, you heavens;
rejoice, you earth;
burst into song, you mountains![a]
For the LORD comforts[b] his people
and will have compassion on his afflicted ones.
[14] But Zion said, "The LORD has forsaken me,
the Lord has forgotten me."
[15] "Can a mother forget the baby at her breast
and have no compassion on the child she has borne?
Though she may forget,
I will not forget you![c]
[16] See, I have engraved[d] you on the palms of my hands;
your walls[e] are ever before me.
[17] Your children hasten back,
and those who laid you waste[f] depart from you.
[18] Lift up your eyes and look around;
all your children gather[g] and come to you.
As surely as I live,"[h] declares the LORD,
"you will wear[i] them all as ornaments;
you will put them on, like a bride.

[19] "Though you were ruined and made desolate[j]
and your land laid waste,[k]
now you will be too small for your people,[l]
and those who devoured you will be far away.
[20] The children born during your bereavement
will yet say in your hearing,
'This place is too small for us;
give us more space to live in.'[m]
[21] Then you will say in your heart,
'Who bore me these?
I was bereaved and barren;
I was exiled and rejected.[n]
Who brought these up?

49:11 [x] Isa 11:16 [y] Isa 40:4
49:12 [z] Isa 43:5-6
49:13 [a] Isa 44:23 [b] Isa 40:1
49:15 [c] Isa 44:21
49:16 [d] SS 8:6 [e] Ps 48:12-13; Isa 62:6
49:17 [f] Isa 10:6
49:18 [g] Isa 43:5; 54:7; Isa 60:4 [h] Isa 45:23 [i] Isa 52:1
49:19 [j] Isa 54:1,3 [k] Isa 5:6 [l] Zec 10:10
49:20 [m] Isa 54:1-3
49:21 [n] Isa 5:13

a 12 Dead Sea Scrolls; Masoretic Text *Sinim*

49:12 Because of the ministry of the servant, God's people come to him from all over the earth (cf. 2:1–5; 11:10–12,15–16; 43:5–7; 60:1–9).
49:13—50:3 *Zion Is Not Forgotten.* As with 42:10–17 and 44:23, a call to praise (49:13) follows the announcement of salvation. But here Zion is unwilling to join in the praise because she believes that God has forgotten her and does not wish to be reconciled to her (49:14). But God asserts that this is not the case: he has both the desire (49:15) and ability (50:1–3) to restore her to himself (49:16–26).
49:13 comforts. Encourages; the first occurrence of the word since 40:1. As there, the issue is encouraging despondent people to believe in God's grace (see 51:3,12,19; 57:18).
49:14 Cf. 40:27. They think God does not care whether or not they continue to exist as a people.
49:15–16 God's love for his people is deeper than a nursing mother's for her baby. Their name is "engraved" on his "hands."
49:17–23 God will restore Israel's children to them. On the theme of widowhood and childlessness, see note on 29:23. This restoration will not be minimal. The nation's expansion will be astounding. So it was when the nations were integrated into the people of God through the ministry of Christ (cf. Eph 2:11–22). In a few short years, the number of the people of God grew exponentially.

49:21 [o]Isa 1:8
49:22 [p]Isa 11:10 [q]Isa 60:4
49:23 [r]Isa 60:3,10-11 [s]Isa 60:16 [t]Ps 72:9 [u]Mic 7:17
49:24 [v]Mt 12:29; Lk 11:21
49:25 [w]Isa 14:2 [x]Jer 50:33-34 [y]Isa 25:9; 35:4
49:26 [z]Isa 9:4 [a]Isa 9:20 [b]Rev 16:6 [c]Eze 39:7
50:1 [d]Dt 24:1; Jer 3:8; Hos 2:2 [e]Ne 5:5; Mt 18:25 [f]Dt 32:30; Isa 52:3
50:2 [g]Isa 41:28 [h]Nu 11:23; Isa 59:1 [i]Ge 18:14

I was left[o] all alone,
but these — where have they come from?' "

22 This is what the Sovereign LORD says:

"See, I will beckon to the nations,
I will lift up my banner[p] to the peoples;
they will bring your sons in their arms
and carry your daughters on their hips.[q]
23 Kings[r] will be your foster fathers,
and their queens your nursing mothers.[s]
They will bow down before you with their faces to the ground;
they will lick the dust[t] at your feet.
Then you will know that I am the LORD;[u]
those who hope in me will not be disappointed."

24 Can plunder be taken from warriors,[v]
or captives be rescued from the fierce[a]?

25 But this is what the LORD says:

"Yes, captives[w] will be taken from warriors,[x]
and plunder retrieved from the fierce;
I will contend with those who contend with you,
and your children I will save.[y]
26 I will make your oppressors[z] eat[a] their own flesh;
they will be drunk on their own blood,[b] as with wine.
Then all mankind will know[c]
that I, the LORD, am your Savior,
your Redeemer, the Mighty One of Jacob."

Israel's Sin and the Servant's Obedience

50 This is what the LORD says:

"Where is your mother's certificate of divorce[d]
with which I sent her away?
Or to which of my creditors
did I sell[e] you?
Because of your sins you were sold;[f]
because of your transgressions your mother was sent away.
2 When I came, why was there no one?
When I called, why was there no one to answer?[g]
Was my arm too short[h] to deliver you?
Do I lack the strength[i] to rescue you?

[a] *24* Dead Sea Scrolls, Vulgate and Syriac (see also Septuagint and verse 25); Masoretic Text *righteous*

49:22 banner. See notes on 5:26; 11:10–16.
49:23 See 60:4,16. As elsewhere, the former oppressing nations will come to Zion as supplicants, either to serve them as here (also in 61:4–5) or to join in worshiping their God (see 2:1–5; 66:18–24). **Then you will know.** Language not only of the exodus (Exod 7:5; 10:2) but also of the exile and the return (Ezek 12:15; 36:11). Yahweh's power is convincing.
49:24–26 God is stronger than Israel's plunderers and captors. He can cause the enemies to destroy themselves (v. 26; cf. Judg 7:22; 1 Sam 14:20; 2 Chr 20:23) and can take his people from their hands.
49:26 On the piling up of epithets for God, see notes on 1:24; 41:11–14; 43:14–15; 44:6–8.
50:1–3 The people feel that Yahweh had been forced to exile them, as though someone compelled him to "divorce" their mother (v. 1) or "sell" them into captivity to pay off a debt (v. 1). Yahweh asserts that nothing of the kind is true. It is only because of their "transgressions" (v. 1) that the exile will have occurred and only then because there were not sufficient intercessors (v. 2; cf. Ezek 22:30). So there is no compelling reason that he cannot restore them to himself. It is certainly not a matter of strength: the "arm" he raised in judgment (v. 2; see "hand" in 9:12) can also stretch out to save (51:5,9; 52:10; 53:1). The cosmos is at his command.
50:2–3 dry up the sea ... clothe the heavens with darkness. Possibly allusions to the exodus and God's deliverance of his people at that time.

By a mere rebuke I dry up the sea,[j]
I turn rivers into a desert;
their fish rot for lack of water
and die of thirst.
3 I clothe the heavens with darkness
and make sackcloth[k] its covering."

4 The Sovereign LORD has given me a well-instructed tongue,[l]
to know the word that sustains the weary.[m]
He wakens me morning by morning,[n]
wakens my ear to listen like one being instructed.
5 The Sovereign LORD has opened my ears;[o]
I have not been rebellious,[p]
I have not turned away.
6 I offered my back to those who beat[q] me,
my cheeks to those who pulled out my beard;
I did not hide my face
from mocking and spitting.[r]
7 Because the Sovereign LORD helps[s] me,
I will not be disgraced.
Therefore have I set my face like flint,[t]
and I know I will not be put to shame.
8 He who vindicates me is near.
Who then will bring charges against me?[u]
Let us face each other![v]
Who is my accuser?
Let him confront me!
9 It is the Sovereign LORD who helps[w] me.
Who will condemn me?
They will all wear out like a garment;
the moths[x] will eat them up.

10 Who among you fears the LORD
and obeys the word of his servant?[y]
Let the one who walks in the dark,
who has no light,
trust[z] in the name of the LORD
and rely on their God.
11 But now, all you who light fires
and provide yourselves with flaming torches,[a]
go, walk in the light of your fires[b]
and of the torches you have set ablaze.
This is what you shall receive from my hand:
You will lie down in torment.[c]

50:2 [j] Ex 14:22; Jos 3:16
50:3 [k] Rev 6:12
50:4 [l] Ex 4:12 [m] Mt 11:28 [n] Ps 5:3; 119:147; 143:8
50:5 [o] Isa 35:5 [p] Mt 26:39; Jn 8:29; 14:31; 15:10; Ac 26:19; Heb 5:8
50:6 [q] Isa 53:5; Mt 27:30; Mk 14:65; 15:19; Lk 22:63 [r] La 3:30; Mt 26:67
50:7 [s] Isa 42:1 [t] Eze 3:8-9
50:8 [u] Isa 43:26; Ro 8:32-34 [v] Isa 41:1
50:9 [w] Isa 41:10 [x] Job 13:28; Isa 51:8
50:10 [y] Isa 49:3 [z] Isa 26:4
50:11 [a] Pr 26:18 [b] Jas 3:6 [c] Isa 65:13-15

50:4–9 *The Third Revelation of the Ministering Servant.* The servant once more speaks of the instrument of his "tongue" (v. 4; see note on 49:2). He emphasizes both his sensitivity and submissiveness (50:4–5), characteristics distinctly lacking in servant Israel. He is submissive not only to God but also to humans (v. 6). Here dismissal (49:4) turns to actual opposition and abuse. The descriptions of the abuse correspond very closely to what happened to Jesus (cf. Matt 26:67; 27:26; Mark 14:65; John 18:22). But the servant is confident in the "Sovereign LORD" (Isa 50:7,9) and knows that he will be vindicated in the end (v. 8) and that his "accuser" (v. 8) will disappear.

50:7 set my face like flint. The servant will carry out his ministry at all costs. Cf. Luke 9:51: "Jesus resolutely set out for Jerusalem."

50:10—51:8 *Obey the Voice of the Ministering Servant.* This segment is marked by repetitions of the call to listen to (and act upon; see note on 48:1) what God is saying through these revelations of his servant (50:10; 51:1,4,7). They must have faith in his ability to deliver not only them but the whole world from the alienation of sin.

50:10 obeys the word. Persons who have "no light" in themselves can either hear the servant's word (equated with "fears the LORD") or try to create their own light and consequently "lie down in torment" (v. 11). Salvation is through the servant.

51:1 [d]Isa 46:3 [e]ver 7; Ps 94:15; Ro 9:30-31
51:2 [f]Isa 29:22; Ro 4:16; Heb 11:11 [g]Ge 12:2
51:3 [h]Isa 40:1 [i]Isa 52:9 [j]Ge 2:8 [k]Isa 25:9; 66:10
51:4 [l]Ps 50:7 [m]Isa 2:4 [n]Isa 42:4,6
51:5 [o]Isa 46:13 [p]Isa 40:10; 63:1,5
51:6 [q]Mt 24:35; 2Pe 3:10 [r]Ps 102:25-26
51:7 [s]ver 1 [t]Ps 37:31 [u]Mt 5:11; Ac 5:41
51:8 [v]Isa 50:9 [w]ver 6

Everlasting Salvation for Zion

51 "Listen[d] to me, you who pursue righteousness[e]
and who seek the LORD:
Look to the rock from which you were cut
and to the quarry from which you were hewn;
2 look to Abraham,[f] your father,
and to Sarah, who gave you birth.
When I called him he was only one man,
and I blessed him and made him many.[g]
3 The LORD will surely comfort[h] Zion
and will look with compassion on all her ruins;[i]
he will make her deserts like Eden,[j]
her wastelands like the garden of the LORD.
Joy and gladness[k] will be found in her,
thanksgiving and the sound of singing.

4 "Listen to me, my people;[l]
hear me, my nation:
Instruction will go out from me;
my justice[m] will become a light to the
nations.[n]
5 My righteousness draws near speedily,
my salvation is on the way,[o]
and my arm[p] will bring justice to the nations.
The islands will look to me
and wait in hope for my arm.
6 Lift up your eyes to the heavens,
look at the earth beneath;
the heavens will vanish like smoke,[q]
the earth will wear out like a garment[r]
and its inhabitants die like flies.
But my salvation will last forever,
my righteousness will never fail.

7 "Hear me, you who know what is right,[s]
you people who have taken my instruction
to heart:[t]
Do not fear the reproach of mere mortals
or be terrified by their insults.[u]
8 For the moth will eat them up like a garment;[v]
the worm will devour them like wool.
But my righteousness will last forever,[w]
my salvation through all generations."

51:1–3 This addresses the first group in 50:10–11, those who "trust in the name of the LORD" (50:10), "who pursue righteousness and who seek the LORD" (51:1). Isaiah counsels them not to lose hope but to remember that just as Abraham received God's undeserved grace and became a great nation (v. 2), so it will be with Abraham's descendants when Yahweh makes the "ruins" and "wastelands" of Zion/Jerusalem "like Eden" (v. 3; cf. Gen 2:8–14). This is fulfilled in the new Jerusalem (Rev 22:1–5).

51:3 Joy and gladness. See 35:10.

51:4–6 Through the servant (Yahweh's "arm," v. 5), Yahweh will extend "instruction" (v. 4; see 2:3), "justice" (v. 4; cf. 42:1), and righteous "salvation" (v. 5) to the whole world. This righteous salvation will outlast the physical world (v. 6; cf. 50:2–3). On referring to salvation as divine "righteousness" (v. 5), see note on 45:8.

51:5 islands. Ends of the earth. **hope.** The same Hebrew word as in 40:31. To wait in confidence on the Lord is to trust him (see note on 30:18).

51:7–8 God concludes by admonishing those "who know what is right." They should not allow fear of mortals to cause them to lose faith in what Yahweh will do for them through his servant. Just as the abusers of the servant would disappear like a garment eaten by moths (v. 8; see 50:9), so will those who would abuse God's people.

9 Awake, awake, arm of the LORD,
clothe yourself with strength![x]
Awake, as in days gone by,
as in generations of old.[y]
Was it not you who cut Rahab to pieces,
who pierced that monster[z] through?
10 Was it not you who dried up the sea,[a]
the waters of the great deep,
who made a road in the depths of the sea
so that the redeemed might cross over?
11 Those the LORD has rescued[b] will return.
They will enter Zion with singing;
everlasting joy will crown their heads.
Gladness and joy[c] will overtake them,
and sorrow and sighing will flee away.[d]

12 "I, even I, am he who comforts[e] you.
Who are you that you fear mere mortals,[f]
human beings who are but grass,[g]
13 that you forget[h] the LORD your Maker,[i]
who stretches out the heavens[j]
and who lays the foundations of the earth,
that you live in constant terror[k] every day
because of the wrath of the oppressor,
who is bent on destruction?
For where is the wrath of the oppressor?
14 The cowering prisoners will soon be set free;
they will not die in their dungeon,
nor will they lack bread.[l]
15 For I am the LORD your God,
who stirs up the sea[m] so that its waves roar—
the LORD Almighty is his name.
16 I have put my words in your mouth[n]
and covered you with the shadow of my hand[o]—
I who set the heavens in place,
who laid the foundations of the earth,
and who say to Zion, 'You are my people.'"

51:9 [x] Isa 52:1 [y] Dt 4:34 [z] Ps 74:13
51:10 [a] Ex 14:22
51:11 [b] Isa 35:9 [c] Jer 33:11 [d] Rev 7:17
51:12 [e] 2Co 1:4 [f] Ps 118:6; Isa 2:22 [g] Isa 40:6-7; 1Pe 1:24
51:13 [h] Isa 17:10 [i] Isa 45:11 [j] Ps 104:2; Isa 48:13 [k] Isa 7:4
51:14 [l] Isa 49:10
51:15 [m] Jer 31:35
51:16 [n] Dt 18:18; Isa 59:21 [o] Ex 33:22
51:17 [p] Isa 52:1

The Cup of the LORD's Wrath

17 Awake, awake![p]
Rise up, Jerusalem,

51:9—52:12 *Awake and Be Delivered.* The people are now convinced that God can deliver them and indeed wants to. So they call upon him to do it, to bare his "arm" (51:9). But God responds that it is they who need to wake up to a genuine and active faith (51:17; 52:1). He is ready to save (51:11–16); their punishment is at an end (51:17–23); the hour for Jerusalem to rise up out of the dust (contrast Babylon, 47:1–3) has come (52:1–6); and the Lord is on his way to relieve the besieged city (52:7–12). In this segment the anticipation of salvation reaches its height (see note on 49:1—55:13).
51:9–16 The Lord is ready to save. The people call for God to act (vv. 9–10), and he responds that he is more than ready to do so if they will put their faith in him and not cower in fear before the oppressors (vv. 11–16).
51:9 arm of the LORD. The servant as the agent of Yahweh's salvation (cf. v. 5; 40:10; 50:2; 52:10; 53:1; 59:1,16). This utilizes the language of the pagan myth to show Yahweh's incomparable power. Here it is his redeeming power, as in the exodus, that is in view (see note on 27:1). **Rahab.** See 30:7 and note.
51:10 waters of the great deep. See note on 44:27.
51:11 Cf. 35:10.
51:12–16 Instead of living in fear of what "mere mortals" might be able to do to them (v. 12), the people should remember that God has put his very "words" in their mouths (i.e., made them the recipients of divine revelation, v. 16; cf. Ps 56). They should focus on their Maker, who is also the Maker of the cosmos (vv. 13,15–16).
51:17–23 It is not Yahweh's arm that should awaken (v. 9), but it is Jerusalem, fearful that she is condemned to suffer for her sins forever.

51:17 [q] Job 21:20; Rev 14:10; 16:19 [r] Ps 60:3
51:18 [s] Ps 88:18 [t] Isa 49:21
51:19 [u] Isa 47:9 [v] Isa 14:30
51:20 [w] Isa 5:25; Jer 14:16
51:21 [x] ver 17; Isa 29:9
51:22 [y] Isa 49:25 [z] ver 17
51:23 [a] Isa 49:26; Jer 25:15-17,26,28; 49:12 [b] Zec 12:2 [c] Jos 10:24
52:1 [d] Isa 51:17 [e] Isa 51:9 [f] Ex 28:2,40; Ps 110:3; Zec 3:4 [g] Ne 11:1; Mt 4:5; Rev 21:2 [h] Na 1:15; Rev 21:27
52:2 [i] Isa 29:4

you who have drunk from the hand of the LORD
the cup of his wrath,[q]
you who have drained to its dregs
the goblet that makes people stagger.[r]
18 Among all the children[s] she bore
there was none to guide her;[t]
among all the children she reared
there was none to take her by the hand.
19 These double calamities[u] have come upon you —
who can comfort you? —
ruin and destruction, famine[v] and sword —
who can[a] console you?
20 Your children have fainted;
they lie at every street corner,[w]
like antelope caught in a net.
They are filled with the wrath of the LORD,
with the rebuke of your God.

21 Therefore hear this, you afflicted one,
made drunk,[x] but not with wine.
22 This is what your Sovereign LORD says,
your God, who defends[y] his people:
"See, I have taken out of your hand
the cup[z] that made you stagger;
from that cup, the goblet of my wrath,
you will never drink again.
23 I will put it into the hands of your tormentors,[a]
who said to you,
'Fall prostrate[b] that we may walk[c] on you.'
And you made your back like the ground,
like a street to be walked on."

52

Awake, awake,[d] Zion,
clothe yourself with strength![e]
Put on your garments of splendor,[f]
Jerusalem, the holy city.[g]
The uncircumcised and defiled
will not enter you again.[h]
2 Shake off your dust;[i]
rise up, sit enthroned, Jerusalem.
Free yourself from the chains on your neck,
Daughter Zion, now a captive.

[a] *19* Dead Sea Scrolls, Septuagint, Vulgate and Syriac; Masoretic Text / *how can I*

She is bereft of her children (vv. 18–20; see note on 29:23) and fears she will die alone, the end of her family line. But God, as a result of his own grace (cf. 44:21–22; 48:9–11) and by means of the servant's self-sacrifice, has taken "the cup of his wrath" (v. 17) out of her hand (v. 22) and "put it into the hands of [her] tormentors" (v. 23). But even they would not have to drink it if they would put their faith in the servant (53:5; Luke 22:42–44).

52:1–6 The hour has come for Jerusalem to rise up out of the dust. Unlike Babylon, whose pride drove them off their throne and into the dust (47:1–3), Jerusalem may rise up and "sit enthroned" (v. 2) because they have been "redeemed" by free grace, i.e., "without money" (v. 3). Again, this refers to physical release, but Israel needs to be redeemed from far more than physical captivity; the Israelites need to be delivered from alienation from God (see note on 49:1—55:13; cf. Ezek 36:20–27). Yahweh's name is "blasphemed" (v. 5) because of Israel's condition, so he is going to take action for the sake of his "name" (v. 6; cf. 12:4; 18:7; 24:15; 29:23; 59:19).

52:1 uncircumcised. A physical condition that marks a person as non-Israelite and a spiritual condition that applies to both Israelites and non-Israelites. Cf. Exod 12:48; Lev 26:41; Deut 10:16; Jer 9:26; Ezek 31:18; 44:7,9; Gal 5:2–6; Col 2:11–13. Here it refers to the Gentiles who had attacked and destroyed Judah and Jerusalem.

[3]For this is what the LORD says:

"You were sold for nothing,[j]
and without money[k] you will be redeemed."

[4]For this is what the Sovereign LORD says:

"At first my people went down to Egypt[l] to live;
lately, Assyria has oppressed them.

[5]"And now what do I have here?" declares the LORD.

"For my people have been taken away for nothing,
and those who rule them mock,[a]"
declares the LORD.

"And all day long
my name is constantly blasphemed.[m]
[6]Therefore my people will know[n] my name;
therefore in that day they will know
that it is I who foretold it.
Yes, it is I."

[7]How beautiful on the mountains
are the feet of those who bring good news,[o]
who proclaim peace,[p]
who bring good tidings,
who proclaim salvation,
who say to Zion,
"Your God reigns!"[q]
[8]Listen! Your watchmen[r] lift up their voices;
together they shout for joy.
When the LORD returns to Zion,
they will see it with their own eyes.
[9]Burst into songs of joy[s] together,
you ruins[t] of Jerusalem,
for the LORD has comforted his people,
he has redeemed Jerusalem.[u]
[10]The LORD will lay bare his holy arm
in the sight of all the nations,[v]

52:3 [j]Ps 44:12 [k]Isa 45:13
52:4 [l]Ge 46:6
52:5 [m]Eze 36:20; Ro 2:24*
52:6 [n]Isa 49:23
52:7 [o]Isa 40:9; Ro 10:15* [p]Na 1:15; Eph 6:15 [q]Ps 93:1
52:8 [r]Isa 62:6
52:9 [s]Ps 98:4 [t]Isa 51:3 [u]Isa 48:20
52:10 [v]Isa 66:18

[a] 5 Dead Sea Scrolls and Vulgate; Masoretic Text *wail*

52:3 sold for nothing. So also v. 5; see 50:1.
52:4 went down to Egypt. Isaiah compares the sojourn in Egypt to the coming exile. **Assyria.** Isaiah saw the destruction of Samaria in 722 BC and the ensuing exile of the Israelite people as the beginning of a single event incorporating the destruction of Jerusalem and the exile of the people of Judah in 586 BC. Thus, Isaiah treated the Assyrians and the Babylonians as a single oppressing group. The prophecy against Babylon in chs. 13–14 concludes with words spoken against Assyria (14:24–27).
52:7–12 The Lord is on his way to deliver the besieged city. Isa 49:1—52:12 anticipates salvation, and this is the climax of that anticipation. In Isaiah's typical fashion, he graphically illustrates (e.g., 3:16—4:1; 5:1–7): he depicts Israel as a city that an enemy army besieges. In 49:1—55:13, the enemy is the unforgiven sins that separate Israel from Yahweh. But Yahweh and his armies have won a decisive victory (52:9–10), and the "watchmen" on the walls (v. 8) see the herald coming with the "good news" of deliverance (v. 7). So Isaiah calls the people to leave the city deliberately, with God before them and behind them (vv. 11–12). God has accomplished "salvation" (vv. 7,10).
52:7 How beautiful on the mountains. The watchmen see the herald coming from the scene of battle bringing a message of victory (2 Sam 18:24–27; Nah 1:15). **those who bring good news.** See also 61:1–2; Rom 10:15.The Greek word the Septuagint (the pre-Christian Greek translation of the OT) uses to translate this phrase is the same one used in the NT to speak of the "good news" (or "gospel") of Christ's salvation from sin. It is especially frequent in Luke and Acts (e.g., Luke 2:10; 3:18; 4:18; Acts 8:35; 10:36; 13:32; but see also Heb 4:2,6). **peace.** See note on 9:6.
52:8 the LORD returns. Israel's redemption (and the world's) depends on whether God can find a way to restore the relationship with humanity that sin has ruptured. The "watchmen" see the evidence that he has found a way and can return to his people with blessing and not curse in his hands. Thus, "they shout for joy." The Jerusalem from which the "glory of the LORD" departed (Ezek 10:18) is now Zion, the city of God, to which the Spirit has returned (Ezek 37:14).
52:9 comforted. See note on 66:13.
52:10 arm. See 40:10; 50:2; 51:5,9; 53:1; 59:1,16. **ends of the earth.** See note on 12:4–6.

52:10 [w]Ps 98:2-3; Lk 3:6
52:11 [x]Isa 48:20 [y]Isa 1:16; 2Co 6:17* [z]2Ti 2:19
52:12 [a]Ex 12:11 [b]Mic 2:13 [c]Ex 14:19
52:13 [d]Isa 42:1 [e]Isa 57:15; Php 2:9
52:15 [f]Ro 15:21*; Eph 3:4-5
53:1 [g]Ro 10:16* [h]Jn 12:38*
53:2 [i]Isa 52:14
53:3 [j]ver 4,10; Lk 18:31-33

and all the ends of the earth will see
the salvation[w] of our God.

11 Depart,[x] depart, go out from there!
Touch no unclean thing![y]
Come out from it and be pure,[z]
you who carry the articles of the LORD's house.
12 But you will not leave in haste[a]
or go in flight;
for the LORD will go before you,[b]
the God of Israel will be your rear guard.[c]

The Suffering and Glory of the Servant

13 See, my servant[d] will act wisely[a];
he will be raised and lifted up and highly exalted.[e]
14 Just as there were many who were appalled at him[b]—
his appearance was so disfigured beyond that of any human being
and his form marred beyond human likeness—
15 so he will sprinkle many nations,[c]
and kings will shut their mouths because of him.
For what they were not told, they will see,
and what they have not heard, they will understand.[f]

53

Who has believed our message[g]
and to whom has the arm of the LORD been revealed?[h]
2 He grew up before him like a tender shoot,
and like a root out of dry ground.
He had no beauty or majesty to attract us to him,
nothing in his appearance[i] that we should desire him.
3 He was despised and rejected by mankind,
a man of suffering, and familiar with pain.[j]

[a] 13 Or *will prosper* [b] 14 Hebrew *you* [c] 15 Or *so will many nations be amazed at him* (see also Septuagint)

52:11 articles of the LORD's house. When the Babylonians captured Jerusalem, Nebuchadnezzar took them (2 Kgs 25:14–15); Belshazzar drank from them (Dan 5:2–4); and Cyrus restored them (Ezra 1:7–8).
52:13—53:12 *The Final Revelation of the Ministering Servant.* This is the fullest statement in Isaiah of the means by which Yahweh would restore his people to himself, making it possible for him to fulfill his assertions in chs. 41–48 that they are his chosen servants. The servant is "the arm of the LORD" (53:1; see also 50:2; 51:5,9), but a very unexpected one. His power for deliverance is in surrender, both to Yahweh and to his abusers. But that self-sacrifice for the sins of his people and all people will make victory possible over the sin that holds the world in bondage. It is apparent both from Jesus' own statements and those of the NT writers that all of them understood this passage to be speaking of Jesus' life and ministry (Matt 8:17; Acts 8:30–35; Rom 10:15–17; 15:21; 1 Pet 2:22,24–25). The pronouns in the passage are very important: "I" generally refers to Yahweh; "he" refers to the servant; "we," "us," and "our" refer to the prophet and his audience; "you" refers to the audience. There is no reason to limit the scope of the audience. As noted above, the servant's work is not only for "Jacob" but for all the nations (49:6). The poem is carefully structured in five stanzas with three sentences each (52:13–15; 53:1–3,4–6,7–9,10–12).
52:13–15 *The Triumph and the Shock of the Servant's Work.* The poem begins on a note of triumph.
52:13 act wisely. The Hebrew connotes being successful (see NIV text note), i.e., the servant will successfully accomplish his mission. Furthermore, this describes him in terms used only of God elsewhere in the book: "raised and lifted up" (cf. 6:1; 57:15).
52:14–15 The servant's appearance will be a shock, especially to the great ones ("kings") of the earth. They expected a godlike mighty man; instead, he is "disfigured" (see note on v. 14).
52:14 disfigured. In Mal 1:14 the term refers to a blemished animal that is not an acceptable sacrifice (cf. 50:6; Matt 27:26–31) and is apparently weak (cf. 53:1–3).
52:15 sprinkle many nations. See NIV text note. "Amazed" may be a better poetic parallel with "shut their mouths." Elsewhere the object of "sprinkle" is specified. Perhaps blood is intended (Lev 4:6,17; 16:14). **what they have not heard.** The message of deliverance through self-sacrifice, which they had not previously comprehended, will now be demonstrated before their eyes (cf. Rom 15:21).
53:1–3 *The Rejection of the Servant.* The sense of rejection that emerges in the second and third revelations of the servant (49:4; 50:6–9) here comes to the fore. "The arm of the LORD" (v. 1) was not supposed to look like a spindly plant in "dry ground" (v. 2); he was not supposed to suffer, but was to impose suffering on others (cf. Mark 8:27–33). God's strength was manifested in weakness. This is the same theme that appeared in chs. 7–12, especially in the recurring references to children.
53:1 Cf. John 12:38; Rom 10:16.
53:3 despised. Not so much an emotional response as a judgment that something or someone is not worthy of attention or respect.

Like one from whom people hide their faces
he was despised,[k] and we held him in low esteem.

4 Surely he took up our pain
and bore our suffering,[l]
yet we considered him punished by God,[m]
stricken by him, and afflicted.
5 But he was pierced for our transgressions,[n]
he was crushed for our iniquities;
the punishment that brought us peace was on him,
and by his wounds we are healed.[o]
6 We all, like sheep, have gone astray,
each of us has turned to our own way;
and the LORD has laid on him
the iniquity of us all.

7 He was oppressed and afflicted,
yet he did not open his mouth;[p]
he was led like a lamb to the slaughter,
and as a sheep before its shearers is
silent,
so he did not open his mouth.
8 By oppression[a] and judgment he was
taken away.
Yet who of his generation protested?
For he was cut off from the land of the
living;[q]
for the transgression[r] of my people he
was punished.[b]

[a] 8 Or *From arrest* [b] 8 Or *generation considered / that he was cut off from the land of the living, / that he was punished for the transgression of my people?*

53:3 [k] Ps 22:6; Jn 1:10-11
53:4 [l] Mt 8:17* [m] Jn 19:7
53:5 [n] Ro 4:25; 1Co 15:3; Heb 9:28 [o] 1Pe 2:24-25
53:7 [p] Mk 14:61
53:8 [q] Da 9:26; Ac 8:32-33* [r] ver 12

53:4–6 *The Substitutionary Suffering of the Servant.* The suffering that caused us to despise the servant was in fact ours. The first-person pronouns throughout this stanza are impressive. Everything that happened to the servant was in fact what should have happened to us (cf. Rom 4:25; 2 Cor 5:21; 1 Pet 2:24–25). "We" thought he was being "punished by God" (v. 4), but we were wrong; it was our "punishment ... on him" (v. 5). Not only did he take our punishment, but in taking it, he made us whole ("brought us peace," v. 5; see 9:6 and note). He was beaten, and we became healthy. This stanza carries the basic thrust of the entire poem.
53:5 pierced. See Ps 22:16; Zech 12:10; John 19:34 and notes. **crushed ... punishment ... wounds.** All speak of the agony that the servant had to undergo because of our sins. Atonement is not achieved through a mere religious sleight of hand; it is a matter of death.
53:6–7 These verses provide two contrasting comparisons involving sheep. In us, it is the tendency to go "astray" (v. 6; cf. Ps 119:176; Jer 50:6; Ezek 34:4–6,16; 1 Pet 2:25). In him, it is defenselessness (v. 7).
53:6 laid on him. Similar to the action of the high priest on the Day of Atonement when he laid the sins of the people on the scapegoat (Lev 16:21).
53:7–9 *The Apparent Outcome of the Servant's Suffering.* It appears on the surface that the servant has suffered in vain (cf. 49:4). "He was oppressed and afflicted" (v. 7), but no one spoke up on his behalf—neither he himself (v. 7) nor anyone else (v. 8). He was denied a fair trial (the phrase "by oppression and judgment" in v. 8 is likely "oppressive judgment"). He was "cut off" (v. 8) without children, and no one seemed to recognize what he was actually doing (see NIV text note on v. 8). The final insult was that he was buried with the rich (v. 9). The context here shows that this was not a place of honor. The Bible often associates the rich with wickedness, because many times their wealth was acquired through oppression or dishonesty (see 1 Sam 25:2–3; Prov 22:16; 28:6; Jer 5:27). This prophecy was fulfilled when Joseph of Arimathea, himself a righteous man, buried Jesus among the rich. Verses 7–8 were those troubling the Ethiopian eunuch when Philip met him (Acts 8:32–34).
53:7 lamb to the slaughter. This the picture of the Lamb in Revelation, "looking as if it had been slain" (Rev 5:6). John the Baptist described Jesus as "the Lamb of God" (John 1:29,36). **did not open his mouth.** Jesus did not respond to the charges of the Sanhedrin (Mark 14:60–61) nor to the questions of Pilate (Mark 15:4–5) and Herod (Luke 23:8–9).

QUOTATIONS FROM AND REFERENCES TO ISAIAH 53 IN THE NEW TESTAMENT

ISAIAH	NEW TESTAMENT
vv. 1–12	Luke 24:27,46; 1 Pet 1:11
v. 1	John 12:38; Rom 10:16
v. 2	Matt 2:23
v. 3	Mark 9:12
v. 4	Matt 8:17; 1 Pet 2:24
vv. 4–5	Rom 4:25
v. 5	Matt 26:67; 1 Pet 2:24
vv. 5–6	Acts 10:43
v. 6	1 Pet 2:25
vv. 6–7	John 1:29
v. 7	Matt 26:63; 27:12,14; Mark 14:60–61; 15:4–5; 1 Cor 5:7; 1 Pet 2:23; Rev 5:6,12; 13:8
vv. 7–8 (Septuagint)	Acts 8:32–33
vv. 8–9	1 Cor 15:3
v. 9	Matt 26:24; 1 Pet 2:22; 1 John 3:5; Rev 14:5
v. 11	Rom 5:19
v. 12	Matt 27:38; Luke 22:37; 23:33–34; Heb 9:28; 1 Pet 2:24

Taken from *The Zondervan Encyclopedia of the Bible*: Vol. 5 by MOISÉS SILVA.

53:9 [s] Mt 27:57-60 [t] Isa 42:1-3 [u] 1Pe 2:22*
53:10 [v] Isa 46:10 [w] ver 5 [x] ver 3 [y] Ps 22:30
53:11 [z] Jn 10:14-18 [a] Ro 5:18-19
53:12 [b] Php 2:9 [c] Mt 26:28,38,39,42 [d] Mk 15:27*; Lk 22:37*; 23:32
54:1 [e] Isa 49:20 [f] 1Sa 2:5; Gal 4:27*

9 He was assigned a grave with the wicked,
and with the rich[s] in his death,
though he had done no violence,[t]
nor was any deceit in his mouth.[u]

10 Yet it was the LORD's will[v] to crush[w] him and cause him to suffer,[x]
and though the LORD makes[a] his life an offering for sin,
he will see his offspring[y] and prolong his days,
and the will of the LORD will prosper in his hand.
11 After he has suffered,[z]
he will see the light of life[b] and be satisfied[c];
by his knowledge[d] my righteous servant will justify[a] many,
and he will bear their iniquities.
12 Therefore I will give him a portion among the great,[e][b]
and he will divide the spoils with the strong,[f]
because he poured out his life unto death,[c]
and was numbered with the transgressors.[d]
For he bore the sin of many,
and made intercession for the transgressors.

The Future Glory of Zion

54

"Sing, barren woman,
you who never bore a child;
burst into song, shout for joy,
you who were never in labor;
because more are the children[e] of the desolate woman
than of her who has a husband,[f]"
says the LORD.

[a] 10 Hebrew *though you make* [b] 11 Dead Sea Scrolls (see also Septuagint); Masoretic Text does not have *the light of life.* [c] 11 Or (with Masoretic Text) *11He will see the fruit of his suffering / and will be satisfied* [d] 11 Or *by knowledge of him* [e] 12 Or *many* [f] 12 Or *numerous*

53:10–12 *The Real Outcome of the Servant's Suffering.* These things happened not accidentally or merely because this is an unjust world but because "it was the LORD's will" (v. 10). On the surface this seems terrible. But this expresses not cruelty but love for a lost world. When "his life" is made "an offering for sin" (v. 10), then the children and the long life that he was deprived of will be amply repaid, because he will have progeny in faith over the whole world (v. 10). This accomplishes Yahweh's will ("prosper," v. 10; see note on 52:13) and satisfies the servant (v. 11). The mission ends in victory since the servant divides "the spoils with the strong" (v. 12). The victory is surprising: the victor "poured out his life unto death," but in dying he carries the "sin of many" and intercedes "for the transgressors" (v. 12), thereby justifying "many" (v. 11). Therein is victory.
53:10 the LORD makes. See NIV text note. Interpretations vary; the subject could be Yahweh, the servant, or even the sinner.
53:11 The servant will be "satisfied" because he will see that his suffering has achieved its redemptive purpose. **light of life.** Points to his resurrection from death (vv. 9,12; cf. Rom 1:4). **knowledge.** Not intellectual but experiential. It could be the servant's relationship with the Father, but in the context it is probably what he has undergone in bearing the sins of the world (cf. 1 John 2:2). **justify.** Because the servant has suffered in "our" place (vv. 4–6), we need not suffer for our sins but can be declared innocent (Rom 3:20–24).
53:12 unto death. See Phil 2:8. **transgressors.** Includes the idea of rebellion, an important concept in Isaiah (1:2,20,23,28; 24:20; 43:27; 46:8; 66:24). The servant would identify himself with these rebels, bearing their "sin" (cf. Luke 22:37; 2 Cor 5:21) and making "intercession" for them so that they could once again become faithful servants of the King (cf. Rom 8:34).
54:1—55:13 *Invitation to Deliverance.* The final revelation of the servant (52:13—53:12) enables the move from anticipation (49:1—52:12) to this two-part invitation in 54:1—55:13. In light of what the servant enabled, God invites Israel to move back into the relationship with him that he first offered at Mount Sinai (cf. Exod 19:5–6).
54:1–17 *The Heritage of the Lord's Servants.* Chs. 41–48 repeat benefits that would accrue to Yahweh's servants, and ch. 54 reiterates and expands those benefits (see v. 17). This is the only place in 49:1—55:13 where the idea of the nation as God's servant appears; the other occurrences are all of the ministering servant who makes Israel's servanthood possible. The benefits that his service make possible are restoring Israel's marriage with Yahweh (vv. 1–8) and protecting Israel from enemies (vv. 9–17).
54:1–8 *Restoration of Marriage With Yahweh.* Israel, who thought herself a "barren woman" (v. 1), is restored to her "husband" (v. 1), who is also her "Maker" (v. 5; cf. 17:7: 45:9,11; 51:13), with the result that she will have many children again (54:1–3). The nation will not disappear under the wrath of God, but will grow and multiply as Yahweh had promised to Abraham. The return from exile is a preliminary and partial fulfillment of the final ingathering of all God's people that has been inaugurated by Christ.
54:1 On the grief of barrenness, see 1 Sam 1:6–11. The first three mothers of Israel (Sarah, Rebekah, and Rachel) were all barren until God gave them fertility (Gen 11:30; 25:21; 30:1,22), symbolizing humanity's

[2] "Enlarge the place of your tent,[g]
stretch your tent curtains wide,
do not hold back;
lengthen your cords,
strengthen your stakes.[h]
[3] For you will spread out to the right and to the left;
your descendants will dispossess nations
and settle in their desolate[i] cities.

[4] "Do not be afraid; you will not be put to shame.
Do not fear disgrace; you will not be humiliated.
You will forget the shame of your youth
and remember no more the reproach[j] of your
widowhood.
[5] For your Maker is your husband[k]—
the LORD Almighty is his name—
the Holy One of Israel is your Redeemer;[l]
he is called the God of all the earth.[m]
[6] The LORD will call you back[n]
as if you were a wife deserted[o] and distressed
in spirit—
a wife who married young,
only to be rejected," says your God.
[7] "For a brief moment[p] I abandoned you,
but with deep compassion I will bring you back.[q]
[8] In a surge of anger[r]
I hid my face from you for a moment,
but with everlasting kindness[s]
I will have compassion on you,"
says the LORD your Redeemer.

[9] "To me this is like the days of Noah,
when I swore that the waters of Noah would never
again cover the earth.[t]
So now I have sworn not to be angry[u] with you,
never to rebuke you again.
[10] Though the mountains be shaken[v]
and the hills be removed,
yet my unfailing love for you will not be shaken[w]
nor my covenant[x] of peace be removed,"
says the LORD, who has compassion[y] on you.

54:2 [g] Isa 49:19-20 [h] Ex 35:18; 39:40
54:3 [i] Isa 49:19
54:4 [j] Isa 51:7
54:5 [k] Jer 3:14 [l] Isa 48:17 [m] Isa 6:3
54:6 [n] Isa 49:14-21 [o] Isa 50:1-2; 62:4,12
54:7 [p] Isa 26:20 [q] Isa 49:18
54:8 [r] Isa 60:10 [s] ver 10
54:9 [t] Ge 8:21 [u] Isa 12:1
54:10 [v] Ps 46:2 [w] Isa 51:6 [x] Ps 89:34 [y] ver 8

inability to ensure its own survival, not only physically but (more important) spiritually (Gal 4:26–27).
54:3 God will use his people in the judgment of their oppressors (see notes on 30:23–33; 41:15–16).
54:4 shame ... disgrace. See note on 25:8. It will be evident that Israel's trust in Yahweh was not misplaced. God will erase the shame of the exile ("widowhood").
54:5 On the piling up of divine epithets for Yahweh, see notes on 1:4,9,24; 41:11–14.
54:7–8 Yahweh *becomes* angry, but he *is* love (see Exod 34:6–7; Pss 30:5; 103:8–14; 1 John 4:7–8). His "compassion" is "deep" because it expresses his "everlasting kindness" (see note on v. 8).
54:8 everlasting kindness. Hebrew *ḥesed*, translated "unfailing love" in v. 10 and elsewhere (e.g., Pss 13:5; 36:7; 51:1).
54:9–17 *Protection From Enemies.* For those who trust in the work of the servant, "there is now no condemnation" (Rom 8:1; see Rom 8:33–34). There will be need for discipline and correction but not condemnation.
54:9–10 The servant's work inaugurates a new era, like that after "the waters of Noah." He has taken God's anger away, expressing that unshakable "unfailing love" (see note on v. 8).
54:10 covenant of peace. Expresses the *šālôm* (see note on 9:6) that God intends for his people (cf. John 14:27; Rom 5:1–2). This is the new covenant (Jer 33:20–21), which is the climax of all God intended to accomplish through the Abrahamic, Sinaitic, and Davidic covenants. The description of this covenant in Ezek 34:25–31 makes it clear that the return from exile was only the beginning of all that God was promising to accomplish for his people.

54:11 [z]Isa 14:32 [a]Isa 28:2; 29:6 [b]Isa 51:19 [c]1Ch 29:2; Rev 21:18 [d]Isa 28:16; Rev 21:19-20
54:13 [e]Jn 6:45* [f]Isa 48:18
54:14 [g]Isa 9:4
54:15 [h]Isa 41:11-16
54:17 [i]Isa 29:8 [j]Isa 45:24-25
55:1 [k]Jn 4:14; 7:37 [l]La 5:4; Mt 13:44; Rev 3:18 [m]SS 5:1 [n]Hos 14:4; Mt 10:8; Rev 21:6
55:2 [o]Ps 22:26; Ecc 6:2; Hos 8:7 [p]Isa 1:19
55:3 [q]Lev 18:5; Ro 10:5 [r]Isa 61:8 [s]Isa 54:8 [t]Ac 13:34*

11 "Afflicted[z] city, lashed by storms[a] and not comforted,[b]
I will rebuild you with stones of turquoise,[a][c]
your foundations[d] with lapis lazuli.
12 I will make your battlements of rubies,
your gates of sparkling jewels,
and all your walls of precious stones.
13 All your children will be taught by the LORD,[e]
and great will be their peace.[f]
14 In righteousness you will be established:
Tyranny[g] will be far from you;
you will have nothing to fear.
Terror will be far removed;
it will not come near you.
15 If anyone does attack you, it will not be my doing;
whoever attacks you will surrender[h] to you.

16 "See, it is I who created the blacksmith
who fans the coals into flame
and forges a weapon fit for its work.
And it is I who have created the destroyer to wreak havoc;
17 no weapon forged against you will prevail,[i]
and you will refute[j] every tongue that accuses you.
This is the heritage of the servants of the LORD,
and this is their vindication from me,"
declares the LORD.

Invitation to the Thirsty

55 "Come, all you who are thirsty,[k]
come to the waters;
and you who have no money,
come, buy[l] and eat!
Come, buy wine and milk[m]
without money and without cost.[n]
2 Why spend money on what is not bread,
and your labor on what does not satisfy?[o]
Listen, listen to me, and eat what is good,[p]
and you will delight in the richest of fare.
3 Give ear and come to me;
listen, that you may live.[q]
I will make an everlasting covenant[r] with you,
my faithful love[s] promised to David.[t]

[a] *11* The meaning of the Hebrew for this word is uncertain.

54:11–12 Cf. the city of salvation (26:1–4). See also Rev 21:10–21.
54:13 taught by the LORD. Cf. 45:1–4; see also John 6:45.
54:14–17 Zion need fear no "terror" so long as the people are in a trusting relationship with Yahweh (v. 14), because he is the one who forged the "weapon" used against them (v. 16) and any other "weapon" raised against them must ultimately fail (v. 17; cf. Rom 8:31–34).
55:1–13 *Seek the Lord.* In light of the benefits of the servant's work (ch. 54), the people of Israel should avail themselves of this salvation now. They should not imagine that they can purchase it (vv. 1–2) but should obey the call to believe what God says (vv. 3–5). They should not wait to understand it all (vv. 6–11) but should immediately act (vv. 6–7) on the glorious promise (vv. 12–13).
55:1–2 God's gracious provision through the death of the servant is priceless, and people can do nothing to earn it (cf. Eph 2:8–9). They must simply act upon it.
55:2 Listen, listen. See note on 48:1.
55:3–5 God offers an "everlasting covenant," the "faithful love promised to David" (v. 3). This promise may have a double meaning: (1) the new covenant made available to us through Jesus Christ, the son of David, who fulfilled the promise of an eternal dynasty (2 Sam 7:14–16), and (2) the kind of covenant God made with David, namely, through David and his descendant, Yahweh would give an endless "witness" to all the world (v. 4) that Yahweh is the only Savior (v. 5). So too the church will be such a witness (cf. Acts 1:8).

4 See, I have made him a witness to the peoples,
a ruler and commander[u] of the peoples.
5 Surely you will summon nations[v] you know not,
and nations you do not know will come running to you,
because of the LORD your God,
the Holy One of Israel,
for he has endowed you with splendor."[w]

6 Seek the LORD while he may be found;[x]
call[y] on him while he is near.
7 Let the wicked forsake their ways
and the unrighteous their thoughts.[z]
Let them turn[a] to the LORD, and he will have mercy[b]
on them,
and to our God, for he will freely pardon.[c]

8 "For my thoughts are not your thoughts,
neither are your ways my ways,"[d]
declares the LORD.

9 "As the heavens are higher than the earth,[e]
so are my ways higher than your ways
and my thoughts than your thoughts.
10 As the rain[f] and the snow
come down from heaven,
and do not return to it
without watering the earth
and making it bud and flourish,
so that it yields seed for the sower and bread for
the eater,[g]
11 so is my word that goes out from my mouth:
It will not return to me empty,[h]
but will accomplish what I desire
and achieve the purpose[i] for which I sent it.
12 You will go out in joy
and be led forth in peace;[j]
the mountains and hills
will burst into song before you,
and all the trees[k] of the field
will clap their hands.[l]
13 Instead of the thornbush will grow the juniper,
and instead of briers[m] the myrtle[n] will grow.
This will be for the LORD's renown,[o]
for an everlasting sign,
that will endure forever."

55:4 [u] Jer 30:9; Eze 34:23-24
55:5 [v] Isa 49:6 [w] Isa 60:9
55:6 [x] Ps 32:6; Isa 49:8; 2Co 6:1-2 [y] Isa 65:24
55:7 [z] Isa 32:7; 59:7 [a] Isa 44:22 [b] Isa 54:10 [c] Isa 1:18; 40:2
55:8 [d] Isa 53:6
55:9 [e] Ps 103:11
55:10 [f] Isa 30:23 [g] 2Co 9:10
55:11 [h] Isa 45:23 [i] Isa 44:26
55:12 [j] Isa 54:10,13 [k] 1Ch 16:33 [l] Ps 98:8
55:13 [m] Isa 5:6 [n] Isa 41:19 [o] Isa 63:12

55:5 splendor. Glory (see note on 6:3); see also 46:13; 49:3; 52:1; 60:9,21; 61:1–3.
55:6–7 This briefly explains how to enter a saving relationship with the Lord: earnestly pursue ("seek") God and his ways in his opportune time; "forsake" all "wicked" behavior ("ways") and "unrighteous" attitudes ("thoughts"); cast oneself on the "mercy" of Yahweh, knowing that nothing we have done merits his "pardon."
55:8–11 We should not attempt to reduce God's works for our salvation to an explanation that we can understand. His ways are higher than ours (v. 9). Isa 52:13—53:12 created many questions for Isaiah's hearers and perhaps for Isaiah himself (cf. 1 Pet 1:10–12). Even after Christ appeared and fulfilled the prophecy, theories of the atonement abound. A saving relationship with God depends not on our complete understanding what he has done but on our complete acceptance of his "word" (v. 11). Note the emphasis on God's unfailing word in ch. 40 at the beginning of this section (40:1—55:13).
55:12–13 See 35:1–2,6–10. Salvation is a journey: we walk with the Lord to the accompaniment of joyous song. Ultimately, nature will also benefit from God's salvation of Adam and Eve's children.

56:1 [p]Isa 1:17 [q]Ps 85:9
56:2 [r]Ps 119:2 [s]Ex 20:8, 10; Isa 58:13
56:3 [t]Jer 38:7 *fn*; Ac 8:27
56:5 [u]Isa 26:1; 60:18 [v]Isa 48:19; 55:13
56:6 [w]Isa 60:7,10; 61:5 [x]ver 2,4

Salvation for Others

56 This is what the LORD says:

"Maintain justice[p]
and do what is right,
for my salvation[q] is close at hand
and my righteousness will soon be revealed.
2 Blessed[r] is the one who does this—
the person who holds it fast,
who keeps the Sabbath[s] without desecrating it,
and keeps their hands from doing any evil."

3 Let no foreigner who is bound to the LORD say,
"The LORD will surely exclude me from his people."
And let no eunuch[t] complain,
"I am only a dry tree."

4 For this is what the LORD says:

"To the eunuchs who keep my Sabbaths,
who choose what pleases me
and hold fast to my covenant—
5 to them I will give within my temple and its walls[u]
a memorial and a name
better than sons and daughters;
I will give them an everlasting name
that will endure forever.[v]
6 And foreigners who bind themselves to the LORD
to minister[w] to him,
to love the name of the LORD,
and to be his servants,
all who keep the Sabbath[x] without desecrating it
and who hold fast to my covenant—

56:1—66:24 *Righteousness: The Character of Servanthood.* This last division of the book, especially its central unit (60:1—62:12), reveals the completion of Israel's mission to be a light to the nations (just as Isaiah's declaration of God's word to the nation fulfilled his experience of revelation and cleansing). However, the people's inability to live righteous lives hinders their completing that mission (56:9—59:15a; 63:7—66:17). It is only as God enables them to live such lives by his mighty power that they are able to complete the mission (59:15b–21; 63:1–6). The goal of that mission is to produce righteous, worshiping Gentiles, which the opening and closing units signal (56:1–8; 66:18–24). While it is probable that Isaiah wrote this with the return from exile in mind, its primary purpose is completing the book's theological message. Thus, while we could understand 56:9—59:15a and 63:7—66:17 as describing sinful behavior by the unregenerate, the order of the materials in the book makes it more likely that it describes the behavior of those who have been restored to fellowship with God (54:1—55:13) but have not availed themselves of the Servant-Warrior's power to give them victory over sin in their lives.

56:1–8 *Righteous Foreigners and Eunuchs.* Redemption is not primarily a judicial proclamation; it is a spiritual rebirth issuing in changed behavior. Thus, people who are not part of the community by birth (foreigners) but yet keep the terms of God's covenant for love's sake are fully pleasing to God, as are persons who have no hope of ever having children to carry on the national heritage (eunuchs, v. 3). This corrects a possible misunderstanding of 40:1—55:13, namely, that grace is available to Israel merely because of election and therefore the people need not concern themselves with godly behavior.

56:1 This verse synthesizes the points of chs. 1–39 (righteousness is required but not achieved) and chs. 40–55 (redemption is through grace alone). **Maintain justice and do what is right.** The requirement for justice is still in place. **my salvation ... my righteousness.** See note on 45:8. God makes righteous living possible through his grace.

56:2 The twin emphases on Sabbath-keeping (vv. 4,6; cf. 58:13; 66:23) and refraining "from doing any evil" ("righteousness" occurs 14 times in 56:1—66:24; e.g., 57:12; 59:14; 61:3; 62:1,2 ["vindication"]) express in concrete form the righteous behavior that should result from gracious salvation and that will constitute a witness to a watching world (cf. Ezek 36:23).

56:3 foreigner. See Exod 12:48–49; Num 9:14; Eph 2:11–13. **eunuch.** See Deut 23:1.

56:4 For such a person, see Acts 8:27. The ceremonial laws of the OT were God-designed symbols to teach spiritual truths. So physical wholeness was required of the worshiper as a symbol of spiritual wholeness. When the Holy Spirit wrote the new covenant on the heart (Jer 31:33; 2 Cor 3:3), the symbols, such as the prohibition in Deut 23:1, were no longer needed.

56:6 This is not Pharisaic righteousness but glad conformity to God's wishes as conveyed through the "covenant" and all for the sake of "love." Sabbath-keeping was a particular sign of the Sinai covenant (Exod 20:8–11; 31:12–17; 35:1–3).

[7] these I will bring to my holy mountain[y]
and give them joy in my house of prayer.
Their burnt offerings and sacrifices[z]
will be accepted on my altar;
for my house will be called
a house of prayer for all nations.[a]"[b]
[8] The Sovereign LORD declares—
he who gathers the exiles of Israel:
"I will gather[c] still others to them
besides those already gathered."

God's Accusation Against the Wicked

[9] Come, all you beasts of the field,[d]
come and devour, all you beasts of the forest!
[10] Israel's watchmen[e] are blind,
they all lack knowledge;
they are all mute dogs,
they cannot bark;
they lie around and dream,
they love to sleep.[f]
[11] They are dogs with mighty appetites;
they never have enough.
They are shepherds[g] who lack understanding;[h]
they all turn to their own way,
they seek their own gain.[i]
[12] "Come," each one cries, "let me get wine!
Let us drink our fill of beer!
And tomorrow will be like today,
or even far better."[j]

57
The righteous perish,[k]
and no one takes it to heart;[l]
the devout are taken away,
and no one understands
that the righteous are taken away
to be spared from evil.[m]
[2] Those who walk uprightly[n]
enter into peace;
they find rest as they lie in death.

56:7 [y] Isa 2:2 [z] Ro 12:1; Heb 13:15 [a] Mt 21:13*; Lk 19:46* [b] Mk 11:17*
56:8 [c] Isa 11:12; 60:3-11; Jn 10:16
56:9 [d] Isa 18:6; Jer 12:9
56:10 [e] Eze 3:17 [f] Na 3:18
56:11 [g] Eze 34:2 [h] Isa 1:3 [i] Isa 57:17; Eze 13:19; Mic 3:11
56:12 [j] Ps 10:6; Lk 12:18-19
57:1 [k] Ps 12:1 [l] Isa 42:25 [m] 2Ki 22:20
57:2 [n] Isa 26:7

56:7–8 The purpose of restoring "the exiles" and rebuilding God's "house" is that the "nations" (i.e., the Gentiles) might also be "gathered" to worship God in his "house of prayer" (66:18–24).

56:7 my holy mountain. The temple; people in the ancient world thought the gods lived on mountains. Since Yahweh is the only God, then his place in Jerusalem is the only "holy mountain." See 2:2; 11:9; 27:13; 57:13; 65:11,25; 66:20.

56:9—59:21 *Israel's Inability to Do Righteousness.* This strongly contrasts with 56:1–8. Despite the command of 56:1, Israel is unable to live a righteous life in its own strength. This has four parts: 56:9—57:13; 57:14–21; 58:1—59:15a; 59:15b–21.

56:9—57:13 *God's Accusation Against the Wicked.* These descriptions of Israel's behavior would have resonated with persons of Isaiah's own day as well as those of later times. Their leaders, their "watchmen" (56:10), have failed them (56:9–12; cf. 28:7–8,14–15). The "righteous" (57:1) have perished (57:1–2), and all those who remain worship idols (57:3–13; cf. 2:20; 17:8; 30:22).

56:9–12 *Blind Watchmen.* The "beasts" of sin (v. 9) are devouring Israel, because those who should be warning them of the danger are like "mute dogs" (v. 10; cf. Ezek 3:16–19). They do not give the alarm because they themselves have fallen prey to the temptation to self-indulgence: "sleep," "appetites," "their own way," and "their own gain" (vv. 10–11).

57:1–2 *A Righteous Generation Quietly Disappears.* Although this could refer to any righteous generation, Isaiah might have had in mind the one that would return from exile full of faith and determination to live for God only to be replaced by a new generation that fell back into the self-indulgent paganism of the past. Some may have seen their deaths as some sort of judgment, but it was actually a blessing: they have been "spared" from the coming "evil."

57:3 [o]Mt 16:4 [p]Isa 1:21
57:5 [q]2Ki 16:4 [r]Lev 18:21; Ps 106:37-38; Eze 16:20
57:6 [s]Jer 3:9 [t]Jer 7:18 [u]Jer 5:9,29; 9:9
57:7 [v]Jer 3:6; Eze 16:16
57:8 [w]Eze 16:26; 23:7 [x]Eze 23:18
57:9 [y]Eze 23:16,40
57:10 [z]Jer 2:25; 18:12
57:11 [a]Pr 29:25

3 "But you — come here, you children of a sorceress,
you offspring of adulterers[o] and prostitutes![p]
4 Who are you mocking?
At whom do you sneer
and stick out your tongue?
Are you not a brood of rebels,
the offspring of liars?
5 You burn with lust among the oaks
and under every spreading tree;[q]
you sacrifice your children[r] in the ravines
and under the overhanging crags.
6 The idols[s] among the smooth stones of the ravines are your portion;
indeed, they are your lot.
Yes, to them you have poured out drink offerings[t]
and offered grain offerings.
In view of all this, should I relent?[u]
7 You have made your bed on a high and lofty hill;[v]
there you went up to offer your sacrifices.
8 Behind your doors and your doorposts
you have put your pagan symbols.
Forsaking me, you uncovered your bed,
you climbed into it and opened it wide;
you made a pact with those whose beds you love,[w]
and you looked with lust on their naked bodies.[x]
9 You went to Molek[a] with olive oil
and increased your perfumes.
You sent your ambassadors[b][y] far away;
you descended to the very realm of the dead!
10 You wearied yourself by such going about,
but you would not say, 'It is hopeless.'[z]
You found renewal of your strength,
and so you did not faint.

11 "Whom have you so dreaded and feared[a]
that you have not been true to me,

[a] 9 Or *to the king* [b] 9 Or *idols*

57:3–13 *A Diatribe Against Worshipers of Idols.* Idolatry opposes joyously submitting to the transcendent God (v. 13b). It attempts to manipulate the forces of nature for one's own ends. For attacks on idolatry, see 40:18–20; 44:6–20; 45:20; 46:1–2; see also 65:3–7; 66:1–3. It is not clear that Isaiah is actually accusing the people of these specific practices. Clearly Judahites were doing these things in Isaiah's own day, and they may have been ignorant enough of the Torah to be unaware of how contrary paganism is to worshiping Yahweh. That was certainly true of Manasseh (cf. 2 Kgs 21:2–7). But to the extent that chs. 56–66 look forward to the postexilic period, when explicitly pagan practices seem not as common, it is at least possible that the prophet is saying that a manipulative, cultic religiosity that laboriously conforms to certain legislated practices is nothing other than paganism of the grossest kind. Isa 65:2–5 and 66:1–3 seem to point in this direction.

57:3 But you. In contrast to the righteous dead. Elsewhere the OT calls worshiping other gods rather than Yahweh adultery and prostitution, because rejecting his covenant love compares to marital infidelity (e.g., Jer 5:7–9; Ezek 16; Hos 2:2–5; 4:10–14). **children of a sorceress.** Israel (cf. 2 Chr 33:6; Hos 5:7; Mal 3:5).

57:4 Who are you mocking? The righteous dead or perhaps the prophet. **rebels.** See note on 1:2.

57:5 among the oaks. See 1:29–30. **spreading tree.** See notes on 1:29; 17:8. **sacrifice your children.** Cf. 2 Kgs 3:27; Ezek 23:37–39.

57:7 bed on a high and lofty hill. Not only did idolatry involve spiritual adultery; it also involved actual sexual activities. Cf. Gen 38:15–22; Jer 3:6.

57:8 pagan symbols. Cf. Ezek 8:9–10. **those whose beds you love.** Cf. Ezek 23:5,11–12,19–21, which describe covenanted alliances with pagan nations in terms of sexual behavior.

57:9 Molek. The Ammonite god (cf. 1 Kgs 11:7). **ambassadors ... dead!** Probably a reference to occult attempts to make some arrangement to defeat death (cf. 28:14–15).

57:11 dreaded. Cf. 8:12–13. **true ... remembered ... taken ... to heart.** Thoughtful faithfulness. If Israel in the future would carefully consider all that Yahweh had done for them, especially through the servant (52:13—53:12), they would not have anything to do with idols. **been silent.** Not rushed to judgment. Cf. 26:9–10; Matt 13:24–30.

and have neither remembered[b] me
nor taken this to heart?
Is it not because I have long been silent[c]
that you do not fear me?
12 I will expose your righteousness and your works,[d]
and they will not benefit you.
13 When you cry out[e] for help,
let your collection of idols save you!
The wind will carry all of them off,
a mere breath will blow them away.
But whoever takes refuge in me
will inherit the land[f]
and possess my holy mountain."[g]

Comfort for the Contrite

14 And it will be said:

"Build up, build up, prepare the road!
Remove the obstacles out of the way of my people."[h]
15 For this is what the high and exalted[i] One says—
he who lives forever,[j] whose name is holy:
"I live in a high and holy place,
but also with the one who is contrite[k] and lowly in spirit,[l]
to revive the spirit of the lowly
and to revive the heart of the contrite.[m]
16 I will not accuse them forever,
nor will I always be angry,[n]
for then they would faint away because of me—
the very people I have created.
17 I was enraged by their sinful greed;[o]
I punished them, and hid my face in anger,
yet they kept on in their willful ways.[p]
18 I have seen their ways, but I will heal[q] them;
I will guide them and restore comfort[r] to Israel's mourners,
19 creating praise on their lips.[s]
Peace, peace,[t] to those far and near,"[u]
says the LORD. "And I will heal them."
20 But the wicked[v] are like the tossing sea,
which cannot rest,
whose waves cast up mire and mud.
21 "There is no peace,"[w] says my God, "for the wicked."[x]

57:11 [b] Jer 2:32; 3:21 [c] Ps 50:21
57:12 [d] Isa 29:15; Mic 3:2-4,8
57:13 [e] Jer 22:20; 30:15 [f] Ps 37:9 [g] Isa 65:9-11
57:14 [h] Isa 62:10; Jer 18:15
57:15 [i] Isa 52:13 [j] Dt 33:27 [k] Ps 147:3 [l] Ps 34:18; 51:17; Isa 66:2 [m] Isa 61:1
57:16 [n] Ps 85:5; 103:9; Mic 7:18
57:17 [o] Isa 56:11 [p] Isa 1:4
57:18 [q] Isa 30:26 [r] Isa 61:1-3
57:19 [s] Isa 6:7; Heb 13:15 [t] Eph 2:17 [u] Ac 2:39
57:20 [v] Job 18:5-21
57:21 [w] Isa 59:8 [x] Isa 48:22

57:12 your righteousness. Actually, their lack of righteousness. God is mocking them.
57:13 This is transitional. The first two sentences conclude vv. 5–12 (the futility of idolatry), and the last sentence points ahead to vv. 14–21 (the "refuge" that Yahweh is for those who trust in him). **my holy mountain.** Jerusalem and the temple (see notes on 2:2; 56:7).
57:14–21 *Comfort for the Contrite.* Those who are "contrite" (v. 15), who confess their inability to live righteous lives and their attempts to exalt themselves through their idolatry, will find Yahweh more than ready to "revive" them (v. 15), "heal" them (v. 19), and encourage ("comfort") them (v. 18). But the "wicked" will not find it so (vv. 20,21).
57:14 road. See notes on 11:16; 35:8–10; 40:3–5.
57:15 A beautiful contrast: the "high and exalted One" (cf. 6:1; 52:13) dwells with the "contrite and lowly in spirit." This is the other side of the theme that ch. 2 first introduces: those who attempt to exalt themselves (in part through worshiping idols) will only humiliate themselves (2:9,11,17–21). On the other hand, Yahweh will graciously lift up those who reverently affirm his incomparable holiness and will give them eternity to share his glory (see note on 55:5).
57:16–19 In this statement of divine grace, Yahweh is angered at the "willful" sin of humans (v. 17), but he chooses not to retain that anger (see note on 54:7–8). In Christ and through the Holy Spirit, he has made a way to "heal" those who mourn over their sin (v. 18) and give to them the wholeness ("peace," v. 19) that he alone can offer. All that will necessarily issue in "praise" (v. 19; cf. 60:18; Exod 15:2; Pss 96:2; 116:13; Heb 13:15).
57:20–21 In typical fashion, Isaiah will not allow hopeful words to deafen his hearers to the real alternatives that exist in life (see note on 32:9–14).
57:21 See 48:22 and note. **no peace.** Those who persist in wickedness cannot know the "peace" that "my [Isaiah's] God" offers (v. 21).

True Fasting

58

"Shout it aloud,[y] do not hold back.
Raise your voice like a trumpet.
Declare to my people their rebellion[z]
and to the descendants of Jacob their sins.
2 For day after day they seek[a] me out;
they seem eager to know my ways,
as if they were a nation that does what is right
and has not forsaken the commands of its God.
They ask me for just decisions
and seem eager for God to come near[b] them.
3 'Why have we fasted,'[c] they say,
'and you have not seen it?
Why have we humbled ourselves,
and you have not noticed?'[d]

"Yet on the day of your fasting, you do as you please[e]
and exploit all your workers.
4 Your fasting ends in quarreling and strife,[f]
and in striking each other with wicked fists.
You cannot fast as you do today
and expect your voice to be heard[g] on high.
5 Is this the kind of fast[h] I have chosen,
only a day for people to humble[i] themselves?
Is it only for bowing one's head like a reed
and for lying in sackcloth and ashes?[j]
Is that what you call a fast,
a day acceptable to the LORD?

6 "Is not this the kind of fasting I have chosen:
to loose the chains of injustice[k]
and untie the cords of the yoke,
to set the oppressed[l] free
and break every yoke?
7 Is it not to share your food with the hungry[m]
and to provide the poor wanderer with shelter[n]—
when you see the naked, to clothe[o] them,
and not to turn away from your own flesh and blood?[p]
8 Then your light will break forth like the dawn,[q]
and your healing[r] will quickly appear;

58:1 [y]Isa 40:6 [z]Isa 48:8
58:2 [a]Isa 48:1; Titus 1:16; Jas 4:8 [b]Isa 29:13
58:3 [c]Lev 16:29 [d]Mal 3:14 [e]Isa 22:13; Zec 7:5-6
58:4 [f]1Ki 21:9-13; Isa 59:6 [g]Isa 59:2
58:5 [h]Zec 7:5 [i]1Ki 21:27 [j]Job 2:8
58:6 [k]Ne 5:10-11 [l]Jer 34:9
58:7 [m]Eze 18:16; Lk 3:11 [n]Isa 16:4; Heb 13:2 [o]Job 31:19-20; Mt 25:36 [p]Ge 29:14; Lk 10:31-32
58:8 [q]Job 11:17 [r]Isa 30:26

58:1—59:15a *Declare Their Rebellion.* After briefly revealing that God can enable people to be righteous, the prophet returns to describing how the people dismally failed to be so. This has four parts: an introduction (58:1–2), an example of their false religiosity in insincere fasting (58:3–12), an example of true religion in contrast (58:13–14), and a condemnation for and confession of their utter failure (59:1–15a).
58:1–2 *The Sin of Hypocrisy.* "The descendants of Jacob" act as though they really want to know God and his "ways." But what they want is to have *their* way and God's blessing at the same time. They do not seem able to understand that "for God to come near them" while they are in that state would mean disaster (cf. Mal 3:2–3).
58:3–12 *False Versus True Fasting.* Their fasting has been simply self-affliction in order to get favors from God. It has made them harsh and quarrelsome (vv. 3–5). True fasting involves forgetting oneself in caring for others (vv. 6–7,9–10). That would be a God-produced "righteousness" (v. 8) that would be the "light" (vv. 8,10; cf. 60:1–3) that Yahweh promised would shine out of them. Then Israel would be truly restored (vv. 11–12).
58:3 Their relationship with God is solely selfish and has not changed the way they relate to others, especially those under them ("your workers").
58:5 humble themselves. They were not humbling themselves but seeking to exalt themselves for their rigorous religiosity (cf. Matt 6:16).
58:6–7 If they are going to stop doing something, God instructs them to stop being unjust and greedy in their relations with others, particularly with those weaker than themselves (cf. Matt 25:34–46).
58:8 rear guard. Language of the exodus and the return from exile (cf. 52:12; Exod 14:19–20). "Righteousness" lived out in relation to others, especially to those who cannot repay, is the true fruit of God's gracious deliverance in such events as the exodus and the return from exile.

then your righteousness[a] will go before you,
and the glory of the LORD will be your rear guard.[s]
9 Then you will call,[t] and the LORD will answer;
you will cry for help, and he will say: Here am I.

"If you do away with the yoke of oppression,
with the pointing finger[u] and malicious talk,[v]
10 and if you spend yourselves in behalf of the hungry
and satisfy the needs of the oppressed,[w]
then your light[x] will rise in the darkness,
and your night will become like the noonday.[y]
11 The LORD will guide you always;
he will satisfy your needs[z] in a sun-scorched land
and will strengthen your frame.
You will be like a well-watered garden,[a]
like a spring[b] whose waters never fail.
12 Your people will rebuild the ancient ruins[c]
and will raise up the age-old foundations;[d]
you will be called Repairer of Broken Walls,
Restorer of Streets with Dwellings.

13 "If you keep your feet from breaking the Sabbath[e]
and from doing as you please on my holy day,
if you call the Sabbath a delight[f]
and the LORD's holy day honorable,
and if you honor it by not going your own way
and not doing as you please or speaking idle words,
14 then you will find your joy[g] in the LORD,
and I will cause you to ride in triumph on the heights[h] of the land
and to feast on the inheritance of your father Jacob."
For the mouth of the LORD has spoken.[i]

Sin, Confession and Redemption

59 Surely the arm of the LORD is not too short[j] to save,
nor his ear too dull to hear.[k]
2 But your iniquities have separated
you from your God;
your sins have hidden his face from you,
so that he will not hear.[l]
3 For your hands are stained with blood,[m]
your fingers with guilt.

[a] 8 Or *your righteous One*

58:8 [s] Ex 14:19
58:9 [t] Ps 50:15 [u] Pr 6:13 [v] Ps 12:2; Isa 59:13
58:10 [w] Dt 15:7-8 [x] Isa 42:16 [y] Job 11:17
58:11 [z] Ps 107:9 [a] SS 4:15 [b] Jn 4:14
58:12 [c] Isa 49:8 [d] Isa 44:28
58:13 [e] Isa 56:2 [f] Ps 84:2,10
58:14 [g] Job 22:26 [h] Dt 32:13 [i] Isa 1:20
59:1 [j] Nu 11:23; Isa 50:2 [k] Isa 58:9; 65:24
59:2 [l] Isa 1:15; 58:4
59:3 [m] Isa 1:15

58:9–12 Unlike those whom vv. 1–2 describe, these persons who are manifesting godly character in how they treat others will have instant access to Yahweh, and his "light" (v. 10) will be visible to everyone. Furthermore, under his provision they will be "like a well-watered garden" (v. 11; contrast 1:29–31). They will be the true rebuilders of the nation (v. 12).
58:13–14 *Sabbath-Keeping.* Though it can become ritualistic, as it did for many in NT times (cf. Col 2:16), sincerely and gladly separating one day in the week for worshiping God and resting from one's work can both express spiritual sincerity and be a source of renewed spiritual life (v. 14). It concretely expresses "not going your own way." It also was a particular sign of faithfulness to the covenant (see 56:6 and note).
58:14 ride in triumph on the heights of the land. Cf. Hab 3:19.

59:1–15a *Failure to Do Righteousness.* The prophet condemns the people for failing to live righteous lives (vv. 1–8) and then speaks with them as together they admit the truth of the condemnation (vv. 9–15a). This confession is comparable to Isaiah's own in 6:5.
59:1–2 Similar to 58:1–2; 64:12—65:1. It is not God's fault that the people are not experiencing the reality of a saving relationship; they are not sincere. They prefer to live in their sin while having the appearance of a relationship with God.
59:1 arm of the LORD. His divine power as especially manifested in his servant (cf. 51:5).
59:3 stained with blood. Metaphorically true and perhaps actually so (see vv. 6–7; cf. 1:15).

59:4 [n] Job 15:35; Ps 7:14
59:5 [o] Job 8:14
59:6 [p] Isa 28:20 [q] Isa 58:4
59:7 [r] Pr 6:17 [s] Mk 7:21-22 [t] Ro 3:15-17*
59:8 [u] Isa 57:21; Lk 1:79
59:9 [v] Isa 5:30; 8:20
59:10 [w] Dt 28:29 [x] Isa 8:15 [y] La 3:6
59:11 [z] Isa 38:14; Eze 7:16
59:12 [a] Ezr 9:6 [b] Isa 3:9
59:13 [c] Pr 30:9; Mt 10:33; Titus 1:16 [d] Isa 5:7 [e] Mk 7:21-22
59:14 [f] Isa 1:21

Your lips have spoken falsely,
and your tongue mutters wicked things.
4 No one calls for justice;
no one pleads a case with integrity.
They rely on empty arguments, they utter lies;
they conceive trouble and give birth to evil.[n]
5 They hatch the eggs of vipers
and spin a spider's web.[o]
Whoever eats their eggs will die,
and when one is broken, an adder is hatched.
6 Their cobwebs are useless for clothing;
they cannot cover themselves with what they make.[p]
Their deeds are evil deeds,
and acts of violence[q] are in their hands.
7 Their feet rush into sin;
they are swift to shed innocent blood.[r]
They pursue evil schemes;[s]
acts of violence mark their ways.[t]
8 The way of peace they do not know;
there is no justice in their paths.
They have turned them into crooked roads;
no one who walks along them will know peace.[u]

9 So justice is far from us,
and righteousness does not reach us.
We look for light, but all is darkness;[v]
for brightness, but we walk in deep shadows.
10 Like the blind[w] we grope along the wall,
feeling our way like people without eyes.
At midday we stumble[x] as if it were twilight;
among the strong, we are like the dead.[y]
11 We all growl like bears;
we moan mournfully like doves.[z]
We look for justice, but find none;
for deliverance, but it is far away.

12 For our offenses[a] are many in your sight,
and our sins testify[b] against us.
Our offenses are ever with us,
and we acknowledge our iniquities:
13 rebellion and treachery against the LORD,
turning our backs[c] on our God,
inciting revolt and oppression,[d]
uttering lies[e] our hearts have conceived.
14 So justice is driven back,
and righteousness[f] stands at a distance;

59:5–6 Graphically illustrates futile and deadly behavior.
59:7–8 Paul quotes v. 7 and the first phrase of v. 8 in Rom 3:15–17 as part of his collection of OT passages showing how thoroughly sin has corrupted humanity.
59:8 peace. See notes on 9:6; 57:16–19. **paths ... roads.** See notes on 11:16; 35:8–10; 40:3–5.
59:9 Although Yahweh commanded the people to keep "justice" and do "righteousness" to express the salvation that is theirs through the work of the servant (56:1), they confess that such behavior is "far from" them (see v. 14)—so is the "light" that was supposed to shine out of them to the world (cf. 42:16; 60:3). They are in the "darkness," like those in 8:20–22.
59:12 offenses ... sins ... iniquities. Translate the three most significant Hebrew terms for sin in the OT (see Ps 32:5 and note). Incorporating all three makes this confession comprehensive.
59:13 The sinful behavior is intentional.

truth[g] has stumbled in the streets,
honesty cannot enter.
15 Truth is nowhere to be found,
and whoever shuns evil becomes a prey.

The LORD looked and was displeased
that there was no justice.
16 He saw that there was no one,[h]
he was appalled that there was no one to intervene;
so his own arm achieved salvation[i] for him,
and his own righteousness sustained him.
17 He put on righteousness as his breastplate,[j]
and the helmet[k] of salvation on his head;
he put on the garments[l] of vengeance
and wrapped himself in zeal[m] as in a cloak.
18 According to what they have done,
so will he repay
wrath to his enemies
and retribution to his foes;
he will repay the islands their due.
19 From the west,[n] people will fear the name
of the LORD,
and from the rising of the sun,[o] they
will revere his glory.
For he will come like a pent-up flood
that the breath of the LORD drives along.[a]

20 "The Redeemer will come to Zion,
to those in Jacob who repent of their
sins,"[p]
declares the LORD.

21 "As for me, this is my covenant with them," says the
LORD. "My Spirit,[q] who is on you, will not depart from you,
and my words that I have put in your mouth will always
be on your lips, on the lips of your children and on the lips
of their descendants—from this time on and forever," says
the LORD.

[a] *19* Or *When enemies come in like a flood, / the Spirit of the LORD will put them to flight*

59:14 [g] Isa 48:1
59:16 [h] Isa 41:28 [i] Ps 98:1; Isa 63:5
59:17 [j] Eph 6:14 [k] Eph 6:17; 1Th 5:8 [l] Isa 63:3 [m] Isa 9:7
59:19 [n] Isa 49:12 [o] Ps 113:3
59:20 [p] Ac 2:38-39; Ro 11:26-27*
59:21 [q] Isa 11:2; 44:3

Assyrian soldier with scaled breastplate and helmet. "He put on righteousness as his breastplate, and the helmet of salvation on his head" (Isa 59:17).

59:15b–21 *The Divine Warrior, Solution to the Problem.* This passage stands between dramatically contrasting sections (56:9—59:15a; 60:1—62:12) and explains the difference. When the mighty Warrior does his full work in the life of the believer, then the people of God, helpless in themselves, will indeed be the lamps through which the light of God will shine in the world.

59:15 This verse is transitional (cf. 57:13): the first sentence concludes the former thought, and the second sentence introduces the following one.

59:16 no one to intervene. Cf. Gen 18:27–33; Ezek 22:30. **arm.** This person is the servant of 49:1—55:13 in whom God's power of salvation is displayed. See notes on 40:10–11; 51:9.

59:17 breastplate ... helmet ... garments. These accoutrements of battle depict the "arm" of the Lord (v. 16) in starkly different terms than those of 52:13—53:12. Perhaps the difference is that there he deals with the guilt of sin; here, the power of sin. Salvation must address both. See Eph 6:10–17, where Paul pictures the Christian believer putting on this kind of armor to "stand against the devil's schemes" (Eph 6:11).

59:18 enemies. In the context of the preceding chapters, the sins of the restored people are what need to be defeated.

59:19 As a result of the Warrior's work on behalf of his people, the whole world from west to east ("rising") will come to worship Yahweh ("fear the name ... revere his glory," cf. 60:2–3; 66:18–24). The Warrior will accomplish his work through the power of the Lord's Spirit ("breath"; see NIV text note; cf. v. 21; 11:2; 61:1).

59:20 repent of their sins. Means not only confessing sin but intentionally turning from it (cf. Rev 2:5; 3:3).

59:21 you. Perhaps (1) the prophet and his metaphoric "children" (see 8:18; cf. "offspring" in 53:10) or (2) the Messiah. In view of 42:5–9 and 49:8–12 and the reference to the "Spirit" (as in "breath of the LORD" in v. 19), the second view seems more likely than the first.

60:1 [r]Isa 52:2 [s]Eph 5:14
60:2 [t]Jer 13:16; Col 1:13
60:3 [u]Isa 45:14; Rev 21:24 [v]Isa 49:23
60:4 [w]Isa 11:12 [x]Isa 43:6 [y]Isa 49:20-22
60:6 [z]Ge 25:2 [a]Ge 25:4 [b]Ps 72:10 [c]Isa 43:23; Mt 2:11 [d]Isa 42:10
60:7 [e]Ge 25:13 [f]ver 13; Hag 2:3,7,9
60:8 [g]Isa 49:21
60:9 [h]Isa 11:11 [i]Isa 2:16 *fn* [j]Isa 14:2; 43:6 [k]Isa 55:5

The Glory of Zion

60 "Arise,[r] shine, for your light[s] has come,
and the glory of the LORD rises upon you.
2 See, darkness covers the earth
and thick darkness[t] is over the peoples,
but the LORD rises upon you
and his glory appears over you.
3 Nations[u] will come to your light,
and kings[v] to the brightness of your dawn.

4 "Lift up your eyes and look about you:
All assemble[w] and come to you;
your sons come from afar,
and your daughters[x] are carried on the hip.[y]
5 Then you will look and be radiant,
your heart will throb and swell with joy;
the wealth on the seas will be brought to you,
to you the riches of the nations will come.
6 Herds of camels will cover your land,
young camels of Midian[z] and Ephah.[a]
And all from Sheba[b] will come,
bearing gold and incense[c]
and proclaiming the praise[d] of the LORD.
7 All Kedar's[e] flocks will be gathered to you,
the rams of Nebaioth will serve you;
they will be accepted as offerings on my altar,
and I will adorn my glorious temple.[f]

8 "Who are these[g] that fly along like clouds,
like doves to their nests?
9 Surely the islands[h] look to me;
in the lead are the ships of Tarshish,[a][i]
bringing[j] your children from afar,
with their silver and gold,
to the honor of the LORD your God,
the Holy One of Israel,
for he has endowed you with splendor.[k]

[a] 9 Or *the trading ships*

lips. Significant in light of 6:5. **from this time on.** The time of the coming of the Messiah.

60:1—62:12 *Light to the Nations.* Because of the Warrior's work, the light of God shines through redeemed Israel, and all the nations see it. Some come to worship with Israel (56:1–8; 66:18–24). Those who do not come to worship will come to serve the redeemed or to perish (60:12). The Spirit-anointed Messiah accomplishes all this. There are three sections: 60:1–22; 61:1–3; 61:4—62:12.

60:1–22 *The Lord's Light Shines on the Nations.* In dramatic contrast to the descriptions of the darkness of sin in Israel in 56:9—59:15a, here Israel is a bearer of Yahweh's "light" (vv. 1,3,19,20). That light will draw the nations to his "sanctuary" (v. 13). They will bring back Israel's children (vv. 4,9), bring wealth to adorn the temple (vv. 5–9), and help to rebuild the city (vv. 10–14). As a result it will be apparent that Zion is the place of God's favor (vv. 15–22).

60:1–3 Yahweh gives "light" (v. 1) in place of "darkness" (v. 2; cf. 8:21—9:1). Israel is not the source of the light; that light is "the glory of the LORD" displayed in them (see note on v. 1).

60:1 glory. Forms of the Hebrew word translated "glory" appear eight times in vv. 1–22. God intends to share his glory with his people (see notes on 6:3; 49:3; 55:5).

60:4 The nations will restore Zion's children (see v. 9). If Isaiah wrote chs. 56–66 with those returned from exile in mind, this would refer to those who did not respond to the first invitation but would come later (Ezra 7:7). But it is likely that the address is more general, referring to the continuation of the nation in spite of the attempts by enemies to destroy them (see note on 29:23).

60:5–7 The nations will come to praise the Lord and use their wealth both to adorn his temple and provide offerings for it.

60:6–7 These are lands in the desert to the south and east of Judah: Midian (Exod 2:15), Ephah (Gen 25:4), Sheba (2 Chr 9:1), Kedar (21:16), and Nebaioth (Gen 25:13).

60:9 look to. The Hebrew means "wait for" (cf. 40:31 ["hope in"]; 51:5; see note on 8:17). The world will trust Yahweh.

10 "Foreigners[l] will rebuild your walls,
and their kings[m] will serve you.
Though in anger I struck you,
in favor I will show you compassion.[n]
11 Your gates[o] will always stand open,
they will never be shut, day or night,
so that people may bring you the wealth of the nations[p] —
their kings[q] led in triumphal procession.
12 For the nation or kingdom that will not serve[r] you will perish;
it will be utterly ruined.

13 "The glory of Lebanon[s] will come to you,
the juniper, the fir and the cypress together,[t]
to adorn my sanctuary;
and I will glorify the place for my feet.[u]
14 The children of your oppressors[v] will come bowing before you;
all who despise you will bow down[w] at your feet
and will call you the City of the LORD,
Zion[x] of the Holy One of Israel.

15 "Although you have been forsaken[y] and hated,
with no one traveling[z] through,
I will make you the everlasting pride[a]
and the joy[b] of all generations.
16 You will drink the milk of nations
and be nursed[c] at royal breasts.
Then you will know that I, the LORD, am your Savior,
your Redeemer,[d] the Mighty One of Jacob.
17 Instead of bronze I will bring you gold,
and silver in place of iron.
Instead of wood I will bring you bronze,
and iron in place of stones.
I will make peace your governor
and well-being your ruler.
18 No longer will violence be heard in your land,
nor ruin or destruction within your borders,
but you will call your walls Salvation[e]
and your gates Praise.
19 The sun will no more be your light by day,
nor will the brightness of the moon shine on you,
for the LORD will be your everlasting light,[f]
and your God will be your glory.[g]
20 Your sun[h] will never set again,
and your moon will wane no more;
the LORD will be your everlasting light,
and your days of sorrow[i] will end.

60:10 [l] Isa 14:1-2 [m] Isa 49:23; Rev 21:24 [n] Isa 54:8
60:11 [o] ver 18; Isa 62:10; Rev 21:25 [p] ver 5; Rev 21:26 [q] Ps 149:8
60:12 [r] Isa 14:2
60:13 [s] Isa 35:2 [t] Isa 41:19 [u] 1Ch 28:2; Ps 132:7
60:14 [v] Isa 14:2 [w] Isa 49:23; Rev 3:9 [x] Heb 12:22
60:15 [y] Isa 1:7-9; 6:12 [z] Isa 33:8 [a] Isa 4:2 [b] Isa 65:18
60:16 [c] Isa 49:23; 66:11, 12 [d] Isa 59:20
60:18 [e] Isa 26:1
60:19 [f] Rev 22:5 [g] Zec 2:5; Rev 21:23
60:20 [h] Isa 30:26 [i] Isa 35:10

60:10 anger … compassion. See note on 57:16–19.
60:11–12 Nations that will not join in worship will be brought in chains, either to "serve" or to "perish," just as they once led the Israelites.
60:13 juniper … fir … cypress. Expensive wood, desirable for decoration.
60:15–22 This series of contrasts between what was and what will be demonstrates that Zion is the place of Yahweh's favor: no longer "forsaken" but the "joy of all generations" (v. 15); not "hated" but nursing at "royal breasts" (vv. 15–16); built not of "bronze" but of "gold" (v. 17); not a victim of "violence" but a place of "Salvation" and "Praise" (v. 18; see 54:11–15); no longer the "light" of the sun but the "everlasting light" of Yahweh (vv. 19–20). While the language is a metaphor of the life of the believer, it also speaks of the conditions of the new Jerusalem (Rev 21:23–27).

60:21 [j]Rev 21:27 [k]Ps 37:11,22; Isa 57:13; 61:7 [l]Mt 15:13 [m]Isa 19:25; 29:23; Eph 2:10 [n]Isa 52:1
61:1 [o]Isa 11:2 [p]Ps 45:7 [q]Mt 11:5; Lk 7:22 [r]Isa 57:15 [s]Isa 42:7; 49:9
61:2 [t]Isa 49:8; Lk 4:18-19* [u]Isa 34:8 [v]Isa 57:18; Mt 5:4
61:3 [w]Isa 60:20-21
61:4 [x]Isa 49:8; Eze 36:33; Am 9:14

21 Then all your people will be righteous[j]
and they will possess[k] the land forever.
They are the shoot I have planted,[l]
the work of my hands,[m]
for the display of my splendor.[n]
22 The least of you will become a thousand,
the smallest a mighty nation.
I am the LORD;
in its time I will do this swiftly."

The Year of the LORD's Favor

61 The Spirit[o] of the Sovereign LORD is on me,
because the LORD has anointed[p] me
to proclaim good news to the poor.[q]
He has sent me to bind up[r] the brokenhearted,
to proclaim freedom for the captives[s]
and release from darkness for the prisoners,[a]
2 to proclaim the year of the LORD's favor[t]
and the day of vengeance[u] of our God,
to comfort[v] all who mourn,
3 and provide for those who grieve in Zion—
to bestow on them a crown of beauty
instead of ashes,
the oil of joy
instead of mourning,
and a garment of praise
instead of a spirit of despair.
They will be called oaks of righteousness,
a planting of the LORD
for the display of his splendor.[w]
4 They will rebuild the ancient ruins[x]
and restore the places long devastated;

[a] *1* Hebrew; Septuagint *the blind*

60:21–22 This conclusion describes the character and nature of the nation that is a light to the nations. They are now "righteous" (contrast the previous chapters)—because of Yahweh's work, not theirs. They are a "shoot" that Yahweh himself has "planted." The connection with 11:1 is not coincidental. It is the "shoot" from the "stump of Jesse" (11:1) that enables God's people to also be such a "shoot." As such, they will display his "splendor" (i.e., "glory"; see note on 6:3) before the world. All this is true for one reason: the God of Israel is I AM ("I am the LORD," v. 22; see note on 1:2). No one else could do this.

61:1–3 *The Messiah Announces Good News of Deliverance.* This leaves the reader in no doubt about how it is that Yahweh sets his people free from both the guilt and the power of sin: the Spirit-anointed Servant-Messiah. Jesus Christ uses vv. 1–2 to announce his ministry (Luke 4:16–21)—just as the text intends. He is the servant who has taken upon himself the condemnation of our sins (52:13—53:12), and he is the Warrior (59:15b–21; 63:1–6) who has broken the power of sin. As such he is the King who comes to establish the kingdom of peace (9:1–7; 11:1–16). This passage is the climactic center of chs. 56–66. From this point to the end of the book, Isaiah recapitulates the points in 56:1—60:22 in reverse order, beginning with Israel among the nations in 61:4—62:12. This structure highlights the central importance of 61:1–3 and reinforces the two end points (56:1–8; 66:18–24): the Messiah made Israel Yahweh's chosen servant so that the nations might be brought to him.

61:1 anointed. This term refers to the action of pouring sacred oil on the head of someone particularly set apart for service (cf. Exod 29:29; 1 Sam 10:1; see 45:1 and note). **proclaim good news.** Cf. 52:7. **freedom.** Cf. 42:7; 49:9.

61:2 vengeance. See note on 34:8. **mourn.** Cf. 57:18; 66:10.

61:3 oaks of righteousness. Contrast "sacred oaks" in 1:29 (see note there). On trees, see notes on 1:29–31; 10:28–34. **display of his splendor.** See 60:21.

61:4—62:12 *The Lord's Righteousness Is Displayed to the Nations.* This begins to recapitulate earlier points in reverse order (see note on 61:1–3). There is some variation, but the main points are the same. So this unit matches 60:1–22 by emphasizing Israel's witness to the nations. "Righteousness" (not "light") is the repeated word (as prepared for by 61:3: "oaks of righteousness"; 61:10,11; 62; 1,2 ["vindication"]). This is not Israel's righteousness that they produced but Yahweh's righteousness displayed in them.

61:4–11 *The People Whom the Lord Has Blessed.* Yahweh will keep his ancient promises and demonstrate his nature to the world through Israel (vv. 4–9), and Israel's testimony confirms that (vv. 10–11).

61:4 As in 58:12, this renewal has both literal and metaphoric signifi-

they will renew the ruined cities
that have been devastated for generations.
5 Strangers[y] will shepherd your flocks;
foreigners will work your fields and vineyards.
6 And you will be called priests[z] of the LORD,
you will be named ministers of our God.
You will feed on the wealth[a] of nations,
and in their riches you will boast.

7 Instead of your shame
you will receive a double[b] portion,
and instead of disgrace
you will rejoice in your inheritance.
And so you will inherit a double portion in your land,
and everlasting joy will be yours.

8 "For I, the LORD, love justice;[c]
I hate robbery and wrongdoing.
In my faithfulness I will reward my people
and make an everlasting covenant[d] with them.
9 Their descendants will be known among the nations
and their offspring among the peoples.
All who see them will acknowledge
that they are a people the LORD has blessed."

10 I delight greatly in the LORD;
my soul rejoices[e] in my God.
For he has clothed me with garments of salvation
and arrayed me in a robe of his righteousness,[f]
as a bridegroom adorns his head like a priest,
and as a bride[g] adorns herself with her jewels.
11 For as the soil makes the sprout come up
and a garden causes seeds to grow,
so the Sovereign LORD will make righteousness[h]
and praise spring up before all nations.

Zion's New Name

62 For Zion's sake I will not keep silent,
for Jerusalem's sake I will not remain quiet,
till her vindication[i] shines out like the dawn,
her salvation like a blazing torch.

61:5 [y] Isa 14:1-2
61:6 [z] Ex 19:6; 1Pe 2:5 [a] Isa 60:11
61:7 [b] Isa 40:2; Zec 9:12
61:8 [c] Ps 11:7; Isa 5:16 [d] Isa 55:3
61:10 [e] Isa 25:9; Hab 3:18 [f] Ps 132:9; Isa 52:1 [g] Isa 49:18; Rev 21:2
61:11 [h] Ps 85:11
62:1 [i] Isa 1:26

cance. In the literal sense it refers to the rebuilding of Jerusalem in the postexilic period as well as to the building of the new Jerusalem at the end of the age. In a metaphoric sense it speaks of the spiritual renewal of people who are enabled to live in godly ways.

61:5–6 "Strangers" (i.e., foreigners) will carry on the menial work so that Israel will be free to fulfill the promise of Exod 19:6: they will be "a kingdom of priests and a holy nation" (cf. 1 Pet 2:9). But that priesthood is not merely to God; it is also for the world.

61:7–9 Instead of the nations mocking Israel because Yahweh apparently failed them (v. 7), the nations will recognize that Yahweh has uniquely "blessed" Israel (v. 9), as demonstrated through their multitude of "descendants" (v. 9).

61:7 shame. See note on 25:8. **double portion.** The right of a firstborn son. Israel is God's "firstborn" (Exod 4:22). **everlasting joy.** See 35:10.

61:8 robbery and wrongdoing. Probably have a double significance: (1) the unjust things the nations did to Israel when Yahweh had assigned them to only discipline his people (cf. 47:6); and (2) the crimes the people themselves were committing against one another (cf. 59:1–15; Neh 5:1–5). God will demonstrate his "faithfulness" and his "covenant" by enabling them to live according to his patterns for a rewarding life ("justice"; see notes on 33:22; 42:1).

61:10–11 Yahweh will clothe Israel with his "righteousness" before the nations, and it will be a cause for praise to him. This righteousness is not something Israel produces; it is something with which Yahweh clothes his "bride" (v. 10; cf. Eph 5:27; Rev 21:2,9). Thus, it defines a new status (v. 10) and at the same time defines a new pattern of behavior (v. 11), enabled by his grace (see note on 58:9–12). This two-pronged understanding also appears in 62:1–2.

62:1–12 *Zion's New Name.* These verses expand on the thoughts of 60:15; 61:7. They describe the new condition of Israel that the

62:2 [j]Isa 52:10; 60:3 [k]ver 4,12
62:3 [l]Isa 28:5; Zec 9:16; 1Th 2:19
62:4 [m]Isa 54:6 [n]Jer 32:41; Zep 3:17 [o]Jer 3:14; Hos 2:19
62:5 [p]Isa 65:19
62:6 [q]Isa 52:8; Eze 3:17
62:7 [r]Mt 15:21-28; Lk 18:1-8
62:8 [s]Dt 28:30-33; Isa 1:7; Jer 5:17
62:10 [t]Isa 60:11 [u]Isa 11:16; 57:14 [v]Isa 11:10

2 The nations[j] will see your vindication,
and all kings your glory;
you will be called by a new name[k]
that the mouth of the LORD will bestow.
3 You will be a crown[l] of splendor in the LORD's hand,
a royal diadem in the hand of your God.
4 No longer will they call you Deserted,[m]
or name your land Desolate.
But you will be called Hephzibah,[a]
and your land Beulah[b];
for the LORD will take delight[n] in you,
and your land will be married.[o]
5 As a young man marries a young woman,
so will your Builder marry you;
as a bridegroom rejoices over his bride,
so will your God rejoice[p] over you.

6 I have posted watchmen[q] on your walls, Jerusalem;
they will never be silent day or night.
You who call on the LORD,
give yourselves no rest,
7 and give him no rest[r] till he establishes Jerusalem
and makes her the praise of the earth.

8 The LORD has sworn by his right hand
and by his mighty arm:
"Never again will I give your grain[s]
as food for your enemies,
and never again will foreigners drink the new wine
for which you have toiled;
9 but those who harvest it will eat it
and praise the LORD,
and those who gather the grapes will drink it
in the courts of my sanctuary."

10 Pass through, pass through the gates![t]
Prepare the way for the people.
Build up, build up the highway![u]
Remove the stones.
Raise a banner[v] for the nations.

11 The LORD has made proclamation
to the ends of the earth:

[a] 4 *Hephzibah* means *my delight is in her.* [b] 4 *Beulah* means *married.*

world sees. She will no longer be seen as "Deserted" and "Desolate" (v. 4), but will be a source of special delight to the Lord ("Hephzibah," v. 4; see NIV text note there). A sign of his favor is that foreigners will not steal what Israelites have planted (vv. 8–9; cf. 1:7; see also Jer 5:17). Their "salvation" (v. 1) will be a sign ("banner," v. 10) to all the world.

62:1,2 vindication. The Hebrew word is often rendered "righteousness." Yahweh's saving his people displays his righteousness (cf. 56:1; see notes on 45:8; 46:12–13). "Vindication" focuses on the new status conferred by God's salvation of his people. But this "vindication" may also include a new Spirit-endowed pattern of behavior. "The nations will see ... your glory" (v. 2) expresses both of these ideas (see notes on 55:5; 60:1–3).

62:3–5 Yahweh rejoices over his bride. See 52:1; 54:6–7. On Jerusalem as Yahweh's bride, see Rev 21:2,9.

62:6 watchmen. Cf. 52:7–10. They look expectantly for the realization of Yahweh's promises.

62:10–12 This proclaims salvation for Israel and the nations. Israel's restoration to the Lord ("highway," v. 10; see 11:16; 35:8; 49:11) is a signal to the nations of their salvation ("banner," v. 10; see 11:10,12; 49:22).

62:11 Daughter Zion. See 1:8 and note; 10:32: 16:1; 37:22; 52:2. **reward ... recompense.** See 40:10.

"Say to Daughter Zion,[w]
'See, your Savior comes![x]
See, his reward is with him,
and his recompense accompanies him.'"[y]
12 They will be called[z] the Holy People,[a]
the Redeemed[b] of the LORD;
and you will be called Sought After,
the City No Longer Deserted.[c]

62:11 [w]Zec 9:9; Mt 21:5 [x]Rev 22:12 [y]Isa 40:10
62:12 [z]ver 4 [a]1Pe 2:9 [b]Isa 35:9 [c]Isa 42:16
63:1 [d]Am 1:12 [e]Zep 3:17
63:3 [f]Rev 14:20; 19:15 [g]Isa 22:5 [h]Rev 19:13
63:5 [i]Isa 41:28 [j]Ps 44:3; 98:1 [k]Isa 59:16
63:6 [l]Isa 29:9 [m]Isa 34:3
63:7 [n]Isa 54:8

God's Day of Vengeance and Redemption

63 Who is this coming from Edom,
from Bozrah,[d] with his garments stained crimson?
Who is this, robed in splendor,
striding forward in the greatness of his strength?

"It is I, proclaiming victory,
mighty to save."[e]

2 Why are your garments red,
like those of one treading the winepress?

3 "I have trodden the winepress[f] alone;
from the nations no one was with me.
I trampled them in my anger
and trod them down in my wrath;[g]
their blood spattered my garments,[h]
and I stained all my clothing.
4 It was for me the day of vengeance;
the year for me to redeem had come.
5 I looked, but there was no one[i] to help,
I was appalled that no one gave support;
so my own arm[j] achieved salvation for me,
and my own wrath sustained me.[k]
6 I trampled the nations in my anger;
in my wrath I made them drunk[l]
and poured their blood[m] on the ground."

Praise and Prayer

7 I will tell of the kindnesses[n] of the LORD,
the deeds for which he is to be praised,
according to all the LORD has done for us—

62:12 Holy People. Reflects both a status (they belong to God) and condition (they share his character). The Jerusalem of the future will be very different from the city of Isaiah's day (cf. 1:2–15,21–23).

63:1—66:17 *Israel's Inability to Do Righteousness.* This is a mirror image of 56:9—59:21, and it begins in the same way the other ends: by revealing the Warrior, whose work solves the problem (63:1–6). This second treatment of the theme more sharply contrasts God's ability to save with Israel's inability to be righteous, especially in how it pictures the new heaven and earth (65:17–25), but the main point is to reveal that human strength cannot produce the transformed lives that will attract the nations to God. It has four parts: 63:1–6; 63:7—65:16; 65:17–25; 66:1–17.

63:1–6 *The Divine Warrior.* He defeats his people's enemies in an act of vengeance and redemption (v. 4; cf. 61:2). As in 34:5–15, "Edom" (v. 1) symbolizes human pride that defies Yahweh. But the Warrior has defeated it, trampling it down like grapes in a "winepress" (v. 3). As a result, his "garments" are "stained" with the "blood" of his enemies (v. 3). But the Bible shows us that it is the Warrior's own blood, for he became one with his enemies (cf. 2 Cor 5:21; Eph 2:13; Heb 9:12,14; 13:12; 1 Pet 1:2; 1 John 1:7; Rev 1:5). But in the final judgment, it is the blood of those who have refused the Savior's grace that will stain his garments (cf. Rev 19:13).

63:5 This verse almost exactly duplicates 59:16 except that it is in first person instead of third person. It confirms that the two passages are intended to be read in light of each other.

63:7—65:16 *A History of Redemption and Rebellion.* Israel's unrighteous attitudes and behavior go far back into its history and have persisted in spite of God's acts of deliverance. After an opening résumé of redemption and rebellion (63:7–14), the prophet cries to Yahweh on behalf of the people to change this situation (63:15—64:12), and Yahweh responds (65:1–16).

63:7–14 *A Résumé of Redemption and Rebellion.* Yahweh showed "kindnesses" (v. 7; see notes on 54:7,8) to Israel as he became their Savior (vv. 7–9). He "lifted them up and carried them" (v. 9; cf. 46:3–4)

63:7 [o]Ps 51:1; Eph 2:4
63:8 [p]Isa 51:4
63:9 [q]Ex 33:14 [r]Dt 7:7-8 [s]Dt 1:31
63:10 [t]Ps 78:40 [u]Ps 51:11; Ac 7:51; Eph 4:30 [v]Ps 106:40
63:11 [w]Ex 14:22,30 [x]Nu 11:17
63:12 [y]Ex 14:21-22; Isa 11:15
63:13 [z]Dt 32:12 [a]Jer 31:9
63:15 [b]Dt 26:15; Ps 80:14 [c]Ps 123:1 [d]Isa 9:7; 26:11 [e]Jer 31:20; Hos 11:8
63:16 [f]Job 14:21

yes, the many good things
he has done for Israel,
according to his compassion[o] and many kindnesses.
8 He said, "Surely they are my people,[p]
children who will be true to me";
and so he became their Savior.
9 In all their distress he too was distressed,
and the angel of his presence[q] saved them.[a]
In his love and mercy he redeemed[r] them;
he lifted them up and carried[s] them
all the days of old.
10 Yet they rebelled[t]
and grieved his Holy Spirit.[u]
So he turned and became their enemy[v]
and he himself fought against them.

11 Then his people recalled[b] the days of old,
the days of Moses and his people —
where is he who brought them through the sea,[w]
with the shepherd of his flock?
Where is he who set
his Holy Spirit[x] among them,
12 who sent his glorious arm of power
to be at Moses' right hand,
who divided the waters[y] before them,
to gain for himself everlasting renown,
13 who led[z] them through the depths?
Like a horse in open country,
they did not stumble;[a]
14 like cattle that go down to the plain,
they were given rest by the Spirit of the LORD.
This is how you guided your people
to make for yourself a glorious name.

15 Look down from heaven[b] and see,
from your lofty throne,[c] holy and glorious.
Where are your zeal[d] and your might?
Your tenderness and compassion[e] are withheld from us.
16 But you are our Father,
though Abraham does not know us
or Israel acknowledge[f] us;

[a] 9 Or *Savior* [9]*in their distress. / It was no envoy or angel / but his own presence that saved them*
[b] 11 Or *But may he recall*

as though they were his "children" (v. 8). But the people "rebelled," and God "fought against them" (v. 10). Only then did they begin to wonder: Where was Yahweh who had "brought them through the sea" (v. 11) and "guided" them (v. 14) by "his Holy Spirit" (v. 11)?

63:9 angel of his presence. Expresses God's personal involvement in time and space with the people; probably identical to the Holy Spirit (vv. 10,11,14).

63:10 grieved his Holy Spirit. Cf. Num 14:11; Ps 78:40; Acts 7:51; Eph 4:30.

63:11–14 These verses recall the exodus from Egypt and point to the great deliverance to come.

63:14 name. Character or reputation (12:4; 30:27; 52:5; cf. Exod 34:14; 1 Kgs 8:42; Ps 135:13).

63:15—64:12 *A Cry for Yahweh to Intervene.* The prophet speaks for the people, confessing that they are helpless in their sins unless God takes action (through the Warrior, 59:15b–21; 63:1–6). The people wonder why God has not done this sooner (63:15,17; 64:12). The desolation of the land and sanctuary (63:18; 64:10–11) that occurred during the exile symbolizes the people's spiritual desolation (64:5–7). There is almost an accusatory tone: the people have not repented because Yahweh has not made them do so (63:17; 64:9,12).

63:15 your lofty throne. Cf. 6:1–2; 57:15.

63:16 our Father. Not the one who caused them to be born, as in pagan literature, but their caregiver and protector. Cf. 1:2; 9:6; 30:1,9; 45:11; 64:8.

you, LORD, are our Father,
our Redeemer[g] from of old is your name.
17 Why, LORD, do you make us wander from your ways
and harden our hearts so we do not revere[h] you?
Return[i] for the sake of your servants,
the tribes that are your inheritance.
18 For a little while your people possessed your holy place,
but now our enemies have trampled down your sanctuary.[j]
19 We are yours from of old;
but you have not ruled over them,
they have not been called[a] by your name.

64 [b] Oh, that you would rend the heavens[k] and come down,[l]
that the mountains[m] would tremble before you!
2 As when fire sets twigs ablaze
and causes water to boil,
come down to make your name known to your enemies
and cause the nations to quake[n] before you!
3 For when you did awesome[o] things that we did not expect,
you came down, and the mountains trembled before you.
4 Since ancient times no one has heard,
no ear has perceived,
no eye has seen any God besides you,
who acts on behalf of those who wait for him.[p]
5 You come to the help of those who gladly do right,[q]
who remember your ways.
But when we continued to sin against them,
you were angry.
How then can we be saved?
6 All of us have become like one who is unclean,
and all our righteous[r] acts are like filthy rags;
we all shrivel up like a leaf,[s]
and like the wind our sins sweep us away.
7 No one[t] calls on your name
or strives to lay hold of you;
for you have hidden[u] your face from us
and have given us over[v] to[c] our sins.

8 Yet you, LORD, are our Father.[w]
We are the clay, you are the potter;[x]
we are all the work of your hand.

63:16 [g] Isa 41:14; 44:6
63:17 [h] Isa 29:13 [i] Nu 10:36
63:18 [j] Ps 74:3-8
64:1 [k] Ps 18:9; 144:5 [l] Mic 1:3 [m] Ex 19:18
64:2 [n] Ps 99:1; Jer 5:22; 33:9
64:3 [o] Ps 65:5
64:4 [p] Isa 30:18; 1Co 2:9*
64:5 [q] Isa 26:8
64:6 [r] Isa 46:12; 48:1 [s] Ps 90:5-6
64:7 [t] Isa 59:4 [u] Dt 31:18; Isa 1:15; 54:8 [v] Isa 9:18
64:8 [w] Isa 63:16 [x] Isa 29:16

[a] *19* Or *We are like those you have never ruled, / like those never called* [b] In Hebrew texts 64:1 is numbered 63:19b, and 64:2-12 is numbered 64:1-11. [c] *7* Septuagint, Syriac and Targum; Hebrew *have made us melt because of*

63:17 For God's response to the veiled charge in this question, see 65:1–16.
63:18 See note on 63:15—64:12.
63:19 See NIV text note. If the alternate reading is taken, then the people are saying in their despair that it appears as though they really are not God's people and that he does not care about them.
64:1–4 An appeal for Yahweh to take dramatic action to change his people's attitudes and behavior. Cf. 51:6; Pss 18:9; 144:5.
64:1 mountains. Cf. Exod 19:18–20; Judg 5:4–5; Mic 1:3–4; Hab 3:3–7.
64:2 name. See note on 63:14.
64:4 wait. Expresses trust (see note on 8:17).
64:5–7 A confession of sin. While God responds to those "who gladly do right" (v. 5), that is not the case with these people. Because of their continued sins, even their "righteous acts are like filthy rags" (v. 6). Emphasizing righteous actions confirms the note of this entire division (56:1—66:24): unless God's servants manifest God's character in their behavior, their mission to the nations will be abortive. Equally important is recognizing that such actions are impossible unless Yahweh makes them possible.
64:7 calls on your name. Seeks God on the basis of his character and nature (63:14).
64:8–12 Surely God cannot "hold [himself] back" (v. 12) in view of his

64:9 [y] Isa 57:17; 60:10 [z] Isa 43:25
64:11 [a] Ps 74:3-7 [b] La 1:7,10
64:12 [c] Ps 74:10-11; Isa 42:14 [d] Ps 83:1
65:1 [e] Hos 1:10; Ro 9:24-26; 10:20* [f] Eph 2:12
65:2 [g] Isa 1:2,23; Ro 10:21* [h] Ps 81:11-12; Isa 66:18
65:3 [i] Job 1:11 [j] Isa 1:29
65:4 [k] Lev 11:7
65:5 [l] Mt 9:11; Lk 7:39; 18:9-12
65:6 [m] Ps 50:3 [n] Jer 16:18 [o] Ps 79:12

9 Do not be angry[y] beyond measure, LORD;
do not remember our sins[z] forever.
Oh, look on us, we pray,
for we are all your people.
10 Your sacred cities have become a wasteland;
even Zion is a wasteland, Jerusalem a desolation.
11 Our holy and glorious temple,[a] where our ancestors praised you,
has been burned with fire,
and all that we treasured[b] lies in ruins.
12 After all this, LORD, will you hold yourself back?[c]
Will you keep silent[d] and punish us beyond measure?

Judgment and Salvation

65 "I revealed myself to those who did not ask for me;
I was found by those who did not seek me.[e]
To a nation[f] that did not call on my name,
I said, 'Here am I, here am I.'
2 All day long I have held out my hands
to an obstinate people,[g]
who walk in ways not good,
pursuing their own imaginations[h]—
3 a people who continually provoke me
to my very face,[i]
offering sacrifices in gardens[j]
and burning incense on altars of brick;
4 who sit among the graves
and spend their nights keeping secret vigil;
who eat the flesh of pigs,[k]
and whose pots hold broth of impure meat;
5 who say, 'Keep away; don't come near me,
for I am too sacred[l] for you!'
Such people are smoke in my nostrils,
a fire that keeps burning all day.

6 "See, it stands written before me:
I will not keep silent[m] but will pay back[n] in full;
I will pay it back into their laps[o]—

people's spiritual desolation, which the destruction of Jerusalem and the temple symbolize (vv. 10–11).
64:8 Father ... potter. Cf. 1:2; 29:16; 45:9. These appeals have a double edge: they have not been submissive to their Father or their Potter.
64:10–11 The appearance of the word "holy" in relation to the "temple" and the word "sacred" in relation to "cities" is ironic since the people's behavior is anything but holy.
64:12 This intimates that Yahweh might be reluctant to take action to deliver his people from their continued sinning.
65:1–16 *Yahweh's Response.* In strong words, like those of 58:1–2 and 59:1–3, Yahweh charges that there has been no reluctance on his part to take action on his people's behalf. The problem has been their hypocrisy. They have pagan hearts (vv. 3–7; cf. 57:3–13; 66:3–4) in that they want to manipulate God to gain his blessing for themselves while still being free to have their own way. God will indeed act on behalf of his "servants" (vv. 8,13–15) who "seek" him (v. 10). But to the hypocrites ("you," vv. 11–15), who say they are seeking him while they actually "forsake" him (v. 11), he promises only "death" (v. 15).
65:1–2 God bluntly asserts that he has not been "silent" (64:12) or far away (63:17) but was making himself known ("revealed myself") even before anyone was calling.
65:1 did not seek. Refers in its context here to rebellious Israel but ultimately can be seen also to include Gentiles (cf. Rom 10:20). The problem is not divine reluctance but human obstinacy.
65:3–7 As to whether or not Isaiah is actually accusing the people of these specific practices, see note on 57:3–13. He may be using figurative speech to accuse them of a manipulative cultic religiosity that is truly pagan in spirit.
65:3 gardens. Here, places of pagan worship (see 1:29–30). For gardens as places of divine blessing, see 51:3; 58:11.
65:4–5 This appears to be sarcasm. It is hard to believe that any Israelite with any awareness of the Torah would think these practices made one holy ("sacred"). But it is equally ludicrous to believe that careful, cultic religion makes one holy in spite of a hard, selfish heart (cf. Luke 11:42).
65:6–7 Perhaps Isaiah's audience decried the open paganism of their "ancestors" who "burned sacrifices on the mountains" (v. 7; see Deut

7 both your sins[p] and the sins of your ancestors,"[q]
says the LORD.
"Because they burned sacrifices on the mountains
and defied me on the hills,[r]
I will measure into their laps
the full payment for their former deeds."

8 This is what the LORD says:

"As when juice is still found in a cluster of grapes
and people say, 'Don't destroy it,
there is still a blessing in it,'
so will I do in behalf of my servants;
I will not destroy them all.
9 I will bring forth descendants[s] from Jacob,
and from Judah those who will possess[t] my mountains;
my chosen people will inherit them,
and there will my servants live.[u]
10 Sharon[v] will become a pasture for flocks,
and the Valley of Achor[w] a resting place for herds,
for my people who seek[x] me.

11 "But as for you who forsake[y] the LORD
and forget my holy mountain,
who spread a table for Fortune
and fill bowls of mixed wine for Destiny,
12 I will destine you for the sword,[z]
and all of you will fall in the slaughter;
for I called but you did not answer,[a]
I spoke but you did not listen.[b]
You did evil in my sight
and chose what displeases me."

13 Therefore this is what the Sovereign LORD says:

"My servants will eat,[c]
but you will go hungry;
my servants will drink,
but you will go thirsty;[d]
my servants will rejoice,
but you will be put to shame.[e]

65:7 [p] Isa 22:14 [q] Ex 20:5 [r] Isa 57:7
65:9 [s] Isa 45:19 [t] Am 9:11-15 [u] Isa 32:18
65:10 [v] Isa 35:2 [w] Jos 7:26 [x] Isa 51:1
65:11 [y] Dt 29:24-25; Isa 1:28
65:12 [z] Isa 27:1 [a] Pr 1:24-25; Isa 41:28; 66:4 [b] 2Ch 36:15-16; Jer 7:13
65:13 [c] Isa 1:19 [d] Isa 41:17 [e] Isa 44:9

12:2; 2 Kgs 16:4; Jer 2:20; Ezek 6:13) while thinking themselves better. If so, Isaiah would be saying that if the heart, the core of one's being, is wrong, the behavior is wrong, whatever the behavior may be.

65:8–12 The fates of those who seek the Lord and those who forsake him differ.

65:8–10 The Lord blesses those who seek him. He will not extinguish them as a people, but they will have "descendants" (v. 9; see notes on 43:5–7; 54:1–8) who will "inherit" the land (v. 9).

65:10 Sharon. A fertile plain on the shore of the Mediterranean northwest of Jerusalem. **Valley of Achor.** Despite its sad history (Josh 7:26), it was fertile and productive (cf. Hos 2:15). It was located on the west side of the Jordan Valley, northeast of Jerusalem.

65:11–12 Slaughter for those who forsake the Lord. The direct address ("you"; cf. 57:3–13) probably links this, as well as vv. 13–15, to the appeal of 63:7—64:12 and indicates that the appeal was not sincerely motivated. The people wanted Yahweh's blessings, but not Yahweh himself. They thought he was not listening, but he actually was calling them all the time (v. 12). They could not hear because he was asking them to give themselves to him, something they were unwilling to do.

65:11 Fortune ... Destiny. They were not interested in what a biblical prophet might have to say to them about their moral behavior; they wanted only to know the future so they could have some illusion of control over their lives (cf. 8:18–20). But Yahweh has a destiny for them: "the sword" (v. 12).

65:13–15 This further states blessing for those who obey and curses for those who do not. "My servants" implies an obedient relationship. Servants will "eat ... drink ... rejoice ... [and] sing" (vv. 13–14) and have "another name" (v. 15; cf. 62:4). But "you," the disobedient, will be "hungry ... thirsty ... [and] put to shame" (v. 13) and will "cry out ... [and] leave your name" (vv. 14–15) to be used in "curses" (v. 15).

65:14 [f]Mt 8:12; Lk 13:28
65:15 [g]Zec 8:13
65:16 [h]Ps 31:5 [i]Isa 19:18
65:17 [j]Isa 66:22; 2Pe 3:13 [k]Isa 43:18; Jer 3:16
65:18 [l]Ps 98:1-9; Isa 25:9
65:19 [m]Isa 35:10; 62:5 [n]Isa 25:8; Rev 7:17
65:20 [o]Ecc 8:13
65:21 [p]Isa 32:18 [q]Isa 37:30; Am 9:14

14 My servants will sing
out of the joy of their hearts,
but you will cry out[f]
from anguish of heart
and wail in brokenness of spirit.
15 You will leave your name
for my chosen ones to use in their curses;[g]
the Sovereign LORD will put you to death,
but to his servants he will give another name.
16 Whoever invokes a blessing in the land
will do so by the one true God;[h]
whoever takes an oath in the land
will swear[i] by the one true God.
For the past troubles will be forgotten
and hidden from my eyes.

New Heavens and a New Earth

17 "See, I will create
new heavens and a new earth.[j]
The former things will not be remembered,[k]
nor will they come to mind.
18 But be glad and rejoice[l] forever
in what I will create,
for I will create Jerusalem to be a delight
and its people a joy.
19 I will rejoice[m] over Jerusalem
and take delight in my people;
the sound of weeping and of crying[n]
will be heard in it no more.

20 "Never again will there be in it
an infant who lives but a few days,
or an old man who does not live out his years;[o]
the one who dies at a hundred
will be thought a mere child;
the one who fails to reach[a] a hundred
will be considered accursed.
21 They will build houses[p] and dwell in them;
they will plant vineyards and eat their fruit.[q]

[a] 20 Or *the sinner who reaches*

65:16 by the one true God. Implies that during the times of judgment, people had been afraid to use the name of Yahweh for fear that doing so would bring down further disaster (cf. Amos 6:10).

65:17–25 *New Heavens and a New Earth.* This poetically states God's power on behalf of the contrite, his "chosen ones" (v. 22; cf. 57:14–21; 66:2). Expressed in the language of Isaiah's day, it is a beautiful statement of the blessings that God has for his people. Interpreters disagree over the precise reference. There are three main positions: (1) a metaphoric statement about a restored but ideal Jerusalem, and more literal statements about (2) the millennial kingdom, or (3) eternity. Each of these has certain inconsistencies. Whereas the "new heavens and a new earth" (v. 17) most easily speak of eternity (Rev 21), the references to old age and dying do not accord with that view, nor do they accord with a millennial kingdom. These difficulties have led some to the first interpretation, describing in physical terms the benefits that come to those in fellowship with God: peace, security, abundance, freedom from sorrow and destruction. At the same time, as with other such poetic statements in the book (cf. 11:6–9,12–16; 54:11–12), literal fulfillment of some or all of the elements described here—perhaps in ways we cannot now imagine—should not be ruled out.

65:17–19 The Creator will do new things; he is not hampered by any restrictions the past may impose (see note on 43:18). The Jerusalem of the past was a place of weeping but not so the Jerusalem to come. Salvation is not mere renovation; it is transformation.

65:20–24 Metaphors of blessedness: long life (v. 20), enjoying the fruits of one's labor (vv. 21–23), instant access to Yahweh and his power (v. 24; cf. 58:9).

[22] No longer will they build houses and others live in them,
or plant and others eat.
For as the days of a tree,[r]
so will be the days[s] of my people;
my chosen ones will long enjoy
the work of their hands.
[23] They will not labor in vain,
nor will they bear children doomed to misfortune;
for they will be a people blessed[t] by the LORD,
they and their descendants[u] with them.
[24] Before they call[v] I will answer;
while they are still speaking[w] I will hear.
[25] The wolf and the lamb[x] will feed together,
and the lion will eat straw like the ox,
and dust will be the serpent's[y] food.
They will neither harm nor destroy
on all my holy mountain,"
says the LORD.

65:22 [r] Ps 92:12-14 [s] Ps 21:4; 91:16
65:23 [t] Dt 28:3-12; Isa 61:9 [u] Ac 2:39
65:24 [v] Isa 55:6 [w] Da 9:20-23; 10:12
65:25 [x] Isa 11:6 [y] Ge 3:14; Mic 7:17
66:1 [z] Mt 23:22 [a] 1Ki 8:27; Mt 5:34-35 [b] 2Sa 7:7; Jn 4:20-21; Ac 7:49*; 17:24
66:2 [c] Isa 40:26; Ac 7:50* [d] Isa 57:15; Mt 5:3-4; Lk 18:13-14 [e] Ezr 9:4
66:3 [f] Isa 1:11 [g] Lev 2:2 [h] Isa 57:17

Judgment and Hope

66 This is what the LORD says:

"Heaven is my throne,[z]
and the earth is my footstool.[a]
Where is the house[b] you will build for me?
Where will my resting place be?
[2] Has not my hand made all these things,[c]
and so they came into being?"
declares the LORD.

"These are the ones I look on with favor:
those who are humble and contrite in spirit,[d]
and who tremble at my word.[e]
[3] But whoever sacrifices a bull[f]
is like one who kills a person,
and whoever offers a lamb
is like one who breaks a dog's neck;
whoever makes a grain offering
is like one who presents pig's blood,
and whoever burns memorial incense[g]
is like one who worships an idol.
They have chosen their own ways,[h]
and they delight in their abominations;

65:25 They will neither harm nor destroy on all my holy mountain. Directly quotes 11:9a, connecting these promises to the work of the Messiah (see 11:6–8). It is his power that will enable his chosen ones, those who seek him in sincerity, to live the kinds of lives that result in true blessedness.

66:1–17 *Unrighteousness and Redemption.* This concluding section of 63:1—66:17 combines both judgment (vv. 1–4,15–17) and hope (vv. 5–14), just as did the introductory chapters (judgment: 1:2–15,21–25,28–31; 2:6—4:1; 5:1–30; hope: 1:16–20,26–27; 2:1–5; 4:2–6). In this way it caps one of the book's important themes: hope for a sinful people comes through judgment.

66:1–4 Correct ritual behavior without a changed heart and "spirit" (v. 2)—as shown in how people treat others (cf. 58:6–10)—is only a collection of "abominations" (v. 3; cf. 1:10–15; Ps 50:7–23). Verse 3 suggests that the extravagant descriptions of pagan behavior in v. 17; 57:3–13; 65:3–5 may be symbolic in the same ways.

66:1–2a To think that Yahweh actually dwells in an earthly temple is to think in pagan ways. He transcends creation (cf. 40:22; 1 Kgs 8:27; Ps 2:4); he is its Maker (cf. 17:7; 51:13; 54:5). The whole cosmos is his palace.

66:2b humble and contrite in spirit. The only appropriate response of humans before the Holy One (57:15).

66:3 have chosen their own ways. They are using the sacrifices God commanded to manipulate him for their own purposes (cf. Amos 4:4–5).

66:4 [i] Pr 10:24 [j] Pr 1:24; Jer 7:13 [k] 2Ki 21:2, 4, 6 [l] Isa 65:12
66:5 [m] Ps 38:20; Isa 60:15 [n] Lk 13:17
66:6 [o] Isa 65:6; Joel 3:7
66:7 [p] Isa 54:1 [q] Rev 12:5
66:8 [r] Isa 64:4
66:9 [s] Isa 37:3
66:10 [t] Dt 32:43; Ro 15:10 [u] Ps 26:8
66:11 [v] Isa 60:16
66:12 [w] Isa 48:18 [x] Ps 72:3; Isa 60:5; 61:6

4 so I also will choose harsh treatment for them
and will bring on them what they dread.[i]
For when I called, no one answered,[j]
when I spoke, no one listened.
They did evil[k] in my sight
and chose what displeases me."[l]

5 Hear the word of the LORD,
you who tremble at his word:
"Your own people who hate[m] you,
and exclude you because of my name, have said,
'Let the LORD be glorified,
that we may see your joy!'
Yet they will be put to shame.[n]
6 Hear that uproar from the city,
hear that noise from the temple!
It is the sound of the LORD
repaying[o] his enemies all they deserve.

7 "Before she goes into labor,[p]
she gives birth;
before the pains come upon her,
she delivers a son.[q]
8 Who has ever heard of such things?
Who has ever seen[r] things like this?
Can a country be born in a day
or a nation be brought forth in a moment?
Yet no sooner is Zion in labor
than she gives birth to her children.
9 Do I bring to the moment of birth[s]
and not give delivery?" says the LORD.
"Do I close up the womb
when I bring to delivery?" says your God.
10 "Rejoice[t] with Jerusalem and be glad for her,
all you who love[u] her;
rejoice greatly with her,
all you who mourn over her.
11 For you will nurse[v] and be satisfied
at her comforting breasts;
you will drink deeply
and delight in her overflowing abundance."

12 For this is what the LORD says:

"I will extend peace to her like a river,[w]
and the wealth[x] of nations like a flooding stream;

66:4 when I called. Cf. 65:12, contrast 58:9; Jer 29:12.

66:5–13 Yahweh will empower those who "tremble at his word" (v. 5; see v. 2). He will protect them from their "enemies" (v. 6), give them "children" (v. 8), and make Jerusalem a place of "abundance" (v. 11), like a nursing mother (vv. 10–14).

66:5 Your own people. Probably the self-righteous who are so proud of their own religious achievements and who hold in contempt those who are passionate to do God's will. Those passionate ones are mockingly enjoined to have "joy" in the Lord while being systematically excluded from any place of influence.

66:7–9 For the importance of descendants, see notes on 29:23; 43:5–7; 44:1–5; 54:1–8.

66:8 gives birth. Contrast 26:18; 37:3.

66:10–13 Historically, Jerusalem in the short term would become a red-hot cauldron scorching to death everyone in her (Ezek 24:3–14), but Isaiah focuses on Yahweh's transforming power that will change her into a mother of nursing children from around the world. As elsewhere, this is probably a metaphor both of spiritual reality and of ultimate reality in the new Jerusalem (cf. 65:17–25).

you will nurse and be carried[y] on her arm
and dandled on her knees.
13 As a mother comforts her child,
so will I comfort[z] you;
and you will be comforted over Jerusalem."

14 When you see this, your heart will rejoice
and you will flourish like grass;
the hand of the LORD will be made known to his servants,
but his fury[a] will be shown to his foes.
15 See, the LORD is coming with fire,
and his chariots[b] are like a whirlwind;
he will bring down his anger with fury,
and his rebuke[c] with flames of fire.
16 For with fire[d] and with his sword[e]
the LORD will execute judgment on all people,
and many will be those slain by the LORD.

17 "Those who consecrate and purify themselves to go into the gardens,[f] following one who is among
those who eat the flesh of pigs,[g] rats and other unclean things — they will meet their end[h] together
with the one they follow," declares the LORD.
18 "And I, because of what they have planned and done, am about to come[a] and gather the people
of all nations and languages, and they will come and see my glory.
19 "I will set a sign[i] among them, and I will send some of those who survive to the nations — to
Tarshish,[j] to the Libyans[b] and Lydians[k] (famous as archers), to Tubal[l] and Greece, and to the distant
islands[m] that have not heard of my fame or seen my glory.[n] They will proclaim my glory among the
nations. 20 And they will bring all your people, from all the nations, to my holy mountain in Jerusalem
as an offering to the LORD — on horses, in chariots and wagons, and on mules and camels," says the
LORD. "They will bring them, as the Israelites bring their grain offerings, to the temple of the LORD in ceremonially clean vessels.[o] 21 And I will select some of them also to be priests[p] and Levites," says the LORD.

22 "As the new heavens and the new earth[q] that I make will endure before me," declares the LORD, "so
will your name and descendants endure.[r] 23 From one New Moon to another and from one Sabbath[s] to
another, all mankind will come and bow down[t] before me," says the LORD. 24 "And they will go out and
look on the dead bodies of those who rebelled against me; the worms[u] that eat them will not die, the
fire that burns them will not be quenched,[v] and they will be loathsome to all mankind."

a *18* The meaning of the Hebrew for this clause is uncertain. *b* *19* Some Septuagint manuscripts *Put* (Libyans); Hebrew *Pul*

66:12 [y] Isa 60:4
66:13 [z] Isa 40:1; 2Co 1:4
66:14 [a] Isa 10:5
66:15 [b] Ps 68:17 [c] Ps 9:5
66:16 [d] Isa 30:30 [e] Isa 27:1
66:17 [f] Isa 1:29 [g] Lev 11:7 [h] Ps 37:20; Isa 1:28
66:19 [i] Isa 11:10; 49:22 [j] Isa 2:16 [k] Eze 27:10 [l] Ge 10:2 [m] Isa 11:11 [n] 1Ch 16:24; Isa 24:15
66:20 [o] Isa 52:11
66:21 [p] Ex 19:6; Isa 61:6; 1Pe 2:5,9
66:22 [q] Isa 65:17; Heb 12:26-27; 2Pe 3:13; Rev 21:1 [r] Jn 10:27-29; 1Pe 1:4-5
66:23 [s] Eze 46:1-3 [t] Isa 19:21
66:24 [u] Isa 14:11 [v] Isa 1:31; Mk 9:48*

66:13 comfort. Cf. 12:1; 22:4; 40:1; 49:13; 51:3,12,19; 52:9; 54:11; 57:18; 61:2.
66:14–17 As throughout the book, Isaiah will not allow his hearers to use hopeful promises to evade the realities of judgment. So the section on Israel's inability to do righteousness concludes with this stark reality in view.
66:14 The only alternatives open to people: Are we "servants" or "foes" of the Lord?
66:15,16 fire. Cf. 10:17; 29:6; 30:27,30.
66:16 slain by the LORD. Not the result of arbitrary rage or personal pique, but a righteous judgment on evil, the logical and necessary effect of human choices, just as in the natural world.
66:17 See notes on vv. 1–4; 57:3–13. **gardens.** See notes on 1:29–31.
66:18–24 *Righteous Gentiles.* This final segment of 56:1—66:24 mirrors the opening one (56:1–8). It emphasizes the division's central theme: Israel has a mission to bear God's light to the world because God intends to restore to himself not only Israel but all peoples (cf. 56:7–8). This segment makes the redemption of the world very explicit: "all nations and languages" (v. 18); "all mankind will come" (v. 23). But the promises are not indiscriminate: they apply to those who "bow down before [the LORD]" (v. 23), *not* to "those who rebelled against [him]" (v. 24).
66:18 See NIV text note. An alternative rendering based on the Septuagint (the pre-Christian Greek translation of the OT): "For I know their works and thoughts, and I am coming to gather all the nations." **my glory.** Yahweh's character and nature, which Israel must display to the world (see notes on 49:3; 55:5; see also v. 19).
66:20 they will bring. Cf. 60:4,9.
66:21 them. This naturally refers to the nations. Like the approval of eunuchs in 56:3–5, this is a revolutionary idea but one that the NT fully endorses (cf. 1 Pet 2:9–10; Rev 1:6; 5:9–10).
66:22 your name. This seems to refer to Israel: Israel's identity will not be lost in the "new heavens and the new earth" (cf. 65:17–25).
66:24 rebelled. The book ends as it begins (cf. 1:2). The great issue is whether human creatures will allow Yahweh, the "I AM" (see Exod 3:14 and note), to be who he is, the Holy One of Israel, in their lives. If they persist in their rebellion, then fiery destruction awaits. This approach is typical of Isaiah. Hope is never allowed to obscure the reality that unless we avail ourselves of God's grace, judgment will not be refining, but destructive (see 14:11; 48:22; 50:11; 57:21). This verse is quoted in Mark 9:48, where Jesus speaks of the judgment to come upon sinners (cf. Matt 5:22; 25:41; Rev 20:11–15).

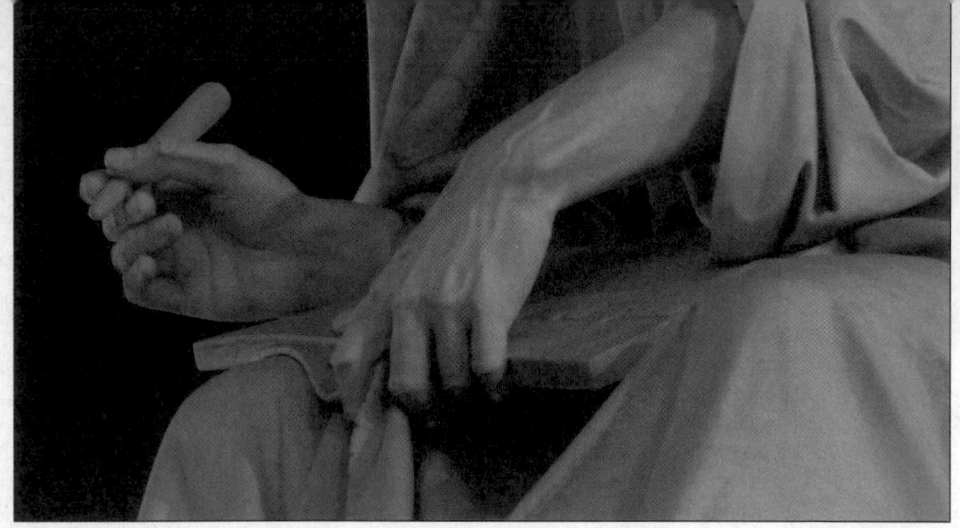

INTRODUCTION TO JEREMIAH

AUTHOR AND DATE

The book of Jeremiah records the ministry of a prophet who lived through some of the most traumatic events of Israel's history. He was called to communicate God's words of judgment and hope during the turbulent years that led up to the destruction of Jerusalem by the Babylonians. The book that bears his name includes not only his prophecies but also a window into his own personal struggles as a prophet. It is the longest book of the Bible.

Jeremiah was born to a priestly family in the town of Anathoth (1:1), a few miles/kilometers from Jerusalem, probably around 650 BC. His call to be a prophet came in 628/27 BC, in the 13th year of King Josiah (1:2), at a time when, along with the hope brought by Josiah's reforms, there was a growing threat from the rising power of the Babylonians. The bulk of his ministry took place between then and the fall of Jerusalem to the Babylonians in 586 BC (39:1 – 10). Jeremiah was not deported with those taken to exile in Babylon but initially remained in Judah and was taken down to Egypt against his will by those who fled there after the death of the Babylonian-appointed governor, Gedaliah (chs. 42 – 44). He presumably died in Egypt. The last event recorded in the book is Jehoiachin's release from a Babylonian prison, which took place in 561/560 BC (52:31 – 34; 2 Kgs 25:27 – 30). The last chapter of the book of Jeremiah summarizes the events surrounding the fall of Jerusalem and provides a historical framework demonstrating the fulfillment of Jeremiah's words.

The book itself was probably written in several stages. God instructed Jeremiah to commit some of his prophecies to writing in 605 BC, using Baruch as his scribe (36:1 – 4). This was done so the words of judgment could be read to the people (36:2 – 6) and eventually to King Jehoiakim, who responded by burning them (36:23). This scroll was then rewritten (36:28,32). This early edition was expanded to include many of Jeremiah's later prophecies, along with various biographical accounts of incidents from his life, whether written by the prophet himself or by Baruch or another scribe.

This multistage expansion of the book of Jeremiah may account for the differences between the present Hebrew text and the Greek translation of Jeremiah that is found in the Septuagint (the pre-Christian Greek translation of the OT). The Greek version is much shorter than the Hebrew text, and the messages against the nations are placed after 25:13 rather than toward the end of the book. Hebrew equivalents of both versions have been found among the manuscripts at Qumran. The Greek version may represent an earlier edition of the book, though some scholars have argued that it is an abridged version of the Masoretic Text, omitting material that is redundant or repeated elsewhere.

JEREMIAH'S LIFE AND TIMES

Jeremiah lived during a time of great stress and upheaval in the life of God's people. King Josiah came to the throne in 641/40 BC as a boy of only eight years old (2 Kgs 22:1), inheriting a nation that his father, Amon, and his grandfather, Manasseh (2 Kgs 21), had led away from the Lord. Josiah set his heart on following the Lord, and external factors initially helped him to pursue that goal. The major power in the region, the Assyrian Empire, was then in its last days under Ashurbanipal. Ashurbanipal was able to retain power and maintain the boundaries of his empire until his death in 627 BC, but the empire then began to fragment. Nabopolassar took over the province of Babylon, which became independent in 626 BC. In 614 the Medes captured the old capital of Ashur, and in 612 Nineveh itself fell to the Medes and the Babylonians. The remaining Assyrian forces retreated to Harran, where they were subsequently routed.

The turmoil within Assyria left King Josiah free to pursue his own path in Judah, and he took full advantage of the opportunity. In 622 BC, an old law book was discovered during temple renovation work (2 Kgs 22:8). This book must have been or contained parts of the book of Deuteronomy, for its rediscovery led to a renewed focus on reforming worship in line with the teachings of that book. Local altars were torn down, non-Levitical priests were dismissed, and the other priests were relocated closer to Jerusalem so that they could properly carry out their ministry in the temple (2 Kgs 23). The nation renewed the covenant and memorably celebrated the Passover (2 Kgs 23:21 – 23). In his early prophetic ministry, in keeping with these reforms, Jeremiah sought to bring this covenant message back to the center of his people's life. Yet even during Josiah's days, it appears that Jeremiah's message was out of step with popular sentiment. As a result, there were plots against Jeremiah's life, and the community greeted him with broad ostracism. The lack of support for Jeremiah's message highlights the difficulty that the reform movement faced in Judah, even with royal support.

Judah's independence movement did not last long. In 609 BC, the Egyptians marched out in support of the Assyrians, hoping to prop them up as a buffer against the rising tide of Babylonian power. For reasons that are not entirely clear, Josiah marched out to try to block their advance at Megiddo (2 Kgs 23:29 – 30). It was a catastrophic error: he was killed in the battle, and the Egyptians controlled Judah for the next four years. They replaced the new Judahite king, Jehoahaz, with his brother Jehoiakim, during whose reign all of the reforms of Josiah were suspended or reversed (2 Kgs 23:34 – 37).

The Egyptians were defeated by the Babylonian king Nebuchadnezzar at Carchemish in 605 BC. From then on, the Judahites had to pay tribute to Babylon instead of Egypt. In 602, Jehoiakim rebelled against the Babylonians, only to be swiftly defeated (2 Kgs 24:1 – 5). Four years later, Jehoiakim died and was replaced by his son Jehoiachin, who also adopted an anti-Babylonian stance. Nebuchadnezzar returned and besieged Jerusalem. He captured the city, deposed Jehoiachin, and deported him to Babylon, replacing him with his uncle, Zedekiah (2 Kgs 24:10 – 17). The Babylonians treated Jehoiachin himself kindly in exile, and he remained the true king of Judah in the eyes of some Judahites. Far from being grateful to the Babylonians who had placed him on the throne, Zedekiah led a revolt against them when the opportunity presented itself in 589 BC. Nebuchadnezzar subsequently returned in force with the Babylonian army and besieged Jerusalem (2 Kgs 25). After a long siege, which was only briefly lifted to deal with an Egyptian advance, the Babylonians broke through the walls in 586 BC and Zedekiah and his troops fled. The Babylonians captured Zedekiah near Jericho, forced him to watch as they slaughtered his sons, and then put out his eyes (2 Kgs 25:7).

TOWNS AND CITIES ASSOCIATED WITH JEREMIAH AND THE NEO-BABYLONIAN EMPIRE

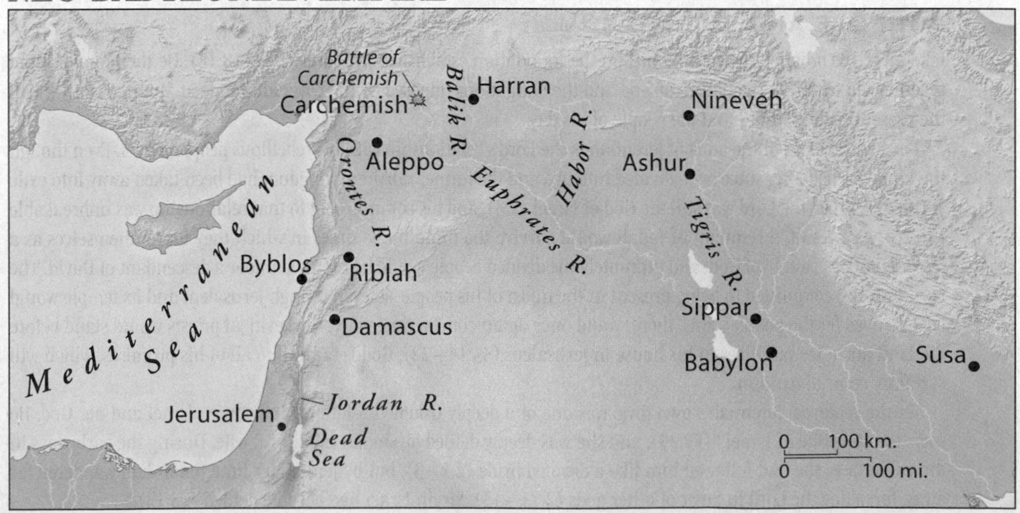

ASSYRIAN, BABYLONIAN, AND JUDAHITE KINGS

YEAR	ASSYRIAN KINGS	NEO-BABYLONIAN KINGS	JUDAHITE KINGS
675	Ashurbanipal 669–627 BC		
650	Ashur-etil-ilani 627–622 BC		Josiah 641/40–609 BC
625	Sin-shar-ishkun 622–612 BC Ashur-uballit 612–608 BC	Nabopolassar 626–605 BC Nebuchadnezzar 605–562 BC	Jehoahaz 609 BC Jehoiakim 609–598 BC
600			Jehoiachin 598–597 BC Zedekiah 597–586 BC
575		Amel-Marduk 562–560 BC Neriglissar 560–556 BC Labashi-Marduk 556 BC Nabonidus 556–539 BC	

Jerusalem itself was destroyed, the temple was burned to the ground, and the vast majority of the remaining population was taken off to exile in Babylon.

Jeremiah lived through all of these terrible events. If life was difficult for him in the days of Josiah (when he was at least in line with official royal policy), it must have been far more difficult under Josiah's successors. Jeremiah's prophecies of the coming of the Babylonian army from the north (e.g., 1:13–15) and the certainty of the Babylonian victory (e.g., 37:7–10) would have sounded deeply treasonous. He advocated that Judah immediately submit to the Babylonians at a time when the king was trying to persuade people to make the necessary sacrifices to endure the great ordeal of the Babylonian siege. As a result, Jeremiah spent a considerable time imprisoned for his convictions. When a group of men went to Zedekiah seeking Jeremiah's death for his morale-sapping message, the king responded, "He is in your hands ... The king can do nothing to oppose you" (38:5). The men then took Jeremiah and tossed him into a cistern, where Jeremiah sank "into the mud" (38:6). They intended for him to die there and only the intervention of Ebed-Melek, a Cushite eunuch, saved his life (38:7–11).

After Jerusalem fell to the Babylonians, the new rulers offered Jeremiah a comfortable retirement in Babylon (40:4), yet he chose to remain in his homeland with the lowest ranks of the people, whom the Babylonians had left behind to tend the soil. But the respite for Jeremiah was brief: a failed coup attempt ended with the assassination of Gedaliah, the Judahite governor whom the Babylonians had appointed (41:1–3). Those who remained in the land determined to flee to Egypt, and though the Lord's word through Jeremiah warned against such action (42:9–22), he was carried to Egypt against his will. Presumably he died there, before his prophecies were fulfilled and the exiles in Babylon were allowed to return home (Ezra 1:1–3). In confirmation of Jeremiah's warnings to his fellow countrymen, as far as we know, very few of those who went down to Egypt ever came back to the province of Judah.

PURPOSE AND THEMES

Like all of the prophets, Jeremiah built on the foundation established by Moses (Deut 18:18). He therefore brought together old truths — the nature of God and the obligations imposed by the covenant made at Mount Sinai — with the present realities that faced the people of his day.

The central focus of the book of Jeremiah is the Lord's relationship with his rebellious people, Israel. Even though the kingdom had long since been divided into two and the former northern kingdom had been taken away into exile 100 years earlier, the Lord was still the God of Israel (7:3), and his commitment to that relationship was unbreakable (33:26). As a result, a remnant of Judah would survive the tumultuous times in which they found themselves as a representative "Israel" of God, and ultimately the divided people would be reunited under a descendant of David. The Lord was also committed to being present in the midst of his people, so even though Jerusalem and its temple would be destroyed for the people's sins, there would once again come a time when the Levitical priests would stand before the Lord and offer sacrifices in his house in Jerusalem (33:14–22). God is faithful to all of his promises, which will certainly come to fruition.

Yet the reality in Jeremiah's own time was one of a deeply troubled relationship between Israel and her God. He was "the Holy One of Israel" (50:29), and she was deeply defiled by sin, an unfaithful wife. During the early days in the wilderness, she had followed him like a devoted bride (2:2–3), but by Jeremiah's time Judah had wandered far away, forsaking the Lord in favor of other gods (2:11–13). Virgin Israel had become defiled (18:13).

The result of that unfaithfulness on Judah's part was inevitably judgment and disaster. Their idols could not protect them when the Lord brought upon them the judgment they deserved (2:18–19). This was a central part of Jeremiah's message: the Lord had appointed him "to uproot and tear down, to destroy and overthrow" (1:10). Jeremiah's opening vision depicted a flowering almond tree, the first tree to blossom in the spring, indicating that the Lord was about to act against Judah and Jerusalem (1:11–12). Immediately afterward he saw a boiling pot tilting from the north, about to pour its scalding contents over the unprepared people (1:13–16). The Babylonians were about to invade Judah from the north as a judgment from God against Judah's idolatry.

Jeremiah's hearers were, for the most part, unresponsive. They rejected his message, preferring to trust in the symbols of their religion rather than the reality of a living relationship with God. They believed that the presence of the temple in Jerusalem meant that they were secure, no matter how they lived (7:4). Yet Jeremiah reminded the people that the Lord had earlier abandoned Shiloh, even though the ark of the covenant had been housed there (7:12–14), and he told them that Jerusalem would share Shiloh's fate if they did not change their ways (7:3–8). The covenant the Lord had made with his people at Mount Sinai promised blessing to those who obeyed its terms and curses on those who disobeyed (11:3–5). The stubborn disobedience of Judah's ancestors had led to disaster before (11:6–8) and would do so again in their own day (11:9–17).

Yet in the midst of an unresponsive people destined for judgment, some responded to the prophet's message and heard words of hope. God did not instruct Jeremiah merely to uproot and tear down but also "to build and to plant" (1:10). Though many of the people were like bad figs, too rotten to eat, there were others who were like good figs (24:2–3). In Jeremiah's day, most of the "good figs" were not in Jerusalem but among those already taken into exile (24:5). Though those who remained at home regarded the exiles as being under God's curse, the exiles were actually the ones for whom God had a positive future, a plan to prosper and bless them (29:11). Their exile would be protracted, extending for 70 years (25:11) — an entire lifetime. Nonetheless, they were to seek the prosperity of the place where God had put them while they awaited the distant day of their return to Judah (29:4–10). In contrast, God planned an immediate future of dire judgment on those who remained in Jerusalem, along with their king (29:16–19). God's purpose was not purely linked to a person's geographic location: those among the exiles who were false prophets or who rejected Jeremiah's message faced the same fate as those back in Jerusalem (29:20–32), while others who lived in Jerusalem but supported Jeremiah's ministry, like Ebed-Melek and Baruch, heard words of comfort and life (39:16–18; 45:5).

Opposition from false prophets was a continual challenge for Jeremiah. Many preached words of a peaceful and prosperous future in spite of the gathering storm clouds (8:11). While Jeremiah prophesied a lengthy period of exile, others spoke of an imminent return for both the people and the sacred property that had been carried off to Babylon (27:16). When Jeremiah made a wooden yoke for himself to wear as a sign of the coming yoke of Babylon, the false prophet Hananiah broke it, proclaiming that the Lord would break Nebuchadnezzar's yoke within two years (28:10–11). Jeremiah then prophesied that the Lord would replace it with an unbreakable iron yoke and declared Hananiah's imminent death, which happened within a few months (28:12–17). But the false prophets remained popular with the people who resented or resisted Jeremiah's messages. In the face of such hostility, Jeremiah frequently got his message across by resorting to dramatic sign-acts, such as buying and burying an expensive linen belt so that it would be ruined (13:1–11), shattering a clay jar in front of witnesses (19:1–11), and buying a field located in enemy-held territory (32:7–12). Each of these actions communicated Jeremiah's message in an unforgettable way to a reluctant audience.

Even though the immediate future was bleak for God's people, nonetheless the Lord had made an unbreakable promise to bless them and their king. That did not mean that the present Davidic kings could rest secure. Jehoiachin had been comprehensively rejected by God and would be recorded as if childless (22:24–30). Yet the Lord would eventually raise up a "righteous Branch" (23:5) to take Jehoiachin's place, a good shepherd who would rule in place of the oppressive shepherds of Jeremiah's day (23:1–6). The Lord would accomplish a new act of salvation that would eclipse even the exodus from Egypt (23:7–8). In place of the old covenant, which failed because the people broke it through their long history of sin, the Lord would enact a new covenant that would succeed because he would put the law in the people's minds and write it on their hearts (31:32–33). In place of the old external obedience that merely covered hypocritical hearts, now there would be true heart-motivated obedience that would bring with it the Lord's blessing in place of his curse. This new covenant anticipates the restored relationship between God and human beings promised in Gen 3:15 and accomplished through the ministry of Jesus Christ.

The unbreakable commitment of God to his people, first given to Abraham, is also evident in the various messages against the nations (chs. 46–51). In Gen 12:1–3, God promised to bless those who blessed his people and curse those who cursed or assaulted them. Even when the nations attacked Judah as the agents of the Lord's wrath, as the Babylonians did, they were not exempt from punishment under the terms of the Abrahamic covenant. Because the Lord is the "Holy One of Israel" (50:29; 51:5), he would not only punish his own people when they strayed but also bring judgment upon those who harmed his people, as he had promised to do. The Babylonians, with their pride and their trust in their own gods, would be humbled once they had served the Lord's purposes of judgment. This certainty also reassured God's people that the positive purposes of the Abrahamic covenant would be accomplished. In the end, the Lord would establish a people belonging to him, in whom all nations on earth would ultimately find their blessing.

This promise reaches its goal in the NT, where the new covenant finds its fulfillment in the coming of Jesus Christ. Jesus is the promised righteous Branch, the new shoot from David's broken line (Luke 1:32 – 33), who establishes his kingdom in justice and righteousness. Like Jeremiah (7:9 – 11), Jesus warned against turning the temple into a "den of robbers" (Matt 21:12 – 13), yet also like Jeremiah (9:1), Jesus wept over those who were condemned by his words of judgment (Luke 19:41). Jesus is himself the Good Shepherd of whom Jeremiah spoke (23:3 – 4), the shepherd who laid down his life for the sheep instead of abusing them and taking advantage of them (John 10:11). The new covenant is established in Jesus' own blood (Luke 22:20) and is made effective through the work of the Holy Spirit in giving believers hearts of flesh that now desire to keep God's holy law; this is something the old covenant could never do (2 Cor 3:2 – 6; cf. Jer 31:33). Those who have the Spirit's anointing have no need for anyone to teach them, just as Jeremiah anticipated (1 John 2:27; cf. Jer 31:34), though God still gives pastors and teachers as a gift to his church (Eph 4:11). The covenant of which Christ is the high priest now brings the blessings that God promised, in ch. 31 to the house of Israel and the house of Judah, to the new Israel of God, the church (Heb 8), for in Christ we have access to the heavenly reality toward which the OT types and shadows pointed.

OUTLINE

Unlike the book of Ezekiel, the messages in Jeremiah are not arranged in chronological order. Insofar as it would be possible to put the messages in chronological sequence, the sections within the book would be ordered approximately as follows: 1:1 — 7:15; 26:1 – 24; 7:16 — 20:18; 25:1 – 38; 46:1 — 51:64; 36:1 – 8; 45:1 – 5; 36:9 – 32; 35:1 – 19; 21:1 — 24:10; 27:1 — 31:40; 34:1 – 7; 37:1 – 10; 34:8 – 22; 37:11 — 38:13; 39:15 – 18; 32:1 — 33:26; 38:14 — 39:14; 52:1 – 30; 40:1 — 44:30; 52:31 – 34. The outline below represents an analysis of the book of Jeremiah in its present canonical order.

I. The Call of Jeremiah (1:1 – 19)
- A. Historical Setting (1:1 – 3)
- B. Call Narrative (1:4 – 19)

II. Crime and Punishment (2:1 — 6:30)
- A. Israel Forsakes the Lord (2:1 — 3:5)
- B. Unfaithful Israel (3:6 — 4:4)
- C. Disaster From the North (4:5 – 31)
- D. Not One Is Upright (5:1 – 31)
- E. Jerusalem Under Siege (6:1 – 30)

III. False Religion and a Deluded People (7:1 — 10:25)
- A. False Religion Worthless (7:1 – 29)
- B. The Valley of Slaughter (7:30 — 8:3)
- C. Sin and Punishment (8:4 — 9:26)
- D. The Lord and Idols (10:1 – 16)
- E. Coming Destruction (10:17 – 22)
- F. Jeremiah's Prayer (10:23 – 25)

IV. The Broken Covenant and Its Consequences (11:1 — 15:21)
- A. The Covenant Is Broken (11:1 – 17)
- B. Plot Against Jeremiah (11:18 – 23)
- C. Jeremiah's Complaint (12:1 – 4)
- D. The Lord's Answer (12:5 – 17)
- E. A Linen Belt (13:1 – 11)
- F. Wineskins (13:12 – 14)
- G. Threat of Captivity (13:15 – 27)
- H. Drought, Famine, Sword (14:1 — 15:21)

V. Opposition to Jeremiah's Messages of Judgment (16:1—29:32)
- A. Day of Disaster (16:1—17:18)
- B. Keeping the Sabbath Day Holy (17:19–27)
- C. At the Potter's House (18:1—19:15)
- D. Jeremiah and Pashhur (20:1–6)
- E. Jeremiah's Complaint (20:7–18)
- F. The Lord Rejects Zedekiah's Request (21:1–14)
- G. Judgment Against Wicked Kings (22:1–30)
- H. The Righteous Branch (23:1–8)
- I. Lying Prophets (23:9–32)
- J. False Prophecy (23:33–40)
- K. Two Baskets of Figs (24:1–10)
- L. Seventy Years of Captivity (25:1–14)
- M. The Cup of the Lord's Wrath (25:15–38)
- N. Jeremiah Threatened With Death (26:1–24)
- O. Judah to Serve Nebuchadnezzar (27:1–22)
- P. The False Prophet Hananiah (28:1–17)
- Q. A Letter to the Exiles (29:1–23)
- R. Message to Shemaiah (29:24–32)

VI. Restoration and a New Covenant (30:1—33:26)
- A. Restoration of Israel (30:1—31:40)
- B. Jeremiah Buys a Field (32:1–44)
- C. Promise of Restoration (33:1–26)

VII. The Last Days of Jehoiakim and Zedekiah (34:1—39:18)
- A. Warning to Zedekiah (34:1–7)
- B. Freedom for Slaves (34:8–22)
- C. The Rekabites (35:1–19)
- D. Jehoiakim Burns Jeremiah's Scroll (36:1–32)
- E. Jeremiah in Prison (37:1–21)
- F. Jeremiah Thrown Into a Cistern (38:1–13)
- G. Zedekiah Questions Jeremiah Again (38:14–28)
- H. The Fall of Jerusalem (39:1–18)

VIII. The Aftermath of Jerusalem's Destruction (40:1—45:5)
- A. Jeremiah Freed (40:1–6)
- B. Gedaliah Assassinated (40:7—41:15)
- C. Flight to Egypt (41:16—43:13)
- D. Disaster Because of Idolatry (44:1–30)
- E. A Message to Baruch (45:1–5)

IX. Messages Against the Nations (46:1—51:64)
- A. A Message About Egypt (46:1–28)
- B. A Message About the Philistines (47:1–7)
- C. A Message About Moab (48:1–47)
- D. A Message About Ammon (49:1–6)
- E. A Message About Edom (49:7–22)
- F. A Message About Damascus (49:23–27)
- G. A Message About Kedar and Hazor (49:28–33)
- H. A Message About Elam (49:34–39)
- I. A Message About Babylon (50:1—51:64)

X. The Fall of Jerusalem and Its Aftermath (52:1–34)
- A. The Fall of Jerusalem (52:1–30)
- B. Jehoiachin Released (52:31–34)

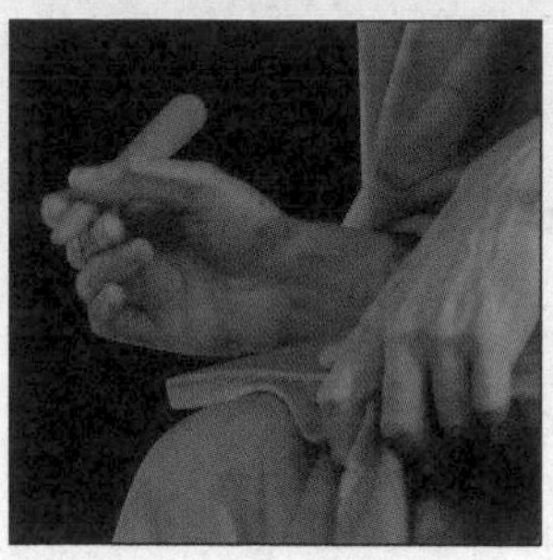

JEREMIAH

1:1 [a]Jos 21:18; 1Ch 6:60; Jer 32:7-9
1:3 [b]2Ki 23:34 [c]2Ki 24:17; Jer 39:2 [d]Jer 52:15
1:5 [e]Ps 139:16 [f]Isa 49:1 [g]ver 10; Jer 25:15-26
1:6 [h]Ex 4:10; 6:12 [i]1Ki 3:7

1 The words of Jeremiah son of Hilkiah, one of the priests at Anathoth[a] in the territory of Benjamin.
2 The word of the LORD came to him in the thirteenth year of the reign of Josiah son of Amon king of
Judah, 3 and through the reign of Jehoiakim[b] son of Josiah king of Judah, down to the fifth month of the
eleventh year of Zedekiah[c] son of Josiah king of Judah, when the people of Jerusalem went into exile.[d]

The Call of Jeremiah

4 The word of the LORD came to me, saying,

> 5 "Before I formed you in the womb I knew[a][e] you,
> before you were born[f] I set you apart;
> I appointed you as a prophet to the nations.[g]"

6 "Alas, Sovereign LORD," I said, "I do not know how to speak;[h] I am too young."[i]
7 But the LORD said to me, "Do not say, 'I am too young.' You must go to everyone I send you to and

[a] 5 Or *chose*

1:1–19 *The Call of Jeremiah.* Like many of the OT prophets, Jeremiah describes his call to that office. True prophets were not self-appointed; God raised them up (Deut 18:18). In that way, they followed the pattern of Moses, the archetypal prophet (Deut 18:15), whom God dramatically called to serve him (Exod 3). The call narrative thus authenticates the prophet.
1:1–3 *Historical Setting.* Jeremiah's prophetic ministry occurs in a particular historical context: the southern kingdom of Judah during the reigns of the last several kings before the exile to Babylon in 586 BC. Since his prophetic career begins in "the thirteenth year of the reign of Josiah" (627 BC) and continues until after Jerusalem's destruction, he prophesies for more than 40 years (2 Chr 36:12,21–22).
1:1 The words of Jeremiah. The words of the book are both Jeremiah's and the Lord's (v. 2): the Holy Spirit divinely reveals them (2 Pet 1:21), but they also reflect the experiences and style of the human author. Like Ezekiel and Zechariah, Jeremiah comes from a priestly family, which is significant in his ministry. **Anathoth.** Only a few miles/kilometers from Jerusalem, one of the towns assigned to the priests in Josh 21:18.
1:2–3 Jeremiah's work begins during the reign of Josiah (641/40–609 BC), a reforming king who brings Judah back toward faithfulness to the Lord. It continues during the reigns of Jehoiakim (609–598 BC) and Zedekiah (597–586 BC), as well as the unmentioned Jehoahaz (reigned for three months in 609 BC), and Jehoiachin (reigned for three months in 598–597 BC). All of these later kings, under considerable political pressure from Egypt and Babylon, follow policies that are out of step with the warnings of the prophets whom the Lord sends. The end result of their failed policies is the near total destruction of Jerusalem by the Babylonian king Nebuchadnezzar in 586 BC, just as Jeremiah had warned.
1:4–19 *Call Narrative.* The Lord chooses his messengers carefully and sovereignly. The call is not an invitation but a draft notice: there is no option of refusing to serve, as Jonah discovered (see Jonah 1:1–3; 3:3). The call narrative often highlights a reason the prophet feels unqualified, as with the archetypal prophet Moses (Exod 3:11), but the Lord always overrules the objection with the assurance that he will be with the prophet, empowering them for their task. It also often orients the reader to the nature of the particular ministry to which God has called the prophet.
1:5 knew. More than merely an awareness of who Jeremiah was; the Lord specifically chose Jeremiah for this task before he was even born (see NIV text note). The Hebrew word used here is used in Amos 3:2 to describe the Lord's unique relationship with his people: "You only have I chosen of all the families of the earth." **prophet.** The Lord's ambassador, bringing his words of judgment and consolation for both the present and the future (Deut 18:18–22). Most prophets address Israel and Judah primarily as the Lord's covenant people, often charging them with breaking the terms of the covenant God had made with the Israelites at Mount Sinai (Zech 1:4). But God calls Jeremiah to be a "prophet to the nations," which underlines his broader ministry. God calls him, like some other prophets, to deliver messages of judgment against the nations for their assaults on God's people, confirming that the covenant with Abraham is still intact in spite of Israel's sin and rebellion (chs. 46–51).
1:6–8 Jeremiah objects to his call on the grounds of his youth and inexperience. However, God identifies the real issue: fear (v. 8). If the Lord knew and chose him before he was formed in the womb (v. 5), then he is a better judge of Jeremiah's readiness for ministry than Jeremiah himself. The answer to Jeremiah's fear is to remember that the Lord is with him, even though he will face great conflict and opposition (cf. Ps 46).

say whatever I command you. 8Do not be afraid[j] of them, for I am with you[k] and will rescue you,"
declares the LORD.
9Then the LORD reached out his hand and touched[l] my mouth and said to me, "I have put my words
in your mouth.[m] 10See, today I appoint you over nations and kingdoms to uproot and tear down, to
destroy and overthrow, to build and to plant."[n]
11The word of the LORD came to me: "What do you see, Jeremiah?"[o]
"I see the branch of an almond tree," I replied.
12The LORD said to me, "You have seen correctly, for I am watching[a] to see that my word is fulfilled."
13The word of the LORD came to me again: "What do you see?"[p]
"I see a pot that is boiling," I answered. "It is tilting toward us from the north."
14The LORD said to me, "From the north disaster will be poured out on all who live in the land. 15I
am about to summon all the peoples of the northern kingdoms," declares the LORD.

"Their kings will come and set up their thrones
  in the entrance of the gates of Jerusalem;
they will come against all her surrounding walls
  and against all the towns of Judah.[q]
16I will pronounce my judgments on my people
  because of their wickedness[r] in forsaking me,[s]
in burning incense to other gods[t]
  and in worshiping what their hands have made.

17"Get yourself ready! Stand up and say to them whatever I command you. Do not be terrified[u] by
them, or I will terrify you before them. 18Today I have made you[v] a fortified city, an iron pillar and a
bronze wall to stand against the whole land — against the kings of Judah, its officials, its priests and
the people of the land. 19They will fight against you but will not overcome you, for I am with you[w] and
will rescue[x] you," declares the LORD.

Israel Forsakes God

2 The word of the LORD came to me: 2"Go and proclaim in the hearing of Jerusalem:

"This is what the LORD says:

" 'I remember the devotion of your youth,[y]
  how as a bride you loved me

[a] 12 The Hebrew for *watching* sounds like the Hebrew for *almond tree.*

1:8 [j] Eze 2:6 [k] Jos 1:5; Jer 15:20
1:9 [l] Isa 6:7 [m] Ex 4:12
1:10 [n] Jer 18:7-10; 24:6; 31:4,28
1:11 [o] Jer 24:3; Am 7:8
1:13 [p] Zec 4:2
1:15 [q] Jer 4:16; 9:11
1:16 [r] Dt 28:20 [s] Jer 17:13 [t] Jer 7:9; 19:4
1:17 [u] Eze 2:6
1:18 [v] Isa 50:7
1:19 [w] Jer 20:11 [x] ver 8
2:2 [y] Eze 16:8-14,60; Hos 2:15

1:9 put my words in your mouth. Though the words are Jeremiah's, in a more profound sense they are the Lord's.
1:10 to uproot and tear down, to destroy and overthrow, to build and to plant. Expresses the dual nature of Jeremiah's ministry. Four negatives ("uproot," "tear down," "destroy," "overthrow") describe his declarations of certain judgment to come. If the people do not repent and turn to the Lord, they face certain destruction for their sins. Yet God has good plans for a future and a hope for a remnant of his people who will go into exile in Babylon (29:11). Even in the darkest of days, the prophet's ministry is not purely a word of judgment but illuminates God's purpose for the remnant of his people, whom he will preserve throughout the great tribulation, ultimately rebuilding what he destroys and replanting what he uproots. Jeremiah's words of destruction are not merely for God's sinful and rebellious people but are also for those whom the Lord raises up against them. The Lord will easily defeat Babylon once its usefulness is over.
1:11–14 The Lord shows Jeremiah two visions: a branch of an almond tree and a boiling pot.
1:11 almond tree. One of the first trees to blossom in the spring and therefore a sign of changing seasons. **almond.** The Hebrew (*šāqēd*) sounds like the word for watching (*šōqēd*). The Lord is watching to bring into effect his words of judgment, symbolized by the pot of boiling water about to tip over (v. 13).
1:13–14 from the north ... From the north. The direction from which the judgment will come. Though Babylon is east of Judah as the crow flies, there is a desert between them, which means that invaders from Babylon threaten Judah from the north, as did the Assyrians before them.
1:15 all the ... northern kingdoms. The enemy is coming from the north. The overwhelming scale of the invasion is clear; it is an alliance of which Babylon will be the head.
1:16 in forsaking [the LORD], in burning incense to other gods and in worshiping what their hands have made. This breach of the covenant relationship demands that God apply the covenant curses (cf. Deut 28).
1:17 Get yourself ready! The image used here describes preparing for action by tucking the long, flowing robe worn in those days into a belt to make it easier to run or fight.
1:18 a fortified city, an iron pillar and a bronze wall. Even though Jeremiah will face fierce opposition, he must stand firm like an immovable object.
1:19 I am with you. The decisive factor in the conflict.
2:1—6:30 *Crime and Punishment.* Jeremiah's call is to "uproot and tear down" (1:10) and to warn of coming disaster (1:14–15). This terrible fate

2:2 [z]Dt 2:7
2:3 [a]Dt 7:6 [b]Ex 19:6 [c]Jas 1:18; Rev 14:4 [d]Isa 41:11; Jer 30:16 [e]Jer 50:7
2:5 [f]2Ki 17:15
2:6 [g]Hos 13:4 [h]Dt 8:15 [i]Dt 32:10
2:7 [j]Nu 13:27; Dt 8:7-9; 11:10-12 [k]Ps 106:34-39; Jer 16:18
2:8 [l]Jer 4:22 [m]Jer 23:13 [n]Jer 16:19
2:9 [o]Eze 20:35-36; Mic 6:2

and followed me through the wilderness,[z]
through a land not sown.
3 Israel was holy[a] to the LORD,[b]
the firstfruits[c] of his harvest;
all who devoured[d] her were held guilty,[e]
and disaster overtook them,' "
declares the LORD.

4 Hear the word of the LORD, you descendants of Jacob,
all you clans of Israel.

5 This is what the LORD says:

"What fault did your ancestors find in me,
that they strayed so far from me?
They followed worthless idols
and became worthless[f] themselves.
6 They did not ask, 'Where is the LORD,
who brought us up out of Egypt[g]
and led us through the barren wilderness,
through a land of deserts[h] and ravines,[i]
a land of drought and utter darkness,
a land where no one travels and no one lives?'
7 I brought you into a fertile land
to eat its fruit and rich produce.[j]
But you came and defiled my land
and made my inheritance detestable.[k]
8 The priests did not ask,
'Where is the LORD?'
Those who deal with the law did not know me;[l]
the leaders rebelled against me.
The prophets prophesied by Baal,[m]
following worthless idols.[n]

9 "Therefore I bring charges[o] against you again,"
declares the LORD.
"And I will bring charges against your children's children.

is not a coincidence but the necessary consequence of Israel's covenant unfaithfulness. Under the terms of the covenant made at Sinai, the Lord will bless Israel if they are faithful, but if they are unfaithful, he will curse them (Deut 28). Jeremiah's role is to build a case showing Judah that the reason for the coming disaster is their chronic unfaithfulness, not the power of the Babylonians and their gods (2 Chr 36:15–17).

2:1—3:5 *Israel Forsakes the Lord.* Jeremiah compares Israel's early years, when they were devoted to the Lord and the Lord blessed and protected them, to their subsequent history of rebellion. Of course, Israel's 40 years of wandering in the wilderness were hardly unmarked by sin (cf. Num 12–17), and that reality serves to highlight all the more the intensity of their later unfaithfulness.

2:2 devotion. Faithfulness (Hebrew *ḥesed*). During this honeymoon period in the wilderness, Israel showed devotion and love to her "husband" (3:14; i.e., the Lord), even though her pathway lay through difficult terrain. **bride.** Israel as God's bride is a common image in Scripture, highlighting the expectation of single-hearted devotion to God (Isa 54:5; 62:4–5; Ezek 16:8). The reverse image of Israel as an adulterous and unfaithful wife often describes her attraction to idolatry (see Ezek 6:9; 16:32; see also Hos 1:2 and note).

2:3 holy. Set apart (see Introduction to Leviticus: Major Theological Themes [Holiness and Purity]; see also "Holiness," p. 2676). Israel is uniquely set apart to the Lord, as precious to him as the "firstfruits of his harvest." He therefore protects her against her enemies.

2:5 worthless … worthless. Instead of being holy (see note on v. 3), Israel's ancestors abandoned the Lord to pursue worthless idols, and they themselves became as worthless as the idols they worshiped.

2:7 fertile land. The promised land. **detestable.** By worshiping idols, they defiled the holy land God gave them.

2:8 priests … leaders … prophets. The leaders, including the religious leaders (the "priests" and "prophets"), who should have called them to faithfulness, were unfaithful. **priests.** Their primary ministry was to teach the law (Deut 33:10). **leaders.** Political leaders. **prophets.** They were to declare the word of the Lord, but instead they even prophesied by Baal, the Canaanite fertility god. This was especially prominent in the time of King Ahab, whom Elijah confronted at Mount Carmel (see 1 Kgs 16:29—18:46).

2:9–13 Israel's faithlessness was utterly irrational. No other nation in antiquity so easily abandoned their gods, even though their gods were merely worthless idols.

10 Cross over to the coasts of Cyprus and look,
send to Kedar[a] and observe closely;
see if there has ever been anything like this:
11 Has a nation ever changed its gods?
(Yet they are not gods[p] at all.)
But my people have exchanged their glorious[q] God
for worthless idols.
12 Be appalled at this, you heavens,
and shudder with great horror,"
declares the LORD.

13 "My people have committed two sins:
They have forsaken me,
the spring of living water,[r]
and have dug their own cisterns,
broken cisterns that cannot hold water.
14 Is Israel a servant, a slave[s] by birth?
Why then has he become plunder?
15 Lions[t] have roared;
they have growled at him.
They have laid waste[u] his land;
his towns are burned and deserted.
16 Also, the men of Memphis[v] and Tahpanhes[w]
have cracked your skull.
17 Have you not brought this on yourselves[x]
by forsaking the LORD your God
when he led you in the way?
18 Now why go to Egypt[y]
to drink water from the Nile[b]?[z]
And why go to Assyria
to drink water from the Euphrates?
19 Your wickedness will punish you;
your backsliding[a] will rebuke[b] you.
Consider then and realize
how evil and bitter[c] it is for you
when you forsake the LORD your God
and have no awe[d] of me,"
declares the Lord, the LORD Almighty.

20 "Long ago you broke off your yoke[e]
and tore off your bonds;
you said, 'I will not serve you!'

2:11 [p] Isa 37:19; Jer 16:20 [q] Ps 106:20; Ro 1:23
2:13 [r] Ps 36:9; Jn 4:14
2:14 [s] Ex 4:22
2:15 [t] Jer 4:7; 50:17 [u] Isa 1:7
2:16 [v] Isa 19:13 [w] Jer 43:7-9
2:17 [x] Jer 4:18
2:18 [y] Isa 30:2 [z] Jos 13:3
2:19 [a] Jer 3:11,22 [b] Isa 3:9; Hos 5:5 [c] Job 20:14; Am 8:10 [d] Ps 36:1
2:20 [e] Lev 26:13

[a] *10* In the Syro-Arabian desert [b] *18* Hebrew *Shibor*; that is, a branch of the Nile

2:10 Cyprus. An island west of Israel. **Kedar.** A land of desert dwellings to the east of Israel. The people in these lands remained faithful to their gods, while Israel alone rebelled (v. 11).
2:12 The Lord calls the "heavens" as a witness of this covenant breaking since they witnessed the original covenant making (Deut 30:19; 31:28).
2:13 forsaken me, the ... living water ... dug their own cisterns. In abandoning the Lord, Israel abandoned the source of "living" (i.e., running) water in favor of stagnant "cisterns" that could not even hold the water that was put in them. In other words, they exchanged the source of true life and peace for empty and deceptive promises, which is all that idols can give (see Isa 44:9–20).
2:14 Is Israel a servant ... by birth? This rhetorical question expects a negative answer. Jeremiah has already declared that Israel is the Lord's bride, not a slave (see v. 2 and note). So why are foreign nations attacking and plundering Israel like roaring "lions" (v. 15)?
2:16 Memphis ... Tahpanhes. Leading cities in Egypt, which along with Assyria, were a constant threat to the peace and existence of Israel.
2:18 why ... drink water from the Nile? ... from the Euphrates? Instead of trusting in the Lord, Israel's diplomatic policy has been to seek an alliance with either Egypt (whose national river is the Nile) or Assyria (whose national river is the Euphrates), whichever of these is not currently a threat.
2:19 when you forsake the LORD. By seeking help from Egypt or Assyria, nations that never deliver the help they promise (v. 13; cf. Ezek 29:6–7).
2:20 Israel's servitude to Egypt and Assyria was the result of rejecting

2:20 [f] Isa 57:7; Jer 17:2 [g] Dt 12:2
2:21 [h] Ex 15:17 [i] Ps 80:8 [j] Isa 5:4
2:23 [k] Pr 30:12 [l] Jer 9:14 [m] Jer 7:31 [n] ver 33; Jer 31:22
2:24 [o] Jer 14:6
2:25 [p] Dt 32:16; Jer 3:13; 14:10
2:26 [q] Jer 48:27
2:27 [r] Jer 3:9 [s] Jer 18:17; 32:33 [t] Jdg 10:10; Isa 26:16
2:28 [u] Isa 45:20 [v] Dt 32:37 [w] 2Ki 17:29; Jer 11:13

Indeed, on every high hill[f]
and under every spreading tree[g]
you lay down as a prostitute.
21 I had planted[h] you like a choice vine[i]
of sound and reliable stock.
How then did you turn against me
into a corrupt,[j] wild vine?
22 Although you wash yourself with soap
and use an abundance of cleansing powder,
the stain of your guilt is still before me,"
declares the Sovereign LORD.
23 "How can you say, 'I am not defiled;[k]
I have not run after the Baals'?[l]
See how you behaved in the valley;[m]
consider what you have done.
You are a swift she-camel
running[n] here and there,
24 a wild donkey[o] accustomed to the desert,
sniffing the wind in her craving—
in her heat who can restrain her?
Any males that pursue her need not tire themselves;
at mating time they will find her.
25 Do not run until your feet are bare
and your throat is dry.
But you said, 'It's no use!
I love foreign gods,[p]
and I must go after them.'
26 "As a thief is disgraced[q] when he is caught,
so the people of Israel are disgraced—
they, their kings and their officials,
their priests and their prophets.
27 They say to wood, 'You are my father,'
and to stone,[r] 'You gave me birth.'
They have turned their backs to me
and not their faces;[s]
yet when they are in trouble,[t] they say,
'Come and save us!'
28 Where then are the gods[u] you made for yourselves?
Let them come if they can save you
when you are in trouble![v]
For you, Judah, have as many gods
as you have towns.[w]

submission to the Lord. Like the Gentile nations in Ps 2, Israel sought to tear off the Lord's "bonds." **high hill ... spreading tree.** Locations of pagan fertility cults (Deut 12:2). **prostitute.** Instead of being a pure bride (see v. 2 and note), Israel committed adultery (i.e., worshiped idols).

2:21 choice vine. An image for Israel that links with Isa 5, where it similarly shows the completeness of the Lord's care for his people as the divine gardener and their unfaithful response. Ultimately, God provides the true vine in Jesus Christ, who is himself the new Israel who responds faithfully to his Father's calling (see John 15:1–17 and note; see also note on John 15:1).

2:22 soap ... cleansing powder. There were various kinds available in the ancient world. They were made from vegetable and mineral alkalis.

2:23–24 she-camel ... wild donkey. In order to cut through Israel's denial (see note on v. 23), Jeremiah uses graphic imagery to describe Israel's sins (cf. Ezek 16; 23) of spiritual adultery. These images represent unrestrained pursuit of passion. Far from needing to be seduced and bought, Israel desperately pursued her foreign lovers at her own cost.

2:23 I am not defiled. The Israelites deny their sins. Until they recognize and confess their sins, they will remain guilty, even if they perform ritual acts of cleansing (v. 22).

2:27 wood ... stone. Canaanite deities were often depicted in their sanctuaries by a wooden pole or tree representing Asherah and a stone representing Baal.

[29]"Why do you bring charges against me?
You have all[x] rebelled against me,"
declares the LORD.
[30]"In vain I punished your people;
they did not respond to correction.
Your sword has devoured your prophets[y]
like a ravenous lion.

[31]"You of this generation, consider the word of the LORD:

"Have I been a desert to Israel
or a land of great darkness?[z]
Why do my people say, 'We are free to roam;
we will come to you no more'?
[32]Does a young woman forget her jewelry,
a bride her wedding ornaments?
Yet my people have forgotten me,
days without number.
[33]How skilled you are at pursuing love!
Even the worst of women can learn from your ways.
[34]On your clothes is found
the lifeblood[a] of the innocent poor,
though you did not catch them breaking in.[b]
Yet in spite of all this
[35] you say, 'I am innocent;
he is not angry with me.'
But I will pass judgment[c] on you
because you say, 'I have not sinned.'[d]
[36]Why do you go about so much,
changing[e] your ways?
You will be disappointed by Egypt[f]
as you were by Assyria.
[37]You will also leave that place
with your hands on your head,[g]
for the LORD has rejected those you trust;
you will not be helped[h] by them.

3 "If a man divorces[i] his wife
and she leaves him and marries another man,
should he return to her again?
Would not the land be completely defiled?
But you have lived as a prostitute with many lovers[j]—
would you now return to me?"
declares the LORD.

2:29 [x]Jer 5:1; 6:13; Da 9:11
2:30 [y]Ne 9:26; Ac 7:52; 1Th 2:15
2:31 [z]Isa 45:19
2:34 [a]2Ki 21:16 [b]Ex 22:2
2:35 [c]Jer 25:31 [d]1Jn 1:8,10
2:36 [e]Jer 31:22 [f]Isa 30:2,3,7
2:37 [g]2Sa 13:19 [h]Jer 37:7
3:1 [i]Dt 24:1-4 [j]Jer 2:20, 25; Eze 16:26,29

2:29 bring charges. Since false deities are powerless to act, in time of trouble the Israelites still seek help from the Lord but not in a spirit of repentance. The Lord has not been the unfaithful one; they have rebelled against him, forgetting their own husband (v. 32; see v. 2 and note).
2:34 On your clothes ... lifeblood of the innocent poor. Their abandonment of God is revealed not only by their idolatry but also by their abuse of the poor. Their clothing is stained with the blood of the poor, who committed no offense against them. **did not catch them breaking in.** The law declares that killing a thief in the act of entering a house does not constitute murder (Exod 22:2); however, Israel has shed the blood of the poor even though they did not catch them breaking in.
2:35 pass judgment. The Lord is bringing charges against them (v. 9), for which he will certainly pass judgment on them.
2:36 disappointed by Egypt ... Assyria. Alliance with Egypt will no more help the Judahites resist the coming Babylonians than alliance with Assyria helped them resist the Egyptians in the days of Josiah (2 Kgs 23:29). Trusting these nations is as futile as trusting idols of wood and stone: the people will leave their land as captives.
2:37 with your hands on your head. A posture of prisoners of war.
3:1 The law forbids a man from remarrying his divorced wife after she

3:2 [k]Ge 38:14; Eze 16:25 [l]Jer 2:7
3:3 [m]Lev 26:19 [n]Jer 14:4 [o]Jer 6:15; 8:12; Zep 3:5
3:4 [p]ver 19 [q]Jer 2:2
3:5 [r]Ps 103:9; Isa 57:16
3:6 [s]Jer 17:2 [t]Jer 2:20
3:7 [u]Eze 16:46
3:8 [v]Eze 16:47; 23:11
3:9 [w]ver 2 [x]Isa 57:6 [y]Jer 2:27
3:10 [z]Jer 12:2
3:11 [a]Eze 16:52; 23:11 [b]ver 7
3:12 [c]2Ki 17:3-6 [d]ver 14; Jer 31:21,22; Eze 33:11 [e]Ps 86:15
3:13 [f]Dt 30:1-3; Jer 14:20; 1Jn 1:9

2 "Look up to the barren heights and see.
Is there any place where you have not been ravished?
By the roadside[k] you sat waiting for lovers,
sat like a nomad in the desert.
You have defiled the land[l]
with your prostitution and wickedness.
3 Therefore the showers have been withheld,[m]
and no spring rains[n] have fallen.
Yet you have the brazen look of a prostitute;
you refuse to blush with shame.[o]
4 Have you not just called to me:
'My Father,[p] my friend from my youth,[q]
5 will you always be angry?[r]
Will your wrath continue forever?'
This is how you talk,
but you do all the evil you can."

Unfaithful Israel

6 During the reign of King Josiah, the LORD said to me, "Have you seen what faithless Israel has done?
She has gone up on every high hill and under every spreading tree[s] and has committed adultery[t] there.
7 I thought that after she had done all this she would return to me but she did not, and her unfaithful
sister[u] Judah saw it. 8 I gave faithless Israel her certificate of divorce and sent her away because of all
her adulteries. Yet I saw that her unfaithful sister Judah had no fear;[v] she also went out and committed
adultery. 9 Because Israel's immorality mattered so little to her, she defiled the land[w] and committed
adultery with stone[x] and wood.[y] 10 In spite of all this, her unfaithful sister Judah did not return to me
with all her heart, but only in pretense,[z]" declares the LORD.
11 The LORD said to me, "Faithless Israel is more righteous[a] than unfaithful[b] Judah. 12 Go, proclaim
this message toward the north:[c]

" 'Return,[d] faithless Israel,' declares the LORD,
'I will frown on you no longer,
for I am faithful,' declares the LORD,
'I will not be angry[e] forever.
13 Only acknowledge[f] your guilt—
you have rebelled against the LORD your God,

has married another man (Deut 24:1–4). Could Israel then casually live a prostitute's life with so many men and then simply return to the Lord whenever she wished, as if nothing had happened?

3:2 By the roadside. Where prostitutes waited for clients (Gen 38:14).

3:3 showers … withheld, and no spring rains. The covenant curses have befallen Israel: the seasonal rainfalls on which their harvests depend have been withheld, as Deut 11:16–17 warns.

3:4 called to me. Israel thinks that all they have to do is call out the Lord's name and everything will be forgotten. Genuine repentance is necessary, not merely saying the right words (cf. Hos 6:6).

3:6—4:4 *Unfaithful Israel.* Thus far, the prophet has addressed Israel as a single entity. However, long before Jeremiah's time, the country had broken up into two distinct kingdoms, the northern kingdom of Israel and the southern kingdom of Judah. Because the northern kingdom rebelled against God, the Assyrians subjugated it in 722 BC and dispersed its population. In this section, Jeremiah distinguishes between the former northern kingdom and the southern kingdom, in which he lives.

3:6 faithless Israel. The northern kingdom committed spiritual adultery with idols "on every high hill and under every spreading tree" (see also 2:20 and note).

3:8 certificate of divorce … sent her away. Because of Israel's spiritual adultery, the Lord gave them a "certificate of divorce" and sent them away (Deut 24:1); this refers to the northern kingdom's destruction and the exile of its people in 722 BC. **Judah had no fear.** The Lord's judgment of the northern kingdom of Israel should have acted as a warning to the southern kingdom of Judah, but Judah did the same thing as Israel.

3:10 did not return … with all her heart. Even when Judah seemed to repent (e.g., the reforms of Hezekiah [2 Kgs 18] and Josiah [2 Kgs 23]), there was no true heart change, as evidenced by how quickly the people returned to their idolatry after the death of the reforming king.

3:12 faithless … faithful. There is hope for the remnant of the scattered northern tribes of Israel. Even though they had been faithless, the Lord remains faithful.

3:13 If Judah will "acknowledge [their] guilt," they will be forgiven and received back. There is an implicit message here for the inhabitants of "unfaithful Judah" (v. 11), who are still pretending not to need forgiveness (see 2:23 and note). They too can trust the Lord's faithfulness to forgive, if only they return with all their hearts. Yet to fail to repent, even after seeing what happened to Israel, will prove that Judah is even more corrupt than her sister (v. 11).

you have scattered your favors to foreign gods[g]
under every spreading tree,[h]
and have not obeyed[i] me,' "
declares the LORD.

14"Return,[j] faithless people," declares the LORD, "for I am your husband. I will choose you — one
from a town and two from a clan — and bring you to Zion. 15Then I will give you shepherds[k] after
my own heart, who will lead you with knowledge and understanding. 16In those days, when your
numbers have increased greatly in the land," declares the LORD, "people will no longer say, 'The ark
of the covenant of the LORD.' It will never enter their minds or be remembered;[l] it will not be missed,
nor will another one be made. 17At that time they will call Jerusalem The Throne[m] of the LORD, and
all nations will gather in Jerusalem to honor[n] the name of the LORD. No longer will they follow the
stubbornness of their evil hearts.[o] 18In those days the people of Judah will join the people of Israel,[p]
and together[q] they will come from a northern[r] land to the land[s] I gave your ancestors as an
inheritance.

19"I myself said,

" 'How gladly would I treat you like my children
and give you a pleasant land,
the most beautiful inheritance of any nation.'
I thought you would call me 'Father'[t]
and not turn away from following me.
20But like a woman unfaithful to her husband,
so you, Israel, have been unfaithful to me,"
declares the LORD.

21A cry is heard on the barren heights,[u]
the weeping and pleading of the people of Israel,
because they have perverted their ways
and have forgotten the LORD their God.

22"Return,[v] faithless people;
I will cure[w] you of backsliding."

"Yes, we will come to you,
for you are the LORD our God.
23Surely the idolatrous commotion on the hills
and mountains is a deception;
surely in the LORD our God
is the salvation[x] of Israel.
24From our youth shameful[y] gods have consumed
the fruits of our ancestors' labor —

3:13 [g] Jer 2:25 [h] Dt 12:2 [i] ver 25
3:14 [j] Hos 2:19
3:15 [k] Ac 20:28
3:16 [l] Isa 65:17
3:17 [m] Jer 17:12; Eze 43:7 [n] Isa 60:9 [o] Jer 11:8
3:18 [p] Hos 1:11 [q] Isa 11:13; Jer 50:4 [r] Jer 16:15; 31:8 [s] Am 9:15
3:19 [t] ver 4; Isa 63:16
3:21 [u] ver 2
3:22 [v] Hos 14:4 [w] Jer 33:6; Hos 6:1
3:23 [x] Ps 3:8; Jer 17:14
3:24 [y] Hos 9:10

3:14 I am your husband. Even though the Lord gave the northern kingdom of Israel a certificate of divorce and sent her inhabitants away (v. 8), he remains her husband. He will sovereignly gather a small remnant from the north — "one from a town and two from a clan" — and bring them to Zion, the spiritual center of Judah and the home of the temple. **3:15 shepherds.** Translated "leaders" in 2:8. In place of their rebellious leaders, God will give them "shepherds after [his] own heart," like David, Israel's greatest king (1 Sam 13:14; cf. Ezek 34:23–24). **3:16** The Lord's presence will be so tangible that people will no longer remember its former representation: the ark of the covenant. **nor will another one be made.** Suggests that the original ark no longer existed in Jeremiah's time. Yet the absence of the ark of the covenant, regarded as the divine footstool (1 Chr 28:2), will not prevent Jerusalem from being "The Throne of the LORD" (v. 17), the place from which he exercises his dominion over the nations.

3:18 God will purify (see 31:33) and reunite the former northern and southern kingdoms, fulfilling the promises he made to Abraham in Gen 12:2–3. This anticipates the gathering of Jews and Samaritans, together with the Gentiles, into the church (Acts 1:8; 8:1b–17) and ultimately into the new Jerusalem (Heb 12:22–24; Rev 21:24–26). **3:19–20** The Lord gave them a "pleasant land," expecting them to respond to his kindness with favor (cf. Ps 106:24; Zech 7:14); however, they rejected him not only as their husband but also as their father. **3:22 Return.** If the people of Israel will turn their backs on the "idolatrous commotion" (v. 23) of the pagan rituals in favor of the "weeping and pleading" of true repentance (v. 21), acknowledging the Lord as their God and their salvation, confessing their sin and its shameful consequences, then the Lord will "cure [them] of backsliding." See also 4:1–4. Yet these words express an attitude that Israel does not feel.

3:25 [z] Ezr 9:6 [a] Jer 22:21
4:1 [b] Jer 3:1,22; Joel 2:12 [c] Jer 35:15
4:2 [d] Dt 10:20; Isa 65:16 [e] Jer 12:16 [f] Ge 22:18; Gal 3:8
4:3 [g] Hos 10:12 [h] Mk 4:18
4:4 [i] Dt 10:16; Jer 9:26; Ro 2:28-29 [j] Zep 2:2 [k] Am 5:6
4:5 [l] Jos 10:20; Jer 8:14
4:6 [m] Jer 1:13-15; 50:3

their flocks and herds,
  their sons and daughters.
25 Let us lie down in our shame,[z]
  and let our disgrace cover us.
We have sinned against the LORD our God,
  both we and our ancestors;
from our youth[a] till this day
  we have not obeyed the LORD our God."

4

"If you, Israel, will return,[b]
  then return to me,"
declares the LORD.
"If you put your detestable idols[c] out of my sight
  and no longer go astray,
2 and if in a truthful, just and righteous way
  you swear,[d] 'As surely as the LORD lives,'[e]
then the nations will invoke blessings[f] by him
  and in him they will boast."

3 This is what the LORD says to the people of Judah and to Jerusalem:

"Break up your unplowed ground[g]
  and do not sow among thorns.[h]
4 Circumcise yourselves to the LORD,
  circumcise your hearts,[i]
  you people of Judah and inhabitants of Jerusalem,
or my wrath[j] will flare up and burn like fire
  because of the evil you have done—
  burn with no one to quench[k] it.

Disaster From the North

5 "Announce in Judah and proclaim in Jerusalem and say:
  'Sound the trumpet throughout the land!'
Cry aloud and say:
  'Gather together!
  Let us flee to the fortified cities!'[l]
6 Raise the signal to go to Zion!
  Flee for safety without delay!
For I am bringing disaster from the north,[m]
  even terrible destruction."

4:1–4 True repentance—for both Israel (vv. 1–2) and Judah (vv. 3–4)—is more than simply lamenting the consequences of sin.
4:2 As surely as the LORD lives. Such an oath acknowledges the Lord as the sole deity. Such oaths had to be made "in a truthful, just and righteous way" and be backed up by faithful behavior to God and to one's fellow human beings. Such repentance will lead to "blessings" not merely for Israel but for the nations as well, for when Israel is what she is supposed to be, the nations will find blessings in God, just as God promised Abraham (Gen 12:1–3; Isa 49:6). This is true not just for the northern kingdom but for Judah as well.
4:3 Break up your unplowed ground. The people need to reclaim and restore spiritual "ground" that they had left fallow and unfruitful, abandoned to the thorns.
4:4 circumcise your hearts. Externally, they may have been circumcised—marked out as belonging distinctively to the Lord as a holy nation, as God commanded Abraham (Gen 17:10–14). But they need to match that external mark of the covenant with internal commitment to the Lord, as Deut 10:16 commands. Failure to keep the terms of the covenant in this way will lead to certain judgment, as the prophetess Huldah warned Josiah when they rediscovered the Book of the Law in the temple (2 Kgs 22:17).
4:5–31 *Disaster From the North.* After the passionate plea for the people to repent, which apparently falls on deaf ears, the prophet comprehensively announces judgment on Judah and its capital city, Jerusalem.
4:5–6 Sound the trumpet ... Raise the signal. When danger approached in ancient times, the watchman would sound the trumpet (more precisely, the ram's horn) and raise a signal to warn everyone to flee to the safety of the walled cities. This image became a symbol for the work of the prophet (Ezek 3:16–21).
4:6 The danger comes "from the north," the direction from which Assyrian armies came and from which Babylonian armies will come.

[7]A lion[n] has come out of his lair;
a destroyer of nations has set out.
He has left his place
to lay waste[o] your land.
Your towns will lie in ruins[p]
without inhabitant.
[8]So put on sackcloth,[q]
lament and wail,
for the fierce anger[r] of the LORD
has not turned away from us.

[9]"In that day," declares the LORD,
"the king and the officials will lose heart,
the priests will be horrified,
and the prophets will be appalled."[s]

[10]Then I said, "Alas, Sovereign LORD! How completely you have deceived[t] this people and Jerusalem
by saying, 'You will have peace,'[u] when the sword is at our throats!"
[11]At that time this people and Jerusalem will be told, "A scorching wind[v] from the barren heights in
the desert blows toward my people, but not to winnow or cleanse; [12]a wind too strong for that comes
from me. Now I pronounce my judgments[w] against them."

[13]Look! He advances like the clouds,[x]
his chariots[y] come like a whirlwind,[z]
his horses are swifter than eagles.[a]
Woe to us! We are ruined!
[14]Jerusalem, wash[b] the evil from your heart and be saved.
How long will you harbor wicked thoughts?
[15]A voice is announcing from Dan,[c]
proclaiming disaster from the hills of Ephraim.
[16]"Tell this to the nations,
proclaim concerning Jerusalem:
'A besieging army is coming from a distant land,
raising a war cry[d] against the cities of Judah.
[17]They surround[e] her like men guarding a field,
because she has rebelled[f] against me,' "
declares the LORD.

4:7 [n]2Ki 24:1; Jer 2:15 [o]Isa 1:7 [p]Jer 25:9
4:8 [q]Isa 22:12; Jer 6:26 [r]Jer 30:24
4:9 [s]Isa 29:9
4:10 [t]2Th 2:11 [u]Jer 14:13
4:11 [v]Eze 17:10; Hos 13:15
4:12 [w]Jer 1:16
4:13 [x]Isa 19:1 [y]Isa 66:15 [z]Isa 5:28 [a]Dt 28:49; Hab 1:8
4:14 [b]Jas 4:8
4:15 [c]Jer 8:16
4:16 [d]Eze 21:22
4:17 [e]2Ki 25:1,4 [f]Jer 5:23

4:7 lion. Judah's enemy is seeking its prey (2:15) and will totally devastate the land, depopulating and destroying the towns. **destroyer.** Frequently alludes to Babylon in the book of Jeremiah (6:26; 15:8; 48:8,32), though in ch. 51 it refers to the similar role that Persia and its allies will play against Babylon (51:1,48,53,56).
4:8 sackcloth. A traditional Near Eastern cultural symbol of mourning (see note on 1 Kgs 20:31). Such a comprehensive disaster will lead everyone in Judah to mourn. **the fierce anger of the LORD.** The coming assault is not merely the result of the Babylonians' expansionist policies; the Lord's judgment lies behind the brutality of the human agents.
4:9 king ... officials ... priests ... prophets. All of the leaders of the people, both religious and political (as in 2:26), will be powerless and terrified in the face of the onslaught.
4:10 you have deceived this people. The people refuse to repent (and thus the impending disaster comes upon Jerusalem and Judah) because they remain attached to the words of the false prophets who insist they will have "peace" when there is no peace to find (see 6:13–14). Yet Jeremiah recognizes that this false prophecy is itself a fitting judgment that the Lord sends on people who reject the truth (cf. 1 Kgs 22:22–23; Ezek 14:9). Since Judah has rejected the Lord's message and killed the true prophets he sent (2:30), he will turn the people over to believe the deceitful lies of the false prophets.
4:11 scorching wind. In Israel, hot, dry winds blow from the eastern desert at certain times of the year, drying up everything in their path. **winnow.** Separate the heavy grain from the lighter chaff, which the wind disperses. The Lord's judgment will be like such a hot wind—not purifying the people (by winnowing), but destroying them.
4:13 He ... his ... his. The identity of the destroying army is left blank, perhaps because they are a mere tool in the Lord's hands. **chariots ... like a whirlwind.** Similar to how Isa 5:28 describes the Assyrian army. **Woe.** Prophetically declares God's judgment, which Jeremiah pronounces on himself as well as his contemporaries. **We.** Jeremiah both identifies with his suffering people and represents the Lord, who is judging them (v. 8; cf. Isa 6:5).
4:15 Dan ... hills of Ephraim. The northern outposts of Israel. Since the invading army will come from the north (v. 6), the first glimpse of their arrival will be from there.

4:18 [g]Ps 107:17; Isa 50:1 [h]Jer 2:17 [i]Jer 2:19
4:19 [j]Isa 16:11; 22:4; Jer 9:10 [k]Jer 20:9 [l]Nu 10:9
4:20 [m]Ps 42:7; Eze 7:26 [n]Jer 10:20
4:22 [o]Jer 10:8 [p]Jer 2:8 [q]Jer 13:23; 1Co 14:20 [r]Ro 16:19
4:23 [s]Ge 1:2
4:24 [t]Isa 5:25; Eze 38:20
4:25 [u]Jer 9:10; 12:4; Zep 1:3
4:27 [v]Jer 5:10,18; 12:12; 30:11; 46:28
4:28 [w]Jer 12:4,11; 14:2; Hos 4:3 [x]Isa 5:30; 50:3 [y]Nu 23:19 [z]Jer 23:20; 30:24

18 "Your own conduct and actions[g]
have brought this on you.[h]
This is your punishment.
How bitter[i] it is!
How it pierces to the heart!"

19 Oh, my anguish, my anguish![j]
I writhe in pain.
Oh, the agony of my heart!
My heart pounds within me,
I cannot keep silent.[k]
For I have heard the sound of the trumpet;
I have heard the battle cry.[l]
20 Disaster follows disaster;[m]
the whole land lies in ruins.
In an instant my tents[n] are destroyed,
my shelter in a moment.
21 How long must I see the battle standard
and hear the sound of the trumpet?

22 "My people are fools;[o]
they do not know me.[p]
They are senseless children;
they have no understanding.
They are skilled in doing evil;[q]
they know not how to do good."[r]

23 I looked at the earth,
and it was formless and empty;[s]
and at the heavens,
and their light was gone.
24 I looked at the mountains,
and they were quaking;[t]
all the hills were swaying.
25 I looked, and there were no people;
every bird in the sky had flown away.[u]
26 I looked, and the fruitful land was a desert;
all its towns lay in ruins
before the LORD, before his fierce anger.

27 This is what the LORD says:

"The whole land will be ruined,
though I will not destroy[v] it completely.
28 Therefore the earth will mourn[w]
and the heavens above grow dark,[x]
because I have spoken and will not relent,[y]
I have decided and will not turn back.[z]"

4:18–19 the heart! . . . my heart! The judgment will be comprehensive, reaching even the heart, the seat of thinking and feeling. Yet it is the heart of the prophet himself that first registers the pain of the coming judgment, causing him agony.

4:22 Since "the fear of the LORD is the beginning of knowledge" (Prov 1:7), those who reject the Lord have become "fools," implying moral deficiency as much as intellectual weakness (see note on Prov 1:7). Having abandoned their father (3:19), they are "children" who are turned loose to express the full extent of their depravity.

4:23 formless and empty. Hebrew *tōhû wābōhû* (see Gen 1:2 and note). The coming judgment on Judah will be so great that it will be as if the entire universe has been returned to a state of barren uncreation, a formless and uninhabited wilderness, without light or human occupants to cultivate it. Other than here, this Hebrew phrase occurs only in Gen 1:2, before the creation of light or humans. In other words, the destruction will make the land as if Gen 1 had never happened.

4:27 I will not destroy it completely. In the midst of the devastation, there is a tiny glimmer of hope. The Lord will preserve a remnant.

[29] At the sound of horsemen and archers[a]
every town takes to flight.[b]
Some go into the thickets;
some climb up among the rocks.
All the towns are deserted;[c]
no one lives in them.

[30] What are you doing,[d] you devastated one?
Why dress yourself in scarlet
and put on jewels[e] of gold?
Why highlight your eyes with makeup?[f]
You adorn yourself in vain.
Your lovers[g] despise you;
they want to kill you.

[31] I hear a cry as of a woman in labor,[h]
a groan as of one bearing her first child—
the cry of Daughter Zion gasping for breath,[i]
stretching out her hands[j] and saying,
"Alas! I am fainting;
my life is given over to murderers."

Not One Is Upright

5 "Go up and down[k] the streets of Jerusalem,
look around and consider,
search through her squares.
If you can find but one person[l]
who deals honestly and seeks the truth,
I will forgive[m] this city.
[2] Although they say, 'As surely as the LORD lives,'[n]
still they are swearing falsely."

[3] LORD, do not your eyes[o] look for truth?
You struck[p] them, but they felt no pain;
you crushed them, but they refused correction.[q]
They made their faces harder than stone[r]
and refused to repent.
[4] I thought, "These are only the poor;
they are foolish,
for they do not know[s] the way of the LORD,
the requirements of their God.
[5] So I will go to the leaders[t]
and speak to them;
surely they know the way of the LORD,
the requirements of their God."

4:29 [a] Jer 6:23 [b] 2Ki 25:4 [c] ver 7
4:30 [d] Isa 10:3-4 [e] Eze 23:40 [f] 2Ki 9:30 [g] La 1:2; Eze 23:9,22
4:31 [h] Jer 13:21 [i] Isa 42:14 [j] Isa 1:15; La 1:17
5:1 [k] 2Ch 16:9; Eze 22:30 [l] Ge 18:32 [m] Ge 18:24
5:2 [n] Jer 4:2
5:3 [o] 2Ch 16:9 [p] Isa 9:13 [q] Jer 2:30; Zep 3:2 [r] Jer 7:26; 19:15; Eze 3:8-9
5:4 [s] Jer 8:7
5:5 [t] Mic 3:1,9

4:30 scarlet … gold. Instead of repenting and dressing in sackcloth (see v. 8 and note), Jerusalem responds by putting on her finery in a last appeal to her former "lovers," Assyria and Egypt. She seeks political solutions that involve fruitlessly trusting in human help rather than the Lord. **4:31** The metaphor shifts from a prostitute (v. 30) to a "woman in labor," gasping and panting in intense pain. **Daughter Zion.** Zion herself is the daughter in question (some translations render this "daughter of Zion"). **Zion.** Another name for Jerusalem.
5:1–31 *Not One Is Upright.* The challenge to find "one person who deals honestly" (v. 1) echoes Abraham's challenge to God over Sodom (Gen 18:20–33). For Sodom, a minimum number of ten righteous people would have saved the city. On this occasion, God offers to spare Jerusalem if a single righteous person can be brought forth, but not even one can be found.
5:2 they say, 'As surely as the LORD lives.' The people take oaths in the Lord's name but perjure themselves.
5:4 only the poor. If only the uneducated poor were sinning like this, it might be blamed on a lack of education. But a settled attitude of rebellion pervades every class.
5:5 broken off the yoke and torn off the bonds. They have rejected the Lord's requirements as a burdensome "yoke" and restrictive "bonds" that must be removed as soon as possible (see 2:20).

5:5 [u]Ps 2:3; Jer 2:20
5:6 [v]Hos 13:7 [w]Jer 30:14
5:7 [x]Jos 23:7; Zep 1:5 [y]Dt 32:21; Jer 2:11; Gal 4:8 [z]Nu 25:1
5:8 [a]Jer 29:23; Eze 22:11
5:9 [b]ver 29; Jer 9:9
5:10 [c]Jer 4:27
5:11 [d]Jer 3:20
5:12 [e]Jer 23:17 [f]2Ch 36:16; Jer 14:13
5:13 [g]Jer 14:15
5:14 [h]Jer 1:9; Hos 6:5 [i]Jer 23:29
5:15 [j]Dt 28:49; Isa 5:26; Jer 4:16 [k]Isa 28:11

But with one accord they too had broken off the yoke
and torn off the bonds.[u]
6 Therefore a lion from the forest will attack them,
a wolf from the desert will ravage them,
a leopard[v] will lie in wait near their towns
to tear to pieces any who venture out,
for their rebellion is great
and their backslidings many.[w]

7 "Why should I forgive you?
Your children have forsaken me
and sworn[x] by gods that are not gods.[y]
I supplied all their needs,
yet they committed adultery[z]
and thronged to the houses of prostitutes.
8 They are well-fed, lusty stallions,
each neighing for another man's wife.[a]
9 Should I not punish them for this?"[b]
declares the LORD.
"Should I not avenge myself
on such a nation as this?

10 "Go through her vineyards and ravage them,
but do not destroy them completely.[c]
Strip off her branches,
for these people do not belong to the LORD.
11 The people of Israel and the people of Judah
have been utterly unfaithful[d] to me,"
declares the LORD.

12 They have lied about the LORD;
they said, "He will do nothing!
No harm will come to us;[e]
we will never see sword or famine.[f]
13 The prophets[g] are but wind
and the word is not in them;
so let what they say be done to them."

14 Therefore this is what the LORD God Almighty says:

"Because the people have spoken these words,
I will make my words in your mouth[h] a fire[i]
and these people the wood it consumes.
15 People of Israel," declares the LORD,
"I am bringing a distant nation[j] against you —
an ancient and enduring nation,
a people whose language[k] you do not know,
whose speech you do not understand.

5:6 a lion ... a wolf ... a leopard. The result of their rebellion will be comprehensive destruction. Who can escape from such a fearsome trio?
5:8 well-fed, lusty stallions. Various fertility cults ("houses of prostitutes," v. 7) are central in Jeremiah's indictment, leading to Judah disregarding the commandments against adultery and coveting their neighbor's wife.
5:9–10 The Lord must punish them for rejecting the terms of the covenant, yet he will still not destroy them completely.
5:13 wind. Hebrew *rûaḥ* may be translated as both "Spirit" and "wind." The people mock the words of the prophet with a pun: instead of being words of the Spirit, they are merely empty "wind."
5:14 The people mistake the Lord's patience and forbearance as inactivity or indifference (v. 12; cf. Ezek 12:22). But when the Lord acts, he will vindicate the prophet's words.

16 Their quivers are like an open grave;
all of them are mighty warriors.
17 They will devour[l] your harvests and food,
devour[m] your sons and daughters;
they will devour[n] your flocks and herds,
devour your vines and fig trees.
With the sword they will destroy
the fortified cities in which you trust.[o]

18 "Yet even in those days," declares the LORD, "I will not destroy[p] you completely. 19 And when the
people ask,[q] 'Why has the LORD our God done all this to us?' you will tell them, 'As you have forsaken
me and served foreign gods[r] in your own land, so now you will serve foreigners[s] in a land not your
own.'

20 "Announce this to the descendants of Jacob
and proclaim it in Judah:
21 Hear this, you foolish and senseless people,
who have eyes[t] but do not see,
who have ears but do not hear:[u]
22 Should you not fear[v] me?" declares the LORD.
"Should you not tremble in my presence?
I made the sand a boundary for the sea,
an everlasting barrier it cannot cross.
The waves may roll, but they cannot prevail;
they may roar, but they cannot cross it.
23 But these people have stubborn and rebellious[w] hearts;
they have turned aside and gone away.
24 They do not say to themselves,
'Let us fear the LORD our God,
who gives autumn and spring rains[x] in season,
who assures us of the regular weeks of harvest.'[y]
25 Your wrongdoings have kept these away;
your sins have deprived you of good.

26 "Among my people are the wicked
who lie in wait[z] like men who snare birds
and like those who set traps to catch people.
27 Like cages full of birds,
their houses are full of deceit;[a]
they have become rich[b] and powerful
28 and have grown fat[c] and sleek.
Their evil deeds have no limit;
they do not seek justice.
They do not promote the case of the fatherless;[d]
they do not defend the just cause of the poor.[e]

5:17 [l] Lev 26:16; Jer 8:16 [m] Dt 28:32; Jer 50:7, 17 [n] Dt 28:31 [o] Dt 28:33
5:18 [p] Jer 4:27
5:19 [q] Dt 29:24-26; 1Ki 9:9 [r] Jer 16:13 [s] Dt 28:48
5:21 [t] Isa 6:10; Eze 12:2 [u] Mt 13:15; Mk 8:18
5:22 [v] Dt 28:58
5:23 [w] Dt 21:18
5:24 [x] Ps 147:8; Joel 2:23 [y] Ge 8:22; Ac 14:17
5:26 [z] Ps 10:8; Pr 1:11
5:27 [a] Jer 9:6 [b] Jer 12:1
5:28 [c] Dt 32:15 [d] Zec 7:10 [e] Isa 1:23; Jer 7:6

5:19 you have forsaken me and served foreign gods in your own land. Because of this, the Lord will judge them fittingly: they will "serve foreigners" in a distant land, namely, Babylon. Yet the Lord will maintain a remnant through the judgment so that he can still fulfill his promises to Abraham.
5:21 do not see ... do not hear. The people have become like the idols they serve: blind and deaf (see Isa 44:18).
5:22 The Lord created the universe and set the limits for the powerful sea.
5:24 autumn and spring rains. Given by God, the rains were necessary in that dry climate if they were to have an abundant harvest. The Baal cult claimed that Baal was the one who brought these rains, yet the Lord controls the rainfall, as he demonstrated in Elijah's days (1 Kgs 17–18). It was the people's covenantal unfaithfulness that deprived them of these routine necessities (v. 25; see Lev 26:4).
5:26–29 The rich were oppressing the weak, especially the "fatherless" and the "poor" (v. 28)—sections of society that had no one to advocate their cause and therefore often found it hard to gain justice. Yet such people could cry out to the Lord, who would certainly answer their plea for justice (Prov 22:22–23).

5:30 [f] Jer 23:14; Hos 6:10
5:31 [g] Eze 13:6; Mic 2:11
6:1 [h] 2Ch 11:6 [i] Ne 3:14 [j] Jer 4:6
6:3 [k] Jer 12:10 [l] 2Ki 25:4; Lk 19:43
6:4 [m] Jer 15:8
6:6 [n] Dt 20:19-20 [o] Jer 32:24
6:7 [p] Ps 55:9; Eze 7:11, 23 [q] Jer 20:8

29 Should I not punish them for this?"
declares the LORD.
"Should I not avenge myself
on such a nation as this?

30 "A horrible[f] and shocking thing
has happened in the land:
31 The prophets prophesy lies,[g]
the priests rule by their own authority,
and my people love it this way.
But what will you do in the end?

Jerusalem Under Siege

6 "Flee for safety, people of Benjamin!
Flee from Jerusalem!
Sound the trumpet in Tekoa![h]
Raise the signal over Beth Hakkerem![i]
For disaster looms out of the north,[j]
even terrible destruction.
2 I will destroy Daughter Zion,
so beautiful and delicate.
3 Shepherds[k] with their flocks will come against her;
they will pitch their tents around[l] her,
each tending his own portion."
4 "Prepare for battle against her!
Arise, let us attack at noon![m]
But, alas, the daylight is fading,
and the shadows of evening grow long.
5 So arise, let us attack at night
and destroy her fortresses!"

6 This is what the LORD Almighty says:

"Cut down the trees[n]
and build siege ramps[o] against Jerusalem.
This city must be punished;
it is filled with oppression.
7 As a well pours out its water,
so she pours out her wickedness.
Violence[p] and destruction[q] resound in her;
her sickness and wounds are ever before me.

5:31 prophets. They should warn the people of the coming punishment; instead, they prophesy "lies." **priests.** They should teach the people the law; instead, they teach their own ideas. Such teaching might be very popular with God's people, but it is deadly because it fails to take into account what will happen "in the end."

6:1–30 *Jerusalem Under Siege.* Normally, people would flee *to* a city for safety when danger threatened, but here Jeremiah advises the reverse behavior, because Jerusalem will fall after a devastating siege.

6:1 Benjamin. The one remaining tribe that along with Judah comprise the southern kingdom. **Tekoa.** It and (probably) Beth Hakkerem lie to the south of Jerusalem, so if they give the alarm to signal an approaching enemy, then an army approaching from the north must have Jerusalem surrounded. **Beth Hakkerem.** Likely Ramat Rahel, which was previously an Assyrian fortress and may have been a natural place to seek safety now that the Assyrians had left.

6:2 Daughter Zion. See note on 4:31.

6:3 Shepherds ... flocks. Kings and their armies.

6:4 Prepare for battle. The kings are preparing for battle against Jerusalem, a process which often involved divination to seek the best time to attack. But they are so impatient for victory that they will consider a nighttime attack, a rare event in those days.

6:6–9 The real enemy is not the opposition kings and armies that surround Jerusalem but the Lord, who commands and directs the siege to punish the city for their sins.

6:6 siege ramps. A common way of counteracting high defensive walls.

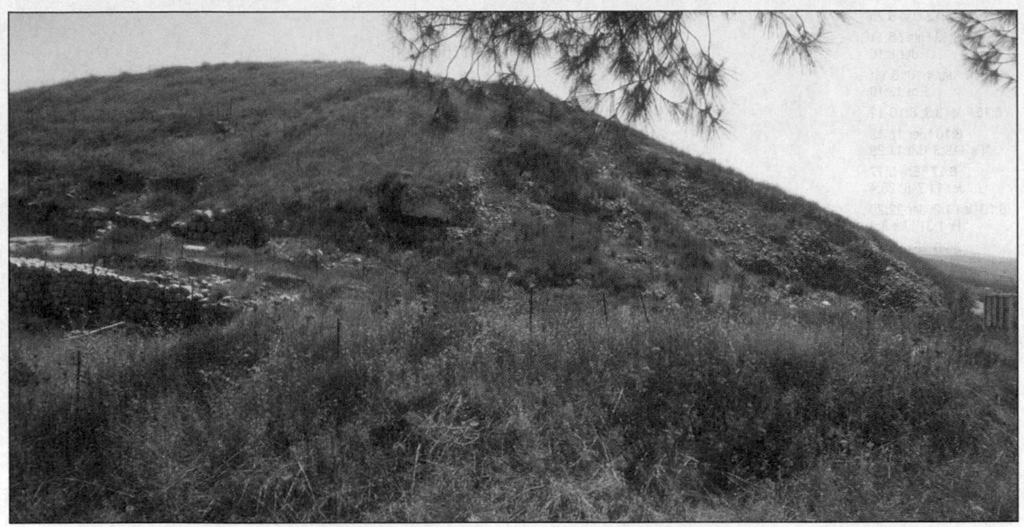

The Assyrian siege ramp (Jer 6:6) at Lachish from the siege and conquest in 701 BC.

8 Take warning, Jerusalem,
or I will turn away[r] from you
and make your land desolate
so no one can live in it."

9 This is what the LORD Almighty says:

"Let them glean the remnant of Israel
as thoroughly as a vine;
pass your hand over the branches again,
like one gathering grapes."

10 To whom can I speak and give warning?
Who will listen to me?
Their ears are closed[a][s]
so they cannot hear.
The word[t] of the LORD is offensive to them;
they find no pleasure in it.
11 But I am full of the wrath[u] of the LORD,
and I cannot hold it in.[v]

"Pour it out on the children in the street
and on the young men[w] gathered together;
both husband and wife will be caught in it,
and the old, those weighed down with years.
12 Their houses will be turned over to others,[x]
together with their fields and their wives,[y]

6:8 [r] Eze 23:18; Hos 9:12
6:10 [s] Ac 7:51 [t] Jer 20:8
6:11 [u] Jer 7:20 [v] Job 32:20; Jer 20:9 [w] Jer 9:21
6:12 [x] Dt 28:30 [y] Jer 8:10; 38:22

[a] 10 Hebrew *uncircumcised*

6:9 glean ... as thoroughly as a vine. The destruction is to be as thorough as "gathering grapes": normally, the few leftover grapes from the initial harvest were supposed to be left for the poor (Deut 24:21), but here there is to be a second gathering process to make sure that no one escapes the Lord's judgment. God will preserve only a very small "remnant" through the siege.

6:10 closed. See NIV text note. Judah has been as unresponsive to the Lord's word as one would expect pagans to be. Yet their refusal to listen to God's word does not protect them from the consequences of their sin.

6:11 the wrath of the LORD. Judgment will affect everyone from the youngest "children in the street" to the "old," men and women alike.

6:12 [z]Isa 5:25
6:13 [a]Isa 56:11 [b]Jer 8:10
6:14 [c]Jer 4:10; 8:11; Eze 13:10
6:15 [d]Jer 3:3; 8:10-12
6:16 [e]Jer 18:15 [f]Ps 119:3 [g]Mt 11:29
6:17 [h]Eze 3:17 [i]Jer 11:7-8; 25:4
6:19 [j]Isa 1:2; Jer 22:29 [k]Pr 1:31 [l]Jer 8:9
6:20 [m]Ex 30:23 [n]Am 5:22 [o]Ps 50:8-10; Jer 7:21; Mic 6:7-8 [p]Isa 1:11

when I stretch out my hand[z]
against those who live in the land,"
declares the LORD.

13 "From the least to the greatest,
all are greedy for gain;[a]
prophets and priests alike,
all practice deceit.[b]
14 They dress the wound of my people
as though it were not serious.
'Peace, peace,' they say,
when there is no peace.[c]
15 Are they ashamed of their detestable conduct?
No, they have no shame at all;
they do not even know how to blush.[d]
So they will fall among the fallen;
they will be brought down when I punish them,"
says the LORD.

16 This is what the LORD says:

"Stand at the crossroads and look;
ask for the ancient paths,[e]
ask where the good way[f] is, and walk in it,
and you will find rest[g] for your souls.
But you said, 'We will not walk in it.'
17 I appointed watchmen[h] over you and said,
'Listen to the sound of the trumpet!'
But you said, 'We will not listen.'[i]
18 Therefore hear, you nations;
you who are witnesses,
observe what will happen to them.
19 Hear, you earth:[j]
I am bringing disaster on this people,
the fruit of their schemes,[k]
because they have not listened to my words
and have rejected my law.[l]
20 What do I care about incense from Sheba
or sweet calamus[m] from a distant land?
Your burnt offerings are not acceptable;[n]
your sacrifices[o] do not please me."[p]

21 Therefore this is what the LORD says:

6:13–15 The reason for this comprehensive judgment is comprehensive sin: "all are greedy for gain" (v. 13).
6:13 prophets and priests. Those whom the Lord appointed to warn the people. **practice deceit.** Instead of declaring the unpopular truth.
6:14 'Peace, peace,' they say, when there is no peace. Instead of warning of the wrath to come. **Peace, peace.** Repetition is a form of emphasis in Hebrew, so "Peace, peace" affirms a certain future of comfort and wholeness.
6:15 The false priests and prophets will fall along with those whom they deceived.
6:16 ancient paths. The ways of obedience revealed to Moses, toward which priests and prophets alike were to direct the people. But the people rejected those ways.
6:17 watchmen. The prophets (Ezek 3:17). The people refused to listen to those who did faithfully warn them.
6:18–19 The Lord summons the nations and the earth itself as witnesses in his legal action against his own people, who have refused to listen to him.
6:20 incense. Frankincense (see note on Song 3:6). **Sheba.** In southwest Arabia (modern Yemen). **calamus.** Aromatic sweet cane. **burnt offerings ... sacrifices.** The usual sacrificial offerings could not atone for their defiant sin (see Num 15:30–31), even if accompanied by expensive spices. The problem was not with the sacrificial system but with the people: if the hands that brought the offering were defiled, the offering itself was defiled and therefore unacceptable to God (see Hag 2:11–14).

"I will put obstacles before this people.
Parents and children alike will stumble[q] over them;
neighbors and friends will perish."

22 This is what the LORD says:

"Look, an army is coming
from the land of the north;[r]
a great nation is being stirred up
from the ends of the earth.
23 They are armed with bow and spear;
they are cruel and show no mercy.[s]
They sound like the roaring sea
as they ride on their horses;[t]
they come like men in battle formation
to attack you, Daughter Zion."

24 We have heard reports about them,
and our hands hang limp.
Anguish[u] has gripped us,
pain like that of a woman in labor.[v]
25 Do not go out to the fields
or walk on the roads,
for the enemy has a sword,
and there is terror on every side.[w]
26 Put on sackcloth,[x] my people,
and roll in ashes;[y]
mourn with bitter wailing
as for an only son,[z]
for suddenly the destroyer
will come upon us.

27 "I have made you a tester[a] of metals
and my people the ore,
that you may observe
and test their ways.
28 They are all hardened rebels,[b]
going about to slander.[c]
They are bronze and iron;[d]
they all act corruptly.
29 The bellows blow fiercely
to burn away the lead with fire,
but the refining goes on in vain;
the wicked are not purged out.
30 They are called rejected silver,
because the LORD has rejected them."[e]

6:21 [q] Isa 8:14
6:22 [r] Jer 1:15; 10:22
6:23 [s] Isa 13:18 [t] Jer 4:29
6:24 [u] Jer 4:19 [v] Jer 4:31; 50:41-43
6:25 [w] Jer 49:29
6:26 [x] Jer 4:8 [y] Jer 25:34; Mic 1:10 [z] Zec 12:10
6:27 [a] Jer 9:7
6:28 [b] Jer 5:23 [c] Jer 9:4 [d] Eze 22:18
6:30 [e] Ps 119:119; Jer 7:29; Hos 9:17

6:21 obstacles. People who try to approach the Lord when their hearts are somewhere else will find obstacles in their paths, preventing them from access (cf. Ezek 14:1–5).
6:22 land of the north; a great nation. Babylon. From an Israelite perspective, the Babylonians lived at "the ends of the earth."
6:23 cruel … no mercy. Though the Lord summons Babylon, knowing that it is a cruel invader, he does not sanction their cruelty. **Daughter Zion.** See note on 4:31.
6:24 hands hang limp. The news of this fearsome enemy will totally demoralize the defenders.
6:25 terror on every side. A slogan Jeremiah repeats often (see 20:3,10; 46:5; 49:29; cf. Ps 31:13).
6:26 wailing as for an only son. A particularly intense mourning, for with the death of the sole heir, the family name seems certain to die out (cf. Zech 12:10).
6:27 tester of metals. The image depicts the prophet as a refiner, separating the pure metal from the dross (cf. Mal 3:2–3).
6:28–29 In this case, the refining process is a failure: the refiner is unable to separate any silver from the bronze, iron, and lead. The people are altogether dross and will be burned up entirely in the fire of God's wrath.

7:2 [f] Jer 17:19
7:3 [g] Jer 18:11; 26:13
7:4 [h] Mic 3:11
7:5 [i] Jer 22:3
7:6 [j] Jer 2:34; 19:4 [k] Dt 8:19
7:7 [l] Dt 4:40
7:9 [m] Jer 11:13,17 [n] Ex 20:3
7:10 [o] Jer 32:34; Eze 23:38-39
7:11 [p] Isa 56:7 [q] Mt 21:13*; Mk 11:17*; Lk 19:46* [r] Jer 29:23
7:12 [s] Jos 18:1 [t] 1Sa 4:10-11,22; Ps 78:60-64

False Religion Worthless

7 This is the word that came to Jeremiah from the LORD: 2"Stand[f] at the gate of the LORD's house and
there proclaim this message:
" 'Hear the word of the LORD, all you people of Judah who come through these gates to worship the
LORD. 3This is what the LORD Almighty, the God of Israel, says: Reform your ways[g] and your actions, and
I will let you live in this place. 4Do not trust in deceptive[h] words and say, "This is the temple of the LORD,
the temple of the LORD, the temple of the LORD!" 5If you really change your ways and your actions and
deal with each other justly,[i] 6if you do not oppress the foreigner, the fatherless or the widow and do not
shed innocent blood[j] in this place, and if you do not follow other gods[k] to your own harm, 7then I will
let you live in this place, in the land[l] I gave your ancestors for ever and ever. 8But look, you are trusting
in deceptive words that are worthless.
9" 'Will you steal and murder, commit adultery and perjury,[a] burn incense to Baal[m] and follow other
gods[n] you have not known, 10and then come and stand before me in this house,[o] which bears my Name,
and say, "We are safe"—safe to do all these detestable things? 11Has this house,[p] which bears my Name,
become a den of robbers[q] to you? But I have been watching![r] declares the LORD.
12" 'Go now to the place in Shiloh[s] where I first made a dwelling for my Name, and see what I did[t] to

[a] 9 Or *and swear by false gods*

7:1—10:25 *False Religion and a Deluded People.* The people of Jerusalem and Judah are content with a form of orthodox religion while rejecting true devotion to the Lord. Such a relationship to the Lord cannot save them any more than it saved their ancestors who tried the same approach.

7:1–29 *False Religion Worthless.* Jeremiah confronts the people as they enter the temple of the Lord in Jerusalem. This is the place where God himself told them to come and worship, yet mere attendance at his house is not enough if they continually despise him by breaking his commandments.

7:1–3 It appears that worshipers may have recited passages like Ps 15 as they entered "the gate of the LORD's house" (v. 2), stressing the need for purity of life among those who came before the Lord. If the Israelites are to be saved, they need to reform their ways and their actions, not merely offer the required sacrifices. This is not because OT believers were saved by works but because their actions exposed the true commitments of their hearts. As Jesus said, a good tree cannot bear bad fruit, and a bad tree cannot bear good fruit (Matt 7:16–18).

7:4 This is the temple of the LORD. The inhabitants of Jerusalem repeat this formula as if the temple is a magic amulet that will protect them no matter how they live. This superstitious belief may have been reinforced by the dramatic deliverance of Jerusalem from the Assyrian army in the time of Hezekiah, 100 years earlier (2 Kgs 18:13—19:37). Psalms also speaks of the Lord's protecting his city (e.g., Ps 46).

7:5–6 True religion can never divorce faith from obedience, especially care for the weak and helpless, the "fatherless" and the "widow" (cf. Jas 1:27).

7:6 foreigner. One who temporarily stayed in Jerusalem; they were likewise often subject to abuse and ill-treatment since they had no advocate. God's law protected them, along with widows and the fatherless (Deut 24:19–21), but these laws were often broken in ancient Israel. Those who broke these covenant stipulations, as well as the commandment prohibiting "other gods" (see Exod 20:3), could not expect the Lord to give them the covenantal blessing of long life in the land (see v. 7 and note).

7:7 let you live in this place. God had warned that if the Israelites broke the covenant, they would lose the promised land and go into exile (Deut 28:25–68).

7:9 The Ten Commandments (Exod 20:1–17) form the heart of the covenant made at Mount Sinai, yet in this verse alone violations of five commandments are listed.

7:10 It is folly to recklessly break the covenant's terms and yet expect to find acceptance at the house on which the Lord placed his Name (1 Kgs 8:29).

Arad letter inscribed with "temple of the LORD" (probably referring to the Jerusalem temple) from a southern Judahite fortress, from the same time as Jeremiah. A message against false religion is given near the temple in Jer 7.

Z. Radovan/www.BibleLandPictures.com

7:11 den of robbers. A place to which thieves return after they have committed their evil deeds; they feel safe there (cf. Matt 21:13; Mark 11:17; Luke 19:46).

7:12–15 The history of Shiloh should make them think twice: in 1 Sam 4, the Israelites treated the ark of the covenant as an amulet that would grant them victory, even though the priesthood was defiled and corrupt. Yet the ark went into exile among the Philistines, and the glory of God

it because of the wickedness of my people Israel. 13While you were doing all these things, declares the
LORD, I spoke to you again and again,[u] but you did not listen;[v] I called you, but you did not answer.[w]
14Therefore, what I did to Shiloh I will now do to the house that bears my Name,[x] the temple you trust
in, the place I gave to you and your ancestors. 15I will thrust you from my presence, just as I did all your
fellow Israelites, the people of Ephraim.'[y]

16"So do not pray for this people nor offer any plea[z] or petition for them; do not plead with me, for
I will not listen to you. 17Do you not see what they are doing in the towns of Judah and in the streets of
Jerusalem? 18The children gather wood, the fathers light the fire, and the women knead the dough and
make cakes to offer to the Queen of Heaven.[a] They pour out drink offerings[b] to other gods to arouse[c]
my anger. 19But am I the one they are provoking? declares the LORD. Are they not rather harming themselves, to their own shame?[d]

20" 'Therefore this is what the Sovereign LORD says: My anger[e] and my wrath will be poured out on
this place—on man and beast, on the trees of the field and on the crops of your land—and it will
burn and not be quenched.

21" 'This is what the LORD Almighty, the God of Israel, says: Go ahead, add your burnt offerings to your
other sacrifices[f] and eat[g] the meat yourselves! 22For when I brought your ancestors out of Egypt and spoke
to them, I did not just give them commands about burnt offerings and sacrifices,[h] 23but I gave them this
command: Obey[i] me, and I will be your God and you will be my people.[j] Walk in obedience to all I command you, that it may go well[k] with you. 24But they did not listen or pay attention;[l] instead, they followed
the stubborn inclinations of their evil hearts. They went backward and not forward. 25From the time your
ancestors left Egypt until now, day after day, again and again I sent you my servants the prophets.[m] 26But
they did not listen to me or pay attention. They were stiff-necked and did more evil than their ancestors.'[n]

27"When you tell[o] them all this, they will not listen[p] to you; when you call to them, they will not
answer. 28Therefore say to them, 'This is the nation that has not obeyed the LORD its God or responded
to correction. Truth has perished; it has vanished from their lips.

29" 'Cut off[q] your hair and throw it away; take up a lament on the barren heights, for the LORD has
rejected and abandoned[r] this generation that is under his wrath.

The Valley of Slaughter

30" 'The people of Judah have done evil in my eyes, declares the LORD. They have set up their detestable idols[s] in the house that bears my Name and have defiled[t] it. 31They have built the high places of

7:13 [u] 2Ch 36:15 [v] Isa 65:12 [w] Jer 35:17
7:14 [x] 1Ki 9:7
7:15 [y] Ps 78:67
7:16 [z] Ex 32:10; Dt 9:14; Jer 15:1
7:18 [a] Jer 44:17-19 [b] Jer 19:13 [c] 1Ki 14:9
7:19 [d] Jer 9:19
7:20 [e] Jer 42:18; La 2:3-5
7:21 [f] Isa 1:11; Am 5:21-22 [g] Hos 8:13
7:22 [h] 1Sa 15:22; Ps 51:16; Hos 6:6
7:23 [i] Ex 19:5 [j] Lev 26:12 [k] Ex 15:26
7:24 [l] Ps 81:11-12; Jer 11:8
7:25 [m] Jer 25:4
7:26 [n] Jer 16:12
7:27 [o] Eze 2:7 [p] Eze 3:7
7:29 [q] Job 1:20; Isa 15:2; Mic 1:16 [r] Jer 6:30
7:30 [s] Eze 7:20-22 [t] Jer 32:34

departed from Shiloh, resulting in a loss of its central status. So the glory of God will now depart from his dwelling place in Jerusalem (see Ezek 10), leaving the temple unprotected; the people will likewise be "thrust" (v. 15) from the Lord's presence into exile, just as the northern kingdom ("the people of Ephraim," v. 15) had been in 722 BC.

7:16 do not pray ... do not plead. A key element of the deliverance of Jerusalem in the time of Hezekiah was Isaiah's intercession (2 Kgs 19:5–7,20–34). Jeremiah, however, is not permitted to pray or plead for Jerusalem; their fate is virtually sealed.

7:18 the Queen of Heaven. Ishtar to the Assyrians and Babylonians; Astarte to the Canaanites. The women made "cakes" stamped with her image as offerings (44:19). They also offered "drink offerings" to other deities as part of their fertility rituals.

7:19–20 The Lord declares that far from assuring blessing, these practices (see note on v. 18) are harming the people. Instead of bringing fertility to humans, beasts, trees, and crops, these practices will bring the Lord's wrath.

7:21 Go ahead, add your burnt offerings ... eat the meat yourselves! Grain and incense could legitimately be offered in various places (though not to various gods), because these offerings did not involve shedding blood. Jeremiah shockingly suggests that they might as well add whole "burnt offerings" to their sacrifices (even though only the priests in the temple could offer such offerings; see Lev 1:8 and note) and that they might as well go ahead and "eat the meat" of these sacrifices (even though the law demanded that whole burnt offerings be completely consumed by the fire; see Lev 1:9 and note). His point is that it is hypocritical of the people to scrupulously obey some of the ritual laws in the temple while transgressing others so comprehensively in their daily lives. The Lord's commands in the time of Moses concerned not (just) "burnt offerings and sacrifices" (v. 22) but also a relationship that would affect every aspect of their lives (v. 23).

7:24–27 The Lord tells Jeremiah that the people will not listen to this message any more than their ancestors listened to the law Moses gave them. To ignore the Lord's servants, the prophets, is to refuse to listen to the Lord who sent them.

7:29 Cut off ... throw it away. During a Nazirite vow, allowing one's hair to grow was a mark of consecration (see Num 6:1–8 and note); if that is the allusion here, then cutting off and throwing away the hair seems to symbolize the deconsecration and rejection of God's people because of their defilement. The Lord has "rejected and abandoned" them. Alternatively, the hair cutting could simply be a sign of mourning.

7:30—8:3 *The Valley of Slaughter.* Idolatry has penetrated even to Jerusalem in the form of the cult of child sacrifice. Child sacrifice was associated with several ancient Near Eastern religions, and the people of Jerusalem practiced it during the time of Manasseh (2 Kgs 21:6). In 2 Kgs 23:10, Topheth was one of the places destroyed by Manasseh's grandson Josiah in his reforms, but worship may have been revived there by Jeremiah's day.

7:31 built. Can mean "rebuilt" in Hebrew. **Topheth.** High places had been set up nearby for pagan worship in the Valley of Ben Hinnom, just

7:31 [u]2Ki 23:10 [v]Ps 106:38 [w]Jer 19:5
7:32 [x]Jer 19:6 [y]Jer 19:11
7:33 [z]Dt 28:26
7:34 [a]Isa 24:8; Eze 26:13 [b]Rev 18:23 [c]Lev 26:34
8:2 [d]2Ki 23:5; Ac 7:42
8:3 [e]Job 3:22; Rev 9:6
8:4 [f]Pr 24:16
8:5 [g]Jer 5:27 [h]Jer 7:24; 9:6
8:6 [i]Rev 9:20 [j]Ps 14:1-3
8:7 [k]Isa 1:3; Jer 5:4-5
8:8 [l]Ro 2:17

Topheth[u] in the Valley of Ben Hinnom to burn their sons and daughters[v] in the fire—something I did
not command, nor did it enter my mind.[w] 32 So beware, the days are coming, declares the LORD, when
people will no longer call it Topheth or the Valley of Ben Hinnom, but the Valley of Slaughter,[x] for they
will bury[y] the dead in Topheth until there is no more room. 33 Then the carcasses of this people will
become food[z] for the birds and the wild animals, and there will be no one to frighten them away. 34 I
will bring an end to the sounds[a] of joy and gladness and to the voices of bride and bridegroom[b] in the
towns of Judah and the streets of Jerusalem, for the land will become desolate.[c]

8 "'At that time, declares the LORD, the bones of the kings and officials of Judah, the bones of the
priests and prophets, and the bones of the people of Jerusalem will be removed from their graves.
2 They will be exposed to the sun and the moon and all the stars of the heavens, which they have loved
and served[d] and which they have followed and consulted and worshiped. They will not be gathered up
or buried, but will be like dung lying on the ground. 3 Wherever I banish them, all the survivors of this
evil nation will prefer death to life,[e] declares the LORD Almighty.'

Sin and Punishment

4 "Say to them, 'This is what the LORD says:

"'When people fall down, do they not get up?[f]
  When someone turns away, do they not return?
5 Why then have these people turned away?
  Why does Jerusalem always turn away?
They cling to deceit;[g]
  they refuse to return.[h]
6 I have listened attentively,
  but they do not say what is right.
None of them repent[i] of their wickedness,
  saying, "What have I done?"
Each pursues their own course[j]
  like a horse charging into battle.
7 Even the stork in the sky
  knows her appointed seasons,
and the dove, the swift and the thrush
  observe the time of their migration.
But my people do not know[k]
  the requirements of the LORD.

8 "'How can you say, "We are wise,
  for we have the law[l] of the LORD,"

west of Jerusalem. Since the west is where the sun goes down, it was the direction connected with death in the ancient Near East, which is why in Egypt burial sites and tombs were all located west of the Nile. **nor did it enter my mind.** An anthropomorphism indicating how contrary it is to the Lord's will for his people.

7:32 Valley of Slaughter. Topheth and the Valley of Ben Hinnom will be called this when they become the dumping ground for the bodies of the slain. Such an act is both a fitting judgment (the bodies of those who killed their own firstborn would end up in the same place) and a way to defile the location so that it could not be used again for its pagan purpose.

7:33 carcasses ... food for the birds. Leaving bodies exposed to the attentions of scavengers was a covenantal curse (Deut 28:26).

8:1–3 This same judgment (7:30–34) will apply to all the leaders of Judah: the "kings and officials," the "priests and prophets," even those who had already been buried (v. 1). They will have their bones exposed like so much "dung" (v. 2).

8:2 sun ... moon ... stars. Worshiped as deities by many in the ancient world, yet they have no power to protect their worshipers.

8:3 survivors ... will prefer death to life. Life in exile will be so hard that even death will seem preferable (Deut 28:64–68).

8:4—9:26 *Sin and Punishment.* If God's people will repent, they will find forgiveness and mercy from the Lord. But instead, they are utterly committed to their path and completely unrepentant, which makes their destruction inevitable.

8:5 turned away ... return. The Hebrew (*šûb*) can also mean "repent." Just as getting back up is the normal response to falling down (v. 4), so repenting should be the normal response to sin. Judah, however, is defiantly set on their course like a warhorse in full flight (v. 6).

8:7 What we call "the laws of nature" actually manifest God's order, which creation perfectly obeys (see Ps 19:1–6). **the stork ... the dove, the swift and the thrush.** Migratory birds never refuse to travel their appointed routes at their "appointed seasons." These birds know and obey the patterns of behavior the Lord laid down for them, while God's people "do not know the requirements of the LORD." **do not know.** See note on v. 8, "law."

8:8 Compounding their blindness, the people claim to be "wise" because

when actually the lying pen of the scribes
has handled it falsely?
9 The wise[m] will be put to shame;
they will be dismayed and trapped.
Since they have rejected the word[n] of the LORD,
what kind of wisdom do they have?
10 Therefore I will give their wives to other men
and their fields to new owners.[o]
From the least to the greatest,
all are greedy for gain;[p]
prophets and priests alike,
all practice deceit.
11 They dress the wound of my people
as though it were not serious.
"Peace, peace," they say,
when there is no peace.[q]
12 Are they ashamed of their detestable conduct?
No, they have no shame[r] at all;
they do not even know how to blush.
So they will fall among the fallen;
they will be brought down when they are punished,[s]
says the LORD.[t]

13 " 'I will take away their harvest,
declares the LORD.

There will be no grapes on the vine.[u]
There will be no figs[v] on the tree,
and their leaves will wither.[w]
What I have given them
will be taken[x] from them.[a]' "

14 Why are we sitting here?
Gather together!
Let us flee to the fortified cities[y]
and perish there!
For the LORD our God has doomed us to perish
and given us poisoned water[z] to drink,
because we have sinned[a] against him.

8:9 [m] Jer 6:15 [n] Jer 6:19
8:10 [o] Jer 6:12 [p] Isa 56:11
8:11 [q] Jer 6:14
8:12 [r] Jer 3:3 [s] Ps 52:5-7; Isa 3:9 [t] Jer 6:15
8:13 [u] Joel 1:7 [v] Lk 13:6 [w] Mt 21:19 [x] Jer 5:17
8:14 [y] Jer 4:5; 35:11 [z] Dt 29:18; Jer 9:15; 23:15 [a] Jer 14:7,20

a 13 The meaning of the Hebrew for this sentence is uncertain.

they have "the law of the LORD." **law.** Hebrew *tôrâ*; includes instruction and teaching within its semantic range. This shows that "do not know" in v. 7 is not ignorance but willfully refusing to submit. **scribes.** Their job was to interpret and apply the law. They have "handled it falsely," leading the people astray through their writings. Jesus says similar things of the religious leaders of his day (Matt 23:13–36).

8:10–13 The "prophets and priests" (v. 10), as well as the "scribes" (v. 8), pretend that the people's condition is not serious, declaring that there is "peace" (v. 11; i.e., "wholeness") in the relationship between Israel and the Lord when in reality the covenant is profoundly broken and destruction is imminent. Their judgment will be to experience personally the covenant curses whose reality they deny. They will lose "their wives to other men and their fields to new owners" (v. 10), and there will be "no grapes on the vine ... no figs on the tree" (v. 13; see Deut 28:30–45). All of these things are gifts from the Lord, and he can take them away as well as give them. Much of this passage is identical to 6:12–15.

8:10 greedy. The motivation for Judah's religious leaders is simple self-interest.

8:11 my people. Alternate translation: "the daughter of my people." This term of affection that heightens the poignancy of the appeal to repent that falls on deaf ears. **Peace, peace.** See note on 6:14.

8:14–17 When it becomes plain that the teaching of the prophets and priests is false and that there is no peace or healing (v. 15), the people will be left in despair. The arrival of the enemy's horses in the northern city of Dan will expose the delusion (v. 16), but there will be no time to do anything other than flee to the fortified cities and die there (v. 14). In that day, they will make (too late) the connection between their sin and the Lord's judgment.

8:14 poisoned water. The fitting punishment for those who sought their water from poisonous sources (2:13), especially since "poison" elsewhere connects with idolatry (Deut 29:17–18; 32:32).

8:15 [b]ver 11 [c]Jer 14:19
8:16 [d]Jer 4:15
8:17 [e]Nu 21:6; Dt 32:24 [f]Ps 58:5
8:18 [g]La 5:17
8:19 [h]Jer 9:16 [i]Dt 32:21
8:21 [j]Jer 14:17
8:22 [k]Ge 37:25 [l]Jer 30:12
9:1 [m]Jer 13:17; La 2:11, 18 [n]Isa 22:4

15 We hoped for peace[b]
but no good has come,
for a time of healing
but there is only terror.[c]
16 The snorting of the enemy's horses
is heard from Dan;[d]
at the neighing of their stallions
the whole land trembles.
They have come to devour
the land and everything in it,
the city and all who live there.

17 "See, I will send venomous snakes[e] among you,
vipers that cannot be charmed,[f]
and they will bite you,"
declares the LORD.

18 You who are my Comforter[a] in sorrow,
my heart is faint[g] within me.
19 Listen to the cry of my people
from a land far away:[h]
"Is the LORD not in Zion?
Is her King no longer there?"

"Why have they aroused my anger with their images,
with their worthless foreign idols?"[i]

20 "The harvest is past,
the summer has ended,
and we are not saved."

21 Since my people are crushed, I am crushed;
I mourn,[j] and horror grips me.
22 Is there no balm in Gilead?[k]
Is there no physician there?
Why then is there no healing[l]
for the wound of my people?

9[b]

1 Oh, that my head were a spring of water
and my eyes a fountain of tears!
I would weep[m] day and night
for the slain of my people.[n]
2 Oh, that I had in the desert
a lodging place for travelers,

[a] *18* The meaning of the Hebrew for this word is uncertain. [b] In Hebrew texts 9:1 is numbered 8:23, and 9:2-26 is numbered 9:1-25.

8:17 venomous snakes. In the wilderness, the Lord sent these to bite the people, but on that occasion he provided deliverance (Num 21:6–9).
8:18–20 Though Judah is justly condemned, neither the prophet nor the Lord delights in their downfall. The prophet mourns over the coming exile of his people and also gives voice to the Lord's anguish. The people feel abandoned by their God, yet in reality their idolatry drove him away, leaving the land unprotected.
8:19 my people. See note on v. 11.
8:20 we are not saved. The false confidence of 7:10 has now been exposed. The Lord will not always remain in a defiled house, and their assumed safety is an empty boast.
8:22 Is there no balm in Gilead? A proverbial expression to which the answer is, "Of course there is." Gilead was well-known for aromatic resin, which was used in a variety of medicines. Yet there is no remedy there for Judah's sickness; their idolatry will lead to their judgment.
9:1,10 weep. It is because of verses like these that Jeremiah has been called the "weeping prophet." The prophets were not detached and aloof from the people to whom they spoke but were often caught up in the emotion of the messages they delivered (cf. Ezek 3:14–15).
9:1 my people. See note on 8:11.

so that I might leave my people
and go away from them;
for they are all adulterers,[o]
a crowd of unfaithful people.

3 "They make ready their tongue
like a bow, to shoot lies;[p]
it is not by truth
that they triumph[a] in the land.
They go from one sin to another;
they do not acknowledge me,"
declares the LORD.

4 "Beware of your friends;
do not trust anyone in your clan.[q]
For every one of them is a deceiver,[b r]
and every friend a slanderer.
5 Friend deceives friend,
and no one speaks the truth.
They have taught their tongues to lie;
they weary themselves with sinning.
6 You[c] live in the midst of deception;[s]
in their deceit they refuse to acknowledge me,"
declares the LORD.

7 Therefore this is what the LORD Almighty says:

"See, I will refine[t] and test[u] them,
for what else can I do
because of the sin of my people?
8 Their tongue[v] is a deadly arrow;
it speaks deceitfully.
With their mouths they all speak cordially to their neighbors,
but in their hearts they set traps[w] for them.
9 Should I not punish them for this?"
declares the LORD.
"Should I not avenge[x] myself
on such a nation as this?"

10 I will weep and wail for the mountains
and take up a lament concerning the wilderness grasslands.
They are desolate and untraveled,
and the lowing of cattle is not heard.
The birds[y] have all fled
and the animals are gone.

11 "I will make Jerusalem a heap of ruins,
a haunt of jackals;[z]

9:2 [o] Jer 5:7-8; 23:10; Hos 4:2
9:3 [p] Ps 64:3
9:4 [q] Mic 7:5-6 [r] Ge 27:35
9:6 [s] Jer 5:27
9:7 [t] Isa 1:25 [u] Jer 6:27
9:8 [v] ver 3 [w] Jer 5:26
9:9 [x] Jer 5:9,29
9:10 [y] Jer 4:25; 12:4; Hos 4:3
9:11 [z] Isa 34:13

[a] 3 Or *lies; / they are not valiant for truth* [b] 4 Or *a deceiving Jacob* [c] 6 That is, Jeremiah (the Hebrew is singular)

9:3–9 These verses focus on the sins of the tongue, depicted as a deadly weapon: a bow (v. 3) and an arrow (v. 8). The central sin is deceitfulness, which includes lying about God (refusing to "acknowledge" [v. 3], or "know," the Lord) as well as lying to their neighbors. Even the closest relations (friends, clan members, neighbors) are not trustworthy. They speak "cordially," (v. 8) but plot evil against them (cf. 8:11,15). Though such duplicity may seem temporarily to be triumphing, it demands God's judgment.

9:7 refine. See 6:27–30 and notes.

9:10–11 the mountains … the towns of Judah. The prophet combines the genres of lament and judgment speech, expressing his grief over the Lord's determination to follow through with judgment to the point that the countryside will be left abandoned and the cities ruined, devoid not just of humans but of animals as well.

9:11 [a]Isa 25:2; Jer 26:9
9:12 [b]Ps 107:43; Hos 14:9
9:13 [c]2Ch 7:19; Ps 89:30-32
9:14 [d]Jer 2:8,23 [e]Jer 7:24
9:15 [f]La 3:15 [g]Jer 8:14
9:16 [h]Lev 26:33 [i]Dt 28:64 [j]Eze 5:2 [k]Jer 44:27; Eze 5:12
9:17 [l]2Ch 35:25; Ecc 12:5; Am 5:16
9:18 [m]Jer 14:17
9:19 [n]Jer 4:13
9:20 [o]Isa 32:9-13
9:21 [p]2Ch 36:17
9:22 [q]Jer 8:2
9:23 [r]Ecc 9:11 [s]1Ki 20:11 [t]Eze 28:4-5

and I will lay waste the towns of Judah
so no one can live there."[a]

12 Who is wise[b] enough to understand this? Who has been instructed by the LORD and can explain it?
Why has the land been ruined and laid waste like a desert that no one can cross?
13 The LORD said, "It is because they have forsaken my law, which I set before them; they have not
obeyed me or followed my law.[c] 14 Instead, they have followed[d] the stubbornness of their hearts;[e] they
have followed the Baals, as their ancestors taught them." 15 Therefore this is what the LORD Almighty,
the God of Israel, says: "See, I will make this people eat bitter food[f] and drink poisoned water.[g] 16 I will
scatter them among nations[h] that neither they nor their ancestors have known,[i] and I will pursue them
with the sword[j] until I have made an end of them."[k]

17 This is what the LORD Almighty says:

"Consider now! Call for the wailing women[l] to come;
send for the most skillful of them.
18 Let them come quickly
and wail over us
till our eyes overflow with tears
and water streams from our eyelids.[m]
19 The sound of wailing is heard from Zion:
'How ruined[n] we are!
How great is our shame!
We must leave our land
because our houses are in ruins.'"

20 Now, you women, hear the word of the LORD;
open your ears to the words of his mouth.
Teach your daughters how to wail;
teach one another a lament.[o]
21 Death has climbed in through our windows
and has entered our fortresses;
it has removed the children from the streets
and the young men[p] from the public squares.

22 Say, "This is what the LORD declares:

" 'Dead bodies will lie
like dung[q] on the open field,
like cut grain behind the reaper,
with no one to gather them.' "

23 This is what the LORD says:

"Let not the wise boast of their wisdom[r]
or the strong boast of their strength[s]
or the rich boast of their riches,[t]

9:12 Jeremiah has repeatedly explained the reason for this state of affairs. Yet such truths can be grasped only by those who have been "instructed by the LORD" and have received his wisdom.
9:14 – 16 Israel's rebellion and idolatry are what "their ancestors taught them" (v. 14). Yet the result of such a way of life is "bitter food" (v. 15) and "poisoned water" (v. 15; see note on 8:14): they will experience the bitterness of God's judgment, as Deut 29:18 warns.
9:16 nations that neither they nor their ancestors have known. This does not mean that they did not know of their existence; rather, they had no relationships with them that might have provided shelter and support in their exile (see Deut 28:36).
9:17 wailing women. Semiprofessional mourners who led the dirges. Mourning a death was an important social rite in antiquity.
9:20 hear the word of the LORD. Be open to receive God's wisdom (see v. 12 and note). They will prepare for that awful day by learning and teaching laments to their daughters and friends.
9:21 Death. Pictured as a thief stealthily climbing in the window or as a victorious army triumphantly entering a fortress. Death typically carried off the old, but now it will remove the "children" and the "young men," the future of the community.
9:22 lie … on the open field. A sign of judgment; it was a dishonor for a body to be left unburied.
9:23 wise … strong … rich. Natural sources of human confidence.

[24]but let the one who boasts boast[u] about this:
that they have the understanding to know me,
that I am the LORD,[v] who exercises kindness,[w]
justice and righteousness[x] on earth,
for in these I delight,"
declares the LORD.

[25]"The days are coming," declares the LORD, "when I will punish all who are circumcised only in the
flesh[y]— [26]Egypt, Judah, Edom, Ammon, Moab and all who live in the wilderness in distant places.[a z] For
all these nations are really uncircumcised, and even the whole house of Israel is uncircumcised in heart.[a]"

9:24 [u] 1Co 1:31*; Gal 6:14 [v] 2Co 10:17* [w] Ps 51:1; Mic 7:18 [x] Ps 36:6
9:25 [y] Ro 2:8-9
9:26 [z] Jer 25:23 [a] Lev 26:41; Ac 7:51; Ro 2:28
10:2 [b] Lev 20:23
10:3 [c] Isa 40:19
10:4 [d] Isa 41:7
10:5 [e] 1Co 12:2 [f] Ps 115:5,7 [g] Isa 41:24; 46:7
10:6 [h] Ps 48:1
10:7 [i] Ps 22:28; Rev 15:4

God and Idols

10:12-16pp — Jer 51:15-19

10 Hear what the LORD says to you, people of Israel. [2]This is what the LORD says:

"Do not learn the ways of the nations[b]
or be terrified by signs in the heavens,
though the nations are terrified by them.
[3]For the practices of the peoples are worthless;
they cut a tree out of the forest,
and a craftsman[c] shapes it with his chisel.
[4]They adorn it with silver and gold;
they fasten it with hammer and nails
so it will not totter.[d]
[5]Like a scarecrow in a cucumber field,
their idols cannot speak;[e]
they must be carried
because they cannot walk.[f]
Do not fear them;
they can do no harm
nor can they do any good."[g]

[6]No one is like you, LORD;
you are great,[h]
and your name is mighty in power.
[7]Who should not fear you,
King of the nations?[i]
This is your due.
Among all the wise leaders of the nations
and in all their kingdoms,
there is no one like you.

[a] 26 Or *wilderness and who clip the hair by their foreheads*

But none of these things will avail anything in the impending outpouring of God's wrath.

9:24 Anyone who wishes to "boast" should boast in knowing the Lord (contrast v. 6), especially his kindness (Hebrew *ḥesed*; i.e., covenant faithfulness), justice, and righteousness. These attributes are the delight and the favorite topic of conversation for such people, because it is in these characteristics that there is hope for the faithful remnant of God's people. In the NT, Paul quotes this verse as he admonishes the Corinthians to boast in Jesus Christ alone, who is our righteousness, holiness, and redemption (1 Cor 1:30–31).

9:25 circumcised only in the flesh. Israel was not the only ancient nation that practiced circumcision. What made them unique was the significance of circumcision as a sign of the covenant with their God (Gen 17:9–14). Yet Israel became like these other nations: circumcised in the flesh but not in heart (see Deut 10:16). Some of these pagan nations also clipped the hair by their foreheads (see NIV text note on v. 26) in honor of their deities, something Israel was forbidden to do (Lev 19:27).

10:1–16 *The Lord and Idols.* Israel has been constantly attracted to the ways of the surrounding nations, especially their idolatry.

10:2 signs in the heavens. Israel's attraction to idolatry often manifest itself in an interest in astrology.

10:3 worthless. Idols have no power to speak or act (v. 5).

10:5 scarecrow. Set up to terrify dumb birds but powerless to actually harm or bless anyone (cf. Isa 40:19–20; 41:7).

10:6 No one is like you, LORD. No idol is like the Lord in his greatness, power, name, and wisdom (v. 7). **name.** Reputation and character.

Ruins of Dor, where a purple dye refinery has been found. "What the craftsman and goldsmith have made is then dressed in blue and purple—all made by skilled workers" (Jer 10:9).

Todd Bolen/www.BiblePlaces.com

10:8 [j] Isa 40:19; Jer 4:22
10:9 [k] Ps 115:4; Isa 40:19
10:10 [l] Ps 76:7
10:11 [m] Ps 96:5; Isa 2:18
10:12 [n] Ge 1:1,8; Job 9:8; Isa 40:22
10:13 [o] Job 36:29 [p] Ps 135:7

8 They are all senseless and foolish;[j]
they are taught by worthless wooden idols.
9 Hammered silver is brought from Tarshish
and gold from Uphaz.
What the craftsman and goldsmith have made[k]
is then dressed in blue and purple—
all made by skilled workers.
10 But the LORD is the true God;
he is the living God, the eternal King.
When he is angry, the earth trembles;
the nations cannot endure his wrath.[l]

11 "Tell them this: 'These gods, who did not make the heavens and the earth, will perish[m] from the
earth and from under the heavens.'"[a]

12 But God made the earth by his power;
he founded the world by his wisdom
and stretched out the heavens[n] by his understanding.
13 When he thunders,[o] the waters in the heavens roar;
he makes clouds rise from the ends of the earth.
He sends lightning with the rain[p]
and brings out the wind from his storehouses.

[a] *11* The text of this verse is in Aramaic.

10:9 Tarshish. In the far west, possibly Spain. **Uphaz.** Location unknown. Together, these places give the impression of particularly choice and therefore expensive silver and gold. **blue and purple.** Colors connected with wealth and royalty because they were the most expensive dyes at that time.

10:11–13 The doctrine of creation is central to the polemic against idolatry. The idols "did not make the heavens and the earth" (v. 11); God did. The doctrine of creation is likewise crucial to maintain against modern idolatries that claim to explain the origin of the universe apart from the Creator.

10:12 power … wisdom … understanding. Creation is a living testimony to these attributes of the Lord.

10:13 waters in the heavens … clouds … lightning … rain … wind. God is behind these natural processes. These are not a random selection of natural phenomena but precisely those that the Canaanite god Baal allegedly controlled, phenomena that were essential to fertility and agricultural success in Canaan. See note on vv. 11–13.

14 Everyone is senseless and without knowledge;
every goldsmith is shamed by his idols.
The images he makes are a fraud;
they have no breath in them.
15 They are worthless,[q] the objects of mockery;
when their judgment comes, they will perish.
16 He who is the Portion[r] of Jacob is not like these,
for he is the Maker of all things,[s]
including Israel, the people of his inheritance[t] —
the LORD Almighty is his name.[u]

Coming Destruction

17 Gather up your belongings[v] to leave the land,
you who live under siege.
18 For this is what the LORD says:
"At this time I will hurl[w] out
those who live in this land;
I will bring distress on them
so that they may be captured."

19 Woe to me because of my injury!
My wound[x] is incurable!
Yet I said to myself,
"This is my sickness, and I must endure[y] it."
20 My tent[z] is destroyed;
all its ropes are snapped.
My children are gone from me and are no more;[a]
no one is left now to pitch my tent
or to set up my shelter.
21 The shepherds are senseless
and do not inquire of the LORD;
so they do not prosper
and all their flock is scattered.[b]
22 Listen! The report is coming —
a great commotion from the land of the north!
It will make the towns of Judah desolate,
a haunt of jackals.[c]

Jeremiah's Prayer

23 LORD, I know that people's lives are not their own;
it is not for them to direct their steps.[d]
24 Discipline me, LORD, but only in due measure —
not in your anger,[e]
or you will reduce me to nothing.[f]

10:15 [q] Isa 41:24; Jer 14:22
10:16 [r] Dt 32:9; Ps 119:57 [s] ver 12 [t] Ps 74:2 [u] Jer 31:35; 32:18
10:17 [v] Eze 12:3-12
10:18 [w] 1Sa 25:29
10:19 [x] Jer 14:17 [y] Mic 7:9
10:20 [z] Jer 4:20 [a] Jer 31:15; La 1:5
10:21 [b] Jer 23:2
10:22 [c] Jer 9:11
10:23 [d] Pr 20:24
10:24 [e] Ps 6:1; 38:1 [f] Jer 30:11

10:16 Creation is intricately connected with redemption in the OT. The same God who created the universe also called Israel into existence so that they could be "the people of his inheritance" and so that he could be their "Portion" (cf. Deut 32:9). God is our inheritance, and we are his (see Eph 1:18), which means that we belong together for all eternity.
10:17–22 *Coming Destruction.* Exile is now inevitable, so the inhabitants of the land should prepare whatever they can carry.
10:17–19 Jeremiah so identifies with his people that he feels the pain of this coming disaster like an incurable "wound" (v. 19).
10:20 tent. An image of Israel (also in 4:20).
10:21 shepherds. See note on 2:8 ("leaders").
10:22 land of the north. Babylon. See notes on 1:13–15.
10:23–25 *Jeremiah's Prayer.* Identifying with his people (as he has throughout this passage), Jeremiah pleads for limits on the Lord's judgment.
10:23 direct their steps. The Lord is sovereign over their steps (see Prov 20:24).
10:24 in due measure. Jeremiah asks for the Lord to discipline his people in justice, not in anger. This reflects the distinction between a judgment designed to restore someone to a renewed covenant rela-

10:25 [g]Zep 3:8 [h]Job 18:21; Ps 14:4 [i]Ps 79:7; Jer 8:16 [j]Ps 79:6-7
11:3 [k]Dt 27:26; Gal 3:10
11:4 [l]Dt 4:20; 1Ki 8:51 [m]Ex 24:8 [n]Jer 7:23; 31:33
11:5 [o]Ex 13:5; Dt 7:12; Ps 105:8-11
11:6 [p]Dt 15:5; Ro 2:13; Jas 1:22
11:7 [q]2Ch 36:15
11:8 [r]Jer 7:26 [s]Lev 26:14-43
11:9 [t]Eze 22:25
11:10 [u]Dt 9:7 [v]Jdg 2:12-13
11:11 [w]2Ki 22:16 [x]Jer 14:12; Eze 8:18 [y]ver 14; Pr 1:28; Isa 1:15; Zec 7:13
11:12 [z]Jer 44:17 [a]Dt 32:37
11:13 [b]Jer 7:9 [c]Jer 3:24
11:14 [d]Ex 32:10 [e]ver 11

25Pour out your wrath on the nations[g]
that do not acknowledge you,
on the peoples who do not call on your name.[h]
For they have devoured[i] Jacob;
they have devoured him completely
and destroyed his homeland.[j]

The Covenant Is Broken

11 This is the word that came to Jeremiah from the LORD: 2"Listen to the terms of this covenant
and tell them to the people of Judah and to those who live in Jerusalem. 3Tell them that
this is what the LORD, the God of Israel, says: 'Cursed[k] is the one who does not obey the terms of this
covenant— 4the terms I commanded your ancestors when I brought them out of Egypt, out of the
iron-smelting furnace.[l] I said, 'Obey[m] me and do everything I command you, and you will be my people,[n] and I will be your God. 5Then I will fulfill the oath I swore[o] to your ancestors, to give them a land
flowing with milk and honey'—the land you possess today."
I answered, "Amen, LORD."
6The LORD said to me, "Proclaim all these words in the towns of Judah and in the streets of Jerusalem:
'Listen to the terms of this covenant and follow[p] them. 7From the time I brought your ancestors up
from Egypt until today, I warned them again and again,[q] saying, "Obey me." 8But they did not listen or
pay attention;[r] instead, they followed the stubbornness of their evil hearts. So I brought on them all the
curses[s] of the covenant I had commanded them to follow but that they did not keep.' "
9Then the LORD said to me, "There is a conspiracy[t] among the people of Judah and those who
live in Jerusalem. 10They have returned to the sins of their ancestors,[u] who refused to listen to my
words. They have followed other gods[v] to serve them. Both Israel and Judah have broken the covenant I made with their ancestors. 11Therefore this is what the LORD says: 'I will bring on them a
disaster[w] they cannot escape. Although they cry[x] out to me, I will not listen[y] to them. 12The towns of
Judah and the people of Jerusalem will go and cry out to the gods to whom they burn incense,[z] but
they will not help them at all when disaster[a] strikes. 13You, Judah, have as many gods as you have
towns; and the altars you have set up to burn incense[b] to that shameful[c] god Baal are as many as
the streets of Jerusalem.'
14"Do not pray[d] for this people or offer any plea or petition for them, because I will not listen[e] when
they call to me in the time of their distress.

---

tionship and a judgment designed to cast off that person (Ps 6:1; 38:1). This restorative judgment is what God promised David in 2 Sam 7:14–15.

10:25 Pour out your wrath on the nations. The nations deserve God's punitive wrath because they do not acknowledge him. But how can God's people escape his judgment since they practice that same sin (see 9:6)?

11:1—15:21 *The Broken Covenant and Its Consequences.* God made a covenant with his people at Mount Sinai when he brought them out of the land of Egypt. Attached to that covenant were blessings and curses: blessings for obedience and curses for disobedience (Deut 28). The impending judgment upon Judah and Jerusalem is the consequence of their long history of breaking that covenant, and it is now inevitable.

11:1–17 *The Covenant Is Broken.* The task of the prophets was to remind the people of the stipulations of the covenant made between God and his people at Mount Sinai (Exod 19–24), and to warn of the consequences of disobedience (2 Chr 36:15–16).

11:4–5 Even though the Israelites were not saved by works, possessing their land was conditional on obeying the God who graciously brought them out of Egypt.

11:4 iron-smelting furnace. Reminds the people of their painful experiences in Egypt, the place from which the Lord delivered them into the land of Canaan (Deut 4:20; 1 Kgs 8:51). **you will be my people, and I will be your God.** The goal of the covenant. It could not be reached if they were persistently idolatrous, following other gods.

11:5 flowing with milk and honey. A proverbial expression of plenty that describes the promised land of Canaan (see note on Exod 3:8). **Amen.** "May it be so."

11:8 the curses of the covenant. See Lev 26; Deut 28. In Exod 24:3–7, the people bound themselves to keep the terms of the covenant and were sprinkled with the blood of the sacrifices as a reminder of the consequences of disobedience.

11:9 conspiracy. Has the overtones of rebellion against a king (2 Kgs 15:30; 17:4). The Israelites rebelled against the Lord, their true king.

11:10 returned to the sins of their ancestors. After the temporary reforms of King Josiah (2 Kgs 22:1—23:25), the people of Judah returned to various forms of pagan idolatry.

11:11 I will not listen to them. In their difficulty, the people will finally cry out to the Lord for help, only to find his ears deaf because of their idolatry.

11:12 They will "cry out" to their many idols, but their idols "will not" (or more precisely, cannot) "help them." **burn incense.** One of the simplest and most common acts of devotion.

11:14 Do not pray for this people. Since the Lord is determined not to listen to the people, there is no point in Jeremiah's interceding for them, even though this was normally part of a prophet's role (see 7:16).

15 "What is my beloved doing in my temple
as she, with many others, works out her evil schemes?
Can consecrated meat avert your punishment?
When you engage in your wickedness,
then you rejoice.[a]"
16 The Lord called you a thriving olive tree
with fruit beautiful in form.
But with the roar of a mighty storm
he will set it on fire,[f]
and its branches will be broken.[g]

17 The Lord Almighty, who planted[h] you, has decreed disaster for you, because the people of both Israel
and Judah have done evil and aroused my anger by burning incense to Baal.[i]

Plot Against Jeremiah

18 Because the Lord revealed their plot to me, I knew it, for at that time he showed me what they were doing.
19 I had been like a gentle lamb led to the slaughter; I did not realize that they had plotted[j] against me, saying,

"Let us destroy the tree and its fruit;
let us cut him off from the land of the living,[k]
that his name be remembered[l] no more."
20 But you, Lord Almighty, who judge righteously
and test the heart and mind,[m]
let me see your vengeance on them,
for to you I have committed my cause.

21 Therefore this is what the Lord says about the people of Anathoth who are threatening to kill you,[n]
saying, "Do not prophesy in the name of the Lord or you will die[o] by our hands"— 22 therefore this is
what the Lord Almighty says: "I will punish them. Their young men[p] will die by the sword, their sons
and daughters by famine. 23 Not even a remnant[q] will be left to them, because I will bring disaster on
the people of Anathoth in the year of their punishment.'"

Jeremiah's Complaint

12 You are always righteous,[s] Lord,
when I bring a case before you.
Yet I would speak with you about your justice:
Why does the way of the wicked prosper?[t]
Why do all the faithless live at ease?

[a] 15 Or *Could consecrated meat avert your punishment? / Then you would rejoice*

11:16 [f] Jer 21:14 [g] Isa 27:11; Ro 11:17-24
11:17 [h] Isa 5:2; Jer 12:2 [i] Jer 7:9
11:19 [j] Jer 18:18; 20:10 [k] Job 28:13; Isa 53:8 [l] Ps 83:4
11:20 [m] Ps 7:9
11:21 [n] Jer 12:6 [o] Jer 26:8,11; 38:4
11:22 [p] Jer 18:21
11:23 [q] Jer 6:9 [r] Jer 23:12
12:1 [s] Ezr 9:15 [t] Jer 5:27-28

11:15 In spite of the "evil schemes" that they pursue, Israel is still the Lord's "beloved" (cf. Isa 5:1); but because of their sin, the sacrifices that they continue to offer at the temple are worthless.
11:16 thriving olive tree. A beautiful symbol of prosperity (Ps 52:8); but the tree that the Lord planted has become dry and barren and will now be burned. **branches.** Represent the people. Paul adopts a similar image in Rom 11:17–24, where the olive tree represents the true people of God: dead branches can be broken off from the tree, and other wild olive branches (the Gentiles) can be grafted in to take their place.
11:18–23 *Plot Against Jeremiah.* This is the first of Jeremiah's six "confessions" (see 12:1–4; 15:10–21; 17:12–18; 18:18–23; 20:7–18). Like some of the other prophets before him, Jeremiah is the target of plots because of his unpopular words. In his case, the Lord warns him of the danger, enabling him to escape.
11:20 let me see your vengeance. Jeremiah prays that those who plot against him will receive their just punishment. He is praying not for vengeance on his personal enemies but that the Lord will judge the wicked justly, a common theme in lament psalms (see note on Ps 69:22–28). Such judgment will publicly vindicate Jeremiah as the Lord's messenger.
11:21 Anathoth. Jeremiah's hometown and the location of his enemies (see 1:1 and note). As a priestly city, Jeremiah's prophecies against the priests have not been well received. They are threatening him with death if he continues to prophesy.
11:22–23 False prophets, who faced little opposition (see Mic 2:11), will receive a fitting punishment (death), with no remnant left to them.
12:1–4 *Jeremiah's Complaint.* Jeremiah asks the same question as that in Ps 37 and Ps 73: "Why does the way of the wicked prosper?" (v. 1; cf. Ps 37:1–2,35–36; 73:3–20). In Jeremiah's case, the plot against his life probably triggers this concern (Jer 11:19–23). Yet Jeremiah's concern for justice and for righteous punishment for those of his own family who betray him is a small matter compared to the Lord's anger at his people's betrayal of him.
12:1–2 As a prophet, Jeremiah declared the Lord's case against his

12:2 [u]Jer 11:17 [v]Isa 29:13; Jer 3:10; Mt 15:8; Titus 1:16
12:3 [w]Ps 7:9; 11:5; 139:1-4; Jer 11:20 [x]Jer 17:18
12:4 [y]Jer 4:28 [z]Joel 1:10-12 [a]Jer 4:25; 9:10
12:5 [b]Jer 49:19; 50:44
12:6 [c]Pr 26:24-25; Jer 9:4 [d]Ps 12:2
12:7 [e]Jer 7:29
12:8 [f]Hos 9:15; Am 6:8

2 You have planted[u] them, and they have taken root;
they grow and bear fruit.
You are always on their lips
but far from their hearts.[v]
3 Yet you know me, LORD;
you see me and test[w] my thoughts about you.
Drag them off like sheep to be butchered!
Set them apart for the day of slaughter![x]
4 How long will the land lie parched[y]
and the grass in every field be withered?[z]
Because those who live in it are wicked,
the animals and birds have perished.[a]
Moreover, the people are saying,
"He will not see what happens to us."

God's Answer

5 "If you have raced with men on foot
and they have worn you out,
how can you compete with horses?
If you stumble[a] in safe country,
how will you manage in the thickets[b] by[b]
the Jordan?
6 Your relatives, members of your own family—
even they have betrayed you;
they have raised a loud cry against you.[c]
Do not trust them,
though they speak well of you.[d]
7 "I will forsake my house,
abandon[e] my inheritance;
I will give the one I love
into the hands of her enemies.
8 My inheritance has become to me
like a lion in the forest.
She roars at me;
therefore I hate her.[f]

[a] 5 Or *you feel secure only* [b] 5 Or *the flooding of*

people (2:9); but here he lays out his own case before God, the righteous judge. If "the wicked prosper," it must be because the Lord has "planted them" since the Lord is sovereign (cf. 1:10), enabling them to grow like the fruitful tree that represents the righteous in Ps 1 (see Ps 1:3 and note). Yet they are hypocrites in their service to God. The Lord promises judgment "in the year of their punishment" (11:23), yet in the meantime, they seem to continue to prosper.

12:3 Drag them off like sheep. Since the wicked regard Jeremiah as a "lamb led to the slaughter" (11:19), it is only fitting that they share a similar fate. Yet the longer they continue untouched in their wickedness, the more people are emboldened in their sin and the more they deny the seriousness of Jeremiah's words of impending judgment. Instead, they say, "He [Jeremiah] will not see what happens to us" (v. 4; i.e., they believe Jeremiah's predictions of the future are false). Jeremiah's attitude is similar to that of James and John, who ask Jesus if they can call down fire on those who oppose him (Luke 9:54).

12:5–17 *The Lord's Answer.* The Lord gently rebukes Jeremiah. If Jeremiah is struggling like this when he has raced against only human adversaries, how will he fare if things get worse, metaphorically described as if he races against horses, which run much faster (v. 5)?

12:5 So far Jeremiah has operated in "safe country"; how will he survive in the more dangerous "thickets by the Jordan," the home of lions and other dangerous wild animals (see Zech 11:3)? Jeremiah will face far greater challenges in the future than anything he has faced so far.

12:6 they have betrayed you. Just as Jeremiah cannot trust the members of his own family, the Lord has been betrayed by his own people and must "forsake" and "abandon" them (v. 7), giving his people into the hands of their enemies.

12:7–11 Poignantly, first person forms occur frequently in these verses, as if to emphasize the close relationship between the Lord and the nation and land that are now to be destroyed.

12:7 forsake my house. Foreshadows the departure of God's glory from the Jerusalem temple in Ezek 8–11 and the ultimate abandonment of Christ, the true temple (John 2:19), on the cross.

[9]Has not my inheritance become to me
like a speckled bird of prey
that other birds of prey surround and attack?
Go and gather all the wild beasts;
bring them to devour.[g]
[10]Many shepherds[h] will ruin my vineyard
and trample down my field;
they will turn my pleasant field
into a desolate wasteland.[i]
[11]It will be made a wasteland,
parched and desolate before me;[j]
the whole land will be laid waste
because there is no one who cares.
[12]Over all the barren heights in the desert
destroyers will swarm,
for the sword of the LORD[k] will devour
from one end of the land to the other;[l]
no one will be safe.
[13]They will sow wheat but reap thorns;
they will wear themselves out but gain nothing.[m]
They will bear the shame of their harvest
because of the LORD's fierce anger."[n]

[14]This is what the LORD says: "As for all my wicked neighbors who seize the inheritance I gave my
people Israel, I will uproot[o] them from their lands and I will uproot the people of Judah from among
them. [15]But after I uproot them, I will again have compassion and will bring[p] each of them back to
their own inheritance and their own country. [16]And if they learn well the ways of my people and swear
by my name, saying, 'As surely as the LORD lives'[q]—even as they once taught my people to swear by
Baal[r]—then they will be established among my people.[s] [17]But if any nation does not listen, I will
completely uproot and destroy[t] it," declares the LORD.

A Linen Belt

13 This is what the LORD said to me: "Go and buy a linen belt and put it around your waist, but
do not let it touch water." [2]So I bought a belt, as the LORD directed, and put it around my waist.
[3]Then the word of the LORD came to me a second time: [4]"Take the belt you bought and are wearing
around your waist, and go now to Perath[a] and hide it there in a crevice in the rocks." [5]So I went and
hid it at Perath, as the LORD told me.[u]
[6]Many days later the LORD said to me, "Go now to Perath and get the belt I told you to hide there."

[a] 4 Or possibly *to the Euphrates*; similarly in verses 5-7

12:9 [g] Isa 56:9; Jer 15:3; Eze 23:25
12:10 [h] Jer 23:1 [i] Isa 5:1-7
12:11 [j] ver 4; Isa 42:25; Jer 23:10
12:12 [k] Jer 47:6 [l] Jer 3:2
12:13 [m] Lev 26:20; Dt 28:38; Mic 6:15; Hag 1:6 [n] Jer 4:26
12:14 [o] Zec 2:7-9
12:15 [p] Am 9:14-15
12:16 [q] Jer 4:2 [r] Jos 23:7 [s] Isa 49:6; Jer 3:17
12:17 [t] Isa 60:12
13:5 [u] Ex 40:16

12:9 speckled bird of prey. This pictures doom and death, with the carcasses of the people left exposed (see note on 7:33). **birds of prey ... wild beasts.** The nations the Lord is calling against Judah.
12:10 shepherds. Kings of the nations who wreak destruction on the land and the people.
12:13 sow wheat but reap thorns. The idea of sowing but not reaping what you sowed and toiling for nothing are well-known futility curses in ancient Near Eastern covenants (cf. Hag 2:19).
12:14–17 The Abrahamic covenant is foundational, and Israel's subsequent unfaithfulness cannot nullify it: those who harm Israel will do so to their own ultimate harm (Gen 12:1–3). After judging his people, the Lord will bring them back from exile. More than that, he will show compassion on the nations as well, as the Abrahamic covenant anticipated. They too will be restored if they turn from their idols and join the Lord's people. But if they continue to be rebelliously committed to their idolatry, God will permanently destroy them. Just as Judah became like the nations and had to be judged, so too there is hope for the nations if they will repent.
13:1–11 *A Linen Belt.* Several prophets were instructed to perform sign-acts and speak in parables symbolizing the Lord's plans for his people. This was particularly true of Jeremiah and Ezekiel, perhaps because both spoke to resistant audiences. The dramatic format engaged even those who did not want to listen to the prophet's words.
13:1 a linen belt. An undergarment. Linen was costly, so this was a valuable item. Jeremiah uses it to perform the sign. It is to be worn once but is not to "touch water" to rule out the possibility of any damage.
13:4 Perath. The Hebrew name for the Euphrates River. But it is unlikely that the prophet would travel 350 miles (563 kilometers) to perform this action. More likely, this refers to a similarly named spring four miles (six kilometers) outside Anathoth. The similarity of the names deliberately highlights the region from which the symbolic destruction will come.

13:9 [v]Lev 26:19 **13:10** [w]Jer 11:8; 16:12 [x]Jer 9:14 **13:11** [y]Jer 32:20; 33:9 [z]Ex 19:5-6 [a]Jer 7:26 **13:13** [b]Ps 60:3; 75:8; Isa 51:17; 63:6; Jer 51:57 **13:14** [c]Jer 16:5 [d]Dt 29:20; Eze 5:10 **13:16** [e]Jos 7:19 [f]Jer 23:12 [g]Isa 59:9 **13:17** [h]Mal 2:2 [i]Jer 9:1 [j]Ps 80:1; Jer 23:1 [k]Jer 14:18

7 So I went to Perath and dug up the belt and took it from the place where I had hidden it, but now it was ruined and completely useless.
8 Then the word of the LORD came to me:
9 "This is what the LORD says: 'In the same way I will ruin the pride of Judah and the great pride[v] of Jerusalem.
10 These wicked people, who refuse to listen to my words, who follow the stubbornness of their hearts[w] and go after other gods[x] to serve and worship them, will be like this belt — completely useless!
11 For as a belt is bound around the waist, so I bound all the people of Israel and all the people of Judah to me,' declares the LORD, 'to be my people for my renown[y] and praise and honor.[z] But they have not listened.'[a]

Wineskins

12 "Say to them: 'This is what the LORD, the God of Israel, says: Every wineskin should be filled with wine.' And if they say to you, 'Don't we know that every wineskin should be filled with wine?'
13 then tell them, 'This is what the LORD says: I am going to fill with drunkenness[b] all who live in this land, including the kings who sit on David's throne, the priests, the prophets and all those living in Jerusalem.
14 I will smash them one against the other, parents and children alike, declares the LORD. I will allow no pity or mercy or compassion[c] to keep me from destroying[d] them.' "

Threat of Captivity

15 Hear and pay attention,
do not be arrogant,
for the LORD has spoken.
16 Give glory[e] to the LORD your God
before he brings the darkness,
before your feet stumble[f]
on the darkening hills.
You hope for light,
but he will turn it to utter darkness
and change it to deep gloom.[g]
17 If you do not listen,[h]
I will weep in secret
because of your pride;
my eyes will weep bitterly,
overflowing with tears,[i]
because the LORD's flock[j] will be taken captive.[k]

18 Say to the king and to the queen mother,
"Come down from your thrones,
for your glorious crowns
will fall from your heads."

13:7 ruined. Predictably, the garment is spoiled when Jeremiah goes back to retrieve it.

13:9 In the same way. A sign-act is not a scientific experiment to uncover new facts but rather a demonstration of existing facts by means of a vivid analogy. Just as the belt was closely attached to Jeremiah's waist (vv. 1,11), the Lord closely attached Israel and Judah to himself (v. 11). But their pride, self-will, and idolatry ruined them, and they became as useless as the ruined garment (v. 10). The nation the Lord created for his "renown and praise and honor" (v. 11) became "useless" (v. 10).

13:12–14 *Wineskins.* As with the sign-act (vv.1–11), this parable states the obvious: "every wineskin should be filled with wine" (v. 12). What is less obvious is the application to Jeremiah's hearers: God will fill the people and all their leaders with wine to the point of "drunkenness" (v. 13), i.e., he will make them act like drunkards, stumbling and reeling around (cf. Zech 9:15). Then he will "smash them one against the other" (v. 14), shattering them like clay wine jars, with "no pity or mercy or compassion" (v. 14).

13:15–27 *Threat of Captivity.* This message is tied together with the sign-act (vv. 1–11) and the parable (vv. 12–14) by the themes of pride and stumbling.

13:16 Give glory to the LORD your God. Sometimes a charge to confess sin (Josh 7:19; John 9:24). **utter darkness.** The same Hebrew word occurs in Ps 23:4 ("darkest valley") to describe the trials through which the psalmist must go.

13:17 pride. Resists the call to confess, so the prophet laments the pride that will result in Judah's exile.

13:18 king. Likely Jehoiachin. **queen mother.** Often exercised considerable power behind the scenes (1 Kgs 15:13). The Babylonians took both Jehoiachin and his mother into exile in 597 BC (2 Kgs 24:15). This poem is in the form of a lament, mourning the royal family's downfall before it even occurs.

[19]The cities in the Negev will be shut up,
and there will be no one to open them.
All Judah[l] will be carried into exile,
carried completely away.

[20]Look up and see
those who are coming from the north.[m]
Where is the flock[n] that was entrusted to you,
the sheep of which you boasted?
[21]What will you say when the LORD sets over you
those you cultivated as your special allies?[o]
Will not pain grip you
like that of a woman in labor?[p]
[22]And if you ask yourself,
"Why has this happened to me?" —
it is because of your many sins[q]
that your skirts have been torn off
and your body mistreated.[r]
[23]Can an Ethiopian[a] change his skin
or a leopard its spots?
Neither can you do good
who are accustomed to doing evil.

[24]"I will scatter you like chaff[s]
driven by the desert wind.[t]
[25]This is your lot,
the portion[u] I have decreed for you,"
declares the LORD,

"because you have forgotten me
and trusted in false gods.
[26]I will pull up your skirts over your face
that your shame may be seen[v] —
[27]your adulteries and lustful neighings,
your shameless prostitution![w]

[a] 23 Hebrew *Cushite* (probably a person from the upper Nile region)

13:19 [l] Jer 20:4; 52:30
13:20 [m] Jer 6:22; Hab 1:6 [n] Jer 23:2
13:21 [o] Jer 38:22 [p] Jer 4:31
13:22 [q] Jer 9:2-6; 16:10-12 [r] Eze 16:37; Na 3:5-6
13:24 [s] Ps 1:4 [t] Lev 26:33
13:25 [u] Job 20:29; Mt 24:51
13:26 [v] La 1:8; Eze 16:37; Hos 2:10
13:27 [w] Jer 2:20

13:19 Negev. Southern region of Judah. Since the enemy is coming from the north, the whole country is overrun. The king was supposed to shepherd his flock (Ezek 34:1 – 24), but he failed in that mission.
13:21 Judah's attempts to form political alliances against the Babylonians will be fruitless; indeed, the very nations they pursue as "special allies" will turn against them and join with the Babylonians.
13:22 your skirts have been torn off and your body mistreated. Describes Jerusalem's destruction as a sexual assault. Since she has been so eager to commit spiritual adultery, prostituting herself with the surrounding nations, the punishment will fit the crime (cf. 3:8 – 9).
13:23 Ethiopian. See NIV text note; ancient Ethiopia-Cush is equivalent to modern Sudan. **change his skin ... its spots?** These rhetorical questions expect a negative answer. Equally implausible is a change in Judah's moral character.
13:24 chaff driven by the desert wind. A proverbial image of impermanence and destruction (see Ps 83:13).
13:26 – 27 Public exposure was part of the punishment for adultery (see Ezek 16:36 – 37; Nah 3:5).

Image from the Tomb of Sebekhotep shows Nubians (Ethiopians) carrying trade goods, including a leopard skin (Jer 13:23).

Heritage Images/Glow Images

13:27 [x]Eze 6:13 [y]Hos 8:5
14:2 [z]Isa 3:26; Jer 8:21
14:3 [a]2Ki 18:31; Job 6:19-20 [b]2Sa 15:30
14:4 [c]Jer 3:3
14:5 [d]Isa 15:6
14:6 [e]Job 39:5-6; Jer 2:24
14:7 [f]Hos 5:5 [g]Jer 5:6 [h]Jer 8:14
14:8 [i]Jer 17:13
14:9 [j]Isa 50:2 [k]Jer 8:19 [l]Isa 63:19; Jer 15:16

I have seen your detestable acts
on the hills and in the fields.[x]
Woe to you, Jerusalem!
How long will you be unclean?"[y]

Drought, Famine, Sword

14 This is the word of the LORD that came to Jeremiah concerning the drought:

2 "Judah mourns,[z]
her cities languish;
they wail for the land,
and a cry goes up from Jerusalem.
3 The nobles send their servants for water;
they go to the cisterns
but find no water.[a]
They return with their jars unfilled;
dismayed and despairing,
they cover their heads.[b]
4 The ground is cracked
because there is no rain in the land;[c]
the farmers are dismayed
and cover their heads.
5 Even the doe in the field
deserts her newborn fawn
because there is no grass.[d]
6 Wild donkeys stand on the barren heights[e]
and pant like jackals;
their eyes fail
for lack of food."

7 Although our sins testify[f] against us,
do something, LORD, for the sake of your name.
For we have often rebelled;[g]
we have sinned[h] against you.
8 You who are the hope[i] of Israel,
its Savior in times of distress,
why are you like a stranger in the land,
like a traveler who stays only a night?
9 Why are you like a man taken by surprise,
like a warrior powerless to save?[j]
You are among[k] us, LORD,
and we bear your name;[l]
do not forsake us!

10 This is what the LORD says about this people:

14:1—15:21 *Drought, Famine, Sword.* Israel had been warned about the consequences of disobedience to the Mosaic covenant. These included drought, the sword, famine, and plague (Lev 26:19–20,25–26). Jeremiah's responsibility is to help the people understand the reason for these events.
14:1 This is the word of the LORD. The opening section of this chapter is a message from the Lord in which he describes the effect of the drought he has brought on his people.
14:4 cover their heads. A sign of grief and shame.
14:5–6 the doe ... Wild donkeys. Were accustomed to the usual ebbs and flows in the water supply, but this drought will be so severe that even they cannot survive.
14:7 do something, LORD. Having described the situation of need in vv. 2–6, the prophet identifies with the people in confessing their sins and appealing to the Lord for help.
14:8 Since Israel bears God's name (they belong to him), surely he will act to deliver them. Jeremiah asks why the Lord, "the hope of Israel," has started acting distantly to his people.
14:10–12 At this point in a lament, after confession and supplication, there is sometimes an assurance of deliverance. But in this case, there

"They greatly love to wander;
  they do not restrain their feet.[m]
So the LORD does not accept[n] them;
  he will now remember[o] their wickedness
  and punish them for their sins."[p]

11 Then the LORD said to me, "Do not pray[q] for the well-being of this people. 12 Although they fast,
I will not listen to their cry;[r] though they offer burnt offerings[s] and grain offerings, I will not accept[t]
them. Instead, I will destroy them with the sword, famine and plague."

13 But I said, "Alas, Sovereign LORD! The prophets keep telling them, 'You will not see the sword or
suffer famine.[u] Indeed, I will give you lasting peace in this place.'"

14 Then the LORD said to me, "The prophets are prophesying lies[v] in my name. I have not sent[w] them
or appointed them or spoken to them. They are prophesying to you false visions,[x] divinations,[y] idolatries[a] and the delusions of their own minds. 15 Therefore this is what the LORD says about the prophets
who are prophesying in my name: I did not send them, yet they are saying, 'No sword or famine will
touch this land.' Those same prophets will perish[z] by sword and famine.[a] 16 And the people they are
prophesying to will be thrown out into the streets of Jerusalem because of the famine and sword. There
will be no one to bury[b] them, their wives, their sons and their daughters.[c] I will pour out on them the
calamity they deserve.[d]

17 "Speak this word to them:

"'Let my eyes overflow with tears[e]
  night and day without ceasing;
for the Virgin Daughter, my people,
  has suffered a grievous wound,
  a crushing blow.[f]
18 If I go into the country,
  I see those slain by the sword;
if I go into the city,
  I see the ravages of famine.[g]
Both prophet and priest
  have gone to a land they know not.'"

19 Have you rejected Judah completely?[h]
  Do you despise Zion?
Why have you afflicted us
  so that we cannot be healed?[i]
We hoped for peace
  but no good has come,
for a time of healing
  but there is only terror.[j]

[a] 14 Or *visions, worthless divinations*

14:10 [m] Ps 119:101; Jer 2:25 [n] Jer 6:20; Am 5:22 [o] Hos 9:9 [p] Jer 44:21-23; Hos 8:13
14:11 [q] Ex 32:10
14:12 [r] Isa 1:15; Jer 11:11 [s] Jer 7:21 [t] Jer 6:20
14:13 [u] Jer 5:12
14:14 [v] Jer 27:14 [w] Jer 23:21,32 [x] Jer 23:16 [y] Eze 12:24
14:15 [z] Eze 14:9 [a] Jer 5:12-13
14:16 [b] Ps 79:3 [c] Jer 7:33 [d] Pr 1:31
14:17 [e] Jer 9:1 [f] Jer 8:21
14:18 [g] Eze 7:15
14:19 [h] Jer 7:29 [i] Jer 30:12-13 [j] Jer 8:15

is a confirmation of judgment. In place of Jeremiah's "we," the Lord responds with "they."

14:12 fast ... offerings. There is no real repentance in the hearts of the people, and so even if they were to undertake the appropriate religious mourning rituals of fasting and sacrifice, the Lord would not accept them. There is therefore no point in the prophet interceding any further for them (v. 11). **sword, famine and plague.** The classic curse triad that will be the punishment for their sins (1 Chr 21:12).

14:13–15 The false prophets continue to confuse the people by sending a message opposite to Jeremiah's message (see 6:14–15; 8:10–11), declaring that there will be "lasting peace in this place" (v. 13). But this is not the Lord's message to his people at this time, and the false prophets are therefore "prophesying lies" in the Lord's name (v. 14). The Lord warned his people of this danger in Deut 18:20–22. The test of the true prophet was that his words would come true, and false prophets were to be put to death. The Lord will ultimately vindicate Jeremiah when his message of sword and famine comes true. In the process, the Lord will also cause the false prophets to die by the sword and the famine that they now deny.

14:17 Let my eyes overflow with tears. Jeremiah weeps over the effects of the Lord's curse that he has just announced, just as Jesus later weeps over Jerusalem (Matt 23:37). **Virgin Daughter.** Israel. God describes her as she was in the beginning rather than as the adulterous woman she has become (13:26–27).

14:20 [k]Da 9:7-8
14:21 [l]ver 7 [m]Jer 3:17
14:22 [n]Ps 135:7
15:1 [o]Ex 32:11; Nu 14:13-20 [p]1Sa 7:9 [q]Jer 7:16; Eze 14:14,20 [r]2Ki 17:20
15:2 [s]Jer 43:11 [t]Jer 14:12 [u]Rev 13:10
15:3 [v]Lev 26:16 [w]Dt 28:26 [x]Lev 26:22; Eze 14:21
15:4 [y]Jer 24:9; 29:18 [z]Dt 28:25 [a]2Ki 21:2; 23:26-27
15:5 [b]Isa 51:19; Jer 13:14; 21:7; Na 3:7
15:6 [c]Jer 6:19; 7:24 [d]Zep 1:4
15:7 [e]Jer 18:21
15:8 [f]Jer 6:4
15:9 [g]1Sa 2:5

20 We acknowledge our wickedness, LORD,
and the guilt of our ancestors;
we have indeed sinned[k] against you.
21 For the sake of your name[l] do not despise us;
do not dishonor your glorious throne.[m]
Remember your covenant with us
and do not break it.
22 Do any of the worthless idols of the nations bring rain?[n]
Do the skies themselves send down showers?
No, it is you, LORD our God.
Therefore our hope is in you,
for you are the one who does all this.

15 Then the LORD said to me: "Even if Moses[o] and Samuel[p] were to stand before me, my heart
would not go out to this people.[q] Send them away from my presence![r] Let them go! 2 And if they
ask you, 'Where shall we go?' tell them, 'This is what the LORD says:

" 'Those destined for death, to death;
those for the sword, to the sword;[s]
those for starvation, to starvation;[t]
those for captivity, to captivity.'[u]

3 "I will send four kinds of destroyers[v] against them," declares the LORD, "the sword to kill and the
dogs to drag away and the birds[w] and the wild animals to devour and destroy.[x] 4 I will make them abhorrent[y] to all the kingdoms of the earth[z] because of what Manasseh[a] son of Hezekiah king of Judah
did in Jerusalem.

5 "Who will have pity[b] on you, Jerusalem?
Who will mourn for you?
Who will stop to ask how you are?
6 You have rejected[c] me," declares the LORD.
"You keep on backsliding.
So I will reach out[d] and destroy you;
I am tired of holding back.
7 I will winnow them with a winnowing fork
at the city gates of the land.
I will bring bereavement and destruction on my people,[e]
for they have not changed their ways.
8 I will make their widows more numerous
than the sand of the sea.
At midday I will bring a destroyer[f]
against the mothers of their young men;
suddenly I will bring down on them
anguish and terror.
9 The mother of seven will grow faint[g]
and breathe her last.

14:20–22 Jeremiah confesses the people's sins and asks the Lord to intervene and deliver them. But God cannot accept Jeremiah's intercession because the people do not share Jeremiah's sorrow over sin, as the Lord said in vv. 11–12.

15:1–4 Even if Moses and Samuel, two archetypal prophets, were to intercede on behalf of the people, it would not change their fate. They are set in their course of sin, so their destiny is determined in one of four judgments: death, the sword, starvation, or captivity. The low point of Judah's disobedience was Manasseh's abominations (2 Kgs 21:1–16; 2 Chr 33:1–9), and from that point on the Babylonian exile was inevitable (2 Kgs 23:26–27).

15:6 You have rejected me. The Hebrew is emphatic. The problem is not that the Lord has rejected Judah, as the people claim (14:19); it is that they have rejected the Lord.

15:7 winnowing fork. Separates the grain from the chaff when they are thrown into the air; the wind carries the lighter chaff away. Judah is the "chaff" (13:24).

15:8 midday. Shows the supreme confidence of the invaders; they do not even attempt to conceal their attack.

Her sun will set while it is still day;
she will be disgraced and humiliated.
I will put the survivors to the sword[h]
before their enemies,"
declares the LORD.

10 Alas, my mother, that you gave me birth,[i]
a man with whom the whole land strives and contends![j]
I have neither lent[k] nor borrowed,
yet everyone curses me.

11 The LORD said,

"Surely I will deliver you[l] for a good purpose;
surely I will make your enemies plead[m] with you
in times of disaster and times of distress.

12 "Can a man break iron—
iron from the north[n]—or bronze?

13 "Your wealth and your treasures
I will give as plunder, without charge,[o]
because of all your sins
throughout your country.[p]
14 I will enslave you to your enemies
in[a] a land you do not know,[q]
for my anger will kindle a fire[r]
that will burn against you."

15 LORD, you understand;
remember me and care for me.
Avenge me on my persecutors.[s]
You are long-suffering—do not take me away;
think of how I suffer reproach for your sake.[t]
16 When your words came, I ate[u] them;
they were my joy and my heart's delight,[v]
for I bear your name,[w]
LORD God Almighty.
17 I never sat[x] in the company of revelers,
never made merry with them;
I sat alone because your hand was on me
and you had filled me with indignation.
18 Why is my pain unending
and my wound grievous and incurable?[y]

15:9 [h] Jer 21:7
15:10 [i] Job 3:1 [j] Jer 1:19 [k] Lev 25:36
15:11 [l] Jer 40:4 [m] Jer 21:1-2; 37:3; 42:1-3
15:12 [n] Jer 28:14
15:13 [o] Ps 44:12 [p] Jer 17:3
15:14 [q] Dt 28:36; Jer 16:13 [r] Dt 32:22; Ps 21:9
15:15 [s] Jer 12:3 [t] Ps 69:7-9
15:16 [u] Eze 3:3; Rev 10:10 [v] Ps 119:72, 103 [w] Jer 14:9
15:17 [x] Ps 1:1; 26:4-5; Jer 16:8
15:18 [y] Jer 30:15; Mic 1:9

[a] *14* Some Hebrew manuscripts, Septuagint and Syriac (see also 17:4); most Hebrew manuscripts *I will cause your enemies to bring you / into*

15:10 Jeremiah laments that he was even born. Had he "lent" or "borrowed" money, there might be reason for people to hate him; financial obligations often complicate relationships. Yet he is universally hated without any reason, viewed as a man "with whom the whole land strives and contends"—an ironic reversal, since Jeremiah was the prosecuting attorney of the Lord's contention against his people (see 2:9).
15:11 The Lord gently rebukes Jeremiah by assuring him that he has a good purpose for him (cf. 29:11) and will protect him until he accomplishes that good purpose.
15:12–14 The singular "you" (v. 14) is Judah. The Lord reminds Jeremiah of the message that he must still deliver to the people. Their confidence in their own strength is misplaced; they will be unable to break the "iron from the north" (v. 12). North is the direction from which their enemies will come (cf. 28:10–13).
15:15–18 The prophet is still disturbed and complains about his assignment.
15:16 When your words came, I ate them. Jeremiah internalized the Lord's message that he had to deliver. Like Ezekiel (Ezek 2:8—3:3), Jeremiah found the message initially sweet. Yet his prophetic role isolated him from normal human companionship, and the message he received made him start to feel God's own "indignation" toward the people (v. 17).
15:18 pain unending. Identifying both with the Lord and with his people, Jeremiah experiences unremitting pain. Whereas in 2:13 he

15:18 [z] Job 6:15
15:19 [a] Zec 3:7
15:20 [b] Jer 20:11; Eze 3:8
15:21 [c] Jer 50:34 [d] Ge 48:16
16:2 [e] 1Co 7:26-27
16:3 [f] Jer 6:21
16:4 [g] Jer 25:33 [h] Ps 83:10; Jer 9:22 [i] Ps 79:1-3; Jer 15:3; 34:20
16:6 [j] Eze 9:5-6 [k] Lev 19:28 [l] Jer 41:5; 47:5
16:7 [m] Eze 24:17; Hos 9:4
16:8 [n] Ecc 7:2-4; Jer 15:17
16:9 [o] Isa 24:8; Eze 26:13; Hos 2:11 [p] Rev 18:23

You are to me like a deceptive brook,
  like a spring that fails.[z]

19 Therefore this is what the LORD says:

"If you repent, I will restore you
  that you may serve[a] me;
if you utter worthy, not worthless, words,
  you will be my spokesman.
Let this people turn to you,
  but you must not turn to them.
20 I will make you a wall to this people,
  a fortified wall of bronze;
they will fight against you
  but will not overcome you,
for I am with you
  to rescue and save you,"[b]

declares the LORD.

21 "I will save you from the hands of the wicked
  and deliver[c] you from the grasp of the cruel."[d]

Day of Disaster

16 Then the word of the LORD came to me: 2 "You must not marry[e] and have sons or daughters in
this place." 3 For this is what the LORD says about the sons and daughters born in this land and
about the women who are their mothers and the men who are their fathers:[f] 4 "They will die of deadly
diseases. They will not be mourned or buried[g] but will be like dung lying on the ground.[h] They will perish by sword and famine, and their dead bodies will become food for the birds and the wild animals."[i]
5 For this is what the LORD says: "Do not enter a house where there is a funeral meal; do not go to
mourn or show sympathy, because I have withdrawn my blessing, my love and my pity from this people," declares the LORD. 6 "Both high and low will die in this land.[j] They will not be buried or mourned,
and no one will cut[k] themselves or shave[l] their head for the dead. 7 No one will offer food to comfort
those who mourn[m] for the dead—not even for a father or a mother—nor will anyone give them a
drink to console them.
8 "And do not enter a house where there is feasting and sit down to eat and drink.[n] 9 For this is what
the LORD Almighty, the God of Israel, says: Before your eyes and in your days I will bring an end to the
sounds[o] of joy and gladness and to the voices of bride and bridegroom in this place.[p]

---

described the Lord as a "spring of living water," he now accuses God of being like a "deceptive brook," a watercourse that dries up in the heat of summer and is not there when most needed. It seems to Jeremiah as if God has abandoned him in his hour of need.

15:19 If you repent. Jeremiah must lead the people in repentance and continue his prophetic work, uttering worthy words, unlike the false prophets. Then the Lord will deliver and protect him, making him into an impenetrable "wall of bronze" (v. 20). If the people only had ears to hear, they would likewise repent and be protected from the forthcoming day of disaster.

16:1—29:32 *Opposition to Jeremiah's Messages of Judgment.* Jeremiah's ministry faces constant opposition from kings, priests, and false prophets, as well as ordinary people. In particular, his message that the temple will be destroyed and the people taken into exile in Babylon seems at odds with earlier assurances of the Lord's presence with Jerusalem (e.g., Ps 46), which makes the message of the false prophets even more attractive to the people.

16:1—17:18 *Day of Disaster.* The prophets were sometimes called to be signs themselves in their personal lives. Ezekiel was instructed not to mourn publicly when his wife died (Ezek 24:15–24) as a sign of the coming judgment, when there would be too many dead people for the proper mourning rites to be undertaken. Jeremiah's highly unusual actions of not getting married and not engaging in mourning for the dead will be signs to the people of the certainty of his message.

16:2 You must not marry and have sons or daughters. Celibacy was not regarded as a more holy state in Israel; priests could marry, as could those who had taken a Nazirite vow of holiness to the Lord. Yet Jeremiah is not to marry or have children as a sign of the terrible fate that is coming on the land—a day when it will be easier not to have any close relationships, so as not to have to endure the pain of seeing loved ones suffer (v. 4). Also, when the Babylonians come they will make many childless.

16:5 funeral meal ... mourn ... show sympathy. Conventional cultural mourning practices. By not following these practices, Jeremiah will embody the Lord's lack of love and pity toward his people. In the days to come, such practices will be suspended because of the scale of the disaster to come on Judah (vv. 6–7).

16:6 cut themselves ... shave their head for the dead. Pagan rituals that Deut 14:1 forbids; including them in this list shows the extent to which paganism had invaded the culture.

16:8 feasting ... eat and drink. These occur at celebrations such as weddings. The Lord will bring all such celebrations to an end (v. 9).

10 "When you tell these people all this and they ask you, 'Why has the LORD decreed such a great disaster against us? What wrong have we done? What sin have we committed against the LORD our God?'[q]
11 then say to them, 'It is because your ancestors forsook me,' declares the LORD, 'and followed other gods
and served and worshiped them. They forsook me and did not keep my law.[r] 12 But you have behaved
more wickedly than your ancestors.[s] See how all of you are following the stubbornness of your evil
hearts[t] instead of obeying me. 13 So I will throw you out of this land into a land neither you nor your ancestors have known,[u] and there you will serve other gods[v] day and night, for I will show you no favor.'[w]

14 "However, the days are coming," declares the LORD, "when it will no longer be said, 'As surely as
the LORD lives, who brought the Israelites up out of Egypt,'[x] 15 but it will be said, 'As surely as the LORD
lives, who brought the Israelites up out of the land of the north and out of all the countries where he
had banished them.'[y] For I will restore[z] them to the land I gave their ancestors.

16 "But now I will send for many fishermen," declares the LORD, "and they will catch them.[a] After that I
will send for many hunters, and they will hunt[b] them down on every mountain and hill and from the crevices of the rocks.[c] 17 My eyes are on all their ways; they are not hidden[d] from me, nor is their sin concealed
from my eyes.[e] 18 I will repay them double[f] for their wickedness and their sin, because they have defiled my
land[g] with the lifeless forms of their vile images and have filled my inheritance with their detestable idols."

19 LORD, my strength and my fortress,
  my refuge in time of distress,
to you the nations will come[h]
  from the ends of the earth and say,
"Our ancestors possessed nothing but false gods,[i]
  worthless idols that did them no good.
20 Do people make their own gods?
  Yes, but they are not gods!"[j]

21 "Therefore I will teach them —
  this time I will teach them
  my power and might.
Then they will know
  that my name is the LORD.

17 "Judah's sin is engraved with an iron tool,[k]
  inscribed with a flint point,
on the tablets of their hearts[l]
  and on the horns of their altars.
2 Even their children remember
  their altars and Asherah poles[a][m]

[a] 2 That is, wooden symbols of the goddess Asherah

16:10 [q] Dt 29:24; Jer 5:19
16:11 [r] Dt 29:25-26; 1Ki 9:9; Ps 106:35-43; Jer 22:9
16:12 [s] Jer 7:26 [t] Ecc 9:3; Jer 13:10
16:13 [u] Dt 28:36; Jer 5:19 [v] Dt 4:28 [w] Jer 15:5
16:14 [x] Dt 15:15; Jer 23:7-8
16:15 [y] Isa 11:11; Jer 23:8 [z] Jer 24:6
16:16 [a] Am 4:2; Hab 1:14-15 [b] Am 9:3; Mic 7:2 [c] 1Sa 26:20
16:17 [d] 1Co 4:5; Heb 4:13 [e] Pr 15:3
16:18 [f] Isa 40:2; Rev 18:6 [g] Nu 35:34; Jer 2:7
16:19 [h] Isa 2:2; Jer 3:17 [i] Ps 4:2
16:20 [j] Ps 115:4-7; Isa 37:19; Jer 2:11
17:1 [k] Job 19:24 [l] Pr 3:3; 2Co 3:3
17:2 [m] 2Ch 24:18

16:10 When ... they ask you. The purpose of Jeremiah's announcement is to make people ask him questions about why the Lord will bring such judgment upon them.
16:11 The reason for judgment is twofold: (1) their ancestors sinned when they "followed other gods," "forsook" the Lord, and "did not keep [his] law"; and (2) more significant, the present generation is sinning in exactly the same way (v. 12). Serving other gods in exile is a fitting judgment for their sin of serving other gods in the land the Lord gave them (v. 13).
16:14 the days are coming. This message of judgment will not be the Lord's last word in his relationship with his people. Instead, it is the precursor for a new and greater exodus in which he will bring his people back "out of the land of the north" (v. 15; i.e., Babylon; see notes on 1:13–15) and "out of all the countries" where they will be scattered. He will return them to their own land (v. 15).
16:16 fishermen ... hunters. The Babylonians, whom the Lord will employ to relentlessly hunt his people down.
16:17 My eyes are on all their ways. It would normally be good news to hear the Lord say this (2 Chr 16:9), but here this means that they will be unable to hide from his judgment.
16:18 double. May mean "ample" or "full" punishment; however, it could also mean "an exact match," as today we speak of an actor's "double." Deut 17:18 uses the same Hebrew word for an exact "copy" of the law. **lifeless.** In contrast to the living and life-giving God.
16:19–20 In contrast to the idolatry of his people (v. 18), Jeremiah himself proclaims the Lord alone as his "refuge." In addition to the new exodus of the people, Jeremiah anticipates the day when the "nations" also will abandon their worthless idols and come to the Lord (Isa 2:2–4).
16:21 By bringing his people back from Babylon, the Lord will "teach" the nations his "power and might." **know that my name is the LORD.** Recognize and acknowledge the Lord as the true God.
17:1 iron ... flint. Hard materials, hard enough even to write on Judah's stony "hearts" as well as on their "altars," on which they offered their sinful sacrifices.
17:2 Asherah poles. Either living trees or wooden symbols representing

17:2 [n]Jer 2:20
17:3 [o]2Ki 24:13 [p]Jer 26:18; Mic 3:12 [q]Jer 15:13
17:4 [r]La 5:2 [s]Dt 28:48; Jer 12:7 [t]Jer 16:13 [u]Jer 7:20; 15:14
17:5 [v]Isa 2:22; 30:1-3
17:6 [w]Dt 29:23; Job 39:6
17:7 [x]Ps 34:8; 40:4; Pr 16:20
17:8 [y]Jer 14:1-6 [z]Ps 1:3; 92:12-14
17:9 [a]Ecc 9:3; Mt 13:15; Mk 7:21-22
17:10 [b]1Sa 16:7; Rev 2:23 [c]Ps 17:3; 139:23; Jer 11:20; 20:12; Ro 8:27 [d]Ps 62:12; Jer 32:19 [e]Ro 2:6

beside the spreading trees
    and on the high hills.[n]
3 My mountain in the land
    and your[a] wealth and all your treasures
I will give away as plunder,[o]
    together with your high places,[p]
    because of sin throughout your country.[q]
4 Through your own fault you will lose
    the inheritance[r] I gave you.
I will enslave you to your enemies[s]
    in a land[t] you do not know,
for you have kindled my anger,
    and it will burn[u] forever."

5 This is what the LORD says:

"Cursed is the one who trusts in man,[v]
    who draws strength from mere flesh
    and whose heart turns away from the LORD.
6 That person will be like a bush in the wastelands;
    they will not see prosperity when it comes.
They will dwell in the parched places of the desert,
    in a salt[w] land where no one lives.

7 "But blessed is the one who trusts[x] in the LORD,
    whose confidence is in him.
8 They will be like a tree planted by the water
    that sends out its roots by the stream.
It does not fear when heat comes;
    its leaves are always green.
It has no worries in a year of drought[y]
    and never fails to bear fruit."[z]

9 The heart[a] is deceitful above all things
    and beyond cure.
    Who can understand it?

10 "I the LORD search the heart[b]
    and examine the mind,[c]
to reward[d] each person according to their conduct,
    according to what their deeds deserve."[e]

[a] 2,3 Or *hills / 3and the mountains of the land. / Your*

the green trees that were associated with the fertility goddess Asherah (see NIV text note; see photo, p. 180). **spreading trees ... high hills.** See note on 2:20.

17:3 My mountain. This refers to Zion, the sacred home of the temple in Jerusalem. Some translations render it as "the mountains," linking it with the "high hills" in v. 2.

17:5 man ... mere flesh. The Hebrew words focus on human mortality as opposed to the matchless power of the living God.

17:6–8 bush in the wastelands ... tree planted by the water. Ps 1 similarly contrasts the blessed person (who is like a "tree planted by streams of water" [Ps 1:3] that has leaves that are always green and that bears fruit in season) and the cursed person (who is dry and barren and whom the wind "blows away" [Ps 1:4]). In this context, it is also a reminder that true fertility and fruitfulness come from the Lord, not from Asherah (v. 2).

17:9 The heart is deceitful above all things and beyond cure. The heart is not simply the seat of the emotions in the OT; it is the location of a person's thoughts and beliefs (cf. Ezek 28:2). Because it is hidden, the heart is hard to understand (Prov 14:10).

17:10 mind. This word often occurs together with "heart" to indicate the most hidden recesses of a person. The Lord is a judge who searches both the "heart" and the "mind"; therefore, he is able to judge with absolute justice, rewarding "each person according to their conduct." This is not good news given the deceitfulness of the human heart (see v. 9 and note; Ezek 9:10). However, the Lord is able to heal and transform even such a broken and dysfunctional organ, and he promises to do so under the new covenant (Jer 31:33; 32:40; cf. Ezek 36:26; Rom 5:5; Heb 10:22). That process is begun in the present in believers and will be completed on the "day of Christ Jesus" (Phil 1:6).

[11]Like a partridge that hatches eggs it did not lay
are those who gain riches by unjust means.
When their lives are half gone, their riches will desert them,
and in the end they will prove to be fools.[f]

[12]A glorious throne,[g] exalted from the beginning,
is the place of our sanctuary.
[13]LORD, you are the hope[h] of Israel;
all who forsake[i] you will be put to shame.
Those who turn away from you will be written in the dust
because they have forsaken the LORD,
the spring of living water.
[14]Heal me, LORD, and I will be healed;
save me and I will be saved,
for you are the one I praise.[j]
[15]They keep saying to me,
"Where is the word of the LORD?
Let it now be fulfilled!"[k]
[16]I have not run away from being your shepherd;
you know I have not desired the day of despair.
What passes my lips is open before you.
[17]Do not be a terror[l] to me;
you are my refuge[m] in the day of disaster.
[18]Let my persecutors be put to shame,
but keep me from shame;
let them be terrified,
but keep me from terror.
Bring on them the day of disaster;
destroy them with double destruction.[n]

17:11 [f]Lk 12:20
17:12 [g]Jer 3:17
17:13 [h]Jer 14:8 [i]Isa 1:28; Jer 2:17
17:14 [j]Ps 109:1
17:15 [k]Isa 5:19; 2Pe 3:4
17:17 [l]Ps 88:15-16 [m]Jer 16:19; Na 1:7
17:18 [n]Ps 35:1-8
17:19 [o]Jer 7:2; 26:2
17:20 [p]Jer 19:3

Keeping the Sabbath Day Holy

[19]This is what the LORD said to me: "Go and stand at the Gate of the People,[a] through which the kings
of Judah go in and out; stand also at all the other gates of Jerusalem.[o] [20]Say to them, 'Hear the word
of the LORD, you kings of Judah and all people of Judah and everyone living in Jerusalem[p] who come

[a] *19* Or *Army*

17:11 The proverbial inverse of the cuckoo, which lays eggs for others to raise, is the "partridge," which reputedly hatches eggs that it did not lay. The point: people "who gain riches by unjust means" will find that, like fledglings, their riches will fly away from them and leave them abandoned and alone. These people are "fools," which in the Bible points to moral (not intellectual) deficiency (see Ps 14:1 and NIV text note there).

17:12 sanctuary. The temple in Jerusalem, where the Lord reigned on his glorious throne (Isa 6:1); a place of refuge for those who trust in the Lord but not for those who forsake the Lord.

17:13 written in the dust. Perhaps (1) written down in insubstantial dust only to be blown away, or (2) written down for the judgment of death and decay. Either way, it is clear that God will judge those who forsake "the spring of living water" (see 2:13 and note).

17:14 Heal me. Psalms sometimes describe personal difficulty or trials in the metaphoric language of sickness, with deliverance then being an act of healing by the Lord (e.g., Ps 6). Unlike those who forsake the Lord, Jeremiah looks to the Lord for deliverance.

17:15 Jeremiah's trial is that the words that he prophesies have not yet come true, which leads to skepticism about his message.

17:16 not run away from being your shepherd. Jeremiah has not shirked his responsibility as a prophet. **not desired the day of despair.** Jeremiah has not gloated over the message of destruction that he has been delivering.

17:17 Even though his hearers mock him, Jeremiah believes wholeheartedly in his message, so he prays that when the disaster he has been called to prophesy comes, the Lord will be his "refuge."

17:18 double. See note on 16:18.

17:19–27 *Keeping the Sabbath Day Holy.* The Sabbath command was a key part of the Lord's covenant with Israel (Exod 20:8–11; 31:12–18) as well as perhaps part of God's design for humanity in the beginning (Gen 2:2–3). As the people of Israel submitted their time to the Lord's kingship, the Sabbath was a sign that distinguished Israel from the surrounding nations. The coming exile will be in part a punishment for Israel's failure to keep the Sabbath (Lev 26:34–35); the exile will be a time for the land to enjoy the Sabbath rests that it never experienced during Israel's time of residence (2 Chr 36:21).

17:19 Gate of the People. Not mentioned elsewhere in Scripture; it must have been one of the many gates into Jerusalem. **the kings of Judah.** Probably included the royal princes.

17:20 [q]Jer 22:2
17:21 [r]Nu 15:32-36; Ne 13:15-21; Jn 5:10
17:22 [s]Ex 20:8; 31:13; Isa 56:2-6; Eze 20:12
17:23 [t]Jer 7:26 [u]Jer 19:15 [v]Jer 7:28
17:25 [w]2Sa 7:13; Isa 9:7; Jer 22:2,4; Lk 1:32
17:26 [x]Jer 32:44; 33:13; Zec 7:7
17:27 [y]Jer 22:5 [z]Jer 7:20 [a]2Ki 25:9; Am 2:5
18:6 [b]Isa 45:9; Ro 9:20-21
18:7 [c]Jer 1:10
18:8 [d]Jer 26:13; Jnh 3:8-10 [e]Eze 18:21; Hos 11:8-9
18:9 [f]Jer 1:10; 31:28
18:10 [g]Eze 33:18 [h]1Sa 2:29-30
18:11 [i]Jer 4:6 [j]2Ki 17:13; Isa 1:16-19 [k]Jer 7:3
18:12 [l]Isa 57:10; Jer 2:25

through these gates.[q] 21This is what the LORD says: Be careful not to carry a load on the Sabbath[r] day or bring it through the gates of Jerusalem. 22Do not bring a load out of your houses or do any work on the Sabbath, but keep the Sabbath day holy, as I commanded your ancestors.[s] 23Yet they did not listen or pay attention;[t] they were stiff-necked[u] and would not listen or respond to discipline.[v] 24But if you are careful to obey me, declares the LORD, and bring no load through the gates of this city on the Sabbath, but keep the Sabbath day holy by not doing any work on it, 25then kings who sit on David's throne[w] will come through the gates of this city with their officials. They and their officials will come riding in chariots and on horses, accompanied by the men of Judah and those living in Jerusalem, and this city will be inhabited forever. 26People will come from the towns of Judah and the villages around Jerusalem, from the territory of Benjamin and the western foothills, from the hill country and the Negev,[x] bringing burnt offerings and sacrifices, grain offerings and incense, and bringing thank offerings to the house of the LORD. 27But if you do not obey[y] me to keep the Sabbath day holy by not carrying any load as you come through the gates of Jerusalem on the Sabbath day, then I will kindle an unquenchable fire[z] in the gates of Jerusalem that will consume her fortresses.' "[a]

At the Potter's House

18 This is the word that came to Jeremiah from the LORD: 2"Go down to the potter's house, and there I will give you my message." 3So I went down to the potter's house, and I saw him working at the wheel. 4But the pot he was shaping from the clay was marred in his hands; so the potter formed it into another pot, shaping it as seemed best to him.

5Then the word of the LORD came to me. 6He said, "Can I not do with you, Israel, as this potter does?" declares the LORD. "Like clay[b] in the hand of the potter, so are you in my hand, Israel. 7If at any time I announce that a nation or kingdom is to be uprooted,[c] torn down and destroyed, 8and if that nation I warned repents of its evil, then I will relent[d] and not inflict on it the disaster[e] I had planned. 9And if at another time I announce that a nation or kingdom is to be built[f] up and planted, 10and if it does evil[g] in my sight and does not obey me, then I will reconsider[h] the good I had intended to do for it.

11"Now therefore say to the people of Judah and those living in Jerusalem, 'This is what the LORD says: Look! I am preparing a disaster[i] for you and devising a plan against you. So turn[j] from your evil ways,[k] each one of you, and reform your ways and your actions.' 12But they will reply, 'It's no use.[l] We will continue with our own plans; we will all follow the stubbornness of our evil hearts.' "

17:21 carry a load. Forbidden on the Sabbath day since it was a form of work. In this case, it also served to advance another form of Sabbath breaking: trading on the Sabbath.

17:24–26 Jerusalem will continue to be the home of David's descendants forever, as God promised (2 Sam 7:12–16), if the people carefully obey the Sabbath command. It will also remain the home of the temple, "the house of the LORD" (v. 26), the place to which people bring sacrifices from areas around Jerusalem.

17:26 hill country. The area of Judah west of Jerusalem. **Negev.** The area of Judah south of Jerusalem.

17:27 Covenantal unfaithfulness in Sabbath keeping will lead to the destruction of Jerusalem, including the temple and the house of David (ch. 22).

18:1—19:15 *At the Potter's House.* Just as a potter has the right to shape the clay and reshape it if the first design doesn't please him, so too the Lord has the right to deal with his rebellious people, whom he created.

18:3 wheel. A circular stone that was turned by foot so that the potter could produce round objects such as bowls and jugs.

18:4 marred. Malformed, so the potter simply presses the clay back into a lump and starts again.

18:6 Like clay in the hand of the potter. The object of the analogy in vv. 6–10 is Judah and Jerusalem's relationship with the Lord.

18:7–10 The people of Judah assume that because the Lord entered a covenant with them, they can behave however they wish and still call on him in time of trouble. Yet the Lord declares that his relationship with a "nation or kingdom" (v. 7) can change based on the behavior of its people. He can threaten to uproot, tear down, and destroy a kingdom (v. 7) but then relent if the nation "repents of its evil" (v. 8). Alternatively, he can promise to build up or plant a kingdom but reconsider if they do not obey (vv. 9–10). The verbs in vv. 7,9 ("uprooted, torn down and destroyed ... built up and planted") are all drawn from Jeremiah's call in 1:10. This does not mean that God changes his mind, for he is outside time and does not change (Num 23:19). Yet we should not therefore think our actions have no significance. On the contrary, God's dealings with a people, though foreordained from all eternity, nonetheless reflect their response to him. Hard-heartedness will lead to destruction, while repentance will lead to blessing. Of course, the specific application of the passage refers to nations receiving a prophetic word of blessing or curse, so it is not directly applicable to modern nation states, though it remains generally true that "righteousness exalts a nation, but sin condemns any people" (Prov 14:34).

18:11–12 Although the theoretical scenario sketched out in vv. 7–10 (see note on vv. 7–10) could result in blessing or curse, the immediate situation is bleak. The Lord warns his people that he is preparing a "plan" for their doom, but instead of repenting, they will stubbornly determine to continue with their own evil "plans." There is no hope for them as long as they persist in this rebellion: the good promises of God will remain unfulfilled. However, the Lord's words provide hope for the next generation. Though they will inherit the destruction of the exile, there can still be a positive outcome if they respond with repentance.

13 Therefore this is what the LORD says:

"Inquire among the nations:
Who has ever heard anything like this?[m]
A most horrible[n] thing has been done
by Virgin Israel.
14 Does the snow of Lebanon
ever vanish from its rocky slopes?
Do its cool waters from distant sources
ever stop flowing?[a]
15 Yet my people have forgotten me;
they burn incense to worthless idols,[o]
which made them stumble in their ways,
in the ancient paths.[p]
They made them walk in byways,
on roads not built up.[q]
16 Their land will be an object of horror[r]
and of lasting scorn;[s]
all who pass by will be appalled
and will shake their heads.[t]
17 Like a wind[u] from the east,
I will scatter them before their enemies;
I will show them my back and not my face[v]
in the day of their disaster."

18 They said, "Come, let's make plans[w] against Jeremiah; for the teaching of the law by the priest[x]
will not cease, nor will counsel from the wise, nor the word from the prophets.[y] So come, let's attack
him with our tongues[z] and pay no attention to anything he says."

19 Listen to me, LORD;
hear what my accusers are saying!
20 Should good be repaid with evil?
Yet they have dug a pit[a] for me.
Remember that I stood before you
and spoke in their behalf[b]
to turn your wrath away from them.
21 So give their children over to famine;[c]
hand them over to the power of the sword.
Let their wives be made childless and widows;[d]
let their men be put to death,
their young men slain by the sword in battle.

18:13 [m] Isa 66:8; Jer 2:10 [n] Jer 5:30
18:15 [o] Jer 10:15 [p] Jer 6:16 [q] Isa 57:14; 62:10
18:16 [r] Jer 25:9 [s] Jer 19:8 [t] Ps 22:7
18:17 [u] Jer 13:24 [v] Jer 2:27
18:18 [w] Jer 11:19 [x] Mal 2:7 [y] Jer 5:13 [z] Ps 52:2
18:20 [a] Ps 35:7; 57:6 [b] Ps 106:23
18:21 [c] Jer 11:22 [d] Ps 109:9

[a] *14* The meaning of the Hebrew for this sentence is uncertain.

18:13 Virgin Israel. See note on 14:17.
18:14–15 The exact meaning of v. 14 is uncertain, though its point is clear: snow is consistently visible on the slopes of Mount Lebanon, and waters consistently flow from springs and the melting snows; nature is reliable in obeying the Lord's laws (Ps 19:1–6). But Israel forgot the Lord, turning to "worthless idols" and abandoning "the ancient paths" (see note on 6:16).
18:16 lasting scorn. Reflects a gesture of astonishment and derision.
18:17 a wind from the east. A scorching wind from the desert that dries up and devastates the crops; it symbolizes destruction (see 4:11 and note). As Judah turned its back to the Lord (2:27), so he will now turn his back to them.
18:18 Instead of listening to Jeremiah's words and repenting, the people's response is to "make plans against Jeremiah," proving the Lord's assertion in v. 12. Jeremiah tells them that the Lord will turn his back to them (v. 17), which will terminate the communication between him and his people through the priest's teaching of the law (Deut 33:10), the wise man's thoughtful reflections on the nature of God's world, and the prophets' declaration of the word. They deny the truth of Jeremiah's prophecy (17:15) and instead of submitting to the unwelcome truth, they determine to attack the messenger.
18:19 my accusers. This is often legal terminology. Jeremiah understands that their intention is more than merely to attack him with their tongues (v. 18). Their real intent is to put him to death (v. 23; see 11:19), perhaps on the grounds that he is a false prophet (Deut 18:20–22).
18:20–23 Jeremiah asks that the Lord vindicate the truth of his message by bringing upon his adversaries the righteous judgment that the Lord has announced will fall upon their children: "famine" and "the sword" (v. 21; see 14:15).

18:22 [e] Jer 6:26 [f] Ps 140:5
18:23 [g] Jer 11:21 [h] Ps 109:14
19:1 [i] Jer 18:2 [j] Nu 11:17
19:2 [k] Jos 15:8
19:3 [l] Jer 17:20 [m] Jer 6:19 [n] 1Sa 3:11
19:4 [o] Dt 28:20; Isa 65:11 [p] Lev 18:21 [q] 2Ki 21:16; Jer 2:34
19:5 [r] Lev 18:21; Ps 106:37-38 [s] Jer 7:31; 32:35
19:6 [t] Jos 15:8 [u] Jer 7:32
19:7 [v] Lev 26:17; Dt 28:25 [w] Jer 16:4; 34:20 [x] Ps 79:2
19:8 [y] Jer 18:16
19:9 [z] Lev 26:29; Dt 28:49-57; La 4:10 [a] Isa 9:20
19:10 [b] ver 1
19:11 [c] Ps 2:9; Isa 30:14 [d] Jer 7:32
19:13 [e] Jer 32:29; 52:13 [f] Dt 4:19; Ac 7:42 [g] Jer 7:18; Eze 20:28
19:14 [h] 2Ch 20:5; Jer 26:2

22 Let a cry[e] be heard from their houses
  when you suddenly bring invaders against them,
for they have dug a pit to capture me
  and have hidden snares[f] for my feet.
23 But you, LORD, know
  all their plots to kill[g] me.
Do not forgive[h] their crimes
  or blot out their sins from your sight.
Let them be overthrown before you;
  deal with them in the time of your anger.

19 This is what the LORD says: "Go and buy a clay jar from a potter.[i] Take along some of the elders[j]
of the people and of the priests 2 and go out to the Valley of Ben Hinnom,[k] near the entrance of
the Potsherd Gate. There proclaim the words I tell you, 3 and say, 'Hear the word of the LORD, you kings[l]
of Judah and people of Jerusalem. This is what the LORD Almighty, the God of Israel, says: Listen! I am
going to bring a disaster[m] on this place that will make the ears of everyone who hears of it tingle.[n] 4 For
they have forsaken[o] me and made this a place of foreign gods; they have burned incense[p] in it to gods
that neither they nor their ancestors nor the kings of Judah ever knew, and they have filled this place
with the blood of the innocent.[q] 5 They have built the high places of Baal to burn their children[r] in the
fire as offerings to Baal—something I did not command or mention, nor did it enter my mind.[s] 6 So
beware, the days are coming, declares the LORD, when people will no longer call this place Topheth or
the Valley of Ben Hinnom,[t] but the Valley of Slaughter.[u]

7 " 'In this place I will ruin[a] the plans of Judah and Jerusalem. I will make them fall by the sword
before their enemies,[v] at the hands of those who want to kill them, and I will give their carcasses[w] as
food[x] to the birds and the wild animals. 8 I will devastate this city and make it an object of horror and
scorn;[y] all who pass by will be appalled and will scoff because of all its wounds. 9 I will make them eat[z]
the flesh of their sons and daughters, and they will eat one another's flesh because their enemies[a] will
press the siege so hard against them to destroy them.'

10 "Then break the jar[b] while those who go with you are watching, 11 and say to them, 'This is what the
LORD Almighty says: I will smash[c] this nation and this city just as this potter's jar is smashed and cannot
be repaired. They will bury[d] the dead in Topheth until there is no more room. 12 This is what I will do to
this place and to those who live here, declares the LORD. I will make this city like Topheth. 13 The houses[e] in
Jerusalem and those of the kings of Judah will be defiled like this place, Topheth—all the houses where
they burned incense on the roofs to all the starry hosts[f] and poured out drink offerings[g] to other gods.' "

14 Jeremiah then returned from Topheth, where the LORD had sent him to prophesy, and stood in the
court[h] of the LORD's temple and said to all the people, 15 "This is what the LORD Almighty, the God of

[a] 7 The Hebrew for *ruin* sounds like the Hebrew for *jar* (see verses 1 and 10).

19:1 clay jar. Unlike wet clay that the potter can easily reshape into something else, a hardened vessel cannot be repaired once it is broken. In 1 Kgs 14:3, this kind of jar is used to carry honey. **some ... elders.** They will be witnesses of Jeremiah's sign-act.
19:2 Valley of Ben Hinnom. Where the people have been performing idolatrous child sacrifices (see 7:31). **Potsherd Gate.** A fitting location for the events that follow; potters may have dumped their broken vessels outside this gate, though there is no other reference to it in the Bible.
19:3 make the ears ... tingle. A Hebrew idiom for a shocking catastrophe (1 Sam 3:11).
19:5 burn their children. See 7:31. Child sacrifice is normally associated with the god Molek, but here it is linked with the worship of Baal, the Canaanite fertility god. It is also possible that Baal (which means "lord") functions here more as a title than a name and thus encompasses Molek.
19:6,11,12 Topheth. See note on 7:31.
19:7 plans. Recalls the people's confidence that "counsel from the wise," as well as their own plots to kill Jeremiah, will continue (18:18). Such plans will come to nothing; instead, they themselves will die, and their bodies will be left shamefully exposed for "the birds and the wild animals" (see 7:33 and note; cf. Deut 28:26).
19:9 A fitting judgment: instead of offering their children as sacrifices, their desperate hunger will be so great as a result of the Babylonian siege that they will eat their own "sons and daughters" (cf. Deut 28:53; Lam 2:20).
19:10–11 As a sign of what will happen to Judah and Jerusalem, Jeremiah is to "break" the clay jar. The symbolism is self-evident: just as the smashed jar could not be "repaired," so too the city and nation will be destroyed.
19:13 defiled. By the presence of many corpses. The Lord cannot remain in such a defiled city. **burned incense on the roofs to all the starry hosts.** Probably related to worshiping Astarte/Ishtar, the Queen of Heaven (see 7:18 and note).
19:14 Since only a small number of the leaders were present at Topheth to witness the sign-act (v. 1), Jeremiah goes back to "the court of the LORD's temple," the spiritual center of Jerusalem, to repeat the central theme.

Merneptah relief of Ashkelon where Canaanites stand on the roof and burn incense and pray to their god for aid, ca. 1207 BC. "They burned incense on the roofs" (Jer 19:13).

Todd Bolen/www.BiblePlaces.com

Israel, says: 'Listen! I am going to bring on this city and all the villages around it every disaster I pronounced against them, because they were stiff-necked[i] and would not listen to my words.' "

Jeremiah and Pashhur

20 When the priest Pashhur son of Immer,[j] the official[k] in charge of the temple of the LORD,
heard Jeremiah prophesying these things, 2 he had Jeremiah the prophet beaten[l] and put in the
stocks[m] at the Upper Gate of Benjamin[n] at the LORD's temple. 3 The next day, when Pashhur released him
from the stocks, Jeremiah said to him, "The LORD's name for you is not Pashhur, but Terror on Every
Side.[o] 4 For this is what the LORD says: 'I will make you a terror to yourself and to all your friends; with
your own eyes[p] you will see them fall by the sword of their enemies. I will give[q] all Judah into the hands
of the king of Babylon, who will carry[r] them away to Babylon or put them to the sword. 5 I will deliver
all the wealth[s] of this city into the hands of their enemies — all its products, all its valuables and all
the treasures of the kings of Judah. They will take it away[t] as plunder and carry it off to Babylon. 6 And
you, Pashhur, and all who live in your house will go into exile to Babylon. There you will die and be
buried, you and all your friends to whom you have prophesied[u] lies.' "

19:15 [i] Ne 9:16; Jer 7:26; 17:23
20:1 [j] 1Ch 24:14 [k] 2Ki 25:18
20:2 [l] Jer 1:19 [m] Job 13:27 [n] Jer 37:13; 38:7; Zec 14:10
20:3 [o] ver 10
20:4 [p] Jer 29:21 [q] Jer 21:10 [r] Jer 52:27
20:5 [s] Jer 17:3 [t] 2Ki 20:17
20:6 [u] Jer 14:15; La 2:14

20:1–6 *Jeremiah and Pashhur.* Priests are at the center of the opposition to Jeremiah (see 11:21 and note) partly because they are one of the targets of his sharpest criticism (1:18). They are part of the central power structures in Jerusalem that Jeremiah declares are about to come to an end (18:18).

20:1 Pashhur. A common name; possibly the father of Gedaliah (38:1). **official in charge of the temple of the LORD.** Maintained order within the sacred precincts. Ironically, Pashhur chooses to maintain order by persecuting the Lord's prophet rather than deal with the practices defiling the temple (identified by Jeremiah in ch. 7). The opposition endured by all the OT prophets foreshadows the opposition faced by Jesus as the final prophet (Luke 11:49–51).

20:2 in the stocks. Or possibly in a small, confined room. **Upper Gate of Benjamin.** A prominent gate into the temple area.

20:3–4 Jeremiah makes a wordplay between the name "Pashhur" (which sounds like the Aramaic phrase meaning "torn in pieces all around") and the new name that God gives to the priest: *Māgôr-missābîb* (meaning "Terror on Every Side"; see note on 6:25). The new name describes the fate of Pashhur and all his friends.

20:5–6 Because Pashhur refuses to believe the Lord's message, he and his friends will become living examples of its veracity: at the Lord's decree, they will "go into exile to Babylon," where they will die and be buried. Pashhur's treatment of Jeremiah is functionally equivalent to the work of the false prophets who "prophesied lies," denying the truth of Jeremiah's words.

20:8 [v] Jer 6:7 [w] 2Ch 36:16; Jer 6:10
20:9 [x] Ps 39:3 [y] Job 32:18-20; Ac 4:20
20:10 [z] Ps 31:13; Jer 6:25 [a] Isa 29:21 [b] Ps 41:9 [c] Lk 11:53-54 [d] 1Ki 19:2
20:11 [e] Jer 1:8; Ro 8:31 [f] Jer 17:18 [g] Jer 15:20 [h] Jer 23:40
20:12 [i] Jer 17:10 [j] Ps 54:7; 59:10 [k] Ps 62:8; Jer 11:20
20:13 [l] Ps 35:10
20:14 [m] Job 3:3; Jer 15:10

Jeremiah's Complaint

7 You deceived[a] me, LORD, and I was deceived[a];
you overpowered me and prevailed.
I am ridiculed all day long;
everyone mocks me.
8 Whenever I speak, I cry out
proclaiming violence and destruction.[v]
So the word of the LORD has brought me
insult and reproach[w] all day long.
9 But if I say, "I will not mention his word
or speak anymore in his name,"
his word is in my heart like a fire,[x]
a fire shut up in my bones.
I am weary of holding it in;[y]
indeed, I cannot.
10 I hear many whispering,
"Terror[z] on every side!
Denounce[a] him! Let's denounce him!"
All my friends[b]
are waiting for me to slip,[c] saying,
"Perhaps he will be deceived;
then we will prevail[d] over him
and take our revenge on him."

11 But the LORD[e] is with me like a mighty warrior;
so my persecutors[f] will stumble and not prevail.[g]
They will fail and be thoroughly disgraced;[h]
their dishonor will never be forgotten.
12 LORD Almighty, you who examine the righteous
and probe the heart and mind,[i]
let me see your vengeance[j] on them,
for to you I have committed[k] my cause.
13 Sing to the LORD!
Give praise to the LORD!
He rescues[l] the life of the needy
from the hands of the wicked.

14 Cursed be the day I was born![m]
May the day my mother bore me not be blessed!

[a] 7 Or *persuaded*

20:7–18 *Jeremiah's Complaint.* Jeremiah cries out to God, lamenting his difficulties. Typically in laments the poet is wrestling with three subjects: God, his enemies, and himself. All three are present in vv. 7–9.
20:7 Jeremiah's central struggle is with God: "You deceived me." Jeremiah begins to question the Lord's purpose in his call. **deceived.** In 1 Kgs 22:20–22 the same Hebrew verb (translated "entice") describes the Lord's strategy of employing the false prophets who told Ahab what he wanted to hear instead of the unwelcome truth that Micaiah brought. God is able to use sinful agents to accomplish his holy purposes. The verb's use here shows that Jeremiah is not reading the situation rightly. He accuses God of using him like one of those false prophets, perhaps because none of his prophecies have yet been fulfilled. In reality, his role is to be like Micaiah, telling the truth in a hostile situation (1 Kgs 22:13–14).
20:8–9 Jeremiah struggles with his own body: if he tries not to speak the words God has given him, it feels like a fire burning in his bones.
20:10 Jeremiah's struggle is not just with God and his own body (see notes on 20:7–9); it is also with the enemies who mock him and ridicule him. The prophet brings out all of these difficulties with which he is wrestling and lays them out before the Lord. **Terror on every side!** See 20:3 and note on 20:3–4. **Denounce him!** They hope that he is "deceived" and that his predictions are false, which means that they can take action against him ("take our revenge").
20:11–13 As with many laments, the prophet turns from describing his own difficult situation to expressing confidence in the Lord and his protection as "a mighty warrior" (v. 11). He has entrusted his cause to the Lord and will wait to see the Lord act to vindicate him (v. 12). After the words of confidence, there are words of praise to the Lord, words that anticipate already the Lord's answer to his petitions (v. 13).
20:14 Cursed be the day I was born! Uttering his lament does not resolve Jeremiah's painful feelings. At the end of his earlier laments

[15]Cursed be the man who brought my father the news,
who made him very glad, saying,
"A child is born to you — a son!"
[16]May that man be like the towns[n]
the LORD overthrew without pity.
May he hear wailing in the morning,
a battle cry at noon.
[17]For he did not kill me in the womb,[o]
with my mother as my grave,
her womb enlarged forever.
[18]Why did I ever come out of the womb
to see trouble and sorrow
and to end my days in shame?[p]

God Rejects Zedekiah's Request

21 The word came to Jeremiah from the LORD when King Zedekiah[q] sent to him Pashhur[r] son of
Malkijah and the priest Zephaniah[s] son of Maaseiah. They said: [2]"Inquire[t] now of the LORD for
us because Nebuchadnezzar[a][u] king of Babylon is attacking us. Perhaps the LORD will perform wonders[v]
for us as in times past so that he will withdraw from us."
[3]But Jeremiah answered them, "Tell Zedekiah, [4]'This is what the LORD, the God of Israel, says: I am
about to turn[w] against you the weapons of war that are in your hands, which you are using to fight the
king of Babylon and the Babylonians[b] who are outside the wall besieging[x] you. And I will gather them
inside this city. [5]I myself will fight against you with an outstretched hand[y] and a mighty arm in furious
anger and in great wrath. [6]I will strike down those who live in this city — both man and beast — and
they will die of a terrible plague.[z] [7]After that, declares the LORD, I will give Zedekiah[a] king of Judah,
his officials and the people in this city who survive the plague, sword and famine, into the hands of
Nebuchadnezzar king of Babylon[b] and to their enemies who want to kill them. He will put them to the
sword; he will show them no mercy or pity or compassion.'[c]
[8]"Furthermore, tell the people, 'This is what the LORD says: See, I am setting before you the way of life
and the way of death. [9]Whoever stays in this city will die by the sword, famine or plague.[d] But whoever goes
out and surrenders to the Babylonians who are besieging you will live; they will escape with their lives.[e]

[a] 2 Hebrew *Nebuchadrezzar,* of which *Nebuchadnezzar* is a variant; here and often in Jeremiah and Ezekiel
[b] 4 Or *Chaldeans*; also in verse 9

20:16 [n]Ge 19:25
20:17 [o]Job 10:18-19
20:18 [p]Ps 90:9
21:1 [q]2Ki 24:18; Jer 52:1 [r]Jer 38:1 [s]2Ki 25:18; Jer 29:25; 37:3
21:2 [t]Jer 37:3,7 [u]2Ki 25:1 [v]Ps 44:1-4; Jer 32:17
21:4 [w]Jer 32:5 [x]Jer 37:8-10
21:5 [y]Jer 6:12
21:6 [z]Jer 14:12
21:7 [a]2Ki 25:7; Jer 52:9 [b]Jer 37:17; 39:5 [c]2Ch 36:17; Eze 7:9; Hab 1:6
21:9 [d]Jer 14:12 [e]Jer 38:2,17; 39:18; 45:5

(11:18–20; 15:10), there were words of encouragement from the Lord, but here the prophet is plunged back into depression and despair. He pronounces a curse on the day on which he was born.

20:15 Jeremiah pronounces a curse on the man who brought his father the news of Jeremiah's birth. Normally, one bringing such joyous tidings could expect a blessing for it.

20:16 towns the LORD overthrew without pity. Probably Sodom and Gomorrah (Gen 18:24–25).

20:17 Jeremiah claims it would have been better for him to have been killed before birth than to face such a difficult life. Job made a similar wish in Job 3:11–19.

21:1–14 *The Lord Rejects Zedekiah's Request.* Zedekiah wants Jeremiah to inquire of the Lord on his behalf — not because he is repentant but because he is desperate for any possible source of help.

21:1 Zedekiah. The last king of Judah (597–586 BC; see 2 Kgs 24:18–25:21). He foolishly rebels against Babylon, trusting in Egypt to come to his aid; in the aftermath, Jerusalem itself is destroyed. **Pashhur son of Malkijah.** A different person than Pashhur son of Immer (20:1–6). **Zephaniah.** Called "the priest next in rank" to the chief priest in 2 Kgs 25:18. This is not the same person as the prophet Zephaniah.

21:2 Inquire now of the LORD. People seeking direction could go to a prophet and ask him to inquire of God on their behalf (e.g., 2 Kgs 3:11; 22:13). But such inquiries were not always acceptable since they might be viewed as a form of pagan divination (Ezek 20:1–3). Repentance was necessary if God was to receive the inquiry. **Nebuchadnezzar.** The original Hebrew spelling is Nebuchadrezzar (see NIV text note), which more closely reflects the ancient Babylonian form of the name. **wonders.** Miraculous acts of deliverance. **in times past.** For example, in the days of Hezekiah (2 Kgs 19:35–36).

21:4–7 The Lord rebuffs Zedekiah's appeal because Zedekiah rebelled against the Lord as well as Babylon (2 Kgs 24:19). As a result, the Lord will not fight for Zedekiah; he will fight against him (v. 5), assuring his defeat (v. 7).

21:5 with an outstretched hand and a mighty arm. Recalls the wonders the Lord did for his people in the exodus (Deut 5:15). This time that same marvelous power will be used against his people, not for them.

21:7 plague, sword and famine. See note on 14:12. Even those who survive these curses will be handed over to their enemies.

21:8 I am setting before you the way of life and the way of death. This echoes Deut 30:19, where the choice is between obeying the Lord (leading to fullness of life) or turning away from the Lord (leading to death). Having already chosen the latter path, the people's only choice now is between death (if they remain in the city) or a prisoner's life (if they surrender to the Babylonians). Nonetheless, those who make the latter choice will at least live, while those who continue their rebellion within the city will face certain death (v. 9).

21:10 [f] Jer 44:11,27; Am 9:4 [g] Jer 32:28; 38:2-3 [h] Jer 52:13
21:11 [i] Jer 13:18
21:12 [j] Jer 22:3 [k] Isa 1:31
21:13 [l] Eze 13:8 [m] Ps 125:2 [n] Jer 49:4; Ob 3-4
21:14 [o] Isa 3:10-11 [p] 2Ch 36:19; Jer 52:13 [q] Eze 20:47
22:2 [r] Jer 17:25; Lk 1:32 [s] Jer 17:20
22:3 [t] Mic 6:8; Zec 7:9 [u] Ps 72:4; Jer 21:12 [v] Ex 22:22
22:4 [w] Jer 17:25
22:5 [x] Jer 17:27 [y] Heb 6:13
22:6 [z] Mic 3:12
22:7 [a] Jer 4:7

10 I have determined to do this city harm[f] and not good, declares the LORD. It will be given into the hands[g]
of the king of Babylon, and he will destroy it with fire.'[h]
11 "Moreover, say to the royal house[i] of Judah, 'Hear the word of the LORD. 12 This is what the LORD
says to you, house of David:

"'Administer justice[j] every morning;
rescue from the hand of the oppressor
the one who has been robbed,
or my wrath will break out and burn like fire
because of the evil you have done—
burn with no one to quench[k] it.
13 I am against[l] you, Jerusalem,
you who live above this valley[m]
on the rocky plateau, declares the LORD—
you who say, "Who can come against us?
Who can enter our refuge?"[n]
14 I will punish you as your deeds[o] deserve,
declares the LORD.
I will kindle a fire[p] in your forests[q]
that will consume everything around you.'"

Judgment Against Wicked Kings

22 This is what the LORD says: "Go down to the palace of the king of Judah and proclaim this message
there: 2 'Hear the word of the LORD to you, king of Judah, you who sit on David's throne[r]—you,
your officials and your people who come through these gates.[s] 3 This is what the LORD says: Do what is just[t]
and right. Rescue from the hand of the oppressor[u] the one who has been robbed. Do no wrong or violence
to the foreigner, the fatherless or the widow,[v] and do not shed innocent blood in this place. 4 For if you are
careful to carry out these commands, then kings[w] who sit on David's throne will come through the gates
of this palace, riding in chariots and on horses, accompanied by their officials and their people. 5 But if you
do not obey[x] these commands, declares the LORD, I swear[y] by myself that this palace will become a ruin.'"
6 For this is what the LORD says about the palace of the king of Judah:

"Though you are like Gilead to me,
like the summit of Lebanon,
I will surely make you like a wasteland,[z]
like towns not inhabited.
7 I will send destroyers[a] against you,
each man with his weapons,

21:10 The ultimate agent of their destruction will be not the Babylonians but the Lord, who has "determined to do this city harm" because of all the sins of its inhabitants. The book of Lamentations witnesses to the brutal effects of the Babylonian siege of Jerusalem.
21:11 the royal house of Judah. The current king in the line of David embodied the sin of the people. How tragic!
21:12 Administer justice … rescue from … the oppressor. The job of the king (Ps 72:1–2; see introduction to Ps 72). Since Judah's kings have failed to do this, the Lord's wrath burns against them.
21:13 Their confidence in Jerusalem's inaccessible location "on the rocky plateau" is misplaced. The Jebusites had a similarly misplaced confidence in David's day (see 2 Sam 5:6–7).
22:1–30 *Judgment Against Wicked Kings.* In these next chapters, Jeremiah interacts very directly with the kings of Judah, as many other prophets had done before him (e.g., Isa 7), warning that the line of David will be judged and brought to an end before ultimately being restored.
22:1 the king of Judah. Which king is not clear, perhaps because the following messages address several kings (Jehoahaz, Jehoiakim, Jehoiachin, and Zedekiah) who all failed in essentially the same ways. They sat on David's throne but didn't follow David's ways. Isa 11:1–3 anticipates the coming of a future king of David's line who will rule with justice and righteousness, unlike these final kings of Judah.
22:3 foreigner … fatherless … widow. Vulnerable groups of society without a strong protector and therefore the objects of the Lord's special care (see Exod 22:22–24 and note).
22:4,5 palace. Can denote the king's family as well as the royal residence. The future of the Davidic line was dependent upon their continued faithfulness (cf. 17:25). If they were unfaithful, the king's palace would "become a ruin."
22:6 Gilead … Lebanon. Famous for their forests, which produced the finest cedars, including those that made the palace of the king so beautiful (1 Kgs 7:2–3).
22:7 send. The language of holy war (see Introduction to Deuteronomy: Themes and Theology [Holy War]). **destroyers.** See note on 4:7; they will turn the palace into firewood (Ps 74:4–8).

and they will cut[b] up your fine cedar beams
and throw them into the fire.

8"People from many nations will pass by this city and will ask one another, 'Why has the LORD done
such a thing to this great city?'[c] 9And the answer will be: 'Because they have forsaken the covenant of
the LORD their God and have worshiped and served other gods.[d]'"

10 Do not weep for the dead[e] king or mourn[f] his loss;
rather, weep bitterly for him who is exiled,
because he will never return
nor see his native land again.

11For this is what the LORD says about Shallum[a][g] son of Josiah, who succeeded his father as king of
Judah but has gone from this place: "He will never return. 12He will die[h] in the place where they have
led him captive; he will not see this land again."

13 "Woe to him who builds[i] his palace by unrighteousness,
his upper rooms by injustice,
making his own people work for nothing,
not paying[j] them for their labor.
14 He says, 'I will build myself a great palace[k]
with spacious upper rooms.'
So he makes large windows in it,
panels it with cedar[l]
and decorates it in red.
15 "Does it make you a king
to have more and more cedar?
Did not your father have food and drink?
He did what was right and just,[m]
so all went well[n] with him.
16 He defended the cause of the poor and needy,[o]
and so all went well.
Is that not what it means to know me?"
declares the LORD.
17 "But your eyes and your heart
are set only on dishonest gain,
on shedding innocent blood[p]
and on oppression and extortion."

18Therefore this is what the LORD says about Jehoiakim son of Josiah king of Judah:

"They will not mourn for him:
'Alas, my brother! Alas, my sister!'

[a] *11* Also called *Jehoahaz*

22:7 [b] Isa 10:34
22:8 [c] Dt 29:25-26; 1Ki 9:8-9; Jer 16:10-11
22:9 [d] 2Ki 22:17; 2Ch 34:25
22:10 [e] Ecc 4:2 [f] ver 18
22:11 [g] 2Ki 23:31
22:12 [h] 2Ki 23:34
22:13 [i] Mic 3:10; Hab 2:9 [j] Lev 19:13; Jas 5:4
22:14 [k] Isa 5:8-9 [l] 2Sa 7:2
22:15 [m] 2Ki 23:25 [n] Ps 128:2; Isa 3:10
22:16 [o] Ps 72:1-4,12-13
22:17 [p] 2Ki 24:4

22:10–12 People mourned and wept intensely at the death of King Josiah, who died in battle at Megiddo (2 Chr 35:24), yet Jeremiah declares that there should be greater mourning for Josiah's son Shallum (also known as Jehoahaz, see NIV text note; 2 Kgs 23:31–34), who was exiled to Egypt after reigning for only three months as king in 609 BC. He will never return.
22:13–14 Jehoahaz followed the oppressive practice of forced labor in order to rebuild and enlarge his palace, which he paneled with expensive cedar and painted in extravagant red, or vermillion. For all its beauty, it will not last for long (see vv. 6–7).
22:15 He did what was right and just. Josiah, Jehoahaz's father, was a righteous king, doing what was right and defending the weak and the helpless (v. 16), as the Lord commanded (v. 3).
22:16 what it means to know me. Josiah's actions (v. 15) demonstrated that he knew the Lord, i.e., that he had a relationship with the Lord as his servant.
22:17 Unlike his father Josiah (v. 16), Jehoahaz had no interest in such knowledge of God. As a result, he oppressed the poor and needy, shedding the blood of those he was supposed to protect, so that he could multiply his possessions.
22:18 Jehoiakim. An oppressive ruler (609–598 BC) put on the throne by the Egyptians after they defeated his brother Jehoahaz. He was the exact opposite of the model of justice and righteousness the Lord desired (v. 3; 21:12). No one will lament Jehoiakim's death in the way one laments the death of family members ("brother ... sister") or even a worthy employer ("master"). Instead, his body will be treated like the

22:19 [q] Jer 36:30
22:20 [r] Nu 27:12
22:21 [s] Jer 3:25; 32:30 [t] Jer 7:23-28
22:23 [u] Jer 4:31
22:24 [v] 2Ki 24:6,8; Jer 37:1
22:25 [w] 2Ki 24:16; Jer 34:20
22:26 [x] 2Ki 24:8; 2Ch 36:10
22:28 [y] Ps 31:12; Jer 48:38; Hos 8:8 [z] Jer 15:1 [a] Jer 17:4
22:29 [b] Jer 6:19; Mic 1:2

They will not mourn for him:
'Alas, my master! Alas, his splendor!'
19 He will have the burial of a donkey —
dragged away and thrown[q]
outside the gates of Jerusalem."

20 "Go up to Lebanon and cry out,
let your voice be heard in Bashan,
cry out from Abarim,[r]
for all your allies are crushed.
21 I warned you when you felt secure,
but you said, 'I will not listen!'
This has been your way from your youth;[s]
you have not obeyed[t] me.
22 The wind will drive all your shepherds away,
and your allies will go into exile.
Then you will be ashamed and disgraced
because of all your wickedness.
23 You who live in 'Lebanon,[a]'
who are nestled in cedar buildings,
how you will groan when pangs come upon you,
pain[u] like that of a woman in labor!

24 "As surely as I live," declares the LORD, "even if you, Jehoiachin[b][v] son of Jehoiakim king of Judah,
were a signet ring on my right hand, I would still pull you off. 25 I will deliver[w] you into the hands of
those who want to kill you, those you fear — Nebuchadnezzar king of Babylon and the Babylonians.[c]
26 I will hurl[x] you and the mother who gave you birth into another country, where neither of you was
born, and there you both will die. 27 You will never come back to the land you long to return to."

28 Is this man Jehoiachin a despised, broken pot,[y]
an object no one wants?
Why will he and his children be hurled[z] out,
cast into a land[a] they do not know?
29 O land,[b] land, land,
hear the word of the LORD!

[a] *23* That is, the palace in Jerusalem (see 1 Kings 7:2) [b] *24* Hebrew *Koniah,* a variant of *Jehoiachin*; also in verse 28 [c] *25* Or *Chaldeans*

carcass of a "donkey" (v. 19), an unclean animal, which is dumped unceremoniously outside the city gate.
22:20–23 The prophecy broadens out to address all of the inhabitants of Judah. They should go up on a high mountain to lament their fate.
22:20 Lebanon. In the north. **Bashan.** To the northeast. **Abarim.** To the southeast. **allies.** The nations Judah trusted to help them rebel against Babylon.
22:21 Because of their political alliances, Judah felt secure even though the Lord sent his prophets repeatedly to warn them.
22:22 wind. Often represents the Lord's judgment; here it extends to all "the shepherds" (kings) of Judah.
22:23 Lebanon. The cedar-paneled buildings of the palace (see NIV text note; see also v. 14), named after the place from which the cedar came. Yet they will provide no protection (vv. 6–7).
22:24 As surely as I live. The Lord swears an oath by himself to underscore how certain this event is (see Heb 6:16–17). **Jehoiachin.** Hebrew Coniah; also called Jeconiah (24:1 and NIV text note there); the "son of Jehoiakim." He succeeded Jehoiakim as king, though he reigned for only three months (598–597 BC) before being exiled to Babylon (2 Kgs 24:8–17). **signet ring.** A precious and carefully protected object since it was used to seal documents and certify the authenticity of contracts and edicts. Jehoiachin, as a Davidic king, ought to have the special, protected status of a royal signet ring before the Lord; however, the Lord declares that Jehoiachin will be cast off and handed over to Nebuchadnezzar and the Babylonians (v. 25).
22:26 The Babylonians will take Jehoiachin and his mother to Babylon (fulfilled in 2 Kgs 24:15), where both will die (though Jehoiachin is eventually released from prison; 2 Kgs 25:27–30). After he is taken into exile, the Babylonians place Jehoiachin's uncle, Zedekiah, on the throne. Zedekiah, however, dies in the aftermath of the final destruction of Jerusalem, while Jehoiachin lives on in exile. Yet God's promise of a lasting royal line for David is not forgotten (23:5), and Hag 2:23 reverses the prophecy of the signet ring (see note on v. 24): the postexilic Davidic governor Zerubbabel is restored to that same protected status (Hag 2:23).
22:28 despised, broken pot. Like the shattered vessel of ch. 19.
22:29 land, land, land. The triple repetition adds emphasis, like the triple repetition of the word "holy" in Isa 6:3. The land is called as a witness of the impending judgment.

30 This is what the LORD says:
"Record this man as if childless,[c]
a man who will not prosper[d] in his lifetime,
for none of his offspring will prosper,
none will sit on the throne[e] of David
or rule anymore in Judah."

The Righteous Branch

23 "Woe to the shepherds[f] who are destroying and scattering[g] the sheep of my pasture!"[h] declares
the LORD. 2 Therefore this is what the LORD, the God of Israel, says to the shepherds who tend my
people: "Because you have scattered my flock and driven them away and have not bestowed care on them,
I will bestow punishment on you for the evil[i] you have done," declares the LORD. 3 "I myself will gather the
remnant[j] of my flock out of all the countries where I have driven them and will bring them back to their
pasture, where they will be fruitful and increase in number. 4 I will place shepherds[k] over them who will
tend them, and they will no longer be afraid[l] or terrified, nor will any be missing,[m]" declares the LORD.

5 "The days are coming," declares the LORD,
"when I will raise up for David[a] a righteous Branch,[n]
a King who will reign[o] wisely
and do what is just and right[p] in the land.
6 In his days Judah will be saved
and Israel will live in safety.
This is the name[q] by which he will be called:
The LORD Our Righteous Savior.[r]

7 "So then, the days are coming," declares the LORD, "when people will no longer say, 'As surely as the
LORD lives, who brought the Israelites up out of Egypt,'[s] 8 but they will say, 'As surely as the LORD lives,
who brought the descendants of Israel up out of the land of the north and out of all the countries where
he had banished them.' Then they will live in their own land."[t]

22:30 [c] 1Ch 3:18; Mt 1:12 [d] Jer 10:21 [e] Ps 94:20
23:1 [f] Jer 10:21; Eze 34:1-10; Zec 11:15-17 [g] Isa 56:11 [h] Eze 34:31
23:2 [i] Jer 21:12
23:3 [j] Isa 11:10-12; Jer 32:37; Eze 34:11-16
23:4 [k] Jer 3:15; 31:10; Eze 34:23 [l] Jer 30:10; 46:27-28 [m] Jn 6:39
23:5 [n] Isa 4:2 [o] Isa 9:7 [p] Isa 11:1; Zec 6:12
23:6 [q] Jer 33:16; Mt 1:21-23 [r] Ro 3:21-22; 1Co 1:30
23:7 [s] Jer 16:14
23:8 [t] Isa 43:5-6; Am 9:14-15

[a] 5 Or *up from David's line*

22:30 Jehoiachin will be recorded as "childless" even though he has seven sons (1 Chr 3:17–18), because he and all of his children die in exile. His grandson, Zerubbabel, later becomes the governor of Judah after the return from exile, but he is not a king (Hag 1:1).
23:1–8 *The Righteous Branch.* In spite of the declaration of an end to the rule of the Davidic line in Jehoiachin, God nonetheless still has a future for that line in the person of a future Messianic king, the Branch.
23:1,2 shepherds. Leaders (see note on 2:8), especially the kings of Judah, who failed to take care of God's people. Without a caring shepherd, the sheep are scattered and left vulnerable to predators (cf. Ezek 34).
23:2 bestowed care on ... bestow punishment on. A play on words: this uses a single Hebrew verb with two meanings. In English, the phrase "to take care of someone" can have the same positive or negative connotations.
23:3 I myself will gather ... my flock. The Lord is himself the good shepherd (Ps 23:1; Ezek 34:11). Judah's kings reigned as representatives of the Lord. Jesus declares that he is the Good Shepherd (John 10:14), claiming to fulfill this Messianic promise. The good shepherd's job is to protect and care for the sheep, gathering them safely together (v. 4; John 10:14–16).
23:5 righteous Branch. Zedekiah means "the LORD is righteous," but Zedekiah is anything but righteous. After him there are no more Davidic kings on the throne of Judah. In his place, the Lord ultimately brings a new offspring from the line of David, a "righteous Branch," i.e., a new growth that is not the main stem. Isaiah speaks in similar terms of a new beginning for the line of David, a "shoot ... from the stump of Jesse" (Isa 11:1). Other passages also promise a coming "Branch" (33:15; Isa 4:2; Zech 3:8; 6:12). This "Branch" was already recognized as a Messianic figure in the Targum (an ancient Aramaic paraphrase). In contrast to Zedekiah and Jehoiakim, he will "reign wisely" and "do what is just and right" (22:3; cf. 22:13).
23:6 This righteous king (see note on v. 5) will save his people (see Zech 9:9), unlike the Davidic kings of those days whose folly and sin brought catastrophe upon Jerusalem (22:20–23). He will not be called Zedekiah ("the LORD is righteous") but Yahweh Tsidkenu ("the LORD is our righteousness"). The righteousness that the Lord will provide will enable the people to "live in safety," experiencing the blessings promised in the Sinai covenant (Lev 26:5; see Deut 28:1–14) rather than the curses they had merited through their own disobedience (Deut 28:15–68).

This promise finds its fulfillment in Jesus, the true son of David (Matt 1:1), in whom we are "blessed ... with every spiritual blessing" (Eph 1:3). He is "the Holy and Righteous One" (Acts 3:14), the Lord who clothes us with his righteousness (Rev 7:13–14). Yet in Matthew's Gospel it is the blind, Gentiles, and children who recognize that Jesus is indeed the Son of David (Matt 9:27; 15:22; 20:30–31; 21:9), while the influential Pharisees cannot see it (Matt 12:23–24; 22:41–46).
23:7–8 This act of salvation by God in bringing the remnant of his people back from exile will be so dramatic that it will eclipse even the exodus. As a result, people will no longer swear oaths by "the LORD ... who brought the Israelites up out of Egypt" but by "the LORD ... who brought the descendants of Israel up out of the land of the north." In Luke 9:31, the redemption that Christ accomplished on the cross is explicitly called his "exodus" in Greek (NIV "departure"; see NIV text note on Luke 9:31).
23:8 land of the north. Babylon (see notes on 1:13–15), as well as the other countries where the Judahites are scattered.

23:9 [u] Jer 20:8-9
23:10 [v] Jer 9:2 [w] Ps 107:34; Jer 9:10 [x] Hos 4:2-3
23:11 [y] Jer 6:13; 8:10; Zep 3:4 [z] Jer 7:10
23:12 [a] Ps 35:6; Jer 13:16 [b] Jer 11:23
23:13 [c] Jer 2:8
23:14 [d] Jer 5:30 [e] Jer 29:23 [f] Eze 13:22 [g] Ge 18:20 [h] Isa 1:9-10; Jer 20:16
23:15 [i] Jer 8:14; 9:15

Lying Prophets

9 Concerning the prophets:

My heart is broken within me;
all my bones tremble.
I am like a drunken man,
like a strong man overcome by wine,
because of the LORD
and his holy words.[u]
10 The land is full of adulterers;[v]
because of the curse[a] the land lies parched
and the pastures[w] in the wilderness are withered.[x]
The prophets follow an evil course
and use their power unjustly.
11 "Both prophet and priest are godless;[y]
even in my temple[z] I find their wickedness,"
declares the LORD.
12 "Therefore their path will become slippery;[a]
they will be banished to darkness
and there they will fall.
I will bring disaster on them
in the year they are punished,[b]"
declares the LORD.

13 "Among the prophets of Samaria
I saw this repulsive thing:
They prophesied by Baal[c]
and led my people Israel astray.
14 And among the prophets of Jerusalem
I have seen something horrible:[d]
They commit adultery and live a lie.[e]
They strengthen the hands of evildoers,[f]
so that not one of them turns from their wickedness.
They are all like Sodom[g] to me;
the people of Jerusalem are like Gomorrah."[h]

15 Therefore this is what the LORD Almighty says concerning the prophets:

"I will make them eat bitter food
and drink poisoned water,[i]

[a] 10 Or *because of these things*

23:9–32 *Lying Prophets.* The Lord warned his people in Deut 18:20–22 that false prophets would come. Yet Jeremiah is distraught at the ease with which they deceive the people. The people prefer to listen to false prophets because, rather than announce the difficult truth, they tell the people what they want to hear. These false prophets did not stand in the Lord's council; the Lord did not commission them to go and contend with the nation and declare words of judgment and hope. The Lord did not send them, yet they speak as if he did. Their fate and the fate of those who listen to them is deserved.

23:9 The Lord's words are "holy," unlike the unholy words of the false prophets (vv. 16–18), and they consume Jeremiah, making his "bones tremble" (cf. 20:9). This is an experience about which the false prophets know nothing.

23:10 adulterers. Those who are spiritually unfaithful to the Lord. They bring a "curse" upon the land in the shape of drought (14:1–6).

23:11 prophet and priest. They should represent the Lord to the people, but they are "godless" (14:8). This message (vv. 9–32) focuses on the prophets.

23:13 prophets of Samaria ... prophesied by Baal. The prophets of the former northern kingdom of Israel had been perverted in the time of Ahab and Jezebel (and other kings) and had led Israel astray (1 Kgs 16:31; 18:18–40; 2 Kgs 17:16–20). Jeremiah's hearers (Judahites) likely agreed with this assessment of their former neighbors.

23:14 prophets of Jerusalem. Jeremiah compares them to the former false prophets of Samaria (see note on v. 13)—a comparison his hearers (Judahites) find offensive. Instead of seeking to turn people from their sins, which was the work of true prophets (Ezek 3:18–19), false prophets simply confirmed "evildoers" in their wickedness. Not only are the prophets of Jerusalem like the prophets of Israel, but the "people of Jerusalem" are like the inhabitants of Sodom and Gomorrah, whom the Lord destroyed for their sins (Gen 19:1–29).

23:15 bitter food ... poisoned water. See 9:15.

because from the prophets of Jerusalem
ungodliness has spread throughout the land."

16 This is what the LORD Almighty says:

"Do not listen[j] to what the prophets are prophesying
to you;
they fill you with false hopes.
They speak visions[k] from their own minds,
not from the mouth[l] of the LORD.
17 They keep saying to those who despise me,
'The LORD says: You will have peace.'[m]
And to all who follow the stubbornness[n] of their hearts
they say, 'No harm[o] will come to you.'
18 But which of them has stood in the council of
the LORD
to see or to hear his word?
Who has listened and heard his word?
19 See, the storm[p] of the LORD
will burst out in wrath,
a whirlwind swirling down
on the heads of the wicked.
20 The anger[q] of the LORD will not turn back[r]
until he fully accomplishes
the purposes of his heart.
In days to come
you will understand it clearly.
21 I did not send[s] these prophets,
yet they have run with their message;
I did not speak to them,
yet they have prophesied.
22 But if they had stood in my council,
they would have proclaimed my words to my people
and would have turned[t] them from their evil ways
and from their evil deeds.

23 "Am I only a God nearby,[u]"
declares the LORD,
"and not a God far away?
24 Who can hide[v] in secret places
so that I cannot see them?"
declares the LORD.
"Do not I fill heaven and earth?"[w]
declares the LORD.

23:16 [j] Jer 27:9-10,14; Mt 7:15 [k] Jer 14:14 [l] Jer 9:20
23:17 [m] Jer 8:11 [n] Jer 13:10 [o] Jer 5:12; Am 9:10; Mic 3:11
23:19 [p] Jer 25:32; 30:23
23:20 [q] 2Ki 23:26 [r] Jer 30:24
23:21 [s] Jer 14:14; 27:15
23:22 [t] Jer 25:5; Zec 1:4
23:23 [u] Ps 139:1-10
23:24 [v] Job 22:12-14 [w] 1Ki 8:27

23:16 false hopes. Hebrew *hebel*, translated "vanity" (KJV) or "meaningless" (NIV) in Ecclesiastes (see, e.g., Eccl l:2). **visions from their own minds.** See 14:14.
23:17 The false prophets declare "peace" to those at enmity with the Lord (see 6:14; 8:11). In this respect, they are like the preachers of a "different gospel" in Gal 1:6.
23:18 council of the LORD. The heavenly courtroom where the Lord commissions his servants and gives them their marching orders (1 Kgs 22:19–23; Isa 6:1–13). Only those whom he called into his presence had an authentic message to declare.
23:19 The Bible often depicts the Lord's awesome presence as a "storm" or "whirlwind" (see Job 38:1; Ezek 1:4), though here it could simply be a storm sent by God.
23:20 In days to come. God will vindicate the message of the true prophet when the prophecy comes true (Deut 18:22). The imminent destruction of Jerusalem will vindicate Jeremiah's words of wrath and reveal the false prophets' words of peace to be lies.
23:23 a God nearby ... a God far away. The Lord is not, like the pagan gods, tied to one locality. He rules over near and far.
23:24 God rules over the entire universe, filling "heaven and earth." There will be nowhere safe for the false prophets to run and "hide" on the day of judgment.

23:25 [x] Jer 14:14 [y] ver 28,32; Jer 29:8
23:26 [z] 1Ti 4:1-2
23:27 [a] Dt 13:1-3; Jer 29:8 [b] Jdg 3:7; 8:33-34
23:29 [c] Jer 5:14
23:30 [d] Ps 34:16 [e] Dt 18:20; Jer 14:15
23:31 [f] ver 17
23:32 [g] ver 25 [h] Jer 7:8; La 2:14
23:33 [i] Mal 1:1 [j] ver 39
23:34 [k] La 2:14 [l] Zec 13:3
23:35 [m] Jer 33:3; 42:4
23:36 [n] Gal 1:7-8; 2Pe 3:16
23:39 [o] Jer 7:15
23:40 [p] Jer 20:11; Eze 5:14-15
24:1 [q] 2Ki 24:16; 2Ch 36:9; Jer 29:2 [r] Am 8:1-2
24:2 [s] Isa 5:4

25 "I have heard what the prophets say who prophesy lies[x] in my name. They say, 'I had a dream![y] I had a dream!' 26 How long will this continue in the hearts of these lying prophets, who prophesy the delusions[z] of their own minds? 27 They think the dreams they tell one another will make my people forget[a] my name, just as their ancestors forgot[b] my name through Baal worship. 28 Let the prophet who has a dream recount the dream, but let the one who has my word speak it faithfully. For what has straw to do with grain?" declares the LORD. 29 "Is not my word like fire,"[c] declares the LORD, "and like a hammer that breaks a rock in pieces?

30 "Therefore," declares the LORD, "I am against[d] the prophets[e] who steal from one another words supposedly from me. 31 Yes," declares the LORD, "I am against the prophets who wag their own tongues and yet declare, 'The LORD declares.'[f] 32 Indeed, I am against those who prophesy false dreams,[g]" declares the LORD. "They tell them and lead my people astray with their reckless lies, yet I did not send or appoint them. They do not benefit[h] these people in the least," declares the LORD.

False Prophecy

33 "When these people, or a prophet or a priest, ask you, 'What is the message[i] from the LORD?' say to them, 'What message? I will forsake[j] you, declares the LORD.' 34 If a prophet or a priest or anyone else claims, 'This is a message[k] from the LORD,' I will punish[l] them and their household. 35 This is what each of you keeps saying to your friends and other Israelites: 'What is the LORD's answer?'[m] or 'What has the LORD spoken?' 36 But you must not mention 'a message from the LORD' again, because each one's word becomes their own message. So you distort[n] the words of the living God, the LORD Almighty, our God. 37 This is what you keep saying to a prophet: 'What is the LORD's answer to you?' or 'What has the LORD spoken?' 38 Although you claim, 'This is a message from the LORD,' this is what the LORD says: You used the words, 'This is a message from the LORD,' even though I told you that you must not claim, 'This is a message from the LORD.' 39 Therefore, I will surely forget you and cast[o] you out of my presence along with the city I gave to you and your ancestors. 40 I will bring on you everlasting disgrace[p] — everlasting shame that will not be forgotten."

Two Baskets of Figs

24 After Jehoiachin[a][q] son of Jehoiakim king of Judah and the officials, the skilled workers and the artisans of Judah were carried into exile from Jerusalem to Babylon by Nebuchadnezzar king of Babylon, the LORD showed me two baskets of figs[r] placed in front of the temple of the LORD. 2 One basket had very good figs, like those that ripen early; the other basket had very bad[s] figs, so bad they could not be eaten.

[a] *1* Hebrew *Jeconiah,* a variant of *Jehoiachin*

23:25–27 The false prophets claim to have had dreams. God did sometimes reveal himself through dreams in those days (Num 12:6), but the proof that their dreams were false is that their effect was intended to make the people forget the Lord's name. Such dreamers were subject to the death penalty (Deut 13:1–5).
23:28–29 Their dreams are as different from the true revelation of God's word as valueless straw is different from precious grain. God's word is like "fire" and a crushing "hammer" compared to their insipid and irrelevant pronouncements.
23:30 Their false pronouncements are not even original: they steal words from one another and pretend that they come from the Lord.
23:33–40 *False Prophecy.* The people's constant desire for a new message from the Lord might sound spiritual, but it is an act of rebellion since they are refusing to listen to the clear message he has already given them through the prophets. For that reason, the Lord will punish anyone who falsely claims to have a new message from him.
23:33 message. Can mean "burden"; it is typically used of judgment messages. There is a play on words here: when the people ask, "What is the message [burden] from the LORD?" Jeremiah is to reply, in effect, "'What is the burden? *You* are the burden, and I will put you down,' declares the LORD." **declares the LORD.** Occurs more often in the book of Jeremiah than it does in the other prophetic books, perhaps precisely because of the intensity of Jeremiah's conflict with false prophecy.
24:1–10 *Two Baskets of Figs.* Many people, including the king himself, were carried into exile by the Babylonians in the days of Jehoiachin. Those who remain in Jerusalem regard those in exile as under the curse of God and as morally inferior to themselves. Jeremiah declares that the reverse is true: the better people have gone into exile, while God's curse is about to fall on all those left in Jerusalem.
24:1 In 597 BC a significant group of "officials" and "skilled workers" were taken to exile in Babylon along with King Jehoiachin (e.g., 2 Kgs 24:12–14). It was standard Babylonian policy to remove leaders and artisans from captured territories to make it harder for those conquered nations to rebel in the future. The prophet Ezekiel was among those exiled at this time.
24:2 Jeremiah compares the groups taken and left behind to two baskets of figs. One basket has "very good figs"—the kind that "ripen early," while the other basket contains "very bad figs," so bad they cannot be eaten. The description of these figs and the location of the baskets "in front of the temple" (v. 1) suggest that this is a kind of firstfruits offering: the good figs are an acceptable offering, while the bad figs are rejected (see note on Num 15:20).

3Then the LORD asked me, "What do you see,[t] Jeremiah?"
"Figs," I answered. "The good ones are very good, but the bad ones are so bad they cannot be eaten."
4Then the word of the LORD came to me: 5"This is what the LORD, the God of Israel, says: 'Like these
good figs, I regard as good the exiles from Judah, whom I sent away from this place to the land of the
Babylonians.[a] 6My eyes will watch over them for their good, and I will bring them back[u] to this land. I
will build[v] them up and not tear them down; I will plant them and not uproot them. 7I will give them
a heart to know me, that I am the LORD. They will be my people,[w] and I will be their God, for they will
return[x] to me with all their heart.[y]
8" 'But like the bad[z] figs, which are so bad they cannot be eaten,' says the LORD, 'so will I deal with
Zedekiah king of Judah, his officials[a] and the survivors[b] from Jerusalem, whether they remain in this
land or live in Egypt.[c] 9I will make them abhorrent[d] and an offense to all the kingdoms of the earth,
a reproach and a byword,[e] a curse[b][f] and an object of ridicule, wherever I banish[g] them. 10I will send
the sword,[h] famine and plague[i] against them until they are destroyed from the land I gave to them
and their ancestors.' "

Seventy Years of Captivity

25 The word came to Jeremiah concerning all the people of Judah in the fourth year of Jehoiakim[j]
son of Josiah king of Judah, which was the first year of Nebuchadnezzar[k] king of Babylon. 2So
Jeremiah the prophet said to all the people of Judah[l] and to all those living in Jerusalem: 3For twenty-
three years—from the thirteenth year of Josiah[m] son of Amon king of Judah until this very day—the
word of the LORD has come to me and I have spoken to you again and again,[n] but you have not listened.[o]
4And though the LORD has sent all his servants the prophets[p] to you again and again, you have not
listened or paid any attention. 5They said, "Turn now, each of you, from your evil ways and your evil
practices, and you can stay in the land the LORD gave to you and your ancestors for ever and ever. 6Do
not follow other gods[q] to serve and worship them; do not arouse my anger with what your hands have
made. Then I will not harm you."
7"But you did not listen to me," declares the LORD, "and you have aroused my anger with what your
hands have made,[r] and you have brought harm[s] to yourselves."
8Therefore the LORD Almighty says this: "Because you have not listened to my words, 9I will summon[t]
all the peoples of the north[u] and my servant[v] Nebuchadnezzar king of Babylon," declares the LORD, "and
I will bring them against this land and its inhabitants and against all the surrounding nations. I will

[a] *5* Or *Chaldeans* [b] *9* That is, their names will be used in cursing (see 29:22); or, others will see that they are cursed.

24:3 [t] Jer 1:11; Am 8:2
24:6 [u] Jer 29:10; Eze 11:17 [v] Jer 33:7; 42:10
24:7 [w] Isa 51:16; Jer 31:33; Heb 8:10 [x] Jer 32:40 [y] Eze 11:19
24:8 [z] Jer 29:17 [a] Jer 39:6 [b] Jer 39:9 [c] Jer 44:1,26
24:9 [d] Jer 15:4; 34:17 [e] Dt 28:25; 1Ki 9:7 [f] Jer 29:18 [g] Dt 28:37
24:10 [h] Isa 51:19 [i] Jer 27:8
25:1 [j] 2Ki 24:2; Jer 36:1 [k] 2Ki 24:1
25:2 [l] Jer 18:11
25:3 [m] Jer 1:2 [n] Jer 11:7; 26:5 [o] Jer 7:26
25:4 [p] Jer 7:25
25:6 [q] Dt 8:19
25:7 [r] Dt 32:21 [s] 2Ki 21:15
25:9 [t] Isa 13:3-5 [u] Jer 1:15 [v] Jer 27:6

24:5 good figs. The exiles, whom the Lord will protect in exile and bring back.
24:6 build ... plant ... not uproot. God's plan for the exiles (see 1:10 and note).
24:7 a heart to know me. The Lord will transform the exiles through their experience of exile, giving them a new heart and establishing a new covenant relationship with them (see 31:31–33 and notes).
24:8 bad figs. Those who "remain in this land" (Judah) or flee to Egypt (see ch. 43). They are under the Lord's curse and will die by "the sword, famine and plague" (v. 10; see 14:12 and note).
25:1–14 *Seventy Years of Captivity.* Though the coming judgment will be devastating for those who remain in the land of Judah, it will not be the end of God's purposes for his people. At the end of 70 years—a full lifetime (Ps 90:10)—the Lord will bring back those who are in exile.
25:1 fourth year of Jehoiakim. 605 BC. This same year Jeremiah dictates a scroll of prophecies to his scribe Baruch, which is then subsequently read to Jehoiakim, who rejects its message (36:4–25).
25:3 thirteenth year of Josiah. 628/27 BC, when Jeremiah's own ministry began (see 1:2; Introduction: Author and Date). He has been preaching fruitlessly now for 23 years. He is not the only true prophet in Judah at this time: Uriah (26:20–23), Zephaniah, and Habakkuk also prophesy during this same approximate period, but the people do not listen.
25:5–6 A summary of the message of all the prophets.
25:7 you have brought harm to yourselves. In the past, the door was open for the people to repent and be restored, but since they did not listen, they are now responsible for the negative outcome.
25:9 all the peoples of the north. Allies of Babylon. Because the Lord is the living God who controls all of history, he can pronounce doom in specific terms, naming the man who will bring devastation on his people: Nebuchadnezzar (cf. Isa 44:24–28, which announces the rise of Cyrus). **my servant.** Though Nebuchadnezzar, ruler of a vast and powerful empire, has his own sinful reasons for waging war, those are subject to the Lord's purposes. He is merely the Lord's vassal king who must do his overlord's bidding. **completely destroy.** As they were supposed to have destroyed the earlier inhabitants of Canaan during the conquest of the land (Deut 7:2). Judah has become like the Canaanites in their worship and behavior, so they will suffer the same fate as the Canaanites. See Introduction to Deuteronomy: Themes and Theology (Holy War). **everlasting.** Hebrew *ʿôlām*; often means "everlasting" but occasionally means simply a lengthy period of time. In this case, the subsequent verses make it clear that after 70 years, those in exile will come back and begin to restore the land.

25:9 [w]Jer 18:16
25:10 [x]Isa 24:8; Eze 26:13 [y]Jer 7:34 [z]Ecc 12:3-4 [a]Rev 18:22-23
25:11 [b]Jer 4:26-27; 12:11-12 [c]2Ch 36:21
25:12 [d]Jer 29:10 [e]Isa 13:19-22; 14:22-23
25:14 [f]Jer 27:7 [g]Jer 50:9; 51:27-28 [h]Jer 51:6
25:15 [i]Isa 51:17; Ps 75:8; Rev 14:10
25:16 [j]Na 3:11 [k]Jer 51:7
25:17 [l]Jer 1:10
25:18 [m]Jer 24:9 [n]Jer 44:22
25:20 [o]Job 1:1 [p]Jer 47:5
25:21 [q]Jer 49:1
25:22 [r]Jer 47:4 [s]Jer 31:10
25:23 [t]Jer 9:26; 49:32
25:24 [u]2Ch 9:14
25:25 [v]Ge 10:22
25:26 [w]Jer 50:3,9 [x]Jer 51:41
25:27 [y]ver 16,28; Hab 2:16 [z]Eze 21:4
25:29 [a]Jer 13:12-14 [b]1Pe 4:17 [c]Pr 11:31 [d]ver 30-31

completely destroy*[a]* them and make them an object of horror and scorn,[w] and an everlasting ruin. 10 I will banish from them the sounds[x] of joy and gladness, the voices of bride and bridegroom,[y] the sound of millstones[z] and the light of the lamp.[a] 11 This whole country will become a desolate wasteland,[b] and these nations will serve the king of Babylon seventy years.[c]

12 "But when the seventy years[d] are fulfilled, I will punish the king of Babylon and his nation, the land of the Babylonians,*[b]* for their guilt," declares the LORD, "and will make it desolate[e] forever. 13 I will bring on that land all the things I have spoken against it, all that are written in this book and prophesied by Jeremiah against all the nations. 14 They themselves will be enslaved[f] by many nations[g] and great kings; I will repay[h] them according to their deeds and the work of their hands."

The Cup of God's Wrath

15 This is what the LORD, the God of Israel, said to me: "Take from my hand this cup[i] filled with the wine of my wrath and make all the nations to whom I send you drink it. 16 When they drink it, they will stagger[j] and go mad[k] because of the sword I will send among them."

17 So I took the cup from the LORD's hand and made all the nations to whom he sent[l] me drink it: 18 Jerusalem and the towns of Judah, its kings and officials, to make them a ruin and an object of horror and scorn, a curse*[c]*[m] — as they are today;[n] 19 Pharaoh king of Egypt, his attendants, his officials and all his people, 20 and all the foreign people there; all the kings of Uz;[o] all the kings of the Philistines (those of Ashkelon,[p] Gaza, Ekron, and the people left at Ashdod); 21 Edom, Moab and Ammon;[q] 22 all the kings of Tyre and Sidon;[r] the kings of the coastlands[s] across the sea; 23 Dedan, Tema, Buz and all who are in distant places;*[d]*[t] 24 all the kings of Arabia[u] and all the kings of the foreign people who live in the wilderness; 25 all the kings of Zimri, Elam[v] and Media; 26 and all the kings of the north,[w] near and far, one after the other — all the kingdoms on the face of the earth. And after all of them, the king of Sheshak*[e]*[x] will drink it too.

27 "Then tell them, 'This is what the LORD Almighty, the God of Israel, says: Drink, get drunk[y] and vomit, and fall to rise no more because of the sword[z] I will send among you.' 28 But if they refuse to take the cup from your hand and drink, tell them, 'This is what the LORD Almighty says: You must drink it! 29 See, I am beginning to bring disaster[a] on the city that bears my Name,[b] and will you indeed go unpunished?[c] You will not go unpunished, for I am calling down a sword on all[d] who live on the earth, declares the LORD Almighty.'

30 "Now prophesy all these words against them and say to them:

a *9* The Hebrew term refers to the irrevocable giving over of things or persons to the LORD, often by totally destroying them. *b* *12* Or *Chaldeans* *c* *18* That is, their names to be used in cursing (see 29:22); or, to be seen by others as cursed *d* *23* Or *who clip the hair by their foreheads* *e* *26* *Sheshak* is a cryptogram for Babylon.

25:10 sounds of joy and gladness ... sound of millstones ... light of the lamp. Marks of routine life that the coming invasion will thoroughly disrupt.

25:11 seventy years. Represents a full lifetime (Ps 90:10), indicating that none of those who go into exile can expect to return alive. The immediate context applies the 70 years to the time from the first deportation in 605 BC to the fall of Babylon in 539 BC (see Dan 9:1–2). For other possibilities, see note on 2 Chr 36:21.

25:12 I will punish the king of Babylon and his nation ... for their guilt. Even though the Lord will employ Babylon as his agent of destruction, the Babylonians will be responsible for their own brutal actions, which will incur a debt of "guilt." The result will be that just as the Babylonians make the land of Judah desolate forever, so also their land will be made "desolate forever."

25:13 Jeremiah's prophecies will be vindicated not merely in the fall of Jerusalem but also a lifetime later when the Medes and Persians destroy Babylon. Those who assault the Lord's people will pay the penalty, as the Abrahamic covenant requires (Gen 12:1–3). **this book.** Suggests that Jeremiah's prophecies are to be written down as a permanent record.

25:15–38 *The Cup of the Lord's Wrath.* Judgment is often compared to drinking a cup filled with an intoxicating beverage, resulting in disorientation and confusion (cf. Isa 51:17–23; Hab 2:16), which foreshadows God's final judgment on the nations, represented by Babylon (Rev 18:6). This is the cup that Christ drained for us on the cross (Matt 26:39,42) so that we might drink the cup of blessing instead (1 Cor 10:16).

25:17–26 Jerusalem and Judah must drink this cup first, and then it will be passed to their neighbors. The list of nations is the same as that in the messages against the nations in chs. 46–51, except for Damascus. The list runs from south to north, beginning with Egypt, which will be Judah's hope for deliverance from the Babylonian assault. It includes nations that ally themselves to the Babylonians, such as Edom (see the book of Obadiah), as well as those who join Judah in rebelling against them.

25:26 Sheshak. Babylon, according to a simple cryptogram in which the first letter of the alphabet is switched with the last, the second with the second-to-last, and so on (the Hebrew consonants for Babylon, *bbl,* become *ššk*; see NIV text note).

25:28 You must drink it! If judgment begins with the house of God for their sins, judgment must also be carried out on the other nations for their sins (1 Pet 4:17). No one can refuse to drink this cup. This historical judgment foreshadows the final judgment, when the Lord will crush all remaining opposition to his rule.

25:30 tread the grapes. To squeeze out the wine. Those doing so become covered with red juice, which becomes a potent image for

"'The LORD will roar[e] from on high;
he will thunder[f] from his holy dwelling
and roar mightily against his land.
He will shout like those who tread the grapes,
shout against all who live on the earth.
31 The tumult will resound to the ends of the earth,
for the LORD will bring charges[g] against the nations;
he will bring judgment on all mankind
and put the wicked to the sword,'"
declares the LORD.

32This is what the LORD Almighty says:

"Look! Disaster is spreading
from nation to nation;[h]
a mighty storm[i] is rising
from the ends of the earth."

33At that time those slain[j] by the LORD will be everywhere—from one end of the earth to the other. They
will not be mourned or gathered[k] up or buried,[l] but will be like dung lying on the ground.

34 Weep and wail, you shepherds;
roll[m] in the dust, you leaders of the flock.
For your time to be slaughtered[n] has come;
you will fall like the best of the rams.[a]
35 The shepherds will have nowhere to flee,
the leaders of the flock no place to escape.[o]
36 Hear the cry of the shepherds,
the wailing of the leaders of the flock,
for the LORD is destroying their pasture.
37 The peaceful meadows will be laid waste
because of the fierce anger of the LORD.
38 Like a lion[p] he will leave his lair,
and their land will become desolate
because of the sword[b] of the oppressor
and because of the LORD's fierce anger.

Jeremiah Threatened With Death

26 Early in the reign of Jehoiakim[q] son of Josiah king of Judah, this word came from the LORD:
2"This is what the LORD says: Stand in the courtyard[r] of the LORD's house and speak to all the
people of the towns of Judah who come to worship in the house of the LORD. Tell[s] them everything I

[a] 34 Septuagint; Hebrew *fall and be shattered like fine pottery* [b] 38 Some Hebrew manuscripts and Septuagint (see also 46:16 and 50:16); most Hebrew manuscripts *anger*

25:30 [e] Isa 16:10; 42:13 [f] Joel 3:16; Am 1:2
25:31 [g] Hos 4:1; Joel 3:2; Mic 6:2
25:32 [h] Isa 34:2 [i] Jer 23:19
25:33 [j] Isa 66:16; Eze 39:17-20 [k] Jer 16:4 [l] Ps 79:3
25:34 [m] Jer 6:26 [n] Isa 34:6; Jer 50:27
25:35 [o] Job 11:20
25:38 [p] Jer 4:7
26:1 [q] 2Ki 23:36
26:2 [r] Jer 19:14 [s] Jer 1:17; Mt 28:20; Ac 20:27

judgment in the Scriptures (Isa 63:1–6; Rev 14:19–20). It is a time of great celebration that is associated with singing, cheering, and shouting for joy (cf. Isa 16:10). **shout.** Here linked with the Lord's roaring like a lion that has captured its prey (Amos 3:4).

25:32 Ezekiel also depicts the Lord's coming judgment as a "mighty storm" (Ezek 1:4; cf. Jer 23:19).

25:33 The devastation will be so overwhelming that no one will be able to mourn or bury the dead (8:2).

25:34,35,36 shepherds. Kings and leaders of the nations.

25:34 roll in the dust. To symbolize mourning and grief. **you will fall like the best of the rams.** See NIV text note, but in this context speaking about shepherds, the imagery of rams seems more likely.

25:38 Like a lion. See v. 30 and note ("shout"). There will be no escape from the Lord's wrath. The "sword" of judgment is coming on all nations, first in the form of Babylon (v. 9) and then in judgment upon Babylon itself (v. 26).

26:1–24 *Jeremiah Threatened With Death.* In ch. 7, Jeremiah preaches a powerful message against the temple in Jerusalem. This passage records how the people respond to that message and how the Lord protects his servant from death.

26:1 Early in the reign of Jehoiakim. Sometime in 609 BC. Ch. 25 describes events in the "fourth year of Jehoiakim" (25:1), so the prophecies are not recorded chronologically (see Introduction: Outline).

26:2–6 This summarizes Jeremiah's sermon in ch. 7. If the Judahites do not listen to Jeremiah's message, the Lord will make the temple in Jerusalem "like Shiloh" (v. 6), the earlier home of the ark of the

26:2 [t]Dt 4:2
26:3 [u]Jer 36:7 [v]Jer 18:8
26:4 [w]Lev 26:14 [x]1Ki 9:6
26:5 [y]Jer 25:4
26:6 [z]Jos 18:1 [a]2Ki 22:19
26:9 [b]Jer 9:11
26:11 [c]Dt 18:20; Jer 18:23; 38:4; Mt 26:66; Ac 6:11
26:12 [d]Jer 1:18 [e]Am 7:15; Ac 4:18-20; 5:29 [f]ver 2,15
26:13 [g]Jer 7:5; Joel 2:12-14
26:14 [h]Jer 38:5
26:16 [i]Ac 23:9 [j]Ac 5:34-39; 23:29
26:18 [k]Mic 1:1 [l]Isa 2:3 [m]Ne 4:2; Jer 9:11 [n]Mic 4:1; Zec 8:3 [o]Jer 17:3
26:19 [p]2Ch 32:24-26; Isa 37:14-20 [q]Ex 32:14; 2Sa 24:16 [r]Jer 44:7 [s]Hab 2:10
26:20 [t]Jos 9:17

command you; do not omit[t] a word. [3]Perhaps they will listen and each will turn[u] from their evil ways. Then I will relent[v] and not inflict on them the disaster I was planning because of the evil they have done. [4]Say to them, 'This is what the LORD says: If you do not listen[w] to me and follow my law,[x] which I have set before you, [5]and if you do not listen to the words of my servants the prophets, whom I have sent to you again and again (though you have not listened[y]), [6]then I will make this house like Shiloh[z] and this city a curse[*a*][a] among all the nations of the earth.' "

[7]The priests, the prophets and all the people heard Jeremiah speak these words in the house of the LORD. [8]But as soon as Jeremiah finished telling all the people everything the LORD had commanded him to say, the priests, the prophets and all the people seized him and said, "You must die! [9]Why do you prophesy in the LORD's name that this house will be like Shiloh and this city will be desolate and deserted?"[b] And all the people crowded around Jeremiah in the house of the LORD.

[10]When the officials of Judah heard about these things, they went up from the royal palace to the house of the LORD and took their places at the entrance of the New Gate of the LORD's house. [11]Then the priests and the prophets said to the officials and all the people, "This man should be sentenced to death[c] because he has prophesied against this city. You have heard it with your own ears!"

[12]Then Jeremiah said to all the officials[d] and all the people: "The LORD sent me to prophesy[e] against this house and this city all the things you have heard.[f] [13]Now reform[g] your ways and your actions and obey the LORD your God. Then the LORD will relent and not bring the disaster he has pronounced against you. [14]As for me, I am in your hands;[h] do with me whatever you think is good and right. [15]Be assured, however, that if you put me to death, you will bring the guilt of innocent blood on yourselves and on this city and on those who live in it, for in truth the LORD has sent me to you to speak all these words in your hearing."

[16]Then the officials[i] and all the people said to the priests and the prophets, "This man should not be sentenced to death![j] He has spoken to us in the name of the LORD our God."

[17]Some of the elders of the land stepped forward and said to the entire assembly of people, [18]"Micah[k] of Moresheth prophesied in the days of Hezekiah king of Judah. He told all the people of Judah, 'This is what the LORD Almighty says:

" 'Zion[l] will be plowed like a field,
Jerusalem will become a heap of rubble,[m]
the temple hill[n] a mound overgrown with thickets.'[*b*][o]

[19]"Did Hezekiah king of Judah or anyone else in Judah put him to death? Did not Hezekiah[p] fear the LORD and seek his favor? And did not the LORD relent,[q] so that he did not bring the disaster[r] he pronounced against them? We are about to bring a terrible disaster[s] on ourselves!"

[20](Now Uriah son of Shemaiah from Kiriath Jearim[t] was another man who prophesied in the name

a *6* That is, its name will be used in cursing (see 29:22); or, others will see that it is cursed. *b* *18* Micah 3:12

covenant. When the priests and the people in those days were unfaithful, the Lord abandoned them, sent the ark into exile among the Philistines, and gave Shiloh over to destruction (1 Sam 4; see note on Jer 7:12–15). If the Judahites do not listen to the Lord's "servants the prophets" (v. 5), the same fate will befall Jerusalem.

26:8 You must die! The people display their attitude to the Lord's message by how they respond to the Lord's messenger (see 20:1–2 and note on 20:1; Matt 21:35–36). They are ready to kill Jeremiah for speaking the Lord's words. Death was the appropriate punishment for a false prophet (Deut 13:5), but these people leave false prophets unharmed while seeking to kill the true prophet.

26:10 officials. They come to restore order. **entrance of the New Gate.** The place of judgment. A trial is immediately convened there.

26:11 "The priests and the prophets" again demand Jeremiah's death.

26:12 The LORD sent me. Jeremiah's defense rests in the Lord's sending him to prophesy these things. Of course, only subsequent history can vindicate that defense, so the court may or may not believe him.

26:15 To execute Jeremiah at this point is to risk bringing "the guilt of innocent blood" on themselves and the city. The Lord condemned such unjust killings (e.g., Deut 19:13).

26:16 The people are initially on the side of the priests and prophets, who are against Jeremiah (v. 8). But once the people have time to consider, they join the officials against the priests and prophets in defending Jeremiah since he spoke "in the name of the LORD."

26:17–19 Jeremiah's case is assisted by some of the elders, who remind the people of the prophecy of Mic 3:12, which warned centuries earlier of the coming day when Zion would be "plowed like a field." Far from putting Micah to death, Hezekiah heeded Micah's warning and repented, which delivered the city from immediate destruction. If they put Jeremiah to death and he is indeed a messenger of the Lord, they will "bring a terrible disaster" on themselves (v. 19). Unfortunately, even though the people spare Jeremiah's life, they don't follow Hezekiah's example of repentance.

26:20–23 Jeremiah is fortunate. Uriah, another prophet with a similar message in those days, was put to death by King Jehoiakim, who sent envoys to hunt Uriah down in Egypt, where he had fled. Since the Egyptians had put Jehoiakim in his position as king, he was able to get

Benches and throne area at the gate of Dan. This is where the elders sat and held court. The gate area was a common place for officials to meet (Jer 26:10).

of the LORD; he prophesied the same things against this city and this land as Jeremiah did. [21]When
King Jehoiakim[u] and all his officers and officials heard his words, the king was determined to put him
to death. But Uriah heard of it and fled[v] in fear to Egypt. [22]King Jehoiakim, however, sent Elnathan[w]
son of Akbor to Egypt, along with some other men. [23]They brought Uriah out of Egypt and took him
to King Jehoiakim, who had him struck down with a sword and his body thrown into the burial place
of the common people.)
[24]Furthermore, Ahikam[x] son of Shaphan supported Jeremiah, and so he was not handed over to the
people to be put to death.

26:21 [u] 1Ki 19:2 [v] Mt 10:23
26:22 [w] Jer 36:12,25
26:24 [x] 2Ki 22:12
27:1 [y] 2Ch 36:11
27:2 [z] Jer 28:10,13
27:3 [a] Jer 25:21

Judah to Serve Nebuchadnezzar

27 Early in the reign of Zedekiah[a][y] son of Josiah king of Judah, this word came to Jeremiah from
the LORD: [2]This is what the LORD said to me: "Make a yoke[z] out of straps and crossbars and
put it on your neck. [3]Then send word to the kings of Edom, Moab, Ammon,[a] Tyre and Sidon through
the envoys who have come to Jerusalem to Zedekiah king of Judah. [4]Give them a message for their

[a] *1* A few Hebrew manuscripts and Syriac (see also 27:3,12 and 28:1); most Hebrew manuscripts *Jehoiakim* (Most Septuagint manuscripts do not have this verse.)

Uriah extradited to stand trial for treason. Jeremiah could easily have suffered a similar fate.

26:24 Shaphan. A key leader in the reforms of Josiah's days (2 Kgs 22:3–14). He had at least three sons who followed in his footsteps: Ahikam, Elasah (29:3), and Gemariah (who later tries to persuade Jehoiakim to heed the scroll of Jeremiah's prophecies; 36:11–26). Shaphan's grandson, Gedaliah, later becomes governor of Judah after the fall of Jerusalem (39:14; 40:5–16). Ahikam's support helps keep Jeremiah alive in this dangerous environment.

27:1–22 *Judah to Serve Nebuchadnezzar.* This chapter covers events eight years after the events of ch. 26. The common theme is the fierce opposition to Jeremiah's consistent message of Jerusalem's destruction.

27:1 Zedekiah. See NIV text note. Zedekiah is clearly the correct name from what follows (see vv. 3,12; 28:1). The scribal error ("Jehoiakim" rather than "Zedekiah") is probably due to the close similarity of this verse and 26:1.

27:2 Make a yoke. Another prophetic sign-act (cf. chs. 13; 19). Its power is in its simplicity and self-explanatory nature.

27:3 send word. Alternatively this phrase can mean "send them," perhaps suggesting that Jeremiah make individual yokes to be delivered to each of the envoys, which would send a clear message for them to take home. The kings of the surrounding nations come to Judah to discuss rebelling against Nebuchadnezzar, possibly because of internal dissension in the Babylonian Empire at this time.

27:4–7 The prophet does not soften his message to these foreigners: he asserts that the Lord made the earth, along with its people and animals; therefore, it is his to give to whomever he chooses. The Lord is giving them into the hand of Nebuchadnezzar (v. 6).

27:5 [b]Dt 9:29 [c]Ps 115:16
27:6 [d]Jer 25:9 [e]Jer 21:7; Eze 29:18-20 [f]Jer 28:14; Da 2:37-38
27:7 [g]2Ch 36:20 [h]Jer 25:12 [i]Jer 25:14; Da 5:28
27:9 [j]Dt 18:11
27:10 [k]Jer 23:25
27:11 [l]Jer 21:9
27:13 [m]Eze 18:31
27:14 [n]Jer 14:14
27:15 [o]Jer 23:21 [p]Jer 29:9 [q]Jer 6:15
27:16 [r]2Ki 24:13; 2Ch 36:7,10; Jer 28:3; Da 1:2
27:18 [s]1Sa 7:8
27:19 [t]2Ki 25:13 [u]Jer 52:17-23
27:20 [v]2Ch 36:10; Jer 24:1 [w]Jer 22:24
27:22 [x]2Ki 25:13

masters and say, 'This is what the LORD Almighty, the God of Israel, says: "Tell this to your masters:
5 With my great power and outstretched arm[b] I made the earth and its people and the animals that are
on it, and I give[c] it to anyone I please. 6 Now I will give all your countries into the hands of my servant[d]
Nebuchadnezzar[e] king of Babylon; I will make even the wild animals subject to him.[f] 7 All nations will
serve[g] him and his son and his grandson until the time[h] for his land comes; then many nations and
great kings will subjugate[i] him.

8 " ' "If, however, any nation or kingdom will not serve Nebuchadnezzar king of Babylon or bow
its neck under his yoke, I will punish that nation with the sword, famine and plague, declares the
LORD, until I destroy it by his hand. 9 So do not listen to your prophets, your diviners, your interpreters
of dreams, your mediums[j] or your sorcerers who tell you, 'You will not serve the king of Babylon.'
10 They prophesy lies[k] to you that will only serve to remove you far from your lands; I will banish
you and you will perish. 11 But if any nation will bow its neck under the yoke[l] of the king of Babylon
and serve him, I will let that nation remain in its own land to till it and to live there, declares the
LORD." ' "

12 I gave the same message to Zedekiah king of Judah. I said, "Bow your neck under the yoke of the
king of Babylon; serve him and his people, and you will live. 13 Why will you and your people die[m] by
the sword, famine and plague with which the LORD has threatened any nation that will not serve the
king of Babylon? 14 Do not listen to the words of the prophets who say to you, 'You will not serve the king
of Babylon,' for they are prophesying lies[n] to you. 15 'I have not sent[o] them,' declares the LORD. 'They
are prophesying lies in my name.[p] Therefore, I will banish you and you will perish,[q] both you and the
prophets who prophesy to you.' "

16 Then I said to the priests and all these people, "This is what the LORD says: Do not listen to the
prophets who say, 'Very soon now the articles[r] from the LORD's house will be brought back from Babylon.' They are prophesying lies to you. 17 Do not listen to them. Serve the king of Babylon, and you will
live. Why should this city become a ruin? 18 If they are prophets and have the word of the LORD, let them
plead[s] with the LORD Almighty that the articles remaining in the house of the LORD and in the palace
of the king of Judah and in Jerusalem not be taken to Babylon. 19 For this is what the LORD Almighty
says about the pillars, the bronze Sea,[t] the movable stands and the other articles[u] that are left in this
city, 20 which Nebuchadnezzar king of Babylon did not take away when he carried[v] Jehoiachin[a][w] son of
Jehoiakim king of Judah into exile from Jerusalem to Babylon, along with all the nobles of Judah and
Jerusalem — 21 yes, this is what the LORD Almighty, the God of Israel, says about the things that are left
in the house of the LORD and in the palace of the king of Judah and in Jerusalem: 22 'They will be taken[x]

[a] *20* Hebrew *Jeconiah,* a variant of *Jehoiachin*

27:6 my servant. See note on 25:9. **make even the wild animals subject to him.** Nebuchadnezzar's power is likened to the power Adam possessed before the fall. If Nebuchadnezzar is given power to tame such untamable creatures, how much more easily will he crush human rebellions?
27:7 his son and his grandson. May refer to those who succeeded Nebuchadnezzar as king, not necessarily those physically descended from him. Though two of his sons did indeed succeed him, the dynasty came to an end with them. **subjugate him.** Babylon's reign will not be forever: its time too will come.
27:8 Any nation that refuses to submit to Babylon will be cursed with "the sword, famine and plague," just like rebellious Judah (see 14:12 and note).
27:9 prophets ... diviners ... interpreters of dreams ... mediums ... sorcerers. These will prove no more reliable than Judah's own false prophets. Deut 18:9–13 forbids Israel to use these means of discerning the future.
27:10–11 If the nations resist Nebuchadnezzar, they will be banished to Babylon, but if they submit to his God-given authority, the Lord (not merely Nebuchadnezzar!) will allow them to remain in their own land.
27:12–15 The message to Zedekiah is exactly the same as the one delivered to the surrounding nations.
27:16 articles from the LORD's house. The gold, silver, and bronze utensils that Nebuchadnezzar took in 605 BC (Dan 1:1–2) and 597 BC (2 Kgs 24:10–13). These were highly symbolic because they were dedicated to the Lord. They will remain in Babylon until the Lord retrieves them (v. 22), which will not happen until the days of the Persian king Cyrus. That is still almost 70 years away at this point, not "very soon" as the false prophets claim. The return of these items will provide an important element of continuity between those who return from exile and the preexilic community, a tangible point of contact with the temple Solomon built.
27:18 If they are prophets. True prophets will spend their time interceding with the Lord (see note on 7:16) so that the remaining articles from the temple do not go to Babylon also.
27:19–22 The Lord has already decided the fate of these articles. When Nebuchadnezzar destroys Jerusalem in 586 BC, he will take away the articles that were too big to remove earlier.
27:19 bronze Sea. A massive basin (see 1 Kgs 7:23 and note) that held the water used by the priests to wash (see note on Exod 30:17–21). It was called the "Sea" because it represented the Lord's victory over the chaotic forces of nature, which had been symbolically domesticated within his dwelling place. Many articles from the temple will return from Babylon with those who return to Jerusalem in the time of Cyrus (Ezra 1:7–8; 5:13–17).

to Babylon and there they will remain until the day[y] I come for them,' declares the LORD. 'Then I will
bring[z] them back and restore them to this place.' "

The False Prophet Hananiah

28 In the fifth month of that same year, the fourth year, early in the reign of Zedekiah[a] king of
Judah, the prophet Hananiah son of Azzur, who was from Gibeon,[b] said to me in the house
of the LORD in the presence of the priests and all the people: 2"This is what the LORD Almighty, the God of
Israel, says: 'I will break the yoke[c] of the king of Babylon. 3Within two years I will bring back to this
place all the articles[d] of the LORD's house that Nebuchadnezzar king of Babylon removed from here
and took to Babylon. 4I will also bring back to this place Jehoiachin[a][e] son of Jehoiakim king of Judah
and all the other exiles from Judah who went to Babylon,' declares the LORD, 'for I will break the yoke
of the king of Babylon.' "

5Then the prophet Jeremiah replied to the prophet Hananiah before the priests and all the
people who were standing in the house of the LORD. 6He said, "Amen! May the LORD do so! May
the LORD fulfill the words you have prophesied by bringing the articles of the LORD's house and
all the exiles back to this place from Babylon. 7Nevertheless, listen to what I have to say in your
hearing and in the hearing of all the people: 8From early times the prophets who preceded you
and me have prophesied war, disaster and plague[f] against many countries and great kingdoms.
9But the prophet who prophesies peace will be recognized as one truly sent by the LORD only if his
prediction comes true.[g]"

10Then the prophet Hananiah took the yoke[h] off the neck of the prophet Jeremiah and broke it, 11and
he said[i] before all the people, "This is what the LORD says: 'In the same way I will break the yoke of
Nebuchadnezzar king of Babylon off the neck of all the nations within two years.' " At this, the prophet
Jeremiah went on his way.

12After the prophet Hananiah had broken the yoke off the neck of the prophet Jeremiah, the word
of the LORD came to Jeremiah: 13"Go and tell Hananiah, 'This is what the LORD says: You have broken a wooden yoke, but in its place you will get a yoke of iron. 14This is what the LORD Almighty, the
God of Israel, says: I will put an iron yoke[j] on the necks of all these nations to make them serve[k]
Nebuchadnezzar king of Babylon, and they will serve him. I will even give him control over the wild
animals.[l] ' "

15Then the prophet Jeremiah said to Hananiah the prophet, "Listen, Hananiah! The LORD has not
sent[m] you, yet you have persuaded this nation to trust in lies.[n] 16Therefore this is what the LORD says: 'I

27:22 [y] 2Ch 36:21 [z] Ezr 1:7; 7:19
28:1 [a] Jer 27:1,3 [b] Jos 9:3
28:2 [c] Jer 27:12
28:3 [d] 2Ki 24:13
28:4 [e] Jer 22:24-27
28:8 [f] Lev 26:14-17; Isa 5:5-7
28:9 [g] Dt 18:22
28:10 [h] Jer 27:2
28:11 [i] Jer 14:14; 27:10
28:14 [j] Dt 28:48 [k] Jer 25:11 [l] Jer 27:6
28:15 [m] Jer 29:31 [n] Jer 20:6; 29:21; La 2:14; Eze 13:6

[a] *4* Hebrew *Jeconiah,* a variant of *Jehoiachin*

28:1–17 *The False Prophet Hananiah.* This chapter contains a specific example of Jeremiah's confrontation with false prophecy in the person of Hananiah, who declares the imminent return of the temple vessels and the people who are already in exile.

28:1 that same year. The events of ch. 28 are linked with those of ch. 27. **Gibeon.** A few miles/kilometers west of Anathoth, Jeremiah's hometown.

28:2 yoke of the king of Babylon. See 27:2–6 and note on 27:2.

28:3 articles of the LORD's house. See 27:16 and note. This prophecy directly contradicts Jeremiah's prophecy, which means that one of them must be a false prophet. Jeremiah has prophesied a 70-year exile (25:11), while Hananiah expects the temple articles to be brought back "within two years."

28:4 Jeremiah has declared that Jehoiachin will die in exile (22:27); Hananiah says that Jehoiachin and all the other exiles will return home soon.

28:6 Amen! "May it be so!" Jeremiah wishes Hananiah's prophecy were true. He takes no pleasure in predicting the destruction of his own people. Since it was always much more popular to be a prophet of good news than a prophet of bad news, a prophet bringing bad news was less likely to make up his message than one bringing news of peace and plenty, especially if that bad news was in line with the words of earlier true prophets.

28:10–11 Jeremiah is wearing a yoke that he was told to make as a sign of the coming bondage to Babylon (27:2). Hananiah now performs a sign-act of his own: he breaks the yoke off Jeremiah's neck to picture the freedom that his message proclaims.

28:11 went on his way. Jeremiah does not immediately respond. A false prophet, who invents his message as he goes along, needs never be at a loss for words. As a true prophet, Jeremiah needs instruction from the Lord about how he should respond.

28:12–14 The Lord reiterates his message in even stronger terms: in place of a wooden yoke, Jeremiah is to make an unbreakable iron yoke and deliver it to "all these nations" to symbolize the irresistible power of the Babylonians. Not only Judah but all these nations (v. 14; see 27:3) will serve the king of Babylon.

28:14 control over the wild animals. Even the created order will serve him (see note on 27:6).

28:16 you are going to die. The difference between a true and a false prophet is this: what the true prophet says actually happens. The Lord condemns Hananiah to death because of his false prophecy. Hananiah will not even live for the two years necessary to prove his own prophecies false; he will die within one year. Two months later, in that year's "seventh month" (v. 17), Hananiah dies, vindicating Jeremiah's message and his identity as a true prophet.

28:16 [o] Ge 7:4 [p] Dt 13:5; Jer 29:32
29:1 [q] 2Ch 36:10
29:2 [r] 2Ki 24:12; Jer 22:24-28
29:4 [s] Jer 24:5
29:5 [t] ver 28
29:7 [u] Ezr 6:10; 1Ti 2:1-2
29:8 [v] Jer 37:9 [w] Jer 23:27
29:9 [x] Jer 14:14; 27:15
29:10 [y] 2Ch 36:21; Jer 25:12; Da 9:2 [z] Jer 21:22
29:11 [a] Ps 40:5
29:12 [b] Ps 145:19
29:13 [c] Mt 7:7 [d] Dt 4:29; Jer 24:7
29:14 [e] Dt 30:3; Jer 30:3 [f] Jer 23:3-4

am about to remove you from the face of the earth.[o] This very year you are going to die, because you
have preached rebellion[p] against the LORD.' "
17 In the seventh month of that same year, Hananiah the prophet died.

A Letter to the Exiles

29 This is the text of the letter that the prophet Jeremiah sent from Jerusalem to the surviving
elders among the exiles and to the priests, the prophets and all the other people Nebuchadnezzar had carried into exile from Jerusalem to Babylon.[q] 2 (This was after King Jehoiachin[a][r] and the
queen mother, the court officials and the leaders of Judah and Jerusalem, the skilled workers and the
artisans had gone into exile from Jerusalem.) 3 He entrusted the letter to Elasah son of Shaphan and
to Gemariah son of Hilkiah, whom Zedekiah king of Judah sent to King Nebuchadnezzar in Babylon.
It said:

4 This is what the LORD Almighty, the God of Israel, says to all those I carried[s] into exile from
Jerusalem to Babylon: 5 "Build[t] houses and settle down; plant gardens and eat what they produce.
6 Marry and have sons and daughters; find wives for your sons and give your daughters in marriage, so that they too may have sons and daughters. Increase in number there; do not decrease.
7 Also, seek the peace and prosperity of the city to which I have carried you into exile. Pray[u] to the
LORD for it, because if it prospers, you too will prosper." 8 Yes, this is what the LORD Almighty, the
God of Israel, says: "Do not let the prophets and diviners among you deceive[v] you. Do not listen
to the dreams you encourage them to have.[w] 9 They are prophesying lies[x] to you in my name. I
have not sent them," declares the LORD.

10 This is what the LORD says: "When seventy years[y] are completed for Babylon, I will come to
you and fulfill my good promise to bring you back[z] to this place. 11 For I know the plans[a] I have for
you," declares the LORD, "plans to prosper you and not to harm you, plans to give you hope and a
future. 12 Then you will call on me and come and pray to me, and I will listen[b] to you. 13 You will
seek[c] me and find me when you seek me with all your heart.[d] 14 I will be found by you," declares
the LORD, "and will bring you back[e] from captivity.[b] I will gather you from all the nations and
places where I have banished you," declares the LORD, "and will bring you back to the place from
which I carried you into exile."[f]

[a] 2 Hebrew *Jeconiah,* a variant of *Jehoiachin*   [b] 14 Or *will restore your fortunes*

29:1–23 *A Letter to the Exiles.* Jeremiah earlier declared that the future of God's people lies with the exiles, not with those still in Jerusalem (ch. 24). He therefore writes a letter encouraging the exiles to settle down in Babylon in the meantime, recognizing that they will be there for 70 years, not the brief period that Hananiah and other prophets predicted (28:3–4).

29:2 after King Jehoiachin ... had gone into exile. In 597 BC, Nebuchadnezzar took many of the "leaders," "skilled workers," and "artisans" from Judah to Jerusalem. This included many of the "priests" and "prophets" (v. 1), since they would normally have been educated, able to read and write.

29:3 Elasah son of Shaphan. See note on 26:24. **Gemariah son of Hilkiah.** Possibly the son of the high priest at the time of Josiah's reforms (this is not the Gemariah who later tries to persuade Jehoiakim to heed the scroll of Jeremiah's prophecies [ch. 36]). For connections between Shaphan and Hilkiah, see 2 Kgs 22.

29:4 I carried into exile. The Lord (not the Babylonians) is sovereign over the entire process.

29:5 Build houses ... plant gardens. These are long-term activities that would not be worthwhile if the people were coming back to Judah immediately.

29:6 Marry ... find wives. They are to look beyond the immediate challenges to the needs of the next generation and the one after that. The Babylonians resettled the Jews in their own communities, so the Jews could still marry other Jews and remain a distinct people.

29:7 seek the peace and prosperity of the city ... Pray ... for it. They are used to doing this for Jerusalem (Ps 122:6–9). Shockingly, the Lord tells them to transfer their prayers and energies from Jerusalem to Babylon, the pagan capital, because for the next 70 years their "peace and prosperity" (Hebrew *šālôm*) will be connected with Babylon's "peace and prosperity." This message is the exact opposite of what the false prophets among them in Babylon are saying; they are falsely predicting a speedy return home to Judah.

29:10–14 The Lord will not abandon the exiles in Babylon forever. After 70 years (25:11), he will fulfill his "good promise" (v. 10) from Deut 30:3–5 to bring them back to their homeland. God is the ultimate source of blessings and curses. The plans he has for those in exile are for a good future (unlike the plans he has for those in Judah; see vv. 16–19). He is willing to listen to their prayers and allow them to call upon his name (Deut 4:29).

29:13 You will seek me and find me. In antiquity, gods were typically connected with particular lands, so it is a remarkable encouragement to those in exile in Babylon that they can approach the Lord (cf. Ezek 11:16). It is also a profound encouragement to contemporary believers who may feel cut off from God by their sins or by difficult circumstances.

15 You may say, "The LORD has raised up prophets for us in Babylon," 16 but this is what the LORD
says about the king who sits on David's throne and all the people who remain in this city, your
fellow citizens who did not go with you into exile— 17 yes, this is what the LORD Almighty says: "I
will send the sword, famine and plague[g] against them and I will make them like figs[h] that are so
bad they cannot be eaten. 18 I will pursue them with the sword, famine and plague and will make
them abhorrent[i] to all the kingdoms of the earth, a curse[a] and an object of horror,[j] of scorn and
reproach, among all the nations where I drive them. 19 For they have not listened to my words,"[k]
declares the LORD, "words that I sent to them again and again by my servants the prophets.[l] And
you exiles have not listened either," declares the LORD.

20 Therefore, hear the word of the LORD, all you exiles whom I have sent[m] away from Jerusalem
to Babylon. 21 This is what the LORD Almighty, the God of Israel, says about Ahab son of Kolaiah
and Zedekiah son of Maaseiah, who are prophesying lies[n] to you in my name: "I will deliver them
into the hands of Nebuchadnezzar king of Babylon, and he will put them to death before your
very eyes. 22 Because of them, all the exiles from Judah who are in Babylon will use this curse:
'May the LORD treat you like Zedekiah and Ahab, whom the king of Babylon burned[o] in the fire.'
23 For they have done outrageous things in Israel; they have committed adultery[p] with their neighbors' wives, and in my name they have uttered lies—which I did not authorize. I know[q] it and
am a witness to it," declares the LORD.

29:17 [g] Jer 27:8 [h] Jer 24:8-10
29:18 [i] Jer 15:4 [j] Dt 28:25; Jer 42:18
29:19 [k] Jer 6:19 [l] Jer 25:4
29:20 [m] Jer 24:5
29:21 [n] ver 9; Jer 14:14
29:22 [o] Da 3:6
29:23 [p] Jer 23:14 [q] Heb 4:13
29:25 [r] 2Ki 25:18; Jer 21:1
29:26 [s] 2Ki 9:11; Hos 9:7; Jn 10:20 [t] Jer 20:2
29:28 [u] ver 1 [v] ver 10 [w] ver 5
29:31 [x] ver 24 [y] Jer 14:14; 28:15
29:32 [z] 1Sa 2:30-33 [a] ver 10 [b] Jer 28:16

Message to Shemaiah

24 Tell Shemaiah the Nehelamite, 25 "This is what the LORD Almighty, the God of Israel, says: You
sent letters in your own name to all the people in Jerusalem, to the priest Zephaniah[r] son of Maaseiah, and to all the other priests. You said to Zephaniah, 26 'The LORD has appointed you priest
in place of Jehoiada to be in charge of the house of the LORD; you should put any maniac[s] who
acts like a prophet into the stocks[t] and neck-irons. 27 So why have you not reprimanded Jeremiah
from Anathoth, who poses as a prophet among you? 28 He has sent this message[u] to us in Babylon:
It will be a long time.[v] Therefore build[w] houses and settle down; plant gardens and eat what they
produce.'"

29 Zephaniah the priest, however, read the letter to Jeremiah the prophet. 30 Then the word of the
LORD came to Jeremiah: 31 "Send this message to all the exiles: 'This is what the LORD says about
Shemaiah[x] the Nehelamite: Because Shemaiah has prophesied to you, even though I did not send[y]
him, and has persuaded you to trust in lies, 32 this is what the LORD says: I will surely punish Shemaiah the Nehelamite and his descendants.[z] He will have no one left among this people, nor will he
see the good[a] things I will do for my people, declares the LORD, because he has preached rebellion[b]
against me.'"

[a] *18* That is, their names will be used in cursing (see verse 22); or, others will see that they are cursed.

29:15–19 The exiles are not to listen to those claiming to be the Lord's prophets in Babylon.
29:16 the king who sits on David's throne. Zedekiah. God's word concerning Zedekiah and those who remain in Jerusalem is judgment: "the sword, famine and plague" (v. 17; see 14:12 and note).
29:17 figs. See ch. 24 and notes. Those in Jerusalem had failed repeatedly to listen to the words of God's prophets, as indeed the exiles had.
29:21 put them to death. The penalty for false prophecy was death, a sentence that was carried out on Hananiah (28:17) and that would now befall two of the false prophets among the exiles, Ahab and Zedekiah.
29:22 Proving the Lord's sovereign control over his instruments of judgment, Nebuchadnezzar will burn the false prophets in the fire, as he later tries to do unsuccessfully to Shadrach, Meshach, and Abednego (Dan 3).
29:23 outrageous things. Particularly offensive crimes (see Gen 34:7; Josh 7:15 and note). In this case, they compounded the sin of false prophecy with marital infidelity.
29:24–32 *Message to Shemaiah.* Although located among the exiles, Shemaiah shares the negative perspective of many of the leaders back home in Jerusalem with regard to Jeremiah's messages.
29:24 Shemaiah the Nehelamite. One of the exiles who disapproves of Jeremiah's letter and seeks to have the authorities back in Jerusalem take action against him. Shemaiah wants Jeremiah put in "the stocks and neck-irons" (v. 26), as if he were a "maniac" (v. 26), as Pashhur had done in 20:2.
29:25 Zephaniah son of Maaseiah. A priest apparently in charge of temple security; a trusted envoy of King Zedekiah (see 21:1); possibly the brother of the false prophet Zedekiah, who is prophesying in Babylon (v. 21), since their fathers' names are the same.
29:29–32 Zephaniah takes no action beyond showing Jeremiah the letter. In turn, the Lord declares that even though Shemaiah is physically located among the exiles, he will not share the good future the Lord has planned for the exiles. Instead, "because he has preached rebellion against [the LORD]" (v. 32) by inciting violence against one of the Lord's servants, he will share the fate of those still in Jerusalem and be left without descendants.

30:2 [c] Isa 30:8
30:3 [d] Jer 29:14 [e] Jer 16:15
30:5 [f] Jer 6:25
30:6 [g] Jer 4:31
30:7 [h] Isa 2:12; Joel 2:11 [i] Zep 1:15 [j] ver 10
30:8 [k] Isa 9:4 [l] Eze 34:27
30:9 [m] Isa 55:3-4; Lk 1:69; Ac 2:30; 13:23 [n] Eze 34:23-24; 37:24; Hos 3:5
30:10 [o] Isa 43:5; Jer 46:27-28 [p] Isa 44:2 [q] Jer 29:14 [r] Isa 35:9

Restoration of Israel

30 This is the word that came to Jeremiah from the LORD: [2]"This is what the LORD, the God of Israel, says: 'Write[c] in a book all the words I have spoken to you. [3]The days are coming,' declares
the LORD, 'when I will bring[d] my people Israel and Judah back from captivity[a] and restore[e] them to the
land I gave their ancestors to possess,' says the LORD."
[4]These are the words the LORD spoke concerning Israel and Judah: [5]"This is what the LORD says:

"'Cries of fear[f] are heard —
terror, not peace.
[6]Ask and see:
Can a man bear children?
Then why do I see every strong man
with his hands on his stomach like a woman in labor,[g]
every face turned deathly pale?
[7]How awful that day[h] will be!
No other will be like it.
It will be a time of trouble[i] for Jacob,
but he will be saved[j] out of it.

[8]"'In that day,' declares the LORD Almighty,
'I will break the yoke[k] off their necks
and will tear off their bonds;
no longer will foreigners enslave them.[l]
[9]Instead, they will serve the LORD their God
and David[m] their king,[n]
whom I will raise up for them.

[10]"'So do not be afraid,[o] Jacob my servant;[p]
do not be dismayed, Israel,'
declares the LORD.
'I will surely save[q] you out of a distant place,
your descendants from the land of their exile.
Jacob will again have peace and security,[r]
and no one will make him afraid.

[a] 3 Or *will restore the fortunes of my people Israel and Judah*

30:1—33:26 *Restoration and a New Covenant.* Having consistently preached the destruction of Jerusalem for many years, Jeremiah now turns to speak words of comfort and consolation to the faithful remnant of his people. The few references to such hope in the earlier messages become the central focus in these chapters. The covenant relationship between Israel and the Lord has not been a blessing to Israel because of its unfaithfulness. That will change in the years ahead.
30:1—31:40 *Restoration of Israel.* The Lord's judgment of his people is not merely venting his wrath. Its goal is to establish a pure and holy people who will belong to him in faithfulness, restored to the land that he promised to their ancestors.
30:2 a book. That is, a scroll. Jeremiah is to preserve the words for future generations.
30:3 The Lord will bring Israel and Judah back together, reuniting what was separated in the time of Rehoboam (cf. Ezek 37:15–28). This finds fulfillment in the NT as the gospel goes to Samaria as well as to Jerusalem and Judea before going out to the ends of the earth (Acts 1:8). In Christ, all God's scattered people are brought together into a new unity (Rev 7:4–10).
30:6 a woman in labor. This image of pain and anguish is one of the OT's most potent descriptions of powerful emotions such as terror (cf. Isa 13:8; 21:3). The men who face the Babylonian onslaught of Jerusalem will finally recognize that, contrary to the message of the false prophets, there is no peace, and they will be in profound anguish. There is no way of bypassing the coming judgment.
30:7 that day. The day of the Lord's judgment on Jerusalem (see note on Amos 2:16). It will be a time of almost unbearable distress for God's people, yet the end of the process will not be utter destruction but new life, as in childbirth (see v. 6 and note; cf. Rom 8:22). **No other will be like it.** Cf. Dan 12:1; Joel 2:2; Matt 24:19–21. **Jacob.** Recalls the story of their forefather in Genesis: even though he was a cheat and a deceiver, he ultimately came to inherit the blessing that he so desired by God's undeserved grace.
30:8–9 In chs. 27–28, the Lord uses the image of a yoke to describe the people's bondage to Babylon. Now he promises that in "that day" (the day of their deliverance) he will break the unbreakable iron yoke of Babylon (28:14) and "tear off their bonds," setting his people free (cf. Ps 2:3). Whereas previously they sought freedom by rebelling against God (2:20; 5:5), now freedom will mean freedom to "serve the LORD" and the promised descendant of David, a king after God's own heart (3:15; 1 Sam 13:14; Ezek 34:23–24). This promise finds its fulfillment in Jesus' invitation to take up his easy yoke (Matt 11:29), which is in contrast to the harsh rule of Nebuchadnezzar and the unfaithful rules of Jehoiachin and Zedekiah.
30:10 do not be afraid, Jacob my servant. See note on 46:27–28; see also note on Isa 42:1–9.

[11] I am with you and will save you,'
declares the LORD.
'Though I completely destroy all the nations
among which I scatter you,
I will not completely destroy[s] you.
I will discipline[t] you but only in due measure;
I will not let you go entirely unpunished.'[u]

[12] "This is what the LORD says:

" 'Your wound is incurable,
your injury beyond healing.[v]
[13] There is no one to plead your cause,
no remedy for your sore,
no healing[w] for you.
[14] All your allies[x] have forgotten you;
they care nothing for you.
I have struck you as an enemy[y] would
and punished you as would the cruel,[z]
because your guilt is so great
and your sins[a] so many.
[15] Why do you cry out over your wound,
your pain that has no cure?
Because of your great guilt and many sins
I have done these things to you.

[16] " 'But all who devour[b] you will be devoured;
all your enemies will go into exile.[c]
Those who plunder[d] you will be plundered;
all who make spoil of you I will despoil.
[17] But I will restore you to health
and heal your wounds,'

declares the LORD,

'because you are called an outcast,[e]
Zion for whom no one cares.'

[18] "This is what the LORD says:

" 'I will restore the fortunes[f] of Jacob's tents
and have compassion[g] on his dwellings;
the city will be rebuilt[h] on her ruins,
and the palace will stand in its proper place.
[19] From them will come songs[i] of thanksgiving[j]
and the sound of rejoicing.[k]
I will add to their numbers,[l]
and they will not be decreased;

30:11 [s] Jer 4:27; 46:28 [t] Jer 10:24 [u] Am 9:8
30:12 [v] Jer 15:18
30:13 [w] Jer 8:22; 14:19; 46:11
30:14 [x] Jer 22:20; La 1:2 [y] Job 13:24 [z] Job 30:21 [a] Jer 5:6
30:16 [b] Isa 33:1; Jer 2:3; 10:25 [c] Isa 14:2; Joel 3:4-8 [d] Jer 50:10
30:17 [e] Jer 33:24
30:18 [f] ver 3; Jer 31:23 [g] Ps 102:13 [h] Jer 31:4, 24,38
30:19 [i] Isa 35:10; 51:11 [j] Isa 51:3 [k] Ps 126:1-2; Jer 31:4 [l] Jer 33:22

30:11 completely destroy all the nations. In contrast to Judah (see 4:27; 5:10,18). See note on 12:14–17. **in due measure.** With justice. The Lord is with his people to save and deliver them.
30:12 Your wound is incurable … beyond healing. Humanly speaking, because the Lord will inflict judgment on them (8:22).
30:14 allies. They all desert Judah and leave the Judahites to their fate; this includes both the nations from which Judah seeks help, such as Egypt, and the false gods with whom they commit spiritual adultery.
30:16–17 Paradoxically, since it is the Lord who will strike them, he can restore them to health (Lam 3:31–32). The great physician can heal their incurable wound. The one who is slow to anger and abounding in steadfast love can forgive their guilt and sin (Exod 34:6–7). Then the ones who plunder and spoil Judah will in turn be plundered and spoiled, in accordance with the terms of the Abrahamic covenant (Gen 12:1–3), which even the people's sin cannot render invalid.
30:18 fortunes of Jacob's tents. Israel's origins before she made a shipwreck of her position (Num 24:5). **city.** Jerusalem. **ruins.** The term used here reflects the ancient practice of rebuilding ruined cities on the rubble of preexisting sites.
30:19 In place of laments and mourning, there will be "songs of thanksgiving and the sound of rejoicing."

30:19 [m]Isa 60:9
30:20 [n]Isa 54:13; Jer 31:17 [o]Isa 54:14
30:21 [p]ver 9 [q]Nu 16:5
30:23 [r]Jer 23:19
30:24 [s]Jer 4:8 [t]Jer 4:28 [u]Jer 23:19-20
31:1 [v]Jer 30:22
31:2 [w]Nu 14:20 [x]Ex 33:14
31:3 [y]Dt 4:37 [z]Hos 11:4

I will bring them honor,[m]
and they will not be disdained.
20 Their children[n] will be as in days of old,
and their community will be established[o] before me;
I will punish all who oppress them.
21 Their leader[p] will be one of their own;
their ruler will arise from among them.
I will bring him near[q] and he will come close to me—
for who is he who will devote himself
to be close to me?'
declares the LORD.

22 " 'So you will be my people,
and I will be your God.' "

23 See, the storm[r] of the LORD
will burst out in wrath,
a driving wind swirling down
on the heads of the wicked.
24 The fierce anger[s] of the LORD will not turn back[t]
until he fully accomplishes
the purposes of his heart.
In days to come
you will understand[u] this.

31 "At that time," declares the LORD, "I will be the God[v] of all the families of Israel, and they will be my people."

2 This is what the LORD says:

"The people who survive the sword
will find favor[w] in the wilderness;
I will come to give rest[x] to Israel."

3 The LORD appeared to us in the past,[a] saying:

"I have loved[y] you with an everlasting love;
I have drawn[z] you with unfailing kindness.
4 I will build you up again,
and you, Virgin Israel, will be rebuilt.

[a] *3* Or *LORD has appeared to us from afar*

30:21 In place of foreign rulers like Nebuchadnezzar, Israel will once again be ruled by "one of their own" people. **Their leader ... their ruler.** The promised new David (v. 9). He will have a close relationship with the Lord, unlike Jehoiachin, whom the Lord cast away (22:24–30). The result will be a renewed relationship with God for the entire people, the goal of the covenant with Israel (Exod 6:7).

30:23 storm of the LORD. His anger previously raged against Judah (11:16; 25:32), but now it will come down on "the heads of the wicked" instead. The Lord's wrath against his own people will be completely satisfied, and he will turn to protect his people.

30:24 the purposes of his heart. The Lord's plan to save a people for himself.

31:1–40 The old covenant ends in disaster and exile, as Moses anticipated (Deut 30:1–5). But God will do a new work, as he promised in Deut 30:6, giving the people a hope and a future.

31:1 At that time. The day when the Lord acts to redeem his people (see note on 30:8–9) and finally reaches the covenant's goal: "all the families of Israel" reunite as the one people of God (see 30:3 and note; see also 30:22) instead of straying after idols. **they will be my people.** The Lord's purpose to have a holy people for himself remains unshakable in spite of Israel's repeated sin and rebellion. If this purpose is to reach fruition, however, a new covenant is needed in which the Lord himself undertakes to ensure that the conditions of the covenant are fulfilled; this occurs through Christ (Matt 5:17–18; Rom 8:1–4; Gal 4:4–5).

31:2 The people who survive the sword. The exiles. They will find themselves in a situation like that of Israel "in the wilderness" in the book of Numbers. There too one generation was cut off because of sin, but a new generation found favor and experienced rest as a gift from the Lord as they began to enter the promised land.

31:3 everlasting love ... unfailing kindness. Covenantal terms that express God's continued care for his bride ("you" is feminine singular in Hebrew).

31:4 Though "Virgin Israel" (see note on 14:17) has been repeatedly unfaithful, the Lord will not abandon his commitment to her (see Hos 1–3). In place of her mourning and sadness, she will again show her

Again you will take up your timbrels
and go out to dance with the joyful.[a]
5 Again you will plant vineyards
on the hills of Samaria;[b]
the farmers will plant them
and enjoy their fruit.[c]
6 There will be a day when watchmen cry out
on the hills of Ephraim,
'Come, let us go up to Zion,
to the LORD our God.' "[d]

7 This is what the LORD says:

"Sing with joy for Jacob;
shout for the foremost[e] of the nations.
Make your praises heard, and say,
'LORD, save[f] your people,
the remnant[g] of Israel.'
8 See, I will bring them from the land of the north[h]
and gather[i] them from the ends of the earth.
Among them will be the blind[j] and the lame,[k]
expectant mothers and women in labor;
a great throng will return.
9 They will come with weeping;[l]
they will pray as I bring them back.
I will lead[m] them beside streams of water
on a level[n] path where they will not stumble,
because I am Israel's father,[o]
and Ephraim is my firstborn son.

10 "Hear the word of the LORD, you nations;
proclaim it in distant coastlands:[p]
'He who scattered Israel will gather[q] them
and will watch over his flock like a shepherd.'[r]
11 For the LORD will deliver Jacob
and redeem[s] them from the hand of those stronger[t] than they.
12 They will come and shout for joy on the heights[u] of Zion;
they will rejoice in the bounty[v] of the LORD—

31:4 [a] Jer 30:19
31:5 [b] Jer 50:19 [c] Isa 65:21; Am 9:14
31:6 [d] Isa 2:3; Jer 50:4-5; Mic 4:2
31:7 [e] Dt 28:13; Isa 61:9 [f] Ps 14:7; 28:9 [g] Isa 37:31
31:8 [h] Jer 3:18; 23:8 [i] Dt 30:4; Eze 34:12-14 [j] Isa 42:16 [k] Eze 34:16; Mic 4:6
31:9 [l] Ps 126:5 [m] Isa 63:13 [n] Isa 49:11 [o] Ex 4:22; Jer 3:4
31:10 [p] Isa 66:19; Jer 25:22 [q] Jer 50:19 [r] Isa 40:11; Eze 34:12
31:11 [s] Isa 44:23; 48:20 [t] Ps 142:6
31:12 [u] Eze 17:23; Mic 4:1 [v] Joel 3:18

joy in the way typical of young women dancing with timbrels. **timbrels.** Decorative pieces of metal that jingle when moved (Exod 15:20).

31:5 The restoration in view here speaks primarily of the former northern kingdom. **hills of Samaria.** The region around the former capital of the northern kingdom.

31:6 Ephraim. Another name for the northern kingdom. **Zion.** The home of the temple in Jerusalem (Isa 2:3). Instead of crying out a warning about oncoming enemies, the watchmen will encourage the people once again to go up to Jerusalem. In the past, Jeroboam had established temples at Bethel and Dan to dissuade the people from making the journey to Jerusalem (1 Kgs 12:28–30). The prophecy implicitly requires the restoration of the southern kingdom of Judah in order for Zion to become a place of pilgrimage once again.

31:7 foremost of the nations. Title for Israel once the Lord saves them (cf. Amos 6:1). **the remnant of Israel.** Those who survive the holocaust of exile.

31:8 land of the north. Babylon. **the blind and the lame, expectant mothers and women in labor.** Even those weakest and least able to endure the rigors of travel will be able to journey safely home (cf. Isa 40:11).

31:9 with weeping ... will pray. Marks of repentance. The physical return will also be an act of spiritual turning, for in place of the hard and unresponsive hearts of the past, they will now come with repentance. **beside streams of water on a level path.** The Lord, like a good shepherd, will lead them (cf. Ps 23:2).

31:10 nations ... distant coastlands. Reminiscent of Isa 41:1. The news must be proclaimed to the most distant parts so that all of the scattered exiles may be brought back. **scattered ... gather.** As widely as the Lord disperses them, he will also bring them back like a good shepherd.

31:12 grain ... new wine ... olive oil. Three staple crops. These, together with multiplying "the young of the flocks and herds," are how the Lord promised to bless Israel in Deut 7:13 if they kept the terms of the Sinai covenant. Here the Lord promises to establish these blessings in spite of their long history of disobedience and covenant breaking.

31:12 [w]Hos 2:21-22 [x]Isa 58:11 [y]Isa 65:19; Jn 16:22; Rev 7:17
31:13 [z]Isa 61:3 [a]Ps 30:11; Isa 51:11
31:14 [b]ver 25
31:15 [c]Jos 18:25 [d]Ge 37:35 [e]Jer 10:20; Mt 2:17-18*
31:16 [f]Isa 25:8; 30:19 [g]Ru 2:12 [h]Jer 30:3; Eze 11:17
31:18 [i]Job 5:17 [j]Hos 4:16 [k]Ps 80:3
31:19 [l]Eze 36:31 [m]Eze 21:12; Lk 18:13

the grain, the new wine and the olive oil,[w]
the young of the flocks and herds.
They will be like a well-watered garden,[x]
and they will sorrow[y] no more.
13 Then young women will dance and be glad,
young men and old as well.
I will turn their mourning[z] into gladness;
I will give them comfort and joy[a] instead of sorrow.
14 I will satisfy[b] the priests with abundance,
and my people will be filled with my bounty,"
declares the LORD.

15 This is what the LORD says:

"A voice is heard in Ramah,[c]
mourning and great weeping,
Rachel weeping for her children
and refusing to be comforted,[d]
because they are no more."[e]

16 This is what the LORD says:

"Restrain your voice from weeping
and your eyes from tears,[f]
for your work will be rewarded,[g]"
declares the LORD.
"They will return[h] from the land of the enemy.
17 So there is hope for your descendants,"
declares the LORD.
"Your children will return to their own land.

18 "I have surely heard Ephraim's moaning:
'You disciplined[i] me like an unruly calf,[j]
and I have been disciplined.
Restore[k] me, and I will return,
because you are the LORD my God.
19 After I strayed,[l]
I repented;
after I came to understand,
I beat[m] my breast.
I was ashamed and humiliated
because I bore the disgrace of my youth.'
20 Is not Ephraim my dear son,
the child in whom I delight?

31:13 The Lord's blessings will result in joy for all classes of people—men and women, young and old alike. "Mourning" will be transformed into "gladness," and "sorrow" into "comfort and joy."
31:14 priests … people. The frequent targets of rebuke and threats of judgment in the earlier messages (e.g., 26:8). Now they will be satisfied with "abundance" and "bounty."
31:15 Ramah. A few miles/kilometers north of Jerusalem and a place from which exiles were dispatched to Babylon (see 40:1). Matt 2:18 quotes this verse, connecting it with the mourning of the mothers of Bethlehem over the deaths of their young sons at the hands of Herod. Herod, the king of Judea, took Nebuchadnezzar's place in reenacting the painful losses of the exile. **Rachel.** The favored wife of Jacob and the mother of Joseph and Benjamin. She represents all of the mothers of Israel "mourning" and "weeping" for their exiled offspring.
31:16 Restrain your voice. The Lord urges the mothers to cease their mourning, for he will ultimately return their children from exile; the labor and heartache they invested in their children will not be in vain.
31:18 Ephraim's moaning. If the northern kingdom repents, the Lord will be ready and eager to welcome them back as his "dear son" (v. 20). **unruly calf.** The northern kingdom had rebelled like an unbroken calf. The Lord disciplined them through their sufferings, and they changed.
31:19 beat my breast. A symbol of sorrow and grief. Their sorrow evokes compassion in the Lord's heart.

Though I often speak against him,
I still remember[n] him.
Therefore my heart yearns for him;
I have great compassion[o] for him,"
declares the LORD.

21 "Set up road signs;
put up guideposts.
Take note of the highway,[p]
the road that you take.
Return,[q] Virgin[r] Israel,
return to your towns.
22 How long will you wander,[s]
unfaithful[t] Daughter Israel?
The LORD will create a new thing on earth—
the woman will return to[a] the man."

23 This is what the LORD Almighty, the God of Israel, says: "When I bring them back from captivity,[b][u]
the people in the land of Judah and in its towns will once again use these words: 'The LORD bless you,
you prosperous city,[v] you sacred mountain.'[w] 24 People will live[x] together in Judah and all its towns—
farmers and those who move about with their flocks. 25 I will refresh the weary and satisfy the faint."[y]
26 At this I awoke[z] and looked around. My sleep had been pleasant to me.
27 "The days are coming," declares the LORD, "when I will plant[a] the kingdoms of Israel and Judah
with the offspring of people and of animals. 28 Just as I watched over them to uproot and tear down, and
to overthrow, destroy and bring disaster,[b] so I will watch over them to build and to plant,"[c] declares the
LORD. 29 "In those days people will no longer say,

'The parents[d] have eaten sour grapes,
and the children's teeth are set on edge.'[e]

30 Instead, everyone will die for their own sin;[f] whoever eats sour grapes—their own teeth will be set
on edge.

31 "The days are coming," declares the LORD,
"when I will make a new covenant[g]
with the people of Israel
and with the people of Judah.

[a] *22* Or *will protect* [b] *23* Or *I restore their fortunes*

31:20 [n] Hos 4:4; 11:8 [o] Isa 55:7; 63:15; Mic 7:18
31:21 [p] Jer 50:5 [q] Isa 52:11 [r] ver 4
31:22 [s] Jer 2:23 [t] Jer 3:6
31:23 [u] Jer 30:18 [v] Isa 1:26 [w] Ps 48:1; Zec 8:3
31:24 [x] Zec 8:4-8
31:25 [y] Jn 4:14
31:26 [z] Zec 4:1
31:27 [a] Eze 36:9-11; Hos 2:23
31:28 [b] Jer 18:8; 44:27 [c] Jer 1:10
31:29 [d] La 5:7 [e] Eze 18:2
31:30 [f] Isa 3:11; Gal 6:7
31:31 [g] Jer 32:40; Eze 37:26; Lk 22:20; Heb 8:8-12*; 10:16-17

31:21 road signs ... guideposts. Perhaps stone memorials or other markers along the road as a testimony that their trip to Babylon will not be simply a one-way journey. **guideposts.** The Hebrew word sounds like the word for "great weeping" in v. 15, underlining the return from exile as an answer to the tears and sorrow of the present generation. **Virgin Israel.** See note on 14:17. Israel will return to her own towns. She will no longer be an "unfaithful Daughter" (v. 22).

31:22 In place of her errant past, the Lord will create a new and different future for her. **the woman will return to the man.** An obscure Hebrew idiom that may refer to a woman's faithful embrace of her husband, in contrast to Israel's past history of affairs with idols.

31:23 When I bring them back. The section of the message that begins by speaking of Ephraim's return (vv. 1–22) concludes by speaking of Judah's return, underlining that both peoples will ultimately return and be reunited. **sacred mountain.** Jerusalem. The people will once again call down the Lord's blessing on Jerusalem as a "prosperous city." In the OT, mountains were often places of encounter with God (e.g., Gen 22:14; Ezek 40:2; cf. Rev 21:10), and so the city of Jerusalem, which contains God's temple, can be described as his "holy mountain" (Ps 48:1).

31:26 My sleep had been pleasant. Jeremiah received the message as a dream—a refreshing dream of hope in contrast to the threatening portents of many prophetic dreams (e.g., Dan 8:27).

31:28 to build and to plant. God originally commissioned Jeremiah "to uproot and tear down, to destroy and overthrow, to build and to plant" (1:10; see note there). Now, after many messages of destruction, he also has words of encouragement for the future.

31:29 Ezek 18 also quotes and refutes this proverb. People used it to claim that it was not fair for the Lord to bring judgment upon the present generation ("the children") for the sins of past generations ("the parents"). However, the underlying assumption that the present generation is without blame for the coming destruction of Jerusalem is false, as should be clear to all of Jeremiah's hearers. The Lord never judges unjustly: this generation too has contributed their own sin by rebelling against the Lord (v. 30). Positively, though, this refutation also leads to hope that a new generation may see a different future ahead of them, but only if they repent and turn to the Lord.

31:31–34 This passage is quoted in its entirety in Heb 8:8–12.

31:31 The days are coming. In the Messianic era. **new covenant.** This is the only explicit OT reference to the new covenant.

31:32 [h]Ex 24:8 [i]Dt 5:3
31:33 [j]2Co 3:3 [k]Jer 24:7; Heb 10:16
31:34 [l]1Jn 2:27 [m]Jn 6:45 [n]Isa 54:13; Jer 33:8; 50:20 [o]Mic 7:19; Ro 11:27; Heb 10:17*
31:35 [p]Ps 136:7-9 [q]Ge 1:16 [r]Jer 10:16
31:36 [s]Isa 54:9-10; Jer 33:20-26 [t]Ps 89:36-37
31:37 [u]Jer 33:22

32 It will not be like the covenant[h]
I made with their ancestors[i]
when I took them by the hand
to lead them out of Egypt,
because they broke my covenant,
though I was a husband to[a] them,[b]"
declares the LORD.

33 "This is the covenant I will make with the people of Israel
after that time," declares the LORD.
"I will put my law in their minds
and write it on their hearts.[j]
I will be their God,
and they will be my people.[k]
34 No longer will they teach[l] their neighbor,
or say to one another, 'Know the LORD,'
because they will all know[m] me,
from the least of them to the greatest,"
declares the LORD.
"For I will forgive[n] their wickedness
and will remember their sins[o] no more."

35 This is what the LORD says,

he who appoints[p] the sun
to shine by day,
who decrees the moon and stars
to shine by night,[q]
who stirs up the sea
so that its waves roar—
the LORD Almighty is his name:[r]
36 "Only if these decrees[s] vanish from my sight,"
declares the LORD,
"will Israel[t] ever cease
being a nation before me."

37 This is what the LORD says:

"Only if the heavens above can be measured[u]
and the foundations of the earth below be searched out

[a] *32* Hebrew; Septuagint and Syriac */ and I turned away from* [b] *32* Or *was their master*

31:32 The new covenant is not like the old covenant made "with their ancestors" at Mount Sinai (Exod 19–24; cf. 2 Cor 3:14), which inevitably ended in judgment for Israel. The problem with the old covenant was that Israel repeatedly broke it, even though the Lord was a faithful "husband" to them.
31:33 minds ... hearts. The new covenant involves a promise that the Lord will write his law on the hearts and minds of his people. In contrast to the old covenant, which gave the law to Israel written on tablets of stone (Exod 24:12), the new covenant will transform them internally and result in real change (2 Cor 5:17). Deut 30 already anticipated the prospect that the old covenant would end in the curse of exile through Israel's disobedience and that God would subsequently change ("circumcise") the hearts of his people (Deut 30:6). **my people.** Some interpreters focus the fulfillment of this prophecy specifically on ethnic Israel ("the people of Israel" in this verse and "the people of Judah" in v. 31). Others, in light of the usage in Hebrews, apply its reference more broadly to a redefined Israel that includes Gentiles alongside Jews as God's people through union with Christ (Rom 11:11–27; Gal 3:9,14,27–29).

The new covenant is inaugurated through the shedding of Christ's blood (Matt 26:28; Heb 9:15) and fulfills the purpose of the old covenant (Matt 5:17). Through the work of the Spirit, God's people will know the Lord (Isa 54:13) and will respond to Christ (John 6:45). In Christ, our sins are forgiven and our wickedness is remembered no more (Ps 103:12; Rom 8:1–2).
31:35–37 The impending exile looks like the end of Israel as a people because of their unfaithfulness. Yet their existence as a nation before the Lord depends on *his* faithfulness, not theirs. The Lord who ordered the sun, moon, stars, and sea is capable of preserving his people. He will not "reject all the descendants of Israel" (v. 37). So too Paul affirms that Israel's unfaithfulness in his own day was not the end of the story (Rom 11). The Lord will not abandon his people even though he adds the Gentiles as new branches of the family tree.

will I reject[v] all the descendants of Israel
because of all they have done,"
declares the LORD.

38 "The days are coming," declares the LORD, "when this city will be rebuilt[w] for me from the Tower of Hananel[x] to the Corner Gate.[y] 39 The measuring line will stretch from there straight to the hill of Gareb and then turn to Goah. 40 The whole valley[z] where dead bodies[a] and ashes are thrown, and all the terraces out to the Kidron Valley[b] on the east as far as the corner of the Horse Gate,[c] will be holy[d] to the LORD. The city will never again be uprooted or demolished."

Jeremiah Buys a Field

32 This is the word that came to Jeremiah from the LORD in the tenth[e] year of Zedekiah king of Judah, which was the eighteenth[f] year of Nebuchadnezzar. 2 The army of the king of Babylon was then besieging Jerusalem, and Jeremiah the prophet was confined in the courtyard of the guard[g] in the royal palace of Judah.

3 Now Zedekiah king of Judah had imprisoned him there, saying, "Why do you prophesy[h] as you do? You say, 'This is what the LORD says: I am about to give this city into the hands of the king of Babylon, and he will capture[i] it. 4 Zedekiah king of Judah will not escape[j] the Babylonians[a] but will certainly be given into the hands of the king of Babylon, and will speak with him face to face and see him with his own eyes. 5 He will take[k] Zedekiah to Babylon, where he will remain until I deal with him, declares the LORD. If you fight against the Babylonians, you will not succeed.'"[l]

6 Jeremiah said, "The word of the LORD came to me: 7 Hanamel son of Shallum your uncle is going to come to you and say, 'Buy my field at Anathoth, because as nearest relative it is your right and duty[m] to buy it.'

8 "Then, just as the LORD had said, my cousin Hanamel came to me in the courtyard of the guard and said, 'Buy my field at Anathoth in the territory of Benjamin. Since it is your right to redeem it and possess it, buy it for yourself.'

"I knew that this was the word of the LORD; 9 so I bought the field at Anathoth from my cousin Hanamel and weighed out for him seventeen shekels[b] of silver.[n] 10 I signed and sealed the deed, had it witnessed,[o] and weighed out the silver on the scales. 11 I took the deed of purchase — the sealed copy containing the terms and conditions, as well as the unsealed copy — 12 and I gave this deed to Baruch[p] son of Neriah,[q] the son of Mahseiah, in the presence of my cousin Hanamel and of the witnesses who had signed the deed and of all the Jews sitting in the courtyard of the guard.

13 "In their presence I gave Baruch these instructions: 14 'This is what the LORD Almighty, the God of Israel, says: Take these documents, both the sealed and unsealed copies of the deed of purchase, and put them in a clay jar so they will last a long time. 15 For this is what the LORD Almighty, the God of Israel, says: Houses, fields and vineyards will again be bought in this land.'[r]

[a] 4 Or *Chaldeans*; also in verses 5, 24, 25, 28, 29 and 43 [b] 9 That is, about 7 ounces or about 200 grams

31:37 [v] Jer 33:24-26; Ro 11:1-5
31:38 [w] Jer 30:18 [x] Ne 3:1 [y] 2Ki 14:13; Zec 14:10
31:40 [z] Jer 7:31-32 [a] Jer 8:2 [b] 2Sa 15:23; Jn 18:1 [c] 2Ki 11:16 [d] Joel 3:17; Zec 14:21
32:1 [e] 2Ki 25:1 [f] Jer 25:1; 39:1
32:2 [g] Ne 3:25; Jer 37:21
32:3 [h] Jer 26:8-9 [i] ver 28; Jer 34:2-3
32:4 [j] Jer 38:18,23; 39:5-7; 52:9
32:5 [k] Jer 39:7; Eze 12:13 [l] Jer 21:4
32:7 [m] Lev 25:24-25; Ru 4:3-4; Mt 27:10*
32:9 [n] Ge 23:16
32:10 [o] Ru 4:9
32:12 [p] ver 16; Jer 36:4; 43:3,6; 45:1 [q] Jer 51:59
32:15 [r] ver 43-44; Jer 30:18; Am 9:14-15

31:38–40 The city of Jerusalem also has a future in the Lord's plan (see Gal 4:26; Rev 21:1–5). Though Nebuchadnezzar will destroy it, it will be completely rebuilt from the "Tower of Hananel" (probably close to the northwest corner of the temple mount [Neh 3:1], where the Antonia fortress stood in the time of Jesus) to the "Corner Gate" (possibly on the northwest side).
31:39 Gareb … Goah. Unknown; perhaps south of the city.
31:40 valley where dead bodies and ashes are thrown. Presumably the Ben Hinnom Valley (see 7:31 and note ["Topheth"]); it will be transformed into a location sacred to the Lord.
32:1–44 *Jeremiah Buys a Field.* The Lord tells Jeremiah to perform another sign-act, this time buying a field in enemy-controlled territory as a sign of confidence in the Lord's promise that the people will return to the land in peace and freedom.
32:1 tenth year of Zedekiah. 588–587 BC, shortly before Jerusalem falls to the Babylonians.
32:2–5 Jeremiah's persistent messages of doom against the city and the king have made him unpopular with King Zedekiah. Zedekiah sees Jeremiah's words as treasonous and bad for morale, so he imprisons Jeremiah within the royal palace, though he also consults him privately (37:11–21).
32:7 Anathoth. Jeremiah's hometown (see 1:1 and note). **your right and duty to buy it.** When someone fell into debt and sold their property, their nearest kinsman was supposed to purchase the field on their behalf so that the family could retain the property (Lev 25:25–28). At this point, Anathoth is already in Babylonian-held territory, so it seems an act of folly to purchase a property that appears lost forever. Yet because Jeremiah knows this is "the word of the LORD" (v. 8b), he buys the property (v. 9), paying the purchase price and having the transaction formally witnessed (vv. 9–10)
32:11–15 Jeremiah gives the title deeds to his scribe, Baruch, with instructions to carefully preserve the documents in a sealed clay jar, safely protected from moisture and insects. He declares that his action is a sign from the Lord that people will once again buy and sell property in Israel. The Babylonian invasion will not last forever, though it will also not be over in the immediate future.

16“After I had given the deed of purchase to Baruch son of Neriah, I prayed to the LORD:

17“Ah, Sovereign LORD,[s] you have made the heavens and the earth by your great power and outstretched arm.[t] Nothing is too hard[u] for you. 18You show love[v] to thousands but bring the punishment for the parents' sins into the laps of their children[w] after them. Great and mighty God,
whose name is the LORD Almighty,[x] 19great are your purposes and mighty are your deeds.[y] Your
eyes are open to the ways of all mankind;[z] you reward each person according to their conduct
and as their deeds deserve.[a] 20You performed signs and wonders in Egypt[b] and have continued
them to this day, in Israel and among all mankind, and have gained the renown that is still yours.
21You brought your people Israel out of Egypt with signs and wonders, by a mighty hand[c] and an
outstretched arm and with great terror.[d] 22You gave them this land you had sworn to give their
ancestors, a land flowing with milk and honey.[e] 23They came in and took possession[f] of it, but
they did not obey you or follow your law;[g] they did not do what you commanded them to do. So
you brought all this disaster[h] on them.

24“See how the siege ramps are built up to take the city. Because of the sword, famine and
plague,[i] the city will be given into the hands of the Babylonians who are attacking it. What you
said[j] has happened, as you now see. 25And though the city will be given into the hands of the
Babylonians, you, Sovereign LORD, say to me, 'Buy the field with silver and have the transaction
witnessed.'”

26Then the word of the LORD came to Jeremiah: 27“I am the LORD, the God of all mankind.[k] Is anything too hard for me? 28Therefore this is what the LORD says: I am about to give this city into the hands
of the Babylonians and to Nebuchadnezzar[l] king of Babylon, who will capture it.[m] 29The Babylonians
who are attacking this city will come in and set it on fire; they will burn it down,[n] along with the houses[o]
where the people aroused my anger by burning incense on the roofs to Baal and by pouring out drink
offerings[p] to other gods.

30“The people of Israel and Judah have done nothing but evil in my sight from their youth;[q] indeed, the people of Israel have done nothing but arouse my anger[r] with what their hands have made,[s]
declares the LORD. 31From the day it was built until now, this city has so aroused my anger and wrath
that I must remove[t] it from my sight. 32The people of Israel and Judah have provoked me by all the
evil[u] they have done — they, their kings and officials, their priests and prophets, the people of Judah
and those living in Jerusalem. 33They turned their backs[v] to me and not their faces; though I taught[w]
them again and again, they would not listen or respond to discipline. 34They set up their vile images
in the house that bears my Name and defiled[x] it. 35They built high places for Baal in the Valley of Ben
Hinnom to sacrifice their sons and daughters to Molek,[y] though I never commanded — nor did it enter
my mind[z] — that they should do such a detestable thing and so make Judah sin.

36“You are saying about this city, 'By the sword, famine and plague[a] it will be given into the hands of
the king of Babylon'; but this is what the LORD, the God of Israel, says: 37I will surely gather[b] them from
all the lands where I banish them in my furious anger and great wrath; I will bring them back to this
place and let them live in safety.[c] 38They will be my people,[d] and I will be their God. 39I will give them
singleness[e] of heart and action, so that they will always fear me and that all will then go well for them

32:17 [s] Jer 1:6 [t] 2Ki 19:15; Ps 102:25 [u] Mt 19:26
32:18 [v] Dt 5:10 [w] Ex 20:5 [x] Jer 10:16
32:19 [y] Isa 28:29 [z] Pr 5:21; Jer 16:17 [a] Jer 17:10; Mt 16:27
32:20 [b] Ex 9:16
32:21 [c] Ex 6:6; 1Ch 17:21; Da 9:15 [d] Dt 26:8
32:22 [e] Ex 3:8; Jer 11:5
32:23 [f] Ps 44:2; 78:54-55 [g] Ne 9:26; Jer 11:8 [h] Da 9:14
32:24 [i] Jer 14:12 [j] Dt 4:25-26; Jos 23:15-16
32:27 [k] Nu 16:22
32:28 [l] 2Ch 36:17 [m] ver 3
32:29 [n] 2Ch 36:19; Jer 21:10; 37:8,10; 52:13 [o] Jer 19:13 [p] Jer 44:18
32:30 [q] Jer 22:21 [r] Jer 8:19 [s] Jer 25:7
32:31 [t] 2Ki 23:27; 24:3
32:32 [u] Isa 1:4-6; Da 9:8
32:33 [v] Jer 2:27; Eze 8:16 [w] Jer 7:13
32:34 [x] Jer 7:30
32:35 [y] Lev 18:21 [z] Jer 7:31; 19:5
32:36 [a] ver 24
32:37 [b] Jer 23:3,6 [c] Dt 30:3; Eze 34:28
32:38 [d] Jer 24:7; 2Co 6:16*
32:39 [e] Eze 11:19

32:17 you have made the heavens. Jeremiah's prayer expresses his confidence in God's power. He confesses the truth that the Lord is the Creator of all things, which means that nothing is too hard for him to accomplish. He is sovereign over every molecule of the universe, including humanity.
32:18 You show love … but bring … punishment. God is both just and gracious: he shows love to thousands but also brings the consequences of the parents' sins on the next generation (Exod 34:6–7). Yet at the same time, he rewards each according to their own conduct: it is not that the parents ate sour grapes and the innocent children's teeth are set on edge (see 31:29 and note); rather, the next generation inherits the sinful patterns of their fathers, often in magnified form.
32:20 You performed signs and wonders. The Lord's sovereignty is evident not only in creation but also in redemption: he brought his people out of Egypt and into the promised land. Yet Jeremiah is also puzzled by the Lord's plans: since the Babylonians are assaulting the city, which must fall to them because of Israel's unfaithfulness (v. 24), why does the Lord command Jeremiah to buy property at a time like this (v. 25)?
32:27 Is anything too hard for me? The Lord's answer begins in the same place as Jeremiah's prayer (see v. 17). The Lord is indeed going to give the city to the Babylonians because of Israel's sins, especially their sin of idolatry (vv. 29,34–35).
32:35 Valley of Ben Hinnom. See note on 7:31 ("Topheth").
32:37 I will surely gather them. The Lord not only has the power to bring the Babylonians as agents of judgment but also the power to gather his people and bring them back.
32:39 The Lord also (see note on v. 37) has the power to "give them singleness of heart and action," uniting thought and deed in the Lord's service, "so that they will always fear [him]."

and for their children after them. 40 I will make an everlasting covenant[f] with them: I will never stop doing good to them, and I will inspire them to fear me, so that they will never turn away from me.[g] 41 I will rejoice in doing them good[h] and will assuredly plant[i] them in this land with all my heart and soul.

42 "This is what the LORD says: As I have brought all this great calamity on this people, so I will give them all the prosperity I have promised[j] them. 43 Once more fields will be bought[k] in this land of which you say, 'It is a desolate waste, without people or animals, for it has been given into the hands of the Babylonians.' 44 Fields will be bought for silver, and deeds[l] will be signed, sealed and witnessed in the territory of Benjamin, in the villages around Jerusalem, in the towns of Judah and in the towns of the hill country, of the western foothills and of the Negev,[m] because I will restore[n] their fortunes,[a] declares the LORD."

Promise of Restoration

33 While Jeremiah was still confined in the courtyard[o] of the guard, the word of the LORD came to him a second time: 2 "This is what the LORD says, he who made the earth,[p] the LORD who formed it and established it—the LORD is his name:[q] 3 'Call[r] to me and I will answer you and tell you great and unsearchable things you do not know.' 4 For this is what the LORD, the God of Israel, says about the houses in this city and the royal palaces of Judah that have been torn down to be used against the siege[s] ramps[t] and the sword 5 in the fight with the Babylonians[b]: 'They will be filled with the dead bodies of the people I will slay in my anger and wrath.[u] I will hide my face[v] from this city because of all its wickedness.

6 " 'Nevertheless, I will bring health and healing to it; I will heal my people and will let them enjoy abundant peace and security. 7 I will bring Judah[w] and Israel back from captivity[c][x] and will rebuild them as they were before.[y] 8 I will cleanse[z] them from all the sin they have committed against me and will forgive[a] all their sins of rebellion against me. 9 Then this city will bring me renown, joy, praise[b] and honor[c] before all nations on earth that hear of all the good things I do for it; and they will be in awe and will tremble at the abundant prosperity and peace I provide for it.'

10 "This is what the LORD says: 'You say about this place, "It is a desolate waste, without people or animals."[d] Yet in the towns of Judah and the streets of Jerusalem that are deserted, inhabited by neither people nor animals, there will be heard once more 11 the sounds of joy and gladness,[e] the voices of bride and bridegroom, and the voices of those who bring thank offerings[f] to the house of the LORD, saying,

> "Give thanks to the LORD Almighty,
> for the LORD is good;[g]
> his love endures forever."[h]

For I will restore the fortunes of the land as they were before,' says the LORD.

12 "This is what the LORD Almighty says: 'In this place, desolate[i] and without people or animals—in all its towns there will again be pastures for shepherds to rest their flocks.[j] 13 In the towns of the hill country, of the western foothills and of the Negev,[k] in the territory of Benjamin, in the villages around

[a] 44 Or *will bring them back from captivity* [b] 5 Or *Chaldeans* [c] 7 Or *will restore the fortunes of Judah and Israel*

32:40 [f] Isa 55:3 [g] Jer 24:7
32:41 [h] Dt 30:9 [i] Jer 24:6; 31:28; Am 9:15
32:42 [j] Jer 31:28
32:43 [k] ver 15
32:44 [l] ver 10 [m] Jer 17:26 [n] Jer 33:7,11,26
33:1 [o] Jer 32:2-3; 37:21; 38:28
33:2 [p] Jer 10:16 [q] Ex 3:15; 15:3
33:3 [r] Isa 55:6; Jer 29:12
33:4 [s] Eze 4:2 [t] Jer 32:24; Hab 1:10
33:5 [u] Jer 21:4-7 [v] Isa 8:17
33:7 [w] Jer 32:44 [x] Jer 30:3; Am 9:14 [y] Isa 1:26
33:8 [z] Heb 9:13-14 [a] Jer 31:34; Mic 7:18; Zec 13:1
33:9 [b] Jer 13:11 [c] Isa 62:7; Jer 3:17
33:10 [d] Jer 32:43
33:11 [e] Isa 51:3 [f] Lev 7:12 [g] 1Ch 16:8; Ps 136:1 [h] 1Ch 16:34; 2Ch 5:13; Ps 100:4-5
33:12 [i] Jer 32:43 [j] Isa 65:10; Eze 34:11-15
33:13 [k] Jer 17:26

32:40 This new relationship of peace and blessing will be "an everlasting covenant" in which the Lord will constantly bless his people and they will constantly serve him.

32:43–44 The land that is desolate on account of the people's sins will be restored so that once again people will buy and sell property there.

33:1–26 *Promise of Restoration.* In the OT context, a restoration of the people and the land is incomplete without a corresponding restoration of the line of David to the kingship and the line of Levi to the priesthood.

33:1 confined in the courtyard of the guard. See note on 32:2–5.

33:2 made the earth. God's power as Creator of everything assures his ability to judge and redeem his people. **the LORD is his name.** God's name is not merely a title that he bears; it denotes his character as well (see notes on Exod 3:14,15).

33:3 Because the Lord is sovereign over the future, he can reveal to his prophets "unsearchable things"—things that no human can know by themselves.

33:4 houses ... royal palaces. Torn down to provide the materials needed to internally reinforce walls that were being assaulted by siege ramps on the outside. Yet all of these human efforts to ward off divine judgment are in vain: the city will be filled with "dead bodies" (v. 5).

33:6–9 Though human attempts to save the city will fail, the Lord still has good plans for its future beyond the time of judgment. The people's sin has brought judgment (see 32:30–35), but the Lord will "bring Judah and Israel back from captivity" in Babylon (v. 7), "cleanse them" and "forgive all their sins" (v. 8; see 31:34). The result of this new act of salvation will be "praise and honor" for the Lord "before all nations on earth" (v. 9). The nations will be astonished at the people's new prosperity (v. 9).

33:11 sounds of joy and gladness. Specifically, celebrations at weddings and the feasting that accompanied giving "thank offerings." **thank offerings.** Part of the sacrificial animal was given back to the person making the offering so that they could celebrate with family and friends.

33:12 pastures ... to rest their flocks. The open country will again be safe.

33:13 The image of the shepherd counting his sheep as they pass under

33:13 [l]Lev 27:32
33:14 [m]Jer 29:10
33:15 [n]Ps 72:2 [o]Isa 4:2; 11:1; Jer 23:5
33:16 [p]Isa 45:17 [q]1Co 1:30
33:17 [r]2Sa 7:13; 1Ki 2:4; Ps 89:29-37; Lk 1:33
33:18 [s]Dt 18:1 [t]Heb 13:15
33:20 [u]Ps 89:36
33:21 [v]Ps 89:34 [w]2Ch 7:18
33:22 [x]Ge 15:5
33:24 [y]Eze 37:22 [z]Ne 4:4 [a]Jer 30:17
33:25 [b]Jer 31:35-36 [c]Ps 74:16-17
33:26 [d]Jer 31:37 [e]Isa 14:1 [f]ver 7
34:1 [g]Jer 27:7 [h]2Ki 25:1; Jer 39:1
34:2 [i]2Ch 36:11

Jerusalem and in the towns of Judah, flocks will again pass under the hand[l] of the one who counts
them,' says the LORD.
14"'The days are coming,' declares the LORD, 'when I will fulfill the good promise[m] I made to the
people of Israel and Judah.

15"'In those days and at that time
I will make a righteous[n] Branch[o] sprout from David's line;
he will do what is just and right in the land.
16In those days Judah will be saved[p]
and Jerusalem will live in safety.
This is the name by which it[a] will be called:
The LORD Our Righteous Savior.'[q]

17For this is what the LORD says: 'David will never fail[r] to have a man to sit on the throne of Israel, 18nor
will the Levitical[s] priests ever fail to have a man to stand before me continually to offer burnt offerings,
to burn grain offerings and to present sacrifices.[t]'"
19The word of the LORD came to Jeremiah: 20"This is what the LORD says: 'If you can break my covenant with the day[u] and my covenant with the night, so that day and night no longer come at their
appointed time, 21then my covenant[v] with David my servant—and my covenant with the Levites who
are priests ministering before me—can be broken and David will no longer have a descendant to reign
on his throne.[w] 22I will make the descendants of David my servant and the Levites who minister before
me as countless[x] as the stars in the sky and as measureless as the sand on the seashore.'"
23The word of the LORD came to Jeremiah: 24"Have you not noticed that these people are saying, 'The
LORD has rejected the two kingdoms[b][y] he chose'? So they despise[z] my people and no longer regard them
as a nation.[a] 25This is what the LORD says: 'If I have not made my covenant with day and night[b] and
established the laws of heaven and earth,[c] 26then I will reject[d] the descendants of Jacob[e] and David my
servant and will not choose one of his sons to rule over the descendants of Abraham, Isaac and Jacob.
For I will restore their fortunes[c][f] and have compassion on them.'"

Warning to Zedekiah

34 While Nebuchadnezzar king of Babylon and all his army and all the kingdoms and peoples[g] in
the empire he ruled were fighting against Jerusalem[h] and all its surrounding towns, this word
came to Jeremiah from the LORD: 2"This is what the LORD, the God of Israel, says: Go to Zedekiah[i] king

[a] 16 Or *he* [b] 24 Or *families* [c] 26 Or *will bring them back from captivity*

his hand into the sheepfold reveals the intimate connection between a shepherd and his flock.

33:14–16 Talk of restoring literal shepherds leads naturally into a discussion of the restoration of Israel's shepherd, their king. This language is very similar to the language of 23:5–6, yet now the focus shifts to the city of Jerusalem.

33:15 righteous Branch. See note on 23:5. He will reign over his city.

33:16 The LORD Our Righteous Savior. See note on 23:6. Not only will the "righteous Branch" be called this but so will the city.

33:17–18 David will never fail ... nor will the Levitical priests ever fail. The kingship and priesthood will continue and reach their goal. Though God has already promised the rejection of the reigning Davidic kings (22:30) and the destruction of the Jerusalem temple, which will leave no place for priests to offer sacrifices, that cannot be the end of the story.

33:17 David. Represents the kingship (2 Sam 7).

33:18 Levitical priests. Represent the priesthood (Mal 2:4–8).

33:22 descendants ... as countless as the stars ... as measureless as the sand. Recalls the covenant with Abraham (Gen 22:17). The fulfillment of these promises for David and Levi is found in the new covenant, in which believers are kings and priests who reign and serve with Christ (1 Pet 2:5,9; Rev 20:4–6).

33:24 these people. Either the surrounding nations or unbelievers within the Jewish community. Either way, their conclusion that the Lord has rejected the northern and southern kingdoms is false.

33:25–26 The Lord's election of the descendants of Jacob as his people is as secure as the regular transition from day to night and back again.

34:1—39:18 *The Last Days of Jehoiakim and Zedekiah.* In the last years of Judah before the final Babylonian invasion leading to the fall of Jerusalem, Jeremiah repeatedly speaks to Judah's kings, first Jehoiakim and then Zedekiah. Sometimes his messages are messages of encouragement, but mostly they are messages of judgment. The kings repeatedly fail to listen to Jeremiah, leading to the inevitable destruction of Jerusalem, which the last part of this section records.

34:1–7 *Warning to Zedekiah.* This section and the one that follows (vv. 8–22) contain two contrasting messages addressed to King Zedekiah. Both speak of the certain fall of Jerusalem to Nebuchadnezzar, but the first speaks in positive terms of Zedekiah's own fate, while the second is much bleaker.

34:1 all the kingdoms and peoples in the empire he ruled. Nebuchadnezzar has an overwhelming force arrayed against tiny Jerusalem. Nothing short of divine deliverance can rescue them from his hand.

34:2–3 Jeremiah makes it clear that no deliverance will be forthcoming this time. Zedekiah will have an uncomfortable face-to-face interview with his overlord that will result in his exile to Babylon (2 Kgs 25:6–7).

of Judah and tell him, 'This is what the LORD says: I am about to give this city into the hands of the king
of Babylon, and he will burn it down.[j] [3]You will not escape from his grasp but will surely be captured
and given into his hands.[k] You will see the king of Babylon with your own eyes, and he will speak with
you face to face. And you will go to Babylon.
[4]" 'Yet hear the LORD's promise to you, Zedekiah king of Judah. This is what the LORD says concerning
you: You will not die by the sword; [5]you will die peacefully. As people made a funeral fire[l] in honor of
your predecessors, the kings who ruled before you, so they will make a fire in your honor and lament,
"Alas,[m] master!" I myself make this promise, declares the LORD.' "
[6]Then Jeremiah the prophet told all this to Zedekiah king of Judah, in Jerusalem, [7]while the army of
the king of Babylon was fighting against Jerusalem and the other cities of Judah that were still holding
out — Lachish[n] and Azekah.[o] These were the only fortified cities left in Judah.

Freedom for Slaves

[8]The word came to Jeremiah from the LORD after King Zedekiah had made a covenant with all the
people[p] in Jerusalem to proclaim freedom[q] for the slaves. [9]Everyone was to free their Hebrew slaves,
both male and female; no one was to hold a fellow Hebrew in bondage.[r] [10]So all the officials and people
who entered into this covenant agreed that they would free their male and female slaves and no longer
hold them in bondage. They agreed, and set them free. [11]But afterward they changed their minds and
took back the slaves they had freed and enslaved them again.
[12]Then the word of the LORD came to Jeremiah: [13]"This is what the LORD, the God of Israel, says: I made
a covenant with your ancestors[s] when I brought them out of Egypt, out of the land of slavery. I said, [14]'Every seventh year each of you must free any fellow Hebrews who have sold themselves to you. After they
have served you six years, you must let them go free.'[a][t] Your ancestors, however, did not listen to me or
pay attention[u] to me. [15]Recently you repented and did what is right in my sight: Each of you proclaimed
freedom to your own people.[v] You even made a covenant before me in the house that bears my Name.[w]
[16]But now you have turned around[x] and profaned[y] my name; each of you has taken back the male and
female slaves you had set free to go where they wished. You have forced them to become your slaves again.
[17]"Therefore this is what the LORD says: You have not obeyed me; you have not proclaimed freedom
to your own people. So I now proclaim 'freedom' for you,[z] declares the LORD — 'freedom' to fall by the
sword, plague and famine. I will make you abhorrent to all the kingdoms of the earth.[a] [18]Those who
have violated my covenant and have not fulfilled the terms of the covenant they made before me, I

34:2 [j] ver 22; Jer 32:29; 37:8
34:3 [k] 2Ki 25:7; Jer 21:7; 32:4
34:5 [l] 2Ch 16:14; 21:19 [m] Jer 22:18
34:7 [n] Jos 10:3 [o] Jos 10:10; 2Ch 11:9
34:8 [p] 2Ki 11:17 [q] Ex 21:2; Lev 25:10, 39-41; Ne 5:5-8
34:9 [r] Lev 25:39-46
34:13 [s] Ex 24:8
34:14 [t] Ex 21:2 [u] Dt 15:12; 2Ki 17:14
34:15 [v] ver 8 [w] Jer 7:10-11; 32:34
34:16 [x] Eze 3:20; 18:24 [y] Ex 20:7; Lev 19:12
34:17 [z] Mt 7:2; Gal 6:7 [a] Dt 28:25,64; Jer 29:18

a 14 Deut. 15:12

Jer 32:3 – 5 records Zedekiah's earlier response to a similar prediction by Jeremiah.

34:5 die peacefully. Zedekiah will "not die by the sword" (v. 4) in battle, and the people will mourn him in death. This is a mark of God's mercy in judgment (cf. the similar case of Hezekiah in Isa 39). Yet it is only a limited mercy: Hezekiah died knowing that the Babylonians would make his own offspring eunuchs; Zedekiah's eyes will be put out after he sees his sons put to death (2 Kgs 25:7). Had Zedekiah listened to Jeremiah and surrendered to Nebuchadnezzar earlier, things might have gone better for him. Zedekiah's stubborn refusal to listen to the prophet's words of counsel prove very costly.

34:7 Lachish. About 30 miles (48 kilometers) southwest of Jerusalem. **Azekah.** Slightly farther north than Lachish, guarding the strategic Valley of Elah. Archaeologists have discovered letters from the ruins of Lachish that describe the increasingly desperate situation in that city, including a poignant note that the signal fire from Azekah was no longer visible.

34:8 – 22 *Freedom for Slaves.* The Judahites have been conveniently ignoring the laws of the Pentateuch about periodically freeing Hebrew slaves. Under the pressure of the Babylonian assault, they covenant to fulfill their obligations under the law, but when the Babylonians temporarily withdraw, they go back on their commitments.

34:8 – 11 During the desperate days of the siege, the king and the people agree to free their Hebrew slaves. This language explicitly invokes the law requiring the freeing of such slaves every seven years (Exod 21:2 – 6; Deut 15:12 – 18). Since the agreement is a solemn covenant, it invokes the Lord as witness of the agreement (v. 15). There may be a dual motivation: (1) attempting to win God's favor by following his law and (2) attempting to increase the available manpower to fight the Babylonians. Yet afterward, probably when the Babylonians withdraw from Jerusalem temporarily to deal with an Egyptian relief force, the Judahites go back on their solemn promise and again enslave their former Hebrew slaves.

34:13 – 16 If the people had been following the laws of Exodus and Deuteronomy, they would not have had to make such a covenant. Nevertheless, the Lord endorses their action as repenting and doing "what is right in [his] sight" (v. 15). Coming to obedience late is better than continuing in disobedience. However, events prove that their repentance was not sincere. Taking back their Hebrew slaves is not merely an offense against their fellow men and women, it profanes the Lord's name since he was named as witness in the covenant.

34:17 'freedom' to fall by the sword, plague and famine. A fitting punishment (see note on 14:12).

34:18 like the calf they cut in two. In ancient Near Eastern covenant making, animals were divided in two and the parties making the covenant passed between the pieces. It was an acted out oath of

34:18 [b]Ge 15:10
34:19 [c]Zep 3:3-4
34:20 [d]Jer 21:7 [e]Jer 11:21 [f]Dt 28:26; Jer 7:33; 19:7
34:21 [g]Jer 32:4 [h]Jer 39:6; 52:24-27 [i]Jer 37:5
34:22 [j]Jer 39:1-2 [k]Jer 39:8
35:1 [l]2Ch 36:5
35:2 [m]2Ki 10:15; 1Ch 2:55 [n]1Ki 6:5
35:4 [o]Dt 33:1 [p]1Ch 9:19 [q]2Ki 12:9
35:6 [r]2Ki 10:15 [s]Lev 10:9; Nu 6:2-4; Lk 1:15
35:7 [t]Heb 11:9 [u]Ex 20:12; Eph 6:2-3
35:8 [v]Pr 1:8; Col 3:20
35:9 [w]1Ti 6:6
35:11 [x]2Ki 24:1 [y]Jer 8:14
35:13 [z]Jer 6:10; 32:33

will treat like the calf they cut in two and then walked between its pieces.[b] 19 The leaders of Judah and
Jerusalem, the court officials,[c] the priests and all the people of the land who walked between the pieces
of the calf, 20 I will deliver[d] into the hands of their enemies who want to kill them.[e] Their dead bodies
will become food for the birds and the wild animals.[f]
21 "I will deliver Zedekiah[g] king of Judah and his officials[h] into the hands of their enemies who want
to kill them, to the army of the king of Babylon, which has withdrawn[i] from you. 22 I am going to give
the order, declares the LORD, and I will bring them back to this city. They will fight against it, take[j] it and
burn[k] it down. And I will lay waste the towns of Judah so no one can live there."

The Rekabites

35 This is the word that came to Jeremiah from the LORD during the reign of Jehoiakim[l] son of
Josiah king of Judah: 2 "Go to the Rekabite[m] family and invite them to come to one of the side
rooms[n] of the house of the LORD and give them wine to drink."
3 So I went to get Jaazaniah son of Jeremiah, the son of Habazziniah, and his brothers and all his
sons — the whole family of the Rekabites. 4 I brought them into the house of the LORD, into the room of
the sons of Hanan son of Igdaliah the man of God.[o] It was next to the room of the officials, which was
over that of Maaseiah son of Shallum[p] the doorkeeper.[q] 5 Then I set bowls full of wine and some cups
before the Rekabites and said to them, "Drink some wine."
6 But they replied, "We do not drink wine, because our forefather Jehonadab[a][r] son of Rekab gave us
this command: 'Neither you nor your descendants must ever drink wine.[s] 7 Also you must never build
houses, sow seed or plant vineyards; you must never have any of these things, but must always live in
tents.[t] Then you will live a long time in the land[u] where you are nomads.' 8 We have obeyed everything
our forefather[v] Jehonadab son of Rekab commanded us. Neither we nor our wives nor our sons and
daughters have ever drunk wine 9 or built houses to live in or had vineyards, fields or crops.[w] 10 We have
lived in tents and have fully obeyed everything our forefather Jehonadab commanded us. 11 But when
Nebuchadnezzar king of Babylon invaded[x] this land, we said, 'Come, we must go to Jerusalem[y] to escape
the Babylonian[b] and Aramean armies.' So we have remained in Jerusalem."
12 Then the word of the LORD came to Jeremiah, saying: 13 "This is what the LORD Almighty, the God
of Israel, says: Go and tell the people of Judah and those living in Jerusalem, 'Will you not learn a lesson[z] and obey my words?' declares the LORD. 14 'Jehonadab son of Rekab ordered his descendants not

[a] 6 Hebrew *Jonadab*, a variant of *Jehonadab*; here and often in this chapter [b] 11 Or *Chaldean*

self-imprecation, saying, "May I become like these animals if I break my word" (see Gen 15:9–17 and note).
34:20 dead bodies … food for the birds and the wild animals. The Lord will bring upon the leaders of Judah and Jerusalem the curse they pronounced so that after death their bodies will not be decently buried (see note on 7:33).
34:21–22 Zedekiah will also be subject to judgment. Though he will not personally die in battle (v. 5), God will give him into the hand of his enemies. The juxtaposition of these two messages (see note on vv. 1–7) tempers the good news of the first because of Zedekiah's broken covenant. Though God is always faithful to his word, sin has consequences.
35:1–19 *The Rekabites.* One family in Judah, the Rekabites, have faithfully kept a command from one of their ancestors not to drink wine or establish permanent residences in the land. Their faithfulness is a living counter example to Judah and Jerusalem's persistent unfaithfulness to their spiritual father, the Lord. It is not that drinking wine, planting vineyards, or building houses is evil: these are part of the life of blessing as God intended it in the land (Deut 28:2–8). The commitment of the Rekabites seems to be a reminder that the promised land and its blessings merely symbolize the real inheritance that God has prepared for his people.
35:1 during the reign of Jehoiakim. This took place earlier than the material in the previous chapters that deal with Zedekiah (see Introduction: Outline).
35:2 Rekabite family. Little is known about them; 1 Chr 2:55 links them with the Kenites, who descended from Moses' father-in-law (Judg 1:16). Jehonadab son of Rekab (v. 8) was a key supporter of Jehu's purging of the house of King Ahab in 841 BC as judgment for Ahab's Baal worship (2 Kgs 10:15–17). **give them wine to drink.** In those days water was often undrinkable, so wine was a common beverage.
35:4 the house of the LORD. The temple. The Rekabites were in Jerusalem because the Babylonian invasion made their nomadic lifestyle impossible (v. 11). There were a number of living areas connected to the temple. **Igdaliah.** A "man of God," i.e., a prophet (1 Kgs 13:1; 2 Kgs 4:9). His family may have been sympathetic to Jeremiah. **Maaseiah.** His family occupied the neighboring room. He was very close to the king (21:1; 29:21,25; 37:3). **doorkeeper.** An important office in the temple; in 2 Kgs 25:18, the three doorkeepers are listed right after the high priest and his second-in-command.
35:6 Jehonadab. An ancestor of the Rekabites who had commanded them over 200 years earlier not to drink wine or settle permanently in any one place (see note on vv. 1–19). He had even framed his command in a way that echoed the style of Deuteronomy, promising that they would "live a long time in the land" (v. 7; cf. Deut 11:9; 25:15; 32:47).
35:8 We have obeyed … Jehonadab. So they refuse Jeremiah's invitation.
35:13 Will you not learn a lesson …? The faithfulness of the Rekabites to their forefather's command visibly condemns the people's continual unfaithfulness to the Lord's commands.

to drink wine and this command has been kept. To this day they do not drink wine, because they obey
their forefather's command. But I have spoken to you again and again,[a] yet you have not obeyed[b] me.
15 Again and again I sent all my servants the prophets[c] to you. They said, "Each of you must turn[d] from
your wicked ways and reform[e] your actions; do not follow other gods to serve them. Then you will live
in the land[f] I have given to you and your ancestors." But you have not paid attention or listened[g] to
me. 16 The descendants of Jehonadab son of Rekab have carried out the command their forefather[h] gave
them, but these people have not obeyed me.'
17 "Therefore this is what the LORD God Almighty, the God of Israel, says: 'Listen! I am going to bring
on Judah and on everyone living in Jerusalem every disaster[i] I pronounced against them. I spoke to
them, but they did not listen;[j] I called to them, but they did not answer.' "[k]
18 Then Jeremiah said to the family of the Rekabites, "This is what the LORD Almighty, the God of
Israel, says: 'You have obeyed the command of your forefather Jehonadab and have followed all his
instructions and have done everything he ordered.' 19 Therefore this is what the LORD Almighty, the God
of Israel, says: 'Jehonadab son of Rekab will never fail[l] to have a descendant to serve[m] me.' "

Jehoiakim Burns Jeremiah's Scroll

36 In the fourth year of Jehoiakim[n] son of Josiah king of Judah, this word came to Jeremiah from
the LORD: 2 "Take a scroll[o] and write on it all the words I have spoken to you concerning Israel,
Judah and all the other nations from the time I began speaking to you in the reign of Josiah[p]
till now. 3 Perhaps[q] when the people of Judah hear[r] about every disaster I plan to inflict
on them, they will each turn[s] from their wicked ways; then I will forgive[t] their
wickedness and their sin."
4 So Jeremiah called Baruch[u] son of Neriah, and while Jeremiah dictated[v] all the words the LORD had spoken to him, Baruch wrote them
on the scroll.[w] 5 Then Jeremiah told Baruch, "I am restricted; I am
not allowed to go to the LORD's temple. 6 So you go to the house of
the LORD on a day of fasting[x] and read to the people from the
scroll the words of the LORD that you wrote as I dictated. Read
them to all the people of Judah who come in from their towns.
7 Perhaps they will bring their petition before the LORD and will
each turn[y] from their wicked ways, for the anger[z] and wrath pronounced against this people by the LORD are great."
8 Baruch son of Neriah did everything Jeremiah the prophet told him
to do; at the LORD's temple he read the words of the LORD from the scroll.
9 In the ninth month[a] of the fifth year of Jehoiakim son of Josiah king of
Judah, a time of fasting[b] before the LORD was proclaimed for all the people
in Jerusalem and those who had come from the towns of Judah. 10 From the
room of Gemariah son of Shaphan the secretary,[c] which was in the upper

Hebrew seal impression written of Baruch son of Neriah (Jer 36:4).

Z. Radovan/www.BibleLandPictures.com

35:14 [a] Jer 7:13; 25:3 [b] Isa 30:9
35:15 [c] Jer 7:25 [d] Jer 26:3 [e] Isa 1:16-17; Jer 4:1; 18:11; Eze 18:30 [f] Jer 25:5 [g] Jer 7:26
35:16 [h] Mal 1:6
35:17 [i] Jos 23:15; Jer 21:4-7 [j] Pr 1:24; Ro 10:21 [k] Isa 65:12; 66:4; Jer 7:13
35:19 [l] Jer 33:17 [m] Jer 15:19
36:1 [n] 2Ch 36:5
36:2 [o] Ex 17:14; Jer 30:2; Hab 2:2 [p] Jer 1:2; 25:3
36:3 [q] ver 7; Eze 12:3 [r] Mk 4:12 [s] Jer 26:3; Jnh 3:8; Ac 3:19 [t] Jer 18:8
36:4 [u] Jer 32:12 [v] ver 18 [w] Eze 2:9
36:6 [x] ver 9
36:7 [y] Jer 26:3 [z] Dt 31:17
36:9 [a] ver 22 [b] 2Ch 20:3
36:10 [c] Jer 52:25

35:17–19 Because of the faithfulness of the Rekabites, their fate will be different from that of the rest of the people. The Judahites will not live long in the land; the Lord will bring the curses upon them that he had threatened. But the Rekabites will receive rewards for their continued faithfulness; they will have continued descendants serving the Lord. At least one of the Rekabites is later involved in rebuilding the wall of Jerusalem in the days of Nehemiah (Neh 3:14).
36:1–32 *Jehoiakim Burns Jeremiah's Scroll.* Apparently at the very same time that the Rekabites are demonstrating their faithfulness (ch. 35), Jehoiakim is refusing to listen to the Lord's word through his prophet. Juxtaposing ch. 35 and ch. 36 makes the contrast very stark.
36:1 fourth year of Jehoiakim. 605 BC, shortly before Nebuchadnezzar subjugates Judah and takes the first captives to Babylon.
36:2 Take a scroll. The prophets generally delivered their messages verbally, but this passage demonstrates that they sometimes wrote down their messages; in this case it was dictated to a scribe (v. 4; cf. 30:2). This is how the words of the prophets were preserved, which would have been necessary to vindicate their predictions of future events (Deut 18:22).
36:3 turn from their wicked ways. The Lord's desire is always that people repent and turn from their sin so that they might find forgiveness. The Lord takes no pleasure in punishing the guilty (Ezek 18:23).
36:4 Baruch. Jeremiah's scribe (32:12). His role in the process is to transmit the words Jeremiah dictates to him, just as Jeremiah faithfully conveys the words the Lord gives him (see v. 6).
36:5 restricted. From going to the temple, probably because he prophesied judgment against it. But the Lord's word cannot be so easily restrained.
36:6 Baruch is to read the message to the people in the hope that they will repent.
36:9 time of fasting before the LORD. A time that brings large crowds to the temple; it is an auspicious time to call people to repentance.
36:10 Gemariah. Not the Gemariah of 29:3. A son of Shaphan (see note on 26:24). **the upper courtyard.** Where the crowds below could

36:10 [d]Jer 26:10
36:12 [e]Jer 26:22
36:14 [f]ver 21
36:18 [g]ver 4
36:19 [h]1Ki 17:3
36:21 [i]ver 14 [j]2Ki 22:10
36:22 [k]Am 3:15
36:23 [l]1Ki 22:8
36:24 [m]Ps 36:1 [n]Ge 37:29; 2Ki 22:11; Isa 37:1
36:26 [o]Mt 23:34 [p]Jer 15:21
36:27 [q]ver 4
36:29 [r]Isa 30:10
36:30 [s]Jer 22:19
36:31 [t]Pr 29:1

courtyard at the entrance of the New Gate[d] of the temple, Baruch read to all the people at the LORD's
temple the words of Jeremiah from the scroll.
11When Micaiah son of Gemariah, the son of Shaphan, heard all the words of the LORD from the
scroll, 12he went down to the secretary's room in the royal palace, where all the officials were sitting:
Elishama the secretary, Delaiah son of Shemaiah, Elnathan[e] son of Akbor, Gemariah son of Shaphan,
Zedekiah son of Hananiah, and all the other officials. 13After Micaiah told them everything he had
heard Baruch read to the people from the scroll, 14all the officials sent Jehudi[f] son of Nethaniah, the
son of Shelemiah, the son of Cushi, to say to Baruch, "Bring the scroll from which you have read to
the people and come." So Baruch son of Neriah went to them with the scroll in his hand. 15They said
to him, "Sit down, please, and read it to us."
So Baruch read it to them. 16When they heard all these words, they looked at each other in fear and
said to Baruch, "We must report all these words to the king." 17Then they asked Baruch, "Tell us, how
did you come to write all this? Did Jeremiah dictate it?"
18"Yes," Baruch replied, "he dictated[g] all these words to me, and I wrote them in ink on the scroll."
19Then the officials said to Baruch, "You and Jeremiah, go and hide.[h] Don't let anyone know where
you are."
20After they put the scroll in the room of Elishama the secretary, they went to the king in the courtyard and reported everything to him. 21The king sent Jehudi[i] to get the scroll, and Jehudi brought it
from the room of Elishama the secretary and read it to the king[j] and all the officials standing beside
him. 22It was the ninth month and the king was sitting in the winter apartment,[k] with a fire burning
in the firepot in front of him. 23Whenever Jehudi had read three or four columns of the scroll, the king
cut them off with a scribe's knife and threw them into the firepot, until the entire scroll was burned in
the fire.[l] 24The king and all his attendants who heard all these words showed no fear,[m] nor did they tear
their clothes.[n] 25Even though Elnathan, Delaiah and Gemariah urged the king not to burn the scroll,
he would not listen to them. 26Instead, the king commanded Jerahmeel, a son of the king, Seraiah son
of Azriel and Shelemiah son of Abdeel to arrest[o] Baruch the scribe and Jeremiah the prophet. But the
LORD had hidden[p] them.
27After the king burned the scroll containing the words that Baruch had written at Jeremiah's dictation,[q] the word of the LORD came to Jeremiah: 28"Take another scroll and write on it all the words
that were on the first scroll, which Jehoiakim king of Judah burned up. 29Also tell Jehoiakim king of
Judah, 'This is what the LORD says: You burned that scroll and said, "Why did you write on it that the
king of Babylon would certainly come and destroy this land and wipe from it[r] both man and beast?"
30Therefore this is what the LORD says about Jehoiakim king of Judah: He will have no one to sit on the
throne of David; his body will be thrown out[s] and exposed to the heat by day and the frost by night.
31I will punish him and his children and his attendants for their wickedness; I will bring on them and
those living in Jerusalem and the people of Judah every disaster[t] I pronounced against them, because
they have not listened.' "

see and hear Baruch. **the New Gate.** Where judicial cases were heard (see 26:10).
36:11 Micaiah son of Gemariah. From the family of Shaphan (see note on 26:24).
36:12 Elnathan son of Akbor. From a family that was involved in the rediscovery of the Book of the Law in Josiah's day (2 Kgs 22:12). Perhaps the officials hoped for a similar outcome.
36:19 go and hide. Indicates the kind of response the officials anticipated while also showing that not all of the court officials were opposed to Jeremiah's message. This king had already brought the prophet Uriah back from Egypt and executed him (26:23).
36:22 ninth month. December, so the king is in "the winter apartment" with a "fire burning in the firepot."
36:23 As the scroll is being read, the king systematically cuts sections of it off and throws them into the fire, symbolizing his utter disregard for its message. The scene dramatically contrasts with how Jehoiakim's father, Josiah, responded to the reading of the rediscovered Book of the Law (2 Kgs 22:11). Josiah tore his clothes and repented because of the Lord's great wrath against his people for not keeping the law's demands. Jehoiakim neither tears his clothes nor shows any fear at all (v. 24).
36:26 a son of the king. Not necessarily a son of the reigning king but a person of royal blood. **arrest Baruch . . . and Jeremiah.** Instead of seeking reform (see note on v. 23). **the LORD had hidden them.** Normally a king could find and arrest dissidents in his own capital, but in this instance, the Lord enables them to remain concealed.
36:28 Take another scroll. Jehoiakim's display of disdain will not prevent the prophecies from being fulfilled. The Lord commands Jeremiah to prepare a new scroll; it contains the previous warnings of coming judgment as well as the addition of "many similar words" (v. 32).
36:30 The Lord reiterates one of the key judgment prophecies: Jehoiakim will not have a lasting dynasty to follow him on the throne of David (see 22:24–30 and note on 22:26), and his body will come to a dishonorable end. Jehoiakim's son Jehoiachin reigns for merely three months before Nebuchadnezzar carries Jehoiachin off to Babylon, never to return.

32 So Jeremiah took another scroll and gave it to the scribe Baruch son of Neriah, and as Jeremiah
dictated,[u] Baruch wrote[v] on it all the words of the scroll that Jehoiakim king of Judah had burned[w] in
the fire. And many similar words were added to them.

Jeremiah in Prison

37 Zedekiah[x] son of Josiah was made king[y] of Judah by Nebuchadnezzar king of Babylon; he
reigned in place of Jehoiachin[a][z] son of Jehoiakim. 2 Neither he nor his attendants nor the
people of the land paid any attention[a] to the words the LORD had spoken through Jeremiah the prophet.
3 King Zedekiah, however, sent Jehukal son of Shelemiah with the priest Zephaniah[b] son of Maaseiah
to Jeremiah the prophet with this message: "Please pray[c] to the LORD our God for us."
4 Now Jeremiah was free to come and go among the people, for he had not yet been put in prison.[d]
5 Pharaoh's army had marched out of Egypt,[e] and when the Babylonians[b] who were besieging Jerusalem heard the report about them, they withdrew[f] from Jerusalem.[g]
6 Then the word of the LORD came to Jeremiah the prophet: 7 "This is what the LORD, the God of Israel,
says: Tell the king of Judah, who sent you to inquire[h] of me, 'Pharaoh's army, which has marched out
to support you, will go back to its own land, to Egypt.[i] 8 Then the Babylonians will return and attack
this city; they will capture it and burn[j] it down.'
9 "This is what the LORD says: Do not deceive[k] yourselves, thinking, 'The Babylonians will surely leave
us.' They will not! 10 Even if you were to defeat the entire Babylonian[c] army that is attacking you and
only wounded men were left in their tents, they would come out and burn this city down."
11 After the Babylonian army had withdrawn[l] from Jerusalem because of Pharaoh's army, 12 Jeremiah started to leave the city to go to the territory of Benjamin to get his share of the property[m] among
the people there. 13 But when he reached the Benjamin Gate, the captain of the guard, whose name
was Irijah son of Shelemiah, the son of Hananiah, arrested him and said, "You are deserting to the
Babylonians!"
14 "That's not true!" Jeremiah said. "I am not deserting to the Babylonians." But Irijah would not
listen to him; instead, he arrested[n] Jeremiah and brought him to the officials. 15 They were angry with
Jeremiah and had him beaten[o] and imprisoned in the house[p] of Jonathan the secretary, which they
had made into a prison.
16 Jeremiah was put into a vaulted cell in a dungeon, where he remained a long time. 17 Then King
Zedekiah sent for him and had him brought to the palace, where he asked[q] him privately,[r] "Is there
any word from the LORD?"
"Yes," Jeremiah replied, "you will be delivered[s] into the hands of the king of Babylon."

[a] *1* Hebrew *Koniah,* a variant of *Jehoiachin* [b] *5* Or *Chaldeans*; also in verses 8, 9, 13 and 14
[c] *10* Or *Chaldean*; also in verse 11

36:32 [u] ver 4 [v] Ex 34:1 [w] ver 23
37:1 [x] 2Ki 24:17 [y] Eze 17:13 [z] 2Ki 24:8, 12; 2Ch 36:10; Jer 22:24
37:2 [a] 2Ki 24:19; 2Ch 36:12, 14
37:3 [b] Jer 29:25; 52:24 [c] 1Ki 13:6; Jer 21:1-2; 42:2
37:4 [d] ver 15; Jer 32:2
37:5 [e] Eze 17:15 [f] Jer 34:21 [g] 2Ki 24:7
37:7 [h] 2Ki 22:18 [i] Jer 2:36; La 4:17
37:8 [j] Jer 34:22; 39:8
37:9 [k] Jer 29:8
37:11 [l] ver 5
37:12 [m] Jer 32:9
37:14 [n] Jer 40:4
37:15 [o] Jer 20:2 [p] Jer 38:26
37:17 [q] Jer 15:11 [r] Jer 38:16 [s] Jer 21:7

37:1–21 *Jeremiah in Prison.* Chs. 37–39 cover the painful last days of Jerusalem after the Babylonians surround it. Jeremiah himself is the target of assault and persecution because of his prophecies about the city's impending fall. Even while charting a public course that will end in disaster, King Zedekiah has several private interviews with Jeremiah, seeking to discover the Lord's word concerning the city's future. Yet he is unwilling or unable to change his direction in response to Jeremiah's clear warnings.

37:1–3 This fulfills the prophecy in 36:30 (see note there). Instead of Jehoiachin succeeding his father, Jehoiakim, Nebuchadnezzar places Jehoiakim's brother Zedekiah on the throne.

37:2 the people of the land. The wealthy landowners and ruling class. Neither they nor the king nor the king's officials pay attention to the Lord's words.

37:3 pray to the LORD our God for us. See 21:2 and note. Such a request in the absence of repentance is doomed to fail; in any event, the Lord has already instructed Jeremiah not to pray for this people, perhaps precisely because of this attitude (7:16).

37:4 free to come and go. This will soon change (see vv. 12–15). In 588 BC, the Egyptians march out to threaten the Babylonians, who have already begun to besiege Jerusalem. The siege is temporarily lifted while Nebuchadnezzar deals with the Egyptians, but the respite for Jerusalem is only temporary, just as Jeremiah prophesied.

37:9 Do not deceive yourselves. The people of Jerusalem greet the Babylonian withdrawal as the Lord's deliverance, but the Lord is still set on their destruction.

37:10 wounded men. Even they would be sufficient to capture and burn the city. The Lord doesn't need the Babylonian power to accomplish his purposes.

37:12 the territory of Benjamin. Where Jeremiah came from (see 1:1). **his share of the property.** May refer to the portion of land he purchased from Hanamel in 32:1–15.

37:13 deserting to the Babylonians! The "captain of the guard" arrests Jeremiah, assuming that since his prophecies about the fall of the city have not come true, he is escaping the city.

37:16 cell in a dungeon. Apparently a damp underground cell.

37:17 word from the LORD. See note on 21:2. Perhaps Zedekiah hopes Jeremiah will be more inclined to give him good news after his lengthy confinement, but Jeremiah's message to the king is unchanged.

37:18 [t]1Sa 26:18; Jn 10:32; Ac 25:8
37:21 [u]Isa 33:16; Jer 38:9 [v]2Ki 25:3; Jer 52:6 [w]Jer 32:2; 38:6,13,28
38:1 [x]Jer 37:3
38:2 [y]Jer 34:17 [z]Jer 21:9; 39:18; 45:5
38:3 [a]Jer 21:4,10; 32:3
38:4 [b]Jer 36:12 [c]Jer 26:11
38:6 [d]Jer 37:21
38:7 [e]Jer 39:16 [f]Ac 8:27 [g]Job 29:7
38:9 [h]Jer 37:21
38:13 [i]Jer 37:21

18 Then Jeremiah said to King Zedekiah, "What crime[t] have I committed against you or your attendants
or this people, that you have put me in prison? 19 Where are your prophets who prophesied to you, 'The
king of Babylon will not attack you or this land'? 20 But now, my lord the king, please listen. Let me bring
my petition before you: Do not send me back to the house of Jonathan the secretary, or I will die there."
21 King Zedekiah then gave orders for Jeremiah to be placed in the courtyard of the guard and given
a loaf of bread from the street of the bakers each day until all the bread[u] in the city was gone.[v] So Jeremiah remained in the courtyard of the guard.[w]

Jeremiah Thrown Into a Cistern

38 Shephatiah son of Mattan, Gedaliah son of Pashhur, Jehukal[a][x] son of Shelemiah, and Pashhur
son of Malkijah heard what Jeremiah was telling all the people when he said, 2 "This is what
the LORD says: 'Whoever stays in this city will die by the sword, famine or plague,[y] but whoever goes
over to the Babylonians[b] will live. They will escape with their lives; they will live.'[z] 3 And this is what
the LORD says: 'This city will certainly be given into the hands of the army of the king of Babylon, who
will capture it.'"[a]
4 Then the officials[b] said to the king, "This man should be put to death.[c] He is discouraging the soldiers who are left in this city, as well as all the people, by the things he is saying to them. This man is
not seeking the good of these people but their ruin."
5 "He is in your hands," King Zedekiah answered. "The king can do nothing to oppose you."
6 So they took Jeremiah and put him into the cistern of Malkijah, the king's son, which was in the
courtyard of the guard.[d] They lowered Jeremiah by ropes into the cistern; it had no water in it, only
mud, and Jeremiah sank down into the mud.
7 But Ebed-Melek,[e] a Cushite,[c] an official[d][f] in the royal palace, heard that they had put Jeremiah
into the cistern. While the king was sitting in the Benjamin Gate,[g] 8 Ebed-Melek went out of the palace
and said to him, 9 "My lord the king, these men have acted wickedly in all they have done to Jeremiah
the prophet. They have thrown him into a cistern, where he will starve to death when there is no longer
any bread[h] in the city."
10 Then the king commanded Ebed-Melek the Cushite, "Take thirty men from here with you and lift
Jeremiah the prophet out of the cistern before he dies."
11 So Ebed-Melek took the men with him and went to a room under the treasury in the palace. He
took some old rags and worn-out clothes from there and let them down with ropes to Jeremiah in the
cistern. 12 Ebed-Melek the Cushite said to Jeremiah, "Put these old rags and worn-out clothes under your
arms to pad the ropes." Jeremiah did so, 13 and they pulled him up with the ropes and lifted him out of
the cistern. And Jeremiah remained in the courtyard of the guard.[i]

[a] *1* Hebrew *Jukal,* a variant of *Jehukal* [b] *2* Or *Chaldeans*; also in verses 18, 19 and 23 [c] *7* Probably from the upper Nile region [d] *7* Or *a eunuch*

37:18 What crime have I committed ...? Jeremiah asks the king to detail the charges against him for which he has been imprisoned. Jeremiah merely told the truth, unlike the false prophets who declared, "The king of Babylon will not attack you or this land" (v. 19).

37:21 courtyard of the guard. Next to the palace (32:2). **bread ... was gone.** Because of the siege.

38:1–13 *Jeremiah Thrown Into a Cistern.* The weakness of King Zedekiah is on full display in ch. 38. When one group of his officials wants to kill Jeremiah, Zedekiah does nothing to prevent them from doing so, but when another of his servants wants to rescue Jeremiah, he supports him. Zedekiah once again seeks a private audience with Jeremiah to find out the Lord's word concerning his future, but Zedekiah still refuses to change his behavior in response to it. There are many similarities between the events of ch. 37 and those of ch. 38.

38:1 Jehukal. Also mentioned in 37:3.

38:2 sword, famine or plague. See note on 14:12.

38:4 put to death. Jeremiah's prophecies thus far have proven entirely accurate, but instead of listening to his words, these officials want to silence him. **discouraging the soldiers.** Jeremiah's continued message of the certain demise of Jerusalem is, unsurprisingly, demoralizing to those who hear it.

38:5 He is in your hands. Zedekiah's position as king is not strong because the Babylonians placed him on the throne when they exiled his nephew, Jehoiachin, and because of the rigors of the Babylonian siege. In the face of powerful court opposition, he chooses not to do anything to protect Jeremiah.

38:6 cistern. Normally stores water but is presently empty. They intend for Jeremiah to slowly starve to death in this muddy pit. **king's son.** See note on 36:26.

38:7 Cushite. A foreigner from southern (Upper) Egypt (see NIV text note). **official in the royal palace.** He may have been a eunuch since the Hebrew word translated "official" can also mean "eunuch" (see NIV text note). Eunuchs held many important positions in royal households. **Benjamin Gate.** Also mentioned in 37:13.

38:10 thirty men. A sizeable force, suggesting the expectation of possible opposition from Jeremiah's enemies.

38:13 Jeremiah is not freed from imprisonment but is returned to the safety of the "courtyard of the guard" (see note on 37:21).

Zedekiah Questions Jeremiah Again

[14]Then King Zedekiah sent for Jeremiah the prophet and had him brought to the third entrance to the temple of the LORD. "I am going to ask you something," the king said to Jeremiah. "Do not hide[j] anything from me."

[15]Jeremiah said to Zedekiah, "If I give you an answer, will you not kill me? Even if I did give you counsel, you would not listen to me."

[16]But King Zedekiah swore this oath secretly[k] to Jeremiah: "As surely as the LORD lives, who has given us breath,[l] I will neither kill you nor hand you over to those who want to kill you."[m]

[17]Then Jeremiah said to Zedekiah, "This is what the LORD God Almighty, the God of Israel, says: 'If you surrender to the officers of the king of Babylon, your life will be spared and this city will not be burned down; you and your family will live.[n] [18]But if you will not surrender to the officers of the king of Babylon, this city will be given into the hands[o] of the Babylonians and they will burn[p] it down; you yourself will not escape[q] from them.' "

[19]King Zedekiah said to Jeremiah, "I am afraid[r] of the Jews who have gone over[s] to the Babylonians, for the Babylonians may hand me over to them and they will mistreat me."

[20]"They will not hand you over," Jeremiah replied. "Obey[t] the LORD by doing what I tell you. Then it will go well with you, and your life[u] will be spared. [21]But if you refuse to surrender, this is what the LORD has revealed to me: [22]All the women[v] left in the palace of the king of Judah will be brought out to the officials of the king of Babylon. Those women will say to you:

" 'They misled you and overcame you—
 those trusted friends of yours.
Your feet are sunk in the mud;
 your friends have deserted you.' "

[23]"All your wives and children[w] will be brought out to the Babylonians. You yourself will not escape from their hands but will be captured[x] by the king of Babylon; and this city will[a] be burned down."

[24]Then Zedekiah said to Jeremiah, "Do not let anyone know about this conversation, or you may die. [25]If the officials hear that I talked with you, and they come to you and say, 'Tell us what you said to the king and what the king said to you; do not hide it from us or we will kill you,' [26]then tell them, 'I was pleading with the king not to send me back to Jonathan's house[y] to die there.' "

[27]All the officials did come to Jeremiah and question him, and he told them everything the king had ordered him to say. So they said no more to him, for no one had heard his conversation with the king.

[28]And Jeremiah remained in the courtyard of the guard[z] until the day Jerusalem was captured.

The Fall of Jerusalem

39:1-10pp — 2Ki 25:1-12; Jer 52:4-16

39 This is how Jerusalem was taken: [1]In the ninth year of Zedekiah king of Judah, in the tenth month, Nebuchadnezzar king of Babylon marched against Jerusalem with his whole army and laid siege[a] to it. [2]And on the ninth day of the fourth month of Zedekiah's eleven year, the city wall

a 23 Or *and you will cause this city to*

38:14 [j]1Sa 3:17
38:16 [k]Jer 37:17 [l]Isa 42:5; 57:16 [m]ver 4
38:17 [n]2Ki 24:12; Jer 21:9
38:18 [o]ver 3; Jer 34:3 [p]Jer 37:8 [q]Jer 24:8; 32:4
38:19 [r]Isa 51:12; Jn 12:42 [s]Jer 39:9
38:20 [t]Jer 11:4 [u]Isa 55:3
38:22 [v]Jer 6:12
38:23 [w]2Ki 25:6 [x]Jer 41:10
38:26 [y]Jer 37:15
38:28 [z]Jer 37:21; 39:14
39:1 [a]2Ki 25:1; Jer 52:4; Eze 24:2

38:14–28 *Zedekiah Questions Jeremiah Again.* This is now the second time that Zedekiah asks to meet with Jeremiah (see 37:16–17).
38:15 will you not kill me? Jeremiah is understandably suspicious of Zedekiah's intentions, given Zedekiah's earlier failure to protect him and Zedekiah's lack of response to Jeremiah's earlier messages.
38:16 As surely as the LORD lives. A standard oath formula.
38:17–18 Jeremiah has no new words for King Zedekiah; Jeremiah simply repeats what he told him before (27:1–15).
38:19 I am afraid of the Jews who have gone over to the Babylonians. Zedekiah fears the wrong things. He should fear and obey the Lord (v. 20).
38:22 sunk in the mud. Just like Jeremiah in v. 6.
38:24 Do not let anyone know about this conversation. Zedekiah's weakness is striking. He is unable to guarantee Jeremiah's safety, which he swore in v. 16, unless his own officials are kept in the dark. Yet the Lord continues to protect Jeremiah (1:8).
39:1–18 *The Fall of Jerusalem.* All of Jeremiah's words of judgment are finally and painfully vindicated in 586 BC when Nebuchadnezzar captures Jerusalem after a long siege. This is the fullest account in the OT of the Babylonian conquest of Jerusalem.
39:1 ninth year ... tenth month. On the tenth day (52:4), i.e., Jan. 15, 588 BC.
39:2 ninth day ... fourth month ... eleventh year. July 18, 586 BC. The siege of Jerusalem lasts about 18 months (Jan. 15, 588–July 18, 586 BC) before the city wall is broken through.

Babylonian tablet naming Nebo-Sarsekim and his title (Jer 39:3).

39:3 [b] Jer 21:4
39:5 [c] Jer 32:4 [d] 2Ki 23:33
39:7 [e] Eze 12:13 [f] Jer 32:5
39:8 [g] Jer 38:18 [h] Ne 1:3
39:9 [i] Jer 40:1
39:12 [j] Pr 16:7; 1Pe 3:13

was broken through. 3 Then all the officials[b] of the king of Babylon came and took seats in the Middle
Gate: Nergal-Sharezer of Samgar, Nebo-Sarsekim a chief officer, Nergal-Sharezer a high official and
all the other officials of the king of Babylon. 4 When Zedekiah king of Judah and all the soldiers saw
them, they fled; they left the city at night by way of the king's garden, through the gate between the two
walls, and headed toward the Arabah.[a]

5 But the Babylonian[b] army pursued them and overtook Zedekiah[c] in the plains of Jericho. They
captured him and took him to Nebuchadnezzar king of Babylon at Riblah[d] in the land of Hamath,
where he pronounced sentence on him. 6 There at Riblah the king of Babylon slaughtered the sons of
Zedekiah before his eyes and also killed all the nobles of Judah. 7 Then he put out Zedekiah's eyes[e] and
bound him with bronze shackles to take him to Babylon.[f]

8 The Babylonians[c] set fire[g] to the royal palace and the houses of the people and broke down the
walls[h] of Jerusalem. 9 Nebuzaradan commander of the imperial guard carried into exile to Babylon the
people who remained in the city, along with those who had gone over to him, and the rest of the people.[i] 10 But Nebuzaradan the commander of the guard left behind in the land of Judah some of the poor
people, who owned nothing; and at that time he gave them vineyards and fields.

11 Now Nebuchadnezzar king of Babylon had given these orders about Jeremiah through Nebuzaradan commander of the imperial guard: 12 "Take him and look after him; don't harm[j] him but do for
him whatever he asks." 13 So Nebuzaradan the commander of the guard, Nebushazban a chief officer,

[a] 4 Or *the Jordan Valley* [b] 5 Or *Chaldean* [c] 8 Or *Chaldeans*

39:3 Middle Gate. Where the Babylonians hold the victory celebration, with the officials of the king of Babylon taking their seats of authority and rule. City gates were often places where officials made decisions and issued judgments. **Nergal-Sharezer.** Perhaps Nebuchadnezzar's son-in-law, who ultimately succeeded him as king. **Nebo-Sarsekim.** Archaeologists have uncovered a tablet from Babylon from 595 BC mentioning this man and his title. See photo, this page.

39:4 they fled. As the Babylonians breach the wall, probably on the northern side, King Zedekiah and the remnant of his army flee at night to the east and south, toward the Arabah. **Arabah.** A region that includes the Jordan Valley. There they hope to disappear into the wilderness.

39:5 the plains of Jericho. Less than 20 miles (32 kilometers) from Jerusalem. See note on 2 Kgs 25:5. **Riblah.** Nebuchadnezzar's command center; a town 65 miles (105 kilometers) north of Damascus.

39:6–8 slaughtered ... before his eyes ... put out Zedekiah's eyes ... broke down the walls. See notes on 2 Kgs 25:7,10.

39:9 carried into exile. This is the third deportation to Babylon (see note on 2 Kgs 25:11; see also "Nebuchadnezzar's Campaigns Against Judah," pp. 708–709). This deportation includes the majority of the remaining inhabitants of Judah, including all those with skills or wealth.

39:10 some of the poor people. Left behind to work the "vineyards and fields" so that the Babylonians can continue to receive their tribute.

39:11 orders about Jeremiah. The Babylonians had heard of Jeremiah's prophecies. Though they didn't believe in the Lord, they protected Jeremiah, whether out of superstition or a politically motivated desire to be able to claim that Judah's own god had turned against them. Ironically, Jeremiah receives much better treatment at the hands of the Babylonians than he received from his own people.

Nergal-Sharezer a high official and all the other officers of the king of Babylon 14 sent and had Jeremiah
taken out of the courtyard of the guard.[k] They turned him over to Gedaliah son of Ahikam,[l] the son of
Shaphan, to take him back to his home. So he remained among his own people.[m]
15 While Jeremiah had been confined in the courtyard of the guard, the word of the LORD came to
him: 16 "Go and tell Ebed-Melek[n] the Cushite, 'This is what the LORD Almighty, the God of Israel, says:
I am about to fulfill my words against this city—words concerning disaster,[o] not prosperity. At that
time they will be fulfilled before your eyes. 17 But I will rescue[p] you on that day, declares the LORD; you
will not be given into the hands of those you fear. 18 I will save you; you will not fall by the sword[q] but
will escape with your life,[r] because you trust[s] in me, declares the LORD.' "

Jeremiah Freed

40 The word came to Jeremiah from the LORD after Nebuzaradan commander of the imperial
guard had released him at Ramah. He had found Jeremiah bound in chains among all the captives from Jerusalem and Judah who were being carried into exile to Babylon. 2 When the commander
of the guard found Jeremiah, he said to him, "The LORD your God decreed this disaster for this place.[t]
3 And now the LORD has brought it about; he has done just as he said he would. All this happened because you people sinned[u] against the LORD and did not obey[v] him. 4 But today I am freeing you from the
chains on your wrists. Come with me to Babylon, if you like, and I will look after you; but if you do not
want to, then don't come. Look, the whole country lies before you; go wherever you please."[w] 5 However,
before Jeremiah turned to go,[a] Nebuzaradan added, "Go back to Gedaliah[x] son of Ahikam, the son of
Shaphan, whom the king of Babylon has appointed over the towns of Judah, and live with him among
the people, or go anywhere else you please."[y]

Then the commander gave him provisions and a present and let him go. 6 So Jeremiah went to Gedaliah son of Ahikam at Mizpah[z] and stayed with him among the people who were left behind in the land.

Gedaliah Assassinated

40:7-9; 41:1-3pp — 2Ki 25:22-26

7 When all the army officers and their men who were still in the open country heard that the king of
Babylon had appointed Gedaliah son of Ahikam as governor over the land and had put him in charge
of the men, women and children who were the poorest[a] in the land and who had not been carried
into exile to Babylon, 8 they came to Gedaliah at Mizpah[b]—Ishmael[c] son of Nethaniah, Johanan and
Jonathan the sons of Kareah, Seraiah son of Tanhumeth, the sons of Ephai the Netophathite,[d] and
Jaazaniah[b] the son of the Maakathite,[e] and their men. 9 Gedaliah son of Ahikam, the son of Shaphan,

[a] 5 Or *Jeremiah answered* [b] 8 Hebrew *Jezaniah,* a variant of *Jaazaniah*

39:14 [k] Jer 38:28 [l] 2Ki 22:12 [m] Jer 40:5
39:16 [n] Jer 38:7 [o] Jer 21:10; Da 9:12
39:17 [p] Ps 41:1-2
39:18 [q] Jer 45:5 [r] Jer 21:9; 38:2 [s] Jer 17:7
40:2 [t] Jer 50:7
40:3 [u] Da 9:11 [v] Dt 29:24-28; Ro 2:5-9
40:4 [w] Ge 13:9; Jer 39:11-12
40:5 [x] 2Ki 25:22 [y] Jer 39:14
40:6 [z] Jdg 20:1; 1Sa 7:5-17
40:7 [a] Jer 39:10
40:8 [b] ver 13 [c] ver 14; Jer 41:1,2 [d] 2Sa 23:28 [e] Dt 3:14

39:14 Gedaliah son of Ahikam. A Judahite whom the Babylonians appointed as governor of the new province (see 40:7). As part of the family of Shaphan, he is sympathetic to Jeremiah (see note on 26:24).

39:15–18 Jeremiah is not the only one to escape death or exile. Ebed-Melek the Cushite (see note on 38:7) is likewise rewarded for trusting in the Lord and faithfully rescuing Jeremiah (38:7–13).

40:1—45:5 *The Aftermath of Jerusalem's Destruction.* Even after the fall of Jerusalem vindicates Jeremiah's prophecies, some Judahites continue to resist the Babylonians. This resistance culminates in a successful plot to assassinate Gedaliah, the governor whom the Babylonians appointed. When the Babylonians apprehend and execute the culprits, the remaining Judahites fear Babylonian reprisals and flee to Egypt. Jeremiah encourages them to stay in Judah and warns them that going down to Egypt will lead to further judgment from the Lord. But the destruction of Jerusalem has not changed the stubborn and rebellious hearts of the people, who do not heed his words. They leave for Egypt, forcibly taking Jeremiah with them.

40:1–6 *Jeremiah Freed.* Although Nebuchadnezzar gave orders to release and protect Jeremiah (39:11–12), in the chaos following the fall of Jerusalem, Jeremiah is caught up with other prisoners and taken in chains to the staging center at Ramah. Nebuchadnezzar's orders were explicit enough to bring Nebuzaradan, the commander of the Babylonian imperial guard, to personally seek out and release Jeremiah from bondage. From a Babylonian perspective, Jeremiah's prophecies are useful propaganda, for they declare that Judah's own God handed them over to the Babylonians because of their sins. But Jeremiah has no personal sympathy for the Babylonians nor any reason to wish to go and live in Babylon (cf. 25:12). Nebuzaradan therefore encourages Jeremiah to go back to help Gedaliah's new administration, located in the relatively unscathed town of Mizpah.

40:1 Ramah. About five miles (eight kilometers) north of Jerusalem (see 31:15; Matt 2:18)

40:6 Mizpah. About eight miles (13 kilometers) north of Jerusalem.

40:7—41:15 *Gedaliah Assassinated.* Some in the community who remain in Judah plot to kill Gedaliah. This is a useless gesture of rebellion against Babylon, and it tragically removes from a position of influence a good man who has supported Jeremiah's prophecies (see 38:1).

40:7–10 The population remaining in Judah is made up of small military groups that have been hiding in the open country, the wilderness areas where it was hard for the invaders to track them down alongside "the poorest in the land" (v. 7), whom the Babylonians left behind to take care of the farmland (39:10).

Seal impression of Gedaliah "servant of the king," probably the Gedaliah of Jer 40:5 before he was appointed governor.

Z. Radovan/www.BibleLandPictures.com

took an oath to reassure them and their men. "Do not be afraid to serve[f]
the Babylonians,[a]" he said. "Settle down in the land and serve the king
of Babylon, and it will go well with you.[g] 10I myself will stay at Mizpah[h] to represent you before the Babylonians who come to us, but
you are to harvest the wine, summer fruit and olive oil, and
put them in your storage jars, and live in the towns you have
taken over."[i]
11When all the Jews in Moab,[j] Ammon, Edom and all the
other countries heard that the king of Babylon had left a remnant in Judah and had appointed Gedaliah son of Ahikam, the
son of Shaphan, as governor over them, 12they all came back to
the land of Judah, to Gedaliah at Mizpah, from all the countries
where they had been scattered.[k] And they harvested an abundance of
wine and summer fruit.
13Johanan son of Kareah and all the army officers still in the open country came to Gedaliah at Mizpah[l] 14and said to him, "Don't you know that
Baalis king of the Ammonites[m] has sent Ishmael son of Nethaniah to take
your life?" But Gedaliah son of Ahikam did not believe them.
15Then Johanan son of Kareah said privately to Gedaliah in Mizpah, "Let
me go and kill Ishmael son of Nethaniah, and no one will know it. Why should he take your life and
cause all the Jews who are gathered around you to be scattered and the remnant of Judah to perish?"
16But Gedaliah son of Ahikam said to Johanan son of Kareah, "Don't do such a thing! What you are
saying about Ishmael is not true."

41 In the seventh month Ishmael[n] son of Nethaniah, the son of Elishama, who was of royal blood
and had been one of the king's officers, came with ten men to Gedaliah son of Ahikam at Mizpah. While they were eating together there, 2Ishmael[o] son of Nethaniah and the ten men who were with
him got up and struck down Gedaliah son of Ahikam, the son of Shaphan, with the sword, killing the
one whom the king of Babylon had appointed[p] as governor over the land.[q] 3Ishmael also killed all the
men of Judah who were with Gedaliah at Mizpah, as well as the Babylonian[b] soldiers who were there.
4The day after Gedaliah's assassination, before anyone knew about it, 5eighty men who had shaved
off their beards,[r] torn their clothes and cut themselves came from Shechem,[s] Shiloh[t] and Samaria,[u]
bringing grain offerings and incense with them to the house of the LORD.[v] 6Ishmael son of Nethaniah
went out from Mizpah to meet them, weeping[w] as he went. When he met them, he said, "Come to Gedaliah son of Ahikam." 7When they went into the city, Ishmael son of Nethaniah and the men who were
with him slaughtered them and threw them into a cistern. 8But ten of them said to Ishmael, "Don't
kill us! We have wheat and barley, olive oil and honey, hidden in a field."[x] So he let them alone and did
not kill them with the others. 9Now the cistern where he threw all the bodies of the men he had killed
along with Gedaliah was the one King Asa[y] had made as part of his defense[z] against Baasha[a] king of
Israel. Ishmael son of Nethaniah filled it with the dead.

[a] *9* Or *Chaldeans*; also in verse 10 [b] *3* Or *Chaldean*

40:9 [f]Jer 27:11 [g]Jer 38:20 **40:10** [h]ver 6 [i]Dt 1:39 **40:11** [j]Nu 25:1 **40:12** [k]Jer 43:5 **40:13** [l]ver 8 **40:14** [m]2Sa 10:1-19; Jer 25:21; 41:10 **41:1** [n]Jer 40:8 **41:2** [o]Ps 41:9; 109:5 [p]Jer 40:5 [q]2Sa 3:27; 20:9-10 **41:5** [r]Lev 19:27 [s]Ge 33:18; Jdg 9:1-57; 1Ki 12:1 [t]Jos 18:1 [u]1Ki 16:24 [v]2Ki 25:9 **41:6** [w]2Sa 3:16 **41:8** [x]Isa 45:3 **41:9** [y]1Ki 15:22; 2Ch 16:6 [z]Jdg 6:2 [a]2Ch 16:1

40:11–12 Jews who had fled to the surrounding nations, such as Moab, Ammon, and Edom, return to Judah after hearing that a "remnant" is left in Judah. Not all those who fled found safe refuge: Edom, in particular, had a policy of handing back fugitives to the Babylonians (Obad 14). Those who did return "harvested an abundance of wine and summer fruit," justifying their faith in making the difficult journey back.

40:14 Ammonites. Lived east of the Jordan River and were anti-Babylonian.

41:1 Ishmael ... was of royal blood. He may have had ambitions to claim the throne. **While they were eating together.** Killing one's host while sharing a meal together was regarded as a particularly heinous and cowardly breach of hospitality.

41:5 had shaved off their beards, torn their clothes and cut themselves. Forms of mourning, not all of which were considered legitimate in Mosaic law (see Deut 14:1). **cut themselves.** Ritual wounds. **Shechem, Shiloh and Samaria.** Cities in the former northern kingdom. **offerings and incense.** They probably intended to go to Jerusalem for the Festival of Tabernacles, which occurred in the "seventh month" (v. 1). **the house of the LORD.** The temple, which was now in ruins. A similar entourage later comes to Jerusalem from Bethel shortly after the end of the exile (Zech 7:2–3).

41:8 Out of the 80 pilgrims (v. 5), 10 escape by claiming to have access to hidden supplies.

41:9 cistern ... King Asa had made. Part of Judah's defensive preparations made during the wars with Baasha king of Israel (see 1 Kgs 15:16–22).

10Ishmael made captives of all the rest of the people[b] who were in Mizpah — the king's daughters
along with all the others who were left there, over whom Nebuzaradan commander of the imperial
guard had appointed Gedaliah son of Ahikam. Ishmael son of Nethaniah took them captive and set out
to cross over to the Ammonites.[c]

11When Johanan[d] son of Kareah and all the army officers who were with him heard about all the
crimes Ishmael son of Nethaniah had committed, 12they took all their men and went to fight Ishmael
son of Nethaniah. They caught up with him near the great pool[e] in Gibeon. 13When all the people[f]
Ishmael had with him saw Johanan son of Kareah and the army officers who were with him, they were
glad. 14All the people Ishmael had taken captive at Mizpah turned and went over to Johanan son of
Kareah. 15But Ishmael son of Nethaniah and eight of his men escaped[g] from Johanan and fled to the
Ammonites.

Flight to Egypt

16Then Johanan son of Kareah and all the army officers who were with him led away all the people
of Mizpah who had survived,[h] whom Johanan had recovered from Ishmael son of Nethaniah after
Ishmael had assassinated Gedaliah son of Ahikam — the soldiers, women, children and court officials
he had recovered from Gibeon. 17And they went on, stopping at Geruth Kimham[i] near Bethlehem on
their way to Egypt[j] 18to escape the Babylonians.[a] They were afraid[k] of them because Ishmael son of
Nethaniah had killed Gedaliah[l] son of Ahikam, whom the king of Babylon had appointed as governor
over the land.

42 Then all the army officers, including Johanan[m] son of Kareah and Jezaniah[b] son of Hoshaiah,
and all the people from the least to the greatest[n] approached 2Jeremiah the prophet and said
to him, "Please hear our petition and pray[o] to the LORD your God for this entire remnant.[p] For as you
now see, though we were once many, now only a few[q] are left. 3Pray that the LORD your God will tell us
where we should go and what we should do."[r]

4"I have heard you," replied Jeremiah the prophet. "I will certainly pray[s] to the LORD your God as
you have requested; I will tell you everything the LORD says and will keep nothing back from you."[t]

5Then they said to Jeremiah, "May the LORD be a true and faithful witness[u] against us if we do not
act in accordance with everything the LORD your God sends you to tell us. 6Whether it is favorable or
unfavorable, we will obey the LORD our God, to whom we are sending you, so that it will go well[v] with
us, for we will obey[w] the LORD our God."

7Ten days later the word of the LORD came to Jeremiah. 8So he called together Johanan son of Kareah and all the army officers[x] who were with him and all the people from the least to the greatest. 9He
said to them, "This is what the LORD, the God of Israel, to whom you sent me to present your petition,

41:10 [b] Jer 40:7,12 [c] Jer 40:14
41:11 [d] Jer 40:8
41:12 [e] 2Sa 2:13
41:13 [f] ver 10
41:15 [g] Job 21:30; Pr 28:17
41:16 [h] Jer 43:4
41:17 [i] 2Sa 19:37 [j] Jer 42:14
41:18 [k] Isa 51:12; Jer 42:16; Lk 12:4-5 [l] Jer 40:5
42:1 [m] Jer 40:13; 41:11 [n] Jer 6:13; 44:12
42:2 [o] Jer 36:7; Ac 8:24; Jas 5:16 [p] Isa 1:9 [q] Lev 26:22; La 1:1
42:3 [r] Ps 86:11; Pr 3:6
42:4 [s] Ex 8:29; 1Sa 12:23 [t] 1Ki 22:14; 1Sa 3:17
42:5 [u] Ge 31:50
42:6 [v] Dt 5:29; 6:3; Jer 7:23 [w] Ex 24:7; Jos 24:24
42:8 [x] ver 1

[a] *18* Or *Chaldeans* [b] *1* Hebrew; Septuagint (see also 43:2) *Azariah*

41:10 the king's daughters. They may have been intended as hostages. They are not mentioned elsewhere in the accounts of Jerusalem's fate and seem not to have been put to death like their brothers or exiled like their father. **the Ammonites.** Had supported Ishmael in his rebellion against Babylon (see 40:14 and note).

41:11 Johanan son of Kareah. He tried earlier to persuade Gedaliah to allow him to assassinate Ishmael (see 40:15).

41:12 the great pool in Gibeon. The site of a bloody encounter between the forces of Ish-Bosheth and David after the death of Saul (2 Sam 2:13–17). **Gibeon.** Three miles (five kilometers) south of Mizpah.

41:16—43:13 *Flight to Egypt.* After the death of Gedaliah at the hands of a Judahite revolutionary, those who remain in Judah are concerned about the risk of Babylonian reprisals. For that reason, they decide to flee to Egypt. Although they ask Jeremiah to inquire of the Lord for them, they have already decided what their course of action will be, so they ignore the Lord's word when it comes.

41:16–18 The mantle of leadership now passes to the army officers, led by Johanan, who decide to flee to Egypt for safety.

41:17 Geruth Kimham. Otherwise unknown. **Bethlehem.** Five miles (eight kilometers) south of Jerusalem.

42:1 Jezaniah son of Hoshaiah. The same person 43:2 identifies as Azariah.

42:2 pray to the LORD your God. Before the people abandon the promised land and go to Egypt, they and their leaders decide to inquire of the Lord through Jeremiah. It appears that Jeremiah was not in Mizpah at the time of the massacre. Jacob made an inquiry of the Lord at Beersheba in Gen 46:1–3 before Jacob went down to Egypt in the time of Joseph. Perhaps the people expect to receive an encouraging word from the Lord similar to the one Jacob received (Gen 46:3–4).

42:5 Jeremiah calls the Lord as a witness against them if they fail to do what he says.

42:6 favorable or unfavorable. Indicates that they already prefer a course of action, namely, going down to Egypt.

42:7 Ten days later. The word of the Lord did not come to Jeremiah immediately, which must have tested the patience of the people waiting to hear him speak. But unlike the false prophets, he could not manufacture an instant response.

42:9 [y] 2Ki 22:15
42:10 [z] Jer 24:6 [a] Jer 31:28 [b] Eze 36:36 [c] Jer 18:8
42:11 [d] Jer 27:11 [e] Nu 14:9 [f] Isa 43:5 [g] Jer 1:8; Ro 8:31
42:12 [h] Ps 106:44-46
42:13 [i] Jer 44:16
42:14 [j] Nu 11:4-5
42:16 [k] Eze 11:8
42:17 [l] ver 22; Jer 44:13
42:18 [m] Dt 29:18-20; Jer 7:20 [n] 2Ch 36:19; Jer 39:1-9 [o] Jer 29:18 [p] Jer 22:10
42:19 [q] Dt 17:16; Isa 30:7
42:20 [r] ver 2
42:21 [s] Eze 2:7; Zec 7:11-12
42:22 [t] ver 17; Eze 6:11 [u] Hos 9:6
43:1 [v] Jer 26:8; 42:9-22
43:2 [w] Jer 42:1
43:3 [x] Jer 38:4
43:4 [y] Jer 42:5-6 [z] Jer 42:10
43:5 [a] Jer 40:12
43:7 [b] Jer 2:16; 44:1
43:8 [c] Jer 2:16

says:[y] 10‘If you stay in this land, I will build[z] you up and not tear you down; I will plant[a] you and not
uproot you,[b] for I have relented concerning the disaster I have inflicted on you.[c] 11Do not be afraid of
the king of Babylon,[d] whom you now fear.[e] Do not be afraid of him, declares the LORD, for I am with
you and will save[f] you and deliver you from his hands.[g] 12I will show you compassion so that he will
have compassion on you and restore you to your land.’[h]

13“However, if you say, ‘We will not stay in this land,’ and so disobey[i] the LORD your God, 14and if you
say, ‘No, we will go and live in Egypt,[j] where we will not see war or hear the trumpet or be hungry for
bread,’ 15then hear the word of the LORD, you remnant of Judah. This is what the LORD Almighty, the
God of Israel, says: ‘If you are determined to go to Egypt and you do go to settle there, 16then the sword[k]
you fear will overtake you there, and the famine you dread will follow you into Egypt, and there you
will die. 17Indeed, all who are determined to go to Egypt to settle there will die by the sword, famine and
plague;[l] not one of them will survive or escape the disaster I will bring on them.’ 18This is what the LORD
Almighty, the God of Israel, says: ‘As my anger and wrath[m] have been poured out on those who lived in
Jerusalem,[n] so will my wrath be poured out on you when you go to Egypt. You will be a curse*a* and an
object of horror,[o] a curse*a* and an object of reproach; you will never see this place again.’[p]

19“Remnant of Judah, the LORD has told you, ‘Do not go to Egypt.’[q] Be sure of this: I warn you today
20that you made a fatal mistake when you sent me to the LORD your God and said, ‘Pray to the LORD our
God for us; tell us everything he says and we will do it.’[r] 21I have told you today, but you still have not
obeyed the LORD your God in all he sent me to tell you.[s] 22So now, be sure of this: You will die by the
sword, famine and plague[t] in the place where you want to go to settle.”[u]

43 When Jeremiah had finished telling the people all the words of the LORD their God—everything the LORD had sent him to tell them[v]— 2Azariah son of Hoshaiah and Johanan[w] son of
Kareah and all the arrogant men said to Jeremiah, “You are lying! The LORD our God has not sent you
to say, ‘You must not go to Egypt to settle there.’ 3But Baruch son of Neriah is inciting you against us to
hand us over to the Babylonians,*b* so they may kill us or carry us into exile to Babylon.”[x]

4So Johanan son of Kareah and all the army officers and all the people disobeyed the LORD’s command[y] to stay in the land of Judah.[z] 5Instead, Johanan son of Kareah and all the army officers led away
all the remnant of Judah who had come back to live in the land of Judah from all the nations where
they had been scattered.[a] 6They also led away all those whom Nebuzaradan commander of the imperial
guard had left with Gedaliah son of Ahikam, the son of Shaphan—the men, the women, the children
and the king’s daughters. And they took Jeremiah the prophet and Baruch son of Neriah along with
them. 7So they entered Egypt in disobedience to the LORD and went as far as Tahpanhes.[b]

8In Tahpanhes[c] the word of the LORD came to Jeremiah: 9“While the Jews are watching, take some

a 18 That is, your name will be used in cursing (see 29:22); or, others will see that you are cursed.
b 3 Or *Chaldeans*

42:10 When the word comes, it is not what the people had hoped: the Lord promises that if they stay in the land, he will “build [them] up and not tear [them] down” (cf. 1:10). **relented.** Changed his attitude toward them. The judgment already inflicted by the king of Babylon is sufficient.

42:11 Do not be afraid of the king of Babylon. Because the Lord will “deliver [them] from his hands.” This demonstrates that Nebuzaradan’s claim in 40:2–3 was incomplete. At that time, the Lord *had* decreed disaster upon Jerusalem; but now the day of judgment is over, and the Lord will once again show compassion to his people (v. 12; contrast 13:14).

42:13–22 This word of compassion from the Lord (see note on v. 11) is conditional upon their responding in faith. In ch. 38, the prophet’s words about the safety of surrendering to Babylon in view of the impending destruction of Jerusalem called for faith; here too it is counterintuitive to believe that staying in Judah is safer than fleeing to Egypt. If they act in unbelief once again, they will find that the Lord’s triple judgment of “sword, famine and plague” (v. 17; see note on 14:12) will continue to pursue them. The same fate that had befallen the inhabitants of Jerusalem will meet them in Egypt for the very same reason: they refuse to listen to and heed the word of the Lord through his prophet. Yet it is evident to Jeremiah even as he speaks the Lord’s word to the people that they are determined to disobey it, whatever the consequences (vv. 19–22).

43:2 Azariah son of Hoshaiah. See note on 42:1. **You are lying!** In spite of their solemn vow (42:5–6), the people refuse to listen to Jeremiah. Previously, they delighted in false prophets who promised peace for Judah; now they refuse to listen to the true prophet when he promises blessing, accusing him instead of lying as the false prophets had (cf. 5:31).

43:3 Baruch ... is inciting you. It is not clear why they think Jeremiah’s scribe, Baruch, is behind this or what he would gain by it.

43:4 disobeyed the LORD’s command. Johanan and the army officers lead all the people with them, willingly or unwillingly, down to Egypt (vv. 5–7), disregarding Jeremiah’s counsel. Those who began as liberators became as oppressive as Ishmael, the rebel from whom they supposedly freed the people (see 41:10–15). The group going to Egypt includes Jeremiah and Baruch.

43:7 Tahpanhes. A town in northern Egypt not far across the border. The Jews settle there, close to the region of Goshen, where the Israelites settled under Joseph.

43:9 take some large stones. There in Egypt the Lord sends a mes-

large stones with you and bury them in clay in the brick pavement at the entrance to Pharaoh's palace
in Tahpanhes. 10 Then say to them, 'This is what the LORD Almighty, the God of Israel, says: I will send for
my servant[d] Nebuchadnezzar king of Babylon, and I will set his throne over these stones I have buried
here; he will spread his royal canopy above them. 11 He will come and attack Egypt,[e] bringing death to
those destined for death, captivity to those destined for captivity, and the sword to those destined for the
sword.[f] 12 He will set fire to the temples of the gods[g] of Egypt; he will burn their temples and take their
gods captive. As a shepherd picks[h] his garment clean of lice, so he will pick Egypt clean and depart.
13 There in the temple of the sun[a] in Egypt he will demolish the sacred pillars and will burn down the
temples of the gods of Egypt.' "

Disaster Because of Idolatry

44 This word came to Jeremiah concerning all the Jews living in Lower Egypt — in Migdol,[i] Tahpanhes[j] and Memphis[k] — and in Upper Egypt:[l] 2 "This is what the LORD Almighty, the God of
Israel, says: You saw the great disaster I brought on Jerusalem and on all the towns of Judah. Today
they lie deserted and in ruins[m] 3 because of the evil they have done. They aroused my anger by burning
incense to and worshiping other gods[n] that neither they nor you nor your ancestors[o] ever knew. 4 Again
and again[p] I sent my servants the prophets,[q] who said, 'Do not do this detestable thing that I hate!' 5 But
they did not listen or pay attention; they did not turn from their wickedness or stop burning incense to
other gods.[r] 6 Therefore, my fierce anger was poured out; it raged against the towns of Judah and the
streets of Jerusalem and made them the desolate ruins they are today.

7 "Now this is what the LORD God Almighty, the God of Israel, says: Why bring such great disaster[s]
on yourselves by cutting off from Judah the men and women,[t] the children and infants, and so leave
yourselves without a remnant? 8 Why arouse my anger with what your hands have made,[u] burning
incense to other gods in Egypt, where you have come to live?[v] You will destroy yourselves and make
yourselves a curse[b] and an object of reproach[w] among all the nations on earth. 9 Have you forgotten
the wickedness committed by your ancestors and by the kings and queens of Judah and the wickedness
committed by you and your wives in the land of Judah and the streets of Jerusalem?[x] 10 To this day they
have not humbled themselves or shown reverence, nor have they followed my law[y] and the decrees I
set before you and your ancestors.[z]

11 "Therefore this is what the LORD Almighty, the God of Israel, says: I am determined to bring disaster[a] on you and to destroy all Judah. 12 I will take away the remnant[b] of Judah who were determined to
go to Egypt to settle there. They will all perish in Egypt; they will fall by the sword or die from famine.
From the least to the greatest, they will die by sword or famine.[c] They will become a curse and an object
of horror, a curse and an object of reproach.[d] 13 I will punish those who live in Egypt with the sword,

[a] *13* Or *in Heliopolis* [b] *8* That is, your name will be used in cursing (see 29:22); or, others will see that you are cursed; also in verse 12; similarly in verse 22.

43:10 [d] Isa 44:28; Jer 25:9; 27:6
43:11 [e] Jer 46:13-26; Eze 29:19-20 [f] Jer 15:2; 44:13; Zec 11:9
43:12 [g] Jer 46:25; Eze 30:13 [h] Ps 104:2; 109:18-19
44:1 [i] Ex 14:2 [j] Jer 43:7,8 [k] Isa 19:13 [l] Isa 11:11; Jer 46:14
44:2 [m] Isa 6:11; Jer 9:11; 34:22
44:3 [n] ver 8; Dt 13:6-11; 29:26 [o] Dt 32:17; Jer 19:4
44:4 [p] Jer 7:13 [q] Jer 7:25; 25:4; 26:5
44:5 [r] Jer 11:8-10
44:7 [s] Jer 26:19 [t] Jer 51:22
44:8 [u] Jer 25:6-7 [v] 1Co 10:22 [w] Jer 42:18
44:9 [x] ver 17,21
44:10 [y] Jos 1:7 [z] 1Ki 9:6-9
44:11 [a] Jer 21:10; Am 9:4
44:12 [b] ver 7 [c] Isa 1:28 [d] Jer 29:18; 42:15-18

sage for Jeremiah to communicate by means of a sign-act, similar to the ones he had performed earlier in Jerusalem (see notes on 13:1 – 14). **Pharaoh's palace.** This may have been a government building belonging to Pharaoh rather than a royal residence.

43:10 Jeremiah declares that these stones will become the location where Nebuchadnezzar will set up his throne, with its royal canopy protecting him from the sun. In other words, fleeing to Egypt will not put the Jews outside the reach of Nebuchadnezzar and the Babylonian military. Instead, he will arrive right on their doorstep there in Egypt.

43:12 picks his garment clean of lice. Nebuchadnezzar's victory will be as one-sided as a shepherd picking annoying vermin off his clothing. In 568 BC, Nebuchadnezzar invaded Egypt as Jeremiah predicted, though it is not clear whether Jeremiah remained alive to see the fulfillment of his prophecy.

43:13 temple of the sun. Located in Heliopolis, a few miles/kilometers south of Tahpanhes. The gods of Egypt will be powerless to protect their sacred objects. **sacred pillars.** Obelisks.

44:1 – 30 *Disaster Because of Idolatry.* Nothing has changed in the hearts of the Judahites simply by relocating them to Egypt. Their old idolatrous practices continue to haunt them, dooming them inevitably to face the same curse that pursued them in Judah.

44:1 Migdol, Tahpanhes and Memphis. Where groups of Jews were living in Egypt at this time: in Lower (northern) Egypt and in Upper (southern) Egypt, notably at Elephantine (Syene), where the Jewish settlers built their own temple to the Lord. We know a great deal about this community because they later carried out extensive correspondence with the postexilic authorities in Jerusalem, and some of these papyri have survived. Yet all of them were under God's curse because they followed the example of their ancestors in pursuing idols and ignoring the words of the prophets.

44:3 gods that neither they nor you nor your ancestors ever knew. They had never had a relationship with these gods before. The people will share the same fate as those who rebelled in Jerusalem.

44:8 Why arouse my anger ...? Pursuing idolatry will result in the same outcome as before: those who escaped from Jerusalem will be completely cut off, leaving no remnant of the Jewish people except those who are in exile in Babylon and a "few fugitives" (v. 14) from Egypt.

44:13 sword, famine and plague. Those "determined to go to Egypt"

44:13 [e]Jer 42:17
44:14 [f]ver 28; Jer 22:24-27; Ro 9:27
44:16 [g]Jer 11:8-10
44:17 [h]Dt 23:23 [i]ver 25; Jer 7:18 [j]Hos 2:5-13
44:18 [k]Mal 3:13-15
44:19 [l]Jer 7:18
44:21 [m]Isa 64:9; Jer 14:10 [n]Jer 11:13 [o]ver 9 [p]Ps 79:8
44:22 [q]Jer 25:18 [r]Ge 19:13; Ps 107:33-34
44:23 [s]Jer 40:2 [t]1Ki 9:9; Jer 7:13-15; Da 9:11-12
44:24 [u]ver 15 [v]Jer 43:7
44:25 [w]ver 17 [x]Eze 20:39
44:26 [y]Ge 22:16; Isa 48:1; Heb 6:13-17 [z]Dt 32:40; Ps 50:16
44:27 [a]Jer 31:28
44:28 [b]ver 13-14; Isa 10:19 [c]ver 17,25-26
44:29 [d]Pr 19:21
44:30 [e]Jer 46:26; Eze 30:21 [f]2Ki 25:1-7 [g]Jer 39:5

famine and plague,[e] as I punished Jerusalem. [14]None of the remnant of Judah who have gone to live in
Egypt will escape or survive to return to the land of Judah, to which they long to return and live; none
will return except a few fugitives."[f]

[15]Then all the men who knew that their wives were burning incense to other gods, along with all the
women who were present—a large assembly—and all the people living in Lower and Upper Egypt,
said to Jeremiah, [16]"We will not listen[g] to the message you have spoken to us in the name of the LORD!
[17]We will certainly do everything we said we would:[h] We will burn incense to the Queen of Heaven[i] and
will pour out drink offerings to her just as we and our ancestors, our kings and our officials did in the
towns of Judah and in the streets of Jerusalem. At that time we had plenty of food and were well off and
suffered no harm.[j] [18]But ever since we stopped burning incense to the Queen of Heaven and pouring out
drink offerings to her, we have had nothing and have been perishing by sword and famine.[k]"

[19]The women added, "When we burned incense to the Queen of Heaven[l] and poured out drink offerings to her, did not our husbands know that we were making cakes impressed with her image and
pouring out drink offerings to her?"

[20]Then Jeremiah said to all the people, both men and women, who were answering him, [21]"Did not
the LORD remember[m] and call to mind the incense[n] burned in the towns of Judah and the streets of Jerusalem[o] by you and your ancestors,[p] your kings and your officials and the people of the land? [22]When the
LORD could no longer endure your wicked actions and the detestable things you did, your land became
a curse[q] and a desolate waste without inhabitants, as it is today.[r] [23]Because you have burned incense
and have sinned against the LORD and have not obeyed him or followed his law or his decrees or his
stipulations, this disaster[s] has come upon you, as you now see."[t]

[24]Then Jeremiah said to all the people, including the women,[u] "Hear the word of the LORD, all you
people of Judah in Egypt.[v] [25]This is what the LORD Almighty, the God of Israel, says: You and your wives
have done what you said you would do when you promised, 'We will certainly carry out the vows we
made to burn incense and pour out drink offerings to the Queen of Heaven.'[w]

"Go ahead then, do what you promised! Keep your vows![x] [26]But hear the word of the LORD, all you
Jews living in Egypt: 'I swear[y] by my great name,' says the LORD, 'that no one from Judah living anywhere in Egypt will ever again invoke my name or swear, "As surely as the Sovereign LORD lives."[z] [27]For
I am watching over them for harm,[a] not for good; the Jews in Egypt will perish by sword and famine
until they are all destroyed. [28]Those who escape the sword and return to the land of Judah from Egypt
will be very few.[b] Then the whole remnant of Judah who came to live in Egypt will know whose word
will stand—mine or theirs.[c]

[29]" 'This will be the sign to you that I will punish you in this place,' declares the LORD, 'so that you
will know that my threats of harm against you will surely stand.'[d] [30]This is what the LORD says: 'I am
going to deliver Pharaoh[e] Hophra king of Egypt into the hands of his enemies who want to kill him,
just as I gave Zedekiah[f] king of Judah into the hands of Nebuchadnezzar king of Babylon, the enemy
who wanted to kill him.' "[g]

(v. 12) will die by these covenantal curses (see note on 14:12). Instead of being blessed by God and being a blessing, as Gen 12:1–3 promised, they will become a "curse" (v. 12), a living example of God's judgment in action.

44:15 wives were burning incense to other gods. Idolatry seems to have affected particularly the women. We know from archaeological sources that women's religious concerns in antiquity often revolved around basic concerns such as fertility, to which pagan religions often appealed.

44:17,18,19 Queen of Heaven. Astarte (see note on 7:18).

44:18 ever since we stopped. The women deny that the Lord is the one who brought judgment on Jerusalem and instead claim that the cessation of their idolatrous worship practices at the time of Josiah's reforms is the reason (see 2 Kgs 23).

44:19 did not our husbands know ...? The men knew that their wives were burning incense to idols, so they were not blameless in this apostasy. Not only did they not stop them; they supported their denunciation of Jeremiah.

44:22 When the LORD could no longer endure. The previous delay between Judah's sin and God's judgment was due to God's mercy, but he eventually judged Judah (v. 23) and will do so again (vv. 26–27).

44:25 Keep your vows! If they consider their vows to the idols so precious, they should go ahead and keep them, but the Lord will also take a vow by himself to ensure that they never take another vow (v. 26).

44:27 I am watching over them for harm. In contrast to the exiles in Babylon, whom he is watching over for good (24:6).

44:29 the sign. The Lord will deliver Pharaoh Hophra into the hands of his enemies to share the fate of his former ally, King Zedekiah of Judah, as a sign to the Jews that the Lord's word (not theirs) will stand. The Jews in Egypt will be punished!

44:30 Pharaoh Hophra. He tried unsuccessfully in 588 BC to relieve the siege of Jerusalem (see 37:5) and was subsequently deposed in 570 BC in an internal coup. He was executed a few years later.

A Message to Baruch

45 When Baruch[h] son of Neriah wrote on a scroll the words Jeremiah the prophet dictated in the
fourth year of Jehoiakim[i] son of Josiah king of Judah, Jeremiah said this to Baruch: 2“This is
what the LORD, the God of Israel, says to you, Baruch: 3You said, ‘Woe to me! The LORD has added sorrow
to my pain; I am worn out with groaning[j] and find no rest.’ 4But the LORD has told me to say to you, ‘This
is what the LORD says: I will overthrow what I have built and uproot what I have planted,[k] throughout
the earth.[l] 5Should you then seek great things for yourself? Do not seek them.[m] For I will bring disaster
on all people, declares the LORD, but wherever you go I will let you escape with your life.’ ”[n]

A Message About Egypt

46 This is the word of the LORD that came to Jeremiah the prophet concerning the nations:[o]

2Concerning Egypt:

This is the message against the army of Pharaoh Necho[p] king of Egypt, which was defeated at Carchemish[q] on the Euphrates River by Nebuchadnezzar king of Babylon in the fourth year of Jehoiakim[r]
son of Josiah king of Judah:

3“Prepare your shields,[s] both large and small,
  and march out for battle!
4Harness the horses,
  mount the steeds!
Take your positions
  with helmets on!
Polish[t] your spears,
  put on your armor![u]
5What do I see?
  They are terrified,
they are retreating,
  their warriors are defeated.

45:1 [h] Jer 32:12; 36:4, 18,32 [i] 2Ch 36:5
45:3 [j] Ps 69:3
45:4 [k] Jer 11:17 [l] Isa 5:5-7; Jer 18:7-10
45:5 [m] Mt 6:25-27,33 [n] Jer 21:9; 38:2; 39:18
46:1 [o] Jer 1:10; 25:15-38
46:2 [p] 2Ki 23:29 [q] 2Ch 35:20 [r] Jer 45:1
46:3 [s] Isa 21:5; Jer 51:11-12
46:4 [t] Eze 21:9-11 [u] 1Sa 17:5,38; 2Ch 26:14; Ne 4:16

45:1–5 *A Message to Baruch.* Baruch, Jeremiah’s faithful scribe, has been carried off with Jeremiah to Egypt. Yet the Lord’s earlier word of blessing to him, recorded here, remains true in the midst of impending judgment on those around him. Apart from the messages against the nations (46:1—51:64), this is the end of Jeremiah’s own prophecies (see 51:64b and note). By locating this short message here, it allows the prophecy to end with words of blessing rather than cursing and shows how God’s words came true. A clay impression from the seal of a scribe named “Berechiahu, son of Neriahu” has been recovered by archaeologists. Most scholars believe this came from the seal of Jeremiah’s scribe, providing independent verification of his existence.

45:1 fourth year of Jehoiakim. 605 BC. Ch. 36 describes in more detail the burning of the scroll by Jehoiakim.

45:3 Woe to me! Like Jeremiah (see 15:10), Baruch finds the hostile reception of his message hard to bear and pronounces the covenant curse on himself (cf. Isa 6:5). Yet at a time when the Lord is overthrowing what he built and uprooting what he planted (v. 4), is any other reception likely? The servant is not greater than the master: if they rejected the Lord, they will reject his servants also (John 15:20).

45:5 At a time when the Lord is bringing “disaster on all people,” Baruch should not expect to see “great things” for himself, whether in terms of a responsive audience and personal popularity or great deliverances by the Lord. Baruch is living in a “day of small things” (Zech 4:10), a time in which it is a remarkable blessing for him merely to “escape with [his] life” (v. 5), the same promise given to Ebed-Melek (39:18).

46:1—51:64 *Messages Against the Nations.* Like other prophets (e.g., Ezek 25–32), Jeremiah delivers a series of messages against the nations around God’s people. These are not necessarily intended to be delivered exclusively to these nations, however; the messages are far more for God’s own people, reminding them of the Lord’s sovereignty over the whole world. The Lord raises nations up for his own purposes and then brings them down in turn. In addition, these messages often declare judgment on the nations for their assault on God’s people, reassuring them that the negative aspect of the Abrahamic covenant is still in place: “whoever curses you I will curse” (Gen 12:3). Even though the nations came against Judah at the Lord’s direction, they brought their own agendas and will pay the price for their enmity toward Israel and Judah.

46:1–28 *A Message About Egypt.* Since chs. 42–44 end with Jews who are fleeing to Egypt taking Jeremiah there, it is fitting that the message against Egypt comes first.

46:1 concerning the nations. This covers chs. 46–51 (cf. 1:5).

46:2 fourth year of Jehoiakim. 605 BC; the date links this passage to ch. 45. Pharaoh Necho defeated and killed King Josiah at Megiddo in 609 BC (2 Kgs 23:29–30) and for a brief period controlled Judah. The Babylonians defeat him in 605 BC at the battle of Carchemish. Subsequently, the Judahites become vassals of the Babylonians, yet they continue to harbor hope for help from the Egyptians, hopes that the prophets declare are futile (e.g., Ezek 29).

46:3–5 The extensive preparations of the Egyptians for battle are in vain. They have all of the necessary military equipment (“shields … horses … helmets … spears … armor,” vv. 3–4), but they end up retreating in disarray (v. 5).

46:5 [v] ver 21 [w] Jer 49:29
46:6 [x] Isa 30:16 [y] ver 12, 16; Da 11:19
46:7 [z] Jer 47:2
46:9 [a] Jer 47:3 [b] Isa 66:19
46:10 [c] Joel 1:15 [d] Dt 32:42 [e] Zep 1:7
46:11 [f] Jer 8:22 [g] Isa 47:1 [h] Jer 30:13; Mic 1:9
46:12 [i] Isa 19:4; Na 3:8-10
46:13 [j] Isa 19:1
46:14 [k] Jer 43:8

They flee[v] in haste
without looking back,
and there is terror[w] on every side,"
declares the LORD.
6 "The swift cannot flee[x]
nor the strong escape.
In the north by the River Euphrates
they stumble and fall.[y]

7 "Who is this that rises like the Nile,
like rivers of surging waters?[z]
8 Egypt rises like the Nile,
like rivers of surging waters.
She says, 'I will rise and cover the earth;
I will destroy cities and their people.'
9 Charge, you horses!
Drive furiously, you charioteers![a]
March on, you warriors — men of Cush[a] and Put who carry shields,
men of Lydia[b] who draw the bow.
10 But that day[c] belongs to the Lord, the LORD Almighty —
a day of vengeance, for vengeance on his foes.
The sword will devour[d] till it is satisfied,
till it has quenched its thirst with blood.
For the Lord, the LORD Almighty, will offer sacrifice[e]
in the land of the north by the River Euphrates.

11 "Go up to Gilead and get balm,[f]
Virgin[g] Daughter Egypt.
But you try many medicines in vain;
there is no healing[h] for you.
12 The nations will hear of your shame;
your cries will fill the earth.
One warrior will stumble over another;
both will fall[i] down together."

13 This is the message the LORD spoke to Jeremiah the prophet about the coming of Nebuchadnezzar king of Babylon to attack Egypt:[j]

14 "Announce this in Egypt, and proclaim it in Migdol;
proclaim it also in Memphis and Tahpanhes:[k]

[a] 9 That is, the upper Nile region

46:6 swift ... strong. This proves the dictum of Eccl 9:11: "The race is not to the swift or the battle to the strong." The reason for their defeat is that the Lord is against them, inducing "terror on every side" (v. 5), as he earlier did to his own people (6:25).
46:7–8 Every year the Nile rises and overflows its banks, surging across the countryside. In the same way, Egypt seeks to rise and cover the earth.
46:9 horses ... charioteers. Elite troops. **men of Cush ... Put ... Lydia.** Mercenaries. **Cush.** Southern Egypt; modern Sudan. **Put ... Lydia.** These locations are debated, ranging from Somalia to Libya to Asia Minor. More important, they were recognized sources of hired soldiers (Isa 66:19; Ezek 27:10; 30:5).
46:10 Egypt's ambitions will be frustrated at Carchemish, for "that day belongs to the Lord" as a "day of vengeance" on Egypt, a day when the sword will quench "its thirst with blood." **that day.** The "day of the LORD" is the time when he saves his people and judges their enemies (see note on Amos 2:16). Both salvation and judgment are sure and certain, but they may be carried out at different times and in different stages. **offer sacrifice.** A victory feast. **land of the north.** Babylon.
46:11 Gilead. Just as Judah earlier sought in vain for "balm in Gilead" (8:22), though it was famed for its medicines, so now Egypt will find no remedy. **Virgin Daughter.** See note on 14:17, where the title describes the Lord's people.
46:13–17 Ezek 29:17–21 also describes Nebuchadnezzar's attack on Egypt the year after the 605 BC battle of Carchemish.
46:14 Migdol ... Memphis ... Tahpanhes. Fortified Egyptian settlements close to the northeastern border (see note on 44:1); Nebuchadnezzar's early targets. All their preparations will be unavailing, and their mercenaries (see v. 9) will decide to return to their "native lands" (v. 16).

Cushite warriors (Jer 46:9).
Frederick J. Mabie

'Take your positions and get ready,
for the sword devours those around you.'
15 Why will your warriors be laid low?
They cannot stand, for the LORD will push them down.[l]
16 They will stumble[m] repeatedly;
they will fall[n] over each other.
They will say, 'Get up, let us go back
to our own people and our native lands,
away from the sword of the oppressor.'
17 There they will exclaim,
'Pharaoh king of Egypt is only a loud noise;
he has missed his opportunity.[o]'
18 "As surely as I live," declares the King,[p]
whose name is the LORD Almighty,
"one will come who is like Tabor[q] among the mountains,
like Carmel[r] by the sea.
19 Pack your belongings for exile,[s]
you who live in Egypt,
for Memphis will be laid waste
and lie in ruins without inhabitant.

20 "Egypt is a beautiful heifer,
but a gadfly is coming
against her from the north.[t]

46:15 [l] Isa 66:15-16
46:16 [m] Lev 26:37 [n] ver 6
46:17 [o] Isa 19:11-16
46:18 [p] Jer 48:15 [q] Jos 19:22 [r] 1Ki 18:42
46:19 [s] Isa 20:4
46:20 [t] ver 24; Jer 47:2

46:15 your warriors … cannot stand. Against the might of the Lord.
46:17 Pharaoh could talk impressively, but he could not back it up with actions: there is a pun between the Egyptian name of Pharaoh Hophra and the Hebrew phrase "he has missed his opportunity."
46:18–24 Hophra might be king of Egypt, but the Lord is the true "King" (v. 18).
46:18 the King. The Lord. **LORD Almighty.** A title that focuses on God's power. The Lord swears on oath ("As surely as I live") that he will bring an opponent against Egypt who will overshadow Egypt as comprehensively as Mount Tabor and Mount Carmel rise impressively above their surroundings in Israel.
46:19 Memphis, Egypt's capital; it will be left as desolate as Judah's capital, Jerusalem (see 9:12).
46:20 heifer. A young female cow; may be an ironic comment on Egypt's real weakness: they are nothing like the powerful bull that depicts their god Apis.

46:21 [u]2Ki 7:6 [v]ver 5 [w]Ps 37:13
46:23 [x]Jdg 7:12
46:24 [y]Jer 1:15
46:25 [z]Eze 30:14; Na 3:8 [a]Jer 43:12 [b]Isa 20:6
46:26 [c]Jer 44:30 [d]Eze 32:11 [e]Eze 29:11-16
46:27 [f]Isa 41:13; 43:5 [g]Isa 11:11; Jer 50:19
46:28 [h]Isa 8:9-10 [i]Jer 4:27
47:1 [j]Ge 10:19; Am 1:6; Zec 9:5-7

21 The mercenaries[u] in her ranks
are like fattened calves.
They too will turn and flee[v] together,
they will not stand their ground,
for the day[w] of disaster is coming upon them,
the time for them to be punished.
22 Egypt will hiss like a fleeing serpent
as the enemy advances in force;
they will come against her with axes,
like men who cut down trees.
23 They will chop down her forest,"
declares the LORD,
"dense though it be.
They are more numerous than locusts,[x]
they cannot be counted.
24 Daughter Egypt will be put to shame,
given into the hands of the people of the north.[y]"

25 The LORD Almighty, the God of Israel, says: "I am about to bring punishment on Amon god of
Thebes,[z] on Pharaoh, on Egypt and her gods[a] and her kings, and on those who rely[b] on Pharaoh. 26 I
will give them into the hands[c] of those who want to kill them — Nebuchadnezzar king[d] of Babylon and
his officers. Later, however, Egypt will be inhabited[e] as in times past," declares the LORD.

27 "Do not be afraid,[f] Jacob my servant;
do not be dismayed, Israel.
I will surely save you out of a distant place,
your descendants from the land of their exile.[g]
Jacob will again have peace and security,
and no one will make him afraid.
28 Do not be afraid, Jacob my servant,
for I am with you,"[h] declares the LORD.
"Though I completely destroy[i] all the nations
among which I scatter you,
I will not completely destroy you.
I will discipline you but only in due measure;
I will not let you go entirely unpunished."

A Message About the Philistines

47 This is the word of the LORD that came to Jeremiah the prophet concerning the Philistines before Pharaoh attacked Gaza:[j]

2 This is what the LORD says:

46:21 fattened calves. Egypt's mercenaries; they are ripe for the slaughter (see v. 10).
46:22 serpent. Symbol of Egypt and an emblem on the Egyptian crown. But the "serpent" will flee away, powerless against the Babylonian forces.
46:25 Amon. The patron deity of Thebes, the capital of Upper (southern) Egypt. Like Memphis, Thebes will be handed over to destruction (v. 19). Yet after this devastation, the Lord promises to restore a remnant from Egypt (v. 26), just as he promised Judah. This anticipation of hope for Egypt also occurs in Isa 19:19–25; 27:13. **Egypt and her gods.** As in the exodus, the Lord's judgment is not only upon Pharaoh and Egypt but also upon the gods of Egypt.
46:27–28 This passage is almost identical to 30:10–11. The prophecy of the destruction of Egypt is designed to encourage Judah to trust in the Lord. The day when the Lord destroys "all the nations" is full of hope for his people. God's people are being disciplined like children, not utterly destroyed like enemies. So they should bear patiently their sufferings and not be afraid that their banishment means that God has abandoned them. On the contrary, though their sojourn in the world might be difficult, like that of their forefather "Jacob" (see Gen 47:9), their ultimate destiny is to be "Israel," God's chosen people.
46:27 Jacob my servant. Recalls Isa 41:8–14; 43:1–5.
47:1–7 *A Message About the Philistines.* The Philistines are among Israel's oldest enemies. Even though they do not aid the Babylonians in their assault on Judah, the Philistines will be destroyed along with Judah. The city of Ashkelon was destroyed by Nebuchadnezzar in 604 BC.
47:1 Pharaoh. Necho; he may have attacked the Philistine city of Gaza

"See how the waters are rising in the north;[k]
they will become an overflowing torrent.
They will overflow the land and everything in it,
the towns and those who live in them.
The people will cry out;
all who dwell in the land will wail
3 at the sound of the hooves of galloping steeds,
at the noise of enemy chariots
and the rumble of their wheels.
Parents will not turn to help their children;
their hands will hang limp.
4 For the day has come
to destroy all the Philistines
and to remove all survivors
who could help Tyre[l] and Sidon.[m]
The LORD is about to destroy the Philistines,[n]
the remnant from the coasts of Caphtor.[a][o]
5 Gaza will shave[p] her head in mourning;
Ashkelon[q] will be silenced.
You remnant on the plain,
how long will you cut yourselves?

6 " 'Alas, sword[r] of the LORD,
how long till you rest?
Return to your sheath;
cease and be still.'
7 But how can it rest
when the LORD has commanded it,
when he has ordered it
to attack Ashkelon and the coast?"

47:2 [k]Isa 8:7; 14:31
47:4 [l]Am 1:9-10; Zec 9:2-4 [m]Jer 25:22 [n]Ge 10:14; Joel 3:4 [o]Dt 2:23
47:5 [p]Jer 41:5; Mic 1:16 [q]Jer 25:20
47:6 [r]Jer 12:12
48:1 [s]Nu 32:38 [t]Nu 32:37

A Message About Moab

48:29-36pp — Isa 16:6-12

48 Concerning Moab:

This is what the LORD Almighty, the God of Israel, says:

"Woe to Nebo,[s] for it will be ruined.
Kiriathaim[t] will be disgraced and captured;
the stronghold[b] will be disgraced and shattered.

[a] 4 That is, Crete [b] 1 Or *captured; / Misgab*

on several occasions, including prior to engaging Josiah at Megiddo in 609 BC and during 601 BC when he briefly recaptured some of the territory lost to Babylon.

47:2 waters ... rising in the north. Babylon, not Egypt, is the real enemy for Philistia (see notes on 1:13–14,15). The Babylonians will overflow the land, as Egypt aspired to do (see 46:8).

47:3 This vividly depicts the sounds of warfare: Babylon will utterly demoralize the Philistines so that their "hands will hang limp" and even the strongest natural bond, that between parents and their children, will be broken.

47:4 the day. Of the Lord's judgment. **Tyre and Sidon.** Phoenician cities north of Philistia; they seem to have had an alliance with Philistia. **Caphtor.** Most likely Crete (see NIV text note), the original homeland of the Sea Peoples who first settled the coastal plain.

47:5 shave her head ... cut yourselves. See note on 41:5.

47:6 sword of the LORD. The instrument of God's judgment, which cannot be sheathed until it completes its destructive work (v. 7).

48:1–47 *A Message About Moab.* Moab also has been one of Israel's enemies from the time of the exodus onward (Num 22–25). Located east of Judah on the far side of the Dead Sea, Moab does not side with Judah against Babylon in the days of Zedekiah but rebels in 582 BC, at which time Nebuchadnezzar invades it. Shortly after, Arabs overrun them, and they cease to exist as a nation.

48:1 Nebo ... Kiriathaim. Two northern towns in Moab; they will be first to experience the Babylonian invasion of Moab.

48:2 [u] Isa 16:14 [v] Nu 21:25
48:3 [w] Isa 15:5
48:5 [x] Isa 15:5
48:6 [y] Jer 17:6
48:7 [z] Nu 21:29 [a] Isa 46:1-2; Jer 49:3
48:10 [b] Jer 47:6 [c] 1Ki 20:42; 2Ki 13:15-19
48:11 [d] Zec 1:15 [e] Zep 1:12

[2] Moab will be praised[u] no more;
in Heshbon[a][v] people will plot her downfall:
'Come, let us put an end to that nation.'
You, the people of Madmen,[b] will also be silenced;
the sword will pursue you.
[3] Cries of anguish arise from Horonaim,[w]
cries of great havoc and destruction.
[4] Moab will be broken;
her little ones will cry out.[c]
[5] They go up the hill to Luhith,[x]
weeping bitterly as they go;
on the road down to Horonaim
anguished cries over the destruction are heard.
[6] Flee! Run for your lives;
become like a bush[d] in the desert.[y]
[7] Since you trust in your deeds and riches,
you too will be taken captive,
and Chemosh[z] will go into exile,[a]
together with his priests and officials.
[8] The destroyer will come against every town,
and not a town will escape.
The valley will be ruined
and the plateau destroyed,
because the LORD has spoken.
[9] Put salt on Moab,
for she will be laid waste[e];
her towns will become desolate,
with no one to live in them.

[10] "A curse on anyone who is lax in doing the LORD's work!
A curse on anyone who keeps their sword[b] from
bloodshed![c]

[11] "Moab has been at rest[d] from youth,
like wine left on its dregs,[e]
not poured from one jar to another—
she has not gone into exile.
So she tastes as she did,
and her aroma is unchanged.
[12] But days are coming,"
declares the LORD,

[a] 2 The Hebrew for *Heshbon* sounds like the Hebrew for *plot*. [b] 2 The name of the Moabite town Madmen sounds like the Hebrew for *be silenced*. [c] 4 Hebrew; Septuagint / *proclaim it to Zoar* [d] 6 Or *like Aroer* [e] 9 Or *Give wings to Moab, / for she will fly away*

48:2 Heshbon. Northeast of Mount Nebo (cf. Num 21:25–30).
48:3 Horonaim. This place is mentioned on the Moabite Stone (Mesha Stele), which dates back to the ninth century BC.
48:5 Luhith. Location unknown.
48:6 bush in the desert. Probably the juniper, a short, stubby evergreen that clings to life in marginal areas.
48:7 Chemosh. The patron deity of Moab and their northern neighbors, the Ammonites (Judg 11:24); he was known as a god who demanded human sacrifice (2 Kgs 3:27). Yet he had no power to defend his people.
48:9 salt ... laid waste. Spreading salt on captured territory as a sign of its permanent destruction is attested elsewhere (Judg 9:45) and fits well in this context.
48:10 Destroying Moab was nothing less than "doing the LORD's work."
48:11 at rest. While the surrounding nations endure invasion and exile, Moab remains secure in its remote location. **left on its dregs.** The Moabites are like wine that has been left to settle rather than carefully transferred into a new container, leaving the dregs behind. But to adjust the metaphor, they will not be poured from "one jar to another" in order to mature properly; rather, the invaders will "empty her pitchers" and "smash her jars" (v. 12), destroying Moab's entire community.

"when I will send men who pour from pitchers,
and they will pour her out;
they will empty her pitchers
and smash her jars.
13 Then Moab will be ashamed[f] of Chemosh,
as Israel was ashamed
when they trusted in Bethel.

14 "How can you say, 'We are warriors,[g]
men valiant in battle'?
15 Moab will be destroyed and her towns invaded;
her finest young men will go down in the slaughter,[h]"
declares the King,[i] whose name is the LORD Almighty.[j]
16 "The fall of Moab is at hand;[k]
her calamity will come quickly.
17 Mourn for her, all who live around her,
all who know her fame;
say, 'How broken is the mighty scepter,
how broken the glorious staff!'

18 "Come down from your glory
and sit on the parched ground,[l]
you inhabitants of Daughter Dibon,[m]
for the one who destroys Moab
will come up against you
and ruin your fortified cities.[n]
19 Stand by the road and watch,
you who live in Aroer.[o]
Ask the man fleeing and the woman escaping,
ask them, 'What has happened?'
20 Moab is disgraced, for she is shattered.
Wail[p] and cry out!
Announce by the Arnon[q]
that Moab is destroyed.
21 Judgment has come to the plateau —
to Holon, Jahzah[r] and Mephaath,[s]
22 to Dibon,[t] Nebo and Beth Diblathaim,
23 to Kiriathaim, Beth Gamul and Beth Meon,[u]
24 to Kerioth[v] and Bozrah —
to all the towns of Moab, far and near.
25 Moab's horn[a][w] is cut off;
her arm[x] is broken,"
declares the LORD.

26 "Make her drunk,[y]
for she has defied the LORD.

48:13 [f] Hos 10:6
48:14 [g] Ps 33:16
48:15 [h] Jer 50:27 [i] Jer 46:18 [j] Jer 51:57
48:16 [k] Isa 13:22
48:18 [l] Isa 47:1 [m] Nu 21:30; Jos 13:9 [n] ver 8
48:19 [o] Dt 2:36
48:20 [p] Isa 16:7 [q] Nu 21:13
48:21 [r] Nu 21:23; Isa 15:4 [s] Jos 13:18
48:22 [t] Jos 13:9,17
48:23 [u] Jos 13:17
48:24 [v] Am 2:2
48:25 [w] Ps 75:10 [x] Ps 10:15; Eze 30:21
48:26 [y] Jer 25:16,27

[a] 25 *Horn* here symbolizes strength.

48:13 The result will be that Moab will abandon trust in their god Chemosh, just as the northern kingdom of Israel became ashamed of their confidence in the high place that Jeroboam set up at Bethel (1 Kgs 12:26–33).

48:14–16 This disaster will come in spite of Moab's confidence in their "warriors" (v. 14). Like Egypt, they will discover the emptiness of military might (46:3–6) when pitted against the sovereign decree of the King, the Lord Almighty (46:18).

48:17 Mourn for her. The nations around Moab are called to join in mourning for her. A call to mourn for someone who has not yet died is a rhetorical device to affirm the utter certainty of the prophecy of their doom (cf. Ezek 19). **mighty scepter ... glorious staff!** Symbols of Moab's power. They will be broken, leaving Moab utterly defenseless.

48:25 horn is cut off. Another symbol of Moab's broken power (see note on v. 17). **horn.** See NIV text note.

48:27 [z] Jer 2:26 [a] Job 16:4; Jer 18:16 [b] Mic 7:8-10
48:28 [c] Ps 55:6-7 [d] Jdg 6:2
48:29 [e] Job 40:12; Isa 16:6
48:31 [f] Isa 15:5-8 [g] 2Ki 3:25
48:32 [h] Isa 16:8-9
48:33 [i] Isa 16:10 [j] Joel 1:12
48:34 [k] Nu 32:3 [l] Isa 15:4 [m] Ge 13:10 [n] Isa 15:5 [o] Isa 15:6
48:35 [p] Isa 15:2; 16:12 [q] Jer 11:13

Let Moab wallow in her vomit;
let her be an object of ridicule.
27 Was not Israel the object of your ridicule?[z]
Was she caught among thieves,
that you shake your head[a] in scorn[b]
whenever you speak of her?
28 Abandon your towns and dwell among the rocks,
you who live in Moab.
Be like a dove[c] that makes its nest
at the mouth of a cave.[d]
29 "We have heard of Moab's pride[e] —
how great is her arrogance! —
of her insolence, her pride, her conceit
and the haughtiness of her heart.
30 I know her insolence but it is futile,"
declares the LORD,
"and her boasts accomplish nothing.
31 Therefore I wail[f] over Moab,
for all Moab I cry out,
I moan for the people of Kir Hareseth.[g]
32 I weep for you, as Jazer weeps,
you vines of Sibmah.[h]
Your branches spread as far as the sea*[a]*;
they reached as far as*[b]* Jazer.
The destroyer has fallen
on your ripened fruit and grapes.
33 Joy and gladness are gone
from the orchards and fields of Moab.
I have stopped the flow of wine[i] from the presses;
no one treads them with shouts of joy.[j]
Although there are shouts,
they are not shouts of joy.
34 "The sound of their cry rises
from Heshbon to Elealeh[k] and Jahaz,[l]
from Zoar[m] as far as Horonaim[n] and Eglath
Shelishiyah,
for even the waters of Nimrim are dried up.[o]
35 In Moab I will put an end
to those who make offerings on the high places[p]
and burn incense[q] to their gods,"
declares the LORD.

a 32 Probably the Dead Sea *b* 32 Two Hebrew manuscripts and Septuagint; most Hebrew manuscripts *as far as the Sea of*

48:27 ridicule. Moab ridiculed the sufferings of Israel. **caught among thieves.** Moab suggested that Judah's fate was purely the result of the Judahites' own folly. The Lord will make Moab herself the object of ridicule by making her "drunk" (v. 26), just as he made Judah drink the cup of his wrath (see 25:15–38 and note).
48:29 arrogance ... insolence ... pride ... conceit ... haughtiness. Resulted from Moab's confidence in its safety and strength (see Isa 25:10–11; Zeph 2:8–10).
48:31 I wail over Moab. The prophet himself joins in the mourning song for Moab.
48:32 Jazer ... Sibmah. At the northern end of the Dead Sea; famous for their vineyards and orchards, but these would be destroyed.
48:33 shouts. The shouts that resound will no longer be the joyful shouts of people treading the grapes but rather the fierce shouts of battle.
48:35 put an end to those who make offerings on the high places and burn incense to their gods. The goal of Moab's destruction; the same reason the Lord will destroy Judah (17:3).

[36] "So my heart laments[r] for Moab like the music of a pipe;
it laments like a pipe for the people of Kir Hareseth.
The wealth they acquired[s] is gone.
[37] Every head is shaved[t]
and every beard cut off;
every hand is slashed
and every waist is covered with sackcloth.[u]
[38] On all the roofs in Moab
and in the public squares
there is nothing but mourning,
for I have broken Moab
like a jar[v] that no one wants,"
declares the LORD.
[39] "How shattered she is! How they wail!
How Moab turns her back in shame!
Moab has become an object of ridicule,
an object of horror to all those around her."

[40] This is what the LORD says:

"Look! An eagle is swooping[w] down,
spreading its wings[x] over Moab.
[41] Kerioth[a] will be captured
and the strongholds taken.
In that day the hearts of Moab's warriors
will be like the heart of a woman in labor.[y]
[42] Moab will be destroyed[z] as a nation[a]
because she defied[b] the LORD.
[43] Terror and pit and snare[c] await you,
you people of Moab,"
declares the LORD.
[44] "Whoever flees[d] from the terror
will fall into a pit,
whoever climbs out of the pit
will be caught in a snare;
for I will bring on Moab
the year[e] of her punishment,"
declares the LORD.

[45] "In the shadow of Heshbon
the fugitives stand helpless,
for a fire has gone out from Heshbon,
a blaze from the midst of Sihon;[f]
it burns the foreheads of Moab,
the skulls[g] of the noisy boasters.
[46] Woe to you, Moab![h]
The people of Chemosh are destroyed;

48:36 [r] Isa 16:11 [s] Isa 15:7
48:37 [t] Isa 15:2; Jer 41:5 [u] Ge 37:34
48:38 [v] Jer 22:28
48:40 [w] Dt 28:49; Hab 1:8 [x] Isa 8:8
48:41 [y] Isa 21:3
48:42 [z] Ps 83:4; Isa 16:14 [a] ver 2 [b] ver 26
48:43 [c] Isa 24:17
48:44 [d] 1Ki 19:17; Isa 24:18 [e] Jer 11:23
48:45 [f] Nu 21:21,26-28 [g] Nu 24:17
48:46 [h] Nu 21:29

[a] 41 Or *The cities*

48:36 music of a pipe. Often accompanied mourning (e.g., Job 30:31).
48:37 A reference to various mourning practices (see note on 41:5).
48:38–39 See 19:11; 22:28.
48:40 eagle. Often represents the threat of foreign powers in the prophetic books (Ezek 17:3; Hab 1:8).
48:42 she defied the LORD. The reason for Moab's fate. No one can escape the Lord's wrath.
48:44 fall into a pit. Like hunted animals. If they escape the pit, they will be taken in a "snare."

48:47 [i] Jer 12:15; 49:6,39
49:1 [j] Am 1:13; Zep 2:8-9
49:2 [k] Jer 4:19 [l] Dt 3:11 [m] Isa 14:2; Eze 21:28-32; 25:2-11
49:3 [n] Jos 8:28 [o] Jer 48:7
49:4 [p] Jer 9:23; 1Ti 6:17 [q] Jer 21:13

your sons are taken into exile
and your daughters into captivity.
47 "Yet I will restore[i] the fortunes of Moab
in days to come,"
declares the LORD.

Here ends the judgment on Moab.

A Message About Ammon

49 Concerning the Ammonites:[j]

This is what the LORD says:

"Has Israel no sons?
Has Israel no heir?
Why then has Molek[a] taken possession of Gad?
Why do his people live in its towns?
2 But the days are coming,"
declares the LORD,
"when I will sound the battle cry[k]
against Rabbah[l] of the Ammonites;
it will become a mound of ruins,
and its surrounding villages will be set on fire.
Then Israel will drive out
those who drove her out,[m]"
says the LORD.

3 "Wail, Heshbon, for Ai[n] is destroyed!
Cry out, you inhabitants of Rabbah!
Put on sackcloth and mourn;
rush here and there inside the walls,
for Molek will go into exile,[o]
together with his priests and officials.
4 Why do you boast of your valleys,
boast of your valleys so fruitful?
Unfaithful Daughter Ammon,
you trust in your riches[p] and say,
'Who will attack me?'[q]
5 I will bring terror on you
from all those around you,"
declares the Lord, the LORD Almighty.

[a] *1* Or *their king*; also in verse 3

48:47 There will be a day when the Lord "will restore the fortunes of Moab" (cf. Egypt in 46:26). Even Moab can repent and be added to the kingdom of the Lord.
49:1–6 *A Message About Ammon.* The Ammonites are Moab's northern neighbors and have been Israel's enemies since the time of the exodus (Judg 11:15–27). They too will face coming destruction.
49:1 Molek. The god of the Ammonites. The name may combine the consonants of *melek* ("king"; see NIV text note) with the vowels of *bōšet* ("shame"), which is elsewhere substituted for the name of the god Baal (see, e.g., 2 Sam 2:8; 1 Chr 8:33 and text note). **Gad.** An Israelite tribe that settled east of the Jordan River at the time of the conquest (see Num 32). Since the Lord gave the land to them, it should have been passed on to their offspring as an inalienable inheritance, but the Ammonites took it over after the Assyrian invasion of 734–732 BC, claiming that it belonged to their god, Molek.
49:2 Rabbah. The capital city of the Ammonites. It will be reduced to ruins, allowing the Israelites to reclaim their old heritage.
49:3 Heshbon. On the border between Moab and Ammon, which accounts for its appearing in both messages (48:2; 49:3). **Ai.** Not the same as the village destroyed in Josh 7, which was close to Jericho. The judgment is not merely on Ammon but also on their god, Molek, who will "go into exile" with Ammon. The gods of the nations were regional deities, unlike the Lord, who is the God of the whole earth.
49:5 terror on you from all those around you. Recalls the refrain "Terror on every side" (6:25; 20:3; 46:5).

"Every one of you will be driven away,
and no one will gather the fugitives.

6 "Yet afterward, I will restore[r] the fortunes of the Ammonites,"
declares the LORD.

A Message About Edom

49:9-10pp — Ob 5-6
49:14-16pp — Ob 1-4

7 Concerning Edom:[s]

This is what the LORD Almighty says:

"Is there no longer wisdom in Teman?[t]
Has counsel perished from the prudent?
Has their wisdom decayed?
8 Turn and flee, hide in deep caves,
you who live in Dedan,[u]
for I will bring disaster on Esau
at the time when I punish him.
9 If grape pickers came to you,
would they not leave a few grapes?
If thieves came during the night,
would they not steal only as much as they wanted?
10 But I will strip Esau bare;
I will uncover his hiding places,
so that he cannot conceal himself.
His armed men are destroyed,
also his allies and neighbors,
so there is no one[v] to say,
11 'Leave your fatherless children;[w] I will keep them alive.
Your widows too can depend on me.' "

12 This is what the LORD says: "If those who do not deserve to drink the cup[x] must drink it, why should
you go unpunished?[y] You will not go unpunished, but must drink it. 13 I swear[z] by myself," declares
the LORD, "that Bozrah[a] will become a ruin and a curse,[a] an object of horror and reproach; and all its
towns will be in ruins forever."

14 I have heard a message from the LORD;
an envoy was sent to the nations to say,

49:6 [r] ver 39; Jer 48:47
49:7 [s] Ge 25:30; Eze 25:12 [t] Ge 36:11, 15,34
49:8 [u] Jer 25:23
49:10 [v] Mal 1:2-5
49:11 [w] Hos 14:3
49:12 [x] Jer 25:15 [y] Jer 25:28-29
49:13 [z] Ge 22:16 [a] Ge 36:33; Isa 34:6

[a] *13* That is, its name will be used in cursing (see 29:22); or, others will see that it is cursed.

49:6 In the end, God will restore the fortunes of Ammon just as he promised to do for Egypt (46:26) and Moab (48:47). This theme is important to the prophet's Judahite hearers: if God will restore Ammon, Moab, and Egypt after destroying them, how much more will that be the case for Israel and Judah?

49:7–22 *A Message About Edom.* The Edomites seem to have celebrated with joy and even participated in Judah's downfall at the hands of Nebuchadnezzar (Obad 13–14), for which reason they are sometimes singled out for judgment messages (the book of Obadiah, e.g., shares much in common with this passage).

49:7–8 Teman … Dedan. Represent the northern and southern limits of Edom, respectively (Ezek 25:13), so a disaster that strikes both will engulf the whole land.

49:7 Edom. The Edomites were the descendants of "Esau" (v. 8), Jacob's brother, who was also known as "Edom" (Gen 25:30). The Edomites lived in the region to the south and east of the Dead Sea, and by the time of Jeremiah they had expanded northwest from there into Judahite territory. **wisdom.** The link between Edom and wisdom also occurs in Obad 8.

49:9 grape pickers … thieves. Metaphors virtually identical to Obad 5. The point of the metaphors: while both of these groups will take everything of value, they will usually leave something behind. Not so when the Babylonians come: the destruction will be so complete that there will be no intact families to whom the many widows and fatherless can look for support.

49:12 drink the cup. Drinking the cup of the Lord's wrath is a common image in the prophetic books (25:15–17; Isa 51:17–23), but the idea of it being given to those who do not deserve it is unusual. Perhaps it reflects the fact that the Lord's faithful followers (like Jeremiah and Baruch) share the exile's judgment and pain with those who actively opposed God. If these people share the pain in Judah, why should the actively wicked outside their borders escape unpunished? Lam 4:21 also refers to the cup coming to Edom.

49:13 Bozrah. The capital of Edom; it will be destroyed, like the chief cities of its neighbors.

49:14–16 These verses are very similar to Obad 1–4.

49:16 [b]Job 39:27; Am 9:2
49:17 [c]ver 13 [d]Jer 50:13; Eze 35:7
49:18 [e]Ge 19:24; Dt 29:23 [f]ver 33
49:19 [g]Jer 12:5 [h]Jer 50:44
49:20 [i]Isa 14:27 [j]Jer 50:45
49:21 [k]Eze 26:15 [l]Jer 50:46; Eze 26:18
49:22 [m]Hos 8:1 [n]Isa 13:8; Jer 48:40-41
49:23 [o]Ge 14:15; 2Ch 16:2; Ac 9:2 [p]Isa 10:9; Am 6:2; Zec 9:2 [q]2Ki 18:34

"Assemble yourselves to attack it!
Rise up for battle!"

15 "Now I will make you small among the nations,
despised by mankind.
16 The terror you inspire
and the pride of your heart have deceived you,
you who live in the clefts of the rocks,
who occupy the heights of the hill.
Though you build your nest[b] as high as the eagle's,
from there I will bring you down,"
declares the LORD.

17 "Edom will become an object of horror;[c]
all who pass by will be appalled and will scoff
because of all its wounds.[d]
18 As Sodom and Gomorrah[e] were overthrown,
along with their neighboring towns,"
says the LORD,
"so no one will live there;
no people will dwell[f] in it.

19 "Like a lion coming up from Jordan's thickets[g]
to a rich pastureland,
I will chase Edom from its land in an instant.
Who is the chosen one I will appoint for this?
Who is like me and who can challenge me?[h]
And what shepherd can stand against me?"
20 Therefore, hear what the LORD has planned against Edom,
what he has purposed[i] against those who live in Teman:
The young of the flock[j] will be dragged away;
their pasture will be appalled at their fate.
21 At the sound of their fall the earth will tremble;[k]
their cry[l] will resound to the Red Sea.[a]
22 Look! An eagle will soar and swoop[m] down,
spreading its wings over Bozrah.
In that day the hearts of Edom's warriors
will be like the heart of a woman in labor.[n]

A Message About Damascus

23 Concerning Damascus:[o]

"Hamath[p] and Arpad[q] are dismayed,
for they have heard bad news.

[a] 21 Or *the Sea of Reeds*

49:16 Much of Edom's confidence came from its inaccessible rocky location: in some cases, like the ancient city of Petra, the Edomites literally lived "in the clefts of the rocks." But this will not save them from the Lord's judgment.
49:18 Sodom and Gomorrah. These archetypal wicked cities that faced destruction (Gen 19:24–25) were geographically not far away from the territory of Edom.
49:19 lion. In Bible times, lions were found in the lush thickets around the Jordan River and were a constant threat to shepherds (1 Sam 17:37; Amos 3:12). In 4:7, the lion represents Nebuchadnezzar, but here it represents the one who sent Nebuchadnezzar: the Lord himself. Who is like him or can stand against him?
49:22 Almost exactly parallel to 48:40–41; however, unlike the other nations, there is no mention of restoration for Edom (cf. 46:26; 48:47).
49:23–27 *A Message About Damascus.* Damascus was the capital of Aram, to the north of Israel. Babylon will destroy Aram like the rest of Israel's neighbors. Since Aram was at a distance from Judah, the Arameans were not usually an immediate threat. But in the days of Isaiah, an alliance between the northern kingdom of Israel and Aram sought to invade Judah and replace King Ahaz of Judah with a puppet king (Isa 7).

They are disheartened,
troubled like[a] the restless sea.[r]
24 Damascus has become feeble,
she has turned to flee
and panic has gripped her;
anguish and pain have seized her,
pain like that of a woman in labor.
25 Why has the city of renown not been abandoned,
the town in which I delight?
26 Surely, her young men will fall in the streets;
all her soldiers will be silenced[s] in that day,"
declares the LORD Almighty.
27 "I will set fire[t] to the walls of Damascus;
it will consume the fortresses of Ben-Hadad.[u]"

A Message About Kedar and Hazor

28 Concerning Kedar[v] and the kingdoms of Hazor, which Nebuchadnezzar king of Babylon attacked:

This is what the LORD says:

"Arise, and attack Kedar
and destroy the people of the East.[w]
29 Their tents and their flocks will be taken;
their shelters will be carried off
with all their goods and camels.
People will shout to them,
'Terror[x] on every side!'

30 "Flee quickly away!
Stay in deep caves, you who live in Hazor,"
declares the LORD.
"Nebuchadnezzar king of Babylon has plotted against you;
he has devised a plan against you.

31 "Arise and attack a nation at ease,
which lives in confidence,"
declares the LORD,
"a nation that has neither gates nor bars;[y]
its people live far from danger.
32 Their camels will become plunder,
and their large herds will be spoils of war.
I will scatter to the winds those who are in distant places[b][z]
and will bring disaster on them from every side,"
declares the LORD.

49:23 [r] Ge 49:4; Isa 57:20
49:26 [s] Jer 50:30
49:27 [t] Jer 43:12; Am 1:4 [u] 1Ki 15:18
49:28 [v] Ge 25:13 [w] Jdg 6:3
49:29 [x] Jer 6:25; 46:5
49:31 [y] Eze 38:11
49:32 [z] Jer 9:26

[a] 23 Hebrew *on* or *by* [b] 32 Or *who clip the hair by their foreheads*

49:23 Hamath and Arpad. North of Damascus; they would be first to experience the assault of an invader from the north.
49:27 Ben-Hadad. Not a personal name but the title of the ruler of Aram, meaning "the son of [the storm-god] Hadad" (cf. 1 Kgs 15:18; 20:1; 2 Kgs 6:24; 13:3). The last part of v. 27 echoes Amos 1:4.
49:28–33 *A Message About Kedar and Hazor.* Kedar was a nomadic tribe of shepherds who lived in the Arabian desert, east of the Ammonites. This Hazor was a collection of villages or nomadic tribes in the desert, not the town in northern Israel. Nebuchadnezzar conducted a campaign in this region in 599/598 BC.
49:28 the people of the East. The nomadic desert tribes.
49:29 tents ... flocks ... camels. Sources of wealth for nomads. **Terror on every side!** They will experience the same terror as the other victims of the Babylonians (6:25; 20:3; 46:5).
49:30 plotted ... devised a plan against you. Just as the Lord did against Jerusalem (18:11). Yet even though it is Nebuchadnezzar's plan, he can do nothing apart from God's purpose.
49:31 a nation that has neither gates nor bars. Since these people were nomads, there were no significant cities to sack.
49:32 bring disaster on them from every side. Sums up the Lord's purpose.

49:33 [a] Jer 10:22 [b] ver 18; Jer 51:37
49:34 [c] Ge 10:22 [d] 2Ki 24:18
49:35 [e] Isa 22:6
49:36 [f] ver 32
49:37 [g] Jer 30:24 [h] Jer 9:16
49:39 [i] Jer 48:47
50:1 [j] Ge 10:10; Isa 13:1
50:2 [k] Jer 4:16

33 "Hazor will become a haunt of jackals,
a desolate[a] place forever.
No one will live there;
no people will dwell[b] in it."

A Message About Elam

34 This is the word of the LORD that came to Jeremiah the prophet concerning Elam,[c] early in the
reign of Zedekiah[d] king of Judah:

35 This is what the LORD Almighty says:

"See, I will break the bow[e] of Elam,
the mainstay of their might.
36 I will bring against Elam the four winds[f]
from the four quarters of heaven;
I will scatter them to the four winds,
and there will not be a nation
where Elam's exiles do not go.
37 I will shatter Elam before their foes,
before those who want to kill them;
I will bring disaster on them,
even my fierce anger,"[g]

declares the LORD.

"I will pursue them with the sword[h]
until I have made an end of them.
38 I will set my throne in Elam
and destroy her king and officials,"

declares the LORD.

39 "Yet I will restore[i] the fortunes of Elam
in days to come,"

declares the LORD.

A Message About Babylon

51:15-19pp — Jer 10:12-16

50 This is the word the LORD spoke through Jeremiah the prophet concerning Babylon[j] and the land of the Babylonians[a]:

2 "Announce and proclaim[k] among the nations,
lift up a banner and proclaim it;
keep nothing back, but say,

[a] *1* Or *Chaldeans*; also in verses 8, 25, 35 and 45

49:33 jackals. Known to haunt desert ruins (cf. Mal 1:3).

49:34–39 *A Message About Elam.* Elam, an ancient kingdom southeast of Babylon, was brought under Assyrian control during the days of Ashurbanipal (669–627 BC) before regaining its independence. That freedom did not last: it was brought under the yoke of the Babylonians in ca. 594 BC.

49:34 early in the reign of Zedekiah. Zedekiah began his reign in 597 BC. Unlike the other messages against the nations, this message is dated. At this time, Elam is a source of hope for those in Judah who believe that Babylonian power will soon come to an end, resulting in a swift return of those who had been exiled there (28:1–4). Jeremiah's words in this message, like those in his other messages, show that hope to be empty.

49:35 bow. The symbol of Elam's strength, since they were noted for their archers.

49:36 the four winds. All four points of the compass; they will be utterly destroyed before Nebuchadnezzar.

49:38 set my throne. The defeat of Elam and its allies by the Babylonians will not be on account of the strength of the Babylonian god Marduk. It will be the means by which the Lord will "set [his] throne in Elam." Pagan powers cannot triumph without the express permission and direction of the sovereign Lord of the universe.

49:39 Like Egypt (46:26), Moab (48:47), and Ammon (49:6), the Lord will "restore" Elam after destroying them. The God who uproots and tears down also plants and builds (1:10).

50:1—51:64 *A Message About Babylon.* The last and longest message against the nations is reserved for Babylon. The Lord will in due course bring low and punish the nation that he raised up and used to judge the other nations, including Judah, because the Babylonians are arrogant

'Babylon will be captured;[l]
Bel[m] will be put to shame,
Marduk[n] filled with terror.
Her images will be put to shame
and her idols filled with terror.'
3 A nation from the north will attack her
and lay waste her land.
No one will live[o] in it;
both people and animals[p] will flee away.

4 "In those days, at that time,"
declares the LORD,
"the people of Israel and the people of Judah together[q]
will go in tears[r] to seek[s] the LORD their God.
5 They will ask the way to Zion
and turn their faces toward it.
They will come[t] and bind themselves to the LORD
in an everlasting covenant[u]
that will not be forgotten.

6 "My people have been lost sheep;[v]
their shepherds have led them astray
and caused them to roam on the mountains.
They wandered over mountain and hill[w]
and forgot their own resting place.[x]
7 Whoever found them devoured them;
their enemies said, 'We are not guilty,[y]
for they sinned against the LORD, their verdant pasture,
the LORD, the hope[z] of their ancestors.'

8 "Flee[a] out of Babylon;
leave the land of the Babylonians,
and be like the goats that lead the flock.
9 For I will stir up and bring against Babylon
an alliance of great nations from the land of the north.
They will take up their positions against her,
and from the north she will be captured.
Their arrows will be like skilled warriors
who do not return empty-handed.

50:2 [l] Jer 51:31 [m] Isa 46:1 [n] Jer 51:47
50:3 [o] ver 13; Isa 14:22-23 [p] Zep 1:3
50:4 [q] Jer 3:18; Hos 1:11 [r] Ezr 3:12; Jer 31:9 [s] Hos 3:5
50:5 [t] Jer 33:7 [u] Isa 55:3; Jer 32:40; Heb 8:6-10
50:6 [v] Isa 53:6; Mt 9:36; 10:6 [w] Jer 3:6; Eze 34:6 [x] ver 19
50:7 [y] Jer 2:3 [z] Jer 14:8
50:8 [a] Isa 48:20; Jer 51:6; Rev 18:4

and cruel. As prophesied, Babylon fell in 539 BC to an alliance of the Medes and the Persians (Dan 5:30).

50:2 Bel ... Marduk. The gods of Babylon, to whom the Babylonians attribute their great victories. Yet they are nothing more than "images" and "idols," unable to protect their people from the "shame" and "terror" they had inflicted on other nations.

50:3 A nation from the north. In the book of Jeremiah, this usually indicates Babylon coming to attack Judah (e.g., 1:13–15 and notes on 1:13–14,15), but here it ironically refers to the Medes and Persians, who will destroy Babylon.

50:4 the people of Israel and the people of Judah together. See 31:31. The Lord does not direct these messages primarily to the nations about which he speaks; rather, the news of the impending fall of Babylon is good news for his people, who in those days "will go in tears [of repentance] to seek the LORD."

50:5 turn ... come ... bind. God's people will return to the site of the temple on Mount Zion and "bind themselves to the LORD in an everlasting covenant" (cf. 32:37–40). Unlike the old covenant, which the people broke (31:32), this one "will not be forgotten": the law will now be written on their hearts (31:33).

50:6 God's people were previously "lost sheep," led astray by bad "shepherds" (see 23:1,2 and note).

50:7 Enemies freely assaulted God's people and claimed the people's sins "against the LORD" as the reason for their actions (40:2–3). Yet the location of this message within the message against Babylon shows that the Lord does not accept that argument. Even though he judged Israel and Judah for their sins, their enemies are still culpable under the terms of the Abrahamic covenant (Gen 12:2–3), which was "the hope of their ancestors."

50:8 Flee ... leave. When the day of judgment against Babylon comes, it will be time for the remnant of God's people to go back to Judah (Isa 48:20; Zech 2:6; Rev 18:4).

50:9–10 The Lord will bring against Babylon "an alliance of great nations from the land of the north" (see note on v. 3) that will "plunder" Babylon as they once "plundered" others (20:5).

50:11 [b] Isa 47:6
50:13 [c] Jer 18:16 [d] Jer 49:17
50:14 [e] ver 29,42
50:15 [f] Jer 51:14 [g] Jer 51:44,58 [h] Jer 51:6 [i] Ps 137:8; Rev 18:6
50:16 [j] Jer 25:38 [k] Isa 13:14 [l] Jer 51:9
50:17 [m] Jer 2:15 [n] 2Ki 17:6 [o] 2Ki 24:10,14 [p] 2Ki 25:7
50:18 [q] Isa 10:12 [r] Eze 31:3
50:19 [s] Jer 31:10; Eze 34:13

10 So Babylonia[a] will be plundered;
all who plunder her will have their fill,"
declares the LORD.

11 "Because you rejoice and are glad,
you who pillage my inheritance,[b]
because you frolic like a heifer threshing grain
and neigh like stallions,
12 your mother will be greatly ashamed;
she who gave you birth will be disgraced.
She will be the least of the nations —
a wilderness, a dry land, a desert.
13 Because of the LORD's anger she will not be inhabited
but will be completely desolate.
All who pass Babylon will be appalled;
they will scoff[c] because of all her wounds.[d]

14 "Take up your positions around Babylon,
all you who draw the bow.[e]
Shoot at her! Spare no arrows,
for she has sinned against the LORD.
15 Shout[f] against her on every side!
She surrenders, her towers fall,
her walls[g] are torn down.
Since this is the vengeance[h] of the LORD,
take vengeance on her;
do to her[i] as she has done to others.
16 Cut off from Babylon the sower,
and the reaper with his sickle at harvest.
Because of the sword[j] of the oppressor
let everyone return to their own people,[k]
let everyone flee to their own land.[l]

17 "Israel is a scattered flock
that lions[m] have chased away.
The first to devour them
was the king[n] of Assyria;
the last to crush their bones
was Nebuchadnezzar[o] king[p] of Babylon."

18 Therefore this is what the LORD Almighty, the God of Israel, says:

"I will punish the king of Babylon and his land
as I punished the king[q] of Assyria.[r]
19 But I will bring[s] Israel back to their own pasture,
and they will graze on Carmel and Bashan;

[a] 10 Or *Chaldea*

50:11 my inheritance. God's people. The Lord regards an attack on Judah as pillaging his "inheritance." To do so with delight and joy, like a cow allowed to eat its fill on the threshing floor, inevitably stirs "the LORD's anger" (v. 13) against them, which must result in their judgment.
50:14 Even though the Lord brings Babylon against Judah, the way Babylon carries out its calling means that "she has sinned against the LORD." As a result, the Lord will bring others to "take vengeance on her" (v. 15).
50:17 Israel. Not simply the former northern kingdom but the original people of God consisting of the 12 tribes, the Lord's special possession (Zech 2:8). **lions.** Assyria scattered the former northern kingdom, while Nebuchadnezzar will crush the southern kingdom of Judah.
50:18–19 The Lord will punish both Babylon and Assyria, and the Good Shepherd will bring Israel back to the green pastures of Carmel and Bashan, famous for producing fat livestock (Ezek 39:18; Amos 4:1).

their appetite will be satisfied
on the hills[t] of Ephraim and Gilead.
20 In those days, at that time,"
declares the LORD,
"search will be made for Israel's guilt,
but there will be none,
and for the sins[u] of Judah,
but none will be found,
for I will forgive[v] the remnant[w] I spare.

21 "Attack the land of Merathaim
and those who live in Pekod.[x]
Pursue, kill and completely destroy[a] them,"
declares the LORD.
"Do everything I have commanded you.
22 The noise[y] of battle is in the land,
the noise of great destruction!
23 How broken and shattered
is the hammer of the whole earth!
How desolate[z] is Babylon
among the nations!
24 I set a trap[a] for you, Babylon,
and you were caught before you knew it;
you were found and captured[b]
because you opposed[c] the LORD.
25 The LORD has opened his arsenal
and brought out the weapons[d] of his wrath,
for the Sovereign LORD Almighty has work to do
in the land of the Babylonians.[e]
26 Come against her from afar.
Break open her granaries;
pile her up like heaps of grain.
Completely destroy[f] her
and leave her no remnant.
27 Kill all her young bulls;
let them go down to the slaughter!
Woe to them! For their day has come,
the time for them to be punished.
28 Listen to the fugitives and refugees from Babylon
declaring in Zion[g]
how the LORD our God has taken vengeance,[h]
vengeance for his temple.

29 "Summon archers against Babylon,
all those who draw the bow.[i]

50:19 [t] Jer 31:5; 33:12
50:20 [u] Mic 7:18,19 [v] Jer 31:34 [w] Isa 1:9
50:21 [x] Eze 23:23
50:22 [y] Jer 4:19-21; 51:54
50:23 [z] Isa 14:16
50:24 [a] Da 5:30-31 [b] Jer 51:31 [c] Job 9:4
50:25 [d] Isa 13:5 [e] Jer 51:25,55
50:26 [f] Isa 14:22-23
50:28 [g] Isa 48:20; Jer 51:10 [h] ver 15
50:29 [i] ver 14

[a] *21* The Hebrew term refers to the irrevocable giving over of things or persons to the LORD, often by totally destroying them; also in verse 26.

50:20 In contrast to Babylon's sins that cry out for judgment (v. 14), in that day the Lord will completely remove ("forgive") the "guilt" of Israel and Judah, as he does ultimately in Christ (Col 1:14; Heb 10:1–14).
50:21 Merathaim. An area of Babylon where the Tigris and Euphrates Rivers come together at the head of the Persian Gulf; but in Hebrew it also sounds like "[the land of] Double Rebellion." **Pekod.** An area in eastern Babylon that sounds in Hebrew like "punished" (v. 18).
50:23 hammer of the whole earth! Babylon. Hammers were used for breaking up rocks (23:29), but now Babylon itself will be shattered.
50:28 fugitives and refugees from Babylon. Those who return from exile in Babylon. They will give their testimonies of how "the LORD [their] God has taken vengeance ... for his temple." **Zion.** The site of the temple in Jerusalem.
50:29 let no one escape. There will be no remnant from Babylon.

50:29 [j] Rev 18:6 [k] Jer 51:56 [l] Isa 47:10
50:30 [m] Isa 13:18; Jer 49:26
50:31 [n] Jer 21:13
50:32 [o] Jer 21:14; 49:27
50:33 [p] Isa 58:6 [q] Isa 14:17
50:34 [r] Jer 51:19 [s] Jer 15:21; 51:36 [t] Isa 14:7
50:35 [u] Jer 47:6 [v] Da 5:7
50:36 [w] Jer 49:22
50:37 [x] Jer 51:21 [y] Jer 51:30; Na 3:13
50:38 [z] Jer 51:36

Encamp all around her;
let no one escape.
Repay[j] her for her deeds;[k]
do to her as she has done.
For she has defied[l] the LORD,
the Holy One of Israel.
30 Therefore, her young men[m] will fall in the streets;
all her soldiers will be silenced in that day,"
declares the LORD.

31 "See, I am against[n] you, you arrogant one,"
declares the Lord, the LORD Almighty,
"for your day has come,
the time for you to be punished.
32 The arrogant one will stumble and fall
and no one will help her up;
I will kindle a fire[o] in her towns
that will consume all who are around her."

33 This is what the LORD Almighty says:

"The people of Israel are oppressed,[p]
and the people of Judah as well.
All their captors hold them fast,
refusing to let them go.[q]
34 Yet their Redeemer is strong;
the LORD Almighty[r] is his name.
He will vigorously defend their cause[s]
so that he may bring rest[t] to their land,
but unrest to those who live in Babylon.

35 "A sword[u] against the Babylonians!"
declares the LORD—
"against those who live in Babylon
and against her officials and wise[v] men!
36 A sword against her false prophets!
They will become fools.
A sword against her warriors![w]
They will be filled with terror.
37 A sword against her horses and chariots[x]
and all the foreigners in her ranks!
They will become weaklings.[y]
A sword against her treasures!
They will be plundered.
38 A drought on[a] her waters!
They will dry[z] up.

[a] 38 Or *A sword against*

Repay her. Doing to her what she did to Jerusalem (cf. Dan 6:24). When she praised her gods for giving the victory (Hab 1:15–17), she "defied the LORD, the Holy One of Israel." There will be no one left to help her on the day when her arrogance is finally exposed as empty posturing.
50:34 Redeemer. The kinsman whose responsibility it was to buy back a relative who had been sold into slavery or to bring justice to a relative who was oppressed (Lev 25:25). The Lord's concern for his people—both Israel and Judah—motivates him to help them, and when he decides to act, no one can stay his hand. **defend their cause.** As Israel's legal advocate, the Lord will certainly win their case, which means "rest" for their land but "unrest" for those who oppressed them (Zech 1:8–17).
50:35–38 When the Lord summons a "sword" against the Babylonians (v. 35), everything in which they might trust will prove hollow: the "false prophets" will have no wisdom (v. 36); the "warriors," no courage (v. 36); the "horses and chariots" and "foreigners" (mercenaries), no strength (v. 37). "Her treasures … will be plundered" (v. 37). Even her

For it is a land of idols,[a]
idols that will go mad with terror.

39 "So desert creatures and hyenas will live there,
and there the owl will dwell.
It will never again be inhabited
or lived in from generation to generation.[b]
40 As I overthrew Sodom and Gomorrah[c]
along with their neighboring towns,"
declares the LORD,
"so no one will live there;
no people will dwell in it.

41 "Look! An army is coming from the north;[d]
a great nation and many kings
are being stirred up from the ends of the earth.[e]
42 They are armed with bows[f] and spears;
they are cruel and without mercy.[g]
They sound like the roaring sea[h]
as they ride on their horses;
they come like men in battle formation
to attack you, Daughter Babylon.[i]
43 The king of Babylon has heard reports about them,
and his hands hang limp.
Anguish has gripped him,
pain like that of a woman in labor.
44 Like a lion coming up from Jordan's thickets
to a rich pastureland,
I will chase Babylon from its land in an instant.
Who is the chosen[j] one I will appoint for this?
Who is like me and who can challenge me?[k]
And what shepherd can stand against me?"
45 Therefore, hear what the LORD has planned against Babylon,
what he has purposed[l] against the land of the
Babylonians:
The young of the flock will be dragged away;
their pasture will be appalled at their fate.
46 At the sound of Babylon's capture the earth will tremble;
its cry[m] will resound among the nations.

50:38 [a] ver 2
50:39 [b] Isa 13:19-22; 34:13-15; Jer 51:37; Rev 18:2
50:40 [c] Ge 19:24
50:41 [d] Jer 6:22 [e] Isa 13:4; Jer 51:22-28
50:42 [f] ver 14 [g] Isa 13:18 [h] Isa 5:30 [i] Jer 6:23
50:44 [j] Nu 16:5 [k] Job 41:10; Isa 46:9; Jer 49:19
50:45 [l] Ps 33:11; Isa 14:24; Jer 51:11
50:46 [m] Rev 18:9-10

51

This is what the LORD says:

"See, I will stir up the spirit of a destroyer
against Babylon and the people of Leb Kamai.[a]

[a] *1 Leb Kamai* is a cryptogram for Chaldea, that is, Babylonia.

"waters" (v. 38), the source of her intricate irrigation canals, will dry up. Their "idols" that inspired such fear in their devotees will themselves be driven "mad with terror" (v. 38).
50:39 hyenas. Desert scavengers. **owl.** Possibly "ostrich"; the exact identification of the bird in view is not clear.
50:40 Sodom and Gomorrah. See note on 49:18. Babylon's downfall will be complete and permanent.
50:41 from the north. See note on v. 3. **ends of the earth.** Jer 6:22–24 depicts the armies of Babylon coming from the ends of the earth against Judah. Now exactly the same kind of fierce foe is coming against Babylon.
50:44–46 A parallel message in 49:19–22 describes Babylon's advance against Edom. Now Babylon is the one who is defenseless against "what the LORD has planned" (v. 45). What the Babylonians did to others will now be done to them (v. 15).
51:1 Leb Kamai. This name means "the heart of those who rise against me"; see NIV text note (the same device is used in the name Sheshak in v. 41; 25:26 [see NIV text notes there]).

51:2 [n] Isa 41:16; Jer 15:7; Mt 3:12
51:3 [o] Jer 50:29 [p] Jer 46:4
51:4 [q] Isa 13:15 [r] Jer 49:26; 50:30
51:5 [s] Isa 54:6-8 [t] Hos 4:1
51:6 [u] Jer 50:8 [v] Nu 16:26; Rev 18:4 [w] Jer 50:15 [x] Jer 25:14
51:7 [y] Jer 25:15-16; Rev 14:8-10; 17:4
51:8 [z] Isa 21:9; Rev 14:8 [a] Jer 46:11
51:9 [b] Isa 13:14; Jer 50:16 [c] Rev 18:4-5
51:10 [d] Mic 7:9 [e] Jer 50:28
51:11 [f] Jer 50:9 [g] Jer 46:4

2 I will send foreigners to Babylon
to winnow[n] her and to devastate her land;
they will oppose her on every side
in the day of her disaster.
3 Let not the archer string his bow,[o]
nor let him put on his armor.[p]
Do not spare her young men;
completely destroy[a] her army.
4 They will fall[q] down slain in Babylon,[b]
fatally wounded in her streets.[r]
5 For Israel and Judah have not been forsaken[s]
by their God, the LORD Almighty,
though their land[c] is full of guilt[t]
before the Holy One of Israel.

6 "Flee[u] from Babylon!
Run for your lives!
Do not be destroyed because of her sins.[v]
It is time for the LORD's vengeance;[w]
he will repay[x] her what she deserves.
7 Babylon was a gold cup[y] in the LORD's hand;
she made the whole earth drunk.
The nations drank her wine;
therefore they have now gone mad.
8 Babylon will suddenly fall[z] and be broken.
Wail over her!
Get balm[a] for her pain;
perhaps she can be healed.

9 " 'We would have healed Babylon,
but she cannot be healed;
let us leave[b] her and each go to our own land,
for her judgment[c] reaches to the skies,
it rises as high as the heavens.'

10 " 'The LORD has vindicated[d] us;
come, let us tell in Zion
what the LORD our God has done.'[e]

11 "Sharpen the arrows,[f]
take up the shields![g]

[a] *3* The Hebrew term refers to the irrevocable giving over of things or persons to the LORD, often by totally destroying them. [b] *4* Or *Chaldea* [c] *5* Or *Almighty, / and the land of the Babylonians*

51:2 winnow her ... devastate her land. The nations are coming to destroy Babylon because "the LORD Almighty" has not forsaken his people (v. 5).

51:3 completely destroy. See NIV text note; see also Introduction to Deuteronomy: Themes and Theology (Holy War). Babylon's army will be treated according to the rules of war during the conquest of Canaan, according to which no one was to be left alive (cf. Josh 6:17).

51:5 land. It is unclear which land is in view, Judah or Babylon (see NIV text note).

51:6 Flee from Babylon! Those Judahites who remain in Babylon when Babylon's judgment finally comes should flee back to Judah at once and not be caught up in her demise for her sins (see Isa 48:20; Rev 18:5). This does not mean that people like Daniel should have left in Jeremiah's day: they were not free to return to Judah until the edict of Cyrus in 539 BC.

51:7 gold cup. Containing the wine of God's vengeance on other nations (25:15; see note on 25:15–38). Now the Babylonians themselves will have to drink the cup of God's judgment.

51:8 balm. The Babylonians are wounded and cannot be healed (cf. 8:22; see note there).

51:9 as high as the heavens. In Ps 103:11, this describes the extent of the Lord's faithfulness to his people. Here Babylon's judgment will be of the same magnitude, leading the Lord's people to sing of his salvation at his temple in Zion (v. 10).

51:11 kings of the Medes. Includes Darius the Mede, who ruled Babylon immediately after its downfall (Dan 5:30–31). The destruction of

The LORD has stirred up the kings of the Medes,[h]
because his purpose[i] is to destroy Babylon.
The LORD will take vengeance,
vengeance for his temple.[j]
12 Lift up a banner against the walls of Babylon!
Reinforce the guard,
station the watchmen,
prepare an ambush!
The LORD will carry out his purpose,
his decree against the people of Babylon.
13 You who live by many waters[k]
and are rich in treasures,[l]
your end has come,
the time for you to be destroyed.
14 The LORD Almighty has sworn by himself:[m]
I will surely fill you with troops, as with a swarm of locusts,[n]
and they will shout[o] in triumph over you.

15 "He made the earth by his power;
he founded the world by his wisdom
and stretched[p] out the heavens by his understanding.
16 When he thunders,[q] the waters in the heavens roar;
he makes clouds rise from the ends of the earth.
He sends lightning with the rain
and brings out the wind from his storehouses.[r]

17 "Everyone is senseless and without knowledge;
every goldsmith is shamed by his idols.
The images he makes are a fraud;[s]
they have no breath in them.
18 They are worthless,[t] the objects of mockery;
when their judgment comes, they will perish.
19 He who is the Portion of Jacob is not like these,
for he is the Maker of all things,
including the people of his inheritance —
the LORD Almighty is his name.

20 "You are my war club,[u]
my weapon for battle —
with you I shatter[v] nations,
with you I destroy kingdoms,

51:11 [h]ver 28 [i]Jer 50:45 [j]Jer 50:28
51:13 [k]Rev 17:1,15 [l]Isa 45:3; Hab 2:9
51:14 [m]Am 6:8 [n]ver 27; Na 3:15 [o]Jer 50:15
51:15 [p]Ge 1:1; Job 9:8; Ps 104:2
51:16 [q]Ps 18:11-13 [r]Ps 135:7; Jnh 1:4
51:17 [s]Isa 44:20; Hab 2:18-19
51:18 [t]Jer 18:15
51:20 [u]Isa 10:5 [v]Mic 4:13

Babylon by the Medes and the Persians was the Lord's judgment for the Babylonian destruction of his temple (50:28).

51:13 live by many waters. Babylon's location was a source of both pride and prosperity; the waters fed her irrigation canals. But none of those natural assets would help her when the time came for her to be destroyed. In the same way, the great prostitute of Rev 17:1 is a kind of new Babylon who also sits on many waters.

51:15–19 Almost identical to 10:12–16, where the Lord brings his power and wisdom to bear against Israel; here, a virtually identical judgment is brought against Babylon.

51:17–19 In contrast to the Creator God, idols have no power. They are made by mere humans and have "no breath" (v. 17) with which to speak or accomplish anything. Those who trust in them are "senseless and without knowledge" (v. 17). But the Lord is "the Maker of all things" (v. 19), the one who made everything out of nothing and who chose Israel as his people.

51:19 the people of his inheritance. In Eph 1:18 Paul applies this to Christians. Because God chose us to belong to him, no one and nothing can separate us from his love (Rom 8:38–39).

51:20–24 The Lord addresses his "war club" (v. 20), which comes to shatter the Babylonians as the hammer of God's wrath (50:23). The Persian king Cyrus now takes up the role that Nebuchadnezzar previously held (Isa 41:2–4). Babylon's punishment is not for their crimes against humanity as a whole but specifically "for all the wrong they have done in Zion" (v. 24).

51:21 [w]Ex 15:1
51:22 [x]2Ch 36:17; Isa 13:17-18
51:23 [y]ver 57
51:24 [z]Jer 50:15
51:25 [a]Zec 4:7
51:26 [b]ver 29; Isa 13:19-22; Jer 50:12
51:27 [c]Isa 13:2; Jer 50:2 [d]Jer 25:14 [e]Ge 8:4 [f]Ge 10:3
51:28 [g]ver 11
51:29 [h]ver 43; Isa 13:20
51:30 [i]Jer 50:36 [j]Isa 19:16 [k]Isa 45:2; La 2:9; Na 3:13
51:31 [l]2Sa 18:19-31

21 with you I shatter horse and rider,[w]
with you I shatter chariot and driver,
22 with you I shatter man and woman,
with you I shatter old man and youth,
with you I shatter young man and young woman,[x]
23 with you I shatter shepherd and flock,
with you I shatter farmer and oxen,
with you I shatter governors and officials.[y]

24 "Before your eyes I will repay[z] Babylon and all who live in Babylonia[a] for all the wrong they have
done in Zion," declares the LORD.

25 "I am against you, you destroying mountain,
you who destroy the whole earth,"
declares the LORD.

"I will stretch out my hand against you,
roll you off the cliffs,
and make you a burned-out mountain.[a]
26 No rock will be taken from you for a cornerstone,
nor any stone for a foundation,
for you will be desolate[b] forever,"
declares the LORD.

27 "Lift up a banner[c] in the land!
Blow the trumpet among the nations!
Prepare the nations for battle against her;
summon against her these kingdoms:[d]
Ararat,[e] Minni and Ashkenaz.[f]
Appoint a commander against her;
send up horses like a swarm of locusts.
28 Prepare the nations for battle against her—
the kings of the Medes,[g]
their governors and all their officials,
and all the countries they rule.
29 The land trembles and writhes,
for the LORD's purposes against Babylon stand—
to lay waste the land of Babylon
so that no one will live there.[h]
30 Babylon's warriors[i] have stopped fighting;
they remain in their strongholds.
Their strength is exhausted;
they have become weaklings.[j]
Her dwellings are set on fire;
the bars[k] of her gates are broken.
31 One courier[l] follows another
and messenger follows messenger

[a] *24* Or *Chaldea*; also in verse 35

51:25–26 This is the reverse of Dan 2:31–35, where a stone becomes a mountain that fills the whole earth, representing the kingdom of God. In contrast, the kingdom of Babylon starts out as a mountain that destroys the whole earth but shrinks to become small enough to be rolled off the cliffs and then burned. It will not contribute a "cornerstone" or "stone for a foundation" but will remain desolate forever. But the Lord declares in Isa 28:16 that he will lay in Zion "a precious cornerstone for a sure foundation." Mount Zion will endure in spite of Israel's sin, while the kingdoms of this world will all pass away.

51:27 Ararat, Minni and Ashkenaz. Districts of the kingdom of Media; the Lord summons them, along with their kings (v. 28), to fight against Babylon.

51:29 the LORD's purposes against Babylon stand. The outcome is certain.

to announce to the king of Babylon
that his entire city is captured,
32 the river crossings seized,
the marshes set on fire,
and the soldiers terrified.[m]"

33 This is what the LORD Almighty, the God of Israel, says:

"Daughter Babylon is like a threshing floor[n]
at the time it is trampled;
the time to harvest[o] her will soon come."

34 "Nebuchadnezzar[p] king of Babylon has devoured us,
he has thrown us into confusion,
he has made us an empty jar.
Like a serpent he has swallowed us
and filled his stomach with our delicacies,
and then has spewed us out.
35 May the violence done to our flesh[a] be on Babylon,"
say the inhabitants of Zion.
"May our blood be on those who live in Babylonia,"
says Jerusalem.[q]

36 Therefore this is what the LORD says:

"See, I will defend your cause[r]
and avenge[s] you;
I will dry up[t] her sea
and make her springs dry.
37 Babylon will be a heap of ruins,
a haunt[u] of jackals,
an object of horror and scorn,
a place where no one lives.[v]
38 Her people all roar like young lions,
they growl like lion cubs.
39 But while they are aroused,
I will set out a feast for them
and make them drunk,
so that they shout with laughter—
then sleep forever and not awake,"
declares the LORD.[w]

40 "I will bring them down
like lambs to the slaughter,
like rams and goats.

41 "How Sheshak[b][x] will be captured,[y]
the boast of the whole earth seized!
How desolate Babylon will be
among the nations!

51:32 [m] Jer 50:36
51:33 [n] Isa 21:10 [o] Isa 17:5; Hos 6:11
51:34 [p] Jer 50:17
51:35 [q] ver 24; Ps 137:8
51:36 [r] Ps 140:12; Jer 50:34; La 3:58 [s] ver 6; Ro 12:19 [t] Jer 50:38
51:37 [u] Isa 13:22; Rev 18:2 [v] Jer 50:13,39
51:39 [w] ver 57
51:41 [x] Jer 25:26 [y] Isa 13:19

[a] 35 Or *done to us and to our children* [b] 41 *Sheshak* is a cryptogram for Babylon.

51:32 marshes. Possible hiding places.
51:33 like a threshing floor. Where wheat was beaten with sticks and "trampled" to separate the grain from the chaff.
51:34 serpent. Hebrew *tannîn*, which describes the great sea creatures in Gen 1:21 and the sea monsters in Ps 74:13 (see note on Ps 74:13–17). It is thus much more than an ordinary snake that has "swallowed" God's people.
51:39 drunk ... sleep forever. The Babylonians will sink into a drunken stupor from which they will never awake.
51:41 Sheshak. See NIV text note; see also note on 25:26.

51:42 [z]Isa 8:7
51:43 [a]ver 29,62; Isa 13:20; Jer 2:6
51:44 [b]Isa 46:1 [c]ver 34 [d]ver 58; Jer 50:15
51:45 [e]Rev 18:4 [f]ver 6; Isa 48:20; Jer 50:8
51:46 [g]Jer 46:27 [h]2Ki 19:7
51:47 [i]ver 52; Isa 46:1-2; Jer 50:2 [j]Jer 50:12
51:48 [k]Isa 44:23; Rev 18:20 [l]ver 11
51:49 [m]Ps 137:8; Jer 50:29
51:50 [n]ver 45 [o]Ps 137:6
51:51 [p]Ps 44:13-16; 79:4 [q]La 1:10

42 The sea will rise over Babylon;
its roaring waves[z] will cover her.
43 Her towns will be desolate,
a dry and desert land,
a land where no one lives,
through which no one travels.[a]
44 I will punish Bel[b] in Babylon
and make him spew out[c] what he has swallowed.
The nations will no longer stream to him.
And the wall[d] of Babylon will fall.

45 "Come out[e] of her, my people!
Run[f] for your lives!
Run from the fierce anger of the LORD.
46 Do not lose heart or be afraid[g]
when rumors[h] are heard in the land;
one rumor comes this year, another the next,
rumors of violence in the land
and of ruler against ruler.
47 For the time will surely come
when I will punish the idols[i] of Babylon;
her whole land will be disgraced[j]
and her slain will all lie fallen within her.
48 Then heaven and earth and all that is in them
will shout[k] for joy over Babylon,
for out of the north[l]
destroyers will attack her,"
declares the LORD.

49 "Babylon must fall because of Israel's slain,
just as the slain in all the earth
have fallen because of Babylon.[m]
50 You who have escaped the sword,
leave[n] and do not linger!
Remember[o] the LORD in a distant land,
and call to mind Jerusalem."

51 "We are disgraced,[p]
for we have been insulted
and shame covers our faces,
because foreigners have entered
the holy places of the LORD's house."[q]

51:44 Bel. One of the gods of the Babylonians (50:2), here identified with the serpent that swallows Zion in v. 34. The nations will no longer "stream" to this idol. According to Isa 2:2, in the last days the nations will instead stream to Zion, the home of the Lord. **wall of Babylon.** Famous in antiquity; it was reputedly wide enough for several chariots to drive side by side on its top.
51:45 Come out of her ... Run for your lives! When Babylon's demise comes, the Lord's people should be ready to leave and escape for their lives (see v. 6 and note).
51:46 Even though it will be some time coming and there will be conflicting "rumors" and reports in the meantime, the Lord's victory over the "idols"(v. 47) will surely arrive.
51:48 shout for joy. All creation will rejoice in Babylon's fall. **out of the north.** See note on 50:3.
51:50 Remember the LORD in a distant land. See Ps 137:4 and note. Even though God's people are to settle down and seek Babylon's peace in the short term (29:4–7), they are never to forget that Babylon is not their home.
51:51 It might seem that Babylon's gods are powerful because their soldiers have been allowed to enter "the holy places of the LORD's house," but the situation will soon be reversed: God will punish Babylon's idols and expose their powerlessness (v. 52).

52 "But days are coming," declares the LORD,
"when I will punish her idols,[r]
and throughout her land
the wounded will groan.
53 Even if Babylon ascends to the heavens[s]
and fortifies her lofty stronghold,
I will send destroyers[t] against her,"
declares the LORD.

54 "The sound of a cry comes from Babylon,
the sound of great destruction[u]
from the land of the Babylonians.[a]
55 The LORD will destroy Babylon;
he will silence her noisy din.
Waves[v] of enemies will rage like great waters;
the roar of their voices will resound.
56 A destroyer[w] will come against Babylon;
her warriors will be captured,
and their bows will be broken.[x]
For the LORD is a God of retribution;
he will repay[y] in full.
57 I will make her officials and wise men drunk,
her governors, officers and warriors as well;
they will sleep[z] forever and not awake,"
declares the King,[a] whose name is the LORD Almighty.

58 This is what the LORD Almighty says:

"Babylon's thick wall[b] will be leveled
and her high gates set on fire;
the peoples[c] exhaust themselves for nothing,
the nations' labor is only fuel for the flames."[d]

59 This is the message Jeremiah the prophet gave to the staff officer Seraiah son of Neriah,[e] the son
of Mahseiah, when he went to Babylon with Zedekiah[f] king of Judah in the fourth[g] year of his reign.
60 Jeremiah had written on a scroll[h] about all the disasters that would come upon Babylon—all that
had been recorded concerning Babylon. 61 He said to Seraiah, "When you get to Babylon, see that you
read all these words aloud. 62 Then say, 'LORD, you have said you will destroy this place, so that neither
people nor animals will live in it; it will be desolate[i] forever.' 63 When you finish reading this scroll, tie
a stone to it and throw it into the Euphrates. 64 Then say, 'So will Babylon sink to rise no more because
of the disaster I will bring on her. And her people[j] will fall.' "

The words of Jeremiah end[k] here.

[a] 54 Or *Chaldeans*

51:52 [r] ver 47
51:53 [s] Ge 11:4; Isa 14:13-14 [t] Jer 49:16
51:54 [u] Jer 50:22
51:55 [v] Ps 18:4
51:56 [w] ver 48 [x] Ps 46:9 [y] ver 6; Ps 94:1-2; Hab 2:8
51:57 [z] Ps 76:5; Jer 25:27 [a] Jer 46:18; 48:15
51:58 [b] ver 44 [c] ver 64 [d] Hab 2:13
51:59 [e] Jer 36:4 [f] Jer 52:1 [g] Jer 28:1
51:60 [h] Jer 30:2; 36:2
51:62 [i] Isa 13:20; Jer 50:13,39
51:64 [j] ver 58 [k] Job 31:40

51:53 ascends to the heavens. Reminiscent of Gen 11:1–9.

51:56 the LORD is a God of retribution. Babylon's sins against Jerusalem and the Lord's people cry out for vindication (v. 35), and that cry must be answered.

51:58 Babylon's thick wall. See note on v. 44.

51:59 fourth year of [Zedekiah's] reign. 594/593 BC, several years before Babylon conquers Jerusalem. Jeremiah is under no illusions as to the ultimate fate of Babylon, even while he urges his fellow countrymen to surrender to them (38:1–3).

51:60 Jeremiah had written on a scroll about all the disasters that would come upon Babylon. A dramatic sign-act attesting the veracity of these words.

51:61 Seraiah. May have been Baruch's brother. When Seraiah accompanies Zedekiah on a visit to Babylon, he is to read the contents of the scroll aloud.

51:64a sink. After reading the scroll aloud, Seraiah is to attach it to a stone (v. 63) and throw it into the Euphrates River. Just as the scroll will sink without a trace, so Babylon will "sink" forever under God's judgment.

51:64b The words of Jeremiah end here. Ch. 52 is a postscript that records the fulfillment of some of Jeremiah's prophecies.

52:1 [l] 2Ki 24:17 [m] Jos 10:29; 2Ki 8:22
52:2 [n] Jer 36:30
52:3 [o] Isa 3:1 [p] Eze 17:12-16
52:4 [q] Zec 8:19 [r] 2Ki 25:1-7; Jer 39:1 [s] Eze 24:1-2
52:6 [t] Isa 3:1
52:9 [u] Jer 32:4 [v] Nu 34:11 [w] Nu 13:21
52:10 [x] Jer 22:30
52:11 [y] Eze 12:13
52:12 [z] Zec 7:5; 8:19 [a] Jer 39:9
52:13 [b] 2Ch 36:19; Ps 74:8; La 2:6 [c] Ps 79:1; Mic 3:12
52:14 [d] Ne 1:3
52:16 [e] Jer 40:6
52:17 [f] 1Ki 7:15 [g] 1Ki 7:27-37 [h] 1Ki 7:23 [i] Jer 27:19-22
52:18 [j] Ex 27:3; 1Ki 7:45
52:19 [k] 1Ki 7:50

The Fall of Jerusalem

52:1-3pp — 2Ki 24:18-20; 2Ch 36:11-16
52:4-16pp — Jer 39:1-10
52:4-21pp — 2Ki 25:1-21; 2Ch 36:17-20

52 Zedekiah[l] was twenty-one years old when he became king, and he reigned in Jerusalem eleven years. His mother's name was Hamutal daughter of Jeremiah; she was from Libnah.[m] 2He did evil in the eyes of the LORD, just as Jehoiakim[n] had done. 3It was because of the LORD's anger that all this happened to Jerusalem and Judah,[o] and in the end he thrust them from his presence.

Now Zedekiah rebelled[p] against the king of Babylon.

4So in the ninth year of Zedekiah's reign, on the tenth[q] day of the tenth month, Nebuchadnezzar king of Babylon marched against Jerusalem[r] with his whole army. They encamped outside the city and built siege works all around it.[s] 5The city was kept under siege until the eleventh year of King Zedekiah.

6By the ninth day of the fourth month the famine in the city had become so severe that there was no food for the people to eat.[t] 7Then the city wall was broken through, and the whole army fled. They left the city at night through the gate between the two walls near the king's garden, though the Babylonians[*a*] were surrounding the city. They fled toward the Arabah,[*b*] 8but the Babylonian[*c*] army pursued King Zedekiah and overtook him in the plains of Jericho. All his soldiers were separated from him and scattered, 9and he was captured.[u]

He was taken to the king of Babylon at Riblah[v] in the land of Hamath,[w] where he pronounced sentence on him. 10There at Riblah the king of Babylon killed the sons[x] of Zedekiah before his eyes; he also killed all the officials of Judah. 11Then he put out Zedekiah's eyes, bound him with bronze shackles and took him to Babylon, where he put him in prison till the day of his death.[y]

12On the tenth day of the fifth[z] month, in the nineteenth year of Nebuchadnezzar king of Babylon, Nebuzaradan[a] commander of the imperial guard, who served the king of Babylon, came to Jerusalem. 13He set fire[b] to the temple[c] of the LORD, the royal palace and all the houses of Jerusalem. Every important building he burned down. 14The whole Babylonian army, under the commander of the imperial guard, broke down all the walls[d] around Jerusalem. 15Nebuzaradan the commander of the guard carried into exile some of the poorest people and those who remained in the city, along with the rest of the craftsmen[*d*] and those who had deserted to the king of Babylon. 16But Nebuzaradan left behind[e] the rest of the poorest people of the land to work the vineyards and fields.

17The Babylonians broke up the bronze pillars,[f] the movable stands[g] and the bronze Sea[h] that were at the temple of the LORD and they carried all the bronze to Babylon.[i] 18They also took away the pots, shovels, wick trimmers, sprinkling bowls, dishes and all the bronze articles used in the temple service.[j] 19The commander of the imperial guard took away the basins, censers,[k] sprinkling bowls, pots, lampstands, dishes and bowls used for drink offerings — all that were made of pure gold or silver.

[*a*] *7* Or *Chaldeans*; also in verse 17 [*b*] *7* Or *the Jordan Valley* [*c*] *8* Or *Chaldean*; also in verse 14
[*d*] *15* Or *the populace*

52:1 – 34 *The Fall of Jerusalem and Its Aftermath.* The book concludes with an account of historical events drawn from 2 Kgs 24 – 25; some of these events are already recorded in ch. 39. This omits the section from 2 Kings dealing with the assassination of Gedaliah, probably because chs. 40 – 41 already recount that story. There are many echoes of ch. 52 in Rev 18, where the city made by humans opposes God's people in all ages and times (called "Babylon"); it reflects many of the characteristics of ancient Babylon and therefore shares the same ultimate fate of destruction (see note on Rev 18:1 – 3).

52:1 – 30 *The Fall of Jerusalem.* This is a historical account of the fall of Jerusalem.

52:1 eleven years. 597 – 586 BC. Zedekiah, the uncle of the previous king (Jehoiachin), was placed on the throne by Nebuchadnezzar, who carried off Jehoiachin to exile in Babylon.

52:2 – 3a did evil in the eyes of the LORD. In 1 – 2 Kings, all of the kings of Israel and Judah are rated as good or evil largely based on their commitment to encouraging and maintaining faithful worship in Jerusalem (see note on 1 Kgs 15:26). Zedekiah failed to do this. Since he is the last in a long series of kings who mostly "did evil in the eyes of the LORD," the Lord's anger is stirred up against Jerusalem and Judah.

52:3b – 16 Zedekiah rebels against the king of Babylon (see note on 2 Kgs 24:20b), and so Nebuchadnezzar lays siege to Jerusalem for about 18 months (see note on Jer 39:2), leading to a severe famine (see note on 2 Kgs 25:3). When the walls are finally breached (see note on 2 Kgs 25:10), Zedekiah tries to flee the city but is quickly captured and taken to Riblah (see notes on Jer 39:4,5), where his sons are executed and his eyes put out (see note on 2 Kgs 25:7). Meanwhile, Jerusalem is burned to the ground (see note on 2 Kgs 25:9).

52:4 ninth year … tenth day of the tenth month. Jan. 15, 588 BC.

52:17 – 23 The sacred objects of the temple are taken away into exile to Babylon rather than destroyed in the temple fire (see note on 2 Kgs 25:13). They are later brought out for Belshazzar's ill-fated feast (Dan 5:1 – 4) before being repatriated with the returning exiles during the reign of Cyrus (Ezra 1:7). They thus provide an element of continuity between the first temple and its successor.

[20]The bronze from the two pillars, the Sea and the twelve bronze bulls under it, and the movable
stands, which King Solomon had made for the temple of the LORD, was more than could be weighed.[l]
21Each pillar was eighteen cubits high and twelve cubits in circumference[a]; each was four fingers
thick, and hollow.[m] 22The bronze capital[n] on top of one pillar was five cubits[b] high and was decorated
with a network and pomegranates of bronze all around. The other pillar, with its pomegranates, was
similar. 23There were ninety-six pomegranates on the sides; the total number of pomegranates[o] above
the surrounding network was a hundred.

24The commander of the guard took as prisoners Seraiah[p] the chief priest, Zephaniah[q] the priest
next in rank and the three doorkeepers. 25Of those still in the city, he took the officer in charge of the
fighting men, and seven royal advisers. He also took the secretary who was chief officer in charge of
conscripting the people of the land, sixty of whom were found in the city. 26Nebuzaradan[r] the commander took them all and brought them to the king of Babylon at Riblah. 27There at Riblah, in the
land of Hamath, the king had them executed.

So Judah went into captivity, away[s] from her land. 28This is the number of the people Nebuchadnezzar carried into exile:[t]

in the seventh year, 3,023 Jews;
29 in Nebuchadnezzar's eighteenth year,
832 people from Jerusalem;
30 in his twenty-third year,
745 Jews taken into exile by Nebuzaradan the commander of the imperial guard.
There were 4,600 people in all.

52:20 [l]1Ki 7:47
52:21 [m]1Ki 7:15
52:22 [n]1Ki 7:16
52:23 [o]1Ki 7:20
52:24 [p]2Ki 25:18 [q]Jer 21:1; 37:3
52:26 [r]ver 12
52:27 [s]Jer 20:4
52:28 [t]2Ki 24:14-16; 2Ch 36:20
52:33 [u]2Sa 9:7
52:34 [v]2Sa 9:10

Jehoiachin Released

52:31-34pp — 2Ki 25:27-30

31In the thirty-seventh year of the exile of Jehoiachin king of Judah, in the year Awel-Marduk became king of Babylon, on the twenty-
fifth day of the twelfth month, he released Jehoiachin king of Judah
and freed him from prison. 32He spoke kindly to him and gave him
a seat of honor higher than those of the other kings who were with
him in Babylon. 33So Jehoiachin put aside his prison clothes and for
the rest of his life ate regularly at the king's table.[u] 34Day by day the king
of Babylon gave Jehoiachin a regular allowance[v] as long as he lived, till the
day of his death.

[a] *21* That is, about 27 feet high and 18 feet in circumference or about 8.1 meters high and 5.4 meters in circumference [b] *22* That is, about 7 1/2 feet or about 2.3 meters

Babylonian Chronicles that mention how Jehoiachin was fed rations at the table of the later Babylonian king, as in Jer 52:33.
Todd Bolen/www.BiblePlaces.com taken at the British Museum

52:24–30 The people are not as fortunate as the temple's sacred objects (see note on vv. 17–23).
52:24 Seraiah the chief priest. Not the same Seraiah as in 51:61.
52:27 executed. Babylon executes many of the leading officials of the king, including "Seraiah the chief priest, Zephaniah the priest next in rank and the three doorkeepers [of the temple]" (v. 24). **Judah went into captivity.** The remainder of the people, with the exception of the poorest (v. 16), are taken into exile.
52:28–30 These verses mention three deportations, but the first deportation was actually in 605 BC, shortly after Nebuchadnezzar came to the throne. The deportation in 605 BC probably included Daniel. The first deportation mentioned here (but the second deportation) refers to the largest deportation, which took place in Nebuchadnezzar's "seventh year" (597 BC), when Nebuchadnezzar took away Jehoiachin and replaced him with Zedekiah. The deportation of 597 BC probably included Ezekiel. The number given here ("3,023") is much smaller than that in 2 Kgs 24:14 (10,000), so it may count only the leaders. The second deportation mentioned here (but the third deportation) was in 586 BC, in the "eighteenth year" of Nebuchadnezzar. The third deportation mentioned here (but the fourth deportation) was in 581 BC. It may have come in response to the assassination of Gedaliah.
52:31–34 *Jehoiachin Released.* The book of Jeremiah, like 2 Kings, ends on a hopeful note: the good treatment extended to Jehoiachin in Babylon.
52:31 Awel-Marduk. Traditionally known as Evil-Merodach (which means "devotee of Marduk"). He releases Jehoiachin from prison on his accession in 561/60 BC and gives Jehoiachin royal clothing and a place at the royal table (vv. 32–33).
52:34 till the day of his death. Jeremiah prophesied that Jehoiachin would die in exile (22:24–30) and that the Davidic line would continue (23:5). Since this vindication of Jeremiah's prophecies does not refer to the return from exile, it is reasonable to suppose that the book reached its present form prior to the decree of Cyrus allowing the Jews to return in 539 BC (Ezra 1:1–4).

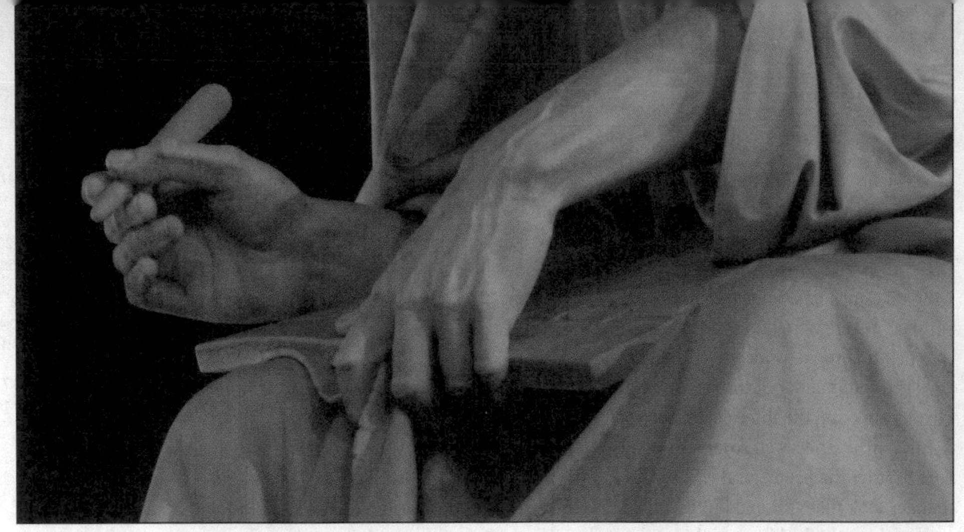

INTRODUCTION TO LAMENTATIONS

The book of Lamentations is comprised of five poems responding to the destruction of Jerusalem by the Babylonians in 586 BC. A deep sense of grief pervades the whole book. At the same time, each of the five poems makes a distinctive contribution to the collection.

AUTHOR

The tradition that Jeremiah is the author of the collection of five poems we know as Lamentations goes back at least to the brief prologue in the Septuagint (the pre-Christian Greek translation of the OT): "And so it was, after Israel had been taken captive and Jerusalem laid waste, that Jeremiah sat weeping; he sang this dirge over Jerusalem ..." Jeremiah announced his intention to raise a lament in response to God's judgment of his people (Jer 9:10), and the prophet invited his hearers to do likewise (Jer 7:29). It was therefore natural to draw a connection between the weeping prophet (Jer 9:1) and the weeping author of these laments (Lam 2:11; 3:48).

The poems themselves are anonymous, however, and in the Hebrew tradition the book is found among the "Writings" of the Hebrew canon, with no immediate connection to the book of Jeremiah among the "Prophets." Also, there are some tensions between the books of Lamentations and Jeremiah. For example, the pit of Lamentations is full of water (3:53–54), whereas Jeremiah's pit is not (Jer 38:6b). Lamentations appears to condone assistance from foreign nations (4:17; 5:6), while for Jeremiah this was consistently an anathema (Jer 2:18; 37:6–10; 42:15–17). And while 2 Chr 35:25 was sometimes invoked to bolster the case for Jeremiah's authorship of Lamentations, it relates to the death of Josiah, not to the fall of Jerusalem a number of years later.

Even if the Jeremianic authorship is set aside, most students of the book today would not name any author for the book that the book itself does not identify. Scholars also debate whether a single poet is responsible for all five laments or whether stylistic variations from poem to poem suggest a plurality of authors, making a collection on the model of the Psalms. On the other hand, Lamentations has a consistency of tone and outlook—the variations in poetry notwithstanding—that means sole authorship remains plausible, and the name of Jeremiah is the only viable possibility if that author is to be identified.

DATE, OCCASION, PLACE

Each of the five poems of Lamentations relates to the fall of Jerusalem in the Babylonian period. This, however, was a complex phase in Judah's history, and Jerusalem's destruction has a succession of focal points. The subjection of Judah and deportation of the elite to Babylon occurred in stages: the first deportation under Jehoiakim occurred in 605 BC; the second under Jehoiachin in 597 BC; the third under Zedekiah in 586 BC, which included the razing of the city and the destruction of the temple. This was not the final outcome, however, as Gedaliah's subsequent governorship ended several years later with his assassination and another deportation in 581 BC, leaving the fragmented members of any remnant in disarray (Jer 41–43).

How, then, do we relate Lamentations to the events of this period? The vivid and poignant poetic observations on the ruined city have suggested to many a date close to the events, penned by an eyewitness, at least in the first four poems. The conditions in view in the first chapter — people in exile but not an emphatic sense of a city in ruins — have allowed some to suggest a composition in response to the 597 BC fall of the city rather than its destruction in 586 BC. On the other hand, ch. 5 lacks the immediacy of the earlier poems and hints at a date deeper into the period of exile. Linguistic arguments provide a firm setting for the book in the exilic period, undercutting speculative claims that the poems could have come from the postexilic period.

As for the occasion of their composition, in the simplest terms, lament for the holy city almost inevitably would call forth a creative response from Zion's poets. The tradition of lamentation over a ruined city has a very old pedigree in Mesopotamian literature, reaching back as far as 2000 BC. But the literary effort was much more than an outpouring of grief. The lament over the ruined city served ritual purposes and grappled forthrightly with the anger of the deity toward the sanctuary and its city in the light of the devastation experienced by the inhabitants.

While it is difficult to believe these poems were written from anywhere but Judah, this cannot be proven. Some have suggested that composition took place elsewhere or that we simply cannot assume a Palestinian origin. Still, the poems reflect a Jerusalem setting: the personified city speaks and watches callous passersby, her remaining inhabitants are summoned to repentance, and so on. These might be the product of a literary imagination at work in Egypt or Babylon, but in biblical writings such settings tend to be reflected in the literature itself (e.g., cf. Ps 137; Ezek 8 – 11).

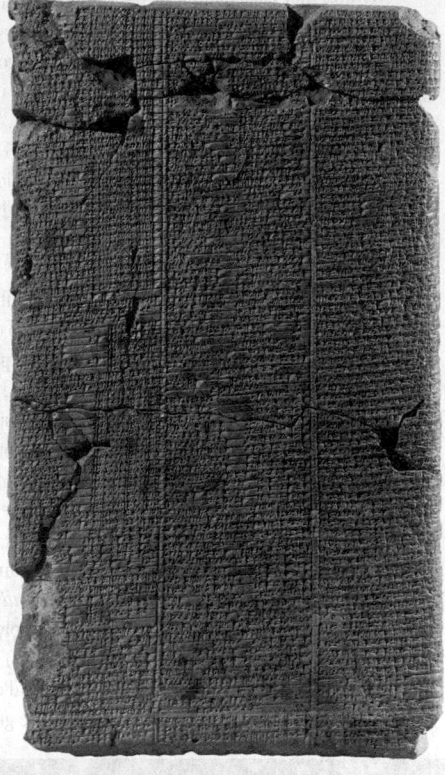

"Hymn of Nidaba," an ancient Sumerian lament on the destruction of Ur, 2112–2004 BC. The book of Lamentations similarly focuses on the trauma experienced by the kingdom of Judah.

Erich Lessing/Art Resource, NY

LITERARY STYLE AND GENRE

Lamentations' poems mostly use an alphabetic acrostic pattern. The precise form of the acrostic differs from chapter to chapter. Ch. 1 and ch. 2 begin every three-line verse with the successive letter of the 22-letter Hebrew alphabet. Ch. 3 extends this by beginning every three-line unit with the same Hebrew letter, with each line here numbered as a separate verse. Thus, in spite of ch. 1 and ch. 2 having 22 verses and ch. 3 having 66, the poems are the same length. Like ch. 1 and ch. 2, ch. 4 is again 22 verses long, but each verse is made up of two poetic lines each rather than three (so a 44-line poem). Ch. 5 abandons the acrostic discipline of beginning lines with the successive letter of the alphabet, but it maintains the constraint of 22 lines/verses overall. There is a further variation between poems in that ch. 1 alone uses the order of the alphabet familiar to us, while chs. 2; 3; 4 reverse the order of the letters *pe* and *ayin* (vv. 16 – 17 in ch. 2 and ch. 4, but vv. 46 – 51 in ch. 3). This variant order is known from inscriptions, and rather than holding deep significance, it simply reflects a different sequence of letters known in the period.

The distinctive artistry of Lamentations also has a metrical aspect. Hebrew poetry typically resists classification by "meter," but the limping 3:2 stress pattern that predominates in Lamentations has a strong (although not exclusive) association with lament, so much so that it is often referred to as *qinah* ("dirge") meter.

It is at first jarring that such a highly disciplined poetic structure should be used for such intensely emotive content. On reflection, however, it is not greatly different from using the highly prescriptive sonnet form for a poem from lover to beloved. The alphabetic acrostic form is not unique in the Hebrew Bible to these laments: there are eight acrostic psalms (Pss 9 – 10 [together they form an acrostic poem]; 25; 34; 37; 111; 112; 119; 145), and the ode to a wife of noble character in Prov 31:10 – 31 is also an alphabetic acrostic. There seem to be some shared motifs and word choices among these acrostic poems that intersect with the interests of the sages and address aspects of life before God, although this is not so clearly the case for the ode in Proverbs. Observing this formal constraint demonstrates that Lamentations is not simply a gush of grief but a highly reflective and considered response to trauma: in literary terms, the ordered nature of the poetry contrasts with the chaos it portrays.

This does not offer as much guidance for consideration of genre as might be supposed. The acrostic structure has associations with wisdom literature, but here it is filled with lamentation. The hallmark of the psalms of lament are the questions "Why?" and "How long?" (e.g., Pss 10:1,13; 13:1 – 2), and these are conspicuous by their absence in Lamentations until they finally appear in ch. 5 at the collection's end. This combination might be expected to produce a theodicy — an argument justifying the actions of a good and all-powerful God in the face of some evil — but no argument is mounted, and the poems themselves arrive at no resolution on this question.

PURPOSE AND THEMES AND THEOLOGY

The laments give expression to and grapple with the distance the community feels away from their God, who alone can bring relief to the suffering of which he is also ultimately the cause. The few dominant themes that carry this purpose forward are widely dispersed throughout the poems. This is no tightly argued case; that is not the nature of lament. As noted (see Literary Style and Genre), these laments should be regarded not as simply an emotional outpouring but as a deliberate attempt to explore the possibility that the relationship between God and people can be restored.

1. *God is sovereign.* God's sovereignty is not simply a platitude for these laments. Rather, this truth is the bedrock beneath the shattered foundations of Zion and her broken people, and it carries practical implications — much as the writer to the Hebrews was to explain in Heb 12. Most important, it means that the destruction of Jerusalem was not due to the domineering whim of a violent, foreign aggressor (1:17; 3:38; 4:11) but was the work of the God who had in times past chosen this place to dwell among his people (2:7).

2. *Sin shatters the relationship of God and people.* The violence of God against his own people was not perceived as capricious; it was the just response of a holy God to the sin of those who had rejected him. It is not only observed of Zion (1:8) but also confessed by Zion (1:18). In the pivotal third lament, this admission is found at the moment of possible turning (3:40 – 42). Even if the so-called religious professionals bear a special responsibility (2:14; 4:13), still the whole people, past and present, own the guilt (5:7,16). However, the nature of the sin is not confessed in detail, much like Ps 51, even though the full Hebrew vocabulary for "sin," "guilt," "iniquity," etc. is employed (see note on Ps 32:5).

3. *Cherished institutions are not exempt from God's judgment.* The deep consequences of sin are realized in the judgment on Zion and the line of David. Both were divine choices (Ps 132) and central to Israel's fellowship with the Lord. But neither place nor person was exempt from divine wrath. Lamentations struggles with what this means for the future of God's people, this quandary pointing forward through the postexilic prophets like Haggai and Zechariah and into the NT fulfillment in Christ and the new Jerusalem (cf. Luke 13:34 – 35; Rev 22:12 – 16).

4. *Suffering is real.* This might be so obvious as to not require special mention. And it might also be thought that if God is responsible for the suffering of Zion's people, he is well aware of its nature. Nonetheless, these laments are rife with details, bitter and graphic, of the degradation, violence, and shame that Zion's inhabitants experience. The crying child points at the place of pain for the parent to lavish tender care — and so too these hurting people direct the gaze of God at their wounds (2:20 – 21; 3:43 – 45).

5. *Hope is found in God alone.* There is nowhere else to turn and no one else to turn to besides the Lord (2:18 – 19; 3:32 – 33,37). This is, perhaps, the most practical outworking of God's sovereignty (5:19): even if the suffering community is left without resolution in these poems, resolution cannot be found apart from God.

Egyptian painting of a Nubian and an Asiatic prisoner. Leaders sometimes showed their power by painting images of captives on the soles of their sandals, thus placing their enemies "underfoot" as in Lam 3:34.
Erich Lessing/Art Resource, NY

OUTLINE

I. Lonely Zion (1:1–22)
- A. Zion's Degradation (1:1–11)
- B. Zion's Lament (1:12–22)

II. Knowing the Wrath of God (2:1–22)
- A. The Wrath of God (2:1–10)
- B. The Poet's Grief (2:11–12)
- C. Zion's Plight (2:13–19)
- D. Zion Pleads With the Lord (2:20–22)

III. Hoping Against Hope (3:1–66)
- A. The "Man's" Suffering (3:1–16)
- B. Transition to Hope (3:17–21)
- C. Appealing to the Afflicted (3:22–47)
- D. Prayer on Behalf of the Damaged Community (3:48–66)

IV. Despair (4:1–22)
- A. Zion's Desolations (4:1–16)
- B. Communal Disappointment (4:17–20)
- C. Edom's Retribution (4:21–22)

V. "Remember, Lord" (5:1–22)
- A. Imploring the Lord (5:1)
- B. Catalog of Woe (5:2–18)
- C. Imploring the Lord—Reprise (5:19–22)

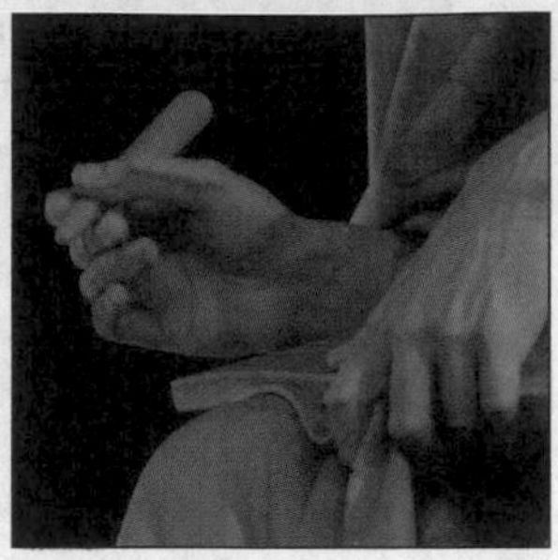

LAMENTATIONS

1:1 [a]Isa 47:8 [b]1Ki 4:21 [c]Isa 3:26; Jer 40:9
1:2 [d]Ps 6:6 [e]Jer 3:1 [f]Jer 4:30; Mic 7:5 [g]ver 16
1:3 [h]Jer 13:19 [i]Dt 28:65

1 [a]

How deserted lies the city,
once so full of people!
How like a widow[a] is she,
who once was great[b] among the nations!
She who was queen among the provinces
has now become a slave.[c]

2 Bitterly she weeps[d] at night,
tears are on her cheeks.
Among all her lovers[e]
there is no one to comfort her.
All her friends have betrayed[f] her;
they have become her enemies.[g]

3 After affliction and harsh labor,
Judah has gone into exile.[h]
She dwells among the nations;
she finds no resting place.[i]
All who pursue her have overtaken her
in the midst of her distress.

[a] This chapter is an acrostic poem, the verses of which begin with the successive letters of the Hebrew alphabet.

1:1 – 22 *Lonely Zion.* The sense of loneliness and abandonment that the suffering city expresses here stands in tension with the realities of passersby and the conversation beginning at v. 12. But the repeated refrain that she is alone ("no one" is used five times in 22 verses) is not about absolute isolation but about lack of comfort, healing, and rescue.

The opening lament divides roughly into two halves: Verses 1 – 11 describe Zion's degradation, punctuated in v. 9 by a brief, prayerful outcry. This is echoed at the end of v. 11, providing the transition to vv. 12 – 22, in which the direct speech of lamenting Zion dominates, addressed first to unmoved onlookers (vv. 12 – 16,18 – 19) before again appealing to the Lord (vv. 20 – 22). Only in v. 17 does third-person narration return with a poignant summary of Zion's distress. The characters that recur throughout the five poems all appear here: the narrator, personified Zion/Jerusalem and her populace, Zion's enemies, the surrounding nations, and Yahweh himself. This lament repeatedly makes clear that responsibility for Zion's fall is to be credited not to any human foe but to God alone in response to Zion's sin.

1:1 – 11 *Zion's Degradation.* The voice of the poet-narrator surveys Zion's current plight, drawing a contrast throughout with her former exalted estate.

1:1 In Hebrew, while the word "nation" is grammatically masculine, "city" is grammatically feminine, and feminine imagery flows naturally and pervades the book's first two poems. Inversions frame this opening verse: from royal status and the security of being a "queen" to the vulnerability of being a "widow" to the degradation of being a "slave." This depiction of a world turned upside down recurs throughout ch. 1. The nature of Zion's "desertion" in particular is explored and qualified in the following verses.

1:2 she weeps … tears. Zion's nighttime tears provide one of the thematic links associating these laments with Jeremiah, whose book, more than any other, portrays a weeping prophet (Jer 9:1; 13:17; 14:17; cf. 31:15 – 16; see also Lam 3:48 – 51). Inversion continues (see note on v. 1) with absent "lovers" and treacherous "friends." **no one to comfort her.** Zion perceives her own isolation. This observation becomes a refrain through the chapter (see vv. 7 ["help"],9,17,21, with a variation in v. 16). **no one.** The exclusivity of "no one" (also in vv. 16 – 17) combines with the inclusivity of "all" her lovers and "all" her friends — the Hebrew word "all" (*kōl*) echoing like a death knell through the rest of the poem (vv. 3 – 4,6 – 11,21).

1:3 After. This glance to the past deviates momentarily from the consistent attention in this poem to Zion's present. **Judah.** Normally, the Hebrew word is grammatically masculine; here, it is taken as feminine, fitting seamlessly with the overarching feminine reference started in v. 1 ("city"; see note on v. 1). See photo, p. 1308.

4 The roads to Zion mourn,
for no one comes to her appointed festivals.
All her gateways are desolate,[j]
her priests groan,
her young women grieve,
and she is in bitter anguish.[k]

5 Her foes have become her masters;
her enemies are at ease.
The LORD has brought her grief[l]
because of her many sins.
Her children have gone into exile,[m]
captive before the foe.

6 All the splendor has departed
from Daughter Zion.[n]
Her princes are like deer
that find no pasture;
in weakness they have fled
before the pursuer.

7 In the days of her affliction and wandering
Jerusalem remembers all the treasures
that were hers in days of old.
When her people fell into enemy hands,
there was no one to help her.[o]
Her enemies looked at her
and laughed at her destruction.

8 Jerusalem has sinned[p] greatly
and so has become unclean.
All who honored her despise her,
for they have all seen her naked;[q]
she herself groans[r]
and turns away.

9 Her filthiness clung to her skirts;
she did not consider her future.[s]
Her fall[t] was astounding;
there was none to comfort[u] her.
"Look, LORD, on my affliction,[v]
for the enemy has triumphed."

10 The enemy laid hands
on all her treasures;[w]

1:4 [j] Jer 9:11 [k] Joel 1:8-13
1:5 [l] Jer 30:15 [m] Jer 39:9; 52:28-30
1:6 [n] Jer 13:18
1:7 [o] Jer 37:7; La 4:17
1:8 [p] ver 20; Isa 59:2-13 [q] Jer 13:22,26 [r] ver 21,22
1:9 [s] Dt 32:28-29; Isa 47:7; Eze 24:13 [t] Jer 13:18 [u] Ecc 4:1; Jer 16:7 [v] Ps 25:18
1:10 [w] Isa 64:11

1:4 no one comes to her appointed festivals. The theme of Zion's loneliness, signaled in v. 1, is deepened by this description. **priests.** Responsible for the celebration of pilgrimage festivals. **young women.** Normally their dance expresses festive joy (Judg 21:21; see Ps 68:25); here they "grieve." Jerusalem is not wholly depopulated; her isolation is of a deeper kind.

1:5 her many sins. Zion's judgment for sin is not only recognized by the poet (also v. 8) but also confessed by Zion herself (vv. 14,18,20). The claim of the poet is that the Lord, rather than a foreign enemy, brought destruction in response to sin (see vv. 12,14–15). **children.** Perhaps Zion's inhabitants or the wider populace of surrounding towns and villages (cf. 2 Sam 20:19).

1:6–7 The poignant contrast between Zion's former "splendor" and her current sorry state provides the theme elaborated in ch. 4.

1:6 Daughter Zion. See note on 2:1.

1:8–10 The dramatic extent of Zion's fall operates also at the cultic level. The combination of sin and purity resonates with the message of the contemporary prophet Ezekiel (cf. Ezek 7:19–20; 23:28–30; 36:22–32). Desecration of the holy place by gloating enemies (v. 10) contributes to her nakedness and shame. Her groans of self-revulsion (v. 8c) anticipate the pithy prayer (v. 9c).

1:9 Look, LORD. We hear Zion's voice directly for the first time as she makes her first plea to the Lord.

1:10 [x]Ps 74:7-8; Jer 51:51 [y]Dt 23:3
1:11 [z]Ps 38:8 [a]Jer 52:6
1:12 [b]Jer 18:16 [c]ver 18 [d]Isa 13:13; Jer 30:24
1:13 [e]Job 30:30 [f]Jer 44:6 [g]Hab 3:16
1:14 [h]Dt 28:48; Isa 47:6 [i]Jer 32:5
1:15 [j]Jer 37:10 [k]Isa 41:2 [l]Isa 28:18; Jer 18:21
1:16 [m]La 2:11,18; 3:48-49 [n]Ps 69:20; Ecc 4:1 [o]ver 2; Jer 13:17; 14:17

she saw pagan nations
enter her sanctuary[x] —
those you had forbidden[y]
to enter your assembly.

11 All her people groan[z]
as they search for bread;[a]
they barter their treasures for food
to keep themselves alive.
"Look, LORD, and consider,
for I am despised."

12 "Is it nothing to you, all you who pass by?[b]
Look around and see.
Is any suffering like my suffering[c]
that was inflicted on me,
that the LORD brought on me
in the day of his fierce anger?[d]

13 "From on high he sent fire,
sent it down into my bones.[e]
He spread a net for my feet
and turned me back.
He made me desolate,[f]
faint[g] all the day long.

14 "My sins have been bound into a yoke[a];[h]
by his hands they were woven together.
They have been hung on my neck,
and the Lord has sapped my strength.
He has given me into the hands[i]
of those I cannot withstand.

15 "The Lord has rejected
all the warriors in my midst;[j]
he has summoned an army[k] against me
to[b] crush my young men.[l]
In his winepress the Lord has trampled
Virgin Daughter Judah.

16 "This is why I weep
and my eyes overflow with tears.[m]
No one is near to comfort[n] me,
no one to restore my spirit.
My children are destitute
because the enemy has prevailed."[o]

[a] 14 Most Hebrew manuscripts; many Hebrew manuscripts and Septuagint *He kept watch over my sins*
[b] 15 Or *has set a time for me / when he will*

1:11 search for bread. Later poems describe in hideous detail the full horror of desperate hunger because of the siege (2:11–12,20; 4:4–5,9–10). **Look, LORD.** Zion's second plea to the Lord.

1:12–22 *Zion's Lament.* Zion's own voice is heard through the remainder of the lament, accounting for her distress and pleading for help.

1:12–15 Zion's second plea to the Lord (see v. 11 and note) initiates her sustained speech that continues throughout most of the second half of ch. 1. In spite of the presence of a human foe (vv. 5,7,9–10), this relentless sequence of statements recognizes that the ultimate source of the people's suffering is none other than the Lord and that it comes in judgment, the theme that dominates ch. 2. In this prayer, lamenting Jerusalem echoes the preaching of the prophets going back at least to Amos (cf. Amos 2:6–13; 5:18) and the prayers of the poets (cf. Pss 44; 89:38–51; 119:67,71,75).

1:16 Zion summarizes: seemingly abandoned by God, she is desolate, vulnerable, and vanquished. Her tears go uncomforted, much as did Jeremiah's (Jer 9:1,17–20; 14:17–22).

Hezekiah's broad wall, an example of a stronghold (Lam 2:2).

[17]Zion stretches out her hands,[p]
but there is no one to comfort her.
The LORD has decreed for Jacob
that his neighbors become his foes;
Jerusalem has become
an unclean thing among them.

[18]"The LORD is righteous,
yet I rebelled[q] against his command.
Listen, all you peoples;
look on my suffering.[r]
My young men and young women
have gone into exile.[s]

[19]"I called to my allies
but they betrayed me.
My priests and my elders
perished[t] in the city
while they searched for food
to keep themselves alive.

[20]"See, LORD, how distressed[u] I am!
I am in torment[v] within,
and in my heart I am disturbed,
for I have been most rebellious.

1:17 [p] Jer 4:31
1:18 [q] 1Sa 12:14 [r] ver 12 [s] Dt 28:32,41
1:19 [t] Jer 14:15; La 2:20
1:20 [u] Jer 4:19 [v] La 2:11

1:17 The narrator briefly interrupts Zion's lament, pointedly affirming Zion's own perceptions that the Lord "decreed" hostility, and offers not a crumb of comfort but rather a word of confirmation.

1:18 The LORD is righteous, yet I rebelled. Not merely a statement of fact; this signals confession and aligns Jerusalem with God's judgment. It could be translated: "The LORD is in the right, for I rebelled," thus acknowledging at once both the fitness of the Lord's actions and the culpability of Zion's rebellion (Ezra 9:15; Jer 12:1).

1:19 allies. A term frequently used by the prophets for spiritual adultery on the part of God's people (e.g., Ezek 23:22; Hos 2:5). The NIV opts for a political nuance. It is difficult to decide between these senses here, and the ambiguity may be deliberate.

1:20 See. Here and in 2:20 ("look"), a concluding plea for the Lord to "see" is the catalyst for turning his wrath to compassion. It serves the same purpose in the introduction of 5:1. **Outside ... inside.** The connection between external and internal realities provides an apt summary for this poem as a whole.

1:20 [w]Dt 32:25; Eze 7:15
1:21 [x]ver 8 [y]ver 4 [z]La 2:15 [a]Isa 47:11; Jer 30:16
1:22 [b]Ne 4:5
2:1 [c]La 3:44 [d]Ps 99:5; 132:7
2:2 [e]La 3:43 [f]Ps 21:9 [g]Ps 89:39-40; Mic 5:11 [h]Isa 25:12
2:3 [i]Ps 75:5,10

Outside, the sword bereaves;
inside, there is only death.[w]

21 "People have heard my groaning,[x]
but there is no one to comfort me.[y]
All my enemies have heard of my distress;
they rejoice[z] at what you have done.
May you bring the day[a] you have announced
so they may become like me.

22 "Let all their wickedness come before you;
deal with them
as you have dealt with me
because of all my sins.[b]
My groans are many
and my heart is faint."

2 [a]

How the Lord has covered Daughter Zion
with the cloud of his anger[b][c]
He has hurled down the splendor of Israel
from heaven to earth;
he has not remembered his footstool[d]
in the day of his anger.

2 Without pity[e] the Lord has swallowed[f] up
all the dwellings of Jacob;
in his wrath he has torn down
the strongholds[g] of Daughter Judah.
He has brought her kingdom and its princes
down to the ground[h] in dishonor.

3 In fierce anger he has cut off
every horn[c,d][i] of Israel.

[a] This chapter is an acrostic poem, the verses of which begin with the successive letters of the Hebrew alphabet. [b] 1 Or *How the Lord in his anger / has treated Daughter Zion with contempt* [c] 3 Or *off / all the strength*; or *every king* [d] 3 *Horn* here symbolizes strength.

1:21–22 Zion's prayer is not only that she be restored but more insistently, that her enemies experience the judgment appropriate for their own sins—a pattern that also concludes ch. 3 and ch. 4.

2:1–22 *Knowing the Wrath of God.* Few passages in the OT share the concentration of references to the wrath of God found in this second lament, framing it at beginning (vv. 1–6) and end (vv. 21–22). If ch. 1 dwells on the result of God's judgment, ch. 2 describes the horror of God's active fury. The intensity deepens when this wrath is juxtaposed with this poem's favored designation for Jerusalem as "Daughter Zion," used repeatedly in this chapter (see note on 2:1). Much as Ps 51 exploits a rich Hebrew vocabulary for sin to frame David's repentance, so this poem finds a range of terms to express the nature of divine wrath as the community recoils in grief.

The poem falls into two large sections, each with a response: (1) vv. 1–10 focus on God's wrath and its effects on people and place, and vv. 11–12 record the poet's own traumatized reaction; (2) the poet confronts Zion with her plight (vv. 13–19), and in response Zion prays to the Lord (vv. 20–22).

2:1–10 *The Wrath of God.* These verses catalog the catastrophic effects of God's anger: God's wrath has turned him into Zion's enemy.

2:1 God in his fury rejects Zion's participation in his heavenly glory. **Daughter Zion.** This designation of Zion runs throughout ch. 2 (vv. 4,8,10,13 ["Daughter Jerusalem"],18); it only appears elsewhere in Lamentations in 1:6; 4:22. Whatever political overtones this style might carry, this lament clearly adds to the pathos as the city, personified as a vulnerable maiden, is subjected to a violent attack. Implicit throughout this verse is the blending of perspectives of heaven and earth that God in his wrath is forcing apart. Israel's "splendor" combined with the reference to God's "footstool" indicates that the Jerusalem temple is in the poet's mind, the place of divine presence on earth (cf. Isa 66:1). **covered ... with the cloud.** The alternate translation suggested in the NIV text note ("treated ... with contempt") arises from uncertainty regarding the meaning of the Hebrew verb that occurs only here. The more evocative "cloud" rendering makes good sense as part of the celestial scenario accompanying the onslaught of the Lord.

2:2 swallowed up. The Hebrew for this devouring metaphor for divine wrath dominates the first part of the poem (also vv. 5 [twice],8 ["destroying"],16) but is found nowhere else in the book. The plummet from the stellar height of v. 1 then continues as Judah's royal splendor crashes earthward. **princes.** Zion's elite hold the poet's eye for a moment, giving way to a survey of the desolation of the place that pervades this section (vv. 6,9b–10 again register the human impact).

2:3 approach of the enemy. To human eyes, the enemy appears in the shape of the Babylonians. But the poet sees the only effective actor in all the destructive activity of this chapter as the Lord alone.

He has withdrawn his right hand[j]
at the approach of the enemy.
He has burned in Jacob like a flaming fire
that consumes everything around it.[k]

4 Like an enemy he has strung his bow;[l]
his right hand is ready.
Like a foe he has slain
all who were pleasing to the eye;[m]
he has poured out his wrath like fire[n]
on the tent of Daughter Zion.

5 The Lord is like an enemy;[o]
he has swallowed up Israel.
He has swallowed up all her palaces
and destroyed her strongholds.[p]
He has multiplied mourning and lamentation
for Daughter Judah.[q]

6 He has laid waste his dwelling like a garden;
he has destroyed his place of meeting.[r]
The LORD has made Zion forget
her appointed festivals and her Sabbaths;[s]
in his fierce anger he has spurned
both king and priest.[t]

7 The Lord has rejected his altar
and abandoned his sanctuary.
He has given the walls of her palaces[u]
into the hands of the enemy;
they have raised a shout in the house of the LORD
as on the day of an appointed festival.

8 The LORD determined to tear down
the wall around Daughter Zion.
He stretched out a measuring line[v]
and did not withhold his hand from destroying.
He made ramparts and walls lament;
together they wasted away.[w]

9 Her gates[x] have sunk into the ground;
their bars he has broken and destroyed.
Her king and her princes are exiled[y] among the nations,
the law[z] is no more,
and her prophets no longer find
visions[a] from the LORD.

2:3 [j] Ps 74:11 [k] Isa 42:25; Jer 21:4-5,14
2:4 [l] Job 16:13; La 3:12-13 [m] Eze 24:16, 25 [n] Isa 42:25; Jer 7:20
2:5 [o] Jer 30:14 [p] ver 2 [q] Jer 9:17-20
2:6 [r] Jer 52:13 [s] La 1:4; Zep 3:18 [t] La 4:16
2:7 [u] Ps 74:7-8; Isa 64:11; Jer 33:4-5
2:8 [v] 2Ki 21:13; Isa 34:11 [w] Isa 3:26
2:9 [x] Ne 1:3 [y] Dt 28:36; 2Ki 24:15 [z] 2Ch 15:3 [a] Jer 14:14

2:4–5 Like an enemy ... Like a foe ... like an enemy. Describes Yahweh's behavior so that the "likeness" here becomes a matter of identity rather than similarity as the poet's description of God's wrath in action hardens and intensifies. This completes the rupture initiated in v. 1 (see note), the effects of which the remainder of ch. 2 observes. **palaces.** See note on 2:7.

2:4 poured out. A metaphor for God's wrath; cf. "swallowed up" (see v. 2 and note) in its inclusive power. It appears again in 4:11 but is most frequently used by the contemporary prophet Ezekiel (12 times versus 2 times by Jeremiah and 1 time by Isaiah).

2:6–10 The mournful tour of destruction begins where the lament begins in v. 1: at the temple, the dwelling place of God on earth. The circle is drawn ever wider from the central temple area to include the walls and gates of the city (vv. 8–9). The trauma of the onlookers matches the physical desolation of the city. Each "class" of people finds their situation the opposite of what it should be: rulers are absent; prophets lack revelation; elders are silent; maidens mourn (see note on 1:4).

2:7 palaces. Hebrew *'armôn* (also in v. 5); best understood as referring to some architectural feature of the temple itself. The focus is not on royal apartments but on the place of Yahweh's dwelling.

2:10 [b]Job 2:12 [c]Isa 15:3 [d]Job 2:13; Isa 3:26
2:11 [e]La 1:16; 3:48-51 [f]La 1:20 [g]ver 19; Ps 22:14 [h]La 4:4
2:12 [i]La 4:4
2:13 [j]Isa 37:22 [k]Jer 14:17; La 1:12
2:14 [l]Isa 58:1 [m]Jer 2:8; 23:25-32,33-40; 29:9; Eze 13:3; 22:28
2:15 [n]Eze 25:6 [o]Jer 19:8 [p]Ps 50:2 [q]Ps 48:2
2:16 [r]Ps 56:2; La 3:46 [s]Job 16:9 [t]Ps 35:25

10 The elders of Daughter Zion
sit on the ground in silence;
they have sprinkled dust on their heads[b]
and put on sackcloth.[c]
The young women of Jerusalem
have bowed their heads to the ground.[d]

11 My eyes fail from weeping,[e]
I am in torment within[f];
my heart is poured out[g] on the ground
because my people are destroyed,
because children and infants faint[h]
in the streets of the city.

12 They say to their mothers,
"Where is bread and wine?"
as they faint like the wounded
in the streets of the city,
as their lives ebb away
in their mothers' arms.[i]

13 What can I say for you?
With what can I compare you,
Daughter Jerusalem?
To what can I liken you,
that I may comfort you,
Virgin Daughter Zion?[j]
Your wound is as deep as the sea.[k]
Who can heal you?

14 The visions of your prophets
were false and worthless;
they did not expose your sin
to ward off your captivity.[l]
The prophecies they gave you
were false and misleading.[m]

15 All who pass your way
clap their hands at you;[n]
they scoff[o] and shake their heads
at Daughter Jerusalem:
"Is this the city that was called
the perfection of beauty,[p]
the joy of the whole earth?"[q]

16 All your enemies open their mouths
wide against you;[r]
they scoff and gnash their teeth[s]
and say, "We have swallowed her up.[t]

2:11–12 *The Poet's Grief.* Elaboration of divine wrath now elicits a first-person response from the lamenting poet.
2:11–12 Poignantly and tenderly observes the suffering of dying children.
2:13–19 *Zion's Plight.* The poet's explanation to Zion of her suffering has a prophetic quality, but it can only bring cold comfort.
2:13 The poet addresses Zion, taking on the impossible task of providing the comfort markedly absent from ch. 1.
2:14 false and worthless. It was not that prophetic sight was blinded (see v. 9); it was actively misleading. Here again Lamentations resonates with Jeremiah's prophecies (cf. Jer 23:9–40).
2:15–16 Derision from onlookers (reported in 1:7,12) is now heard firsthand.
2:16 These gloating words of Zion's enemies presume that their long-laid plans have now come to fruition. See "The City of God," p. 2666.

This is the day we have waited for;
we have lived to see it."

17 The LORD has done what he planned;
he has fulfilled his word,
which he decreed long ago.[u]
He has overthrown you without pity,[v]
he has let the enemy gloat over you,
he has exalted the horn[a] of your foes.[w]

18 The hearts of the people
cry out to the Lord.[x]
You walls of Daughter Zion,
let your tears[y] flow like a river
day and night;[z]
give yourself no relief,
your eyes no rest.[a]

19 Arise, cry out in the night,
as the watches of the night begin;
pour out your heart[b] like water
in the presence of the Lord.[c]
Lift up your hands to him
for the lives of your children,
who faint[d] from hunger
at every street corner.

20 "Look, LORD, and consider:
Whom have you ever treated like this?
Should women eat their offspring,[e]
the children they have cared for?[f]
Should priest and prophet be killed[g]
in the sanctuary of the Lord?

21 "Young and old lie together
in the dust of the streets;
my young men and young women
have fallen by the sword.[h]
You have slain them in the day of your anger;
you have slaughtered them without pity.[i]

22 "As you summon to a feast day,
so you summoned against me terrors[j] on every side.
In the day of the LORD's anger
no one escaped or survived;
those I cared for and reared[k]
my enemy has destroyed."

[a] *17 Horn* here symbolizes strength.

2:17 [u]Dt 28:15-45 [v]ver 2; Eze 5:11 [w]Ps 89:42
2:18 [x]Ps 119:145 [y]La 1:16 [z]Jer 9:1 [a]La 3:49
2:19 [b]1Sa 1:15; Ps 62:8 [c]Isa 26:9 [d]Isa 51:20
2:20 [e]Dt 28:53; Jer 19:9 [f]La 4:10 [g]Ps 78:64; Jer 14:15
2:21 [h]2Ch 36:17; Ps 78:62-63; Jer 6:11 [i]Jer 13:14; La 3:43; Zec 11:6
2:22 [j]Ps 31:13; Jer 6:25 [k]Hos 9:13

2:17 planned ... fulfilled ... decreed. Reveals the enemy's hubris and that Zion's downfall is the result of settled divine determination, elaborating the statement of intent in v. 8. Jerusalem's human foes are mere pawns in the hand of her angry God.

2:18 tears. See note on 1:2.

2:20–22 *Zion Pleads With the Lord.* Zion cries out to God in response to the poet's invitation (v. 19). This lament's conclusion follows a pattern similar to that in 1:20–22. We hear Zion's own plaintive voice in the first-person language. There is nothing here of the energetic plea for payback against the foe that concludes chs. 1; 3; 4. Rather, Zion's energy is spent, and she simply holds before the Lord the appalling suffering that is the outcome of God's calculated wrath and that has left no citizen of Jerusalem untouched. Reading the poems sequentially, this makes an effective transition from the feminine voice in ch. 2 to the man's reflections in ch. 3.

2:20 eat their offspring. See note on 4:10.

3:1 [l] Job 19:21; Ps 88:7
3:2 [m] Jer 4:23
3:3 [n] Isa 5:25
3:4 [o] Ps 51:8; Isa 38:13; Jer 50:17
3:5 [p] ver 19 [q] Jer 23:15
3:6 [r] Ps 88:5-6
3:7 [s] Job 3:23 [t] Jer 40:4
3:8 [u] Job 30:20; Ps 22:2
3:9 [v] Isa 63:17; Hos 2:6

3 [a]

I am the man who has seen affliction
by the rod of the LORD's wrath.[l]
2 He has driven me away and made me walk
in darkness[m] rather than light;
3 indeed, he has turned his hand against me[n]
again and again, all day long.

4 He has made my skin and my flesh grow old
and has broken my bones.[o]
5 He has besieged me and surrounded me
with bitterness[p] and hardship.[q]
6 He has made me dwell in darkness
like those long dead.[r]

7 He has walled me in so I cannot escape;[s]
he has weighed me down with chains.[t]
8 Even when I call out or cry for help,
he shuts out my prayer.[u]
9 He has barred my way with blocks of stone;
he has made my paths crooked.[v]

[a] This chapter is an acrostic poem; the verses of each stanza begin with the successive letters of the Hebrew alphabet, and the verses within each stanza begin with the same letter.

3:1–66 *Hoping Against Hope.* This is the central and most complex poem of the book. It is overtly theological, hopeful, and enigmatic. In contrast to the focus in ch. 2 on Jerusalem as a place and the reaction to its destruction, the poet adopts a personal perspective in ch. 3. In fact, there is little, if anything, in the poem to forge a direct connection between this suffering individual and the destruction of Zion; only the admonitions to the community to turn to the Lord in the latter half of the poem (vv. 40–42) imply that this distress is part of a larger scenario. If, however, this lament was composed as a sequel to ch. 2, then the fate of Zion would form the immediate context for the individual cry. It is noteworthy that the most pronounced expression of hope in the book comes in ch. 3, which directly follows the darkest portrait of God's wrath in ch. 2. Here also the acrostic structure is intensified (see Introduction: Literary Style and Genre), although it remains unclear what significance this has since no compelling explanation for the heightened acrostic technique has been made. At the least, as many note, ch. 3 is the book's central poem, and the acrostic technique has the effect of giving it a certain prominence.

Attention to the dominant voices of ch. 3 provides an effective means of seeing its structure, since changes in voice bring associated shifts in perspective, tone, and focus of thought. (1) Almost every clause of vv. 1–16 describes an act of violence or oppression by some fierce but unnamed opponent against a suffering "man." (2) A remarkable transition unfolds in vv. 17–21 in which the "man" speaks of himself and recalls the hopes he invested in the Lord. (3) With this realization, vv. 22–47 see the man turn to his afflicted community, holding before them the true character of the Lord (vv. 22–38) and what is required by way of response (vv. 39–47). (4) From that point, the voice of the individual returns for the rest of the lament (vv. 48–66), but in a different mood from that in the beginning of the chapter. Now his grief is not only for himself but also for his community, and God is explicitly engaged on their behalf against their enemies. This remains a prayer, however, and a final resolution to personal and social traumas is not realized. On the other hand, the theological strain is relieved as the estrangement from God that launched the poem has been overcome for this "man" by the abiding conviction of God's true redemptive nature.

3:1–16 *The "Man's" Suffering.* The account of communal suffering is now depicted in the agony and misery of a particular, unnamed individual.

3:1 man. Hebrew *geber* (also in vv. 27,35 [people],39 [the living]). Who is this man? If the traditional ascription of authorship to Jeremiah is maintained, he becomes the most natural candidate, and the profile of the sufferer matches that of the prophet in a general way. Others suggest that the "man" is "every man," a representative individual, or even an "ideal man" who comes with eyes of faith to see beyond the present misery. Since a personal identity cannot be attached to this man with confidence, it seems best simply to hear his voice in the terms laid down in the text: he is one whose suffering at the hands of the deity has been acute, who sees in that source of suffering also the source of hope (v. 38), and who, in solidarity with the community in distress, longs to experience the relief that only the Lord can bring. **the LORD's wrath.** For clarification, the NIV has "the LORD's wrath," but the Hebrew has simply "his wrath," and nowhere in the Hebrew of this poem is the assailant directly named. The poet's reticence is remarkable given the willingness of ch. 2 to identify the Lord as Zion's enemy. This reluctance to name the Lord as the oppressor may contribute to the sufferer's capacity to call to mind the Lord's faithfulness and thus find hope (vv. 17–26).

3:2–16 The sequence of third-person verbs describing the violence perpetrated on this man is unrelenting, as is his suffering. Although God is not named, some of these effects—even if metaphoric—would require cosmic power (e.g., v. 8). The metaphors range from the siege to the hunt and settle finally on simple brutality (v. 16).

3:2 darkness rather than light. The same phrase is used in Amos 5:18 to express the judgment of the day of the Lord (see notes on Amos 2:16; 5:18).

3:4 Job also understood that God had fashioned his "skin," "flesh," and "bones" (Job 10:11) and that God had afflicted him in these terms, i.e., in the totality of his being (Job 19:20).

3:7–9 Parallels to Job's experience of suffering at God's hands continue: being "walled ... in" (v. 7; cf. Job 19:8) and feeling that his prayers go unheard (v. 8; cf. Job 9:16).

[10] Like a bear lying in wait,
like a lion in hiding,
[11] he dragged me from the path and mangled[w] me
and left me without help.
[12] He drew his bow[x]
and made me the target[y] for his arrows.[z]

[13] He pierced my heart
with arrows from his quiver.[a]
[14] I became the laughingstock[b] of all my people;
they mock me in song[c] all day long.
[15] He has filled me with bitter herbs
and given me gall to drink.[d]

[16] He has broken my teeth with gravel;[e]
he has trampled me in the dust.
[17] I have been deprived of peace;
I have forgotten what prosperity is.
[18] So I say, "My splendor is gone
and all that I had hoped from the LORD."[f]

[19] I remember my affliction and my wandering,
the bitterness and the gall.
[20] I well remember them,
and my soul is downcast[g] within me.[h]
[21] Yet this I call to mind
and therefore I have hope:

[22] Because of the LORD's great love we are not consumed,
for his compassions never fail.[i]
[23] They are new every morning;
great is your faithfulness.[j]
[24] I say to myself, "The LORD is my portion;[k]
therefore I will wait for him."

[25] The LORD is good to those whose hope is in him,
to the one who seeks him;[l]
[26] it is good to wait quietly
for the salvation of the LORD.[m]
[27] It is good for a man to bear the yoke
while he is young.

3:11 [w] Hos 6:1
3:12 [x] La 2:4 [y] Job 7:20 [z] Ps 7:12-13; 38:2
3:13 [a] Job 6:4
3:14 [b] Jer 20:7 [c] Job 30:9
3:15 [d] Jer 9:15
3:16 [e] Pr 20:17
3:18 [f] Job 17:15
3:20 [g] Ps 42:5 [h] Ps 42:11
3:22 [i] Ps 78:38; Mal 3:6
3:23 [j] Zep 3:5
3:24 [k] Ps 16:5
3:25 [l] Isa 25:9; 30:18
3:26 [m] Ps 37:7; 40:1

3:10 bear … lion. Far from a protective presence, this again resonates with Amos's description of the day of the Lord (see note on v. 2).
3:14 laughingstock. Similar to Job (Job 12:4), Jeremiah (Jer 20:7), and even Jesus (Matt 27:41; Mark 15:31; Luke 23:35–36).
3:17–21 *Transition to Hope.* The "man" turns from the actions of his assailant to consider his own response. His despair is palpable, but a remarkable transformation unfolds.
3:18–21 The very act of facing disappointment is the occasion for recalling the source of hope, triggered it seems by the first articulation of the Lord's name in this poem (v. 18). This, it seems, is enough to pierce the darkness, as a reflection on the Lord's true nature inspires renewed hope—even if that hope is partially dashed by the end of ch. 3. Nonetheless, the contrast effected between what precedes and what follows is both stark and startling.
3:22–47 *Appealing to the Afflicted.* The perspective throughout these verses is informed by a reflection on God's nature (vv. 31–33) that has strong resonances with one of the OT's foundational theological texts: Exod 34:6–7 (cf. Num 14:18). Several prophets drew on that confession of God's character (e.g., Hos 14:2–4; Joel 2:13–14; Jonah 3:9—4:2; Mic 7:18–20), and this lament stands with them. A full understanding of who God is brings hopeful insight both to the nature of his wrath and consequently to what is required by the community of faith: they must turn to the Lord in repentance, hoping for gracious restoration (v. 40).
3:22–24 A passage of central importance—the significance of its subject matter matched by its actual location at the center of the book. This is one of the great statements of the "great love" (Hebrew *ḥesed*) of God's covenant loyalty, but it does not nullify feeling the force of his wrath. The psalmist also forges this clear-sighted connection in Ps 30:5, where a sufferer also issues an invitation to the wider community. The same dynamic can be discerned in the apostle Paul's experience (2 Cor 4:8–9). As the sufferer turns to invite the community to share his insight, there is also a tacit response to the "swallowing" of ch. 2 (see note on 2:2). There is, at least, a remnant.
3:27 bear the yoke. Context suggests this is more a matter of

3:28 [n] Jer 15:17
3:29 [o] Jer 31:17
3:30 [p] Job 16:10; Isa 50:6
3:31 [q] Ps 94:14; Isa 54:7
3:32 [r] Ps 78:38; Hos 11:8
3:33 [s] Eze 33:11
3:36 [t] Jer 22:3; Hab 1:13
3:37 [u] Ps 33:9-11
3:38 [v] Job 2:10; Isa 45:7; Jer 32:42
3:39 [w] Jer 30:15; Mic 7:9
3:40 [x] 2Co 13:5 [y] Ps 119:59; 139:23-24
3:41 [z] Ps 25:1; 28:2
3:42 [a] Da 9:5 [b] Jer 5:7-9
3:43 [c] La 2:2,17,21
3:44 [d] Ps 97:2 [e] ver 8
3:45 [f] 1Co 4:13
3:46 [g] La 2:16

28 Let him sit alone in silence,[n]
for the LORD has laid it on him.
29 Let him bury his face in the dust —
there may yet be hope.[o]
30 Let him offer his cheek to one who would strike him,[p]
and let him be filled with disgrace.

31 For no one is cast off
by the Lord forever.[q]
32 Though he brings grief, he will show compassion,
so great is his unfailing love.[r]
33 For he does not willingly bring affliction
or grief to anyone.[s]

34 To crush underfoot
all prisoners in the land,
35 to deny people their rights
before the Most High,
36 to deprive them of justice —
would not the Lord see such things?[t]

37 Who can speak and have it happen
if the Lord has not decreed it?[u]
38 Is it not from the mouth of the Most High
that both calamities and good things come?[v]
39 Why should the living complain
when punished for their sins?[w]

40 Let us examine our ways and test them,[x]
and let us return to the LORD.[y]
41 Let us lift up our hearts and our hands
to God in heaven,[z] and say:
42 "We have sinned and rebelled[a]
and you have not forgiven.[b]

43 "You have covered yourself with anger and pursued us;
you have slain without pity.[c]
44 You have covered yourself with a cloud[d]
so that no prayer[e] can get through.
45 You have made us scum[f] and refuse
among the nations.

46 "All our enemies have opened their mouths
wide against us.[g]

suffering than discipline, although both are implied by the metaphor. This idea resonates with the sense of the poet of Ps 119 (Ps 119:10,50,67,71,75), while for Jeremiah the "yoke" invariably refers to the Babylonian subjection of Judah (Jer 27:8 – 11; 28:14). See the note on v. 39.

3:28 In the light of the transition from hopelessness (v. 18) to hope (v. 21), counsel is offered on how to respond to suffering. **the LORD**. The source is unnamed in Hebrew despite the density of references in the immediate context (vv. 22,24,25,26). See note on v. 1.

3:31 – 38 The poet's call to his people refers to God now in terms appropriate to the relationship: **Lord** or "master" (Hebrew *'ădônây*, vv. 31,36,37) and **Most High** (Hebrew *'elyôn*, vv. 35,38).

3:33 The conviction that in some mysterious sense God **does not willingly bring affliction** resonates with Ezekiel's repeated claim that God takes "no pleasure in the death of the wicked" (Ezek 18:23,32; 33:11). His nature is both holy and compassionate.

3:39 An alternate translation of this verse (emphasis added) would be: "Why should a survivor complain, a *man* about his punishment?" At the transition from reflection on God's character to the community's response, the experience of the "man" (Hebrew *geber*, see v. 1 and note) is revisited. The Hebrew term *geber* is also used in vv. 27 ("man") and 35 ("people"). Together vv. 1,27,35,39 plot the sufferer's path from despairing anguish to hopeful repentance, as he now calls the community to join in this posture before the sovereign God.

3:42 – 47 The community's prayer forthrightly owns the responsibility for their sin, but it does not shrink from detailing the blows they have suffered at God's hand in terms that echo at points the experience of the "man" in vv. 1 – 16.

47 We have suffered terror and pitfalls,[h]
ruin and destruction.[i]"
48 Streams of tears flow from my eyes[j]
because my people are destroyed.[k]

49 My eyes will flow unceasingly,
without relief,[l]
50 until the LORD looks down
from heaven and sees.[m]
51 What I see brings grief to my soul
because of all the women of my city.

52 Those who were my enemies without cause
hunted me like a bird.[n]
53 They tried to end my life in a pit[o]
and threw stones at me;
54 the waters closed over my head,[p]
and I thought I was about to perish.

55 I called on your name, LORD,
from the depths of the pit.[q]
56 You heard my plea:[r] "Do not close your ears
to my cry for relief."
57 You came near when I called you,
and you said, "Do not fear."[s]

58 You, Lord, took up my case;[t]
you redeemed my life.[u]
59 LORD, you have seen the wrong done to me.[v]
Uphold my cause!
60 You have seen the depth of their vengeance,
all their plots against me.[w]

61 LORD, you have heard their insults,
all their plots against me—
62 what my enemies whisper and mutter
against me all day long.[x]
63 Look at them! Sitting or standing,
they mock me in their songs.
64 Pay them back what they deserve, LORD,
for what their hands have done.[y]
65 Put a veil over their hearts,[z]
and may your curse be on them!
66 Pursue them in anger and destroy them
from under the heavens of the LORD.

3:47 [h] Jer 48:43 [i] Isa 24:17-18; 51:19
3:48 [j] La 1:16 [k] La 2:11
3:49 [l] Jer 14:17
3:50 [m] Isa 63:15
3:52 [n] Ps 35:7
3:53 [o] Jer 37:16
3:54 [p] Ps 69.2, Jnh 2.3-5
3:55 [q] Ps 130:1; Jnh 2:2
3:56 [r] Ps 55:1
3:57 [s] Isa 41:10
3:58 [t] Jer 51:36 [u] Ps 34:22; Jer 50:34
3:59 [v] Jer 18:19-20
3:60 [w] Jer 11:20; 18:18
3:62 [x] Eze 36:3
3:64 [y] Ps 28:4
3:65 [z] Isa 6:10

3:48–66 *Prayer on Behalf of the Damaged Community.* First-person language returns for the remainder of the poem. Although some have resisted making the connection to the individual whose voice is heard in the first part of the lament, this identification makes good sense. The lament tradition both here and in the Psalms typically sees renewed confidence in God's saving nature as the fulcrum allowing the person praying to move from pain to praise. The terms have shifted from the beginning of the poem: it is no longer the isolated, personal conflict of a man with a (divine) assailant but rather the intercession of a man with God against some external enemy on behalf of the community. The earlier reluctance to explicitly invoke Yahweh has also now vanished: the poet addresses the Lord by name (vv. 50,55,59,61,64,66).

3:48 tears. See note on 1:2.

3:64–66 The imprecation (i.e., curse) against the enemy resonates with the conclusions of the first and fourth laments (see notes on 1:21–22; Ps 69:22–28). This is not simply a request for revenge; it is also a request for justice: the call is for punishment commensurate with the enemy's action. For God to ignore the enemy's actions would be injustice of another kind.

4:1 [a]Eze 7:19
4:3 [b]Job 39:16
4:4 [c]Ps 22:15 [d]La 2:11,12
4:5 [e]Jer 6:2 [f]Am 6:3-7
4:6 [g]Ge 19:25
4:8 [h]Job 30:28 [i]Ps 102:3-5

4 [a]

How the gold has lost its luster,
 the fine gold become dull!
The sacred gems are scattered
 at every street corner.[a]

2 How the precious children of Zion,
 once worth their weight in gold,
are now considered as pots of clay,
 the work of a potter's hands!

3 Even jackals offer their breasts
 to nurse their young,
but my people have become heartless
 like ostriches in the desert.[b]

4 Because of thirst the infant's tongue
 sticks to the roof of its mouth;[c]
the children beg for bread,
 but no one gives it to them.[d]

5 Those who once ate delicacies
 are destitute in the streets.
Those brought up in royal purple[e]
 now lie on ash heaps.[f]

6 The punishment of my people
 is greater than that of Sodom,[g]
which was overthrown in a moment
 without a hand turned to help her.

7 Their princes were brighter than snow
 and whiter than milk,
their bodies more ruddy than rubies,
 their appearance like lapis lazuli.

8 But now they are blacker[h] than soot;
 they are not recognized in the streets.
Their skin has shriveled on their bones;[i]
 it has become as dry as a stick.

[a] This chapter is an acrostic poem, the verses of which begin with the successive letters of the Hebrew alphabet.

4:1–22 *Despair.* This patient, ominous, depressing observation of suffering on every side gives a human face to the travelogue of trauma in ch. 2. In vv. 1–16, the poet's voice is a dispassionate third person, flickering with identity to Zion herself in the fleeting first-person references in vv. 3,6,10. Verses 17–20 add to the catalog of woe but through the eyes of the dispossessed and defeated people themselves; the language is consistently in the first-person plural: the collective voice of the community. Finally, vv. 21–22 predict Edom's fate by way of contrast with Zion's. There is little room for reminiscence: the brief glances to the past only exacerbate present distress.

This lament holds out no hope for the future (though see v. 22). There is no prayer (this is the only poem in the book that does not directly address God). Strikingly, a mute note of hope embedded in the wish for the enemy's destruction at the end of the poem is not spoken as a prayer but is addressed directly to Edom. This pervasive mood of despair contrasts sharply with the active hope of ch. 3. It finds its closest echo in the OT in the bleak Ps 88, although in that psalm, Heman's direct addresses to God maintain at least some semblance of relationship. The poet of this lament cannot even rise to that in his somber account of annihilation. Still, a fundamental theological foundation is visible regarding God's agency (vv. 11,16) and the community's responsibility (v. 13). This prepares for a further contrast with ch. 5, which is entirely addressed to God.

4:1–16 *Zion's Desolations.* This sad survey of Jerusalem's ravished cityscape is dominated by the bleak scene surveyed by the poet but includes reflections on causes as well as effects.

4:1–2 Literalistic readers stumble over the notion that gold does not tarnish, but that is to miss the point. The picture is that of the aftermath of destruction: charred embers and settling dust. This figurative overlaying of the temple rubble (the focus of the second poem) with the fate of human victims, reinforced by the insistent language of these opening verses, creates a powerful effect. Place plus people, both formerly blessed by God's presence, are now bereft of life and hope.

4:5 streets. This scene is constantly held before the reader's eyes; the Hebrew word (*ḥûṣ*) is repeated in vv. 1,8,14 (and a related Hebrew term occurs in the first-person plural section in v. 18). This is a relentlessly public display.

9 Those killed by the sword are better off
than those who die of famine;
racked with hunger, they waste away
for lack of food from the field.[j]

10 With their own hands compassionate women
have cooked their own children,[k]
who became their food
when my people were destroyed.

11 The LORD has given full vent to his wrath;
he has poured out his fierce anger.
He kindled a fire[l] in Zion
that consumed her foundations.[m]

12 The kings of the earth did not believe,
nor did any of the peoples of the world,
that enemies and foes could enter
the gates of Jerusalem.[n]

13 But it happened because of the sins of her prophets
and the iniquities of her priests,[o]
who shed within her
the blood of the righteous.

14 Now they grope through the streets
as if they were blind.[p]
They are so defiled with blood[q]
that no one dares to touch their garments.

15 "Go away! You are unclean!" people cry to them.
"Away! Away! Don't touch us!"
When they flee and wander about,
people among the nations say,
"They can stay here no longer."[r]

16 The LORD himself has scattered them;
he no longer watches over them.[s]
The priests are shown no honor,
the elders[t] no favor.

17 Moreover, our eyes failed,
looking in vain[u] for help;[v]

4:9 [j] Jer 15:2; 16:4
4:10 [k] Lev 26:29; Dt 28:53-57; Jer 19:9; La 2:20; Eze 5:10
4:11 [l] Jer 17:27 [m] Dt 32:22; Jer 7:20; Eze 22:31
4:12 [n] 1Ki 9:9; Jer 21:13
4:13 [o] Jer 5:31; 6:13; Eze 22:28; Mic 3:11
4:14 [p] Isa 59:10 [q] Jer 2:34; 19:4
4:15 [r] Lev 13:46
4:16 [s] Isa 9:14-16 [t] La 5:12
4:17 [u] Isa 20:5; Eze 29:16 [v] La 1:7

4:9–10 This quietly contemplates the full horror of the effects of famine.
4:10 women have cooked their own children. Mothers cannibalizing their children is shocking, but the poet simply registers it as a further facet of Zion's plight. An outcome of covenant infidelity (Lev 26:27–29; Deut 28:53–57), it compares with the earlier siege of Samaria (2 Kgs 6:26–29) and is mentioned in the preaching of Jeremiah (Jer 19:9).
4:11,16 The LORD. As in ch. 2, the only effective actor in the destruction of Jerusalem is God alone (see note on 2:3).
4:13 because of. This nuanced ethical assessment develops the guilt implied by "punishment" in v. 6. Sin in the city has occasioned divine destruction, but it is not generalized. Failures of "prophets" and "priests" led to shedding "the blood of the righteous"—for such are still to be found in the community. The more typical formulation is "innocent blood," which Jeremiah uses five times (Jer 7:6; 19:4; 22:3,17; 26:15) following the pattern of Deuteronomy (five times: Deut 19:10,13; 21:8,9; 27:25 "innocent person"). The issue here, however, is not so much standing in law as right standing before God.
4:14 defiled with blood. The "iniquities" of v. 13 provoke the outcry of v. 15. Priests were responsible for the maintenance of purity (Ezek 22:26; 44:23); their own actions render them unfit for service (Num 19:20) and abhorrent to the community.
4:17–20 *Communal Disappointment.* These verses are couched in insistently first-person plural language, deepening the depressed affect by expressing the community's demoralized disappointment.
4:17–20 What "we" did or thought (vv. 17,20) frames observations on what others did (vv. 18–19). The poetic formulation of these lines is especially intricate, as the discipline of the poet's art gives shape to his grief. If these details are taken as autobiographical, then the poet could have been among those who fled with Zedekiah (2 Kgs 25:4–5).
4:17 a nation that could not save us. The vain hope they looked to was likely Egypt (cf. Jer 37:4–10). If external support was absent, internal support (v. 20) also failed.

4:17 [w] Jer 37:7
4:18 [x] Eze 7:2-12; Am 8:2
4:19 [y] Dt 28:49 [z] Isa 5:26-28
4:20 [a] 2Sa 19:21 [b] Jer 39:5; Eze 12:12-13; 19:4,8
4:21 [c] Jer 25:15 [d] Isa 34:6-10; Am 1:11-12; Ob 16
4:22 [e] Isa 40:2; Jer 33:8 [f] Ps 137:7; Mal 1:4
5:1 [g] Ps 44:13-16; 89:50
5:2 [h] Ps 79:1 [i] Zep 1:13
5:3 [j] Jer 15:8; 18:21

from our towers we watched
for a nation[w] that could not save us.

18 People stalked us at every step,
so we could not walk in our streets.
Our end was near, our days were numbered,
for our end had come.[x]

19 Our pursuers were swifter
than eagles[y] in the sky;
they chased us[z] over the mountains
and lay in wait for us in the desert.

20 The LORD's anointed,[a] our very life breath,
was caught in their traps.[b]
We thought that under his shadow
we would live among the nations.

21 Rejoice and be glad, Daughter Edom,
you who live in the land of Uz.
But to you also the cup[c] will be passed;
you will be drunk and stripped naked.[d]

22 Your punishment will end, Daughter Zion;[e]
he will not prolong your exile.
But he will punish your sin, Daughter Edom,
and expose your wickedness.[f]

5

Remember, LORD, what has happened to us;
look, and see our disgrace.[g]
2 Our inheritance[h] has been turned over to strangers,
our homes[i] to foreigners.
3 We have become fatherless,
our mothers are widows.[j]

4:20 The LORD's anointed. The identity of the particular Davidic possibility in mind here is obscure, although Zedekiah is one candidate; the phrase is used most often by David of Saul (e.g., 1 Sam 24:6,10).
4:21–22 *Edom's Retribution.* Zion's distress occasions a reflection on neighbor Edom's fate.
4:21–22 The voice changes once again, but to whom does it belong? Since it addresses both Edom and Zion and refers to God in the third person, it may well be the voice of a prophet or at least the poet speaking with prophetic overtones.
4:21 Daughter. Echoes the frequent use in ch. 2 (see note on 2:1). **Edom.** Viewed as especially culpable for exposing Judah to the ravages of the Babylonians (Ps 137:7; Obad 1,10–11). **cup.** This motif provides a further link to the language of Jeremiah (e.g., Jer 25:15–29). The strains of confidence in these verses jar against the morose tone of the rest of the poem.
5:1–22 *"Remember, LORD."* The fourth poem uniquely does not address God at all, and the fifth and final poem is addressed wholly to God, although this does not mean that God is the focus of attention. The voice of the community ("us," "our," "we") is heard throughout: vv. 1,19–22 implore God directly to consider his suffering people, leaving vv. 2–18 as a continuous litany of woe. Although ch. 5 is linked by theme and vocabulary to the preceding chapters, its outlook implies a situation of settled domination rather than the fresh conquest that the preceding chapters envisage. Theologically it coheres with the rest of the book, as the confessions in vv. 7,16–18 share the conviction expressed throughout Lamentations that sin in the community is responsible for the disaster. Its form echoes that of laments found in the Psalms in which the community calls on God to respond to its suffering cry (cf. Pss 44; 80). This is by far the shortest poem in the book, its 22 verses being a single line each: the length required for an acrostic poem but without using the alphabetic acrostic technique itself. The literary shape of the poem—the loss of both the acrostic pattern and the *qinah* meter (see Introduction: Literary Style and Genre)—thus reflects its content, as hope ebbs away (cf. v. 17).
5:1 *Imploring the Lord.* The lack of any direct address to God in ch. 4 contrasts sharply with the opening invocation of this final lament.
5:1 Remember. Does not imply that God's memory is faulty (see note on Gen 8:1). It is one of the typical ways the psalmists of lament invite God to attend to a situation of distress and respond appropriately (e.g., Ps 137:7 specifies the Edomite atrocities by this means; cf. Ps 74, a communal lament in which "remember" occurs three times [Ps 74:2,18,22]). **look, and see our disgrace.** Recalls 1:9,11,20, deliberately linking the first and fifth poems as a frame for the book.
5:2–18 *Catalog of Woe.* Earlier surveys combined place and populace, but this litany attends almost solely to the troubles and traumas suffered by the inhabitants of Judah and Jerusalem.
5:2 Our inheritance ... our homes. This pained overview of communal suffering continues throughout the chapter in the first-person plural language that is featured toward the end of ch. 4 (see note on 4:17–20).

Assyrians impaling and dismembering their enemies as shown on the Balawat Gate. Lam 5 also mentions violence and abuse of God's people.

A. D. Riddle/www.BiblePlaces.com, taken at the British Museum

4 We must buy the water we drink;
our wood can be had only at a price.[k]
5 Those who pursue us are at our heels;
we are weary[l] and find no rest.
6 We submitted to Egypt and Assyria[m]
to get enough bread.
7 Our ancestors sinned and are no more,
and we bear their punishment.[n]
8 Slaves[o] rule over us,
and there is no one to free us from their hands.[p]
9 We get our bread at the risk of our lives
because of the sword in the desert.
10 Our skin is hot as an oven,
feverish from hunger.[q]
11 Women have been violated[r] in Zion,
and virgins in the towns of Judah.
12 Princes have been hung up by their hands;
elders are shown no respect.[s]
13 Young men toil at the millstones;
boys stagger under loads of wood.
14 The elders are gone from the city gate;
the young men have stopped their music.[t]

5:4 [k] Isa 3:1
5:5 [l] Ne 9:37
5:6 [m] Hos 9:3
5:7 [n] Jer 14:20; 16:12
5:8 [o] Ne 5:15 [p] Zec 11:6
5:10 [q] La 4:8-9
5:11 [r] Zec 14:2
5:12 [s] La 4:16
5:14 [t] Isa 24:8; Jer 7:34

5:6 submitted. Given warnings from the prophets, neither Egypt (Isa 30:1–2) nor Assyria (Jer 2:18) ought to have been a source of sustenance for God's people. Ironically, of the ancient Near Eastern "superpowers" that vied for supremacy at this time, only the Babylonians were resisted—but Judah should have submitted to them (Jer 29).

5:7 Ancestral responsibility and cumulative guilt became contentious notions during the exilic period. The movement from Jeremiah's use of the "sour grapes" proverb (Jer 31:29–30) to its elaboration by Ezekiel (Ezek 18) illustrates this shifting perspective. The books of Chronicles teach that individuals pay for their own sin (e.g., 10:13; 2 Chr 26:16). But at this point the poet still envisages the present plight of the community as the result of generational sin (see note on v. 16).

5:12 hung. The action and intent is unclear, especially since "their hands" could refer to the enemy's hands rather than the princes' hands (cf. v. 8). It is unlikely that hanging as a form of execution is in mind, at least not by noose, as the exposure of bodies by impalement was the more typical practice. Perhaps, then, in parallel with treatment of elders, this is some form of shaming action, akin to being put in the stocks.

5:15 [u] Jer 25:10
5:16 [v] Ps 89:39 [w] Isa 3:11
5:17 [x] Isa 1:5 [y] Ps 6:7
5:18 [z] Mic 3:12
5:19 [a] Ps 45:6; 102:12,24-27
5:20 [b] Ps 13:1; 44:24
5:21 [c] Ps 80:3
5:22 [d] Isa 64:9

15 Joy is gone from our hearts;
our dancing has turned to mourning.[u]
16 The crown[v] has fallen from our head.
Woe to us, for we have sinned![w]
17 Because of this our hearts[x] are faint,
because of these things our eyes[y] grow dim
18 for Mount Zion, which lies desolate,[z]
with jackals prowling over it.

19 You, LORD, reign forever;
your throne endures[a] from generation to generation.
20 Why do you always forget us?[b]
Why do you forsake us so long?
21 Restore[c] us to yourself, LORD, that we may return;
renew our days as of old
22 unless you have utterly rejected us
and are angry with us beyond measure.[d]

5:15 dancing ... mourning. An inversion of Jeremiah's hope (Jer 31:13; cf. Ps 30:11).
5:16 This lament equally recognizes the sin of the present generation; the destructive inheritance of ancestral guilt that v. 7 claims does not absolve the contemporary generation. In the mind of the poet, it is not a matter of *either* ancestral sin *or* contemporary sin but rather both/and, just as the Jerusalem community would later confess under Nehemiah (Neh 9:2; cf. Ezra 9:6–7; Dan 9:6,8,16).
5:19–22 *Imploring the Lord—Reprise.* With the summary statement of the desolation of Mount Zion (v. 18) concluding the account of the oppressive suffering now experienced in Judah and Jerusalem, the explicit plea to God to respond continues from v. 1.
5:19 reign forever. The plea for God to bring relief is rooted in recognizing his sovereignty. This declaration echoes the confessions of Pss 9:7; 102:12, where God's eternal rule implies also the exercise of divine justice.
5:20–22 The hallmark of lament is the plaintive and protesting "Why?" This is not a request for an explanation but a means of registering the community's need of divine intervention. Like the psalmist in Ps 89, the poet cannot reconcile a future in which the community's current plight continues with knowledge of God and his promises.
5:22 From the ancient versions onward, there has been no consensus on understanding how v. 22 connects to what precedes it. Of several possibilities, two have the most merit. (1) The NIV's "unless" is among the most common translations given the vehemence of the language in the rest of the verse. At the same time, this rendering seems to retreat from the plea the community has embarked on. Are they prepared to give up on God if God has given up on them? (2) The Hebrew particles may be translated "although." This aligns well with the spirit of the request—forthrightly owning guilt and acknowledging God's just anger—but pleading for restoration nonetheless. This option, however, stands in some tension with the finality expressed in the remainder of the verse. This linguistic ambiguity is telling, deepening the sense of God's utter sovereignty and the precarious status of the suffering community. The struggle for hope can find a resolution nowhere else but in God himself.

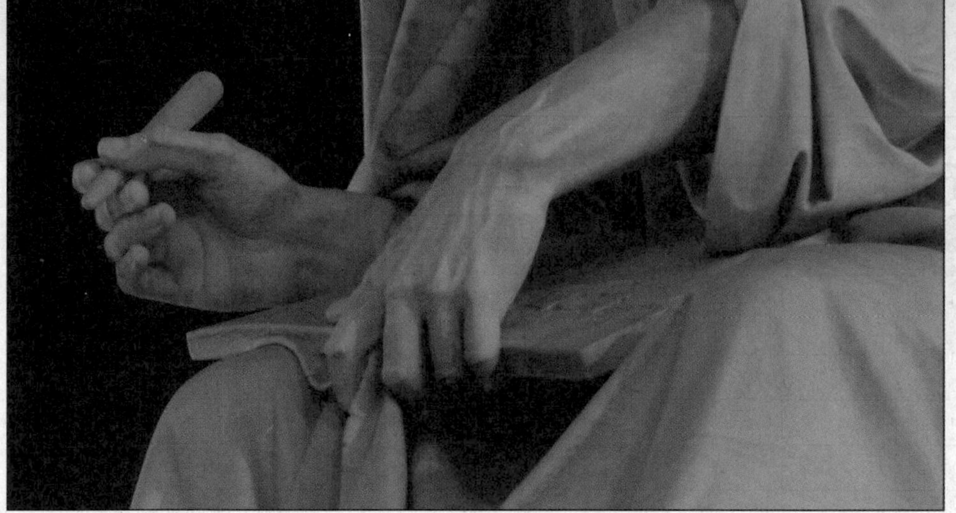

INTRODUCTION TO EZEKIEL

The book of Ezekiel highlights Israel's unrelenting sins of rebellion and idolatry that lead to Yahweh's unrelenting anger and culminates in the fall of Jerusalem. Sin results in death, and Ezekiel repeatedly portrays the death and destruction that await Israel. Ultimately, death brings lamentation, mourning, and woe; yet out of death restored life will come. In both the death and the life of his people, God will get the glory he desires and deserves.

AUTHOR

A dominant autobiographical style suggests that Ezekiel is the author of the book bearing his name. Besides the reference in 1 Chr 24:16 of another Ezekiel (called "Jehezkel") who existed in an earlier generation, the designation does not occur elsewhere in the Bible. The name in Hebrew means, "may God strengthen" or "God strengthens." Although his given name is Ezekiel, he is designated as "son of man" 93 times (e.g., 2:1) and as Ezekiel only twice (1:3; 24:24). Ezekiel is Israel's prophet (2:5; 33:33), watchman (3:17; 33:7), sign (12:6,11; 24:24,27), judge (20:4; 22:2), and funeral director (19:1; 27:1–11,26–36; 28:11; 32:1). He comes from priestly stock (1:3), is a married exile (1:1–3; 3:11,15; 24:15–24), and is grief-stricken (2:9—3:15).

DATE

The biblical record does not often give dates. Ezekiel contains more dates (see "Dates in Ezekiel," p. 1598) than any other OT prophetic book. Its prophecies can be dated with considerable precision. This is so because modern scholarship, using archaeology (Babylonian annals on cuneiform tablets) and astronomy (accurate dating of eclipses referred to in ancient archives), provides relatively precise modern calendar equivalents. Of the 13 dates mentioned, 12 specify times when Ezekiel received a divine message. The other is the date of the arrival of the messenger who reported Jerusalem's fall (33:21). Ezekiel's call came on July 31, 593 BC, and he ministered for 22 years; his last dated message was received on April 26, 571 BC (see 29:17). Ezekiel's ministry began 7 years before Jerusalem's 586 BC destruction and continued for 14 years after the city's fall.

AUDIENCE

Ezekiel's preaching targeted those whom Nebuchadnezzar exiled to Babylon in 597 BC (2 Kgs 24:10–16; Dan 1:1). A few years into their exile, God called Ezekiel, who was among those exiled at that time, to speak to his fellow exiles concerning unfolding events back in Jerusalem (1:1—3:15). The Kebar River locates him and his audience (1:1), but he probably preached and shared the visions from his house (3:24–27; 8:1). Ezekiel and the exilic community (at the Kebar River) were within a close suburb of Nippur, a city that for centuries was a renowned hub of Mesopotamian religion.

In preparation for commencing his ministry, God repeatedly communicated important information about Ezekiel's audience. The Israelites in exile (2:3; 3:1,4–5,7) were rebellious, obstinate, stubborn, and hardened (2:3–8; 3:7). They were like their stiff-necked (stubborn) ancestors who rebelled (2:3; cf. Exod 32:1–12). Ezekiel's audience, after some 800 years of blatant, stubborn misconduct, was no better: they had not only stiff necks but also stiff hearts (3:8).

DATES IN EZEKIEL

REFERENCE	YEAR	MONTH	DAY	APPROXIMATE MODERN RECKONING	EVENT
1. 1:1	30	4	5	July 31, 593 BC	Inaugural vision
1:2	5	—	5		
3:16	"At the end of seven days"				
2. 8:1	6	6	5	Sept. 17, 592	The temple vision
3. 20:1–2	7	5	10	Aug. 14, 591	Negative view of Israel's history
4. 24:1	9	10	10	Jan. 15, 588	Beginning of siege (see also 2 Kgs 25:1)
5. 26:1	11	—	1	between Apr. 23, 587, and Apr. 13, 586; or alternatively Feb. 3, 585	Prophecy against Tyre (see note on 26:1)
6. 29:1	10	10	12	Jan. 7, 587	Prophecy against Egypt
7. 29:17	27	1	1	Apr. 26, 571	Egypt as plunder for Nebuchadnezzar
8. 30:20	11	1	7	Apr. 29, 587	Prophecy against Pharaoh
9. 31:1	11	3	1	June 21, 587	Prophecy against Pharaoh
10. 32:1	12	12	1	Mar. 3, 585	Lament over Pharaoh
11. 32:17	12	—	15	between Apr. 13, 586, and Apr. 1, 585	Egypt's burial
12. 33:21	12	10	5	Jan. 8, 585	Arrival of first fugitive
13. 40:1	25	1	10	Apr. 28, 573	Vision of new spiritual center
40:1	"fourteenth year after the fall of the city"				

PARTICULAR INTERPRETIVE CHALLENGES

Among the challenges of reading any prophetic book, but especially Ezekiel, is the identification of certain places and figures. Gog and Magog (chs. 38–39) and the new temple (chs. 40–48) are the two examples that most interest readers in this regard. When will these prophecies be fulfilled? And by whom?

Chs. 38–39, along with parts of Isaiah, Daniel, Zechariah, and Revelation, are apocalyptic literature. By nature this type of literature is highly figurative, symbolic, and futuristic (see Introduction to Revelation: Literary Genre [Apocalypse]). When reading these texts, one must keep the larger meaning in mind rather than strive to interpret their details. Reading the book in this way, chs. 38–39 teach that in order for God's glory to be revealed, he must act decisively and powerfully against all opposition to that goal. The battle that unfolds in the Gog narrative represents such a reality and should be the interpreter's prime focus. Chs. 38–39 would have encouraged the exiles to know that their enemies would be dealt with by God in the future. Although the starting point of God dealing with his enemies unfolds in the prophecies against the nations (chs. 25–32) and begins in 539 BC with the defeat of Babylon by Persia, the Gog narrative points beyond this time frame to future realities. The battle points to the end of the age, when God will destroy the "Babylon" of this age, along with the beast and the devil (Rev 18–20).

Likewise, the vision of restored worship in a new "temple-city" (chs. 40–48) describes worship in terms familiar to a Judahite, but it does not demand literalism. The worship that unfolds through the rebuilt "temple-city" envisions a relationship with God, one even better than past experiences, and it should be the interpreter's focus. Chs. 40–48 would have encouraged the exiles to have hope in the character and promises of God for an even better future. The reader should realize that although the starting point for the fulfillment of restored worship is 539 BC (when the exiles began to return to Jerusalem), the vision points beyond this to future realities. The picture of restored worship that unfolds in chs. 40–48 points to the covenantal promises of God realized in Jesus. In Jesus one finds complete restoration. The vision of restored worship points to the age to come, when worship of God will be unhindered, undefiled, and unmediated — the ultimate restoration.

HISTORICAL SETTING, PURPOSE, AND OCCASION

In 593 BC, God's people were living out the consequences of their failures. Because they chose to turn away from the Lord and not trust in him, Judah experienced a military takeover. The Babylonians had already displaced two waves of Judahites from the promised land to Babylon (605 BC and 597 BC), and they soon would reduce the temple in Jerusalem — the object of Judah's affection — to rubble when they besieged and destroyed Jerusalem in 586 BC. All of this would lead to many people of Judah living on foreign soil for 70 long years. Their markers of identity as God's people (the temple and the land) were being stripped away before their very eyes. They seemed separated from God and his promises. Thus, Judah was paying a price for sins and idolatry that could have been avoided. Years later Ezra would look back on the sum of these events and conclude that their guilt had mounted to the heavens; for their sins, Israel's and Judah's kings, priests, and people were subjected to the sword, captivity, plundering, and utter humiliation (Ezra 9:6 – 7).

In the middle of this mess, God raised up Ezekiel not merely to warn that the siege and fall of Jerusalem were inevitable but also to help those in exile interpret these events. Through Ezekiel, God placed a corrective lens on their faulty interpretation of the Babylonian invasions of Jerusalem. The situation back in Jerusalem demanded that the exiles in Babylon be anchored in reality. It was not a time to deny the death of the community (12:27), heed false prophets assuring the community's preservation (ch. 13), pass blame for their suffering on to others (18:1 – 4), question Yahweh's justice (18:25,29), or hope for the city's preservation or for the safety of loved ones. It was a time to sigh, groan, and mourn (21:6 – 7,12 – 13; 24:17).

But hardened, disobedient people such as the exiles in Babylon were unable to grasp the gravity and theological realities of their circumstances. They were incapable of mourning because they believed God would rescue them; indeed, they thought he was *obliged* to rescue them. After all, they were his people, Jerusalem was his holy dwelling, and the land was theirs due to divine promise. They failed to recognize that their suffering was not because God had faltered but because *they* had faltered. They thought that God would save and shield them even from the consequences of their own rebellion. Death and destruction of this religious community, as Ezekiel predicted, did not fit their theological grid.

For this reason, Ezekiel's prophetic act of mourning was crucial. By his mourning he prophetically indicated the coming and necessary mourning God's people would experience. By eating a scroll containing lamentation, mourning, and woe, Ezekiel became what he ate (2:8 – 10). His posture of mourning immediately expressed this: sitting in stunned silence for a period of seven days (3:15). Many of his actions in chs. 3 – 24 also showed that he had become a

EZEKIEL IN BABYLON

mourner. For example, his sentence to house confinement and a speechlessness that persisted until the city fell could indicate an extended mourning period (3:24 — 4:17). Various gestures that God had commanded — e.g., cutting hair from his beard and head (5:1), clapping his hands, stomping his feet, and saying "alas" in response to the people's "detestable practices" (6:11) — further indicate mourning. On two occasions Ezekiel utilized words associated with grief and mourning when asking God to spare Israel further destruction (9:8 – 10; 11:13). He mourned for Jerusalem's princes (ch. 19). He mourned for the city of Jerusalem by striking his hands together (21:17). Ezekiel symbolically reenacted Israel's funeral procession and mourned inwardly when his wife died (24:15 – 24). He even mourned the downfall of the kings of Tyre and Egypt (27:1 — 28:19; 32:1 – 16). In this way, the man became the message and the means by which the exiles were to interpret their circumstances. God's aim through Ezekiel was for the exiles to lament over their situation *before* the events of 586 BC. Such an attitude would have led them to acknowledge wrongdoing. But had they adopted such a posture, not even mournful pleas and petitions by Ezekiel could have reversed Yahweh's decision, one secured by the scroll. Thus, Ezekiel's actions communicated to the exiles that it was a time to mourn (see 21:6 – 7,12 – 13; 24:17).

LITERARY FEATURES

The book of Ezekiel follows the pattern of other prophetic books (i.e., Isaiah, Jeremiah, and Zephaniah) in that it contains prophecies of judgment and restoration. Particular to Ezekiel, however, is how the book is patterned after the well-known city lament genre in the ancient Near East. As that genre title indicates, Ezekiel laments for the city of Jerusalem throughout the book (see Historical Setting, Purpose, and Occasion). Important elements of the genre include the themes of death and destruction and the anger of God manifested by his abandonment of the temple because of the people's sin and guilt. Also included in the city lament genre is the theme of restoration. The imprint of this genre for the entire collection of Ezekiel's prophecies, dated over a period of years, is illustrated in how the mourning theme unfolds in the book.

Chs. 1 – 24 (see Outline: A Time to Mourn: Prophecies Against Israel) begin with the scroll incident (2:8 — 3:3) and end with the death of Ezekiel's wife (24:15 – 18). The section starts with a prediction of the city's siege (4:1 – 17) and closes with a prediction of its fall (24:20 – 27). Responsibility for Jerusalem's fall is assigned to God's people. Ezekiel's repeated use of terms for guilt and abominations, the repeated "because ... therefore" indictment pattern (e.g., 5:9 – 12), and the recollection and description of Israelite history unpack Israel's guilt. This explains the book's numerous demonstrations of God's seemingly unrestrained anger that leads to divine abandonment (God physically leaves the temple in ch. 10). Accordingly, Yahweh will destroy the city. Yahweh himself will call for his agents of destruction, the Babylonians, who through the sword will destroy Jerusalem in 586 BC. These chapters repeatedly show how Yahweh, together with his authorized agents, will bring wide-scale destruction and devastation to Jerusalem.

The finale to this fate is the death of Ezekiel's own wife (24:15 – 27). Her death was an immediate sign of the city's fall. However, embedded in this tragedy was another sign. The command to put on festive garments at a time of grief indicated that mourning would come to an end. The death of Ezekiel's wife and the associated symbolism of wearing festive garments at an unexpected time created anticipation among the exiles (24:19). Once the city fell, there would be no reason to mourn because God would have dealt with the problem; his anger would be spent. Putting on festive garments, therefore, would be a sign to anticipate a hopeful future.

In chs. 25 – 32 (see Outline: Signs Mourning Will End: Prophecies Against the Nations), the prophecies of Yahweh's punishment of Israel's neighbors are other signs that mourning would end. The prophecies against these cities and nations (those who made Israel's grief worse) provide Israel with necessary comfort and represent a necessary first step in Israel's forthcoming restoration. When Israel's oppressors received their punishment, Israel would be comforted. The mourning period would cease when comfort came, giving way to restoration.

In chs. 33 – 48 (see Outline: A Time to Rejoice: Words of Restoration and Hope), the sequence of events moves from death to life. When the fugitive brought word that Jerusalem had fallen (33:21 – 22), mourning would officially end and restoration would be possible. This is so because Yahweh would have a change of heart. He would provide new and faithful leadership (ch. 34), cleansing Israel and giving life (chs. 36 – 37), cleansing the land from the enemy both near and far (chs. 35; 38 – 39), rebuilding his sanctuary, and dwelling once again in a new temple-city where his seat of sovereignty would be firmly established (chs. 40 – 48). Ezek 48:35 best summarizes this permanent and ideal condition: "And the name of the city from that time on will be: THE LORD IS THERE." The name of the city reflects the fullness of the restoration due to Yahweh's presence. Accordingly, Yahweh will be exalted as sovereign over all the earth (37:28). Thus, it is a time to rejoice; out of death comes restored life.

THEOLOGICAL SIGNIFICANCE

The driving force behind the city's fall and rise is Yahweh's desire and intention to be known and acknowledged as sovereign over all. Approximately 65 occurrences or variations of the clause "they will know that I am the LORD" (e.g., 6:10,13,14) testify to this divine desire and intention. In fact, the phrase punctuates the vast majority of Ezekiel's prophecies. Yahweh's desire is to vindicate his glory and character, the holiness of his name, as he interacts with people.

The book reveals that both internal and external challenges threaten this purpose. With respect to the internal threat, God's own people are guilty of idolatry: "you continue to defile yourselves with all your idols to this day" (20:31) and "I had concern for my holy name, which the people of Israel profaned among the nations where they had gone" (36:21). More than any other prophet, Ezekiel helps us understand how idolatry arouses God to anger. Idolatry diminishes the glory that is Yahweh's due. God is utterly opposed to sharing his glory with idols (Isa 48:11). To ignore this is to bring judgment: "When I have spent my wrath on them, they will know that I the LORD have spoken in my zeal" (5:13). This divine word formula, coupled with his merciless gaze ("I will not look on you with pity" [5:11; 7:9]), is lethal for Israel.

The outpouring of Yahweh's fury on Israel requires divine abandonment, God turning his face away in judgment (39:24). The results are death and destruction through exile, the promised covenantal curses. This judgment, however, is, ironically, accompanied by deeper knowledge of God: "then you will know that it is I the LORD who strikes you" (7:9c) and "they will know that I am the LORD, when their people lie slain among their idols" (6:13).

But once Yahweh's wrath is poured out, once justice is served through the exile, God's anger subsides (24:13). This produces another divine confrontation: as part of the restoration, divine compassion (39:25) confronts Israel's uncleanness acquired from idolatry (24:13). Ezekiel promises that God will "save" Israel from her uncleanness by performing heart surgery (36:25–26), a supernatural act requiring no human assistance. In so doing hardened hearts become pliable — a heart surgery that with God's Spirit enables a spiritually transformed life. This transformation entails keeping God's law, enjoying the promises of God (the land as an inheritance), and a renewed relationship with him forever. Indeed, Ezekiel uses resurrection language (the return from exile) to describe this transformation from death to life. This act too, Ezekiel says, is driven out of concern for Yahweh's own reputation: "It is not for your sake, people of Israel, that I am going to do these things, but for the sake of my holy name, which you have profaned ... I will show the holiness of my great name ... Then the nations will know that I am the LORD ... I will gather you from all the countries and bring you back into your own land ... I will cleanse you ... from all your idols" (36:22–25). Thus, through a divine confrontation of compassion, God cleanses his people and resolves the internal threat.

There is also an external threat to God's desire and intention to be known and acknowledged as sovereign, namely, the surrounding nations. God must confront all of Israel's enemies. He must make a public spectacle of them because of their gross misunderstanding of his character (chs. 25–32; 38–39). Israel's idolatry, which led to exile, mars God's reputation among the nations; i.e., negative and false views about Yahweh exist as long as Israel remains in exile. The nations view Yahweh as impotent. But as outside observers, the nations are not aware of the human causation (idolatry) that led to the exile. In this way, idolatry robs God of the glory due his name. Hence God invites a battle on his land in Israel and defeats the enemy (39:21–24). Thus, through another divine confrontation of judgment God guarantees that his power and uniqueness will never again be questioned; he proves his holiness among the nations.

From a biblical-theological point of view, Ezekiel points forward to the bigger picture of redemptive history. The driving force behind humankind's fall and restoration is God's desire to be known and acknowledged as sovereign over all. Humankind's idolatry and guilt continued to pose an internal threat to God's purposes of achieving glory. As Paul says, "All have sinned and fall short of the glory of God" (Rom 3:23). In this condition people lack the ability to live holy lives and to demonstrate God's holy character to the world. People rob God of his glory, reputation, and character. This angers God, resulting in divine judgment, for only divine intervention can put a stop to this ongoing problem. The cross ultimately confronts this internal threat: God intervenes and pours out his wrath on Jesus rather than on us. Jesus experienced divine abandonment from the Father, the ultimate covenantal curse.

The cross also confronts our uncleanness. Jesus' blood cleanses us from all sin and unrighteousness (1 John 1:9); in so doing he saves us by performing heart surgery, fills us with the new life of his Spirit, who empowers us for holy living to enjoy his promises forever in a renewed relationship. Indeed the resurrection enables the supernatural transformation from death to life. This saving act of cleansing and restoration requires no human assistance. For it is "in Christ" that we are holy and blameless before God (Rom 8:1; 1 Cor 1:30). As a direct result of this act, God receives all the glory, "to the praise of his glorious grace" (Eph 1:6).

The cross and resurrection confront the external threat to God's desire to be known and acknowledged as sovereign over all. Jesus triumphs over the devil and the powers of darkness, humiliating the enemy and revealing God's holiness and sovereign power over sin and death (Col 2:13–15). This decisive victory ensures his glory for all time, something that he will fully secure at the end of the age.

Ultimately, Ezekiel points us to the consummation of God's kingdom (see "The Consummation," p. 2695). Judgment and restoration of the city in Ezekiel prepare us for the restored city that culminates in Revelation (see "The City of God," p. 2666). John sees "the Holy City, the new Jerusalem, coming down out of heaven from God" (Rev 21:2). The new Jerusalem is the true spiritual center of God's eternal kingdom (Rev 21:1–3). In the new Jerusalem, mourning has turned to joy and death becomes life (Rev 21:4). The new Jerusalem is the seat of Yahweh's sovereignty, which is no longer challenged but stands forever. Idolatry is no longer a threat. The new Jerusalem is holy and pure (Rev 22:3–5). Through the praise and adoration of those present, Yahweh will receive continual glory and honor. The new Jerusalem is the seat of the divine presence (Rev 21:3–4,22). Yahweh has provided a way for our mourning to turn to joy. Is it any wonder that the heavenly anthem that resounds in Revelation is all about proclaiming God's glory? The four living creatures, the 24 elders, myriads of angels, and people from every tongue and language are around the throne of God, his seat of sovereignty over the universe, giving him unending praise and adoration (Rev 4:8–11). Thus, in this respect, Ezekiel anticipates the cross, the resurrection, and the consummation of God's kingdom, when at long last God's desire to be known and acknowledged will be fulfilled (Phil 2:9–11).

OUTLINE

I. A Time to Mourn: Prophecies Against Israel (1:1—24:27)

- A. Ezekiel's First and Formative Vision (1:1—3:27)
  1. Ezekiel Experiences God's Presence in Babylon (1:1–28)
  2. Ezekiel's Call as Prophet and Mourner (2:1—3:15)
  3. Ezekiel's Call as Watchman (3:16–21)
  4. Ezekiel's Confinement and Speechlessness (3:22–27)
- B. Visual Aids of Jerusalem's Upcoming Siege (4:1—5:17)
  1. Ezekiel's Drawing, Posture, and Dietary Restrictions (4:1–17)
  2. Shaving as a Sign of Humiliation and Mourning (5:1–17)
- C. Descriptions of Upcoming Total Destruction (6:1—7:27)
  1. Doom for the Mountains of Israel (6:1–14)
  2. The End for the Entire Land (7:1–27)
- D. The Temple Vision (8:1—11:25)
  1. Tour of Temple Violations (8:1–18)
  2. Temple Owner's Response (9:1–11)
  3. God's Presence Departs the Temple (10:1–22)
  4. God's Certain Judgment on Jerusalem (11:1–13)
  5. Those in Exile to Be Restored (11:14–21)
  6. Conclusion of Temple Vision (11:22–25)
- E. Ezekiel Symbolizes the Exile of Jerusalem (12:1–28)
  1. Packed and Ready to Go (12:1–16)
  2. Unfavorable Outcomes (12:17–28)
- F. False Prophets and Idolatry (13:1—14:23)
  1. Condemnation of False Prophets (13:1–23)
  2. Condemnation for Consulting Prophets (14:1–11)
  3. Inescapable Judgment (14:12–23)
- G. Three Allegories (15:1—17:24)
  1. Jerusalem a Useless Vine (15:1–8)
  2. Jerusalem an Adulterous Wife (16:1–63)
  3. Two Eagles and a Vine (17:1–24)
- H. Individual Responsibility (18:1–32)
  1. The One Who Sins Will Die (18:1–18)
  2. Objections to God's Justice (18:19–32)

- I. Lamenting Leadership (19:1–14)
    - 1. Lament Over Jerusalem's Kings: A Lament for the Lion (19:1–9)
    - 2. Lament Over David's Dynasty: A Lament for the Vine (19:10–14)
- J. History of Idolatry (20:1–44)
    - 1. Cycles of Rebellion (20:1–32)
        - a. Guilty in Egypt (20:1–12)
        - b. Guilty in the Wilderness (20:13–26)
        - c. Guilty in Canaan and Exile (20:27–32)
    - 2. A Shocking Exodus (20:33–38)
    - 3. Holy on My Holy Mountain (20:39–44)
- K. The Lord's Sword of Destruction (20:45—21:32)
    - 1. Forest Fire Parable and Interpretation (20:45—21:7)
    - 2. God's Sharpened and Polished Sword (21:8–17)
    - 3. The King of Babylon's Sword (21:18–27)
    - 4. The Sword Wielded Against Ammon (21:28–29)
    - 5. The Lord's Sword Returned to Its Sheath (21:30–32)
- L. History of Bloodshed (22:1–31)
    - 1. Indictment of the City (22:1–16)
    - 2. The Furnace of God's Fury (22:17–22)
    - 3. Corruption Across Classes (22:23–31)
- M. Story of Two Depraved Sisters (23:1–49)
    - 1. Samaria: Oholah's Story (23:1–10)
    - 2. Jerusalem: Oholibah's Story (23:11–21)
    - 3. The End of the Story for Oholibah (23:22–35)
    - 4. The End of the Story for Both Sisters (23:36–49)
- N. Jerusalem's Siege and the Fall Vividly Predicted (24:1–27)
    - 1. City Under Siege: Jerusalem Cooked Over the Fire (24:1–14)
    - 2. Ezekiel's Wife Dies (24:15–27)

II. Signs Mourning Will End: Prophecies Against the Nations (25:1—32:32)

- A. Prophecy Against Ammon (25:1–7)
- B. Prophecy Against Moab (25:8–11)
- C. Prophecy Against Edom (25:12–14)
- D. Prophecy Against Philistia (25:15–17)
- E. Prophecy Against Tyre and Sidon (26:1—28:26)
    - 1. Tyre's Destruction Announced (26:1–21)
    - 2. Lament Over Tyre the Ship (27:1–36)
    - 3. Lament Over Tyre's King (28:1–19)
    - 4. Prophecy Against Sidon (28:20–24)
    - 5. Israel's Restoration (28:25–26)
- F. Prophecy Against Egypt (29:1—32:32)
    - 1. Egypt a Doomed Monster (29:1–16)
    - 2. Egypt a Payment to Nebuchadnezzar (29:17–21)
    - 3. The Day of the Lord for Egypt and Her Allies (30:1–19)
    - 4. Pharaoh's Arms Broken (30:20–26)
    - 5. Pharaoh a Fallen Tree (31:1–18)
    - 6. Lament Over Pharaoh (32:1–16)
    - 7. Egypt's Descent to the Realm of the Dead (32:17–32)

III. A Time to Rejoice: Words of Restoration and Hope (33:1—48:35)

- A. Renewed Responsibilities (33:1–20)
- B. Jerusalem's Fall Reported: Ezekiel's Speech Returns (33:21–33)
- C. Restoration of Righteous Leadership (34:1–31)

D. The Mountains of Edom and Israel (35:1—36:15)
   1. Desolation for Mount Seir (35:1–15)
   2. Restoration for the Mountains of Israel (36:1–15)
E. Restoration Assured (36:16–38)
F. Restoration of People (37:1–14)
G. Restoration of Unity (37:15–28)
H. Restoration Permanent: Enemies Abroad Destroyed (38:1—39:29)
I. Restoration of Worship in the New Spiritual Center (40:1—48:35)
   1. Restoration of the Temple Area, Temple, Presence of God, and Altar (40:1—43:27)
   2. Restoration of Restricted Access for People and Priests (44:1–31)
   3. Restoration of Social Justice, Worship Calendar, and Procedures (45:1—46:24)
   4. Restoration of Land: Living Water (47:1–12)
   5. Restoration of Land Boundaries (47:13–23)
   6. Restoration of Tribal Allotments (48:1–29)
   7. Restoration of God's Sovereign Name (48:30–35)

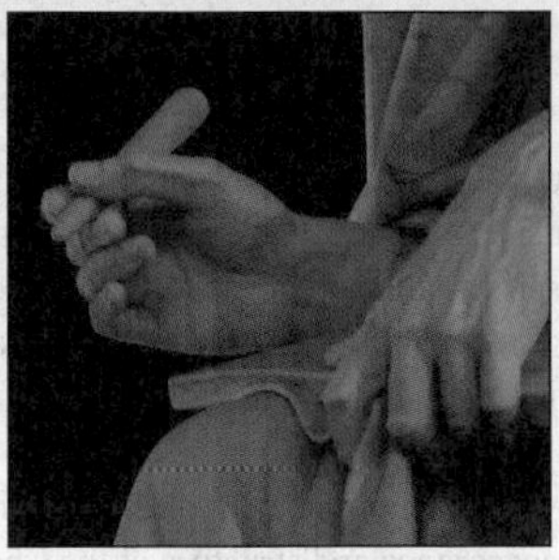

EZEKIEL

Ezekiel's Inaugural Vision

1 In my thirtieth year, in the fourth month on the fifth day, while I was among the exiles[a] by the
Kebar River, the heavens were opened[b] and I saw visions[c] of God.
[2]On the fifth of the month — it was the fifth year of the exile of King Jehoiachin[d] — [3]the word of
the LORD came to Ezekiel the priest, the son of Buzi, by the Kebar River in the land of the Babylonians.[a]
There the hand of the LORD was on him.[e]
[4]I looked, and I saw a windstorm coming out of the north[f] — an immense cloud with flashing
lightning and surrounded by brilliant light. The center of the fire looked like glowing metal,[g] [5]and in
the fire was what looked like four living creatures.[h] In appearance their form was human,[i] [6]but each
of them had four faces[j] and four wings. [7]Their legs were straight; their feet were like those of a calf and
gleamed like burnished bronze.[k] [8]Under their wings on their four sides they had human hands.[l] All
four of them had faces and wings, [9]and the wings of one touched the wings of another. Each one went
straight ahead; they did not turn as they moved.[m]
[10]Their faces looked like this: Each of the four had the face of a human being, and on the right
side each had the face of a lion, and on the left the face of an ox; each also had the face of an eagle.[n]

[a] *3* Or *Chaldeans*

1:1 [a]Eze 11:24-25 [b]Mt 3:16; Ac 7:56 [c]Ex 24:10
1:2 [d]2Ki 24:15
1:3 [e]2Ki 3:15; Eze 3:14,22
1:4 [f]Jer 1:14 [g]Eze 8:2
1:5 [h]Rev 4:6 [i]ver 26
1:6 [j]Eze 10:14
1:7 [k]Da 10:6; Rev 1:15
1:8 [l]Eze 10:8
1:9 [m]Eze 10:22
1:10 [n]Eze 10:14; Rev 4:7

1:1 — 24:27 *A Time to Mourn: Prophecies Against Israel.* Two related matters shape and frame chs. 1 – 24: the mourning motif and the city's prominence. (1) Ezekiel becomes a mourner by virtue of eating a scroll containing lamentation, mourning, and woe (2:8 – 10), and he symbolically enacts Israel's funeral procession as he mourns inwardly after his wife dies (24:15 – 24). (2) Ezekiel portrays the city's siege (ch. 4) and the city's fall, which his wife's death symbolizes (24:15 – 24). See Introduction: Literary Features.

1:1 — 3:27 *Ezekiel's First and Formative Vision.* This opening vision sets the tone for the entire book. Overcome by the supernatural, Ezekiel partially sees God and hears God's voice as he is propelled into God's service. In the context of exile, Ezekiel is the recipient of bad news. The scroll Ezekiel must eat communicates the irrevocable nature of the news, provides the main subject matter for most of the book, and sets the heavy tone of both his book and his ministry.

1:1 – 28 *Ezekiel Experiences God's Presence in Babylon.* Through a remarkable vision on foreign territory, Ezekiel experiences God's presence outside the temple in Jerusalem. He attempts to describe the indescribable: the radiant splendor of God's glory. His experience is stunning and perplexing, yet it communicates much about God.

1:1 my thirtieth year ... fourth month ... fifth day. July 31, 593 BC. The Babylonians had forcibly carried Ezekiel away from Jerusalem to Babylon in 597. **my thirtieth year.** Possibly refers to the prophet's age. Instead of entering the priestly ministry (Num 4:3), God gives him a prophetic ministry. **I saw visions of God.** Introduces the first of Ezekiel's four visions (see 8:1 – 2; 37:1 – 14; 40:1 – 2).

1:2 King Jehoiachin. This Judahite king reigned for three months (2 Kgs 24:8) in 598 – 597 BC.

1:4 I saw a windstorm. Ezekiel describes his vision. He sees a storm cloud roll in. But this is no ordinary cloud; it is both "immense" and "surrounded by brilliant light." **coming out of the north.** The cloud's direction and immensity signal disaster (cf. 23:23 – 24; 26:7; Isa 41:25; Jer 1:13 – 15; 4:6; see notes on Isa 14:31; Jer 1:13 – 14).

1:5 four living creatures. It is not until his second vision (chs. 8 – 11) that Ezekiel realizes that these living creatures are cherubim (10:15 – 17). Knowing now that these are cherubim helps the reader understand the nature of the vision as it unfolds. Cherubim are guardians and bearers of the things of God (Gen 3:24; Exod 25:18 – 22).

1:6 four ... four. Likely expresses a geographic totality, comparable to the four directions on a compass (Gen 13:14; Isa 11:12). **four faces.** Enables the living creatures to see at once in any direction. **faces.** See note on v. 10.

1:9 the wings of one touched the wings of another. Spatially the creatures' outstretched wings formed a square-like perimeter. This is similar to the cherubim described in the Most Holy Place in Solomon's temple (1 Kgs 6:27). **they did not turn as they moved.** They were multidirectional. This reflects their supernatural mobility, which enabled them to move "straight ahead" in any direction.

1:10 face of a human being ... a lion ... an ox ... an eagle. This reveals the composite nature of one face. Suggestions abound relative to the symbolism here. At the very minimum, the lion, ox, eagle, and human represent the most majestic of creatures in their respective

1:11 [o]Isa 6:2
1:13 [p]Rev 4:5
1:14 [q]Ps 29:7
1:16 [r]Eze 10:9-11; Da 10:6
1:17 [s]ver 9
1:18 [t]Eze 10:12; Rev 4:6
1:20 [u]ver 12
1:21 [v]Eze 10:17
1:22 [w]Eze 10:1
1:24 [x]Eze 10:5; 43:2; Da 10:6; Rev 1:15; 19:6 [y]2Ki 7:6
1:26 [z]Ex 24:10; Eze 10:1 [a]Rev 1:13
1:27 [b]Eze 8:2
1:28 [c]Ge 9:13; Rev 10:1 [d]Rev 4:2 [e]Eze 8:4 [f]Eze 3:23; Da 8:17; Rev 1:17

11 Such were their faces. They each had two wings[o] spreading out upward, each wing touching that of
the creature on either side; and each had two other wings covering its body. 12 Each one went straight
ahead. Wherever the spirit would go, they would go, without turning as they went. 13 The appearance
of the living creatures was like burning coals of fire or like torches. Fire moved back and forth among
the creatures; it was bright, and lightning[p] flashed out of it. 14 The creatures sped back and forth like
flashes of lightning.[q]

15 As I looked at the living creatures, I saw a wheel on the ground beside each creature with its four
faces. 16 This was the appearance and structure of the wheels: They sparkled like topaz,[r] and all four
looked alike. Each appeared to be made like a wheel intersecting a wheel. 17 As they moved, they would
go in any one of the four directions the creatures faced; the wheels did not change direction[s] as the
creatures went. 18 Their rims were high and awesome, and all four rims were full of eyes[t] all around.

19 When the living creatures moved, the wheels beside them moved; and when the living creatures
rose from the ground, the wheels also rose. 20 Wherever the spirit would go, they would go,[u] and the
wheels would rise along with them, because the spirit of the living creatures was in the wheels. 21 When
the creatures moved, they also moved; when the creatures stood still, they also stood still; and when
the creatures rose from the ground, the wheels rose along with them, because the spirit of the living
creatures was in the wheels.[v]

22 Spread out above the heads of the living creatures was what looked something like a vault,[w] sparkling like crystal, and awesome. 23 Under the vault their wings were stretched out one toward the other,
and each had two wings covering its body. 24 When the creatures moved, I heard the sound of their
wings, like the roar of rushing waters, like the voice[x] of the Almighty,[a] like the tumult of an army.[y]
When they stood still, they lowered their wings.

25 Then there came a voice from above the vault over their heads as they stood with lowered wings.
26 Above the vault over their heads was what looked like a throne of lapis lazuli,[z] and high above on
the throne was a figure like that of a man.[a] 27 I saw that from what appeared to be his waist up he
looked like glowing metal, as if full of fire, and that from there down he looked like fire; and brilliant
light surrounded him.[b] 28 Like the appearance of a rainbow[c] in the clouds on a rainy day, so was the
radiance around him.[d]

This was the appearance of the likeness of the glory[e] of the LORD. When I saw it, I fell facedown,[f] and
I heard the voice of one speaking.

[a] *24* Hebrew *Shaddai*

---

realms. In the wild, the lion represents the most ferocious (Prov 30:30). Of domestic animals, the ox represents the strongest beast (Prov 14:4). In the air, an eagle's might is undisputed (Prov 23:5; cf. Obad 4). On earth, humans have dominion over all creation (Gen 1:26–28).

1:12 Wherever the spirit would go, they would go. The cherubim depended on the "spirit," not the "Spirit," for mobility (see also v. 20 and note). Given 3:12, that which directs the cherubim derives from the divine spirit. They had an orientation in all directions.

1:15 I saw a wheel on the ground beside each creature. The wheel description (vv. 15–21) depicts the mobility of the cherubim. The close proximity of the wheels to the creatures, or "cherubim," reflects the readiness of the wheels to follow the lead of the creatures.

1:20 the spirit of the living creatures was in the wheels. Indicates speed of movement. The description of the cherubim highlights their supernatural ability to see in any direction and move with speed at a moment's notice anytime and anywhere.

1:22 something like a vault. A gemlike platform supported by the cherubim, whose noisy wings were heard as they flew around, bearing the platform.

1:25–26 above the vault ... like a throne. The vault (see note on v. 22) functioned as a platform for a throne, upon which an unidentified male figure sat. But this was no ordinary human.

1:27 fire; and brilliant light surrounded him. In the Bible, God's presence is often symbolically revealed in the form of fire and light (Exod 13:21; 19:18; 24:17; 40:34,38; Isa 66:15).

1:28 the likeness of the glory of the LORD. Ezekiel's interpretation of what he sees in this vision. The glory is God's manifested presence with his people that was first visible as a cloud in the wilderness (see Exod 16:10 and note) and later in the tabernacle (see Exod 40:34–38 and note) and the temple (see 1 Kgs 8:10–12 and notes). See "The Glory of God," p. 2640. The architecture of the Most Holy Place indicates that the Lord dwelled there in the midst of the cherubim (see Exod 25:20–22 and note on 25:22; 2 Sam 6:2). Thus, in this vision, the cherubim were supporting, transporting, and guarding the throne chariot of God. These heavenly attendants have escorted God to Ezekiel and the exiles in Babylon. **fell facedown.** Because he is face to face with the living God. In other words, God is on the move, no longer content to disclose himself only in Jerusalem in the Most Holy Place. What Ezekiel sees and experiences anticipates God appearing in human form (Heb 1:3) and the experience of the disciples (John 1:14). That Ezekiel sees God outside God's expected habitation (the temple) points to the reality that as redemptive history moves forward, God will no longer dwell in houses made with human hands. God is now with the exiles in Babylon, and in this way, the appearance is positive (11:16). However, since the Lord's presence emerges from an immense cloud out of the north, it seems that the storm of the Lord's presence is advancing like an enemy, clearly a threatening indicator (see note on v. 4 ["coming out of the north"]). This is further established in the ominous nature of the Lord's speech that immediately follows.

Ezekiel's Call to Be a Prophet

2 He said to me, "Son of man,[a] stand[g] up on your feet and I will speak to you." 2As he spoke, the
Spirit came into me and raised me[h] to my feet, and I heard him speaking to me.
3He said: "Son of man, I am sending you to the Israelites, to a rebellious nation that has rebelled
against me; they and their ancestors have been in revolt against me to this very day.[i] 4The people to
whom I am sending you are obstinate and stubborn.[j] Say to them, 'This is what the Sovereign LORD
says.' 5And whether they listen or fail to listen[k]—for they are a rebellious people[l]—they will know
that a prophet has been among them.[m] 6And you, son of man, do not be afraid[n] of them or their words.
Do not be afraid, though briers and thorns[o] are all around you and you live among scorpions. Do not
be afraid of what they say or be terrified by them, though they are a rebellious people.[p] 7You must
speak my words to them, whether they listen or fail to listen, for they are rebellious.[q] 8But you, son of
man, listen to what I say to you. Do not rebel like that rebellious people;[r] open your mouth and eat[s]
what I give you."
9Then I looked, and I saw a hand[t] stretched out to me. In it was a scroll, 10which he unrolled before
me. On both sides of it were written words of lament and mourning and woe.[u]

3 And he said to me, "Son of man, eat what is before you, eat this scroll; then go and speak to the
people of Israel." 2So I opened my mouth, and he gave me the scroll to eat.
3Then he said to me, "Son of man, eat this scroll I am giving you and fill your stomach with it." So
I ate[v] it, and it tasted as sweet as honey[w] in my mouth.
4He then said to me: "Son of man, go now to the people of Israel and speak my words to them. 5You
are not being sent to a people of obscure speech and strange language,[x] but to the people of Israel—
6not to many peoples of obscure speech and strange language, whose words you cannot understand.

[a] *1* The Hebrew phrase *ben adam* means *human being*. The phrase *son of man* is retained as a form of address here and throughout Ezekiel because of its possible association with "Son of Man" in the New Testament.

2:1 [g] Da 10:11
2:2 [h] Eze 3:24; Da 8:18
2:3 [i] Jer 3:25; Eze 20:8-24
2:4 [j] Eze 3:7
2:5 [k] Eze 3:11 [l] Eze 3:27 [m] Eze 33:33
2:6 [n] Jer 1:8,17 [o] Isa 9:18; Mic 7:4 [p] Eze 3:9
2:7 [q] Jer 1:7; Eze 3:10-11
2:8 [r] Isa 50:5 [s] Jer 15:16; Rev 10:9
2:9 [t] Eze 8:3
2:10 [u] Rev 8:13
3:3 [v] Jer 15:16 [w] Ps 19:10; Ps 119:103; Rev 10:9-10
3:5 [x] Isa 28:11; Jnh 1:2

2:1—3:15 *Ezekiel's Call as Prophet and Mourner.* Ezekiel's prophetic role, its outcome, his audience, and his mourning role merge as God speaks to him and reveals the serious call on his life.

2:1 Son of man. Human (see NIV text note). This is how the Lord addresses Ezekiel 93 times in the book. The designation emphasizes Ezekiel's humanity (as creature), which identifies him closely with his audience, and starkly contrasts him with the Lord (as Creator)—even though Ezekiel and the Lord seem to function as one in the book. Daniel is also addressed this way (Dan 8:17).

2:2 the Spirit came into me and raised me to my feet. After falling facedown upon experiencing God's presence, Ezekiel is placed on his feet. The Spirit of God supernaturally empowers Ezekiel to stand and hear God's words (Isa 48:15–16; cf. Gen 1:2–3). Without the empowerment of the Spirit of God, the word of the Lord cannot energize. The speaking voice that Ezekiel hears comes from the throne (1:25–26) and continues to reveal the lifelike nature of the storm.

2:3 I am sending you ... to a rebellious nation. As a prophet of God (v. 5). Ezekiel's assignment is difficult because of his audience. See Introduction: Audience; Historical Setting, Purpose, and Occasion. God's people in exile are like those who commit crimes against the state, bent on doing wrong.

2:5 they will know that a prophet has been among them. "[Then] they will know" is a refrain that recurs throughout Ezekiel; this is its first occurrence. The test for whether one is a true prophet is the fulfillment of their predictions (Deut 18:20–22). When Jerusalem falls in seven years, Ezekiel's audience will know he is a true prophet. This is directly tied to knowing the Lord; God will reveal his character and vindicate his name when Ezekiel's predictions come to pass, because God is the one speaking. The dominant biblical-theological theme of knowing the Lord through judgment begins to surface (see Exod 5:2; 6:3; 7:5; 14:4; 16:6; 18:11; 20:19; 33:12–13; see also "Sin," p. 2644). See Introduction: Theological Significance.

2:6 briers and thorns ... scorpions. Vivid descriptions of his audience show how their deep-seated rebellion makes them prickly and even dangerous. The people will welcome neither the messenger nor the message.

2:8 open your mouth and eat what I give you. The command to eat without any indication of what he will be eating is meant to test Ezekiel's character and obedience. **eat.** Symbolizes the appropriation of God's words (e.g., Jer 15:16).

3:1,3 eat this scroll. This event appears to be more than just a test of Ezekiel's obedience. Both the description of the scroll and Ezekiel's response to it are indicators. The scroll's nature is fixed since its origin is divine (2:9) and it is fully written upon (2:10); any additions or changes are impossible. It concerns "lament and mourning and woe" (2:10) due to Jerusalem's upcoming downfall. The Lord has decreed anguish and severe emotional turmoil, ongoing cries likened to death pangs—a destiny that is nonnegotiable on the basis of the scroll's content. On the one hand, the scroll sets a specific and undeniable tone for Ezekiel's ministry. On the other, it seems to describe some of the contents of Ezekiel's book, even if not all of it reads like a lament. Internalizing the scroll is equivalent to internalizing the divine message. Ezekiel becomes what he eats. He becomes a mourner as a result of eating a scroll containing lamentation, mourning, and woes. In this way, the event represents more than just a test of obedience.

3:3 sweet as honey in my mouth. A surprising contrast with what one might expect from eating words of mourning. Following God's command touches Ezekiel's sense of taste in a positive way (see Pss 19:10; 119:103; Rev 10:9–10), probably indicating that God's justice, however severe, is incomparably better than injustice.

3:5 You are not being sent to a people of obscure speech. God is not sending the prophet to serve in a foreign land, where he would have to learn another language and culture. In one sense, however, a cross-cultural mission would have been easier for Ezekiel. This is so because foreigners (those not a part of God's covenantal community) would not be as rebellious as God's covenantal people. Foreigners would actually listen and, in fact, might be more ready to hear and heed the word of God (Jonah 3:5; Mal 1:10–11; Rom 10:20–21).

3:6 [y] Mt 11:21-23
3:7 [z] Eze 2:4; Jn 15:20-23
3:8 [a] Jer 1:18
3:9 [b] Isa 50:7; Eze 2:6; Mic 3:8
3:11 [c] Eze 2:4-5,7
3:12 [d] Eze 8:3; Ac 8:39
3:13 [e] Eze 1:24; 10:5,16-17
3:15 [f] Ps 137:1 [g] Job 2:13
3:16 [h] Jer 42:7
3:17 [i] Isa 52:8; Jer 6:17; Eze 33:7-9
3:18 [j] ver 20; Eze 33:6
3:19 [k] 2Ki 17:13; Eze 14:14,20; Ac 18:6; 20:26; 1Ti 4:14-16
3:20 [l] Ps 125:5; Eze 18:24; 33:12,18
3:21 [m] Ac 20:31
3:22 [n] Eze 1:3 [o] Ac 9:6 [p] Eze 8:4

Surely if I had sent you to them, they would have listened to you.[y] 7But the people of Israel are not willing to listen to you because they are not willing to listen to me, for all the Israelites are hardened and obstinate.[z] 8But I will make you as unyielding and hardened as they are.[a] 9I will make your forehead like the hardest stone, harder than flint. Do not be afraid of them or terrified by them, though they are a rebellious people.[b]"

10And he said to me, "Son of man, listen carefully and take to heart all the words I speak to you. 11Go now to your people in exile and speak to them. Say to them, 'This is what the Sovereign LORD says,' whether they listen or fail to listen.[c]"

12Then the Spirit lifted me up,[d] and I heard behind me a loud rumbling sound as the glory of the LORD rose from the place where it was standing.[a] 13It was the sound of the wings of the living creatures brushing against each other and the sound of the wheels beside them, a loud rumbling sound.[e] 14The Spirit then lifted me up and took me away, and I went in bitterness and in the anger of my spirit, with the strong hand of the LORD on me. 15I came to the exiles who lived at Tel Aviv near the Kebar River.[f] And there, where they were living, I sat among them for seven days[g]—deeply distressed.

Ezekiel's Task as Watchman

16At the end of seven days the word of the LORD came to me:[h] 17"Son of man, I have made you a watchman[i] for the people of Israel; so hear the word I speak and give them warning from me. 18When I say to a wicked person, 'You will surely die,' and you do not warn them or speak out to dissuade them from their evil ways in order to save their life, that wicked person will die for[b] their sin, and I will hold you accountable for their blood.[j] 19But if you do warn the wicked person and they do not turn from their wickedness or from their evil ways, they will die for their sin; but you will have saved yourself.[k]

20"Again, when a righteous person turns from their righteousness and does evil, and I put a stumbling block before them, they will die. Since you did not warn them, they will die for their sin. The righteous things that person did will not be remembered, and I will hold you accountable for their blood.[l] 21But if you do warn the righteous person not to sin and they do not sin, they will surely live because they took warning, and you will have saved yourself.[m]"

22The hand of the LORD[n] was on me there, and he said to me, "Get up and go[o] out to the plain,[p] and

[a] 12 Probable reading of the original Hebrew text; Masoretic Text *sound—may the glory of the LORD be praised from his place* [b] 18 Or *in*; also in verses 19 and 20

3:12–15 The dramatic conclusion of the vision. God's glory is escorted away in the same manner it appeared: by the loud sound of the cherubim's wings (1:24).
3:14 I went in bitterness and in the anger of my spirit. Upon leaving the vision and beginning his prophetic task under God's compelling hand, Ezekiel comes to the exiles. A description of Ezekiel's reaction to the scroll incident unfolds in first-person narrative. He is filled with strong emotions and expresses deep dissatisfaction, consistent with the scroll he swallowed (2:10). Ezekiel has God's perspective on the people's rebellion.
3:15 Tel Aviv. The name means "mound of the deluge" in Babylonian, but its exact location is uncertain. The designation was used to refer to ancient cities that had been reduced to mere mounds (*tells*). **I sat among them for seven days—deeply distressed.** Typical posture and length of time for the ritual period of mourning (Gen 50:10; 1 Sam 31:13; 1 Chr 10:12). Part of the mourning period was a time of stunned silence, shock, despair, and distress. Ezekiel describes himself as one participating in mourning rites. He is sitting among his peers, the exiles, in stunned silence and is motionless for a week as a result of the shocking news of the Lord (Job 2:13). By becoming what he ate, he becomes a mourner and subsequently does what mourners do.
3:16–21 *Ezekiel's Call as Watchman.* Not only does God call Ezekiel to be a prophet and mourner, but his call also entails a related task as Israel's watchman, one who warns of impending danger. A watchman was responsible to protect, defend, and care for the people (33:1–6; cf. Isa 21:6–9; Hos 9:8; Hab 2:1). While it is not uncommon to designate Israelite prophets as watchmen, Ezekiel is charged with carrying out his prophetic task or he will share in the punishment that will come upon the people. Thus, his own life is threatened. Ezekiel becomes responsible for people's life and death.
3:16 seven days. See note on v. 15. The mourner usually returned to normal life after seven days, but Ezekiel does not (see note on v. 17): the Lord makes Ezekiel Israel's watchman (vv. 16–21) and appears to extend Ezekiel's mourning period (vv. 22–27). **the word of the LORD came to me.** As in 1:3.
3:17 watchman. Stationed in a lookout tower on the city wall, a watchman was responsible to sound a trumpet for soldiers and civilians in the city at the sight of approaching danger or attack. God asks Ezekiel to give people fair warning of the present crisis: they will experience the consequences for being a rebellious nation. As a prophet Ezekiel spoke about these things to this nation of rebels as a whole. But the nation is made up of individuals whom he must warn. His watchman role for the "people of Israel" zooms in on individuals: "a wicked person" (v. 18) or "a righteous person [who] turns from their righteousness and does evil" (v. 20). These individuals need fair warning—not of enemy invasion but that death awaits those who oppose God. This warning of death ties into Ezekiel's mourning role (see note on vv. 1,3).
3:20 I put a stumbling block before them. Those who have abandoned righteousness and embraced what is evil will be put to the test by God personally (14:9; Deut 13:3; 2 Sam 24:1).
3:22–27 *Ezekiel's Confinement and Speechlessness.* God places severe limitations on Ezekiel, limitations in line with his call to be a mourner.

there I will speak to you." 23So I got up and went out to the plain. And the glory of the LORD was standing
there, like the glory I had seen by the Kebar River,[q] and I fell facedown.[r]
24Then the Spirit came into me and raised me[s] to my feet. He spoke to me and said: "Go, shut yourself inside your house. 25And you, son of man, they will tie with ropes; you will be bound so that you
cannot go out among the people.[t] 26I will make your tongue stick to the roof of your mouth so that you
will be silent and unable to rebuke them, for they are a rebellious people.[u] 27But when I speak to you,
I will open your mouth and you shall say to them, 'This is what the Sovereign LORD says.'[v] Whoever
will listen let them listen, and whoever will refuse let them refuse; for they are a rebellious people.[w]

Siege of Jerusalem Symbolized

4 "Now, son of man, take a block of clay, put it in front of you and draw the city of Jerusalem on it.
2Then lay siege to it: Erect siege works against it, build a ramp[x] up to it, set up camps against it
and put battering rams around it.[y] 3Then take an iron pan, place it as an iron wall between you and
the city and turn your face toward it. It will be under siege, and you shall besiege it. This will be a sign[z]
to the people of Israel.[a]
4"Then lie on your left side and put the sin of the people of Israel upon yourself.[a] You are to bear
their sin for the number of days you lie on your side. 5I have assigned you the same number of days as
the years of their sin. So for 390 days you will bear the sin of the people of Israel.
6"After you have finished this, lie down again, this time on your right side, and bear the sin of the
people of Judah. I have assigned you 40 days, a day for each year.[b] 7Turn your face toward the siege of
Jerusalem and with bared arm prophesy against her. 8I will tie you up with ropes so that you cannot
turn from one side to the other until you have finished the days of your siege.[c]
9"Take wheat and barley, beans and lentils, millet and spelt;[d] put them in a storage jar and use
them to make bread for yourself. You are to eat it during the 390 days you lie on your side. 10Weigh out
twenty shekels[b] of food to eat each day and eat it at set times. 11Also measure out a sixth of a hin[c] of

3:23 [q] Eze 1:1 [r] Eze 1:28
3:24 [s] Eze 2:2
3:25 [t] Eze 4:8
3:26 [u] Eze 2:5; 24:27; 33:22
3:27 [v] ver 11 [w] Eze 12:3; 24:27; 33:22
4:2 [x] Jer 6:6 [y] Eze 21:22
4:3 [z] Isa 8:18; 20:3; Eze 12:3-6; 24:24,27 [a] Jer 39:1
4:6 [b] Nu 14:34; Da 9:24-26; 12:11-12
4:8 [c] Eze 3:25
4:9 [d] Isa 28:25

[a] *4* Or *upon your side* [b] *10* That is, about 8 ounces or about 230 grams [c] *11* That is, about 2/3 quart or about 0.6 liter

3:24 shut yourself inside your house. The Lord demands Ezekiel's seclusion and seems to secure it by having him bound with ropes (v. 25).
3:26 you will be silent. God secures Ezekiel's silence by making him speechless unless he needs to deliver a word from the Lord (v. 27). Generally, to be motionless is connected to silence as a sign of mourning. Furthermore, his silence is coterminous with the fate of Jerusalem. The Lord later promises that on the day the fugitive arrives with the news of Jerusalem's fall, Ezekiel will again speak (24:25–27), and that happens (33:21–23). The prophet's confinement and speechlessness encompass about a seven-and-a-half-year period (ca. 593–586 BC) and should be understood in terms of an extended mourning period.
4:1—5:17 *Visual Aids of Jerusalem's Upcoming Siege.* By means of a series of symbolic acts, Ezekiel is to portray the siege of Jerusalem and its outcome. In 4:1–3 the siege itself is portrayed; in 4:4–8 Ezekiel symbolically bears the punishment of the people of Israel and Judah; in 4:9–17 Ezekiel's diet symbolizes both the limitations of food that those under siege will suffer and that they and the exiles will be forced to eat food the law specified as "unclean" and therefore prohibited; in 5:1–4 Ezekiel is instructed to shave off his hair and use it to symbolize that only a small remnant of Israel will be left after God's judgment. In 5:5–17 these symbolic acts are interpreted.
4:1–17 *Ezekiel's Drawing, Posture, and Dietary Restrictions.* With the city's destruction as the focal point, God asks Ezekiel to engage his audience with actions rather than words. In order to symbolize the upcoming siege on Jerusalem for his rebellious audience, God requires Ezekiel to use three elaborate visual aids (vv. 1–3,4–8,9–15)—nonverbal communication for non-hearing people.
4:1 take a block of clay. Ezekiel must build a model of Jerusalem under siege, with all the accompanying features of a city's defense system.
4:3 iron wall. Represents the ironclad barrier between God and his people, one that people cannot penetrate. **you shall besiege it.** That Ezekiel takes action in the mock siege shows God's deliberate hostility toward the city rather than his passive neglect. **sign.** See 12:6,11; 24:24,27.
4:4 You are to bear their sin. As a priest (1:3) Ezekiel must bear the weight of the nation's sin (Exod 28:38; Num 18:1) by lying first on his left side for 390 days (v. 5) and then on his right side for 40 days (v. 6). This is a representative, not substitutionary, bearing of sin. The actions symbolize not the removal of sin but the punishment Israel will suffer for sin. Although the prophet must dramatize this, the context (vv. 9–17) assumes that it requires not an around-the-clock demonstration but a periodic demonstration—one that will capture the attention of his non-hearing audience.
4:5 for 390 days. Likely represents the years of the nation's misconduct that started early in Solomon's reign (1 Kgs 11:1–10; 14:21–24) and will end when Jerusalem falls in 586 BC.
4:6 40 days. May represent the long and wicked reign of Manasseh (his sole reign was 687/86–643/42 BC; see 2 Kgs 21:11–15; 23:26–27; 24:3). It could also represent the 40 years that the nation wandered in the wilderness for their unbelief (Num 14:33–34).
4:7 prophesy against her. By means of this symbolic action.
4:9–15 The dietary restrictions here represent the severe famine that will hit Jerusalem as a result of the siege. Ezekiel must make bread from limited and unusual ingredients that amount to a daily allotment (see NIV text note on v. 10), and his water supply is also limited (see NIV text note on v. 11). The food and its repulsive preparation indicate the level of contamination the people will experience by living in places outside of Israel, places God considered defiled and unclean on account of idolatrous religious practices.
4:9 wheat and barley, beans and lentils, millet and spelt. Meager vegetarian provisions of a besieged city.

4:12 [e]Isa 36:12
4:13 [f]Hos 9:3
4:14 [g]Jer 1:6; Eze 9:8; 20:49 [h]Lev 11:39 [i]Ex 22:31; Dt 14:3; Ac 10:14
4:16 [j]Ps 105:16; Eze 5:16 [k]ver 10-11; Lev 26:26; Isa 3:1; Eze 12:19
4:17 [l]Lev 26:39; Eze 24:23; 33:10
5:1 [m]Isa 7:20 [n]Eze 44:20 [o]Lev 21:5
5:2 [p]ver 12; Lev 26:33
5:3 [q]Jer 39:10
5:6 [r]Jer 11:10; Eze 16:47-51; Zec 7:11
5:7 [s]2Ch 33:9; Jer 2:10-11; Eze 16:47
5:8 [t]Eze 15:7
5:9 [u]Da 9:12; Mt 24:21
5:10 [v]Lev 26:29; La 2:20 [w]Lev 26:33; Ps 44:11; Eze 12:14; Zec 2:6

water and drink it at set times. 12 Eat the food as you would a loaf of barley bread; bake it in the sight of the people, using human excrement[e] for fuel." 13 The LORD said, "In this way the people of Israel will eat defiled food among the nations where I will drive them."[f]

14 Then I said, "Not so, Sovereign LORD![g] I have never defiled myself. From my youth until now I have never eaten anything found dead[h] or torn by wild animals. No impure meat has ever entered my mouth.[i]"

15 "Very well," he said, "I will let you bake your bread over cow dung instead of human excrement."

16 He then said to me: "Son of man, I am about to cut off[j] the food supply in Jerusalem. The people will eat rationed food in anxiety and drink rationed water in despair,[k] 17 for food and water will be scarce. They will be appalled at the sight of each other and will waste away because of[a] their sin.[l]

God's Razor of Judgment

5 "Now, son of man, take a sharp sword and use it as a barber's razor[m] to shave[n] your head and your beard.[o] Then take a set of scales and divide up the hair. 2 When the days of your siege come to an end, burn a third of the hair inside the city. Take a third and strike it with the sword all around the city. And scatter a third to the wind. For I will pursue them with drawn sword.[p] 3 But take a few hairs and tuck them away in the folds of your garment.[q] 4 Again, take a few of these and throw them into the fire and burn them up. A fire will spread from there to all Israel.

5 "This is what the Sovereign LORD says: This is Jerusalem, which I have set in the center of the nations, with countries all around her. 6 Yet in her wickedness she has rebelled against my laws and decrees more than the nations and countries around her. She has rejected my laws and has not followed my decrees.[r]

7 "Therefore this is what the Sovereign LORD says: You have been more unruly than the nations around you and have not followed my decrees or kept my laws. You have not even[b] conformed to the standards of the nations around you.[s]

8 "Therefore this is what the Sovereign LORD says: I myself am against you, Jerusalem, and I will inflict punishment on you in the sight of the nations.[t] 9 Because of all your detestable idols, I will do to you what I have never done before and will never do again.[u] 10 Therefore in your midst parents will eat their children, and children will eat their parents.[v] I will inflict punishment on you and will scatter all your survivors to the winds.[w] 11 Therefore as surely as I live, declares the Sovereign LORD, because you

[a] *17* Or *away in* [b] *7* Most Hebrew manuscripts; some Hebrew manuscripts and Syriac *You have*

4:15 cow dung instead of human excrement. Rather than use a defiling substance, something ceremonially unclean for a priest, God allows Ezekiel to use animal dung, a common fuel used for baking in the ancient Near East.

4:16–17 Verbally interprets the dramatic performance in vv. 9–15 in the event his non-hearing audience might be tempted to listen. The Lord is the agent of destruction behind the siege; he is dispensing the covenantal curses on his rebellious people.

5:1–17 *Shaving as a Sign of Humiliation and Mourning.* With the city's destruction as the focal point, God asks Ezekiel to engage his audience in another gesture that affects Ezekiel personally.

5:1 shave your head. An external, nonverbal gesture that symbolizes the upcoming sword that will fall upon Jerusalem for its rebellion and the associated humiliation. The treatment of the shaved hair (vv. 1–4) symbolizes the treatment of the population of Jerusalem when the Babylonians invade (vv. 11–12). Shaving one's head was also associated with mourning (Jer 47:5; Mic 1:16). If by eating the scroll Ezekiel becomes a mourner (see note on 3:1,3), then this shaving might also be a visual aid of mourning over Jerusalem's destruction.

5:5 This is Jerusalem. God interprets Ezekiel's nonverbal communication. What is shocking is not that Ezekiel's actions refer to Jerusalem but that God would allow Jerusalem to be destroyed. God assigned a special status to the city among the nations (Deut 12:1–28), and his sanctuary and name dwelled there (v. 11; 1 Kgs 8:29). **center of the nations.** God chose for his people Israel and his earthly temple to be at the crossroads of the continents of Africa, Asia, and Europe so that what he did for them might be visible to the nations.

5:7 You have been more unruly than the nations around you. Although God chose to dwell in Jerusalem (1 Kgs 11:36; 2 Kgs 21:4,7; 2 Chr 33:7), Jerusalem was worse and "more unruly" than her neighbors in that the people rebelled against God and engaged in worship practices in the Lord's temple that he did not authorize (v. 11).

5:8 I myself am against you. Ezekiel's audience gets short, shocking reminders of this fact (13:8; 21:3; 26:3; 28:22; 29:3,10; 34:10; 38:3; 39:1; cf. 30:22; 35:3).

5:9–11 Because ... Therefore ... Therefore. Because they have acted in a certain way, God will act in a certain way. A cause-and-effect pattern prevails. Jerusalem has failed and will fall and experience the unspeakable horrors threatened in the covenant (Lev 26:25–26,29; Deut 28:53–57).

5:10 parents will eat their children. Cannibalism, the most gruesome extremity of life under siege (see 2 Kgs 6:28), was threatened as a consequence of breaking the covenant (Deut 28:53; see Jer 19:9 and note; Lam 2:20; Zech 11:9 and note).

5:11 as surely as I live. A divine oath communicating God's unalterable intentions. **I myself will shave you.** This aftershock is worse than the unfathomable and sobering announcement in v. 8. **shave you.** Humiliation; here associated with the sword.

have defiled my sanctuary with all your vile images[x] and detestable practices,[y] I myself will shave you;
I will not look on you with pity or spare you.[z] 12 A third of your people will die of the plague or perish
by famine inside you; a third will fall by the sword outside your walls; and a third I will scatter to the
winds and pursue with drawn sword.[a]
13 "Then my anger will cease and my wrath[b] against them will subside, and I will be avenged.[c] And
when I have spent my wrath on them, they will know that I the LORD have spoken in my zeal.
14 "I will make you a ruin and a reproach among the nations around you, in the sight of all who
pass by.[d] 15 You will be a reproach and a taunt, a warning and an object of horror to the nations around
you when I inflict punishment on you in anger and in wrath and with stinging rebuke.[e] I the LORD
have spoken.[f] 16 When I shoot at you with my deadly and destructive
arrows of famine, I will shoot to destroy you. I will bring more and
more famine upon you and cut off your supply of food.[g] 17 I will
send famine and wild beasts against you, and they will leave you
childless. Plague and bloodshed[h] will sweep through you, and I will
bring the sword against you. I the LORD have spoken.[i]"

Doom for the Mountains of Israel

6 The word of the LORD came to me: 2 "Son of man, set your face
against the mountains[j] of Israel; prophesy against them 3 and say:
'You mountains of Israel, hear the word of the Sovereign LORD. This is
what the Sovereign LORD says to the mountains and hills, to the ravines
and valleys:[k] I am about to bring a sword against you, and I will destroy
your high places.[l] 4 Your altars will be demolished and your incense altars[m] will be smashed; and I will slay your people in front of your idols.
5 I will lay the dead bodies of the Israelites in front of their idols, and I
will scatter your bones[n] around your altars. 6 Wherever you live, the
towns will be laid waste and the high places demolished, so that
your altars will be laid waste and devastated, your idols[o] smashed
and ruined, your incense altars[p] broken down, and what you
have made wiped out.[q] 7 Your people will fall slain among you,
and you will know that I am the LORD.

Incense altar found at Megiddo. "Your incense altars will be smashed" (Ezek 6:4).
Kim Walton, taken at the Oriental Institute Museum

5:11 [x] Eze 7:20 [y] 2Ch 36:14; Eze 8:6 [z] Eze 7:4,9
5:12 [a] ver 2,17; Jer 15:2; 21:9; Eze 6:11-12; 12:14
5:13 [b] Eze 21:17; 36:6 [c] Isa 1:24
5:14 [d] Lev 26:32; Ne 2:17; Ps 74:3-10; 79:1-4
5:15 [e] 1Ki 9:7; Jer 22:8-9; 24:9 [f] Eze 25:17
5:16 [g] Dt 32:24
5:17 [h] Eze 38:22 [i] Eze 14:21
6:2 [j] Eze 36:1
6:3 [k] Eze 36:4 [l] Lev 26:30
6:4 [m] 2Ch 14:5
6:5 [n] Jer 8:1-2
6:6 [o] Mic 1:7; Zec 13:2 [p] Lev 26:30 [q] Isa 6:11; Eze 5:14

5:13 I will be avenged. The outcome for God relative to his just judgment. This happens once God's wrath is used up on guilty covenant-breakers. Israel violated their relationship with God and tarnished his reputation. God's punishment of his rebellious people reasserts his holiness; his reputation is thereby avenged and his anger ceases. **they will know that I the LORD have spoken in my zeal.** Driven by passion for recognition as the sovereign Lord, his judgment produces such knowledge of him. See Introduction: Theological Significance.

5:15 when I inflict punishment on you in anger and in wrath and with stinging rebuke. More expressions of divine hostility and punishment for sin. The punishment includes horrific judgment on Jerusalem (vv. 16–17), in line with earlier warnings of catastrophic judgment (Deut 32:22–25). Although the reader may be uneasy with such Bible verses, Ezekiel does not downplay God's anger over sin. The outpouring and dispensing of God's anger through the exile is a visual reality of what later came when he poured out his wrath on Jesus at the cross. It is a picture of the anger of God being satisfied for sin and its consequences. See Introduction: Theological Significance.

6:1—7:27 *Descriptions of Upcoming Total Destruction.* After the dramatic performances signaling Jerusalem's end (4:1—5:17), God gives Ezekiel portraits of destruction using the topography of the land to describe the complete and utter destruction that awaits the people of Judah.

6:1–14 *Doom for the Mountains of Israel.* The Lord first draws attention to Israel's highlands.

6:2 set your face against. Indicates hostility; elsewhere refers to how the Lord opposes the nation (4:3,7; 14:8; 15:7; cf. Lev 17:10; 20:3,5–6; Jer 21:10; 44:11), which suggests that divine abandonment or alienation is in view. **mountains of Israel.** The central highlands, but the whole land is in view since v. 3 mentions hills, ravines, and valleys. Singling out the mountains refers to where the people set up pagan sanctuaries and worshiped idolatrous images (see note on v. 3).

6:3 high places. Open-air sanctuaries. Some are associated with the Lord, others with foreign deities. Consistent activities at both included sacrificing and burning incense. Objects typically associated with these sanctuaries were "altars," "incense altars," and "idols" (v. 4; see note on v. 4).

6:4 altars. Used for cooking animal meat. **incense altars.** Made of clay and standing two feet (0.6 meters) tall, they were small stands that burned sweet-smelling fragrances. Yahweh's high places varied in size and location. They were legitimate before Solomon's temple (1 Sam 9:1—10:16; 1 Kgs 3:1–4) but not afterward (1 Kgs 15:14; 22:43; 2 Kgs 12:3; 14:4; 15:4,35). The Lord himself is going to demolish the illegitimate cultic sites and all things associated with them, and many Israelite worshipers will fall victim to God's wrath (vv. 3–7). What they think is so powerful is, in reality, impotent.

6:7 you will know that I am the LORD. Knowledge of God's character and reputation will ripple throughout the surviving community, thereby giving him name recognition (cf. vv. 10,13,14), God's main goal when

6:8 [r] Jer 44:28
[s] Isa 6:13; Jer 44:14; Eze 12:16; 14:22
6:9 [t] Ps 78:40; Isa 7:13
[u] Eze 20:7,24
[v] Eze 20:43; 36:31
6:11 [w] Eze 5:12; 21:14,17; 25:6
6:12 [x] Eze 5:12
6:13 [y] Isa 57:5
[z] 1Ki 14:23; Jer 2:20; Eze 20:28; Hos 4:13
6:14 [a] Isa 5:25
[b] Eze 14:13
7:2 [c] Am 8:2,10
[d] Rev 7:1; 20:8
7:4 [e] Eze 5:11

8 " 'But I will spare some, for some of you will escape[r] the sword when you are scattered among the
lands and nations.[s] 9 Then in the nations where they have been carried captive, those who escape will
remember me — how I have been grieved[t] by their adulterous hearts, which have turned away from
me, and by their eyes, which have lusted after their idols.[u] They will loathe themselves for the evil they
have done and for all their detestable practices.[v] 10 And they will know that I am the LORD; I did not
threaten in vain to bring this calamity on them.

11 " 'This is what the Sovereign LORD says: Strike your hands together and stamp your feet and cry out
"Alas!" because of all the wicked and detestable practices of the people of Israel, for they will fall by the
sword, famine and plague.[w] 12 One who is far away will die of the plague, and one who is near will fall
by the sword, and anyone who survives and is spared will die of famine. So will I pour out my wrath on
them.[x] 13 And they will know that I am the LORD, when their people lie slain among their idols around
their altars, on every high hill and on all the mountaintops, under every spreading tree and every leafy
oak[y] — places where they offered fragrant incense to all their idols.[z] 14 And I will stretch out my hand[a]
against them and make the land a desolate waste from the desert to Diblah[a] — wherever they live.
Then they will know that I am the LORD.[b] ' "

The End Has Come

7 The word of the LORD came to me: 2 "Son of man, this is what the Sovereign LORD says to the land
of Israel:

" 'The end![c] The end has come
    upon the four corners[d] of the land!
3 The end is now upon you,
    and I will unleash my anger against you.
I will judge you according to your conduct
    and repay you for all your detestable practices.
4 I will not look on you with pity;[e]
    I will not spare you.
I will surely repay you for your conduct
    and for the detestable practices among you.

" 'Then you will know that I am the LORD.'

a *14* Most Hebrew manuscripts; a few Hebrew manuscripts *Riblah*

he judges Israel. The theme of the Lord's judgment and restoration, which results in his being known and acknowledged by Israel and the nations, echoes throughout chs. 6–39 (see Introduction: Theological Significance; see also note on 5:13).

6:9 those who escape will remember me. Those who survive the divine sword but are taken captive in a foreign land will acknowledge that God's judgment is just. The escapees represent the promise of a remnant; complete annihilation will not take place (5:3; Rom 9:27; 11:5). **grieved.** God's anger is mournful. **adulterous.** Idolatrous. By giving affection to something or someone other than the Lord, Israel has acted like an unfaithful marriage partner (cf. chs. 16; 23). God is grieved yet justified in his punitive actions (v. 10).

6:11 Strike your hands together and stamp your feet. Ezekiel must display mournful anger. This fits his mourning role that the scroll established (see note on 3:1,3). This mirrors the Lord's sentiments since Ezekiel can do nothing apart from the Lord's bidding (see notes on ch. 3). See Introduction: Literary Features.

7:1–27 *The End for the Entire Land.* Ch. 7 vividly describes destruction on the entire land and the inability to escape such destruction because of God's wrath poured out on wrongdoing and wrongdoers. Both the places where one would typically find refuge in the day of trouble and the people who would typically furnish protection will not provide safe haven. Escape, a defense, hope for deliverance, a reversal of the decreed end — none of these is possible because the agent of destruction is the Lord (v. 9). God's patience with his stubborn people has run out.

7:1–9 Announces "the end" (vv. 2,3,6) as an unleashing (v. 3) and outpouring (v. 8) of God's anger, judging and repaying them for misconduct (9:8; 14:13–14; 20:8,13,21; 22:31; 36:18; cf. 30:15).

7:2 The end! The end. A repetition that communicates finality (see also v. 6). This creates a strong emotional reaction. The audience must take the threats seriously, for the end is imminent. **the four corners of the land!** Expresses totality; an idiomatic way of communicating "the whole land."

7:4,9 I will not look on you with pity. Suggests that God is hardening his heart in order to carry out judgment. When God revealed himself to Moses, he made himself known as a gracious and merciful God but one who would not let the guilty go unpunished (Exod 34:5–7). For about 800 years God had given the nation numerous chances to change, but their opportunities for change have run out.

7:4 Then you will know that I am the LORD. The intended outcome of God's furious unleashing of anger is not only the promised consequences for their misconduct (Deut 28) but also that Israel acknowledge and recognize his power. See also v. 27.

5 "This is what the Sovereign LORD says:

" 'Disaster![f] Unheard-of[a] disaster!
See, it comes!
6 The end has come!
The end has come!
It has roused itself against you.
See, it comes!
7 Doom has come upon you,
upon you who dwell in the land.
The time has come! The day is near![g]
There is panic, not joy, on the mountains.
8 I am about to pour out my wrath[h] on you
and spend my anger against you.
I will judge you according to your conduct
and repay you for all your detestable practices.[i]
9 I will not look on you with pity;
I will not spare you.
I will repay you for your conduct
and for the detestable practices among you.

" 'Then you will know that it is I the LORD who strikes you.

10 " 'See, the day!
See, it comes!
Doom has burst forth,
the rod[j] has budded,
arrogance has blossomed!
11 Violence has arisen,[b]
a rod to punish the wicked.
None of the people will be left,
none of that crowd—
none of their wealth,
nothing of value.[k]
12 The time has come!
The day has arrived!
Let not the buyer rejoice
nor the seller grieve,
for my wrath is on the whole crowd.[l]
13 The seller will not recover
the property that was sold—
as long as both buyer and seller live.
For the vision concerning the whole crowd
will not be reversed.
Because of their sins, not one of them
will preserve their life.[m]

14 " 'They have blown the trumpet,
they have made all things ready,

7:5 [f] 2Ki 21:12
7:7 [g] Eze 12:23; Zep 1:14
7:8 [h] Isa 42:25; Eze 9:8; 14:19; Na 1:6 [i] Eze 20:8, 21; 36:19
7:10 [j] Ps 89:32; Isa 10:5
7:11 [k] Jer 16:6; Zep 1:18
7:12 [l] ver 7; Isa 5:13-14; Eze 30:3
7:13 [m] Lev 25:24-28

[a] *5* Most Hebrew manuscripts; some Hebrew manuscripts and Syriac *Disaster after has become*   [b] *11* Or *The violent one*

7:10 the day! Another notification of "the end" (vv. 2,3,6) but without using the term. It refers to an outpouring of God's wrath using language of totality with respect to the people in the land (vv. 11–12,14) on "the day" (also in vv. 7,12,19). Instead of it being a day when people would experience God's goodness (Amos 5:18–20), people will experience his judgment and justice as a time of "doom" (also v. 7), "violence" (v. 11), "calamity" (v. 26), and "rumor" (v. 26). The effects will be economic and emotional (vv. 12–18), religious (vv. 19–24), and political (vv. 25–27). See note on Amos 2:16.

7:15 [n] Dt 32:25; Jer 14:18; La 1:20; Eze 5:12
7:16 [o] Isa 59:11 [p] Ezr 9:15; Eze 6:8
7:17 [q] Isa 13:7; Eze 21:7; 22:14
7:18 [r] Ps 55:5 [s] Isa 15:2-3; Eze 27:31; Am 8:10
7:19 [t] Eze 13:5; Zep 1:7, 18 [u] Eze 14:3 [v] Pr 11:4
7:20 [w] Jer 7:30
7:21 [x] 2Ki 24:13
7:22 [y] Eze 39:23-24
7:23 [z] 2Ki 21:16
7:24 [a] Eze 24:21 [b] 2Ch 7:20; Eze 28:7
7:25 [c] Eze 13:10, 16
7:26 [d] Jer 4:20

but no one will go into battle,
for my wrath is on the whole crowd.
15 Outside is the sword;
inside are plague and famine.
Those in the country
will die by the sword;
those in the city
will be devoured by famine and plague.[n]
16 The fugitives who escape
will flee to the mountains.
Like doves[o] of the valleys,
they will all moan,
each for their own sins.[p]
17 Every hand will go limp;[q]
every leg will be wet with urine.
18 They will put on sackcloth
and be clothed with terror.[r]
Every face will be covered with shame,
and every head will be shaved.[s]

19 " 'They will throw their silver into the streets,
and their gold will be treated as a thing unclean.
Their silver and gold
will not be able to deliver them
in the day of the LORD's wrath.[t]
It will not satisfy their hunger
or fill their stomachs,
for it has caused them to stumble[u] into sin.[v]
20 They took pride in their beautiful jewelry
and used it to make their detestable idols.
They made it into vile images;[w]
therefore I will make it a thing unclean for them.
21 I will give their wealth as plunder to foreigners
and as loot to the wicked of the earth,
who will defile it.[x]
22 I will turn my face[y] away from the people,
and robbers will desecrate the place I treasure.
They will enter it
and will defile it.

23 " 'Prepare chains!
For the land is full of bloodshed,[z]
and the city is full of violence.
24 I will bring the most wicked of nations
to take possession of their houses.
I will put an end to the pride of the mighty,
and their sanctuaries[a] will be desecrated.[b]
25 When terror comes,
they will seek peace in vain.[c]
26 Calamity upon calamity[d] will come,
and rumor upon rumor.

7:18 They will put on sackcloth ... every head will be shaved. Signs of mourning (Gen 37:34; Job 1:20; Isa 15:2; Rev 11:3).

7:22 the place I treasure. Jerusalem's temple (Deut 12).

7:26 vision ... law ... counsel. Guidance from God through the expected

They will go searching for a vision from the prophet,
priestly instruction in the law will cease,
the counsel of the elders will come to an end.[e]
27The king will mourn,
the prince will be clothed with despair,[f]
and the hands of the people of the land will tremble.
I will deal with them according to their conduct,[g]
and by their own standards I will judge them.

" 'Then they will know that I am the LORD.[h]' "

Idolatry in the Temple

8 In the sixth year, in the sixth month on the fifth day, while I was sitting in my house and the elders[i]
of Judah were sitting before[j] me, the hand of the Sovereign LORD came on me there.[k] 2I looked,
and I saw a figure like that of a man.[a] From what appeared to be his waist down he was like fire, and
from there up his appearance was as bright as glowing metal.[l] 3He stretched out what looked like a
hand and took me by the hair of my head. The Spirit lifted me up[m] between earth and heaven and in
visions of God he took me to Jerusalem, to the entrance of the north gate of the inner court, where the
idol that provokes to jealousy[n] stood. 4And there before me was the glory[o] of the God of Israel, as in the
vision I had seen in the plain.[p]

5Then he said to me, "Son of man, look toward the north." So I looked, and in the entrance north
of the gate of the altar I saw this idol[q] of jealousy.

6And he said to me, "Son of man, do you see what they are doing—the utterly detestable[r] things
the Israelites are doing here, things that will drive me far from my sanctuary? But you will see things
that are even more detestable."

7Then he brought me to the entrance to the court. I looked, and I saw a hole in the wall. 8He said to
me, "Son of man, now dig into the wall." So I dug into the wall and saw a doorway there.

9And he said to me, "Go in and see the wicked and detestable things they are doing here." 10So I

7:26 [e] Isa 47:11; Eze 20:1-3; Mic 3:6
7:27 [f] Ps 109:19; Eze 26:16 [g] Eze 18:20 [h] ver 4
8:1 [i] Eze 14:1 [j] Eze 33:31 [k] Eze 1:1-3
8:2 [l] Eze 1:4,26-27
8:3 [m] Eze 3:12; 11:1 [n] Ex 20:5; Dt 32:16
8:4 [o] Eze 1:28 [p] Eze 3:22
8:5 [q] Ps 78:58; Jer 32:34
8:6 [r] Eze 5:11

[a] 2 Or *saw a fiery figure*

means of prophet, priest, and elder, respectively, will not be available (1 Sam 28:6; Amos 8:11–12; Mic 3:6–7; see note on Jer 18:18).

7:27 king ... prince. Refer to the same person: King Jehoiachin.

8:1—11:25 *The Temple Vision.* This is the second of four dream-like visions the prophet receives. It culminates tragically with God's presence leaving the Jerusalem temple (11:22–23). Because of Israel's relentless idolatry, God is angry and justified in abandoning his temple, people, and land. Divine abandonment is the ultimate curse of the covenantal curses that Deuteronomy promises (see Introduction: Literary Features).

8:1–18 *Tour of Temple Violations.* Ezekiel sees escalating snapshots of idolatrous worship. He "sees" with "spiritual eyes" the detestable things that people are doing, justifying the Lord's departure.

8:1–6 The Spirit supernaturally transports Ezekiel from exile (v. 1) to the Jerusalem temple (v. 3). When he arrives at the temple entrance, two opposing images capture his attention: "the idol that provokes to jealousy" (v. 3) and "the glory of the God of Israel" (v. 4). The "glory" represents God's presence (see 1:28 and note). The "idol" intrudes on the Lord's property; ownership and sovereignty of the temple belong to "the God of Israel," hence the vision highlights this important reality through the repeated designation "the glory of the God of Israel." This "idol" with which the people have associated themselves has caused a serious rift in their relationship with God; God is a jealous God and will not share his glory with another (Exod 20:5). Ezekiel is about to see up close and personal "things that are even more detestable" (vv. 6,13,15).

8:1 sixth year ... sixth month ... fifth day. The second of 13 dates (see Introduction: Date). The date is Sept. 17, 592 BC, just over a year from the inaugural vision (see note on 1:1). The "elders" seek a word from Ezekiel.

8:2 figure like that of a man. Similar to the vision of God in 1:26–27. **like fire ... as bright as glowing metal.** A description of the blinding brightness of the divine presence.

8:3 The Spirit lifted me up between earth and heaven. Hovering between two realities, physically with the exiles in Babylon but spiritually seeing events in Jerusalem. An experience unique to Ezekiel (see 3:12,14; 11:1,24; 43:5).

8:4 glory of the God of Israel. See also 9:3; 10:19; 11:22. A designation that communicates that Israel's God supremely owns the temple and city (see vv. 1–6 and note). Ezekiel experiences the glory of God's presence outside of the Jerusalem temple (1:28; 3:23).

8:5 idol of jealousy. An unidentified figure. The focus is not the image itself but the divine outrage it provokes.

8:6,13,15 even more detestable. What Ezekiel is about to see will be even worse than what he sees now. The people's actions are altogether hateful and dishonoring before God.

8:7 Then he brought me to the entrance to the court. As Ezekiel is escorted through the temple, the spotlight is on those involved in the detestable practices: 70 elders (vv. 7–13), women (vv. 14–15), and 25 men (v. 16).

8:9–13 The leadership is engaged in polytheistic religious practices in a dark, secret room. Tragically, Israel's leaders are crying out to the animal spirits, revealed by the images on the walls as they use incense smoke to symbolize the animals' glory (v. 10). This might reflect Egyptian influence (2 Kgs 23:31–35).

8:10 [s]Ex 20:4
8:11 [t]Nu 16:17 [u]Nu 16:35
8:12 [v]Ps 10:11; Isa 29:15; Eze 9:9
8:16 [w]Joel 2:17 [x]Dt 4:19; 17:3; Job 31:28; Jer 2:27; Eze 11:1,12
8:17 [y]Eze 9:9 [z]Eze 16:26
8:18 [a]Eze 9:10; 24:14 [b]Isa 1:15; Jer 11:11; Mic 3:4; Zec 7:13
9:2 [c]Lev 16:4; Eze 10:2; Rev 15:6
9:3 [d]Eze 10:4 [e]Eze 11:22
9:4 [f]Ex 12:7; 2Co 1:22; Rev 7:3; 9:4 [g]Ps 119:136; Jer 13:17; Eze 21:6 [h]Ps 119:53
9:5 [i]Eze 5:11
9:6 [j]Eze 8:11-13,16 [k]2Ch 36:17; Jer 25:29; 1Pe 4:17

went in and looked, and I saw portrayed all over the walls all kinds of crawling things and unclean
animals and all the idols of Israel.[s] 11In front of them stood seventy elders of Israel, and Jaazaniah
son of Shaphan was standing among them. Each had a censer[t] in his hand, and a fragrant cloud of
incense[u] was rising.
12He said to me, "Son of man, have you seen what the elders of Israel are doing in the darkness, each
at the shrine of his own idol? They say, 'The LORD does not see[v] us; the LORD has forsaken the land.' "
13Again, he said, "You will see them doing things that are even more detestable."
14Then he brought me to the entrance of the north gate of the house of the LORD, and I saw women
sitting there, mourning the god Tammuz. 15He said to me, "Do you see this, son of man? You will see
things that are even more detestable than this."
16He then brought me into the inner court of the house of the LORD, and there at the entrance to
the temple, between the portico and the altar,[w] were about twenty-five men. With their backs toward
the temple of the LORD and their faces toward the east, they were bowing down to the sun in the east.[x]
17He said to me, "Have you seen this, son of man? Is it a trivial matter for the people of Judah to do
the detestable things they are doing here? Must they also fill the land with violence[y] and continually
arouse my anger?[z] Look at them putting the branch to their nose! 18Therefore I will deal with them
in anger; I will not look on them with pity[a] or spare them. Although they shout in my ears, I will not
listen[b] to them."

Judgment on the Idolaters

9 Then I heard him call out in a loud voice, "Bring near those who are appointed to execute judgment on the city, each with a weapon in his hand." 2And I saw six men coming from the direction
of the upper gate, which faces north, each with a deadly weapon in his hand. With them was a man
clothed in linen[c] who had a writing kit at his side. They came in and stood beside the bronze altar.
3Now the glory[d] of the God of Israel went up from above the cherubim,[e] where it had been, and
moved to the threshold of the temple. Then the LORD called to the man clothed in linen who had the
writing kit at his side 4and said to him, "Go throughout the city of Jerusalem and put a mark[f] on the
foreheads of those who grieve and lament[g] over all the detestable things that are done in it.[h]"
5As I listened, he said to the others, "Follow him through the city and kill, without showing pity[i] or
compassion. 6Slaughter the old men, the young men and women, the mothers and children, but do
not touch anyone who has the mark. Begin at my sanctuary." So they began with the old men[j] who
were in front of the temple.[k]

8:11 Jaazaniah son of Shaphan. Perhaps a shock that he was among the traitors, because his family was staunchly loyal to the Lord during Jeremiah's ministry (2 Kgs 22:8–10; Jer 26:24).

8:12 The LORD does not see us; the LORD has forsaken the land. Their rationale for going astray; a reflection of faulty theology. Perhaps they understood the Babylonian invasion in 597 BC to mean that the Babylonian gods had defeated Yahweh and that Yahweh had been driven away from his land.

8:14 Tammuz. The Hebrew spelling of Dumuzi, the dying and rising Sumerian-Babylonian god. His followers mourned his death, which supposedly happened seasonally at the height of the summer heat and which they thought caused the annual die-off of vegetation. "Mourning" this god may mean that the women are equating the Lord with Tammuz (cf. v. 12) or that syncretism is taking place in the Lord's temple; hence, the women are weeping because Tammuz is gone too.

8:16 between the portico and the altar. Normally reserved for priests. At this sacred place — the very entrance to the Holy Place — these men are venerating the sun and turning their backs on the Holy Place of the temple, which Deut 4:19 prohibits (see Deut 17:3; 2 Kgs 23:5,11). **bowing down to the sun.** Worshiping the sun as it rose required people to turn their backs to the temple because ancient temples faced east.

8:17 putting the branch to their nose! Probably a gesture of derision.

8:18 I will not look on them with pity. God has hardened himself against them. This is another reminder that there are no more chances for them to change (see 7:4,9 and note; 9:10). The behavior that ch. 8 describes has justifiably angered the God of Israel, who has a rationale for judging the idolaters and abandoning the temple, people, and city. As the Lord shows Ezekiel all these detestable practices, stage by stage, a growing tension builds in the vision.

9:1–11 *Temple Owner's Response.* As the owner of the temple, God communicates how he intends to deal decisively with the detestable practices of the people (8:1–18). Before his official departure from the city (11:22–23), which is his ultimate response, he will clean house with a citywide slaughter of the idolaters.

9:2 a man clothed in linen. The garment helps identify him more specifically than the "six men." He is a heavenly attendant associated with righteousness (44:17–18; Dan 12:6–7; Rev 19:8,14). **writing kit.** Pen and ink for marking (see note on v. 4).

9:4 mark ... those who grieve and lament. The man's role is to spare from execution those who grieve over the people's rebellion (see Introduction: Historical Setting, Purpose, and Occasion). The mark happily sets the righteous apart from the rebels. It preserves a faithful remnant for God. **foreheads.** The most visible part of their bodies.

9:5 kill, without showing pity or compassion. This execution is not taking place literally but anticipates the upcoming brutality of the Babylonian invasion in 587 BC. The killing is thorough, indiscriminate, and merciless. It mirrors the Lord's attitude toward their sins (v. 10; 8:18).

7Then he said to them, "Defile the temple and fill the courts with the slain. Go!" So they went out and
began killing throughout the city. 8While they were killing and I was left alone, I fell facedown,[l] crying
out, "Alas, Sovereign LORD! Are you going to destroy the entire remnant of Israel in this outpouring of
your wrath on Jerusalem?[m]"
9He answered me, "The sin of the people of Israel and Judah is exceedingly great; the land is full of
bloodshed and the city is full of injustice.[n] They say, 'The LORD has forsaken the land; the LORD does not
see.'[o] 10So I will not look on them with pity[p] or spare them, but I will bring down on their own heads
what they have done.[q]"
11Then the man in linen with the writing kit at his side brought back word, saying, "I have done as
you commanded."

God's Glory Departs From the Temple

10 I looked, and I saw the likeness of a throne[r] of lapis lazuli[s] above the vault[t] that was over the
heads of the cherubim. 2The LORD said to the man clothed in linen,[u] "Go in among the wheels[v]
beneath the cherubim. Fill[w] your hands with burning coals from among the cherubim and scatter them
over the city." And as I watched, he went in.
3Now the cherubim were standing on the south side of the temple when the man went in, and a
cloud filled the inner court. 4Then the glory of the LORD[x] rose from above the cherubim and moved to
the threshold of the temple. The cloud filled the temple, and the court was full of the radiance of the
glory of the LORD. 5The sound of the wings of the cherubim could be heard as far away as the outer
court, like the voice[y] of God Almighty[a] when he speaks.
6When the LORD commanded the man in linen, "Take fire from among the wheels, from among
the cherubim," the man went in and stood beside a wheel. 7Then one of the cherubim reached out
his hand to the fire that was among them. He took up some of it and put it into the hands of the man
in linen, who took it and went out. 8(Under the wings of the cherubim could be seen what looked like
human hands.)[z]
9I looked, and I saw beside the cherubim four wheels, one beside each of the cherubim; the wheels

9:8 [l]Jos 7:6 [m]Eze 11:13; Am 7:1-6
9:9 [n]Eze 22:29 [o]Job 22:13; Eze 8:12
9:10 [p]Eze 7:4; 8:18 [q]Isa 65:6; Eze 11:21
10:1 [r]Rev 4:2 [s]Ex 24:10 [t]Eze 1:22
10:2 [u]Eze 9:2 [v]Eze 1:15 [w]Rev 8:5
10:4 [x]Eze 1:28; 9:3
10:5 [y]Job 40:9; Eze 1:24
10:8 [z]Eze 1:8

[a] 5 Hebrew *El-Shaddai*

The first to experience God's wrath are the leaders who have done detestable things at God's "sanctuary" (v. 6; see 8:16).

9:7 Defile the temple. Beyond the defilements already present in the temple (8:4–18), the dead bodies of the slain will further defile the Lord's sanctuary (cf. 6:4–5,13).

9:8 I fell facedown, crying out, "Alas ... " As a mourner, Ezekiel utilizes words associated with mourning and grief (cf. 11:13). This is a voluntary human response to bad news, as he is asking the Lord to have mercy and spare some. But it is a time not for mercy but for God's just judgment. See Introduction: Literary Features.

9:10 bring down on their own heads what they have done. Although some might be spared this fate due to the work of the man in linen (vv. 4,6), the vision focuses on the realities and justness of God's actions carried out through the six men. See 16:43; Jer 50:15.

10:1–22 *God's Presence Departs the Temple.* God judges the city with fire, but the ultimate judgment and focal point is God's departure from his earthly home. This is the curse God promised in Deut 31:17–18: God said he would hide his face from his people because they turned to other gods. God's glory departs slowly and even reluctantly at several stages. The departure is like that of a bird due to the movement of the cherubim as they escort the "glory" throughout the vision. The glory of the Lord goes up from the ark of the covenant to the temple's entrance (9:3) to the east gate (10:19) and eventually to the mountain in the east (11:22–23). The initial step is Yahweh's departure from the Most Holy Place, the place of his earthly throne, to the temple's entrance (9:3). After the destruction of the idolaters (9:4–10), Yahweh joins up again with the waiting cherubim at the temple's entrance, then moves out of the temple to the east gate of the temple complex, and temporarily stops there (10:4,18–19). This pause is at the "east gate" (v. 19), i.e., the gate at the very edge of the temple complex (the outer court gate), where the "glory" would be best positioned to leave the city (11:23).

10:1–8 These verses describe the setting for the coals of judgment hurled on the city. Judgment by fire derives from God's very throne. The man in linen has to enact judgment now (contrast ch. 9).

10:1 the likeness of a throne ... over the heads of the cherubim. See notes on 1:22–28. **cherubim.** Creatures that guard and transport the divine presence (Gen 3:24; Exod 25:18–22; 1 Kgs 6:23–28). Here they provide conveyance for the Lord as he makes his way around and out of the temple complex (v. 18; 9:3; 11:22–23). They move by flying (vv. 5,16,19; 11:22; cf. 1:19,24), and their wings generate noise when they move (v. 5; cf. 1:24), probably indicating that they are ready to act or anticipate the departure. They also provide the man in linen with the fire to hurl onto the city (vv. 7–8).

10:3 cloud. Enclosed the "glory of the LORD" (v. 4). At their respective completions, the tabernacle and temple were filled with the "cloud," i.e., the glory of God's presence (Exod 40:34–35,38; 1 Kgs 8:10–12). In those structures the cloud visually declared the reality that God was in Israel's midst. The cloud was also associated with Israel's guidance while in the wilderness (Num 9:15–17). In the NT John says of Jesus (God in human form) that by seeing him the disciples actually saw the glory of God (John 1:14). Jesus reveals God to humankind and gives guidance to believers through the Holy Spirit. At the end of the age, Christ will come again, but it will be in the clouds and all will see him (Matt 24:30; Rev 1:7).

10:9 wheels. Called "the whirling wheels" (v. 13). See notes 1:12,15,20. Along with the wings of the cherubim, the wheels help the cherubim move. The wheels keep pace with the cherubim, and the movements of the wheels

Likely a picture of two cherubim on a tenth-century BC cult stand from the city of Taanach. Ezek 10:1–5 mentions the cherubim in God's temple.

Z. Radovan/www.BibleLandPictures.com

10:9 [a]Eze 1:15-16; Rev 21:20 10:12 [b]Rev 4:6-8 [c]Eze 1:15-21 10:14 [d]1Ki 7:36 [e]Eze 1:6 [f]Eze 1:10; Rev 4:7 10:15 [g]Eze 1:3,5 10:17 [h]Eze 1:20-21 10:18 [i]Ps 18:10 10:19 [j]Eze 11:1,22 10:20 [k]Eze 1:1 10:21 [l]Eze 41:18 [m]Eze 1:6 11:1 [n]Eze 8:16; 10:19; 43:4-5

sparkled like topaz.[a] 10As for their appearance, the four of them looked alike; each was like a wheel
intersecting a wheel. 11As they moved, they would go in any one of the four directions the cherubim
faced; the wheels did not turn about[a] as the cherubim went. The cherubim went in whatever direction
the head faced, without turning as they went. 12Their entire bodies, including their backs, their hands
and their wings, were completely full of eyes,[b] as were their four wheels.[c] 13I heard the wheels being
called "the whirling wheels." 14Each of the cherubim[d] had four faces:[e] One face was that of a cherub,
the second the face of a human being, the third the face of a lion, and the fourth the face of an eagle.[f]
15Then the cherubim rose upward. These were the living creatures[g] I had seen by the Kebar River.
16When the cherubim moved, the wheels beside them moved; and when the cherubim spread their
wings to rise from the ground, the wheels did not leave their side. 17When the cherubim stood still,
they also stood still; and when the cherubim rose, they rose with them, because the spirit of the living
creatures was in them.[h]
18Then the glory of the LORD departed from over the threshold of the temple and stopped above the
cherubim.[i] 19While I watched, the cherubim spread their wings and rose from the ground, and as they
went, the wheels went with them.[j] They stopped at the entrance of the east gate of the LORD's house, and
the glory of the God of Israel was above them.
20These were the living creatures I had seen beneath the God of Israel by the Kebar River,[k] and I
realized that they were cherubim. 21Each had four faces[l] and four wings,[m] and under their wings was
what looked like human hands. 22Their faces had the same appearance as those I had seen by the Kebar
River. Each one went straight ahead.

God's Sure Judgment on Jerusalem

11 Then the Spirit lifted me up and brought me to the gate of the house of the LORD that faces
east. There at the entrance of the gate were twenty-five men, and I saw among them Jaazaniah son of Azzur and Pelatiah son of Benaiah, leaders of the people.[n] 2The LORD said to me, "Son of

[a] *11* Or *aside*

are synchronized with those of the cherubim (v. 16) because "the spirit of the living creatures was in them" (v. 17). Through his flying throne chariot (see note on 1:28), God is infinitely mobile and presently on the move.

10:14 four faces. See notes on 1:6,10.

10:15 These were the living creatures I had seen. See also v. 20. Ezekiel realizes that the cherubim in this second vision are the same as the "living creatures" in his first vision (see 1:5–15 and notes).

10:19 east gate. See note on vv. 1–22.

11:1–13 *God's Certain Judgment on Jerusalem.* Before God leaves Jerusalem (vv. 22–23), he confronts through the prophet the people's erroneous theology.

11:2 men ... giving wicked advice in this city. Refers to the 25 leaders in v. 1. The nature of their advice follows in v. 3.

man, these are the men who are plotting evil and giving wicked advice in this city. 3They say, 'Haven't
our houses been recently rebuilt? This city is a pot,[o] and we are the meat in it.'[p] 4Therefore prophesy[q]
against them; prophesy, son of man."
5Then the Spirit of the LORD came on me, and he told me to say: "This is what the LORD says: That
is what you are saying, you leaders in Israel, but I know what is going through your mind.[r] 6You have
killed many people in this city and filled its streets with the dead.[s]
7"Therefore this is what the Sovereign LORD says: The bodies you have thrown there are the meat
and this city is the pot, but I will drive you out of it.[t] 8You fear the sword, and the sword is what I will
bring against you, declares the Sovereign LORD.[u] 9I will drive you out of the city and deliver you into
the hands[v] of foreigners and inflict punishment on you.[w] 10You will fall by the sword, and I will execute
judgment on you at the borders of Israel.[x] Then you will know that I am the LORD. 11This city will not
be a pot[y] for you, nor will you be the meat in it; I will execute judgment on you at the borders of Israel.
12And you will know that I am the LORD, for you have not followed my decrees[z] or kept my laws but have
conformed to the standards of the nations around you.[a]"
13Now as I was prophesying, Pelatiah[b] son of Benaiah died. Then I fell facedown and cried out in a
loud voice, "Alas, Sovereign LORD! Will you completely destroy the remnant of Israel?[c]"

The Promise of Israel's Return

14The word of the LORD came to me: 15"Son of man, the people of Jerusalem have said of your fellow exiles
and all the other Israelites, 'They are far away from the LORD; this land was given to us as our possession.'[d]
16"Therefore say: 'This is what the Sovereign LORD says: Although I sent them far away among the
nations and scattered them among the countries, yet for a little while I have been a sanctuary[e] for them
in the countries where they have gone.'
17"Therefore say: 'This is what the Sovereign LORD says: I will gather you from the nations and
bring you back from the countries where you have been scattered, and I will give you back the land
of Israel again.'[f]
18"They will return to it and remove all its vile images[g] and detestable idols.[h] 19I will give them an
undivided heart[i] and put a new spirit in them; I will remove from them their heart of stone[j] and give
them a heart of flesh.[k] 20Then they will follow my decrees and be careful to keep my laws.[l] They will
be my people, and I will be their God.[m] 21But as for those whose hearts are devoted to their vile images

11:3 [o] Jer 1:13; Eze 24:3 [p] ver 7,11
11:4 [q] Eze 3:4,17
11:5 [r] Jer 17:10
11:6 [s] Eze 7:23; 22:6
11:7 [t] Eze 24:3-13; Mic 3:2-3
11:8 [u] Pr 10:24
11:9 [v] Ps 106:41 [w] Dt 28:36; Eze 5:8
11:10 [x] 2Ki 14:25
11:11 [y] ver 3
11:12 [z] Lev 18:4; Eze 18:9 [a] Eze 8:10
11:13 [b] ver 1 [c] Eze 9:8
11:15 [d] Eze 33:24
11:16 [e] Ps 90:1; 91:9; Isa 8:14
11:17 [f] Jer 3:18; 24:5-6; Eze 28:25; 34:13
11:18 [g] Eze 5:11 [h] Eze 37:23
11:19 [i] Jer 32:39 [j] Zec 7:12 [k] Eze 18:31; 36:26; 2Co 3:3
11:20 [l] Ps 105:45 [m] Eze 14:11; 36:26-28

11:3 Owing to the obscure nature of the Hebrew of this verse, the "wicked advice" of the leaders (v. 2) is not clear. Verse 3a may be either a statement or a question. If it is a statement, the "pot" and "meat" metaphor is negative ("we're cooked!"); but if it is a question, the metaphor is positive ("we won't be burned!"). Most likely, the metaphor is positive. As meat belongs in a pot, so the current leaders think they are safe and belong in Jerusalem. The city is theirs (v. 15); it cannot be taken away because God made an ironclad promise. This reveals the theology of Jerusalem's leaders, but it is way off base (v. 4).
11:7 The bodies you have thrown there are the meat. This is the theological reality the leaders must face. The meat, redefined by the prophet, is not the leaders in Jerusalem (who will be driven out of it) but the innocent people they killed.
11:13 Pelatiah son of Benaiah died. This leader's sudden death tangibly demonstrates that God will judge the people of the city. Ezekiel mourns over the loss and pleads mercy for the remnant of Israel (see 5:3; 6:9). Pelatiah means "the LORD delivers"; Benaiah means "the LORD builds"; therefore, "The LORD delivers"—the son of "The LORD builds"—has died.
11:14–21 *Those in Exile to Be Restored.* The prophet brings a message of hope for a return to the land of Canaan. This message of hope, however, is not for Jerusalem's current residents, who think of themselves as more privileged than those in Babylon.
11:15 They are far away from the LORD; this land was given to us as our possession. A wrong theological boast. The people of Jerusalem arrogantly and self-confidently think the promises of God exclude the exiles.
11:16 I have been a sanctuary for them in the countries where they have gone. God's corrective to the residents of Jerusalem (v. 15) and encouragement to the exiles. God redefines his relationship with the exiles, his remnant. God is present with the exiles even though they were driven away from Jerusalem and the temple (the symbol of God's presence). This is so because the real sanctuary is a person, not a symbolic place or building. Ezekiel's first vision underscores this fact: "above on the throne was a figure like that of a man" (1:26). This anticipates the person of Jesus, who refers to himself as a temple (John 2:19).
11:19 undivided heart … new spirit. A description of the new relationship with the remnant. The mark of the relationship is a single-minded commitment to God that produces faithfulness in the relationship (36:26). **remove … their heart of stone and give them a heart of flesh.** A spiritual heart transplant performed by God. Points to the new covenant in Christ (see Jer 31:31–34; Heb 8:8–13; 10:15–18 and notes; see also 2 Cor 3:3).
11:20 They will be my people, and I will be their God. An exclusive and possessive relationship. The heart of God's covenant promise (see Exod 6:7 and note; Jer 7:23; Zech 8:8 and note). This covenantal relationship derives from Exod 6:2–8, yet it points back to Gen 17. The exiled population, "the remnant of Israel" (v. 13), will return to the land. They will be cleansed and become the new people of God. Ironically, those facing death in exile will experience life. Not only does this statement correct the faulty theology of the present inhabitants of Jerusalem about the land, but it also answers Ezekiel's question in v. 13. God will not destroy all the remnant of Israel. In wrath God will remember mercy (Hab 3:2).

11:21 [n]Eze 9:10; 16:43
11:22 [o]Eze 10:19
11:23 [p]Eze 8:4; 10:4 [q]Zec 14:4
11:24 [r]Eze 8:3 [s]2Co 12:2-4
11:25 [t]Eze 3:4,11
12:2 [u]Isa 6:10; Eze 2:6-8; Mt 13:15
12:3 [v]Jer 36:3 [w]Jer 26:3 [x]2Ti 2:25-26
12:4 [y]ver 12; Jer 39:4
12:6 [z]ver 12; Isa 8:18; 20:3; Eze 4:3; 24:24
12:7 [a]Eze 24:18; 37:10
12:9 [b]Eze 17:12; 20:49; 24:19
12:11 [c]2Ki 25:7; Jer 15:2; 52:15
12:12 [d]Jer 39:4 [e]Jer 52:7
12:13 [f]Eze 17:20; 19:8; Hos 7:12 [g]Isa 24:17-18 [h]Jer 39:7 [i]Jer 52:11; Eze 17:16
12:14 [j]2Ki 25:5; Eze 5:10,12

and detestable idols, I will bring down on their own heads what they have done, declares the Sovereign
LORD.[n]"
22 Then the cherubim, with the wheels beside them, spread their wings, and the glory of the God of
Israel was above them.[o] 23 The glory[p] of the LORD went up from within the city and stopped above the
mountain[q] east of it. 24 The Spirit[r] lifted me up and brought me to the exiles in Babylonia[a] in the vision[s]
given by the Spirit of God.

Then the vision I had seen went up from me, 25 and I told the exiles everything the LORD had
shown me.[t]

The Exile Symbolized

12 The word of the LORD came to me: 2 "Son of man, you are living among a rebellious people. They
have eyes to see but do not see and ears to hear but do not hear, for they are a rebellious people.[u]
3 "Therefore, son of man, pack your belongings for exile and in the daytime, as they watch, set out
and go from where you are to another place. Perhaps[v] they will understand,[w] though they are a rebellious people.[x] 4 During the daytime, while they watch, bring out your belongings packed for exile.
Then in the evening, while they are watching, go out like those who go into exile.[y] 5 While they watch,
dig through the wall and take your belongings out through it. 6 Put them on your shoulder as they are
watching and carry them out at dusk. Cover your face so that you cannot see the land, for I have made
you a sign[z] to the Israelites."

7 So I did as I was commanded.[a] During the day I brought out my things packed for exile. Then in
the evening I dug through the wall with my hands. I took my belongings out at dusk, carrying them
on my shoulders while they watched.

8 In the morning the word of the LORD came to me: 9 "Son of man, did not the Israelites, that rebellious people, ask you, 'What are you doing?'[b]

10 "Say to them, 'This is what the Sovereign LORD says: This prophecy concerns the prince in Jerusalem and all the Israelites who are there.' 11 Say to them, 'I am a sign to you.'

"As I have done, so it will be done to them. They will go into exile as captives.[c]

12 "The prince among them will put his things on his shoulder at dusk[d] and leave, and a hole will
be dug in the wall for him to go through. He will cover his face so that he cannot see the land.[e] 13 I will
spread my net[f] for him, and he will be caught in my snare;[g] I will bring him to Babylonia, the land of
the Chaldeans, but he will not see[h] it, and there he will die.[i] 14 I will scatter to the winds all those around
him—his staff and all his troops—and I will pursue them with drawn sword.[j]

[a] 24 Or *Chaldea*

11:22–25 *Conclusion of Temple Vision.* The vision ends tragically, with the Lord's presence departing the city of Jerusalem. The last mention of the "glory" was its position at the east gate of the temple complex (10:19). The throne chariot flies away (v. 22), and Ezekiel sees it at the city limits (v. 23). Now the "glory" is positioned on a mountain east of the city. This is a stunning reversal of 1 Kgs 8:10, which describes the glory of the Lord filling the temple at its dedication in the time of Solomon (cf. Exod 40:35). In sum, chs. 4–11 anticipate desolation to the city, people (chs. 4–5), its environs and whole land (chs. 6–7), and the temple proper (chs.8–11). Thus, there has been a progression in chs. 4–11 as it relates to descriptions of total destruction.

12:1–28 *Ezekiel Symbolizes the Exile of Jerusalem.* Although already exiled in 597 BC during Jehoiachin's reign (1:1–3), Ezekiel predicts a future exile through two symbolic acts (vv. 3–16,17–20). This reference to future exile concerns events that unfold between 597 (when Ezekiel was exiled) and 586 BC (the final fall of Jerusalem, during Zedekiah's reign).

12:1–16 *Packed and Ready to Go.* Upon returning to his fellow exiles in mind and spirit from his second visionary experience (chs. 8–11), God commands Ezekiel to utilize another visual aid (pack his belongings) to prepare the people for future exile and its effects on the present Judahite puppet king and those who remain in the land. See photo, p. 1308.

12:2 do not see … do not hear. Malfunctioning body parts symbolize spiritual blindness and deafness due to rebellion (cf. Isa 6:9). Physically they will see Ezekiel's visual aid, but spiritually they will not understand it (v. 9). They are lifeless, like the idols they worship.

12:3 pack your belongings. Ezekiel must prepare for future exile by packing something portable to take on the journey. In the evening he must depart as if going into exile.

12:5 dig through the wall. Probably of his house. Invading armies entered cities by breaking down walls at various locations (Amos 4:3).

12:6 Cover your face. Ezekiel is not supposed to see where he is going: he is in darkness, walking away from his home and leaving the city through a breach in the wall. **sign.** A repeated term used in the book for the visual aids God has Ezekiel perform (v. 11; 24:24,27).

12:8–15 The interpretation of the visual aid concerns Zedekiah and those remaining in Jerusalem.

12:10 prince in Jerusalem. Zedekiah, Judah's last king, whom the Babylonians installed in 597 BC. He rebels against Babylon (2 Kgs 25:1), so the Babylonians capture him, kill his sons in front of him, gouge out his eyes, and take him blind to Babylon, where he later dies (2 Kgs 25:6–7). **all … who are there.** Babylon will carry off the remaining Israelites.

12:11 sign. A visual aid (vv. 6,11) of the "end times" for Judah as an independent state.

15"They will know that I am the LORD, when I disperse them among the nations and scatter them
through the countries. 16But I will spare a few of them from the sword, famine and plague, so that in
the nations where they go they may acknowledge all their detestable practices. Then they will know
that I am the LORD.[k]"

17The word of the LORD came to me: 18"Son of man, tremble as you eat your food,[l] and shudder
in fear as you drink your water. 19Say to the people of the land: 'This is what the Sovereign LORD says
about those living in Jerusalem and in the land of Israel: They will eat their food in anxiety and drink
their water in despair, for their land will be stripped of everything[m] in it because of the violence of all
who live there.[n] 20The inhabited towns will be laid waste and the land will be desolate. Then you will
know that I am the LORD.[o]' "

There Will Be No Delay

21The word of the LORD came to me: 22"Son of man, what is this proverb you have in the land of Israel:
'The days go by and every vision comes to nothing'?[p] 23Say to them, 'This is what the Sovereign LORD says:
I am going to put an end to this proverb, and they will no longer quote it in Israel.' Say to them, 'The days
are near when every vision will be fulfilled.[q] 24For there will be no more false visions or flattering divinations[r] among the people of Israel. 25But I the LORD will speak what I will, and it shall be fulfilled without
delay. For in your days, you rebellious people, I will fulfill whatever I say, declares the Sovereign LORD.[s]' "

26The word of the LORD came to me: 27"Son of man, the Israelites are saying, 'The vision he sees is
for many years from now, and he prophesies about the distant future.'[t]

28"Therefore say to them, 'This is what the Sovereign LORD says: None of my words will be delayed
any longer; whatever I say will be fulfilled, declares the Sovereign LORD.' "

False Prophets Condemned

13 The word of the LORD came to me: 2"Son of man, prophesy against the prophets of Israel who are
now prophesying. Say to those who prophesy out of their own imagination: 'Hear the word of the
LORD![u] 3This is what the Sovereign LORD says: Woe to the foolish[a] prophets[v] who follow their own spirit

[a] 3 Or *wicked*

12:16 [k] Jer 22:8-9; Eze 6:8-10; 14:22
12:18 [l] La 5:9; Eze 4:16
12:19 [m] Eze 6:6-14; Mic 7:13; Zec 7:14 [n] Eze 4:16; 23:33
12:20 [o] Isa 7:23-24; Jer 4:7
12:22 [p] Eze 11:3; Am 6:3; 2Pe 3:4
12:23 [q] Ps 37:13; Joel 2:1; Zep 1:14
12:24 [r] Jer 14:14; Eze 13:23; Zec 13:2-4
12:25 [s] Isa 14:24; Hab 1:5
12:27 [t] Da 10:14
13:2 [u] ver 17; Jer 23:16; 37:19
13:3 [v] La 2:14

12:15,16 They will know that I am the LORD. God's goal in exiling the remaining rebellious Judahite population and yet sparing some. God is about gaining glory. He wants the exiles to recognize his true character (v. 15). Their rebellion and spiritual poverty brought a contrast between God and his people (see note on v. 16). If they are his people and he is their God, then they will display his character. Rebellious people cannot acknowledge God's holy and just character. The humiliation and suffering of exile would help to correct this. God also wants those he spares to recognize his true character (v. 16).

12:16 sword, famine and plague. Covers the full range of divine agents of destruction; a standard way of speaking about divine punishment (5:12; 7:15). The Lord desires that the group of people he graciously spares (Lev 26:42–45; Deut 4:30–31) publically (in the nations where they go) acknowledge their sinful past. As they acknowledge him, they will restore God's reputation for what appeared to be harsh and unjust dealings with his people. Then there will no longer be a contrast between the character of God's people and that of their God (see note on vv. 15,16). The exile will expose the truth about Israel and her God. See Introduction: Theological Significance.

12:17–28 *Unfavorable Outcomes.* After the sign of an exile packing their belongings, its interpretation, and purpose (vv. 1–16), ch. 12 concludes with one more visual aid and another theological correction, this one pertaining to the people's understanding of prophets and prophecy.

12:18 tremble ... shudder. Another prophetic visual aid symbolizing the emotional turmoil that people will experience in the siege leading up to the exile. **tremble.** The same Hebrew term is used of an earthquake in 1 Kgs 19:11; Amos 1:1.

12:22 The days go by and every vision comes to nothing. A mocking slogan. This includes the prophetic words about the nation's demise from the time of Amos (ca. 760 BC; cf. Amos 2:4–5) to the time of Ezekiel. Jerusalem had remained untouched for almost 200 years since Amos's words, and people did not really believe that Jerusalem would fall. They could not see that the delay in fulfilling these prophetic words was an undeserved extension of Yahweh's loyalty and grace.

12:23 The Lord refutes the mocking slogan (see note on v. 22) of the people that dismissed his prophet's announcements of impending judgment.

12:24 no more false visions. False prophecies will come to an end (see ch. 13).

12:25 in your days. God corrects their false security. The Judahites *are* going to experience the "end times," and those proclaiming anything different are false (see ch. 13). The corrective, therefore, is that Ezekiel's generation will witness the destruction.

12:27–28 Another dismissive slogan about Ezekiel's revelations concerning Jerusalem's fall that reveal belief and unbelief. The people acknowledge that Ezekiel's revelation is from God, but they think Ezekiel's timing is off.

12:28 None of my words will be delayed. God's response to the people's false sense of security.

13:1—14:23 *False Prophets and Idolatry.* Ezekiel must speak to false prophets who sound like true ones. Linked to this brutal word to the false prophets is a word to idolatrous elders who are consulting both these false prophets and Ezekiel, the true prophet, at the same time.

13:1–23 *Condemnation of False Prophets.* This section targets male prophets (vv. 1–16) and female prophets (vv. 17–23).

13:2 out of their own imagination. Unlike true prophets, who repeat what God said, false prophets make up the words in their own minds and for their own gain.

13:3 Ironically, the false prophets are seers (i.e., prophets) who "have

13:3 [w] Jer 23:25-32
13:5 [x] Isa 58:12; Eze 22:30 [y] Eze 7:19
13:6 [z] Jer 28:15; Eze 22:28
13:9 [a] Jer 17:13 [b] Eze 20:38
13:10 [c] Jer 50:6 [d] Eze 7:25; 22:28
13:11 [e] Eze 38:22
13:13 [f] Rev 11:19; 16:21 [g] Ex 9:25; Isa 30:30
13:14 [h] Mic 1:6 [i] Jer 6:15
13:16 [j] Isa 57:21; Jer 6:14
13:17 [k] Rev 2:20 [l] ver 2
13:19 [m] Eze 20:39; 22:26

and have seen nothing![w] 4 Your prophets, Israel, are like jackals
among ruins. 5 You have not gone up to the breaches in the wall
to repair[x] it for the people of Israel so that it will stand firm in the
battle on the day of the LORD.[y] 6 Their visions are false and their
divinations a lie. Even though the LORD has not sent them, they
say, "The LORD declares," and expect him to fulfill their words.[z]
7 Have you not seen false visions and uttered lying divinations
when you say, "The LORD declares," though I have not spoken?
8 " 'Therefore this is what the Sovereign LORD says: Because
of your false words and lying visions, I am against you, declares
the Sovereign LORD. 9 My hand will be against the prophets who
see false visions and utter lying divinations. They will not belong to the council of my people or be listed in the records[a] of
Israel, nor will they enter the land of Israel. Then you will know
that I am the Sovereign LORD.[b]

10 " 'Because they lead my people astray,[c] saying, "Peace,"
when there is no peace, and because, when a flimsy wall is
built, they cover it with whitewash,[d] 11 therefore tell those who
cover it with whitewash that it is going to fall. Rain will come in
torrents, and I will send hailstones hurtling down, and violent
winds will burst forth.[e] 12 When the wall collapses, will people
not ask you, "Where is the whitewash you covered it with?"

13 " 'Therefore this is what the Sovereign LORD says: In my
wrath I will unleash a violent wind, and in my anger hailstones[f]
and torrents of rain will fall with destructive fury.[g] 14 I will tear
down the wall you have covered with whitewash and will level it
to the ground so that its foundation[h] will be laid bare. When it[a] falls,[i] you will be destroyed in it; and you
will know that I am the LORD. 15 So I will pour out my wrath against the wall and against those who covered it with whitewash. I will say to you, "The wall is gone and so are those who whitewashed it, 16 those
prophets of Israel who prophesied to Jerusalem and saw visions of peace for her when there was no peace,
declares the Sovereign LORD.[j]" '

17 "Now, son of man, set your face against the daughters[k] of your people who prophesy out of their
own imagination. Prophesy against them[l] 18 and say, 'This is what the Sovereign LORD says: Woe to the
women who sew magic charms on all their wrists and make veils of various lengths for their heads
in order to ensnare people. Will you ensnare the lives of my people but preserve your own? 19 You have
profaned[m] me among my people for a few handfuls of barley and scraps of bread. By lying to my people,

Magical amulet of goddess Lamashtu, to ward off evil, from eighth-century BC Babylonia. Ezek 13:18 warns against women who make magic charms.
Kim Walton, taken at the British Museum

[a] 14 Or *the city*

seen nothing." God has not given them a message, yet they are deceiving people with a message of hope.
13:4 jackals. Wild scavenger dogs. **ruins.** Of abandoned cities (Isa 13:20–21; Jer 50:39; 51:37; Lam 5:18). The imagery is that Israel's false prophets are running around loose and providing no help in rebuilding the nation.
13:5 not gone up to the breaches in the wall. The inability of the false prophets to defend the city. They are not strengthening the weak spiritual fortifications of the nation by speaking out against its evils.
13:8 I am against you. God personally opposes and confronts the false prophets (see 5:8 and note). The false prophets will be excluded and isolated from the community of faith (v. 9).
13:10 saying, "Peace," when there is no peace. A false sense of security or well-being. **flimsy wall ... whitewash.** The false prophets "fix" poorly constructed walls by cosmetically covering up the problem areas, but the walls are structurally still weak and vulnerable. Their messages are worthless (cf. Jer 6:14; 8:11; Mic 3:5).
13:12 When the wall collapses. When Jerusalem's destruction becomes a reality.
13:13 I will unleash a violent wind. God's judgment comes in storm imagery (cf. 1:4–9; see, e.g., Ps 18:7–15; Isa 28:17; Jer 23:19) to rain down on the faulty structure and those who built it. He is his own agent of destruction.
13:17 daughters. The fraudulent counterpart to the male prophets (v. 2). They make up the words in their own minds and for their own gain. A contrast with other Israelite women who function as true agents of God (Exod 15:20; Judg 4:4; 2 Kgs 22:14; Neh 6:14; Isa 8:3).
13:18 magic charms ... veils. Associated with black magic and sorcery of witches or fortunetellers. They aim to trap people, like hunters stalking their prey (v. 20). They hunt the souls of God's people who consult with them.
13:19 a few handfuls of barley and scraps of bread. The price for their services (1 Sam 9:7).

who listen to lies, you have killed those who should not have died and have spared those who should not live.[n]

20“ ‘Therefore this is what the Sovereign LORD says: I am against your magic charms with which you ensnare people like birds and I will tear them from your arms; I will set free the people that you ensnare like birds. 21I will tear off your veils and save my people from your hands, and they will no longer fall prey to your power. Then you will know that I am the LORD.[o] 22Because you disheartened the righteous with your lies, when I had brought them no grief, and because you encouraged the wicked not to turn from their evil ways and so save their lives,[p] 23therefore you will no longer see false visions or practice divination.[q] I will save my people from your hands. And then you will know that I am the LORD.[r] ’ ”

Idolaters Condemned

14 Some of the elders of Israel came to me and sat down in front of me.[s] 2Then the word of the LORD came to me: 3“Son of man, these men have set up idols in their hearts and put wicked stumbling blocks[t] before their faces. Should I let them inquire of me at all?[u] 4Therefore speak to them and tell them, ‘This is what the Sovereign LORD says: When any of the Israelites set up idols in their hearts and put a wicked stumbling block before their faces and then go to a prophet, I the LORD will answer them myself in keeping with their great idolatry. 5I will do this to recapture the hearts of the people of Israel, who have all deserted[v] me for their idols.’[w]

6“Therefore say to the people of Israel, ‘This is what the Sovereign LORD says: Repent! Turn from your idols and renounce all your detestable practices![x]

7“ ‘When any of the Israelites or any foreigner[y] residing in Israel separate themselves from me and set up idols in their hearts and put a wicked stumbling block before their faces and then go to a prophet to inquire of me, I the LORD will answer them myself. 8I will set my face against[z] them and make them an example and a byword.[a] I will remove them from my people. Then you will know that I am the LORD.

9“ ‘And if the prophet[b] is enticed[c] to utter a prophecy, I the LORD have enticed that prophet, and I will stretch out my hand against him and destroy him from among my people Israel.[d] 10They will bear their guilt—the prophet will be as guilty as the one who consults him. 11Then the people of Israel will no longer stray[e] from me, nor will they defile themselves anymore with all their sins. They will be my people, and I will be their God, declares the Sovereign LORD.[f] ’ ”

Jerusalem’s Judgment Inescapable

12The word of the LORD came to me: 13“Son of man, if a country sins against me by being unfaithful and I stretch out my hand against it to cut off its food supply[g] and send famine upon it and kill its people and their animals,[h] 14even if these three men—Noah,[i] Daniel[a][j] and Job[k]—were in it, they could save only themselves by their righteousness,[l] declares the Sovereign LORD.

a *14* Or *Danel*, a man of renown in ancient literature; also in verse 20

13:19 [n]Pr 28:21
13:21 [o]Ps 91:3
13:22 [p]Jer 23:14; Eze 33:14-16
13:23 [q]ver 6; Eze 12:24 [r]Mic 3:6
14:1 [s]Eze 8:1; 20:1
14:3 [t]ver 7; Eze 7:19 [u]Isa 1:15; Eze 20:31
14:5 [v]Zec 11:8 [w]Jer 2:11
14:6 [x]Isa 2:20; 30:22
14:7 [y]Ex 12:48; 20:10
14:8 [z]Eze 15:7 [a]Eze 5:15
14:9 [b]Jer 14:15 [c]Jer 4:10 [d]1Ki 22:23
14:11 [e]Eze 48:11 [f]Eze 11:19-20; 37:23
14:13 [g]Lev 26:26 [h]Eze 5:16; 6:14; 15:8
14:14 [i]Ge 6:8 [j]ver 20; Eze 28:3; Da 1:6; 6:13 [k]Job 1:1 [l]Job 42:9; Jer 15:1; Eze 18:20

13:20–23 God will end the cult of the false female prophets and rescue victims from the snares of these powerful women and thus get glory. Both the male and female prophets starkly contrast with Ezekiel.

14:1–11 *Condemnation for Consulting Prophets.* The condemnation now turns to the leaders of the exiled community, the recipients rather than the creators of false prophecies. The elders approach Ezekiel during a time of crisis in hopes of achieving the Lord’s perspective (8:1; cf. Num 22:8; 2 Kgs 4:38).

14:3 idols in their hearts. The elders internalize idolatry even in exile. They allow their new circumstances in pagan Babylon to compromise their loyalty to God. **Should I let them inquire of me at all?** How can people bent on idolatry expect to hear from the one true God (Exod 20:4–5)?

14:4 I the LORD will answer them myself. Instead of giving them his perspective about the Jerusalem crisis, God surprisingly “answers” them by personally confronting their idolatry.

14:6 Repent! If the exiles renew their loyalties to the Lord and discard their idolatrous alliances, they may have a chance, unlike those in Jerusalem. Ezekiel’s call to “repent” must be understood in light of the differing circumstances of the exiles (18:30; 33:11).

14:9 I the LORD have enticed that prophet. As a form of judgment, the Lord will force a false prophet to falsely prophesy to an idolatrous inquirer (cf. 1 Kgs 22:19–23; Jer 20:7,10). The Lord gives people over to their own desires (Rom 1:18–32; 2 Thess 2:9–12). God will then destroy both, resulting in a cleansing that leads to restoration of the covenantal relationship that once was (vv. 10–11).

14:11 my people ... their God. Terminology that suggests an exclusive and possessive relationship (see note on 11:20, cf. Exod 6:2–8).

14:12–23 *Inescapable Judgment.* “Salvation” (see vv. 14,16,18,20) from the upcoming judgment is not possible and cannot be achieved by another’s righteousness.

14:13 famine. A covenantal curse promised for disobedience (Lev 26:26,29; Deut 28:53–56; 32:24). A city’s inhabitants die when isolated from food sources in a siege.

14:14 Noah ... Job. Well-known individuals from the past who found favor with God in the midst of adversity (Gen 6:9; Job 1:1). **Daniel.** Cf. 28:3. This could refer to the prophet Daniel, the author of the book bearing his name. Alternatively, if the name is spelled “Danel” (see NIV text note), it could refer to an ancient sage of the Syrian region known from

14:15 [m]Eze 5:17 [n]Lev 26:22
14:16 [o]Eze 18:20
14:17 [p]Lev 26:25; Eze 5:12; 21:3-4 [q]Eze 25:13; Zep 1:3
14:19 [r]Eze 7:8 [s]Eze 38:22
14:20 [t]ver 14
14:21 [u]Jer 15:3; Eze 5:17; 33:27; Am 4:6-10; Rev 6:8
14:22 [v]Eze 12:16 [w]Eze 20:43
14:23 [x]Jer 22:8-9
15:2 [y]Isa 5:1-7; Jer 2:21; Hos 10:1
15:4 [z]Eze 19:14; Jn 15:6
15:7 [a]Ps 34:16; Eze 14:8 [b]Isa 24:18; Am 9:1-4
15:8 [c]Eze 14:13 [d]Eze 17:20

15 “Or if I send wild beasts[m] through that country and they leave it childless and it becomes desolate so that no one can pass through it because of the beasts,[n] 16 as surely as I live, declares the Sovereign LORD, even if these three men were in it, they could not save their own sons or daughters. They alone would be saved, but the land would be desolate.[o]

17 “Or if I bring a sword[p] against that country and say, ‘Let the sword pass throughout the land,’ and I kill its people and their animals,[q] 18 as surely as I live, declares the Sovereign LORD, even if these three men were in it, they could not save their own sons or daughters. They alone would be saved.

19 “Or if I send a plague into that land and pour out my wrath[r] on it through bloodshed, killing its people and their animals,[s] 20 as surely as I live, declares the Sovereign LORD, even if Noah, Daniel and Job were in it, they could save neither son nor daughter. They would save only themselves by their righteousness.[t]

21 “For this is what the Sovereign LORD says: How much worse will it be when I send against Jerusalem my four dreadful judgments—sword and famine and wild beasts and plague—to kill its men and their animals![u] 22 Yet there will be some survivors—sons and daughters who will be brought out of it.[v] They will come to you, and when you see their conduct[w] and their actions, you will be consoled regarding the disaster I have brought on Jerusalem—every disaster I have brought on it. 23 You will be consoled when you see their conduct and their actions, for you will know that I have done nothing in it without cause, declares the Sovereign LORD.[x]”

Jerusalem as a Useless Vine

15 The word of the LORD came to me: 2 “Son of man, how is the wood of a vine[y] different from that of a branch from any of the trees in the forest? 3 Is wood ever taken from it to make anything useful? Do they make pegs from it to hang things on? 4 And after it is thrown on the fire as fuel and the fire burns both ends and chars the middle, is it then useful for anything?[z] 5 If it was not useful for anything when it was whole, how much less can it be made into something useful when the fire has burned it and it is charred?

6 “Therefore this is what the Sovereign LORD says: As I have given the wood of the vine among the trees of the forest as fuel for the fire, so will I treat the people living in Jerusalem. 7 I will set my face against[a] them. Although they have come out of the fire, the fire will yet consume them. And when I set my face against them, you will know that I am the LORD.[b] 8 I will make the land desolate[c] because they have been unfaithful,[d] declares the Sovereign LORD.”

extrabiblical texts found at Ugarit. God spared these individuals from the full impact of hardship because of “their righteousness.” Although God spared Lot due to Abraham’s prayer (Gen 18:20–33), this is not possible now for Jerusalem because her “end” (7:2) has been decreed (see note on 7:1–27).

14:15 wild beasts. Ravenous animals that inhabit desolate cities as a result of a siege; it was a covenantal curse for disobedience (Lev 26:22; Deut 32:24).

14:17 sword. Suffering in war; a covenantal curse for disobedience (Lev 26:25,33; Deut 32:25,41–42).

14:19 plague. Sickness and disease due to living conditions during a siege; a covenantal curse for disobedience (Lev 26:25; Deut 28:21–22; 32:24).

14:21 when I send against Jerusalem my ... judgments. Not “if” but “when” God confronts the city. It summarizes and concludes the hypothetical scenarios that vv. 12–20 outline about an unidentified country, now identified as “Jerusalem.”

14:22 survivors. Random people who escape the devastation but are not delivered by anyone’s righteousness; these are not the righteous remnant God promises Ezekiel.

14:23 The wicked conduct of the survivors (v. 22) amid the exiles will confirm to the exiles that God’s judgment on the city was just.

15:1—17:24 *Three Allegories.* God gives Ezekiel three word pictures, fictional stories that creatively illustrate true events concerning Jerusalem’s fall: the useless vine (ch. 15), the adulterous wife (ch. 16), and the two eagles (ch. 17).

15:1–8 *Jerusalem a Useless Vine.* This is the first of three allegories in chs. 15–17 illustrating Jerusalem’s guilt. The surprise factor is the nation’s fruitlessness, which equates to having no value. Cf. Ps 80:8–16.

15:2 wood of a vine. The wood that remains after a grapevine’s fruit is useless; it cannot be used to make furniture because it is not strong enough (v. 3). It is only slightly useful when supplying fuel for a fire (v. 4). And when burned up it is even less valuable (v. 5).

15:6–7 Interprets the vine story (cf. Gen 49:22; Deut 32:32; Isa 5:1–7; Jer 2:21). In 586 BC the Babylonians will exile Jerusalem’s inhabitants that were not exiled in 597 BC (see 2 Kgs 24:14; 2 Chr 36:9–10 and notes).

15:6 fire. An agent of destruction along with the fourfold package of sword, famine, wild beasts, and plague (10:2,6–7; Gen 19:24; Amos 7:4). Although the invading Babylonians will be the ones to actually burn the city, this represents God’s fury against the people of Jerusalem, whom God has rejected as useless to him because they have been unfaithful. The land, as a result, will lie desolate, as promised in covenantal curses for disobedience (Lev 26:32–35,43; Deut 29:23).

15:7 you will know that I am the LORD. When the fire of God strikes the inhabitants of Jerusalem in 586 BC, those already in exile will acknowledge the divine hand of judgment as a revelation of the Lord. See Introduction: Theological Significance.

Jerusalem as an Adulterous Wife

16 The word of the LORD came to me: [2]"Son of man, confront Jerusalem with her detestable practices[e] [3]and say, 'This is what the Sovereign LORD says to Jerusalem: Your ancestry[f] and birth
were in the land of the Canaanites; your father was an Amorite and your mother a Hittite.[g] [4]On the day
you were born[h] your cord was not cut, nor were you washed with water to make you clean, nor were
you rubbed with salt or wrapped in cloths. [5]No one looked on you with pity or had compassion enough
to do any of these things for you. Rather, you were thrown out into the open field, for on the day you
were born you were despised.

[6]" 'Then I passed by and saw you kicking about in your blood, and as you lay there in your blood I
said to you, "Live!"[a][i] [7]I made you grow[j] like a plant of the field. You grew and developed and entered
puberty. Your breasts had formed and your hair had grown, yet you were stark naked.[k]

[8]" 'Later I passed by, and when I looked at you and saw that you were old enough for love, I spread
the corner of my garment[l] over you and covered your naked body. I gave you my solemn oath and entered into a covenant with you, declares the Sovereign LORD, and you became mine.[m]

[9]" 'I bathed you with water and washed[n] the blood from you and put ointments on you. [10]I clothed
you with an embroidered[o] dress and put sandals of fine leather on you. I dressed you in fine linen[p]
and covered you with costly garments.[q] [11]I adorned you with jewelry:[r] I put bracelets[s] on your arms
and a necklace[t] around your neck, [12]and I put a ring on your nose,[u] earrings on your ears and a
beautiful crown[v] on your head. [13]So you were adorned with gold and silver; your clothes were of fine
linen and costly fabric and embroidered cloth. Your food was honey, olive oil[w] and the finest flour.
You became very beautiful and rose to be a queen.[x] [14]And your fame[y] spread among the nations on
account of your beauty,[z] because the splendor I had given you made your beauty perfect, declares
the Sovereign LORD.

[15]" 'But you trusted in your beauty and used your fame to become a prostitute. You lavished your
favors on anyone who passed by[a] and your beauty became his.[b] [16]You took some of your garments to
make gaudy high places, where you carried on your prostitution.[c] You went to him, and he possessed

[a] 6 A few Hebrew manuscripts, Septuagint and Syriac; most Hebrew manuscripts repeat *and as you lay there in your blood I said to you, "Live!"*

16:2 [e]Eze 20:4; 22:2
16:3 [f]Eze 21:30 [g]ver 45
16:4 [h]Hos 2:3
16:6 [i]Ex 19:4
16:7 [j]Dt 1:10 [k]Ex 1:7
16:8 [l]Ru 3:9 [m]Jer 2:2; Hos 2:7,19-20
16:9 [n]Ru 3:3
16:10 [o]Ex 26:36 [p]Eze 27:16 [q]ver 18
16:11 [r]Eze 23:40 [s]Isa 3:19; Eze 23:42 [t]Ge 41:42
16:12 [u]Isa 3:21 [v]Isa 28:5; Jer 13:18
16:13 [w]1Sa 10:1 [x]Dt 32:13-14; 1Ki 4:21
16:14 [y]1Ki 10:24 [z]La 2:15
16:15 [a]ver 25 [b]Isa 57:8; Jer 2:20; Eze 23:3; 27:3
16:16 [c]2Ki 23:7

16:1–63 *Jerusalem an Adulterous Wife.* This is the second of three allegories in chs. 15–17 illustrating Jerusalem's guilt. It narrates the city's past through the story of an unfaithful wife. It portrays Jerusalem as a professional prostitute who for personal gain gives her affections to numerous others. Not only is this the longest single prophecy in the book, but it is also the hardest and most shocking to read, given the sexual language used and the violence portrayed. Ezekiel does not attempt to water down the offensive nature of Jerusalem's sin, because that is precisely the point. Jerusalem's conduct is just as shocking as the language used to describe it. Ch. 16 has two parts. The first part addresses idolatry and illustrates the problem with the analogy of the unfaithful wife (vv. 1–43). The second part addresses social injustices and illustrates this by a familial analogy of an older and younger sister (vv. 44–52). The two metaphors rely heavily on irony to expose the nation's guilt. Ch. 16 concludes with a glimmer of hope for restoration (vv. 53–63).
16:3 Your ancestry and birth were in the land of the Canaanites. Jerusalem had a centuries-old, pre-Israelite history, and the city long resisted Israelite conquest (Josh 15:63) until David's conquest (2 Sam 5:6–9). **father ... mother.** A reference to Jerusalem's non-Israelite origin (cf. v. 45). **Amorite.** Like the Canaanites, the Amorites were pre-Israelite, Semitic inhabitants of Canaan (see notes on Gen 10:15–19; 15:16; Josh 5:1; Judg 1:34–36). **Hittite.** Non-Semitic residents of Canaan who flourished in Asia Minor during the second millennium BC (see notes on Gen 10:15–19; Josh 1:4). Israel intermarried with the population of the land and served the Canaanite gods (Judg 3:6), which diluted their tribal identity and compromised their bloodline, so Jerusalem's ancestry is dubious.
16:4 the day you were born. Jerusalem's birthday. Instead of receiving the expected care at birth, Jerusalem was abandoned as a baby girl, an unwanted child.
16:5 thrown out into the open field. Abandoned to die. Exposure of infants, common in ancient pagan societies, was abhorrent to Israel.
16:6 Then I passed by and saw you. God, unlike negligent birth parents, had compassion on the abandoned, unwashed baby (covered with amniotic fluid and blood at birth), and with one word of his mouth, God rescued, adopted, and took in the baby (i.e., Jerusalem). He graciously gave her life and growth.
16:8 God married the girl when he saw that she was ready for lovemaking. **spread the corner of my garment.** Signified establishing a new relationship that entailed protecting and sustaining the wife (cf. Ruth 3:9). **gave you my solemn oath.** The Lord pledged his commitment, probably entailed in the gesture of raising his hand (20:5), a covenantal basis for the marriage metaphor. **mine.** A very special status and possession. Jerusalem became Yahweh's wife (Mal 2:14). This was always God's intention, but Jerusalem did not realize that special status until David's time (2 Sam 5:7–9).
16:9–14 Portrays Jerusalem as a world-renowned beautiful queen and a bride who was cleansed, perfumed (perhaps a wedding ritual), adorned with lavish garments and fine jewelry, and given the choicest of food—all lavish provisions that her loving and committed husband provided her.
16:15–34 Highlights the queen and how she responded to God's gracious, life-giving provisions and reputation.
16:15 Ironically, the bride used her reputation and all the lavish gifts she received "to become a prostitute." **anyone who passed by.** Her sexual "favors" were numerous and indiscriminate.

16:17 [d] Eze 7:20
16:19 [e] Hos 2:8
16:20 [f] Jer 7:31 [g] Ex 13:2 [h] Ps 106:37-38; Isa 57:5; Eze 23:37
16:21 [i] 2Ki 17:17; Jer 19:5
16:22 [j] Jer 2:2; Hos 11:1 [k] ver 6
16:24 [l] ver 31; Isa 57:7 [m] Ps 78:58; Jer 2:20; 3:2; Eze 20:28
16:25 [n] ver 15; Pr 9:14
16:26 [o] Eze 8:17 [p] Eze 20:8; 23:19-21
16:27 [q] Eze 20:33 [r] 2Ch 28:18
16:28 [s] 2Ki 16:7
16:29 [t] Eze 23:14-17
16:30 [u] Jer 3:3
16:31 [v] ver 24
16:33 [w] Isa 30:6; 57:9 [x] Hos 8:9-10
16:36 [y] Jer 19:5; Eze 23:10
16:37 [z] Jer 13:22
16:38 [a] Eze 23:45 [b] Lev 20:10; Eze 23:25
16:39 [c] Eze 23:26; Hos 2:3
16:40 [d] Jn 8:5,7
16:41 [e] Dt 13:16 [f] Eze 23:10 [g] Eze 23:27,48
16:42 [h] Isa 54:9; Eze 5:13; 39:29

your beauty.[a] 17 You also took the fine jewelry I gave you, the jewelry made of my gold and silver, and
you made for yourself male idols and engaged in prostitution with them.[d] 18 And you took your embroidered clothes to put on them, and you offered my oil and incense before them. 19 Also the food I
provided for you — the flour, olive oil and honey I gave you to eat — you offered as fragrant incense
before them. That is what happened, declares the Sovereign LORD.[e]

20 " 'And you took your sons and daughters[f] whom you bore to me[g] and sacrificed them as food to
the idols. Was your prostitution not enough?[h] 21 You slaughtered my children and sacrificed them to the
idols.[i] 22 In all your detestable practices and your prostitution you did not remember the days of your
youth,[j] when you were naked and bare, kicking about in your blood.[k]

23 " 'Woe! Woe to you, declares the Sovereign LORD. In addition to all your other wickedness, 24 you
built a mound for yourself and made a lofty shrine[l] in every public square.[m] 25 At every street corner
you built your lofty shrines and degraded your beauty, spreading your legs with increasing promiscuity
to anyone who passed by.[n] 26 You engaged in prostitution with the Egyptians, your neighbors with large
genitals, and aroused my anger[o] with your increasing promiscuity.[p] 27 So I stretched out my hand[q]
against you and reduced your territory; I gave you over to the greed of your enemies, the daughters of
the Philistines,[r] who were shocked by your lewd conduct. 28 You engaged in prostitution with the Assyrians[s] too, because you were insatiable; and even after that, you still were not satisfied. 29 Then you
increased your promiscuity to include Babylonia,[b][t] a land of merchants, but even with this you were
not satisfied.

30 " 'I am filled with fury against you,[c] declares the Sovereign LORD, when you do all these things,
acting like a brazen prostitute![u] 31 When you built your mounds at every street corner and made your
lofty shrines[v] in every public square, you were unlike a prostitute, because you scorned payment.

32 " 'You adulterous wife! You prefer strangers to your own husband! 33 All prostitutes receive gifts, but
you give gifts[w] to all your lovers, bribing them to come to you from everywhere for your illicit favors.[x]
34 So in your prostitution you are the opposite of others; no one runs after you for your favors. You are
the very opposite, for you give payment and none is given to you.

35 " 'Therefore, you prostitute, hear the word of the LORD! 36 This is what the Sovereign LORD says:
Because you poured out your lust and exposed your naked body in your promiscuity with your
lovers, and because of all your detestable idols, and because you gave them your children's blood,[y]
37 therefore I am going to gather all your lovers, with whom you found pleasure, those you loved as
well as those you hated. I will gather them against you from all around and will strip you in front
of them, and they will see you stark naked.[z] 38 I will sentence you to the punishment of women who
commit adultery and who shed blood;[a] I will bring on you the blood vengeance of my wrath and
jealous anger.[b] 39 Then I will deliver you into the hands of your lovers, and they will tear down your
mounds and destroy your lofty shrines. They will strip you of your clothes and take your fine jewelry
and leave you stark naked.[c] 40 They will bring a mob against you, who will stone[d] you and hack you
to pieces with their swords. 41 They will burn down[e] your houses and inflict punishment on you in
the sight of many women.[f] I will put a stop[g] to your prostitution, and you will no longer pay your
lovers. 42 Then my wrath against you will subside and my jealous anger will turn away from you; I
will be calm and no longer angry.[h]

[a] *16* The meaning of the Hebrew for this sentence is uncertain. [b] *29* Or *Chaldea* [c] *30* Or *How feverish is your heart,*

16:20–21 She sacrificed her children, born out of wedlock. God condemned the vile practice of child sacrifice (Lev 18:21; Deut 18:10; 2 Kgs 21:6; cf. Jer 7:31).

16:23 Woe! Woe. Announces the uncontrollable nature of her promiscuity, which included multiple partners because of her insatiable sexual appetite.

16:26–29 Egyptians ... Philistines ... Assyrians ... Babylonia. Represent Jerusalem's political alliances that caused her to turn away from and forget God (v. 22). Her heart was so feverish for folly that exclusive loyalty to God was not possible, expressed as infidelity in marriage and multiple sexual partners associated with prostitution.

16:26 neighbors with large genitals. Egyptians; strongly expresses the nature of Jerusalem's lust and God's disgust with it (cf. 23:20).

16:33 you give gifts to all your lovers. Jerusalem's acts of prostitution and adultery are worse than what is considered "normal" for such an act.

16:35–42 God personally prosecutes the prostitute Jerusalem for her idolatry (vv. 37,39). Initially, God provided a garment to cover her nakedness, symbolizing marriage (vv. 4,7–8), but now he will remove that garment ("strip you," v. 37), exposing her to open shame, symbolizing divorce (see Hos 2:2 and note).

43" 'Because you did not remember[i] the days of your youth but enraged me with all these things, I
will surely bring down[j] on your head what you have done, declares the Sovereign LORD. Did you not add
lewdness to all your other detestable practices?[k]
44" 'Everyone who quotes proverbs will quote this proverb about you: "Like mother, like daughter."
45You are a true daughter of your mother, who despised her husband and her children; and you are a
true sister of your sisters, who despised their husbands and their children. Your mother was a Hittite
and your father an Amorite.[l] 46Your older sister was Samaria, who lived to the north of you with her
daughters; and your younger sister, who lived to the south of you with her daughters, was Sodom.[m]
47You not only followed their ways and copied their detestable practices, but in all your ways you soon
became more depraved than they.[n] 48As surely as I live, declares the Sovereign LORD, your sister Sodom
and her daughters never did what you and your daughters have done.[o]
49" 'Now this was the sin of your sister Sodom:[p] She and her daughters were arrogant,[q] overfed and
unconcerned; they did not help the poor and needy.[r] 50They were haughty and did detestable things
before me. Therefore I did away with them as you have seen.[s] 51Samaria did not commit half the sins
you did. You have done more detestable things than they, and have made your sisters seem righteous by
all these things you have done.[t] 52Bear your disgrace, for you have furnished some justification for your
sisters. Because your sins were more vile than theirs, they appear more righteous than you. So then, be
ashamed and bear your disgrace, for you have made your sisters appear righteous.
53" 'However, I will restore[u] the fortunes of Sodom and her daughters and of Samaria and her daughters, and your fortunes along with them, 54so that you may bear your disgrace[v] and be ashamed of all
you have done in giving them comfort. 55And your sisters, Sodom with her daughters and Samaria with
her daughters, will return to what they were before; and you and your daughters will return to what
you were before.[w] 56You would not even mention your sister Sodom in the day of your pride, 57before
your wickedness was uncovered. Even so, you are now scorned by the daughters of Edom[a][x] and all her
neighbors and the daughters of the Philistines — all those around you who despise you. 58You will bear
the consequences of your lewdness and your detestable practices, declares the LORD.[y]
59" 'This is what the Sovereign LORD says: I will deal with you as you deserve, because you have despised my oath by breaking the covenant.[z] 60Yet I will remember the covenant I made with you in the
days of your youth, and I will establish an everlasting covenant[a] with you. 61Then you will remember
your ways and be ashamed[b] when you receive your sisters, both those who are older than you and those
who are younger. I will give them to you as daughters, but not on the basis of my covenant with you.
62So I will establish my covenant with you, and you will know that I am the LORD.[c] 63Then, when I make
atonement[d] for you for all you have done, you will remember and be ashamed and never again open
your mouth[e] because of your humiliation, declares the Sovereign LORD.[f] ' "

[a] 57 Many Hebrew manuscripts and Syriac; most Hebrew manuscripts, Septuagint and Vulgate *Aram*

16:43 [i] Ps 78:42 [j] Eze 22:31 [k] ver 22; Eze 11:21
16:45 [l] Eze 23:2
16:46 [m] Ge 13:10-13; Eze 23:4
16:47 [n] 2Ki 21:9; Eze 5:7
16:48 [o] Mt 10:15; 11:23-24
16:49 [p] Ge 13:13 [q] Ps 138:6 [r] Eze 18:7,12, 16; Lk 12:16-20
16:50 [s] Ge 18:20-21; 19:5
16:51 [t] Jer 3:8-11
16:53 [u] Isa 19:24-25
16:54 [v] Jer 2:26; Eze 14:22
16:55 [w] Mal 3:4
16:57 [x] 2Ki 16:6
16:58 [y] Eze 23:49
16:59 [z] Eze 17:19
16:60 [a] Jer 32:40; Eze 37:26
16:61 [b] Eze 20:43
16:62 [c] Jer 24:7; Eze 20:37,43-44; Hos 2:19-20
16:63 [d] Ps 65:3; 79:9 [e] Ro 3:19 [f] Ps 39:9; Da 9:7-8

16:43 did not remember the days of your youth. Forgot God's care.

16:44–52 Traces family traits passed to Jerusalem's two siblings—daughters of a Hittite mother (see note on v. 46).

16:45 Your mother was a Hittite and your father an Amorite. Swaps the order in v. 3 to highlight Jerusalem's Hittite mother. **Hittite ... Amorite.** See note on v. 3.

16:46 Samaria ... Sodom. Jerusalem's siblings, both known proverbially for their wickedness. The inhabitants of Samaria were related to the inhabitants of Jerusalem; both descended from the patriarch Israel. Along with idolatry, Samaria was known for social crimes against humanity (2 Kgs 17:6–17; Amos 3:9–11; 4:1; 8:14). But Jerusalem and Sodom were not related. Sodom was the pinnacle of social and moral evil (Gen 13:10; 19:4–9; Deut 29:23; Isa 1:9–10). Calling Sodom Jerusalem's sister would have shocked Ezekiel's audience.

16:51 Jerusalem is doubly guilty.

16:53 I will restore the fortunes. God promises family restoration. The siblings will return to their former state of well-being (v. 55). More shock and irony unfold: God will restore wicked Sodom. By doing so he will cut to the core of Jerusalem's pride (vv. 56–57). Sodom was a dirty word. The shock is that God can restore the vilest of the vile.

16:59–63 God's concluding word concerning Jerusalem's future reformation and restoration. The city's role as representative of Israel is foregrounded so that his words about remembering the covenant and establishing an everlasting covenant parallel what is elsewhere said of Israel itself (37:26; Isa 55:3; Jer 32:40).

16:59–60 breaking the covenant ... remember the covenant. See v. 8 and note. Covenant is mentioned three times in these two verses. Although Jerusalem failed to remember its obligations in the relationship, God will not fail to remember his.

16:60 remember ... establish an everlasting covenant. When God remembers his covenant, it translates into action (Gen 9:15–16; Exod 2:24; 6:5; Lev 26:42; Ps 105:8). This refers to the new covenant (Isa 59:21; Jer 31:31–34) and fulfills elements of the Abrahamic covenant (Isa 55:3; Jer 32:40).

16:63 when I make atonement for you. God himself will do for faithless Jerusalem what she cannot do for herself (cf. Rom 3:23). God's forgiveness will cover shame and humiliation for sin. The action described here helps to identify more specifically the "everlasting covenant" (v. 60). God will graciously intervene to purge and purify his people (36:22–38; Deut 21:8).

17:2 [g]Eze 20:49
17:3 [h]Hos 8:1 [i]Jer 22:23
17:5 [j]Dt 8:7-9; Isa 44:4
17:7 [k]Eze 31:4
17:10 [l]Hos 13:15
17:12 [m]Eze 12:9 [n]2Ki 24:15 [o]Eze 24:19
17:13 [p]2Ch 36:13
17:14 [q]Eze 29:14
17:15 [r]Jer 52:3 [s]Dt 17:16 [t]Jer 34:3; 38:18
17:16 [u]Jer 52:11; Eze 12:13 [v]2Ki 24:17
17:17 [w]Jer 37:7 [x]Eze 4:2 [y]Isa 36:6; Jer 37:5; Eze 29:6-7
17:18 [z]1Ch 29:24
17:19 [a]Eze 16:59
17:20 [b]Eze 12:13; 32:3 [c]Jer 2:35; Eze 20:36
17:21 [d]Eze 12:14 [e]2Ki 25:11 [f]2Ki 25:5

Two Eagles and a Vine

17 The word of the LORD came to me: 2“Son of man, set forth an allegory and tell it to the Israelites as a parable.[g] 3Say to them, ‘This is what the Sovereign LORD says: A great eagle[h] with
powerful wings, long feathers and full plumage of varied colors came to Lebanon.[i] Taking hold of the
top of a cedar, 4he broke off its topmost shoot and carried it away to a land of merchants, where he
planted it in a city of traders.
5“ ‘He took one of the seedlings of the land and put it in fertile soil. He planted it like a willow by
abundant water,[j] 6and it sprouted and became a low, spreading vine. Its branches turned toward him,
but its roots remained under it. So it became a vine and produced branches and put out leafy boughs.
7“ ‘But there was another great eagle with powerful wings and full plumage. The vine now sent out
its roots toward him from the plot where it was planted and stretched out its branches to him for water.[k] 8It had been planted in good soil by abundant water so that it would produce branches, bear fruit
and become a splendid vine.’
9“Say to them, ‘This is what the Sovereign LORD says: Will it thrive? Will it not be uprooted and
stripped of its fruit so that it withers? All its new growth will wither. It will not take a strong arm or many
people to pull it up by the roots. 10It has been planted,[l] but will it thrive? Will it not wither completely
when the east wind strikes it — wither away in the plot where it grew?’ ”
11Then the word of the LORD came to me: 12“Say to this rebellious people, ‘Do you not know what
these things mean?[m]’ Say to them: ‘The king of Babylon went to Jerusalem and carried off her king and
her nobles,[n] bringing them back with him to Babylon.[o] 13Then he took a member of the royal family
and made a treaty with him, putting him under oath.[p] He also carried away the leading men of the
land, 14so that the kingdom would be brought low,[q] unable to rise again, surviving only by keeping
his treaty. 15But the king rebelled[r] against him by sending his envoys to Egypt to get horses and a large
army.[s] Will he succeed? Will he who does such things escape? Will he break the treaty and yet escape?[t]
16“ ‘As surely as I live, declares the Sovereign LORD, he shall die[u] in Babylon, in the land of the king
who put him on the throne, whose oath he despised and whose treaty he broke.[v] 17Pharaoh[w] with his
mighty army and great horde will be of no help to him in war, when ramps[x] are built and siege works
erected to destroy many lives.[y] 18He despised the oath by breaking the covenant. Because he had given
his hand in pledge[z] and yet did all these things, he shall not escape.
19“ ‘Therefore this is what the Sovereign LORD says: As surely as I live, I will repay him for despising
my oath and breaking my covenant.[a] 20I will spread my net[b] for him, and he will be caught in my snare.
I will bring him to Babylon and execute judgment[c] on him there because he was unfaithful to me. 21All
his choice troops will fall by the sword,[d] and the survivors[e] will be scattered to the winds.[f] Then you will
know that I the LORD have spoken.

17:1 – 24 *Two Eagles and a Vine.* This is the third of three allegories in chs. 15 – 17 illustrating Jerusalem’s guilt. Here its guilt is due to King Zedekiah’s vacillating royal policy. Ezekiel must deliver a riddle, an allegory (vv. 3 – 10; see also 20:49; cf. Judg 14:12 – 19); then God interprets this mysterious story (vv. 12b – 21). Ch. 17 ends on a surprising note of hope, utilizing the imagery of the allegory (vv. 22 – 24).
17:3 great eagle. Nebuchadnezzar (v. 12). **Lebanon.** Jerusalem (v. 12). **cedar.** David’s dynasty (i.e., his royal family).
17:4 topmost shoot. Jehoiachin. **land of merchants.** The country of Babylonia (v. 12; 16:29). **city of traders.** The city of Babylon.
17:5 one of the seedlings. Zedekiah (see 2 Kgs 23 – 24). **planted it.** Made him king (2 Kgs 24:17).
17:6 low, spreading vine. Because of the deportation (2 Kgs 24:15 – 16; Jer 52:28), it is no longer a tall cedar.
17:7 another great eagle. An Egyptian pharaoh, either Psammetichus II (595 – 589 BC) or Hophra (589 – 570 BC). **sent out its roots.** Zedekiah’s appeal to Egypt for military aid.
17:9 Will it thrive? The riddle raises questions that demand the audience’s judgment. The audience’s judgment or answer reveals their guilt. This is the first of four questions in vv. 9 – 10. The implied answer to each question is no, thereby showing that the vine cannot thrive.
17:10 east wind. Nebuchadnezzar and his Babylonian forces. A wind from the east was a hot, dry wind that withers vegetation (vv. 16,18).
17:12 – 18 God explains the riddle. The first eagle is Nebuchadnezzar, the “king of Babylon” (v. 12b). He “carried off [Jerusalem’s] king” (v. 12b), King Jehoiachin of Judah, the “topmost shoot” (v. 4), to the “city of traders” (v. 4), i.e., Babylon, in 597 BC. He also took Zedekiah, “a member of the royal family” (v. 13), the “seedling” (v. 5), and installed him as a puppet king after carrying off Jehoiachin (2 Kgs 24:15). Zedekiah’s installation as puppet king put him unwillingly “under oath” (v. 13) to keep his “treaty” (v. 14), i.e., to keep political alliances with the king of Babylon. Zedekiah “rebelled” (v. 15). He broke his oath by turning to Pharaoh and Egypt for help, the second “eagle” (v. 7; see 2 Chr 36:13; Jer 44:30; 52:11).
17:19 I will repay him for despising my oath. Zedekiah was not loyal to God (vv. 19 – 20; cf. 2 Chr 36:11 – 14). He pledged his allegiance to Nebuchadnezzar in God’s name, which meant that Israel’s God would hold Zedekiah liable unto death if Zedekiah did not keep his side of the bargain. The form of the oath might have been as follows: “May the LORD kill me if I do not do what I promised” (an oath that promises harm to the one making the oath if he breaks his word; see Gen 15:9 – 17; 1 Sam 20:12 – 13; 2 Sam 3:9 – 10 and notes).

22“ ‘This is what the Sovereign LORD says: I myself will take a shoot from the very top of a cedar and
plant it; I will break off a tender sprig from its topmost shoots and plant it on a high and lofty mountain.[g] 23On the mountain heights of Israel I will plant it; it will produce branches and bear fruit and
become a splendid cedar. Birds of every kind will nest in it; they will find shelter in the shade of its
branches.[h] 24All the trees of the forest[i] will know that I the LORD bring down the tall tree and make the
low tree grow tall. I dry up the green tree and make the dry tree flourish.

“ ‘I the LORD have spoken, and I will do it.[j]’ ”

The One Who Sins Will Die

18 The word of the LORD came to me: 2“What do you people mean by quoting this proverb about
the land of Israel:

> “ ‘The parents eat sour grapes,
> and the children’s teeth are set on edge’?[k]

3“As surely as I live, declares the Sovereign LORD, you will no longer quote this proverb in Israel.
4For everyone belongs to me, the parent as well as the child—both alike belong to me. The one who
sins is the one who will die.[l]

> 5“Suppose there is a righteous man
> who does what is just and right.
> 6He does not eat at the mountain[m] shrines
> or look to the idols[n] of Israel.
> He does not defile his neighbor’s wife
> or have sexual relations with a woman during her period.
> 7He does not oppress[o] anyone,
> but returns what he took in pledge[p] for a loan.
> He does not commit robbery
> but gives his food to the hungry
> and provides clothing for the naked.[q]
> 8He does not lend to them at interest
> or take a profit from them.[r]
> He withholds his hand from doing wrong
> and judges fairly[s] between two parties.

17:22 [g] Jer 23:5; Eze 20:40; 36:1,36; 37:22
17:23 [h] Ps 92:12; Isa 2:2; Eze 31:6; Da 4:12; Hos 14:5-7; Mt 13:32
17:24 [i] Ps 96:12 [j] Eze 19:12; 21:26; 22:14; Am 9:11
18:2 [k] Isa 3:15; Jer 31:29; La 5:7
18:4 [l] ver 20; Isa 42:5; Ro 6:23
18:6 [m] Eze 22:9 [n] Dt 4:19; Eze 6:13; 20:24
18:7 [o] Ex 22:21 [p] Ex 22:26; Dt 24:12 [q] Dt 15:11; Mt 25:36
18:8 [r] Ex 22:25; Lev 25:35-37; Dt 23:19-20 [s] Zec 8:16

17:22–24 These verses explain the riddle’s surprising future consequence. They use the previous imagery but in a new and unexpected way. At God’s own initiative he will replant a shoot on Israel’s mountain heights that will grow into a cedar that provides shelter for birds. “Shoot” or “Branch” is used to speak of a Messianic figure, a son of David, who will revive the royal line and under whose branches one will find safety (see Isa 4:2; 11:1; Jer 23:5; Zech 3:8 and notes). The new king from David’s line is Christ. He will rule over a renewed and mighty kingdom, which the mountain on which the cedar is planted symbolizes (Isa 2:2; Mic 4:1).

18:1–32 *Individual Responsibility.* The people of Jerusalem accuse God of being unjust. They believe that their present sufferings are due not to their own sins but to the sins of their ancestors. That they are guilty of wrongdoing is far from their minds. Ch. 18 brings a needed corrective to their wrong interpretive framework. Through the prophet they learn that God’s justice visits individuals across the generations.

18:1–18 *The One Who Sins Will Die.* This section exposes the problem (v. 1–3) and then follows with the corrective based on Deut 24:16, utilizing three hypothetical scenarios about a father, his son, and his grandson to illustrate God’s views on generational guilt and innocence (vv. 4–18).

18:2 this proverb. A popular belief that commenced in Jeremiah’s time (Jer 31:29) and was circulating among those who experienced the exile of 597 BC. **parents … children’s teeth are set on edge.** A statement of inherited guilt and self-pity, one that mocks God’s justice. It presents an undesirable and uncontrollable situation given to children by their parents and reveals a fatalistic approach to life. It may have derived from a misunderstanding of Exod 20:5, which states that God punishes the children for the sins of the parents to the third and fourth generation. **set on edge.** Though the meaning of this rare Hebrew word is uncertain, here may refer to a bitter or sour taste.

18:4 The one who sins is the one who will die. God corrects the proverb (see v. 2 and note). Individuals are not in the hand of fate but in the hand of God, who looks at each individual in a group. What follows describes three men (vv. 5–9,10–13,14–18), standing for three generations, who break the three/four-generation pattern.

18:5 a righteous man. Represents the first generation and refers to one who “faithfully keeps [God’s] laws” (v. 9), which includes ceremonial and moral injunctions. A person’s righteousness is credited individually and does not depend on parental influence.

18:6 eat at the mountain shrines. Eating meat sacrificed to idols at the high places (see 6:3; Hos 4:13 and notes).

18:7 oppress anyone. Speaks of the rich taking advantage of the poor. **returns what he took in pledge.** See Exod 22:26. **commit robbery.** See the commandment against stealing (Exod 20:15).

18:9 [t]Hab 2:4 [u]Lev 18:5; Eze 20:11; Am 5:4
18:10 [v]Ex 21:12
18:12 [w]Am 4:1 [x]2Ki 21:11; Isa 59:6-7; Jer 22:17; Eze 8:6,17
18:13 [y]Ex 22:25 [z]Eze 33:4-5
18:14 [a]2Ch 34:21; Pr 23:24
18:16 [b]Ps 41:1; Isa 58:10
18:19 [c]Ex 20:5; Dt 5:9; Jer 15:4; Zec 1:3-6
18:20 [d]Dt 24:16; 1Ki 8:32; 2Ki 14:6; Isa 3:11; Mt 16:27; Ro 2:9

9 He follows my decrees
and faithfully keeps my laws.
That man is righteous;[t]
he will surely live,[u]
declares the Sovereign LORD.

10 "Suppose he has a violent son, who sheds blood[v] or does any of these other things[a] 11 (though the
father has done none of them):

"He eats at the mountain shrines.
He defiles his neighbor's wife.
12 He oppresses the poor[w] and needy.
He commits robbery.
He does not return what he took in pledge.
He looks to the idols.
He does detestable things.[x]
13 He lends at interest and takes a profit.[y]

Will such a man live? He will not! Because he has done all these detestable things, he is to be put to death; his blood will be on his own head.[z]
14 "But suppose this son has a son who sees all the sins his father commits, and though he sees them,
he does not do such things:[a]

15 "He does not eat at the mountain shrines
or look to the idols of Israel.
He does not defile his neighbor's wife.
16 He does not oppress anyone
or require a pledge for a loan.
He does not commit robbery
but gives his food to the hungry
and provides clothing for the naked.[b]
17 He withholds his hand from mistreating the poor
and takes no interest or profit from them.
He keeps my laws and follows my decrees.

He will not die for his father's sin; he will surely live. 18 But his father will die for his own sin, because
he practiced extortion, robbed his brother and did what was wrong among his people.
19 "Yet you ask, 'Why does the son not share the guilt of his father?' Since the son has done what is
just and right and has been careful to keep all my decrees, he will surely live.[c] 20 The one who sins is the
one who will die. The child will not share the guilt of the parent, nor will the parent share the guilt of the child. The righteousness of the righteous will be credited to them, and the wickedness of the wicked will be charged against them.[d]
21 "But if a wicked person turns away from all the sins they have committed and keeps all my decrees

[a] *10* Or *things to a brother*

18:9 That man is righteous; he will surely live. The verdict for the man of this first generation. **live.** Includes fellowship with God (see Pss 63:3; 73:27–28) and anticipates life that comes through Christ's perfect righteousness (Rom 3:23–26; 6:23).

18:10 a violent son. Represents the second generation and refers to one who does not faithfully keep God's commands. A person's unrighteousness is credited individually, regardless of positive parental conduct. This proves v. 4.

18:13 his blood will be on his own head. A clear statement of owning responsibility for sin.

18:14 a son. Represents the third generation. He is the opposite of the son in vv. 10–13. This son has not done detestable things contrary to God's law. His righteousness is credited individually, regardless of negative parental conduct. This proves v. 4.

18:19–32 *Objections to God's Justice.* Even though the three men, standing for three generations, show the proverb (v. 2) to be false, the second half of ch. 18 anticipates several questions and objections that Ezekiel's audience may have.

18:19 Why does the son not share the guilt of his father? A logical question. Samaria fell because successive generations of Israelites engaged in idolatry (2 Kgs 17:6–23).

18:20 The one who sins ... will die. The answer to the question in v. 19.

18:21 Verses 1–20 illustrate that the chain of inherited guilt can be broken, and vv. 21–29 teach that guilt can be overcome in a person's life.

and does what is just and right, that person will surely live; they will not die.[e] 22 None of the offenses
they have committed will be remembered against them. Because of the righteous things they have done,
they will live.[f] 23 Do I take any pleasure in the death of the wicked? declares the Sovereign LORD. Rather,
am I not pleased[g] when they turn from their ways and live?[h]

24 "But if a righteous person turns from their righteousness and commits sin and does the same
detestable things the wicked person does, will they live? None of the righteous things that person has
done will be remembered. Because of the unfaithfulness they are guilty of and because of the sins they
have committed, they will die.[i]

25 "Yet you say, 'The way of the Lord is not just.' Hear, you Israelites: Is my way unjust?[j] Is it not your
ways that are unjust? 26 If a righteous person turns from their righteousness and commits sin, they will
die for it; because of the sin they have committed they will die. 27 But if a wicked person turns away from
the wickedness they have committed and does what is just and right, they will save their life.[k] 28 Because
they consider all the offenses they have committed and turn away from them, that person will surely
live; they will not die. 29 Yet the Israelites say, 'The way of the Lord is not just.' Are my ways unjust, people
of Israel? Is it not your ways that are unjust?

30 "Therefore, you Israelites, I will judge each of you according to your own ways, declares the Sovereign
LORD. Repent![l] Turn away from all your offenses; then sin will not be your downfall.[m] 31 Rid yourselves of
all the offenses you have committed, and get a new heart[n] and a new spirit. Why will you die, people of
Israel?[o] 32 For I take no pleasure in the death of anyone, declares the Sovereign LORD. Repent and live![p]

A Lament Over Israel's Princes

19 "Take up a lament[q] concerning the princes[r] of Israel 2 and say:

"'What a lioness was your mother
among the lions!
She lay down among them
and reared her cubs.
3 She brought up one of her cubs,
and he became a strong lion.
He learned to tear the prey
and he became a man-eater.
4 The nations heard about him,
and he was trapped in their pit.
They led him with hooks
to the land of Egypt.[s]

18:21 [e] Eze 33:12,19
18:22 [f] Ps 18:20-24; Isa 43:25; Mic 7:19
18:23 [g] Ps 147:11 [h] Eze 33:11; 1Ti 2:4
18:24 [i] 1Sa 15:11; 2Ch 24:17-20; Eze 3:20; 20:27; 2Pe 2:20-22
18:25 [j] Ge 18:25; Jer 12:1; Eze 33:17; Zep 3:5; Mal 2:17; 3:13-15
18:27 [k] Isa 1:18
18:30 [l] Mt 3:2 [m] Eze 7:3; 33:20; Hos 12:6
18:31 [n] Ps 51:10 [o] Isa 1:16-17; Eze 11:19; 36:26
18:32 [p] Eze 33:11
19:1 [q] Eze 26:17; 27:2, 32 [r] 2Ki 24:6
19:4 [s] 2Ki 23:33-34; 2Ch 36:4

18:23 Do I take any pleasure in the death of the wicked? God denies any accusations to this effect. The evidence is v. 21. God allows for a person to change the direction of their life. Thus, God will not factor in a person's wicked past in light of a visible lifestyle change. This answers the charge that God lacks mercy, prefers judgment over mercy, or punishes the unrighteous on a whim. What pleases God is life, not death (v. 32; 16:6; 33:11; Jonah 4:11).

18:25 Is my way unjust? Is it not your ways that are unjust? Cf. 33:17. *Their* character and behavior is in question, not God's.

18:30 Therefore ... I will judge each of you. A conclusion and summary to ch. 18. **Repent!** See note on 14:6.

18:31 get a new heart and a new spirit. An appeal to live right before God. Contrasts 11:19; 36:26, where the new heart and new spirit are gifts from God.

18:32 Repent and live! The third and final call to repentance in the book (v. 30; 14:6); a charge to take moral responsibility (see v. 31). Although reversing God's judgment on Jerusalem is impossible (2:8; 7:1–4), the exiles are being urged to make lifestyle changes that will benefit them in their present circumstances.

19:1–14 *Lamenting Leadership.* In line with Ezekiel's role as a mourner (see note on 3:1,3), ch. 19 is a funeral song (vv. 1,14). Ironically, Ezekiel adapts this common ancient Near Eastern lament genre for his exilic audience. Just as he must mourn the death of the nation (due to their guilt and upcoming judgment), so too he mourns the deaths of the nation's princes (due to their guilt and imminent judgment) from the line of David (vv. 1–9) along with the demise of the dynasty (vv. 10–14). He holds individual monarchs (not just individual Israelites, cf. ch. 18) accountable and illustrates some of the principles in ch. 18. Using the lament genre encourages Ezekiel's audience not to have false hopes about their protection.

19:1–9 *Lament Over Jerusalem's Kings: A Lament for the Lion.* This section of the lament specifically concerns Jehoahaz, and either Jehoiachin or Zedekiah, two out of four of Judah's last kings.

19:2 mother. A figurative way of speaking about the nation as a whole, which produced the two kings described in vv. 1–9.

19:3 one of her cubs ... man-eater. Jehoahaz's policies were oppressive.

19:4 trapped ... led him with hooks to ... Egypt. This is cause for mourning because the free and dangerous lion became trapped: in one of his Egyptian campaigns into the Syria-Palestine region, Pharaoh Necho (610–595 BC) captured Jehoahaz and exiled him to Egypt, where Jehoahaz died (2 Kgs 23:34).

19:5 [t]2Ki 23:34
19:6 [u]2Ki 24:9; 2Ch 36:9
19:7 [v]Eze 30:12
19:8 [w]2Ki 24:2 [x]2Ki 24:11
19:9 [y]2Ch 36:6 [z]2Ki 24:15
19:10 [a]Ps 80:8-11
19:11 [b]Eze 31:3; Da 4:11
19:12 [c]Eze 17:10 [d]Isa 27:11; Eze 28:17; Hos 13:15
19:13 [e]Eze 20:35 [f]Hos 2:3
19:14 [g]Eze 20:47

5 "'When she saw her hope unfulfilled,
her expectation gone,
she took another of her cubs
and made him a strong lion.[t]
6 He prowled among the lions,
for he was now a strong lion.
He learned to tear the prey
and he became a man-eater.[u]
7 He broke down[a] their strongholds
and devastated[v] their towns.
The land and all who were in it
were terrified by his roaring.
8 Then the nations[w] came against him,
those from regions round about.
They spread their net for him,
and he was trapped in their pit.[x]
9 With hooks they pulled him into a cage
and brought him to the king of Babylon.[y]
They put him in prison,
so his roar was heard no longer
on the mountains of Israel.[z]

10 "'Your mother was like a vine in your vineyard[b]
planted by the water;
it was fruitful and full of branches
because of abundant water.[a]
11 Its branches were strong,
fit for a ruler's scepter.
It towered high
above the thick foliage,
conspicuous for its height
and for its many branches.[b]
12 But it was uprooted[c] in fury
and thrown to the ground.
The east wind made it shrivel,
it was stripped of its fruit;
its strong branches withered
and fire consumed them.[d]
13 Now it is planted in the desert,[e]
in a dry and thirsty land.[f]
14 Fire spread from one of its main[c] branches
and consumed[g] its fruit.

[a] *7* Targum (see Septuagint); Hebrew *He knew your blood* [b] *10* Two Hebrew manuscripts; most Hebrew manuscripts *your blood* [c] *14* Or *from under its*

19:5 another of her cubs. Either (1) Jehoiachin (2 Kgs 24:8–15), who reigned for three months in 598–597 BC before his exile to Babylon and who was Judah's last legitimate ruler, or (2) Zedekiah (597–586 BC), Judah's puppet king whom Nebuchadnezzar installed (2 Kgs 24:16—25:7).
19:10–14 *Lament Over David's Dynasty: A Lament for the Vine.* Mourning will take place over the end of Judah and its Davidic kings. The imagery for the princes of Israel changes from lion (vv. 1–9) to vine (cf. 15:1–8; 17:5–10).
19:10 mother ... a vine. The tribe of Judah, which produced kings ("branches," v. 11) from David to Zedekiah (cf. Gen 49:9–11). The kingdom was fruitful and highly visible.
19:12 east wind. The Babylonian king Nebuchadnezzar (see note on 17:10).
19:13 in the desert. In Babylonia. Nebuchadnezzar's Babylonian army will capture Zedekiah and bring him to Babylon, "a dry and thirsty land" in the east (2 Kgs 25; Jer 52).
19:14 Fire. A symbol often used for destruction and annihilation (e.g., Gen 19:24; Rev 20:14). **one of its main branches.** Zedekiah, the final

No strong branch is left on it
fit for a ruler's scepter.'[h]

"This is a lament and is to be used as a lament."

Rebellious Israel Purged

20 In the seventh year, in the fifth month on the tenth day, some of the elders of Israel came to
inquire of the LORD, and they sat down in front of me.[i]
2 Then the word of the LORD came to me: 3 "Son of man, speak to the elders of Israel and say to them,
'This is what the Sovereign LORD says: Have you come to inquire[j] of me? As surely as I live, I will not let
you inquire of me, declares the Sovereign LORD.'[k]
4 "Will you judge them? Will you judge them, son of man? Then confront them with the detestable
practices of their ancestors[l] 5 and say to them: 'This is what the Sovereign LORD says: On the day I chose[m]
Israel, I swore with uplifted hand to the descendants of Jacob and revealed myself to them in Egypt.
With uplifted hand I said to them, "I am the LORD your God."[n] 6 On that day I swore to them that I
would bring them out of Egypt into a land I had searched out for them, a land flowing with milk and
honey,[o] the most beautiful of all lands.[p] 7 And I said to them, "Each of you, get rid of the vile images[q]
you have set your eyes on, and do not defile yourselves with the idols of Egypt. I am the LORD your God."[r]
8 " 'But they rebelled against me and would not listen to me; they did not get rid of the vile images
they had set their eyes on, nor did they forsake the idols of Egypt.[s] So I said I would pour out my wrath
on them and spend my anger against them in Egypt.[t] 9 But for the sake of my name, I brought them
out of Egypt.[u] I did it to keep my name from being profaned in the eyes of the nations among whom
they lived and in whose sight I had revealed myself to the Israelites. 10 Therefore I led them out of Egypt
and brought them into the wilderness.[v] 11 I gave them my decrees and made known to them my laws,
by which the person who obeys them will live.[w] 12 Also I gave them my Sabbaths as a sign[x] between us,
so they would know that I the LORD made them holy.
13 " 'Yet the people of Israel rebelled[y] against me in the wilderness. They did not follow my decrees

19:14 [h]Eze 15:4
20:1 [i]Eze 8:1
20:3 [j]Eze 14:3 [k]Mic 3:7
20:4 [l]Eze 16:2; 22:2; Mt 23:32
20:5 [m]Dt 7:6 [n]Ex 6:7
20:6 [o]Ex 3:8; Jer 32:22 [p]Dt 8:7; Ps 48:2; Da 8:9
20:7 [q]Ex 20:4 [r]Ex 20:2; Lev 18:3; Dt 29:18
20:8 [s]Eze 7:8 [t]Isa 63:10
20:9 [u]Eze 36:22; 39:7
20:10 [v]Ex 13:18
20:11 [w]Lev 18:5; Dt 4:7-8; Ro 10:5
20:12 [x]Ex 31:13
20:13 [y]Ps 78:40

king of Judah, whose godless reign furthered the ruin of the nation (2 Kgs 24:18—25:7). The cause for mourning is the upcoming removal of the Davidic dynasty in 586 BC. But removing the royal scepter as a consequence for sin is only temporary (ch. 34; Gen 49:10), because out of death will come life.

20:1–44 *History of Idolatry.* This section narrates Israel's guilt from the day God chose the Israelites (sometime prior to the exodus event) to the time God exiled them from the promised land. It is part of the literary unit comprising chs. 16–23 that highlights individual and national guilt. Rather than use allegory or metaphor, it uses straightforward historical recollection.

20:1–32 *Cycles of Rebellion.* This section identifies cycles of rebellion in Egypt (vv. 1–12), the wilderness (vv. 13–26), and Canaan (vv. 27–32). The general pattern is the rebellion, the nature of the rebellion, wrath threatened, and wrath withheld for the sake of God's name. Each cycle concludes with a statement about God graciously giving something to his people so that they will know he is the Lord.

20:1–12 *Guilty in Egypt.* Israel's history of apostasy goes back to the days when she lived under Egyptian servitude and got entangled with the gods of the land. This is the first cycle of rebellion (see note on vv. 1–32).

20:1 seventh year … fifth month … tenth day. Aug. 14, 591 BC. **elders.** The representative group in the community. It is their third visit to Ezekiel (8:1; 14:1). **inquire of the LORD.** Access God's guidance through the prophet.

20:3 I will not let you inquire of me. Owing to their idolatry, God resists giving the people guidance (see note on 14:3).

20:4 Will you judge them? … Then confront them. God calls for a confrontation instead of answering their concerns. Ezekiel must confront his exilic audience. The confrontation begins by looking at the detestable practices of their ancestors.

20:5 the day I chose Israel. An undefined time prior to the exodus event (Exod 12:33—14:31). God saw Israel's plight and announced that he would remember his covenant (Exod 2:23–25). **uplifted hand.** A symbolic action accompanying God's oath that reinforced to the exodus generation that God would keep his promises (Gen 12:1–3). **I am the LORD your God.** A statement demonstrating the exclusive and possessive relationship God would have with his people.

20:7 get rid of the vile images. A required action in response to God's oath. **vile images.** A Hebrew term routinely used by Ezekiel to reflect his attitude toward such practices; perhaps understood as excrement (cf. vv. 8,30; 5:11; 7:20; 11:18,21; 37:23). **the idols of Egypt.** Improper worship and ways of reaching the deity.

20:8 rebelled. An action that marked the relationship (vv. 13,21). Israel was unable to say no to idols and yes to the Lord. **So I said I would pour out my wrath on them.** A repeated refrain punctuating the historical recollection of apostasy in ch. 20 (vv. 13,21). God threatened to dispense his anger by calling off the long-awaited rescue mission from Egypt.

20:9 for the sake of my name, I brought them out. The conclusion to the first cycle of rebellion in Egypt (see note on vv. 1–12). God acted and delivered them out of concern for his own reputation and character, not because of Israel's merit. **name.** Signals both identity and character. God's acts of deliverance in the past and in the future reveal his nature (see 36:22).

20:11 my decrees … by which the person who obeys them will live. Speaks of the life-giving power of obedience to the commandments (see note on 18:9, cf. Rom 10:5; Gal 3:12).

20:12 Sabbaths. Days of required rest in the calendar year. **sign.** A visual reality of Israel's relationship to God.

20:13–26 *Guilty in the Wilderness.* Israel's history of apostasy goes back to the first and second wilderness generations. This is the second of three rebellion cycles (see note on vv. 1–32).

20:13–20 The first generation rebelled by rejecting God's laws. They

20:13 [z] Dt 9:8 [a] Nu 14:29; Ps 95:8-10; Isa 56:6
20:14 [b] Eze 36:23
20:15 [c] Ps 95:11; 106:26
20:16 [d] Nu 15:39 [e] Am 5:26
20:18 [f] Zec 1:4
20:19 [g] Ex 20:2 [h] Dt 5:32-33; 6:1-2; 8:1; 11:1; 12:1
20:20 [i] Jer 17:22
20:22 [j] Ps 78:38
20:23 [k] Lev 26:33; Dt 28:64
20:24 [l] ver 13 [m] Eze 6:9 [n] ver 16
20:25 [o] Ps 81:12 [p] 2Th 2:11
20:26 [q] 2Ki 17:17
20:27 [r] Ro 2:24 [s] Eze 18:24
20:28 [t] Ps 78:55,58 [u] Eze 6:13
20:30 [v] ver 43 [w] Jer 16:12
20:31 [x] Eze 16:20 [y] Ps 106:37-39; Jer 7:31

but rejected my laws — by which the person who obeys them will live — and they utterly desecrated
my Sabbaths. So I said I would pour out my wrath[z] on them and destroy them in the wilderness.[a]
14 But for the sake of my name I did what would keep it from being profaned in the eyes of the
nations in whose sight I had brought them out.[b] 15 Also with uplifted hand I swore to them in the
wilderness that I would not bring them into the land I had given them — a land flowing with milk
and honey, the most beautiful of all lands[c] — 16 because they rejected my laws and did not follow
my decrees and desecrated my Sabbaths. For their hearts[d] were devoted to their idols.[e] 17 Yet I looked
on them with pity and did not destroy them or put an end to them in the wilderness. 18 I said to their
children in the wilderness, "Do not follow the statutes of your parents[f] or keep their laws or defile
yourselves with their idols. 19 I am the LORD your God;[g] follow my decrees and be careful to keep my
laws.[h] 20 Keep my Sabbaths holy, that they may be a sign between us. Then you will know that I am
the LORD your God.[i]"

21 " 'But the children rebelled against me: They did not follow my decrees, they were not careful to
keep my laws, of which I said, "The person who obeys them will live by them," and they desecrated
my Sabbaths. So I said I would pour out my wrath on them and spend my anger against them in the
wilderness. 22 But I withheld[j] my hand, and for the sake of my name I did what would keep it from
being profaned in the eyes of the nations in whose sight I had brought them out. 23 Also with uplifted
hand I swore to them in the wilderness that I would disperse them among the nations and scatter[k]
them through the countries, 24 because they had not obeyed my laws but had rejected my decrees and
desecrated my Sabbaths,[l] and their eyes lusted after[m] their parents' idols.[n] 25 So I gave[o] them other
statutes that were not good and laws through which they could not live;[p] 26 I defiled them through
their gifts — the sacrifice of every firstborn — that I might fill them with horror so they would know
that I am the LORD.[q]'

27 "Therefore, son of man, speak to the people of Israel and say to them, 'This is what the Sovereign
LORD says: In this also your ancestors blasphemed[r] me by being unfaithful to me:[s] 28 When I brought
them into the land[t] I had sworn to give them and they saw any high hill or any leafy tree, there they
offered their sacrifices, made offerings that aroused my anger, presented their fragrant incense and
poured out their drink offerings.[u] 29 Then I said to them: What is this high place you go to?' " (It is
called Bamah[a] to this day.)

Rebellious Israel Renewed

30 "Therefore say to the Israelites: 'This is what the Sovereign LORD says: Will you defile yourselves[v]
the way your ancestors did and lust after their vile images?[w] 31 When you offer your gifts — the sacrifice of your children[x] in the fire — you continue to defile yourselves with all your idols to this day.
Am I to let you inquire of me, you Israelites? As surely as I live, declares the Sovereign LORD, I will not
let you inquire of me.[y]

32 " 'You say, "We want to be like the nations, like the peoples of the world, who serve wood and stone."

[a] *29 Bamah* means *high place.*

loved idols, not the Lord. God threatened to dispense his anger by destroying them in the wilderness and by withholding the promised land. He withheld wrath out of concern for his reputation and because he "looked on them with pity" (v. 17). He graciously warned their children (vv. 18–20).

20:21–26 The second generation also rebelled — regardless of God's warning (vv. 18–20) — by rejecting God's laws. They also loved idols. God threatened to dispense his anger but withheld wrath out of concern for his reputation (v. 22).

20:25 So I gave them ... laws through which they could not live. An act of judgment. Instead of keeping God's good laws, they followed pagan laws that could produce only death. As a consequence of their sin, God gave them over to their idolatry by giving them more of what they wanted (Deut 4:28; cf. Rom 1:21–27; 2 Thess 2:9–12).

20:26 I defiled them through their gifts. Rather than dedicate every firstborn to God (Exod 13:2; 22:29), a law that produced life, he gave them over to their sin — "the sacrifice of every firstborn" in the fire (see v. 31 and note) — as an act of judgment producing death.

20:27–32 *Guilty in Canaan and Exile.* Israel's history of apostasy goes back to living in the land of promise and includes present apostasy in exile. This is the third and final cycle of rebellion (see note on vv. 1–32).

20:28 made offerings that aroused my anger. Those in the promised land "blasphemed" God (v. 27), probably through child sacrifice, an act of devotion and adoration to a pagan deity (see v. 31; 16:20–21 and notes).

20:31 sacrifice of your children in the fire. See 2 Kgs 16:3; 17:17; 21:6; 23:10; Jer 32:35; see also notes on Lev 18:21; Jer 7:30 — 8:3. This practice was condemned (Lev 18:21; 20:2–5).

20:32 like the nations. Rather than resist this temptation, they fell into the trap (1 Sam 8:5); this suggests a loss of their uniqueness as a people of God (Exod 19). This aroused God's anger and instead of withholding wrath, it is now about to be dispensed.

But what you have in mind will never happen. 33As surely as I live, declares the Sovereign LORD, I will
reign over you with a mighty hand and an outstretched arm and with outpoured wrath.[z] 34I will bring
you from the nations[a] and gather you from the countries where you have been scattered—with a
mighty hand and an outstretched arm and with outpoured wrath.[b] 35I will bring you into the wilderness
of the nations and there, face to face, I will execute judgment[c] upon you. 36As I judged your ancestors in
the wilderness of the land of Egypt, so I will judge you, declares the Sovereign LORD.[d] 37I will take note
of you as you pass under my rod,[e] and I will bring you into the bond of the covenant.[f] 38I will purge[g]
you of those who revolt and rebel against me. Although I will bring them out of the land where they are
living, yet they will not enter the land of Israel. Then you will know that I am the LORD.[h]
39" 'As for you, people of Israel, this is what the Sovereign LORD says: Go and serve your idols,[i] every one of you! But afterward you will surely listen to me and no longer profane my holy name with
your gifts and idols.[j] 40For on my holy mountain, the high mountain of Israel, declares the Sovereign
LORD, there in the land all the people of Israel will serve me, and there I will accept them. There I will
require your offerings[k] and your choice gifts,[a] along with all your holy sacrifices.[l] 41I will accept you
as fragrant incense when I bring you out from the nations and gather you from the countries where
you have been scattered, and I will be proved holy[m] through you in the sight of the nations.[n] 42Then
you will know that I am the LORD,[o] when I bring you into the land of Israel,[p] the land I had sworn with
uplifted hand to give to your ancestors. 43There you will remember your conduct and all the actions by
which you have defiled yourselves, and you will loathe yourselves for all the evil you have done.[q] 44You
will know that I am the LORD, when I deal with you for my name's sake[r] and not according to your evil
ways and your corrupt practices, you people of Israel, declares the Sovereign LORD.[s] ' "

Prophecy Against the South

45The word of the LORD came to me: 46"Son of man, set your face toward the south; preach against
the south and prophesy against[t] the forest of the southland.[u] 47Say to the southern forest: 'Hear the
word of the LORD. This is what the Sovereign LORD says: I am about to set fire to you, and it will consume all your trees, both green and dry. The blazing flame will not be quenched, and every face from

20:33 [z]Jer 21:5
20:34 [a]2Co 6:17* [b]Isa 27:12-13; Jer 44:6; La 2:4
20:35 [c]Jer 2:35
20:36 [d]Nu 11:1-35; 1Co 10:5-10
20:37 [e]Lev 27:32; Jer 33:13 [f]Eze 16:62
20:38 [g]Eze 34:17-22; Am 9:9-10 [h]Ps 95:11; Jer 44:14; Eze 13:9; Mal 3:3; Heb 4:3
20:39 [i]Jer 44:25 [j]Isa 1:13; Eze 43:7; Am 4:4
20:40 [k]Isa 60:7 [l]Isa 56:7; Mal 3:4
20:41 [m]Eze 28:25; 36:23 [n]Eze 11:17
20:42 [o]Eze 38:23 [p]Eze 34:13; 36:24
20:43 [q]Eze 6:9; 16:61; Hos 5:15
20:44 [r]Eze 36:22 [s]Eze 24:24
20:46 [t]Eze 21:2; Am 7:16 [u]Isa 30:6; Jer 13:19

[a] *40* Or *and the gifts of your firstfruits*

20:33–38 *A Shocking Exodus.* Utilizes imagery and language from the book of Exodus but with an ironic twist. After about 800 years of Israel's blatant misconduct and God's continual display of his long-suffering patience, God reveals himself here as one who will by no means clear the guilty (Exod 34:5–7); he will visit on them the consequences of their idolatry.
20:33 mighty hand ... outstretched arm. A statement of power and might. It was language of redemption in Exodus (Exod 6:6) but is now language of judgment in Ezekiel.
20:35 I will bring you into the wilderness of the nations. Exile among the nations is likened to the first wilderness experience. He is bringing them out "from the nations" (v. 34) and into "the wilderness" to experience wrath. **face to face.** Expresses the personal and direct nature of this "visitation" of judgment God promised (Exod 32:34).
20:37 I will take note of you as you pass under my rod. An idiom that comes from animal husbandry—the shepherd's rod guided and counted the sheep—expressing a time of examination and accountability. God is weighing their actions against the covenant, a legal document binding both God (vv. 5–6) and Israel (vv. 11–12) to a certain course of action. God swore to give the land, and Israel swore to keep God's laws, decrees, and Sabbaths (cf. Exod 20; 24). After close scrutiny the king/shepherd asserts his authority by stating that he will remove the rebels (v. 38); they will not enter the land. These actions will produce knowledge of the Lord (v. 38).
20:39–44 *Holy on My Holy Mountain.* After this shocking new exodus described in vv. 33–38, there will be a reversal of idolatry as the norm. Holiness, not profane behavior, will characterize God's people. Acceptance, not rejection, will characterize God's response. This renewed relationship will unfold on a sacred and high mountain found not in Egypt, the wilderness, or in exile but "in the land" (v. 40). In the land of promise Israel will wholeheartedly serve the Lord, not idols. God will require and accept their sacrifices because now those sacrifices are set apart solely for him (v. 40), and God will accept the people *themselves* like a pleasing sacrifice (v. 41). Thus, in the restoration, when God returns people to Jerusalem in 539 BC (Ezra 1), he will be shown as holy (different from other gods) and faithful to his word (v. 42). The restoration to the land will recall shame for past behavior (v. 43). God will restore them to the land in spite of their misconduct (v. 44). All this will help his people acknowledge him as the one true Lord with whom they have covenantal obligations (vv. 42,44). Though this anticipates 539 BC, it points beyond it to a permanent restoration (ch. 36). See Introduction: Theological Significance.
20:40 holy mountain. Jerusalem, or Zion (Ps 2:6; Isa 2:2–4; 27:13; 56:7; Jer 31:23).
20:45—21:32 *The Lord's Sword of Destruction.* This section uses language and imagery for warfare to further describe God's judgment on the nation. Destruction will come by way of the sword (i.e., war). Although the Lord is the primary agent of destruction, he hands his sword over to the king of Babylon to wield.
20:45—21:7 *Forest Fire Parable and Interpretation.* This section describes Yahweh's metaphoric fire, a blaze he sets off that consumes all that is in its path as divine punishment (Deut 28:24; 32:22). It expresses his divine anger (21:31–32). This "parable" is not clear to Ezekiel's audience (20:49), so it is interpreted in 21:1–7.
20:46 set your face. Represents hostility (e.g., 6:2; 13:17; 21:1; 25:2; 28:21; 29:2; 35:2). **toward the south.** Toward Judah and Jerusalem. The Babylonian invaders traverse Israel from north to south.
20:47 trees, both green and dry. Expresses comprehensive judgment.

20:47 [v]Isa 9:18-19; 13:8; Jer 21:14
20:48 [w]Jer 7:20
20:49 [x]Mt 13:13; Jn 16:25
21:2 [y]Eze 20:46
21:3 [z]Jer 21:13 [a]ver 9-11; Job 9:22
21:4 [b]Eze 20:47
21:5 [c]ver 30 [d]Na 1:9
21:6 [e]Isa 22:4
21:7 [f]Eze 22:14; 7:17
21:10 [g]Ps 110:5-6; Isa 34:5-6
21:11 [h]Jer 46:4
21:12 [i]Jer 31:19
21:14 [j]Nu 24:10 [k]Eze 6:11; 30:24

south to north will be scorched by it.[v] 48Everyone will see that I the LORD have kindled it; it will not be
quenched.[w]"

49Then I said, "Sovereign LORD, they are saying of me, 'Isn't he just telling parables?[x]' "[a]

Babylon as God's Sword of Judgment

21 [b] The word of the LORD came to me: 2"Son of man, set your face against Jerusalem and preach
against the sanctuary. Prophesy against[y] the land of Israel 3and say to her: 'This is what the
LORD says: I am against you.[z] I will draw my sword from its sheath and cut off from you both the righteous and the wicked.[a] 4Because I am going to cut off the righteous and the wicked, my sword will be
unsheathed against everyone from south to north.[b] 5Then all people will know that I the LORD have
drawn my sword from its sheath; it will not return[c] again.'[d]

6"Therefore groan, son of man! Groan before them with broken heart and bitter grief.[e] 7And when
they ask you, 'Why are you groaning?' you shall say, 'Because of the news that is coming. Every heart
will melt with fear and every hand go limp;[f] every spirit will become faint and every leg will be wet with
urine.' It is coming! It will surely take place, declares the Sovereign LORD."

8The word of the LORD came to me: 9"Son of man, prophesy and say, 'This is what the Lord says:

" 'A sword, a sword,
sharpened and polished—
10sharpened for the slaughter,[g]
polished to flash like lightning!

" 'Shall we rejoice in the scepter of my royal son? The sword despises every such stick.

11" 'The sword is appointed to be polished,[h]
to be grasped with the hand;
it is sharpened and polished,
made ready for the hand of the slayer.
12Cry out and wail, son of man,
for it is against my people;
it is against all the princes of Israel.
They are thrown to the sword
along with my people.
Therefore beat your breast.[i]

13" 'Testing will surely come. And what if even the scepter, which the sword despises, does not continue? declares the Sovereign LORD.'

14"So then, son of man, prophesy
and strike your hands[j] together.
Let the sword strike twice,
even three times.
It is a sword for slaughter—
a sword for great slaughter,
closing in on them from every side.[k]

[a] *49* In Hebrew texts 20:45-49 is numbered 21:1-5. [b] In Hebrew texts 21:1-32 is numbered 21:6-37.

21:2 Jerusalem ... sanctuary ... land of Israel. Judah, the south (20:46–47).
21:3 sword. Of warfare; Yahweh's fire (20:47). **cut off ... the righteous and the wicked.** Describes completeness of judgment. No one will escape the final and upcoming attack by the Babylonians in 586 BC (see notes on ch. 7). All (see 20:47 and note) will be carried away in war.
21:6 Groan ... with broken heart and bitter grief. In line with his mourning role (see note on 3:1,3), Ezekiel outwardly mourns in their midst, anticipating the bad news of Jerusalem's death. The Jerusalem invasion will involve grief, pain, and suffering.
21:8–17 *God's Sharpened and Polished Sword.* This section reveals God's main agent of destruction. Like the storm of Yahweh's presence in ch. 1, the sword is lifelike.
21:10 sharpened ... polished. Razorlike readiness for fierce slaughter, creating an atmosphere of dread. **Shall we rejoice in the scepter of my royal son?** A rhetorical question; the answer is no. It is a time to mourn, not rejoice, because the reigning king of David's house cannot escape judgment (see Introduction: Literary Features).
21:12–14 Cry out and wail ... strike your hands together. Mournful gestures of grief and anger that communicate dread.

[15] So that hearts may melt with fear[l]
and the fallen be many,
I have stationed the sword for slaughter[a]
at all their gates.
Look! It is forged to strike like lightning,
it is grasped for slaughter.[m]
[16] Slash to the right, you sword,
then to the left,
wherever your blade is turned.
[17] I too will strike my hands[n] together,
and my wrath[o] will subside.
I the LORD have spoken."

[18]The word of the LORD came to me: [19]"Son of man, mark out two roads for the sword of the king
of Babylon to take, both starting from the same country. Make a signpost where the road branches off
to the city. [20]Mark out one road for the sword to come against Rabbah of the Ammonites[p] and another
against Judah and fortified Jerusalem. [21]For the king of Babylon will stop at the fork in the road, at
the junction of the two roads, to seek an omen: He will cast lots[q] with arrows, he will consult his idols,
he will examine the liver.[r] [22]Into his right hand will come the lot for Jerusalem, where he is to set up
battering rams, to give the command to slaughter, to sound the battle cry, to set battering rams against
the gates, to build a ramp and to erect siege works.[s] [23]It will seem like a false omen to those who have
sworn allegiance to him, but he will remind[t] them of their guilt and take them captive.

[24]"Therefore this is what the Sovereign LORD says: 'Because you people have brought to mind your
guilt by your open rebellion, revealing your sins in all that you do—because you have done this, you
will be taken captive.

[25]" 'You profane and wicked prince of Israel, whose day has come, whose time of punishment has
reached its climax,[u] [26]this is what the Sovereign LORD says: Take off the turban, remove the crown.[v] It
will not be as it was: The lowly will be exalted and the exalted will be brought low.[w] [27]A ruin! A ruin! I
will make it a ruin! The crown will not be restored until he to whom it rightfully belongs shall come;
to him I will give it.'[x]

[28]"And you, son of man, prophesy and say, 'This is what the Sovereign LORD says about the Ammonites[y] and their insults:

" 'A sword,[z] a sword,
drawn for the slaughter,
polished to consume
and to flash like lightning!
[29] Despite false visions concerning you
and lying divinations about you,

[a] *15* Septuagint; the meaning of the Hebrew for this word is uncertain.

21:15 [l] 2Sa 17:10 [m] Ps 22:14
21:17 [n] ver 14; Eze 22:13 [o] Eze 5:13
21:20 [p] Dt 3:11; Jer 49:2; Am 1:14
21:21 [q] Pr 16:33 [r] Nu 22:7; 23:23
21:22 [s] Eze 4:2; 26:9
21:23 [t] Nu 5:15
21:25 [u] Eze 35:5
21:26 [v] Jer 13:18 [w] Ps 75:7; Eze 17:24
21:27 [x] Ps 2:6; Jer 23:5-6; Eze 37:24; Hag 2:21-22
21:28 [y] Zep 2:8 [z] Jer 12:12

21:18–27 *The King of Babylon's Sword.* Ezekiel role-plays as the Babylonian king Nebuchadnezzar. Faced with a military choice to attack an Ammonite or Judahite city, the king seeks an omen for advice (v. 21). His guidance is governed by the sovereign God.
21:21 cast lots with arrows ... consult his idols ... examine the liver. Babylonian omen-seeking methods to get guidance from the gods. **cast lots with arrows.** Arrows were labeled (e.g., "Rabbah," "Jerusalem"), placed into a quiver, and drawn out, one with each hand. The selection in the right hand was seen as a good omen (v. 22). **idols.** Cultic objects, or "household gods" (Gen 31:34; Judg 18:14; Hos 3:4), were consulted. **examine the liver.** Observation of line patterns on sheep livers to indicate a certain course of action—a common practice in ancient Babylon and Rome. Taken together the "luck of the draw" fell to Jerusalem. The city will undergo siege, and its inhabitants will be captured regardless of a previous allegiance (2 Chr 36:13).
21:25 wicked prince of Israel. Zedekiah (597–586 BC).
21:26 turban ... crown. Royal headwear also worn by the high priest (Exod 28:36–37; 29:6; 39:31; cf. Isa 62:3). Zedekiah no longer possesses the right to wear kingly garments. Jerusalem no longer possesses the right to kingship, a clear reversal of the norm (17:24; 1 Sam 2:7–8).
21:27 The crown will not be restored until he ... shall come. The fall of Jerusalem brings a temporary interruption of the promises of God relative to Davidic kingship (see ch. 34).
21:28–29 *The Sword Wielded Against Ammon.* As with Zedekiah (v. 25), "punishment has reached its climax" for the Ammonites (v. 29), because they gloated over Jerusalem's demise (v. 28; 25:1–7). The Ammonites and their capital of Rabbah (v. 20; Jer 49:2) will feel the effects of the Babylonian sword that Nebuchadnezzar wields.

21:29 [a]ver 25; Eze 22:28; 35:5
21:30 [b]Jer 47:6
[c]Eze 16:3
21:31 [d]Eze 22:20-21
[e]Jer 51:20-23
21:32 [f]Mal 4:1
[g]Eze 25:10
22:2 [h]Eze 24:6,9; Na 3:1
[i]Eze 16:2
22:3 [j]ver 6,13,27; Eze 23:37,45
22:4 [k]2Ki 21:16
[l]Eze 21:25 [m]Eze 5:14
22:6 [n]Isa 1:23
22:7 [o]Dt 5:16; 27:16
[p]Ex 22:21-22
22:8 [q]Eze 23:38-39
22:9 [r]Lev 19:16
[s]Eze 18:11 [t]Hos 4:10,14
22:10 [u]Lev 18:8,19
22:11 [v]Lev 18:15
[w]Lev 18:9; 2Sa 13:14
22:12 [x]Dt 27:25; Mic 7:3
[y]Lev 19:13
22:13 [z]Eze 21:17
[a]Isa 33:15 [b]ver 3
22:14 [c]Eze 24:14
[d]Eze 17:24; 21:7
22:15 [e]Dt 4:27; Zec 7:14

it will be laid on the necks
    of the wicked who are to be slain,
whose day has come,
    whose time of punishment has reached its climax.[a]

30 " 'Let the sword return to its sheath.[b]
    In the place where you were created,
in the land of your ancestry,[c]
    I will judge you.
31 I will pour out my wrath on you
    and breathe out my fiery anger[d] against you;
I will deliver you into the hands of brutal men,
    men skilled in destruction.[e]
32 You will be fuel for the fire,[f]
    your blood will be shed in your land,
you will be remembered[g] no more;
    for I the LORD have spoken.' "

Judgment on Jerusalem's Sins

22 The word of the LORD came to me:
2 "Son of man, will you judge her? Will you judge this city of bloodshed?[h] Then confront her with all
her detestable practices[i] 3 and say: 'This is what the Sovereign LORD says: You city that brings on herself
doom by shedding blood[j] in her midst and defiles herself by making idols, 4 you have become guilty
because of the blood you have shed[k] and have become defiled by the idols you have made. You have
brought your days to a close, and the end of your years has come.[l] Therefore I will make you an object
of scorn to the nations and a laughingstock to all the countries.[m] 5 Those who are near and those who
are far away will mock you, you infamous city, full of turmoil.
6 " 'See how each of the princes of Israel who are in you uses his power to shed blood.[n] 7 In you they
have treated father and mother with contempt;[o] in you they have oppressed the foreigner and mistreated the fatherless and the widow.[p] 8 You have despised my holy things and desecrated my Sabbaths.[q]
9 In you are slanderers[r] who are bent on shedding blood; in you are those who eat at the mountain
shrines[s] and commit lewd acts.[t] 10 In you are those who dishonor their father's bed; in you are those
who violate women during their period, when they are ceremonially unclean.[u] 11 In you one man commits a detestable offense with his neighbor's wife, another shamefully defiles his daughter-in-law,[v] and
another violates his sister,[w] his own father's daughter. 12 In you are people who accept bribes[x] to shed
blood; you take interest and make a profit from the poor. You extort unjust gain from your neighbors.[y]
And you have forgotten me, declares the Sovereign LORD.
13 " 'I will surely strike my hands[z] together at the unjust gain[a] you have made and at the blood[b] you
have shed in your midst. 14 Will your courage endure or your hands be strong in the day I deal with
you? I the LORD have spoken,[c] and I will do it.[d] 15 I will disperse you among the nations and scatter[e] you

21:30–32 *The Lord's Sword Returned to Its Sheath.* These verses complete the story of the unsheathed sword that begins in v. 3.
21:30 in the land ... I will judge you. Anticipates the real end of the story: Babylon will experience the Lord's wrath but only after God uses them to destroy Jerusalem (Jer 50:15,27,29,31; 51:6; Hab 2:4–20; cf. Isa 10:5–19).
22:1–31 *History of Bloodshed.* The topic of Israel's guilt continues to shape Ezekiel's discussion. From the covenantal perspective, guilt provides the legal rationale for the demise of the city (see chs. 16–23). Ezekiel takes on the role of judge, one of his many roles in the book (see Introduction: Author). His charge is against the city (vv. 1–16), all classes of people (vv. 17–22), and the land (vv. 23–31), and it concerns widespread bloodshed and idolatry. As a result, the city is defiled and a sentence is on it. Jerusalem will experience the fiery furnace of God's fury (vv. 13–22,30–31).
22:1–16 *Indictment of the City.* The city has fostered bloodshed and idolatry. It has been a receptacle for a pattern of sin (vv. 6–12), so it is dirty, or defiled.
22:2 bloodshed. Jerusalem's characteristic sin (vv. 3–4,6,9,12–13). This refers not necessarily to physically taking life but to harming and exploiting people.
22:6 in you. In Jerusalem; repeated in vv. 7–12. Jerusalem is "sin city," a dirty container filled to the brim with every sort of defilement.
22:13 strike my hands together. Expresses mournful anger (cf. 6:11; 21:14); a gesture signifying that God has had enough of their sins.
22:14–15 In the upcoming exile God will demonstrate that their stub-

through the countries; and I will put an end to your uncleanness.[f] 16When you have been defiled[a] in
the eyes of the nations, you will know that I am the LORD.' "
17Then the word of the LORD came to me: 18"Son of man, the people of Israel have become dross[g] to
me; all of them are the copper, tin, iron and lead left inside a furnace. They are but the dross of silver.[h]
19Therefore this is what the Sovereign LORD says: 'Because you have all become dross, I will gather you
into Jerusalem. 20As silver, copper, iron, lead and tin are gathered into a furnace to be melted with a
fiery blast, so will I gather you in my anger and my wrath and put you inside the city and melt you.[i]
21I will gather you and I will blow on you with my fiery wrath, and you will be melted inside her. 22As
silver is melted[j] in a furnace, so you will be melted inside her, and you will know that I the LORD have
poured out my wrath on you.' "[k]
23Again the word of the LORD came to me: 24"Son of man, say to the land, 'You are a land that has
not been cleansed or rained on in the day of wrath.'[l] 25There is a conspiracy[m] of her princes[b] within
her like a roaring lion tearing its prey; they devour people,[n] take treasures and precious things and
make many widows[o] within her. 26Her priests do violence to my law[p] and profane my holy things; they
do not distinguish between the holy and the common;[q] they teach that there is no difference between
the unclean and the clean;[r] and they shut their eyes to the keeping of my Sabbaths, so that I am profaned among them.[s] 27Her officials within her are like wolves tearing their prey; they shed blood and
kill people to make unjust gain.[t] 28Her prophets whitewash[u] these deeds for them by false visions and
lying divinations. They say, 'This is what the Sovereign LORD says'—when the LORD has not spoken.[v]
29The people of the land practice extortion and commit robbery; they oppress the poor and needy and
mistreat the foreigner,[w] denying them justice.[x]
30"I looked for someone among them who would build up the wall[y] and stand before me in the gap
on behalf of the land so I would not have to destroy it, but I found no one.[z] 31So I will pour out my
wrath on them and consume them with my fiery anger, bringing down[a] on their own heads all they
have done, declares the Sovereign LORD.[b]"

Two Adulterous Sisters

23 The word of the LORD came to me: 2"Son of man, there were two women, daughters of the same
mother.[c] 3They became prostitutes in Egypt,[d] engaging in prostitution[e] from their youth. In
that land their breasts were fondled and their virgin bosoms caressed. 4The older was named Oholah,

[a] 16 Or *When I have allotted you your inheritance* [b] 25 Septuagint; Hebrew *prophets*

22:15 [f] Eze 23:27
22:18 [g] Ps 119:119; Isa 1:22 [h] Jer 6:28-30
22:20 [i] Mal 3:2
22:22 [j] Isa 1:25 [k] Eze 20:8,33
22:24 [l] Eze 24:13
22:25 [m] Jer 11:9 [n] Hos 6:9 [o] Jer 15:8
22:26 [p] Mal 2:7-8 [q] Eze 44:23 [r] Lev 10:10 [s] 1Sa 2:12-17; Jer 2:8,26; Hag 2:11-14
22:27 [t] Isa 1:23
22:28 [u] Eze 13:10 [v] Eze 13:2,6-7
22:29 [w] Ex 22:21; 23:9 [x] Isa 5:7
22:30 [y] Eze 13:5 [z] Ps 106:23; Jer 5:1
22:31 [a] Eze 16:43 [b] Eze 7:8-9; 9:10; Ro 2:8
23:2 [c] Jer 3:7; Eze 16:45
23:3 [d] Jos 24:14 [e] Lev 17:7

born "courage" to continue in sin is no match for his own character that will put an end to their "uncleanness."

22:16 you will know that I am the LORD. See notes on 6:7; 7:4; 12:15,16; 15:7; see also Introduction: Theological Significance.

22:17–22 *The Furnace of God's Fury.* Appropriately, the place where sin was fostered, i.e., in Jerusalem (see note on v. 6), becomes the place where God's anger will burn in order to rid the city of its impurities. Jerusalem, the container of sin, will become God's furnace. Due to their sin, the people are as useless to God as the by-products produced when metals undergo the refining process (v. 18). As punishment God will "melt down" all those in and around the city in this severe and atypical purification process (Isa 1:22–25; Jer 6:27–30).

22:23–31 *Corruption Across Classes.* This section addresses the land. Collectively, the city, people, and land are impure. Much like in 7:23–27, the systemic nature of their corruption cuts through the covenantal administrative leadership structure.

22:25–29 princes ... priests ... officials ... prophets ... people of the land. They all negatively influenced society and abused their leadership roles. Kings abused widows for more wealth; priests misrepresented God (Lev 10:10–11); government officials mishandled finances; false prophets misled; rich land owners abused the poor.

22:30 I looked for someone ... who would build up the wall ... so I would not have to destroy it. Confirms God does not delight in death (cf. ch. 18). No line of defense was in place against the city's sins (13:5; Ps 106:23). There was no one to help avert the destruction. **before me.** Suggests that this standing in the gap in defense of the city is in fact intercessory prayer before God. This pictures a vulnerable city that is open to attack because its wall is broken.

23:1–49 *Story of Two Depraved Sisters.* Ch. 23 climactically bookends chs. 16–23, which begin with the nation being addressed as an adulterous wife (ch. 16). Ch. 23 is an allegory of two sisters, representing Samaria and Jerusalem. They prostituted themselves largely by forging political alliances with pagans (vv. 1–35). They were unfaithful (vv. 36–49; see ch. 16 and notes). Samaria was bad, but Jerusalem was worse (vv. 11,14). Jerusalem's promiscuity escalated with no end in sight (v. 19), and her passions were so out of control that only divine intervention could stop it (v. 27; cf. 22:15).

23:1–10 *Samaria: Oholah's Story.* This section introduces both sisters and their prostitution (vv. 1–4) and recounts Oholah's story (vv. 5–10).

23:3 Egypt. Where Israel was enslaved to Pharaoh. The sisters early depended on a pagan power for provision, protection, and security. Their continual desire to return to Egypt revealed a codependence God would not tolerate. The exodus revealed that they did not need to rely on a pagan power, because Yahweh miraculously saved them and provided for their needs in the wilderness (20:5–8; Exod 17:3; Num 11:5,18; 14:2–4). **fondled ... caressed.** Sexually suggestive language for political prostitution, which is as disgusting in God's eyes as religious prostitution, because it is a personal affront to God.

and her sister was Oholibah. They were mine and gave birth to sons and daughters. Oholah is Samaria, and Oholibah is Jerusalem.

5 "Oholah engaged in prostitution while she was still mine; and she lusted after her lovers, the Assyrians[f]—warriors[g] 6 clothed in blue, governors and commanders, all of them handsome young men, and mounted horsemen. 7 She gave herself as a prostitute to all the elite of the Assyrians and defiled herself with all the idols of everyone she lusted after.[h] 8 She did not give up the prostitution she began in Egypt,[i] when during her youth men slept with her, caressed her virgin bosom and poured out their lust on her.[j]

9 "Therefore I delivered her into the hands[k] of her lovers, the Assyrians, for whom she lusted.[l] 10 They stripped[m] her naked, took away her sons and daughters and killed her with the sword. She became a byword among women,[n] and punishment was inflicted on her.[o]

11 "Her sister Oholibah saw this, yet in her lust and prostitution she was more depraved than her sister.[p] 12 She too lusted after the Assyrians—governors and commanders, warriors in full dress, mounted horsemen, all handsome young men.[q] 13 I saw that she too defiled herself; both of them went the same way.

14 "But she carried her prostitution still further. She saw men portrayed on a wall,[r] figures of Chaldeans[a] portrayed in red,[s] 15 with belts around their waists and flowing turbans on their heads; all of them looked like Babylonian chariot officers, natives of Chaldea.[b] 16 As soon as she saw them, she lusted after them and sent messengers to them in Chaldea. 17 Then the Babylonians came to her, to the bed of love, and in their lust they defiled her. After she had been defiled by them, she turned away from them in disgust. 18 When she carried on her prostitution openly and exposed her naked body, I turned away[t] from her in disgust, just as I had turned away from her sister.[u] 19 Yet she became more and more promiscuous as she recalled the days of her youth, when she was a prostitute in Egypt. 20 There she lusted after her lovers, whose genitals were like those of donkeys and whose emission was like that of horses. 21 So you longed for the lewdness of your youth, when in Egypt your bosom was caressed and your young breasts fondled.[c][v]

22 "Therefore, Oholibah, this is what the Sovereign LORD says: I will stir up your lovers against you, those you turned away from in disgust, and I will bring them against you from every side[w]— 23 the Babylonians[x] and all the Chaldeans, the men of Pekod[y] and Shoa and Koa, and all the Assyrians with them, handsome young men, all of them governors and commanders, chariot officers and men of high rank, all mounted on horses.[z] 24 They will come against you with weapons,[d] chariots and wagons[a] and with a throng of people; they will take up positions against you on every side with large and small shields and with helmets. I will turn you over to them for punishment,[b] and they will punish you according to their standards. 25 I will direct my jealous anger against you, and they will deal with you in fury. They will cut off your noses and your ears, and those of you who are left will fall by the sword. They will take away your sons and daughters,[c] and those of you who are left will be consumed by fire.[d] 26 They will also strip[e] you of your clothes and take your fine jewelry.[f] 27 So I will put a stop[g] to the lewdness and prostitution you began in Egypt. You will not look on these things with longing or remember Egypt anymore.

[a] *14* Or *Babylonians* [b] *15* Or *Babylonia*; also in verse 16 [c] *21* Syriac (see also verse 3); Hebrew *caressed because of your young breasts* [d] *24* The meaning of the Hebrew for this word is uncertain.

23:5 [f] 2Ki 16:7; Hos 5:13 [g] Hos 8:9
23:7 [h] Hos 5:3; 6:10
23:8 [i] Ex 32:4 [j] Eze 16:15
23:9 [k] 2Ki 18:11 [l] Hos 11:5
23:10 [m] Hos 2:10 [n] Eze 16:41 [o] Eze 16:36
23:11 [p] Jer 3:8-11; Eze 16:51
23:12 [q] 2Ki 16:7-15; 2Ch 28:16
23:14 [r] Eze 8:10 [s] Jer 22:14
23:18 [t] Ps 78:59; 106:40; Jer 6:8 [u] Jer 12:8; Am 5:21
23:21 [v] Eze 16:26
23:22 [w] Eze 16:37
23:23 [x] 2Ki 20:14-18 [y] Jer 50:21 [z] 2Ki 24:2
23:24 [a] Jer 47:3; Eze 26:7,10; Na 2:4 [b] Jer 39:5-6
23:25 [c] ver 47 [d] Eze 20:47-48
23:26 [e] Jer 13:22 [f] Isa 3:18-23; Eze 16:39
23:27 [g] Eze 16:41

23:5–10 Samaria's political prostitution continued with the Assyrians, with whom Samaria made political alliances. But God made these "lovers" (vv. 5,9) turn against Samaria (vv. 9–10). The Assyrians captured the city and deported the people in 722 BC (2 Kgs 15–17).

23:11–21 *Jerusalem: Oholibah's Story.* Jerusalem, like Samaria, was enticed by the power of not only the Assyrians but also the Chaldeans (Babylonians) to solve her problems (2 Kgs 20:12–13; 24:1,8–12). Jerusalem's prostitution surpassed Samaria's (v. 14).

23:14–18 Jerusalem's political prostitution continued with the Babylonians when Babylon conquered Assyria in 612–605 BC. Hopeful that alliances with Babylon would help to solve her problems, Judah metaphorically got into bed with Babylon. But Jerusalem's new partner abandoned and defiled her (2 Kgs 23:29–30).

23:19–21 Judah attempted to solve her own problems through international diplomacy (2 Kgs 23:29—24:20). These verses mock her relentless pursuit of looking for "love" in all the wrong places (other nations) with a gross and exaggerated description of her lover's reproductive organs.

23:22–35 *The End of the Story for Oholibah.* Although Jerusalem could not end her insatiable appetite for love (a codependence on Assyria and Babylon and not a dependence on the Lord), God takes the initiative and ends her political prostitution (v. 27). God stirs up Jerusalem's lovers and uses them to punish Jerusalem. He gives his people more of what they want but with an ironic twist: Jerusalem's lovers will come not to love her but to abuse her.

23:23 Babylonians ... Chaldeans. Two designations for the same nation along with those assimilated into their army (Aramean tribal people and Assyrians). God stirs them up.

23:24 God describes and sanctions the enemy's severe warfare tactics.

28“For this is what the Sovereign LORD says: I am about to deliver you into the hands[h] of those you hate, to those you turned away from in disgust. 29They will deal with you in hatred and take away everything you have worked for. They will leave you stark naked, and the shame of your prostitution will be exposed. Your lewdness and promiscuity[i] 30have brought this on you, because you lusted after the nations and defiled yourself with their idols.[j] 31You have gone the way of your sister; so I will put her cup[k] into your hand.[l]

32“This is what the Sovereign LORD says:

“You will drink your sister’s cup,
a cup large and deep;
it will bring scorn and derision,
for it holds so much.[m]
33You will be filled with drunkenness and sorrow,
the cup of ruin and desolation,
the cup of your sister Samaria.[n]
34You will drink it[o] and drain it dry
and chew on its pieces—
and you will tear your breasts.

I have spoken, declares the Sovereign LORD.

35“Therefore this is what the Sovereign LORD says: Since you have forgotten[p] me and turned your back on me,[q] you must bear the consequences of your lewdness and prostitution.”

36The LORD said to me: “Son of man, will you judge Oholah and Oholibah? Then confront[r] them with their detestable practices,[s] 37for they have committed adultery and blood is on their hands. They committed adultery with their idols; they even sacrificed their children, whom they bore to me, as food for them.[t] 38They have also done this to me: At that same time they defiled my sanctuary and desecrated my Sabbaths. 39On the very day they sacrificed their children to their idols, they entered my sanctuary and desecrated[u] it. That is what they did in my house.[v]

40“They even sent messengers for men who came from far away,[w] and when they arrived you bathed yourself for them, applied eye makeup[x] and put on your jewelry.[y] 41You sat on an elegant couch,[z] with a table[a] spread before it on which you had placed the incense and olive oil that belonged to me.

42“The noise of a carefree crowd was around her; drunkards were brought from the desert along with men from the rabble, and they put bracelets[b] on the wrists of the woman and her sister and beautiful crowns on their heads.[c] 43Then I said about the one worn out by adultery, ‘Now let them use her as a prostitute,[d] for that is all she is.’ 44And they slept with her. As men sleep with a prostitute, so they slept with those lewd women, Oholah and Oholibah. 45But righteous judges will sentence them to the punishment of women who commit adultery and shed blood, because they are adulterous and blood is on their hands.[e]

23:28 [h] Jer 34:20
23:29 [i] Dt 28:48
23:30 [j] Eze 6:9
23:31 [k] Jer 25:15 [l] 2Ki 21:13
23:32 [m] Ps 60:3; Isa 51:17; Jer 25:15
23:33 [n] Jer 25:15-16
23:34 [o] Ps 75:8; Isa 51:17
23:35 [p] Isa 17:10; Jer 3:21 [q] 1Ki 14:9
23:36 [r] Eze 16:2 [s] Isa 58:1; Eze 22:2; Mic 3:8
23:37 [t] Eze 16:36
23:39 [u] 2Ki 21:4 [v] Jer 7:10
23:40 [w] Isa 57:9 [x] 2Ki 9:30 [y] Jer 4:30; Eze 16:13-19
23:41 [z] Est 1:6; Pr 7:17; Am 6:4 [a] Isa 65:11; Eze 44:16
23:42 [b] Ge 24:30 [c] Eze 16:11-12
23:43 [d] ver 3
23:45 [e] Lev 20:10; Eze 16:38; Hos 6:5

23:29 leave you stark naked. Punishment for adultery included stripping an adulterous wife naked—to expose in public what she had done in private (see note on 16:35–42). The Babylonians similarly will strip Jerusalem and Judah of everything valuable (2 Kgs 25:8–17) and expose them, to their own shame.
23:31 put her cup into your hand. Jerusalem’s fate will be like that of her sister. **cup.** Signifies an outpouring of God’s anger (Ps 75:8; Isa 51:17,22; see Jer 25:15–38 and note).
23:32–34 The cup’s size, contents, and shattered state after being emptied mock Jerusalem’s promiscuity (see Isa 37:22–29; Jer 25:15–29).
23:34 tear your breasts. In anguish; a sign of mourning (21:12) and an attempt to find relief. These were once fondled for pleasure (vv. 3,8,21).
23:35 They scorned God’s love (cf. 22:12).
23:36–49 *The End of the Story for Both Sisters.* This section addresses both Samaria and Jerusalem and again portrays Ezekiel as their judge (v. 36; 22:2). Their combined religious prostitution is murder and adultery.
23:37–38 sacrificed their children … defiled my sanctuary. See notes on 16:20–21; 20:31.
23:40–44 Trusting international diplomacy rather than the Lord was political prostitution. Oholah and Oholibah invited their lovers from all walks of life to engage them sexually until they were “worn out” (v. 43).
23:41 incense and olive oil that belonged to me. Items they beautified themselves with in anticipation of their lover’s arrival. The level of callousness toward the husband manifests itself by misusing his gifts to attract the attention of their lovers.
23:45–49 The judge’s gavel comes down on the conduct of Oholah and Oholibah: guilty as charged; their two crimes are adultery and murder (v. 45). The sentence is the death penalty (vv. 46–47), as the Mosaic law prescribed (Lev 20:10; 24:17,21; Deut 22:22). Thus, God will “put an end” (v. 48) to the uncontrolled passions of Samaria and Jerusalem (vv. 27,48), and knowledge of who he is will be apparent (v. 49). An end to sin will come, but only by God’s initiative.

23:46 [f]Eze 16:40
23:47 [g]2Ch 36:19 [h]2Ch 36:17; Eze 16:40-41
23:48 [i]2Pe 2:6
23:49 [j]Eze 7:4; 9:10; 20:38
24:1 [k]Eze 8:1
24:2 [l]2Ki 25:1; Jer 39:1; 52:4
24:3 [m]Isa 1:2; Eze 2:3,6 [n]Eze 17:2; 20:49 [o]Jer 1:13; Eze 11:3
24:5 [p]Jer 52:10 [q]Jer 52:24-27
24:6 [r]Eze 22:2 [s]Ob 11; Na 3:10
24:7 [t]Lev 17:13

46 "This is what the Sovereign LORD says: Bring a mob[f] against them and give them over to terror and
plunder. 47 The mob will stone them and cut them down with their swords; they will kill their sons and
daughters and burn[g] down their houses.[h]

48 "So I will put an end to lewdness in the land, that all women may take warning and not imitate
you.[i] 49 You will suffer the penalty for your lewdness and bear the consequences of your sins of idolatry.
Then you will know that I am the Sovereign LORD.[j]"

Jerusalem as a Cooking Pot

24 In the ninth year, in the tenth month on the tenth day, the word of the LORD came to me:[k]
2 "Son of man, record this date, this very date, because the king of Babylon has laid siege to
Jerusalem this very day.[l] 3 Tell this rebellious people[m] a parable[n] and say to them: 'This is what the
Sovereign LORD says:

"'Put on the cooking pot;[o] put it on
    and pour water into it.
4 Put into it the pieces of meat,
    all the choice pieces—the leg and the shoulder.
Fill it with the best of these bones;
5   take the pick of the flock.[p]
Pile wood beneath it for the bones;
    bring it to a boil
    and cook the bones in it.[q]

6 "'For this is what the Sovereign LORD says:

"'Woe to the city of bloodshed,[r]
    to the pot now encrusted,
    whose deposit will not go away!
Take the meat out piece by piece
    in whatever order[s] it comes.

7 "'For the blood she shed is in her midst:
    She poured it on the bare rock;
she did not pour it on the ground,
    where the dust would cover it.[t]
8 To stir up wrath and take revenge
    I put her blood on the bare rock,
    so that it would not be covered.

9 "'Therefore this is what the Sovereign LORD says:

"'Woe to the city of bloodshed!
    I, too, will pile the wood high.

24:1–27 *Jerusalem's Siege and the Fall Vividly Predicted.* This points back to the two related matters that shape and frame the book: the mourning motif and the city's prominence (see note on 1:1—24:27). Attention to the city via Ezekiel's dramatic performances functions as a framing device. Ezekiel's ministry commenced with a "sign" reflecting the siege on the city (4:3). Now God tells Ezekiel that Babylon has laid siege to Jerusalem (vv. 1–2). Ch. 24 concludes with the city's fall dramatically portrayed in the death of Ezekiel's wife and his response to it, another "sign" for the people (vv. 15–17). Ironically, when Ezekiel's wife dies he must "groan quietly" (v. 17) rather than mourn outwardly, as he would be expected to do.

24:1–14 *City Under Siege: Jerusalem Cooked Over the Fire.* The prophet has revealed the people's misconceptions about Jerusalem and the safety of its people (see 11:3–11 and note on 11:3). The imagery of Jerusalem as a pot protecting the meat (inhabitants) gives way to this parable of plunder. Siege not safety, plundering not protection, will be Jerusalem's lot as God uses the Babylonians, his agent of destruction, to fulfill his purposes.

24:1 ninth year ... tenth month ... tenth day. Of King Zedekiah's reign, Jan. 15, 588 BC (2 Kgs 25:1; Jer 52:4), the beginning of the Babylonian siege on the city.

24:4 choice pieces. People remaining in the city who think that they were spared the exile of 597 BC because of their goodness (see 11:3 and note). The pot is to boil and cook the meat pieces (vv. 3–5). The scum that remains will be burned away by burning the pot clean of its filth (vv. 10–11).

24:6 pot now encrusted. Represents Jerusalem's irredeemable situation.

[10] So heap on the wood
and kindle the fire.
Cook the meat well,
mixing in the spices;
and let the bones be charred.
[11] Then set the empty pot on the coals
till it becomes hot and its copper glows,
so that its impurities may be melted
and its deposit burned away.[u]
[12] It has frustrated all efforts;
its heavy deposit has not been removed,
not even by fire.

[13] " 'Now your impurity is lewdness. Because I tried to cleanse you but you would not be cleansed
from your impurity, you will not be clean again until my wrath against you has subsided.[v]

[14] " 'I the LORD have spoken. The time has come for me to act. I will not hold back; I will not have
pity, nor will I relent. You will be judged according to your conduct and your actions,[w] declares the
Sovereign LORD.[x] ' "

Ezekiel's Wife Dies

[15] The word of the LORD came to me: [16] "Son of man, with one blow I am about to take away from you
the delight of your eyes. Yet do not lament or weep or shed any tears.[y] [17] Groan quietly; do not mourn
for the dead. Keep your turban fastened and your sandals on your feet; do not cover your mustache and
beard or eat the customary food of mourners.[z] "

[18] So I spoke to the people in the morning, and in the evening my wife died. The next morning I did
as I had been commanded.

[19] Then the people asked me, "Won't you tell us what these things have to do with us?[a] Why are you
acting like this?"

[20] So I said to them, "The word of the LORD came to me: [21] Say to the people of Israel, 'This is what
the Sovereign LORD says: I am about to desecrate my sanctuary—the stronghold in which you take
pride, the delight of your eyes,[b] the object of your affection. The sons and daughters[c] you left behind
will fall by the sword.[d] [22] And you will do as I have done. You will not cover your mustache and beard
or eat the customary food of mourners.[e] [23] You will keep your turbans on your heads and your sandals
on your feet. You will not mourn[f] or weep but will waste away because of[a] your sins and groan among

[a] *23* Or *away in*

24:11 [u] Jer 21:10; Eze 22:15
24:13 [v] Jer 6:28-30; Eze 16:42; 22:24
24:14 [w] Eze 36:19 [x] Eze 18:30
24:16 [y] Jer 13:17; 16:5; 22:10
24:17 [z] Jer 16:7
24:19 [a] Eze 12:9; 37:18
24:21 [b] Ps 27:4 [c] Eze 23:25 [d] Jer 7:14,15; Eze 23:47
24:22 [e] Jer 16:7
24:23 [f] Job 27:15

24:11 empty pot. Jerusalem, emptied of inhabitants. **its impurities ... melted.** Jerusalem's punishment. The Babylonians will cleanse the city and burn away its impurity, commencing with the siege.

24:14 I the LORD have spoken. The certainty of Jerusalem's end rests on the power of Yahweh's word. **The time has come.** See ch. 7 and notes. God will unleash his fury. **I will not hold back.** The certainty of Jerusalem's destruction involves a lack of restraint from Yahweh. **I will not have pity, nor will I relent.** Unrestrained judgment materializes because Yahweh detaches himself emotionally from his people (e.g., 5:11). **You will be judged.** God takes sin seriously.

24:15–27 *Ezekiel's Wife Dies.* The sudden death of Ezekiel's wife, along with the command not to mourn outwardly, shockingly demonstrates that Jerusalem will die and reveals how the people must respond when they hear the news (v. 24). Connected to hearing the news of Jerusalem's fall is the promise that Ezekiel will regain his speech, another "sign" (v. 27) intended to reveal God's character. Unless delivering a word from God, however, Ezekiel is made speechless (see note on 3:26).

24:16 with one blow I am about to take away from you. Suggests a sudden fatal sickness that God allows to strike Ezekiel's wife (Exod 9:14; Num 14:37). **the delight of your eyes.** Ezekiel's wife (v. 18). Ezekiel's strong affection for his wife mirrors the affection people have for the Jerusalem temple and the city itself (vv. 21,25).

24:17 Groan quietly; do not mourn for the dead. Outwardly showing his grief would be expected (Josh 7:6; 1 Sam 4:12; 2 Sam 15:30; Jer 16:7), but at her death he may groan only inwardly.

24:21 my sanctuary ... the delight of your eyes. The Jerusalem temple, which Nebuchadnezzar will strike down as God planned. The people have strong affection for the temple and city, but their affection, false pride, and confidence in the temple are misplaced (Jer 7). Therefore, these things too will be destroyed metaphorically when the temple burns down. Rather than outwardly showing grief when the people hear the dreaded news, they will groan inwardly (vv. 23–24), and it will remind them of their sins.

24:23 keep your turbans on your heads. Rather than discarding this garment, as one would do in mourning rites (Josh 7:6; 1 Sam 4:12), the command is to keep it on. The turban was also a festive garment related to wedding imagery and the election of priests (44:18; see Isa 61:10; Zech 3:5). By wearing a festive garment or a garment associated with a special religious status at a time of grief, Ezekiel's sign manifests hope

24:23 [g]Ps 78:64
24:24 [h]Isa 20:3; Eze 4:3; 12:11
24:25 [i]Jer 11:22
24:26 [j]1Sa 4:12; Job 1:15-19
24:27 [k]Eze 3:26; 33:22
25:2 [l]Eze 21:28; Zep 2:8-9 [m]Jer 49:1-6
25:3 [n]Eze 26:2; 36:2 [o]Pr 17:5
25:4 [p]Jdg 6:3 [q]Dt 28:33,51; Jdg 6:33
25:5 [r]Dt 3:11; Eze 21:20 [s]Isa 17:2
25:6 [t]Ob 12; Zep 2:8
25:7 [u]Zep 1:4 [v]Eze 21:31 [w]Am 1:14-15
25:8 [x]Jer 48:1; Am 2:1

yourselves.[g] 24 Ezekiel will be a sign[h] to you; you will do just as he has done. When this happens, you
will know that I am the Sovereign LORD.'
25 "And you, son of man, on the day I take away their stronghold, their joy and glory, the delight of
their eyes, their heart's desire, and their sons and daughters[i] as well— 26 on that day a fugitive will
come to tell you[j] the news. 27 At that time your mouth will be opened; you will speak with him and will
no longer be silent. So you will be a sign to them, and they will know that I am the LORD.[k]"

A Prophecy Against Ammon

25 The word of the LORD came to me: 2 "Son of man, set your face against the Ammonites[l] and
prophesy against them.[m] 3 Say to them, 'Hear the word of the Sovereign LORD. This is what the
Sovereign LORD says: Because you said "Aha!"[n] over my sanctuary when it was desecrated and over the
land of Israel when it was laid waste and over the people of Judah when they went into exile,[o] 4 therefore I am going to give you to the people of the East[p] as a possession. They will set up their camps and
pitch their tents among you; they will eat your fruit and drink your milk.[q] 5 I will turn Rabbah[r] into a
pasture for camels and Ammon into a resting place for sheep.[s] Then you will know that I am the LORD.
6 For this is what the Sovereign LORD says: Because you have clapped your hands and stamped your feet,
rejoicing with all the malice of your heart against the land of Israel,[t] 7 therefore I will stretch out my
hand[u] against you and give you as plunder to the nations. I will wipe you out from among the nations
and exterminate you from the countries. I will destroy[v] you, and you will know that I am the LORD.[w]' "

A Prophecy Against Moab

8 "This is what the Sovereign LORD says: 'Because Moab[x] and Seir said, "Look, Judah has become like
all the other nations," 9 therefore I will expose the flank of Moab, beginning at its frontier towns—Beth

for their restoration, a new status for prophet and people alike. This explains why mourning will not be necessary.

24:25 the day I take away their stronghold. The day Jerusalem falls.

24:26 a fugitive. A fugitive from the events of 586 BC in Jerusalem will trek about 880 miles (about 1,400 kilometers) to tell Ezekiel the news in Babylon (33:21). Upon hearing that Jerusalem has fallen, Ezekiel the mourner can expect a return to normal life. He will be able to speak again (v. 27; see note on 3:26), a sign reflecting a change in Ezekiel's mourning role (cf. 2 Sam 12). The time for mourning will be over when the city finally falls.

25:1—32:32 *Signs Mourning Will End: Prophecies Against the Nations.* Readers expect to hear of Jerusalem's fall immediately following the death of Ezekiel's wife (24:15–27). But this does not come until approximately two years after her death (33:21–22). Sandwiched in between are a series of prophecies condemning seven surrounding nations that, at first glance, seem misplaced. If one understands the actual news of Jerusalem's fall as inaugurating a new era of hope (turning mourning to joy), the latter can only be realized when Israel's enemies are destroyed. Given Israel's vulnerable condition, it would be expected that friends and neighbors would come and offer comfort. In Israel's case, her neighbors act like enemies. Rather than share in the mourner's grief by bringing comfort, her enemies rejoice. The way Ammon and Tyre gloat over the ruination of the house of Judah and the less than neighborly ways of Moab, Edom, and Philistia cause Israel further grief. As a result, when Israel's oppressors receive punishment from God, God's people will be comforted. Only then, when comfort arrives, will the mourning period cease and full restoration begin. Thus, the literary placement of these prophecies has a distinct function in the book's overall message (see Introduction: Literary Features). From a biblical-theological point of view, the prophecies are a reminder that a day is coming when God will confront all those who oppose him and his people (see Introduction: Theological Significance).

25:1–17 The judgment sequence "because [they are evil] ... therefore [God will judge them]," used previously for Israel (e.g., 5:7–11), repeats itself in the prophecies against the nations (e.g., vv. 3–4). This grammatical sequence, with a clear cause-and-effect pattern, exposes the guilt of each nation. The promised punishment will comfort Ezekiel's Judahite audience. Judah's four immediate neighbors, moving clockwise: Ammon to the northeast (vv. 1–7), Moab to the east (vv. 8–11), Edom to the south (vv. 12–14), and Philistia to the west (vv. 15–17).

25:1–7 *Prophecy Against Ammon.* God confronts Israel's neighbors to the northeast. The Ammonites descended from Lot and his incestuous relationship with his daughter (Gen 19:30–38). They are characterized by idolatry (1 Kgs 11:7,33) and especially by their opposition to God's people (Deut 23:3–4; Judg 3:13; 1 Sam 11:1–3; 2 Sam 10:1–14; 2 Kgs 24:2; Neh 4:3,7–8). Although they are relatives, Israel must treat the Ammonites as foreigners due to their conflicting religious practices (20:28–29). Moreover, malicious joy (vv. 3,6) characterizes their demeanor toward God's temple and land in time of trouble (2 Kgs 24:2). All of this requires a direct confrontation with God.

25:2 set your face against. See note on 6:2.

25:4 people of the East. Either desert nomads or the Babylonian army (see 21:31). They are God's agents of destruction on Ammon.

25:5 Rabbah. The Ammonite capital. God will tear down this built-up city, reversing human ingenuity.

25:7 stretch out my hand against. Destroy (cf. Zeph 2:13–15).

25:8–11 *Prophecy Against Moab.* God confronts Israel's neighbors to the east. As the Ammonites (see note on vv. 1–7), the Moabites also descended from Lot and his incestuous relationship with his daughter (Gen 19:30–38). They polluted God's people by introducing them to Baal worship (Num 21:1–25; 31:16). As with the Ammonites, Israel must treat the Moabites as foreigners (even though they are distant relatives) owing to their idolatrous religious practices (Deut 23:3–4; 1 Kgs 11). The Moabites join forces with the Babylonians and attack Judah and delight at Judah's downfall (2 Kgs 24:2; Jer 48:29; Zeph 2:8–9). Rather than offer comfort, they mock Israel's God.

25:8 Judah has become like all the other nations. From the mouth of the enemy comes this shocking reality. Moab accuses God as powerless, insulting God's character and distinctness among the gods of the nations (Josh 2:8–11; Lam 4:12). God's people wanted to be like the

Jeshimoth[y], Baal Meon[z] and Kiriathaim[a]—the glory of that land. 10 I will give Moab along with the
Ammonites to the people of the East as a possession, so that the Ammonites will not be remembered[b]
among the nations; 11 and I will inflict punishment on Moab. Then they will know that I am the LORD.' "

A Prophecy Against Edom

12 "This is what the Sovereign LORD says: 'Because Edom[c] took revenge on Judah and became very
guilty by doing so, 13 therefore this is what the Sovereign LORD says: I will stretch out my hand against
Edom and kill both man and beast.[d] I will lay it waste, and from Teman to Dedan[e] they will fall by the
sword. 14 I will take vengeance on Edom by the hand of my people Israel, and they will deal with Edom in
accordance with my anger[f] and my wrath; they will know my vengeance, declares the Sovereign LORD.' "

A Prophecy Against Philistia

15 "This is what the Sovereign LORD says: 'Because the Philistines[g] acted in vengeance and took revenge with malice in their hearts, and with ancient hostility sought to destroy Judah, 16 therefore this
is what the Sovereign LORD says: I am about to stretch out my hand against the Philistines,[h] and I will
wipe out the Kerethites[i] and destroy those remaining along the coast. 17 I will carry out great vengeance
on them and punish them in my wrath. Then they will know that I am the LORD, when I take vengeance
on them.' "

A Prophecy Against Tyre

26 In the eleventh month of the twelfth[a] year, on the first day of the month, the word of the
LORD came to me: 2 "Son of man, because Tyre[j] has said of Jerusalem, 'Aha![k] The gate to the
nations is broken, and its doors have swung open to me; now that she lies in ruins I will prosper,'

25:9 [y] Nu 33:49 [z] Nu 32:3; Jos 13:17 [a] Nu 32:37; Jos 13:19
25:10 [b] Eze 21:32
25:12 [c] 2Ch 28:17
25:13 [d] Eze 29:8 [e] Jer 25:23
25:14 [f] Eze 35:11
25:15 [g] 2Ch 28:18
25:16 [h] Jer 47:1-7 [i] 1Sa 30:14; Zep 2:4-5
26:2 [j] 2Sa 5:11; Isa 23 [k] Eze 25:3

[a] *1* Probable reading of the original Hebrew text; Masoretic Text does not have *month of the twelfth*.

nations (20:32; 1 Sam 8:5), but God mandated a distinction and separation (Exod 19:5–6; Deut 17:14–20; 18:9–16).

25:10 people of the East. The same agents of destruction on Ammon (see note on v. 4). The lineup of cities in the Moabite heartland will be exposed to the enemy (v. 9).

25:12–14 *Prophecy Against Edom.* God confronts Israel's neighbors to the south. The Edomites descended from Esau, Jacob's twin brother born to Rebekah (Gen 25:21–34). The Israelites descended from Jacob. The early struggle between these twins intensifies to hatred in the biblical narrative (v. 12). See also 35:1—36:15.

25:12 revenge. Instead of helping Judah's refugees after the fall of Jerusalem in 586 BC, they attack those fleeing and gloat over the downfall of the Jerusalem temple (Ps 137:7; Lam 4:21–22; Obad 11–14).

25:15–17 *Prophecy Against Philistia.* God confronts Israel's neighbors to the west. The Philistines were inhabitants on the coastal plain of the Mediterranean Sea. These people were constant adversaries of Israel as early as the time of the judges as they fought over contested territory (Judg 3:31; 10:7,13–16; 1 Sam 4; 2 Sam 5; 2 Kgs 18:8). The Philistines were eventually conquered by David (2 Sam 5:17–25), but they remained hostile until their own encounter with the Babylonians (Isa 14:29–31; Jer 47; Amos 1:6–8; Zeph 2:4–7).

25:16 Kerethites. Coastal dwellers probably related to and perhaps identical to the Philistines (1 Sam 30:14; 2 Sam 8:18; 15:18; 20:7). The name might also relate to their origin from Crete (see second NIV text note on Amos 9:7 ["Caphtor"]).

26:1—28:26 *Prophecy Against Tyre and Sidon.* This section contains a lengthy judgment on Tyre (26:1—28:19) and a short statement concerning Sidon's end (28:20–24). Tyre and Sidon were two wealthy and influential seafaring Phoenician cities, and the Bible often speaks of them together (Isa 23:1–4; Jer 25:22; 47:4; Joel 3:4; Zech 9:2). With respect to Tyre, the repeated phrase "I will bring you to a horrible end and you will be no more" (26:21; cf. 27:36; 28:19) divides the prophecy into three parts. Tyre, the chief seaport of Phoenicia, rejoices rather than comforts Jerusalem and gloats over Jerusalem's problems (26:2). Therefore, God is against them (26:3). As an economic superpower, they played a key role in international trade due to their location. Tyre was an island. It was wealthy and renowned, and, as a result, arrogant. The Lord assures the end of Tyre's arrogance by sending the king of Babylon as his instrument of judgment (26:7). Ezekiel poetically and appropriately describes Tyre's end with sea-faring language. God will reduce Tyre to a "bare rock" (26:4,14), good only for fishing (26:5,14). God will "sink" Tyre, "the ship" (27:25–27). He will also demolish the pride of its king (28:1–19). The prophecy ends with a brief word of judgment on Sidon (28:20–23).

26:1–21 *Tyre's Destruction Announced.* Three images dominate: Tyre is made a "bare rock" (vv. 4,14) out in the open seas (vv. 1–14); the coastlands are personified as mourners over the city's destruction (vv. 15–18); and the pit becomes Tyre's eternal dwelling place (vv. 19–21). These three images communicate Tyre's fall, lament, and burial. See also Isa 23; Jer 25:22; 47:4; Joel 3:4–5; Amos 1:9–10; Zech 9:2–4.

26:1 eleventh month of the twelfth year ... first day of the month. The fifth date in the book (1:1; 8:1; 20:1; 24:1). As the NIV text note indicates, the Masoretic Text (the traditional Hebrew text) does not have "month of the twelfth." Thus, it reads "eleventh year," which dates between Apr. 23, 587 and Apr. 13, 586 BC. If the Masoretic Text is the correct text, the prophecy must date from the end of that year, i.e., in the 11th (Feb. 13, 586) or the 12th month (Mar. 15, 586). But there is a problem with these dates: this prophecy describes Tyre's gloating over the destruction of Jerusalem (v. 2), yet Jerusalem did not fall until July 18, 586 (see note on 2 Kgs 25:3) and was not burned until Aug. 14, 586 (see note on 2 Kgs 25:8)—several months after the date given here for Tyre's celebration of the fact that Jerusalem "now ... lies in ruins" (v. 2). To solve the problem, many interpreters believe that the probable reading of the original Hebrew text is "in the eleventh month of the twelfth year, on the first day of the month" and that the words "month of the twelfth" must have been inadvertently omitted by a copyist (hence

26:3 [l]Isa 5:30; Jer 50:42; 51:42
26:4 [m]Isa 23:1,11 [n]Am 1:10
26:5 [o]Eze 27:32 [p]Eze 29:19
26:7 [q]Jer 27:6 [r]Ezr 7:12; Da 2:37 [s]Eze 23:24; Na 2:3-4
26:8 [t]Jer 6:6 [u]Eze 21:22
26:10 [v]Jer 4:13
26:11 [w]Isa 5:28 [x]Jer 43:13 [y]Isa 26:5
26:12 [z]Isa 23:8; Eze 27:3-27; 28:8
26:13 [a]Jer 7:34 [b]Isa 14:11 [c]Jer 25:10; Rev 18:22
26:14 [d]Job 12:14; Mal 1:4
26:15 [e]Eze 27:35 [f]Jer 49:21
26:16 [g]Job 8:22 [h]Hos 11:10 [i]Eze 32:10
26:17 [j]Eze 19:1; 27:32 [k]Isa 14:12

3 therefore this is what the Sovereign LORD says: I am against you, Tyre, and I will bring many nations
against you, like the sea[l] casting up its waves. 4 They will destroy[m] the walls of Tyre[n] and pull down
her towers; I will scrape away her rubble and make her a bare rock. 5 Out in the sea[o] she will become
a place to spread fishnets, for I have spoken, declares the Sovereign LORD. She will become plunder[p]
for the nations, 6 and her settlements on the mainland will be ravaged by the sword. Then they will
know that I am the LORD.

7 "For this is what the Sovereign LORD says: From the north I am going to bring against Tyre Nebuchadnezzar[a][q] king of Babylon, king of kings,[r] with horses and chariots,[s] with horsemen and a great
army. 8 He will ravage your settlements on the mainland with the sword; he will set up siege works[t]
against you, build a ramp[u] up to your walls and raise his shields against you. 9 He will direct the blows
of his battering rams against your walls and demolish your towers with his weapons. 10 His horses will
be so many that they will cover you with dust. Your walls will tremble at the noise of the warhorses,
wagons and chariots[v] when he enters your gates as men enter a city whose walls have been broken
through. 11 The hooves[w] of his horses will trample all your streets; he will kill your people with the
sword, and your strong pillars[x] will fall to the ground.[y] 12 They will plunder your wealth and loot your
merchandise; they will break down your walls and demolish your fine houses and throw your stones,
timber and rubble into the sea.[z] 13 I will put an end[a] to your noisy songs, and the music of your harps[b]
will be heard no more.[c] 14 I will make you a bare rock, and you will become a place to spread fishnets.
You will never be rebuilt,[d] for I the LORD have spoken, declares the Sovereign LORD.

15 "This is what the Sovereign LORD says to Tyre: Will not the coastlands[e] tremble[f] at the sound of your
fall, when the wounded groan and the slaughter takes place in you? 16 Then all the princes of the coast
will step down from their thrones and lay aside their robes and take off their embroidered garments.
Clothed[g] with terror, they will sit on the ground, trembling[h] every moment, appalled[i] at you. 17 Then
they will take up a lament[j] concerning you and say to you:

"'How you are destroyed, city of renown,
 peopled by men of the sea!
You were a power on the seas,
 you and your citizens;
you put your terror
 on all who lived there.[k]
18 Now the coastlands tremble
 on the day of your fall;

[a] 7 Hebrew *Nebuchadrezzar,* of which *Nebuchadnezzar* is a variant; here and often in Ezekiel and Jeremiah

the NIV reading). The restored reading would yield the date Feb. 3, 585, which would nicely fit the chronology in 33:21 (see note there). If, on the other hand, the Masoretic Text is correct, then the Lord (through Ezekiel) was prophesying what Tyre's response to Jerusalem's fall would be and how the Lord, in turn, would judge Tyre.

26:3 I will bring many nations against you. God's agents of destruction against Tyre are "like the sea casting up its waves." The great army blends together the nations Babylon conquered (v. 7).

26:4 a bare rock. Tyre, an easily defendable, preeminent center of sea trade, the most powerful city on the Phoenician coast, will become "a bare rock" (Tyre in Hebrew means "rock").

26:5 a place to spread fishnets. Tyre will be reduced to nothing more than a place to fish.

26:7 From the north. The direction from which the enemy usually comes in Ezekiel (see note on 1:4). Nebuchadnezzar's army will move up the Euphrates River valley into Syria in a northward direction to descend on Tyre (Jer 1:13). **king of kings.** Nebuchadnezzar (605–562 BC). He leads a military force merged from the nations he conquered. This title amplifies his power over a powerful nation (29:18–19; 30:10).

26:13 noisy songs ... heard no more. Expresses the curse of a city's desolation (Lev 26; Deut 28–32; Isa 24:8).

26:14 never be rebuilt. Tyre will never be built up again in the same way; its heyday has come and gone, only a modest population with little influence will remain. This is fulfilled by Alexander the Great's devastating siege of Tyre in 332 BC.

26:16 Mainland cities and their princes (or kings; 27:35) respond to Tyre's fall. **lay aside their robes ... Clothed with terror.** A fear-based grief grips the coastlands as they dread Nebuchadnezzar yet mourn the loss of the most influential and defendable city of the Mediterranean world. Mourning typically involved tearing clothing, a change in posture, and speechlessness (see 3:15; Ezra 9:3–4; Job 2:8,12; Isa 3:26; Lam 2:10; 3:28; Jonah 3:6). **sit on the ground.** A posture of ritual mourning. **appalled.** Speechless and in shock because of the distress of Tyre's fall.

26:17–18 This short lament song was a typical way to express grief (cf. 19:1; 27:2; 28:12). Lament songs, especially those for destroyed cities, often included eulogy-like words about the city's great past (v. 17). But they also included words about the city's present devastation (see ch. 27 for a fuller lament). As was customary, this lament song utilizes the second person ("you"/"your") to address dead Tyre.

the islands in the sea
are terrified at your collapse.'[l]

19"This is what the Sovereign LORD says: When I make you a desolate city, like cities no longer inhabited, and when I bring the ocean depths over you and its vast waters cover you,[m] 20then I will bring
you down with those who go down to the pit,[n] to the people of long ago. I will make you dwell in the
earth below, as in ancient ruins, with those who go down to the pit, and you will not return or take your
place[a] in the land of the living.[o] 21I will bring you to a horrible end and you will be no more. You will
be sought, but you will never again be found, declares the Sovereign LORD."[p]

26:18 [l] Isa 23:5; 41:5; Eze 27:35
26:19 [m] Isa 8:7-8
26:20 [n] Eze 32:18; Am 9:2; Jnh 2:2,6 [o] Eze 32:24,30
26:21 [p] Eze 27:36; 28:19; Rev 18:21
27:3 [q] ver 33 [r] Eze 28:2

A Lament Over Tyre

27 The word of the LORD came to me: 2"Son of man, take up a lament concerning Tyre. 3Say to
Tyre, situated at the gateway to the sea,[q] merchant of peoples on many coasts, 'This is what
the Sovereign LORD says:

" 'You say, Tyre,
"I am perfect in beauty."[r]
4Your domain was on the high seas;
your builders brought your beauty to perfection.

[a] 20 Septuagint; Hebrew *return, and I will give glory*

26:19–21 Tyre's burial place is appropriate for this port and trading city: the ocean depths. Tyre drowns at sea and plunges to the pit, or grave, where she shares the fate of those long dead (Ps 143:3; Lam 3:6). The "pit" (v. 20; 32:18; see note on Ps 88:4) is a synonym for hell, reserved for those whom death has separated from communion with God (Isa 38:18). Thus, Tyre's fall, lament, and burial is secured.
27:1–36 *Lament Over Tyre the Ship.* Portrays Tyre as a proud, self-exalting, spectacular merchant ship. This lauds the ship's beauty and crew and discusses the lands with which the ship trades.
27:2 take up a lament. God prophetically anticipates the lament song that will be sung when Tyre "dies." It illumines Ezekiel's mourning role, established in 3:1–15 (see note on 3:1,3).
27:3–11 This passage personifies Tyre as a beautiful ship. Her "beauty" (vv. 3b,11) frames vv. 3b–11.

NATIONS AND CITIES UNDER JUDGMENT IN EZEKIEL

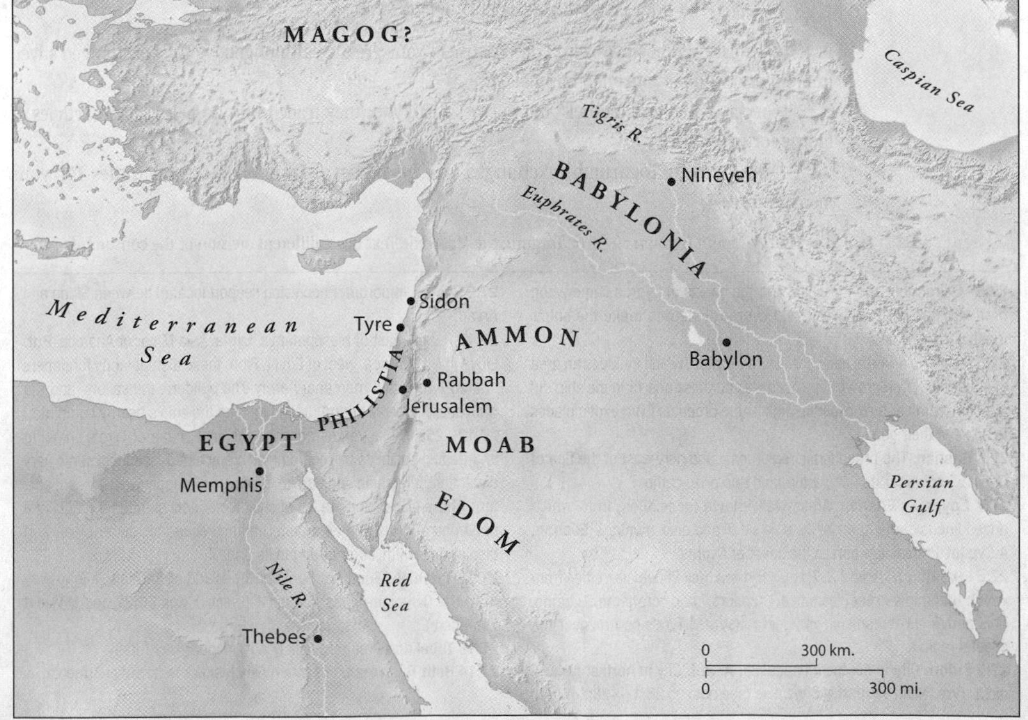

27:5 [s] Dt 3:9
27:6 [t] Nu 21:33; Jer 22:20; Zec 11:2 [u] Ge 10:4; Isa 23:12
27:7 [v] Ex 25:4; Jer 10:9
27:8 [w] Ge 10:18 [x] 1Ki 9:27
27:9 [y] Jos 13:5; 1Ki 5:18
27:10 [z] Eze 38:5 [a] Eze 30:5
27:12 [b] Ge 10:4 [c] ver 18,33
27:13 [d] Ge 10:2; Isa 66:19; Eze 38:2 [e] Rev 18:13
27:14 [f] Ge 10:3; Eze 38:6

5 They made all your timbers
of juniper from Senir[a];[s]
they took a cedar from Lebanon
to make a mast for you.
6 Of oaks[t] from Bashan
they made your oars;
of cypress wood[b] from the coasts of Cyprus[u]
they made your deck, adorned with ivory.
7 Fine embroidered linen from Egypt was your sail
and served as your banner;
your awnings were of blue and purple[v]
from the coasts of Elishah.
8 Men of Sidon and Arvad[w] were your oarsmen;
your skilled men, Tyre, were aboard as your sailors.[x]
9 Veteran craftsmen of Byblos[y] were on board
as shipwrights to caulk your seams.
All the ships of the sea and their sailors
came alongside to trade for your wares.

10 " 'Men of Persia,[z] Lydia and Put[a]
served as soldiers in your army.
They hung their shields and helmets on your walls,
bringing you splendor.
11 Men of Arvad and Helek
guarded your walls on every side;
men of Gammad
were in your towers.
They hung their shields around your walls;
they brought your beauty to perfection.

12 " 'Tarshish[b] did business with you because of your great wealth of goods;[c] they exchanged silver,
iron, tin and lead for your merchandise.
13 " 'Greece, Tubal and Meshek[d] did business with you; they traded human beings[e] and articles of
bronze for your wares.
14 " 'Men of Beth Togarmah[f] exchanged chariot horses, cavalry horses and mules for your
merchandise.

[a] *5* That is, Mount Hermon [b] *6* Targum; the Masoretic Text has a different division of the consonants.

27:5–6 From Lebanon, Bashan, and the coasts of Cyprus came wood products (juniper, cedar, oak, and cypress wood) to make the ship's mast, oars, and deck.
27:5 Senir. An Amorite name for Mount Hermon, which includes an area of substantial tree growth. The builders and those adorning the ship did not compromise; they exported high-value products from exotic places to achieve their goals.
27:6 Bashan. The broad fertile region east and northeast of the Sea of Galilee; known for its rich pastureland and prize cattle.
27:7 Egypt ... Elishah. Areas well-known for textiles, from which prized linens came to make the ship's sail and deck awnings. **Elishah.** A Cypriot-Phoenician port on the coast of Cyprus.
27:8–9 Sidon ... Arvad ... Tyre ... Byblos. Key Phoenician cities from which the ship's crew ("oarsmen," "sailors," and "craftsmen") came. This native, all-Phoenician crew demonstrates Tyre's control over the coastal region.
27:8 Sidon. City in southern Phoenicia. **Arvad.** City in northern Phoenicia. **Tyre.** Main seaport of Phoenicia (see note on 26:1—28:26).
27:9 Byblos. Important Phoenician seaport located between Sidon and Arvad.
27:10 Persia. East of Mesopotamia. **Lydia.** Asia Minor or Anatolia. **Put.** Libya in North Africa, west of Egypt. From these distant lands foreigners staffed Tyre with a mercenary army. The builders, the sailors, and the mercenary army all contributed in making the ship's beauty complete.
27:12–25a These verses describe the vast scope of Tyre's shipping and trading business by recording as many as 23 locations, some very distant (e.g., Tarshish and Persia), following a roughly west-to-east pattern. These places and the list of choice products shuttled through Tyre underscore Tyre's role as an international economic superpower and display its wealth, contributing to its pride.
27:12 Tarshish. Southern Spain or the island of Sardinia, a long way from the Canaanite coast (Jonah 1:3; see 1 Kgs 10:22 and NIV text note there).
27:13 Tubal and Meshek. Asia Minor; modern-day Turkey.
27:14 Beth Togarmah. In eastern Asia Minor; modern-day Armenia.

15 " 'The men of Rhodes[a][g] traded with you, and many coastlands[h] were your customers; they paid
you with ivory[i] tusks and ebony.
16 " 'Aram[b][j] did business with you because of your many products; they exchanged turquoise,[k] purple
fabric, embroidered work, fine linen, coral and rubies for your merchandise.
17 " 'Judah and Israel traded with you; they exchanged wheat from Minnith[l] and confections,[c] honey,
olive oil and balm for your wares.
18 " 'Damascus[m] did business with you because of your many products and great wealth of goods.
They offered wine from Helbon, wool from Zahar 19 and casks of wine from Izal in exchange for your
wares: wrought iron, cassia and calamus.
20 " 'Dedan traded in saddle blankets with you.
21 " 'Arabia and all the princes of Kedar[n] were your customers; they did business with you in lambs,
rams and goats.
22 " 'The merchants of Sheba[o] and Raamah traded with you; for your merchandise they exchanged
the finest of all kinds of spices[p] and precious stones, and gold.
23 " 'Harran,[q] Kanneh and Eden[r] and merchants of Sheba, Ashur and Kilmad traded with you. 24 In
your marketplace they traded with you beautiful garments, blue fabric, embroidered work and multicolored rugs with cords twisted and tightly knotted.

25 " 'The ships of Tarshish[s] serve
as carriers for your wares.
You are filled with heavy cargo
as you sail the sea.
26 Your oarsmen take you
out to the high seas.
But the east wind[t] will break you to pieces
far out at sea.
27 Your wealth,[u] merchandise and wares,
your mariners, sailors and shipwrights,
your merchants and all your soldiers,
and everyone else on board
will sink into the heart of the sea
on the day of your shipwreck.
28 The shorelands will quake[v]
when your sailors cry out.
29 All who handle the oars
will abandon their ships;
the mariners and all the sailors
will stand on the shore.
30 They will raise their voice
and cry bitterly over you;

27:15 [g] Ge 10:7 [h] Jer 25:22 [i] 1Ki 10:22; Rev 18:12
27:16 [j] Jdg 10:6; Isa 7:1-8 [k] Eze 28:13
27:17 [l] Jdg 11:33
27:18 [m] Ge 14:15; Eze 47:16-18
27:21 [n] Ge 25:13; Isa 60:7
27:22 [o] Ge 10:7,28; 1Ki 10:1-2; Isa 60:6 [p] Ge 43:11
27:23 [q] 2Ki 19:12 [r] Isa 37:12
27:25 [s] Isa 2:16 *fn*
27:26 [t] Ps 48:7; Jer 18:17
27:27 [u] Pr 11:4
27:28 [v] Eze 26:15

[a] *15* Septuagint; Hebrew *Dedan* [b] *16* Most Hebrew manuscripts; some Hebrew manuscripts and Syriac *Edom* [c] *17* The meaning of the Hebrew for this word is uncertain.

27:15 Rhodes. An eastern Mediterranean island; a gateway to the Aegean islands.
27:16 Aram. Modern-day Syria. Since Damascus, the capital of Aram, is mentioned in v. 18, perhaps Edom is meant here (see NIV text note).
27:18 Damascus. Capital of Aram.
27:19 Izal. Area between Harran and the Tigris River. **cassia.** Like the cinnamon tree; it is in a list of aromatic plants in Exod 30:24. **calamus.** An aromatic reed.
27:20–22 Dedan ... Arabia ... Kedar ... Sheba ... Raamah. Regions in Arabia (see note on Gen 10:7).
27:23 Harran, Kanneh. In northern Mesopotamia (modern-day Iraq).
27:25b–28 Because of its great prestige through trade, the ship Tyre is "filled with heavy cargo" (v. 25). But the ship and all its crew will sink—not because of the heavy cargo but because of "the east wind" (v. 26). From ship to shore their cries for help will be heard (v. 28). The imagery of the shipwreck speaks of the disaster that Nebuchadnezzar, coming from the east (17:10; 19:12; Jonah 4:8), will bring upon Tyre.
27:29–36 These verses develop 26:17–18 (see note there) and describe mourning the sunken ship. As a mourner, Ezekiel prophetically creates this lament (v. 2). He envisions mourners arriving for Tyre's funeral and singing the accompanying lament song. The lament song has notes of fear-based grief as funeral participants anticipate their own end (v. 35; cf. 26:18). But the "merchants among the nations" (v. 36), those vying for business alongside Tyre, gloat over the city's death.

27:30 [w]2Sa 1:2 [x]Jer 6:26 [y]Rev 18:18-19
27:31 [z]Isa 16:9 [a]Isa 22:12; Eze 7:18
27:32 [b]Eze 26:17
27:33 [c]ver 12; Eze 28:4-5
27:34 [d]Zec 9:4
27:35 [e]Eze 26:15
27:36 [f]Jer 18:16; 19:8; 49:17; 50:13; Zep 2:15 [g]Ps 37:10,36; Eze 26:21
28:2 [h]Isa 14:13 [i]Ps 9:20; 82:6-7; Isa 31:3; 2Th 2:4
28:3 [j]Da 1:20; 5:11-12
28:4 [k]Zec 9:3
28:5 [l]Job 31:25; Ps 52:7; 62:10; Hos 12:8; 13:6

they will sprinkle dust[w] on their heads
    and roll[x] in ashes.[y]
31 They will shave their heads because of you
    and will put on sackcloth.
They will weep[z] over you with anguish of soul
    and with bitter mourning.[a]
32 As they wail and mourn over you,
    they will take up a lament[b] concerning you:
"Who was ever silenced like Tyre,
    surrounded by the sea?"
33 When your merchandise went out on the seas,
    you satisfied many nations;
with your great wealth[c] and your wares
    you enriched the kings of the earth.
34 Now you are shattered by the sea
    in the depths of the waters;
your wares and all your company
    have gone down with you.[d]
35 All who live in the coastlands[e]
    are appalled at you;
their kings shudder with horror
    and their faces are distorted with fear.
36 The merchants among the nations scoff at you;
    you have come to a horrible end
    and will be no more.[g]' "

A Prophecy Against the King of Tyre

28 The word of the LORD came to me: 2 "Son of man, say to the ruler of Tyre, 'This is what the Sovereign LORD says:

" 'In the pride of your heart
    you say, "I am a god;
I sit on the throne[h] of a god
    in the heart of the seas."
But you are a mere mortal and not a god,
    though you think you are as wise as a god.[i]
3 Are you wiser than Daniel[a]?[j]
    Is no secret hidden from you?
4 By your wisdom and understanding
    you have gained wealth for yourself
and amassed gold and silver
    in your treasuries.[k]
5 By your great skill in trading
    you have increased your wealth,
and because of your wealth
    your heart has grown proud.[l]

[a] 3 Or *Danel*, a man of renown in ancient literature

28:1–19 *Lament Over Tyre's King.* This section concerns Tyre's arrogant king; it uses images mainly from Gen 1–3 (creation and Eden), as well as the mountain of God image (the location of God's dwelling), to expose the arrogance of the king of Tyre (Ittobaal III).

28:2 I am a god. The king's prideful heart frames this literary section (vv. 2,5). The elevation of his pride is comparable to deity-like claims about himself, noted by the repetition of the term "god" (four times in v. 2).

28:3 Are you wiser than Daniel? See note on 14:14. This rhetorical question anticipates no answer. It exposes the king's pride. The question and indictment that follow, therefore, acknowledge the king's wisdom, natural leadership abilities, and their benefit to Tyre (vv. 4–5)—but in a tongue-in-cheek fashion.

6 " 'Therefore this is what the Sovereign LORD says:

" 'Because you think you are wise,
as wise as a god,
7 I am going to bring foreigners against you,
the most ruthless of nations;[m]
they will draw their swords against your beauty and wisdom
and pierce your shining splendor.
8 They will bring you down to the pit,[n]
and you will die a violent death
in the heart of the seas.[o]
9 Will you then say, "I am a god,"
in the presence of those who kill you?
You will be but a mortal, not a god,
in the hands of those who slay you.
10 You will die the death of the uncircumcised[p]
at the hands of foreigners.

I have spoken, declares the Sovereign LORD.' "

11 The word of the LORD came to me: 12 "Son of man, take up a lament[q] concerning the king of Tyre
and say to him: 'This is what the Sovereign LORD says:

" 'You were the seal of perfection,
full of wisdom and perfect in beauty.[r]
13 You were in Eden,[s]
the garden of God;[t]
every precious stone adorned you:
carnelian, chrysolite and emerald,
topaz, onyx and jasper,
lapis lazuli, turquoise[u] and beryl.[a]
Your settings and mountings[b] were made of gold;
on the day you were created they were prepared.
14 You were anointed[v] as a guardian cherub,[w]
for so I ordained you.
You were on the holy mount of God;
you walked among the fiery stones.
15 You were blameless in your ways
from the day you were created
till wickedness was found in you.

28:7 [m] Eze 30:11; 31:12; 32:12; Hab 1:6
28:8 [n] Eze 32:30 [o] Eze 27:27
28:10 [p] Eze 31:18; 32:19,24
28:12 [q] Eze 19:1 [r] Eze 27:2-4
28:13 [s] Ge 2:8 [t] Eze 31:8-9 [u] Eze 27:16
28:14 [v] Ex 30:26; 40:9 [w] Ex 25:17-20

a 13 The precise identification of some of these precious stones is uncertain. *b 13* The meaning of the Hebrew for this phrase is uncertain.

28:6–10 The consequences of pride and wrong self-perceptions.
28:7 foreigners … the most ruthless of nations. The Babylonians, whom God employs as his agents of destruction (cf. 30:11; 31:12; 32:12). They will kill the king (cf. 26:19–21).
28:10 uncircumcised. Those not part of God's covenantal people. Used here in the sense of "barbarian."
28:11–19 The final word to the king of Tyre. Although this passage describes his pride and fall, the imagery of creation causes some to understand these verses as a reference to Satan's pride, fall, and curse (Gen 3:1–15; cf. Isa 14:12–15). The king of Tyre is compared to a second Adam, a created being (vv. 13,15), and also to a cherub (v. 14) dwelling in the garden (v. 13) and on the mountain of God (v. 14). A proud heart causes his downfall (v. 17). Ezekiel adapts the Genesis passage for use in this lament because it fits the general characteristic of the lament genre, which magnifies the life of the deceased and then describes the magnitude of the loss.
28:12 take up a lament. See also 19:1; 27:2. **seal of perfection.** Mark of authority and authenticity (Jer 22:24; Hag 2:23).
28:13 You were in Eden. A created, Adam-like figure placed in God's Eden sanctuary. The king of Tyre owes his entire existence to God as creator and sovereign over all.
28:14 as a guardian cherub. God's ordained purpose for the king is likened to cherubim guarding the way to the divine presence in the garden (Gen 3:24) and God's dwelling "on the holy mount of God" (Exod 19:16–23). God's purpose for his creation was to serve the Creator. Both Adam and the king of Tyre failed.
28:15 You were blameless. An allusion to the pre-fall conditions of Gen 1–2; the king of Tyre's character before wealth and arrogance marked him.

28:16 [x] Hab 2:17 [y] Ge 3:24
28:17 [z] Eze 31:10
28:18 [a] Mal 4:3
28:19 [b] Jer 51:64; Eze 26:21; 27:36
28:21 [c] Eze 6:2 [d] Ge 10:15; Jer 25:22
28:22 [e] Eze 39:13 [f] Eze 30:19
28:23 [g] Eze 38:22
28:24 [h] Nu 33:55; Jos 23:13; Eze 2:6
28:25 [i] Ps 106:47; Jer 32:37

16 Through your widespread trade
you were filled with violence,[x]
and you sinned.
So I drove you in disgrace from the mount of God,
and I expelled you, guardian cherub,[y]
from among the fiery stones.
17 Your heart became proud[z]
on account of your beauty,
and you corrupted your wisdom
because of your splendor.
So I threw you to the earth;
I made a spectacle of you before kings.
18 By your many sins and dishonest trade
you have desecrated your sanctuaries.
So I made a fire come out from you,
and it consumed you,
and I reduced you to ashes[a] on the ground
in the sight of all who were watching.
19 All the nations who knew you
are appalled at you;
you have come to a horrible end
and will be no more.[b]' "

A Prophecy Against Sidon

20 The word of the LORD came to me: 21 "Son of man, set your face against[c] Sidon;[d] prophesy against
her 22 and say: 'This is what the Sovereign LORD says:

" 'I am against you, Sidon,
and among you I will display my glory.[e]
You will know that I am the LORD,
when I inflict punishment[f] on you
and within you am proved to be holy.
23 I will send a plague upon you
and make blood flow in your streets.
The slain will fall within you,
with the sword against you on every side.
Then you will know that I am the LORD.[g]

24 " 'No longer will the people of Israel have malicious neighbors who are painful briers and sharp
thorns.[h] Then they will know that I am the Sovereign LORD.
25 " 'This is what the Sovereign LORD says: When I gather[i] the people of Israel from the nations where

28:16 you sinned. The king of Tyre is a fallen, Adam-like figure. This attributes his fall to dishonest trade that led to pride and arrogance. **28:17 I threw you to the earth.** The consequence of his sin: being driven away to experience death. As with the expulsion of Adam from the garden (cf. Gen 3:1 – 19), pride came before the king of Tyre's fall. The judgment on Tyre represents more than just God's wrath on Tyre for its treatment of Jerusalem when it fell. The figurative and exaggerated language about Tyre's wealth and pride suggests the possibility of something more. Moreover, Tyre's judgment is lengthy, second only to the subsequent prophecy against Egypt (chs. 29 – 32). This lengthy judgment represents the culmination of God's judgment on the Canaanites. The coastal Canaanite city of Tyre personifies Canaan's pride and arrogance, a negative influence on God's people.

28:19 horrible end ... be no more. The fall of this economic superpower shocks observers.

28:20 – 24 *Prophecy Against Sidon.* God will also judge Sidon, another important Phoenician city, along with Tyre. This passage does not specify why God is against Sidon other than calling Sidon one of Israel's "malicious neighbors" (v. 24). But it does specify what happens when God confronts Sidon and all of Israel's neighbors: God's glory and holiness are displayed (vv. 22 – 23), God gets name recognition (vv. 22 – 24), and God comforts Israel (v. 24; cf. Num 33:55; Josh 23:13). Only after Israel receives comfort can mourning end and Israel's restoration process begin. **28:25 – 26** *Israel's Restoration.* This restoration, placed unexpectedly after prophecies against the nations, points forward to this theme in chs. 33 – 48. This restoration includes holiness, safety in the land, and God's name recognition. Once God destroys Israel's enemies, God's covenantal

they have been scattered,[j] I will be proved holy[k] through them in the sight of the nations. Then they will
live in their own land, which I gave to my servant Jacob.[l] 26They will live there in safety[m] and will build
houses and plant vineyards; they will live in safety when I inflict punishment on all their neighbors
who maligned them. Then they will know that I am the LORD their God.[n]' "

A Prophecy Against Egypt

Judgment on Pharaoh

29 In the tenth year, in the tenth month on the twelfth day, the word of the LORD came to me:[o]
2"Son of man, set your face against Pharaoh king of Egypt[p] and prophesy against him and
against all Egypt.[q] 3Speak to him and say: 'This is what the Sovereign LORD says:

" 'I am against you, Pharaoh[r] king of Egypt,
you great monster[s] lying among your streams.
You say, "The Nile belongs to me;
I made it for myself."
4But I will put hooks[t] in your jaws
and make the fish of your streams stick to your scales.
I will pull you out from among your streams,
with all the fish sticking to your scales.[u]
5I will leave you in the desert,
you and all the fish of your streams.
You will fall on the open field
and not be gathered or picked up.
I will give you as food
to the beasts of the earth and the birds of the sky.[v]

6Then all who live in Egypt will know that I am the LORD.

" 'You have been a staff of reed[w] for the people of Israel. 7When they grasped you with their hands,
you splintered[x] and you tore open their shoulders; when they leaned on you, you broke and their backs
were wrenched.[a][y]

8" 'Therefore this is what the Sovereign LORD says: I will bring a sword against you and kill both man
and beast.[z] 9Egypt will become a desolate wasteland. Then they will know that I am the LORD.

" 'Because you said, "The Nile is mine; I made it,[a]" 10therefore I am against you and against your
streams, and I will make the land of Egypt a ruin and a desolate waste from Migdol to Aswan,[b] as far

28:25 [j]Isa 11:12 [k]Eze 20:41 [l]Jer 23:8; Eze 11:17; 34:27; 37:25
28:26 [m]Jer 23:6 [n]Isa 65:21; Jer 32:15; Eze 38:8; Am 9:14-15
29:1 [o]ver 17; Eze 26:1
29:2 [p]Jer 25:19 [q]Isa 19:1-17; Jer 46:2; Eze 30:1-26; 31:1-18; 32:1-32
29:3 [r]Jer 44:30 [s]Ps 74:13; Isa 27:1; Eze 32:2
29:4 [t]2Ki 19:28 [u]Eze 38:4
29:5 [v]Jer 7:33; 34:20; Eze 32:4-6; 39:4
29:6 [w]2Ki 18:21; Isa 36:6
29:7 [x]Isa 36:6 [y]Eze 17:15-17
29:8 [z]Eze 14:17; 32:11-13
29:9 [a]Eze 30:7-8,13-19
29:10 [b]Eze 30:6

[a] 7 Syriac (see also Septuagint and Vulgate); Hebrew *and you caused their backs to stand*

promises can advance. People will observe that God is manifesting his holiness because his people will be gathered, not scattered. Israel will be safe and secure in the promised land. Above all, God's people will recognize and acknowledge afresh his loyalties as their God (v. 26).

29:1—32:32 *Prophecy Against Egypt.* The prophecy against Egypt is the largest of the prophecies against the nations in the book. The date formula (ranging from 587 to 571 BC) separates the prophecy into seven literary units (with the exception of 30:1, which has no date). The prophecy (actually seven small prophecies) begins with Pharaoh's fall (ch. 29) and concludes with his burial in "the pit" (32:18), the final resting place reserved for God's enemies (ch. 32). During some of these years, the Egyptian king encouraged Zedekiah to rebel against Nebuchadnezzar (17:15; Jer 37:5–8; 42:1—43:13). Egypt was Israel's early oppressor and Babylon's continual enemy. As a military superpower Egypt flexed its muscles to control Canaan, as did Babylon. Israel was landlocked between these two powers fighting for international control on their soil. This is why Israel repeatedly appealed to Egypt for either military or economic help against the Babylonians, which displeased God (e.g., see 17:7; 19:4 and notes; 1 Kgs 3:1; 2 Kgs 18:21; Isa 30:1–3). Egypt's military power also explains its deep-seated national pride.

29:1–16 *Egypt a Doomed Monster.* The first of seven prophecies against Egypt addresses why God is against Egypt and its king, Hophra (589–570 BC). As with Tyre's king (28:1–10), God confronts Egypt's elevated pride.

29:3 you great monster. The metaphor pictures Pharaoh as a large fish or sea animal, possibly a crocodile (cf. 32:2), dwelling in the Nile delta and its canals (Isa 7:18; 19:6; 37:25). God will go "fishing" in the Nile and "catch a big one" (v. 4). Pharaoh will be food for land and air creatures (v. 5). **You say, "The Nile belongs to me."** The rationale for the fishing trip is the king's arrogant boasting as creator and owner of the Nile (v. 9).

29:6 all who live in Egypt will know that I am the LORD. The result of God's "fishing trip" (see v. 3 and note). **staff of reed.** Hophra's limp, useless support when Jerusalem was under siege (Jer 37:5–11; cf. 2 Kgs 18:21–22).

29:10 from Migdol to Aswan. Suggests geographic totality of the land's desolation (from north to south; see 30:6), similar to "from Dan to Beersheba" to describe all Israel (see Judg 20:1; 1 Sam 3:20 and notes).

29:11 [c]Eze 32:13
29:12 [d]Jer 46:19; Eze 30:7,23,26
29:14 [e]Eze 30:14 [f]Eze 17:14
29:15 [g]Zec 10:11
29:16 [h]Isa 36:4,6 [i]Isa 30:2; Hos 8:13
29:17 [j]Eze 24:1
29:18 [k]Jer 27:6; Eze 26:7-8 [l]Jer 48:37
29:19 [m]Jer 43:10-13; Eze 30:4,10,24-25
29:20 [n]Isa 10:6-7; 45:1; Jer 25:9
29:21 [o]Ps 132:17 [p]Eze 33:22 [q]Eze 24:27
30:2 [r]Isa 13:6
30:3 [s]Eze 7:7; Joel 2:1, 11; Ob 15 [t]ver 18; Eze 7:12,19

as the border of Cush.[a] 11 The foot of neither man nor beast will pass through it; no one will live there
for forty years.[c] 12 I will make the land of Egypt desolate among devastated lands, and her cities will
lie desolate forty years among ruined cities. And I will disperse the Egyptians among the nations and
scatter them through the countries.[d]

13 "'Yet this is what the Sovereign LORD says: At the end of forty years I will gather the Egyptians
from the nations where they were scattered. 14 I will bring them back from captivity and return them
to Upper Egypt,[e] the land of their ancestry. There they will be a lowly[f] kingdom. 15 It will be the lowliest
of kingdoms and will never again exalt itself above the other nations.[g] I will make it so weak that it
will never again rule over the nations. 16 Egypt will no longer be a source of confidence[h] for the people
of Israel but will be a reminder of their sin in turning to her for help. Then they will know that I am
the Sovereign LORD.[i]'"

Nebuchadnezzar's Reward

17 In the twenty-seventh year, in the first month on the first day, the word of the LORD came to me:[j]
18 "Son of man, Nebuchadnezzar[k] king of Babylon drove his army in a hard campaign against Tyre;
every head was rubbed bare[l] and every shoulder made raw. Yet he and his army got no reward from
the campaign he led against Tyre. 19 Therefore this is what the Sovereign LORD says: I am going to give
Egypt to Nebuchadnezzar king of Babylon, and he will carry off its wealth. He will loot and plunder the
land as pay for his army.[m] 20 I have given him Egypt as a reward for his efforts because he and his army
did it for me, declares the Sovereign LORD.[n]

21 "On that day I will make a horn[b][o] grow for the Israelites, and I will open your mouth[p] among
them. Then they will know that I am the LORD.[q]"

A Lament Over Egypt

30 The word of the LORD came to me: 2 "Son of man, prophesy and say: 'This is what the Sovereign LORD says:

"'Wail[r] and say,
    "Alas for that day!"
3 For the day is near,[s]
    the day of the LORD[t] is near—
a day of clouds,
    a time of doom for the nations.
4 A sword will come against Egypt,
    and anguish will come upon Cush.[c]

[a] *10* That is, the upper Nile region [b] *21* *Horn* here symbolizes strength. [c] *4* That is, the upper Nile region; also in verses 5 and 9

29:11,12 forty years. The duration of Egypt's desolation and exile is reminiscent of Israel's wandering in the wilderness; it symbolizes a long period of hardship to counter rebellion (cf. 4:6 and note).
29:13–15 God will return the Egyptians to Upper Egypt (southern Egypt; 30:14; Isa 11:11), where Egypt will be a weak nation unable to rule again, an act of humiliation more than an act of mercy. This return occurs under Cyrus in 539 BC.
29:16 Purposes for restoring Egypt: humiliating Egypt, warning others, and recognizing God's sovereign hand over the nations.
29:17–21 *Egypt a Payment to Nebuchadnezzar.* This is the second of seven prophecies against Egypt but the latest prophecy in the book, dated to spring 571 BC.
29:17 twenty-seventh year ... first month ... first day. Apr. 26, 571 BC, during the 27th year of exile.
29:18 hard campaign. The Babylonians besieged Tyre for 13 years (586–573 BC). **got no reward.** Gained little plunder because the siege was so long (cf. 26:12).
29:19–20 as pay ... as a reward. God will pay the Babylonian army at Egypt's expense. Nebuchadnezzar attacks Egypt in 568 BC (Jer 43–44).
29:21 On that day. Suggests a general but unspecified time associated with the punishment of Egypt by Babylon (see vv. 19–20 and note). **horn.** See NIV text note. God will restore his people. **I will open your mouth among them.** Even after 571 BC (when Ezekiel gives this prophecy) and after 568 Ezekiel will have a word for Israel, suggesting the ongoing nature of Ezekiel's ministry to the exiles.
30:1–19 *The Day of the Lord for Egypt and Her Allies.* This is the third of seven prophecies against Egypt. Through imagery of the day of the Lord, a day when God breaks through to deal with his enemies (see note on Amos 2:16), this prophecy describes the shock waves in the land when the Babylonians confront this military superpower.
30:2 Wail. This is a time for lamenting, because God will negatively intervene in Egypt's affairs.
30:3 day is near. Announces the day of the Lord (cf. 7:10–27; Isa 2:12–17; Joel 2:1–11; Amos 5:18–20; Zeph 1:14–18). **day of clouds.** Disaster will roll in (cf. Joel 2:2; Zeph 1:15).
30:4 sword. Symbolizes war, which will sweep across the country, slaying Egypt and its neighbors.

When the slain fall in Egypt,
her wealth will be carried away
and her foundations torn down.[u]

5 Cush and Libya,[v] Lydia and all Arabia, Kub and the people[w] of the covenant land will fall by the sword
along with Egypt.

6 "'This is what the LORD says:

"'The allies of Egypt will fall
and her proud strength will fail.
From Migdol to Aswan[x]
they will fall by the sword within her,
declares the Sovereign LORD.

7 "'They will be desolate
among desolate lands,
and their cities will lie
among ruined cities.[y]
8 Then they will know that I am the LORD,
when I set fire to Egypt
and all her helpers are crushed.

9 "'On that day messengers will go out from me in ships to frighten Cush[z] out of her complacency.
Anguish[a] will take hold of them on the day of Egypt's doom, for it is sure to come.[b]

10 "'This is what the Sovereign LORD says:

"'I will put an end to the hordes of Egypt
by the hand of Nebuchadnezzar king of Babylon.[c]
11 He and his army—the most ruthless of nations[d]—
will be brought in to destroy the land.
They will draw their swords against Egypt
and fill the land with the slain.
12 I will dry up[e] the waters of the Nile[f]
and sell the land to an evil nation;
by the hand of foreigners
I will lay waste the land and everything in it.

I the LORD have spoken.

13 "'This is what the Sovereign LORD says:

"'I will destroy the idols[g]
and put an end to the images in Memphis.[h]
No longer will there be a prince in Egypt,[i]
and I will spread fear throughout the land.
14 I will lay[j] waste Upper Egypt,
set fire to Zoan[k]
and inflict punishment on Thebes.[l]
15 I will pour out my wrath on Pelusium,
the stronghold of Egypt,
and wipe out the hordes of Thebes.

30:4 [u] Eze 29:19
30:5 [v] Eze 27:10 [w] Jer 25:20
30:6 [x] Eze 29:10
30:7 [y] Eze 29:12
30:9 [z] Isa 18:1-2 [a] Isa 23:5 [b] Eze 32:9-10
30:10 [c] Eze 29:19
30:11 [d] Eze 28:7
30:12 [e] Isa 19:6 [f] Eze 29:9
30:13 [g] Jer 43:12 [h] Isa 19:13 [i] Zec 10:11
30:14 [j] Eze 29:14 [k] Ps 78:12,43 [l] Jer 46:25

30:5 people of the covenant land. Jewish mercenaries apparently living in Egypt (Jer 24:8; 44).

30:6 allies of Egypt will fall. Reflects the effects of Egyptian military power. No one in association with Egypt is safe from the sword and fire, not even those far from Egypt. God's far-reaching judgment mirrors Egypt's far-reaching military power. **From Migdol to Aswan.** See note on 29:10.

30:11 most ruthless of nations. Babylonia (see note on 28:7; cf. Hab 1:6).

30:13–19 God emphasizes his initiative in Egypt's fall by repeatedly saying, "I will" (vv. 13,14,15,16,19). The list of geographic locations unpacks the scope of the devastation and illustrates the meaning of the day of the Lord for Egypt. Devastation will be total: from Egypt's largest city (Memphis, v. 13) to its strategically located fortress cities (Pelusium and Tahpanhes, vv. 15,18), and God will get the glory he deserves (v. 19).

The monumental entrance to the Luxor temple at Thebes. This temple, built by Pharaohs Amenhotep III (1387–1350 BC) and Rameses II (1279–1212 BC), was later besieged by Nebuchadnezzar.

30:17 [m] Ge 41:45
30:18 [n] Lev 26:13 [o] ver 3
30:20 [p] Eze 26:1; 29:17; 31:1
30:21 [q] Jer 48:25 [r] Jer 30:13; 46:11
30:22 [s] Jer 46:25 [t] Ps 37:17
30:23 [u] Eze 29:12
30:24 [v] Zec 10:6,12 [w] Eze 21:14; Zep 2:12

16 I will set fire to Egypt;
    Pelusium will writhe in agony.
Thebes will be taken by storm;
    Memphis will be in constant distress.
17 The young men of Heliopolis[m] and Bubastis
    will fall by the sword,
    and the cities themselves will go into captivity.
18 Dark will be the day at Tahpanhes
    when I break the yoke of Egypt;[n]
    there her proud strength will come to an end.
She will be covered with clouds,
    and her villages will go into captivity.[o]
19 So I will inflict punishment on Egypt,
    and they will know that I am the LORD.' "

Pharaoh's Arms Are Broken

20 In the eleventh year, in the first month on the seventh day, the word of the LORD came to me:[p]
21 "Son of man, I have broken the arm[q] of Pharaoh king of Egypt. It has not been bound up to be
healed[r] or put in a splint so that it may become strong enough to hold a sword. 22 Therefore this is
what the Sovereign LORD says: I am against Pharaoh king of Egypt.[s] I will break both his arms, the
good arm as well as the broken one, and make the sword fall from his hand.[t] 23 I will disperse the
Egyptians among the nations and scatter them through the countries.[u] 24 I will strengthen[v] the arms
of the king of Babylon and put my sword[w] in his hand, but I will break the arms of Pharaoh, and
he will groan before him like a mortally wounded man. 25 I will strengthen the arms of the king of
Babylon, but the arms of Pharaoh will fall limp. Then they will know that I am the LORD, when I put

30:20–26 *Pharaoh's Arms Broken.* This is the fourth of seven prophecies against Egypt.
30:20 eleventh year ... first month ... seventh day. Apr. 29, 587 BC.
30:21 arm. Symbolizes power. Pharaoh Hophra offered help to Judah when Nebuchadnezzar was besieging Jerusalem (Jer 37:5–11), but Hophra gave only temporary relief (588 BC) to Judah (Jer 37:17; 38:2). The Babylonian resistance weakened Egypt (Pharaoh's arm was "broken"). That was the beginning of the end for Egypt, the first "break."
30:22 God will break Pharaoh's "good arm" in 568 BC (cf. 29:12).
30:24 God will transfer power from Egypt to Babylon (cf. ch. 21).

my sword into the hand of the king of Babylon and he brandishes it against Egypt. 26 I will disperse
the Egyptians among the nations and scatter them through the countries. Then they will know that
I am the LORD.[x]"

Pharaoh as a Felled Cedar of Lebanon

31 In the eleven year,[y] in the third month on the first day, the word of the LORD came to me:[z]
2 "Son of man, say to Pharaoh king of Egypt and to his hordes:

"'Who can be compared with you in majesty?
3 Consider Assyria, once a cedar in Lebanon,
with beautiful branches overshadowing the forest;
it towered on high,
its top above the thick foliage.[a]
4 The waters nourished it,
deep springs made it grow tall;
their streams flowed
all around its base
and sent their channels
to all the trees of the field.
5 So it towered higher
than all the trees of the field;
its boughs increased
and its branches grew long,
spreading because of abundant waters.[b]
6 All the birds of the sky
nested in its boughs,
all the animals of the wild
gave birth under its branches;
all the great nations
lived in its shade.[c]
7 It was majestic in beauty,
with its spreading boughs,
for its roots went down
to abundant waters.
8 The cedars[d] in the garden of God
could not rival it,
nor could the junipers
equal its boughs,
nor could the plane trees
compare with its branches—
no tree in the garden of God
could match its beauty.[e]
9 I made it beautiful
with abundant branches,
the envy of all the trees of Eden[f]
in the garden of God.[g]

30:26 [x] Eze 29:12
31:1 [y] Jer 52:5 [z] Eze 30:20
31:3 [a] Isa 10:34
31:5 [b] Eze 17:5
31:6 [c] Eze 17:23; Mt 13:32
31:8 [d] Ps 80:10 [e] Ge 2:8-9
31:9 [f] Ge 2:8 [g] Ge 13:10; Eze 28:13

31:1–18 *Pharaoh a Fallen Tree.* This is the fifth of seven prophecies against Egypt, dated to early summer 587 BC. Rhetorical questions to Pharaoh frame the passage (vv. 2b,18). An allegory provides the answer: Assyria was once a great cedar in Lebanon (vv. 3,10,17), but it was cut down because it was proud (vv. 10–12). It will be buried and mourned in "the realm of the dead" (v. 17). For trees symbolizing nations, see chs. 17; 19; Dan 4.

31:1 eleventh year … third month … first day. June 21, 587 BC.

31:3 Consider Assyria. Compares Egypt to Assyria, a beautiful cedar, another allegory (see ch. 17). As the cedar was well-known for its glory and majesty in the forest of Lebanon (Isa 35:2), so too Assyria's glory and majesty was well-known among the nations. But Assyria was proud, forgetting that God was responsible for her creation and beauty (vv. 8–9; cf. Isa 10:15–19).

31:10 [h]Isa 14:13-14; Eze 28:17
31:11 [i]Da 5:20
31:12 [j]Eze 28:7 [k]Eze 32:5; 35:8 [l]Eze 32:11-12; Da 4:14
31:13 [m]Isa 18:6; Eze 29:5; 32:4
31:14 [n]Ps 82:7 [o]Ps 63:9; Eze 26:20; 32:24
31:16 [p]Eze 26:15 [q]Isa 14:8 [r]Eze 14:22; 32:31 [s]Isa 14:15; Eze 32:18
31:17 [t]Ps 9:17
31:18 [u]Jer 9:26; Eze 32:19,21
32:1 [v]Eze 31:1; 33:21
32:2 [w]Eze 19:1; 27:2 [x]Eze 19:3,6; Na 2:11-13 [y]Eze 29:3; 34:18
32:3 [z]Eze 12:13

10“ ‘Therefore this is what the Sovereign LORD says: Because the great cedar towered over the thick
foliage, and because it was proud[h] of its height, 11I gave it into the hands of the ruler of the nations, for
him to deal with according to its wickedness. I cast it aside,[i] 12and the most ruthless of foreign nations[j]
cut it down and left it. Its boughs fell on the mountains and in all the valleys;[k] its branches lay broken
in all the ravines of the land. All the nations of the earth came out from under its shade and left it.[l] 13All
the birds settled on the fallen tree, and all the wild animals lived among its branches.[m] 14Therefore no
other trees by the waters are ever to tower proudly on high, lifting their tops above the thick foliage.
No other trees so well-watered are ever to reach such a height; they are all destined for death,[n] for the
earth below, among mortals who go down to the realm of the dead.[o]

15“ ‘This is what the Sovereign LORD says: On the day it was brought down to the realm of the dead
I covered the deep springs with mourning for it; I held back its streams, and its abundant waters were
restrained. Because of it I clothed Lebanon with gloom, and all the trees of the field withered away. 16I
made the nations tremble[p] at the sound of its fall when I brought it down to the realm of the dead to
be with those who go down to the pit. Then all the trees[q] of Eden, the choicest and best of Lebanon,
the well-watered trees, were consoled[r] in the earth below.[s] 17They too, like the great cedar, had gone
down to the realm of the dead, to those killed by the sword,[t] along with the armed men who lived in
its shade among the nations.

18“ ‘Which of the trees of Eden can be compared with you in splendor and majesty? Yet you, too, will
be brought down with the trees of Eden to the earth below; you will lie among the uncircumcised,[u]
with those killed by the sword.

“ ‘This is Pharaoh and all his hordes, declares the Sovereign LORD.’ ”

A Lament Over Pharaoh

32 In the twelfth year, in the twelfth month on the first day, the word of the LORD came to me:[v]
2“Son of man, take up a lament[w] concerning Pharaoh king of Egypt and say to him:

“ ‘You are like a lion[x] among the nations;
  you are like a monster in the seas
thrashing about in your streams,
  churning the water with your feet
  and muddying the streams.[y]

3“ ‘This is what the Sovereign LORD says:

“ ‘With a great throng of people
  I will cast my net over you,
  and they will haul you up in my net.[z]
4I will throw you on the land
  and hurl you on the open field.

31:10 because it was proud of its height. Assyria's pride caused God to hand that "great cedar" over to the Babylonians, "the most ruthless of foreign nations" (v. 12).
31:12 cut it down. Refers to the defeat of Assyria by Babylon in 612–605 BC.
31:15 the realm of the dead. The OT likeness of hell (also vv. 14,16), a destiny of death. As Assyria was brought down (see v. 10 and note), so too will Egypt be "brought down" (v. 18).
31:16 the pit. The realm of the dead (see note on v. 15). **all the trees of Eden ... were consoled.** Because the mightiest of trees had joined them in the realm of the dead.
31:18 Which of the trees of Eden can be compared with you ...? A repeated rhetorical question that frames the passage (cf. v. 2). **you, too, will be brought down.** As Egypt's "splendor and majesty" (her arrogant pride) are compared to Assyria's (and to any of Eden's trees), so too Egypt's fate will be like Assyria's. **uncircumcised.** Those outside God's community.
32:1–16 *Lament Over Pharaoh.* The sixth of seven prophecies against Egypt, dated to spring 585 BC. This highlights Ezekiel's mourning role once again (see note on 3:1,3) with the command to write a lament for Pharaoh king of Egypt (v. 2; cf. 28:11). The sea monster metaphor that describes Pharaoh and his end in 29:1–6 is developed more fully here. God will "catch" the sea monster with a net and bring it to its death on land (vv. 3–4). Pharaoh's death will cause national mourning (v. 9); the sword of Babylon will devastate Egypt (v. 10).
32:1 twelfth year ... twelfth month ... first day. Mar. 3, 585 BC.
32:2 lion ... monster. Two images for Pharaoh. Only descriptions of large animals could fit Pharaoh's larger-than-life view of himself, Egypt, and its influence. The size of these animals is the point. The description here favors the sea-dwelling monster, perhaps the crocodile (29:3; Job 41).
32:3 cast my net. The "crocodile," or monster (see note on v. 2), gets caught by God's net and is left to die on land (cf. 12:13; 17:20; 19:8).
32:4 I will throw ... and hurl you ... let all the birds ... settle on you. God's violent action against the monster (see 29:3–5).

I will let all the birds of the sky settle on you
and all the animals of the wild gorge themselves
on you.[a]
5 I will spread your flesh on the mountains
and fill the valleys[b] with your remains.
6 I will drench the land with your flowing blood[c]
all the way to the mountains,
and the ravines will be filled with your flesh.
7 When I snuff you out, I will cover the heavens
and darken their stars;
I will cover the sun with a cloud,
and the moon will not give its light.[d]
8 All the shining lights in the heavens
I will darken over you;
I will bring darkness over your land,
declares the Sovereign LORD.
9 I will trouble the hearts of many peoples
when I bring about your destruction among the nations,
among[a] lands you have not known.
10 I will cause many peoples to be appalled at you,
and their kings will shudder with horror because of you
when I brandish my sword before them.
On the day[e] of your downfall
each of them will tremble
every moment for his life.[f]

11 " 'For this is what the Sovereign LORD says:
" 'The sword of the king of Babylon[g]
will come against you.
12 I will cause your hordes to fall
by the swords of mighty men —
the most ruthless of all nations.[h]
They will shatter the pride of Egypt,
and all her hordes will be overthrown.[i]
13 I will destroy all her cattle
from beside abundant waters
no longer to be stirred by the foot of man
or muddied by the hooves of cattle.[j]
14 Then I will let her waters settle
and make her streams flow like oil,
declares the Sovereign LORD.
15 When I make Egypt desolate
and strip the land of everything in it,

32:4 [a] Isa 18:6; Eze 31:12-13
32:5 [b] Eze 31:12
32:6 [c] Isa 34:3
32:7 [d] Isa 13:10; 34:4; Eze 30:3; Joel 2:2,31; 3:15; Mt 24:29; Rev 8:12
32:10 [e] Jer 46:10 [f] Eze 26:16; 27:35
32:11 [g] Jer 46:26
32:12 [h] Eze 28:7 [i] Eze 31:11-12
32:13 [j] Eze 29:8,11

[a] 9 Hebrew; Septuagint *bring you into captivity among the nations, / to*

32:6 drench the land with your flowing blood. Language describing violent death.
32:7–8 The description is cataclysmic: a blood-soaked land covered with darkness. This is the day of the Lord for Pharaoh (see 30:3,18 and note on 30:1–19; cf. Joel 2:2,10,31; Amos 5:18).
32:9 trouble the hearts. Describes how people feel about the monster's death (see note on 32:2). As with Tyre (26:16–18; 27:35; 28:19), so with Egypt. Fear prevails as onlookers are horrified by the destruction Babylon will bring to Egypt and possibly to them.
32:11–15 The sword metaphor replaces the monster metaphor (see note on 32:2). The agent of destruction is the king of Babylon (cf. 29:8–9; 30:4,11,17,20–26; 31:17–18; see also 21:3–5 and note on 21:3). The purpose of the sword is to shatter Pharaoh's pride.
32:14 streams flow like oil. Their surface undisturbed by any form of life, the result after God finishes with Egypt.
32:15 strip the land of everything. A nakedness that leaves the land free of humans and animals.

32:15 [k]Ex 7:5; 14:4,18; Ps 107:33-34; Eze 6:7
32:16 [l]2Sa 1:17; 2Ch 35:25; Eze 26:17
32:17 [m]ver 1
32:18 [n]Jer 1:10 [o]Eze 31:14,16; Mic 1:8
32:19 [p]ver 29-30; Eze 28:10; 31:18
32:20 [q]Ps 28:3
32:21 [r]Isa 14:9
32:23 [s]Isa 14:15
32:24 [t]Ge 10:22 [u]Jer 49:37 [v]Job 28:13 [w]Eze 26:20
32:26 [x]Ge 10:2; Eze 27:13
32:29 [y]Isa 34:5-15; Jer 49:7; Eze 35:15; Ob 1 [z]Eze 25:12-14
32:30 [a]Jer 25:26; Eze 38:6; 39:2 [b]Jer 25:22; Eze 28:21
32:31 [c]Eze 14:22; 31:16

when I strike down all who live there,
then they will know that I am the LORD.[k]'

16 "This is the lament[l] they will chant for her. The daughters of the nations will chant it; for Egypt
and all her hordes they will chant it, declares the Sovereign LORD."

Egypt's Descent Into the Realm of the Dead

17 In the twelfth year, on the fifteenth day of the month, the word of the LORD came to me:[m] 18 "Son
of man, wail for the hordes of Egypt and consign[n] to the earth below both her and the daughters of
mighty nations, along with those who go down to the pit.[o] 19 Say to them, 'Are you more favored than
others? Go down and be laid among the uncircumcised.'[p] 20 They will fall among those killed by the
sword. The sword is drawn; let her be dragged[q] off with all her hordes. 21 From within the realm of
the dead[r] the mighty leaders will say of Egypt and her allies, 'They have come down and they lie with
the uncircumcised, with those killed by the sword.'

22 "Assyria is there with her whole army; she is surrounded by the graves of all her slain, all who have
fallen by the sword. 23 Their graves are in the depths of the pit[s] and her army lies around her grave. All
who had spread terror in the land of the living are slain, fallen by the sword.

24 "Elam[t] is there, with all her hordes around her grave. All of them are slain, fallen by the sword.[u]
All who had spread terror in the land of the living[v] went down uncircumcised to the earth below. They
bear their shame with those who go down to the pit.[w] 25 A bed is made for her among the slain, with all
her hordes around her grave. All of them are uncircumcised, killed by the sword. Because their terror
had spread in the land of the living, they bear their shame with those who go down to the pit; they are
laid among the slain.

26 "Meshek and Tubal[x] are there, with all their hordes around their graves. All of them are uncircumcised, killed by the sword because they spread their terror in the land of the living. 27 But they do
not lie with the fallen warriors of old,[a] who went down to the realm of the dead with their weapons of
war — their swords placed under their heads and their shields[b] resting on their bones — though these
warriors also had terrorized the land of the living.

28 "You too, Pharaoh, will be broken and will lie among the uncircumcised, with those killed by the
sword.

29 "Edom[y] is there, her kings and all her princes; despite their power, they are laid with those killed
by the sword. They lie with the uncircumcised, with those who go down to the pit.[z]

30 "All the princes of the north[a] and all the Sidonians[b] are there; they went down with the slain in
disgrace despite the terror caused by their power. They lie uncircumcised with those killed by the sword
and bear their shame with those who go down to the pit.

31 "Pharaoh — he and all his army — will see them and he will be consoled[c] for all his hordes that
were killed by the sword, declares the Sovereign LORD. 32 Although I had him spread terror in the land of

[a] 27 Septuagint; Hebrew *warriors who were uncircumcised* [b] 27 Probable reading of the original Hebrew text; Masoretic Text *punishment*

32:16 daughters of the nations will chant. The end of Egypt, a military superpower, will be such that women worldwide will sing the lament song that Ezekiel writes.

32:17–32 *Egypt's Descent to the Realm of the Dead.* The last of seven prophecies against Egypt, dated between spring 586 and spring 585 BC (see note on v. 17). As with Pharaoh in vv. 1–16, Ezekiel is now commanded to wail again, but this time for "the hordes of Egypt" (v. 18). This envisions the slain armies of nations that rejected God laid to rest in the pit. The list begins with Assyria (v. 22; cf. 31:16) and ends with Egypt (v. 31).

32:17 twelfth year ... fifteenth day. The month is missing; therefore, this prophecy is dated between Apr. 13, 586, and Apr. 1, 585 BC.

32:21 within the realm of the dead. A welcoming committee awaits Egypt and her allies, assuring their arrival at the right place. This is not surprising given 26:20, which anticipated the occupancy of the pit.

32:22–30 Egypt's destiny is shared ("surrounded by the graves of all her slain," v. 22). The name of the deceased, previously deceased family members, cause of death ("killed by the sword," v. 21), and specific burial places within the pit are mentioned.

32:22 Assyria. In northern Mesopotamia along the Tigris River (modern-day Iraq).

32:24 Elam. In the plains of Susa, lowlands of southern Mesopotamia (modern-day Iran).

32:26 Meshek and Tubal. Peoples and territories in Asia Minor (27:13; 38:2).

32:29 Edom. Southernmost region of Transjordan (modern-day Jordan).

32:30 Sidonians. Sidon was a coastal Phoenician city-state (modern-day Lebanon).

32:31–32 The entire collection of prophecies against the nations (chs. 25–32) climaxes with the death, mourning, and burial of Egypt, Israel's archenemy.

the living, Pharaoh and all his hordes will be laid among the uncircumcised, with those killed by the
sword, declares the Sovereign LORD."

Renewal of Ezekiel's Call as Watchman

33 The word of the LORD came to me: 2"Son of man, speak to your people and say to them:
'When I bring the sword[d] against a land, and the people of the land choose one of their
men and make him their watchman,[e] 3and he sees the sword coming against the land and blows
the trumpet[f] to warn the people, 4then if anyone hears the trumpet but does not heed the warning[g]
and the sword comes and takes their life, their blood will be on their own head.[h] 5Since they heard
the sound of the trumpet but did not heed the warning, their blood will be on their own head. If they
had heeded the warning, they would have saved themselves. 6But if the watchman sees the sword
coming and does not blow the trumpet to warn the people and the sword comes and takes someone's
life, that person's life will be taken because of their sin, but I will hold the watchman accountable
for their blood.'[i]

7"Son of man, I have made you a watchman for the people of Israel; so hear the word I speak and
give them warning from me.[j] 8When I say to the wicked, 'You wicked person, you will surely die,'[k]
and you do not speak out to dissuade them from their ways, that wicked person will die for[a] their
sin, and I will hold you accountable for their blood.[l] 9But if you do warn the wicked person to turn
from their ways and they do not do so, they will die for their sin, though you yourself will be saved.[m]

10"Son of man, say to the Israelites, 'This is what you are saying: "Our offenses and sins weigh us
down, and we are wasting away[n] because of[b] them. How then can we live?"'[o] 11Say to them, 'As surely
as I live, declares the Sovereign LORD, I take no pleasure in the death of the wicked, but rather that they
turn from their ways and live.[p] Turn! Turn from your evil ways! Why will you die, people of Israel?'[q]

12"Therefore, son of man, say to your people, 'If someone who is righteous disobeys, that person's
former righteousness will count for nothing. And if someone who is wicked repents, that person's former wickedness will not bring condemnation. The righteous person who sins will not be allowed to
live even though they were formerly righteous.'[r] 13If I tell a righteous person that they will surely live,
but then they trust in their righteousness and do evil, none of the righteous things that person has
done will be remembered; they will die for the evil they have done.[s] 14And if I say to a wicked person,
'You will surely die,' but they then turn away from their sin and do what is just[t] and right— 15if
they give back what they took in pledge for a loan, return what they have stolen,[u] follow the decrees
that give life, and do no evil—that person will surely live; they will not die.[v] 16None of the sins that
person has committed will be remembered against them. They have done what is just and right; they
will surely live.[w]

17"Yet your people say, 'The way of the Lord is not just.' But it is their way that is not just. 18If a
righteous person turns from their righteousness and does evil, they will die for it.[x] 19And if a wicked
person turns away from their wickedness and does what is just and right, they will live by doing so.
20Yet you Israelites say, 'The way of the Lord is not just.' But I will judge each of you according to
your own ways."

[a] *8* Or *in*; also in verse 9 [b] *10* Or *away in*

33:2 [d] Jer 12:12 [e] Eze 3:11
33:3 [f] Hos 8:1
33:4 [g] 2Ch 25:16 [h] Jer 6:17; Eze 18:13; Zec 1:4; Ac 18:6
33:6 [i] Eze 3:18
33:7 [j] Jer 26:2; Eze 3:17
33:8 [k] ver 14 [l] Eze 18:4
33:9 [m] Eze 3:17-19
33:10 [n] Eze 24:23 [o] Lev 26:39; Eze 4:17
33:11 [p] Eze 18:32; 2Pe 3:9 [q] Eze 18:23
33:12 [r] 2Ch 7:14; Eze 3:20
33:13 [s] Eze 18:24; Heb 10:38; 2Pe 2:20-21
33:14 [t] Eze 18:27
33:15 [u] Ex 22:1-4; Lev 6:2-5 [v] Eze 20:11; Lk 19:8
33:16 [w] Isa 43:25; Eze 18:22
33:18 [x] Eze 3:20; Eze 18:26

33:1—48:35 *A Time to Rejoice: Words of Restoration and Hope.* After judgment against Israel (chs. 1–24) and the nations (chs. 25–32), a drastic transition occurs: the prophet offers mostly words of hope (chs. 33–48). In this section ch. 33 is key because Ezekiel gets word that the city has fallen (v. 21). This news provides a preface to the theme of restoration that follows in chs. 34–48, emphasizing that life will come out of death. See Introduction: Literary Features.

33:1–20 *Renewed Responsibilities.* Given that Ezekiel's message shifts from death to life, his watchman role is renewed (see 3:16–21 and note).

33:3 sees the sword ... blows the trumpet. The watchman must act and warn of danger. **sword.** See ch. 21 and notes.

33:4 if anyone hears the trumpet. The people are responsible to attend to the watchman's warnings.

33:7–9 Parallels 3:17–19.

33:10 Our offenses and sins weigh us down ... How then can we live? The Israelites recognize their sin and humbly acknowledge its consequences. For the first time in the book, they take ownership of their problem instead of blaming their ancestors (18:2) or God (18:19,25).

33:11 As surely as I live. God's sworn statement backing his word (see 5:11 and note). **Turn! Turn from your evil ways!** God's answer to the question of v. 10. This is a possibility because God delights in life, not death (14:6; 18:23,30).

33:12–20 Cf. 18:19–32 and notes.

33:17 The way of the Lord is not just. See note on 18:25. They are still skeptical about God's ways, even after God's statement in vv. 11–16. This contrasts their human ideas of justice with God's.

33:21 [y]Eze 24:26 [z]2Ki 25:4,10; Jer 39:1-2; Eze 32:1
33:22 [a]Eze 1:3 [b]Lk 1:64 [c]Eze 3:26-27; 24:27
33:24 [d]Eze 36:4 [e]Isa 51:2; Jer 40:7; Eze 11:15; Ac 7:5
33:25 [f]Ge 9:4; Dt 12:16 [g]Jer 7:9-10; Eze 22:6,27
33:26 [h]Eze 22:11
33:27 [i]1Sa 13:6; Isa 2:19; Jer 42:22; Eze 39:4
33:31 [j]Eze 8:1 [k]Ps 78:36-37; Isa 29:13; Eze 22:27; Mt 13:22; 1Jn 3:18
33:32 [l]Mk 6:20
33:33 [m]1Sa 3:20; Jer 28:9; Eze 2:5
34:2 [n]Ps 78:70-72; Isa 40:11; Jer 3:15; 23:1; Mic 3:11; Jn 10:11; 21:15-17

Jerusalem's Fall Explained

21 In the twelfth year of our exile, in the tenth month on the fifth day, a man who had escaped[y] from Jerusalem came to me and said, "The city has fallen![z]" 22 Now the evening before the man arrived, the hand of the LORD was on me,[a] and he opened my mouth[b] before the man came to me in the morning. So my mouth was opened and I was no longer silent.[c]

23 Then the word of the LORD came to me: 24 "Son of man, the people living in those ruins[d] in the land of Israel are saying, 'Abraham was only one man, yet he possessed the land. But we are many; surely the land has been given to us as our possession.'[e] 25 Therefore say to them, 'This is what the Sovereign LORD says: Since you eat meat with the blood[f] still in it and look to your idols and shed blood, should you then possess the land?[g] 26 You rely on your sword, you do detestable things, and each of you defiles his neighbor's wife.[h] Should you then possess the land?'

27 "Say this to them: 'This is what the Sovereign LORD says: As surely as I live, those who are left in the ruins will fall by the sword, those out in the country I will give to the wild animals to be devoured, and those in strongholds and caves will die of a plague.[i] 28 I will make the land a desolate waste, and her proud strength will come to an end, and the mountains of Israel will become desolate so that no one will cross them. 29 Then they will know that I am the LORD, when I have made the land a desolate waste because of all the detestable things they have done.'

30 "As for you, son of man, your people are talking together about you by the walls and at the doors of the houses, saying to each other, 'Come and hear the message that has come from the LORD.' 31 My people come to you, as they usually do, and sit before[j] you to hear your words, but they do not put them into practice. Their mouths speak of love, but their hearts are greedy for unjust gain.[k] 32 Indeed, to them you are nothing more than one who sings love songs with a beautiful voice and plays an instrument well, for they hear your words but do not put them into practice.[l]

33 "When all this comes true — and it surely will — then they will know that a prophet has been among them.[m]"

The LORD Will Be Israel's Shepherd

34 The word of the LORD came to me: 2 "Son of man, prophesy against the shepherds of Israel; prophesy and say to them: 'This is what the Sovereign LORD says: Woe to you shepherds of Israel who only take care of yourselves! Should not shepherds take care of the flock?[n] 3 You eat the curds,

33:21 – 33 *Jerusalem's Fall Reported: Ezekiel's Speech Returns.* From a chronological perspective, the reader does not expect to hear the news of Jerusalem's fall and the return of Ezekiel's speech *after* the literary interruption of the prophecies against the nations (chs. 25 – 32). The reader expects this news to immediately follow the death of Ezekiel's wife (24:15 – 27). The news of Jerusalem's fall marks a new phase for the remnant (see notes on 24:23,26), a transition from mourning to joy. Joy and restoration could not be realized until Israel's enemies were destroyed (chs. 25 – 32). The fact that Yahweh breaks Ezekiel's "mourning silence" with the news he hears of the city's end signals that the time to mourn has passed. See Introduction: Literary Features.

33:21 twelfth year ... tenth month ... fifth day. Jan. 8, 585 BC, five months after the temple was burned. **The city has fallen!** A fulfillment of 24:20 – 21, which indicates that Ezekiel is a true prophet (v. 33).

33:22 my mouth was opened and I was no longer silent. A fulfillment of 24:25 – 27. Yahweh does what he said he would do: he destroys the city and releases Ezekiel from the divine imposition of speechlessness (see 3:26 – 27) the night before the fugitive arrives (several months after Jerusalem's destruction, due to travel from Judah to Babylon) with the news.

33:24 people living in those ruins. People living in Jerusalem who did not experience the 586 BC exile (2 Kgs 25:12). **Abraham was only one man ... But we are many.** A slogan coined by those remaining in Jerusalem. By "name-dropping" they are expressing an arrogant entitlement to the land (Gen 12:1 – 3; 15; 17).

33:30 – 33 God informs Ezekiel about his exilic audience.

33:31 hear your words ... do not put them into practice. Rather than do the hard work and apply God's word to their lives, they are like classroom auditors. This is a sad reality now that Ezekiel has been proven to be a true prophet (see note on v. 21).

33:32 one who sings love songs with a beautiful voice. Metaphor that shows Ezekiel's message is like entertainment to his audience.

34:1 – 31 *Restoration of Righteous Leadership.* Now that God has destroyed Israel's local enemies (chs. 25 – 32) and Jerusalem has fallen (33:21), all threats are gone; restoration can take place. It starts with the promise of a true shepherd to lead Israel and encapsulates other elements of restoration that radiate throughout the larger section (chs. 35 – 48). Ch. 34 shows how Yahweh's change in disposition will revitalize the religious life of his people. Indeed, he will cause Israel's mourning to turn to joy. The failure of human shepherds (vv. 1 – 10) gives way to the success of Israel's true shepherd, God, who will care for and hold the sheep accountable (vv. 11 – 24). Through a David-like human figure, a righteous ruler, the sheep will be saved (vv. 20 – 24), and the Lord's gracious favors will flow, as the covenant of peace articulates (vv. 25 – 31).

34:2 shepherds of Israel. The leadership, especially the kings and their officials (see 2 Sam 7:7 and note; Jer 25:18 – 19) but also the prophets and priests (Isa 56:11; Jer 23:9 – 11). Ezekiel had earlier singled out the princes, priests, and prophets for special rebuke (ch. 22). To call a king a shepherd was common throughout the ancient Near East. For David's rise from shepherd to shepherd-king, see Ps 78:70 – 72 and note. For condemnation of the shepherds, cf. Jer 23:1 – 4 and note on 23:1,2.

34:3 eat the curds ... slaughter the choice animals. The benefits of

clothe yourselves with the wool and slaughter the choice animals, but you do not take care of the flock.[o]
4You have not strengthened the weak or healed the sick or bound up the injured. You have not brought
back the strays or searched for the lost. You have ruled them harshly and brutally.[p] 5So they were scattered because there was no shepherd,[q] and when they were scattered they became food for all the wild
animals.[r] 6My sheep wandered over all the mountains and on every high hill. They were scattered over
the whole earth, and no one searched or looked for them.[s]

7" 'Therefore, you shepherds, hear the word of the LORD: 8As surely as I live, declares the Sovereign
LORD, because my flock lacks a shepherd and so has been plundered and has become food for all the
wild animals, and because my shepherds did not search for my flock but cared for themselves rather
than for my flock, 9therefore, you shepherds, hear the word of the LORD: 10This is what the Sovereign
LORD says: I am against[t] the shepherds and will hold them accountable for my flock. I will remove them
from tending the flock so that the shepherds can no longer feed themselves. I will rescue[u] my flock from
their mouths, and it will no longer be food for them.[v]

11" 'For this is what the Sovereign LORD says: I myself will search for my sheep and look after them.
12As a shepherd[w] looks after his scattered flock when he is with them, so will I look after my sheep. I
will rescue them from all the places where they were scattered on a day of clouds and darkness.[x] 13I will
bring them out from the nations and gather them from the countries, and I will bring them into their
own land. I will pasture them on the mountains of Israel, in the ravines and in all the settlements in
the land.[y] 14I will tend them in a good pasture, and the mountain heights of Israel[z] will be their grazing land. There they will lie down in good grazing land, and there they will feed in a rich pasture[a] on
the mountains of Israel.[b] 15I myself will tend my sheep and have them lie down, declares the Sovereign
LORD.[c] 16I will search for the lost and bring back the strays. I will bind up the injured and strengthen
the weak,[d] but the sleek and the strong I will destroy. I will shepherd the flock with justice.[e]

17" 'As for you, my flock, this is what the Sovereign LORD says: I will judge between one sheep and
another, and between rams and goats.[f] 18Is it not enough for you to feed on the good pasture? Must you
also trample the rest of your pasture with your feet? Is it not enough for you to drink clear water? Must
you also muddy the rest with your feet? 19Must my flock feed on what you have trampled and drink
what you have muddied with your feet?

20" 'Therefore this is what the Sovereign LORD says to them: See, I myself will judge between the fat
sheep and the lean sheep. 21Because you shove with flank and shoulder, butting all the weak sheep with
your horns[g] until you have driven them away, 22I will save my flock, and they will no longer be plundered. I will judge between one sheep and another.[h] 23I will place over them one shepherd, my servant
David, and he will tend[i] them; he will tend them and be their shepherd. 24I the LORD will be their God,[j]
and my servant David will be prince among them. I the LORD have spoken.[k]

25" 'I will make a covenant of peace with them and rid the land of savage beasts[l] so that they may

34:3 [o] Isa 56:11; Eze 22:27; Zec 11:16
34:4 [p] Zec 11:15-17
34:5 [q] Nu 27:17 [r] ver 28; Isa 56:9
34:6 [s] Ps 142:4; 1Pe 2:25
34:10 [t] Jer 21:13 [u] Ps 72:14 [v] 1Sa 2:29-30; Zec 10:3
34:12 [w] Isa 40:11; Jer 31:10; Lk 19:10 [x] Eze 30:3
34:13 [y] Jer 23:3
34:14 [z] Eze 20:40 [a] Ps 23:2 [b] Eze 36:29-30
34:15 [c] Ps 23:1-2
34:16 [d] Mic 4:6 [e] Isa 10:16; Lk 5:32
34:17 [f] Mt 25:32-33
34:21 [g] Dt 33:17
34:22 [h] Ps 72:12-14; Jer 23:2-3
34:23 [i] Isa 40:11
34:24 [j] Eze 36:28 [k] Jer 30:9
34:25 [l] Lev 26:6

being a shepherd. Israel's leaders benefited from their titles and official roles but did not do their job of caring for the flock.

34:4 have not ... searched for the lost. Have had no concern for the good of the people. Cf. Jer 50:6; Zech 11:15–17; Matt 18:12–13; Luke 15:4–6; 19:10.

34:5 scattered. Because they were neglected; a term often used by Ezekiel to describe Israel's exile and dispersion (11:16,17; 12:15; 20:23,34,41; 22:15; 28:25). **no shepherd.** That is, no true shepherd (cf. Mark 6:34).

34:10 I am against the shepherds. God requires their removal.

34:11 I myself will search for my sheep. Reveals the Lord's tender demeanor toward his lost flock. God is on a rescue mission. He uses forms of "I will," 12 times in vv. 11–16, showing that God is taking the initiative.

34:12 from all the places. Reveals the far-reaching nature of God's rescue mission. Babylonia was not the only place where the Israelites had gone in exile (Jer 43:1–7).

34:16 the sleek and the strong I will destroy. God will carry out justice among those who had fattened themselves by oppressing other "sheep" (vv. 17–22).

34:17 rams and goats. People of influence and power who were oppressing poor Israelites. Social justice within the covenantal community was not valued.

34:22–24 Yahweh will save and unite the scattered, whom he will gather under one new ruler.

34:23–24 one shepherd ... my servant David will be prince. A ruler like David and from his line: the Messiah. He is a shepherd-servant and prince (37:24–28; Jer 23:5–6) who rules with justice. This points to Jesus the Messiah, the "good shepherd" (John 10:11–18), and a kingdom in which God will be King and the earthly Davidic king will be "prince" (cf. 37:25; 44:3; 45:7,16–17,22; 46:2–18; 48:21–22).

34:24 I the LORD will be their God. God's commitment to Israel, first articulated when he rescued them from Egyptian bondage (Exod 6:7) and reaffirmed now that he has rescued them from the wicked shepherds.

34:25 covenant of peace. Cf. 37:26. God's covenants aim at peace (Gen 26:28–31; Num 25:12; Isa 54:10; Mal 2:5). This covenant (the "new covenant" spoken of by Jeremiah in Jer 31:31–34 [see notes there]) looks to the final peace, initiated by Christ (Phil 4:7) and still awaiting final fulfillment. The "peace" (Hebrew *šālôm*) envisioned here

34:25 [m]Isa 11:6-9; Hos 2:18
34:26 [n]Ge 12:2 [o]Ps 68:9 [p]Dt 11:13-15; Isa 44:3
34:27 [q]Lev 26:13 [r]Jer 30:8
34:28 [s]Jer 30:10; Eze 39:26
34:29 [t]Isa 4:2 [u]Eze 36:29 [v]Eze 36:6 [w]Eze 36:15
34:30 [x]Eze 14:11; 37:27
34:31 [y]Ps 100:3; Jer 23:1
35:3 [z]Jer 6:12 [a]Eze 25:12-14
35:4 [b]ver 9
35:5 [c]Ps 137:7; Eze 21:29
35:6 [d]Isa 63:2-6
35:8 [e]Eze 31:12
35:9 [f]Jer 49:13
35:10 [g]Ps 83:12; Eze 36:2,5
35:11 [h]Eze 25:14 [i]Ps 9:16; Mt 7:2
35:12 [j]Jer 50:7
35:13 [k]Da 11:36
35:14 [l]Jer 51:48
35:15 [m]Ob 12 [n]ver 3 [o]Isa 34:5-6,11; Jer 50:11-13; La 4:21

live in the wilderness and sleep in the forests in safety.[m] 26 I will make them and the places surrounding
my hill a blessing.[a][n] I will send down showers in season;[o] there will be showers of blessing.[p] 27 The trees
will yield their fruit and the ground will yield its crops; the people will be secure in their land. They will
know that I am the LORD, when I break the bars of their yoke[q] and rescue them from the hands of those
who enslaved them.[r] 28 They will no longer be plundered by the nations, nor will wild animals devour
them. They will live in safety, and no one will make them afraid.[s] 29 I will provide for them a land renowned[t] for its crops, and they will no longer be victims of famine[u] in the land or bear the scorn[v] of the
nations.[w] 30 Then they will know that I, the LORD their God, am with them and that they, the Israelites,
are my people, declares the Sovereign LORD.[x] 31 You are my sheep, the sheep of my pasture,[y] and I am
your God, declares the Sovereign LORD.' "

A Prophecy Against Edom

35 The word of the LORD came to me: 2 "Son of man, set your face against Mount Seir; prophesy
against it 3 and say: 'This is what the Sovereign LORD says: I am against you, Mount Seir, and
I will stretch out my hand[z] against you and make you a desolate waste.[a] 4 I will turn your towns into
ruins and you will be desolate. Then you will know that I am the LORD.[b]

5 " 'Because you harbored an ancient hostility and delivered the Israelites over to the sword at the
time of their calamity, the time their punishment reached its climax,[c] 6 therefore as surely as I live,
declares the Sovereign LORD, I will give you over to bloodshed and it will pursue you.[d] Since you did not
hate bloodshed, bloodshed will pursue you. 7 I will make Mount Seir a desolate waste and cut off from
it all who come and go. 8 I will fill your mountains with the slain; those killed by the sword will fall on
your hills and in your valleys and in all your ravines.[e] 9 I will make you desolate forever; your towns
will not be inhabited. Then you will know that I am the LORD.[f]

10 " 'Because you have said, "These two nations and countries will be ours and we will take possession[g] of them," even though I the LORD was there, 11 therefore as surely as I live, declares the Sovereign
LORD, I will treat you in accordance with the anger[h] and jealousy you showed in your hatred of them
and I will make myself known among them when I judge you.[i] 12 Then you will know that I the LORD
have heard all the contemptible things you have said against the mountains of Israel. You said, "They
have been laid waste and have been given over to us to devour."[j] 13 You boasted against me and spoke
against me without restraint, and I heard it.[k] 14 This is what the Sovereign LORD says: While the whole
earth rejoices, I will make you desolate.[l] 15 Because you rejoiced[m] when the inheritance of Israel became
desolate, that is how I will treat you. You will be desolate, Mount Seir,[n] you and all of Edom.[o] Then they
will know that I am the LORD.' "

[a] 26 Or *I will cause them and the places surrounding my hill to be named in blessings* (see Gen. 48:20); or *I will cause them and the places surrounding my hill to be seen as blessed*

is that of a restored relationship with God and the secure enjoyment of a life made full and rich through his blessings. None of the threats to life experienced under God's judgments will mar this "peace" (cf. vv. 25–29 with 5:16–17 and note on 5:15).

34:26 showers in season. Autumn rains, which signal the beginning of the rainy season, and spring rains, which come at the end (cf. Jer 5:24). **showers of blessing.** Blessing, the power of life promised to God's people through Abraham (Gen 12:1–3), is beautifully symbolized in the life-giving effects of rain.

34:27 break the bars of their yoke. Symbolizes freedom from foreign oppressors. **bars.** Wooden pegs inserted down through holes in the yoke and tied with cords below the animal's neck (Isa 58:6) to form a collar (cf. 30:18; Lev 26:13; Jer 27:2; 28:10–13).

34:30 Then they will know that I ... am with them. The true goal and result of the covenant of peace: the awareness of the divine presence, a reversal of divine abandonment due to the exile (see chs. 8–11). Jesus, the Prince of Peace, is the exact representation of God's glory and presence (Heb 1:3).

35:1—36:15 *The Mountains of Edom and Israel.* Edom here is representative of the enemy (36:5). Edom (descendants of Esau) treated their twin brother, Israel (descendants of Jacob; Gen 25:21–30), with spite at the time Jerusalem fell (Obad 8). The outcome for Edom (Esau) is destruction (ch. 35), but the outcome for Israel (Jacob) is restoration (ch. 36).

35:1–15 *Desolation for Mount Seir.* Comfort and restoration will come to Israel when God ends the "ancient hostility" Edom has toward Israel (v. 5; cf. v. 11). God will do this by making Edom desolate (vv. 3,7,9,14,15). The hatred, anger, and jealousy Edom had toward Israel manifested itself as murder (v. 5). God "heard" Edom's heart (vv. 12,13) toward Israel, and the Sovereign Lord took it personally (vv. 1–3).

35:5 ancient hostility. Started with Jacob's treatment of Esau (Gen 27) and continued well into their history (Num 20:14–21; 2 Sam 8:13–14; 1 Kgs 9:26–28). **delivered the Israelites over to the sword.** Edomites sat in waiting to kill Israelites fleeing the Babylonian siege of Jerusalem in 588–586 BC (Obad 10,14).

35:6 bloodshed ... will pursue you. God's retaliation (Gen 9:6). This reveals his justice and anticipates his treatment of the enemy at the end of the age (Rev 20:11–15).

35:10 two nations and countries. Israel and Judah before they reunite.

Hope for the Mountains of Israel

36 "Son of man, prophesy to the mountains of Israel and say, 'Mountains of Israel, hear the word
of the LORD. 2This is what the Sovereign LORD says: The enemy said of you, "Aha![p] The ancient
heights[q] have become our possession.[r]"' 3Therefore prophesy and say, 'This is what the Sovereign LORD
says: Because they ravaged and crushed you from every side so that you became the possession of the
rest of the nations and the object of people's malicious talk and slander,[s] 4therefore, mountains of Israel, hear the word of the Sovereign LORD: This is what the Sovereign LORD says to the mountains and
hills, to the ravines and valleys,[t] to the desolate ruins and the deserted towns that have been plundered
and ridiculed by the rest of the nations around you[u] — 5this is what the Sovereign LORD says: In my
burning zeal I have spoken against the rest of the nations, and against all Edom, for with glee and with
malice in their hearts they made my land their own possession so that they might plunder its pastureland.'[v] 6Therefore prophesy concerning the land of Israel and say to the mountains and hills, to the
ravines and valleys: 'This is what the Sovereign LORD says: I speak in my jealous wrath because you
have suffered the scorn of the nations.[w] 7Therefore this is what the Sovereign LORD says: I swear with
uplifted hand that the nations around you will also suffer scorn.

8" 'But you, mountains of Israel, will produce branches and fruit[x] for my people Israel, for they will
soon come home. 9I am concerned for you and will look on you with favor; you will be plowed and
sown, 10and I will cause many people to live on you — yes, all of Israel. The towns will be inhabited
and the ruins rebuilt.[y] 11I will increase the number of people and animals living on you, and they will
be fruitful and become numerous. I will settle people on you as in the past[z] and will make you prosper more than before.[a] Then you will know that I am the LORD. 12I will cause people, my people Israel,
to live on you. They will possess you, and you will be their inheritance;[b] you will never again deprive
them of their children.

13" 'This is what the Sovereign LORD says: Because some say to you, "You devour people[c] and deprive
your nation of its children," 14therefore you will no longer devour people or make your nation childless,
declares the Sovereign LORD. 15No longer will I make you hear the taunts of the nations, and no longer
will you suffer the scorn of the peoples or cause your nation to fall, declares the Sovereign LORD.[d]' "

Israel's Restoration Assured

16Again the word of the LORD came to me: 17"Son of man, when the people of Israel were living in
their own land, they defiled it by their conduct and their actions. Their conduct was like a woman's
monthly uncleanness in my sight.[e] 18So I poured out[f] my wrath on them because they had shed blood
in the land and because they had defiled it with their idols. 19I dispersed them among the nations, and

36:2 [p] Eze 25:3 [q] Dt 32:13 [r] Eze 35:10
36:3 [s] Ps 44:13-14
36:4 [t] Eze 6:3 [u] Dt 11:11; Ps 79:4; Eze 34:28
36:5 [v] Jer 50:11; Eze 25:12-14; 35:10,15
36:6 [w] Ps 123:3-4; Eze 34:29
36:8 [x] Isa 27:6
36:10 [y] ver 33; Isa 49:17-23
36:11 [z] Mic 7:14 [a] Jer 31:28; Eze 16:55
36:12 [b] Eze 47:14,22
36:13 [c] Nu 13:32
36:15 [d] Ps 89:50-51; Eze 34:29
36:17 [e] Jer 2:7
36:18 [f] 2Ch 34:21

36:1 – 15 *Restoration for the Mountains of Israel.* God swears to the mountains that he is against Israel's enemy, the nations (v. 5), and announces renewal of the land's prosperity in the future. This is the comforting counterpart to ch. 6.

36:2 Aha! ... ancient heights ... our possession. The temporary boast of those who conquered the promised land. They possessed the land only temporarily (vv. 8 – 15). **ancient heights.** The highlands sandwiched between the Jordan River and the Mediterranean Sea (vv. 3,5; 35:10).

36:5 with glee and with malice ... made my land their own. The enemy plundered God's land, and he took offense at their mockery. Here Edom is singled out because of its history of hatred toward Israel (see ch. 35 and notes).

36:6 – 7 in my jealous wrath ... the nations around you will also suffer. God is angry toward those who treated Israel badly (see also chs. 25 – 32).

36:7 with uplifted hand. God vows to deal with these enemies of Israel (see 20:5 and note).

36:9 look on you with favor. God's new disposition (Lev 26:9). A favorable look leads to restoration; this contrasts God's unfavorable look, which brought destruction. God's favor translates into repossession of the land.

36:10 all of Israel. The rightful inhabitants (not only exiled Judah), who will repossess the land according to God's promises (Exod 6:6 – 8).

36:11 be fruitful and become numerous ... prosper more than before. A mark of God's favor; terminology reminiscent of God's blessing at creation (Gen 1:22,28) and at Abraham's covenant (Gen 17:6; cf. Exod 1:7). **you will know that I am the LORD.** The goal of God in restoration; corresponds to his goal in rendering his just judgment noted throughout the book (see Introduction: Theological Significance).

36:12 live on you. Live on the mountains of Israel. **never again deprive them of their children.** Fruitfulness. This is a poetic picture of the mountains having contributed to the depopulation brought by the exile and could refer to the influence of the Canaanites that led Israel astray.

36:16 – 38 *Restoration Assured.* Because sin and its consequence of exile negatively affected God's reputation among the nations, he must act to restore his holy name (vv. 16 – 23). He does so by cleansing his people, with a life-giving outcome (vv. 24 – 38). This act ultimately brings him glory among the nations (v. 36). This is a key restoration passage in the book.

36:17 The nature of Israel's ritual defilement is graphically compared to that of a woman's monthly period (Lev 15:19 – 30).

36:19 [g]Dt 28:64 [h]Eze 39:24
36:20 [i]Ro 2:24 [j]Isa 52:5; Jer 33:24; Eze 12:16
36:21 [k]Ps 74:18; Isa 48:9
36:22 [l]Ro 2:24* [m]Ps 106:8
36:23 [n]Eze 20:41 [o]Ps 126:2; Isa 5:16
36:24 [p]Eze 34:13; 37:21
36:25 [q]Heb 9:13; 10:22 [r]Ps 51:2,7 [s]Zec 13:2
36:26 [t]Jer 24:7 [u]Ps 51:10; Eze 11:19
36:27 [v]Eze 37:14
36:28 [w]Jer 30:22 [x]Eze 14:11; 37:14,27
36:29 [y]Eze 34:29
36:30 [z]Lev 26:4-5; Eze 34:27; Hos 2:21-22
36:31 [a]Eze 6:9; 20:43
36:32 [b]Dt 9:5
36:35 [c]Joel 2:3 [d]Isa 51:3
36:36 [e]Eze 17:22; 22:14; 37:14; 39:27-28
36:38 [f]1Ki 8:63; 2Ch 35:7-9

they were scattered[g] through the countries; I judged them according to their conduct and their actions.[h]
20 And wherever they went among the nations they profaned[i] my holy name, for it was said of them,
'These are the LORD's people, and yet they had to leave his land.'[j] 21 I had concern for my holy name,
which the people of Israel profaned among the nations where they had gone.[k]
22 "Therefore say to the Israelites, 'This is what the Sovereign LORD says: It is not for your sake, people
of Israel, that I am going to do these things, but for the sake of my holy name, which you have profaned[l]
among the nations where you have gone.[m] 23 I will show the holiness of my great name, which has been
profaned among the nations, the name you have profaned among them. Then the nations will know
that I am the LORD, declares the Sovereign LORD, when I am proved holy[n] through you before their eyes.[o]
24 " 'For I will take you out of the nations; I will gather you from all the countries and bring you back
into your own land.[p] 25 I will sprinkle[q] clean water on you, and you will be clean; I will cleanse[r] you from
all your impurities and from all your idols.[s] 26 I will give you a new heart[t] and put a new spirit in you; I will
remove from you your heart of stone and give you a heart of flesh.[u] 27 And I will put my Spirit[v] in you and
move you to follow my decrees and be careful to keep my laws. 28 Then you will live in the land I gave your
ancestors; you will be my people,[w] and I will be your God.[x] 29 I will save you from all your uncleanness. I
will call for the grain and make it plentiful and will not bring famine[y] upon you. 30 I will increase the fruit
of the trees and the crops of the field, so that you will no longer suffer disgrace among the nations because
of famine.[z] 31 Then you will remember your evil ways and wicked deeds, and you will loathe yourselves for
your sins and detestable practices.[a] 32 I want you to know that I am not doing this for your sake, declares
the Sovereign LORD. Be ashamed and disgraced for your conduct, people of Israel![b]
33 " 'This is what the Sovereign LORD says: On the day I cleanse you from all your sins, I will resettle
your towns, and the ruins will be rebuilt. 34 The desolate land will be cultivated instead of lying desolate
in the sight of all who pass through it. 35 They will say, "This land that was laid waste has become like
the garden of Eden;[c] the cities that were lying in ruins, desolate and destroyed, are now fortified and
inhabited.[d]" 36 Then the nations around you that remain will know that I the LORD have rebuilt what
was destroyed and have replanted what was desolate. I the LORD have spoken, and I will do it.'[e]
37 "This is what the Sovereign LORD says: Once again I will yield to Israel's plea and do this for them:
I will make their people as numerous as sheep, 38 as numerous as the flocks for offerings[f] at Jerusalem

36:20 the LORD's people, and yet they had to leave his land. The nations that were looking on thought Yahweh was unable to protect his people, since another people's god plundered God's land and temple. But the nations did not know that the exile was God's punishment for Israel's idolatry.

36:22 It is not for your sake ... but for the sake of my holy name. A statement that reveals why God is offering them restoration. The fundamental reason given is not grace and mercy (though it *is* gracious and merciful) but to uphold the sanctity and greatness of God's reputation. God promises action to prove he is different from other deities. His goal is to reverse the false verdict about his character brought on by Israel's exile. The reason given in ch. 20 for the withholding of divine punishment (see 20:9,14,22 and note on 20:9) is here given as the reason for divine restoration.

36:23 show the holiness of my great name. To hallow God's great name (Matt 6:9). **my great name ... has been profaned.** God's name (and so he himself) was treated as not holy. **Then the nations will know that I am the LORD.** God's goal in Israel's restoration is to have worldwide recognition that he is the true God. Although this "recognition formula" is used repeatedly throughout the book of Ezekiel, its significance here is made plain. It is not just that Israel's God is "great" and "holy"; it is also imperative that God be given the recognition and respect, indeed the honor, that he is due. See Introduction: Theological Significance.

36:24–27 Key elements to the promised restoration: (1) return of the exiles (v. 24), (2) cleansing from sin (v. 25), (3) renewal of heart (v. 26), and (4) enablement by God's Spirit to live God's way (v. 27).

36:25 sprinkle clean water on you. A ritual act of cleansing symbolizing a renewed readiness for worship (Exod 30:19–20; Lev 14:51; Num 19:18; Heb 10:22). **I will cleanse you.** A God-initiated act (v. 33; 37:23; Jer 33:8). Ezekiel does not highlight human participation or cooperation in this cleansing process (spiritual regeneration).

36:26–32 The outcome of the cleansing entails a surgery of sorts, a "new heart ... of flesh" (v. 26); i.e., teachable, not hard like stone. This is "new covenant" terminology (see Jer 31:33–34 and note on 31:33).

36:26 new heart. See notes on 11:19; 18:31.

36:27 my Spirit. A bestowal of the divine presence to enable the human spirit to do God's will (see 37:14 and note).

36:28 my people ... your God. Covenant language (see 11:20 and note). Ultimately, the cleansing means a restored relationship between God and his people.

36:32 I am not doing this for your sake. Repeats v. 22 for emphasis (see note on v. 22). Yahweh's motivation brings further disgrace to the "people of Israel." **Be ashamed and disgraced.** Recalling their guilt will make them feel "disgraced" in light of God's grace.

36:33 On the day I cleanse you. An unspecified time in the future that connects the promise of cleansing (vv. 24–32) with the promise of repopulation (vv. 33–36).

36:35 garden of Eden. Expresses a return to pristine conditions (cf. 28:13; 31:9).

36:36 the nations ... will know. On the "day" (v. 33) of cleansing, the nations will feel the impact of Israel's restoration (v. 23). The physical return in 539 BC will be only the beginning of the fulfillment of the restoration promised, as evidenced by the language that seems to go beyond ethnic Israel. The cleansing anticipates the inward work of God's Spirit in the new covenant.

36:37 I will yield to Israel's plea. Reverses God's previous refusals to hear (14:3; 20:3,31).

36:38 numerous as the flocks for offerings. A population increase

during her appointed festivals. So will the ruined cities be filled with flocks of people. Then they will
know that I am the LORD."

The Valley of Dry Bones

37 The hand of the LORD was on me,[g] and he brought me out by the Spirit[h] of the LORD and set
me in the middle of a valley;[i] it was full of bones.[j] [2]He led me back and forth among them,
and I saw a great many bones on the floor of the valley, bones that were very dry. [3]He asked me, "Son
of man, can these bones live?"
I said, "Sovereign LORD, you alone know.[k]"
[4]Then he said to me, "Prophesy to these bones and say to them, 'Dry bones, hear the word of the
LORD![l] [5]This is what the Sovereign LORD says to these bones: I will make breath[a] enter you, and you will
come to life.[m] [6]I will attach tendons to you and make flesh come upon you and cover you with skin; I
will put breath in you, and you will come to life. Then you will know that I am the LORD.[n]'"
[7]So I prophesied as I was commanded. And as I was prophesying, there was a noise, a rattling sound,
and the bones came together, bone to bone. [8]I looked, and tendons and flesh appeared on them and
skin covered them, but there was no breath in them.
[9]Then he said to me, "Prophesy to the breath;[o] prophesy, son of man, and say to it, 'This is what the
Sovereign LORD says: Come, breath, from the four winds and breathe into these slain, that they may
live.'" [10]So I prophesied as he commanded me, and breath entered them; they came to life and stood
up on their feet—a vast army.[p]
[11]Then he said to me: "Son of man, these bones are the people of Israel. They say, 'Our bones are
dried up and our hope is gone; we are cut off.'[q] [12]Therefore prophesy and say to them: 'This is what the
Sovereign LORD says: My people, I am going to open your graves and bring you up from them; I will bring
you back to the land of Israel.[r] [13]Then you, my people, will know that I am the LORD, when I open your
graves and bring you up from them. [14]I will put my Spirit[s] in you and you will live, and I will settle you in
your own land. Then you will know that I the LORD have spoken, and I have done it, declares the LORD.[t]'"

One Nation Under One King

[15]The word of the LORD came to me: [16]"Son of man, take a stick of wood and write on it, 'Belonging
to Judah and the Israelites[u] associated with him.'[v] Then take another stick of wood, and write on it,

[a] 5 The Hebrew for this word can also mean *wind* or *spirit* (see verses 6-14).

37:1 [g]Eze 1:3; 8:3 [h]Eze 11:24; Lk 4:1; Ac 8:39 [i]Jer 7:32 [j]Jer 8:2; Eze 40:1
37:3 [k]Dt 32:39; 1Sa 2:6; Isa 26:19
37:4 [l]Jer 22:29
37:5 [m]Ge 2:7; Ps 104:29-30
37:6 [n]Eze 38:23; Joel 2:27; 3:17
37:9 [o]Ps 104:30
37:10 [p]Rev 11:11
37:11 [q]La 3:54
37:12 [r]Dt 32:39; 1Sa 2:6; Isa 26:19; Hos 13:14; Am 9:14-15
37:14 [s]Joel 2:28-29 [t]Eze 36:27-28,36
37:16 [u]1Ki 12:20; 2Ch 10:17-19 [v]Nu 17:2-3; 2Ch 15:9

that will allow for festivals unto God (1 Kgs 8:63; 1 Chr 29:21; 2 Chr 35:7). This summarizes Israel's full restoration with God.

37:1–14 *Restoration of People.* This is the third of four visions Ezekiel sees (1:1; 8:4; 40:2). The imagery is that of a large slain army that miraculously comes to life on the battlefield; an open graveyard suggests an undignified "burial." The imagery refers to the death-like nature of exile but promises the impossible: out of death comes life (see 36:26–27). God again commands Ezekiel to do something (vv. 1–10) and interprets the vision (vv. 11–14). The exiles' hopelessness and detachment from the promises of God (v. 11) fuels this vision's purpose.

37:2 many bones. The entire exiled community (see v. 11). **very dry.** Suggests they were long dead. The imagery of scattered bones on a battlefield magnifies hopelessness and the impossibility of change.

37:3 can these bones live? A rhetorical question whose logical answer is no. It challenges Ezekiel to look beyond the natural circumstances to God's sovereignty.

37:4 Prophesy to these bones. This command, together with the notion that the bones can "hear" God's word, strikes a hopeful note about the possibility of life. Ezekiel prophesies to lifeless bones and to "the breath" (v. 9).

37:8 but there was no breath. Bodies reassembled but without breath.

37:10 breath entered them. See NIV text note on v. 5. The dry bones will become bodies with breath, full of life. The divine breath ("wind" or "spirit") will give new life to these bones. Breath and life are connected numerous times in the passage (vv. 5–6,9–10). God re-creates, as he did with Adam, a twofold process (Gen 2:7). A "vast army" comes into formation on their feet. The vastness of the army matches the numerous slain bodies (vv. 1–2).

37:12 I am going to open your graves. The imagery changes from a battlefield to a cemetery. God causes life to come out of death (a resurrection of sorts). This speaks of the physical return from exile and the restoration under Cyrus in 539 BC, using resurrection language. In this sense, Ezekiel contributes to OT teaching on resurrection. Although clear statements of bodily life after death are not common in the OT, one of the clearest comes in Dan 12:2–3. In addition, there are hints in earlier texts that prepare the way. The influence of a number of these texts (e.g., Isa 26:19; Hos 6:1–2; 13:14) is immediately apparent in the NT. For the biblical-theological significance, see v. 14 and note.

37:14 I will put my Spirit in you and you will live. A clear connection between breath (vv. 5,6,8,9 [twice],10) and God's Spirit reflects the life-giving power of God. Without God's presence there is no hope for God's people. Although Israel's national revival is in view, this act points beyond it to the resurrected life through the Spirit of Christ (John 11:25–26; Rom 8:9–17; Col 3:1–4).

37:15–28 *Restoration of Unity.* Connected to the promise of renewed life back in the land (vv. 1–14), restoration also includes unifying the nation under one king. Through another dramatic performance (vv. 15–17) and its subsequent interpretation (vv. 18–28), Ezekiel illustrates the unity God intends in the restoration.

37:16 take a stick. The last visual aid involves writing on a material

37:17 [w]ver 24; Isa 11:13; Jer 50:4; Hos 1:11
37:18 [x]Eze 24:19
37:19 [y]Zec 10:6
37:21 [z]Isa 43:5-6; Eze 36:24; 39:27
37:22 [a]Isa 11:13; Jer 3:18; Hos 1:11
37:23 [b]Eze 36:25; 43:7 [c]Eze 11:18; 36:28
37:24 [d]Hos 3:5 [e]Isa 40:11; Eze 34:23 [f]Ps 78:70-71
37:25 [g]Eze 28:25 [h]Am 9:15 [i]Isa 11:1
37:26 [j]Isa 55:3 [k]Jer 30:19 [l]Eze 16:62
37:27 [m]Lev 26:11; Jn 1:14 [n]2Co 6:16*
37:28 [o]Ex 31:13; Eze 20:12
38:2 [p]Ge 10:2 [q]Rev 20:8
38:3 [r]Eze 39:1

'Belonging to Joseph (that is, to Ephraim) and all the Israelites associated with him.' 17 Join them together into one stick so that they will become one in your hand.[w]

18 "When your people ask you, 'Won't you tell us what you mean by this?'[x] 19 say to them, 'This is what the Sovereign LORD says: I am going to take the stick of Joseph—which is in Ephraim's hand—and of the Israelite tribes associated with him, and join it to Judah's stick. I will make them into a single stick of wood, and they will become one in my hand.'[y] 20 Hold before their eyes the sticks you have written on 21 and say to them, 'This is what the Sovereign LORD says: I will take the Israelites out of the nations where they have gone. I will gather them from all around and bring them back into their own land.[z] 22 I will make them one nation in the land, on the mountains of Israel. There will be one king over all of them and they will never again be two nations or be divided into two kingdoms.[a] 23 They will no longer defile[b] themselves with their idols and vile images or with any of their offenses, for I will save them from all their sinful backsliding,[a] and I will cleanse them. They will be my people, and I will be their God.[c]

24 " 'My servant David[d] will be king over them, and they will all have one shepherd.[e] They will follow my laws and be careful to keep my decrees.[f] 25 They will live in the land I gave to my servant Jacob, the land where your ancestors lived.[g] They and their children and their children's children will live there forever,[h] and David my servant will be their prince forever.[i] 26 I will make a covenant of peace[j] with them; it will be an everlasting covenant. I will establish them and increase their numbers,[k] and I will put my sanctuary among them forever.[l] 27 My dwelling place[m] will be with them; I will be their God, and they will be my people.[n] 28 Then the nations will know that I the LORD make Israel holy,[o] when my sanctuary is among them forever.' "

The LORD's Great Victory Over the Nations

38 The word of the LORD came to me: 2 "Son of man, set your face against Gog, of the land of Magog,[p] the chief prince of[b] Meshek and Tubal;[q] prophesy against him 3 and say: 'This is what the Sovereign LORD says: I am against you, Gog, chief prince of[c] Meshek and Tubal.[r] 4 I will turn you around,

[a] *23* Many Hebrew manuscripts (see also Septuagint); most Hebrew manuscripts *all their dwelling places where they sinned* [b] *2* Or *the prince of Rosh,* [c] *3* Or *Gog, prince of Rosh,*

object. **Judah.** Represents the entire southern kingdom. **Joseph.** Represents the entire northern kingdom. Joseph was the father of Ephraim (Gen 48:5,8–20).

37:19 one in my hand. The interpretation of the visual aid: unity (see also vv. 17,22). The two kingdoms have been separated since Solomon's death (1 Kgs 12).

37:21–22 their own land ... one king. The renewal includes a secure national homeland with a national leader, the future Messianic ruler (see v. 24; cf. "prince" in v. 25).

37:23 no longer defile themselves with their idols. The king will lead law-abiding citizens who are moral and pure (cf. 36:27) because of God. **my people ... their God.** A repetition of the covenant formula (cf. v. 27; see 11:20 and note).

37:24–26 These verses echo the Davidic covenant (the promise of eternal kingship), the Sinaitic covenant (expectations of holy living), and the Abrahamic covenant (the promise of land)—all will be fulfilled in the covenant of peace (v. 26).

37:24 My servant David. See note on 34:23–24.

37:26 covenant of peace ... everlasting covenant. Previously mentioned individually (16:60; 34:25); merged here as the charter for the renewed nation. David's unified rule will be characterized by permanent peace (34:25; cf. Gen 9:16; 17:7; 2 Sam 23:5; Jer 32:40).

37:27 My dwelling place will be with them. God's desire from the beginning of time (Gen 1–3). **dwelling place.** Recalls the wilderness tabernacle (see Lev 15:31 and NIV text note there).

37:28 sanctuary. Recalls Solomon's temple. Mentioning the "dwelling place" (i.e., the tabernacle, see v. 27 and note) and the "sanctuary" (the temple) together anticipates the rebuilt temple (chs. 40–48) necessary for restored worship. Thus, restoration reaches a climactic point.

38:1—39:29 *Restoration Permanent: Enemies Abroad Destroyed.* Before the covenant of peace (34:25–31; 37:26–28) can become a reality and God's permanent sanctuary can be rebuilt (chs. 40–48), God must destroy his enemies who live outside the promised land: Gog of Magog and all his hoards (38:2). Chs. 38–39 describe a major attack by Gog and his allies (38:4–6) on God's restored people. The battle brings great peril to God's people and upheavals in the natural world. Ezekiel predicts this army's downfall at the Lord's command (38:1–3,7–13) with three prophecies (38:1–13,14–23; 39:1–16). The number of the fallen warriors is such that this "sacrifice" provides a feast for predators (39:17–20). God's victory over Gog will reveal God's supremacy and sovereignty. The nations will know the real cause of Israel's exile: God purposefully withdrew due to Israel's unfaithfulness (39:21–24). The victory will also reveal that Israel's God is truly the Holy One (39:25–29). For the exiled Israelites, their protection against an enemy even more perilous than the Babylonians will give them great assurance and hope as they anticipate the future. See Introduction: Particular Interpretive Challenges.

38:2 Gog. Apparently a leader or king. His name appears only in chs. 38–39; Rev 20:8. Several identifications have been attempted, notably Gyges, king of Lydia (ca. 660 BC). Possibly the name is purposely vague, standing for a mysterious, as yet undisclosed, enemy of God's people. **of the land of Magog.** In Gen 10:2 and 1 Chr 1:5, Magog is one of the sons of Japheth, thus the name of a people. In Ezek 39:6 it appears to refer to a people. But since the prefix *ma-* can mean "place of," Magog may here simply mean "land of Gog." Israel had long experienced the hostility of the Hamites and other Semitic peoples; the future coalition here envisioned will include—and in fact be led by—peoples descended from Japheth (cf. Gen 10). **chief prince.** Military commander-in-chief. The NIV text note gives the possible translation "prince of Rosh," and if it is correct, Rosh is probably the name of an

put hooks[s] in your jaws and bring you out with your whole army — your horses, your horsemen fully
armed, and a great horde with large and small shields, all of them brandishing their swords.[t] 5Persia,
Cush[a][u] and Put[v] will be with them, all with shields and helmets, 6also Gomer[w] with all its troops, and
Beth Togarmah[x] from the far north with all its troops — the many nations with you.
7"'Get ready; be prepared,[y] you and all the hordes gathered about you, and take command of them.
8After many days[z] you will be called to arms. In future years you will invade a land that has recovered
from war, whose people were gathered from many nations[a] to the mountains of Israel, which had long
been desolate. They had been brought out from the nations, and now all of them live in safety.[b] 9You
and all your troops and the many nations with you will go up, advancing like a storm;[c] you will be like
a cloud[d] covering the land.
10"'This is what the Sovereign LORD says: On that day thoughts will come into your mind and you will

38:4 [s]2Ki 19:28 [t]Eze 29:4; Da 11:40
38:5 [u]Ge 10:6 [v]Eze 27:10
38:6 [w]Ge 10:2 [x]Eze 27:14
38:7 [y]Isa 8:9
38:8 [z]Isa 24:22 [a]Isa 11:11 [b]Jer 23:6
38:9 [c]Isa 28:2 [d]Jer 4:13; Joel 2:2

[a] 5 That is, the upper Nile region

unknown people or place. Identification with Russia is unlikely and in any case cannot be proven. **Meshek and Tubal.** Sons of Japheth in Gen 10:2 (see note); 1 Chr 1:5. Here they are peoples and territories probably located in eastern Asia Minor (see 27:13; 32:26 and notes), to the north of Israel (cf. vv. 6,15; 39:2). As in the days of the Assyrians and Babylonians, the major attack will come from the north. See Introduction: Particular Interpretive Challenges.

38:4 I will ... bring you out. A clear statement of God's initiative and control over Gog in this battle. **put hooks in your jaws.** The manner in which God will bring Gog out (like Pharaoh in 29:4).

38:5 Cush. The upper Nile region (south of Egypt; modern-day Sudan). The invading forces from the north (v. 2) are joined by forces from the south. **Put.** Libya.

38:6 Gomer. Another northern ally (named as a son of Japheth in Gen 10:2; 1 Chr 1:5). **Beth Togarmah.** See note on 27:14. Togarmah is named as a child of Gomer in Gen 10:3 (see note); 1 Chr 1:6.

38:8 After many days ... In future years. Not the near future but an unspecified time following the events of Israel's restoration (chs. 34–37).

38:9 your troops ... like a cloud. An enormous army from abroad that God summons. It is not possible to identify the invaders further. To attempt to associate the invaders with modern countries is to misunderstand the symbolism in this type of prophecy and miss what is certain: God will arouse a foe in the future from faraway places (vv. 4,16) to spring a vicious attack on God's people.

38:10 thoughts will come into your mind. Gog's human action parallels divine initiative (v. 4). Cf. Cyrus in Ezra 1; Isa 45:1–13; and Assyria in Isa 10:6–7.

TERRITORIES IN EZEKIEL 38

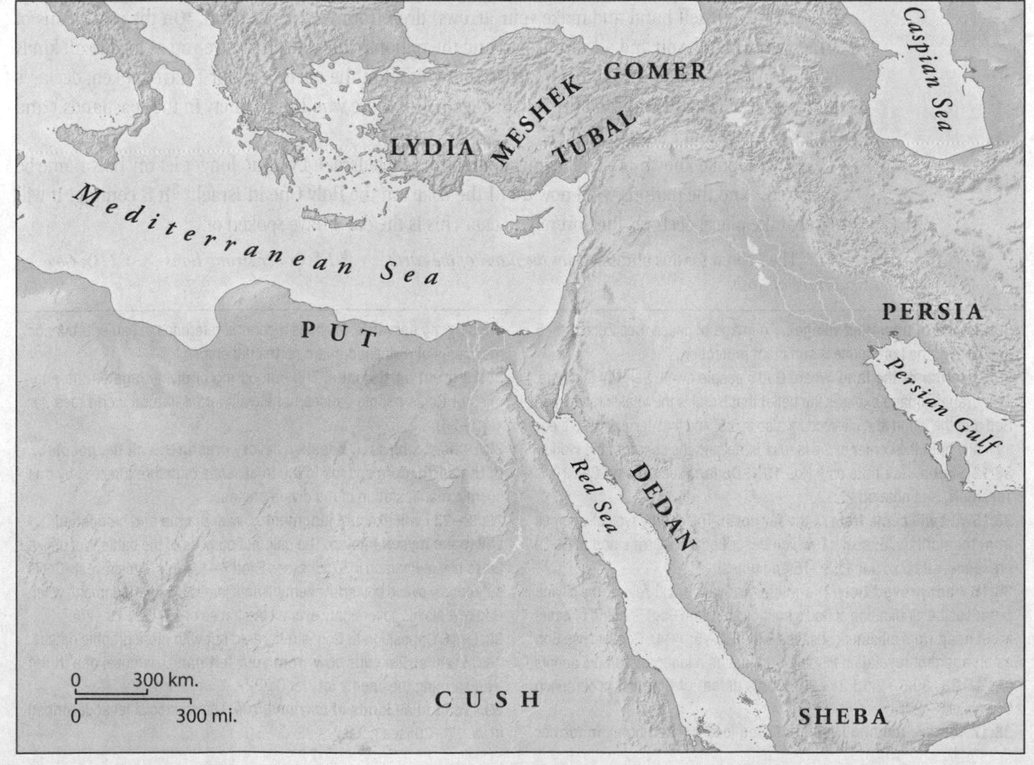

38:10 [e]Ps 36:4; Mic 2:1
38:11 [f]Jer 49:31; Zec 2:4
38:13 [g]Eze 27:22 [h]Isa 10:6; Jer 15:13
38:14 [i]ver 8; Zec 2:5
38:15 [j]Eze 39:2
38:16 [k]ver 9 [l]Isa 29:23; Eze 39:21
38:19 [m]Ps 18:7; Eze 5:13; Hag 2:6,21
38:20 [n]Hos 4:3; Na 1:5
38:21 [o]Eze 14:17 [p]1Sa 14:20; 2Ch 20:23; Hag 2:22
38:22 [q]Isa 66:16; Jer 25:31 [r]Ps 18:12; Rev 16:21
38:23 [s]Eze 36:23
39:1 [t]Eze 38:2,3
39:3 [u]Hos 1:5 [v]Ps 76:3
39:4 [w]ver 17-20; Eze 29:5; 33:27
39:6 [x]Eze 30:8; Am 1:4 [y]Jer 25:22
39:7 [z]Ex 20:7 [a]Isa 12:6; Eze 36:16,23

devise an evil scheme.[e] 11 You will say, "I will invade a land of unwalled villages; I will attack a peaceful
and unsuspecting people — all of them living without walls and without gates and bars.[f] 12 I will plunder and loot and turn my hand against the resettled ruins and the people gathered from the nations,
rich in livestock and goods, living at the center of the land.[a]" 13 Sheba[g] and Dedan and the merchants
of Tarshish and all her villages[b] will say to you, "Have you come to plunder? Have you gathered your
hordes to loot, to carry off silver and gold, to take away livestock and goods and to seize much plunder?[h]"'

14 "Therefore, son of man, prophesy and say to Gog: 'This is what the Sovereign LORD says: In that
day, when my people Israel are living in safety,[i] will you not take notice of it? 15 You will come from your
place in the far north, you and many nations with you, all of them riding on horses, a great horde, a
mighty army.[j] 16 You will advance against my people Israel like a cloud[k] that covers the land. In days to
come, Gog, I will bring you against my land, so that the nations may know me when I am proved holy
through you before their eyes.[l]

17 "'This is what the Sovereign LORD says: You are the one I spoke of in former days by my servants
the prophets of Israel. At that time they prophesied for years that I would bring you against them. 18 This
is what will happen in that day: When Gog attacks the land of Israel, my hot anger will be aroused, declares the Sovereign LORD. 19 In my zeal and fiery wrath I declare that at that time there shall be a great
earthquake in the land of Israel.[m] 20 The fish in the sea, the birds in the sky, the beasts of the field, every
creature that moves along the ground, and all the people on the face of the earth will tremble at my presence. The mountains will be overturned, the cliffs will crumble and every wall will fall to the ground.[n] 21 I
will summon a sword[o] against Gog on all my mountains, declares the Sovereign LORD. Every man's sword
will be against his brother.[p] 22 I will execute judgment[q] on him with plague and bloodshed; I will pour
down torrents of rain, hailstones[r] and burning sulfur on him and on his troops and on the many nations
with him. 23 And so I will show my greatness and my holiness, and I will make myself known in the sight
of many nations. Then they will know that I am the LORD.[s]'

39 "Son of man, prophesy against Gog and say: 'This is what the Sovereign LORD says: I am against
you, Gog, chief prince of[c] Meshek and Tubal.[t] 2 I will turn you around and drag you along. I
will bring you from the far north and send you against the mountains of Israel. 3 Then I will strike your
bow[u] from your left hand and make your arrows[v] drop from your right hand. 4 On the mountains of
Israel you will fall, you and all your troops and the nations with you. I will give you as food to all kinds
of carrion birds and to the wild animals.[w] 5 You will fall in the open field, for I have spoken, declares
the Sovereign LORD. 6 I will send fire[x] on Magog and on those who live in safety in the coastlands,[y] and
they will know that I am the LORD.

7 "'I will make known my holy name among my people Israel. I will no longer let my holy name be
profaned,[z] and the nations will know that I the LORD am the Holy One in Israel.[a] 8 It is coming! It will
surely take place, declares the Sovereign LORD. This is the day I have spoken of.

[a] *12* The Hebrew for this phrase means *the navel of the earth.* [b] *13* Or *her strong lions* [c] *1* Or *Gog, prince of Rosh,*

38:11 land of unwalled villages. An image of peace (see Zech 2:4–5 and notes); the Lord alone is sufficient protection.
38:12 center of the land. Where God's people dwell. See NIV text note. This graphic image explains the belief that Israel is the vital link between God and the world (the idea occurs also in 5:5) and that Jerusalem is theologically both the center of the land of Israel and the center of the world.
38:13 Sheba. See note on 1 Kgs 10:1. **Dedan.** See note on Gen 10:7. **Tarshish.** See note on 27:12.
38:15 You will come from ... the far north. The enemy typically comes from the north (v. 6; see 1:4, which describes the storm cloud of God's presence; see also Jer 1:13–15 and notes).
38:16 I am proved holy. The military advance will reveal the divine purpose: the vindication of God's holiness through Gog. The God of Israel is set apart from all other gods (see Exod 7:3–5; 14:4). God will use Gog as an agent of revelation to the world, not as a judgment on his people (vv. 16,23; 39:6–7,13,21–29). God's defeat of Gog will accomplish this (vv. 18–23).
38:17 You are the one I spoke of. Gog (see v. 2 and note). **in former days by my servants.** Perhaps a general reference to earlier prophetic messages of divine judgment on the nations.
38:19 great earthquake. The outpouring of divine rage on the enemies of God's people causes upheavals in the natural world (see Jer 4:23–26).
38:20 fish ... birds ... beasts ... every creature ... all the people ... of the earth. Corresponds to the total scope of nature affected by this cosmic manifestation of the divine presence.
38:22–23 I will execute judgment ... with plague and bloodshed ... I will make myself known. The ultimate purpose of the battle. Not unlike God's use of Pharaoh in Exodus (see Exod 7–14), this battle reveals God's supremacy over a powerful enemy. It anticipates the final judgment, when God reveals his sovereignty over all the forces of evil (Rev 19–20).
39:1–16 Opposition to Gog is reiterated but with more graphic details.
39:3 I will strike your bow from your left hand. Removal of a threat by disarming the enemy (cf. Jer 6:23).
39:4 food to all kinds of carrion birds. The sacrificial feast described in vv. 17–20 (see notes).

9“ ‘Then those who live in the towns of Israel will go out and use the weapons for fuel and burn them
up—the small and large shields, the bows and arrows, the war clubs and spears. For seven years they
will use them for fuel.[b] 10They will not need to gather wood from the fields or cut it from the forests,
because they will use the weapons for fuel. And they will plunder those who plundered them and loot
those who looted them, declares the Sovereign LORD.[c]
11“ ‘On that day I will give Gog a burial place in Israel, in the valley of those who travel east of the
Sea. It will block the way of travelers, because Gog and all his hordes will be buried there. So it will be
called the Valley of Hamon Gog.[a][d]
12“ ‘For seven months the Israelites will be burying them in order to cleanse the land.[e] 13All the
people of the land will bury them, and the day I display my glory[f] will be a memorable day for them, declares the Sovereign LORD. 14People will be continually employed in cleansing the land. They will spread
out across the land and, along with others, they will bury any bodies that are lying on the ground.
“ ‘After the seven months they will carry out a more detailed search. 15As they go through the land,
anyone who sees a human bone will leave a marker beside it until the gravediggers bury it in the Valley
of Hamon Gog, 16near a town called Hamonah.[b] And so they will cleanse the land.’
17“Son of man, this is what the Sovereign LORD says: Call out to every kind of bird[g] and all the wild
animals: ‘Assemble and come together from all around to the sacrifice I am preparing for you, the great
sacrifice on the mountains of Israel. There you will eat flesh and drink blood. 18You will eat the flesh
of mighty men and drink the blood of the princes of the earth as if they were rams and lambs, goats
and bulls—all of them fattened animals from Bashan.[h] 19At the sacrifice I am preparing for you, you
will eat fat till you are glutted and drink blood till you are drunk. 20At my table you will eat your fill of
horses and riders, mighty men and soldiers of every kind,’ declares the Sovereign LORD.[i]
21“I will display my glory among the nations, and all the nations will see the punishment I inflict
and the hand I lay on them.[j] 22From that day forward the people of Israel will know that I am the LORD
their God. 23And the nations will know that the people of Israel went into exile for their sin, because
they were unfaithful to me. So I hid my face from them and handed them over to their enemies, and
they all fell by the sword.[k] 24I dealt with them according to their uncleanness and their offenses, and
I hid my face from them.[l]
25“Therefore this is what the Sovereign LORD says: I will now restore the fortunes of Jacob[c][m] and

39:9 [b] Ps 46:9
39:10 [c] Isa 14:2; 33:1; Hab 2:8
39:11 [d] Eze 38:2
39:12 [e] Dt 21:23
39:13 [f] Eze 28:22
39:17 [g] Rev 19:17
39:18 [h] Ps 22:12; Jer 51:40
39:20 [i] Rev 19:17-18
39:21 [j] Ex 9:16; Isa 37:20; Eze 38:16
39:23 [k] Isa 1:15; 59:2; Jer 22:8-9; 44:23
39:24 [l] Jer 2:17,19; 4:18; Eze 36:19
39:25 [m] Jer 33:7; Eze 34:13

[a] *11 Hamon Gog* means *hordes of Gog.* [b] *16 Hamonah* means *horde.* [c] *25* Or *now bring Jacob back from captivity*

39:9 seven years. The number seven symbolizing completeness. **for fuel.** The enemies' weaponry becomes useful for God's people.
39:11–16 Gog's burial finalizes the removal of the threat.
39:11 I will give Gog a burial place … in the valley. God's control of Gog continues. He selects and names the burial site. **valley.** Probably that of Jezreel/Megiddo (the site of many epic battles in the history of the southern Levant, e.g., 2 Kings 23:29). It will be filled to the brim with dead bodies, blocking travel and underscoring the large threat this enemy posed.
39:12 seven months … burying them. The task requires all the people; it reflects the importance of the "holy land," the task's size, and the burial's thoroughness. **seven months.** Cf. v. 9 and note. **cleanse the land.** The burial's purpose. Dead bodies contaminated people and the land (Num 19:11–22). Cleansed people (36:24–32) need to live in a cleansed land.
39:13 the day I display my glory … a memorable day. The burial process (v. 12) and the site (v. 11) function as a permanent reminder of "the day" God defeated the enemy (v. 13), "the day" when God demonstrates who he is in all his splendor.
39:14 People will be continually employed. A special search party seeks any human remains to ensure a total and complete cleansing. Total ritual purity is the goal.
39:17 Assemble and come … to the sacrifice. A summons to a huge banquet meal for predators in celebration of Gog's defeat. The metaphor of sacrifice suggests consecration, or devotion, to God in judgment (cf. Jericho in Josh 6:17; see NIV text note and note there).
39:18 You will eat the flesh of mighty men … as if they were rams. The corpses of the victims are compared to animals used for sacrifices (see note on Gen 22:13). This portrays an undignified end for the enemies of God (Isa 34:6–8; Zeph 1:7; Rev 19:17–21).
39:19–20 At the sacrifice I am preparing … At my table. The one preparing the sacrifice is God. His "table" represents the sacrificial altar.
39:19 eat fat … drink blood. When offering a sacrifice, these were reserved for God (44:15; Lev 3:16; 1 Sam 2:15; cf. Isa 34:6). Another indicator that this feast is for the Lord.
39:22–23 Israel will know … the nations will know. The theological significance of Gog's defeat. For Israel it will reaffirm God's commitment to them. For the nations, they will know why God exiled his people: his justice, not powerlessness or cowardice, sealed Israel's fate (cf. Deut 31:16–18). Pharaoh's demise and defeat functioned similarly (Exod 6:6–7; 7:5; 14:18).
39:23 I hid my face. An expression of divine abandonment (see note on Ps 27:9; contrast v. 29 and note).
39:25–29 God's message to the exiles. His compassion will set the story line of restoration into motion. But his drive for glory fuels his grace (and fury). Thus, the exile is temporary, and a return home is their hope. The basis for confidence is the supernatural work of God.
39:25 restore the fortunes of Jacob. Conditions before their judgment, indicating a reversal of the judgment; cf. Sodom and Samaria in 16:53 and Egypt in 29:13–14.

39:25 [n]Jer 30:18 [o]Isa 27:12-13
39:26 [p]1Ki 4:25 [q]Isa 17:2; Eze 34:28; Mic 4:4
39:27 [r]Eze 36:23-24; 37:21; 38:16
39:29 [s]Joel 2:28; Ac 2:17
40:1 [t]2Ki 25:7; Jer 39:1-10; 52:4-11; Eze 33:21 [u]Eze 1:3
40:2 [v]Da 7:1,7 [w]Eze 17:22; Rev 21:10
40:3 [x]Eze 1:7; Da 10:6; Rev 1:15 [y]Eze 47:3; Zec 2:1-2; Rev 11:1; 21:15
40:4 [z]Jer 26:2 [a]Eze 44:5

will have compassion[n] on all the people of Israel, and I will be zealous for my holy name.[o] [26]They
will forget their shame and all the unfaithfulness they showed toward me when they lived in safety[p]
in their land with no one to make them afraid.[q] [27]When I have brought them back from the nations
and have gathered them from the countries of their enemies, I will be proved holy through them in
the sight of many nations.[r] [28]Then they will know that I am the LORD their God, for though I sent
them into exile among the nations, I will gather them to their own land, not leaving any behind. [29]I
will no longer hide my face from them, for I will pour out my Spirit[s] on the people of Israel, declares
the Sovereign LORD."

The Temple Area Restored

40 In the twenty-fifth year of our exile, at the beginning of the year, on the tenth of the month, in
the fourteenth year after the fall of the city[t]—on that very day the hand of the LORD was on
me[u] and he took me there. [2]In visions[v] of God he took me to the land of Israel and set me on a very high
mountain,[w] on whose south side were some buildings that looked like a city. [3]He took me there, and I
saw a man whose appearance was like bronze;[x] he was standing in the gateway with a linen cord and
a measuring rod[y] in his hand. [4]The man said to me, "Son of man, look carefully and listen closely
and pay attention to everything I am going to show you, for that is why you have been brought here.
Tell[z] the people of Israel everything you see.[a]"

39:26 They will forget their shame. The result of God's compassion (v. 25). See 6:9; 20:43; 36:31, where remembrance of shame comes because of God's judgment.

39:29 I will pour out my Spirit. Contrasts with God's hidden face (v. 23) and reflects the reality of the divine presence in the restoration process (36:27; 37:14; see Joel 2:28).

40:1—48:35 *Restoration of Worship in the New Spiritual Center.* The book of Ezekiel ends on a powerful note. This is the last of four visions experienced by the prophet (see 1:1; 8:4; 37:1). Ezekiel sees familiar things but with new eyes. This section concludes with the return of the Lord to his temple, city, and land, an event that enables his people to worship him forever in an unhindered, unmediated, and undefiled relationship.

The book ends by summarizing this permanent ideal condition in 48:35b: "THE LORD IS THERE," which reflects the fullness of the restoration due to God's presence. The city of God is the seat of the divine presence. The re-creation of a new spiritual center (chs. 40–43), along with a renewed system of worship (chs. 44–48), is the subject of Ezekiel's last vision.

Because the language of the vision merges well-known physical realities with idealized ones (for example, the description of tribal allocations), the meaning is not evident. Should one expect to see a literal temple constructed in the future, or is it figurative, or perhaps even both? A general rule when interpreting predictive prophecy is to look for the nearest fulfillment in history. Perhaps what Ezekiel saw was the post-exilic temple of Ezra's day. However, the divine glory does not return to Ezra's rebuilt temple at its dedication. From Ezra's day to the present, there has been no temple built that matches Ezekiel's vision. The next possible place to see this prophecy fulfilled literally belongs to what some have called a future millennial kingdom on earth based on Rev 20:1–6. In this millennial kingdom animal sacrifices will be offered at a rebuilt temple and will function as reminders of the sufficiency of Christ's sacrifice (a different function from OT sacrifices). Figurative interpretations also exist. Some interpret the temple vision to predict the New Covenant and the presence of God through the Holy Spirit among his people (see 1 Cor 3:16–17). Others see Ezekiel's temple as part of the new heavens and new earth (2 Pet 3:13; Rev 21:1) in the eschatological age. Accordingly, the physical details described in the vision (and their notable lack of direct correspondence with Pentateuchal legislation) are symbolic indications of the great blessings of that future age of worship.

Regardless of one's interpretation, several things are clear. The vision describes future realities that cannot be fully expressed in terms of Ezekiel's present realities. There are reminders throughout the vision that the future realities described are clearly intended for Ezekiel's audience (Ezek 40:4; 43:9–11; 44:5–6). It is a vision of restoration that features the presence of God within the new worship community. The large scale nature of the "temple-city" complex also tells us something about the scale of restoration promised. Rather than focusing only on the building project itself (literal or figurative), the vision inspires us to anticipate unending worship of the Living God. See Introduction: Particular Interpretive Challenges.

40:1—43:27 *Restoration of the Temple Area, Temple, Presence of God, and Altar.* The guide shows Ezekiel the outer court and its gates and the inner court and its gates (six gates total) and the rooms for priests to do their work related to sacrifices. Only authorized personnel, "the sons of Zadok" (40:46), can lead people to the epicenter of worship and sacrifice. The guide then moves Ezekiel to the temple itself, with a description of its beauty, perfect symmetry (ch. 41–42), and courtyards. The climactic point of this building project, as it was with the tabernacle and then Solomon's temple, is the presence of God. The glory comes from the east (the direction it moved when leaving the temple in the vision of abandonment in chs. 8–11) to make this habitation holy (43:1–11). The description of the new altar (43:13–27) ensures a God-given means for unbroken fellowship with him through the shedding of blood. The first phase of the new spiritual center is complete.

40:1 twenty-fifth year ... beginning of the year ... tenth of the month, in the fourteenth year after the fall of the city. Apr. 28, 573 BC.

40:2 In visions of God he took me to the land of Israel. Cf. 1:1; 8:3 and notes. What unfolds for Ezekiel is supernatural in light of the context of the fallen city. **set me on a very high mountain.** Height ensures visibility. Mount Zion is the earthly seat of God's reign (17:22; Isa 2:2; Mic 4:1; Zech 14:10). **buildings that looked like a city.** The fact that he sees what appears to be a city complex 14 years after Jerusalem's fall emphasizes hope in a future restoration.

40:3 I saw a man ... with a linen cord and a measuring rod. An angelic guide similar to the one mentioned in chs. 8–11 (see also Dan 10:5–6; Rev 1:13–15). He carries standard measuring tools for construction purposes. This man contrasts with the "man clothed in linen" in 9:2, whose tools (a writing kit) were for destruction.

The East Gate to the Outer Court

[5]I saw a wall completely surrounding the temple area. The length of the measuring rod in the man's hand was six long cubits,[a] each of which was a cubit and a handbreadth. He measured[b] the wall; it was one measuring rod thick and one rod high.

[6]Then he went to the east gate.[c] He climbed its steps and measured the threshold of the gate; it was one rod deep. [7]The alcoves[d] for the guards were one rod long and one rod wide, and the projecting walls between the alcoves were five cubits[b] thick. And the threshold of the gate next to the portico facing the temple was one rod deep.

[8]Then he measured the portico of the gateway; [9]it[c] was eight cubits[d] deep and its jambs were two cubits[e] thick. The portico of the gateway faced the temple.

[10]Inside the east gate were three alcoves on each side; the three had the same measurements, and the faces of the projecting walls on each side had the same measurements. [11]Then he measured the width of the entrance of the gateway; it was ten cubits and its length was thirteen cubits.[f] [12]In front of each alcove was a wall one cubit high, and the alcoves were six cubits square. [13]Then he measured the gateway from the top of the rear wall of one alcove to the top of the opposite one; the distance was twenty-five cubits[g] from one parapet opening to the opposite one. [14]He measured along the faces of the projecting walls all around the inside of the gateway—sixty cubits.[h] The measurement was up to the portico[i] facing the courtyard.[j][e] [15]The distance from the entrance of the gateway to the far end of its portico was fifty cubits.[k] [16]The alcoves and the projecting walls inside the gateway were surmounted by narrow parapet openings all around, as was the portico; the openings all around faced inward. The faces of the projecting walls were decorated with palm trees.[f]

The Outer Court

[17]Then he brought me into the outer court.[g] There I saw some rooms and a pavement that had been constructed all around the court; there were thirty rooms[h] along the pavement.[i] [18]It abutted the sides of the gateways and was as wide as they were long; this was the lower pavement. [19]Then he measured the distance from the inside of the lower gateway to the outside of the inner court;[j] it was a hundred cubits[l][k] on the east side as well as on the north.

The North Gate

[20]Then he measured the length and width of the north gate, leading into the outer court. [21]Its alcoves[l]—three on each side—its projecting walls and its portico had the same measurements as those of the first gateway. It was fifty cubits long and twenty-five cubits wide. [22]Its openings, its

40:5 [b]Eze 42:20
40:6 [c]Eze 8:16
40:7 [d]ver 36
40:14 [e]Ex 27:9
40:16 [f]ver 21-22; 2Ch 3:5; Eze 41:26
40:17 [g]Rev 11:2 [h]Eze 41:6 [i]Eze 42:1
40:19 [j]Eze 46:1 [k]ver 23,27
40:21 [l]ver 7

[a] *5* That is, about 11 feet or about 3.2 meters; also in verse 12. The long cubit of about 21 inches or about 53 centimeters is the basic unit of measurement of length throughout chapters 40–48. [b] *7* That is, about 8 3/4 feet or about 2.7 meters; also in verse 48 [c] *8,9* Many Hebrew manuscripts, Septuagint, Vulgate and Syriac; most Hebrew manuscripts *gateway facing the temple; it was one rod deep. [9]Then he measured the portico of the gateway; it* [d] *9* That is, about 14 feet or about 4.2 meters [e] *9* That is, about 3 1/2 feet or about 1 meter [f] *11* That is, about 18 feet wide and 23 feet long or about 5.3 meters wide and 6.9 meters long [g] *13* That is, about 44 feet or about 13 meters; also in verses 21, 25, 29, 30, 33 and 36 [h] *14* That is, about 105 feet or about 32 meters [i] *14* Septuagint; Hebrew *projecting wall* [j] *14* The meaning of the Hebrew for this verse is uncertain. [k] *15* That is, about 88 feet or about 27 meters; also in verses 21, 25, 29, 33 and 36 [l] *19* That is, about 175 feet or about 53 meters; also in verses 23, 27 and 47

40:5–27 Description of the outer court and its gates.

40:5 a wall completely surrounding the temple area. The outer court had a defined space. The wall separating the area outside the temple from the holy area inside the wall was 11 feet (3.2 meters) high and 11 feet (3.2 meters) thick.

40:6 east gate. One of three gates (east, north, south) of the outer court. It was the most important gate, since it provided a direct path to the temple itself. East, not north, oriented ancient cultures of the Near East. God's glory moved east when departing the temple, a sign of judgment (10:18–19; 11:22–23). God's glory will return through the east gate (43:1–5), a reversal of the judgment.

40:9 The portico of the gateway. A porch-like structure leading to the building.

40:10 alcoves. Recesses in the wall of the gate (on each side) for the guards, which thus demonstrates their defensive importance.

40:17 he brought me into the outer court. Ezekiel's guide takes him beyond the east gate and into the outer court proper, the main place of worship for an Israelite and the area farthest away from the temple proper. **thirty rooms.** Perhaps used by worshipers for various functions (see Jer 35:2,4).

40:19 a hundred cubits. The width of the court. About 175 feet (about 53 meters) separated the outer wall from the inner wall.

40:20 north gate. Identical to the south (v. 24) and east gates (v. 6). These gates prohibited the unauthorized from approaching.

40:22 [m]ver 49
40:23 [n]ver 19
40:25 [o]ver 33
40:26 [p]ver 22
40:27 [q]ver 32
40:28 [r]ver 35
40:30 [s]ver 21
40:31 [t]ver 22
40:34 [u]ver 22
40:35 [v]Eze 44:4; 47:2
40:36 [w]ver 7
40:38 [x]2Ch 4:6; Eze 42:13
40:39 [y]Eze 46:2 [z]Lev 4:3,28 [a]Lev 7:1
40:42 [b]Ex 20:25 [c]ver 39

portico[m] and its palm tree decorations had the same measurements as those of the gate facing east. Seven steps led up to it, with its portico opposite them. [23]There was a gate to the inner court facing the north gate, just as there was on the east. He measured from one gate to the opposite one; it was a hundred cubits.[n]

The South Gate

[24]Then he led me to the south side and I saw the south gate. He measured its jambs and its portico, and they had the same measurements as the others. [25]The gateway and its portico had narrow openings all around, like the openings of the others. It was fifty cubits long and twenty-five cubits wide.[o] [26]Seven steps led up to it, with its portico opposite them; it had palm tree decorations on the faces of the projecting walls on each side.[p] [27]The inner court[q] also had a gate facing south, and he measured from this gate to the outer gate on the south side; it was a hundred cubits.

The Gates to the Inner Court

[28]Then he brought me into the inner court through the south gate, and he measured the south gate; it had the same measurements[r] as the others. [29]Its alcoves, its projecting walls and its portico had the same measurements as the others. The gateway and its portico had openings all around. It was fifty cubits long and twenty-five cubits wide. [30](The porticoes[s] of the gateways around the inner court were twenty-five cubits wide and five cubits deep.) [31]Its portico[t] faced the outer court; palm trees decorated its jambs, and eight steps led up to it.

[32]Then he brought me to the inner court on the east side, and he measured the gateway; it had the same measurements as the others. [33]Its alcoves, its projecting walls and its portico had the same measurements as the others. The gateway and its portico had openings all around. It was fifty cubits long and twenty-five cubits wide. [34]Its portico[u] faced the outer court; palm trees decorated the jambs on either side, and eight steps led up to it.

[35]Then he brought me to the north gate[v] and measured it. It had the same measurements as the others, [36]as did its alcoves,[w] its projecting walls and its portico, and it had openings all around. It was fifty cubits long and twenty-five cubits wide. [37]Its portico[a] faced the outer court; palm trees decorated the jambs on either side, and eight steps led up to it.

The Rooms for Preparing Sacrifices

[38]A room with a doorway was by the portico in each of the inner gateways, where the burnt offerings[x] were washed. [39]In the portico of the gateway were two tables on each side, on which the burnt offerings,[y] sin offerings[b][z] and guilt offerings[a] were slaughtered. [40]By the outside wall of the portico of the gateway, near the steps at the entrance of the north gateway were two tables, and on the other side of the steps were two tables. [41]So there were four tables on one side of the gateway and four on the other — eight tables in all — on which the sacrifices were slaughtered. [42]There were also four tables of dressed stone[b] for the burnt offerings, each a cubit and a half long, a cubit and a half wide and a cubit high.[c] On them were placed the utensils for slaughtering the burnt offerings and the other sacrifices.[c] [43]And double-pronged hooks, each a handbreadth[d] long, were attached to the wall all around. The tables were for the flesh of the offerings.

a *37* Septuagint (see also verses 31 and 34); Hebrew *jambs* *b* *39* Or *purification offerings* *c* *42* That is, about 2 2/3 feet long and wide and 21 inches high or about 80 centimeters long and wide and 53 centimeters high *d* *43* That is, about 3 1/2 inches or about 9 centimeters

40:28 the inner court. A smaller version of the outer court, but it served a different purpose. The priests helped the worshipers with their sacrifices in this area; it was the area closest to the temple proper. **the south gate.** Provided access to the inner court (vv. 28–49).

40:38 A room ... in each of the inner gateways. Places for preparing sacrifices. **burnt offerings.** One of the oldest kinds of sacrifice (Gen 8:20; 22:2; see note on Gen 22:13). As a consecration to God, the entire animal was burned (see Lev 1:3–17 and note; see also note on Lev 1:9).

40:39 sin offerings. See note on Lev 4:1 — 5:13. **guilt offerings.** See note on Lev 5:14 — 6:7. Offering sacrifices was the main function of this new temple. Restored fellowship is made possible between the worshiper and God. Ezekiel's audience would have been comforted by this fact. Although Ezekiel's visions were for the exiles (v. 4; 43:9–11; 44:5–6), the symbolism here points beyond that time to Christ's sacrifice, which provides ultimate restoration of fellowship with God (see Heb 9:11–14 and notes).

The Rooms for the Priests

44 Outside the inner gate, within the inner court, were two rooms, one[a] at the side of the north gate
and facing south, and another at the side of the south[b] gate and facing north. 45 He said to me, “The
room facing south is for the priests who guard the temple,[d] 46 and the room facing north[e] is for the
priests who guard the altar.[f] These are the sons of Zadok,[g] who are the only Levites who may draw near
to the LORD to minister before him.[h]”

47 Then he measured the court: It was square—a hundred cubits long and a hundred cubits wide.
And the altar was in front of the temple.

The New Temple

48 He brought me to the portico of the temple[i] and measured the jambs of the portico; they were five
cubits wide on either side. The width of the entrance was fourteen cubits[c] and its projecting walls were[d]
three cubits[e] wide on either side. 49 The portico[j] was twenty cubits[f] wide, and twelve[g] cubits[h] from front
to back. It was reached by a flight of stairs,[i] and there were pillars[k] on each side of the jambs.

41 Then the man brought me to the main hall[l] and measured the jambs; the width of the jambs
was six cubits[j] on each side.[k] 2 The entrance was ten cubits[l] wide, and the projecting walls
on each side of it were five cubits[m] wide. He also measured the main hall; it was forty cubits long and
twenty cubits wide.[n][m]

3 Then he went into the inner sanctuary and measured the jambs of the entrance; each was two
cubits[o] wide. The entrance was six cubits wide, and the projecting walls on each side of it were seven
cubits[p] wide. 4 And he measured the length of the inner sanctuary; it was twenty cubits, and its width
was twenty cubits across the end of the main hall.[n] He said to me, “This is the Most Holy Place.[o]”

5 Then he measured the wall of the temple; it was six cubits thick, and each side room around the
temple was four cubits[q] wide. 6 The side rooms were on three levels, one above another, thirty[p] on each
level. There were ledges all around the wall of the temple to serve as supports for the side rooms, so that
the supports were not inserted into the wall of the temple.[q] 7 The side rooms all around the temple were
wider at each successive level. The structure surrounding the temple was built in ascending stages, so
that the rooms widened as one went upward. A stairway[r] went up from the lowest floor to the top floor
through the middle floor.

8 I saw that the temple had a raised base all around it, forming the foundation of the side rooms. It
was the length of the rod, six long cubits. 9 The outer wall of the side rooms was five cubits thick. The

[a] 44 Septuagint; Hebrew *were rooms for singers, which were* [b] 44 Septuagint; Hebrew *east* [c] 48 That is, about 25 feet or about 7.4 meters [d] 48 Septuagint; Hebrew *entrance was* [e] 48 That is, about 5 1/4 feet or about 1.6 meters [f] 49 That is, about 35 feet or about 11 meters [g] 49 Septuagint; Hebrew *eleven* [h] 49 That is, about 21 feet or about 6.4 meters [i] 49 Hebrew; Septuagint *Ten steps led up to it* [j] 1 That is, about 11 feet or about 3.2 meters; also in verses 3, 5 and 8 [k] 1 One Hebrew manuscript and Septuagint; most Hebrew manuscripts *side, the width of the tent* [l] 2 That is, about 18 feet or about 5.3 meters [m] 2 That is, about 8 3/4 feet or about 2.7 meters; also in verses 9, 11 and 12 [n] 2 That is, about 70 feet long and 35 feet wide or about 21 meters long and 11 meters wide [o] 3 That is, about 3 1/2 feet or about 1.1 meters; also in verse 22 [p] 3 That is, about 12 feet or about 3.7 meters [q] 5 That is, about 7 feet or about 2.1 meters

40:45 [d] 1Ch 9:23
40:46 [e] Eze 42:13 [f] Nu 18:5 [g] 1Ki 2:35 [h] Nu 16:5; Eze 43:19; 44:15; 45:4; 48:11
40:48 [i] 1Ki 6:2
40:49 [j] ver 22; 1Ki 6:3 [k] 1Ki 7:15
41:1 [l] ver 23
41:2 [m] 2Ch 3:3
41:4 [n] 1Ki 6:20 [o] Ex 26:33; Heb 9:3-8
41:6 [p] Eze 40:17 [q] 1Ki 6:5
41:7 [r] 1Ki 6:8

40:46 the priests . . . the sons of Zadok. The stipulated personnel for proper worship. From the time of Solomon's reign, only the relatives of Zadok were authorized to offer sacrifices (see note on 1 Kgs 4:4). All priests had to be descendants of Aaron (see notes on Num 3:1–51; 18:1–7; see also “Priest,” p. 2654).

40:47 the altar was in front of the temple. The altar, used daily for worship (43:13–17), takes center stage in the inner court.

40:48 He brought me to the portico of the temple. Ezekiel has finally arrived at the temple entrance, more specifically, the porch attached to the temple.

41:1 the main hall. The central part of the temple building, or the outer sanctuary, the largest of the three rooms comprising the temple (1 Kgs 6:3–5). The dimensions are the same as those in Solomon's main hall (1 Kgs 6:17).

41:3 the inner sanctuary. The Most Holy Place (v. 4; Exod 26:31–35; 1 Kgs 6:19–28; 2 Chr 3:8; Ps 28:2; Matt 27:51; Heb 8:2; 9:3–5,7; 10:19–20). Only the angelic guide, not Ezekiel, enters the Most Holy Place to measure it, which suggests restricted access as one approaches God, reminiscent of the restrictions in Lev 16 that forbid anyone but the high priest to enter it, and then only once a year (Lev 16:2,32–34; Heb 9:7). Likewise, the decreasing width of the three openings (see 40:48; v. 2; here) to the inner sanctuary further illustrates the need for restricted and controlled access as one gets closer to God.

41:5 the wall of the temple. Verses 5–11 describe side storage chambers along the wall of the temple.

41:6 thirty on each level. These 90 side rooms stored the Lord's treasures and utensils for worship (see Mal 3:10 and note). See v. 12 for a large storage building on the west side.

41:14 [s]Eze 40:47
41:15 [t]Eze 42:3
41:16 [u]1Ki 6:4 [v]ver 25-26; 1Ki 6:15; Eze 42:3
41:18 [w]1Ki 6:18 [x]Ex 37:7; 2Ch 3:7 [y]1Ki 6:29; 7:36 [z]Eze 10:21
41:19 [a]Eze 10:14
41:21 [b]ver 1
41:22 [c]Ex 30:1 [d]Ex 25:23; Eze 23:41; 44:16; Mal 1:7,12
41:23 [e]ver 1 [f]1Ki 6:32
41:24 [g]1Ki 6:34
41:26 [h]ver 15-16; Eze 40:16
42:1 [i]ver 13 [j]Eze 41:12-14 [k]Eze 40:17
42:3 [l]Eze 41:15 [m]Eze 41:16
42:4 [n]Eze 46:19

open area between the side rooms of the temple 10 and the priests' rooms was twenty cubits wide all around the temple. 11 There were entrances to the side rooms from the open area, one on the north and another on the south; and the base adjoining the open area was five cubits wide all around.

12 The building facing the temple courtyard on the west side was seventy cubits[a] wide. The wall of the building was five cubits thick all around, and its length was ninety cubits.[b]

13 Then he measured the temple; it was a hundred cubits[c] long, and the temple courtyard and the building with its walls were also a hundred cubits long. 14 The width of the temple courtyard on the east, including the front of the temple, was a hundred cubits.[s]

15 Then he measured the length of the building facing the courtyard at the rear of the temple, including its galleries[t] on each side; it was a hundred cubits.

The main hall, the inner sanctuary and the portico facing the court, 16 as well as the thresholds and the narrow windows[u] and galleries around the three of them—everything beyond and including the threshold was covered with wood. The floor, the wall up to the windows, and the windows were covered.[v] 17 In the space above the outside of the entrance to the inner sanctuary and on the walls at regular intervals all around the inner and outer sanctuary 18 were carved[w] cherubim[x] and palm trees.[y] Palm trees alternated with cherubim. Each cherub had two faces:[z] 19 the face of a human being toward the palm tree on one side and the face of a lion toward the palm tree on the other. They were carved all around the whole temple.[a] 20 From the floor to the area above the entrance, cherubim and palm trees were carved on the wall of the main hall.

21 The main hall[b] had a rectangular doorframe, and the one at the front of the Most Holy Place was similar. 22 There was a wooden altar[c] three cubits[d] high and two cubits square[e]; its corners, its base[f] and its sides were of wood. The man said to me, "This is the table[d] that is before the LORD." 23 Both the main hall[e] and the Most Holy Place had double doors.[f] 24 Each door had two leaves—two hinged leaves[g] for each door. 25 And on the doors of the main hall were carved cherubim and palm trees like those carved on the walls, and there was a wooden overhang on the front of the portico. 26 On the sidewalls of the portico were narrow windows with palm trees carved on each side. The side rooms of the temple also had overhangs.[h]

The Rooms for the Priests

42 Then the man led me northward into the outer court and brought me to the rooms[i] opposite the temple courtyard[j] and opposite the outer wall on the north side.[k] 2 The building whose door faced north was a hundred cubits long and fifty cubits wide.[g] 3 Both in the section twenty cubits[h] from the inner court and in the section opposite the pavement of the outer court, gallery[l] faced gallery at the three levels.[m] 4 In front of the rooms was an inner passageway ten cubits wide and a hundred cubits[i] long.[j] Their doors were on the north.[n] 5 Now the upper rooms were narrower, for the galleries took more space from them than from the rooms on the lower and middle floors of the building. 6 The rooms on the top floor had no pillars, as the courts had; so they were smaller in floor space than those on the lower and middle floors. 7 There was an outer wall parallel to the rooms and the outer court; it extended in front of the rooms for fifty cubits. 8 While the row of rooms on the side next to the outer court was fifty cubits long, the row on the side nearest the sanctuary

[a] *12* That is, about 123 feet or about 37 meters [b] *12* That is, about 158 feet or about 48 meters [c] *13* That is, about 175 feet or about 53 meters; also in verses 14 and 15 [d] *22* That is, about 5 1/4 feet or about 1.5 meters [e] *22* Septuagint; Hebrew *long* [f] *22* Septuagint; Hebrew *length* [g] *2* That is, about 175 feet long and 88 feet wide or about 53 meters long and 27 meters wide [h] *3* That is, about 35 feet or about 11 meters [i] *4* Septuagint and Syriac; Hebrew *and one cubit* [j] *4* That is, about 18 feet wide and 175 feet long or about 5.3 meters wide and 53 meters long

41:16 everything ... was covered with wood. Ezekiel sees the overall beauty of the temple's interior. **wood.** A costly material.

41:18,20 cherubim and palm trees. Designs associated with peace and heavenly protection of the temple. See also 1:5–24; Gen 3:24 and notes.

41:22 wooden altar. The only furnishing inside the sanctuary. As the altar of burnt offering stood outside the temple proper (43:13–17), so a smaller altar (see NIV text notes) stood outside the Most Holy Place. It served as a table to hold the bread of the Presence, laid out daily by the priests (Exod 25:30; Lev 24:5–9; 1 Kgs 7:48). This table-like altar underscores the important role of sacrifice in these visions.

41:23 double doors. Possibly folding doors; suggests restricted or narrow access of entry.

42:1 rooms opposite the temple courtyard. Large chambers on the sides of the building; used by priests. Their purpose is stated in vv. 13–14 (see notes).

was a hundred cubits long. 9 The lower rooms had an entrance[o] on the east side as one enters them
from the outer court.
10 On the south side[a] along the length of the wall of the outer court, adjoining the temple courtyard
and opposite the outer wall, were rooms[p] 11 with a passageway in front of them. These were like the
rooms on the north; they had the same length and width, with similar exits and dimensions. Similar
to the doorways on the north 12 were the doorways of the rooms on the south. There was a doorway at
the beginning of the passageway that was parallel to the corresponding wall extending eastward, by
which one enters the rooms.
13 Then he said to me, "The north[q] and south rooms facing the temple courtyard are the priests'
rooms, where the priests who approach the LORD will eat the most holy offerings. There they will put the
most holy offerings — the grain offerings, the sin offerings[b][r] and the guilt offerings[s] — for the place is
holy.[t] 14 Once the priests enter the holy precincts, they are not to go into the outer court until they leave
behind the garments[u] in which they minister, for these are holy. They are to put on other clothes before
they go near the places that are for the people.[v]"
15 When he had finished measuring what was inside the temple area, he led me out by the east gate[w]
and measured the area all around: 16 He measured the east side with the measuring rod; it was five
hundred cubits.[c,d] 17 He measured the north side; it was five hundred cubits[e] by the measuring rod.
18 He measured the south side; it was five hundred cubits by the measuring rod. 19 Then he turned to the
west side and measured; it was five hundred cubits by the measuring rod. 20 So he measured[x] the area
on all four sides. It had a wall around it,[y] five hundred cubits long and five hundred cubits wide,[z] to
separate the holy from the common.[a]

God's Glory Returns to the Temple

43 Then the man brought me to the gate facing east,[b] 2 and I saw the glory of the God of Israel
coming from the east. His voice was like the roar of rushing waters,[c] and the land was radiant
with his glory.[d] 3 The vision I saw was like the vision I had seen when he[f] came to destroy the city and
like the visions I had seen by the Kebar River, and I fell facedown. 4 The glory[e] of the LORD entered the
temple through the gate facing east.[f] 5 Then the Spirit[g] lifted me up[h] and brought me into the inner
court, and the glory of the LORD filled the temple.
6 While the man was standing beside me, I heard someone speaking to me from inside the temple. 7 He said: "Son of man, this is the place of my throne and the place for the soles of my feet. This

[a] *10* Septuagint; Hebrew *Eastward* [b] *13* Or *purification offerings* [c] *16* See Septuagint of verse 17; Hebrew *rods*; also in verses 18 and 19. [d] *16* Five hundred cubits equal about 875 feet or about 265 meters; also in verses 17, 18 and 19. [e] *17* Septuagint; Hebrew *rods* [f] *3* Some Hebrew manuscripts and Vulgate; most Hebrew manuscripts *I*

42:9 [o] Eze 44:5; 46:19
42:10 [p] ver 1
42:13 [q] Eze 40:46 [r] Lev 10:17; 6:25 [s] Lev 14:13 [t] Ex 29:31; Lev 6:29; 7:6; 10:12-13; Nu 18:9-10
42:14 [u] Eze 44:19 [v] Ex 29:9; Lev 8:7-9
42:15 [w] Eze 43:1
42:20 [x] Eze 40:5 [y] Zec 2:5 [z] Eze 45:2; Rev 21:16 [a] Eze 22:26
43:1 [b] Eze 10:19; 42:15; 44:1; 46:1
43:2 [c] Rev 1:15 [d] Isa 6:3; Eze 11:23; Rev 18:1
43:4 [e] Eze 1:28 [f] Eze 10:19
43:5 [g] Eze 11:24 [h] Eze 3:12; 8:3

42:13 priests' rooms. Used by the priest to store their clothing (see v. 14 and note) and to "eat the most holy offerings," i.e., the sacrificial meal cooked on the altar (Lev 2:3; 5:13; 6:16,26,29; 7:6,10).
42:14 the garments. The holy garments, which were exchanged for street clothes after serving the Lord in this holy place.
42:20 five hundred cubits long and five hundred cubits wide. The dimensions of the entire exterior temple area (875 feet by 875 feet or 270 meters by 270 meters); note the perfect symmetry of this sacred space. The construction of the sacred space is now complete; however, the climax of the building project follows in 43:5 (see note).
43:1 the man brought me to the gate facing east. Where the visions started (see 40:5–6 and note on 40:6). This is the primary temple entrance.
43:2 I saw the glory of the God of Israel coming from the east. Corresponds to the direction of God's departure from Solomon's temple (10:19; 11:23). Ezekiel experiences the divine presence approaching the new temple, similar to that of his first vision (1:27–28). **God of Israel.** An important designation: God is reclaiming ownership of his people, land, and temple (see note on 8:4). **like the roar of rushing waters.** The approach was not only loud but overpowering (1:24; Rev 1:15; 14:2; 19:6) and luminous, "the land was radiant with his glory" (10:4; Luke 2:9; Rev 21:11,23).
43:3 the vision I saw … like the visions I had seen. A comparison with Ezekiel's two previous experiences of God's presence. **when he came to destroy the city.** When God appeared for purposes of judgment, he was the divine agent of destruction (see chs. 8–11). **by the Kebar River.** When God appeared to call Ezekiel into prophetic ministry (chs. 1–3). Now he appears for other purposes.
43:5 the glory of the LORD filled the temple. God appears for the purposes of restoration. He is reclaiming ownership of his land. This is the crowning moment in this building project. God occupies this architectural structure and gives meaning to it, analogous to the dedications of the tabernacle and Solomon's temple (Exod 40:34; 1 Kgs 8:10–11; cf. Isa 6:4). This prepares us for God's restoration work in us. When God builds the temple of his church corporately and individually (Eph 2:21), he fills us with his Spirit (Eph 1:13) and our bodies become temples of the Holy Spirit (1 Cor 6:19).
43:6 I heard someone speaking to me from inside the temple. As before (ch. 2) God's speaks directly to the prophet.
43:7 the place of my throne … place for the soles of my feet. The restored temple is God's palace. God is reclaiming his seat of kingship (1 Sam 4:4; Ps 47:8). God possesses this place; it marks his dominion and rule (1 Chr 28:2; Pss 99:5; 132:7; Isa 60:13; Lam 2:1).

43:7 [i] Lev 26:30
43:9 [j] Eze 37:26-28
43:10 [k] Eze 16:61
43:11 [l] Eze 44:5
43:12 [m] Eze 40:2
43:13 [n] 2Ch 4:1
43:15 [o] Ex 27:2
43:17 [p] Ex 20:26
43:18 [q] Ex 40:29 [r] Lev 1:5,11; Heb 9:21-22
43:19 [s] Lev 4:3; Eze 45:18-19 [t] Eze 44:15 [u] Nu 16:40; Eze 40:46
43:20 [v] ver 17 [w] Lev 16:19
43:21 [x] Ex 29:14; Heb 13:11

is where I will live among the Israelites forever. The people of Israel will never again defile my holy name—neither they nor their kings—by their prostitution and the funeral offerings[a] for their kings at their death.[b][i] 8 When they placed their threshold next to my threshold and their doorposts beside my doorposts, with only a wall between me and them, they defiled my holy name by their detestable practices. So I destroyed them in my anger. 9 Now let them put away from me their prostitution and the funeral offerings for their kings, and I will live among them forever.[j]

10 "Son of man, describe the temple to the people of Israel, that they may be ashamed[k] of their sins. Let them consider its perfection, 11 and if they are ashamed of all they have done, make known to them the design of the temple—its arrangement, its exits and entrances—its whole design and all its regulations[c] and laws. Write these down before them so that they may be faithful to its design and follow all its regulations.[l]

12 "This is the law of the temple: All the surrounding area[m] on top of the mountain will be most holy. Such is the law of the temple.

The Great Altar Restored

13 "These are the measurements of the altar[n] in long cubits,[d] that cubit being a cubit and a handbreadth: Its gutter is a cubit deep and a cubit wide, with a rim of one span[e] around the edge. And this is the height of the altar: 14 From the gutter on the ground up to the lower ledge that goes around the altar it is two cubits high, and the ledge is a cubit wide.[f] From this lower ledge to the upper ledge that goes around the altar it is four cubits high, and that ledge is also a cubit wide.[g] 15 Above that, the altar hearth is four cubits high, and four horns[o] project upward from the hearth. 16 The altar hearth is square, twelve cubits[h] long and twelve cubits wide. 17 The upper ledge also is square, fourteen cubits[i] long and fourteen cubits wide. All around the altar is a gutter of one cubit with a rim of half a cubit.[e] The steps[p] of the altar face east."

18 Then he said to me, "Son of man, this is what the Sovereign LORD says: These will be the regulations for sacrificing burnt offerings[q] and splashing blood[r] against the altar when it is built: 19 You are to give a young bull[s] as a sin offering[j] to the Levitical priests of the family of Zadok,[t] who come near[u] to minister before me, declares the Sovereign LORD. 20 You are to take some of its blood and put it on the four horns of the altar and on the four corners of the upper ledge[v] and all around the rim, and so purify the altar[w] and make atonement for it. 21 You are to take the bull for the sin offering and burn it in the designated part of the temple area outside the sanctuary.[x]

[a] *7* Or *the memorial monuments*; also in verse 9 [b] *7* Or *their high places* [c] *11* Some Hebrew manuscripts and Septuagint; most Hebrew manuscripts *regulations and its whole design* [d] *13* That is, about 21 inches or about 53 centimeters; also in verses 14 and 17. The long cubit is the basic unit for linear measurement throughout Ezekiel 40–48. [e] *13,17* That is, about 11 inches or about 27 centimeters
[f] *14* That is, about 3 1/2 feet high and 1 3/4 feet wide or about 105 centimeters high and 53 centimeters wide
[g] *14* That is, about 7 feet high and 1 3/4 feet wide or about 2.1 meters high and 53 centimeters wide
[h] *16* That is, about 21 feet or about 6.4 meters [i] *17* That is, about 25 feet or about 7.4 meters
[j] *19* Or *purification offering*; also in verses 21, 22 and 25

I will live among the Israelites forever. The longevity of his possession and dominion. God is reclaiming his eternal seat of sovereignty; thus this constitutes a renewal of the promise of 37:26–28 (see 43:9; 1 Kgs 6:13; Zech 2:11). **funeral offerings.** See first NIV text note. Fourteen kings of Judah were buried near the temple in Jerusalem (e.g., 2 Kgs 21:18,26; 23:30). God's presence brings correction to past behaviors. These memorials, not prescribed by God, were designed to honor human kings.

43:8 detestable practices. Practices that brought about Jerusalem's destruction (e.g., 5:11; 18:10–12; and especially 22:1–15). God is without rivals; he alone reigns as king. This part of the vision prepares us for what is known about God's reign in the book of Revelation (Rev 4; 7:9–17). In the new Jerusalem, when all things are fully restored, when God has made all things new (Rev 21:5), God's possession of the Holy City and his rulership will be eternal. See Introduction: Theological Significance; see also "The City of God," p. 2666.

43:10 describe the temple to the people of Israel, that they may be ashamed of their sins. God intends that Ezekiel's visions convict Ezekiel's audience of sin. Such conviction would make them ashamed and thus steer them away from the sins of the past. Ezekiel's generation is not so much given a blueprint to build a temple as they are given a plan to keep them pure.

43:12 law of the temple. The requirement of holiness outlined in chs. 40–42.

43:13 the altar. First mentioned in 40:47 and now described in detail in vv. 13–27. It is square (vv. 13–17) and has stone projections at each corner (v. 15) to contain the wood and animal sacrifices (Exod 29:12; Ps 118:27). It emphasizes the importance of performing sacrifices in the new temple.

43:18 regulations ... when it is built. The altar had to be consecrated to God before it could be used. This required cleansing with animal blood (Exod 29:16; Lev 4:7; 5:9). What begins as common, or ordinary, is consecrated to God and assigned a God-designated function.

43:21 bull for the sin offering ... burn it. The animal meat was to be burned completely, not in part. Similar stipulations exist for the goat (v. 22) and the young bull and ram (vv. 23–24).

22“On the second day you are to offer a male goat without defect for a sin offering, and the altar is
to be purified as it was purified with the bull. 23When you have finished purifying it, you are to offer a
young bull and a ram from the flock, both without defect.[y] 24You are to offer them before the LORD, and
the priests are to sprinkle salt[z] on them and sacrifice them as a burnt offering to the LORD.
25“For seven days[a] you are to provide a male goat daily for a sin offering; you are also to provide a
young bull and a ram from the flock, both without defect.[b] 26For seven days they are to make atonement
for the altar and cleanse it; thus they will dedicate it. 27At the end of these days, from the eighth day[c] on,
the priests are to present your burnt offerings and fellowship offerings[d] on the altar. Then I will accept
you, declares the Sovereign LORD.”

The Priesthood Restored

44 Then the man brought me back to the outer gate of the sanctuary, the one facing east,[e] and
it was shut. 2The LORD said to me, “This gate is to remain shut. It must not be opened; no one
may enter through it.[f] It is to remain shut because the LORD, the God of Israel, has entered through it.
3The prince himself is the only one who may sit inside the gateway to eat in the presence[g] of the LORD.
He is to enter by way of the portico of the gateway and go out the same way.[h]”
4Then the man brought me by way of the north gate to the front of the temple. I looked and saw the
glory of the LORD filling the temple[i] of the LORD, and I fell facedown.[j]
5The LORD said to me, “Son of man, look carefully, listen closely and give attention to everything I
tell you concerning all the regulations and instructions regarding the temple of the LORD. Give attention
to the entrance to the temple and all the exits of the sanctuary.[k] 6Say to rebellious Israel,[l] ‘This is what
the Sovereign LORD says: Enough of your detestable practices, people of Israel! 7In addition to all your
other detestable practices, you brought foreigners uncircumcised in heart[m] and flesh into my sanctuary,
desecrating my temple while you offered me food, fat and blood, and you broke my covenant.[n] 8Instead
of carrying out your duty in regard to my holy things, you put others in charge of my sanctuary.[o] 9This
is what the Sovereign LORD says: No foreigner uncircumcised in heart and flesh is to enter my sanctuary,
not even the foreigners who live among the Israelites.[p]
10“ ‘The Levites who went far from me when Israel went astray[q] and who wandered from me after
their idols must bear the consequences of their sin.[r] 11They may serve in my sanctuary, having charge
of the gates of the temple and serving in it; they may slaughter the burnt offerings[s] and sacrifices for
the people and stand before the people and serve them.[t] 12But because they served them in the presence
of their idols and made the people of Israel fall into sin, therefore I have sworn with uplifted hand[u]
that they must bear the consequences of their sin, declares the Sovereign LORD.[v] 13They are not to come
near to serve me as priests or come near any of my holy things or my most holy offerings; they must

43:23 [y]Ex 29:1
43:24 [z]Lev 2:13; Mk 9:49-50
43:25 [a]Lev 8:33 [b]Ex 29:37
43:27 [c]Lev 9:1 [d]Lev 17:5
44:1 [e]Eze 43:1
44:2 [f]Eze 43:4-5
44:3 [g]Ex 24:9-11 [h]Eze 46:2,8
44:4 [i]Isa 6:4; Rev 15:8 [j]Eze 1:28; 3:23
44:5 [k]Eze 40:4; 43:10-11
44:6 [l]Eze 3:9
44:7 [m]Lev 26:41 [n]Ge 17:14; Ex 12:48; Lev 22:25
44:8 [o]Lev 22:2; Nu 18:7
44:9 [p]Joel 3:17; Zec 14:21
44:10 [q]2Ki 23:8 [r]Nu 18:23
44:11 [s]2Ch 29:34 [t]Nu 3:5-37; 16:9; 1Ch 26:12-19
44:12 [u]Ps 106:26 [v]2Ki 16:10-16

43:26 atonement for the altar. Required “seven days” of purification. Only after this would the people’s offerings be accepted by God. All is in place for people to approach God through sacrifice on this altar. Their offerings would ensure communion and peace with a holy God abiding in their midst. The new altar and the sacrifices made on it are a reminder that God provides a way for people to become holy. Christ’s blood sacrifice is God’s provision for our holiness (Heb 9:11–14; 10:12–14). Cleansing from sin through sacrifice (sin offering) produces peace (fellowship offering) with God.

44:1–31 *Restoration of Restricted Access for People and Priests.* Only the true people of God have access to worship a holy God (vv. 1–14). The priests, together with the other worshipers, must have clear lines of separation between the holy and unholy in their worship (vv. 15–31).

44:2 This gate is to remain shut. The gate facing east, the main entrance to the temple, was closed (v. 1). God entered through the east gate, thus making it holy. Human accessibility would defile it. Since God is living permanently with his people (43:7), he will not need access to this gate for exiting, as he did in the past (10:19; 11:23).

44:3 prince. Ezekiel’s word for king, used here for the first time in chs. 40–48 (see 34:24). Restricted access applies even to the king. He could only eat at this gate. The restriction emphasizes God’s character of holiness. **eat.** Presumably the prince’s part of the fellowship meal (Lev 7:15; Deut 12:7; see 43:27).

44:4 to the front of the temple ... the glory of the LORD filling the temple. Another visible manifestation of the divine presence but now at the north gate, the gate used by the priests (40:44–45). As in 43:4–12, after the divine presence approaches, God gives a word of correction that Ezekiel is to speak.

44:5 look carefully, listen closely. Another reminder that these visions have implications for Ezekiel’s generation (see 40:4).

44:6 Say to rebellious Israel. Even 14 years after the fall of Jerusalem (see 40:1 and note), God still describes his people as law breakers (see Introduction: Audience). Owing to past abuses, correction is still needed.

44:9 foreigner uncircumcised. Non-Israelites. In the past the authorities had allowed uncircumcised foreigners access to the Lord’s temple (v. 7). As a result, the temple was not kept pure. Illegitimate temple access will not be tolerated in the new spiritual center.

44:13 They. The Levites (v. 10). **are not to come near to serve me as priests.** In the new order the Levites will serve only as gatekeepers and temple attendants (v. 14). This Levitical limitation is due to the fact that in the past, their sin of idolatry led the nation into sin (cf. Num 18:23; Ezek 8).

44:13 [w]Eze 16:61 [x]Nu 18:3
44:14 [y]Nu 18:4; 1Ch 23:28-32
44:15 [z]Jer 33:18; Eze 40:46; Zec 3:7
44:16 [a]Eze 41:22 [b]Nu 18:5
44:17 [c]Ex 39:27-28; Rev 19:8
44:18 [d]Ex 28:39; Isa 3:20 [e]Ex 28:42 [f]Lev 16:4
44:19 [g]Lev 6:27; Eze 46:20 [h]Lev 6:10-11; Eze 42:14
44:20 [i]Lev 21:5; Nu 6:5
44:21 [j]Lev 10:9
44:22 [k]Lev 21:7
44:23 [l]Eze 22:26 [m]Mal 2:7
44:24 [n]Dt 17:8-9; 1Ch 23:4 [o]2Ch 19:8
44:25 [p]Lev 21:1-4
44:26 [q]Nu 19:14
44:28 [r]Nu 18:20; Dt 10:9; 18:1-2; Jos 13:33
44:29 [s]Lev 27:21 [t]Nu 18:9,14
44:30 [u]Nu 18:12-13 [v]Nu 15:18-21 [w]Mal 3:10 [x]Ne 10:35-37
44:31 [y]Ex 22:31; Lev 22:8
45:1 [z]Eze 47:21-22 [a]Eze 48:8-9,29
45:2 [b]Eze 42:20

bear the shame[w] of their detestable practices.[x] 14 And I will appoint them to guard the temple for all the work that is to be done in it.[y]

15 " 'But the Levitical priests, who are descendants of Zadok and who guarded my sanctuary when the Israelites went astray from me, are to come near to minister before me; they are to stand before me to offer sacrifices of fat and blood, declares the Sovereign LORD.[z] 16 They alone are to enter my sanctuary; they alone are to come near my table[a] to minister before me and serve me as guards.[b]

17 " 'When they enter the gates of the inner court, they are to wear linen clothes;[c] they must not wear any woolen garment while ministering at the gates of the inner court or inside the temple. 18 They are to wear linen turbans[d] on their heads and linen undergarments[e] around their waists. They must not wear anything that makes them perspire.[f] 19 When they go out into the outer court where the people are, they are to take off the clothes they have been ministering in and are to leave them in the sacred rooms, and put on other clothes, so that the people are not consecrated[g] through contact with their garments.[h]

20 " 'They must not shave their heads or let their hair grow long, but they are to keep the hair of their heads trimmed.[i] 21 No priest is to drink wine when he enters the inner court.[j] 22 They must not marry widows or divorced women; they may marry only virgins of Israelite descent or widows of priests.[k] 23 They are to teach my people the difference between the holy and the common[l] and show them how to distinguish between the unclean and the clean.[m]

24 " 'In any dispute, the priests are to serve as judges[n] and decide it according to my ordinances. They are to keep my laws and my decrees for all my appointed festivals, and they are to keep my Sabbaths holy.[o]

25 " 'A priest must not defile himself by going near a dead person; however, if the dead person was his father or mother, son or daughter, brother or unmarried sister, then he may defile himself.[p] 26 After he is cleansed, he must wait seven days.[q] 27 On the day he goes into the inner court of the sanctuary to minister in the sanctuary, he is to offer a sin offering[a] for himself, declares the Sovereign LORD.

28 " 'I am to be the only inheritance[r] the priests have. You are to give them no possession in Israel; I will be their possession. 29 They will eat the grain offerings, the sin offerings and the guilt offerings; and everything in Israel devoted[b] to the LORD[s] will belong to them.[t] 30 The best of all the firstfruits[u] and of all your special gifts will belong to the priests. You are to give them the first portion of your ground meal[v] so that a blessing[w] may rest on your household.[x] 31 The priests must not eat anything, whether bird or animal, found dead or torn by wild animals.[y]

Israel Fully Restored

45 " 'When you allot the land as an inheritance,[z] you are to present to the LORD a portion of the land as a sacred district, 25,000 cubits[c] long and 20,000[d] cubits[e] wide; the entire area will be holy.[a] 2 Of this, a section 500 cubits[f] square[b] is to be for the sanctuary, with 50 cubits[g] around it for

[a] *27* Or *purification offering*; also in verse 29 [b] *29* The Hebrew term refers to the irrevocable giving over of things or persons to the LORD. [c] *1* That is, about 8 miles or about 13 kilometers; also in verses 3, 5 and 6 [d] *1* Septuagint (see also verses 3 and 5 and 48:9); Hebrew *10,000* [e] *1* That is, about 6 1/2 miles or about 11 kilometers [f] *2* That is, about 875 feet or about 265 meters [g] *2* That is, about 88 feet or about 27 meters

44:15 descendants of Zadok ... are to come near to minister. The ministry distinction between the Levites and the priests. The ministry of serving at the altar and in the sanctuary, nearest to God, is to be carried out by the Zadokite priests. Zadok was a prominent priest during David's reign (2 Sam 20:25). Later he supported Solomon, not Adonijah. In so doing he secured for himself and his descendants the honor of serving in the Jerusalem temple (1 Kgs 1:8,32–35). Because of their faithfulness, the Zadokites receive special consideration in chs. 40–48.

44:16 They alone are to enter my sanctuary. An exclusivity based on God's holy character and the concern to maintain this uncompromising standard.

44:17 they are to wear linen clothes. Linen breathes; wool does not. The point is to restrict perspiration (v. 18).

44:19 take off the clothes. Take off the sacred wardrobe for the sake of maintaining God's distinction between the holy and the common (vv. 17–19).

44:20–27 This section restricts certain behaviors that threaten purity. The main concern for such restrictions is voiced specifically in v. 23.

44:20 must not shave their heads. This ritual mourning practice for the dead was to be avoided (7:18; see Lev 21:1–5).

44:23 difference between the holy and the common. By distinguishing between the holy and the common, the Zadokite priests would model to God's people that a radical distinction exists between everyday things and the things of God. See Introduction to Leviticus: Major Theological Themes (Holiness and Purity).

44:28 I am to be the only inheritance the priests have ... give them no possession in Israel. Another restriction. Priestly provisions (such as land and temporal needs) derive from and are met by God as the priests serve him (see Num 18:20,23–24; Deut 10:9; Josh 13:14,33; 18:7).

45:1 — 46:24 *Restoration of Social Justice, Worship Calendar, and Procedures.* The key elements for worship at the new spiritual center

open land. 3 In the sacred district, measure off a section 25,000 cubits long and 10,000 cubits[a] wide. In it will be the sanctuary, the Most Holy Place. 4 It will be the sacred portion of the land for the priests,[c] who minister in the sanctuary and who draw near to minister before the LORD. It will be a place for their houses as well as a holy place for the sanctuary.[d] 5 An area 25,000 cubits long and 10,000 cubits wide will belong to the Levites, who serve in the temple, as their possession for towns to live in.[b][e]

6 " 'You are to give the city as its property an area 5,000 cubits[c] wide and 25,000 cubits long, adjoining the sacred portion; it will belong to all Israel.[f]

7 " 'The prince will have the land bordering each side of the area formed by the sacred district and the property of the city. It will extend westward from the west side and eastward from the east side, running lengthwise from the western to the eastern border parallel to one of the tribal portions.[g] 8 This land will be his possession in Israel. And my princes will no longer oppress my people but will allow the people of Israel to possess the land according to their tribes.[h]

9 " 'This is what the Sovereign LORD says: You have gone far enough, princes of Israel! Give up your violence and oppression and do what is just and right.[i] Stop dispossessing my people, declares the Sovereign LORD. 10 You are to use accurate scales,[j] an accurate ephah[d][k] and an accurate bath.[e] 11 The ephah[l] and the bath are to be the same size, the bath containing a tenth of a homer and the ephah a tenth of a homer; the homer is to be the standard measure for both. 12 The shekel[f] is to consist of twenty gerahs.[m] Twenty shekels plus twenty-five shekels plus fifteen shekels equal one mina.[g]

13 " 'This is the special gift you are to offer: a sixth of an ephah[h] from each homer of wheat and a sixth of an ephah[i] from each homer of barley. 14 The prescribed portion of olive oil, measured by the bath, is a tenth of a bath[j] from each cor (which consists of ten baths or one homer, for ten baths are equivalent to a homer). 15 Also one sheep is to be taken from every flock of two hundred from the well-watered pastures of Israel. These will be used for the grain offerings, burnt offerings[n] and fellowship offerings to make atonement[o] for the people, declares the Sovereign LORD. 16 All the people of the land will be required to give this special offering to the prince in Israel. 17 It will be the duty of the prince to provide the burnt offerings, grain offerings and drink offerings at the festivals, the New Moons and the Sabbaths[p]—at all the appointed festivals of Israel. He will provide the sin offerings,[k] grain offerings, burnt offerings and fellowship offerings to make atonement for the Israelites.[q]

18 " 'This is what the Sovereign LORD says: In the first month[r] on the first day you are to take a young bull without defect[s] and purify the sanctuary.[t] 19 The priest is to take some of the blood of the sin offering and put it on the doorposts of the temple, on the four corners of the upper ledge[u] of the altar[v] and on the gateposts of the inner court. 20 You are to do the same on the seventh day of the month for anyone who sins unintentionally[w] or through ignorance; so you are to make atonement for the temple.

21 " 'In the first month on the fourteenth day you are to observe the Passover,[x] a festival lasting seven

45:4 [c] Eze 40:46 [d] Eze 48:10-11
45:5 [e] Eze 48:13
45:6 [f] Eze 48:15-18
45:7 [g] Eze 48:21
45:8 [h] Nu 26:53; Eze 46:18
45:9 [i] Jer 22:3; Zec 7:9-10; 8:16
45:10 [j] Dt 25:15; Pr 11:1; Am 8:4-6; Mic 6:10-11 [k] Lev 19:36
45:11 [l] Isa 5:10
45:12 [m] Ex 30:13; Lev 27:25; Nu 3:47
45:15 [n] Lev 1:4 [o] Lev 6:30
45:17 [p] Lev 23:38; Isa 66:23 [q] 1Ki 8:62; 2Ch 31:3; Eze 46:4-12
45:18 [r] Ex 12:2 [s] Lev 22:20; Heb 9:14 [t] Lev 16:16,33
45:19 [u] Eze 43:17 [v] Lev 16:18-19; Eze 43:20
45:20 [w] Lev 4:27
45:21 [x] Ex 12:11; Lev 23:5-6

[a] *3* That is, about 3 1/3 miles or about 5.3 kilometers; also in verse 5 [b] *5* Septuagint; Hebrew *temple; they will have as their possession 20 rooms* [c] *6* That is, about 1 2/3 miles or about 2.7 kilometers [d] *10* An ephah was a dry measure having the capacity of about 3/5 bushel or about 22 liters. [e] *10* A bath was a liquid measure equaling about 6 gallons or about 22 liters. [f] *12* A shekel weighed about 2/5 ounce or about 12 grams. [g] *12* That is, 60 shekels; the common mina was 50 shekels. Sixty shekels were about 1 1/2 pounds or about 690 grams. [h] *13* That is, probably about 6 pounds or about 2.7 kilograms [i] *13* That is, probably about 5 pounds or about 2.3 kilograms [j] *14* That is, about 2 1/2 quarts or about 2.2 liters [k] *17* Or *purification offerings*; also in verses 19, 22, 23 and 25

include fair land distribution (45:1–8), economic justice (45:9–12), offerings (45:13–17), keeping the new worship calendar (45:18–25), and the prince's observance of law and order (46:1–18).

45:1–8 Allotment of land provides boundaries for service and work. The emphasis here is on the division of sacred districts in the holy land (v. 1). These districts include (1) a central piece of land given for the sanctuary (v. 2; see 42:16–20); (2) a parcel of land to the north of this for the priests to live on but not own (v. 5; cf. 44:28); (3) a parcel of land to the south for the city that belonged to "all Israel" (v. 6), not to one tribe; and (4) a generous portion that remained for the prince (vv. 7–8).

45:7 prince. The Messiah-like ruler in this new spiritual center.

45:9 You have gone far enough, princes of Israel! A reference to Israel's past kings, who ruled without equity and justice. This contrasts the prince mentioned in v. 8.

45:10 accurate scales. Accurate measurements; a symbol of economic justice (Lev 19:35; Deut 25:13–16; Mic 6:10–12). Rather than "fix" the scales for personal benefit, the prince is to be honest.

45:13–17 A description of offering amounts. These are given as fees, or taxes, for temple services. The prince was responsible for these fees so that he might provide daily, weekly, and annual or seasonal offerings.

45:18–25 A calendar schedule to follow regarding distinctive festivals. This worship calendar indicates that everything belongs to God and that purification from sin is ongoing.

45:18 first month ... first day. Early spring (March or April).

45:21 first month ... fourteenth day. Late March or April.

45:22 [y]Lev 4:14
45:23 [z]Job 42:8 [a]Nu 28:16-25
45:24 [b]Nu 28:12-13 [c]Eze 46:5-7
45:25 [d]Dt 16:13 [e]Lev 23:34-43; Nu 29:12-38
46:1 [f]Eze 40:19 [g]1Ch 9:18 [h]ver 6; Isa 66:23
46:2 [i]ver 8 [j]ver 12; Eze 44:3
46:3 [k]Lk 1:10
46:5 [l]ver 11; Eze 45:24
46:6 [m]ver 1; Nu 10:10
46:7 [n]Eze 45:24
46:8 [o]ver 2 [p]Eze 44:3
46:9 [q]Ex 23:14; 34:20
46:10 [r]2Sa 6:14-15; Ps 42:4
46:11 [s]ver 5
46:12 [t]Eze 45:17 [u]Lev 7:16 [v]ver 2
46:13 [w]Ex 29:38; Nu 28:3
46:14 [x]Da 8:11
46:15 [y]Ex 29:42 [z]Ex 29:38; Nu 28:5-6
46:16 [a]2Ch 21:3

days, during which you shall eat bread made without yeast. 22 On that day the prince is to provide a bull
as a sin offering for himself and for all the people of the land.[y] 23 Every day during the seven days of
the festival he is to provide seven bulls and seven rams[z] without defect as a burnt offering to the LORD,
and a male goat for a sin offering.[a] 24 He is to provide as a grain offering[b] an ephah for each bull and
an ephah for each ram, along with a hin[*a*] of olive oil for each ephah.[c]

25 " 'During the seven days of the festival,[d] which begins in the seventh month on the fifteenth day, he
is to make the same provision for sin offerings, burnt offerings, grain offerings and oil.[e]

46 " 'This is what the Sovereign LORD says: The gate of the inner court[f] facing east[g] is to be shut
on the six working days, but on the Sabbath day and on the day of the New Moon[h] it is to be
opened. 2 The prince is to enter from the outside through the portico[i] of the gateway and stand by the
gatepost. The priests are to sacrifice his burnt offering and his fellowship offerings. He is to bow down
in worship at the threshold of the gateway and then go out, but the gate will not be shut until evening.[j]
3 On the Sabbaths and New Moons the people of the land are to worship in the presence of the LORD at
the entrance of that gateway.[k] 4 The burnt offering the prince brings to the LORD on the Sabbath day is
to be six male lambs and a ram, all without defect. 5 The grain offering given with the ram is to be an
ephah,[*b*] and the grain offering with the lambs is to be as much as he pleases, along with a hin[*c*] of olive
oil for each ephah.[l] 6 On the day of the New Moon[m] he is to offer a young bull, six lambs and a ram, all
without defect. 7 He is to provide as a grain offering one ephah with the bull, one ephah with the ram,
and with the lambs as much as he wants to give, along with a hin of oil for each ephah.[n] 8 When the
prince enters, he is to go in through the portico[o] of the gateway, and he is to come out the same way.[p]

9 " 'When the people of the land come before the LORD at the appointed festivals,[q] whoever enters by
the north gate to worship is to go out the south gate; and whoever enters by the south gate is to go out
the north gate. No one is to return through the gate by which they entered, but each is to go out the
opposite gate. 10 The prince is to be among them, going in when they go in and going out when they
go out.[r] 11 At the feasts and the appointed festivals, the grain offering is to be an ephah with a bull, an
ephah with a ram, and with the lambs as much as he pleases, along with a hin of oil for each ephah.[s]

12 " 'When the prince provides[t] a freewill offering[u] to the LORD—whether a burnt offering or fellowship offerings—the gate facing east is to be opened for him. He shall offer his burnt offering or his
fellowship offerings as he does on the Sabbath day. Then he shall go out, and after he has gone out,
the gate will be shut.[v]

13 " 'Every day you are to provide a year-old lamb without defect for a burnt offering to the LORD;
morning by morning you shall provide it.[w] 14 You are also to provide with it morning by morning a
grain offering, consisting of a sixth of an ephah[*d*] with a third of a hin[*e*] of oil to moisten the flour. The
presenting of this grain offering to the LORD is a lasting ordinance.[x] 15 So the lamb and the grain offering
and the oil shall be provided morning by morning for a regular[y] burnt offering.[z]

16 " 'This is what the Sovereign LORD says: If the prince makes a gift from his inheritance to one of his
sons, it will also belong to his descendants; it is to be their property by inheritance.[a] 17 If, however, he makes

a *24* That is, about 1 gallon or about 3.8 liters *b* *5* That is, probably about 35 pounds or about 16 kilograms; also in verses 7 and 11 *c* *5* That is, about 1 gallon or about 3.8 liters; also in verses 7 and 11 *d* *14* That is, probably about 6 pounds or about 2.7 kilograms *e* *14* That is, about 1 1/2 quarts or about 1.3 liters

45:25 seventh month ... fifteenth day. Late September or October.

46:1 gate of the inner court facing east ... is to be opened. While the east gate of the outer court was permanently closed (44:1–2), the east gate between the inner and outer court could be opened once a week (on the Sabbath), once a month (on the day of the New Moon), and for the prince to present his offerings (v. 12).

46:2 The prince is to ... worship at the threshold of the gateway. He can enter the east gate but must keep his distance from the altar. He can only observe the priestly mediation being performed on the altar of burnt offering in the inner court.

46:3 the people of the land. A reference to lay Israelites, the common people. They may offer their worship on the Sabbath and on the first day of the month.

46:4–7 The new temple provides an opportunity for new regulations to be introduced. The prince provides and presents the offerings (45:17) for the weekly and monthly festivals.

46:9 whoever enters by the north gate to worship is to go out the south gate. An orderly way to circulate large groups of people coming for religious festivals.

46:10 The prince is to be among them. He leads the worshipers in procession and recession.

46:13,14,15 morning by morning. Suggests a commanded regularity to worship.

46:16–18 These verses describe legitimate land distribution to family and nonfamily members of the community as a demonstration of social justice. The gift of the land was to be in the hands of the prince and his descendants and was only a temporary gift to his servants (see note on v. 17).

a gift from his inheritance to one of his servants, the servant may keep it until the year of freedom;[b] then
it will revert to the prince. His inheritance belongs to his sons only; it is theirs. [18]The prince must not take
any of the inheritance[c] of the people, driving them off their property. He is to give his sons their inheritance
out of his own property, so that not one of my people will be separated from their property.' "
[19]Then the man brought me through the entrance[d] at the side of the gate to the sacred rooms facing
north, which belonged to the priests, and showed me a place at the western end. [20]He said to me, "This
is the place where the priests are to cook the guilt offering and the sin offering[a] and bake the grain
offering, to avoid bringing them into the outer court and consecrating[e] the people."[f]
[21]He then brought me to the outer court and led me around to its four corners, and I saw in each
corner another court. [22]In the four corners of the outer court were enclosed[b] courts, forty cubits long
and thirty cubits wide;[c] each of the courts in the four corners was the same size. [23]Around the inside of
each of the four courts was a ledge of stone, with places for fire built all around under the ledge. [24]He
said to me, "These are the kitchens where those who minister at the temple are to cook the sacrifices
of the people."

The River From the Temple

47 The man brought me back to the entrance to the temple, and I saw water[g] coming out from
under the threshold of the temple toward the east (for the temple faced east). The water was
coming down from under the south side of the temple, south of the altar.[h] [2]He then brought me out
through the north gate and led me around the outside to the outer gate facing east, and the water was
trickling from the south side.
[3]As the man went eastward with a measuring line[i] in his hand, he measured off a thousand cubits[d]
and then led me through water that was ankle-deep. [4]He measured off another thousand cubits and led
me through water that was knee-deep. He measured off another thousand and led me through water
that was up to the waist. [5]He measured off another thousand, but now it was a river that I could not
cross, because the water had risen and was deep enough to swim in — a river that no one could cross.[j]
[6]He asked me, "Son of man, do you see this?"
Then he led me back to the bank of the river. [7]When I arrived there, I saw a great number of trees on
each side of the river.[k] [8]He said to me, "This water flows toward the eastern region and goes down into
the Arabah,[e][l] where it enters the Dead Sea. When it empties into the sea, the salty water there becomes
fresh.[m] [9]Swarms of living creatures will live wherever the river flows. There will be large numbers of fish,
because this water flows there and makes the salt water fresh; so where the river flows everything will live.[n]
[10]Fishermen[o] will stand along the shore; from En Gedi[p] to En Eglaim there will be places for spreading
nets.[q] The fish will be of many kinds[r] — like the fish of the Mediterranean Sea.[s] [11]But the swamps and

[a] *20* Or *purification offering* [b] *22* The meaning of the Hebrew for this word is uncertain. [c] *22* That is, about 70 feet long and 53 feet wide or about 21 meters long and 16 meters wide [d] *3* That is, about 1,700 feet or about 530 meters [e] *8* Or *the Jordan Valley*

46:17 [b]Lev 25:10
46:18 [c]Lev 25:23; Eze 45:8; Mic 2:1-2
46:19 [d]Eze 42:9
46:20 [e]Lev 6:27 [f]Zec 14:20
47:1 [g]Isa 55:1 [h]Ps 46:4; Joel 3:18; Rev 22:1
47:3 [i]Eze 40:3
47:5 [j]Isa 11:9; Hab 2:14
47:7 [k]ver 12; Rev 22:2
47:8 [l]Dt 3:17; Jos 3:16 [m]Isa 41:18
47:9 [n]Isa 12:3; 55:1; Jn 4:14; 7:37-38
47:10 [o]Mt 4:19 [p]Jos 15:62 [q]Eze 26:5 [r]Ps 104:25; Mt 13:47 [s]Nu 34:6

46:17 the year of freedom. The Year of Jubilee, or every 50th year (see Lev 25:8–15, especially v. 13), when the original family owners had claims to the land once again. Inheritance issues were in the hands of the Lord, not the hands of the prince.
46:19–24 These verses describe the kitchens where the priests cooked the sacrifices offered by the people (see also 42:13–14).
47:1–12 *Restoration of Land: Living Water.* The prophet sees a water source that originates from the temple of God (vv. 1,12) with a surprising increase in its depth — from a trickle (v. 2) to a river depth suitable for swimming (v. 5) as it flows out to the sea (v. 8). Verses 8–12 explain this supernatural water source. It is the means by which life comes out of death. This living water promises abundance of life, supernatural fruitfulness, and sustainability in the land (nutritionally and medicinally) for its inhabitants (Pss 36:8; 46:4; see Joel 3:18; Zech 13:1; 14:8; John 7:37–38; Rev 22:1–2).
47:1 back to the entrance to the temple. Ezekiel is back at the front of the sanctuary. **water coming out from ... the temple.** The source of the water comes from the divine presence (Gen 2:10–14; Ps 46:4).
47:2 trickling. Initially a small amount of water.
47:3–5 water ... ankle-deep ... a river that no one could cross. The water source grows from a stream into a river. The river symbolizes fruitfulness and abundance (Ps 65:9; Isa 33:21; Joel 3:18; Zech 14:8; Rev 22:1–2).
47:7 great number of trees. Evidence of the river's fruitfulness.
47:8 flows ... goes down ... enters the Dead Sea. The water's movement indicates its capacity not only to bring life but to bring life to places devoid of life: to the salty waters of the Dead Sea. **the Dead Sea.** The lowest and saltiest substantial body of water in the world, incapable of sustaining life owing to its heavy salt and mineral content. The scene provides a vivid picture of life coming out death, as "salty water there becomes fresh."
47:9 Swarms of living creatures ... large numbers of fish. Language expressive of fruitfulness, reminiscent of the fruitfulness of creation in Genesis.
47:10 from En Gedi to En Eglaim. A stretch of land on the shores of the Dead Sea that will provide a thriving fishing industry — another picture of abundance.
47:11 swamps and marshes ... left for salt. Although the salty water

47:11 [t]Dt 29:23
47:12 [u]ver 7; Rev 22:2 [v]Ps 1:3 [w]Ge 2:9; Jer 17:8
47:13 [x]Nu 34:2-12 [y]Ge 48:5
47:14 [z]Ge 12:7; Dt 1:8; Eze 20:5-6
47:15 [a]Eze 48:1
47:16 [b]2Sa 8:8 [c]Nu 13:21; Eze 48:1
47:17 [d]Eze 48:1
47:19 [e]Dt 32:51 [f]Isa 27:12 [g]Eze 48:28
47:20 [h]Eze 48:1 [i]Nu 34:6
47:22 [j]Isa 14:1 [k]Nu 26:55-56; Isa 56:6-7; Ro 10:12; Eph 2:12-16; 3:6; Col 3:11
48:1 [l]Ge 30:6 [m]Eze 47:15-17 [n]Eze 47:20

marshes will not become fresh; they will be left for salt.[t] 12 Fruit trees of all kinds will grow on both banks of the river.[u] Their leaves will not wither, nor will their fruit[v] fail. Every month they will bear fruit, because the water from the sanctuary flows to them. Their fruit will serve for food and their leaves for healing.[w]"

The Boundaries of the Land

13 This is what the Sovereign LORD says: "These are the boundaries[x] of the land that you will divide among the twelve tribes of Israel as their inheritance, with two portions for Joseph.[y] 14 You are to divide it equally among them. Because I swore with uplifted hand to give it to your ancestors, this land will become your inheritance.[z]

15 "This is to be the boundary of the land:

"On the north side it will run from the Mediterranean Sea by the Hethlon road[a] past Lebo Hamath to Zedad, 16 Berothah[a][b] and Sibraim (which lies on the border between Damascus and Hamath),[c] as far as Hazer Hattikon, which is on the border of Hauran. 17 The boundary will extend from the sea to Hazar Enan,[b] along the northern border of Damascus, with the border of Hamath to the north. This will be the northern boundary.[d]

18 "On the east side the boundary will run between Hauran and Damascus, along the Jordan between Gilead and the land of Israel, to the Dead Sea and as far as Tamar.[c] This will be the eastern boundary.

19 "On the south side it will run from Tamar as far as the waters of Meribah Kadesh,[e] then along the Wadi of Egypt[f] to the Mediterranean Sea.[g] This will be the southern boundary.

20 "On the west side, the Mediterranean Sea will be the boundary to a point opposite Lebo Hamath.[h] This will be the western boundary.[i]

21 "You are to distribute this land among yourselves according to the tribes of Israel. 22 You are to allot it as an inheritance for yourselves and for the foreigners[j] residing among you and who have children. You are to consider them as native-born Israelites; along with you they are to be allotted an inheritance among the tribes of Israel.[k] 23 In whatever tribe a foreigner resides, there you are to give them their inheritance," declares the Sovereign LORD.

The Division of the Land

48 "These are the tribes, listed by name: At the northern frontier, Dan[l] will have one portion; it will follow the Hethlon road[m] to Lebo Hamath;[n] Hazar Enan and the northern border of Damascus next to Hamath will be part of its border from the east side to the west side.

[a] *15,16* See Septuagint and 48:1; Hebrew *road to go into Zedad, 16Hamath, Berothah.* [b] *17* Hebrew *Enon,* a variant of *Enan* [c] *18* See Syriac; Hebrew *Israel. You will measure to the Dead Sea.*

becomes fresh (v. 8), God graciously leaves some salt, perhaps for food preparation purposes and for use with sacrifices (43:24).

47:12 Fruit trees … Every month they will bear fruit … leaves for healing. An ongoing fruitfulness and abundance that never ends. The complete nature of this fruitfulness is seen in that even the leaves have a purpose. An extension of the promises in 34:27; 36:30; see also Amos 9:13. Thus, the supernatural source, growth, and stunning effects of this "river of life" anticipate Jesus as the believer's source of life (John 7:38). Likewise, a supernatural water source, "the river of the water of life" (Rev 22:1), flows from God's throne in the new Jerusalem. The water symbolizes the fruitful life of abundance enjoyed in God's presence (Rev 22:1–2).

47:13–23 *Restoration of Land Boundaries.* This envisions the proper boundaries of the land in the new spiritual center.

47:13 two portions for Joseph. Each of Joseph's sons, Ephraim and Manasseh (Gen 48:5,17–20), receives a portion (48:4–5). This maintains 12 portions of land because the tribe of Levi receives none (44:28). **Joseph.** Understood to be the firstborn (1 Chr 5:1–2), he receives a double portion. Accordingly, he is honored among the patriarchs.

47:14 Because I swore. A reference to the covenant made with Abram (see Gen 15:9–21; cf. Ezek 20:5; 36:28). **with uplifted hand.** Reaffirms God's unending relational loyalties to his people.

47:15–21 These boundaries are similar to but different from the original land boundaries mapped out in Num 34:1–12. The northern, eastern, southern, and western boundaries are described. The Transjordan boundaries are not mentioned. The northern border is marked by Lebo Hamath and the eastern is marked by the Jordan River and Dead Sea. The southern border is not entirely clear but is likely the Wadi of Egypt. The western border is the Mediterranean Sea.

47:22 an inheritance … for the foreigners residing among you. Territorial provisions are made for resident foreigners. **You are to consider them as native-born Israelites.** An amazing statement of inclusion. It assumes that they discard their national deities and embrace the Lord as their God, much like Ruth did (Ruth 1:16; 2:12; 4:13–22). The vision is understandable in light of v. 14 and the allusion to inheritance rights associated with the Abrahamic blessings (Gal 3:9,14,26–29; 4:28–31).

48:1–29 *Restoration of Tribal Allotments.* These verses describe distribution of the land in the new spiritual center. The land division for the tribes is a configuration meant to emphasize a new reality through the literary means of symmetry. For this reason, allotment of land is broken up into 12 horizontal (east-west) pieces running from north

2“Asher[o] will have one portion; it will border the territory of Dan from east to west.

3“Naphtali[p] will have one portion; it will border the territory of Asher from east to west.

4“Manasseh[q] will have one portion; it will border the territory of Naphtali from east to west.

5“Ephraim[r] will have one portion; it will border the territory of Manasseh[s] from east to west.[t]

6“Reuben[u] will have one portion; it will border the territory of Ephraim from east to west.

7“Judah[v] will have one portion; it will border the territory of Reuben from east to west.

8“Bordering the territory of Judah from east to west will be the portion you are to present as a special gift. It will be 25,000 cubits[a] wide, and its length from east to west will equal one of the tribal portions; the sanctuary will be in the center of it.[w]

9“The special portion you are to offer to the LORD will be 25,000 cubits long and 10,000 cubits[b] wide.[x] 10This will be the sacred portion for the priests. It will be 25,000 cubits long on the north side, 10,000 cubits wide on the west side, 10,000 cubits wide on the east side and 25,000 cubits long on the south side. In the center of it will be the sanctuary of the LORD.[y] 11This will be for the consecrated priests, the Zadokites,[z] who were faithful in serving me[a] and did not go astray as the Levites did when the Israelites went astray.[b] 12It will be a special gift to them from the sacred portion of the land, a most holy portion, bordering the territory of the Levites.

13“Alongside the territory of the priests, the Levites will have an allotment 25,000 cubits long and 10,000 cubits wide. Its total length will be 25,000 cubits and its width 10,000 cubits.[c] 14They must not sell or exchange any of it. This is the best of the land and must not pass into other hands, because it is holy to the LORD.[d]

15“The remaining area, 5,000 cubits[c] wide and 25,000 cubits long, will be for the common use of the city, for houses and for pastureland. The city will be in the center of it 16and will have these measurements: the north side 4,500 cubits,[d] the south side 4,500 cubits, the east side 4,500 cubits, and the west side 4,500 cubits.[e] 17The pastureland for the city will be 250 cubits[e] on the north, 250 cubits on the south, 250 cubits on the east, and 250 cubits on the west. 18What remains of the area, bordering on the sacred portion and running the length of it, will be 10,000 cubits on the east side and 10,000 cubits on the west side. Its produce will supply food for the workers of the city.[f] 19The workers from the city who farm it will come from all the tribes of Israel. 20The entire portion will be a square, 25,000 cubits on each side. As a special gift you will set aside the sacred portion, along with the property of the city.

21“What remains on both sides of the area formed by the sacred portion and the property of the city will belong to the prince. It will extend eastward from the 25,000 cubits of the sacred portion to the eastern border, and westward from the 25,000 cubits to the western border. Both these areas running the length of the tribal portions will belong to the prince, and the sacred portion with the temple sanctuary will be in the center of them.[g] 22So the property of the Levites and the property of the city will lie in the center of the area that belongs to the prince. The area belonging to the prince will lie between the border of Judah and the border of Benjamin.

23“As for the rest of the tribes: Benjamin[h] will have one portion; it will extend from the east side to the west side.

[a] *8* That is, about 8 miles or about 13 kilometers; also in verses 9, 10, 13, 15, 20 and 21 [b] *9* That is, about 3 1/3 miles or about 5.3 kilometers; also in verses 10, 13 and 18 [c] *15* That is, about 1 2/3 miles or about 2.7 kilometers [d] *16* That is, about 1 1/2 miles or about 2.4 kilometers; also in verses 30, 32, 33 and 34 [e] *17* That is, about 440 feet or about 135 meters

48:2 [o] Jos 19:24-31
48:3 [p] Jos 19:32-39
48:4 [q] Jos 17:1-11
48:5 [r] Jos 16:5-9 [s] Jos 17:7-10 [t] Jos 17:17
48:6 [u] Jos 13:15-21
48:7 [v] Jos 15:1-63
48:8 [w] ver 21
48:9 [x] Eze 45:1
48:10 [y] ver 21; Eze 45:3-4
48:11 [z] 2Sa 8:17 [a] Lev 8:35 [b] Eze 14:11; 44:15
48:13 [c] Eze 45:5
48:14 [d] Lev 25:34; 27:10,28
48:16 [e] Rev 21:16
48:18 [f] Eze 45:6
48:21 [g] ver 8,10; Eze 45:7
48:23 [h] Jos 18:11-28

to south. The description here also emphasizes a nameless “city” (vv. 15,17,18,19,20,21,22) attached to Levite territory (vv. 15–20) that has a flow of traffic from each of the 12 tribes, giving it prominence in the land. The name of the city, however, is not revealed until the final section of the chapter (vv. 30–35), in the last verse of the book (v. 35).

48:1–8 The northern frontier includes the tribes of Dan, Asher, Naphtali, Manasseh, Ephraim, Reuben, and Judah.

48:7 Judah. Has a prestigious location, bordering the central territory that contains the sanctuary (v. 8). This is so because the Messiah was promised to come from the tribe of Judah (Gen 35:23; 49:8–12).

48:9–22 Verses 9–14,15–22 repeat and expand the material found in 45:1–8.

48:9–14 This section concerns territories for the Levites and priests.

48:15–22 In this section the “city” is given prominence. It is a visible hub (square in shape, v. 20) uniting the tribes. Together with the territory for the Levites and priests, this area could be considered centrally located. To the north of it are seven tribes (vv. 1–8) and to the south are the five remaining tribes (vv. 23–29).

48:22 Benjamin. Borders the temple area to the south. Judah and Benjamin flank the land’s spiritual center, the place where the sanctuary is located.

48:23–29 The southern frontier includes Benjamin, Simeon, Issachar, Zebulun, and Gad.

48:24 [i] Ge 29:33; Jos 19:1-9
48:25 [j] Jos 19:17-23
48:26 [k] Jos 19:10-16
48:27 [l] Jos 13:24-28
48:28 [m] Ge 14:7 [n] Eze 47:19
48:35 [o] Isa 12:6; 24:23; Jer 3:17; 14:9; 33:16; Joel 3:21; Zec 2:10; Rev 21:3

24 "Simeon[i] will have one portion; it will border the territory of Benjamin from east to west.
25 "Issachar[j] will have one portion; it will border the territory of Simeon from east to west.
26 "Zebulun[k] will have one portion; it will border the territory of Issachar from east to west.
27 "Gad[l] will have one portion; it will border the territory of Zebulun from east to west.
28 "The southern boundary of Gad will run south from Tamar[m] to the waters of Meribah Kadesh, then along the Wadi of Egypt to the Mediterranean Sea.[n]
29 "This is the land you are to allot as an inheritance to the tribes of Israel, and these will be their portions," declares the Sovereign LORD.

The Gates of the New City

30 "These will be the exits of the city: Beginning on the north side, which is 4,500 cubits long, 31 the
gates of the city will be named after the tribes of Israel. The three gates on the north side will be the gate of Reuben, the gate of Judah and the gate of Levi.
32 "On the east side, which is 4,500 cubits long, will be three gates: the gate of Joseph, the gate of Benjamin and the gate of Dan.
33 "On the south side, which measures 4,500 cubits, will be three gates: the gate of Simeon, the gate of Issachar and the gate of Zebulun.
34 "On the west side, which is 4,500 cubits long, will be three gates: the gate of Gad, the gate of Asher and the gate of Naphtali.
35 "The distance all around will be 18,000 cubits.[a]

"And the name of the city from that time on will be:

THE LORD IS THERE.[o]"

[a] *35* That is, about 6 miles or about 9.5 kilometers

48:30–35 *Restoration of God's Sovereign Name.* The universal, even personal, access to the city and the unfolding of its name bring the vision and book to a climactic end.

48:30–34 Providing access to the city are 12 gates that are associated with the 12 tribes, emphasizing the unity of the entire people of God. The gates are named after Jacob's original sons, not the tribal territories. As a result, Levi's name appears in the list (v. 31) when one does not expect it (the Levites were not granted tribal allotments, cf. Num 1:49; Deut 10:9; Josh 13:14). Likewise, Joseph's name appears (v. 32) instead of Ephraim and Manasseh (vv. 4–5). This maintains the number 12 and may emphasize the city's accessibility to all (cf. Rev 21:12–14). The number 12, because of its origin with Israel and God's promises to him and his family (Gen 49:28), is used repeatedly in the OT (Exod 24:4; Num 13:1–16; Josh 3–4; 1 Kgs 10:20; etc.). The NT writers make great use of its symbolism (Matt 19:28; Mark 4:10; Jas 1:1; Rev 7:1–8; 21:12). Thus, Ezekiel's audience would be reminded of God's character. God will fulfill his promises of redemption.

48:35 the city. The new spiritual center *is* a city. By the end of the vision, Ezekiel is finally able to make a clear identification of what he sees and initially identified as "buildings that looked like a city" (40:2). **THE LORD IS THERE.** The name of the city; it is pregnant with significance. The Hebrew for this clause is *yhwh šāmmâ* and means "The LORD is there" or "Yahweh is there." The reality of God's permanent presence in Israel's midst is the ultimate covenantal blessing. Ezekiel's audience would be reminded of God's gracious and merciful character. God's blessing awaits them. Without the divine presence the city, people, and temple were destroyed (chs. 8–11); there was no hope for the people of God. With the divine presence the city, people, and temple are restored (chs. 40–48); there is hope again for God's people. From Genesis to Revelation, from Eden to eternity, the promise of the divine presence thematically unites the Bible. His presence guarantees that life will come out of death. The name of the city, the city of God, reflects the fullness of the restoration due to the divine presence. Restoration is complete (cf. Rev 21:9–27). See Introduction: Theological Significance; see also "The City of God," p. 2666.

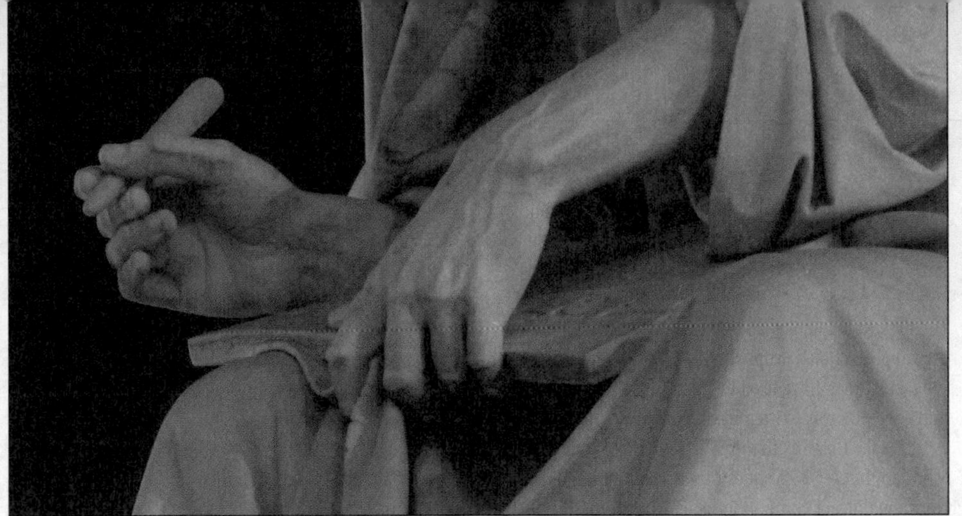

INTRODUCTION TO DANIEL

The book of Daniel contains two parts. Chs. 1 – 6 present accounts of Daniel and his three friends in a foreign court; chs. 7 – 12 contain four apocalyptic visions. Each account and each vision expresses the same important message: in spite of present circumstances that make it appear as if evil is winning the day, God is in control and will have the final victory. This message has brought comfort to God's people throughout history and up to the present day.

AUTHOR

Until the twentieth century, Christian and Jewish scholars agreed that Daniel, the book's main protagonist, wrote the book. Daniel speaks in the first person in the four visions of the second half of the book (7:2,4,6,28; 8:1,15; 9:2; 10:2), and it is Daniel who is told to "seal the words of the scroll" (12:4). At a minimum, the internal evidence of the book claims that Daniel received the visions. However, since the first six chapters of the book are stories about Daniel and since the visions themselves often have a third-person introduction (7:1; 10:1), this allows for but does not require the possibility that a later editor could have written the final form of the book. Though the NT often cites the book of Daniel, only Matt 24:15 – 16 (speaking of the "abomination that causes desolation" [Dan 9:27; 11:31; 12:11]) names Daniel as the author. The real controversy concerning authorship concerns the visions that the book connects to Daniel's personal experience (see Date).

DATE

The stories and the visions of Daniel are firmly set in the context of events that occur between 605 (see 1:1 and note) and 537/536 BC (see 10:1 and note). Nebuchadnezzar, Belshazzar, Cyrus, and Jehoiakim are well-known figures from this time period. This period of time is crucial in the history of God's people, stretching from the beginning of Babylonian encroachment into Judah and covering the time of the destruction of Jerusalem (though not mentioned in the book) and the end of the exile. The book has its foundation in events and visions that occur in the sixth century BC.

Some, however, claim that a sixth-century dating for the book is impossible due to the contents of the visions, particularly that of the vision in ch. 11. As the notes on ch. 11 show, it contains prophecies connected to the Seleucid (king of the north) and Ptolemaic (king of the south) kingdoms of the late fourth to mid-second centuries BC. To some, precisely predicting these future events is simply impossible and this points to a date of writing in the second century BC. Furthermore, these people point to 11:36 – 45 as an example of a failed prophecy of the death of the climactic king of the south (Antiochus IV) thus being an indication that the book was written just before his death (ca. 164 BC). Not all who opt for this late date of the writing of the book do so because they reject the idea of true prophecy, but many do. (For more on this issue, see note on 11:36 – 45.) The discovery of a second-century BC partial copy of Dan 11 among the Dead Sea Scrolls (4QDan[c]) lends strong support to those who argue that this passage was composed much earlier than the time the predictions describe. The notes in this study Bible assume that Daniel received these visions from God in the sixth century BC.

PLACE OF COMPOSITION

While God may have used an editor to bring the book of Daniel to its inspired final form, the book originates with Daniel, who lived in the royal court in Babylon.

PARTICULAR CHALLENGES

The biggest challenge, addressed above (see Date) and in the notes (see note on 11:36–45), concerns the charge that the supposed failed prophecy in 11:36–45 exposes that the precise predictions in 11:5–35 are really prophecies after the fact. Others have used two additional issues to challenge the book's historical reliability and to support the view that the book was written in the second century BC with a murky knowledge of earlier events.

1. Dan 1:1 claims that Nebuchadnezzar besieged Jerusalem during the third year of the reign of Jehoiakim, king of Judah; but Jer 25:1 states that Nebuchadnezzar's first year was Jehoiakim's fourth, and Jer 36:9 says that the Babylonians did not come to Jerusalem until the fifth year of Jehoiakim. To some, the Babylonian Chronicle supports Jeremiah's chronology. However, there were two systems of dating in place at this time. Jeremiah used the Judahite method that reckons the first year of a king's reign as his first year, while Daniel used the Babylonian system, which counts the first year as his "accession year."

2. Mystery surrounds the figure of Darius the Mede (5:31; 9:1), who became king when Belshazzar was executed (5:30) and was the one who was forced to send Daniel to the lions' den (ch. 6). Darius is not known in the extrabiblical sources of the day, and one would expect the book to name the "king of Babylon" as Cyrus the Persian (who defeated Babylon), not Darius the Mede. While certainty on this matter is not possible at this time, solutions exist. Perhaps, for instance, Darius is to be identified as a man named Gubaru, who is known from Babylonian texts as the governor of Babylon. More likely is the idea that Darius is a second name for none other than Cyrus. Historical sources attest to the practice of a king ruling two nations under two different names (see note on 6:28).

OCCASION AND PURPOSE

The book was written to encourage those living during times of oppression and persecution. Its stories and visions show that it is possible not only to survive but to thrive as a faithful follower of God under the most difficult conditions. While not every Christian today faces the severe persecution that Daniel and his friends encountered, they do

DANIEL IN BABYLON

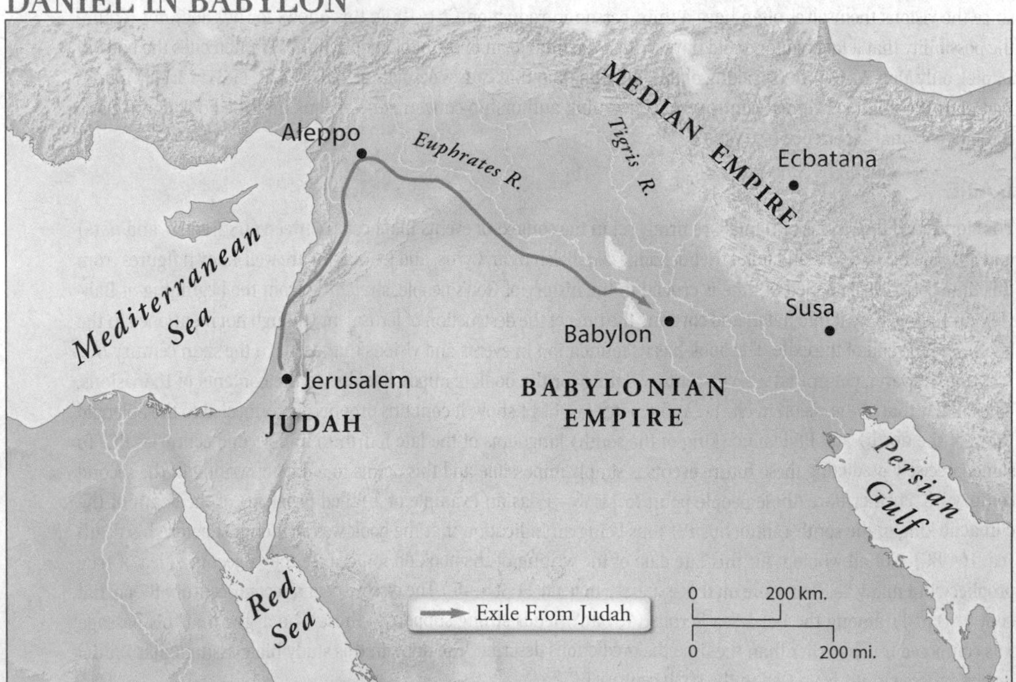

live in a culture that is toxic or hostile to the faith, and the book's reminder that God is in control and will win the final victory provides confidence for living in the present and hope to face the future. The book does not intend to give information that would allow readers to predict the time period when Jesus will return at the end of the age.

GENRE AND STRUCTURE

The book of Daniel has two major parts. Chs. 1–6 contain court narratives (stories about Daniel and his three friends living in a foreign court); chs. 7–12 present four visions that contain apocalyptic prophecies. Interestingly, the book is written in two different languages, though the Hebrew (1:1—2:3; chs. 8–12) and Aramaic (2:4—7:28) do not coincide with the genre division.

The court narratives focus on the interaction between Daniel and/or his three friends and members of the Babylonian or Persian court. Ch. 1 narrates how the four men come to Babylon and how they preserve their faith as they are forced to prepare for service in the Babylonian royal court. Chs. 2, 4, and 5 tell stories of court contests. In ch. 5, for example, when the king has a problem of interpretation, his Babylonian wise men cannot provide a solution. Where they fail, Daniel succeeds, thus demonstrating the superiority of Daniel's God, which leads to Daniel's promotion. Chs. 3 and 6 contain stories of court conflicts. In ch. 3, e.g., the three friends are set up by their court rivals and accused of not bowing down to Nebuchadnezzar's golden statue. God delivers them from the fiery furnace, and those who challenged them are thrown into it. The three friends are then promoted.

Artist's rendition of Babylon.
Painting by Maurice Bardin; photo from the Oriental Institute Museum, University of Chicago

The four visions in chs. 7–12 are apocalyptic in nature. Apocalyptic and prophetic books share many features but differ in key areas. While prophetic texts like Jeremiah focus on the near future, Daniel looks beyond the near future to events of the end times. While God commissions a prophet to preach to the people to elicit repentance, Daniel receives visions that intend to comfort the people of God who suffer oppression. Daniel's apocalytic texts share intense imagery that often baffles modern readers, for the imagery is drawn from the symbolic world of the ancient Near East (see notes in chs. 7–12). The use of numbers in apocalyptic texts tends to be symbolic as well and should not be used to create a calendar of the end times. While prophecy is often conditional based on the response of the audience, apocalyptic visions like Daniel's announce the certain destruction of evil forces, an encouraging message to the faithful who suffer at their hands.

THEMES AND THEOLOGY

A focus on God's sovereignty unites the six stories and four visions. Though it looks like evil is in control, God really is. From a human perspective, Nebuchadnezzar took the city of Jerusalem in the third year of Jehoiakim, but the book of Daniel reveals that he did so only because God allowed him to do so (1:1–2). Furthermore, it looks like the evil forces of the world will win the victory, but at the end of the stories it is God's people who come out on top, and at the end of the visions it is God who defeats the evil human kingdoms that oppress his people.

No OT book has a more pronounced picture of the kingdom of God versus the kingdoms of this world than the book of Daniel. The kingdom of God (the rock not formed by human hands) will destroy the kingdoms of the world (the multi-metaled statue; 2:31–45). The "one like a son of man coming with the clouds" (7:13) will lead the saints of the Most High in battle and win the victory over the beasts and their horns. God's kingdom, an everlasting kingdom, will succeed the kingdoms of the world (7:27).

Thus, the book of Daniel models how God's people should live in this world torn by evil forces. Knowing that God's victory is assured and that his kingdom will prevail, they should share the courage, confidence, and hope of Daniel and his three friends. While God's persecuted people can survive and even prosper in a toxic culture, they should be ready to face death (3:16–18), knowing that even death is not beyond God's rescue. Perhaps for this reason, Daniel has the OT's clearest statement of personal, physical resurrection (12:1–3).

The book of Daniel anticipates the coming of God as a warrior who will defeat the forces of evil and establish his kingdom. The NT depicts Jesus Christ as the one who wins the battle, first by defeating Satan on the cross (Col 2:13–15) and then completing the victory when he returns in his second coming. In this connection, the book of Revelation, the NT's apocalyptic book, frequently alludes to the book of Daniel. For instance, the image of ultimate evil in the book of Revelation is the beast that arises out of the sea (Rev 13), reminiscent of the four beasts that arise out of the sea in Dan 7. Jesus is the one who, "like a son of man" (Rev 1:13; see Dan 7:13), rides the clouds to battle the powers of evil (Matt 24:30; Mark 13:26; 14:62; Luke 21:27; see Dan 7:13–14). Daniel's description of the Ancient of Days in Dan 7:9 resembles the description of the one "like a son of man" in Rev 1:12–16.

OUTLINE

I. Daniel and the Three Friends in a Foreign Court (1:1—6:28)

- A. Daniel's Training in Babylon (1:1–21)
    1. The Subjugation of Judah (1:1–2)
    2. Nebuchadnezzar's Training Program (1:3–5)
    3. Name Change (1:6–7)
    4. Refusing the King's Food (1:8–16)
    5. Valedictorians (1:17–21)
- B. God's Wisdom Versus Babylonian Wisdom (2:1–49)
    1. The King's Disturbing Dream (2:1–13)
    2. God's Wisdom (2:14–30)
    3. The King's Dream (2:31–35)
    4. The Interpretation of the Dream (2:36–45)
    5. Nebuchadnezzar Praises the True God (2:46–49)
- C. The Image of Gold and the Blazing Furnace (3:1–30)
    1. The Image of Gold (3:1–7)
    2. The Three Friends Accused (3:8–18)
    3. God's Miraculous Rescue (3:19–27)
    4. Nebuchadnezzar Worships God (3:28–30)
- D. The King's Pride Humbled (4:1–37)
    1. The King Praises God (4:1–3)
    2. The Dream Report (4:4–18)
    3. Daniel Interprets the Dream (4:19–27)
    4. The Dream Is Fulfilled (4:28–37)
- E. The Writing on the Wall (5:1–31)
    1. The King Profanes the Holy Goblets (5:1–4)
    2. The Writing on the Wall (5:5–12)
    3. Daniel's Interpretation (5:13–28)
    4. Daniel's Reward and Babylon's Punishment (5:29–31)
- F. Daniel in the Den of Lions (6:1–28)
    1. The Plot Against Daniel (6:1–9)
    2. Darius Reluctantly Punishes Daniel (6:10–18)
    3. Daniel's Rescue (6:19–24)
    4. Darius's Decree (6:25–28)

II. Four Apocalyptic Visions (7:1—12:13)

- A. The First Vision (7:1–28)
    1. Daniel's Dream of Four Beasts (7:1–14)
    2. The Interpretation of the Dream (7:15–28)

- B. The Second Vision (8:1 – 27)
  1. Daniel's Vision of a Ram and a Goat (8:1 – 14)
  2. The Interpretation of the Vision (8:15 – 27)
- C. The Third Vision (9:1 – 27)
  1. Daniel's Prayer (9:1 – 19)
  2. The Seventy "Sevens" (9:20 – 27)
- D. The Fourth Vision (10:1 — 12:13)
  1. Daniel's Vision of a Man (10:1 — 11:1)
  2. The Kings of the South and the North (11:2 — 12:4)
  3. Final Words (12:5 – 13)

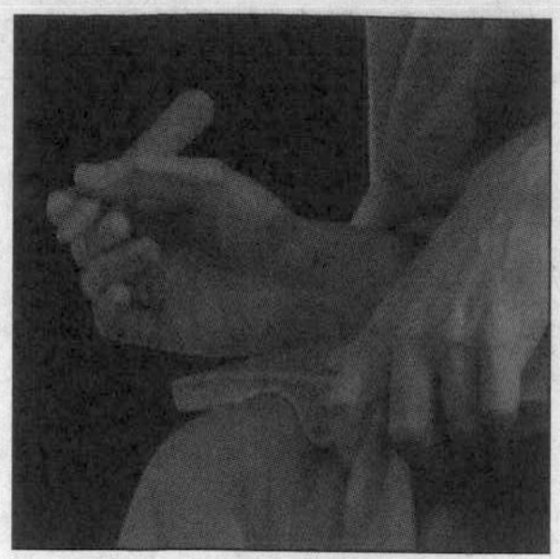

DANIEL

1:1 [a]2Ki 24:1 [b]2Ch 36:6
1:2 [c]2Ch 36:7; Jer 27:19-20; Zec 5:5-11
1:3 [d]2Ki 20:18; 24:15; Isa 39:7
1:5 [e]ver 8, 10 [f]ver 19

Daniel's Training in Babylon

1 In the third year of the reign of Jehoiakim king of Judah, Nebuchadnezzar[a] king of Babylon came
to Jerusalem and besieged it.[b] 2And the Lord delivered Jehoiakim king of Judah into his hand,
along with some of the articles from the temple of God. These he carried off to the temple of his god in
Babylonia[a] and put in the treasure house of his god.[c]

3Then the king ordered Ashpenaz, chief of his court officials, to bring into the king's service some of
the Israelites from the royal family and the nobility[d] — 4young men without any physical defect, handsome, showing aptitude for every kind of learning, well informed, quick to understand, and qualified to
serve in the king's palace. He was to teach them the language and literature of the Babylonians.[b] 5The
king assigned them a daily amount of food and wine[e] from the king's table. They were to be trained for
three years, and after that they were to enter the king's service.[f]

[a] 2 Hebrew *Shinar* [b] 4 Or *Chaldeans*

1:1—6:28 *Daniel and the Three Friends in a Foreign Court.* Chs. 1–6 present six separate accounts of Daniel and his three friends in a foreign court. They span from the third year of the reign of Jehoiakim king of Judah (ca. 605 BC) to the reign of Cyrus the Persian (post 539 BC). The first four stories take place during the reign of the Babylonian king Nebuchadnezzar (605–562 BC), the fifth story during what looks like the last year of the reign of Belshazzar of Babylon (539 BC), and the final story during the time of Darius the Mede (for his relationship to Cyrus the Persian, see note on 6:28), thus dating sometime after Persia took over Babylon in 539 BC. Each of these stories illustrates the book's main theme: in spite of present troubles, God is in control, and he will have the victory. These accounts teach later readers how to live in a culture that is toxic to faith and not only survive but even prosper. Further, these young men have been exiled from Jerusalem (thought to be the place that God would establish his kingdom on earth) to Babylon (which symbolizes human resistance to God's plan). Their surviving and thriving in Babylon show that God is still with his people and that his redemptive plans have not ended.

1:1–21 *Daniel's Training in Babylon.* The first of the six accounts describes how Daniel and his three friends came to Babylon and Nebuchadnezzar's efforts to mold them into servants of the Babylonian Empire. While on the surface it looks like Nebuchadnezzar is in control of their lives, the book reveals that God is the one who is in control.

1:1–2 *The Subjugation of Judah.* Daniel begins with a brief account of Jerusalem's yielding to Babylon and its king Nebuchadnezzar. From this point, Judah is a tribute-paying vassal state of the Babylonian Empire.

1:1 third year. Using the Babylonian method of dating a king's rule (Jer 25:1; 46:2 call this his "fourth year" since Jeremiah uses the Judahite method), this was probably 605 BC, the same year Nebuchadnezzar became king of Babylon. **Jehoiakim.** Became king of Judah in 609 BC after his father, Josiah, died on the battlefield at the hands of Egyptian forces (2 Kgs 23:29–30; 2 Chr 35:20–27). Pharaoh Necho placed Jehoiakim on the throne, and Jehoiakim foolishly hoped that Egypt would help him against the Babylonians. Since Jehoiakim did not trust in God, Jeremiah announced his eventual judgment (Jer 22:18–23).

1:2 the Lord delivered. On a human level, it appears that Nebuchadnezzar took Jerusalem due to his superior strength. Perhaps the Babylonians also credited their gods for the victory. But the book of Daniel explains that God is in charge and that the only reason Nebuchadnezzar succeeded is that "the Lord delivered Jehoiakim ... into his hand." This deportation in 605 BC is the first of three; Daniel and his three friends are included in this deportation. Due to Judah's continued sin, there would be further deportations in 597 BC (2 Kgs 24:12b–17) and in 586 BC, at which time the Babylonians destroyed Jerusalem, burned the temple, and brought the monarchy to a close (2 Kgs 25:1–26). **articles from the temple.** In the ancient Near East, it was typical for a victorious army to take the idol of the chief god of a vanquished people back to their home temple. Since Judah did not have an idol of their God, Yahweh, Nebuchadnezzar settled for "some of the articles from the temple of God." These articles included the gold and silver goblets that feature in the story in ch. 5. The first group of returnees from Babylon after the edict of Cyrus returns these objects to the temple, which signals the end of the exile (Ezra 1:7–11).

1:3–5 *Nebuchadnezzar's Training Program.* According to ancient Near Eastern custom, the victors would take young men from the ruling class to train them in their ways so they could serve the imperialistic purposes of their conquerors.

1:3 court officials. Might also be translated "eunuchs." Many palace officials were eunuchs. Daniel and his three friends may also have been made eunuchs as anticipated by Isaiah's words to Hezekiah in Isa 39:7.

1:4 language ... of the Babylonians. Aramaic. The scholarly language of the Babylonians was Akkadian. Daniel and his three friends likely learned both. **literature of the Babylonians.** Included pagan myths praising the

[6]Among those who were chosen were some from Judah: Daniel,[g] Hananiah, Mishael and Azariah.
[7]The chief official gave them new names: to Daniel, the name Belteshazzar;[h] to Hananiah, Shadrach;
to Mishael, Meshach; and to Azariah, Abednego.[i]
[8]But Daniel resolved not to defile[j] himself with the royal food and wine, and he asked the chief official for permission not to defile himself this way. [9]Now God had caused the official to show favor[k] and compassion[l] to Daniel, [10]but the official told Daniel, "I am afraid of my lord the king, who has assigned your[a] food and drink. Why should he see you looking worse than the other young men your age? The king would then have my head because of you."
[11]Daniel then said to the guard whom the chief official had appointed over Daniel, Hananiah, Mishael and Azariah, [12]"Please test your servants for ten days: Give us nothing but vegetables to eat and water to drink. [13]Then compare our appearance with that of the young men who eat the royal food, and treat your servants in accordance with what you see." [14]So he agreed to this and tested them for ten days.
[15]At the end of the ten days they looked healthier and better nourished than any of the young men who ate the royal food.[m] [16]So the guard took away their choice food and the wine they were to drink and gave them vegetables instead.[n]
[17]To these four young men God gave knowledge and understanding[o] of all kinds of literature and learning.[p] And Daniel could understand visions and dreams of all kinds.[q]
[18]At the end of the time[r] set by the king to bring them into his service, the chief official presented them to Nebuchadnezzar. [19]The king talked with them, and he found none equal to Daniel, Hananiah, Mishael and Azariah; so they entered the king's service.[s] [20]In every matter of wisdom and understanding about which the king questioned them, he found them ten times better than all the magicians and enchanters in his whole kingdom.[t]
[21]And Daniel remained there until the first year of King Cyrus.[u]

Nebuchadnezzar's Dream

2 In the second year of his reign, Nebuchadnezzar had dreams;[v] his mind was troubled[w] and he could not sleep.[x] [2]So the king summoned the magicians,[y] enchanters, sorcerers[z] and astrologers[b][a] to tell him what he had dreamed.[b] When they came in and stood before the king, [3]he said to them, "I have had a dream that troubles[c] me and I want to know what it means.[c]"

[a] *10* The Hebrew for *your* and *you* in this verse is plural. [b] *2* Or *Chaldeans*; also in verses 4, 5 and 10
[c] *3* Or *was*

1:6 [g]Eze 14:14
1:7 [h]Da 4:8; 5:12 [i]Da 2:49; 3:12
1:8 [j]Eze 4:13-14
1:9 [k]Ge 39:21; Pr 16:7 [l]1Ki 8:50; Ps 106:46
1:15 [m]Ex 23:25
1:16 [n]ver 12-13
1:17 [o]1Ki 3:12 [p]Da 2:23; Jas 1:5 [q]Da 2:19,30; 7:1; 8:1
1:18 [r]ver 5
1:19 [s]Ge 41:46
1:20 [t]1Ki 4:30; Da 2:13,28
1:21 [u]Da 6:28; 10:1
2:1 [v]Job 33:15,18; Da 4:5 [w]Ge 41:8 [x]Est 6:1; Da 6:18
2:2 [y]Ge 41:8 [z]Ex 7:11 [a]ver 10; Da 5:7 [b]Da 4:6
2:3 [c]Da 4:5

deeds of false gods and divination texts of various sorts, such as astrological texts and commentaries on dream interpretation.

1:6–7 *Name Change.* As part of their attempt to reprogram these young men, the Babylonians change the names of Daniel and his three friends. Their Hebrew names praise the true God, and their Babylonian names praise pagan gods. Daniel ("God is my judge") becomes Belteshazzar ("the divine lady protects the king"). Azariah ("The LORD is my help") becomes Abednego (probably a jumbled form of "servant of Nabu"). Hananiah ("The LORD has been gracious") and Mishael ("Who is what God is?") become Shadrach and Meshach, respectively, names of debated meaning, but the latter may refer to the god Marduk.

1:8–16 *Refusing the King's Food.* The king determined a specific diet for the young men so that they might look the part of court wise men. Ancient Babylonian art depicts wise men as pudgy and well fed. The king's choice food and wine would achieve that result, and as Ashpenaz recognizes, the vegetables and water that Daniel desires would have the opposite effect. We know from 10:3 that at least Daniel refused the royal food only temporarily, so this refusal of the royal diet has nothing to do with keeping kosher, avoiding political connections, or refusing food offered to idols; rather, they are giving God room to work. Their healthy appearance at the end of the chapter is the result not of diet but of God's grace.

1:8 Daniel goes through the proper channels to adopt a different diet.

1:11–12 Rather than becoming discouraged at his failure to convince Ashpenaz, the wise Daniel simply seeks another means to his desired end. The guard would have less to lose, especially considering that Daniel began his requested diet plan with a ten-day trial.

1:13–14 A diet of vegetables and water rather than the royal food and wine would naturally make the four men look worse (v. 10; see note on 1:8–16). Such a diet gives God space to demonstrate that he, not the king, is the reason the young men succeed.

1:17–21 *Valedictorians.* The four young Israelites were at the top of their class even though the curriculum was repellent to their faith. It included mythological and divination texts, including those used for interpreting dreams. Though thrown into a situation that was dangerous, Daniel and his friends not only survive but thrive in captivity, thanks to God.

1:18 chief official. Ashpenaz (see v. 3 and note).

1:19 they entered the king's service. Their training prepared them to serve as advisors to Nebuchadnezzar.

1:20 They far exceeded ("ten times better") all the other graduates in their training class. Nebuchadnezzar surely attributes their nourished appearance and academic achievement to his training program, but Daniel and his friends, as well as the reader, know that their appearance is not because of the king's diet but is God's doing.

2:1–49 *God's Wisdom Versus Babylonian Wisdom.* In ch. 1, Nebuchadnezzar subjects Daniel and his three friends to a rigorous diet and academic curriculum in order to shape them to be proper wise men in service to his court. At the end of the chapter, they are found to be the best of their class. While Nebuchadnezzar thinks that their

2:4 [d]Ezr 4:7 [e]Da 3:9; 5:10
2:5 [f]ver 12 [g]Ezr 6:11; Da 3:29
2:6 [h]ver 48; Da 5:7,16
2:9 [i]Est 4:11 [j]Isa 41:22-24
2:10 [k]ver 27
2:11 [l]Da 5:11
2:12 [m]Da 3:13,19 [n]ver 5
2:13 [o]Da 1:20
2:17 [p]Da 1:6
2:18 [q]Isa 37:4 [r]Jer 33:3
2:19 [s]ver 28 [t]Job 33:15; Da 1:17
2:20 [u]Ps 113:2; 145:1-2 [v]Jer 32:19
2:21 [w]Da 7:25 [x]Job 12:19; Ps 75:6-7

4 Then the astrologers answered the king,[a][d] "May the king live forever![e] Tell your servants the dream,
and we will interpret it."
5 The king replied to the astrologers, "This is what I have firmly decided: If you do not tell me what
my dream was and interpret it, I will have you cut into pieces[f] and your houses turned into piles of
rubble.[g] 6 But if you tell me the dream and explain it, you will receive from me gifts and rewards and
great honor.[h] So tell me the dream and interpret it for me."
7 Once more they replied, "Let the king tell his servants the dream, and we will interpret it."
8 Then the king answered, "I am certain that you are trying to gain time, because you realize that
this is what I have firmly decided: 9 If you do not tell me the dream, there is only one penalty[i] for you.
You have conspired to tell me misleading and wicked things, hoping the situation will change. So then,
tell me the dream, and I will know that you can interpret it for me."[j]
10 The astrologers answered the king, "There is no one on earth who can do what the king asks! No
king, however great and mighty, has ever asked such a thing of any magician or enchanter or astrol-
oger.[k] 11 What the king asks is too difficult. No one can reveal it to the king except the gods,[l] and they
do not live among humans."
12 This made the king so angry and furious[m] that he ordered the execution[n] of all the wise men of
Babylon. 13 So the decree was issued to put the wise men to death, and men were sent to look for Daniel
and his friends to put them to death.[o]
14 When Arioch, the commander of the king's guard, had gone out to put to death the wise men of
Babylon, Daniel spoke to him with wisdom and tact. 15 He asked the king's officer, "Why did the king
issue such a harsh decree?" Arioch then explained the matter to Daniel. 16 At this, Daniel went in to the
king and asked for time, so that he might interpret the dream for him.
17 Then Daniel returned to his house and explained the matter to his friends Hananiah, Mishael and
Azariah.[p] 18 He urged them to plead for mercy[q] from the God of heaven concerning this mystery,[r] so that
he and his friends might not be executed with the rest of the wise men of Babylon. 19 During the night
the mystery[s] was revealed to Daniel in a vision.[t] Then Daniel praised the God of heaven 20 and said:

> "Praise be to the name of God for ever and ever;[u]
> wisdom and power[v] are his.
> 21 He changes times and seasons;[w]
> he deposes[x] kings and raises up others.

a *4* At this point the Hebrew text has *in Aramaic*, indicating that the text from here through the end of chapter 7 is in Aramaic.

robust appearance is a result of their diet of choice food and wine, the reader knows that they have not been eating the king's food and that their looks are due to God's intervention. But their great knowledge and understanding does not seem to be the result of Nebuchadnezzar's training. Ch. 2 demonstrates that their true wisdom comes not from the Babylonians, who are unable to interpret Nebuchadnezzar's troubling dream, but from God, illustrating the contrast that Paul later describes as the ineffective "wisdom of this age or of the rulers of this age" (1 Cor 2:6) with the wisdom of God. Daniel is able to describe and interpret the dream that disturbs the king in a way that anticipates God's victory over evil human kingdoms and the establishment of the kingdom of God.

2:1–13 *The King's Disturbing Dream.* In ancient Babylon, as through much of the ancient world, dreams were often thought to communicate important messages. After a disturbing dream, Nebuchadnezzar summons his wise men, who are versed in dream interpretation. They ask the king to describe the dream to them. In ancient Babylon, wise men did not pretend to know what a person dreamed. They claimed only that they could interpret dreams, and they accomplished this with "dream books," commentaries on the significance of different types of dreams.

2:1 second year. Approximately 603 BC.

2:4 See NIV text note. The language shifts back to Hebrew in 8:1. Attempts to explain the use of these two different languages have not persuaded the majority of scholars.

2:13 The king's decree of death includes Daniel and his three friends since they are wise men.

2:14–30 *God's Wisdom.* The wisdom of the Babylonians, dependent on knowing the content of a dream to interpret it, is woefully inadequate to answer the king's question. God shows the superiority of his wisdom by revealing the content and the interpretation of the dream to Daniel, who then informs the king.

2:14 commander of the king's guard. Or "chief of the butchers of the king," indicating Arioch's deadly role. Daniel does not panic at the threat of death, but "with wisdom and tact" receives permission from Arioch to consider the matter of the dream.

2:18 mystery. Nebuchadnezzar's dream is beyond human comprehension.

2:19 Daniel praises God because God revealed the dream and its interpretation. What is beyond human ability is not beyond God's. God's action shows that he, unlike the pagan gods of Babylon, makes his saving presence known to his people (cf. v. 11). God comes through to rescue Daniel and the three friends from certain death.

2:20 Daniel responds properly to God's help by praising him for his wisdom and power. The wisdom that counts is not the wisdom taught by the Babylonians but the wisdom God reveals.

2:21 deposes kings and raises up others. Nebuchadnezzar's position and power depend on Daniel's God, who deposes and raises up

He gives wisdom[y] to the wise
and knowledge to the discerning.
22 He reveals deep and hidden things;[z]
he knows what lies in darkness,[a]
and light[b] dwells with him.
23 I thank and praise you, God of my ancestors:[c]
You have given me wisdom[d] and power,
you have made known to me what we asked of you,
you have made known to us the dream of the king."

Daniel Interprets the Dream

24 Then Daniel went to Arioch,[e] whom the king had appointed to execute the wise men of Babylon,
and said to him, "Do not execute the wise men of Babylon. Take me to the king, and I will interpret
his dream for him."
25 Arioch took Daniel to the king at once and said, "I have found a man among the exiles from Judah[f]
who can tell the king what his dream means."
26 The king asked Daniel (also called Belteshazzar),[g] "Are you able to tell me what I saw in my dream
and interpret it?"
27 Daniel replied, "No wise man, enchanter, magician or diviner can explain to the king the mystery
he has asked about,[h] 28 but there is a God in heaven who reveals mysteries.[i] He has shown King Nebuchadnezzar what will happen in days to come.[j] Your dream and the visions that passed through your
mind[k] as you were lying in bed are these:
29 "As Your Majesty was lying there, your mind turned to things to come, and the revealer of mysteries
showed you what is going to happen. 30 As for me, this mystery has been revealed[l] to me, not because I
have greater wisdom than anyone else alive, but so that Your Majesty may know the interpretation and
that you may understand what went through your mind.
31 "Your Majesty looked, and there before you stood a large statue — an enormous, dazzling statue,[m] awesome in appearance. 32 The head of the statue was made of pure gold, its chest and arms of
silver, its belly and thighs of bronze, 33 its legs of iron, its feet partly of iron and partly of baked clay.
34 While you were watching, a rock was cut out, but not by human hands.[n] It struck the statue on its
feet of iron and clay and smashed them.[o] 35 Then the iron, the clay, the bronze, the silver and the gold
were all broken to pieces and became like chaff on a threshing floor in the summer. The wind swept
them away[p] without leaving a trace. But the rock that struck the statue became a huge mountain[q]
and filled the whole earth.
36 "This was the dream, and now we will interpret it to the king. 37 Your Majesty, you are the king of
kings.[r] The God of heaven has given you dominion[s] and power and might and glory; 38 in your hands

2:21 [y] Jas 1:5
2:22 [z] Job 12:22; Ps 25:14; Da 5:11 [a] Ps 139:11-12; Jer 23:24; Heb 4:13 [b] Isa 45:7; Jas 1:17
2:23 [c] Ex 3:15 [d] Da 1:17
2:24 [e] ver 14
2:25 [f] Da 1:6; 5:13; 6:13
2:26 [g] Da 1:7
2:27 [h] ver 10
2:28 [i] Ge 40:8; Am 4:13 [j] Ge 49:1; Da 10:14 [k] Da 4:5
2:30 [l] Isa 45:3; Da 1:17; Am 4:13
2:31 [m] Hab 1:7
2:34 [n] Zec 4:6 [o] ver 44-45; Ps 2:9; Isa 60:12; Da 8:25
2:35 [p] Ps 1:4; 37:10; Isa 17:13 [q] Isa 2:3; Mic 4:1
2:37 [r] Eze 26:7 [s] Jer 27:7

kings. **gives wisdom ... and knowledge.** Humans are wise and powerful only if God makes them so.
2:24 Daniel becomes an instrument of common grace for the Babylonian wise men, calling on Arioch to stop their execution.
2:27 – 28 Daniel makes it absolutely clear to Nebuchadnezzar that he is able to reveal the dream and its interpretation only because God revealed it to him. In this way, Daniel contrasts his God to the pagan gods the Babylonians worship.
2:30 Daniel boasts not in his own wisdom but in God's wisdom.
2:31 – 35 *The King's Dream.* From head down, the preciousness of the materials diminishes. A rock is cut out but not by human hands, implying that God chiseled it out.
2:35 chaff. The external husk that protects the grain. Without the grain, chaff is useless and easily blown away. Chaff often, as here, represents something worthless and temporary (see Job 21:18; Pss 1:4; 35:5; Jer 13:24).
2:36 – 45 *The Interpretation of the Dream.* Unlike the Babylonian wise men, Daniel is able to reveal the contents of the dream as well as its interpretation. The different parts of the statue represent different kingdoms that succeed each other. With the exception of the head of gold, Daniel does not name the kingdoms represented by the parts of the statue, and opinions differ over their identification. Some interpreters believe that the sequence represents first the Babylonian Empire (the head of gold), followed by the Medo-Persian Empire (the chest and arms of silver), the Greek Empire (the belly and thighs of bronze), and then the Roman Empire (legs of iron). Others identify the sequence after Babylon as the Medes, the Persians, and ending with the Greeks. It is possible, perhaps even probable, that these parts of the statue do not refer to specific kingdoms, the point being that evil human kingdoms will succeed each other until God's kingdom decisively intrudes. The "rock" (vv. 34,45) represents the kingdom of God that will destroy and displace these evil human kingdoms. The dream thus represents the conflict between the kingdoms of this world and the kingdom of God and announces that God will have the final victory.
2:38 head of gold. Nebuchadnezzar, representing the Babylonian Empire. Though the kingdom will eventually pass away, at the moment Nebuchadnezzar's empire surpasses all other human kingdoms.

2:38 [t]Jer 27:6; Da 4:21-22
2:40 [u]Da 7:7,23
2:44 [v]Ps 2:9; 1Co 15:24 [w]Isa 60:12 [x]Ps 145:13; Isa 9:7; Da 4:34; 6:26; 7:14,27; Mic 4:7,13; Lk 1:33
2:45 [y]Isa 28:16 [z]Da 8:25
2:46 [a]Da 8:17; Ac 10:25 [b]Ac 14:13
2:47 [c]Da 11:36 [d]Da 4:25 [e]ver 22,28
2:48 [f]ver 6; Da 4:9; 5:11
2:49 [g]Da 1:7
3:1 [h]Isa 46:6; Jer 16:20; Hab 2:19
3:2 [i]ver 27; Da 6:7
3:4 [j]Da 4:1; 6:25

he has placed all mankind and the beasts of the field and the birds in the sky. Wherever they live, he has made you ruler over them all.[t] You are that head of gold.

39 "After you, another kingdom will arise, inferior to yours. Next, a third kingdom, one of bronze, will rule over the whole earth. 40 Finally, there will be a fourth kingdom, strong as iron — for iron breaks and smashes everything — and as iron breaks things to pieces, so it will crush and break all the others.[u] 41 Just as you saw that the feet and toes were partly of baked clay and partly of iron, so this will be a divided kingdom; yet it will have some of the strength of iron in it, even as you saw iron mixed with clay. 42 As the toes were partly iron and partly clay, so this kingdom will be partly strong and partly brittle. 43 And just as you saw the iron mixed with baked clay, so the people will be a mixture and will not remain united, any more than iron mixes with clay.

44 "In the time of those kings, the God of heaven will set up a kingdom that will never be destroyed, nor will it be left to another people. It will crush[v] all those kingdoms[w] and bring them to an end, but it will itself endure forever.[x] 45 This is the meaning of the vision of the rock[y] cut out of a mountain, but not by human hands[z] — a rock that broke the iron, the bronze, the clay, the silver and the gold to pieces.

"The great God has shown the king what will take place in the future. The dream is true and its interpretation is trustworthy."

46 Then King Nebuchadnezzar fell prostrate[a] before Daniel and paid him honor and ordered that an offering[b] and incense be presented to him. 47 The king said to Daniel, "Surely your God is the God of gods[c] and the Lord of kings[d] and a revealer of mysteries,[e] for you were able to reveal this mystery."

48 Then the king placed Daniel in a high position and lavished many gifts on him. He made him ruler over the entire province of Babylon and placed him in charge of all its wise men.[f] 49 Moreover, at Daniel's request the king appointed Shadrach, Meshach and Abednego administrators over the province of Babylon,[g] while Daniel himself remained at the royal court.

The Image of Gold and the Blazing Furnace

3 King Nebuchadnezzar made an image[h] of gold, sixty cubits high and six cubits wide,[a] and set it up on the plain of Dura in the province of Babylon. 2 He then summoned the satraps, prefects, governors, advisers, treasurers, judges, magistrates and all the other provincial officials[i] to come to the dedication of the image he had set up. 3 So the satraps, prefects, governors, advisers, treasurers, judges, magistrates and all the other provincial officials assembled for the dedication of the image that King Nebuchadnezzar had set up, and they stood before it.

4 Then the herald loudly proclaimed, "Nations and peoples of every language,[j] this is what you are

[a] *1* That is, about 90 feet high and 9 feet wide or about 27 meters high and 2.7 meters wide

2:39 another kingdom. As silver (v. 32) is "inferior" to gold, so the second kingdom (perhaps Persia) is inferior to Babylon; Daniel does not indicate the precise nature of its inferiority. **third kingdom ... of bronze.** It will rule the whole earth and may refer to Greece, which displaced Persia with a vastly larger empire.

2:40 fourth kingdom. Traditionally thought to be Rome; like the "iron" that represents it, it will treat other nations with violence.

2:41–43 The feet made partly of iron and partly of baked clay represent a weakening of these human kingdoms as time progresses. Like the statue's feet, "the people will be a mixture" (v. 43) that lacks unity.

2:44–45a God's kingdom (the rock not made with human hands) will destroy human kingdoms (the statue). Throughout Scripture, evil human powers resist God's rule, but Daniel anticipates God's final victory.

2:45b True wisdom comes from God, not from human resources, including the training that Daniel and his three friends received in Babylon (1:3–5).

2:46–49 *Nebuchadnezzar Praises the True God.* God receives the glory from none other than the pagan Nebuchadnezzar, the king who defeated Jerusalem. Historical records, as well as later chapters in Daniel (see note on 4:8), imply that the king never became an exclusive worshiper of the true God.

2:46 Nebuchadnezzar reveals his ignorance by prostrating himself before Daniel and offering sacrifices to him. Even so, later readers of Daniel, especially those who were themselves persecuted, would derive great comfort in seeing this great king paying honor to Daniel the exile.

2:47–49 This story teaches that God's people can survive and even thrive while experiencing exile and persecution.

3:1–30 *The Image of Gold and the Blazing Furnace.* The faith of the three friends (ch. 3 does not mention Daniel) is tested when Nebuchadnezzar sets up a golden image and demands that his officials worship it on pain of death. This story illustrates that God's power even transcends death. The repeated long list of officials (vv. 2,3,27) and musical instruments (vv. 5,7,10,15) gives the story a mood of pomposity and heightens the tension, focusing on the moment of obedience or disobedience.

3:1–7 *The Image of Gold.* The image of gold represents either a false god (like Marduk the chief god of the Babylonians) or Nebuchadnezzar himself. In either case, Nebuchadnezzar appears to be demanding a test of loyalty to himself and his reign.

3:1 sixty cubits ... six cubits. See NIV text notes. **plain of Dura.** Location unknown, though Dura means "fortress" in Akkadian, the language of the Babylonians.

3:4 The Babylonian Empire incorporated "nations and peoples of every language."

commanded to do: [5]As soon as you hear the sound of the horn, flute, zither, lyre, harp, pipe and all kinds of music, you must fall down and worship the image of gold that King Nebuchadnezzar has set up.[k] [6]Whoever does not fall down and worship will immediately be thrown into a blazing furnace."[l]

[7]Therefore, as soon as they heard the sound of the horn, flute, zither, lyre, harp and all kinds of music, all the nations and peoples of every language fell down and worshiped the image of gold that King Nebuchadnezzar had set up.[m]

[8]At this time some astrologers[a][n] came forward and denounced the Jews. [9]They said to King Nebuchadnezzar, "May the king live forever![o] [10]Your Majesty has issued a decree[p] that everyone who hears the sound of the horn, flute, zither, lyre, harp, pipe and all kinds of music must fall down and worship the image of gold,[q] [11]and that whoever does not fall down and worship will be thrown into a blazing furnace. [12]But there are some Jews whom you have set over the affairs of the province of Babylon—Shadrach, Meshach and Abednego[r]—who pay no attention[s] to you, Your Majesty. They neither serve your gods nor worship the image of gold you have set up."[t]

[13]Furious[u] with rage, Nebuchadnezzar summoned Shadrach, Meshach and Abednego. So these men were brought before the king, [14]and Nebuchadnezzar said to them, "Is it true, Shadrach, Meshach and Abednego, that you do not serve my gods[v] or worship the image[w] of gold I have set up? [15]Now when you hear the sound of the horn, flute, zither, lyre, harp, pipe and all kinds of music, if you are ready to fall down and worship the image I made, very good. But if you do not worship it, you will be thrown immediately into a blazing furnace. Then what god[x] will be able to rescue[y] you from my hand?"

[16]Shadrach, Meshach and Abednego[z] replied to him, "King Nebuchadnezzar, we do not need to defend ourselves before you in this matter. [17]If we are thrown into the blazing furnace, the God we serve is able to deliver[a] us from it, and he will deliver[b] us[b] from Your Majesty's hand. [18]But even if he does not, we want you to know, Your Majesty, that we will not serve your gods or worship the image of gold you have set up.[c]"

[19]Then Nebuchadnezzar was furious with Shadrach, Meshach and Abednego, and his attitude toward them changed. He ordered the furnace heated seven[d] times hotter than usual [20]and commanded some of the strongest soldiers in his army to tie up Shadrach, Meshach and Abednego and throw them into the blazing furnace. [21]So these men, wearing their robes, trousers, turbans and other clothes, were bound and thrown into the blazing furnace. [22]The king's command was

Musicians play on a lyre, a vertical harp, and double pipes in this Assyrian relief from the North Palace at Nineveh, 645–635 BC.

Kim Walton, taken at the British Museum

[a] 8 Or *Chaldeans* [b] 17 Or *If the God we serve is able to deliver us, then he will deliver us from the blazing furnace and*

3:5 [k] ver 10,15
3:6 [l] ver 11,15,21; Jer 29:22; Da 6:7; Mt 13:42,50; Rev 13:15
3:7 [m] ver 5
3:8 [n] Da 2:10
3:9 [o] Ne 2:3; Da 5:10; 6:6
3:10 [p] Da 6:12 [q] ver 4-6
3:12 [r] Da 2:49 [s] Da 6:13 [t] Est 3:3
3:13 [u] Da 2:12
3:14 [v] Isa 46:1; Jer 50:2 [w] ver 1
3:15 [x] Isa 36:18-20 [y] Ex 5:2; 2Ch 32:15
3:16 [z] Da 1:7
3:17 [a] Ps 27:1-2 [b] Job 5:19; Jer 1:8
3:18 [c] ver 28; Jos 24:15
3:19 [d] Lev 26:18-28

3:5 Most people of the ancient Near East would have no problem bowing to an image of a god or even of the king. As worshipers of many gods, they could easily incorporate the worship of one more.

3:8–18 *The Three Friends Accused.* Rivals of the three friends inform the king that the three friends did not bow to the image of gold, thus failing the loyalty test in the eyes of the king. The three friends thus demonstrate that their ultimate loyalty is to God alone.

3:12 Jews whom you have set over the affairs of the province of Babylon. May imply the motivation of the astrologers, native Babylonians who were likely jealous of the status and power of the men from Judah.

3:15 what god will be able to rescue you ...? Nebuchadnezzar believes that no god can save the three friends from his judgment. Those who know the true God know Nebuchadnezzar's claim is pathetic (Ps 2:1–6).

3:17–18 The three friends know that God is able to rescue them if he so wills. Even so, if God for his reasons chooses not to rescue them, they are ready to die for their God rather than surrender to the evil powers of this world.

3:19–27 *God's Miraculous Rescue.* God demonstrates his loyalty to the three friends and his power to Nebuchadnezzar and the Babylonians by rescuing the three friends from the furnace.

3:19 his attitude toward them changed. Or "the image of his face changed." The word "image" also describes the large statue that Nebuchadnezzar set up on the plain of Dura (vv. 1–3,5,7,10,12,14–15, 18). The one who in his pride has created an image with the purpose of assuring uniform loyalty finds his own image provoked beyond his control. **seven times hotter than usual.** Since seven is a number that signifies completeness, this means as hot as it can get.

3:22 [e] Da 1:7
3:26 [f] Da 4:2,34
3:27 [g] ver 2 [h] Isa 43:2; Heb 11:32-34 [i] Da 6:23
3:28 [j] Ps 34:7; Da 6:22; Ac 5:19 [k] Job 13:15; Ps 26:1; 84:12; Jer 17:7 [l] ver 18
3:29 [m] Da 6:26 [n] Ezr 6:11 [o] Da 6:27
3:30 [p] Da 2:49
4:1 [q] Da 3:4 [r] Da 6:25
4:2 [s] Ps 74:9 [t] Da 3:26
4:3 [u] Ps 105:27; Da 6:27 [v] Da 2:44
4:4 [w] Ps 30:6
4:5 [x] Da 2:1 [y] Da 2:28
4:6 [z] Da 2:2
4:7 [a] Ge 41:8 [b] Isa 44:25; Da 2:2 [c] Da 2:10
4:8 [d] Da 1:7 [e] Da 5:11,14

so urgent and the furnace so hot that the flames of the fire killed the soldiers who took up Shadrach,
Meshach and Abednego,[e] 23 and these three men, firmly tied, fell into the blazing furnace.
24 Then King Nebuchadnezzar leaped to his feet in amazement and asked his advisers, "Weren't there
three men that we tied up and threw into the fire?"
They replied, "Certainly, Your Majesty."
25 He said, "Look! I see four men walking around in the fire, unbound and unharmed, and the fourth
looks like a son of the gods."
26 Nebuchadnezzar then approached the opening of the blazing furnace and shouted, "Shadrach,
Meshach and Abednego, servants of the Most High God,[f] come out! Come here!"
So Shadrach, Meshach and Abednego came out of the fire, 27 and the satraps, prefects, governors
and royal advisers[g] crowded around them.[h] They saw that the fire[i] had not harmed their bodies, nor
was a hair of their heads singed; their robes were not scorched, and there was no smell of fire on them.
28 Then Nebuchadnezzar said, "Praise be to the God of Shadrach, Meshach and Abednego, who has sent
his angel[j] and rescued his servants! They trusted[k] in him and defied the king's command and were willing to
give up their lives rather than serve or worship any god except their own God.[l] 29 Therefore I decree[m] that the
people of any nation or language who say anything against the God of Shadrach, Meshach and Abednego
be cut into pieces and their houses be turned into piles of rubble,[n] for no other god can save[o] in this way."
30 Then the king promoted Shadrach, Meshach and Abednego in the province of Babylon.[p]

Nebuchadnezzar's Dream of a Tree

4 [a] King Nebuchadnezzar,

To the nations and peoples of every language,[q] who live in all the earth:

May you prosper greatly![r]

2 It is my pleasure to tell you about the miraculous signs[s] and wonders that the Most High
God[t] has performed for me.

3 How great are his signs,
how mighty his wonders![u]
His kingdom is an eternal kingdom;
his dominion endures[v] from generation to generation.

4 I, Nebuchadnezzar, was at home in my palace, contented[w] and prosperous. 5 I had a dream[x]
that made me afraid. As I was lying in bed, the images and visions that passed through my mind[y]
terrified me. 6 So I commanded that all the wise men of Babylon be brought before me to interpret[z] the dream for me. 7 When the magicians,[a] enchanters, astrologers[b] and diviners[b] came,
I told them the dream, but they could not interpret it for me.[c] 8 Finally, Daniel came into my
presence and I told him the dream. (He is called Belteshazzar,[d] after the name of my god, and
the spirit of the holy gods[e] is in him.)

[a] In Aramaic texts 4:1-3 is numbered 3:31-33, and 4:4-37 is numbered 4:1-34. [b] 7 Or *Chaldeans*

3:25 like a son of the gods. The exact identity of the rescuer is unclear. Whether he is God himself in human form or an angel sent by God, the deliverance no doubt comes from God himself. Christians cannot help but see a prefigurement of Jesus, who came to dwell in an evil and dangerous world and who died so that we might have victory over death.

3:28–30 *Nebuchadnezzar Worships God.* The pagan king Nebuchadnezzar praises God, though he probably never became an exclusive worshiper of the true God (see note on 2:46–49).

3:28 his angel. Though Nebuchadnezzar refers to the fourth man in the furnace as God's "angel," he does not resolve the issue of the figure's exact identity (see note on v. 25) since he speaks from his pagan background.

4:1–37 *The King's Pride Humbled.* Nebuchadnezzar has a second dream that only Daniel can interpret (see ch. 2), thus again demonstrating the superiority of God's wisdom over Babylonian wisdom (see note on 2:1–49). Nebuchadnezzar and everyone who reads this story comes to recognize that God is vastly more powerful than even this most powerful of all human beings.

4:1–3 *The King Praises God.* Ch. 4 begins with a letter or an official proclamation from Nebuchadnezzar to the inhabitants of all the earth and proclaims the greatness of God. The letter is written in response to the events narrated in vv. 4–33. See note on 2:46–49.

4:4–18 *The Dream Report.* In ch. 2, Nebuchadnezzar demanded that the Babylonian wise men tell him the content of his dream as well as its interpretation. In this story, they cannot even interpret the dream once Nebuchadnezzar tells them what the dream was about.

4:8 Though Nebuchadnezzar earlier praised the true God (2:47; 3:28–29), he retains his polytheistic beliefs as indicated by his calling

[9]I said, "Belteshazzar, chief[f] of the magicians, I know that the spirit of the holy gods[g] is in you, and no mystery is too difficult for you. Here is my dream; interpret it for me. [10]These are the visions I saw while lying in bed:[h] I looked, and there before me stood a tree in the middle of the land. Its height was enormous.[i] [11]The tree grew large and strong and its top touched the sky; it was visible to the ends of the earth. [12]Its leaves were beautiful, its fruit abundant, and on it was food for all. Under it the wild animals found shelter, and the birds lived in its branches;[j] from it every creature was fed.

[13]"In the visions I saw while lying in bed,[k] I looked, and there before me was a holy one,[l] a messenger,[a] coming down from heaven. [14]He called in a loud voice: 'Cut down the tree and trim off its branches; strip off its leaves and scatter its fruit. Let the animals flee from under it and the birds from its branches.[m] [15]But let the stump and its roots, bound with iron and bronze, remain in the ground, in the grass of the field.

" 'Let him be drenched with the dew of heaven, and let him live with the animals among the plants of the earth. [16]Let his mind be changed from that of a man and let him be given the mind of an animal, till seven times[b] pass by for him.[n]

[17]" 'The decision is announced by messengers, the holy ones declare the verdict, so that the living may know that the Most High[o] is sovereign[p] over all kingdoms on earth and gives them to anyone he wishes and sets over them the lowliest[q] of people.'

[18]"This is the dream that I, King Nebuchadnezzar, had. Now, Belteshazzar, tell me what it means, for none of the wise men in my kingdom can interpret it for me.[r] But you can,[s] because the spirit of the holy gods is in you."[t]

Daniel Interprets the Dream

[19]Then Daniel (also called Belteshazzar) was greatly perplexed for a time, and his thoughts terrified[u] him. So the king said, "Belteshazzar, do not let the dream or its meaning alarm you."

Belteshazzar answered, "My lord, if only the dream applied to your enemies and its meaning to your adversaries! [20]The tree you saw, which grew large and strong, with its top touching the sky, visible to the whole earth, [21]with beautiful leaves and abundant fruit, providing food for all, giving shelter to the wild animals, and having nesting places in its branches for the birds— [22]Your Majesty, you are that tree![v] You have become great and strong; your greatness has grown until it reaches the sky, and your dominion extends to distant parts of the earth.[w]

[23]"Your Majesty saw a holy one,[x] a messenger, coming down from heaven and saying, 'Cut down the tree and destroy it, but leave the stump, bound with iron and bronze, in the grass of the field, while its roots remain in the ground. Let him be drenched with the dew of heaven; let him live with the wild animals, until seven times pass by for him.'[y]

[24]"This is the interpretation, Your Majesty, and this is the decree[z] the Most High has issued against my lord the king: [25]You will be driven away from people and will live with the wild animals; you will eat grass like the ox and be drenched with the dew of heaven. Seven times will pass by for you until you acknowledge that the Most High[a] is sovereign over all kingdoms on earth and gives them to anyone he wishes.[b] [26]The command to leave the stump of the tree with its roots[c] means that your kingdom will be restored to you when you acknowledge that Heaven

4:9 [f]Da 2:48 [g]Da 5:11-12
4:10 [h]ver 5 [i]Eze 31:3-4
4:12 [j]Eze 17:23; Mt 13:32
4:13 [k]Da 7:1 [l]ver 23; Dt 33:2; Da 8:13
4:14 [m]Eze 31:12; Mt 3:10
4:16 [n]ver 23,32
4:17 [o]ver 2,25; Ps 83:18 [p]Jer 27:5-7; Da 2:21; 5:18-21 [q]Da 11:21
4:18 [r]Ge 41:8; Da 5:8,15 [s]Ge 41:15 [t]ver 7-9
4:19 [u]Da 7:15,28; 8:27; 10:16-17
4:22 [v]2Sa 12:7 [w]Jer 27:7; Da 2:37-38; 5:18-19
4:23 [x]ver 13 [y]Da 5:21
4:24 [z]Job 40:12; Ps 107:40
4:25 [a]ver 17; Ps 83:18 [b]Jer 27:5; Da 5:21
4:26 [c]ver 15

[a] *13* Or *watchman*; also in verses 17 and 23 [b] *16* Or *years*; also in verses 23, 25 and 32

Daniel "Belteshazzar" (see note on 1:6–7) and describing Daniel as one who has "the spirit of the holy gods."

4:13 messenger. A supernatural being, probably an angel, reminding us that intertestamental literature used "watchers" to refer to angels (see NIV text note).

4:15 The function and symbolic meaning of the band of iron and bronze around the stump is not explained here or in the interpretation (v. 23), though it may have protected what was left of the tree.

4:16 seven times. Either seven years (see NIV text note) or an indefinite but long period of time.

4:19–27 *Daniel Interprets the Dream.* Daniel shows compassion toward the king, even though the king was responsible for Daniel's deportation from Judah.

4:20–22 The tree represents Nebuchadnezzar, whose empire has exceeded all previous world empires.

4:23 The magnificent tree that represents the king would transform into a mindless wild animal by divine decree. **seven times**. See note on v. 16.

4:25 Due to his pride, Nebuchadnezzar will be reduced to an animal-like condition. **like the ox.** A rare mental disorder that today goes by the name boanthropy causes its victims to assume the appearance, habits, and posture of cattle.

4:26 acknowledge that Heaven rules. God wants the king, as powerful as he is, to know and acknowledge that he is no match for God.

4:26 [d]Da 2:37
4:27 [e]Isa 55:6-7 [f]1Ki 21:29; Ps 41:3; Eze 18:22
4:28 [g]Nu 23:19
4:30 [h]Isa 37:24-25; Da 5:20; Hab 2:4
4:33 [i]Da 5:20-21
4:34 [j]Da 12:7; Rev 4:10 [k]Ps 145:13; Da 2:44; 5:21; 6:26; Lk 1:33
4:35 [l]Isa 40:17 [m]Ps 115:3; 135:6 [n]Isa 45:9; Ro 9:20
4:36 [o]Pr 22:4
4:37 [p]Dt 32:4; Ps 33:4-5 [q]Ex 18:11; Job 40:11-12; Da 5:20,23
5:1 [r]Est 1:3
5:2 [s]2Ki 24:13; Jer 52:19

rules.[d] 27 Therefore, Your Majesty, be pleased to accept my advice: Renounce your sins by doing
what is right, and your wickedness by being kind to the oppressed.[e] It may be that then your
prosperity will continue.[f]"

The Dream Is Fulfilled

28 All this happened[g] to King Nebuchadnezzar. 29 Twelve months later, as the king was walking
on the roof of the royal palace of Babylon, 30 he said, "Is not this the great Babylon I have built as
the royal residence, by my mighty power and for the glory of my majesty?"[h]
31 Even as the words were on his lips, a voice came from heaven, "This is what is decreed for
you, King Nebuchadnezzar: Your royal authority has been taken from you. 32 You will be driven
away from people and will live with the wild animals; you will eat grass like the ox. Seven times
will pass by for you until you acknowledge that the Most High is sovereign over all kingdoms on
earth and gives them to anyone he wishes."

33 Immediately what had been said about Nebuchadnezzar was fulfilled. He was driven away
from people and ate grass like the ox. His body was drenched with the dew of heaven until his
hair grew like the feathers of an eagle and his nails like the claws of a bird.[i]

34 At the end of that time, I, Nebuchadnezzar, raised my eyes toward heaven, and my sanity was
restored. Then I praised the Most High; I honored and glorified him who lives forever.[j]

His dominion is an eternal dominion;
his kingdom endures from generation to generation.[k]
35 All the peoples of the earth
are regarded as nothing.[l]
He does as he pleases[m]
with the powers of heaven
and the peoples of the earth.
No one can hold back his hand
or say to him: "What have you done?"[n]

36 At the same time that my sanity was restored, my honor and splendor were returned to me
for the glory of my kingdom.[o] My advisers and nobles sought me out, and I was restored to my
throne and became even greater than before. 37 Now I, Nebuchadnezzar, praise and exalt and glorify the King of heaven, because everything he does is right and all his ways are just.[p] And those
who walk in pride he is able to humble.[q]

The Writing on the Wall

5 King Belshazzar gave a great banquet[r] for a thousand of his nobles and drank wine with them.
2 While Belshazzar was drinking his wine, he gave orders to bring in the gold and silver goblets[s]
that Nebuchadnezzar his father[a] had taken from the temple in Jerusalem, so that the king and his

[a] 2 Or *ancestor*; or *predecessor*; also in verses 11, 13 and 18

4:27 Daniel hopes that the dream contains a provisional judgment that the king could avoid by repenting of wickedness and exhibiting right behavior toward the "oppressed," perhaps including the Judahite people. Nebuchadnezzar must resist the idea that he is more powerful than God himself.

4:28–37 *The Dream Is Fulfilled.* Though warned, Nebuchadnezzar attributes to himself God-like status, so God reduces this arrogant human into a mindless animal for a period of time. Skeptics point out that though we have Babylonian records from the time of Nebuchadnezzar, they give no hint of a period of extended illness during his life. It is unlikely, however, that ancient sources would preserve memory of an embarrassing episode in the great king's life.

4:30 the great Babylon I have built. From historical records and archaeological investigation, we know that the city of Babylon was indeed great, including the legendary hanging gardens and magnificent walls. Rather than praising God for its greatness, Nebuchadnezzar praises himself.

4:32–33 Thinking himself a god, Nebuchadnezzar the man becomes an animal.

4:34 With a mind like that of an ox, Nebuchadnezzar could not verbally acknowledge God's sovereignty, but the simple gesture of raising his eyes toward heaven was sufficient to show that he had learned his lesson.

4:37 pride … humble. Nebuchadnezzar recognizes that his experience illustrates the principle that God will humble the proud (Prov 3:34; 29:23; Jas 4:6,10; 1 Pet 5:5–6).

5:1–31 *The Writing on the Wall.* Nebuchadnezzar has died (in 562 BC) and the story now shifts forward to the very end of the Babylonian period when Belshazzar is ruling in Babylon (the year is now 539 BC). Belshazzar demonstrates his blasphemous arrogance by toasting his gods using

nobles, his wives and his concubines might drink from them.[t] 3 So they brought in the gold goblets
that had been taken from the temple of God in Jerusalem, and the king and his nobles, his wives and
his concubines drank from them. 4 As they drank the wine, they praised the gods of gold and silver, of
bronze, iron, wood and stone.[u]
5 Suddenly the fingers of a human hand appeared and wrote on the plaster of the wall, near the
lampstand in the royal palace. The king watched the hand as it wrote. 6 His face turned pale and he was
so frightened[v] that his legs became weak[w] and his knees were knocking.
7 The king summoned the enchanters, astrologers[a] and diviners.[x] Then he said to these wise[y] men
of Babylon, "Whoever reads this writing and tells me what it means will be clothed in purple and have
a gold chain placed around his neck,[z] and he will be made the third highest ruler in the kingdom."[a]
8 Then all the king's wise men came in, but they could not read the writing or tell the king what
it meant.[b] 9 So King Belshazzar became even more terrified[c] and his face grew more pale. His nobles
were baffled.
10 The queen,[b] hearing the voices of the king and his nobles, came into the banquet hall. "May the
king live forever!"[d] she said. "Don't be alarmed! Don't look so pale! 11 There is a man in your kingdom
who has the spirit of the holy gods[e] in him. In the time of your father he was found to have insight and
intelligence and wisdom[f] like that of the gods. Your father, King Nebuchadnezzar, appointed him chief
of the magicians, enchanters, astrologers and diviners.[g] 12 He did this because Daniel, whom the king
called Belteshazzar,[h] was found to have a keen mind and knowledge and understanding, and also the
ability to interpret dreams, explain riddles and solve difficult problems.[i] Call for Daniel, and he will tell
you what the writing means."
13 So Daniel was brought before the king, and the king said to him, "Are you Daniel, one of the exiles
my father the king brought from Judah?[j] 14 I have heard that the spirit of the gods is in you and that
you have insight, intelligence and outstanding wisdom. 15 The wise men and enchanters were brought
before me to read this writing and tell me what it means, but they could not explain it. 16 Now I have
heard that you are able to give interpretations and to solve difficult problems. If you can read this writing and tell me what it means, you will be clothed in purple and have a gold chain placed around your
neck, and you will be made the third highest ruler in the kingdom."
17 Then Daniel answered the king, "You may keep your gifts for yourself and give your rewards to
someone else.[k] Nevertheless, I will read the writing for the king and tell him what it means.
18 "Your Majesty, the Most High God gave your father Nebuchadnezzar sovereignty and greatness and
glory and splendor.[l] 19 Because of the high position he gave him, all the nations and peoples of every

5:2 [t] Est 1:7; Da 1:2
5:4 [u] Ps 135:15-18; Hab 2:19; Rev 9:20
5:6 [v] Da 4:5 [w] Eze 7:17
5:7 [x] Isa 44:25 [y] Da 4:6-7 [z] Ge 41:42 [a] Da 2:5-6, 48; 6:2-3
5:8 [b] Da 2:10, 27
5:9 [c] Isa 21:4
5:10 [d] Da 3:9
5:11 [e] Da 4:8-9, 19 [f] ver 14; Da 1:17 [g] Da 2:47-48
5:12 [h] Da 1:7 [i] ver 14-16; Da 6:3
5:13 [j] Da 6:13
5:17 [k] 2Ki 5:16
5:18 [l] Jer 27:7; Da 2:37-38

[a] 7 Or *Chaldeans*; also in verse 11 [b] *10* Or *queen mother*

the sacred vessels taken from the temple. God will not let Belshazzar go unchallenged.

5:1–4 *The King Profanes the Holy Goblets.* While Nebuchadnezzar stole the goblets from the temple, he never appears to have gone as far as Belshazzar, who actually used them.

5:1 King Belshazzar. While Babylonian records list Nabonidus as the final king of Babylon (556–539 BC), other historical texts report that he ruled from Teima in what is today Saudi Arabia, setting his son Belshazzar up as coregent in Babylon. Greek historians (Herodotus and Xenophon) mention drinking parties that took place on the eve of the fall of Babylon to the Persians.

5:2 father. See NIV text note. Historical records from Babylon indicate that "father" here likely is used in the sense of predecessor.

5:4 gods. Belshazzar's gods are lifeless, being made of metals, wood, and stone.

5:5–12 *The Writing on the Wall.* God announces his judgment against Belshazzar's blasphemy. The hand that writes the message on the wall is likely the hand of God himself.

5:5 fingers of a human hand. Though God does not have a body, his actions are often metaphorically described as accomplished by his "hand" (Pss 37:24; 95:4; Isa 5:25). Indeed, the "finger" of God wrote the Ten Commandments on the stone tablets (Exod 31:18).

5:7 clothed in purple ... gold chain. Symbols of royal power. **third highest.** After Nabonidus and Belshazzar (see note on v. 1).

5:10 queen. Likely the queen mother (see NIV text note) since Belshazzar's wives are already present (v. 2) and she vividly remembers Nebuchadnezzar's reign (vv. 11–12). She is perhaps Adad-guppi, the long-lived mother of Nabonidus, known from extrabiblical historical records.

5:11 has the spirit of the holy gods in him. The queen mother's description of Daniel from her pagan point of view, though the reader knows his wisdom comes from the true God. **father**. See note on v. 2.

5:13–28 *Daniel's Interpretation.* By interpreting the writing on the wall, Daniel again (chs. 2; 4) succeeds where the Babylonian wise men fail.

5:13 Belshazzar attempts to put Daniel in his place by calling him "one of the exiles my father the king brought from Judah."

5:14 I have heard. Belshazzar is not yet willing to endorse Daniel's God-given ability (contrast Nebuchadnezzar's "I know" in 4:9). **spirit of the gods**. See note on v. 11.

5:16 clothed in purple ... gold chain. See note on v. 7.

5:17 keep your gifts. Noting Belshazzar's pride and condescension, Daniel refuses the reward and proceeds to deliver a stinging rebuke to the king.

5:18–21 Nebuchadnezzar, like Belshazzar, was a man of pride, but in the light of God's rebuke, he humbled himself. These verses summarize the content of ch. 4.

5:19 [m]Da 2:12-13; 3:6
5:20 [n]Da 4:30 [o]Jer 13:18 [p]Job 40:12; Isa 14:13-15
5:21 [q]Eze 17:24 [r]Da 4:16-17,35
5:22 [s]Ex 10:3; 2Ch 33:23
5:23 [t]Jer 50:29 [u]Ps 115:4-8; Hab 2:19 [v]Job 12:10 [w]Job 31:4; Jer 10:23
5:26 [x]Jer 27:7 [y]Isa 13:6
5:27 [z]Ps 62:9
5:28 [a]Isa 13:17 [b]Da 6:28
5:30 [c]ver 1 [d]Isa 21:9; Jer 51:31
5:31 [e]Da 6:1; 9:1
6:1 [f]Da 5:31 [g]Est 1:1
6:2 [h]Da 2:48-49 [i]Ezr 4:22

language dreaded and feared him. Those the king wanted to put to death, he put to death;[m] those he
wanted to spare, he spared; those he wanted to promote, he promoted; and those he wanted to humble,
he humbled. [20]But when his heart became arrogant and hardened with pride,[n] he was deposed from
his royal throne and stripped[o] of his glory.[p] [21]He was driven away from people and given the mind of
an animal; he lived with the wild donkeys and ate grass like the ox; and his body was drenched with
the dew of heaven, until he acknowledged that the Most High God is sovereign[q] over all kingdoms on
earth and sets over them anyone he wishes.[r]

[22]"But you, Belshazzar, his son,[a] have not humbled[s] yourself, though you knew all this. [23]Instead,
you have set yourself up against[t] the Lord of heaven. You had the goblets from his temple brought to
you, and you and your nobles, your wives and your concubines drank wine from them. You praised the
gods of silver and gold, of bronze, iron, wood and stone, which cannot see or hear or understand.[u] But
you did not honor the God who holds in his hand your life[v] and all your ways.[w] [24]Therefore he sent the
hand that wrote the inscription.

[25]"This is the inscription that was written:

MENE, MENE, TEKEL, PARSIN

[26]"Here is what these words mean:

Mene[b]: God has numbered the days[x] of your reign and brought it to an end.[y]
[27]*Tekel*[c]: You have been weighed on the scales and found wanting.[z]
[28]*Peres*[d]: Your kingdom is divided and given to the Medes[a] and Persians."[b]

[29]Then at Belshazzar's command, Daniel was clothed in purple, a gold chain was placed around his
neck, and he was proclaimed the third highest ruler in the kingdom.

[30]That very night Belshazzar,[c] king of the Babylonians,[e] was slain,[d] [31]and Darius[e] the Mede took
over the kingdom, at the age of sixty-two.[f]

Daniel in the Den of Lions

6 [g] It pleased Darius[f] to appoint 120 satraps[g] to rule throughout the kingdom, [2]with three administrators over them, one of whom was Daniel.[h] The satraps were made accountable[i] to them so
that the king might not suffer loss. [3]Now Daniel so distinguished himself among the administrators and

[a] 22 Or *descendant*; or *successor* [b] 26 *Mene* can mean *numbered* or *mina* (a unit of money). [c] 27 *Tekel* can mean *weighed* or *shekel.* [d] 28 *Peres* (the singular of *Parsin*) can mean *divided* or *Persia* or *a half mina* or *a half shekel.* [e] 30 Or *Chaldeans* [f] 31 In Aramaic texts this verse (5:31) is numbered 6:1. [g] In Aramaic texts 6:1-28 is numbered 6:2-29.

5:22–24 Belshazzar did not learn from Nebuchadnezzar's experience, though he "knew all this" (v. 22). God will not let the proud go unhumbled. Belshazzar expresses his immense arrogance by using the goblets from the Jerusalem temple for a drinking party and to praise his false gods. He thus combines arrogance, idolatry, and blasphemy.

5:25–28 The writing on the wall may have more than one layer of meaning. Daniel takes the three nouns in their verbal meanings: "*Mene*" (v. 26) is connected to the verb *m-n-h* ("to number"). "*Tekel*" (v. 27) is related to the verb *t-q-l* ("to weigh"). "*Peres*" (v. 28) is from the verb *p-r-s* ("to divide"). All three verbs anticipate Babylon's fall to the Medes and Persians: (1) Babylon's days are numbered; (2) Babylon has been evaluated and found wanting; and (3) the Medes and Persians are the human agents of Babylon's fall. *Peres* also sounds like the name of the Persians. In addition, the noun *mene* can also mean mina, while *tekel* can mean shekel (both are units of money; the mina is more valuable than the shekel), while *parsin* can mean "half." Thus, "mina, mina, shekel, and a half" denotes Babylon's decline.

5:29–31 *Daniel's Reward and Babylon's Punishment.* In spite of his refusal (v. 17), Daniel is promoted to third most important ruler in the kingdom (v. 7).

5:31 Darius the Mede. His identity remains a mystery. Historical records indicate that Babylon fell to Cyrus the Persian in October 539 BC. Cyrus had earlier incorporated the kingdom of the Medes into his empire. Perhaps Darius was a Median ruler who ruled Babylon for a short period of time under the greater authority of Cyrus; perhaps Darius was the man known as Gubaru, the governor of Babylon. Alternatively, Darius could be another name for Cyrus (6:28). See Introduction: Particular Challenges.

6:1–28 *Daniel in the Den of Lions.* The sixth and final story of Daniel in a foreign court once again illustrates the book's main message: in spite of present troubles, God is in control, and he will win the victory. The story of Daniel in the lions' den shares many elements in common with the account of Nebuchadnezzar's golden statue (ch. 3), though ch. 3 features the three friends, while ch. 6 focuses on Daniel. In both chapters the king forces his subjects to demonstrate their loyalty to him in a way that is noxious to the faith of Daniel and his friends, who consequently refuse to comply. Jealous foreign wise men use the refusal of these faithful men as a pretense to force the king to execute them. In both stories, God intercedes to rescue Daniel and his friends while punishing their rivals, and the foreign kings praise the true God.

6:1–9 *The Plot Against Daniel.* Even though there is a change of empire (from Babylonian to Persian), Daniel continues to be held in high regard due to his integrity and wisdom. Out of jealousy the other wise men devise a plan to rid themselves of Daniel.

the satraps by his exceptional qualities that the king planned to set him over the whole kingdom.[j] 4At this, the administrators and the satraps tried to find grounds for charges against Daniel in his conduct of government affairs, but they were unable to do so. They could find no corruption in him, because he was trustworthy and neither corrupt nor negligent. 5Finally these men said, "We will never find any basis for charges against this man Daniel unless it has something to do with the law of his God."[k]

6So these administrators and satraps went as a group to the king and said: "May King Darius live forever![l] 7The royal administrators, prefects, satraps, advisers and governors[m] have all agreed that the king should issue an edict and enforce the decree that anyone who prays to any god or human being during the next thirty days, except to you, Your Majesty, shall be thrown into the lions' den.[n] 8Now, Your Majesty, issue the decree and put it in writing so that it cannot be altered — in accordance with the law of the Medes and Persians, which cannot be repealed."[o] 9So King Darius put the decree in writing.

10Now when Daniel learned that the decree had been published, he went home to his upstairs room where the windows opened toward[p] Jerusalem. Three times a day he got down on his knees[q] and prayed, giving thanks to his God, just as he had done before.[r] 11Then these men went as a group and found Daniel praying and asking God for help. 12So they went to the king and spoke to him about his royal decree: "Did you not publish a decree that during the next thirty days anyone who prays to any god or human being except to you, Your Majesty, would be thrown into the lions' den?"

The king answered, "The decree stands — in accordance with the law of the Medes and Persians, which cannot be repealed."[s]

13Then they said to the king, "Daniel, who is one of the exiles from Judah,[t] pays no attention[u] to you, Your Majesty, or to the decree you put in writing. He still prays three times a day." 14When the king heard this, he was greatly distressed;[v] he was determined to rescue Daniel and made every effort until sundown to save him.

15Then the men went as a group to King Darius and said to him, "Remember, Your Majesty, that according to the law of the Medes and Persians no decree or edict that the king issues can be changed."[w]

16So the king gave the order, and they brought Daniel and threw him into the lions' den.[x] The king said to Daniel, "May your God, whom you serve continually, rescue[y] you!"

17A stone was brought and placed over the mouth of the den, and the king sealed[z] it with his own signet ring and with the rings of his nobles, so that Daniel's situation might not be changed. 18Then the king returned to his palace and spent the night without eating[a] and without any entertainment being brought to him. And he could not sleep.[b]

19At the first light of dawn, the king got up and hurried to the lions' den. 20When he came near the den, he called to Daniel in an anguished voice, "Daniel, servant of the living God, has your God, whom you serve continually, been able to rescue you from the lions?"[c]

21Daniel answered, "May the king live forever![d] 22My God sent his angel,[e] and he shut the mouths

6:3 [j] Ge 41:41; Est 10:3; Da 5:12-14
6:5 [k] Ac 24:13-16
6:6 [l] Ne 2:3; Da 2:4
6:7 [m] Da 3:2 [n] Ps 59:3; 64:2-6; Da 3:6
6:8 [o] Est 1:19
6:10 [p] 1Ki 8:48-49 [q] Ps 95:6 [r] Ac 5:29
6:12 [s] Est 1:19; Da 3:8-12
6:13 [t] Da 2:25; 5:13 [u] Est 3:8; Da 3:12
6:14 [v] Mk 6:26
6:15 [w] Est 8:8
6:16 [x] ver 7 [y] Job 5:19; Ps 37:39-40
6:17 [z] Mt 27:66
6:18 [a] 2Sa 12:17 [b] Est 6:1; Da 2:1
6:20 [c] Da 3:17
6:21 [d] Da 2:4
6:22 [e] Da 3:28

6:4 Daniel's integrity testifies to the vitality of his faith in God.

6:5 The wise men know that Daniel places God's law above human law.

6:7 Since Daniel, one of the three highest administrators in the kingdom (v. 2), would never have agreed with this proposal, the administrators and satraps are lying to the king when they claim that "all" support the idea of such a decree. The decree to pray only to the king is unusual from what we know about Persian religion, which did not consider the king a deity. Perhaps this envisions the king as a mediator to the gods. In any case, the decree is likely a loyalty test (see note on 3:1 – 7). If so, Darius feels insecure in his reign at this time.

6:8 cannot be repealed. Not even the king is above the law. Once he issues a decree, it cannot be changed (Esth 8:8). While God's law perfectly expresses his will, the Persian king could find himself trapped by his own law (v. 14).

6:10 – 18 *Darius Reluctantly Punishes Daniel.* Daniel prays not to or through Darius but to God. He doesn't worry; he simply remains obedient to God.

6:10 Daniel continues his practice of praying three times a day while facing Jerusalem. While not making a public display, Daniel must obey God rather than a human ruler (Acts 5:29). 1 Kgs 8:35 – 36 calls for prayer in the direction of the temple in Jerusalem in response to God's judgment against his people's sin. Daniel prays in the direction of Jerusalem even though it is now gone.

6:16 The king realizes that rescue is beyond human help, so he encourages Daniel to appeal to God for deliverance.

6:17 his own signet ring ... rings of his nobles. Each ring has a design or inscription that identifies the ring's owner. Pressed into soft clay, it serves as a means of identification. The impressions of the rings assure all that no one could tamper with the stone to allow Daniel to escape even for a moment.

6:19 – 24 *Daniel's Rescue.* While God spares Daniel, his accusers meet the fate they intended for him. This story illustrates the teaching of Proverbs that wicked people often suffer the horrible fate they plan for the innocent (Prov 1:18 – 19; see Pss 9:15; 35:7 – 8).

6:19 That the king checks on Daniel first thing in the morning indicates that he thinks that Daniel's God might indeed have saved him.

6:22 In the ancient Near East, to survive an ordeal like a night in a lions' den indicated the innocence of the accused. As he did for the three friends in the fiery furnace (3:25), God sent an angel to protect Daniel in the lions' den.

6:22 [f]Ps 91:11-13; Heb 11:33 [g]Ac 12:11; 2Ti 4:17
6:23 [h]Da 3:27 [i]1Ch 5:20
6:24 [j]Dt 19:18-19; Est 7:9-10; Ps 54:5 [k]Dt 24:16; 2Ki 14:6 [l]Isa 38:13
6:25 [m]Da 4:1
6:26 [n]Ps 99:1-3; Da 3:29 [o]Da 2:44; 4:34
6:27 [p]Da 4:3 [q]ver 22
6:28 [r]2Ch 36:22; Da 1:21
7:1 [s]Da 5:1 [t]Da 1:17 [u]Jer 36:4
7:2 [v]Rev 7:1
7:3 [w]Rev 13:1
7:4 [x]Jer 4:7 [y]Eze 17:3
7:5 [z]Da 2:39
7:6 [a]Rev 13:2

of the lions.[f] They have not hurt me, because I was found innocent in his sight.[g] Nor have I ever done any wrong before you, Your Majesty."

23 The king was overjoyed and gave orders to lift Daniel out of the den. And when Daniel was lifted from the den, no wound[h] was found on him, because he had trusted[i] in his God.

24 At the king's command, the men who had falsely accused Daniel were brought in and thrown into the lions' den,[j] along with their wives and children.[k] And before they reached the floor of the den, the lions overpowered them and crushed all their bones.[l]

25 Then King Darius wrote to all the nations and peoples of every language in all the earth:

"May you prosper greatly![m]

26 "I issue a decree that in every part of my kingdom people must fear and reverence the God of Daniel.[n]

"For he is the living God
and he endures forever;
his kingdom will not be destroyed,
his dominion will never end.[o]
27 He rescues and he saves;
he performs signs and wonders[p]
in the heavens and on the earth.
He has rescued Daniel
from the power of the lions."[q]

28 So Daniel prospered during the reign of Darius and the reign of Cyrus[a][r] the Persian.

Daniel's Dream of Four Beasts

7 In the first year of Belshazzar[s] king of Babylon, Daniel had a dream, and visions passed through his mind[t] as he was lying in bed. He wrote[u] down the substance of his dream.

2 Daniel said: "In my vision at night I looked, and there before me were the four winds of heaven[v] churning up the great sea. 3 Four great beasts,[w] each different from the others, came up out of the sea.

4 "The first was like a lion,[x] and it had the wings of an eagle.[y] I watched until its wings were torn off and it was lifted from the ground so that it stood on two feet like a human being, and the mind of a human was given to it.

5 "And there before me was a second beast, which looked like a bear. It was raised up on one of its sides, and it had three ribs in its mouth between its teeth. It was told, 'Get up and eat your fill of flesh!'[z]

6 "After that, I looked, and there before me was another beast, one that looked like a leopard.[a] And

[a] 28 Or *Darius, that is, the reign of Cyrus*

6:24 While Daniel was able to spend the entire night in the den unharmed, the accusers and their families meet their fate before they even hit the ground. This illustrates that those who wish to harm others will themselves be harmed (see note on vv. 19–24).

6:25–28 *Darius's Decree.* Like Nebuchadnezzar before him (2:47; 3:28–29; 4:2–3), Darius responds to the display of God's power by praising God.

6:26 Contrary to human empires, God's kingdom will last forever (see 2:44–45a and note).

6:28 Darius. See note on 5:31. If Darius and Cyrus are different names for the same king, then the alternative reading presented in the NIV text note is correct.

7:1—12:13 *Four Apocalyptic Visions.* The last six chapters of Daniel present four apocalyptic visions (chs. 7; 8; 9; 10–12). All four visions recognize that the people of God experience oppression now and into the future but that at the end of time God will intervene to rescue them.

7:1–28 *The First Vision.* Daniel's first vision begins with four beasts arising out of a chaotic sea and wreaking great damage (vv. 1–8). The second scene is a judgment room where one like the son of man comes into the presence of the Ancient of Days (vv. 9–14). The second half of ch. 7 interprets the vision (vv. 15–28).

7:1–14 *Daniel's Dream of Four Beasts.* Early in Belshazzar's reign (see note on 5:1), Daniel has a dream that begins with four fearsome beasts arising out of a turbulent sea. While the first scene of Daniel's vision concerns beasts that represent human kings/kingdoms (v. 17), the second scene presents the divine realm using human figures.

7:1 first year. The exact date of the start of Belshazzar's coregency with his father, Nabonidus, is uncertain, but it was likely sometime between 553 and 550 BC.

7:2–3 The "sea" (v. 2) and its "beasts" (v. 3) often represent the forces of chaos and evil (Ps 18:15; Isa 27:1; Jer 5:22; Nah 1:4; Hab 3:15).

7:4 The first beast is a hybrid—part lion, part eagle—that transforms into a human. Like many mixed elements (Deut 22:9–11), Israelites considered hybrid animals unclean and thus repulsive.

7:6 The third beast is also a hybrid (see v. 4 and note)—part leopard, part bird. Its unnatural condition is highlighted by its four wings and four heads.

on its back it had four wings like those of a bird. This beast had four heads, and it was given authority
to rule.

7“After that, in my vision at night I looked, and there before me was a fourth beast—terrifying
and frightening and very powerful. It had large iron[b] teeth; it crushed and devoured its victims and
trampled underfoot whatever was left. It was different from all the former beasts, and it had ten horns.[c]

8“While I was thinking about the horns, there before me was another horn, a little[d] one, which came
up among them; and three of the first horns were uprooted before it. This horn had eyes like the eyes
of a human being[e] and a mouth that spoke boastfully.[f]

9“As I looked,

> “thrones were set in place,
> and the Ancient of Days took his seat.
> His clothing was as white as snow;
> the hair of his head was white like wool.[g]
> His throne was flaming with fire,
> and its wheels[h] were all ablaze.
> 10A river of fire[i] was flowing,
> coming out from before him.[j]
> Thousands upon thousands attended him;
> ten thousand times ten thousand stood before him.
> The court was seated,
> and the books[k] were opened.

11“Then I continued to watch because of the boastful words the horn was speaking. I kept looking
until the beast was slain and its body destroyed and thrown into the blazing fire.[l] 12(The other beasts
had been stripped of their authority, but were allowed to live for a period of time.)

13“In my vision at night I looked, and there before me was one like a son of man,[a][m] coming with
the clouds of heaven.[n] He approached the Ancient of Days and was led into his presence. 14He was given
authority,[o] glory and sovereign power; all nations and peoples of every language worshiped him.[p] His
dominion is an everlasting dominion that will not pass away, and his kingdom is one that will never
be destroyed.[q]

The Interpretation of the Dream

15“I, Daniel, was troubled in spirit, and the visions that passed through my mind disturbed me.[r] 16I
approached one of those standing there and asked him the meaning of all this.

“So he told me and gave me the interpretation[s] of these things: 17“The four great beasts are four

7:7 [b]Da 2:40 [c]Rev 12:3
7:8 [d]Da 8:9 [e]Rev 9:7 [f]Ps 12:3; Rev 13:5-6
7:9 [g]Rev 1:14 [h]Eze 1:15; 10:6
7:10 [i]Ps 50:3; 97:3; Isa 30:27 [j]Dt 33:2; Ps 68:17; Rev 5:11 [k]Rev 20:11-15
7:11 [l]Rev 19:20
7:13 [m]Mt 8:20*; Rev 1:13* [n]Mt 24:30; Rev 1:7
7:14 [o]Mt 28:18 [p]Ps 72:11; 102:22; 1Co 15:27; Eph 1:22 [q]Da 2:44; Heb 12:28; Rev 11:15
7:15 [r]Da 4:19
7:16 [s]Da 8:16; 9:22; Zec 1:9

a *13* The Aramaic phrase *bar enash* means *human being*. The phrase *son of man* is retained here because of its use in the New Testament as a title of Jesus, probably based largely on this verse.

7:7 The fourth beast is metallic with “iron teeth” (and “bronze claws” [v. 19]) and thus unnatural and fearsome. **horns.** Symbolize power and authority. The image of a lifted-up horn often describes pride and honor, whether godly (1 Sam 2:1; Ps 89:17) or ungodly (Ps 75:5), stemming from the idea of a powerful animal lifting its head high.
7:8 The vision climaxes in the appearance of a little horn that sees and speaks like a human.
7:9 Ancient of Days. Pictures God as a powerful, aged king rendering judgment in court. Much of the imagery in this verse is not uncommonly associated with God’s appearance and signals his wisdom (white hair), righteousness (white clothing), and power in judgment (fire). Elements of this description are used in reference to “a man” in 10:5–6, an angel in Matt 28:3, and Jesus in Rev 1:14.
7:10 Thousands of God’s angelic creatures attend him.
7:13 son of man. A well-known phrase in the OT that means “human being” (Ezek 2:1,3,6,8 and throughout Ezekiel). However, this figure is not a human being but is “like” a human being, and in the OT riding on clouds indicates divinity (Pss 68:4; 104:3–4; Isa 19:1; Nah 1:3). The description of this figure left no doubt in the minds of the NT authors that this refers to Jesus Christ. Indeed, many believe that this passage is the source of Jesus’ self-designation as the Son of Man (e.g., Matt 8:20). The NT also cites these verses when envisioning Christ’s future return at the end of history when he rides the clouds to defeat the forces of evil (e.g., Matt 24:30; Mark 13:26; 14:62; Luke 21:27; Rev 1:7).
7:15–28 *The Interpretation of the Dream.* Daniel does not understand the import of his vision, and he approaches a figure nearby who interprets the vision for him.
7:16 one of those standing there. His identity is not given, but it is clear from other examples (8:16; 9:21; probably 10:16—11:1) that he is an angel, likely Gabriel.
7:17–18 The vision concerns the conflict between the kingdoms of this world (represented by the beasts) and the heavenly kingdom. God will defeat evil human powers and establish his kingdom forever.
7:17 Similar to Nebuchadnezzar’s vision of the multi-metaled statue in 2:31–45, the four great beasts represent four kings or kingdoms. Debate surrounds the exact identification of the kingdoms. One school

7:18 [t] Isa 60:12-14; Rev 2:26; 20:4
7:21 [u] Rev 13:7
7:23 [v] Da 2:40
7:24 [w] Rev 17:12
7:25 [x] Isa 37:23; Da 11:36 [y] Da 2:21 [z] Da 8:24; 12:7; Rev 12:14
7:27 [a] Da 2:44; 4:34; Lk 1:33; Rev 11:15; 22:5 [b] Ps 22:27; 72:11; 86:9
7:28 [c] Da 4:19
8:2 [d] Est 1:2 [e] Ge 10:22

kings that will rise from the earth. 18 But the holy people of the Most High will receive the kingdom and
will possess it forever — yes, for ever and ever.'[t]
19 "Then I wanted to know the meaning of the fourth beast, which was different from all the others
and most terrifying, with its iron teeth and bronze claws — the beast that crushed and devoured its
victims and trampled underfoot whatever was left. 20 I also wanted to know about the ten horns on its
head and about the other horn that came up, before which three of them fell — the horn that looked
more imposing than the others and that had eyes and a mouth that spoke boastfully. 21 As I watched,
this horn was waging war against the holy people and defeating them,[u] 22 until the Ancient of Days
came and pronounced judgment in favor of the holy people of the Most High, and the time came when
they possessed the kingdom.
23 "He gave me this explanation: 'The fourth beast is a fourth kingdom that will appear on earth. It
will be different from all the other kingdoms and will devour the whole earth, trampling it down and
crushing it.[v] 24 The ten horns[w] are ten kings who will come from this kingdom. After them another king will arise, different from the earlier ones; he will subdue three kings. 25 He will
speak against the Most High[x] and oppress his holy people and try to change the set
times[y] and the laws. The holy people will be delivered into his hands for a time,
times and half a time.[a][z]
26 " 'But the court will sit, and his power will be taken away and completely destroyed forever. 27 Then the sovereignty, power and greatness of all the kingdoms
under heaven will be handed over to the holy people of the Most High. His kingdom will be an everlasting[a] kingdom, and all rulers will worship[b] and obey him.'
28 "This is the end of the matter. I, Daniel, was deeply troubled[c] by my
thoughts, and my face turned pale, but I kept the matter to myself."

Some believe that the fourth kingdom (Dan 7:23) is Greece and that the little horn is Antiochus IV Epiphanes (215–164 BC).

Kim Walton, taken at the Bode Museum, Berlin

Daniel's Vision of a Ram and a Goat

8 In the third year of King Belshazzar's reign, I, Daniel, had a vision, after
the one that had already appeared to me. 2 In my vision I saw myself in
the citadel of Susa[d] in the province of Elam;[e] in the vision I was beside the Ulai

[a] 25 Or *for a year, two years and half a year*

of thought identifies the first beast as Babylon, followed by the Medes, the Persians, and the Greeks. Another view sees the first beast as Babylon, but then identifies the next three as the Medo-Persian Empire, followed by the Greeks and the Romans. It is more likely that these beasts and the horns do not represent actual kingdoms (with the exception of the first) but rather point to one evil human kingdom succeeding another until God intervenes at the end of time to defeat them and establish his eternal kingdom.

7:18 holy people of the Most High. May refer to God's human followers or perhaps to angels (4:13; 8:13). A spiritual war stands behind human conflicts, so perhaps this refers to both humans and angels; God will win this great cosmic battle.

7:19–22 Daniel focuses attention on the fourth beast and the horns that emanate from it. This beast is particularly violent. For the significance of the horns, see note on v. 7. The ultimate battle takes place between the little horn and the holy people (see note on v. 18).

7:23–25 The interpreting angel goes no further than to say that the fourth beast represents a kingdom and that the ten horns and the little horn represent kings. Some believe that the fourth kingdom is Greece and that the little horn is Antiochus IV Epiphanes (215–164 BC), who unleashed atrocities against the Jews in the middle of the second century BC; others believe that the fourth kingdom is Rome and that the little horn anticipates the antichrist at the end of the age. Even if we are not to identify the beasts with specific nations like Greece or Rome, the image of God defeating the little horn to usher in his eternal kingdom gives credence to the idea that it anticipates his victory over evil at the end of the age.

7:25 a time, times and half a time. See NIV text note. The significance of this chronological reference is debated. Those who believe that the fourth beast is Greece and the little horn Antiochus (see note on vv. 23–25) connect this three-and-a-half-year period to the time this king wreaked havoc on the Jews (167–164 BC). Those who believe that the fourth beast is Rome and the little horn the antichrist think this refers to a three-and-a-half-year tribulation. More likely this is intentionally vague and symbolizes the little horn's fast start: it looks like it is building momentum but then is suddenly cut off.

7:26–27 The ultimate message of Daniel's vision concerns God's ultimate victory over the forces of evil, which is good news for God's people presently experiencing the oppression of evil human kingdoms.

7:28 deeply troubled. The vision's interpretation does nothing to calm Daniel's thoughts (v. 15). He has just looked into the abyss of human evil and seen the glorious victory of God.

8:1–27 *The Second Vision.* While much debate surrounds the interpretation of Daniel's other visions, the second vision garners little disagreement. Daniel receives a vision concerning a ram and a goat, and the angel's interpretation indicates that the vision concerns events that culminate in the reign of the evil king Antiochus IV Epiphanes.

8:1–14 *Daniel's Vision of a Ram and a Goat.* Similar to the previous vision of ch. 7, ch. 8 begins with a description of the vision, followed by its interpretation.

8:1 third year. Two years after the vision in ch. 7; sometime between 550 and 547 BC (see note on 7:1). The fall of Babylon is still almost a decade away (539 BC).

8:2 Susa. Will become an important city in the Persian Empire (Esth 1:2),

Canal. 3 I looked up,[f] and there before me was a ram with two horns, standing beside the canal, and the
horns were long. One of the horns was longer than the other but grew up later. 4 I watched the ram as
it charged toward the west and the north and the south. No animal could stand against it, and none
could rescue from its power. It did as it pleased[g] and became great.
5 As I was thinking about this, suddenly a goat with a prominent horn between its eyes came from the
west, crossing the whole earth without touching the ground. 6 It came toward the two-horned ram I had
seen standing beside the canal and charged at it in great rage. 7 I saw it attack the ram furiously, striking
the ram and shattering its two horns. The ram was powerless to stand against it; the goat knocked it
to the ground and trampled on it,[h] and none could rescue the ram from its power. 8 The goat became
very great, but at the height of its power the large horn was broken off,[i] and in its place four prominent
horns grew up toward the four winds of heaven.[j]
9 Out of one of them came another horn, which started small but grew in power to the south and to
the east and toward the Beautiful Land.[k] 10 It grew until it reached[l] the host of the heavens, and it threw
some of the starry host down to the earth[m] and trampled[n] on them. 11 It set itself up to be as great as the
commander of the army of the LORD;[o] it took away the daily sacrifice[p] from the LORD, and his sanctuary
was thrown down.[q] 12 Because of rebellion, the LORD's people[a] and the daily sacrifice were given over to
it. It prospered in everything it did, and truth was thrown to the ground.
13 Then I heard a holy one[r] speaking, and another holy one said to him, "How long will it take for the
vision to be fulfilled[s] — the vision concerning the daily sacrifice, the rebellion that causes desolation,
the surrender of the sanctuary and the trampling underfoot[t] of the LORD's people?"
14 He said to me, "It will take 2,300 evenings and mornings; then the sanctuary will be reconsecrated."[u]

8:3 [f]Da 10:5
8:4 [g]Da 11:3,16
8:7 [h]Da 7:7
8:8 [i]2Ch 26:16-21; Da 5:20 [j]Da 7:2; Rev 7:1
8:9 [k]Da 11:16
8:10 [l]Isa 14:13 [m]Rev 12:4 [n]Da 7:7
8:11 [o]Da 11:36-37 [p]Eze 46:13-14 [q]Da 11:31; 12:11
8:13 [r]Da 4:23 [s]Da 12:6 [t]Lk 21:24; Rev 11:2
8:14 [u]Da 12:11-12
8:15 [v]ver 1 [w]Da 10:16-18
8:16 [x]Da 9:21; Lk 1:19
8:17 [y]Eze 1:28; Da 2:46; Rev 1:17 [z]Hab 2:3
8:18 [a]Da 10:9 [b]Eze 2:2; Da 10:16-18
8:19 [c]Hab 2:3

The Interpretation of the Vision

15 While I, Daniel, was watching the vision[v] and trying to understand it, there before me stood one
who looked like a man.[w] 16 And I heard a man's voice from the Ulai calling, "Gabriel,[x] tell this man
the meaning of the vision."
17 As he came near the place where I was standing, I was terrified and fell prostrate.[y] "Son of man,"[b]
he said to me, "understand that the vision concerns the time of the end."[z]
18 While he was speaking to me, I was in a deep sleep, with my face to the ground.[a] Then he touched
me and raised me to my feet.[b]
19 He said: "I am going to tell you what will happen later in the time of wrath, because the vision
concerns the appointed time of the end.[c] 20 The two-horned ram that you saw represents the kings of

[a] *12* Or *rebellion, the armies* [b] *17* The Hebrew phrase *ben adam* means *human being*. The phrase *son of man* is retained as a form of address here because of its possible association with "Son of Man" in the New Testament. [c] *19* Or *because the end will be at the appointed time*

which plays an important role in the following vision. **Ulai Canal.** A human-made waterway that later classical writings call the Eulaeus.
8:8 four winds of heaven. From the north, south, east, and west.
8:9 Beautiful Land. Israel, the land of milk and honey (Ezek 20:6,15).
8:10 host of the heavens ... starry host. Both refer to God's angelic army. Daniel's vision concerns a battle that is not only earthly but cosmic in scope.
8:11 daily sacrifice. The morning and evening sacrifices at the temple (Exod 29:38–41; Num 28:3–8).
8:12 LORD's people. Can be translated "armies" (see NIV text note) and refer to either the heavenly army or an army of people or both. **It prospered.** The horn achieves some measure of success against its rivals, calling to mind Gen 3:15, where the serpent (representing the forces of evil and ultimately Satan) "will strike" the heel of the offspring of the woman (representing those who follow God and ultimately the Messiah [Rom 16:20; Rev 12:9]).
8:14 2,300 evenings and mornings. The number can refer to 2,300 days if the language is used similar to Gen 1; or if the evening and morning sacrifices are counted separately, it can refer to 1,150 days; the number could also be symbolic. Whichever the correct interpretation, the message is clear: there is a limit to the amount of time God will permit Antiochus to perpetrate atrocities against his people (see note on v. 23). **sanctuary will be reconsecrated.** While the moment this period of time begins is unclear, it is clear that the end point is the rededication of the temple in Jerusalem after Antiochus IV profaned it. The rededication of temple in 165 BC is the origin of the Jewish holiday Hanukkah, still celebrated by Jews today.
8:15–27 *The Interpretation of the Vision.* Like ch. 7, the presentation of the vision is followed by its interpretation. In contrast to the vision of ch. 7, Gabriel identifies the ram and the goat with specific kingdoms, but not the four horns. The focus is on the small horn identified as an evil king.
8:15–16 The voice, though not identified, is that of God; he instructs Gabriel, an angel commissioned to deliver messages (see 9:21–22; Luke 1:19,26–37), to interpret the vision for Daniel.
8:17 Son of man. The NIV text note indicates that this means human being; here it is likely not connected with Jesus' title in the NT. **time of the end.** While some take this (see also v. 19) to refer to the end of history associated with Christ's return, it more likely refers to the end of the persecution described in this chapter (see notes on vv. 14,23).
8:19 time of the end. See note on v. 17.
8:20 Unlike the vision of ch. 7, Gabriel identifies the animals with

8:21 [d] Da 10:20 [e] Da 11:3
8:24 [f] Da 7:25; 11:36
8:25 [g] Da 11:36
[h] Da 2:34; 11:21
8:26 [i] Da 10:1 [j] Rev 22:10
[k] Da 10:14
8:27 [l] Da 2:48 [m] Da 7:28
9:1 [n] Da 5:31

Media and Persia. 21 The shaggy goat is the king of Greece,[d] and the large horn between its eyes is the
first king.[e] 22 The four horns that replaced the one that was broken off represent four kingdoms that
will emerge from his nation but will not have the same power.

23 "In the latter part of their reign, when rebels have become completely wicked, a fierce-looking
king, a master of intrigue, will arise. 24 He will become very strong, but not by his own power. He will
cause astounding devastation and will succeed in whatever he does. He will destroy those who are
mighty, the holy people.[f] 25 He will cause deceit to prosper, and he will consider himself superior. When
they feel secure, he will destroy many and take his stand against the Prince of princes.[g] Yet he will be
destroyed, but not by human power.[h]

26 "The vision of the evenings and mornings that has been given you is true,[i] but seal[j] up the vision,
for it concerns the distant future."[k]

27 I, Daniel, was worn out. I lay exhausted for several days. Then I got up and went about the king's
business.[l] I was appalled[m] by the vision; it was beyond understanding.

Daniel's Prayer

9 In the first year of Darius[n] son of Xerxes[a] (a Mede by descent), who was made ruler over the Babylonian[b] kingdom — 2 in the first year of his reign, I, Daniel, understood from the Scriptures,
according to the word of the LORD given to Jeremiah the prophet, that the desolation of Jerusalem would

[a] 1 Hebrew *Ahasuerus* [b] 1 Or *Chaldean*

specific nations. **two-horned ram.** The ram's two horns (for horn imagery, see note on 7:7) symbolize Media and Persia, kingdoms from the Iranian highlands. One horn was larger than the other (v. 3), indicating Persia's eventual dominance over Media.
8:21 – 22 The goat represents Greece, whose first king was Alexander the Great, who conquered the Persian Empire and extended its boundaries. He died young (thus the broken horn), and his kingdom was eventually divided among four of his generals (the "four horns").
8:23 fierce-looking king. Antiochus IV Epiphanes (215 – 164 BC). He persecuted the Jews, particularly toward the end of his life. **master of intrigue.** He manipulated his way to the throne of the Seleucid kingdom centered in Antioch. He profaned the worship of God in Jerusalem by setting up a holy object sacred to the Greek god Zeus in the Jerusalem temple, and beginning in 167 BC, he also ordered the end to the daily sacrifice.
8:25 His arrogant attacks against the worship of God ("the Prince of princes") lead to his defeat and death.
8:26 evenings and mornings. The "2,300 evenings and mornings" (see v. 14 and note), the time during which the wicked king Antiochus commits his atrocities.
9:1 – 27 *The Third Vision.* Approximately a decade after the events of ch. 8, Daniel has a third vision. The vision takes place while he is studying the book of Jeremiah, particularly where it announces a 70-year exile. Thinking he lives at the end of the 70 years, Daniel turns to God to ask forgiveness on behalf of his people's sin. In response, Gabriel, the interpreting angel, comes to him to explain the "vision" (v. 23) to him.
9:1 – 19 *Daniel's Prayer.* After reading the prophecy of Jeremiah that the exile would last 70 years, Daniel turns to God in prayer with the hope of God's forgiveness and restoration.
9:1 first year of Darius. 539 BC, the year Cyrus delivered an edict allowing the Jews to return to Jerusalem (2 Chr 36:22 – 23; Ezra 1:1 – 4). For the relationship between Darius and Cyrus, see note on 5:31. Daniel's prayer (vv. 4 – 19) seems to have taken place in anticipation of this decree. His witness to the fall of Babylon may have caused him to turn to the Scriptures with new eyes.

Ruins of ancient Susa.

last seventy[o] years. 3So I turned to the Lord God and pleaded with him in prayer and petition, in fasting,
and in sackcloth and ashes.[p]
4I prayed to the LORD my God and confessed:

"Lord, the great and awesome God,[q] who keeps his covenant of love[r] with those who love him
and keep his commandments, 5we have sinned and done wrong.[s] We have been wicked and have
rebelled; we have turned away[t] from your commands and laws.[u] 6We have not listened to your
servants the prophets,[v] who spoke in your name to our kings, our princes and our ancestors, and
to all the people of the land.

7"Lord, you are righteous, but this day we are covered with shame[w] — the people of Judah
and the inhabitants of Jerusalem and all Israel, both near and far, in all the countries where you
have scattered[x] us because of our unfaithfulness to you.[y] 8We and our kings, our princes and our
ancestors are covered with shame, LORD, because we have sinned against you. 9The Lord our God
is merciful and forgiving,[z] even though we have rebelled against him;[a] 10we have not obeyed
the LORD our God or kept the laws he gave us through his servants the prophets.[b] 11All Israel has
transgressed your law and turned away, refusing to obey you.

"Therefore the curses and sworn judgments written in the Law of Moses, the servant of God,
have been poured out on us, because we have sinned[c] against you. 12You have fulfilled[d] the words
spoken against us and against our rulers by bringing on us great disaster. Under the whole heaven
nothing has ever been done like what has been done to Jerusalem.[e] 13Just as it is written in the
Law of Moses, all this disaster has come on us, yet we have not sought the favor of the LORD our
God by turning from our sins and giving attention to your truth.[f] 14The LORD did not hesitate to
bring the disaster[g] on us, for the LORD our God is righteous in everything he does; yet we have
not obeyed him.[h]

15"Now, Lord our God, who brought your people out of Egypt with a mighty hand[i] and who
made for yourself a name[j] that endures to this day, we have sinned, we have done wrong. 16Lord,
in keeping with all your righteous acts,[k] turn away your anger and your wrath from Jerusalem,[l]
your city, your holy hill.[m] Our sins and the iniquities of our ancestors have made Jerusalem and
your people an object of scorn[n] to all those around us.

17"Now, our God, hear the prayers and petitions of your servant. For your sake, Lord, look
with favor[o] on your desolate sanctuary. 18Give ear, our God, and hear; open your eyes and see[p]
the desolation of the city that bears your Name.[q] We do not make requests of you because we are
righteous, but because of your great mercy. 19Lord, listen! Lord, forgive![r] Lord, hear and act! For
your sake, my God, do not delay, because your city and your people bear your Name."

9:2 [o] 2Ch 36:21; Jer 29:10; Zec 7:5
9:3 [p] Ne 1:4; Jer 29:12
9:4 [q] Dt 7:21 [r] Dt 7:9
9:5 [s] Ps 106:6 [t] Isa 53:6 [u] ver 11; La 1:20
9:6 [v] 2Ch 36:16; Jer 44:5
9:7 [w] Ps 44:15 [x] Dt 4:27; Am 9:9 [y] Jer 3:25
9:9 [z] Ps 130:4 [a] Ne 9:17; Jer 14:7
9:10 [b] 2Ki 17:13-15; 18:12
9:11 [c] Isa 1:4-6; Jer 8:5-10
9:12 [d] Isa 44:26; Zec 1:6 [e] Jer 44:2-6; Eze 5:9
9:13 [f] Isa 9:13; Jer 2:30
9:14 [g] Jer 44:27 [h] Ne 9:33
9:15 [i] Jer 32:21 [j] Ne 9:10
9:16 [k] Ps 31:1 [l] Jer 32:32 [m] Zec 8:3 [n] Eze 5:14
9:17 [o] Nu 6:24-26; Ps 80:19
9:18 [p] Ps 80:14 [q] Isa 37:17; Jer 7:10-12; 25:29
9:19 [r] Ps 44:23

9:2 seventy years. Jer 25:11 – 12 (see note on Jer 25:11) and Jer 29:10 speak of a 70-year exile as Judah's punishment for breaking the covenant. Daniel himself was exiled in 605 BC, though Jerusalem was defeated in 586 BC. If the 70 years is a round number for the exile that begins in 605 BC, then the end of the period is 539 BC, when Persia defeats Babylon and allows the Jews to return to Jerusalem. But some believe the 70-year period begins in 586 BC with the destruction of Jerusalem, which means that the end point is the rebuilding of the temple in 516 or 515 BC.
9:3 Daniel prays to God for forgiveness and restoration in the light of judgment according to the instructions given in 1 Kgs 8:33 – 34,46 – 51. **fasting ... sackcloth and ashes.** Expresses deep grief and mourning over the sins of God's people.
9:4 – 19 Daniel's prayer is a prayer of penitence that confesses sin, petitions for restoration, and praises God. While such prayers are found in the book of Psalms (e.g., Ps 51), they are poetic, not in prose. For similar prayers, see Ezra 9:6 – 15; Neh 1:5 – 11; 9:5b – 37.
9:4 – 6 Daniel appeals to God on the basis of his "covenant of love" (v. 4) with his people. In the covenant, God promises to protect his faithful people ("those who love him and keep his commandments" [v. 4]), though Daniel acknowledges that the people have broken covenant with God by disobeying his laws and neglecting to listen to his spokespersons, the prophets.
9:7 Daniel prays on behalf of all the people of God who are scattered all over the known world, not just those in Babylon but also those who fled to Egypt and other small nations surrounding Israel.
9:9 The "covenant of love" (v. 4) includes the promise that God will restore his sinful people if they repent (Deut 30:1 – 10). God indeed is "merciful and forgiving" (see Exod 34:6 – 7; Deut 4:31).
9:11 – 14 Daniel appears to have in mind the covenant as renewed on the plains of Moab and recorded particularly in the book of Deuteronomy. Deut 27 – 28 enumerates the blessings that follow obeying the covenant law (found in Deut 4 – 26) as well as the curses that result from disobeying it. A number of the curses describe the specific judgment that came on Judah with the destruction of Jerusalem and the deportation of its leading citizens (Deut 28:25 – 26,36 – 37,49 – 57,64 – 68).
9:15 – 19 Daniel appeals for God's mercy.
9:15 Daniel evokes the memory of God's great act of rescue at the time of the exodus. Isaiah (Isa 40:3 – 5), Hosea (Hos 2:14 – 15), and other prophets spoke of God's restoration after his judgment as a second exodus.
9:18 not ... because we are righteous. The people are still sinful. If there is any hope for them, it is because of God's mercy and in his righteousness (v. 16), not their own.

9:20 [s]ver 3; Ps 145:18; Isa 58:9
9:21 [t]Da 8:16; Lk 1:19 [u]Ex 29:39
9:23 [v]Da 10:19; Lk 1:28 [w]Da 10:11-12; Mt 24:15
9:24 [x]Isa 53:10 [y]Isa 56:1
9:25 [z]Ezr 4:24 [a]Jn 4:25
9:26 [b]Isa 53:8 [c]Na 1:8
9:27 [d]Isa 10:22
10:1 [e]Da 1:21 [f]Da 1:7 [g]Da 8:26

The Seventy "Sevens"

20 While I was speaking and praying, confessing my sin and the sin of my people Israel and making
my request to the LORD my God for his holy hill[s]— 21 while I was still in prayer, Gabriel,[t] the man I
had seen in the earlier vision, came to me in swift flight about the time of the evening sacrifice.[u] 22 He
instructed me and said to me, "Daniel, I have now come to give you insight and understanding. 23 As
soon as you began to pray, a word went out, which I have come to tell you, for you are highly esteemed.[v]
Therefore, consider the word and understand the vision:[w]

24 "Seventy 'sevens'[a] are decreed for your people and your holy city to finish[b] transgression, to put
an end to sin, to atone[x] for wickedness, to bring in everlasting righteousness,[y] to seal up vision and
prophecy and to anoint the Most Holy Place.[c]

25 "Know and understand this: From the time the word goes out to restore and rebuild[z] Jerusalem
until the Anointed One,[d][a] the ruler, comes, there will be seven 'sevens,' and sixty-two 'sevens.' It will
be rebuilt with streets and a trench, but in times of trouble. 26 After the sixty-two 'sevens,' the Anointed
One will be put to death[b] and will have nothing.[e] The people of the ruler who will come will destroy
the city and the sanctuary. The end will come like a flood:[c] War will continue until the end, and desolations have been decreed. 27 He will confirm a covenant with many for one 'seven.'[f] In the middle of the
'seven'[f] he will put an end to sacrifice and offering. And at the temple[g] he will set up an abomination
that causes desolation, until the end that is decreed[d] is poured out on him.[h]"[i]

Daniel's Vision of a Man

10 In the third year of Cyrus[e] king of Persia, a revelation was given to Daniel (who was called
Belteshazzar).[f] Its message was true[g] and it concerned a great war.[j] The understanding of the
message came to him in a vision.

[a] 24 Or *'weeks'*; also in verses 25 and 26 [b] 24 Or *restrain* [c] 24 Or *the most holy One* [d] 25 Or *an anointed one*; also in verse 26 [e] 26 Or *death and will have no one*; or *death, but not for himself* [f] 27 Or *'week'* [g] 27 Septuagint and Theodotion; Hebrew *wing* [h] 27 Or *it* [i] 27 Or *And one who causes desolation will come upon the wing of the abominable temple, until the end that is decreed is poured out on the desolated city* [j] 1 Or *true and burdensome*

9:20–27 *The Seventy "Sevens."* Gabriel comes to Daniel in order to interpret the significance of Jeremiah's prophecy of 70 years of exile.
9:20 his holy hill. Mount Zion, the location of the temple, where God made his presence known among his people.
9:21 Gabriel. See note on 8:15–16. **evening sacrifice.** It was not being offered at the time due to the destruction of the temple, but Daniel still uses it to reckon the time of day.
9:24 Seventy "sevens." Much debate surrounds its exact significance, but one thing is clear: Gabriel suggests that the end of the 70-year exile begins a process, one that will last for 70 "sevens," or weeks of years—usually understood as 490 years. Though Jews will be allowed to return to the land, the exile will not come to a definitive end with anything approaching full restoration. **to finish transgression, to put an end to sin, to atone for wickedness.** At the end of the 70 "sevens," perhaps 70 seven-year periods of time and thus 490 years, sin and its consequences will come to an end. While these three actions remove the negative, the next three actions are positive. **everlasting righteousness.** The positive side of removing sin. **seal up vision and prophecy.** This is not a sealing away but is best understood as a mark of approval, authenticating the prophetic word (perhaps specifically Jeremiah's prophecy concerning the end of the exile; see note on v. 2). **anoint the Most Holy Place.** This is unclear; it refers to the temple and perhaps to its cleansing by the Maccabeans after Antiochus IV Epiphanes desecrated the temple (see note on 8:23), but others suggest that Gabriel refers to anointing the most holy one: the Messiah (see NIV text note). Though the details of these actions are debatable, the overall point is that at the end of the 70 "sevens," God will remove sin and establish righteousness.
9:25–27 Gabriel divides the period of 70 "sevens" into three parts: (1) 7 "sevens," (2) 62 "sevens," and (3) a final "seven." Gabriel treats the first two, comprising 69 "sevens," as a single unit that begins with the decree to rebuild Jerusalem and ends with the coming of the Anointed One. Some take the 69 "sevens" to refer to 483 years that stretch from the decree to rebuild Jerusalem until the time of the Messiah, though this creates problems of when the period begins. Advocates of this approach might point to Ezra's commission to reestablish the law in Judah in 458 BC, though the decree to rebuilt Jerusalem the city was issued by Cyrus in 539 BC. Still others connect it to Artaxerxes' decree allowing Nehemiah to rebuild the walls of Jerusalem (Neh 2:1–10), and they believe it culminates with Jesus' coming to Jerusalem before his crucifixion (Matt 21:1–11). The final "seven" is divided in the middle, beginning when an individual "will confirm a covenant with many" (Dan 9:27). This individual will cause great havoc until the end, when God will judge his activities. Some interpret these numbers as pointing to the atrocities and end of Antiochus IV Epiphanes, while others believe that they anticipate Christ's coming, the temple's destruction, and the antichrist's arrival and defeat. Still others believe these numbers indicate periods of time that are symbolic and should not be pressed into an absolute chronology of future events. Though the details are obscure, the point is clear: God will eventually bring an end to sin and establish his righteous rule.
9:27 abomination that causes desolation. See note on 11:31.
10:1—12:13 *The Fourth Vision.* The book continues with a fourth and final vision: 10:1—11:1 introduces the vision, 11:2—12:4 presents it, and 12:5–13 concludes with God's final instructions to Daniel.
10:1—11:1 *Daniel's Vision of a Man.* An introduction prefaces the final vision by describing Daniel's reaction to receiving a vision of a great war. Daniel's vision deeply disturbs him. He prays for divine

2At that time I, Daniel, mourned[h] for three weeks. 3I ate no choice food; no meat or wine touched
my lips; and I used no lotions at all until the three weeks were over.
4On the twenty-fourth day of the first month, as I was standing on the bank of the great river,
the Tigris,[i] 5I looked up and there before me was a man dressed in linen,[j] with a belt of fine gold[k]
from Uphaz around his waist. 6His body was like topaz, his face like lightning,[l] his eyes like flaming
torches,[m] his arms and legs like the gleam of burnished bronze,[n] and his voice like the sound of a
multitude.
7I, Daniel, was the only one who saw the vision; those who were with me did not see it,[o] but such
terror overwhelmed them that they fled and hid themselves. 8So I was left alone,[p] gazing at this great
vision; I had no strength left,[q] my face turned deathly pale and I was helpless.[r] 9Then I heard him
speaking, and as I listened to him, I fell into a deep sleep, my face to the ground.[s]
10A hand touched me[t] and set me trembling on my hands and knees.[u] 11He said, "Daniel, you who
are highly esteemed,[v] consider carefully the words I am about to speak to you, and stand up,[w] for I have
now been sent to you." And when he said this to me, I stood up trembling.
12Then he continued, "Do not be afraid, Daniel. Since the first day that you set your mind to gain
understanding and to humble[x] yourself before your God, your words were heard, and I have come in
response to them.[y] 13But the prince of the Persian kingdom resisted me twenty-one days. Then Michael,[z]
one of the chief princes, came to help me, because I was detained there with the king of Persia. 14Now
I have come to explain[a] to you what will happen to your people in the future, for the vision concerns
a time yet to come.[b]"
15While he was saying this to me, I bowed with my face toward the ground and was speechless.[c]
16Then one who looked like a man[a] touched my lips, and I opened my mouth and began to speak.[d]
I said to the one standing before me, "I am overcome with anguish[e] because of the vision, my lord,
and I feel very weak. 17How can I, your servant, talk with you, my lord? My strength is gone and I can
hardly breathe."[f]
18Again the one who looked like a man touched[g] me and gave me strength. 19"Do not be afraid, you
who are highly esteemed," he said. "Peace![h] Be strong now; be strong."[i]

When he spoke to me, I was strengthened and said, "Speak, my lord, since you have given me
strength."[j]

a *16* Most manuscripts of the Masoretic Text; one manuscript of the Masoretic Text, Dead Sea Scrolls and Septuagint *Then something that looked like a human hand*

10:2 [h]Ezr 9:4
10:4 [i]Ge 2:14
10:5 [j]Eze 9:2; Rev 15:6 [k]Jer 10:9
10:6 [l]Mt 17:2 [m]Rev 19:12 [n]Rev 1:15
10:7 [o]2Ki 6:17-20; Ac 9:7
10:8 [p]Ge 32:24 [q]Da 8:27 [r]Hab 3:16
10:9 [s]Da 8:18
10:10 [t]Jer 1:9 [u]Rev 1:17
10:11 [v]Da 9:23 [w]Eze 2:1
10:12 [x]Da 9:3 [y]Da 9:20
10:13 [z]ver 21; Da 12:1; Jude 1:9
10:14 [a]Da 9:22 [b]Da 2:28; 8:26; Hab 2:3
10:15 [c]Eze 24:27; Lk 1:20
10:16 [d]Isa 6:7; Jer 1:9; Da 8:15-18 [e]Isa 21:3
10:17 [f]Da 4:19
10:18 [g]ver 16
10:19 [h]Jdg 6:23; Isa 35:4 [i]Jos 1:9 [j]Isa 6:1-8

help, but he suffers mental anguish for three weeks until he has a vision of a heavenly figure (10:5–21). There is a cosmic battle behind the earthly one, which explains the three-week delay of the angelic interpreter (perhaps Gabriel again). The prince of Persia resisted the heavenly figure until Michael came and rendered help in the fight. After encouraging Daniel to be strong, the angel prepares to explain the vision.

10:1 third year of Cyrus. 537 BC. For a possible connection with Darius, see note on 6:28. **Belteshazzar.** Mentioning Daniel's Babylonian name reminds us he is still in exile (see note on 1:6–7).

10:3 no choice food; no meat or wine. See note on 1:8–16. **lotions.** Used for relief from the effects of the dry, hot climate on the skin. Daniel "lets himself go" because he is in a state of spiritual turmoil.

10:4 Tigris. One of two great rivers (along with the Euphrates) that ran through Mesopotamia. The Tigris was northeast of the city of Babylon.

10:5–6 Daniel sees a heavenly figure, described as a man "dressed in linen," the material worn by priests (Lev 6:10). The figure's features are statue-like: "his body was like topaz … like the gleam of burnished bronze." Other parts are hard to visualize: "his face [was] like lightning, his eyes like flaming torches." His voice is resonant and deep, "like the sound of a multitude." While the figure's dress is similar to that of an angel in Ezek 9:2, the rest of the description connects to Ezekiel's experience of God's presence in Ezek 1 as well as John's depiction of Christ in Rev 1:14–15. On the basis of the Ezekiel parallels, one might think this figure is God himself, but if he is the same as the heavenly figure who speaks in 10:11—11:1, then he is more likely an angel (see note on v. 13).

10:9–10 my face to the ground … set me trembling. Like Paul in Acts 9:1–9, Daniel's private encounter with the heavenly figure overwhelms him.

10:10 touched me. The supernatural figure ministers to Daniel. See also vv. 16,18.

10:11 highly esteemed. A relatively rare Hebrew word found in the tenth commandment and sometimes translated "coveted." Daniel is a highly desired, precious man whom God covets (v. 19a; 9:23). The words of the supernatural figure are meant to encourage Daniel.

10:13 Michael. An archangel known from the NT to engage in conflict with the devil (Jude 9; Rev 12:7). Spiritual beings are associated with nation-states. God distributed the nations among "the sons of God" (Deut 32:8; see NIV text note, widely considered the superior reading), which refer to spiritual beings or angels. Michael ("your prince," v. 21) fights for God's people, while the "prince of Persia" (v. 20) is a spiritual being, a demonic power, who fights for the Persian Empire. Since the prince of Persia could have blocked the arrival of the heavenly figure and since the heavenly figure requires Michael's help to get to Daniel, the heavenly figure speaking is not God but a powerful (not all-powerful) angel, perhaps Gabriel, who is often God's spokesperson (8:16; 9:21; Luke 1:19,26).

10:18 touched me. For the third time (see vv. 10,16), the heavenly figure ministers to Daniel, who is overwhelmed by his vision.

10:20 [k]Da 8:21; 11:2
10:21 [l]Da 11:2
[m]ver 13; Jude 1:9
11:1 [n]Da 5:31
11:2 [o]Da 10:21
[p]Da 10:20
11:3 [q]Da 8:4,21
11:4 [r]Da 7:2; 8:22
11:7 [s]ver 6
11:8 [t]Isa 37:19; 46:1-2
[u]Jer 43:12
11:10 [v]Isa 8:8; Jer 46:8;
Da 9:26
11:11 [w]Da 8:7-8

20 So he said, "Do you know why I have come to you? Soon I will return to fight against the prince of
Persia, and when I go, the prince of Greece[k] will come; 21 but first I will tell you what is written in the
11 Book of Truth.[l] (No one supports me against them except Michael,[m] your prince. 1 And in the
first year of Darius[n] the Mede, I took my stand to support and protect him.)

The Kings of the South and the North

2 "Now then, I tell you the truth:[o] Three more kings will arise in Persia, and then a fourth, who will
be far richer than all the others. When he has gained power by his wealth, he will stir up everyone
against the kingdom of Greece.[p] 3 Then a mighty king will arise, who will rule with great power and
do as he pleases.[q] 4 After he has arisen, his empire will be broken up and parceled out toward the four
winds of heaven.[r] It will not go to his descendants, nor will it have the power he exercised, because his
empire will be uprooted and given to others.

5 "The king of the South will become strong, but one of his commanders will become even stronger
than he and will rule his own kingdom with great power. 6 After some years, they will become allies. The
daughter of the king of the South will go to the king of the North to make an alliance, but she will not
retain her power, and he and his power[a] will not last. In those days she will be betrayed, together with
her royal escort and her father[b] and the one who supported her.

7 "One from her family line will arise to take her place. He will attack the forces of the king of the
North[s] and enter his fortress; he will fight against them and be victorious. 8 He will also seize their gods,[t]
their metal images and their valuable articles of silver and gold and carry them off to Egypt.[u] For some
years he will leave the king of the North alone. 9 Then the king of the North will invade the realm of
the king of the South but will retreat to his own country. 10 His sons will prepare for war and assemble
a great army, which will sweep on like an irresistible flood[v] and carry the battle as far as his fortress.

11 "Then the king of the South will march out in a rage and fight against the king of the North, who
will raise a large army, but it will be defeated.[w] 12 When the army is carried off, the king of the South
will be filled with pride and will slaughter many thousands, yet he will not remain triumphant. 13 For
the king of the North will muster another army, larger than the first; and after several years, he will
advance with a huge army fully equipped.

[a] 6 Or *offspring* [b] 6 Or *child* (see Vulgate and Syriac)

10:20 Persia ... Greece. At the time of the vision, Persia oppresses Judah, but the time is coming when Greece will defeat Persia and take control of God's people.

10:21 Book of Truth. Mentioned nowhere else in Scripture. In this context, it is a book that contains the course of future events. God is truly sovereign over history.

11:2—12:4 *The Kings of the South and the North.* The fourth vision is unlike the highly figurative visions that precede it. The heavenly figure gives a lengthy prophecy about unnamed kings and their actions. While these kings reign in the future from Daniel's sixth-century BC perspective, readers today recognize that the prophecy identifies events through the Persian period and into the Greek period. The prophecy ends with a look to the far distant future, the end of time, when God will reward those who follow him with everlasting life and consign those who resist him to everlasting contempt.

11:2 Three more kings. We cannot be dogmatic about which of the 13 known Persian kings this refers to. Some think this refers to the next three kings after the founder Cyrus: Cambyses (530–522 BC), Pseudo-Smerdis, also known as Gaumata (523–522 BC), and Darius I (522–486 BC). **a fourth.** Either Xerxes I (486–465 BC), who attacked the Greeks, leading to the eventual defeat of Persia a century later, or Darius III (336–333 BC), whom the Greeks conquered.

11:3 a mighty king. Alexander the Great, the Greek who defeated the Persians. He died at a young age in 323 BC, relatively soon after Persia's defeat. His four leading generals ("the four winds of heaven" [v. 4]) then carved up his kingdom. See "The Maccabean-Hasmonean Period," p. 1897.

11:5–20 Focus shifts to the kingdoms established by two of Alexander's generals: "the king of the North" (v. 6) is the head of the Seleucid realm, headquartered in Antioch in Syria; "the king of the South" (v. 5) is the head of the Ptolemaic kingdom, headquartered in Alexandria in Egypt. They fought over controlling Jerusalem, which lay between them, though in these early years the Ptolemaic kingdom held it.

11:5–6 The first king of the South is Ptolemy I (322–285 BC) and the first king of the North is Seleucus I (321–280 BC). At first they were allies, but tensions over controlling Palestine led to a rift. At a later time, their successors attempted to resolve the conflict by a dynastic marriage (ca. 250 BC). Ptolemy II Philadelphus (285–246 BC) gave his daughter Berenice to Antiochus II (261–246 BC) as a wife. But Antiochus reconciled with his first wife, Laodice, who poisoned her husband, Berenice, and their son.

11:7–10 Tensions flared again. Berenice's brother, Ptolemy III Euergetes (246–221 BC), came to the throne in 246 BC. He waged war against the son of Laodice, Seleucus II Callinicus (246–226 BC), who now reigned in the north. Ptolemy III seized their gods and took them to Egypt, but Seleucus II attacked the south and regained his lost land. The sons of Seleucus II were Seleucus III (226–223 BC) and the successful Antiochus III the Great (226–187 BC, 226–223 being a coregency); the latter won back great tracts of land.

11:10 fortress. Either Gaza or Egypt itself.

11:11–19 These verses describe the reign of Antiochus III, who successfully wrests control of Palestine (the Beautiful Land; see note on 8:9), including Jerusalem, from the south.

11:11 Antiochus III fought Ptolemy IV in the Battle of Raphia (in southern Palestine) in 217 BC, which the latter won.

14"In those times many will rise against the king of the South. Those who
are violent among your own people will rebel in fulfillment of the vision,
but without success. 15Then the king of the North will come and build
up siege ramps[x] and will capture a fortified city. The forces of the
South will be powerless to resist; even their best troops will not have
the strength to stand. 16The invader will do as he pleases;[y] no one
will be able to stand against him.[z] He will establish himself in
the Beautiful Land and will have the power to destroy it.[a] 17He
will determine to come with the might of his entire kingdom
and will make an alliance with the king of the South. And he
will give him a daughter in marriage in order to overthrow the
kingdom, but his plans[a] will not succeed[b] or help him. 18Then
he will turn his attention to the coastlands[c] and will take many
of them, but a commander will put an end to his insolence and will
turn his insolence back on him.[d] 19After this, he will turn back toward the fortresses of his own country but will stumble and fall,[e] to
be seen no more.[f]

20"His successor will send out a tax collector to maintain the royal
splendor.[g] In a few years, however, he will be destroyed, yet not in
anger or in battle.

21"He will be succeeded by a contemptible[h] person who has not been given the honor of royalty.[i] He
will invade the kingdom when its people feel secure, and he will seize it through intrigue. 22Then an
overwhelming army will be swept away before him; both it and a prince of the covenant will be destroyed.[j] 23After coming to an agreement with him, he will act deceitfully,[k] and with only a few people
he will rise to power. 24When the richest provinces feel secure, he will invade them and will achieve
what neither his fathers nor his forefathers did. He will distribute plunder, loot and wealth among his
followers.[l] He will plot the overthrow of fortresses—but only for a time.

25"With a large army he will stir up his strength and courage against the king of the South. The king
of the South will wage war with a large and very powerful army, but he will not be able to stand because
of the plots devised against him. 26Those who eat from the king's provisions will try to destroy him; his
army will be swept away, and many will fall in battle. 27The two kings, with their hearts bent on evil,[m]
will sit at the same table and lie[n] to each other, but to no avail, because an end will still come at the
appointed time.[o] 28The king of the North will return to his own country with great wealth, but his heart
will be set against the holy covenant. He will take action against it and then return to his own country.

29"At the appointed time he will invade the South again, but this time the outcome will be different

The king of the South (Dan 11:11) was Ptolemy IV Philopator.
Wikimedia Commons

11:15 [x]Eze 4:2
11:16 [y]Da 8:4 [z]Jos 1:5; Da 8:7 [a]Da 8.9
11:17 [b]Ps 20:4
11:18 [c]Isa 66:19; Jer 25:22 [d]Hos 12:14
11:19 [e]Ps 27:2 [f]Ps 37:36; Eze 26:21
11:20 [g]Isa 60:17
11:21 [h]Da 4:17 [i]Da 8:25
11:22 [j]Da 8:10-11
11:23 [k]Da 8:25
11:24 [l]Ne 9:25
11:27 [m]Ps 64:6 [n]Ps 12:2; Jer 9:5 [o]Hab 2:3

[a] 17 Or *but she*

11:14 among your own people. Though the details are obscure, there were political intrigues going on in Jerusalem. For example, the Oniad family (who supported the Ptolemaic kingdom) vied with the Tobiad family (who supported the Seleucid kingdom) for the high priesthood. Perhaps Daniel's vision even encouraged some to rebel.
11:15 Antiochus pursued the Seleucid general Scopas to Sidon and defeated him there.
11:16 Beautiful Land. See note on 8:9.
11:17 Antiochus III gave his daughter Cleopatra I (not the famous Cleopatra VII, who was connected to Julius Caesar and Mark Antony) to Ptolemy V with the hope that she would serve as a spy in the south, but Cleopatra aligned her interests with her husband. Thus, Antiochus's plans did not succeed.
11:18–19 Antiochus III started annexing parts of Asia Minor and some Greek islands, but when he encroached on Thrace in 196 BC, the Roman consul Lucius Cornelius Scipio defeated him at Thermopylae in 191 BC and Magnesia in 190 BC. Antiochus retreated to Antioch and died in 187 BC.
11:21–35 There is wide agreement that these verses describe Antiochus IV Epiphanes (175–164 BC; see notes on 7:23–25; 8:23), who oppressed and persecuted the Jews. He is described in the Apocrypha in 1 Maccabees 1:7—6:16; 2 Maccabees 1:1—10:9; and in the OT pseudepigrapha in 4 Maccabees 4:15—18:5.
11:21 Antiochus IV took the throne from his nephew by intrigue.
11:22 a prince of the covenant. The high priest Onias III. Antiochus IV deposed him and replaced him with the more amenable Jason.
11:25 Antiochus IV successfully warred against Ptolemy VI Philometor (180–145 BC) near Pelusium, near Gaza.
11:26–27 Ptolemy VI's brother Ptolemy VII declared himself king in Alexandria while his brother reigned from Memphis.
11:28 against the holy covenant. Antiochus IV began aggressive acts toward true worship in Jerusalem.
11:29–30 Antiochus IV invaded the south again in 168 BC, but this time Rome interceded through the agency of the consul Popillius Laenas ("ships of the western coastlands"), who ordered Antiochus IV to turn back. Antiochus then vented his rage against the Jews in Jerusalem.

11:30 [p] Ge 10:4
11:31 [q] Da 8:11-13; 9:27; Mt 24:15*; Mk 13:14*
11:32 [r] Mic 5:7-9
11:33 [s] Mal 2:7 [t] Mt 24:9; Jn 16:2; Heb 11:32-38
11:34 [u] Mt 7:15; Ro 16:18
11:35 [v] Ps 78:38; Da 12:10; Zec 13:9; Jn 15:2
11:36 [w] Rev 13:5-6 [x] Dt 10:17; Isa 14:13-14; Da 7:25; 8:11-12,25; 2Th 2:4 [y] Isa 10:25; 26:20

from what it was before. 30 Ships of the western coastlands[p] will oppose him, and he will lose heart.
Then he will turn back and vent his fury against the holy covenant. He will return and show favor to
those who forsake the holy covenant.

31 "His armed forces will rise up to desecrate the temple fortress and will abolish the daily sacrifice.
Then they will set up the abomination that causes desolation.[q] 32 With flattery he will corrupt those who
have violated the covenant, but the people who know their God will firmly resist[r] him.

33 "Those who are wise will instruct[s] many, though for a time they will fall by the sword or be burned
or captured or plundered.[t] 34 When they fall, they will receive a little help, and many who are not sincere[u] will join them. 35 Some of the wise will stumble, so that they may be refined,[v] purified and made
spotless until the time of the end, for it will still come at the appointed time.

The King Who Exalts Himself

36 "The king will do as he pleases. He will exalt and magnify himself above every god and will say
unheard-of things[w] against the God of gods.[x] He will be successful until the time of wrath[y] is completed,
for what has been determined must take place. 37 He will show no regard for the gods of his ancestors

11:31 abolish the daily sacrifice. Antiochus IV stopped the daily sacrifice at the temple and substituted the sacrifice of pigs, considered unclean (1 Maccabees 1:44–47). **abomination that causes desolation.** A meteorite dedicated to Baal Shamem, the Syrian equivalent of the Greek god Zeus, that Antiochus IV set up in the temple. The NT uses the phrase to describe a future sacrilege at the time of Christ's return (Matt 24:15; Mark 13:14).
11:32 Conflict existed between two parties among God's people: those who supported Antiochus's program of Hellenization ("those who have violated the covenant") and those who resisted it.
11:33 Those who are wise. Those who follow God and obey his law in the face of increasing persecution from Antiochus IV and from those who want to Hellenize Jewish religion and culture. The "wise" may refer to or at least include the Hasmoneans, who fought to rid the land of this foreign influence. But perhaps the Hasmoneans/Maccabees are the "little help" (v. 34) that aids the wise. The Hasmoneans led a revolt against the Seleucid kingdom and Antiochus. They recaptured and purified the polluted temple in 164 BC.
11:36–45 Controversy swirls around the interpretation of these verses. There are those who believe the text is a true prophecy and those who believe it is a failed one. The latter believe that these verses continue to describe Antiochus IV since there is no formal break between v. 35 and v. 36. If so, then v. 45, which describes the death of Antiochus IV, conflicts with what we know from other historical records. Others, however, believe that there is a subtle shift to the end of time (v. 40) and to a description of the antichrist. They make the break between v. 39 and v. 40, taking vv. 36–39 as a transition from Antiochus IV to a future figure who is larger than life (see vv. 40–45 and note). For those who hold this view, Antiochus IV's evil was so intense that he is an appropriate model for the antichrist.
11:36 This king combines power and arrogance. He will even blaspheme the true God.
11:37 This king will blaspheme not only the true God but even his own pagan religion. **the one desired by women.** Adonis, the Syrian version of Tammuz, the Mesopotamian god whose worship reserves an important place for women.

THE GEOGRAPHY OF DANIEL 11

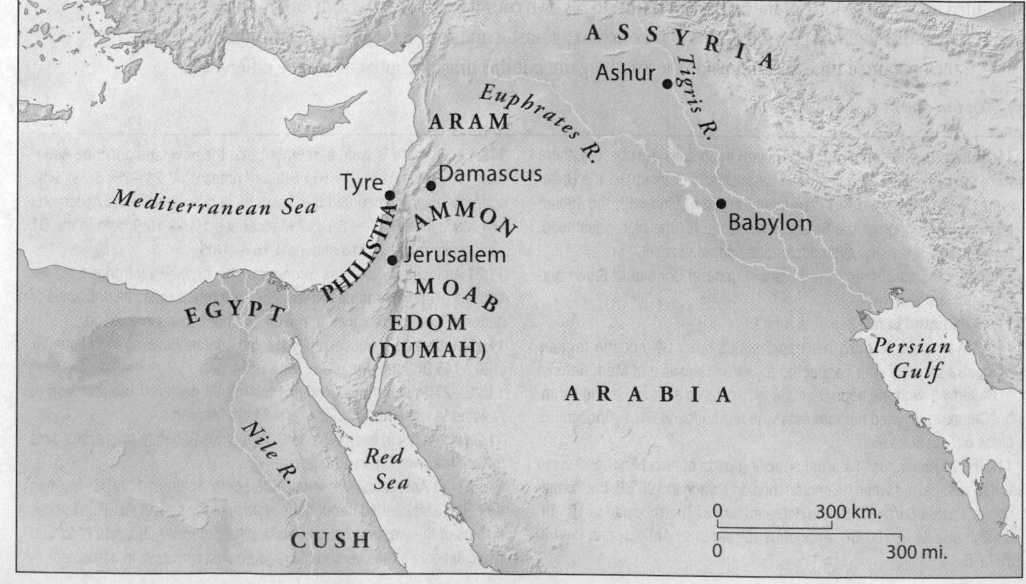

or for the one desired by women, nor will he regard any god, but will exalt himself above them all. 38 Instead of them, he will honor a god of fortresses; a god unknown to his ancestors he will honor with gold and silver, with precious stones and costly gifts. 39 He will attack the mightiest fortresses with the help of a foreign god and will greatly honor those who acknowledge him. He will make them rulers over many people and will distribute the land at a price.[a]

40 "At the time of the end the king of the South[z] will engage him in battle, and the king of the North will storm[a] out against him with chariots and cavalry and a great fleet of ships. He will invade many countries and sweep through them like a flood.[b] 41 He will also invade the Beautiful Land. Many countries will fall, but Edom,[c] Moab[d] and the leaders of Ammon will be delivered from his hand. 42 He will extend his power over many countries; Egypt will not escape. 43 He will gain control of the treasures of gold and silver and all the riches of Egypt,[e] with the Libyans[f] and Cushites[b] in submission. 44 But reports from the east and the north will alarm him, and he will set out in a great rage to destroy and annihilate many. 45 He will pitch his royal tents between the seas at[c] the beautiful holy mountain. Yet he will come to his end, and no one will help him.

The End Times

12 "At that time Michael,[g] the great prince who protects your people, will arise. There will be a time of distress[h] such as has not happened from the beginning of nations until then. But at that time your people—everyone whose name is found written in the book[i]—will be delivered.[j] 2 Multitudes who sleep in the dust of the earth will awake: some to everlasting life, others to shame and everlasting contempt.[k] 3 Those who are wise[d][l] will shine[m] like the brightness of the heavens, and those who lead many to righteousness, like the stars for ever and ever.[n] 4 But you, Daniel, roll up and seal[o] the words of the scroll until the time of the end.[p] Many will go here and there to increase knowledge."

5 Then I, Daniel, looked, and there before me stood two others, one on this bank of the river and one on the opposite bank.[q] 6 One of them said to the man clothed in linen,[r] who was above the waters of the river, "How long will it be before these astonishing things are fulfilled?"[s]

7 The man clothed in linen, who was above the waters of the river, lifted his right hand and his left hand toward heaven, and I heard him swear by him who lives forever,[t] saying, "It will be for a time, times and half a time.[e][u] When the power of the holy people[v] has been finally broken, all these things will be completed.[w]"

11:40 [z] Isa 21:1 [a] Isa 5:28 [b] Eze 38:4
11:41 [c] Isa 11:14 [d] Jer 48:47
11:43 [e] Eze 30:4 [f] 2Ch 12:3; Na 3:9
12:1 [g] Da 10:13 [h] Da 9:12; Mt 24:21; Mk 13:19; Rev 16:18 [i] Ex 32:32; Ps 56:8 [j] Jer 30:7
12:2 [k] Isa 26:19; Mt 25:46; Jn 5:28-29
12:3 [l] Da 11:33 [m] Mt 13:43; Jn 5:35 [n] 1Co 15:42
12:4 [o] Isa 8:16 [p] ver 9,13; Rev 22:10
12:5 [q] Da 10:4
12:6 [r] Eze 9:2 [s] Da 8:13
12:7 [t] Rev 10:5-6 [u] Da 7:25 [v] Da 8:24 [w] Lk 21:24; Rev 10:7

[a] *39* Or *land for a reward* [b] *43* That is, people from the upper Nile region [c] *45* Or *the sea and*
[d] *3* Or *who impart wisdom* [e] *7* Or *a year, two years and half a year*

11:38 a god of fortresses. Exact identification unknown. It indicates the trust this king puts in his military apparatus.
11:40–45 This describes "the end" (v. 40) of the arrogant king and the end of time when God will bring evil to an end.
11:41 Beautiful Land. Israel. **Edom, Moab … Ammon.** Nations on Israel's eastern border.
11:43 Cushites. Inhabitants of the area south of Egypt, the upper Nile region, associated with Sudan.
11:45 the seas. Or "the sea" (see NIV text note), i.e., the Mediterranean Sea. **beautiful holy mountain.** Zion in Jerusalem.
12:1–4 These verses further support reading 11:36–45 (or 11:40–45) as referring to the end (see note on 11:36–45). After the events narrated there, the dead will rise up, some to everlasting life and others to everlasting shame. This is the clearest OT teaching on the physical resurrection and the different fates of the righteous and the wicked.
12:1 At that time. The time of the end of Antiochus IV and the one whom he foreshadows, the antichrist. **Michael.** See 10:13,21 and note on 10:13.
12:2 This is the first reference in the Bible to the physical resurrection of the righteous and the wicked (see Isa 26:19 for a reference to the resurrection of the righteous). The NT's description of heaven and hell expands and deepens this teaching on the afterlife (see John 5:24–29).
12:3 wise. See note on 11:33. When they are raised from the dead, they will "shine like the brightness of the heavens" and be "like the stars for ever and ever"—reminiscent of descriptions of celestial beings (Judg 5:20; Job 38:7; 1 Enoch 104; Testament of Moses 10:9; 2 Baruch 51:3,10).
12:4 seal. See note on 9:24. **Many will go here and there to increase knowledge.** This picture is likely negative (Amos 8:12): people will try to find knowledge by their own power but fail in the attempt.
12:5–13 *Final Words.* Daniel has a final encounter with three heavenly beings: one asks about the time period before the events will be fulfilled, and another responds.
12:5–6 The scene returns to the bank of the river (see 10:4–21). The heavenly figures are not specifically identified, but the man clothed in linen is either God or an angel (see note on 10:5–6), while the other two, one on each side of the river, are clearly angels, perhaps Gabriel and Michael.
12:7 While only one hand is typically raised for an oath (Deut 32:40), the heavenly figure raises both hands for emphasis. **a time, times and half a time.** See note on 7:25. This is not a precise time period (though it may point to three and a half years); rather, it indicates that just as wickedness seems to be gaining momentum, it will be slowed and then stop. Rev 11:2 ("42 months"), Rev 11:3 ("1,260 days"), and Rev 12:6 ("1,260 days") likely derive from this verse and vv. 11–12 (see note there).

12:9 [x]ver 4
12:10 [y]Da 11:35 [z]Isa 32:7; Rev 22:11 [a]Hos 14:9
12:11 [b]Da 8:11; 9:27; Mt 24:15*; Mk 13:14*
12:12 [c]Isa 30:18 [d]Da 8:14
12:13 [e]Isa 57:2 [f]Ps 16:5; Rev 14:13

8 I heard, but I did not understand. So I asked, "My lord, what will the outcome of all this be?"
9 He replied, "Go your way, Daniel, because the words are rolled up and sealed until the time of the
end.[x] 10 Many will be purified, made spotless and refined,[y] but the wicked will continue to be wicked.[z]
None of the wicked will understand, but those who are wise will understand.[a]
11 "From the time that the daily sacrifice is abolished and the abomination that causes desolation[b]
is set up, there will be 1,290 days. 12 Blessed is the one who waits[c] for and reaches the end of the 1,335
days.[d]
13 "As for you, go your way till the end. You will rest,[e] and then at the end of the days you will rise to
receive your allotted inheritance.[f]"

12:10 The wicked do not understand that God will win the victory over evil at the end.
12:11–12 1,290 ... 1,335. The exact significance and meaning of these numbers is enigmatic, though both numbers point to a period of about three and a half years (see 12:7 and note). The numbers are likely symbolic and impart a sense of mystery (though some see them connected to events in the reign of Antiochus IV). They impart the impression that God has determined an end to evil, but they do not allow us to predict when this end will actually come.
12:11 abomination that causes desolation. See note on 11:31.
12:13 go your way. The heavenly figure ends by telling Daniel to get on with his life in the assurance that he will receive his reward when the end does come (v. 2).

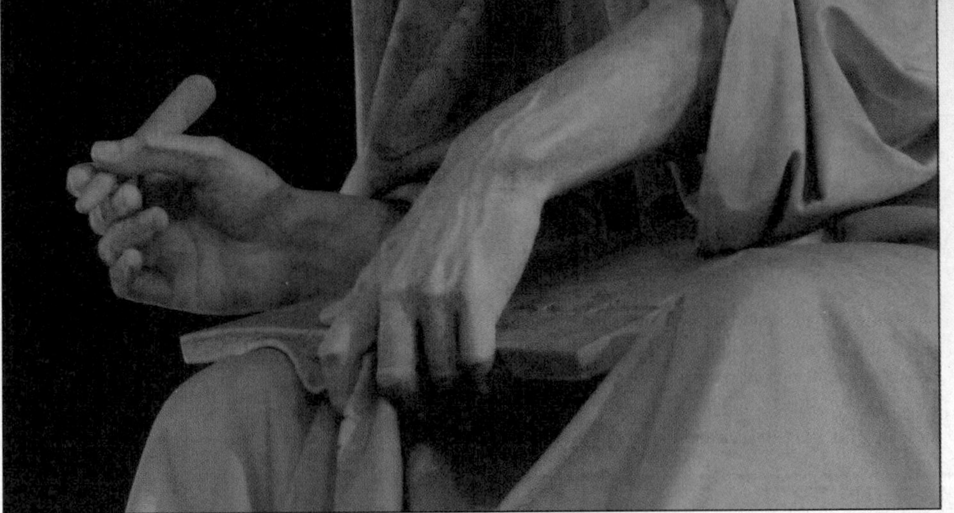

INTRODUCTION TO HOSEA

Hosea announces God's repeated, passionate warnings to both Israel and Judah that their disobedience to God's covenant is leading to well-deserved conquest, decimation, and exile by foreign powers. But that will not be the end of God's people. God will rebuild them from a remnant and give them a new covenant with a new and better relationship to himself in a new age characterized by true faith and true obedience to God's word.

AUTHOR

The book records the prophecies preached by a northern kingdom prophet named Hosea, but personal details about him are limited and intertwined so closely with the message of the book that attempts to write his biography fail. All we know about the person Hosea is found in chs. 1 and 3, which describe symbolic actions in which the prophet acts out revelations from God so as to make them especially memorable. These two chapters appear to describe separate marriages, though many commentators take them to portray an original marriage and a reconciliation. Both marriage stories appear to involve heavy prophetic symbolism. Ch. 1 offers few details about the prophet other than the name of his first wife and the names of his children. Ch. 3 tells us only that he did not consummate the marriage described there but entered into it mainly as a symbolic prophetic act.

In both ch. 1 and ch. 3 Hosea's actions illustrate God's revelations about Israel's future punishments for sin. In 1:2, the NIV terms "promiscuous," "adulterous," and "guilty of unfaithfulness" used in connection with Hosea's wife are all renderings of a single Hebrew word that throughout the OT refers strictly to prostitution, i.e., the selling of sex. "Prostitution" is Hosea's (and other prophets') most common metaphor for infidelity to God's covenant via idolatry and polytheism. Chs. 1–3 focus on this covenant-breaking "prostitution" (cheating on God by seeking payment from other gods, as it were) in contrast to God's faithfulness in his relationship to Israel. Thus, the quality of Hosea's family life and his personal attitudes, feelings, or success as a husband or father, and Gomer's character, are not primarily in view. What is in view in these symbolic actions is Israel's willingness to sell itself to false gods for the gain they thought came from worshiping those gods. Here, the "land" (i.e., the nation as a whole) is "guilty" before the Lord. Hosea's marriage, especially via the symbolic names of his three children, provides a vivid way to act out the sad truth that everyone in Israel is tainted by the way that the nation has sold itself to false gods.

DATE

Hosea began preaching as early as 760 BC, when both the northern kingdom (Israel) and the southern kingdom (Judah) enjoyed prosperity. Unfortunately, this prosperity was accompanied by widespread idolatry (4:17; 8:4–6; cf. Isa 10:11; Amos 5:26; Mic 1:7) and social injustice (Hos 4:2; 12:7) as well as general disobedience to God's covenant law (4:1–2; 6:7; 8:1). Hosea's prophetic ministry seems to have ended no later than 722, when the last unconquered part of the northern kingdom (Ephraim) was captured and annexed by Assyria. The book's message is not limited to events in Hosea's time: it looks backward to the days of the patriarchs (e.g., 12:3–4,12), Moses (e.g., 9:10; 11:1; 12:13; 13:4–5), the judges (e.g., 9:9; 10:9), and the monarchy (e.g., 4:15; 5:1–2; 7:7; 9:15; 13:1–2,10–11); and it looks forward to the destruction of Israel and Judah and their respective exiles (e.g., 1:4–5; 2:3–13; 3:4; 4:3,19; 5:5,10,14–15; 7:16; 8:10,13; 9:6; 10:10; 13:15–16). Wonderfully, it looks beyond these tragedies to the great blessings of the new covenant age to come (e.g., 1:10–11; 2:14–23; 3:5; 6:1–3; 11:8–11; 13:14; 14:1–9).

EARLIEST AUDIENCE

After the death of Solomon, the formerly unified nation of Israel divided into two parts: the northern kingdom of Israel and the southern kingdom of Judah, each with separate kings and worship centers. Hosea preached in and mostly about the northern kingdom, Israel, but he frequently mentioned the southern kingdom, Judah, as well (e.g., 1:7,11; 4:15; 5:5,10,12–14; 6:4,11; 8:14; 10:11; 11:12; 12:2). His initial audience was the population of the northern kingdom. But since the northern kingdom fell to the Assyrians in 722 BC, within one or two years of the conclusion

ISRAEL IN 750 BC

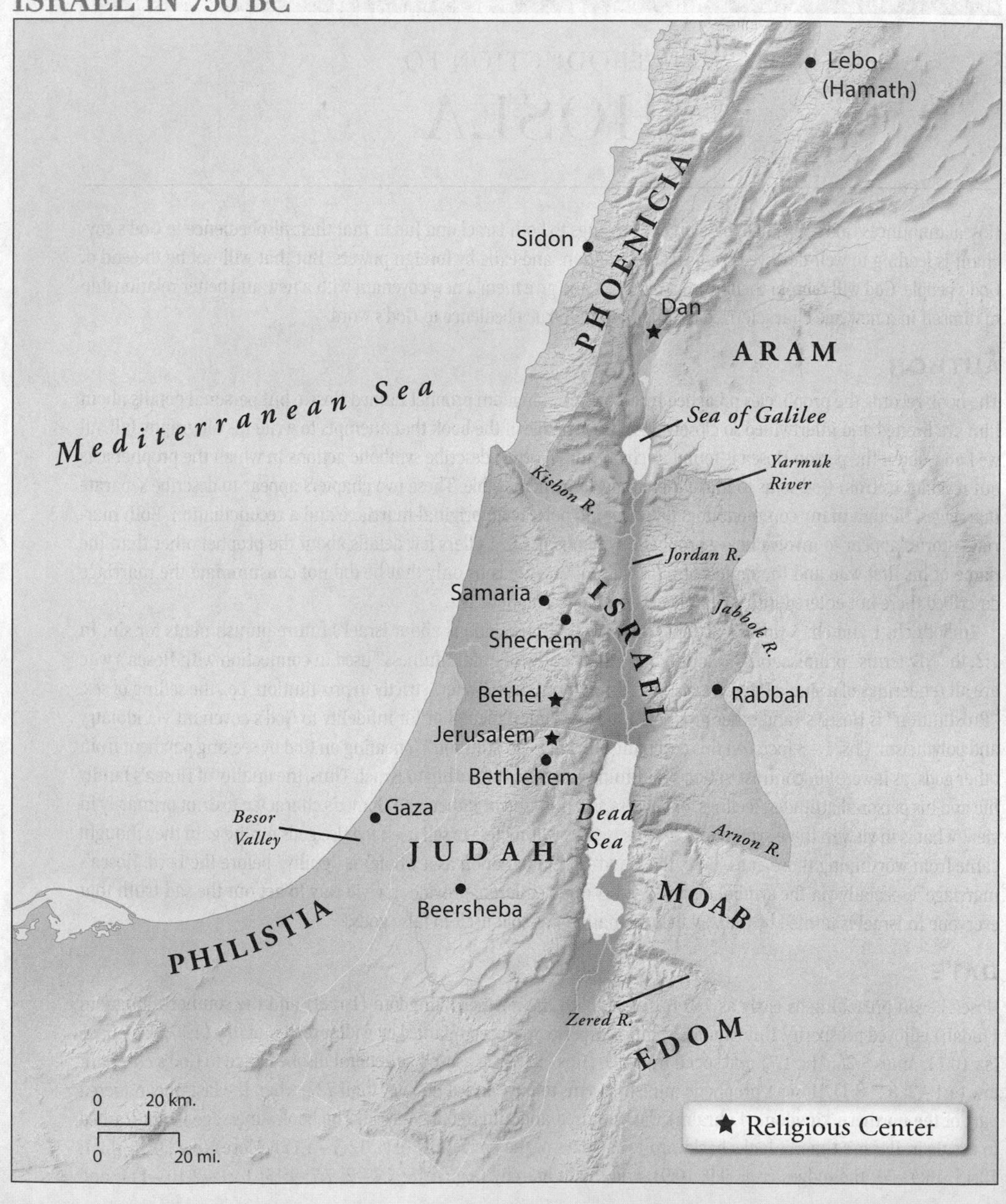

of his preaching there, the people of Judah, who survived the Assyrian conquest, would immediately have valued his words for both their truth about the north and their frequent focus on the south — as well as the long-term future of all of God's people.

The book never indicates the locations of Hosea's preaching. He may have preached frequently at the northern capital, Samaria (8:5), and at the main worship center, Bethel (10:15) — at least prior to 733 BC when Bethel probably fell temporarily under Judahite control. Amos, a contemporary of Hosea early in Hosea's career, also preached at Bethel (e.g., Amos 7:10 – 13). We may be fairly confident of the dating of some of Hosea's preaching (see 1:2 – 9; 5:5 – 10) and of the approximate chronological ordering of most (from ca. 760 to ca. 722 BC).

Hosea directs God's word to several groups. Most often, he addresses the northern kingdom in general, indicated by various terms, including "Israel," "Ephraim," or simply "you" or "your" (see 2:2; 4:1,4,15; 5:1,8; 6:4; 9:1,5,7; 10:9,12; 11:8; 12:9; 13:4,9 – 13; 14:1,8). God's word is directed to Hosea himself twice (1:2; 3:1), though this ultimately points to the people of the northern kingdom as a whole in the context of a symbolic action report. Hosea addresses priests twice (4:6 – 9; 5:1), the royalty once (5:1), Samaria once (8:5), Bethel once (10:15), and Judah twice (6:4,11; but Judah is mentioned often via indirect address, as noted above). What we cannot tell, however, is whether Hosea spoke to these people and places in their presence or simply rhetorically.

The comparatively few faithful people of the northern kingdom who still believed the Mosaic covenant and valued Hosea's preaching in spite of its descriptions of coming doom would have formed a supportive audience for Hosea. But he preached doom to his people so often that he must have been generally unpopular in the north. Nevertheless, his messages eventually proved true, and the collection of his words that we call the book of Hosea was thereafter taken seriously by godly individuals seeking to understand God's plan for their people and their world.

HISTORICAL SETTING AND PURPOSE

God called Hosea to predict the destruction and exile of Israel at a time when Israel was at the height of its material prosperity. The Jehu dynasty of the north, begun in 841 BC, came to an end with the death of Jeroboam II in 753. Thereafter, beginning with the accession of Zechariah to the throne in Samaria in 753, no more dynasties were possible, because the most common way to get rid of a king was assassination. Political instability prevailed. Hosea prophesied during the reigns of Israel's last seven kings — more kings than any other OT prophet. Life in Israel became increasingly precarious; the nation's fortunes waned progressively. The book reflects these developments as it proceeds more or less chronologically from the 750s to the 720s. The complacency of the early days (2:5,8,13) gives way to desperation in foreign (7:8 – 12; 12:1) and domestic (7:3 – 7; 13:10 – 11) affairs, evidenced in the latter chapters. The Syro-Ephraimite war (ca. 734 – 732 BC) represented the beginning of the end for Hosea's native country; it ended with the capitulation of the north to the Assyrian Empire after Israel was reduced to a rump state by Assyrian conquest and by an opportunistic Judahite invasion from the south at the same time (5:8 – 10; cf. 2 Kgs 16:5 – 9).

Sadly, by Hosea's day the Mosaic law (recorded within the books of Exodus, Leviticus, Numbers, and Deuteronomy) had fallen into a limbo of neglect in the northern kingdom. Hosea had to rely upon a limited awareness of that law — its basics only — in proclaiming the enforcement of the divine covenant. Fortunately, many Israelites still knew that the law forbade idolatry and polytheism (even though both were common in the northern kingdom), insisted upon exclusive, national worship of Yahweh at a single sanctuary (even though the first northern king, Jeroboam I, had set up rival sanctuaries to that of Jerusalem), required a life of ethical righteousness (even though prominent kings such as Ahab and his wife Jezebel had defied such standards), and provided blessings for obedience and curses for disobedience. This common knowledge of a few main tenets of the Mosaic law partially explains the frequent repetition of certain themes in prophetic passages. By reminding the people (through his prophets) that they had violated even these well-known foundational stipulations, God gave more than sufficient notice of justification for the coming judgment. Prophets, in other words, did not need to recite for their audiences every instance of Israelite infidelity to the various covenant provisions. It was enough to demonstrate major violations (e.g., idolatry, polytheism, disloyalty to God via foreign entanglements, multiple sanctuary worship, dishonesty, governmental and/or priestly corruption, economic oppression). The presence of such violations proved that the covenant was broken. In fact, any one of them would have sufficed for that purpose (cf. Jas 2:10).

HOSEA'S INTEREST IN JUDAH

Hosea was from the northern kingdom and probably preached exclusively to people of the northern kingdom. Nevertheless, he made many references to Judah and its capital, Jerusalem, in the south. Hosea and his audience had a keen interest in the fate of Judah precisely in contrast to, and separate from, the fate of Israel. The only two writing prophets who preached in the north (Hosea and Amos) make many references to the southern kingdom among their prophecies, and these are firmly entrenched in the structures and messages of each book. Clearly, God wanted his people in the north to understand his will for all his people, north and south, and not merely to focus narrowly on their own self-defined concerns.

GENRE AND STRUCTURE

Through Hosea, God inspired messages of divine judgment on northern Israel (often including Judah) as well as promises of restoration to God's favor in a united Israel of the future. Hosea does not always use prophetic literary forms in standard ways, but he does employ both allegories and symbolic action reports in the same way various other prophets do.

The editorial arranging of Hosea's messages, whether done by Hosea himself or perhaps a disciple, often results in an absence of sharp delineations between individual prophecies, so deciding where one passage in Hosea leaves off and another begins can be challenging. As a result, Hosea's prophecy is best considered as a whole. If we accept the rapid and often unpredictable shifts in person, subject matter, and tone that occur frequently within verses and from verse to verse in the book, we can usually appreciate how these variations fit into a coherent message. The overall message and its effectiveness are no less sure than would be the case if Hosea always used common prophetic speech patterns. This is the sort of divine creativity that makes the book such a rich literary treasure: a mixing of familiar clarity of message with challenging creativity in structure and style, producing truth conveyed in beautiful and often novel wordings. Hosea delivered most of his prophecies in poetry. The symbolic action reports in chs. 1 and 3, however, are prose, as is normally the case with such reports in other prophetical books.

THEMES AND THEOLOGY

Like all true prophets, Hosea understood that he was a messenger from God, entrusted with God's word, bringing matters related to God's covenant with Israel to people who needed reminders about that covenant. His references to the Mosaic covenant in 6:7 and 8:1 indicate that his audience understood, at least broadly, the terms of the covenant since otherwise he would have had to characterize it in more detail. The book contains a variety of blessings and curses for Israel, each based upon a corresponding type in the Mosaic law (see especially Lev 26:3–45; Deut 28:1–68; 29:18–28; 30:1–20; 31:17–23; 32:5–43). Some blessings and curses so closely parallel the wordings in the Mosaic law that they border on "citation," while others merely allude generally to those wordings. Hosea's style is in some ways original, but his message is consistent with the overall message of the OT. He warns that God intends to enforce his covenant (including the punishments of subjugation to and exile by foreigners) but also redeem his people, after punishment, to a better relationship with him than ever before.

Hosea often characterizes Israel's unfaithfulness or potential for redemption by citing either positive or negative images from family life, community life, and the world of nature. Among the things to which he likens Israel are: a prostitute (1:2), an unloved daughter (1:6), a rejected wife and mother (2:2–13) , a wife denied her marital rights (3:3), neglected children (4:6), a stubborn heifer (4:16), illegitimate children (5:7), incurably sick people (5:13), criminals (7:1) a blazing oven (7:4,6–7), a senseless dove (7:11–12), grapes in the desert (9:10), wanderers (9:17), a spreading vine (10:1), an trained heifer (10:11), a beloved child (11:1–4), fearful birds (11:11), mist, chaff, smoke (13:3), a child without wisdom (13:13), a lily (14:5), and an olive tree (14:6). Yet whatever the description of Israel's often vacillating nature, God still loves his wayward people and continues to invite them to abandon their rebellion and return to him and his redemptive love, a love that is far more generous than his people deserve (11:8–11; 13:14; 14:1–8).

Hosea's predictions of punishment and destruction outnumber his predictions of restoration. This is common in preexilic prophets. Promises of hope do appear, but they come somewhat unpredictably, and the book speaks more often of Israel's bleak short-term future. Hosea tells Israel that prior to the exile there is still a measure of divine blessing; during the exile there will be great woe, but later, after exile, there will come a time of great abundant blessings greater than those experienced previously. The blessings portions of the book are, accordingly, mainly eschatological (referring especially to the new covenant) in their orientation, while the curses are more immediate. Hosea holds out no hope that Israel can actually escape from the wrath of God that will lead to their capture and exile. Israel's future blessing must await the full measure of divine punishment. Encouragingly, however, Hosea preaches that the eventual restoration blessing from God will be grander than anything yet experienced — a new age to come, characterized by a special and better relationship with God. These restoration blessings foreshadow in part the NT's promises of the permanent joy of eternal life in heaven.

Aerial view of Tel Jezreel (Hos 1:4–5).
Todd Bolen/www.BiblePlaces.com

HOSEA'S FAMILY

Hosea's prophecies often blend literal and figurative descriptions. Using metaphors and similes, images from daily life and nature, he helps his readers see, by analogy, what Israel was really like. Some of these descriptions are outlined in the Themes and Theology section.

This same sort of blending of literal and figurative occurs in the descriptions of Hosea's family life in chs. 1 and 3, so that what these chapters say about Hosea's family is literal and also points symbolically to God's relationship with Israel — the real concern of the book. In 1:2, for example, a marriage to a woman named Gomer occurs, but a symbolic purpose is also revealed: to explain Israel's departure from faithfulness to God ("for … this land is guilty of unfaithfulness to the LORD"). Likewise, the negative children's names in 1:4 (Jezreel, meaning "God scatters," a massacre site), 1:6 (Lo-Ruhamah, meaning "not loved") and 1:9 (Lo-Ammi, meaning "not my people") refer to real children given unpleasant names so as to symbolize Israel's coming rejection and destruction. In Gomer's case (1:2) it is not her name that is unpleasant but her title ("promiscuous woman"), again, symbolic. The verse links her and her children to the Israelite idolatrous apostasy of Hosea's day. It is a metaphoric way of saying, in effect, that idolatry and unfaithfulness to God were everywhere.

In ch. 3, Hosea marries again, but this time he must not consummate the marriage (3:3). This marriage appears to be real, but again, biography is not the primary purpose. The goal of the passage is to symbolize by an enactment prophecy the immediate deprivations and later reacceptance (3:4–5) the Israelites would experience when their nation would first be conquered and taken into exile, but ultimately restored as God's people.

So we know little about Hosea's family life. He was married, had three children, and was married again at some later point. Their story is used by God with an ominous and figurative purpose: to predict the future of God's family (Israel) — a future of trouble and deprivation, but one nonetheless culminating in hope (1:10–11; 3:5).

CANONICITY AND POSITION IN THE MINOR PROPHETS AND THE BIBLE

Ancient versions of the Bible arrange the Minor Prophets in various orders, but Hosea is always first. This is probably due to four factors: (1) its date is early (only Amos and Jonah among the prophets are as early); (2) its size is long (the Minor Prophets are organized partly from longer to shorter, though not as strictly as Paul's letters in the NT); (3) Hosea preaches to both northern Israel and southern Judah repeatedly; and (4) its extensive sweep of historical references spans from the days of the OT patriarchs to the NT era. No other minor prophet is quite so comprehensive. The NT cites or alludes to Hosea 40 times, perhaps most notably in Matt 2:15 (Hos 11:1 includes a Messianic prediction in its overall intent) and in Rom 9:25–26 (the great reversal of fortunes for God's people predicted in Hos 1:10, 2:1, and 2:23 have been accomplished in Christ).

SPECIAL PROBLEMS SURROUNDING THE INTERPRETATION OF HOSEA

Readers of the book of Hosea often raise two questions: How could God command Hosea in 1:2 to marry a "promiscuous" woman? And how could God command Hosea in 3:1 to take her back after she had relations with another man (contrary to Deut 24:1–4)? These questions have been answered in various ways in the past.

The questions arise partly from the way that Hos 1:2 uses metaphoric language that modern people don't easily recognize. We know that "The country's going to the dogs!" or "Everybody's becoming a couch potato!" are metaphoric statements, figurative rather than literal in intent. But we don't automatically recognize that "wife of prostitution" and "children of prostitution" were metaphors in Hosea's day, based on the well-established scriptural idea that idolatry and polytheism were likened to prostitution because they represented betrayal of God for material gain (e.g., Exod 34:15–16; Lev 20:4–6; Deut 31:16). Israelite idolaters thought that religious intimacy with other gods could deliver more wealth and blessings than a monogamous relationship with the true God could.

The questions above also arise partly from the way that chs. 1–3 group together different prophecies that contain marriage themes and love-sex-marriage vocabulary, sometimes directly mentioning Hosea and his family, causing some readers to focus on the personal lives of Hosea and Gomer, rather than on the real topic: God and his relationship with Israel.

The questions also arise because of a prophetic technique that Hosea uses, easy for his audience to understand, but not obvious to a modern reader: the enactment prophecy (prophetic action report). This technique adds memorable actions to prophetic words as visual aids to symbolize truths God wants his people to remember. Hosea uses this technique to compare the divine covenant of God and Israel to the human covenant of marriage. Symbolic rather than literal language is often employed in the process.

Hosea performs two enactment prophecies. In 1:2—2:1 his own marriage is used to symbolize the way that all Israel is affected by idolatry and polytheism, which Hosea calls "unfaithfulness" ("prostitution"). Since there aren't any wives or children in Israel untouched by these sins in some way (the whole "land is guilty," v. 2), anyone Hosea marries and any children he has would be, in the strict translation of 1:2, "a wife of 'prostitution' and 'children of 'prostitution.'" Jeremiah performed a similar enactment prophecy (see Jer 5:1–11). No matter how hard he searched throughout Jerusalem, he couldn't find a single righteous person. The point in each case? That Hosea's Israel and Jeremiah's Judah were so corrupt that God was planning to bring an end to each—as both prophecies go on to say explicitly. Hosea's second enactment prophecy is found in 3:1–5. It too involves a marriage, used symbolically to represent Israel's unfaithfulness and God's resulting judgment, and not necessarily a remarriage to Gomer.

The special language and style of chs. 1–3 have resulted in a variety of interpretations by godly, thoughtful scholars. These notes follow one line of reasoning: symbolic actions and words tell the story of Israel's unfaithfulness to God, but do not suggest actual personal immorality on the part of Hosea's wife or children, or any violation of God's prior commands about marriage.

OUTLINE

I. Superscription: Hosea's Ministry Timed to the Reigns of Several Kings (1:1)

II. Marriage Themes: Israel as God's Wayward Wife (1:2—3:5)

- A. Hosea's Wife and Children (1:2—2:1)
  1. Wife, Children, and Land Symbolize Pervasive Idolatry (1:2–3)
  2. Three Unpleasant Children's Names Predict Judgment (1:4–9)
  3. Reversal of Names: Restoration in "the Day of Jezreel" (1:10—2:1)
- B. Israel Punished and Restored (2:2–23)
  1. Divorce Proceedings: An Allegory of God and Israel (2:2–13)
  2. Restoration of the Marriage: God's Future Covenant With His People (2:14–23)

C. Hosea's Reconciliation With His Wife (3:1–5)
1. Another Marriage, This Time Unconsummated (3:1–3)
2. Israel's Exile as Punishment for Covenant Infidelity (3:4–5)

III. Judgment Warnings Involving Israel's Present and Future (4:1—9:8)
A. The Charge Against Israel (4:1–19)
1. Another Covenant Lawsuit Against Israel (4:1–14)
2. Israel's Guilt a Warning to Judah (4:15–19)
B. Judgment Against Israel (5:1–15)
1. Indictment of People and Leaders for "Prostitution" (Idolatry) and Evil Deeds (5:1–7)
2. War Between Israel and Judah and Its Aftermath (5:8–15)
C. Israel Unrepentant (6:1—7:16)
1. A Glimpse of What Could Be: God's Healing of a Future Repentant People (6:1–3)
2. God's Frustration With His People (6:4–11a)
3. Israel's Foolish Sinfulness in National and International Affairs (6:11b—7:16)
D. Israel to Reap the Whirlwind (8:1–14)
1. Punishments for Political Intrigue and Idolatry (8:1–6)
2. Israel Under Foreign Control (8:7–10)
3. False Worship and Misplaced Trust Bring Disaster (8:11–14)
E. Punishment for Israel (9:1–8)
1. Multiple Sins (9:1–4)
2. Multiple Deprivations (9:5–8)

IV. Judgment Warnings With a Retrospective Tone (9:9—13:16)
A. Ephraim Rejected, Exiled, and Unloved (9:9–17)
B. No More Cult, Kingship, or Capital (10:1–8)
C. Inevitable War Against Israel for Its History of Wickedness (10:9–15)
D. God's Love for Israel (11:1–11)
1. Out of Captivity in the Past and Back Again in the Future (11:1–7)
2. Rescue by Grace From Captivity (11:8–11)
E. Israel's Sin (11:12—12:14)
1. Israel's Deceit in Contrast to the Lord's Faithfulness (11:12—12:10)
2. Present Sins Against the Backdrop of Jacob and Moses (12:11–14)
F. The Lord's Anger Against Israel (13:1–16)
1. Israel's Tragic Fall via Idolatry and Coming Punishment (13:1–9)
2. Divine Judgment on a People Who Have No Sense (13:10–16)

V. Repentance to Bring Blessing (14:1–9)
A. Promise to the Remnant That Will Return (14:1–8)
B. A Challenge to the Wise Reader (14:9)

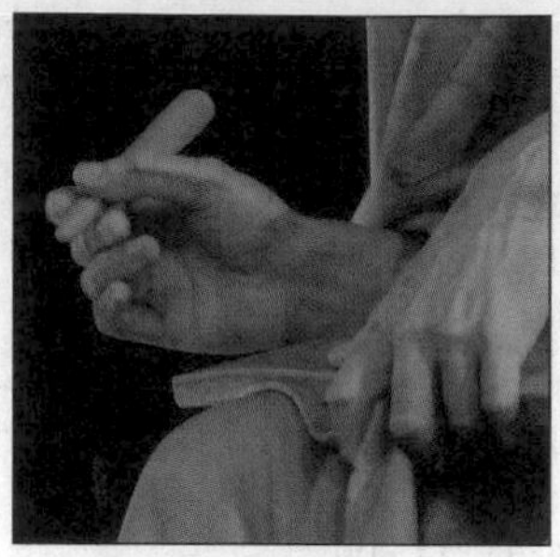

HOSEA

1:1 [a]Isa 1:1; Mic 1:1 [b]2Ki 13:13 [c]Am 1:1
1:2 [d]Jer 3:1; Hos 2:2,5; 3:1 [e]Dt 31:16; Jer 3:14; Eze 23:3-21; Hos 5:3
1:4 [f]2Ki 10:1-14; Hos 2:22

1 The word of the LORD that came to Hosea son of Beeri during the reigns of Uzziah, Jotham, Ahaz and Hezekiah, kings of Judah,[a] and during the reign of Jeroboam[b] son of Jehoash[a] king of Israel:[c]

Hosea's Wife and Children

[2]When the LORD began to speak through Hosea, the LORD said to him, "Go, marry a promiscuous[d] woman and have children with her, for like an adulterous wife this land is guilty of unfaithfulness[e] to the LORD." [3]So he married Gomer daughter of Diblaim, and she conceived and bore him a son.

[4]Then the LORD said to Hosea, "Call him Jezreel,[f] because I will soon punish the house of Jehu for

[a] *1* Hebrew *Joash,* a variant of *Jehoash*

1:1 *Superscription: Hosea's Ministry Timed to the Reigns of Several Kings.* The superscription is fairly extensive for a prophetic book (for a shorter example, see Mal 1:1; for a longer example, see Jer 1:1–3). By coordination to the reigns of four kings of Judah and one king of Israel, it dates Hosea's prophetic ministry to the mid- and late eighth century BC, the time of events described in 2 Kgs 15–20 and 2 Chr 26–32.

1:2—3:5 *Marriage Themes: Israel as God's Wayward Wife.* The first three chapters of the book each contain symbolic marriage stories that illustrate God's covenant with Israel and are part of the widely attested biblical analogy of the people of God as his "bride" (cf. Rev 21:2). In all cultures, people have understood that marriage, properly practiced, is the most intimate and long-lasting human contractual arrangement (covenant). Thus, marriage serves as an analogy for Israel's covenant relationship with God. Both the OT and NT liken God's people to his bride: beloved to him, special in his plans, and by reason of his gracious love, called into his eternal compassion and care. Indeed, God's people are worthy of his Son's death on a cruel cross for the redemption of their sins. In chs. 1–3 that sort of covenant love is foreshadowed in three detailed stories that tell of God's love, his people's rejecting him, his efforts to win them back, and his great favor toward them after they return. In each of the three symbolic stories, he punishes his people for their infidelity to his covenant, so he is not a "soft" or standardless God; but he also restores and forgives them completely when they return to him.

1:2—2:1 *Hosea's Wife and Children.* God instructs Hosea to perform a symbolic action (also called enactment prophecy or dramatized prophecy). Its purpose is to illustrate that all Israelites, without exception, were tainted by Israel's moral corruption via idolatry and associated evils. Symbolic action reports combine vivid illustrative actions with divine pronouncements so as to impress God's word on a prophet's audience. Similar examples include Isaiah's going stripped and barefoot to symbolize how the Cushites would go into Assyrian exile (Isa 20:1–4), Ezekiel's building a model of the siege of Jerusalem and acting out related prophecies of the coming Babylonian siege and eventual capture of Jerusalem (Ezek 4:1—5:17), and Jeremiah's buying a field to symbolize the eventual restoration of normal life in Judah after its exile (Jer 32:1–15). Hos 3:1–5 is also such a symbolic action report, using a marriage relationship in which there was no intimacy to illustrate God's coming confinement of Israel via exile.

1:2–3 *Wife, Children, and Land Symbolize Pervasive Idolatry.* The NIV uses three different English terms ("promiscuous," "adulterous," "guilty of unfaithfulness") to render a single Hebrew term that describes Hosea's wife (see note on v. 2).

1:2 promiscuous woman. Other prophets use the term translated here "promiscuous" figuratively, in parallel to its usage in Hosea (e.g., Jer 3:1–3; Ezek 16; 23; Mic 1:7). In a marriage covenant, the practice of adultery by a spouse is an extreme form of unfaithfulness. In Israel's covenant with God, idolatry is an extreme form of unfaithfulness on the part of his "bride." A marriage covenant requires fidelity, and likewise, the Mosaic covenant begins with the requirement to "have no other gods" and prohibits making "an image in the form of anything" (Exod 20:3–4). "Promiscuity," "adultery," "prostitution," and similar terms connote idolatry and polytheism in both the OT (e.g., Judg 2:17) and the NT (e.g., Rev 17:1–18; 19:1–3). But why apply such language to Hosea's wife, children, and indeed the whole land of Israel? The reason is that *everyone* in Israel was being affected by idolatry in one way or another. In other words, *any* woman Hosea marries and *any* children he has will be or will have the potential to be tainted by the ubiquitous idolatry that already taints *everyone* in northern Israel. It is not sexual immorality but spiritual unfaithfulness that is in view here, and its widespread nature (cf. Judg 8:27: "all Israel prostituted themselves") is symbolized by what God commands Hosea to do.

1:4–9 *Three Unpleasant Children's Names Predict Judgment.* God commanded that all three children receive abnormal (negative) names—unusual in any culture—so that all who met them would likely ask about the reason for their unusual names and would learn from those names about God's plans for Israel via this enactment prophecy—an effective way of spreading the message throughout Hosea's homeland.

1:4–5 The enactment prophecy continues with a symbolic naming of the first child. The name **Jezreel** ("God scatters") recalls the location

the massacre at Jezreel, and I will put an end to the kingdom of Israel. 5In that day I will break Israel's
bow in the Valley of Jezreel.[g]"
6Gomer[h] conceived again and gave birth to a daughter. Then the LORD said to Hosea, "Call her
Lo-Ruhamah (which means "not loved"), for I will no longer show love to Israel,[i] that I should at all
forgive them. 7Yet I will show love to Judah; and I will save them — not by bow,[j] sword or battle, or by
horses and horsemen, but I, the LORD their God,[k] will save them."
8After she had weaned Lo-Ruhamah, Gomer had another son. 9Then the LORD said, "Call him Lo-
Ammi (which means "not my people"), for you are not my people, and I am not your God.[a]
10"Yet the Israelites will be like the sand on the seashore, which cannot be measured or counted.[l] In
the place where it was said to them, 'You are not my people,' they will be called 'children of the living
God.'[m] 11The people of Judah and the people of Israel will come together;[n] they will appoint one leader[o]
and will come up out of the land,[p] for great will be the day of Jezreel.[b]

2 [c] "Say of your brothers, 'My people,' and of your sisters, 'My loved one.'[q]

Israel Punished and Restored

2"Rebuke your mother,[r] rebuke her,
for she is not my wife,
and I am not her husband.
Let her remove the adulterous[s] look from her face
and the unfaithfulness from between her breasts.
3Otherwise I will strip her naked
and make her as bare as on the day she was born;[t]

1:5 [g] 2Ki 15:29
1:6 [h] ver 3 [i] Hos 2:4
1:7 [j] Ps 44:6 [k] Zec 4:6
1:10 [l] Ge 22:17; Jer 33:22 [m] ver 9; Ro 9:26*
1:11 [n] Isa 11:12,13 [o] Jer 23:5-8 [p] Eze 37:15-28
2:1 [q] ver 23
2:2 [r] ver 5; Isa 50:1; Hos 1:2 [s] Eze 23:45
2:3 [t] Eze 16:4,22

[a] 9 Or *your I AM* [b] 11 In Hebrew texts 1:10,11 is numbered 2:1,2. [c] In Hebrew texts 2:1-23 is numbered 2:3-25.

of a great slaughter in Israel's past (2 Kgs 10:11) and predicts an even greater one in the future for Israel. The predicted slaughter will be fulfilled in the Assyrian conquest of northern Israel in 722 BC.

1:6–7 Their second child, a girl, also gets a symbolic negative name: **Lo-Ruhamah.** means "not loved." The statement **for I will no longer show love to Israel** predicts God's coming rejection of northern Israel for its idolatry and overall covenant unfaithfulness. That rejection will spare Judah, which survived by God's grace for another century and a half until its demise in 586 BC (2 Kgs 25:1–26; 2 Chr 36:15–21).

1:8–9 The last child, another son, receives a name that also symbolizes rejection: **Lo-Ammi.** That name means "not my people." The statement **for you are not my people, and I am not your God** parallels ancient divorce formulas and connotes divine rejection as predicted in the covenant curses of Lev 26 and Deut 28–32. Here the first symbolic action report ends.

1:10—2:1 *Reversal of Names: Restoration in "the Day of Jezreel."* These verses are kept together in the Hebrew rather than divided between chapters as in the later tradition that produced the English chapter system. They constitute a restoration blessing based solely on the grace of God, by faith and not by works of the law (Gen 15:5–6; Rom 4:1–3; Gal 3:6). Instead of a "scattered," "unloved," people who are "not God's," they will "come together" as the "loved" "children of the living God." Paul cites these verses in detail in Rom 9:25–26, confirming that Christ's death and resurrection brought about this reversal.

1:10 like the sand on the seashore. This wording echoes predictions in the promises to Abraham that one day the Israelites would again be as numerous as "the sand on the seashore" (Gen 22:17; see Gen 32:12).

1:11 will come together ... will come up out of the land. After the respective exiles of Israel and Judah, God's people would be reunited and restored (cf. Ezek 37), reversing the curses described in Hos 1:2–9. This prediction that God's people will return from exile and be reunited was not fully accomplished in OT times but is fulfilled in Christ. The unity of all God's people — including the Gentiles who believe — is a major theme in NT teaching (e.g., John 17:23; Eph 4:13). **one leader.** The key person in this scenario is Jesus, who notably drew to himself both northerners (Samaritans) and southerners (Jews/Judahites).

2:1 your brothers ... your sisters. The previously negative names are changed to positive names and applied to all Israel, confirming the reversal of the curses contained in 1:2–9.

2:2–23 *Israel Punished and Restored.* The literary form is a prophetic covenant lawsuit (in this case, a symbolic divorce trial). Hosea uses the covenant lawsuit device in other places as well, including ch. 4 (cf. also Isa 1–3; Jer 2; Amos 3–4; Mic 6). Such prophecies imagine God playing several roles in a court trial (plaintiff, prosecutor, judge, jailer) and summoning Israel (the defendant) into court. God presents the evidence of Israel's crimes (ways they have broken God's covenant law), finds Israel guilty, pronounces the judgment sentence (various forms of deprivation and discipline, most commonly exile), and announces Israel's future as a convicted covenant-breaker. In the short term, that future will involve great hardship and confinement as Israel is conquered by a foreign power and exiled; in the long term, God's people are eventually shown great mercy because God never forgets his promises.

2:2–13 *Divorce Proceedings: An Allegory of God and Israel.* The divorce trial is based on Israel's infidelity to the divine covenant, symbolized by her "adulterous look" and "unfaithfulness" described in v. 2.

2:2 your mother. Throughout the allegory, the children and the mother are simply ways of referring to Israel (children = citizens; mother = corporate nation). God orders the children to testify in court against their mother, symbolizing the need for the people of Israel to bring about godly change in their nation, which God is currently in the process of "divorcing" — rejecting and exiling ("she is not my wife, and I am not her husband").

2:3 strip her naked. A play on the Hebrew concept of exile, which is usually rendered by a word that literally means "strip" (away from one's land). **desert ... parched land.** Israel's coming deprivation would be so severe it is compared to changing a fruitful country into a desert, a parched land.

2:3 [u]Isa 32:13-14
2:4 [v]Eze 8:18
2:5 [w]Jer 3:6 [x]Jer 44:17-18
2:6 [y]Job 3:23; 19:8; La 3:9
2:7 [z]Hos 5:13 [a]Jer 2:2; 3:1 [b]Eze 16:8
2:8 [c]Isa 1:3 [d]Eze 16:15-19; Hos 8:4
2:9 [e]Hos 8:7 [f]Hos 9:2
2:10 [g]Eze 16:37
2:11 [h]Jer 7:34 [i]Isa 1:14; Jer 16:9; Hos 3:4; Am 8:10
2:12 [j]Isa 7:23; Jer 8:13 [k]Isa 5:6 [l]Hos 13:8
2:13 [m]Hos 11:2 [n]Eze 16:17 [o]Hos 4:13 [p]Hos 4:6; 8:14; 13:6

I will make her like a desert,[u]
turn her into a parched land,
and slay her with thirst.
4 I will not show my love to her children,[v]
because they are the children of adultery.
5 Their mother has been unfaithful
and has conceived them in disgrace.
She said, 'I will go after my lovers,[w]
who give me my food and my water,
my wool and my linen, my olive oil and my drink.'[x]
6 Therefore I will block her path with thornbushes;
I will wall her in so that she cannot find her way.[y]
7 She will chase after her lovers but not catch them;
she will look for them but not find them.[z]
Then she will say,
'I will go back to my husband as at first,[a]
for then I was better off[b] than now.'
8 She has not acknowledged[c] that I was the one
who gave her the grain, the new wine and oil,
who lavished on her the silver and gold—
which they used for Baal.[d]

9 "Therefore I will take away my grain[e] when it ripens,
and my new wine[f] when it is ready.
I will take back my wool and my linen,
intended to cover her naked body.
10 So now I will expose her lewdness
before the eyes of her lovers;
no one will take her out of my hands.[g]
11 I will stop[h] all her celebrations:
her yearly festivals, her New Moons,
her Sabbath days—all her appointed festivals.[i]
12 I will ruin her vines[j] and her fig trees,
which she said were her pay from her lovers;
I will make them a thicket,[k]
and wild animals will devour them.[l]
13 I will punish her for the days
she burned incense to the Baals;[m]
she decked herself with rings and jewelry,[n]
and went after her lovers,[o]
but me she forgot,[p]"

declares the LORD.

2:4–7 God's covenant punishments will produce deprivation designed to cause Israel to repent of idolatry. The "children of adultery" ("prostitution," Hosea's standard metaphor for idolatry) and their "mother" who "has been unfaithful" must have their freedom taken away so that Israel will have no choice but to "go back" to the Lord, her "husband as at first" (v. 7).
2:6 Therefore. This word introduces the first of three verdicts of the divine Judge, the Lord. The first two (vv. 6–8,9–13) involve punishments, but the final "therefore" (v. 14) mercifully reverses Israel's fortunes, yet only *after* the coming exile.
2:8 I was the one who gave her the grain, new wine and oil. It was the Lord who actually gave Israel any blessings they had. Worship of Baal had been promoted by the northern king Ahab (1 Kgs 16:29–33) and had been fought by the prophet Elijah (1 Kgs 18:16–40), but it had once again become popular in northern Israel in Hosea's day. **Baal.** This Canaanite deity was thought to be a fertility god whose blessing brought wealth ("silver and gold") to an agrarian society.
2:9–13 Therefore. This introduces the second verdict (see note on v. 6). **grain … wine … wool … linen … celebrations … vines … fig trees.** Things the Israelites held dear; they would be stopped and/or taken away.
2:12 which she said were her pay from her lovers. Again, Israelites attributed their blessings to false gods ("her lovers").
2:13 the Baals. A way of referring to various gods, including multiple aspects of Baal.

[14] "Therefore I am now going to allure her;
I will lead her into the wilderness
and speak tenderly to her.
[15] There I will give her back her vineyards,
and will make the Valley of Achor[a][q] a door of hope.
There she will respond[b][r] as in the days of her youth,[s]
as in the day she came up out of Egypt.[t]

[16] "In that day," declares the LORD,
"you will call me 'my husband';
you will no longer call me 'my master.[c]'
[17] I will remove the names of the Baals from her lips;[u]
no longer will their names be invoked.[v]
[18] In that day I will make a covenant for them
with the beasts of the field, the birds in the sky
and the creatures that move along the ground.[w]
Bow and sword and battle
I will abolish[x] from the land,
so that all may lie down in safety.[y]
[19] I will betroth[z] you to me forever;
I will betroth you in[d] righteousness and justice,[a]
in[d] love and compassion.
[20] I will betroth you in[d] faithfulness,
and you will acknowledge[b] the LORD.

[21] "In that day I will respond,"
declares the LORD —
"I will respond[c] to the skies,
and they will respond to the earth;
[22] and the earth will respond to the grain,
the new wine and the olive oil,[d]
and they will respond to Jezreel.[e]
[23] I will plant[e] her for myself in the land;
I will show my love to the one I called 'Not my loved one.[f][f]'
I will say to those called 'Not my people,[g]' 'You are my people';[g]
and they will say, 'You are my God.[h]' "

[a] *15* *Achor* means *trouble.* [b] *15* Or *sing* [c] *16* Hebrew *baal* [d] *19,20* Or *with* [e] *22* *Jezreel* means *God plants.* [f] *23* Hebrew *Lo-Ruhamah* (see 1:6) [g] *23* Hebrew *Lo-Ammi* (see 1:9)

2:15 [q] Jos 7:24,26 [r] Ex 15:1-18 [s] Jer 2:2 [t] Hos 12:9
2:17 [u] Ex 23:13; Ps 16:4 [v] Jos 23:7
2:18 [w] Job 5:22 [x] Isa 2:4 [y] Jer 23:6; Eze 34:25
2:19 [z] Isa 62:4 [a] Isa 1:27
2:20 [b] Jer 31:34; Hos 6:6; 13:4
2:21 [c] Isa 55:10; Zec 8:12
2:22 [d] Jer 31:12; Joel 2:19
2:23 [e] Jer 31:27 [f] Hos 1:6 [g] Hos 1:10 [h] Ro 9:25*; 1Pe 2:10

2:14–23 *Restoration of the Marriage: God's Future Covenant With His People.* "Therefore" (v. 14) introduces the final verdict (see note on v. 6) and looks far beyond the punishments of exile and deprivation. In contrast to what has preceded, this verdict announces hope and promise. God's merciful plan for his people includes redemption and restoration on a scale not found in any OT era but available abundantly in Christ (1 Cor 2:7–10).
2:14–15 wilderness. The term may recall the early years ("as in the days of her youth"), after Israel "came up out of Egypt" when God directly led his people through the wilderness and they followed him closely (Exod 12:1 — Deut 34:12). **Valley of Achor.** A notorious instance of disobedience from the past (Josh 7); now it will yield to future obedience ("she will respond") and "hope."
2:16–17 husband. One meaning of the name Baal was "husband," so God predicts the day when his people won't say "Baal" anymore, avoiding the way of saying "my husband" that uses the word "Baal" and saying "my husband" via other Hebrew wordings. They will give God undivided loyalty and will reject the falsehood and folly that worship of the Baals represented.
2:18 I will make a covenant for them with the beasts ... the birds ... the creatures. The new covenant will change everything, bringing peace and safety, and bringing back the original idyllic harmony with nature once enjoyed in Eden (Gen 1:28–30).
2:19–20 God will "betroth" his people in a covenant relationship so that they will finally "acknowledge the LORD," as they should have been doing in Hosea's time.
2:21–23 A glorious renewal in the new covenant age. God will undo and transform various facets of Israel's prior corruption (vv. 2–14) into good things, so that even the names of Hosea's children (1:4–8) will be endowed with new meaning (see note on 2:23).
2:23 The names Jezreel (1:4), Lo-Ruhamah (1:6), and Lo-Ammi (1:9) are changed to positive forms: **I will plant her for myself.** Jezreel, though a reminder of a massacre, means "God plants." **I will show my love.** Lo-Ruhamah means "not loved." **You are my people.** Lo-Ammi means "not my people." In Rom 9:25–26 and 1 Pet 2:10, the expansive wording of this verse is shown not only to describe repentant Israelites but to predict the inclusion of converted Gentiles in the church.

3:1 [i]Hos 1:2 [j]2Sa 6:19
3:4 [k]Hos 13:11
[l]Da 11:31; Hos 2:11
[m]Jdg 17:5-6; Zec 10:2
3:5 [n]Eze 34:23-24
[o]Jer 50:4-5
4:1 [p]Jer 7:28

Hosea's Reconciliation With His Wife

3 The LORD said to me, "Go, show your love to your wife again, though she is loved by another man
and is an adulteress.[i] Love her as the LORD loves the Israelites, though they turn to other gods and
love the sacred raisin cakes.[j]"
2So I bought her for fifteen shekels[a] of silver and about a homer and a lethek[b] of barley. 3Then I
told her, "You are to live with me many days; you must not be a prostitute or be intimate with any man,
and I will behave the same way toward you."
4For the Israelites will live many days without king or prince,[k] without sacrifice[l] or sacred stones,
without ephod or household gods.[m] 5Afterward the Israelites will return and seek the LORD their God
and David their king.[n] They will come trembling to the LORD and to his blessings in the last days.[o]

The Charge Against Israel

4 Hear the word of the LORD, you Israelites,
because the LORD has a charge to bring
against you who live in the land:
"There is no faithfulness, no love,
no acknowledgment[p] of God in the land.

[a] *2* That is, about 6 ounces or about 170 grams [b] *2* A homer and a lethek possibly weighed about 430 pounds or about 195 kilograms.

3:1–5 *Hosea's Reconciliation With His Wife.* This chapter contains a second symbolic action report, which, with the symbolic action report contained in 1:2—2:1, surrounds the marriage allegory of God and Israel found in 2:2–23. Thus, marriage themes dominate the first three chapters of the book, after which other themes are introduced.

3:1–3 *Another Marriage, This Time Unconsummated.* The NIV section heading, "Hosea's Reconciliation With His Wife," is carefully worded so as to refer potentially either to Gomer (1:3) or to another wife married either actually or symbolically after Gomer's death. If it is the latter, then 3:4 would represent the reconciliation with that second wife. No evidence exists to fill in the details or to resolve the questions, but the message for God's people of 3:1–5 is not in doubt. The passage describes a marriage without intimacy, in contrast to that of 1:2–9, as a prediction of Israel's confinement via its coming exile, again using the human covenant of marriage to illustrate the covenant of God with his people.

3:1 Go, show your love to your wife again. Here again, God's love for Israel—the key theme and promise of the book of Hosea—is vividly on display, foreshadowing the way God, in Christ, willingly forgives and accepts sinners (Rom 4:7–8; 5:6–11). "Go again, love a woman" is the literal translation of the original, thus not necessarily pointing to the wife named in 1:3. This symbolic action report describes a second marriage under different circumstances from Hosea's first marriage. Now, the anonymous woman nevertheless has an immoral past ("adulteress") whose personal history of infidelity thus parallels Israel's ("as the LORD loves the Israelites"). **raisin cakes.** These were often eaten in pagan religious feasts; their mention suggests Israel's willingness to sell out cheaply to other gods (via idolatry and polytheism).

3:2 A bride-price, paid in this case via silver and barley, signified a woman's value to her family. It was a compensation paid in OT times to the family a woman left when she married and went to live with her husband. It did not mean that her husband owned her like property, but it did symbolize her great worth both to the family she left and to her husband. Israel is very precious to God; his love for her is not casual. In the NT, the "price" God pays to redeem his people is high indeed: the death of his own beloved Son (1 Cor 6:20; 7:23).

3:3 not ... be intimate. Since this marriage seems to be primarily symbolic, in contrast to what would typically happen after a new marriage, it will not be consummated. Hosea tells his bride that they can have no intimate relations. For those who take this marriage to be a recommitment by Hosea to Gomer, the original marriage having been consummated, these words represent a prohibition of sexual relations going forward. In either case, the wording points to Israel's confinement, like a shunned wife, in exile.

3:4–5 *Israel's Exile as Punishment for Covenant Infidelity.* The wording now makes clear that the previous enactment symbolized the coming exile.

3:4 without king or prince. Israel will be under foreign domination in exile, without its own government. **sacred stones ... ephod ... household gods.** These are items Israel revered in a pagan fashion in Hosea's day. They will be forced to live and worship in a foreign religious setting, without these familiar possessions (Deut 4:28; 28:36,64).

3:5 return ... in the last days. After the punishments, including Israel's exile, have ended, the return to the Lord in the last days (the new covenant era) will include reunification of all of God's people in Christ's kingdom. **David.** Jesus is the new David of prophecy (cf. 2 Sam 7:11b–16; Isa 9:7; 55:3; Jer 23:5; Ezek 34:23–24; Matt 22:42; Rev 22:16). Israel will have learned her lesson and will be restored to God in Christ in a way not yet experienced in the old covenant (Deut 30:5–6). Israel and Judah were politically and religiously divided from one another in Hosea's day and had been so for two centuries, since the death of Solomon (1 Kgs 12). **David their king.** The idea of reunification with David as their king may have seemed out of the question to Hosea's contemporaries, but just as Israel and Judah had been united under the first David (2 Sam 5:1–5), they would again be united under David's greater Son (Matt 22:41–45) in fulfillment of God's covenant promise to David himself (2 Sam 7:16).

4:1—9:8 *Judgment Warnings Involving Israel's Present and Future.* This central section of the book contains a variety of prophecies in various styles warning that the nation will continue to deteriorate in the short term, and it will not be spared but will be conquered and exiled. Only eventually, after much trial and deprivation, will Israel be restored to God by his grace.

4:1–19 *The Charge Against Israel.* As in 2:2–23, this imagines Israel on trial. This is more a general criminal trial than a divorce proceeding, but it is for the same sorts of crimes: idolatry, polytheism, and related covenant violations.

4:1–14 *Another Covenant Lawsuit Against Israel.* This section is structured in such a way that the evidence for Israel's covenant-breaking is interspersed with judgment sentences (verdicts) that are pronounced on the basis of that evidence.

4:1–2 no love, no acknowledgment of God. A way of indicating general disobedience to the covenant. **murder, stealing and adultery.** Specific violations of the Ten Commandments.

2 There is only cursing,[a] lying[q] and murder,[r]
stealing[s] and adultery;
they break all bounds,
and bloodshed follows bloodshed.
3 Because of this the land dries up,[t]
and all who live in it waste away;[u]
the beasts of the field, the birds in the sky
and the fish in the sea are swept away.[v]

4 "But let no one bring a charge,
let no one accuse another,
for your people are like those
who bring charges against a priest.[w]
5 You stumble[x] day and night,
and the prophets stumble with you.
So I will destroy your mother[y] —
6 my people are destroyed from lack of knowledge.[z]

"Because you have rejected knowledge,
I also reject you as my priests;
because you have ignored the law[a] of your God,
I also will ignore your children.
7 The more priests there were,
the more they sinned against me;
they exchanged their glorious God[b][b] for something disgraceful.[c]
8 They feed on the sins of my people
and relish their wickedness.[d]
9 And it will be: Like people, like priests.[e]
I will punish both of them for their ways
and repay them for their deeds.[f]

10 "They will eat but not have enough;[g]
they will engage in prostitution but not flourish,
because they have deserted[h] the LORD
to give themselves 11 to prostitution;[i]
old wine and new wine
take away their understanding.[j]
12 My people consult a wooden idol,[k]
and a diviner's rod speaks to them.[l]
A spirit of prostitution leads them astray;[m]
they are unfaithful to their God.
13 They sacrifice on the mountaintops
and burn offerings on the hills,

4:2 [q] Hos 7:3; 10:4 [r] Hos 6:9 [s] Hos 7:1
4:3 [t] Jer 4:28 [u] Isa 33:9 [v] Jer 4:25; Zep 1:3
4:4 [w] Dt 17:12; Eze 3:26
4:5 [x] Eze 14:7 [y] Hos 2:2
4:6 [z] Hos 2:13; Mal 2:7-8 [a] Hos 8:1,12
4:7 [b] Hab 2:16 [c] Hos 10:1,6; 13:6
4:8 [d] Isa 56:11; Mic 3:11
4:9 [e] Isa 24:2 [f] Jer 5:31; Hos 8:13; 9:9,15
4:10 [g] Lev 26:26; Mic 6:14 [h] Hos 7:14; 9:17
4:11 [i] Hos 5:4 [j] Pr 20:1
4:12 [k] Jer 2:27 [l] Hab 2:19 [m] Isa 44:20

[a] *2* That is, to pronounce a curse on [b] *7* Syriac (see also an ancient Hebrew scribal tradition); Masoretic Text *me; / I will exchange their glory*

4:3 dries up ... waste away ... swept away. These predictions recall the covenant curses of Deut 28–32, including drought, famine, and decimation (cf. Jer 14).
4:4–9 No citizen can rightfully "bring a charge" (v. 4) against "mother" Israel (v. 5; cf. 2:2) because they are all guilty: the prophets, the priests, the people.
4:5 prophets. In this case, false prophets, who led the people away from the Lord.
4:6 reject you as my priests. Israel was to be a nation of priests to the world (Exod 19:6), but their sins disqualify them.
4:7 they exchanged their glorious God for something disgraceful. A description of idolatry. Both the temple priests and the people collaborated in ignoring and/or breaking God's law, especially by condoning and practicing idolatry, so God will punish both people and priests (v. 9).
4:10–14 Once again Hosea's favorite metaphor for idolatry, "prostitution," conveys the idea of infidelity to God's covenant law, including the often alcohol-fueled (v. 11) pagan practices of idolatry and divination (v. 12), showing that they are "unfaithful" (v. 12).
4:13 on the hills. Pagan idolatry typically took place at hilltop shrines (cf. Jer 3:6).

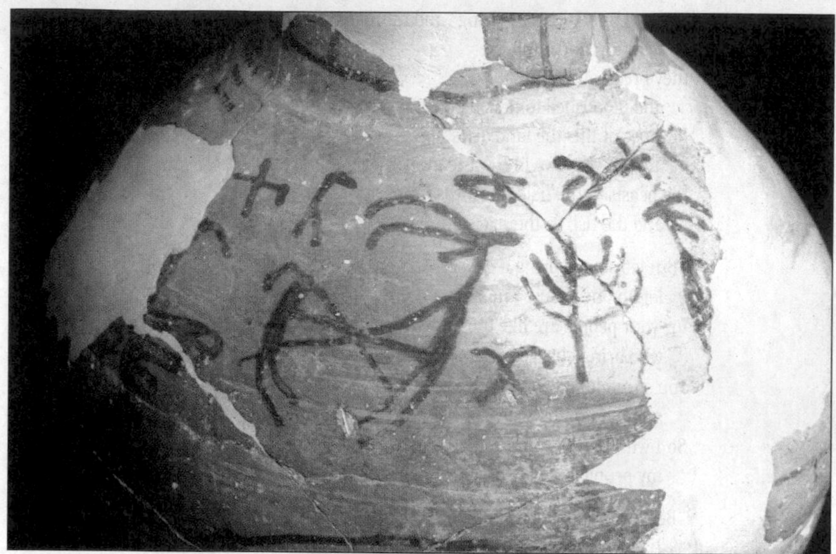

Lachish ewer with ca. 1200 BC picture of tree associated with goddess worship. Hos 4:13 describes some of the pagan rituals being practiced by the Israelites.
Z. Radovan/www.BibleLandPictures.com

4:13 [n]Isa 1:29 [o]Jer 3:6; Hos 11:2 [p]Jer 2:20; Am 7:17 [q]Hos 2:13
4:14 [r]ver 11
4:15 [s]Hos 9:15; 12:11; Am 4:4
4:16 [t]Isa 5:17; 7:25

under oak,[n] poplar and terebinth,
where the shade is pleasant.[o]
Therefore your daughters turn to prostitution[p]
and your daughters-in-law to adultery.[q]

14 "I will not punish your daughters
when they turn to prostitution,
nor your daughters-in-law
when they commit adultery,
because the men themselves consort with harlots[r]
and sacrifice with shrine prostitutes—
a people without understanding will come to ruin!

15 "Though you, Israel, commit adultery,
do not let Judah become guilty.

"Do not go to Gilgal;[s]
do not go up to Beth Aven.[a]
And do not swear, 'As surely as the LORD lives!'
16 The Israelites are stubborn,
like a stubborn heifer.
How then can the LORD pasture them
like lambs[t] in a meadow?

[a] 15 *Beth Aven* means *house of wickedness* (a derogatory name for Bethel, which means *house of God*).

4:14 I will not punish your daughters. This does not mean that the women who chose to "turn to prostitution" bore no guilt, but indicates that God would not punish *only* the women without also punishing the whole "people without understanding." **sacrifice with shrine prostitutes.** Idolatry sometimes included actual ritual prostitution with cult prostitutes who may have represented fertility goddesses. In this context Hosea uses the term "prostitution" literally to describe such debauchery practiced in the name of religion (cf. Lev 19:29; 2 Kgs 23:7; Amos 2:7–8).

4:15–19 *Israel's Guilt a Warning to Judah.* Even though Hosea preached in the north, his message showed concern from time to time for Judah as well. He warns that Judah must stay away from the places and practices that corrupted and doomed (northern) Israel.
4:15 Israel … Judah. The "adultery" (idolatry) of northern Israel did not yet infect Judah as mortally as it did Israel. But in another century and a half, when Judah's own sins would bring them into exile, Judah would "become guilty" as well. **Gilgal.** See note on 9:15. **Beth Aven.** See note on 10:5.

[17]Ephraim is joined to idols;
leave him alone!
[18]Even when their drinks are gone,
they continue their prostitution;
their rulers dearly love shameful ways.
[19]A whirlwind[u] will sweep them away,
and their sacrifices will bring them shame.[v]

Judgment Against Israel

5 "Hear this, you priests!
Pay attention, you Israelites!
Listen, royal house!
This judgment is against you:
You have been a snare[w] at Mizpah,
a net spread out on Tabor.
[2]The rebels are knee-deep in slaughter.[x]
I will discipline all of them.[y]
[3]I know all about Ephraim;
Israel is not hidden from me.
Ephraim, you have now turned to prostitution;
Israel is corrupt.[z]

[4]"Their deeds do not permit them
to return to their God.
A spirit of prostitution[a] is in their heart;
they do not acknowledge[b] the LORD.
[5]Israel's arrogance testifies[c] against them;
the Israelites, even Ephraim, stumble in their sin;
Judah also stumbles with them.
[6]When they go with their flocks and herds
to seek the LORD,[d]
they will not find him;
he has withdrawn[e] himself from them.
[7]They are unfaithful[f] to the LORD;
they give birth to illegitimate[g] children.
When they celebrate their New Moon feasts,
he will devour[a][h] their fields.

[a] 7 Or *Now their New Moon feasts / will devour them and*

4:19 [u]Hos 12:1; 13:15 [v]Isa 1:29
5:1 [w]Hos 6:9; 9:8
5:2 [x]Hos 4:2 [y]Hos 9:15
5:3 [z]Hos 6:10
5:4 [a]Hos 4:11 [b]Hos 4:6
5:5 [c]Hos 7:10
5:6 [d]Mic 6:6-7 [e]Pr 1:28; Isa 1:15; Eze 8:6
5:7 [f]Hos 6:7 [g]Hos 2:4 [h]Hos 2:11-12

4:17 Ephraim. Northern Israel. This is the first of 37 times in the book that Israel is called Ephraim, partly because Ephraim was the northern tribe most associated with leadership from Genesis to Judges and also because Ephraim was the central and most populous tribal territory that managed to survive the Syro-Ephraimite war, ca. 734–732 BC (see 5:5–8 and note on 5:8–15). But Ephraim fell to the Assyrians in 722 BC. The last of the people and even their "rulers" (v. 18) would be swept away by the Assyrian conquest because of their idolatrous sacrifices and the syndrome of disobedience to God that such sacrifices represented (v. 19).

5:1–15 *Judgment Against Israel.* Not only are the leaders of the nation and the population in general guilty of disobedience so great that "their deeds do not permit them to return to their God" (v. 4), but Israel and Judah find themselves fighting against each other in a war (vv. 8–15) that represented God's "wrath on them like a flood of water" (v. 10).

5:1–7 *Indictment of People and Leaders for "Prostitution" (Idolatry) and Evil Deeds.* When a nation's religious leaders ("priests," v. 1) and government leaders ("royal house," v. 1) are corrupt, they help turn the population in general ("Israelites," v. 1) toward corrupt ways.

5:1 Mizpah … Tabor. These cities serve as examples of cult centers where pagan worship took place, and memorably so, because in Hebrew the word for "snare" sounds similar to the last syllable of Mizpah, and part of the words for "net spread" sound similar to "Tabor."

5:4 deeds … spirit of prostitution. This pattern keeps Israel away from the only one who can forgive them and restore them: the Lord.

5:6 flocks and herds. Sacrificial animals. Since both northern Israel and Judah were practicing idolatry and false worship, it was unacceptable to bring sacrificial animals to try to mollify God by going through the motions of worshiping him while also worshiping other gods.

5:7 unfaithful … illegitimate children. In the manner of unfaithful women, the Israelites produce illegitimate children (yet more citizens devoted to pagan idolatry) whose practices will, in effect, allow others to take over their country ("devour their fields") when God exiles them from their homeland.

5:8 [i]Hos 9:9; 10:9 [j]Isa 10:29 [k]Hos 4:15
5:9 [l]Isa 37:3; Hos 9:11-17 [m]Isa 46:10; Zec 1:6
5:10 [n]Dt 19:14 [o]Eze 7:8
5:11 [p]Hos 9:16; Mic 6:16
5:12 [q]Isa 51:8
5:13 [r]Hos 7:11; 8:9 [s]Hos 10:6 [t]Hos 14:3 [u]Jer 30:12
5:14 [v]Am 3:4 [w]Mic 5:8
5:15 [x]Hos 3:5 [y]Jer 2:27 [z]Isa 64:9
6:1 [a]Hos 5:14

8 "Sound the trumpet in Gibeah,[i]
the horn in Ramah.[j]
Raise the battle cry in Beth Aven[a],[k]
lead on, Benjamin.
9 Ephraim will be laid waste
on the day of reckoning.[l]
Among the tribes of Israel
I proclaim what is certain.[m]
10 Judah's leaders are like those
who move boundary stones.[n]
I will pour out my wrath[o] on them
like a flood of water.
11 Ephraim is oppressed,
trampled in judgment,
intent on pursuing idols.[b][p]
12 I am like a moth[q] to Ephraim,
like rot to the people of Judah.

13 "When Ephraim saw his sickness,
and Judah his sores,
then Ephraim turned to Assyria,[r]
and sent to the great king for help.[s]
But he is not able to cure[t] you,
not able to heal your sores.[u]
14 For I will be like a lion[v] to Ephraim,
like a great lion to Judah.
I will tear them to pieces and go away;
I will carry them off, with no one to rescue them.[w]
15 Then I will return to my lair
until they have borne their guilt
and seek my face[x]—
in their misery[y]
they will earnestly seek me.[z]"

Israel Unrepentant

6 "Come, let us return to the LORD.
He has torn us to pieces[a]
but he will heal us;

[a] 8 *Beth Aven* means *house of wickedness* (a derogatory name for Bethel, which means *house of God*).
[b] 11 The meaning of the Hebrew for this word is uncertain.

5:8–15 *War Between Israel and Judah and Its Aftermath.* In ca. 734 BC northern Israel and Syria (Aram) went to war ("raise the battle cry," v. 8) against Judah because Judah refused to join them in a war against their common enemy Assyria (2 Kgs 16:5–9). Judah's king Ahaz appealed to Assyria for help, in effect saying, "Israel and Syria are attacking us because we won't attack you." Assyria quickly intervened, invaded Syria and northern Israel, and annexed their territory except for the part of Israel that belonged to the tribe of Ephraim. Thereafter, northern Israel was often called just Ephraim. Too late, Ephraim "turned to Assyria" (Hos 5:13) and tried to patch things up by paying tribute (2 Kgs 17:3), but Assyria soon conquered and annexed Ephraim anyway (2 Kgs 17:5–6).
5:10 move boundary stones. In effect stealing land; it was a serious crime (Deut 19:14; 27:17; Job 24:2). Some archaeological evidence indicates that Judah took advantage of the Assyrian attack on her neighbors by invading northern Israel and temporarily annexing the territory of Benjamin and the city of Bethel in Ephraim, thus acting like land thieves.
5:13–14 turned to Assyria. Israel was reduced to Ephraim but was not conquered totally only because it paid Assyria's "great king," Tiglath-Pileser III, tribute money. **not able to heal.** Paying tribute to Assyria could not really heal Israel's sores because God would exile them ("I will carry them off, with no one to rescue them," v. 14) for their continuing sins ("guilt," v. 15), including the foolish notion that they could stop paying tribute once Tiglath-Pileser was dead and his son Shalmaneser reigned in his stead (2 Kgs 17:3–4).
5:15 earnestly seek me. Israel's only future hope, as is ultimately the case with any person or nation, is to seek God's forgiveness when in exile from him and his favor.
6:1—7:16 *Israel Unrepentant.* With a variety of descriptions of Israel's

he has injured us
but he will bind up our wounds.[b]
2 After two days he will revive us;[c]
on the third day he will restore us,
that we may live in his presence.
3 Let us acknowledge the LORD;
let us press on to acknowledge him.
As surely as the sun rises,
he will appear;
he will come to us like the winter rains,[d]
like the spring rains that water the earth.[e]"

4 "What can I do with you, Ephraim?[f]
What can I do with you, Judah?
Your love is like the morning mist,
like the early dew that disappears.[g]
5 Therefore I cut you in pieces with my prophets,
I killed you with the words of my mouth[h]—
then my judgments go forth like the sun.[a][i]
6 For I desire mercy, not sacrifice,[j]
and acknowledgment[k] of God rather than burnt offerings.
7 As at Adam,[b] they have broken the covenant;[l]
they were unfaithful[m] to me there.
8 Gilead is a city of evildoers,
stained with footprints of blood.
9 As marauders lie in ambush for a victim,
so do bands of priests;

6:1 [b] Dt 32:39; Jer 30:17; Hos 14:4
6:2 [c] Ps 30:5
6:3 [d] Joel 2:23 [e] Ps 72:6
6:4 [f] Hos 11:8 [g] Hos 7:1; 13:3
6:5 [h] Jer 1:9-10; 23:29 [i] Heb 4:12
6:6 [j] Isa 1:11; Mt 9:13*; 12:7* [k] Hos 2:20
6:7 [l] Hos 8:1 [m] Hos 5:7

[a] 5 The meaning of the Hebrew for this line is uncertain. [b] 7 Or *Like Adam*; or *Like human beings*

stubborn disobedience, God shows how the nation is inexorably headed for destruction because it rebelled against him.

6:1–3 *A Glimpse of What Could Be: God's Healing of a Future Repentant People.* It might seem that the opening line of this chapter promises a quick resolution of Israel's problems and an almost immediate nullification of the consequences of their sins, but the book makes very clear that such a possibility is long past (e.g., 5:4,6,14; 6:11—7:2,13–16; 9:3,9,11–12).

6:1 Come, let us return to the LORD. These words, like all restoration promises in the book, are about future redemption *after* Israel's exile. They remind Hosea's hearers and readers that there is hope beyond the dire predictions of the immediate future. Like all the OT prophets, Hosea looks beyond the coming time of deprivation (3:4) to the great era of the Spirit, the time of the new covenant, when God will "heal" what he has "torn" and "revive" and "restore" his people (vv. 1–2) that he once had "injured" (v. 1).

6:2 on the third day. This wording does not suggest that Hosea was trying specifically to describe Christ's resurrection after three days; it is an idiomatic expression for God's readiness and eagerness to show mercy to those who ask for it. Nevertheless, NT statements that Jesus was resurrected "on the third day" (Luke 24:46; 1 Cor 15:4) may have this wording in mind, since a close connection exists between Jesus the Messiah and his people (his "body"). So a three-day process for Israel's "resurrection"—from being "torn ... to pieces" (Hos 6:1) to being able to "live in [God's] presence" (v. 2)—is a fitting model for the resurrection of Jesus. Jesus himself made the connection of his resurrection on the third day to the story of Jonah (Matt 12:40).

6:3 he will appear; he will come. Amid predictions of disaster and judgment, this reminds us that God comes to any who "acknowledge the LORD."

6:4–11a *God's Frustration With His People.* Both the north (Ephraim) and south (Judah) have shown a long history of "prostitution" (idolatry, polytheism), ignoring the warnings of God's prophets and breaking his covenant.

6:5 Therefore I cut ... I killed. God's word has real consequences, even to the extent of death for those who ignore or disobey it.

6:6 not sacrifice. Sacrifices, even the special sacrifices given to cover sins ("burnt offerings"), are essentially hypocritical if the worship is not matched by behavior (cf. Amos 5:21–24; Jas 2:18).

6:7 As at Adam ... unfaithful to me there. Adam was a city located along the Jordan River, which Israel crossed to enter Canaan (Josh 3:16). Referring to Adam in this way would remind listeners and readers that Israel had begun to violate God's covenant from the moment they entered the promised land. An alternative translation is "like Adam" (see NIV text note), in which case it is the serious disobedience of the first human (Gen 3:17–19) that Israel's disobedience is compared to. In either case, a long history of unfaithfulness to God is described. **they have broken the covenant.** Hosea refers to the Mosaic covenant, as found in Exodus through Deuteronomy (Hos 2:18; 8:1). Hosea regularly alludes to the blessings and curses of that covenant (see especially Lev 26; Deut 28–32) and makes it clear that Israel's failure to live up to the covenant—which gave the nation its standards, laws, and, above all, its relationship to God—meant that it would lose its divine protection and be rejected by God, the people becoming "wanderers among the nations" (Hos 9:17).

6:8–9 Gilead ... Shechem. Popular worship centers that were illegal under the covenant. Priests at these shrines were in effect guilty of "murder" (v. 9) for leading the people away from God. Jerusalem was the only proper place for worship (Deut 12:5–7; 1 Kgs 11:36; 14:21; Zech 14:17).

6:9 [n]Jer 7:9-10; Eze 22:9; Hos 7:1
6:10 [o]Jer 5:30 [p]Hos 5:3
6:11 [q]Jer 51:33; Joel 3:13
7:1 [r]Hos 6:4 [s]ver 13 [t]Hos 4:2
7:2 [u]Jer 14:10; Hos 8:13 [v]Jer 2:19
7:3 [w]Hos 4:2; Mic 7:3
7:4 [x]Jer 9:2
7:5 [y]Isa 28:1,7
7:6 [z]Ps 21:9
7:7 [a]ver 16
7:8 [b]ver 11; Ps 106:35; Hos 5:13

they murder on the road to Shechem,
carrying out their wicked schemes.[n]
10 I have seen a horrible[o] thing in Israel:
There Ephraim is given to prostitution,
Israel is defiled.[p]

11 "Also for you, Judah,
a harvest[q] is appointed.

7

"Whenever I would restore the fortunes of my people,
1 whenever I would heal Israel,
the sins of Ephraim are exposed
and the crimes of Samaria revealed.[r]
They practice deceit,[s]
thieves break into houses,[t]
bandits rob in the streets;
2 but they do not realize
that I remember[u] all their evil deeds.
Their sins engulf them;[v]
they are always before me.

3 "They delight the king with their wickedness,
the princes with their lies.[w]
4 They are all adulterers,[x]
burning like an oven
whose fire the baker need not stir
from the kneading of the dough till it rises.
5 On the day of the festival of our king
the princes become inflamed with wine,[y]
and he joins hands with the mockers.
6 Their hearts are like an oven;[z]
they approach him with intrigue.
Their passion smolders all night;
in the morning it blazes like a flaming fire.
7 All of them are hot as an oven;
they devour their rulers.
All their kings fall,
and none of them calls[a] on me.

8 "Ephraim mixes[b] with the nations;
Ephraim is a flat loaf not turned over.

6:10 prostitution … defiled. Israelites and Judahites worshiped the Lord as their national God but practiced idolatry with other gods at the same time and so defiled themselves.
6:11a Judah, though perhaps less corrupt than Ephraim, was still more than minimally guilty of breaking the covenant and would therefore eventually reap its own "harvest" of judgment.
6:11b — 7:16 *Israel's Foolish Sinfulness in National and International Affairs.* God loved his people Israel (here with the focus on Ephraim, the remnant of northern Israel after 734 BC), but they were more concerned with finding success and power via internal political intrigues and international diplomatic maneuvers than with trusting him to protect and benefit them. Thus, the nation spiraled downward during its last years of monarchy (753–722), when no fewer than six kings reigned, most coming to power by assassination of a predecessor (see 8:1–6 and note). Kings ruled for life, so an average of only five years per king is evidence of civil unrest and instability.
6:11b — 7:2 Lawlessness prevailed in the north under weak and immoral kings. In the chaos of such times, people can forget that God is never distracted but remembers "all their evil deeds" (7:2).
7:1 Samaria. Placed here in poetic parallelism with "Ephraim," it was yet another way to refer to the northern kingdom, since Samaria was the capital city of the north during most of its history. "Samaria" became a shorthand way to refer to (northern) Israel in general (see also 8:5–6; 10:5,7; 13:16).
7:3–7 The northern Israelite political maneuvering at the end of its history as a nation, including intrigues, assassinations, and forced abdications of kings (see 2 Kgs 15:8–30), was far from God's will and resulted from a failure to seek his favor and aid ("none of them calls on me," v. 7).
7:5–6 inflamed with wine … flaming fire. In the ancient world, plotters of coups and planners of war often emboldened themselves with alcohol, thinking that it helped them plan more decisively (cf. Esth 1:10).
7:8–16 mixes with the nations … do not turn to the Most High.

[9] Foreigners sap his strength,[c]
but he does not realize it.
His hair is sprinkled with gray,
but he does not notice.
[10] Israel's arrogance testifies against him,[d]
but despite all this
he does not return to the LORD his God
or search[e] for him.

[11] "Ephraim is like a dove,[f]
easily deceived and senseless—
now calling to Egypt,
now turning to Assyria.[g]
[12] When they go, I will throw my net[h] over them;
I will pull them down like the birds in the sky.
When I hear them flocking together,
I will catch them.
[13] Woe[i] to them,
because they have strayed[j] from me!
Destruction to them,
because they have rebelled against me!
I long to redeem them
but they speak about me[k] falsely.
[14] They do not cry out to me from their hearts[l]
but wail on their beds.
They slash themselves,[a] appealing to their gods
for grain and new wine,[m]
but they turn away from me.[n]
[15] I trained them and strengthened their arms,
but they plot evil[o] against me.
[16] They do not turn to the Most High;
they are like a faulty bow.[p]
Their leaders will fall by the sword
because of their insolent words.
For this they will be ridiculed[q]
in the land of Egypt.[r]

7:9 [c] Isa 1:7; Hos 8:7
7:10 [d] Hos 5:5 [e] Isa 9:13
7:11 [f] Hos 11:11 [g] Hos 5:13; 12:1
7:12 [h] Eze 12:13
7:13 [i] Hos 9:12 [j] Jer 14:10; Eze 34:4-6; Hos 9:17 [k] ver 1; Mt 23:37
7:14 [l] Jer 3:10 [m] Am 2:8 [n] Hos 13:16
7:15 [o] Na 1:9,11
7:16 [p] Ps 78:9,57 [q] Eze 23:32 [r] Hos 9:3
8:1 [s] Dt 28:49; Jer 4:13 [t] Hos 4:6; 6:7

Israel to Reap the Whirlwind

8 "Put the trumpet to your lips!
An eagle[s] is over the house of the LORD
because the people have broken my covenant
and rebelled against my law.[t]

[a] *14* Some Hebrew manuscripts and Septuagint; most Hebrew manuscripts *They gather together*

Desperate attempts to avoid defeat at the hands of the menacing Assyrian Empire reveal Israel's assumption that their God would not save them but that they could save themselves by diplomacy and alliances.
7:11 Egypt ... Assyria. The superpowers of Hosea's day. The Israelites tried to play them against one another. It was a desperate strategy, one doomed to fail (cf. Isa 30:2–7; 31:1–6; Jer 2:17–19; Lam 5:6).
7:12–16 God would not allow his people to escape their well-deserved punishment for ignoring him and disobeying his covenant, both over the centuries and during their last decades. Nevertheless, he always longs to "redeem" (rescue, reclaim, repossess) those who have turned away from him (Rom 10:21). But for northern Israel in Hosea's day, it was too late.
7:16 They do not turn to the Most High. Their stubbornness meant exile. **Egypt.** The land of Israel's original captivity, so in the OT it sometimes symbolizes any enslavement (e.g., 8:13; 11:5; Deut 28:68). Israel was not literally exiled to Egypt at this time, but was exiled to Mesopotamia (2 Kgs 17:23).
8:1–14 *Israel to Reap the Whirlwind.* This section of the prophecy predicts punishments that God would mete out to Israel for various covenant violations, including ignoring and/or rejecting God, political

8:4 [u]Hos 13:10 [v]Hos 2:8 **8:5** [w]Hos 10:5 [x]Jer 13:27 **8:7** [y]Pr 22:8; Isa 66:15; Hos 10:12-13; Na 1:3 [z]Hos 2:9 **8:8** [a]Jer 51:34 [b]Jer 22:28 **8:10** [c]Eze 16:37; 22:20 [d]Jer 42:2 **8:11** [e]Hos 10:1; 12:11

2 Israel cries out to me,
'Our God, we acknowledge you!'
3 But Israel has rejected what is good;
an enemy will pursue him.
4 They set up kings without my consent;
they choose princes without my approval.[u]
With their silver and gold
they make idols[v] for themselves
to their own destruction.
5 Samaria, throw out your calf-idol![w]
My anger burns against them.
How long will they be incapable of purity?[x]
6 They are from Israel!
This calf — a metalworker has made it;
it is not God.
It will be broken in pieces,
that calf of Samaria.

7 "They sow the wind
and reap the whirlwind.[y]
The stalk has no head;
it will produce no flour.
Were it to yield grain,
foreigners would swallow it up.[z]
8 Israel is swallowed up;[a]
now she is among the nations
like something no one wants.[b]
9 For they have gone up to Assyria
like a wild donkey wandering alone.
Ephraim has sold herself to lovers.
10 Although they have sold themselves among the nations,
I will now gather them together.[c]
They will begin to waste away[d]
under the oppression of the mighty king.

11 "Though Ephraim built many altars for sin offerings,
these have become altars for sinning.[e]

intrigue that relied on human maneuvering and not on God's protection, idolatry, dependence on alliances with foreign powers rather than the Lord, improper worship, and trusting in material and military assets rather than God.

8:1–6 *Punishments for Political Intrigue and Idolatry.* In the political sphere, Israel had sought national stability by changing kings via assassination (e.g., 2 Kgs 15:10,14,25,30). In the religious sphere, manufacture and worship of idols was being counted on to save the nation — something it could never do.

8:1 trumpet. An instrument used to announce danger or war (as in 5:8). **eagle.** A bird of prey; it was not differentiated in Hebrew from the vulture, and either one can be in view here as a metaphor of danger "over the house of the LORD," a way of saying that Israel's relationship to God was in trouble.

8:3 enemy. Assyria.

8:4a They set up kings without my consent. God alone expected to choose Israel's kings, who were to be obedient to his covenant (Deut 17:14–20). The last several kings of (northern) Israel, however, had been chosen by political intrigue of one sort or another without concern for such requirements. This was sometimes true of earlier kings as well, but not so consistently as in the case of the final six kings of Israel (2 Kgs 15:8 — 17:4).

8:4b Idols. Including the calf-idols that Jeroboam I introduced to northern Israel (1 Kgs 12:28–30). **destruction.** The result of idolatry.

8:5 Samaria. Northern Israel, here designated by the name of its most prominent city. **incapable of purity.** This describes idolaters; their idolatry polluted their worship (cf. Ps 135:15–18).

8:7–10 *Israel Under Foreign Control.* Relying on foreigners, who cared nothing for them, was fatal for Israel and led to their complete conquest by Assyria in 722 BC.

8:8–10 Although it temporarily bought off Assyria in 732 BC to save part of its territory from annexation (see 5:13–14 and note), northern Israel eventually ran out of tribute money (2 Kgs 17:4) and was more useful to Assyria as part of its empire than as an independent nation, so by 722 BC it was "swallowed up ... among the nations" (Hos 8:8). Thereafter, each successive mighty king of Assyria, beginning with Shalmaneser (2 Kgs 17:3–6), ruled Israel.

8:11–14 *False Worship and Misplaced Trust Bring Disaster.* The offering

[12] I wrote for them the many things of my law,
but they regarded them as something foreign.
[13] Though they offer sacrifices as gifts to me,
and though they eat[f] the meat,
the LORD is not pleased with them.
Now he will remember[g] their wickedness
and punish their sins:[h]
They will return to Egypt.[i]
[14] Israel has forgotten[j] their Maker
and built palaces;
Judah has fortified many towns.
But I will send fire on their cities
that will consume their fortresses."[k]

8:13 [f] Jer 7:21 [g] Hos 7:2 [h] Hos 4:9 [i] Hos 9:3,6
8:14 [j] Dt 32:18; Hos 2:13 [k] Jer 17:27
9:1 [l] Isa 22:12-13 [m] Hos 10:5
9:2 [n] Hos 2:9
9:3 [o] Lev 25:23 [p] Hos 8:13 [q] Eze 4:13; Hos 7:11
9:4 [r] Jer 6:20; Hos 8:13 [s] Hag 2:13-14
9:5 [t] Isa 10:3; Jer 5:31 [u] Hos 2:11
9:6 [v] Isa 19:13

Punishment for Israel

9 Do not rejoice, Israel;
do not be jubilant[l] like the other nations.
For you have been unfaithful[m] to your God;
you love the wages of a prostitute
at every threshing floor.
[2] Threshing floors and winepresses will not feed the people;
the new wine[n] will fail them.
[3] They will not remain[o] in the LORD's land;
Ephraim will return to Egypt[p]
and eat unclean food in Assyria.[q]
[4] They will not pour out wine offerings to the LORD,
nor will their sacrifices please[r] him.
Such sacrifices will be to them like the bread of mourners;
all who eat them will be unclean.[s]
This food will be for themselves;
it will not come into the temple of the LORD.

[5] What will you do[t] on the day of your appointed festivals,[u]
on the feast days of the LORD?
[6] Even if they escape from destruction,
Egypt will gather them,
and Memphis[v] will bury them.

altar at the Jerusalem temple was legitimate, but pagan altars were forbidden by God. Sacrifices made to God on these altars displeased God (v. 13). The result: Israel would go into exile.

8:11 altars for sinning. Pagan altars.

8:13 return to Egypt. A metaphor for going into foreign exile (see 7:16 and note).

8:14 palaces ... fortresses. People often trust in political, material, and military power rather than in God (cf. Pss 20:7; 49:6–7; 1 Tim 6:7; Rev 18:19). The results are temporary; they bring false security instead of true refuge. When the time came, the Assyrians broke down and burned the palaces and the fortresses that both Israel and Judah had erected at great effort and expense (cf. Mic 1:8–16).

9:1–8 *Punishment for Israel.* The culture of northern Israel had become sufficiently pagan by Hosea's day that the country was generally characterized by sin, not decency (1:2; 4:1–2). Since the Mosaic covenant predicted exile for just such a situation (e.g., Lev 26:33–44; Deut 4:27; 28:36–37,63–68), various images of exile and its sad consequences appear here.

9:1–4 *Multiple Sins.* As in 2:5,8,12, Israel attributed its successful harvests (a main source of wealth in any agrarian society) to its idolatry and thus was "unfaithful to ... God" (9:1). God's blessing by abundant harvests in northern Israel will soon be a thing of the past, when their threshing floors and winepresses will lie empty and the people will be exiled to Assyria.

9:1 wages of a prostitute. Tainted money in ancient Israel (Deut 23:18), so the phrase is sometimes used to refer to improperly earned wealth (cf. Mic 1:7), but in this context the image contributes to the theme of unfaithfulness to God that runs throughout the prophecy.

9:3 Egypt ... Assyria. Israel will be exiled figuratively to Egypt (see note on 7:16) and literally to Assyria. **unclean food.** Food prohibited by the dietary laws of the covenant (cf. Lev 11; Deut 14).

9:4 not come into the temple of the LORD. In Assyria the people would have no place to offer sacrifices to the Lord.

9:5–8 *Multiple Deprivations.* Little was left of true religious practice once the Assyrians fully conquered Israel.

9:5 festivals. The three great annual festivals (Passover, Pentecost/Weeks, and Tabernacles), as well as other "feast days" beloved to the Israelites (see Lev 23), could no longer be celebrated during the exile.

9:6 [w] Isa 5:6; Hos 10:8
9:7 [x] Isa 34:8; Jer 10:15; Mic 7:4 [y] Jer 16:18 [z] Isa 44:25; La 2:14; Eze 14:9-10
9:8 [a] Hos 5:1
9:9 [b] Jdg 19:16-30; Hos 5:8; 10:9 [c] Hos 8:13
9:10 [d] Nu 25:1-5; Ps 106:28-29 [e] Jer 11:13; Hos 4:14
9:11 [f] Hos 4:7; 10:5 [g] ver 14
9:12 [h] Hos 7:13 [i] Dt 31:17
9:13 [j] Eze 27:3

Their treasures of silver will be taken over by briers,
and thorns[w] will overrun their tents.
7 The days of punishment[x] are coming,
the days of reckoning are at hand.
Let Israel know this.
Because your sins[y] are so many
and your hostility so great,
the prophet is considered a fool,[z]
the inspired person a maniac.
8 The prophet, along with my God,
is the watchman over Ephraim,[a]
yet snares[a] await him on all his paths,
and hostility in the house of his God.
9 They have sunk deep into corruption,
as in the days of Gibeah.[b]
God will remember[c] their wickedness
and punish them for their sins.

10 "When I found Israel,
it was like finding grapes in the desert;
when I saw your ancestors,
it was like seeing the early fruit on the fig tree.
But when they came to Baal Peor,[d]
they consecrated themselves to that shameful idol[e]
and became as vile as the thing they loved.
11 Ephraim's glory will fly away like a bird[f]—
no birth, no pregnancy, no conception.[g]
12 Even if they rear children,
I will bereave them of every one.
Woe[h] to them
when I turn away from them![i]
13 I have seen Ephraim, like Tyre,
planted in a pleasant place.[j]
But Ephraim will bring out
their children to the slayer."

[a] 8 Or *The prophet is the watchman over Ephraim, / the people of my God*

9:7 days of punishment. The time in exile.
9:8 The prophet ... is the watchman. In the late eighth century BC, the Israelites were so paganized that they ignored the watchman-like warnings of any true prophet (not merely Hosea) and instead showed him only hostility. **hostility in the house of his God.** Probably the Jerusalem temple, since it is unlikely that the temple at Bethel would have been described by Hosea as a legitimate house of God. This was where, of all places, prophets should have been honored.
9:9—13:16 *Judgment Warnings With a Retrospective Tone.* From 9:9 onward, the book continues to remind Israel of their covenant-violating sin and their impending doom via exile, but it does so with a special focus on the past. What *might* have been (obeying God) is often compared to what *actually* happened (repeatedly rejecting God). The long history of Israel's rebellion against her divine savior is sampled, showing that God was always faithful even though Israel rarely was.
9:9–17 *Ephraim Rejected, Exiled, and Unloved.* Gibeah (cf. 10:9), Baal Peor, and Gilgal exemplify places where false worship by Israelites flourished in past times. Israel's history reveals that they have long been a nation that ignored their potential to love and serve the true God; instead they were typically rebellious and sinful.
9:9 Gibeah. A city in Benjamin and the site of the horrendous gang rape and murder of the wife of a Levite who expected safety there in the days of the judges (Judg 19). When the tribe of Benjamin actually defended Gibeah's sin, the rest of Israel was at first unable to bring them to justice, but then imposed judgment so severe it brought the tribe of Benjamin to the edge of extinction (Judg 20–21). This demonstrated the general corruption of the chosen people.
9:10 Baal Peor. The site of an idolatrous orgy during the days of the wandering in the wilderness (Num 25); there Israelite men had ritual sex with Moabite women, obviously violating God's law. Again a past sin shows that Israelite rebellion against God in Hosea's day is nothing new.
9:11 no birth, no pregnancy, no conception. Infertility was one of the predicted punishments for failure to keep the Mosaic covenant (e.g., Deut 28:18). That it would be widespread in Israel signaled God's judgment in the old covenant.
9:12 I will bereave them of every one. Losing children in this instance is the result of national sin and fulfills a common Mosaic covenant prediction (Deut 28:32,41; 32:25). Conquest often resulted in infant deaths (Hos 10:14; 13:16; 2 Kgs 8:12; Isa 13:16), and exile typically separated children from their parents.

[14] Give them, LORD—
what will you give them?
Give them wombs that miscarry
and breasts that are dry.[k]

[15] "Because of all their wickedness in Gilgal,[l]
I hated them there.
Because of their sinful deeds,[m]
I will drive them out of my house.
I will no longer love them;
all their leaders are rebellious.[n]
[16] Ephraim[o] is blighted,
their root is withered,
they yield no fruit.[p]
Even if they bear children,
I will slay[q] their cherished offspring."

[17] My God will reject them
because they have not obeyed[r] him;
they will be wanderers among the nations.[s]

10
Israel was a spreading vine;[t]
he brought forth fruit for himself.
As his fruit increased,
he built more altars;[u]
as his land prospered,
he adorned his sacred stones.[v]
[2] Their heart is deceitful,[w]
and now they must bear their guilt.[x]
The LORD will demolish their altars[y]
and destroy their sacred stones.[z]

[3] Then they will say, "We have no king
because we did not revere the LORD.
But even if we had a king,
what could he do for us?"
[4] They make many promises,
take false oaths[a]
and make agreements;[b]
therefore lawsuits spring up
like poisonous weeds in a plowed field.
[5] The people who live in Samaria fear
for the calf-idol of Beth Aven.[a][c]

9:14 [k] ver 11; Lk 23:29
9:15 [l] Hos 4:15 [m] Hos 7:2 [n] Isa 1:23; Hos 4:9; 5:2
9:16 [o] Hos 5:11 [p] Hos 8:7 [q] ver 12
9:17 [r] Hos 4:10 [s] Dt 28:65; Hos 7:13
10:1 [t] Eze 15:2 [u] 1Ki 14:23 [v] Hos 8:11; 12:11
10:2 [w] 1Ki 18:21 [x] Hos 13:16 [y] ver 8 [z] Mic 5:13
10:4 [a] Hos 4:2 [b] Eze 17:19; Am 5:7
10:5 [c] Hos 5:8

[a] 5 *Beth Aven* means *house of wickedness* (a derogatory name for Bethel, which means *house of God*).

9:15 Gilgal. The first place west of the Jordan where the Israelites set their feet in their conquest of the promised land (Josh 4:19–24). They eventually turned it into an illegitimate worship center that still functioned in Hosea's day (Hos 4:15; 12:11; cf. Amos 4:4).
9:17 wanderers among the nations. The land of Israel, including Judah, was the only true home of God's chosen people in OT times. For the (northern) Israelites to be exiled from it meant being homeless ("wanderers"), forcibly relocated to a foreign place.
10:1–8 *No More Cult, Kingship, or Capital.* This section of Hosea's prophecies concentrates on how God would destroy central factors in the life of northern Israel—its religion, its government, and even its capital city Samaria—in consequence of a long history of national sin.
10:1 As his fruit increased, he built more altars. Instead of using their agricultural success in Canaan to glorify God as the land prospered, the Israelites attributed it to polytheistic idolatry and built forbidden altars for the worship of pagan gods in violation of Deut 12:1–14 (cf. 2 Kgs 21:3–4).
10:2 sacred stones. Objects of worship, including idols made of stone.
10:3 no king … what could he do for us? In exile the Israelites will not have a king of their own but will suffer under foreign domination so complete that even if they had a king, he would be powerless.
10:4 false oaths … lawsuits. Because so many in Israel had ignored the honesty and fair dealings required by the Mosaic covenant, the people's moral and legal problems multiplied.
10:5 Beth Aven. The name means "house of wickedness" and mockingly

10:5 [d]2Ki 23:5 [e]Hos 8:5; 9:1,3,11 **10:6** [f]Hos 11:5 [g]Hos 5:13 [h]Isa 30:3; Hos 4:7 **10:7** [i]Hos 13:11 **10:8** [j]1Ki 12:28-30; Hos 4:13 [k]Hos 9:6 [l]ver 2; Isa 32:13 [m]Lk 23:30*; Rev 6:16 **10:9** [n]Hos 5:8 **10:10** [o]Eze 5:13; Hos 4:9 **10:12** [p]Pr 11:18 [q]Jer 4:3 [r]Hos 12:6 [s]Isa 45:8

Its people will mourn over it,
  and so will its idolatrous priests,[d]
those who had rejoiced over its splendor,
  because it is taken from them into exile.[e]
6 It will be carried to Assyria[f]
  as tribute for the great king.[g]
Ephraim will be disgraced;[h]
  Israel will be ashamed of its foreign alliances.
7 Samaria's king will be destroyed,[i]
  swept away like a twig on the surface of the
    waters.
8 The high places of wickedness[a][j] will be destroyed—
  it is the sin of Israel.
Thorns[k] and thistles will grow up
  and cover their altars.[l]
Then they will say to the mountains, "Cover us!"
  and to the hills, "Fall on us!"[m]

9 "Since the days of Gibeah,[n] you have sinned, Israel,
  and there you have remained.[b]
Will not war again overtake
  the evildoers in Gibeah?
10 When I please, I will punish[o] them;
  nations will be gathered against them
  to put them in bonds for their double sin.
11 Ephraim is a trained heifer
  that loves to thresh;
so I will put a yoke
  on her fair neck.
I will drive Ephraim,
  Judah must plow,
  and Jacob must break up the ground.
12 Sow righteousness[p] for yourselves,
  reap the fruit of unfailing love,
and break up your unplowed ground;[q]
  for it is time to seek[r] the LORD,
until he comes
  and showers his righteousness[s] on you.

[a] *8* Hebrew *aven,* a reference to Beth Aven (a derogatory name for Bethel); see verse 5. [b] *9* Or *there a stand was taken*

refers to Bethel (see NIV text note), where the people worshiped a golden calf-idol (1 Kgs 12:28–30).

10:6 tribute. Conquerors routinely required gold and other payments from their victims, so the calf-idol will be "taken from them" (v. 5) to Assyria.

10:7 Samaria's king. Israel's last king, Hoshea (2 Kgs 17:1–6), will be "swept away."

10:8 high places. Pagan worship centers were usually located on hills (as most habitations in ancient Israel were, for safety) and constituted "places of wickedness" for Israelites. Ironically, God's coming judgment would cause people to wish for instant death by burial under "mountains" or "hills," as will also be the case when Christ returns in judgment (Luke 23:30).

10:9–15 *Inevitable War Against Israel for Its History of Wickedness.* Although northern Israel's destruction was certain, Hosea still urges righteous individuals to repent and seek the Lord since a future larger and longer than merely earthly life is regularly in view in the Bible. The temporal judgment of a nation is not the same as the eternal judgment of each of its individuals (cf. Ezek 33:1–20; Acts 2:40).

10:9 war ... evildoers in Gibeah. War followed the past sins of the people of Gibeah (Judg 19–21), and that historical model serves to illustrate the coming conquest by Assyria.

10:10 nations will be gathered against them. Assyria had people from many nations in its army. **double sin.** Very great sin.

10:11 yoke ... plow. Both Ephraim and later Judah will be made to toil in exile like animals bound by a yoke and forced to plow.

10:12 Sow righteousness ... seek the LORD. Individuals and groups could still repent in faith and keep God's covenant while awaiting return from exile.

[13]But you have planted wickedness,
you have reaped evil,[t]
you have eaten the fruit of deception.
Because you have depended on your own strength
and on your many warriors,[u]
[14]the roar of battle will rise against your people,
so that all your fortresses will be devastated[v] —
as Shalman devastated Beth Arbel on the day of battle,
when mothers were dashed to the ground with their children.[w]
[15]So will it happen to you, Bethel,
because your wickedness is great.
When that day dawns,
the king of Israel will be completely destroyed.[x]

God's Love for Israel

11 "When Israel was a child, I loved him,
and out of Egypt I called my son.[y]
[2]But the more they were called,
the more they went away from me.[a]
They sacrificed to the Baals[z]
and they burned incense to images.[a]
[3]It was I who taught Ephraim to walk,
taking them by the arms;[b]
but they did not realize
it was I who healed[c] them.
[4]I led them with cords of human kindness,
with ties of love.[d]
To them I was like one who lifts
a little child to the cheek,
and I bent down to feed[e] them.

[5]"Will they not return to Egypt[f]
and will not Assyria[g] rule over them
because they refuse to repent?
[6]A sword[h] will flash in their cities;
it will devour their false prophets
and put an end to their plans.

10:13 [t] Job 4:8; Hos 7:3; 11:12; Gal 6:7-8 [u] Ps 33:16
10:14 [v] Isa 17:3 [w] Hos 13:16
10:15 [x] ver 7
11:1 [y] Ex 4:22; Hos 12:9,13; 13:4; Mt 2:15*
11:2 [z] Hos 2:13 [a] 2Ki 17:15; Isa 65:7; Jer 18:15
11:3 [b] Dt 1:31; Hos 7:15 [c] Jer 30:17
11:4 [d] Jer 31:2-3 [e] Ex 16:32; Ps 78:25
11:5 [f] Hos 7:16 [g] Hos 10:6
11:6 [h] Hos 13:16

a 2 Septuagint; Hebrew *them*

10:14–15 Beth Arbel. The story of Beth Arbel's destruction by someone named Shalman, whose identity is not known today but who was obviously well-known to Hosea's audience, was a fitting reminder of the sort of thing God was about to do to northern Israel's chief worship center, Bethel (1 Kgs 12:32–33; Amos 3:14; 7:13), as well as all its "fortresses," when "the king of Israel will be completely destroyed" and the nation subjugated by its enemies.

11:1–11 *God's Love for Israel.* The nation's long history with Egypt provides a backdrop for past and future blessings, apostasy, and coming punishment. "Egypt" thus appears at the beginning (v. 1), middle (v. 5) and end (v. 11) of this section of prophecy.

11:1–7 *Out of Captivity in the Past and Back Again in the Future.* At many places in the OT, God's deliverance of his people from Egypt is remembered as a signature indication of his mercy and of Israel's indebtedness to him, as it is here. But the OT also tells the story of how the Israelites eventually squandered that mercy, rebelled against their deliverer, and so were handed over to foreign oppressors, as Hosea predicts here.

11:1 out of Egypt I called my son. Although the immediate focus of this passage is Israel's exodus from Egypt (Israel is God's "son"; cf. Exod 4:22–23), Matt 2:15 shows us that it also has a future, typological focus: Jesus' return from Egypt as a child identified him with his people and their deliverance through him.

11:3–4 I … taught … healed … led. Israel's rebellion could not be blamed on God. He had done nothing but good for them as a faithful and loving father, even while they "went away" from him (v. 2) to believe in and worship other gods.

11:5 return to Egypt. The coming exile, again expressed symbolically as if the destination were Egypt, took Israelites mainly to Assyria (see 7:16; 9:3 and notes). But some Judahites did flee voluntarily to Egypt (Jer 41:16–18).

11:6 sword. A symbol of war (cf. Rev 6:8). It would all start with war.

11:7 [i] Jer 3:6-7; 8:5
11:8 [j] Hos 6:4 [k] Ge 14:8
11:9 [l] Dt 13:17; Jer 30:11 [m] Mal 3:6 [n] Nu 23:19
11:10 [o] Hos 6:1-3
11:11 [p] Isa 11:11 [q] Eze 28:26
11:12 [r] Hos 4:2
12:1 [s] Eze 17:10

7 My people are determined to turn from me.[i]
Even though they call me God Most High,
I will by no means exalt them.

8 "How can I give you up, Ephraim?[j]
How can I hand you over, Israel?
How can I treat you like Admah?
How can I make you like Zeboyim?[k]
My heart is changed within me;
all my compassion is aroused.
9 I will not carry out my fierce anger,[l]
nor will I devastate[m] Ephraim again.
For I am God, and not a man[n]—
the Holy One among you.
I will not come against their cities.
10 They will follow the LORD;
he will roar like a lion.
When he roars,
his children will come trembling from the west.[o]
11 They will come from Egypt,
trembling like sparrows,
from Assyria,[p] fluttering like doves.
I will settle them in their homes,"[q]
declares the LORD.

Israel's Sin

12 Ephraim has surrounded me with lies,[r]
Israel with deceit.
And Judah is unruly against God,
even against the faithful Holy One.[a]

12[b]
1 Ephraim feeds on the wind;[s]
he pursues the east wind all day
and multiplies lies and violence.

[a] *12* In Hebrew texts this verse (11:12) is numbered 12:1. [b] In Hebrew texts 12:1-14 is numbered 12:2-15.

11:7 God Most High. The Israelites hypocritically flattered their national God with perfectly good terms but also trusted in the overly positive words of "false prophets" (v. 6) and turned from the Lord to idolatry and polytheism.

11:8–11 *Rescue by Grace From Captivity.* Hosea reminds Israel of future blessing even in the broader context of predicting dire judgments. Restoration promises like these reveal how great God's love is, since he is willing, according to his grace and not any deeds that the Israelites could perform, to redeem to himself people who had once rebelled against him in all sorts of ways. God's holiness shines brightly here as well: Lest his audience think that the only thing in store for God's people in the future is destruction and rejection, Hosea conveys God's plan for restoration after the coming exile—not because his people will have made themselves holy, but because he will credit them with the holiness of his beloved Son. Promises of return and reunification are encouraging prophetic assurances about the latter days, i.e., the time of the new covenant.

11:8 Admah ... Zeboyim. Cities near Sodom and Gomorrah (Gen 10:19), destroyed for their outrageous sins during the time of Lot and Abraham (Gen 19:1–29; Deut 29:23).

11:10 They will follow the LORD. Although these verses are primarily about the restoration of Israel/Ephraim, the hope expressed in these verses does not end there. Restoration is something available now as well, only by following Christ as taught in the NT. **from the west ... from Egypt ... from Assyria.** God's people are no longer merely ethnic Israel but are "from the west" (including distant lands across the sea) and "from Egypt" (the south) and "from Assyria" (the east), all idiomatic ways of describing a worldwide people not limited by location or nationality.

11:12—12:14 *Israel's Sin.* Using a variety of images for Israel's rebellion against God and his covenant, Hosea continues to show how deeply the nation remained mired in their disobedience to "the faithful Holy One" (11:12).

11:12—12:10 *Israel's Deceit in Contrast to the Lord's Faithfulness.* Three extended examples of Israel's deceit against the Lord are combined with three extended examples of the Lord's faithfulness to them in a covenant "lawsuit" (see 2:2–23; 4:1–19 and notes) that results in judgment for the wayward people of God.

11:12—12:1 lies ... deceit ... unruly ... multiplies lies. Israel/Ephraim (cf. 4:16–17; 5:3; 11:8) and Judah repeatedly promised to keep God's covenant, so when they broke it by idolatry, polytheism, and forbidden foreign alliances and business dealings (Exod 34:12,15; Deut 17:16) with Assyria and Egypt, they opened themselves to the covenant lawsuit charges that follow in 12:2–14.

He makes a treaty with Assyria
and sends olive oil to Egypt.[t]
2 The LORD has a charge[u] to bring against Judah;
he will punish Jacob[a] according to his ways
and repay him according to his deeds.[v]
3 In the womb he grasped his brother's heel;[w]
as a man he struggled[x] with God.
4 He struggled with the angel and overcame him;
he wept and begged for his favor.
He found him at Bethel[y]
and talked with him there—
5 the LORD God Almighty,
the LORD is his name![z]
6 But you must return to your God;
maintain love and justice,[a]
and wait for your God always.[b]

7 The merchant uses dishonest scales[c]
and loves to defraud.
8 Ephraim boasts,
"I am very rich; I have become wealthy.[d]
With all my wealth they will not find in me
any iniquity or sin."

9 "I have been the LORD your God
ever since you came out of Egypt;[e]
I will make you live in tents[f] again,
as in the days of your appointed festivals.
10 I spoke to the prophets,
gave them many visions
and told parables[g] through them."[h]

11 Is Gilead wicked?[i]
Its people are worthless!
Do they sacrifice bulls in Gilgal?[j]
Their altars will be like piles of stones
on a plowed field.[k]
12 Jacob fled to the country of Aram[b];[l]
Israel served to get a wife,
and to pay for her he tended sheep.[m]
13 The LORD used a prophet to bring Israel up from Egypt,
by a prophet he cared for him.[n]

12:1 [t] 2Ki 17:4
12:2 [u] Mic 6:2 [v] Hos 4:9
12:3 [w] Ge 25:26 [x] Ge 32:24-29
12:4 [y] Ge 28:12-15; 35:15
12:5 [z] Ex 3:15
12:6 [a] Mic 6:8 [b] Hos 6:1-3; 10:12; Mic 7:7
12:7 [c] Am 8:5
12:8 [d] Ps 62:10; Rev 3:17
12:9 [e] Lev 23:43; Hos 11:1 [f] Ne 8:17
12:10 [g] Eze 20:49 [h] 2Ki 17:13; Jer 7:25
12:11 [i] Hos 6:8 [j] Hos 4:15 [k] Hos 8:11
12:12 [l] Ge 28:5 [m] Ge 29:18
12:13 [n] Ex 13:3; Isa 63:11-14

[a] 2 *Jacob* means *he grasps the heel*, a Hebrew idiom for *he takes advantage of* or *he deceives*. [b] 12 That is, Northwest Mesopotamia

12:2 Judah … Jacob. Denotes all Israel.
12:3–5 These verses describe how Jacob, Israel's famous ancestor, returned to God, and all Israel must do the same. The "charge" (v. 2) begins with a reminder that God specially chose his people in the days of the patriarch Jacob. They should have returned to God in righteous obedience and been willing to trust ("wait for," v. 6) him always.
12:7–8 dishonest scales … defraud. Financial and economic corruption taints any society, and yet those who are corrupt and exploit others often hope to get away with it; (thus the words of Ephraim, "They will not find in me any iniquity"). But God is not fooled.
12:9 I will make you live in tents again. This recalls 2:14–15 (see note there) and predicts a time, after the exile, when God will again be as close to a repentant Israel as he had been during the wilderness years following the exodus from Egypt.
12:11–14 *Present Sins Against the Backdrop of Jacob and Moses.* This concludes the covenant lawsuit. Hosea contrasts Israel's sin and the resulting destruction with what Israel might have been, as shown in the former days of Jacob's blessed and protected life in "Aram" (Syria) and Moses' faithful leading of Israel "up from Egypt" (vv. 12–13).
12:11 Their altars. Where false worship took place. Israel worshiped at illegal shrines like the one at Gilgal (see 4:15; 9:15 and note), with the result that God will destroy them and their altars.

12:14 [o]Eze 18:13 [p]Da 11:18
13:1 [q]Jdg 12:1 [r]Jdg 8:1 [s]Hos 11:2
13:2 [t]Isa 46:6; Jer 10:4 [u]Isa 44:17-20
13:3 [v]Hos 6:4 [w]Isa 17:13 [x]Da 2:35 [y]Ps 68:2
13:4 [z]Hos 12:9 [a]Ex 20:3 [b]Isa 43:11; 45:21-22
13:6 [c]Dt 32:12-15; Hos 2:13
13:8 [d]2Sa 17:8 [e]Ps 50:22

14 But Ephraim has aroused his bitter anger;
his Lord will leave on him the guilt of his bloodshed[o]
and will repay him for his contempt.[p]

The Lord's Anger Against Israel

13 When Ephraim spoke, people trembled;[q]
he was exalted[r] in Israel.
But he became guilty of Baal worship[s] and died.
2 Now they sin more and more;
they make idols for themselves from their silver,[t]
cleverly fashioned images,
all of them the work of craftsmen.
It is said of these people,
"They offer human sacrifices!
They kiss[a] calf-idols![u]"
3 Therefore they will be like the morning mist,
like the early dew that disappears,[v]
like chaff[w] swirling from a threshing floor,[x]
like smoke[y] escaping through a window.

4 "But I have been the Lord your God
ever since you came out of Egypt.[z]
You shall acknowledge no God but me,[a]
no Savior[b] except me.
5 I cared for you in the wilderness,
in the land of burning heat.
6 When I fed them, they were satisfied;
when they were satisfied, they became proud;
then they forgot me.[c]
7 So I will be like a lion to them,
like a leopard I will lurk by the path.
8 Like a bear robbed of her cubs,[d]
I will attack them and rip them open;
like a lion I will devour them—
a wild animal will tear them apart.[e]

[a] 2 Or *"Men who sacrifice / kiss*

12:14 bloodshed. This term often denotes crime in general (cf. 1:4 [there translated "massacre"]; 4:2; 5:2; 6:8). It can refer to violence against people, including human sacrifice (13:2). Israel's crimes showed her contempt for God and had to be punished. This is in line with such passages as Lev 20:11–27, where the phrase "their blood will be on their own heads" describes guilt.

13:1–16 *The Lord's Anger Against Israel.* This section links Israel's tragic fall from earlier faithfulness to God to the practice of idolatry especially and to a variety of related sins that violate the Mosaic covenant.

13:1–9 *Israel's Tragic Fall via Idolatry and Coming Punishment.* Great potential may yield little without faithfulness to God's purposes since God controls the destinies of people and nations (cf. Exod 19:5–6; 1 Chr 16:14; Prov 16:9; Dan 4:35).

13:1 When Ephraim spoke, people trembled. Ephraim, both as a tribe and as a territory, was dominant ("exalted") in Israel. But Ephraim's Baal worship constituted open unfaithfulness to a faithful God and resulted in conquest, decimation, annexation, and exile so that Israel "died" as a nation. Fortunately, they would be reborn in the future via the new covenant (v. 14; 14:1–9; cf. Jer 31:31–34).

13:2 kiss calf-idols. When people in (northern) Israel sacrificed to the calf-idols at Bethel and Dan (1 Kgs 12:28–30), they would kiss them as their pagan way of displaying homage to the gods that those idols represented (cf. 1 Kgs 19:18). The NIV text note, "Men who sacrifice/kiss [calf-idols]," is a good alternative rendering of the original since the focus here seems to be not on human sacrifice but on the folly of doing something so ridiculous as "kissing cows" in order to receive a blessing.

13:3 morning mist … dew that disappears … chaff … smoke. This language describes God's judgment on Israel and is not a general statement about all humans but relates to the larger biblical teaching that human life on earth is fleeting (cf. Ps 90:3–10) compared to the eternal life God offers.

13:4–6 God's history of loving care for Israel contrasts sharply with their history of abandoning him.

13:7–9 God is the righteous Judge of all the earth (Gen 18:25; Ps 7:11; 2 Tim 4:8), who saves forever those who place their trust in him but who removes from his presence those who defy him. Various metaphoric comparisons to devouring animals ("lion," "leopard" "bear") graphically make that point.

9 "You are destroyed, Israel,
because you are against me,[f] against your helper.[g]
10 Where is your king,[h] that he may save you?
Where are your rulers in all your towns,
of whom you said,
'Give me a king and princes'?[i]
11 So in my anger I gave you a king,
and in my wrath I took him away.[j]
12 The guilt of Ephraim is stored up,
his sins are kept on record.[k]
13 Pains as of a woman in childbirth[l] come to him,
but he is a child without wisdom;
when the time arrives,
he doesn't have the sense to come out of the womb.[m]

14 "I will deliver this people from the power of the grave;[n]
I will redeem them from death.
Where, O death, are your plagues?
Where, O grave, is your destruction?[o]

"I will have no compassion,
15 even though he thrives[p] among his brothers.
An east wind[q] from the LORD will come,
blowing in from the desert;
his spring will fail
and his well dry up.[r]
His storehouse will be plundered[s]
of all its treasures.
16 The people of Samaria must bear their guilt,[t]
because they have rebelled[u] against their God.
They will fall by the sword;[v]
their little ones will be dashed[w] to the ground,
their pregnant women[x] ripped open."[a]

13:9 [f] Jer 2:17-19 [g] Dt 33:29
13:10 [h] 2Ki 17:4 [i] 1Sa 8:6; Hos 8:4
13:11 [j] 1Ki 14:10; Hos 10:7
13:12 [k] Dt 32:34
13:13 [l] Isa 13:8; Mic 4:9-10 [m] Isa 66:9
13:14 [n] Ps 49:15; Eze 37:12-13 [o] 1Co 15:55*
13:15 [p] Hos 10:1 [q] Eze 19:12 [r] Jer 51:36 [s] Jer 20:5
13:16 [t] Hos 10:2 [u] Hos 7:14 [v] Hos 11:6 [w] 2Ki 8:12; Hos 10:14 [x] 2Ki 15:16; Isa 13:16
14:1 [y] Hos 5:5

Repentance to Bring Blessing

14 [b] Return, Israel, to the LORD your God.
Your sins have been your downfall![y]
2 Take words with you
and return to the LORD.

[a] 16 In Hebrew texts this verse (13:16) is numbered 14:1. [b] In Hebrew texts 14:1-9 is numbered 14:2-10.

13:10–16 *Divine Judgment on a People Who Have No Sense.* Likening Israel to a "child without wisdom" who doesn't even have the "sense to come out of the womb" (v. 13), Hosea portrays the nation (as one might say it today) as "missing the boat" of God's goodness, and instead incurring his wrath by reason of willful disobedience.
13:10–12 God's wrath against sin is not a trifling matter. Israel's civil leaders were unable to prevent the last unconquered parts of northern Israel—those around Samaria—from being seized and annexed by the Assyrians in 722 BC. **Where is your king ... your rulers ...?** The last king of (northern) Israel, Hoshea (732/31–723/22 BC), was already in an Assyrian prison (2 Kgs 17:4–6) when the nation succumbed; its "princes" (i.e., officials) were deposed as well.
13:14 I will deliver ... I will redeem. The Hebrew original allows for either assertions or questions (Shall I deliver? ... Shall I redeem?), and the context may seem to offer little hope ("I will have no compassion"). **Where, O death ... Where, O grave.** In the new covenant, these words can be understood very differently because Christ's death on the cross has conquered death for us, and thus the wording of 1 Cor 15:55 centers on the positive sense of this verse. There, Paul helps us see that death no longer has its "plagues" and "destruction" (eternal judgment) but gives way to a blessed resurrection to eternal life.
13:15–16 east wind ... sword. These symbolize the Assyrian armies and the war of conquest and plunder that will strike Samaria. Once again, God makes abundantly clear that all this could have been avoided, but it came about because Israel "rebelled against their God."
13:16 little ones will be dashed ... pregnant women ripped open. The horrors of war, including brutality against women and children, would mark the end of the nation.
14:1–9 *Repentance to Bring Blessing.* The final section of Hosea's prophecies promises abundant blessing to the remnant of Israel

14:2 [z]Mic 7:18-19 [a]Heb 13:15
14:3 [b]Ps 33:17; Isa 31:1 [c]Hos 8:6 [d]Ps 10:14; 68:5
14:4 [e]Hos 6:1 [f]Zep 3:17
14:5 [g]SS 2:1 [h]Isa 35:2 [i]Job 29:19
14:6 [j]Ps 52:8; Jer 11:16 [k]SS 4:11
14:7 [l]Ps 91:1-4 [m]Hos 2:22 [n]Eze 17:23
14:8 [o]ver 3

Say to him:
"Forgive all our sins
and receive us graciously,[z]
that we may offer the fruit of our lips.[a][a]
3 Assyria cannot save us;
we will not mount warhorses.[b]
We will never again say 'Our gods'[c]
to what our own hands have made,
for in you the fatherless[d] find compassion."

4 "I will heal[e] their waywardness
and love them freely,[f]
for my anger has turned away from them.
5 I will be like the dew to Israel;
he will blossom like a lily.[g]
Like a cedar of Lebanon[h]
he will send down his roots;[i]
6 his young shoots will grow.
His splendor will be like an olive tree,[j]
his fragrance like a cedar of Lebanon.[k]
7 People will dwell again in his shade;[l]
they will flourish like the grain,
they will blossom like the vine—
Israel's fame will be like the wine[m] of
Lebanon.[n]
8 Ephraim, what more have I[b] to do with idols?[o]
I will answer him and care for him.
I am like a flourishing juniper;
your fruitfulness comes from me."

[a] *2* Or *offer our lips as sacrifices of bulls* [b] *8* Or Hebrew; Septuagint *What more has Ephraim*

that will one day return to God. Israel's future words of true worship (vv. 2–3) are followed by God's promise of forgiveness and great blessing (vv. 4–8).

14:1–8 *Promise to the Remnant That Will Return.* Hosea's prophecies are replete with predictions of doom for Israel in the immediate future, but by no means does this imply that the ultimate future must also be bleak. On the contrary, it will be glorious for all who repent, turn to God in faith, and place their trust in him.

14:1 Return. The Hebrew word also conveys the concept of repentance and conversion, as the NT teaches and encourages.

14:2 Forgive all our sins. Notes the comprehensiveness of the promise that all our sins can be forgiven in the wonderful era this depicts (cf. Matt 12:31). Forgiveness comes no longer by required offerings of animals, since Christ's sacrifice makes all others unnecessary. Forgiveness by faith means that worship sacrifice can include "the fruit of our lips," i.e., offerings of praise and glory to God, who alone can save us.

14:3 Assyria ... warhorses ... what our own hands have made. The repentant Israelites of the future, i.e., all who are in Christ (cf. Rom 9:6–8; Gal 3:29), will acknowledge that neither human power (e.g., "Assyria") nor military might ("warhorses") nor idols ("what our own hands have made") nor any power except the one true God can save from sin and its severe consequences. **fatherless.** Hosea metaphorically depicts God's salvation as lovingly accepting people like needy children ("fatherless"), thus showing them his eternal "compassion."

14:4 heal their waywardness and love them freely. Once God's "anger has turned away from them," repentant Israel will see his favor in great measure.

14:5–8 blossom ... cedar ... roots ... shoots ... olive tree ... grain ... vine ... wine ... juniper ... fruitfulness. Like other OT prophets, Hosea expresses God's future spiritual blessings for his people in terms of agricultural abundance. Such imagery connotes divine blessing in a vivid, tangible, memorable way (cf. Joel 3:18; Amos 9:13–15; Mic 7:14). The dry east wind from the desert (13:15) will disappear, and fruitfulness will prevail. In other words, the new covenant age will be far better than the days of the old covenant, with its failures of faith and practice (e.g., "idols," v. 8) and resulting punishments.

14:5,6,7 Lebanon. A symbol of agricultural abundance used three times in this passage because its highlands were verdant year round, even in times of drought elsewhere (Deut 3:25; 2 Kgs 19:23; Pss 72:16; 104:16), as a result of the relatively high rainfall there brought by moist westerly air from the Mediterranean.

14:8 Ephraim. The northern kingdom of Israel (see note on 4:17). This is the final time (of 37 times, the first being in 4:17) that Hosea calls northern Israel by the name of the tribe that was expected to lead Israel (note its leadership blessing in Gen 48:19–20). It was also the last tribal territory to be annexed to the Assyrian Empire. Israel had assumed that its material prosperity in Hosea's day had come from its idolatry (see Hos 2:5,8,12), but in the end the people would learn that all good things come from the one true God alone. Paul makes the same point in different words: "In him we live and move and have our being" (Acts 17:28).

9 Who is wise?[p] Let them realize these things.
Who is discerning? Let them understand.[q]
The ways of the LORD are right;[r]
the righteous walk[s] in them,
but the rebellious stumble in them.

14:9 [p] Ps 107:43 [q] Pr 10:29; Isa 1:28 [r] Ps 111:7-8; Zep 3:5; Ac 13:10 [s] Isa 26:7

14:9 *A Challenge to the Wise Reader.* The final verse of Hosea employs vocabulary often found in Proverbs and other wisdom sections of the OT ("wise," "discerning," "righteous," "rebellious") to remind readers that God's revelation through his prophet has very practical purposes: it guides people in "the ways of the LORD" so that they can live for him rather than against him (cf. 2 Tim 3:16–17). Most ancient Israelites who heard Hosea preach did not take him seriously and ran afoul of this very warning, to their sorrow. God's people must be sure that they never ignore God's Word but that it is always at work in them (1 Thess 2:13).

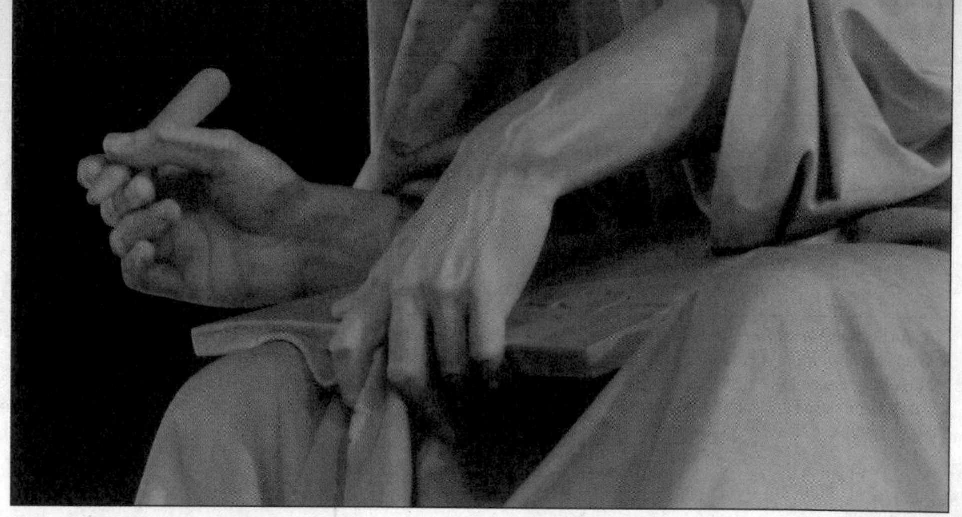

INTRODUCTION TO JOEL

God, through his prophet, uses a natural catastrophe to call his people to repentance, reminding them that they are not alone in suffering, since all the nations are under God's judgment. Israel's economy was mainly agricultural during the OT period, so locusts were a catastrophe for them. These voracious insects strip all green vegetation, leaving nothing to harvest to provide food for either people or livestock. But repentance will lead to restoration, and blessing will replace barrenness.

AUTHOR

Joel, whose name means "the LORD [Yah(weh)] is God," is the prophet through whom God speaks. He cannot be identified with any of the 12 others with the same name in the OT. His only identification in the book is through his father, who is otherwise unknown, but no date or geographic location is given. He does not appear to be strictly a court or temple prophet but one for the people since the woes he describes and the blessing he envisions affect all levels of society. His only mention outside this book is the reference to his prophecy in Acts 2:16.

DATE

The book is extremely difficult to date since its main event is an ecological crisis, a locust swarm, which was, unfortunately, too common an occurrence to provide help in dating the book. Since the prophecy mentions "Israel" so rarely, the northern kingdom of Israel had probably already suffered its exile in 722 BC, as supported by 3:2. Since the temple and its rituals were still in operation (2:17), the prophecy either precedes its destruction in 586 BC or follows its rebuilding in 516 or 515 BC. Even though its exact chronology is unclear, the book's message is timeless.

OCCASION AND PURPOSE

A natural catastrophe such as this locust swarm, threatening Judah's very existence, would have driven them to their knees, literally and theologically. How could God let this happen to his chosen people? Joel affirms the people in their emotional reaction, telling them to not only lament but repent. God will restore his people while also judging their enemies. The end focus of the prophecy is not on despair but on the God who dwells among his people.

Rather than simply being the reminder of a catastrophe, the prophecy also serves as a model. Destruction, lamentation, and repentance leading to restoration are steps applicable to many periods of existence, both for a nation and for an individual. The prophecy can well serve as a liturgy for life.

GENRE AND STRUCTURE

As prophecy, Joel is mainly poetic, and as such employs techniques such as simile (1:8,15; 2:2,3b – 5,7,9) and metaphor (1:6,10,12,19; 2:3a,13,21,25,28 – 29; 3:13,16,18). It remembers times of calamity past (1:2 — 2:27) in anticipation of future judgment (2:28 — 3:21), frequently reusing words and motifs throughout the book, showing its conceptual unity. It twice details the precipitating event for Judah, a devastating swarm of locusts (1:2–12; 2:1–11), with subsequent calls to lament and repent (1:13–20; 2:12–17), after which the Lord promises restoration and blessing (2:18–27). The pattern is modified, though on a more global scale, with the impending judgment upon the nations (2:28—3:16). This judgment is not mitigated since there is no mention of international repentance, though God will restore and bless his people who repent (3:17–21).

THEMES AND THEOLOGY

The Lord, Yahweh, the God of Israel, unites this book from beginning (twice in 1:1 [once within the prophet's name, see Author]) to end (3:21). His name occurs 33 times, and the common noun "God" occurs 11 times. He is referred to in other ways over 50 times. This averages more than one reference to Israel's God per verse of the book. The book highlights specific areas of God's activities that relate to time (the "day of the LORD") and to place (Zion).

The "day of the LORD" plays an important part in the theology of Joel (1:15; 2:1,11,31; 3:14; see also 2:2,29; 3:1,18). Israel anticipated it as a time for God to bless his people (Amos 5:18). False prophets twisted the concept, suggesting that simply being God's chosen people, Israel, was sufficient to trigger this blessing. It did not matter how the people acted in relation to the covenant requirements (Jer 14:13–15; Mic 3:5); sinner or saint, Israel would be blessed. But faithfulness, not ancestry, brings blessing. A lack of faithfulness, whether by Israel (2:31–32) or anyone else (3:11–16), brings judgment and punishment. The day can focus on different time periods, depending on its context. In some cases it refers to an eschatological, epoch-changing event at the end of this age that ushers in the age to come (2:31), while at other times it refers to smaller and closer cataclysmic events in which God intervenes in history (1:15; 2:1,11; 3:14; 1 Cor 1:8; 2 Thess 2:2; 2 Pet 3:10). The latter prefigure and anticipate the former.

A key location is Zion (2:1,15,23,32; 3:16,17,21) the location of the temple in Jerusalem (2:32; 3:1,6,16,17,20). As the site of God's dwelling (3:17), the temple is the source of blessing when God's people follow him (2:15,23,32; 3:1,17,20–21). The prophecy also warns of destructive judgment when God's people turn their back on their covenant promises to him (2:1; 3:16,21).

LOCATIONS IN JOEL

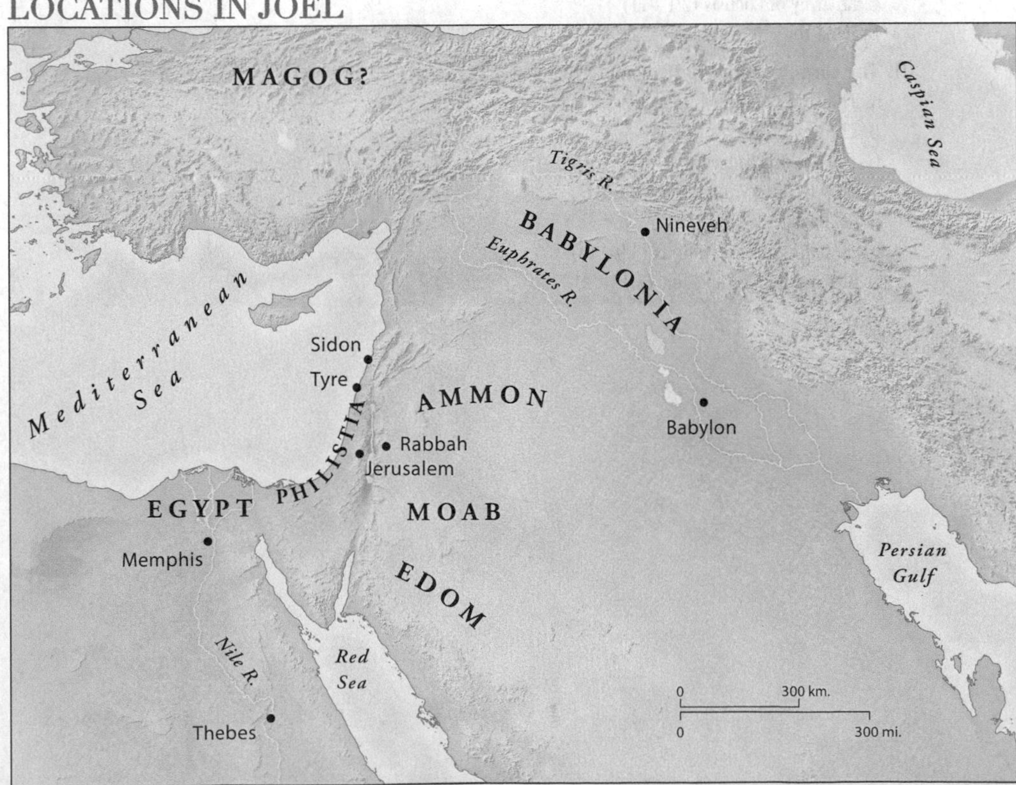

Fifteenth-century BC Tomb of Nahkt of Thebes showing an abundant grape harvest. The Lord took pity on his people and promised that their "vats will overflow with new wine" (Joel 2:24).

Z. Radovan/www.BibleLandPictures.com

OUTLINE

I. Heading (1:1)

II. The Lord's Call to Judah to Lament and Repent (1:2 — 2:17)

- A. An Invasion of Locusts (1:2 – 12)
- B. A Call to Lamentation (1:13 – 20)
- C. An Army of Locusts (2:1 – 11)
- D. Rend Your Heart (2:12 – 17)

III. The Lord Responds to His People (2:18 — 3:21)

- A. The Lord's Answer (2:18 – 27)
- B. The Day of the Lord (2:28 – 32)
- C. The Nations Judged (3:1 – 16)
  1. Why They Are Judged (3:1 – 3)
  2. Payback (3:4 – 8)
  3. Calling to the Nations (3:9 – 16)
- D. Blessing for God's People (3:17 – 21)

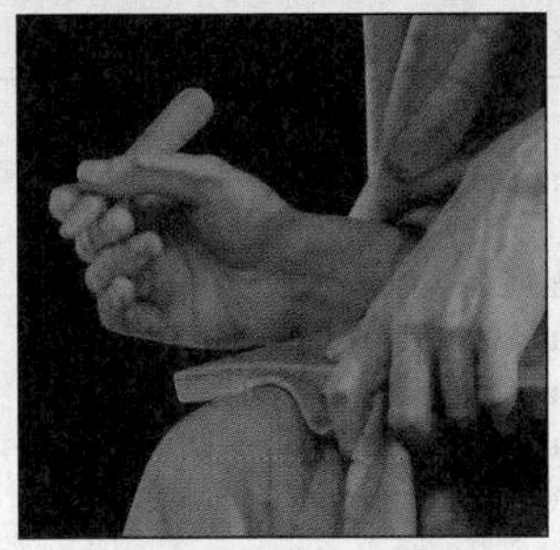

JOEL

1 The word of the Lord that came[a] to Joel[b] son of Pethuel.

An Invasion of Locusts

[2] Hear this,[c] you elders;
listen, all who live in the land.[d]
Has anything like this ever happened in your days
or in the days of your ancestors?[e]
[3] Tell it to your children,[f]
and let your children tell it to their children,
and their children to the next generation.
[4] What the locust swarm has left
the great locusts have eaten;
what the great locusts have left
the young locusts have eaten;
what the young locusts have left
other locusts[a] have eaten.[g]

[5] Wake up, you drunkards, and weep!
Wail, all you drinkers of wine;[h]
wail because of the new wine,
for it has been snatched from your lips.
[6] A nation has invaded my land,
a mighty army without number;[i]

1:1 [a] Jer 1:2 [b] Ac 2:16
1:2 [c] Hos 5:1 [d] Hos 4:1 [e] Joel 2:2
1:3 [f] Ex 10:2; Ps 78:4
1:4 [g] Dt 28:39; Na 3:15
1:5 [h] Joel 3:3
1:6 [i] Joel 2:2,11,25

[a] 4 The precise meaning of the four Hebrew words used here for locusts is uncertain.

1:1 *Heading.* This verse introduces both the source and recipient of the message of the book.
1:1 The word of the Lord. The divine origin of the prophetic message of challenge and comfort is Israel's God. This description of origin is common, occurring in every prophetic book except Daniel, Obadiah, Nahum, and Habakkuk.
1:2—2:17 *The Lord's Call to Judah to Lament and Repent.* God uses a natural disaster that threatens their very existence in order to call them back to himself.
1:2–12 *An Invasion of Locusts.* The Lord addresses the entire nation, leaders at the top of the social scale (vv. 2,9), workers in the middle (v. 11), and drunks at the bottom (v. 5). He describes in painful detail the havoc wrought by a scourge of locusts, affecting not only their physical livelihood but also their religious ritual.
1:2 elders. Old folk among those "who live in the land" (possibly leaders). They hear a message relevant not only to them but also to generations far into the future (v. 3). **Has ... this ever happened ...?** A rhetorical question inviting them to participate in the sermon by acknowledging that something unprecedented has happened.
1:4 locusts. A species of grasshopper that migrates in massive swarms, devouring fields and crops. Farmers like the Israelites were especially vulnerable to natural pests such as locusts since they had few preventive measures against them. The various locust types mentioned could be different species, but they more likely describe different stages of the locust life cycle. These are actual insects like those that plagued the Egyptians (Exod 10:1–20), not allegorical depictions of invading nations as some interpreters hold.
1:5 drunkards. Likely not the town alcoholics, but all those who are "drinkers of wine," a drink regularly accompanying Israelite meals. This not only condemns excessive use, but also laments the loss of new wine production to the locusts, which will affect almost everyone.
1:6 The literal locusts are metaphorically compared to a "mighty army"

1:6 [j] Rev 9:8
1:7 [k] Isa 5:6 [l] Am 4:9
1:8 [m] ver 13; Isa 22:12; Am 8:10
1:9 [n] Hos 9:4; Joel 2:14,17
1:10 [o] Isa 24:4 [p] Hos 9:2
1:11 [q] Jer 14:3-4; Am 5:16 [r] Isa 17:11
1:12 [s] Hag 2:19
1:13 [t] Jer 4:8 [u] Joel 2:17 [v] ver 9
1:14 [w] 2Ch 20:3

it has the teeth[j] of a lion,
the fangs of a lioness.
7 It has laid waste[k] my vines
and ruined my fig trees.[l]
It has stripped off their bark
and thrown it away,
leaving their branches white.

8 Mourn like a virgin in sackcloth[m]
grieving for the betrothed of her youth.
9 Grain offerings and drink offerings[n]
are cut off from the house of the LORD.
The priests are in mourning,
those who minister before the LORD.
10 The fields are ruined,
the ground is dried up;[o]
the grain is destroyed,
the new wine[p] is dried up,
the olive oil fails.

11 Despair, you farmers,[q]
wail, you vine growers;
grieve for the wheat and the barley,
because the harvest of the field is destroyed.[r]
12 The vine is dried up
and the fig tree is withered;
the pomegranate, the palm and the apple[a] tree —
all the trees of the field — are dried up.[s]
Surely the people's joy
is withered away.

A Call to Lamentation

13 Put on sackcloth,[t] you priests, and mourn;
wail, you who minister[u] before the altar.
Come, spend the night in sackcloth,
you who minister before my God;
for the grain offerings and drink offerings[v]
are withheld from the house of your God.
14 Declare a holy fast;[w]
call a sacred assembly.
Summon the elders
and all who live in the land

[a] 12 Or possibly *apricot*

(2:11,25), just as in other places an army is compared to a locust swarm (Jer 46:23), both vast in number and leaving devastation in its wake.
1:7 Israel's food supply depended not only on grains, but also on vines and the grapes they produced, which in turn were used for wine. When locusts destroyed them, "drunkards" (v. 5) would have nothing to drink. By removing all leaves from the fig trees, the locusts also deprived the people of their next fruit crop. These elements of a good life (Mic 4:4) are no longer available.
1:8 Mourn. A call to Judah to grieve "like a virgin" who is engaged but has lost her beloved, "the betrothed of her youth," before the marriage is consummated. Mourners wore course sackcloth to accompany their tears (see Gen 37:34).
1:9 Grain offerings. The second of the sacrifice types described in Leviticus (see Lev 2 and notes); they are difficult to produce when the crops and olives, whose oil forms part of the offering, have been devastated. Israel is unable to participate in these twice-daily elements of Israelite ritual (Exod 29:38–41; Num 28:3–8). **drink offerings.** This category of offering includes wine (Exod 29:40), which is also in jeopardy (v. 5). The inability to sacrifice directly affected the food supply of the priests, part of which was their due from the offerings presented (Lev 2:3,10). See "Grain and Drink Offerings That Accompany Animal Sacrifices," p. 273.
1:13–20 *A Call to Lamentation.* The locust's destruction calls for a response.
1:14 holy fast. Accompanied national mourning and was dedicated to God by willful choice rather than simply being forced upon Israel through the lack of food. While such fasts could be private (2 Sam 12:16), this

to the house of the LORD your God,
and cry out[x] to the LORD.

15 Alas for that[y] day!
For the day of the LORD[z] is near;
it will come like destruction from the Almighty.[a]

16 Has not the food been cut off[a]
before our very eyes—
joy and gladness
from the house of our God?[b]
17 The seeds are shriveled
beneath the clods.[b][c]
The storehouses are in ruins,
the granaries have been broken down,
for the grain has dried up.
18 How the cattle moan!
The herds mill about
because they have no pasture;
even the flocks of sheep are suffering.

19 To you, LORD, I call,[d]
for fire[e] has devoured the pastures[f] in the wilderness
and flames have burned up all the trees of the field.
20 Even the wild animals pant for you;[g]
the streams of water have dried up[h]
and fire has devoured the pastures in the wilderness.

1:14 [x]Jnh 3:8
1:15 [y]Jer 30:7 [z]Isa 13:6,9; Joel 2:1,11,31
1:16 [a]Isa 3:7 [b]Dt 12:7
1:17 [c]Isa 17:10-11
1:19 [d]Ps 50:15 [e]Am 7:4 [f]Jer 9:10
1:20 [g]Ps 104:21 [h]1Ki 17:7
2:1 [i]Jer 4:5 [j]ver 15 [k]Joel 1:15; Zep 1:14-16 [l]Ob 15
2:2 [m]Am 5:18 [n]Da 9:12 [o]Joel 1:6 [p]Joel 1:2

An Army of Locusts

2 Blow the trumpet[i] in Zion;[j]
sound the alarm on my holy hill.

Let all who live in the land tremble,
for the day of the LORD[k] is coming.
It is close at hand[l]—
2 a day of darkness[m] and gloom,[n]
a day of clouds and blackness.
Like dawn spreading across the mountains
a large and mighty army[o] comes,
such as never was in ancient times[p]
nor ever will be in ages to come.

3 Before them fire devours,
behind them a flame blazes.

[a] *15* Hebrew *Shaddai* [b] *17* The meaning of the Hebrew for this word is uncertain.

was a public affair (Lev 16:29; Num 29:7); everyone was affected, so everyone needed to respond.
1:15 day of the LORD. A time of either national blessing for those who followed God or destruction for those who set themselves against his will (see Introduction: Themes and Theology). Though no specific wrongs are attributed to Israel, their responses here indicate the need for national repentance.
1:19–20 Destruction is also brought by fire, which at times symbolizes God's wrathful judgment (Isa 66:15–16) but here could well be the culmination of the natural progression: land that is stripped by locusts and suffers drought (v. 12) is then susceptible to fire.
2:1–11 *An Army of Locusts.* The suffering is not over; disaster follows disaster. Locust swarms are cyclical, not onetime events, and another catastrophe is coming.
2:1 trumpet. Made of a ram's horn, it was used to signal important events such as fast-approaching attacks (Judg 7:18). In this case, what is close and approaching is "the day of the LORD," a day to be feared (1:15).
2:2 darkness and gloom. Caused by the dense locust swarms (cf. Exod 10:22); they will be metaphorically present in the grief accompanying God's judgment (Zeph 1:15). **large and mighty army.** Likely refers still to the locusts since they are compared to human warriors (v. 7), whose coming and destruction are as feared as an overwhelming military advance.
2:3 A stark before-and-after picture contrasts the lush, fertile condition

2:3 [q]Ge 2:8 [r]Ps 105:34-35
2:4 [s]Rev 9:7
2:5 [t]Rev 9:9 [u]Isa 5:24; 30:30
2:6 [v]Isa 13:8 [w]Na 2:10
2:7 [x]Isa 5:27
2:9 [y]Jer 9:21
2:10 [z]Ps 18:7 [a]Mt 24:29 [b]Isa 13:10; Eze 32:8
2:11 [c]Joel 1:15 [d]Zep 1:14; Rev 18:8 [e]Eze 22:14
2:12 [f]Jer 4:1; Hos 12:6
2:13 [g]Ps 34:18; Isa 57:15 [h]Job 1:20

Before them the land is like the garden of Eden,[q]
behind them, a desert waste[r] —
nothing escapes them.
4 They have the appearance of horses;[s]
they gallop along like cavalry.
5 With a noise like that of chariots[t]
they leap over the mountaintops,
like a crackling fire[u] consuming stubble,
like a mighty army drawn up for battle.

6 At the sight of them, nations are in anguish;[v]
every face turns pale.[w]
7 They charge like warriors;
they scale walls like soldiers.
They all march in line,
not swerving[x] from their course.
8 They do not jostle each other;
each marches straight ahead.
They plunge through defenses
without breaking ranks.
9 They rush upon the city;
they run along the wall.
They climb into the houses;
like thieves they enter through the windows.[y]

10 Before them the earth shakes,[z]
the heavens tremble,
the sun and moon are darkened,[a]
and the stars no longer shine.[b]
11 The LORD[c] thunders
at the head of his army;
his forces are beyond number,
and mighty is the army that obeys his command.
The day of the LORD is great;[d]
it is dreadful.
Who can endure it?[e]

Rend Your Heart

12 "Even now," declares the LORD,
"return[f] to me with all your heart,
with fasting and weeping and mourning."

13 Rend your heart[g]
and not your garments.[h]

of the land, a blessing from God much as it was in the "garden of Eden" (Gen 2:8–9; Lev 25:18–19; Ps 107:37–38), with the scorched-earth denudation following the insatiable locusts.

2:11 The destruction befalling Israel is not caused by inanimate nature or by an enemy of them and their God. Rather, the locusts are "his army," under the bidding and control of God himself just as the human armies of Assyria and Babylonia served as God's instruments of punishment (Isa 10:5; Jer 25:9). The prophet asks, in light of the coming ruin, "Who can endure it?" On a natural level, none can (Nah 1:6; Rev 6:17); it is possible only through repentance and God's grace.

2:12–17 *Rend Your Heart.* God is willing to relent, showing grace by withholding judgment, but only at the sign of true repentance. This repentance must be more than an outward show; it must reflect an inner reality, a true change of direction.

2:12 Even now ... return to me. While Israel already experiences God's judgment, they must not give up hope; there is still a window of opportunity. God calls them, even at this late date, to show three traditional outward signs of repentance: fasting (1:14; 2:15), weeping (Jer 3:21), and mourning (Amos 5:16–17). There also needs to be an inner transformation of the heart, the center of human will.

2:13 Rend your heart and not your garments. A traditional response to distress was to tear one's clothing (Gen 37:34), but God requests a

Return to the LORD your God,
for he is gracious and compassionate,
slow to anger and abounding in love,[i]
and he relents from sending calamity.[j]
14 Who knows? He may turn[k] and relent
and leave behind a blessing[l] —
grain offerings and drink offerings[m]
for the LORD your God.

15 Blow the trumpet[n] in Zion,
declare a holy fast,[o]
call a sacred assembly.[p]
16 Gather the people,
consecrate[q] the assembly;
bring together the elders,
gather the children,
those nursing at the breast.
Let the bridegroom[r] leave his room
and the bride her chamber.
17 Let the priests, who minister before the LORD,
weep between the portico and the altar.[s]
Let them say, "Spare your people, LORD.
Do not make your inheritance an object
of scorn,[t]
a byword among the nations.
Why should they say among the peoples,
'Where is their God?[u]' "

2:13 [i] Ex 34:6 [j] Jer 18:8
2:14 [k] Jer 26:3 [l] Hag 2:19 [m] Joel 1:13
2:15 [n] Nu 10:2 [o] Jer 36:9 [p] Joel 1:14
2:16 [q] Ex 19:10,22 [r] Ps 19:5
2:17 [s] Eze 8:16; Mt 23:35 [t] Dt 9:26-29; Ps 44:13 [u] Ps 42:3
2:18 [v] Zec 1:14

The LORD's Answer

18 Then the LORD was jealous[v] for his land
and took pity on his people.

19 The LORD replied[a] to them:

[a] *18,19* Or *LORD will be jealous . . . / and take pity . . . / [19]The LORD will reply*

more intimate, personal, and permanent response. There needs to be an inner conversion, not just a public spectacle. Even though Israel wronged their holy and just God, God is both "gracious and compassionate," as God revealed to Moses at Sinai (Exod 34:6). **relents.** God's love is at times shown when he relents, changing plans to avert the calamity he had proposed. More problematic are some translations describing God as "repenting" from "evil." "Repent" describes turning from sin, which is not applicable to a sinless God who does no evil (i.e., what is morally unacceptable). In Hebrew the term here translated "relent" also indicates a divine response to moral evil when the perpetrator comes to repentance. Following this, God, who wants to temper judgment because of his gracious love, can choose to withhold promised punishment.

2:14 God's grace is a gift that sinners should not take for granted, thinking that God will always forgive sin. Even following repentance, who knows if God will forgive? While it is in God's very nature to do so, sinners must never assume forgiveness; it should always be a blessed surprise. This surprise can advance beyond forgiveness to include blessing, restoring the grain and grapes that locusts devoured. God thus restores the ability for his repentant people to offer him their offerings.

2:15 For the second time people from every life stage are called by a trumpet blast (v. 1), not as a warning but as an invitation to a fast of mourning (see 1:14 and note).

2:17 Priests perform their service to God between the "portico" (the temple vestibule or entryway; 1 Kgs 6:3; 7:6) and the "altar" (upon which offerings are burned; Lev 1–7). In this dire situation, their ministry is to weep there in petition on behalf of God's wayward children. Israel's sin and subsequent punishment reflects poorly on the priests themselves, making them "an object of scorn" in the eyes of their neighbors, a "byword" or term of derision. But God is also affected since if God cannot protect his people from calamity, their neighbors will ask, "Where is their God?" Scorn on God's people makes the nations doubt God's very existence.

2:18—3:21 *The Lord Responds to His People.* God in his grace showers his repentant people with unparalleled blessing.

2:18–27 *The Lord's Answer.* A literary pivot turns the book in a new direction, from pain to promise. God now speaks, showing concern for his land and his people (v. 18) by promising to bless them (vv. 19–24), restoring what the locusts had consumed (vv. 25–26) along with his own reputation (v. 27). In the midst of this, they are still to call on him (vv. 21–24).

2:18 God is "jealous" (see note on Exod 20:5) for a permanent, exclusive, and unique relationship with his land and his people, used here as synonyms (cf. Isa 9:19), as laid out in the nation's foundational constitution (Exod 20:5; Deut 5:9).

2:19 grain, new wine and olive oil. Elements vital for existence. God will restore what the locusts had destroyed (1:10). Israel worries no longer about the "perhaps" of God's grace (2:14) but can rest in his "I will."

2:19 [w] Jer 31:12 [x] Eze 34:29
2:20 [y] Jer 1:14-15 [z] Isa 34:3
2:21 [a] Isa 54:4; Zep 3:16-17 [b] Ps 126:3
2:22 [c] Ps 65:12 [d] Joel 1:18-20
2:23 [e] Ps 149:2; Isa 12:6; 41:16; Hab 3:18; Zec 10:7 [f] Lev 26:4
2:24 [g] Lev 26:10; Mal 3:10 [h] Am 9:13
2:26 [i] Lev 26:5 [j] Isa 62:9 [k] Ps 126:3; Isa 25:1
2:27 [l] Joel 3:17

"I am sending you grain, new wine and olive oil,[w]
enough to satisfy you fully;
never again will I make you
an object of scorn[x] to the nations.

20 "I will drive the northern horde[y] far from you,
pushing it into a parched and barren land;
its eastern ranks will drown in the Dead Sea
and its western ranks in the Mediterranean Sea.
And its stench[z] will go up;
its smell will rise."

Surely he has done great things!
21 Do not be afraid,[a] land of Judah;
be glad and rejoice.
Surely the LORD has done great things![b]
22 Do not be afraid, you wild animals,
for the pastures in the wilderness are becoming green.[c]
The trees are bearing their fruit;
the fig tree and the vine yield their riches.[d]
23 Be glad, people of Zion,
rejoice[e] in the LORD your God,
for he has given you the autumn rains
because he is faithful.
He sends you abundant showers,
both autumn and spring rains,[f] as before.
24 The threshing floors will be filled with grain;
the vats will overflow[g] with new wine[h] and oil.

25 "I will repay you for the years the locusts have eaten —
the great locust and the young locust,
the other locusts and the locust swarm[a] —
my great army that I sent among you.
26 You will have plenty to eat, until you are full,[i]
and you will praise[j] the name of the LORD your God,
who has worked wonders[k] for you;
never again will my people be shamed.
27 Then you will know that I am in Israel,
that I am the LORD[l] your God,
and that there is no other;
never again will my people be shamed.

[a] 25 The precise meaning of the four Hebrew words used here for locusts is uncertain.

2:20 northern horde. Either the locust swarm or an attacking army. Israel was used to armies attacking from the north as they moved through the Fertile Crescent, since crossing the Arabian desert to Israel's east was extremely difficult. The locusts denuded the land of every growing thing (1:10), so it is fitting that the encroaching army will be sent "into a parched and barren land." **Dead Sea ... Mediterranean Sea.** Israel is bounded on two sides by these bodies of water — the former to its east and the latter to its west. The huge locust army will span the area between them.

2:23 autumn and spring rains. Rather than using rivers like the neighboring Egyptians (the Nile) and Mesopotamians (the Tigris and Euphrates), Israel depended on rain to provide water to irrigate its fields (Lev 26:4). The early autumn rains in September – October softened the soil for plowing after the summer dry season, while the later spring rains allowed spring and summer crops to mature. They both are God's blessing (Jer 5:24).

2:24 Abundant grain and grapes will replace the loss of produce. **threshing floors.** Where people separated the useless husks from the nutritious kernels (see Ruth 3:2 and note). **vats.** Winepresses that processed grapes into wine.

2:26 God is not simply a magician, working wonders in order to dazzle. Rather, he presents his works as a witness to his power over both nations and nature (Exod 15:11; Isa 25:1), leading those who see them to revere and obey him.

The Day of the LORD

[28] "And afterward,
I will pour out my Spirit[m] on all people.
Your sons and daughters will prophesy,
your old men will dream dreams,
your young men will see visions.
[29] Even on my servants,[n] both men and women,
I will pour out my Spirit in those days.
[30] I will show wonders in the heavens[o]
and on the earth,[p]
blood and fire and billows of smoke.
[31] The sun will be turned to darkness[q]
and the moon to blood
before the coming of the great and dreadful day of the LORD.[r]
[32] And everyone who calls
on the name of the LORD will be saved;[s]
for on Mount Zion[t] and in Jerusalem
there will be deliverance,[u]
as the LORD has said,
even among the survivors[v]
whom the LORD calls.[a]

The Nations Judged

3 [b] "In those days and at that time,
when I restore the fortunes[w] of Judah and Jerusalem,
[2] I will gather all nations
and bring them down to the Valley of Jehoshaphat.[c]

2:28 [m] Eze 39:29
2:29 [n] 1Co 12:13; Gal 3:28
2:30 [o] Lk 21:11 [p] Mk 13:24-25
2:31 [q] Mt 24:29 [r] Isa 13:9-10; Mal 4:1,5
2:32 [s] Ac 2:17-21*; Ro 10:13* [t] Isa 46:13 [u] Ob 17 [v] Isa 11:11; Mic 4:7; Ro 9:27
3:1 [w] Jer 16:15

[a] *32* In Hebrew texts 2:28-32 is numbered 3:1-5. [b] In Hebrew texts 3:1-21 is numbered 4:1-21.
[c] *2* *Jehoshaphat* means *the LORD judges*; also in verse 12.

2:28–32 *The Day of the Lord.* Not only does God restore what has been lost (2:18–27), but he will bring about a new thing, not only for Judah in its time of immediate need but also ultimately for all of creation. This includes bestowing his Spirit on all humanity (Acts 2:1–13) with accompanying heavenly displays (Matt 24:29; Rev 6:12–13).

2:28 And afterward. Marks a transition from restoration of Judah's physical environment to a discussion of a new thing that will happen to humanity itself. **pour out.** Like water poured from a container, God promises to pour out his Spirit (Isa 44:3). This gift from God, which in certain contexts can be translated "wind" or "breath," not only gives life where there was desert and destruction (Ezek 37), but the Spirit also facilitates communication with God. Previously given to kings, prophets, priests, and others to enable them to minister in God's name, God promises the Spirit to "all people." Israel could have misheard this as referring only to their own nation, but the term is broader, encompassing all of humanity (Acts 2:32,38–39). **sons and daughters.** In Israel, prophet, priest, and king were roles usually reserved for males, but not so this divine gift of the Spirit, which falls on men and women equally. **old ... young.** There is no age preference. Everyone will be enabled to prophesy. **prophesy.** Communicating divine revelation, which could come through dreams or visions (2 Sam 7:17; Dan 2:1), terms with overlapping meaning. The new element here is not the means of the messages from God, but their recipients.

2:29 servants. There are also no socioeconomic restrictions to the Spirit, whom God gives to servants of both genders as well as to their masters and mistresses.

2:30 As natural phenomena accompanied the locust swarm (2:10), so they accompany the gift of the Spirit. These "wonders" also showed God's earth-shattering power over both "the heavens" and "the earth" during the exodus of his people from Egypt and their encounter with God when they became a nation at Mount Sinai. **blood and fire and billows of smoke.** Visible signs (not only to Israel but also to their enemies) of God's power working to free and restore his followers and to destroy and judge his enemies within the experience of Israel (Exod 3:2; 19:18; 20:18) and also in the future (Rev 8–9) when Christ returns to establish his rule over the entire earth.

2:32 everyone. God's salvation and blessing, while available to all (v. 28), is not automatic. To receive it, one must call on the Lord. **the name of the LORD.** God's personal name of covenant relationship (Exod 20:2). This is not only pleading to him for help but also declaring one's covenant allegiance to him (Isa 44:5). Paul writes that everyone, both Gentiles and Jews, can be saved through Christ (Rom 10:13). This will take place "on Mount Zion and in Jerusalem" (see Introduction: Themes and Theology; see also "The City of God," p. 2666).

3:1–16 *The Nations Judged.* God looks beyond his people to the nations, speaking about them (vv. 1–3,12–16) and then speaking directly to them (vv. 4–11).

3:1–3 *Why They Are Judged.* Turning from a focus on God's people, the prophet turns to the nations, who face a court case.

3:1 In those days and at that time. Ties the anticipated blessing that will come upon faithful Judah (Jer 33:15) and all peoples with a future judgment upon those who mistreated Israel.

3:2 God will judge the gathered nations. **the Valley of Jehoshaphat.** Means "the Lord judged" (see v. 12). There is a wordplay in Hebrew here since "put ... on trial" is related to the judgment in the Hebrew name. All nations had mistreated Israel, and now God repays them.

3:2 [x]Eze 36:5
3:3 [y]Am 2:6
3:4 [z]Mt 11:21 [a]Isa 34:8
3:5 [b]2Ch 21:16-17
3:7 [c]Isa 43:5-6; Jer 23:8
3:8 [d]Isa 60:14 [e]Isa 14:2
3:9 [f]Isa 8:9 [g]Jer 46:4
3:10 [h]Isa 2:4; Mic 4:3 [i]Zec 12:8
3:11 [j]Eze 38:15-16; Zep 3:8 [k]Isa 13:3

There I will put them on trial[x]
for what they did to my inheritance, my people Israel,
because they scattered my people among the nations
and divided up my land.
3 They cast lots for my people
and traded boys for prostitutes;
they sold girls for wine[y] to drink.

4 "Now what have you against me, Tyre and Sidon[z] and all you regions of Philistia? Are you repaying
me for something I have done? If you are paying me back, I will swiftly and speedily return on your own
heads what you have done.[a] 5 For you took my silver and my gold and carried off my finest treasures to
your temples.[a][b] 6 You sold the people of Judah and Jerusalem to the Greeks, that you might send them
far from their homeland.
7 "See, I am going to rouse them out of the places to which you sold them,[c] and I will return on your
own heads what you have done. 8 I will sell your sons[d] and daughters to the people of Judah,[e] and they
will sell them to the Sabeans, a nation far away." The LORD has spoken.

9 Proclaim this among the nations:
Prepare for war![f]
Rouse the warriors![g]
Let all the fighting men draw near and attack.
10 Beat your plowshares into swords
and your pruning hooks[h] into spears.
Let the weakling[i] say,
"I am strong!"
11 Come quickly, all you nations from every side,
and assemble[j] there.
Bring down your warriors,[k] LORD!

[a] 5 Or *palaces*

3:3 cast lots. A form of gambling using something like a small stone thrown in some way to determine a yes or no response. The nations would use this method to randomly select among various options. They had such little regard for people as to treat them in this way. This evil is heightened even further by how they treat children: they "traded boys" and "sold girls" as slaves but for pitifully small amounts—just enough to engage in sexual perversion and debauchery.

3:4–8 *Payback.* One cannot oppress people, especially God's people, with impunity. What others inflicted on Israel will return on their own heads.

3:4 God confronts three of Israel's opponents. **Tyre and Sidon.** Phoenician cities often mentioned together (Isa 23); located to the northwest of Israel on the Mediterranean coast in what is now Lebanon. They were involved in the trafficking of humans (Amos 1:9), as was Israel's southern neighbor and longtime enemy Philistia (Judg 3:1–3; 1 Sam 4; Amos 1:6–8). **Philistia.** The coastal plain along the Mediterranean west of Judah. Its inhabitants, the Philistines (see notes on Gen 21:32; 1 Sam 4:1b), strove for control of Canaan until subdued by David. Their hostility to Israel continued, however (see Isa 14:29–31; Jer 47; Amos 1:6–8; Zeph 2:4–7), until Nebuchadnezzar deported them.

3:5 Israel's enemies took Israel's national treasures that were kept in the temple of the Lord in Jerusalem for their own temples. A disgrace to Israel and God, the pagan gods would have looked more powerful than the Lord himself.

3:6 Impoverished Israelites were at times separated from their homeland (2:20) and sold as slaves to the Greeks, who had a large slave population. They thus suffered poverty, servitude, and exile.

3:7 return on your own heads. Still speaking directly to the nations who harmed Israel, God warns that they will get back what they inflicted; what they sowed, they will now reap. Unlike the gods of Israel's neighbors (whom pagans viewed as territorial, having control over only a single people and geographic area), Israel's God exercises universal authority.

3:8 sell your sons and daughters. In making the punishment fit the crime, God himself sells the nations' offspring to Judah, who in turn will sell these offspring to the Sabeans. **Sabeans.** Probably coming from the southwest portion of the Arabian peninsula, elsewhere known as "Seba" (Gen 10:7).

3:9–16 *Calling to the Nations.* The Lord now describes his retribution against the nations, revisiting a theme that vv. 1–3 introduce. With a sense of irony, God summons the enemy nations to prepare for an unwinnable conflict with him.

3:9 Prepare for. Apparently Israel's neighbors shared with Israel the concept of "holy war" (Jer 6:4; Mic 3:5; see Introduction to Deuteronomy: Themes and Theology [Holy War]), fighting on behalf and through the assistance of the national deity, whom they summoned through prayer and fasting. Reversing v. 5, the pagan divinities will prove unable to withstand the God of Israel.

3:10 Beat your plowshares into swords. See also Isa 2:4; Mic 4:3. During the final, anticipated time of universal peace, all nations can safely convert implements of war for peaceful, agricultural use since a military need has passed. This is probably a well-known formulation that Joel ironically and powerfully turns on its head, capturing the attention of his audience. Before there can be universal peace, there must be universal punishment by God for wrongs done against him, from which the nations, even though they amass great military resources, will not be able to escape.

Remains of the Philistine temple at Tell Qasile showing pillar bases from Stratum X, and a stone threshold, walls, and benches from Stratum XII. Israel's enemies took Israel's national treasures that were kept in the temple of the Lord in Jerusalem and used them in their own temples (Joel 3:5).

Kim Walton, taken at the Eretz Israel Museum

12 "Let the nations be roused;
let them advance into the Valley of Jehoshaphat,
for there I will sit
to judge[l] all the nations on every side.
13 Swing the sickle,
for the harvest[m] is ripe.
Come, trample the grapes,
for the winepress[n] is full
and the vats overflow—
so great is their wickedness!"

14 Multitudes, multitudes
in the valley of decision!
For the day of the LORD[o] is near
in the valley of decision.
15 The sun and moon will be darkened,
and the stars no longer shine.
16 The LORD will roar from Zion
and thunder from Jerusalem;[p]
the earth and the heavens will tremble.[q]

3:12 [l]Isa 2:4
3:13 [m]Hos 6:11; Mt 13:39; Rev 14:15-19 [n]Rev 14:20
3:14 [o]Isa 34:2-8; Joel 1:15
3:16 [p]Am 1:2 [q]Eze 38:19

3:14 the valley of decision. The valley previously identified with Jehoshaphat (see v. 2 and note; see also v. 12). **decision.** Or "verdict," a decision being reached resulting in judgment, as indicated by another possible translation of "threshing" (see Amos 1:3). The Lord will judge the nations here.
3:15 God's judgments affect the natural world in addition to the nations. **The sun and moon … and the stars.** They will again cease their light-giving functions at the coming day of the Lord (2:10).
3:16 roar … thunder. God is like a fearsome lion, like a frightening storm (Amos 1:2), terrorizing the nations. **refuge.** For those who follow him, God is a place of safety from natural forces such as locust swarms (Isa 4:6). **stronghold.** Protection from fear (Ps 27:1).

3:16 [r] Jer 16:19
3:17 [s] Joel 2:27 [t] Isa 4:3
3:18 [u] Ex 3:8 [v] Isa 30:25; 35:6 [w] Rev 22:1-2 [x] Eze 47:1; Am 9:13
3:19 [y] Ob 10
3:20 [z] Am 9:15
3:21 [a] Eze 36:25

But the LORD will be a refuge for his people,
a stronghold[r] for the people of Israel.

Blessings for God's People

17 "Then you will know that I, the LORD your God,[s]
dwell in Zion,[t] my holy hill.
Jerusalem will be holy;
never again will foreigners invade her.

18 "In that day the mountains will drip new wine,
and the hills will flow with milk;[u]
all the ravines of Judah will run with water.[v]
A fountain will flow out of the LORD's house[w]
and will water the valley of acacias.[a][x]
19 But Egypt will be desolate,
Edom a desert waste,
because of violence[y] done to the people of Judah,
in whose land they shed innocent blood.
20 Judah will be inhabited forever[z]
and Jerusalem through all generations.
21 Shall I leave their innocent blood unavenged?
No, I will not.[a]"

The LORD dwells in Zion!

[a] 18 Or *Valley of Shittim*

3:17–21 *Blessings for God's People.* For the faithful, the day of the Lord brings blessing (vv. 17–18) rather than the judgment awaiting God's enemies (v. 19). Through it the Lord vindicates his righteousness (vv. 20–21).

3:17 Zion. The mountain on which the temple was built; God is not simply a visitor, but an eternal resident (v. 21; Ps 132:13–14). **holy.** Separate from any pollution, natural or human. While Zion/Jerusalem falls and the temple is destroyed in 586 BC due to the rebellion of God's people (2 Kgs 25:1–21), they are physically restored after the exile (Ezra, Neh; Ezek 40–48). In the NT, Christ fulfills the temple's role, providing access to God (John 2:19–21), while the church (his people) has become the place where God dwells through the Spirit (1 Cor 3:16). Eschatologically, God will establish a new Jerusalem where he and the Lamb will be the temple (Rev 21). See "The City of God," p. 2666 and "Temple," p. 2652.

3:18 God restores the vineyards the locusts stripped (1:5,7), thereby restoring their wine. **mountains.** What had been the source of alarm at the approaching enemy (2:1,5) will now "drip new wine," replacing what was lost. **milk.** Cattle, whose fodder was destroyed, now produce abundant milk, a dietary staple (Isa 7:22). **run with water.** Even more important for an agricultural society living in a semi-arid climate is the presence of water, which will run as a natural source of life where it previously dried up (1:20). **flow out of the LORD's house.** Water metaphorically will flow from God's house since God is the source of both physical life (Gen 2:7) and spiritual life (John 3:16; Rev 21:6). Jesus portrays himself as the source of life-giving water (John 4:14). **valley of acacias.** A pleasant valley, in contrast to the valleys of judgment (vv. 2,12,14), will benefit from the Lord's provision (Ezek 47:1–12).

3:19 Two of Israel's southern neighbors not yet mentioned in the book are included among the enemy nations: **Egypt.** A foreign nation with which Israel had a long and unpleasant history (Exod 1:8–22; 1 Kgs 14:25; 2 Kgs 23:29). **Edom.** Though Israel's blood relatives through Esau (Gen 36), Edom treated Israel with hostility (Num 20:14–21). **desolate ... waste.** Like Israel was after the passing locusts, so these two countries will be following God's judgment: uninhabitable and uninhabited.

3:20 Judah will be inhabited forever. In contrast to her two neighbors (see v. 19 and note). The destruction Judah endured was unknown since time immemorial (1:3; 2:2), but their restoration will continue through the future.

3:21 innocent. Judah, responding to God's call to repentance (2:12–16), is declared innocent, and God brings to account those who wronged Judah. **The LORD dwells in Zion!** The prophecy closes with this ringing reminder (see also v. 17). The approaching judgment on God's people and their land is thus not the last word; the last word is hope and reassurance that the King is still in control.

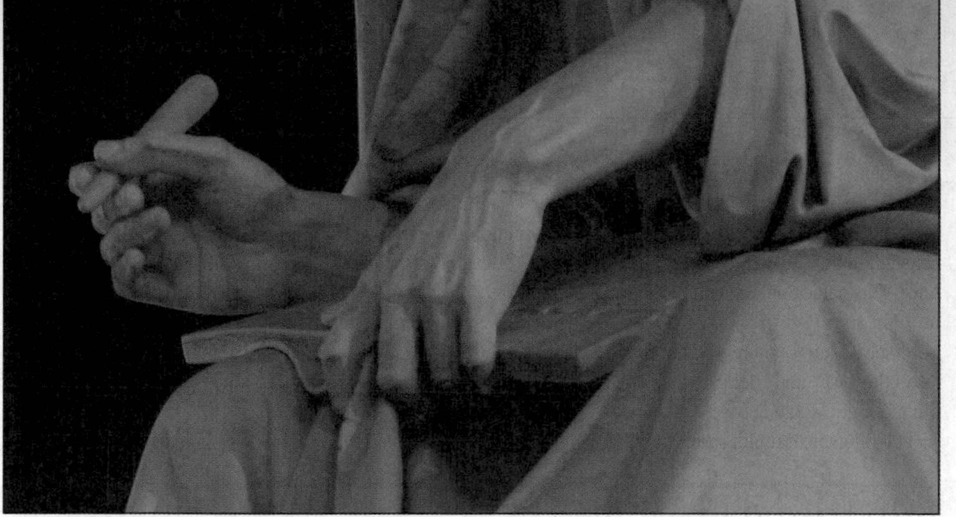

INTRODUCTION TO AMOS

The book of Amos is well known for its demand for socioeconomic justice, although there is much more to its message than this. Many individuals and groups have appealed to this prophetic book in their struggle against discrimination and oppression. Martin Luther King Jr., for instance, quoted 5:24, perhaps the book's best-known verse, in his famous "I Have a Dream" speech at the Washington Memorial on August 28, 1963.

AUTHOR

Based on 1:1, the prophet Amos traditionally has been taken to be the author of the book that bears his name. While a good case can be made that the book comes from the time of the prophet, nowhere is it said that he wrote down its words. The book is well organized and exhibits the author's great literary skill, which suggests that it was a literary work from the beginning and is not simply a loose collection of messages.

The book itself suggests that Amos was relatively well-to-do, not a poor peasant (1:1; 7:14). Chs. 1 – 2 reveal an awareness of the international scene, and the quality of the poetry indicates that the prophet was an educated man. Amos clearly was versed in the traditions of Israel and was no stranger to the sanctuaries and spheres of economic and political power. Although neither a priest nor a professional prophet, he must have been an impressive individual to merit the accusation of being a conspirator against the king of Israel (7:10). His message found particular opposition because he was from the southern kingdom of Judah.

DATE AND BACKGROUND

The opening verse dates the ministry of Amos during the reigns of King Uzziah (also known as Azariah) in Judah and King Jeroboam II in Israel (2 Kgs 14:23 — 15:7). Although there are disagreements as to the exact dates of these two kings, all agree that the time frame of Amos's ministry is about 760 – 750 BC. There is evidence of a powerful earthquake at Hazor (Stratum VI), Gezer, and Lachish that has been dated to about 760. This probably is the earthquake that 1:1 mentions (also 8:8; perhaps 6:9 – 10; 9:1). People still remembered its violent effect over two centuries later (Zech 14:5). Amos 8:9 might refer to a lunar eclipse that is dated by the Assyrian Eponym Chronicle to June 16, 763. The evidence of these natural disasters, along with the lack of any mention of the political turmoil in Israel after the death of Jeroboam II or of the Assyrians (who enjoyed a resurgence under Tiglath-Pileser III beginning in 744), indicate a date for the ministry of Amos around 760. The prophet's predictions about a foreign invasion were fulfilled when Israel fell to the Assyrian armies in 722 (2 Kgs 17:3 – 5). Israel then ceased to exist as an independent country and became a province of the Assyrian Empire. Many were taken into exile at that time, as well as in 720 BC after another Assyrian campaign into the region (2 Kgs 17:6,18 – 20; 18:11; see map, p. 687).

THEMES AND THEOLOGY

The focus of the theology of the book of Amos is Yahweh ("the LORD"). The name Yahweh appears by itself or in combination with other names and epithets over 80 times in the book. Lord (*ʾădōnāy*) occurs alone 3 times and in combination some 22 times. God (*ʾĕlōhîm*) occurs alone twice and in combination with other names for God 9 times. Three doxology passages climax with the declaration "The LORD [God Almighty] is his name" (4:13; 5:8; 9:6). Amos portrays the Lord as sovereign over the nations and history and as the Creator of the earth and the constellations. The epithet "LORD God Almighty" ("Yahweh God of hosts") appears 8 times, and "LORD Almighty" once. This name and title combination could refer to the heavenly host of angels (1 Kgs 22:19; Neh 9:6; Ps 148:2) or to the stars (Deut 4:19; 2 Kgs 17:16; Jer 8:2). It also can mean the troops of Israel (1 Sam 17:45), though this is not likely in Amos. There is also a strong emphasis on divine speech. God's voice is like thunder (1:2); the phrases "says the LORD" and "declares the LORD" permeate the book, and God's oath taking underscores the seriousness of the messages (4:2; 6:8; 8:7).

The fundamental obligation that the God of Israel places on his people is that they practice justice and righ-

LOCATIONS IN AMOS

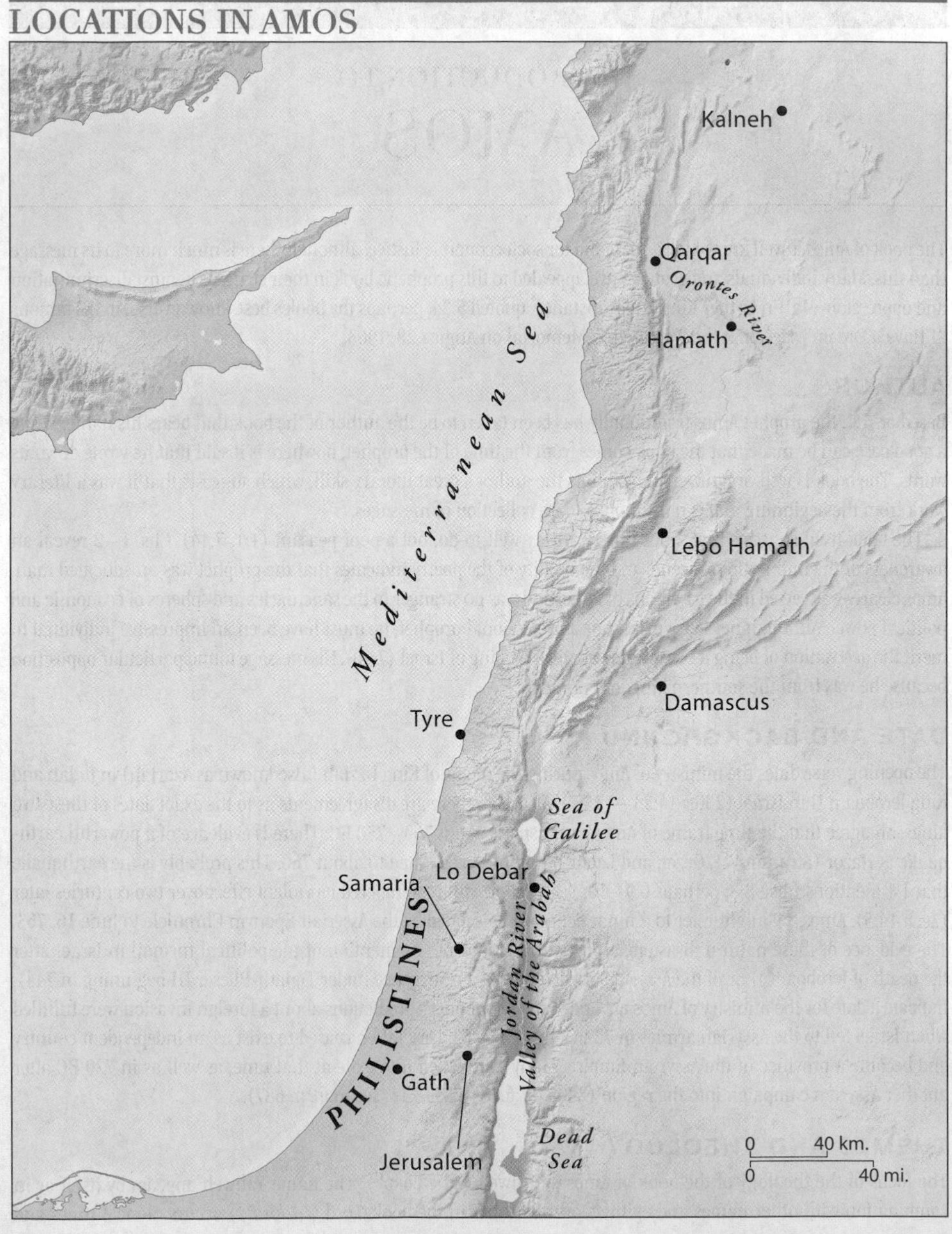

teousness. This combination of terms appears in 5:7,24; 6:12. God demands the proper ordering of society, especially as it pertains to the vulnerable (2:6–8; 3:9–10; 4:1; 5:10–15; 6:3–6; 8:4–6). Although the term "covenant" does not appear in the book, Amos's message is grounded in Israel's unique relationship with God, which looked back to the deliverance from Egypt (2:10; 3:1–2) and even earlier to the patriarchs Jacob (6:8; 7:2,5; 8:7; 9:8) and Isaac (7:9,16).

Sheep grazing at Tekoa, Amos's hometown. There he earned his living from the flock and the sycamore-fig grove (Amos 1:1; 7:14–15).

Todd Bolen/www.BiblePlaces.com

The religious ideology of the northern kingdom of Israel sanctioned its unjust government and social order and thereby presented a distorted view of the Lord (7:13). The roots of this system went back to the division of the united monarchy over a century before, when Jeroboam I established an alternative to the worship of the Lord, which was centered in Jerusalem (1 Kgs 12:25–33). Israel crowded the sanctuaries to worship their god, but the Lord rejected this self-serving nationalistic faith that ignored his ethical demands (Amos 4:4–5; 5:4–6,21–25; 7:9–17). This society and its theology were unacceptable to the Lord. As judgment, God would send an unnamed enemy to invade the northern kingdom (3:11; 6:14). Its fortresses and dwellings would be destroyed (3:15; 6:8–10) and the temple at Bethel torn down (9:1; cf. 3:14; 5:5–6; 8:3). The day of the Lord, which the people believed would be a time of victory, instead would bring defeat and sorrow (5:18–20; cf. 2:14–16; 5:1–3,16–17; 8:9–14). Many, in particular the leaders, would be taken far from the land (4:2–3; 5:5,26–27; 6:7; 9:9).

The prophetic call to turn to God was given in the hope that a remnant, a faithful few, might respond and survive this fate (5:4–6,14–15). Sometime after the devastation, the exiles would return, rebuild the cities, and work their fields once more (9:13–15). The northern kingdom of Israel and its rulers were illegitimate in God's sight and had no place in his plans for that future day. This is clear from the fact that the Lord had roared from Jerusalem and its temple (1:2) and that final restoration would come under a Davidic monarchy (9:11).

Judgment was not limited to Israel. The nations were accountable to the Lord for their treatment of his people and their cruelty in war (1:3—2:3). Their deserved punishment would be defeat in battle and exile. God's sovereignty over other peoples also extends to his involvement in their migrations (9:7). In the future they will come under his rule more directly in that eschatological day of peace and abundance (9:12).

STRUCTURE AND LITERARY FEATURES

The book of Amos can be separated into four parts: the inscription and summary words of the preface (1:1–2), the judgments directed against the nations (chs. 1–2), the messages directed against the northern kingdom (chs. 3–6), and the visions of chs. 7–9.

These large sections can be subdivided. The command to "Hear this word," coupled with further specification at 3:1 and 5:1, marks the start of two major segments. As the notes will make clear, chs. 5–6 are composed of three concentric literary structures or chiasms. The section of visions can be organized into three sequences of visions (7:1–9; 8:1–3; 9:1–10), each of which is followed by theological expansion (7:10–17; 8:4–14; 9:11–15).

There are several other outstanding literary features of the book. These include the penchant for series of five (e.g., the fivefold refrain "'yet you have not returned to me,' declares the LORD" in 4:4–11; the five descriptors of 4:13; the five visions in chs. 7–9) and seven items (e.g., the list of seven types of soldiers in 2:14–16). The messages of 1:3—2:16, which all begin with "For three sins ... even for four" (1:3,6,9,11,13; 2:1,4,6), exhibit an x/x+1 structure (here x is 3). This pattern was not uncommon in the ancient Near East and also appears in Prov 30:15–16,18–19, 21–23,29–31. Amos's imagery is powerful and the language direct.

OUTLINE

I. Preface (1:1 – 2)

II. Judgment on the Nations (1:3 — 2:16)
- A. Judgment on Israel's Neighbors (1:3 — 2:3)
- B. Judgment on Judah (2:4 – 5)
- C. Judgment on Israel (2:6 – 16)

III. More Details About Israel's Sin and Fate (3:1 — 6:14)
- A. Divine Exposure of Israel's Guilt (3:1 — 4:13)
  1. Witnesses Summoned Against Israel (3:1 – 15)
  2. Israel Has Not Returned to God (4:1 – 13)
- B. Lament for the Death of Israel (5:1 — 6:14)
  1. A Lament and Call to Repentance (5:1 – 17)
  2. The Day of the Lord (5:18 – 27)
  3. Woe to the Complacent (6:1 – 7)
  4. The Lord Abhors the Pride of Israel (6:8 – 14)

IV. Five Visions of Israel's Future (7:1 — 9:15)
- A. Three Visions of Disaster (7:1 – 9)
- B. Expansion: Amos and Amaziah (7:10 – 17)
- C. The Fourth Vision: A Basket of Ripe Fruit (8:1 – 3)
- D. Expansion: The Cost of Religious Perversion (8:4 – 14)
- E. The Fifth Vision: Israel to Be Destroyed (9:1 – 10)
- F. Expansion: Israel's Restoration (9:11 – 15)

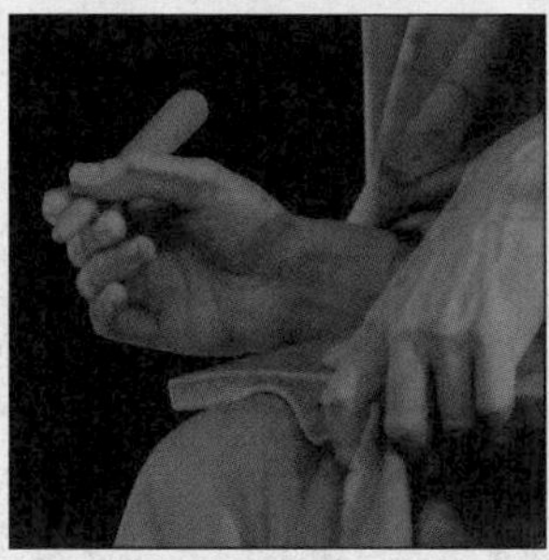

AMOS

1 The words of Amos, one of the shepherds of Tekoa[a]—the vision he saw concerning Israel two
years before the earthquake,[b] when Uzziah[c] was king of Judah and Jeroboam[d] son of Jehoash[a]
was king of Israel.[e]
[2]He said:

"The LORD roars[f] from Zion
  and thunders from Jerusalem;[g]
the pastures of the shepherds dry up,
  and the top of Carmel[h] withers."[i]

1:1 [a]2Sa 14:2 [b]Zec 14:5 [c]2Ch 26:23 [d]2Ki 14:23 [e]Hos 1:1
1:2 [f]Isa 42:13 [g]Joel 3:16 [h]Am 9:3 [i]Jer 12:4
1:3 [j]Isa 8:4; 17:1-3 [k]Am 2:6

Judgment on Israel's Neighbors

[3]This is what the LORD says:

"For three sins of Damascus,[j]
  even for four, I will not relent.[k]

[a] *1* Hebrew *Joash,* a variant of *Jehoash*

1:1–2 *Preface.* This sets the historical context for the prophet's message, identifies Amos's hometown, and establishes the tone of judgment that characterizes the book.
1:1 shepherds. Not the typical Hebrew word for shepherd (cf. 3:12). The Hebrew word occurs elsewhere only in 2 Kgs 3:4, referring to King Mesha of Moab and his huge flocks. The implication is that Amos was not poor, which 7:14 reinforces. He was not a professional prophet but rather a layperson called to deliver God's word (7:14–15). **Tekoa.** Modern Khirbet Tequ'a, a town in Judah about ten miles (16 kilometers) south of Jerusalem and five miles (8 kilometers) southeast of Bethlehem. For other background material, see Introduction: Author; Date and Background.
1:2 roars. Suggests the prey has been caught by the divine lion (3:4,8,12; cf. Isa 31:4; Hos 5:14–15; 13:7–8). That God "thunders" also is ominous. From the beginning, the word of the Lord is powerful. This verse sets a threatening tone for the rest of the book. **Zion ... Jerusalem.** The site of the temple and the capital of Judah, which communicates that the Lord does not identify with the northern kingdom of Israel. **dry up.** The Hebrew term is often translated "mourn." Inanimate objects grieve in the OT (e.g., Isa 3:26; Lam 2:8; Hos 4:3). This verb recurs in contexts of death (5:16; 8:8,10; 9:5). It alerts the reader that this prophetic message is about loss.
1:3—2:16 *Judgment on the Nations.* This section is a series of judgments on Israel and seven other peoples. These messages demonstrate consistent patterns in structure and content. Amos prefaces each word to a nation with the phrase "This is what the LORD says" (1:3,6,9,11,13; 2:1,4,6) and closes several with the formula "says the LORD" (1:5,8 [with the addition of "Sovereign"],15; 2:3,16 [has "declares the LORD"]). The reasons for God's displeasure at the northern kingdom will be made clear in the judgment on Israel (2:6–16), the climax of this series. The inclusion of Israel conveys that it was no better than nations that did not have the Lord as their God and that it too would be punished for its sins. This indictment surely was a shock to those in the northern kingdom, who believed that they enjoyed God's favor.
1:3—2:3 *Judgment on Israel's Neighbors.* God condemns seven nations surrounding the northern kingdom of Israel, including Judah. If we leave Judah aside, the transgression is violence against Israel and other peoples. These atrocities probably occurred toward the end of the reign of Jeroboam II, who early on enjoyed success (2 Kgs 14:25–27). Judgment corresponds to these violations: these nations will be overcome in war. Defeat involves sending fire (1:4,7,10,12,14; 2:2,5), demolishing strongholds and capital cities (1:4–5,7,10,12,14; 2:2,5), and removing rulers (1:5,8,15; 2:3). These inspired utterances teach that God will punish those who mistreat his people and others. He does not tolerate brutality. Humans are made in the image of God. To mistreat so horrifically another person is a strike against the Lord and is worthy of punishment. As throughout the Prophets, leaders are singled out as particularly responsible for the sins of their people and the judgment that ensues.
1:3 For three sins ... even for four. See also vv. 6,9,11,13; 2:1,4,6. This three-four pattern is also found in Proverbs (30:15–16,18–19,21–23, 29–31). Unlike the Proverbs passages, however, these messages do not list four items. Some suppose that the purpose is to highlight the worst sins or those that finally triggered God's wrath. Others argue that the

A threshing sledge was made of boards with stones or metal embedded in it. It was used to thresh grain (Amos 1:3).

Z. Radovan/www.BibleLandPictures.com

1:4 [l] Jer 49:27 [m] Jer 17:27 [n] 1Ki 20:1; 2Ki 6:24
1:5 [o] Jer 51:30 [p] 2Ki 16:9
1:6 [q] 1Sa 6:17; Zep 2:4 [r] Ob 11

Because she threshed Gilead
with sledges having iron teeth,
4 I will send fire[l] on the house of Hazael
that will consume the fortresses[m] of Ben-Hadad.[n]
5 I will break down the gate[o] of Damascus;
I will destroy the king who is in[a] the Valley of Aven[b]
and the one who holds the scepter in Beth Eden.
The people of Aram will go into exile to Kir,[p]"
says the LORD.

6 This is what the LORD says:

"For three sins of Gaza,[q]
even for four, I will not relent.
Because she took captive whole communities
and sold them to Edom,[r]

[a] 5 Or *the inhabitants of* [b] 5 *Aven* means *wickedness.*

numbers three and four should be added together to produce the number seven, suggesting that these nations have reached the fullness of sin. **Damascus.** Capital of Aram (Syria), Israel's northern neighbor. **I will not relent.** A wooden translation of the Hebrew yields: "I will not cause it to turn back" (see also vv. 6,9,11,13; 2:1,4,6), where "it" could refer to God's word of judgment or the judgment itself. Either way, the meaning is that these punishments are irrevocable. **threshed.** Could refer to the physical torture of dragging a sledge with iron teeth over victims or be a metaphor for ruthlessness (Isa 41:15; Mic 4:13; Hab 3:12). This same language is used to depict Aram's attacks on Israel years before (2 Kgs 13:7). **Gilead.** Territory of the tribes of Reuben and Gad in Transjordan between the Arnon and Yarmuk Rivers (cf. v. 13). Israel and Aram had long contested this area.
1:4 send fire. Most likely refers to devastation in war, with defeated cities being burned. "Fire" and the destruction of the "fortresses" are a constant theme in these judgments (see vv. 7,10,12,14; 2:2,5). **Hazael ... Ben-Hadad.** Rulers of Aram in the ninth and eighth centuries BC.
1:5 king. Hebrew *yôšēb* ("one [sitting or] dwelling"); some translate this "inhabitants" (see NIV text note). The parallelism with "holds the scepter" suggests that this person is sitting on a throne and thus is a royal figure (cf. v. 8). **Valley of Aven.** Could be a geographic name or a derogatory reference (see NIV text note). **go into exile.** The judgment on Aram, a punishment later decreed for Israel (5:5,27; 6:7; 7:11,17; cf. 4:2). **Kir.** The place of the origin of the Arameans (9:7). Aram's judgment will reverse its history.
1:6–8 This message mentions four of the five cities commonly associated with the Philistines. The fifth, Gath, appears in 6:2. Unlike the other nations, Philistia did not have a set capital city. The strongest ruler of the moment was the leader over the region.
1:6 God denounces trafficking in slaves ("took captive whole communities and sold them"), who would have been taken in war—a war most likely with Israel, Philistia's eastern neighbor. These captives were sold to Edom. The repetition of this indictment in v. 9 could suggest that Tyre participated in this crime. Humans are valuable in God's sight, not a commodity to be bought and sold.

7 I will send fire on the walls of Gaza
that will consume her fortresses.
8 I will destroy the king[a] of Ashdod[s]
and the one who holds the scepter in Ashkelon.
I will turn my hand[t] against Ekron,
till the last of the Philistines[u] are dead,"
says the Sovereign LORD.[v]

9 This is what the LORD says:

"For three sins of Tyre,[w]
even for four, I will not relent.
Because she sold whole communities of captives to Edom,
disregarding a treaty of brotherhood,
10 I will send fire on the walls of Tyre
that will consume her fortresses.[x]"

11 This is what the LORD says:

"For three sins of Edom,[y]
even for four, I will not relent.
Because he pursued his brother with a sword
and slaughtered the women of the land,
because his anger raged continually
and his fury flamed unchecked,[z]
12 I will send fire on Teman[a]
that will consume the fortresses of Bozrah."

13 This is what the LORD says:

"For three sins of Ammon,[b]
even for four, I will not relent.
Because he ripped open the pregnant women[c] of Gilead
in order to extend his borders,
14 I will set fire to the walls of Rabbah[d]
that will consume her fortresses
amid war cries[e] on the day of battle,
amid violent winds on a stormy day.
15 Her king[b] will go into exile,
he and his officials together,"
says the LORD.

1:8 [s]2Ch 26:6 [t]Ps 81:14 [u]Eze 25:16 [v]Isa 14:28-32; Zep 2:4-7
1:9 [w]1Ki 5:1; 9:11-14; Isa 23:1-18; Jer 25:22; Joel 3:4; Mt 11:21
1:10 [x]Zec 9:1-4
1:11 [y]Nu 20:14-21; 2Ch 28:17; Jer 49:7-22 [z]Eze 25:12-14
1:12 [a]Ob 9-10
1:13 [b]Jer 49:1-6; Eze 21:28; 25:2-7 [c]Hos 13:16
1:14 [d]Dt 3:11 [e]Am 2:2

[a] 8 Or *inhabitants* [b] 15 Or / *Molek*

1:8 king. See note on v. 5.
1:9 Tyre. A Phoenician kingdom northwest of Israel. The language of this indictment echoes the judgment against the Philistines. **disregarding a treaty of brotherhood.** Most likely refers to violating an agreement with Israel. **treaty.** A covenant. It is difficult to identify this treaty. David established ties with Hiram of Tyre (2 Sam 5:11), who supplied materials to Solomon for the building of the temple in Jerusalem (1 Kgs 5; 9:10–14). Years later Ahab of Israel married Jezebel, a princess of Sidon, another Phoenician city (1 Kgs 16:31); she was killed in Jehu's coup (2 Kgs 9:30–37). Possibly the relationship with Phoenicia had been restored in Jeroboam's time but now had been broken in this act of violence.
1:11 Edom. Located south of the Dead Sea; a historic enemy of Israel. In the eighth century BC, King Amaziah of Judah subdued it for a time (2 Kgs 14:7), but this alludes to armed conflict with a debilitated Israel. **brother.** The nation of Israel. Edom is Israel's "brother" because the relationship between the two peoples went back to the patriarchal period: the tensions between Jacob, the ancestor of the Israelites, and Esau, the older twin brother of Jacob and the ancestor of the Edomites (Gen 25:21–34; 27; 32–33; 36). **slaughtered the women of the land.** This possible rendering of a difficult Hebrew phrase is based on the Septuagint (the pre-Christian Greek translation of the OT). The term translated "women" can also be rendered "compassion." The phrase could be read "cast off his compassion." Either option emphasizes Edom's unrestrained cruelty, another instance of violence not acceptable to God.
1:12 Teman. Synonym for Edom (Jer 49:7,20). **Bozrah.** A principal city of Edom (cf. Isa 34:6; Jer 49:13–22). Excavations at Khirbat en-Nahas demonstrate the viability of this kingdom at an earlier date than many scholars thought possible.
1:13 Ammon. Located east of Israel, across the Jordan. **Gilead.** A zone disputed by Israel and Ammon (cf. v. 3). That Ammon "ripped open the pregnant women" to extend its territory speaks of unspeakable barbarity in war.
1:14 Rabbah. The capital city of Ammon, modern Amman in Jordan.

2:3 [f]Ps 2:10 [g]Isa 40:23
2:4 [h]2Ki 17:19; Hos 12:2 [i]Jer 6:19 [j]Eze 20:24 [k]Isa 9:16 [l]Isa 28:15 [m]2Ki 22:13; Jer 16:12
2:5 [n]Jer 17:27; Hos 8:14
2:6 [o]Joel 3:3; Am 8:6

2 This is what the LORD says:

"For three sins of Moab,
even for four, I will not relent.
Because he burned to ashes
the bones of Edom's king,
2 I will send fire on Moab
that will consume the fortresses of Kerioth.[a]
Moab will go down in great tumult
amid war cries and the blast of the trumpet.
3 I will destroy her ruler[f]
and kill all her officials with him,"[g]
says the LORD.

4 This is what the LORD says:

"For three sins of Judah,[h]
even for four, I will not relent.
Because they have rejected the law[i] of the LORD
and have not kept his decrees,[j]
because they have been led astray[k] by false gods,[b][l]
the gods[c] their ancestors followed,[m]
5 I will send fire on Judah
that will consume the fortresses of Jerusalem.[n]"

Judgment on Israel

6 This is what the LORD says:

"For three sins of Israel,
even for four, I will not relent.
They sell the innocent for silver,
and the needy for a pair of sandals.[o]
7 They trample on the heads of the poor
as on the dust of the ground
and deny justice to the oppressed.

[a] 2 Or *of her cities* [b] 4 Or *by lies* [c] 4 Or *lies*

2:1 Moab. In Transjordan, south of Ammon and Israelite territory. **burned to ashes the bones of Edom's king.** Another instance of a lack of restraint in war. **burned to ashes.** This was done to desecrate the dead, the leftover substance perhaps to be used as plaster (cf. Deut 27:2,4). The judgment of God is not limited to those who commit violence against his people. Respect of persons is a universal divine demand.

2:4–5 *Judgment on Judah.* The southern kingdom, like the northern kingdom of Israel, is numbered among the condemned nations, although Judah's transgression is not atrocity in warfare. Though Amos is from Judah, he is not reticent about denouncing his own people. He is not a narrow nationalist. The northern kingdom may have cheered this indictment of Judah, but theirs quickly follows.

2:4 rejected the law of the LORD. Refused to bring every area of national life under God's guidelines as expressed in the law (cf. Isa 5:24). This is not limited to religious practices. It is common to render the Hebrew as "false gods." The term also could be translated "lies" (see NIV text note). In that case, the reference most likely is to the teachings of false prophets or corrupt national leaders (cf. Isa 28:15,17; Hos 7:13; Mic 2:11). This sin was habitual and longstanding; Judah's ancestors followed these errant messages as well.

2:6–16 *Judgment on Israel.* The transgressions of the northern kingdom of Israel center primarily on social injustice and rebellion against the Lord, not atrocities committed in war. Nevertheless, the judgment is the same as that of all the other nations. As the final and longest message, this is the climax to the entire series.

2:6–8 This inspired utterance begins with the same formula as all the others (see note on 1:3). The northern kingdom of Israel is included with all the other nations deserving of punishment. It is possible to count seven sins in these verses; if understood this way, it is the only judgment that provides a complete listing of transgressions and implies that Israel exhibits the fullness of sin.

2:6 The meaning of these transgressions is disputed. **sell the innocent.** This could mean that the judges are bought off with bribes so that the poor cannot get a fair hearing (5:12; cf. Exod 23:6–8; Isa 5:23; Mic 3:9–11). A better option is that the destitute are sold into debt slavery for owing a creditor "silver" (see 8:4–6; cf. Exod 21:1–11; Lev 25:39–40; Neh 5:1–8) or even for something as paltry as "a pair of sandals."

2:7 This verse lists three additional sins. **trample on the heads of the poor as on the dust of the ground.** A powerful metaphor for the callous disregard of the needy. **deny justice to the oppressed.** Another reference to irregularities in the legal process directed against the

Father and son use the same girl
and so profane my holy name.[p]
8 They lie down beside every altar
on garments taken in pledge.[q]
In the house of their god
they drink wine[r] taken as fines.

9 "Yet I destroyed the Amorites[s] before them,
though they were tall as the cedars
and strong as the oaks.
I destroyed their fruit above
and their roots[t] below.
10 I brought you up out of Egypt[u]
and led you forty years in the wilderness[v]
to give you the land of the Amorites.[w]

11 "I also raised up prophets[x] from among your children
and Nazirites[y] from among your youths.
Is this not true, people of Israel?"
declares the LORD.
12 "But you made the Nazirites drink wine
and commanded the prophets not to prophesy.[z]

13 "Now then, I will crush you
as a cart crushes when loaded with grain.
14 The swift will not escape,
the strong[a] will not muster their strength,
and the warrior will not save his life.[b]
15 The archer[c] will not stand his ground,
the fleet-footed soldier will not get away,
and the horseman will not save his life.
16 Even the bravest warriors[d]
will flee naked on that day,"
declares the LORD.

2:7 [p] Am 5:11-12; 8:4
2:8 [q] Ex 22:26 [r] Am 4:1; 6:6
2:9 [s] Nu 21:23-26; Jos 10:12 [t] Eze 17:9; Mal 4:1
2:10 [u] Ex 20:2; Am 3:1 [v] Dt 2:7 [w] Ex 3:8; Am 9:7
2:11 [x] Dt 18:18; Jer 7:25 [y] Nu 6:2-3; Jdg 13:5
2:12 [z] Isa 30:10; Jer 11:21; Am 7:12-13; Mic 2:6
2:14 [a] Jer 9:23 [b] Ps 33:16; Isa 30:16-17
2:15 [c] Eze 39:3
2:16 [d] Jer 48:41

powerless, or a more general description of making their life miserable. **Father and son use the same girl**. Or "go to." It is difficult to specify what is meant by this. The reference may be to some form of incest (Lev 18:6–18) or to taking advantage of a servant girl who is working in the household, perhaps due to debt slavery (v. 6; cf. Neh 5:5). However, the Hebrew verb used here is not the one usually employed for sexual activity. Whatever the correct interpretation, the result is that God's name is put in disrepute. Unacceptable actions of God's people project a distorted image of his person and damage their mission to be an example to the nations.

2:8 The final two transgressions could refer to worshiping either the Lord or other deities (cf. 5:26; 8:14). **every altar.** Possibly household or local shrines (7:9; 8:14). **garments taken in pledge.** Items either (1) taken as security for a loan (Exod 22:26–27) or (2) confiscated when a loan was defaulted (cf. 2 Kgs 4:1). **house of their god [or gods].** Perhaps refers to religious sites or the temple at Bethel (7:13). **fines.** Could be unjust taxes (cf. 5:11), thereby expanding the web of injustice beyond unscrupulous creditors to include corrupt government officials.

2:9–12 In contrast to the sinful behavior of Israel, the Lord continually demonstrates grace. He brought them out from slavery in Egypt, led them in the wilderness for 40 years, and defeated their powerful foes. God also "raised up prophets" from among them to be his spokespersons and "Nazirites" as models of commitment (v. 11). Israel tried to compromise the Nazirite vow not to drink wine (Num 6:1–4) and silenced the prophetic voice (7:10–13). At the center of vv. 11–12 is an indictment in the form of a rhetorical question: "Is this not true, people of Israel?"

2:13–16 This judgment closes with a list of seven kinds of soldiers who will suffer defeat in the invasion that will be God's judgment. There will be no escape (3:11; 5:2,19; 6:14; 9:1–4).

2:13 cart … loaded with grain. The overloaded cart symbolizes the weight of sin.

2:16 that day. This possibly is the earliest mention of the day of the Lord in the Prophets (see also 5:18,20). It is a key theme in Isaiah, Jeremiah, Ezekiel, and in the Minor Prophets, especially Joel, Obadiah, and Zephaniah. This day can refer to a severe judgment on particular nations (Isa 23:15; Jer 46:10; 47:4; Ezek 30:2–3; Obad 8) or on the people of God (vv. 1–2; Jer 4:9; Lam 1:21; Obad 11–14; Hab 3:16; Zeph 1:15–16). While these devastating judgments could happen in the near future, the prophets also announce a final day of the Lord when all the nations of the earth will be judged (Joel 3:14; Obad 15; Zeph 3:8; Zech 14:1–4; Mal 4:5). This climactic event is followed by a global restoration of peace and plenty (Isa 2:2–5; 4:2–6; Zech 14:8–21). The book of Amos speaks of both an imminent day of punishment (here; 3:14; 5:18–20; 6:3; 8:3,9–11,13) and an end-time renewal (9:11–15).

3:1 [e]Am 2:10
3:2 [f]Dt 7:6; Lk 12:47 [g]Jer 14:10
3:4 [h]Ps 104:21; Hos 5:14
3:6 [i]Isa 14:24-27; 45:7
3:7 [j]Ge 18:17; Da 9:22; Jn 15:15; Rev 10:7 [k]Jer 23:22
3:8 [l]Jer 20:9; Jnh 1:1-3; 3:1-3; Ac 4:20
3:9 [m]Am 4:1; 6:1

Witnesses Summoned Against Israel

3 Hear this word, people of Israel, the word the LORD has spoken against you—against the whole family I brought up out of Egypt:[e]

2 "You only have I chosen[f]
of all the families of the earth;
therefore I will punish you
for all your sins.[g]"

3 Do two walk together
unless they have agreed to do so?
4 Does a lion roar in the thicket
when it has no prey?[h]
Does it growl in its den
when it has caught nothing?
5 Does a bird swoop down to a trap on the ground
when no bait is there?
Does a trap spring up from the ground
if it has not caught anything?
6 When a trumpet sounds in a city,
do not the people tremble?
When disaster comes to a city,
has not the LORD caused it?[i]

7 Surely the Sovereign LORD does nothing
without revealing his plan[j]
to his servants the prophets.[k]

8 The lion has roared—
who will not fear?
The Sovereign LORD has spoken—
who can but prophesy?[l]

9 Proclaim to the fortresses of Ashdod
and to the fortresses of Egypt:
"Assemble yourselves on the mountains of Samaria;[m]
see the great unrest within her
and the oppression among her people."

3:1—6:14 *More Details About Israel's Sin and Fate.* This section provides additional details concerning the transgressions of Israel. It can be divided into two large parts of two chapters each. The first part (chs. 3–4) broadens the indictment of Israel and its judgment (2:6–16) by exposing more transgressions. The second part (chs. 5–6) is characterized by lament over the coming judgment.

3:1—4:13 *Divine Exposure of Israel's Guilt.* This first part of the condemnation of chs. 3–6 presents the sin and judgment of Israel with powerful images drawn from different spheres of national life.

3:1–15 *Witnesses Summoned Against Israel.* This passage begins by calling the entire nation to account (vv. 1–8), moves on to concentrate its attention on the capital city (vv. 9–12), and narrows its accusation further to the sanctuary at Bethel and the royal house (vv. 13–15).

3:1–2 As also at 4:1 and 5:1, the nation is commanded to "hear this word." The unique election of Israel as the people of God brought singular responsibility. This exceptional choice and charge are emphasized by the repetition of "whole" and "all" (the same word in Hebrew). Their special status made judgment that more certain.

3:3–6 This sequence of questions can be broken down into a series of five ("Do ... Does ... Does ... Does ... Does" [vv. 3–5]) and two ("When ... When" [v. 6]), which add up to seven. This is another example of the lists of five and seven that characterize the book (see Introduction: Structure and Literary Features). This passage teaches that actions bring inevitable consequences. It also demonstrates an ominous progression from the vague statement of a meeting in v. 3 to a variety of encounters with death that culminate with the Lord's action against a city.

3:7–8 A prophet's participation in the divine council of angelic beings in the heavenly court (or temple) confirmed that the Lord truly had called that person to be a prophet (1 Kgs 22:19–21; Isa 6:1–3; Jer 23:16–22; cf. Job 1–2; Ps 82:1).

3:8 The lion has roared. Connects with the roar of 1:2 and signals that the lion has taken its prey (v. 4; cf. v. 12). In judgment the Lord is a devouring lion (e.g., Isa 31:4; Jer 4:7; 25:38; Hos 5:14; 13:7–8).

3:9–11 This is a rhetorical call for Ashdod (1:8) and Egypt (2:10) to witness the transgressions of Samaria, the capital of Israel, whose fortresses have been filled with the plunder gained through oppression. The sin of God's people will surprise even their enemies. An enemy will "overrun [the] land" in judgment (v. 11) and expose the nation's misplaced confidence in its fortifications (4:3; 6:13–14; 7:7–8).

10 "They do not know how to do right,[n]" declares the LORD,
"who store up in their fortresses[o]
what they have plundered[p] and looted."

11 Therefore this is what the Sovereign LORD says:

"An enemy will overrun your land,
pull down your strongholds
and plunder your fortresses.[q]"

12 This is what the LORD says:

"As a shepherd rescues from the lion's[r] mouth
only two leg bones or a piece of an ear,
so will the Israelites living in Samaria be rescued,
with only the head of a bed
and a piece of fabric[a] from a couch.[b][s]"

13 "Hear this and testify[t] against the descendants of Jacob," declares the Lord, the LORD God Almighty.

14 "On the day I punish Israel for her sins,
I will destroy the altars of Bethel;[u]
the horns of the altar will be cut off
and fall to the ground.
15 I will tear down the winter house[v]
along with the summer house;[w]
the houses adorned with ivory[x] will be destroyed
and the mansions will be demolished,"

declares the LORD.

3:10 [n] Jer 4:22; Am 5:7; 6:12 [o] Zep 1:9 [p] Hab 2:8
3:11 [q] Am 2:5; 6:14
3:12 [r] 1Sa 17:34 [s] Am 6:4
3:13 [t] Eze 2:7
3:14 [u] Am 5:5-6
3:15 [v] Jer 36:22 [w] Jdg 3:20 [x] 1Ki 22:39
4:1 [y] Ps 22:12; Eze 39:18 [z] Am 3:9 [a] Am 2:8; 5:11; 8:6

Israel Has Not Returned to God

4 Hear this word, you cows of Bashan[y] on Mount Samaria,[z]
you women who oppress the poor and crush the needy
and say to your husbands, "Bring us some drinks![a]"

[a] 12 The meaning of the Hebrew for this phrase is uncertain. [b] 12 Or *Israelites be rescued, / those who sit in Samaria / on the edge of their beds / and in Damascus on their couches.*

3:12 A shepherd was required to present some remains of the sheep to its owner as evidence that he had not stolen or lost the animal (Exod 22:10–13; cf. Gen 31:39). The point here is either that only a few in Israel will survive the invasion or that the northern kingdom will be left with little by the enemy. **bed … couch.** Both reoccur in 6:4. **a piece of fabric from a couch.** This is difficult to translate. The rendering "fabric" is based on a different spelling of the Hebrew text, as is the alternative "Damascus" (see NIV text note; cf. 1:3; 5:27). It is possible that the term rendered "a piece of fabric" refers to a piece of furniture, in parallel with the preceding phrase, yielding "a part of a couch."
3:13–15 One of the targets of judgment is Bethel, where the northern kingdom's most important sanctuary was located. It was associated with Jacob's vision (Gen 28:10–22) and was one of the two religious sites (along with Dan) established by Jeroboam I when the northern kingdom separated from Judah (1 Kgs 12:25—13:34). A golden calf was placed in each sanctuary, a sin that became the standard of condemnation of the kings of the northern kingdom (1 Kgs 15:34; 16:2,19,26; 2 Kgs 17:21; 23:15). Bethel is a focus of judgment because the religious system defended the regime's actions and the society's unjust structures. Those who came to the sanctuaries believed that the Lord had authorized this oppressive kingdom (Amos 7:9–17; cf. 4:4–5; 5:4–6,21–27). God will not tolerate being portrayed as supportive of such injustice. The prophet Hosea mocked Bethel (which means "house of God") by calling it Beth Aven ("house of iniquity") in Hos 4:15; 5:8; 10:5.
3:14 horns of the altar. A place of mercy and protection (1 Kgs 1:50; 2:28), but for Israel there would be no escape from divine wrath (v. 11; 2:14–16; 5:2; 6:14; 9:1–4).
3:15 houses … mansions. Amos's other targets are the luxurious dwellings of the royal family or powerful individuals who enjoyed the fruits of their exploitation of the defenseless (v. 9; cf. 4:1; 6:3–6). **ivory.** A precious commodity in the ancient world. Its presence starkly contrasts with the poverty of many in Israel (6:4).
4:1–13 *Israel Has Not Returned To God.* The central concern of this prophetic book is a proper understanding of God, which should have been made evident in just social relationships and acceptable worship. Neither was the case in Israel. This section begins with a judgment on the self-indulgent elite (vv. 1–3) and then points out how the nation's religion ignored the losses the people had endured (vv. 4–11). A dreadful meeting with the Lord lay ahead (vv. 12–13). The opening verse begins with "Hear this word," but unlike those at 3:1 and 5:1, this command is not followed by an explanatory phrase (cf. 3:13). This lack could indicate that it is not a heading for a new set of verses; i.e., vv. 1–3 may continue the diatribe against Israel's elite, with vv. 4–13 beginning the next indictment.
4:1 cows of Bashan. A sarcastic reference to the overindulgent wives of the leaders denounced in 3:15, who drink to excess (6:6). Bashan was

4:2 [b]Am 6:8
4:3 [c]Eze 12:5
4:4 [d]Hos 4:15 [e]Nu 28:3 [f]Dt 14:28 [g]Eze 20:39; Am 5:21-22
4:5 [h]Lev 7:13 [i]Lev 22:18-21
4:6 [j]Isa 3:1; Jer 5:3; Hag 2:17
4:7 [k]Ex 9:4,26; Dt 11:17; 2Ch 7:13
4:8 [l]Eze 4:16-17 [m]Jer 3:7 [n]Jer 14:4
4:9 [o]Dt 28:22 [p]Joel 1:7 [q]Jer 3:10; Hag 2:17

2 The Sovereign LORD has sworn by his holiness:
"The time will surely come
when you will be taken away[b] with hooks,
the last of you with fishhooks.[a]
3 You will each go straight out
through breaches in the wall,[c]
and you will be cast out toward Harmon,[b]"
declares the LORD.

4 "Go to Bethel and sin;
go to Gilgal[d] and sin yet more.
Bring your sacrifices every morning,[e]
your tithes[f] every three years.[c][g]
5 Burn leavened bread[h] as a thank offering
and brag about your freewill offerings[i]—
boast about them, you Israelites,
for this is what you love to do,"
declares the Sovereign LORD.

6 "I gave you empty stomachs in every city
and lack of bread in every town,
yet you have not returned to me,"
declares the LORD.[j]

7 "I also withheld rain from you
when the harvest was still three months away.
I sent rain on one town,
but withheld it from another.[k]
One field had rain;
another had none and dried up.
8 People staggered from town to town for water[l]
but did not get enough to drink,
yet you have not returned[m] to me,"
declares the LORD.[n]

9 "Many times I struck your gardens and vineyards,
destroying them with blight and mildew.[o]
Locusts devoured your fig and olive trees,[p]
yet you have not returned[q] to me,"
declares the LORD.

[a] 2 Or *away in baskets, / the last of you in fish baskets* [b] 3 Masoretic Text; with a different word division of the Hebrew (see Septuagint) *out, you mountain of oppression* [c] 4 Or *days*

located in Transjordan and was famous for its pastures and cattle (Deut 32:14; Ps 22:12; Jer 50:19; Ezek 39:18).

4:2–3 The seriousness of the announcement of judgment is emphasized by the oath sworn by the Sovereign Lord. The punishment on these women is portrayed graphically. They will be led out to exile like fish on "hooks" or "fishhooks" (or in a basket; see NIV text note) through the holes in the wall caused by the attack on Samaria (3:11; 5:26–27; 6:7; 7:17).

4:3 Harmon. Does not match any known place-name. See NIV text note for an alternative reading.

4:4–5 The language of these verses is surprising and ironic. Israel is encouraged to go to the historic religious centers of Bethel and Gilgal, but their worship was sin. The significance of Bethel extended back to the experiences of Abraham and Jacob (Gen 12:8; 28:10–22; 35:1–15). Jeroboam I, the founder of the northern kingdom, set up a golden calf there and instituted a religious system alternative to that at the temple in Jerusalem (1 Kgs 12:28—13:6).

4:4 Gilgal. Associated with Joshua's conquest (Josh 4–5; 10) and Saul's anointing (1 Sam 11:14–15). The ceremonies cited here (cf. Lev 3; 7:11–21; 27:30–33), of which the Israelites were proud, express gratitude to God but do not include sacrifices for sin. This religion of celebration fulfilled their spiritual impulses, but it was rejected by God. What they "love to do" (v. 5) the Lord hates (5:21).

4:6–13 This passage explains in part the grounds of God's dissatisfaction with the religion of Israel (cf. 5:4–6,21–26). This religion of celebration was disconnected from the harsh realities that Israel was enduring. The nation brought the Lord offerings of thanksgiving, but he had given them "empty stomachs" (v. 6), drought (vv. 7–8), ruined crops (v. 9), and death in battle (v. 10). Israel had suffered a fate almost akin to "Sodom and Gomorrah" (v. 11). These disasters were designed to bring the nation to true repentance. The fivefold refrain "'yet you have not returned to me,' declares the LORD" makes it abundantly clear that Israel had not responded. The nation preferred a religion formulated according to its own tastes.

[10] "I sent plagues[r] among you
as I did to Egypt.
I killed your young men with the sword,
along with your captured horses.
I filled your nostrils with the stench of your camps,
yet you have not returned to me,"
declares the LORD.[s]

[11] "I overthrew some of you
as I overthrew Sodom and Gomorrah.[t]
You were like a burning stick snatched from the fire,
yet you have not returned to me,"
declares the LORD.

[12] "Therefore this is what I will do to you, Israel,
and because I will do this to you, Israel,
prepare to meet your God."

[13] He who forms the mountains,[u]
who creates the wind,
and who reveals his thoughts[v] to mankind,
who turns dawn to darkness,
and treads on the heights of the earth[w]—
the LORD God Almighty is his name.[x]

4:10 [r] Ex 9:3; Dt 28:27 [s] Isa 9:13
4:11 [t] Ge 19:24; Jer 23:14
4:13 [u] Ps 65:6 [v] Da 2:28 [w] Mic 1:3 [x] Isa 47:4; Am 5:8,27; 9:6
5:1 [y] Eze 19:1
5:2 [z] Jer 14:17 [a] Jer 50:32; Am 8:14

A Lament and Call to Repentance

5 Hear this word, Israel, this lament[y] I take up concerning you:

[2] "Fallen is Virgin[z] Israel,
never to rise again,
deserted in her own land,
with no one to lift her up.[a]"

[3] This is what the Sovereign LORD says to Israel:

"Your city that marches out a thousand strong
will have only a hundred left;

4:12–13 Israel believed that arriving at the sanctuaries with offerings guaranteed a genuine encounter with God. Verse 12 forcefully announces that such was not the case. Now the people would surely meet him, but it would be a terrible confrontation with the all-powerful Creator. Continuing the use of lists of five in the book (see Introduction: Structure and Literary Features), v. 13 gives a fivefold description of God. The third portrait is that the Lord "reveals his thoughts to mankind." Some contend that this refers to God's knowledge of human thoughts (e.g., Ps 139:2; Dan 2:27–28), but it also can mean that God communicates his word to his people so that they are without excuse. The climax of vv. 4–13 is the announcement that "the LORD God Almighty is his name." He is omnipotent and will not tolerate a self-absorbed religion that will not grapple with reality or address his demands. This closing formula is found in the other two doxologies (5:8–9; 9:5–6; cf. 5:27).

5:1—6:14 *Lament for the Death of Israel.* This long section is composed of three long chiasms, or inverted structures with corresponding passages (5:1–17; 5:18–27; 6:1–14), the centers of which are their climax. Though there is a call to seek God and his ways (5:4–6,14–15), there is no avoiding imminent punishment at God's hand.

5:1–17 *A Lament and Call to Repentance.* This is the best-known chiasm of the book. The focal point, "the LORD is his name," is imbedded in the doxology of vv. 8–9.

5:1–3 Lament for Israel
5:4–6 Seek the Lord and live
5:7 Accusation against Israel
5:8a The power of the Lord to create
5:8b "The LORD is his name"
5:9 The power of the Lord to destroy
5:10–13 Accusation against the powerful
5:14–15 Seek the Lord and live
5:16–17 Lament for Israel

5:1 Hear this word, Israel. Signals the beginning of another section (cf. 3:1; 4:1). The tone is tragic (cf. vv. 16–17). Following on the challenge of 4:12–13, this dirge anticipates that the meeting with the Lord would be disastrous. The past tense communicates that this tragic future is as good as accomplished. It would come via a devastating military defeat (2:14–16; 3:11; 6:14) that decimated the troops sent out by a city (cf. 6:9–10; 8:3; 9:8).

5:2 Virgin. This epithet is used elsewhere of Zion and Judah (e.g., Isa 37:22; Lam 1:15; 2:13). Israel, like an unfortunate young woman, is

5:3 [b]Isa 6:13; Am 6:9
5:4 [c]Isa 55:3; Jer 29:13
5:5 [d]1Sa 11:14; Am 4:4 [e]Am 8:14 [f]1Sa 7:16
5:6 [g]Isa 55:6 [h]ver 14 [i]Dt 4:24 [j]Am 3:14
5:7 [k]Am 6:12
5:8 [l]Job 9:9 [m]Isa 42:16 [n]Ps 104:20; Am 8:9 [o]Ps 104:6-9; Am 4:13
5:9 [p]Mic 5:11
5:10 [q]Isa 29:21 [r]1Ki 22:8
5:11 [s]Am 8:6

your town that marches out a hundred strong
will have only ten left.[b]"

4 This is what the LORD says to Israel:

"Seek me and live;[c]
5 do not seek Bethel,
do not go to Gilgal,[d]
do not journey to Beersheba.[e]
For Gilgal will surely go into exile,
and Bethel will be reduced to nothing.[a][f]"
6 Seek[g] the LORD and live,[h]
or he will sweep through the tribes of Joseph like a fire;[i]
it will devour them,
and Bethel[j] will have no one to quench it.
7 There are those who turn justice into bitterness[k]
and cast righteousness to the ground.

8 He who made the Pleiades and Orion,[l]
who turns midnight into dawn[m]
and darkens day into night,[n]
who calls for the waters of the sea
and pours them out over the face of the land—
the LORD is his name.[o]
9 With a blinding flash he destroys the stronghold
and brings the fortified city to ruin.[p]

10 There are those who hate the one who upholds justice in court[q]
and detest the one who tells the truth.[r]

11 You levy a straw tax on the poor[s]
and impose a tax on their grain.

[a] 5 Hebrew *aven,* a reference to Beth Aven (a derogatory name for Bethel); see Hosea 4:15.

pictured as already having been slain. This image of her discarded body would evoke sadness and dismay.

5:4–6 As at 4:4, the Lord turns Israel's attention away from the sanctuaries. The mention of Beersheba (v. 5), another historic site in southern Judah (Gen 21:14,31; 26:23,33), may indicate that some from Israel were crossing into the southern kingdom to observe their popular religion. All the holy places will be judged (3:14; 7:9; 8:3,14; 9:1). **Seek ... Seek.** While this Hebrew verb can be used of going to holy places (Deut 12:5; 2 Chr 1:5) or of consulting God through a prophet (1 Sam 9:9; Jer 37:7), it can also refer to pleasing God through obedience (Isa 55:6; Hos 10:12; cf. Isa 9:13). That is the best option here. Its meaning is explained in the mirror passage (vv. 14–15).

5:4,6 live. Can mean a quality of life for those who obey God (Deut 30:6; Prov 9:6; 21:21), but here it probably refers to the possibility of surviving the coming invasion (2 Kgs 7:4,12), the fire of divine judgment (cf. 1:4–5) that none will be able to "quench." Repentance is no guarantee of avoiding exile or death at the hands of the enemy, as the parallel passage emphasizes (v. 15), but the demand on Israel to follow the Lord stands.

5:6 Joseph. Refers to the northern kingdom (v. 15; 6:6; cf. Ps 80:1–2; Ezek 37:16,19; Zech 10:6). He was the father of Ephraim, from whom arose the strongest of the northern tribes.

5:7 justice ... righteousness. This combination occurs again in v. 24; 6:12. It is not easy to distinguish the two terms (Gen 18:19; Prov 1:3). Justice can be appreciated as the "fruit of righteousness" (6:12) made concrete in every dimension of a community's life—in dealings between individuals, equitable laws, a properly functioning judicial process, as well as fair and charitable legal decisions. Ultimately, justice and righteousness are grounded in the character of God (Ps 97:2; Isa 30:18; Zeph 3:5). The Lord expects his moral standards to be followed by societies and their rulers, especially by his chosen people (Ps 72:1–2; Isa 1:21; Jer 22:15–16; cf. Matt 25:31–46; Jas 2; 5). **bitterness.** A term based on the word for the wormwood plant, which has an unpleasant odor and taste.

5:8–9 This second doxology (cf. 4:13; 9:5–6) extols the Lord as the Creator of the constellations, the one who controls the rhythms of the day and of the rain, and the omnipotent deity who "destroys the stronghold" and brings to ruin "the fortified city." The divine judge's power is incomparable. The focus of the chiasm of vv. 1–17 (see note there) is "the LORD is his name."

5:10–13 As does the matching passage for v. 7, these verses supply details of the injustice in Israel. The setting is the "court" (see v. 10 and note). Local leaders, merchants, and government officials loathed those who spoke up for justice and the truth, intimidating the prudent to silence. Their many "offenses" (v. 12) included imposing an unfair tax on the vulnerable and using bribes to secure gain. The powerful benefited greatly from these fraudulent dealings, enjoying "stone mansions" and "lush vineyards" (v. 11), but these would be taken away.

5:10 court. The gate of the city, the place for the administration of justice by elders or other officials (Deut 21:19; 25:7; 2 Sam 15:1–4), for business dealings (Gen 23:10–11; Ruth 4:1–12), and for community gatherings (Neh 8:1; Jer 17:19).

Therefore, though you have built stone mansions,[t]
you will not live in them;
though you have planted lush vineyards,
you will not drink their wine.[u]
12 For I know how many are your offenses
and how great your sins.

There are those who oppress the innocent and take bribes
and deprive the poor of justice in the courts.[v]
13 Therefore the prudent keep quiet in such times,
for the times are evil.

14 Seek good, not evil,
that you may live.
Then the LORD God Almighty will be with you,
just as you say he is.
15 Hate evil,[w] love good;
maintain justice in the courts.
Perhaps the LORD God Almighty will have mercy[x]
on the remnant[y] of Joseph.

16 Therefore this is what the Lord, the LORD God Almighty, says:

"There will be wailing[z] in all the streets
and cries of anguish in every public square.
The farmers[a] will be summoned to weep
and the mourners to wail.
17 There will be wailing in all the vineyards,
for I will pass through[b] your midst,"

says the LORD.[c]

5:11 [t]Am 3:15 [u]Mic 6:15
5:12 [v]Isa 5:23; Am 2:6-7
5:15 [w]Ps 97:10; Ro 12:9 [x]Joel 2:14 [y]Mic 5:7,8
5:16 [z]Jer 9:17 [a]Joel 1:11
5:17 [b]Ex 12:12 [c]Isa 16:10; Jer 48:33
5:18 [d]Joel 1:15 [e]Joel 2:2 [f]Isa 5:19,30; Jer 30:7

The Day of the LORD

18 Woe to you who long
for the day of the LORD![d]
Why do you long for the day of the LORD?
That day will be darkness,[e] not light.[f]

5:14–15 These verses develop the meaning of "seek the LORD" in vv. 4–6. **Seek good, not evil ... Hate evil, love good.** The good is defined tangibly as establishing "justice in the courts" (see note on v. 10) in Israel's social, legal, economic, and familial spheres (see note on vv. 10–13). Only by truly following God's demand for justice could the nation expect the presence of the Lord to be with them. God had not been present at the ceremonies held at the sanctuaries (4:4–5,12), no matter their desires or claims. All they could hope was that God would show mercy on them.

5:15 remnant. Those who would survive the judgment (vv. 1–3; 4:2–3; 6:9–10; 8:3; 9:8). **Joseph.** See v. 6 and note; 6:6.

5:16–17 Vividly portrays the pain of the losses in vv. 1–3. The repetitive vocabulary emphasizes the comprehensive impact of the coming war. There will be "wailing ... cries of anguish ... wailing," and many will be called "to weep" and "to wail." The laments would be heard everywhere: in "all the streets ... in every public square ... in all the vineyards." The encounter with the Lord would have frightening consequences (v. 15; 3:6; 4:12). God would "pass through" them in judgment as he had done with the Egyptians (Exod 12:12).

5:18–27 *The Day of the Lord.* Verses 18–27 form a chiasm, or concentric pattern, that exposes the foundationless self-assurance of Israel's religion, which is betrayed by a lack of ethical concern. The erroneous perception of the day of the Lord as a time of victory (vv. 18–20) is matched by an announcement of future exile (vv. 26–27). God's rejection of Israel's worship in the present (vv. 21–23) has its parallel in their past worship in the wilderness (v. 25). The center of the structure is v. 24.

5:18 Woe. The first of two woe passages (cf. 6:1). Woes arise in contexts of mourning (the Hebrew is translated "alas," rather than "woe," in 1 Kgs 13:30; Jer 22:18), which is appropriate after vv. 1–17. On occasion woes can introduce an ironic announcement of doom on those who violate God's laws (e.g., Isa 5:8,11,18,21,22). There may be an element of this nuance here and in 6:1. What follows continues the litany of terrible errors of Israel, here in relationship to "the day of the LORD." **day of the LORD.** This passage reveals that Israel had a false understanding of that day. They believed it would bring "light" (i.e., victory over their enemies). Instead, that day would be "darkness" and "pitch-dark" (v. 20), an inescapable disaster sent by God (2:16; 3:14; 6:3; 8:3,9–11,13). Israel already had begun to experience defeat (4:10), but nothing on this scale. History tells us that this disaster came at the hands of the Assyrians in 722 BC. Israel would be like someone who had fled deadly animals without success (v. 19), so to "long for" that day was foolish. The prediction of exile (vv. 26–27) confirms how wrong the northern kingdom was in its sense of security. The NT develops the concept of

5:19 [g] Job 20:24; Isa 24:17-18; Jer 15:2-3; 48:44
5:20 [h] Isa 13:10; Zep 1:15
5:21 [i] Lev 26:31 [j] Isa 1:11-16
5:22 [k] Isa 66:3; Am 4:4; Mic 6:6-7
5:23 [l] Am 6:5
5:24 [m] Jer 22:3 [n] Mic 6:8
5:25 [o] Isa 43:23 [p] Dt 32:17
5:27 [q] Am 4:13; Ac 7:42-43*

19 It will be as though a man fled from a lion
only to meet a bear,
as though he entered his house
and rested his hand on the wall
only to have a snake bite him.[g]
20 Will not the day of the LORD be darkness, not light —
pitch-dark, without a ray of brightness?[h]

21 "I hate, I despise your religious festivals;[i]
your assemblies[j] are a stench to me.
22 Even though you bring me burnt offerings and grain offerings,
I will not accept them.
Though you bring choice fellowship offerings,
I will have no regard for them.[k]
23 Away with the noise of your songs!
I will not listen to the music of your harps.[l]
24 But let justice[m] roll on like a river,
righteousness like a never-failing stream![n]

25 "Did you bring me sacrifices[o] and offerings
forty years[p] in the wilderness, people of Israel?
26 You have lifted up the shrine of your king,
the pedestal of your idols,
the star of your god[a] —
which you made for yourselves.
27 Therefore I will send you into exile beyond Damascus,"
says the LORD, whose name is God Almighty.[q]

[a] 26 Or *lifted up Sakkuth your king / and Kaiwan your idols, / your star-gods*; Septuagint *lifted up the shrine of Molek / and the star of your god Rephan, / their idols*

this day: believers must live a life of faithfulness and obedience in the light of Christ's second coming and the final judgment (e.g., Rom 2:16; 1 Cor 1:8; Phil 1:10; 2 Thess 1:10; 2 Pet 3:10; Jude 6).

5:21–23 The verbs that open this passage communicate the Lord's deep reaction against Israel's worship. God spurns the northern kingdom's hypocritical worship (v. 5; 4:4). The imagery of divine distaste is made vivid by the reference to the Lord's senses: smell ("stench," v. 21), sight ("regard," v. 22), sound ("listen," v. 23). The seven religious practices listed here reflect God's comprehensive rebuff of the nation's worship. Ceremonies and sacrifices to atone for sin and establish communion with God were now unacceptable. The corresponding verse, v. 25, relates Israel's worship to its history. The Lord also refuses to accept worship in other prophetic books (e.g., Isa 1:11–20; 58:1–14; Jer 7; Ezek 8; Mic 6:1–8; Zech 7; Mal 1–3). In all of these passages, the rejection is connected to the disregard of social justice, a theme v. 24 underscores.

5:24 This is the center and climax of vv. 18–27. In a land where water can be scarce, the image of abundant water is powerful. That region has many wadis, or riverbeds, that are dry except during seasons of rain or immediately after a downpour. God's desire is that justice and righteousness always characterize his people (v. 7) like a "never-failing stream" continually fills ravines.

5:25 This verse corresponds to vv. 21–23 but is difficult to interpret. If the answer to the rhetorical question about Israel's history is "yes," then the lesson is that offering sacrifices in "the wilderness" did not protect that rebellious generation from judgment and would not save Israel now. A response of "no" would appear to contradict the biblical account (Exod 24:4–8; Num 7). Perhaps the assumption is that the conditions for those "forty years" did not allow for sacrifices (due to lack of appropriate animals), yet their limited resources yielded a relationship with God in contrast to the extravagant hypocritical rituals of the northern kingdom. An alternative is that Israel did not have to offer sacrifices then because sacrifices are not necessary to worship God. A religion without rituals, however, would have made no sense in the ancient world. Others focus on "me" for the negative answer: Israel brought sacrifices not to the Lord but to other gods; i.e., illegitimate worship had characterized their history from the beginning (cf. Acts 7:42–43). Another option is to argue that a qualifier is presupposed: Did you bring me *only* sacrifices in the desert? The idea would be that the rituals "in the wilderness" had been accompanied by righteous devotion, unlike the northern kingdom's religious practices. This may be an idealized view of the wilderness period (see Exod 32; Num 25; cf. Hos 2:14–15), but it would serve as a call to follow the model of Israel's ancestors (cf. 2:10).

5:26–27 These verses match vv. 18–20 in the chiasm of vv. 18–27 (see note there) and announce the consequences of the northern kingdom's misplaced religious confidence. This is one of the most challenging passages in the book. The first issue is the tense of the opening verb: "You have lifted up." It puts the action in the past, possibly in connection with v. 25, or describes what Israel was now doing. Another option is to interpret the verb as a future tense, linking v. 26 to v. 27 and Israel's trek into exile. The second issue is the translation of several terms: (1) The word "shrine" reflects the Septuagint (the pre-Christian Greek translation of the OT), and "pedestal" is an uncommon translation choice. Most versions identify these words with Mesopotamian astral ("star") deities and render the terms "Sikkut" (or Sakkuth) and "Kiyyun" (or Kiyun or Kaiwan), respectively (see NIV text note on v. 26). Verse 26 establishes a level of syncretism in Israel due to foreign religious influences (cf.

Samarian ivory furniture inlays, ninth–eighth century BC. Ivory furniture was a sign of opulence (Amos 6:4).

A. D. Riddle/www.BiblePlaces.com, taken at the Israel Museum

Woe to the Complacent

6 Woe to you[r] who are complacent in Zion,
and to you who feel secure on Mount Samaria,
you notable men of the foremost nation,
to whom the people of Israel come![s]
2 Go to Kalneh[t] and look at it;
go from there to great Hamath,[u]
and then go down to Gath[v] in Philistia.
Are they better off than[w] your two kingdoms?
Is their land larger than yours?
3 You put off the day of disaster
and bring near a reign of terror.[x]
4 You lie on beds adorned with ivory
and lounge on your couches.
You dine on choice lambs
and fattened calves.[y]
5 You strum away on your harps[z] like David
and improvise on musical instruments.[a]
6 You drink wine[b] by the bowlful
and use the finest lotions,
but you do not grieve[c] over the ruin of Joseph.
7 Therefore you will be among the first to go into exile;
your feasting and lounging will end.

6:1 [r] Lk 6:24 [s] Isa 32:9-11
6:2 [t] Ge 10:10 [u] 2Ki 18:34 [v] 2Ch 26:6 [w] Na 3:8
6:3 [x] Isa 56:12; Am 9:10
6:4 [y] Eze 34:2-3; Am 3:12
6:5 [z] Isa 5:12; Am 5:23 [a] 1Ch 15:16
6:6 [b] Am 2:8 [c] Eze 9:4

2:8; 7:9; 8:14). Those gods, which Israel had "made," will be carried into an exile decreed by the Lord, the Creator of the stars (v. 8), who is the incomparable "God Almighty." This threat was fulfilled when Assyria took many Israelites into exile (see Introduction: Date and Background; cf. v. 5; 4:3; 6:7; 7:11,17; 9:9).

6:1–7 *Woe to the Complacent.* This is the second woe (cf. 5:18). This mourning cry again heralds doom. The prophet concentrates on the elite of the northern kingdom. They indulge themselves in total disregard of the needs of the people. Therefore, they will lead the way into judgment. These verses and the next passage (vv. 8–14) form the third chiastic structure within 5:1—6:14 (see note there). Misplaced pride (vv. 1–3) finds its echo in a false confidence in Israel's military (vv. 13–14); the callous behavior of the elite (vv. 4–7) is mirrored by v. 12; and the decree of v. 8 is matched by the command of v. 11. The destruction in vv. 9–10 is the center of the concentric pattern.

6:1–3 The prophetic denunciation shifts its target from the nation's worship (5:18–27) to those in power. The prophet includes Zion (i.e., Jerusalem, Judah's capital) in his criticism (2:4–5). The leaders in both Judah and Israel were "complacent" (v. 1). They were self-deceived, not appreciating that other important cities (e.g., Kalneh, capital of the neo-Hittite state of Pattin, to the north; Hamath also to the north, on the Orontes River; and Gath of the Philistines to the west) had suffered defeat in the previous century. This flawed self-assurance would be contradicted by an invasion (vv. 13–14).

6:4–7 The arrogance of the powerful was accompanied by licentious living. They indulged in choice meat (v. 4), "wine by the bowlful" (v. 6), and the "finest lotions" (v. 6). Their repose on "beds adorned with ivory" (v. 4; cf. 3:15) and on "couches" (v. 4) reveals an inexcusable callousness about the "ruin of Joseph" (v. 6; see note on 5:6)—the scarcity endured by the general population (4:6–9), the misery suffered by the poor, and the military defeats. Elements in these verses suggest that they describe a *marzeah* feast, a sumptuous banquet of the wealthy in the ancient world that was apparently related to mourning. It is debated whether pagan rituals were involved. If they were, then this scene is witness to a syncretism of the affluent. This callous debauchery "will end" (v. 7), for this group will be the first to go into exile (5:27; cf. 4:3). The corresponding passage of v. 12 condemns the injustice of the leaders.

6:6 Joseph. See 5:6 and note.

6:8 [d]Ge 22:16; Heb 6:13 [e]Lev 26:30 [f]Ps 47:4 [g]Am 4:2 [h]Dt 32:19
6:9 [i]Am 5:3
6:10 [j]1Sa 31:12 [k]Am 8:3
6:11 [l]Am 3:15 [m]Isa 55:11
6:12 [n]Hos 10:4 [o]Am 5:7
6:13 [p]Job 8:15; Isa 28:14-15
6:14 [q]Jer 5:15 [r]1Ki 8:65 [s]Am 3:11
7:1 [t]Am 8:1 [u]Joel 1:4
7:2 [v]Ex 10:15 [w]Isa 37:4 [x]Eze 11:13

The LORD Abhors the Pride of Israel

8 The Sovereign LORD has sworn by himself[d]—the LORD God Almighty declares:

"I abhor[e] the pride of Jacob[f]
and detest his fortresses;
I will deliver up[g] the city
and everything in it.[h]"

9 If ten[i] people are left in one house, they too will die. 10 And if the relative who comes to carry the
bodies out of the house to burn them[a][j] asks anyone who might be hiding there, "Is anyone else with
you?" and he says, "No," then he will go on to say, "Hush![k] We must not mention the name of the LORD."

11 For the LORD has given the command,
and he will smash the great house[l] into pieces
and the small house into bits.[m]

12 Do horses run on the rocky crags?
Does one plow the sea[b] with oxen?
But you have turned justice into poison[n]
and the fruit of righteousness into bitterness[o]—
13 you who rejoice in the conquest of Lo Debar[c]
and say, "Did we not take Karnaim[d] by our own strength?[p]"

14 For the LORD God Almighty declares,
"I will stir up a nation[q] against you, Israel,
that will oppress you all the way
from Lebo Hamath[r] to the valley of the Arabah.[s]"

Locusts, Fire and a Plumb Line

7 This is what the Sovereign LORD showed me:[t] He was preparing swarms of locusts[u] after the king's
share had been harvested and just as the late crops were coming up. 2 When they had stripped the
land clean,[v] I cried out, "Sovereign LORD, forgive! How can Jacob survive?[w] He is so small![x]"

[a] 10 Or *to make a funeral fire in honor of the dead* [b] 12 With a different word division of the Hebrew; Masoretic Text *plow there* [c] 13 *Lo Debar* means *nothing.* [d] 13 *Karnaim* means *horns*; *horn* here symbolizes strength.

6:8–14 *The Lord Abhors the Pride of Israel.* The confidence of the northern kingdom rests on its defenses and strength. These verses expose how deeply God despises this presumption. Israel's illogical confidence will not be able to deter the sweeping invasion of divine judgment.

6:8 The divine oath and the various ways of referring to God accentuate the seriousness of the declaration of judgment (4:2; 8:7; cf. Gen 22:16; Isa 45:23; Jer 22:5; Heb 6:13). Once again (cf. 5:21) the Lord repudiates the northern kingdom. The parallelism in the verse discloses the source of Israel's pride: their "fortresses" (in context, probably of the city of Samaria [v. 1; cf. 3:9; 4:1]). A national ideology of military might masked the transgressions that filled the centers of power (3:9–10) and blinded Israel to the coming destruction of their defenses (vv. 13–14; 3:11; 4:3; 7:7–8). Such arrogance is unacceptable to God (v. 1; cf. 5:18–20; 9:10). This announcement to "deliver up" the city is matched by the declaration of judgment in v. 11.

6:9–10 This is the center of the chiasm of vv. 1–14 (see note on vv. 1–7). The scene is difficult to understand. The ruins may be due to an earthquake (1:1; 8:8; cf. 9:1) or to the devastation caused by an enemy invasion. Apparently, relatives are searching through the rubble for the dead in order to burn the corpses either to avoid an epidemic or as an expression of mourning (see NIV text note on v. 10; cf. 5:16–17).

6:10 We must not mention the name of the LORD. This line may have been motivated by a superstitious fear that the Lord might return with more disaster. Or it may express deep frustration that the God of their nationalistic theology had failed them by allowing this catastrophe to happen.

6:11 As in v. 8, the Lord decrees destruction on the entire city.

6:12 justice ... righteousness. The combination occurs for a second time (see 5:7). The self-destructive absurdity of reversing the moral order is made manifest by the rhetorical questions. This ethical irrationality corresponds to the insensitivity of those who use wrongdoing to support a luxurious lifestyle (vv. 4–7).

6:13 Lo Debar ... Karnaim. Both located in Transjordan. Lo Debar was north of the Jabbok River in Gilead (2 Sam 9:4–5; 17:27); Karnaim was located in Bashan (4:1). Lo Debar allows for sarcasm: the supposedly mighty armies of Israel had taken a town whose name means "nothing" (see NIV text note). On the other hand, Karnaim (whose name means "horns" [see NIV text note]) may have fed the nation's military pride as horns symbolized power or authority. These were hollow victories.

6:14 "The LORD God Almighty" (also in 5:16; cf. 5:27) was sending an unstoppable foe who would "oppress" the nation from the northern border ("Lebo Hamath"; see Num 13:21) to the southern border ("the valley of the Arabah"; see Deut 3:17). This parody of 2 Kgs 14:25 reveals that the judgment would be comprehensive (vv. 8,11): the breadth of Jeroboam II's success was to be the extent of Israel's defeat.

7:1—9:15 *Five Visions of Israel's Future.* This final section of the book is comprised of five visions. The number of visions is another example of

3So the LORD relented.[y]
"This will not happen," the LORD said.[z]
4This is what the Sovereign LORD showed me: The Sovereign LORD was calling for judgment by fire;[a]
it dried up the great deep and devoured[b] the land. 5Then I cried out, "Sovereign LORD, I beg you, stop!
How can Jacob survive? He is so small![c]"
6So the LORD relented.[d]
"This will not happen either," the Sovereign LORD said.

7This is what he showed me: The Lord was standing by a wall that had been built true to plumb,[a]
with a plumb line[b] in his hand. 8And the LORD asked me, "What do you see,[e] Amos?[f]"
"A plumb line,[g]" I replied.
Then the Lord said, "Look, I am setting a plumb line among my people Israel; I will spare them no
longer.[h]

9"The high places of Isaac will be destroyed
 and the sanctuaries[i] of Israel will be ruined;
with my sword I will rise against the house of Jeroboam.[j]"

Amos and Amaziah

10Then Amaziah the priest of Bethel[k] sent a message to Jeroboam[l] king of Israel: "Amos is raising a
conspiracy[m] against you in the very heart of Israel. The land cannot bear all his words.[n] 11For this is
what Amos is saying:

[a] *7* The meaning of the Hebrew for this phrase is uncertain. [b] *7* The meaning of the Hebrew for this phrase is uncertain; also in verse 8.

7:3 [y] Dt 32:36; Jer 26:19; Jnh 3:10 [z] Hos 11:8
7:4 [a] Isa 66:16 [b] Dt 32:22
7:5 [c] ver 1-2; Joel 2:17
7:6 [d] Jnh 3:10
7:8 [e] Jer 1:11,13 [f] Isa 28:17; La 2:8; Am 8:2 [g] 2Ki 21:13 [h] Jer 15:6; Eze 7:2-9
7:9 [i] Lev 26:31 [j] 2Ki 15:9; Isa 63:18; Hos 10:8
7:10 [k] 1Ki 12:32 [l] 2Ki 14:23 [m] Jer 38:4 [n] Jer 26:8-11

lists of five or seven items (see Introduction: Structure and Literary Features). In three places commentary follows a vision (7:10–17; 8:4–14; 9:11–15). The five visions describe the coming inescapable judgment.

7:1–9 *Three Visions of Disaster.* Amos intercedes for Israel after the first and second visions (vv. 1–3,4–6), but the third lacks any petition (vv. 7–9).

7:1 The first vision concerns a locust plague. Locusts were one of the plagues of Egypt (Exod 10:1–20) and are listed as one of the covenant curses for disobedience (Deut 28:38–42). **swarms of locusts.** Devastating in an ancient agrarian economy like Israel's (cf. Joel 1). God had sent locusts before as a warning (4:9), but this would be larger in scope. **the king's share.** The royal prerogative of claiming a portion of the harvest (cf. 1 Sam 8:15; 1 Kgs 4:7–28). **the late crops.** Vegetables sown after the rains of March and April. The timing was catastrophic. The locusts would leave nothing for the general populace to eat. After the king had taken his share, these insects would destroy the earlier planting of grain that was maturing and the vegetable crop that was beginning to sprout.

7:2–3 The intercessory prayer is a plea for forgiveness. The prophet has a realistic grasp of Israel's condition. Though it might boast of its prosperity and victories, the northern kingdom was vulnerable. Israel would be weak not only because of the hunger brought on by the locusts but also because of its delusions of military strength (vv. 7–9; 6:13; cf. 2:14–16; 3:11; 4:3,11). The Lord responds to the prophet's entreaty and changes his mind about the judgment (cf. Jer 18:5–10; Joel 2:13–14; Jonah 3:9–10). God's willingness to not implement punishment is based on his patient compassion (Exod 34:6–7; Joel 2:12–14). The God of judgment also is the God of mercy.

7:4–6 The second vision concerns an all-consuming fire that devours the subterranean waters (cf. Gen 7:11; Isa 51:10), or perhaps the sea (cf. Jonah 2:5), and the tillable land. Instead of asking for forgiveness, as in the previous vision, Amos asks God to restrain his hand of judgment. Once again the Lord relents, and disaster is averted.

7:7–9 The third vision is different than the previous two. The prophet no longer intercedes for Israel. The primary interpretive problem concerns the Hebrew term *ʾănāk*. This is the only passage in the OT where the term occurs, so its meaning is debated (see NIV text notes on v. 7). It is usually translated "plumb line." Like a builder who uses a plumb line to check to see if a wall is properly vertical, so God will assess whether the nation matches the standards of the law, his "plumb line." This Hebrew word, however, may be a cognate of an Akkadian term for "tin." The scene then would portray God standing on a wall of tin, i.e., one that from a distance might deceivingly look like it is made of strong metal. He rips out a piece of this flimsy wall with his hand and throws it into the midst of the people, mocking the military arrogance of Israel. Its armies cannot protect the holy places or the monarchy (cf. 6:13).

7:9 high places ... sanctuaries. Could refer to the historic sanctuaries of Bethel and Gilgal, where the northern kingdom gathered to worship the Lord, or could be another indication of syncretism among the people (2:8; 5:26; 8:14).

7:10–17 *Expansion: Amos and Amaziah.* This is the first of three amplifications that develop a theme in the preceding vision. This scene at Bethel, Israel's most important national sanctuary, follows naturally after the announcement of the destruction of Israel's holy places (v. 9). Amaziah, the chief priest at Bethel, challenges Amos. To predict doom for Israel's king and its religious centers was to undermine the national theology, which claimed that the Lord would guard and bless Israel (cf. 5:18–20). This belief was celebrated especially at Bethel.

7:10–13 Amaziah considers Amos's questioning of the legitimacy of the Israelite crown (cf. 1:2 and note; 9:11) and of the popular belief in God's unwavering protection of the nation a seditious "conspiracy" (v. 10). Is Bethel not "the king's sanctuary and the temple of the kingdom" (v. 13)? Surely, the Lord is on their side! Perhaps Amaziah is worried that Amos might trigger a coup, like Elisha's disciple had done years before (2 Kgs 9:1–10; cf. 1 Kgs 21:20–24). Accordingly, he reports the prophet to the king and demands that the prophet leave Israel. What right does Amos, a foreigner from Judah, have to denounce their country? Amaziah calls Amos a "seer" (v. 12), which may relate to Amos having visions (cf. 1:1). The priest believes that prophets give messages for hire, since he tells Amos to "earn" his support in his homeland (v. 12).

7:12 [o]Mt 8:34
7:13 [p]Am 2:12; Ac 4:18
7:14 [q]2Ki 2:5; 4:38
7:15 [r]2Sa 7:8 [s]Jer 7:1-2; Eze 2:3-4
7:16 [t]Eze 20:46; Mic 2:6
7:17 [u]Hos 4:13 [v]2Ki 17:6; Eze 4:13; Hos 9:3
8:2 [w]Jer 24:3 [x]Am 7:8 [y]Eze 7:2-9
8:3 [z]Am 5:16 [a]Am 5:23; 6:10
8:4 [b]Pr 30:14 [c]Ps 14:4; Am 2:7

" 'Jeroboam will die by the sword,
and Israel will surely go into exile,
away from their native land.' "

12Then Amaziah said to Amos, "Get out, you seer! Go back to the land of Judah. Earn your bread
there and do your prophesying there.[o] 13Don't prophesy anymore at Bethel, because this is the king's
sanctuary and the temple of the kingdom.[p]"
14Amos answered Amaziah, "I was neither a prophet[q] nor the son of a prophet, but I was a shepherd,
and I also took care of sycamore-fig trees. 15But the LORD took me from tending the flock[r] and said to
me, 'Go, prophesy to my people Israel.'[s] 16Now then, hear the word of the LORD. You say,

" 'Do not prophesy against[t] Israel,
and stop preaching against the descendants of Isaac.'

17"Therefore this is what the LORD says:

" 'Your wife will become a prostitute[u] in the city,
and your sons and daughters will fall by the sword.
Your land will be measured and divided up,
and you yourself will die in a pagan[a] country.
And Israel will surely go into exile,
away from their native land.[v]' "

A Basket of Ripe Fruit

8 This is what the Sovereign LORD showed me: a basket of ripe fruit. 2"What do you see,[w] Amos?[x]"
he asked.
"A basket of ripe fruit," I answered.
Then the LORD said to me, "The time is ripe for my people Israel; I will spare them no longer.[y]
3"In that day," declares the Sovereign LORD, "the songs in the temple will turn to wailing.[b][z] Many,
many bodies—flung everywhere! Silence![a]"

4Hear this, you who trample the needy
and do away with the poor[b] of the land,[c]

5saying,

"When will the New Moon be over
that we may sell grain,
and the Sabbath be ended
that we may market wheat?"—

[a] *17* Hebrew *an unclean* [b] *3* Or *"the temple singers will wail*

7:14–17 Amos responds that his profession had been taking care of his animals and property. He had not aspired to proclaim this harsh message. He was "neither a prophet nor the son of a prophet" (v. 14). He had come to Israel solely because of the irresistible call of the Lord.
7:14 shepherd. Or "herdsman" as the Hebrew word (used only here in the OT) can suggest ownership of herds, not just flocks of sheep. Amos apparently was a prosperous individual (see Introduction: Author; see also 1:1).
7:17 With a fivefold curse, Amos applies the prediction of national exile to Amaziah's family. As chief priest, Amaziah was most responsible for propagating false views of God at the national sanctuary. His wife would be disgraced, his family killed, the inheritance of his land lost, and he banished to die in an unclean land in exile along with the rest of the nation (see Introduction: Date and Background; see also 5:27).
8:1–3 *The Fourth Vision: A Basket of Ripe Fruit.* Once again, the Lord shows something to Amos (cf. 7:1,4,7). The vision utilizes a wordplay in vv. 1–2 between "ripe fruit" (Hebrew *qâyiṣ*) and "the time is ripe" (Hebrew *qēṣ*). God's patience has run out. Now is the day of judgment, a central theme of the chapter (vv. 9,10,11,13). Death and destruction will cause "the songs in the temple" (or palace) to "turn to wailing" (v. 3; see 5:1–3,16–17). Exposure of the dead to the elements and animals of prey was a source of shame (e.g., 1 Kgs 14:11; 2 Kgs 9:26; Jer 22:19). The impact would be so terrible that everyone would be reduced to "silence" (v. 3; cf. 6:10).
8:4–14 *Expansion: The Cost of Religious Perversion.* This is the second amplification of a vision (cf. 7:10–17). This section describes the divorce of worship from ethical responsibility (vv. 4–6) and the judgment that this brings (vv. 7–14).
8:4–6 This passage highlights the economic greed of the merchants who manipulate the weights, scales, and prices in the marketplace—even as they continue with their religious practices. They could not wait for these gatherings to end in order to profit from their corruption. Tampering with weights and scales is prohibited in the law and elsewhere (Lev 19:35–36; Deut 25:13–15; Prov 11:1; 16:11; 20:10,23). The language of vv. 4,6 is reminiscent of 2:6–7, but here victims of injustice are bought as debt slaves (in 2:6 the poor are sold).

skimping on the measure,
boosting the price
and cheating with dishonest scales,[d]
6 buying the poor with silver
and the needy for a pair of sandals,
selling even the sweepings with the wheat.[e]

7 The LORD has sworn by himself, the Pride of Jacob:[f] "I will never forget[g] anything they have done.

8 "Will not the land tremble[h] for this,
and all who live in it mourn?
The whole land will rise like the Nile;
it will be stirred up and then sink
like the river of Egypt.[i]

9 "In that day," declares the Sovereign LORD,

"I will make the sun go down at noon
and darken the earth in broad daylight.[j]
10 I will turn your religious festivals into mourning
and all your singing into weeping.
I will make all of you wear sackcloth[k]
and shave your heads.
I will make that time like mourning for an only son[l]
and the end of it like a bitter day.[m]

11 "The days are coming," declares the Sovereign LORD,
"when I will send a famine through the land —
not a famine of food or a thirst for water,
but a famine of hearing the words of the LORD.[n]
12 People will stagger from sea to sea
and wander from north to east,
searching for the word of the LORD,
but they will not find it.[o]

13 "In that day

"the lovely young women and strong young men
will faint because of thirst.[p]
14 Those who swear by the sin of Samaria —
who say, 'As surely as your god lives, Dan,'[q]
or, 'As surely as the god[a] of Beersheba[r] lives' —
they will fall, never to rise again.[s]"

8:5 [d] 2Ki 4:23; Ne 13:15-16; Hos 12:7; Mic 6:10-11
8:6 [e] Am 2:6
8:7 [f] Am 6:8 [g] Hos 8:13
8:8 [h] Hos 4:3 [i] Ps 18:7; Jer 46:8; Am 9:5
8:9 [j] Job 5:14; Isa 59:9-10; Jer 15:9; Am 5:8; Mic 3:6
8:10 [k] Jer 48:37 [l] Jer 6:26; Zec 12:10 [m] Eze 7:18
8:11 [n] 1Sa 3:1; 2Ch 15:3; Eze 7:26
8:12 [o] Eze 20:3,31
8:13 [p] Isa 41:17; Hos 2:3
8:14 [q] 1Ki 12:29 [r] Am 5:5 [s] Am 5:2

[a] 14 Hebrew *the way*

8:7–10 The seriousness of the charges is underlined by God's swearing by himself (v. 7; see 4:2). In 6:8 "the pride of Jacob" refers to Israel's misplaced confidence in its fortresses, but here in v. 7 it appears to refer to the Lord. That the land will "tremble" (v. 8) like the powerful twisting and surging of the Nile suggests that an earthquake would be part of the divine judgment (1:1; 2:13; cf. 9:1,5). Other vocabulary echoes earlier passages: darkness (v. 9; see 5:18–20) and mourning for the losses suffered (v. 10; see v. 3; 5:16–17).
8:9 darken the earth in broad daylight. Some suggest this refers to an eclipse that occurred in 763 BC.
8:11–14 Rejection of God's messengers (2:11; 7:12–13) yields "a famine of hearing the words of the LORD" (v. 11). This rebuff of the prophets is made worse by the nation's three oaths. These oaths connect a place with a deity; they could refer to other gods or to what some thought to be different manifestations of the Lord at various sanctuaries. If these oaths refer to other deities, this would be more evidence of syncretism (cf. 2:8; 5:26; 7:9). To swear by other gods is prohibited (Josh 23:7). Israel must make its oaths only in the name of the Lord (Deut 6:13; 10:20). Whichever is the case, the nation "will fall, never to rise again" (v. 14; cf. 5:3).
8:14 the sin of Samaria. A disputed phrase. **sin.** Or guilt. Some versions view "sin" as a wordplay on the name of a goddess, Asherah or Ashima (cf. 2 Kgs 17:16,30), who may have been worshiped in the capital.

9:1 [t]Ps 68:21
9:2 [u]Ps 139:8 [v]Jer 51:53 [w]Ob 4
9:3 [x]Am 1:2 [y]Ps 139:8-10 [z]Jer 16:16-17
9:4 [a]Lev 26:33; Eze 5:12 [b]Jer 21:10 [c]Jer 39:16 [d]Jer 44:11
9:5 [e]Ps 46:2; Mic 1:4 [f]Am 8:8
9:6 [g]Ps 104:1-3, 5-6,13; Am 5:8
9:7 [h]Isa 20:4; 43:3 [i]Dt 2:23; Jer 47:4 [j]2Ki 16:9; Isa 22:6; Am 1:5; 2:10

Israel to Be Destroyed

9 I saw the Lord standing by the altar, and he said:

"Strike the tops of the pillars
so that the thresholds shake.
Bring them down on the heads[t] of all the people;
those who are left I will kill with the sword.
Not one will get away,
none will escape.
2 Though they dig down to the depths below,[u]
from there my hand will take them.
Though they climb up to the heavens above,[v]
from there I will bring them down.[w]
3 Though they hide themselves on the top of Carmel,[x]
there I will hunt them down and seize them.[y]
Though they hide from my eyes at the bottom of the sea,
there I will command the serpent to bite them.[z]
4 Though they are driven into exile by their enemies,
there I will command the sword[a] to slay them.

"I will keep my eye on them
for harm[b] and not for good.[c]"[d]

5 The Lord, the LORD Almighty—
he touches the earth and it melts,[e]
and all who live in it mourn;
the whole land rises like the Nile,
then sinks like the river of Egypt;[f]
6 he builds his lofty palace[a] in the heavens
and sets its foundation[b] on the earth;
he calls for the waters of the sea
and pours them out over the face of the land—
the LORD is his name.[g]

7 "Are not you Israelites
the same to me as the Cushites[c]?"[h]

declares the LORD.

"Did I not bring Israel up from Egypt,
the Philistines from Caphtor[d][i]
and the Arameans from Kir?[j]

[a] *6* The meaning of the Hebrew for this phrase is uncertain. [b] *6* The meaning of the Hebrew for this word is uncertain. [c] *7* That is, people from the upper Nile region [d] *7* That is, Crete

9:1–10 *The Fifth Vision: Israel to Be Destroyed.* The fifth and final vision depicts the destruction of a temple, most likely the chief sanctuary at Bethel (cf. 3:14; 5:5; 7:9,13). This was the primary place where the unacceptable national theology was celebrated and perpetuated.

9:1–4 Unlike the previous four, this vision begins with "I saw the Lord." As in other passages (e.g., 6:9–10), it is difficult to know whether the destruction is wrought by an earthquake (1:1; 8:8) or by an invading army (3:11; 4:3). Either way, the religious center of Israel was to be no more (3:14; 5:5; 7:9). The inescapability of divine judgment is expressed poetically in vv. 2–4 by literary merisms (totality expressed by two extremes); everywhere between the two extremes is included in the judgment's scope.

9:4 for harm and not for good. The nation's fate is sealed.

9:5–6 This is the third doxology, and it also closes with the declaration "the LORD is his name" (cf. 4:13; 5:8–9; see notes on 4:12–13; 5:8–9). The vocabulary recalls earlier passages—God is Creator (4:13) and shaker of the land (8:8)—and the various descriptions emphasize the power of the divine Judge.

9:6 lofty palace. Can be translated "steps" and could be a reference to the steps of the Lord's temple (cf. Ezek 40:6), throne (cf. 1 Kgs 10:19–20), or palace (cf. 2 Kgs 20:9–11) "in the heavens." The idea of steps may echo Jacob's dream of the ladder connecting the earth with heaven (Gen 28:10–22).

9:7 Once again the language of the exodus is used in a surprising way. In 3:1–2 the text declares that Israel's unique position as the Lord's chosen people would in no way spare them from judgment. Here, God declares that he also was involved in the history of other nations, even two of Israel's enemies (Philistia and Aram, 1:3–8). **Cushites.** From the southern Nile region, today identified with Sudan.

[8]"Surely the eyes of the Sovereign LORD
are on the sinful kingdom.
I will destroy it
from the face of the earth.
Yet I will not totally destroy
the descendants of Jacob,"
declares the LORD.[k]
[9]"For I will give the command,
and I will shake the people of Israel
among all the nations
as grain[l] is shaken in a sieve,[m]
and not a pebble will reach the ground.
[10]All the sinners among my people
will die by the sword,
all those who say,
'Disaster will not overtake or meet us.'[n]

9:8 [k]Jer 44:27
9:9 [l]Lk 22:31 [m]Isa 30:28
9:10 [n]Am 6:3
9:11 [o]Ps 80:12
9:12 [p]Nu 24:18 [q]Isa 43:7 [r]Ac 15:16-17*

Israel's Restoration

[11]"In that day

"I will restore David's fallen shelter—
I will repair its broken walls
and restore its ruins—
and will rebuild it as it used to be,[o]
[12]so that they may possess the remnant of Edom[p]
and all the nations that bear my name,[a][q]"
declares the LORD, who will do these things.[r]

[13]"The days are coming," declares the LORD,

[a] 12 Hebrew; Septuagint *so that the remnant of people / and all the nations that bear my name may seek me*

9:8 eyes of the Sovereign LORD. Recalls v. 4. Although the judgment on the northern kingdom of Israel was inevitable (vv. 1–4; 2:14–16; 5:19) and would be severe, a remnant would survive (3:12; 5:15).

9:10 the sinners. Those who brought this ruin upon the nation. They had a misplaced confidence in God's protection (5:18–20; 6:13; 7:13).

9:11–15 *Expansion: Israel's Restoration.* The book closes with a brief word of hope that announces a glorious future for Israel and the rest of the world. Judgment is not God's final word; beyond divine chastisement lies wonderful restoration.

9:11 restore David's fallen shelter. "Shelter" (meaning "booth" or "tabernacle") in this context probably refers to the monarchy of Judah. In Amos's time it was not as impressive as it had been in the past, and a few decades later Isaiah and Micah would condemn Judah for its sin and announce judgment. Nevertheless, the ultimate future for the northern kingdom of Israel lay to the south in Judah, not in Jeroboam II's regime or dynasty. "In that day" the promise of a global kingdom under a Davidic king would be fulfilled (2 Sam 7:8–16; cf. Isa 9:6–7; Jer 23:5–8; 33:14–26; Ezek 37:24–28; Hos 3:4–5). For the original audience, these words would have brought to mind this kingdom as a concrete political entity headquartered in its promised land. Some Christian eschatological systems hold that this prediction will find its fulfillment in a millennial age after the second coming of Christ, at which time Israel will turn to its Messiah (cf. Acts 3:19–21; Rom 11:25–27). Several Christian traditions, however, do not contemplate such a future for ethnic Israel. They propose that with the coming of Jesus, the Son of David (Rom 1:3), distinctions between Jew and Gentile have been done away with (Gal 3:26–29; 6:16; Eph 2:11—3:6), and because Jesus "tabernacled" among us (John 1:14), he is the new temple (John 2:18–22), and established believers and the church as temples (1 Cor 3:16–17; 6:19; Eph 2:21). So in this theory, there is now no place for a separate sociopolitical destiny for Israel nor will there be an earthly Davidic kingdom instituted at Jesus' second coming. Rather, at Jesus' second coming the new heavens and new earth of Rev 21–22 will be ushered in.

9:12 The neighboring nations that had attacked Israel (1:3–15), Edom in particular and assumedly even the one that was to invade Israel, would become part of that Davidic kingdom. The inclusion of Gentiles among the people of God finds its roots in the Abrahamic promise (Gen 12:1–3; cf. Deut 28:9–10; 1 Kgs 8:41–43) and was predicted by several prophets (Isa 2:2–4; 19:19–25; Jer 12:15–16; Zech 2:11; 8:22). It is not surprising that at the Jerusalem council of Acts 15:1–29, James introduced his citation of Amos 9:11–12 by saying that "the words of the prophets are in agreement" (Acts 15:15) with the idea of allowing believing Gentiles to be brought into the people of God (Acts 15:13–17). Interestingly, James quotes primarily from the Septuagint (the pre-Christian Greek translation of the OT), whose wording differs from the Hebrew text (i.e., the Masoretic text). The Septuagint of this verse reads "that the rest of mankind may seek the Lord, even all the Gentiles who bear my name" (Acts 15:17). A slight change to the Hebrew is required for this translation, but this rendering does capture the inclusive spirit of the prophetic message and serves as an appropriate summary. Some Christian interpreters relate this verse to the global mission of the church (Matt 28:19–20; Luke 24:45–49; Acts 1:8) and its multinational character.

9:13–15 The vision of restoration starkly contrasts with the hunger,

9:13 [s]Lev 26:5 [t]Joel 3:18
9:14 [u]Isa 61:4 [v]Jer 30:18; 31:28; Eze 28:25-26
9:15 [w]Isa 60:21 [x]Jer 24:6; Eze 34:25-28; 37:12,25

"when the reaper will be overtaken by the plowman[s]
and the planter by the one treading grapes.
New wine will drip from the mountains
and flow from all the hills,[t]
14 and I will bring my people Israel back from exile.[a]

"They will rebuild the ruined cities[u] and live in them.
They will plant vineyards and drink their wine;
they will make gardens and eat their fruit.[v]
15 I will plant[w] Israel in their own land,
never again to be uprooted
from the land I have given them,"
says the LORD your God.[x]

[a] 14 Or *will restore the fortunes of my people Israel*

drought, and destruction that most of the northern kingdom already had endured (4:6–11; cf. 4:1; 6:4–6). The suffering that Amos had announced was imminent. What awaited the faithful remnant and the survivors of God's judgment were abundant crops, food, and drink, which the prophet describes with hyperbolic language. The destruction would pass, and the "ruined cities" (v. 14) would be rebuilt; Israel would return from exile and rest secure in "their own land" (v. 15). This Edenic hope is foundational to the prophets' vision of the future for Israel and the world (e.g., Isa 11:6–9; 35:1–10; 65:17–25). As at v. 11 (see note there), some Christian interpreters connect this prediction with the millennial kingdom and the special promises to ethnic Israel for its future return to the land. Others argue that the historical fulfillment of return occurred when Israel came back from Babylonian exile with the permission of the Persian Empire (2 Chr 36:22–23; Ezra 1:1–4); they hold that the further realization of these promises can be found in the spiritual blessings enjoyed by the church.

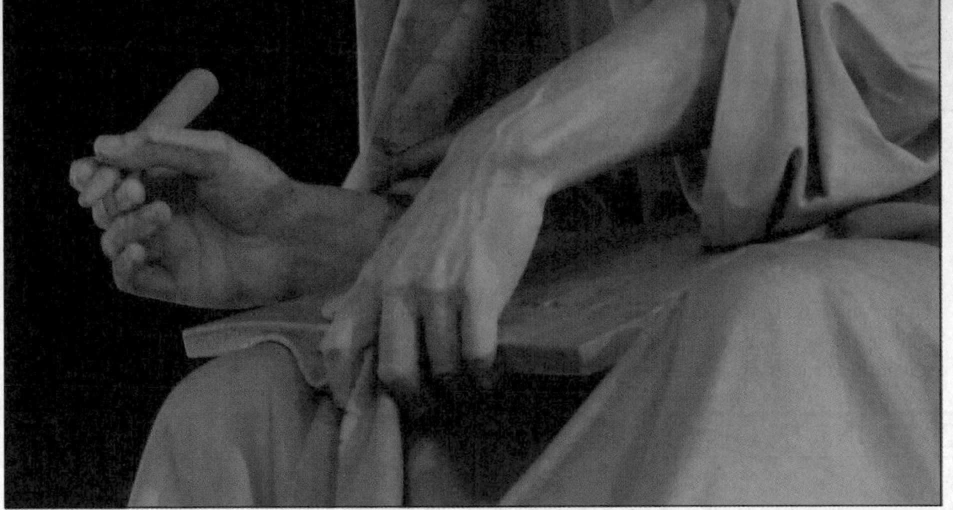

INTRODUCTION TO OBADIAH

Though the shortest OT book (only 292 Hebrew words), Obadiah's prophecy is a powerful, two-pronged message from God: those oppressing God's people will suffer the consequences, and his people will triumph. All is in the hand of the Lord.

AUTHOR

The narrator is identified only by name, Obadiah (which means "the Lord's servant"), with no information concerning time or parentage, though his parents must have been pious followers of Israel's God to give Obadiah his name. At least 11 other OT characters have this name.

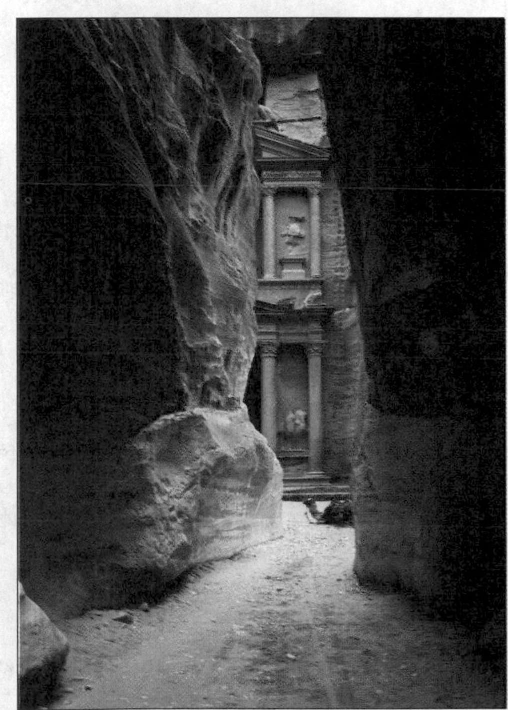

Narrow entrance to ancient Petra, Jordan. Obadiah warns those who "live in the clefts of the rocks" (Obad 3).

© Dimos/Shutterstock

DATE

The book does not mention any specific date indicators such as kings' reigns, so one must use detective work, analyzing the events mentioned. Verses 10 – 14 most likely refer to either the second deportation in 597 BC (2 Kgs 24:8 – 13) or the fall of Jerusalem and the exile of Judah's leaders to Babylon in 586 BC (2 Kgs 25:1 – 9). Therefore, the prophecy is certainly later than the earlier date, probably later than the later date, and most likely from the middle decade of the sixth century BC.

OCCASION AND PURPOSE

Edom, Israel's eastern neighbor (Gen 36:6 – 8), had been mistreating their relatives, the people of Judah, for which God calls them to account. God also takes this opportunity to speak against any nation that acts against his people. Judah, humiliated by their enemy's actions, can now take hope since God will restore what they had lost.

GENRE AND STRUCTURE

The poetic prophecies, which make up the majority of the book, are introduced and interrupted by prose elements in which the author identifies the broad literary genre of the book as a vision (v. 1) and its source being the Lord (vv. 4,8,18). The poetry includes a battle call, which begins the prophecy (v. 1), judgment speeches against Edom (vv. 2 – 14) and every nation (vv. 15 – 18), and ends with a salvation promise to Israel (vv. 19 – 21).

THEMES AND THEOLOGY

The lordship of God encompasses the book (vv. 1,21), as well as his sovereignty over all humanity. God shows his justice by calling people, even pagan Edom and the nations, to account for their hurtful actions against his chosen nation. The Edomites are specifically singled out due to their kinship relationship with Israel, which should demand

LOCATIONS IN OBADIAH

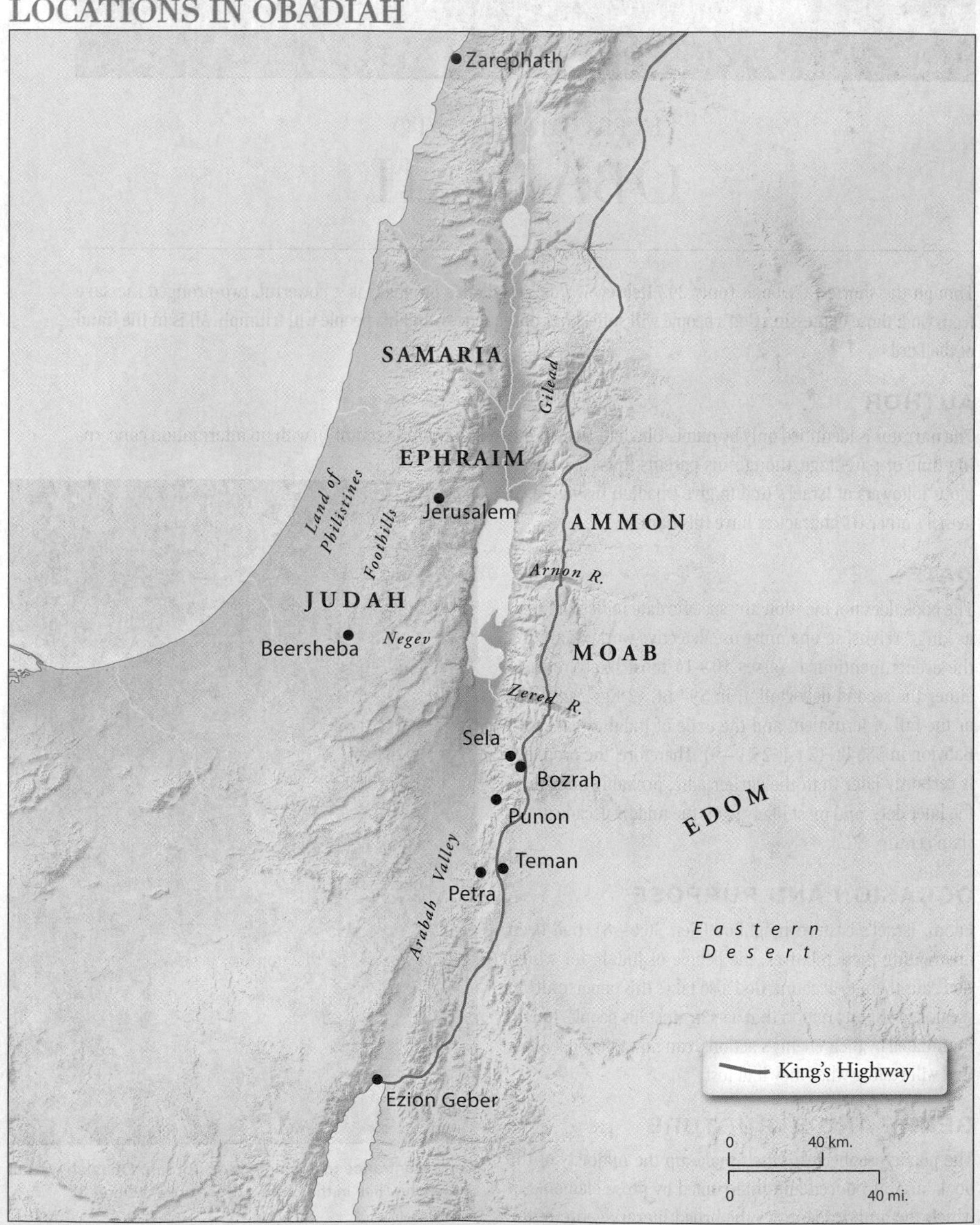

support rather than opposition. While Israel's punishment through defeat and exile is justified since they broke their covenant with God (Deut 29:28; 1 Kgs 14:15–16), God's grace and faithfulness to his own covenant obligations toward Israel (Deut 30) lead him to restore them (vv. 17–21). God does not make a blanket, permanent judgment of punishment on the nations, but makes judgment or blessing dependent on their response to God and his people (v. 15). The time for this judgment is the day of the Lord. This day is a final, eschatological event (2 Pet 3:12–13) when the faithful are blessed (Joel 2:28–32) but sinners are punished (Amos 5:18–20). Prior to this culminating event there are also times of judgment throughout Israel's history—anticipatory days of the Lord (Joel 1–2).

OUTLINE

I. Heading (1)
- A. Title (1a)
- B. The Lord Against Edom (1b)

II. Messages Against Edom (2–14)
- A. Pride's Downfall (2–4)
- B. Hurtful Enemies and Friends (5–7)
- C. In That Day (8–10)
- D. Why You Suffer, Edom (11–14)

III. The Nations and Israel (15–21)
- A. A Reversal (15–18)
- B. Israel Will Return (19–21)

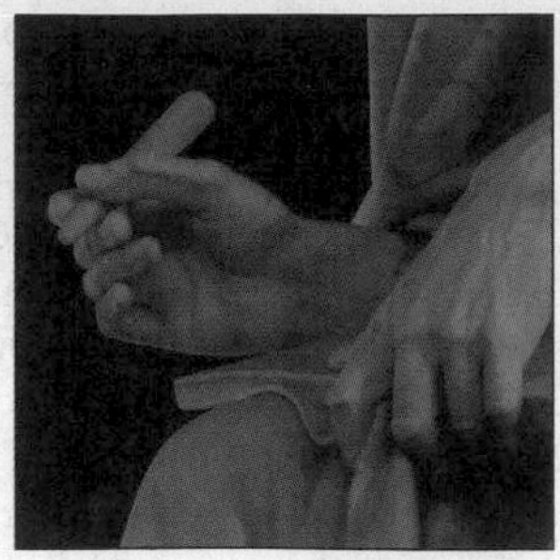

OBADIAH

1 [a]Isa 63:1-6; Jer 49:7-22; Eze 25:12-14; Am 1:11-12 [b]Isa 18:2 [c]Jer 6:4-5
3 [d]Isa 16:6 [e]Isa 14:13-15; Rev 18:7
4 [f]Hab 2:9 [g]Isa 14:13 [h]Job 20:6

Obadiah's Vision

1-4pp — Jer 49:14-16
5-6pp — Jer 49:9-10

1 The vision of Obadiah.

This is what the Sovereign LORD says about Edom[a]—

We have heard a message from the LORD:
An envoy[b] was sent to the nations to say,
"Rise, let us go against her for battle"[c]—

2 "See, I will make you small among the nations;
you will be utterly despised.
3 The pride[d] of your heart has deceived you,
you who live in the clefts of the rocks[a]
and make your home on the heights,
you who say to yourself,
'Who can bring me down to the ground?'[e]
4 Though you soar like the eagle
and make your nest[f] among the stars,
from there I will bring you down,"[g]

declares the LORD.[h]

[a] 3 Or *of Sela*

1 *Heading.* This introduces the prophet, the literary form of his book, and the Lord's commission of him to preach against a neighboring enemy (see Introduction).
1a *Title.* The literary genre of the book is a "vision," something known through either physical sight (Isa 1:1) or other means of prophetic perception. This prophet is Obadiah (see Introduction: Author).
1b *The Lord Against Edom.* The narrator introduces the speaker, Israel's God, and the nation against whom he urged his people to join him in battle.
1b This is what ... says. A messenger formula found also in contemporary documents to indicate who commissioned the messenger. **Edom.** Located in southern Transjordan, from the tip of the Dead Sea south to the Gulf of Aqaba. Esau is their founding ancestor (Gen 36). Edom opposed Israel after the exodus (Num 20:14–21) and at others times in Israel's history (2 Sam 8:13–14; 2 Kgs 16:6). They moved into southern Judah when Edom fell to the Arabs in the fifth century BC, as shown by archaeological remains. Their new location was later named after them: Idumea (Mark 3:8).
2–14 *Messages Against Edom.* God holds the Edomites, longtime opponents of Israel, responsible for how they have mistreated their neighbors. Even non-Israelites fall under God's judgment, receiving punishment for the evil they inflict.
2–4 *Pride's Downfall.* Living high among the rocky plateaus rising up to 5,000 feet (1,525 meters) above sea level to the south and east of the Dead Sea, the Edomites felt pride in their security against attack from human enemies. They forgot that God is not stopped by such fortifications. They are condemned in almost the same words in Jer 49:14–16.
2 small. Compared even to Israel (and more so to the major nations of the period: Babylonia and Egypt), Edom is "small" numerically and geographically, and God will diminish their honor even further.
3 clefts of the rocks. Narrow mountain passages where a few soldiers could easily hold off an attacking army. They were common in western Edom. "Rock" can also be translated "Sela," a fortress captured by Amaziah king of Judah in the early eighth century BC (2 Kgs 14:7).
4 The cliffs of Edom provide good nesting for the eagle or griffin vulture (Job 39:27–28), large birds of prey that fly swiftly and high (2 Sam 1:23; Prov 23:5), though not literally to the "stars," which emphasizes height through hyperbole.

5 "If thieves came to you,
if robbers in the night—
oh, what a disaster awaits you!—
would they not steal only as much as they wanted?
If grape pickers came to you,
would they not leave a few grapes?[i]
6 But how Esau will be ransacked,
his hidden treasures pillaged!
7 All your allies[j] will force you to the border;
your friends will deceive and overpower you;
those who eat your bread[k] will set a trap for you,[a]
but you will not detect it.

8 "In that day," declares the LORD,
"will I not destroy[l] the wise men of Edom,
those of understanding in the mountains of Esau?
9 Your warriors, Teman,[m] will be terrified,
and everyone in Esau's mountains
will be cut down in the slaughter.
10 Because of the violence[n] against your brother Jacob,[o]
you will be covered with shame;
you will be destroyed forever.[p]
11 On the day you stood aloof
while strangers carried off his wealth
and foreigners entered his gates
and cast lots[q] for Jerusalem,
you were like one of them.
12 You should not gloat over your brother
in the day of his misfortune,

5 [i] Dt 24:21
7 [j] Jer 30:14 [k] Ps 41:9
8 [l] Job 5:12; Isa 29:14
9 [m] Ge 36:11,34
10 [n] Joel 3:19 [o] Ps 137:7; Am 1:11-12 [p] Eze 35:9
11 [q] Na 3:10

[a] 7 The meaning of the Hebrew for this clause is uncertain.

5–7 *Hurtful Enemies and Friends.* The Edomites became rich both from trade routes passing through their land (Num 20:17) and from sea traffic (1 Kgs 9:26–28), but both enemy and friend find them open to plunder.
5 leave a few grapes. Israelite law required farmers to leave some grapes at the harvest to supply food for the poor of the land who did not have their own vineyards to harvest (Lev 19:10). Edom was known for its grapes and wine (cf. Isa 63:1–3), but these, and all other things of value, will be pillaged.
6 hidden treasures. Their wealth and vulnerable family members. The ancient Greek historian Diodorus Siculus mentions the Edomites using their mountain fortresses as protection for their treasures.
7 allies. Or "those of your covenant." Edom will be abandoned by those with whom they had a formal relationship as "friends." **those who eat your bread.** This group would have also been at peace with Edom since only friends and partners (not enemies) eat together (Gen 14:18; 31:51–54).
8–10 *In That Day.* When the Edomites are violent toward their neighbor, even those who should help them are unable to withstand God. They will find themselves vulnerable even in their mountain fortress.
8 In that day. Though referring to Edom's imminent destruction, it also anticipates the eschatological day of the Lord (see Introduction: Themes and Theology), when all humanity will be judged. **Edom.** Famed for its "wise men" (see Jer 49:7), whose human insights are unable to help them any more than Egypt's wise men were able to help Pharaoh (Exod 7:11). Using poetic variation, three terms identify Israel's enemy: they designate the nation through its geographic location (Edom), through what could be either another name for the land as a whole (Teman, "southland"; v. 9; Job 2:11; Jer 49:7) or one of its cities (Tawilan, in southern Jordan just north of Petra), and through its ancestral founder (Esau; Gen 36).
9 warriors. The elite force of Teman (2 Sam 20:7). They will be anything but heroic; they will cower in terror (cf. 1 Sam 17:51).
10 your brother Jacob. The Edomites descended from Esau, who is first called "Edom" when he sells his birthright to his brother (Gen 25:30). Violence against anyone is wicked, but it is even more so when it ignores kinship bonds.
11–14 *Why You Suffer, Edom.* The Edomites gradually increased their evil against Judah, starting out as spectators gloating at its misfortune, becoming plunderers, and finally turning refugees back to their enemy. This will all come back against them.
11,13 gates. For protection, towns had walls to keep enemies and animals out. Entry was through the "gates," which were closed at night. Unguarded and open gates show that the town was humiliated, no longer under its own control.
11 stood aloof. The Edomites were indifferent (cf. 2 Sam 18:13; Ps 38:11) rather than defending their brothers and standing beside them when they were under attack as is expected of a family. This event is probably in conjunction with an onslaught by the Babylonians under Nebuchadnezzar in which Jerusalem was plundered and many people were taken into exile, though no mention of such a role for Edom is found either in the Bible or elsewhere. **cast lots.** Conquerors cast lots to divide booty in a way that would not favor one party over another or to decide what was to be taken and what was to be destroyed (Ps 22:18; Joel 2:3; Mark 15:24).
12 gloat ... rejoice ... boast. The response of Edom to their brother's difficulties was not neutral: they took perverse pleasure, stopping to

12 [r] Eze 35:15 [s] Pr 17:5 [t] Mic 4:11
13 [u] Eze 35:5
15 [v] Eze 30:3 [w] Jer 50:29; Hab 2:8
16 [x] Jer 25:15; 49:12
17 [y] Am 9:11-15 [z] Isa 4:3
18 [a] Zec 12:6

nor rejoice[r] over the people of Judah
in the day of their destruction,[s]
nor boast so much
in the day of their trouble.[t]
13 You should not march through the gates of my people
in the day of their disaster,
nor gloat over them in their calamity[u]
in the day of their disaster,
nor seize their wealth
in the day of their disaster.
14 You should not wait at the crossroads
to cut down their fugitives,
nor hand over their survivors
in the day of their trouble.

15 "The day of the LORD is near[v]
for all nations.
As you have done, it will be done to you;
your deeds[w] will return upon your own head.
16 Just as you drank on my holy hill,
so all the nations will drink[x] continually;
they will drink and drink
and be as if they had never been.
17 But on Mount Zion will be deliverance;[y]
it will be holy,[z]
and Jacob will possess his inheritance.
18 Jacob will be a fire
and Joseph a flame;
Esau will be stubble,
and they will set him on fire and destroy[a] him.
There will be no survivors
from Esau."

The LORD has spoken.

"gloat" (an internal response), "rejoice" (showing their attitude outwardly; cf. Prov 24:17), and even "boast" (taking national credit for their perversity).

13 The Edomites should not have "marched" into the conquered city, entering what was not theirs, or "gloat over them," or "seizing" what the demoralized Israelites could no longer protect.

14 wait ... cut down ... hand over. The culminating act of betrayal against their brothers was to lie in wait, capturing any "fugitives" who escaped, any "survivors" of the battle for Jerusalem, and turning them over to their conquerors. This fits the period of Edomite expansion into southern Judah (v. 1b). The Edomites, who prided themselves in their geographic protection from attack, do not protect their own kin but show them treachery instead, handing them over to defeat and slavery (Amos 1:6,9).

15–21 *The Nations and Israel.* Judgment day, when it comes, will not be only for Edom; God will judge every nation that oppresses his people, the Israelites. Israel gladly receives this news of judgment on their enemies since that means that God will restore what they lost.

15–18 *A Reversal.* The Lord's day of judgment will turn the mistreated Israelites into the means through which God will bring about his just punishment.

15 The day of the LORD. An important prophetic theme (e.g., Amos 2:16; 5:18; Zeph). It has two aspects: It will bring (1) judgment upon the enemies of God and his people and (2) blessing upon those who follow God's ways. Edom, and now "all nations," will be among the former group because they mistreated Israel. The Edomites ("you") are specifically told that they will receive the same kind of indignities that they rained on their brothers.

16 drank ... drink ... drink and drink. Celebrating a successful military campaign often involved an excess of drink, from which Edom (Lam 4:21) and the nations will become drunk and stupefied, losing all ability to aid themselves. This refers not only to literal alcohol, which could be part of their plunder, but also to the metaphoric cup of God's wrath that would bring not joy but suffering (Jer 49:12; Hab 2:16; Rev 14:10). **holy hill.** Commonly called "Mount Zion" (v. 17; Ps 48:2; Joel 2:32), it was the location of the temple and the center not only of Jerusalem but of all Israel. Cf. Jer 31:23.

17–18 But. A major contrast and change in focus comes in the course of events. Restoring an "inheritance" that Judah will "possess" will replace defeat and loss (Gen 15:7–8; Isa 54:3). Two titles represent Israel: (1) **Jacob.** Esau's brother, appropriate in this context in which Jacob's descendants, the people of Judah, are in conflict with Esau's descendants, Edom. It represents the southern kingdom. (2) **Joseph.** Represents the northern kingdom of Israel. Israel is often called "Ephraim" after the son of its founder, Joseph (Gen 41:50–52; see Obad 19 and note). This suggests that though the northern kingdom had been previously exiled, the northern and southern kingdoms will be reunited,

[19] People from the Negev will occupy
the mountains of Esau,
and people from the foothills will possess
the land of the Philistines.[b]
They will occupy the fields of Ephraim and Samaria,[c]
and Benjamin will possess Gilead.
[20] This company of Israelite exiles who are in Canaan
will possess the land as far as Zarephath;[d]
the exiles from Jerusalem who are in Sepharad
will possess the towns of the Negev.[e]
[21] Deliverers will go up on[a] Mount Zion
to govern the mountains of Esau.
And the kingdom will be the LORD's.[f]

19 [b] Isa 11:14 [c] Jer 31:5
20 [d] 1Ki 17:9-10 [e] Jer 33:13
21 [f] Ps 22:28; Zec 14:9, 16; Rev 11:15

[a] 21 Or *from*

restoring both the nation and the temple (Ezek 40–48). **no survivors.** This claim of the complete extermination of the Edomites, like that of the Canaanites (Josh 10:40), is literary hyperbole (see Amos 9:12, noting the comparison with Acts 15:17).

19–21 *Israel Will Return.* While a message of judgment on their enemies can encourage Israel, hearing that Israel will get back what they lost to their enemies is even better news. God does remember his people in their need!

19 Negev. Southwest of the Dead Sea (Gen 20:1). Edomites who had encroached upon Judah's territory (to Edom's west) will now receive the same treatment from Judah. Israel will also dispossess other "nations" (v. 15), including the Philistines. **Philistines.** Longtime enemies of Israel (1 Sam 7:3; 17:1); their land lay in the southwest of Judah's territory. Judah's expansion will also move into the territory of the exiled northern kingdom of Ephraim. **Samaria.** Ephraim's capital. **Benjamin.** One of the two tribes (Josh 18:11) north of Judah's territory. They will take the area of "Gilead," across the Jordan to Benjamin's east.

20 Israelite restoration expands, including "Canaan" (the promised land; Num 34:2–12), as far north as Zarephath. **Zarephath.** South of Sidon in Lebanon (1 Kgs 17:9), a territory Israel never completely occupied (Josh 13:1–6). **Sepharad.** The Lydian capital in western Turkey. It was a distant place of exile. The returnees to the Negev will complete the restoration to Israel of the entire promised land.

21 the kingdom will be the LORD's. In the midst of joy at the restoration of the land, Israel needs reminding that it all belongs to God. He is the "King of all the earth" (Ps 47:7) and most specifically the king of Israel. He reigns from his sanctuary on Mount Zion (see v. 16 and note; see also Exod 15:17–18). This eschatological kingdom will be reestablished by God and his Son, Jesus the Messiah (Rev 11:15).

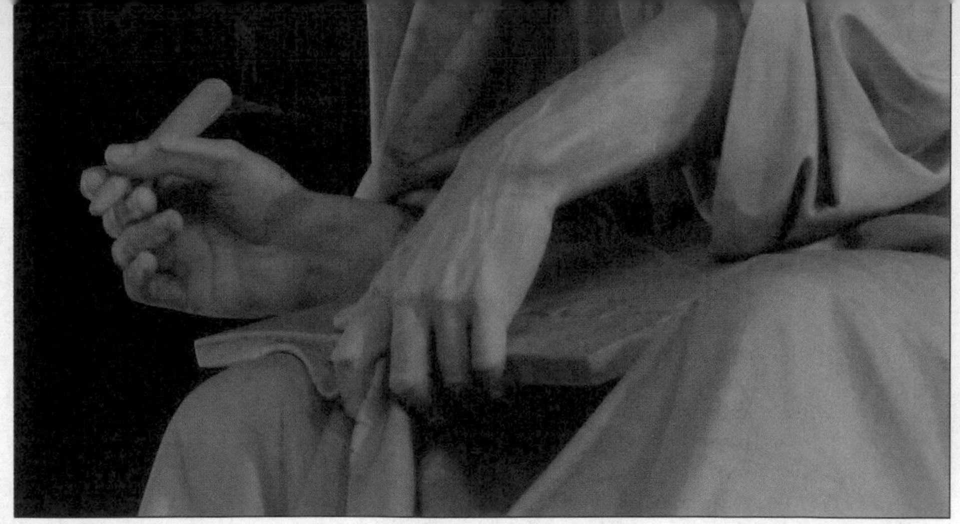

INTRODUCTION TO JONAH

The short account of Jonah's mission to the city of Nineveh presents a challenging message to its readers. Once we look beyond the popular image of Jonah and the "whale," we discover a deeply profound story that explores the complex relationship between divine justice and mercy.

AUTHOR

Although its central character, "Jonah son of Amittai" (1:1), is credited with composing the song of thanksgiving in 2:2 – 9, we cannot be certain that he is the book's author. As it comes to us, the book of Jonah is anonymous. While we may not be able to identify the author, he was clearly a gifted writer, because the story displays an extensive use of literary devices (e.g., concentric structures, key words, wordplay).

DATE

Scholars have debated at length when the book of Jonah was composed. According to 2 Kgs 14:25, a prophet by the name of "Jonah son of Amittai" was active during the reign of Jeroboam II (793/92 – 753 BC). There is good reason to equate that Jonah with the one mentioned in the book of Jonah. This implies that the book cannot have been composed before the middle of the eighth century BC. The earliest known references to the book come from the second century BC. In the absence of further evidence, the majority of scholars tend to favor a date of composition in the fifth or fourth centuries BC, arguing that this is the most likely option on the basis of linguistic features and supposedly historical inaccuracies. However, a strong case can be made for an earlier date of composition.

GENRE

Much discussion centers on how the book of Jonah should be understood. Does it report real historical events, or is it a fictional account created to teach an important truth? Those who support the latter understanding point to the series of miraculous events recorded in the book as evidence against its being factually accurate. Could Jonah have possibly survived inside a fish for 72 hours? Would the entire city of Nineveh, both people and animals, have repented at the preaching of a foreign prophet? Could the plant that sheltered Jonah have grown up in one day? Such questions need to be asked and carefully considered. Unfortunately, there are no easy answers. Many modern scholars are drawn toward explanations that avoid affirming the historical nature of the book of Jonah, suggesting that it could be a parable-like story that seeks to communicate a profound truth through a fictional account. While this is a possibility, it cannot be overlooked that Jesus, in common with all the earliest readers of Jonah, assumed the historicity of the story (Matt 12:39 – 42; 16:4; Luke 11:29 – 32). For Christians, Jesus' testimony ought to be viewed as decisive on this issue. To dismiss these exceptional occurrences as utterly impossible simply because they are miraculous automatically excludes belief in an all-powerful God. Yet such a God lies at the heart of the Christian faith, for we believe that this same God raised Jesus Christ to life, an even more miraculous event.

HISTORICAL SETTING

To appreciate the book's message, readers need to have some understanding of its historical context. 2 Kings 14:25 identifies Jonah as an eighth-century BC prophet originating from the village of Gath Hepher in the Galilee region. Unlike his contemporaries Amos and Hosea, Jonah grew up in the northern kingdom of Israel and appears to have been loyal to his homeland, prophesying that its borders would extend under King Jeroboam II, during a period when the elite classes prospered. But all was far from well within Israel, and the nation continued to move further and further from serving God during the eighth century BC.

While the Assyrians had been an aggressive enemy against Israel a century earlier, by Jonah's time their power had waned. However, all this was about to change. In 722 BC the Assyrians would capture Samaria, the capital of Israel, and deport over 27,000 inhabitants before repopulating the region with foreigners. Early readers of Jonah, aware of Samaria's downfall, likely associated Jonah's reluctance to go to Nineveh with this traumatic event. Jonah possibly knew from Hosea's preaching that the Assyrians were a threat to the future well-being of Israel (see Hos 9:3; 10:6; 11:5; cf. Amos 5:27). Conscious from the outset that God would pardon the Assyrians of Nineveh and not destroy their city, Jonah tried to prevent this from happening. By fleeing from God's presence, he hoped to secure the future safety of Israel. To this end, he was willing to sacrifice his own life rather than be the prophet whose message would cause the Ninevites to repent.

PURPOSE

Why was the story composed? The plentiful answers to this question generally fall into one of four categories.

1. *To encourage repentance.* At the heart of the book's plot is the repentance of the Ninevites at Jonah's preaching.

JONAH AND NINEVEH

When Jonah announces the city's destruction, the Ninevites repent of their wickedness, thus averting God's judgment. The repentance of wicked pagans provides an example for Jews to follow. For this reason, Jews read the book of Jonah on the Day of Atonement, when they fast and repent of their sins.

2. *To show that prophecies of judgment can be conditional.* As a story that centers on an unfulfilled prophetic pronouncement of judgment, the book of Jonah highlights the conditional nature of prophecies. In the opinion of some scholars, the book was composed to show that all prophecies of judgment are essentially conditional, spoken by a prophet with the intention of summoning people to repentance. It is claimed that the story of Jonah acts as a counterbalance to the assertion in Deut 18:22: "If what a prophet proclaims in the name of the LORD does not take place or come true, that is a message the LORD has not spoken." In the case of Jonah, his message was indeed from the Lord.

3. *To show how Jews should view Gentiles.* Throughout the book, Jonah's disobedience and anger toward God contrast with the positive actions of pagan Gentiles. In ch. 1 the sailors, in spite of their precarious situation, display compassion for Jonah during the storm. In ch. 3 the people of Nineveh respond immediately by fasting and mourning for their wrongdoing. In marked contrast, Jonah defiantly and stubbornly opposes God's compassion toward Gentiles.

4. *To explore the complex relationship between God's justice and mercy.* Through exploring the very differing attitudes of God and Jonah toward the repentant people of Nineveh, the book of Jonah provides an important insight into the relationship between divine justice and mercy. This is especially true in ch. 4, where Jonah complains to God about the nondestruction of Nineveh and then about the destruction of the plant that shelters him. In both instances, Jonah is so angry with God that he considers life not worth living. Jonah appraises God's actions in terms of how they will impact him personally. As a prophet, he anticipates that sparing the Ninevites will result in the destruction of his own nation, Israel. Any temporary comfort that he derives from the plant swiftly ends when it wilts. Jonah's self-centered evaluation of God's actions reveals that Jonah wants justice for his enemies but mercy for himself (cf. his song of praise in 2:2–9). But God, unlike Jonah, is totally impartial. As a gracious and forgiving God, his mercy may extend to the most unlikely of people.

In assessing why the book of Jonah was composed, all of these ideas merit consideration and each may possibly contribute something toward a final answer. Ultimately, the most appropriate solution will explain why the author of Jonah has included every element within the story. Some answers listed above go much further toward doing this than others.

JONAH IN THE NEW TESTAMENT

There are three brief references to Jonah in the Gospels (Matt 12:39–42; 16:4; Luke 11:29–32). In all three passages Jesus speaks of "the sign of [the prophet] Jonah" in the context of a "wicked [and adulterous] generation" asking for a sign. The intended sign, according to Luke 11:30, involves some kind of resemblance between Jonah and Jesus, although with Jesus "something greater than Jonah" occurs (Luke 11:32).

The parallels between Jonah and Jesus must not be pushed too far, for they are in many ways very different. Of the possible parallels between them, four are most apparent: (1) Jonah and Jesus call people to repent. (2) As Jonah was "three days and three nights in the belly of a huge fish," so Jesus will be "three days and three nights in the heart of the earth" (Matt 12:40). (3) The activities of Jonah and Jesus result in repentant Gentiles being saved but wicked Israelites/Jews being punished. (4) Both Jonah and Jesus sacrifice themselves in order to save others, but God delivers them from death. The "sign of Jonah" may consist of some or all of these elements.

OUTLINE

I. Jonah Flees From the Lord (1:1–16)

II. Jonah's Prayer (1:17—2:10)

III. Jonah Goes to Nineveh (3:1–10)

IV. Jonah's Anger at the Lord's Compassion (4:1–11)

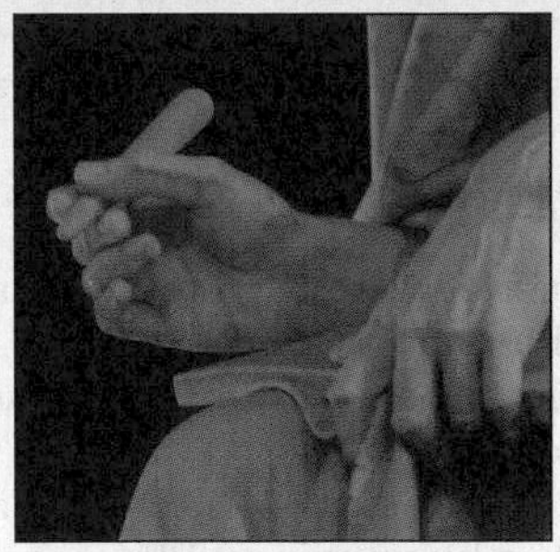

JONAH

Jonah Flees From the LORD

1 The word of the LORD came to Jonah[a] son of Amittai:[b] 2 "Go to the great city of Nineveh[c] and preach
against it, because its wickedness has come up before me."
3 But Jonah ran[d] away from the LORD and headed for Tarshish. He went down to Joppa,[e] where he
found a ship bound for that port. After paying the fare, he went aboard and sailed for Tarshish to flee
from the LORD.
4 Then the LORD sent a great wind on the sea, and such a violent storm arose that the ship threatened
to break up.[f] 5 All the sailors were afraid and each cried out to his own god. And they threw the cargo
into the sea to lighten the ship.[g]
But Jonah had gone below deck, where he lay down and fell into a deep sleep. 6 The captain went
to him and said, "How can you sleep? Get up and call[h] on your god! Maybe he will take notice of us so
that we will not perish."[i]
7 Then the sailors said to each other, "Come, let us cast lots to find out who is responsible for this
calamity."[j] They cast lots and the lot fell on Jonah. 8 So they asked him, "Tell us, who is responsible for
making all this trouble for us? What kind of work do you do? Where do you come from? What is your
country? From what people are you?"

1:1 [a] Mt 12:39-41 [b] 2Ki 14:25
1:2 [c] Ge 10:11
1:3 [d] Ps 139:7 [e] Jos 19:46; Ac 9:36,43
1:4 [f] Ps 107:23-26
1:5 [g] Ac 27:18-19
1:6 [h] Jnh 3:8 [i] Ps 107:28
1:7 [j] Jos 7:10-18; 1Sa 14:42

1:1–16 *Jonah Flees From the Lord.* Jonah deliberately evades God's instruction to preach against the Assyrian city of Nineveh. Jonah does not merely ignore the command; he sets out to get as far away from God and Nineveh as possible. To add to the sense of Jonah's rebellion against God, the pagan sailors respond in ways that put Jonah to shame.

1:1 The word of the LORD came to. Frequently introduces divine communication. While this often introduces the message a prophet proclaims (e.g., Joel 1:1; Mic 1:1), sometimes, as here, it introduces an instruction for a prophet to obey (e.g., 2 Sam 7:4–5; 1 Kgs 17:2–3). **Jonah son of Amittai.** See Introduction: Author; Date.

1:2 great city. See note on 3:3. **Nineveh.** An important provincial city in Assyria during the eighth century BC. It was located on the Tigris River about 500 miles (800 kilometers), or a month's journey, from Israel. It later became the capital of the Assyrian Empire during the reign of Sennacherib (705–681 BC), who redeveloped the city considerably. The ruins of the ancient city, which the Medes destroyed in 612 BC, are close to the modern city of Mosul in northern Iraq. **preach against it, because its wickedness has come up before me.** The message is condemnation. While Israelite prophets often denounced the sins of other nations, they rarely preached directly to them.

1:3 ran away. An unexpected response. The story does not explain Jonah's decision to disobey God until 4:2. **Tarshish.** Associated with a distant location that may be reached by ship (cf. Ps 72:10; Isa 66:19). One possible candidate is Tartessos on the southern Atlantic coast of Spain. Jonah decides to get as far away from Nineveh as is physically possible. **went down.** At each stage of his flight from God, Jonah goes downward in elevation (see note on 2:6). **Joppa.** A port on the Mediterranean coast; now called Jaffa.

1:4 the LORD sent a great wind. The Hebrew text says that God threw the wind at the sea. Later, the sailors will throw the cargo (v. 5) and eventually Jonah (v. 15) into the sea in response to God's action. This is the first of a series of events that highlight God's sovereign power at work in nature: providing the fish (v. 17), returning Jonah to dry land (2:10), providing the plant (4:6), providing the worm (4:7), and providing the east wind (4:8).

1:5 afraid. The first of three references to the sailors' fear (see vv. 10,16). While their fear of the storm intensifies in v. 10, by v. 16 their fear focuses on the one who initiated the storm. **his own god.** The sailors, possibly of different nationalities, apparently worshiped several different pagan gods. They later cry out to the Lord (v. 14). **below deck.** Descending yet again (see note on v. 3), Jonah is oblivious to the danger of the storm.

1:6 Maybe he will take notice of us. Acknowledges that gods are free to act as they wish (see also 3:9). In contrast, Jonah struggles to accept that God is free to act as he pleases. **so that we will not perish.** The captain rebukes Jonah for his indifference toward the plight of those around him. A similar indifference surfaces later regarding Jonah's feelings concerning the citizens of Nineveh.

1:7 calamity. Translates the same Hebrew word (*raʿâ*) rendered "wickedness" in v. 2. Jonah's actions place him on a par with the Ninevites.

1:9 [k]Ac 17:24 [l]Ps 146:6
1:12 [m]2Sa 24:17; 1Ch 21:17
1:13 [n]Pr 21:30
1:14 [o]Dt 21:8 [p]Ps 115:3
1:15 [q]Ps 107:29; Lk 8:24
1:16 [r]Mk 4:41
1:17 [s]Mt 12:40; 16:4; Lk 11:30
2:2 [t]Ps 18:6; 120:1
2:3 [u]Ps 88:6 [v]Ps 42:7
2:4 [w]Ps 31:22

9 He answered, "I am a Hebrew and I worship the LORD, the God of heaven,[k] who made the sea and
the dry land.[l]"
10 This terrified them and they asked, "What have you done?" (They knew he was running away from
the LORD, because he had already told them so.)
11 The sea was getting rougher and rougher. So they asked him, "What should we do to you to make
the sea calm down for us?"
12 "Pick me up and throw me into the sea," he replied, "and it will become calm. I know that it is my
fault that this great storm has come upon you."[m]
13 Instead, the men did their best to row back to land. But they could not, for the sea grew even wilder
than before.[n] 14 Then they cried out to the LORD, "Please, LORD, do not let us die for taking this man's life.
Do not hold us accountable for killing an innocent man,[o] for you, LORD, have done as you pleased."[p]
15 Then they took Jonah and threw him overboard, and the raging sea grew calm.[q] 16 At this the men
greatly feared[r] the LORD, and they offered a sacrifice to the LORD and made vows to him.

Jonah's Prayer

2 [a] 17 Now the LORD provided a huge fish to swallow Jonah,[s] and Jonah was in the belly of the fish
three days and three nights. 1 From inside the fish Jonah prayed to the LORD his God. 2 He said:

"In my distress I called to the LORD,[t]
and he answered me.
From deep in the realm of the dead I called for help,
and you listened to my cry.
3 You hurled me into the depths,[u]
into the very heart of the seas,
and the currents swirled about me;
all your waves and breakers
swept over me.[v]
4 I said, 'I have been banished
from your sight;[w]

[a] In Hebrew texts 2:1 is numbered 1:17, and 2:1-10 is numbered 2:2-11.

1:9 Hebrew. In foreign contexts often designates an Israelite (e.g., Gen 40:15; Exod 1:19). **worship.** Closely links to the Hebrew verb that reports the sailors' fear in vv. 5,10,16. Whereas their fear results in frantic action, Jonah's confession that he fears/worships God rings hollow in the light of his disobedience. **the God of heaven, who made the sea and the dry land.** By emphasizing the Lord's authority over the whole creation, Jonah makes it very clear that his God is responsible for the storm.

1:10 terrified. Jonah's response in v. 9 increases the sailors' fear (see note on v. 5).

1:12 throw me into the sea. While Jonah is prepared to sacrifice his life, there is no reason to assume that this action is primarily driven by a concern for the safety of the sailors.

1:13 The sailors try in vain to return to shore, hoping to save Jonah. Their desire to rescue Jonah from divine punishment contrasts sharply with Jonah's lack of compassion for the people of Nineveh.

1:14 for you, LORD, have done as you pleased. The sailors readily recognize God's right to act as he wishes; this contrasts with the attitude of Jonah, who later challenges God's compassionate forgiveness of the Ninevites.

1:16 greatly feared the LORD. As Jonah claimed to do (see v. 9 and note). **sacrifice ... vows.** Presumably showing commitment to God (cf. Ps 116:17–18). Jonah himself later responds to God's deliverance with a sacrifice and vows (2:9). Even when rebelling against God, Jonah is used by God to bring salvation to others.

1:17—2:10 *Jonah's Prayer.* Jonah reacts to his unexpected rescue from drowning. To thank God, he composes a song (2:2–9); existing psalms of praise influence the poetry (e.g., cf. 2:3 with Ps 42:7). In ch. 2, vv. 2–7, which are framed by references to God's hearing Jonah's cry for help (2:1,10), describe Jonah's distress as he sinks downward (see note on 2:6); vv. 8–9 briefly contrast the fates of those who either reject or trust the Lord.

1:17 provided. Reappears three times in 4:6–8: God's providing a plant, a worm, and an east wind. Each instance illustrates God's authority over nature, as already evident in the great storm (see note on v. 4). **fish.** The text does not identify the type of fish; it states merely that it was "huge." Given the exceptional nature of this event, the wording of the report is remarkably low-key. **three days and three nights.** See Introduction: Jonah in the New Testament.

2:1 inside the fish. Since the fish saves Jonah from drowning, Jonah praises God from inside it.

2:2 Summarizes what happens after Jonah is thrown into the sea. **I called to the LORD.** In spite of having fled from God's presence (1:3), Jonah cries to him for help. As his later confession in 4:2 reveals, he believes in a God of mercy and forgiveness. **realm of the dead.** Hebrew *šĕʾôl*, which probably designates the place where the wicked go after dying. In *šĕʾôl* people are separated from God's presence, so the righteous ask God to deliver them from *šĕʾôl* (e.g., Ps 49:15).

2:3 You hurled. Though the sailors threw Jonah into the water (1:15), God is ultimately responsible for the action.

2:4 banished from your sight. Ironically, Jonah had set out to escape from God's presence (1:3). **yet I will look again toward your holy temple.** The NIV takes these words as continuing what Jonah says while drowning in the sea, before the fish swallows him. If so, this is an extraordinary statement of faith given Jonah's circumstances. Alterna-

Philistine ships shown on a drawing of the Medinet Habu relief, 1195–1164 BC. These are likely similar to the one Jonah boarded (Jonah 1:3).

yet I will look again
  toward your holy temple.'
5 The engulfing waters threatened me,[a]
  the deep surrounded me;
  seaweed was wrapped around my head.[x]
6 To the roots of the mountains I sank down;
  the earth beneath barred me in forever.
But you, LORD my God,
  brought my life up from the pit.

7 "When my life was ebbing away,
  I remembered[y] you, LORD,
and my prayer[z] rose to you,
  to your holy temple.[a]

8 "Those who cling to worthless idols[b]
  turn away from God's love for them.
9 But I, with shouts of grateful praise,
  will sacrifice[c] to you.
What I have vowed[d] I will make good.
  I will say, 'Salvation[e] comes from the LORD.' "

10 And the LORD commanded the fish, and it vomited Jonah onto dry land.

2:5 [x] Ps 69:1-2
2:7 [y] Ps 77:11-12 [z] 2Ch 30:27 [a] Ps 11:4; 18:6
2:8 [b] 2Ki 17:15; Jer 10:8
2:9 [c] Ps 50:14,23; Hos 14:2 [d] Ecc 5:4-5 [e] Ps 3:8

[a] 5 Or *waters were at my throat*

tively, since the Hebrew text lacks quotation marks, Jonah could have composed these words while within the fish. In this case, his rescue by the fish gives Jonah confidence that God has not permanently expelled Jonah from his presence. Jonah associated God's presence with the temple in Jerusalem (see "Temple," p. 2652).

2:6 I sank down. At every stage on his journey away from God, Jonah goes downward (1:3,5,15; 2:2). **earth.** Probably the underworld, which Jonah views as a city with a gate. **barred.** As he descends closer and closer to death, Jonah pictures himself being imprisoned in the realm of the dead. **brought my life up.** God reverses Jonah's descent. **the pit.** *Šĕ'ôl* (see note on v. 2).

2:8 Indicts those who serve other gods.

2:9 sacrifice … vowed. Like the sailors (1:16), Jonah will worship God through offering a sacrifice and fulfilling a vow. **Salvation comes from**

3:1 [f]Jnh 1:1
3:5 [g]Da 9:3; Lk 11:32
3:6 [h]Job 2:8,13; Eze 27:30-31
3:7 [i]2Ch 20:3
3:8 [j]Ps 130:1; Jnh 1:6
3:9 [k]2Sa 12:22 [l]Joel 2:14
3:10 [m]Am 7:6 [n]Jer 18:8 [o]Ex 32:14
4:1 [p]ver 4; Lk 15:28
4:2 [q]Jer 20:7-8 [r]Ex 34:6; Ps 86:5,15 [s]Joel 2:13
4:3 [t]1Ki 19:4 [u]Job 7:15

Jonah Goes to Nineveh

3 Then the word of the LORD came to Jonah[f] a second time: 2“Go to the great city of Nineveh and
proclaim to it the message I give you.”
3Jonah obeyed the word of the LORD and went to Nineveh. Now Nineveh was a very large city; it took
three days to go through it. 4Jonah began by going a day’s journey into the city, proclaiming, “Forty
more days and Nineveh will be overthrown.” 5The Ninevites believed God. A fast was proclaimed, and
all of them, from the greatest to the least, put on sackcloth.[g]
6When Jonah’s warning reached the king of Nineveh, he rose from his throne, took off his royal robes,
covered himself with sackcloth and sat down in the dust.[h] 7This is the proclamation he issued in Nineveh:

“By the decree of the king and his nobles:

Do not let people or animals, herds or flocks, taste anything; do not let them eat or drink.[i] 8But
let people and animals be covered with sackcloth. Let everyone call[j] urgently on God. Let them
give up their evil ways and their violence. 9Who knows?[k] God may yet relent and with compassion
turn[l] from his fierce anger so that we will not perish.”

10When God saw what they did and how they turned from their evil ways, he relented[m] and did not
bring on them the destruction[n] he had threatened.[o]

Jonah’s Anger at the LORD’s Compassion

4 But to Jonah this seemed very wrong, and he became angry.[p] 2He prayed to the LORD, “Isn’t this
what I said, LORD, when I was still at home? That is what I tried to forestall by fleeing to Tarshish.
I knew[q] that you are a gracious and compassionate God, slow to anger and abounding in love,[r] a God
who relents from sending calamity.[s] 3Now, LORD, take away my life,[t] for it is better for me to die[u] than
to live.”

---

the LORD. The climax of Jonah’s psalm concludes the first half of the book. Even though he rebelled against God’s command, Jonah experiences forgiveness, and God rescues him from death. But the Lord’s decision to save the Ninevites from destruction later fills Jonah with anger (4:1–3).

3:1–10 *Jonah Goes to Nineveh.* The opening words repeat God’s instructions to Jonah, offering Jonah a fresh start. Obediently, Jonah goes and proclaims God’s judgment to the population of Nineveh. Remarkably, his mission prompts an exceptionally positive reaction as the people publicly acknowledge with genuine contrition their terrible wickedness, and God pardons them.

3:1 the word of the LORD came to. See note on 1:1. **second time.** Verse 2 echoes Jonah’s first call (1:2). God gives the repentant prophet a second chance.

3:3 obeyed. Unlike Jonah’s previous response (1:3). **very large city.** Can also be translated “a great city to God.” Most English translations view the Hebrew word *ʾĕlōhîm* (“God”) as functioning in this context as a superlative. While this is a possibility, it is also possible that the expression means “important to God,” an interpretation that would be in keeping with the overall message of the book. **three days to go through it.** Archaeological evidence shows that in the eighth century BC the walled city of Nineveh was about a mile (1.5 kilometers) across at its widest part. Some scholars, therefore, take “three days” to refer to the time necessary for Jonah to go from place to place within the city as he proclaimed his message. Alternatively, the expression “the great city” (v. 2; 1:2; 4:11) may refer to “Greater Nineveh,” a region that also included the cities of Rehoboth Ir, Calah, and Resen (see Gen 10:11–12).

3:4 Forty more days and Nineveh will be overthrown. Summarizes Jonah’s message.

3:5 fast … sackcloth. The normal method of expressing repentance (cf. 1 Kgs 21:27; Joel 1:13–14).

3:6 king of Nineveh. Not the usual designation “king of Assyria” (e.g., 2 Kgs 19:36); possibly the governor of the region of Nineveh. During the first half of the eighth century BC, the king of Assyria’s power was considerably reduced.

3:7 and his nobles. It was not typical for the king of Assyria to include his nobles when he issued a decree. This may reflect the unique circumstances of this occasion and that the “king” is actually the governor (see note on v. 6).

3:8 and animals. Emphasizes the seriousness with which the people received Jonah’s message. **call urgently on God.** Cf. 1:6,14; 2:2.

3:9–10 relent … relented. God’s decision not to destroy the Ninevites parallels the repentance of the Ninevites. Prophetic denouncements were meant to produce repentance, leading to forgiveness (Jer 18:7–8). Even Jonah recognizes this in 4:2.

4:1–11 *Jonah’s Anger at the Lord’s Compassion.* Structurally, this corresponds with 1:17—2:10. But whereas in ch. 2 Jonah rejoices over how God has forgiven and saved him, in ch. 4 he is distraught that God should forgive the Ninevites. This incongruity lies at the heart of the book’s message. While Jonah welcomes salvation for himself, he does not welcome it for others, especially for those whom he perceives to be his enemy.

4:1 seemed very wrong. Jonah strongly disapproves of God’s response to the Ninevites’ repentance. The Hebrew text possibly implies that Jonah perceived this as a great evil. As a possible contemporary of Hosea, Jonah may have realized that the Ninevites would in a few decades destroy the northern kingdom of Israel (Hos 9:3; 10:6; 11:5). This being so, how could God spare the Ninevites? **angry.** See also vv. 4,9.

4:2 Jonah now explains why he originally disobeyed God’s command and fled to Tarshish (1:3): aware of God’s forgiving nature, Jonah did not want God to pardon the Ninevites. **prayed to the LORD.** As he did when inside the fish (2:1). **gracious and compassionate.** Briefly summarizes God’s nature as God stated it to Moses at Mount Sinai (see Exod 34:6–7; cf. Neh 9:17; Pss 86:15; 103:8; Joel 2:13).

4:3 Shows how strongly Jonah feels about this.

[4]But the LORD replied, "Is it right for you to be angry?"[v]
[5]Jonah had gone out and sat down at a place east of the city. There he made himself a shelter, sat in
its shade and waited to see what would happen to the city. [6]Then the LORD God provided a leafy plant[a]
and made it grow up over Jonah to give shade for his head to ease his discomfort, and Jonah was very
happy about the plant. [7]But at dawn the next day God provided a worm, which chewed the plant so that
it withered.[w] [8]When the sun rose, God provided a scorching east wind, and the sun blazed on Jonah's
head so that he grew faint. He wanted to die, and said, "It would be better for me to die than to live."
[9]But God said to Jonah, "Is it right for you to be angry about the plant?"

"It is," he said. "And I'm so angry I wish I were dead."

[10]But the LORD said, "You have been concerned about this plant, though you did not tend it or make
it grow. It sprang up overnight and died overnight. [11]And should I not have concern[x] for the great city
of Nineveh,[y] in which there are more than a hundred and twenty thousand people who cannot tell their
right hand from their left—and also many animals?"

4:4 [v] Mt 20:11-15
4:7 [w] Joel 1:12
4:11 [x] Jnh 3:10
[y] Jnh 1:2; 3:2

[a] *6* The precise identification of this plant is uncertain; also in verses 7, 9 and 10.

4:4 Is it right for you to be angry? God challenges Jonah's attitude. Jonah's anger receives an angry response from God (v. 8).
4:5 shelter. Possibly made from branches and leaves. **waited to see.** Perhaps Jonah hopes that his vigil will persuade God to reverse his decision to forgive the Ninevites.
4:6,7,8 provided. See note on 1:17.
4:6 leafy plant. Probably a climbing plant, perhaps a gourd (see NIV text note).
4:7 worm. God deliberately destroys the plant that was shading Jonah. Verses 6–7 display two opposite sides of God's sovereign power: his ability both to protect and to destroy. In a book that emphasizes God's compassion, the destruction of the plant seems out of place. The plant may symbolize the northern kingdom of Israel, which Jonah would have viewed as "sheltering" him.
4:8 scorching east wind. An extremely hot wind that adds greatly to Jonah's discomfort. As his body temperature rises, so does his anger. In v. 3 Jonah wanted to die because God did not destroy Nineveh; now he wants to die because God has destroyed a plant. Jonah is intensely distraught at God's actions.
4:9 Is it right for you to be angry about the plant? Again God questions Jonah regarding Jonah's anger (see v. 4). This time Jonah replies.
4:10–11 God has the final say, contrasting Jonah's passionate concern for a mere plant with Jonah's hardheartedness toward the great city of Nineveh.
4:11 should I not have concern for the great city of Nineveh ...? Highlights Jonah's misplaced concern for the plant. God was legitimately concerned for the well-being of the Ninevites. **a hundred and twenty thousand people.** Scholars have estimated the population of the eighth-century BC walled city of Nineveh to be about 36,000, so 120,000 is more appropriate to "Greater Nineveh" (see note on 3:3). **who cannot tell their right hand from their left.** Possibly young children, but probably all the people of Nineveh, who cannot distinguish clearly between right and wrong. **many animals.** Even if Jonah has no compassion for the people of Nineveh, God ironically challenges him to have compassion for the animals of the region. Jonah must learn that God is ultimately free to forgive those who repent, for as Jonah affirms in his psalm of praise, "Salvation comes from the LORD" (2:9).

Artist's depiction of central Nineveh, ca. 700 BC.

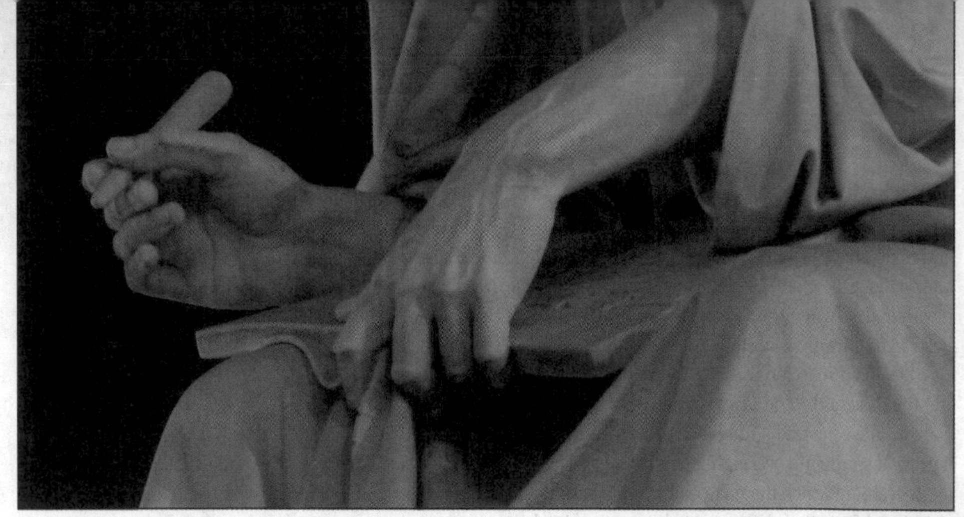

INTRODUCTION TO MICAH

AUTHOR

The book opens with a thunderclap: "the word of the LORD" (1:1). God's message "came" through Micah's personality, spirit, language, and voice. Micah was also the Lord's pen. His name frames the book. "Micah" (1:1) means "who is like the LORD?" and in the book's last stanza the author asks, "Who is a God like you ...?" (7:18). If this pun is intentional, Micah probably authored this unified book. Two more obvious sutures, besides those mentioned in the notes, show that Micah compiled and arranged his prophesies delivered over a span of years (see Date and Addressees): "Then I said" (3:1a) stitches together two cycles of prophecies (chs. 1 – 2 and chs. 3 – 4). "But as for me" (7:7) provides a smooth transition from the Lord's dirge in (7:1 – 6) to Zion's song of victory (7:8 – 20). Unlike Isaiah and Amos, Micah does not mention his call to be a prophet, but he does testify that he is "filled with power, with the Spirit of the LORD, and with justice and might" (3:8). His use of "we," "us," and "our" (e.g., 5:6; 7:19) identifies him with Israel's faithful remnant (see 2:12). He is a man of prayer and of faith (7:7). Against the normal custom of identifying oneself as the son of a father, Micah identifies himself by his hometown, Moresheth Gath (1:1,14), suggesting he was an outsider to Jerusalem. The fulfillment of his prophecies validates him as a true prophet (cf. Deut 18:22; Jer 26:17 – 19). This validation and the convincing work of the Holy Spirit led God's people immediately to recognize his book as the inspired "word of the LORD" (1:1), as is true of all the canonical books (2 Tim 3:16).

DATE AND ADDRESSEES

Micah prophesied between 750 and 686 BC and into the seventh century to the leaders of Samaria (the capital of the northern kingdom) and of Jerusalem (the capital of the southern kingdom). The kings of Samaria were pretenders to the throne, lacking prophetic sanction (cf. Hos 8:4), so Micah names only the kings of Jerusalem: Jotham (750 – 732/31 BC), Ahaz (735 – 716/15), and Hezekiah (729 – 687/86). His contemporaries were Hosea in Samaria (Hos 1:1) and Isaiah in Jerusalem (Isa 1:1). In his prophecies Micah names neither the leaders of Israel nor Israel's enemies, except for "Babylon" (see 4:10 and note) and "Assyria" and the "land of Nimrod" (see 5:6 and note). This lack of historical specificity evokes more elevated sentiments and facilitates a more universal application. Nevertheless, some prophecies can be better understood by creating scenarios for them from Micah's historical background. Micah predicts the fall of Samaria to Assyria (1:2 – 7), which happened in 722 BC. His judgment-prophecies reflect social conditions prior to Hezekiah's reforms about 701 (Jer 26:19). Micah's naming of "Assyria" and the "land of Nimrod" in 5:6 reflect Micah's time, when Assyria reigned over Babylonia. His language is preexilic Hebrew. No scientific evidence disputes the claims of the book's title.

Micah originally addressed Samaria and Jerusalem. His prophecy "Jerusalem will become a heap of rubble" (3:12) led Hezekiah to repent (Jer 26:19). In its canonical form, his prophecy about the Messiah's birthplace guided the Magi to Bethlehem (5:2; Matt 2:1 – 11). The book of Micah still speaks. When the Library of Congress in Washington DC was rebuilt in the late nineteenth century, prominent religious leaders, after considering notable quotes from all known religious literature, chose Mic 6:8 as the motto for the alcove of religion. His book comforts the church in sorrow, restrains her from temptation, and nerves her to fidelity in testing.

HISTORICAL BACKGROUND

Assyrian annals give us firsthand knowledge of the Assyrian invasions of Israel at this time. Matching those annals with biblical texts (cf. 2 Kgs 15:29 — 20:21) this relevant picture emerges:

1. Tiglath-Pileser III (745 – 727 BC) in 733 took Gilead and much of Galilee and deported the people to Assyria (2 Kgs 15:29).

2. Shalmaneser V (727 – 722 BC) besieged Samaria for three years and captured it in 722 (2 Kgs 17:5 – 6).

3. Sargon II (722 – 705 BC) claims to have captured Samaria, but it was more likely a mopping-up operation. He deported the large property holders, rulers, and religious leaders from Samaria.

4. Sennacherib (705 – 681 BC) in 701 overran Judah because Hezekiah had joined Babylon and Egypt in a revolt against the Assyrian king (2 Kgs 18 – 20; Isa 38 – 39).

MESSAGE

In a nutshell, the Lord's message through Micah is that God's kingdom comes through his keeping his covenants with Abraham (Gen 22:17 – 18), Moses (Deut 5 – 28), David (2 Sam 7:12 – 16) and all Israel in coming days (Jer 31:31 – 34). Micah accuses Israel's civil and religious leaders of crimes against the Mosaic covenant (Deut 5:6 – 21) and sentences them to punishment according to its curses (Deut 28:15 – 68). Micah's salvation-prophecies fulfill the Lord's oath to Abraham (7:20) and also fulfill his prophecy through Moses regarding Israel's restoration after exile (Deut 30:1 – 10). Micah's prophecy, that Messiah's origins are in the loins of David (see 5:2 and note), fulfills the Davidic covenant (5:1 – 6; Isa 11:1). As for the people of Israel, Micah prophesies that their sins will be forgiven (7:18) and they will know the Lord (cf. 6:5) and keep his law within their hearts (cf. 6:8) — all of which fulfill the promises of the new covenant and Moses' prophecy. Spiritually strengthened by Micah's salvation-prophecies, God's people walk in a way becoming God's name (4:5) and wait in hope for the triumph of God's kingdom (7:7).

Today the seed of Abraham is the church, those who have been baptized into Jesus Christ (Gal 3:29). Christ took the curse of God's judgment in the church's stead, and through his church Christ is making disciples of all nations (Matt 28:18 – 20). According to the apostle Paul's theology of the remnant, it is possible that at the end of salvation-history all of ethnic Israel will experience the blessings of God's covenants (Rom 11:1 – 32).

REGION OF THE SHEPHELAH

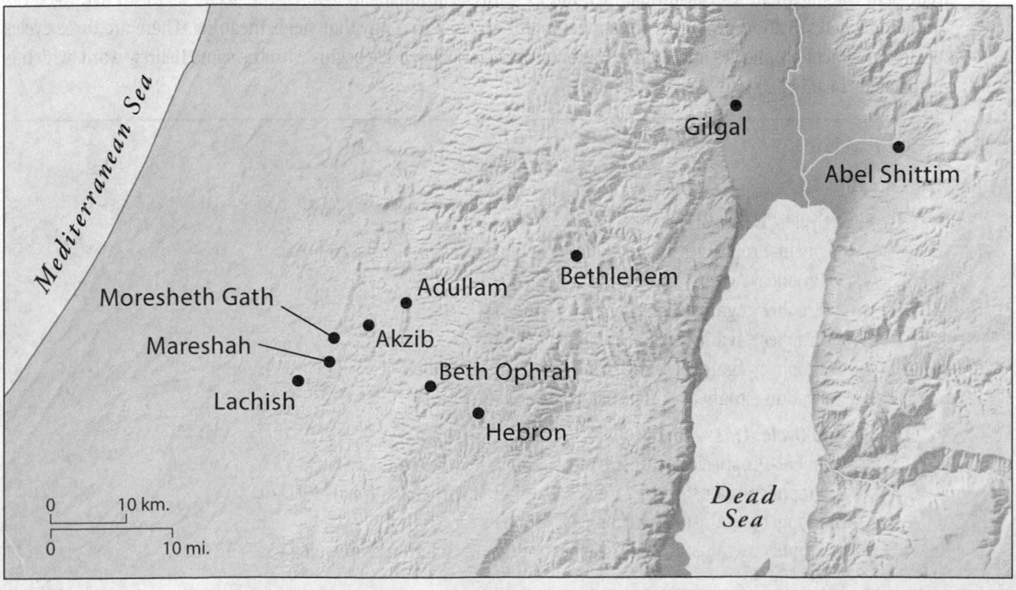

Aerial view of Tell Judeideh (Moresheth Gath), Micah's probable hometown (Mic 1:14).
Todd Bolen/www.BiblePlaces.com

CONTENT

The book consists of about 20 judgment and salvation prophecies. Judgment-prophecies consist of two essential motifs: accusation and judicial sentence. Their function is to lead God's people to repentance (Jer 18:7; 26:17–19). Salvation-prophecies promise God's people salvation "in the last days" (4:1). If they speak of God's judgment, they represent the judgment as a historical fact, not as a threat of judgment against the accused. Micah arranged his judgment- and salvation-prophecies in a meaningful way and in a way that yields meaning. There are three cycles of first judgment prophecies and then salvation prophecies. Each cycle begins with the same Hebrew word, which is translated "hear" (1:2) and "listen" (3:1; 6:1).

OUTLINE

I. Title (1:1)

II. First Cycle (1:2—2:13)

A. Judgment-Prophecies Against Samaria and Jerusalem (1:2—2:11)

1. Prophecy Against Samaria (1:2–7)
2. Prophecy Against Jerusalem (1:8–16)
3. Prophecy Against Land-Grabbers (2:1–5)
4. Prophecy Against Land-Grabbers and False Prophets (2:6–11)

B. A Salvation-Prophecy: A Remnant Delivered (2:12–13)

III. Second Cycle: (3:1—5:15)

A. Judgment-Prophecies Against Israel's Leaders (3:1–12)

1. Prophecy Against Unjust Rulers: Shepherds Turned Cannibals (3:1–4)
2. Prophecy Against False Prophets: Prophets for Profit (3:5–8)
3. Prophecy Against Rulers, Prophets, and Priests: Jerusalem Leveled (3:9–12)

B. Salvation-Prophecies (4:1 — 5:15)
   1. Exaltation of Zion (4:1 – 5)
   2. Restoration of the Remnant: Lame Become Strong (4:6 – 7)
   3. Restoration of Zion (4:8)
   4. The Lord's Secret Strategy: Captivity to Freedom; Besieged to Victory (4:9 – 13)
   5. A Promised Ruler From Bethlehem (5:1 – 6)
   6. The Remnant Among the Nations: Life and Death (5:7 – 9)
   7. The Lord Purges and Protects His Kingdom (5:10 – 15)

IV. Third Cycle: (6:1 — 7:20)

A. Judgment-Prophecies (6:1 — 7:7)
   1. The Lord's Case Against Israel (6:1 – 8)
   2. Covenant Curses Fulfilled (6:9 – 16)
   3. A Dirge: Israel's Misery (7:1 – 6)

B. Personal Testimony: Hope in Darkness (7:7)

C. Salvation-Prophecies: A Song of Victory (7:8 – 20)

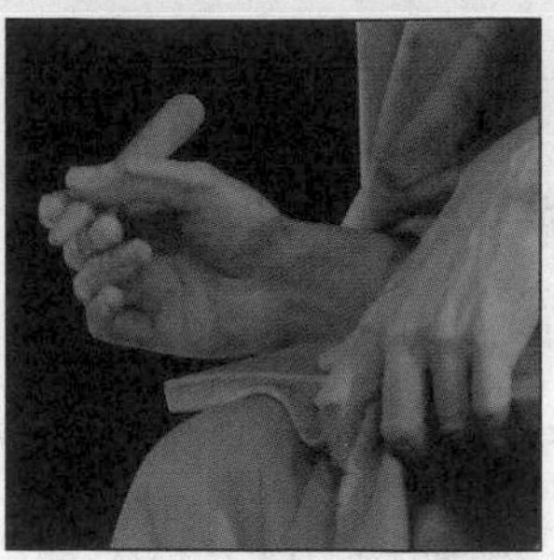

MICAH

1:1 [a]Jer 26:18 [b]1Ch 3:12 [c]1Ch 3:13 [d]Hos 1:1 [e]Isa 1:1
1:2 [f]Ps 50:7 [g]Jer 6:19 [h]Ge 31:50; Dt 4:26; Isa 1:2 [i]Ps 11:4
1:3 [j]Isa 18:4 [k]Am 4:13
1:4 [l]Ps 46:2,6 [m]Nu 16:31; Na 1:5
1:5 [n]Am 8:14

1 The word of the LORD that came to Micah of Moresheth[a] during the reigns of Jotham,[b] Ahaz[c] and
Hezekiah, kings of Judah[d] — the vision[e] he saw concerning Samaria and Jerusalem.

2 Hear, you peoples, all of you,[f]
listen, earth[g] and all who live in it,
that the Sovereign LORD may bear witness[h] against you,
the Lord from his holy temple.[i]

Judgment Against Samaria and Jerusalem

3 Look! The LORD is coming from his dwelling[j] place;
he comes down and treads on the heights of the earth.[k]
4 The mountains melt[l] beneath him
and the valleys split apart,[m]
like wax before the fire,
like water rushing down a slope.
5 All this is because of Jacob's transgression,
because of the sins of the people of Israel.
What is Jacob's transgression?
Is it not Samaria?[n]
What is Judah's high place?
Is it not Jerusalem?

1:1 *Title.* See Introduction.
1:1 Samaria and Jerusalem. Figures for the leaders: kings, judges, priests, and prophets of the northern kingdom and Judah, respectively.
1:2—2:13 *First Cycle.* The first cycle's four judgment-prophecies are against Samaria and Jerusalem, and against land-grabbers and the prophets who are in cahoots with them. Samaria will be destroyed and Jerusalem sent into exile. The land-grabbers will lose their land. The cycle ends with a salvation-prophecy that a remnant will survive.
1:2—2:11 *Judgment-Prophecies Against Samaria and Jerusalem.* Micah accuses the leaders of both Samaria and Jerusalem of leading their kingdoms into sin and idolatry (1:5). The Lord sentences Samaria to destruction (1:6–7), and Micah laments Judah's sentence to exile (1:8–16). In particular Micah sentences land-grabbers to lose the land from which they drove off its rightful heirs (2:1–5) and condemns false prophets for not preaching justice (2:6–11).
1:2–7 *Prophecy Against Samaria.* It consists of four parts: (1) *Introduction.* Micah summons Israel to a trial as defendants (v. 2). (2) *Vision.* The Lord descends in a punitive epiphany (v. 3) to convulse the land (v. 4). (3) *Accusation.* Samaria (v. 5a) and Jerusalem (v. 5b) broke covenant. (4) *Sentence.* Samaria will be leveled (v. 6) and its idols reused in another cult (v. 7).
1:2 earth. Or "land" [of Israel] (see 1:1). **bear witness against you.** Cf. 6:1–6. **temple.** God's royal residence, where his throne of judgment was located. The ark of the covenant in Jerusalem is linked inseparably to the Lord's throne in heaven (1 Kgs 8:30; 1 Chr 28:2). See "Temple," p. 2652.
1:3 the LORD is coming. The punitive epiphany depicts God's wrath against the land, and may depict the fall of Samaria in particular (see v. 6). If so, the epiphany probably represents the Lord's march behind the Assyrian army. **heights.** Possibly "high places" for pagan shrines (see v. 5b).
1:4 mountains ... valleys. Topographical extremes for the entire land. **rushing down a slope.** Removing vineyards and any place for humans to live.
1:5 Israel. The alternate name for Jacob. It may refer to the northern kingdom (see v. 13), to Judah (3:1,8–9; 5:1,3; 6:2), or to the entire nation (2:12–13; 5:2). The parallel "Jacob's transgression ... is it not Samaria" favors the first meaning. **Samaria ... Jerusalem.** See v. 1. The judgment-prophecy in vv. 1–7 sentences only Samaria to destruction and the judgment prophecy against Jerusalem in vv. 8–16 lacks the expected motif of accusation. By putting the accusation motif against Jerusalem in this verse, Micah weaves the two prophecies into a unity,

[6] "Therefore I will make Samaria a heap of rubble,
a place for planting vineyards.
I will pour her stones[o] into the valley
and lay bare her foundations.[p]
[7] All her idols[q] will be broken to pieces;
all her temple gifts will be burned with fire;
I will destroy all her images.[r]
Since she gathered her gifts from the wages of prostitutes,[s]
as the wages of prostitutes they will again be used."

1:6 [o] Am 5:11 [p] Eze 13:14
1:7 [q] Eze 6:6 [r] Dt 9:21 [s] Dt 23:17-18
1:8 [t] Isa 15:3
1:9 [u] Jer 46:11 [v] 2Ki 18:13 [w] Isa 3:26
1:11 [x] Eze 23:29
1:12 [y] Jer 14:19

Weeping and Mourning

[8] Because of this I will weep[t] and wail;
I will go about barefoot and naked.
I will howl like a jackal
and moan like an owl.
[9] For Samaria's plague[u] is incurable;
it has spread to Judah.[v]
It has reached the very gate[w] of my people,
even to Jerusalem itself.
[10] Tell it not in Gath[a];
weep not at all.
In Beth Ophrah[b]
roll in the dust.
[11] Pass by naked[x] and in shame,
you who live in Shaphir.[c]
Those who live in Zaanan[d]
will not come out.
Beth Ezel is in mourning;
it no longer protects you.
[12] Those who live in Maroth[e] writhe in pain,
waiting for relief,[y]
because disaster has come from the LORD,
even to the gate of Jerusalem.

[a] 10 *Gath* sounds like the Hebrew for *tell.* [b] 10 *Beth Ophrah* means *house of dust.* [c] 11 *Shaphir* means *pleasant.* [d] 11 *Zaanan* sounds like the Hebrew for *come out.* [e] 12 *Maroth* sounds like the Hebrew for *bitter.*

implying that Jerusalem is no better than notoriously wicked Samaria (cf. 6:16; see "because of this," v. 8).

1:6 I. The Lord. **Samaria a heap of rubble.** Some of Samaria's superbly cut stones for its walls and fortifications are still visible. **stones into the valley.** Samaria was built on a hill over 300 feet (100 meters) high.

1:7 temple gifts. The gold and silver "gifts" paid to temple prostitutes were used to make idols. **will again be used.** As wages for the temple prostitutes in Assyria, from which new idols will be made.

1:8–16 *Prophecy Against Jerusalem.* It consists of three parts. (1) *Introduction.* Intention to mourn (vv. 8–9). (2) *Dirge.* A lament song for exiles (vv. 10–15). (3) *Conclusion.* Call to the house of David to join in mourning rites (v. 16).

1:8 Micah mimics the captives going into exile (2 Kgs 17). **this.** The accusation against Jerusalem (v. 5) and the exemplary punishment of Samaria (vv. 6–7). **barefoot.** Or "stripped."

1:9 plague. Probably Sennacherib's blows. **incurable.** Nothing survives because Sennacherib's invasion reaches right to Jerusalem's "gate" (see 2 Kgs 18:27).

1:10–15 Micah's song of lament uses several wordplays on names (see NIV text notes). These towns lie in Judah's Shephelah (the foothills between the Mediterranean and Judah's high mountains where Jerusalem was located). They form a circle with a radius of about a day's journey by foot (ca. 10 miles or 16 kilometers) from Moresheth Gath. To capture Jerusalem, Sennacherib had to conquer these fortified cities. He boasted about them: "I laid siege to 46 of Hezekiah's strong cities" (from "The Prism of Sennacherib").

1:10 Tell it not in Gath. From David's eulogy of Saul and Jonathan (2 Sam 1:20), linking the defeat of the house of David with the death of the house of Saul. Judah's defeat must not be mentioned in the hostile Philistine city, lest the city gloat over Israel's dead (cf. 7:8). **roll in the dust.** Symbolizes lamenting death.

1:11 Pass by. Into exile. **naked.** See v. 8. **will not come out.** From behind their walls to battle because they fear death and/or exile. **Ezel.** May mean "taken away."

1:13 [z] Jos 10:3
1:14 [a] 2Ki 16:8 [b] Jos 15:44 [c] Jer 15:18
1:15 [d] Jos 15:44 [e] Jos 12:15
1:16 [f] Job 1:20
2:1 [g] Ps 36:4
2:2 [h] Isa 5:8 [i] Jer 22:17
2:3 [j] Jer 18:11; Am 3:1-2 [k] Isa 2:12

13 You who live in Lachish,[z]
harness fast horses to the chariot.
You are where the sin of Daughter Zion began,
for the transgressions of Israel were found in you.
14 Therefore you will give parting gifts[a]
to Moresheth Gath.
The town of Akzib[a][b] will prove deceptive[c]
to the kings of Israel.
15 I will bring a conqueror against you
who live in Mareshah.[b][d]
The nobles of Israel
will flee to Adullam.[e]
16 Shave[f] your head in mourning
for the children in whom you delight;
make yourself as bald as the vulture,
for they will go from you into exile.

Human Plans and God's Plans

2 Woe to those who plan iniquity,
to those who plot evil on their beds![g]
At morning's light they carry it out
because it is in their power to do it.
2 They covet fields[h] and seize them,
and houses, and take them.
They defraud[i] people of their homes,
they rob them of their inheritance.

3 Therefore, the LORD says:

"I am planning disaster[j] against this people,
from which you cannot save yourselves.
You will no longer walk proudly,[k]
for it will be a time of calamity.

[a] *14 Akzib* means *deception.* [b] *15 Mareshah* sounds like the Hebrew for *conqueror.*

1:13 Lachish. In the British Museum one can see Sennacherib's palace reliefs that celebrate this triumph. **fast horses.** War horses may be fast but not as face as race horses. The irony of hitching race horses to chariots emphasizes the speed with which the people of Lachish must flee. **sin.** Probably of relying on military might, not on the Lord (cf. 5:10–11; Deut 17:16; 2 Chr 26:9,11–15; Isa 2:7; 31:1–2; Hos 10:13–15; 14:4). **Daughter Zion.** Jerusalem. Cities are personified as women because the Hebrew word for "city" is a feminine noun.
1:14 Therefore. Without the protection of Lachish, Micah's home town of Moresheth Gath is doomed (see 1:1). **you.** Feminine form, for Daughter Zion. The rulers of Israel, not Lachish, paid tribute to Sennacherib (2 Kgs 18:14; cf. 2 Kgs 16:8). **parting gifts.** May refer to a dowry. Jerusalem's greedy rulers not only lose the income of Moresheth but also pay tribute (cf. 2 Kgs 18:16). **Moresheth.** Sounds like the Hebrew word for "bride." **town.** Or "workshops." The tribute the leaders of Jerusalem counted on from the workshops of Akzib (see NIV text note) proved "deceptive" because they counted on it but did not receive it.
1:15 Adullam. As David fled to Adullam as a fugitive from Saul (1 Sam 22:1; 2 Sam 23:13), now his descendants must flee there as fugitives from the Assyrians.
1:16 Shave ... head. Part of a mourning ritual to conform one's outer appearance with one's inner feelings (cf. Isa 3:24; 15:2; 22:12; Jer 47:5; 48:37; Ezek 7:18; 27:31). **your.** Feminine form, for Daughter Zion. Probably not Mareshah (v. 15) because v. 15b separates v. 16 from v. 15a. **children in whom you delight.** Israel's future nobles.
2:1–5 *Prophecy Against Land-Grabbers.* It consists of three parts. (1) *Accusation.* Greedy and violent land-grabbers seize sacred property (vv. 1–2). (2) *Puns.* Two wordplays between accusation and sentence show that the punishment is just: (a) "those who plot *rāʿ*" (Hebrew for "evil," v. 1) and "I am planning *rāʿ*" (Hebrew for "disaster," v. 3); (b) "they covet fields" (v. 2) and "he assigns our fields" (v. 4). (3) *Sentence.* Land-grabbers consigned to eternal death but hope for remnant (v. 5).
2:1 iniquity. The Hebrew signifies negative power and deception. **morning's light.** Ironic because in the biblical world, court was held at sunrise, symbolizing that light dispels darkness (cf. Job 38:12–13; possibly Ps 101:8). These "legal sharks" who plotted their unlawful deeds at night perverted the legal system in the morning light.
2:2 defraud. By dishonest scales (Hos 12:7–8) or extortion (Isa 52:4; Jer 50:33) or, as here, manipulating the legal system (Amos 5:7,10–17). **people.** Or "man" (Hebrew *geber*). *Geber* signifies a strong and capable man. **inheritance.** Land that was to be the permanent possession of a particular family (cf. Lev 25:13; Num 27:1–11; 36:1–12; 1 Kgs 21:3).
2:3 disaster. The Assyrian invasion.

[4] In that day people will ridicule you;
they will taunt you with this mournful song:
'We are utterly ruined;[l]
my people's possession is divided up.
He takes it from me!
He assigns our fields to traitors.'"
[5] Therefore you will have no one in the assembly of
the LORD
to divide the land[m] by lot.

False Prophets

[6] "Do not prophesy," their prophets say.
"Do not prophesy about these things;
disgrace[n] will not overtake us.[o]"
[7] You descendants of Jacob, should it be said,
"Does the LORD become[a] impatient?
Does he do such things?"

"Do not my words do good[p]
to the one whose ways are upright?[q]
[8] Lately my people have risen up
like an enemy.
You strip off the rich robe
from those who pass by without a care,
like men returning from battle.
[9] You drive the women of my people
from their pleasant homes.[r]
You take away my blessing
from their children forever.
[10] Get up, go away!
For this is not your resting place,[s]
because it is defiled,[t]
it is ruined, beyond all remedy.
[11] If a liar and deceiver[u] comes and says,
'I will prophesy for you plenty of wine and beer,'
that would be just the prophet for this people![v]

2:4 [l] Jer 4:13
2:5 [m] Jos 18:4
2:6 [n] Mic 6:16 [o] Am 2:12
2:7 [p] Ps 119:65 [q] Ps 15:2; 84:11
2:9 [r] Jer 10:20
2:10 [s] Dt 12:9 [t] Lev 18:25-29; Ps 106:38-39
2:11 [u] Jer 5:31 [v] Isa 30:10

[a] 7 Or *Is the Spirit of the LORD*

2:4 takes it from me! The Lord gave Israel their land as a gift to be used and enjoyed as long as it was not abused (cf. Lev 25:23; 26:33; Deut 28:49–68). **traitors.** The Assyrians.

2:5 assembly of the LORD. Composed of the faithful remnant. **to divide the land by lot.** As Joshua did at the beginning of Israel's settlement of the Holy Land (Josh 14:1–2).

2:6–11 *Prophecy Against Land-Grabbers and False Prophets.* It consists of four parts: (1) *Setting.* Micah rebuffs false prophets (v. 6). (2) *Accusation.* False prophets misrepresent the Lord's patience and his justice (v. 7) and the people exploit the defenseless (vv. 8–9). (3) *Sentence.* Exile. (4) *Conclusion.* People choose liars for prophets (v. 11).

2:6 Do not prophesy. Plural verb addressed to Micah and prophets such as Hosea and Isaiah. **their.** The greedy land-grabbers. **us.** "Descendants of Jacob" (v. 7).

2:7 should it be said. Expects a negative answer. **Do not.** Expects a positive answer. **my.** The Lord's (God is now speaking). **words.** Delivered through true prophets.

2:8–9 rich robe ... pleasant homes ... blessing from their children. Accusation expands v. 2. The oppressed belong to Israel's middle class.

2:8 like an enemy. As an invading army plunders Israel from without, the greedy people plunder the defenseless from within. **without a care, like men returning from battle.** Soldiers returning from battle do not expect to be attacked by their own people.

2:10 Get up, go away! Ironically, the Lord sentences the greedy to exile by using the same words they used to drive the women from their pleasant homes (v. 9). **For ... remedy.** Or "For this is not a resting place! Because it is defiled, it will bring destruction beyond all remedy." **resting place.** Alludes to a family's well-being in their own possession (Deut 3:20; Josh 21:43–44; 22:4). **defiled.** An abhorrent, ritually unclean thing that must be removed from God's presence.

2:12 [w]Mic 4:7; 5:7; 7:18
2:13 [x]Isa 52:12
3:1 [y]Jer 5:5
3:2 [z]Ps 53:4; Eze 22:27
3:3 [a]Ps 14:4 [b]Zep 3:3 [c]Eze 11:7
3:4 [d]Ps 18:41; Isa 1:15 [e]Dt 31:17
3:5 [f]Isa 3:12; 9:16

Deliverance Promised

12 "I will surely gather all of you, Jacob;
I will surely bring together the remnant[w] of Israel.
I will bring them together like sheep in a pen,
like a flock in its pasture;
the place will throng with people.
13 The One who breaks open the way will go up before[x] them;
they will break through the gate and go out.
Their King will pass through before them,
the LORD at their head."

Leaders and Prophets Rebuked

3 Then I said,

"Listen, you leaders[y] of Jacob,
you rulers of Israel.
Should you not embrace justice,
2 you who hate good and love evil;
who tear the skin from my people
and the flesh from their bones;[z]
3 who eat my people's flesh,[a]
strip off their skin
and break their bones in pieces;[b]
who chop them up like meat for the pan,
like flesh for the pot?[c]"

4 Then they will cry out to the LORD,
but he will not answer them.[d]
At that time he will hide his face[e] from them
because of the evil they have done.

5 This is what the LORD says:

"As for the prophets
who lead my people astray,[f]

2:12–13 *A Salvation-Prophecy: A Remnant Delivered.* It consists of two parts: Israel's Shepherd-King gathers the remnant within protective walls (v. 12) and then leads them out triumphantly (v. 13).
2:12 I. The Lord. **Jacob ... Israel.** The entire nation (see note on 1:5). **remnant.** The relatively few faithful people who survive the Lord's judgment on Israel (see 4:7; 5:7–8; 7:18). The remnant will become a strong nation (4:7b; Isa 60:22), bringing life and death to the nations (5:7–8). **in a pen.** Jerusalem, during Sennacherib's siege.
2:13 The release from besieged Jerusalem occurs in three stages: (1) the Shepherd-King "breaks open the way"; (2) the masses "break through the gate [of Jerusalem] and go out"; (3) "the LORD" takes his rightful place "at their head" (cf. 5:4).
3:1—5:15 *Second Cycle.* The second cycle's three judgment-prophecies are against Jerusalem's leaders: rulers, prophets, and priests. The climax in the prophecy is that Jerusalem will be destroyed. Seven salvation-prophecies pertain to Israel's future golden age, when Zion will be exalted and the remnant will rule the nations under the Messiah, and Israel will be purged of its sins.
3:1–12 *Judgment-Prophecies Against Israel's Leaders.* The next three judgment-prophecies, each four verses, share a common form: (1) *Address.* Leaders (rulers and judges, v. 1), prophets (v. 5), and leaders plus priests (vv. 9,11). The addressed leaders, prophets and priests represent the same branches of Israel's government as those stipulated in Israel's so-called constitution (Deut 16:18—18:22). (2) *Accusation.* Introduced by "who" (vv. 2b,5,9b). (3) *Sentence.* Introduced by "then"/"therefore" (vv. 4,6,12). Instead of working together to foster justice, the constituted leaders are all in cahoots to plunder the helpless. The judicial sentences escalate from God's silence (v. 4) to his silence plus darkness (vv. 6–7) to his absence when he destroys his temple (v. 12).
3:1–4 *Prophecy Against Unjust Rulers: Shepherds Turned Cannibals.* The Lord will turn a deaf ear to the cannibalistic rulers at the time of judgment.
3:1 Jacob ... Israel. The entire nation (see note on 1:5). **justice.** As codified in the Mosaic law.
3:2–3 The grinding poverty the greedy magistrates inflicted on the innocent led to their early death. Micah, in a sustained, grotesque metaphor depicts them as cannibals.
3:4 they will cry out to the LORD. For salvation when disaster comes (cf. Prov 1:26; Matt 25:11–13; Luke 16:26; Heb 10:31; 12:17). **will not answer them.** As the corrupt judges turned a deaf ear to the pleas of the oppressed.
3:5–8 *Prophecy Against False Prophets: Prophets for Profit.* The Lord will make the future dark for the false prophets, who bite like serpents.
3:5 This is what the LORD says. A messenger formula. **prophets.** Are like angels, who are God's messengers from his heavenly court to earth,

they proclaim 'peace'
if they have something to eat,
but prepare to wage war against anyone
who refuses to feed them.
6 Therefore night will come over you, without visions,
and darkness, without divination.[g]
The sun will set for the prophets,[h]
and the day will go dark for them.
7 The seers will be ashamed[i]
and the diviners disgraced.[j]
They will all cover their faces
because there is no answer from God."
8 But as for me, I am filled with power,
with the Spirit of the LORD,
and with justice and might,
to declare to Jacob his transgression,
to Israel his sin.[k]
9 Hear this, you leaders of Jacob,
you rulers of Israel,
who despise justice
and distort all that is right;[l]
10 who build[m] Zion with bloodshed,[n]
and Jerusalem with wickedness.[o]
11 Her leaders judge for a bribe,
her priests teach for a price,
and her prophets tell fortunes for money.[p]
Yet they look for the LORD's support and say,
"Is not the LORD among us?
No disaster will come upon us."[q]
12 Therefore because of you,
Zion will be plowed like a field,
Jerusalem will become a heap of rubble,[r]
the temple hill a mound overgrown with thickets.

3:6 [g] Isa 8:19-22 [h] Isa 29:10
3:7 [i] Mic 7:16 [j] Isa 44:25
3:8 [k] Isa 58:1
3:9 [l] Ps 58:1-2; Isa 1:23
3:10 [m] Jer 22:13 [n] Hab 2:12 [o] Eze 22:27
3:11 [p] Isa 1:23; Jer 6:13; Hos 4:8,18 [q] Jer 7:4
3:12 [r] Jer 26:18

especially to the rulers of Samaria and Jerusalem. In both calls of Isaiah, the prophet envisions himself in the heavenly court with other potential messengers (cf. Isa 6:1–8; 40:1–3). As messengers from God, prophets are vested with the full authority of the one who commissions them. **lead my people astray.** By preaching only God's patience, never his justice. (cf. v. 7). **if they have something to eat.** Or "bite [Hebrew *n-š-k*] with their teeth." Ten of the eleven uses of the Hebrew root *n-š-k* have to do with snakes that kill their victims to feed themselves. If that nuance is intended, the grotesque picture of biting snakes matches the grizzly picture of cannibalism in the preceding prophecy. **prepare to wage war.** Along with the greedy rich (see 2:8–9).

3:6 without visions. False prophets, like Balaam, may be able to see beyond the ordinary range of human perception (cf. Num 22:5–41; Deut 23:1–5). **sun will set.** Symbolizes their losing their exceptional perception.

3:7 disgraced. When a prophet was exposed as a fraud, he was regarded as unclean (cf. Lam 4:13–15). **faces.** Or "mustache," "lower part of their face" (i.e., the place of their gift), like unclean lepers (Lev 13:45).

3:8 filled with. A sign of being filled with the Spirit of the Lord is a zeal for justice. **power.** Spirit-directed energy and dynamism (cf. Ezek 2:2; 3:12,14,24). **might.** Valor, making Micah equal to formidable adversaries.

3:9–12 *Prophecy Against Rulers, Prophets, and Priests: Jerusalem Leveled.* The Lord will level Jerusalem because of its greedy leaders: rulers, prophets, and priests.

3:10 Zion. A poetic parallel to "Jerusalem" (cf. Isa 2:3; 4:3). The title invests the capital with a theological quality: it was regarded as the center of the nations in the biblical world and the place where God uniquely dwelled (Ezek 5:5; cf. Ezek 5:7–8). **bloodshed.** See Exod 20:13 (cf. Mic 2:2–3; 3:2–3). Micah saw beneath Jerusalem's grandeur its bloody economic base (2:9–10: 3:1–4). "Bloodshed" recalls payment in kind (cf. Gen 4:10; 9:6; Num 35:33; Deut 19:11–13; 21:9; 2 Sam 1:16; 4:11; 1 Kgs 2:31–33; 2 Kgs 9:7).

3:11 judge. Give specific judicial verdicts. **teach [the law].** On which judgments were to be based. **tell fortunes.** The same Hebrew word as "divination" in v. 6; special revelations in deciding options. **money.** Love of money is the "root of all kinds of evil" (1 Tim 6:10). **LORD among us.** See notes on 1:2 ("temple"); 3:10 ("Zion").

3:12 temple. Not the "house of the LORD" (unlike 4:1). By omitting "the LORD" Micah implies the Lord has left the temple and handed it over to destruction. Ezekiel envisioned God's glory departing from the temple to the Mount of Olives before he handed over the city and its temple to destruction (Ezek 10:1–22; 11:22–23). After Jesus denounced the religious leaders for misusing their positions of leadership, he also departed

4:1 [s]Zec 8:3 [t]Eze 17:22 [u]Ps 22:27; 86:9; Jer 3:17
4:2 [v]Jer 31:6 [w]Zec 2:11; 14:16 [x]Ps 25:8-9; Isa 54:13
4:3 [y]Isa 11:4 [z]Joel 3:10 [a]Isa 2:4
4:4 [b]1Ki 4:25 [c]Lev 26:6 [d]Isa 1:20; Zec 3:10
4:5 [e]2Ki 17:29 [f]Jos 24:14-15; Isa 26:8; Zec 10:12

The Mountain of the LORD

4:1-3pp — Isa 2:1-4

4 In the last days
the mountain[s] of the LORD's temple will be established
as the highest of the mountains;
it will be exalted above the hills,[t]
and peoples will stream to it.[u]

2 Many nations will come and say,

"Come, let us go up to the mountain of the LORD,[v]
to the temple of the God of Jacob.[w]
He will teach us his ways,[x]
so that we may walk in his paths."
The law will go out from Zion,
the word of the LORD from Jerusalem.
3 He will judge between many peoples
and will settle disputes for strong nations far and wide.[y]
They will beat their swords into plowshares
and their spears into pruning hooks.[z]
Nation will not take up sword against nation,
nor will they train for war anymore.[a]
4 Everyone will sit under their own vine
and under their own fig tree,[b]
and no one will make them afraid,[c]
for the LORD Almighty has spoken.[d]
5 All the nations may walk
in the name of their gods,[e]
but we will walk in the name of the LORD
our God for ever and ever.[f]

to the Mount of Olives before handing over Jerusalem to destruction (Matt 23–24). Micah's prophecy was not fulfilled because Hezekiah repented (Jer 26:16–19). The fulfillment of a prophecy is contingent upon human behavior (Jer 18:7–8).

4:1—5:15 *Salvation-Prophecies.* The three prophecies of judgment in the first section of the second cycle (ch. 3) give way to seven prophecies of salvation for the remnant. The cycle's two halves (see Introduction: Content) are woven together by references to Zion and its temple. In a breathtaking shift, as sudden as a resurrection, the dismantled Zion (3:9–12) is transformed into a temple mountain that, towering over the earth, becomes a magnet drawing nations to it (4:1–4).

4:1–5 *Exaltation of Zion.* These verses are almost identical to Isa 2:2–4. It makes no difference in meaning if Micah is quoting Isaiah or vice versa, or if both are quoting an earlier prophecy. The prophecy is inspired and meaningful in both contexts. The prophet first sees "the mountain of the LORD's temple" (v. 1) exalted above other mountains, drawing to itself many people (v. 1). Then he overhears the nations exhorting one another to go up the Lord's temple mountain to receive the law and the divine word (v. 2). He reflects on this vision and relates in detail the life of this pacified world, the fruit of converted hearts, which issues into three unfolding benefits: (1) God arbitrates among the peoples (v. 3a). (2) Disputes are no longer settled by war (v. 3b). (3) Every individual enjoys the fruit of their own labor (v. 4a). The prophecy ends with a twofold conclusion: (1) "the LORD Almighty has spoken," guaranteeing the prophecy's fulfillment (v. 4b), and (2) a liturgical response to the vision by Micah and the faithful congregation (v. 5).

4:1 last days. See note on v. 6. In the unfolding drama of salvation-history, there seems to be a certain chronological series of events contained in this prophetic term, of which the prophet was unaware. If so, this prophecy found a partial fulfillment when the temple was rebuilt, is finding a much more intense fulfillment in the heavenly Mount Zion to which the church now comes (Heb 12:22–24), and will find its consummation when the new Jerusalem comes down from heaven (Rev 21:1,10,22–27). Some salvation-prophecies can be fitted into different epochs in salvation-history. The untroubled peace for which people hope does not lie exclusively in a presently unattainable utopia but is available now to all who come to Jesus in the heavenly Jerusalem, but the faithful wait for consummate peace in a new heaven and earth. **highest of the mountains.** Because of Zion's association with the living God, it was viewed as towering above all other temple mountains, though in terms of topography it was lower (cf. Ps 68:16–17). Great and powerful nations began to discern its true heavenly quality when the Lord raised Zion out of its ashes. Today people learn of its heavenly quality when they hear that God raised his Son from the dead in a heavenly body and set him at his right hand in the heavenly Jerusalem. Here people from many nations worship Israel's incomparable God (7:18; cf. John 2:20–21; 4:24; 12:32; Heb 12:22–24). **stream.** May be a polemic against Babylon, which was located on the Euphrates River. It was the historic, religious center of Micah's world, to which people "streamed" by boat (see Jer 51:44).

4:4 own vine ... fig tree. Symbolizes peace and prosperity (cf. 1 Kgs 4:25; Zech 3:10). **LORD Almighty.** A military title.

4:5 we. Micah and the remnant (2:12; see Introduction: Message).

The LORD's Plan

6"In that day," declares the LORD,

"I will gather the lame;
I will assemble the exiles[g]
and those I have brought to grief.[h]
7 I will make the lame my remnant,[i]
those driven away a strong nation.
The LORD will rule over them in Mount Zion
from that day and forever.[j]
8 As for you, watchtower of the flock,
stronghold[a] of Daughter Zion,
the former dominion will be restored[k] to you;
kingship will come to Daughter Jerusalem."

9 Why do you now cry aloud—
have you no king[b][l]?
Has your ruler[c] perished,
that pain seizes you like that of a woman in labor?[m]
10 Writhe in agony, Daughter Zion,
like a woman in labor,
for now you must leave the city
to camp in the open field.
You will go to Babylon;[n]
there you will be rescued.
There the LORD will redeem[o] you
out of the hand of your enemies.

11 But now many nations
are gathered against you.
They say, "Let her be defiled,
let our eyes gloat[p] over Zion!"
12 But they do not know
the thoughts of the LORD;

4:6 [g] Ps 147:2 [h] Eze 34:13, 16; 37:21; Zep 3:19
4:7 [i] Mic 2:12 [j] Da 7:14; Lk 1:33; Rev 11:15
4:8 [k] Isa 1:26
4:9 [l] Jer 8:19 [m] Jer 30:6
4:10 [n] 2Ki 20:18; Isa 43:14 [o] Isa 48:20
4:11 [p] La 2:16; Ob 12

[a] *8* Or *hill* [b] *9* Or *King* [c] *9* Or *Ruler*

4:6–7 *Restoration of the Remnant: Lame Become Strong.* The Lord will transform the remnant into a strong nation and rule over them.
4:6 In that day. Unlike the word "tomorrow," the phrase refers not to a 24-hour period but to a time that is beyond humankind's immediate reach and that is in the hand of God. It probably should be associated with "in the last days" (4:1) and interpreted as the first of the following six salvation-prophecies that unpack the grand vision of Zion's restoration in 4:1–5. **lame.** A rare word in Hebrew, probably alluding to the laming (same Hebrew word) of Jacob (Gen 32:31), when his name was changed to Israel, which means "you have struggled with God and with humans and have overcome" (Gen 32:28). The transformation of Jacob to Israel through laming foreshadows the history of his offspring
4:7 remnant. See 2:12; Isa 1:9. **strong nation.** Cf. 1 Pet 2:9,10.
4:8 *Restoration of Zion.* The Lord will restore Zion as an impregnable fortress.
4:8 you. Jerusalem. **watchtower.** A fortified tower to which people ran for protection. **stronghold.** Hebrew *ʿōpel*, an architectural term, denotes the acropolis on which the city's fortress was built. It was located on the north end of the city, just south of the temple mount (2 Chr 27:3; 33:14).
4:9–13 *The Lord's Secret Strategy: Captivity to Freedom; Besieged to Victory.* Two originally distinct prophecies of salvation (vv. 9–10,11–13) are unified by form—"now [the time of distress]" (vv. 9,11), "Daughter Zion" (vv. 10,13), and a command (vv. 10,13)—and movement from present distress to future deliverance. "Now" in 5:1 links the salvation-prophecy of the Messiah (5:1–6) with the two salvation-prophecies in 4:9–13.
4:9 you. Feminine form; for Daughter Zion. **now.** Present distress. **cry aloud.** Probably because of Sennacherib's blockade of Jerusalem. **king ... ruler** Or "counselor" or "planner." The NIV text interprets this verse as a judgment-prophecy (and as Micah using sarcasm). Alternatively, this could read "King ... Ruler" (see NIV text notes on v. 9), interpreting the verse as a salvation-prophecy. It contains neither accusation nor threatened punishment but assumes the reality of a present distress (see Introduction: Content). Moreover, the formally parallel prophecy in vv. 11–13 (see note on vv. 9–13) clearly states that *the Lord* has a "plan" (*ʿēṣâ*, v. 12), from the same Hebrew root as "Ruler" in 4:9, identifying the Ruler/Planner in v. 9 as the Lord.
4:10 woman in labor. Through her distress Zion will give birth to a new age (see 5:1–6). **Babylon.** The relatively unique naming of the enemy may highlight this amazing prophecy that will be fulfilled more than a century after Micah prophesied it.
4:12 the LORD. He has a secret plan behind the Assyrian siege of Jerusalem in 701 BC (vv. 11–13) and Israel's exile. **plan.** God arranges history

4:12 [q]Isa 55:8; Ro 11:33-34
4:13 [r]Da 2:44
5:1 [s]La 3:30
5:2 [t]Jn 7:42 [u]Ge 48:7 [v]Ps 102:25 [w]Mt 2:6*
5:4 [x]Isa 40:11; 49:9; Eze 34:11-15,23; Mic 7:14 [y]Isa 52:13; Lk 1:32

they do not understand his plan,[q]
that he has gathered them like sheaves to the threshing floor.
13 "Rise and thresh, Daughter Zion,
for I will give you horns of iron;
I will give you hooves of bronze,
and you will break to pieces many nations."[r]
You will devote their ill-gotten gains to the LORD,
their wealth to the Lord of all the earth.

A Promised Ruler From Bethlehem

5[a] Marshal your troops now, city of troops,
for a siege is laid against us.
They will strike Israel's ruler
on the cheek[s] with a rod.

2 "But you, Bethlehem[t] Ephrathah,[u]
though you are small among the clans[b] of Judah,
out of you will come for me
one who will be ruler over Israel,
whose origins are from of old,[v]
from ancient times."[w]

3 Therefore Israel will be abandoned
until the time when she who is in labor bears a son,
and the rest of his brothers return
to join the Israelites.

4 He will stand and shepherd his flock[x]
in the strength of the LORD,
in the majesty of the name of the LORD his God.
And they will live securely, for then his greatness[y]
will reach to the ends of the earth.

[a] In Hebrew texts 5:1 is numbered 4:14, and 5:2-15 is numbered 5:1-14. [b] *2* Or *rulers*

so that what appears to the enemy as victory leads to their defeat in the war for the meaning of history (cf. 1 Cor 2:6–9).
4:13 Rise and thresh. Jerusalem's destruction of her enemies is likened to a fearsome animal. **horns of iron ... hooves of bronze.** None can stop Zion from totally thrashing her enemy. **many nations.** Assyria's imperial army was composed of mercenaries from many nations.
5:1–6 *A Promised Ruler From Bethlehem.* The prophecy is framed by "us" (i.e., Micah and the faithful remnant) and the Assyrian invaders (vv. 1,6). Like the two preceding salvation-prophecies (4:9–10,11–13), it envisions Israel's historic tragedy (v. 1) being transformed into her triumph, but it adds the transformation of her helpless ruler (v. 1) into the Messiah—theological shorthand for Israel's ideal future king whose rule extends to the ends of the earth (v. 4).
5:1 troops. Connotes the smallness of the army in her distress (cf. 2 Kgs 18:23). **now.** See note on 4:9–13. **city of troops.** Jerusalem. **siege.** By Sennacherib (see 4:9–13). **strike ... on the cheek.** The humiliated ruler cannot defend himself (cf. Job 16:10; Ps 3:7; Isa 50:6; Lam 3:30).
5:2 Bethlehem. Chosen by the Lord to exhibit paradoxically both the Messiah's inauspicious and most auspicious origins. Jesus of Nazareth's birth in Bethlehem fulfills this prophecy (Matt 2:6). **Ephrathah ... Judah.** Associated with David's origins (1 Sam 17:12; cf. Ruth 1:2; 2 Sam 7:8–16). **small.** In quantity and quality, signifying the Messiah's inauspicious origin. **from ancient times.** Hebrew *ʿôlām,* which signifies the Messiah's humble origins from Jesse and David (cf. 1 Sam 16:1). Hebrew *ʿôlām* may mean "eternal," but when qualified by "days," "years," or "generations," the phrase always refers to remote historical times, not to eternity (cf. 7:14; Deut 32:7; Ps 77:6; Isa 51:9; 61:9,11; Amos 9:11; Mal 3:4). The phrase here alludes to the covenantal promises to David (2 Sam 7:11b–16). The NT reveals that the origin of Jesus Christ, who is so much greater than his biological father, is from eternity, implying his divinity as also the Son of God (see John 1:1,14,18; 8:58; 17:5; Phil 2:5–11; Col 1:15–20; Heb 1:1–3; cf. Isa 11:1).
5:3 will be abandoned. Will be without a shepherd-king. Israel was without a king from her exile until the birth of Jesus Christ. **she who is in labor.** The remnant of Zion who survive the Babylonian exile will birth the Messiah (see 4:9–10; cf. Luke 1:5—2:40). **a son.** The Messiah. **the rest of his brothers return to join.** The rest of nominal Israel will unite with the faithful remnant under the Messiah's rule in his coming kingdom.
5:4 stand. Endure forever. **shepherd.** The figure here refers to his protection (cf. John 10:11; Heb 13:20). **in the strength ... in the majesty of the name.** The Messiah lives by faith in "the LORD his God." **they will live securely.** For his kingdom "will reach to the ends of the earth" (cf. 4:1–6; Matt 28:16–20; Acts 28:30–31).

[5]And he will be our peace[z]
when the Assyrians invade[a] our land
and march through our fortresses.
We will raise against them seven shepherds,
even eight commanders,[b]
[6]who will rule[a] the land of Assyria with the sword,
the land of Nimrod[c] with drawn sword.[bd]
He will deliver us from the Assyrians
when they invade our land
and march across our borders.[e]

[7]The remnant[f] of Jacob will be
in the midst of many peoples
like dew from the LORD,
like showers on the grass,[g]
which do not wait for anyone
or depend on man.
[8]The remnant of Jacob will be among the nations,
in the midst of many peoples,
like a lion among the beasts of the forest,[h]
like a young lion among flocks of sheep,
which mauls and mangles[i] as it goes,
and no one can rescue.[j]
[9]Your hand will be lifted up[k] in triumph over your enemies,
and all your foes will be destroyed.

[10]"In that day," declares the LORD,

"I will destroy your horses from among you
and demolish your chariots.[l]
[11]I will destroy the cities[m] of your land
and tear down all your strongholds.[n]
[12]I will destroy your witchcraft
and you will no longer cast spells.[o]
[13]I will destroy your idols
and your sacred stones from among you;
you will no longer bow down
to the work of your hands.[p]

5:5 [z]Isa 9:6; Lk 2:14; Col 1:19-20 [a]Isa 8:7 [b]Isa 10:24-27
5:6 [c]Ge 10:8 [d]Zep 2:13 [e]Na 2:11-13
5:7 [f]Mic 2:12 [g]Isa 44:4
5:8 [h]Ge 49:9 [i]Mic 4:13; Zec 10:5 [j]Ps 50:22; Hos 5:14
5:9 [k]Ps 10:12
5:10 [l]Hos 14:3; Zec 9:10
5:11 [m]Isa 6:11 [n]Hos 10:14; Am 5:9
5:12 [o]Dt 18:10-12; Isa 2:6; 8:19
5:13 [p]Eze 6:9; Zec 13:2

[a] 6 Or *crush* [b] 6 Or *Nimrod in its gates*

5:5 our ... We. Micah and the faithful community. **peace.** Hebrew *šālôm* is often associated with prosperity, but this context pertains primarily to conflict. Faith in the Messiah unifies and fortifies his people for battle (cf. Isa 9:6; Luke 2:14; Eph 2:14). **the Assyrians.** Symbolize the enemy of God's people (cf. Isa 11:11; Zech 10:10). **seven ... eight.** Typical Hebrew poetry for the real number, here "eight." There will be more than a perfect number of under-shepherds (cf. Eph 4:7–12; 1 Pet 5:4).
5:6 Assyria. This relatively rare specification of the enemy dates this salvation-prophecy to the time of Micah. **sword.** Prophets often describe the future in terms of their own historical context. The NT uses "sword" as a figure for the Spirit and the Word of God (cf. Eph 6:17). **the land of Nimrod.** This phrase could mean either "even" or "also" the land of Nimrod. The latter interpretation fits Micah's historical context, for at that time Babylon was a subordinate of Assyria. Also, Gen 10:8–12 associates Nimrod with both Babylon and Nineveh.
5:7–9 *The Remnant Among the Nations: Life and Death.* Using the similes of dew and of a lion, two similarly structured verses present the paradox that the remnant, "in the midst of many peoples," will bring life to some (v. 7) and death to others (v. 8; cf. John 3:18; 6:28–29; 2 Cor 2:14–16). The prophecy ends with the promise that the remnant will be triumphant (v. 9; cf. 5:5).
5:7 from the LORD. The remnant's life-giving ministry does not depend on impotent "man." **wait for.** Or "wait upon" (see the parallel "depend on").
5:9 Your. The remnant's.
5:10–15 *The Lord Purges and Protects His Kingdom.* The Lord promises to purge Israel of her false reliance on military might, witchcraft, and idolatry (vv. 10–14). But he will punish the disobedient nations (v. 15).
5:10 In that day. See notes on 4:1,6. **destroy.** Hebrew *kārat,* here with the connotation "to purge." *Kārat* is used for purging the nation of persons who have violated the holiness of Israel (see Lev 17:10; cf. Lev 10:2–6).
5:13 sacred stones. Symbols of male deities. **work of your hands.** Military arms and fortifications (v. 10; cf. 1:13; Deut 17:16), witchcraft (see note on v. 10; cf. Deut 18:10), and idolatry (vv. 13–14; Rom 1:22–23).

Standing stones worshiped at Canaanite Hazor. God tells the people he will destroy their sacred stones (Mic 5:13).

Kim Walton, taken at the Israel Museum, Jerusalem

5:14 [q]Ex 34:13
5:15 [r]Isa 65:12
6:1 [s]Ps 50:1; Eze 6:2
6:2 [t]Dt 32:1 [u]Hos 12:2 [v]Ps 50:7
6:3 [w]Jer 2:5
6:4 [x]Dt 7:8

14 I will uproot from among you your Asherah poles[a][q]
when I demolish your cities.
15 I will take vengeance[r] in anger and wrath
on the nations that have not obeyed me."

The LORD's Case Against Israel

6 Listen to what the LORD says:

"Stand up, plead my case before the mountains;[s]
let the hills hear what you have to say.

2 "Hear,[t] you mountains, the LORD's accusation;[u]
listen, you everlasting foundations of the earth.
For the LORD has a case against his people;
he is lodging a charge[v] against Israel.

3 "My people, what have I done to you?
How have I burdened[w] you? Answer me.
4 I brought you up out of Egypt
and redeemed you from the land of slavery.[x]

[a] *14* That is, wooden symbols of the goddess Asherah

5:14 Asherah poles. Symbols of female deities.

6:1—7:20 *Third Cycle.* The third cycle consists of three judgment-prophecies in diverse forms: a lawsuit, a typical judgment-prophecy, and a dirge. The dirge is replaced in a concluding salvation-prophecy by a song of victory.

6:1—7:7 *Judgment-Prophecies.* The three judgment-prophecies in the first half of the third cycle are presented in the form of (1) a lawsuit (6:1–8), (2) a typical judgment-prophecy (6:9–16), and a dirge (7:1–6). Micah's personal testimony of faith in this dark hour (7:7) forms a smooth transition from the dirge to the song of victory (7:8–20). The song consists of four probably originally independent salvation-prophecies of about equal length. The dirge, Micah's testimony, and the song of victory each begins with the catchword "I" (7:1,7,8), probably referring to the Lord, Micah, and Daughter Zion, respectively. Possibly, Micah should be regarded as in corporate solidarity with the Lord and with Zion.

6:1–8 *The Lord's Case Against Israel.* Cf. Deut 32; Ps 50; Isa 1:2–3. It consists of four parts: (1) *Setting.* The Lord summons Micah to plead the Lord's case (see v. 1a) and the mountains are summoned as witnesses for the Lord (v. 2). (2) *Accusation.* Israel did not reciprocate the Lord's love (v. 3), supported by two exhibits of his love in his saving acts at the beginning (v. 4) and end (v. 5) of Israel's formation as a nation. The Lord's complaint aims to bring Israel to its senses, to "remember" his saving and to "know" him personally (v. 5). (3) *Israel's Response Repudiated.* An apostate worshiper, representing the nation, responds by bribing God with sacrifices to gain his favor. Using absurd extremes, Micah sarcastically denounces their bribe: sacrifices by themselves can never establish a proper relationship with God (vv. 6–7). A proper relationship with God depends on heartfelt obedience to God's law (v. 8). Such a standard condemns implicitly religious, but unrepentant, Israel.

6:1,2 mountains. Called upon as witnesses because these "everlasting foundations" (v. 2) were firsthand witnesses of the Lord's saving acts (see Deut 32:1).

6:4–5 Egypt ... Gilgal. Extremes, representing all of God's saving acts

I sent Moses[y] to lead you,
also Aaron[z] and Miriam.[a]
5 My people, remember
what Balak[b] king of Moab plotted
and what Balaam son of Beor answered.
Remember your journey from Shittim[c] to Gilgal,[d]
that you may know the righteous acts[e] of the LORD."

6 With what shall I come before the LORD
and bow down before the exalted God?
Shall I come before him with burnt offerings,
with calves a year old?[f]
7 Will the LORD be pleased with thousands of rams,[g]
with ten thousand rivers of olive oil?[h]
Shall I offer my firstborn[i] for my transgression,
the fruit of my body for the sin of my soul?[j]
8 He has shown you, O mortal, what is good.
And what does the LORD require of you?
To act justly[k] and to love mercy
and to walk humbly[a][l] with your God.[m]

Israel's Guilt and Punishment

9 Listen! The LORD is calling to the city—
and to fear your name is wisdom—
"Heed the rod and the One who appointed it.[b]
10 Am I still to forget your ill-gotten treasures, you wicked house,
and the short ephah,[c] which is accursed?[n]
11 Shall I acquit someone with dishonest scales,[o]
with a bag of false weights?
12 Your rich people are violent;[p]
your inhabitants are liars[q]
and their tongues speak deceitfully.[r]

6:4 [y]Ex 4:16 [z]Ps 77:20 [a]Ex 15:20
6:5 [b]Nu 22:5-6 [c]Nu 25:1 [d]Jos 5:9-10 [e]Jdg 5:11; 1Sa 12:7
6:6 [f]Ps 40:6-8; 51:16-17
6:7 [g]Isa 40:16 [h]Ps 50:8-10 [i]Lev 18:21 [j]2Ki 16:3
6:8 [k]Isa 1:17; Jer 22:3 [l]Isa 57:15 [m]Dt 10:12-13; 1Sa 15:22; Hos 6:6
6:10 [n]Eze 45:9-10; Am 3:10; 8:4-6
6:11 [o]Lev 19:36; Hos 12:7
6:12 [p]Isa 1:23 [q]Isa 3:8 [r]Jer 9:3

[a] *8* Or *prudently* [b] *9* The meaning of the Hebrew for this line is uncertain. [c] *10* An ephah was a dry measure.

during Israel's formative period as a nation. Today, reciting and accepting God's saving acts includes the gospel message of Jesus Christ (1 Cor 15:3–5).

6:5 remember. Hebrew *zākar*, which means to actualize the past into the present by "re-membering" oneself to the past, not merely recalling as on a history exam. This re-identification with salvation-history entails a faith commitment (cf. Luke 22:19). **know.** Personal knowledge: the human spirit resonates with God's Spirit.

6:6 With what. Micah charges the questions in vv. 6–7 with escalating, absurd hyperboles to show he is using sarcasm. Each question demands a resounding negative answer. Micah is not denying the desirability of offering sacrifices but is asserting they are worthless without obedience (cf. 1 Sam 15:22; Ps 51:17; Isa 1:11–15; Hos 6:6). **I.** Either a representative false worshiper or corporate Israel represented as an individual (see "mortal," v. 8). **come before the LORD.** To find protection in his temple.

6:7 thousands of rams. Only kings can offer this amount (1 Kgs 3:4; cf. 1 Kgs 8:63). **ten thousand rivers of olive oil.** An absurd amount that none can offer. **my firstborn.** An outrage in God's sight.

6:8 This famous standard defining a proper relationship with God (cf. Jer 22:3; Hos 6:6; Jas 1:27) must be read within the lawsuit context (6:1–8). The accusing plaintiff asked his people to "re-member" themselves to his saving act (6:5). Without repentance and a new heart to identify with God's salvation-history, one cannot satisfy the standard of a heartfelt obedience. **mortal.** See v. 6 and note. **humbly.** Or "prudently" (see NIV text note). "Humbly" is the traditional translation of a Hebrew word that occurs only here, but new philological evidence argues for "prudently."

6:9–16 *Covenant Curses Fulfilled.* This section consists of four parts. (1) *Address.* Jerusalem (v. 9). (2) *Accusation.* Unethical business practices and false, violent speech (vv. 10–12). (3) *Sentence.* Diseases (vv. 13–14) and pillaging of crops (v. 15). (4) *Summary.* Recapitulates the accusation and the judicial sentence, adding "the scorn of the nations" (v. 16; cf. Deut 28:37). The judicial sentence fulfills the futility curses threatened in the Mosaic covenant (Lev 26:16,26; Deut 28:18,40,51).

6:10 Am I. If the Lord turned a blind eye to unscrupulous business practices, he would be an accomplice in the crime. **ephah.** This dry measure varied from place to place but weighed about 285 pounds (about 130 kilograms).

6:11 scales. The Lord stands behind standard weights and measures (Lev 19:35–36; Deut 25:13–16; Ezek 45:10–12). During the monarchy the king set the standard (cf. 2 Sam 14:26; Prov 16:10–13).

6:13 [s] Isa 1:7; 6:11 **6:14** [t] Isa 9:20 [u] Isa 30:6 **6:15** [v] Dt 28:38; Jer 12:13 [w] Am 5:11; Zep 1:13 **6:16** [x] 1Ki 16:25 [y] 1Ki 16:29-33 [z] Jer 7:24 [a] Jer 25:9 [b] Jer 51:51 **7:2** [c] Ps 12:1 [d] Mic 3:10 [e] Jer 5:26 **7:3** [f] Pr 4:16

13 Therefore, I have begun to destroy[s] you,
to ruin[a] you because of your sins.
14 You will eat but not be satisfied;[t]
your stomach will still be empty.[b]
You will store up but save nothing,[u]
because what you save[c] I will give to the sword.
15 You will plant but not harvest;[v]
you will press olives but not use the oil,
you will crush grapes but not drink the wine.[w]
16 You have observed the statutes of Omri[x]
and all the practices of Ahab's[y] house;
you have followed their traditions.[z]
Therefore I will give you over to ruin[a]
and your people to derision;
you will bear the scorn[b] of the nations.[d]"

Israel's Misery

7 What misery is mine!
I am like one who gathers summer fruit
at the gleaning of the vineyard;
there is no cluster of grapes to eat,
none of the early figs that I crave.
2 The faithful have been swept from the land;[c]
not one upright person remains.
Everyone lies in wait to shed blood;[d]
they hunt each other with nets.[e]
3 Both hands are skilled in doing evil;[f]
the ruler demands gifts,

[a] *13* Or *Therefore, I will make you ill and destroy you; / I will ruin* [b] *14* The meaning of the Hebrew for this word is uncertain. [c] *14* Or *You will press toward birth but not give birth, / and what you bring to birth* [d] *16* Septuagint; Hebrew *scorn due my people*

6:13 See NIV text note.
6:14 your stomach will still be empty. See NIV text note. Or "dysentery will strike you." **store up ... save.** See NIV text note.
6:16 Omri ... Ahab's house. Kings of Israel a century before Micah who were legendary for apostasy (1 Kgs 16:25,30–33), immorality, and injustice (cf. 1 Kgs 21).
7:1–6 *A Dirge: Israel's Misery.* It consists of: (1) *Accusation.* Total corruption (vv. 1–4a). (2) *Punishment.* Social anarchy (vv. 4b–6). The accusation and consequences are linked by the alliteration of "hedge" (Hebrew *měsûkâ*, v. 4a) and "confusion" (Hebrew *měbûkâ*, v. 4b).
7:1–4a The accusation has two parts: an allegory (v. 1) with its interpretation (v. 2), and a figurative depiction of the judge's malpractices (vv. 3–4).
7:1 mine. The Lord or Micah speaking for him (cf. Isa 5:1–3). **vineyard.** The "land" of Israel (v. 2). **grapes ... figs.** The "faithful" and "upright" (see v. 2), especially a faithful "ruler" and a just "judge" (v. 3).
7:2 not one upright person remains. General accusation narrowed down to the ruler and judge in v. 3. **Everyone.** Does not include true prophets who inveighed against these crimes (see 3:8) and the righteous remnant (see note on 2:12; cf. 7:8). **lies in wait.** Tactics are sinister and covert (cf. Prov 1:10–14). **hunt ... with nets.** So none escape. **hunt.** Cf. 3:1–3.
7:3 Both hands. The king and the judge.
7:4a best of them. The officials. **hedge.** Obstruction of justice.
7:4b–6 See note on 7:1–6. A general statement (v. 4b) and specific illustrations (vv. 5–6).
7:4b The day. The time (see 4:6) of judgment prophets warned about. It may be a reference to Sennacherib's invasion. **watchmen.** Lookouts posted on city walls to warn of approaching danger; a figure for the prophets (Ezek 3:16–21; 33:7–9; Hos 9:8). **time of your confusion.** Social anarchy.
7:5 Corrupt officials have torn the fabric of national solidarity; now the invasion snaps the strongest ties of social solidarity: closest friends (v. 5a) and intimate lovers (v. 5b) They dare not confide in one another how they hope to cope with the crisis of Sennacherib's siege of Jerusalem; otherwise, their confidant will abuse their trust to ensure their own survival.
7:6 Micah pictures a world turned upside-down. Normally, the father had authority over his sons and the men of his household, and the mother had authority over her unmarried daughters and married daughters-in-law. Jesus uses v. 6 to illustrate the divisions that his advent would produce (cf. Matt 10:35–39; Luke 12:53).
7:7 *Personal Testimony: Hope in Darkness.* Micah's confident hope in God's promises turns the dirge into a song of victory.
7:7 I. Micah. The pronoun is a suture linking the "I" of the preceding dirge (v. 1) to the "I" of the climactic victory song (v. 8). **watch.** The "watchmen" foresaw the judgment (v. 4), but now Micah watches "in hope" for salvation (cf. v. 20). **wait.** The same Hebrew word is translated "depend" in 5:7. The persevering faith of Micah, who represents the faithful remnant, preserves the lamented Israel (vv. 1–6) until it becomes triumphant Israel (vv. 8–20). **God will hear.** The living God, not death, will have the last word.

the judge accepts bribes,
the powerful dictate what they desire —
they all conspire together.
4 The best of them is like a brier,[g]
the most upright worse than a thorn hedge.
The day God visits you has come,
the day your watchmen sound the alarm.
Now is the time of your confusion.[h]
5 Do not trust a neighbor;
put no confidence in a friend.[i]
Even with the woman who lies in your embrace
guard the words of your lips.
6 For a son dishonors his father,
a daughter rises up against her mother,[j]
a daughter-in-law against her mother-in-law —
a man's enemies are the members of his own
household.[k]

7 But as for me, I watch in hope[l] for the LORD,
I wait for God my Savior;
my God will hear[m] me.

Israel Will Rise

8 Do not gloat over me,[n] my enemy!
Though I have fallen, I will rise.[o]
Though I sit in darkness,
the LORD will be my light.[p]
9 Because I have sinned against him,
I will bear the LORD's wrath,[q]
until he pleads my case
and upholds my cause.
He will bring me out into the light;
I will see his righteousness.[r]
10 Then my enemy will see it
and will be covered with shame,[s]
she who said to me,
"Where is the LORD your God?"
My eyes will see her downfall;[t]
even now she will be trampled[u] underfoot
like mire in the streets.

7:4 [g] Eze 2:6 [h] Isa 22:5; Hos 9:7
7:5 [i] Jer 9:4
7:6 [j] Eze 22:7 [k] Mt 10:35-36*
7:7 [l] Ps 130:5; Isa 25:9 [m] Ps 4:3
7:8 [n] Pr 24:17 [o] Ps 37:24; Am 9:11 [p] Isa 9:2
7:9 [q] La 3:39-40 [r] Isa 46:13
7:10 [s] Ps 35:26 [t] Isa 51:23 [u] Zec 10:5

7:8–20 *Salvation-Prophecies: A Song of Victory.* Probably four or five original prophecies have been stitched together as four escalating stanzas — almost equal in length — in a unified song: (1) Jerusalem's confession of faith in the Lord (vv. 8–10). (2) Micah's promise of restoration (vv. 11–13). (3) Micah's petition to the Lord to again shepherd his people (v. 14), and the Lord's response that he will again show them his wonders by vanquishing the hostile nations (vv. 16–17). (4) The remnant's climactic song of praise to the Lord (vv. 18–20). The song is framed by Jerusalem's confession of its sin (v. 9) and Micah's praise to God for forgiving their sins (v. 18). There are striking textual connections with Moses' "Song of the Sea," Israel's first victory song (Exod 15): the vanquished "tremble" (Exod 15:14; cf. Mic 7:17b) and become mute (Exod 15:16; cf. Mic 7:16); the Lord does "wonders" (Exod 15:11; cf. Mic 7:15) and is praised as incomparable in similar rhetorical questions (Exod 15:11; cf. Mic 7:18), and in a unique metaphor "hurled [the enemy/Israel's sins] into the sea" (Exod 15:1; cf. Mic 7:19).

7:8 me. Personification of Jerusalem. The addressed "you" of the second stanza probably has as its antecedent the speaker of the first stanza. This "you" has "walls" (v. 11) and so personifies a city, undoubtedly Jerusalem. The speaker of the second stanza is a prophet vested with the authority of God to command the rulers of Jerusalem and its people to rebuild its walls and in so doing infers their confessions are accepted by God. **enemy.** Probably Nineveh. **will rise.** Continues Micah's theme of hope (v. 7). **sit in darkness.** In a dungeon. **the LORD will be my light.** A confession of faith.

7:9 I have sinned against. Another confession on the part of the prophet. **bear the LORD's wrath.** Because it is just and temporary ("until") and restorative. Micah goes on to acknowledge that Assyria is the Lord's disciplinary agent (cf. Isa 10:5).

7:11 [v]Isa 54:11
7:12 [w]Isa 19:23-25
7:13 [x]Isa 3:10-11
7:14 [y]Mic 5:4 [z]Ps 23:4 [a]Jer 50:19
7:15 [b]Ex 3:20; Ps 78:12
7:16 [c]Isa 26:11
7:17 [d]Isa 25:3; 49:23; 59:19
7:18 [e]Isa 43:25; Jer 50:20 [f]Ps 103:8-13 [g]Mic 2:12 [h]Ex 34:9 [i]Ps 103:9 [j]Jer 32:41

11 The day for building your walls[v] will come,
the day for extending your boundaries.
12 In that day people will come to you
from Assyria and the cities of Egypt,
even from Egypt to the Euphrates
and from sea to sea
and from mountain to mountain.[w]
13 The earth will become desolate because of its inhabitants,
as the result of their deeds.[x]

Prayer and Praise

14 Shepherd[y] your people with your staff,[z]
the flock of your inheritance,
which lives by itself in a forest,
in fertile pasturelands.[a]
Let them feed in Bashan and Gilead[a]
as in days long ago.

15 "As in the days when you came out of Egypt,
I will show them my wonders.[b]"

16 Nations will see and be ashamed,[c]
deprived of all their power.
They will put their hands over their mouths
and their ears will become deaf.
17 They will lick dust like a snake,
like creatures that crawl on the ground.
They will come trembling out of their dens;
they will turn in fear[d] to the LORD our God
and will be afraid of you.
18 Who is a God like you,
who pardons sin[e] and forgives[f] the transgression
of the remnant[g] of his inheritance?[h]
You do not stay angry[i] forever
but delight to show mercy.[j]

[a] *14* Or *in the middle of Carmel*

7:11–13 Micah's command to confessing Jerusalem consists of two parts: (1) a command to rebuild her walls (v. 11) and (2) an explanation (vv. 12–13).
7:11 The day. See note on 4:6. **building ... walls.** Assurance that God accepted Jerusalem's confessions. **your.** Feminine form of "your," refers to Jerusalem.
7:12 that day. The prophets seemingly do not see the historical chronological gap between Israel's restoration from the Babylonian exile and her final restoration (see note on 4:1). **people.** The remnant (cf. v. 14) and/or the nations (cf. 4:1–5; Isa 19:23–25). **Assyria.** See notes on 5:5,6. **Egypt.** The periphery of Micah's world, representing all who are saved from the Lord's coming wrath on all the earth (v. 15).
7:13 earth will become desolate. Outside of Zion there will be universal judgment.
7:14 Shepherd. Probably addressed to the Lord (see v. 18), because "your people" are probably the same as "my people" in 6:4–5 and the song mentions "God" (v. 18), not the Messiah. The figure depicts the love and trust between the people and their protector. **staff.** Symbolizes rule. **inheritance.** Israel's permanent possession of the land by virtue of ancient right. **Bashan and Gilead.** Extremes of Transjordan, famous for rich pasture lands (Gen 31:21; Ps 22:12; Ezek 39:18; Amos 4:1) that Moses gave to Israel "in days long ago" (see Deut 3:12–17; Josh 13).
7:16 will put their hands over their mouths. Will no longer taunt Zion (cf. v. 8). **will become deaf.** Will no longer listen to the vain boast of others.
7:17 lick dust. A figure of humiliating defeat (cf. Gen 3:14; Ps 44:25).
7:18–20 The concluding stanza of the victory song, and so of the book, praises God's gracious attributes (v. 18; cf. Exod 34:6), his consequent deeds (v. 19), and his fulfilling his covenant obligations to the patriarchs (v. 20).
7:18 Who is a God like you ...? See Introduction: Author, where it is noted that Micah's name means "Who is like the LORD?" No other gods, who are manufactured in the imaginations of the nations, have the sublime attributes of Israel's God to present the message of this book (cf. Exod 34:6–7; see Introduction: Message). **You do not stay angry forever.** If that is not true, Micah's ministry is pointless, for otherwise people would become hardened in sin and despair of hope (cf. Ps 130:3–4).

19 You will again have compassion on us;
  you will tread our sins underfoot
  and hurl all our iniquities[k] into the depths of the sea.[l]
20 You will be faithful to Jacob,
  and show love to Abraham,
 as you pledged on oath to our ancestors[m]
  in days long ago.

7:19 [k] Isa 43:25 [l] Jer 31:34
7:20 [m] Dt 7:8; Lk 1:72

7:19 tread our sins underfoot. When God takes away sin's guilt so that it does not condemn (v. 18), he also takes away its power so that it does not rule (cf. Ps 19:13; Rom 6:14). **our.** Micah and the faithful remnant. **hurl … into the depths of the sea.** As Israel began its journey as a nation with God hurling the Egyptians into the sea, so too it will end with God hurling Israel's iniquities into the metaphoric "depths of the sea."

7:20 faithful. In his word and in his deeds. **to Abraham.** See Introduction: Message. God keeps his promise to Abraham by raising Christ from the dead and by giving him a spiritual seed from all the nations (cf. Rom 4:17; Gal 3:6–29).

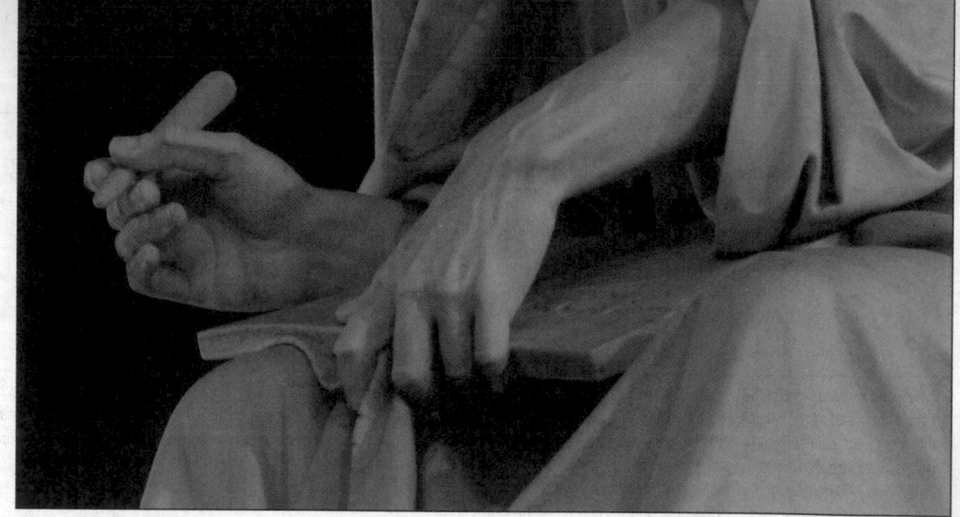

INTRODUCTION TO NAHUM

NAME, DATE, AND OCCASION

This short book is named for the prophet Nahum, whose vision comprises prophecies of woe against Nineveh sometime between 663 and 612 BC. Nahum's name sounds like a Hebrew word associated with "comfort" and may be short for "(God) comforts" (see note on 1:1). For a first-time reader, however, the book of Nahum, with its emphasis on divine wrath and severe judgment, may seem anything but comforting.

The key is to note that the book's "woes" are directed against the immeasurably cruel Assyrians and their great city Nineveh. If a century earlier the Ninevites had repented under the ministry of Jonah, their repentance clearly did not continue. And so Nahum's message that their "endless cruelty" (3:19) will be brought to an end is comforting indeed. For more on the date and occasion, see Historical Context.

CANONICAL CONTEXT

The book of Nahum comes near the middle of the Book of the Twelve (also called the Minor Prophets). While Jonah's mission, set in the early eighth century BC, leads to the Ninevites' repentance and escape from judgment (much to Jonah's dismay; see Jonah 3:6—4:5), Nahum's late seventh-century prophecies foretell in graphic detail the judgment soon to befall Nineveh and the Assyrians, who have returned to their former wickedness and cruelty (see Historical Context).

The order of the central four books of the Twelve in Hebrew and English is Jonah, Micah, Nahum, Habakkuk. Not only does this order follow the assumed chronological order in which the respective prophets ministered, but it also suggests a certain symmetry in which the outer books, Jonah and Habakkuk, involve direct interaction between God and his prophet, while the inner books, Micah and Nahum, focus on judgment against Israel/Judah and Nineveh, respectively. Taken together, the four books emphasize that God is both just and merciful (cf. the Lord's explicit self-description in Exod 34:6–7).

HISTORICAL CONTEXT

Nahum 3:8 refers to the defeat of the Egyptian city of Thebes, which occurred in 663 BC at the hands of the Assyrian king Ashurbanipal (669–627). That establishes the earliest possible date for the composition of the book. The latest possible date is the fall of Nineveh itself to the Medes and Babylonians in 612 BC, which Nahum anticipates. Within this range, an early date seems the more likely since the book presents Assyria as still strong. After the death of Ashurbanipal in 627 BC, Assyrian power waned rapidly.

In its heyday, Assyria was infamous for its cruelty (see notes on 3:3,10,19). During the reign of Tiglath-Pileser III (745–727 BC), the northern kingdom of Israel was forced to pay tribute and eventually, toward the end of the reign of the next Assyrian king (Shalmaneser V, 727–722), was conquered (in 722) and its leading citizens sent into exile, never to return. Now, in Nahum's day, the surviving southern kingdom of Judah faces the same threat. Manasseh, the ruinously wicked king of Judah, has already experienced exile to Babylon under the Assyrian king Esarhaddon (2 Kgs 21:1 – 18; 2 Chr 33:1 – 20), and fear of further Assyrian aggression is rife in Judah. To Nahum's contemporaries, prophetic messages of Nineveh's impending doom would indeed have been words of "comfort."

LITERARY CHARACTERISTICS

The book's one-verse introduction names its genre (prophetic utterance and vision), topic (the fate of Nineveh), and spokesman (Nahum, the Elkoshite). Apart from that, the book consists entirely of poetry. And brilliant poetry it is! In places clipped, rapid, and immediate, the prophetic woes, taunts, and prophecies of judgment bombard readers/hearers with image after image (cf. 3:2 – 3), conveying the sense of being eyewitnesses to the anticipated fall of Nineveh.

THEMES AND THEOLOGY

1. *An Avenging God.* To readers accustomed to thinking first and foremost of God's grace and mercy, the opening lines of Nahum's first prophecy seem shocking: the Lord is "jealous ... avenging ... filled with wrath," one who "vents his wrath against his enemies" (1:2). But the reader is quickly reminded that the Lord is also "good" (1:7).

2. *A Good God.* "Slow to anger" (1:3), "the Lord is good" and "a refuge in times of trouble" (1:7). Indeed, "he cares for those who trust in him" (1:7). For all who bend the knee to him, the goodness of God is a comfort, for he is "great in power" (1:3).

3. *A Powerful and Active God.* Far from remaining aloof and removed from the world and its affairs, the Lord controls the forces of nature (1:3 – 5) and oversees the affairs of humankind. He is a terrifying presence to his enemies (1:6) and a comforter to his own people (1:12 – 13).

4. *A God of Good News.* God's good news is not just for Israel and Judah but for all who experience the "endless cruelty" (3:19) of the Assyrians or other tyrannical oppressors. Nahum's powerful message, that Nineveh is doomed, with its broader implication that tyranny and cruel injustice will not always endure, is good news indeed: "All who hear the news [of Nineveh's doom] ... clap their hands" (3:19). From his ancient vantage point, Nahum sees a day coming when "messengers" of cruel injustice "will no longer be heard" (2:13). Instead, he sees "the feet of one who brings good news, who proclaims peace" (1:15). For Nahum, this would be a messenger of the final end of Nineveh. But in the fullness of time Nahum's words grew in significance and were linked with the Good News of Christ's defeat of the most tyrannical oppressors of all: sin and death (Rom 8:1 – 2; see Rom 10:14 – 15 and note the context).

LOCATIONS IN NAHUM

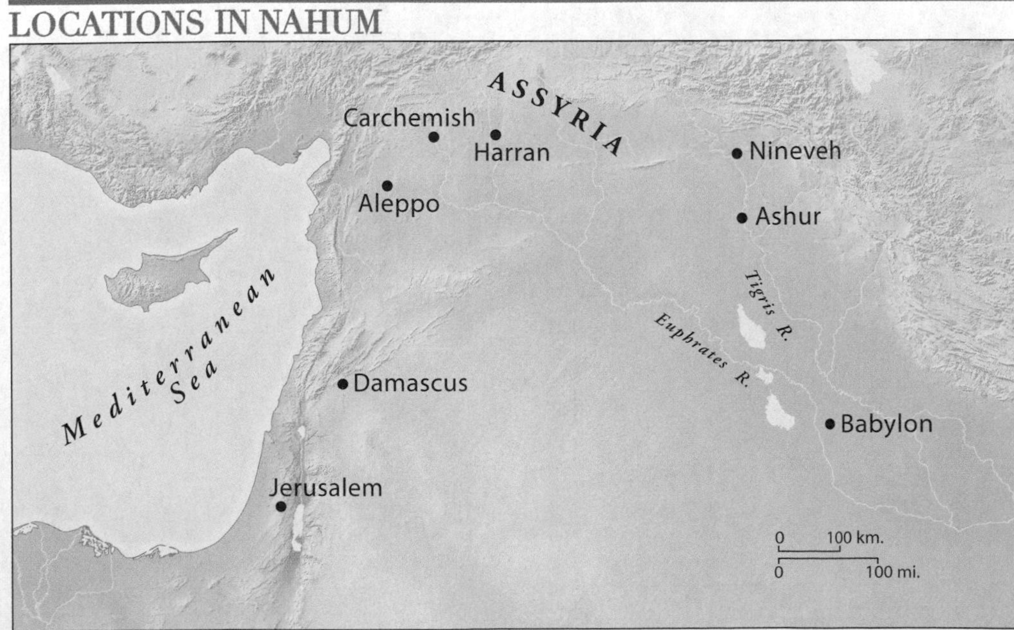

OUTLINE

I. Opening (1:1)

II. The Lord's Anger Against Nineveh (1:2 – 15)

III. Nineveh to Fall (2:1 – 13)

IV. Woe to Nineveh (3:1 – 19)

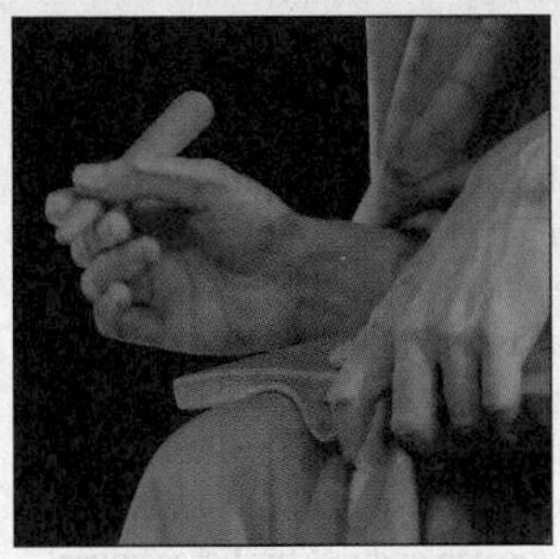

NAHUM

1 A prophecy[a] concerning Nineveh.[b] The book of the vision of Nahum the Elkoshite.

The Lord's Anger Against Nineveh

[2] The Lord is a jealous[c] and avenging God;
the Lord takes vengeance[d] and is filled with wrath.
The Lord takes vengeance on his foes
and vents his wrath against his enemies.
[3] The Lord is slow to anger[e] but great in power;
the Lord will not leave the guilty unpunished.[f]
His way is in the whirlwind and the storm,
and clouds[g] are the dust of his feet.
[4] He rebukes the sea and dries it up;
he makes all the rivers run dry.

1:1 [a] Isa 13:1; 19:1; Jer 23:33-34 [b] Jnh 1:2; Na 2:8; Zep 2:13
1:2 [c] Ex 20:5 [d] Dt 32:41; Ps 94:1
1:3 [e] Ne 9:17 [f] Ex 34:7 [g] Ps 104:3

1:1 *Opening.* The introduction to the book of Nahum is unusual in the Bible (but cf. Isa 13:1). It mentions not only the book's human source (Nahum the prophet) but also its chief subject (Nineveh, i.e., the Assyrians). We know little about Nahum. His name was fairly common in the ancient Near East but is not mentioned elsewhere in the Bible, apart from one uncertain reference in Jesus' Lukan genealogy (Luke 3:25). The name recalls the Hebrew word for "comfort." "Elkoshite" may refer to an unknown location or may be Nahum's clan name or may involve a wordplay in Hebrew suggesting the sense "God is severe." In any event, the book conveys a sense of both the severity of God's judgments against those who oppose him and the comfort that he affords those who trust him (v. 7).

1:2–15 *The Lord's Anger Against Nineveh.* Nahum powerfully and poetically describes God's justice and mercy (vv. 2–8) and then turns to Assyria's impending doom (vv. 9–11) and Judah's deliverance (vv. 12–15).

1:2 jealous. Although jealousy sometimes carries a negative connotation, this need not always be the case. To be jealous to protect a good reputation or a right relationship is very positive. In the Bible, God's jealousy is concerned with both his good name and his relationship with his people (see Exod 20:5 and note). **avenging ... vengeance.** Like jealousy, these terms may at first glance seem negative, conjuring up notions of cruel and unnecessary reprisals. But while there are instances of wrongful vengeance in the OT (Lev 19:18; Pss 8:2; 44:16; Lam 3:60; Ezek 25:12,15–16), most of the time vengeance is positive, having to do with establishing lawful justice. In some 85 percent of occurrences, God is the worker of vengeance, either directly or through his appointed instruments (kings, judges, etc.). God may execute vengeance against those, even among his own people, who break the covenant (Lev 26:25), but most often his vengeance is against power-hungry enemies such as Egypt (Jer 46:2–12), Babylon (Isa 47:1–3; Jer 50–51), or, as in the present case, Assyria. The purpose of God's vengeance is normally to restore his own honor, his people's honor, or both. Lawful vengeance is a divine, not human, prerogative (Rom 12:19; cf. Deut 32:35; Heb 10:29–31).

1:3a slow to anger. Following hard on the insistence that the Lord is an "avenging God" (v. 2) is the equal insistence that he is patient. God himself first fully articulates this divine patience by declaring his name (i.e., character) to Moses in Exod 34:6–7 (see note on Exod 34:5–7), after which it becomes a dominant theme in both the OT (e.g., Num 14:18; Neh 9:17; Pss 86:15; 103:8; 145:8; Joel 2:13) and NT (e.g., Rom 2:4; 9:22; 2 Pet 3:9,15). Ironically, the prophet Jonah cites the Lord's patience and likely forbearance as the very reasons he initially refused to go to the Ninevites as God commanded him (Jonah 4:2). **great in power.** It would be a mistake to interpret God's patience as impotence (see note on vv. 3b–6). **not leave the guilty unpunished.** See Exod 34:6,7 and notes. God's commitment to righting wrongs and effecting justice is as certain as any of his divine attributes.

1:3b–6 His way ... He rebukes ... His wrath is poured out. The Lord's attributes give rise to actions, here described in dramatic, even cosmic, terms. Such figurative language occurs also in extrabiblical ancient Near Eastern literature (e.g., Baal is described as the storm-god who rides on the clouds). The Bible's ascribing such imagery exclusively to the Lord (see also Deut 33:26; Ps 68:4) may suggest a polemic against false gods and false religious notions. But more than that, the specific images invoked here recall particular events in Israel's history, such as passing through the sea at the time of the exodus from Egypt (v. 4; cf. Exod 14:21) and through the river at the time of Israel's entry into Canaan (v. 4; cf. Josh 3:13) and the theophany at Mount Sinai (v. 5; cf. Exod 19:18).

1:4 [h]Isa 33:9
1:5 [i]Ex 19:18 [j]Mic 1:4
1:6 [k]Mal 3:2 [l]Jer 10:10 [m]1Ki 19:11
1:7 [n]Jer 33:11 [o]Ps 1:6
1:10 [p]2Sa 23:6 [q]Isa 5:24; Mal 4:1
1:12 [r]Isa 10:34 [s]Isa 54:6-8; La 3:31-32
1:13 [t]Isa 9:4

Bashan and Carmel[h] wither
and the blossoms of Lebanon fade.
5 The mountains quake[i] before him
and the hills melt away.[j]
The earth trembles at his presence,
the world and all who live in it.
6 Who can withstand his indignation?
Who can endure[k] his fierce anger?
His wrath is poured out like fire;[l]
the rocks are shattered[m] before him.

7 The LORD is good,[n]
a refuge in times of trouble.
He cares for[o] those who trust in him,
8 but with an overwhelming flood
he will make an end of Nineveh;
he will pursue his foes into the realm of darkness.

9 Whatever they plot against the LORD
he will bring[a] to an end;
trouble will not come a second time.
10 They will be entangled among thorns[p]
and drunk from their wine;
they will be consumed like dry stubble.[b][q]
11 From you, Nineveh, has one come forth
who plots evil against the LORD
and devises wicked plans.

12 This is what the LORD says:

"Although they have allies and are numerous,
they will be destroyed[r] and pass away.
Although I have afflicted you, Judah,
I will afflict you no more.[s]
13 Now I will break their yoke[t] from your neck
and tear your shackles away."

[a] 9 Or *What do you foes plot against the LORD? / He will bring it* [b] 10 The meaning of the Hebrew for this verse is uncertain.

1:4 Bashan ... Carmel ... Lebanon. Often cited as emblems of fertility and fruitfulness (Isa 33:9; 35:2).
1:6 rocks are shattered before him. God is sovereign over all things, including the natural world, and even its strongest elements cannot withstand his wrath—how much less those who defy him (cf. Rom 2:3–5; Heb 10:26–31).
1:7 good. Just as God displays his goodness in vengeance against wrongdoers, his patience (v. 3) and care "for those who trust in him" confirm it. He is a "refuge in times of trouble" for his followers (cf. Ps 37:39–40) but "an overwhelming flood" (v. 8) for his foes.
1:9 they. The Hebrew has "you" (plural), addressing the Assyrians directly (see NIV text note).
1:10 entangled ... drunk ... consumed like dry stubble. The Hebrew of this verse is difficult, but the general sense is clear enough: Nineveh's doom is sure! Faced with God's righteous judgment, the Assyrians are as defenseless as those "entangled among thorns" (cf. Gen 22:13 and perhaps 2 Sam 18:9), as soldiers "drunk" on the day of battle, and as "dry stubble" before the flame. To be made drunk by the cup of God's wrath is devastating (Hab 2:16; cf. Isa 49:26; Jer 25:15–17,27; 51:57; Lam 4:21).
1:11 one ... who plots evil against the LORD. While v. 9 charges the Assyrians as a people with plotting against the Lord, here the plotter is an individual, perhaps a king or archetypal king (see 3:18). Suggested candidates for this plotter of evil include Sennacherib, famous for his failed siege of Jerusalem ca. 701 BC (see 2 Kgs 18:13—19:37; cf. 2 Chr 32:1–23; Isa 36–37), and Ashurbanipal, the Assyrian king during Nahum's ministry who succeeded in subduing Egypt (cf. 3:8–10) and taking Judah's king Manasseh as a prisoner to Babylon (2 Chr 33:11).
1:12 you, Judah. Just as vv. 8,11 directly address the Assyrians, vv.12–13 directly address Judah. **I will afflict you no more.** The message of hope promises to break the Assyrian "yoke from your neck and tear your shackles away" (see v. 13 and note).
1:13 yoke ... shackles. Appropriate metaphors for subjugation to an enemy power; in the ancient Near East, conquered kings were sometimes humiliated by being forced to wear a yoke. Nahum's prophecy was fulfilled during the reign of King Nabopolassar (626–605 BC) of Babylonia, who conquered Nineveh and, in his words, "threw off [the] yoke" of the Assyrians. The call of God's people has always been to accept willingly a very different yoke, the yoke of the Divine King; in the NT Jesus links accepting his "yoke" with receiving "rest" (Matt 11:28–29).

[14]The Lord has given a command concerning you, Nineveh:
"You will have no descendants to bear your name.[u]
I will destroy the images[v] and idols
that are in the temple of your gods.
I will prepare your grave,[w]
for you are vile."

[15]Look, there on the mountains,
the feet of one who brings good news,[x]
who proclaims peace![y]
Celebrate your festivals,[z] Judah,
and fulfill your vows.
No more will the wicked invade you;[a]
they will be completely destroyed.[a]

1:14 [u]Isa 14:22 [v]Mic 5:13 [w]Eze 32:22-23
1:15 [x]Isa 40:9; Ro 10:15 [y]Isa 52:7 [z]Lev 23:2-4 [a]Isa 52:1
2:1 [b]Jer 51:20
2:2 [c]Eze 37:23 [d]Isa 60:15
2:3 [e]Eze 23:14-15
2:4 [f]Jer 4:13

Nineveh to Fall

2[b] An attacker[b] advances against you, Nineveh.
Guard the fortress,
watch the road,
brace yourselves,
marshal all your strength!

[2]The Lord will restore[c] the splendor[d] of Jacob
like the splendor of Israel,
though destroyers have laid them waste
and have ruined their vines.

[3]The shields of the soldiers are red;
the warriors are clad in scarlet.[e]
The metal on the chariots flashes
on the day they are made ready;
the spears of juniper are brandished.[c]
[4]The chariots[f] storm through the streets,
rushing back and forth through the squares.
They look like flaming torches;
they dart about like lightning.

[a] *15* In Hebrew texts this verse (1:15) is numbered 2:1. [b] In Hebrew texts 2:1-13 is numbered 2:2-14.
[c] *3* Hebrew; Septuagint and Syriac *ready; / the horsemen rush to and fro*.

1:14 descendants. One's descendants carried on one's name, protected sacred precincts and the divine images, and properly prepared one for burial — all values of ancient societies. Nineveh was to be deprived not only of descendants but also of their "images and idols." The destruction of Nineveh and its temples in 612 BC by a coalition of Medes and Babylonians is confirmed by the archeological evidence.
1:15 feet of one who brings good news. A phrase familiar from Isa 52:7 (where the "good news" is release from exile in Babylon) and ultimately from Rom 10:15 (where the "good news" is release from the power and penalty of sin). Here it celebrates the coming "peace" that will arrive with the fall of Assyria. The image is of a running messenger first sighted as he crests a nearby mountain. **festivals ... vows.** With the destruction of idolatrous Assyrian worship (v. 14), true Israelite worship can be restored. With the return of peace, Judah will be able to resume its worship practices, which in turn will serve as reminders of the Lord's many acts of deliverance in the past and perhaps prepare them for even greater acts of deliverance to come.
2:1–13 *Nineveh to Fall.* Assyria's doom is sure. Defenses will fail, warriors will fall. Why? Because the Lord Almighty has declared himself against the cruel Assyrians, and their "gods" (1:14) will prove as impotent as they are false. The crisp poetry of this judgment-prophecy brilliantly captures Nineveh's doom; a shaft of bright hope for Israel pierces the darkness only once (v. 2).
2:1 An attacker advances. While Judah can anticipate a messenger of good news advancing (1:15), Assyria can anticipate an "attacker," or "scatterer," advancing. **Guard ... watch ... brace ... marshal.** In a mocking tone, the prophet charges Nineveh to shore up its defenses. But all will be to no avail, as the next verse makes clear.
2:2 Jacob ... Israel. By the time of Nahum, the northern kingdom of Israel had long since fallen to the Assyrians. Thus, the reference to "Israel" most likely refers to Judah (Jacob) as representing all "Israel." **ruined their vines.** An effective means of depriving enemies of liquid sustenance; environmental depredation was a typical Assyrian tactic.
2:3–4 shields ... chariots ... spears ... flaming torches. Brilliant poetic imagery captures a sense of immediacy, as if Nahum is witnessing Nineveh's frantic preparations before its fall in 612 BC.

2:5 [g] Jer 46:12
2:6 [h] Na 3:13
2:7 [i] Isa 59:11 [j] Isa 32:12
2:10 [k] Isa 29:22
2:11 [l] Isa 5:29
2:12 [m] Jer 51:34

5 Nineveh summons her picked troops,
yet they stumble[g] on their way.
They dash to the city wall;
the protective shield is put in place.
6 The river gates[h] are thrown open
and the palace collapses.
7 It is decreed[a] that Nineveh
be exiled and carried away.
Her female slaves moan[i] like doves
and beat on their breasts.[j]
8 Nineveh is like a pool
whose water is draining away.
"Stop! Stop!" they cry,
but no one turns back.
9 Plunder the silver!
Plunder the gold!
The supply is endless,
the wealth from all its treasures!
10 She is pillaged, plundered, stripped!
Hearts melt, knees give way,
bodies tremble, every face grows pale.[k]

11 Where now is the lions' den,[l]
the place where they fed their young,
where the lion and lioness went,
and the cubs, with nothing to fear?
12 The lion killed[m] enough for his cubs
and strangled the prey for his mate,
filling his lairs with the kill
and his dens with the prey.

[a] 7 The meaning of the Hebrew for this word is uncertain.

2:5 Nineveh. The name is not actually present in the Hebrew text, so some suggest that perhaps the attacker summons his troops. If so, then this pictures them rushing toward the city wall from outside the city, stumbling in their haste, and then erecting "the protective shield," a kind of defensive structure to deflect projectiles raining down from the city walls. Conversely, and more likely, the stumbling soldiers are Ninevites, and "the protective shield" hangs from the walls themselves; reliefs of the Assyrian siege of Lachish depict such shields on the battlements. The imagery of Jer 46:10–12 tends to support the second interpretation. **picked troops ... stumble.** Neither special troops nor advanced weaponry (cf. vv. 3–4) will be of any use in the day of God's judgment.
2:6 river gates. By Nahum's day, a system of canals and reservoirs had been constructed in and around Nineveh, and the Khosr River (a tributary of the Tigris River) ran through the city. Gates (dams) controlled these waterways, and by breaching these dams, attackers could release floodwaters to threaten the city. **collapses.** The Hebrew verb can mean "melt," and the sense may be either that the structural integrity of the palace is undercut by the floodwaters or that the palace's inhabitants "melt" with fear. Archaeological excavation at Nineveh seems to support the former interpretation, though the two are not mutually exclusive. "Melting" of hearts is frequently associated with impending divine judgment (e.g., Josh 2:11; 5:1; Isa 13:7; 19:1; Ezek 21:7; cf. also Ps 22:14, which anticipates Christ's experience on the cross).
2:7 exiled and carried away. The Assyrians are to be treated as they have treated so many others; one Assyrian king, Sennacherib, boasted of relocating some 500,000 conquered foes. **like doves.** The Hebrew word for "dove" sounds like the name Jonah, suggesting a subtle reminder of a better time in Nineveh's history, though the image is elsewhere also used of mourners (Isa 38:14; 59:11).
2:8 Nineveh. The name occurs for the first time explicitly since 1:1 (it appears once more in 3:7). **like a pool ... draining away.** The poet deftly combines the earlier reference to uncontrolled waters with a metaphor of Nineveh as a pool whose waters (i.e., inhabitants) are dispersing uncontrollably.
2:9 Plunder ... Plunder ... The supply is endless. Drained of defenders and inhabitants, Nineveh's legendary wealth is there for the taking.
2:10 She is pillaged, plundered, stripped! The translation partially captures the sonorous effect of the Hebrew text: *bûkâ ûmĕbûkâ ûmĕbulākâ*. **Hearts ... knees ... bodies ... every face.** The rapid piling up of images of dismay contrasts sharply with the earlier string of military images in vv. 3–4 on the eve of Nineveh's collapse.
2:11 lions' den. The lion functions in ancient Near Eastern iconography as a powerful symbol of threat to humans and animals. Scenes of royal lion hunts, in which the king demonstrates superior prowess by killing lions, are commonplace. Sometimes Assyrian kings themselves boast of being lions. **lioness.** Ishtar (Astarte), a major goddess in Assyria and throughout the ancient Near East, is often associated with a lioness. Nahum ridicules Assyrian power and false religion. The once mighty lion and lioness can no longer care for their own. As the Lord had discredited the false gods of the Egyptians (Exod 12:12; Isa 19:1) and

13 "I am against[n] you,"
declares the LORD Almighty.
"I will burn up your chariots in smoke,[o]
and the sword will devour your young lions.
I will leave you no prey on the earth.
The voices of your messengers
will no longer be heard."

Woe to Nineveh

3 Woe to the city of blood,[p]
full of lies,
full of plunder,
never without victims!
2 The crack of whips,
the clatter of wheels,
galloping horses
and jolting chariots!
3 Charging cavalry,
flashing swords
and glittering spears!
Many casualties,
piles of dead,
bodies without number,
people stumbling over the corpses[q] —
4 all because of the wanton lust of a prostitute,
alluring, the mistress of sorceries,[r]
who enslaved nations by her prostitution[s]
and peoples by her witchcraft.

5 "I am against[t] you," declares the LORD Almighty.
"I will lift your skirts[u] over your face.
I will show the nations your nakedness[v]
and the kingdoms your shame.
6 I will pelt you with filth,[w]
I will treat you with contempt[x]
and make you a spectacle.[y]

2:13 [n] Jer 21:13; Na 3:5 [o] Ps 46:9
3:1 [p] Eze 22:2; Mic 3:10
3:3 [q] 2Ki 19:35; Isa 34:3
3:4 [r] Isa 47:9 [s] Isa 23:17; Eze 16:25-29
3:5 [t] Na 2:13 [u] Jer 13:22 [v] Isa 47:3
3:6 [w] Job 9:31 [x] 1Sa 2:30; Jer 51:37 [y] Isa 14:16

Canaanites (cf. Josh 4:24), so now he discredits the false gods of the Assyrians.
2:13 I am against you. This divine pronouncement says it all. The final verse of ch. 2 recalls earlier images in the chapter: chariots (vv. 3–4), now up in smoke; young lions (vv. 11–12), now themselves prey to the sword; and messengers, now "no longer ... heard" (v. 1 in the Hebrew text [1:15 in the English text]). The Lord's vengeance (righteous judgment; see note on 1:2), when it comes, is irresistible and final.
3:1–19 *Woe to Nineveh.* Nahum's pronouncement of "woe to the city of blood" (v. 1) is another poetic masterpiece (cf. 2:3–10). Its cascade of clipped images gives the reader an impression of immediacy, as if one were inside the city with all its chaotic cruelty.
3:1 full of plunder. Recalls the well-supplied lions' den of 2:11–12.
3:2–3 crack ... clatter ... galloping ... flashing swords. Rapid-fire images capture the frenetic cruelty of Nineveh in its heyday. They also foreshadow what the Assyrian city will soon experience.
3:3 piles of dead, bodies without number. Assyrian cruelty to its defeated foes is legendary, attested in both word and image. One Assyrian king (Ashurnasirpal) boasts of piling up both living captives and severed heads before his gate, impaling hundreds of soldiers, and burning to death adolescent boys and girls. Such rampant cruelty is attested in Assyrian reliefs.
3:4 wanton lust of a prostitute ... the mistress of sorceries. Whether or not this alludes to Ishtar (see note on 2:11), cities themselves—as "mothers" of their inhabitants—were often referred to using feminine metaphors. Wicked cities such as Nineveh, capable of seducing or bewitching others through their wanton luxury, were considered guilty of "prostitution" and "sorceries." The book of Revelation refers to "Babylon" as the "MOTHER OF PROSTITUTES" (Rev 17:5).
3:5–6 lift your skirts over your face ... make you a spectacle. Continuing the metaphors of v. 4, the Lord describes Nineveh's shaming in keeping with standard ancient Near Eastern practice that sought a punishment appropriate to the crime: the prostitute (city) who exposes her "nakedness" wantonly will be publicly exposed in "shame." Correspondence of crime and punishment is a typical feature of prophetic judgment speeches in the OT (cf. Isa 47:3; Jer 13:22; Hos 2:3,10).
3:5 I am against you. Cf. 2:13.

3:7 [z] Na 1:1 [a] Jer 15:5 [b] Isa 51:19
3:8 [c] Am 6:2 [d] Jer 46:25 [e] Isa 19:6-9
3:9 [f] 2Ch 12:3 [g] Eze 27:10 [h] Eze 30:5
3:10 [i] Isa 20:4 [j] Isa 13:16; Hos 13:16
3:11 [k] Isa 49:26 [l] Isa 2:10
3:12 [m] Isa 28:4
3:13 [n] Isa 19:16; Jer 50:37 [o] Na 2:6 [p] Isa 45:2
3:14 [q] 2Ch 32:4 [r] Na 2:1

7 All who see you will flee from you and say,
'Nineveh[z] is in ruins—who will mourn for her?'[a]
Where can I find anyone to comfort[b] you?"

8 Are you better than[c] Thebes,[d]
situated on the Nile,[e]
with water around her?
The river was her defense,
the waters her wall.
9 Cush[a][f] and Egypt were her boundless strength;
Put[g] and Libya[h] were among her allies.
10 Yet she was taken captive[i]
and went into exile.
Her infants were dashed[j] to pieces
at every street corner.
Lots were cast for her nobles,
and all her great men were put in chains.
11 You too will become drunk;[k]
you will go into hiding[l]
and seek refuge from the enemy.

12 All your fortresses are like fig trees
with their first ripe fruit;
when they are shaken,
the figs[m] fall into the mouth of the eater.
13 Look at your troops—
they are all weaklings.[n]
The gates[o] of your land
are wide open to your enemies;
fire has consumed the bars of your gates.[p]

14 Draw water for the siege,[q]
strengthen your defenses![r]
Work the clay,
tread the mortar,
repair the brickwork!

[a] 9 That is, the upper Nile region

3:7 All who see. The Hebrew text deftly links "seeing" (spectating) with the "spectacle" of v. 6. Revulsion and flight will be the response of those who witness Nineveh's disgrace. **Where can I find anyone to comfort you?** Underscores the finality of Nineveh's ruin and subtly echoes Nahum's name ("comfort").
3:8–11 This refers to Egypt, specifically to the city of Thebes on the Nile (modern Luxor). The Assyrian king Ashurbanipal ransacked Thebes in 663 BC. Nahum argues from the lesser to the greater: if Thebes, with all its fine defenses, could not withstand Assyrian attack, how can Nineveh stand when the Lord Almighty is against it (2:13; 3:5; cf. 1:6)?
3:9 Cush. Probably south of Egypt (in modern Sudan). **Put.** Difficult to locate; some suggest that it may be an alternate name for Libya, to Egypt's west.
3:10 infants were dashed to pieces. Such had been the violent actions of the Assyrian conquerors of Thebes, underscoring yet again Nineveh's history of cruelty and aggression (on the action generally, cf. 2 Kgs 8:12; Isa 13:16). **Lots were cast for her nobles.** In the ancient Near East, captives were sometimes distributed among the conquering troops by casting lots (similar to rolling dice). In Nineveh's case, the nobles themselves will be treated as the lowliest captives. **great men ... in chains.** The Assyrian king Ashurbanipal boasted of collaring and chaining like a dog a defeated enemy leader. Soon it will be Nineveh's turn to suffer such humiliation.
3:11 become drunk. See 1:10 and note. The drunkenness in view may result from being forced to drink the cup of God's wrath.
3:12 fortresses ... like fig trees. Nahum explains the simile: Nineveh's fortresses will give up their inhabitants as readily as ripe figs fall from a shaken branch.
3:13 Look at your troops—they are all weaklings. In essence the prophet is saying, "Your troops are all women in your midst." In the ancient world of hand-to-hand combat, women were considered weaklings in battle (Isa 19:16; Jer 50:37; 51:30), and an effeminacy-curse was occasionally pronounced on enemy troops (Assyrian kings are on record imploring the goddess Ishtar to turn enemy soldiers "from a man into a woman").
3:14–15 strengthen your defenses ... the fire will consume you; the sword will cut you down. All Nineveh's attempts to withstand attack will be to no avail. Archaeological excavations at Nineveh have discovered evidence of (1) defensive construction efforts within the city's ancient gateways, (2) fire, and (3) defeat, as evidenced by the skeletons of many fallen defenders in the gateway.

[15]There the fire will consume you;
the sword will cut you down—
they will devour you like a swarm of locusts.
Multiply like grasshoppers,
multiply like locusts![s]
[16]You have increased the number of your merchants
till they are more numerous than the stars in the sky,
but like locusts they strip the land
and then fly away.
[17]Your guards are like locusts,[t]
your officials like swarms of locusts
that settle in the walls on a cold day—
but when the sun appears they fly away,
and no one knows where.

[18]King of Assyria, your shepherds[a] slumber;[u]
your nobles lie down to rest.[v]
Your people are scattered[w] on the mountains
with no one to gather them.
[19]Nothing can heal you;[x]
your wound is fatal.
All who hear the news about you
clap their hands[y] at your fall,
for who has not felt
your endless cruelty?

3:15 [s]Joel 1:4
3:17 [t]Jer 51:27
3:18 [u]Ps 76:5-6 [v]Isa 56:10 [w]1Ki 22:17
3:19 [x]Jer 30:13; Mic 1:9 [y]Job 27:23; La 2:15; Zep 2:15

[a] *18* That is, rulers

3:15 they will devour you like a swarm of locusts. Massive swarms of locusts are known to appear periodically in the Near East, literally blocking out the sun and denuding the landscape of all vegetation. Such will be the consuming power of the fire and sword to be turned against Nineveh. **multiply like locusts!** Hebrew grammar suggests that this charge addresses the fire and sword, which Nahum just compared to a swarm of locusts; some suggest that it addresses the Ninevites themselves.
3:16 your merchants ... like locusts. The locust metaphor continues. Just like locusts, Nineveh's innumerable merchants "strip the land and then fly away."
3:17 guards ... officials. These titles are rare in Hebrew usage but common in the Assyrian language. Many of these officials would have been, like Daniel, displaced foreigners, and so they were as likely as locusts to take flight when a situation got hot. There is some documentary evidence from the period before the fall of Nineveh of officials fleeing westward toward Harran.
3:18 King of Assyria. The identity of this king depends on the date of Nahum's prophecy and the date of Nineveh's fall (see Introduction: Historical Context; see also note on 1:11). **shepherds.** Often refers to ruling officials since their duty was to guide and care for the people. **Your people are scattered ... no one to gather them.** Because shepherds and nobles are lying down on the job, the king of Assyria can expect little help from his scattered people. Or possibly we should understand that the shepherds and nobles are dead and the people scattered in the aftermath of defeat. Either way, the king of Assyria is doomed.
3:19 your wound is fatal. Healing is no longer possible for the king of Assyria. **All who hear ... clap their hands.** A certain joyful relief on the part of those who have felt the "endless cruelty" naturally accompanies the moment when justice is finally done. Like the book of Jonah but unlike any other biblical book, Nahum concludes with a rhetorical question.

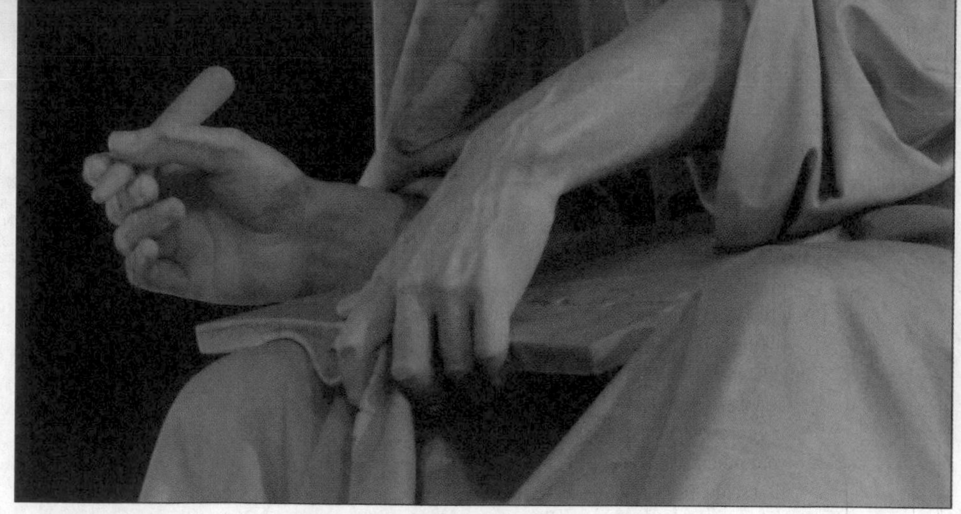

INTRODUCTION TO HABAKKUK

AUTHOR

Some prophetic books open with identifications and even dates (e.g., Jer 1:1–3), but Habakkuk says merely that he is a prophet (1:1). A prophet's function included (1) analyzing the shape of evil in a society (1:2–4; 2:6–19; Mic 2:1–2; 3:1–4); (2) proclaiming God's message for the present and sometimes for the future (1:5–11; Isa 1:27–31; 2:1–4); and (3) interceding for God's people (3:2; 1 Sam 12:23; Amos 7:1–6). Habakkuk has social sensitivities. He is direct and forthright in his dialogue with God, but he also listens (2:1; 3:16). His contemporaries included Jeremiah, Zephaniah, Daniel, and possibly Ezekiel.

DATE

Habakkuk, who ministered in Judah, witnessed a shift in the balance of international powers. The Assyrians, who dominated the Holy Land in the eighth and seventh centuries BC, were defeated with the overthrow of their capital Nineveh by the Babylonians (612 BC). The Babylonians then marched westward, defeating Egypt in the battle of Carchemish (605 BC) at the Euphrates River. Under the command of King Nebuchadnezzar, the Babylonians, now moving southward, threatened the lands of Syria, Israel, and Edom. The Babylonians attacked Judah in 605, 597, and 586 BC.

Given his prediction of the approaching Babylonian invasion (1:6), Habakkuk likely lived toward the end of Josiah's reign (641/40–609 BC) and the beginning of Jehoiakim's rule (609–598). An approximate date for his book is 612–605 BC.

MESSAGE AND THEMES

The book opens with questions: Why is God silent, allowing gross evil to increase within a society? Why would God use an evil nation, Babylon, to punish Judah, which is presumably less evil? As an answer to such questions, the message of the book is that God will do what is just and right. Sooner or later, God will hold evil nations and individuals to account (chs. 1–2). God, who is mighty in power (3:1–15), is nevertheless merciful and attentive to a person's cry for answers. Believers live by steadfast trust in God. They embrace God's ways and so are enabled to move from lament to song. The prophet, initially perplexed and frustrated, in the end exults, ready to press on with confidence.

The book touches on themes of unrighteousness, spiritual struggle, national consciousness, God's ways in the world, trust, personal lament, and cosmic victory. The book of Job wrestles with similar questions, though on a personal rather than a national scale. In ch. 3 God's glory in creation and in history informs prayer and worship (cf. Ps 136). The key verses, 2:4–5, are referenced in the NT three times (Rom 1:17; Gal 3:11; Heb 10:38–39).

LITERARY FEATURES

The book, cast in poetry, reports a dialogue with God and ends with a prayer, part of which is a description of God's appearing (a theophany). The dialogue consists of two sets of questions (1:1–4; 1:12—2:1), each answered by a divine response (1:5–11; 2:2–20). God's activity is described in chs. 1–2; more vivid and heightened descriptions of God's action and person are given in ch. 3. The book, akin to a spiritual journal, ends with a personal testimony (3:16–19).

Ruins of Babylon. The book of Habakkuk (Hab 1:6) predicts the coming Babylonian invasion.
Wikimedia Commons

OUTLINE

- **I. Heading (1:1)**
- **II. Habakkuk's First Complaint (1:2 – 4)**
- **III. The Lord's Answer (1:5 – 11)**
- **IV. Habakkuk's Second Complaint (1:12 — 2:1)**
- **V. The Lord's Answer (2:2 – 20)**
  - A. Instructions for Living (2:2 – 5)
  - B. Taunt Songs (2:6 – 20)
- **VI. Habakkuk's Prayer (3:1 – 19)**
  - A. Heading (3:1)
  - B. Adoration and Petition (3:2)
  - C. Report of God's Coming (Theophany) (3:3 – 15)
  - D. The Prophet's Response of Confidence and Joy (3:16 – 19)

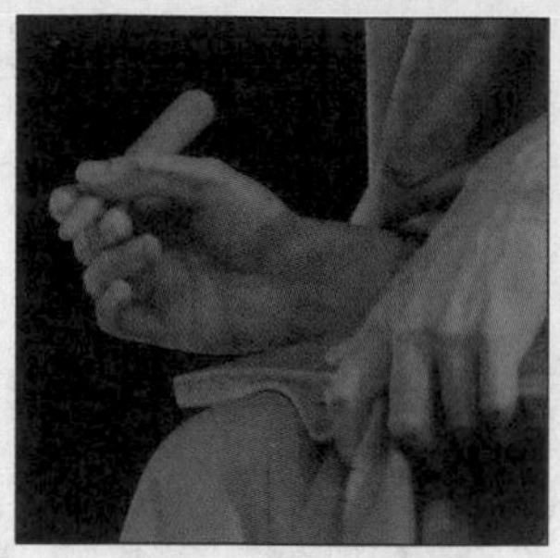

HABAKKUK

1:1 [a]Na 1:1
1:2 [b]Ps 13:1-2; 22:1-2 [c]Jer 14:9
1:3 [d]ver 13 [e]Jer 20:8 [f]Ps 55:9
1:4 [g]Ps 119:126 [h]Job 19:7; Isa 1:23; 5:20; Eze 9:9
1:5 [i]Isa 29:9

1 The prophecy[a] that Habakkuk the prophet received.

Habakkuk's Complaint

[2]How long, LORD, must I call for help,
but you do not listen?[b]
Or cry out to you, "Violence!"
but you do not save?[c]
[3]Why do you make me look at injustice?
Why do you tolerate[d] wrongdoing?
Destruction and violence[e] are before me;
there is strife,[f] and conflict abounds.
[4]Therefore the law[g] is paralyzed,
and justice never prevails.
The wicked hem in the righteous,
so that justice is perverted.[h]

The LORD's Answer

[5]"Look at the nations and watch —
and be utterly amazed.[i]

1:1 *Heading.* The heading does not specify the subject, which is the moral problem of evil and the report of God's answer (1:2 — 2:20). A second heading (3:1) is designated a prayer; it too reports responses, both God's and the prophet's.
1:1 prophecy. A weighty message, usually of judgment (Isa 13:1; Nah 1:1 – 2) but sometimes of hope (Zech 9:1). Prophecies were received as revelations (1:5 – 11; 2:2 – 3; 3:3 – 15) or as pronouncements (2:4 – 19). **Habakkuk the prophet.** The author is identified by name and vocation. No other information such as genealogy (cf. Zeph 1:1) or date (cf. Amos 1:1) is given. See Introduction: Author.
1:2 – 4 *Habakkuk's First Complaint.* The frustrated prophet complains to God about having to tolerate gross societal injustice. The age-old problem of social evil is compounded by God's failure to answer the prophet's prayer.
1:2 How long ... ? Common to laments (Pss 6:3; 13:1 – 2). For similar cries, essentially "Emergency! Urgent!" see Pss 22:1 – 2; 107:13; 142:1 – 6; Jonah 1:5. The bluntness of the prophet's reproach — a daring move — is at the same time a testimony to the prophet's intimacy with God. **save.** In this context it is deliverance out of a nasty situation. Assurances and testimonies that God hears and answers prayer are many (e.g., Pss 50:15; 91:15; 145:18 – 19; see Matt 7:7; John 15:7).
1:3 injustice. Whether it is brought on by the ruling Assyrians or by the corruption of the judicial process within Judah, Habakkuk is troubled by God's indifference and inaction. Contention and quarreling characterize Habakkuk's society; law enforcement, if not absent, is questionable and perverted, as when the wealthy in Micah's time controlled the courts through bribery (Mic 3:11; 7:3).
1:4 justice. This concept is dominant in the OT: the Hebrew word occurs 425 times. Its meaning is broader than "fairness"; it entails something like "honorable relations," as defined by God's character and will. **wicked.** Or godless (2:4 – 19). The wicked run circles around the righteous. **righteous.** Those who live in faithfulness (2:4).
1:5 – 11 *The Lord's Answer.* God answers by taking the prophet backstage, informing him that he is at work. In what is a surprise move, God is preparing a pagan army, the Babylonians, to overrun Judah's fortifications. Similes set the scene: horses "swifter than leopards" (v. 8), an army "like a desert wind" (v. 9), swift movements "like an eagle" (v. 8), and captives "like sand" in number (v. 9). For God to enlist a decadent nation (Babylon) to punish a less decadent people (Judah) will raise further perplexing questions (vv. 12 – 17).
1:5 The unidentified speaker is God. He urges Habakkuk to broaden his horizons. Paul quotes this verse in his sermon in Pisidian Antioch (Acts 13:41). God controls nations (Ps 67:4; Prov 21:1; Dan 2:21); they are his agents (Deut 28:32 – 57; Judg 2:21 — 3:4).

1:5 [j] Ac 13:41*
1:6 [k] 2Ki 24:2 [l] Jer 13:20
1:7 [m] Isa 18:7; Jer 39:5-9
1:8 [n] Jer 4:13
1:9 [o] Hab 2:5
1:10 [p] 2Ch 36:6
1:11 [q] Jer 4:11-12 [r] Da 4:30
1:12 [s] Isa 31:1 [t] Isa 10:6
1:13 [u] La 3:34-36

For I am going to do something in your days
that you would not believe,
even if you were told.[j]
6 I am raising up the Babylonians,[a][k]
that ruthless and impetuous people,
who sweep across the whole earth
to seize dwellings not their own.[l]
7 They are a feared and dreaded people;[m]
they are a law to themselves
and promote their own honor.
8 Their horses are swifter[n] than leopards,
fiercer than wolves at dusk.
Their cavalry gallops headlong;
their horsemen come from afar.
They fly like an eagle swooping to devour;
9 they all come intent on violence.
Their hordes[b] advance like a desert wind
and gather prisoners[o] like sand.
10 They mock kings
and scoff at rulers.[p]
They laugh at all fortified cities;
by building earthen ramps they capture them.
11 Then they sweep past like the wind[q] and go on—
guilty people, whose own strength is their god."[r]

Habakkuk's Second Complaint

12 LORD, are you not from everlasting?
My God, my Holy One,[s] you[c] will never die.
You, LORD, have appointed[t] them to execute judgment;
you, my Rock, have ordained them to punish.
13 Your eyes are too pure to look on evil;
you cannot tolerate wrongdoing.[u]
Why then do you tolerate the treacherous?
Why are you silent while the wicked
swallow up those more righteous than themselves?

a 6 Or *Chaldeans* *b* 9 The meaning of the Hebrew for this word is uncertain. *c* 12 An ancient Hebrew scribal tradition; Masoretic Text *we*

1:6 Babylonians. The Chaldeans, an alternative name (see NIV note), were located far east of Palestine between the Euphrates and Tigris Rivers (in modern Iraq). Their rapid and unexpected rise to power was utterly amazing. The speed of their conquests was proverbial. God raises up nations and leaders to fulfill his purposes (cf. the Assyrians in Isa 10:5–6; Cyrus in Isa 44:28—45:13).

1:7–9 The Babylonians were cavalier, self-promoting, and pompous. That the invaders were given to violence even more than the prophet's own society (vv. 2–3) compounded Habakkuk's problem about justice and God's ways.

1:9 like a desert wind. Translates a problem phrase about a large number of faces approaching.

1:10 mock ... scoff ... laugh. The invaders snub their noses at those in power. **fortified cities.** Among them in Israel/Judah would be Gezer, Megiddo, and Hazor, all built by Solomon with conscripted labor (1 Kgs 9:15). They had thick walls, which is corroborated by archaeology. **earthen ramps.** Warfare tactics included building siege ramps of earth so that movable towers could be pushed close to the city walls (Jer 32:24).

1:12—2:1 *Habakkuk's Second Complaint.* The prophet wonders how God is justified in using an evil empire to bring judgment on Judah, which is not as evil as Babylon. Isn't using a wicked people to punish Judah contrary to God's holiness and justice (1:12–13a)? How can God be silent when the very wicked triumph over the less wicked (1:13b; see also 1:3a)? Habakkuk resolves to wait for a response.

1:12 are you not from everlasting? Like the first prayer (v. 2a), this complaint begins with a rhetorical question prompted by Israel's creed: Does not God exist eternally (Ps 90:1–2)? His death is unthinkable (see NIV text note). Habakkuk acknowledges that God appoints nations like Babylon as his agents (cf. Isa 7:18–20; 44:28—45:1). **Holy One.** See Lev 19:2; Isa 6:3; 43:3,15. Holiness is associated with cleanliness and purity (v. 13). **Rock.** This metaphor signifies God's great might (Gen 49:24; Deut 32:4,31; 1 Sam 2:2; Pss 18:31; 89:26).

1:13 silent. For the question about God's silence and inaction, see vv. 2–3 (cf. Ps 13:1). The issue of evil is a classic one. Why would God, described as holy and powerful, not deal with the obvious unholiness in the world (see Pss 37; 73)? The stories of Joseph (Gen 37–50) and

1:15 [v]Isa 19:8 [w]Jer 16:16
1:16 [x]Jer 44:8
1:17 [y]Isa 14:6; 19:8
2:1 [z]Isa 21:8 [a]Ps 48:13 [b]Ps 85:8 [c]Ps 5:3
2:2 [d]Rev 1:19
2:3 [e]Da 8:17; 10:14 [f]Ps 27:14 [g]Eze 12:25; Heb 10:37-38
2:4 [h]Ro 1:17*; Gal 3:11*; Heb 10:37-38*

14 You have made people like the fish in the sea,
like the sea creatures that have no ruler.
15 The wicked foe pulls all of them up with hooks,[v]
he catches them in his net,[w]
he gathers them up in his dragnet;
and so he rejoices and is glad.
16 Therefore he sacrifices to his net
and burns incense[x] to his dragnet,
for by his net he lives in luxury
and enjoys the choicest food.
17 Is he to keep on emptying his net,
destroying nations without mercy?[y]

2 I will stand at my watch[z]
and station myself on the ramparts;[a]
I will look to see what he will say[b] to me,
and what answer I am to give to this complaint.[a][c]

The LORD's Answer

2 Then the LORD replied:

"Write[d] down the revelation
and make it plain on tablets
so that a herald[b] may run with it.
3 For the revelation awaits an appointed time;
it speaks of the end[e]
and will not prove false.
Though it linger, wait[f] for it;
it[c] will certainly come
and will not delay.[g]

4 "See, the enemy is puffed up;
his desires are not upright—
but the righteous person will live by his faithfulness[d][h]—

[a] *1* Or *and what to answer when I am rebuked* [b] *2* Or *so that whoever reads it* [c] *3* Or *Though he linger, wait for him; / he* [d] *4* Or *faith*

Job (Job 1–42) highlight the problem and point to considerations for a solution.

1:14–15 Leaderless, like fish, Habakkuk's society is disorganized and vulnerable. Rock reliefs in Mesopotamia portray prisoners taken to captivity in nets. The enemy's rejoicing in the victory, possibly with exuberant shrieks and malicious glee, adds to the pathos of defeat (cf. Ezek 36:5).

1:16 sacrifices to his net. The idolatrous Babylonians credit their fishing gear for the catch. **burns incense.** Part of sacrificing (1 Kgs 3:3; Jer 18:15).

1:17 The complaint ends as it begins: with a question (v. 12). It highlights the unending merciless and murderous actions of the invader (cf. v. 9).

2:1 stand … station myself … look to see. Envisioning the coming invasion, the prophet, like a sentinel, mounts the ramparts, the walls of Jerusalem. **complaint.** See NIV text note. It translates a word with a range of meanings: protest, correction, reprimand, reproach.

2:2–20 *The Lord's Answer.* God's reply to Habakkuk's questions is in two parts. God first instructs the prophet about practical living in the face of his questions. The five-stanza taunt song that follows underscores God's dealing in judgment with all those who do wickedly.

2:2–5 *Instructions for Living.* These instructions are to be carefully put in writing (vv. 2–3; cf. Jer 30:2), likely in the interests of permanence and wider accessibility.

2:2,3 revelation. Or vision; it is about the life of the righteous and the destiny of the evildoers, and it is to be plainly written (cf. Deut 27:8), perhaps in large letters.

2:2 herald. From a root in Hebrew that can mean both "to call out" and "to read" (as in Exod 24:7; Deut 17:19; 2 Kgs 5:7; Jer 36:6,8,10). Possible meanings then are: "so that he who runs may be able to read" (stressing "tablets" for clarity) or "so that the one reading the message may run," either in the sense of delivering the message or in a metaphoric sense of running well, living one's life (cf. Isa 40:31).

2:3 appointed time. Though unspecified, it may refer to the fall of Babylon some six decades later (539 BC). The expression points to a God-ordained plan (Isa 14:26). **the end.** Likely refers to the end of Babylonian supremacy. Some suggest it refers to the end times (Dan 12:1–3) or even to the time when God's redemptive purposes will be consummated. **wait for it.** With patience and expectancy, since the revelation is time sensitive.

2:4–5 The contrast is between "the enemy" and "the righteous person."

2:4 the enemy. Babylon (either collectively or its king) or anyone who is arrogant and follows evil desires (elaborated in vv. 6–19). **puffed up.**

5 indeed, wine[i] betrays him;
he is arrogant and never at rest.
Because he is as greedy as the grave
and like death is never satisfied,[j]
he gathers to himself all the nations
and takes captive all the peoples.

6 "Will not all of them taunt[k] him with ridicule and scorn, saying,

"'Woe to him who piles up stolen goods
and makes himself wealthy by extortion![l]
How long must this go on?'
7 Will not your creditors suddenly arise?
Will they not wake up and make you tremble?
Then you will become their prey.[m]
8 Because you have plundered many nations,
the peoples who are left will plunder you.[n]
For you have shed human blood;[o]
you have destroyed lands and cities and everyone in them.

9 "Woe to him who builds[p] his house by unjust gain,
setting his nest on high
to escape the clutches of ruin!
10 You have plotted the ruin[q] of many peoples,
shaming[r] your own house and forfeiting your life.
11 The stones[s] of the wall will cry out,
and the beams of the woodwork will echo it.

12 "Woe to him who builds a city with bloodshed[t]
and establishes a town by injustice!
13 Has not the LORD Almighty determined
that the people's labor is only fuel for the fire,[u]
that the nations exhaust themselves for nothing?[v]

2:5 [i]Pr 20:1 [j]Pr 27:20; 30:15-16
2:6 [k]Isa 14:4 [l]Am 2:8
2:7 [m]Pr 29:1
2:8 [n]Isa 33:1; Zec 2:8-9 [o]ver 17
2:9 [p]Jer 22:13
2:10 [q]Jer 26:19 [r]ver 16
2:11 [s]Jos 24:27; Lk 19:40
2:12 [t]Mic 3:10
2:13 [u]Isa 50:11 [v]Isa 47:13

A person who is haughty, arrogant, self-sufficient, and presumptuous (Num 14:44). **desires are not upright.** Examples are listed in v. 5 (see note). **the righteous person.** The one whose faithfulness (see NIV text note) is anchored in the God who triumphs over evil (3:3–15, especially v. 13; cf. Gen 15:6; Isa 26, especially vv. 1–8; Ezek 18:9). The righteous person trusts God in the darkest of times, holding fast to the conviction that God's promises will be fulfilled (2 Cor 1:20). The teaching that people are saved by grace through faith (Rom 1:17; Gal 3:11; Eph 2:8) includes the call to live by faith (Heb 10:38–39; 11:17; Jas 2:22–23). "Justification by faith," part of the book's message and central to NT teaching, became the rallying cry of the Protestant Reformation in the sixteenth century.

2:5 wine ... arrogant ... greedy ... takes captive. Examples of "desires [that] are not upright" (v. 4; cf. vv. 6–19). **never at rest.** A life style of restlessness is opposite to that of the serenity that characterizes those who patiently wait for God (v. 3, Isa 26:3). **greedy as the grave.** As the grave never says, "Enough!" (Prov 30:15–16; cf. Job 24:19; Isa 5:14), so evil persons are never satisfied with what they acquire.

2:6–20 *Taunt Songs.* A taunt is a tirade, often with innuendos of satire and sarcasm. The taunt songs may have Babylon in focus but extend to empires and individuals universally. Each of the five taunt songs (vv. 6–8,9–11,12–14,15–17,18–20) has three elements: a woe (a term used in funeral laments), a reason for the woe, and an announcement of doom. The taunts are about the unscrupulous, the covetous, the violent, perverted manipulators, and idolaters. The taunts are in two series (vv. 6–14; 15–20); each ends with a statement about God's glory. For other "woe" messages see Isa 5:8–23; Mic 2:1; Zeph 2:5; Matt 23:13–30; Rev 18:10.

2:6–8 "All of them" (v. 6) refers to the victims of theft, plunder, extortion by irresponsible entrepreneurs (e.g., Jehoiakim, Jer 22:18–19), and all who have been unscrupulously mistreated. The victimizer (to whom money is owed) will become the victim (vv. 7–8; cf. Prov 22:16; 28:8). Babylon, the implied object of the woe, is guilty of havoc of all kinds, including the wanton destruction of lands. On environmental violence to the earth, see Rev. 11:18.

2:9–11 "House" may have a double meaning: a building or a dynasty. As an eagle builds a nest to insure against ruin, so the Babylonians built their empire to be unconquerable (Isa 14:4, 13–15; cf. Edom, Obad 3–4). Covetous persons resort to "unjust gain" (v. 9), which may entail bribes (Exod 23:6,8). Those who scheme the ruin of others (genocide?) will be held responsible; they will forfeit their life (Prov 1:18–19). Cheating in construction or using stolen materials is eventually brought to light and will have consequences.

2:12 injustice. Includes evil tactics by builders (cf. Mic 3:9–10). God's surveillance includes examination of the business practices of both nations and private contractors.

2:13–14 That for which the Babylonians labored in an unprincipled way will be burned (Jer 51:58; cf. Ps 127:1). God may cut short what people hope will be permanent (Luke 12:16–21).

2:14 [w] Nu 14:21 [x] Isa 11:9
2:16 [y] ver 10 [z] La 4:21 [a] Isa 51:22
2:17 [b] Jer 51:35 [c] Jer 50:15 [d] ver 8
2:18 [e] Jer 5:21 [f] Ps 115:4-5; Jer 10:14
2:19 [g] 1Ki 18:27 [h] Jer 10:4
2:20 [i] Ps 11:4 [j] Isa 41:1
3:2 [k] Ps 44:1 [l] Ps 119:120 [m] Ps 85:6 [n] Isa 54:8

14 For the earth will be filled with the knowledge of the glory[w] of the LORD
as the waters cover the sea.[x]

15 "Woe to him who gives drink to his neighbors,
pouring it from the wineskin till they are drunk,
so that he can gaze on their naked bodies!
16 You will be filled with shame[y] instead of glory.
Now it is your turn! Drink and let your nakedness be exposed[a]![z]
The cup[a] from the LORD's right hand is coming around to you,
and disgrace will cover your glory.
17 The violence[b] you have done to Lebanon will overwhelm you,
and your destruction of animals will terrify you.[c]
For you have shed human blood;[d]
you have destroyed lands and cities and everyone in them.

18 "Of what value is an idol[e] carved by a craftsman?
Or an image that teaches lies?
For the one who makes it trusts in his own creation;
he makes idols that cannot speak.[f]
19 Woe to him who says to wood, 'Come to life!'
Or to lifeless stone, 'Wake up!'[g]
Can it give guidance?
It is covered with gold and silver;[h]
there is no breath in it."

20 The LORD is in his holy temple;[i]
let all the earth be silent[j] before him.

Habakkuk's Prayer

3 A prayer of Habakkuk the prophet. On *shigionoth*.[b]

2 LORD, I have heard[k] of your fame;
I stand in awe[l] of your deeds, LORD.
Repeat[m] them in our day,
in our time make them known;
in wrath remember mercy.[n]

[a] *16* Masoretic Text; Dead Sea Scrolls, Aquila, Vulgate and Syriac (see also Septuagint) *and stagger*
[b] *1* Probably a literary or musical term

2:14 knowledge of the glory of the LORD. Habakkuk quotes and expands Isaiah's vision (Isa 11:9). That glory is God's presence: in the desert tent (Exod 40:34), the temple (1 Kgs 8:10; Ezek 43:4), and even in the whole earth (Isa 6:3; cf. Hab 3:3–6). The knowledge of that glory will someday be universal (Exod 14:4,17–18; Rev 17:1—19:4).
2:15–17 God denounces perverted manipulators who abet evil in others; they assist in intoxicating others with wine, a practice not unlike helping drug addicts maintain their habit.
2:15 gaze on their naked bodies. A dishonorable act (Gen 9:20–25) and in this context may suggest perverse sexual practices.
2:16 The cup from the Lord's right hand. Symbolic of God's authority to render retribution (Jer 25:15–29; Rev 16:1–21).
2:17 violence ... done to Lebanon. May refer to ravaging the terrain in order to adorn foreign temples and palaces. Environmental damage extends to animals (cf. Jonah 4:11) and lands (cf. 2:8; Rev 11:18). **Lebanon.** A region north of Israel known for its cedar trees (1 Kgs 5:6; 2 Kgs 19:23; Ps 104:16; Isa 14:8).
2:18–20 idols. Though God forbade idols (Exod 20:4–6), the critique of idolatry appeals first to human reasoning. Idols (cf. Lev 19:4), whether carved of stone or wood (2 Kgs 21:7) or cast from metals (2 Kgs 17:16), by their very presence taught the lie that someone other than God was to be worshiped.
2:19 Wake up! God is vigilant compared to idols that need to be awakened (cf. Elijah's taunt, 1 Kgs 18:27). The clincher to the taunt series is the assertion that God rules and judges righteously from his "holy temple" (v. 20; Isa 6:1–3; Jonah 2:7).
2:20 be silent. Out of reverence and respect (Zeph 1:7).
3:1–19 *Habakkuk's Prayer.* Into this psalm-like prayer, which opens with a petition and ends with a testimony, is inserted the report of God's appearance. The moods are several: earnest pleas, excitement, perplexity, nervousness, confidence, and joy.
3:1 *Heading.* The new heading divides the book (chs. 1–2; 3). Both divisions include first-person style as well as questions and answers about God's way in the world. The intensity is greater in part two. Some regard ch. 3 as the content of the revelation in 2:2. Ch. 3 is bracketed by references to music (see vv. 1,19b and notes).
3:1 ***shigionoth.*** May be a type of psalm (lament has been suggested; see Ps 7 superscript) or a rhythm or cadence.
3:2 *Adoration and Petition.* The "deeds" may refer to those noted earlier (1:5–11; 2:4–19) or to others in history, such as the exodus, in which

3 God came from Teman,
the Holy One from Mount Paran.[a]
His glory covered the heavens
and his praise filled the earth.[o]
4 His splendor was like the sunrise;
rays flashed from his hand,
where his power was hidden.
5 Plague went before him;
pestilence followed his steps.
6 He stood, and shook the earth;
he looked, and made the nations tremble.
The ancient mountains crumbled
and the age-old hills collapsed[p] —
but he marches on forever.
7 I saw the tents of Cushan in distress,
the dwellings of Midian[q] in anguish.[r]
8 Were you angry with the rivers,[s] LORD?
Was your wrath against the streams?
Did you rage against the sea
when you rode your horses
and your chariots to victory?[t]
9 You uncovered your bow,
you called for many arrows.[u]
You split the earth with rivers;
10 the mountains saw you and writhed.
Torrents of water swept by;
the deep roared[v]
and lifted its waves[w] on high.

11 Sun and moon stood still[x] in the heavens
at the glint of your flying arrows,[y]
at the lightning of your flashing spear.
12 In wrath you strode through the earth
and in anger you threshed[z] the nations.

3:3 [o] Ps 48:10
3:6 [p] Ps 114:1-6
3:7 [q] Judg 7:24-25 [r] Ex 15:14
3:8 [s] Ex 7:20 [t] Ps 68:17
3:9 [u] Ps 7:12-13
3:10 [v] Ps 98:7 [w] Ps 93:3
3:11 [x] Jos 10:13 [y] Ps 18:14
3:12 [z] Isa 41:15

[a] *3* The Hebrew has *Selah* (a word of uncertain meaning) here and at the middle of verse 9 and at the end of verse 13.

God intervened in judgment and salvation. Repeat ("make alive" or "enliven" or "revive") is found in other petitions for God's renewal work (Pss 80:18; 85:6; cf. Isa 57:15; Hos 6:2). An earlier request for judgment (1:3–4) is now tempered by a plea for mercy (cf. Exod 34:6–7).

3:3–15 *Report of God's Coming (Theophany).* The poetic account of God's appearance may restate what Habakkuk had heard (v. 2), the stories of exodus and conquest as suggested by "plague" (v. 5), and the standing still of the sun and moon (v. 11); or Habakkuk may be relating a personal visionary experience, one he was instructed to record (2:2). God approaches the battle scene, surveys the situation, and engages in battle to deliver his people. Divine appearances disturb nature (cf. Exod 19:16–25; Judg 5:4–5,20–21; 1 Kgs 19:11–18; Ps 18:7–15). Not only is the Lord in full control of nature and nations, but he is powerful enough to overcome opposition of whatever kind.

3:3 Teman. A city or region in northern Edom, south of the Dead Sea (Jer 49:20; Ezek 25:13). **Holy One.** This designation is frequent in Isaiah (e.g., Isa 43:15; 45:11). **Mount Paran.** A wilderness in the Sinai region (Deut 33:2; cf. 1 Kgs 11:18) or a peak in a more eastern mountain range or the mountain range itself.

3:4 where his power was hidden. Elaborated in vv. 6–15. God is on the march with an entourage of "plague" and "pestilence" (v. 5), personified as soldiers (cf. Exod 7:10—11:9; Deut 32:24).

3:6 nations tremble. Cf. Exod 15:14–16; 1 Sam 5:11. **mountains crumbled.** Cf. Pss 18:7; 46:3; 97:4–5. The portrait is of an irresistible force approaching a battle.

3:7 Cushan. Possibly a shortened form of "Cush-Rishathaim," a king of Aram Naharaim who oppressed Israel (Judg 3:8–11). **Midian.** A region east and south of the Dead Sea. Gideon defeated the Midianites (Judg 6–8).

3:8 Were you angry with the rivers, Lord? Hardly. God's anger is against evil nations (v. 12), but nature feels the effect. **rode.** For God as rider, see Ps 18:10.

3:9 bow … arrows. Continues the imagery of a mighty warrior who subdues and rearranges nature, as in creation (Ps 74:12–15) and in the parting of waters in Israel's history (Exod 14:21–22; Josh 3:14–17).

3:10 Torrents of water. Denotes cloudbursts.

3:11 Sun and moon. God's powerful intervention extends to the cosmos (cf. Josh 10:5–14). Nature too is in the service of fulfilling God's purposes.

3:12 you threshed the nations. God judicially separates wheat from chaff (cf. 2 Kgs 13:7; Amos 1:3).

3:13 [a]Ps 20:6; 28:8 [b]Ps 68:21; 110:6 **3:14** [c]Jdg 7:22 [d]Ps 64:2-5 **3:15** [e]Ex 15:8; Ps 77:19 **3:17** [f]Joel 1:10-12,18 [g]Jer 5:17 **3:18** [h]Isa 61:10; Php 4:4 **3:19** [i]Dt 33:29; Ps 46:1-5 [j]Dt 32:13; 2Sa 22:34; Ps 18:33

13 You came out to deliver[a] your people,
to save your anointed one.
You crushed[b] the leader of the land of wickedness,
you stripped him from head to foot.
14 With his own spear you pierced his head
when his warriors stormed out to scatter us,[c]
gloating as though about to devour
the wretched[d] who were in hiding.
15 You trampled the sea with your horses,
churning the great waters.[e]

16 I heard and my heart pounded,
my lips quivered at the sound;
decay crept into my bones,
and my legs trembled.
Yet I will wait patiently for the day of calamity
to come on the nation invading us.
17 Though the fig tree does not bud
and there are no grapes on the vines,
though the olive crop fails
and the fields produce no food,[f]
though there are no sheep in the pen
and no cattle in the stalls,[g]
18 yet I will rejoice in the LORD,[h]
I will be joyful in God my Savior.

19 The Sovereign LORD is my strength;[i]
he makes my feet like the feet of a deer,
he enables me to tread on the heights.[j]

For the director of music. On my stringed instruments.

3:13 anointed one. Israel's king (1 Sam 10:1); a frequent designation for the Davidic king (2 Chr 6:42; Pss 89: 50–51; 132:10). God marches to deliver Israel's king and crush leaders "of wickedness," even heads of world empires (e.g., Egypt, Exod 15:4; Assyria, Isa 10:5–6).
3:15 the sea. A symbol of chaos. In a final poetic flourish, it is "trampled" with "horses" (cf. v. 8) to establish that God, the mighty warrior, is invincible and victorious over all (Exod 15:1–18; Ps 18), even death (1 Cor 15:54–55).
3:16–19 *The Prophet's Response of Confidence and Joy.* The tone of Habakkuk's response after meeting God is radically different from his opening complaint (1:2–4). He is left exhausted, if not also ill and anxious about the future destruction, whether of Jerusalem or of the enemy as previewed in 1:11. His dialogue with God opens with a challenge; it ends with trust and joy. Other responses to divine appearances include worship (Josh 5:13–15), humility (Isa 6:5), awe (Ezek 1:28b), and fear (Luke 1:30). The prophet is ready to "wait patiently" (v. 16) as instructed (2:3).
3:18–19a Joy is a natural response to God's Word (Jer 15:16) and God's salvation (Isa 12:1–6). Initially problem-centered, the prophet is now God-centered. He will not be diverted from his trust and joy in God, even in times of bad economy, crop failures, and lost assets. Nimble and sure-footed "like the feet of a deer" (v. 19), he has embraced the "Sovereign LORD," and so is empowered to live the lesson learned about living by faith (2:4). Along with Job's sturdy expression of hope in his redeemer (Job 19:25), Habakkuk's closing statement is one of the finest affirmations of faith (cf. Rom 8:31–39; 2 Tim 1:12).
3:19b the director of music. Likely the chief chorister or conductor of temple musicians (see superscripts for Pss 4; 5). **stringed instruments.** Among them would be the harp and lyre (Pss 33:2; 92:3; 144:9). This notation suggests that the prayer-poem (see note on 3:1) was to be sung in community.

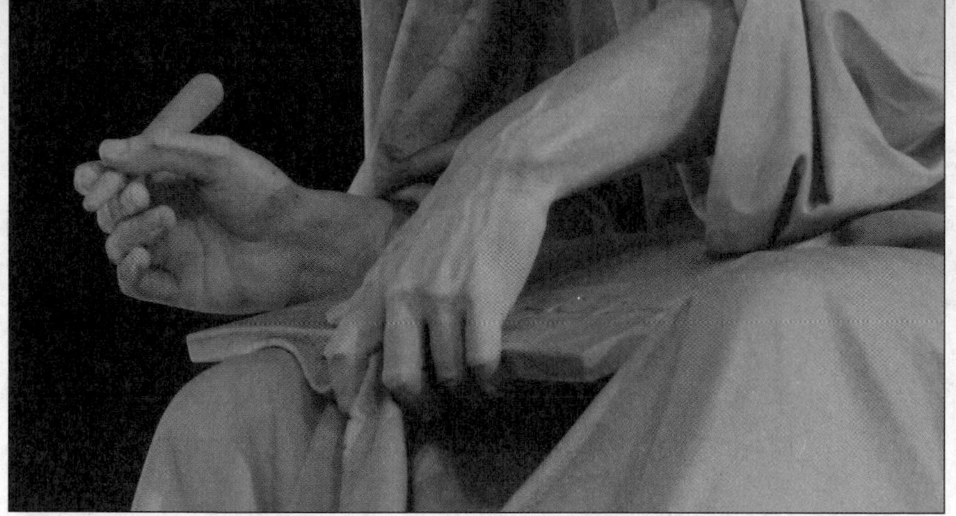

INTRODUCTION TO
ZEPHANIAH

AUTHOR

Because the prophet Zephaniah was the "son of Cushi" (1:1) and uniquely interested in the sin and future restoration of the Cushites (i.e., black Africans from ancient Ethiopia, today modern Sudan, 2:12; 3:9–10), he may have been a black Jew. Books like Genesis, Deuteronomy, Amos, and Isaiah apparently influenced him, and he may have been aware of the ministries of his contemporaries Nahum, Habakkuk, and young Jeremiah.

Zephaniah means "Yahweh hides." Perhaps his parents prayed that God would protect him at his birth during the shadowy reign of Manasseh (2 Kgs 20:21—21:18), who was son of King Hezekiah (2 Kgs 18–20; Isa 36–38), Zephaniah's great-great-grandfather (Zeph 1:1). As part of the royal family, Zephaniah was part of the Messianic-Davidic hope that still burned in the darkness. His social status may explain how he was aware of the international climate (2:5–15) and the ethics of Jerusalem's political and religious leadership (1:4,8–9; 3:3–4).

DATE

Zephaniah prophesied during the reign of King Josiah of Judah (641/40–609 BC) (1:1). In about 628 BC, Josiah started removing all pagan Canaanite shrines and emblems (2 Chr 34:3–7), and around 622 BC he recovered the Book of the Law and instituted a mass religious reform throughout the land (2 Kgs 22:3—23:25; 2 Chr 34:8—35:19). Because Zephaniah's message shows signs of Deuteronomy's influence while stressing a high need for spiritual growth, he likely ministered early in 622 BC after Josiah found the Book of the Law but before the reform movement was fully underway.

MESSAGE

Zephaniah provides a summons to satisfaction—a call to persevering trust in God in order to experience personal and divine pleasure in the future. In light of the impending day of Yahweh's wrath, the prophet urges his listeners to join the remnant in patiently pursuing Yahweh (i.e., "seek" [2:3] and "wait" [3:8]); this alone will preserve them through judgment and secure consummate joy in God (3:14) and the experience of God's delight in saved sinners (3:17). Three main messages are evident.

Basic Training for Satisfaction

Because Yahweh's day of fury is coming, Judah must repent and wait upon God. The prophet calls the people back to the basics as the only means for experiencing salvation through judgment (2:1,3; 3:8). Two judgments are certain: (1) near judgment against Judah through Babylon (1:4–13; 2:2; 3:7), and (2) future judgment against the entire world due to pervasive sin against the God of all the earth (1:1–3,14–18; 3:8; cf. Deut 30:7; Isa 24:5–6).

These warnings provide the context for the book's main purpose: to exhort Judah to trust God to faithfully preserve and ultimately satisfy them—even through judgment. What we hope for or fear tomorrow changes who we are

LOCATIONS IN ZEPHANIAH

today. Zephaniah motivates his audience with hope and dread as basic training for finding satisfaction in the Lord (2:1,3; 3:8,14–15).

Yahweh's War Equated With Sacrifice

The fires of Yahweh's retributive war will destroy the entire old creation order, including unbelieving humanity (1:3,18; 3:8), yet Yahweh will protect those who have humbled themselves and called on his name (2:3; 3:9,11). How can a righteous God who does no injustice (3:5) pardon, preserve, and bring pleasure to former sinful rebels (3:9–20)?

Zephaniah says little explicitly about the saving work of the Messiah, probably to portray that the Judahites were deep in darkness and almost fully separated from hope. But he hints that the means for understanding salvation through judgment and the inauguration of new creation is penal substitutionary atonement. He associates the fires of God's judgment with sacrifice (1:7; cf. 1:18; 3:8), which appeases God's righteous wrath. He also urges his audience to "draw near" to Yahweh (3:2), the exact language for approaching God by faith through a substitute sacrifice (Lev 9:1—10:3), which points to Christ (Heb 9:11–14,27–28; 10:11–14). Jesus took upon himself the sacrificial fires of God's judgment on behalf of all who believe (1:7,18; 3:8; cf. Isa 53:5,7,11); thus God is both just and the justifier (Rom 3:24–26). See "Sacrifice," p. 2656, and "Wrath," p. 2681.

Global Salvation

While Zephaniah focuses on a righteous remnant from Judah, he also highlights that God will save other peoples of the world (3:9–10; cf. 2:11). He thus anticipates the church age and the fulfillment of the Abrahamic covenant in blessing Jews and Gentiles alike in Christ (Gal 3:8,14,29; Eph 2:14–16). Together they will worship the King, the "Mighty Warrior who saves" (3:17; cf. 3:14–15). All these features have been inaugurated already in Christ and his church, and they now await complete consummation at Christ's second coming. See "People of God," p. 2672.

OUTLINE

I. Superscription (1:1)

II. Judgment on the Whole Earth in the Day of the Lord: A Call to Dreadful Silence Before God (1:2–18)

A. The Reason for the Call to Silence (1:2–6)

B. The Nature of the Call to Silence (1:7–18)

III. Judah and Jerusalem Judged Along With the Nations: Calls to Repent and to Wait for God (2:1—3:8)

A. Judah Summoned to Repent Before the Lord to Avoid Judgment (2:1–3)

B. Reasons for the Summons to Repent and Wait (2:4—3:7)

1. The Lamentable State and Fate of the Rebels From the Foreign Nations (2:4–15)
2. The Lamentable State and Fate of the Rebels From Jerusalem (3:1–7)

C. Judah Summoned to Wait for the Lord, Ultimately to Enjoy Satisfaction (3:8)

IV. Restoration of Israel's Remnant: Lasting Joy as Motivation for Waiting on God (3:9–20)

A. The Motivation: Global Salvation (3:9–10)

B. The Impact of Global Salvation for the Remnant of Judah: Lasting Joy (3:11–20)

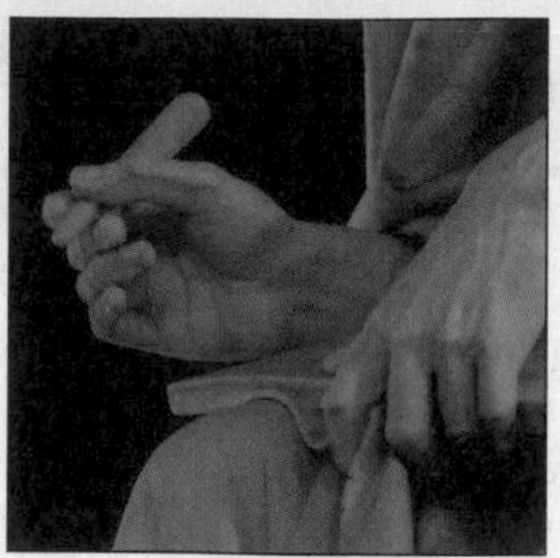

ZEPHANIAH

1:1 [a]2Ki 22:1; 2Ch 34:1-35:25
1:2 [b]Ge 6:7
1:3 [c]Jer 4:25 [d]Hos 4:3
1:4 [e]Jer 6:12 [f]Mic 5:13 [g]Hos 10:5
1:5 [h]Jer 5:7
1:6 [i]Isa 1:4; Jer 2:13 [j]Isa 9:13 [k]Hos 7:7

1 The word of the Lord that came to Zephaniah son of Cushi, the son of Gedaliah, the son of Amariah, the son of Hezekiah, during the reign of Josiah[a] son of Amon king of Judah:

Judgment on the Whole Earth in the Day of the Lord

2 "I will sweep away everything
from the face of the earth,"[b]

declares the Lord.

3 "I will sweep away both man and beast;
I will sweep away the birds in the sky[c]
and the fish in the sea —
and the idols that cause the wicked to stumble."[a]

"When I destroy all mankind
on the face of the earth,"[d]

declares the Lord,

4 "I will stretch out my hand[e] against Judah
and against all who live in Jerusalem.
I will destroy every remnant of Baal worship in this place,[f]
the very names of the idolatrous priests[g] —
5 those who bow down on the roofs
to worship the starry host,
those who bow down and swear by the Lord
and who also swear by Molek,[b][h]
6 those who turn back from following[i] the Lord
and neither seek[j] the Lord nor inquire[k] of him."

[a] 3 The meaning of the Hebrew for this line is uncertain. [b] 5 Hebrew *Malkam*

1:1 *Superscription.* See Introduction: Author; Date.
1:2–18 *Judgment on the Whole Earth in the Day of the Lord: A Call to Dreadful Silence Before God.* This sets a context for the book's main exhortations in chs. 2–3. Zephaniah's listeners must pause in silence since Yahweh's impending judgment is near.
1:2–6 *The Reason for the Call to Silence.* Yahweh will judge the world in general (vv. 2–3) and Judah in particular (vv. 4–6) because of their idolatrous rebellion.
1:2 sweep away everything. Echoes the flood judgment (Gen 6:7). Yahweh will destroy the proud rebel majority by fire (3:8b; cf. 1:18) but preserve and bless the penitent few (3:9–10,20).
1:3 man ... beast ... birds ... fish. Specifies "everything" (v. 2) in the reverse order that God created them (Gen 1:20–28), suggesting that the impending judgment will be a de-creation, parallel to the flood but now with fire (see note on v. 2).
1:4 remnant of Baal worship. Remaining pagan apostasy. **idolatrous priests.** Priests were supposed to preserve holiness and teach God's law (Lev 10:10–11). The Hebrew raises the possibility of two corrupt groups of priests: foreign and Israelite.
1:5 worship the starry host. A sin that corrupted the northern kingdom (2 Kgs 17:16) and characterized the reigns of Manasseh and Amon (2 Kgs 21:3,5–6,21; cf. 2 Kgs 23:4–5,24). **swear by the Lord and ... by Molek.** Make promises to Yahweh by Molek (cf. Deut 6:13; 10:20; Josh 23:7; 2 Kgs 23:10). God strongly condemned syncretism (2 Kgs 17:7–18; 21:2–9; 23:4–25).
1:6 those who turn back. Covenant disloyalty (Pss 44:18; 78:56–57; Isa 59:13). Following God is the only means to life (Matt 7:13–14; John 14:6).

7 Be silent[l] before the Sovereign LORD,
for the day of the LORD[m] is near.
The LORD has prepared a sacrifice;[n]
he has consecrated those he has invited.

8 "On the day of the LORD's sacrifice
I will punish[o] the officials
and the king's sons[p]
and all those clad
in foreign clothes.
9 On that day I will punish
all who avoid stepping on the threshold,[a]
who fill the temple of their gods
with violence and deceit.[q]

10 "On that day,"
declares the LORD,
"a cry will go up from the Fish Gate,[r]
wailing from the New Quarter,
and a loud crash from the hills.
11 Wail,[s] you who live in the market district[b];
all your merchants will be wiped out,
all who trade with[c] silver will be destroyed.[t]
12 At that time I will search Jerusalem with lamps
and punish those who are complacent,[u]
who are like wine left on its dregs,[v]
who think, 'The LORD will do nothing,[w]
either good or bad.'
13 Their wealth will be plundered,[x]
their houses demolished.
Though they build houses,
they will not live in them;
though they plant vineyards,
they will not drink the wine."[y]

14 The great day of the LORD[z] is near[a] —
near and coming quickly.

1:7 [l] Hab 2:20; Zec 2:13 [m] ver 14; Isa 13:6 [n] Isa 34:6; Jer 46:10
1:8 [o] Isa 24:21 [p] Jer 39:6
1:9 [q] Am 3:10
1:10 [r] 2Ch 33:14
1:11 [s] Jas 5:1 [t] Hos 9:6
1:12 [u] Am 6:1 [v] Jer 48:11 [w] Eze 8:12
1:13 [x] Jer 15:13 [y] Dt 28:30,39; Am 5:11; Mic 6:15
1:14 [z] ver 7; Joel 1:15 [a] Eze 7:7

[a] *9* See 1 Samuel 5:5. [b] *11* Or *the Mortar* [c] *11* Or *in*

1:7–18 *The Nature of the Call to Silence.* Like a herald readying an audience for an angry king's arrival, Zephaniah charges his audience to become quiet (v. 7a) because Yahweh will imminently judge Judah (vv. 7b–13) and the whole world (vv. 14–18).
1:7 silent. A reverent hush demanded of courtiers in an earthly king's presence (cf. Judg 3:19) or of humans before Yahweh (Hab 2:20; Zech 2:13 ["be still"]). **day of the LORD.** See note on Amos 2:16. **prepared a sacrifice.** To appease Yahweh's just wrath against sin. For the day of the Lord as a sacrifice, see Jer 46:10; Ezek 39:17,20–21. Christ's death combines Yahweh's day of judgment imagery with substitutionary sacrifice (see "Sacrifice," p. 2656). **those he has invited.** Either (1) the enemy invaders (i.e., Babylon) whom Yahweh consecrated as agents in Judah's destruction (Isa 13:3) or (2) the sacrificial victims devoted to slaughter (Jer 12:3), first from Judah (vv. 8–13) and then from the rest of the earth (vv. 14–18).
1:8 officials … king's sons. Judah's public leaders and royal court. Their rebellion caused the nation's destruction (cf. 3:3–4). **foreign clothes.** Signify pagan influence.
1:9 avoid stepping on the threshold. Probably associated with pagan superstitious activity (see 1 Sam 5:3–5 and note on 5:5).
1:10 Fish Gate … New Quarter. A main gate (2 Chr 33:14; Neh 3:3) and important district (2 Kgs 22:14; 2 Chr 34:22) on the north side of Jerusalem, implying enemies would invade from the north.
1:11 market district. Where "violence and deceit" flourished (v. 9; cf. 3:1) as the rich exploited the poor (cf. vv. 13,18).
1:12 search … with lamps. Yahweh will find his enemies in the dark when least expected. **complacent.** Cf. Amos 6:1; Mic 3:11; Mal 2:17. Rather than diminishing fear of punishment or desire for blessing, God's delayed judgment should cause people to be humble and in awe of his longsuffering mercy (see Exod 34:6–7).
1:13 wealth … houses … vineyards. God's judgment targets false securities (cf. vv. 11,18), likely gained by oppressing the weak (v. 9; cf. 3:1–4). **not live in … not drink.** Covenant curses (Deut 28:30–31,39), reversing the original blessings (Deut 6:10–11).
1:14 great day. Not merely the "day" as in vv. 7–10. This moves from Yahweh's impending punishment of Jerusalem to his final judgment of the

1:15 [b]Isa 22:5; Joel 2:2
1:16 [c]Jer 4:19 [d]Isa 2:15
1:17 [e]Isa 59:10 [f]Ps 79:3 [g]Jer 9:22
1:18 [h]Eze 7:19 [i]ver 2-3; Zep 3:8 [j]Ge 6:7
2:1 [k]2Ch 20:4; Joel 1:14 [l]Jer 3:3; 6:15
2:2 [m]Isa 17:13; Hos 13:3 [n]La 4:11
2:3 [o]Am 5:6

The cry on the day of the LORD is bitter;
the Mighty Warrior shouts his battle cry.
15 That day will be a day of wrath—
a day of distress and anguish,
a day of trouble and ruin,
a day of darkness and gloom,
a day of clouds and blackness[b]—
16 a day of trumpet and battle cry[c]
against the fortified cities
and against the corner towers.[d]

17 "I will bring such distress on all people
that they will grope about like those who are blind,[e]
because they have sinned against the LORD.
Their blood will be poured out[f] like dust
and their entrails like dung.[g]
18 Neither their silver nor their gold
will be able to save them
on the day of the LORD's wrath."[h]

In the fire of his jealousy
the whole earth will be consumed,[i]
for he will make a sudden end
of all who live on the earth.[j]

Judah and Jerusalem Judged Along With the Nations

Judah Summoned to Repent

2 Gather together,[k] gather yourselves together,
you shameful[l] nation,
2 before the decree takes effect
and that day passes like windblown chaff,[m]
before the LORD's fierce anger[n]
comes upon you,
before the day of the LORD's wrath
comes upon you.
3 Seek[o] the LORD, all you humble of the land,
you who do what he commands.

world (cf. Joel 2:11,31; Mal 4:5; Acts 2:20; Rev 6:17; 16:14). Its inauguration is Christ's death and resurrection (Acts 2:19–20), and its consummation will come at his second coming (cf. Rom 2:5; 2 Pet 3:7,10,12). **near.** With respect to eternity and God's timeline. **Mighty Warrior.** Likely Yahweh (cf. 3:17) but possibly a valiant soldier crying in defeat.

1:15 darkness and gloom ... clouds and blackness. Common cataclysmic images (likely figurative) associated with the day of the Lord that express God's fierce presence and the reversal of creation for those he judges (i.e., a move back to the state of Gen 1:2). Cf. Joel 2:2,30–31; 3:15; Acts 2:20.

1:16 trumpet and battle cry. Alarms that ready people for war, often associated with Yahweh's judgment (Joel 2:1; Zech 9:14; cf. 1 Thess 4:16).

1:17 blind. A covenant curse (Deut 28:28–29) that may point to spiritual disability and suggest that sin not only *deserves* judgment but *is* judgment (cf. Rom 1:24,26,28).

1:18 silver ... gold. Either money (vv. 8,11,13) or idols shaped from it (vv. 3,5). **save.** Cf. 1 Pet 1:18–19. **fire of his jealousy.** Cf. 3:8. Yahweh's passion for highest allegiance (Deut 5:7–10) is often associated with his inflamed zeal for worship (Deut 4:24; 6:15; Ps 79:5), which would soon burst forth in unquenchable fires of wrath against the ungodly of the earth (Deut 32:21–22; Heb 10:27; 2 Pet 3:10–13; Rev 20:14–15), paralleling the flood judgment by water (see notes on 1:2–3; 2 Pet 3:5–7).

2:1—3:8 *Judah and Jerusalem Judged Along With the Nations: Calls to Repent and to Wait for God.* The book's main section calls the remnant of Judah to repent (2:1–3) and wait for God (3:8). These two charges frame 2:4—3:7, which highlights the lamentable state and fate of the rebels from the foreign nations (2:4–15) and from Jerusalem (3:1–7) in order to clarify why Judah should turn to Yahweh.

2:1–3 *Judah Summoned to Repent Before the Lord to Avoid Judgment.* Repentance entails *gathering* together (vv. 1–2) and *seeking* Yahweh (v. 3).

2:1 Gather. Like desirable straw or grain is collected after being separated from the chaff (cf. v. 2), the remnant of the faithful must join in unity (cf. Heb 3:13; 10:24–25). **shameful.** Since the word for silver (cf. 1:18) is based on the same three Hebrew letters as "shameful," the prophet acknowledges that part of their "shame" is that they were relying on silver instead of on God.

2:2 There is still opportunity to repent, but it is fleeting.

2:3 Seek the LORD. Pursue God (cf. 1:6; 3:2; Pss 27:8; 105:3). **humble.** Earnestly and dependently trusting Yahweh (3:12). **righteousness.** Cor-

Seek righteousness, seek humility;[p]
perhaps you will be sheltered[q]
on the day of the LORD's anger.

Philistia

4 Gaza[r] will be abandoned
and Ashkelon left in ruins.
At midday Ashdod will be emptied
and Ekron uprooted.
5 Woe to you who live by the sea,
you Kerethite[s] people;
the word of the LORD is against you,[t]
Canaan, land of the Philistines.
He says, "I will destroy you,
and none will be left."[u]
6 The land by the sea will become pastures
having wells for shepherds
and pens for flocks.[v]
7 That land will belong
to the remnant of the people of Judah;
there they will find pasture.
In the evening they will lie down
in the houses of Ashkelon.
The LORD their God will care for them;
he will restore their fortunes.[a][w]

Moab and Ammon

8 "I have heard the insults[x] of Moab
and the taunts of the Ammonites,
who insulted[y] my people
and made threats against their land.
9 Therefore, as surely as I live,"
declares the LORD Almighty,
the God of Israel,

2:3 [p] Ps 45:4; Am 5:14-15 [q] Ps 57:1
2:4 [r] Am 1:6,7-8; Zec 9:5-7
2:5 [s] Eze 25:16 [t] Am 3:1 [u] Isa 14:30
2:6 [v] Isa 5:17
2:7 [w] Ps 126:4; Jer 32:44
2:8 [x] Jer 48:27 [y] Eze 25:3

[a] 7 Or *will bring back their captives*

rect order in the cosmos (Ps 89:14) and community (Deut 16:20), thus commonly associated with acts of justice, especially for the marginalized (cf. 1:9; 3:1–5). See Matt 6:33.

2:4—3:7 *Reasons for the Summons to Repent and Wait.* Beginning with a statement of judgment in 2:4, this two-part unit provides the logical basis for the charges to "seek" Yahweh (2:3) and "wait" for him (3:8) that frame it. Judah should repent and patiently trust Yahweh for two reasons: he will judge his enemies from the foreign nations where Judah might seek protection (2:4–15) and the rebels from Jerusalem itself (3:1–7). After the initial punishment declared in 2:4, each reason begins with "woe" (2:5; 3:1).

2:4–15 *The Lamentable State and Fate of the Rebels From the Foreign Nations.* God will punish those surrounding Judah: the Philistines to the west (vv. 4–7), the Moabites and Ammonites to the east (vv. 8–11), and the Cushites and Assyrians to the south and north (vv. 12–15). God's judgment encircles Judah, so they cannot escape; therefore, their only hope is to repent.

2:4 Judah must repent *because* Yahweh's judgment will fall very close to home, including on the foreign rebels from nearby Philistia. (In Hebrew, v. 4 begins with "Because.") **Gaza ... Ashkelon ... Ashdod ... Ekron.** Four of the five main Philistine cities, listed from south to north.

2:5 Woe. Parallels the "woe" of 3:1; used to express disgust over covenant rebellion (e.g., Hab 2:12,19) or dismay over impending doom (e.g., Jer 30:7). **Kerethite people.** The Philistines (Ezek 25:16).

2:6 pastures. Depicts fertility and peace, which God's people will enjoy (v. 7), ultimately through the one great shepherd in the line of Judah (Ezek 34:23; Mic 5:4; John 10:14–16; Rev 7:16–17).

2:7 remnant. Humble, faithful, God-trusting Judahites (v. 9; 3:12–13, 17–20; cf. 2 Kgs 19:31). Yahweh will preserve them through the destruction and satisfy them. **lie down in the houses of Ashkelon.** Restores original covenant blessings (Deut 6:10–11; see note on 1:13) but outside the original promised land. This suggests that God's earthly sovereignty, manifest first in the Garden of Eden and then in Zion and the promised land (Exod 15:17; Ps 78:54), is now beginning to expand to include the whole earth, which was the goal from the beginning (Gen 1:28; cf. Jer 3:16–17; Matt 5:5; Rom 4:13; Rev 21:2,10–27). See "Temple," p. 2652, and "The City of God," p. 2666. **restore their fortunes.** Bless them irreversibly in the future age of new creation and new covenant (see 3:20; cf. Deut 30:3; Jer 30:18; Joel 3:1).

2:8 Cf. Jer 48:27–30. **Moab ... Ammonites.** Judah's "cousins" (see Gen 19:36–38). They were proud (see note on v. 10).

2:9 like Sodom ... like Gomorrah. See Gen 19 and notes. This

2:9 [z]Isa 15:1-16:14; Jer 48:1-47 [a]Dt 29:23 [b]Jer 49:1-6; Eze 25:1-7 [c]Isa 11:14 [d]Am 2:1-3
2:10 [e]Isa 16:6 [f]Jer 48:27
2:11 [g]Joel 2:11 [h]Zep 1:4 [i]Zep 3:9
2:12 [j]Isa 18:1; 20:4 [k]Jer 46:10
2:13 [l]Na 1:1 [m]Mic 5:6
2:14 [n]Isa 14:23
2:15 [o]Isa 32:9 [p]Isa 47:8 [q]Eze 28:2 [r]Na 3:19

"surely Moab[z] will become like Sodom,[a]
  the Ammonites[b] like Gomorrah—
a place of weeds and salt pits,
  a wasteland forever.
The remnant of my people will plunder[c] them;
  the survivors of my nation will inherit their land.[d]"

10 This is what they will get in return for their pride,[e]
  for insulting[f] and mocking
  the people of the LORD Almighty.
11 The LORD will be awesome[g] to them
  when he destroys all the gods[h] of the earth.
Distant nations will bow down to him,[i]
  all of them in their own lands.

Cush

12 "You Cushites,[a][j] too,
  will be slain by my sword.[k]"

Assyria

13 He will stretch out his hand against the north
  and destroy Assyria,
leaving Nineveh[l] utterly desolate
  and dry as the desert.[m]
14 Flocks and herds will lie down there,
  creatures of every kind.
The desert owl[n] and the screech owl
  will roost on her columns.
Their hooting will echo through the windows,
  rubble will fill the doorways,
  the beams of cedar will be exposed.
15 This is the city of revelry[o]
  that lived in safety.[p]
She said to herself,
  "I am the one! And there is none besides me."[q]
What a ruin she has become,
  a lair for wild beasts!
All who pass by her scoff[r]
  and shake their fists.

[a] *12* That is, people from the upper Nile region

comparison stresses the ominous severity of Yahweh's judgment against the Moabites and Ammonites by ironically linking it with the very cities he destroyed in the days of Lot (Gen 19:24–25), the progenitor of these people groups (see note on 2:8). Again Zephaniah portrays the day of the Lord as reversing the created order (see note on 1:3). Biblical authors make similar comparisons elsewhere when addressing God's judgment against the ungodly (2 Pet 2:6; Rev 11:8)—be they from Israel (Deut 29:23; 32:32; Lam 4:6; Amos 4:11; Matt 10:15; 11:24; cf. Isa 1:9–10; 3:9; Jer 23:14; Ezek 16:46–56) or the nations (Isa 13:19; Jer 49:18; 50:40). **inherit their land.** See note on v. 7.

2:10 pride. Self-reliance or self-exaltation, a regular problem for Israel's neighbors to the east (see v. 8; Isa 16:6). See Prov 16:18; Jas 4:6; 1 Pet 5:5.

2:11 all the gods. Cf. Pss 95:3; 96:4–5; 97:7,9. **Distant nations will bow down.** Foreigners will pay homage to Yahweh, whether as defeated rebels (Isa 45:14) or the worshiping remnant (3:9–10). Cf. Phil 2:10–11.

2:12 Cushites. Black Africans from ancient Ethiopia in the region of modern Sudan, the southernmost empire of the known world at that time (see NIV text note). They controlled Egypt ca. 715–663 BC.

2:13 Assyria ... Nineveh. See Introduction to Nahum.

2:14–15 Such will be the devastation of the city that fails to surrender to Yahweh. Animals will replace humans as the inhabitants of what was the center of human power.

2:15 Speaks as if God has *already* destroyed Assyria. **safety.** False security (see Ps 118:8–9; Jer 17:5; cf. 1:18). **none besides me.** Cf. Isa 45:5–6,18,21–22; 46:9.

Jerusalem

3

Woe to the city of oppressors,[s]
rebellious and defiled![t]
2 She obeys[u] no one,
she accepts no correction.[v]
She does not trust in the LORD,
she does not draw near[w] to her God.
3 Her officials within her
are roaring lions;
her rulers are evening wolves,[x]
who leave nothing for the morning.
4 Her prophets are unprincipled;
they are treacherous people.[y]
Her priests profane the sanctuary
and do violence to the law.[z]
5 The LORD within her is righteous;
he does no wrong.[a]
Morning by morning he dispenses his justice,
and every new day he does not fail,
yet the unrighteous know no shame.

Jerusalem Remains Unrepentant

6 "I have destroyed nations;
their strongholds are demolished.
I have left their streets deserted,
with no one passing through.
Their cities are laid waste;[b]
they are deserted and empty.
7 Of Jerusalem I thought,
'Surely you will fear me
and accept correction!'
Then her place of refuge[a] would not be destroyed,
nor all my punishments come upon[b] her.
But they were still eager
to act corruptly[c] in all they did.
8 Therefore wait[d] for me,"
declares the LORD,
"for the day I will stand up to testify.[c]

3:1 [s] Jer 6:6 [t] Eze 23:30
3:2 [u] Jer 22:21 [v] Jer 7:28 [w] Ps 73:28; Jer 5:3
3:3 [x] Eze 22:27
3:4 [y] Jer 9:4 [z] Eze 22:26
3:5 [a] Dt 32:4
3:6 [b] Lev 26:31
3:7 [c] Hos 9:9
3:8 [d] Ps 27:14

[a] 7 Or *her sanctuary* [b] 7 Or *all those I appointed over to plunder* [c] 8 Septuagint and Syriac; Hebrew *will rise up*

3:1–7 *The Lamentable State and Fate of the Rebels From Jerusalem.* God will judge not only those surrounding Israel (2:4–15) but Jerusalem itself. **3:1 Woe.** See 2:5. **city of oppressors.** Cf. vv. 3–5; 1:9; Ezek 22:6–7,29. Cf. also Jas 1:27. **rebellious and defiled!** Though God called Israel to be holy (see "Holiness," p. 2676).
3:2 obeys no one. Cf. Jer 7:28; 22:21. **accepts no correction.** Stubborn and unlearning (v. 7). **does not trust.** Cf. Pss 62:8; 115:9–11; cf. also Jer 17:5–8. **draw near.** Probably shorthand (when paired with trusting God and linked to the imagery of sacrifice in 1:7–8) for approaching Yahweh through his provision of sacrificial atonement. As the supreme savior, sovereign, and satisfier of the world, God promises to meet all who draw near to him (Jas 4:8). In the new covenant, we draw near to God only through Jesus' blood and righteousness (Eph 2:13; Heb 7:19).
3:3 Rather than guarding the people like shepherds protect sheep, the rulers abused them like wild beasts devour prey (Ezek 22:25,27; Mic 3:1–3).
3:4 Rather than representing Yahweh accurately, as his mouthpiece or his ambassador, the (false) prophets spread lies (cf. Ezek 13) and the priests failed to preserve holiness and teach God's law (Lev 10:10–11).
3:5 righteous. Preserves and displays right order (see note on 2:3). See Deut 32:4.
3:6 destroyed nations. Cf. 2:4–15. This destruction should motivate Judah to fear Yahweh (v. 7).
3:7 fear. Respect or worship (see note on Prov 1:7; cf. Eccl 12:13; Matt 10:28). **my punishments.** The covenant curses, which remove all provision and protection (Lev 26:14–33; Deut 28:15–68). **act corruptly.** Parallels what brought about the flood (Gen 6:11–12). See notes on 1:2,18.
3:8 *Judah Summoned to Wait for the Lord, Ultimately to Enjoy*

3:8 [e] Joel 3:2 [f] Zep 1:18
3:9 [g] Zep 2:11 [h] Isa 19:18
3:10 [i] Ps 68:31 [j] Isa 60:7
3:11 [k] Joel 2:26-27
3:12 [l] Isa 14:32 [m] Na 1:7

I have decided to assemble the nations,[e]
to gather the kingdoms
and to pour out my wrath on them—
all my fierce anger.
The whole world will be consumed[f]
by the fire of my jealous anger.

Restoration of Israel's Remnant

9 "Then I will purify the lips of the peoples,
that all of them may call[g] on the name of the LORD
and serve[h] him shoulder to shoulder.
10 From beyond the rivers of Cush[a][i]
my worshipers, my scattered people,
will bring me offerings.[j]
11 On that day you, Jerusalem, will not be put to shame[k]
for all the wrongs you have done to me,
because I will remove from you
your arrogant boasters.
Never again will you be haughty
on my holy hill.
12 But I will leave within you
the meek[l] and humble.
The remnant of Israel
will trust[m] in the name of the LORD.

[a] *10* That is, the upper Nile region

Satisfaction. The "therefore" signals that Zephaniah is now drawing an inference from the bilateral ground of 2:4—3:7 and returning to the primary line of command begun at 2:1–3 (see note at 2:4—3:7). The charge to wait for Yahweh in 3:8 stands as a counterpart to the plea to repent in 2:1–3, and those who obey the call will experience lasting joy on the other side of judgment (vv. 9–20).

3:8 Therefore. Likely introduces a necessary, appropriate logical inference from the ground in 2:4—3:7 (see note there). **wait.** Possibly dread of future punishment but probably patient, persistent hoping for salvation through judgment (e.g., Ps 33:20). Judah must continue to "wait" for Yahweh *because* his judgment on the rebel nations is coming but delayed. (In Hebrew, "because" precedes "I have decided.") **testify.** As both righteous accuser and judge. **fire of my jealous anger.** See note on 1:18.

3:9–20 *Restoration of Israel's Remnant: Lasting Joy as Motivation for Waiting on God.* The ultimate motivation for waiting for God (v. 8) is eternal joy. The vision of a redeemed community of worshipers made up of ethnic Israelites and others from the nations points to the re-creation of a unified humanity fulfilling its purpose, now eternally realized in the church (Matt 28:18–20; Rom 11; Eph 2:11–22; Rev 5:9–10; 7:9–10).

3:9–10 *The Motivation: Global Salvation.* Judah must continue to "wait" for Yahweh (v. 8) because, when he judges as covenant witness, he will transform peoples from all over the world into true worshipers. (In Hebrew, "because" or "for" precedes "then" in v. 9.)

3:9 Then. Corresponds to "on that day" in vv. 11,16. **purify the lips.** Cleanse speech (cf. Isa 6:5–7). This likely alludes to a reversal of the tower of Babel episode, where Yahweh confused the world's languages because of the people's pride (Gen 11:7–9). **the peoples.** Those from Judah and the nations whom Yahweh preserved through judgment. **call on.** Depend on Yahweh as the savior, sovereign, and satisfier (Ps 116:4,13,17; Joel 2:32; Acts 2:21; Rom 10:13; cf. Zeph 3:12).

3:10 rivers. Likely the White Nile and Blue Nile, the two main tributaries of the Nile River in northeast Africa, the region of modern Sudan (cf. Isa 18:1–2). **Cush my worshipers.** Even the most distant lands will have a remnant of worshipers (see NIV text note), as if following the rivers of life back up to the Garden of Eden for fellowship with the great King (Gen 2:13). The Ethiopian eunuch (from the area of modern Sudan) in Acts 8:26–39 gives evidence of the initial fulfillment of this prophecy. **my scattered.** Yahweh reverses Israel's exile (Deut 30:3; Ezek 11:17) and the tower of Babel episode (Gen 11:8–9; see note on v. 9). Cf. John 11:51–52. **offerings.** Tangible gifts of praise. Those who were once enemies of God now gather to pay homage to their King (Isa 18:7; 60:4–7; 66:20; Zech 14:16), with some even serving as priests (Isa 66:21; cf. Isa 56:6; 60:7). The NT treats all Christians as priests who, in light of the completed and sufficient sacrificial and priestly work of Christ (Heb 2:17; 9:7,11–14), now offer God spiritual sacrifices of praise expressed in doing good, sharing, and using their spiritual gifts (Rom 12:1; Heb 13:15–16; 1 Pet 2:5; cf. 1 Pet 2:9; Rev 5:10).

3:11–20 *The Impact of Global Salvation for the Remnant of Judah: Lasting Joy.* This is what the global transformation in vv. 8–10 implies: God will remove the proud and preserve the God-dependent (vv. 11–13), who will joyfully sing in the wake of his irreversible victory (vv. 14–15), and he will deliver and delight in them (vv. 16–20). So the call to patiently pursue Yahweh that shapes the book's body (2:1–3; 3:8) is nothing less than a summons to satisfaction (see Introduction: Message).

3:11 On that day. When Yahweh carries out his judicial decision (v. 8; also v. 16). **put to shame.** Humiliated, dishonored (v. 19). **because.** Introduces two reasons that Yahweh's judgment will not disgrace Jerusalem: he will remove the proud (v. 11b) and preserve the humble (v. 12).

3:12 remnant. See note on 2:7. **trust.** See note on v. 9.

[13] They[n] will do no wrong;[o]
they will tell no lies.[p]
A deceitful tongue
will not be found in their mouths.
They will eat and lie down[q]
and no one will make them afraid.[r]"

[14] Sing, Daughter Zion;[s]
shout aloud,[t] Israel!
Be glad and rejoice with all your heart,
Daughter Jerusalem!
[15] The LORD has taken away your punishment,
he has turned back your enemy.
The LORD, the King of Israel, is with you;[u]
never again will you fear[v] any harm.
[16] On that day
they will say to Jerusalem,
"Do not fear, Zion;
do not let your hands hang limp.[w]
[17] The LORD your God is with you,
the Mighty Warrior who saves.[x]
He will take great delight[y] in you;
in his love he will no longer rebuke you,
but will rejoice over you with singing."

[18] "I will remove from you
all who mourn over the loss of your appointed festivals,
which is a burden and reproach for you.
[19] At that time I will deal
with all who oppressed you.
I will rescue the lame;
I will gather the exiles.[z]
I will give them praise[a] and honor
in every land where they have suffered shame.

3:13 [n] Isa 10:21; Mic 4:7 [o] Ps 119:3 [p] Rev 14:5 [q] Eze 34:15; Zep 2:7 [r] Eze 34:25-28
3:14 [s] Zec 2:10 [t] Isa 12:6
3:15 [u] Eze 37:26-28 [v] Isa 54:14
3:16 [w] Job 4:3; Isa 35:3-4; Heb 12:12
3:17 [x] Isa 63:1 [y] Isa 62:4
3:19 [z] Eze 34:16; Mic 4:6 [a] Isa 60:18

3:13 no lies. Because of Yahweh's speech-purifying work (v. 9; see Rev 14:5). **eat and lie down and no one will make them afraid.** Like sheep under the care of a good shepherd (Ps 23).
3:14–15 An ode to joy expressing wholehearted delight in all God has won (cf. Isa 65:18).
3:14 Daughter Zion ... Daughter Jerusalem. No longer "the city of oppressors" (v. 1); now the object of Yahweh's saving love.
3:15 Jerusalem should celebrate (v. 14) because judgment day is over (stated as if it is already accomplished). **has taken away your punishment.** God ultimately removes his wrath and curse through Christ (Rom 5:9; 8:1; Gal 3:13–14). **King of Israel.** See Introduction to Psalms: Theology of the Psalms. Highlights Yahweh's reign over a restored, unified people. The rulers of Israel and Judah were always to represent, rather than replace, Yahweh's kingship (cf. Num 23:21; Deut 33:5; 1 Sam 8:7; Ezek 20:33). While the OT never refers to the Messianic royal deliverer with the title "King of Israel," it clearly declares that Yahweh's reign will be realized through his royal son (e.g., Gen 49:8; Num 24:17–19; 1 Sam 2:10; Ps 2:8,12; Isa 9:5–7; 11:1–4; Jer 23:5–6; Ezek 34:23–24). Furthermore, the NT applies the title to Jesus the Messiah (Matt 27:42; Mark 15:32; John 1:49; 12:13; cf. Matt 2:2; 28:18; Luke 1:32–33; Heb 1:8), and when speaking of Jesus' Triumphal Entry into Jerusalem in John 12:13, John appears to apply to Jesus the mention of Yahweh's reign in Zeph 3:15–16. **with you.** The eschatological promise of God's enduring Spirit-presence in the midst of his people that enables holiness and brings security (Ezek 36:27; 37:26–28; Zech 2:10). Jesus has inaugurated the fulfillment of these promises, for he is "God with us" (Matt 1:23; John 1:14) and indwells the church through his Spirit (Matt 28:20; John 14:16–20; Rom 8:9–10; cf. Rev 21:3).
3:16 hands hang limp. Symbolizes discouragement.
3:17 Mighty Warrior. Cf. 1:14. Yahweh is the supreme soldier (Ps 24:8). **take great delight.** Rejoice like a bridegroom delights in his bride (Isa 62:4–5). **with singing.** Cf. 3:14. Yahweh delights in his beloved (cf. Isa 65:18–19).
3:18 The suffering rebels that Yahweh removed from his remnant were a reproach to Jerusalem (cf. v. 11). **appointed festivals.** Possibly refers to a festival (e.g., Isa 33:20) but could also be a time of judgment like the day of the Lord (Hab 2:3). An alternative rendering of this verse is: "Those mourning/suffering from the appointed time [i.e., the day of judgment] I removed from you; they were a burden on her [i.e., Jerusalem], a reproach" (cf. v. 11).
3:19 rescue the lame. The weak and humble that the rebel majority abused (1:9; 3:1–2; cf. Ezek 34:21) are the very ones upon whom Yahweh's justice would shine (3:5; cf. 2:3; 3:12; Deut 10:17–18). God would deliver the broken (Mic 4:6–7; cf. Isa 35:6; Jer 31:8; Ezek 34:16), for to them belong the kingdom and its comfort (Matt 5:3–4). Christ's own ministry of mercy proved that he was inaugurating this eschatological

3:20 [b] Jer 29:14; Eze 37:12 [c] Isa 56:5; 66:22 [d] Joel 3:1

[20] At that time I will gather you;
at that time I will bring[b] you home.
I will give you honor[c] and praise
among all the peoples of the earth
when I restore your fortunes[a][d]
before your very eyes,"
says the LORD.

[a] 20 Or *I bring back your captives*

age of rescue (Matt 11:5; Luke 7:22; cf. Isa 42:3; 61:1–3; Matt 15:30–31; 21:14; Luke 14:21), and through his church comparable acts of healing and restoration are to continue until the consummation (Acts 3:1–10; 8:5–8; 14:8–10; 20:35; 1 Thess 5:14; Heb 12:13; Jas 1:27). **praise and honor.** The Hebrew can also be translated "*for* praise and *for* honor," which suggests that admiration and acclaim would be given not to the remnant of Judah but to God (Jer 33:9; cf. Ezek 36:23).

3:20 restore your fortunes. See note on 2:7. **says the LORD.** The book ends where it began (1:1): these words are from God and are therefore utterly trustworthy.

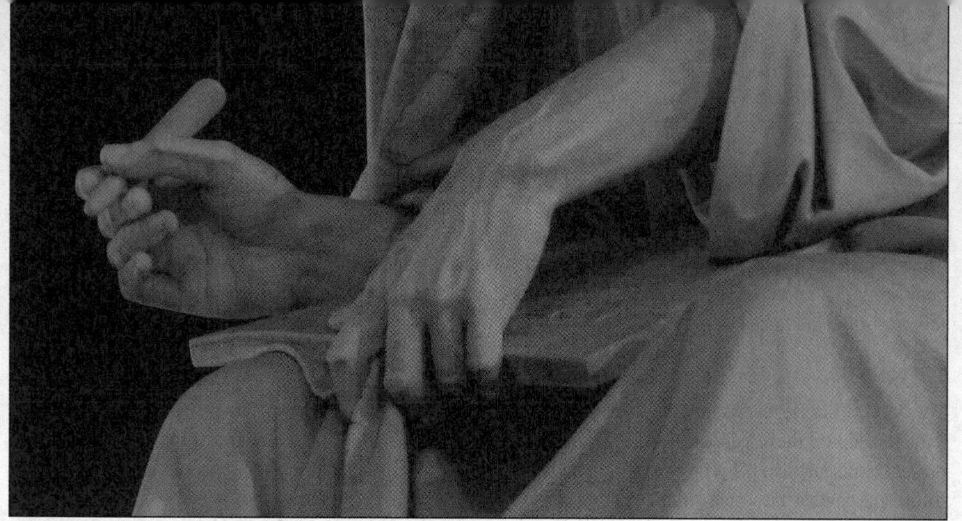

INTRODUCTION TO HAGGAI

AUTHOR

Haggai is remembered outside his book for the vital role he played as a prophet, along with Zechariah, in rebuilding the temple after the Babylonians destroyed it almost 70 years earlier (Ezra 5:1–2; 6:14; Zech 8:9). In Hebrew, his name means "festal."

DATE

The book of Haggai contains six precise dates, all in the second year of the Persian king Darius (520 BC). The dates structure the book and identify key moments in the temple reconstruction.

The book was most likely written shortly after the final date in 2:20, since it does not record the completion of the temple (in 516 or 515 BC; cf. Ezra 6:15). Additionally, Zech 8 (dated two years after Haggai's last prophecy), contains many echoes of Haggai.

OCCASION AND PURPOSE

In 539 BC the Persian king Cyrus (reigned 539–530 BC) decreed that the Jewish exiles in Babylonia could return to Jerusalem and rebuild the temple (cf. Ezra 1:1–4). The book of Ezra records that many Jews returned under Sheshbazzar and began the difficult task of rebuilding. Yet vigorous opposition from the neighboring Samaritans soon brought the work to a standstill (Ezra 4:1–5,24). Haggai's prophetic ministry began in 520 BC, almost 20 years after the first exiles returned. At this time, Darius I Hystaspes (cf. 1:1) was the Persian king who had just consolidated his rule after a series of rebellions following the death of the previous king, Cambyses (reigned 530–522 BC). Darius brought a measure of peace to the region and supported the temple rebuilding (Ezra 5:3–6; 6:6–12).

Yet this period proved to be a time of great hardship for God's people (e.g., 1:6,10–11; Zech 8:10). Earlier proph-

DATES IN HAGGAI

REFERENCE	DATE	SIGNIFICANCE	ADDRESSEE(S)
1:1	1st day of sixth month (Aug. 29)	The date of the first prophecy	Zerubbabel, Joshua (1:1), the people (implied in 1:12–14)
1:15	24th day of sixth month (Sept. 21)	Beginning of the work on the temple	
2:1	21st day of seventh month (Oct. 17)	The date of the second prophecy	Zerubbabel, Joshua, the remnant of the people (2:2)
2:10	24th day of nineth month (Dec. 18)	The date of the third prophecy	The priests (presumably including Joshua) (2:11)
2:18	24th day of nineth month (Dec. 18)	Foundation of the temple laid	
2:20	24th day of nineth month (Dec. 18)	The date of the fourth prophecy	Zerubbabel (2:21)

ets had promised a glorious restoration after exile (e.g., Zeph 3:20). For those in Jerusalem the reality fell far short of this hope. Haggai understands that the temple is central to God's restoration purposes and speaks God's word of rebuke, challenge, and comfort to get its construction back on track. He also speaks of a future work of God to "shake the heavens and the earth" (2:6,21) and establish his kingdom, moving from disappointment to hope. The book continues to encourage God's people about this coming kingdom and to challenge all readers about whether their priorities in life line up with God's.

GENRE

The book of Haggai reports four prophecies of Haggai (1:1–11; 2:1–9; 2:10–19; 2:20–23), each introduced by a date. In addition, the response to the first prophecy is reported (1:12–15). The first and third prophecies focus on the present and admonish the people to work to build the temple. The second and fourth prophecies focus more on the future and console the people with the promise that God will "shake the heavens and the earth" (2:6,21) and establish his kingdom. A feature of Haggai is the use of questions to raise key issues (1:4,9; 2:3,12,13,19).

THEMES

1. *Covenant.* The book of Haggai must be read against the background of the Mosaic covenant; otherwise, there is a real danger of distorting its message into one that seeks to manipulate God by human-centered religion (i.e., build the temple to win God's blessing), a distortion that denies God's grace and twists the message into a "prosperity gospel." In Exodus, God saved his people by grace and gave them the law to show them how to live as his saved people. At the end of Leviticus and Deuteronomy, Moses spells out not only the blessings that will continue if God's people obey but also the curses that will come should his people disobey, the ultimate curse being exile from the promised land (e.g., Deut 28:63–68). Even then, God promises restoration and blessing when they repent ("return") and "obey" (Deut 30:1–3). In Deuteronomy, this repentance is ultimately a work of God (Deut 30:6), highlighting his grace. Haggai does not say, "Give to the temple, and God will make you rich." Rather, he calls the people back to covenant obedience and promises the blessings of the covenant. Furthermore, when the people heed the call to obey, Haggai explains this as God working in their midst by his Spirit through his powerful word (1:12–14; 2:4–5). This response in Haggai's day anticipates the new covenant (cf. Jer 24:7; 31:33; Ezek 11:19–20; 2 Cor 3:3; Heb 8:10).

2. *Temple.* The temple is a central theme in Haggai and one that traverses the Bible. God's intention since creation was to dwell in the midst of his people. Indeed, Eden is portrayed as a garden sanctuary (see note on Gen 2:8; see also "Temple," p. 2652). After the exodus, God established the tabernacle as the visible representation of his presence and rule (Exod 25–31; 35–40; see note on Exod 25:1—40:38), and he promised that the goal of the Israelites' journey from Egypt would be his "sanctuary" (Exod 15:17). After King David built his house of cedar in Jerusalem, he desired to build a permanent house for God (2 Sam 7:2). This temple was built by David's son Solomon (1 Kgs 5–8). When God later judged his people by the Babylonians in 586 BC, the temple was destroyed (2 Kgs 25:8–17). Yet the prophets promised a key role for the temple in the restoration of God's people (e.g., Isa 2:2–3; 44:28; Ezek 40–48; Joel 3:18; Mic 4:1–2). Hence, when the people returned to the land, rebuilding the temple was to be their priority, and Haggai reminds the people of this. God's ultimate purposes for the temple find their fulfillment in Jesus (e.g., John 2:19–21), the people of the church (e.g., 1 Cor 3:16–17; Eph 2:21; 1 Pet 2:4–5), and the new creation (e.g., Rev 21–22). See "Temple," p. 2652.

3. *Messiah.* Along with God's purposes for the temple, Haggai also confirms that God's covenant with David and the hope for a future king (Messiah) still stand (2:23).

OUTLINE

I. First Prophecy: A Call to Build the House of the Lord (1:1–11)

II. Response: Obedience, Assurance, and Action (1:12–15a)

III. Second Prophecy: The Promised Glory of the New House (1:15b—2:9)

IV. Third Prophecy: Blessings for a Defiled People (2:10–19)

V. Fourth Prophecy: Zerubbabel the Lord's Signet Ring (2:20–23)

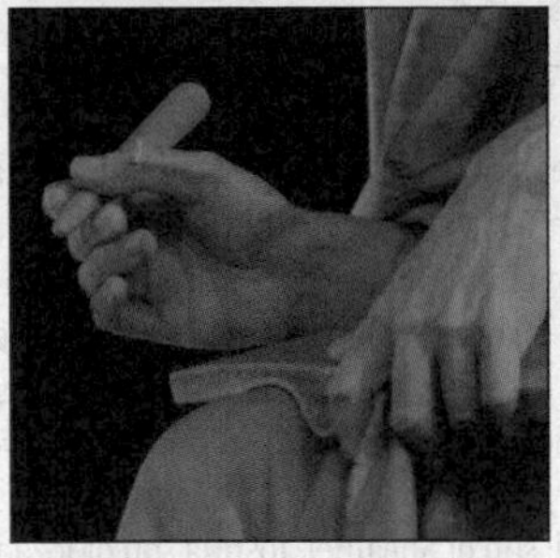

HAGGAI

A Call to Build the House of the Lord

1 In the second year of King Darius,[a] on the first day of the sixth month, the word of the LORD came
through the prophet Haggai[b] to Zerubbabel[c] son of Shealtiel, governor[d] of Judah, and to Joshua[e]
son of Jozadak,[a][f] the high priest:

[2]This is what the LORD Almighty says: "These people say, 'The time has not yet come to rebuild the
LORD's house.'"

[3]Then the word of the LORD came through the prophet Haggai:[g] [4]"Is it a time for you yourselves to
be living in your paneled houses,[h] while this house remains a ruin?[i]"

[5]Now this is what the LORD Almighty says: "Give careful thought[j] to your ways. [6]You have planted
much, but harvested little.[k] You eat, but never have enough. You drink, but never have your fill. You put
on clothes, but are not warm. You earn wages,[l] only to put them in a purse with holes in it."

[7]This is what the LORD Almighty says: "Give careful thought to your ways. [8]Go up into the mountains

1:1 [a]Ezr 4:24 [b]Ezr 5:1 [c]Mt 1:12-13 [d]Ezr 5:3 [e]Ezr 2:2 [f]1Ch 6:15; Ezr 3:2
1:3 [g]Ezr 5:1
1:4 [h]2Sa 7:2 [i]ver 9; Jer 33:12
1:5 [j]La 3:40
1:6 [k]Dt 28:38 [l]Hag 2:16; Zec 8:10

[a] *1* Hebrew *Jehozadak*, a variant of *Jozadak*; also in verses 12 and 14

1:1–11 *First Prophecy: A Call to Build the House of the Lord.* Haggai challenges the people of Judah to reorder their priorities and rebuild the temple.
1:1 In the second year of King Darius. Cf. v. 15b; 2:10. See Introduction: Occasion and Purpose. **first day of the sixth month.** Aug. 29, 520 BC. **through.** Indicates Haggai's status as a "prophet" of God, like Moses (cf. v. 3; 2:1; 1 Kgs 8:53). **Zerubbabel.** Had earlier returned from Babylon, rebuilt the altar, and laid the foundation of the temple under the authority of Sheshbazzar (see Ezra 1:8 and note; Ezra 2:2; 3:2,8–10; 5:16; Neh 12:1). **son of Shealtiel.** His Davidic lineage qualifies him to rebuild the temple (cf. 1 Chr 3:17). **governor of Judah.** A Persian-appointed administrator. **Joshua son of Jozadak.** A priest from the line of Levi (cf. 1 Chr 6:15), responsible for the temple and sacrificial system (cf. Ezra 2:2; Zech 3:1; 6:11 and notes).
1:2 LORD Almighty. Or "Yahweh of armies." This title, which occurs 14 times in Haggai, speaks of God's might and universal rule; here it underlines why the people should listen to his word (cf. 2 Sam 7:8). **These people.** Possibly reflects God's displeasure by not calling them "my people." **The time has not yet come.** Perhaps they were making excuses, saying that the end of Jeremiah's 70 years had not come (cf. Jer 25:11–12; 29:10; Zech 1:12; 7:5) or that a Davidic king would come and build the temple (cf. Ezek 37:24–28). In any case, their failure "to rebuild the LORD's house" is the problem that Haggai addresses.
1:4 paneled. Possibly internal wood lining walls or ceilings (cf. 1 Kgs 6:9; 7:3,7; Jer 22:14). **this house.** The temple. **a ruin.** See also v. 9. Verse 11 translates the same Hebrew root as "drought." "Desolate" is used to described the destruction of Jerusalem in 586 BC in Jer 33:12 and Ezek 36:35. While some 20 years earlier Israelites attempted to rebuild the temple, enemy opposition brought it to a standstill (cf. Ezra 4:1–5,24). The people's failure to rebuild it demonstrates that they have lost track of God's priorities as revealed in his word. God's ultimate purposes for the temple find their fulfillment in Jesus, and his kingdom is to be the Christian's first priority (Matt 6:33). See Introduction: Themes.
1:5 Give careful thought to your ways. A challenge (repeated in v. 7; 2:15,18) to consider how failing to rebuild the temple has adversely impacted their lives.
1:6 The essential background is the Mosaic covenant and the curses for disobedience (see, e.g., Lev 26:26; Deut 28:18,38–39). **purse with holes in it.** Wages were often carried in a small pouch attached to a waist cord. The phrase indicates that prices were high since resources were scarce. While the people have returned from exile, they are still suffering the curses for disobedience since they do not demonstrate that they have returned to the Lord to love and obey him with all their heart and soul (cf. Deut 30:1–6; Zech 1:3).
1:8 Go up into the mountains and bring down timber. The "mountain" (singular in Hebrew) is best understood as the temple mount (cf. Isa 2:2–3). Timber in the surrounding "mountains" was not suitable for temple construction (Neh 8:15), so provision had earlier been made to acquire timber from Lebanon (Ezra 3:7; cf. 1 Kgs 5:6–11), which Haggai now calls them to bring to build the temple. Perhaps it was some of this timber that they used in their own houses (v. 4). While not mentioned here, the stones from the earlier temple were probably still located at the site (cf. 2:15). **take pleasure.** Often describes God's favorable acceptance of a sacrifice (Ps 51:19; Mic 6:7). **honored.** Or "glorified." This hints at the return of God's glory to the temple (cf. Ezek 43:1–4). Ultimately, the people must build the temple for the pleasure and glory of God (cf. 1 Cor 10:31; Rev 4:11).

1:8 [m]Ps 132:13-14
1:9 [n]ver 4
1:10 [o]Lev 26:19; Dt 28:23
1:11 [p]Dt 28:22; 1Ki 17:1 [q]Hag 2:17
1:12 [r]ver 1 [s]ver 14; Isa 1:9; Hag 2:2 [t]Isa 50:10 [u]Dt 31:12
1:13 [v]Mt 28:20; Ro 8:31
1:14 [w]Ezr 5:2 [x]ver 12
1:15 [y]ver 1
2:3 [z]Ezr 3:12 [a]Zec 4:10
2:4 [b]1Ch 28:20; Zec 8:9; Eph 6:10 [c]2Sa 5:10; Ac 7:9
2:5 [d]Ex 29:46 [e]Ne 9:20; Isa 63:11

and bring down timber and build my house, so that I may take pleasure[m] in it and be honored," says the
LORD. 9"You expected much, but see, it turned out to be little. What you brought home, I blew away. Why?"
declares the LORD Almighty. "Because of my house, which remains a ruin,[n] while each of you is busy
with your own house. 10Therefore, because of you the heavens have withheld their dew and the earth its
crops.[o] 11I called for a drought[p] on the fields and the mountains, on the grain, the new wine, the olive oil
and everything else the ground produces, on people and livestock, and on all the labor of your hands.[q]"

12Then Zerubbabel[r] son of Shealtiel, Joshua son of Jozadak, the high priest, and the whole remnant[s]
of the people obeyed[t] the voice of the LORD their God and the message of the prophet Haggai, because
the LORD their God had sent him. And the people feared[u] the LORD.

13Then Haggai, the LORD's messenger, gave this message of the LORD to the people: "I am with[v] you,"
declares the LORD. 14So the LORD stirred up the spirit of Zerubbabel[w] son of Shealtiel, governor of Judah,
and the spirit of Joshua son of Jozadak, the high priest, and the spirit of the whole remnant[x] of the
people. They came and began to work on the house of the LORD Almighty, their God, 15on the twenty-
fourth day of the sixth month.[y]

The Promised Glory of the New House

2 In the second year of King Darius, 1on the twenty-first day of the seventh month, the word of the
LORD came through the prophet Haggai: 2"Speak to Zerubbabel son of Shealtiel, governor of Judah,
to Joshua son of Jozadak,[a] the high priest, and to the remnant of the people. Ask them, 3'Who of you is
left who saw this house[z] in its former glory? How does it look to you now? Does it not seem to you like
nothing?[a] 4But now be strong, Zerubbabel,' declares the LORD. 'Be strong,[b] Joshua son of Jozadak, the
high priest. Be strong, all you people of the land,' declares the LORD, 'and work. For I am with[c] you,'
declares the LORD Almighty. 5'This is what I covenanted with you when you came out of Egypt.[d] And my
Spirit[e] remains among you. Do not fear.'

[a] 2 Hebrew *Jehozadak*, a variant of *Jozadak*; also in verse 4

1:9 You expected much. Earlier prophets held out a glorious hope of agricultural abundance after returning from exile (see, e.g., Jer 31:11–14; Amos 9:13–15). The people's experience is nothing like this; as they bring home the harvest, God blows it away. This is God's punishment for their skewed priorities since they are busy with their own houses rather than God's house.

1:10–11 Like v. 6, the curses of the Mosaic covenant are in the background (Lev 26:19–20; Deut 28:24,30,38–40,48). There are also echoes of Gen 1–3 and the curse on the "ground" that results from disobedience (Gen 3:17; cf. Rom 8:20–22). As the sovereign Creator, God's displeasure with his people is unmistakably evident, and Haggai implicitly calls on them to repent (cf. 2:17). While the rain falls on "the righteous and the unrighteous" (Matt 5:45) and not all suffering and adversity is a direct result of a particular sin (e.g., Job; John 9:1–3), sometimes adversity is God's punishment or "discipline" as a warning to repent (Luke 13:1–5; 1 Cor 11:30; Heb 12:4–13; Jas 5:14–15; Rev 2:22).

1:12–15a *Response: Obedience, Assurance, and Action.* The people turn to God in obedience (v. 12). God assures them (v. 13), and moves them to action to build the temple (vv. 14–15a).

1:12 remnant. Those who survive the exile and emerge as a purified, faithful people (cf. Isa 10:20–22). They show themselves to be the "remnant" (cf. "these people" in v. 2) because they "obeyed." **the voice of the LORD their God and the message of the prophet Haggai.** These are one and the same. Like Moses, Haggai is "sent" by God as the mediator of his word.

1:13 I am with you. An assurance of covenant relationship in light of the people's fear (v. 12; cf. 2:4–5). God's presence will uphold them (cf. Isa 41:10; 43:5; Jer 30:10–11).

1:14 stirred up the spirit. God moved the will of his people to respond to his word so that they began to rebuild the temple (cf. Ezra 1:1,5). See Introduction: Themes.

1:15a the twenty-fourth day of the sixth month. They begin the work 23 days after Haggai's first prophecy (Sept. 21, 520 BC; cf. v. 1), possibly using this time to complete their harvests and assemble the required materials.

1:15b—2:9 *Second Prophecy: The Promised Glory of the New House.* Haggai further exhorts and encourages the people to rebuild the temple. He applies God's past dealings with his people to the present and future.

2:1 the twenty-first day of the seventh month. Oct. 17, 520 BC (cf. 1:1,15). The seventh month included several festivals (cf. Lev 23:23–43). This is the seventh day of the Festival of Tabernacles, a festival of joy and thanksgiving for the harvest and God's goodness. The tabernacles were a reminder of the tents the Israelites lived in when they came out of Egypt (cf. v. 5). The festival is associated with the temple and includes the foreigner (Deut 16:13–15; 1 Kgs 8:2,41–43,65). See note on Lev 23:34; Deut 16:13–17; see also "The Lord's Appointed Festivals," p. 229.

2:2 Cf. 1:1,12,14.

2:3 The temple had been destroyed about 66 years earlier in 586 BC, so those left were likely to be few. **former glory.** The glory of Solomon's temple; both its splendor and the presence of God's "glory" before its destruction (cf. 1:4). **Does it not seem to you like nothing?** The present state of the temple cannot be compared with its earlier one (cf. Ezra 3:12–13).

2:4 be strong. Echoes God's exhortation to an earlier Joshua to trust his word of promise (Josh 1:6,7,9,18). **work.** Rebuild the temple, the central command of this passage. **I am with you.** God will support them in their efforts (cf. 1:13; 1 Chr 22:16; 28:10,20).

2:5 This is what I covenanted with you. God dwelling among his people (v. 4) was a central promise of the covenant with Israel at Sinai (cf. Exod 25:8; 29:45–46). **remains among you.** God's Spirit empowered his people in the past, and he will continue to do so (cf.

[6]"This is what the LORD Almighty says: 'In a little while[f] I will once more shake the heavens and the
earth,[g] the sea and the dry land. [7]I will shake all nations, and what is desired by all nations will come,
and I will fill this house[h] with glory,' says the LORD Almighty. [8]'The silver is mine and the gold is mine,'
declares the LORD Almighty. [9]'The glory[i] of this present house will be greater than the glory of the former house,' says the LORD Almighty. 'And in this place I will grant peace,' declares the LORD Almighty."

Blessings for a Defiled People

[10]On the twenty-fourth day of the ninth month,[j] in the second year of Darius, the word of the LORD
came to the prophet Haggai: [11]"This is what the LORD Almighty says: 'Ask the priests[k] what the law says:
[12]If someone carries consecrated meat in the fold of their garment, and that fold touches some bread
or stew, some wine, olive oil or other food, does it become consecrated?[l]'"

The priests answered, "No."

[13]Then Haggai said, "If a person defiled by contact with a dead body touches one of these things,
does it become defiled?"

"Yes," the priests replied, "it becomes defiled.[m]"

[14]Then Haggai said, "'So it is with this people and this nation in my sight,' declares the LORD. 'Whatever they do and whatever they offer[n] there is defiled.

[15]"'Now give careful thought[o] to this from this day on[a]—consider how things were before one

[a] 15 Or *to the days past*

2:6 [f]Isa 10:25 [g]Heb 12:26* **2:7** [h]Isa 60:7 **2:9** [i]Ps 85:9 **2:10** [j]ver 1 **2:11** [k]Lev 10:10-11; Dt 17:8-11; Mal 2:7 **2:12** [l]Lev 6:27; Mt 23:19 **2:13** [m]Lev 22:4-6 **2:14** [n]Isa 1:13 **2:15** [o]Hag 1:5

Isa 63:11; Zech 4:6). **Do not fear.** Fear can hinder obedience (cf. 1:12–13; Isa 41:10).

2:6 In a little while. Indicates imminence. **once more.** Like God's appearance at Sinai when the mountain "trembled violently" (Exod 19:18), God will "shake" the cosmos ("the heavens and the earth"), the world ("the sea and the dry land"), and "all nations" (v. 7).

2:7 what is desired by all nations. A long tradition interprets this to refer to the Messiah. While there is a strong hope expressed by the prophets for a future Davidic king (cf. vv. 20–23), the Hebrew syntax and immediate context argue against this interpretation. Instead, it refers to the wealth that will come to the temple when God shakes "all nations" (cf. Isa 60:5,11; 61:6; 66:12,20; Zech 14:14). **glory.** Primarily wealth (like v. 3). Yet it also implicitly refers to God's presence since the same expression elsewhere refers to God's "glory" filling the tabernacle and temple (Exod 40:34–35; 1 Kgs 8:10–11; Ezek 43:5; 44:4). The provision of wealth was fulfilled to some extent through the decree of Darius (cf. 1:1) to provide from the royal treasury (Ezra 6:8) and some 60 years later when the Persian king Artaxerxes and the surrounding nations gave silver and gold to Ezra for the temple (Ezra 7:15–23). Yet Heb 12:26 quotes v. 6 to speak of a greater fulfillment in Jesus, where the shaking of the earth and the heavens will result in a kingdom that "cannot be shaken" (Heb 12:28). The Gospels also claim that Jesus' glory surpasses the temple and that the coming of his kingdom shakes the heavens (cf. Matt 24:1–2,29–30; Mark 13:1–2,25–26; Luke 21:5–6,26–27). Rev 21:22–27 also develops the themes of vv. 6–7 in relation to Jesus. Hence there is a "now" and "not yet" aspect to the fulfillment of these promises as they are fulfilled to some extent in the Persian period and then finally in the first and second comings of Jesus (cf. 2:21–23).

2:8 God is entitled to claim the wealth of the nations (v. 7) because he owns it (cf. Job 41:11).

2:9 this place. Either the temple or Jerusalem. **peace.** Hebrew *šālôm*, meaning wholeness, well-being, prosperity, right relationships; see "Shalom," p. 2693. Ultimately this promise of "greater glory" and "peace" is fulfilled through the prince of peace, Jesus (Zech 9:9–10; John 20:19–21; Col 1:20). Jesus' temple (the church) includes people from all nations (Eph. 2:11–22). See Introduction: Themes, 2.

2:10–19 *Third Prophecy: Blessings for a Defiled People.* Haggai involves the priests in a lesson (vv. 10–14) that further encourages the people to rebuild the temple so that curse might turn to blessing (vv. 15–19).

2:10 the twenty-fourth day of the ninth month. Dec. 18, 520 BC, exactly three months after they "began to work on the house of the LORD Almighty" (1:14–15; cf. 2:18,20).

2:11 Ask the priests what the law says. Priests were responsible to give instruction in the law and to "distinguish between the holy and the common, between the unclean and the clean" (Lev 10:10; see also Deut 17:8–13; 33:10; Jer 18:18; Ezek 7:26; 22:26; see further the Introduction to Leviticus: Major Theological Themes [Holiness and Purity] and "Holiness," p. 2676).

2:12 consecrated meat. Meat made holy through sacrifice; probably a fellowship offering since it could be eaten by the one who offered it (Lev 7:15–16). **the fold of their garment.** People wore long robes that they could fold up to carry goods in. Haggai's first question is about the transmission of holiness. Consecrated meat made the garment holy (see Lev 6:27), but the garment could not then pass on the holiness to another object.

2:13 defiled. Or unclean. People who are defiled are to be isolated from the community until cleansed by washing and/or sacrifice; they are not to enter God's presence (e.g., Lev 15:31). **by contact with a dead body.** Death defiles people and objects that come in contact with it (e.g., Lev 7:19; 21:11; Num 5:2; 9:6–7; 19:22). **these things.** The foods in v. 12. Haggai's second question is about the transmission of defilement. Defilement is transmitted much more easily than holiness.

2:14 this people and this nation. The people of Judah. Haggai applies the lesson on consecration and defilement (vv. 12–13) to them: because they are defiled, so are their deeds and their offerings. Haggai does not state why the people are defiled; it could be their earlier sin (cf. 1:9–12), or perhaps they remain defiled from the exile (cf. the defilement of Joshua in Zech 3:1–4). An implication of Haggai's lesson is that the temple is crucial to solving this problem of defilement and they should build it. The problem of defilement is ultimately solved in Jesus. Heb 9:11 explains how Jesus' sacrifice in the "more perfect tabernacle that is not made with human hands" is God's ultimate act of cleansing and forgiveness for sin. **there.** Probably the altar on the temple site (cf. Ezra 3:1–3).

2:15 give careful thought. To the future in view of their experience over the past two decades (cf. 1:5,7; 2:18). **before one stone was laid on another.** Most likely when the "foundation ... was laid" in the ninth month (v. 18) rather than the beginning of the work (probably including transporting supplies, clearing the site, etc.) in the sixth month (1:14).

2:15 [p]Ezr 3:10 [q]Ezr 4:24
2:16 [r]Hag 1:6
2:17 [s]Hag 1:11 [t]Dt 28:22; 1Ki 8:37; Am 4:9 [u]Am 4:6
2:18 [v]Zec 8:9
2:21 [w]Ezr 5:2
2:22 [x]Da 2:44 [y]Mic 5:10 [z]Jdg 7:22
2:23 [a]Isa 43:10

stone was laid[p] on another in the LORD's temple.[q] 16When anyone came to a heap of twenty measures,
there were only ten. When anyone went to a wine vat to
draw fifty measures, there were only twenty.[r] 17I struck
all the work of your hands[s] with blight,[t] mildew and
hail, yet you did not return to me,' declares the LORD.[u]
18'From this day on, from this twenty-fourth day of the
ninth month, give careful thought to the day when the
foundation[v] of the LORD's temple was laid. Give careful
thought: 19Is there yet any seed left in the barn? Until
now, the vine and the fig tree, the pomegranate and the
olive tree have not borne fruit.

"'From this day on I will bless you.'"

Zerubbabel the LORD's Signet Ring

20The word of the LORD came to Haggai a second time
on the twenty-fourth day of the month: 21"Tell Zerubbabel[w] governor of Judah that I am going to shake the
heavens and the earth. 22I will overturn royal thrones
and shatter the power of the foreign kingdoms.[x] I will
overthrow chariots[y] and their drivers; horses and their
riders will fall, each by the sword of his brother.[z]
23"'On that day,' declares the LORD Almighty, 'I will
take you, my servant[a] Zerubbabel son of Shealtiel,' declares the LORD, 'and I will make you like my signet ring,
for I have chosen you,' declares the LORD Almighty."

Signet ring of Hanan, son of Hilkiah the priest. Hilkiah was the high priest in the days of King Josiah in the seventh century BC. See note on Hag 2:23.

Z. Radovan/www.BibleLandPictures.com

2:16–17 Like 1:6,9–11, the curses of the Mosaic covenant are in view (cf. Deut 28:22). This also echoes Amos 4:9: God "struck ... with blight and mildew" so that his people might "return" to him (cf. 1:10–11).
2:16 a heap. Probably a store or pile of grain (cf. Jer 50:26).
2:17 blight. Browning of plant leaves by dry heat. **mildew.** A fungal infection from excessive moisture. **hail.** Cf. Exod 9:13–32.
2:18 when the foundation of the LORD's temple was laid. This was an important event. Exactly two months later (cf. Zech 1:7), the governor Zerubbabel is said to have been responsible for it (Zech 4:9). Since the foundation of the temple was laid on two separate occasions by Zerubbabel (earlier in 538 BC and now in 520 BC), this suggests that it was more than just an act of construction, but involved some kind of ceremony, since presumably the foundation from the first occasion remained (Ezra 3:8–13; see notes on Hag 1:1; Zech 8:9).
2:19 The date in v. 18 is mid-December 520 BC, after sowing seed for the next year's crops. The lack of fruit (fruit elsewhere is mostly associated with peace, prosperity, and blessing) speaks again of God's curse (cf. 2:16–17). Haggai now promises God's blessing. God's purpose since creation was to dwell among his people and bless them (Gen 1:28; 12:2–3). Now that the people have heeded his word through Haggai, God restates his commitment (cf. Zech 8, which echoes Haggai).
2:20–23 *Fourth Prophecy: Zerubbabel the Lord's Signet Ring.* With the restoration of God's house under way, God reaffirms the earlier promise to David concerning his house (i.e., his dynasty; cf. 2 Sam 7:11–16). The prophecy coming on the same day strengthens the link between the two houses (vv. 10,18,20).
2:21–22 Addressed to Zerubbabel (cf. 1:1).
2:21 shake the heavens and the earth. Cf. v. 6.
2:22 royal thrones. The kings of the nations. God will devastate their kingdoms and destroy their military might. These images resonate with many OT passages (Gen 19:25,29; Exod 15:1,4,19,21; Judg 7:22; Pss 2:10–12; 110:5–6; Ezek 38:21; Amos 4:11; Zech 12:4; 14:13).
2:23 On that day. The "day of the LORD" (cf. Joel 1:15; Zech 2:11); when God will establish his kingdom on earth in glory. Four terms in this verse are associated with King David: (1) **take.** Cf. 2 Sam 7:8; Ps 78:70. (2) **my servant.** See 2 Sam 3:18; 7:5,8; 1 Kgs 11:32,34,36; 1 Chr 17:4; 2 Chr 32:16; Pss 78:70; 89:3; 132:10; Isa 42:1; 52:13; Ezek 34:23; 37:24. (3) **son of Shealtiel.** Cf. 1:1. (4) **chosen.** See 1 Sam 16:8–12; 2 Sam 6:21; Ps 78:70; Isa 42:1. **signet ring.** Used by a king to seal royal documents; a sign of his authority. The background to this promise is the judgment pronounced against King Jehoiachin in Jer 22:24: "Even if you ... were a signet ring on my right hand, I would still pull you off." As the human representative of God's authority, Jehoiachin is told that his immediate offspring will not rule in Jerusalem (Jer 22:24–30), yet Jeremiah also promises a righteous Davidic king (the Branch/Messiah) in coming days (Jer 23:5–6; 33:15–16). Haggai is promising here that the judgment against Jehoiachin will be over and God will make Zerubbabel "like my signet ring." This means that as well as overseeing the rebuilding of the temple (v. 18; Zech 4:9), Zerubbabel will reestablish the Davidic line in Jerusalem (cf. Matt 1:12–13; Luke 3:27). This prophecy raises the expectation for the coming Branch/Messiah, a hope reiterated by Zechariah (Zech 3:8; 6:12). King Jesus realizes Haggai's hope for God's presence and blessing among his people.

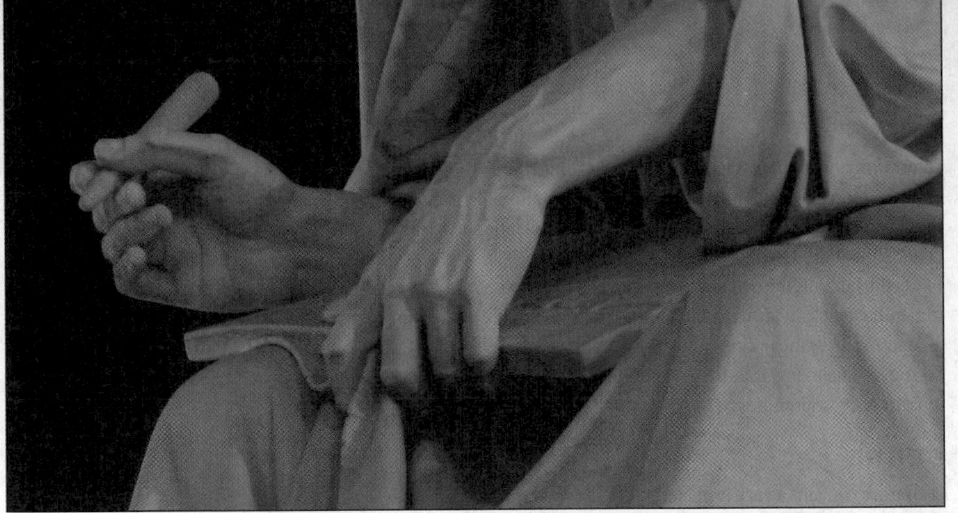

INTRODUCTION TO ZECHARIAH

OVERVIEW

The book of Zechariah looks to the coming kingdom of God. Zechariah deals in the first instance with the rebuilding of the city of Jerusalem and the temple after they were destroyed by the Babylonians almost 70 years earlier. The high priest Joshua and the governor Zerubbabel, along with the prophets, have important roles to play in this project. The book also looks beyond this reconstruction to the return of God, so that a cleansed Jerusalem will become the center of worship for all nations. Central to this latter project is a future Davidic king.

AUTHORSHIP

The prophet Zechariah is known outside his book for the key role he played, along with Haggai, in rebuilding the temple (Ezra 5:1; 6:14). His genealogy places him in a priestly family (Zech 1:1,7; Neh 12:4,16). If he is the "Zechariah son of Berekiah" of Matt 23:35, then he was later "murdered between the temple and the altar."

Since the seventeenth century, some scholars have challenged the traditional view of Zecharian authorship. While most scholars see much of chs. 1 – 8 coming from the prophet, the different literary style of chs. 9 – 14 and some of the historical references (such as "Greece" in 9:13) are taken to indicate that another author wrote chs. 9 – 14 (some propose even further authors for different parts). However, there is no evidence outside the book that it ever circulated in parts. In the earliest extant manuscripts from Qumran, Zechariah is a single work (though the manuscripts are quite fragmentary). Recent research supports reading the book as a unit and taking the book as it presents itself — essentially as the product of the prophet Zechariah. The development and coherence of many themes across the book provide evidence for this. The often unstated assumption that Zechariah was able to write in only one literary genre is unsustainable. The different genres may simply reflect different stages in Zechariah's ministry, with chs. 1 – 8 coming before the temple's completion and chs. 9 – 14 coming after it. Historical references in chs. 9 – 14 can be understood as consistent with Zechariah's time.

DATE

There are three dates in the book (1:1,7; 7:1). They correspond to the years 520, 519, and 518 BC, some 20 years after Cyrus decreed (in 539 BC) that the Jewish exiles could return from Babylon to Jerusalem to rebuild the temple, which was completed in 515 or possibly 516 BC.

For further details of the historical setting, see Introduction to Haggai.

OCCASION AND PURPOSE

Zechariah's prophetic ministry, like Haggai's, began some 20 years after some Jews returned from exile in Babylon. The earlier prophets had promised that after the exile there would be a glorious restoration (e.g., Isa 51:11). For the exiles who returned to Jerusalem in Zechariah's day, the reality fell far short of the earlier prophetic hope. The community faced many challenges: financial hardship (Hag 1:6), opposition from outside enemies (Ezra 4:1 – 3), and low morale (Hag 1:14). There were also social problems (Zech 8:10), possibly on account of disputes between those who returned and those who remained in the land. It was a time of disappointment, disillusionment, despondency, and guilt.

Zechariah calls the people to trust and obey God's word. He calls on them to get on with and complete the rebuilding of the temple in anticipation of God's return to establish his kingdom, a kingdom in which God will throw down all opposition by the nations and bring forgiveness and cleansing through his Messiah. In proclaiming this message, Zechariah maintains that the restoration hopes of the earlier prophets still stand, and he calls God's people to live in light of these promises.

GENRE

Zechariah contains a variety of literary genres. Zechariah 1 – 6 contains eight night visions. In each vision the prophet is shown a scene, and in most, an angel interprets its key features. It is important to read these against the backdrop of the earlier OT writings as they provide keys to interpretation.

Zechariah also contains one prophetic sign-action in 6:9 – 15 and two sign-actions in 11:4 – 17. Sign-actions were visible representations of the prophet's message.

Zechariah 7 – 8 begins with a short report about a delegation from Bethel seeking instruction about fasting. It provides an occasion for Zechariah to reapply pertinent covenant requirements to the people and restate the hope for restoration. These chapters transition the two main parts of the book.

Zechariah 9 – 14 comprises two prophetic messages that dramatically portray God returning to his people and establishing his kingdom. These chapters depict a future battle and explore what God's coming will mean from different perspectives: for the nations, for God's people, for those who are leaders, for God's king, for Jerusalem, and for all creation.

THEMES

A key theme of Zechariah is God's return to his people after the judgment of exile. Ezekiel depicts God's glory departing from the temple and Jerusalem on account of sin (Ezek 8 – 11), but it also anticipates God's return to the temple after the exile (Ezek 43:1 – 5) accompanied by covenant restoration and blessing. Zechariah says that God has now turned from judgment to mercy (1:16; 8:3 and notes) and will return to dwell among his people (1:3; 2:5,10 – 11; 4:9 – 10;

THE PERSIAN EMPIRE IN THE TIME OF DARIUS I

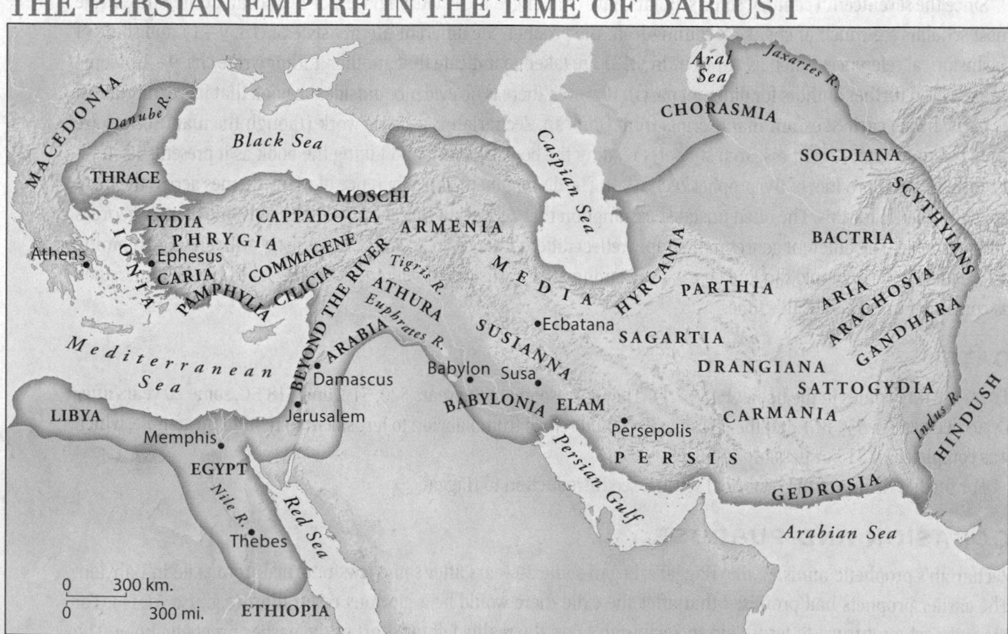

8:3; 9:8; 14:5). In view of God's return, God's people are to rebuild the temple and obey God's covenant requirements.

Other important themes of Zechariah include the sovereign rule of God (the book consistently calls him the "LORD Almighty"). As king over all the earth (14:9), he will judge enemy nations (1:21; 2:9; 6:7–8; 9:1—14:21) and save his people (Jerusalem/Zion) and those from the nations who seek him (2:11; 8:20; 9:7; 14:16). While God's people have an important role to play in the restoration, it is ultimately God's work (e.g., 4:6; 9:16; 12:7–9). The restoration of covenant relationship with all of its ensuing blessings also underlies much of Zechariah's hope (e.g., 8:8; 13:9).

Closely associated with God's return is a future Davidic king (Messiah) who will serve as a priest (6:13) by cleansing sin and reversing its consequences (3:9; 13:1). The NT identifies this king as Jesus, who fulfills the hopes for God's return (e.g., John 1:14). After the Psalms, Zechariah is the most quoted part of the OT in the passion narratives of the Gospels. Zechariah understood, like Isaiah before him, that God's kingdom would come only with the atoning death of God's Messiah (12:10; 13:7; cf. Luke 24:25–27). Zechariah anticipates the coming of Jesus, who won the victory over the enemies of God's people through his death on the cross and who will fully realize this victory when he returns, when those from all nations will join God's chosen people to worship and to feast in his presence. The book of Revelation richly mines Zechariah's treasures.

Darius I enthroned, from the Apadana staircase at Persepolis. The word of the Lord came to Zechariah in the eighth month of the second year of Darius (Zech 1:1).

Zechariah describes his time as a "day of small things" (Zech 4:10), yet this "day" is significant in that it anticipates a much greater day. Zechariah contains a vital message for the church today living in similar circumstances. The restoration has been inaugurated: God's Messiah, Jesus, has come and established God's kingdom, and yet those who acknowledge Jesus are a minority and often face opposition in this age. The progress in the work of God's kingdom is often slow and discouraging. Yet God has promised that he is building an eternal kingdom. Zechariah challenges the church not to despise the day of small things; rather, "Let your hands be strong" (8:9,13). Get on with Jesus' commission to build his church. Be people who reflect God's character, for his glorious kingdom is coming.

OUTLINE

I. Introduction: A Call to Return to the Lord (1:1–6)

II. Eight Night Visions of Zechariah (1:7—6:8)
- A. The Man Among the Myrtle Trees (1:7–17)
- B. Four Horns and Four Craftsmen (1:18–21)
- C. A Man With a Measuring Line (2:1–13)
- D. Clean Garments for the High Priest (3:1–10)
- E. The Gold Lampstand and the Two Olive Trees (4:1–14)
- F. The Flying Scroll (5:1–4)
- G. The Woman in a Basket (5:5–11)
- H. Four Chariots (6:1–8)

III. A Crown for Joshua (6:9–15)

IV. From Fasting to Feasting (7:1—8:23)
- A. Justice and Mercy, Not Fasting (7:1–14)
- B. The Lord Promises to Bless Jerusalem (8:1–23)

V. First Prophetic Message (9:1 — 11:17)
- A. The Lord Returns (9:1 – 17)
  - 1. Judgment on Israel's Enemies (9:1 – 8)
  - 2. The Coming of Zion's King (9:9 – 13)
  - 3. The Lord Will Appear (9:14 – 17)
- B. The Lord Will Care for Judah (10:1 — 11:3)
- C. Two Shepherds (11:4 – 17)

VI. Second Prophetic Message (12:1 — 14:21)
- A. Jerusalem's Enemies to Be Destroyed (12:1 – 9)
- B. Mourning for the One They Pierced (12:10 – 14)
- C. Cleansing From Sin (13:1 – 6)
- D. The Shepherd Struck, the Sheep Scattered (13:7 – 9)
- E. The Lord Comes and Reigns (14:1 – 21)

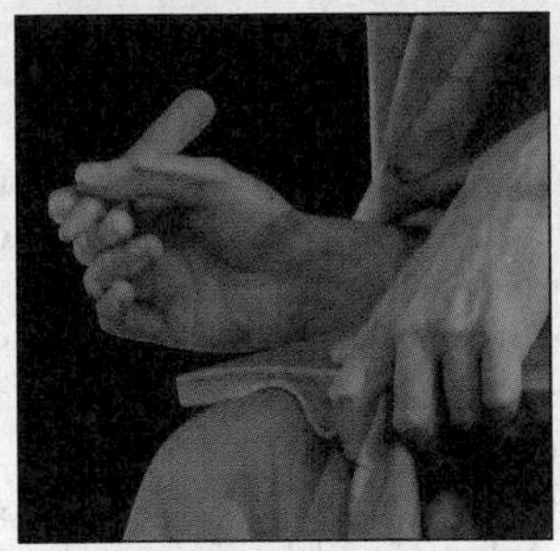

ZECHARIAH

A Call to Return to the LORD

1 In the eighth month of the second year of Darius,[a] the word of the LORD came to the prophet Zechariah[b] son of Berekiah,[c] the son of Iddo:[d]
2“The LORD was very angry[e] with your ancestors. 3Therefore tell the people: This is what the LORD
Almighty says: ‘Return to me,’ declares the LORD Almighty, ‘and I will return to you,’[f] says the LORD
Almighty. 4Do not be like your ancestors,[g] to whom the earlier prophets proclaimed: This is what the
LORD Almighty says: ‘Turn from your evil ways[h] and your evil practices.’ But they would not listen or
pay attention to me,[i] declares the LORD. 5Where are your ancestors now? And the prophets, do they live
forever? 6But did not my words and my decrees, which I commanded my servants the prophets, overtake your ancestors?
“Then they repented and said, ‘The LORD Almighty has done to us what our ways and practices deserve,[j] just as he determined to do.’ ”

1:1 [a]Ezr 4:24; 6:15 [b]Ezr 5:1 [c]Mt 23:35; Lk 11:51 [d]ver 7; Ne 12:4
1:2 [e]2Ch 36:16
1:3 [f]Mal 3:7; Jas 4:8
1:4 [g]2Ch 36:15 [h]Ps 106:6 [i]2Ch 24:19; Ps 78:8; Jer 6:17
1:6 [j]Jer 12:14-17; La 2:17

The Man Among the Myrtle Trees

7On the twenty-fourth day of the eleventh month, the month of Shebat, in the second year of Darius,
the word of the LORD came to the prophet Zechariah son of Berekiah, the son of Iddo.

1:1–6 *Introduction: A Call to Return to the Lord.* Zechariah begins with a call to return to God. The subsequent night visions (1:7—6:8), sign-action (6:9–15), and response to a question about fasting (7:1—8:23) indicate what this “return” (v. 3), or repentance (see v. 6), should look like in view of God’s return. The two prophetic messages of chs. 9–14 vividly portray the impact of God’s return.

1:1 In the eighth month of the second year of Darius. Cf. v. 7; 7:1. Darius was the Persian king who succeeded Cambyses (who reigned 530–522 BC) and Cyrus (who reigned 559–530 BC). In 539 BC, Cyrus decreed that the Judean exiles in Babylonia could return to Jerusalem and rebuild the temple (cf. Ezra 1:1–4). However, an initial attempt to rebuild the temple came to a standstill (cf. Ezra 4:24). The date in this verse is some 20 years later (520 BC) and “the eighth month” is late October/early November, two months after temple building had recommenced (cf. Hag 1:14–15). **the word of the LORD came to.** A technical phrase that indicates Zechariah’s status as a prophet of God (cf. 7:1). **son of Berekiah, the son of Iddo.** Places Zechariah in a priestly family (Ezra 5:1; 6:14; Neh 12:4–7,16).

1:2 very angry with your ancestors. God’s anger with the sins of their preexilic ancestors resulted in the destruction of Jerusalem and the experience of exile (cf. v. 4).

1:3 LORD Almighty. Or “Yahweh of armies.” This title, which occurs 53 times in Zechariah, speaks of God’s might and universal rule; here it underlines why the people should listen to his word. **Return to me.** A call to repentance and covenant obedience. **I will return to you.** Promises full restoration of covenant blessing. In the wider context of the book, it also speaks of God’s return to the temple to dwell among his people, a key motif in Zechariah (cf. 1:16; 8:3; 9:8–9; 14:16–21) and a promise that Jesus ultimately fulfills (e.g., John 1:14; 2:21).

1:4–5 God was very angry (v. 2) because their ancestors refused to obey his word spoken through the “earlier prophets” (v. 4), a word which called them to repentance (e.g., Isa 45:22; Jer 18:11; 25:5; Ezek 33:11). Zechariah wants his contemporaries to learn from the example of their ancestors and not repeat their mistake.

1:6 they repented. Since judgment overtook their ancestors and they were no more (see v. 5), “they” must refer to Zechariah’s contemporaries rather than their ancestors. Those who heard God’s word proclaimed by Zechariah repented and acknowledged the rightness of God’s ways (cf. Hag 1:12–14). The challenge is for later readers of Zechariah also to repent, not as a one-time act, but as an ongoing response to God’s word.

1:7—6:8 *Eight Night Visions of Zechariah.* These visions portray God returning to his people and establishing his kingdom. This is significant given God’s earlier abandonment of the Jerusalem temple, his palace. Having given Jerusalem over to the Babylonians, God will reestablish his control over the city.

1:7–17 *The Man Among the Myrtle Trees.* The first vision proclaims the end of the exile, God’s coming judgment of the nations, and his return to Jerusalem.

1:7 A second dating formula (cf. v. 1; 7:1) introduces the visions. It is about three months after the date of v. 1 (see note there). **Shebat.** A Babylonian month name (cf. 7:1). Whereas the dates in the earlier prophets relate to the kings of Judah (e.g., Isa 1:1; Jer 1:2–3; Hos

1:8 [k]Rev 6:4 [l]Zec 6:2-7
1:9 [m]Zec 4:1,4-5
1:10 [n]Zec 6:5-8
1:11 [o]Isa 14:7
1:12 [p]Da 9:2
1:13 [q]Zec 4:1
1:14 [r]Joel 2:18; Zec 8:2
1:15 [s]Jer 48:11 [t]Ps 123:3-4; Am 1:11
1:16 [u]Zec 8:3 [v]Zec 2:1-2
1:17 [w]Isa 51:3 [x]Isa 14:1 [y]Zec 2:12
1:19 [z]Am 6:13
1:21 [a]Ps 75:4 [b]Ps 75:10

8 During the night I had a vision, and there before me was a man mounted on a red[k] horse. He was
standing among the myrtle trees in a ravine. Behind him were red, brown and white horses.[l]
9 I asked, "What are these, my lord?"
The angel[m] who was talking with me answered, "I will show you what they are."
10 Then the man standing among the myrtle trees explained, "They are the ones the LORD has sent
to go throughout the earth."[n]
11 And they reported to the angel of the LORD who was standing among the myrtle trees, "We have
gone throughout the earth and found the whole world at rest and in peace."[o]
12 Then the angel of the LORD said, "LORD Almighty, how long will you withhold mercy from Jerusalem and from the towns of Judah, which you have been angry with these seventy[p] years?" 13 So the LORD
spoke kind and comforting words to the angel who talked with me.[q]
14 Then the angel who was speaking to me said, "Proclaim this word: This is what the LORD Almighty
says: 'I am very jealous[r] for Jerusalem and Zion, 15 and I am very angry with the nations that feel secure.[s] I was only a little angry, but they went too far with the punishment.'[t]
16 "Therefore this is what the LORD says: 'I will return[u] to Jerusalem with mercy, and there my house
will be rebuilt. And the measuring line[v] will be stretched out over Jerusalem,' declares the LORD Almighty.
17 "Proclaim further: This is what the LORD Almighty says: 'My towns will again overflow with prosperity, and the LORD will again comfort[w] Zion and choose[x] Jerusalem.' "[y]

Four Horns and Four Craftsmen

18 Then I looked up, and there before me were four horns. 19 I asked the angel who was speaking to
me, "What are these?"
He answered me, "These are the horns[z] that scattered Judah, Israel and Jerusalem."
20 Then the LORD showed me four craftsmen. 21 I asked, "What are these coming to do?"
He answered, "These are the horns that scattered Judah so that no one could raise their head, but
the craftsmen have come to terrify them and throw down these horns of the nations who lifted up their
horns[a] against the land of Judah to scatter its people."[a][b]

[a] *21* In Hebrew texts 1:18-21 is numbered 2:1-4.

1:1), God's people are now reckoning their history with reference to the pagan king, Darius (cf. 1:1). This situation is less than ideal.

1:8 "The word of the LORD" (v. 7) comes to Zechariah as a vision or a series of visions during the night. A vision is distinct from a dream in that the recipient is awake (cf. 4:1). Zechariah sees "a man mounted on a red horse." Horses were used for military or royal purposes and have great speed. There were "red, brown and white horses." In Hebrew, the colors are plural, which indicates multiple horses of each color. Verse 11 suggests that the horses have riders since they "reported to the angel of the LORD." The significance of the colors and the "myrtle trees in a ravine" is not stated. These features may only contribute to the vision's picture rather than its meaning.

1:9–10 The angel features in seven of the eight visions and explains the important features of the visions. "The man standing among the myrtle trees" (v. 10; cf. v. 8) explains the function of the horses: They "go throughout the earth" (v. 10) to patrol or provide surveillance for God and express his sovereign rule.

1:11–12 The "man" of v. 8 is "the angel of the LORD" (v. 11), a different figure from the interpreting angel of v. 9. He represents God and speaks for God and yet is distinct from God (cf. 3:1,5–6). The riders report that they have "found the whole world at rest and in peace" (v. 11). By his second year, and after some years of uncertainty when one might suppose Jewish expectation of freedom from Persian control was heightened, Darius was able to establish control over the Persian Empire. The report of "rest" and "peace" suggests a return of the status quo and provokes the complaint "how long . . . ?" (v. 12). Indeed, God had promised his people "rest" and "peace" after being restored to the land (see, e.g., Jer 30:10).

1:12 seventy years. The years of exile and temple desolation prophesied in Jer 25:11–12; 29:10 (cf. Zech 7:5). The exact beginning and end points are debated (cf. Dan 9:2,24–27). However, the period between the destruction of the temple (in 586 BC) and its reconstruction (in 516/15 BC) is almost exactly 70 years.

1:13 kind and comforting words. A description of the contents of vv. 14–17. Cf. Isa 40:1.

1:14 very jealous. God is concerned for what is rightly his, and he is willing to overthrow all opposition to defend it (e.g., Exod 20:5). While God used the nations to judge his people for their sin (cf. Isa 27:6–7; Jer 25:9–14), the nations "went too far with the punishment" (v. 15). God's judgment of the nations is the theme of the next two visions.

1:16 I will return. Can also be translated "I have turned" (cf. 8:3). God has turned back to his people with mercy; the judgment of exile is over. God promises a rebuilt temple (his "house") and city ("the measuring line will be stretched out over Jerusalem").

1:17 towns will again overflow with prosperity. Cf. 7:7. **will again comfort Zion.** See v. 13. **choose Jerusalem.** Cf. 2:12; 3:2; Deut 12:5; Ps 78:68–70.

1:18–21 *Four Horns and Four Craftsmen.* The second vision connects the rebuilding of Jerusalem and the temple (v. 16) with the judgment of the nations (v. 15).

1:18–19 four horns. Animal horns were a common image of military and political power (see, e.g., Deut 33:17; 1 Sam 2:1; Ps 132:17; Jer 48:25; Dan 7–8). The number "four" elsewhere symbolizes north, south, east, and west (cf. 2:6; 6:1,5–6). Hence, the "four horns" (v. 18) represent all the surrounding nations that "scattered Judah, Israel and Jerusalem" (v. 19), primarily Assyria and Babylon, but also Egypt, Edom, Ammon, and Philistia. "Scattered" (v. 19) refers to the exiles of the northern and southern kingdoms (cf. vv. 5–6,15).

1:20–21 craftsmen. Helped construct (Exod 35:35; 1 Kgs 7:14) and

A Man With a Measuring Line

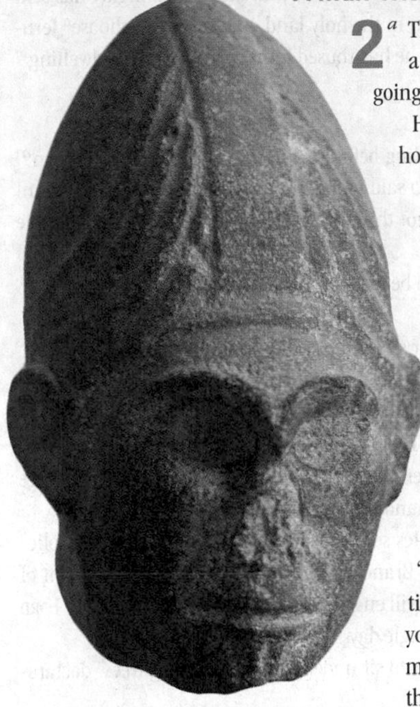

Head of a deity from the end of the Middle Bronze Age, found in Djabul, Syria. Horns (represented here schematically with the helmet's curved lines) are often used in the Bible as the image of power (Zech 1:18–19).
Wikimedia Commons

2 [a] Then I looked up, and there before me was a man with
a measuring line in his hand. [2]I asked, "Where are you
going?"
He answered me, "To measure Jerusalem, to find out
how wide and how long it is."[c]
[3]While the angel who was speaking to me was leaving, another angel came to meet him [4]and said to him:
"Run, tell that young man, 'Jerusalem will be a city
without walls[d] because of the great number[e] of people and animals in it. [5]And I myself will be a wall[f] of
fire around it,' declares the LORD, 'and I will be its
glory[g] within.'
[6]"Come! Come! Flee from the land of the
north," declares the LORD, "for I have scattered you
to the four winds of heaven,"[h] declares the LORD.
[7]"Come, Zion! Escape, you who live in Daughter
Babylon!"[i] [8]For this is what the LORD Almighty says:
"After the Glorious One has sent me against the nations that have plundered you—for whoever touches
you touches the apple of his eye[j]— [9]I will surely raise
my hand against them so that their slaves will plunder
them.[bk] Then you will know that the LORD Almighty has
sent me.[l]
[10]"Shout and be glad, Daughter Zion.[m] For I am com
ing,[n] and I will live among you,"[o] declares the LORD.
[11]"Many nations will be joined with the LORD in that day

[a] In Hebrew texts 2:1-13 is numbered 2:5-17.
[b] 8,9 Or *says after . . . eye:* [9]*"I . . . plunder them."*

2:2 [c]Eze 40:3; Rev 21:15
2:4 [d]Eze 38:11 [e]Isa 49:20; Jer 30:19; 33:22
2:5 [f]Isa 26:1 [g]Rev 21:23
2:6 [h]Eze 17:21
2:7 [i]Isa 48:20
2:8 [j]Dt 32:10
2:9 [k]Isa 14:2 [l]Zec 4:9
2:10 [m]Zep 3:14 [n]Zec 9:9 [o]Lev 26:12; Zec 8:3

repair (2 Kgs 12:11; 22:6) the tabernacle and temple. There are "four" to match the horns. They will do to the horns what the horns have done to others: "terrify" and "throw down" (v. 21). In context, the craftsmen are best understood as temple workers, who by their rebuilding will bring about the reversal promised in the first vision as God returns to judge the nations (an element of the third vision).

2:1–13 *A Man With a Measuring Line.* The third vision of a glorious new Jerusalem (vv. 1–5) serves as the basis for a call to exiles in Babylon to return to Jerusalem (vv. 6–9) and rejoice in God's return to his people (vv. 10–13).

2:1 a man with a measuring line. He surveys Jerusalem for its rebuilding (cf. 1:16; Jer 31:39; Ezek 40:3).

2:4 Run. The second angel's message is urgent. The young man's conception of the restored Jerusalem is too small. **without walls.** Walls will not be able to contain Jerusalem because its human and animal populations will be overflowing (cf. 1:17).

2:5 Since a wall functioned to protect and secure a city, God promises to be "a wall of fire" (cf. Gen 3:24; Exod 14:19–20,24; Deut 5:23–24; 2 Kgs 6:17; Pss 46; 48) and "its glory within" (cf. 1:3,16). God's glory was associated with the tabernacle and the temple (Exod 40:34–35; 1 Kgs 8:11). Ezekiel envisions God's glory returning to Jerusalem (Ezek 43:1–5) after departing in judgment (Ezek 1; 8–11).

2:6 Flee. The exiles in Babylon must return to Jerusalem. **land of the north.** Babylon (cf. Jer 3:18; 50:8). **scattered.** God judged his people's sin by exiling them among the nations.

2:7 Daughter Babylon. Personifies the inhabitants of the city (cf. "Daughter Zion" in v. 10). In the Bible, "Babylon" comes to typify human opposition to God. For instance, in Rev 18, Babylon is a seductive prostitute who deceives the nations. She represents the glitz and glamour of an anti-God world. Likewise, Christians must flee from her or be destroyed (Rev 18:4; see also "City of God," p. 2666).

2:8 After the Glorious One has sent me against the nations that have plundered you. The Hebrew of this verse is difficult to understand. An alternative rendering is "After glory sent me to the nations that have plundered you," where "glory" refers to God's own character that compelled him to depart the defiled temple and dwell with his people among the nations (cf. Ezek 8:6). **apple of his eye.** God's people are precious (cf. Exod 19:5).

2:9 I will surely raise my hand. God will judge the nations that have touched his people (cf. 1:15). **plunder.** God's judgment will be like how the Israelites plundered the Egyptians (cf. Exod 12:35–36). This will underline Zechariah's authority as a prophet.

2:10 Shout and be glad. Cf. 9:9; Zeph 3:14. **Daughter Zion.** Inhabitants of Jerusalem (cf. "Daughter Babylon," v. 7). **For.** The reason for this jubilation is God's promise to come and "live among" them, presumably once the temple is rebuilt.

2:11 Many nations will be joined with the LORD. Fulfills God's promise to Abraham (Gen 12:3; 18:18; 22:18; cf. Zech 8:22–23; 14:16; Isa 2:1–4; 14:1; 56:3,6). **in that day.** The day when God will establish his kingdom on earth in glory (cf. 3:10 and note on 12:1—14:21). Fulfillment will confirm Zechariah's message (cf. 4:8–10). **will become my people.** A covenant privilege (cf. Jer 31:33).

2:12 [p] Dt 32:9; Ps 33:12; Jer 10:16 [q] Zec 1:17
2:13 [r] Hab 2:20
3:1 [s] Hag 1:1; Zec 6:11 [t] Ps 109:6
3:2 [u] Jude 1:9 [v] Isa 14:1 [w] Am 4:11; Jude 1:23
3:4 [x] Eze 36:25; Mic 7:18 [y] Isa 52:1; Rev 19:8
3:5 [z] Ex 29:6
3:7 [a] Dt 17:8-11; Eze 44:15-16
3:8 [b] Eze 12:11 [c] Isa 4:2
3:9 [d] Isa 28:16 [e] Jer 50:20
3:10 [f] 1Ki 4:25; Mic 4:4

and will become my people. I will live among you and you will know that the LORD Almighty has sent
me to you. 12 The LORD will inherit[p] Judah as his portion in the holy land and will again choose[q] Jerusalem. 13 Be still[r] before the LORD, all mankind, because he has roused himself from his holy dwelling."

Clean Garments for the High Priest

3 Then he showed me Joshua[s] the high priest standing before the angel of the LORD, and Satan[a][t]
standing at his right side to accuse him. 2 The LORD said to Satan, "The LORD rebuke you,[u] Satan!
The LORD, who has chosen[v] Jerusalem, rebuke you! Is not this man a burning stick snatched from the
fire?"[w]

3 Now Joshua was dressed in filthy clothes as he stood before the angel. 4 The angel said to those who
were standing before him, "Take off his filthy clothes."

Then he said to Joshua, "See, I have taken away your sin,[x] and I will put fine garments[y] on you."

5 Then I said, "Put a clean turban[z] on his head." So they put a clean turban on his head and clothed
him, while the angel of the LORD stood by.

6 The angel of the LORD gave this charge to Joshua: 7 "This is what the LORD Almighty says: 'If you will
walk in obedience to me and keep my requirements, then you will govern my house[a] and have charge
of my courts, and I will give you a place among these standing here.

8 " 'Listen, High Priest Joshua, you and your associates seated before you, who are men symbolic[b]
of things to come: I am going to bring my servant, the Branch.[c] 9 See, the stone I have set in front of
Joshua! There are seven eyes[b] on that one stone,[d] and I will engrave an inscription on it,' says the LORD
Almighty, 'and I will remove the sin[e] of this land in a single day.

10 " 'In that day each of you will invite your neighbor to sit under your vine and fig tree,[f]' declares
the LORD Almighty."

[a] *1* Hebrew *satan* means *adversary.* [b] *9* Or *facets*

2:12–13 Judah and Jerusalem have a privileged place: Judah is the tribe of king David, and Jerusalem is the city of David and the location of the temple (the next two visions feature the king and temple).
2:12 holy. The land is "holy" because God is present (cf. v. 13; 14:21; Ps 78:54). **choose.** Expresses God's sovereignty (cf. Deut 12).
2:13 Be still. Or silent, anticipating God's return. The return of God's glory came with Jesus, who "made his dwelling among us" (John 1:14) and brought salvation for Israel and the nations (cf. Acts 1:8; Eph 2:13–18). John's vision of the new Jerusalem in Rev 21–22 draws on many aspects of Zechariah's vision.
3:1–10 *Clean Garments for the High Priest.* The fourth vision pictures a heavenly court scene (cf. Job 1–2) where the high priest Joshua is cleansed for service in the new temple (vv. 1–5). This priestly service anticipates the day of the Branch (Messiah), a day of forgiveness and prosperity (vv. 8–10).
3:1 Joshua the high priest. He was responsible for ensuring the purity of God's people through temple sacrifice. **standing before.** Indicates coming before a judge (cf. Num 27:2). **the angel of the LORD.** Represents and speaks for God yet is distinct from God (cf. 1:11; see note on 1:11–12). **Satan.** Means "the accuser." The Hebrew is definite ("the Satan") and implies a title (cf. Job 1:6–12; 2:1–7). From a canonical perspective, he can be identified as "the devil" (Rev 12:9). He stands ready "to accuse" Joshua. **accuse.** The Hebrew for "accuse" has the same root as "Satan."
3:2 The LORD rebuke you, Satan! God silences Satan before he can make any accusation. **chosen Jerusalem.** God's sovereign purposes will come to pass (cf. 1:17; 2:12; Deut 12:5). **burning stick snatched from the fire.** God has delivered Joshua from the judgment of exile, but the image implies that he is charred and unclean (cf. Amos 4:11).
3:3 filthy clothes. In Hebrew, the adjective "filthy" when used as a noun denotes excrement (see, e.g., Deut 23:13). Hence, there were grounds for Satan's accusation as Joshua is ritually unclean and unfit for temple service.
3:4 those who were standing before him. Probably angels in the heavenly court. **taken away your sin.** This qualifies and reinstates Joshua to serve as the high priest. **fine.** Or "clean" or "pure."
3:5 clean turban. The high priest's head-wear (cf. Exod 28:39). Joshua is cleansed by God's grace and clothed with clean garments so that he might serve God. Christians are set free from the accusations of Satan similarly. By grace and through the cross, Jesus cleanses and clothes his people with a righteousness not their own in order to serve God (Rom 3:21–26; 8:33–34; 12:1).
3:6–7 If Joshua, now cleansed and clothed, obeys God in covenant faithfulness (cf. Deut 11:1; 28:9), then God will give him the privilege of governing his temple ("house"), guarding the purity of his temple "courts," and being admitted to his presence ("a place among these standing here"), the high priest's privilege on the Day of Atonement (cf. Lev 16).
3:8 associates. Likely Joshua's fellow priests. As they serve in the new temple, they will function as a sign that God will bring "my servant," a title used 31 times of David. **the Branch.** Or "Shoot." This is a future Davidic king of humble origins who is associated with the coming kingdom of God with all its blessings (cf. 6:12; Jer 23:5–6; 33:14–18). The promise of a servant is ultimately fulfilled in Jesus the Messiah.
3:9 stone. Given the focus on the high priest's garments in vv. 4–5, this "stone" with seven facets (see NIV text note) is likely an inscribed gemstone (cf. Exod 28:9–11,21). It functions as a reminder of God's promise to "remove the sin of this land in a single day," which brings to mind the Day of Atonement. Yet the connection of this day with the coming Messiah (v. 8) and prosperity (v. 10) suggests an even greater day than this: the day when the great high priest Jesus offered the once-for-all sacrifice that cleanses consciences from acts that lead to death so that people can serve the living God (Heb 9:14).
3:10 sit under your vine and fig tree. An image of peace and prosperity (cf. 1 Kgs 4:25; Mic 4:4).

The Gold Lampstand and the Two Olive Trees

4 Then the angel who talked with me returned and woke[g] me up, like someone awakened from
sleep.[h] 2He asked me, "What do you see?"[i]
I answered, "I see a solid gold lampstand[j] with a bowl at the top and seven lamps[k] on it, with seven
channels to the lamps. 3Also there are two olive trees[l] by it, one on the right of the bowl and the other
on its left."
4I asked the angel who talked with me, "What are these, my lord?"
5He answered, "Do you not know what these are?"
"No, my lord," I replied.[m]
6So he said to me, "This is the word of the LORD to Zerubbabel:[n] 'Not by might nor by power, but by
my Spirit,'[o] says the LORD Almighty.
7"What are you, mighty mountain? Before Zerubbabel you will become level ground.[p] Then he will
bring out the capstone[q] to shouts of 'God bless it! God bless it!' "
8Then the word of the LORD came to me: 9"The hands of Zerubbabel have laid the foundation[r] of this
temple; his hands will also complete it.[s] Then you will know that the LORD Almighty has sent me[t] to you.
10"Who dares despise the day of small things,[u] since the seven eyes[v] of the LORD that range throughout the earth will rejoice when they see the chosen capstone[a] in the hand of Zerubbabel?"
11Then I asked the angel, "What are these two olive trees[w] on the right and the left of the lampstand?"
12Again I asked him, "What are these two olive branches beside the two gold pipes that pour out
golden oil?"
13He replied, "Do you not know what these are?"
"No, my lord," I said.
14So he said, "These are the two who are anointed[x] to[b] serve the Lord of all the earth."

4:1 [g]Da 8:18 [h]Jer 31:26
4:2 [i]Jer 1:13 [j]Ex 25:31; Rev 1:12 [k]Rev 4:5
4:3 [l]ver 11; Rev 11:4
4:5 [m]Zec 1:9
4:6 [n]Ezr 5:2 [o]Isa 11:2-4; Hos 1:7
4:7 [p]Jer 51:25 [q]Ps 118:22
4:9 [r]Ezr 3:11 [s]Ezr 3:8; 6:15; Zec 6:12 [t]Zec 2:9
4:10 [u]Hag 2:3 [v]Zec 3:9; Rev 5:6
4:11 [w]ver 3; Rev 11:4
4:14 [x]Ex 29:7; 40:15; Da 9:24-26; Zec 3:1-7

[a] 10 Or *the plumb line* [b] 14 Or *two who bring oil and*

4:1–14 *The Gold Lampstand and the Two Olive Trees.* The fifth vision (vv. 1–5,11–14) centers on a message to Zerubbabel (vv. 6–10) that he will build the temple by the power of God's Spirit.

4:1 The angel returns and rouses Zechariah for another vision.

4:2 solid gold lampstand. Hebrew of "lampstand" is *mĕnôrâ*; brings to mind the lampstand of the tabernacle and temple (Exod 25:31–40; 1 Kgs 7:49), which has tree-like qualities that evoke the Garden of Eden (Gen 2:9). Fire is often associated with God's presence (see, e.g., Gen 15:17; Exod 3:2–6), and this suggests that the lampstand with "seven lamps" represents God's presence in the temple. Zechariah's lampstand has several additional features: "seven channels" to a "bowl" (v. 3) and also "gold pipes" and "golden oil" (v. 12), which means that it is supplied with oil from "two olive trees by it" (v. 3) and is therefore without the need for priests.

4:4–5 Zechariah fails to understand the significance of the olive trees, so the angel gives him two prophetic messages concerning Zerubbabel in vv. 6–7 and vv. 8–10.

4:6 Zerubbabel. He returned from Babylon, rebuilt the altar, and laid the foundation of the temple (Ezra 2:2; 3:2,8; Neh 12:1). He was the "governor of Judah" (Hag 1:1) and the "son of Shealtiel" (Hag 1:1), which indicates his Davidic lineage and qualification to rebuild the temple (Hag 1:1,14; 2:2,21,23; cf. 1 Chr 3:17). In the first prophetic message, Zechariah must tell Zerubbabel that the temple will be built "not by might nor by power" (v. 6; cf. Ps 33:16), but by God's Spirit. Like the lampstand that is supplied with resources from outside itself, Zerubbabel will rebuild the temple in the power of God's Spirit.

4:7 mighty mountain . . . will become level ground. Obstacles such as spiritual and economic difficulties (cf. Hag 1) will be overcome (cf. Isa 40:4). Zerubbabel will complete the temple with a "capstone" accompanied by shouts requesting God to "bless" the building.

4:8–10 A second prophetic message assures Zechariah that Zerubbabel will complete the temple. This will demonstrate that Zechariah's message is authentic (cf. 1:16; 2:9,11; 8:9).

4:10 Who dares despise the day of small things. May indicate that the community is frustrated over the slow and painful progress of the rebuilding. It implies that their present experience is "small" compared to what lay in the future. **seven eyes of the LORD that range throughout the earth.** Cf. 2 Chr 16:9; Ezra 5:5. God's presence among his people to strengthen them to complete the temple connects the vision of the lampstand, which represents God's presence in the temple (cf. v. 2), with the message to Zerubbabel. **capstone.** Derision will turn to joy when Zerubbabel completes the temple with the "chosen capstone." It is difficult to see how the alternative translation "plumb line" (see NIV text note) would inspire joy.

4:11–13 Zechariah asks the angel twice more about the significance of the "two olive trees" (v. 11) and "two olive branches" (v. 12; cf. vv. 3–5).

4:12 two gold pipes that pour out golden oil. The pipes presumably pour the oil into the "bowl" of vv. 2–3.

4:14 two who are anointed. The translation "two who bring oil" (see NIV text note) is definitely preferred. The olive trees "bring" oil rather than receive it ("are anointed"). **two.** While commonly identified as Joshua and Zerubbabel, they are better understood as the prophets Haggai and Zechariah. **serve.** Alternatively rendered "stand by." This heavenly access indicates a privilege of the prophet (1 Kgs 22:19; Jer 23:18–22). In addition, the OT often connects the work of the Spirit with prophecy (7:12) and attributes the reconstruction of the temple to the prophets Haggai and Zechariah (8:9; Ezra 5:1–2; 6:14–15). Revelation 11:3–4 creatively uses this vision, and the two olive trees are prophets. This identification also connects the vision with the two prophetic messages about Zerubbabel (vv. 6–7,8–10): The main driving force behind the completion of the temple will be God's Spirit as he rouses the people to action through the preaching of his prophets. This side of the coming of Jesus, God builds his temple the church in exactly the same way: by his word through his Spirit (Eph 2:19–22).

5:1 [y]Eze 2:9; Rev 5:1
5:3 [z]Isa 24:6; 43:28; Mal 3:9; 4:6 [a]Ex 20:15; Mal 3:8 [b]Isa 48:1
5:4 [c]Lev 14:34-45; Hab 2:9-11; Mal 3:5
5:8 [d]Mic 6:11
5:9 [e]Lev 11:19
5:11 [f]Ge 10:10 [g]Jer 29:5,28 [h]Da 1:2
6:1 [i]ver 5
6:2 [j]Rev 6:5
6:3 [k]Rev 6:2

The Flying Scroll

5 I looked again, and there before me was a flying scroll.[y] [2]He asked me, "What do you see?"

I answered, "I see a flying scroll, twenty cubits long and ten cubits wide.[a]"

[3]And he said to me, "This is the curse[z] that is going out over the whole land; for according to what it says on one side, every thief[a] will be banished, and according to what it says on the other, everyone who swears falsely[b] will be banished. [4]The LORD Almighty declares, 'I will send it out, and it will enter the house of the thief and the house of anyone who swears falsely by my name. It will remain in that house and destroy it completely, both its timbers and its stones.[c]'"

The Woman in a Basket

[5]Then the angel who was speaking to me came forward and said to me, "Look up and see what is appearing."

[6]I asked, "What is it?"

He replied, "It is a basket." And he added, "This is the iniquity[b] of the people throughout the land."

[7]Then the cover of lead was raised, and there in the basket sat a woman! [8]He said, "This is wickedness," and he pushed her back into the basket and pushed its lead cover down on it.[d]

[9]Then I looked up—and there before me were two women, with the wind in their wings! They had wings like those of a stork,[e] and they lifted up the basket between heaven and earth.

[10]"Where are they taking the basket?" I asked the angel who was speaking to me.

[11]He replied, "To the country of Babylonia[c][f] to build a house[g] for it. When the house is ready, the basket will be set there in its place."[h]

Four Chariots

6 I looked up again, and there before me were four chariots[i] coming out from between two mountains—mountains of bronze. [2]The first chariot had red horses, the second black,[j] [3]the third white,[k] and the fourth dappled—all of them powerful. [4]I asked the angel who was speaking to me, "What are these, my lord?"

[a] *2* That is, about 30 feet long and 15 feet wide or about 9 meters long and 4.5 meters wide
[b] *6* Or *appearance* [c] *11* Hebrew *Shinar*

5:1–4 *The Flying Scroll.* After envisioning God's return in visions 1–5, visions 6–7 picture God judging the wicked and driving iniquity and wickedness far from the land.

5:2 flying scroll. It is extraordinary in its activity and dimensions. Scrolls are generally associated with God's written words (cf. Ps 40:7; Jer 36; Ezek 2–3). God sends this scroll (cf. v. 4), and it is clear for all to see, like a huge banner. **twenty cubits long and ten cubits wide.** See NIV text note.

5:3 The "curse" and the crimes of theft and swearing falsely suggest that the scroll represents "the Book [scroll] of the Law of Moses" (Josh 8:31,34; 23:6; cf. Exod 24:4,7; 1 Kgs 2:3; Dan 9:11). The Hebrew indicates that these crimes have gone unpunished ("been acquitted" rather than "banished"), and hence there has been a corruption of justice. God has sent the scroll to put things right and ensure that the guilty will not be acquitted, an action consistent with his character (cf. Exod 20:7; 34:7).

5:4 In contrast to God's "house" (the temple) that will be built (1:16; 3:7; 4:9), the curse of the scroll will enter and destroy the houses of the guilty. This implies the death of the inhabitants (cf. Deut 30:15). There is an echo of this vision in Revelation with the scroll in the hands of the risen Lord Jesus that judges his enemies (Rev 5:9; 6:12–17).

5:5–11 *The Woman in a Basket.* The seventh vision pictures wickedness being removed from the land and transported to Babylon.

5:6 basket. Or "ephah," a vessel holding about 22 liters and used in worship and commerce (e.g., Lev 5:11; 19:36). It represents "the iniquity of the people throughout the land."

5:7–8 Concealed in the basket is a woman who represents "wickedness" (v. 8), which in Hebrew is a near anagram for "Asherah," a foreign god worshiped up until the Babylonian exile (2 Kgs 23:4,6–7). She is restrained in the basket with a "cover of lead" (v. 7) and cannot escape.

5:9 wind in their wings. Indicates flight (cf. Ezek 1:11–12). **between heaven and earth.** The sky. The basket is transported to the country of God's enemies, Babylonia (cf. 2:7; see also "City of God," p. 2666), where a house is built for it, and it is set up like an idol. There are many elements of this vision that suggest the basket is a parody of the ark of the covenant (cf. Ezek 1; 8–11). In Hebrew "cover of lead" (v. 7) sounds like "mercy seat." The two cherubim of the ark are paralleled by the two women with stork-like wings. Where God was enthroned on the ark, the woman sits beneath the lead cover (v. 7). As God's house is built in Jerusalem and he returns (visions 1–5), wickedness is carried far away and a house is built for it (v. 11). Jesus' second coming will see the final judgment and removal of wickedness in the world (cf. 2 Thess 1:6–10).

6:1–8 *Four Chariots.* In the final vision, God's heavenly army subdues the nations and gives his Spirit rest.

6:1 four chariots. Recalls the horses in the first vision, though the colors are not all the same. "Four" may represent the scope of their mission to "the whole world" (v. 5; cf. 1:19–20). Chariots were primarily military vehicles used in open country for rapid movement. These are heavenly chariots since they come from God's presence (v. 5). **two mountains ... of bronze.** They represent the entrance to the heavens in the vision. Solomon's temple, which represented the heavens in its layout (cf. Heb 8:5), had two bronze pillars at its entrance (1 Kgs 7:15–22).

6:2–3 Each chariot has different colored horses, though no significance is given to the colors. The horses are "powerful" (cf. vv. 3,7).

[5]The angel answered me, "These are the four spirits[a][l] of heaven, going out from standing in the presence of the Lord of the whole world. [6]The one with the black horses is going toward the north country,
the one with the white horses toward the west,[b] and the one with the dappled horses toward the south."
[7]When the powerful horses went out, they were straining to go throughout the earth.[m] And he said,
"Go throughout the earth!" So they went throughout the earth.
[8]Then he called to me, "Look, those going toward the north country have given my Spirit[c] rest[n] in
the land of the north."

6:5 [l]Eze 37:9; Mt 24:31; Rev 7:1
6:7 [m]Zec 1:10
6:8 [n]Eze 5:13; 24:13
6:10 [o]Ezr 7:14-16; Jer 28:6

A Crown for Joshua

[9]The word of the LORD came to me: [10]"Take silver and gold from the exiles Heldai, Tobijah and
Jedaiah, who have arrived from Babylon.[o] Go the same day to the house of Josiah son of Zephaniah.

[a] 5 Or *winds* [b] 6 Or *horses after them* [c] 8 Or *spirit*

6:5 four spirits. The chariots are characterized as "four spirits," or "winds" (see NIV text note), of heaven, which suggests swift and wide-ranging movement (cf. Ps 104:4). **going out from standing in the presence of the Lord of the whole world.** See the description of God in 4:14, which indicates they go from his heavenly court. They are the army of "the LORD Almighty" or "the Yahweh of armies" (see note on 1:3). **world.** Or "earth."

6:6 Two chariots go "toward the north country." The word translated "west" can also be read as "after them" (see NIV text note); in other words, the chariot with the white horses goes "after them," namely, after the chariot with the black horses. They go to Babylon, where God's people had been taken as captives (cf. 2:6–7) and where the woman in the basket had been taken (5:11). Another chariot travels "south" (there is no need to travel elsewhere since to the east is desert and to the west is sea). The fourth chariot is possibly held in reserve.

6:7–8 The horses and chariots go out at God's command "throughout the earth" (v. 7). Whereas the horses in the first vision did surveillance, these subdue the nations as God's heavenly army. In the first vision, the "whole world" was "at rest" (1:11), rather than God's people. This vision pictures the judgment of the nations, particularly Babylon, with God's Spirit "given … rest" (v. 8). God's "spirit" (see NIV text note on v. 8), or "wind" (see NIV text note on v. 5), could refer to his anger or wrath (cf. Eccl 10:4; Ezek 13:13; 21:17). Rev 19:11–16 develops this imagery: Jesus and the armies of heaven ride white horses and strike down rebellious nations.

6:9–15 *A Crown for Joshua.* Zechariah is to perform a symbolic action that looks beyond Zerubbabel's temple to the coming Branch and the temple that he will build.

6:9–11 Many exiles returned from Babylon with wealth (cf. Ezra 2:68–69).

THE EIGHT VISIONS OF ZECHARIAH

VISION	PASSAGE	IMAGE(S)	ZECHARIAH'S QUESTION(S)	SUMMARY OUTCOME
1	1:7–17	Horsemen on red, brown, and white horses who patrol the earth	What are these, my lord? (v. 9)	God will judge the nations for he has turned to Jerusalem with mercy. The temple and city will be rebuilt and the surrounding towns will become prosperous.
2	1:18–21	Four horns and four craftsmen	What are these? (v. 19) What are these coming to do? (v. 21)	The nations who exiled Judah, Israel, and Jerusalem will be terrified and thrown down after the temple reconstruction.
3	2:1–13	Man with a measuring line	Where are you going? (v. 2)	Jerusalem's population will expand. Exiles are to flee from Babylon. The glory of God will return to Jerusalem and protect the city. Nations will be judged and saved.
4	3:1–10	The high priest Joshua is cleansed, re-clothed, and commissioned		Joshua will serve in the temple and be a sign of the coming of "my servant, the Branch" (v. 8).
5	4:1–14	The temple menorah supplied with oil from two olive trees	What are these, my lord? (v. 4) What are these two olive trees … ? (v. 11) What are these two olive branches … ? (v. 12)	Zerubbabel will build the temple, not in his own strength, but by God's Spirit through the agency of the prophets.
6	5:1–4	A flying scroll		The curses of the covenant will bring God's judgment on covenant breakers.
7	5:5–11	A woman in a basket carried by two women with stork-like wings	What is it? (v. 6) Where are they taking the basket? (v. 10)	The woman represents "wickedness" (v. 8) and is removed far from the land and housed in Babylon.
8	6:1–8	Four chariots with red, black, white, and dappled horses	What are these, my lord? (v. 4)	God's heavenly army subdues the nations.

6:11 [p]Ps 21:3 [q]Zec 3:1 [r]Ezr 3:2
6:12 [s]Isa 4:2; Zec 3:8 [t]Ezr 3:8-10; Zec 4:6-9
6:13 [u]Ps 110:4
6:15 [v]Isa 60:10 [w]Zec 2:9-11 [x]Isa 58:12; Jer 7:23; Zec 3:7
7:1 [y]Ne 1:1
7:2 [z]Jer 26:19; Zec 8:21
7:3 [a]Zec 12:12-14 [b]Jer 52:12-14; Zec 8:19
7:5 [c]Isa 58:5
7:7 [d]Zec 1:4 [e]Jer 22:21 [f]Jer 17:26

11 Take the silver and gold and make a crown,[p] and set it on the head of the high priest, Joshua[q] son of
Jozadak.[a r] 12 Tell him this is what the LORD Almighty says: 'Here is the man whose name is the Branch,[s]
and he will branch out from his place and build the temple of the LORD.[t] 13 It is he who will build the
temple of the LORD, and he will be clothed with majesty and will sit and rule on his throne. And he[b] will
be a priest[u] on his throne. And there will be harmony between the two.' 14 The crown will be given to
Heldai,[c] Tobijah, Jedaiah and Hen[d] son of Zephaniah as a memorial in the temple of the LORD. 15 Those
who are far away will come and help to build the temple of the LORD,[v] and you will know that the LORD
Almighty has sent me to you.[w] This will happen if you diligently obey[x] the LORD your God."

Justice and Mercy, Not Fasting

7 In the fourth year of King Darius, the word of the LORD came to Zechariah on the fourth day of the
ninth month, the month of Kislev.[y] 2 The people of Bethel had sent Sharezer and Regem-Melek,
together with their men, to entreat[z] the LORD 3 by asking the priests of the house of the LORD Almighty
and the prophets, "Should I mourn[a] and fast in the fifth[b] month, as I have done for so many years?"
4 Then the word of the LORD Almighty came to me: 5 "Ask all the people of the land and the priests, 'When
you fasted[c] and mourned in the fifth and seventh months for the past seventy years, was it really for me
that you fasted? 6 And when you were eating and drinking, were you not just feasting for yourselves? 7 Are
these not the words the LORD proclaimed through the earlier prophets[d] when Jerusalem and its surrounding towns were at rest[e] and prosperous, and the Negev and the western foothills[f] were settled?' "
8 And the word of the LORD came again to Zechariah: 9 "This is what the LORD Almighty said:

[a] *11* Hebrew *Jehozadak*, a variant of *Jozadak* [b] *13* Or *there* [c] *14* Syriac; Hebrew *Helem*
[d] *14* Or *and the gracious one, the*

6:11 the high priest, Joshua. Cf. 3:1. In the exile, the Davidic king was removed from the throne and his crown was defiled in the dust (Ps 89:39; Jer 22:24–30; Ezek 21:26–27). The crown is possibly placed on the high priest to sanctify it in preparation for a king to wear it again.
6:12–13 Zechariah is to speak to Joshua, who represents the future "Branch" (or "Shoot") in this symbolic action (see note on 3:8 concerning the Messianic significance of this title).
6:12 he will branch out from his place. The Branch will literally "shoot up" in place of Joshua and take the crown (in the Hebrew "branch out" is a wordplay on "Branch" or "Shoot"). **build the temple of the LORD.** Repeated for emphasis in v. 13. This is the temple that earlier prophets expected—much greater than Zerubbabel's temple (e.g., Isa 2:2–4; Jer 3:16–18; Ezek 40–42; Mic 4:1–5).
6:13 clothed with majesty. Appropriate for a king. **sit and rule on his throne ... be a priest.** Ps 110 is the conceptual background: The Messiah sits by the Lord's throne (Ps 110:1) and rules (Ps 110:2–3) and is designated as a priest in the order of Melchizedek (Ps 110:4; cf. Heb 5:1–10; 6:20—8:2). The reign of the Lord and his Messiah ("the two") will issue in "harmony," or "peace" (Hebrew *šālôm*)—a peace that ultimately comes in the priest-king Jesus (cf. 9:9–10; John 14:27; Eph 2:14), who is building God's temple, the church (Matt 16:18; Eph 2:19–22).
6:14 The crown will be given. Given to the exiles for safekeeping in Zerubbabel's temple "as a memorial," presumably pointing to the coming Branch (cf. the symbols of 3:8–9).
6:15 Those who are far away. May be Gentiles (cf. 2:11; 8:20–23; 14:16–19), but more likely exiles (cf. 2:6) who will come to help complete Zerubbabel's temple and thereby authenticate Zechariah's message. The challenge is to "obey" (cf. 1:3).
7:1—8:23 *From Fasting to Feasting.* A question about fasting provides an occasion for Zechariah to reapply pertinent covenant requirements to the people and restate the hope for restoration. This section forms a bridge between chs. 1–6 and chs. 9–14.
7:1–14 *Justice and Mercy, Not Fasting.* Zechariah calls for covenant obedience in view of past sin and judgment.
7:1 A third dating formula (cf. 1:1,7 and notes) introduces this section. **fourth year ... fourth day of the ninth month.** Dec. 7, 518 BC. Almost two years after the night visions and two years before the temple is completed (cf. Ezra 6:14–16). **Kislev.** A Babylonian month name (see note on 1:7).
7:2 Bethel. Located about 12 miles (20 kilometers) north of Jerusalem. Before the exile it had been a northern town (1 Kgs 12:29–33; Hos 10:15; Amos 3:14); after the exile it appears to have been part of Judah (Ezra 2:28; Neh 7:32). **entreat the LORD.** The delegation went to seek God's favor.
7:3 mourn and fast. Doing so "in the fifth month" may recall Nebuchadnezzar's destruction of the temple in 586 BC (2 Kgs 25:8–9). It was a sign of penitence and lamentation over sin (cf. 2 Sam 12:21–22). With the near completion of the temple, the delegation asks if they must continue to mourn and fast.
7:5 The fast of the "seventh" month apparently commemorated the assassination of Gedaliah, whom Nebuchadnezzar appointed as governor (2 Kgs 25:25). **seventy years.** The time of exile and temple desolation that Jeremiah prophesies (Jer 25:11–12; 29:10; cf. Zech 1:12 and note). **was it really for me that you fasted?** Zechariah challenges the people about their motives. Furthermore, did they eat and drink at their religious festivals (e.g., Passover, Weeks, Tabernacles) for God or for their own benefit? The implication is that their motives have been selfish and insincere. Jesus likewise teaches (e.g., Luke 18:9–14) that repentance and humility before God is more important than fasting.
7:7 the earlier prophets. They proclaimed that having a relationship with God and obeying his word is more important than religious ritual (e.g., Isa 1:10–11; 58:3–6; Jer 7; Joel 2:12–13; Mic 6:6–8). **Negev.** About 50 miles (80 kilometers) south of Jerusalem. Used for grazing and agriculture. **Western foothills.** Or "Shephelah," the tract of low hills between the high central ranges of Judea and the coastal plains. Zechariah implies that these regions are not inhabited as they were in preexilic times.
7:8–10 God summarizes what the earlier prophets said: God values justice more than religious ritual (e.g., 1 Sam 15:22–23; Amos 5:21–27; Mic 6:7–8).
7:9 Administer true justice. Broader than ruling in legal cases (cf. 8:16–17; see also "Justice," p. 2679). **justice.** It is first and fore-

'Administer true justice;[g] show mercy and compassion to one another. 10Do not oppress the widow or
the fatherless, the foreigner[h] or the poor. Do not plot evil against each other.'[i]
11"But they refused to pay attention; stubbornly they turned their backs and covered their ears.[j]
12They made their hearts as hard as flint[k] and would not listen to the law or to the words that the LORD
Almighty had sent by his Spirit through the earlier prophets.[l] So the LORD Almighty was very angry.[m]
13" 'When I called, they did not listen;[n] so when they called, I would not listen,'[o] says the LORD Almighty.[p] 14'I scattered[q] them with a whirlwind[r] among all the nations, where they were strangers. The
land they left behind them was so desolate that no one traveled through it. This is how they made the
pleasant land desolate.[s]' "

The LORD Promises to Bless Jerusalem

8 The word of the LORD Almighty came to me.
2This is what the LORD Almighty says: "I am very jealous for Zion; I am burning with jealousy for
her."
3This is what the LORD says: "I will return[t] to Zion and dwell in Jerusalem.[u] Then Jerusalem will
be called the Faithful City, and the mountain of the LORD Almighty will be called the Holy Mountain."
4This is what the LORD Almighty says: "Once again men and women of ripe old age will sit in the
streets of Jerusalem,[v] each of them with cane in hand because of their age. 5The city streets will be filled
with boys and girls playing there.[w]"
6This is what the LORD Almighty says: "It may seem marvelous to the remnant of this people at that
time,[x] but will it seem marvelous to me?[y]" declares the LORD Almighty.
7This is what the LORD Almighty says: "I will save my people from the countries of the east and the
west.[z] 8I will bring them back[a] to live in Jerusalem; they will be my people,[b] and I will be faithful and
righteous to them as their God."
9This is what the LORD Almighty says: "Now hear these words, 'Let your hands be strong[c] so that
the temple may be built.' This is also what the prophets[d] said who were present when the foundation

7:9 [g]Zec 8:16
7:10 [h]Ex 22:21 [i]Ex 22:22; Isa 1:17
7:11 [j]Jer 8:5; 11:10; 17:23
7:12 [k]Jer 17:1; Eze 11:19 [l]Ne 9:29 [m]Da 9:12
7:13 [n]Pr 1:24 [o]Isa 1:15; Jer 11:11; 14:12; Mic 3:4 [p]Pr 1:28
7:14 [q]Dt 4:27; 28:64-67 [r]Jer 23:19 [s]Jer 44:6
8:3 [t]Zec 1:16 [u]Zec 2:10
8:4 [v]Isa 65:20
8:5 [w]Jer 30:20; 31:13
8:6 [x]Ps 118:23; 126:1-3 [y]Jer 32:17,27
8:7 [z]Ps 107:3; Isa 11:11; 43:5
8:8 [a]Zec 10:10 [b]Eze 11:19-20; 36:28; Zec 2:11
8:9 [c]Hag 2:4 [d]Ezr 5:1

most found in God, but for people it represents right relationships as enshrined in the Mosaic covenant and encompasses "mercy and compassion" (cf. Jer 9:24; Hos 2:19; 12:6). Justice includes not oppressing the weak and vulnerable (the "widow ... fatherless ... foreigner ... poor" [v. 10]; cf. Isa 1:17; Jer 7:6), and it extends to thoughts and motivations ("Do not plot evil" [v. 10]). This is a universal biblical emphasis (e.g., Matt 9:13; 1 Cor 11:17–34; Gal 6:10; 1 Tim 5:8–16; 1 John 3:17).

7:11–12 The ancestors refused to obey God's words through the "law [and] ... the earlier prophets" (v. 12; see 1:4; Isa 6:10; Jer 6:28; 7:24; 17:1). God's words came through the prophets "by his Spirit" (v. 12; cf. 4:6; Ezek 11:5; Mic 3:8; 1 Pet 1:10–12). God judged the ancestors (vv. 13–14) because he "was very angry" (v. 12; cf. 1:2).

7:13 they did not listen. Because they refused to listen to God, God shut his ears to their prayers. He also "scattered them with a whirlwind among all the nations" (v. 14), one of the covenant curses (Lev 26:31–33; Deut 28:64).

7:14 they made the pleasant land desolate. Their disobedience reversed the prosperous situation of v. 7.

8:1–23 *The Lord Promises to Bless Jerusalem.* This section contains ten promises of blessing, each beginning with "This is what the LORD (Almighty) says" (vv. 2,3,4,6,7,9,14,19,20,23).

8:2 very jealous for Zion. Cf. 1:14; see note there. God's concern for what is rightly his is the grounds for his return (v. 3).

8:3 will return. Could be translated "have turned" (cf. 1:16; 2:10). Like 1:16, God has turned to his people with mercy (the exile is over), and he will dwell in Jerusalem after the temple's completion when his glory returns (cf. Ezek 43:4). Malachi 3:1 anticipates the coming of God to his temple, a dwelling that is fulfilled in Jesus (John 1:14). Then Jerusalem will be "the Faithful City" as its inhabitants reflect God's character (cf. the transformation of Jerusalem in Isaiah [e.g., Isa 1:21—2:5]). **mountain.** Mount Zion, the temple site in Jerusalem. It will be "the Holy Mountain" because God will dwell upon it (cf. Jer 31:23; Ezek 20:40). This holiness expands from the temple through Jerusalem and Judah (14:20–21; cf. Rev 21:2).

8:4–5 A picture of great prosperity. The elderly and children were the first to perish when cities were besieged, and they had to work in times of adversity. Here the elderly are "of ripe old age" (v. 4) and have time to "sit" (v. 4), and "boys and girls" (v. 5) play in the "city streets" (v. 5), which are not transport routes but open places between houses.

8:6 marvelous. This future may seem incredible to "the remnant" (those who had returned from exile) but not to God because of his power to save (cf. 4:10).

8:7 will save. God will bring his people back from the countries to which they had been scattered. Presumably they are saved from the coming judgment on the nations (1:21; 6:7–8).

8:8 to live in Jerusalem. Cf. 2:6; 7:14. **they will be my people, and I will be ... their God.** Classic covenant terminology expressing the intimate fellowship between God and his people (cf. 13:9; Exod 6:7; Lev 26:12). This language is also associated with the promised new covenant (e.g., Jer 24:7; 31:33; Ezek 11:20). Salvation and restoration express God's faithfulness (keeping his word) and righteousness (doing what is right).

8:9–11 This section has many echoes of Haggai and speaks of difficult times: "no wages for people or hire for animals" (v. 10; cf. Hag 1:11), no safety because of "their enemies" (v. 10; see Ezra 4:1–5), and conflict within the community with "everyone against their neighbor" (v. 10). Again God promises a great reversal for the "remnant" (v. 11; cf. v. 6; Hag 1:12,14; 2:2).

8:9 Let your hands be strong. A call for courage (cf. v. 13) so that they can finish building the temple. **foundation was laid.** Not what happened under Zerubbabel some 20 years earlier (Ezra 3:10), but the recommenced building under Haggai and Zechariah, "the prophets ... who were present."

8:10 [e]Hag 1:6
8:11 [f]Isa 12:1
8:12 [g]Joel 2:22 [h]Ps 67:6 [i]Ge 27:28 [j]Ob 17
8:13 [k]Jer 42:18 [l]Ge 12:2
8:14 [m]Jer 31:28; Eze 24:14
8:15 [n]ver 13; Jer 29:11; Mic 7:18-20
8:16 [o]Ps 15:2; Eph 4:25 [p]Zec 7:9
8:17 [q]Pr 3:29 [r]Pr 6:16-19
8:19 [s]Jer 39:2 [t]Jer 52:12 [u]2Ki 25:25 [v]Jer 52:4 [w]Ps 30:11 [x]ver 16
8:21 [y]Zec 7:2
8:22 [z]Ps 117:1; Isa 60:3; Zec 2:11
8:23 [a]Isa 45:14; 1Co 14:25
9:1 [b]Isa 17:1

was laid for the house of the LORD Almighty. 10 Before that time there were no wages[e] for people or hire
for animals. No one could go about their business safely because of their enemies, since I had turned
everyone against their neighbor. 11 But now I will not deal with the remnant of this people as I did in
the past,"[f] declares the LORD Almighty.

12 "The seed will grow well, the vine will yield its fruit,[g] the ground will produce its crops,[h] and the
heavens will drop their dew.[i] I will give all these things as an inheritance[j] to the remnant of this people.
13 Just as you, Judah and Israel, have been a curse[a][k] among the nations, so I will save you, and you will
be a blessing.[b][l] Do not be afraid, but let your hands be strong."

14 This is what the LORD Almighty says: "Just as I had determined to bring disaster[m] on you and
showed no pity when your ancestors angered me," says the LORD Almighty, 15 "so now I have determined
to do good[n] again to Jerusalem and Judah. Do not be afraid. 16 These are the things you are to do: Speak
the truth[o] to each other, and render true and sound judgment in your courts;[p] 17 do not plot evil[q] against
each other, and do not love to swear falsely.[r] I hate all this," declares the LORD.

18 The word of the LORD Almighty came to me.

19 This is what the LORD Almighty says: "The fasts of the fourth,[s] fifth,[t] seventh[u] and tenth[v] months
will become joyful[w] and glad occasions and happy festivals for Judah. Therefore love truth[x] and peace."

20 This is what the LORD Almighty says: "Many peoples and the inhabitants of many cities will yet
come, 21 and the inhabitants of one city will go to another and say, 'Let us go at once to entreat[y] the LORD
and seek the LORD Almighty. I myself am going.' 22 And many peoples and powerful nations will come to
Jerusalem to seek the LORD Almighty and to entreat him."[z]

23 This is what the LORD Almighty says: "In those days ten people from all languages and nations will
take firm hold of one Jew by the hem of his robe and say, 'Let us go with you, because we have heard
that God is with you.' "[a]

Judgment on Israel's Enemies

9 A prophecy:

> The word of the LORD is against the land of Hadrak
> and will come to rest on Damascus[b] —

[a] 13 That is, your name has been used in cursing (see Jer. 29:22); or, you have been regarded as under a curse.
[b] 13 Or *and your name will be used in blessings* (see Gen. 48:20); or *and you will be seen as blessed*

8:12–13 The covenant blessings (cf. Deut 28:4,11–12) are a reversal of the curse in Hag 1:10–11. They are the remnant's "inheritance" in the land (v. 12; cf. Jer 3:18; Ezek 47:14). Curse will turn to blessing. **8:14 disaster on ... your ancestors.** In the past God was angry with their ancestors and brought disaster (i.e., exile) on them (cf. 1:2,6,12,15–16; cf. 8:2–3). **8:15 Jerusalem and Judah.** They are at the center of God's purpose "to do good" (cf. 1:17; Josh 24:20; Ezek 36:11) that will then spread out to include the nations (vv. 20–23). **8:16–17** The words of the earlier prophets (cf. 7:9–10) continue to apply. **Speak the truth ... do not plot evil.** Uphold honesty in personal relationships. **render true and sound judgment in your courts ... do not love to swear falsely.** Administer justice in the community. The two negative commands involve things that God hates (cf. 5:3–4,8). While God wants the temple rebuilt, it is not an end in itself. Ethical transformation is essential. **8:19 fasts.** God mentions two additional fasts (cf. 7:3,5; see notes there) not referred to elsewhere in the OT. **fourth.** Commemorates the Babylonian army breaching the walls of Jerusalem (2 Kgs 25:2–4). **tenth.** Recalls the beginning of the siege against Jerusalem (2 Kgs 25:1). These will all become "joyful and glad occasions" (cf. Isa 35:10; 51:3,11; Jer 31:13; 33:10–11) and "happy festivals" (cf. 14:18; Isa 33:20). Hence, feasting will replace fasting. **love truth and peace.** Summarizes God's concern for the social dimensions of life. These are the opposite of the things that God hates (v. 17). **8:20 inhabitants of many cities.** Perhaps the towns surrounding Jerusalem (like Bethel; cf. 7:2,7). It seems that they will be caught up in the excitement of what God is doing in Jerusalem and tell others (v. 21). **8:22 many peoples.** Cf. v. 23. **powerful nations.** The powerful will recognize true power and will come to Jerusalem. **to seek the LORD Almighty and to entreat him.** To seek God's mercy (cf. 7:2). **8:23 In those days.** The future day of salvation (cf. 2:11; 3:10). The ratio of "ten" to "one" speaks of a great multitude "from all languages and nations" (cf. Rev 7:9). At Babel, humanity united together against God. In judgment, God confused their language and scattered them (Gen 11:7–8). Here Babel is reversed as all languages and nations seek God on his terms and join together in the "happy festivals" (v. 19) in Jerusalem. **take firm hold of one Jew by the hem of his robe.** This custom lays claim to a desired relationship or outcome (cf. Ruth 3:9; 1 Sam 15:27; Matt 9:20–22). **God is with you.** Cf. "Immanuel" in Isa 7:14 (see NIV text note there); Isa 8:10. This summarizes Zechariah's hope: God will return to dwell among his people. It will turn the nations from enemies to friends. God's promise to Abraham includes blessing for the nations (Gen 12:3; 17:4–7). This is a major theme of Isaiah (e.g., 2:2–4; 42:1–7; 66:18–24) and Zechariah (2:11; 9:7; 14:16–19). It is fulfilled in the coming of Jesus (e.g., Acts 11:18; Gal 3:14; Rev 5:9). **9:1—11:17** *First Prophetic Message.* The first of two prophecies that dramatically picture God's return and its outcome in terms drawn from Israel's past history. Many texts from chs. 9–14 are applied to Jesus in the NT. The first prophetic message (chs. 9–11) presents God subduing enemy nations and their kings.

for the eyes of all people and all the tribes of Israel
are on the LORD — [a]
2 and on Hamath[c] too, which borders on it,
and on Tyre[d] and Sidon, though they are very skillful.
3 Tyre has built herself a stronghold;
she has heaped up silver like dust,
and gold like the dirt of the streets.[e]
4 But the Lord will take away her possessions
and destroy her power on the sea,
and she will be consumed by fire.[f]
5 Ashkelon will see it and fear;
Gaza will writhe in agony,
and Ekron too, for her hope will wither.
Gaza will lose her king
and Ashkelon will be deserted.
6 A mongrel people will occupy Ashdod,
and I will put an end to the pride of the Philistines.
7 I will take the blood from their mouths,
the forbidden food from between their teeth.
Those who are left will belong to our God
and become a clan in Judah,
and Ekron will be like the Jebusites.
8 But I will encamp at my temple
to guard it against marauding forces.
Never again will an oppressor overrun my people,
for now I am keeping watch.[g]

The Coming of Zion's King

9 Rejoice greatly, Daughter Zion!
Shout, Daughter Jerusalem!
See, your king comes to you,
righteous and victorious,[h]
lowly and riding on a donkey,
on a colt, the foal of a donkey.[i]

[a] 1 Or *Damascus. / For the eye of the* LORD *is on all people, / as well as on the tribes of Israel,*

9:2 [c] Jer 49:23 [d] Eze 28:1-19
9:3 [e] Job 27:16; Eze 28:4
9:4 [f] Isa 23:1; Eze 26:3-5; 28:18
9:8 [g] Isa 52:1; 54:14
9:9 [h] Isa 9:6-7; 43:3-11; Jer 23:5-6; Zep 3:14-15; Zec 2:10 [i] Mt 21:5*; Jn 12:15*

9:1–17 *The Lord Returns.* God's coming will claim the land (vv. 1–8) through his king (vv. 9–13) for his people (vv. 14–17).
9:1–8 *Judgment on Israel's Enemies.* God comes to subdue the nations and return to his temple (v. 8). The movement from north to south mirrors earlier enemy campaigns. The cities in this section mark out the ideal land of Israel. King David incorporated many of these cities into his empire, and some paid him tribute. They existed during Zechariah's time but did not threaten Judah. Hence, Zechariah draws on Israel's past to portray the future. In addition, Jeremiah prophesied the downfall of many of these cities before restoration would take place (e.g., Jer 25).
9:1 land of Hadrak. Not mentioned elsewhere in the OT. Probably a "land" that relates to the city of Hatarikka (known from Assyrian sources); a region that borders Damascus, the capital of Syria (Aram). David subdued Damascus, and they paid him tribute (2 Sam 8:6).
9:2 Hamath. Hostile to Israel until David subdued it (2 Sam 8:9–10). **Tyre and Sidon.** Trade ports that possessed great wealth and security (v. 3). The king of Tyre helped build palaces for David and Solomon (2 Sam 5:11; 1 Kgs 9:11). God will judge all these cities in the northern regions (cf. 6:1–8).
9:5–7 Moving south, God mentions four cities associated with the Philistines. They defined the borders of the territory of Judah (Josh 15:11,45–46), but Israel did not subdue them until David's time (2 Sam 5:17–25; 21:15–22). God will subdue them once again and remove what is unclean (v. 7). God will incorporate "those who are left" (v. 7) into his people, just like the Jebusites who inhabited Jerusalem before David captured it were absorbed into Judah (2 Sam 5:6–9; 24:18–24). Hence, Zechariah envisages God judging and saving the nations (cf. 8:22–23).
9:8 God will return to "encamp" at his "temple" to protect his people (cf. 7:14). This also brings David to mind since it was only in his time when God "camped" in his house (the tabernacle tent) in Jerusalem.
9:9–13 *The Coming of Zion's King.* Along with Israel's enemies being subdued and God returning to his temple, Jerusalem's king will come.
9:9 Rejoice greatly ... Shout. Cf. 2:10; Zeph 3:14. **Daughter Zion ... Daughter Jerusalem.** Inhabitants of Jerusalem. The Davidic king whom the earlier prophets expected will come (cf. 3:8; 6:12). Unlike many kings of the past, this king will be "righteous" (cf. Jer 23:5). **victorious.** The Hebrew can also be translated "saved" (cf. Ps 33:16–17). **lowly.** Or "afflicted" (cf. Isa 53:4,7). The background to this picture is the suffering David of 2 Samuel and the Psalms, along with the suffering servant of

9:10 [j] Hos 1:7; 2:18; Mic 4:3; 5:10; Zec 10:4 [k] Ps 72:8
9:11 [l] Ex 24:8 [m] Isa 42:7
9:12 [n] Joel 3:16
9:13 [o] Isa 49:2 [p] Joel 3:6 [q] Jer 51:20
9:14 [r] Isa 31:5 [s] Ps 18:14; Hab 3:11 [t] Isa 21:1; 66:15
9:15 [u] Isa 37:35; Zec 12:8 [v] Ex 27:2
9:16 [w] Isa 62:3; Jer 31:11

10 I will take away the chariots from Ephraim
and the warhorses from Jerusalem,
and the battle bow will be broken.[j]
He will proclaim peace to the nations.
His rule will extend from sea to sea
and from the River[a] to the ends of the earth.[k]
11 As for you, because of the blood of my covenant[l] with you,
I will free your prisoners[m] from the waterless pit.
12 Return to your fortress,[n] you prisoners of hope;
even now I announce that I will restore twice as much to you.
13 I will bend Judah as I bend my bow
and fill it with Ephraim.[o]
I will rouse your sons, Zion,
against your sons, Greece,[p]
and make you like a warrior's sword.[q]

The LORD Will Appear

14 Then the LORD will appear over them;[r]
his arrow will flash like lightning.[s]
The Sovereign LORD will sound the trumpet;
he will march in the storms[t] of the south,
15 and the LORD Almighty will shield[u] them.
They will destroy
and overcome with slingstones.
They will drink and roar as with wine;
they will be full like a bowl
used for sprinkling[b] the corners[v] of the altar.
16 The LORD their God will save his people on that day
as a shepherd saves his flock.
They will sparkle in his land
like jewels in a crown.[w]
17 How attractive and beautiful they will be!
Grain will make the young men thrive,
and new wine the young women.

[a] *10* That is, the Euphrates [b] *15* Or *bowl, / like*

Isaiah. **riding on a donkey.** During David's exile from Jerusalem, when he was nearly defeated by his enemies, he rode on a donkey (cf. 2 Sam 16:2). God saved David in battle and delivered him back to Jerusalem as king. Isaiah's suffering servant is "afflicted" not for his own sins (like David) but for the sins of others (Isa 53). Zechariah combines the images here to speak of the future Messiah who will return to Jerusalem on a donkey and "proclaim peace to the nations" (v. 10; cf. the "harmony" of 6:13). (The forgiveness of sin associated with Isaiah's servant is the focus of Zech 12:10—13:1; cf. 3:9.) The king's rule will extend over all the earth (v. 10; cf. Gen 49:10–11; Ps 72:8). All four Gospels record that Jesus rode a donkey into Jerusalem claiming to be this king (Matt 21:1–11; Mark 11:1–11; Luke 19:28–38; John 12:12–19). His righteousness and his affliction as a servant to the point of death (Phil 2:6–11) meant that God "saved" him in his resurrection, and now through his gospel he proclaims "peace to the nations" (v. 10; cf. Eph 2:14–18; Col 1:20).

9:11 blood of my covenant. The Sinai covenant was ratified with blood, indicating God's commitment to his people (cf. Exod 24:8; Matt 26:28). Like Joseph (Gen 37:24) and Jeremiah (Jer 38:6), the "prisoners" (exiles) will be set "free … from the waterless pit" (an image of exile).

9:12 fortress. Jerusalem. They are to return to Jerusalem with hope for a double restoration (cf. 2:6–7).

9:13 Greece. The Philistines had sold the people of Jerusalem and Judah to the Greeks (Joel 3:4–6). God will use Judah as his bow and Ephraim (the northern kingdom) as his arrow. This image points to a reunited kingdom (cf. 9:1; 10:6–7).

9:14–17 *The Lord Will Appear.* God will fight for, save, and bless his people.

9:14–15 Like God's salvation in the exodus (Exod 15:1–21) and his appearance at Sinai with "lightning" and "trumpet" (Exod 19:16), God will appear to save his people. He will come as an army on the "march" with "arrow" and "trumpet" (v. 14; cf. 6:1–8; 9:1–8). He will "shield" (v. 15), or protect, his people, who "will destroy and overcome with slingstones" (v. 15) as did David (cf. 12:8; 1 Sam 17). The battle will sound like the "roar" (v. 15) of those drunk with wine, and its sight will be like blood at a sacrifice.

9:16–17 Shepherd imagery is prominent in chs. 10–13.

9:16 jewels in a crown. Cf. the "treasured possession" of Exod 19:5; Mal 3:17.

9:17 Grain … new wine. Agricultural abundance is a covenant blessing (Deut 33:28; Joel 2:19; Amos 9:13).

The LORD Will Care for Judah

10 Ask the LORD for rain in the springtime;
it is the LORD who sends the thunderstorms.
He gives showers of rain to all people,
and plants of the field to everyone.
2 The idols[x] speak deceitfully,
diviners see visions that lie;
they tell dreams that are false,
they give comfort in vain.
Therefore the people wander like sheep
oppressed for lack of a shepherd.[y]

3 "My anger burns against the shepherds,
and I will punish the leaders;[z]
for the LORD Almighty will care
for his flock, the people of Judah,
and make them like a proud horse in battle.
4 From Judah will come the cornerstone,
from him the tent peg,[a]
from him the battle bow,[b]
from him every ruler.
5 Together they[a] will be like warriors in battle
trampling their enemy into the mud of the streets.[c]
They will fight because the LORD is with them,
and they will put the enemy horsemen to shame.[d]

6 "I will strengthen Judah
and save the tribes of Joseph.
I will restore them
because I have compassion on them.[e]
They will be as though
I had not rejected them,
for I am the LORD their God
and I will answer[f] them.
7 The Ephraimites will become like warriors,
and their hearts will be glad as with wine.[g]

10:2 [x] Eze 21:21 [y] Eze 34:5; Hos 3:4; Mt 9:36
10:3 [z] Jer 25:34
10:4 [a] Isa 22:23 [b] Zec 9:10
10:5 [c] 2Sa 22:43 [d] Am 2:15; Hag 2:22
10:6 [e] Zec 8:7-8 [f] Zec 13:9
10:7 [g] Zec 9:15

[a] *4,5* Or *ruler, all of them together. / [5]They*

10:1 — 11:3 *The Lord Will Care for Judah.* In view of God's future coming (ch. 9), this section deals with the present leadership of God's oppressed people (10:1–2). God will raise up a new leadership who will overthrow the enemies of his people and save and restore them (10:3–12). Foreign leaders will be judged (11:1–3). It is another perspective on the battle of ch. 9.

10:1 Ask the LORD for rain. Yahweh, not the false gods, controls the weather. **springtime.** The season of rain, crucial for crops and survival. In times of drought (cf. Hag 1:10–11), the temptation would be to turn to "idols" and "diviners" (v. 2) to predict the future (which Deut 5:8–9; 18:9–14 forbids), but these deceive. Following them is what led to exile and removal of the kings of Israel and Judah.

10:2 shepherd. Metaphor for a leader, particularly a king (e.g., Ps 78:70–72). Without a king, "the people wander like sheep oppressed" (cf. Isa 53:6; Jer 50:6–7; Ezek 34:5). Hence, the importance of godly leaders (cf. 1 Tim 3:1–13; 1 Pet 5:1–6).

10:3 God is coming to judge the present rulers of his people, probably foreign rulers since the people lacked a shepherd of their own (v. 2). **leaders.** Elsewhere this word can refer to foreign kings (e.g., Isa 14:9; Ezek 39:18). They are likely the same rulers destroyed in 11:1–3. **the LORD Almighty.** See note on 1:3. **will care for his flock.** Cf. 9:16. They will no longer be like sheep but will be "like a proud horse in battle."

10:4–5 God will raise up an alternative leadership for his people.

10:4 From Judah. Or "from the LORD" (the Hebrew is simply "from him"). God will send these leaders. **cornerstone ... tent peg ... battle bow.** Leadership metaphors conveying strength and stability.

10:5 the LORD is with them. Ensures the certainty of victory (cf. 9:14–16).

10:6 With a new leadership, God will "strengthen Judah" and "save the tribes of Joseph" (the southern and northern houses of Israel). In his "compassion" he will "restore" their covenant relationship and answer his people's prayers (cf. 7:13; 13:9).

10:7 Ephraimites. Another name for the northern house of Israel (cf. "Ephraim" in 9:13 and "tribes of Joseph" in v. 6). God is committed to strengthen and save all his people (cf. "all the tribes of Israel" in 9:1), which will result in "joyful" celebration (cf. 9:9).

10:8 [h]Isa 5:26 [i]Jer 33:22; Eze 36:11
10:9 [j]Eze 6:9
10:10 [k]Isa 11:11 [l]Jer 50:19 [m]Isa 49:19
10:11 [n]Isa 19:5-7; 51:10 [o]Zep 2:13 [p]Eze 30:13
10:12 [q]Mic 4:5
11:1 [r]Eze 31:3
11:2 [s]Isa 32:19
11:3 [t]Jer 2:15; 50:44

Their children will see it and be joyful;
their hearts will rejoice in the LORD.
8 I will signal[h] for them
and gather them in.
Surely I will redeem them;
they will be as numerous[i] as before.
9 Though I scatter them among the peoples,
yet in distant lands they will remember me.[j]
They and their children will survive,
and they will return.
10 I will bring them back from Egypt
and gather them from Assyria.[k]
I will bring them to Gilead[l] and Lebanon,
and there will not be room[m] enough for them.
11 They will pass through the sea of trouble;
the surging sea will be subdued
and all the depths of the Nile will dry up.[n]
Assyria's pride[o] will be brought down
and Egypt's scepter[p] will pass away.
12 I will strengthen them in the LORD
and in his name they will live securely,[q]"
declares the LORD.

11 Open your doors, Lebanon,[r]
so that fire may devour your cedars!
2 Wail, you juniper, for the cedar has fallen;
the stately trees are ruined!
Wail, oaks of Bashan;
the dense forest[s] has been cut down!
3 Listen to the wail of the shepherds;
their rich pastures are destroyed!
Listen to the roar of the lions;
the lush thicket of the Jordan is ruined![t]

Two Shepherds

4 This is what the LORD my God says: "Shepherd the flock marked for slaughter. 5 Their buyers slaughter them and go unpunished. Those who sell them say, 'Praise the LORD, I am rich!' Their own shepherds

10:8–12 This passage echoes Moses' prophecy in Deut 30:1–10. God will "gather" (v. 8) his people from the nations, pictured as a new exodus. God will "redeem them" (v. 8; cf. Deut 7:8), and "they will be as numerous as before" (v. 8; cf. Deut 30:5; Jer 23:3; Ezek 36:11). God scattered them (or, "sowed" them like seeds) in exile, where they grew (having "children," v. 9). In exile, God's people "will remember" him (v. 9; cf. Deut 30:2), and God will bring them back from Egypt and Assyria, traditional enemies of God's people and countries to which the Ephraimites had been exiled. **Gilead.** In the Transjordan region; the territory through which Moses first approached the promised land from Egypt (Deut 3:10,12–13,15). **Lebanon.** The northernmost extent of the promised land from which Assyrian exiles would return. The people will fill these lands, which historically had been relatively empty. The exodus imagery continues as they will "pass through the sea" (v. 11)—this time through "the Nile" (v. 11) rather than the Red Sea. God promises to humble the proud and powerful nations (cf. Deut 30:7) and "strengthen" (v. 12) his people.

11:1–3 Kings are often portrayed as mighty trees (e.g., 2 Kgs 14:9; Dan 4:10–27). In this taunt song, foreign kings—"cedars" (v. 1), "juniper" (v. 2), "oaks" (v. 2)—are cut down and devoured by fire so that God's people might return to the land, just as ch. 10 portrays. "Lebanon" (v. 1; 10:10) and "Bashan" (v. 2) epitomize pride (e.g., Isa 2:12–13), and here their kings are the objects of God's wrath. Mixing metaphors, the "shepherds" (v. 3) of the foreign nations are like "lions" (v. 3) that ravage and feed on God's people (cf. Jer 25:36). They will "wail" and "roar" (v. 3) as God saves and takes away their resources, namely, God's people.

11:4–17 *Two Shepherds.* God tells Zechariah to perform two sign-actions that represent two very different shepherds (vv. 4–14; 15–17). These sign-actions explain why foreign shepherds currently rule and oppress God's people (cf. v. 3).

11:4–6 The first sign-action looks backward as Zechariah portrays what led to the Babylonian exile. He does so by playing the role of a "shepherd" who represents God. **flock.** The nation of Israel (cf. Jer 12:3). **marked for slaughter.** The experience of exile because "their own shepherds" (v. 5), i.e., leaders, failed (cf. 10:2). Rather than feeding and protecting the flock, the leaders used the flock for their own gain

do not spare them.[u] 6For I will no longer have pity on the people of the land," declares the LORD. "I will
give everyone into the hands of their neighbors[v] and their king. They will devastate the land, and I will
not rescue anyone from their hands."[w]
7So I shepherded the flock marked for slaughter, particularly the oppressed of the flock. Then I took
two staffs and called one Favor and the other Union, and I shepherded the flock. 8In one month I got
rid of the three shepherds.
The flock detested me, and I grew weary of them 9and said, "I will not be your shepherd. Let the dying
die, and the perishing perish.[x] Let those who are left eat one another's flesh."
10Then I took my staff called Favor[y] and broke it, revoking[z] the covenant I had made with all the
nations. 11It was revoked on that day, and so the oppressed of the flock who were watching me knew it
was the word of the LORD.
12I told them, "If you think it best, give me my pay; but if not, keep it." So they paid me thirty pieces
of silver.[a]
13And the LORD said to me, "Throw it to the potter"—the handsome price at which they valued me!
So I took the thirty pieces of silver and threw them to the potter at the house of the LORD.[b]
14Then I broke my second staff called Union, breaking the family bond between Judah and Israel.
15Then the LORD said to me, "Take again the equipment of a foolish shepherd. 16For I am going to
raise up a shepherd over the land who will not care for the lost, or seek the young, or heal the injured,
or feed the healthy, but will eat the meat of the choice sheep, tearing off their hooves.

17"Woe to the worthless shepherd,[c]
who deserts the flock!
May the sword strike his arm[d] and his right eye!
May his arm be completely withered,
his right eye totally blinded!"[e]

Jerusalem's Enemies to Be Destroyed

12 A prophecy: The word of the LORD concerning Israel.

The LORD, who stretches out the heavens,[f] who lays the foundation of the earth,[g] and who forms
the human spirit within a person,[h] declares: 2"I am going to make Jerusalem a cup[i] that sends all the

11:5 [u] Jer 50:7; Eze 34:2-3
11:6 [v] Zec 14:13 [w] Isa 9:19-21; Jer 13:14; Mic 5:8; 7:2-6
11:9 [x] Jer 15:2; 43:11
11:10 [y] ver 7 [z] Ps 89:39; Jer 14:21
11:12 [a] Ex 21:32; Mt 26:15
11:13 [b] Mt 27:9-10*; Ac 1:18-19
11:17 [c] Jer 23:1 [d] Eze 30:21-22 [e] Jer 23:1
12:1 [f] Isa 42:5; Jer 51:15 [g] Ps 102:25; Heb 1:10 [h] Isa 57:16
12:2 [i] Ps 75:8

by buying and selling them and then mocking God, saying, "Praise the LORD, I am rich!" (v. 5). Cf. Jer 23:1–2; Ezek 34. God's patience finally ran out; he would "no longer have pity" (v. 6) but would hand them over to their enemies. The judgment of v. 6 came with the Babylonian king Nebuchadnezzar in 586 BC.

11:7–9 Acting this out, Zechariah takes up two shepherd staffs. Verses 10 and 14 explain the names "Favor" and "Union."

11:8 one month. When Jerusalem fell (see Jer 52:6,12) and its leadership was exiled or killed. **three shepherds.** Probably king, priest, and prophet (Jer 52:10,15,24–27). The people "detested" God, whose patience ran thin ("grew weary"), so he ceased shepherding his people and handed them over to the destruction of exile.

11:9 eat one another's flesh. Cannibalism occurred during the siege of Jerusalem (cf. Deut. 28:53; Jer 19:9; Lam 2:20; 4:10).

11:10–11 Zechariah breaks the first staff, called "Favor," which represents "the covenant [God] had made with all the nations" (the Hebrew is "all the peoples," where "peoples" may refer to the whole nation of Israel [cf. Isa 3:13; Mic 1:1–2], hence the Mosaic covenant). The judgment of exile for rejecting God was a curse of the Mosaic covenant (e.g., Deut 28:36,45–68). **knew it was the word of the LORD.** In Deuteronomy (28:36,63–64), God promises exile if his people reject him, a message the earlier prophets reiterate.

11:12–13 thirty pieces of silver. The price of a slave in Exod 21:32. This payoff is an insult that utterly rejects God as shepherd. Zechariah throws the money to the potter in the temple, the place of idolatrous worship that earlier prophets condemn (e.g., Ezek 8–11). Matthew sees this same scenario of rejecting God played out again when Judas betrays Jesus, the Good Shepherd, for 30 pieces of silver (Matt 26:14–15; 27:9–10). See note on 13:7.

11:14 broke. Represents dividing the kingdom into Israel under Jeroboam and Judah under Rehoboam (cf. 1 Kgs 12). Elsewhere, Zechariah promises reunion (e.g., 10:6–7; 12:12–14; cf. Ezek 37:15–28). This first sign-action explains that the division of the kingdom and the exile came about because the people rejected the Lord as their Shepherd.

11:15–17 The second sign-action explains how the people received the leadership they deserved. Zechariah acts as a "foolish shepherd" who oppresses and devours the flock. **eat the meat of the choice sheep, tearing off their hooves.** Like a lion; the "foolish shepherd" represents foreign kings who presently oppress and feed off God's people (cf. v. 3). Yet the last word judges this "worthless shepherd" (v. 17). This connects back to vv. 1–3 and 10:3, which also look forward to the destruction of foreign shepherds. In stark contrast, Jesus is the Good Shepherd who rescues and reunites the flock by laying down his life (John 10:11–18; Rev 7:17).

12:1—14:21 *Second Prophetic Message.* A second prophecy (cf. 9:1; see note on 9:1—11:17) reveals that God's kingdom will not come without great cost. There will be another exile-like experience for Jerusalem, but its outcome will be glorious. The phrase "on that day" runs through this section and refers to the day when God will establish his kingdom on earth in glory. In the NT, this "day" is expanded to encompass both the first and second comings of Jesus.

12:2 [j] Isa 51:23 [k] Zec 14:14
12:3 [l] Zec 14:2 [m] Da 2:34-35 [n] Mt 21:44
12:4 [o] Ps 76:6
12:6 [p] Isa 10:17-18; Zec 11:1 [q] Ob 18
12:7 [r] Jer 30:18; Am 9:11
12:8 [s] Joel 3:16; Zec 9:15 [t] Ps 82:6 [u] Mic 7:8
12:9 [v] Zec 14:2-3
12:10 [w] Isa 44:3; Eze 39:29; Joel 2:28-29 [x] Jn 19:34,37*; Rev 1:7
12:11 [y] 2Ki 23:29
12:12 [z] Mt 24:30; Rev 1:7

surrounding peoples reeling.[j] Judah[k] will be besieged as well as Jerusalem. [3]On that day, when all the
nations[l] of the earth are gathered against her, I will make Jerusalem an immovable rock[m] for all the
nations. All who try to move it will injure[n] themselves. [4]On that day I will strike every horse with panic
and its rider with madness," declares the LORD. "I will keep a watchful eye over Judah, but I will blind
all the horses of the nations.[o] [5]Then the clans of Judah will say in their hearts, 'The people of Jerusalem
are strong, because the LORD Almighty is their God.'

[6]"On that day I will make the clans of Judah like a firepot[p] in a woodpile, like a flaming torch
among sheaves. They will consume[q] all the surrounding peoples right and left, but Jerusalem will
remain intact in her place.

[7]"The LORD will save the dwellings of Judah first, so that the honor of the house of David and of Jerusalem's inhabitants may not be greater than that of Judah.[r] [8]On that day the LORD will shield[s] those
who live in Jerusalem, so that the feeblest among them will be like David, and the house of David will
be like God,[t] like the angel of the LORD going before[u] them. [9]On that day I will set out to destroy all the
nations that attack Jerusalem.[v]

Mourning for the One They Pierced

[10]"And I will pour out on the house of David and the inhabitants of Jerusalem a spirit[a] of grace and
supplication.[w] They will look on[b] me, the one they have pierced,[x] and they will mourn for him as one
mourns for an only child, and grieve bitterly for him as one grieves for a firstborn son. [11]On that day the
weeping in Jerusalem will be as great as the weeping of Hadad Rimmon in the plain of Megiddo.[y] [12]The
land will mourn,[z] each clan by itself, with their wives by themselves: the clan of the house of David and
their wives, the clan of the house of Nathan and their wives, [13]the clan of the house of Levi and their
wives, the clan of Shimei and their wives, [14]and all the rest of the clans and their wives.

[a] *10* Or *the Spirit* [b] *10* Or *to*

12:1–9 *Jerusalem's Enemies to Be Destroyed.* Zechariah prophesies a future offensive by the nations against Jerusalem. God promises to save and strengthen his people.
12:1 God's work in creation demonstrates his power and dominion over all nations of the earth (cf. 14:9).
12:2–4 The Hebrew allows for the possibility that Judah (the region around Jerusalem) was initially also opposed to Jerusalem (see also 14:14). When Jerusalem is "besieged" (v. 2), God will repel the nations who attack: He will "make Jerusalem a cup that sends all the surrounding peoples reeling" (v. 2) as if drunk; Jerusalem will be "an immovable rock" (v. 3) that injures all those "who try to move it" (v. 3); and "the horses of the nations" (v. 4; used in warfare) will be put out of action, thwarting their attack. Yet God promises to "keep a watchful eye over Judah" (v. 4), who was initially caught up with the nations in this attack.
12:5–6 When the "clans of Judah" (v. 5) see God protecting them and defending Jerusalem, they have a change of heart and turn against the surrounding peoples and "consume" them (v. 6). The outcome is that "Jerusalem will remain intact in her place" (v. 6); it will be saved (cf. 9:9,16; 10:6).
12:7–9 This day of salvation will be glorious for Jerusalem and the house of David. So that the "dwellings of Judah" (v. 7) do not miss out on this honor, they are saved "first" (v. 7).
12:8 like David. Who defeated the mighty Goliath and the Philistines in God's strength. **the angel of the LORD.** Cf. 1:11; see note on 1:11–12. The angel of the Lord led and protected God's people on many occasions, particularly in the exodus (Exod 13:21; 14:19; 33:2). David was likened to an "angel of God," enabling him to lead his people (2 Sam 14:17,20; 19:27). Hence, the house of David will once again lead and protect God's people like God himself (cf. 9:9). The promises of the Davidic covenant, including an eternal throne (2 Sam 7:13,16; cf. 23:5), explain the focus on the house of David here.
12:9 destroy all the nations that attack Jerusalem. Summarizes vv. 1–9. The day when the nations and the people of Israel gathered against Jerusalem (represented by God and his anointed king in Ps 2) was when God's holy servant Jesus, the Messiah, was crucified (Acts 4:24–28; notice how they conspire "in this city," i.e., Jerusalem). This was the day of salvation for God's people.
12:10–14 *Mourning for the One They Pierced.* In the aftermath of this battle, the people will mourn and grieve the one they have pierced.
12:10 a spirit of grace. The Spirit (see NIV text note; cf. Isa 44:3–5; Ezek 39:29; Joel 2:28–29). **supplication.** Prayer for mercy; a sign of repentance. **me … him … him.** Suggests that the people "pierced" God (metaphorically) and a closely associated third party (literally). The immediate and wider contexts of Zechariah suggest that this third party is the future king of the "house of David" (see 3:8; 6:12; 9:9), the shepherd of 13:7–9. **pierced.** Piercing with a weapon normally meant death (cf. Isa 13:15). The close connection between God and his anointed (cf. Ps 45:6; Isa 9:6) explains how the death of the Messiah also "pierced" God. This prophecy gains even greater clarity for Christians who see its fulfillment in the piercing of Jesus on the cross by a Roman soldier's spear (John 19:34–37). After Jesus' death, God's Spirit was poured out on the God-fearing Jews in Jerusalem, who were "cut to the heart" and repented (Acts 2:32–37). At his return, all the nations will mourn the one who was pierced (Rev 1:7). **as one mourns for an only child.** Immense sorrow. **firstborn.** The heir.
12:11 weeping in Jerusalem. Cf. 2 Chr 35:20–25, where another Davidic king, Josiah, was pierced in a battle at Megiddo. **Hadad Rimmon.** Likely a place in the plain of Megiddo (otherwise unknown) rather than a reference to Baal, since a reference to pagan mourning is unlikely in this context.
12:12–14 The extent of the mourning suggests the one who died is royalty. **house of David … house of Levi.** The royal and priestly lines. **house of Nathan … clan of Shimei.** Likely subsidiary lines of David (2 Sam 5:14) and Levi (Num 3:21), respectively. **wives.** The whole community is involved.

Cleansing From Sin

13 "On that day a fountain[a] will be opened to the house of David and the inhabitants of Jerusalem, to cleanse[b] them from sin and impurity.
2 "On that day, I will banish the names of the idols[c] from the land, and they will be remembered no
more," declares the LORD Almighty. "I will remove both the prophets[d] and the spirit of impurity from
the land. 3 And if anyone still prophesies, their father and mother, to whom they were born, will say to
them, 'You must die, because you have told lies in the LORD's name.' Then their own parents will stab
the one who prophesies.[e]
4 "On that day every prophet will be ashamed[f] of their prophetic vision. They will not put on a prophet's garment[g] of hair[h] in order to deceive. 5 Each will say, 'I am not a prophet. I am a farmer; the land
has been my livelihood since my youth.[a]'[i] 6 If someone asks, 'What are these wounds on your body[b]?'
they will answer, 'The wounds I was given at the house of my friends.'

The Shepherd Struck, the Sheep Scattered

7 "Awake, sword,[j] against my shepherd,[k]
against the man who is close to me!"
declares the LORD Almighty.
"Strike the shepherd,
and the sheep will be scattered,[l]
and I will turn my hand against the little ones.
8 In the whole land," declares the LORD,
"two-thirds will be struck down and perish;
yet one-third will be left in it.[m]

[a] 5 Or *farmer; a man sold me in my youth* [b] 6 Or *wounds between your hands*

13:1 [a] Jer 17:13 [b] Ps 51:2; Heb 9:14
13:2 [c] Ex 23:13; Eze 36:25; Hos 2:17 [d] 1Ki 22:22; Jer 23:14-15
13:3 [e] Dt 13:6-11; 18:20; Jer 23:34; Eze 14:9
13:4 [f] Jer 6:15; Mic 3:6-7 [g] Mt 3:4 [h] 2Ki 1:8; Isa 20:2
13:5 [i] Am 7:14
13:7 [j] Jer 47:6 [k] Isa 40:11; 53:4; Eze 37:24 [l] Mt 26:31*; Mk 14:27*
13:8 [m] Eze 5:2-4,12

13:1–6 *Cleansing From Sin.* Mourning and grief give way to cleansing God's people "from sin and impurity" (v. 1) and removing impurity from the land (vv. 2–6).

13:1 Water was used for cleansing in the Torah (e.g., Num 8:5–14). **fountain.** Suggests an abundant and ongoing supply. The sequence implies that cleansing "from sin and impurity" follows the death of the Messiah and the pouring out of the Spirit (12:10–11; cf. 3:8–9). The NT shows how this is at the heart of the gospel message about Jesus (e.g., Titus 3:4–7).

13:2–6 Idols and the powers attributed to them are to be "banished" (v. 2), i.e., eliminated. Idolatry and false prophecy are often associated (e.g., Jer 6:13–14). They were the chief sins that led to the exile, and their seriousness is underscored by the penalty: Even "parents will stab" their children if they prophesy (v. 3; cf. Deut 13:6–11). The Hebrew for "stab" (v. 3) is the same as the verb for "pierced" in 12:10. False prophets will be "ashamed" (v. 4) and eschew their past. They will no longer dress in pretense (cf. 2 Kgs 1:8) but will pretend to have always been a "farmer" (v. 5). They will explain in another way the "wounds" (v. 6) they may have received from their false prophetic activity (cf. 1 Kgs 18:28). Idolatry, false prophecy, and impurity have no place in God's kingdom, and hence no place in the church (e.g., Eph 5:5–6; Rev 2:14–16,20–23).

13:7–9 *The Shepherd Struck, the Sheep Scattered.* Judgment lies ahead for God's people with the shepherd struck, but it will refine and renew those who emerge.

13:7 Awake, sword. God charges a sword to be drawn and strike his "shepherd ... the man who is close to me." Indicates a close relationship with God, hence a different shepherd from the "foolish" and "worthless shepherd" of 11:15–17. Striking the shepherd will result in scattering "the sheep," including "the little ones" coming under God's judgment. The wider expectation of the book of Zechariah suggests this shepherd is the future Davidic king who will be pierced in the battle that will usher in God's kingdom (3:8; 6:12; 9:9; 12:10). His death will be God's intent and design. There are many similarities with Isaiah's presentation of the suffering servant, who suffers death on behalf of God's people by God's intent (cf. Isa 53:6,10). Jesus quotes this verse with reference to his own imminent death (Matt 26:31; Mark 14:27), which will establish the new covenant, an idea also present in 13:9.

13:8–9 The extent of this judgment "in the whole land" (v. 8) will be devastating: "Two-thirds [of the flock] will be struck down and perish" (v. 8). The "third" (v. 9) that remains will be refined and tested in "fire ... like silver and ... gold" (v. 9; cf. Isa 1:24–26).

QUOTATIONS OF ZECHARIAH IN THE GOSPELS

ZECH PASSAGE	SUMMARY OF CONTENT	NT PASSAGES
9:9	The king comes to Jerusalem riding on a donkey	Matt 21:5; John 12:15
11:12–13	God insultingly paid off for 30 pieces of silver	Matt 27:9–10
12:10	Mourning for the One they pierced	John 19:37
13:7	The shepherd struck, the sheep scattered	Matt 26:31; Mark 14:27

13:9 [n]Mal 3:2 [o]Isa 48:10; 1Pe 1:6-7 [p]Ps 50:15 [q]Zec 10:6 [r]Jer 30:22 [s]Jer 29:12
14:1 [t]Isa 13:9; Mal 4:1
14:2 [u]Isa 13:6; Zec 13:8
14:3 [v]Zec 9:14-15
14:4 [w]Eze 11:23
14:5 [x]Am 1:1 [y]Isa 29:6; 66:15-16 [z]Mt 16:27; 25:31
14:6 [a]Isa 13:10; Jer 4:23
14:7 [b]Jer 30:7 [c]Rev 21:23-25; 22:5 [d]Isa 30:26
14:8 [e]Eze 47:1-12; Jn 7:38; Rev 22:1-2 [f]Joel 2:20
14:9 [g]Dt 6:4; Isa 45:24; Rev 11:15 [h]Eph 4:5-6
14:10 [i]1Ki 15:22 [j]Jer 30:18; Am 9:11 [k]Zec 12:6
14:11 [l]Eze 34:25-28

9 This third I will put into the fire;[n]
  I will refine them like silver[o]
  and test them like gold.
They will call[p] on my name
  and I will answer[q] them;
I will say, 'They are my people,'[r]
  and they will say, 'The LORD is our God.[s]' "

The LORD Comes and Reigns

14 A day of the LORD[t] is coming, Jerusalem, when your possessions will be plundered and divided
up within your very walls.
2 I will gather all the nations to Jerusalem to fight against it; the city will be captured, the houses ransacked, and the women raped. Half of the city will go into exile, but the rest of the people will not be taken
from the city.[u] 3 Then the LORD will go out and fight[v] against those nations, as he fights on a day of battle. 4 On
that day his feet will stand on the Mount of Olives,[w] east of Jerusalem, and the Mount of Olives will be split in
two from east to west, forming a great valley, with half of the mountain moving north and half moving south.
5 You will flee by my mountain valley, for it will extend to Azel. You will flee as you fled from the earthquake[a][x]
in the days of Uzziah king of Judah. Then the LORD my God will come,[y] and all the holy ones with him.[z]
6 On that day there will be neither sunlight[a] nor cold, frosty darkness. 7 It will be a unique[b] day — a
day known only to the LORD — with no distinction between day and night.[c] When evening comes, there
will be light.[d]
8 On that day living water[e] will flow out from Jerusalem, half of it east[f] to the Dead Sea and half of
it west to the Mediterranean Sea, in summer and in winter.
9 The LORD will be king over the whole earth.[g] On that day there will be one LORD, and his name the
only name.[h]
10 The whole land, from Geba[i] to Rimmon, south of Jerusalem, will become like the Arabah. But
Jerusalem will be raised up[j] high from the Benjamin Gate to the site of the First Gate, to the Corner
Gate, and from the Tower of Hananel to the royal winepresses, and will remain in its place.[k] 11 It will be
inhabited; never again will it be destroyed. Jerusalem will be secure.[l]
12 This is the plague with which the LORD will strike all the nations that fought against Jerusalem: Their

[a] 5 Or [5] *My mountain valley will be blocked and will extend to Azel. It will be blocked as it was blocked because of the earthquake*

13:9 They are my people ... The LORD is our God. Those who emerge will enjoy a new covenant relationship with God, including answered prayer (cf. 2:11; 8:8; 9:16; 10:6; Jer 31:33).

14:1–21 *The Lord Comes and Reigns.* God will return to his people to save them from their enemies and bring in a new creation. Zechariah uses well-known images from Israel's past and present to picture God's future kingdom. The NT applies the language and images in this chapter to both the first and second comings of Jesus. Hence there is a "now and not yet" perspective on the fulfillment of this chapter. The kingdom has come with Jesus' death and resurrection and will come at his return.

14:1–2 This gives another perspective on the future battle of 12:2–9, revealing great devastation to Jerusalem's inhabitants (cf. Ezek 38–39). This picture replays the past when they were "plundered" (v. 1) by the nations and taken into "exile" (v. 2; cf. 2 Kgs 25).

14:3 fight. Cf. 12:2–9. God's salvation will shake the heavens and the earth (cf. Hag 2:21–22).

14:4 forming a great valley. Through which God's people will flee to escape. This echoes the exodus-salvation of the parting of the Red Sea (Exod 14:21–22).

14:5 Azel. Location unknown. **earthquake in the days of Uzziah.** Occurred over 200 years earlier and left a lasting impression (Amos 1:1). **holy ones.** Could be angels or the people who are saved and now return to Jerusalem (cf. 1 Thess 3:13; Jude 14). According to Matt 27:51–54, when Jesus died on the cross, "the earth shook, the rocks split" in an "earthquake" and "many holy people ... were raised to life ... and went into the holy city" (Jerusalem). Matthew connects these apocalyptic signs with the salvation that came in Jesus' death.

14:6–8 The language of these verses reflects the Genesis creation account (cf. 12:1). However, this will be a new creation with a single day of "light" (v. 7; cf. Isa 60:19–20; Rev 21:25; 22:5). "Darkness" (v. 6) precedes the "light" (v. 7) and is also associated with Jesus' death (Matt 27:45; cf. Joel 2:31; Amos 8:9). Just as life-giving water flowed from Eden (Gen 2:10), this day will bring a new supply of "living water" (v. 8) to the world from Jerusalem (cf. Ps 36:8–9; Ezek 47:1–12; Joel 3:18). Jesus gives this "living water" (John 4:10; see Rev 21:6; 22:17), which is also a feature of the new Jerusalem (Rev 22:1–2).

14:9 king over the whole earth. The climax of Zechariah's vision of the future. Since the names of the idols will be banished (cf. 13:2), God's "name" will be "the only name," expressing his uniqueness (cf. 13:9; Deut 6:4). This reality will be finally experienced at Jesus' return, when he hands the kingdom to his Father (1 Cor 15:23–28).

14:10–11 Geba ... Rimmon. The northern and southern boundaries of the land of Judah, respectively. **Arabah.** A desert plain to the south of the Dead Sea. Hence, the land will be flattened, and "Jerusalem will be raised up high" (v. 10; cf. Isa 2:1–4; Ezek 40:1–2; Mic 4:1–5). The city "will be inhabited" (v. 11; cf. 1:17; 2:4) and "secure" (v. 11; cf. 2:5; Ps 46:5).

14:12–13 God will defeat the nations who fight against Jerusalem (cf. v. 2) by causing "plague" (v. 12) and "panic" (v. 13) to come on them

flesh will rot while they are still standing on their feet, their eyes will rot in their sockets, and their tongues
will rot in their mouths.[m] 13On that day people will be stricken by the LORD with great panic. They will seize
each other by the hand and attack one another.[n] 14Judah[o] too will fight at Jerusalem. The wealth of all
the surrounding nations will be collected[p] — great quantities of gold and silver and clothing. 15A similar
plague[q] will strike the horses and mules, the camels and donkeys, and all the animals in those camps.
16Then the survivors from all the nations that have attacked Jerusalem will go up year after year to
worship the King, the LORD Almighty, and to celebrate the Festival of Tabernacles.[r] 17If any of the peoples
of the earth do not go up to Jerusalem to worship the King, the LORD Almighty, they will have no rain.[s]
18If the Egyptian people do not go up and take part, they will have no rain. The LORD[a] will bring on
them the plague he inflicts on the nations that do not go up to celebrate the Festival of Tabernacles.[t]
19This will be the punishment of Egypt and the punishment of all the nations that do not go up to celebrate the Festival of Tabernacles.
20On that day HOLY TO THE LORD will be inscribed on the bells of the horses, and the cooking pots[u] in
the LORD's house will be like the sacred bowls[v] in front of the altar. 21Every pot in Jerusalem and Judah
will be holy[w] to the LORD Almighty, and all who come to sacrifice will take some of the pots and cook
in them. And on that day[x] there will no longer be a Canaanite[b][y] in the house of the LORD Almighty.[z]

14:12 [m] Lev 26:16; Dt 28:22
14:13 [n] Zec 11:6
14:14 [o] Zec 12:2 [p] Isa 23:18
14:15 [q] ver 12
14:16 [r] Isa 60:6-9
14:17 [s] Jer 14:4; Am 4:7
14:18 [t] ver 12
14:20 [u] Eze 46:20 [v] Zec 9:15
14:21 [w] Ro 14:6-7; 1Co 10:31 [x] Ne 8:10 [y] Zec 9:8 [z] Eze 44:9

[a] *18* Or *part, then the LORD* [b] *21* Or *merchant*

(cf. Rev 19:11–21). This recalls earlier military victories (cf. Exod 7–11; Judg 7:22; 1 Sam 5:9; 14:15–20).

14:14 Judah too will fight at Jerusalem. Reflects the circumstances in 12:2–5 (see notes on 12:2–4,5–6). **wealth.** Reverses the situation in 14:1 (cf. Hag 2:6–9; Rev 21:26).

14:15 A destroying "plague" (cf. v. 12) will strike the animals used in war (present in the "camps" of those who fight).

14:16 Including "all the nations" in worship mirrors the end of ch. 8 (see note on 8:23). **Festival of Tabernacles.** *Sukkôt*, a seven-day festival of joy and thanksgiving for the harvest and God's goodness. The tabernacles were a reminder of the tents the Israelites lived in when they came out of Egypt (cf. Lev 23:33–43). The festival is associated with the temple and includes the foreigner (Deut 16:13–15; 1 Kings 8:2,41–43,65). The reality to which this festival points is found in Christ, who has won an even greater salvation and blessings (Col 2:16–17).

14:17–19 The alternative for those who do not "worship the King" (v. 16) is "no rain" (vv. 17–18) and "plague" (v. 18) as "punishment" (v. 19; cf. vv. 12–15). A lack of rain would devastate the harvest and is a classic covenant curse (e.g., Deut 28:22–24). The "Egyptian people" (v. 18) are singled out, possibly because they were not so dependent on rain on account of the Nile or to indicate that this salvation will be a new exodus.

14:20–21 Zechariah finishes with a picture of the holiness that will result from God's presence among his people. **HOLY TO THE LORD.** Engraved on the gold plate attached to the turban of the high priest (Exod 28:36–38; see also "Holiness," p. 2676). The holiness that once belonged to the priesthood and the Lord's "house" (v. 20; the temple) will spread to all "Jerusalem and Judah" (see v. 21 and note), from "the bells of the horses" (v. 20) to "the cooking pots" (v. 20; cf. 2:12–13). Everything impure, including the idolatrous "Canaanite" (see v. 21 and note), will be removed from the land (cf. 3:9; 5:5–11; 13:1–6; Rev 21:27).

14:21 Canaanite. May also be translated "merchant" (see NIV text note). This verse may lie behind Jesus' cleansing of the temple (Matt 21:12–13; Mark 11:15–17; Luke 19:45–46; John 2:13–16). In John's vision of the new Jerusalem there is no temple (Rev 21:22), for all that the temple symbolized (God's presence and rule) will be realized in the city. This "Holy City, the new Jerusalem" (Rev 21:2) is the bride of the Lamb, the church.

THE PERSON AND WORK OF ZECHARIAH'S SHEPHERD-KING COMPARED WITH ISAIAH'S SERVANT

ZECHARIAH REF.	ISAIAH REF.	SIMILARITY
9:9	53:4,7	Lowly or afflicted (same Hebrew word)
9:10	42:1,4,6; 49:6	Blessing to the nations
9:11–12	42:7; 61:1	Release prisoners or captives
9:12; 10:8	49:5–6	Gather those scattered
10:2	53:6	People wander like sheep, gone astray
12:10	44:3–5	Spirit poured out
12:10	53:5	Pierced (different Hebrew word)
12:10; 13:7	53:3	Rejected
13:1	53:4–6	Death results in forgiveness
13:7	53:6,10	Suffers by the LORD's intent
13:7	53:4	Struck (same Hebrew word)
14:1	53:12	Results in spoil being divided

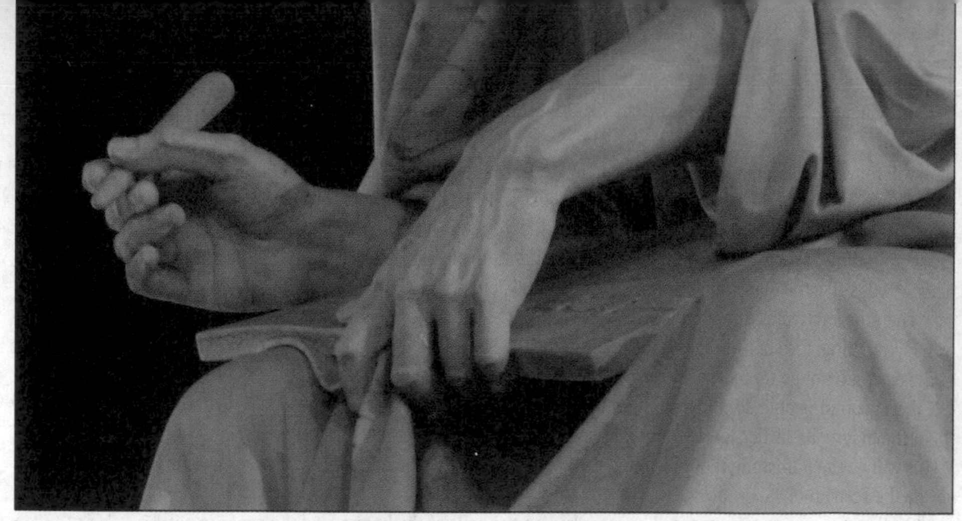

INTRODUCTION TO MALACHI

Malachi was a prophet and a preacher called to minister to a diverse crowd. His audience included doubters (1:2–3), cynics (1:7; 2:2), the cold-hearted (2:16), cheaters (3:5), the indifferent (3:14–15), faithful (3:16–18), and the openly wicked (4:1). What does God's prophet say to this flock? Malachi's message is a variation on an old prophetic theme: God's covenant love for Israel (1:2–3). As a stern prophet, he rebukes and warns priests and people alike of God's impending judgment (3:2–4,17–18; 4:1). As a compassionate pastor, he calls his audience to repentance and closes his sermon with words of encouragement and hope (2:10; 3:7; 4:1–3).

AUTHOR

The book is traditionally ascribed to a prophet named Malachi. His name means "my messenger," and the form is repeated in 3:1. Since both prophets and priests were messengers of the Lord (cf. 2:7), some regard the term "Malachi" to be a title rather than a proper name. The Greek translation of the OT supports this view, translating "his messenger" in 1:1. The grammatical construction of 1:1 ("the word of the LORD to Israel by the hand of Malachi") suggests that Malachi was the prophet's name. Either Malachi himself or his disciples or others associated with the guild of the prophets composed the book in Jerusalem. Malachi's audience included the leaders, priests, and people of postexilic Judah, essentially anyone within earshot.

DATE

Malachi includes no date formula linking the prophet's message to the reign of any particular king, unlike many other prophetic books (e.g., Hag 1:1; Zech 1:1). The book may be broadly dated between the completion of the second temple (516 or 515 BC) and the reforms of Ezra and Nehemiah (ca. 450–430 BC). Traditionally, the book of Malachi is dated between 450 and 430 BC. It is assumed that Malachi was a contemporary of Ezra and Nehemiah because he addressed the same religious concerns (e.g., a lax and corrupt priesthood, abuses in the sacrificial liturgy, neglect of the tithe) and social ills (e.g., mixed marriages, divorce, economic injustices) confronted by these two postexilic reformers. The Elephantine papyri (ca. 410–390 BC) portray a similar situation in terms of heterodoxy and marriage and divorce issues in the Jewish mercenary colony in Egypt.

The language of Malachi and the theological context of his message are similar to that of Haggai and Zechariah. Alternatively, it may be that Malachi was a later contemporary of these two prophets. His message may have been prompted by the titanic wars between the Persians and the Greeks, perhaps between 490 and 470 BC, in response to Haggai's forecast of God's overthrow of royal thrones (Hag 2:22).

OCCASION AND PURPOSE

The Jerusalem temple had been rebuilt at the encouragement of the prophets Haggai and Zechariah (Ezra 5:1–2; 6:14), but the corrupt worship offered there prompted God to raise up Malachi and call for its closure (1:10). The

SETTING OF MALACHI

Jerusalem
Dead Sea
Arnon R.
Beersheba
MOAB
Zoar
Zered R.
Tamar
Sela
Bozrah
Punon
Arabah
EDOM
Arabian Desert
Petra
Mount Seir
King's Highway
Ezion Geber
Gulf of Aqaba
0 20 km.
0 20 mi.

Nahal Zered from the north. Edom was Esau's inheritance (Mal 1:3).
Todd Bolen/www.BiblePlaces.com

prophet goads the lax priesthood and apathetic people to restore pure temple worship by turning to God in repentance (3:7). This redirection of community loyalty will renew temple worship, transform social relationships, and bring about the covenant blessings the people have looked for since their return from exile (3:14; cf. Hag 1:6).

GENRE AND STRUCTURE

Like Haggai and Zechariah, Malachi's sermons are broadly classified as prophetic literature. The setting and tone of the book is that of a courtroom. The discourse units are judgment or trial speeches since they accuse, indict, and pronounce God's verdict against his audience in confrontational dialogue. As God's spokesman, Malachi's disputations generally feature four elements: (1) Malachi declares a truth claim; (2) the audience hypothetically (or actually?) rebuts the claim in the form of a question; (3) Malachi answers the audience's rebuttal by restating his initial premise; and (4) Malachi presents additional supporting evidence.

THEOLOGY AND THEMES

The prophet reminds the people that God is a Covenant-maker who loves and has chosen Israel (1:2–3) and that he is a Father (1:6; 2:10) as well as Lord and King over the nations (1:6,14).

Malachi's message centers on the theme of Yahweh's covenants, specifically the covenants of Jacob (1:2; cf. Gen 12:1–3; 28:10–15), the covenant of Levi (2:4–5), the covenant of marriage (2:14), and the covenant of Moses (4:4).

OUTLINE

I. Superscription: Introducing the Prophet and His Message (1:1)

II. First Message: Israel Doubts God's Love (1:2–5)

III. Second Message (1:6—2:9)
- A. Breaking Covenant Through Blemished Sacrifices (1:6–14)
- B. Additional Warning to the Priests (2:1–9)

IV. Third Message: Breaking Covenant Through Divorce (2:10–16)

V. Fourth Message: Breaking Covenant Through Injustice (2:17—3:5)

VI. Fifth Message: Breaking Covenant by Withholding Tithes (3:6–12)

VII. Sixth Message: The Coming Day of Judgment (3:13 — 4:3)

- A. Israel Speaks Arrogantly Against God (3:13 – 15)
- B. The Faithful Remnant (3:16 – 18)
- C. Judgment and Covenant Renewal (4:1 – 3)

VIII. Conclusion: Remember the Law of Moses, Look for Elijah (4:4 – 6)

Alternate Outline:

The messages or disputations of Malachi may also be outlined rhetorically. The book demonstrates a chiasmic structure in which the emphases of the prophet's disputes with the priests and the people are arranged in an inverted mirror pattern.

Superscription: Introducing the Prophet and His Message (1:1)

- *a* First Disputation: God Declares His Covenant Love for Israel and Rejection of Esau (1:2 – 5)
  - *b* Second Disputation: Call to Restore Proper Sacrificial Worship in God's Temple (1:6 — 2:9)
    - *c* Third Disputation: Indictment of Faithless People for Injustice of Divorce (2:10 – 16)
    - *c´* Fourth Disputation: Indictment of Faithless People for Social Injustices (2:17 — 3:5)
  - *b´* Fifth Disputation: Call to Return to God and Restore the Tithe in Worship (3:6 – 12)
- *a´* Sixth Disputation: God Declares His Compassion for the Righteous and Judgment for the Wicked (3:13 — 4:3)

Conclusion (4:4 – 6)

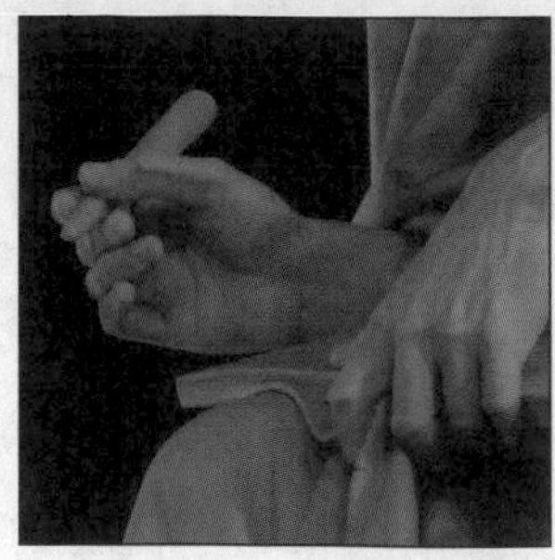

MALACHI

1:1 [a]Na 1:1 [b]1Pe 4:11
1:2 [c]Dt 4:37 [d]Ro 9:13*
1:3 [e]Isa 34:10 [f]Eze 35:3-9
1:4 [g]Isa 9:10 [h]Eze 25:12-14
1:5 [i]Ps 35:27; Mic 5:4 [j]Am 1:11-12
1:6 [k]Isa 1:2 [l]Job 5:17

1 A prophecy:[a] The word[b] of the LORD to Israel through Malachi.[a]

Israel Doubts God's Love

[2]"I have loved[c] you," says the LORD.

"But you ask, 'How have you loved us?'

"Was not Esau Jacob's brother?" declares the LORD. "Yet I have loved Jacob,[d] [3]but Esau I have hated, and I have turned his hill country into a wasteland[e] and left his inheritance to the desert jackals.[f]"

[4]Edom may say, "Though we have been crushed, we will rebuild[g] the ruins."

But this is what the LORD Almighty says: "They may build, but I will demolish. They will be called the Wicked Land, a people always under the wrath of the LORD.[h] [5]You will see it with your own eyes and say, 'Great[i] is the LORD—even beyond the borders of Israel!'[j]

Breaking Covenant Through Blemished Sacrifices

[6]"A son honors his father, and a slave his master. If I am a father, where is the honor due me? If I am a master, where is the respect[k] due me?" says the LORD Almighty.[l]

[a] *1 Malachi* means *my messenger.*

1:1 *Superscription: Introducing the Prophet and His Message.* The superscription classifies the book of Malachi as prophetic literature and revelation from God. It identifies the writer and the audience but does not mention the date and occasion of the messages.
1:1 prophecy. Can be rendered "oracle," and infuses Malachi's message with divine authority and urgency, a cue to the audience to listen and respond (cf. Nah 1:1; Hab 1:1; Zech 9:1; 12:1).
1:2–5 *First Message: Israel Doubts God's Love.* Malachi's first sermon presents the thesis for the entire book: the Lord loves Israel (v. 2). The prophet debates this thesis with the audience in the five speeches that follow. The Israelites are being contrasted with the Edomites in order to establish the fact that God loves them. The nations of Israel and Edom are descended from the twin sons of Isaac—Jacob and Esau, respectively. The one nation has survived, while the other has perished. This is a sign of God's love for Israel.
1:3 Esau. Ancestor of the Edomite nation. Edom was a "brother" nation to Israel (Obad 10–12). Edom became a prototype of hostility toward Israel and haughtiness toward God (Num 20:14–21; Deut 2:8; Jer 49:7–22; Ezek 25:12–14; Amos 1:11–12; Obad). **hated.** Can mean "rejected" in covenant contexts. God has rejected Esau and his descendants, the Edomites. Previously Esau despised and rejected a covenant relationship with Yahweh (cf. Gen 25:34; 26:34–35). **wasteland.** Denotes desolation, a land conquered by an enemy, ruined, and abandoned. Earlier prophets had predicted Edom's utter destruction (Isa 34:5–15; Jer 49:7–22; Ezek 25:12–14; 35:1–15; Obad). The historical details are unclear, but a coalition of Nabatean Arab tribes gradually displaced the Edomites and took control of their territory between 550 and 400 BC. **his inheritance.** The territory of Edom, located on the southeastern corner of the Dead Sea (from the Brook Zered in the north toward the Gulf of Aqaba in the south). Contrasting Jacob and Esau calls to mind the twin brothers' rivalry (cf. Gen 25:23–26). Paul appeals to Mal 1:2–3 to confirm the mystery of Israel's election, the divine adoption of Jacob as the free decision of God, apart from any human merit (Rom 9:13–14).
1:4 Edom. Land or territory synonymous with the people of Edom, the descendants of Esau. **LORD Almighty.** The divine name means "the LORD of [heaven's] armies." This epithet for God is prominent in the OT prophets (Isa 1:9; Jer 2:19; Hag 1:2; Zech 1:3) and is a favorite of Malachi (found 24 times in 55 verses). It emphasizes Yahweh's invincible power as the commander of heaven's angelic armies. **Wicked Land.** The nation of Edom personified pride in self-centered existence, foolishly assuming that they could avoid divine judgment by their strategic location and human achievement (cf. Jer 49:7–18). Edom was also an ally of the Babylonians in the sack of Jerusalem, giving further cause for God's wrath against the nation (cf. Ps 137:7; Lam 4:21–22; Obad 10–14).
1:5 Great is the LORD. Perhaps a liturgical expression from the Zion tradition of the Psalter calling attention to Yahweh's universal kingship over all the earth and over all gods (cf. Pss 35:27; 40:16; 48:1).
1:6—2:9 *Second Message.* The second disputation contains two speeches (1:6–14; 2:1–9), and the theme of worship joins them: the great king God is worthy of worship (1:14), but the priests have cor-

“It is you priests who show contempt for my name.
“But you ask, ‘How have we shown contempt for your name?’
7“By offering defiled food[m] on my altar.
“But you ask, ‘How have we defiled you?’
“By saying that the LORD’s table is contemptible. 8When you offer blind animals for sacrifice, is that
not wrong? When you sacrifice lame or diseased animals,[n] is that not wrong? Try offering them to your
governor! Would he be pleased with you? Would he accept you?” says the LORD Almighty.[o]
9“Now plead with God to be gracious to us. With such offerings[p] from your hands, will he accept
you?”—says the LORD Almighty.
10“Oh, that one of you would shut the temple doors, so that you would not light useless fires on my
altar! I am not pleased[q] with you,” says the LORD Almighty, “and I will accept no offering[r] from your
hands. 11My name will be great among the nations, from where the sun rises to where it sets. In every
place incense[s] and pure offerings will be brought to me, because my name will be great among the
nations,” says the LORD Almighty.
12“But you profane it by saying, ‘The Lord’s table is defiled,’ and, ‘Its food[t] is contemptible.’ 13And you
say, ‘What a burden!’[u] and you sniff at it contemptuously,” says the LORD Almighty.
“When you bring injured, lame or diseased animals and offer them as sacrifices, should I accept
them from your hands?” says the LORD. 14“Cursed is the cheat who has an acceptable male in his flock
and vows to give it, but then sacrifices a blemished animal[v] to the Lord. For I am a great king,[w]” says
the LORD Almighty, “and my name is to be feared among the nations.

Additional Warning to the Priests

2 “And now, you priests, this warning is for you.[x] 2If you do not listen, and if you do not resolve to
honor my name,” says the LORD Almighty, “I will send a curse[y] on you, and I will curse your blessings. Yes, I have already cursed them, because you have not resolved to honor me.
3“Because of you I will rebuke your descendants[a]; I will smear on your faces the dung[z] from your

1:7 [m] ver 12; Lev 21:6
1:8 [n] Lev 22:22; Dt 15:21 [o] Isa 43:23
1:9 [p] Lev 23:33-44
1:10 [q] Hos 5:6 [r] Isa 1:11-14; Jer 14:12
1:11 [s] Isa 60:6-7; Rev 8:3
1:12 [t] ver 7
1:13 [u] Isa 43:22-24
1:14 [v] Lev 22:18-21 [w] 1Ti 6:15
2:1 [x] ver 7
2:2 [y] Dt 28:20
2:3 [z] Ex 29:14

[a] 3 Or *will blight your grain*

rupted that worship (2:8). The real issue is not God’s love for Israel but Israel’s love for God.

1:6–14 *Breaking Covenant Through Blemished Sacrifices.* The prophet exposes the improper worship of Yahweh, indicts the corrupt Levitical priesthood responsible, and affirms God’s role as Father, Lord, and sovereign Ruler of the nations.

1:6 my name. Embodies the essence of God’s being, character, and reputation (cf. Ezek 36:19–23). The priests who “show contempt” for, or despise, God’s name shame him by sacrilegiously disregarding the laws that regulate sacrificial worship of him.

1:7 defiled food. Offerings presented on the Lord’s table, the altar of sacrifice (cf. Lev 3:16; Ezek 44:6–8,15–16). The animal and grain sacrifices were “food” for God only symbolically (cf. Lev 21:8,21), as the priests and Levites were permitted to eat portions of the offerings (Num 18:17–19; Deut 18:1–4).

1:8 blind ... lame or diseased animals. Priests and people have disobeyed the Mosaic commandments concerning acceptable animal sacrifices (cf. Lev 22:17–25; Deut 15:21).

1:10 shut the temple doors. Better to close the temple and halt the worship of Yahweh than to offer defiled and contemptible sacrifices (see v. 12; cf. Isa 1:10–15; Jer 7:21–26; Amos 5:21–23). True worship of God has always been a matter of the heart, not form or ritual (Isa 29:13; cf. Matt 5:8; 12:30,33).

1:11 My name will be great among the nations. Perhaps a liturgical refrain affirming God as the creator and ruler of the nations (cf. Pss 76:12; 86:9; Jer 10:6). Sadly, the nations will instruct postexilic Judah in the greatness of God in their worship rituals of burning “incense” and giving “pure offerings.”

1:13 sniff at it contemptuously. The priests find their duties irksome and tiresome. The act of sniffing, or turning up their noses, at the sacrificial offerings was a gesture of insolence and derision (cf. 1 Sam 2:17).

1:14 Cursed. Cursing an individual delivered them over to adversity as divine punishment for a serious crime against the community (cf. Deut 27:15–26; Jer 48:10). People who swear “vows” to Yahweh must keep them or risk incurring guilt (cf. Deut 23:21–23); they must sacrifice an unblemished male animal in fulfillment of a vow (cf. Lev 22:18–23). **I am a great king.** Perhaps alludes to Ps 47:2 or Ps 95:3. The climactic declaration completes the triad of references to the great Lord of the Hebrews and ruler of all the nations (vv. 5,11,14). **my name is to be feared among the nations.** The universal worship of Yahweh is a central theme of the second disputation as well as the OT prophets generally (cf. Isa 42:4; 49:6; 66:22–23; Hag 2:7,22; Zech 8:22–23; 14:16–17). The NT concludes with the nations surrounding God’s throne in worship (Rev 7:9).

2:1–9 *Additional Warning to the Priests.* The second speech of the disputation rebukes the priests for liturgical malpractice and threatens them and their descendants with divine judgment.

2:2 curse on you. The total destruction God threatened against those who break the Mosaic covenant (cf. Deut 28:20). **your blessings.** The duties of the priests included pronouncing God’s blessing upon the people (cf. Num 6:23–27).

2:3 dung. The dung or entrails of the sacrificial animals that were burned outside the camp along with the hide and flesh (cf. Exod 29:14; Lev 8:17; 16:27). Since the priests had defiled God (1:7), he will figuratively defile and disqualify them for priestly ministry. The humiliating act of God rubbing dung on the faces of the priests rendered them unfit for temple service since they were ritually unclean (cf. Lev 4:11; 8:17; Num 19:5–7). Like the dung taken away from the sanctuary and burned, they too will be carried off (e.g., Exod 29:14; Lev 4:11–12,21).

2:3 [a]1Ki 14:10
2:4 [b]Nu 3:12
2:5 [c]Dt 33:9 [d]Nu 25:12
2:6 [e]Dt 33:10 [f]Jer 23:22; Jas 5:19-20
2:7 [g]Jer 18:18 [h]Nu 27:21 [i]Lev 10:11
2:8 [j]Jer 18:15
2:9 [k]1Sa 2:30
2:10 [l]1Co 8:6 [m]Ex 19:5
2:11 [n]Ne 13:23 [o]Ezr 9:1; Jer 3:7-9
2:12 [p]Eze 24:21 [q]Mal 1:10
2:13 [r]Jer 14:12
2:14 [s]Pr 5:18
2:15 [t]Ge 2:24; Mt 19:4-6 [u]1Co 7:14

festival sacrifices, and you will be carried off with it.[a] 4 And you will know that I have sent you this warning so that my covenant with Levi[b] may continue," says the LORD Almighty. 5 "My covenant was with
him, a covenant[c] of life and peace,[d] and I gave them to him; this called for reverence and he revered
me and stood in awe of my name. 6 True instruction[e] was in his mouth and nothing false was found on
his lips. He walked with me in peace and uprightness, and turned many from sin.[f]
7 "For the lips of a priest[g] ought to preserve knowledge, because he is the messenger[h] of the LORD
Almighty and people seek instruction from his mouth.[i] 8 But you have turned from the way and by your
teaching have caused many to stumble;[j] you have violated the covenant with Levi," says the LORD Almighty. 9 "So I have caused you to be despised[k] and humiliated before all the people, because you have
not followed my ways but have shown partiality in matters of the law."

Breaking Covenant Through Divorce

10 Do we not all have one Father[a]? Did not one God create us? Why do we profane the covenant[m] of
our ancestors by being unfaithful to one another?
11 Judah has been unfaithful. A detestable thing has been committed in Israel and in Jerusalem:
Judah has desecrated the sanctuary the LORD loves by marrying[n] women who worship a foreign god.[o]
12 As for the man who does this, whoever he may be, may the LORD remove[p] him from the tents of Jacob[b]—even though he brings an offering[q] to the LORD Almighty.
13 Another thing you do: You flood the LORD's altar with tears. You weep and wail because he no longer
looks with favor[r] on your offerings or accepts them with pleasure from your hands. 14 You ask, "Why?"
It is because the LORD is the witness between you and the wife of your youth.[s] You have been unfaithful
to her, though she is your partner, the wife of your marriage covenant.
15 Has not the one God made you?[t] You belong to him in body and spirit. And what does the one
God seek? Godly offspring.[c][u] So be on your guard, and do not be unfaithful to the wife of your youth.

[a] *10* Or *father* [b] *12* Or *12 May the LORD remove from the tents of Jacob anyone who gives testimony in behalf of the man who does this* [c] *15* The meaning of the Hebrew for the first part of this verse is uncertain.

2:4 my covenant with Levi. Perhaps an allusion to the "covenant of life and peace" (v. 5) between Yahweh and Phinehas for his zeal in defending God's honor against those involved in idolatry and immorality at Baal of Peor (Num 25:1–13; cf. Num 3:12–13; Jer 33:21) or more generally to the blessing of Levi by Moses (Deut 33:8–11). The ancient priestly ideal is contrasted with the disgraceful reality of an irreverent priesthood.
2:6,7 instruction. The priests were charged with teaching the people the knowledge of God as revealed in the law of Moses (Lev 10:8–11; Deut 33:10).
2:7 messenger. A title usually reserved for prophets, but Malachi ascribes prophetic duties to the priests as teachers and interpreters of God's law (cf. Deut 33:8–11).
2:8 violated. By their false teaching (and perhaps by their hypocritical example in intermarrying with foreign women, see v. 11; cf. Ezra 9:1–2; 10:18–22; Neh 13:27–29), the priests have corrupted "the covenant of Levi" (see note on v. 4).
2:9 shown partiality. The charges of corruption are unspecified, but the priests have failed to administer the law with kindness and fairness. They were to be impartial (Lev 19:15), like God (Deut 10:17).
2:10–16 *Third Message: Breaking Covenant Through Divorce.* The prophet traces covenant failure in Judah from the priests (v. 8) to the people (v. 10). His lofty view of the marriage covenant hearkens back to the marriage ideal announced in Gen 2:23–24. Divorce is an act of violence against the marriage partner and a form of social injustice, a topic the fourth sermon addresses (3:5).
2:10 one … one. The repetition echoes what will become the Shema in later Judaism, the affirmation of Hebrew monotheism (Deut 6:4–5). **Father … God.** The divine titles emphasize the Lord's special role as Israel's Father and his unique function as Creator (cf. Isa 63:16). **covenant of our ancestors.** The Sinai covenant (Exod 19–24), reminding postexilic Judah that the law of Moses specified their responsibilities to God and to one another (e.g., the Ten Commandments, Exod 20:1–17).
2:11 detestable thing. Abomination, a grave indictment. The term also applies to the offensive and loathsome practices of the Canaanites, including idolatry, perverse sexual acts, and human sacrifice (cf. Lev 18:21,24,29–30; 19:4). **desecrated the sanctuary … by marrying women who worship a foreign god.** Hebrew men were divorcing their wives to marry other women who practiced idolatry. Presumably these marriages were contracted to gain economic advantage in the established merchant guilds and trading cartels. The practice violated the law of Moses, which prohibits marriage to foreigners. Such intermarriage had led Israel into idolatry (cf. Deut 7:3–4; 1 Kgs 11:1–6).
2:12 remove. In the sense of blotting out or destroying evildoers in the form of executing them. The Lord himself is the executioner, not the people. Others understand the term as banishing evildoers from the Hebrew community or cursing them so that they have no descendants (cf. Lev 7:20,25; 20:17–18).
2:14 partner. The root word is used for a seam or a joint in construction contexts (e.g., Exod 26:6–11), suggesting that the marriage bond is permanent (perhaps alluding to "one flesh" in Gen 2:24).
2:15 See NIV text note. The first portion of the verse is extremely difficult, and the Hebrew may be understood in various ways, which the English versions attest. The NIV captures the gist of the verse. God has made male and female one by ordaining marriage, and the life force of humanity belongs to God. **Godly offspring.** The prophet answers his own question. Divorcing and then marrying other idolatrous women threatened the training of children in the righteousness of the Torah, undermining the loyalty of the next generation to Yahweh's covenant (cf. Exod 13:8; Deut 6:4–9; Josh 4:6–7). **be on your guard, and do not be unfaithful.** Verse 16 develops this warning and admonition; the prophet combats an entrenched practice.

16 "The man who hates and divorces his wife,[v]" says the LORD, the God of Israel, "does violence to the one he should protect,"[a] says the LORD Almighty.

So be on your guard, and do not be unfaithful.

Breaking Covenant Through Injustice

17 You have wearied[w] the LORD with your words.

"How have we wearied him?" you ask.

By saying, "All who do evil are good in the eyes of the LORD, and he is pleased with them" or "Where is the God of justice?"

3 "I will send my messenger, who will prepare the way before me.[x] Then suddenly the Lord you are seeking will come to his temple; the messenger of the covenant, whom you desire, will come," says the LORD Almighty.

2 But who can endure[y] the day of his coming? Who can stand when he appears? For he will be like
a refiner's fire[z] or a launderer's soap. 3 He will sit as a refiner and purifier of silver;[a] he will purify[b] the Levites and refine them like gold and silver. Then the LORD will have men who will bring offerings in righteousness, 4 and the offerings[c] of Judah and Jerusalem will be acceptable to the LORD, as in days gone by, as in former years.[d]

5 "So I will come to put you on trial. I will be quick to testify against sorcerers, adulterers and perjurers,[e] against those who defraud laborers of their wages,[f] who oppress the widows[g] and the fatherless, and deprive the foreigners among you of justice, but do not fear me," says the LORD Almighty.

[a] 16 Or *"I hate divorce," says the LORD, the God of Israel, "because the man who divorces his wife covers his garment with violence,"*

2:16 [v] Dt 24:1; Mt 5:31-32; 19:4-9
2:17 [w] Isa 43:24
3:1 [x] Isa 40:3; Mt 11:10*; Mk 1:2*; Lk 7:27*
3:2 [y] Eze 22:14; Rev 6:17 [z] Zec 13:9; Mt 3:10-12
3:3 [a] Da 12:10 [b] Isa 1:25
3:4 [c] 2Ch 7:12; Ps 51:19; Mal 1:11 [d] 2Ch 7:3
3:5 [e] Jer 7:9 [f] Lev 19:13; Jas 5:4 [g] Ex 22:22

2:16 See NIV text note. **The man who hates.** The clause is difficult and may be understood in reference to God as the one who hates divorce (e.g., "I hate divorce" in other translations like NRSV or NASB), or in reference to the man who hates and divorces his wife. Regardless, God hates a broken covenant (cf. 1:3; Hos 9:15). The context suggests that the subject of the sentence is the man who divorces his wife, since it is he, not God, who has done violence to the wife. **divorces.** Contractually expels a marriage partner (whether divorce or separation). Malachi attempts to correct abuses resulting from misapplying the Mosaic divorce laws (cf. Deut 24:1–4). The NT allows for divorce in two situations: Jesus condemned divorce except for the grounds of marital unfaithfulness (Matt 19:1–12), and Paul allows for divorce in the case of abandonment in 1 Cor 7:15. **does violence.** Divorce is a cruel social crime since it fractures the divinely ordained marriage covenant and robs the woman of the dignity and protection afforded by the legal agreement. To divorce one's wife is an act of treachery against her and the God who made her. Divorce breaks the heart, destroys relationships, violates family integrity, damages the children's well-being, and makes for an uncertain future.

2:17—3:5 *Fourth Message: Breaking Covenant Through Injustice.* The fourth sermon addresses the inequities between God's justice and human perspectives of justice. The prophet assures his audience that God is indeed just (2:17—3:1) and then threatens the people with the impending experience of divine judgment (3:2–5). Like Amos's audience, the people are not fully aware that in asking for God's justice they bring judgment upon themselves (cf. Amos 5:18–20).

2:17 wearied. The people have worn out God with their accusations that he has not loved them (1:2) and that he condones wickedness.

3:1 my messenger. Plays on the meaning of the name Malachi (see Introduction, Author). "Messenger" may indicate either an angelic being or a human being functioning as a divine forerunner. The NT identifies John the Baptist as the Messiah's herald who fulfills this passage (Matt 11:10; Mark 1:2; Luke 7:27). **prepare the way.** The imagery of clearing obstacles from the roadway for the procession of the king comes from Isa 40:3; 57:14; 62:10. Malachi applies the road-construction motif figuratively to the ministry of the messenger who will remove the obstructions preventing spiritual renewal in God's people. **Lord.** Yahweh himself (cf. Zech 4:14; 6:5). Pairing the title "Lord" with "the LORD Almighty" at the end of the verse emphasizes God's role as sovereign over all creation (cf. Isa 10:16,33; 19:4). **will come to his temple.** The prophet anticipates the divine judgment associated with the sudden and unexpected second coming of Christ (Matt 24:36–51; 25:1–13). **messenger of the covenant.** Malachi's audience would have understood this as a divine being or an angelic being on the basis of the parallel with the angel of Yahweh in Exod 23:20–23. Christian interpretation has long understood Jesus the Messiah to be the messenger of the new covenant (cf. Isa 42:6; Luke 2:29–32; 22:20).

3:2 day of his coming. Another expression for the day of the Lord. It establishes the future-oriented theme of the fourth disputation. In the OT this future day is always an imminent era of unspecified duration in which the God of justice will break into human history to establish his kingdom among the nations (cf. Dan 2:44–45). The first advent of Jesus the Messiah inaugurated the coming of the kingdom of God (Matt 4:23; 9:35; Luke 4:43; 10:9,11). The day of God's judgment occurs at the second coming of Christ (Matt 13; 24). For Malachi, it purifies, vindicates, and restores the righteous (vv. 2–5,17–18; 4:2–3), and it judges and destroys the wicked (4:1). **refiner's fire.** Malachi borrows the image of God purifying his people in the smelter's furnace from Isa 1:25; Jer 6:29; Ezek 22:22. **launderer's soap.** Laundry detergent or fuller's lye in the form of alkali powder made from certain plants or herbs (cf. Jer 2:22). White clothes signified purity (cf. Mark 9:3; Rev 3:5). The dual images of cleansing by fire and washing indicate the extent of the people's wickedness and the degree of purification necessary to restore the proper worship of the Lord.

3:5 put you on trial. The setting and tone of the courtroom persist: God serves as prosecuting attorney, expert witness, and trial judge. **sorcerers.** Practitioners of occult arts such as witchcraft, black magic, and fortune-telling for profit (cf. Deut 18:10; Isa 47:9; Mic 5:12). **widows ... fatherless ... foreigners.** The Mosaic covenant repeatedly prescribes the practice of social justice, especially to those on the margins of society (e.g., Exod 22:22; 23:6; Deut 10:18–19; 24:17; 26:12–13; 27:19).

3:6 [h] Nu 23:19; Jas 1:17
3:7 [i] Jer 7:26; Ac 7:51 [j] Zec 1:3
3:8 [k] Ne 13:10-12
3:10 [l] Ne 13:12 [m] 2Ki 7:2

Breaking Covenant by Withholding Tithes

6 "I the LORD do not change.[h] So you, the descendants of Jacob, are not destroyed. 7 Ever since the time
of your ancestors you have turned away[i] from my decrees and have not kept them. Return to me, and
I will return to you,"[j] says the LORD Almighty.

"But you ask, 'How are we to return?'

8 "Will a mere mortal rob God? Yet you rob me.

"But you ask, 'How are we robbing you?'

"In tithes[k] and offerings. 9 You are under a curse—your whole nation—because you are robbing me.
10 Bring the whole tithe into the storehouse,[l] that there may be food in my house. Test me in this," says the
LORD Almighty, "and see if I will not throw open the floodgates[m] of heaven and pour out so much blessing
that there will not be room enough to store it. 11 I will prevent pests from devouring your crops, and the

3:6–12 *Fifth Message: Breaking Covenant by Withholding Tithes.* Malachi's fifth message contains two disputations: the charge to bring the tithe (vv. 8–10) is tied to the call to repentance (vv. 6–7), the heart of the message. The speech echoes the first sermon by underscoring God's covenant faithfulness (1:2–5).

3:6 I ... do not change. Indirectly a theological commentary on the nature of God's being, as his holy character and eternal purposes are immutable. God is not static in his actions, as the call to repentance in v. 7 indicates. He responds to those who respond to him as the situation merits (as Jonah learned, Jonah 3:9–10; cf. Jonah 2:9–10). Explicitly the statement affirms God's integrity as a covenant-maker and his faithfulness as a covenant-keeper with Israel (cf. Exod 2:24; Lev 26:42; Num 23:19; Pss 105:8; 111:5; Jas 1:17).

3:7 Return. Signifies repentance; repeats Zech 1:3. Repentance is an "about face," a complete change of direction. In this case it is a shift in loyalty, a reorientation back to the God of Israel (cf. 1 Kgs 8:33; Jer 24:7). Preaching repentance characterizes the ministry of John the Baptist, forerunner of the Messiah (Matt 3:2,11; Luke 3:3–6). The church still proclaims a gospel that calls everyone to repent and turn to God (Acts 3:19; Rom 2:4; 2 Cor 7:10; 2 Pet 3:9).

3:8–9 rob ... rob ... robbing ... robbing. The people cheat God by failing to give the required tithes and by stinginess in bringing additional offerings. Repeating the word indicates the gravity of the offense of defrauding God of his due (cf. Lev 27:30; Zech 5:3).

List of names of Jewish settlers used for taxation in 419 BC. The list contains Jewish first names of men and women who had to pay two pounds of silver to "the god Yahweh." God tells the people they are robbing him in tithes and offerings (Mal 3:8).

bpk, Berlin/Aegyptisches Museum/Jürgen Liepe/Art Resource, NY

3:8 tithes. Required tithe offerings in the OT included: a tenth of the produce of the land (Lev 27:30–33; Deut 12:6,11,17); the tenth of the tithe required of the priests and Levites (Num 18:21–32); and the third-year tithe given to the socially disadvantaged in Israel (Deut 14:28–29; 26:12–15). Malachi's ambiguity with reference to specific tithes may be intentional. The giving of tithes was an act of worship acknowledging Yahweh as the Lord of the earth and the provider for Israel. **offerings.** Including freewill, or voluntary, offerings and mandatory gifts to the Lord or his sanctuary that may include agricultural produce, material goods, or personal valuables (e.g., Exod 25:2; 29:27; Num 5:9; 31:29; Deut 12:6). Such contributions were thank-offerings recognizing God's goodness and generosity (see "whole tithe" in v. 10 [see also note]).

3:9 under a curse. Cryptically alludes to the covenant curses of Deut 28 (the same Hebrew word for "curse" appears in Deut 28:20).

3:10 whole tithe. Perhaps the tenth-part tithe and the tithe tax (or "tenth of the tithe" that the Levites were required to give on the tithes they received from the Israelites, Num 18:26; cf. Neh 10:38). If so, Malachi may be calling for reinstating the tithe tax (not the giving of additional offerings). **food in my house.** Food and other goods received as tithes and offerings were stockpiled in the treasury rooms ("storehouse") of the temple (1 Kgs 7:51; 2 Chr 31:11–12; Neh 13:12). The sacrificial gifts were literally "food" for the priests and Levites, whom the gifts supported (cf. Num 18:8–21; Deut 18:1–4). **Test me.** The prophet's challenge does not contradict the prohibition against testing God (Deut 6:16). It offers the priests and the people an opportunity to prove Yahweh's covenant-faithfulness by personal experience through obedience to God's commands. The passage is not a formula for achieving personal wealth, as some claim, although it is possible to give freely and attain more wealth (as a general principle, not a promise, cf. Prov 11:24). Context indicates Malachi has the blessings of the Mosaic covenant in mind (see Deut 28:12). These blessings are national, or corporate, in character, rather than individually centered. They are primarily agricultural benefits, but are not without moral and spiritual counterparts. The prophet recognized that turning to God in repentance and reasserting fidelity in covenant relationship with him must begin somewhere—in this case, the practical act of obedience to the Mosaic laws regulating tithes. The point of the "testing" is to probe the willingness of the community to respond to God in faith and obedience, not to manipulate God's blessing through the giving of tithes. The theme of God's testing and providing runs through the Bible, giving rise to names for God like "The LORD Will Provide" (Gen 22:14; cf. Deut 8:2,16; Ps 81:7; 1 Thess 2:4. **throw open the floodgates of heaven.** Abundant rainfall would yield bumper crops (cf. Deut 28:12), overturning the drought and poor harvests that Haggai reports (Hag 1:6; 2:16,19).

3:11 prevent. God will intervene in such a way that the agricultural bounty of covenant-blessing will become a reality (cf. Deut 28:3–5,11–12). **pests.** The ambiguous word may refer to insects (like locusts) or worms that would infest and destroy produce (cf. Deut 28:39–40).

vines in your fields will not drop their fruit before it is ripe," says the LORD Almighty. 12"Then all the nations
will call you blessed,[n] for yours will be a delightful land,"[o] says the LORD Almighty.

3:12 [n]Isa 61:9 [o]Isa 62:4
3:13 [p]Mal 2:17
3:14 [q]Ps 73:13 [r]Isa 58:3
3:15 [s]Jer 7:10
3:16 [t]Ps 34:15 [u]Ps 56:8

Israel Speaks Arrogantly Against God

13"You have spoken arrogantly[p] against me," says the LORD.

"Yet you ask, 'What have we said against you?'

14"You have said, 'It is futile[q] to serve God. What do we gain by carrying out his requirements and
going about like mourners[r] before the LORD Almighty? 15But now we call the arrogant blessed. Certainly
evildoers[s] prosper, and even when they put God to the test, they get away with it.'"

The Faithful Remnant

16Then those who feared the LORD talked with each other, and the LORD listened and heard.[t] A scroll[u] of
remembrance was written in his presence concerning those who feared the LORD and honored his name.

3:12 all the nations will call you blessed. Abundant harvests would indicate God's covenant-blessing on Israel (Deut 28:4,11) and tangibly demonstrate the return of his favor upon his people. **delightful land.** Recalls the description of the promised land as one "flowing with milk and honey" (Exod 3:8,17) and serves as a foil to Edom as the "Wicked Land" (1:4). The reversal overturns the taunting and jeering of fallen Jerusalem by the nations at the time of the Babylonian exile (Jer 18:16; Lam 2:15; cf. Deut 28:37).

3:13—4:3 *Sixth Message: The Coming Day of Judgment.* The prophet's final sermon distills the teaching of the previous speeches, especially highlighting the contrast between the evildoers and the righteous.

3:13–15 *Israel Speaks Arrogantly Against God.* Malachi rebukes the people for denying any value in obeying God in an effort to persuade them to return to Yahweh in repentance (v. 7).

3:13 spoken arrogantly. The people accused God of being unjust (2:17), even favoring evildoers (v. 15). They have chosen to ignore the truth that God loves justice (Pss 9:16; 37:28), blinded by their preoccupation with immediate economic concerns.

3:14 gain. The people assume that their acts of righteousness should result in corresponding material blessing (cf. Deut 28:1–14). **going about like mourners.** Parading in funeral garb or dressing in sackcloth and ashes as if mourning the dead (cf. Job 30:28; Ps 35:13–14). The people lament that their penitence seemingly has no effect upon God. The prophet's call to repentance in 3:7 suggests their contrition was more show than substance (cf. Matt 6:16–18).

3:15 evildoers prosper. The people contend that the covenant principle of retribution (i.e., God curses the wicked [cf. Deut 28]) has been ignored. The psalmist also wrestles with the incongruity of how the wicked prosper and the righteous suffer (Ps 73:3,9–12,15–17). **they put God to the test.** Malachi challenged the people to "test" God from the posture of faith (v. 10), but the people accuse God of failing to judge those who dare him to punish them. **they get away with it.** Those insolent evildoers who try God's patience and justice seem to escape, which contradicts the retribution principle (cf. Deut 28:15; Ezek 17:15).

3:16–18 *The Faithful Remnant.* This portion of Malachi's final sermon suggests that some responded to the prophet's message (v. 16) and assures people that divine justice will prevail (vv. 17–18).

3:16 feared. Revered. This signifies covenant loyalty to Yahweh, indicating that Malachi's audience includes a core of faithful people. The term connotes the response of covenant obedience to God's

Jewish marriage contract from Elephantine, 449 BC. Writing the scroll of remembrance (Mal 3:16) in the presence of the Lord suggests a formal agreement, signed by those who took counsel together, affirming covenant loyalty (cf. Ezra 10:3; Neh 9:38).

Marriage document in Aramaic, 3rd July 449 BC, Egyptian/Brooklyn Museum of Art, New York, USA/Bequest of Theodora Wilbour from the collection of her father, Charles Edwin Wilbour/Bridgeman Images

3:17 [v] Dt 7:6 [w] Ps 103:13; Isa 26:20
3:18 [x] Ge 18:25
4:1 [y] Joel 2:31 [z] Isa 5:24; Ob 18
4:2 [a] Lk 1:78; Eph 5:14 [b] Isa 30:26 [c] Isa 35:6
4:3 [d] Job 40:12 [e] Eze 28:18

17 "On the day when I act," says the LORD Almighty, "they will be my treasured possession.[v] I will
spare[w] them, just as a father has compassion and spares his son who serves him. 18 And you will again
see the distinction between the righteous[x] and the wicked, between those who serve God and those who
do not.

Judgment and Covenant Renewal

4 [a] "Surely the day is coming;[y] it will burn like a furnace. All the arrogant and every evildoer will
be stubble,[z] and the day that is coming will set them on fire," says the LORD Almighty. "Not a
root or a branch will be left to them. 2 But for you who revere my name, the sun of righteousness[a]
will rise with healing[b] in its rays. And you will go out and frolic[c] like well-fed calves. 3 Then you will
trample[d] on the wicked; they will be ashes[e] under the soles of your feet on the day when I act," says
the LORD Almighty.

[a] In Hebrew texts 4:1-6 is numbered 3:19-24.

commands, resulting in righteous conduct and genuine worship (cf. Exod 20:20; Deut 5:29; 10:12; Ps 34:9,11; Isa 33:6). The early church lived in this "fear of the Lord" (Acts 9:31; cf. 1 Pet 2:17; Rev 14:7). **listened.** Emphasizes Yahweh's high level of interest in his people (cf. Jer 8:6; Dan 10:12). His ability to hear and respond to his people distinguishes him from the idols of the nations (cf. Ps 115:4–7; Isa 44:18–20; 46:1–7; Hab 2:18–19); he tends to the prayers of the righteous (cf. Prov 15:29; Matt 6:6; Jas 5:16). **scroll of remembrance.** A document, following Persian tradition, containing a catalog of names and a record of events associated with those individuals (cf. Esth 6:1). Writing the document in the presence of the Lord suggests a formal agreement affirming covenant loyalty signed by those who took council together (cf. Ezra 10:3; Neh 9:38).

3:17 treasured possession. A covenant expression describing the privileged status of Israel as God's elect people (1:2–3; Exod 19:5; Deut 7:6; 14:2). **a father has compassion.** Further emphasizes the theme of God's role as Father (1:6; 2:10); it may allude to Exod 34:6–7; Ps 103:13.

3:18 you will again see. Segregating the righteous from the wicked in the day of the Lord will provide convincing evidence that God is indeed just (cf. 2:17) since the people failed to recognize the fall of Edom as an act of God's justice (1:5). This future day of God's judgment is also the answer to the problem of evil for the psalmist (Ps 73:15–17).

4:1–3 *Judgment and Covenant Renewal.* Here Malachi breaks away from the disputation format of his sermon, bluntly warning the people that God's judgment is inescapable. This decisively answers the people's charge that God does not distinguish between the righteous and the wicked (cf. 3:15,18).

4:1–3 The first speech unit confirms the opening sermon (1:2–5): Yahweh has "loved Jacob" (1:2). Those who revere God are assured of God's blessing: "the sun of righteousness" will shine upon them (v. 2).

4:1 the day. Shorthand for the day of the Lord (see v. 5; 3:2 and note). **burn like a furnace.** The imagery of using a furnace as an incinerator for destroying wicked people in the day of Yahweh's judgment is both graphic and frightening (see 3:2–3; cf. Ps 21:9; Isa 1:31; 66:15–16). **arrogant.** The proud and "haughty" (Isa 13:11) who challenge God and escape, both by doing evil and then flaunting it (3:15; cf. Isa 2:12). **stubble.** Useless grain stalks; it is found in combination with fire in the OT as an image of divine judgment (cf. Isa 5:24; 33:11; Joel 2:5; Obad 18). **fire.** A frequent symbol of divine judgment (e.g., Isa 66:15; Amos 1:4; Zeph 1:18; Zech 12:6) and one aspect of Jesus' ministry according to John the Baptist's preaching (Matt 3:12; cf. Matt 13:30).

4:2 sun of righteousness. Usually understood as a solar epithet for Yahweh (cf. Ps 84:11; Isa 60:19–20). The expression is a word picture describing the restoration and healing that will characterize the day of the Lord, when God will vindicate his people, as bright and sure as daybreak (2 Sam 23:4; Isa 30:26; 60:1,3). It is a title for Christ in Zechariah's song, the "rising sun ... from heaven" that shines "on those living in darkness" (Luke 1:78–79; see note on Luke 1:78). The source for this title may have been the winged sun disk that is ubiquitous in ancient Near Eastern iconography. **righteousness ... healing.** Connotes salvation and restoration, vindicating the faithful people of God. Jeremiah longed for and promised such divine "healing" (Jer 8:15; 33:6). **rays.** In other contexts, this Hebrew word is often translated "wings." The outstretched wings of a bird and the extended rays of the sun were symbols of divine protection and deliverance in the biblical world (Exod 19:4; Deut 32:10–11; Pss 17:8; 18:10). **frolic like well-fed calves.** The imagery suggests the freshness and renewal of divine blessing, confirming the promise of 3:10 and overturning the lament of 3:14.

4:3 trample on the wicked. Like grain "crushed on the threshing floor" (Isa 21:10) and burned as stubble (v. 1). **soles of your feet.** Perhaps alludes to Israel's covenant destiny to possess the land upon which they had set foot (Deut 11:24).

LMLK (Hebrew abbreviation meaning "belonging to the king") stamped jar handle with two-winged sun disk, from Gibeon, 900–701 BC. The "sun of righteousness" (Mal 4:2) may have been the winged sun disk that is ubiquitous in ancient Near Eastern iconography.

Kim Walton, taken at the University of Pennsylvania Museum of Archaeology and Anthropology

[4]"Remember the law[f] of my servant Moses, the decrees and laws I gave him at Horeb for all
Israel.
[5]"See, I will send the prophet Elijah[g] to you before that great and dreadful day of the LORD comes.[h]
[6]He will turn the hearts of the parents to their children,[i] and the hearts of the children to their parents;
or else I will come and strike[j] the land with total destruction."[k]

4:4 [f]Ps 147:19
4:5 [g]Mt 11:14; Lk 1:17 [h]Joel 2:31
4:6 [i]Lk 1:17 [j]Isa 11:4; Rev 19:15 [k]Zec 5:3

4:4–6 *Conclusion: Remember the Law of Moses, Look for Elijah.* Some consider vv. 4–6 postscripts to the book that feature Moses and Elijah as two exemplary models of OT faith. Moses and Elijah also represent the ideals of the OT Law and the Prophets. The first postscript (v. 4) reminds the people to obey the law of Moses since Israel's identity was rooted in their exodus from Egypt and defined by the Sinai covenant that Moses mediated (cf. Exod 34:10–12). The second postscript (vv. 5–6) warns that divine judgment of the wicked is impending but that deliverance and restoration remains an open possibility for the righteous.
4:4 Remember the law. Implies recalling and applying the words and deeds of the God of Sinai to behavior (Deut 4:9–10; Ps 103:18). **my servant.** A title of honor, idealizing Moses' role as Israel's leader and recognizing his intimate relationship with Yahweh (Exod 33:11; Deut 34:10–12). **Horeb.** Another name for Mount Sinai, the mountain of God (Exod 3:1).
4:5 Elijah. The supreme example of an OT prophet of God: he boldly rebuked kings (1 Kgs 21:17–29), preached repentance (1 Kgs 18:18–21,36–39), and validated his messages with signs and miracles (1 Kgs 17:17–23; cf. Luke 1:17; Jas 5:17–18). The NT identifies John the Baptist as the Elijah figure who ministered "in the spirit and power of Elijah" (Luke 1:17) and prepared the way for Jesus the Messiah by calling people to repentance (see note on 3:1; see also Matt 11:9–15 and notes). Some identify Elijah as one of the two witnesses in Rev 11:3.
4:6 turn. The word for repentance, indicating a reversal of attitude, loyalty, and behavior. Turning hearts and the ministry of reconciliation are key themes in the OT Prophets (Isa 44:22; Jer 24:7; Hos 6:1–3; 14:1–2). Turning toward God in repentance results in intergenerational reconciliation (cf. Luke 1:17). Christ gives this ministry of reconciliation to the church (2 Cor 5:18–20). **total destruction.** The Hebrew word refers to objects set apart or devoted to utter destruction by God, as in the case of the nations living in the land of Canaan (cf. Deut 7:1–11; 20:16–18; see Introduction to Deuteronomy: Themes and Theology [Holy War]). The people of Israel who did not respond to God's prophet faced oblivion—the fate of their Edomite neighbors (1:3–4) and Canaanite predecessors (Josh 6:17).

FROM MALACHI TO CHRIST

THE PERSIAN PERIOD
450–330 BC
For about 200 years after Nehemiah's time the Persians controlled Judah, but the Jews were allowed to carry on their religious observances and were not interfered with. During this time Judah was ruled by high priests, who answered to the Persian authorities.

THE HELLENISTIC PERIOD
330–166 BC
In the late fourth century BC, Alexander the Great defeated the Persians repeatedly in battle and quickly conquered the eastern Mediterranean region, including Syria, Egypt, Persia, and Babylonia. Alexander believed in the superiority of Greek culture and was convinced that it was the one force that could unify the world. Alexander permitted the Jews to observe their laws and even granted them exemption from tribute or tax during their sabbath years. When he built Alexandria in Egypt, he encouraged Jews to live there. The Greek conquest prepared the way for the translation of the Hebrew Old Testament into Greek (Septuagint version), beginning ca. 250 BC.

THE HASMONEAN PERIOD
166–63 BC
When this historical period began, the Jews were being greatly oppressed. The Ptolemies of Egypt had been tolerant of the Jews and their religious practices, but the Seleucid rulers of Syria were determined to force Hellenism on them. Copies of the Scriptures were ordered destroyed, and laws were enforced banning circumcision and other Jewish practices. The oppressed Jews revolted, led by Judas Maccabeus.

THE ROMAN PERIOD
BEGINS IN 63 BC
In the year 63 BC, Pompey, the Roman general, captured Jerusalem, and the provinces in the Holy Land became subject to Rome. The Romans ruled at times through local vassal kings and at other times through Roman governors who were appointed by the emperors. Herod the Great was ruler of that whole region at the time of Jesus' birth.

	410	Malachi ca. 430 BC
	400 BC	
	390	
	380	
	370	
	360	
	350	
	340	
	330	334–323 Alexander the Great conquers the East; 330–328 Alexander's years of power
Rule of Alexander the Great	320	320 Ptolemy (I) Soter conquers Jerusalem
	310	311 Seleucus conquers Babylon; Seleucid dynasty begins
	300	
	290	
	280	
	270	
Rule of the Ptolemies of Egypt	260	ca. 270-200 Translation of the Old Testament into Greek (Septuagint)
	250	
	240	
	230	226 Antiochus (III) of Syria conquers the Holy Land
	220	223–187 Antiochus becomes Seleucid ruler of Syria
	210	
	200	198 Antiochus defeats Egypt and gains control of the Holy Land
	190	
Rule of the Seleucids of Syria	180	175–164 Antiochus (IV) Epiphanes rules Syria; Judaism is prohibited
	170	167 Mattathias and his sons rebel against Antiochus; Maccabean revolt begins
	160	166–160 Judas Maccabeus's leadership
	150	160–143 Jonathan is high priest
	140	142–134 Simon becomes high priest; establishes Hasmonean dynasty
	130	
	120	134–104 John Hyrcanus enlarges the independent Jewish state
Hasmonean Dynasty	110	
	100	103 Aristobulus's rule
	90	102–76 Alexander Janneus's rule
	80	75–67 Rule of Salome Alexandra with Hyrcanus II as high priest
	70	66–63 Battle between Aristobulus II and Hyrcanus II
	60	63 Pompey invades the Holy Land; Roman rule begins
	50	63–40 Hyrcanus II governs but is subject to Rome
	40	40–37 Parthians conquer Jerusalem
	30	37 Herod becomes ruler of the Holy Land
Herod the Great rules as king; subject to Rome	20	19 Herod's temple begun
	10	4 Herod dies; Archelaus succeeds him
		20 BC–AD 50 Philo of Alexandria, Jewish philospher
	10	
	20	
	AD 30	

THE TIME BETWEEN THE TESTAMENTS

Douglas J. Moo

INTRODUCTION

A gap exists in our biblical canon between the Old and New Testaments. The OT historical record ends about 430 BC with the return of a small number of exiles to their own land (see Introductions to Ezra and Nehemiah). The latest prophetic book (probably Malachi) was written at about this time. Over 400 years therefore separate the OT and the NT. Because no canonical book was written during these years, they are sometimes called "the silent years."

But from other perspectives these four centuries were far from silent. They were filled with significant historical, social, and religious developments that help us understand the NT much more accurately. The Gospels bring to the stage a host of characters whom the OT never mentions: Pharisees, Sadducees, teachers of the law, and officials from the Roman Empire (e.g., Caesar Augustus and Pontius Pilate). Who are these people? How can we understand their roles in the gospel story? Even more vital to accurately understanding the NT, however, are the religious developments. The Judaism that Jesus and the NT writers related to stands in continuity with the OT on many basic points, but it also developed beyond the OT in a bewildering variety of ways. Appreciating these developments helps explain the nature of the NT interface with early Judaism and therefore sheds light on key NT teachings that relate to Jewish perspectives.

HISTORY

Our sources for the history of Israel during these centuries are varied. The Jewish historian Josephus (AD 37 – ca. 100) wrote several long histories that, while not without bias, are invaluable. Some Apocryphal and pseudepigraphical books (especially 1 and 2 Maccabees) cover selected periods of time in considerable detail (see Literature). Other writings touch on events or indirectly suggest perspectives on them. Apart from several allusions in Heb 11:33 – 38, the NT does not refer to this period.

The history of Israel during these years may be usefully organized according to the world powers that successively dominated the ancient Near East.

The Persian Period

As the OT ends, the nation of Israel exists as a small "temple state" within the Persian Empire. Ezra and Nehemiah, along with the prophets Zechariah, Haggai, and Malachi, shed some light on this early period (as does Esther from a very different perspective). But we know little about the life of Israel during the century from about 430 to 330 BC.

FOREIGN DOMINATION OF ISRAEL (722 BC–AD 135)

OLD TESTAMENT PERIOD	**The Assyrian Empire** (722 – 605 BC)
	The Babylonian Empire (605 – 539 BC)
	The Persian Empire (539 – 333 BC)
INTERTESTAMENTAL PERIOD	**The Macedonian-Greek Empire** (333 – 166 BC) • Alexander the Great (334 – 323 BC) • Ptolemaic domination (323 – 198 BC) • Seleucid domination (198 – 166 BC)
	Jewish Independence (166 – 63 BC) • The Maccabees • The Hasmonean Dynasty
NEW TESTAMENT PERIOD	**The Roman Empire** (63 BC – AD 135) • The Herodian Dynasty • Roman governors • Destruction of Jerusalem (AD 70) • Second revolt ends the Jewish state (AD 135)

The Greek Period

Alexander the Great mosaic from Pompeii.

The conquests by Alexander the Great in 334–331 BC brought Israel under the influence of the Greeks. No single Greek empire emerged from Alexander's conquests. His death at age 32 in 323 led to a scramble for power among his generals. Two of them managed to establish kingdoms that affected Israel.

Ptolemy consolidated power in Egypt, and the Ptolemies ruled Israel for over a century (323–198 BC). Little is known about life in Israel during this century, but one development proved especially significant. Although Alexander failed to establish Greek political dominance, his conquest did have two consequences that were important for Jewish history and the NT. First, a simplified version of the Greek language, called koine ("common") Greek, became the dominant lingua franca. Most Jews living in Palestine would have learned this koine Greek as their second language. In God's providence, then, the NT missionaries and the writers of the NT could use koine Greek to communicate to most people in the world of their day. Second, the armies of Alexander exported to the ancient Near East the Greek worldview and way of life—in a word, "Hellenism." Hellenism, in contrast to Eastern thought, greatly emphasized human beings and their rational abilities. Its view of life was enshrined in certain institutions, such as the gymnasium, where naked (*gymnos*) men enjoyed athletic contests and community. Hellenism proved attractive to many people, especially the elite, in the territories that Alexander conquered.

The Maccabees and Jewish Independence

A Greek papyrus of Gal 1:23—2:9, second or third century AD.

The influence of Hellenism within Israel became a key issue in the tumultuous years 200–160 BC. In 198, Israel became part of the empire that Seleucus, another of Alexander's generals, founded. The Seleucid Empire, headquartered in Babylonia, was more fragile than the stable Ptolemaic Empire. The Seleucid rulers were accordingly less tolerant of deviant religions and pursued a policy of Hellenization in order to consolidate their diverse territories—including Israel. Matters came to a head under the rule of the tyrannical Antiochus IV Epiphanes (175–164 BC), who in 167–164 attempted to eradicate the Jewish faith. Possessing a copy of the Torah or circumcising one's son became punishable by death. He demanded offerings to the Greek god Zeus and went so far as to sacrifice a pig in the Jerusalem temple. Antiochus's persecution led to the famous Maccabean revolt. An elderly Jew named Mattathias sparked the revolt, which was led by a succession of his sons, especially Judas "Maccabeus" (probably meaning "the hammer"). Under Judas's leadership, Jewish partisans won battle after battle against the Seleucid forces, eventually retaking and rededicating the temple in 165 (an event that Jews celebrate during the festival of Hanukkah). Two brothers of Judas, Jonathan and Simon, successively led the revolt, which succeeded in gaining Israel's independence from the Seleucids in 166 BC. The Maccabean revolt preserved the Jewish faith in the face of Antiochus's persecution. But perhaps just as important was the battle for the faith within Israel. Hellenism had penetrated Judaism to

PALESTINE OF THE MACCABEES AND HASMONEAN DYNASTY

Judea at the beginning of the revolt
Additions of Jonathan, 160–142 BC
Additions of Simon, 142–134 BC
Additions of Hyrcanus I, 134–104 BC
Additions of Aristobulus I, 104–103 BC
Additions of Alexander Jannaeus, 103–76 BC
Kingdom of Alexander Jannaeus
Sidon
PHOENICIA
COELE-SYRIA
Damascus
Tyre
Dan (Antiochia)
Paneas
Cadasa
Seleucia
Hazor
Bascama
Ptolemais
Bethsaida
Gamala
Gennesaret
Dathema
Taricheae
Sea of Galilee
Arbela
Hippus
GALILEE
Philoteria
Sepphoris
Mt. Carmel
Jezreel Valley
Dora
Mediterranean Sea
GALAADITIS
Strato's Tower
Scythopolis
Pella
SAMARIA
Jordan R.
Gerasa
Samaria
Ammathus
Apollonia
Mt. Gerizim
Shechem
Acrabeta
PEREA
Alexandrium
Joppa
Gadora
Arimathea
Apherema
Philadelphia
Lydda
Modein
Docus
Jamnia
Gazara
JUDEA
Jericho
Esbus
Azotus
Accaron
Samaga
PHILISTIA
Jerusalem
Hyrcania
Ascalon
Medeba
Herodium
Beth Zur
Machaerus
Anthedon
Marisa
Gaza
Adora
Hebron
MOABITIS
En Gedi
Dead Sea
Gerar
Orda
IDUMEA
Masada
Raphia
Beersheba
Malatha
NABATEANS
Rhinocorura
Wadi of Egypt
Petra
0 10 km.
0 10 miles

Judas Maccabeus pursuing Timotheus.
Planet Art

the degree that some Jews were, in effect, turning from their ancestral faith. The "faithful ones" (*hasidim*) who successfully fought the Seleucids just as successfully fought off the creeping Hellenism that would have eviscerated the Jewish faith. For all their success, however, the *hasidim* did not fulfill OT promises of restoration, leaving the Jewish people still hoping for much more to come.

The Roman Period

A series of rulers in the Hasmonean dynasty, which Jonathan and Simon established, tried to consolidate Israel's position in the succeeding decades. However, a new world power was taking its place on the historical scene: Rome. Greece had become a Roman province in 146 BC and Pergamum (in Asia Minor) in 136 BC. In 63 BC, Israel, considered part of the larger province of Syria, came under Roman rule. Herod the Great (in power 37–4 BC) was a "client king" of Rome, answerable to Roman authority. All of NT history takes place in the larger context of the Roman Empire. It was the Romans who invaded Israel in the years AD 66–73 to put down a Jewish revolt, destroying the temple in AD 70 and winning the final victory at the fortress of Masada in AD 73.

LITERATURE

While no canonical books emerged during these four centuries, the Jewish people produced a sizable body of other kinds of literature—particularly in the tumultuous years from 170 BC on. This literature falls into five basic categories.

Scripture Translations

As generations of Jewish people lived outside the land of Israel, their ability to understand Hebrew was lost. They needed translations. Greek, which had become the common language of much of the eastern Mediterranean area, was a natural choice for a translation. Jewish legend (see the *Letter of Aristeas*), probably written more than a century after the event, claimed that 72 translators assembled at the command of the Ptolemaic ruler around 250 BC to produce a translation of the Torah (the Pentateuch). The alleged number of translators has given this translation its name: "Septuagint," Latin for "70" (a rounding of "72"). This tradition is probably right to locate the origins of the translation in Alexandria, with its large Greek-speaking population, but the tradition is otherwise unreliable. The translation was probably generated by the needs of the Jewish population, with the five books of Moses being translated as early as the third century BC and the other parts of the OT (the Prophets and the Writings) being translated over the next two centuries. Moreover, other Greek translations of at least parts of the OT were probably circulating as well.

Another language that was widespread in and around Israel was Aramaic. Parts of Daniel and Ezra were written in Aramaic, and Aramaic was likely the language Jesus most often used. Jewish teachers probably began translating the Hebrew Scriptures into Aramaic, and from those initial translation attempts arose the "targums," Aramaic paraphrases of parts of the OT.

The Apocrypha

The Apocrypha (which means "hidden") is a collection of books the Roman Catholic and Eastern Orthodox churches recognize as canonical (or "Deuterocanonical"), though they differ over which books they include in this collection. Most of these books appear in the Septuagint. Most early Christians read the Bible in this Greek version, and they therefore tended to put these books on a par with other books of Scripture. Protestants, however, following the lead of the Reformers, reject the canonical status of these books because they are not part of the Hebrew canon. When and how the Hebrew OT took on its official canonical shape is debated, but evidence points to the recognition of a collection of books identical to the Protestant canon sometime before the time of Christ.

While not having canonical status among Protestants, the books of the Apocrypha, almost all of which were written in the time between the Testaments, are valuable sources for understanding Jewish life and thought during these years. They include histories (e.g., 1–2 Maccabees), expansions of Scripture (e.g., Additions to Daniel), stories of God's faithfulness (e.g., Judith and Tobit), wisdom books (e.g., Sirach), and an apocalypse (2 Esdras).

THE MACCABEAN-HASMONEAN PERIOD

SELEUCID KINGS		JEWISH LEADERS		PTOLEMAIC KINGS	
Seleucus I (Nicator)	321–280			Ptolemy I (Soter)	322–285
Antiochus I (Soter)	280–261				
Antiochus II (Theos)	261–246			Ptolemy II (Philadelphus)	285–246
Seleucus II (Callinicus)	246–226			Ptolemy III (Euergetes)	246–221
Seleucus III (Soter)	226–223			Ptolemy IV (Philopator)	221–205
Antiochus III (the Great)	223–187			Ptolemy V (Epiphanes)	204–180
Seleucus IV (Philopator)	187–175			Ptolemy VI (Philometor)	180–145
Antiochus IV (Epiphanes)	175–164	Mattathias Judas	166 166–160		
Antiochus V (Eupator)	164–162				
Demetrius I (Soter)	162–150	Jonathan	160–143		
Alexander Balas	150–145			Ptolemy VII (Neos Philopator)	145
Demetrius II (Nicator)	145–139	Simon	143–135	Ptolemy VII (Neos Philopator)	145
(Antiochus VI [Epiphanes Dionysus])	145–142			Ptolemy VIII (Euergetes II or Physcon)	145–116
Antiochus VII (Sidetes)	139–129	John Hyrcanus I	135–104		
Demetrius II (Nicator)	129–125				
Antiochus VIII (Grypus)	125/4–113			Ptolemy IX (Soter II or Lathyrus)	116–110
Antiochus IX (Philopator Cyzicenus)	113–111				
Antiochus VIII (Grypus)	111–95	Aristobulus	104–103	Ptolemy X (Alexander)	110–109 108–88
Seleucus VI	95–54	Alexander Jannaeus	103–76		
Antiochus X (Eusebes)	94–83			Ptolemy IX (Soter II or Lathyrus)	88–80
Tigranes, King of Armenia	83–69	Salome Alexandra	76–67	Ptolemy XI (Alexander II)	80 (20 days)
				Ptolemy XII (Philopator Philadelphus Neos Dionysus or Auletes)	80–51
Antiochus XIII (Asiaticus)	69–65	Hyrcanus II Aristobulus	67 (3 months) 67–63	Cleopatra VII	51–30

The Dead Sea Scrolls

In the late 1940s and early 1950s, a shepherd boy stumbled across some ancient scrolls in a cave near the Dead Sea. Over the next years, a treasure trove of almost 1,000 ancient scrolls were discovered in this area. They are written mainly in Hebrew and include many different kinds of books (and often only fragments of books): biblical texts, apocalyptic works, interpretations of biblical texts, hymns, and directions for the life of a community. The community that produced the scrolls is almost certainly the community whose remains are found at Khirbet Qumran. The scrolls suggest that a group of Jews (perhaps from the *hasidim* of the Maccabean period) split off from the main body of Judaism and relocated in the wilderness to establish a true and faithful Jewish remnant. Most scholars think these Jews belonged to the Essenes (see The Parties: Jewish Diversity [Essenes]). The community flourished during the first century BC, and the members of the community probably wrote most of the books found on the scrolls.

The scrolls have had a great impact on three areas of study. First, the biblical texts push back written evidence for much of the Hebrew OT by 1,000 years. On the whole, the scrolls confirm that the Hebrew text that forms the basis for our English Bibles (the Masoretic Text) is old and reliable. Second, the scrolls portray a variant form of Judaism,

The Great Isaiah Scroll of the Dead Sea Scrolls.
Wikimedia Commons

Aerial view of Qumran and its caves.
© 1995 by Phoenix Data Systems

helping us better understand the diversity of Jewish belief and practice at the time of Christ. Third, because the scrolls come from Jews who used the OT to prove that they were the righteous remnant preparing for the coming of the Messiah, they provide intriguing parallels to (and substantial differences from) the early Christian church.

The Pseudepigrapha

The Jews produced many other books in the time between the Testaments. These books vary considerably in genre, origin, and theology, so they are difficult to categorize. They range from collections of psalms (e.g., *The Psalms of Solomon*) to rewritings of Scripture (e.g., *Jubilees*) to collections of speeches from famous OT people on their deathbeds (e.g., *Testaments of the Twelve Patriarchs*). Especially frequent are apocalypses, books of visions that are usually attributed to well-known biblical characters (e.g., Adam, Abraham, Moses). The falsely attributed authorship of these books has led to the title for this general collection: "pseudepigrapha," which means "false writings." This collection of writings provides invaluable insight into the nature and diversity of Judaism just before and during the time of Christ. But they must be used with caution because some of the books are very difficult to date. Many of the books in the pseudepigrapha were written after (some of them long after) the NT period. And other books in the collection have probably gone through a series of editions, making it difficult to determine which parts may have been in existence in the NT period. Thus, for instance, *The Testament of the Twelve Patriarchs*, while available in some form during the first century AD, probably did not reach its final form until the second century.

Philo and Josephus

Two Jewish writers responsible for a large body of literature related to the period between the Testaments were Philo and Josephus. Philo (ca. 20 BC – ca. AD 50), a native of Alexandria in Egypt, wrote many treatises about the OT and the Jewish faith. Keen to explain and defend the Jewish faith to his Greek-educated contemporaries, Philo extensively used allegory to interpret the OT in terms of contemporary philosophical categories. Josephus (AD 37 – ca. 100) was a historian who took part in the Jewish revolt against Rome in AD 66 – 73 and later moved to Rome, where he wrote extensive histories of Israel. Although not without his own bias, Josephus provides a lot of information about the time between the Testaments that we would not otherwise possess.

CULTURAL AND RELIGIOUS DEVELOPMENTS

Diaspora

"Diaspora" comes from the Greek for "scatter." It refers to the "scattering" of Jews throughout the world, initially through exile and later through emigration as well. More Jews lived in the Diaspora than in the Holy Land during the NT period (see map, p. 2523). The contrast between the pagan culture in which Diaspora Jews were immersed and their Jewish faith created special challenges for them. Many undoubtedly assimilated their Judaism to their surroundings. But many others remained faithful to their heritage, maintaining ties to the Holy Land and the temple by sending regular contributions and making occasional pilgrimage trips.

The Synagogue

The many Jews who lived in the Diaspora were cut off from the vital community forming and shaping ceremonies of the Jerusalem temple and therefore had to develop other means of maintaining faithfulness to Judaism. It is possible that the synagogue had its origins in this Diaspora context. Jews would gather on the Sabbath to read the Torah, pray, and generally encourage one another in their faith. We cannot be sure when synagogues were first established, but they were widespread by the NT period (e.g., Matt 4:23; Acts 13:5).

The main room of the Delos Synagogue in Greece. It has been suggested that use of this synagogue started in the second century BC.

www.HolyLandPhotos.org

Josephus.
Wikimedia Commons

THE PARTIES: JEWISH DIVERSITY

The Jewish historian Josephus refers to three "philosophies" that were popular among the Jews of his day: the Essenes, the Sadducees, and the Pharisees (*Antiquities*, 18.11). By calling them "philosophies," he hoped to make Judaism understandable for his Roman readers, but they are better called "parties." The existence of these parties is a reminder that the Jewish faith in Jesus' day was very diverse. At the same time, most first-century Jews belonged to no party. Those who prided themselves on their party affiliation sometimes labeled these average people the "people of the land" (the *am ha-eretz*).

Sadducees

The Sadducees were Jews, probably few in number, who were willing to work closely with the governing Romans. They controlled the priesthood through much of the NT period (cf. Acts 5:17). In theology, they insisted that doctrine had to be built on only the five books of Moses, and they rejected the increasingly popular belief in resurrection (Luke 20:27).

Essenes

Little was known about the Essenes until the Dead Sea Scrolls were discovered. The NT does not mention the Essenes (at least by name). Most scholars now agree that the Essenes produced most of the scrolls. But we need to use caution concerning sweeping conclusions since there may have been other Essenes who did not hold all the beliefs of the Dead Sea Scrolls community. The group of Essenes who established the community at Khirbet Qumran was disenchanted with the temple establishment of their day, so they moved to the wilderness to reestablish a pure worship of the Lord. They were devoted to strict interpretation of the law and to personal purity, eagerly anticipating the appearance of the Lord to fulfill OT prophecies.

Pharisees

Jesus debated the Pharisees more than any other Jewish party—probably because the Pharisees lived among the people and were very influential. They practiced strict purity, often taking the form of separation from anything they considered impure. They tried to convince average Jews to pursue a similar purity. They sought to direct the life of the Jews through their interpretation of the law. These interpretations became so authoritative that they were viewed as a second law, an "oral" law. The Pharisees were the only party to survive the destruction of the temple in AD 70 and were the precursors to the rabbis.

Zealots

Although Josephus does not include them in his list of Jewish "philosophies," the Zealots deserve mention. Their hero was Phinehas, who preserved Israel's purity by killing an Israelite and his Midianite lover (Num 25:6–8). The Zealots embraced violence against the Romans as a way of purifying Israel from foreign influence. They sparked the rebellion against Rome that brought upon Israel the disaster of Roman invasion in AD 66–73. The NT does not mention the Zealots as a group, but one of the Twelve may have been a devotee of this movement: "Simon the Zealot" (Matt 10:4).

THEOLOGICAL DEVELOPMENTS

Jewish beliefs during the intertestamental period were firmly rooted in the OT but also underwent significant revision. These revisions were made in response to three key factors:

1. The Jewish people needed to figure out how to live under relatively constant subjugation to foreign powers.
2. The many Jews living outside the Holy Land needed to develop a theology that enabled them to live in the midst of pagans and worship God apart from the temple.

The Pharisees question Jesus.
The Pharisees Question Jesus, ca 1886–96, Tissot, James Jacques Joseph/Brooklyn Museum of Art, New York, USA/Bridgeman Images

3. The Jewish people of the intertestamental period were exposed to new ways of thinking that inevitably affected their beliefs. The most important of these was Hellenism, the dominant worldview of the period. Some Jews sought to syncretize their faith with Hellenistic ideas, while others resisted Hellenistic influence.

The existence of several different "parties" within Judaism reminds us that these theological developments were not uniform. Theological diversity characterized this period. This diversity is important to keep in mind when we assess "the Jewish background" to the NT. We might more accurately refer to "the Jewish backgrounds."

Within this diversity, however, we also find certain beliefs that almost all Jews held in common. Four were particularly important: monotheism, election, the centrality of torah, and eschatology.

Monotheism

The idea that there is ultimately only one true, supreme God, who alone must be worshiped, was carried over from the OT into the intertestamental period. This monotheism distinguished Judaism from most of the other religions of the intertestamental and NT epochs. To be sure, some Jews during this time engaged in considerable speculation about the existence and influence of other powers closely related to God. They extensively developed the OT teaching about angels and sometimes gave important roles to OT concepts such as wisdom and the word in mediating God and his purposes to humans. These mediators became important partly because God was being viewed as increasingly transcendent and removed from the everyday lives of Jewish people. These speculations have left their mark on the NT, although the theory that these figures paved the way for the early Christians to ascribe deity to Christ goes beyond the evidence.

Election

Jews of the intertestamental period strongly maintained one of the central teachings of the OT: God chose Israel to be his special people. At his own gracious initiative, God entered into a covenant with this people. Indeed, this conviction became increasingly important as persecution (such as that under Antiochus IV Epiphanes) and dispersion forced the Jewish people to reaffirm and guard their unique identity. At the same time, the division of Judaism into competing parties meant that these groups entered into competition with one another for the distinction of being "true Israel." Election, then, became not simply a matter of God's choice of a nation. Election also became tied to certain kinds of behavior that marked those Jews who were truly "the elect ones." In some Jewish circles, what one did, or one's merits, became important as a basis for election. NT Christians entered into this debate, claiming that adherence to Jesus, the Messiah, was the only true mark of election.

The Centrality of Torah

When God chose Israel, he gave the people a series of commandments and prohibitions setting forth their obligations to him within the covenant. This covenant law (Hebrew *torah*), mediated through Moses, was central to the life of Israel. Israel's stubborn refusal to live by this law led to her exile. The Jewish people of the intertestamental period were united in affirming the importance of living under the torah in order to maintain their place within God's covenant and as a means of separating themselves from the hostile cultures in which they lived. But two developments in the Jewish view of torah during this period are important to note.

First, the content of torah was debated. While almost all Jews affirmed the continuing validity of the law of Moses, the conditions in which they lived (in the midst of pagans and for many away from the Holy Land) led to certain revisions. Groups such as the Sadducees insisted that only the written laws of Moses should govern the people. But others, such as the Pharisees, sought to give the people guidance for their lives by extending the written law of Moses. Their interpretations and applications of the written law morphed into virtually a second law, an "oral" law, standing alongside the written law. Many Pharisees claimed that this law originated with Moses himself. It is this extended law that Jesus had in view when he criticized some Pharisees and teachers of the law for insisting on obedience to "the tradition of the elders" even when that tradition undercut the written law (Matt 15:1–9).

Second, the great stress placed on torah obedience during this period fostered among some Jews a kind of legalism. The balance between God's gracious choice and human response in salvation is a delicate one that is easy to tip too far one way or the other. The Jewish people in the intertestamental period maintained a lively conviction about the importance of God's gracious election. But since so much emphasis was placed on obedience to torah as the expected means of accessing and living within this gracious election, a certain reliance on this obedience for one's status before God became all too common. Diversity over the relative importance of God's grace and human obedience to the law marked this period of Jewish history. But most Jews were united in insisting that "doing the law" was a necessary *basis* for securing God's election. It is probably this tendency that Paul has in mind when he warns about seeking to be justified by "the works of the law" (e.g., Rom 3:28; Gal 2:16).

Moses with the Ten Commandments.
Wikimedia Commons

Eschatology

Most of the Jews during this period were anticipating a time when God would intervene decisively to reward his people and punish evildoers. The return of some Jews to the land of Israel made a start in the fulfillment of the prophetic promises. But many of those promises remained unfulfilled: Israel languished under Gentile domination, and the people were far from the righteousness that the prophets predicted (e.g., Isa 54; Ezek 34:20–31). Considerable diversity marked this general eschatological expectation. Groups who enjoyed positions of power and privilege, such as the Sadducees, did not have a strong eschatological hope. Those Jews who did entertain a robust expectation of the future differed considerably about how God would fulfill that expectation. Many looked for a royal, warrior Messiah, in the model of David, whom God would use to bring in his final kingdom (see especially the *Psalms of Solomon*). This expectation explains why the people tried to make Jesus their "king" after his spectacular miracle of feeding the 5,000 (John 6:15). Other Jews expected two Messiahs, one royal and one priestly (see The Parties: Jewish Diversity [Essenes]). Still others did not expect a Messiah at all, thinking that God would intervene directly or through an angelic intermediary. These diverse ideas about the Messiah made it particularly difficult for Jesus to identify himself as the Messiah without creating confusion or misunderstanding. It is probably for this reason that he was reluctant to use the title often.

Sixth-century mosaic of a warrior Christ. Many Jews of the Bible looked for a royal, warrior Messiah, in the model of David, whom God would use to bring in his final kingdom.

Warrior Christ, 6th century AD/Cappella Arcivescovile, Ravenna, Italy/Ancient Art and Architecture Collection Ltd./Bridgeman Images

One important intertestamental development related to eschatology was apocalyptic literature. Apocalyptic writing has its roots in the OT, especially in the book of Daniel. Apocalyptic is often associated with a certain kind of eschatology, one that focuses on a sudden and dramatic turn of events in which the present evil age gives way to an age of righteousness. This division of history into two epochs is fundamental to NT eschatology. However, the revelation that the Messiah would be coming twice requires an important modification in the scheme. The first coming of Christ inaugurates the new age but without eradicating the old age. It is with the second coming of Christ that this old age will cease to exist and the new age will be consummated. Though using "apocalyptic" to describe this kind of eschatology is appropriate, it is too narrow. The word *apocalyptic* comes from a Greek word meaning "revelation," and its essence is the revelation of divine mysteries as a human being is given access to heavenly realities. Our world, with its sin and evil, is often hard to square with the realities of a powerful and loving God. The apocalyptic seers are taken behind the scenes of this world and given a vision of what is really going on. They see the reality and power of God and receive insight into his purposes in history. Books taking this form were often themselves called "apocalypses." Written in the name of a great figure in Israel's history (thus pseudonymous), apocalypses were an important literary genre in the intertestamental period. The book of Revelation shares many characteristics with these apocalypses (see Introduction to Revelation: Genre [Apocalypse]). While not pseudonymous (John writes in his own name), the book of Revelation takes God's people behind the distressed scenes of this world to a vision of our God on his throne, infallibly working through the slain Lamb of God to accomplish his good and holy purposes for his entire creation.

NEW TESTAMENT CHRONOLOGY

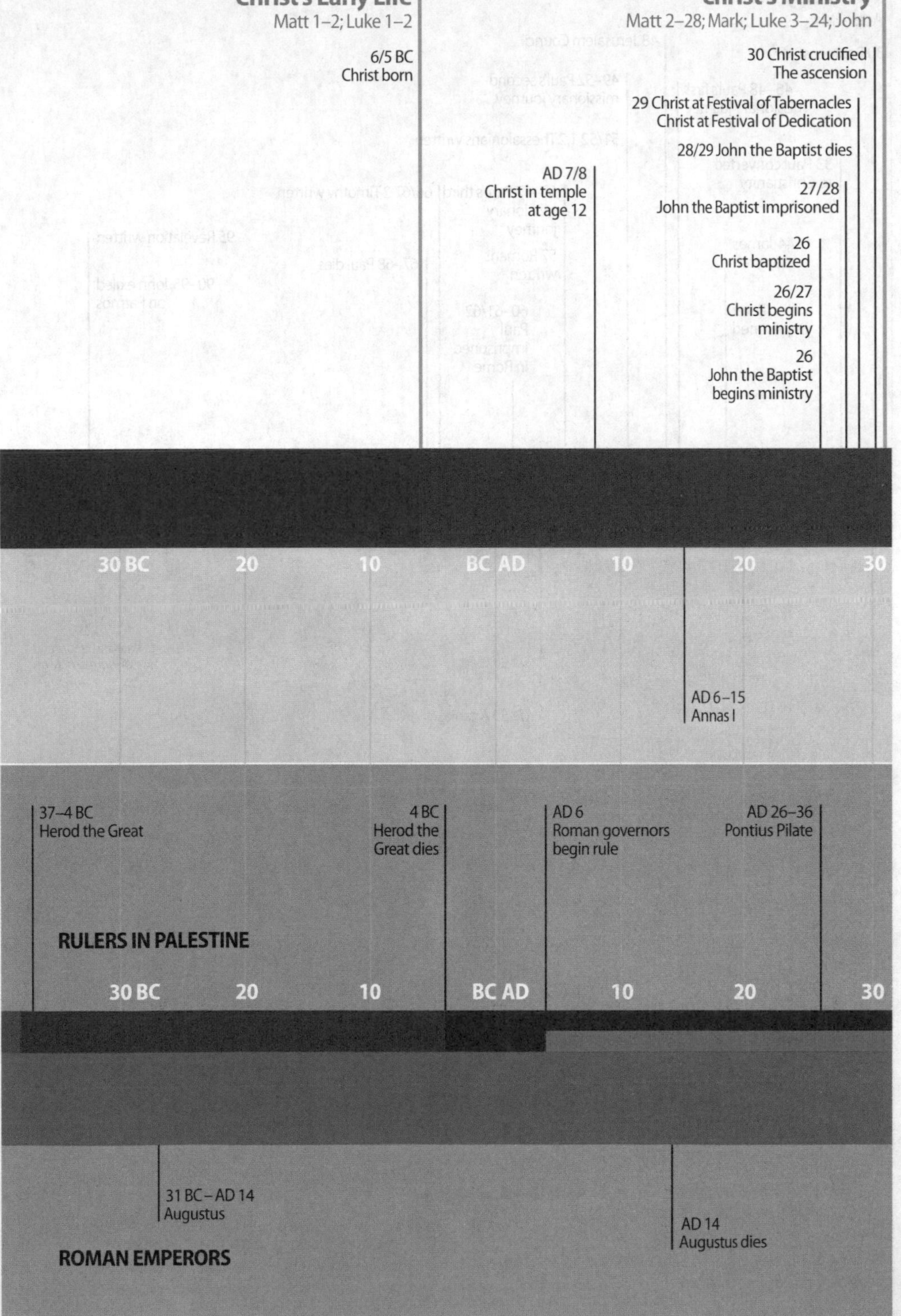
Christ's Early Life
Matt 1–2; Luke 1–2
6/5 BC
Christ born
Christ's Ministry
Matt 2–28; Mark; Luke 3–24; John
30 Christ crucified
The ascension
29 Christ at Festival of Tabernacles
Christ at Festival of Dedication
28/29 John the Baptist dies
AD 7/8
Christ in temple
at age 12
27/28
John the Baptist imprisoned
26
Christ baptized
26/27
Christ begins
ministry
26
John the Baptist
begins ministry
30 BC
20
10
BC AD
10
20
30
AD 6–15
Annas I
37–4 BC
Herod the Great
4 BC
Herod the
Great dies
AD 6
Roman governors
begin rule
AD 26–36
Pontius Pilate
RULERS IN PALESTINE
30 BC
20
10
BC AD
10
20
30
31 BC – AD 14
Augustus
AD 14
Augustus dies
ROMAN EMPERORS

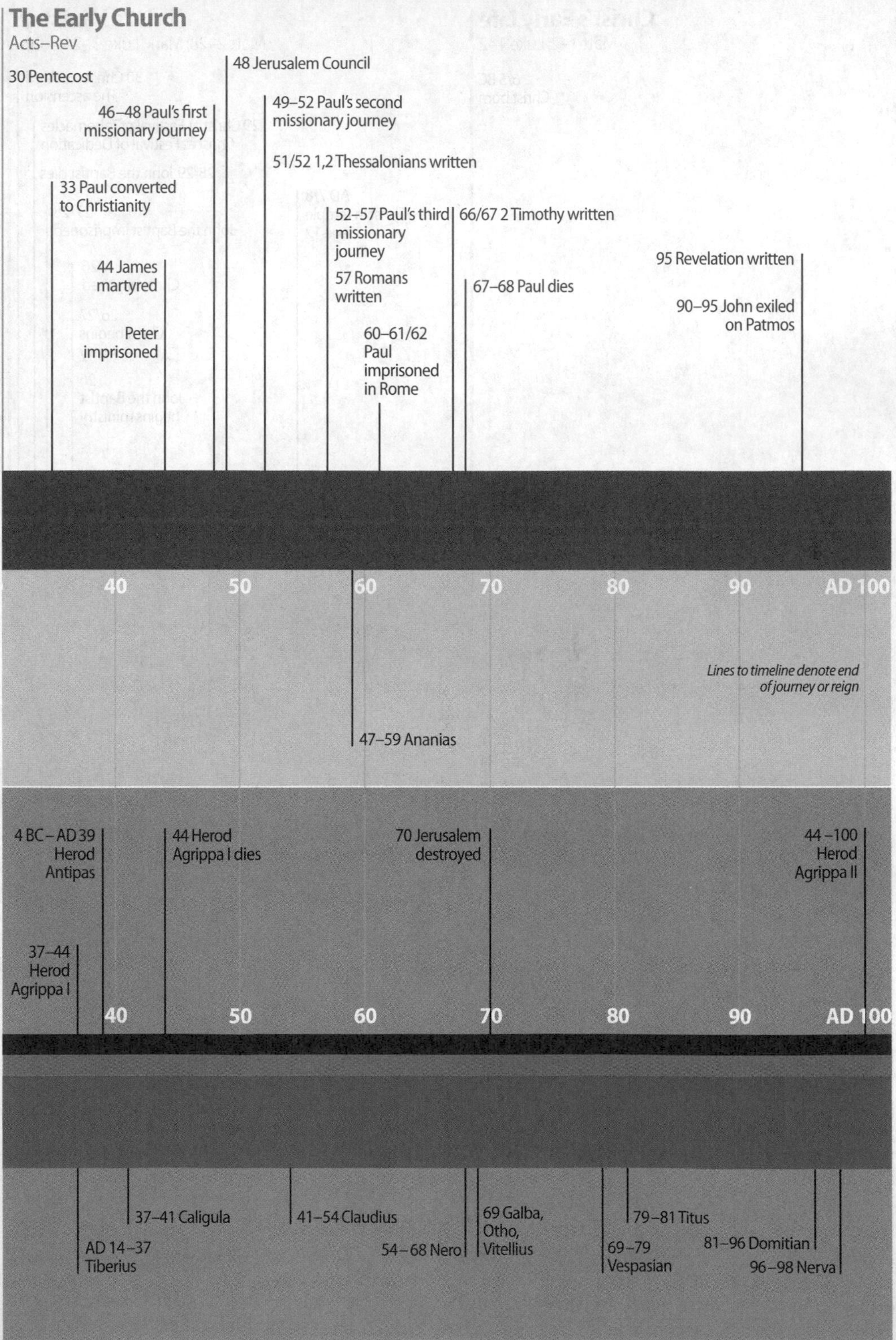
The Early Church
Acts–Rev
30 Pentecost
33 Paul converted to Christianity
44 James martyred
Peter imprisoned
46–48 Paul's first missionary journey
48 Jerusalem Council
49–52 Paul's second missionary journey
51/52 1,2 Thessalonians written
52–57 Paul's third missionary journey
57 Romans written
60–61/62 Paul imprisoned in Rome
66/67 2 Timothy written
67–68 Paul dies
95 Revelation written
90–95 John exiled on Patmos
40
50
60
70
80
90
AD 100
Lines to timeline denote end of journey or reign
47–59 Ananias
4 BC – AD 39 Herod Antipas
37–44 Herod Agrippa I
44 Herod Agrippa I dies
70 Jerusalem destroyed
44 –100 Herod Agrippa II
40
50
60
70
80
90
AD 100
AD 14–37 Tiberius
37–41 Caligula
41–54 Claudius
54 – 68 Nero
69 Galba, Otho, Vitellius
69–79 Vespasian
79–81 Titus
81–96 Domitian
96–98 Nerva

THE NEW TESTAMENT

INTRODUCTION TO THE NEW TESTAMENT

Douglas J. Moo

"New Testament" is the name given to the collection of 27 books that comprise the second part of the Christian Bible. "Testament" is the English equivalent of the Latin *testamentum*, which translates the Greek *diathēkē* (Hebrew *berit*). The Bible uses this Greek word in a rather technical sense to designate the "covenants" that God enters into with his people. In a covenant, God pledges to act on behalf of his people in certain ways, and his people, in turn, commit themselves to respond to God as he requires. Although the Bible refers to several covenants, it also suggests the idea of two basic covenants. God, through the prophet Jeremiah, contrasts the "covenant" he entered into with Israel when he brought them out of Egypt with a "new covenant" (Jer 31:31–32; see Heb 8:8–9). The sacrifice of Jesus on the cross enacts this new covenant: in Jesus' words over the cup at the Last Supper, he calls the cup "the new covenant in my blood" (Luke 22:20). The extension of covenant language to a collection of books that describes the covenant has roots in the NT itself: the apostle Paul refers to reading "the old covenant" (2 Cor 3:14; cf. "new covenant" in 2 Cor 3:6). Building on these biblical texts, Christians were referring to the work of God in history in terms of two covenants by the end of the second century AD. Applying this language to the two collections of books that Christians recognized as inspired and authoritative Scripture was a natural step.

The Two-Testament Shape of the Bible

The two-testament form of our Bibles reflects the two basic stages in the unfolding of God's grand program of redemption. The OT tells the story of creation, the fall into sin, and God's inauguration of his single plan to conquer the evil that invaded his good creation and to reassert his sovereignty over the entire cosmos. God hints at his plan immediately after the fall (Gen 3:15) and sets it into motion by entering into a covenant with Abraham. God promises that he will establish Abraham's many descendants in a land of their own and that he will use Abraham and his descendants to bless the world. Those descendants are the people of Israel. God renews his covenant with Israel, promising them that they will live securely and prosperously in the land he will give them as long as they turn their hearts to the Lord and obey his law. But despite the many blessings God bestows on Israel, the people prove again and again to be faithless, lapsing into idolatry and refusing to obey God's law. God therefore visits his people with the judgment that he had threatened when he first gave the law: he uses pagan nations to force the people from their land, sending them into exile. Yet in the midst of his peoples' unfaithfulness, God proves himself to be both faithful and gracious, promising to bring the people back to their land and to change the hearts of his people so that they will be fully able to obey him and bring glory to his name. This deliverance is often associated with a redeemer figure, often portrayed as a warrior-king like David. God promises to use this redeemer figure to punish Israel's enemies, save the people of Israel, and extend God's blessing to the nations.

The NT is the story of how God fulfills this promise of salvation. Jesus is the redeemer whom God had promised. Jesus is the "Christ," the "anointed one," or "Messiah." Yet the program of redemption does not initially take the shape that most Jews in Jesus' day were expecting. While Jesus manifested his power in miraculous works, he did not gather the armies of Israel to battle the pagan nations oppressing the people. Instead, he allowed himself to be condemned and put to death by those pagans. Yet this startling turn in the history of redemption was, in fact, anticipated in many OT passages. God's raising Jesus from the dead announced to the world that Jesus was, in fact, God's "anointed one," the one through whom God was bringing salvation to his people. Moreover, the Christ who went humbly to his death is also the Christ who will return again in glory to judge the world and fully establish God's sovereignty over all creation. These two "comings" of Jesus provide the two fundamental linchpins of the NT story. Jesus' first coming inaugurates the "last days," the time when God fulfills his promises of judgment and salvation. Jesus' second coming will culminate the end-time work of redemption. Much of the NT is devoted to helping believers understand the nature of this time in which they live: "already" brought into God's kingdom by the work of Christ, but "not yet" enjoying the full benefits of God's redemptive program.

One of the most significant storylines in the NT is a redefinition of the people of God. In the OT, God's people are by and large identified by their descent from Abraham: the people of Israel. To be sure, the OT itself plainly indicates that God's people cannot ultimately be confined to Israel. Yet the NT announces a new and revolutionary step in this direction: God's people are now defined by their relationship to Christ, *the* descendant of Abraham. Only Jews who place their faith in Christ are the true people of God; and Gentiles, through that same faith, can now join believing Jews as full and equal members of God's people. A "new covenant" has been inaugurated through the redemption won by Christ and sealed by the pouring out of God's Spirit with new power on all his people.

The two-testament format of our Bibles therefore reflects the contrast between "promise" and "fulfillment" that is the central storyline of the story of the Bible. This story is one continuous story that falls into two basic parts; there is both continuity and discontinuity. We err if we do not recognize the fundamental shift in salvation history that Christ's coming created; as Jesus himself put it, he has brought "new wine" that cannot be confined in the "old wineskins" (Mark 2:22). But we also err if we fail to recognize that the two stages of salvation history are part of one continuous story, a single plan of God to reclaim his creation: two "testaments" but one Bible.

THE BOOKS OF THE NEW TESTAMENT

BOOK	DATES OF WRITING
The Gospels Matthew Mark Luke John	Late 50s to late 80s
Acts	Early to middle 60s
The Letters *Letters of Paul* Romans 1 Corinthians 2 Corinthians Galatians Ephesians Philippians Colossians 1 Thessalonians 2 Thessalonians 1 Timothy 2 Timothy Titus Philemon *The General Letters* Hebrews James 1 Peter 2 Peter 1 John 2 John 3 John Jude	Middle 40s to early 90s
Revelation	90s (or late 60s)

The Books of the New Testament

Gospels

The first four books of the NT are named "Gospels." The word "gospel" comes from the Old English *god spell*, a phrase that means "good news." In the NT this word never refers to a book; it denotes the coming of Christ and the message about him (e.g., Mark 1:1 ["good news"]; Rom 1:16; 1 Thess 1:5). By the early second century, however, Christians were calling the books that recorded the life of Jesus "Gospels." But the original application of the word was not left behind. The titles of our Gospels take the form "[the Gospel] according to Matthew," etc. — that is, the story of the good news as related by Matthew, etc. (The titles are abbreviated in the NIV.) While our Gospels are not biographies in the modern sense, their obvious focus on the life and significance of one person, Jesus Christ, suggests that they fit comfortably in the ancient genre of *bios*, or "biography." The fourfold Gospel was explicitly recognized by the end of the second century.

The four Gospels tell the same basic story: Jesus ministers in several regions of Israel, teaching and performing miracles; he gathers followers and makes enemies (especially in the Jewish religious establishment); this opposition leads to his death by crucifixion at the hands of the Romans in Jerusalem; he is resurrected from the grave. All four accounts relate that Jesus' followers recognized him to be God's Messiah, the one through whom God's plan of salvation was reaching its climax. For all their basic agreement, the four Gospels also differ, sometimes significantly, in their presentations of the life of Jesus. These differences are especially marked between the first three Gospels, on the one hand, and John, on the other. The many parallels between Matthew, Mark, and Luke — extending even to specific wording at many places — suggest that they are closely related. Accordingly, they are labeled the "Synoptic" Gospels (*synoptic* is Greek for "seen together"). Mark's Gospel may have been the first to be written, with both Matthew and Luke using Mark's account to compose their own Gospels. John's Gospel differs significantly from the first three, and it is not clear if it depends on any of the first three. The diversity in our Gospels can prove challenging at times, but a careful and charitable reading reveals that they do not contradict one another. Rather, they complement one another: God has used four different early Christian leaders to help his people understand the many facets of Jesus' life and teaching.

Acts

The "Acts of the Apostles" serves as a bridge between the stories of Jesus' life and the letters that instruct churches about Jesus' significance. This book tells the story of the expansion of the early church, from the 120 disciples gathered together on the day of Pentecost in Jerusalem to significant numbers of believers scattered all over the Mediterranean world — including the great center of that world, Rome. The title "Acts of the Apostles" (abbreviated to "Acts" in the NIV) was given to the book not by its author but by later Christians who recognized the prominence of Peter (chs. 1 – 12) and Paul (chs. 13 – 28) in the book. Yet a better title might be "Acts of the Holy Spirit" because the author is especially keen to show how God's Spirit, poured out on the church at Pentecost, is the power behind the apostolic preaching of the word of God. As the similarity between Acts 1:1 and Luke 1:1 – 4 reveals, the author of the third Gospel, Luke, the companion of Paul, wrote Acts also. Some key plotlines and theological themes bind these two volumes together.

Letters

The next major section of the NT comprises 21 letters. These may be divided into two basic parts: 13 letters written by the apostle Paul and 8 written by five other early Christian leaders. Most of them were written to churches but four of them were written to church leaders (1 and 2 Timothy, Titus, and 3 John; Philemon is addressed not only to a man named Philemon but to other Christians and the church in Colossae). The "letter" form was a popular means of communication in the ancient world that Christians adapted to maintain relationships among the widely scattered Christian communities (see The Letters of the New Testament, p. 2282). Written over the course of about 50 years to churches and individuals scattered all over the Mediterranean world, these letters deal with an incredible number of issues. Yet they are united in their concern to help believers understand how Jesus Christ must be the center and touchstone of all that believers think and do. Believers today read them with profit, not only to understand the many facets of Christian truth and to know how to live out the gospel in specific circumstances but also to appreciate how the gospel must be integrated into every aspect of the believer's life.

Revelation

As the last book of the NT, Revelation appropriately focuses on the end of history. The climax of the book is the coming of Jesus Christ in glory to reward believers, punish unbelievers, and usher in the new heaven and the new earth (chs. 19 – 22). Yet Revelation is about much more than just the end of history. The book utilizes a popular Jewish genre called the "apocalypse" to take John (and us) into the unseen spiritual realm where the ultimate realities that dictate the course of our history are revealed. The visions that God gave to John provide believers with a vital perspective on all of history. These visions remind the church that, however difficult our circumstances might be, God is indeed on his throne (ch. 4); God has a definite plan for his people; God is infallibly carrying out this plan through Jesus, "the Lamb, who was slain" (5:12; see ch. 5); and believers must remain faithful to God in order to receive their ultimate reward from him.

How the New Testament Came Into Being

All of the NT books were written in koine, or "common," Greek. This Greek was the lingua franca in most of the countries surrounding the Mediterranean Sea. It was the language that people with many different native languages would use to communicate with one another (much like English in our day). Jews who grew up in Palestine, for instance, would often learn Greek in addition to the Aramaic that was their native language at the time. Jesus and the apostles would have learned Greek so that they could interact with the many Gentiles who lived in their own country and surrounding regions. Greek was so widely used that when Paul, a Roman citizen, wrote a letter to the believers in the capital of the Roman Empire, he wrote not in the Latin of the empire but in Greek.

Papyrus 46 (known by the siglum P46) is among the oldest surviving NT manuscripts written in Greek (typically dated to around AD 200). Pictured here is a folio (or sheet) from P46 containing 2 Cor 10:11 — 11:2.

Image digitally reproduced with the permission of the Papyrology Collection, Graduate Library, University of Michigan, MS 6238

This widespread, common language smoothed the way for the early evangelists, who could travel almost anywhere in the Roman Empire and effectively communicate the gospel in the Greek they already knew.

We do not know how soon the early Christians began to write about their faith. It is quite possible that Christians committed to writing some of the details about Jesus' life and ministry shortly after the resurrection. But the earliest NT letter was written probably in the middle 40s, and the earliest NT Gospel was probably written in the late 50s or early 60s. These Christian authors would have used sharpened reeds or quills to transfer ink to papyrus, a paper made from the reeds of the papyrus plant. In the NT period, papyrus was rolled up to form scrolls; later in Christian history the codex, or book form as we know it, began to be used. We do not possess the original written text of any NT book. As the books of the NT were written and sent to their destinations, Christians undoubtedly came to realize how valuable these books would be if distributed more widely. Indeed, we see the beginnings of the wider distribution of the NT books in the NT itself; Paul encourages the Colossians to read the letter he sent to the Laodiceans and the Laodiceans, conversely, to read the letter he sent to the Colossians (Col 4:16). As this process continued, we can imagine early Christians wanting collections of several similar NT books, such as the letters of Paul or the Gospels. In order to preserve and to disseminate these books or collections of books, copies of the originals would have been made.

Today we possess over 5,000 manuscripts containing a part of (in most cases) or the whole NT. Some of these manuscripts contain only a few verses. Many of them contain several NT books, usually organized by type of book: Gospels, Acts, the letters of Paul, the "catholic" (i.e., general) letters, and Revelation. The earliest manuscript containing part of the NT dates from the early second century, but the most significant come from the fourth and fifth centuries. Scholars have devoted many centuries to studying these manuscripts in an effort to identity the "original text" of the NT. The fruit of this labor (called "textual criticism") is a Greek text of the NT, called the modern critical text, that is without doubt very close to what the NT authors originally wrote. The sheer mass of evidence, the text's origins from many parts of the ancient world, and its comparatively early date enable us to have great confidence that when we read this text, we are reading the words that God himself inspired their authors to record. Most modern translations of the Bible, such as the NIV, work from this reconstructed text, using text notes to signal places where the text may be somewhat uncertain.

The Canon of the New Testament

The NT itself refers to books written by early Christians that are not part of the NT (e.g., Paul's letter to the Laodiceans [Col 4:16]). And there are many books written in the late first century and second century by apostolic fathers that were popular among early Christians but are not now found in our NT (e.g., The First Letter of Clement, The Shepherd of Hermas, The Letter of Barnabas). How did it come to be that the NT contains only the 27 books that we are familiar with?

This question involves what we call the canon. The Greek word *kanon* referred originally to a reed, and then to a rod, or bar, and eventually a rod used for measuring something. Hence *kanon* came to have the sense of a

Papyrus plants along the Nile River.

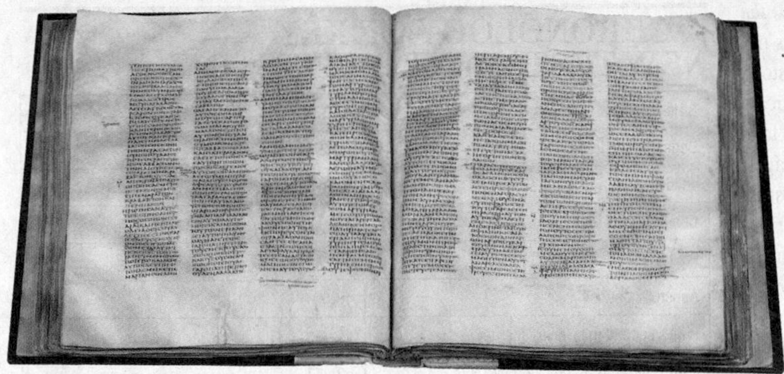

Codex Sinaiticus is a fourth-century manuscript of the Greek Bible, written between AD 330–350. Originally it contained the whole of both testaments; today only portions of the Greek OT or Septuagint survive, along with a complete NT. It was discovered in 1844 by Constantine Tischendorf in St. Catherine's Monastery in Sinai, where parts of it are preserved today.

Z. Radovan/www.BibleLandPictures.com

"standard." The "canon" of the NT is the collection of those books that have been deemed to meet the standard for inclusion in Scripture. These books, and only these books, are the ones that the church has recognized as inspired by God and therefore providing authoritative divine guidance about Christian belief and practice.

The recognition that some early Christian books had the same status as the existing books of Scripture (the OT) can be traced back to the NT itself. In 1 Tim 5:18 Paul cites a saying of Jesus — "The worker deserves his wages" (Luke 10:7) — as "Scripture" along with a quotation from the OT. In 2 Pet 3:16 Peter criticizes people for twisting the meaning of some of the letters of Paul, "as they do the other Scriptures" — "the other" implying that Peter thinks of these Pauline letters as Scripture. But aside from these few references, the NT provides little guidance for deciding what books should belong to the canon of NT Scripture. Partly as a result of this silence, it took early Christians some time to settle on the limits of the NT canon.

Christians everywhere clearly recognized many NT books, such as the Gospels, Acts, and most of Paul's letters, as Scripture at an early date. Other books took them longer to widely embrace as part of the NT canon, especially James, 2 Peter, 2–3 John, Jude, and Revelation. But these doubts are not surprising. Doubts about Revelation were due mainly to the animus against the apocalyptic style of the book shared by many early believers. The brevity of some letters meant that the church did not widely use them, which made them difficult to distinguish from the many forgeries circulating in the names of the apostles. Considering these historical circumstances and the diversity of the early church, what is remarkable is that virtually the entire early Christian movement came to agree on the identity of NT canonical books. The first list containing all (and only) the 27 canonical NT books is found in the Easter letter written by the famous early church theologian Athanasius in 367. The Third Council of Carthage (397) provided official church recognition of the 27 books of the NT canon.

Finally, it is especially important to emphasize that the early church did not *create* the canon; it *recognized* the canon. Early Christians used several criteria in their judgments. Apostolic authorship or connection with an apostle was important (Mark, for instance, was viewed as a disciple of Peter). More important, however, was conformity to the apostolic teaching, the "rule of faith" (Latin *regula fidei*). But most important of all was inspiration. God, in a sense, created the canon by inspiring what human authors wrote as they wrote certain books. He entered into this special work of inspiration, for instance, as Paul wrote Colossians, but not as he wrote to the Laodiceans. Early Christians recognized the unique significance and authority of certain books, and this recognition led to the decision to include them in the canon.

Reading the New Testament

God inspired the books of the NT so that people would have an authoritative record of his climactic revelation in his Son, the Lord Jesus. The NT has been translated into hundreds of languages so that people around the world can access this revelation in their own tongue. Whether you are a seasoned believer or someone who has picked up the Bible for the very first time, the message God has for you is (in the words Augustine heard long ago): "Take up, read!"

Some simple principles will help you as you read:

1. *Ask God to help you understand.* The NT itself warns that sin has affected the ability of humans to understand God's truth (Rom 1:28; 1 Cor 2:14; Eph 4:18). Pray for illumination from the Spirit of God.

2. *Look for connections with the OT.* The NT is part of one large "book" (the Bible), and we should always seek to understand how a particular passage fits into this single story of God's redemptive work. The NT authors themselves, soaked in this story, constantly point us to these connections. They make use of the basic categories of the OT (sacrifice, covenant, law, etc.), they quote the OT, they pick up language from the OT. NIV text notes, cross references, and study notes in this Bible will help readers identify many of these points of contact.

3. *Recognize the different ways the NT communicates.* The NT books use different genres — biography, history, letter, apocalypse — to communicate with us, and a good reader will take these into account. Some passages, such as Jesus' teaching in the Gospels or the apostles' teachings in the letters, address us quite directly, telling us what to believe or what to do (or not to do). Other passages, such as stories about Jesus in the Gospels or about the early church in Acts, give us insight into the nature of reality as God sees it, challenging us to adjust our worldview to align it with the worldview seen in these stories.

4. *Remember that the NT books are occasional.* While God designed the NT to speak to every generation of believers in every part of the world, a particular first-century person wrote each NT book to a particular first-century audience with first-century concerns in view. Fortunately, most of those first-century concerns involve basic spiritual realities that transcend time and place. But some of those first-century issues are different than ours, and we will understand and apply the NT message more effectively if we know something about that world. The notes on biblical passages in this study Bible are designed precisely to help the reader navigate these issues.

5. *Compare Scripture with Scripture.* Because NT books address specific issues in the first century, they will sometimes give advice that is directly relevant only for that time and place. Readers should follow the cross references provided in this Bible to see what the Bible says elsewhere about a particular topic. If, for instance, what the Bible says elsewhere contradicts a particular teaching, that teaching may have been limited to a special circumstance or period of time. If, on the other hand, parallel passages say much the same thing, we may conclude that the teaching applies generally. ■

A CHRONOLOGY OF KEY NEW TESTAMENT EVENTS

Birth of Jesus	6–5 BC
Beginning of Jesus' public ministry	AD 27 or 28
Jesus' death and resurrection	30 (or 31 or 33)
Conversion of Paul	33
Paul's first missionary journey	46–47
Apostolic Council	48
Paul's second missionary journey	49–52
Paul's third missionary journey	52–57
Paul's voyage to Rome	Fall 59–Spring 60
Imprisonment of Paul in Rome	60–62
Death of Paul and Peter	64–65 (or 67)

INTRODUCTION TO

THE GOSPELS AND ACTS

MATTHEW

MARK

LUKE

JOHN

ACTS

THE GOSPELS AND ACTS

D. A. Carson

The first four books of the NT are commonly called Gospels. The fifth book, the Acts of the Apostles, is tied to Luke by common authorship: the same man wrote both Luke's Gospel and Acts. Although these five books convey great theological truths, they are also historical books: they aim to give readers a historical and theological account of the life, ministry, death, and resurrection of Jesus, and of the early decades of the Christian church. The other 22 books of the NT disclose many historical details, but unlike these first five books, they do not set out to tell a story.

What Does "Gospel" Mean?

The word *gospel* reflects the Greek word for "good news" or "momentous news" (see "The Gospel," p. 2686). The good news is what God has done in Jesus Christ, supremely in Jesus' life, death, and resurrection. This God did in fulfillment of all that he had promised to do (Luke 24:44) to reconcile lost and guilty human beings to himself, powerfully transforming them by his Spirit in anticipation of their resurrection existence in the new heaven and the new earth.

When Christians used the word "gospel" in the first century AD, it always referred to this message about Jesus; it did not refer to the writings of Matthew, Mark, Luke, or John — books that tell the story about Jesus. At that time, Christians spoke of the gospel *according to* Matthew, Mark, or the others. In other words, there was *one* gospel, the gospel of Jesus Christ, *according to* Matthew, Mark, Luke, or John. Only in the second century and beyond did Christians start talking about these books themselves as Gospels — Matthew's Gospel (or the Gospel of Matthew), Mark's Gospel, and so on. In the first century, "gospel" referred to the *message*, not the *book* that conveyed it.

Two things follow. (1) This way of speaking emphasizes that there is only *one* gospel, only one message. The individual writers doubtless bear witness to Jesus in somewhat different and complementary ways, but there is only one gospel. (2) If Matthew, Mark, Luke, and John all tell about the one gospel, we gain a clearer idea of what this gospel is by observing what these four books have in common. In all four books (we may refer to them as four Gospels provided we recognize that doing so is to use the word "Gospel" in its second-century sense), we learn that the one gospel, the one message, focuses on Jesus and emphasizes that his coming and mission fulfill what God promised in the past. These books say something about Jesus' origin, his teaching and preaching, his miracles, and his interactions with very diverse people — and always the story moves inexorably to Jesus' death and resurrection. Always there is some explanation of what these stupendous events mean, of what God is doing through Jesus to save his people, to bring in the kingdom, to move history toward its consummation at the end of the age. Without this amalgam of elements, there is no gospel.

That is why certain second-century documents should not be considered Gospels at all. For example, the pseudepigraphical *Gospel of Thomas*, published in the second century, is a collection of 114 statements ascribed to Jesus and two very small historical snippets. The document says nothing of Jesus' origin, miracles, death, or resurrection. In short, it does not tell the good news, the gospel, at all. It cannot claim to relate the one gospel of Jesus Christ according to Thomas — not only because Thomas did not write the document but also because what it relates is not the gospel.

The Relationships Among These Five Books

In this study Bible, the book introductions on these five books provide information on the individual writers, when each book was written, and each book's structure and themes. Here it is enough to say something about how these books relate to one another.

Although these five books convey great theological truths, they are also historical books: they aim to give readers a historical and theological account of the life, ministry, death, and resurrection of Jesus, and of the early decades of the Christian church.

Resurrection of Jesus.
Wikimedia Commons

The first four NT books are the Gospels (we shall continue to call them that). They are historical narratives that tell the story of the life, ministry, death, and resurrection of Jesus. In style they are not completely different from other biographies (called "lives") written about that time. However, because they relate the story of Jesus, collectively they are utterly unique: Jesus is the Son of God in a unique sense, the Messiah who is crucified and rises from the dead.

Even a casual reading discloses that John differs considerably from Matthew, Mark, and Luke. These three (Matthew, Mark, and Luke) are often referred to as the Synoptic Gospels (*syn*, "together with"; *optic*, "seeing"; hence, *synoptic* is "seeing together"). That is because Matthew, Mark, and Luke present Jesus in a similar way: they often choose to include the same material; they share much common vocabulary; and they frequently relate incidents in Jesus' life in the same order (which is sometimes a topical order rather than a chronological one). For example, they relate quite a few of Jesus' parables, tell of occasions when Jesus casts out demons, and with minor variations describe the death of Jesus in very similar ways. From the Synoptics it is difficult to draw conclusions about the length of Jesus' ministry, but Jesus' emphasis on the kingdom of God or the kingdom of heaven is unmistakable.

By contrast, the Gospel according to John is rather different in its use of words and in some of the material covered. Its vocabulary is much more limited. John relates no narrative parables or exorcisms. He says relatively little about the kingdom of God (though admittedly the three instances when he talks of the kingdom are highly significant; see John 3:3,5; 18:36), preferring to speak of eternal life. The first five chapters of John's book, about one quarter of its length, describe Jesus' ministry in the south of the country, in Jerusalem and Judea, before Jesus' ministry in Galilee begins — the Galilean ministry with which the Synoptics begin. John's structured references to specific Jewish festival days enable us to infer that Jesus' public ministry was either two and a half or three and a half years long. John lays great emphasis on Jesus' sonship to God (e.g., 5:16 – 30; 20:30 – 31). Obviously there are points in common among all four books (e.g., all four relate the feeding of the 5,000). But John records several discourses not found elsewhere, including John 14 – 17, a long passage that comprises Jesus' words to his disciples on the evening he was betrayed and his own remarkable prayer on that same evening.

If of the four Gospels John stands out in these ways, the Gospel of Luke stands out in another way: it alone is tied to a second book, the Acts of the Apostles. Luke and Acts comprise about one quarter of the NT. Acts picks up where Luke ends. Acts provides a selective narrative of the first decades of the church, focusing especially on the ministries of the apostles Peter and Paul. It says little about what the other apostles were doing, though from other sources we can glimpse their extensive ministries. Acts shows how the gospel crosses one boundary after another: from Jerusalem to far corners of the Roman Empire, from Jew to Samaritan to Gentile, from the old covenant to the new, from the eastern end of the Mediterranean to Rome, the capital city.

Acts is tied to Luke not only by much common vocabulary and many common themes (e.g., an emphasis on prayer and on the work of the Holy Spirit) but also by common reference to Theophilus in the opening verses of each book (Luke 1:3; Acts 1:1). More dramatically, while Luke tells of Jesus' earthly life, ministry, death, and resurrection — it is, after all, telling the one gospel and will itself later be called a Gospel — Acts insists that Luke relates but what Jesus *began* to do (Acts 1:1), giving the impression that what Acts relates is what Jesus *continues* to do. Acts extends the story beyond Jesus' resurrection and ascension. This is a powerful way of reminding readers that the Jesus of history continues to reign as the Lord of the church, the Ruler over history, bringing about his sovereign, gracious purposes in the wake of his triumphant resurrection.

The Relationships Among the Synoptics

Although the Synoptic Gospels (Matthew, Mark, and Luke) display many similarities, they are certainly not identical: careful reading shows how each differs from the other two. Matthew appears to be written in a dominantly Jewish context. Matthew quotes extensively from the OT, and he is eager to show that Jesus is the promised Messiah (or Christ). Matthew's work is carefully structured, with speeches and narratives alternating. Mark carries the story forward with breathless speed: Mark's book is characterized by urgent drama as he demonstrates that Jesus is the suffering Son of God. Luke is measured and polished. Luke repeatedly shows that the good news is that Jesus is the Savior not only for Jews but for all people, especially the poor and oppressed.

One should not think that each of these respective historical and theological emphases in the Synoptic Gospels is restricted to its own Gospel. All three themes — Jesus is the Messiah (Matthew), Jesus is the suffering Son of God (Mark), Jesus is the Savior of Jews and Gentiles alike (Luke) — are found in all three Gospels. Differences in emphasis should not be confused with mutual exclusiveness.

The degree of overlap in these three Gospels invites readers to try to work out how, in God's providence, they came to be written. About 91 percent of Mark is found in Matthew; about 53 percent of Mark is found in Luke. Matthew and Luke contain some common material that is not found in Mark. Did one or more of the writers have access to the work of the other(s), borrowing freely? After all, before the invention of the printing press, free borrowing was not viewed as plagiarism (which is why, for example, some kind of borrowing is going on between 2 Peter and Jude). In fact, Luke tells us that he carefully studied other sources when he composed his book (Luke 1:1 – 3). There is no particular reason to think that Matthew and Mark refrained from the same practice. Apparently both oral and written accounts of Jesus' words and deeds circulated freely before the NT Gospels came to be written. And what explains the fact that sometimes one of the Synoptic Gospels uses exactly the same Greek words as another (e.g., "hate[d]" in Matt 10:22a; Mark 13:13a; Luke 21:17), sometimes there is close agreement in content but not in exact wording (e.g., Matt 9:2 – 8; Mark 2:3 – 12; Luke 5:18 – 26), and sometimes the order of events is quite different (e.g., miracles that are grouped thematically in Matt 8 – 9 are distributed throughout Mark's book)?

All four of the Gospels relate the feeding of the 5,000.

Feeding the multitude, Hole, William Brassey (1846 – 1917)/Private Collection/© Look and Learn/Bridgeman Images

Questions of this sort, called forth by the tight but highly variable relationships among the Synoptics, constitute what is today called the Synoptic Problem. Scholars have proposed many solutions. The most important ones are these:

1. *The priority and use of Matthew.* This was the most common view in the first centuries of the early church. This view held that the Gospel according to Matthew was written first and that Mark and Luke used Matthew. Though most of Mark was drawn from Matthew, Mark added some independent material. Luke drew on Matthew and Mark and supplemented this material with other sources.

2. *Two-source theory.* This is the most popular view today. It argues that Mark was written first. At roughly the same time, another source, des-

Paul preaching at Ephesus.
WikiArt

ignated Q (from the German word *Quelle*, "source"), was circulating. Q is comprised of sayings of Jesus, and much of its material is found in Matthew and Luke, but little of its material is found in Mark. (Thus to refer to it as the Q Gospel, as some do, is highly misleading.) Q is hypothetical: no written manuscript has been found. It is an inference drawn from the many parallels between Matthew and Luke. It is quite possible that there was no one Q. Instead, there may have been several documents that reported miscellaneous sayings of Jesus on which both Matthew and Luke drew, and these documents can for convenience be jointly labeled Q. In the two-source theory, Mark and Q were the sources used by Matthew and Luke, who used them in somewhat different ways.

This two-source theory is sometimes also called the four-source theory because in addition to Mark and Q, Matthew has some material found only in Matthew (designated M), and Luke has some material found only in Luke (designated L).

3. *The Griesbach hypothesis.* This theory, named after the man who first articulated it in detail, again argues that Matthew was written first, but it holds that Luke drew on Matthew, and Mark drew on Matthew and Luke.

Several other theories have circulated. For example, a handful of people argue that the three Synoptic Gospels were independently written. Others have advocated modifications and revisions of the theories already indicated. The complexity of the issues is compounded by such additional factors as the following:

1. *Date of composition.* If the second theory (the "two-source theory") is right, Mark was written first; but if we assume the priority of Matthew (the first theory), then clearly Matthew was written first. Questions surrounding the dating of these documents are themselves rather tricky, and these dating questions are addressed in the book introductions of each book.

2. *Language.* There is at least some evidence that Matthew first wrote his book in Aramaic and then later produced it in Greek. Some have speculated that Mark or Luke may have relied on Aramaic Matthew. But by the time Matthew produced his Greek version, Mark and Luke were already circulating, so the lines of dependence then went the other way. If anything like this happened, clearly the lines of dependence become so complex that people living in the twenty-first century cannot possibly retrieve them.

3. *Eyewitnesses.* It appears that Matthew and John were eyewitnesses; Mark, for the most part, was not (though he depended on the testimony of the eyewitness Peter), and Luke was not. How much did personal memory play into the writing of these books?

4. *Readers.* At one time many commentators held that Matthew was written for a rather narrow collection

Matthew writing his Gospel.
Wikimedia Commons

of churches associated with Matthew, Mark was written for another collection of churches, and so forth. If this is correct, then it might have taken a while in the nondigital world of the first century for any one Gospel book to circulate and be used in diverse circles. Increasingly, however, students of the first century have shown that the four NT Gospels were designed from the first to be widely disseminated and read. If that is the case, the possibility of borrowing, in one direction or another, would take very little time because the books were circulated rapidly and extensively.

Even if we do not have enough information to finally resolve the Synoptic Problem, the subtle differences we find among the Gospels testify to something important. In giving us these accounts of his Son through the hands of four different men, God ensured two things: (1) multiple witnesses and (2) the richness of slightly different portraits. That suggests that when we teach and preach these four Gospels, we ought to study them with such reverent attention to details that we preserve their individual flavors. It is not wrong, of course, to try to put their details together into one organic whole — that is, to create a "harmony" of the Gospels. Christian thinkers have been constructing harmonies of the Gospels since at least the second century: the first one we know about was prepared by a man called Tatian. Such harmonies tend to focus on the historical cohesion of the four books. Nevertheless, these four books originally circulated separately, and it is important that we not lose the distinctive theological flavor of each work.

John and Other Writings by John

Just as Luke is tied by common authorship to another book of the NT, i.e., Acts (see The Relationships Among These Five Books), so the Gospel according to John is tied by common authorship to other NT books: 1 John, 2 John, 3 John, and Revelation. 1, 2, and 3 John are letters sent to churches several decades after Jesus had risen from the dead; they deal with pastoral issues arising from rejection of the gospel. Revelation, mostly written in the highly symbol-laden language of apocalyptic literature (see Introduction to Revelation), describes the conflict of the ages between God and the devil. Jesus achieves unqualified victory over death and the devil by his death and resurrection, and the rest of history is nothing other than the remaining conflict that continues until the church arrives at the end of the age and the consummation of all things. In other words, all the NT books refer to the gospel, the momentous news of what God has done in Jesus Christ, but only the four books we call Gospels concentrate all their attention on the life, ministry, death, and resurrection of the Savior.

From this we must infer two things, one of them obvious and the other important.

1. The obvious thing is that at least some of the writers whom God used to give us the NT were capable of writing books of quite different sorts — in John's case, a Gospel, three short letters, and an apocalyptic work.

2. The important thing is to recognize that the crucial issue is what *kind* of book was written, not *when* it was written. Matthew and John, for example, were written after most of the letters of the NT were written. This has led some scholars to argue that the theology found in Matthew and John is necessarily later theology than, say, the theology found in Paul's early letters. But *when* they are writing is not as important as *what* they are writing. Paul is clearly writing to churches that have been established in the wake of the death and resurrection of Jesus, and part of his purpose is to add understanding to the significance of those momentous events. By contrast, the Gospel writers describe the events that lead up to and are climaxed by Jesus' death and resurrection. Although they (especially Matthew and John) write long after the events they describe, they have a deep understanding of the significance of those events and take great pains to portray the confusion, partial understanding, and even misunderstanding of the apostles themselves as the events unfolded in history.

During the days of Jesus' life on earth, the apostles confront a Messiah very different from the one they expected — a Messiah who is not only descended from David but is one with God, a Messiah who is not only sovereign king but suffering servant, a Messiah who demands full submission and allegiance but who came not "to be served, but to serve, and to give his life as a ransom for many" (Matt 20:28; Mark 10:45). The four NT Gospel writers bear witness to that story with a God-given combination of historical faithfulness and theological nuance as the full impact of the gospel is fully understood only after the events themselves. ■

John receiving the revelation on the island of Patmos.
The British Library Catalogue of Illuminated Manuscripts

INTRODUCTION TO MATTHEW

AUTHOR

The unanimous tradition of the early church ascribed this Gospel to Matthew, one of Jesus' 12 closest followers and a former tax collector, also named Levi (cf. 9:9 – 13 with Mark 2:14 – 17). Strictly speaking, however, all four Gospels are anonymous. No statement within them anywhere identifies their authors; in contrast, Paul's name appears in the opening greetings of each of his letters. It is likely that the titles were added only after there was more than one Gospel, thus necessitating a need to distinguish them from one another. So the author of this Gospel (Greek *euangelion kata Maththaion*) probably was not the person to give his document this title.

At the same time, no other names ever competed with Matthew's as this Gospel's author. The oldest known testimony comes from an early second-century Christian writer named Papias, whom Eusebius, an early fourth-century church historian, quoted as saying, "Matthew composed his Gospel in the Hebrew [or Aramaic] language, and everyone translated as they were able" (*Ecclesiastical History*, 3.39.16). Of the 12 apostles (except for Judas, who betrayed Jesus), it is not likely that anyone would have chosen to ascribe this Gospel to Matthew, the once hated tax collector, unless they knew that he actually wrote it.

Some modern scholars think Matthew is not the author for four main reasons: (1) We have discovered no ancient text of this Gospel in Hebrew (see the Eusebius quotation above), and most of Matthew in Greek does not read like a

Stone depiction of a Roman lease payment. Matthew was a tax collector before Jesus called him into ministry.

direct translation from a Semitic tongue. (2) Matthew appears to have relied on Mark's Gospel for his content and wording at numerous places, but an apostle would not have had to depend on a Gospel written by a lesser-known Christian who was not an eyewitness to most of what he penned. (3) Matthew appears to refer to himself in 13:52 as an early Christian scribe, not a tax collector. (4) Some of Matthew appears too anti-Jewish to have been written by a Jewish follower of Jesus the Jew.

On the other hand, (1) writers translating from one language to another in the ancient Mediterranean world often translated freely, putting their own stylistic stamp on their work. The Gospel as we have it does contain a lot of parallelism in its literary style, a regular feature of both Semitic prose and poetry. (2) Early church tradition affirmed that Mark got much of the contents of his Gospel from the apostle Peter, the leader of the apostles in the mid-first century, which would make his narrative one of great interest to Matthew. (3) It is not at all clear that 13:52 is the author's self-reference, but even if it is, the unusual literacy of tax collectors would have made it natural for Matthew as a follower of Jesus to turn to scribal activity. (4) Finally, a careful reading of his Gospel shows that while Matthew depicts Jesus as sharply challenging certain Jewish leaders and more general national trends, he does so as a devoted insider, not as an outsider to the movement. There is no compelling reason, then, to reject the early church's uniform conviction that Matthew was the author of this narrative. Little interpretive significance necessarily changes, however, if one rejects this conclusion and attributes the book, as many today do, to an otherwise anonymous first-century Christian.

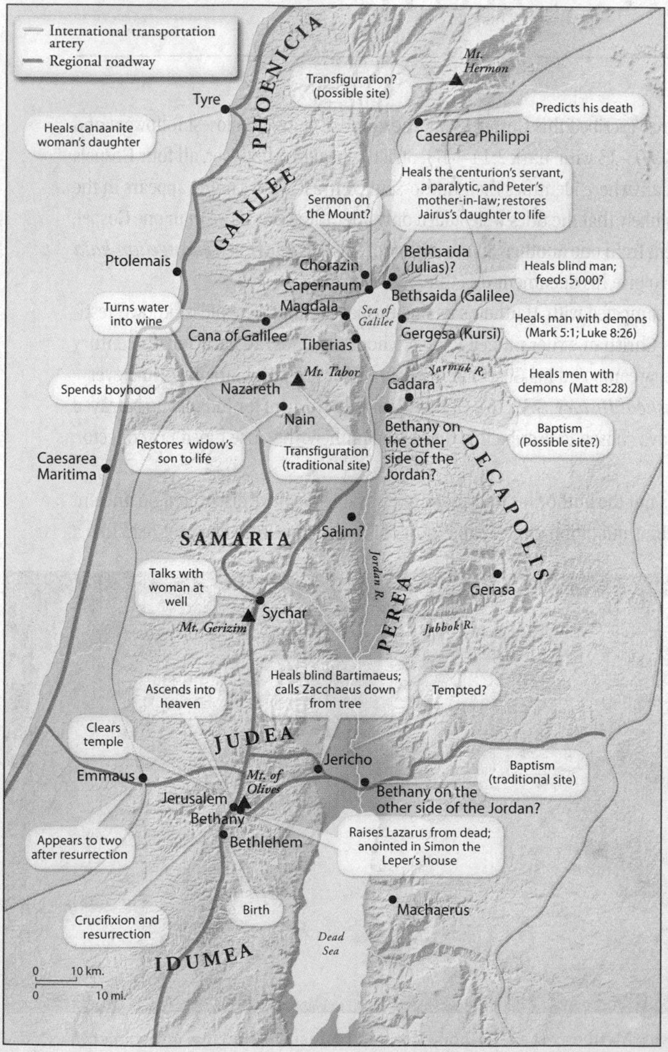

DATE

The second-century Christian writer Irenaeus declared that Matthew wrote "while Peter and Paul were preaching the Gospel and founding the church in Rome" (*Against Heresies*, 3.1.1). If this is accurate, Matthew was probably written in the early to mid-60s, because this is the one time before the martyrdoms of these two Christian leaders that we know they were together in the capital of the first-century Roman Empire.

There are at least three objections to this line of reasoning: (1) Matt 22:6–7 is "prophecy" after the fact, reflecting knowledge of the destruction of Jerusalem in AD 70 by the Romans. (2) The tensions with Pharisaic Judaism recurring throughout the Gospel reflect conditions in the latter decades of the first century, when Christian Judaism and rabbinic Judaism were competing to be the one true remaining form of Judaism after the destruction of the others due to the war with Rome. (3) Matthew was written after Mark, and Mark was written either just before or after AD 70, so Matthew must have been written later still.

HIGHLIGHTS OF JESUS' MINISTRY

In reply: (1) The first objection holds only if Jesus could not have actually predicted the coming fall of Jerusalem, which seems to require unwarranted antisupernatural presuppositions. (2) The competition described was beginning already in the 60s, and the numerous references to the Sadducees (not the Pharisees) and the larger Jerusalem temple leadership as Jesus' primary antagonists, especially during his passion, could support a pre-70 debate (before the Pharisees alone were left). (3) Mark may well have been written in the early 60s, so that Matthew's use of Mark poses no problem for a date in the early or mid-60s. Whether one dates Matthew to the 60s (which more conservative scholars prefer) or the 80s (which more liberal scholars prefer), we are still well within a 60-year period of time from the events narrated. Most ancient history that has survived and is deemed to be reasonably trustworthy was written considerably longer after the events happened than this. Matthew merits all the more trust.

BACKGROUND, OCCASION, AND PURPOSE

What little ancient testimony we have (Irenaeus, Eusebius, Jerome) suggests that Matthew wrote in the Holy Land or to Jewish believers in the Holy Land. Most of the tradition affirms simply that he addressed predominantly Jewish Christians without specifying their location or a place from which he wrote. Modern scholars have frequently suggested Antioch of Syria because of its large Jewish and Jewish-Christian population and because it was a city outside of Israel that would have needed a Greek rather than Hebrew or Aramaic account. Beyond these basic points it is difficult to add much with any confidence.

It may well be, as a consensus of modern scholarship has increasingly suggested, that Matthew was writing primarily to Jewish-Christians who had broken from the synagogue (or been excommunicated by their local synagogues) because they accepted Jesus as Messiah and Lord. But they were not so far removed from their Jewish roots that the tensions of this break had dissipated. Believers wanted their purely Jewish friends and family to join them in worshiping Jesus. Non-Christian Jews increasingly feared that God was punishing Israel for tolerating this "apostasy" in its ranks. Such "sibling rivalry" could naturally have produced some of the strong language in Matthew's Gospel about the Jews of Jesus' day and accounted for the emphasis on some of Jesus' equally strong invective against various Jewish leaders (e.g., 15:3–9; ch. 23). Conflict with key Jewish leaders also probably hastened the shift to a multiethnic church of Jew and Gentile alike (e.g., 21:43; 28:18–20).

So Matthew's central purpose is to commend following Jesus as the true way for a Jew to continue as one of God's elect people. But he doubtless has multiple purposes. His distinctive inclusion of five large blocks of Jesus' teaching (chs. 5–7; 10:5–42; 13:1–52; ch. 18; chs. 23–25) suggests catechetical designs, especially since so much of this teaching involves ethical matters, and discipleship is a major theme in Matthew as well. With unique references to the "church" (16:18; 18:17) and to God's people living in community, along with warnings against false teachers, Matthew may also be trying to take some of the first steps in implementing organization and criteria for leadership in the Christian church.

GENRE

Despite some claims to the contrary, Matthew is still more like Mark in literary genre than any other known work of its time, and Mark still reads more like theological biography than any other known genre of its time. Like *all* ancient historians, the Gospel writers' main reason for writing was not to chronicle unadorned facts about the person of Jesus of Nazareth like some modern dispassionate historians. Biographers in antiquity selected paradigmatic events. Though the evangelists had theology they wished to stress, that does not impugn their reliability. After all, the very nature of certain ideologies requires factual support in order to be persuasive! Matthew, like Christians more generally, had an uphill battle in convincing monotheistic Jews that Jesus is God, so he would have had no reason to create additional problems for his cause by playing fast and loose with the history on which it was built. Competing Jewish movements would have quickly debunked the fledgling church, given the care with which Jews in general passed on by oral tradition information that was important to them. Strikingly, the traditions about Jesus that were preserved from ancient Jewish sources regularly called him a "sorcerer who led Israel astray." In other words, they acknowledged his wondrous feats but disputed which supernatural power inspired him.

At the same time, this is a "gospel," an account of good news. Like Mark, Matthew is convinced that Jesus of Nazareth was God's heaven-sent envoy to proclaim good news to Israel and to fulfill all of Scripture's prophecies, even if by unconventional and unexpected methods—dying for the sins of the world rather than fighting to rid the land of the Romans. Christians ever since have believed that this is the most important good news that anyone can receive or share.

THEOLOGY

In light of the circumstances that led to Matthew's Gospel described in Background, Occasion, and Purpose on p. 1923, the dominant and distinctive themes of this book occasion no surprise. Matthew stresses how a message that is the fulfillment of the hopes of Israel is increasingly rejected by many within the nation and how Jesus prepares the way for the Gentile mission his disciples will embark on. Only Matthew has Jesus' comments about being sent just to Israel during his earthly life (10:5–6; 15:24), and only Matthew has Jesus sending the disciples to all the nations (28:18–20) and the kingdom being taken from the current Jewish leadership and "given to a people who will produce its fruit" (21:43).

Matthew's depiction of Jesus focuses on his roles as Teacher (especially with Matthew's five main sermons; see Outline, p. 1925) and Son of David (the Messianic king from David's lineage who would rule Israel). In common with the other Gospels, Matthew portrays Jesus as preferring the title "Son of Man" for himself, alluding to the exalted human who is ushered into God's presence to receive universal authority over the peoples of the earth (Dan 7:13–14). He is also the "Son of God," a title that in Jewish circles could mean merely Messiah, but which, especially in Matthew, came more and more to have overtones of divinity (e.g., 14:33; 16:16). The most significant title for Jesus in Matthew is probably "Lord"—Jesus as both Master and God (e.g., 8:2,6,25; 9:28). Somewhat distinctive to Matthew, though less common, are Jesus as "wisdom" (e.g., 11:19) and "Immanuel" (that is, "God with us"; 1:23; see 28:20).

Matthew further highlights discipleship and often discloses a little more understanding on the part of the Twelve than does Mark (cf. 14:33 with Mark 6:52). Only Matthew uses the word "church" among the four Gospels (16:18; 18:17), with teaching about its foundation and its discipline. Matthew calls more attention to Peter, although the distinctive passages in which he appears include both positive and negative traits (14:28–31; 15:15; 16:18–19; 17:24–27; 18:21), so it is clear that Matthew is not trying to overly exalt Peter as some in the history of the church have done.

Aerial view of Capernaum, along the northern shore of the Sea of Galilee. Matthew was a tax collector in Capernaum and was met there and called by Jesus (Matt 9:9).

OUTLINE

I. Introduction to Jesus' Ministry (1:1—4:16)
- A. Jesus' Birth Narrative (1:1—2:23)
- B. Other Introductory Events in Jesus' Ministry (3:1—4:17)

II. The Major Phase of Jesus' Public Ministry (4:18—16:20)
- A. Introduction to the Galilean Ministry (4:18–25)
- B. Jesus' Authoritative Teaching: The Sermon on the Mount (5:1—7:29)
- C. Jesus' Authoritative Miracle-Working Ministry (8:1—9:34)
- D. Missionary Discourse (9:35—10:42)
- E. Increasing Hostility toward Jesus (11:1—12:50)
- F. Parables of the Kingdom (13:1–52)
- G. Progressive Polarization (13:53—16:20)

III. The Road to the Cross and the Resurrection (16:21—28:20)
- A. Preparation for the Passion (16:21—17:27)
- B. Sermon on Humility and Forgiveness (18:1–35)
- C. Journeying to the Temple (19:1—22:46)
- D. Woes and Warnings (23:1—25:46)
- E. Jesus' Passion, Death, and Resurrection (26:1—28:20)

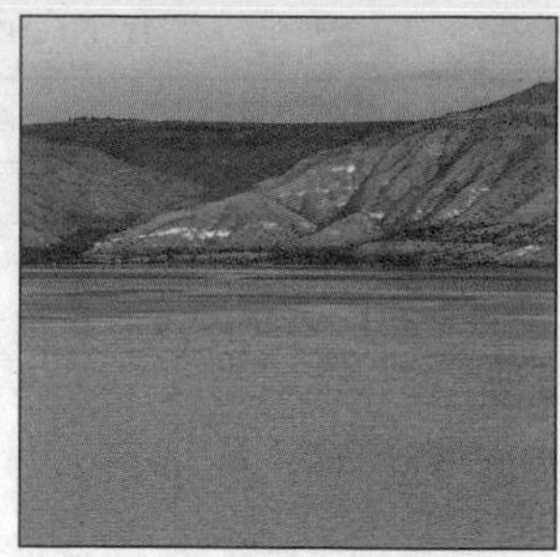

MATTHEW

1:1 [a]2Sa 7:12-16; Isa 9:6,7; 11:1; Jer 23:5, 6; Mt 9:27; Lk 1:32,69; Ro 1:3; Rev 22:16 [b]Ge 22:18; Gal 3:16
1:2 [c]Ge 21:3,12 [d]Ge 25:26 [e]Ge 29:35
1:3 [f]Ge 38:27-30

The Genealogy of Jesus the Messiah

1:1-17pp — Lk 3:23-38
1:3-6pp — Ru 4:18-22
1:7-11pp — 1Ch 3:10-17

1 This is the genealogy[a] of Jesus the Messiah[b] the son of David,[a] the son of Abraham:[b]

2 Abraham was the father of Isaac,[c]
Isaac the father of Jacob,[d]
Jacob the father of Judah and his brothers,[e]
3 Judah the father of Perez and Zerah, whose mother was Tamar,[f]
Perez the father of Hezron,
Hezron the father of Ram,
4 Ram the father of Amminadab,
Amminadab the father of Nahshon,
Nahshon the father of Salmon,
5 Salmon the father of Boaz, whose mother was Rahab,
Boaz the father of Obed, whose mother was Ruth,

[a] *1* Or *is an account of the origin* [b] *1* Or *Jesus Christ. Messiah* (Hebrew) and *Christ* (Greek) both mean *Anointed One*; also in verse 18.

1:1—4:16 *Introduction to Jesus' Ministry.* Prior to narrating Jesus' main public ministry, Matthew provides Jesus' genealogy, selected events surrounding his birth and childhood, his association with John the Baptist, and his temptations by the devil.

1:1—2:23 *Jesus' Birth Narrative.* Chs. 1–2 depict Jesus' origins. His family tree shows that he has the right credentials for his God-appointed ministry. His fulfilling prophecy points to him as the only possible descendant of David who qualifies to be the Messiah. Ch. 1 also identifies who Jesus is: "the Messiah the son of David, the son of Abraham" (1:1) and "Immanuel" (1:23). Ch. 2 highlights key locations associated with his youngest days: Bethlehem (2:5), Egypt (2:13), Ramah (2:18), and Nazareth (2:23).

1:1–17 This genealogy introduces a select list of Jesus' ancestors from Abraham onward in the style of OT genealogies (especially Gen 5:1–32). Luke 3:23–38 contains a longer but still selective list moving backward from Jesus all the way to Adam and then to God. Matthew probably provides the legal or royal line; Luke, the biological line.

1:1 This is the genealogy. The genealogy demonstrates that Jesus was qualified to be the Messiah, the prophesied liberator of Israel (Greek *christos*, "anointed one"). 2 Sam 7:14 requires him to be a descendant of David, the great king of Israel a millennium earlier, which also makes him a descendant of Abraham, the founder of the Israelite nation, through whose offspring all the peoples of the world would be blessed (Gen 12:1–3). Jesus will rule as king on earth when he returns (Rev 19:11—20:4), but first he must die as the suffering servant (Isa 52:13—53:12).

1:2–16 The list of names follows the conventional Jewish practice of itemizing fathers. **the father of.** Could also mean "the ancestor of." Matthew skips generations at times (see also, e.g., 1 Chr 3:10–14).

1:2 Judah and his brothers. The 12 sons of Jacob, the ancestors of the 12 tribes of Israel.

1:3 Perez and Zerah. Both mentioned probably because they were twins. **Tamar.** The daughter-in-law of Judah. She was a Canaanite who disguised herself as a prostitute to trick Judah into impregnating her so that she could bear children for the family line after his successive sons had failed to do so (Gen 38). She is the first of five mothers included in the genealogy. All, including Mary, were shrouded in suspicions, founded or unfounded, of sexual sin. Jesus will thus be the Messiah for the least, the last, and the lost of the world as well as for the righteous in Israel.

1:5 Rahab. The famous Canaanite prostitute who harbored the Israelite spies (Josh 2). **Ruth.** A Moabite who followed her mother-in-law, Naomi, back to Israel. By lying down at Boaz's feet in the middle of the night while he was sleeping—an ancient custom apparently equivalent to a marriage proposal (Ruth 3)—she left herself open to suspicions of illicit sex, even though the charge would have been unfounded.

Obed the father of Jesse,
6 and Jesse the father of King David.[g]

David was the father of Solomon, whose mother had been Uriah's wife,[h]
7 Solomon the father of Rehoboam,
Rehoboam the father of Abijah,
Abijah the father of Asa,
8 Asa the father of Jehoshaphat,
Jehoshaphat the father of Jehoram,
Jehoram the father of Uzziah,
9 Uzziah the father of Jotham,
Jotham the father of Ahaz,
Ahaz the father of Hezekiah,
10 Hezekiah the father of Manasseh,[i]
Manasseh the father of Amon,
Amon the father of Josiah,
11 and Josiah the father of Jeconiah[a] and his brothers at the time of the exile to Babylon.[j]

12 After the exile to Babylon:
Jeconiah was the father of Shealtiel,[k]
Shealtiel the father of Zerubbabel,[l]
13 Zerubbabel the father of Abihud,
Abihud the father of Eliakim,
Eliakim the father of Azor,
14 Azor the father of Zadok,
Zadok the father of Akim,
Akim the father of Elihud,
15 Elihud the father of Eleazar,
Eleazar the father of Matthan,
Matthan the father of Jacob,
16 and Jacob the father of Joseph, the husband of Mary,[m] and Mary was the mother of Jesus who is called the Messiah.[n]

17 Thus there were fourteen generations in all from Abraham to David, fourteen from David to the exile to Babylon, and fourteen from the exile to the Messiah.

Joseph Accepts Jesus as His Son

18 This is how the birth of Jesus the Messiah came about[b]: His mother Mary was pledged to be married to Joseph, but before they came together, she was found to be pregnant through the Holy Spirit.[o]

a 11 That is, Jehoiachin; also in verse 12 *b 18* Or *The origin of Jesus the Messiah was like this*

1:6 [g] 1Sa 16:1; 17:12 [h] 2Sa 12:24
1:10 [i] 2Ki 20:21
1:11 [j] 2Ki 24:14-16; Jer 27:20; Da 1:1,2
1:12 [k] 1Ch 3:17 [l] 1Ch 3:19; Ezr 3:2
1:16 [m] Lk 1:27 [n] Mt 27:17
1:18 [o] Lk 1:35

1:6 Uriah's wife. Bathsheba; probably called "Uriah's wife" to recall not only David's adultery with Solomon's mother but also his indirect murder of her husband (2 Sam 11).

1:8 Jehoram the father. Matthew calls Jehoram the father of Uzziah, but from 2 Chr 21:4—26:23 it is clear that several generations were assumed (Ahaziah, Joash, and Amaziah) and that "father" is used in the sense of "forefather" or "ancestor."

1:16 husband of Mary. Matthew does not say that Joseph was the father of Jesus but only that he was the husband of Mary and that Jesus was born of her.

1:17 fourteen generations. By counting both inclusively and exclusively, Matthew selects enough members of Jesus' lineage to create three segments of 14 names. Because Hebrew used letters for numerals, the consonants of every Hebrew word added up to a certain number. This practice was called *gematria.* The *gematria* for the Hebrew consonants for at least one spelling of "David" was 14 (D + V + D = 4 + 6 + 4). Matthew is probably using a Jewish device for highlighting David as Jesus' key ancestor; David also appears as the 14th name in this genealogy.

1:18—2:23 Matthew chooses to narrate five episodes from the events surrounding the conception, birth, and infancy of Jesus, all of which fulfill OT prophecy. He continues to demonstrate that Jesus is the Messiah (Christ) who has come to save his people.

1:18–25 Christians have traditionally labeled this account as "the virgin birth," but the important point, theologically, is not that Mary was a virgin at the time Jesus was born but that she was a virgin at the time Jesus was conceived.

1:18 pledged to be married. Engagement, a legally binding commitment in ancient Judaism. Jewish couples often wed when the young man was about 18 and the young woman was in her very early teens. Prior to marriage they would not live together and were expected to refrain from sexual relations until after their wedding ceremony. **pregnant through the Holy Spirit.** Jesus had no human paternity but was

1:19 [p] Dt 24:1
1:21 [q] Lk 1:31 [r] Lk 2:11; Ac 5:31; 13:23,28
1:23 [s] Isa 7:14; 8:8,10
1:25 [t] ver 21
2:1 [u] Lk 2:4-7 [v] Lk 1:5
2:2 [w] Jer 23:5; Mt 27:11; Mk 15:2; Jn 1:49; 18:33-37 [x] Nu 24:17
2:5 [y] Jn 7:42

19 Because Joseph her husband was faithful to the law, and yet[a] did not want to expose her to public
disgrace, he had in mind to divorce[p] her quietly.
20 But after he had considered this, an angel of the Lord appeared to him in a dream and said, "Joseph son of David, do not be afraid to take Mary home as your wife, because what is conceived in her is
from the Holy Spirit. 21 She will give birth to a son, and you are to give him the name Jesus,[b][q] because
he will save his people from their sins."[r]
22 All this took place to fulfill what the Lord had said through the prophet: 23 "The virgin will conceive
and give birth to a son, and they will call him Immanuel"[c][s] (which means "God with us").
24 When Joseph woke up, he did what the angel of the Lord had commanded him and took Mary
home as his wife. 25 But he did not consummate their marriage until she gave birth to a son. And he
gave him the name Jesus.[t]

The Magi Visit the Messiah

2 After Jesus was born in Bethlehem in Judea,[u] during the time of King Herod,[v] Magi[d] from the east
came to Jerusalem 2 and asked, "Where is the one who has been born king of the Jews?[w] We saw
his star[x] when it rose and have come to worship him."
3 When King Herod heard this he was disturbed, and all Jerusalem with him. 4 When he had called
together all the people's chief priests and teachers of the law, he asked them where the Messiah was to
be born. 5 "In Bethlehem[y] in Judea," they replied, "for this is what the prophet has written:

[a] *19* Or *was a righteous man and* [b] *21* *Jesus* is the Greek form of *Joshua,* which means *the LORD saves.*
[c] *23* Isaiah 7:14 [d] *1* Traditionally *wise men*

supernaturally conceived by the power of God. **the Holy Spirit.** The common NT way of referring to the divine Spirit, who in the OT was almost always called "the Spirit of God" or "the Spirit of the LORD" (but see Ps 51:11). Christian reflection on the Biblical word about him (see 3:16–17; 28:19; 2 Cor 13:14) led to the understanding that he is one of the three persons of the Trinity.

1:19 to divorce her quietly. Jewish tradition required divorce in the case of adultery. (Sexual relations with another partner even during engagement constituted adultery.) Joseph does not initially believe Mary's story that she is pregnant without another man having been involved. Joseph wanted to fulfill the law but also show compassion to his fiancée.

1:20–21 Not surprisingly, it takes a supernatural appearance of an angel to convince Joseph that Mary has not been unfaithful and that they may proceed with their wedding plans. The angel addresses Joseph as "son of David" to prepare him for the promise that Mary "will give birth to a son" who will fulfill the role of Messiah. But instead of the political liberator for which many Jews longed, this child will grow up to die and bring spiritual salvation to Israel.

1:22 to fulfill. Twelve times (here; 2:15,23; 3:15; 4:14; 5:17; 8:17; 12:17; 13:14,35; 21:4; 27:9) Matthew speaks of the OT being fulfilled in the events of Jesus' life. Some of these prophecies are uniquely fulfilled by Jesus, while others are typological, where Jesus is the ultimate fulfillment of an OT type (see note on 2:15). Here the OT text in question is Isa 7:14. The immediate OT context suggests a partial fulfillment in Isaiah's day: "Before the boy knows enough to reject the wrong and choose the right, the land of the two kings you dread will be laid waste" (Isa 7:16) refers back to Rezin and Pekah (Isa 7:1).

1:23 virgin. The word in Hebrew can also mean any young woman of marriageable age. But the larger context in Isaiah promises a child who "will be called Wonderful Counselor, Mighty God, Everlasting Father, Prince of Peace," and of "his government ... there will be no end" (Isa 9:6–7). This was never true of any previous Jewish king. The Greek word Matthew uses for "virgin" (*parthenos*) more consistently refers to a woman who has never had sex. The Septuagint (the pre-Christian Greek translation of the OT) had already chosen it in translating the Hebrew text. Apparently at least some pre-Christian Jewish circles thought that this passage would have a double fulfillment. **Immanuel.** Means "God with us," which also points to more than just an ordinary child in Isaiah's day (see note on v. 22).

1:24–25 Joseph obeys the angel's instructions. We do not know when Mary and he had their actual wedding ceremony, but they remain chaste until after Jesus is born.

1:25 did not consummate their marriage until she gave birth. The most natural interpretation is that after Jesus' birth they have normal marital relations.

2:1–12 Matthew seems to presuppose his audience's knowledge of the circumstances of Jesus' birth in Bethlehem (cf. Luke 2:1–20), moving immediately to the account of the visit of the Magi.

2:1 Bethlehem in Judea. A small village about five miles (eight kilometers) south of Jerusalem, the birthplace of King David of old. **the time of King Herod.** 37 to 4 BC. **King Herod.** Herod the Great, he was an Idumean, unqualified by lineage for his position. But he was a shrewd diplomat, funding many public works in Judea, and began a dynasty that accounts for various descendants also called "Herod" later in the NT. **Magi from the east.** Astronomers or astrologers who served in royal courts in Persia and Arabia. The appearance of a new celestial light above a certain land was often believed to portend the birth of a king in that country. Although various attempts have been made to equate the "star" with a comet, a conjunction of planets, or some other natural phenomena, a supernatural explanation is better, especially because the star guides the Magi from Jerusalem to Bethlehem (v. 9).

2:2 when it rose. Lit. "from the dawn," which is a more likely translation than "in the east" because Magi from the east would have seen the star in their west.

2:3 disturbed. Herod was concerned because he was not a legitimate king of Israel by birth, as Jesus was. **all Jerusalem.** May refer particularly to the many political and religious leaders Herod installed, who were equally illegitimate according to Jewish law.

2:4 chief priests. The ruling priests in charge of worship at the temple in Jerusalem. **teachers of the law.** The Jewish scholars of the day, professionally trained in the teaching and application of OT law. Herod's ignorance of the Mic 5 prophecy shows that his supposed conversion to Judaism did not involve acquainting himself with the Hebrew Scriptures.

2:5–6 Jesus' birth in Bethlehem fulfills a direct predictive prophecy

6 "'But you, Bethlehem, in the land of Judah,
are by no means least among the rulers of Judah;
for out of you will come a ruler
who will shepherd my people Israel.'[a]"[z]

7 Then Herod called the Magi secretly and found out from them the exact time the star had appeared.
8 He sent them to Bethlehem and said, "Go and search carefully for the child. As soon as you find him,
report to me, so that I too may go and worship him."
9 After they had heard the king, they went on their way, and the star they had seen when it rose went
ahead of them until it stopped over the place where the child was. 10 When they saw the star, they were
overjoyed. 11 On coming to the house, they saw the child with his mother Mary, and they bowed down
and worshiped him.[a] Then they opened their treasures and presented him with gifts[b] of gold, frankincense and myrrh. 12 And having been warned[c] in a dream[d] not to go back to Herod, they returned to
their country by another route.

The Escape to Egypt

13 When they had gone, an angel[e] of the Lord appeared to Joseph in a dream.[f] "Get up," he said, "take
the child and his mother and escape to Egypt. Stay there until I tell you, for Herod is going to search
for the child to kill him."
14 So he got up, took the child and his mother during the night and left for Egypt, 15 where he stayed
until the death of Herod. And so was fulfilled what the Lord had said through the prophet: "Out of
Egypt I called my son."[b][g]
16 When Herod realized that he had been outwitted by the Magi, he was furious, and he gave orders to
kill all the boys in Bethlehem and its vicinity who were two years old and under, in accordance with the
time he had learned from the Magi. 17 Then what was said through the prophet Jeremiah was fulfilled:

18 "A voice is heard in Ramah,
weeping and great mourning,
Rachel weeping for her children
and refusing to be comforted,
because they are no more."[c][h]

2:6 [z] 2Sa 5:2; Mic 5:2
2:11 [a] Isa 60:3 [b] Ps 72:10
2:12 [c] Heb 11:7 [d] ver 13, 19,22; Mt 27:19
2:13 [e] Ac 5:19 [f] ver 12,19,22
2:15 [g] Ex 4:22,23; Hos 11:1
2:18 [h] Jer 31:15

[a] *6* Micah 5:2,4 [b] *15* Hosea 11:1 [c] *18* Jer. 31:15

from Mic 5:2 and may also allude to 2 Sam 5:2. Matthew adds the words "by no means" to the prophecy, not to contradict Micah but to reflect that once the Messiah is born in this small village, it will no longer be "least among the rulers of Judah," as it had been.

2:7–8 Herod does not really want to worship the Christ-child (vv. 12–18). This is all a ruse.

2:11 the house. Shows that the Magi did not visit the baby Jesus at the manger the night of his birth when the shepherds were present. The Magi would have come months later. **worshiped him.** The Magi, unlike Herod, do worship the baby. Gentile pagans come to know the true king of the universe, whereas key leaders in Israel reject him. **gold, frankincense and myrrh.** Gifts fit for a king but not necessarily having additional symbolism. There may, however, be an allusion to Isa 60, with its picture of foreigners, including kings, streaming to Jerusalem along with their great wealth (including gold) in the age to come. Frankincense (an aromatic resin) and myrrh (a similar fragrant spice) appear in Song 3:6 as desired spices sold by traveling merchants. We are not told how many Magi came; the tradition that there were three probably arose from the mention of three gifts.

2:13–18 Two fulfillments of Scripture appear here (vv. 14–15 and vv. 16–18).

2:13 escape to Egypt. A sizable Jewish community existed in Egypt, outside of Herod's jurisdiction, so this is a natural place for the angel to command the young family to find refuge from Herod's murderous assaults.

2:15 Out of Egypt I called my son. This quotation from Hos 11:1 originally referred to God's calling the nation of Israel out of Egypt in the time of Moses. But Matthew, under the inspiration of the Spirit, applies it also to Jesus. He sees the history of Israel (God's "son") recapitulated in the life of Jesus (God's unique Son). Just as Israel as an infant nation went down into Egypt, so the child Jesus went there. And as Israel was led by God out of Egypt, so also was Jesus.

2:16–18 While not recorded in other ancient histories that have survived, Herod's slaughter of the babies is perfectly in keeping with his executing his wife Mariamne and two of his sons for perceived threats on his kingdom. That perhaps as few as 20 babies were involved could explain its lack of notice elsewhere.

2:16 two years old and under. This suggests that more than a year has elapsed from Jesus' birth to the Magi's visit. Since Herod died in 4 BC, Jesus may have been born in 6 or 5 BC. Ancient calculations leading to the division of the calendar into BC and AD did not consult the work of the first-century Jewish historian Josephus, from which we now derive more accurate dates.

2:18 Double typology is at work with this quotation of Jer 31:15. Jeremiah had already likened the mothers in Israel who mourned over the loss of their sons at the time of the Babylonian exile to "Rachel [Jacob's wife] weeping for her children." Matthew sees the same pattern repeating itself with the Bethlehem mothers' laments. **Ramah.** About five miles (eight kilometers) north of Jerusalem, so not far from Bethlehem. It is along the road to Bethlehem that Rachel was buried (Gen 35:19) and that the young men at the time of the Babylonian captivity were led off into exile.

2:19 [l] ver 12,13,22

The Return to Nazareth

19 After Herod died, an angel of the Lord appeared in a dream[l] to Joseph in Egypt 20 and said, "Get
up, take the child and his mother and go to the land of Israel, for those who were trying to take the
child's life are dead."
21 So he got up, took the child and his mother and went to the land of Israel. 22 But when he heard

2:19–23 Once it was safe to return to Israel, the family chose to go to Nazareth, a Galilean village of about 500 people, because they had previously lived there (Luke 1:26). Matthew's use of both "Judea" (v. 22) and "Israel" (v. 21) may suggest that Jesus is viewed as reuniting the once divided kingdoms of Judah and Israel.

2:22 Archelaus. Herod's kingdom was divided among three of his

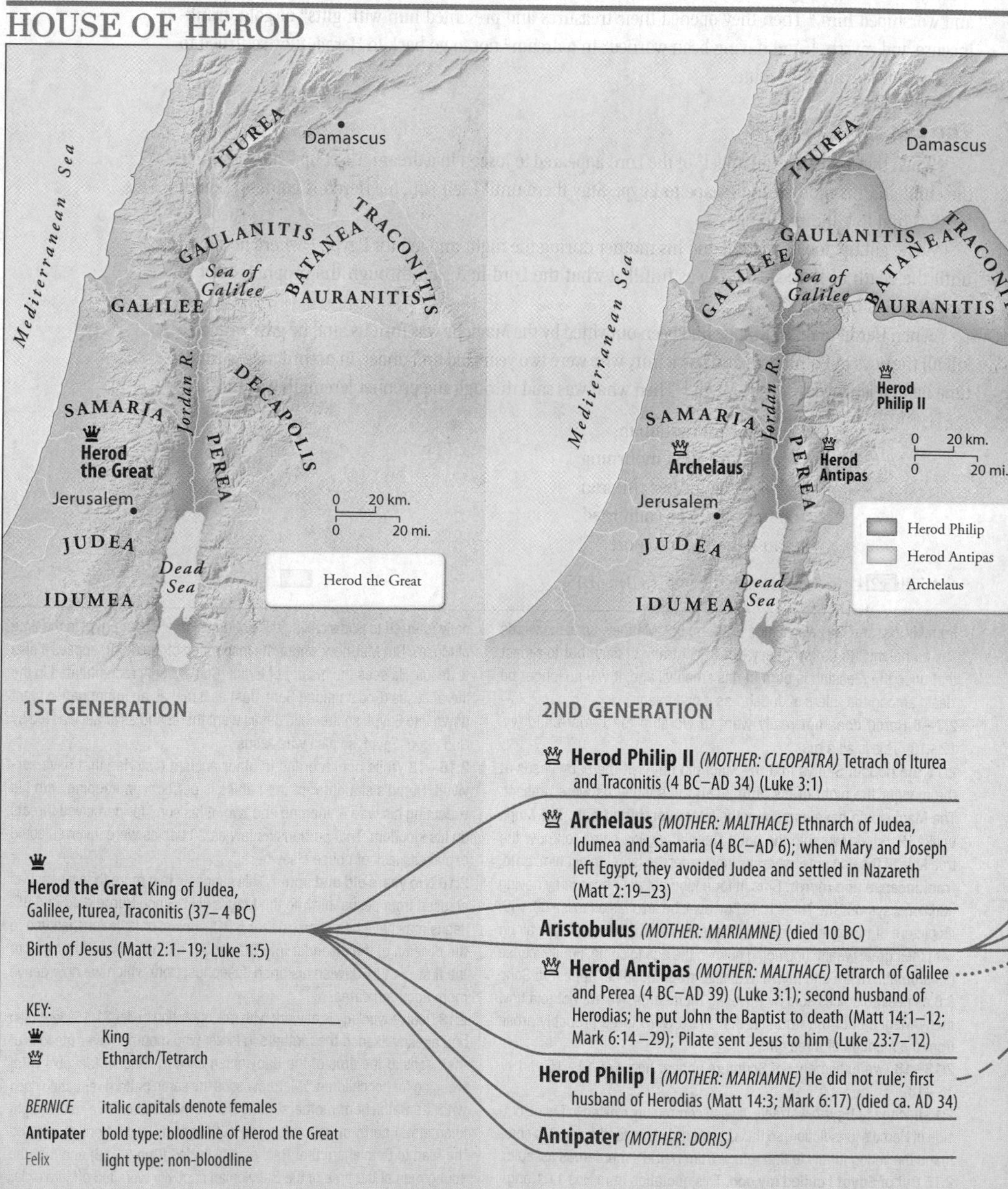

that Archelaus was reigning in Judea in place of his father Herod, he was afraid to go there. Having been warned in a dream,[j] he withdrew to the district of Galilee,[k] 23 and he went and lived in a town called Nazareth.[l] So was fulfilled[m] what was said through the prophets, that he would be called a Nazarene.[n]

2:22 [j] ver 12,13,19; Mt 27:19 [k] Lk 2:39
2:23 [l] Lk 1:26; Jn 1:45, 46 [m] Mt 1:22 [n] Mk 1:24

sons. Archelaus received Judea and Samaria; Antipas, Galilee and Perea; and Philip, only various regions outside of Israel. Archelaus was the worst of the three, such that Rome deposed him after a Jewish embassy in AD 6 complained of his cruelty. Judea then became a Roman province, administered by governors appointed by the emperor. See "House of Herod" for the second generation of Herods. **2:23 called a Nazarene.** No OT text contains this "quotation," but Matthew indicates that he is referring to multiple passages or a larger biblical theme by referring to "the prophets" (in the plural). Matthew may be making a play on the Hebrew word *nēṣer* for

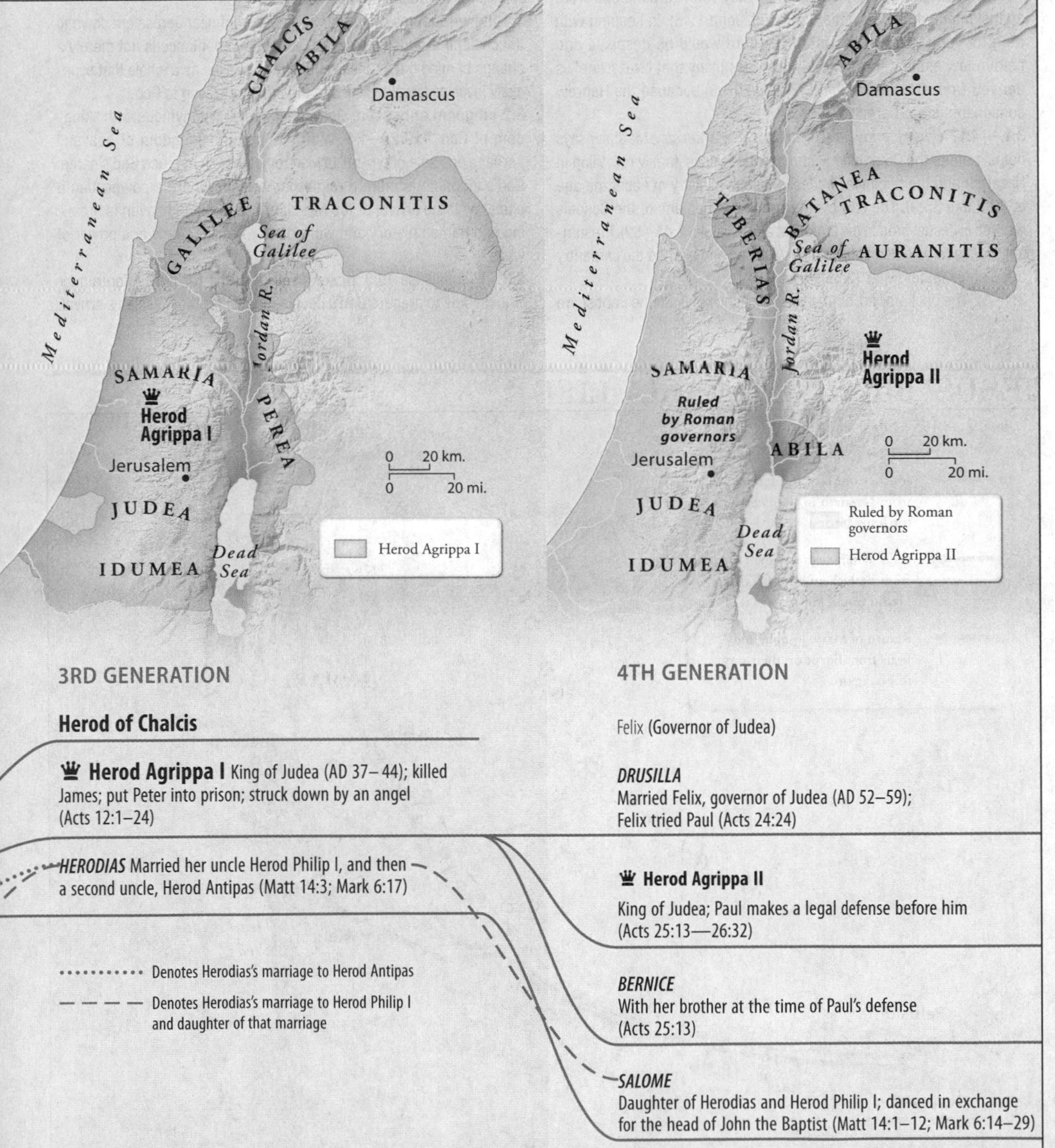

3RD GENERATION

Herod of Chalcis

Herod Agrippa I King of Judea (AD 37–44); killed James; put Peter into prison; struck down by an angel (Acts 12:1–24)

HERODIAS Married her uncle Herod Philip I, and then a second uncle, Herod Antipas (Matt 14:3; Mark 6:17)

.... Denotes Herodias's marriage to Herod Antipas

– – – – Denotes Herodias's marriage to Herod Philip I and daughter of that marriage

4TH GENERATION

Felix (Governor of Judea)

DRUSILLA
Married Felix, governor of Judea (AD 52–59); Felix tried Paul (Acts 24:24)

Herod Agrippa II
King of Judea; Paul makes a legal defense before him (Acts 25:13—26:32)

BERNICE
With her brother at the time of Paul's defense (Acts 25:13)

SALOME
Daughter of Herodias and Herod Philip I; danced in exchange for the head of John the Baptist (Matt 14:1–12; Mark 6:14–29)

3:1 [o]Lk 1:13,57-66; 3:2-19
3:2 [p]Da 2:44; Mt 4:17; 6:10; Lk 11:20; 21:31; Jn 3:3,5; Ac 1:3,6
3:3 [q]Isa 40:3; Mal 3:1; Lk 1:76; Jn 1:23

John the Baptist Prepares the Way

3:1-12pp — Mk 1:3-8; Lk 3:2-17

3 In those days John the Baptist[o] came, preaching in the wilderness of Judea 2and saying, "Repent,
for the kingdom of heaven[p] has come near." 3This is he who was spoken of through the prophet
Isaiah:

"A voice of one calling in the wilderness,
'Prepare the way for the Lord,
make straight paths for him.' "[a][q]

[a] *3* Isaiah 40:3

"Branch," a Messianic title in Isa 11:1, or *nāzîr* for "prince" (Gen 49:26; Deut 33:16). Or a "Nazarene" may refer to someone from an insignificant place of little repute (cf. John 1:46), in keeping with the prophecy that the servant of the Lord would be despised and held in low esteem (Isa 53:2–3). It is less likely that "Nazarene" is derived from "Nazirite" (Num 6:2; Judg 13:5) because the Hebrew consonants are different.

3:1—4:17 *Other Introductory Events in Jesus' Ministry.* Matthew says nothing about the 25 or more years between Jesus' family resettling in Nazareth and the beginning of Jesus' public ministry at about the age of 30 (Luke 3:23). The only event from this period any of the Gospels records is Jesus' time in the temple at age 12 (Luke 2:41–52). Presumably Jesus remained an obedient Jewish son and learned the carpentry trade of his father (Matt 13:55).

3:1–12 The background, birth, and significance of John the Baptist are described in detail in Luke 1:5–25,57–80. Matthew focuses on John's role as the forerunner for the Messiah.

3:1 the wilderness of Judea. Stretches from near Jerusalem down to Jericho and includes points farther south. Repentance is not merely a change of mind but a radical change in one's life as a whole that especially involves forsaking sin and turning or returning to God.

3:2 kingdom of heaven. God's kingly rule, synonymous with "kingdom of God" (19:23–24). Matthew prefers "kingdom of heaven" perhaps because of typical Jewish reluctance to overuse God's name. God's kingdom is more a reign than a realm, more a power than a place. With the arrival of the Messiah, God's rule in heaven is breaking into human history and will extend to earth in new and powerful ways.

3:3 This fulfills Isa 40:3. **make straight paths for him.** A forerunner would come to prepare God's people morally for the Messiah's arrival.

JESUS' BIRTH AND EARLY LIFE

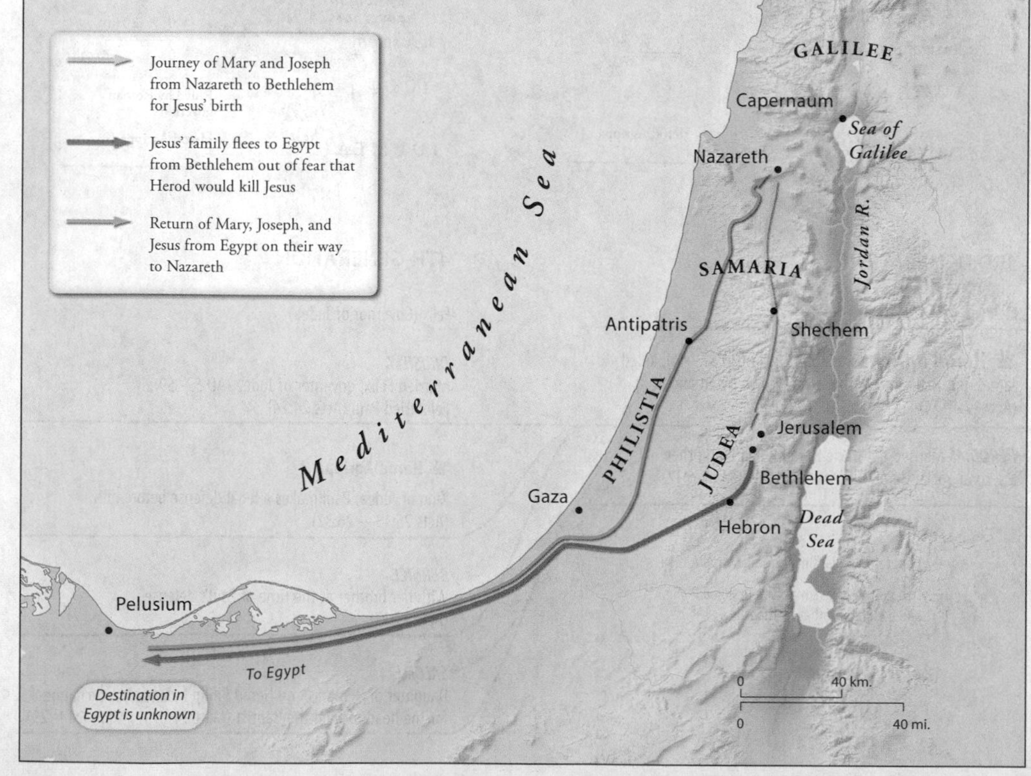

4John's clothes were made of camel's hair, and he had a leather belt around his waist.[r] His food was locusts[s] and wild honey. 5People went out to him from Jerusalem and all Judea and the whole region of the Jordan. 6Confessing their sins, they were baptized by him in the Jordan River.

7But when he saw many of the Pharisees and Sadducees coming to where he was baptizing, he said to them: "You brood of vipers![t] Who warned you to flee from the coming wrath?[u] 8Produce fruit in keeping with repentance.[v] 9And do not think you can say to yourselves, 'We have Abraham as our father.' I tell you that out of these stones God can raise up children for Abraham. 10The ax is already at the root of the trees, and every tree that does not produce good fruit will be cut down and thrown into the fire.[w]

11"I baptize you with[a] water for repentance. But after me comes one who is more powerful than I, whose sandals I am not worthy to carry. He will baptize you with[a] the Holy Spirit[x] and fire.[y] 12His winnowing fork is in his hand, and he will clear his threshing floor, gathering his wheat into the barn and burning up the chaff with unquenchable fire."[z]

3:4 [r] 2Ki 1:8 [s] Lev 11:22
3:7 [t] Mt 12:34; 23:33 [u] Ro 1:18; 1Th 1:10
3:8 [v] Ac 26:20
3:10 [w] Mt 7:19; Lk 13:6-9; Jn 15:2,6
3:11 [x] Mk 1:8 [y] Isa 4:4; Ac 2:3,4
3:12 [z] Mt 13:30
3:13 [a] Mk 1:4
3:16 [b] Isa 11:2; 42:1
3:17 [c] Mt 17:5; Jn 12:28 [d] Ps 2:7; 2Pe 1:17,18 [e] Isa 42:1; Mt 12:18; 17:5; Mk 1:11; 9:7; Lk 9:35
4:2 [f] Ex 34:28; 1Ki 19:8
4:3 [g] 1Th 3:5 [h] Mt 3:17; Jn 5:25; Ac 9:20

The Baptism of Jesus

3:13-17pp — Mk 1:9-11; Lk 3:21,22; Jn 1:31-34

13Then Jesus came from Galilee to the Jordan to be baptized by John.[a] 14But John tried to deter him, saying, "I need to be baptized by you, and do you come to me?"

15Jesus replied, "Let it be so now; it is proper for us to do this to fulfill all righteousness." Then John consented.

16As soon as Jesus was baptized, he went up out of the water. At that moment heaven was opened, and he saw the Spirit of God[b] descending like a dove and alighting on him. 17And a voice from heaven[c] said, "This is my Son,[d] whom I love; with him I am well pleased."[e]

Jesus Is Tested in the Wilderness

4:1-11pp — Mk 1:12,13; Lk 4:1-13

4 Then Jesus was led by the Spirit into the wilderness to be tempted[b] by the devil. 2After fasting forty days and forty nights,[f] he was hungry. 3The tempter[g] came to him and said, "If you are the Son of God,[h] tell these stones to become bread."

[a] *11* Or *in* [b] *1* The Greek for *tempted* can also mean *tested.*

3:4 John's clothes. Reminds people of Elijah the OT prophet (2 Kgs 1:8). **His food.** Reflects the simple, austere fare of poor wilderness dwellers.
3:5 People went out to him. Because his preaching is powerful.
3:6 Confessing their sins. Evidence of repentance. **they were baptized.** "Baptize" means to dip or immerse. John most likely immersed people in the Jordan River to symbolize their death to sin and the spiritual cleansing associated with the new way of life they were beginning.
3:7 Pharisees and Sadducees. Two key Jewish leadership sects. Pharisees scrupulously obeyed the biblical laws and the traditions that had grown up around them. Sadducees tended to be in the majority among temple authorities and were willing to accommodate Rome to keep the peace. These leaders are coming not to be baptized (cf. Luke 7:30) but to check up on John. **brood of vipers.** Suggests that their teaching is spiritually poisonous. John's response in vv. 7–10 drips with sarcasm: he speaks as if they *were* pretending to follow him, and he points out that their lifestyle does not demonstrate repentance. They are in danger of trusting solely in their ethnicity and thus coming under God's judgment.
3:11–12 John predicts the coming Messiah, whose baptism will involve the purifying work of the Holy Spirit or the judgment associated with "fire," depending on how people respond to him.
3:12 winnowing fork. See Ruth 3:2. Here winnowing is figurative for the separation of the righteous ("wheat") from the wicked ("chaff").
3:13–17 The ministries of John and Jesus now intersect. John 1:19–36 and 3:22—4:3 show how extensive this intersection was. Here Matthew focuses solely on Jesus' baptism.
3:13–15 John the Baptist recognizes that his role and Jesus' role seem reversed: the inferior immerses the superior. John sees no need for Jesus to submit to a rite symbolizing a person's repentance from sin. But Jesus recognizes his baptism will "fulfill all righteousness" (v. 15). He models God's will for his people and puts his stamp of approval on John's ministry.
3:16–17 Jesus' baptism becomes the occasion for God himself to testify to Jesus. The Holy Spirit anoints him, commissioning him for his ministry, and the heavenly voice combines snippets of Ps 2:7 and Isa 42:1 to indicate Jesus' regal and suffering servant roles. All three persons of the Trinity appear, united but distinct.
4:1–11 Instead of moving immediately to his public ministry, Jesus must be tested first. Adam and Eve yielded to temptation so that sin entered this world (Gen 3). The Israelites failed their test and wandered in the wilderness for 40 years—another kind of testing (Deut 8:2–3). How would the Messiah-designate respond? He resists temptation, thereby remaining qualified for his mission of being a sinless sacrifice for the sins of humanity. Luke 4:1–13 narrates topically, not chronologically, reversing the last two temptations.
4:1 The Spirit of God always guides Jesus, but only the devil (not God, see Jas 1:13) actually tempts him. Jesus goes to the wilderness just as John frequently ministered there (3:1).
4:2–4 The first of three temptations appeals to Jesus' intense hunger after not eating for 40 days. But Jesus must never use his miracle-working abilities for self-serving reasons. God will sustain him, and spiritual nourishment takes priority over physical sustenance (Deut 8:3).

HEROD'S TEMPLE

20 BC–AD 70

Begun in 20 BC, Herod's new structure towered 15 stories high, following the floor dimensions of the former temples in the Holy Place and the Most Holy Place. The high sanctuary shown here was built on the site of the former temples of Solomon and Zerubbabel.

The outer courts surrounding the temple mount were not completed until AD 64. The entire structure was demolished by the Romans in AD 70.

Dimensions of rooms, steps, doorways, cornices, and exterior measurements are mentioned in history (Josephus and the Mishnah) but are subject to interpretation.

[4]Jesus answered, "It is written: 'Man shall not live on bread alone, but on every word that comes
from the mouth of God.'[a]"[i]
[5]Then the devil took him to the holy city[j] and had him stand on the highest point of the temple. [6]"If
you are the Son of God," he said, "throw yourself down. For it is written:

> " 'He will command his angels concerning you,
> and they will lift you up in their hands,
> so that you will not strike your foot against a stone.'[b]"[k]

[7]Jesus answered him, "It is also written: 'Do not put the Lord your God to the test.'[c]"[l]
[8]Again, the devil took him to a very high mountain and showed him all the kingdoms of the world
and their splendor. [9]"All this I will give you," he said, "if you will bow down and worship me."
[10]Jesus said to him, "Away from me, Satan![m] For it is written: 'Worship the Lord your God, and serve
him only.'[d]"[n]
[11]Then the devil left him, and angels came and attended him.[o]

Jesus Begins to Preach

[12]When Jesus heard that John had been put in prison,[p] he withdrew to Galilee.[q] [13]Leaving Nazareth,
he went and lived in Capernaum,[r] which was by the lake in the area of Zebulun and Naphtali— [14]to
fulfill what was said through the prophet Isaiah:

> [15]"Land of Zebulun and land of Naphtali,
> the Way of the Sea, beyond the Jordan,
> Galilee of the Gentiles—
> [16]the people living in darkness
> have seen a great light;
> on those living in the land of the shadow of death
> a light has dawned."[e][s]

[17]From that time on Jesus began to preach, "Repent, for the kingdom of heaven[t] has come near."

Jesus Calls His First Disciples

4:18-22pp — Mk 1:16-20; Lk 5:2-11; Jn 1:35-42

[18]As Jesus was walking beside the Sea of Galilee,[u] he saw two brothers, Simon called Peter[v] and
his brother Andrew. They were casting a net into the lake, for they were fishermen. [19]"Come, follow

4:4 [i]Dt 8:3
4:5 [j]Ne 11:1; Da 9:24; Mt 27:53
4:6 [k]Ps 91:11,12
4:7 [l]Dt 6:16
4:10 [m]1Ch 21:1 [n]Dt 6:13
4:11 [o]Mt 26:53; Lk 22:43; Heb 1:14
4:12 [p]Mt 14:3 [q]Mk 1:14
4:13 [r]Mk 1:21; Lk 4:23, 31; Jn 2:12; 4:46,47
4:16 [s]Isa 9:1,2; Lk 2:32
4:17 [t]Mt 3:2
4:18 [u]Mt 15:29; Mk 7:31; Jn 6:1 [v]Mt 16:17,18

[a] *4* Deut. 8:3 [b] *6* Psalm 91:11,12 [c] *7* Deut. 6:16 [d] *10* Deut. 6:13 [e] *16* Isaiah 9:1,2

4:5–7 The second temptation appeals to the desire to have one's life saved spectacularly. Satan quotes Scripture (Ps 91:11–12) but applies it in exactly the wrong context. Jesus again counters with the more relevant Scripture for this setting (Deut 6:16). One must never manipulate God by trying to force his hand.
4:8–10 The third temptation may occur in a vision (though no less real a test), since there are no places from which one can literally see "all the kingdoms of the world" (v. 8). Worshiping Satan is by far the worst of his three demands since "the Lord your God" alone (v. 10) should be adored (Deut 6:13). Jesus does claim authority over all the cosmos but cannot do so if he bypasses the cross. Scripture has already demonstrated this. He will rescue those who want salvation but not those implacably opposed to him.
4:11 Now that Christ has passed his tests, it *is* appropriate for the angels to minister to his needs.
4:12 in prison. For John's imprisonment, see 14:1–12.
4:13 Capernaum. A slightly larger town than Nazareth on the northwest shore of the Sea of Galilee. The last preparatory event before Jesus' public ministry is to relocate here. The location, along with the highway from Damascus to the Mediterranean Sea, makes Matthew recall another OT prophecy (Isa 9:1–2).
4:14–16 In the context of Isa 9:6, this is a fairly direct prediction that could be fulfilled only by a divine Messiah.
4:15 Galilee of the Gentiles. Since the eighth century BC, Galilee had often had proportionally more Gentile residents than Judea had (cf. Luke 1:79; 2:32).
4:17 Matthew summarizes Jesus' message with the identical words he used in headlining John's (3:2). But 11:16–19 notes key differences between the two. **From that time on Jesus began to.** Marks the end of the first major section of Matthew, just as it will begin the third and last major section (cf. 16:21).
4:18—16:20 *The Major Phase of Jesus' Public Ministry.* Here appear the highlights of Jesus' public ministry, especially in Galilee.
4:18–25 *Introduction to the Galilean Ministry.* Calling his first disciples and announcing the arrival of God's kingdom via preaching, teaching, and healing set the stage for Jesus' great sermon, beginning in ch. 5.
4:18–22 Two pairs of fishermen brothers are the first Jesus calls to follow him (see photos, pp. 2009, 2081). Rabbis typically selected disciples from among those who wanted to learn from them. Jesus reverses this process. John 1:35–51 shows that some of his disciples had previous exposure to him. Matthew stresses the immediacy of their response to Jesus' call.
4:18 Simon called Peter. See 16:18.

4:19 [w]Mk 10:21,28,52
4:21 [x]Mt 20:20
4:23 [y]Mk 1:39; Lk 4:15, 44 [z]Mt 9:35; 13:54; Mk 1:21; Lk 4:15; Jn 6:59 [a]Mk 1:14 [b]Mt 3:2; Ac 20:25 [c]Mt 8:16; 15:30; Ac 10:38

me,"[w] Jesus said, "and I will send you out to fish for people." 20 At once they left their nets and followed him.

21 Going on from there, he saw two other brothers, James son of Zebedee and his brother John.[x] They were in a boat with their father Zebedee, preparing their nets. Jesus called them, 22 and immediately they left the boat and their father and followed him.

Jesus Heals the Sick

23 Jesus went throughout Galilee,[y] teaching in their synagogues,[z] proclaiming the good news[a] of the kingdom,[b] and healing every disease and sickness among the people.[c] 24 News about him spread

4:23–25 Jesus' travels, along with the lands from which people came to see and hear him, show the extraordinary extent of his ministry and reputation.

JESUS IN GALILEE

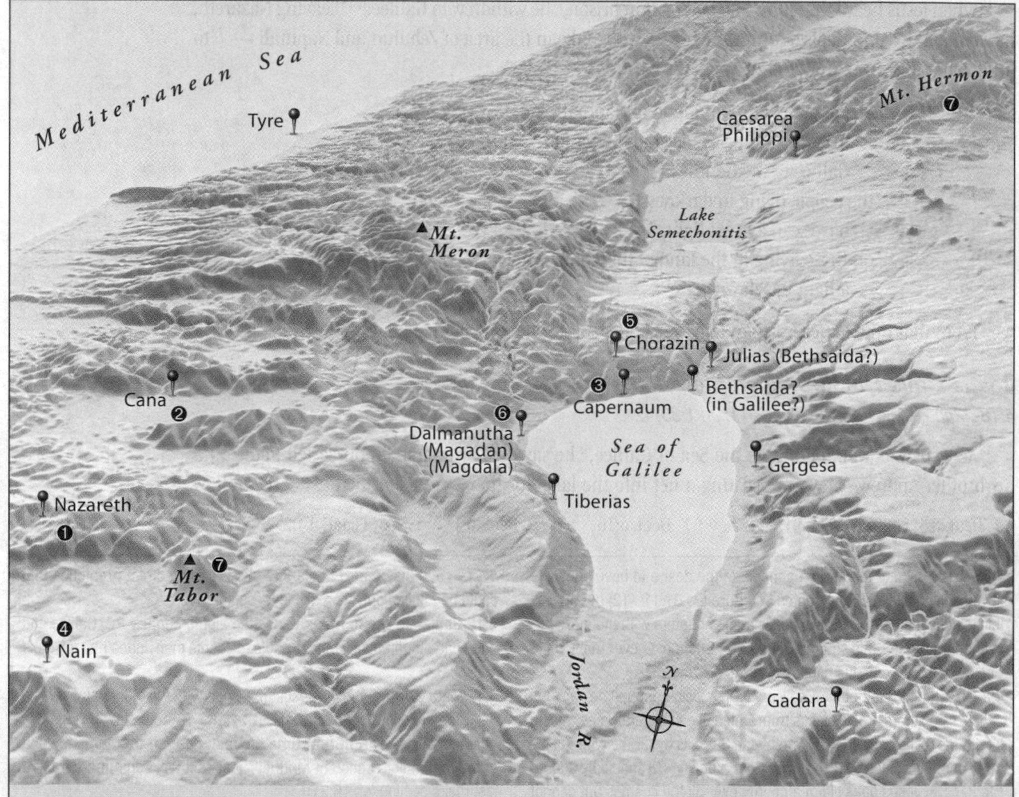

❶ Town where Jesus grew up. He was rejected in the synagogue here and people sought to kill him (Luke 4:16).

❷ Here at Cana Jesus performed his first miracle by turning water into wine at a wedding feast (John 2:1,11). Home of Nathanael (John 21:2).

❸ Site of many miracles of Jesus (Matt 8:5; Mark 2:1 and Luke 7:1; Matt 17:24; Mark 1:21 and Luke 4:31; John 4:46; 6:17). Jesus taught in the synagogue here at Capernaum (John 6:59).

❹ Here at Nain, Jesus raised a widow's son from the dead (Luke 7:11).

❺ One of the cities against which Jesus pronounced a woe (Matt 11:21; Luke 10:13).

❻ Fishing town and home of Mary Magdalene (Matt 15:39; Mark 8:10).

❼ Mount Tabor, the traditional Mount of Transfiguration (Matt 17:1–8; Mark 9:2–8; Luke 9:28–36). However, many scholars identify Mount Hermon as the most likely site of the transfiguration.

all over Syria,[d] and people brought to him all who were ill with various diseases, those suffering
severe pain, the demon-possessed,[e] those having seizures,[f] and the paralyzed;[g] and he healed them.
25 Large crowds from Galilee, the Decapolis,[a] Jerusalem, Judea and the region across the Jordan followed him.[h]

Introduction to the Sermon on the Mount

5 Now when Jesus saw the crowds, he went up on a mountainside and sat down. His disciples came
to him, 2 and he began to teach them.

The Beatitudes

5:3-12pp — Lk 6:20-23

He said:

3 "Blessed are the poor in spirit,
for theirs is the kingdom of heaven.[i]
4 Blessed are those who mourn,
for they will be comforted.[j]
5 Blessed are the meek,
for they will inherit the earth.[k]
6 Blessed are those who hunger and thirst
for righteousness,
for they will be filled.[l]
7 Blessed are the merciful,
for they will be shown mercy.
8 Blessed are the pure in heart,[m]
for they will see God.[n]
9 Blessed are the peacemakers,
for they will be called children of God.[o]
10 Blessed are those who are persecuted because
of righteousness,[p]
for theirs is the kingdom of heaven.

11 "Blessed are you when people insult you,[q] persecute you and falsely say all kinds of evil against
you because of me. 12 Rejoice and be glad,[r] because great is your reward in heaven, for in the same way
they persecuted the prophets who were before you.[s]

[a] *25* That is, the Ten Cities

4:24 [d] Lk 2:2 [e] Mt 8:16, 28; 9:32; 15:22; Mk 1:32; 5:15,16,18 [f] Mt 17:15 [g] Mt 8:6; 9:2; Mk 2:3
4:25 [h] Mk 3:7,8; Lk 6:17
5:3 [i] ver 10,19; Mt 25:34
5:4 [j] Isa 61:2,3; Rev 7:17
5:5 [k] Ps 37:11; Ro 4:13
5:6 [l] Isa 55:1,2
5:8 [m] Ps 24:3,4 [n] Heb 12:14; Rev 22:4
5:9 [o] ver 44,45; Ro 8:14
5:10 [p] 1Pe 3:14
5:11 [q] 1Pe 4:14
5:12 [r] Ac 5:41; 1Pe 4:13,16 [s] Mt 23:31,37; Ac 7:52; 1Th 2:15

5:1—7:29 *Jesus' Authoritative Teaching: The Sermon on the Mount.* Possibly the most famous sermon in all religious literature, Jesus here offers his "kingdom manifesto." Like the "already but not yet" reign of God, this is the ideal ethic for which believers must strive, even while recognizing they will fall far short of living up to it. Luke 6:20–49 is an extract of what appears to be the same sermon.

5:1–2 on a mountainside. Means simply "into the hill country," including level places for the crowds to gather (cf. Luke 6:17). **His disciples came to him, and he began to teach them.** This message is primarily for those already committed to following Christ or learning from him.

5:3–12 These kingdom blessings (beatitudes) disclose God's gracious favor toward his followers for traits that are opposite of what usually garners acclaim and popularity. The rewards for this countercultural behavior include present membership in "the kingdom of heaven" (vv. 3,10) and future recompense for this life's lack of glamour (vv. 4–9,11–12).

5:3 poor. In the OT "poor" often refers to the economically destitute among God's people (cf. Luke 6:20) who trusted in God as their only hope (cf. Luke 6:22).

5:4 those who mourn. Over both personal and corporate sins (see Ezra 9:1–4).

5:5 the meek ... will inherit the earth. Alludes to Ps 37:11. In the OT faithful Israelites would occupy the land of Israel in peace and prosperity, but in the NT Jesus' humble followers encompass the entire globe and receive spiritual blessings.

5:6 hunger and thirst for righteousness. Have a deep longing for both personal holiness and justice for the oppressed.

5:8 heart. The center of one's being, including mind, will, and emotions. **see God.** Experience his presence in this life and know him intimately in the life to come.

5:9 peacemakers. Those who promote peace, as far as it depends on them (Rom 12:18). In so doing they reflect the character of their heavenly Father and so are called "children of God" (see Jas 3:17–18).

5:10 Blessed are those who are persecuted. Righteous living is often offensive to others (v. 11). Persecution provides an opportunity for believers to prove their fitness for the kingdom (Heb 12:4–11).

5:13 [t]Mk 9:50; Lk 14:34,35
5:14 [u]Jn 8:12
5:15 [v]Mk 4:21; Lk 8:16
5:16 [w]Mt 9:8
5:17 [x]Ro 3:31
5:18 [y]Lk 16:17
5:19 [z]Jas 2:10
5:21 [a]Ex 20:13; Dt 5:17
5:22 [b]1Jn 3:15 [c]Mt 26:59 [d]Jas 3:6

Salt and Light

[13]"You are the salt of the earth. But if the salt loses its saltiness, how can it be made salty again? It is no longer good for anything, except to be thrown out and trampled underfoot.[t]

[14]"You are the light of the world.[u] A town built on a hill cannot be hidden. [15]Neither do people light a lamp and put it under a bowl. Instead they put it on its stand, and it gives light to everyone in the house.[v] [16]In the same way, let your light shine before others, that they may see your good deeds and glorify[w] your Father in heaven.

The Fulfillment of the Law

[17]"Do not think that I have come to abolish the Law or the Prophets; I have not come to abolish them but to fulfill them.[x] [18]For truly I tell you, until heaven and earth disappear, not the smallest letter, not the least stroke of a pen, will by any means disappear from the Law until everything is accomplished.[y] [19]Therefore anyone who sets aside one of the least of these commands[z] and teaches others accordingly will be called least in the kingdom of heaven, but whoever practices and teaches these commands will be called great in the kingdom of heaven. [20]For I tell you that unless your righteousness surpasses that of the Pharisees and the teachers of the law, you will certainly not enter the kingdom of heaven.

Murder

5:25,26pp — Lk 12:58,59

[21]"You have heard that it was said to the people long ago, 'You shall not murder,[*a*][a] and anyone who murders will be subject to judgment.' [22]But I tell you that anyone who is angry with a brother or sister[*b,c*] will be subject to judgment.[b] Again, anyone who says to a brother or sister, 'Raca,'[*d*] is answerable to the court.[c] And anyone who says, 'You fool!' will be in danger of the fire of hell.[d]

[23]"Therefore, if you are offering your gift at the altar and there remember that your brother or sister has something against you, [24]leave your gift there in front of the altar. First go and be reconciled to them; then come and offer your gift.

a 21 Exodus 20:13 *b 22* The Greek word for *brother or sister* (*adelphos*) refers here to a fellow disciple, whether man or woman; also in verse 23. *c 22* Some manuscripts *brother or sister without cause* *d 22* An Aramaic term of contempt

5:13–16 salt ... light. The point of both metaphors is that Jesus' followers should positively impact the world. While salt was used for various purposes in Jesus' day, its preservative power is probably the point of the comparison here. After the countercultural beatitudes, the salt and light sayings remind Jesus' followers not to isolate themselves from other people but to model discipleship in the midst of a fallen world.
5:14 light. Illuminates one's way.
5:16 This verse does not contradict 6:1–4 because the point here of others seeing "your good deeds" is that they "glorify your Father in heaven," not that they praise you. Here Jesus' main point is about the result of one's actions; in 6:1–4 it is more about one's purpose.
5:17–20 Jesus' teaching is radical enough that he has to assure his Jewish audience that he has "not ... come to abolish the Law or the Prophets" (v. 17)—the two major, earliest divisions of their Scriptures, standing for their whole Bible. But neither is he preserving all of its principles unchanged; he has come "to fulfill them" (v. 17).
5:17 fulfill. As in Matthew's earlier use of prophecies, "fulfill" means to complete an intended purpose. It can refer to articulating the final and complete intention of a commandment (Gal 5:14), the typological recurrence of a significant pattern of God's actions (Jas 2:23), or the occurrence of something previously promised (Acts 7:17).
5:18 Some regulations, like those involving animal sacrifices, *were* done away with by Christ's death precisely because, as the once-for-all sacrifice for sinners (cf. Heb 8–10), he accomplished everything to which these laws had pointed forward. All OT texts, therefore, must be filtered through the grid of NT teaching to see how, if at all, their laws or principles have changed. But the OT remains binding for Christians once it is understood how each part of it is fulfilled in Christ.
5:20 teachers of the law. Scribes who became lawyers because of their familiarity with the law from copying Scripture. Together with the Pharisees, they were among the most law-abiding Jews of the day. Thus, to have a "righteousness [that] surpasses" theirs cannot mean a more perfect obedience to the OT. Instead it refers to doing God's will, as newly defined in Jesus, made possible by his indwelling Spirit (cf. 10:20).
5:21–48 Six times Jesus contrasts traditional interpretations of OT texts or themes with his understanding of their meaning and application. In five of the six antitheses, he also prescribes proactive, positive action as an antidote to what is prohibited. Presumably similar action is implied in the remaining instance (to prevent divorce) as well.
5:21 murder. The sixth commandment (Exod 20:13) prohibits the taking of another human life. The verb refers to all killing except in war, capital punishment, or self-defense. Jesus' assertion internalizes the command so that one who harbors rage or spews out spiteful words is also guilty of sin and its consequences (v. 22). The matter is so serious that one should leave a worship service, if necessary, to be "reconciled" (v. 24) to a fellow believer and "settle matters" (v. 25) out of court if at all possible to avoid any chance of conviction and imprisonment.
5:22 Raca. "Empty-headed" (an Aramaic swear word). **fool.** Has overtones of immorality as well as stupidity. **fire.** See note on 8:12. **hell.** Greek *ge(h)enna*; the Hinnom Valley near Jerusalem was used for child

25 "Settle matters quickly with your adversary who is taking you to court. Do it while you are still
together on the way, or your adversary may hand you over to the judge, and the judge may hand you
over to the officer, and you may be thrown into prison. 26 Truly I tell you, you will not get out until you
have paid the last penny.

Adultery

27 "You have heard that it was said, 'You shall not commit adultery.'[a][e] 28 But I tell you that anyone
who looks at a woman lustfully has already committed adultery with her in his heart.[f] 29 If your right
eye causes you to stumble,[g] gouge it out and throw it away. It is better for you to lose one part of your
body than for your whole body to be thrown into hell. 30 And if your right hand causes you to stumble,
cut it off and throw it away. It is better for you to lose one part of your body than for your whole body
to go into hell.

Divorce

31 "It has been said, 'Anyone who divorces his wife must give her a certificate of divorce.'[b][h] 32 But I tell
you that anyone who divorces his wife, except for sexual immorality, makes her the victim of adultery,
and anyone who marries a divorced woman commits adultery.[i]

Oaths

33 "Again, you have heard that it was said to the people long ago, 'Do not break your oath,[j] but fulfill
to the Lord the vows you have made.'[k] 34 But I tell you, do not swear an oath at all:[l] either by heaven, for
it is God's throne;[m] 35 or by the earth, for it is his footstool; or by Jerusalem, for it is the city of the Great
King.[n] 36 And do not swear by your head, for you cannot make even one hair white or black. 37 All you
need to say is simply 'Yes' or 'No';[o] anything beyond this comes from the evil one.[c][p]

Eye for Eye

38 "You have heard that it was said, 'Eye for eye, and tooth for tooth.'[d][q] 39 But I tell you, do not resist an evil person. If anyone slaps you on the right cheek, turn to them the other cheek also.[r] 40 And if

5:27 [e] Ex 20:14; Dt 5:18
5:28 [f] Pr 6:25
5:29 [g] Mt 18:6,8,9; Mk 9:42-47
5:31 [h] Dt 24:1-4
5:32 [i] Lk 16:18
5:33 [j] Lev 19:12 [k] Nu 30:2; Dt 23:21; Mt 23:16-22
5:34 [l] Jas 5:12 [m] Isa 66:1; Mt 23:22
5:35 [n] Ps 48:2
5:37 [o] Jas 5:12 [p] Mt 6:13; 13:19,38; Jn 17:15; 2Th 3:3; 1Jn 2:13,14; 3:12; 5:18,19
5:38 [q] Ex 21:24; Lev 24:20; Dt 19:21
5:39 [r] Lk 6:29; Ro 12:17,19; 1Co 6:7; 1Pe 3:9

[a] *27* Exodus 20:14 [b] *31* Deut. 24:1 [c] *37* Or *from evil* [d] *38* Exodus 21:24; Lev. 24:20; Deut. 19:21

sacrifice by fire in OT times (2 Chr 28:3; Jer 7:31) and became a natural metaphor for a place of eternal punishment.

5:26 penny. Quadrans, 1/64 of a day's minimum wage (a denarius), the smallest Roman copper coin. Prisoners in Jesus' world had no opportunity to earn money in jail. Paying a fine for which they had insufficient funds would require that a benefactor from outside provide the money.

5:27 adultery. Sexual infidelity to one's spouse violates the seventh commandment (Exod 20:14), and adultery can even be committed in one's "heart" (v. 28). The two are not equally bad, but they are both sinful.

5:29–30 gouge it out … cut it off. Because unchecked lust can lead to literal adultery, Jesus counsels drastic action to remove sources of temptation. These are classic examples of hyperbole, not meant to be taken literally. After all, blind and injured people can still lust.

5:31 divorces. Deut 24:1, cited here, spawned a debate between the two main Pharisaic rabbis in Jesus' day, Shammai and Hillel. Shammai required divorce (and permitted remarriage) only for sexual infidelity; Hillel permitted divorce for "any good cause." Typically, only men could initiate divorce. Jesus is actually stricter than Shammai because he only *permits* divorce and remarriage; he does not *require* them, even for marital unfaithfulness (v. 32), as both Pharisaic positions did.

5:32 sexual immorality. Greek *porneia*, the broadest term for sexual sin. It refers to sexual relations with any other person besides one's monogamous heterosexual spouse. **makes her the victim of adultery.** Greek *moicheuthēnai*, a passive-voice form not used elsewhere in an active sense. **anyone who marries a divorced woman.** This exception from the previous clause carries over, i.e., unless she was divorced legitimately. See also 19:1–9.

5:33 oath. The OT reference here resembles Lev 19:12. While the OT insisted that people must fulfill their vows, Jesus says not to take vows at all (vv. 34–37). He is particularly concerned about the Pharisaic practice of swearing by something other than God himself to create a lesser degree of accountability. Verses 34–35 give examples of how even lesser objects by which some swore were still closely related to God. The prohibition apparently does not rule out all solemn statements about the truth of a matter, since Paul assures his readers "before God" that he does not lie (Gal 1:20), and God himself confirms his promises with oaths (e.g., Heb 6:17). The problem here was that oaths were being used as occasions for deceitfulness, depending on by what they were sworn.

5:38 Eye for eye. The *lex talionis*, or law of retaliation, which appears in several OT contexts (e.g., Exod 21:23–24; Lev 24:19–20; Deut 19:21), prohibited personal revenge and required law courts to hand down sentences stricter than were appropriate. It was never applied literally. Jesus gives examples of doing more than one's enemies or oppressors ask (vv. 39–42).

5:39 do not resist an evil person. The context suggests Jesus is prohibiting retaliation for wrongs experienced. Jas 4:7 commands one to resist the devil, and Jesus and Paul both exorcise demons that possessed people. **slaps you on the right cheek.** A slap by a person presumed to be right-handed would be a backhanded cuff, a common Jewish insult by a superior to a subordinate, not an aggressor's blow.

5:40 shirt. Tunic, an undergarment. **coat.** Cloak, an outer piece of clothing. For a poor person wearing only these two basic forms of dress, giving away both, especially in a law court, where the shirt could be held

5:42 [s]Dt 15:8; Lk 6:30
5:43 [t]Lev 19:18 [u]Dt 23:6
5:44 [v]Lk 6:27,28; 23:34; Ac 7:60; Ro 12:14; 1Co 4:12; 1Pe 2:23
5:45 [w]ver 9 [x]Job 25:3
5:46 [y]Lk 6:32
5:48 [z]Lev 19:2; 1Pe 1:16
6:1 [a]Mt 23:5
6:4 [b]ver 6,18; Col 3:23,24
6:5 [c]Mk 11:25; Lk 18:10-14
6:6 [d]2Ki 4:33
6:7 [e]Ecc 5:2 [f]1Ki 18:26-29
6:8 [g]ver 32

anyone wants to sue you and take your shirt, hand over your coat as well. 41 If anyone forces you to go one mile, go with them two miles. 42 Give to the one who asks you, and do not turn away from the one who wants to borrow from you.[s]

Love for Enemies

43 "You have heard that it was said, 'Love your neighbor[a][t] and hate your enemy.'[u] 44 But I tell you, love your enemies and pray for those who persecute you,[v] 45 that you may be children[w] of your Father in heaven. He causes his sun to rise on the evil and the good, and sends rain on the righteous and the unrighteous.[x] 46 If you love those who love you, what reward will you get?[y] Are not even the tax collectors doing that? 47 And if you greet only your own people, what are you doing more than others? Do not even pagans do that? 48 Be perfect, therefore, as your heavenly Father is perfect.[z]

Giving to the Needy

6 "Be careful not to practice your righteousness in front of others to be seen by them.[a] If you do, you will have no reward from your Father in heaven.

2 "So when you give to the needy, do not announce it with trumpets, as the hypocrites do in the synagogues and on the streets, to be honored by others. Truly I tell you, they have received their reward in full. 3 But when you give to the needy, do not let your left hand know what your right hand is doing, 4 so that your giving may be in secret. Then your Father, who sees what is done in secret, will reward you.[b]

Prayer

6:9-13pp — Lk 11:2-4

5 "And when you pray, do not be like the hypocrites, for they love to pray standing[c] in the synagogues and on the street corners to be seen by others. Truly I tell you, they have received their reward in full. 6 But when you pray, go into your room, close the door and pray to your Father,[d] who is unseen. Then your Father, who sees what is done in secret, will reward you. 7 And when you pray, do not keep on babbling[e] like pagans, for they think they will be heard because of their many words.[f] 8 Do not be like them, for your Father knows what you need[g] before you ask him.

9 "This, then, is how you should pray:

"'Our Father in heaven,
hallowed be your name,

[a] *43* Lev. 19:18

as collateral, would leave the defendant naked and mock the justice of the court.

5:41 Going the extra mile suggests the context of Roman soldiers conscripting Jewish civilians to carry their heavy packs for up to a mile. Jesus commands voluntarily duplicating the legal limit.

5:42 Give to the one who asks you. Jesus does not say *what* to give. Sometimes what a person really needs is not what they request. Positively, Jesus encourages a spirit of generosity.

5:43 Love your neighbor. Appears in Lev 19:18. **hate your enemy.** Found nowhere in the OT but might have been inferred from commands like those to exterminate certain Canaanite towns or peoples. Jesus commands enemy love instead. Loving only one's friends or those who reciprocate one's good will makes a person no better than a complete pagan—someone who is neither Jewish nor Christian (vv. 46–47). Of the six antitheses in 5:21–48 (see note there), enemy love has the least Jewish precedent.

5:46 tax collectors. See notes on 9:9,11.

5:48 This verse rounds out the entire set of six antitheses (see note on vv. 21–48). **Be perfect.** Christ sets up the high ideal of perfect love (vv. 43–47)—not that we can fully attain it in this life. That, however, is God's high standard for us. **perfect.** Could also be translated "mature" and echoes Lev 19:2 on being holy as God is holy. Luke 6:36 offers another partial equivalent—"Be merciful, just as your Father is merciful"—which may be a synecdoche (part for the whole) for Matthew's version.

6:1–18 Jesus turns to address three common Jewish practices of devotion to God: giving to the needy, prayer, and fasting. His point is to warn against calling attention to one's good behavior for the sake of earning human praise.

6:2 announce it with trumpets. May be a metaphor for ostentatiously displaying one's giving.

6:3 do not let your left hand know what your right hand is doing. Emphasizing that one should not call attention to one's giving. Self-glorification is always a present danger.

6:5–15 Like giving to the needy, public prayer should not call undue attention to the one praying. Most prayer should be personal and done in a private place. It is particularly hypocritical to parade one's piety in prayer since, by definition, to "pray" means to talk to God, not other people.

6:7 babbling. Onomatopoetic in both Greek and English. The term does not forbid reciting fixed prayers or repeating the same concerns, but it excludes trying to manipulate God through prescribed formulas or meaningless verbiage. **like pagans.** They used long lists of the names of their gods in their prayers, hoping that by constantly repeating them they would call on the name of the god that could help them.

6:9–13 Commonly known as "the Lord's Prayer," this prayer of Jesus models the kinds of issues that prayer should prioritize and their relative value. Verses 9–10 focus on God first; only then do vv. 11–13 turn to people.

6:9 Father. Probably reflects the underlying Aramaic *Abba* (as in Mark

[10]your kingdom[h] come,
your will be done,[i]
on earth as it is in heaven.
[11]Give us today our daily bread.[j]
[12]And forgive us our debts,
as we also have forgiven our debtors.[k]
[13]And lead us not into temptation,[a][l]
but deliver us from the evil one.[b][m]

[14]For if you forgive other people when they sin against you, your heavenly Father will also forgive you.[n]
[15]But if you do not forgive others their sins, your Father will not forgive your sins.[o]

Fasting

[16]"When you fast, do not look somber[p] as the hypocrites do, for they disfigure their faces to show
others they are fasting. Truly I tell you, they have received their reward in full. [17]But when you fast,
put oil on your head and wash your face, [18]so that it will not be obvious to others that you are fasting, but only to your Father, who is unseen; and your Father, who sees what is done in secret, will
reward you.[q]

Treasures in Heaven

6:22,23pp — Lk 11:34-36

[19]"Do not store up for yourselves treasures on earth,[r] where moths and vermin destroy,[s] and where
thieves break in and steal. [20]But store up for yourselves treasures in heaven,[t] where moths and vermin
do not destroy, and where thieves do not break in and steal.[u] [21]For where your treasure is, there your
heart will be also.[v]

[22]"The eye is the lamp of the body. If your eyes are healthy,[c] your whole body will be full of light.
[23]But if your eyes are unhealthy,[d] your whole body will be full of darkness. If then the light within you
is darkness, how great is that darkness!

[24]"No one can serve two masters. Either you will hate the one and love the other, or you will be devoted to the one and despise the other. You cannot serve both God and money.[w]

[a] *13* The Greek for *temptation* can also mean *testing*. [b] *13* Or *from evil*; some late manuscripts *one, / for yours is the kingdom and the power and the glory forever. Amen.* [c] *22* The Greek for *healthy* here implies *generous.* [d] *23* The Greek for *unhealthy* here implies *stingy*.

6:10 [h]Mt 3:2 [i]Mt 26:39
6:11 [j]Pr 30:8
6:12 [k]Mt 18:21-35
6:13 [l]Jas 1:13 [m]Mt 5:37
6:14 [n]Mt 18:21-35; Mk 11:25,26; Eph 4:32; Col 3:13
6:15 [o]Mt 18:35
6:16 [p]Isa 58:5
6:18 [q]ver 4,6
6:19 [r]Pr 23:4; Heb 13:5 [s]Jas 5:2,3
6:20 [t]Mt 19:21; Lk 12:33; 18:22; 1Ti 6:19 [u]Lk 12:33
6:21 [v]Lk 12:34
6:24 [w]Lk 16:13

14:36), almost but not quite "Daddy." **hallowed.** Regarded as holy. Thus a unique intimacy with God ("Father") is then balanced with proper reverence ("hallowed be your name").

6:10 your kingdom come. Not in the sense of "come into existence" but in the sense of "come more completely" until its full and final consummation. **your will.** What humans already know God wants them to do, especially through the Scriptures.

6:11 daily bread. The necessities of life. Food is central, but all basic physical needs are probably in view.

6:12 forgive us our debts. Means not that we lose our salvation every time we sin but that our fellowship with God is hindered when we fail to repent of our misdeeds. **as we also have forgiven our debtors.** Is explained by vv. 14–15. Jesus means not "to the same extent as" but "just as." The prayer assumes that those whom God forgives in turn forgive others.

6:13 lead us not into temptation. God never tempts anyone (Jas 1:13); therefore, this probably means "Do not allow us to succumb to temptation." **the evil one.** Could also be translated "evil."

6:16–18 To "fast" means to refrain from food for a longer than normal period. Those fasting to free up more time for prayer or other spiritual disciplines should not dress or groom themselves so as to let others know what they are doing.

6:19–24 Materialism may be God's greatest rival competing for the allegiance of human hearts, not the least because constantly striving to secure one's life via possessions produces anxiety. These verses set up the fundamental contrast; vv. 25–34 tell those committed to God not to worry about the basics of physical life. Far from promising prosperity, the NT calls believers to give generously from any surplus (2 Cor 8:13–15) and assumes fellow believers will come to their aid should they become needy by giving away too much (see note on vv. 33–34).

6:19–21 The issue is not one's net worth, but how one is using material possessions. Unused surplus is eventually destroyed or stolen.

6:22–23 Just as a "healthy" eye lets in "light" to guide an entire person, an eye focused on God will see clearly everything spiritual. Just as a blind person sees only "darkness," one worshiping possessions will get everything wrong from God's perspective.

6:22 healthy. Can also be translated "generous."

6:23 unhealthy. Can also be translated "stingy." Stewardship of possessions is a key barometer of spiritual health.

6:24 A slave, owned entirely by one master, cannot serve two masters, and both God and money are masters that make all-consuming demands. **money.** Greek *mamōna* ("mammon") refers to material possessions that have become an idol.

6:25 [x]ver 27,28,31,34; Lk 10:41; 12:11,22; Php 4:6; 1Pe 5:7
6:26 [y]Job 38:41; Ps 147:9 [z]Mt 10:29-31
6:27 [a]Ps 39:5
6:29 [b]1Ki 10:4-7
6:30 [c]Mt 8:26; 14:31; 16:8
6:32 [d]ver 8
6:33 [e]Mt 19:29; Mk 10:29-30
7:1 [f]Lk 6:37; Ro 14:4,10, 13; 1Co 4:5; Jas 4:11,12
7:2 [g]Mk 4:24; Lk 6:38
7:7 [h]Mt 21:22; Mk 11:24; Jn 14:13,14; 15:7,16; 16:23,24; Jas 1:5-8; 4:2,3; 1Jn 3:22; 5:14,15
7:8 [i]Pr 8:17; Jer 29:12,13

Do Not Worry

6:25-33pp — Lk 12:22-31

[25]"Therefore I tell you, do not worry[x] about your life, what you will eat or drink; or about your body, what you will wear. Is not life more than food, and the body more than clothes? [26]Look at the birds of the air; they do not sow or reap or store away in barns, and yet your heavenly Father feeds them.[y] Are you not much more valuable than they?[z] [27]Can any one of you by worrying add a single hour to your life[a]?[a]

[28]"And why do you worry about clothes? See how the flowers of the field grow. They do not labor or spin. [29]Yet I tell you that not even Solomon in all his splendor[b] was dressed like one of these. [30]If that is how God clothes the grass of the field, which is here today and tomorrow is thrown into the fire, will he not much more clothe you—you of little faith?[c] [31]So do not worry, saying, 'What shall we eat?' or 'What shall we drink?' or 'What shall we wear?' [32]For the pagans run after all these things, and your heavenly Father knows that you need them.[d] [33]But seek first his kingdom and his righteousness, and all these things will be given to you as well.[e] [34]Therefore do not worry about tomorrow, for tomorrow will worry about itself. Each day has enough trouble of its own.

Judging Others

7:3-5pp — Lk 6:41,42

7 "Do not judge, or you too will be judged.[f] [2]For in the same way you judge others, you will be judged, and with the measure you use, it will be measured to you.[g]

[3]"Why do you look at the speck of sawdust in your brother's eye and pay no attention to the plank in your own eye? [4]How can you say to your brother, 'Let me take the speck out of your eye,' when all the time there is a plank in your own eye? [5]You hypocrite, first take the plank out of your own eye, and then you will see clearly to remove the speck from your brother's eye.

[6]"Do not give dogs what is sacred; do not throw your pearls to pigs. If you do, they may trample them under their feet, and turn and tear you to pieces.

Ask, Seek, Knock

7:7-11pp — Lk 11:9-13

[7]"Ask and it will be given to you;[h] seek and you will find; knock and the door will be opened to you. [8]For everyone who asks receives; the one who seeks finds;[i] and to the one who knocks, the door will be opened.

[9]"Which of you, if your son asks for bread, will give him a stone? [10]Or if he asks for a fish, will give

a 27 Or *single cubit to your height*

6:25 do not worry. Means not that we should not think about or plan ahead but that we are not to be anxious.

6:26–27 God provides food and drink for birds, so he will surely provide them for his people. Of course, birds often work hard to find their food, so this is scarcely a call to laziness.

6:28–32 Even wild flowers and grass are beautifully dressed, so God will surely clothe his people much more wonderfully. Unbelievers worry about the basics of life such as food, drink, and clothing.

6:33–34 seek first his kingdom and his righteousness. By definition includes sharing one's surplus with fellow Christians who lack the basic necessities of life or the ability to acquire them. When God's people worldwide do this, "all these things" (food, drink, clothing) will be given to them as well. This is not a promise that faithful believers will never starve to death, but there *need* never be any poor among them (Deut 15:4). Only the disobedience of God's people makes it inevitable that at least a few poor believers remain (Deut 15:11). Moreover, each day has too many unavoidable worries of its own for us to indulge in worries about the future as well.

7:1–12 Verses 1–6 are tied together by the theme of judging others, while vv. 7–11 have to do with petitioning God. Verse 12 summarizes both themes as well as the entire section.

7:1 judge. Greek *krinō* can mean to condemn or judge overly harshly; that is what it means here in v. 1 because, following the *lex talionis* (see note on 5:38), God will judge accordingly. Jesus condemns censoriousness and judgmentalism (v. 1), but judgment in the sense of analysis or discernment is always necessary, once one has examined oneself first (vv. 2–6). Verses 5–6 make it clear that Jesus' followers must analyze situations and correct people when they err (cf. vv. 15–20; John 7:24).

7:5 Once one has dealt with an area in which they have sinned greatly, they can and must offer sincere help for others struggling in that area.

7:6 Do not give dogs what is sacred; do not throw your pearls to pigs. Probably refers to the prolonged offering of the gospel and its holy truths and practices to those who spitefully mock and reject it, especially given that dogs were wild scavengers in Israel and pigs were the most unclean of animals.

7:7 Ask … seek … knock. The commands are all in the present tense in Greek, suggesting continuous or frequent action. Jesus expects his audience to remember "your will be done" in his model prayer (6:10). These verses are not quite the "blank check" they may first seem to be.

7:9–10 stone … snake. Small, hand-size loaves of bread often resembled stones in shape and color, and some eel-shaped fish could look like

him a snake? 11 If you, then, though you are evil, know how to give good gifts to your children, how
much more will your Father in heaven give good gifts to those who ask him! 12 So in everything, do to
others what you would have them do to you,[j] for this sums up the Law and the Prophets.[k]

The Narrow and Wide Gates

13 "Enter through the narrow gate.[l] For wide is the gate and broad is the road that leads to destruction, and many enter through it. 14 But small is the gate and narrow the road that leads to life, and
only a few find it.

True and False Prophets

15 "Watch out for false prophets.[m] They come to you in sheep's clothing, but inwardly they are ferocious wolves.[n] 16 By their fruit you will recognize them.[o] Do people pick grapes from thornbushes, or figs
from thistles?[p] 17 Likewise, every good tree bears good fruit, but a bad tree bears bad fruit. 18 A good tree
cannot bear bad fruit, and a bad tree cannot bear good fruit. 19 Every tree that does not bear good fruit
is cut down and thrown into the fire.[q] 20 Thus, by their fruit you will recognize them.

True and False Disciples

21 "Not everyone who says to me, 'Lord, Lord,'[r] will enter the kingdom of heaven, but only the one
who does the will of my Father who is in heaven.[s] 22 Many will say to me on that day,[t] 'Lord, Lord, did
we not prophesy in your name and in your name drive out demons and in your name perform many
miracles?'[u] 23 Then I will tell them plainly, 'I never knew you. Away from me, you evildoers!'[v]

The Wise and Foolish Builders

7:24-27pp — Lk 6:47-49

24 "Therefore everyone who hears these words of mine and puts them into practice[w] is like a wise
man who built his house on the rock. 25 The rain came down, the streams rose, and the winds blew and
beat against that house; yet it did not fall, because it had its foundation on the rock. 26 But everyone
who hears these words of mine and does not put them into practice is like a foolish man who built
his house on sand. 27 The rain came down, the streams rose, and the winds blew and beat against that
house, and it fell with a great crash."

28 When Jesus had finished saying these things,[x] the crowds were amazed at his teaching,[y] 29 because
he taught as one who had authority, and not as their teachers of the law.

7:12 [j] Lk 6:31 [k] Ro 13:8-10; Gal 5:14
7:13 [l] Lk 13:24
7:15 [m] Jer 23:16; Mt 24:24; Mk 13:22; Lk 6:26; 2Pe 2:1; 1Jn 4:1; Rev 16:13 [n] Ac 20:29
7:16 [o] Mt 12:33; Lk 6:44 [p] Jas 3:12
7:19 [q] Mt 3:10
7:21 [r] Hos 8:2; Mt 25:11 [s] Ro 2:13; Jas 1:22
7:22 [t] Mt 10:15 [u] 1Co 13:1-3
7:23 [v] Ps 6:8; Mt 25:12, 41; Lk 13:25-27
7:24 [w] Jas 1:22-25
7:28 [x] Mt 11:1; 13:53; 19:1; 26:1 [y] Mt 13:54; Mk 1:22; 6:2; Lk 4:32; Jn 7:46

snakes. Normally, parents do not intentionally deceive their children in these potentially harmful ways.

7:11 though you are evil. Refers simply to the inherent sinfulness of all, even the best of parents.

7:12 The "Golden Rule" summarizes Jesus' ethics in this sermon. Other teachers, ancient and modern, including Hillel (see note on 5:31), made similar statements negatively: "Don't do to others what you don't want them to do to you." Jesus' positive phrasing makes obedience something that can never be complete.

7:13–27 The conclusion of Jesus' great sermon employs three analogies to illustrate there are only two ways—a right way and a wrong way—to respond to his message: narrow versus broad gates and roads, good versus bad fruit, and building on rock versus building on sand.

7:13–14 narrow. The narrow way involves constraint and hardship. **many … few.** This does not mean that only a tiny percentage of the world's population of all time will ever be saved, but it does suggest the number will not be large.

7:15 false prophets. Claimed to speak on behalf of God when in fact they did not. **sheep's clothing.** Implies that they looked harmless, like part of the "flock" of Jesus' followers. **ferocious wolves.** Depict the damage they will actually do to God's people through their teaching and/or behavior (cf. Ezek 22:27).

7:16–20 fruit. Works or behavior. The focus on good versus bad works or behavior could suggest that doctrine or beliefs are irrelevant, but v. 23 makes it clear that one must have a relationship with Jesus as well.

7:21–22 The good works that false prophets can perform may include even what we associate with Christian leadership, what appears to be miraculous, and what is alleged to be done in Jesus' name (i.e., by his power). Still, none of these is a foolproof criterion for determining what truly comes from God.

7:24–27 *The Parable of the Wise and Foolish Builders.* Numerous wadis, or dry gulches, in and around Israel made this parable particularly apt. Those tempted to erect even temporary shelters in the flat, parched stream beds might find themselves swept away in the flash floods that a sudden downpour could create. Jesus is not teaching salvation by works because v. 23 has just stressed the need for an actual relationship with him. Jesus is commanding what John the Baptist calls "fruit in keeping with repentance" (3:8).

7:28–29 Jesus' audience is astonished at the "authority" with which Christ preaches—"not as their teachers of the law," who wielded considerable authority but normally quoted Scripture or other rabbis to support their perspectives. Jesus rarely does the first and never does the second. His sovereign pronouncements reflect direct, divine declarations. Only someone viewing himself as a divine spokesman would likely speak in such a fashion.

8:2 [z]Lk 5:12 [a]Mt 9:18; 15:25; 18:26; 20:20
8:4 [b]Mt 9:30; Mk 5:43; 7:36; 8:30 [c]Lev 14:2-32
8:8 [d]Ps 107:20
8:10 [e]Mt 15:28
8:11 [f]Ps 107:3; Isa 49:12; 59:19; Mal 1:11 [g]Lk 13:29
8:12 [h]Mt 13:38 [i]Mt 13:42,50; 22:13; 24:51; 25:30; Lk 13:28
8:13 [j]Mt 9:22

Jesus Heals a Man With Leprosy

8:2-4pp — Mk 1:40-44; Lk 5:12-14

8 When Jesus came down from the mountainside, large crowds followed him. [2]A man with leprosy[a][z]
came and knelt before him[a] and said, "Lord, if you are willing, you can make me clean."
[3]Jesus reached out his hand and touched the man. "I am willing," he said. "Be clean!" Immediately
he was cleansed of his leprosy. [4]Then Jesus said to him, "See that you don't tell anyone.[b] But go, show
yourself to the priest and offer the gift Moses commanded,[c] as a testimony to them."

The Faith of the Centurion

8:5-13pp — Lk 7:1-10

[5]When Jesus had entered Capernaum, a centurion came to him, asking for help. [6]"Lord," he said,
"my servant lies at home paralyzed, suffering terribly."
[7]Jesus said to him, "Shall I come and heal him?"
[8]The centurion replied, "Lord, I do not deserve to have you come under my roof. But just say the
word, and my servant will be healed.[d] [9]For I myself am a man under authority, with soldiers under
me. I tell this one, 'Go,' and he goes; and that one, 'Come,' and he comes. I say to my servant, 'Do this,'
and he does it."
[10]When Jesus heard this, he was amazed and said to those following him, "Truly I tell you, I have
not found anyone in Israel with such great faith.[e] [11]I say to you that many will come from the east
and the west,[f] and will take their places at the feast with Abraham, Isaac and Jacob in the kingdom of
heaven.[g] [12]But the subjects of the kingdom[h] will be thrown outside, into the darkness, where there will
be weeping and gnashing of teeth."[i]
[13]Then Jesus said to the centurion, "Go! Let it be done just as you believed it would."[j] And his servant
was healed at that moment.

Jesus Heals Many

8:14-16pp — Mk 1:29-34; Lk 4:38-41

[14]When Jesus came into Peter's house, he saw Peter's mother-in-law lying in bed with a fever. [15]He
touched her hand and the fever left her, and she got up and began to wait on him.
[16]When evening came, many who were demon-possessed were brought to him, and he drove out the

a 2 The Greek word traditionally translated *leprosy* was used for various diseases affecting the skin.

8:1—9:34 *Jesus' Authoritative Miracle-Working Ministry.* Matt 9:35 forms a "bookend" with 4:23. The Sermon on the Mount illustrates Jesus' authoritative preaching and teaching, as mentioned in these two framing verses. Most of chs. 8–9 illustrate his authoritative healing (and other miracles), which these two verses likewise highlight.

8:1–17 The first three miracles Matthew narrates in this section show Jesus healing the ritually outcast: a leper, a centurion's servant, and Peter's mother-in-law. The highly defiling sickness, the probable Gentile background of the commander of the hated occupying army, and the symptoms of Peter's mother-in-law's fever make all three individuals ritually impure. The section ends with Jesus' broader ministry of healing, which Matthew indicates is another fulfillment of prophecy (v. 17).

8:4 See that you don't tell anyone. The first of several occurrences in Matthew of the "Messianic secret," a phenomenon even more common in Mark. Jesus frequently tells people not to talk about him, even in contexts in which it is highly unlikely he will be obeyed, probably to avoid stirring up even more hope for a militaristic and royal Messiah who would rid the land of the Romans. **as a testimony to them.** Could mean showing that Jesus follows the law of sacrifice after a leper has been cleansed (Lev 13–14). But fresh on the heels of a sermon that stresses Jesus' distinctive approach to the law, the testimony is more likely to Jesus' power and identity.

8:5 centurion. A commanding officer of up to 100 soldiers.

8:7 Shall I come and heal him? Most translations treat this as a statement: "I shall come and heal him." But Jesus makes no similar declarations elsewhere, while the emphatic Greek pronoun *egō* ("I") may make better sense in a question. In other words, Jesus is asking if he, a Jew, should go to the home of a Gentile and risk ritual impurity. In so doing he draws out the man's extraordinary belief that Jesus can heal from a distance.

8:10–12 Jesus doubtless enrages the Jewish crowd in Capernaum (v. 5) by claiming (1) that this foreign officer of the hated occupying Roman forces has greater faith than anyone in Israel (v. 10), and (2) that many will come from the ends of the earth to partake in the heavenly banquet of all God's redeemed people, while many Israelites will be excluded (vv. 11–12).

8:12 darkness ... weeping and gnashing of teeth. Whether or not the darkness or gnashing is literal, Jesus' words powerfully depict hell as exclusion from God and all things good. As recently as 5:22, Jesus speaks of the "fire of hell," which does conflict with darkness if taken literally. The agony, however, remains very real.

8:14–17 Matthew generalizes from the final specific example of healing to large numbers of other sick who were brought to Christ. **Peter's house.** See photo, p. 2076.

8:16 Jesus did not heal every sick person he encountered (cf. John 5:1–15), but on *this* occasion, he heals "all" who were brought to him.

spirits with a word and healed all the sick.[k] 17This was to fulfill[l] what was spoken through the prophet
Isaiah:

> "He took up our infirmities
> and bore our diseases."[a][m]

8:16 [k]Mt 4:23,24
8:17 [l]Mt 1:22 [m]Isa 53:4
8:18 [n]Mk 4:35
8:20 [o]Da 7:13; Mt 12:8, 32,40; 16:13,27,28; 17:9; 19:28; Mk 2:10; 8:31

The Cost of Following Jesus

8:19-22pp — Lk 9:57-60

18When Jesus saw the crowd around him, he gave orders to cross to the other side of the lake.[n] 19Then
a teacher of the law came to him and said, "Teacher, I will follow you wherever you go."
20Jesus replied, "Foxes have dens and birds have nests, but the Son of Man[o] has no place to lay his
head."

[a] *17* Isaiah 53:4 (see Septuagint)

8:17 This fulfills Isa 53:4, part of the most famous suffering servant passage. Isaiah has primarily forgiveness of sin in mind, and Matthew applies it to physical diseases as well. There *is* healing in the atonement, but in this life it is only partial and on God's terms and when he desires. The death rate remains 100 percent. Given vv. 1–16, cleansing from ritual impurity may also be in view.

8:18–22 Two brief exchanges between Jesus and would-be disciples interrupt the succession of miracles to highlight the cost of following Jesus. Apparently, in each case Jesus' commands prove too demanding for the inquirers. First, a scribe promises more than he can actually deliver (vv. 19–20); then another person refuses to follow wholeheartedly (vv. 21–22).

8:20 the Son of Man. A key title Jesus uses for himself. Throughout Ezekiel, God uses the term to address the prophet as a mere mortal. But in Dan 7:13–14, "one like a son of man" (i.e., a human being) is ushered into God's presence on the clouds of heaven and given universal and eternal authority over the kingdoms of the earth. Some of Jesus' "Son of Man" sayings, like this one, emphasize his role as a humble, earthly figure, especially in his passion and death, but many reflect his exalted, Messianic role. **has no place to lay his head.** Does not mean Jesus no longer has a home or friends who will take him in, but reflects the arduous nature of his itinerant ministry without a regular residence.

Northwestern shore of the Sea of Galilee where Jesus spent much of his ministry.

8:22 [p] Mt 4:19
8:26 [q] Mt 6:30 [r] Ps 65:7; 89:9; 107:29
8:28 [s] Mt 4:24
8:29 [t] Jdg 11:12; 2Sa 16:10; 1Ki 17:18; Mk 1:24; Lk 4:34; Jn 2:4 [u] 2Pe 2:4
8:34 [v] Lk 5:8; Ac 16:39
9:1 [w] Mt 4:13
9:2 [x] Mt 4:24 [y] ver 22 [z] Jn 16:33 [a] Lk 7:48

21 Another disciple said to him, "Lord, first let me go and bury my father."
22 But Jesus told him, "Follow me,[p] and let the dead bury their own dead."

Jesus Calms the Storm

8:23-27pp — Mk 4:36-41; Lk 8:22-25
8:23-27Ref — Mt 14:22-33

23 Then he got into the boat and his disciples followed him. 24 Suddenly a furious storm came up on
the lake, so that the waves swept over the boat. But Jesus was sleeping. 25 The disciples went and woke
him, saying, "Lord, save us! We're going to drown!"
26 He replied, "You of little faith,[q] why are you so afraid?" Then he got up and rebuked the winds and
the waves, and it was completely calm.[r]
27 The men were amazed and asked, "What kind of man is this? Even the winds and the waves obey him!"

Jesus Restores Two Demon-Possessed Men

8:28-34pp — Mk 5:1-17; Lk 8:26-37

28 When he arrived at the other side in the region of the Gadarenes,[a] two demon-possessed[s] men
coming from the tombs met him. They were so violent that no one could pass that way. 29 "What do you
want with us,[t] Son of God?" they shouted. "Have you come here to torture us before the appointed time?"[u]
30 Some distance from them a large herd of pigs was feeding. 31 The demons begged Jesus, "If you
drive us out, send us into the herd of pigs."
32 He said to them, "Go!" So they came out and went into the pigs, and the whole herd rushed down
the steep bank into the lake and died in the water. 33 Those tending the pigs ran off, went into the town
and reported all this, including what had happened to the demon-possessed men. 34 Then the whole
town went out to meet Jesus. And when they saw him, they pleaded with him to leave their region.[v]

Jesus Forgives and Heals a Paralyzed Man

9:2-8pp — Mk 2:3-12; Lk 5:18-26

9 Jesus stepped into a boat, crossed over and came to his own town.[w] 2 Some men brought to him
a paralyzed man,[x] lying on a mat. When Jesus saw their faith,[y] he said to the man, "Take heart,[z]
son; your sins are forgiven."[a]

[a] *28* Some manuscripts *Gergesenes*; other manuscripts *Gerasenes*

8:21 let me go and bury my father. Could mean staying around for up to a year when the coffin was exhumed and the bones reburied in a much smaller ossuary.

8:22 let the dead bury their own dead. Probably means letting the spiritually dead bury the physically dead. The point is the urgency of discipleship, not literal disrespect for one's parents or for a culture's burial practices. Contrast 1 Kgs 19:20–21.

8:23—9:8 The second triad of miracles in chs. 8–9 demonstrates Jesus' authority over disaster, demons, and disease.

8:23–27 This passage does not promise that Jesus will calm all the "storms" of life; often he does not. Rather, it highlights his authority over nature (v. 27).

8:26 rebuked. The same verb is sometimes used in the Gospels when Jesus casts out demons (e.g., 17:18) and may suggest that Matthew sees a demonic influence behind what we would call a natural event. Biblically, discord between humans and "nature" ultimately stems from sin entering the world (Gen 3:17–19) and is thus unnatural.

8:27 What kind of man is this? This is the question this miracle should raise for everyone who hears of it. In Ps 89:9 God alone rules "over the surging sea" and stills it "when its waves mount up." Jesus demonstrates his divinity.

8:28–34 Mark refers to one demonized individual rather than two (Mark 5:1–20). But Mark does not say there is *only* one, and he may focus on the spokesman and/or the more distressed of the two.

8:28 the region of the Gadarenes. A large province east and southeast of the Sea of Galilee (see map, p. 2876). A city within Gadara directly across the lake from Tiberias was Khersa, which could easily have been put into Greek as "Gerasa." Hence Mark 5:1 has "Gerasenes." Textual variants sometimes substituted "Gergesenes" as yet another translation for residents of Khersa. **tombs.** Demonized individuals were so unclean and destructive that they were attracted to tombs.

8:29 What do you want with us, Son of God? Demons in the NT regularly recognize Jesus' identity but fear him and try to ward him off. Because Jesus' ministry will deal the death blow to the demonic realm but not yet entirely vanquish it—that remains for after his return—these demons ask if he has come "to torture [them] before the appointed time."

8:30–32 In keeping with this timetable, Jesus does not destroy the demons but permits them to enter a herd of pigs, which the demons in turn destroy.

8:30 herd of pigs. Typical Jewish reaction to this story, in a culture in which pigs were the most unclean of animals, probably ranged from laughter to a quiet recognition that the farmers, who should not have been raising pigs for food in the first place, got their appropriate comeuppance.

8:34 pleaded with him to leave their region. Reasons likely ranged from anger over the loss of the farmers' livelihood to fear of Jesus' power.

9:1–8 For the third straight time, a miracle calls even more attention to the question of Jesus' identity than to what he will do for people.

9:1 own town. Capernaum (Mark 2:1), not Nazareth (cf. Matt 4:13).

9:2 sins. Sometimes Jesus links a person's affliction directly to their sins (e.g., John 5:14); sometimes he denies such a link (e.g., John 9:3). Neither relationship applies in all situations.

3 At this, some of the teachers of the law said to themselves, "This fellow is blaspheming!"[b]
4 Knowing their thoughts,[c] Jesus said, "Why do you entertain evil thoughts in your hearts? 5 Which
is easier: to say, 'Your sins are forgiven,' or to say, 'Get up and walk'? 6 But I want you to know that the
Son of Man[d] has authority on earth to forgive sins." So he said to the paralyzed man, "Get up, take your
mat and go home." 7 Then the man got up and went home. 8 When the crowd saw this, they were filled
with awe; and they praised God,[e] who had given such authority to man.

The Calling of Matthew

9:9-13pp — Mk 2:14-17; Lk 5:27-32

9 As Jesus went on from there, he saw a man named Matthew sitting at the tax collector's booth.
"Follow me," he told him, and Matthew got up and followed him.
10 While Jesus was having dinner at Matthew's house, many tax collectors and sinners came and ate
with him and his disciples. 11 When the Pharisees saw this, they asked his disciples, "Why does your
teacher eat with tax collectors and sinners?"[f]
12 On hearing this, Jesus said, "It is not the healthy who need a doctor, but the sick. 13 But go and learn
what this means: 'I desire mercy, not sacrifice.'[a][g] For I have not come to call the righteous, but sinners."[h]

Jesus Questioned About Fasting

9:14-17pp — Mk 2:18-22; Lk 5:33-39

14 Then John's disciples came and asked him, "How is it that we and the Pharisees fast often,[i] but
your disciples do not fast?"
15 Jesus answered, "How can the guests of the bridegroom mourn while he is with them?[j] The time
will come when the bridegroom will be taken from them; then they will fast.[k]
16 "No one sews a patch of unshrunk cloth on an old garment, for the patch will pull away from the
garment, making the tear worse. 17 Neither do people pour new wine into old wineskins. If they do, the
skins will burst; the wine will run out and the wineskins will be ruined. No, they pour new wine into
new wineskins, and both are preserved."

[a] *13* Hosea 6:6

9:3 [b] Mt 26:65; Jn 10:33
9:4 [c] Ps 94:11; Mt 12:25; Lk 6:8; 9:47; 11:17
9:6 [d] Mt 8:20
9:8 [e] Mt 5:16; 15:31; Lk 7:16; 13:13; 17:15; 23:47; Jn 15:8; Ac 4:21; 11:18; 21:20
9:11 [f] Mt 11:19; Lk 5:30; 15:2; Gal 2:15
9:13 [g] Hos 6:6; Mic 6:6-8; Mt 12:7 [h] 1Ti 1:15
9:14 [i] Lk 18:12
9:15 [j] Jn 3:29 [k] Ac 13:2,3; 14:23

9:3 blaspheming. Simply declaring a person's sins forgiven would not have meant one was blaspheming. Priests did it regularly. But making such a declaration while bypassing the temple authorities and the biblical requirements for animal sacrifices was something only God could do.
9:5 easier. It is far easier to *say*, "Your sins are forgiven" than "Get up and walk" because the first of these commands cannot be disproved as easily. So to show that Jesus has the authority to make the easier claim, he demonstrates his miracle-working power that vindicates the harder claim.
9:8 The onlookers do not necessarily draw the correct conclusions about Jesus' identity, concluding only that God had given remarkable "authority to man."
9:9–17 As in 8:18–22, Matthew punctuates his collection of miracles with teachings on discipleship: his own call to be an apostle and Jesus' teaching about fasting.
9:9–13 Unlike the fishermen in 4:18–22, there is no indication in any of the Gospels that Matthew had any prior exposure to Jesus, though of course he may have.
9:9 Matthew. Mark 2:14 refers to him as Levi. It was common for people in Jesus' day to have two or three names. Matthew may be using the name by which he became better known. **the tax collector's booth.** It was probably on the edge of Capernaum as a place for collecting tolls and/or customs duties. Jews would have despised Matthew, a Jewish middleman collecting levies for Rome. He may also have made his own living by charging higher fees than required and skimming the extra off the top for himself.
9:11 tax collectors and sinners. Lumped together, showing how notorious the former had become.
9:12 Jesus reapplies well-known proverbial wisdom from the physical world to the spiritual realm. Like medical doctors attending to the most ill, Jesus must minister to the most unrighteous.
9:13 I desire mercy, not sacrifice. The contrasts are not absolute, as the context in Hos 6:6 shows. The point is one of priorities. The neediest often require the most attention.
9:14–17 A difference among the practices of the followers of various Jewish leaders, including Jesus, leads to a question about fasting.
9:14 fast often. Although most Jews understood the OT to command fasting only on the Day of Atonement (Lev 23:26–32), Pharisees fasted twice a week as well. John the Baptist's asceticism naturally led his followers to refrain from food periodically, though we do not know with what frequency.
9:15 Jesus calls himself the "bridegroom"; his followers will thus be the bride. With his presence, wedding-like celebration rather than self-denial is in order. After he has died, they will mourn and fast. In Isa 62:5 God is depicted as a bridegroom; Jesus may be using a similarly exalted picture for himself here.
9:16–17 unshrunk cloth. Many types of cloth shrink after their first washing, so one would not want to patch an "old garment" with new, unshrunk cloth. **new wine.** Unfermented wine expands as it ferments, so one would not want to put it in brittle "old wineskins" that could break in the process. **both are preserved.** Refers to both the "new wine" and the "new wineskins." Jesus' message is new enough compared to the old ways of Judaism that it requires new attitudes and behaviors, including less fasting. After his death and resurrection, believers do occasionally fast (Acts 13:2–3) but not with the regularity of the Jewish leaders.

9:18 [l]Mt 8:2 [m]Mk 5:23
9:20 [n]Mt 14:36; Mk 3:10
9:22 [o]Mk 10:52; Lk 7:50; 17:19; 18:42 [p]Mt 15:28
9:23 [q]2Ch 35:25; Jer 9:17,18
9:24 [r]Ac 20:10 [s]Jn 11:11-14
9:26 [t]Mt 4:24
9:27 [u]Mt 15:22; Mk 10:47; Lk 18:38-39
9:29 [v]ver 22
9:30 [w]Mt 8:4
9:31 [x]ver 26; Mk 7:36
9:32 [y]Mt 4:24 [z]Mt 12:22-24
9:33 [a]Mk 2:12
9:34 [b]Mt 12:24; Lk 11:15
9:35 [c]Mt 4:23
9:36 [d]Mt 14:14 [e]Nu 27:17; Eze 34:5,6; Zec 10:2; Mk 6:34

Jesus Raises a Dead Girl and Heals a Sick Woman

9:18-26pp — Mk 5:22-43; Lk 8:41-56

18 While he was saying this, a synagogue leader came and knelt before him[l] and said, "My daughter has just died. But come and put your hand on her,[m] and she will live." 19 Jesus got up and went with him, and so did his disciples.

20 Just then a woman who had been subject to bleeding for twelve years came up behind him and touched the edge of his cloak.[n] 21 She said to herself, "If I only touch his cloak, I will be healed."

22 Jesus turned and saw her. "Take heart, daughter," he said, "your faith has healed you."[o] And the woman was healed at that moment.[p]

23 When Jesus entered the synagogue leader's house and saw the noisy crowd and people playing pipes,[q] 24 he said, "Go away. The girl is not dead[r] but asleep."[s] But they laughed at him. 25 After the crowd had been put outside, he went in and took the girl by the hand, and she got up. 26 News of this spread through all that region.[t]

Jesus Heals the Blind and the Mute

27 As Jesus went on from there, two blind men followed him, calling out, "Have mercy on us, Son of David!"[u]

28 When he had gone indoors, the blind men came to him, and he asked them, "Do you believe that I am able to do this?"

"Yes, Lord," they replied.

29 Then he touched their eyes and said, "According to your faith let it be done to you";[v] 30 and their sight was restored. Jesus warned them sternly, "See that no one knows about this."[w] 31 But they went out and spread the news about him all over that region.[x]

32 While they were going out, a man who was demon-possessed[y] and could not talk[z] was brought to Jesus. 33 And when the demon was driven out, the man who had been mute spoke. The crowd was amazed and said, "Nothing like this has ever been seen in Israel."[a]

34 But the Pharisees said, "It is by the prince of demons that he drives out demons."[b]

The Workers Are Few

35 Jesus went through all the towns and villages, teaching in their synagogues, proclaiming the good news of the kingdom and healing every disease and sickness.[c] 36 When he saw the crowds, he had compassion on them,[d] because they were harassed and helpless, like sheep without a shepherd.[e] 37 Then he

9:18–34 Four final miracles of chs. 8–9 appear in three discrete episodes, rounding out this section on Jesus' authoritative healing (see note on 8:1—9:34).
9:18–26 Jesus' countercultural concern for women continues, while his overcoming ritual uncleanness associates him closely with God.
9:18 synagogue leader. Mark 5:22 gives the name of the synagogue leader (the chief elder) as Jairus. Mark's much fuller version shows that Jesus was informed twice, first that the girl was dying (Mark 5:23) and then that she was dead (Mark 5:35). Matthew condenses the entire story considerably, here using a different verb for "died" that means "came to an end."
9:20 bleeding. Greek *haimorroeō* ("to hemorrhage"), implying an unnatural bodily discharge. The malady would have been intermittent if she had been afflicted for 12 years and was still alive. It would have made her ritually unclean; normally, anything she touched would have also become unclean.
9:21–22 The woman has undoubtedly heard about Jesus' other miracles and hopes that by secretly touching him, she can also avail herself of his healing power. But Jesus praises her "faith" (v. 22), teaching that trusting in him as the great healer is the key to salvation, spiritual and physical. **healed.** Greek *sōzō*, which often means "to save."
9:23 the noisy crowd. Probably included those mourning loudly. **people playing pipes.** Refers to flutists or oboists performing dirges.
9:24 The girl is not dead but asleep. Probably denies the permanence of her death. The crowds take Jesus literally and thus mock his claim. By touching the corpse, Jesus again shows he cannot be defiled but has the power to make the unclean clean.
9:27 Son of David. The Messiah (see note on 1:1—2:23).
9:29 According to your faith. That is, "because you have faith," not "in proportion to your faith." But in vv. 32–34 Jesus heals someone who is probably prevented by demons from believing, so we cannot generalize and make faith a prerequisite for every miracle.
9:30 See that no one knows. For Jesus' stern warning, see note on 8:4. Not surprisingly, many just ignore Christ's command.
9:32 demon-possessed and could not talk. Although the demons had caused *this* affliction, not all sickness was attributed to demon possession. The crowd's response (v. 33) highlights Jesus' incomparable power and authority. But an ominous, contrary explanation by the Pharisees foreshadows growing hostility toward Jesus by many Jewish leaders. For their specific charge, see 12:24 and note on 12:22–37.
9:35—10:42 *Missionary Discourse.* After a three-verse introduction (9:36–38) and the formal call of the 12 apostles (10:1–4), Matthew presents the second of five major sermons of Jesus that punctuate this Gospel (10:5–42).
9:35 See 4:23 and note on 8:1—9:34.
9:37 the workers are few. The shepherd imagery in vv. 35–38 is akin

said to his disciples, "The harvest[f] is plentiful but the workers are few.[g] 38Ask the Lord of the harvest,
therefore, to send out workers into his harvest field."

Jesus Sends Out the Twelve

10:2-4pp — Mk 3:16-19; Lk 6:14-16; Ac 1:13
10:9-15pp — Mk 6:8-11; Lk 9:3-5; 10:4-12
10:19-22pp — Mk 13:11-13; Lk 21:12-17
10:26-33pp — Lk 12:2-9
10:34,35pp — Lk 12:51-53

10 Jesus called his twelve disciples to him and gave them authority to drive out impure spirits[h]
and to heal every disease and sickness.
2These are the names of the twelve apostles: first, Simon (who is called Peter) and his brother Andrew; James son of Zebedee, and his brother John; 3Philip and Bartholomew; Thomas and Matthew
the tax collector; James son of Alphaeus, and Thaddaeus; 4Simon the Zealot and Judas Iscariot, who
betrayed him.[i]
5These twelve Jesus sent out with the following instructions: "Do not go among the Gentiles or enter
any town of the Samaritans.[j] 6Go rather to the lost sheep of Israel.[k] 7As you go, proclaim this message:
'The kingdom of heaven[l] has come near.' 8Heal the sick, raise the dead, cleanse those who have leprosy,[a] drive out demons. Freely you have received; freely give.
9"Do not get any gold or silver or copper to take with you in your belts[m]— 10no bag for the journey
or extra shirt or sandals or a staff, for the worker is worth his keep.[n] 11Whatever town or village you
enter, search there for some worthy person and stay at their house until you leave. 12As you enter the
home, give it your greeting.[o] 13If the home is deserving, let your peace rest on it; if it is not, let your
peace return to you. 14If anyone will not welcome you or listen to your words, leave that home or town
and shake the dust off your feet.[p] 15Truly I tell you, it will be more bearable for Sodom and Gomorrah[q]
on the day of judgment[r] than for that town.[s]

9:37 [f] Jn 4:35 [g] Lk 10:2
10:1 [h] Mk 3:13-15; Lk 9:1
10:4 [i] Mt 26:14-16,25, 47; Jn 13:2,26,27
10:5 [j] 2Ki 17:24; Lk 9:52; Jn 4:4-26,39,40; Ac 8:5,25
10:6 [k] Jer 50:6; Mt 15:24
10:7 [l] Mt 3:2
10:9 [m] Lk 22:35
10:10 [n] 1Ti 5:18
10:12 [o] 1Sa 25:6
10:14 [p] Ne 5:13; Lk 10:11; Ac 13:51
10:15 [q] 2Pe 2:6 [r] Mt 12:36; 2Pe 2:9; 1Jn 4:17 [s] Mt 11:22,24

[a] *8* The Greek word traditionally translated *leprosy* was used for various diseases affecting the skin.

to Ezek 34 with its prophecy against evil shepherds. Too many of the Jewish leaders were offering their people inadequate or improper guidance. Good leaders in large quantities were acutely needed.

10:1–42 Jesus instructs his 12 closest followers to replicate his ministry.

10:1 impure spirits. Another way of referring to demons.

10:2–4 Jesus may have already designated his closest followers, but Matthew gives the full list of their names for the first time here. Twelve men were chosen, probably on an analogy to the twelve tribes of Israel (cf. the council of twelve at Qumran, 1QS 8:1ff.), and they point to the renewal of the people of God in the Messianic age.

10:2 apostles. Those disciples closest to Jesus whom he called to follow him throughout his ministry. The term is used for people sent on a mission. The first four appeared already in 4:18–22. Peter begins all the lists of the apostles (Mark 3:16–19; Luke 6:14–16; Acts 1:13) and often plays the role of spokesman. Peter, along with James and John, formed an inner circle of leadership for the Twelve.

10:3 Bartholomew. Meaning "son of Tolmai," he may be the same person as Nathanael (his actual name) in John 1:45–51, since both are paired with Philip. **Thomas.** Best known, sadly, for his one episode of doubt in John 20:24–25 (but see John 20:26–29). **Matthew.** Introduced in 9:9–13. **James son of Alphaeus.** Called "James the younger" in Mark 15:40. **Thaddaeus.** A nickname of endearment, since it comes from Aramaic *taday* ("breast"). Appears to be the same person as "Judas son of James" in Luke 6:16.

10:4 Simon the Zealot. See also Luke 16:15. He is possibly a former freedom fighter; here he is literally a Cananean (from an Aramaic word for "zealous"). **Iscariot.** The name distinguishes this Judas from the one mentioned in the note on v. 3 and probably means "man of Kerioth." For his betrayal, see 26:47–50.

10:5–42 In these verses Jesus gives instructions for the Twelve. Verses 5–15 itemize conditions of their immediate missionary travels within Israel. Verses 17–42 look beyond this short-term mission to what they will experience after Jesus' death. Verse 16 forms a transition, linking the two main sections.

10:5–15 Jesus sends out the Twelve to replicate his ministry: to proclaim the arrival of the kingdom and to heal the sick (vv. 7–8; cf. 9:35). Their immediate mission is within Israel.

10:5–6 Jesus lifts these restrictions after his resurrection (28:18–20). The gospel is offered "first to the Jew" (Rom 1:16) because Israel is God's "treasured possession" (Exod 19:5).

10:9–10 Mark 6:8–9 gives slightly different instructions, which some harmonize by taking "Do not get" as meaning not to acquire *extra* provisions. Alternately, because Luke includes accounts of the sending of both the Twelve (Luke 9:1–6) and the Seventy-two (which may have included the Twelve; Luke 10:1–24) with similar but not identical regulations, Matthew may have included some of the information from the latter occasion in this sermon.

10:10 the worker is worth his keep. Jesus reverses the typical rabbinic practice of not receiving material possessions for ministry. But precisely because he expects others to provide for the disciples as they journey, he can command them to travel light.

10:13 let your peace rest on it. Give the household a blessing. **let your peace return to you.** Retract (or do not give) the blessing.

10:14 shake the dust off your feet. A ceremonial gesture that means one has no further responsibility or relationship with the places or people involved.

10:15 more bearable. Implies degrees of judgment, based on degrees of wickedness, in eternal punishment (cf. Luke 12:47–48). **Sodom and Gomorrah.** The extremely wicked towns that God destroyed in the time of Abraham and Lot (Gen 19:1–29).

10:16 [t]Lk 10:3 [u]Ro 16:19
10:17 [v]Mt 5:22 [w]Mt 23:34; Mk 13:9; Ac 5:40; 26:11
10:18 [x]Ac 25:24-26
10:19 [y]Ex 4:12
10:20 [z]Ac 4:8
10:21 [a]ver 35,36; Mic 7:6
10:22 [b]Mt 24:13; Mk 13:13
10:24 [c]Lk 6:40; Jn 13:16; 15:20
10:25 [d]Mk 3:22

16 "I am sending you out like sheep among wolves.[t] Therefore be as shrewd as snakes and as innocent
as doves.[u] 17 Be on your guard; you will be handed over to the local councils[v] and be flogged in the synagogues.[w] 18 On my account you will be brought before governors and kings[x] as witnesses to them and to the
Gentiles. 19 But when they arrest you, do not worry about what to say or how to say it.[y] At that time you will
be given what to say, 20 for it will not be you speaking, but the Spirit of your Father[z] speaking through you.
21 "Brother will betray brother to death, and a father his child; children will rebel against their
parents[a] and have them put to death. 22 You will be hated by everyone because of me, but the one who
stands firm to the end will be saved.[b] 23 When you are persecuted in one place, flee to another. Truly I
tell you, you will not finish going through the towns of Israel before the Son of Man comes.
24 "The student is not above the teacher, nor a servant above his master.[c] 25 It is enough for students
to be like their teachers, and servants like their masters. If the head of the house has been called Beelzebul,[d] how much more the members of his household!

10:16 This verse serves as a transition. Both in the short and long terms, the disciples must recognize the danger from those who will reject them and even prove hostile to them like "wolves." **like sheep.** Suggests that the disciples do not fight back.
10:17–42 The disciples did not experience before Jesus' death and resurrection most of what Jesus predicts in this section, so he is looking to a time further in the future that reveals long-term reactions to the Christian mission.
10:17 councils. The disciples are arraigned before councils in Acts 4:1–22; 5:17–41. **flogged in the synagogues.** Paul is flogged with 39 lashes on five different occasions (2 Cor 11:24).
10:18 governors and kings. Paul appears before various Roman "governors" (regional rulers, e.g., Acts 18:12–17) and "kings" (including the emperor, Acts 25:10–12).
10:19–20 These verses promise the empowerment of the Spirit in situations such as sudden arrest when one cannot prepare ahead of time what to say.
10:21 betray. The betrayal will occur because not all members of a given family will share the same loyalties to Jesus.
10:22 everyone. All who are not true believers.
10:23 Some have imagined that Jesus initially thought his death, resurrection, and return would occur before the Twelve had finished even their short-term ministry. But because the rest of vv. 17–42 has long-term ministry in view, it is more likely that he means the mission to the Jews will never be completed before his second coming. Still other options include his coming in his resurrection, in his sending of the Spirit at Pentecost, or invisibly in his judgment on Israel in AD 70.
10:24–25 There are plenty of contexts in which students can eclipse their teachers, but they are not greater in ways that exempt them from persecution.
10:25 Beelzebul. From the Hebrew "lord of the high abode" or "prince Baal," it was a name for Satan, or the devil (cf. 9:34).

THE TWELVE APOSTLES

MATTHEW 10:2–4	MARK 3:16–19	LUKE 6:14–16	ACTS 1:13
Simon Peter	Simon Peter	Simon Peter	(Simon) Peter
Andrew	James	Andrew	John
James	John	James	James
John	Andrew	John	Andrew
Philip	Philip	Philip	Philip
Bartholomew	Bartholomew (Nathanael)	Bartholomew	Thomas
Thomas	Matthew (Levi)	Matthew	Bartholomew
Matthew	Thomas	Thomas	Matthew
James (of Alphaeus)	James (of Alphaeus)	James (of Alphaeus)	James (of Alphaeus)
Thaddaeus[1]	Thaddaeus	Simon (the Zealot)	Simon (the Zealot)
Simon (the Zealot)	Simon (the Zealot)	Judas (of James)	Judas (of James)
Judas Iscariot	Judas Iscariot	Judas Iscariot	....

[1] Matthew and Mark have the name Thaddaeus while Luke, in his two lists (Luke 6 and Acts 1), has Judas (of James). Some think Judas may have been his original name and that it was changed later to Thaddaeus (meaning perhaps "warmhearted") in order to avoid the stigma attached to the name Judas Iscariot.

It is interesting that all four lists begin with Simon Peter and end with Judas Iscariot (except the Acts 1 list, for Judas had already killed himself). Also, the names would appear to be in groups of four. Peter, Andrew, James, and John are always in the first group—though not always in that order—and Philip, Bartholomew, Thomas, and Matthew are in the second group in all four lists.

In all four lists, Peter's name heads the first group, Philip heads the second, and James (of Alphaeus) heads the third. John's Gospel does not contain a listing of the apostles.

26“So do not be afraid of them, for there is nothing concealed that will not be disclosed, or hidden
that will not be made known.[e] 27What I tell you in the dark, speak in the daylight; what is whispered
in your ear, proclaim from the roofs. 28Do not be afraid of those who kill the body but cannot kill the
soul. Rather, be afraid of the One[f] who can destroy both soul and body in hell. 29Are not two sparrows
sold for a penny? Yet not one of them will fall to the ground outside your Father’s care.[a] 30And even
the very hairs of your head are all numbered.[g] 31So don’t be afraid; you are worth more than many
sparrows.[h]

32“Whoever acknowledges me before others,[i] I will also acknowledge before my Father in heaven.
33But whoever disowns me before others, I will disown before my Father in heaven.[j]

34“Do not suppose that I have come to bring peace to the earth. I did not come to bring peace, but
a sword. 35For I have come to turn

> “ ‘a man against his father,
> a daughter against her mother,
> a daughter-in-law against her mother-in-law[k]—
> 36 a man’s enemies will be the members of his own household.’[b][l]

37“Anyone who loves their father or mother more than me is not worthy of me; anyone who loves
their son or daughter more than me is not worthy of me.[m] 38Whoever does not take up their cross and
follow me is not worthy of me.[n] 39Whoever finds their life will lose it, and whoever loses their life for
my sake will find it.[o]

40“Anyone who welcomes you welcomes me,[p] and anyone who welcomes me welcomes the one who
sent me.[q] 41Whoever welcomes a prophet as a prophet will receive a prophet’s reward, and whoever
welcomes a righteous person as a righteous person will receive a righteous person’s reward. 42And if
anyone gives even a cup of cold water to one of these little ones who is my disciple, truly I tell you, that
person will certainly not lose their reward.”[r]

Jesus and John the Baptist

11:2-19pp — Lk 7:18-35

11 After Jesus had finished instructing his twelve disciples,[s] he went on from there to teach and
preach in the towns of Galilee.[c]

2When John, who was in prison,[t] heard about the deeds of the Messiah, he sent his disciples 3to ask
him, “Are you the one who is to come,[u] or should we expect someone else?”

4Jesus replied, “Go back and report to John what you hear and see: 5The blind receive sight, the lame

10:26 [e]Mk 4:22; Lk 8:17
10:28 [f]Isa 8:12,13; Heb 10:31
10:30 [g]1Sa 14:45; 2Sa 14:11; Lk 21:18; Ac 27:34
10:31 [h]Mt 12:12
10:32 [i]Ro 10:9
10:33 [j]Mk 8:38; 2Ti 2:12
10:35 [k]ver 21
10:36 [l]Mic 7:6
10:37 [m]Lk 14:26
10:38 [n]Mt 16:24; Lk 14:27
10:39 [o]Lk 17:33; Jn 12:25
10:40 [p]Mt 18:5; Gal 4:14 [q]Lk 9:48; Jn 12:44; 13:20
10:42 [r]Mt 25:40; Mk 9:41; Heb 6:10
11:1 [s]Mt 7:28
11:2 [t]Mt 14:3
11:3 [u]Ps 118:26; Jn 11:27; Heb 10:37

[a] *29* Or *will*; or *knowledge* [b] *36* Micah 7:6 [c] *1* Greek *in their towns*

10:26–27 All wrongs will be made right at the final judgment (v. 26), so don’t be afraid to proclaim the gospel boldly and widely (v. 27).
10:27 roofs. Flat roofs were sometimes used for making announcements to people below.
10:28 the One. God, not Satan.
10:32–33 Jesus makes the astonishing claim that it is people’s response to *him* that will make the difference as to how God treats them on judgment day. Only one who shares divinity with his Father in heaven can legitimately make such a claim.
10:34–36 Jesus does not mean he came to start wars but that, by the very fact that some in certain families would follow him whereas others would not, there would be interpersonal hostility (“a sword,” v. 34).
10:37 An important explanation of the much harsher statement in Luke 14:26.
10:38 take up their cross. Be prepared to follow Jesus all the way to martyrdom if necessary.
10:39 This verse means “Whoever finds their life [spiritually] will lose it [physically], and whoever loses their life [physically] for my sake will find it [spiritually].”
10:40 Providing hospitality for itinerant religious teachers in Jesus’ world usually meant accepting their message as well.
10:41–42 Because they are accepting the gospel announced by God’s messengers, all those who offer physical or material help to God’s people will receive a spiritual “reward” (v. 41).
11:1—12:50 *Increasing Hostility toward Jesus.* Each of these two chapters is dominated by the people’s growing doubts, rejection, and even overt hostility toward Jesus—although each ends with a reminder of the magnificent relationships Christ makes possible (11:25–30; 12:46–50).
11:1–19 John the Baptist has doubts about Jesus (vv. 2–6), Jesus testifies about John (vv. 7–15), and Jesus tells a short parable depicting the crowds’ reactions to John and him (vv. 16–19).
11:2–3 in prison. See 14:3–5. **deeds of the Messiah.** Jesus’ deeds, especially his miracles, reinforce John’s earlier convictions about Jesus’ identity. But Jesus has not set *this* prisoner free, and God has probably not revealed to John that he will have to languish in prison. So John is understandably confused and sends his followers to ask Jesus directly about his role.
11:4–6 Although Jesus does not answer John’s question directly, he implies that his miracles and concern for the poor demonstrate his Messiahship (cf. Isa 35:5–6; 61:1), which is illustrated already in Matt 5–9. The beatitude in v. 6 encourages John not to “stumble” in his faith just because Jesus’ Messianic ministry is not entirely what he expected.

11:5 [v]Isa 35:4-6; 61:1; Lk 4:18,19
11:6 [w]Mt 13:21
11:7 [x]Mt 3:1
11:9 [y]Mt 21:26; Lk 1:76
11:10 [z]Mal 3:1; Mk 1:2
11:14 [a]Mal 4:5; Mt 17:10-13; Mk 9:11-13; Lk 1:17; Jn 1:21
11:15 [b]Mt 13:9,43; Mk 4:23; Lk 14:35; Rev 2:7
11:18 [c]Mt 3:4 [d]Lk 1:15
11:19 [e]Mt 9:11
11:21 [f]Mk 6:45; Lk 9:10; Jn 12:21 [g]Mt 15:21; Lk 6:17; Ac 12:20 [h]Jnh 3:5-9
11:22 [i]ver 24; Mt 10:15
11:23 [j]Mt 4:13 [k]Isa 14:13-15

walk, those who have leprosy[a] are cleansed, the deaf hear, the dead are raised, and the good news is
proclaimed to the poor.[v] 6 Blessed is anyone who does not stumble on account of me."[w]
7 As John's[x] disciples were leaving, Jesus began to speak to the crowd about John: "What did you go
out into the wilderness to see? A reed swayed by the wind? 8 If not, what did you go out to see? A man
dressed in fine clothes? No, those who wear fine clothes are in kings' palaces. 9 Then what did you go out
to see? A prophet?[y] Yes, I tell you, and more than a prophet. 10 This is the one about whom it is written:

> "'I will send my messenger ahead of you,
> who will prepare your way before you.'[b][z]

11 Truly I tell you, among those born of women there has not risen anyone greater than John the Baptist;
yet whoever is least in the kingdom of heaven is greater than he. 12 From the days of John the Baptist
until now, the kingdom of heaven has been subjected to violence,[c] and violent people have been raiding
it. 13 For all the Prophets and the Law prophesied until John. 14 And if you are willing to accept it, he is
the Elijah who was to come.[a] 15 Whoever has ears, let them hear.[b]
16 "To what can I compare this generation? They are like children sitting in the marketplaces and
calling out to others:

> 17 "'We played the pipe for you,
> and you did not dance;
> we sang a dirge,
> and you did not mourn.'

18 For John came neither eating[c] nor drinking,[d] and they say, 'He has a demon.' 19 The Son of Man came
eating and drinking, and they say, 'Here is a glutton and a drunkard, a friend of tax collectors and
sinners.'[e] But wisdom is proved right by her deeds."

Woe on Unrepentant Towns

11:21-23pp — Lk 10:13-15

20 Then Jesus began to denounce the towns in which most of his miracles had been performed, because they did not repent. 21 "Woe to you, Chorazin! Woe to you, Bethsaida![f] For if the miracles that
were performed in you had been performed in Tyre and Sidon,[g] they would have repented long ago in
sackcloth and ashes.[h] 22 But I tell you, it will be more bearable for Tyre and Sidon on the day of judgment than for you.[i] 23 And you, Capernaum,[j] will you be lifted to the heavens? No, you will go down to
Hades.[d][k] For if the miracles that were performed in you had been performed in Sodom, it would have

[a] *5* The Greek word traditionally translated *leprosy* was used for various diseases affecting the skin.
[b] *10* Mal. 3:1 [c] *12* Or *been forcefully advancing* [d] *23* That is, the realm of the dead

11:7 A reed swayed by the wind. A weak person whose mind is easily changed. John's consistently austere prophecy hardly fits that picture.
11:8 dressed in fine clothes … kings' palaces. A pampered person benefiting from positions of power and privilege. Again John scarcely fits the mold.
11:9–10,14 Matt 3:1–6 depicts John's prophetic ministry. But Mal 3:1 promises a messenger—whom Mal 4:5 equates with Elijah—who would immediately precede the Messiah. As this unique forerunner, John is "more than a prophet" (Matt 11:9).
11:11 those born of women. An idiom for human beings. **greater than he.** John the Baptist is greater than all OT prophets, because he most clearly points to Jesus as the Messiah, but he will not live to see the inauguration of the new covenant after Christ's death and resurrection. In that sense, even the least significant Christian (the "least in the kingdom of heaven") is "greater than he."
11:12 the days of John the Baptist. The time before John's imprisonment. **subjected to violence.** The hostility to Christ's ministry, almost from its outset (e.g., 9:34; Mark 3:6; John 5:16), is the "violence" to which the kingdom of heaven has been "subjected."
11:13 Much of this hostility is related to the shift in ages between old and new covenants that Jesus brings but that many do not understand or accept.
11:16–19 Jesus' ministry involved celebration, like playing the pipe so that people could dance (v. 17). John's ministry called others to "mourn" in repentance, like singing a funeral "dirge" (v. 17). But a fair number in the audiences of each of these two ("this generation," v. 16) rejected both overtures, like recalcitrant "children" (v. 16) who refused to play the various games their playmates suggested.
11:19 wisdom. God's wisdom in all of this will nevertheless be "proved right" by the good "deeds" of John, Jesus, and their disciples.
11:20–24 The inhabitants of Chorazin and Bethsaida, small villages near the northern end of the Sea of Galilee, had witnessed Christ's miracles, like the people of Capernaum had (v. 23). So they would be more accountable on judgment day than even the most wicked cities in the OT, like "Tyre and Sidon" (v. 22; see especially Ezek 28), because those cities "would have repented long ago in sackcloth and ashes" (the outward garb and symbols of mourning, v. 21). Degrees of punishment in hell (or "Hades" [v. 23], the OT place of the wicked who have died) are consistent with the principle of judgment according to works (see note on 10:15).

remained to this day. 24But I tell you that it will be more bearable for Sodom on the day of judgment
than for you."[l]

The Father Revealed in the Son

11:25-27pp — Lk 10:21,22

25At that time Jesus said, "I praise you, Father,[m] Lord of heaven and earth, because you have hidden
these things from the wise and learned, and revealed them to little children.[n] 26Yes, Father, for this is
what you were pleased to do.

27"All things have been committed to me[o] by my Father.[p] No one knows the Son except the Father,
and no one knows the Father except the Son and those to whom the Son chooses to reveal him.[q]

28"Come to me,[r] all you who are weary and burdened, and I will give you rest. 29Take my yoke upon
you and learn from me,[s] for I am gentle and humble in heart, and you will find rest for your souls.[t]
30For my yoke is easy and my burden is light."[u]

Jesus Is Lord of the Sabbath

12:1-8pp — Mk 2:23-28; Lk 6:1-5
12:9-14pp — Mk 3:1-6; Lk 6:6-11

12 At that time Jesus went through the grainfields on the Sabbath. His disciples were hungry and
began to pick some heads of grain[v] and eat them. 2When the Pharisees saw this, they said to
him, "Look! Your disciples are doing what is unlawful on the Sabbath."[w]

3He answered, "Haven't you read what David did when he and his companions were hungry?[x] 4He
entered the house of God, and he and his companions ate the consecrated bread—which was not lawful for them to do, but only for the priests.[y] 5Or haven't you read in the Law that the priests on Sabbath
duty in the temple desecrate the Sabbath[z] and yet are innocent? 6I tell you that something greater than
the temple is here.[a] 7If you had known what these words mean, 'I desire mercy, not sacrifice,'[ab] you
would not have condemned the innocent. 8For the Son of Man[c] is Lord of the Sabbath."

9Going on from that place, he went into their synagogue, 10and a man with a shriveled hand was there.
Looking for a reason to bring charges against Jesus, they asked him, "Is it lawful to heal on the Sabbath?"[d]

11He said to them, "If any of you has a sheep and it falls into a pit on the Sabbath, will you not take

a 7 Hosea 6:6

11:24 [l] Mt 10:15
11:25 [m] Lk 22:42; Jn 11:41 [n] 1Co 1:26-29
11:27 [o] Mt 28:18 [p] Jn 3:35; 13:3; 17:2 [q] Jn 10:15
11:28 [r] Jn 7:37
11:29 [s] Jn 13:15; Php 2:5; 1Pe 2:21; 1Jn 2:6 [t] Jer 6:16
11:30 [u] 1Jn 5:3
12:1 [v] Dt 23:25
12:2 [w] ver 10; Lk 13:14; 14:3; Jn 5:10; 7:23; 9:16
12:3 [x] 1Sa 21:6
12:4 [y] Lev 24:5,9
12:5 [z] Nu 28:9,10; Jn 7:22,23
12:6 [a] ver 41,42
12:7 [b] Hos 6:6; Mic 6:6-8; Mt 9:13
12:8 [c] Mt 8:20
12:10 [d] ver 2; Lk 13:14; 14:3; Jn 9:16

11:25–30 Jesus beautifully summarizes the biblical balance between divine sovereignty and human responsibility. God initiates, revealing himself to his Son and thus to "those to whom the Son chooses to reveal him" (v. 27), and humans must respond—"Come to me" (v. 28). Those who think themselves too wise for God lose out to those who know their true need.

11:25 Those who esteem themselves "wise and learned" will often find God's truth hidden from them. Those who recognize their dependence on God, just as little children depend on adults, will discover he has revealed himself to them.

11:27 Cf. John 14:6. Jesus is the only way to the Father, and God reveals himself to his chosen people through Jesus.

11:28–30 All who are weary and burdened may come to Christ for rest. His is not the yoke of the law (a common rabbinic expression), which made demands without adequate empowerment for obedience. Jesus also offers a yoke (commands that restrict and guide), but with the greater demand comes a greater empowerment through the Spirit, so that his "yoke is easy" and his "burden is light" (v. 30).

12:1–14 Both plucking grain and healing a man whose life was not at risk violated the Pharisaic laws that had sprung up around Sabbath-keeping. Jesus justifies his behavior by claiming that he is "Lord of the Sabbath" (v. 8), a claim that makes sense only coming from one who is divine.

12:1–8 Pharisees considered plucking grain to be work, because it was a form of harvesting and led to the preparation of a meal. These were two of the many activities that the Pharisees decided involved work, which the Scriptures forbade on the Sabbath, the seventh day of the week (Exod 20:10).

12:3–4 Jesus, the greater son (descendant) of David, justifies his disciples' lawbreaking behavior by appealing to the OT example of David eating the sacred bread of the Presence when his men were hungry and nothing else was available (1 Sam 21:1–6).

12:5–6 For a second OT example of justifiable lawbreaking, and one that even involved the Sabbath, Jesus reminds his critics that priests who administered the sacrificial rites in the temple on the Sabbath (e.g., Num 28:9–10) were at work but were not considered to be sinning. Now "something greater than the temple is here" (the kingdom and Jesus' ministry of ushering it in), so he has even greater authority to determine what does and does not violate the Sabbath.

12:7 I desire mercy, not sacrifice. Hos 6:6 shows the priority of moral law over ritual law. Applied to the behavior of Jesus' disciples, satisfying hunger takes precedence over adhering to unwritten Sabbath traditions.

12:8 Lord. Need not mean more than "Master," but who has sovereignty over God's law but God himself? So Jesus may be indirectly pointing to his deity as well.

12:9–14 This time certain Pharisees provoke the controversy by asking if it is "lawful to heal" (v. 10) on the Sabbath, the day of rest. Jesus answers by another "from the lesser to the greater" argument and then heals a man whose hand is either atrophied or paralyzed ("shriveled," v. 10).

12:11–12 Although the Dead Sea Scrolls community at Qumran forbade rescuing animals on the Sabbath, all other Jews permitted it. So

12:11 [e]Lk 14:5
12:12 [f]Mt 10:31
12:14 [g]Mt 26:4; 27:1; Mk 3:6; Lk 6:11; Jn 5:18; 11:53
12:15 [h]Mt 4:23
12:16 [i]Mt 8:4
12:18 [j]Mt 3:17
12:21 [k]Isa 42:1-4
12:22 [l]Mt 4:24; 9:32-33
12:23 [m]Mt 9:27
12:24 [n]Mk 3:22 [o]Mt 9:34
12:25 [p]Mt 9:4
12:26 [q]Mt 4:10
12:27 [r]Ac 19:13

hold of it and lift it out?[e] [12]How much more valuable is a person than a sheep![f] Therefore it is lawful
to do good on the Sabbath."

[13]Then he said to the man, "Stretch out your hand." So he stretched it out and it was completely
restored, just as sound as the other. [14]But the Pharisees went out and plotted how they might kill Jesus.[g]

God's Chosen Servant

[15]Aware of this, Jesus withdrew from that place. A large crowd followed him, and he healed all who
were ill.[h] [16]He warned them not to tell others about him.[i] [17]This was to fulfill what was spoken through
the prophet Isaiah:

[18] "Here is my servant whom I have chosen,
  the one I love, in whom I delight;[j]
I will put my Spirit on him,
  and he will proclaim justice to the nations.
[19] He will not quarrel or cry out;
  no one will hear his voice in the streets.
[20] A bruised reed he will not break,
  and a smoldering wick he will not snuff out,
till he has brought justice through to victory.
[21] In his name the nations will put their hope."[a][k]

Jesus and Beelzebul

12:25-29pp — Mk 3:23-27; Lk 11:17-22

[22]Then they brought him a demon-possessed man who was blind and mute, and Jesus healed him,
so that he could both talk and see.[l] [23]All the people were astonished and said, "Could this be the Son
of David?"[m]

[24]But when the Pharisees heard this, they said, "It is only by Beelzebul,[n] the prince of demons, that
this fellow drives out demons."[o]

[25]Jesus knew their thoughts[p] and said to them, "Every kingdom divided against itself will be ruined,
and every city or household divided against itself will not stand. [26]If Satan[q] drives out Satan, he is divided against himself. How then can his kingdom stand? [27]And if I drive out demons by Beelzebul, by
whom do your people[r] drive them out? So then, they will be your judges. [28]But if it is by the Spirit of
God that I drive out demons, then the kingdom of God has come upon you.

[a] *21* Isaiah 42:1-4

they should be all the more concerned to heal a human being on God's holy day. **it is lawful to do good on the Sabbath.** This statement opens the door for sweeping changes in the understanding of this day because there are countless forms of helpful, constructive behavior that can be seen as doing good.

12:14 Legalists of all eras put obedience to rules above love for people. In extreme instances, this misguided passion leads to murderous rage. Matthew may hint here at their hypocrisy as they condemn Jesus for doing good on the Sabbath but are willing to plot his death on the same day.

12:15–21 It was not yet time for Jesus to die so he "withdrew" (v. 15) from the hostility, but his ministry of healing continued. To avoid provoking even more premature opposition, he tried to silence the crowds and "warned them not to tell others about him" (v. 16). Characteristically, Matthew finds a fulfillment of prophecy here; this time from Isa 42:1–4. In context, the servant appears to be Israel (Isa 42:18–19; 43:1; 44:1), but Jesus typologically fulfills the prophecy on an even grander scale. He too is God's "chosen" one, who will "proclaim justice" not just to Israel but to all "the nations" (Matt 12:18). Still, he will do so gently and without fighting (vv. 19–20). But it is possible that the "servant" in Isa 42:1 is an individual within Israel, in which case Matthew sees more direct fulfillment of prophecy.

12:22–37 An exorcism leads to the accusation that Jesus himself is demon-possessed (vv. 22–24). Jesus replies by first pointing out the absurdity of Satan attacking his own hordes, just as civil wars weaken nations (vv. 25–27). Christ's exorcisms point instead to the arrival of *God's* kingdom (vv. 28–29). Indeed, someone who so misjudges the source of Jesus' power is in danger of committing an unpardonable sin (see vv. 31–32 and note). It shows how thoroughly evil such people are and outlines the nature of their coming judgment (vv. 33–37).

12:23 Could this be the Son of David? A grammatical form that usually anticipates a negative answer to a question but could also indicate a hopeful but very hesitant inquiry.

12:24 Beelzebul. See note on 10:25.

12:27 Numerous other Jewish exorcists, including Pharisaic ones, existed in Jesus' day. Surely these Pharisees were not prepared to attribute to Satan the power working through all these other exorcists, were they?

12:28 The alternative is that "the kingdom of God has come upon you." Perhaps to make the contrast between God and the devil clear, Matthew avoids his otherwise preferred expression, "kingdom of heaven." Jesus does exhibit special power, but it is divine, not diabolical. His miracles combine with his supernatural origin to show that he is not just another Elijah or Elisha but is the Messiah himself.

29"Or again, how can anyone enter a strong man's house and carry off his possessions unless he first
ties up the strong man? Then he can plunder his house.
30"Whoever is not with me is against me, and whoever does not gather with me scatters.[s] 31And so
I tell you, every kind of sin and slander can be forgiven, but blasphemy against the Spirit will not be
forgiven.[t] 32Anyone who speaks a word against the Son of Man will be forgiven, but anyone who speaks
against the Holy Spirit will not be forgiven, either in this age[u] or in the age to come.[v]
33"Make a tree good and its fruit will be good, or make a tree bad and its fruit will be bad, for a tree
is recognized by its fruit.[w] 34You brood of vipers,[x] how can you who are evil say anything good? For the
mouth speaks[y] what the heart is full of. 35A good man brings good things out of the good stored up in
him, and an evil man brings evil things out of the evil stored up in him. 36But I tell you that everyone
will have to give account on the day of judgment for every empty word they have spoken. 37For by your
words you will be acquitted, and by your words you will be condemned."

The Sign of Jonah

12:39-42pp — Lk 11:29-32
12:43-45pp — Lk 11:24-26

38Then some of the Pharisees and teachers of the law said to him, "Teacher, we want to see a sign
from you."[z]
39He answered, "A wicked and adulterous generation asks for a sign! But none will be given it except
the sign of the prophet Jonah.[a] 40For as Jonah was three days and three nights in the belly of a huge
fish,[b] so the Son of Man[c] will be three days and three nights in the heart of the earth.[d] 41The men of
Nineveh[e] will stand up at the judgment with this generation and condemn it; for they repented at the
preaching of Jonah,[f] and now something greater than Jonah is here. 42The Queen of the South will rise
at the judgment with this generation and condemn it; for she came[g] from the ends of the earth to listen
to Solomon's wisdom, and now something greater than Solomon is here.
43"When an impure spirit comes out of a person, it goes through arid places seeking rest and does
not find it. 44Then it says, 'I will return to the house I left.' When it arrives, it finds the house unoccu-
pied, swept clean and put in order. 45Then it goes and takes with it seven other spirits more wicked than
itself, and they go in and live there. And the final condition of that person is worse than the first.[h] That
is how it will be with this wicked generation."

12:30 [s] Mk 9:40; Lk 11:23
12:31 [t] Mk 3:28,29; Lk 12:10
12:32 [u] Titus 2:12 [v] Mk 10:30; Lk 20:34,35; Eph 1:21; Heb 6:5
12:33 [w] Mt 7:16,17; Lk 6:43,44
12:34 [x] Mt 3:7; 23:33 [y] Mt 15:18; Lk 6:45
12:38 [z] Mt 16:1; Mk 8:11, 12; Lk 11:16; Jn 2:18; 6:30; 1Co 1:22
12:39 [a] Mt 16:4; Lk 11:29
12:40 [b] Jnh 1:17 [c] Mt 8:20 [d] Mt 16:21
12:41 [e] Jnh 1:2 [f] Jnh 3:5
12:42 [g] 1Ki 10:1; 2Ch 9:1
12:45 [h] 2Pe 2:20

12:29 ties up the strong man ... plunder his house. This implies that Jesus is in the process of vanquishing the devil: Jesus is transforming people who have been demonized into disciples.
12:30 Contrast Mark 9:40 ("For whoever is not against us is for us"). Each proverb is true in its context. Here Jesus is responding to his opponents, stressing that they need to support him instead of slander him.
12:31–32 not be forgiven. The only unforgivable sin in the Bible is "blasphemy against the Spirit" (v. 31). It is repudiating Christ to such a degree that someone attributes his divine power to the devil and never repents of that attitude. It is a sin that can be discerned only with 20/20 hindsight; many whom we might have imagined committed this sin later become Christians. Anyone who anxiously fears that they *have* committed it demonstrates by their concern (quite the opposite of the Pharisees' rancor here) that they have not done so. **speaks a word against the Son of Man.** May refer to rejecting Jesus without truly sensing the *Spirit's* power in him.
12:33 Cf. 7:16–20.
12:34 Cf. 3:7.
12:35 Despite all the gradations in humanity we perceive, ultimately there are only two kinds of people: "good" and "evil." The distinguishing criterion is their response to Jesus.
12:36–37 Our whole lives come under review on judgment day. Particularly telling, however, is our speech, because it reflects what exists in our hearts. See Jas 3:1–12.
12:36 empty word. A careless one that somehow does damage.
12:38–45 Ironically, the Jewish leaders opposed to Jesus ask him for a sign to prove he is heaven sent. What more could they possibly want after all the miracles he has already worked? The only new kind of sign they will receive will be "the sign of the prophet Jonah" (v. 39), i.e., Jesus' death and resurrection. These Israelites who are rejecting Jesus are worse than the pagan Ninevites in the OT who eventually repented.
12:40 three days and three nights. Any parts of three consecutive 24-hour periods of time in Jewish idiom. Hence Jesus' death on Friday afternoon through his resurrection on Sunday morning can be spoken of this way. The language is used to match Jonah 1:17. Jonah appeared as if he had died and been raised up in order to save Israel from future destruction by the Assyrians.
12:41 greater than Jonah. After Jonah preached, the Ninevites repented (Jonah 3:5–10). But Jesus and his ministry are "greater than Jonah," so all the more worthy of acceptance.
12:42 The Queen of the South. The queen of Sheba (probably in Ethiopia) who came to learn from Solomon's wisdom and praised Israel's God as a result (1 Kgs 10:1–13). But Jesus and his ministry are "greater than Solomon," so all the more worthy of acceptance.
12:43 impure spirit. See note on 10:1. It cannot find "rest" in "arid places" because demons are associated with watery regions (cf. 8:26,32).
12:44 The word picture suggests a person from whom a demon has been cast out but who has not replaced the spiritual vacuum with Christ.
12:45 worse than the first. Even those from whom Jesus has cast out demons must become true disciples or they will revert to an even worse condition than before: they will be inhabited by even more demonic spirits.

12:46 [i]Mt 1:18; 2:11,13, 14,20; Lk 1:43; 2:33,34, 48,51; Jn 2:1,5; 19:25, 26 [j]Mt 13:55; Jn 2:12; 7:3,5; Ac 1:14; 1Co 9:5; Gal 1:19
12:50 [k]Jn 15:14
13:1 [l]ver 36; Mt 9:28
13:2 [m]Lk 5:3
13:8 [n]Ge 26:12
13:9 [o]Mt 11:15
13:11 [p]Mt 11:25; 16:17; 19:11; Jn 6:65; 1Co 2:10,14; Col 1:27; 1Jn 2:20,27
13:12 [q]Mt 25:29; Lk 19:26

Jesus' Mother and Brothers

12:46-50pp — Mk 3:31-35; Lk 8:19-21

46 While Jesus was still talking to the crowd, his mother[i] and brothers[j] stood outside, wanting to
speak to him. 47 Someone told him, "Your mother and brothers are standing outside, wanting to speak
to you."
48 He replied to him, "Who is my mother, and who are my brothers?" 49 Pointing to his disciples, he
said, "Here are my mother and my brothers. 50 For whoever does the will of my Father in heaven[k] is my
brother and sister and mother."

The Parable of the Sower

13:1-15pp — Mk 4:1-12; Lk 8:4-10
13:16,17pp — Lk 10:23,24
13:18-23pp — Mk 4:13-20; Lk 8:11-15

13 That same day Jesus went out of the house[l] and sat by the lake. 2 Such large crowds gathered
around him that he got into a boat[m] and sat in it, while all the people stood on the shore.
3 Then he told them many things in parables, saying: "A farmer went out to sow his seed. 4 As he was
scattering the seed, some fell along the path, and the birds came and ate it up. 5 Some fell on rocky
places, where it did not have much soil. It sprang up quickly, because the soil was shallow. 6 But when
the sun came up, the plants were scorched, and they withered because they had no root. 7 Other seed
fell among thorns, which grew up and choked the plants. 8 Still other seed fell on good soil, where
it produced a crop — a hundred,[n] sixty or thirty times what was sown. 9 Whoever has ears, let them
hear."[o]
10 The disciples came to him and asked, "Why do you speak to the people in parables?"
11 He replied, "Because the knowledge of the secrets of the kingdom of heaven has been given to
you,[p] but not to them. 12 Whoever has will be given more, and they will have an abundance. Whoever does not have, even what they have will be taken from them.[q] 13 This is why I speak to them in
parables:

12:46–50 The one who becomes a Christ-follower receives a new, extended (and extensive) spiritual family, with intimacy and allegiance that should transcend even ties to biological family members, and this in a culture of honor and shame that highly prized family loyalty and honor.
12:46 brothers. Actually half brothers, most likely the children that Mary and Joseph subsequently conceived, though some ancient traditions suggest that Joseph had children by a previous marriage. Still others — usually only in circles that believe in Mary's perpetual virginity — assume they were cousins, but this is a rare usage of the Greek *adelphoi.* At this stage it does not appear that Jesus' brothers believed in him yet.
12:50 Having biological siblings and other close relatives who are also Christ-followers creates the potential for having the best of both worlds: spiritual and genealogical families in sync with each other.
13:1–52 *Parables of the Kingdom.* Jesus employs the parable, a characteristic rabbinic teaching device, to illustrate spiritual truths about God's reign. Parables are stories or analogies involving people and activities familiar to one's audience. But often they contain surprising twists that help listeners understand God's ways with humanity from new perspectives. This is Christ's third extended discourse in Matthew (cf. chs. 5–7 and 10:5–42).
13:1–23 *The Parable of the Sower.* Farmers used broadcast sowing, taking a bag of seeds in their hands and scattering them across the ground in which they wanted them to grow, often plowing them into the dirt afterward. Thus not every seed would take root in good soil, and there would be varied growth based on the kind of soil in which each seed landed (vv. 3–9). Jesus explains this parable in vv. 18–23. Matthew probably places this parable here to explain the different reactions to Jesus found in chs. 11–12. This parable also explains that Jesus has not come to bring an immediate end to evil, something which John the Baptist may have expected.
13:2 into a boat. More people could hear Jesus teaching from a boat secured in the shallow water in one of the coves of the Sea of Galilee, especially if the wind was blowing from behind, than if he were on the beach with people crowded around him. **sat.** Rabbis regularly sat on a raised platform to teach.
13:8 produced a crop. The only result the farmer desired. **a hundred … times what was sown.** Would have been an outstanding harvest by ancient standards. Cf. Gen 26:12.
13:10–17 Although parables illustrate spiritual truths, their meanings are not always self-evident. Throughout church history commentators have swung the pendulum from treating them as detailed allegories to simple stories making only one point, with many intermediate options also suggested. Jesus' own remarks here are also somewhat puzzling.
13:11 given to you, but not to them. There are certain insights into the nature of God's kingdom that only Jesus' disciples will understand. These insights do not appear to involve the basic truths of the parables, since v. 36 shows the disciples asking for an explanation of these, while 21:45 has Christ's opponents recognizing that he was identifying them as the wicked tenants in that parable. Rather, the "secrets" that the disciples alone grasp must involve Jesus' identity, so that they are drawn to keep following him, whereas others are not.
13:12 See note on 25:28–30.
13:13–15 Seeing the general reaction of too many in Israel (their hard hearts and rebellious behavior against God's decrees), Jesus quotes Isa 6:9–10, seeing it fulfilled again as in the prophet's day. But Isa 6 ends on a note of hope, with "the holy seed" being "the stump in the land" from which new life would yet emerge (Isa 6:13). So Jesus is leaving open the possibility that some of those whose hearts are presently hard will yet be softened to the gospel of grace.

"Though seeing, they do not see;
though hearing, they do not hear or understand.[r]

14In them is fulfilled the prophecy of Isaiah:

"'You will be ever hearing but never understanding;
you will be ever seeing but never perceiving.
15For this people's heart has become calloused;
they hardly hear with their ears,
and they have closed their eyes.
Otherwise they might see with their eyes,
hear with their ears,
understand with their hearts
and turn, and I would heal them.'[a][s]

16But blessed are your eyes because they see, and your ears because they hear.[t] 17For truly I tell you,
many prophets and righteous people longed to see what you see[u] but did not see it, and to hear what
you hear but did not hear it.

18"Listen then to what the parable of the sower means: 19When anyone hears the message about
the kingdom[v] and does not understand it, the evil one[w] comes and snatches away what was sown in
their heart. This is the seed sown along the path. 20The seed falling on rocky ground refers to someone who hears the word and at once receives it with joy. 21But since they have no root, they last only a
short time. When trouble or persecution comes because of the word, they quickly fall away.[x] 22The seed
falling among the thorns refers to someone who hears the word, but the worries of this life and the
deceitfulness of wealth[y] choke the word, making it unfruitful. 23But the seed falling on good soil refers
to someone who hears the word and understands it. This is the one who produces a crop, yielding a
hundred, sixty or thirty times what was sown."[z]

The Parable of the Weeds

24Jesus told them another parable: "The kingdom of heaven is like[a] a man who sowed good seed in
his field. 25But while everyone was sleeping, his enemy came and sowed weeds among the wheat, and
went away. 26When the wheat sprouted and formed heads, then the weeds also appeared.

27"The owner's servants came to him and said, 'Sir, didn't you sow good seed in your field? Where
then did the weeds come from?'

28"'An enemy did this,' he replied.

"The servants asked him, 'Do you want us to go and pull them up?'

29"'No,' he answered, 'because while you are pulling the weeds, you may uproot the wheat with

a 15 Isaiah 6:9,10 (see Septuagint)

13:13 [r] Dt 29:4; Jer 5:21; Eze 12:2
13:15 [s] Isa 6:9,10; Jn 12:40; Ac 28:26,27; Ro 11:8
13:16 [t] Mt 16:17
13:17 [u] Jn 8:56; Heb 11:13; 1Pe 1:10-12
13:19 [v] Mt 4:23 [w] Mt 5:37
13:21 [x] Mt 11:6
13:22 [y] Mt 19:23; 1Ti 6:9,10,17
13:23 [z] ver 8
13:24 [a] ver 31,33,45,47; Mt 18:23; 20:1; 22:2; 25:1; Mk 4:26,30

13:18–23 Jesus proceeds to explain that the parable he has just told refers to four main ways people respond to "the message about the kingdom" (v. 19).
13:19 the seed sown along the path. Stands for those who completely fail to grasp Jesus' person and teaching so that the gospel takes no root at all.
13:20 The seed falling on rocky ground. It may find just enough soil to produce a plant, but it will not grow nearly enough to yield the crop intended. While many think that "one who hears the word and at once receives it with joy" must be a Christian, this seems unlikely.
13:21 trouble or persecution comes. It comes for being identified with the Christian community and leads them to "quickly fall away." These appear to be people who are attracted to the benefits of the gospel but are not willing to endure the hardships associated with it, and hence they are not true believers.
13:22 The seed falling among the thorns. The seed apparently grows for a longer period of time but ultimately proves "unfruitful" as well. It has produced no crop for the farmer to harvest. It too appears to represent a spurious believer. These people may make a profession of faith and continue in Christian circles or activities longer than the second group (vv. 20–21), but they eventually show their true colors as "the worries of this life and the deceitfulness of wealth" overcome their interest in the One who calls people to serve him rather than money (cf. 6:24).
13:23 Parables frequently contrast two or three bad examples with one climactic good one (or vice versa). Here the sole positive example to imitate is the fruit-bearing seed. **crop.** Nothing suggests that this refers to one specific form of Christian behavior; true believers generate many different kinds of "produce" of highly varying quantities, but they do produce *something* of value in keeping with kingdom priorities.
13:24–30 *The Parable of the Weeds.* Although the actions in this parable may seem implausible today, there are recorded examples in antiquity of people behaving exactly like this, using a primitive form of what today would be called bioterrorism.
13:25 weeds. Darnel (Greek *zizanion*), which often looked somewhat like wheat as the plants grew. Jesus explains this parable in vv. 36–43.
13:28–29 The surprising twist in this parable is that the farmer forbids his servants to do any weeding at all. Although there was the real danger

13:30 [b]Mt 3:12
13:31 [c]ver 24 [d]Mt 17:20; Lk 17:6
13:32 [e]Ps 104:12; Eze 17:23; 31:6; Da 4:12
13:33 [f]ver 24 [g]Ge 18:6 [h]Gal 5:9
13:34 [i]Mk 4:33; Jn 16:25
13:35 [j]Ps 78:2; Ro 16:25,26; 1Co 2:7; Eph 3:9; Col 1:26
13:36 [k]Mt 15:15
13:37 [l]Mt 8:20
13:38 [m]Jn 8:44,45; 1Jn 3:10
13:39 [n]Joel 3:13 [o]Mt 24:3; 28:20 [p]Rev 14:15
13:41 [q]Mt 8:20 [r]Mt 24:31
13:42 [s]ver 50; Mt 8:12
13:43 [t]Da 12:3 [u]Mt 11:15
13:44 [v]ver 24 [w]Isa 55:1; Php 3:7,8

them. 30 Let both grow together until the harvest. At that time I will tell the harvesters: First collect
the weeds and tie them in bundles to be burned; then gather the wheat and bring it into my barn.' "[b]

The Parables of the Mustard Seed and the Yeast

13:31,32pp — Mk 4:30-32
13:31-33pp — Lk 13:18-21

31 He told them another parable: "The kingdom of heaven is like[c] a mustard seed,[d] which a man
took and planted in his field. 32 Though it is the smallest of all seeds, yet when it grows, it is the largest
of garden plants and becomes a tree, so that the birds come and perch in its branches."[e]
33 He told them still another parable: "The kingdom of heaven is like[f] yeast that a woman took and
mixed into about sixty pounds[a] of flour[g] until it worked all through the dough."[h]
34 Jesus spoke all these things to the crowd in parables; he did not say anything to them without using
a parable.[i] 35 So was fulfilled what was spoken through the prophet:

"I will open my mouth in parables,
I will utter things hidden since the creation of the world."[b][j]

The Parable of the Weeds Explained

36 Then he left the crowd and went into the house. His disciples came to him and said, "Explain to
us the parable[k] of the weeds in the field."
37 He answered, "The one who sowed the good seed is the Son of Man.[l] 38 The field is the world, and
the good seed stands for the people of the kingdom. The weeds are the people of the evil one,[m] 39 and the
enemy who sows them is the devil. The harvest[n] is the end of the age,[o] and the harvesters are angels.[p]
40 "As the weeds are pulled up and burned in the fire, so it will be at the end of the age. 41 The Son
of Man[q] will send out his angels,[r] and they will weed out of his kingdom everything that causes sin
and all who do evil. 42 They will throw them into the blazing furnace, where there will be weeping and
gnashing of teeth.[s] 43 Then the righteous will shine like the sun[t] in the kingdom of their Father. Whoever has ears, let them hear.[u]

The Parables of the Hidden Treasure and the Pearl

44 "The kingdom of heaven is like[v] treasure hidden in a field. When a man found it, he hid it again,
and then in his joy went and sold all he had and bought that field.[w]

a 33 Or about 27 kilograms   *b 35* Psalm 78:2

of uprooting the wheat while pulling the weeds out, the far greater danger is to do nothing and lose the entire crop.

13:30 The farmer remains confident, nevertheless, that he will have an adequate harvest, and then he will instruct his harvesters to pull out the weeds and burn them.

13:31–33 *The Parables of the Mustard Seed and the Yeast.* Scientists today know of smaller seeds than the mustard seed, but it was "the smallest of all seeds" (v. 32) that anyone cultivated in first-century fields or gardens in Israel. Normally the plant grows into a medium-size bush, but eight-foot high small "trees" have been discovered, even if rarely. The "kingdom" (v. 31) too will begin as insignificant in size and impact but become surprisingly large and powerful. The "birds [that] ... perch in its branches" (v. 32) may be the Gentiles, especially if Jesus is alluding to Ezek 17:23.

Closely paired with the parable of the mustard seed (vv. 31–32), the second parable (v. 33) makes much the same point as the first. Just as small amounts of yeast, or leaven, make dough rise to produce large amounts of bread, so too the tiny, inauspicious kingdom will one day have a surprisingly great impact.

If there is a difference between the two parables, it may be that the mustard seed portrays extensive growth and the yeast depicts intensive growth. No Jew would have made these comparisons. How could God's kingdom be compared to the smallest of seeds? Jesus deliberately uses this shocking illustration to challenge how most Jews thought about the coming of God's kingdom.

13:34–35 Matthew again finds a typological fulfillment of a biblical passage (Ps 78:2). Asaph the psalmist, like Jesus, made once "hidden" things known.

13:36–43 Jesus explains the parable of the weeds. Other than the parable of the sower in vv. 3–9,18–23, this is the only time in all the Gospels that Jesus interprets one of his parables in elaborate detail. Like the sower (vv. 3–9,18–23) and the mustard seed (vv. 31–32) and yeast (v. 33), this parable is about the growth of the kingdom. Despite all the obstacles it faces, and without necessarily removing them, God's purposes will be accomplished throughout his creation. As more explicitly in Luke 9:54–55, Jesus forbids his followers from trying to exterminate his opponents.

13:38 The field is the world. Therefore, when Jesus says that "his angels ... will weed out of his kingdom everything that causes sin" (v. 41), he is not referring to a mixed church of believers and unbelievers but to the entire human community, which combines good and evil people. Jesus will be their final judge; for now, the kingdom does not come with irresistible power but leaves room for those who want to reject it to do so.

13:41 angels ... will weed out. See note on v. 38.

13:42 See notes on 5:22; 8:12.

13:43 the righteous will shine like the sun. Probably alludes to Dan 12:3 and the splendor of eternal life.

13:44–46 *The Parables of the Hidden Treasure and the Valuable Pearl.* The kingdom is worth sacrificing whatever is necessary in order to be a part of it. This does not mean one literally purchases eternal life or

[45]"Again, the kingdom of heaven is like[x] a merchant looking for fine pearls. [46]When he found one
of great value, he went away and sold everything he had and bought it.

The Parable of the Net

[47]"Once again, the kingdom of heaven is like[y] a net that was let down into the lake and caught
all kinds[z] of fish. [48]When it was full, the fishermen pulled it up on the shore. Then they sat down and
collected the good fish in baskets, but threw the bad away. [49]This is how it will be at the end of the age.
The angels will come and separate the wicked from the righteous[a] [50]and throw them into the blazing
furnace, where there will be weeping and gnashing of teeth.[b]

[51]"Have you understood all these things?" Jesus asked.

"Yes," they replied.

[52]He said to them, "Therefore every teacher of the law who has become a disciple in the kingdom
of heaven is like the owner of a house who brings out of his storeroom new treasures as well as old."

A Prophet Without Honor

13:54-58pp — Mk 6:1-6

[53]When Jesus had finished these parables,[c] he moved on from there. [54]Coming to his hometown, he
began teaching the people in their synagogue,[d] and they were amazed.[e] "Where did this man get this
wisdom and these miraculous powers?" they asked. [55]"Isn't this the carpenter's son?[f] Isn't his mother's[g]
name Mary, and aren't his brothers James, Joseph, Simon and Judas? [56]Aren't all his sisters with us?
Where then did this man get all these things?" [57]And they took offense[h] at him.

But Jesus said to them, "A prophet is not without honor except in his own town and in his own home."[i]

[58]And he did not do many miracles there because of their lack of faith.

John the Baptist Beheaded

14:1-12pp — Mk 6:14-29

14 At that time Herod[j] the tetrarch heard the reports about Jesus,[k] [2]and he said to his attendants,
"This is John the Baptist;[l] he has risen from the dead! That is why miraculous powers are at
work in him."

13:45 [x]ver 24
13:47 [y]ver 24 [z]Mt 22:10
13:49 [a]Mt 25:32
13:50 [b]Mt 8:12
13:53 [c]Mt 7:28
13:54 [d]Mt 4:23 [e]Mt 7:28
13:55 [f]Lk 3:23; Jn 6:42 [g]Mt 12:46
13:57 [h]Jn 6:61 [i]Lk 4:24; Jn 4:44
14:1 [j]Mk 8:15; Lk 3:1, 19; 13:31; 23:7,8; Ac 4:27; 12:1 [k]Lk 9:7-9
14:2 [l]Mt 3:1

exercises duplicity in coming to Christ. The parable of the pearl "of great value" (vv. 45–46) is a twin with the previous parable (v. 44). The only difference is that the pearl merchant was clearly looking for his treasure, whereas the man in v. 44 may have discovered it by surprise.

13:47–50 *The Parable of the Net.* Like the parable of the wheat and weeds, but without the period of growth, this little narrative envisions a large seine net being dragged across portions of a lake, scooping up whatever comes into its path. Fish that were too small or inedible would be cast aside; those that could be sold or eaten would be collected. So too all people will be judged "at the end of the age" (v. 49), divided into "wicked" and "righteous" (v. 49), and assigned to their eternal destinies. See also notes on 5:22; 8:12.

13:52 *The Parable of the Owner of a House.* The disciples claim to have understood all these things (v. 51) despite their initial questions. There is still continuity between the "old" and "new" eras, even as there are fresh items that require explanation, just like the "owner of a house" who "brings out" valuable items of both ancient and recent vintage from "his storeroom."

13:53—16:20 *Progressive Polarization.* Reactions to the parables in ch. 13 highlight the growing polarization of responses to Jesus' ministry. The next narrative segment of Matthew's Gospel does so as well. Jesus and John are rejected (13:53—14:12); Jesus reveals himself to Israel—the crowds and his disciples (14:13–36)—and to the Gentiles (15:1—16:12); and the disciples recognize Jesus' identity in Gentile territory (16:13–20).

13:53—14:12 Both Jesus and John are rejected. Jesus' hometown acquaintances find it hard to believe he is so special (13:53–58), while Herod Antipas imprisons and executes John (14:1–12).

13:53–58 This appears to be a briefer version of the episode that Luke frontloads in his Gospel (Luke 4:16–30) as a headline over Jesus' Galilean ministry.

13:54 his hometown. Nazareth. See 2:23 and note on 2:19–23; see also 4:13 and note on 4:13.

13:55–56 his brothers ... his sisters. See note on 12:46.

13:55 carpenter's son. Greek *tektōn* (here translated "carpenter") could be a stonemason besides just a woodworker.

13:57 A prophet ... without honor. Family members, childhood friends, and others who have known a person for a long time are often the last to acknowledge special powers or abilities that suddenly emerge to make a person appear like a prophet to others.

13:58 because of their lack of faith. But see note on 9:29. There is no consistent relationship between faith and miracles throughout the Gospels more generally. God is sovereign and works miracles whenever he chooses.

14:1–12 Matthew explains the reason for and result of John's imprisonment (11:2).

14:1 Herod the tetrarch. Herod Antipas, one of the three sons of Herod the Great among whom his kingdom was divided (see chart/map, pp. 1930–1931). Antipas received the provinces of Galilee and Perea. See note on 2:22.

14:2 risen from the dead. Matthew begins with Antipas's reaction to Jesus sometime after John the Baptist died, and then Matthew moves back in time to explain how John had come to be executed. Jews did not normally believe in reincarnation, but some ancient pagans did, from whom Antipas must have gotten the notion. Why that would have given

14:3 [m]Mt 4:12; 11:2 [n]Lk 3:19,20
14:4 [o]Lev 18:16; 20:21
14:5 [p]Mt 11:9
14:10 [q]Mt 17:12
14:12 [r]Ac 8:2
14:14 [s]Mt 9:36 [t]Mt 4:23
14:17 [u]Mt 16:9
14:19 [v]1Sa 9:13; Mt 26:26; Mk 8:6; Lk 24:30; Ac 2:42; 27:35; 1Ti 4:4

3Now Herod had arrested John and bound him and put him in prison[m] because of Herodias, his
brother Philip's wife,[n] 4for John had been saying to him: "It is not lawful for you to have her."[o]
5Herod wanted to kill John, but he was afraid of the people, because they considered John a prophet.[p]
6On Herod's birthday the daughter of Herodias danced for the guests and pleased Herod so much
7that he promised with an oath to give her whatever she asked. 8Prompted by her mother, she said,
"Give me here on a platter the head of John the Baptist." 9The king was distressed, but because of his
oaths and his dinner guests, he ordered that her request be granted 10and had John beheaded[q] in
the prison. 11His head was brought in on a platter and given to the girl, who carried it to her mother.
12John's disciples came and took his body and buried it.[r] Then they went and told Jesus.

Jesus Feeds the Five Thousand

14:13-21pp — Mk 6:32-44; Lk 9:10-17; Jn 6:1-13
14:13-21Ref — Mt 15:32-38

13When Jesus heard what had happened, he withdrew by boat privately to a solitary place. Hearing
of this, the crowds followed him on foot from the towns. 14When Jesus landed and saw a large crowd,
he had compassion on them[s] and healed their sick.[t]
15As evening approached, the disciples came to him and said, "This is a remote place, and it's already getting late. Send the crowds away, so they can go to the villages and buy themselves some food."
16Jesus replied, "They do not need to go away. You give them something to eat."
17"We have here only five loaves[u] of bread and two fish," they answered.
18"Bring them here to me," he said. 19And he directed the people to sit down on the grass. Taking the
five loaves and the two fish and looking up to heaven, he gave thanks and broke the loaves.[v] Then he
gave them to the disciples, and the disciples gave them to the people. 20They all ate and were satisfied,
and the disciples picked up twelve basketfuls of broken pieces that were left over. 21The number of those
who ate was about five thousand men, besides women and children.

Jesus Walks on the Water

14:22-33pp — Mk 6:45-51; Jn 6:16-21
14:34-36pp — Mk 6:53-56

22Immediately Jesus made the disciples get into the boat and go on ahead of him to the other side,
while he dismissed the crowd. 23After he had dismissed them, he went up on a mountainside by himself

Jesus the ability to work miracles that John never performed is unclear, but superstitious beliefs are often illogical. At any rate, Herod recognized similarities between the two men.

14:3 This Philip appears to be a different Philip than the one who received part of Herod the Great's kingdom (Luke 3:1). Herodias divorced this Philip to marry his brother Antipas, and John dared to rebuke Herod publicly for it.

14:6–7 the daughter of Herodias. Called a "girl" (Greek *korasion*) in Mark 6:22, a term often used for a young teenager. Given the reputation of the Herodian family for throwing debauched parties, the girl's dance may have been sexually suggestive, and Antipas may have uttered his oath when he was drunk.

14:8 Mark 6:19 explains that Herodias was the one most upset over John's rebuke of her divorce and remarriage. An underage daughter would naturally turn to her when Antipas made his lavish promise, so Herodias requests John's beheading and the public proof of it.

14:9 Antipas's moral weakness and cowardice are reflected in his refusal to go back on the rash vow he had made in front of his guests, probably some of the elite of his society.

14:13–36 In contrast to those who refuse to recognize who Jesus and John truly are in 13:53—14:12, here Jesus shows himself to be the bread of life for Israel (vv. 13–21; cf. John 6:25–59) and reveals his divine nature to the Twelve (vv. 22–36).

14:13–21 The feeding of the 5,000 is the only miracle recorded in all four Gospels, which signals its importance. Jesus appears as a new and greater Moses, who fed the crowds with supernatural bread in the wilderness (cf. Exod 16), and as a new and greater Elisha, who fed a hundred people with 20 hand-size loaves of bread and still had leftovers (2 Kgs 4:42–44).

14:13 withdrew. From the potential hostility that had led to John's martyrdom. **privately to a solitary place.** Perhaps also for prayer and respite. In light of v. 22, it appears Jesus is on the northeast side of the Sea of Galilee. But the crowds quickly catch up with him.

14:16 You give them something to eat. Perhaps Jesus is merely setting up the disciples for the next stage of the conversation.

14:17 loaves of bread. Hand-size loaves. The bread and fish were probably intended for one boy's (or possibly one family's) dinner (cf. John 6:9), not for the multitudes.

14:19 None of the Gospels describes how the miracle occurred. Jesus "gave thanks" to God and "broke the loaves" in preparation for distributing them to those present, just as a Jewish father typically would do at the start of any main meal. Many have seen a foreshadowing of the Last Supper here (cf. 26:26), but this is less certain.

14:20 They all ate and were satisfied. The heart of the miracle. Indeed, the multiplication of the loaves was so bountiful and overflowing that there were "twelve basketfuls of broken pieces ... left over."

14:21 women and children. Would have been less likely to follow Jesus a long distance from their villages, but with 5,000 "men" present and large families the norm, the total number could easily have ranged from 10,000 to 20,000 people.

14:22–33 The miracle of Jesus walking on the water highlights Jesus' identity. Only God "treads on the waves of the sea" (Job 9:8; cf. Ps 77:19).

14:23 to pray. Even if his earlier withdrawal from the crowds (v. 13) had

to pray.[w] Later that night, he was there alone, 24and the boat was already a considerable distance from
land, buffeted by the waves because the wind was against it.
25Shortly before dawn Jesus went out to them, walking on the lake. 26When the disciples saw him
walking on the lake, they were terrified. "It's a ghost,"[x] they said, and cried out in fear.
27But Jesus immediately said to them: "Take courage![y] It is I. Don't be afraid."[z]
28"Lord, if it's you," Peter replied, "tell me to come to you on the water."
29"Come," he said.
Then Peter got down out of the boat, walked on the water and came toward Jesus. 30But when he saw
the wind, he was afraid and, beginning to sink, cried out, "Lord, save me!"
31Immediately Jesus reached out his hand and caught him. "You of little faith,"[a] he said, "why did
you doubt?"
32And when they climbed into the boat, the wind died down. 33Then those who were in the boat worshiped him, saying, "Truly you are the Son of God."[b]
34When they had crossed over, they landed at Gennesaret. 35And when the men of that place recognized Jesus, they sent word to all the surrounding country. People brought all their sick to him
36and begged him to let the sick just touch the edge of his cloak,[c] and all who touched it were healed.

14:23 [w]Lk 3:21
14:26 [x]Lk 24:37
14:27 [y]Mt 9:2; Ac 23:11 [z]Da 10:12; Mt 17:7; 28:10; Lk 1:13,30; 2:10; Ac 18:9; 23:11; Rev 1:17
14:31 [a]Mt 6:30
14:33 [b]Ps 2:7; Mt 4:3
14:36 [c]Mt 9:20
15:2 [d]Lk 11:38
15:4 [e]Ex 20:12; Dt 5:16; Eph 6:2 [f]Ex 21:17; Lev 20:9

That Which Defiles

15:1-20pp — Mk 7:1-23

15 Then some Pharisees and teachers of the law came to Jesus from Jerusalem and asked, 2"Why do
your disciples break the tradition of the elders? They don't wash their hands before they eat!"[d]
3Jesus replied, "And why do you break the command of God for the sake of your tradition? 4For God said,
'Honor your father and mother'[a][e] and 'Anyone who curses their father or mother is to be put to death.'[b][f]
5But you say that if anyone declares that what might have been used to help their father or mother is 'devoted to God,' 6they are not to 'honor their father or mother' with it. Thus you nullify the word of God for
the sake of your tradition. 7You hypocrites! Isaiah was right when he prophesied about you:

[a] *4* Exodus 20:12; Deut. 5:16 [b] *4* Exodus 21:17; Lev. 20:9

not been to pray, Jesus needs to do so now. He sends even the disciples on ahead of him back across the lake.

14:25 Shortly before dawn. Lit. "in the fourth watch of the night," i.e., sometime between 3:00 and 6:00 a.m.

14:26 ghost. Many Jews believed that after a person died, the person's ghost inhabited areas nearby. This was apparently the only way the disciples could explain Jesus appearing on top of the water.

14:27 It is I. Could also be translated "I am," the divine name of Exod 3:14 revealed by God to Moses in the burning bush. This is a theophany, a revelation of God's divinity in Christ.

14:28–29 Unique to Matthew's account of this miracle is Peter's attempt to walk on the water as well. His willingness to step out of the boat is amazing; the faith represented should not be minimized.

14:30–31 The fury of the storm quickly undermines Peter's faith, so he begins to sink. Had he fully realized that Jesus was helping him do the far harder task of walking on the lake, he would not have been afraid of the wind. Thus, after rescuing him, Jesus chastises him for his "little faith" (v. 31).

14:33 worshiped him. The miracle was so spectacular that otherwise monotheistic Jews actually worshiped Jesus. **Son of God.** Whereas in a Jewish context this could sometimes be a synonym for Messiah and not carry hints of divinity, this context doubtless implies a more awe-inspired declaration. Still, Peter reaches a new stage of understanding in 16:16–17 (see note there), and even then he is not prepared for the Messiah to suffer (16:22–23). So we must not overestimate how much the disciples grasp the meaning of the miracle here in vv. 22–33. In this light, the strikingly different aftermath of Mark 6:52 that "their hearts were hardened" becomes complementary rather than contradictory.

14:34–36 Blown well off course, the disciples land at Gennesaret, on the west-central shores of Galilee. Jesus responds to the townspeople's faith with more healings.

14:36 edge. Could mean "fringe," and is probably a reference to the prayer tassels at the bottom of a rabbi's robe. Cf. 9:20–21.

15:1—16:12 While still in Galilee, Jesus makes his sharpest break from conventional Judaism thus far (15:1–20). Not surprisingly, Matthew next narrates Jesus leaving Jewish territory for an extended period of time to minister in Gentile provinces. Israel has increasingly rejected him, and Gentiles begin to accept him (15:21–39). When he returns to Galilee (16:1–4), tensions resume, so he leaves again (16:5–12).

15:1–20 Questions about the oral law that offered rulings about how to apply the law of Moses to numerous modern settings ("the tradition of the elders," v. 2) lead Jesus to berate the Pharisees and scribes for breaking the written law of Moses through their interpretive traditions (vv. 3–9) and then prompt Jesus to make more sweeping claims about external rituals versus inward purity (vv. 10–20).

15:2 wash their hands. Ritual hand washing was not a requirement for Jews before every meal, but the Pharisees were trying to extend the level of purity demanded of priests (cf. Exod 30:17–21) to the entire people of Israel.

15:4 Honor your father and mother. The fifth of the Ten Commandments (Exod 20:12). Severe infringements of it could lead even to the death penalty in OT times (Exod 21:17).

15:5–6 These were laws of "Corban" ("devoted to God"; cf. Mark 7:11), somewhat like an irrevocable trust, in which monetary gifts donated to the temple treasury could still be used by their owners before they died but in very limited ways and not to help others.

15:7–9 Matthew again sees Scripture fulfilled typologically as the circumstances of Isaiah's day recur in striking fashion (Isa 29:13). Religion has degenerated into "merely human rules" (Matt 15:9) characterized

15:9 [g]Col 2:20-22 [h]Isa 29:13; Mal 2:2
15:11 [i]Ac 10:14,15 [j]ver 18
15:13 [k]Isa 60:21; 61:3; Jn 15:2
15:14 [l]Mt 23:16,24; Ro 2:19 [m]Lk 6:39
15:15 [n]Mt 13:36
15:16 [o]Mt 16:9
15:18 [p]Mt 12:34; Lk 6:45; Jas 3:6
15:19 [q]Gal 5:19-21
15:20 [r]Ro 14:14
15:21 [s]Mt 11:21
15:22 [t]Mt 9:27 [u]Mt 4:24
15:24 [v]Mt 10:6,23; Ro 15:8
15:25 [w]Mt 8:2
15:28 [x]Mt 9:22

8 "These people honor me with their lips,
but their hearts are far from me.
9 They worship me in vain;
their teachings are merely human rules.[g] [a][h]"

10 Jesus called the crowd to him and said, "Listen and understand. 11 What goes into someone's mouth
does not defile them,[i] but what comes out of their mouth, that is what defiles them."[j]
12 Then the disciples came to him and asked, "Do you know that the Pharisees were offended when
they heard this?"
13 He replied, "Every plant that my heavenly Father has not planted[k] will be pulled up by the roots.
14 Leave them; they are blind guides.[b][l] If the blind lead the blind, both will fall into a pit."[m]
15 Peter said, "Explain the parable to us."[n]
16 "Are you still so dull?"[o] Jesus asked them. 17 "Don't you see that whatever enters the mouth goes
into the stomach and then out of the body? 18 But the things that come out of a person's mouth come
from the heart,[p] and these defile them. 19 For out of the heart come evil thoughts—murder, adultery,
sexual immorality, theft, false testimony, slander.[q] 20 These are what defile a person;[r] but eating with
unwashed hands does not defile them."

The Faith of a Canaanite Woman

15:21-28pp — Mk 7:24-30

21 Leaving that place, Jesus withdrew to the region of Tyre and Sidon.[s] 22 A Canaanite woman from
that vicinity came to him, crying out, "Lord, Son of David,[t] have mercy on me! My daughter is demon-
possessed and suffering terribly."[u]
23 Jesus did not answer a word. So his disciples came to him and urged him, "Send her away, for she
keeps crying out after us."
24 He answered, "I was sent only to the lost sheep of Israel."[v]
25 The woman came and knelt before him.[w] "Lord, help me!" she said.
26 He replied, "It is not right to take the children's bread and toss it to the dogs."
27 "Yes it is, Lord," she said. "Even the dogs eat the crumbs that fall from their master's table."
28 Then Jesus said to her, "Woman, you have great faith![x] Your request is granted." And her daughter
was healed at that moment.

[a] *9* Isaiah 29:13 [b] *14* Some manuscripts *blind guides of the blind*

by lip service, and the people's hearts are far from God. No matter how good their worship appears externally, God declares it futile.

15:10–12 Matthew does not include as explicitly revolutionary a statement as Mark 7:19 ("Jesus declared all foods clean"), but the logical implications of "what goes into someone's mouth does not defile them" amounts to the same thing. Little wonder these Pharisees are offended or scandalized

15:13–14 These particular Jewish leaders are the plants the Father "has not planted" (v. 13) and "blind guides" (v. 14). Their end is therefore destruction: they will be uprooted (v. 13) and "fall into a pit" (v. 14).

15:15–20 In light of Jesus' reply, the "parable" (v. 15)—here more of an analogy—must refer to v. 11. Although Jesus berates the disciples as "still so dull" (v. 16), they probably did not imagine that Jesus was overturning even the OT dietary laws (Lev 11; Deut 14:4–21; cf. Peter's hesitancy in Acts 10:13–16). So he expands on his "parable" to stress that food simply passes through the digestive system (v. 17), whereas "evil thoughts" (v. 19) can produce truly harmful actions, violating even fundamental moral commandments (v. 19). These evil thoughts—not ritual impurities—are what "defile a person" (v. 20).

15:21–28 A woman from Syrian Phoenicia (coastal Lebanon; cf. Mark 7:26) demonstrates great faith that Jesus can heal her daughter.

15:21 Tyre and Sidon. See note on 11:20–24.

15:22 Canaanite. This archaic term is used deliberately by Matthew to highlight her Gentile, pagan background and her descent from ancient Israel's enemies. **Lord, Son of David.** A double title found elsewhere in this combination only in 20:30–31, where it is also used in the context of a request for healing.

15:23 The disciples reflect the typically ethnocentric and chauvinist attitudes of many of their Jewish contemporaries.

15:24 At first Jesus seems to agree with the disciples, echoing his command to the Twelve in 10:5–6. His mission "only to the lost sheep of Israel" was a temporary restriction, however, as even this episode demonstrates. The Good News comes first to Israel as God's uniquely elect nation, but it will soon extend to all peoples throughout the earth (28:18–20).

15:25–26 The woman is undaunted and keeps pleading for help. Reflecting the Jewish perspective that Israelites alone, not Gentiles ("dogs"), are God's children, Jesus appears to continue to reject her plea. But he likely recognizes her tenacious faith and wants to draw it out so that he can publicly praise her (v. 28) and show his disciples that their prejudices are inappropriate.

15:26 dogs. Gentiles. Among Jews, dogs were not household pets but wild scavengers.

15:27 Gentiles, unlike Jews, sometimes did have dogs as household pets, so the woman thinks of their eating "crumbs that fall from their master's table." Instead of disputing the conventional Jewish worldview, she argues her case from within it.

15:28 The woman's faith wins her the healing of her demon-possessed daughter (v. 22), even from a distance. Both of these features recall the story of the centurion in 8:5–13.

Jesus Feeds the Four Thousand

15:29-31pp — Mk 7:31-37
15:32-39pp — Mk 8:1-10
15:32-39Ref — Mt 14:13-21

29Jesus left there and went along the Sea of Galilee. Then he went up on a mountainside and sat down.
30Great crowds came to him, bringing the lame, the blind, the crippled, the mute and many others, and
laid them at his feet; and he healed them.[y] 31The people were amazed when they saw the mute speaking,
the crippled made well, the lame walking and the blind seeing. And they praised the God of Israel.[z]
32Jesus called his disciples to him and said, "I have compassion for these people;[a] they have already
been with me three days and have nothing to eat. I do not want to send them away hungry, or they
may collapse on the way."
33His disciples answered, "Where could we get enough bread in this remote place to feed such a crowd?"
34"How many loaves do you have?" Jesus asked.
"Seven," they replied, "and a few small fish."
35He told the crowd to sit down on the ground. 36Then he took the seven loaves and the fish, and
when he had given thanks, he broke them[b] and gave them to the disciples, and they in turn to the
people. 37They all ate and were satisfied. Afterward the disciples picked up seven basketfuls of broken
pieces that were left over.[c] 38The number of those who ate was four thousand men, besides women and
children. 39After Jesus had sent the crowd away, he got into the boat and went to the vicinity of Magadan.

15:30 [y] Mt 4:23
15:31 [z] Mt 9:8
15:32 [a] Mt 9:36
15:36 [b] Mt 14:19
15:37 [c] Mt 16:10

15:29–39 The miracle of the feeding of the 4,000 strikingly resembles the feeding of the 5,000 (see note on 14:13–21). But here the crowds appear to be Gentile, not those who have followed Jesus around the lake from Galilee as before. The teaching period is longer and the need for food more acute (v. 32). The close duplication of the earlier miracle may intentionally demonstrate that Jesus is the bread of life for Gentiles as well as Jews (see note on 14:13–36).

15:31 they praised the God of Israel. Makes more sense if it describes a Gentile, rather than a Jewish, response. Jews would praise just "God," but Gentiles would have to specify that it was not their god(s) but the Jewish one.

15:33 The disciples' question seems extremely obtuse after the previous feeding miracle. But because the Greek for "we" may be emphatic, perhaps they think Jesus is now asking *them* to provide the food. Perhaps the question also illustrates the hardness of heart (see note on 14:33) that blinds even Jesus' closer followers before the resurrection and the gift of the Spirit at Pentecost.

15:34–38 The "seven loaves" (v. 36) and the "four thousand men, besides women and children" (v. 38) may be merely the numbers counted. But Matthew may see symbolic, as well as literal, meaning in the "seven basketfuls" of leftovers in v. 37 as opposed to the "twelve basketfuls" in 14:20, because seven was the universal number (as in seven days of creation), appropriate for all nations, while twelve was the distinctively Jewish number (as in twelve tribes of Israel). That the word for "basket" in the Greek also changes from a typical Jewish lunch pack (*kophinos* in 14:20) to a larger Gentile hamper (*spyris* here in v. 37) could support this suggestion.

15:39 Magadan. Probably a variant of Magdala, on the west-central shore of the Sea of Galilee, confirming that Jesus had been on the Gentile, eastern side before they crossed over.

Aerial view of Magdala (Magadan), the home of Mary Magdalene and where Jesus spent some of his time (Matt 15:39). In 2009, the remains of a first-century synagogue were discovered.

16:1 [d]Ac 4:1 [e]Mt 12:38
16:3 [f]Lk 12:54-56
16:4 [g]Mt 12:39
16:6 [h]Lk 12:1
16:8 [i]Mt 6:30
16:9 [j]Mt 14:17-21
16:10 [k]Mt 15:34-38
16:12 [l]Ac 4:1
16:14 [m]Mt 3:1; 14:2 [n]Mk 6:15; Jn 1:21
16:16 [o]Mt 4:3; Ps 42:2; Jn 11:27; Ac 14:15; 2Co 6:16; 1Th 1:9; 1Ti 3:15; Heb 10:31; 12:22
16:17 [p]1Co 15:50; Gal 1:16; Eph 6:12; Heb 2:14
16:18 [q]Jn 1:42

The Demand for a Sign

16:1-12pp — Mk 8:11-21

16 The Pharisees and Sadducees[d] came to Jesus and tested him by asking him to show them a
sign from heaven.[e]
2 He replied, "When evening comes, you say, 'It will be fair weather, for the sky is red,' 3 and in the
morning, 'Today it will be stormy, for the sky is red and overcast.' You know how to interpret the appearance of the sky, but you cannot interpret the signs of the times.[a][f] 4 A wicked and adulterous generation
looks for a sign, but none will be given it except the sign of Jonah."[g] Jesus then left them and went away.

The Yeast of the Pharisees and Sadducees

5 When they went across the lake, the disciples forgot to take bread. 6 "Be careful," Jesus said to them.
"Be on your guard against the yeast of the Pharisees and Sadducees."[h]
7 They discussed this among themselves and said, "It is because we didn't bring any bread."
8 Aware of their discussion, Jesus asked, "You of little faith,[i] why are you talking among yourselves
about having no bread? 9 Do you still not understand? Don't you remember the five loaves for the five
thousand, and how many basketfuls you gathered?[j] 10 Or the seven loaves for the four thousand, and
how many basketfuls you gathered?[k] 11 How is it you don't understand that I was not talking to you
about bread? But be on your guard against the yeast of the Pharisees and Sadducees." 12 Then they understood that he was not telling them to guard against the yeast used in bread, but against the teaching
of the Pharisees and Sadducees.[l]

Peter Declares That Jesus Is the Messiah

16:13-16pp — Mk 8:27-29; Lk 9:18-20

13 When Jesus came to the region of Caesarea Philippi, he asked his disciples, "Who do people say
the Son of Man is?"
14 They replied, "Some say John the Baptist;[m] others say Elijah; and still others, Jeremiah or one of
the prophets."[n]
15 "But what about you?" he asked. "Who do you say I am?"
16 Simon Peter answered, "You are the Messiah, the Son of the living God."[o]
17 Jesus replied, "Blessed are you, Simon son of Jonah, for this was not revealed to you by flesh and
blood,[p] but by my Father in heaven. 18 And I tell you that you are Peter,[b][q] and on this rock I will build

[a] *2,3* Some early manuscripts do not have *When evening comes . . . of the times.* [b] *18* The Greek word for *Peter* means *rock.*

16:1–12 There is danger in Israel as Jewish leaders test Jesus further by requesting a sign (vv. 1–4), and Jesus warns his disciples about them and their influence as he returns to Gentile territory (vv. 5–12).

16:1–4 The demand for a sign closely resembles the episode in 12:38–42. This time some of the otherwise rival groups, the Pharisees and Sadducees (see note on 3:7), "tested him" (v. 1). Perhaps the request for "a sign from heaven" (v. 1) made Jesus think of the "appearance of the sky" (v. 3). Verses 2–3 reflect common weather patterns: clouds in the west at dawn portend rain for later in the day; clouds (only) in the east at dusk mean bad weather has passed.

16:4 the sign of Jonah. See note on 12:38–45.

16:6 yeast of the Pharisees and Sadducees. The "teaching of the Pharisees and Sadducees" (v. 12). It could have pervasive influence, like yeast in bread (see note on 13:31–33). Misguided teaching is damaging.

16:7–8 The disciples' obtuseness continues as they try to interpret an obvious metaphor literally. Jesus' rebuke is well deserved.

16:9–12 If they thought about the feedings of the 5,000 and 4,000, the disciples would know that Jesus could provide the necessary food. They would also recall the symbolism in those events, especially with Jesus as the bread of life, and they would be looking for the metaphoric meaning in Christ's warning about the "yeast of the Pharisees and Sadducees" (v. 6; see note there).

16:13–20 The narrative segment that began with the people of Nazareth failing to acknowledge Jesus' true identity (13:53–58) now ends with Peter correctly recognizing that Jesus is the Messiah.

16:13 Caesarea Philippi. North of Israel. The city had formerly been named Paneas, after Pan, the Greek god of the forest. Renamed for Augustus Caesar and Herod Philip early in the first century, the area was an appropriate one in which to ask people about Jesus' identity. The correct answer would show Jesus as rival and superior to those other gods and rulers.

16:14 John the Baptist ... Elijah ... Jeremiah ... one of the prophets. All of the suggested options represent prophetic forerunners to the Messiah, but not the Messiah himself.

16:16–17 Simon gives the correct answer. Jesus is "the Messiah, the Son of the living God" (v. 16). He is not just the prophesied Jewish liberator but one in a uniquely intimate relationship with the only true God of the universe. Simon's understanding has improved even from 14:33 (see note there), hence Jesus' declaration that this insight was divinely disclosed and not from human beings ("flesh and blood," v. 17).

16:18 Peter ... rock. Greek *petros* and *petra*, respectively, a play on words. Some have thought the difference in endings of the two words distinguishes Peter from the rock, with the rock being Christ or Peter's confession *about* Jesus. But the word for "rock" in Greek is the feminine

my church,[r] and the gates of Hades[a] will not overcome it. [19]I will give you the keys[s] of the kingdom of heaven; whatever you bind on earth will be[b] bound in heaven, and whatever you loose on earth will be[b] loosed in heaven."[t] [20]Then he ordered his disciples not to tell anyone[u] that he was the Messiah.

Jesus Predicts His Death

16:21-28pp — Mk 8:31–9:1; Lk 9:22-27

[21]From that time on Jesus began to explain to his disciples that he must go to Jerusalem and suffer many things[v] at the hands of the elders, the chief priests and the teachers of the law, and that he must be killed and on the third day[w] be raised to life.[x]

[22]Peter took him aside and began to rebuke him. "Never, Lord!" he said. "This shall never happen to you!"

[23]Jesus turned and said to Peter, "Get behind me, Satan![y] You are a stumbling block to me; you do not have in mind the concerns of God, but merely human concerns."

[24]Then Jesus said to his disciples, "Whoever wants to be my disciple must deny themselves and take up their cross and follow me.[z] [25]For whoever wants to save their life[c] will lose it, but whoever loses their life for me will find it.[a] [26]What good will it be for someone to gain the whole world, yet forfeit their soul?

[a] *18* That is, the realm of the dead [b] *19* Or *will have been* [c] *25* The Greek word means either *life* or *soul*; also in verse 26.

16:18 [r]Eph 2:20
16:19 [s]Isa 22:22; Rev 3:7 [t]Mt 18:18; Jn 20:23
16:20 [u]Mk 8:30
16:21 [v]Mk 10:34; Lk 17:25 [w]Jn 2:19 [x]Mt 17:22,23; 27:63; Mk 9:31; Lk 9:22; 18:31-33; 24:6,7
16:23 [y]Mt 4:10
16:24 [z]Mt 10:38; Lk 14:27
16:25 [a]Jn 12:25

noun *petra*, whereas "Peter," a man's name, is the masculine *petros*. The play on words requires the change in gender, even if Peter *is* the rock. And the wordplay makes best sense this way, because in v. 23 it is Peter himself who suddenly becomes a quite different kind of rock—a "stumbling block." **build.** Most likely refers to those activities Peter undertakes in the rest of the NT—especially leading the church in Jerusalem (Acts 2; 8; 10) and writing authoritative letters to congregations he helped to evangelize (1–2 Peter). Eph 2:20 speaks of the foundation of the church as all of the NT prophets and apostles, suggesting that Peter is merely the chief or representative apostle, with nothing here or elsewhere in the Bible suggesting he is infallible or beginning a process of "apostolic succession" of church leadership. **my church.** The assembly (Greek *ekklēsia*) of God's people, akin to the assembly of the children of Israel throughout the OT. That Jesus can speak of it as *his* church sets him apart from the church's members as its Lord.

16:19 the keys of the kingdom. Seems to allude to Isa 22:22 and to refer to the process of ratifying God's will on earth by recognizing new Christians and disciplining those who rebel against Jesus. **will be bound ... will be loosed.** Heaven is in accord with church authority properly exercised. Matt 18:18 gives this same privilege to all the apostles, not just to Peter.

16:20 The "Messianic secret" has appeared before (see 8:4 and note). In light of Peter's imminent failure to accept the passion prediction (vv. 21–22), it makes good sense for Jesus to caution his audience not to talk too much about him.

16:21—28:20 *The Road to the Cross and the Resurrection.* Jesus now begins to travel under the shadow of the cross but with resurrection hope on the other side.

16:21—17:27 *Preparation for the Passion.* Jesus teaches about his need to die at the hands of the Jewish authorities in Jerusalem (16:21–28; 17:22–23; 20:17–20). Yet to sustain his disciples, his transfiguration (17:1–13) and further miracle-working ministry (17:14–21,24–27) give them glimpses of his glory to sustain them through the dark days.

16:21–28 When Jesus predicts his coming death, Peter rebukes him (v. 22). But Jesus explains not only that *he* must suffer but that anyone who would *follow* him must suffer too. Nevertheless, resurrection follows crucifixion. See notes on 17:22–23; 20:17–19.

16:21 From that time on Jesus began to. Again this signals a new major section in Matthew (cf. 4:17; see note there). **he must ... suffer ... be killed ... be raised to life.** This assertion by Jesus was contrary to virtually all Jewish expectation, yet it was in accordance with the OT (see especially Isa 52:13—53:12). **the elders, the chief priests and the teachers of the law.** The three main groups of temple authorities in Jerusalem who oppose Jesus (see also 17:22–23; 20:17–19).

16:22 never happen. Peter still has a triumphant, conquering Messiah in mind.

16:23 Get behind me, Satan. Jesus is not claiming that Peter is demon-possessed but that his rejection of the way of the cross reflects the attitude of Satan. **Get behind me.** Means "Get away from me." Peter, the "rock" (v. 18), has quickly become a "stumbling block."

16:24–25 See notes on 10:38,39.

16:26 What good will it be ... ? All the material possessions and privilege in this world cannot compensate for spending an eternity in hell. Nor can any human offer anything to God to redeem themselves. Eternal life must be received as God's free gift. But this context reminds people that it may cost them their lives.

CAESAREA PHILIPPI

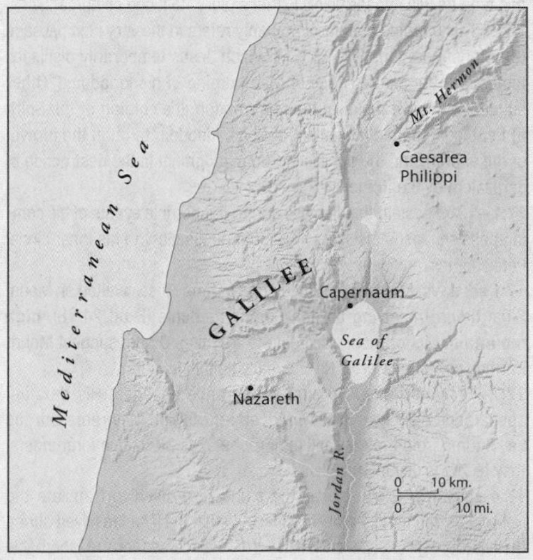

16:27 [b]Mt 8:20 [c]Ac 1:11 [d]Job 34:11; Ps 62:12; Jer 17:10; Ro 2:6; 2Co 5:10; Rev 22:12
17:5 [e]Mt 3:17; 2Pe 1:17 [f]Ac 3:22,23
17:7 [g]Mt 14:27
17:9 [h]Mk 8:30 [i]Mt 8:20 [j]Mt 16:21
17:11 [k]Mal 4:6; Lk 1:16,17
17:12 [l]Mt 11:14 [m]Mt 14:3,10 [n]Mt 16:21
17:15 [o]Mt 4:24

Or what can anyone give in exchange for their soul? 27 For the Son of Man[b] is going to come[c] in his
Father's glory with his angels, and then he will reward each person according to what they have done.[d]
28 "Truly I tell you, some who are standing here will not taste death before they see the Son of Man
coming in his kingdom."

The Transfiguration

17:1-8pp — Lk 9:28-36
17:1-13pp — Mk 9:2-13

17 After six days Jesus took with him Peter, James and John the brother of James, and led them
up a high mountain by themselves. 2 There he was transfigured before them. His face shone
like the sun, and his clothes became as white as the light. 3 Just then there appeared before them Moses
and Elijah, talking with Jesus.
4 Peter said to Jesus, "Lord, it is good for us to be here. If you wish, I will put up three shelters — one
for you, one for Moses and one for Elijah."
5 While he was still speaking, a bright cloud covered them, and a voice from the cloud said, "This is
my Son, whom I love; with him I am well pleased.[e] Listen to him!"[f]
6 When the disciples heard this, they fell facedown to the ground, terrified. 7 But Jesus came and
touched them. "Get up," he said. "Don't be afraid."[g] 8 When they looked up, they saw no one except
Jesus.
9 As they were coming down the mountain, Jesus instructed them, "Don't tell anyone[h] what you have
seen, until the Son of Man[i] has been raised from the dead."[j]
10 The disciples asked him, "Why then do the teachers of the law say that Elijah must come first?"
11 Jesus replied, "To be sure, Elijah comes and will restore all things.[k] 12 But I tell you, Elijah has
already come,[l] and they did not recognize him, but have done to him everything they wished.[m] In the
same way the Son of Man is going to suffer[n] at their hands." 13 Then the disciples understood that he
was talking to them about John the Baptist.

Jesus Heals a Demon-Possessed Boy

17:14-19pp — Mk 9:14-28; Lk 9:37-42

14 When they came to the crowd, a man approached Jesus and knelt before him. 15 "Lord, have mercy
on my son," he said. "He has seizures[o] and is suffering greatly. He often falls into the fire or into the
water. 16 I brought him to your disciples, but they could not heal him."

16:27 come ... and then. Jesus himself will return after his death, resurrection, and ascension. Unlike his coming as a baby in humiliation, this time he will appear "in his Father's glory" to judge all humanity.

16:28 This puzzling statement probably refers to the very next passage (the transfiguration, 17:1–13), in which Jesus temporarily discloses himself as the exalted "Son of Man coming in his kingdom." Other suggestions have included the resurrection, the coming of the Spirit at Pentecost, the advancement of God's kingdom through the growth of the church, and the coming of God in judgment in the destruction of Jerusalem by the Romans in AD 70.

17:1–13 To sustain the disciples during the horrible events of his coming passion, Jesus discloses himself in all his glory to his inner circle: Peter, James, and John.

17:1 six days. May allude to the period of time Moses waited on Mount Sinai before receiving the Ten Commandments (Exod 24:16). **high mountain.** Mount Tabor, according to tradition. Others suggest Mount Hermon or Mount Meron. No one really knows for sure.

17:2–3 transfigured. Jesus' appearance changes. His dazzling appearance displays his deity. **Moses and Elijah.** May represent the key figures from the Law and the Prophets; as Messianic forerunners, they testify to Jesus' true identity.

17:4 shelters. Greek *skēnē*, the same term used to translate the Hebrew for the tents, or tabernacles, in which the Israelites lived during their wilderness wanderings. This term is also used for the tabernacle and the tent of meeting that became the means for God's continuing presence with Israel after Sinai (Exod 25–40). Peter proposes prolonging this amazing experience by erecting these.

17:5 voice from the cloud. It echoes the words from Ps 2:7 and Isa 42:1 as at Jesus' baptism (see Matt 3:17 and note on 3:16–17).

17:6–8 The entire scene would leave most anyone terrified. Jesus, though, does not want to scare his followers but wants to encourage them so that they can face the challenges ahead. At the same time, this experience is not to be prolonged, so Moses and Elijah disappear as suddenly as they appeared.

17:9 Don't tell anyone. Here is the final injunction to keep quiet about Jesus' Messiahship. Jesus also clarifies that the restriction is lifted after the resurrection. Then it will be much clearer what type of ministry Christ came to fulfill.

17:10–13 Having seen Elijah reminds the disciples of Mal 4:5–6. If Jesus is the Messiah, what about the prophecies that Elijah will be his forerunner? John the Baptist has already played that role in his ministry and martyrdom (see 3:4 and note; 14:3–12), foreshadowing Jesus' own mission.

17:14–21 The inability of the nine remaining disciples to deal with a demon-possessed boy — one of the maladies they were commissioned to handle (10:8) — contrasts sharply with the mountaintop experience of the three who accompanied Jesus. But Jesus salvages the situation.

17:15 has seizures. Perhaps caused by epilepsy.

17“You unbelieving and perverse generation,” Jesus replied, “how long shall I stay with you? How long shall I put up with you? Bring the boy here to me.” 18Jesus rebuked the demon, and it came out of the boy, and he was healed at that moment.

19Then the disciples came to Jesus in private and asked, “Why couldn’t we drive it out?”

20He replied, “Because you have so little faith. Truly I tell you, if you have faith[p] as small as a mustard seed,[q] you can say to this mountain, ‘Move from here to there,’ and it will move.[r] Nothing will be impossible for you.” [21][a]

Jesus Predicts His Death a Second Time

22When they came together in Galilee, he said to them, “The Son of Man[s] is going to be delivered into the hands of men. 23They will kill him,[t] and on the third day[u] he will be raised to life.”[v] And the disciples were filled with grief.

The Temple Tax

24After Jesus and his disciples arrived in Capernaum, the collectors of the two-drachma temple tax[w] came to Peter and asked, “Doesn’t your teacher pay the temple tax?”

25“Yes, he does,” he replied.

When Peter came into the house, Jesus was the first to speak. “What do you think, Simon?” he asked. “From whom do the kings of the earth collect duty and taxes[x]—from their own children or from others?”

26“From others,” Peter answered.

“Then the children are exempt,” Jesus said to him. 27“But so that we may not cause offense,[y] go to the lake and throw out your line. Take the first fish you catch; open its mouth and you will find a four-drachma coin. Take it and give it to them for my tax and yours.”

The Greatest in the Kingdom of Heaven

18:1-5pp — Mk 9:33-37; Lk 9:46-48

18 At that time the disciples came to Jesus and asked, “Who, then, is the greatest in the kingdom of heaven?”

2He called a little child to him, and placed the child among them. 3And he said: “Truly I tell you, unless you change and become like little children,[z] you will never enter the kingdom of heaven.[a] 4Therefore, whoever takes the lowly position of this child is the greatest in the kingdom of heaven.[b] 5And whoever welcomes one such child in my name welcomes me.[c]

[a] *21* Some manuscripts include here words similar to Mark 9:29.

17:20 [p] Mt 21:21 [q] Mt 13:31; Mk 11:23; Lk 17:6 [r] 1Co 13:2
17:22 [s] Mt 8:20
17:23 [t] Ac 2:23; 3:13 [u] Mt 16:21 [v] Mt 16:21
17:24 [w] Ex 30:13
17:25 [x] Mt 22:17-21; Ro 13:7
17:27 [y] Jn 6:61
18:3 [z] Mt 19:14; 1Pe 2:2 [a] Mt 3:2
18:4 [b] Mk 9:35
18:5 [c] Mt 10:40

17:17 Interestingly, Jesus rebukes the crowd for their “unbelieving and perverse” nature, not the disciples for their failure. Perhaps the general spiritual malaise of this “generation” was also a cause of the number of demonized people afflicted at this time.

17:18 Not all seizures were the result of demon possession, but these were.

17:20 With only a very little faith, the disciples could have exorcised this demon. No spiritually elite status is necessary. **mustard seed.** See note on 13:31–33. To “move a mountain” was proverbial for a great accomplishment (cf. 1 Cor 13:2).

17:22–23 Jesus predicts his death a second time. The disciples have moved from denial to grief. See notes on 16:21–28; 20:17–19.

17:24–27 The temple tax will no longer be incumbent on Jesus’ followers because he is inaugurating a new age in which the law is fulfilled (5:17) and something greater than the temple is here (12:6).

17:24 two-drachma temple tax. A half-shekel temple tax was levied on all Israelites 20 years of age or older (Exod 30:13–16; see photo, p. 2295). A drachma, like a denarius, was one day’s minimum wage.

17:25–26 Just as kings do not tax their own children, but only their subjects, Jesus’ followers should not have to pay a religious tax to their heavenly King and Father.

17:27 Jesus gives Peter a creative way to obey the law and not cause unnecessary “offense” without financially inconveniencing the Twelve. **fish.** Greek *ichthys.* This particular fish found in the Sea of Galilee frequently scoops up objects fallen on the lake bed. People have caught fish with coins in their mouths in this lake even in modern times. **four-drachma coin.** See note on v. 24. It could pay the tax for both Jesus and Peter.

18:1–35 *Sermon on Humility and Forgiveness.* The fourth major block of Jesus’ teaching (after chs. 5–7; 10:5–42; 13:1–52). Verses 1–14 show the lengths to which God humbles himself to save the lost, while vv. 15–35 define the extent to which we should humble ourselves to forgive others.

18:1–14 Those who would “enter the kingdom” (v. 3) must exercise childlike humility (vv. 1–5) and avoid causing other little ones to stumble (vv. 6–9). After all, God himself is a good shepherd who will seek out even one lost sheep (vv. 10–14).

18:1–5 Positively, to be the greatest in the kingdom of heaven, the disciples must mirror the humble position of children.

18:1 Kingdoms typically have hierarchies, so the disciples wonder who will be closest to the top. Cf. note on 20:20–28.

18:3–4 Jesus’ reign, however, is an upside-down kingdom. Even to enter, people must “become like little children” (v. 3). This does not imply being childish, but being childlike in recognizing one’s vulnerability and dependence—in this case on God.

18:4 takes the lowly position of. Equivalent to “humbles himself as.”

18:5 See 10:42.

18:6 [d] Mk 9:42; Lk 17:2
18:7 [e] Lk 17:1
18:8 [f] Mt 5:29; Mk 9:43,45
18:9 [g] Mt 5:29 [h] Mt 5:22
18:10 [i] Ge 48:16; Ps 34:7; Ac 12:11,15; Heb 1:14
18:15 [j] Lev 19:17; Lk 17:3; Gal 6:1; Jas 5:19,20
18:16 [k] Nu 35:30; Dt 17:6; 19:15; Jn 8:17; 2Co 13:1; 1Ti 5:19; Heb 10:28
18:17 [l] 1Co 6:1-6 [m] Ro 16:17; 2Th 3:6,14
18:18 [n] Mt 16:19; Jn 20:23
18:19 [o] Mt 7:7

Causing to Stumble

6 “If anyone causes one of these little ones—those who believe in me—to stumble, it would be better
for them to have a large millstone hung around their neck and to be drowned in the depths of the sea.[d]
7 Woe to the world because of the things that cause people to stumble! Such things must come, but woe
to the person through whom they come![e] 8 If your hand or your foot causes you to stumble,[f] cut it off
and throw it away. It is better for you to enter life maimed or crippled than to have two hands or two feet
and be thrown into eternal fire. 9 And if your eye causes you to stumble,[g] gouge it out and throw it away.
It is better for you to enter life with one eye than to have two eyes and be thrown into the fire of hell.[h]

The Parable of the Wandering Sheep

18:12-14pp — Lk 15:4-7

10 “See that you do not despise one of these little ones. For I tell you that their angels[i] in heaven always see the face of my Father in heaven. [11][a]
12 “What do you think? If a man owns a hundred sheep, and one of them wanders away, will he not
leave the ninety-nine on the hills and go to look for the one that wandered off? 13 And if he finds it, truly
I tell you, he is happier about that one sheep than about the ninety-nine that did not wander off. 14 In
the same way your Father in heaven is not willing that any of these little ones should perish.

Dealing With Sin in the Church

15 “If your brother or sister[b] sins,[c] go and point out their fault,[j] just between the two of you. If they listen
to you, you have won them over. 16 But if they will not listen, take one or two others along, so that ‘every matter may be established by the testimony of two or three witnesses.’[d][k] 17 If they still refuse to listen, tell it to the
church;[l] and if they refuse to listen even to the church, treat them as you would a pagan or a tax collector.[m]
18 “Truly I tell you, whatever you bind on earth will be[e] bound in heaven, and whatever you loose
on earth will be[e] loosed in heaven.[n]
19 “Again, truly I tell you that if two of you on earth agree about anything they ask for, it will be done
for them[o] by my Father in heaven. 20 For where two or three gather in my name, there am I with them.”

[a] *11* Some manuscripts include here the words of Luke 19:10. [b] *15* The Greek word for *brother or sister* (*adelphos*) refers here to a fellow disciple, whether man or woman; also in verses 21 and 35. [c] *15* Some manuscripts *sins against you* [d] *16* Deut. 19:15 [e] *18* Or *will have been*

18:6–9 Negatively, disciples must refrain from causing those who believe in Jesus to stumble, i.e., they must not spiritually harm other fledgling followers of Jesus.
18:6 stumble. Here in the sense of committing the worst sin of all: complete apostasy. **a large millstone.** A heavy wheel-shaped stone tied to a pole that was turned by a donkey as it walked around a birdbath shaped structure into which grain was poured, causing the stone to crush the grain. **sea.** To be thrown into the open sea with a large millstone around one's neck would certainly cause drowning.
18:8–9 See note on 5:29–30.
18:10–14 *The Parable of the Lost Sheep.* Jesus tells a parable similar to the parable of the lost sheep in Luke 15:3–7. In this context, however, the sheep “wanders away” (v. 12), perhaps representing the wayward disciple. In both accounts, God is eager to restore those not in right relationships with him.
18:10 their angels in heaven. Could suggest the concept of guardian angels, but nothing requires that there be a one-to-one correlation between angels and humans.
18:12 Shepherds tended to band together, so other shepherds would watch the 99 left behind.
18:13 Restoration is always a cause for celebration
18:14 is not willing that any of these little ones should perish. Cf. 2 Pet 3:9. But it is also true that God does not override human freedom, so unfortunately many are lost (7:13). Theologians often distinguish between God's sovereign (decretive, secret/hidden) will, i.e., what he decrees, and his moral (preceptive, revealed) will, i.e., what he commands. The Bible preserves a running tension between God's sweeping sovereignty and his personal yearning that his image-bearers repent, believe, and be saved. God is never less than unrelentingly sovereign and unrelentingly personal in his dealings with people. The latter is highlighted here.
18:15–35 Interpersonal sin should be followed by forgiveness and reconciliation whenever possible. Verses 15–20 outline the process and also what to do if someone refuses to repent. Verses 23–35 depict God's lavish forgiveness, limited only by human unwillingness to forgive. Tucked between these two sections, Jesus' commands about unlimited forgiveness (vv. 21–22) must refer to situations when there *is* genuine repentance (cf. Luke 17:3–4).
18:15–20 As throughout the NT, the goal of all Christian discipline is restoration and rehabilitation, not retribution.
18:15 The best manuscripts omit “against you” after “if your brother or sister sins”; however, this inclusion clarifies the text's meaning (cf. v. 21; see the second NIV text note on v. 15).
18:16 This procedure comes from Deut 19:15. Taking “one or two” people with you adds up to “two or three.” **witnesses.** Not eyewitnesses of the sin, but those who can testify as to how the attempt at reconciliation goes.
18:17 pagan ... tax collector. Jesus regularly treats them with remarkable compassion. But he does not treat them as disciples until they repent. The removal of fellowship depicted here does not mean having no further contact with a person; rather it means not allowing them to retain positions reserved for Christians until they repent.
18:18–19 See note on 16:19. Here the application seems restricted to church discipline (cf. John 20:23). Note that the promise given to Peter in 16:19 is here given to the Twelve.
18:20 where two or three gather. While Christ is present in even the

The Parable of the Unmerciful Servant

21 Then Peter came to Jesus and asked, "Lord, how many times shall I forgive my brother or sister
who sins against me?[p] Up to seven times?"[q]
22 Jesus answered, "I tell you, not seven times, but seventy-seven times.[a][r]
23 "Therefore, the kingdom of heaven is like[s] a king who wanted to settle accounts[t] with his servants.
24 As he began the settlement, a man who owed him ten thousand bags of gold[b] was brought to him.
25 Since he was not able to pay,[u] the master ordered that he and his wife and his children and all that
he had be sold[v] to repay the debt.
26 "At this the servant fell on his knees before him.[w] 'Be patient with me,' he begged, 'and I will pay
back everything.' 27 The servant's master took pity on him, canceled the debt and let him go.
28 "But when that servant went out, he found one of his fellow servants who owed him a hundred
silver coins.[c] He grabbed him and began to choke him. 'Pay back what you owe me!' he demanded.
29 "His fellow servant fell to his knees and begged him, 'Be patient with me, and I will pay it back.'
30 "But he refused. Instead, he went off and had the man thrown into prison until he could pay the
debt. 31 When the other servants saw what had happened, they were outraged and went and told their
master everything that had happened.
32 "Then the master called the servant in. 'You wicked servant,' he said, 'I canceled all that debt of yours
because you begged me to. 33 Shouldn't you have had mercy on your fellow servant just as I had on you?'
34 In anger his master handed him over to the jailers to be tortured, until he should pay back all he owed.
35 "This is how my heavenly Father will treat each of you unless you forgive your brother or sister
from your heart."[x]

Divorce

19:1-9pp — Mk 10:1-12

19 When Jesus had finished saying these things,[y] he left Galilee and went into the region of Judea
to the other side of the Jordan. 2 Large crowds followed him, and he healed them[z] there.
3 Some Pharisees came to him to test him. They asked, "Is it lawful for a man to divorce his wife[a]
for any and every reason?"

18:21 [p] Mt 6:14 [q] Lk 17:4
18:22 [r] Ge 4:24
18:23 [s] Mt 13:24 [t] Mt 25:19
18:25 [u] Lk 7:42 [v] Lev 25:39; 2Ki 4:1; Ne 5:5,8
18:26 [w] Mt 8:2
18:35 [x] Mt 6:14; Jas 2:13
19:1 [y] Mt 7:28
19:2 [z] Mt 4:23
19:3 [a] Mt 5:31

[a] 22 Or *seventy times seven* [b] 24 Greek *ten thousand talents*; a talent was worth about 20 years of a day laborer's wages. [c] 28 Greek *a hundred denarii*; a denarius was the usual daily wage of a day laborer (see 20:2).

smallest gathering of his people, his point in this context is that heaven is in accord (v. 19) with believers who follow his instructions regarding church discipline. **two or three.** Corresponds to the two or three witnesses of v. 16.

18:21–35 *The Parable of the Unmerciful Servant.* In light of the teaching on church discipline immediately preceding in vv. 15–20, Peter asks Jesus about the extent of forgiveness (vv. 21–22). In the follow-up parable (vv. 23–35), Jesus' central point is that forgiven people forgive. Those who refuse to forgive comparatively paltry offenses show that they have never truly appropriated God's far more lavish forgiveness.

18:22 seventy-seven times. Seems to be a more likely translation than "seventy times seven." Either way, the point is not to withhold forgiveness on the 78th (or 491st) offense. The numbers 77 and 490 are multiples of 7, the Jewish number of completeness. But Luke 17:3–4 shows that this kind of forgiveness requires repentance, which in turn refers to a change of behavior and not just attitude. Of course, even when there is no repentance, believers must not harbor grudges, plot retaliation, or remain embittered. But without another party's repentance, there can be no full reconciliation.

18:24 ten thousand. Greek *myrios* ("myriad"), the largest numeral. A talent was worth about 20 years of a day laborer's wages. The figures are therefore astronomical, as is the king's forgiveness. **bags of gold.** Greek *talanton* ("talent"), in the ancient sense of a form of money. A talent was the largest unit of currency in the Greco-Roman world.

18:28 a hundred. About four months' earnings, no pittance, except in comparison with 10,000 bags of gold in v. 24. The contrast between the behavior of the king (the "master," v. 32) and that of his "servant" (v. 32) could scarcely be more striking. **silver coins.** Lit. "denarii." A denarius was a day laborer's minimum daily wage.

18:32–34 Now the king discloses his justice, not merely his mercy. A servant so incapable of forgiving another's slight debt after the amazing forgiveness he himself has received merits the very imprisonment he has meted out to his fellow servant.

18:34 until he should pay back all he owed. Amounts to "never" because ancient jails did not allow inmates to earn money and because this debt was virtually unrepayable even had the man been free.

18:35 See note on 6:12.

19:1—22:46 *Journeying to the Temple.* Jesus leaves Galilee to head for Jerusalem but more specifically for the temple at Passover time. Matthew again sandwiches a narrative between two discourses (18:1–35; 23:1–39) as Jesus teaches both his disciples and other people along the way.

19:1—20:34 Seven discrete passages comprise this section on Jesus' final journey, only one of which involves a miracle. Preparing his disciples for his departure by means of teaching them and the others he encounters along the way must take priority.

19:1–12 God intends for married couples to remain together as long as they live. If adultery breaks the one-flesh uniqueness designed for marriage, divorce and remarriage are possible though never ideal. For those who cannot accept these regulations, a celibate, single life is the appropriate alternative.

19:3 Pharisees. Were already debating the interpretation of Deut 24:1. See note on 5:31. **test.** Could also be translated "trap" or "tempt." This and further "testings" associate the religious leaders with Satan.

19:4 [b]Ge 1:27; 5:2
19:5 [c]Ge 2:24; 1Co 6:16; Eph 5:31
19:7 [d]Dt 24:1-4; Mt 5:31
19:9 [e]Mt 5:32; Lk 16:18
19:11 [f]Mt 13:11; 1Co 7:7-9,17
19:13 [g]Mk 5:23
19:14 [h]Mt 25:34 [i]Mt 18:3; 1Pe 2:2
19:16 [j]Mt 25:46 [k]Lk 10:25
19:17 [l]Lev 18:5

4“Haven’t you read,” he replied, “that at the beginning the Creator ‘made them male and female,’[a][b] 5and said, ‘For this reason a man will leave his father and mother and be united to his wife, and the two will become one flesh’[b]?[c] 6So they are no longer two, but one flesh. Therefore what God has joined together, let no one separate.”

7“Why then,” they asked, “did Moses command that a man give his wife a certificate of divorce and send her away?”[d]

8Jesus replied, “Moses permitted you to divorce your wives because your hearts were hard. But it was not this way from the beginning. 9I tell you that anyone who divorces his wife, except for sexual immorality, and marries another woman commits adultery.”[e]

10The disciples said to him, “If this is the situation between a husband and wife, it is better not to marry.”

11Jesus replied, “Not everyone can accept this word, but only those to whom it has been given.[f] 12For there are eunuchs who were born that way, and there are eunuchs who have been made eunuchs by others—and there are those who choose to live like eunuchs for the sake of the kingdom of heaven. The one who can accept this should accept it.”

The Little Children and Jesus

19:13-15pp — Mk 10:13-16; Lk 18:15-17

13Then people brought little children to Jesus for him to place his hands on them[g] and pray for them. But the disciples rebuked them.

14Jesus said, “Let the little children come to me, and do not hinder them, for the kingdom of heaven belongs[h] to such as these.”[i] 15When he had placed his hands on them, he went on from there.

The Rich and the Kingdom of God

19:16-29pp — Mk 10:17-30; Lk 18:18-30

16Just then a man came up to Jesus and asked, “Teacher, what good thing must I do to get eternal life[j]?”[k]

17“Why do you ask me about what is good?” Jesus replied. “There is only One who is good. If you want to enter life, keep the commandments.”[l]

[a] *4* Gen. 1:27   [b] *5* Gen. 2:24

19:4–5 Jesus quotes Gen 1:27 and 2:24, God’s purposes for marriage from the very dawn of creation.

19:5 leave his father and mother and be united to his wife. Transfer their most important human allegiance from parents to spouse. **become one flesh.** Consummate that commitment with sexual intercourse and close, loving fellowship.

19:6 what God has joined together. Applies to the newly formed marital union. Nothing limits this to Christian marriages or any other subset of marriages, as if there were certain married couples that God has not joined. **let no one separate.** Refers to husband, wife, and any other third party.

19:7–8 divorce. Divorce was permitted under various circumstances in OT times, but Jesus says this was a concession to the Israelites, whose “hearts were hard” (v. 8). “But it was not this way from the beginning” (v. 8), before the giving of the law, and so it is not to be this way among Jesus’ followers. Hardheartedness, therefore, cannot be a legitimate reason for divorce in the age of the new covenant. Jesus is reaffirming God’s original intention that marriage be permanent and lifelong.

19:9 See notes on 5:31,32. The person “commits adultery” because divorce in antiquity was typically for the purpose of remarriage. But even the rupture of the first marriage by itself may be a metaphor for adultery, just as faithless Israel was likened to a prostitute throughout the OT (see especially Hosea). **except for sexual immorality.** The followers of both Hillel and Shammai, two Pharisaic contemporaries of Jesus, agreed that sexual infidelity required divorce, as did all known Greco-Roman views of the day. Jesus, however, merely *permits* rather than *requires* divorce. Some have argued that “divorces” here means merely separation; others, that divorce but not remarriage is what is permitted. Others translate “sexual immorality” as “premarital intercourse,” or “incest.” But all of these alternatives appeal to much less common meanings of the words in question and do not fit the context as naturally.

19:10 Jesus’ position is more stringent than either of the two main Pharisaic approaches (see notes on 5:31,32). Little wonder the disciples think it might be “better not to marry.”

19:11 Not everyone can accept this. Jesus acknowledges that some have indeed been given the gift of celibacy, but he recognizes that many cannot accept this lot in life.

19:12 eunuchs. There are literal eunuchs, either born deformed or castrated at some point in their lives, and metaphoric eunuchs, those who voluntarily adopt the (celibate) single life “for the sake of the kingdom” (cf. 1 Cor 7:32–35). Those who can “accept” this last option should do so.

19:13 children. They were second-class citizens in antiquity. A great rabbi shouldn’t be bothered by them, Jesus’ disciples naturally think. Jesus disagrees.

19:14 for the kingdom ... belongs to such as these. The point is not that children are automatically saved but that those who acknowledge their dependence on God, like many children do, can then come to Jesus in the right spirit. Cf. 18:1–5.

19:15 placed his hands on them. Conveyed a blessing from God.

19:16–36 This is the only account in the entire Bible in which someone is asked to sell all their possessions, so it is not a guide for everyone in every circumstance. See, e.g., Luke 19:1–10,11–27 for different approaches to money. But the person who is too quickly relieved by this observation might be precisely the kind of person God *is* calling to imitate this young man.

19:16 The questioner is concerned about a key Jewish issue: the relationship between good works and eternal life.

19:17 Matthew probably phrases this verse to avoid the potential

18“Which ones?” he inquired.
Jesus replied, “‘You shall not murder, you shall not commit adultery,[m] you shall not steal, you shall
not give false testimony, 19honor your father and mother,’[a][n] and ‘love your neighbor as yourself.’[b]”[o]
20“All these I have kept,” the young man said. “What do I still lack?”
21Jesus answered, “If you want to be perfect,[p] go, sell your possessions and give to the poor,[q] and you
will have treasure in heaven.[r] Then come, follow me.”
22When the young man heard this, he went away sad, because he had great wealth.
23Then Jesus said to his disciples, “Truly I tell you, it is hard for someone who is rich[s] to enter the
kingdom of heaven. 24Again I tell you, it is easier for a camel to go through the eye of a needle than for
someone who is rich to enter the kingdom of God.”
25When the disciples heard this, they were greatly astonished and asked, “Who then can be saved?”
26Jesus looked at them and said, “With man this is impossible, but with God all things are
possible.”[t]
27Peter answered him, “We have left everything to follow you![u] What then will there be for us?”
28Jesus said to them, “Truly I tell you, at the renewal of all things, when the Son of Man sits on his
glorious throne,[v] you who have followed me will also sit on twelve thrones, judging the twelve tribes
of Israel.[w] 29And everyone who has left houses or brothers or sisters or father or mother or wife[c] or
children or fields for my sake will receive a hundred times as much and will inherit eternal life.[x] 30But
many who are first will be last, and many who are last will be first.[y]

19:18 [m] Jas 2:11
19:19 [n] Ex 20:12-16; Dt 5:16-20 [o] Lev 19:18; Mt 5:43
19:21 [p] Mt 5:48 [q] Lk 12:33; Ac 2:45; 4:34-35 [r] Mt 6:20
19:23 [s] Mt 13:22; 1Ti 6:9,10
19:26 [t] Ge 18:14; Job 42:2; Jer 32:17; Zec 8:6; Lk 1:37; 18:27; Ro 4:21
19:27 [u] Mt 4:19
19:28 [v] Mt 20:21; 25:31 [w] Lk 22:28-30; Rev 3:21; 4:4; 20:4
19:29 [x] Mt 6:33; 25:46
19:30 [y] Mt 20:16; Mk 10:31; Lk 13:30
20:1 [z] Mt 13:24 [a] Mt 21:28,33

The Parable of the Workers in the Vineyard

20 “For the kingdom of heaven is like[z] a landowner who went out early in the morning to hire
workers for his vineyard.[a] 2He agreed to pay them a denarius[d] for the day and sent them into
his vineyard.
3“About nine in the morning he went out and saw others standing in the marketplace doing nothing. 4He told them, ‘You also go and work in my vineyard, and I will pay you whatever is right.’ 5So
they went.

a 19 Exodus 20:12-16; Deut. 5:16-20 *b 19* Lev. 19:18 *c 29* Some manuscripts do not have *or wife.* *d 2* A denarius was the usual daily wage of a day laborer.

misunderstanding (see Mark 10:18) that imagines Jesus to be denying his goodness.

19:18–20 As in the Sermon on the Mount (especially 5:21–48), the Ten Commandments prove central to God's will. But the young man claims to have kept them all, yet still senses a lack. It could appear that Jesus is suggesting obedience to the law can merit eternal life, but more likely he is setting the man up to realize what he is still missing.

19:21–22 Jesus recognizes the man's great wealth is what is really standing in the way of true discipleship, so he calls him to sell his goods and give to the poor. These commands must not be separated from their positive counterpart: "Then come, follow me" (v. 21). Altruism without faith in Jesus does not lead to "treasure in heaven" (v. 21). That the man "went away sad" (v. 22) demonstrates the accuracy of Jesus' diagnosis and the unwillingness of the man to accept the prescribed treatment for his failings.

19:24 eye of a needle. Some have suggested that there was a narrow "eye of a needle" gate in Jerusalem that camels could go through only with great difficulty. But this notion did not develop until a millennium after the time of Christ. Jesus' words form a metaphor, pure and simple. It is harder for the "rich to enter the kingdom" (v. 23) than for the largest common animal in the ancient Middle East to go through the smallest common aperture. In other words, it is humanly "impossible, but with God all things are possible" (v. 26).

19:27 Unlike the rich young man, the disciples have left their jobs and resources behind to follow Jesus. Peter understandably asks what is in it for them.

19:28 Jesus promises that when he returns ("at the renewal of all things"), the 12 apostles will "sit on twelve thrones, judging the twelve tribes of Israel." How believers help Christ in final judgment is never described, but 1 Cor 6:3 suggests that even the rather immature Corinthian Christians would be involved in judging angels. The context of the apostles' sacrifice versus the rich man's refusal to sacrifice, however, suggests that the judgment here is the condemnation of that portion of Israel that does not believe in Jesus. That the 12 apostles oversee the fate of the 12 tribes suggests that the (still Jewish) leadership of the Jesus movement is replacing the current, corrupt leadership in Israel.

19:29 Even in this life, those who have left family and possessions for Christ's sake "receive a hundred times as much" when the members of the family of God share with each other.

19:30 many who are first will be last. Like the rich young man, those who are first in this life will be last in the next. **many who are last will be first.** Like the disciples, those who are last in this life will be first in the coming fullness of the kingdom.

20:1–16 *The Parable of the Workers in the Vineyard.* Jesus' story further illustrates the great reversal of 19:30. Verses 13–16 enunciate the three lessons of the parable: God is never unfair, he is very generous, and all disciples are fundamentally equal in his sight.

20:1 workers. Many agricultural workers were day laborers, hoping each day that someone would hire them to work on a nearby farm.

20:2 denarius. The minimum day's wage.

20:3–7 If there was a bumper crop and bad weather required a fast harvest, a farmer might need quite a bit of extra help on a given day, though it would be unusual for him to return to a central marketplace this frequently. No specific amount is promised to these partial-day workers other than "whatever is right" (v. 4).

20:8 [b]Lev 19:13; Dt 24:15
20:11 [c]Jnh 4:1
20:12 [d]Jnh 4:8; Lk 12:55; Jas 1:11
20:13 [e]Mt 22:12; 26:50
20:15 [f]Dt 15:9; Mk 7:22
20:16 [g]Mt 19:30
20:18 [h]Lk 9:51 [i]Mt 8:20 [j]Mt 16:21; 27:1,2
20:19 [k]Mt 16:21 [l]Ac 2:23 [m]Mt 16:21 [n]Mt 16:21
20:20 [o]Mt 4:21 [p]Mt 8:2
20:21 [q]Mt 19:28
20:22 [r]Isa 51:17,22; Jer 49:12; Mt 26:39,42; Mk 14:36; Lk 22:42; Jn 18:11
20:23 [s]Ac 12:2; Rev 1:9

"He went out again about noon and about three in the afternoon and did the same thing. 6About five in the afternoon he went out and found still others standing around. He asked them, 'Why have you been standing here all day long doing nothing?'

7" 'Because no one has hired us,' they answered.

"He said to them, 'You also go and work in my vineyard.'

8"When evening came,[b] the owner of the vineyard said to his foreman, 'Call the workers and pay them their wages, beginning with the last ones hired and going on to the first.'

9"The workers who were hired about five in the afternoon came and each received a denarius. 10So when those came who were hired first, they expected to receive more. But each one of them also received a denarius. 11When they received it, they began to grumble[c] against the landowner. 12'These who were hired last worked only one hour,' they said, 'and you have made them equal to us who have borne the burden of the work and the heat[d] of the day.'

13"But he answered one of them, 'I am not being unfair to you, friend.[e] Didn't you agree to work for a denarius? 14Take your pay and go. I want to give the one who was hired last the same as I gave you. 15Don't I have the right to do what I want with my own money? Or are you envious because I am generous?'[f]

16"So the last will be first, and the first will be last."[g]

Jesus Predicts His Death a Third Time

20:17-19pp — Mk 10:32-34; Lk 18:31-33

17Now Jesus was going up to Jerusalem. On the way, he took the Twelve aside and said to them, 18"We are going up to Jerusalem,[h] and the Son of Man[i] will be delivered over to the chief priests and the teachers of the law.[j] They will condemn him to death 19and will hand him over to the Gentiles to be mocked and flogged[k] and crucified.[l] On the third day[m] he will be raised to life!"[n]

A Mother's Request

20:20-28pp — Mk 10:35-45

20Then the mother of Zebedee's sons[o] came to Jesus with her sons and, kneeling down,[p] asked a favor of him.

21"What is it you want?" he asked.

She said, "Grant that one of these two sons of mine may sit at your right and the other at your left in your kingdom."[q]

22"You don't know what you are asking," Jesus said to them. "Can you drink the cup[r] I am going to drink?"

"We can," they answered.

23Jesus said to them, "You will indeed drink from my cup,[s] but to sit at my right or left is not for me to grant. These places belong to those for whom they have been prepared by my Father."

20:8–12 The reversal of order in which the workers are paid enables those who worked longer to see how much those who worked less were paid. The full-day workers expected to receive more than the denarius they were originally promised, so they "grumble[d] against the landowner" (v. 11) when they did not get it.
20:13–15 The employer reminded them that he in no way cheated them out of what he had promised. He was just choosing to be generous to others. Had the full-day workers not known what the partial-day workers received, they would never have felt any injustice.
20:15 are you envious because I am generous? Captures the force of the Greek idiom that literally reads, "Is your eye evil because I am good?" Evil eyes were often believed to be able to place curses on others.
20:16 last will be first ... first will be last. The parable ends with the same two-part saying as in 19:30 (see note there), only the order of the parts has been reversed to correspond to the order of payment in the story. In reality, because all the workers are paid the same, they all wind up equal.
20:17–19 Jesus predicts his death a third time (see notes on 16:21–28; 17:22–23). Here Jesus supplies the fullest details about his coming suffering.
20:20–28 Although Matthew attributes the request for privileged positions in Christ's kingdom to "the mother of Zebedee's sons" (v. 20), Mark 10:35 attributes the request to Zebedee's sons, James and John, who were no doubt the true impetus behind their mother's request. Immediately after Jesus' third passion prediction (see Matt 20:17–19), the request reflects the height of arrogance and misunderstanding. They *will* have a privileged position, but it will be one of suffering, in keeping with Jesus' own mission.
20:21 sit at your right and ... at your left. Means to hold the first and second most powerful and honorable roles in God's reign after Jesus himself.
20:22 drink the cup. In the OT it often means to experience God's wrath (e.g., Job 21:20; Isa 51:17; Jer 25:15). Jesus' disciples will experience the wrath of other humans because of their allegiance to him. James will be martyred (Acts 12:2), and John will be exiled (Rev 1:9).
20:23 drink from my cup. See note on v. 22.

[24]When the ten heard about this, they were indignant[t] with the two brothers. [25]Jesus called them
together and said, "You know that the rulers of the Gentiles lord it over them, and their high officials
exercise authority over them. [26]Not so with you. Instead, whoever wants to become great among you
must be your servant,[u] [27]and whoever wants to be first must be your slave— [28]just as the Son of Man[v]
did not come to be served, but to serve,[w] and to give his life as a ransom[x] for many."

20:24 [t]Lk 22:24,25
20:26 [u]Mt 23:11; Mk 9:35
20:28 [v]Mt 8:20 [w]Lk 22:27; Jn 13:13-16; 2Co 8:9; Php 2:7 [x]Isa 53:10; Mt 26:28; 1Ti 2:6; Titus 2:14; Heb 9:28; 1Pe 1:18,19
20:30 [y]Mt 9:27
21:1 [z]Mt 24:3; 26:30; Mk 14:26; Lk 19:37; 21:37; 22:39; Jn 8:1; Ac 1:12
21:5 [a]Isa 62:11; Zec 9:9

Two Blind Men Receive Sight

20:29-34pp — Mk 10:46-52; Lk 18:35-43

[29]As Jesus and his disciples were leaving Jericho, a large crowd followed him. [30]Two blind men were
sitting by the roadside, and when they heard that Jesus was going by, they shouted, "Lord, Son of David,[y] have mercy on us!"

[31]The crowd rebuked them and told them to be quiet, but they shouted all the louder, "Lord, Son of David, have mercy on us!"

[32]Jesus stopped and called them. "What do you want me to do for you?" he asked.

[33]"Lord," they answered, "we want our sight."

[34]Jesus had compassion on them and touched their eyes. Immediately they received their sight and followed him.

Jesus Comes to Jerusalem as King

21:1-9pp — Mk 11:1-10; Lk 19:29-38
21:4-9pp — Jn 12:12-15

21 As they approached Jerusalem and came to Bethphage on the Mount of Olives,[z] Jesus sent two
disciples, [2]saying to them, "Go to the village ahead of you, and at once you will find a donkey
tied there, with her colt by her. Untie them and bring them to me. [3]If anyone says anything to you, say
that the Lord needs them, and he will send them right away."

[4]This took place to fulfill what was spoken through the prophet:

> [5]"Say to Daughter Zion,
> 'See, your king comes to you,
> gentle and riding on a donkey,
> and on a colt, the foal of a donkey.'"[a][a]

[a] 5 Zech. 9:9

20:24 indignant. The response of the other ten disciples, not because they are more virtuous, but because they would just as much like to hold such supposed places of honor.

20:25–27 Jesus' reign, however, is an upside-down kingdom. Self-serving rule characterizes pagan kingdoms, but God's people should exemplify "servant"—even "slave"—leadership. To follow Christ means to die to self.

20:28 Jesus' own mission was self-giving, not self-serving, as he came to die for the sins of humanity. **ransom.** The price paid to secure a slave's freedom. At the Passover (Exod 11–13) a ransom was paid to rescue the firstborn Israelites. **for many.** Probably alludes to Isa 53:12. **for.** Greek *anti* is a comparatively rare preposition that means "in the place of" or "in exchange for." This succinctly articulates the doctrine of the representative, substitutionary, atoning death of Jesus.

20:29–34 Matthew mentions two blind men, but Mark mentions only one blind man: Bartimaeus (Mark 10:46). But see note on Matt 8:28–34. This is the last miracle of healing Jesus performs during his earthly life. It closely resembles 9:27–31.

20:29 Jericho. Near the Jordan River, east of Jerusalem, just slightly removed from the site of the OT town with the same name. From there Jesus and his disciples would make their ascent to the holy city as the last leg of the journey begun in 19:1.

20:30,31 Lord, Son of David. See note on 15:22.

20:33 we want our sight. The kind of "mercy" (v. 31) the blind men desire is now specified. Many might have asked just for money (cf. Acts 3:3). Matthew does not normally state explicitly that "Jesus had compassion" (v. 34) for a sick person's malady; perhaps these men were in very dire need.

21:1—22:46 The so-called Triumphal Entry into Jerusalem (21:1–11) takes Jesus to the political, economic, and religious heart of first-century Judaism: the temple, where his protest (21:12–13), just like his subsequent curse on the fig tree (21:18–22), symbolizes the building's coming destruction. The temple authorities naturally ask Jesus by what authority he can cause such a disruption in its precincts (21:23–27). Although he does not answer directly, the subsequent triad of parables presents God's indictment on Israel's current leaders (21:28–32), followed by their sentence (21:33–46) and execution (22:1–14). Jesus then avoids a series of questions designed to trap him (22:15–40), after which he poses a question that his audience cannot answer (22:41–46).

21:1–11 To show he is the Messiah, Jesus deliberately fulfills the direct, predictive prophecy of Zech 9:9 by commandeering a donkey to ride as he enters the holy city.

21:1 Bethphage. A small village close to Bethany on the slopes of the Mount of Olives east/southeast of Jerusalem by perhaps less than a mile.

21:2–3 Jesus' instructions could reflect his special insight into people's thoughts or be a prearranged signal with a friend to avoid premature attention to his behavior.

21:5 gentle and riding on a donkey, and on a colt, the foal of a donkey. Some have thought that Matthew misread the parallelism of

21:8 [b] 2Ki 9:13
21:9 [c] ver 15; Mt 9:27 [d] Ps 118:26; Mt 23:39 [e] Lk 2:14
21:11 [f] Lk 7:16,39; 24:19; Jn 1:21,25; 6:14; 7:40
21:12 [g] Dt 14:26 [h] Ex 30:13 [i] Lev 1:14
21:13 [j] Isa 56:7 [k] Jer 7:11
21:14 [l] Mt 4:23
21:15 [m] ver 9; Mt 9:27 [n] Lk 19:39

6The disciples went and did as Jesus had instructed them. 7They brought the donkey and the colt
and placed their cloaks on them for Jesus to sit on. 8A very large crowd spread their cloaks[b] on the road,
while others cut branches from the trees and spread them on the road. 9The crowds that went ahead of
him and those that followed shouted,

> "Hosanna[a] to the Son of David!"[c]
>
> "Blessed is he who comes in the name of the Lord!"[bd]
>
> "Hosanna[a] in the highest heaven!"[e]

10When Jesus entered Jerusalem, the whole city was stirred and asked, "Who is this?"
11The crowds answered, "This is Jesus, the prophet[f] from Nazareth in Galilee."

Jesus at the Temple

21:12-16pp — Mk 11:15-18; Lk 19:45-47

12Jesus entered the temple courts and drove out all who were buying[g] and selling there. He overturned the tables of the money changers[h] and the benches of those selling doves.[i] 13"It is written,"
he said to them, " 'My house will be called a house of prayer,'[cj] but you are making it 'a den of
robbers.'[d]"[k]
14The blind and the lame came to him at the temple, and he healed them.[l] 15But when the chief
priests and the teachers of the law saw the wonderful things he did and the children shouting in the
temple courts, "Hosanna to the Son of David,"[m] they were indignant.[n]

[a] 9 A Hebrew expression meaning "Save!" which became an exclamation of praise; also in verse 15
[b] 9 Psalm 118:25,26 [c] 13 Isaiah 56:7 [d] 13 Jer. 7:11

the prophecy and therefore invented an absurd scene in which Jesus straddles two animals (v. 7). But verses 2 and 7 say there *were* two animals. A previously unridden "colt" (Mark 11:2) would not be ridden easily without its mother present, making Matthew think of the prophecy of Zech 9:9.

21:7 cloaks. Were draped on both animals, but Jesus probably sat only on the colt.

21:8–11 The entire scene recalls the welcoming of Israelite kings in earlier days, especially with the strewing of palm branches (John 12:13). The accolades come from Ps 118:25–26. **Hosanna.** Means "God, save [us]." But those hoping for a liberator from the Romans miss the significance of the humble beast of burden. Residents of Jerusalem unfamiliar with this Galilean "prophet" (v. 11) would naturally wonder about his identity.

21:12–17 The temple area occupied by the money changers was probably a fairly small corner of the court of the Gentiles. Jewish tradition suggests this enterprise had only recently been moved there from the Kidron Valley, which was just below and to the east of the temple. Temple taxes had to be paid and sacrificial animals had to be purchased with Jewish currency, so monies had to be exchanged. But Jesus opposes the practice in the only portion of the temple in which Gentiles could come to pray to the God of Israel (cf. Isa 56:6–7).

The cleansing of the temple by Jesus is reminiscent of how Davidic kings like Hezekiah (2 Chr 29–31) and Josiah (2 Chr 34–35) repaired the temple prior to the celebration of Passover. The unusual reference to the blind and the lame (Matt 21:14) recalls Lev 21:18 and the prohibition there against such entering the sanctuary. By healing them, Jesus removes any barrier to them being within the temple.

In the Synoptic Gospels the clearing of the temple occurs during the last week of Jesus' ministry; in John it takes place during the first few months of Jesus' ministry (John 2:13–17). Two explanations are possible: (1) There were two clearings, one at the beginning and the other at the end of Jesus' public ministry. (2) There was only one clearing, which took place during Passion Week but which John placed at the beginning of his account for theological reasons—to show that God's judgment was operative through the Messiah from the outset of Jesus' ministry. However, different details are present in the two accounts (the selling of cattle and sheep in John 2:14, the whip in John 2:15, and the statements of Jesus in Matt 21:13; John 2:16). From Matthew's and Luke's accounts we might assume that the clearing of the temple took place on Sunday, following the so-called Triumphal Entry (Matt 21:1–11). But Mark 11:12,15–19 clearly indicates that it was on Monday. Matthew often compressed narratives.

21:13 den of robbers. Cf. Jer 7:11. Could mean a place for Jewish freedom fighters to hide out. **robbers.** Translates the same word (*lēstēs*) that is rendered one "leading a rebellion" in 26:55.

21:14 Jesus wants all people—the sick, injured, and even little children—to be able to praise God freely, as in Ps 8:2 (see the Septuagint, the pre-Christian Greek translation of the OT), and be healed.

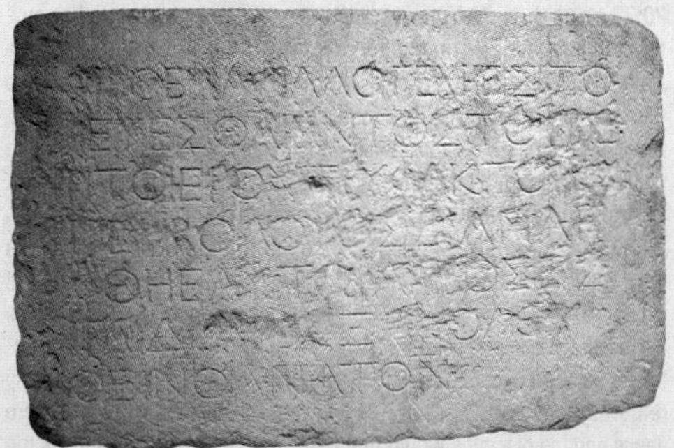

Greek inscription prohibiting Gentiles from entering the inner courtyard of the temple.

Todd Bolen/www.BiblePlaces, taken at the Istanbul Archaeological Museum

[16]"Do you hear what these children are saying?" they asked him.
"Yes," replied Jesus, "have you never read,

"'From the lips of children and infants
you, Lord, have called forth your praise'[a]?"[o]

[17]And he left them and went out of the city to Bethany,[p] where he spent the night.

21:16 [o]Ps 8:2
21:17 [p]Mt 26:6; Mk 11:1; Lk 24:50; Jn 11:1,18; 12:1
21:19 [q]Isa 34:4; Jer 8:13
21:21 [r]Mt 17:20; Lk 17:6; 1Co 13:2; Jas 1:6
21:22 [s]Mt 7:7

Jesus Curses a Fig Tree

21:18-22pp — Mk 11:12-14,20-24

[18]Early in the morning, as Jesus was on his way back to the city, he was hungry. [19]Seeing a fig tree
by the road, he went up to it but found nothing on it except leaves. Then he said to it, "May you never
bear fruit again!" Immediately the tree withered.[q]
[20]When the disciples saw this, they were amazed. "How did the fig tree wither so quickly?" they asked.
[21]Jesus replied, "Truly I tell you, if you have faith and do not doubt,[r] not only can you do what was
done to the fig tree, but also you can say to this mountain, 'Go, throw yourself into the sea,' and it will
be done. [22]If you believe, you will receive whatever you ask for[s] in prayer."

[a] *16* Psalm 8:2 (see Septuagint)

21:17 Bethany. Just slightly farther down the road from Bethphage (see note on v. 1), away from Jerusalem.
21:18–22 Jesus appears to work this rare miracle of destruction solely because he was hungry and the tree had no fruit. Mark 11:13 explains that "it was not the season for figs," suggesting we should look for a less obvious explanation of the action. Sitting under one's own fig tree became a common OT image of the Israelite enjoying freedom and prosperity in the land (e.g., 1 Kgs 4:25; 2 Kgs 18:31; Isa 36:16; Mic 4:4; Zech 3:10). In this context of judgment on Israel, the "withered" fig tree most likely stands for the nation's coming destruction. Mark 11:12–14,20–25 spreads the action over a two-day period, but even if the fig tree did not shrivel up the instant Jesus cursed it (Matt 21:19), a tree withering that quickly could still be said to have withered "immediately."
21:21 this mountain. Refers either to the Mount of Olives or to Mount Zion (the temple mount), depending on where Jesus was on the road between Bethany and Jerusalem. If he is pointing to the Mount of Olives, he may have Zech 14:4 in mind, in which the Messiah stands on the mountain and it splits in two. If, as may be more likely, he is pointing to the temple mount, then he is anticipating the destruction of the temple and its sacrificial system.
21:22 whatever you ask for in prayer. Must be understood in context. Jesus is not offering a "blank check" for those with enough faith but is promising that those with faith will see the end of this age and the coming of the next one.

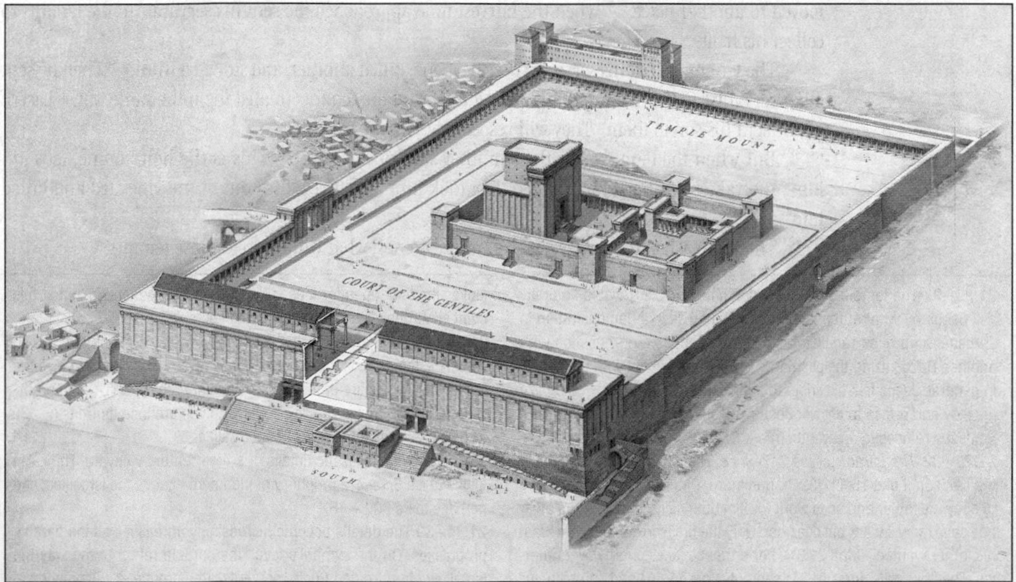

The temple area occupied by the money changers was probably a fairly small corner of the Court of the Gentiles.
Fernando G. Baptista/National Geographic Creative

21:23 [t]Ac 4:7; 7:27
21:26 [u]Mt 11:9; Mk 6:20
21:28 [v]ver 33; Mt 20:1
21:31 [w]Lk 7:29 [x]Lk 7:50
21:32 [y]Mt 3:1-12 [z]Lk 3:12,13; 7:29 [a]Lk 7:36-50 [b]Lk 7:30
21:33 [c]Ps 80:8 [d]Isa 5:1-7 [e]Mt 25:14,15
21:34 [f]Mt 22:3
21:35 [g]2Ch 24:21; Mt 23:34,37; Heb 11:36,37
21:36 [h]Mt 22:4
21:38 [i]Heb 1:2 [j]Mt 12:14 [k]Ps 2:8

The Authority of Jesus Questioned

21:23-27pp — Mk 11:27-33; Lk 20:1-8

23 Jesus entered the temple courts, and, while he was teaching, the chief priests and the elders of the people came to him. "By what authority[t] are you doing these things?" they asked. "And who gave you this authority?"

24 Jesus replied, "I will also ask you one question. If you answer me, I will tell you by what authority I am doing these things. 25 John's baptism — where did it come from? Was it from heaven, or of human origin?"

They discussed it among themselves and said, "If we say, 'From heaven,' he will ask, 'Then why didn't you believe him?' 26 But if we say, 'Of human origin' — we are afraid of the people, for they all hold that John was a prophet."[u]

27 So they answered Jesus, "We don't know."

Then he said, "Neither will I tell you by what authority I am doing these things.

The Parable of the Two Sons

28 "What do you think? There was a man who had two sons. He went to the first and said, 'Son, go and work today in the vineyard.'[v]

29 " 'I will not,' he answered, but later he changed his mind and went.

30 "Then the father went to the other son and said the same thing. He answered, 'I will, sir,' but he did not go.

31 "Which of the two did what his father wanted?"

"The first," they answered.

Jesus said to them, "Truly I tell you, the tax collectors[w] and the prostitutes[x] are entering the kingdom of God ahead of you. 32 For John came to you to show you the way of righteousness,[y] and you did not believe him, but the tax collectors[z] and the prostitutes[a] did. And even after you saw this, you did not repent[b] and believe him.

The Parable of the Tenants

21:33-46pp — Mk 12:1-12; Lk 20:9-19

33 "Listen to another parable: There was a landowner who planted[c] a vineyard. He put a wall around it, dug a winepress in it and built a watchtower.[d] Then he rented the vineyard to some farmers and moved to another place.[e] 34 When the harvest time approached, he sent his servants[f] to the tenants to collect his fruit.

35 "The tenants seized his servants; they beat one, killed another, and stoned a third.[g] 36 Then he sent other servants[h] to them, more than the first time, and the tenants treated them the same way. 37 Last of all, he sent his son to them. 'They will respect my son,' he said.

38 "But when the tenants saw the son, they said to each other, 'This is the heir.[i] Come, let's kill him[j] and take his inheritance.'[k] 39 So they took him and threw him out of the vineyard and killed him.

40 "Therefore, when the owner of the vineyard comes, what will he do to those tenants?"

21:23–27 The temple authorities (see note on 16:21) would naturally ask Jesus by what authority he had initiated such a demonstration in Jerusalem. In good rabbinic fashion, he counters their question with another. Recognizing the popularity of John the Baptist with the people in general, Jesus ties his origin to John's. But the authorities recognize his ploy and refuse to answer Jesus' question, pretending not to know. So Jesus refuses to answer them.

21:28–32 *The Parable of the Two Sons.* This little parable resembles the lost son (Luke 15:11–32) in miniature. One son starts out refusing to obey his father and go to work for him but finally complies. The other one says he will work but does not. Only the first son actually "did what his father wanted" (Matt 21:31). Performance takes priority over promise. The "tax collectors" (v. 31; see notes on 9:9,11) and "prostitutes" (v. 31) are like the first son; the temple authorities (v. 23) were like the second. The phrase "entering the kingdom of God ahead of you" (v. 31) leaves the door open for these religious leaders to come in, but at this point in Matthew's account they remain outside.

21:33–46 *The Parable of the Tenants.* Now Jesus likens the Jewish leaders listening to him to tenants of a vineyard who refuse to give the landowner "his share of the crop at harvest time" (v. 41). Christ promises to replace them with "a people who will produce its fruit" (v. 43): Jewish and Gentile followers of Jesus alike.

21:33 These are realistic details of a first-century vineyard. They also allude to Isa 5:1–7, a prophecy of judgment against the Israelites, and perhaps to Ps 80:8–16.

21:34–39 The details become increasingly unrealistic as the parable progresses. On the symbolic level, the parable refers to the way the Israelites often treated God's "servants" (the prophets), culminating in their execution of God's very "son" (Jesus).

21:40–46 Just as a vineyard owner would replace the wicked tenants

41“He will bring those wretches to a wretched end,”[l] they replied, “and he will rent the vineyard to other tenants,[m] who will give him his share of the crop at harvest time.”

42Jesus said to them, “Have you never read in the Scriptures:

“ ‘The stone the builders rejected
has become the cornerstone;
the Lord has done this,
and it is marvelous in our eyes’[a]?[n]

43“Therefore I tell you that the kingdom of God will be taken away from you[o] and given to a people who will produce its fruit. 44Anyone who falls on this stone will be broken to pieces; anyone on whom it falls will be crushed.”[b][p]

45When the chief priests and the Pharisees heard Jesus’ parables, they knew he was talking about them. 46They looked for a way to arrest him, but they were afraid of the crowd because the people held that he was a prophet.[q]

The Parable of the Wedding Banquet

22:2-14Ref — Lk 14:16-24

22 Jesus spoke to them again in parables, saying: 2“The kingdom of heaven is like[r] a king who prepared a wedding banquet for his son. 3He sent his servants[s] to those who had been invited to the banquet to tell them to come, but they refused to come.

4“Then he sent some more servants[t] and said, ‘Tell those who have been invited that I have prepared my dinner: My oxen and fattened cattle have been butchered, and everything is ready. Come to the wedding banquet.’

5“But they paid no attention and went off — one to his field, another to his business. 6The rest seized his servants, mistreated them and killed them. 7The king was enraged. He sent his army and destroyed those murderers[u] and burned their city.

8“Then he said to his servants, ‘The wedding banquet is ready, but those I invited did not deserve to come. 9So go to the street corners[v] and invite to the banquet anyone you find.’ 10So the servants went out into the streets and gathered all the people they could find, the bad as well as the good,[w] and the wedding hall was filled with guests.

11“But when the king came in to see the guests, he noticed a man there who was not wearing wedding clothes. 12He asked, ‘How did you get in here without wedding clothes, friend[x]?’ The man was speechless.

13“Then the king told the attendants, ‘Tie him hand and foot, and throw him outside, into the darkness, where there will be weeping and gnashing of teeth.’[y]

14“For many are invited, but few are chosen.”[z]

a *42* Psalm 118:22,23 *b* *44* Some manuscripts do not have verse 44.

21:41 [l] Mt 8:11,12 [m] Ac 13:46; 18:6; 28:28
21:42 [n] Ps 118:22,23; Ac 4:11; 1Pe 2:7
21:43 [o] Mt 8:12
21:44 [p] Lk 2:34
21:46 [q] ver 11,26
22:2 [r] Mt 13:24
22:3 [s] Mt 21:34
22:4 [t] Mt 21:36
22:7 [u] Lk 19:27
22:9 [v] Eze 21:21
22:10 [w] Mt 13:47,48
22:12 [x] Mt 20:13; 26:50
22:13 [y] Mt 8:12
22:14 [z] Rev 17:14

with faithful ones, God will replace the Jewish leaders with obedient followers, which for Matthew means all disciples of Jesus. Jesus quotes Ps 118:22–23, understood as Messianic prophecy in at least some Jewish circles, to bolster his claim.

21:42 cornerstone. Could also be a capstone. Both options seem to be in view in v. 44, because it is both a stone one can trip over and a stone that can fall on top of a person.

22:1–14 *The Parable of the Wedding Banquet.* If the parable of the two sons (21:28–32) indicts the Jewish leaders and the parable of the wicked tenants (21:33–44) announces their sentence, then this parable depicts their (spiritual) demise. For a similar parable, see Luke 14:16–24.

22:2–3 Much like a “save the date” wedding invitation, ancient Israelites told invitees the date of the wedding months in advance. The invitees had few legitimate excuses, then, for refusing to attend when that day arrived. The rich and powerful in the country would be the most likely invitees to a prince’s wedding festivities.

22:4–6 The banquet is ready with the finest fare an ancient king could offer. A second summons could scarcely be ignored. But these invitees prove at best extraordinarily rude and at worst murderous. By acting the way they do, they are essentially rejecting the king’s rule.

22:7–10 The insurrection must be squelched, and the king does so violently. But the party must go on, so he orders his servants to fill the wedding hall with whomever they can find, even with the riff-raff off the streets. Some have thought that these verses predict the destruction of Jerusalem in AD 70, but it was primarily the temple that was burned then, not the entire city. More likely these verses anticipate the fire of final judgment (cf., e.g., Amos 1:2,7,12; 2:2,5).

22:11–13 Perhaps the new guests are given time to go home and put on the proper clothes. Perhaps the king has the appropriate wedding attire to loan to those who cannot supply their own. At any rate, the speechless response of the man without the wedding garment suggests he knows he has no excuses. Not only overt rejection but also refusing to come to the banquet in the appropriate way excludes a person from the festivity. One must enter God’s kingdom on his terms rather than ours.

22:14 invited. Can also be “called,” but not in the sense Paul will later use it (e.g., Rom 8:29–30). Jesus’ call here can obviously be

22:16 [a]Mk 3:6
22:17 [b]Mt 17:25
22:21 [c]Ro 13:7
22:22 [d]Mk 12:12
22:23 [e]Ac 4:1 [f]Ac 23:8; 1Co 15:12
22:24 [g]Dt 25:5,6
22:29 [h]Jn 20:9
22:30 [i]Mt 24:38
22:32 [j]Ex 3:6; Ac 7:32
22:33 [k]Mt 7:28
22:34 [l]Ac 4:1
22:35 [m]Lk 7:30; 10:25; 11:45; 14:3

Paying the Imperial Tax to Caesar

22:15-22pp — Mk 12:13-17; Lk 20:20-26

[15]Then the Pharisees went out and laid plans to trap him in his words. [16]They sent their disciples to him along with the Herodians.[a] "Teacher," they said, "we know that you are a man of integrity and that you teach the way of God in accordance with the truth. You aren't swayed by others, because you pay no attention to who they are. [17]Tell us then, what is your opinion? Is it right to pay the imperial tax[ab] to Caesar or not?"

[18]But Jesus, knowing their evil intent, said, "You hypocrites, why are you trying to trap me? [19]Show me the coin used for paying the tax." They brought him a denarius, [20]and he asked them, "Whose image is this? And whose inscription?"

[21]"Caesar's," they replied.

Then he said to them, "So give back to Caesar what is Caesar's,[c] and to God what is God's."

[22]When they heard this, they were amazed. So they left him and went away.[d]

Marriage at the Resurrection

22:23-33pp — Mk 12:18-27; Lk 20:27-40

[23]That same day the Sadducees,[e] who say there is no resurrection,[f] came to him with a question. [24]"Teacher," they said, "Moses told us that if a man dies without having children, his brother must marry the widow and raise up offspring for him.[g] [25]Now there were seven brothers among us. The first one married and died, and since he had no children, he left his wife to his brother. [26]The same thing happened to the second and third brother, right on down to the seventh. [27]Finally, the woman died. [28]Now then, at the resurrection, whose wife will she be of the seven, since all of them were married to her?"

[29]Jesus replied, "You are in error because you do not know the Scriptures[h] or the power of God. [30]At the resurrection people will neither marry nor be given in marriage;[i] they will be like the angels in heaven. [31]But about the resurrection of the dead—have you not read what God said to you, [32]'I am the God of Abraham, the God of Isaac, and the God of Jacob'[b]?[j] He is not the God of the dead but of the living."

[33]When the crowds heard this, they were astonished at his teaching.[k]

The Greatest Commandment

22:34-40pp — Mk 12:28-31

[34]Hearing that Jesus had silenced the Sadducees,[l] the Pharisees got together. [35]One of them, an expert in the law,[m] tested him with this question: [36]"Teacher, which is the greatest commandment in the Law?"

[37]Jesus replied: " 'Love the Lord your God with all your heart and with all your soul and with all your

[a] *17* A special tax levied on subject peoples, not on Roman citizens [b] *32* Exodus 3:6

rejected. **chosen.** In this context refers to those who accept and do so on God's terms.

22:15–48 Three more groups of questioners try to trap Jesus in his words (vv. 15–40), but he turns the tables on them (vv. 41–46). The use of the Greek word for "test/trap/tempt" suggests a link with Satan.

22:15–22 Pharisees objected to paying taxes to Rome. Herodians, who were supporters of the line of Herods Rome had installed as client kings in Israel, supported paying them. However Jesus answered their question, one of these groups would be upset. The preface to their question (v. 16) was simply an attempt to curry favor. Jews paid the imperial tax to Rome as well as their own tithes and temple tax. Jesus' reply "amazed" them (v. 22) as he declared, "So give back to Caesar what is Caesar's, and to God what is God's" (v. 21). While some think that Jesus was prohibiting any form of tribute to the state because ultimately nothing belonged to the emperor but everything belongs to God, this would have meant he sided entirely with the Pharisees. More probably, Jesus was endorsing support of the state as part of obedience to God (cf. Rom 13:1). But if the two conflict, God's will always supersedes the demands of human authorities (Acts 5:29).

22:23–33 Sadducees were the one group of Jews who did not believe in bodily resurrection, just immortality of the soul, because they thought doctrine had to come from the law (Genesis–Deuteronomy). They mock the very concept of bodily resurrection with the extreme example of a woman who had seven husbands, all brothers, because none had fulfilled the intention of the levirate laws by which a childless widow would marry a brother of the deceased to raise up children and preserve the family line (Deut 25:5–10). To whom would she be married in the age to come? Jesus replies with two points: (1) The example is baseless because people will not be married in heaven. Presumably this renders sexual and family relationships obsolete because all God's people will enjoy perfect fellowship with each other. (2) Support for resurrection from the law comes from Exod 3:6,15–16. If God in the time of Moses speaks of himself as the God of the patriarchs, they must be alive, because "he is not the God of the dead but of the living" (Matt 22:31).

22:34–40 The final questioner, an expert in the law, naturally asks what the most important commandment is. Jesus replies with the double love command, which encapsulates the entire Hebrew Bible ("all the Law and the Prophets," v. 40). Loving God with every aspect of one's being (Deut 6:5) and loving one's neighbor as oneself (Lev 19:18) forms the very core of Christian ethics.

mind.'[a][n] [38]This is the first and greatest commandment. [39]And the second is like it: 'Love your neighbor
as yourself.'[b][o] [40]All the Law and the Prophets hang on these two commandments."[p]

Whose Son Is the Messiah?

22:41-46pp — Mk 12:35-37; Lk 20:41-44

[41]While the Pharisees were gathered together, Jesus asked them, [42]"What do you think about the
Messiah? Whose son is he?"

"The son of David,"[q] they replied.

[43]He said to them, "How is it then that David, speaking by the Spirit, calls him 'Lord'? For he says,

[44]" 'The Lord said to my Lord:
"Sit at my right hand
until I put your enemies
under your feet." '[c][r]

[45]If then David calls him 'Lord,' how can he be his son?" [46]No one could say a word in reply, and from
that day on no one dared to ask him any more questions.[s]

A Warning Against Hypocrisy

23:1-7pp — Mk 12:38,39; Lk 20:45,46
23:37-39pp — Lk 13:34,35

23 Then Jesus said to the crowds and to his disciples: [2]"The teachers of the law[t] and the Pharisees
sit in Moses' seat. [3]So you must be careful to do everything they tell you. But do not do what
they do, for they do not practice what they preach. [4]They tie up heavy, cumbersome loads and put them
on other people's shoulders, but they themselves are not willing to lift a finger to move them.[u]

[5]"Everything they do is done for people to see:[v] They make their phylacteries[d][w] wide and the tassels
on their garments[x] long; [6]they love the place of honor at banquets and the most important seats in
the synagogues;[y] [7]they love to be greeted with respect in the marketplaces and to be called 'Rabbi' by
others.[z]

[8]"But you are not to be called 'Rabbi,' for you have one Teacher, and you are all brothers. [9]And do not
call anyone on earth 'father,' for you have one Father,[a] and he is in heaven. [10]Nor are you to be called
instructors, for you have one Instructor, the Messiah. [11]The greatest among you will be your servant.[b]
[12]For those who exalt themselves will be humbled, and those who humble themselves will be exalted.[c]

a 37 Deut. 6:5 *b 39* Lev. 19:18 *c 44* Psalm 110:1 *d 5* That is, boxes containing Scripture verses, worn on forehead and arm

22:37 [n]Dt 6:5
22:39 [o]Lev 19:18; Mt 5:43; 19:19; Gal 5:14
22:40 [p]Mt 7:12
22:42 [q]Mt 9:27
22:44 [r]Ps 110:1; Ac 2:34,35; 1Co 15:25; Heb 1:13; 10:13
22:46 [s]Mk 12:34; Lk 20:40
23:2 [t]Ezr 7:6,25; Ne 8:4
23:4 [u]Lk 11:46; Ac 15:10; Gal 6:13
23:5 [v]Mt 6:1,2,5,16 [w]Ex 13:9; Dt 6:8 [x]Nu 15:38; Dt 22:12
23:6 [y]Lk 11:43; 14:7; 20:46
23:7 [z]ver 8; Mk 9:5; 10:51; Jn 1:38,49
23:9 [a]Mal 1:6; Mt 7:11
23:11 [b]Mt 20:26; Mk 9:35
23:12 [c]Lk 14:11

22:41–46 Having silenced his opponents, Jesus now poses a question himself: Whose son is the Messiah? In Ps 110:1, David, the king and highest human authority in Israel, speaking under inspiration, declares, "The LORD says to my lord." The first "LORD" is naturally God, but who else is above David, except a divine Messiah? Those who argue that the Messiah must be merely an earthly descendant of David (i.e., his son) cannot explain how David can call him his master (i.e., his "lord"). Given Matthew's general interest in Jesus as the Son of David, this passage is very important, drawing attention to the fact that Jesus is someone greater than David.

23:1—25:46 *Woes and Warnings.* The fifth and final extended discourse of Jesus in Matthew (see also chs. 6–7; 10:5–42; 13:1–52; ch. 18) divides into two parts: Jesus' woes against the Jewish leaders in Jerusalem (23:1–39) and his warnings to the disciples about the destruction of the temple and his second coming (24:1—25:46)

23:1–39 Jesus pronounces woes against various religious leaders in Jerusalem. Verses 1–12 contrast the way Jesus' disciples should behave with the way the teachers of the law and the Pharisees act in public. Verses 13–32 contain a series of seven woes against these two groups for their hypocrisy. Verses 33–36 bring to a climax the judgment that will fall on this generation as a result. Verses 37–39 lament how often Jesus wished things could be different but the people were not willing.

23:1–12 Jesus gives a warning against hypocrisy. His followers should exercise servant leadership rather than vie for the greatest amount of public attention.

23:2 Moses' seat. The raised chair in certain synagogues where the rabbi would sit to deliver his sermon.

23:3 everything they tell you. Probably everything that is consistent with the Scripture read and expounded on a given Sabbath in the synagogue. **do not do what they do.** Do not imitate the Jewish leaders' behavior whenever "they do not practice what they preach."

23:4 heavy, cumbersome loads. Probably refers to some of the oral laws that continued to grow around the written law of Moses, especially in the areas of ritual purity, Sabbath-keeping, and separation from sinners.

23:5 phylacteries. See Exod 13:9,16; Deut 6:8; 11:18; however, these verses originally were probably meant to be understood metaphorically. Only later were they interpreted literally. **tassels.** See note on 14:36.

23:8–10 Given the contrast with v. 7, the point is not that Christians can never use honorific titles but that they must not expect or demand them, much less revel in them. To avoid this temptation, it is probably best to use them as little as possible.

23:12 For an excellent illustration, see Luke 18:9–14.

23:13 [d] ver 15,23,25,27, 29 [e] Lk 11:52
23:15 [f] Ac 2:11; 6:5; 13:43 [g] Mt 5:22
23:16 [h] ver 24; Mt 15:14 [i] Mt 5:33-35
23:17 [j] Ex 30:29
23:19 [k] Ex 29:37
23:21 [l] 1Ki 8:13; Ps 26:8
23:22 [m] Ps 11:4; Mt 5:34
23:23 [n] Lev 27:30 [o] Mic 6:8; Lk 11:42
23:24 [p] ver 16
23:25 [q] Mk 7:4 [r] Lk 11:39
23:27 [s] Lk 11:44; Ac 23:3
23:29 [t] Lk 11:47,48

Seven Woes on the Teachers of the Law and the Pharisees

13 "Woe to you, teachers of the law and Pharisees, you hypocrites![d] You shut the door of the kingdom of
heaven in people's faces. You yourselves do not enter, nor will you let those enter who are trying to.[e] [14][a]
15 "Woe to you, teachers of the law and Pharisees, you hypocrites! You travel over land and sea to
win a single convert,[f] and when you have succeeded, you make them twice as much a child of hell[g]
as you are.
16 "Woe to you, blind guides![h] You say, 'If anyone swears by the temple, it means nothing; but anyone
who swears by the gold of the temple is bound by that oath.'[i] 17 You blind fools! Which is greater: the gold,
or the temple that makes the gold sacred?[j] 18 You also say, 'If anyone swears by the altar, it means nothing;
but anyone who swears by the gift on the altar is bound by that oath.' 19 You blind men! Which is greater:
the gift, or the altar that makes the gift sacred?[k] 20 Therefore, anyone who swears by the altar swears
by it and by everything on it. 21 And anyone who swears by the temple swears by it and by the one who
dwells[l] in it. 22 And anyone who swears by heaven swears by God's throne and by the one who sits on it.[m]
23 "Woe to you, teachers of the law and Pharisees, you hypocrites! You give a tenth[n] of your spices—
mint, dill and cumin. But you have neglected the more important matters of the law—justice, mercy
and faithfulness.[o] You should have practiced the latter, without neglecting the former. 24 You blind
guides![p] You strain out a gnat but swallow a camel.
25 "Woe to you, teachers of the law and Pharisees, you hypocrites! You clean the outside of the cup
and dish,[q] but inside they are full of greed and self-indulgence.[r] 26 Blind Pharisee! First clean the inside
of the cup and dish, and then the outside also will be clean.
27 "Woe to you, teachers of the law and Pharisees, you hypocrites! You are like whitewashed tombs,[s]
which look beautiful on the outside but on the inside are full of the bones of the dead and everything
unclean. 28 In the same way, on the outside you appear to people as righteous but on the inside you are
full of hypocrisy and wickedness.
29 "Woe to you, teachers of the law and Pharisees, you hypocrites! You build tombs for the prophets[t]
and decorate the graves of the righteous. 30 And you say, 'If we had lived in the days of our ancestors, we

[a] *14* Some manuscripts include here words similar to Mark 12:40 and Luke 20:47.

23:13–32 Jesus pronounces seven woes on the teachers of the law and the Pharisees. The scribes and Pharisees comprised a very small portion of the Jewish populace, and Jesus is addressing only those present in the temple on this occasion. This one particular group of leaders, not the entire nation, were "hypocrites" (v. 13), i.e., play-actors.

23:13 Woe. "Alas" or "how unfortunate" for someone because of impending doom or judgment. By refusing to help others do God's will and/or by making it harder than God intended, they save neither themselves nor others. See notes on vv. 3,4.

23:15 convert. Jews in general did not proselytize widely, yet they often worked hard to convince a Gentile who showed interest in their religion (especially a "God-fearer" who came to the synagogue) to become a full-fledged convert. But if a person adopted a form of Judaism that could not save them, that convert was still lost, i.e., "a child of hell."

23:16–22 An elaborate hierarchy of oaths or vows grew up in the oral law. Swearing by God himself was completely binding, but swearing by other holy items could leave loopholes by which people might not have to keep their vows. Jesus points out that there should be no difference between swearing "by the temple" (v. 16) or "by the gold of the temple" (v. 16), "by the altar" (v. 18) or "by the gift on the altar" (v. 18). Swearing "by the temple" (v. 21) should be as binding as swearing by God because the temple is where God "dwells" (v. 21), just as swearing "by heaven" (v. 22) should be as binding as swearing by God because "God's throne" (v. 22) on which he sits resides in heaven (v. 22). "Blind guides" (v. 16), "blind fools" (v. 17), and "blind men" (v. 19) all stress how the Pharisees who were supposed to be Israel's teachers were themselves spiritually blind instead.

23:23 mint, dill and cumin. Spices derived from plants. When Israelites cultivated them, a strict interpretation of Lev 27:30 required them to tithe ("give a tenth") on every one of the crops that their land produced. Jesus rejects these Jewish leaders' inversion of the law's priorities because they have "neglected the more important matters of the law—justice, mercy and faithfulness" (cf. Mic 6:8).

23:24 You strain out a gnat but swallow a camel. Involves an Aramaic play on words. "Gnat" is *qalmā*ʾ and "camel" is *gamlā*ʾ. The point is the same as in the previous verse: they scrupulously obey legal minutiae but flagrantly disobey the law's central tenets.

23:25–28 The contrast between the external and internal recalls 15:1–20.

23:25 You clean the outside of the cup and dish. Refers to the ritual washing of containers and plates from which one ate and drank. But if the person using them is internally corrupt ("full of greed and self-indulgence"), the external cleansing proves worthless.

23:27 whitewashed tombs. Decorated or painted tomb entrances or gravestones that nevertheless mask rotting corpses nearby. A person who stepped on a grave became ceremonially unclean (see Nu 19:16), so graves were whitewashed to make them easily visible, especially at night. They appeared clean and beautiful on the outside, but they were unclean on the inside—like these scribes and Pharisees.

23:29–32 By erecting attractive memorials for the prophets their ancestors murdered, these religious leaders appear to dissociate themselves from those heinous sins of the past. But in so doing they acknowledge that they are the biological descendants of these rebellious killers, and their coming involvement with Jesus' execution will demonstrate their spiritual link to their ancestors as well. With biting sarcasm, Jesus thus commands them to get on with their horrific plans and "complete what [their] ancestors started" (v. 32).

would not have taken part with them in shedding the blood of the prophets.' 31So you testify against
yourselves that you are the descendants of those who murdered the prophets.[u] 32Go ahead, then, and
complete[v] what your ancestors started!
33"You snakes! You brood of vipers![w] How will you escape being condemned to hell?[x] 34Therefore I
am sending you prophets and sages and teachers. Some of them you will kill and crucify;[y] others you
will flog in your synagogues[z] and pursue from town to town.[a] 35And so upon you will come all the
righteous blood that has been shed on earth, from the blood of righteous Abel[b] to the blood of Zechariah

23:31 [u] Ac 7:51-52
23:32 [v] 1Th 2:16
23:33 [w] Mt 3:7; 12:34 [x] Mt 5:22
23:34 [y] 2Ch 36:15,16; Lk 11:49 [z] Mt 10:17 [a] Mt 10:23
23:35 [b] Ge 4:8; Heb 11:4

23:33–36 Not only have these leaders not really broken from their ancestors' ways, they will wind up worse than them by crucifying Jesus and persecuting his followers.
23:33 brood of vipers. See note on 3:7.
23:34 prophets and sages and teachers. These include John the Baptist, Jesus, and various other early Christian leaders. Cf. 10:17,23.
23:35 Abel ... Zechariah. It is a coincidence that in English Abel and Zechariah start with the first and last letters of the alphabet (they do not in Greek or Hebrew). But in the order of books in the Hebrew Bible, Abel is the first recorded martyr (Gen 4:8) and Zechariah is the last (2 Chr 24:20–21). **Zechariah son of.** In Matthew, Zechariah is said to be "son of Berekiah," as if he were the writing prophet by that

JEWISH SECTS

PHARISEES	
Their roots can be traced to the Hasidim of the second century BC (see note on Mark 2:16).	(1) Along with the Torah, they accepted as equally inspired and authoritative all the commands set forth in the oral traditions preserved by the rabbis. (2) On free will and determination, they held to a mediating view that did not allow either human free will or the sovereignty of God to cancel out the other. (3) They accepted a rather developed hierarchy of angels and demons. (4) They believed in the immortality of the soul and in reward and retribution after death. (5) They believed in the resurrection of the dead. (6) The main emphasis of their teaching was ethical rather than theological.
SADDUCEES	
They probably had their beginning during the Hasmonean period (166–63 BC). Their demise occurred ca. AD 70 with the fall of Jerusalem and the destruction of the temple.	(1) They considered only the books of Moses to be canonical Scripture, denying that the oral law was authoritative and binding. (2) They were very exacting in Levitical purity. (3) They attributed everything to free will. (4) They argued that there is neither resurrection of the dead nor a future life. (5) They rejected the idea of a spiritual world, including belief in angels and demons.
ESSENES	
They probably originated among the Hasidim, along with the Pharisees, from whom they later separated (1 Maccabees 2:42; 7:13). The Hasidim were a group of zealous Jews who took part with the Maccabeans in a revolt against the Syrians ca. 165–155 BC. A group of Essenes probably moved to Qumran ca. 150 BC, where they copied scrolls and deposited them in nearby caves.	(1) They strictly observed the purity laws of the Torah. (2) They practiced communal ownership of property. (3) They had a strong sense of mutual responsibility. (4) Daily worship was an important feature along with daily study of their sacred scriptures. (5) Solemn oaths of piety and obedience had to be taken. (6) Sacrifices were offered on holy days and during their sacred seasons, but not at the temple, which they considered to be corrupt. (7) Marriage was avoided by some but was not condemned in principle. (8) They attributed to fate everything that happened.
ZEALOTS	
They originated during the reign of Herod the Great ca. 6 BC. A group of Zealots were among the last defenders against the Romans at Masada in AD 73.	(1) They opposed payment of taxes to a pagan emperor because they believed that allegiance was due to God alone. (2) They were fiercely loyal to Jewish tradition. (3) They endorsed the use of violence as long as it accomplished a good end. (4) They were opposed to the influence of Greek pagan culture in the Holy Land.

23:35 [c]Zec 1:1 [d]2Ch 24:21
23:36 [e]Mt 10:23; 24:34
23:37 [f]2Ch 24:21; Mt 5:12
23:38 [g]1Ki 9:7,8; Jer 22:5
23:39 [h]Ps 118:26; Mt 21:9
24:2 [i]Lk 19:44
24:3 [j]Mt 21:1
24:5 [k]ver 11,23,24; 1Jn 2:18
24:7 [l]Isa 19:2 [m]Ac 11:28
24:9 [n]Mt 10:17 [o]Jn 16:2
24:11 [p]Mt 7:15
24:13 [q]Mt 10:22

son of Berekiah,[c] whom you murdered between the temple and the altar.[d] 36 Truly I tell you, all this will come on this generation.[e]

37 "Jerusalem, Jerusalem, you who kill the prophets and stone those sent to you,[f] how often I have longed to gather your children together, as a hen gathers her chicks under her wings, and you were not willing. 38 Look, your house is left to you desolate.[g] 39 For I tell you, you will not see me again until you say, 'Blessed is he who comes in the name of the Lord.'[a]"[h]

The Destruction of the Temple and Signs of the End Times

24:1-51pp — Mk 13:1-37; Lk 21:5-36

24 Jesus left the temple and was walking away when his disciples came up to him to call his attention to its buildings. 2 "Do you see all these things?" he asked. "Truly I tell you, not one stone here will be left on another;[i] every one will be thrown down."

3 As Jesus was sitting on the Mount of Olives,[j] the disciples came to him privately. "Tell us," they said, "when will this happen, and what will be the sign of your coming and of the end of the age?"

4 Jesus answered: "Watch out that no one deceives you. 5 For many will come in my name, claiming, 'I am the Messiah,' and will deceive many.[k] 6 You will hear of wars and rumors of wars, but see to it that you are not alarmed. Such things must happen, but the end is still to come. 7 Nation will rise against nation, and kingdom against kingdom.[l] There will be famines[m] and earthquakes in various places. 8 All these are the beginning of birth pains.

9 "Then you will be handed over to be persecuted[n] and put to death,[o] and you will be hated by all nations because of me. 10 At that time many will turn away from the faith and will betray and hate each other, 11 and many false prophets[p] will appear and deceive many people. 12 Because of the increase of wickedness, the love of most will grow cold, 13 but the one who stands firm to the end will be saved.[q]

[a] *39* Psalm 118:26

name (Zech 1:1,7), and the Zechariah of 2 Chr 24 is said to be "son of Jehoiada" (2 Chr 24:20). So perhaps Zechariah the prophet was murdered in similar fashion to his namesake, which would make the prophet chronologically the last recorded martyr of the OT. "Son" can also mean descendant, and rabbinic traditions point to some pre-Christian confusion concerning the ancestries of these two Zechariahs. Which explanation is best remains unclear.

23:36 generation. Often viewed as about 40 years. In AD 70, 40 years after the death of Jesus (probably in AD 30, though possibly 33), the Romans destroyed the temple and much of Jerusalem. See also v. 38. During this time all these various kinds of deaths likewise occurred at the hands of key Jewish leaders.

23:37–39 Despite the harshness of the rest of his address, Jesus ends with a lament for Jerusalem, which expresses a note of sorrow more than anger.

23:37 how often. Only John's Gospel describes the many times Jesus had previously been in Jerusalem, perhaps explaining "how often." **hen ... chicks.** Jesus wishes he could have spiritually protected and nurtured the people of Jerusalem, like a mother "hen [with] her chicks," but they "were not willing" to let him.

23:38 house. The temple. **desolate.** Bereft of spiritual truth with Jesus' departure in 24:1 and razed by the Romans a generation later (see note on v. 36). The holy city of Israel will, however, see Jesus again when he returns in glory (24:29–31).

23:39 Blessed is he who comes. At Jesus' return Jerusalem's inhabitants will acclaim him with the words of Ps 118:26. Whether this acclamation will reflect genuine repentance and acceptance of Jesus as Messiah or the mournful, grudging acknowledgment of his true identity just before they go away into perdition is more difficult to determine.

24:1—25:46 This passage is called the Olivet discourse. Jesus addresses his followers on the Mount of Olives immediately after he leaves the temple for the last time. He predicts its imminent destruction (24:1–28) and his "coming on the clouds of heaven" (24:30) at some unspecified point after that (24:29–51). The upshot for his followers is that they must live obedient, faithful lives at all times because they cannot know when the end will come. But when it does arrive, everyone will be judged according to their works (25:1–46).

24:1–28 Jesus depicts what must happen in the generation in which he and his followers are living (v. 34). Numerous ominous events will occur, followed finally by the complete razing of the temple in AD 70.

24:2–3 Because Jesus predicts the complete destruction of the temple, the disciples likely assume it must bring about "the end of the age" (v. 3) as they know it. Jesus' reply separates the two events that the disciples have linked.

24:2 not one stone ... will be left on another; every one will be thrown down. Fulfilled literally in AD 70, when the Romans under Titus destroyed Jerusalem and the temple buildings. Stones were even pried apart to collect the gold leaf that melted from the roof when the temple was set on fire. Excavations in 1968 uncovered large numbers of these stones, toppled from the walls by the invaders. The Western Wall in Jerusalem, still standing today, was part of a retaining wall around the temple precincts, not part of the temple itself.

24:4–8 False messiahs, wars, famines, and earthquakes all occurred in the 40 years between Christ's crucifixion (probably AD 30, though possibly 33) and the destruction of the temple in AD 70. Josephus, the first-century Jewish historian, mentions all of them. The NT itself refers to both a famine (Acts 11:27–28) and an earthquake (Acts 16:26). These are *not* the signs the disciples asked about, however, for "the end is still to come" (v. 6). They are merely "the beginning of birth pains" (v. 8). These events are like a pregnant woman's labor pains: they demonstrate there is a baby that the body wants to deliver, but they prove singularly unhelpful in predicting the precise moment of birth.

24:9–13 Persecution, martyrdom, apostasy, false prophets and their deception, an overall increase of wickedness, and a diminution of love will also characterize the years ahead. The NT letters most likely written

14 And this gospel of the kingdom[r] will be preached in the whole world[s] as a testimony to all nations,
and then the end will come.
15 "So when you see standing in the holy place[t] 'the abomination that causes desolation,'[a][u] spoken
of through the prophet Daniel—let the reader understand— 16 then let those who are in Judea flee
to the mountains. 17 Let no one on the housetop[v] go down to take anything out of the house. 18 Let no
one in the field go back to get their cloak. 19 How dreadful it will be in those days for pregnant women
and nursing mothers![w] 20 Pray that your flight will not take place in winter or on the Sabbath. 21 For
then there will be great distress, unequaled from the beginning of the world until now—and never
to be equaled again.[x]
22 "If those days had not been cut short, no one would survive, but for the sake of the elect[y] those
days will be shortened. 23 At that time if anyone says to you, 'Look, here is the Messiah!' or, 'There he
is!' do not believe it.[z] 24 For false messiahs and false prophets will appear and perform great signs and
wonders[a] to deceive, if possible, even the elect. 25 See, I have told you ahead of time.
26 "So if anyone tells you, 'There he is, out in the wilderness,' do not go out; or, 'Here he is, in the
inner rooms,' do not believe it. 27 For as lightning[b] that comes from the east is visible even in the west,
so will be the coming of the Son of Man.[c] 28 Wherever there is a carcass, there the vultures will gather.[d]
29 "Immediately after the distress of those days

"'the sun will be darkened,
and the moon will not give its light;
the stars will fall from the sky,
and the heavenly bodies will be shaken.'[b][e]

a *15* Daniel 9:27; 11:31; 12:11 *b* *29* Isaiah 13:10; 34:4

24:14 [r] Mt 4:23 [s] Lk 2:1; 4:5; Ac 11:28; 17:6; Ro 10:18; Col 1:6,23; Rev 3:10; 16:14
24:15 [t] Ac 6:13 [u] Da 9:27; 11:31; 12:11
24:17 [v] 1Sa 9:25; Mt 10:27; Lk 12:3; Ac 10:9
24:19 [w] Lk 23:29
24:21 [x] Da 12:1; Joel 2:2
24:22 [y] ver 24,31
24:23 [z] Lk 17:23; 21:8
24:24 [a] 2Th 2:9-11; Rev 13:13
24:27 [b] Lk 17:24 [c] Mt 8:20
24:28 [d] Lk 17:37
24:29 [e] Isa 13:10; 34:4; Eze 32:7; Joel 2:10,31; Zep 1:15; Rev 6:12,13; 8:12

between 30 and 70 reflect all of these: Hebrews and 1 Peter are written when persecution against Christians is increasing; Hebrews warns against the dire consequences of apostasy; 2 Peter and Jude combat false prophets; and almost all of Paul's letters emphasize promoting love and avoiding evil. True believers, however, will stand firm to the end and be spiritually saved (v. 13).

24:14 Most think this foreshadows the Great Commission of 28:19–20, in which case Jesus now looks well beyond the first generation of his followers. But it is possible to see this prophecy too fulfilled by AD 70: The "whole world" was viewed by many as roughly contiguous with the Roman Empire (cf. Col 1:23). Paul essentially claims to have completed initial evangelism of the eastern half of the empire (Rom 15:19) as he plants churches in all representative regions to carry on his work by about 57. His subsequent desire to go to Rome and then as far as Spain can be seen as aiming to do the same thing in the western half (Rom 15:28), and he may well have accomplished it before his martyrdom between 64 and 67 if various early Christian traditions are accurate.

24:15 the abomination that causes desolation. Predicted in Dan 9:27; 11:31; 12:11, and some Jews believe that Antiochus IV's desecration of the temple ("the holy place") in 167 BC fulfills it. Jesus obviously sees another fulfillment yet to come as he looks ahead at least to when Rome will destroy the temple of his day in AD 70. Some envision a still future fulfillment in conjunction with Christ's return.

24:16–20 When this time comes, God's people must flee Jerusalem quickly.

24:17 housetop. Roofs were flat so that individuals could work, socialize, and even sleep there.

24:19 pregnant women and nursing mothers. They would find it much harder to travel rapidly.

24:20 in winter. Dirt roads would be muddied by rains and harder to traverse. **on the Sabbath.** There would be travel restrictions.

24:21 great distress. Most think Jesus is foreshadowing the "great distress" (or "tribulation") that will surround his second coming, not talking just of the events of AD 70. But to say that at the end of the age, just before God redeems his creation fully, such misery is never to be equaled again seems so obvious as to be almost pointless. But if Jesus has in mind an event in the "middle" of human history, then the statement makes good sense. The suffering and eventual extinction of the Jews in Jerusalem and the total destruction of the city are well-known. Alternately, the verse is idiomatic for great destruction (cf. Ezek 5:9) or it means that if allowed to continue, such distress would destroy everyone.

24:22 those days. Refers to the time of unequaled distress just described. **no one would survive.** Apparently refers to physical life. **the elect.** Means Jesus' followers.

24:24 false messiahs and false prophets. Repeats the warnings of vv. 4–5,11. **if possible.** Suggests that the deception perpetrated by these individuals is so severe that, were it possible "to deceive" Christ's true followers, even they would be led into apostasy.

24:26–28 The reason not to believe claims that the Messiah has reappeared in one particular place, outdoors or indoors, is that "the coming of the Son of man" (v. 27) will be as universally, publicly, and instantaneously disclosed as "lightning that comes from the east is visible even in the west" (v. 27). Verse 28 is unusually difficult to decipher but appears to be a metaphor about the inevitability of two events following one another. An animal or human "carcass" left in the wild will invariably become carrion for birds of prey. Perhaps Jesus' point is that so too his return will put an end to all this unparalleled wickedness and deception. However, "vultures" (v. 28) could also be "eagles," a symbol for the Roman Empire. So maybe Jesus is recapitulating the inevitability of the destruction of Jerusalem by Rome (as in v. 15; see note there).

24:29–51 These verses describe the return of Christ. "Immediately" in v. 29 could mean that "the distress of those days" (v. 29) surrounding the destruction of the temple in some sense continues all the way until Jesus' second coming (cf. 2 Tim 3:12). Or perhaps the "abomination that causes desolation" (v. 15) will be reenacted on a more awful scale just before Christ's return (cf. Rev 7:14 on those in the last days who will "come out of the great tribulation"). Either way, Jesus now moves ahead to the events surrounding his return in glory. These are signs of the end (vv. 29–35), but the day and hour remain unknown (vv. 36–51).

24:29 This is apocalyptic language taken from texts like Isa 13:10; 34:4.

24:30 [f]Da 7:13; Rev 1:7
24:31 [g]Mt 13:41
[h]Isa 27:13; Zec 9:14; 1Co 15:52; 1Th 4:16; Rev 8:2; 10:7; 11:15
24:33 [i]Jas 5:9
24:34 [j]Mt 16:28; 23:36
24:35 [k]Mt 5:18
24:36 [l]Ac 1:7
24:37 [m]Ge 6:5; 7:6-23
24:38 [n]Mt 22:30
24:40 [o]Lk 17:34
24:41 [p]Lk 17:35
24:42 [q]Mt 25:13; Lk 12:40
24:43 [r]Lk 12:39
24:44 [s]1Th 5:6
24:45 [t]Mt 25:21,23

30 “Then will appear the sign of the Son of Man in heaven. And then all the peoples of the earth[a] will
mourn when they see the Son of Man coming on the clouds of heaven,[f] with power and great glory.[b]
31 And he will send his angels[g] with a loud trumpet call,[h] and they will gather his elect from the four
winds, from one end of the heavens to the other.

32 “Now learn this lesson from the fig tree: As soon as its twigs get tender and its leaves come out,
you know that summer is near. 33 Even so, when you see all these things, you know that it[c] is near,
right at the door.[i] 34 Truly I tell you, this generation will certainly not pass away until all these
things have happened.[j] 35 Heaven and earth will pass away, but my words will never pass away.[k]

The Day and Hour Unknown

24:37-39pp — Lk 17:26,27
24:45-51pp — Lk 12:42-46

36 “But about that day or hour no one knows, not even the angels in heaven, nor the Son,[d] but only
the Father.[l] 37 As it was in the days of Noah,[m] so it will be at the coming of the Son of Man. 38 For in the
days before the flood, people were eating and drinking, marrying and giving in marriage,[n] up to the
day Noah entered the ark; 39 and they knew nothing about what would happen until the flood came
and took them all away. That is how it will be at the coming of the Son of Man. 40 Two men will be in
the field; one will be taken and the other left.[o] 41 Two women will be grinding with a hand mill; one
will be taken and the other left.[p]

42 “Therefore keep watch, because you do not know on what day your Lord will come.[q] 43 But understand this: If the owner of the house had known at what time of night the thief was coming,[r] he would
have kept watch and would not have let his house be broken into. 44 So you also must be ready,[s] because
the Son of Man will come at an hour when you do not expect him.

45 “Who then is the faithful and wise servant,[t] whom the master has put in charge of the servants in
his household to give them their food at the proper time? 46 It will be good for that servant whose master

[a] 30 Or *the tribes of the land* [b] 30 See Daniel 7:13-14. [c] 33 Or *he* [d] 36 Some manuscripts do not have *nor the Son.*

The point is probably not that there are literal cosmic upheavals as depicted or that the universe comes to an end instantly. Rather, the significance of what is about to happen is so great that life as it has been previously experienced cannot continue. A new age is dawning.

24:30 sign. This is the only place where Jesus refers to the “sign” the disciples requested in v. 3, and he does not tell them what it is. Whatever it is—perhaps a “banner” or “standard” (see Isa 11:12; 18:3; 49:22; Jer 4:21; 51:27)—it is part and parcel of Christ’s coming so that it is not something that can enable believers to predict in advance when the second coming will occur. **the Son of Man coming on the clouds of heaven.** Partially recalls Dan 7:13–14, in which a privileged human is ushered into the very presence of God to be given universal authority over the kingdoms of the earth. Here, though, the clouds usher Christ from heaven to earth. It is not clear if “the peoples of the earth will mourn” in repentance or in grief because it is now too late to repent.

24:31 angels ... will gather. Christ’s followers will be gathered together from wherever they reside on earth for protection and reward.

24:32–33 *The Parable of the Fig Tree.* The budding “fig tree” (v. 32) was a crucial barometer for the coming of summer in ancient Israel. Likewise, all of the events Jesus has sketched in this sermon will enable his disciples to know that his return and the fullness of God’s kingdom that it brings are getting close.

24:34 all these things. Must refer to the same events as “all these things” in v. 33, which occur *before* the second coming. So Jesus cannot be predicting his return within “this generation,” i.e., the lifetime of his followers. Instead, he must be promising that all of the preliminary events, including the destruction of Jerusalem—which must take place before he can return—will take place within about a 40-year period of time. From AD 70 on, the church has consistently believed that Christ could return in its day. The events that still remain to be fulfilled can unfold so quickly that believers must be prepared for the end in every generation.

24:35 Jesus’ “words,” especially on the topics of this sermon, are more permanent and certain than even the present universe, which must give way one day to a new heaven and earth.

24:36 that day or hour. Does not mean that people should try to predict the month, year, generation, century, or millennium! After all, Acts 1:7 uses the broadest terms in Greek for “times or dates” when Jesus says his followers will not know when the kingdom will be restored to Israel, i.e., when the remaining OT prophecies that will accompany his return will be fulfilled.

24:37–41 Indeed, for unbelievers (or believers not living with alert faithfulness), the end will come as a complete surprise, just as the flood did for the people who paid no attention to Noah building the ark (Gen 6–7). The rising water “took them all away” (v. 39), i.e., they perished in God’s judgment on the earth. The imagery, therefore, of two men in a field and two women grinding with a hand mill, in which one will in each case be taken and the other left (vv. 40–41), also suggests that the one taken away will be judged. Thus there does not appear to be any secret rapture of believers taken away from the earth in this passage.

24:42 do not know. Jesus repeats the point from v. 36 (see note there) that no one can know when he will return. His followers, however, must always be prepared and alert.

24:43—25:46 Jesus’ sermon concludes with a series of parables that reinforce the need for faithful service for however long or short the interval before Christ’s second coming.

24:43–44 Christ likens himself to a burglar, not in that he comes to steal something, but in terms of the surprise factor. Just as wise homeowners never leave their houses unprotected, Jesus’ followers should never stop being ready for his return.

24:45–51 *The Parable of the Faithful and Wise Servant.* “The faithful and

finds him doing so when he returns.[u] 47Truly I tell you, he will put him in charge of all his possessions.[v]
48But suppose that servant is wicked and says to himself, 'My master is staying away a long time,' 49and he
then begins to beat his fellow servants and to eat and drink with drunkards.[w] 50The master of that servant
will come on a day when he does not expect him and at an hour he is not aware of. 51He will cut him to
pieces and assign him a place with the hypocrites, where there will be weeping and gnashing of teeth.[x]

The Parable of the Ten Virgins

25 "At that time the kingdom of heaven will be like[y] ten virgins who took their lamps[z] and went
out to meet the bridegroom.[a] 2Five of them were foolish and five were wise.[b] 3The foolish ones
took their lamps but did not take any oil with them. 4The wise ones, however, took oil in jars along with
their lamps. 5The bridegroom was a long time in coming, and they all became drowsy and fell asleep.[c]
6"At midnight the cry rang out: 'Here's the bridegroom! Come out to meet him!'
7"Then all the virgins woke up and trimmed their lamps. 8The foolish ones said to the wise, 'Give us
some of your oil; our lamps are going out.'[d]
9" 'No,' they replied, 'there may not be enough for both us and you. Instead, go to those who sell oil
and buy some for yourselves.'
10"But while they were on their way to buy the oil, the bridegroom arrived. The virgins who were
ready went in with him to the wedding banquet.[e] And the door was shut.
11"Later the others also came. 'Lord, Lord,' they said, 'open the door for us!'
12"But he replied, 'Truly I tell you, I don't know you.'
13"Therefore keep watch, because you do not know the day or the hour.[f]

The Parable of the Bags of Gold

25:14-30Ref — Lk 19:12-27

14"Again, it will be like a man going on a journey,[g] who called his servants and entrusted his wealth to
them. 15To one he gave five bags of gold, to another two bags, and to another one bag,[a] each according to
his ability.[h] Then he went on his journey. 16The man who had received five bags of gold went at once and
put his money to work and gained five bags more. 17So also, the one with two bags of gold gained two more.
18But the man who had received one bag went off, dug a hole in the ground and hid his master's money.

a 15 Greek *five talents . . . two talents . . . one talent*; also throughout this parable; a talent was worth about 20 years of a day laborer's wage.

24:46 [u] Rev 16:15
24:47 [v] Mt 25:21,23
24:49 [w] Lk 21:34
24:51 [x] Mt 8:12
25:1 [y] Mt 13:24 [z] Lk 12:35-38; Ac 20:8; Rev 4:5 [a] Rev 19:7; 21:2
25:2 [b] Mt 24:45
25:5 [c] 1Th 5:6
25:8 [d] Lk 12:35
25:10 [e] Rev 19:9
25:13 [f] Mt 24:42,44; Mk 13:35; Lk 12:40
25:14 [g] Mt 21:33; Lk 19:12
25:15 [h] Mt 18:24,25

wise servant" (v. 45) is the slave put in charge of the other slaves during his master's absence. Faithful performance of the tasks delegated to him may lead to his becoming the manager over the entire estate (vv. 45–47). Disorderly and abusive conduct, however, may be interrupted by the master returning home earlier than expected and severely punishing the slave (vv. 48–51). At the spiritual level, this parable refers to heaven and hell as the destinies of the two kinds of servants.

25:1–13 *The Parable of the Ten Virgins.* In the previous two parables, the figure representing Christ (or God) arrives at a time that surprises the owner of the house (24:43–44) and arrives early (24:45–51). In this parable Jesus arrives surprisingly late. Jesus covers all possible options. Christians really must stop pretending to know or trying to predict when Jesus will return.

25:1–5 In an ancient Israelite village wedding, the father of the groom would negotiate the price of the bride's dowry at the bride's parents' home. Then the couple would proceed through the streets, accompanied by the wedding party, to the groom's parents' home, where the festivities would be completed.

25:1 virgins. Bridesmaids. **lamps.** Oil-lit lamps to light the way for the procession. Because they may need to wait awhile before the bridegroom emerges from the bride's home, they need a good supply of extra oil.

25:6–9 In this case, the bridegroom seems to have been considerably delayed. The young women who did not bring extra oil realize, when they trim the wicks of their lamps, that they have already used up all their oil. They ask those with extra to share with them, but the other bridesmaids do not have enough for everyone. At a real wedding, traders would have remained available precisely for last minute provisions like this on the night of a wedding.

25:10–13 By the time the unprepared girls return with their extra oil, the procession has already arrived at the groom's home and gone inside. At a real wedding, the late arrivals would have been publicly shamed but probably let in. But this is a parable, teaching spiritual lessons. Jesus insists that once he has returned it will be too late to repent. One must not wait to choose how to respond to him. And the salvation of one person cannot be transferred, like oil, to another. No bridegroom would ever claim not to know who some of the bridesmaids were (v. 12), but at the spiritual level of the story Christ declares, "I don't know you," perhaps suggesting there was never a genuine relationship at all between God and these alleged disciples. True believers will prepare in case discipleship proves more arduous than they expect.

25:14–30 *The Parable of the Bags of Gold/Talents.* If Jesus' followers can never know when he will return, they must always be good stewards of all the gifts and abilities he has given them.

25:15 bags of gold. "Talents," originally a unit of currency worth about 20 years of a day laborer's wage (see note on 18:24). Not all people receive the same abilities or gifts from God, but everyone is responsible for making good use of what they have been given. For a similar parable, see Luke 19:12–27.

25:18 dug a hole in the ground. People often buried money in the ground under or near their homes for safekeeping. But in so doing there was no chance that their holdings could grow at all.

25:19 [i]Mt 18:23
25:21 [j]ver 23; Mt 24:45, 47; Lk 16:10
25:23 [k]ver 21
25:29 [l]Mt 13:12; Mk 4:25; Lk 8:18; 19:26
25:30 [m]Mt 8:12
25:31 [n]Mt 16:27; Lk 17:30 [o]Mt 19:28
25:32 [p]Mal 3:18 [q]Eze 34:17,20
25:34 [r]Mt 3:2; 5:3,10, 19; 19:14; Ac 20:32; 1Co 15:50; Gal 5:21; Jas 2:5 [s]Heb 4:3; 9:26; Rev 13:8; 17:8
25:35 [t]Job 31:32; Isa 58:7; Eze 18:7; Heb 13:2
25:36 [u]Isa 58:7; Eze 18:7; Jas 2:15,16 [v]Jas 1:27 [w]2Ti 1:16

19“After a long time the master of those servants returned and settled accounts with them.[i] 20The
man who had received five bags of gold brought the other five. ‘Master,’ he said, ‘you entrusted me with
five bags of gold. See, I have gained five more.’
21“His master replied, ‘Well done, good and faithful servant! You have been faithful with a few things;
I will put you in charge of many things.[j] Come and share your master’s happiness!’
22“The man with two bags of gold also came. ‘Master,’ he said, ‘you entrusted me with two bags of
gold; see, I have gained two more.’
23“His master replied, ‘Well done, good and faithful servant! You have been faithful with a few things;
I will put you in charge of many things.[k] Come and share your master’s happiness!’
24“Then the man who had received one bag of gold came. ‘Master,’ he said, ‘I knew that you are a
hard man, harvesting where you have not sown and gathering where you have not scattered seed. 25So
I was afraid and went out and hid your gold in the ground. See, here is what belongs to you.’
26“His master replied, ‘You wicked, lazy servant! So you knew that I harvest where I have not sown
and gather where I have not scattered seed? 27Well then, you should have put my money on deposit with
the bankers, so that when I returned I would have received it back with interest.
28“ ‘So take the bag of gold from him and give it to the one who has ten bags. 29For whoever has will
be given more, and they will have an abundance. Whoever does not have, even what they have will be
taken from them.[l] 30And throw that worthless servant outside, into the darkness, where there will be
weeping and gnashing of teeth.’[m]

The Sheep and the Goats

31“When the Son of Man comes[n] in his glory, and all the angels with him, he will sit on his glorious throne.[o] 32All the nations will be gathered before him, and he will separate[p] the people one from
another as a shepherd separates the sheep from the goats.[q] 33He will put the sheep on his right and
the goats on his left.
34“Then the King will say to those on his right, ‘Come, you who are blessed by my Father; take your
inheritance, the kingdom[r] prepared for you since the creation of the world.[s] 35For I was hungry and
you gave me something to eat, I was thirsty and you gave me something to drink, I was a stranger and
you invited me in,[t] 36I needed clothes and you clothed me,[u] I was sick and you looked after me,[v] I was
in prison and you came to visit me.’[w]
37“Then the righteous will answer him, ‘Lord, when did we see you hungry and feed you, or thirsty
and give you something to drink? 38When did we see you a stranger and invite you in, or needing clothes
and clothe you? 39When did we see you sick or in prison and go to visit you?’

25:20–23 Each of the first two servants makes a 100 percent return on his investment, extraordinary by ancient standards, and each receives the master’s effusive praise.

25:24–25 The third servant claims to have feared losing his master’s money, which can easily happen with investments. He accuses the master of being harsh and unfair, though nothing elsewhere in the parable suggests that this accusation is valid.

25:26–27 The servant stands condemned by his own logic. The master points out that if he really were so harsh, then the man should have feared all the more not trying to earn more money with what had been entrusted to him. At least he could have deposited it with local bankers so it would have earned some modest amount of interest without the risks that accompanied other forms of investment.

25:28–30 Because a “bag of gold” (talent) was more literally a gold ingot, it could not easily be broken in two. The worthless slave’s original talent is given to the first slave, but the second slave was just as faithful, even though he receives no extra talent. So nothing should be read into these details about varying rewards for God’s faithful followers. The point is simply that being ready for Christ’s coming involves more than playing it safe and doing little or nothing. It demands the kind of service that produces results. “Whoever has” and “whoever does not have” (v. 29) must refer to the period of time *after* they have been given their “talents” to steward. Verse 30 makes it clear that Jesus’ real point is a spiritual one since the fate of the faithless slave is eternal punishment (cf. note on 8:12).

25:31–46 *The Parable of the Sheep and the Goats.* This describes in more detail the final judgment that the end of the last two parables depict. Some interpreters view this occurring when Christ returns, just before an earthly, millennial kingdom (Rev 20:4); others equate it with the great white throne judgment (Rev 20:11–15) just prior to the eternal state.

25:32 All the nations. Both Jews and Gentiles. **nations.** Greek *ethnē* (neuter plural) sounds at first as if ethnic or people groups will be judged as a whole. But Jesus will actually “separate the people” (Greek *autous*, “them” [masculine plural]) “one from another,” referring to the personal judgment of each individual. Palestinian sheep and goats often looked similar from a distance and often grazed together. But they needed to be separated at nighttime because the goats required a warmer place to rest.

25:33 right … left. The right hand or side of an individual was considered the more honorable; the left, more disgraceful.

25:34–36 Those who are “blessed” by God (v. 34) are those who have ministered to Jesus. The examples Jesus gives all involve the works of mercy needed by the socially and economically destitute. This is not salvation by works but the fruit of repentance that demonstrates an individual’s right relationship with God through Christ.

25:37–40 The “righteous” (v. 37) are surprised not because they are said to have known Jesus but because Jesus says they have ministered

40“The King will reply, ‘Truly I tell you, whatever you did for one of the least of these brothers and
sisters of mine, you did for me.’[x]
41“Then he will say to those on his left, ‘Depart from me,[y] you who are cursed, into the eternal fire[z]
prepared for the devil and his angels.[a] 42For I was hungry and you gave me nothing to eat, I was thirsty
and you gave me nothing to drink, 43I was a stranger and you did not invite me in, I needed clothes and
you did not clothe me, I was sick and in prison and you did not look after me.’
44“They also will answer, ‘Lord, when did we see you hungry or thirsty or a stranger or needing
clothes or sick or in prison, and did not help you?’
45“He will reply, ‘Truly I tell you, whatever you did not do for one of the least of these, you did not
do for me.’[b]
46“Then they will go away to eternal punishment, but the righteous to eternal life.”[c][d]

The Plot Against Jesus

26:2-5pp — Mk 14:1,2; Lk 22:1,2

26 When Jesus had finished saying all these things,[e] he said to his disciples, 2“As you know, the
Passover[f] is two days away — and the Son of Man will be handed over to be crucified.”
3Then the chief priests and the elders of the people assembled[g] in the palace of the high priest, whose
name was Caiaphas,[h] 4and they schemed to arrest Jesus secretly and kill him.[i] 5“But not during the
festival,” they said, “or there may be a riot[j] among the people.”

Jesus Anointed at Bethany

26:6-13pp — Mk 14:3-9
26:6-13Ref — Lk 7:37,38; Jn 12:1-8

6While Jesus was in Bethany[k] in the home of Simon the Leper, 7a woman came to him with an alabaster jar of very expensive perfume, which she poured on his head as he was reclining at the table.

25:40 [x]Pr 19:17; Mt 10:40,42; Heb 6:10; 13:2
25:41 [y]Mt 7:23 [z]Isa 66:24; Mt 3:12; 5:22; Mk 9:43,48; Lk 3:17; Jude 7 [a]2Pe 2:4
25:45 [b]Pr 14:31; 17:5
25:46 [c]Mt 19:29; Jn 3:15,16,36; 17:2,3; Ro 2:7; Gal 6:8; 5:11,13, 20 [d]Da 12:2; Jn 5:29; Ac 24:15; Ro 2:7,8; Gal 6:8
26:1 [e]Mt 7:28
26:2 [f]Jn 11:55; 13:1
26:3 [g]Ps 2:2 [h]ver 57; Jn 11:47-53; 18:13, 14,24,28
26:4 [i]Mt 12:14
26:5 [j]Mt 27:24
26:6 [k]Mt 21:17

directly to him. Jesus explains that whenever they did these acts of kindness “for one of the least of these brothers and sisters of mine” (v. 40; see note there), they were doing it for him.

25:40 least of these brothers and sisters of mine. Everywhere else in Matthew “brothers and sisters” (Greek *adelphoi*) means either biological siblings or spiritual kin. “Least” is the superlative form of “little,” and “little ones” in Matthew always means either literal children or fellow believers. So while other biblical texts teach the need to help needy people of all religious persuasions (e.g., Luke 10:25–37; Gal 6:10), here the focus is most likely on ministering to the *Christian* needy. The logic is identical to that of Matt 10:40–42: welcoming the Christian messenger implies welcoming the message.

25:41 you ... cursed. Those who have not done any of the previously mentioned acts of mercy (vv. 42–43) toward Christians in need. They show thereby that they have never welcomed the Christian message, i.e., accepted Christ as their Lord and Savior (despite mouthing the title “Lord” in v. 44). **the eternal fire prepared for the devil and his angels.** The destiny of the “cursed”: eternal separation from God and all things good. **his angels.** Demons.

25:46 eternal. Jesus parallels “eternal punishment” and “eternal life.” While the Hebrew underlying the Greek *aiōnios* (“eternal”) can sometimes mean “to the end of the age,” it is clear throughout Jesus’ teaching that he expects *everlasting* life for his followers. Unbelievers, therefore, can expect unending punishment too, not merely some limited period of purgatory or a finite hell.

26:1—28:20 *Jesus’ Passion, Death, and Resurrection.* From here on, Matthew swiftly narrates the events that put Jesus on the cross to die but which could not keep him in his tomb (see map, pp. 2128–2129).

26:1–75 Ch. 26 describes the preparations for Jesus’ death. Most of the events of this chapter take place on the Thursday night before Jesus’ Friday crucifixion. Matthew also includes the plot to betray Jesus begun “two days” earlier (v. 2) and the anointing at Bethany six days earlier (vv. 6–13; cf. John 12:1), because these also directly anticipate Jesus’ execution.

26:1–16 These verses describe Jesus’ arrest and anointing for burial. Jesus reminds his followers one last time of his upcoming crucifixion (vv. 1–2). Although it appears others are in charge of his destiny, his predictions and voluntary surrender (vv. 52–56) demonstrate that he gives his life freely. Judas, who aids Caiaphas and his henchmen in the arrest (vv. 3–5,14–16), and Mary of Bethany, who pours perfume on Jesus’ head (vv. 6–13; cf. John 12:1–8), may have been the first two to believe that Jesus was really going to die. But they reacted in diametrically opposite ways.

26:1–5 More specifically than in his earlier three passion predictions (see notes on 16:21–28; 17:22–23; 20:17–19), Jesus now specifies the very day of his betrayal.

26:3 Caiaphas. Joseph Caiaphas was high priest in Israel from AD 18 to 36. He would have presided over the Sanhedrin (v. 59), the highest Jewish court in the land. In 1990 a first-century tomb with an ornate ossuary (a limestone chest containing the bones of the dead) with his name inscribed on it was discovered near Jerusalem (see photo, p. 2177); it quite possibly is the very box used to rebury his bones (see note on 8:21).

26:4–5 arrest Jesus secretly ... during the festival. As it turns out, the best opportunity to arrest Jesus comes during the festival of Passover. Despite the crowds, the authorities are able to arrest him somewhat secretly under the cloak of night (vv. 47–56).

26:6–13 Jesus’ anointing at Bethany is sandwiched between the two parts of the plot to arrest Jesus, showing that there is a connection between the two (see note on vv. 1–75). John 12:1–8 gives the precise chronological placement of this event; Matthew (following Mark 14:3–9) places it here to create a thematic grouping of passages.

26:6 Bethany. See note on 21:17. **Simon the Leper.** See Mark 14:3. Presumably he was now healed, perhaps even by Jesus himself.

26:7 an alabaster jar of very expensive perfume. Recalls Luke 7:37, but virtually all of the remaining details of that anointing, including its setting, differ from this account. It is most likely a separate event. **reclining.** Refers to the posture of resting one elbow on a cushion next

26:11 [l]Dt 15:11
26:12 [m]Jn 19:40
26:14 [n]ver 25,47; Mt 10:4
26:15 [o]Ex 21:32; Zec 11:12
26:17 [p]Ex 12:18-20
26:18 [q]Jn 7:6,8,30; 12:23; 13:1; 17:1
26:21 [r]Lk 22:21-23; Jn 13:21
26:23 [s]Ps 41:9; Jn 13:18
26:24 [t]Isa 53; Da 9:26; Mk 9:12; Lk 24:25-27, 46; Ac 17:2,3; 26:22,23

8 When the disciples saw this, they were indignant. "Why this waste?" they asked. 9 "This perfume could have been sold at a high price and the money given to the poor."

10 Aware of this, Jesus said to them, "Why are you bothering this woman? She has done a beautiful thing to me. 11 The poor you will always have with you,[a][l] but you will not always have me. 12 When she poured this perfume on my body, she did it to prepare me for burial.[m] 13 Truly I tell you, wherever this gospel is preached throughout the world, what she has done will also be told, in memory of her."

Judas Agrees to Betray Jesus

26:14-16pp — Mk 14:10,11; Lk 22:3-6

14 Then one of the Twelve — the one called Judas Iscariot[n] — went to the chief priests 15 and asked, "What are you willing to give me if I deliver him over to you?" So they counted out for him thirty pieces of silver.[o] 16 From then on Judas watched for an opportunity to hand him over.

The Last Supper

26:17-19pp — Mk 14:12-16; Lk 22:7-13
26:20-24pp — Mk 14:17-21
26:26-29pp — Mk 14:22-25; Lk 22:17-20; 1Co 11:23-25

17 On the first day of the Festival of Unleavened Bread,[p] the disciples came to Jesus and asked, "Where do you want us to make preparations for you to eat the Passover?"

18 He replied, "Go into the city to a certain man and tell him, 'The Teacher says: My appointed time[q] is near. I am going to celebrate the Passover with my disciples at your house.'" 19 So the disciples did as Jesus had directed them and prepared the Passover.

20 When evening came, Jesus was reclining at the table with the Twelve. 21 And while they were eating, he said, "Truly I tell you, one of you will betray me."[r]

22 They were very sad and began to say to him one after the other, "Surely you don't mean me, Lord?"

23 Jesus replied, "The one who has dipped his hand into the bowl with me will betray me.[s] 24 The Son of Man will go just as it is written about him.[t] But woe to that man who betrays the Son of Man! It would be better for him if he had not been born."

a *11* See Deut. 15:11.

to a low-slung table, stretching one's legs out perpendicular to it, and eating with the free hand. It was standard posture for formal banquets.

26:8–9 John 12:4–6 specifies that Judas Iscariot was the primary objector and that his motive was insincere because he was a greedy thief.

26:11–12 Jesus alludes to Deut 15:11, which goes on to remind the Israelites that they may help the poor and needy at any time (and are expected to do so). Jesus' words thus offer no excuse for neglecting the poor but allow for the one-time expenditure of the money often used to perfume a body for burial in a way that allows Jesus to appreciate the gesture before he dies.

26:13 Jesus prophesies that this event will be regularly retold in the preaching of the gospel. Its inclusion in the Gospels forms a large part of the fulfillment of that prophecy.

26:14–16 The motive for Judas seeking to betray his master ("hand him over," v. 16) probably goes beyond the desire for money, although "thirty pieces of silver" (v. 15) may have equaled 120 drachmas, i.e., more than four months' minimum wages. Most likely, he could not accept the fact that Jesus was not going to lead a literal rebellion to help overthrow Rome.

26:17–35 This passage describes what is called the Last Supper, the meal from which Christians developed their practice of the Lord's Supper (communion, the Eucharist). See especially 1 Cor 11:17–34. In this context, it was the Jewish Passover meal, celebrated on the first day (which began at nightfall) of the weeklong Festival of Unleavened Bread (v. 17; see Exod 12). "The first day" was the 14th of Nisan (March-April) and was also called the day of Preparation of the Passover. The Passover meal was eaten the evening of the 14th after sunset — and therefore technically on the 15th, since the Jewish day ended at sunset. The Festival of Unleavened Bread lasted seven days, from the 15th to the 21st of Nisan (see Lev 23:5–6).

26:18–19 As with the securing of the donkey for Jesus' entrance into Jerusalem (21:1–3), this could either be a prearranged strategy or a sign of Jesus' supernatural knowledge and authority.

26:18 My appointed time. Ultimately refers to the time of his death.

26:20 reclining at the table. See note on v. 7.

26:21 As with the previous predictions of his death and resurrection, this one shows that Jesus is not caught off guard by these tragic events.

26:23 The one who has dipped his hand into the bowl with me. Not a clear disclosure of the betrayer's identity because all will have dipped their bread into the sauce as part of the Passover ritual. It was the custom — still practiced by some in the Middle East — to take a piece of bread or a piece of meat wrapped in bread and dip it into a bowl of sauce (made of stewed fruit) on the table.

26:24 Like so many biblical texts, this one juxtaposes divine sovereignty with human responsibility without any hint of tension between the two. The death of the divine Messiah is predicted in Isa 52:13—53:12, but the actual perpetrators are fully accountable. **It would be better for [the betrayer] if he had not been born.** Refutes any notion of universalism (that everyone will eventually be saved) or annihilationism (that the lost simply cease conscious existence after death).

Glass vessels possibly used to store perfume or ointments, AD 66–74.

25Then Judas, the one who would betray him, said, "Surely you don't mean me, Rabbi?"[u]
Jesus answered, "You have said so."
26While they were eating, Jesus took bread, and when he had given thanks, he broke it[v] and gave it
to his disciples, saying, "Take and eat; this is my body."
27Then he took a cup, and when he had given thanks, he gave it to them, saying, "Drink from it, all
of you. 28This is my blood of the[a] covenant,[w] which is poured out for many for the forgiveness of sins.[x]
29I tell you, I will not drink from this fruit of the vine from now on until that day when I drink it new
with you[y] in my Father's kingdom."
30When they had sung a hymn, they went out to the Mount of Olives.[z]

26:25 [u] Mt 23:7
26:26 [v] Mt 14:19; 1Co 10:16
26:28 [w] Ex 24:6-8; Heb 9:20 [x] Mt 20:28; Mk 1:4
26:29 [y] Ac 10:41
26:30 [z] Mt 21:1; Mk 14:26
26:31 [a] Mt 11:6 [b] Zec 13:7; Jn 16:32
26:32 [c] Mt 28:7,10,16

Jesus Predicts Peter's Denial

26:31-35pp — Mk 14:27-31; Lk 22:31-34

31Then Jesus told them, "This very night you will all fall away on account of me,[a] for it is written:

"'I will strike the shepherd,
and the sheep of the flock will be scattered.'[b][b]

32But after I have risen, I will go ahead of you into Galilee."[c]

[a] *28* Some manuscripts *the new* [b] *31* Zech. 13:7

26:25 You have said so. A veiled affirmative, perhaps also implying Judas's self-indictment. John 13:22–30 suggests that most of the disciples did not hear this particular interchange.
26:26–28 When Jesus "took bread" (v. 26) and "took a cup" (v. 27) and declared, "This is my body ... This is my blood" (vv. 26,28), he is adding rich symbolism to the already highly symbolic Passover meal (see notes on vv. 26,27,28).
26:26 took bread ... broke it. The broken bread represents his body, soon to be crucified.
26:27 a cup. The cup of wine, probably the third of four in the Passover meal and symbolizing redemption, stands for the blood shed in his death "for the forgiveness of sins" (v. 28).
26:28 covenant. God's new one, prophesied in Jer 31:31–34.
26:29 Jesus may have left the fourth and final cup of wine of the Passover ceremony undrunk to anticipate the great end-time banquet still to come (Isa 25:6–8).
26:30 hymn. One of the praise psalms or Hallel psalms (Pss 113–118) with which the Passover meal concluded (see note on Mark 14:26). **the Mount of Olives.** Immediately opposite the eastern gate to the temple precincts and the city of Jerusalem, across the Kidron Valley.
26:31–35 Jesus predicts Peter's denial. In v. 31 Jesus interprets Zech 13:7 as predicting an attack on himself as the Messianic "shepherd," leading to "the sheep" (his followers) being "scattered." Verse 56 fulfills v. 31, and 28:7 fulfills v. 32. Peter protests that he will not desert his Lord, but Jesus replies that Peter will "disown" him "three times" that "very night, before the rooster crows," i.e., well before daybreak (vv. 33–34). The disciples deny they could engage in such treachery (v. 35), but vv. 56,69–75 prove Jesus right.

26:34 [d] ver 75; Jn 13:38
26:35 [e] Jn 13:37
26:37 [f] Mt 4:21
26:38 [g] Jn 12:27 [h] ver 40,41
26:39 [i] Mt 20:22 [j] ver 42; Ps 40:6-8; Isa 50:5; Jn 5:30; 6:38

33 Peter replied, "Even if all fall away on account of you, I never will."
34 "Truly I tell you," Jesus answered, "this very night, before the rooster crows, you will disown me
three times."[d]
35 But Peter declared, "Even if I have to die with you,[e] I will never disown you." And all the other
disciples said the same.

Gethsemane

26:36-46pp — Mk 14:32-42; Lk 22:40-46

36 Then Jesus went with his disciples to a place called Gethsemane, and he said to them, "Sit here
while I go over there and pray." 37 He took Peter and the two sons of Zebedee[f] along with him, and he
began to be sorrowful and troubled. 38 Then he said to them, "My soul is overwhelmed with sorrow[g] to
the point of death. Stay here and keep watch with me."[h]
39 Going a little farther, he fell with his face to the ground and prayed, "My Father, if it is possible,
may this cup[i] be taken from me. Yet not as I will, but as you will."[j]

26:36–46 Gethsemane is a garden at the base of the Mount of Olives. The name means "oil press." Olive trees flourished there. No other passage in the Gospels so clearly and poignantly expresses Jesus' humanity. Even having repeatedly predicted the events to come, he longs to avoid such agony. His "soul is overwhelmed with sorrow" (v. 38). But he also surrenders entirely to God's will (v. 39). This pattern of praying is repeated twice more (vv. 42,44).
26:37 Peter and the two sons of Zebedee. These three disciples—Peter, James, and John—form Christ's inner circle (cf. 17:1).
26:39 cup. A metaphor for God's wrath (see note on 20:22). If there

JERUSALEM DURING THE MINISTRY OF JESUS

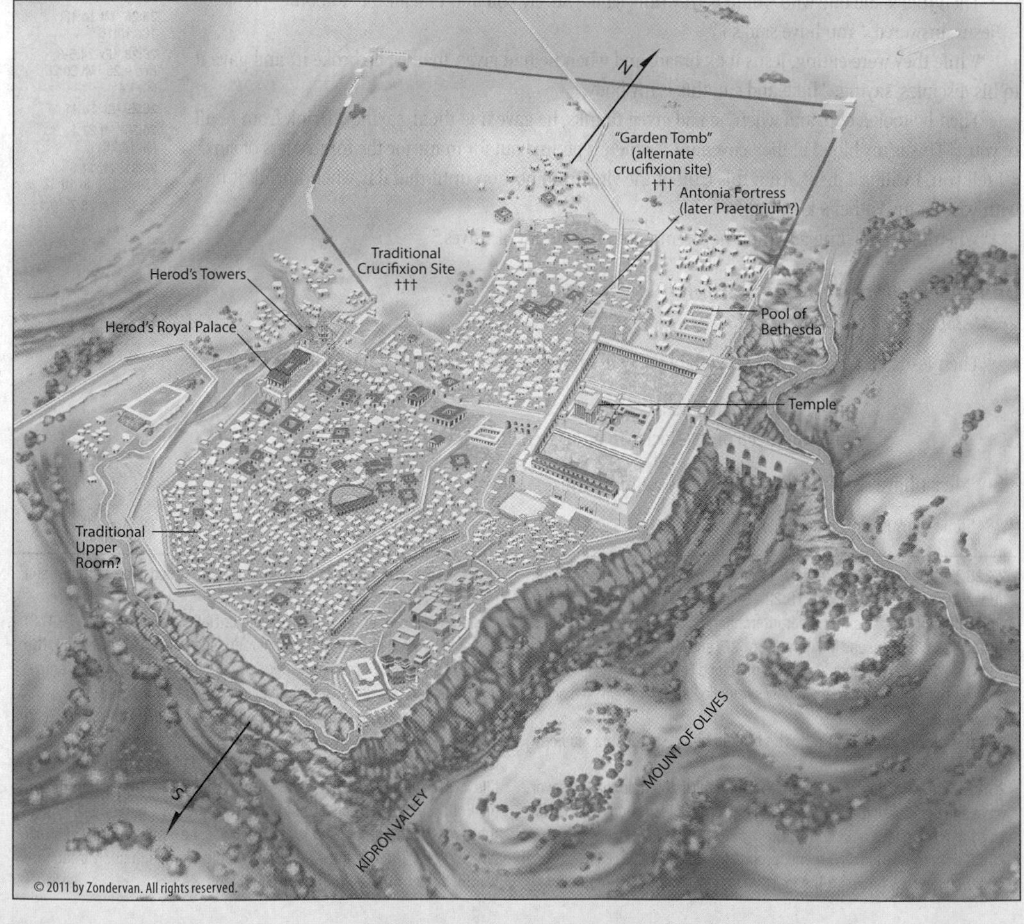

40Then he returned to his disciples and found them sleeping. "Couldn't you men keep watch with
me[k] for one hour?" he asked Peter. 41"Watch and pray so that you will not fall into temptation.[l] The
spirit is willing, but the flesh is weak."

42He went away a second time and prayed, "My Father, if it is not possible for this cup to be taken
away unless I drink it, may your will be done."

43When he came back, he again found them sleeping, because their eyes were heavy. 44So he left
them and went away once more and prayed the third time, saying the same thing.

45Then he returned to the disciples and said to them, "Are you still sleeping and resting? Look, the
hour[m] has come, and the Son of Man is delivered into the hands of sinners. 46Rise! Let us go! Here
comes my betrayer!"

Jesus Arrested

26:47-56pp — Mk 14:43-50; Lk 22:47-53

47While he was still speaking, Judas, one of the Twelve, arrived. With him was a large crowd armed
with swords and clubs, sent from the chief priests and the elders of the people. 48Now the betrayer had
arranged a signal with them: "The one I kiss is the man; arrest him." 49Going at once to Jesus, Judas
said, "Greetings, Rabbi!"[n] and kissed him.

50Jesus replied, "Do what you came for, friend."[a][o]

Then the men stepped forward, seized Jesus and arrested him. 51With that, one of Jesus' companions reached for his sword,[p] drew it out and struck the servant of the high priest, cutting off his ear.[q]

52"Put your sword back in its place," Jesus said to him, "for all who draw the sword will die by the
sword.[r] 53Do you think I cannot call on my Father, and he will at once put at my disposal more than twelve
legions of angels?[s] 54But how then would the Scriptures be fulfilled[t] that say it must happen in this way?"

55In that hour Jesus said to the crowd, "Am I leading a rebellion, that you have come out with
swords and clubs to capture me? Every day I sat in the temple courts teaching,[u] and you did not arrest
me. 56But this has all taken place that the writings of the prophets might be fulfilled."[v] Then all the
disciples deserted him and fled.

Jesus Before the Sanhedrin

26:57-68pp — Mk 14:53-65; Jn 18:12,13,19-24

57Those who had arrested Jesus took him to Caiaphas[w] the high priest, where the teachers of the law

26:40 [k] ver 38
26:41 [l] Mt 6:13
26:45 [m] ver 18
26:49 [n] ver 25
26:50 [o] Mt 20:13; 22:12
26:51 [p] Lk 22:36,38 [q] Jn 18:10
26:52 [r] Ge 9:6; Rev 13:10
26:53 [s] 2Ki 6:17; Da 7:10; Mt 4:11
26:54 [t] ver 24
26:55 [u] Mk 12:35; Lk 21:37; Jn 7:14,28; 18:20
26:56 [v] ver 24
26:57 [w] ver 3

[a] *50* Or *"Why have you come, friend?"*

were any way possible, the completely human Jesus would avert the horrible suffering ahead. Here is the classic example of one not getting what they ask for in prayer, but through no fault of the one praying!

26:41 The spirit is willing, but the flesh is weak. The truth of this principle is illustrated by the disciples, who, with far less at stake than Jesus, cannot stay awake and pray. Even Christ's closest followers may want to obey him, but they find their bodies and/or sinful human natures unable to cooperate.

26:46 my betrayer. At last Judas comes with the authorities. There will be no more time for sleep or prayer.

26:47–56 All of the details of Jesus' arrest highlight how Jesus understands exactly what is happening to him, has the ability to resist, but voluntarily chooses to submit to God's plan.

26:47 Judas, one of the Twelve. It seems odd for Matthew to repeat this so soon after v. 14, but he may be underlining the indignity of one so close to Jesus turning into his betrayer. Roman guards would have brandished the "swords"; Jewish ones, the "clubs."

26:48 kiss. Jesus may have resembled one or more of his disciples in his appearance so that in the darkness of night it would have been hard to be sure which one he was. The kiss would identify him. Men frequently greeted each other with kisses on both cheeks, but as a sign of friendship not hostility! Judas's treachery is turning even more ironic (cf. Luke 22:48).

26:49 Judas cannot bring himself to call Jesus anything more exalted than "Rabbi" ("teacher").

26:50 Do what you came for. The Greek here is terse: lit. "What you came for." "Do" completes the probable sense. **friend.** A surprisingly kind address, given that Judas has come to betray Jesus.

26:51 his sword ... the servant of the high priest. John 18:10 identifies the disciple wielding his sword as Peter and the servant of the high priest as Malchus.

26:52–54 Jesus uses what may have been a commonsense proverb (v. 52) to remind Peter that violence begets violence, whereas he has come so that the Scriptures that predict his atoning death for humanity's sins might be fulfilled (vv. 24,54,56). After all, if he needed violent resistance, he could call on as many as 72,000 ("twelve legions of") angels to annihilate the arresting party (v. 53)! Luke 22:51 adds that Jesus proceeds to heal the servant's ear.

26:55 Am I leading a rebellion ...? Jesus asks if he is being treated as if he were an insurrectionist. He notes there would have been easier times and ways to arrest him (except that it might have inflamed the crowds).

26:57–68 Several irregularities are evident in Jesus' appearance before the Sanhedrin: the court was not to come to a verdict at night, convene during the Festival, meet in the high priest's home, or condemn an accused person without witnesses to testify on behalf of the accused. But desperate leaders sometimes ignore their own laws; some of these may have been formulated only later; and 27:1–2 suggests some pretense of legality after daybreak.

26:57 Caiaphas. See note on v. 3.

26:58 [x]Jn 18:15 [y]Jn 7:32,45,46
26:59 [z]Mt 5:22
26:60 [a]Ps 27:12; 35:11; Ac 6:13 [b]Dt 19:15
26:61 [c]Jn 2:19
26:63 [d]Mt 27:12,14 [e]Lev 5:1 [f]Mt 16:16
26:64 [g]Ps 110:1 [h]Da 7:13; Rev 1:7
26:65 [i]Mk 14:63
26:66 [j]Lev 24:16; Jn 19:7
26:67 [k]Mt 16:21; 27:30
26:68 [l]Lk 22:63-65
26:75 [m]ver 34; Jn 13:38
27:1 [n]Mt 12:14; Mk 15:1; Lk 22:66
27:2 [o]Mt 20:19 [p]Mk 15:1; Lk 13:1; Ac 3:13; 1Ti 6:13

and the elders had assembled. [58]But Peter followed him at a distance, right up to the courtyard of the high priest.[x] He entered and sat down with the guards[y] to see the outcome.

[59]The chief priests and the whole Sanhedrin[z] were looking for false evidence against Jesus so that they could put him to death. [60]But they did not find any, though many false witnesses[a] came forward.

Finally two[b] came forward [61]and declared, "This fellow said, 'I am able to destroy the temple of God and rebuild it in three days.'"[c]

[62]Then the high priest stood up and said to Jesus, "Are you not going to answer? What is this testimony that these men are bringing against you?" [63]But Jesus remained silent.[d]

The high priest said to him, "I charge you under oath[e] by the living God:[f] Tell us if you are the Messiah, the Son of God."

[64]"You have said so," Jesus replied. "But I say to all of you: From now on you will see the Son of Man sitting at the right hand of the Mighty One[g] and coming on the clouds of heaven."[a][h]

[65]Then the high priest tore his clothes[i] and said, "He has spoken blasphemy! Why do we need any more witnesses? Look, now you have heard the blasphemy. [66]What do you think?"

"He is worthy of death,"[j] they answered.

[67]Then they spit in his face and struck him with their fists.[k] Others slapped him [68]and said, "Prophesy to us, Messiah. Who hit you?"[l]

Peter Disowns Jesus

26:69-75pp — Mk 14:66-72; Lk 22:55-62; Jn 18:16-18,25-27

[69]Now Peter was sitting out in the courtyard, and a servant girl came to him. "You also were with Jesus of Galilee," she said.

[70]But he denied it before them all. "I don't know what you're talking about," he said.

[71]Then he went out to the gateway, where another servant girl saw him and said to the people there, "This fellow was with Jesus of Nazareth."

[72]He denied it again, with an oath: "I don't know the man!"

[73]After a little while, those standing there went up to Peter and said, "Surely you are one of them; your accent gives you away."

[74]Then he began to call down curses, and he swore to them, "I don't know the man!"

Immediately a rooster crowed. [75]Then Peter remembered the word Jesus had spoken: "Before the rooster crows, you will disown me three times."[m] And he went outside and wept bitterly.

Judas Hangs Himself

27 Early in the morning, all the chief priests and the elders of the people made their plans how to have Jesus executed.[n] [2]So they bound him, led him away and handed him over[o] to Pilate the governor.[p]

[a] *64* See Psalm 110:1; Daniel 7:13.

26:59 Sanhedrin. See note on Mark 14:55. **looking for false evidence.** Shows that the authorities knew Jesus was innocent of any true violation of their law.
26:60 false witnesses. Mark 14:56 explains why they were initially of no use.
26:61 I am able to destroy the temple of God and rebuild it in three days. Sounds like a distorted version of John 2:19.
26:63 remained silent. Jesus' silence reflects his unwillingness to defend himself because he knows his mission is to die. **Messiah.** See note on 1:1. **Son of God.** See note on 14:33.
26:64 You have said so. Under oath, Jesus has to reply, and he uses the same veiled affirmative as in v. 25. He may also be suggesting that this is Caiaphas's way of phrasing things, but Jesus prefers to call himself the "Son of Man sitting at [God's] right hand." **coming on the clouds of heaven.** Recalls Dan 7:13. Jesus is more than an earthly Messiah, and he will be an ascended and then returning Lord.
26:65 tore his clothes. Represents extreme sorrow at what was perceived as blasphemy. **blasphemy.** In pre-70 Judaism it included not merely pronouncing the divine Name, as was also true later, but also a variety of statements or actions that transgressed a perceived boundary between humanity and deity. For Jesus to associate himself with Daniel's heavenly son of man could have been seen as blasphemy by those who rejected Jesus' claim.
26:66 worthy of death. Blasphemy was a capital offense in ancient Judaism.
26:67–68 The soldiers mock Jesus' reputation. For them he isn't even a prophet (see note on 13:57), much less the Messiah.
26:69–75 Despite his earlier protestation (vv. 33), Peter disowns Jesus. The contrast between Peter's and Jesus' behavior is striking. Jesus gives a true confession of his identity, even though it costs him his life. Peter denies even knowing Jesus, eventually doing so with a self-condemning oath (v. 74), with only two servant girls and some unspecified bystanders listening.
26:73 your accent. When speaking Aramaic Galileans had a different accent than Judeans had.
26:75 Before the rooster crows. Recalls v. 34. Peter remembers his vain boasting and weeps bitterly.
27:1–66 Judas takes his own life while Jesus continues to allow the events to unfold that will culminate in his death and burial.

3When Judas, who had betrayed him,[q] saw that Jesus was condemned, he was seized with remorse
and returned the thirty pieces of silver[r] to the chief priests and the elders. 4"I have sinned," he said,
"for I have betrayed innocent blood."
"What is that to us?" they replied. "That's your responsibility."[s]
5So Judas threw the money into the temple[t] and left. Then he went away and hanged himself.[u]
6The chief priests picked up the coins and said, "It is against the law to put this into the treasury,
since it is blood money." 7So they decided to use the money to buy the potter's field as a burial place for
foreigners. 8That is why it has been called the Field of Blood[v] to this day. 9Then what was spoken by
Jeremiah the prophet was fulfilled:[w] "They took the thirty pieces of silver, the price set on him by the
people of Israel, 10and they used them to buy the potter's field, as the Lord commanded me."[a][x]

Jesus Before Pilate

27:11-26pp — Mk 15:2-15; Lk 23:2,3,18-25; Jn 18:29–19:16

11Meanwhile Jesus stood before the governor, and the governor asked him, "Are you the king of the
Jews?"[y]
"You have said so," Jesus replied.
12When he was accused by the chief priests and the elders, he gave no answer.[z] 13Then Pilate asked
him, "Don't you hear the testimony they are bringing against you?"[a] 14But Jesus made no reply,[b] not
even to a single charge — to the great amazement of the governor.
15Now it was the governor's custom at the festival to release a prisoner[c] chosen by the crowd. 16At
that time they had a well-known prisoner whose name was Jesus[b] Barabbas. 17So when the crowd had
gathered, Pilate asked them, "Which one do you want me to release to you: Jesus Barabbas, or Jesus who
is called the Messiah?"[d] 18For he knew it was out of self-interest that they had handed Jesus over to him.
19While Pilate was sitting on the judge's seat,[e] his wife sent him this message: "Don't have anything
to do with that innocent[f] man, for I have suffered a great deal today in a dream[g] because of him."
20But the chief priests and the elders persuaded the crowd to ask for Barabbas and to have Jesus
executed.[h]

27:3 [q] Mt 10:4 [r] Mt 26:14,15
27:4 [s] ver 24
27:5 [t] Lk 1:9,21 [u] Ac 1:18
27:8 [v] Ac 1:19
27:9 [w] Mt 1:22
27:10 [x] Zec 11:12,13; Jer 32:6-9
27:11 [y] Mt 2:2
27:12 [z] Mt 26:63; Mk 14:61; Jn 19:9
27:13 [a] Mt 26:62
27:14 [b] Mk 14:61
27:15 [c] Jn 18:39
27:17 [d] ver 22; Mt 1:16
27:19 [e] Jn 19:13 [f] ver 24 [g] Ge 20:6; Nu 12:6; 1Ki 3:5; Job 33:14-16; Mt 1:20; 2:12,13,19,22
27:20 [h] Ac 3:14

a *10* See Zech. 11:12,13; Jer. 19:1-13; 32:6-9. *b* *16* Many manuscripts do not have *Jesus*; also in verse 17.

27:1 – 10 If Judas had any thought that his actions might provoke Jesus finally to rebel against Rome, the outcome of the night's events proved otherwise (vv. 1 – 2). Horrified, Judas tries to undo his deed, but he fails. No doubt in great emotional turmoil, he commits suicide (vv. 3 – 10).

27:1 made their plans how to have Jesus executed. Suggests a final wrap-up to the trial after daybreak, creating an aura of legality (see note on 26:57 – 68).

27:2 Pilate. Pontius Pilate, the Roman governor of Judea from AD 26 to 36. Jewish authorities must involve him because under Rome they had lost the right to execute their own condemned (John 18:31).

27:3 seized with remorse. Greek *metamelomai*, not the standard word for repenting. Judas recognizes his horrible mistake but cannot undo the consequences of his actions. The only option he can countenance is hanging himself in despair. See note on Acts 1:18 – 19.

27:6 – 8 Ironically, despite the gross injustice they have perpetrated against Jesus, the chief priests refuse to disobey a minor law about the use of money (cf. 23:23).

27:6 blood money. The silver is called this because it purchases Jesus' bloody death.

27:7 the potter's field. Traditionally believed to have been in the southern end of the Hinnom Valley, just outside Jerusalem. Even when Matthew wrote this Gospel, it was still known as and called "the Field of Blood" (v. 8).

27:9 – 10 Prophecy is again fulfilled typologically (see notes on 1:22; 2:15; 12:15 – 21; 15:7 – 9) as key events related to God's interaction with humanity form parallel patterns to those of their predecessors. Matthew creates a composite quotation from bits of Zech 11:12 – 13; Jer 19:1 – 13; 32:6 – 9. He refers only to Jeremiah in keeping with a convention of referring to the lesser known or less obvious of two passages in such a composite.

27:11 – 26 Jesus appears before Pilate. Like Caiaphas and the Jewish leaders before them, Pilate and the Roman authorities think they have condemned Christ. But they have actually condemned themselves by their actions, although Jesus' death also makes possible their forgiveness, should they repent.

27:11 – 14 A Roman official would care little if a Jew made blasphemous religious claims. But if he aspired to be "king of the Jews" (v. 11; cf. 2:2 – 3; 21:5), the empire would need to take action. Jesus' reply in v. 11 uses the same veiled affirmative as in 26:64, with the same possible additional implications. This time he refuses to say anything more.

27:15 governor's custom. The custom of an annual Passover amnesty is at most only hinted at in other historical sources, but it makes good sense to placate the Jews at the time they celebrate their liberation from Egyptian oppression centuries earlier. Pilate thinks he can pit the crowd against its leaders and free the innocent Jesus, but the people opt for one of their freedom fighters, Barabbas (v. 21; see John 18:40).

27:16 Jesus Barabbas. He is only called this in Matthew, and only in some manuscripts. Still, Jesus was a common name and many scribes might have preferred not to note that the man whose release kept Jesus of Nazareth in prison shared his name. It is hard to imagine any Christian inventing this detail. Ironically, Barabbas means "a son of [his] father," contrasting with Jesus as the heavenly Son of his Father, God.

27:19 dream. Roman rulers often put significant stock in a dream as an omen. This explains why Pilate keeps trying to release Jesus, but to no avail.

27:22 [j]Mt 1:16
27:24 [j]Mt 26:5 [k]Ps 26:6 [l]Dt 21:6-8 [m]ver 4
27:25 [n]Jos 2:19; Ac 5:28
27:26 [o]Isa 53:5; Jn 19:1
27:27 [p]Jn 18:28,33; 19:9
27:28 [q]Jn 19:2
27:29 [r]Isa 53:3; Jn 19:2,3
27:30 [s]Mt 16:21; 26:67
27:31 [t]Isa 53:7
27:32 [u]Heb 13:12 [v]Ac 2:10; 6:9; 11:20; 13:1 [w]Mk 15:21; Lk 23:26
27:33 [x]Jn 19:17
27:34 [y]ver 48; Ps 69:21
27:35 [z]Ps 22:18
27:36 [a]ver 54

21 “Which of the two do you want me to release to you?” asked the governor.
“Barabbas,” they answered.
22 “What shall I do, then, with Jesus who is called the Messiah?”[j] Pilate asked.
They all answered, “Crucify him!”
23 “Why? What crime has he committed?” asked Pilate.
But they shouted all the louder, “Crucify him!”
24 When Pilate saw that he was getting nowhere, but that instead an uproar[j] was starting, he took
water and washed his hands[k] in front of the crowd. “I am innocent of this man’s blood,”[l] he said. “It
is your responsibility!”[m]
25 All the people answered, “His blood is on us and on our children!”[n]
26 Then he released Barabbas to them. But he had Jesus flogged,[o] and handed him over to be crucified.

The Soldiers Mock Jesus

27:27-31pp — Mk 15:16-20

27 Then the governor’s soldiers took Jesus into the Praetorium[p] and gathered the whole company of
soldiers around him. 28 They stripped him and put a scarlet robe on him,[q] 29 and then twisted together
a crown of thorns and set it on his head. They put a staff in his right hand. Then they knelt in front of
him and mocked him. “Hail, king of the Jews!” they said.[r] 30 They spit on him, and took the staff and
struck him on the head again and again.[s] 31 After they had mocked him, they took off the robe and put
his own clothes on him. Then they led him away to crucify him.[t]

The Crucifixion of Jesus

27:33-44pp — Mk 15:22-32; Lk 23:33-43; Jn 19:17-24

32 As they were going out,[u] they met a man from Cyrene,[v] named Simon, and they forced him to
carry the cross.[w] 33 They came to a place called Golgotha (which means “the place of the skull”).[x]
34 There they offered Jesus wine to drink, mixed with gall;[y] but after tasting it, he refused to drink
it. 35 When they had crucified him, they divided up his clothes by casting lots.[z] 36 And sitting down,
they kept watch[a] over him there. 37 Above his head they placed the written charge against him: THIS
IS JESUS, THE KING OF THE JEWS.

27:22–24 The authorities may well have stirred up the crowd to call for Jesus’ crucifixion, just as they persuaded the people to ask for Barabbas’s release.

27:22 Crucify. Usually meant to affix a person to a cross-shaped pair of wooden beams, either with ropes or nails through palms and ankles, with arms outstretched until the person was so fatigued that they could no longer lift their head off their chest enough to breathe. It was a standard but very cruel form of execution the Romans used for slaves and the worst of criminals.

27:24 I am innocent … your responsibility! Pilate finally capitulates to the crowd’s request but symbolically and verbally distances himself from any responsibility in the matter.

27:25 His blood is on us and on our children! Tragically, throughout church history this cry has too often been used to justify many forms of anti-Semitism. Yet only the individuals observing Pilate’s proceedings are condemning themselves. **our children.** Refers to the next generation of offspring. The destruction of Jerusalem in AD 70 could well be the fulfillment of this self-curse. So this verse does not refer to all Jewish people of all time; it does not even refer to all Jews in Jesus’ day.

27:26 flogged. Beating a person’s back for however long the soldiers desired, with a whip embedded with bits of metal or bone on its end, tore the flesh and left searing wounds sufficient to kill some who were thus tortured, even without further punishment. Jesus would have been very weak after he was flogged.

27:27–31 The soldiers mock Jesus by dressing him as a pretend king, with a robe of royal color, a crown (but of thorns to further torture him), and a staff as a scepter. In a culture of honor and shame, the indignity of the mock allegiance to Jesus as king adds psychological torture to the physical abuse they continue to mete out.

27:27 the Praetorium. Housed Pilate’s palace and the Roman guard.

27:32–44 The torment and shame that Jesus has repeatedly predicted would befall him now ensue, culminating in his excruciating death by crucifixion.

27:32 man from Cyrene. The Synoptics all describe the commandeering of Simon of Cyrene (in modern Libya) for this task. It is easy to imagine Jesus, weakened from the flogging, not going very far without collapsing under the heavy weight and needing the help afforded here. **cross.** Typically, this would have meant the crossbeam. Jesus started out for the site of his crucifixion carrying his own cross (John 19:17).

27:33 Golgotha (which means “the place of the skull”). Probably called this because of the skull-like rock formations in the nearby hillside or the number of skulls of other victims that dotted the landscape.

27:34 wine. Functioned as a mild sedative and pain reliever, but Jesus refuses to alleviate the agony he has been called to endure. **gall.** Animal bile, but can refer to some bitter substance more generally.

27:35 divided up his clothes. The condemned were usually crucified naked, which heightened the shame. **casting lots.** Probably resembles modern dice-rolling.

27:37 The inscription on a cross advertised the crime for which someone was executed. Matthew draws attention to Jesus as king because it resonated with his emphasis on Jesus as Son of David.

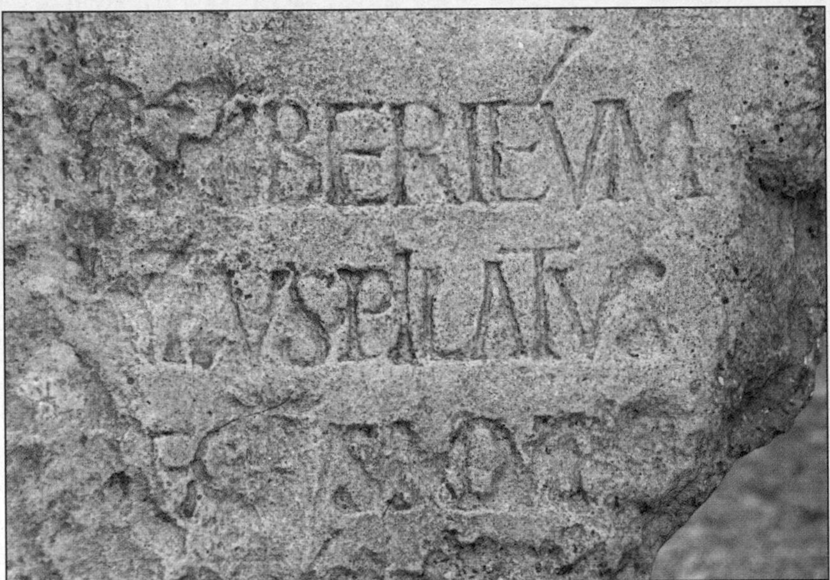

A first-century Roman inscription found at Caesarea Maritima confirms Pilate as the prefect of Judea.

[38]Two rebels were crucified with him,[b] one on his right and one on his left. [39]Those who passed by
hurled insults at him, shaking their heads[c] [40]and saying, "You who are going to destroy the temple
and build it in three days,[d] save yourself![e] Come down from the cross, if you are the Son of God!"[f]
[41]In the same way the chief priests, the teachers of the law and the elders mocked him. [42]"He saved
others," they said, "but he can't save himself! He's the king of Israel![g] Let him come down now from
the cross, and we will believe[h] in him. [43]He trusts in God. Let God rescue him[i] now if he wants him,
for he said, 'I am the Son of God.' " [44]In the same way the rebels who were crucified with him also
heaped insults on him.

27:38 [b]Isa 53:12
27:39 [c]Ps 22:7; 109:25; La 2:15
27:40 [d]Mt 26:61; Jn 2:19 [e]ver 42 [f]Mt 4:3,6
27:42 [g]Jn 1:49; 12:13 [h]Jn 3:15
27:43 [i]Ps 22:8
27:45 [j]Am 8:9
27:46 [k]Ps 22:1
27:48 [l]ver 34; Ps 69:21

The Death of Jesus

27:45-56pp — Mk 15:33-41; Lk 23:44-49; Jn 19:29-30

[45]From noon until three in the afternoon darkness[j] came over all the land. [46]About three in the
afternoon Jesus cried out in a loud voice, *"Eli, Eli,[a] lema sabachthani?"* (which means "My God, my
God, why have you forsaken me?").[bk]

[47]When some of those standing there heard this, they said, "He's calling Elijah."

[48]Immediately one of them ran and got a sponge. He filled it with wine vinegar,[l] put it on a staff,

[a] *46* Some manuscripts *Eloi, Eloi* [b] *46* Psalm 22:1

27:40–44 Despite the mockery, only by not saving himself can Jesus make salvation possible for anyone else, including his enemies.

27:40 destroy the temple and build it in three days. See 26:61.

27:43 He trusts in God. Let God rescue him now if he wants. An allusion to Ps 22:8. Jesus experiences the same treatment his ancestor David experienced.

27:45–56 Jesus' final words, the reaction of nature, and the responses of the onlookers all testify that he was no mere mortal.

27:45 afternoon darkness. Some have linked this with a solar eclipse in AD 33. But nothing prevents it from being considered a more supernatural event in 30, the more likely year for Jesus' death.

27:46 *Eli, Eli, lema sabachthani?* The preservation of these Hebrew words shows how memorable Jesus' cry was. This is the moment Jesus shoulders the sins of humanity and recognizes the rupture of his previously unbroken communion with his heavenly Father — agony worse than his physical suffering. Jesus, as son of David, reuses David's language from Ps 22:1. He too is experiencing abandonment, but the psalm goes on to envision future hope beyond the immediate despair. ***Eli.*** "My God" in Aramaic. It sounds like "Elijah" (v. 47). If Jesus' speech was slurred or unclear or if some of the listeners were unfamiliar with Aramaic, they would not have understood the rest of his words.

27:48 It is uncertain whether this second offer of a drink was meant to assuage his thirst and keep him alive a little longer or dull his senses and hasten his death.

27:50 [m] Jn 19:30
27:51 [n] Ex 26:31-33; Heb 9:3,8 [o] ver 54
27:53 [p] Mt 4:5
27:54 [q] ver 36 [r] Mt 4:3; 17:5
27:55 [s] Lk 8:2,3
27:56 [t] Mk 15:47; Lk 24:10; Jn 19:25
27:60 [u] Mt 27:66; 28:2; Mk 16:4
27:63 [v] Mt 16:21

and offered it to Jesus to drink. 49 The rest said, "Now leave him alone. Let's see if Elijah comes to
save him."
50 And when Jesus had cried out again in a loud voice, he gave up his spirit.[m]
51 At that moment the curtain of the temple[n] was torn in two from top to bottom. The earth shook,
the rocks split[o] 52 and the tombs broke open. The bodies of many holy people who had died were raised
to life. 53 They came out of the tombs after Jesus' resurrection and[a] went into the holy city[p] and appeared to many people.
54 When the centurion and those with him who were guarding[q] Jesus saw the earthquake and all that
had happened, they were terrified, and exclaimed, "Surely he was the Son of God!"[r]
55 Many women were there, watching from a distance. They had followed Jesus from Galilee to care
for his needs.[s] 56 Among them were Mary Magdalene, Mary the mother of James and Joseph,[b] and the
mother of Zebedee's sons.[t]

The Burial of Jesus

27:57-61pp — Mk 15:42-47; Lk 23:50-56; Jn 19:38-42

57 As evening approached, there came a rich man from Arimathea, named Joseph, who had
himself become a disciple of Jesus. 58 Going to Pilate, he asked for Jesus' body, and Pilate ordered
that it be given to him. 59 Joseph took the body, wrapped it in a clean linen cloth, 60 and placed it in
his own new tomb[u] that he had cut out of the rock. He rolled a big stone in front of the entrance
to the tomb and went away. 61 Mary Magdalene and the other Mary were sitting there opposite the
tomb.

The Guard at the Tomb

62 The next day, the one after Preparation Day, the chief priests and the Pharisees went to Pilate.
63 "Sir," they said, "we remember that while he was still alive that deceiver said, 'After three days I will
rise again.'[v] 64 So give the order for the tomb to be made secure until the third day. Otherwise, his disciples may come and steal the body and tell the people that he has been raised from the dead. This last
deception will be worse than the first."

a 53 Or *tombs, and after Jesus' resurrection they*   *b 56* Greek *Joses,* a variant of *Joseph*

27:50 he gave up his spirit. He died. The phrase may also suggest his voluntary submission to his destiny.

27:51 curtain of the temple was torn. A small, localized earthquake (v. 54) ensues, but it is strong enough to rip the curtain of the temple completely in two. God is preparing the way for the period of time in which he will relate to people without the various barriers in the temple that symbolized degrees of access to God. See Heb 10:19–22.

27:52–53 The grammar in the Greek here does not suggest that anyone was raised before Jesus was; the sentence spanning both verses includes both "were raised to life" (v. 52) and "came out of the tombs after Jesus' resurrection" (v. 53). Many mysteries remain: Who were these people? Why did God select them to be raised along with Jesus? To whom did they appear? How long did they stay in "the holy city" (i.e., Jerusalem)? The text answers none of these questions. But it parallels Paul's point that Jesus is the "firstfruits" of the resurrection of all people (1 Cor 15:20) and fulfills OT expectations that many people would be resurrected at the time of the day of the Lord (Dan 12:2).

27:54 Son of God! For a Roman centurion to call someone "the Son of God" may have meant Jesus was unjustly condemned and now deified upon his death. Matthew, however, recognizes testimony to the eternal and exclusive deity of Jesus.

27:55 Many women. Women played a significant role in the ministry of Jesus, in caring for his needs and those of his disciples (see also Luke 8:1–3).

27:56 Mary Magdalene. See Luke 8:2. **James.** "James the younger" (Mark 15:40), probably the same as the apostle James son of Alphaeus (see Matt 10:3 and note), in which case his mother "Mary" is otherwise unknown. **the mother of Zebedee's sons.** Salome, mother of the other apostle James and the apostle John.

27:57–61 Romans typically left the corpses of crucified people unburied for wild animals or birds to scavenge. Jews believed in burying everyone, however modestly. The new, rock-hewn tomb and the devotion Joseph lavishes on the body give Jesus a very honorable burial (vv. 59–60).

27:57 Joseph. From Arimathea and a prominent member of the Sanhedrin (Mark 15:43), he disagreed with its decision to condemn Christ (Luke 23:50–51). John 19:38 says, "Joseph was a disciple of Jesus, but secretly because he feared the Jewish leaders."

27:60 big stone. Sets the stage for 28:2. It is unlikely that the two Marys later go to the wrong tomb since they observe the burial (v. 61).

27:62–66 Various Jewish authorities remember Jesus' predictions of his death and resurrection. Even though they are convinced he was a "deceiver" (v. 63), they don't want to risk the disciples coming to steal his body and claiming he has been raised from the dead. Pilate allows the Jewish authorities access to an imperial guard and a wax seal to secure the tomb.

27:62 The next day ... after Preparation Day. Preparation Day refers to the day preparations were made for the Sabbath (Saturday); thus "Preparation Day" is Friday (Mark 15:42). So the "next day" after this day of preparation is Saturday.

27:63 three days. See 12:40 and note; 16:21; 17:23; 20:19.

65"Take a guard,"[w] Pilate answered. "Go, make the tomb as secure as you know how." 66So they went and made the tomb secure by putting a seal[x] on the stone[y] and posting the guard.[z]

Jesus Has Risen

28:1-8pp — Mk 16:1-8; Lk 24:1-10; Jn 20:1-8

28 After the Sabbath, at dawn on the first day of the week, Mary Magdalene and the other Mary[a] went to look at the tomb.

2There was a violent earthquake,[b] for an angel[c] of the Lord came down from heaven and, going to the tomb, rolled back the stone and sat on it. 3His appearance was like lightning, and his clothes were white as snow.[d] 4The guards were so afraid of him that they shook and became like dead men.

5The angel said to the women, "Do not be afraid,[e] for I know that you are looking for Jesus, who was crucified. 6He is not here; he has risen, just as he said.[f] Come and see the place where he lay. 7Then go quickly and tell his disciples: 'He has risen from the dead and is going ahead of you into Galilee.[g] There you will see him.' Now I have told you."

8So the women hurried away from the tomb, afraid yet filled with joy, and ran to tell his disciples. 9Suddenly Jesus met them.[h] "Greetings," he said. They came to him, clasped his feet and worshiped him. 10Then Jesus said to them, "Do not be afraid. Go and tell my brothers[i] to go to Galilee; there they will see me."

The Guards' Report

11While the women were on their way, some of the guards[j] went into the city and reported to the chief priests everything that had happened. 12When the chief priests had met with the elders and devised a plan, they gave the soldiers a large sum of money, 13telling them, "You are to say, 'His disciples came during the night and stole him away while we were asleep.' 14If this report gets to the governor,[k] we will satisfy him and keep you out of trouble." 15So the soldiers took the money and did as they were instructed. And this story has been widely circulated among the Jews to this very day.

27:65 [w] ver 66; Mt 28:11
27:66 [x] Da 6:17 [y] ver 60; Mt 28:2 [z] Mt 28:11
28:1 [a] Mt 27:56
28:2 [b] Mt 27:51 [c] Jn 20:12
28:3 [d] Da 10:6; Mk 9:3; Jn 20:12
28:5 [e] ver 10; Mt 14:27
28:6 [f] Mt 16:21
28:7 [g] ver 10,16; Mt 26:32
28:9 [h] Jn 20:14-18
28:10 [i] Jn 20:17; Ro 8:29; Heb 2:11-13,17
28:11 [j] Mt 27:65,66
28:14 [k] Mt 27:2

28:1 – 20 Matthew includes three scenes concerning Jesus' resurrection: the foundational appearance (vv. 1 – 10), the debunking of the earliest rival explanation of events (vv. 11 – 15), and Jesus' parting commission of his disciples (vv. 16 – 20).

28:1 the first day of the week. Sunday. **Mary Magdalene and the other Mary.** See 27:56,61. Mark 16:1 includes Salome in the group and gives the reason for their going to the tomb: to provide more embalming spices.

28:2 – 3 violent earthquake. May have been an aftershock from the one two days earlier (27:51,54). **an angel of the Lord ... clothes were white as snow.** Corresponds to the "young man dressed in a white robe" in Mark 16:5. Luke 24:4 has two men "in clothes that gleamed like lightning," but perhaps only one spoke on this occasion — Matthew's and Mark's focus of attention.

28:4 The guards. See 27:62 – 66. **became like dead men.** Suggests they were unable to move for a time, like in a "dead faint." The events of vv. 2 – 4 appear to precede the women's arrival at the tomb.

28:5 Do not be afraid. Given the guards' terror, it is appropriate for the angel to tell the women not to be afraid.

28:6 he has risen. Relying solely on Paul's letters, one can demonstrate that the first post-Easter disciples, who clearly believed in Jesus' bodily resurrection, incorporated the truth of Jesus' resurrection into their earliest teaching and preaching. In other words, Saul of Tarsus, just after his conversion (in ca. AD 32, about 16 years before the council of Gal 2:1 – 10 in 48; see Gal 1:18; 2:1) was taught the list of eyewitnesses to the event (1 Cor 15:3 – 8), already widely agreed upon as fundamental information for new believers. But because Jesus died no earlier than AD 30, resurrection belief is scarcely some slowly evolving myth. **just as he said.** Harks back to Jesus' predictions in 12:40; 16:21; 17:23; 20:19; 26:32. **Come and see the place where he lay.** Offers empirical proof of the empty tomb. This is not just some "spiritual" resurrection that leaves the corpse still in its grave.

28:7 going ahead of you into Galilee. Jesus had promised to go ahead of them into Galilee after he had risen (26:32). His tomb is just outside Jerusalem in Judea. The return to Galilee, which is distinctive to Matthew's Gospel, may well be seen by Matthew as the fulfillment of Isa 9:1 – 2, which he quotes in Matt 4:15 – 16. A light dawns on those living in the land of the shadow of death.

28:8 afraid yet filled with joy. A reasonable response to such wondrous events.

28:9 Jesus met them. Before the women could report back to his disciples, Jesus met them and greeted them. **clasped his feet and worshiped him.** A posture of obeisance by these women and their acknowledgment of Jesus' deity flow from this appearance of Jesus. Note that no ancient legend would have made women the first witnesses to the resurrection, given that a woman's testimony was generally not admitted in legal contexts.

28:10 go and tell. Jesus repeats the command of v. 7. **my brothers.** Jesus treats the disciples as family.

28:11 – 15 This is the sequel to 27:62 – 66. The soldiers could have been executed for shirking their duties, but the Jewish authorities bribe them to tell their superiors the very story about grave-robbing that their presence at the tomb was designed to thwart! Should news of all this reach Pilate, the Jewish authorities would satisfy him, no doubt with a very large bribe, in order to keep the soldiers out of trouble.

28:16 [l] ver 7,10; Mt 26:32
28:18 [m] Da 7:13,14; Lk 10:22; Jn 3:35; 17:2; 1Co 15:27; Eph 1:20-22; Php 2:9,10
28:19 [n] Mk 16:15,16; Lk 24:47; Ac 1:8; 14:21
[o] Ac 2:38; 8:16; Ro 6:3,4
28:20 [p] Ac 2:42
[q] Mt 18:20; Ac 18:10
[r] Mt 13:39

The Great Commission

16 Then the eleven disciples went to Galilee, to the mountain where Jesus had told them to go.[l]
17 When they saw him, they worshiped him; but some doubted. 18 Then Jesus came to them and said,
"All authority in heaven and on earth has been given to me.[m] 19 Therefore go and make disciples of
all nations,[n] baptizing them in the name of the Father and of the Son and of the Holy Spirit,[o] 20 and
teaching[p] them to obey everything I have commanded you. And surely I am with you[q] always, to the
very end of the age."[r]

28:16–20 These verses include the Great Commission (vv. 18–20). The uniquely Jewish mission of 10:5–6 and 15:24 now gives way to the mandate for worldwide, multiethnic ministry. As many as possible, Jew and Gentile alike, must be given opportunity to become part of the "people who will produce [the] fruit" of God's kingdom (21:43).
28:16 the eleven disciples. The Twelve minus Judas. **mountain.** No record is given of Jesus' previous instruction about a specific mountain in Galilee. Perhaps it is the (also unspecified) location of the Sermon on the Mount (chs. 5–7).
28:17 they worshiped him; but some doubted. Could also be translated "they worshiped, but they doubted." For such an unprecedented event as a resurrection, it is easy to envision any or all of the disciples both acclaiming Jesus' deity and being very perplexed as to what exactly had happened and wondering if all this was real.
28:18–20 As a result of his faithfulness to his mission, Jesus once again has returned to his exalted position as divine Son of God with "all authority in heaven and on earth" (v. 18). Christ's program of missions for his followers flowed from this: to "make disciples of all nations" (v. 19). It involves three steps: (1) going, (2) "baptizing them," and (3) "teaching them to obey everything" Christ has commanded.
28:19 make disciples. By his authority, Jesus commands the eleven to "make disciples" of "all nations" (Greek *ethnē*, i.e., all people groups in the world). To begin this process in the first century certainly meant that they would have to "go" to many places, but the main command is "make disciples." While discipling requires bringing people to saving faith in Christ, it involves much more, including all the nurture they need throughout the rest of their lives. **baptizing them.** Jesus singles out for special mention the command to baptize them in the triune name of the Godhead, the earliest known use of this Trinitarian formula. An unbaptized follower of Jesus in the apostolic era would have been viewed as quite an anomaly. **in the name of the Father and of the Son and of the Holy Spirit.** That "the name" is singular of three persons suggests a unity of being of Father, Son, and Holy Spirit.
28:20 teaching them to obey everything I have commanded you. Is never exhausted, even over a lifetime. **with you always.** Jesus promises his (spiritual) presence with them always, empowering them for the task. The One who was introduced near the beginning of the Gospel as "God with us" (1:23) plays precisely that role as the Gospel ends. **to the very end of the age.** Refers to the end of human history as we know it, when Christ will return. Then he will be visibly present with all of his people for all eternity.

INTRODUCTION TO MARK

AUTHOR

Although the Gospel itself lacks any direct internal evidence of its author, its ancient titles and early church tradition unanimously ascribe it to John Mark, or more simply "Mark" without an additional identifier (Acts 12:12). The small number of early Christians, few of whom could write (and even fewer of whom had the community standing and wherewithal to produce this kind of work), suggests that a simple "Mark" sufficed since everyone knew who he was. Our fullest evidence comes from Papias (ca. AD 125). He records John the Elder's claim (ca. AD 90) that Mark was Peter's younger associate who recorded accurately all of Peter's various teachings about Jesus and compiled them into a single work.

JOHN MARK IN THE NT

A bilingual Hellenist—John being his Hebrew name and Mark his Greek one—and relative of the wealthy Cyprian landowner Barnabas (Col 4:10; cf. Acts 4:36), John Mark's well-to-do family occupied a significant place in early Christian communities, first in Jerusalem and later in Antioch. His mother's substantial house provided a focal gathering point for believers in Jerusalem and was the first port of call for a recently escaped Peter (Acts 12:12–16), who when writing later from Rome described Mark as "my son" (1 Pet 5:13). Mark joined his cousin Barnabas and Paul in their early travels from Antioch (Acts 12:25; 13:2–3) and, in spite of a falling-out (Acts 13:13; 15:36–39), later worked closely with Paul (Col 4:10; Phlm 24), even being summoned to Paul's last imprisonment, also in Rome (2 Tim 4:11).

John Mark was therefore well placed to write his Gospel. The great bulk of his oral material would have come through his regular contact with Peter, with perhaps his mother's female friends providing the information for which they are explicitly named: the events surrounding the empty tomb (15:40—16:8). Equally, some of his insights into Jesus' significance may well have come from Paul, to whom Jesus later appeared (cf. 1 Cor 15:8).

DATE

Dating the Gospels is notoriously difficult. But the above scenario is consistent with the bulk of church tradition, which has Mark writing while Peter is yet living. That dates it perhaps in the late AD 50s or early 60s.

PLACE OF COMPOSITION AND DESTINATION

Clear evidence is again lacking, but according to the majority of early tradition, Mark was written in Rome (see 1 Pet 5:13, where Mark is with Peter in "Babylon," usually understood to be Rome). Mark's immediate audience would then include Rome's Jewish and Gentile believers. This explains his various Latinisms, Western terms (e.g., 12:42), and his inclusion of translations of Jesus' Aramaic words (e.g., 3:17; 5:41; 7:11,34; 14:36; 15:34). However, the interrelatedness of the early Christian communities and the fact that many early Christian leaders often traveled between them strongly suggest Mark also envisaged a wider readership.

OCCASION AND PURPOSE

No reason is given either in the Gospel or later sources as to why Mark wrote what he did when he did. The sometimes-cited persecution in Rome under Nero in AD 64–67 seems too late; and in any case other Christians were already suffering long before that time (e.g., Phil 1:29; 1 Thess 2:2,14). But while persecution might explain Mark's emphasis on cross-bearing discipleship, there is much more to his Gospel. Large-scale Jewish rejection of the gospel also raised concerns about the gospel's validity. As Paul does in Rom 9–11, Mark grounds both the gospel and its rejection in Israel's own Scriptural tradition, showing his story's continuity with God's previous promises and Israel's persistent rebellion. It may simply be, however, given the long-standing Jewish commitment to writing down the acts and words of God, that the overwhelming conviction that God himself was uniquely present in Jesus was sufficient reason to record, after some time of reflection, his words and deeds for their own sake.

GENRE

Mark's Gospel best fits the broadly defined ancient genre of biography. Its twin tasks were to preserve the memory and teaching of the subject and to win followers and defend against detractors. But there the similarities end. Lacking the polished sophistication of elite literature, this work with its lively and down-to-earth style was, like its good news, for everyone. But more significantly, Mark impresses his audience with the overwhelming importance and "otherness" of his story, due entirely to the figure of Jesus: his authority and teaching is unlike anything previously experienced in any human being. By deliberately grounding the good news of Jesus in Israel's story, Mark provides the lens for understanding both Jesus' importance and "otherness." Jesus is, however unexpectedly and mysteriously, the long-awaited presence of Israel's unique God come to fulfill his ancient promises to save his people and through them his world.

Designed to be heard rather than read, Mark's gripping immediate style impels his narrative through a range of scenes, often carefully interwoven to enhance their effect. He invites his audience to ponder the significance of these astonishing events by comparing the behaviors of Jesus, his disciples, his opponents, various minor characters, and the crowds—all against the larger backdrop of Israel's ancient narrative of God's historical dealings with his people. In this, Mark's Gospel functions as did Jesus' parables: revealing the condition of his hearers' hearts and opening up the secret of God's kingdom to those who gather around Jesus.

HOLY LAND IN THE TIME OF JESUS

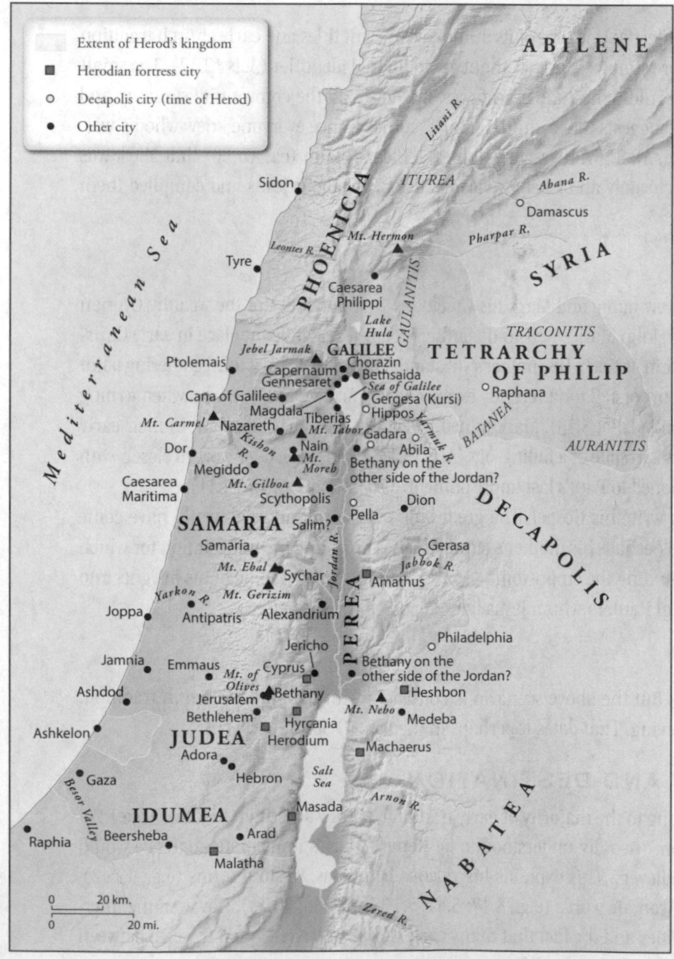

THEMES AND THEOLOGY

1. *The mystery of Jesus.* Although Jesus is clearly human, nevertheless, as God's beloved Son (1:11; 9:7), the Son of Man (e.g., 2:10,28; 14:62), Isaiah's

Chapels located at Bethany on the other side of the Jordan, one of the possible sites of Jesus' baptism (Mark 1:9).

suffering servant (e.g., 8:31; 10:45), and the Davidic Messiah (e.g., 1:11 [see note]; 10:47), he also clearly exercises God's unique authority (1:40–41; 2:10; 4:39; 6:48) and compassion (6:34; 8:2). Since in him "all the fullness of the Deity lives in bodily form" (Col 2:9), doing God's will now means following and listening to Jesus (Mark 3:34–35; 9:7; 10:21).

2. *The character of God.* Since Jesus is divine, his actions reveal clearly who God is. In Jesus' taking on the role of Isaiah's suffering servant, God's exercise of his power must now be understood in the light of the cross and Jesus' death, in weakness and shame, even by his enemies (8:31; 14:16–21,29–31,36; cf. 1 Cor 1:18–25).

3. *Discipleship.* Just as God earlier had called Israel to reflect his character, so too must Jesus' followers reflect his character, especially in self-denying, cross-bearing discipleship (8:34–38). Holiness is a matter of the heart (7:15–23) and is expressed particularly in love of God—and thus love of Jesus—and in how we treat others (9:35–10:16; cf. 12:30–31). Moreover, Jesus' followers must be prepared to face the same kind of rejection he experienced.

4. *The Messianic secret.* Jesus prevents the impure spirits (1:23–25; 3:11–12) and his disciples (8:29–30; 9:9) from revealing his identity until after his resurrection (9:9) because his true nature can be understood only from the foot of the cross (15:39).

5. *Opposition and failure to understand.* From the outset Jesus encounters resistance from Israel's leadership (2:1–3:6,28–29; 11:18) and an increasing lack of understanding in his disciples (4:13,40–41; 6:52; 8:17–21,33; 9:32). Both are addressed through Jesus' parables that speak to the idolatrous blindness and deafness of the human heart that rejects God's ways for its own (4:11–12). Tragically, having refused John's call to repentance (11:29–33), Israel's religious leaders ultimately reject Jesus (14:61–64). As a result, their temple will be destroyed (13:1–2), and the stone they rejected will become the cornerstone of a new temple in which all nations can worship (12:10; see "Temple," p. 2652).

6. *Salvation and Christian identity.* The salvation Jesus brings is deeply grounded in Israel's story and the promises of Israel's unique God. Although Mark appeals particularly to the events of the exodus and Isaiah's promised new

exodus (see "Exile and Exodus," p. 2659), material from Malachi, Daniel, Psalms, Jeremiah, Zechariah, and a range of other Scriptural texts also contribute to the structure and content of Mark's account of Jesus' message and mission. Christian identity, as Paul also declared (Rom 11:13–36), is about the nations joining God's new Israel (cf. Gal 6:16), though now reconstituted around Jesus (Gal 3:13–14).

OUTLINE

I. Beginnings: The Good News of God's Return to His People (1:1–13)
- A. John the Baptist Prepares the Way (1:1–8)
  - 1. Jesus Is Isaiah's Promised Lord (1:1–3)
  - 2. John Is Malachi's Promised Elijah (1:4–8)
- B. The Baptism and Testing of Jesus (1:9–13)

II. The Lord in Strength: Jesus' Mighty Words and Deeds in Galilee and Beyond (1:14—8:21)
- A. Jesus Announces the Good News (1:14–15)
- B. Jesus Calls His First Disciples (1:16–20)
- C. A New Teaching With Authority (1:21–45)
  - 1. Jesus Drives Out an Impure Spirit (1:21–28)
  - 2. Jesus Heals Many (1:29–34)
  - 3. Jesus Prays in a Solitary Place (1:35–39)
  - 4. Jesus Heals a Man With Leprosy (1:40–45)
- D. Emerging Local Opposition: Questions About Jesus' Authority and Holiness (2:1—3:6)
  - 1. Jesus Forgives and Heals a Paralyzed Man (2:1–12)
  - 2. Jesus Calls Levi and Eats With Sinners (2:13–17)
  - 3. Jesus Questioned About Fasting (2:18–22)
  - 4. Jesus Is Lord of the Sabbath (2:23–28)
  - 5. Jesus Heals on the Sabbath (3:1–6)
- E. Jesus Withdraws to Continue His Mission (3:7–19)
  - 1. Crowds Follow Jesus (3:7–12)
  - 2. Jesus Appoints the Twelve (3:13–19)
- F. Jesus Accused by His Family and by Teachers of the Law (3:20–35)
- G. Jesus Responds With Parables of Word and Deed (4:1—5:43)
  - 1. Four Parables of Word (4:1–34)
    - a. The Parable of the Sower (4:1–20)
    - b. A Lamp on a Stand (4:21–25)
    - c. The Parable of the Growing Seed (4:26–29)
    - d. The Parable of the Mustard Seed (4:30–34)
  - 2. Four "Parables" of Deed (4:35—5:43)
    - a. Jesus Calms the Storm (4:35–41)
    - b. Jesus Restores a Demon-Possessed Man (5:1–20)
    - c. Jesus Raises a Dead Girl and Heals a Sick Woman (5:21–43)
- H. Prophets Without Honor ... and More Than a Prophet (6:1–56)
  - 1. A Prophet Without Honor (6:1–6a)
  - 2. Jesus Sends Out the Twelve (6:6b–13)
  - 3. John the Baptist Beheaded (6:14–29)
  - 4. More Than a Prophet (6:30–56)
    - a. Jesus Feeds the Five Thousand (6:30–44)
    - b. Jesus Walks on the Water (6:45–56)
- I. True Holiness and the Inclusion of the Nations (7:1—8:21)
  - 1. That Which Defiles (7:1–23)
    - a. Jesus Rebukes Some Pharisees and Teachers of the Law (7:1–13)
    - b. It Is Not Food but the Heart That Defiles (7:14–23)

2. Salvation to the Gentiles: Healings and a Feeding (7:24—8:13)
   a. Jesus Honors a Syrophoenician Woman's Faith (7:24–30)
   b. Jesus Heals a Deaf and Mute Man (7:31–37)
   c. Jesus Feeds the Four Thousand (8:1–13)
3. The Yeast of the Pharisees and Herod (8:14–21)
   a. Jesus Warns His Disciples (8:14–15)
   b. The Blindness of the Disciples (8:16–21)

III. The New Exodus Way of the Crucified Lord (8:22—10:52)

A. The Beginning of Sight (8:22–30)
   1. Jesus Heals a Blind Man at Bethsaida (8:22–26)
   2. Peter Declares That Jesus Is the Messiah (8:27–30)

B. Following the Crucified Lord (8:31—10:45)
   1. Jesus Predicts His Death (8:31–33)
   2. The Way of the Cross (8:34—9:1)
   3. A New Sinai: God's Affirmation of Jesus and the Disciples' Failure (9:2–29)
      a. The Transfiguration (9:2–13)
      b. Jesus Heals a Boy Possessed by an Impure Spirit (9:14–29)
   4. Jesus Predicts His Death a Second Time (9:30–37)
   5. Jesus' New Law (9:38—10:31)
      a. Whoever Is Not Against Us Is for Us (9:38–41)
      b. Causing to Stumble (9:42–50)
      c. Divorce (10:1–12)
      d. The Little Children and Jesus (10:13–16)
      e. The Rich and the Kingdom of God (10:17–31)
   6. The Disciples' Continued Blindness (10:32–45)
      a. Jesus Predicts His Death a Third Time (10:32–34)
      b. The Request of James and John (10:35–45)

C. Blind Bartimaeus Receives His Sight (10:46–52)

IV. Jerusalem: A New Temple, a New Covenant, and a New Passover (11:1—15:47)

A. The Lord's Return to His Temple (11:1—13:37)
   1. Jesus Comes to Jerusalem as King (11:1–11)
   2. The Lord of the Temple Confronts the Temple Authorities (11:12—12:44).
      a. Jesus Announces Judgment on the Temple (11:12—12:12)
         (1) Jesus Curses a Fig Tree and Clears the Temple Courts (11:12–26)
         (2) The Authority of Jesus Questioned (11:27–33)
         (3) The Parable of the Tenants (12:1–12)
      b. The Temple's Lord Teaches in His House (12:13–44)
         (1) Paying the Imperial Tax to Caesar (12:13–17)
         (2) Marriage at the Resurrection (12:18–27)
         (3) The Greatest Commandment (12:28–34)
         (4) Whose Son Is the Messiah? (12:35–37)
         (5) Warning Against the Teachers of the Law (12:38–40)
         (6) The Widow's Offering (12:41–44).
   3. The End of an Era: God's Judgment on Jerusalem and Its Impure Temple (13:1–37)
      a. The Destruction of the Temple and Signs of the End Times (13:1–31)
      b. The Day and the Hour Unknown (13:32–37)

B. A New Passover and a New Covenant (14:1—15:47)
   1. Jesus Anointed at Bethany (14:1–11)
   2. A New Covenant and a New Regathering (14:12–31)
      a. The Last Supper (14:12–26)
      b. Jesus Predicts Peter's Denial (14:27–31)

3. The Faithful Messianic Son and His Betrayal (14:32–52)
   a. Gethsemane (14:32–42)
   b. Jesus Arrested (14:43–52)
4. Jesus on Trial (14:53—15:20)
   a. Jesus in the Hands of the Chief Priests and Teachers of the Law: God's Son and Israel's Lord (14:53–72)
      (1) Jesus Before the Sanhedrin (14:53–65)
      (2) Peter Disowns Jesus (14:66–72)
   b. Jesus in the Hands of Gentiles: God's Messianic King for the Nations (15:1–20)
      (1) Jesus Before Pilate (15:1–15)
      (2) The Soldiers Mock Jesus (15:16–20)
5. The New Passover Sacrifice (15:21–47)
   a. The Crucifixion of Jesus (15:21–32)
   b. The Death of Jesus (15:33–41)
   c. The Burial of Jesus (15:42–47)

V. Jesus Has Risen (16:1–8)

MARK

John the Baptist Prepares the Way

1:2-8pp — Mt 3:1-11; Lk 3:2-16

1:1 [a]Mt 4:3
1:2 [b]Mal 3:1; Mt 11:10; Lk 7:27
1:3 [c]Isa 40:3; Jn 1:23

1 The beginning of the good news about Jesus the Messiah,[a] the Son of God,[ba] 2 as it is written in
Isaiah the prophet:

> "I will send my messenger ahead of you,
> who will prepare your way"[cb]—
> 3 "a voice of one calling in the wilderness,
> 'Prepare the way for the Lord,
> make straight paths for him.'"[dc]

[a] *1* Or *Jesus Christ. Messiah* (Hebrew) and *Christ* (Greek) both mean *Anointed One.* [b] *1* Some manuscripts do not have *the Son of God.* [c] *2* Mal. 3:1 [d] *3* Isaiah 40:3

1:1–13 *Beginnings: The Good News of God's Return to His People.* These verses serve to introduce the Gospel as both what Jesus himself proclaimed as recorded in the rest of the book and what already had been proclaimed to Mark's hearers. The opening appeal to two prophetic texts establishes the essential outline and themes of Mark's Gospel (vv. 1–3). It also grounds the Gospel in Israel's prophetic hopes and so prepares us first for John, the messenger of whom these prophets spoke (vv. 4–8), and then Jesus, the Lord whose coming the prophets foretold and for whose coming John was to prepare (vv. 9–15).

1:1–8 *John the Baptist Prepares the Way.* While only Matthew and Luke relate the events of Jesus' birth, all four Gospels emphasize John's role in preparing for Jesus. John is indeed a prophet. But more particularly he is Malachi's prophesied Elijah, whose task was to prepare Israel for the long-delayed return of God to Jerusalem and his temple.

1:1–3 *Jesus Is Isaiah's Promised Lord.* These verses locate Jesus' mission and message in the context of Isaiah's great hopes of a new exodus from exile.

1:1 beginning. Perhaps echoing Gen 1:1 (cf. John 1:1), Mark's concern is how the Good News about Jesus, in whom his hearers have believed (Rom 1:1–6), first began. **good news.** Used of the birth of the Roman Emperor Augustus. Here it means the good news of God's intervention on behalf of his people and, through them, the world (see note on v. 14). **Messiah.** The formal title for the anointed son of David whose throne would be established forever when God delivered his people (cf., e.g., Isa 9:7; Jer 23:5; 30:9; Ezek 37:24–25). **Son of God.** Whether these words are original is debated (see second NIV text note on v. 1), their absence being more consistent with other early references to the gospel (e.g., Rom 15:19; 1 Cor 9:12; 2 Cor 2:12; 9:13; 10:14; Gal 1:7; Phil 1:27; 1 Thess 3:2). The designation was first used by God of Israel (Exod 4:22; Hos 11:1; cf. Deut 32:18), then of David and his faithful son (2 Sam 7:14; Ps 2:7; cf. v. 11 and note), and later by others of righteous individuals (in the Apocrypha see Sirach 4:10; Wisdom of Solomon 2:18). In Mark it also takes on the even more important sense of Jesus' unique relationship to God the Father (especially in 1:11; 9:7; cf. 5:7; 12:6; 13:32), which may explain its presence here.

1:2–3 Isaiah is the most influential OT prophetic work in the NT and in Mark. Thus, although the quotation in v. 2 comes from Mal 3:1, it is followed in v. 3 by a quotation from Isa 40:3 (see NIV text notes on vv. 2–3), with Mark's "as it is written in Isaiah" following an ancient convention by introducing the combined citation with its most important source (here, Isaiah). Jesus' story fulfills Isaiah's prophecy that God would rescue his people and restore Jerusalem to be a light to the nations. Both Isa 40:3 and Mal 3:1 promise a messenger who will prepare for the coming, not of the Messiah, but of the Lord himself. In Isaiah the messenger was to encourage exiled Israel to believe the announcement of God's coming in a powerful new exodus (see, e.g., Isa 40:3–11; 42:16; 43:2–7,16–19; 48:20—49:11; 51:10; cf. Isa 11:11–16) to redeem and lead them to a restored Jerusalem (see "Exile and Exodus," p. 2659). However, back in their homeland, Israel's continued disobedience meant God himself had not returned to dwell among them (Isa 59:9–15; 63:15—64:12). Over a century later, Malachi declared that God would send his messenger to purify the priesthood (Mal 3:3) in preparation for the returning Lord and his great and terrible day of judgment against the wicked (Mal 3:5; 4:5). If Israel failed to respond, then when the Lord came "suddenly" to his temple (Mal 3:1), he would curse the land (Mal 4:6). For Mark, John the Baptist is that messenger (vv. 4–8) and Jesus is the Lord whose way John prepares (vv. 9–15). As demonstrated by his mighty words and awesome deeds, Jesus is, in some mysterious way, the long-awaited presence of God himself come to save his people (Col 2:9). But Israel must repent and believe (v. 15). If they and their priesthood fail

1:4 [d]Mt 3:1 [e]Ac 13:24 [f]Lk 1:77
1:6 [g]Lev 11:22
1:7 [h]Ac 13:25
1:8 [i]Isa 44:3; Joel 2:28; Ac 1:5; 2:4; 11:16; 19:4-6
1:9 [j]Mt 2:23
1:10 [k]Jn 1:32
1:11 [l]Mt 3:17

4 And so John the Baptist[d] appeared in the wilderness, preaching a baptism of repentance[e] for the
forgiveness of sins.[f] 5 The whole Judean countryside and all the people of Jerusalem went out to him.
Confessing their sins, they were baptized by him in the Jordan River. 6 John wore clothing made of
camel's hair, with a leather belt around his waist, and he ate locusts[g] and wild honey. 7 And this was
his message: "After me comes the one more powerful than I, the straps of whose sandals I am not
worthy to stoop down and untie.[h] 8 I baptize you with[a] water, but he will baptize you with[a] the Holy
Spirit."[i]

The Baptism and Testing of Jesus

1:9-11pp — Mt 3:13-17; Lk 3:21,22
1:12,13pp — Mt 4:1-11; Lk 4:1-13

9 At that time Jesus came from Nazareth[j] in Galilee and was baptized by John in the Jordan. 10 Just
as Jesus was coming up out of the water, he saw heaven being torn open and the Spirit descending on
him like a dove.[k] 11 And a voice came from heaven: "You are my Son,[l] whom I love; with you I am well
pleased."

[a] 8 Or *in*

---

to respond to the proclamation of Jesus' messenger, the coming of the Lord to his temple will instead mean devastation (cf. ch. 13).

1:4–8 *John Is Malachi's Promised Elijah.* As Malachi's promised Elijah, John, through his preaching and baptism, intends to prepare Israel for the Lord's coming.

1:4 John. Means "the LORD is gracious"; John's call to repentance is God's gracious preparation for his coming (see note on vv. 2–3). **wilderness.** An arid region to the southeast of Jerusalem. The setting evoked memories of the desert where Israel first became God's people (Exod 19) and where God would again purify them (Ezek 20:35–38). Against this backdrop and in the context of the Isa 40:3 quotation found in v. 3, John's location underlines the significance of his mission in preparation for God's new exodus coming (see notes on vv. 2–3,8). **baptism.** Such a distinctively new development (see note on v. 8) that John was identified by it (being called "John the Baptist"). It was an outward sign of heartfelt repentance toward God in preparation for his coming. Israel's prophets, including Isaiah and Malachi, had consistently called Israel to repentance in order that they might know God's gracious forgiveness and be reconciled to him.

1:5 Not having seen a prophet for nearly four centuries, the people's excitement is understandable. **whole ... all.** Hyperbole emphasizing John's impact but at the same time indicating a great hunger among the people and implying that the temple authorities must have been aware of John's preaching (cf. 11:29–32). **Confessing their sins.** A biblical prerequisite for national reconciliation (1 Kgs 8:33–36; Dan 9:19–21; cf. Lev 5:5; Ps 32:5), it indicates the centrality and genuineness of their repentance. John's ministry is presented as inaugurating the fulfillment of Isaiah's new exodus, which Jesus himself would complete through his baptism in the Spirit (1:8) and his death as the suffering servant (see notes on 8:22—10:52; 8:31; 9:12; 10:33,45; 14:22,24).

1:6 Malachi identified God's coming messenger as Elijah (Mal 4:5). This gave rise to a common Jewish tradition that Elijah would prepare God's people for the Lord's return (Mal 3:1; see note on 9:13). **camel's hair ... leather belt.** Identifies John as Malachi's "Elijah" (2 Kgs 1:8; cf. 9:13; Zech 13:4; see note on John 1:21). His rough attire and "clean" desert food (Lev 11:21–22) mark him as one living apart from an impure and self-indulgent Israel (cf. 9:19; Matt 11:8).

1:7 one more powerful. In the context of Mark's opening appeal to Isaiah (vv. 2–3), this echoes the prophet's promise that the mighty God, who was more powerful than Israel's oppressors, would come to judge his foes and restore Zion (Isa 49:24–26; cf. Isa 40:10; 42:13; 50:2; 51:9; 52:10; 53:1; 59:16; 60:16; 62:8; 63:1,5,12; cf. also Gen 49:24; Deut 10:17; Ps 45:3; Isa 1:24; 9:6; 10:21). Israel's deliverance is at hand. **sandals ... not worthy to ... untie.** Servants traditionally untied their master's sandals (see note on John 1:27). John, who as a prophet is God's servant alone, claims he is unworthy of even this lowly service for the one he announces (cf. Luke 17:10).

1:8 he will baptize you with the Holy Spirit. According to Isa 63:11, God sent his Holy Spirit among Israel as they passed through the sea. Several of the prophets declared that in the last days God would pour out his Spirit upon his people (Isa 32:15; 44:3; Ezek 11:18–19; 37:14; 39:29; Joel 2:28–29). The combination of the wilderness, passing through water, and the promised Spirit suggests to some that John's baptism is a reenactment of the exodus, particularly as described in Isa 63:11, in anticipation of God's pouring out of the promised last-days Spirit on his redeemed people (cf. 1 Cor 10:1–2; see "Exile and Exodus," p. 2659). Israel's Messiah and Isaiah's faithful servant would both be especially marked by the Spirit (see note on v. 10; Isa 11:2; 42:1; cf. Isa 61:1–2).

1:9–13 *The Baptism and Testing of Jesus.* Mark introduces the central figure of his Gospel. Whereas God had previously spoken through Scripture (vv. 2–3) and then through his prophet John (vv. 7–8), he himself now speaks directly from heaven to identify Jesus as his beloved Son (v. 11).

1:9 At that time. Probably around AD 28 or 29, when Jesus was in his early 30s. Isa 40:3 and Mal 3:1 (the quotations in vv. 2–3) are concerned primarily with the one whom the messenger heralded, namely, the Lord (see note on vv. 2–3), but here it is Jesus who comes. **Nazareth in Galilee.** A minor town some 70 miles (113 kilometers) to the north of Jerusalem; Jesus spent most of his early life there. **baptized by John.** Not only identifies Jesus with his people Israel—though, unlike them, he has no sins to confess (cf. v. 5)—but shows him to be the one who will save them.

1:10 Recalling the exodus, Isaiah's last great prayer (Isa 63:7—64:12) asked God to again rend the heavens, come down, and make his name known by doing amazing and fearful things that no one expected (Isa 64:1–3). **heaven being torn open.** God has at last answered Isaiah's request through the descent of his Spirit upon Jesus, whose mighty deeds, particularly that of casting out demons, regularly cause amazement and fear (vv. 22,27; 2:12; 4:41; 5:15,33,42; 6:50; 7:37; 9:6; 12:17; 15:5; 16:8). **dove.** The symbolism is unclear; it may represent honesty, integrity, and a nonaggressive nature (cf. Matt 10:16) or, as a traditional symbol for Israel, it could indicate that the Spirit-indwelt Jesus will embody what Israel was always intended to be.

1:11 The rare experience of God's audible voice both attests to and

[12]At once the Spirit sent him out into the wilderness, [13]and he was in the wilderness forty days, being
tempted[a] by Satan.[m] He was with the wild animals, and angels attended him.

1:13 [m]Mt 4:10
1:14 [n]Mt 4:12 [o]Mt 4:23
1:15 [p]Gal 4:4; Eph 1:10 [q]Ac 20:21

Jesus Announces the Good News

1:16-20pp — Mt 4:18-22; Lk 5:2-11; Jn 1:35-42

[14]After John was put in prison, Jesus went into Galilee,[n] proclaiming the good news of God.[o]
[15]"The time has come,"[p] he said. "The kingdom of God has come near. Repent and believe the good
news!"[q]

[a] *13* The Greek for *tempted* can also mean *tested*.

identifies Jesus as God's Son. This introduces the mystery of the incarnation: Jesus is both Lord (vv. 2–3) and Son. The voice draws on Ps 2:7 and Isa 42:1. Ps 2:7 speaks of the hope of a Davidic Messiah who would rule the nations; Isa 42:1 speaks of a faithful and merciful servant who will bring salvation to Israel and be a light to the nations (Isa 42:1–9). Both figures were to be anointed with God's Spirit (see note on v. 8). The prophets promised the restoration of the Davidic kingdom as part of Israel's deliverance from exile (Isa 11:1–9; Jer 23:5–6; 33:15–26; Ezek 34:23–24; 37:24–25; Hos 12:9; Amos 9:11; Zech 12:7–8). Several Jewish traditions read Ps 2 as a promise that the Messiah would drive out the idolatrous nations and wicked Jews from Jerusalem so as to restore the purity of the temple (cf. 11:1–17). God's special personal presence in Jesus enables Jesus to deal with the issues of idolatry, wickedness, and purity but in the unique and utterly unexpected merciful way of Isaiah's servant (see notes on 8:22—10:52; 8:31; 9:12; 10:33,45; 14:22,24).

1:12 At once. Characteristic of Mark's Gospel, the Greek word behind this phrase occurs over 42 times and is especially frequent in the opening chapters. It is variously translated "at once," "without delay," "immediately," "quickly," "just then." The "suddenness" of Mark's story perhaps reflects Mark's opening quotation from Malachi (see v. 2), which goes on to warn that the Lord whom Israel sought would come "suddenly" (Mal 3:1).

1:13 wilderness. See note on v. 4. **forty days.** Just as Israel passed through the sea, was sent the Spirit (Isa 63:10–11), was called God's "son" (Exod 4:22), and was led into the wilderness for 40 years, so too Jesus went through the waters, received the Spirit, was declared God's son, and taken into the wilderness, but for 40 days. However, unlike Israel, Jesus does not betray his sonship when tempted. As Israel's coming Lord and Messianic deliverer, Jesus defeats Satan (see 3:27)—something only God can do—demonstrating that he is both Lord and the true servant of God that Israel failed to be. Having been defeated by him, Satan will never again directly challenge Jesus. **wild animals.** Mentioned here either because they were a threat in the wilderness against which God protects the righteous (cf. Ps 91:11–13) or because Jesus fulfills the Messianic prophecies of renewed peace even with the animals (cf. Isa 11:6–9). **angels.** Whereas God sent Israel one angel to guide them (Exod 23:20,23; 32:34), Jesus is attended by several.

1:14—8:21 *The Lord in Strength: Jesus' Mighty Words and Deeds in Galilee and Beyond.* In keeping with the new exodus pattern—God's coming to deliver, his journey with his people, and his arrival in Jerusalem—Mark's first section from the outset emphasizes God's powerful saving presence in Jesus (1:27–34,40–45). Mark highlights Jesus' miracles (1:21–26,29–34,40–42; 2:3–12; 3:1–5,10; 4:37–39; 5:25–29,35–42; 6:5,35–44,48–51,56; 7:25–30,32–37; 8:1–9) and particularly Jesus' delivering people from their bondage to impure spirits (1:21–27,34,39; 3:11,22; 5:1–20). This causes great amazement (e.g., 1:27; 2:12) and results in Jesus' fame spreading far and wide (1:28,32–33,45; 2:1–4; 3:7–10). Consequently, just as God's self-revelation was central to the first exodus (Exod 3:13–15; 33:19), the fundamental question this Gospel soon poses becomes, "Who is this?" (4:41; cf., e.g., 1:27). Continuing the exodus pattern, just as God called Israel to be his people (Exod 3:12; 6:7) and taught them his ways (Deut 4:1,14; 8:3), so too Jesus calls people to follow him and his teachings—hence Mark's great interest in discipleship (1:16–20; see note on 8:22—10:52). Finally, Jesus' astonishing claims (2:5–10,19,28; cf. 2:21–22; 3:34–35) and his redrawing of the boundaries of holiness (e.g., 1:14–17,23–27; 3:3–5), even to reconstituting Israel around himself (3:13–19 and note on 3:14), quickly create opposition (2:7,16,24; 3:2,22) and lead to an early plot against his life (3:6; cf. 8:31).

1:14–15 *Jesus Announces the Good News.* There is now a dramatic shift in focus. In keeping with John's own emphasis on the coming "one more powerful" (v. 7), John's removal means that all attention is now on Jesus. Using Jesus' own words, Mark summarizes the heart of Jesus' proclamation.

1:14 John was put in prison. Although this seems to follow immediately after Jesus' temptation, John 3:22–36 suggests a longer time frame. Mark's concern, however, is to set Jesus' ministry in the context of John's rejection. Since John was Malachi's "Elijah," who was sent to prepare for the Lord's coming (see notes on vv. 2–3,6), John's imprisonment sounds an ominous note. **good news.** Isaiah's prophesied salvation (Isa 40:9; 52:7). **of God.** It is good news from God since in Jesus God's powerful presence has now come (see note on vv. 2–3; cf. Col 2:9). Thus God in Christ offers forgiveness and restoration to all who repent of their own way of being Israel and believe in his proclamation of what it means to be God's people (2 Cor 5:19). But it is also "of God" in that God's just and merciful character is now fully revealed in Jesus (cf. John 14:9). What is God like? Mark's answer: Jesus (cf. John 14:9–10).

1:15 time has come ... has come near. On the very threshold. This reflects the fulfillment of passages like Dan 7:22, where God promised that his people will inherit his kingdom. However, the combination of the "time" when God acts, its nearness, his inbreaking reign, and calls to repent and believe is uniquely characteristic of Isaiah's announcement of the new exodus (see note on vv. 2–3), which Jesus implies is now fulfilled in him (see Isa 40:9–10; 43:10; 46:13; 49:8; 51:5; 52:7; 53:1; 56:1; 60:22). **kingdom of God.** The fulfillment of Israel's hopes as found in the Law, the Prophets, and the Writings of God's immanent exercise of his kingship over his people, the nations, and creation (e.g., Exod 15:18; Pss 24:8–10; 47:2; Isa 24:21–23; 52:7). Understood differently by various Jewish groups, it often included (1) God's powerful new exodus deliverance of (2) a purified remnant to (3) live in peace under (4) a renewed covenant in (5) true obedience to the law in (6) a restored land with (7) a rebuilt temple in which (8) God's returned presence dwelt, and (9) united under a revived Messianic Davidic monarchy (e.g., Num 24; Isa 11:1–16; Jer 30; 33; Ezek 34:11–31; 37; Dan 7; cf. Pss 2; 110; 118). For several groups it would be accompanied by the outpouring of the Spirit and the resurrection of the dead.

1:21 [r]Mt 4:23; Mk 10:1 **1:22** [s]Mt 7:28,29 **1:24** [t]Mt 8:29 [u]Mt 2:23; Lk 24:19; Ac 24:5 [v]Lk 1:35; Jn 6:69; Ac 3:14 **1:25** [w]ver 34 **1:26** [x]Mk 9:20

Jesus Calls His First Disciples

16 As Jesus walked beside the Sea of Galilee, he saw Simon and his brother Andrew casting a net into
the lake, for they were fishermen. 17 "Come, follow me," Jesus said, "and I will send you out to fish for
people." 18 At once they left their nets and followed him.
19 When he had gone a little farther, he saw James son of Zebedee and his brother John in a boat,
preparing their nets. 20 Without delay he called them, and they left their father Zebedee in the boat with
the hired men and followed him.

Jesus Drives Out an Impure Spirit

1:21-28pp — Lk 4:31-37

21 They went to Capernaum, and when the Sabbath came, Jesus went into the synagogue and began
to teach.[r] 22 The people were amazed at his teaching, because he taught them as one who had authority,
not as the teachers of the law.[s] 23 Just then a man in their synagogue who was possessed by an impure
spirit cried out, 24 "What do you want with us,[t] Jesus of Nazareth?[u] Have you come to destroy us? I know
who you are — the Holy One of God!"[v]
25 "Be quiet!" said Jesus sternly. "Come out of him!"[w] 26 The impure spirit shook the man violently
and came out of him with a shriek.[x]

1:16–20 *Jesus Calls His First Disciples.* As Mark's first detailed account of Jesus' ministry (vv. 14–15 are more of a summary) this paragraph signals the importance of discipleship in Mark's Gospel and testifies to the centrality of Jesus' intention to reconstitute Israel around himself (e.g., 3:13–19; 4:10–12,34; 6:7–12; 8:34–38; 9:2–9,30–50; 10:23–45; 13:3–36; 14:15–42,66–72; 15:40–41; 16:7). The same concern characterizes the first exodus and the new exodus: God forms a people for himself who, in believing in him, are to walk in his ways (e.g., Exod 6:7; Lev 26:12; Num 15:40; Deut 10:12; Isa 35:3–10; 43:3; 48:17; 51:16; 54:1–10; 65:17–19; Mal 3:16–18).

1:16 Much of Mark's early action occurs on and around the beautiful Sea of Galilee, where Simon and Andrew earned their living.

1:17 Come, follow me. Probably not their first encounter with Jesus (cf. John 1:35–42). As Isaiah's faithful servant, much of Jesus' task included teaching (Isa 42:4; 50:4; see note on v. 22), thereby enabling Israel to become the light to the nations God had always intended (Isa 2:2–4; 60:3; cf. especially Isa 49:6 in Acts 13:47; cf. also Deut 4:5–8; Matt 5:14–16; Phil 2:15). **fish for people.** Fulfilling Isaiah's prophecy, the disciples will carry the gospel first to Israel (6:7–13) and then to the nations (cf. 13:10; 14:9).

1:18 At once. See note on v. 12. Peter (i.e., Simon [v. 16]), Andrew (v. 16), and James and John (v. 19) unreservedly obey Jesus' summons by leaving their livelihood ("nets") and families ("their father Zebedee"). This exemplifies the cost of discipleship (cf. 10:28–30). Of these four, Simon Peter, James, and John form an inner circle; Jesus involves them in several critical moments in his life (5:37; 9:2; 14:33; cf. 13:3).

1:21–45 *A New Teaching With Authority.* This series of short episodes describes the remarkable impact of Jesus' early Galilean ministry, with particular emphasis on the growing excitement aroused by his proclamation of the kingdom of God and the restoration he brings. Where Jesus is present, so too is God's power to heal and deliver.

1:21–28 *Jesus Drives Out an Impure Spirit.* This opening scene typifies Jesus' activities during his Galilean ministry: he teaches in the synagogues and effortlessly casts out demons. As the impure spirit immediately recognizes, Jesus is no ordinary teacher; he is the Holy One of God.

1:21 Capernaum. A sizable town on the northwestern shore of the Sea of Galilee. Jesus used Peter's house as his operational base in Galilee (cf. v. 29; 2:1; 9:33). **synagogue.** An important village center for Scriptural study and worship. Recent excavations in Capernaum (Talhum) have revealed evidence of a first-century synagogue. There are also remains of a fourth-century church built by modifying a first-century house, apparently marking the traditional site of Peter's home. As a visiting teacher, Jesus accepted the invitation from the local leadership and began to teach. **teach.** Although Mark's Gospel lacks Matthew's Sermon on the Mount, it has a considerable body of Jesus' teaching in numerous short sayings and in several large blocks (4:1–34; 7:1–23; 9:33—10:45).

1:22 In keeping with God's answering Isaiah's last great prayer (Isa 63:7—64:12)—specifically that God would again come down and do amazing things (Isa 64:1–3; see note on v. 10)—the authority inherent in Jesus' words and deeds constantly amazes his hearers (2:12; 5:20,42; 6:2,51; 7:37; 10:26; 11:18). Isaiah prophesied that when God acted in strength to redeem his people, he would be their teacher (Isa 51:1–5; 54:13; cf. Isa 48:17), the humble would stand in awe of the Holy One, and the wayward would gain understanding (Isa 29:19,23; see note on Mark 1:24). **teachers of the law.** Lit. "scribes," formally trained legal experts in God's law (the Torah) whom Jews respected (cf. 9:7; see notes on Matt 2:4; 5:20). Since God is uniquely present in Jesus, Jesus' authority utterly transcends theirs.

1:23 impure spirit. Stands in contrast to God's Holy Spirit and, as an agent of Satan (3:22–23), its defiling presence radically comprises God's summons to "be holy, because I am holy" (Lev 11:45; cf. Lev 20:7–8; Deut 26:19). Untroubled in a law-centered synagogue, the impure spirit reacts "just then" (see note on v. 12) to Jesus, upon whom the Holy Spirit rests, as Mark's readers know.

1:24 What do you want with us ...? In a situation of unequal power, this implies fear of impending conflict or loss (cf. 5:7; see the Septuagint [the pre-Christian Greek translation of the OT] of Judg 11:12; 1 Kgs 17:18; cf. also 2 Chr 35:21). **Jesus of Nazareth.** Denotes not only Jesus' hometown (v. 9) but also his human origins in this first public identification (cf. 10:47; 14:67; 16:6). **destroy us.** Only God could destroy demons. In Jewish tradition God's inbreaking reign meant the destruction of Satan and his minions. **Holy One of God.** God frequently describes himself as the Holy One of Israel, particularly when delivering his people (e.g., 2 Kgs 19:22; Pss 71:22; 78:41; Isa 29:19; 43:14; Jer 50:29; 51:5). Demons occasionally addressed humans, but never with such exalted language as found here. The impure spirit recognizes Jesus' divine identity—something Mark's readers already know from Mark's introduction—and in the manner of ancient exorcists, who sought to use the name of their spiritual opponents to control them, it attempts to use that knowledge to control Jesus (cf. 5:7).

1:25 Be quiet! Demonstrates Jesus' superior authority. **said ... sternly.** Lit. "rebuked." Only God has the authority to directly rebuke demons (cf. Jude 9). **Come out.** Being made in God's image (Gen 1:26–27), human beings were designed to be indwelt by God's Holy Spirit (cf. Ezek 11:19;

[27]The people were all so amazed[y] that they asked each other, "What is this? A new teaching—and with authority! He even gives orders to impure spirits and they obey him." [28]News about him spread quickly over the whole region[z] of Galilee.

1:27 [y]Mk 10:24,32
1:28 [z]Mt 9:26
1:29 [a]ver 21,23
1:31 [b]Lk 7:14
1:32 [c]Mt 4:24
1:34 [d]Mt 4:23 [e]Mk 3:12; Ac 16:17,18

Jesus Heals Many

1:29-31pp — Mt 8:14,15; Lk 4:38,39
1:32-34pp — Mt 8:16,17; Lk 4:40,41

[29]As soon as they left the synagogue,[a] they went with James and John to the home of Simon and
Andrew. [30]Simon's mother-in-law was in bed with a fever, and they immediately told Jesus about
her. [31]So he went to her, took her hand and helped her up.[b] The fever left her and she began to wait
on them.

[32]That evening after sunset the people brought to Jesus all the sick and demon-possessed.[c] [33]The
whole town gathered at the door, [34]and Jesus healed many who had various diseases.[d] He also drove out
many demons, but he would not let the demons speak because they knew who he was.[e]

36:26) so that they might properly exercise dominion (cf. Ps 8). Jesus' expelling the impure spirit is integral to his restoring the image of God to humanity (cf. Rom 8:9–12,19–21).

1:27 new teaching. See note on v. 22. **authority.** Jesus' authority over impure spirits characterizes his ministry (vv. 32,34,39; 3:11,22; 5:1–20; 7:24–30; 9:14–27; cf. 3:15; 6:7,13; see note on v. 24) and here reinforces the authority of his new teaching. It demonstrates that he has already bound Satan (3:27) and is "the one more powerful" whose coming John proclaimed (v. 7).

1:28 News about him spread quickly. Even in his own lifetime Jesus the proclaimer quickly became the proclaimed (see also v. 45; 5:20; 7:36).

1:29–34 *Jesus Heals Many.* The restoration Jesus announced and effected in the synagogue (vv. 21–28) now spreads to include first Peter's mother-in-law (vv. 29–31) and then "many" as the entire town gathers at the door of the home where Jesus is staying (vv. 32–34).

1:29 went ... to the home of Simon. Probably for the main Sabbath meal, served after the synagogue service (see photo, p. 2076).

1:30 Simon's mother-in-law. Peter (also known as Simon or Cephas) was married (cf. 1 Cor 9:5). **fever.** One of the illnesses associated with God's judgment on Israel for breaking covenant (Lev 26:14–16; Deut 28:15,22). Jesus' healing testifies to God's coming to restore his people.

1:32 Observant Jews would not carry anything before sunset, which marked the end of the Sabbath (cf. Jer 17:21–22).

1:34 healed many ... various diseases. From the beginning Jesus' astonishing power to heal (cf. 5:30) various diseases is a striking

The shore of the Sea of Galilee. Jesus called to Simon (Peter) and Andrew from the shore (Mark 1:16).

1:35 [f] Lk 3:21
1:38 [g] Isa 61:1
1:39 [h] Mt 4:23 [i] Mt 4:24
1:40 [j] Mk 10:17
1:44 [k] Mt 8:4

Jesus Prays in a Solitary Place

1:35-38pp — Lk 4:42,43

35 Very early in the morning, while it was still dark, Jesus got up, left the house and went off to a
solitary place, where he prayed.[f] 36 Simon and his companions went to look for him, 37 and when they
found him, they exclaimed: "Everyone is looking for you!"
38 Jesus replied, "Let us go somewhere else — to the nearby villages — so I can preach there also.
That is why I have come."[g] 39 So he traveled throughout Galilee, preaching in their synagogues[h] and
driving out demons.[i]

Jesus Heals a Man With Leprosy

1:40-44pp — Mt 8:2-4; Lk 5:12-14

40 A man with leprosy[a] came to him and begged him on his knees,[j] "If you are willing, you can
make me clean."
41 Jesus was indignant.[b] He reached out his hand and touched the man. "I am willing," he said. "Be
clean!" 42 Immediately the leprosy left him and he was cleansed.
43 Jesus sent him away at once with a strong warning: 44 "See that you don't tell this to anyone.[k] But

[a] *40* The Greek word traditionally translated *leprosy* was used for various diseases affecting the skin.
[b] *41* Many manuscripts *Jesus was filled with compassion*

and unique characteristic of his ministry. In the first century, medical care was, at best, extremely basic, and infirmities and illnesses were widespread, so Jesus' reputation understandably spreads like wildfire, and people from farther and farther away flock to him (e.g., vv. 40–45; 2:1–12; 3:8–10; 6:54–56). In Israel's Scriptures, God is the one who heals his people of all their diseases (Exod 15:26; Deut 32:39; Ps 103:3), and the absence of illness is a sign of Israel's restoration (e.g., Isa 33:24; 35:5–6). Although the crowds do not understand, Mark's audience already knows that Jesus is the coming "more powerful" Lord (vv. 2–3,7). **drove out many demons.** Mark makes a distinct point of this because it especially testifies to Jesus' having bound Satan (3:27–29). Since this is something only God can do (cf. Rom 16:20; Jude 9), it confirms yet again Jesus' identity as the coming Lord and the presence of God's saving kingdom in him (vv. 14–15; see 4:11). **would not let the demons speak.** In the ancient world the gods were fundamentally about power, and Israel's popular expectation was for a mighty warrior Messiah who would drive out the Romans. Because the demons know who he is, Jesus silences them because their confession would mislead the people. The true nature of his divine Sonship and power could not be properly understood apart from his obedient death on the cross. He later prevents his disciples from proclaiming him as Messiah for the same reason (8:30). The time will come for such public confessions (cf. 14:62; 15:39), but not yet.

1:35–39 *Jesus Prays in a Solitary Place.* In contrast to his disciples, who are swept up in the local excitement, Jesus' priorities are set in private prayer.

1:35 solitary place. Throughout the Gospel, Jesus retreats from the crowds and the demands of the mission (6:31–32,46; 9:30–31; cf. 7:24; 9:2). **prayed.** Although prayer is rarely mentioned in Mark (cf. 6:46; 14:32–39), this short statement underlines its importance for Jesus (cf. Luke 3:21; 6:12; 9:18,28–29; 11:1–4; 18:1; 22:32).

1:36 companions. Probably Andrew, James, and John (see vv. 16–20).

1:37 Everyone is looking for you! Continuing on from the previous evening (vv. 32–33).

1:38 somewhere else. Whereas Simon and his companions are caught up in Jesus' local popularity, his agenda is set by private prayer (cf. 6:46; 14:32–39). Jesus has come to proclaim his message to all Israel.

1:39 The combination of preaching and authority over demons is characteristic of Jesus' ministry (cf. vv. 21–28).

1:40–45 *Jesus Heals a Man With Leprosy.* Already evident in his casting out an impure spirit (vv. 21–28), the concluding account of this section (vv. 21–45) uses the healing of one of the more severe cases of impurity to underline Jesus' authority, power, and intention to bring cleansing to God's people. It will eventually find its fullest expression in his death on the cross (cf. Eph 1:7).

1:40 leprosy. The exact nature of this ailment is unclear (see NIV text note). However, it was regarded as causing grave impurity (see Lev 13–14; see also note there on Lev 13:3), perhaps because it was contagious and/or it particularly defaced the image of God in the individual (cf. Lev 21:16–23 and note on v. 17). Sufferers were regarded as living corpses (Num 12:12; Job 18:13; see note on Lev 13:45) and condemned to lonely isolation from the community (see Lev 13:45,46; 14:3 and notes). **willing.** God alone can do whatever he wants (cf. Pss 115:3; 135:5–6).

1:41 indignant. The text here is uncertain; most manuscripts have the more agreeable "felt compassion" (cf. 6:34; 8:2, which translate the same Greek word as "had/have compassion"). However, "indignant" is so unexpected that it is difficult to explain why anyone would add it. Since Matthew and Luke appear to have relied on Mark's Gospel for the content and wording of their Gospels, that neither Matt 8:1–4 nor Luke 5:12–14 mention either option in their parallel accounts suggests their copies of Mark had "indignant" but they decided to delete it to avoid potential misunderstanding. Jesus' message is that God's gracious deliverance has come (vv. 14–15). His anger could be because the man's "if you are willing" (v. 40) questions both his and God's merciful character. **touched.** God's mercy through Jesus transcends both concerns for strict ritual purity (Lev 13; cf. 5:24b–34; 7:1–23; Hos 6:6) and the man's questioning. **Be clean!** Far from being defiled by the unclean man (see notes on Lev 7:19–21; 13:46; 15:4; 18:19), Jesus' touch cleanses the man (v. 42) and thereby restores him to the community of God's people (see notes on Lev 14:3,8). Healing leprosy, like raising the dead, was something only God could do (2 Kgs 5:7).

1:44 don't tell. News of this particular healing could impede his mission (cf. v. 45). **show yourself to the priest and offer the sacrifices.** This testifies to the Jerusalem priesthood that Jesus both respects the law (cf. Lev 14; see notes on Lev 14:3,8) and does what only God can do (2 Kgs 5:7). However, the man's story also reveals that Jesus disregarded purity regulations by touching the leprous man, an act

go, show yourself to the priest[l] and offer the sacrifices that Moses commanded for your cleansing,[m] as
a testimony to them." 45Instead he went out and began to talk freely, spreading the news. As a result,
Jesus could no longer enter a town openly but stayed outside in lonely places.[n] Yet the people still came
to him from everywhere.[o]

Jesus Forgives and Heals a Paralyzed Man

2:3-12pp — Mt 9:2-8; Lk 5:18-26

2 A few days later, when Jesus again entered Capernaum, the people heard that he had come home.
2They gathered in such large numbers[p] that there was no room left, not even outside the door, and
he preached the word to them. 3Some men came, bringing to him a paralyzed man,[q] carried by four of
them. 4Since they could not get him to Jesus because of the crowd, they made an opening in the roof
above Jesus by digging through it and then lowered the mat the man was lying on. 5When Jesus saw
their faith, he said to the paralyzed man, "Son, your sins are forgiven."[r]

6Now some teachers of the law were sitting there, thinking to themselves, 7"Why does this fellow talk
like that? He's blaspheming! Who can forgive sins but God alone?"[s]

8Immediately Jesus knew in his spirit that this was what they were thinking in their hearts, and he
said to them, "Why are you thinking these things? 9Which is easier: to say to this paralyzed man, 'Your
sins are forgiven,' or to say, 'Get up, take your mat and walk'? 10But I want you to know that the Son of
Man[t] has authority on earth to forgive sins." So he said to the man, 11"I tell you, get up, take your mat
and go home." 12He got up, took his mat and walked out in full view of them all. This amazed everyone
and they praised God,[u] saying, "We have never seen anything like this!"[v]

1:44 [l] Lev 13:49 [m] Lev 14:1-32
1:45 [n] Lk 5:15,16 [o] Mk 2:13; Lk 5:17; Jn 6:2
2:2 [p] ver 13; Mk 1:45
2:3 [q] Mt 4:24
2:5 [r] Lk 7:48
2:7 [s] Isa 43:25
2:10 [t] Mt 8:20
2:12 [u] Mt 9:8 [v] Mt 9:33

that brought defilement (see Lev 13, especially vv. 45–46; see also Lev 5:2), and this was bound to attract criticism.

2:1—3:6 *Emerging Local Opposition: Questions About Jesus' Authority and Holiness.* This section describes a series of five controversies arising from how various Jewish authorities respond to Jesus' mighty words and deeds (see notes on 1:14—8:21 and 1:44). These episodes illustrate the issues that created tension. The hostility that Jesus arouses is so great that the series concludes in very short order with the first plot against his life.

2:1–12 *Jesus Forgives and Heals a Paralyzed Man.* Mark earlier declared that in Jesus the Lord himself was present (1:2–3). Here Jesus demonstrates the truth of that claim by doing what only God can do (v. 7), sparking his first public confrontation with the teachers of the law.

2:4 Houses normally had an outside staircase leading to a flat roof made of packed clay over wooden beams. Demonstrating the kind of commitment God loves, the men go to great lengths to bring their friend to Jesus.

2:5 faith. Central to Jesus' ministry (1:15; 4:40; 5:34,36; 9:23; 10:52; 11:22). The men's audacious faith suffices for their friend. **Son.** Recalls God's fatherly relationship to Israel (Exod 4:22; Hos 11:1), which is the basis of his mercy in the new exodus (Jer 31:20; Hos 11:3–8; cf. 2 Cor 6:16–18; Gal 4:4). Since a broken relationship with God led to a broken world, many Jews believed that sin and sickness went hand in hand (Deut 28:13–27; Pss 41:4; 107:17; John 9:2), as did healing and forgiveness (2 Sam 12:13; 2 Chr 7:14; Ps 103:3; Isa 57:18–19; Jas 5:15). On another occasion, however, Jesus warned his disciples not to assume that behind every illness lay personal sin (John 9:3). **your sins are forgiven.** Restores the man's relationship to God and confirms that Isaiah's promised salvation (Isa 40:3 in Mark 1:2–3), which includes God's forgiving Israel's sins (Isa 44:22; cf. Isa 40:2), has begun. This opening confrontation anticipates what Jesus will do for all in laying down his life (10:45; 14:24).

2:6–7 It is sometimes suggested that the teachers of the law were upset by Jesus' taking the role of someone who could legitimately announce God's forgiveness, e.g., a priest. But if so, why did they not say, "But you are no priest!"? Instead, because the Scriptures state that only God can forgive sins (Exod 34:6–9; Isa 43:25; cf. Num 14:18–19; Pss 25:18; 32:5; 103:3; 130:4; Isa 55:7), the teachers of the law (see note on 1:22) accused Jesus of assuming God's sole prerogatives and thereby directly impinging God's honor.

2:8 Since God alone knows and tests people's hearts (1 Sam 16:7; 1 Kgs 8:39; Ps 7:9; Jer 11:20; Acts 1:24), Jesus' awareness reflects what Mark's readers already know: God himself is mysteriously present in Jesus (see note on 1:2–3).

2:9 say. Not merely to utter words but to effect real change in a situation. The answer to Jesus' question is "neither," for both are equally impossible to all except God.

2:10 the Son of Man. This unusual expression is confined almost entirely to the Gospels (but see Acts 7:56; Rev 1:13; 14:14) and appears only on Jesus' lips. In Mark it is almost a title. But to Jesus' original hearers, who show no reaction at all, it appears to mean something as unremarkable as "I." Apparently Jesus chose the expression precisely because it was ambiguous and allowed him to define its meaning and so control his self-revelation (cf. his silencing the demons in 1:25–26,34). Only later—by adding "holy angels" (8:38), "coming in clouds with ... glory" (13:26) and "coming on the clouds of heaven" (14:62)—does Jesus reveal that he means the Messianic end-time figure of Dan 7:13, to whom God entrusts glory and sovereign authority over all peoples. But none of these additional clues are present here. In some Jewish circles, Daniel's "one like a son of man" (or "human being") was to be God's agent of final judgment on earth, but he is never described as forgiving sins. **forgive sins.** Only God can forgive sins (see notes on vv. 6–7,8), and he dwells in heaven. Jesus' authority reveals the astonishing extent to which God is present, on earth, in him. Confronting the hostile teachers of the law, Jesus performs a mighty deed so that they may know that he not only has the authority to forgive sins but also "wills" to do so (cf. 1:40).

2:11–12 God promised that when he came as Israel's King and Mighty One, the lame would be blessed and their sins forgiven (Isa 33:23–24; 35:6). Jesus, having already forgiven the man's sins (v. 5), demonstrates the truth of his claim by doing the second impossible thing: commanding the man to walk. Jesus does what only God can do. Here again, as Isaiah had prayed, the people are amazed at a mighty deed they did not expect (Isa 64:3; see note on 1:8).

2:13 [w] Mk 1:45; Lk 5:15; Jn 6:2
2:14 [x] Mt 4:19
2:16 [y] Ac 23:9 [z] Mt 9:11
2:17 [a] Lk 19:10; 1Ti 1:15
2:18 [b] Mt 6:16-18; Ac 13:2
2:20 [c] Lk 17:22

Jesus Calls Levi and Eats With Sinners

2:14-17pp — Mt 9:9-13; Lk 5:27-32

13Once again Jesus went out beside the lake. A large crowd came to him,[w] and he began to teach
them. 14As he walked along, he saw Levi son of Alphaeus sitting at the tax collector's booth. "Follow
me,"[x] Jesus told him, and Levi got up and followed him.
15While Jesus was having dinner at Levi's house, many tax collectors and sinners were eating with
him and his disciples, for there were many who followed him. 16When the teachers of the law who were
Pharisees[y] saw him eating with the sinners and tax collectors, they asked his disciples: "Why does he
eat with tax collectors and sinners?"[z]
17On hearing this, Jesus said to them, "It is not the healthy who need a doctor, but the sick. I have
not come to call the righteous, but sinners."[a]

Jesus Questioned About Fasting

2:18-22pp — Mt 9:14-17; Lk 5:33-38

18Now John's disciples and the Pharisees were fasting.[b] Some people came and asked Jesus, "How is
it that John's disciples and the disciples of the Pharisees are fasting, but yours are not?"
19Jesus answered, "How can the guests of the bridegroom fast while he is with them? They cannot,
so long as they have him with them. 20But the time will come when the bridegroom will be taken from
them,[c] and on that day they will fast.
21"No one sews a patch of unshrunk cloth on an old garment. Otherwise, the new piece will pull
away from the old, making the tear worse. 22And no one pours new wine into old wineskins. Otherwise,
the wine will burst the skins, and both the wine and the wineskins will be ruined. No, they pour new
wine into new wineskins."

2:13–17 *Jesus Calls Levi and Eats With Sinners.* Jesus' association with those the Pharisees regarded as impure testifies to the merciful nature of his mission (see note on 1:11).

2:14 Levi. Also known as Matthew (see 3:18; Matt 9:9–13; Luke 5:27–32). He apparently operated a toll booth for Herod Antipas, tetrarch of Galilee, on the major highway from Damascus through Capernaum to Egypt. It is highly likely that he had heard of and perhaps listened to Jesus. His swift response reflects the total demand of discipleship (cf. 10:28–30).

2:15 tax collectors. They routinely demanded inflated payments, and if working for Rome, they were despised as traitors. Their houses were regarded as impure, and they were expelled from the synagogue. **sinners.** The notoriously wicked and those who failed to observe God's law in keeping with how the teachers of the law (see note on 1:22) interpreted it. Jesus' announcement of God's mercy attracted many of them. **eating.** A sign of friendship/fellowship that apparently implied, at least to the Pharisees, a degree of acceptance of the sinners' behavior. Jesus' activity here stands in sharp contrast to the desert-dwelling asceticism of John the Baptist (1:4–6).

2:16 Pharisees. See "The Time Between the Testaments: The Parties: Jewish Diversity," p. 1900. They sought to live out priestly purity in their homes. They promoted studying the law and called Israel to return to its ancestral traditions in the hope of hastening God's promised salvation. The movement included teachers who were experts in the law. In their view, failing to deal with impurity betrayed Israel's calling and merited judgment. Since God would distinguish between his servants and the wicked (Isa 65; Ezek 20:37–38), for Jesus to announce God's reign and yet eat with tax collectors and sinners in their impure houses was deeply offensive to the Pharisees and the teachers of the law.

2:17 Jesus' actions arose not from approval of the actions of the tax collectors and sinners but from his identity as Israel's redeemer come to save those who need saving: doctors visit the sick, not the healthy. This includes the Pharisees, who do not realize that God wants them to trust Jesus, not their own righteousness (cf. Paul's confidence as a Pharisee in Phil 3:4–6).

2:18–22 *Jesus Questioned About Fasting.* Criticism of Jesus' disciples for not fasting leads to Jesus' declaration that not only is he Israel's bridegroom but that his coming requires a new way of being Israel.

2:18 fasting. Required in the law only on the Day of Atonement (Lev 16:29–31; 23:27–32), it was practiced to seek God's blessing (Ezra 8:21) or in times of great mourning (2 Sam 1:12; 3:35) as an expression of self-humbling repentance, particularly in the face of God's judgment (1 Sam 7:6; 1 Kgs 21:27–29; Neh 1:4; Joel 1:13–15; 2:12–15). After the exile the number of prescribed fasts increased (Zech 7:5; 8:19). Here fasting seems to be understood as the righteous response to Israel's present alienation from God and subjugation to the idolatrous Romans (cf., e.g., Luke 2:37). Since John—whose entire lifestyle was, in one sense, a fast—was waiting for the "one more powerful" (1:7), who would effect judgment (1:7; Matt 3:7–12), John's disciples fasted, perhaps with a heightened sense of urgency after John's imprisonment. Likewise, the Pharisees fasted twice a week (Luke 18:12). That Jesus' disciples did not fast raised questions.

2:19 It was unthinkable to fast—a sign of grief or alienation from God—during a wedding's joyful celebration of a new relationship. Isaiah prophesied that God, in merciful forgiveness, would again marry his people (Isa 54:5–6; 62:4–5; cf. Hos 2:19). Mark has already declared that Jesus fulfills the promise of the Lord's coming to save (see 1:2–3 and note). Having just exercised the divine prerogative to forgive sin (vv. 5–12), Jesus now implies that he is Israel's divine husband (cf. Eph 5:32; Rev 19:7).

2:20 Alludes to Jesus' death and subsequent departure (cf. 8:31). Fasting will be appropriate when he is absent.

2:21–22 The same section in Isaiah that speaks of God's remarrying Israel also proclaims that he will do something new (Isa 48:6; 65:17; cf. Isa 42:9; 43:18–19). Ezekiel spoke of God's putting a new heart and new spirit into his people (Ezek 11:19; 18:31; 36:26), and Jeremiah foretold a "new covenant" (Jer 31:31), declaring that the new deliver-

Jesus Is Lord of the Sabbath

2:23-28pp — Mt 12:1-8; Lk 6:1-5
3:1-6pp — Mt 12:9-14; Lk 6:6-11

23 One Sabbath Jesus was going through the grainfields, and as his disciples walked along, they began to pick some heads of grain.[d] 24 The Pharisees said to him, "Look, why are they doing what is unlawful on the Sabbath?"[e]

25 He answered, "Have you never read what David did when he and his companions were hungry and in need? 26 In the days of Abiathar the high priest,[f] he entered the house of God and ate the consecrated bread, which is lawful only for priests to eat.[g] And he also gave some to his companions."[h]

27 Then he said to them, "The Sabbath was made for man,[i] not man for the Sabbath.[j] 28 So the Son of Man[k] is Lord even of the Sabbath."

Jesus Heals on the Sabbath

3 Another time Jesus went into the synagogue,[l] and a man with a shriveled hand was there. 2 Some of them were looking for a reason to accuse Jesus, so they watched him closely[m] to see if he would heal him on the Sabbath.[n] 3 Jesus said to the man with the shriveled hand, "Stand up in front of everyone."

4 Then Jesus asked them, "Which is lawful on the Sabbath: to do good or to do evil, to save life or to kill?" But they remained silent.

5 He looked around at them in anger and, deeply distressed at their stubborn hearts, said to the man, "Stretch out your hand." He stretched it out, and his hand was completely restored. 6 Then the Pharisees went out and began to plot with the Herodians[o] how they might kill Jesus.[p]

2:23 [d] Dt 23:25
2:24 [e] Mt 12:2
2:26 [f] 1Ch 24:6; 2Sa 8:17 [g] Lev 24:5-9 [h] 1Sa 21:1-6
2:27 [i] Ex 23:12; Dt 5:14 [j] Col 2:16
2:28 [k] Mt 8:20
3:1 [l] Mt 4:23; Mk 1:21
3:2 [m] Mt 12:10 [n] Lk 14:1
3:6 [o] Mt 22:16; Mk 12:13 [p] Mt 12:14

ance would be so wonderful that it would replace the exodus as the event by which God was known (Jer 16:14–15; 23:6–8). These two parables (see note on 4:2) explain that the new thing Jesus brings cannot be superimposed on the old. The old patterns of relating to God must give way. Not only will Jesus' teaching become the new norm (e.g., 7:14–15; 9:7; cf. 8:35), but his life and new Passover/new covenant death will become the new way in which God is now to be known throughout the world (cf. 13:10; 15:39).

2:23–28 *Jesus Is Lord of the Sabbath.* In response to the Pharisees' criticism of his disciples, Jesus, claiming God's own authority over the Sabbath, declares that the Sabbath is subordinate to human need.

2:23 Sabbath. A day of rest, the keeping of which was one of the most important expressions of Israel's fidelity to God (see Exod 31:14–16 and notes). According to Deut 23:25, there was nothing wrong with the disciples' action (see note on Deut 23:24–25). But the Pharisees, eager to show the extent of their devotion to God, defined work more stringently.

2:25–26 David's unlawful consumption of consecrated bread (1 Sam 21:1–6) created a problem for the Pharisees. But while they excused their hero David, they criticized Jesus' disciples, who had done nothing wrong.

2:26 days of Abiathar the high priest. According to 1 Sam 21 the priest at the time was Abiathar's father, Ahimelek. Jesus may have mentioned Abiathar because Abiathar was much better known or because Abiathar was the one who subsequently took the ephod—the means by which the king could inquire of God (1 Sam 30:7–8)—to David (1 Sam 22:20; 23:6), thereby confirming David as God's choice.

2:27 Because only people are made in God's image, Jesus declares that true holiness means that caring for people matters more than keeping the Sabbath (see note on 3:4).

2:28 The Sabbath day belonged to the Lord (Exod 20:10; Isa 58:13). If, as "the Son of Man" (see note on v. 10), Jesus has divine authority to forgive sins, then he is also the divine Lord of the Sabbath and the final authority on its true meaning.

3:1–6 *Jesus Heals on the Sabbath.* This fifth and final confrontation of the series (2:1—3:6; see note) sums up what is at stake. On the one hand it demonstrates, on the Sabbath, that Jesus, the Lord of the Sabbath, embodies and brings the life the law offered (v. 4). On the other hand, it reveals the true motivation of Jesus' opponents: a stubbornness of heart (v. 5) that leads to their seeking Jesus' death (v. 6).

3:2 Jesus has already challenged their teachings, so some Pharisees now look to accuse him (i.e., bring formal charges; cf. 15:3–4). Unable to deny his power or compassion (characteristics of God), they seek instead to turn both against him. By permitting work (in this case an act of healing) only if someone's life is at risk, their very different view of the Sabbath reduces the man with a shriveled hand into merely an opportunity to ensnare Jesus.

3:3 By restoring this broken image of God on the day that celebrates the Creator's good provision, Jesus reveals in the synagogue (where the law was taught) God's true character and holiness. **Stand up in front of everyone.** The man's healing in the presence of all will be Jesus' testimony before his accusers.

3:4 Jesus' question takes up Moses' final words to Israel that set out the two ways offered by the law: life and good, or death and evil (see Deut 30:1–20, especially v. 15). Since the law linked life and good, for the Pharisees to force a distinction between them presumes they know better than Moses. Instead, because the Pharisees allowed saving life on the Sabbath, they must also allow doing good. Jesus not only presents his healing as the life and good the law offered but also shows himself to be the coming Lord who makes alive and heals (cf. Deut 32:39; see 2:9).

3:5 anger. Jesus was earlier angered by the man who doubted God's merciful character (see 1:41 and note); here he is angered by those who resist his lawful demonstration of that mercy. **deeply distressed ... stubborn hearts.** Characteristic of God's response (Ps 78:40; Isa 63:10) and Israel's past rebellion (Exod 33:3–5; 34:9; Deut 9:6–27; Judg 2:19), respectively. Jesus, the promised coming Lord (1:2–3), responds similarly to the Pharisees' failure to emulate God's compassion and their rebellious refusal to admit their error.

3:6 Pharisees. See note on 2:16. **plot ... kill.** Whereas the Sabbath testified to God's desire for his people's good, the Pharisees' distorted holiness leads them to do evil, hypocritically plotting with implicit idolaters to kill Jesus. Rejecting the Lord they claim to seek (see note on 1:2–3) leads to serious consequences (Mal 4:6). God had promised

3:7 [q] Mt 4:25
3:8 [r] Mt 11:21
3:10 [s] Mt 4:23 [t] Mt 9:20
3:11 [u] Mt 4:3; Mk 1:23,24
3:12 [v] Mt 8:4; Mk 1:24, 25,34; Ac 16:17,18
3:13 [w] Mt 5:1
3:14 [x] Mk 6:30
3:15 [y] Mt 10:1
3:16 [z] Jn 1:42
3:20 [a] ver 7 [b] Mk 6:31
3:21 [c] Jn 10:20; Ac 26:24

Crowds Follow Jesus

3:7-12pp — Mt 12:15,16; Lk 6:17-19

7 Jesus withdrew with his disciples to the lake, and a large crowd from Galilee followed.[q] 8 When
they heard about all he was doing, many people came to him from Judea, Jerusalem, Idumea, and the
regions across the Jordan and around Tyre and Sidon.[r] 9 Because of the crowd he told his disciples to
have a small boat ready for him, to keep the people from crowding him. 10 For he had healed many,[s] so
that those with diseases were pushing forward to touch him.[t] 11 Whenever the impure spirits saw him,
they fell down before him and cried out, "You are the Son of God."[u] 12 But he gave them strict orders
not to tell others about him.[v]

Jesus Appoints the Twelve

3:16-19pp — Mt 10:2-4; Lk 6:14-16; Ac 1:13

13 Jesus went up on a mountainside and called to him those he wanted, and they came to him.[w] 14 He
appointed twelve[a][x] that they might be with him and that he might send them out to preach 15 and to
have authority to drive out demons.[y] 16 These are the twelve he appointed: Simon (to whom he gave
the name Peter),[z] 17 James son of Zebedee and his brother John (to them he gave the name Boanerges,
which means "sons of thunder"), 18 Andrew, Philip, Bartholomew, Matthew, Thomas, James son of Alphaeus, Thaddaeus, Simon the Zealot 19 and Judas Iscariot, who betrayed him.

Jesus Accused by His Family and by Teachers of the Law

3:23-27pp — Mt 12:25-29; Lk 11:17-22
3:31-35pp — Mt 12:46-50; Lk 8:19-21

20 Then Jesus entered a house, and again a crowd gathered,[a] so that he and his disciples were not
even able to eat.[b] 21 When his family[b] heard about this, they went to take charge of him, for they said,
"He is out of his mind."[c]

[a] *14* Some manuscripts *twelve—designating them apostles—* [b] *21* Or *his associates*

that his return would distinguish between his servants and the rebels (Isa 65–66; cf. Ezek 20:33–38; see note on 11:17). This is now happening in Jesus. Ironically, the Pharisees' hardhearted interpretation of the law puts them, together with the Herodians, on the side of the rebels. **Herodians.** Supporters of Herod's dynasty and indirectly, idolatrous Rome.

3:7–19 *Jesus Withdraws to Continue His Mission.* Leaving his murderous opponents behind and followed by increasingly large crowds (vv. 7–8), Jesus continues his mission to reconstitute Israel around himself (vv. 13–19).

3:7–12 *Crowds Follow Jesus.* In spite of hardening opposition from various local Jewish authorities, Jesus continues to attract ever larger crowds, and people from farther and farther away now flock to him.

3:7–8 God originally intended Israel to be a light to the nations (see note on 1:17). This is now fulfilled in Jesus, God's servant (Isa 42:6; see note on 1:11), as his fame spreads for the first time into the neighboring nations.

3:10 touch. So powerful was God's presence in Jesus that even touching Jesus could heal (see 5:27–28; cf. Acts 19:11–12).

3:11 fell down. A posture of defeat (cf. Ps 72:9; Mic 7:17). Jesus, having already defeated Satan, was the unclean spirits' master (see notes on 1:13; 3:27). **Son of God.** See note on 1:1. In stark contrast to Jesus' obstinate human opponents, the impure spirits, at the mere sight of Jesus, confess what God had already declared concerning him (see 1:11; cf. 1:24).

3:12 Jesus again exercises firm control over his self-revelation (see note on 1:34).

3:13–19 *Jesus Appoints the Twelve.* Jesus chooses 12 of his disciples for two reasons: to "be with him" (v. 14) and to be sent out to Israel (6:6b–13) and eventually the nations (cf. 13:10; 14:9). They are of equal importance.

3:13 called … wanted. The initiative, as with the first four disciples (1:16–20), lies with Jesus (cf. John 15:16).

3:14 twelve. Representing the 12 tribes of Israel. As the one who embodies both God's presence (1:2–3) and the life of God to which the law pointed (vv. 1–6), Jesus is now the center of God's newly reconstituted Israel (see note on 9:2–29; see also notes on 9:2–7). **be with him … send them.** As a precursor to sending the disciples (6:7), Jesus summons the Twelve so that they might know him by sharing intimately in his life. This will later include accepting his coming death and embracing a cross-bearing discipleship (8:31–38).

3:16 Peter. Means "rock" (see Matt 16:18 and note).

3:17 sons of thunder. May indicate their propensity to react harshly to perceived opposition (9:38; Luke 9:54).

3:18 Bartholomew. Apparently the Nathanael John associates with Philip (John 1:45). **Matthew.** Another name for Levi (2:14). **Thaddaeus.** Another name for Judas son of James (Luke 6:16). **Zealot.** Suggests an ardent nationalist.

3:20–35 *Jesus Accused by His Family and by Teachers of the Law.* Concerns about Jesus' words and deeds lead to a climactic confrontation with his family (vv. 21,31–35) and, for the first time, with officials from Jerusalem (vv. 21–30). It centers on Jesus' astonishing authority over the demons. The accusation by Jerusalem's teachers of the law that Jesus is demon-possessed marks a decisive turning point, prompting Mark's first explicit reference to Jesus speaking in parables (v. 23) and a severe warning about blasphemy (vv. 28–29).

3:20 Indicates Jesus' burgeoning popularity (see note on 1:28).

3:21 this. Perhaps refers to Jesus' provocative actions and blasphemous claims to authority (e.g., 2:1—3:6). Notwithstanding Mary's angelic visitation (Luke 1:30–38), Jesus' family seeks to restrain him both for his own sake and for the family's reputation. (John the Baptist was also in danger of being offended by Jesus [cf. Matt 11:2–6].)

22And the teachers of the law who came down from Jerusalem[d] said, "He is possessed by Beelzebul![e]
By the prince of demons he is driving out demons."[f]
23So Jesus called them over to him and began to speak to them in parables:[g] "How can Satan[h] drive
out Satan? 24If a kingdom is divided against itself, that kingdom cannot stand. 25If a house is divided
against itself, that house cannot stand. 26And if Satan opposes himself and is divided, he cannot stand;
his end has come. 27In fact, no one can enter a strong man's house without first tying him up. Then he
can plunder the strong man's house.[i] 28Truly I tell you, people can be forgiven all their sins and every
slander they utter, 29but whoever blasphemes against the Holy Spirit will never be forgiven; they are
guilty of an eternal sin."[j]
30He said this because they were saying, "He has an impure spirit."
31Then Jesus' mother and brothers arrived.[k] Standing outside, they sent someone in to call him. 32A
crowd was sitting around him, and they told him, "Your mother and brothers are outside looking for you."
33"Who are my mother and my brothers?" he asked.
34Then he looked at those seated in a circle around him and said, "Here are my mother and my
brothers! 35Whoever does God's will is my brother and sister and mother."

The Parable of the Sower

4:1-12pp — Mt 13:1-15; Lk 8:4-10
4:13-20pp — Mt 13:18-23; Lk 8:11-15

4 Again Jesus began to teach by the lake.[l] The crowd that gathered around him was so large that he
got into a boat and sat in it out on the lake, while all the people were along the shore at the water's
edge. 2He taught them many things by parables,[m] and in his teaching said: 3"Listen! A farmer went out
to sow his seed.[n] 4As he was scattering the seed, some fell along the path, and the birds came and ate it

3:22 [d]Mt 15:1 [e]Mt 10:25; 11:18; 12:24; Jn 7:20; 8:48,52; 10:20 [f]Mt 9:34
3:23 [g]Mk 4:2 [h]Mt 4:10
3:27 [i]Isa 49:24,25
3:29 [j]Mt 12:31,32; Lk 12:10
3:31 [k]ver 21
4:1 [l]Mk 2:13; 3:7
4:2 [m]ver 11; Mk 3:23
4:3 [n]ver 26

3:22 teachers of the law. See note on 1:22. **Beelzebul.** The ruler of the demons who, according to Jewish tradition, caused demon-worship and provoked wars. If the accusation by the teachers of the law is proved, it could result in Jesus' death by stoning. The accusation may reflect garbled reports of the demons' confessions, alarm over Jesus' attitude toward purity laws, and anxiety that his popularity could cause public disturbances that might provoke Roman reprisals.

3:23a parables. Mark's first explicit mention of parables (see note on 4:2) comes in direct response to the first official denunciation of Jesus by the teachers of the law from Jerusalem. This is critical in understanding Jesus' subsequent explanation of why he uses parables (4:11–12).

3:23b–26 The charge is nonsensical. If Satan were at war with himself, his divided kingdom would self-destruct, and there would be no need for Jesus to cast out the demons.

3:27 Jesus is John's "one more powerful" (1:7). God had promised that as the stronger one he would deliver Zion from its strong oppressors (Isa 49:24–26). In claiming to have tied up the strong man (Satan; see note on 1:13), Jesus implies that his casting out demons fulfills God's promised deliverance of Israel. For Jesus, Israel's fundamental problem is not Rome but Satan, the current "prince of this world" (John 12:31; 14:30; 16:11; see Eph 2:2), and his demons.

3:28 Truly I tell you. Underlines the certainty of the often surprising statement that follows (see 8:12; 9:1,41; 10:15,29; 11:23; 12:43; 13:30; 14:9,18,25).

3:29 Since Jesus is the one in whom God has come to save his people (1:2–3) and in whom God's Spirit dwells (1:10), he is the Holy Son of God (v. 11; 1:11,24) who acts with divine authority (2:10,28). To equate him with Satan (vv. 22,30) is to blaspheme the Holy Spirit of God himself. Isaiah's concluding prayer for God's saving intervention (Isa 63:7—64:12), which was answered at Jesus' baptism (see note on 1:10), began by recalling how in the first exodus Israel grieved God's Holy Spirit and made God their enemy (Isa 63:10). Israel's leadership is making the same mistake in this new exodus. **eternal sin.** Either (1) they are cutting themselves off from the only source of forgiveness by rejecting Jesus, or (2) their identifying what is so obviously from God with Satan is so blasphemous that God will never forgive it (e.g., 1 Sam 3:13–14), or (3) both.

3:31–35 Jesus redefines the meaning of family. While his mother and brothers stand on the outside, the "insiders"—those who listen to Jesus—are his new brother, sister, and mother. Given who Jesus is, doing God's will now means gathering around and obeying Jesus (v. 35; cf. 4:11,34; 9:7,37).

4:1—5:43 *Jesus Responds With Parables of Word and Deed.* Following his first confrontation with the teachers of the law from Jerusalem over the source of his undeniable authority and power (3:20–35), Jesus tells four parables that speak to the divisive impact of the mysterious nature of the kingdom of God. He then performs four mighty deeds that, parable-like, reveal the true source of his authority and what he has come to do.

4:1–34 *Four Parables of Word.* Following Jesus' first explicit use of parables (3:23), Mark provides an extended explanation of why Jesus used parables. Parables serve two purposes: they reveal the truth of the mystery of the kingdom, and, in doing so, they reveal the hearts of the hearers, resulting in life for some and judgment for others.

4:1–20 *The Parable of the Sower.* Understanding this first of the four parables is the key to understanding all of Jesus' parables (v. 13): everything depends on how one hears (vv. 3,9,23–25). Although traditionally known as the parable of the sower (Jesus), it instead concerns the soils (the hearers) and their response to the sown seed (Jesus' proclamation of the kingdom [see 1:14–15]).

4:1 sat. A position typically used by Jewish teachers.

4:2 parables. Vivid proverbial sayings, brief similes, metaphoric phrases, analogies, or short stories drawn from everyday life and designed to communicate important truths. They can be neutral (e.g., vv. 26–29) or provocatively confrontational (e.g., 12:1–12).

4:3 Listen! Jesus' emphatic summons to listen captures the heart of the following parable (cf. vv. 9,23,24).

4:4–8 Taking up the experience of a first-century farmer scattering his seed, Jesus describes the various responses of four different kinds of soils.

4:8 [o] Jn 15:5; Col 1:6
4:9 [p] ver 23; Mt 11:15
4:11 [q] Mt 3:2 [r] 1Co 5:12, 13; Col 4:5; 1Th 4:12; 1Ti 3:7
4:12 [s] Isa 6:9,10; Mt 13:13-15
4:14 [t] Mk 16:20; Lk 1:2; Ac 4:31; 8:4; 16:6; 17:11; Php 1:14
4:15 [u] Mt 4:10
4:19 [v] Mt 19:23; 1Ti 6:9, 10,17; 1Jn 2:15-17
4:21 [w] Mt 5:15
4:22 [x] Jer 16:17; Mt 10:26; Lk 8:17; 12:2
4:23 [y] ver 9; Mt 11:15

up. 5Some fell on rocky places, where it did not have much soil. It sprang up quickly, because the soil
was shallow. 6But when the sun came up, the plants were scorched, and they withered because they
had no root. 7Other seed fell among thorns, which grew up and choked the plants, so that they did not
bear grain. 8Still other seed fell on good soil. It came up, grew and produced a crop, some multiplying
thirty, some sixty, some a hundred times."[o]

9Then Jesus said, "Whoever has ears to hear, let them hear."[p]

10When he was alone, the Twelve and the others around him asked him about the parables. 11He told
them, "The secret of the kingdom of God[q] has been given to you. But to those on the outside[r] everything
is said in parables 12so that,

> " 'they may be ever seeing but never perceiving,
> and ever hearing but never understanding;
> otherwise they might turn and be forgiven!'[a]"[s]

13Then Jesus said to them, "Don't you understand this parable? How then will you understand any
parable? 14The farmer sows the word.[t] 15Some people are like seed along the path, where the word is
sown. As soon as they hear it, Satan[u] comes and takes away the word that was sown in them. 16Others,
like seed sown on rocky places, hear the word and at once receive it with joy. 17But since they have no
root, they last only a short time. When trouble or persecution comes because of the word, they quickly
fall away. 18Still others, like seed sown among thorns, hear the word; 19but the worries of this life, the
deceitfulness of wealth[v] and the desires for other things come in and choke the word, making it unfruitful. 20Others, like seed sown on good soil, hear the word, accept it, and produce a crop—some thirty,
some sixty, some a hundred times what was sown."

A Lamp on a Stand

21He said to them, "Do you bring in a lamp to put it under a bowl or a bed? Instead, don't you put it
on its stand?[w] 22For whatever is hidden is meant to be disclosed, and whatever is concealed is meant to
be brought out into the open.[x] 23If anyone has ears to hear, let them hear."[y]

[a] *12* Isaiah 6:9,10

4:9 One Jewish tradition spoke of God's sowing the law into Israel's hearts at the exodus. But although the people received it, they did not keep it and so came under judgment. Jesus is concerned that this new deliverance does not have the same tragic outcome.

4:10 As in the previous confrontation (3:31–35), full understanding is only for those who gather around Jesus (cf. 3:32). **the Twelve and the others around him.** Jesus' reconstituted Israel (see note on 3:14) and his new family of "insiders" (cf. vv. 33–34; see note on 3:31–35).

4:11 The secret of the kingdom. Primarily Jesus himself, in whose person, mission, and message God's long-awaited mighty saving presence has unexpectedly and surprisingly come. **secret.** Or "mystery." In Jewish tradition it refers to something, often unexpected and hidden in time past, that God now reveals but only on his terms (e.g., Matt 11:25–27; Rom 1:17; 16:25; 1 Cor 2:1; 15:21). For those who—through misunderstanding (e.g., Jesus' family), outright rejection (e.g., the Jerusalem teachers of the law), or indecision (e.g., the crowds)—remain "on the outside," the secret comes only in unexplained parables (cf. vv. 33–34).

4:12 Jesus' parables function like Isaiah's preaching. In the Scriptures, those who reject the living God—who does whatever he pleases (see note on 1:40; cf. Pss 115:3; 135:5–6)—for lifeless idols will become like the idols they worship, neither seeing nor hearing (Pss 115:4–8; 135:15–18). Because Israel refused God's salvation, Isaiah's teaching confirmed that the nation was like the blind and deaf idols it worshiped (Isa 6:9–10). Isaiah gained a few disciples (Isa 8:16), but the majority, including Jerusalem's leadership, pursued their own hypocritical worship (Isa 29:9–16; see 7:6–7), ensuring their destruction (Isa 6:11–13). Because Jesus is faced with an equally stubborn rejection of God's salvation (2:1—3:6,22,28–30), his parables function in the same way as Isaiah's teaching did. Although at this point it is primarily the hypocritical Jerusalem leaders (3:5; 7:6–7; 11:27–33) who will come under God's hardening judgment (12:1–12; ch. 13), the same warning extends to all who fail to respond. However, if people submit to Jesus' teaching (cf. 3:34–35; 12:32–34), then the secret of the kingdom is theirs.

4:13 Failing to understand this parable about the importance of correctly hearing *any* parable is obviously a serious problem.

4:15–20 Jesus offers three characteristic reasons why his word does or does not bear fruit.

4:15 The word makes no impact at all on the hardened, stubborn heart (cf. 3:5); Satan whisks it away.

4:16–17 Shallowness represents a lack of commitment (cf. 8:34–35).

4:18 thorns. The inclination to evil entangles people.

4:19 deceitfulness of wealth. Not only is material prosperity unable to save one's life (8:36; cf. Ps 49:7–9), but it can easily lead to a false sense of self-sufficiency, security, and well-being, making it very difficult to let go when called to follow Jesus (see 10:17–25 but also 10:28–30).

4:20 Although perhaps implied, Jesus makes no specific judgment on whether the soil that produces 100 times more is better than the soil that produces 30 times more. The rates of increase, while certainly good, should not in themselves be seen as miraculous.

4:21–25 *A Lamp on a Stand.* This picks up on the parable of the soils (vv. 3–8) but with the emphasis on Jesus' role. The degree of attention they give will determine their fate.

4:22 Jesus' words and deeds, like a lamp on its stand, will reveal both the secret of the kingdom and the condition of his hearers' hearts. Mark's Gospel, in relating Jesus' story, also does exactly this to its readers.

4:23 Stresses again the importance of hearing correctly (cf. vv. 3,9).

[24]"Consider carefully what you hear," he continued. "With the measure you use, it will be measured
to you—and even more.[z] [25]Whoever has will be given more; whoever does not have, even what they
have will be taken from them."[a]

The Parable of the Growing Seed

[26]He also said, "This is what the kingdom of God is like.[b] A man scatters seed on the ground. [27]Night
and day, whether he sleeps or gets up, the seed sprouts and grows, though he does not know how. [28]All
by itself the soil produces grain—first the stalk, then the head, then the full kernel in the head. [29]As
soon as the grain is ripe, he puts the sickle to it, because the harvest has come."[c]

The Parable of the Mustard Seed

4:30-32pp — Mt 13:31,32; Lk 13:18,19

[30]Again he said, "What shall we say the kingdom of God is like,[d] or what parable shall we use to
describe it? [31]It is like a mustard seed, which is the smallest of all seeds on earth. [32]Yet when planted, it
grows and becomes the largest of all garden plants,
with such big branches that the birds can perch in
its shade."

[33]With many similar parables Jesus spoke the
word to them, as much as they could understand.[e]
[34]He did not say anything to them without using a
parable.[f] But when he was alone with his own disciples, he explained everything.

Jesus Calms the Storm

4:35-41pp — Mt 8:18,23-27; Lk 8:22-25

[35]That day when evening came, he said to his
disciples, "Let us go over to the other side." [36]Leaving the crowd behind, they took him along, just as
he was, in the boat.[g] There were also other boats
with him. [37]A furious squall came up, and the
waves broke over the boat, so that it was nearly
swamped. [38]Jesus was in the stern, sleeping on a
cushion. The disciples woke him and said to him,
"Teacher, don't you care if we drown?"

Jesus compares the kingdom of God to a mustard seed (Mark 4:31).

4:24 [z] Mt 7:2; Lk 6:38
4:25 [a] Mt 13:12; 25:29
4:26 [b] Mt 13:24
4:29 [c] Rev 14:15
4:30 [d] Mt 13:24
4:33 [e] Jn 16:12
4:34 [f] Jn 16:25
4:36 [g] ver 1; Mk 3:9; 5:2, 21; 6:32,45

4:24–25 The receptive among Jesus' hearers will receive more, leading to full and fruitful participation in the kingdom of God (v. 20). From those who do not respond (vv. 15–19) even the little they have will be taken away, resulting finally in their undergoing God's judgment (cf. 8:38; 12:9; 13:5–37).

4:26–29 *The Parable of the Growing Seed.* The growth of the kingdom can neither be forced nor coerced. Although it is not known how, the word contains its own generative power, causing the kingdom to grow steadily and surely in God's time and in God's way.

4:30–34 *The Parable of the Mustard Seed.* The mustard seed was the smallest seed that farmers and gardeners of the day used. Due to the unimpressive beginnings of God's kingdom, some might be tempted to underestimate its power when compared to the great empires of the world. But it will eventually supplant them (cf. Ezek 17:23; Dan 4:12). At the same time, in likening the kingdom to the smallest of all garden plants instead of the expected great cedar (Ezek 17:22–24), Jesus begins implicitly to challenge Israel's traditional Messianic expectations. That challenge will become explicit later in his shocking embrace of the cross (cf. 8:31–38).

4:33–34 Jesus' parables were intended to introduce people to the deeply unsettling secret of the "new wine" of the kingdom (2:22) now present in Jesus. Even so, Jesus gave explicit teaching only "when he was alone" (v. 34) with those already committed to him (see note on v. 11; cf. 3:31–35).

4:35—5:43 *Four "Parables" of Deed.* Jesus' identity has been Mark's primary concern from the opening sentences of his Gospel. After relating four "word" parables (see note on 4:2), Mark records four mighty "deed" parables that raise even more emphatically the question of Jesus' identity (cf. 4:10). Each is accompanied by amazement and fear in response to God's powerful presence in Jesus (see notes on 1:10,11).

4:35–41 *Jesus Calms the Storm.* In commanding the sea and thereby doing what only God can do, Jesus reveals the true source of his authority and power (cf. the scribes' accusation in 3:22).

4:35 That day. Links the parables with the following four deeds.

4:36 Leaving the crowd. Only Jesus' disciples—the "insiders" (see notes on vv. 10,11)—witness the next staggering event.

4:37 The Sea of Galilee is known for its sudden, furious squalls.

4:38 sleeping on a cushion. This is the kind of detail one associates with the recollection of an eyewitness; it indicates the ordinariness of the moment and Jesus' human weariness. In light of Jesus' subsequent command (v. 39), it also testifies to his complete confidence in his power over creation. **Teacher.** The most common form of address for

4:40 [h]Mt 14:31; Mk 16:14
5:2 [i]Mk 4:1 [j]Mk 1:23
5:7 [k]Mt 8:29 [l]Mt 4:3; Lk 1:32; 6:35; Ac 16:17; Heb 7:1
5:9 [m]ver 15

39 He got up, rebuked the wind and said to the waves, "Quiet! Be still!" Then the wind died down and
it was completely calm.
40 He said to his disciples, "Why are you so afraid? Do you still have no faith?"[h]
41 They were terrified and asked each other, "Who is this? Even the wind and the waves obey him!"

Jesus Restores a Demon-Possessed Man

5:1-17pp — Mt 8:28-34; Lk 8:26-37
5:18-20pp — Lk 8:38,39

5 They went across the lake to the region of the Gerasenes.[a] 2 When Jesus got out of the boat,[i] a man
with an impure spirit[j] came from the tombs to meet him. 3 This man lived in the tombs, and no one
could bind him anymore, not even with a chain. 4 For he had often been chained hand and foot, but he
tore the chains apart and broke the irons on his feet. No one was strong enough to subdue him. 5 Night
and day among the tombs and in the hills he would cry out and cut himself with stones.
6 When he saw Jesus from a distance, he ran and fell on his knees in front of him. 7 He shouted at the
top of his voice, "What do you want with me,[k] Jesus, Son of the Most High God?[l] In God's name don't
torture me!" 8 For Jesus had said to him, "Come out of this man, you impure spirit!"
9 Then Jesus asked him, "What is your name?"
"My name is Legion,"[m] he replied, "for we are many." 10 And he begged Jesus again and again not
to send them out of the area.
11 A large herd of pigs was feeding on the nearby hillside. 12 The demons begged Jesus, "Send us
among the pigs; allow us to go into them." 13 He gave them permission, and the impure spirits came
out and went into the pigs. The herd, about two thousand in number, rushed down the steep bank into
the lake and were drowned.

[a] *1* Some manuscripts *Gadarenes*; other manuscripts *Gergesenes*

Jesus in Mark (5:35; 9:17,38; 10:17,20,35; 12:14,19,32; 13:1; 14:14; cf. "Rabbi": 9:5; 10:51; 11:21; 14:45). It indicates that teaching was central to Jesus' ministry. Its use here (the first time in Mark) is specifically in connection with the calming of the storm, indicating why Jesus' teaching has such authority (see note on 1:22).

4:39 Israel's Scriptures are emphatic that God alone controls the sea (Exod 14–15; Pss 65:7; 89:8–10; 107:25–30), which the prophets celebrated as sure evidence of God's power to redeem his people (Isa 63:11–14; see Isa 10:24–26; 43:2,16–17; 50:2; 51:9–11; Zech 10:11). Jesus uses the same language to rebuke the wind as God did when he rebuked the waters at creation (Job 26:10–12) and later the Red Sea (Ps 106:9; the Septuagint [the pre-Christian Greek translation of the OT] of Ps 105:9).

4:40 From Jesus' perspective his disciples had already seen enough to have faith in his power to protect them.

4:41 The disciples had not even begun to grasp the full implications of Jesus' previous words and deeds (e.g., 2:10,28) and so this demonstration of his divine authority leaves them terrified (see note on 1:10). They know who alone calms the sea. Their fear testifies to the inability of the old cloth and the old wineskin to contain what is happening among them (2:21–22). Mark's readers, however, are well prepared by Mark's prologue (see note on 1:2–3) to answer the question "Who is this?" Jesus is not just a powerful teacher (see note on 1:22).

5:1–20 *Jesus Restores a Demon-Possessed Man.* Since in calming the sea Jesus has just done what only God can do, his easy dismissal of the most powerful demonic host in Mark's Gospel underscores Jesus' earlier response to Jerusalem's teachers of the law: in him the mighty God has come to restore his people (3:22–30; see note on 1:2–3).

5:1 region of the Gerasenes. The exact location is unknown, but it could refer to the region of Gergesa or Gadara (see NIV text note).

5:2–4 Mark's focus on the astonishing strength of the man emphasizes the even greater power of Jesus, in whom God has come in strength (see note on 1:7), to bind the strong man and set his captives free (see note on 3:27).

5:5 cut himself. The demons intend to deface God's image and likeness in which God created the man (see notes on 1:25,40; 2:27; 3:3).

5:6 fell on his knees. See note on 3:11.

5:7 What do you want with me ...? See note on 1:24. **Son of the Most High God.** An even more exalted title than seen previously (1:24; 3:11). **In God's name.** Or "I adjure you with respect to God"; adjuring in the name of a more powerful being was normally used by exorcists to control demons. The impure spirit attempts to control Jesus. But the futility of that attempt is already evident in the spirit's submissive posture and in the majesty of Jesus' title. **torture.** Usually associated with imprisonment (Matt 18:34); it anticipates Legion's end-time destiny.

5:9 Legion. The numbers in a Roman legion could vary from as little as 3,000 to as many as 6,000 men. Although some see here an indication of Jesus' opposition to imperial Rome, when the word was applied to other entities, in this case an impure spirit (see note on 1:23), it simply meant a sizable military host in general.

5:10 This probably reflects the demon's fear that Jesus has come to mete out eternal judgment (v. 7).

5:11–12 Pigs were commonly associated with ancient idolatry and were regarded by Jews as impure (Lev 11:7–8). Although from a modern standpoint the destruction of the pigs is problematic, for first-century Jews purity before God was of much greater importance. For them, moving impure spirits from an impure man living among impure tombs to impure animals was fitting.

5:13 He gave them permission. Reflects Jesus' authority. Even so it is the demons who cause the destruction of the pigs, a sobering object lesson of the ultimate outcome of idolatry. Only once has Israel seen someone command the sea and then immediately after witness the drowning of a powerful hostile force within it (Exod 14). Jesus, in this new exodus (see note on 1:2–3), has repeated that iconic moment, but it now involves Israel's true enemies: demons, not nations.

14Those tending the pigs ran off and reported this in the town and countryside, and the people went out to see what had happened. 15When they came to Jesus, they saw the man who had been possessed by the legion[n] of demons,[o] sitting there, dressed and in his right mind; and they were afraid. 16Those who had seen it told the people what had happened to the demon-possessed man — and told about the pigs as well. 17Then the people began to plead with Jesus to leave their region.

18As Jesus was getting into the boat, the man who had been demon-possessed begged to go with him. 19Jesus did not let him, but said, "Go home to your own people and tell them[p] how much the Lord has done for you, and how he has had mercy on you." 20So the man went away and began to tell in the Decapolis[a][q] how much Jesus had done for him. And all the people were amazed.

Jesus Raises a Dead Girl and Heals a Sick Woman

5:22-43pp — Mt 9:18-26; Lk 8:41-56

21When Jesus had again crossed over by boat to the other side of the lake,[r] a large crowd gathered around him while he was by the lake.[s] 22Then one of the synagogue leaders,[t] named Jairus, came, and when he saw Jesus, he fell at his feet. 23He pleaded earnestly with him, "My little daughter is dying. Please come and put your hands on[u] her so that she will be healed and live." 24So Jesus went with him.

A large crowd followed and pressed around him. 25And a woman was there who had been subject to bleeding[v] for twelve years. 26She had suffered a great deal under the care of many doctors and had spent all she had, yet instead of getting better she grew worse. 27When she heard about Jesus, she came up behind him in the crowd and touched his cloak, 28because she thought, "If I just touch his clothes,[w] I will be healed." 29Immediately her bleeding stopped and she felt in her body that she was freed from her suffering.[x]

30At once Jesus realized that power[y] had gone out from him. He turned around in the crowd and asked, "Who touched my clothes?"

31"You see the people crowding against you," his disciples answered, "and yet you can ask, 'Who touched me?' "

a 20 That is, the Ten Cities

5:15 [n] ver 9 [o] ver 16,18; Mt 4:24
5:19 [p] Mt 8:4
5:20 [q] Mt 4:25; Mk 7:31
5:21 [r] Mt 9:1 [s] Mk 4:1
5:22 [t] ver 35,36,38; Lk 13:14; Ac 13:15; 18:8,17
5:23 [u] Mt 19:13; Mk 6:5; 7:32; 8:23; 16:18; Lk 4:40; 13:13; Ac 6:6
5:25 [v] Lev 15:25-30
5:28 [w] Mt 9:20
5:29 [x] ver 34
5:30 [y] Lk 5:17; 6:19

5:15 afraid. Cf. the disciples after Jesus calmed the storm (4:41).
5:16–17 The Gerasenes' dread of Jesus' great power and perhaps their fear of further financial loss lead them to plead with Jesus — not for help (v. 23; 1:40: 6:56; 7:26,32; 8:22) or that they might remain with him (v. 18) but that he might leave. Astonishingly, the same Jesus who has the authority to expel a demonic legion from the region (v. 10) allows the fearful villagers to expel him (cf. 6:1–5). In the same way, the authoritative Lord of the temple will later allow his people and their leaders to reject him. See note on 8:31.
5:19 Probably because Jewish Messianic ideas had little traction in this largely Gentile area, Jesus, in marked contrast to his earlier restrictions (1:34,43–44; 3:12), instructs the man to declare what the Lord has done. **Lord.** Although a title of respect, Mark's readers might see here an allusion to Jesus' divine identity (see notes on 1:2–3; 2:10; 4:41).
5:20 Decapolis. A league of ten highly cultured Greek cities, with all but Scythopolis being east of the Sea of Galilee and the Jordan River. Jesus' amazing power is made known among the Gentiles (see notes on 1:2–3,11; 3:7–8).
5:21–43 *Jesus Raises a Dead Girl and Heals a Sick Woman.* In bringing purity to the impure and effortlessly restoring the dead to life, Jesus not only continues his mission to deliver but again demonstrates the source of his power by doing what only God can do. The interweaving of the two stories highlights their common themes. In the one (vv. 21–24a,35–43), a desperate father and leader appeals to Jesus on behalf of his dying daughter. In the other (vv. 24b–34), an impure, impoverished, isolated, and equally desperate woman, in acting for herself, ends up being affirmed as a daughter. Ignoring their very different social standings, Jesus restores both to "life" in the community (cf. Gal 3:8).
5:21 The immediate appearance of a large crowd emphasizes Jesus' continued popularity (cf. 4:1).
5:22 synagogue leaders. Laypersons usually responsible for various administrative tasks, such as supervising worship and maintaining the building. If the synagogue is in Capernaum, then the man likely comes to Jesus because he knows what Jesus can do. **Jairus.** Means "may Yahweh awaken or enlighten." **fell at his feet.** Indicates both profound deference and desperation.
5:25 The woman's bleeding is due to a menstrual disorder, likely resulting in a state of permanent ritual impurity (Lev 15:25–33). **twelve years.** The only place in Mark's Gospel that mentions the duration of suffering. Herself defiled and at risk of defiling all she touched, the woman had been spiritually and socially isolated the entire time.
5:26 As with the previously mentioned impure demon-controlled man (vv. 3–4), human intervention was of no avail; doctors in the ancient world were not always highly regarded.
5:28 Seeking healing through some kind of physical contact was common in the ancient world, for it was believed that power could be transferred through touch (e.g., Acts 5:15; 19:12). Jesus himself regularly touched people (e.g., 1:41; 7:32; 8:23). Here the woman initiates the process. However, instead of her touch making Jesus temporarily ritually impure, his being indwelt by the Holy Spirit (1:10; 3:28–30) means that his purity renders her permanently clean (cf. 1:41–42).
5:29–31 There is no reason to see anything magical here. Since humans are both body and spirit, it is not surprising that a change in the one can be immediately registered in the other.

5:34 [z]Mt 9:22 [a]Ac 15:33
5:35 [b]ver 22
5:37 [c]Mt 4:21
5:38 [d]ver 22
5:39 [e]Mt 9:24
5:41 [f]Mk 1:31 [g]Lk 7:14; Ac 9:40
5:43 [h]Mt 8:4
6:1 [i]Mt 2:23
6:2 [j]Mk 1:21 [k]Mt 4:23 [l]Mt 7:28
6:3 [m]Mt 12:46 [n]Mt 11:6; Jn 6:61

32But Jesus kept looking around to see who had done it. 33Then the woman, knowing what had happened to her, came and fell at his feet and, trembling with fear, told him the whole truth. 34He said to
her, "Daughter, your faith has healed you.[z] Go in peace[a] and be freed from your suffering."
35While Jesus was still speaking, some people came from the house of Jairus, the synagogue leader.[b]
"Your daughter is dead," they said. "Why bother the teacher anymore?"
36Overhearing[a] what they said, Jesus told him, "Don't be afraid; just believe."
37He did not let anyone follow him except Peter, James and John the brother of James.[c] 38When they
came to the home of the synagogue leader,[d] Jesus saw a commotion, with people crying and wailing
loudly. 39He went in and said to them, "Why all this commotion and wailing? The child is not dead but
asleep."[e] 40But they laughed at him.

After he put them all out, he took the child's father and mother and the disciples who were with him,
and went in where the child was. 41He took her by the hand[f] and said to her, *"Talitha koum!"* (which
means "Little girl, I say to you, get up!").[g] 42Immediately the girl stood up and began to walk around
(she was twelve years old). At this they were completely astonished. 43He gave strict orders not to let
anyone know about this,[h] and told them to give her something to eat.

A Prophet Without Honor

6:1-6pp — Mt 13:54-58

6 Jesus left there and went to his hometown,[i] accompanied by his disciples. 2When the Sabbath
came,[j] he began to teach in the synagogue,[k] and many who heard him were amazed.[l]
"Where did this man get these things?" they asked. "What's this wisdom that has been given him?
What are these remarkable miracles he is performing? 3Isn't this the carpenter? Isn't this Mary's son
and the brother of James, Joseph,[b] Judas and Simon?[m] Aren't his sisters here with us?" And they took
offense at him.[n]

4Jesus said to them, "A prophet is not without honor except in his own town, among his relatives and

[a] *36* Or *Ignoring* [b] *3* Greek *Joses*, a variant of *Joseph*

5:32 Israel's salvation is fundamentally about restoring relationship with a personal God. Jesus' healings are likewise consistently interpersonal (see note on 4:11 where the mystery of the kingdom is the person of Jesus himself). He must speak with whoever touched him.

5:33 fell at his feet. See note on v. 22. **trembling with fear.** Probably because she did not approach Jesus face-to-face with a direct petition. **told him the whole truth.** Her honesty publicly reveals her faith (see v. 28), which Jesus then affirms (v. 34).

5:36 Don't be afraid; just believe. Echoes Jesus' words to the disciples in the boat (4:40). He who exercises God's sole authority over the sea can also command life and death (cf. note on 3:4).

5:37 As with the calming of the storm, the crowds are not to witness this event. In taking with him only the inner circle of Peter, James, and John (see note on 1:18; cf. 9:2; 14:33), Jesus heightens the air of secrecy.

5:38–39 Professional mourners were customarily hired for funerals, but the short time frame suggests that these are relatives, friends, and neighbors.

5:39 asleep. Whereas humans can do nothing about death, for God it is merely a matter of awakening a sleeper (1 Thess 5:10; cf. John 11:11–14; Eph 5:14).

5:40 Jesus' expells all except the parents and his three disciples suggesting they are about to witness a truly remarkable event (see 9:2).

5:41 took her by the hand. A corpse was considered ritually impure. Jesus continues to show his power over impurity (cf. 1:25–26,41–42), this time himself initiating contact (cf. vv. 28,30). ***Talitha koum!*** The original Aramaic of Jesus' simple command reflects the vividness of an eyewitness account. **Little girl.** Indicates her youth and Jesus' tenderness.

5:42 twelve years old. The only time Mark records someone's age; it indicates that she was eligible to be married. **completely astonished.** See note on 1:10. Occurs only here in Mark and highlights the climactic nature of this fourth mighty deed (see note on 4:35—5:43). Not only does Jesus speak to the sea with God's authority, but as with God, his authority over death is merely a matter of a waking word to the sleeper.

5:43 strict orders. See notes on 1:25,34,44. **something to eat.** Demonstrates that she is truly alive (cf. Luke 24:41–43).

6:1–56 *Prophets Without Honor . . . and More Than a Prophet.* Following Jesus' astonishing confirmation of his divine identity and "new exodus" mission to redeem his people, Mark returns to the theme of opposition. After the dishonor shown Jesus in his hometown, Herod's execution of John shows what dishonored prophets can expect (vv. 14–29). The gravity of Jesus' rejection is underlined by his next two mighty deeds, which demonstrate once again that he is far more than a prophet: Israel's leaders are rejecting not just John but the very Lord whose way John prepared (vv. 35–52; see note on 1:2–3). Mark interweaves the disciples being sent (vv. 7–13) and returning (vv. 30–31), implying that their participation in the kingdom will be similarly costly (cf. 8:34–38).

6:1–6a *A Prophet Without Honor.* Jesus' astonishing authority continues to cause offense, this time among those for whom he is merely the local carpenter. That this is the last time in the Gospel where Jesus is associated with a synagogue suggests this rejection marks a significant break in his relationship with the institution and the Judaism it represents.

6:1 hometown. See note on 1:9.

6:2 synagogue. See note on 1:21. **amazed.** See note on 1:22.

6:3 Mark is the only Gospel that describes Jesus as a carpenter. The derogatory question reflects Jesus' hearers' offense at his appearing more special than they felt was warranted. Although Jesus apparently made a favorable impression in his youth (Luke 2:52), they were quite unprepared for his wisdom and mighty deeds (cf. the response of Mary and the family in 3:21).

6:4 prophet ... without honor. A short saying that explains the resistance of the people from Jesus' hometown and prepares for the

in his own home."[o] [5]He could not do any miracles there, except lay his hands on[p] a few sick people and
heal them. [6]He was amazed at their lack of faith.

Jesus Sends Out the Twelve

6:7-11pp — Mt 10:1,9-14; Lk 9:1,3-5

Then Jesus went around teaching from village to village.[q] [7]Calling the Twelve to him,[r] he began to
send them out two by two[s] and gave them authority over impure spirits.[t]

[8]These were his instructions: "Take nothing for the journey except a staff — no bread, no bag, no
money in your belts. [9]Wear sandals but not an extra shirt. [10]Whenever you enter a house, stay there
until you leave that town. [11]And if any place will not welcome you or listen to you, leave that place and
shake the dust off your feet[u] as a testimony against them."

[12]They went out and preached that people should repent.[v] [13]They drove out many demons and
anointed many sick people with oil[w] and healed them.

John the Baptist Beheaded

6:14-29pp — Mt 14:1-12
6:14-16pp — Lk 9:7-9

[14]King Herod heard about this, for Jesus' name
had become well known. Some were saying,[a] "John
the Baptist[x] has been raised from the dead, and that
is why miraculous powers are at work in him."

[15]Others said, "He is Elijah."[y]

And still others claimed, "He is a prophet,[z] like one of
the prophets of long ago."[a]

[16]But when Herod heard this, he said, "John, whom I
beheaded, has been raised from the dead!"

Coins of Herod Antipas, tetrarch of Galilee and Perea (4 BC–AD 39), who put John the Baptist to death. See chart/map, pp. 1930–1931.

Z. Radovan/www.BibleLandPictures.com

[17]For Herod himself had given orders to have John arrested, and he had him bound and put in prison.[b] He did
this because of Herodias, his brother Philip's wife, whom he had married. [18]For John had been saying
to Herod, "It is not lawful for you to have your brother's wife."[c] [19]So Herodias nursed a grudge against
John and wanted to kill him. But she was not able to, [20]because Herod feared John and protected him,

6:4 [o]Lk 4:24; Jn 4:44
6:5 [p]Mk 5:23
6:6 [q]Mt 9:35; Mk 1:39; Lk 13:22
6:7 [r]Mk 3:13 [s]Dt 17:6; Lk 10:1 [t]Mt 10:1
6:11 [u]Mt 10:14
6:12 [v]Lk 9:6
6:13 [w]Jas 5:14
6:14 [x]Mt 3:1
6:15 [y]Mal 4:5 [z]Mt 21:11 [a]Mt 16:14; Mk 8:28
6:17 [b]Mt 4:12; 11:2; Lk 3:19,20
6:18 [c]Lev 18:16; 20:21

[a] *14* Some early manuscripts *He was saying*

immediately following extended account of what happens to such a dishonored prophet: John the Baptist (vv. 14–29).

6:5 Whether expelled, as with the Gerasenes (5:17), or resisted through lack of faith, Jesus, in keeping with his servant calling (cf. Isa 42:2; see note on 1:11), does not override their wishes.

6:6a Others are amazed at Jesus' increasingly mighty deeds. Jesus is amazed at the astonishing lack of faith among the people of his hometown.

6:6b–13 *Jesus Sends Out the Twelve.* In spite of increasing opposition, Jesus not only continues to preach from village to village but intensifies his mission to Israel by sending out his disciples.

6:7 two by two. Provides mutual support (Eccl 4:12) and indicates the judicial nature of the disciples' message (Deut 19:15; cf. Rev 11). In exercising Jesus' own authority over impure spirits, they are God's witnesses, bearing testimony to Jesus and his gospel and, rejected, against Israel (cf. Mal 3:5).

6:8–9 The standard attire of traveling teachers, it stresses their dependence on time-honored Middle Eastern hospitality. Each place the disciples visit is now compelled to make a decision for or against Jesus' message. See note on Matt 10:9–10.

6:11 shake the dust off your feet. Given Jesus' redefinition of Israel and family around him (3:13–19,31–35), this symbolizes that the village, in refusing to offer hospitality to Jesus' disciples, has chosen to remain "outside" of God's offer of salvation (cf. 4:11–12; 9:41).

6:12–13 The disciples replicate Jesus' ministry (cf. 1:14–15,39).

6:13 anointed … with oil. Symbolizes restoration into God's blessing (Isa 61:3).

6:14–29 *John the Baptist Beheaded.* This is the first mention of John since his imprisonment in 1:14. The execution of John — for Jesus, Malachi's promised "Elijah" who was to prepare Israel lest the nation come under God's judgment (see 1:1–8) — does not bode well, either for Israel or for Jesus, himself also a rejected prophet (v. 4).

6:14a King Herod. Antipas, son of Herod the Great; ruler of Galilee and Perea (4 BC–AD 39). He styled himself as a king (cf. "my kingdom" in v. 23), although technically he was only a tetrarch. The title "King" highlights the disparity between Herod's "kingdom" and the kingdom Jesus announced.

6:14b–15 Current speculations surrounding Jesus' identity; all agree that he is some kind of prophet.

6:15 Elijah. Also performed mighty deeds (1 Kgs 17 — 2 Kgs 1) and was associated with Israel's end-time hopes (Mal 4:5; see notes on 1:2–3,6).

6:19–20 A vindictive Herodias and a wavering Herod recall Jezebel and Ahaz, especially Jezebel's murderous hostility toward Elijah (1 Kgs 19:1–2,10,14), to whom Mark has already likened John. Herod's puzzled interest in John is not unlike the crowd's interest in Jesus, though in neither case does curiosity alone save.

6:20 [d]Mt 11:9; 21:26 **6:21** [e]Est 1:3; 2:18 [f]Lk 3:1 **6:23** [g]Est 5:3,6; 7:2 **6:30** [h]Mt 10:2; Lk 9:10; 17:5; 22:14; 24:10; Ac 1:2,26 [i]Lk 9:10 **6:31** [j]Mk 3:20 **6:32** [k]ver 45; Mk 4:36 **6:34** [l]Mt 9:36 **6:37** [m]2Ki 4:42-44

knowing him to be a righteous and holy man.[d] When Herod heard John, he was greatly puzzled[a]; yet
he liked to listen to him.

21 Finally the opportune time came. On his birthday Herod gave a banquet[e] for his high officials and
military commanders and the leading men of Galilee.[f] 22 When the daughter of[b] Herodias came in and
danced, she pleased Herod and his dinner guests.

The king said to the girl, "Ask me for anything you want, and I'll give it to you." 23 And he promised
her with an oath, "Whatever you ask I will give you, up to half my kingdom."[g]

24 She went out and said to her mother, "What shall I ask for?"

"The head of John the Baptist," she answered.

25 At once the girl hurried in to the king with the request: "I want you to give me right now the head
of John the Baptist on a platter."

26 The king was greatly distressed, but because of his oaths and his dinner guests, he did not want to
refuse her. 27 So he immediately sent an executioner with orders to bring John's head. The man went,
beheaded John in the prison, 28 and brought back his head on a platter. He presented it to the girl, and
she gave it to her mother. 29 On hearing of this, John's disciples came and took his body and laid it in
a tomb.

Jesus Feeds the Five Thousand

6:32-44pp — Mt 14:13-21; Lk 9:10-17; Jn 6:5-13
6:32-44Ref — Mk 8:2-9

30 The apostles[h] gathered around Jesus and reported to him all they had done and taught.[i] 31 Then,
because so many people were coming and going that they did not even have a chance to eat,[j] he said
to them, "Come with me by yourselves to a quiet place and get some rest."

32 So they went away by themselves in a boat[k] to a solitary place. 33 But many who saw them leaving
recognized them and ran on foot from all the towns and got there ahead of them. 34 When Jesus landed
and saw a large crowd, he had compassion on them, because they were like sheep without a shepherd.[l]
So he began teaching them many things.

35 By this time it was late in the day, so his disciples came to him. "This is a remote place," they said,
"and it's already very late. 36 Send the people away so that they can go to the surrounding countryside
and villages and buy themselves something to eat."

37 But he answered, "You give them something to eat."[m]

[a] 20 Some early manuscripts *he did many things* [b] 22 Some early manuscripts *When his daughter*

6:21 Herod's banquet provided only for his elites ("high officials and military commanders and the leading men of Galilee"). In sharp contrast, Jesus provides for the large crowd of ordinary people (vv. 34–44).

6:23 Herod's grandiose oath is designed to impress his leading subjects (cf. Esth 5:3,6). On the other hand, when Jesus, Israel's true Shepherd, speaks, he is motivated by compassion and seeks not his own glory but the well-being of the crowds by teaching them (v. 34).

6:26–27 Like the seed choked by the love of this world (4:18–19), this "king," trapped in his own pretensions, chooses the wish of his dancing stepdaughter at the behest of his vindictive wife over a holy prophet who announced God's coming (cf. how the authorities similarly trap Pilate in 15:1–15). The length of the account emphasizes its importance: John was Jesus' forerunner in both his life and his death (cf. 9:11–13).

6:30–56 *More Than a Prophet.* The two following mighty deeds—provision in the wilderness and delivering newly reconstituted Israel (see note on 3:14) through the sea—together provide the most emphatic evidence to this point in Mark of Jesus' divine identity as the Lord come to effect Israel's new exodus deliverance (vv. 32–52; cf. note on 1:2–3). As Israel learned at the first exodus, only God did both.

6:30–44 *Jesus Feeds the Five Thousand.* Whereas Herod's self-promoting feast for his elites led to the death of a prophet, Jesus, Israel's true Shepherd, teaches the crowds and provides for them.

6:30 In spite of John's execution, the gospel forges ahead. **apostles.** Means "sent out ones" (cf. 3:14). As Jesus' representatives they stand in for Jesus himself, preaching his message and performing mighty deeds (vv. 7,12–13) in his name (cf. v. 14). The term also points forward to the disciples' continuing mission after Jesus' departure.

6:31 Jesus' popularity now prevents him and his disciples even from eating (3:20).

6:34 compassion. See note on 1:41. **sheep without a shepherd.** Israel's leaders were to shepherd God's people (Num 27:17; 2 Sam 5:2). Not only is Herod clearly delinquent in this responsibility, but that this self-styled "king" is not even a Jew but an Idumean testifies to Israel's dire state (cf. 1 Kgs 22:17; Jer 23:2).

Just as God gave the law to instruct Israel, Jesus here shepherds the people by teaching them. God promised that with Israel's return from exile he would not only provide a Davidic shepherd after his own heart for his people (Jer 3:15; 23:4–6; Ezek 34:23; 37:24) but he himself would be their Shepherd who fed them (Isa 40:11; 49:9; cf. Pss 23:1; 28:9; 80:1; 95:7) as he had in the wilderness (Ps 78:52). Jesus fulfills both these roles. Although Mark gives first place to Jesus' teaching the crowd "many things" (v. 34), his emphasis lies on Jesus' miraculous provision for them (vv. 35–44).

6:37 By directing the disciples to provide for the crowds, Jesus draws their attention to the significance of what follows. Nevertheless, they will

They said to him, "That would take more than half a year's wages[a]! Are we to go and spend that much on bread and give it to them to eat?"

38 "How many loaves do you have?" he asked. "Go and see."

When they found out, they said, "Five — and two fish."[n]

39 Then Jesus directed them to have all the people sit down in groups on the green grass. 40 So they sat down in groups of hundreds and fifties. 41 Taking the five loaves and the two fish and looking up to heaven, he gave thanks and broke the loaves.[o] Then he gave them to his disciples to distribute to the people. He also divided the two fish among them all. 42 They all ate and were satisfied, 43 and the disciples picked up twelve basketfuls of broken pieces of bread and fish. 44 The number of the men who had eaten was five thousand.

Jesus Walks on the Water

6:45-51pp — Mt 14:22-32; Jn 6:15-21
6:53-56pp — Mt 14:34-36

45 Immediately Jesus made his disciples get into the boat[p] and go on ahead of him to Bethsaida,[q] while he dismissed the crowd. 46 After leaving them, he went up on a mountainside to pray.[r]

47 Later that night, the boat was in the middle of the lake, and he was alone on land. 48 He saw the disciples straining at the oars, because the wind was against them. Shortly before dawn he went out to them, walking on the lake. He was about to pass by them, 49 but when they saw him walking on the lake, they thought he was a ghost.[s] They cried out, 50 because they all saw him and were terrified.

Immediately he spoke to them and said, "Take courage! It is I. Don't be afraid."[t] 51 Then he climbed into the boat[u] with them, and the wind died down.[v] They were completely amazed, 52 for they had not understood about the loaves; their hearts were hardened.[w]

[a] 37 Greek *take two hundred denarii*

6:38 [n] Mt 15:34; Mk 8:5
6:41 [o] Mt 14:19
6:45 [p] ver 32 [q] Mt 11:21
6:46 [r] Lk 3:21
6:49 [s] Lk 24:37
6:50 [t] Mt 14:27
6:51 [u] ver 32 [v] Mk 4:39
6:52 [w] Mk 8:17-21

fail to understand (see v. 52). **more than half a year's wages.** See NIV text note; a denarius was a day's wage for the average person.

6:39 The grass around the Sea of Galilee is green after the early winter or late spring rains. The description evokes the green grass (Ps 23:2) and rich pastures (Ezek 34:14) that symbolize God's provision for his people.

6:40 In a similar setting, "hundreds and fifties" recalls the order of Israel's camp in the wilderness (Exod 18:21,25).

6:42 In answer to popular speculation (vv. 14–15) and in contrast to Herod's "kingdom" with its self-glorifying feast for his elites (v. 21), Jesus, as both the Davidic Messiah (see note on 1:11; cf. Ps 23; Ezek 34:21–24) and God's incarnate presence (see notes on 1:2–3,7; cf. Ezek 34:30–31), is Israel's true Shepherd who compassionately provides for all who come to him. Jesus' superabundant provision, including fish, surpasses that of the manna in the wilderness, where people had only what they needed (Exod 16:16–21).

6:43 twelve. Since this number often symbolizes Israel (cf. 3:13–19), Mark might intend his readers to see here a reference to the fullness of God's end-time provision for his people.

6:44 Based on Israel's experience in the first exodus, several Jewish traditions expected a repetition of the wilderness provision, some even in association with the Messiah, in their end-time deliverance. Of all Jesus' public mighty deeds, this has the most obvious Messianic overtones. But for the first time there is no mention of amazement, suggesting that neither the people nor, more important, the disciples truly perceived what took place (cf. 6:52; 8:17–21).

6:45–56 *Jesus Walks on the Water.* The exodus motif that was begun with the miraculous provision of food continues in what is one of the clearest revelations of Jesus' divine nature: his authority over the sea as he rescues his disciples.

6:46 pray. Only on three occasions does Mark mention Jesus praying (here; 1:35; 14:32–36), and each seems to precede a revelation of something unexpected involving either his mission (1:38; 14:36) or, in this case, his identity.

6:48–50 Various elements of this account echo God's previous self-revelation: it is the time of his deliverance (Exod 14:24; Ps 46:5; Isa 17:14); he alone walks on the water (Job 9:8; Ps 77:19) and says "It is I" (lit. "I am"; Exod 3:14; Isa 41:4,10; 43:10,11,25; 48:12) when encouraging his people not to fear (Isa 41:10,13,14; 43:1,5; 44:2,8); and the phrase "pass by" recalls the revelation of his glory (Exod 33:19–23; 34:6; 1 Kgs 19:11). Even more clearly, Jesus does what only God can do while still controlling when, where, and to whom he reveals his true identity.

6:48 Shortly before dawn. Lit. "before the fourth watch of the night" (cf. note on 13:35); means between 3:00 a.m. and 6:00 a.m. **went out … pass by.** That Jesus goes out, apparently to save his disciples, but then passes them by seems contradictory. However, it is best to see the two as parts of the same action: Jesus' revelation of his divine glory is the moment of their rescue.

6:49 This is so far outside the disciples' experience that they could only think in terms of a "ghost," whose appearance at night brought disaster according to popular Jewish superstition.

6:51 wind died down. Recalls the calming of the storm, though this time the wind dies down at the mere presence of Jesus (see note on 4:39). **completely amazed.** Occurs only here and is even stronger than the response to Jesus' raising of the dead girl (5:42). This even more impressive mighty deed happens before all the disciples.

6:52 hearts were hardened. Used of the disciples for the first time in Mark (see also 8:17; cf. 3:5). Having witnessed Jesus' divine authority on several occasions, the disciples' failure to understand who Jesus is from the "deed parable" of the feedings — it is God who provided for Israel in the wilderness (Pss 78:19–25; 105:40) — reveals their dull hearts (cf. 4:12–13; 8:17–21; see notes on 4:1 — 5:43; 4:35 — 5:43). If they had understood the feedings, they would have understood Jesus' walking on the sea. If the secret of the kingdom is Jesus (see note on 4:11), the disciples are behaving like "outsiders" (see note on 4:12).

6:53 [x]Jn 6:24,25
6:56 [y]Mt 9:20
7:2 [z]Ac 10:14,28; 11:8; Ro 14:14
7:3 [a]ver 5,8,9,13; Lk 11:38
7:4 [b]Mt 23:25; Lk 11:39
7:5 [c]ver 3; Gal 1:14; Col 2:8
7:7 [d]Isa 29:13
7:8 [e]ver 3

[53]When they had crossed over, they landed at Gennesaret and anchored there.[x] [54]As soon as they got out of the boat, people recognized Jesus. [55]They ran throughout that whole region and carried the sick on mats to wherever they heard he was. [56]And wherever he went — into villages, towns or countryside — they placed the sick in the marketplaces. They begged him to let them touch even the edge of his cloak,[y] and all who touched it were healed.

That Which Defiles

7:1-23pp — Mt 15:1-20

7 The Pharisees and some of the teachers of the law who had come from Jerusalem gathered around Jesus [2]and saw some of his disciples eating food with hands that were defiled,[z] that is, unwashed. [3](The Pharisees and all the Jews do not eat unless they give their hands a ceremonial washing, holding to the tradition of the elders.[a] [4]When they come from the marketplace they do not eat unless they wash. And they observe many other traditions, such as the washing of cups, pitchers and kettles.[a])[b]

[5]So the Pharisees and teachers of the law asked Jesus, "Why don't your disciples live according to the tradition of the elders[c] instead of eating their food with defiled hands?"

[6]He replied, "Isaiah was right when he prophesied about you hypocrites; as it is written:

" 'These people honor me with their lips,
but their hearts are far from me.
[7]They worship me in vain;
their teachings are merely human rules.'[bd]

[8]You have let go of the commands of God and are holding on to human traditions."[e]

[9]And he continued, "You have a fine way of setting aside the commands of God in order to observe[c]

[a] 4 Some early manuscripts *pitchers, kettles and dining couches* [b] 6,7 Isaiah 29:13 [c] 9 Some manuscripts *set up*

6:53–56 Mark's final summary statement in this opening section (1:14—8:21) reiterates Jesus' continuing and astonishing popularity. The healing of the sick in the marketplaces prepares for the following confrontation with the Jerusalem authorities (7:1–13).

6:53 Gennesaret. Not a village but the 3.5-mile-long (5.5 kilometer) plain running along the northwestern shore of the Sea of Galilee between Tiberias and Capernaum.

6:55 ran throughout that whole region. Jesus' reputation as a healer continues to draw people in droves (see note on 1:34).

6:56 touch. See note on 5:28.

7:1—8:21 *True Holiness and the Inclusion of the Nations.* At the heart of the first exodus was God's command that Israel be holy as he is holy (Lev 11:44–45). So too in this new exodus. Holiness/purity has been a concern for Mark from the very beginning of his Gospel, expressed by the promised baptism with the Holy Spirit (1:8), Jesus' casting out impure spirits (1:21–28; 3:11), Jesus' curing leprosy (1:40–44), and Jesus' eating with impure sinners (2:16). Now it inevitably becomes prominent in Jesus' replacement of ritual purity with purity of the heart (7:1–23), which prepares the way for his ministry in impure Gentile regions (7:24—8:10) and culminates in his warning to avoid the impure "yeast" that defiles the hearts of Herod and the Pharisees (8:11–21).

7:1–23 *That Which Defiles.* This passage's length, fieriness, and concentration of weighty Scriptures (vv. 6–10) emphasize the importance of Jesus' teaching on ritual purity and food laws. In cancelling them Jesus anticipates the later mission to the Gentiles and their inclusion in God's people simply through faith in him.

7:1–13 *Jesus Rebukes Some Pharisees and Teachers of the Law.* There is now a return of official opposition from Jerusalem not seen since the Beelzebul confrontation (3:22–30). There they accused Jesus of an unholy alliance with the "prince of demons" (3:22). Here their question concerns ritual purity, which was inseparable from Israel's conception of holiness (Lev 11:44) and thus Israel's relationship with God (e.g., Lev 20:25; Num 9:13).

7:1 Pharisees. See note on 2:16. **teachers of the law.** See note on 1:22.

7:3 Pharisees … Jews. Those who made a particular point of their Jewishness. In explaining this practice and later the meaning of Corban (v. 11), Mark reveals that his audience includes a significant number of Gentiles (see Introduction: Place of Composition and Destination). The Pharisees knew that the law required hand washing only of the priests eating the holy food (Exod 30:18–21), but to show their piety, they extended it to ordinary people eating ordinary food (see note on 2:16). The marketplace, from which Jesus and his disciples had just come (6:56), was potentially a major source of ritual contamination.

7:6–8 For the first time, Jesus publicly denounces Jerusalem's teachers. Previous critics from Jerusalem had blasphemed the Holy Spirit, making God their enemy (see note on 3:29). While these teachers of the law (see note on 1:22) see marketplaces as a source of impurity (v. 4) — though they love the praise garnered there (12:38) — Jesus, the true Shepherd-King (see note on 6:34), sees marketplaces as places to bring God's promised restoration to his people (6:56). **Isaiah was right when he prophesied about you.** Israel was already under God's judgment for its idolatrous disobedience (Isa 6:9–10; see notes on 4:12; 8:16–21), and Isaiah had already denounced Israel's faithless and blind leaders (Isa 29:9–10) for pretending to worship God while they pursued their own agendas (Isa 29:13, the text Jesus cites here). For Jesus, Jerusalem's present leaders are in exactly the same position (see note on 3:29). The Pharisees and teachers of the law are "hypocrites" because by requiring people in general to do what God himself had only required of the priests in their temple service, they had put their merely human tradition above the revealed word of God in the Scriptures. Only those whose "hearts are far from [God]" (v. 6) would presume to do such a thing.

your own traditions![f] 10For Moses said, 'Honor your father and mother,'[a][g] and, 'Anyone who curses their
father or mother is to be put to death.'[b][h] 11But you say[i] that if anyone declares that what might have
been used to help their father or mother is Corban (that is, devoted to God) — 12then you no longer
let them do anything for their father or mother. 13Thus you nullify the word of God[j] by your tradition[k]
that you have handed down. And you do many things like that."

14Again Jesus called the crowd to him and said, "Listen to me, everyone, and understand this. 15Noth-
ing outside a person can defile them by going into them. Rather, it is what comes out of a person that
defiles them." [16][c]

17After he had left the crowd and entered the house, his disciples asked him[l] about this parable.
18"Are you so dull?" he asked. "Don't you see that nothing that enters a person from the outside can
defile them? 19For it doesn't go into their heart but into their stomach, and then out of the body." (In
saying this, Jesus declared all foods[m] clean.)[n]

20He went on: "What comes out of a person is what defiles them. 21For it is from within, out of
a person's heart, that evil thoughts come — sexual immorality, theft, murder, 22adultery, greed,[o]
malice, deceit, lewdness, envy, slander, arrogance and folly. 23All these evils come from inside and
defile a person."

Jesus Honors a Syrophoenician Woman's Faith

7:24-30pp — Mt 15:21-28

24Jesus left that place and went to the vicinity of Tyre.[d][p] He entered a house and did not want
anyone to know it; yet he could not keep his presence secret. 25In fact, as soon as she heard about
him, a woman whose little daughter was possessed by an impure spirit[q] came and fell at his feet.
26The woman was a Greek, born in Syrian Phoenicia. She begged Jesus to drive the demon out of
her daughter.

a 10 Exodus 20:12; Deut. 5:16 *b 10* Exodus 21:17; Lev. 20:9 *c 16* Some manuscripts include here the words of 4:23. *d 24* Many early manuscripts *Tyre and Sidon*

7:9 [f] ver 3
7:10 [g] Ex 20:12; Dt 5:16 [h] Ex 21:17; Lev 20:9
7:11 [i] Mt 23:16,18
7:13 [j] Heb 4:12 [k] ver 3
7:17 [l] Mk 9:28
7:19 [m] Ro 14:1-12; Col 2:16; 1Ti 4:3-5 [n] Ac 10:15
7:22 [o] Mt 20:15
7:24 [p] Mt 11:21
7:25 [q] Mt 4:24

7:10 This commandment (Exod 20:12) is the first with a promise: long life in the land (Deut 5:16; cf. Eph 6:2–3). In Jewish tradition honoring parents was the weightiest commandment governing human relationships. Failing to do so risked disinheritance and exile.

7:11–13 "Corban" (v. 11) was the practice of allowing someone to devote something to God (cf. Num 30:1–2). It could result, either by the vower's intention or by legal ruling, in an adult child avoiding or being unable to meet their obligation to support their parents. Either way, the parents were denied what was their due according to Scripture. In Jewish tradition, those who forsake their parents are like blasphemers (cf. 3:28–29); one could only dishonor one's parents if one had already dishonored God (cf. vv. 6–8).

7:14–23 *It Is Not Food but the Heart That Defiles.* That Jesus has just done what only God can do (6:30–56; cf. 2:5,10,28; 4:35–41) demonstrates his divine authority to summon the crowds and to redefine the nature of holiness for God's people (see note on 2:21–22).

7:14 called the crowd ... "Listen to me ..." The first time Jesus does so; it recalls Moses' summons to all Israel to hear the law (Deut 5:1; see Deut 4:1,10; 5:27; 29:2a) and Jesus' warnings to those hearing his parables (Mark 4:3,9,23; cf. 7:14).

7:15 Jesus' sweeping declaration to a Jewish crowd effectively repeals the entire framework of food laws and since nothing exterior can defile, ritual purity (see v. 19; cf. Matt 15:11; Rom 14:14). Since those laws directly related to God's holiness (Lev 11:44), only someone exercising God's own authority could rescind them. Mark's readers already know that Jesus has this authority; he is the authoritative Son of Man (2:10) and embodies God's presence upon the earth (1:2–3).

7:17 Jesus explains the parable (see note on 4:2) privately to his disciples (cf. 4:11,33–34). The numerous parallels with the parable of the sower/soils (4:3–20) suggest that the teaching here is of similar importance for Mark. If that parable concerned the secret of the kingdom (i.e., Jesus' identity; see note on 4:11), then this parable explains the complete and radical implications of Jesus' identity as it relates to the entire system of ritual purity (2:21–22).

7:18–19 The disciples' failure to understand links Jesus' redefinition of purity with his identity (see note on 6:52). It would be several years before the disciples fully understood the implication of Jesus' statement (cf. Acts 10:1 — 11:18). Mark's editorial comment (note the parentheses in v. 19) makes Jesus' intention crystal clear: no longer does food or an unwashed hand "defile" one's relationship with God; only the impure heart does so (cf. Rom 14:14).

7:20–23 Jesus' conformity to God's life-giving character is the hallmark of true purity (cf. 2:27; 3:4). Mark's readers might recall the very different actions of Jesus' opponents (3:5,22).

7:24 — 8:13 *Salvation to the Gentiles: Healings and a Feeding.* At Jesus' baptism God identified Jesus as Isaiah's servant who was to be a light to the nations (see note on 1:11). Here, after his redefinition of the nature of purity, Jesus' journey through Gentile Phoenicia (7:24–30) and the Decapolis (7:31 — 8:10) anticipates the gospel's formation of a new people of God comprised of believing Jews and Gentiles.

7:24–30 *Jesus Honors a Syrophoenician Woman's Faith.* Just as Jesus had earlier rewarded a Jewish woman who dared to put her faith in him above concerns for ritual purity (5:24–30), so here he rewards a Gentile woman whose faith overcomes the boundaries of ritual purity, gender, and ethnicity (cf. Gal 3:28).

7:24 Tyre. One of Israel's most bitter enemies. Jesus' presence cannot be kept secret among the Gentiles any more than it can among his own people (cf. 1:45; 2:1–2; 3:20).

7:25 woman. Respectable Jewish teachers did not associate with a woman, especially a Gentile one (v. 26). **impure spirit.** See note on 1:23. **fell at his feet.** As did the synagogue leader (see note on 5:22) and impure woman (5:33).

A first-century synagogue discovered at Magdala, the main town in the likely region of Dalmanutha (Mark 8:10).

7:31 [r]ver 24; Mt 11:21 [s]Mt 4:18 [t]Mt 4:25; Mk 5:20
7:32 [u]Mt 9:32; Lk 11:14 [v]Mk 5:23

27 “First let the children eat all they want,” he told her, “for it is not right to take the children’s bread
and toss it to the dogs.”

28 “Lord,” she replied, “even the dogs under the table eat the children’s crumbs.”

29 Then he told her, “For such a reply, you may go; the demon has left your daughter.”

30 She went home and found her child lying on the bed, and the demon gone.

Jesus Heals a Deaf and Mute Man

7:31-37pp — Mt 15:29-31

31 Then Jesus left the vicinity of Tyre[r] and went through Sidon, down to the Sea of Galilee[s] and into
the region of the Decapolis.[a][t] 32 There some people brought to him a man who was deaf and could
hardly talk,[u] and they begged Jesus to place his hand on[v] him.

33 After he took him aside, away from the crowd, Jesus put his fingers into the man’s ears. Then he

[a] *31* That is, the Ten Cities

7:27 First let the children eat all they want. Jesus has previously prioritized his inauguration of the kingdom over social convention and ritual purity (cf. 1:43–44; 2:17). But that does not mean contravening God’s plan that salvation should come first to his people Israel. Thus this parable sharply declares Jewish priority (cf. Rom 9:1–5; 11:16–18). **dogs.** Because of the polytheistic idolatry of the Gentiles, Jews likened them to notoriously impure scavenging street “dogs.” But although Jesus speaks strongly when it is warranted (1:43–44; 8:33; cf. Matt 23:27), he changes the metaphor by artfully transforming the wild street dogs into trusted domestic pets gathered around the family table. “First” implies that this is not the final word, especially since the people of Israel just ate with much left over (6:42–43; see notes on 6:30–56; 8:8).

7:28 The woman is the only person in Mark who addresses Jesus as “Lord” (cf. 1:3). While not contesting Jesus’ priorities or her subordinate status, she seizes the opening Jesus offers, and he rewards her for her insight (cf. 5:28–29).

7:29–30 Having earlier raised a Jewish daughter from the dead (5:35–43), Jesus, in driving out an impure spirit, continues his work of restoring the image of God (see note on 1:25), but now in the daughter of a Gentile.

7:31–37 *Jesus Heals a Deaf and Mute Man.* This is the first specific account of this kind of healing in Mark. In yet another Gentile region and again in response to Gentile faith, Jesus this time restores hearing and speech.

7:31 As with his responses to an often less-than-welcoming Israel, Jesus’ earlier rejection in the Decapolis does not dissuade him from a second visit (see 5:17).

7:33 away from the crowd. To avoid either hostile unbelief (5:40; 6:6), unwanted publicity (v. 36; 1:43–45; 5:43), making a spectacle of the man, or perhaps all three. **fingers into ... spit and touched.** Jesus’ use of spittle is unusual, employed only when dealing with hearing, speech, and sight (see 8:23). The significance of Jesus’ actions is debated. First-century people believed that spit had medicinal and even magical properties, but such associations are out of character with Jesus’ healings. Instead, his looking “up to heaven” (v. 34) implies divine action. A better option might be the ancient pagan ritual of enlivening images of the gods, which involved anointing and thus symbolically “opening” the eyes, ears, and mouth of the image (see note on 4:12; cf. Isa 44:18). Since God made humans in his image, giving them the power to speak and hear (Exod 4:11), Jesus’ unusual actions in this Gentile region testify that he is the Lord come to restore the image of God in humanity (see note on 1:25) by opening ears and loosening tongues (Isa 29:18–19; 35:5–6; see notes on v. 37; 8:22–26).

spit[w] and touched the man's tongue. [34]He looked up to heaven[x] and with a deep sigh[y] said to him, *"Eph-*
phatha!" (which means "Be opened!"). [35]At this, the man's ears were opened, his tongue was loosened
and he began to speak plainly.[z]

[36]Jesus commanded them not to tell anyone.[a] But the more he did so, the more they kept talking
about it. [37]People were overwhelmed with amazement. "He has done everything well," they said. "He
even makes the deaf hear and the mute speak."

Jesus Feeds the Four Thousand

8:1-9pp — Mt 15:32-39
8:1-9Ref — Mk 6:32-44
8:11-21pp — Mt 16:1-12

8 During those days another large crowd gathered. Since they had nothing to eat, Jesus called his
disciples to him and said, [2]"I have compassion for these people;[b] they have already been with me
three days and have nothing to eat. [3]If I send them home hungry, they will collapse on the way, because
some of them have come a long distance."

[4]His disciples answered, "But where in this remote place can anyone get enough bread to feed them?"
[5]"How many loaves do you have?" Jesus asked.
"Seven," they replied.
[6]He told the crowd to sit down on the ground. When he had taken the seven loaves and given thanks,
he broke them and gave them to his disciples to distribute to the people, and they did so. [7]They had
a few small fish as well; he gave thanks for them also and told the disciples to distribute them.[c] [8]The
people ate and were satisfied. Afterward the disciples picked up seven basketfuls of broken pieces that
were left over.[d] [9]About four thousand were present. After he had sent them away, [10]he got into the boat
with his disciples and went to the region of Dalmanutha.

[11]The Pharisees came and began to question Jesus. To test him, they asked him for a sign from
heaven.[e] [12]He sighed deeply[f] and said, "Why does this generation ask for a sign? Truly I tell you, no sign
will be given to it." [13]Then he left them, got back into the boat and crossed to the other side.

7:33 [w]Mk 8:23
7:34 [x]Mk 6:41; Jn 11:41 [y]Mk 8:12
7:35 [z]Isa 35:5,6
7:36 [a]Mt 8:4
8:2 [b]Mt 9:36
8:7 [c]Mt 14:19
8:8 [d]ver 20
8:11 [e]Mt 12:38
8:12 [f]Mk 7:34

7:34 deep sigh. Physically expresses the tension between what the world has become and what God initially intended (cf. Rom 8:23,26; 2 Cor 5:2–4). ***Ephphatha.*** Aramaic. See note on 5:41.

7:36 Again, the amazing thing that Jesus has done cannot be kept secret. See note on 1:44.

7:37 done everything well. Echoes Gen 1:31, where God, having just created humanity in his image, sees how exceedingly good is all that he has done. Jesus' restoration of the man in God's image is the beginning of the new creation as promised in Isa 35:5–6 (cf. Isa 29:18–19). This unqualified affirmation in a Gentile region foreshadows the later positive reception of the gospel among the nations (cf. Acts 13:44–49).

8:1–13 *Jesus Feeds the Four Thousand.* This second exodus-like feeding (cf. 6:34–44) is in Gentile territory. It not only testifies again to Jesus' identity and mission but also anticipates the Gentiles later sharing in the "children's bread" (7:27; cf. 7:24–29), i.e., the gospel—to which Mark's Christian community in Rome, comprising believing Jews and Gentiles, now bears witness.

8:2 compassion. See note on 1:41. Jesus earlier reflected God's compassion by providing teaching for leaderless Israel. Here he does so by providing food. Humans live by both the Word of God and bread (cf. Deut 8:3; Matt 4:4; see note on 6:34).

8:4 Not understanding the miraculous nature of the first feeding, the disciples think only in terms of human possibilities (cf. v. 33; 6:52).

8:8 seven basketfuls. The slightly smaller scale (cf. "twelve basketfuls" in 6:43) perhaps signifies Israel's continued priority: to the Jews first but also to the Gentiles (see notes on 7:27–28). The absence of amazement indicates that again neither the crowd nor the disciples understood what had happened (see note on 6:44).

8:10 This time Jesus embarks with his disciples (cf. 6:45) and teaches them instead of performing a mighty deed (vv. 14–21). **Dalmanutha.** Probably on the northwestern shore of Galilee (which was more Jewish than the eastern shore).

8:11 Pharisees. See note on 2:16. **To test him.** Recalls hardhearted Israel's first exodus "testing" of God (Exod 17:1–7; Ps 95:7–11), their true Shepherd, even after all his mighty deeds, including providing food in the desert (Exod 16). It reveals that the Pharisees' question was not sincere but arose from hearts that had similarly gone astray (3:5; see note on 7:6–8; cf. Ps 95:10). **sign.** Several of Israel's prophets—notably Moses (e.g., Exod 4:1–9), Elijah (1 Kgs 18:38), Elisha (2 Kgs 7:2–4,17–20), and Isaiah (2 Kgs 20:8–11; cf. Isa 7:10–11)—performed attesting signs; but not all signs were to be trusted (Deut 13:1–3). Jesus had already sent the man healed of leprosy to the priests as a testimony to them (1:44) and had argued that his casting out demons was from God (3:23–29).

8:12 sighed deeply. Expresses Jesus' frustration with a generation that, because of its stubborn unbelief, fails to understand the significance of his words and deeds (cf. v. 38; 9:19; see note on 7:34). **this generation.** In the current context of Jesus' many mighty deeds, recalls the indictments of the evil generation of the first exodus who refused to believe in spite of God's mighty acts on their behalf (see 9:19; cf. Deut 1:35; 32:5,20; Ps 95:8–10). **Truly I tell you.** Earlier introduced Jesus' warning against blasphemously attributing his casting out demons to Satan (see note on 3:29). Here it solemnly announces judgment; the time for signs is past.

8:13 he left them. Jesus' characteristic response to hardhearted resistance (cf., e.g., 3:6–7). **other side.** The eastern shore of the lake, which was less Jewish than the western shore. Jesus' departure to this region perhaps anticipates that the gospel will, in the future, find greater acceptance among non-Jews.

8:15 [g] 1Co 5:6-8 [h] Lk 12:1 [i] Mt 14:1; Mk 12:13
8:17 [j] Isa 6:9,10; Mk 6:52
8:19 [k] Mt 14:20; Mk 6:41-44; Lk 9:17; Jn 6:13
8:20 [l] ver 6-9; Mt 15:37
8:21 [m] Mk 6:52
8:22 [n] Mt 11:21 [o] Mk 10:46; Jn 9:1
8:23 [p] Mk 7:33 [q] Mk 5:23

The Yeast of the Pharisees and Herod

14 The disciples had forgotten to bring bread, except for one loaf they had with them in the boat. 15 "Be
careful," Jesus warned them. "Watch out for the yeast[g] of the Pharisees[h] and that of Herod."[i]
16 They discussed this with one another and said, "It is because we have no bread."
17 Aware of their discussion, Jesus asked them: "Why are you talking about having no bread? Do you
still not see or understand? Are your hearts hardened?[j] 18 Do you have eyes but fail to see, and ears but
fail to hear? And don't you remember? 19 When I broke the five loaves for the five thousand, how many
basketfuls of pieces did you pick up?"

"Twelve,"[k] they replied.

20 "And when I broke the seven loaves for the four thousand, how many basketfuls of pieces did you
pick up?"

They answered, "Seven."[l]

21 He said to them, "Do you still not understand?"[m]

Jesus Heals a Blind Man at Bethsaida

22 They came to Bethsaida,[n] and some people brought a blind man[o] and begged Jesus to touch him.
23 He took the blind man by the hand and led him outside the village. When he had spit[p] on the man's
eyes and put his hands on[q] him, Jesus asked, "Do you see anything?"
24 He looked up and said, "I see people; they look like trees walking around."

8:14–21 *The Yeast of the Pharisees and Herod.* Jesus' warning both concludes the first major section of Mark's Gospel (1:14—8:21) and prepares for his focus on his uncomprehending and "blind" disciples (vv. 17–18) as he announces his coming death and what it means for discipleship (8:22—10:52).

8:14–15 *Jesus Warns His Disciples.* Theses verses imply that Jesus' disciples are at risk from the same defiling attitudes that have led the Pharisees and Herod astray.

8:14 Recalls the two previous occasions when supplies were insufficient (cf. 6:35–37; 8:4–5).

8:15 yeast. Jewish people had to remove it, on pain of being cut off from Israel, in preparation for the first Passover and for all Passovers thereafter (Exod 12:14–20). In some Jewish traditions the removal of yeast came to symbolize the future purification of God's redeemed people (cf. 1 Cor 5:1–8). The metaphor is appropriate because Jesus' death on Passover (see note on 14:12–26) belongs to his inauguration of Israel's new exodus—in which the impure attitudes of Herod and the Pharisees have, like yeast, no place (see note on 1:2–3). The Pharisees (see note on 2:16) have been the most prominent opponents of Jesus (2:16,18,24; 3:6; 7:1), and Herod executed John (1:14; 6:14–28; cf. 3:6). If Jesus' disciples are to participate in this new redemption, they must rid themselves of the pride and self-deceit—that which comes from the heart is what defiles (7:14–23)—that led the Pharisees and Herod to oppose the inbreaking kingdom of God (cf. 1 Cor 5:6–8). In preparation for the first announcement of Jesus' coming death (v. 31), this warning introduces a major theme in Mark's next section (8:22—10:52). Tragically, confronted by the prospect of a suffering Messiah, Jesus' followers consistently show themselves in jeopardy of the yeast of Herod and the Pharisees (v. 32; 9:34,38; 10:37,41).

8:16–21 *The Blindness of the Disciples.* Jesus' questions concerning seeing, hearing, understanding, and hardening recall both his use of parables (see note on 4:12; cf. Isa 6:10–12) and God's condemnation of idolatrous Israel (Isa 6:10–12; Jer 5:21; Ezek 12:2). In spite of being given the mystery of the kingdom (4:11a), the disciples in failing to perceive Jesus' identity (4:41; 6:49–52) resemble outsiders (4:11b–12) in whom the sown word bears no fruit (4:15–19). It is into this unpromising situation that Jesus must reveal the true nature of his call; thus, he increasingly focuses on instructing his disciples.

8:16 The Greek is difficult. The text presents the disciples' discussion as a response to Jesus' warning, apparently connecting "yeast" with their lack of bread. An alternative translation of this verse would be: "And they continued to discuss with one another that they had no bread." On this reading, the disciples disregard Jesus' warning as of little immediate relevance and continue to confer over what they think is the more pressing matter. Another possibility is that they discuss "why they had no bread" in order to discover who was to blame. In either case Jesus' warning is ignored.

8:20 Recalling the previous two feedings (vv. 8–9; 6:42–43), Jesus explains that the lack of bread is not the issue. Instead, the two feedings are the clearest and most accessible demonstration yet of Jesus' Messianic identity (see note on 6:44).

8:22—10:52 *The New Exodus Way of the Crucified Lord.* This central section of Mark's Gospel shows Jesus leading his increasingly "blind" and uncomprehending disciples (8:16–21,33; 9:6,10, 18–19,32–34,38–40; 10:13–14,24–26,32,35–37,41) on the "way" (8:27; 9:33–34; 10:17,32; see 10:46,52) to Jerusalem. It is also God's new exodus "way" of which Malachi and Isaiah spoke (see notes on 1:2–3,11), now revealed to be the shocking "way" of the cross through which Jesus, Isaiah's suffering servant, will redeem Israel (8:31; 9:31; 10:32–34) and the path true disciples must follow (8:34–38). Furthermore, since Jesus is identified with God's presence, that he embraced suffering reveals the very character of God. It is bracketed by the only two healings of the blind in Mark (8:22–26; 10:46–52), which, in light of Jesus' preceding comments on the disciples' failure to see (8:17–18), symbolize their need to have the "eyes" of their understanding opened and Jesus' ability to do so if they will only listen.

8:22–30 *The Beginning of Sight.* In linking Jesus' two-stage healing of the blind man with Peter's "partial" confession, Mark sets the agenda for what follows (see note on 8:22—10:52). True "sight" means embracing Jesus' declaration that the Messiah must die.

8:22–26 *Jesus Heals a Blind Man at Bethsaida.* Only Mark includes this account, which closely parallels and complements the healing in 7:33 (see note). In both stories Jesus takes the man aside, employs spittle, and seeks to avoid attention. As a pair, these two healings reflect the restoration of the image of God in humanity as Jesus fulfills Isaiah's prophecies of future deliverance (Isa 29:18; 35:5–6; see notes on 4:12; 7:33).

8:22 Bethsaida. On the northeastern side of the Sea of Galilee, which was less Jewish than the western side.

8:24–25 The man's initial partial healing is given no explanation, but in

[25]Once more Jesus put his hands on the man's eyes. Then his eyes were opened, his sight was restored, and he saw everything clearly. [26]Jesus sent him home, saying, "Don't even go into[a] the village."

Peter Declares That Jesus Is the Messiah

8:27-29pp — Mt 16:13-16; Lk 9:18-20

[27]Jesus and his disciples went on to the villages around Caesarea Philippi. On the way he asked them, "Who do people say I am?"

[28]They replied, "Some say John the Baptist;[r] others say Elijah;[s] and still others, one of the prophets."

[29]"But what about you?" he asked. "Who do you say I am?"

Peter answered, "You are the Messiah."[t]

[30]Jesus warned them not to tell anyone about him.[u]

Jesus Predicts His Death

8:31 — 9:1pp — Mt 16:21-28; Lk 9:22-27

[31]He then began to teach them that the Son of Man[v] must suffer many things[w] and be rejected by the elders, the chief priests and the teachers of the law,[x] and that he must be killed[y] and after three days[z] rise again.[a] [32]He spoke plainly[b] about this, and Peter took him aside and began to rebuke him.

[33]But when Jesus turned and looked at his disciples, he rebuked Peter. "Get behind me, Satan!"[c] he said. "You do not have in mind the concerns of God, but merely human concerns."

8:28 [r] Mt 3:1 [s] Mal 4:5
8:29 [t] Jn 6:69; 11:27
8:30 [u] Mt 8:4; 16:20; 17:9; Mk 9:9; Lk 9:21
8:31 [v] Mt 8:20 [w] Mt 16:21 [x] Mt 27:1,2 [y] Ac 2:23; 3:13 [z] Mt 16:21 [a] Mt 16:21
8:32 [b] Jn 18:20
8:33 [c] Mt 4:10

[a] 26 Some manuscripts *go and tell anyone in*

context it parallels Peter's initial but also partial confession (vv. 27–33). Like the man, "blind" Peter and the other disciples (see note on vv.16–21) need a second touch since they understand neither who Jesus really is nor the centrality of the cross to his mission and therefore to their discipleship.

8:27–30 *Peter Declares That Jesus Is the Messiah.* This is one of the high points of Mark's Gospel. Peter's confession, while undoubtedly true, is still a long way from a full comprehension of who Jesus really is (see, e.g., note on 1:2–3).

8:27 Jesus avoided the city of Caesarea Philippi, seeking instead to retreat to the villages of this predominantly non-Jewish region. **Caesarea Philippi.** Some 25 miles (40 kilometers) north of the Sea of Galilee. Rebuilt by Herod's son Philip, it was named for himself and Caesar Augustus and was associated with imperial worship. **Who do people say I am?** For the first time, Jesus himself raises the question of his identity.

8:28 See note on 6:14b–15.

8:29 Jesus is concerned with what his disciples think since they will carry on his work when he is gone. **You are the Messiah.** Although Mark's Christian readers already know this (1:1,11 serve as confirmation), it occurs here for the first time in Mark's narrative. Some Jewish traditions associated a repetition of God's provision of manna with the Messiah's coming (see notes on v. 20; 6:44; cf. John 6:14–15). Peter's confession probably reflects that he finally grasps something of Jesus' pointed questions about the feedings (see vv. 17–20).

8:30 not to tell. As with previous commands to silence (1:25–26,34,44), this implies Jesus' affirmation of Peter's confession. The popular mindset of Jews of the time was that the Messiah would fulfill Israel's nationalistic hopes by military means (see notes on 1:1,11). However, because God will accomplish his purposes through the shameful weakness of the cross, Jesus continues to control his public self-revelation (see notes on 1:34; 2:10). Only at the very end, when events are too far advanced to be subverted, will he publicly affirm his Messiahship (14:62).

8:31 — 10:45 *Following the Crucified Lord.* Intended to reconstitute the disciples' understanding of the Messiah, this section is structured around three blocks of material (8:31–33; 9:30–32; 10:32–41; see note on 8:22 — 10:52). Each begins with a declaration of Jesus' future rejection, death, and vindication (8:31; 9:30–31; 10:32–34), which is followed by his disciples' "leavened" misunderstanding (8:32–33; 9:32; 10:35–41) and then Jesus' corrective instruction (8:34 — 9:1; 9:35–37; 10:42–45). This repetition highlights the centrality of Jesus' suffering service and what it means for discipleship (cf. John 13:3–7).

8:31–33 *Jesus Predicts His Death.* Up to this point Jesus' words and deeds have been characterized by astonishing authority and power. This first declaration of his imminent suffering and death stands in blunt contrast to, and completely undercuts, the Messianic expectations of Peter and the other disciples.

8:31 Son of Man. Jesus' use of this term (not seen since 2:28) implicitly connects his suffering with his divine identity (see notes on 2:10,28). It reveals not just the nature of his Messiahship but more important, the very character of God (see note on 1:2–3; see also 2 Cor 5:19). Jesus' highly compressed declaration combines parts of several Scriptures to make a larger, cohesive point. **must.** Stresses Jesus' conformity to God's will and character as expressed in Scripture (see note on 5:16–17, where Jesus allows the local villages to reject him; and note on 14:36). **suffer many things.** Alludes to Isaiah's servant (Isa 53:3–5,10), who, in bearing Israel's covenant curse, would redeem the nation from bondage, restore them to God, and, himself being a light to the nations, enable Israel to fulfill its similar calling (see note on 1:17). **rejected.** Echoes Ps 118:22's declaration of God's vindication of his rejected but faithful Davidic king over his many enemies by making him the cornerstone of his people. (Ps 118 is cited also in 11:9–10 and especially in 12:10–11.) **by … chief priests.** See 11:18; Matt 3:7. **teachers of the law.** See note on 1:22. **after three days.** Reflects God's promise in Hosea that he will bring to life his covenantally cursed people (Hos 6:2; cf. Deut 32:39; Ezek 37; Gal 3:13), which Jewish tradition took to refer to the final resurrection of the dead at the judgment.

8:32 plainly. The only occurrence in Mark; it underlines the centrality of the cross for Jesus and his mission. **rebuke.** Whatever Peter might have understood by Jesus' earlier "Son of Man" designations (2:10,28), Peter's traditional expectations had no room for any notion of God's glorious Messiah being rejected and executed.

8:33 disciples. Peter was not alone (cf. v. 34), and Jesus' rebuke is directed not at them personally but at their view. **concerns of God.** Anticipated in Jesus' preceding compassionate exercise of his power, God's surprising way is now climactically revealed in Jesus' totally unexpected "suffering servant" embrace of the cross (see notes on

8:34 [d]Mt 10:38; Lk 14:27
8:35 [e]Jn 12:25
8:38 [f]Mt 8:20 [g]Mt 10:33; Lk 12:9 [h]1Th 2:19
9:1 [i]Mk 13:30; Lk 22:18 [j]Mt 24:30; 25:31
9:2 [k]Mt 4:21
9:3 [l]Mt 28:3

The Way of the Cross

[34]Then he called the crowd to him along with his disciples and said: "Whoever wants to be my disciple must deny themselves and take up their cross and follow me.[d] [35]For whoever wants to save their
life[a] will lose it, but whoever loses their life for me and for the gospel will save it.[e] [36]What good is it for
someone to gain the whole world, yet forfeit their soul? [37]Or what can anyone give in exchange for their
soul? [38]If anyone is ashamed of me and my words in this adulterous and sinful generation, the Son of
Man[f] will be ashamed of them[g] when he comes[h] in his Father's glory with the holy angels."

9 And he said to them, "Truly I tell you, some who are standing here will not taste death before they
see that the kingdom of God has come[i] with power."[j]

The Transfiguration

9:2-8pp — Lk 9:28-36
9:2-13pp — Mt 17:1-13

[2]After six days Jesus took Peter, James and John[k] with him and led them up a high mountain, where
they were all alone. There he was transfigured before them. [3]His clothes became dazzling white,[l] whiter

[a] *35* The Greek word means either *life* or *soul*; also in verses 36 and 37.

1:2–3; 8:22—10:52). As Isaiah declared after announcing the role of the servant, God's ways are not human ways (Isa 55:8–9; cf. 1 Cor 1:18–25; 2:6–16). But Jesus will not reveal the full significance of his death until later (10:45; 14:22–25). **merely human concerns.** In particular a love of power and status, as evident earlier in, e.g., the "yeast" of Herod and the Pharisees (see note on v. 15) and later in the disciples' jockeying for greatness (9:34; 10:37,41) and elitist exclusion of others (9:38). These concerns are what occupy Satan (cf. Matt 4:8–10).

8:34—9:1 *The Way of the Cross.* For the first time in Mark, Jesus clearly states the cost of being his disciple. To follow him means one must die to one's own agenda, whether social, political, or spiritual.

8:34 called the crowd. For only the second time in Mark; earlier it was to redefine the law's teaching on purity (7:14–15), and here Jesus makes a similarly startling declaration: the newly remade Israel he is gathering around himself (see note on 3:14) must be characterized by cross-bearing. He addresses his disciples and the crowd together because the disciples' stance (v. 33) puts them back with the crowd. Discipleship has now taken a radical turn, and they must all decide to follow Jesus anew. **deny themselves.** To imitate Jesus in laying down their individual, nationalistic, or religious agendas so as to follow him and his gospel (v. 35). **take up their cross.** Crucifixion was a form of execution Rome used for rebels and runaway slaves (see note on 15:24). The image is of an already-condemned individual carrying the beam of their cross to the site of execution. Jesus would fulfill the role of Isaiah's suffering servant and bring life to his enemies by being crucified for them (cf. 10:45; Rom 5:6–10).

8:35 life ... life. Plays on two meanings of "life." To seek to preserve one's life in this passing adulterous and sinful generation (v. 38; 9:19; see notes on vv. 12,38) by following one's own agenda, as do, e.g., Herod and the Pharisees (see note on v. 15), will mean losing the resurrection life of the world to come (Phil 3:10–11).

8:36 Possessing the entire world means nothing if one does not have eternal life (cf. 10:17–31).

8:37 Echoes Ps 49:7–9, which encourages the poor not to fear the powerful, who, in spite of their riches, cannot ransom themselves from death. Jesus similarly encourages his followers—potentially facing lethal hostility from Israel's powerful leaders (cf. 14:50,66–71; Matt 10:16–25; John 15:20)—to trust in the only one who can give them eternal life.

8:38 ashamed. Crucifixion was an unspeakably weak and shameful death in the eyes of a world fixated on status and power (cf. 1 Cor 1:18–25; Heb 12:2). But the world's standards have no place in God's kingdom, and Jesus will repudiate those who hold them. **adulterous.** A common Scriptural metaphor for idolatry, meaning to be unfaithful in one's relationship to God (Isa 57:3–13; Jer 3:1–21; Hos 1:2; see note on v. 12). Those who reject the way of the cross commit adultery against God; ultimately Jesus, God's authoritative Son, will reject them. **comes ... glory ... angels.** Refers to Dan 7:13–14's prophecy of God's vindication of the Son of Man over against the beastly nations. It is Jesus' first expansion of the Son of Man title (see notes on v. 31; 2:10) and points to his vindication through the resurrection (v. 31). Jesus is the authoritative and glorious figure to whom God will give everlasting dominion over all nations (see note on 13:26).

9:1 Although Jesus denied a sign to this unbelieving generation (see 8:12 and note; see also notes on 3:31–35; 4:11), aware of the shocking nature of his declaration (8:31–38), he announces one now. **Truly I tell you.** See note on 3:28. **some ... standing here.** Probably Peter, James, and John (see note on 1:18), who will see "the kingdom of God" (see note on 1:15) "with power" at the transfiguration. Jesus earlier described himself—including his teaching and mighty deeds—as "the secret of the kingdom" (4:11; see note). They will soon see "the secret" unveiled in all his power and glory.

9:2–29 *A New Sinai: God's Affirmation of Jesus and the Disciples' Failure.* Mark's overall new exodus pattern (see note on 1:2–3) and the many parallels between this event and God's revelation on Sinai (see notes on vv. 3,4,7; cf. Exod 24:9–16; 25:8; 34:1–35) imply that the transfiguration represents a new revelatory Sinai for the newly reconstituted Israel (see note on 3:14).

9:2–13 *The Transfiguration.* It offers divine confirmation of Jesus' identity and teaching, including especially his recent declaration concerning his coming death and the centrality of cross-bearing for the new people of God.

9:2 After six days. The most specific temporal connection in Mark's Gospel; it inseparably links the transfiguration's divine affirmation (v. 7) to Jesus' immediately preceding teaching on his death and on cross-bearing discipleship (8:31–38). **Peter, James and John.** See note on 1:18. **high mountain.** Location unknown, but possibly Mount Hermon (see note on Matt 17:1).

9:3 dazzling white. Since God "wraps himself in light" (Ps 104:2), wears clothing "as white as snow" (Dan 7:9), and according to Jewish tradition, clothed himself in brilliant white at the creation, outshone all on Mount Sinai when he gave the law to Israel, and wore white when he forgave Israel the sins that led to the exile, Jesus' glory testifies to his divine identity and significance. In Jesus God's new exodus presence has uniquely come (see note on 1:2–3). Furthermore, whereas Moses' face shone after meeting God in the cloud (Exod 34:29–35), Jesus radiates his own divine glory long before the cloud appears.

than anyone in the world could bleach them. 4And there appeared before them Elijah and Moses, who
were talking with Jesus.
5Peter said to Jesus, "Rabbi,[m] it is good for us to be here. Let us put up three shelters — one for you,
one for Moses and one for Elijah." 6(He did not know what to say, they were so frightened.)
7Then a cloud appeared and covered them, and a voice came from the cloud:[n] "This is my Son,
whom I love. Listen to him!"[o]
8Suddenly, when they looked around, they no longer saw anyone with them except Jesus.
9As they were coming down the mountain, Jesus gave them orders not to tell anyone[p] what they had
seen until the Son of Man[q] had risen from the dead. 10They kept the matter to themselves, discussing
what "rising from the dead" meant.
11And they asked him, "Why do the teachers of the law say that Elijah must come first?"
12Jesus replied, "To be sure, Elijah does come first, and restores all things. Why then is it written that
the Son of Man[r] must suffer much[s] and be rejected?[t] 13But I tell you, Elijah has come,[u] and they have
done to him everything they wished, just as it is written about him."

9:5 [m] Mt 23:7
9:7 [n] Ex 24:16 [o] Mt 3:17
9:9 [p] Mk 8:30 [q] Mt 8:20
9:12 [r] Mt 8:20 [s] Mt 16:21 [t] Lk 23:11
9:13 [u] Mt 11:14

Jesus Heals a Boy Possessed by an Impure Spirit

9:14-28; 30-32pp — Mt 17:14-19; 22,23; Lk 9:37-45

14When they came to the other disciples, they saw a large crowd around them and the teachers of
the law arguing with them. 15As soon as all the people saw Jesus, they were overwhelmed with wonder
and ran to greet him.
16"What are you arguing with them about?" he asked.
17A man in the crowd answered, "Teacher, I brought you my son, who is possessed by a spirit that has

9:4 Elijah and Moses. Sometimes taken to suggest that Jesus fulfills the Law (Moses) and the Prophets (Elijah; cf. Matt 5:17). The only place in the Scriptures where the two are mentioned together is at the end of Malachi (see note on 1:2–3), where the prophet Elijah, in preparation for the Lord's coming, was to restore Israel to obedience to the Mosaic law (Mal 4:4–5). **talking with.** This expression occurs only here in Mark and once in the exodus account, where it describes Moses talking with God (Exod 34:35; cf. Exod 33:11). Elijah and Moses had individually met with God on Mount Sinai/Horeb (Exod 24; 1 Kgs 19:8–18). Here they talk with Jesus, implying his divine superiority.

9:5–6 Even here Peter's incomprehension continues (see, e.g., 8:32–33; cf. 8:17,21). Jesus is far more than a "Rabbi" (lit. "my teacher"; see note on 4:38), and Peter's suggestion misses Jesus' superiority to Elijah and Moses. Nevertheless, Mark records it because Peter's use of "shelters" (or "tents"), possibly recalling God's presence among his people in the exodus (Exod 25–26; 33:7–11), helps Mark's readers understand Jesus' true significance.

9:7 The voice recalls God's Messianic designation of Jesus at his baptism (1:11; cf. Ps 2:7) and God's speaking from the cloud on Sinai after "six days" (Exod 24:15–16; cf. Mark 9:2). But instead of giving the law and instructions for the tabernacle, God commands them to obey Jesus, who embodies both God's life-giving word and his presence (see notes on 3:1–6 and 3:31–35). **Listen to him!** God had promised to send a prophet like Moses to whom Israel must listen (Deut 18:15), and Jesus has already applied a proverb concerning prophets to himself (6:4). This affirms particularly Jesus' immediately preceding teaching on his death and on discipleship (8:31–38). However, since to listen to Jesus is to do God's will (see note on 3:31–35), it also includes Jesus' past teaching (e.g., on ritual purity [7:1–23]) and later instruction (e.g., on status, divorce, and wealth [9:33—10:31]). In the context of a new Sinai, Jesus' teaching constitutes the reconstituted law of God's reconstituted people.

9:9 not to tell anyone. Jesus continues to control his public self-revelation lest Israel's nationalistic expectations become an obstacle to his mission as the suffering servant (see notes on 1:34; 2:10; 8:30; cf. John 6:15). His transfigured glory can be properly understood only in the light of his suffering, death, and resurrection.

9:10–11 Elijah's appearance seems to have reminded the disciples of the scribal tradition, based on Mal 4:5–6 (cf. Mal 3:1), that Elijah would resolve Israel's divisions prior to God's coming. If so, how could Jesus be rejected and executed in the first place (8:31)? The confused disciples ask Jesus for his assessment of the opinion of the teachers of the law.

9:12 Jesus' answer succinctly states the problem. **suffer much and be rejected.** Jesus again describes his mission in terms of Isaiah's servant, whose suffering will facilitate Israel's redemption (Isa 53:3–5,10; see note on 8:31).

9:13 Elijah has come. Alludes to Malachi's prophecy (1:4; see note on 1:6), which Jesus implies was fulfilled in John the Baptist. **they.** John's enemies, meaning at least Herod and Herodias but also Israel's silent and therefore complicit religious leadership. **as it is written about him.** There is no prediction that Elijah would undergo end-time suffering; on the contrary, Jewish tradition expected him to succeed in preparing Israel for God's coming, hence the disciples' earlier confusion (v. 10). But Jesus draws a parallel between Scripture's account of scheming Jezebel's manipulation of weak King Ahab and Herodias's exploitation of an insecure King Herod, with Herodias succeeding in carrying out Jezebel's wish to kill Elijah (cf. "they" in 1 Kgs 19:10,14; see note on 6:19–20). Since, contrary to all expectation, Elijah-John had been rejected and killed, the disciples should not be surprised that Jesus, for whom John prepared, will suffer the same fate.

9:14–29 *Jesus Heals a Boy Possessed by an Impure Spirit.* Jesus' descent from the glory on the mountain to find an unbelieving generation defeated by an impure spirit recalls Moses' descent to find Israel's apostasy (Exod 32:17–24). Until the disciples fully embrace the way of the cross, their spiritual impurity, exemplified by the yeast of Herod and the Pharisees (8:15), will render them powerless.

9:15 overwhelmed with wonder. Recalls Israel's response to Moses' appearance (Exod 34:29). However, instead of withdrawing in fear (Exod 34:30), the people run to Jesus.

9:20 [v] Mk 1:26
9:23 [w] Mt 21:21; Mk 11:23; Jn 11:40
9:25 [x] ver 15
9:28 [y] Mk 7:17
9:31 [z] Mt 8:20 [a] ver 12; Ac 2:23; 3:13 [b] Mt 16:21 [c] Mt 16:21
9:32 [d] Lk 2:50; 9:45; 18:34; Jn 12:16
9:33 [e] Mt 4:13 [f] Mk 1:29

robbed him of speech. 18 Whenever it seizes him, it throws him to the ground. He foams at the mouth,
gnashes his teeth and becomes rigid. I asked your disciples to drive out the spirit, but they could not."
19 "You unbelieving generation," Jesus replied, "how long shall I stay with you? How long shall I put
up with you? Bring the boy to me."
20 So they brought him. When the spirit saw Jesus, it immediately threw the boy into a convulsion.
He fell to the ground and rolled around, foaming at the mouth.[v]
21 Jesus asked the boy's father, "How long has he been like this?"
"From childhood," he answered. 22 "It has often thrown him into fire or water to kill him. But if you
can do anything, take pity on us and help us."
23 " 'If you can'?" said Jesus. "Everything is possible for one who believes."[w]
24 Immediately the boy's father exclaimed, "I do believe; help me overcome my unbelief!"
25 When Jesus saw that a crowd was running to the scene,[x] he rebuked the impure spirit. "You deaf
and mute spirit," he said, "I command you, come out of him and never enter him again."
26 The spirit shrieked, convulsed him violently and came out. The boy looked so much like a corpse
that many said, "He's dead." 27 But Jesus took him by the hand and lifted him to his feet, and he
stood up.
28 After Jesus had gone indoors, his disciples asked him privately,[y] "Why couldn't we drive it out?"
29 He replied, "This kind can come out only by prayer.[a]"

Jesus Predicts His Death a Second Time

9:33-37pp — Mt 18:1-5; Lk 9:46-48

30 They left that place and passed through Galilee. Jesus did not want anyone to know where they
were, 31 because he was teaching his disciples. He said to them, "The Son of Man[z] is going to be delivered into the hands of men. They will kill him,[a] and after three days[b] he will rise."[c] 32 But they did not
understand what he meant[d] and were afraid to ask him about it.
33 They came to Capernaum.[e] When he was in the house,[f] he asked them, "What were you argu-

[a] *29* Some manuscripts *prayer and fasting*

9:18 The disciples were previously successful in casting out demons (6:13). This is the only detailed account of the disciples failing to drive out an impure spirit, suggesting a significant lapse in their spiritual authority. Since their authority was always dependent on Jesus, this spiritual failure implies that their relationship with him has been seriously compromised by their failure to embrace the newly revealed cross-bearing path of true discipleship (see notes on 8:33; 8:34—9:1).
9:19 unbelieving generation. Echoes Moses' description of faithless Israel during the first exodus (Deut 32:20; cf. Num 14:11) and recalls Jesus' statement in 8:38 but now includes his ineffective disciples.
9:22 into fire or water to kill him. See note on 5:5. **if you can.** If the man truly recognized who Jesus was, everything would be possible since Jesus, in whom God's presence dwells, can do whatever he wills (see notes on 1:40,41).
9:24 help me overcome my unbelief! In immediately admitting his inadequacy and dependence, the man's request stands as an example to the unbelieving generation, including Jesus' disciples.
9:25 saw ... rebuked. To avoid both undue publicity and the boy's becoming a sideshow (see notes on 1:44; 5:43; 7:33; 8:22–26).
9:26 He's dead. Although it appeared that the impure spirit (see note on 1:23) had successfully killed the boy (9:22), Jesus' action (v. 27), recalling his extraordinary authority in the raising of Jairus's daughter (5:41), calmly shows that this is not the case.
9:28 indoors ... privately. See note on 7:17.
9:29 This kind. Some spirits are more difficult to remove than others—though not for Jesus, who commands even the most powerful with a word (5:1–20). **prayer.** Mark has mentioned prayer only twice previously, both occasions describing Jesus communing alone with God and apparently at length (1:35; 6:46). But given the disciples' previous success (6:13), why this failure at this particular moment? Jesus' private (v. 28) explanation suggests there is more at stake. His alienating call to cross-bearing (8:34) constitutes a radical shift in discipleship if Israel and the world are to be truly freed from Satan's power (see note on 8:34; cf. John 12:31; 16:11). Since the disciples' authority depends solely on their relationship to Jesus, their failure to understand and faithfully respond to his call has compromised that authority. Only prayer can align them again with the things of God (see notes on 8:33; 14:36).
9:30–37 *Jesus Predicts His Death a Second Time.* Jesus' first prediction of his death was met by Peter's self-confident rebuke (8:31–32), Jesus' stern response (8:33), God's affirmation of Jesus' declaration (9:2–7), the unexpected rejection of the promised Elijah (vv. 11–13), and the disciples' failure to cast out the impure spirit (vv. 18,28–29). Here, the disciples' failure has left them far less certain and self-assured (v. 32). Jesus' Messiahship is characterized by humble, self-giving service (cf. Luke 22:27).
9:30–31 Jesus continues his instruction of his "blind" and "deaf" disciples (see note on 8:22—10:52), again insisting on his coming suffering, death, and vindication (see note on 8:31—10:45).
9:31 The Son of Man ... will rise. See 2:10; 8:31. **be delivered into the hands of men.** It was God's intention (8:31; cf. Isa 53:6) to use the murderous hostility of the Jewish leaders and wicked Gentiles (Acts 2:23; 4:27–28) to accomplish his redemptive purposes.
9:32 did not understand. See note on 8:22—10:52. **afraid.** In the past the disciples freely asked Jesus questions (e.g., vv. 11,28; 4:10; 7:17). Their reluctance here probably stems from their not wanting to hear what they fear will be a deeply disturbing answer.
9:33 house. Probably Peter's (see note on 1:21); it was a place of private instruction (see note on 7:17).

ing about on the road?" 34But they kept quiet because on the way they had argued about who was
the greatest.[g]
35Sitting down, Jesus called the Twelve and said, "Anyone who wants to be first must be the very last,
and the servant of all."[h]
36He took a little child whom he placed among them. Taking the child in his arms,[i] he said to them,
37"Whoever welcomes one of these little children in my name welcomes me; and whoever welcomes me
does not welcome me but the one who sent me."[j]

9:34 [g] Lk 22:24
9:35 [h] Mt 18:4; 20:26; Mk 10:43; Lk 22:26
9:36 [i] Mk 10:16
9:37 [j] Mt 10:40
9:38 [k] Nu 11:27-29
9:40 [l] Mt 12:30; Lk 11:23
9:41 [m] Mt 10:42
9:42 [n] Mt 5:29 [o] Mt 18:6; Lk 17:2

Whoever Is Not Against Us Is for Us

9:38-40pp — Lk 9:49,50

38"Teacher," said John, "we saw someone driving out demons in your name and we told him to stop,
because he was not one of us."[k]
39"Do not stop him," Jesus said. "For no one who does a miracle in my name can in the next moment
say anything bad about me, 40for whoever is not against us is for us.[l] 41Truly I tell you, anyone who gives
you a cup of water in my name because you belong to the Messiah will certainly not lose their reward.[m]

Causing to Stumble

42"If anyone causes one of these little ones — those who believe in me — to stumble,[n] it would be
better for them if a large millstone were hung around their neck and they were thrown into the sea.[o]

9:34 Status was central to one's honor in ancient societies, whether Jewish or pagan. **kept quiet.** The precise reason is unclear. Perhaps they felt embarrassed or did not want Jesus to interfere until they resolved the pecking order among themselves (cf. 10:35–41). The concern for greatness indicates that the "yeast" of Herod is clearly present in the house (see note on 8:15; cf. 1 Cor 5:6–8).

9:35 Sitting down. See note on 4:1. **the Twelve.** See note on 3:13–19. **very last.** The self-denial of cross-bearing discipleship stands in direct opposition to the "yeast" of a self-promoting Herod and the proud Pharisees (see note on 8:15). **servant of all.** Jesus himself has taken on the role of the "suffering servant" for all (see notes on vv. 30–31; 8:31; 10:45; cf. Isa 53). Cf. John's account of the foot-washing (John 13:3–7) and Paul's reflection on Jesus' humbling himself to deathly service on a cross (Phil 2:6–8), which becomes the pattern of Paul's life (2 Cor 4:10–12).

9:36 little child. As the least important member of ancient society, a child had no power or status and was completely dependent.

9:37 welcomes. Whereas Herod and the Pharisees are concerned with their own honor (cf. 6:21–26; 12:38–39), Jesus' followers should humbly welcome even the least. **one of these little children.** All those of similarly humble standing in the eyes of the world. **in my name.** On Jesus' behalf and with his authority. **one who sent me.** While God is specially present in Jesus, God is also the one who sent him (cf. 1:2). Because Jesus teaches the will of God, to obey Jesus is to welcome God (cf. 3:34–35).

9:38—10:31 *Jesus' New Law.* The longest collection of Jesus' teaching in Mark, these five units (9:38–41,42–50; 10:1–12,13–16,17–31) focus on the centrality of commitment to Jesus (9:39–41; 10:13,21,28; see note on 3:31–35) and the utter importance of treating others, even the least, with radical care (9:36–37,38–41,42,50; 10:5–12,13,21; cf. 12:28–34; Matt 7:12).

9:38–41 *Whoever Is Not Against Us Is for Us.* Verses 33–37 dealt with the disciples' love of status. Here their self-importance leads them to think that they, like the Pharisees and teachers of the law, can define who is "in" and who is "out" of God's people (cf. Luke 11:52).

9:39 in my name. See note on v. 37. However, for Jesus' name to have effect, the man must have already "welcomed" Jesus (cf. Acts 19:13–16).

9:40 The disciples must accept all who follow Jesus, whether or not they belong to the disciples' particular group (cf. Phil 1:17–18). The apparently contradictory statement in Matt 12:30 concerns those who are hostile toward Jesus (Matt 12:24).

9:41 Truly I tell you. See note on 3:28. As the least must be accepted (v. 37), so too the humblest identification with Jesus' followers — offering "a cup of water" — will receive its reward (cf. Matt 25:35–40). **in my name.** See note on v. 37. **Messiah.** Although Jesus customarily employed "Son of Man" (see note on 2:10), the repetitions of "in my name" (vv. 37,39,41; see v. 38) climax in his using "Messiah" for the first time. He *is* the Christ. Confessing Jesus as Messiah (implied by "because you belong to") is to become the distinctive mark of Jesus' disciples.

9:42–50 *Causing to Stumble.* Having forbidden his disciples from hindering another of his followers, Jesus warns against the deadly consequences of causing not only the "little ones ... to stumble" (v. 42) but also themselves.

9:42 little ones. Such as the man mentioned in vv. 38–41. **millstone.** A stone used to grind grain that was so heavy it was usually turned by a donkey. The smallest act of identification (v. 37) is now balanced by the

First-century relief on funerary monument shows a donkey-powered millstone. Jesus says that if anyone causes a little one to stumble, "it would be better for them if a large millstone were hung around their neck and they were thrown into the sea" (Mark 9:42).

9:43 [p] Mt 5:29 [q] Mt 5:30; 18:8 [r] Mt 25:41 **9:45** [s] Mt 5:29 [t] Mt 18:8 **9:47** [u] Mt 5:29 [v] Mt 5:29; 18:9 **9:48** [w] Isa 66:24; Mt 25:41 **9:49** [x] Lev 2:13 **9:50** [y] Mt 5:13; Lk 14:34, 35 [z] Col 4:6 [a] Ro 12:18; 2Co 13:11; 1Th 5:13 **10:1** [b] Mk 1:5; Jn 10:40; 11:7 [c] Mt 4:23; Mk 2:13; 4:2; 6:6,34 **10:2** [d] Mk 2:16

43 If your hand causes you to stumble,[p] cut it off. It is better for you to enter life maimed than with two
hands to go into hell,[q] where the fire never goes out.[r] [44] [a] 45 And if your foot causes you to stumble,[s]
cut it off. It is better for you to enter life crippled than to have two feet and be thrown into hell.[t] [46] [a]
47 And if your eye causes you to stumble,[u] pluck it out. It is better for you to enter the kingdom of God
with one eye than to have two eyes and be thrown into hell,[v] 48 where

> " 'the worms that eat them do not die,
> and the fire is not quenched.'[b][w]

49 Everyone will be salted[x] with fire.

50 "Salt is good, but if it loses its saltiness, how can you make it salty again?[y] Have salt among yourselves,[z] and be at peace with each other."[a]

Divorce

10:1-12pp — Mt 19:1-9

10 Jesus then left that place and went into the region of Judea and across the Jordan.[b] Again crowds of people came to him, and as was his custom, he taught them.[c]

2 Some Pharisees[d] came and tested him by asking, "Is it lawful for a man to divorce his wife?"

[a] *44,46* Some manuscripts include here the words of verse 48. [b] *48* Isaiah 66:24

great offense of causing a little one to stumble in their attempts to follow Jesus. Even a grotesque drowning in the sea is preferable.

9:43–47 hand ... foot ... eye. Various ways a disciple can sin. **cut it off ... cut it off ... pluck it out.** Hyperbole, a figure of speech that stresses the need for dire action. Jesus does not mean the literal removal of body parts since this cannot deal with sin, which, as he has already explained, is a matter of the heart (7:20–23). Physical deformity disqualified priests (Lev 21:17–21) and private individuals from full access to the temple. But in light of Jesus' teaching on ritual purity (7:1–23) and defiling yeast (8:15), sin that deforms the character is far more serious than ritual purity since it disqualifies a person from eternal life in the world to come. Causing oneself to stumble is as serious as causing a little one (v. 42) to stumble and requires radical measures.

9:43,45,47 hell. It was named from the Valley of Ben Hinnom, a deep ravine to the south of Jerusalem in which Ahaz and Manasseh infamously sacrificed their "little ones" (cf. v. 42) to Molek (2 Kgs 16:3; 21:6). Jeremiah prophesied it would be renamed the Valley of Slaughter when, in God's judgment, the Babylonians would discard the unburied bodies of the people of Jerusalem in the very place they had sacrificed their children (Jer 7:30–34; 19:1–15). In later tradition it became a symbol for ultimate punishment. Gehenna's association with abusing children is grimly appropriate (vv. 36–37,42). Though often presented as fact, there is no first-century evidence that Hinnom was used as a rubbish dump.

9:44,46 See NIV text note. Important early manuscripts omit these verses, which are identical to v. 48.

9:47 kingdom of God. See note on 1:15.

9:48 worms ... fire. The final word of Isaiah describes God's awful judgment on Jewish idolaters (Isa 66:24), its imagery evoking Jeremiah's Valley of Slaughter (see note on vv. 43,45,47). If members of Jesus' newly reconstituted Israel (see note on 3:14) continue to cause either these little ones (9:37,42) or themselves to stumble (vv. 43–50), they, like the idolaters of Isa 66:24, will be similarly excluded from salvation.

9:49 This puzzling saying occurs only in Mark and contains one of the most difficult expressions in the NT. **Everyone.** May mean every human being, but at least includes all of Jesus' followers, from the Twelve to the little ones (v. 42), since they are still "in the house" (v. 33) and since vv. 39–48 address the disciples in response to John's question (v. 38). **salted with fire.** A highly compressed mixed metaphor, the meaning of which is more likely allusive rather than precisely literal. Its transitional role suggests that it contains elements of both the preceding threat (v. 48) and subsequent encouragement (v. 50). The main alternatives are: (1) Everyone who enters hell will suffer its flames. This includes those disciples who do not take radical steps against sin (vv. 43–48). "Salted" would then symbolize destruction (Gen 19:24–26; Deut 29:23). (2) Just as some sacrifices needed salt to be acceptable (Lev 2:13), so the disciples (perhaps themselves seen as sacrifices, Rom 12:1) will need to be salted with the purifying fire of suffering (cf. 8:34) or of the Holy Spirit (cf. 1:8) if they are to enter the kingdom of heaven. The saying could encompass both suggestions: everyone, disciple or not, will be salted with fire of either the destructive (the first alternative) or purifying (the second alternative) kind.

9:50 Salt losing its saltiness signals a shift to God's purpose in salting the disciples. Imitating Jesus' cross-bearing character (see note on 8:31), they are to be God's salt in his world (Matt 5:13–16; cf. the dual effect of the "aroma" of Paul's preaching [2 Cor 2:15–16; see note]). For this reason, in contrast to the divisive "yeast" of Herod and the Pharisees (8:15), the disciples' "salty" welcome of the little ones (v. 37) and not causing even the least to stumble (v. 42) maintains the peace that is the hallmark of God's new exodus deliverance (Isa 52:7; 57:19b; see note on 1:15).

10:1–12 *Divorce.* Jesus' teaching on divorce flows directly out of his previous instruction on being a servant of all (see 9:35 and note), welcoming the least (see 9:37 and note), not causing little ones or oneself to stumble (see 9:42 and note on 9:42–50), and being at peace (see 9:50 and note). Foundational to all human society (Gen 1:27; 2:24), the marriage relationship is one of the most important relationships to which these lessons should be applied.

10:1 region of Judea. Along with Galilee, it was controlled by Herod Antipas. John the Baptist's opposition to Herod's unlawful remarriage has already cost him his life (6:16–28). **crowds.** Marks a shift from the private instruction of the disciples. This twofold change in setting alerts the reader to the threatening nature of the Pharisees' question.

10:2 Pharisees. See note on 2:16. **tested.** Appearing for the first time since Jesus' warning against their "yeast" (8:15), their action parallels that of Satan in 1:13 (cf. 8:11; 12:13–15). They apparently hope Jesus' answer will either (1) set him at odds with John, thereby alienating the public, who esteemed John as a prophet (1:5; 11:32), or (2) set him at risk of being Herodias's lethal enmity (6:19). **lawful.** The Scriptures assume divorce's reality (Deut 24:1–4), and all Jews accepted that it was legal; they debated only its grounds. Everyone agreed that adultery and other similarly weighty offenses—e.g., abuse, cruelty, humiliation, persistent refusal to provide requisite food or clothing, willful conjugal or emotional neglect (cf. Exod 21:10–11)—were clear cause for divorce and required the punishment of the offending party (God himself severely

[3]"What did Moses command you?" he replied.
[4]They said, "Moses permitted a man to write a certificate of divorce and send her away."[e]
[5]"It was because your hearts were hard[f] that Moses wrote you this law," Jesus replied. [6]"But at the
beginning of creation God 'made them male and female.'[a][g] [7]'For this reason a man will leave his father
and mother and be united to his wife,[b] [8]and the two will become one flesh.'[c][h] So they are no longer two,
but one flesh. [9]Therefore what God has joined together, let no one separate."
[10]When they were in the house again, the disciples asked Jesus about this. [11]He answered, "Anyone
who divorces his wife and marries another woman commits adultery against her.[i] [12]And if she divorces
her husband and marries another man, she commits adultery."[j]

The Little Children and Jesus

10:13-16pp — Mt 19:13-15; Lk 18:15-17

[13]People were bringing little children to Jesus for him to place his hands on them, but the disciples
rebuked them. [14]When Jesus saw this, he was indignant. He said to them, "Let the little children come
to me, and do not hinder them, for the kingdom of God belongs to such as these.[k] [15]Truly I tell you,
anyone who will not receive the kingdom of God like a little child will never enter it."[l] [16]And he took
the children in his arms,[m] placed his hands on them and blessed them.

The Rich and the Kingdom of God

10:17-31pp — Mt 19:16-30; Lk 18:18-30

[17]As Jesus started on his way, a man ran up to him and fell on his knees[n] before him. "Good teacher,"
he asked, "what must I do to inherit eternal life?"[o]

10:4 [e] Dt 24:1-4; Mt 5:31
10:5 [f] Ps 95:8; Heb 3:15
10:6 [g] Ge 1:27; 5:2
10:8 [h] Ge 2:24; 1Co 6:16
10:11 [i] Mt 5:32; Lk 16:18
10:12 [j] Ro 7:3; 1Co 7:10,11
10:14 [k] Mt 25:34
10:15 [l] Mt 18:3
10:16 [m] Mk 9:36
10:17 [n] Mk 1:40 [o] Lk 10:25; Ac 20:32

[a] *6* Gen. 1:27 [b] *7* Some early manuscripts do not have *and be united to his wife.* [c] *8* Gen. 2:24

punished Israel for such [e.g., Jer 3; Ezek 16; Hos 1–3]). However, many Pharisees also permitted husbands a no-fault divorce for "any matter" (see note on v. 4), such as his wife not accepting his control, his finding a more attractive woman, or even his wife spoiling his meal. From this perspective, the question concerns Jesus' view on the validity not of divorce in general but of the Pharisees' no-fault "any matter" divorce.

10:3 Moses. The Pharisees' highest authority.

10:4 Summarizes Deut 24:1–4, which in regulating remarriage presumes divorce for "something indecent" (Deut 24:1). The Pharisees' case was built on interpreting the "something" of Deut 24:1 as meaning "any matter" and thus constituting a separate category from "indecent" (see note on v. 2).

10:5 hearts were hard. Hardness of heart characteristically refers to Israel's idolatrous resistance to God's will (3:5; see note on 8:16–21; see also Deut 10:16; Jer 4:4; cf. Exod 33:3,5; 34:9). For Jesus, human rebellion against God lies at the heart of all abuse of one's spouse. Without that rebellion there would be no need for the abused party to seek protection through a legally valid divorce (see note on v. 2).

10:6–8 By appealing to Genesis (see NIV text notes on vv. 6,8), Jesus justifies his claim that Moses' permission reflects Israel's hardheartedness, not God's original intention. God's plan in creating two genders ("male and female," v. 6) was precisely so that they would become one flesh and thereby procreate (cf. 12:25; Isa 45:12,18). Since God's intention was oneness and since divorce ruptures that unity, the willful abuse of the other that leads to divorce constitutes idolatrous rebellion.

10:10 See note on 7:17.

10:11–12 divorces his wife ... divorces her husband. Although only a husband could enact a divorce, there were ways for a wife to initiate the process; Jesus addresses both. While on the surface Jesus seems to be rejecting any divorce, the context suggests that he is addressing the Pharisees' advocacy of no-fault "any matter" (see note on v. 2) divorce. **marries another ... marries another.** Jesus affirms John's position: marriage in such cases (including Herod's) is adultery. As to the universally accepted weighty grounds (e.g., adultery, abuse, failing to meet basic marital obligations), the charge of hardheartedness surely also applies. That neither Mark nor Luke (Luke 16:18) have the phrase "except for sexual immorality" (Matt 5:32; 19:9; cf. Paul in 1 Cor 7:15) is most likely because both assume that adultery is a Scripturally valid ground for divorce and that neither Jesus nor the Pharisees are addressing that issue here.

10:13–16 *The Little Children and Jesus.* Jesus, continuing to teach on the basis of entry into the kingdom and thereby confronting the human love of greatness, returns to the theme of "little ones" (9:37,42). Because God's kingdom belongs to people who come to Jesus like status-less children (v. 14), entry into the kingdom is dependent on receiving it like dependent children, as a completely undeserved gift (v. 15; cf. Luke 17:10). This stands in striking contrast to the rich, law-abiding man who cannot let go of his great wealth (vv. 17–31).

10:13 little children. See note on 9:37.

10:14 indignant. The disciples seem not to have heard any of Jesus' previous teaching on welcoming (9:33–37). **kingdom of God.** See note on 1:15. **belongs ... these.** Since "little children" were not considered old enough to understand or obey the law, Jesus also implies that entry into the kingdom depends not on a righteousness that comes from obeying the law but on coming to him in humble trust and complete dependence (see note on 3:31–35; cf. 10:17–31; Gal 2:15–21).

10:15 Returning to the topic of welcoming the least (9:33–37), Jesus declares that only those who realize they are least before God and can do nothing to merit right standing before him can inherit the gift of the kingdom (e.g., 2:17; 4:11; 7:27–29; see Matt 5:3 where the first Beatitude is addressed to those who recognize their spiritual poverty before God).

10:17–31 *The Rich and the Kingdom of God.* In contrast to the completely dependent "little children" (vv. 14–15; 9:37) who have nothing and no standing in the eyes of the world, Mark reports an incident involving a very wealthy and commandment-keeping man whom many Jews of Jesus' day would consider having "great" standing with God and thus a sure claim to salvation.

10:17 fell on his knees. A public act of genuine humility and deference

10:19 [p]Ex 20:12-16; Dt 5:16-20
10:21 [q]Ac 2:45 [r]Mt 6:20; Lk 12:33 [s]Mt 4:19
10:23 [t]Ps 52:7; 62:10; 1Ti 6:9,10,17
10:24 [u]Mt 7:13,14
10:25 [v]Lk 12:16-20
10:27 [w]Mt 19:26
10:28 [x]Mt 4:19
10:30 [y]Mt 6:33 [z]Mt 12:32 [a]Mt 25:46
10:31 [b]Mt 19:30

18 "Why do you call me good?" Jesus answered. "No one is good — except God alone. 19 You know the
commandments: 'You shall not murder, you shall not commit adultery, you shall not steal, you shall
not give false testimony, you shall not defraud, honor your father and mother.'[a]"[p]
20 "Teacher," he declared, "all these I have kept since I was a boy."
21 Jesus looked at him and loved him. "One thing you lack," he said. "Go, sell everything you have
and give to the poor,[q] and you will have treasure in heaven.[r] Then come, follow me."[s]
22 At this the man's face fell. He went away sad, because he had great wealth.
23 Jesus looked around and said to his disciples, "How hard it is for the rich[t] to enter the kingdom
of God!"
24 The disciples were amazed at his words. But Jesus said again, "Children, how hard it is[b] to enter
the kingdom of God![u] 25 It is easier for a camel to go through the eye of a needle than for someone who
is rich to enter the kingdom of God."[v]
26 The disciples were even more amazed, and said to each other, "Who then can be saved?"
27 Jesus looked at them and said, "With man this is impossible, but not with God; all things are possible with God."[w]
28 Then Peter spoke up, "We have left everything to follow you!"[x]
29 "Truly I tell you," Jesus replied, "no one who has left home or brothers or sisters or mother or
father or children or fields for me and the gospel 30 will fail to receive a hundred times as much[y]
in this present age: homes, brothers, sisters, mothers, children and fields — along with persecutions — and in the age to come[z] eternal life.[a] 31 But many who are first will be last, and the last
first."[b]

a *19* Exodus 20:12-16; Deut. 5:16-20   *b* *24* Some manuscripts *is for those who trust in riches*

(cf. 5:22; 7:25–26). **teacher.** See note on 4:38. **what must I do to inherit eternal life?** God's gift of the law, which included provision for dealing with sin, promised life through keeping its commandments (e.g., Lev 18:5). The Pharisees took this to mean eternal life, which led to many debates over what the law required (cf. 2:15–3:6; 7:1–23). The man, also assuming that obedience to the law can merit eternal life, asks Jesus for his opinion.

10:18 good. The life-giving goodness of God is one of the great themes of Scripture (e.g., 1 Chr 16:34; 2 Chr 5:13; 7:3,10; 30:18; Ezra 3:11; Pss 25:7,8; 34:8; 86:5; 100:5; 118:29; 145:9; cf. Deut 10:13; 12:28; Pss 16:2; 34:10). Jesus is not denying his own goodness but wants the man to recognize that since God alone is good and alone gives life (Deut 32:39; 1 Sam 2:6), only God can answer this question (even as only God can forgive sin, cf. 2:7). Hence, Jesus recites the commandments (v. 19). That Jesus then goes on to add his own requirement (vv. 21) implies his equality with God (see notes on 1:2–3,24; 2:10,11–12; 4:39,41; 6:48–50). The man's address ("Good teacher," v. 17) is appropriate only if he realizes this fact.

10:20 all these I have kept. The man's confession (see v. 19 for the meaning of "all these") and the absence of any critique by Jesus, who instead loves him (v. 21), testify to the man's being righteous as far as obedience to the law was concerned (cf. Paul's claim in Phil 3:6). **since I was a boy.** Probably from age 13, at which time a Jewish boy became personally responsible for obeying the commandments.

10:21 sell everything ... give. Jesus nowhere else in Mark requires this of any other follower; although the disciples "left everything" (v. 28), Peter still had a house (1:29). **follow me.** Jewish tradition held that complete obedience to the law would merit eternal life. Here Jesus reveals that eternal life comes only through following him (i.e. the law cannot "impart life," cf. Gal 3:21–22). His requirement thus expresses the two concerns of this section: radical care for others and the utter centrality of following Jesus (see note on 9:38—10:31).

10:22 Only now do Mark's readers learn that the man "had great wealth." While some see this as his secret sin, in Jewish tradition his obedience meant it was God's merited blessing. Jesus' unusual demand (see note on v. 21) means the man must abandon the material signs of God's confirmation of his righteousness and put his confidence entirely in Jesus.

10:23–25 The rich, whether great in righteousness or wealth, find it hard to become least, thereby disqualifying themselves from the kingdom (v. 15).

10:25 camel. As the largest animal in the Holy Land, it simply cannot be threaded through the smallest hole.

10:26 amazed. Given traditional Jewish assumptions, this man, of all people, should have been assured of eternal life.

10:27 It is precisely because salvation is "impossible" for humans that all must accept the kingdom as powerless children (v. 15), trusting only in God's merciful kindness by following Jesus.

10:28–30 Jesus promises the disciples — who, unlike the wealthy man, have left all — a rich harvest of reward (see 4:20). In this new community characterized by generous welcome to all who trust in his name (9:36,41), Jesus appears to refer to the blessings of being received into the houses of other believers.

10:29 Truly I tell you. See note on 3:28.

10:30 present age. The age that since the fall is evil, under the power of Satan, and passing away (John 16:11; 1 Cor 2:6; Gal 1:4). **persecutions.** Just as Jesus arouses hostility and is rejected, so too does his newly reconstituted cross-bearing community (8:34). **age to come eternal life.** The new creation that will never pass away, ushered in by the second coming of Christ. Jesus here puts everything, whether blessings or persecutions, into proper perspective.

10:31 first will be last. Summarizes the main thrust of Jesus' teaching throughout the entire "way" section (8:22—10:52). Eternal life is to be found not on the basis of status, wealth, or obedience to the law (see note on 8:15) but by humble and welcoming cross-bearing discipleship (8:34–39).

Jesus Predicts His Death a Third Time

10:32-34pp — Mt 20:17-19; Lk 18:31-33

32 They were on their way up to Jerusalem, with Jesus leading the way, and the disciples were astonished, while those who followed were afraid. Again he took the Twelve[c] aside and told them what
was going to happen to him. 33 "We are going up to Jerusalem,"[d] he said, "and the Son of Man[e] will be
delivered over to the chief priests and the teachers of the law.[f] They will condemn him to death and will
hand him over to the Gentiles, 34 who will mock him and spit on him, flog him[g] and kill him.[h] Three
days later[i] he will rise."[j]

The Request of James and John

10:35-45pp — Mt 20:20-28

35 Then James and John, the sons of Zebedee, came to him. "Teacher," they said, "we want you to do
for us whatever we ask."

36 "What do you want me to do for you?" he asked.

37 They replied, "Let one of us sit at your right and the other at your left in your glory."[k]

38 "You don't know what you are asking,"[l] Jesus said. "Can you drink the cup[m] I drink or be baptized
with the baptism I am baptized with?"[n]

39 "We can," they answered.

Jesus said to them, "You will drink the cup I drink and be baptized with the baptism I am baptized
with,[o] 40 but to sit at my right or left is not for me to grant. These places belong to those for whom they
have been prepared."

10:32 [c] Mk 3:16-19
10:33 [d] Lk 9:51 [e] Mt 8:20 [f] Mt 27:1,2
10:34 [g] Mt 16:21 [h] Ac 2:23; 3:13 [i] Mt 16:21 [j] Mt 16:21
10:37 [k] Mt 19:28
10:38 [l] Job 38:2 [m] Mt 20:22 [n] Lk 12:50
10:39 [o] Ac 12:2; Rev 1:9

10:32–45 *The Disciples' Continued Blindness.* In spite of Jesus' teaching, the disciples' concern for status continues to blind them to the suffering servant nature of Jesus' Messiahship.

10:32–34 *Jesus Predicts His Death a Third Time.* See note on 8:31—10:45. At the end of Mark's "way" section (8:22—10:52) and on the threshold of Jerusalem, this third and last block of teaching reveals what Jesus' previous allusions to Isaiah's suffering servant actually mean.

10:32 Mark's first clear statement, in keeping with his opening sentence (1:1–3), that the climax of Jesus' "way" is Jerusalem (see notes on 1:2–3; 11:1—15:47). In Isaiah, God's returning presence was expected to result in great joy, glory, and the restoration of the city (Isa 2:1–4; 4:2–6; 35; 54; 60–62). However, because of the hostility of Israel's leadership (see notes on 1:44; 3:29; 9:13), Jerusalem tragically becomes the place of Jesus' rejection and death. Ironically, however, it is Jesus' self-giving that displays the glory of God. To this glory all nations will come (cf. note on 15:39 where the first confession of Jesus as God's son by a human being is made by a Gentile centurion at the foot of the cross). **astonished ... afraid.** Characteristic responses to Jesus' mighty new exodus deeds (see notes on 1:10; 4:35—5:43). Here it suggests that Jesus' "leading the way" had a similar sense of divine presence and authority (cf. Isa 45:2; 52:12).

10:33 Jerusalem. See note on v. 32. **Son of Man.** See note on 2:10. **condemn him to death.** The fate of Isaiah's suffering servant (Isa 53:8,9,12; see note on 8:31). **hand him over to the Gentiles.** Because Rome reserved the right to adjudicate and carry out capital sentences (see note on 14:55), this is a natural progression. But it is also the way God characteristically judges wicked Israel (e.g., Deut 30:1; Neh 1:8; Jer 9:16), which, given the prominence of Isaiah's suffering servant in Jesus' thinking, is consistent with Jesus' taking Israel's judgment upon himself (see note on 8:31).

10:34 spit ... flog. The humiliation suffered by Isaiah's servant (Isa 50:6). **kill.** See note on 8:34. **Three days later he will rise.** See note on 8:31.

10:35–45 *The Request of James and John.* Their request and their fellow disciples' response reveal how the disciples' concern for status continues to blind them to the significance of Jesus' coming suffering-servant death.

10:35 James and John. Earlier it was Peter (8:32–33), but here, even with the benefit of additional teaching, the two remaining members of the inner circle (see note on 1:18) reveal their continued lack of understanding. **Teacher.** The same address used by the wealthy man (vv. 17,20; see note on 4:38). But whereas he asked Jesus what he needed to do, James and John know what they want Jesus to do.

10:37 right ... left. Supreme positions of rank and authority (cf. Pss 80:17; 110:1). **your glory.** It may be that in approaching Jerusalem they were expecting the Son of Man (v. 33; cf. 8:38) to reveal himself as he had at the transfiguration (9:2–10). Despite Jesus' constant teaching on lowly service (8:33—10:16), they are still defiled by the "yeast" of Herod's and the Pharisees' love of status (see note on 8:15).

10:38 don't know. They fail to understand what it means for Jesus to come into his glory (see note on v. 32). **drink the cup I drink.** Share Jesus' fate (14:36). Drinking the cup of wrath was a metaphor for God's judgment on evildoers and especially the nations, including Israel, particularly for their arrogance (Ps 75:8; Jer 25:15–38). This is an appropriate image given James and John's self-seeking request. Jesus earlier alluded to his bearing Israel's covenant curse (see notes on v. 33; 8:31). Here he takes on the nations' judgment as well. **baptism.** Jesus' own striking metaphor, apparently based on John's baptism (cf. Rom 6:3–4), which likened going down into the water to death (cf. 2 Sam 22:5; Ps 69:2–3,15). Having already spoken plainly (8:32), Jesus' use of these parable-like figures of speech (see note on 4:2) suggests that James and John are still thinking like "outsiders" (see note on 8:33).

10:39–40 Though James and John will follow Jesus in the ultimate expression of cross-bearing discipleship (8:34–38), this will not earn them the places they seek.

10:40 those. In keeping with his upside-down vision of the kingdom and continuing the reference to his coming death (v. 38), Jesus might be repudiating their entire way of thinking by referring ironically to the two who will soon be executed "on his right and ... on his left" (15:27), with his glory meaning not a Messianic throne but a cross (8:27–33; John 12:23–28).

10:43 [p]Mk 9:35
10:45 [q]Mt 20:28 [r]Mt 20:28
10:47 [s]Mk 1:24 [t]Mt 9:27
10:51 [u]Mt 23:7
10:52 [v]Mt 9:22 [w]Mt 4:19

41 When the ten heard about this, they became indignant with James and John. 42 Jesus called them
together and said, "You know that those who are regarded as rulers of the Gentiles lord it over them,
and their high officials exercise authority over them. 43 Not so with you. Instead, whoever wants to become great among you must be your servant,[p] 44 and whoever wants to be first must be slave of all. 45 For
even the Son of Man did not come to be served, but to serve,[q] and to give his life as a ransom for many."[r]

Blind Bartimaeus Receives His Sight

10:46-52pp — Mt 20:29-34; Lk 18:35-43

46 Then they came to Jericho. As Jesus and his disciples, together with a large crowd, were leaving the
city, a blind man, Bartimaeus (which means "son of Timaeus"), was sitting by the roadside begging.
47 When he heard that it was Jesus of Nazareth,[s] he began to shout, "Jesus, Son of David,[t] have mercy
on me!"

48 Many rebuked him and told him to be quiet, but he shouted all the more, "Son of David, have
mercy on me!"

49 Jesus stopped and said, "Call him."

So they called to the blind man, "Cheer up! On your feet! He's calling you." 50 Throwing his cloak
aside, he jumped to his feet and came to Jesus.

51 "What do you want me to do for you?" Jesus asked him.

The blind man said, "Rabbi,[u] I want to see."

52 "Go," said Jesus, "your faith has healed you."[v] Immediately he received his sight and followed[w]
Jesus along the road.

10:41 The other disciples' response shows that their hearts are also defiled by the status-seeking "yeast" of Herod and the Pharisees (see note on 8:15). In spite of Jesus' repeated instruction throughout the entire "way" section (8:22—10:52), his uncomprehending disciples are still "blind" and "deaf" (see notes on 8:16–21; 8:22—10:52) to God's surpassing wisdom of the crucified Messiah (cf. 1 Cor 1:18–25).

10:42–45 This is the climax of Mark's "way" section and one of the most important passages in Mark. It shows that Jesus' suffering-servant death (v. 45) is utterly central to the upside-down values of God's kingdom (vv. 42–43).

10:43 Not so with you. In keeping with Jesus' servant calling and teaching throughout the "way" section (8:22—10:52), his disciples must reject the "yeast" of merely human ideas of self-serving and self-promoting leadership. Applying to all of life, Jesus' vision of servant leadership includes politics (in contrast to Herod and the rulers of the nations) and religion and the church (in contrast to the Pharisees) (see notes on 8:15,33; cf. John 13:3–7). **great ... servant.** True greatness is a matter of service for the sake of others.

10:45 Encapsulates the heart and climax of God's "way" of the new exodus (see note on 8:22—10:52) and, for the first time, explains the purpose of Jesus' death. **Son of Man.** See notes on 2:10; 8:31. **serve ... ransom for many.** The necessary conclusion of Jesus' previous allusions to Isaiah's prophesied suffering servant (see notes on v. 33; 8:31; 9:12). In taking a sinful humanity's just penalty upon himself, Jesus' innocent and obedient death fulfills Isaiah's prophecy that God himself would provide a means to redeem both Israel and the nations from their bondage to sin and death (Isa 53:4–6,10–12; see note on 8:22—10:52). **ransom.** The price paid for the release of someone from bondage.

10:46–52 *Blind Bartimaeus Receives His Sight.* This second and last healing of sight in Mark concludes Mark's "way" section. Bartimaeus's "son of David" confession (v. 47) prepares for Jesus' entry into Jerusalem.

10:46 Jericho. Where Israel entered the promised land. **Bartimaeus.** Means "son of impurity," perhaps reflecting a Jewish tradition that blindness was the consequence of sin (cf. John 9:1–3). Bartimaeus sits "by the roadside" of Jesus' new exodus deliverance (see note on v. 52).

10:47 Jesus of Nazareth. This address accompanied the first public confession (1:24) of Jesus' identity by an impure spirit (see note on 1:23), and it appears here for only the second time in this first public Messianic confession by a human. **Son of David.** Already privately identified as the Davidic Messiah by God (1:11; 9:7) and Peter (8:29), this is the only time Jesus is publicly addressed with this Messianic title (cf. Jer 23:5–6; Ezek 37:24–25). **mercy.** Undeserved kindness. The Scriptures overwhelmingly ascribe mercy to God (see especially Exod 33:19; 34:6–7; cf. 5:19). Given Jesus' identification with God's very presence, mercy naturally characterizes Jesus' teaching on how his followers should treat others (9:33—10:12). In contrast to the disciples' concern with status (v. 37; 8:32; 9:34,38), Bartimaeus recognizes his need for mercy, "seeing" what many others do not: Jesus not only is the Messiah but also reflects God's merciful character (see note on 8:33).

10:48 rebuked. Recalls the disciples' response to those bringing children (v. 13). Considering Bartimaeus of no status, the crowd shows no mercy and initially responds in precisely the way Jesus has already forbidden (v. 14).

10:49 Jesus "welcomes" this least one (9:37).

10:50 cloak. His primary protection from the elements, it is probably his most important possession (Exod 22:25–26). In responding to Jesus' call and leaving all behind, the beggar imitates the disciples (v. 28) and does what the rich man could not do (vv. 22–23).

10:51 Rabbi. See note on 9:5–6. Recalls the request of the rich man for eternal life (v. 17) and the request of James and John for power (v. 37). Bartimaeus's request for sight contrasts with the rich man's love of wealth, James and John's self-interest, and Peter's earlier presumption that he "sees" better than Jesus (8:29–31).

10:52 your faith. Bartimaeus's insight into who Jesus is: the merciful Messiah who welcomes the least. **healed.** Or "saved," it reflects the Jewish understanding of the tight link between salvation and physical wholeness (cf. 2:1–12). In healing the blind man, who joyfully follows him on the road into Jerusalem, Jesus fulfills Isaiah's promise that in the new exodus God would come to save his people, prepare a holy way upon which the impure would not walk, and open the eyes of the blind so they could joyfully enter that way into Zion (Isa 35:4–10). Blind Bartimaeus's insistent cry for mercy (v. 47; cf. vv. 26–27) and request

Jesus Comes to Jerusalem as King

11:1-10pp — Mt 21:1-9; Lk 19:29-38
11:7-10pp — Jn 12:12-15

11 As they approached Jerusalem and came to Bethphage and Bethany[x] at the Mount of Olives,[y]
Jesus sent two of his disciples, 2 saying to them, "Go to the village ahead of you, and just as
you enter it, you will find a colt tied there, which no one has ever ridden.[z] Untie it and bring it here. 3 If
anyone asks you, 'Why are you doing this?' say, 'The Lord needs it and will send it back here shortly.' "
4 They went and found a colt outside in the street, tied at a doorway.[a] As they untied it, 5 some people
standing there asked, "What are you doing, untying that colt?" 6 They answered as Jesus had told them
to, and the people let them go. 7 When they brought the colt to Jesus and threw their cloaks over it, he
sat on it. 8 Many people spread their cloaks on the road, while others spread branches they had cut in
the fields. 9 Those who went ahead and those who followed shouted,

"Hosanna![a]"
"Blessed is he who comes in the name of the Lord!"[b][b]

10 "Blessed is the coming kingdom of our father David!"
"Hosanna in the highest heaven!"[c]

a 9 A Hebrew expression meaning "Save!" which became an exclamation of praise; also in verse 10
b 9 Psalm 118:25,26

11:1 [x] Mt 21:17 [y] Mt 21:1
11:2 [z] Nu 19:2; Dt 21:3; 1Sa 6:7
11:4 [a] Mk 14:16
11:9 [b] Ps 118:25,26; Mt 23:39
11:10 [c] Lk 2:14

for sight (v. 51; see note on 8:22—10:52) express the only bases on which one can enter new exodus salvation.

11:1—15:47 *Jerusalem: A New Temple, a New Covenant, and a New Passover.* Mark's third and final section sees various themes converge in climactic fulfillment as Jesus comes to Jerusalem and particularly the temple (see "The City of God," p. 2666, and "Temple," p. 2052). On the one hand, in keeping with God's Ps 2 declarations at Jesus' baptism (1:11) and transfiguration (9:7), the crowds join in Bartimaeus's confession rightly identifying Jesus as Israel's Davidic Messiah come to purify the city (see note on 1:11). But Jesus is also the Lord (1:2–3), the divinely authoritative Son of Man and Lord of the Sabbath (see notes on 2:10,28; 9:3) in whom God's presence returns to his temple, as both Isaiah and Malachi promised (cf. 1:2–3). Because the authorities reject him, what in Isaiah's vision should have resulted in glorious restoration (e.g., Isa 60–62; cf. Mark 11:4–10; see note on 10:32) becomes instead, as Malachi had warned (Mal 4:6b), enacted judgment (11:12—12:12; 12:38–40; 15:38) and a prophecy of destruction (ch. 13). Nevertheless, in keeping with Isaiah's prophecies of a suffering servant, God uses Jesus' innocent and obedient death at the hands of both Jews and Gentiles (14:23–47) to inaugurate a new Passover in which all who believe in him will be redeemed from sin and death (14:12–28; cf. 10:45).

11:1—13:37 *The Lord's Return to His Temple.* This section focuses on the temple, which, as the sign of God's covenantal presence with Israel, embodied the nation's identity (Exod 19:5; 29:45–46; 33:14–15; Lev 26:12). As the opening sentence of Mark's Gospel anticipated (see note on 1:2–3), Jesus, the temple's Lord (Mal 3:1), confronts Israel's rebellious leadership (cf. 3:22–29; 7:1–13) in their barren temple (11:12–21). Having failed to respond to John's preaching, the unrepentant authorities refuse to welcome Jesus, and so they and their temple are doomed (13:1–37). The sequence reflects the ancient practice of royal persons being accorded a lavish welcome before proceeding to the city's primary temple to offer sacrifice as a sign of their authority (cf. Pss 24; 118). Given Jesus' divine and Messianic identity, the authorities' lethal hostility clearly marks them as rebels.

11:1–11 *Jesus Comes to Jerusalem as King.* The crowds welcome Jesus as their Messianic deliverer, little suspecting that his way of being Messiah is radically different from what they envisage. At the same time, Mark's readers know that Jesus also comes as the Lord, Israel's divine king (see note on 1:2–3).

11:1 Bethphage. A little village of unknown location near Jerusalem. **Bethany.** On the eastern slope of the Mount of Olives about two miles (three kilometers) from Jerusalem. It is the last stop on the road from Jericho to Jerusalem. **Mount of Olives.** To the east of the temple mount and about 100 feet (30 meters) higher, it offered a panoramic view of the temple.

11:2 no one has ever ridden. Being unused makes it appropriate for royal or even divine (i.e., religious) use (cf. Num 19:2; Deut 21:3; 1 Sam 6:7). First-century political practice meant that royal figures could make temporary use of someone else's animal if needed. But this may have been prearranged, with Mark's unusual "the Lord" (v. 3) serving as the agreed-upon sign.

11:3 Lord. Since elsewhere this refers to Jesus' divine identity (especially 1:3; see 2:28; 5:19; cf. v. 9), it indicates that he is also the temple's Lord returning to his house (Mal 3:1).

11:7 threw their cloaks over it. Evokes royal homage (cf. 2 Kgs 9:12–13).

11:8 spread branches. Evokes a deliverer's welcome. Since most pilgrims completed the journey on foot, Jesus' entry seems intended to evoke memories of Solomon's coronation (1 Kgs 1:38–48) and the latter's Messianic counterpart (Zech 9:9).

11:9–10 The crowd's acclamation is from Ps 118 (see note on 8:31).

11:9 Hosanna! A shortened form of "Lord, save us" (Ps 118:25); the rest is their Messianic interpretation of Ps 118:26. Ps 118 is a royal thanksgiving for the fulfillment of the kinds of victories promised in Ps 2 (see note on 1:11), which God has twice declared that Jesus fulfills (1:11; 9:7). It was sung on Passover in remembrance of the exodus and in anticipation of the last-days restoration of Israel in a new exodus under a victorious Davidic king. **comes in the name of the Lord.** In the authority and on behalf of God (see note on 9:37). Mark's readers know that Jesus is himself the Lord for whose coming Israel waits (see note on 1:2–3).

11:10 coming kingdom of our father David. The Messianic kingdom of David (see note on 1:1), whom Jewish tradition included among the nation's fathers (Acts 2:29; 4:25). Whereas the crowds anticipate the Messiah's defeat of Rome (see note on 8:30), Jesus' victories are those of God over Satan (see notes on 1:34; 3:27; cf. 5:1–20). The people have no idea that Jesus, in embracing the role of Isaiah's suffering servant, has rejected their militaristic dreams (8:31—9:1). More troubling

11:11 [d]Mt 21:12,17
11:13 [e]Lk 13:6-9
11:17 [f]Isa 56:7 [g]Jer 7:11
11:18 [h]Mt 21:46; Mk 12:12; Lk 20:19 [i]Mt 7:28
11:19 [j]Lk 21:37

11 Jesus entered Jerusalem and went into the temple courts. He looked around at everything, but since it was already late, he went out to Bethany with the Twelve.[d]

Jesus Curses a Fig Tree and Clears the Temple Courts

11:12-14pp — Mt 21:18-22
11:15-18pp — Mt 21:12-16; Lk 19:45-47; Jn 2:13-16
11:20-24pp — Mt 21:19-22

12 The next day as they were leaving Bethany, Jesus was hungry. 13 Seeing in the distance a fig tree in leaf, he went to find out if it had any fruit. When he reached it, he found nothing but leaves, because it was not the season for figs.[e] 14 Then he said to the tree, "May no one ever eat fruit from you again." And his disciples heard him say it.

15 On reaching Jerusalem, Jesus entered the temple courts and began driving out those who were buying and selling there. He overturned the tables of the money changers and the benches of those selling doves, 16 and would not allow anyone to carry merchandise through the temple courts. 17 And as he taught them, he said, "Is it not written: 'My house will be called a house of prayer for all nations'[a]?[f] But you have made it 'a den of robbers.'[b]"[g]

18 The chief priests and the teachers of the law heard this and began looking for a way to kill him, for they feared him,[h] because the whole crowd was amazed at his teaching.[i]

19 When evening came, Jesus and his disciples[c] went out of the city.[j]

[a] *17* Isaiah 56:7 [b] *17* Jer. 7:11 [c] *19* Some early manuscripts *came, Jesus*

is the absence of the priests, highlighted by the crowd's offering the blessing that in Ps 118:26 the priests were supposed to pronounce. In the context of ancient entries, the failure to welcome was an act of high treason—here, against God and Jesus, their Lord and king (see note on 11:1—13:37).

11:11 As its Lord, Jesus surveys the temple, probably in preparation for his action the following day. **went out.** Following an entry, a royal figure would be housed and entertained in the city. That Jesus is not and instead departs suggests that his city and house, as Malachi had warned, are not prepared for him (see note on 1:2–3).

11:12—12:44 *The Lord of the Temple Confronts the Temple Authorities.* Jesus announces judgment on the temple (11:13–14; see notes on 11:13,14,20) and clears the temple (11:15–26). This causes the confrontation between Jesus and the temple authorities to escalate (11:27—12:44), concluding with Jesus' announcement of the temple's coming destruction (ch. 13).

11:12—12:12 *Jesus Announces Judgment on the Temple.* Israel's Lord and Messiah now acts in judgment on a barren nation and the temple's treasonous tenants (see note on 12:9). As Mark's opening sentence warned (1:2–3), the temple authorities' rejection of John the Baptist, the Lord's Elijah sent to prepare the Lord's way (see note on 1:1–8; see also notes on 1:2–3,6), means they are unprepared for the Lord's coming in judgment, so the land is cursed (Mal 3:5; 4:5).

11:12–26 *Jesus Curses a Fig Tree and Clears the Temple Courts.* Jesus' last mighty deed before his death, the disturbing cursing of the fig tree contrasts bleakly with his jubilant welcome. Set on either side of Jesus' action in the temple, this enacted parable (see note on 4:35—5:43) illustrates the true significance of the "cleansing" of the temple (see vv. 15–17).

11:12 hungry. Recalls God's statement that his bringing Israel out of Egypt was like the joy of finding early figs (see note on v. 13) and his later complaint that Israel's idolatry and injustice rendered the nation barren, leaving his hunger for justice unsatisfied (Hos 9:7–17; Mic 6:1—7:6).

11:13 not the season for figs. Fig trees around Jerusalem normally begin to leaf in March or April, producing fruit only in June, when all their leaves are out. This tree is exceptional in that it has already fully leafed at Passover (in April), which aroused the expectation of early figs (see note on v. 12). The issue is not the tree but what Jesus' act symbolizes. In spite of God's gift of his law and the land, and especially his presence now in Jesus, Israel and its leaders have failed to produce the justice and mercy God desires (4:13–19; cf. 3:4–6; 7:6–8; 12:38–40).

11:14 May no one ever eat fruit from you again. Withered fig trees signified God's judgment on rebellious Israel (cf. Jer 8:13; Hos 9:16–17). Jesus, as Israel's Lord, enacts that image in fulfillment of Malachi's threatened curse upon the land (Mal 4:6; see notes on 1:2–3; 11:12—12:12) and hence his following announcement of the destruction of the temple (11:17; 13:2).

11:15,16 temple courts. The outermost court set aside for Gentile worship. The various activities mentioned were deemed necessary because pilgrims needed sacrificial animals and special coins to pay the temple tax; doves were the preferred offering for the poor (Lev 5:7). The problem was not the desire to meet the pilgrim's needs but how and where it was done (see note on v. 17). Jesus' actions evoke Zechariah's prophecy that on the day of the Lord all nations would come to his newly sanctified mountain and that corrupt merchants would no longer defile his holy house (Zech 14:21).

11:17 Quotes both Isa 56:7 and Jer 7:11. **My house.** God's house; but since God is uniquely present in Jesus and since Jesus is Lord of the temple, it is also Jesus' house (see note on 11:1—13:37). **prayer for all nations.** Presupposing Israel's call to be a light to the nations (Isa 42:6; see notes on 1:2–3,11). Turning the Gentile court into a marketplace meant it could no longer properly be the place of prayer for the nations that God had originally intended (Isa 56:7). **den.** Or "cave." **robbers.** Translated "rebels" in 15:27 (those crucified with Jesus). Jesus' use of Jer 7:11 likens the merchants, as well as the temple authorities who permitted their actions, to Jeremiah's generation, whose violent hypocrisy so defiled their worship that the Lord (see note on v. 3) gave his temple over to destruction (Jer 7:1,3,11). For the Lord Jesus (see note on 1:2–3), this present disregard of God's purposes constituted a similar rebellion (cf. 3:6,22–29; 7:6–13) that would similarly lead to the temple's destruction (13:2).

11:18 kill. As Jesus had foretold (8:31; 10:33–34). **feared.** Jesus might inspire the crowds to a popular uprising against them. **amazed.** Characteristically, it is the popular response to Jesus' extraordinary personal authority. See notes on 1:10,22.

11:19 went out. See note on v. 11.

[20]In the morning, as they went along, they saw the fig tree withered from the roots. [21]Peter remembered and said to Jesus, "Rabbi,[k] look! The fig tree you cursed has withered!"
[22]"Have faith in God," Jesus answered. [23]"Truly[a] I tell you, if anyone says to this mountain, 'Go,
throw yourself into the sea,' and does not doubt in their heart but believes that what they say will happen, it will be done for them.[l] [24]Therefore I tell you, whatever you ask for in prayer, believe that you have
received it, and it will be yours.[m] [25]And when you stand praying, if you hold anything against anyone,
forgive them, so that your Father in heaven may forgive you your sins."[n] [26] [b]

11:21 [k]Mt 23:7
11:23 [l]Mt 21:21
11:24 [m]Mt 7:7
11:25 [n]Mt 6:14
11:32 [o]Mt 11:9
12:1 [p]Isa 5:1-7

The Authority of Jesus Questioned

11:27-33pp — Mt 21:23-27; Lk 20:1-8

[27]They arrived again in Jerusalem, and while Jesus was walking in the temple courts, the chief
priests, the teachers of the law and the elders came to him. [28]"By what authority are you doing these
things?" they asked. "And who gave you authority to do this?"
[29]Jesus replied, "I will ask you one question. Answer me, and I will tell you by what authority I am
doing these things. [30]John's baptism — was it from heaven, or of human origin? Tell me!"
[31]They discussed it among themselves and said, "If we say, 'From heaven,' he will ask, 'Then why
didn't you believe him?' [32]But if we say, 'Of human origin' . . ." (They feared the people, for everyone
held that John really was a prophet.)[o]
[33]So they answered Jesus, "We don't know."
Jesus said, "Neither will I tell you by what authority I am doing these things."

The Parable of the Tenants

12:1-12pp — Mt 21:33-46; Lk 20:9-19

12 Jesus then began to speak to them in parables: "A man planted a vineyard.[p] He put a wall
around it, dug a pit for the winepress and built a watchtower. Then he rented the vineyard to
some farmers and moved to another place. [2]At harvest time he sent a servant to the tenants to collect

[a] *22,23* Some early manuscripts *"If you have faith in God," Jesus answered, [23]"truly* [b] *26* Some manuscripts include here words similar to Matt. 6:15.

11:20 withered from the roots. Symbolizes the devastating judgment coming on both Israel (which the fig tree represents, see notes on vv. 12,13; cf. 13:14–19) and its temple (11:15–17; cf. 13:2) for the failure of primarily the leaders but also the nation as a whole to produce the "fruits" of righteousness (see note on 12:1), i.e., to reflect the character of God.
11:21 Rabbi. See note on 4:38.
11:23 Truly I tell you. See note on 3:28. **this mountain.** Since Jesus and his disciples are outside the city, this most likely refers to the temple mount (cf. Pss 30:7; 99:9; Isa 2:2–3; 25:10; Zech 8:3), not the Mount of Olives. If the disciples remain faithful, even this mountain that has consistently blocked God's way through Jesus (see notes on 1:2–3) will be leveled (Isa 40:3–4).
11:24 prayer. See note on 9:29.
11:25 Prayer for God's intervention must be accompanied by extending God's mercy (see note on 10:47; cf. 9:33–50).
11:27–33 *The Authority of Jesus Questioned.* In response to the temple authorities' challenge, Jesus' penetrating question (v. 30) reveals that his justification for cleansing the Gentile court and announcing the temple's judgment stems directly from the authorities' refusal to submit to John's call to repentance (1:4–8).
11:27 walking in the temple courts. The temple's Lord again surveys his house (cf. v. 11). Instead of coming to Jesus to learn (e.g., 3:34–35; 4:10,34), the rebellious temple authorities (cf. vv. 9–10,18) gather to confront him.
11:30 heaven. A respectful substitute for "God." Jesus' question reveals the justification for his action. Since both John's baptism and Jesus are from God (see note on 1:2–3), the authorities' refusal to submit to John, Malachi's preparatory Elijah, means they also refuse to recognize Jesus' authority as the Lord of the temple and the Davidic King; hence their judgment (Mal 3:1–5; 4:5–6; see notes on 3:29; 9:13; 11:12—12:44; see also note on 11:12—12:12).
11:33 We don't know. An admission that ironically reveals their true condition. A few verses after the Isa 56:7 text that Jesus cites in v. 17 to justify his temple action, Isaiah describes Israel's leaders as "shepherds who lack understanding" and "seek their own gain" (Isa 56:11; cf. Jer 3:15 in view of Jer 7:11). This applies equally to the temple authorities who now confront Jesus.
12:1–12 *The Parable of the Tenants.* Jesus' last parable makes explicit the threat inherent in his earlier quotation of Jer 7:11 (see 11:17 and note): God will destroy the rebel temple authorities and give the care of his people and kingdom to others under the leadership of his vindicated Son, Jesus. The parable's pivotal role in moving from Jesus' authority questioned (11:27–33) to his authority demonstrated (12:13–37), its unmatched length (nearly twice as long as the parable of the sower in 4:3–8), and its complexity testify to its climactic importance in summing up God's response to an unrepentant and murderous leadership.
12:1 parables. See note on 4:2. Jesus previously used parables in response to the Jerusalem teachers' original repudiation of his casting out demons (see note on 3:23a). Jesus does so here in response to their final repudiation of John and himself (11:29–33; see note on 6:1–56). Both instances involve a clash over authority (3:22; 11:28). **vineyard.** Closely resembles Isaiah's account of God's loving provision for his "vineyard" Israel (Isa 5:1–2a; cf. Ps 80:8–9). Just as a faithless failure to produce the fruits of justice and righteousness became the grounds for God's judgment in the past, so they are also grounds for judgment in the present (Isa 5:2b–30; cf. 11:12–14; Jer 2:21).
12:2–5 The servants represent God's prophets, whom Israel regularly rejected (e.g., 2 Chr 36:15–16; cf. 1 Kgs 19:10; Matt 23:37).

12:6 [q]Heb 1:1-3
12:10 [r]Ac 4:11
12:11 [s]Ps 118:22,23
12:12 [t]Mk 11:18
[u]Mt 22:22
12:13 [v]Mt 22:16; Mk 3:6
[w]Mt 12:10

from them some of the fruit of the vineyard. 3But they seized him, beat him and sent him away empty-
handed. 4Then he sent another servant to them; they struck this man on the head and treated him
shamefully. 5He sent still another, and that one they killed. He sent many others; some of them they
beat, others they killed.
6"He had one left to send, a son, whom he loved. He sent him last of all,[q] saying, 'They will respect
my son.'
7"But the tenants said to one another, 'This is the heir. Come, let's kill him, and the inheritance will
be ours.' 8So they took him and killed him, and threw him out of the vineyard.
9"What then will the owner of the vineyard do? He will come and kill those tenants and give the
vineyard to others. 10Haven't you read this passage of Scripture:

> " 'The stone the builders rejected
> has become the cornerstone;[r]
> 11the Lord has done this,
> and it is marvelous in our eyes'[a]?"[s]

12Then the chief priests, the teachers of the law and the elders looked for a way to arrest him because they knew he had spoken the parable against them. But they were afraid of the crowd;[t] so they
left him and went away.[u]

Paying the Imperial Tax to Caesar

12:13-17pp — Mt 22:15-22; Lk 20:20-26

13Later they sent some of the Pharisees and Herodians[v] to Jesus to catch him[w] in his words. 14They
came to him and said, "Teacher, we know that you are a man of integrity. You aren't swayed by others,
because you pay no attention to who they are; but you teach the way of God in accordance with the
truth. Is it right to pay the imperial tax[b] to Caesar or not? 15Should we pay or shouldn't we?"
But Jesus knew their hypocrisy. "Why are you trying to trap me?" he asked. "Bring me a denarius and let
me look at it." 16They brought the coin, and he asked them, "Whose image is this? And whose inscription?"

[a] *11* Psalm 118:22,23 [b] *14* A special tax levied on subject peoples, not on Roman citizens

12:6 whom he loved. This phrase appears only twice previously in Mark, both occurring when God declared that Jesus is his Son, "whom I love" (1:11; 9:7). Both statements clearly echo Ps 2:7, wherein God affirms the inheritance of his Messianic son (Ps 2:8) against those who refuse to submit to his rule (Ps 2:9–12). Psalm 2's warnings were directed against the nations that conspired against God's anointed (Ps 2:1,10). To the extent that the temple authorities do the same, they will come under the same judgment.
12:9 kill. Or "destroy" the chief priests, the teachers of the law and the elders (v. 12), in keeping with God's promises in Ps 2 (see note on v. 6), his just character (cf. 1 Kgs 21:17–19), and the judgment implied by Jesus' cursing of the fig tree and his action in the temple (11:12–23). **vineyard.** God's people as reconstituted around Jesus (3:13–19,31–35). If the tenants are the chief priests, the teachers of the law and the elders (v. 12; 11:18), then the "others" are apparently the Twelve (Matt 19:28; Luke 22:30; cf. note on 3:13–19).
12:10–11 Jesus quotes Ps 118:22–23, a psalm the crowds cited earlier as prophesying David's Messianic kingdom (11:9–10, quoting Ps 118:25–26).
12:10 builders. The religious leaders, teachers, and lawyers. **rejected.** The same word occurs in Jesus' first foretelling of his coming death (8:31). **cornerstone.** Probably means the "capstone," used to complete an arch or the pinnacle of a building. In Ps 118 it symbolizes the Davidic king vindicated by God as the nation's rightful leader and therefore the Messiah. In some Jewish traditions the stone also symbolized the Messiah's restoration of the temple in which God's returning presence would dwell (see note on 1:11). Jesus, confident of God's vindication through the resurrection (8:31b), declares the futility of the authorities' plan. As the one in whom God is uniquely present to forgive, heal, and share fellowship, Jesus and his followers will become the new "temple" of prayer for all nations (11:17) in whom God's Spirit dwells (cf. 2 Cor 6:16; Eph 2:21).
12:13–44 *The Temple's Lord Teaches in His House.* The temple courts were where Israel was instructed in God's ways. Echoing earlier confrontations (2:1—3:6), the temple authorities send various groups of Jewish authorities to challenge Jesus' teaching (vv. 12–13). Confounding them with his astonishing answers and his own penetrating questions (vv. 35–37), Jesus demonstrates his unmatched authority as the teacher of Israel. His concluding condemnation of the teachers of the law (vv. 38–40) and the account of the poverty-stricken widow giving her all (vv. 41–44) to maintain a magnificent temple (cf. 13:1) and its functionaries testify to the failure of Israel (the "fig tree") to produce the "fruits" of justice and mercy (see note on 11:13).
12:13–17 *Paying the Imperial Tax to Caesar.* Some Pharisees and Herodians seek to trap Jesus by calling into question his loyalty: was he loyal to God or Caesar?
12:13 Pharisees and Herodians. They very early colluded to seek Jesus' death (see notes on 2:16; 3:6).
12:14 imperial tax. See NIV text note. The Romans introduced direct collection of tribute in AD 6. It was immensely unpopular, with some Jews refusing to pay because it implied that the idolatrous emperor ("Caesar"), not God, was king.
12:15 Identical in intent to their earlier question on divorce (see note on 10:2), the Pharisees calculate that Jesus' answer will either alienate the crowds (11:8–10) or enable them to denounce Jesus to the Roman authorities as a rebel. **hypocrisy.** See 7:6–7. **trap.** See 8:11; 10:2. **denarius.** A silver coin required for paying the tax (see note on 6:37).
12:16 image ... inscription. On one side of the denarius was an image

"Caesar's," they replied.

[17]Then Jesus said to them, "Give back to Caesar what is Caesar's and to God what is God's."[x] And they were amazed at him.

Marriage at the Resurrection

12:18-27pp — Mt 22:23-33; Lk 20:27-38

[18]Then the Sadducees,[y] who say there is no resurrection,[z] came to him with a question. [19]"Teacher," they said, "Moses wrote for us that if a man's brother dies and leaves a wife but no children, the man must marry the widow and raise up offspring for his brother.[a] [20]Now there were seven brothers. The first one married and died without leaving any children. [21]The second one married the widow, but he also died, leaving no child. It was the same with the third. [22]In fact, none of the seven left any children. Last of all, the woman died too. [23]At the resurrection[a] whose wife will she be, since the seven were married to her?"

[24]Jesus replied, "Are you not in error because you do not know the Scriptures[b] or the power of God? [25]When the dead rise, they will neither marry nor be given in marriage; they will be like the angels in heaven.[c] [26]Now about the dead rising — have you not read in the Book of Moses, in the account of the burning bush, how God said to him, 'I am the God of Abraham, the God of Isaac, and the God of Jacob'[b]?[d] [27]He is not the God of the dead, but of the living. You are badly mistaken!"

The Greatest Commandment

12:28-34pp — Mt 22:34-40

[28]One of the teachers of the law[e] came and heard them debating. Noticing that Jesus had given them a good answer, he asked him, "Of all the commandments, which is the most important?"

[29]"The most important one," answered Jesus, "is this: 'Hear, O Israel: The Lord our God, the Lord is one.[c] [30]Love the Lord your God with all your heart and with all your soul and with all your mind and with all your strength.'[d][f] [31]The second is this: 'Love your neighbor as yourself.'[e][g] There is no commandment greater than these."

12:17 [x]Ro 13:7
12:18 [y]Ac 4:1 [z]Ac 23:8; 1Co 15:12
12:19 [a]Dt 25:5
12:24 [b]2Ti 3:15-17
12:25 [c]1Co 15:42,49,52
12:26 [d]Ex 3:6
12:28 [e]Lk 10:25-28; 20:39
12:30 [f]Dt 6:4,5
12:31 [g]Lev 19:18; Mt 5:43

[a] *23* Some manuscripts *resurrection, when people rise from the dead,* [b] *26* Exodus 3:6 [c] *29* Or *The Lord our God is one Lord* [d] *30* Deut. 6:4,5 [e] *31* Lev. 19:18

of Caesar, and on the other side was the inscription "Son of divine Augustus"; both offended pious Jews.

12:17 Jesus rejects their either-or approach. Obligations to God and state are not necessarily in conflict (e.g., Rom 13:1–7; 1 Tim 2:1–3; Titus 3:1–2; 1 Pet 2:13–17), though obedience to God takes unquestioned priority (1 Sam 13:13–14; 2 Sam 12:1–15; 1 Kgs 13:1–3; Jer 20:3–6; Acts 5:29). Jesus might also imply, as he had earlier (see note on 3:27), that Israel's fundamental problem is not Rome but their own need to give God his due, namely, repentance (1:4–5,15) coming from wholehearted love (12:30) of the one whose image they bear (in contrast to image on the coin, cf. note on v. 16).

12:18–27 *Marriage at the Resurrection.* Assuming Jesus' belief in the resurrection, some Sadducees seek to show that the law of Moses implies Jesus is mistaken.

12:18 Sadducees. Comprised of mostly aristocrats and prominent priestly families (8:31; 11:18) who dominated Israel's ruling council, the Sanhedrin (see note on 14:55). Religiously conservative, they recognized only the five books of Moses (Genesis–Deuteronomy) as divinely authoritative and rejected the idea of resurrection since, on their reading, it did not support resurrection.

12:19 Assumes Moses' principle of levirate marriage (Deut 25:5–6), which protected a deceased brother's widow and his family line.

12:25 The angels do not die, and since the resurrection is to eternal life, there is no need for procreation in the world to come (cf. note on 10:6–8).

12:26–27 Book of Moses ... I am the God of Abraham, ... Isaac, and ... Jacob ... not the God of the dead, but of the living. In appealing not only to Moses but to the very words of God at the moment of his first self-revelation to Moses (Exod 3:3–6), Jesus meets the Sadducees' objection on their own ground (see note on v. 18). Because the "I AM" (Exod 3:14; see note there) is everlasting, so are his covenant relationships, which death cannot terminate (cf. Exod 4:1–11 where God demonstrates to a doubting Moses his power over life and death). Since the unchanging and faithful God is the God of the living, the patriarchs, though dead, must one day live; hence, there must be a future resurrection.

12:27 badly mistaken! The Sadducees' assumptions are false (cf. v. 17; 10:5–8). Their theology started with human expectations instead of Scripture's revelation.

12:28–34 *The Greatest Commandment.* This is the last question asked of Jesus during his time in the temple courts (cf. 11:27). In contrast to the preceding hostile questions (vv. 13–27), a passing teacher of the law, impressed by Jesus' response to the Sadducees (vv. 24–27), respectfully (cf. vv. 32,34) seeks Jesus' summation of the law.

12:28 teachers of the law. See note on 1:22. **good answer.** A more neutral expert observer affirms the quality of Jesus' teaching. **most important.** Given the number of regulations (Jewish rabbis counted 613 commandments in the Pentateuch, which could be overwhelming for most common people), various attempts were made to express the heart of the law. Jesus responds with two (vv. 29–31).

12:29 Hear, O Israel. See Deut 6:4–5. This is the central confession of Jewish identity, derived from the heart of Israel's covenant (Deut 6:4–19).

12:30 heart ... soul ... mind ... strength. The entirety of one's being. That Jesus has already demanded this kind of loyalty to himself and his gospel (8:34–35; 10:21,29) further underlines the claim that God's very presence has come in Jesus (see note on 1:2–3).

12:31 Because God loved and showed mercy to Israel, individual Israelites must love and show mercy to each other, which for Jesus includes the least (9:33 — 10:12; see note on 10:47). **neighbor.** The definition is left open, but it is given in Luke 10:29–37.

12:32 [h]Dt 4:35,39; Isa 45:6,14; 46:9
12:33 [i]1Sa 15:22; Hos 6:6; Mic 6:6-8; Heb 10:8
12:34 [j]Mt 3:2 [k]Mt 22:46; Lk 20:40
12:35 [l]Mt 26:55 [m]Mt 9:27
12:36 [n]2Sa 23:2 [o]Ps 110:1; Mt 22:44
12:37 [p]Jn 12:9
12:39 [q]Lk 11:43

32 "Well said, teacher," the man replied. "You are right in saying that God is one and there is no
other but him.[h] 33 To love him with all your heart, with all your understanding and with all your
strength, and to love your neighbor as yourself is more important than all burnt offerings and
sacrifices."[i]

34 When Jesus saw that he had answered wisely, he said to him, "You are not far from the kingdom
of God."[j] And from then on no one dared ask him any more questions.[k]

Whose Son Is the Messiah?

12:35-37pp — Mt 22:41-46; Lk 20:41-44
12:38-40pp — Mt 23:1-7; Lk 20:45-47

35 While Jesus was teaching in the temple courts,[l] he asked, "Why do the teachers of the law say that
the Messiah is the son of David?[m] 36 David himself, speaking by the Holy Spirit,[n] declared:

"'The Lord said to my Lord:
"Sit at my right hand
until I put your enemies
under your feet."'[a][o]

37 David himself calls him 'Lord.' How then can he be his son?"

The large crowd[p] listened to him with delight.

Warning Against the Teachers of the Law

38 As he taught, Jesus said, "Watch out for the teachers of the law. They like to walk around in flowing robes and be greeted with respect in the marketplaces, 39 and have the most important seats in the
synagogues and the places of honor at banquets.[q] 40 They devour widows' houses and for a show make
lengthy prayers. These men will be punished most severely."

[a] *36* Psalm 110:1

12:32 Well said, teacher. Coming from an expert, this testifies to Jesus' orthodoxy. **teacher.** See note on 4:38.

12:33 more important than all burnt offerings and sacrifices. The lawyer's expansion of Jesus' unspecified "no commandment" (v. 31) is appropriate in the temple setting and reflects a major concern of the prophets (e.g., Isa 1:10–23; Jer 7:22–23; Hos 6:6). It implicitly justifies Jesus' earlier cursing of the fig tree and his action in the temple (11:12–25; cf. Jer 7:11 in Mark 11:17).

12:34 wisely. He discerned the core of Jesus' teaching better than the disciples did (9:33–50; 10:35–41). Jesus' earlier linking of his coming sacrifice with how one treats others (see notes on 9:35; 10:42–45) suggests that the same principle applies. For Jesus' followers to confess his death without love of neighbor is equally empty (cf. Matt 7:12; Jas 2:10–23). **not far.** All that he lacks is to follow Jesus, who in himself embodies the secret of the kingdom (see notes on 4:11; 10:21). **kingdom of God.** See note on 1:15. **no one dared ask him any more questions.** Jesus is proved Israel's teacher par excellence not only by answering well but by readily discerning between hypocritical, misconceived, and genuine questions. As the Lord of the temple (see 11:14 and note) and God's "cornerstone" (v. 10), Jesus' claim that doing God's will means listening to him (3:34–35) has been vindicated by God (cf. 9:7) here in the temple's courts before the nation and its authorities (cf. "builders" in v. 10). The lawyer is an important reminder that not every authority in Jerusalem opposed Jesus.

12:35–37 *Whose Son Is the Messiah?* This is Jesus' final engagement with the authorities in the temple courts. His questions challenge the assumption of the teachers of the law that the Messiah is merely David's human son.

12:35 Jesus takes the initiative by asking his own questions, once again revealing the mistaken assumptions of Israel's teachers (cf. vv. 17,26–27). **teachers of the law.** See note on 1:22. **son of David.** See notes on 1:11; 10:47.

12:36 by the Holy Spirit. David was prophesying concerning the Messiah (v. 35). Echoing Ps 2's warnings not to conspire against God's Davidic king (Ps 2:1–6,9–12), Ps 110:1 has God seating David at his right hand while he subdues the rebels. Since Ps 2 is fulfilled in Jesus (see vv. 6,9; 1:11; 9:7; 11:9–10), Ps 110 applies equally to him and its judgments equally to his enemies. His enemies, however, are no longer the nations but the temple authorities.

12:37 Because fathers do not call their sons "Lord," the Messiah must be more than merely David's son. And since Jesus has just declared that there is only one Lord (v. 29), the Messiah must also be that very Lord among them. Jesus is both Lord and Christ (cf. 1 Cor 8:6), as Mark's readers already know well (cf. 1:2–3; 2:10; 4:41).

12:38–40 *Warning Against the Teachers of the Law.* His questions unanswered, Jesus now condemns the "teachers of the law" (v. 38; see note on 1:22; cf. vv. 28,32,35; 11:18,27).

12:38 flowing robes. Long, white linen garments with fringes that signified high status.

12:39 most important seats. A bench at the front of the synagogue nearest the "ark" that contained the Scriptural scrolls.

12:40 devour widows' houses. Employing various shady financial practices, they took advantage of vulnerable widows, eventually leaving them homeless. In defrauding someone else's mother (cf. note on 7:11–13), they have loved neither their neighbor nor God (vv. 28–34), and their lack of mercy has made their prayers empty (see note on 11:25). The prophets condemned such abuses (Isa 1:23; Ezek 22:7), and Malachi includes it in his list of evils that God's coming will set right (Mal 3:5; see note on 1:2–3). Their actions stand in direct opposition to Jesus' teaching on the treatment of others (9:33—10:12).

The Widow's Offering

12:41-44pp — Lk 21:1-4

41 Jesus sat down opposite the place where the offerings were put[r] and watched the crowd putting
their money into the temple treasury. Many rich people threw in large amounts. 42 But a poor widow
came and put in two very small copper coins, worth only a few cents.
43 Calling his disciples to him, Jesus said, "Truly I tell you, this poor widow has put more into the
treasury than all the others. 44 They all gave out of their wealth; but she, out of her poverty, put in
everything—all she had to live on."[s]

The Destruction of the Temple and Signs of the End Times

13:1-37pp — Mt 24:1-51; Lk 21:5-36

13 As Jesus was leaving the temple, one of his disciples said to him, "Look, Teacher! What massive
stones! What magnificent buildings!"
2 "Do you see all these great buildings?" replied Jesus. "Not one stone here will be left on another;
every one will be thrown down."[t]
3 As Jesus was sitting on the Mount of Olives[u] opposite the temple, Peter, James, John[v] and Andrew
asked him privately, 4 "Tell us, when will these things happen? And what will be the sign that they are
all about to be fulfilled?"
5 Jesus said to them: "Watch out that no one deceives you.[w] 6 Many will come in my name, claiming,

12:41 [r] 2Ki 12:9; Jn 8:20
12:44 [s] 2Co 8:12
13:2 [t] Lk 19:44
13:3 [u] Mt 21:1 [v] Mt 4:21
13:5 [w] ver 22; Jer 29:8; Eph 5:6; 2Th 2:3,10-12; 1Ti 4:1; 2Ti 3:13; 1Jn 4:6

12:41–44 *The Widow's Offering.* The treasury was located in the court of women and contained 13 trumpet-shaped receptacles for mandatory tithes and voluntary gifts. The genuine greatness of the widow's humble devotion (yet another sign of the faithfulness of some in Jerusalem, v. 34) contrasts with the ostentatious behavior of the teachers of the law, which Jesus had just denounced.
12:42 small copper coins. The smallest coins in circulation, worth less than one-hundredth of a denarius (see note on 6:37).
12:43–44 Jesus' final word in the temple is to commend this widow's exemplary devotion to God (cf. 10:21–23,28).
12:43 Truly I tell you. See note on 3:28.
13:1–37 *The End of an Era: God's Judgment on Jerusalem and Its Impure Temple.* The coming destruction of the temple flows naturally out of the preceding material. The authorities' failure to welcome their Lord and Messiah (11:9–11,27–33) and their murderous intent (11:18) mark them as rebellious tenants whose fate is sealed (12:9–10), along with that of the temple and Jerusalem (11:12–23). The longest connected block of Jesus' teaching in Mark, this section is commonly known as the Olivet discourse (v. 3; cf. Matt 24:1—25:46). It opens with (1) Jesus' prophecy of the temple's destruction and the disciples' questions concerning its timing and preceding sign (vv. 1–4). Jesus' response interweaves answers to both questions, beginning with (2) warnings against deceivers and false signs that are but the beginning (vv. 5–8) and (3) exhortations to stand firm to the end in proclaiming the gospel to all nations (vv. 9–13). Jesus then offers (4) the particular sign of "the abomination that causes desolation" (v. 14) and the terrible distress it heralds (vv. 14–23), which leads finally to (5) Jerusalem's destruction and the coming of the Son of Man (vv. 24–27). Jesus concludes with (6) the lesson "this generation" (v. 30) should learn from the fig tree (vv. 28–31) and (7) a final summons to watchfulness because the exact time is unknown (vv. 32–37). Jesus' use of imagery that is largely unfamiliar to modern readers has resulted in a wide range of interpretations. But just as the prophets have been central to Jesus' message to this point, so they also are here.
13:1–31 *The Destruction of the Temple and Signs of the End Times.* This is one of the more difficult passages in Mark. There is general agreement that Jesus' initial prophecy (v. 2) concerns the destruction of Jerusalem by the Romans in AD 70. While for some vv. 5–31 continue to deal with that destruction, others see an interwoven reference to the second coming (e.g., vv. 14–27 or vv. 24–27), with some suggesting that vv. 24–27 have a double fulfillment in both the AD 70 destruction and the second coming. Alternatively, some see vv. 5–31 dealing with only the second coming.
13:1 leaving the temple. Although the temple has been the center of his activities since 11:11, Jesus leaves it forever. Soon to be replaced by Jesus and his followers (see note on 12:10), the temple disappears from Mark except for a fleeting comment on its torn curtain (15:38). Jesus' final withdrawal to the Mount of Olives recalls God's departure to the east when he earlier abandoned the temple to the Babylonians (Ezek 10:18–19; 11:22–23; cf. Deut 31:18). **What massive stones!** Some of the temple's foundational stones were up to 37 feet (11 meters) long, 12 feet (3.5 meters) high, and 18 feet (5.5 meters) wide. Seemingly oblivious to Jesus' praise of the humble widow (12:43–44) and his acts signifying the temple's judgment (11:12–23), this unnamed disciple remains impressed by the temple's outward greatness (see notes on 11:12,13,14).
13:2 Not one stone. Over against the temple's apparent permanence, this recalls earlier prophetic judgments upon Jerusalem (Jer 7:14; Mic 3:12; cf. Jer 7:11 in Mark 11:17). Because the temple authorities rejected Jesus, God's "stone" (12:10), all of the temple's stones will be scattered.
13:3 sitting. See note on 4:1. **Mount of Olives.** See note on 11:1. **Peter, James, John and Andrew.** The first disciples Jesus called (1:16–20). As they bore witness to the beginning of Jesus' proclamation of the Lord's return to Jerusalem (see note on 1:2–3), they do the same as that return reaches its tragic climax. **privately.** This teaching is for "insiders" (see note on 3:31–35).
13:4 when ... what. Jesus addresses both the "when" and "the sign" throughout, but he specifically links the two in v. 14. **these things ... all.** The events surrounding the temple's destruction.
13:5 Watch out. A frequent refrain (vv. 9,23,33,35,37). Jesus is concerned that his disciples be neither deceived nor alarmed by earlier events (including persecution, vv. 5–13,21–31) and that they escape the destruction when it finally comes (vv. 14–20).
13:6 I am he. Said by individuals claiming to be Israel's military deliverer (see note on 8:30). Josephus mentions several such pretenders leading up to the temple's destruction in AD 70 (*Antiquities*, 20.97–99,167–172; *Wars*, 2.261–263; 7.437–438; cf. Acts 5:35–37; 21:38).

Lepta, the nearly worthless coins put into the offering by the widow (Mark 12:42).
© Lee Prince/age fotostock

13:9 [x] Mt 10:17
13:11 [y] Mt 10:19,20; Lk 12:11,12
13:12 [z] Mic 7:6; Mt 10:21; Lk 12:51-53
13:13 [a] Jn 15:21 [b] Mt 10:22
13:14 [c] Da 9:27; 11:31; 12:11

'I am he,' and will deceive many. 7When you hear of wars and rumors of wars, do not be alarmed.
Such things must happen, but the end is still to come. 8Nation will rise against nation, and kingdom
against kingdom. There will be earthquakes in various places, and famines. These are the beginning
of birth pains.

9"You must be on your guard. You will be handed over to the local councils and flogged in the
synagogues.[x] On account of me you will stand before governors and kings as witnesses to them.
10And the gospel must first be preached to all nations. 11Whenever you are arrested and brought to
trial, do not worry beforehand about what to say. Just say whatever is given you at the time, for it is not
you speaking, but the Holy Spirit.[y]

12"Brother will betray brother to death, and a father his child. Children will rebel against their parents and have them put to death.[z] 13Everyone will hate you because of me,[a] but the one who stands
firm to the end will be saved.[b]

14"When you see 'the abomination that causes desolation'[a][c] standing where it[b] does not belong—let the reader understand—then let those who are in Judea flee to the mountains. 15Let
no one on the housetop go down or enter the house to take anything out. 16Let no one in the field
go back to get their cloak. 17How dreadful it will be in those days for pregnant women and nursing

[a] *14* Daniel 9:27; 11:31; 12:11 [b] *14* Or *he*

13:7–8 God previously used wars (e.g., Isa 10:28–34; Jer 24:10), earthquakes (e.g., Isa 13:13; 29:6; Nah 1:5–6), and famines (e.g., Isa 14:30; Jer 11:22) as judgments on the nations and Israel. The OT often likens them to birth pains, signifying inescapable distress (e.g., Isa 13:8; Jer 6:24; Mic 4:9–10). But reports of these events occurring, as they did elsewhere in the empire, do not signal "the end" (v. 7), i.e., God's judgment on the temple (cf. Jer 13:19; 49:37; Nah 1:8).

13:9–13 Jesus summarizes what will be the experience of his followers after Pentecost (e.g., Acts 4:8; 5:17; 7:55; 8:1–2; 12:1–4; 13:49–50; 14:19–20; 23:1–11; 2 Cor 11:24).

13:10 gospel ... to all nations. The proclamation of the story of what God has done through Jesus (1:1,14–15) to all people without distinction, such as Acts describes (e.g., Acts 8:4–40; 10:1–48; 11:19–21; 13:44–48). Through Jesus and his renewed people, God's plan to bring blessing and light to the nations (cf. Gen 12:2; Deut 4:5–8; Isa 49:6; 60:3; see note on 1:11) will succeed in spite of Israel's hostility (e.g., Acts 3:25; 10:34–35,45; 11:18; Gal 3:26–29).

13:13 stands firm to the end. Without ever giving in (cf. Lam 3:26; Mic 7:7; Zeph 3:8; Heb 3:6,14; 6:11–12; 10:36).

13:14 abomination that causes desolation. The sign requested in v. 4b. This difficult expression is based on Dan 12:11 (cf. Dan 9:27; 11:31) and describes the setting up an altar to Zeus in the temple by Antiochus IV Epiphanes in 167 BC during the most horrific persecution Israel ever experienced to that time (167–164 BC; in the Apocrypha see 1 Maccabees 1:54–64; see also Josephus, *Antiquities*, 12.248–264). Some see this as a similarly defiling object set up in the temple by either the Romans (e.g., their idolatrous military standards) or the antichrist (cf. 2 Thess 2:3–4; Rev 13:14–15). Others suggest that since (1) throughout Scripture it is Israel's abominations that result in the desolation of the temple and land (2 Chr 26:14–21; Jer 7:30–34; Ezek 5:9–14; cf. Lev 26:30–33), (2) those who reject Jesus are regarded as rebels (see note on 11:17), and (3) "standing" (a masculine participle in the Greek text) indicates something personal, it could refer to an action by one of the false deliverers of v. 6 (perhaps the atrocities of AD 67–68 committed in the temple under John of Gischala and Eleazer son of Simon [Josephus, *Wars*, 4.147–157,160]). On this view, having rejected God's servant-Messiah, Israel's alternatives are as idolatrous and vicious as those of Antiochus. **mountains.** The Judean hills to which the fugitives from the Babylonian armies had previously fled (Ezek 7:16; cf. 1 Sam 26:1). For some, this flight will have a second fulfillment in the end times.

mothers![d] 18 Pray that this will not take place in winter, 19 because those will be days of distress unequaled from the beginning, when God created the world,[e] until now—and never to be equaled
again.[f]
20 "If the Lord had not cut short those days, no one would survive. But for the sake of the elect, whom
he has chosen, he has shortened them. 21 At that time if anyone says to you, 'Look, here is the Messiah!'
or, 'Look, there he is!' do not believe it.[g] 22 For false messiahs and false prophets[h] will appear and perform signs and wonders[i] to deceive, if possible, even the elect. 23 So be on your guard;[j] I have told you
everything ahead of time.
24 "But in those days, following that distress,

"'the sun will be darkened,
and the moon will not give its light;
25 the stars will fall from the sky,
and the heavenly bodies will be shaken.'[a][k]

26 "At that time people will see the Son of Man coming in clouds[l] with great power and glory. 27 And
he will send his angels and gather his elect from the four winds, from the ends of the earth to the ends
of the heavens.[m]
28 "Now learn this lesson from the fig tree: As soon as its twigs get tender and its leaves come out, you
know that summer is near. 29 Even so, when you see these things happening, you know that it[b] is near,
right at the door. 30 Truly I tell you, this generation[n] will certainly not pass away until all these things
have happened.[o] 31 Heaven and earth will pass away, but my words will never pass away.[p]

[a] *25* Isaiah 13:10; 34:4 [b] *29* Or *he*

13:17 [d] Lk 23:29
13:19 [e] Mk 10:6 [f] Da 9:26; 12:1; Joel 2:2
13:21 [g] Lk 17:23; 21:8
13:22 [h] Mt 7:15 [i] Jn 4:48; 2Th 2:9,10
13:23 [j] 2Pe 3:17
13:25 [k] Isa 13:10; 34:4; Mt 24:29
13:26 [l] Da 7:13; Mt 16:27; Rev 1:7
13:27 [m] Zec 2:6
13:30 [n] Lk 17:25 [o] Mk 9:1
13:31 [p] Mt 5:18

13:19 distress unequaled. For some this is a literal statement covering all of human history throughout the millennia. For others, it is a figure of speech (cf. Exod 11:6) deliberately echoing Dan 12:1, which describes the suffering caused by Antiochus. Since Israel's false deliverers (v. 6) are as violent as Antiochus (see note on v. 14), their abominable "salvation" brings equally unparalleled distress, whether directly by their own hands or, as a consequence and in even greater degree, through the Romans. Some locate this distress in the time of the antichrist. **never … again.** This is not in Dan 12:1. For some, Jesus' use of "again" suggests a continuation of history, which means that this event, since it does not usher in the second coming, refers only to the destruction of Jerusalem in AD 70. For others, it is precisely because this distress will never again be equaled that it must immediately precede the second coming.
13:20 cut short. Characteristic of God's mercy even in judgment (cf. Isa 1:9; Zech 13:8). **those days.** The events of vv. 14–19. **no one.** Addressed to those living in Judea at that time, it reflects prophetic hyperbole marking the severity of God's judgments against Jerusalem (Jer 12:12; 13:14; Lam 2:22; cf. "not one stone" in v. 2). **elect.** Chosen; the traditional description first of Israel as a whole (Deut 7:7; 10:15; 14:2; Amos 3:2), then later of the faithful remnant (Isa 41:8; 65:9), and now transferred to the Israel reconstituted around Jesus (see note on 3:14; cf. Rom 8:33; Col 3:12; Rev 17:14).
13:21 Messiah. See notes on v. 6; 1:1; 8:29,30.
13:22 false prophets. Josephus speaks of several first-century prophets who promised to perform various wonders that recalled God's acts in the exodus and conquest (*Antiquities*, 20.97,168,170; *Wars*, 7.438).
13:24–25 "In those days, following that distress" (v. 24) links these verses with the immediately preceding events (vv. 14–23). Some think that Jesus here refers to his second coming; others, that he is speaking of his vindication over a rebellious Jewish leadership when Jerusalem was destroyed by the Romans in AD 70. **that distress.** See vv. 14–19. **sun … shaken.** A combined quotation (see note on 1:2–3) of Isa 13:10 and Isa 34:4 (cf. Ezek 32:3–8; Joel 2:2–10,31; 3:9–15). For some this is a reference to physical cosmic events in the end times; others see it as prophetic imagery using the language of the disintegration of creation to express the overwhelming nature of God's judgments through human armies, in this instance, against Jerusalem. In citing these texts Jesus might imply that Jerusalem has become like arrogant Babylon (Isa 13) and treacherous Edom (Isa 34) and will therefore face similar divine judgment.
13:26 Son of Man coming … glory. Citing Dan 7:13–14 in fulfillment of Jesus' earlier declaration to "this adulterous and sinful generation" (8:38; see note). His earlier entry into Jerusalem having been rejected (see note on 11:1—13:37; see also notes on 11:9,10), Jesus' second coming will be in power and dominion to establish his eternal kingdom over the beast-like nations (Dan 7:2–27). For some this refers to the second coming. Others see it is a prophetic image that Jesus interprets as referring to his vindication as his gospel, having been rejected by a soon-to-be-destroyed Jerusalem (see note on vv. 24–25), spreads throughout the nations (see note on v. 27).
13:27 angels. Or "messengers"; either humans (cf. 1:2; Luke 7:24; 9:52) or angels associated with God's work (Heb 1:14). **gather … winds … heavens.** Scriptural language that describes God's saving redemption of his people from exile (cf. Deut 30:4; Zech 2:6). Jesus, as the glorified Son of Man and in fulfillment of God's promises, will redeem all of God's people, now comprised of believing Jews and Gentiles from every nation (cf. Rom 15:12; Gal 3:8; 1 Tim 3:16; Rev 7:9). This could refer to either the results of proclaiming the gospel (v. 10; see Acts 18:1–11; Gal 4:14) within that generation (see note on v. 30) or the events of the second coming. **elect.** See note on v. 20.
13:29 these things. The events leading up to the time of distress and its dual aftermath (vv. 14–27). **it.** Or "he" (see NIV text note on vv. 14,29), which fits with the previous mention of the coming Son of Man (vv. 26–27). Alternatively, "it" better suits the disciples' initial question concerning the destruction of Jerusalem (v. 2; cf. "you," meaning the disciples, four times in vv. 28–30). **near.** See note on 1:15.
13:30 Truly I tell you. See note on 3:28. **this generation … all these things.** If vv. 5–27 answer the disciples' initial question concerning Jerusalem's destruction (v. 4; see note on vv. 1–31), then "this generation" is straightforwardly the one to which the disciples belong,

13:32 [q] Ac 1:7; 1Th 5:1,2
13:33 [r] 1Th 5:6
13:34 [s] Mt 25:14
13:37 [t] Lk 12:35-40
14:1 [u] Jn 11:55; 13:1
[v] Mt 12:14
14:3 [w] Mt 21:17
[x] Lk 7:37-39

The Day and Hour Unknown

[32]"But about that day or hour no one knows, not even the angels in heaven, nor the Son, but only
the Father.[q] [33]Be on guard! Be alert[a]![r] You do not know when that time will come. [34]It's like a man
going away: He leaves his house and puts his servants[s] in charge, each with their assigned task, and
tells the one at the door to keep watch.
[35]"Therefore keep watch because you do not know when the owner of the house will come back—
whether in the evening, or at midnight, or when the rooster crows, or at dawn. [36]If he comes suddenly,
do not let him find you sleeping. [37]What I say to you, I say to everyone: 'Watch!'"[t]

Jesus Anointed at Bethany

14:1-11pp — Mt 26:2-16
14:1,2,10,11pp — Lk 22:1-6
14:3-8Ref — Jn 12:1-8

14 Now the Passover[u] and the Festival of Unleavened Bread were only two days away, and the chief
priests and the teachers of the law were scheming to arrest Jesus secretly and kill him.[v] [2]"But
not during the festival," they said, "or the people may riot."
[3]While he was in Bethany,[w] reclining at the table in the home of Simon the Leper, a woman came
with an alabaster jar of very expensive perfume, made of pure nard. She broke the jar and poured the
perfume on his head.[x]
[4]Some of those present were saying indignantly to one another, "Why this waste of perfume? [5]It
could have been sold for more than a year's wages[b] and the money given to the poor." And they rebuked her harshly.

[a] *33* Some manuscripts *alert and pray*   [b] *5* Greek *than three hundred denarii*

and "all these things" simply means the events leading up to and including (1) the city's AD 70 judgment, (2) Jesus' vindication through his resurrection and ascension, and (3) his gathering of God's true people from all nations through the gospel. If, however, "all these things" is taken to mean events associated with the second coming, then "this generation" refers to those alive at that time (though "that generation" would be better grammar). For those who see a double fulfillment, both are in view, while others interpret "this generation" to mean either believers, unbelievers (cf. "sinful generation" in 8:38), or the nation of Israel throughout the entire church age.

13:32–37 *The Day and the Hour Unknown.* For most, the specific opening phrase "that day" (v. 32) indicates that Jesus is now speaking of his second coming (cf. note on vv. 24–25). Some, however, find such a shift abrupt and overly subtle and therefore see this as Jesus continuing to address the AD 70 destruction of Jerusalem.

13:32 that day or hour. "That day" is a common prophetic expression for the day of God's decisive intervention, whether in the past (e.g., Isa 7:18; Jer 4:9) or in the future (e.g., Isa 11:10,11; 19:23; 52:6; Jer 30:8; Hos 2:21–23). The "hour" is the precise time when the event happens (see note on 14:35). This rare expression occurs in Dan 12:1, where it refers to the time of unparalleled distress (see note on v. 19) arising as a result of the abomination of Antiochus IV Epiphanes (see note on v. 14). It could also refer to the end times or the Antiochus-like distress caused by Israel's false messiahs that immediately preceded the destruction of AD 70 (see note on vv. 24–25). **no one knows ... nor the Son.** While Jesus' sign is reliable (v. 14), only God knows the precise timing. This should not be seen as undermining Jesus' deity (see note on 1:2–3); it instead reflects Jesus' role as the obedient servant-Son (see note on 1:11) who lived in submission to the Father (cf. 14:36; Heb 10:5–7).

13:35 evening ... midnight ... when the rooster crows ... dawn. The four three-hour periods into which the Romans divided the night.

13:37 Watch! Because the sign (v. 14) will happen with little warning.

14:1—15:47 *A New Passover and a New Covenant.* As Jesus repeatedly predicted (e.g., 8:31; 9:31; 10:32–34), God's plan for his people and Jesus' own confrontation with Jerusalem's hostile authorities come together in this powerful conclusion. Although the Jewish religious authorities (see notes on 1:22; 12:18) believe they have removed a dangerous threat, God, in Jesus, uses their rebellion to establish his new covenant in a new Passover for his newly reconstituted people (see note on 3:14).

14:1–11 *Jesus Anointed at Bethany.* Anointing was traditionally associated with choosing and legitimizing Israel's kings (1 Sam 10:1; 16:1–13; 2 Sam 2:4; 5:3; 1 Kgs 1:34–39; 2 Kgs 9:1–6; 11:12; 23:30); the title "Messiah" means "anointed one." For the first time in Mark, Jesus, Israel's Messianic king (see note on 1:11), is "anointed." But it is for his burial.

14:1 the Passover and the Festival of Unleavened Bread. These two distinct festivals are celebrated together in annual remembrance of Israel's exodus from Egypt (Exod 12). Passover relived the climactic night of God's mighty deliverance with families sharing in the meal of the sacrificial lamb, whose blood protected Israel's firstborn males from the destroying angel (Exod 12:1–27). The Festival of Unleavened Bread, following directly for the next seven days after Passover, recalled Israel's hasty departure and the need for purity (cf. Lev 8:2; 10:12; see note on 8:15). **chief priests ... teachers of the law.** See notes on 1:22; 12:18. **kill him.** As Jesus predicted (8:31).

14:2 people may riot. See note on 11:18. Jerusalem's population increased five- or sixfold during the festival. Combined with the Jewish tradition that anticipated Israel's future deliverance on Passover and a correspondingly increased Roman presence, this made for a highly volatile situation. A riot would bring down swift and violent Roman intervention.

14:3 Bethany. See note on 11:1. **reclining.** The customary posture at a banquet. **Simon the Leper.** Otherwise unknown, but probably healed by Jesus. Arriving after Jesus was at the table, the unnamed woman was likely not an invited guest. **nard.** Highly prized and probably the most expensive perfume mentioned in the Bible (Song 1:12; 4:13–14); made from a plant whose oil was imported at some expense from India.

14:5 rebuked ... harshly. The same Greek word occurs in Jesus' response to the leprous man in 1:43 (rendered "strong warning"). While

[6]"Leave her alone," said Jesus. "Why are you bothering her? She has done a beautiful thing to me.
[7]The poor you will always have with you,[a] and you can help them any time you want.[y] But you will
not always have me. [8]She did what she could. She poured perfume on my body beforehand to prepare
for my burial.[z] [9]Truly I tell you, wherever the gospel is preached throughout the world,[a] what she has
done will also be told, in memory of her."

[10]Then Judas Iscariot, one of the Twelve,[b] went to the chief priests to betray Jesus to them.[c] [11]They
were delighted to hear this and promised to give him money. So he watched for an opportunity to hand
him over.

14:7 [y]Dt 15:11
14:8 [z]Jn 19:40
14:9 [a]Mt 24:14; Mk 16:15
14:10 [b]Mk 3:16-19 [c]Mt 10:4
14:12 [d]Ex 12:1-11; Dt 16:1-4; 1Co 5:7
14:15 [e]Ac 1:13

The Last Supper

14:12-26pp — Mt 26:17-30; Lk 22:7-23
14:22-25pp — 1Co 11:23-25

[12]On the first day of the Festival of Unleavened Bread, when it was customary to sacrifice the Passover lamb,[d] Jesus' disciples asked him, "Where do you want us to go and make preparations for you
to eat the Passover?"

[13]So he sent two of his disciples, telling them, "Go into the city, and a man carrying a jar of water
will meet you. Follow him. [14]Say to the owner of the house he enters, 'The Teacher asks: Where is my
guest room, where I may eat the Passover with my disciples?' [15]He will show you a large room upstairs,[e]
furnished and ready. Make preparations for us there."

[16]The disciples left, went into the city and found things just as Jesus had told them. So they prepared
the Passover.

[17]When evening came, Jesus arrived with the Twelve. [18]While they were reclining at the table eating,
he said, "Truly I tell you, one of you will betray me—one who is eating with me."

[a] 7 See Deut. 15:11.

anointing with less expensive oils was customary at feasts (Ps 23:5; Luke 7:46), this act so exceeded cultural norms that it aroused indignation (v. 4).

14:6–7 Jesus accepts this woman's actions as uninhibited devotion to his person; its very excess intuiting something of his true identity. If he is indeed God's presence among his people, then while one must love one's neighbor, her loving him with all her heart is indeed (lit.) "a good work" (cf. 12:29–31; Matt 5:16; 1 Tim 6:18; Titus 2:7).

14:8 In light of Jesus' Messianic behavior, anointing his head might seem a royal or priestly identification. But this is perfume not oil, the act is offensively excessive, and "poured" is the usual word for anointing not kings but corpses—as Jesus then goes on to explain. Her act is an anticipatory preparation of Jesus, the divinely authoritative yet soon-to-be-crucified Son of Man, for his entombment (see notes on 8:31; 9:31; 10:33,45; cf. 2:10,28).

14:9 Perhaps in her extravagant devotion this woman was one of the first to sense something of who Jesus really is.

14:10 Judas Iscariot, one of the Twelve. See 3:13–19 and notes. Mark never explains why Judas betrays Jesus.

14:11 The chief priests were "delighted" because they had an unexpected opportunity to seize Jesus without arousing the crowds (cf. v. 2).

14:12–31 *A New Covenant and a New Regathering.* One of the key moments in Israel's exodus was God's summoning them into covenant relationship with him (Exod 24). The prophets declared that when God delivered Israel from exile, he would likewise establish a new covenant with them (see especially Jer 31:31–34; cf. Isa 42:6; 49:8; 54:10; 55:3; 61:8; Ezek 34:23–25; 37:24–28). In establishing his covenant, but now through his own body and blood, Jesus fulfills these prophecies and, when his disciples fail and are scattered, he too will regather them (vv. 27–31).

14:12–26 *The Last Supper.* These verses are among the most extraordinary in Mark. Only as the divinely authoritative Lord and Son of Man who exercises God's own prerogatives (see notes on 1:2–3; 2:10,28; 4:39; cf. 9:3,7) could Jesus take up one of Israel's most sacred and inviolable traditions, the Passover, and reconstitute it around himself (as he had with Israel, 3:14–15; see note on 3:14). Perhaps in fulfillment of Jeremiah's prophecies that God would no longer be known by the old exodus but by the new exodus (Jer 16:14–15; 23:7–8), Jesus supplants the exodus as Israel's founding moment, declaring that his person and death will henceforth stand at the center of the new covenant in this new redemption.

14:12 Festival of Unleavened Bread ... Passover. See note on v. 1. Because they were so closely related, Passover was sometimes seen as the first day of the Festival of Unleavened Bread. Whether the Last Supper was the traditional Passover meal is uncertain since John implies that Jesus' trial, and hence the Last Supper, took place the day before Passover (John 13:1; 18:28; 19:14). Part of the difficulty is that Jewish days began after sunset, with the first part of the "day" being the evening and night. For some, vv. 12–16 occur during daylight, the second half of the Jewish "first day," when the lambs were sacrificed (v. 12). The evening (v. 17) then refers to the beginning of the following Jewish day's Passover, with the Last Supper being a traditional Passover meal. For others, "on the first day" means the opening evening and night. Both the minimal preparation (there is no mention of a lamb and the room was ready, v. 15) and the sparse meal (vv. 22–23) then took place during the evening (cf. 6:47, where the Greek word "evening" can mean "later that night") that began the same Jewish day in which the lambs were later sacrificed and at which time Jesus died (cf. again John 13:1; 18:28; 19:14). On this view the Last Supper, which for Jesus was his Passover (vv. 12,16), took place a day earlier than the traditional Passover meal (in agreement with John), and this perhaps explains why they shared bread (v. 22) and not lamb.

14:13 man carrying a jar of water. This was probably a prearranged sign since women traditionally carried jars.

14:15 large room. It would be difficult to find a room so late in a Jerusalem that was awash with pilgrims.

14:18 reclining. See note on v. 3. **Truly I tell you.** See note on 3:28.

14:20 [f] Jn 13:18-27
14:21 [g] Mt 8:20
14:22 [h] Mt 14:19
14:23 [i] 1Co 10:16
14:24 [j] Mt 26:28
14:25 [k] Mt 3:2
14:26 [l] Mt 21:1
14:27 [m] Zec 13:7
14:28 [n] Mk 16:7
14:30 [o] ver 66-72; Lk 22:34; Jn 13:38
14:31 [p] Lk 22:33; Jn 13:37

19 They were saddened, and one by one they said to him, "Surely you don't mean me?"
20 "It is one of the Twelve," he replied, "one who dips bread into the bowl with me.[f] 21 The Son of
Man[g] will go just as it is written about him. But woe to that man who betrays the Son of Man! It would
be better for him if he had not been born."
22 While they were eating, Jesus took bread, and when he had given thanks, he broke it[h] and gave it
to his disciples, saying, "Take it; this is my body."
23 Then he took a cup, and when he had given thanks, he gave it to them, and they all drank from it.[i]
24 "This is my blood of the[a] covenant,[j] which is poured out for many," he said to them. 25 "Truly
I tell you, I will not drink again from the fruit of the vine until that day when I drink it new in the
kingdom of God."[k]
26 When they had sung a hymn, they went out to the Mount of Olives.[l]

Jesus Predicts Peter's Denial

14:27-31pp — Mt 26:31-35

27 "You will all fall away," Jesus told them, "for it is written:

"'I will strike the shepherd,
and the sheep will be scattered.'[b][m]

28 But after I have risen, I will go ahead of you into Galilee."[n]
29 Peter declared, "Even if all fall away, I will not."
30 "Truly I tell you," Jesus answered, "today — yes, tonight — before the rooster crows twice[c] you
yourself will disown me three times."[o]
31 But Peter insisted emphatically, "Even if I have to die with you,[p] I will never disown you." And all
the others said the same.

[a] *24* Some manuscripts *the new* [b] *27* Zech. 13:7 [c] *30* Some early manuscripts do not have *twice.*

14:20 dips … bowl. Participants would dip their pieces of bread into a common bowl of garnish. Since sharing a meal around a common dish symbolized a bond of mutual trust, Judas's act is particularly heinous.
14:21 Son of Man. See notes on 2:10; 8:31. **as it is written.** The Scriptural basis not just of Jesus' declarations of his coming death (see notes on 8:31; 9:30–31; 10:32–34) but also of his betrayal. Jesus could be thinking of Ps 41:9's account of the faithless friend and/or the betrayal of David by Ahithophel (2 Sam 16), who hanged himself, as did Judas (Matt 27:5), when the Lord prevailed against him. Given the crowds and Jesus' evident care in arranging the meal, it would take a faithless insider for his enemies to find him.
14:22 this is my body. Taking the bread that symbolized Israel's departure from Egypt, Jesus interprets his coming death as the new Passover inaugurating God's new exodus. His offering the bread to the disciples, now united to him in sharing this meal, symbolizes his gift of that salvation to and for them.
14:23 they all drank. To drink together expresses mutual obligation to Jesus, as did dipping the bread into the common bowl (see note on v. 20).
14:24 Unlike the bread, which has no explanation, Jesus here invokes two texts (cf. 1:2–3): (1) **my blood of the covenant.** Recalls God's Sinai covenant with Israel (Exod 24:8), whose corporate life, as God's kingdom of priests, was in this act irrevocably tied to him as their Lord and Savior. God's newly reconstituted Israel (see note on 3:14) is henceforth to be similarly united to Jesus, in whom God's long-awaited presence has come (cf. Paul's "in Christ": Rom 12:5; 1 Cor 15:22; Gal 3:26; cf. John 14:23). Whereas in Jewish tradition Exod 24:7's "we will do everything the LORD has said" meant to keep the law, this new covenant means to keep Jesus' teaching (see notes on 3:31–35; 9:7). (2) **poured out for many.** This again recalls Isaiah's prophecy of the suffering servant (Isa 53:12; see note on 10:45). Jesus declares that his death will be the ransom that reconciles an exiled Israel and the nations to God. In these two phrases (the first remembers the first exodus, and the second anticipates the new exodus), Jesus takes up Israel's, and therefore the world's, hope of salvation into himself.
14:25 Jesus' time with them in the present age is coming to an end. The next time they drink together will be in the newly re-created world to come, characterized by the abundance of new wine, a sign of prosperity and life (Isa 25:6–9; cf. Num 13:23–27).
14:26 hymn. Traditionally the Passover meal was accompanied by singing the Hallel psalms (Pss 113–114 before the meal and Pss 115–118 after). They celebrated God's past deliverance in anticipation of the future restoration of Jerusalem and the temple (see notes on 11:9–10; 12:10).
14:27–31 *Jesus Predicts Peter's Denial.* The disciples have been occupied with becoming great ones alongside Israel's Messianic king (cf. 9:34; 10:37,41). Jesus' forthright statement (v. 27) following a meal that confirmed their covenant loyalty (vv. 19–24) reveals how little strength they really have.
14:27 strike … scattered. Zech 13:7 speaks of God's future striking of "my shepherd … who is close to me" in order to purify and regather his "little ones" to a restored Jerusalem. Faced with Jesus' coming death, the confident disciples (cf. 9:33–34; 10:35–41; note "all" in v. 31) will find they too are but little ones who are easily scattered (Zech 13:7b; cf. 9:43–48).
14:28 go ahead of you into Galilee. As the scattering of Zech 13 precedes God's gathering a purified remnant, so Jesus, Zechariah's shepherd, would be resurrected, going ahead of his little ones to Galilee (see 16:7), where it all began.
14:29–30 Since Peter speaks first and most boldly, Jesus addresses him with a prophecy that is fulfilled within a few short hours (vv. 66–72). But three denials are no mere "stumbling" (cf. 9:42–50); they are an emphatic repudiation: "disown" is what disciples must do to themselves in taking up their cross (8:34). The detailed recollection suggests that this searing memory comes from Peter himself.
14:31 Even if I have to die. Peter essentially avows he will "take up [his] cross" (8:34) *if* need be (cf. "must" in 8:31,34). **others.** Cf. "all" in v. 27.

Gethsemane olive trees.

Gethsemane

14:32-42pp — Mt 26:36-46; Lk 22:40-46

[32]They went to a place called Gethsemane, and Jesus said to his disciples, "Sit here while I pray." [33]He
took Peter, James and John[q] along with him, and he began to be deeply distressed and troubled. [34]"My
soul is overwhelmed with sorrow to the point of death,"[r] he said to them. "Stay here and keep watch."
[35]Going a little farther, he fell to the ground and prayed that if possible the hour[s] might pass from
him. [36]"*Abba*,[a] Father,"[t] he said, "everything is possible for you. Take this cup[u] from me. Yet not what
I will, but what you will."[v]
[37]Then he returned to his disciples and found them sleeping. "Simon," he said to Peter, "are you
asleep? Couldn't you keep watch for one hour? [38]Watch and pray so that you will not fall into temptation.[w] The spirit is willing, but the flesh is weak."[x]

14:33 [q]Mt 4:21
14:34 [r]Jn 12:27
14:35 [s]ver 41; Mt 26:18
14:36 [t]Ro 8:15; Gal 4:6 [u]Mt 20:22 [v]Mt 26:39
14:38 [w]Mt 6:13 [x]Ro 7:22,23

[a] *36* Aramaic for *father*

14:32–52 *The Faithful Messianic Son and His Betrayal.* While Jesus remains faithful to the Father in being willing to lay down his life for others, his disciples, as he had just declared (vv. 27–31), all fall away.

14:32–42 *Gethsemane.* From the outset people assumed Jesus' humanity; his divine power and authority is what amazed them. Here Mark's readers encounter a deeply mysterious reminder that Jesus was fully human as he faced the reality of his servant calling (8:31). His vulnerable and humble request contrasts markedly with Peter's earlier bold self-assertion (vv. 29,31).

14:32 Gethsemane. Means "olive press." It was included in greater Jerusalem during the Passover, so the visit complies with the requirement that Passover eve be spent in Jerusalem (cf. Deut 16:1–8; 2 Kgs 23:21–23).

14:33 Peter, James and John. See note on 1:18. Having witnessed Jesus' divine identity in his raising of Jairus's daughter (5:40) and in his transfiguration (9:2), they will also bear witness to his humanity. **deeply distressed.** Previously used of the crowd being overwhelmed by Jesus' presence after the transfiguration (9:15); here it describes how Jesus responds to the awful reality of his coming suffering.

14:34 My soul is overwhelmed with sorrow. A refrain that comes from Pss 42:5a,11a; 43:5a, which first-century Jews thought David wrote. Confronted with a far greater challenge, Jesus, as Israel's Messianic King and Son of God (cf. 1:11; 9:7; 12:10), prays David's prayer of deep agony, doubt, and fear, coming as did David to eventual acceptance and calm trust (Pss 42:9–11; 43:5).

14:35 hour. When Jesus' declarations of his suffering and death (see notes on 8:31; 9:30–31; 10:32–34) are to be fulfilled.

14:36 Although Mark previously mentioned Jesus' habit of private prayer (1:35; 6:46), this is the only example he provides. It might be because, in the context of Jesus' summons to cross-bearing discipleship (8:34–38), it powerfully captures the total submission to the Father that lay at the heart of Jesus' prayer life in general (see note on 9:29) and therefore ought also to characterize that of his followers (cf. the parallels with the Lord's Prayer, Matt 6:9,10b,13). ***Abba.*** Respectful but intimate Aramaic word for father. Jesus' addressing God in this way is unparalleled. **everything is possible.** See note on 1:40. **cup.** See note on 10:38. **what you will.** Because God's will perfectly expresses his character, Jesus' obedience, as God's beloved Son (cf. 1:10–13; 9:7), means reflecting God's character. Jesus' death, then, is a matter not of the Father compelling the Son—an exercise of power wherein God imposes his will on Jesus—but of the Son willingly and intimately embracing and embodying his *Abba*'s self-giving love. In this sense, Jesus' profound anguish testifies to the depth of God's love for his creation.

14:37–38 Simon's sleeping belies his earlier protestations (vv. 29,31); without prayer he will not be able to withstand his "temptation" (v. 38; cf. 1:13).

14:41 [y]ver 35; Mt 26:18
14:43 [z]Mt 10:4
14:45 [a]Mt 23:7
14:49 [b]Mt 26:55
[c]Isa 53:7-12; Mt 1:22
14:50 [d]ver 27
14:54 [e]Mt 26:3
[f]Jn 18:18

[39]Once more he went away and prayed the same thing. [40]When he came back, he again found them
sleeping, because their eyes were heavy. They did not know what to say to him.
[41]Returning the third time, he said to them, "Are you still sleeping and resting? Enough! The hour[y]
has come. Look, the Son of Man is delivered into the hands of sinners. [42]Rise! Let us go! Here comes
my betrayer!"

Jesus Arrested

14:43-50pp — Mt 26:47-56; Lk 22:47-50; Jn 18:3-11

[43]Just as he was speaking, Judas,[z] one of the Twelve, appeared. With him was a crowd armed with
swords and clubs, sent from the chief priests, the teachers of the law, and the elders.
[44]Now the betrayer had arranged a signal with them: "The one I kiss is the man; arrest him and lead
him away under guard." [45]Going at once to Jesus, Judas said, "Rabbi!"[a] and kissed him. [46]The men
seized Jesus and arrested him. [47]Then one of those standing near drew his sword and struck the servant
of the high priest, cutting off his ear.
[48]"Am I leading a rebellion," said Jesus, "that you have come out with swords and clubs to capture
me? [49]Every day I was with you, teaching in the temple courts,[b] and you did not arrest me. But the
Scriptures must be fulfilled."[c] [50]Then everyone deserted him and fled.[d]
[51]A young man, wearing nothing but a linen garment, was following Jesus. When they seized him,
[52]he fled naked, leaving his garment behind.

Jesus Before the Sanhedrin

14:53-65pp — Mt 26:57-68; Jn 18:12,13,19-24
14:61-63pp — Lk 22:67-71

[53]They took Jesus to the high priest, and all the chief priests, the elders and the teachers of the law
came together. [54]Peter followed him at a distance, right into the courtyard of the high priest.[e] There he
sat with the guards and warmed himself at the fire.[f]

14:41 Enough! Could mean (1) the disciples should wake since the time for sleeping is past; (2) the time of preparation is over because the "hour has come"; or (3) there is no more need for Jesus to wrestle in prayer because, in keeping with Pss 42–43 (see note on v. 34), he has fully entrusted himself to the Father's faithful character (cf. Pss 42:5b,11b; 43:5b). From here on, Jesus neither offers resistance nor defends himself against his accusers. **hour.** See note on v. 35. **Son of Man.** See notes on 2:10; 8:31.

14:43–52 *Jesus Arrested.* The "hour" that Jesus previously predicted (8:33; 9:31; 10:33,45) has come. It begins as he had declared: with his being given over (9:31) by one of his own (v. 18).

14:43 Judas, one of the Twelve. See 3:13–19 and notes. **crowd armed.** Jewish temple guards with sundry reinforcements. Their weapons and Jesus' response (v. 48) suggest that they saw Jesus as a potential rebel (see note on 11:18). **chief priests ... teachers of the law.** See notes on 1:22; 12:18.

14:44 kiss. A customary greeting, especially between a rabbi and his disciple (see note on Matt 26:48).

14:45 Going at once. Judas's confident and intimate betrayal of Jesus is his final act in Mark (cf. 3:19).

14:48 leading a rebellion. Or "a rebel." Jesus had publicly distanced himself from rebels (12:13–17) but had applied this label to the temple authorities (see note on 11:17). Nevertheless, Jesus will be crucified between two of them (see 15:27 and note).

14:49 teaching in the temple courts. See 11:27—12:44. **Scriptures must be fulfilled.** No specific text is mentioned, but given the importance of Isa 53 for Jesus' understanding of his death (see note on 8:22—10:52), it perhaps refers to Isaiah's suffering servant being numbered with the "transgressors" (Isa 53:12, where the Hebrew is "rebels"; cf. Luke 22:37). At the same time, the scattering of Jesus' disciples (v. 50) also suggests Zech 13:7.

14:50 Fulfills v. 27.

14:51 young man. Some suggest that this unnamed man is Mark himself. Whoever he is, his naked flight (v. 52) is a far cry from the riot the authorities feared (11:18; 12:12). The lack of an undergarment might imply that he had dressed hurriedly to follow Jesus.

14:53—15:20 *Jesus on Trial.* The "hour" (14:41) continues as Jesus is delivered over to the chief priests and teachers of the law (10:33). Hastily convened, the Sanhedrin, Israel's national court, seeks to establish charges (14:53–72) that warrant a capital trial before Pilate and execution under Rome's authority (15:1–43). On a smaller scale and as Jesus also predicted (14:30), Peter faces his own "trial."

14:53–72 *Jesus in the Hands of the Chief Priests and Teachers of the Law: God's Son and Israel's Lord.* The final confrontation between Jesus and the hostile Jewish religious authorities (see notes on 1:22; 12:18) reflects two of Mark's central themes: (1) In terms of cross-bearing and discipleship, Jesus, who steadfastly goes to his death in hope of the resurrection (cf. 8:31; 9:31; 10:34), starkly contrasts with Peter, who in saving his life in this world betrays his covenant with Jesus (14:20–24) and risks losing his soul (8:34–38). (2) In terms of the long-standing question of Jesus' identity and authority, Jesus himself answers the question in final, dramatic fashion.

14:53–65 *Jesus Before the Sanhedrin.* Having previously challenged Jesus on his home ground (3:22; 7:1) and only recently on theirs (11:27–28,32; 12:13–17), the chief priests, teachers of the law, and elders now have Jesus in a setting they fully control (cf. 11:32; 12:12). Even so Jesus displays an unruffled composure that transcends the increasingly violent agitation that surrounds him.

14:53 Having embraced God's self-giving character (see notes on vv. 36,41), Jesus, perhaps in fulfillment of Isa 53:7, allows himself to be taken (see note on 8:31).

[55]The chief priests and the whole Sanhedrin[g] were looking for evidence against Jesus so that they
could put him to death, but they did not find any. [56]Many testified falsely against him, but their statements did not agree.
[57]Then some stood up and gave this false testimony against him: [58]"We heard him say, 'I will destroy
this temple made with human hands and in three days will build another,[h] not made with hands.'"
[59]Yet even then their testimony did not agree.
[60]Then the high priest stood up before them and asked Jesus, "Are you not going to answer? What is
this testimony that these men are bringing against you?" [61]But Jesus remained silent and gave no answer.[i]
Again the high priest asked him, "Are you the Messiah, the Son of the Blessed One?"[j]
[62]"I am," said Jesus. "And you will see the Son of Man sitting at the right hand of the Mighty One
and coming on the clouds of heaven."[k]
[63]The high priest tore his clothes.[l] "Why do we need any more witnesses?" he asked. [64]"You have
heard the blasphemy. What do you think?"
They all condemned him as worthy of death.[m] [65]Then some began to spit at him; they blindfolded
him, struck him with their fists, and said, "Prophesy!" And the guards took him and beat him.[n]

Peter Disowns Jesus

14:66-72pp — Mt 26:69-75; Lk 22:56-62; Jn 18:16-18,25-27

[66]While Peter was below in the courtyard,[o] one of the servant girls of the high priest came by. [67]When
she saw Peter warming himself,[p] she looked closely at him.
"You also were with that Nazarene, Jesus,"[q] she said.

14:55 [g] Mt 5:22
14:58 [h] Mk 15:29; Jn 2:19
14:61 [i] Isa 53:7; Mt 27:12,14; Mk 15:5; Lk 23:9; Jn 19:9 [j] Mt 16:16; Jn 4:25,26
14:62 [k] Rev 1:7
14:63 [l] Lev 10:6; 21:10; Nu 14:6; Ac 14:14
14:64 [m] Lev 24:16
14:65 [n] Mt 16:21
14:66 [o] ver 54
14:67 [p] ver 54 [q] Mk 1:24

14:55 Sanhedrin. The highest Jewish court in the land. It was comprised of the chief priests, elders, and teachers of the law (see note on 12:18). The high priest presided over it. **looking for evidence against Jesus so that they could put him to death.** This is less a trial than a hearing in search of a viable capital charge; only the Romans could impose the death penalty (cf. 15:1–15). In spite of the agenda, the gathering honored Scriptural guidelines in disallowing false testimony in capital cases (cf. v. 59; Deut 17:6).

14:57–58 Mark nowhere records any such statement by Jesus.

14:57 false testimony. Suggests they presented Jesus' temple denunciation (11:17; cf. John 2:19–20) as a plan to incite a rebellion (cf. vv. 43,48) and, in keeping with Jer 7:11, physically destroy this temple that is "made with human hands" (v. 58; i.e., idolatrous). Jesus would then replace it with a divinely instituted one that would presumably fulfill Isa 56:7.

14:58 in three days. Appears to be a garbled report of Jesus' declarations of his coming death (8:31; 9:31; 10:33). But Mark's readers would likely see here a veiled truth: the resurrected Jesus and his followers themselves would become the new temple in whom God's presence will dwell and where all nations could worship (see note on 12:10).

14:61 remained silent. Given the influence of Isa 53 on his mission (see notes on 8:31; 10:33), Jesus' silence likely reflects the servant's silence when he too was treated unjustly (Isa 53:7). To break the impasse, the high priest intervenes with his limited version of Mark's fundamental question (see notes on 1:14—8:21; 4:41). **Son of the Blessed One.** A respectful substitute for "Son of God" (cf. "heaven" in 11:30 [see note]), which, reflecting God's words to David (Ps 2:7), was another title for the human Messiah, Israel's king (15:32). But "Son" in this title means a special relationship, not deity (cf. Exod 4:22; see note on 1:13).

14:62 A Christological high point of Mark's Gospel. Fittingly before the high priest, Israel's official representative before God, Jesus, for the first time in Mark, publicly declares his identity (see notes on 1:34; 8:30). **I am.** A simple and direct affirmation. However, Jesus' substitution of "Son of Man" again transforms his Messianic affirmation (cf. 8:31)—for Mark's readers, if not for the high priest—by recalling his divine authority as Israel's coming Lord (2:10,28; see note on 1:2–3). **sitting at the right hand of the Mighty One.** From Ps 110:1. This picks up on Jesus' final questions in the temple (see 12:35–37). "Mighty One" is a pious expression for God. **coming on the clouds of heaven.** From Dan 7:13 (see notes on 8:38; 13:26). Jesus is David's Lord, whose enemies God will destroy, and the divinely authoritative Son of Man to whom God will give glory and everlasting dominion over all nations. In responding so directly, Jesus turns the tables on Israel's religious authorities by implicitly putting them on trial. Their response, even if predictable, will determine their fate.

14:63 tore his clothes. The formal response to blasphemy (cf. 2 Kgs 18:37; 19:1).

14:64 blasphemy. This charge readily arises from (1) Jesus' outrageous presumption, as a mere human, to such a close relationship with God; (2) the assertion that he will sit in judgment over the Sanhedrin in their generation ("you [plural] will see" [v. 62; cf. note on 13:30]); and (3) the implication (if the larger contexts of the two passages are in view) that Jesus' opponents are God's enemies (Ps 110) and, even worse, aligned with Daniel's defiling and murderous fourth beast and its blasphemous little horn (Dan 7:7–14,19–27; cf. note on 13:14). This latter point amounts to cursing a leader of God's people, itself equivalent to blasphemy (cf. Exod 22:28). **all condemned him.** The Sanhedrin as a body (with the exception of at least one individual, Joseph of Arimathea, who did not consent to the decision [Luke 23:50–51; cf. 15:43]) achieves the first stage of their agenda (cf. v. 55; 11:18).

14:65 spit at ... blindfolded ... struck ... beat. Conventional acts of social repudiation (cf. Deut 25:9), the violence of which reflects the intensity of the offense. It closely resembles the abuse of Isaiah's servant (Isa 50:6; see note on 10:34). The blindfolding might be related to the demand that he "prophesy"—i.e., identify who struck him (cf. Matt 26:68; Luke 22:64)—itself perhaps reflecting the popular conception that Jesus was a prophet (cf. 6:15). This is ironic because, as Mark's readers know, Jesus has three times predicted this very moment (cf. note on 8:31—10:45).

14:66–72 *Peter Disowns Jesus.* Whereas Jesus, even in the face of death, calmly confirms his true identity, Peter, fearing for his life, denies any association with Jesus.

14:67 Nazarene. See notes on 1:9,24.

14:68 [r] ver 30,72
14:70 [s] ver 30,68,72 [t] Ac 2:7
14:71 [u] ver 30,72
14:72 [v] ver 30,68
15:1 [w] Mt 27:1; Lk 22:66 [x] Mt 5:22 [y] Mt 27:2
15:2 [z] ver 9,12,18,26; Mt 2:2
15:5 [a] Mk 14:61
15:9 [b] ver 2
15:11 [c] Ac 3:14

68 But he denied it. "I don't know or understand what you're talking about,"[r] he said, and went out into the entryway.[a]

69 When the servant girl saw him there, she said again to those standing around, "This fellow is one of them." 70 Again he denied it.[s]

After a little while, those standing near said to Peter, "Surely you are one of them, for you are a Galilean."[t]

71 He began to call down curses, and he swore to them, "I don't know this man you're talking about."[u]

72 Immediately the rooster crowed the second time.[b] Then Peter remembered the word Jesus had spoken to him: "Before the rooster crows twice[c] you will disown me three times."[v] And he broke down and wept.

Jesus Before Pilate

15:2-15pp — Mt 27:11-26; Lk 23:2,3,18-25; Jn 18:29–19:16

15 Very early in the morning, the chief priests, with the elders, the teachers of the law[w] and the whole Sanhedrin,[x] made their plans. So they bound Jesus, led him away and handed him over to Pilate.[y]

2 "Are you the king of the Jews?"[z] asked Pilate.

"You have said so," Jesus replied.

3 The chief priests accused him of many things. 4 So again Pilate asked him, "Aren't you going to answer? See how many things they are accusing you of."

5 But Jesus still made no reply,[a] and Pilate was amazed.

6 Now it was the custom at the festival to release a prisoner whom the people requested. 7 A man called Barabbas was in prison with the insurrectionists who had committed murder in the uprising. 8 The crowd came up and asked Pilate to do for them what he usually did.

9 "Do you want me to release to you the king of the Jews?"[b] asked Pilate, 10 knowing it was out of self-interest that the chief priests had handed Jesus over to him. 11 But the chief priests stirred up the crowd to have Pilate release Barabbas[c] instead.

12 "What shall I do, then, with the one you call the king of the Jews?" Pilate asked them.

[a] *68* Some early manuscripts *entryway and the rooster crowed* [b] *72* Some early manuscripts do not have *the second time.* [c] *72* Some early manuscripts do not have *twice.*

14:68 denied. As Jesus earlier predicted (vv. 30–31; cf. 8:34). **I don't know or understand.** Peter begins to sound like the Jewish religious leaders in their evasion of Jesus' question concerning John (see note on 11:33).

14:70 Peter's Galilean accent was readily identifiable.

14:71 call down curses. Normally people curse something or someone, but neither is specifically mentioned here. Since it is unlikely that Peter is cursing himself, Mark, perhaps to avoid unnecessary affront or embarrassment, has omitted what the context would naturally suggest. In a final, desperate attempt to avoid association with Jesus, Peter possibly begins to curse Jesus.

14:72 As with Judas's betrayal (see note on v. 45), this is Peter's last appearance in Mark. But unlike Judas, Peter's shattered response shows that his betrayal was a matter of weakness (cf. v. 38). There is hope of redemption (cf. 16:7).

15:1–20 *Jesus in the Hands of Gentiles: God's Messianic King for the Nations.* The progression of Jesus' prophecies of his death approaches its climax as he is handed over to the Gentiles (see note on 10:33). The involvement of the Romans, who are world rulers, puts Jesus' death and resurrection in the larger context of God's purposes to save the nations.

15:1–15 *Jesus Before Pilate.* Just as the Sanhedrin represented the nation of Israel (14:53–65) so Pilate acts on behalf of Rome.

15:1 Very early in the morning. Friday of Passion Week. The Roman workday began at dawn. The Jewish religious leaders (see notes on 1:22; 12:18) needed to move quickly because either the Festival of Unleavened Bread or the Passover began that evening (see note on 14:12). **made their plans.** Reworked Jesus' blasphemy into a sufficiently political form to ensure Roman involvement. Since the Messiah was Israel's king (v. 2), this was not difficult, and the heightened tension at Passover and the apparently recently failed insurrection (v. 7) only heightened Roman concerns. **Pilate.** The Roman prefect of the minor province of Judea and under the supervision of the legate of the imperial province of Syria (see photo, p. 1995).

15:2 You have said so. Less direct than Jesus' response to the high priest (14:62), probably because what Pilate assumes and what Jesus means by the title are very different.

15:3 many things. A range of related accusations in order to give the impression of an overwhelming case.

15:5 still made no reply. See note on 14:61. **Pilate was amazed.** At the contrast between the intensity of Jesus' accusers and Jesus' refusal to defend himself, especially when facing crucifixion.

15:6 release a prisoner. Amnesty to display Roman nobility to the crowds. The crowd's demands will increasingly determine the outcome of the proceedings.

15:7 Barabbas. Apparently a popular hero of a local resistance group who was arrested in a recent disturbance.

15:10 self-interest. Lies behind the long-standing clash over authority (cf. 1:22; 2:10; 3:22; 11:28), particularly given Jesus' popularity with the people.

JESUS' TRIALS

BEFORE JEWISH RELIGIOUS AUTHORITIES	
Preliminary hearing before Annas (John 18:12–24)	Although the Romans had deposed Annas, in the eyes of the Jews he still functioned as the high priest because the office was for life. Annas questioned Jesus, but Jesus demanded a legal hearing.
Hearing before Caiaphas (Matt 26:57–68; Mark 14:53–65; Luke 22:54)	Caiaphas was the high priest appointed by the Romans. Two false witnesses testified against Jesus and Caiaphas asked Jesus if he was the Messiah. Jesus answered yes, and Caiaphas concluded that Jesus was guilty of blasphemy.
Trial before the Sanhedrin (Matt 27:1,2; Mark 15:1; Luke 22:66–71)	The council of Jewish religious leaders confirmed Caiaphas's conclusion. In this trial, Jesus admitted he was the Son of God and declared that he would sit on the right hand of God the Father.
BEFORE THE ROMAN AUTHORITIES	
First hearing before Pilate (Matt 27:11–14; Mark 15:2–5; Luke 23:1–5; John 18:28–37)	The Jewish religious leaders brought Jesus to Pilate in order to get permission to execute him. They accused him of treason. Pilate saw Jesus' innocence, but briefly questioned him. In this interview, Jesus revealed to Pilate that his kingdom was not of this earth.
Hearing before Herod (Luke 23:6–12)	Pilate sent Jesus to Herod because Jesus was from Galilee, the region ruled by Herod. Jesus remained silent before Herod.
Final hearing before Pilate (Matt 27:15–26; Mark 15:6–15; Luke 23:13–25; John 18:38—19:16)	Pilate did not want to condemn an innocent man, but he was afraid of another Jewish uprising. Therefore, he finally gave in to the cries of the crowd: "Crucify him!"

13"Crucify him!" they shouted.
14"Why? What crime has he committed?" asked Pilate.
But they shouted all the louder, "Crucify him!"
15Wanting to satisfy the crowd, Pilate released Barabbas to them. He had Jesus flogged,[d] and handed
him over to be crucified.

15:15 [d]Isa 53:6
15:16 [e]Jn 18:28,33; 19:9
15:18 [f]ver 2
15:20 [g]Heb 13:12

The Soldiers Mock Jesus

15:16-20pp — Mt 27:27-31

16The soldiers led Jesus away into the palace[e] (that is, the Praetorium) and called together the whole
company of soldiers. 17They put a purple robe on him, then twisted together a crown of thorns and set
it on him. 18And they began to call out to him, "Hail, king of the Jews!"[f] 19Again and again they struck
him on the head with a staff and spit on him. Falling on their knees, they paid homage to him. 20And
when they had mocked him, they took off the purple robe and put his own clothes on him. Then they
led him out[g] to crucify him.

15:13 Crucify. See notes on v. 24; 8:34. As "king of the Jews" (vv. 12,18) and therefore a rival to Roman authority, a guilty verdict can have only one outcome.

15:14–15 It is important for Mark that a more "neutral" Roman official considers Jesus to be innocent of the charges. But having initiated the custom, Pilate cannot risk inflaming the crowd by ignoring the wishes of the people (v. 6), even if they are manipulated by their leaders (v. 11). All three parties—Pilate, the people, and the Jewish leaders—are complicit in Jesus' death.

15:15 flogged. A brutal torture using whips of leather thongs often tipped with pieces of bone or metal. It severely weakened the prisoner, sometimes proving fatal. **crucified.** See notes on v. 24; 8:34.

15:16–20 *The Soldiers Mock Jesus.* The Jewish verdict was followed by violent mockery of the "prophet" (14:65); now the Roman sentence is followed by a violent mockery of the "king."

15:16 soldiers. Not Roman legionnaires but non-Jewish auxiliaries from neighboring regions. **palace.** Of Herod; Pilate's home while in Jerusalem. **Praetorium.** In this case, barracks.

15:17–18 purple robe ... crown ... "Hail ...!" A parody of imperial garb and salutation ("Ave, Caesar!"). The violent elements complete Jesus' final prediction of his suffering at Gentile hands (10:34), recalling the sufferings of Isaiah's servant (Isa 50:6; cf. 8:34; 14:65). In a few short hours a Roman centurion will address Jesus in a very different manner (v. 39).

15:21 [h]Mt 27:32 [i]Ro 16:13 [j]Mt 27:32; Lk 23:26
15:23 [k]ver 36; Ps 69:21; Pr 31:6
15:24 [l]Ps 22:18
15:26 [m]ver 2
15:29 [n]Ps 22:7; 109:25 [o]Mk 14:58; Jn 2:19
15:31 [p]Ps 22:7
15:32 [q]Mk 14:61 [r]ver 2
15:33 [s]Am 8:9
15:34 [t]Ps 22:1

The Crucifixion of Jesus

15:22-32pp — Mt 27:33-44; Lk 23:33-43; Jn 19:17-24

21 A certain man from Cyrene,[h] Simon, the father of Alexander and Rufus,[i] was passing by on his way
in from the country, and they forced him to carry the cross.[j] 22 They brought Jesus to the place called Golgotha (which means "the place of the skull"). 23 Then they offered him wine mixed with myrrh,[k] but he
did not take it. 24 And they crucified him. Dividing up his clothes, they cast lots[l] to see what each would get.
25 It was nine in the morning when they crucified him. 26 The written notice of the charge against
him read: THE KING OF THE JEWS.[m]
27 They crucified two rebels with him, one on his right and one on his left. [28][a] 29 Those who passed
by hurled insults at him, shaking their heads[n] and saying, "So! You who are going to destroy the temple
and build it in three days,[o] 30 come down from the cross and save yourself!" 31 In the same way the chief
priests and the teachers of the law mocked him[p] among themselves. "He saved others," they said, "but
he can't save himself! 32 Let this Messiah,[q] this king of Israel,[r] come down now from the cross, that we
may see and believe." Those crucified with him also heaped insults on him.

The Death of Jesus

15:33-41pp — Mt 27:45-56; Lk 23:44-49; Jn 19:29-30

33 At noon, darkness came over the whole land until three in the afternoon.[s] 34 And at three in the
afternoon Jesus cried out in a loud voice, *"Eloi, Eloi, lema sabachthani?"* (which means "My God, my
God, why have you forsaken me?").[b][t]

[a] *28* Some manuscripts include here words similar to Luke 22:37. [b] *34* Psalm 22:1

15:21–47 *The New Passover Sacrifice.* In relatively short order, Jesus' predictions concerning his coming death are fulfilled, but ironically each stage already hints toward a very different outcome. Far transcending the conspiracies of the nations against God's beloved Son (cf. 1:11; 9:7; Ps 2:1,7), Jesus' death is God's long-awaited new exodus redemption (see note on 14:24) whereby he finally breaks the power of sin and death that holds humanity in bondage. If, in fact, Jesus dies on Passover eve (see note on 14:12), then, as John implies (John 1:29,36; 19:14) and Paul declares (1 Cor 5:7), Jesus is indeed our new Passover lamb.

15:21–32 *The Crucifixion of Jesus.* Mark's account of the crucifixion passes over Jesus' suffering in silence. Mark focuses instead on the truths expressed ironically in the abuse, Jesus' one statement from the cross, the divine signs that testify to what is really going on, and the first human confession of Jesus' divine Sonship.

15:21 Cyrene. An important city in Libya, North Africa, with a large Jewish population. **father of Alexander and Rufus.** Mentioned only by Mark. Since men are traditionally known by their fathers, Simon's identification by his sons possibly suggests that they are known to Mark's Roman audience (cf. Rom 16:13). This implies that they and perhaps their father had become followers of Jesus as a result of this experience. **forced.** Occupying forces could compel ordinary citizens to carry their baggage (cf. Matt 5:41). **carry the cross.** The condemned normally carried the crossbar, which often weighed 30–40 pounds (13–18 kilograms), to the site of crucifixion. Jesus, weakened by flogging, was incapable of completing (cf. John 19:17) the relatively short journey, some 328 yards (300 meters), to just outside the city walls, so Simon was pressed into service.

15:22 Golgotha. Or "skull"; might reflect its being the site of many executions. The NT nowhere describes it as a hill.

15:23 wine mixed with myrrh. Probably offered by sympathizers to dull the agony. **did not take it.** Jesus was fully resolved to drink the cup of suffering the Father had assigned him (cf. 10:38).

15:24 crucified. One of the most cruel, public, and shameful forms of Roman execution (see photo, p. 2421). Fixed by either nails or ropes, the victim's outstretched arms were pinned to a crossbeam that was raised and attached to a vertical stake. The legs were then similarly attached, either straddling the upright or supported on a foot rest, with the victim often seated on a small support to prevent a premature demise. Damaging no internal organs and causing no serious blood loss, it was designed to prolong suffering for as long as three days (hence, Pilate's surprise, v. 44) before shock or slow asphyxiation due to muscle fatigue resulted in death. Naked—though a loin cloth may have been permitted when Jewish sensibilities were a factor—the humiliated victim was subject to vitriolic abuse, often enduring birds and animals beginning their feast while the victim was still alive. **Dividing up his clothes.** The execution squad had the rights to the victim's minor possessions. Mark's description conforms closely to Ps 22:18, which first-century readers understood as describing David's suffering when abandoned.

15:25 nine in the morning. See note on John 19:14.

15:26 Victims' crosses were sometimes placarded with a statement of their crime.

15:27 rebels. The same word Jesus used of the temple authorities (rendered "robbers" in 11:17). It can also mean "bandit," but the earlier reference to a failed uprising (v. 7) suggests it has a more political connotation here. Jesus is crucified between those whose methods he rejected (12:12–17). **one on his right and one on his left.** Mark's phrasing ironically echoes James and John's request (10:37). Jesus' glory, and thus God's glory, looks very different from human expectations (see notes on 8:33; 10:37). This is possibly an allusion to Isa 53:12, where the servant would be "numbered with the transgressors" (see note on 14:49).

15:29 shaking their heads. Another allusion to Ps 22 (this time Ps 22:7–8; see note on v. 24), similarly mocking Jesus' trust in God. **destroy the temple.** Repeats the accusations presented at the hearing of the Sanhedrin (14:57–58); ironically, the temple's fate is already sealed, and Jesus' death confirms it (cf. v. 38).

15:30–32 Jesus' refusal to save himself is precisely what saves others (10:45).

15:33–41 *The Death of Jesus.* In fulfillment of Jesus' earlier predictions and thus the Scriptures (see notes on 8:31; 10:33,45; 1 Cor 15:3), this is perhaps the greatest mystery at the heart of the gospel. Jesus, the divinely authoritative Lord and fully human Messianic servant (see notes on 1:2–3,11), drinks the cup of God's wrath upon all human rebellion (see notes on 10:38; 2 Cor 5:21). But in taking on our death (2 Cor 5:14), Jesus' offered life (see notes on 14:22,24; Rom 8:3) becomes a ransom for many (10:45).

35 When some of those standing near heard this, they said, "Listen, he's calling Elijah."
36 Someone ran, filled a sponge with wine vinegar,[u] put it on a staff, and offered it to Jesus to drink.
"Now leave him alone. Let's see if Elijah comes to take him down," he said.
37 With a loud cry, Jesus breathed his last.[v]
38 The curtain of the temple was torn in two from top to bottom.[w] 39 And when the centurion,[x] who
stood there in front of Jesus, saw how he died,[a] he said, "Surely this man was the Son of God!"[y]
40 Some women were watching from a distance.[z] Among them were Mary Magdalene, Mary the
mother of James the younger and of Joseph,[b] and Salome.[a] 41 In Galilee these women had followed him
and cared for his needs. Many other women who had come up with him to Jerusalem were also there.[b]

15:36 [u] ver 23; Ps 69:21
15:37 [v] Jn 19:30
15:38 [w] Heb 10:19,20
15:39 [x] ver 45 [y] Mk 1:1, 11; 9:7; Mt 4:3
15:40 [z] Ps 38:11 [a] Mk 16:1; Lk 24:10; Jn 19:25
15:41 [b] Mt 27:55,56; Lk 8:2,3
15:42 [c] Mt 27:62; Jn 19:31
15:43 [d] Mt 5:22 [e] Mt 3:2; Lk 2:25,38

The Burial of Jesus

15:42-47pp — Mt 27:57-61; Lk 23:50-56; Jn 19:38-42

42 It was Preparation Day (that is, the day before the Sabbath).[c] So as evening approached, 43 Joseph
of Arimathea, a prominent member of the Council,[d] who was himself waiting for the kingdom of God,[e]

[a] *39* Some manuscripts *saw that he died with such a cry* [b] *40* Greek *Joses,* a variant of *Joseph*; also in verse 47

15:33 This is the first divine intervention during Jesus' death (see also v. 38). Unnatural darkness signifies God's judgment (e.g., Exod 10:22; Isa 5:30) and a time "like mourning for an only son" (Amos 8:9–10; cf. 1:11; 9:7; 12:6–11). A potent apocalyptic statement, its three-hour duration ("noon ... until three") puts the puny human mockers in true perspective and is the first intimation that Jesus' death is far more significant than they had imagined.

15:34 cried out. The Greek is used by Mark only here and in 1:3 (rendered "calling") of John's proclamation of the Lord's "way." It is appropriate here as Jesus' "way" to the cross reaches its climax and the mystery of Jesus' divine-human identity reemerges (see note on 14:32–42). ***Eloi, Eloi, lema sabachthani?*** Aramaic. Mark very occasionally records Jesus' actual words to heighten the intensity of the moment (5:41; 7:34; 14:36). **My God, my God, why have you forsaken me?** In striking contrast to his settled calm after Gethsemane (14:41) and during his trials and abuse (vv. 2–32; 14:60–65), Jesus' extreme anguish at being separated from God should not be minimized (see note on vv. 33–41). But neither does his anguish nullify his confident declarations of subsequent resurrection (see note on 8:31). His cry is the final and clearest echo of Ps 22 (Ps 22:1; see notes on vv. 24,29), which proceeds from David's certainty of God's faithfulness to hear and vindicate his own (Ps 22:19; see also note on 14:34). Jesus thus sees his death as the Messianic fulfillment of David's deepest experience of divine abandonment (Ps 22:1–18)—in a way that no human could ever understand—but his death will just as surely result in glorious vindication and subsequent universal worship of God (Ps 22:19–31; in ironic fulfillment of the soldiers' mockery, vv. 16–20 and note; cf. v. 39).

15:35,36 Elijah. Some see this as a mishearing of Jesus' "*Eloi*" (v. 34). Additionally, or alternatively, because some Jewish traditions held that Elijah was the savior of the righteous (see note on 9:10–11), those standing near expected the intervention that Jesus cried out for to come through him. Either way, their response confirms that Jesus' cry implied Ps 22's expectation of deliverance (see note on v. 34).

15:37 Mark gives no indication of the content or significance of Jesus' "loud cry" (but see Luke 23:46; John 19:30). However, along with the manner of Jesus' death, his cry was striking enough to cause a hardened centurion to radically change his assessment (v. 39).

15:38 curtain of the temple. There were two curtains in the temple: an outer one between the court and the Holy Place, and an inner one between the Holy Place and the Most Holy Place. Mark does not specify which curtain is in view (but see Heb 9:8–10,12; 10:19–20). **torn.** The second divine intervention during Jesus' death. In divine refutation of the mockers' "You who are going to destroy the temple" (v. 29), Jesus' final cry and sacrificial death (see notes on 10:45; 14:22,24) are accompanied by an already condemned temple (see notes on 11:17; 13:1,2) and its sacrifices being immediately rendered obsolete. It might also symbolize that direct access to God's presence will now be through Jesus. Finally, just as at the beginning of Mark's Gospel the torn heavens were accompanied by God's declaration that Jesus is his Son (1:10–11), so here at the end of Mark's Gospel the torn curtain is accompanied by the first human affirmation of Jesus' divine Sonship.

15:39 centurion. Not a career professional, but a low-ranking non-Jewish auxiliary officer who led the execution squad (see note on v. 16). **Son of God.** See note on 1:1. This is an impressive affirmation from an idolatrous pagan who sees in Jesus what Israel's leaders cannot see. The centurion's confession might also represent the firstfruits of Ps 22's universal worship of God (Ps 22:27–28; see note on v. 34), but now that worship is centered on Jesus (see note on 12:10), himself the light to all nations (see note on 1:11). While perhaps not yet a fully Christian confession, Mark's readers, with the preceding chapters behind them, will rightly hear its full significance.

15:40,41 women. For the first time Mark explicitly mentions the existence of women disciples in Galilee, upon whose care Jesus' ministry depended (Luke 8:1–3; cf. Jesus' use of "sister" and "mother" when looking at those who sat around him in 3:34–35). Presumably Mark's readers know of these women.

15:42–47 *The Burial of Jesus.* The hurried burial explains why the women need to revisit the tomb as soon as the Sabbath is over, and we learn for the first time that not all of the Sanhedrin supported Jesus' execution. One godly and prominent member ensures that Jesus receives an honorable burial.

15:42 Preparation Day. The day before the Sabbath, which means that Jesus died on a Friday. **evening approached.** Deut 21:23 required burial before nightfall, and Sabbath regulations meant it would need to be done before sundown.

15:43 Arimathea. Probably a town in the hill country northwest of Jerusalem. **the Council.** The Sanhedrin (see note on 14:55). This is Mark's first indication that not all the members of the Sanhedrin supported Jesus' execution. **waiting for the kingdom of God.** See note on 1:15. If not a committed disciple, then Joseph was supportive of Jesus. **boldly.** Coming from someone who was not a family member but instead a member of the Sanhedrin, which had condemned Jesus, Joseph's request to provide proper burial for an extremist could have had severe consequences; by appearing to be sympathetic to Jesus and his agenda, he may have been viewed as implicitly critiquing Roman justice.

Artist's reconstruction of a kokhim-style family tomb. A kokhim usually consisted of a central chamber with a bench where the body would be placed for burial prepration. Next the body would be placed into one of the long, narrow shafts extending from the central chamber, and eventually the bones would be collected and placed in an ossuary. See photo, p. 2135.
Leen Ritmeyer

15:45 [f] ver 39
15:46 [g] Mk 16:3
15:47 [h] ver 40
16:1 [i] Lk 23:56; Jn 19:39,40
16:3 [j] Mk 15:46
16:5 [k] Jn 20:12

went boldly to Pilate and asked for Jesus' body. 44 Pilate was surprised to hear that he was already dead.
Summoning the centurion, he asked him if Jesus had already died. 45 When he learned from the centurion[f] that it was so, he gave the body to Joseph. 46 So Joseph bought some linen cloth, took down the
body, wrapped it in the linen, and placed it in a tomb cut out of rock. Then he rolled a stone against
the entrance of the tomb.[g] 47 Mary Magdalene and Mary the mother of Joseph[h] saw where he was laid.

Jesus Has Risen

16:1-8pp — Mt 28:1-8; Lk 24:1-10

16 When the Sabbath was over, Mary Magdalene, Mary the mother of James, and Salome bought
spices[i] so that they might go to anoint Jesus' body. 2 Very early on the first day of the week, just
after sunrise, they were on their way to the tomb 3 and they asked each other, "Who will roll the stone
away from the entrance of the tomb?"[j]

4 But when they looked up, they saw that the stone, which was very large, had been rolled away. 5 As
they entered the tomb, they saw a young man dressed in a white robe[k] sitting on the right side, and
they were alarmed.

15:44 surprised. Cf. 5:20; 6:6. Crucifixions normally lasted several days, yet Jesus expired in just a few hours. Having amazed Pilate with his silence (v. 5), Jesus continues to amaze even in his death. **centurion.** See note on v. 39.

15:45 gave the body. Unusual but perhaps granted because Jesus had impressed Pilate (cf. vv. 5,14–15).

15:46 cut out of rock. Probably a substantial and very expensive family tomb with multiple chambers and stone benches. The entrance was closed off with a large disc-shaped stone that once in place was very difficult to move. Of the two main locations where Jesus is thought to have been buried, early church tradition strongly favors the Church of the Holy Sepulchre, whereas the Garden Tomb is more an OT-era site.

16:1–8 *Jesus Has Risen.* Compared to the events attending Jesus' death, the discovery of the empty tomb is remarkably devoid of spectacle. What is extraordinary, given male dominance in both Jewish and Roman societies, is that with the "strong" males having fled, the only eyewitnesses who can testify to Jesus' death, burial, and empty tomb are these "least," the women disciples (see notes on 9:36,37,41; 10:15,49,52).

16:1 Sabbath was over. Shops could reopen for the evening. **spices … anoint.** A mark of respect; the women are apparently intending to complete the burial rites left undone at the earlier hasty internment.

16:2 first day of the week. See note on John 20:1.

16:3–5 roll … entered. See note on 15:46. The huge stone's removal is the first intimation that something unexpected has happened.

16:5 a young man dressed in a white robe sitting. Even more disturbing than finding the stone rolled away is finding in the tomb someone sitting, the posture of authoritative teaching (9:35; 13:3; cf. Luke 4:20), and clothed in white, normally associated with formal occasions and festivity (Esth 8:15; Eccl 9:7–8) and suggestive of a heavenly visitation (cf. 9:3; Matt 28:3; John 20:12; Acts 1:10; for "young man" as a heavenly messenger, see in the Apocrypha 2 Maccabees 3:26; cf. Matt 28:2–5).

[6]"Don't be alarmed," he said. "You are looking for Jesus the Nazarene,[l] who was crucified. He has
risen! He is not here. See the place where they laid him. [7]But go, tell his disciples and Peter, 'He is going
ahead of you into Galilee. There you will see him,[m] just as he told you.'"[n]
[8]Trembling and bewildered, the women went out and fled from the tomb. They said nothing to anyone, because they were afraid.[a]

[The earliest manuscripts and some other ancient witnesses do not have verses 9–20.]

*[9]When Jesus rose early on the first day of the week, he appeared first to Mary Magdalene,[o] out of whom he
had driven seven demons. [10]She went and told those who had been with him and who were mourning and
weeping. [11]When they heard that Jesus was alive and that she had seen him, they did not believe it.[p]*
[12]Afterward Jesus appeared in a different form to two of them while they were walking in the country.[q]
[13]These returned and reported it to the rest; but they did not believe them either.
*[14]Later Jesus appeared to the Eleven as they were eating; he rebuked them for their lack of faith and their
stubborn refusal to believe those who had seen him after he had risen.[r]*
*[15]He said to them, "Go into all the world and preach the gospel to all creation.[s] [16]Whoever believes and is
baptized will be saved, but whoever does not believe will be condemned.[t] [17]And these signs will accompany
those who believe: In my name they will drive out demons;[u] they will speak in new tongues;[v] [18]they will pick
up snakes[w] with their hands; and when they drink deadly poison, it will not hurt them at all; they will place
their hands on[x] sick people, and they will get well."*
*[19]After the Lord Jesus had spoken to them, he was taken up into heaven[y] and he sat at the right hand of
God.[z] [20]Then the disciples went out and preached everywhere, and the Lord worked with them and confirmed
his word by the signs that accompanied it.*

16:6 [l]Mk 1:24
16:7 [m]Jn 21:1-23 [n]Mk 14:28
16:9 [o]Jn 20:11-18
16:11 [p]ver 13,14; Lk 24:11
16:12 [q]Lk 24:13-32
16:14 [r]Lk 24:36-43
16:15 [s]Mt 28:18-20; Lk 24:47,48
16:16 [t]Jn 3:16,18,36; Ac 16:31
16:17 [u]Mk 9:38; Lk 10:17; Ac 5:16; 8:7; 16:18; 19:13-16 [v]Ac 2:4; 10:46; 19:6; 1Co 12:10, 28,30
16:18 [w]Lk 10:19; Ac 28:3-5 [x]Ac 6:6
16:19 [y]Lk 24:50,51; Jn 6:62; Ac 1:9-11; 1Ti 3:16 [z]Ps 110:1; Ro 8:34; Col 3:1; Heb 1:3; 12:2

[a] *8* Some manuscripts have the following ending between verses 8 and 9, and one manuscript has it after verse 8 (omitting verses 9-20). *Then they quickly reported all these instructions to those around Peter. After this, Jesus himself also sent out through them from east to west the sacred and imperishable proclamation of eternal salvation. Amen.*

16:6 Nazarene. See note on 14:67. **crucified.** See notes on 8:34; 15:24. **He has risen!** One word in Greek. It is hard to imagine anything less grandiose or sensational. The entire gospel and the turning of the ages hangs on this single declaration, delivered so matter-of-factly here. In Christ, death has been conquered!

16:7 The women can testify only to the empty tomb apparently because Jesus, as promised, is already going ahead of his disciples to Galilee (14:28). It is perhaps the failed disciples (14:50) and especially Peter (14:66–72) who most need the assurance of a resurrection appearance, with its hope of forgiveness and restoration (cf. 14:27–28).

16:8 Trembling and bewildered. The typical response to God's mighty deeds, especially at the exodus (Exod 15:15–16), and what Isaiah's last great lament had requested in the new exodus (Isa 64:1–3; see note on 1:10). Just as Jesus' mighty deeds regularly inspired this response, so too this final, mightiest deed. **said nothing to anyone, because they were afraid.** This ending has left readers unsatisfied from the earliest times. Since Mark has already introduced his Gospel as the fulfillment of Isa 40:3 (see note on 1:2–3), perhaps he has in mind Isa 40:9, which is just a few verses further in Isa 40 and the only place in the Scriptures where a command to not "be afraid" is combined with a summons to declare aloud the "good news" (cf. Isa 41:10,13–14; 43:1,5; 44:2; 51:7,12; 54:4). In rejecting Jesus, Jerusalem had refused the summons; even his disciples have fled in fear (14:50; cf. 10:32) and now too the first witnesses. Clearly, silence was not the last word since the gospel has gone out. But in leaving the women's fearful silence hanging, Mark might perhaps be asking his readers a searching question: what will their response be? Will they retreat into fearful silence or proclaim the good news of God's salvation?

16:9–20 Scholars almost universally agree that this section is a later attempt, perhaps by a second-century scribe, to rectify the perceived problem of v. 8 (see note on v. 8). The earliest and best manuscripts do not have these verses; they are unknown to a number of early church fathers; and the vocabulary and style differ from the rest of Mark.

INTRODUCTION TO LUKE

The Gospel of Luke is the first installment of the two-volume work Luke-Acts. This first volume describes God's climactic work in the history of salvation through the life, death, resurrection, and ascension of Jesus Christ; the second volume points to the power of the gospel of Jesus Christ in forming a renewed people of God.

AUTHOR

Although the author does not explicitly identify himself, the evidence points to Luke. The oldest manuscript (late second century AD) names Luke as the author in the attached title, and the roughly contemporary Muratorian Canon and the early church fathers, beginning with Irenaeus, support this identification. The content of both Luke and Acts further confirms this identification. The "we" passages in Acts (Acts 16:10 – 17; 20:5 – 15; 21:1 – 18; 27:1 — 28:16) should best be understood as coming from the pen of a companion of Paul, and Paul's own writings suggest that Luke was one of his co-workers (Col 4:14; 2 Tim 4:11; Phlm 24). Paul's further identification of Luke as a medical doctor (Col 4:14) is consistent with several aspects of this Gospel, such as its prologue (1:1 – 4), which is similar in length and style to contemporary scientific writings.

Luke's familiarity with the wider Greco-Roman cultural and political world, as well as its geographic landscape, suggests that he may have been a Gentile. His interest in the salvation of the Gentiles and his distinct ability to write polished Greek appear to confirm this identification. On the other hand, his knowledge of the OT and his intimate knowledge of the Jewish community point to an intimate connection with the Jews. Perhaps he was a Gentile who was attracted to Jewish religious beliefs and practices. In the first century, Gentiles who worshiped in the synagogue but were not full converts to Judaism were identified as "God-fearers," and Luke's interest in the "God-fearers" (Acts 14:1; 16:13 – 14; 17:2 – 4,10 – 12,17; 18:4; 19:8 – 10) may reflect his own identity as one of them.

DATE

There is a lack of scholarly consensus regarding dating this Gospel, although we can assume that it was written after Mark and before Acts. Those who insist on a pre-AD 70 date note that Luke does not describe Paul's death (mid-60s) in Acts or show an awareness of Paul's letters. Those who argue for a date after AD 70 respond by pointing out that Luke was not writing a biography of Paul but an account of the progress of the gospel, and although Luke does not explicitly quote from Paul's letters, his writings do reflect the influence of Paul's thought. Definitive arguments are lacking to establish a pre-70 dating, but the issues discussed in Luke-Acts do point to the struggles of the first-century church, and the focus of the active work of the Spirit reflects the reality of the early period of the church. Taking into consideration the fact that Luke was a companion of Paul, it is reasonable to assume that Luke wrote his two-volume work around AD 70.

INTENDED AUDIENCE

In the prologue to each of his volumes, Luke mentions a "Theophilus" (Luke 1:3; Acts 1:1). The appellation "most excellent" (Luke 1:3) points to his high social status; in Acts, it is also applied to several Roman officers (Acts 23:26;

24:3; 26:25). It is often assumed that this Theophilus is to be considered the intended reader of this two-volume work, but this narrow identification is doubtful. First, ancient biographies and histories were often public documents written to wider communities, not one individual. Thus, Luke is most likely addressing a wider audience. Second, the content of Luke-Acts addresses a wide variety of issues. To limit this work to the concerns and needs of one individual may not be appropriate.

The content of Luke's writing points to an audience familiar with Jewish customs and culture but still at home in a Gentile environment. This may again point to the "God-fearers" as the possible target audience, although it seems likely that Luke is addressing a wider mixed audience that contains both Jews and Gentiles. These are likely believers who have received "the things [they] have been taught" (1:4), although the evangelistic thrust of Luke's message cannot be denied.

OCCASION AND PURPOSE

Instead of insisting on one particular event or set of circumstances that led to Luke's writing this Gospel, it seems better to read Luke's Gospel as attempting to address a series of issues, even though they are not all equally prominent:

1. Luke's primary purpose is to strengthen and confirm the faith of the early Christians. He writes so that Theophilus (and other readers) "may know the certainty of the things" they have been taught (1:4). As for the exact "things" that require affirmation, one must look further into Luke's writings to find them.

2. One of Luke's main incentives for writing his two-volume work is to emphasize proclaiming the gospel. The first volume establishes the foundation and center of the gospel, while the second volume depicts the power of this gospel as it spread throughout the Roman world.

3. Luke has a particular interest in showing what the coming of Christ means for the identity of God's people (2:30–33; 3:4–6; 4:16–30; 24:46–47; Acts 1:8; 13:46–47; 28:28). Throughout this two-volume work, Luke highlights the powerful work of Jesus the Messiah, whose death and resurrection ushers in a new era in salvation history, an era that witnesses the power of the gospel among both Jews and Gentiles.

4. Other purposes of Luke's two-volume work have been proposed: to explain the delay of Jesus' return, to defend the early Christian movement for the Roman audience, and to combat proto-Gnosticism. None of these, however, can explain the entirety of Luke's two-volume work, even though particular passages may support one of these purposes.

GENRE

In both form and content, this Gospel resembles those of Mark and Matthew. All three can be read as belonging to the broad category of Greco-Roman biographies (see the discussion in "Introduction to the Gospels and Acts," p. 1916). The fact that Luke's second volume (Acts) is to be identified as "history" does not prevent one from reading Luke's Gospel as a biography since early samples of Greco-Roman biographies are often embedded in historical works.

PROVINCES AND TOWNS PERTINENT TO THE BOOK OF LUKE

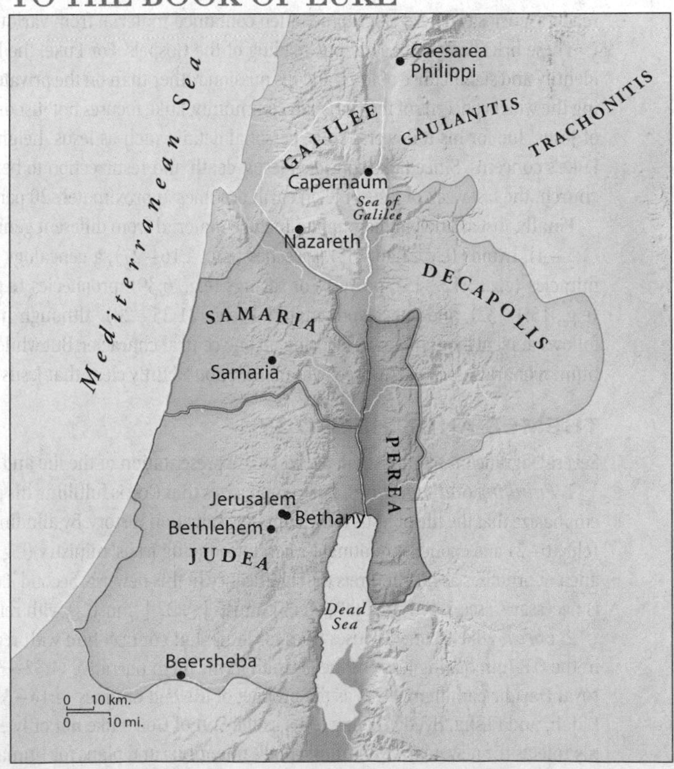

View overlooking the Sea of Galilee from the Mount of Beatitudes where it is thought the Sermon on the Mount (Luke 6:20–49) was preached.

© Jon Arnold Images Ltd/Alamy

Unlike their modern counterparts, ancient biographies focused on the public life and career of a person. Their authors aimed at addressing the concerns of their communities rather than revealing private details to satisfy their readers' curiosity. These biographies often contained material from various subgenres.

These brief descriptions aid our reading of the Gospels. For Luke, the birth narrative (chs. 1–2) focuses on the identity and significance of Jesus and his mission rather than on the private details of his childhood years. In addressing the wider concerns of the Christian community, Luke focuses not just on Jesus himself but also on the significance of Jesus' life for his followers. Thus, personal details such as Jesus' height or appearance are beyond the realm of Luke's concerns. Since Luke considers Jesus' death and resurrection to be the foundational events for the life of the church, the last week of Jesus' life on earth occupies approximately 20 percent of his Gospel.

Finally, just as ancient biographies include material from different genres, Luke's Gospel also includes a prologue (1:1–4), hymns (e.g., 1:46–55), speeches (e.g., 4:16–27), a genealogy (3:23–38), call accounts (e.g., 5:1–11), miracles (e.g., 5:12–15), proverbs or sayings (e.g., 6:39), prophecies (e.g., 9:22), prayers (e.g., 11:2–4), parables (e.g., 15:1–32), and apocalyptic material (e.g., 21:25–28). Although his Gospel contains diverse material, Luke follows ancient biographies in focusing on one central character. But while ancient biographies were concerned with human characters, Luke's Gospel will make it abundantly clear that Jesus is also the Son of God.

THEMES AND THEOLOGY

Several significant themes stand out in Luke's presentation of the life and mission of Jesus:

1. *Fulfilling God's promises.* Luke emphasizes that God is fulfilling his plan of salvation. First, Luke uses the OT to emphasize that the life of Jesus is the climax of salvation history. By alluding to the OT throughout the birth narrative (chs. 1–2) and explicitly quoting it when introducing Jesus' ministry (e.g., 3:4–6; 4:18–19), Luke highlights God's ancient promises as he interprets the significance of this new era. Second, Luke repeatedly uses the Greek word *dei* ("it is necessary"; see 2:49 ["had to"]; 4:43 ["must"]; 9:22 ["must"]) with reference to the predetermined plan of God.

2. *Christ.* Luke frequently uses titles for Jesus that connect him with recurring themes and paradigms that begin in the OT. Introducing Jesus as the Messiah in the birth narrative (1:32–33,68–75; 2:8–14) places him within the royal Davidic paradigm. Jesus as the prophet of the end of times (4:16–31; 13:33; 24:19) fulfills the roles of Moses, Elijah, and Elisha. By identifying Jesus as the Son of God, Luke not only emphasizes Jesus' divinity (22:70) but also his role as the new Adam who fulfills God's intentions and plans for humanity (3:38).

3. *Holy Spirit.* In the birth narrative, Luke draws attention to the Holy Spirit's intensive activity in the announcement that the new eschatological era has arrived (1:15,35,67; 2:25–27). Luke's second volume (Acts) makes this explicit: the outpouring of the Spirit signifies the presence of the "last days" (Acts 2:17). These references to the Spirit pave the way for how Luke portrays Jesus as "anointed" by the Spirit (4:18; 3:22). Not only does the emphasis on the Spirit establish a significant Christological point, it also links Jesus and his disciples because they also experience the outpouring of the Spirit prior to their apostolic mission (Acts 2:1–12).

4. *Salvation.* Luke emphasizes that Jesus saves sinners. Jesus is "the Son of Man [who] came to seek and to save the lost" (19:10). Luke portrays Jesus as the one who saves by using the Greek words *sōzō* ("to save"; see 6:9; 8:12; 9:24; 13:23; 17:19 ["made you well"]; 18:26), *sōtēria* ("salvation"; see 1:69,71,77; 19:9), and *sōtērion* ("salvation"; see 2:30; 3:6).

5. *Including outcasts and Gentiles.* Luke emphasizes how God includes both outcasts and Gentiles. First, he emphasizes marginal groups that are often excluded from Israel. Through acts of table-fellowship, Jesus redefines God's people by including "tax collectors and sinners" (5:30; 7:34; 15:1). This inclusion is based on the principle of divine reversal since in the last days it is the outcasts who will be invited to the eschatological banquet, but "not one of those who were [originally] invited will get a taste of my banquet" (14:24). Second, Luke emphasizes how God includes Gentiles. He introduces this theme in his Gospel (2:32; 3:6; 4:25–27; 7:1–10) and fully develops it in the second volume (Acts 1:8; 10:1—11:18; 15:1–35).

OUTLINE

I. Introduction (1:1–4)

II. Dawn of a New Era (1:5—2:52)
- A. The Birth of John the Baptist Foretold (1:5–25)
- B. The Birth of Jesus Foretold (1:26–38)
- C. Mary Visits Elizabeth (1:39–45)
- D. Mary's Song (1:46–56)
- E. The Birth of John the Baptist (1:57–66)
- F. Zechariah's Song (1:67–80)
- G. The Birth of Jesus (2:1–21)
- H. Jesus Presented in the Temple (2:22–40)
- I. The Boy Jesus at the Temple (2:41–52)

III. Preparation for Jesus' Ministry (3:1—4:13)
- A. John the Baptist Prepares the Way (3:1–20)
- B. The Baptism and Genealogy of Jesus (3:21–38)
- C. Jesus Is Tested in the Wilderness (4:1–13)

IV. The Galilean Ministry (4:14—9:50)
- A. Proclamation in Words and Deeds (4:14–44)
  - 1. Jesus Rejected at Nazareth (4:14–30)
  - 2. Jesus Drives Out an Impure Spirit (4:31–37)
  - 3. Jesus Heals Many (4:38–44)
- B. Formation of a New Community (5:1—6:16)
  - 1. Jesus Calls His First Disciples (5:1–11)
  - 2. Jesus Heals a Man With Leprosy (5:12–16)
  - 3. Jesus Forgives and Heals a Paralyzed Man (5:17–26)
  - 4. Jesus Calls Levi and Eats With Sinners (5:27–32)
  - 5. Jesus Questioned About Fasting (5:33–39)
  - 6. Jesus Is Lord of the Sabbath (6:1–11)
  - 7. The Twelve Apostles (6:12–16)
- C. Teachings for the New Community (6:17–49)
  - 1. Blessings and Woes (6:17–26)
  - 2. Love for Enemies (6:27–36)

3. Judging Others (6:37 – 42)
4. A Tree and Its Fruit (6:43 – 45)
5. The Wise and Foolish Builders (6:46 – 49)

D. Responses to the Gospel (7:1 — 8:21)
1. The Faith of the Centurion (7:1 – 10)
2. Jesus Raises a Widow's Son (7:11 – 17)
3. Jesus and John the Baptist (7:18 – 35)
4. Jesus Anointed by a Sinful Woman (7:36 – 50)
5. The Parable of the Sower (8:1 – 15)
6. A Lamp on a Stand (8:16 – 18)
7. Jesus' Mother and Brothers (8:19 – 21)

E. Authority and Identity of Jesus (8:22 — 9:50)
1. Jesus Calms the Storm (8:22 – 25)
2. Jesus Restores a Demon-Possessed Man (8:26 – 39)
3. Jesus Raises a Dead Girl and Heals a Sick Woman (8:40 – 56)
4. Jesus Sends Out the Twelve (9:1 – 9)
5. Jesus Feeds the Five Thousand (9:10 – 17)
6. Peter Declares That Jesus Is the Messiah (9:18 – 20)
7. Jesus Predicts His Death (9:21 – 27)
8. The Transfiguration (9:28 – 36)
9. Jesus Heals a Demon-Possessed Boy (9:37 – 43a)
10. Jesus Predicts His Death a Second Time (9:43b – 50)

V. Journey to Jerusalem (9:51 — 19:44)

A. Commission and Reception (9:51 — 11:13)
1. Samaritan Opposition (9:51 – 56)
2. The Cost of Following Jesus (9:57 – 62)
3. Jesus Sends Out the Seventy-Two (10:1 – 24)
4. The Parable of the Good Samaritan (10:25 – 37)
5. At the Home of Martha and Mary (10:38 – 42)
6. Jesus' Teaching on Prayer (11:1 – 13)

B. Call to Repentance in the Midst of Opposition (11:14 — 13:35)
1. Jesus and Beelzebul (11:14 – 28)
2. The Sign of Jonah (11:29 – 32)
3. The Lamp of the Body (11:33 – 36)
4. Woes on the Pharisees and the Experts in the Law (11:37 – 54)
5. Warnings and Encouragements (12:1 – 12)
6. The Parable of the Rich Fool (12:13 – 21)
7. Do Not Worry (12:22 – 34)
8. Watchfulness (12:35 – 48)
9. Not Peace but Division (12:49 – 53)
10. Interpreting the Times (12:54 – 59)
11. Repent or Perish (13:1 – 9)
12. Jesus Heals a Crippled Woman on the Sabbath (13:10 – 17)
13. The Parables of the Mustard Seed and the Yeast (13:18 – 21)
14. The Narrow Door (13:22 – 30)
15. Jesus' Sorrow for Jerusalem (13:31 – 35)

C. Identity of God's People (14:1 — 19:27)
1. Jesus at a Pharisee's House (14:1 – 14)
2. The Parable of the Great Banquet (14:15 – 24)
3. The Cost of Being a Disciple (14:25 – 35)
4. The Parable of the Lost Sheep (15:1 – 7)

5. The Parable of the Lost Coin (15:8–10)
6. The Parable of the Lost Son (15:11–32)
7. The Parable of the Shrewd Manager (16:1–15)
8. Additional Teachings (16:16–18)
9. The Rich Man and Lazarus (16:19–31)
10. Sin, Faith, Duty (17:1–10)
11. Jesus Heals Ten Men With Leprosy (17:11–19)
12. The Coming of the Kingdom of God (17:20–37)
13. The Parable of the Persistent Widow (18:1–8)
14. The Parable of the Pharisee and the Tax Collector (18:9–14)
15. The Little Children and Jesus (18:15–17)
16. The Rich and the Kingdom of God (18:18–30)
17. Jesus Predicts His Death a Third Time (18:31–34)
18. A Blind Beggar Receives His Sight (18:35–43)
19. Zacchaeus the Tax Collector (19:1–10)
20. The Parable of the Ten Minas (19:11–27)

D. Jesus Comes to Jerusalem as King (19:28–44)

VI. Death and Vindication of Jesus (19:45—24:53)

A. Controversy With Jerusalem Leaders (19:45—21:38)

1. Jesus at the Temple (19:45–48)
2. The Authority of Jesus Questioned (20:1–8)
3. The Parable of the Tenants (20:9–19)
4. Paying Taxes to Caesar (20:20–26)
5. The Resurrection and Marriage (20:27–40)
6. Whose Son Is the Messiah? (20:41–44)
7. Warning Against the Teachers of the Law (20:45–47)
8. The Widow's Offering (21:1–4)
9. The Destruction of the Temple and Signs of the End Times (21:5–38)

B. Betrayal and Death of Jesus (22:1—23:56)

1. Judas Agrees to Betray Jesus (22:1–6)
2. The Last Supper (22:7–38)
3. Jesus Prays on the Mount of Olives (22:39–46)
4. Jesus Arrested (22:47–53)
5. Peter Disowns Jesus (22:54–62)
6. The Guards Mock Jesus (22:63–65)
7. Jesus Before Pilate and Herod (22:66—23:25)
8. The Crucifixion of Jesus (23:26–43)
9. The Death of Jesus (23:44–49)
10. The Burial of Jesus (23:50–56)

C. Resurrection and Ascension of Jesus (24:1–53)

1. Jesus Has Risen (24:1–12)
2. On the Road to Emmaus (24:13–35)
3. Jesus Appears to the Disciples (24:36–49)
4. The Ascension of Jesus (24:50–53)

LUKE

1:2 [a]Mk 1:1; Jn 15:27; Ac 1:21,22 [b]Heb 2:3; 1Pe 5:1; 2Pe 1:16; 1Jn 1:1 [c]Mk 4:14
1:3 [d]Ac 11:4 [e]Ac 24:3; 26:25 [f]Ac 1:1
1:4 [g]Jn 20:31
1:5 [h]Mt 2:1 [i]1Ch 24:10
1:6 [j]Ge 7:1; 1Ki 9:4

Introduction

1:1-4Ref — Ac 1:1

1 Many have undertaken to draw up an account of the things that have been fulfilled[a] among us,
2just as they were handed down to us by those who from the first[a] were eyewitnesses[b] and servants
of the word.[c] 3With this in mind, since I myself have carefully investigated everything from the beginning, I too decided to write an orderly account[d] for you, most excellent[e] Theophilus,[f] 4so that you may
know the certainty of the things you have been taught.[g]

The Birth of John the Baptist Foretold

5In the time of Herod king of Judea[h] there was a priest named Zechariah, who belonged to the
priestly division of Abijah;[i] his wife Elizabeth was also a descendant of Aaron. 6Both of them were righteous in the sight of God, observing all the Lord's commands and decrees blamelessly.[j] 7But they were
childless because Elizabeth was not able to conceive, and they were both very old.

[a] 1 Or *been surely believed*

1:1–4 *Introduction.* With a long and complex sentence that echoes classical Greek literature, Luke begins by acknowledging his use of existing sources and vouching for their trustworthiness since they are based on eyewitness accounts. He concludes his preface by stating the purpose of his Gospel. The style and content of this preface resemble those found in ancient historical and scientific writings, perhaps reflecting the nature of this work as well as Luke's background as a medical doctor.
1:1 the things that have been fulfilled among us. Luke's Gospel shows how God fulfills OT promises; it recounts his climactic work among his people.
1:2 handed down. A technical term in Greek that draws attention to the tradition's reliable transmission (cf. 1 Cor 11:23; 15:3). **eyewitnesses.** Reaffirms that the traditions about Jesus are reliable. **servants of the word.** Those who proclaimed and submitted to the gospel message (cf. Acts 6:4). **the word.** Paves the way for Luke's later emphasis of the power of the word throughout the Greco-Roman world (Acts 6:7; 12:24; 19:20).
1:3 orderly account. This does not necessarily mean that Luke's Gospel follows a strict chronological order. In some places, Luke appears to use topical rather than chronological organization (e.g., 3:20–21; 4:16–30 [cf. Mark 6:1–6]; 5:1–11 [cf. Mark 1:16–20]). Elsewhere in Luke's writings, the Greek here translated "orderly" refers to systematically and thoughtfully presenting a series of events (Acts 11:4). **Theophilus.** Means "friend of God" and can therefore refer to all friends of God, but in this context it most likely refers to a historical person since the appellation "most excellent" is a title applied to Roman officials in Acts (Acts 23:26; 24:3; 26:25). See Introduction: Intended Audience.
1:4 The purpose of this Gospel includes, but is not limited to, evangelism (see Introduction: Occasion and Purpose). Luke also aims to strengthen the faith of those who have been taught the basic gospel teachings.
1:5—2:52 *Dawn of a New Era.* Luke begins his narrative by presenting the birth and childhood accounts of John the Baptist and Jesus. Parallels between the two highlight the continuity between the old (represented by John the Baptist) and the new (represented by Jesus) ages (cf. 1:5–25 and 1:26–38; cf. 1:57–80 and 2:1–40). Episodes that uniquely apply to Jesus highlight the discontinuity (1:39–56; 2:41–52).

This narrative emphasizes both Jesus' continuity with the prophetic traditions of the past and his unique identity as the Messiah and Son of God.
1:5–25 *The Birth of John the Baptist Foretold.* Like many OT birth stories (e.g., Gen 18; 25; 30; Judg 13; 1 Sam 1–2), this account evokes the theme of barrenness to highlight that God is present among his people. God's reversal for one family signifies that he is present to save and deliver his entire people (Isa 54:1–2). The grace that Zechariah and Elizabeth receive follows the pattern of God's intervention on behalf of his people.
1:5 Herod king of Judea. The same Herod the Great who ruled over Judea, Samaria, Galilee, and the surrounding regions from 37 to 4 BC. **Zechariah.** Means "the Lord has remembered." He very appropriately introduces this narrative. **the priestly division of Abijah.** The 8th of the 24 divisions in charge of managing temple affairs (1 Chr 23:32; 24:10).
1:6 righteous ... blamelessly. Though not without sin, they were faithful in worshiping God and keeping his commandments.
1:7 they were both very old. Recalls the story of Abraham and Sarah (Gen 18:11), particularly as they received the prophecy concerning the birth of their son.

[8]Once when Zechariah's division was on duty and he was serving as priest before God,[k] [9]he was chosen by lot, according to the custom of the priesthood, to go into the temple of the Lord and burn incense.[l] [10]And when the time for the burning of incense came, all the assembled worshipers were praying outside.[m]

[11]Then an angel[n] of the Lord appeared to him, standing at the right side of the altar of incense.[o] [12]When Zechariah saw him, he was startled and was gripped with fear.[p] [13]But the angel said to him: "Do not be afraid,[q] Zechariah; your prayer has been heard. Your wife Elizabeth will bear you a son, and you are to call him John.[r] [14]He will be a joy and delight to you, and many will rejoice because of his birth,[s] [15]for he will be great in the sight of the Lord. He is never to take wine or other fermented drink,[t] and he will be filled with the Holy Spirit even before he is born.[u] [16]He will bring back many of the people of Israel to the Lord their God. [17]And he will go on before the Lord,[v] in the spirit and power of Elijah,[w] to turn the hearts of the parents to their children[x] and the disobedient to the wisdom of the righteous — to make ready a people prepared for the Lord."

[18]Zechariah asked the angel, "How can I be sure of this? I am an old man and my wife is well along in years."[y]

[19]The angel said to him, "I am Gabriel.[z] I stand in the presence of God, and I have been sent to speak to you and to tell you this good news. [20]And now you will be silent and not able to speak[a] until the day this happens, because you did not believe my words, which will come true at their appointed time."

[21]Meanwhile, the people were waiting for Zechariah and wondering why he stayed so long in the temple. [22]When he came out, he could not speak to them. They realized he had seen a vision in the temple, for he kept making signs[b] to them but remained unable to speak.

[23]When his time of service was completed, he returned home. [24]After this his wife Elizabeth became pregnant and for five months remained in seclusion. [25]"The Lord has done this for me," she said. "In these days he has shown his favor and taken away my disgrace[c] among the people."

The Birth of Jesus Foretold

[26]In the sixth month of Elizabeth's pregnancy, God sent the angel Gabriel[d] to Nazareth,[e] a town in Galilee, [27]to a virgin pledged to be married to a man named Joseph,[f] a descendant of David. The virgin's name was Mary. [28]The angel went to her and said, "Greetings, you who are highly favored! The Lord is with you."

[29]Mary was greatly troubled at his words and wondered what kind of greeting this might be. [30]But

1:8 [k] 1Ch 24:19; 2Ch 8:14
1:9 [l] Ex 30:7,8; 1Ch 23:13; 2Ch 29:11
1:10 [m] Lev 16:17
1:11 [n] Ac 5:19 [o] Ex 30:1-10
1:12 [p] Jdg 6:22,23; 13:22
1:13 [q] ver 30; Mt 14:27 [r] ver 60,63
1:14 [s] ver 58
1:15 [t] Nu 6:3; Jdg 13:4; Lk 7:33 [u] Jer 1:5; Gal 1:15
1:17 [v] ver 76 [w] Mt 11:14 [x] Mal 4:5,6
1:18 [y] ver 34; Ge 17:17
1:19 [z] ver 26; Da 8:16; 9:21; Mt 18:10
1:20 [a] Eze 3:26
1:22 [b] ver 62
1:25 [c] Ge 30:23; Isa 4:1
1:26 [d] ver 19 [e] Mt 2:23
1:27 [f] Mt 1:16,18,20; Lk 2:4

1:8–9 Apart from the major pilgrim festivals, each of the priestly divisions served in the temple for just two weeks a year. Because of the large number of priests in each division, each individual priest would burn incense at the daily sacrifice only once in his lifetime. This is an important occasion for Zechariah, and God chooses to appear to him through an angel. **1:11 an angel of the Lord.** Often represents God himself (Gen 16:7–13; Exod 3:2–4; 23:20; Num 20:16; Isa 63:9; see note on Exod 3:2). **1:12 fear.** A common reaction when one encounters God or his agents (Exod 15:15–16; Judg 6:22–23; 13:6,22; 2 Sam 6:9). **1:13 Do not be afraid.** A common response to comfort those who experience such an encounter, especially when announcing the birth of a child (Gen 15:1; 26:24; Judg 6:22–23). **1:14 joy.** A significant theme in Luke (2:10; 10:17; 15:10) and Acts (13:52; 15:3). **1:15 never to take wine or other fermented drink.** John may be a Nazirite (Num 6:1–4; Judg 13:4), or this may point simply to his total devotion to God (Lev 10:9). **1:17 turn the hearts of the parents to their children.** Recalls the prophecy concerning the future Elijah in Mal 4:6. **make ready a people prepared for the Lord.** Points to Isa 40:3, which Mal 3:1 also uses to refer to the future Elijah. Luke 3:4–6 explicitly quotes Isa 40:3–5 to refer to the new era that John's ministry launches. **1:19 Gabriel.** Appears only in Dan 8:16; 9:21 in the OT. His appearance here demonstrates that God is fulfilling his ancient prophecies, which in turn signifies the climax of the history of salvation. **to tell ... good news.** A word group that here depicts an important stage of God's climactic act in history (cf. Isa 40:9–10; 41:27; 52:7). Luke 4:18–19 specifies the content of this Good News or gospel (cf. Isa 58:6; 61:1–2). **1:20 silent ... not able to speak.** A sign of God's punishment for Zechariah's disbelief (cf. Acts 13:11). See also the experience of Daniel, who was "speechless" (Dan 10:15) after he encountered Gabriel. **1:24 remained in seclusion.** This accords with what we know of the cultural practices for a pregnant woman at the time. It may also parallel Zechariah's silence as they both anticipate their son's arrival (cf. v. 64). **1:26–38** *The Birth of Jesus Foretold.* Introducing Mary and Jesus sets this account apart from the previous section. Mary's difficulty lies not in her age but in that she is not married (v. 27) and is a virgin (v. 34). Jesus, on the other hand, is not just a prophet (like John) but is "the Son of the Most High" (v. 32) and "the Son of God" (v. 35) who is also to sit on the throne of David (v. 32). **1:27 virgin.** May evoke Isa 7:14 (cf. Matt 1:23), although Luke does not explicitly quote it. **Joseph, a descendant of David.** Joseph's Davidic descent paves the way for Jesus, who will sit on "the throne of his father" (v. 32). **1:28 The Lord is with you.** Mary has a special role in God's plan (cf. Gen 26:24; 28:15; Exod 3:12; Judg 6:12). This may also allude to Isa 7:14 (see note on v. 27) since Immanuel means "God with us." **1:29 wondered.** Mary is aware of the deeper meaning of what is happening to her (cf. 2:19,51). **1:30 Do not be afraid.** See note on v. 13.

1:30 [g]ver 13; Mt 14:27
1:31 [h]Isa 7:14; Mt 1:21,25; Lk 2:21
1:32 [i]ver 35,76; Mk 5:7
1:33 [j]Mt 28:18 [k]Da 2:44; 7:14,27; Mic 4:7; Heb 1:8
1:35 [l]Mt 1:18 [m]ver 32, 76 [n]Mk 1:24 [o]Mt 4:3
1:37 [p]Mt 19:26
1:39 [q]ver 65
1:42 [r]Jdg 5:24
1:46 [s]Ps 34:2,3
1:47 [t]1Ti 1:1; 2:3
1:48 [u]Ps 138:6 [v]Lk 11:27
1:49 [w]Ps 71:19 [x]Ps 111:9

the angel said to her, "Do not be afraid,[g] Mary; you have found favor with God. 31 You will conceive and
give birth to a son, and you are to call him Jesus.[h] 32 He will be great and will be called the Son of the
Most High.[i] The Lord God will give him the throne of his father David, 33 and he will reign over Jacob's
descendants forever; his kingdom[j] will never end."[k]

34 "How will this be," Mary asked the angel, "since I am a virgin?"
35 The angel answered, "The Holy Spirit will come on you,[l] and the power of the Most High[m] will
overshadow you. So the holy one[n] to be born will be called[a] the Son of God.[o] 36 Even Elizabeth your
relative is going to have a child in her old age, and she who was said to be unable to conceive is in her
sixth month. 37 For no word from God will ever fail."[p]
38 "I am the Lord's servant," Mary answered. "May your word to me be fulfilled." Then the angel
left her.

Mary Visits Elizabeth

39 At that time Mary got ready and hurried to a town in the hill country of Judea,[q] 40 where she entered
Zechariah's home and greeted Elizabeth. 41 When Elizabeth heard Mary's greeting, the baby leaped in
her womb, and Elizabeth was filled with the Holy Spirit. 42 In a loud voice she exclaimed: "Blessed are
you among women,[r] and blessed is the child you will bear! 43 But why am I so favored, that the mother
of my Lord should come to me? 44 As soon as the sound of your greeting reached my ears, the baby in my
womb leaped for joy. 45 Blessed is she who has believed that the Lord would fulfill his promises to her!"

Mary's Song

1:46-53pp — 1Sa 2:1-10

46 And Mary said:

"My soul glorifies the Lord[s]
47 and my spirit rejoices in God my Savior,[t]
48 for he has been mindful
of the humble state of his servant.[u]
From now on all generations will call me blessed,[v]
49 for the Mighty One has done great things[w] for me —
holy is his name.[x]

[a] 35 Or *So the child to be born will be called holy,*

1:31 Jesus. Means "the Lord saves" (Matt 1:21).
1:32–33 These verses recall the depiction of David in 2 Sam 7:8–16: "great" (2 Sam 7:9), "son" (2 Sam 7:14), "throne" (2 Sam 7:13), "David" (2 Sam 7:8), and "kingdom will endure forever" (2 Sam 7:16). These also appear in the later traditions that refer to the future Davidic ruler (Pss 2:7; 89:19–37; Isa 7–9; Jer 23:5–8). In the OT, "the Most High" is a title applied to God (Gen 14:18–22; Deut 32:8; 2 Sam 22:14; Ps 7:17), a title that places him above all created beings.
1:32 the Son of the Most High. Explicitly identifies Jesus as unique and exalted, especially since John is only "a prophet of the Most High" (v. 76).
1:35 This verse alludes to Isa 32:15, which predicts that God will restore his people. Here, God will fulfill this promise through Jesus, "the holy one" and "the Son of God," who uniquely and finally fulfills God's promises to David (cf. Rom 1:3–4).
1:36 relative. Luke does not specify Mary's precise relationship to Elizabeth. The term can refer to a distant relative or merely to someone who comes from the same geographic vicinity (cf. v. 58; 2:44; 14:12; 21:16; Acts 10:24).
1:39–45 *Mary Visits Elizabeth.* This meeting of the two mothers is important in two ways. First, John's leaping in his mother's womb shows that he recognizes that he is in the presence of someone greater than himself; Jesus is not just a prophet like John. Second, the first blessing identifies Mary's blood relationship with Jesus (v. 42), while the second focuses on Mary's faith and obedience (v. 45). Luke later clarifies that faith and obedience are more important than physical relationship (8:19–21; 11:27–28), which paves the way for his later emphasizing that God's people include those who are not related to the Messiah of Israel by blood (i.e., Gentiles).
1:42 Blessed are you among women. This is superlative; i.e., "Among all women, you are the most blessed" (cf. Judg 5:24).
1:43 my Lord. May allude to an important Messianic psalm: "The LORD says to my lord" (Ps 110:1; cf. Luke 20:41–44; Acts 2:34). **Lord.** An exalted Christological title in this context (cf. v. 76; 2:11; 4:12; 13:15,35).
1:44 leaped for joy. This baby is able to experience joy even before his birth.
1:45 has believed. Mary's belief contrasts with Zechariah's disbelief (v. 20).
1:46–56 *Mary's Song.* Based on its opening word in the Latin Vulgate, this song is known as the Magnificat ("glorifies"). Mary's experience is not only a personal one but also reflects the reversal of fortunes that people will experience through her son (vv. 52–55). This song's themes and language resemble those of Hannah's song (1 Sam 2:1–10); both foreshadow God's acts of deliverance. It also echoes OT psalms of thanksgiving that contain both a note of thanksgiving and the reasons for such thanksgiving (Pss 30; 34; 138).
1:47 Savior. An angel later applies this title to Jesus (2:11).
1:49 Mighty One. God is a warrior who can deliver his people through his victorious power (Ps 45:3–5; Zeph 3:17).

[50]His mercy extends to those who fear him,
from generation to generation.[y]
[51]He has performed mighty deeds with his arm;[z]
he has scattered those who are proud in their inmost thoughts.
[52]He has brought down rulers from their thrones
but has lifted up the humble.
[53]He has filled the hungry with good things[a]
but has sent the rich away empty.
[54]He has helped his servant Israel,
remembering to be merciful[b]
[55]to Abraham and his descendants[c] forever,
just as he promised our ancestors."

[56]Mary stayed with Elizabeth for about three months and then returned home.

The Birth of John the Baptist

[57]When it was time for Elizabeth to have her baby, she gave birth to a son. [58]Her neighbors and relatives heard that the Lord had shown her great mercy, and they shared her joy.
[59]On the eighth day they came to circumcise[d] the child, and they were going to name him after his
father Zechariah, [60]but his mother spoke up and said, "No! He is to be called John."[e]
[61]They said to her, "There is no one among your relatives who has that name."
[62]Then they made signs[f] to his father, to find out what he would like to name the child. [63]He asked
for a writing tablet, and to everyone's astonishment he wrote, "His name is John."[g] [64]Immediately his
mouth was opened and his tongue set free, and he began to speak,[h] praising God. [65]All the neighbors
were filled with awe, and throughout the hill country of Judea[i] people were talking about all these
things. [66]Everyone who heard this wondered about it, asking, "What then is this child going to be?" For
the Lord's hand was with him.[j]

Zechariah's Song

[67]His father Zechariah was filled with the Holy Spirit and prophesied:[k]

[68]"Praise be to the Lord, the God of Israel,[l]
because he has come to his people and redeemed them.[m]
[69]He has raised up a horn[a][n] of salvation for us
in the house of his servant David[o]
[70](as he said through his holy prophets of long ago),[p]

[a] *69 Horn* here symbolizes a strong king.

1:50 [y]Ex 20:6; Ps 103:17
1:51 [z]Ps 98:1; Isa 40:10
1:53 [a]Ps 107:9
1:54 [b]Ps 98:3
1:55 [c]Ge 17:19; Ps 132:11; Gal 3:16
1:59 [d]Ge 17:12; Lev 12:3; Lk 2:21; Php 3:5
1:60 [e]ver 13,63
1:62 [f]ver 22
1:63 [g]ver 13,60
1:64 [h]ver 20
1:65 [i]ver 39
1:66 [j]Ge 39:2; Ac 11:21
1:67 [k]Joel 2:28
1:68 [l]Ps 72:18 [m]Ps 111:9; Lk 7:16
1:69 [n]1Sa 2:1,10; Ps 18:2, 89:17, 132:17, Eze 29:21 [o]Mt 1:1
1:70 [p]Jer 23:5

1:52–55 The theme of reversal is important throughout both Luke and Acts. In social terms, the poor and marginalized experience God's blessings (4:18; 6:20–22; 7:22; 14:13,21). In terms of Israel's history, God reverses the fortunes of his people as he remembers his covenant with Abraham (v. 55).
1:56 This verse turns our attention back to the birth of John the Baptist. **returned home.** That is, to Mary's own home.
1:57–66 *The Birth of John the Baptist.* Though often identified as a birth account, this section only briefly describes the birth of John the Baptist (v. 57). It focuses instead on his naming (vv. 58–66), emphasizing his place in God's plan (cf. vv. 68–80).
1:59 The rite of circumcision customarily took place on the eighth day (Gen 17:12; 21:4; Lev 12:3). Usually a child received their name immediately after birth (Gen 25:24–26; 29:31–35), but Abram received the name "Abraham" when he was circumcised (Gen 17:5,23–24). Both John (v. 60) and Jesus (2:21) received their names when they were circumcised, probably to highlight their connection with the Abrahamic promises.
1:60 John. Means "the Lord is merciful."
1:64 praising God. This is repeatedly noted in Luke in recognition of God's decisive acts among human beings (2:13,20,28; 5:25–26; 7:16; 13:13; 17:15,18; 18:43; 19:37; 23:47; 24:53).
1:67–80 *Zechariah's Song.* From its opening word in the Latin Vulgate, this hymn is known as the "Benedictus" ("Praise be"). It praises God for faithfully keeping his promises to David (v. 69) and Abraham (v. 73), and it highlights the relationship between John and Jesus (vv. 76–79).
1:67 was filled with the Holy Spirit and prophesied. Signifies God's renewed presence among his people (cf. Isa 32:14–17; 44:1–4). Luke's later description of the last days makes this significance explicit: "I will pour out my Spirit in those days, and they will prophesy" (Acts 2:18; cf. Joel 2:28).
1:68 redeemed them. Redemption here includes both corporate and individual aspects. Israel as God's people are delivered from their enemies (v. 71), while individual members experience "forgiveness of their sins" (v. 77) that is granted through God's acts of salvation.
1:69 horn of salvation ... in the house of his servant David. Parallels the phrase "horn of my salvation" that appears in the Davidic tradition (2 Sam 22:3; Ps 18:2; cf. Ps 132:17).

1:72 [q]Mic 7:20 [r]Ps 105:8,9; 106:45; Eze 16:60
1:73 [s]Ge 22:16-18
1:74 [t]Heb 9:14
1:75 [u]Eph 4:24
1:76 [v]Mt 11:9 [w]ver 32, 35 [x]ver 17; Mal 3:1
1:77 [y]Jer 31:34; Mk 1:4
1:78 [z]Mal 4:2
1:79 [a]Isa 9:2; 59:9; Mt 4:16; Ac 26:18
1:80 [b]Lk 2:40,52
2:1 [c]Mt 22:17; Lk 3:1 [d]Mt 24:14
2:2 [e]Mt 4:24
2:4 [f]Jn 7:42

71 salvation from our enemies
and from the hand of all who hate us —
72 to show mercy to our ancestors[q]
and to remember his holy covenant,[r]
73 the oath he swore to our father Abraham:[s]
74 to rescue us from the hand of our enemies,
and to enable us to serve him[t] without fear
75 in holiness and righteousness[u] before him all our days.

76 And you, my child, will be called a prophet[v] of the Most High;[w]
for you will go on before the Lord to prepare the way for him,[x]
77 to give his people the knowledge of salvation
through the forgiveness of their sins,[y]
78 because of the tender mercy of our God,
by which the rising sun[z] will come to us from heaven
79 to shine on those living in darkness
and in the shadow of death,[a]
to guide our feet into the path of peace."

80 And the child grew and became strong in spirit[*a*];[b] and he lived in the wilderness until he appeared publicly to Israel.

The Birth of Jesus

2 In those days Caesar Augustus[c] issued a decree that a census should be taken of the entire Roman
world.[d] 2 (This was the first census that took place while[*b*] Quirinius was governor of Syria.)[e] 3 And
everyone went to their own town to register.
4 So Joseph also went up from the town of Nazareth in Galilee to Judea, to Bethlehem[f] the town of
David, because he belonged to the house and line of David. 5 He went there to register with Mary, who
was pledged to be married to him and was expecting a child. 6 While they were there, the time came for

[*a*] 80 Or *in the Spirit* [*b*] 2 Or *This census took place before*

1:73 the oath. Likely refers to God's original promise to Abraham in Gen 22:16–18 (see Deut 4:31; 13:17; 29:13), although the focus here is no longer on the land but on the people of God.

1:76 Jesus is John's superior because he is "the Son of the Most High" (v. 32), while John is "a prophet of the Most High." As in v. 17 (see note there), John's role alludes to Isa 40:3.

1:78 rising sun. Scripture uses imagery of rising/springing forth for God's restoring his people (Isa 42:9; 43:19; 44:4; 61:11), especially in reference to the coming of the Messiah (cf. Mal 4:2). The Greek word that lies behind this phrase (*anatolē*) was also used in Messianic traditions in reference to "branch" (Zech 6:12) or "star" (Num 24:17). In this context, we cannot rule out a secondary reference to these traditions.

1:79 peace. An important term in Luke's Gospel (2:14,29; 7:50; 14:32; 19:38,42; 24:36). It should not be understood exclusively in social and political terms since it also points to the cosmic restoration that God's final saving act will bring about (Isa 11:6–9; 65:17–25).

1:80 wilderness. Likely the region between Jerusalem and the Dead Sea; it may recall the wilderness wanderings of the Israelites who witnessed God's mighty acts in their midst.

2:1–21 *The Birth of Jesus.* Compared to the account of the events surrounding John's birth, the relative length of this account again reflects that Jesus is superior.

For Gentile readers, this section clearly points to Jesus as the only one worthy of honor and respect. Although the Roman emperor appears to be in control, Jesus is the sovereign Lord of all. According to Roman imperial propaganda, Caesar Augustus is the savior who will proclaim the good news of peace. In reality, Jesus is the real "Savior" (v. 11) who will proclaim the "good news" (v. 10) of "peace" (v. 14).

For Jewish readers, Jesus fulfills the ancient promises. There are several parallels to Isa 9:2–7: light and darkness (vv. 8–9; Isa 9:2), joy (v. 10; Isa 9:3), the birth of a child (v. 11; Isa 9:6), a Davidic Messiah (v. 11; Isa 9:7), and a new era of peace (v. 14; Isa 9:6–7). As such, Jesus' "kingdom" will last "forever" (Isa 9:7).

2:1 Caesar Augustus. The title conferred upon Gaius Octavius Thurinus, the first Roman emperor (31 BC–AD 14). Ending a long series of civil wars, he ushered in a period of peace. He decreed a "census" for military and taxation purposes, but the Jews were exempt from Roman military service. Those under Roman rule viewed the census as yet another means of oppression by this foreign power.

2:2 Other sources have dated a census under Quirinius to AD 6 (Josephus, *Antiquities*, 18.26; cf. Acts 5:37), when he began his term as governor of Syria. This census could not be the one noted by Luke since Herod the Great died in 4 BC. It is possible that Quirinius served an earlier term that began before Jesus' birth (often dated at 6 or 5 BC). **while.** Greek *prōtos.* It is possible to translate this as "before" (see NIV text note), which would mean that this census could have taken place before AD 6. Furthermore, inscriptions on ancient coins suggest that there may have been another Quirinius who was governor during the time of Jesus' birth. The presence of two Roman officials of the same name may then explain the historical difficulties here.

2:4 Bethlehem. David's birthplace (1 Sam 17:12; 20:6). Mic 5:1–2 directly connects Bethlehem and the future Davidic king (cf. Matt 2:5–6).

the baby to be born, 7and she gave birth to her firstborn, a son. She wrapped him in cloths and placed
him in a manger, because there was no guest room available for them.
8And there were shepherds living out in the fields nearby, keeping watch over their flocks at night.
9An angel[g] of the Lord appeared to them, and the glory of the Lord shone around them, and they were
terrified. 10But the angel said to them, "Do not be afraid.[h] I bring you good news that will cause great
joy for all the people. 11Today in the town of David a Savior[i] has been born to you; he is the Messiah,[j]
the Lord. 12This will be a sign[k] to you: You will find a baby wrapped in cloths and lying in a manger."
13Suddenly a great company of the heavenly host appeared with the angel, praising God and saying,

14"Glory to God in the highest heaven,
and on earth peace[l] to those on whom his favor rests."

15When the angels had left them and gone into heaven, the shepherds said to one another, "Let's go
to Bethlehem and see this thing that has happened, which the Lord has told us about."
16So they hurried off and found Mary and Joseph, and the baby, who was lying in the manger. 17When
they had seen him, they spread the word concerning what had been told them about this child, 18and
all who heard it were amazed at what the shepherds said to them. 19But Mary treasured up all these
things and pondered them in her heart.[m] 20The shepherds returned, glorifying and praising God[n] for
all the things they had heard and seen, which were just as they had been told.
21On the eighth day, when it was time to circumcise the child,[o] he was named Jesus, the name the
angel had given him before he was conceived.[p]

Jesus Presented in the Temple

22When the time came for the purification rites required by the Law of Moses,[q] Joseph and Mary took
him to Jerusalem to present him to the Lord 23(as it is written in the Law of the Lord, "Every firstborn
male is to be consecrated to the Lord"[a]),[r] 24and to offer a sacrifice in keeping with what is said in the
Law of the Lord: "a pair of doves or two young pigeons."[b][s]
25Now there was a man in Jerusalem called Simeon, who was righteous and devout.[t] He was waiting
for the consolation of Israel,[u] and the Holy Spirit was on him. 26It had been revealed to him by the Holy

[a] *23* Exodus 13:2,12 [b] *24* Lev. 12:8

2:9 [g]Lk 1:11; Ac 5:19
2:10 [h]Mt 14:27
2:11 [i]Mt 1:21; Jn 4:42; Ac 5:31 [j]Mt 1:16; 16:16, 20; Jn 11:27; Ac 2:36
2:12 [k]1Sa 2:34; 2Ki 19:29; Isa 7:14
2:14 [l]Lk 1:79; Ro 5:1; Eph 2:14,17
2:19 [m]ver 51
2:20 [n]Mt 9:8
2:21 [o]Lk 1:59 [p]Lk 1:31
2:22 [q]Lev 12:2-8
2:23 [r]Ex 13:2,12,15; Nu 3:13
2:24 [s]Lev 12:8
2:25 [t]Lk 1:6 [u]ver 38; Isa 52:9; Lk 23:51

2:7 firstborn. May recall the promise in Ps 89:27, where God's "firstborn" is "the most exalted of the kings of the earth." **cloths.** Often used for swaddling newborns. **manger.** Likely a feeding trough for animals. **guest room.** Not necessarily a room at an inn. It could have been simply the guest room of a residential house (cf. 22:11; Mark 14:14).
2:8 shepherds. In later Jewish traditions they were often considered troublemakers, but in the OT God is portrayed as the shepherd who cares for his people (Gen 48:15; 49:24; Ps 23:1; Jer 31:10). David, who was a shepherd, was also called to be the shepherd of God's people (2 Sam 5:2; 7:7; 1 Chr 11:2; 17:6).
2:9 angel of the Lord. May represent God himself (see 1:11 and note).
2:11 Today. Luke uses this word to declare that God's salvation is present (cf. 4:21; 5:26; 13:32–33; 19:5; 23:43). **Savior.** Applies to God himself in 1:47, but the title applies to Jesus here. In the OT, the title also applies to God's servant or messenger (Judg 3:9,15; Neh 9:27). **Messiah.** This Hebrew title, often translated "Christ" in Greek, means "the anointed one." In the OT, the "anointed ones" include kings (1 Sam 9:16; 24:6), priests (Lev 4:3,5,16), and prophets (1 Kgs 19:16; Ps 105:15; Isa 61:1). In intertestamental Jewish literature, "Messiah Lord" refers to the expected royal Messiah (*Psalms of Solomon* 17.32; 18.7).
2:12 sign. Appears to center on the "manger" (vv. 7,16). If so, this may allude to Isa 1:3: "The ox knows its master, the donkey its owner's manger, but Israel does not know, my people do not understand."
2:14 Based on the opening word in the Latin Vulgate, this short song is known as the "Gloria in Excelsis Deo" ("Glory to God in the highest heaven"). **Glory.** The manifestation of God's power and majesty (vv. 9,32; 9:26,32; 24:26; Acts 7:2,55; cf. Acts 22:11). The proper way to respond to witnessing God's power is to give him praise (17:18; cf. Acts 12:23).
2:22–40 *Jesus Presented in the Temple.* Each of the first three verses of this section mentions "the Law"; Luke emphasizes that Jesus both obeys and fulfills the law of Moses. The rest of the section further develops how Jesus' life and ministry is significant for both Jews and Gentiles (vv. 25–40). Temple is a significant theme in Luke (see "Temple," p. 2652).
2:22 purification rites. Was necessary for mothers 40 days after the birth of a son (Lev 12:1–4).
2:23 The quotation paraphrases the consecration rites in Exod 13:2,12,15. Israel's firstborn sons must be consecrated to the Lord to respond to God's sparing the lives of their firstborn sons during the Passover event. Further, Levites serve on behalf of the firstborn sons (Num 18). Luke combines the purification and consecration rites as he focuses on Jesus' total commitment to God.
2:24 Luke returns to the purification rites by quoting Lev 12:8, where a mother who cannot afford to sacrifice a lamb can choose to offer "two doves or two young pigeons." This provides a glimpse of Mary's economic condition and demonstrates her faithfulness to the law.
2:25 the consolation of Israel. God's deliverance of Israel will bring comfort to this people (Isa 40:1; 51:3; 57:18; 66:11), and this comfort includes spiritual, emotional, political, and social elements. **the Holy Spirit.** His presence further confirms the presence of God's climactic act of salvation. These references to God's consolation and the Holy Spirit point forward to 4:18–19, where Jesus quotes Isa 61:1–2.

2:27 [v]ver 22
2:29 [w]ver 26 [x]Ac 2:24
2:30 [y]Isa 52:10; Lk 3:6
2:32 [z]Isa 42:6; 49:6; Ac 13:47; 26:23
2:34 [a]Mt 12:46 [b]Isa 8:14; Mt 21:44; 1Co 1:23; 2Co 2:16; 1Pe 2:7,8
2:36 [c]Ac 21:9
2:37 [d]1Ti 5:9 [e]Ac 13:3; 14:23; 1Ti 5:5
2:38 [f]ver 25; Isa 40:2; Lk 1:68; 24:21
2:39 [g]ver 51; Mt 2:23
2:40 [h]ver 52; Lk 1:80
2:41 [i]Ex 23:15; Dt 16:1-8
2:47 [j]Mt 7:28
2:48 [k]Mt 12:46 [l]Lk 3:23; 4:22

Spirit that he would not die before he had seen the Lord's Messiah. 27 Moved by the Spirit, he went into
the temple courts. When the parents brought in the child Jesus to do for him what the custom of the
Law required,[v] 28 Simeon took him in his arms and praised God, saying:

> 29 "Sovereign Lord, as you have promised,[w]
> you may now dismiss[a] your servant in peace.[x]
> 30 For my eyes have seen your salvation,[y]
> 31 which you have prepared in the sight of all nations:
> 32 a light for revelation to the Gentiles,
> and the glory of your people Israel."[z]

33 The child's father and mother marveled at what was said about him. 34 Then Simeon blessed them
and said to Mary, his mother:[a] "This child is destined to cause the falling[b] and rising of many in Israel,
and to be a sign that will be spoken against, 35 so that the thoughts of many hearts will be revealed. And
a sword will pierce your own soul too."

36 There was also a prophet,[c] Anna, the daughter of Penuel, of the tribe of Asher. She was very old;
she had lived with her husband seven years after her marriage, 37 and then was a widow until she was
eighty-four.[b][d] She never left the temple but worshiped night and day, fasting and praying.[e] 38 Coming
up to them at that very moment, she gave thanks to God and spoke about the child to all who were
looking forward to the redemption of Jerusalem.[f]

39 When Joseph and Mary had done everything required by the Law of the Lord, they returned to Galilee to their own town of Nazareth.[g] 40 And the child grew and became strong; he was filled with wisdom,
and the grace of God was on him.[h]

The Boy Jesus at the Temple

41 Every year Jesus' parents went to Jerusalem for the Festival of the Passover.[i] 42 When he was twelve
years old, they went up to the festival, according to the custom. 43 After the festival was over, while his
parents were returning home, the boy Jesus stayed behind in Jerusalem, but they were unaware of it.
44 Thinking he was in their company, they traveled on for a day. Then they began looking for him among
their relatives and friends. 45 When they did not find him, they went back to Jerusalem to look for him.
46 After three days they found him in the temple courts, sitting among the teachers, listening to them
and asking them questions. 47 Everyone who heard him was amazed[j] at his understanding and his answers. 48 When his parents saw him, they were astonished. His mother[k] said to him, "Son, why have you
treated us like this? Your father[l] and I have been anxiously searching for you."

a 29 Or *promised, / now dismiss* *b* 37 Or *then had been a widow for eighty-four years.*

2:29–32 Based on the opening word in the Latin Vulgate, this song is known as "Nunc Dimittis" ("now dismiss"). Combining the terms "salvation" (v. 30), "prepared" (v. 31), and "all nations" (v. 31)—i.e., the Gentiles who would also witness God's salvation (v. 32)—points forward to 3:4–6, which quotes Isa 40:3–5.
2:34 falling and rising. It could refer to the fall and revival of the entire people of God, but in this context it most likely refers to the Jews' divided response to Jesus. Some will reject the Good News, while others will accept it. **a sign that will be spoken against.** Jesus; his presence causes division and disputes, and those who reject him will be condemned.
2:35 a sword will pierce. Likely the eventual death of Jesus (and the first hint of Jesus' death in Luke's Gospel) that would cause pain and sorrow for his mother, Mary.
2:36 Anna. A "prophet," since she testifies to God's mighty acts (Acts 2:17–21; cf. Joel 2:28–32). **Penuel.** Means "face of God"; it is possible that this person came from the city of Penuel, not too far from Shechem (1 Kgs 12:25; see NIV text note there). **Asher.** Was among the northern tribes (Gen 49:20; Deut 33:24–25), and this reference highlights Anna's northern origin, so her presence represents the northern kingdom as it also witnesses the presence of God's salvation among his entire people.
2:40 Cf. 1:80, which similarly describes John. Unlike John, however, Jesus is "filled with wisdom" and experiences "the grace of God." This may allude to Isa 11:2: "The Spirit of the LORD will rest on him—the Spirit of wisdom and of understanding."
2:41–52 *The Boy Jesus at the Temple.* Because this does not parallel the account of John the Baptist, it demonstrates Jesus' unique status and ability. It highlights Jesus' wisdom (v. 47; cf. vv. 40,52), his ability to interpret the law (vv. 46–47), and his mission and identity (v. 49).
2:41 Passover. The most important of the three major pilgrim festivals (together with Pentecost [Harvest] and Tabernacles [Ingathering]; Exod 23:14–19). It was a celebration and remembrance of how God delivered the Israelites from the hand of Pharaoh (e.g., Exod 12:1–30; cf. 2 Chr 35:1–19).
2:42 Children who turned 13 years old were often considered responsible adults under the law. That Jesus is already to demonstrate his wisdom at the age of 12 highlights his unique ability.
2:46 listening to them and asking them questions. This depicts Jesus not as a lowly student but as one with authority to dialogue with the Jewish teachers, the experts of the law. This explains why people were "amazed at his understanding and his answers" (v. 47).
2:48–49 Your father and I ... my Father's. The mentioning of the two fathers makes it clear that God is Jesus' true Father.

49“Why were you searching for me?” he asked. “Didn’t you know I had to be in my Father’s house?”[a][m]
50But they did not understand what he was saying to them.[n]

51Then he went down to Nazareth with them[o] and was obedient to them. But his mother treasured
all these things in her heart.[p] 52And Jesus grew in wisdom and stature, and in favor with God and man.[q]

John the Baptist Prepares the Way

3:2-10pp — Mt 3:1-10; Mk 1:3-5
3:16,17pp — Mt 3:11,12; Mk 1:7,8

3 In the fifteenth year of the reign of Tiberius Caesar—when Pontius Pilate[r] was governor of Judea, Herod[s] tetrarch of Galilee, his brother Philip tetrarch of Iturea and Traconitis, and Lysanias
tetrarch of Abilene— 2during the high-priesthood of Annas and Caiaphas,[t] the word of God came to
John[u] son of Zechariah[v] in the wilderness. 3He went into all the country around the Jordan, preaching
a baptism of repentance for the forgiveness of sins.[w] 4As it is written in the book of the words of Isaiah
the prophet:

> “A voice of one calling in the wilderness,
> ‘Prepare the way for the Lord,
> make straight paths for him.
> 5Every valley shall be filled in,
> every mountain and hill made low.
> The crooked roads shall become straight,
> the rough ways smooth.
> 6And all people will see God’s salvation.’ ”[b][x]

7John said to the crowds coming out to be baptized by him, “You brood of vipers![y] Who warned you
to flee from the coming wrath?[z] 8Produce fruit in keeping with repentance. And do not begin to say to

2:49 [m] Jn 2:16
2:50 [n] Mk 9:32
2:51 [o] ver 39; Mt 2:23 [p] ver 19
2:52 [q] ver 40; 1Sa 2:26; Lk 1:80
3:1 [r] Mt 27:2 [s] Mt 14:1
3:2 [t] Mt 26:3; Jn 18:13; Ac 4:6 [u] Mt 3:1 [v] Lk 1:13
3:3 [w] ver 16; Mk 1:4
3:6 [x] Ps 98:2; Isa 40:3-5; 42:16; 52:10; Lk 2:30
3:7 [y] Mt 12:34; 23:33 [z] Ro 1:18

[a] *49* Or *be about my Father’s business* [b] *6* Isaiah 40:3-5

2:49 had to be. God’s plan imposed this (cf. 4:43; 9:22; 13:33; 15:32). Jesus’ decision to follow his heavenly Father is not simply a matter of personal preference; he submitted to his Father’s wider plan. **Father’s house.** That is, the temple; it can also be translated as “Father’s business” (see NIV text note).

2:52 Jesus grew … in favor with God and man. Like the OT heroes (1 Sam 2:26; cf. Gen 21:8; Judg 13:24), but Jesus uniquely possesses divine “wisdom.”

3:1—4:13 *Preparation for Jesus’ Ministry.* This section introduces Jesus’ identity and public ministry. In preparation for Jesus’ ministry, John calls God’s people to repent in anticipation of God’s act of fulfilling his promises to Israel (3:1–20). Jesus’ baptism and genealogy present him as both the Son of God and the suffering servant (3:21–38). His faithfulness to God in the wilderness proves him to be unlike Israel as he is truly the faithful Son of God (4:1–13).

3:1–20 *John the Baptist Prepares the Way.* Luke begins describing the ministry of John the Baptist by outlining the political structure of the time (vv. 1–2). John’s prophetic message is relevant for the entire empire. As in the OT, the responsibilities of John the prophet include challenging both the people of God (vv. 7–14) and the corrupt ruler who deviates from his divinely ordained role (vv. 19–20). John is preparing the way for the promised Messiah, who is superior to John (vv. 3–6,15–18).

3:1 Tiberius Caesar. Succeeded Augustus as Roman emperor; his reign began formally in AD 14 so that “the fifteenth year” of his reign may be dated to AD 28–29, although an earlier dating is also possible since his control of the provinces can be dated to a few years before AD 14. After the death of Herod the Great in 4 BC, Herod’s kingdom was divided among his sons: Archelaus, Antipas, and Philip. Archelaus ruled over Judea, Samaria, and Idumea, but his reign ended in AD 6. After that, Roman prefects were assigned to rule these regions. **Pontius Pilate.** The prefect in charge from AD 26 to 36. His official title is confirmed in an inscription discovered in 1961 in Caesarea, identifying him as “Pontius Pilate, Prefect of Judea” (see photo, p. 1995). **Herod tetrarch of Galilee.** Herod’s son Antipas, who ruled over Galilee and Perea from 4 BC to AD 39. **Philip.** Philip II, another son of Herod and the half brother of Antipas; he was “tetrarch of Iturea and Traconitis” from 4 BC to AD 34. **Lysanias tetrarch of Abilene.** Known only from an inscription that describes a person with the same name as a local ruler during the reign of Tiberius Caesar.

3:2 Since the Persian period in the late fifth century BC, high priests had acquired significant political influence in local Judean politics. **Annas.** The high priest from AD 6 to 15. **Caiaphas.** Annas’s son-in-law; he assumed the position of high priest from AD 18 to 36. Luke considers both Annas and Caiaphas high priests, probably recognizing this priestly family’s influence (cf. John 18:13; Acts 4:5–6). **the word of God came to John.** Connects John with OT prophets who had similar experiences (Jer 1:2; Hos 1:1; Joel 1:1; Jonah 1:1; Zeph 1:1; Zech 1:1).

3:3 baptism of repentance. The emphasis is placed on the message conveyed by John’s baptism. **repentance.** Signifies a change of heart that is testified by a change of behavior (vv. 11–14) in anticipation of the judgment that is to come (v. 17). This message prepares the people for God’s decisive work through his Son, who delivers repentant sinners from God’s wrath by dying on the cross.

3:4–6 Luke quotes Isa 40:3–5, which to many Jews describes the final and decisive acts of God on behalf of his people.

3:4 Prepare the way for the Lord. This first part of the quotation focuses on John’s role; the rest situates the story of Jesus and the church within the wider promises of God as found in Isaiah.

3:6 all people will see God’s salvation. This is missing in Mark 1:2–3 (cf. Matt 11:10); it anticipates the gospel spreading among the Gentiles in the book of Acts.

3:7 You brood of vipers! They refused to welcome God’s salvific acts. In Isaiah, these “vipers” (Isa 59:5) are the rebellious people of God who

3:8 [a]Isa 51:2; Lk 19:9; Jn 8:33,39; Ac 13:26; Ro 4:1,11,12,16,17; Gal 3:7
3:9 [b]Mt 3:10
3:10 [c]ver 12,14; Ac 2:37; 16:30
3:11 [d]Isa 58:7
3:12 [e]Lk 7:29
3:13 [f]Lk 19:8
3:14 [g]Ex 23:1; Lev 19:11
3:15 [h]Mt 3:1 [i]Jn 1:19, 20; Ac 13:25
3:16 [j]ver 3; Mk 1:4 [k]Jn 1:26,33; Ac 1:5; 11:16; 19:4
3:17 [l]Isa 30:24 [m]Mt 13:30; 25:41
3:19 [n]ver 1
3:20 [o]Mt 14:3,4; Mk 6:17-18
3:21 [p]Mt 14:23; Mk 1:35; 6:46; Lk 5:16; 6:12; 9:18,28; 11:1
3:22 [q]Isa 42:1; Jn 1:32, 33; Ac 10:38 [r]Mt 3:17 [s]Mt 3:17

yourselves, 'We have Abraham as our father.'[a] For I tell you that out of these stones God can raise up
children for Abraham. 9The ax is already at the root of the trees, and every tree that does not produce
good fruit will be cut down and thrown into the fire."[b]

10"What should we do then?"[c] the crowd asked.

11John answered, "Anyone who has two shirts should share with the one who has none, and anyone
who has food should do the same."[d]

12Even tax collectors came to be baptized.[e] "Teacher," they asked, "what should we do?"

13"Don't collect any more than you are required to,"[f] he told them.

14Then some soldiers asked him, "And what should we do?"
He replied, "Don't extort money and don't accuse people falsely[g]—be content with your pay."

15The people were waiting expectantly and were all wondering in their hearts if John[h] might possibly
be the Messiah.[i] 16John answered them all, "I baptize you with[a] water.[j] But one who is more powerful
than I will come, the straps of whose sandals I am not worthy to untie. He will baptize you with[a] the
Holy Spirit and fire.[k] 17His winnowing fork[l] is in his hand to clear his threshing floor and to gather the
wheat into his barn, but he will burn up the chaff with unquenchable fire."[m] 18And with many other
words John exhorted the people and proclaimed the good news to them.

19But when John rebuked Herod[n] the tetrarch because of his marriage to Herodias, his brother's wife,
and all the other evil things he had done, 20Herod added this to them all: He locked John up in prison.[o]

The Baptism and Genealogy of Jesus

3:21,22pp — Mt 3:13-17; Mk 1:9-11
3:23-38pp — Mt 1:1-17

21When all the people were being baptized, Jesus was baptized too. And as he was praying,[p] heaven
was opened 22and the Holy Spirit descended on him[q] in bodily form like a dove. And a voice came from
heaven: "You are my Son,[r] whom I love; with you I am well pleased."[s]

[a] *16* Or *in*

turned the way of their Lord into "crooked roads" (Isa 59:8). **the coming wrath.** Cf. Isa 13:9; 30:27. It will descend on those who refuse to accept the Good News, and it refers both to the impending destruction of Jerusalem in AD 70 (cf. 21:20–24) and the final judgment at the end of time (21:25–28).

3:9 ax. The OT uses the imagery of its destructive power on plants to picture the enemies of God's people (cf. Isa 10:33–34). John implies that if God's people do not repent, they will suffer the same fate.

3:12 tax collectors. Viewed by Jews as direct or indirect instruments of the Roman oppression and as thieves because they charged a much higher amount in order to pay themselves. In Luke, they are among the marginal and rejected community (5:27–32; 7:34; 15:1; 18:9–14; 19:1–10).

3:14 soldiers. Probably local police rather than members of the Roman army. They may have been personal guards for Herod Antipas. **Don't extort money.** Suggests that the soldiers may be connected with the tax collectors and serve as their police guards. Consistent with biblical teachings elsewhere, a repentant heart must be demonstrated by behavioral changes that have personal and social implications (see note on v. 3).

3:16 with the Holy Spirit and fire. One baptism, not two separate baptisms. In Mark 1:8, John mentions only the baptism of the Holy Spirit. In the OT, the Holy Spirit (Isa 4:4) and fire (Isa 66:24; Joel 2:30; Mal 4:1) can both refer to the future judgment. This reference to judgment is consistent with the imagery in v. 17 of the winnowing fork, which separates the righteous ("wheat") and wicked ("chaff"). This fire can also carry the power to purify God's people in anticipation of the final judgment.

3:17 winnowing fork ... wheat ... chaff. See note on v. 16.

3:19 Herod the tetrarch. Herod Antipas (see v. 1 and note). He had divorced his first wife, the daughter of Aretas IV of Arabia, and married his niece Herodias, who was also the wife of his half brother Philip I (Matt 14:3; Mark 6:17). This Philip (Philip I) did not rule; he is different from the Philip (Philip II) who was tetrarch of Iturea and Traconitis (see v. 1 and note). John's rebuke is based on the Mosaic regulation that prohibits a man from marrying "his brother's wife" (Lev 20:21; cf. Lev 18:16).

3:20 John's imprisonment took place at a later point in time (Mark 6:14–29; John 3:22–24), but Luke follows accepted literary practices of his time by placing this account before Jesus' baptism to conclude his account of John's ministry before moving to Jesus' ministry. This arrangement also highlights the parallelism between John and Jesus: both proclaim the kingdom of God, and both are persecuted for doing so.

3:21–38 *The Baptism and Genealogy of Jesus.* Luke begins portraying Jesus' ministry by describing his baptism, at which time Jesus receives the power of the Holy Spirit, and the Father confirms that Jesus is his Son (vv. 21–22). The genealogy (vv. 23–38) affirms that Jesus will fulfill Adam's role for the new people of God.

3:21–22 The climax of Jesus' baptism is the Holy Spirit descending and the Father declaring that Jesus is his Son. The focus is not as much on the bare fact that John the Baptist baptized Jesus as on what made Jesus' baptism different from the baptism of the crowds.

3:21 heaven was opened. We expect God's revelation to follow (cf. Ezek 1:1; John 1:51; Acts 7:56; 10:11; Rev 19:11).

3:22 the Holy Spirit descended on him. Points to the final age (Acts 2:17–21; cf. Joel 2:28–32) and Jesus' status as the anointed one (Luke 4:18; cf. Isa 61:1). This also fulfills ancient promises such as Isa 11:2: "The Spirit of the LORD will rest on him." The declaration from heaven further identifies Jesus as the promised one. **You are my Son.** Fulfills the Davidic promise in Ps 2:7 (cf. 2 Sam 7:14). **whom I love.** May reinforce the unique ties between the Son and the Father (cf. Gen 22:2,12,16), though it may also allude to the servant figure in Isa 42:1, which also lies behind "with you I am well pleased."

[23]Now Jesus himself was about thirty years old when he began his ministry.[t] He was the son, so it
was thought, of Joseph,[u]

the son of Heli, [24]the son of Matthat,
the son of Levi, the son of Melki,
the son of Jannai, the son of Joseph,
[25] the son of Mattathias, the son of Amos,
the son of Nahum, the son of Esli,
the son of Naggai, [26]the son of Maath,
the son of Mattathias, the son of Semein,
the son of Josek, the son of Joda,
[27] the son of Joanan, the son of Rhesa,
the son of Zerubbabel,[v] the son of Shealtiel,
the son of Neri, [28]the son of Melki,
the son of Addi, the son of Cosam,
the son of Elmadam, the son of Er,
[29] the son of Joshua, the son of Eliezer,
the son of Jorim, the son of Matthat,
the son of Levi, [30]the son of Simeon,
the son of Judah, the son of Joseph,
the son of Jonam, the son of Eliakim,
[31] the son of Melea, the son of Menna,
the son of Mattatha, the son of Nathan,[w]
the son of David, [32]the son of Jesse,
the son of Obed, the son of Boaz,
the son of Salmon,[a] the son of Nahshon,
[33] the son of Amminadab, the son of Ram,[b]
the son of Hezron, the son of Perez,[x]
the son of Judah, [34]the son of Jacob,
the son of Isaac, the son of Abraham,
the son of Terah, the son of Nahor,[y]
[35] the son of Serug, the son of Reu,
the son of Peleg, the son of Eber,
the son of Shelah, [36]the son of Cainan,
the son of Arphaxad,[z] the son of Shem,
the son of Noah, the son of Lamech,[a]
[37] the son of Methuselah, the son of Enoch,
the son of Jared, the son of Mahalalel,
the son of Kenan, [38]the son of Enosh,

3:23 [t]Mt 4:17; Ac 1:1 [u]Lk 1:27
3:27 [v]Mt 1:12
3:31 [w]2Sa 5:14; 1Ch 3:5
3:33 [x]Ru 4:18-22; 1Ch 2:10-12
3:34 [y]Ge 11:24,26
3:36 [z]Ge 11:12 [a]Ge 5:28-32

[a] *32* Some early manuscripts *Sala* [b] *33* Some manuscripts *Amminadab, the son of Admin, the son of Arni*; other manuscripts vary widely.

3:23–38 The genealogy of Jesus in Luke begins with Jesus and ends with Adam, the son of God. The genealogies in Matthew and Luke differ, especially with reference to Jesus and David, and interpreters explain it in different ways: (1) Luke traces the genealogy through the line of Mary; Matthew, through Joseph. (2) Luke traces the "legal" line from David; Matthew traces the physical blood line. (3) Luke considers Nathan (v. 31) rather than Solomon (as in Matthew's genealogy [Matt 1:6]) the heir of David because of the curse upon Jehoiachin, a descendant of Solomon (Jer 22:28–30; 36:30; see note on Luke 3:27).
3:23 about thirty years old. May recall OT characters who assumed significant responsibilities when they turned 30 years old (Gen 41:46; 2 Sam 5:4). **so it was thought.** Reminds readers of the virgin birth.
3:27 In OT accounts, Shealtiel is the son of Jehoiachin, but here he is "the son of Neri." This change is probably based on the curse on Jehoiachin: "Record this man as if childless … for none of his offspring will prosper, none will sit on the throne of David" (Jer 22:30; cf. Jer 36:30). Therefore, in this genealogy of the Davidic Messiah, Shealtiel is no longer considered to be from the line of Jehoiachin.
3:28–31 The names from Melki to Mattatha appear only in this biblical genealogy.
3:31–34 We can trace Jesus through the line of David, Judah, Jacob, Isaac, and Abraham. Jesus fulfilled the Abrahamic and Davidic covenants.
3:37–38 Tracing Jesus' ancestry all the way back to "Adam, the son of God," highlights the universal significance of Jesus' ministry. Luke later emphasizes that all humanity came from God: "We are his [i.e., God's] offspring" (Acts 17:28).

Remains of the fifth-century church that was built over the supposed house of Peter in Capernaum.
www.HolyLandPhotos.org

3:38 [b] Ge 5:1,2,6-9
4:1 [c] ver 14,18 [d] Lk 3:3,21 [e] Lk 2:27
4:2 [f] Ex 34:28; 1Ki 19:8
4:4 [g] Dt 8:3
4:5 [h] Mt 24:14
4:6 [i] Jn 12:31; 14:30; 1Jn 5:19

the son of Seth, the son of Adam,
the son of God.[b]

Jesus Is Tested in the Wilderness

4:1-13pp — Mt 4:1-11; Mk 1:12,13

4 Jesus, full of the Holy Spirit,[c] left the Jordan[d] and was led by the Spirit[e] into the wilderness, 2where
for forty days[f] he was tempted[a] by the devil. He ate nothing during those days, and at the end of
them he was hungry.
3The devil said to him, "If you are the Son of God, tell this stone to become bread."
4Jesus answered, "It is written: 'Man shall not live on bread alone.'[b]"[g]
5The devil led him up to a high place and showed him in an instant all the kingdoms of the world.[h]
6And he said to him, "I will give you all their authority and splendor; it has been given to me,[i] and I
can give it to anyone I want to. 7If you worship me, it will all be yours."

[a] *2* The Greek for *tempted* can also mean *tested.* [b] *4* Deut. 8:3

4:1–13 *Jesus Is Tested in the Wilderness.* Jesus' testing recalls Israel's experience in the wilderness (see note on Matt 4:1–11). Luke explicitly connects them by mentioning "wilderness" and "forty" (vv. 1–2; cf. Num 32:13; Deut 2:7; 29:5; Neh 9:21; Amos 2:10), since the "forty days" (v. 2) recalls Israel's "forty years" in the wilderness (Num 14:34). More important, all three OT passages that Jesus quotes in response to the devil come from Deut 6–8 (Deut 6:13 and Luke 4:8; Deut 6:16 and Luke 4:12; Deut 8:3 and Luke 4:4), a section that calls Israel to be faithful to God in the wilderness (Deut 6:16; 8:2). Moreover, the three specific temptations also parallel three significant instances in which Israel failed in the wilderness, and later traditions such as Ps 106 that recall Israel's faithlessness often point to these three events: (1) Israel failed to remember God in the way "they gave in to their craving" (Ps 106:14; cf. Exod 16:1–3; Num 11:1–6). (2) "They made a calf and worshiped an idol" (Ps 106:19; cf. Exod 32:1–15). (3) They tested and "rebelled against the Spirit of God" (Ps 106:33; cf. Exod 17:1–7; Num 20:1–13). Unlike Israel of old, Jesus the Son of God faithfully resists the devil's temptations.

4:1 This verse mentions the "Spirit" twice. It connects this account with the Spirit's descending on Jesus in the previous section (3:22) and Jesus' proclaiming the anointing of the Spirit in the next section (v. 18). **into the wilderness.** This again refers to the Judean desert (see note on 1:80).

4:2 the devil. Satan (Mark 1:13). Luke often identifies Satan as the evil force that opposes the work of God (10:18; 11:18; 13:16; 22:3,31).

4:3 the Son of God. Adam (3:38), Israel (Exod 4:22), and the ideal Davidic king (Ps 2:7) have been identified as God's sons. Jesus fulfills the role of all three and is uniquely and fully the Son of God (3:22).

4:4 Luke includes only the first part of Jesus' quotation of Deut 8:3. Matthew also includes the second part: "but on every word that comes from the mouth of God" (Matt 4:4).

4:5 a high place. Matthew refers to "a very high mountain" (Matt 4:8). This second temptation appears as the third in Matthew's account. Many argue that Matthew's order is chronological; Luke may have changed the order for various reasons: (1) Luke emphasizes the temple elsewhere and wants this account to climax with the temple. (2) Luke follows the OT account of Israel's experiences in the wilderness. (3) Luke highlights "Do not put the Lord your God to the test" (v. 12) by quoting it last.

8 Jesus answered, "It is written: 'Worship the Lord your God and serve him only.'[a]"[j]

9 The devil led him to Jerusalem and had him stand on the highest point of the temple. "If you are the Son of God," he said, "throw yourself down from here. 10 For it is written:

"'He will command his angels concerning you
to guard you carefully;
11 they will lift you up in their hands,
so that you will not strike your foot against a stone.'[b]"[k]

12 Jesus answered, "It is said: 'Do not put the Lord your God to the test.'[c]"[l]

13 When the devil had finished all this tempting,[m] he left him[n] until an opportune time.

Jesus Rejected at Nazareth

14 Jesus returned to Galilee[o] in the power of the Spirit, and news about him spread through the whole countryside.[p] 15 He was teaching in their synagogues,[q] and everyone praised him.

16 He went to Nazareth,[r] where he had been brought up, and on the Sabbath day he went into the synagogue,[s] as was his custom. He stood up to read, 17 and the scroll of the prophet Isaiah was handed to him. Unrolling it, he found the place where it is written:

18 "The Spirit of the Lord is on me,[t]
because he has anointed me
to proclaim good news to the poor.
He has sent me to proclaim freedom for the prisoners
and recovery of sight for the blind,
to set the oppressed free,
19 to proclaim the year of the Lord's favor."[d][u]

20 Then he rolled up the scroll, gave it back to the attendant and sat down.[v] The eyes of everyone in the synagogue were fastened on him. 21 He began by saying to them, "Today this scripture is fulfilled in your hearing."

22 All spoke well of him and were amazed at the gracious words that came from his lips. "Isn't this Joseph's son?" they asked.[w]

[a] *8* Deut. 6:13 [b] *11* Psalm 91:11,12 [c] *12* Deut. 6:16 [d] *19* Isaiah 61:1,2 (see Septuagint); Isaiah 58:6

4:8 [j] Dt 6:13
4:11 [k] Ps 91:11,12
4:12 [l] Dt 6:16
4:13 [m] Heb 4:15 [n] Jn 14:30
4:14 [o] Mt 4:12 [p] Mt 9:26
4:15 [q] Mt 4:23
4:16 [r] Mt 2:23 [s] Mt 13:54
4:18 [t] Jn 3:34
4:19 [u] Lev 25:10; Isa 61:1,2
4:20 [v] ver 17; Mt 26:55
4:22 [w] Mt 13:54,55; Jn 6:42; 7:15

4:8 This quotation from Deut 6:13 builds on the earlier creedal confession "the LORD our God, the LORD is one" (Deut 6:4).
4:9 the highest point of the temple. Likely the southeast corner of the temple portico below which was a drop of "immense" depth (Josephus, *Antiquities*, 15.412) down the Kidron Valley.
4:10–11 This time the devil also quotes from Scripture (Ps 91:11–12), although he misuses it to challenge Jesus to test the presence of God as Israel did in ancient times. A possible connection between Ps 91 and its present context is the "highest point" (Greek *pterygion*, v. 9) and "wings" (Greek *pterygas*, Ps 91:4; [Septuagint (the pre-Christian Greek translation of the OT) 90:4]).
4:13 left him until an opportune time. The devil challenges Jesus throughout his earthly ministry, but a direct and decisive challenge reappears only during the final week of Jesus' earthly life (22:3).
4:14—9:50 *The Galilean Ministry.* Jesus began his public ministry in Galilee by demonstrating his power in both words and deeds (4:14–44) and by forming a restored community of God's people (5:1—6:16). The teachings that follow outline the behavior that should define this people (6:17–49). After initially presenting Jesus' power and vision for the community, Luke shares responses from different parties (7:1—8:21). Jesus' followers recognize him as the Messiah, while those who oppose him challenge his authority (8:22—9:50).
4:14–44 *Proclamation in Words and Deeds.* In publicly proclaiming the arrival of God's salvation, Jesus reveals his true identity through his powerful words (vv. 14–30) and miracles (vv. 31–44).
4:14–30 *Jesus Rejected at Nazareth.* Unlike Mark, who places this episode in the middle of Jesus' Galilean ministry (Mark 6:1–6), Luke highlights this event by placing it at the beginning of Jesus' public ministry. This account provides lenses through which we can understand the ministry of Jesus: (1) The era that Jesus' life and ministry ushers in fulfills God's ancient promises. (2) Christ is both the anointed one and the rejected one. (3) The gospel message is not limited to Jews, for Gentiles will also see the salvation of God.
4:16 Luke repeats that Jesus was brought up in Nazareth (2:39,51) to pave the way for his account of Jesus' own people rejecting him (v. 24).
4:18–19 Jesus quotes from Isa 61:1–2 and 58:6, which depict the salvation that will come to the suffering people of God.
4:18 the poor ... prisoners ... blind ... oppressed. In their original contexts they refer to the oppressed and exiled people awaiting God's salvation. In this context, they refer to marginalized groups thirsting for God's deliverance.
4:19 the year of the Lord's favor. Alludes to the Jubilee Year (Lev 25:8–55), when once every 50 years debts are canceled and slaves are freed. **favor.** Greek *dekton,* which connects with the word "accepted" (Greek *dektos*) in v. 24; although God has forgiven his people and shown them favor, they did not find this good news acceptable.
4:22 The people are amazed at Jesus' "gracious words" because they are powerful (cf. Acts 6:8). **Isn't this Joseph's son?** This should be understood in a negative sense: "Isn't this the carpenter? Isn't this Mary's son ... ?" (Mark 6:3).

4:23 [x]ver 16 [y]Mk 1:21-28; 2:1-12
4:24 [z]Mt 13:57; Jn 4:44
4:25 [a]1Ki 17:1; 18:1; Jas 5:17,18
4:26 [b]1Ki 17:8-16; Mt 11:21
4:27 [c]2Ki 5:1-14
4:29 [d]Nu 15:35; Ac 7:58; Heb 13:12
4:30 [e]Jn 8:59; 10:39
4:31 [f]ver 23; Mt 4:13
4:32 [g]Mt 7:28 [h]ver 36; Mt 7:29
4:34 [i]Mt 8:29 [j]Mk 1:24 [k]Jas 2:19 [l]ver 41; Mk 1:24
4:35 [m]ver 39,41; Mt 8:26; Lk 8:24
4:36 [n]Mt 7:28 [o]ver 32; Mt 7:29; Mt 10:1
4:37 [p]ver 14; Mt 9:26
4:39 [q]ver 35,41
4:40 [r]Mk 5:23 [s]Mt 4:23

23 Jesus said to them, "Surely you will quote this proverb to me: 'Physician, heal yourself!' And you will tell me, 'Do here in your hometown[x] what we have heard that you did in Capernaum.'"[y]

24 "Truly I tell you," he continued, "no prophet is accepted in his hometown.[z] 25 I assure you that there were many widows in Israel in Elijah's time, when the sky was shut for three and a half years and there was a severe famine throughout the land.[a] 26 Yet Elijah was not sent to any of them, but to a widow in Zarephath in the region of Sidon.[b] 27 And there were many in Israel with leprosy[a] in the time of Elisha the prophet, yet not one of them was cleansed—only Naaman the Syrian."[c]

28 All the people in the synagogue were furious when they heard this. 29 They got up, drove him out of the town,[d] and took him to the brow of the hill on which the town was built, in order to throw him off the cliff. 30 But he walked right through the crowd and went on his way.[e]

Jesus Drives Out an Impure Spirit

4:31-37pp — Mk 1:21-28

31 Then he went down to Capernaum,[f] a town in Galilee, and on the Sabbath he taught the people. 32 They were amazed at his teaching,[g] because his words had authority.[h]

33 In the synagogue there was a man possessed by a demon, an impure spirit. He cried out at the top of his voice, 34 "Go away! What do you want with us,[i] Jesus of Nazareth?[j] Have you come to destroy us? I know who you are[k]—the Holy One of God!"[l]

35 "Be quiet!" Jesus said sternly.[m] "Come out of him!" Then the demon threw the man down before them all and came out without injuring him.

36 All the people were amazed[n] and said to each other, "What words these are! With authority[o] and power he gives orders to impure spirits and they come out!" 37 And the news about him spread throughout the surrounding area.[p]

Jesus Heals Many

4:38-41pp — Mt 8:14-17
4:38-43pp — Mk 1:29-38

38 Jesus left the synagogue and went to the home of Simon. Now Simon's mother-in-law was suffering from a high fever, and they asked Jesus to help her. 39 So he bent over her and rebuked[q] the fever, and it left her. She got up at once and began to wait on them.

40 At sunset, the people brought to Jesus all who had various kinds of sickness, and laying his hands on each one,[r] he healed them.[s] 41 Moreover, demons came out of many people, shouting, "You are the

[a] *27* The Greek word traditionally translated *leprosy* was used for various diseases affecting the skin.

4:23 Physician, heal yourself! In ancient literature this proverb questions a person's power and authority. **yourself.** Can be understood figuratively as "your own people." This explains the contrast between Capernaum and Nazareth, Jesus' hometown (v. 24).

4:24 Jesus expects that people will reject God's prophet, and the people's rejecting Jesus in the following narrative affirms his identity as the true prophet (7:16,39; 13:33–34; 24:19; Acts 3:22–23; 7:37). **hometown.** Nazareth (v. 23), but it may include the wider reference to God's own people (cf. vv. 25–27).

4:25–26 This example from the ministry of Elijah (1 Kgs 17:7–24) illustrates that God's own people reject the prophet and points to the mission to the Gentiles.

4:27 The example of Elisha (2 Kgs 5:1–19) reinforces and extends the connection to Elijah. Not only should the gospel spread to the Gentiles, but in doing so the Jews should in turn "know that there is a prophet in Israel" (2 Kgs 5:8).

4:31–37 *Jesus Drives Out an Impure Spirit.* Jesus' ministry in Capernaum, though recorded here, precedes his sermon in Nazareth (v. 23 hints at it). Mark preserves the temporal order by placing the Capernaum narrative (Mark 1:21–28) before the Nazareth one (Mark 6:1–6). While Jesus did not perform any healing miracles in Nazareth, he did cast out demons in Capernaum (vv. 33–35). Though his own people in Nazareth reject him, the demon here recognizes that he is "the Holy One of God" (v. 34).

4:32 his words had authority. Unlike the magicians of his time, Jesus does not need to rely on elaborate rituals and learned formulas; his own words carry divine authority.

4:33 a demon, an impure spirit. Contrasts with Jesus as "the Holy One of God" (see note on v. 34).

4:34 the Holy One of God. Parallels "the Son of God" (v. 41). Luke 1:35 identifies "the holy one" as "the Son of God."

4:38–44 *Jesus Heals Many.* Luke continues his account of Jesus' ministry in Capernaum by describing Jesus as a physician (cf. v. 23). Unlike those who consider him to be only "Joseph's son" (v. 22), even the demons recognize him to be "the Son of God" (v. 41).

4:38–39 The healing of Simon's mother-in-law paves the way for Simon Peter's call in 5:1–11.

4:39 began to wait on them. Elsewhere in Luke, this refers to the service rendered around the table (10:40; 12:37; 17:8; 22:26–27). As such, this narrative introduces the important theme of table-fellowship in this Gospel, which signifies the formation of a new community of God's people.

4:41 You are the Son of God! Luke earlier introduced Jesus as "the Son of God" (1:35; see 3:22), but here Jesus prevents the demons from

Son of God!"[t] But he rebuked[u] them and would not allow them to speak,[v] because they knew he was
the Messiah.

42 At daybreak, Jesus went out to a solitary place. The people were looking for him and when they
came to where he was, they tried to keep him from leaving them. 43 But he said, "I must proclaim the
good news of the kingdom of God[w] to the other towns also, because that is why I was sent." 44 And he
kept on preaching in the synagogues of Judea.[x]

Jesus Calls His First Disciples

5:1-11pp — Mt 4:18-22; Mk 1:16-20; Jn 1:40-42

5 One day as Jesus was standing by the Lake of Gennesaret,[a] the people were crowding around
him and listening to the word of God.[y] 2 He saw at the water's edge two boats, left there by
the fishermen, who were washing their nets. 3 He got into one of the boats, the one belonging to
Simon, and asked him to put out a little from shore. Then he sat down and taught the people from
the boat.[z]

4 When he had finished speaking, he said to Simon, "Put out into deep water, and let down the nets
for a catch."[a]

5 Simon answered, "Master,[b] we've worked hard all night and haven't caught anything.[c] But because
you say so, I will let down the nets."

6 When they had done so, they caught such a large number of fish that their nets began to break.[d]
7 So they signaled their partners in the other boat to come and help them, and they came and filled both
boats so full that they began to sink.

8 When Simon Peter saw this, he fell at Jesus' knees and said, "Go away from me, Lord; I am a sinful
man!"[e] 9 For he and all his companions were astonished at the catch of fish they had taken, 10 and so
were James and John, the sons of Zebedee, Simon's partners.

Then Jesus said to Simon, "Don't be afraid;[f] from now on you will fish for people." 11 So they pulled
their boats up on shore, left everything and followed him.[g]

[a] *1* That is, the Sea of Galilee

4:41 [t] Mt 4:3 [u] ver 35 [v] Mt 8:4
4:43 [w] Mt 3:2
4:44 [x] Mt 4:23
5:1 [y] Mk 4:14; Heb 4:12
5:3 [z] Mt 13:2
5:4 [a] Jn 21:6
5:5 [b] Lk 8:24,45; 9:33, 49; 17:13 [c] Jn 21:3
5:6 [d] Jn 21:11
5:8 [e] Ge 18:27; Job 42:6; Isa 6:5
5:10 [f] Mt 14:27
5:11 [g] ver 28; Mt 4:19

broadcasting this identity, probably because the demons were attempting to derail Jesus' ministry (see note on Mark 1:34). Earlier the devil had misused this title (4:9), and Jesus later defines his identity as the Son of God as including his death on the cross (9:21–27,28–36).

4:43 must. Jesus submits to God's plan (see 2:49 and note). **kingdom of God.** This is Luke's first use of this term. In the OT, God's people expect the Messiah to reestablish his kingdom (Isa 33:22; 52:7) and renew the Davidic dynasty (Isa 9:1–7; Jer 23:5–8; 33:14–26). In the time of Jesus, Jews often considered this kingdom to be a political and military one; they were looking for God to deliver his people from the hands of the Gentiles. But for Jesus this kingdom represents his victory over the forces of Satan (11:18–20), a victory that affects both the physical (9:2) and spiritual realms (12:31–34). The final consummation remains in the future (11:1–4; 13:18–21).

4:44 Judea. In this context, where Luke is focusing on Jesus' Galilean ministry, it does not refer to the region south of Galilee and Samaria. Rather, it refers to anywhere Jews reside (1:5; 6:17; 7:17; 23:5; Acts 10:37).

5:1—6:16 *Formation of a New Community.* This section begins with Jesus calling his first disciples (5:1–11), and it ends with forming God's restored people, centering on Jesus' 12 apostles (6:12–16). In between, Luke describes this people by focusing on the inclusion of outcasts (5:12–32) and the increasing conflict with the Jewish religious leaders (5:33—6:11).

5:1–11 *Jesus Calls His First Disciples.* After establishing his authority and proclaiming that a new era of God's salvation has arrived, Jesus begins to form his own community of disciples (5:1—6:16). This account shows critical elements of a proper response to encountering Jesus: (1) recognizing Jesus' authority and identity (vv. 1–8a), (2) recognizing one's sinfulness in the presence of the Holy One (v. 8b), and (3) leaving everything to follow him (vv. 9–11).

5:1 Lake of Gennesaret. Elsewhere called the Sea of Galilee (Matt 4:18; Mark 1:16) or the Sea of Tiberias (John 6:1; see NIV text note on John 21:1). Luke's description is comparable to the OT Hebrew term for this body of water: the Sea of Kinnereth (see NIV text note on Num 34:11).

5:2 washing their nets. Preparing for their evening fishing trip (cf. Mark 1:19).

5:3 boats. A typical first-century boat could hold five to seven people. In this story at least two boats are involved. Luke 5:1–11 mentions only Simon and the sons of Zebedee (v. 10) because they are the focus of Jesus' call.

5:8 Simon is now called "Simon Peter," probably to indicate the significance of this experience. It is only later that Jesus calls him Peter (6:14), and Peter becomes the leader of Jesus' disciples (8:51; 9:20,28). Unlike the earlier reference to Jesus as "Master" (v. 5), Peter now recognizes that Jesus is the "Lord." **Go away from me.** The appropriate response from those who realize that they are unworthy to be in God's presence (cf. Exod 3:11; Judg 6:15; Isa 6:5; Jer 1:6). **sinful man.** Reinforces Jesus' mission to reach out to sinners (5:30–32; 7:36–50; 15:1–32).

5:10 James and John. Along with Peter, they form the core of Jesus' group of disciples (8:51; 9:28). **fish for people.** Unlike the act of fishing where the goal is capturing and killing fish, these disciples are called to give life to people through the proclamation of the gospel.

5:11 Those who follow Jesus must leave "everything" (9:3; 12:33; 14:26,33; 18:22).

5:12 [h] Mt 8:2
5:14 [i] Mt 8:4
[j] Lev 14:2-32
5:15 [k] Mt 9:26
5:16 [l] Mt 14:23; Lk 3:21
5:17 [m] Mt 15:1; Lk 2:46
[n] Mk 5:30; Lk 6:19
5:20 [o] Lk 7:48,49
5:21 [p] Isa 43:25
5:24 [q] Mt 8:20
5:26 [r] Mt 9:8

Jesus Heals a Man With Leprosy

5:12-14pp — Mt 8:2-4; Mk 1:40-44

12 While Jesus was in one of the towns, a man came along who was covered with leprosy.[a][h] When he saw Jesus, he fell with his face to the ground and begged him, "Lord, if you are willing, you can make me clean."
13 Jesus reached out his hand and touched the man. "I am willing," he said. "Be clean!" And immediately the leprosy left him.

14 Then Jesus ordered him, "Don't tell anyone,[i] but go, show yourself to the priest and offer the sacrifices that Moses commanded[j] for your cleansing, as a testimony to them."

15 Yet the news about him spread all the more,[k] so that crowds of people came to hear him and to be healed of their sicknesses. 16 But Jesus often withdrew to lonely places and prayed.[l]

Jesus Forgives and Heals a Paralyzed Man

5:18-26pp — Mt 9:2-8; Mk 2:3-12

17 One day Jesus was teaching, and Pharisees and teachers of the law[m] were sitting there. They had come from every village of Galilee and from Judea and Jerusalem. And the power of the Lord was with Jesus to heal the sick.[n] 18 Some men came carrying a paralyzed man on a mat and tried to take him into the house to lay him before Jesus. 19 When they could not find a way to do this because of the crowd, they went up on the roof and lowered him on his mat through the tiles into the middle of the crowd, right in front of Jesus.

20 When Jesus saw their faith, he said, "Friend, your sins are forgiven."[o]

21 The Pharisees and the teachers of the law began thinking to themselves, "Who is this fellow who speaks blasphemy? Who can forgive sins but God alone?"[p]

22 Jesus knew what they were thinking and asked, "Why are you thinking these things in your hearts?
23 Which is easier: to say, 'Your sins are forgiven,' or to say, 'Get up and walk'? 24 But I want you to know that the Son of Man[q] has authority on earth to forgive sins." So he said to the paralyzed man, "I tell you, get up, take your mat and go home." 25 Immediately he stood up in front of them, took what he had been lying on and went home praising God. 26 Everyone was amazed and gave praise to God.[r] They were filled with awe and said, "We have seen remarkable things today."

[a] *12* The Greek word traditionally translated *leprosy* was used for various diseases affecting the skin.

5:12–16 *Jesus Heals a Man With Leprosy.* Embedded in the call narratives (vv. 1–11,27–30; 6:12–16), this event shows that Jesus' mission is to call those whom the Jews view as "unclean" (cf. vv. 12–14).
5:12 leprosy. See NIV text note. Lepers were considered unclean; they were not allowed to come in contact with others or to worship in the temple (Lev 13–14).
5:13 Jesus reached out his hand and touched the man . . . "Be clean!" Jesus risks ceremonial uncleanness (Lev 13:45–46). This not only reflects Jesus' own power and authority but allows the leper to rejoin the community of God's people. In Acts, Luke again uses this clean/unclean word group to refer to those excluded from God's people: We "should not call anyone impure or unclean" (Acts 10:28) whom God has made clean (Acts 10:15).
5:14 Don't tell anyone. Jesus probably does not want to be defined simply by his power to heal (cf. 4:41). **show yourself . . . offer the sacrifices.** Based on Lev 13:9–17; 14:1–20.
5:16 Jesus prayed to his Father as at other critical junctures (3:21; 6:12; 9:28–29; 11:1).
5:17–26 *Jesus Forgives and Heals a Paralyzed Man.* As Jesus continues his healing ministry, he confronts the religious leaders. At issue is Jesus' status and identity. Some who witness Jesus' powerful acts respond by praising God (vv. 25–26), while others whose influence is challenged by Jesus' popularity accuse him of blasphemy (v. 21).
5:17 Pharisees and teachers of the law. Luke portrays them as those who oppose Jesus and his ministry. **Pharisees.** In historical documents, they first appear in the second century BC as a pious group that opposed the Hellenization of Judeans. In the time of Jesus, they are recognized as the religious leaders. Theologically, they relied on oral traditions and affirmed the doctrines of predestination, resurrection, and the immortality of the soul. Sociologically, they were respected by the people of the land. Politically, they were relatively conservative in their attempts to protect the customs of their ancestors. **teachers of the law.** Those who studied and taught the law (cf. vv. 21,30; 6:7). They were often associated with the Pharisees, so both labels can often apply to the same people (cf. Acts 5:34).
5:19 roof. Roofs of houses in the land of Israel were often covered with weeds, branches, and mud, and stairs to the roof were often outside of the house. **tiles.** The building material used on the roofs of Hellenistic urban houses, and for the sake of Gentile readers Luke may have used the term in reference to similar material found on roofs in the Holy Land. It is also possible, however, that tiles were actually used in some well-built houses.
5:20 your sins are forgiven. See note on v. 21.
5:21 who speaks blasphemy. God is the only one who can forgive sins (Ps 103:3; Isa 43:25; Mic 7:18), and in the OT sins cannot be forgiven apart from the temple system (Lev 4:22—5:16; 16:15–16). Jesus' act not only represents his claim to replace the temple cult but is also an implicit claim to divinity.
5:24 To forgive sins appears to be "easier" (v. 23) than to heal, but it is in fact more difficult because the authority to forgive belongs to God alone (see note on v. 21). **Son of Man.** In the OT this is a title that can refer to human beings in general (see Ps 8:4 and NIV text note) or a prophet in particular (Ezek 2:1; 3:3; 4:1). In Daniel, it refers to a heavenly being who is worthy of all honor and glory (Dan 7:13–14). This usage that points to a heavenly being survived in Jewish literature during the time of Jesus. Elsewhere in Luke (21:27,36; 22:69), this title echoes that of Daniel, which may explain why the title appears here when Jesus' authority is at issue.

In 1986, a first-century boat was unearthed from the Sea of Galilee. While there are no direct links to the Gospel stories, it is a good representation of what a generic Sea of Galilee fishing boat looked like in the first century.
© Dr. Shelley Wachsmann

Jesus Calls Levi and Eats With Sinners

5:27-32pp — Mt 9:9-13; Mk 2:14-17

27 After this, Jesus went out and saw a tax collector by the name of Levi sitting at his tax booth. "Follow me,"[s] Jesus said to him, 28 and Levi got up, left everything and followed him.[t]
29 Then Levi held a great banquet for Jesus at his house, and a large crowd of tax collectors[u] and others were eating with them. 30 But the Pharisees and the teachers of the law who belonged to their sect[v]
complained to his disciples, "Why do you eat and drink with tax collectors and sinners?"[w]
31 Jesus answered them, "It is not the healthy who need a doctor, but the sick. 32 I have not come to
call the righteous, but sinners to repentance."[x]

Jesus Questioned About Fasting

5:33-39pp — Mt 9:14-17; Mk 2:18-22

33 They said to him, "John's disciples[y] often fast and pray, and so do the disciples of the Pharisees,
but yours go on eating and drinking."
34 Jesus answered, "Can you make the friends of the bridegroom[z] fast while he is with them? 35 But the
time will come when the bridegroom will be taken from them;[a] in those days they will fast."

5:27 [s] Mt 4:19
5:28 [t] ver 11; Mt 4:19
5:29 [u] Lk 15:1
5:30 [v] Ac 23:9 [w] Mt 9:11
5:32 [x] Jn 3:17
5:33 [y] Lk 7:18; Jn 1:35; 3:25,26
5:34 [z] Jn 3:29
5:35 [a] Lk 9:22; 17:22; Jn 16:5-7

5:27–32 *Jesus Calls Levi and Eats With Sinners.* As in the healing of the man with leprosy (vv. 12–16), this narrative highlights Jesus' ministry among outcasts, as explicitly noted in the concluding saying (v. 32).

5:27 tax collector. See note on 3:12. **Levi.** Another name for Matthew (6:15). **tax booth.** Where customs were collected; this one was located near Capernaum (Mark 2:1,13–14).

5:29 By attending a tax collector's banquet, Jesus identifies with outcasts (cf. 7:34; 15:2). **great banquet.** Elsewhere, Jesus uses this as an image for the kingdom of God (14:16–24).

5:30 complained. The Greek behind this word often appears in the Greek translation of the OT for the Israelites' grumbling in the wilderness (Exod 15:24; 16:7–9,12; 17:3; Num 11:1; 14:2,27,29,36; 16:11; 17:10). Here the Jewish leaders likewise fail to recognize that God is forming his people into a new community.

5:31 May allude to the prophetic critique of the religious leaders of Israel: "You have not strengthened the weak or healed the sick or bound up the injured" (Ezek 34:4).

5:32 the righteous. Those who consider themselves to be righteous (cf. 18:11–12). Jesus implicitly mocks their self-righteousness, which leads to his rejection by the Jewish leaders.

5:33–39 *Jesus Questioned About Fasting.* The OT pointedly critiques those who observe the ritual of fasting even while rebelling against God (cf. Isa 58:4,6). In Jewish tradition, fasting often accompanies acts of lamenting (1 Sam 31:13; 2 Sam 1:12; 1 Chr 10:12) and pleading (Judg 20:26; 1 Sam 7:6; Esth 4:3,16; Dan 9:3) to God in the midst of suffering. Thus, it is an inappropriate response in the presence of the eschatological wedding banquet. A new era has arrived and demands a proper response.

5:33 John's disciples. Those who had received his baptism of repentance (cf. Acts 19:4). **fast and pray.** Represents repentant hearts (1 Sam 7:6; Joel 1:14; Jonah 3:5). **the disciples of the Pharisees.** They fasted twice a week (18:12), but they sought to "exalt themselves" through their fasting (18:14).

5:34 the bridegroom. In the OT describes God (Isa 54:5–6; cf. Isa 62:4–5; Jer 2:2; Ezek 16:8–14; Hos 2:19–20); in the NT applies to Jesus the Messiah (2 Cor 11:2–3; Eph 5:24–27; Rev 19:7–9; 21:2).

5:35 the time will come. Could refer to the time of Jesus' death, but

6:1 [b] Dt 23:25
6:2 [c] Mt 12:2
6:3 [d] 1Sa 21:6
6:4 [e] Lev 24:5,9
6:5 [f] Mt 8:20
6:6 [g] ver 1
6:7 [h] Mt 12:10 [i] Mt 12:2
6:8 [j] Mt 9:4
6:11 [k] Jn 5:18
6:12 [l] Lk 3:21

36 He told them this parable: "No one tears a piece out of a new garment to patch an old one. Otherwise, they will have torn the new garment, and the patch from the new will not match the old. 37 And no one pours new wine into old wineskins. Otherwise, the new wine will burst the skins; the wine will run out and the wineskins will be ruined. 38 No, new wine must be poured into new wineskins. 39 And no one after drinking old wine wants the new, for they say, 'The old is better.' "

Jesus Is Lord of the Sabbath

6:1-11pp — Mt 12:1-14; Mk 2:23–3:6

6 One Sabbath Jesus was going through the grainfields, and his disciples began to pick some heads of grain, rub them in their hands and eat the kernels.[b] 2 Some of the Pharisees asked, "Why are you doing what is unlawful on the Sabbath?"[c]

3 Jesus answered them, "Have you never read what David did when he and his companions were hungry?[d] 4 He entered the house of God, and taking the consecrated bread, he ate what is lawful only for priests to eat.[e] And he also gave some to his companions." 5 Then Jesus said to them, "The Son of Man[f] is Lord of the Sabbath."

6 On another Sabbath[g] he went into the synagogue and was teaching, and a man was there whose right hand was shriveled. 7 The Pharisees and the teachers of the law were looking for a reason to accuse Jesus, so they watched him closely[h] to see if he would heal on the Sabbath.[i] 8 But Jesus knew what they were thinking[j] and said to the man with the shriveled hand, "Get up and stand in front of everyone." So he got up and stood there.

9 Then Jesus said to them, "I ask you, which is lawful on the Sabbath: to do good or to do evil, to save life or to destroy it?"

10 He looked around at them all, and then said to the man, "Stretch out your hand." He did so, and his hand was completely restored. 11 But the Pharisees and the teachers of the law were furious[k] and began to discuss with one another what they might do to Jesus.

The Twelve Apostles

6:13-16pp — Mt 10:2-4; Mk 3:16-19; Ac 1:13

12 One of those days Jesus went out to a mountainside to pray, and spent the night praying to God.[l] 13 When morning came, he called his disciples to him and chose twelve of them, whom he also desig-

elsewhere this phrase implies future judgment (17:22; 21:6; Jer 7:32; Amos 4:2; Zech 14:1). Jesus' death is connected with the future judgment (17:23–36). If this text implies that connection, then Jesus is referring not to the time of the early church (since he is still with them) but to the final judgment, when their fasting will represent their sadness as they encounter God's wrath.

5:36–39 This parable emphasizes the discontinuity between the old age and new age. The new age is brought about by God's decisive revelation in his Son, and it demands full acceptance and obedience to his Son (18:22).

5:39 The old is better. Jewish religious leaders claim this; they refuse to abandon their rules and customs and receive Jesus, the bearer of the new age of salvation. This claim fails to recognize the establishment of the "new covenant" (Jer 31:31), in which the law is now written "on their hearts" (Jer 31:33).

6:1–11 *Jesus Is Lord of the Sabbath.* The two parts of this section (vv. 1–5,6–11) correspond to the two focal points of the Sabbath regulations in the OT: the power and authority of God the Creator (Exod 20:11) and the deliverance brought about by the mighty acts of God (Deut 5:15). Jesus is the Lord of the Sabbath (vv. 1–5) and the healer and life-giver (vv. 6–11).

6:1–2 Mosaic regulations allow Israelites to "pick kernels with [their] hands" (Deut 23:25)—without the use of an instrument for threshing—when they enter their neighbor's field. To the Pharisees, to "rub [heads of grain] in their hands" was threshing; it was therefore "unlawful on the Sabbath."

6:3–5 Jesus makes two points about David (1 Sam 21:1–6): (1) Sabbath regulations should not keep us from attending to human needs. (2) By fulfilling God's promises to David (1:32–33,68–79; 2:11; 3:22,29–32), Jesus surpasses him since he alone is the "Lord of the Sabbath" (v. 5).

6:7 The Mosaic regulations do not forbid healing on the Sabbath. The Pharisees added rules that violated the intent of the Sabbath commandment.

6:10 Stretch out your hand. Neither Jesus' command nor the obedient response of the man to this command is considered work forbidden on the Sabbath. **his hand was completely restored.** Testifies to God's approval of Jesus' act and of his status as the "Lord of the Sabbath" (v. 5).

6:11 Jesus' words and deeds directly challenge the authority of the Jewish religious leaders, especially their interpretation of the law, so they want to get rid of him. A parallel passage in Mark makes their intentions even clearer: "Then the Pharisees went out and began to plot with the Herodians how they might kill Jesus" (Mark 3:6; see Matt 12:14).

6:12–16 *The Twelve Apostles.* This account concludes the large section that began with the call of Peter, James, and John (5:1–11). These twelve, who represent the twelve tribes of Israel, are destined to sit on thrones "judging the twelve tribes of Israel" (22:30).

6:12 spent the night praying to God. Jesus prayed often (3:21; 9:18,28; 11:1; 22:31–32) and taught persistence in prayer (11:5–8; 18:1–8). The significance of what Jesus is about to do in appointing the Twelve is underlined.

6:13 apostles. Those sent to complete a mission (cf. Mark 3:14). In Luke's writings the term often refers to the Twelve (9:10; 17:5; 22:14;

nated apostles:[m] 14Simon (whom he named Peter), his brother Andrew, James, John, Philip, Bartholomew, 15Matthew,[n] Thomas, James son of Alphaeus, Simon who was called the Zealot, 16Judas son of
James, and Judas Iscariot, who became a traitor.

Blessings and Woes

6:20-23pp — Mt 5:3-12

17He went down with them and stood on a level place. A large crowd of his disciples was there and a
great number of people from all over Judea, from Jerusalem, and from the coastal region around Tyre
and Sidon,[o] 18who had come to hear him and to be healed of their diseases. Those troubled by impure
spirits were cured, 19and the people all tried to touch him,[p] because power was coming from him and
healing them all.[q]

20Looking at his disciples, he said:

"Blessed are you who are poor,
for yours is the kingdom of God.[r]
21 Blessed are you who hunger now,
for you will be satisfied.[s]
Blessed are you who weep now,
for you will laugh.[t]
22 Blessed are you when people hate you,
when they exclude you[u] and insult you[v]
and reject your name as evil,
because of the Son of Man.[w]

23"Rejoice in that day and leap for joy,[x] because great is your reward in heaven. For that is how their
ancestors treated the prophets.[y]

24"But woe to you who are rich,[z]
for you have already received your comfort.[a]

6:13 [m]Mk 6:30
6:15 [n]Mt 9:9
6:17 [o]Mt 4:25; 11:21; Mk 3:7,8
6:19 [p]Mt 9:20 [q]Mt 14:36; Mk 5:30; Lk 5:17
6:20 [r]Mt 25:34
6:21 [s]Isa 55:1,2; Mt 5:6 [t]Isa 61:2,3; Mt 5:4; Rev 7:17
6:22 [u]Jn 9:22; 16:2 [v]Isa 51:7 [w]Jn 15:21
6:23 [x]Mt 5:12 [y]Mt 5:12
6:24 [z]Jas 5:1 [a]Lk 16:25

Acts 1:2,26; 2:42–43; 6:6), but it also applies to other followers of Jesus (Luke 11:49; 24:10; Acts 14:4,14).

6:14 Simon (whom he named Peter). The prominence of Peter among the Twelve is reflected in both the placement of his name at the top of the list and the mention that Jesus named him Peter, the name he is known by in the rest of this Gospel (except in 22:31–32; 24:34). **Bartholomew.** Appears only in lists of apostles (Matt 10:3; Mark 3:18; Acts 1:13). He may be the Nathaniel mentioned in John 1:45–49.

6:15 Matthew. Levi, the tax collector (5:27–29; cf. Matt 9:9–10). **James son of Alphaeus.** Appears only in the two lists of disciples in Luke's writings (here; Acts 1:13). Levi is also a son of Alphaeus (Mark 2:14). If this Alphaeus is the same person, then James is Levi's brother. **Zealot.** One zealous for the law. The term later applied to those belonging to an organized party at the center of the Jewish revolts of AD 66–70. Writing after AD 50 (see Introduction: Date), Luke could have been using this term in this semi-technical sense.

6:16 Judas son of James. Elsewhere called Thaddaeus (Matt 10:3; Mark 3:18). **Judas Iscariot.** Always named last in lists of disciples since he "became a traitor."

6:17–49 *Teachings for the New Community.* This long section has often been called the Sermon on the Plain or Sermon on the Plateau, and its content is similar to Matthew's Sermon on the Mount (Matt 5:1—7:29). Matt 5:1 likely describes Jesus entering the hill country, while the "level place" in Luke 6:17 can be understood as a plateau in mountainous regions (see note on Matt 5:1–2). Following the designation of the 12 apostles, Jesus now focuses on the identity and character of those who belong to this new community of God's people. The discussion begins by delineating God's people (vv. 17–26) and centers on their distinct ethic (vv. 27–42). It ends by calling for people to properly respond to Jesus and his gospel (vv. 43–49).

6:17–26 *Blessings and Woes.* The OT considers Israel blessed (Deut 33:29; Pss 33:12; 146:5). Within this covenantal relationship, woes are God's judgment on those who are unfaithful to the covenant (Isa 5:8–25; 31:1; Jer 13:27; Amos 6:1; Hab 2:12–17). This section also reflects the influence of the covenant and the wisdom motif of the two ways, as in Deut 28, Ps 1, and Proverbs. In this context, Jesus uses blessings and woes to describe God's covenantal people. The theme of reversal that depicts the radical change of one's fortunes points to God's gracious deliverance of his people. Equally important is the centrality of Christ (v. 22) that highlights the need for a proper response to God's action through his Son.

6:20–22 In Matthew, Jesus addresses those who are poor "in spirit" (Matt 5:3) and hunger "for righteousness" (Matt 5:6), but even without these qualifying phrases, Luke's version is not merely materialistic. In Isa 61 (quoted in Luke 4:18–19), the "poor" are those who have sinned against God and are deprived as they await God's salvation. Elsewhere in the OT, those who "hunger" are also looking forward to the Messianic banquet, to a time when God's righteousness will be revealed (Isa 25:6). In Luke, the dichotomy between the spiritual and material is not evident; God's salvation reaches both realms.

6:23 in that day. The day of judgment (10:12; 17:31). **how their ancestors treated the prophets.** The persecution of prophets is a recurring theme in OT history (e.g., 1 Kgs 18:4,13; 22:27; 2 Chr 16:10; 24:20–21; Neh 9:26; Jer 2:30; 11:18–22; 37:15–16).

6:24–26 The woes reverse the content of the blessings. Particularly relevant is Isa 65:13, which depicts what will happen to the unfaithful: "My servants will eat, but you will go hungry; my servants will drink, but you will go thirsty; my servants will rejoice, but you will be put to shame." The "rich" (v. 24) and the "well fed" (v. 25) are those who are proud and rely on their own resources (cf. 16:19–31).

6:25 [b]Isa 65:13 [c]Pr 14:13
6:26 [d]Mt 7:15
6:27 [e]ver 35; Mt 5:44; Ro 12:20
6:28 [f]Mt 5:44
6:30 [g]Dt 15:7,8,10; Pr 21:26
6:31 [h]Mt 7:12
6:32 [i]Mt 5:46
6:34 [j]Mt 5:42
6:35 [k]ver 27 [l]Ro 8:14 [m]Mk 5:7
6:36 [n]Jas 2:13 [o]Mt 5:48; 6:1; Lk 11:2; 12:32; Ro 8:15; Eph 4:6; 1Pe 1:17; 1Jn 1:3; 3:1
6:37 [p]Mt 7:1 [q]Mt 6:14
6:38 [r]Ps 79:12; Isa 65:6, 7 [s]Mt 7:2; Mk 4:24
6:39 [t]Mt 15:14
6:40 [u]Mt 10:24; Jn 13:16

25 Woe to you who are well fed now,
for you will go hungry.[b]
Woe to you who laugh now,
for you will mourn and weep.[c]
26 Woe to you when everyone speaks well of you,
for that is how their ancestors treated the false prophets.[d]

Love for Enemies

6:29,30pp — Mt 5:39-42

27 "But to you who are listening I say: Love your enemies, do good to those who hate you,[e] 28 bless
those who curse you, pray for those who mistreat you.[f] 29 If someone slaps you on one cheek, turn to
them the other also. If someone takes your coat, do not withhold your shirt from them. 30 Give to everyone who asks you, and if anyone takes what belongs to you, do not demand it back.[g] 31 Do to others
as you would have them do to you.[h]
32 "If you love those who love you, what credit is that to you?[i] Even sinners love those who love
them. 33 And if you do good to those who are good to you, what credit is that to you? Even sinners do
that. 34 And if you lend to those from whom you expect repayment, what credit is that to you?[j] Even
sinners lend to sinners, expecting to be repaid in full. 35 But love your enemies, do good to them,[k] and
lend to them without expecting to get anything back. Then your reward will be great, and you will be
children[l] of the Most High,[m] because he is kind to the ungrateful and wicked. 36 Be merciful,[n] just as
your Father[o] is merciful.

Judging Others

6:37-42pp — Mt 7:1-5

37 "Do not judge, and you will not be judged.[p] Do not condemn, and you will not be condemned.
Forgive, and you will be forgiven.[q] 38 Give, and it will be given to you. A good measure, pressed down,
shaken together and running over, will be poured into your lap.[r] For with the measure you use, it will
be measured to you."[s]
39 He also told them this parable: "Can the blind lead the blind? Will they not both fall into a pit?[t]
40 The student is not above the teacher, but everyone who is fully trained will be like their teacher.[u]
41 "Why do you look at the speck of sawdust in your brother's eye and pay no attention to the plank
in your own eye? 42 How can you say to your brother, 'Brother, let me take the speck out of your eye,'
when you yourself fail to see the plank in your own eye? You hypocrite, first take the plank out of your
eye, and then you will see clearly to remove the speck from your brother's eye.

6:27–36 *Love for Enemies.* After illustrating the principle of divine reversal, Jesus focuses on the same principle in interpersonal relationships. As people experience God's grace, they must extend that same grace to others.

6:31 Many think that the Golden Rule is merely reciprocal, as if we act based on how we want to be treated. But other parts of this section downplay this focus on reciprocity, and, in fact, reverse it (vv. 27–30,32–35). At the end of the section, Jesus gives a different basis for our actions: we should imitate God the Father (v. 36).

6:35 children of the Most High. In the OT, the people of Israel are the children of God as they rest in their covenantal relationship with their God (Deut 14:1; Hos 1:10; 11:1). In the NT, they are those who respond to the message of Jesus. This includes both Jews and Gentiles, who can now call one another "brothers and sisters" (Acts 1:15–16).

6:36 Be merciful. Not simply an ethical act in the OT, which uses the word to refer to God's faithfulness to his people (1 Chr 21:13; Pss 25:6; 69:16; Isa 63:9; Dan 9:9,18). In Matthew, the focus is the call to be perfect because of God's perfection (Matt 5:48).

6:37–42 *Judging Others.* Building on the principle of loving one's enemies, Jesus calls people to forgive rather than condemn others. The parables provide pointed criticisms against the Jewish leaders of the time (vv. 39–42).

6:37–38 As in the previous section (vv. 27–36), interpersonal relationships should be modeled on God's gracious acts among his people. The illustration is taken from the measuring of grains in the marketplace. A "good measure" is provided abundantly by God, "pressed down" inside the container, and "shaken together" to create room for more until it is "running over." This vividly illustrates the rich blessings God will bestow upon those who are generous toward others.

6:37 Do not judge. This is not a call to abandon a sense of right and wrong (cf. vv. 43–45) nor is it a rejection of the need to encourage one another to walk within the holy will of God (17:3). It is, however, a warning against those who are hypocritical and self-righteous in their condemnation of others (cf. 18:9–14).

6:38 good measure, pressed down, shaken together and running over. See note on vv. 37–38.

6:39 parable. The singular "parable" introduces a three-part parable (vv. 39–42) that depicts the folly of the Jewish leaders who claim to be teachers of the law.

6:41,42 speck ... plank. Jesus uses hyperbolic language to show how ridiculous it is to criticize others without noticing one's own faults.

6:44 [v]Mt 12:33
6:45 [w]Pr 4:23; Mt 12:34,35; Mk 7:20
6:46 [x]Jn 13:13 [y]Mal 1:6; Mt 7:21
6:47 [z]Lk 8:21; 11:28; Jas 1:22-25
7:1 [a]Mt 7:28
7:7 [b]Ps 107:20

A Tree and Its Fruit

6:43,44pp — Mt 7:16,18,20

43“No good tree bears bad fruit, nor does a bad tree bear good fruit. 44Each tree is recognized by its
own fruit.[v] People do not pick figs from thornbushes, or grapes from briers. 45A good man brings good
things out of the good stored up in his heart, and an evil man brings evil things out of the evil stored
up in his heart. For the mouth speaks what the heart is full of.[w]

The Wise and Foolish Builders

6:47-49pp — Mt 7:24-27

46“Why do you call me, ‘Lord, Lord,’[x] and do not do what I say?[y] 47As for everyone who comes to
me and hears my words and puts them into practice,[z] I will show you what they are like. 48They are
like a man building a house, who dug down deep and laid the foundation on rock. When a flood
came, the torrent struck that house but could not shake it, because it was well built. 49But the one
who hears my words and does not put them into practice is like a man who built a house on the
ground without a foundation. The moment the torrent struck that house, it collapsed and its destruction was complete.”

The Faith of the Centurion

7:1-10pp — Mt 8:5-13

7 When Jesus had finished saying all this[a] to the people who were listening, he entered Capernaum. 2There a centurion’s servant, whom his master valued highly, was sick and about to
die. 3The centurion heard of Jesus and sent some elders of the Jews to him, asking him to come
and heal his servant. 4When they came to Jesus, they pleaded earnestly with him, “This man deserves to have you do this, 5because he loves our nation and has built our synagogue.” 6So Jesus
went with them.

He was not far from the house when the centurion sent friends to say to him: “Lord, don’t trouble
yourself, for I do not deserve to have you come under my roof. 7That is why I did not even consider myself worthy to come to you. But say the word, and my servant will be healed.[b] 8For I myself am a man
under authority, with soldiers under me. I tell this one, ‘Go,’ and he goes; and that one, ‘Come,’ and he
comes. I say to my servant, ‘Do this,’ and he does it.”

9When Jesus heard this, he was amazed at him, and turning to the crowd following him, he said, “I
tell you, I have not found such great faith even in Israel.” 10Then the men who had been sent returned
to the house and found the servant well.

6:43–45 *A Tree and Its Fruit.* This parable further illustrates the relationship between source and product. A teacher inevitably produces one kind of student (v. 40); similarly, a heart can produce words and deeds only of the same kind.
6:43 fruit. Can symbolize actions (Prov 1:31; Jer 17:10) or words (Prov 13:2; 18:20–21). Jesus focuses on how words reveal the nature of the heart (v. 45).
6:46–49 *The Wise and Foolish Builders.* This final section of the Sermon on the Plain/Plateau calls hearers to put these words into practice (cf. Lev 26:1–13; Deut 28:1–14). It also contains a word of judgment for those who do not respond to this call to faithfulness (cf. Lev 26:14–46; Deut 28:15–68).
6:47 everyone who comes to me and hears my words. Echoes the opening description of those who come to hear Jesus (vv. 17–18).
7:1—8:21 *Responses to the Gospel.* The first two stories in this section (7:1–10,11–17) echo the programmatic passage in 4:14–30: the healing of a Gentile ruler in 4:27 anticipates this story of the healing of the centurion’s servant (7:1–10), and the care of the widow in 4:25–26 anticipates the raising of a widow’s son (7:11–17). These two stories lead into yet another discussion of Jesus’ identity (7:18–35) and his inclusion of outcasts (7:36–50). Two sets of parables further explain accepting and rejecting Jesus and his message (8:1–15,16–18) before Jesus returns to discussing the true family of God (8:19–21).
7:1–10 *The Faith of the Centurion.* Luke earlier mentions (in 4:27) the healing of Naaman (2 Kgs 5:1–14). As in the case of Naaman, a Gentile ruler here approaches a prophet through an intermediary, and God is gracious to a Gentile. This story may anticipate the conversion of the Gentile centurion Cornelius (Acts 10:1–48).
7:3 centurion. He is likely a member of Herod Antipas’s guard, which was organized according to the Roman military system. Though not necessarily a Roman citizen, this centurion was likely a Gentile (v. 9) who was in charge of about 100 men. Prior to AD 66, the Roman army did not have a significant presence in Judea and Galilee. **elders of the Jews.** Local civic and religious leaders, though these Galilean elders may not have been related to the elders of Jerusalem who are often connected with the rulers of the land (Acts 4:8–9).
7:5 This centurion appears to have been a benefactor of the Jews. He is like the centurion Cornelius, who was “devout and God-fearing” and “gave generously to those in need and prayed to God regularly” (Acts 10:2).
7:9 Luke elsewhere contrasts Jewish disbelief and God’s plan for the Gentiles (4:25–27; Acts 13:46–47; 18:6; 28:26–28).

7:13 [c]ver 19; Lk 10:1; 13:15; 17:5; 22:61; 24:34; Jn 11:2
7:14 [d]Mt 9:25; Mk 1:31; Lk 8:54; Jn 11:43; Ac 9:40
7:16 [e]Lk 1:65 [f]Mt 9:8 [g]ver 39; Mt 21:11 [h]Lk 1:68
7:17 [i]Mt 9:26
7:18 [j]Mt 3:1 [k]Lk 5:33
7:21 [l]Mt 4:23
7:22 [m]Isa 29:18,19; 35:5,6; 61:1,2; Lk 4:18
7:26 [n]Mt 11:9
7:27 [o]Mal 3:1; Mt 11:10; Mk 1:2

Jesus Raises a Widow's Son

7:11-16Ref — 1Ki 17:17-24; 2Ki 4:32-37; Mk 5:21-24,35-43; Jn 11:1-44

11 Soon afterward, Jesus went to a town called Nain, and his disciples and a large crowd went along with him. 12 As he approached the town gate, a dead person was being carried out — the only son of his mother, and she was a widow. And a large crowd from the town was with her. 13 When the Lord[c] saw her, his heart went out to her and he said, "Don't cry."

14 Then he went up and touched the bier they were carrying him on, and the bearers stood still. He said, "Young man, I say to you, get up!"[d] 15 The dead man sat up and began to talk, and Jesus gave him back to his mother.

16 They were all filled with awe[e] and praised God.[f] "A great prophet[g] has appeared among us," they said. "God has come to help his people."[h] 17 This news about Jesus spread throughout Judea and the surrounding country.[i]

Jesus and John the Baptist

7:18-35pp — Mt 11:2-19

18 John's[j] disciples[k] told him about all these things. Calling two of them, 19 he sent them to the Lord to ask, "Are you the one who is to come, or should we expect someone else?"

20 When the men came to Jesus, they said, "John the Baptist sent us to you to ask, 'Are you the one who is to come, or should we expect someone else?' "

21 At that very time Jesus cured many who had diseases, sicknesses[l] and evil spirits, and gave sight to many who were blind. 22 So he replied to the messengers, "Go back and report to John what you have seen and heard: The blind receive sight, the lame walk, those who have leprosy[a] are cleansed, the deaf hear, the dead are raised, and the good news is proclaimed to the poor.[m] 23 Blessed is anyone who does not stumble on account of me."

24 After John's messengers left, Jesus began to speak to the crowd about John: "What did you go out into the wilderness to see? A reed swayed by the wind? 25 If not, what did you go out to see? A man dressed in fine clothes? No, those who wear expensive clothes and indulge in luxury are in palaces. 26 But what did you go out to see? A prophet?[n] Yes, I tell you, and more than a prophet. 27 This is the one about whom it is written:

> " 'I will send my messenger ahead of you,
> who will prepare your way before you.'[b][o]

[a] *22* The Greek word traditionally translated *leprosy* was used for various diseases affecting the skin.
[b] *27* Mal. 3:1

7:11–17 *Jesus Raises a Widow's Son.* This story alludes to the story of Elijah (1 Kgs 17:17–24): a widow (v. 12; 1 Kgs 17:9), the death of the widow's son (v. 12; 1 Kgs 17:17), the prophet's meeting with the widow at "the town gate" (v. 12; 1 Kgs 17:10), the prophet's returning the son to the widow (v. 15; 1 Kgs 17:23), and recognizing that the prophet is from God (v. 16; 1 Kgs 17:24). Luke emphasizes, however, that Jesus is not simply "a great prophet" (v. 16), but "the Lord" (v. 13).
7:11 Nain. Appears only here in the Bible. This town was located on the southern edge of Galilee.
7:14 touched the bier. A "bier" is a stand or a plank used to carry a corpse to its place of burial. Jesus willingly comes in contact with the unclean (cf. 5:12–14; 8:54) with the risk of being "cut off from Israel" (Num 19:13). Instead of being rendered unclean, however, he gives life to the dead.
7:16 great prophet. May refer to the Elijah who is to come in the final age (9:8,19; cf. Mal 4:5) or to the anticipated "prophet like Moses" (Deut 18:15; Acts 3:22; 7:37).
7:18–35 *Jesus and John the Baptist.* Jesus clarifies his relationship with John; Jesus uniquely fulfills the promises of the ancient prophets through his ministry to outcasts (vv. 18–23). Jesus then accuses those who oppose John and himself of rejecting God's plan and compares them to the generation among their ancestors who likewise rejected God's mighty acts (vv. 24–35).
7:19 he sent them. The lack of evidence that Jesus is fulfilling the expected role of the Messiah (it was thought that he would overthrow the rule of the foreign power) and the disappointment caused by his own imprisonment cast doubt in John's mind concerning the identity of Jesus. **the one who is to come.** Refers to John the Baptist's own words in 3:16: "but one who is more powerful than I will come." The OT depicts the royal Messianic figure as "he who comes in the name of the LORD" (Ps 118:26; cf. Mal 3:1).
7:22 Jesus alludes to several passages in Isaiah (Isa 26:19; 29:18–19; 35:5–6; 42:7,18; 61:1). The only clause that cannot be traced back to Isaiah is "those who have leprosy are cleansed," which apparently refers back to Luke 4:27 and 5:12–16, which in turn allude to the healing of Naaman the leper (2 Kgs 5:1–14).
7:24 People would not go to the wilderness to see "a reed swayed by the wind"; nor would they go to see John if he were an insignificant and ordinary person. In Greek literature, a reed is considered weak and fragile. Thus, Jesus' rhetorical question suggests that John was not a weak person, even though he sent his disciples to ask Jesus about Jesus' identity.
7:27 The quotation from Mal 3:1 explains why John is "more than a prophet" (v. 26): John prepared the way for God's act through Jesus.

28 I tell you, among those born of women there is no one greater than John; yet the one who is least in
the kingdom of God[p] is greater than he."
29 (All the people, even the tax collectors, when they heard Jesus' words, acknowledged that God's
way was right, because they had been baptized by John.[q] 30 But the Pharisees and the experts in the law[r]
rejected God's purpose for themselves, because they had not been baptized by John.)
31 Jesus went on to say, "To what, then, can I compare the people of this generation? What are they
like? 32 They are like children sitting in the marketplace and calling out to each other:

"'We played the pipe for you,
and you did not dance;
we sang a dirge,
and you did not cry.'

33 For John the Baptist came neither eating bread nor drinking wine,[s] and you say, 'He has a demon.'
34 The Son of Man came eating and drinking, and you say, 'Here is a glutton and a drunkard, a friend
of tax collectors and sinners.'[t] 35 But wisdom is proved right by all her children."

Jesus Anointed by a Sinful Woman

7:37-39Ref — Mt 26:6-13; Mk 14:3-9; Jn 12:1-8
7:41,42Ref — Mt 18:23-34

36 When one of the Pharisees invited Jesus to have dinner with him, he went to the Pharisee's house
and reclined at the table. 37 A woman in that town who lived a sinful life learned that Jesus was eating
at the Pharisee's house, so she came there with an alabaster jar of perfume. 38 As she stood behind him
at his feet weeping, she began to wet his feet with her tears. Then she wiped them with her hair, kissed
them and poured perfume on them.
39 When the Pharisee who had invited him saw this, he said to himself, "If this man were a prophet,[u]
he would know who is touching him and what kind of woman she is—that she is a sinner."
40 Jesus answered him, "Simon, I have something to tell you."
"Tell me, teacher," he said.
41 "Two people owed money to a certain moneylender. One owed him five hundred denarii,[a] and
the other fifty. 42 Neither of them had the money to pay him back, so he forgave the debts of both. Now
which of them will love him more?"
43 Simon replied, "I suppose the one who had the bigger debt forgiven."
"You have judged correctly," Jesus said.

a 41 A denarius was the usual daily wage of a day laborer (see Matt. 20:2).

7:28 [p] Mt 3:2
7:29 [q] Mt 21:32; Mk 1:5; Lk 3:12
7:30 [r] Mt 22:35
7:33 [s] Lk 1:15
7:34 [t] Lk 5:29,30; 15:1,2
7:39 [u] ver 16; Mt 21:11

7:28 there is no one greater than John. Because he was able to prepare the way for Jesus (cf. vv. 26–27). Uniquely among those who preceded Jesus, John is able to point to the presence of the Messiah and call God's people to prepare for this presence. **the one who is least in the kingdom of God is greater than he.** Because John died before witnessing the death and resurrection of Jesus. Those who come after John are able to understand and appreciate more fully the mission of the Messiah and participate in this new covenantal community that Jesus' death and resurrection bring about.

7:30 experts in the law. Scribes or teachers of the law (both the written law and their oral traditions). They are associated with the Pharisees (see note on 5:17) and are objects of Jesus' criticism (5:17; 11:37–54). **God's purpose.** His saving plan (Acts 2:23; 4:28; 13:36; 20:27).

7:31 this generation. Often appears in judgment texts (9:40–41; 11:29–32,49–51; 17:22–37; Acts 2:40) and recalls the wilderness generation of Israel's past that was unfaithful to God (Deut 32:4–5,20).

7:32 The Jewish leaders were "like children" who demand others to follow their own plans and ideas. When neither John nor Jesus acted according to their expectations (vv. 33–34), they found ways to oppose and destroy them.

7:35 all her children. Primarily Jesus and John (since this passage focuses on them), though "all" may imply whoever follows them as well. In Matt 11:19 Jesus says, "Wisdom is proved right by her deeds"—the deeds of John and Jesus. Their ministries prove that they demonstrate the righteous living that wisdom represents.

7:36–50 *Jesus Anointed by a Sinful Woman.* This story extends the themes of the previous section: (1) Since Jesus is "the one who is to come" (v. 20), he is not simply a "prophet" (v. 39) but is one who has the authority to forgive sins (vv. 48–49; cf. 5:20–24). (2) By interacting with the sinful woman, Jesus shows that he is "a friend of tax collectors and sinners" (v. 34) since his ministry includes these "sinners" (v. 37). (3) By refusing to receive Jesus with love (vv. 44–47), the Pharisees confirm that they have "rejected God's purpose for themselves" (v. 30).

7:37 lived a sinful life. The woman had committed "many sins" (v. 47). Perhaps she was a prostitute (cf. Matt 21:31–32).

7:38 Following the custom of the day, Jesus reclined during the meal, making it possible for the woman to stand "behind him at his feet." **kissed them and poured perfume on them.** Acts of respect (vv. 44–47; cf. John 12:3).

7:41 five hundred denarii. See NIV text note.

7:44 [v]Ge 18:4; 19:2; 43:24; Jdg 19:21; Jn 13:4-14; 1Ti 5:10
7:45 [w]Lk 22:47,48; Ro 16:16
7:46 [x]Ps 23:5; Ecc 9:8
7:48 [y]Mt 9:2
7:50 [z]Mt 9:22; Mk 5:34; Lk 8:48 [a]Ac 15:33
8:1 [b]Mt 4:23
8:2 [c]Mt 27:55,56
8:3 [d]Mt 14:1
8:8 [e]Mt 11:15
8:10 [f]Mt 13:11 [g]Isa 6:9; Mt 13:13,14
8:11 [h]Heb 4:12

44Then he turned toward the woman and said to Simon, "Do you see this woman? I came into your
house. You did not give me any water for my feet,[v] but she wet my feet with her tears and wiped them
with her hair. 45You did not give me a kiss,[w] but this woman, from the time I entered, has not stopped
kissing my feet. 46You did not put oil on my head,[x] but she has poured perfume on my feet. 47Therefore,
I tell you, her many sins have been forgiven—as her great love has shown. But whoever has been
forgiven little loves little."

48Then Jesus said to her, "Your sins are forgiven."[y]

49The other guests began to say among themselves, "Who is this who even forgives sins?"

50Jesus said to the woman, "Your faith has saved you;[z] go in peace."[a]

The Parable of the Sower

8:4-15pp — Mt 13:2-23; Mk 4:1-20

8 After this, Jesus traveled about from one town and village to another, proclaiming the good news
of the kingdom of God.[b] The Twelve were with him, 2and also some women who had been cured of
evil spirits and diseases: Mary (called Magdalene)[c] from whom seven demons had come out; 3Joanna
the wife of Chuza, the manager of Herod's[d] household; Susanna; and many others. These women were
helping to support them out of their own means.

4While a large crowd was gathering and people were coming to Jesus from town after town, he told
this parable: 5"A farmer went out to sow his seed. As he was scattering the seed, some fell along the
path; it was trampled on, and the birds ate it up. 6Some fell on rocky ground, and when it came up,
the plants withered because they had no moisture. 7Other seed fell among thorns, which grew up with
it and choked the plants. 8Still other seed fell on good soil. It came up and yielded a crop, a hundred
times more than was sown."

When he said this, he called out, "Whoever has ears to hear, let them hear."[e]

9His disciples asked him what this parable meant. 10He said, "The knowledge of the secrets of the
kingdom of God has been given to you,[f] but to others I speak in parables, so that,

> " 'though seeing, they may not see;
> though hearing, they may not understand.'[a][g]

11"This is the meaning of the parable: The seed is the word of God.[h] 12Those along the path are the
ones who hear, and then the devil comes and takes away the word from their hearts, so that they may

[a] *10* Isaiah 6:9

7:44–46 In this ancient culture of honor and shame, it was insulting to receive guests improperly (cf. 11:37–38; 14:1). This portrayal of Simon the Pharisee (not to be confused with Simon Peter) is consistent with the description of the Pharisees in general in Luke's Gospel (v. 30; 11:37–54).
7:47 her great love. Evidence of her being forgiven, just as a person who loves little gives evidence of having been forgiven little. The debtor whose forgiven debt is larger should respond with a greater love (vv. 41–43).
7:48–49 Jesus has the authority to forgive sins (cf. 5:20–21).
7:50 faith. An important theme in this Gospel (8:48; 17:19; 18:42); it is the basis of her act. This woman shows her faith by loving and receiving Jesus.
8:1–15 *The Parable of the Sower.* Following a note on Jesus' proclamation of the Good News (v. 1), this parable focuses on the different responses to the ministry of Jesus while demonstrating the particular nature and function of parables. Instead of being simple illustrations, parables are effective in unmasking the behavior and beliefs of the audience. To those who are unwilling to respond to the gospel, however, the deeper meanings of these parables remain hidden from them (see note on Matt 13:11).
8:2 Mary (called Magdalene). Often appears first on lists of the women who followed Jesus (24:10; Matt 27:56,61; 28:1; Mark 15:40,47; 16:1). **Magdalene.** Probably derives from Magadan (Matt 15:39), a village north of Tiberias. Luke does not identify this Mary with the sinful woman of ch. 7.
8:3 By sacrificially supporting Jesus and his disciples, these women participate in gospel ministry and become models for other followers of Jesus (contrast v. 14). The focus on the contributions of women is unique to Luke.
8:5 A farmer in ancient times would "sow his seed" before plowing the field.
8:8 a hundred times more than was sown. The good soil is fruitful (cf. Mark 4:8); this may reflect God's blessings (cf. Gen 26:12).
8:10 the secrets of the kingdom. God's hidden plan (the Greek word for "secrets" is often translated "mystery") now revealed when his people are able to witness his new acts in history (cf. Dan 2:18–19,27–30,47). Jesus quotes from Isa 6:9, which depicts the results of idol worship (cf. Isa 2:6–8,18–22). People become like the idols they worship. This logic is elaborated in Ps 135:15–18. Those who reject the Good News are like idol worshipers: they have become like the objects they worship.
8:11 This parable focuses on "the word of God." This anticipates Luke's second volume (Acts), in which he again uses Isa 6:9–10 to refer to Jews opposing the gospel (Acts 28:26–27), while the word continues to grow among those who receive the gospel (Acts 6:7; 12:24; 19:20).
8:12 the devil. Opposes the work of the gospel, especially because the gospel challenges his power and authority (cf. 10:18).

not believe and be saved. 13 Those on the rocky ground are the ones who receive the word with joy when
they hear it, but they have no root. They believe for a while, but in the time of testing they fall away.[i]
14 The seed that fell among thorns stands for those who hear, but as they go on their way they are choked
by life's worries, riches[j] and pleasures, and they do not mature. 15 But the seed on good soil stands for
those with a noble and good heart, who hear the word, retain it, and by persevering produce a crop.

A Lamp on a Stand

16 "No one lights a lamp and hides it in a clay jar or puts it under a bed. Instead, they put it on
a stand, so that those who come in can see the light.[k] 17 For there is nothing hidden that will not be
disclosed, and nothing concealed that will not be known or brought out into the open.[l] 18 Therefore
consider carefully how you listen. Whoever has will be given more; whoever does not have, even what
they think they have will be taken from them."[m]

Jesus' Mother and Brothers

8:19-21pp — Mt 12:46-50; Mk 3:31-35

19 Now Jesus' mother and brothers came to see him, but they were not able to get near him because of
the crowd. 20 Someone told him, "Your mother and brothers[n] are standing outside, wanting to see you."
21 He replied, "My mother and brothers are those who hear God's word and put it into practice."[o]

Jesus Calms the Storm

8:22-25pp — Mt 8:23-27; Mk 4:36-41
8:22-25Ref — Mk 6:47-52; Jn 6:16-21

22 One day Jesus said to his disciples, "Let us go over to the other side of the lake." So they got into a
boat and set out. 23 As they sailed, he fell asleep. A squall came down on the lake, so that the boat was
being swamped, and they were in great danger.
24 The disciples went and woke him, saying, "Master, Master,[p] we're going to drown!"
He got up and rebuked[q] the wind and the raging waters; the storm subsided, and all was calm.[r]
25 "Where is your faith?" he asked his disciples.
In fear and amazement they asked one another, "Who is this? He commands even the winds and the
water, and they obey him."

8:13 [i] Mt 11:6
8:14 [j] Mt 19:23; 1Ti 6:9,10,17
8:16 [k] Mt 5:15; Mk 4:21; Lk 11:33
8:17 [l] Mt 10:26; Mk 4:22; Lk 12:2
8:18 [m] Mt 13:12; 25:29; Lk 19:26
8:20 [n] Jn 7:5
8:21 [o] Lk 6:47; 11:28; Jn 14:21
8:24 [p] Lk 5:5 [q] Lk 4:35, 39,41 [r] Ps 107:29; Jnh 1:15

8:13 testing. Temptation by Satan (4:13; 11:4; 22:40,46) or persecution by those opposing Jesus and his gospel (22:28; Acts 20:19). These people fall "when trouble or persecution comes because of the word" (Mark 4:17).
8:14 thorns. Used in the OT in reference to idols (Jer 4:3–4); here identified as "life's worries, riches and pleasures." It is striking that in addition to the work of the devil and the threat of persecution, "life's worries, riches and pleasures" are considered powerful forces that prevent people from following Jesus. Jesus also calls his disciples not to be concerned with the worries of this life (12:22) since "you cannot serve both God and money" (16:13).
8:16–18 *A Lamp on a Stand.* After the parable that describes what obstructs the word of God from growing, Jesus emphasizes that this word will shine like a "lamp" (v. 16), and he demands a proper response (vv. 17–18).
8:16 lamp. In a different context, it can stand for the disciples who bear witness to the gospel (Matt 5:15). But here and in Mark 4:21 it refers to the word of God, which reveals what is hidden (v. 17) and judges those who are unfaithful to God (v. 18).
8:17 The word is powerful in the time of judgment (cf. 12:2).
8:18 Jesus now turns to the proper response to the Good News. **what they think they have.** Their status as God's people. With the arrival of God's salvation among his people, the Jews need to repent and accept the Good News embodied in the life and ministry of God's Son.
8:19–21 *Jesus' Mother and Brothers.* After discussing the proper response to the gospel (v. 18), Jesus defines the community of God's people in terms not of physical descent but of their relationship with God.
8:19,20 brothers. "James, Joseph, Judas and Simon" (Mark 6:3, which also mentions Jesus' "sisters"). They are likely his younger half brothers, born of Mary and Joseph.
8:22—9:50 *Authority and Identity of Jesus.* Not unlike what God did in the ancient exodus event, Jesus performs a miracle over the water (8:22–25), several healing miracles (8:26–56), and a feeding miracle (9:10–17). Embedded in this discussion of Christ's power and identity is a section on the mission of the Twelve, who are to extend Jesus' mission (9:1–9). These stories lead to identifying Jesus as the Messiah (9:18–20) who embodies both glory and suffering (9:21–36). However, the disciples fail to comprehend Jesus' mission to the cross (9:37–43a) despite his repeated comments on his coming suffering (9:43b–50).
8:22–25 *Jesus Calms the Storm.* This story begins a cycle of three miracles that highlight Jesus' power and authority (vv. 22–25, 26–39,40–56), and it paves the way for 9:1–9, where Jesus gives his disciples "power and authority to drive out all demons and to cure diseases" (9:1). Jesus' calming of the storm lends insight to the identity of Jesus in light of the OT teaching that God alone can control the waters (Pss 24:1–2; 29:3–4; 33:6–7; 65:5–8; 77:16–20; 104:7–9).
8:22 other side of the lake. The eastern coast of the Lake of Gennesaret (see 5:1 and note), the region of the Gerasenes (v. 26).
8:25 The disciples react "in fear and amazement" even after the storm subsides because they recognize the significance of what has just happened. **fear.** The expected reaction in the presence of God (1:12; 2:9; 5:26; 7:16). **amazement.** The result of witnessing God's mighty acts

8:28 [s]Mt 8:29 [t]Mk 5:7
8:31 [u]Rev 9:1,2,11; 11:7; 17:8; 20:1,3
8:33 [v]ver 22,23
8:35 [w]Lk 10:39
8:36 [x]Mt 4:24
8:37 [y]Ac 16:39
8:41 [z]ver 49; Mk 5:22

Jesus Restores a Demon-Possessed Man

8:26-37pp — Mt 8:28-34
8:26-39pp — Mk 5:1-20

26 They sailed to the region of the Gerasenes,[a] which is across the lake from Galilee. 27 When Jesus
stepped ashore, he was met by a demon-possessed man from the town. For a long time this man had
not worn clothes or lived in a house, but had lived in the tombs. 28 When he saw Jesus, he cried out and
fell at his feet, shouting at the top of his voice, "What do you want with me,[s] Jesus, Son of the Most High
God?[t] I beg you, don't torture me!" 29 For Jesus had commanded the impure spirit to come out of the
man. Many times it had seized him, and though he was chained hand and foot and kept under guard,
he had broken his chains and had been driven by the demon into solitary places.
30 Jesus asked him, "What is your name?"
"Legion," he replied, because many demons had gone into him. 31 And they begged Jesus repeatedly
not to order them to go into the Abyss.[u]
32 A large herd of pigs was feeding there on the hillside. The demons begged Jesus to let them go into
the pigs, and he gave them permission. 33 When the demons came out of the man, they went into the
pigs, and the herd rushed down the steep bank into the lake[v] and was drowned.
34 When those tending the pigs saw what had happened, they ran off and reported this in the town
and countryside, 35 and the people went out to see what had happened. When they came to Jesus, they
found the man from whom the demons had gone out, sitting at Jesus' feet,[w] dressed and in his right
mind; and they were afraid. 36 Those who had seen it told the people how the demon-possessed[x] man
had been cured. 37 Then all the people of the region of the Gerasenes asked Jesus to leave them,[y] because
they were overcome with fear. So he got into the boat and left.
38 The man from whom the demons had gone out begged to go with him, but Jesus sent him away,
saying, 39 "Return home and tell how much God has done for you." So the man went away and told all
over town how much Jesus had done for him.

Jesus Raises a Dead Girl and Heals a Sick Woman

8:40-56pp — Mt 9:18-26; Mk 5:22-43

40 Now when Jesus returned, a crowd welcomed him, for they were all expecting him. 41 Then a man
named Jairus, a synagogue leader,[z] came and fell at Jesus' feet, pleading with him to come to his house
42 because his only daughter, a girl of about twelve, was dying.

[a] *26* Some manuscripts *Gadarenes*; other manuscripts *Gergesenes*; also in verse 37

(1:63–66; 2:18,33; 4:22; 9:43; 11:14). The disciples recognize that they are in the presence of someone great.
8:26–39 *Jesus Restores a Demon-Possessed Man.* Extending the previous presentation on Jesus' power and identity, this account declares that Jesus is the "Son of the Most High God" (v. 28). The place in which Jesus performs this healing miracle highlights his ministry among the Gentiles (see v. 26 and note).
8:26 the region of the Gerasenes. In the area of the Gentiles, as confirmed by the presence of pigs (v. 32). It is difficult to identify its precise location, especially since different names appear in different manuscripts of Luke (see NIV text note) and in the other Gospels (Matt 8:28; Mark 5:1).
8:28 Son of the Most High God. Recalls "Son of the Most High" (1:32).
8:29 Luke's description of this demon-possessed man may allude to Isa 61:1–2, which Luke quotes in 4:18. If so, this man's healing again signifies that God is fulfilling his promises to his people through his Son.
8:30 Legion. Reflects the number and power of these demons over this man. A legion technically refers to a unit in the Roman army consisting of about 1,000 men. In NT times, it can include as many as 5,000 soldiers plus officers.
8:31 Abyss. Can refer to a bottomless pit (i.e., the "deep"; Gen 1:2; Deut 33:13; Job 28:14; Ps 42:7; cf. Rev 20:1,3) or the place of the wicked dead (i.e., the "deep" or "depths"; Ps 71:20; cf. Rom 10:7). In Jewish traditions, this is also the place of demons (cf. Rev 9:1–2,11; 11:7).
8:32,33 pigs. Considered unclean in OT law (Lev 11:7–8; Deut 14:8).
8:33 demons ... went into the pigs ... rushed down ... into the lake. Signifies Jesus' authority over these demons, but his battle with the demonic forces continues until his victory in the final battle.
8:35–37 afraid ... fear. The people recognize the unusual power of Jesus.
8:39 tell how much God has done for you. Allows the gospel to be preached among the Gentiles (cf. v. 56; 4:41).
8:40–56 *Jesus Raises a Dead Girl and Heals a Sick Woman.* This account contains two healing stories that both address issues of ritual purity. Women with a regular or irregular flow of blood were considered unclean (Lev 15), and "anyone who touches them will be unclean" (Lev 15:27). Touching these women or touching a human corpse rendered a person unclean (Num 19:11–13). Transcending these rules, Jesus allows the bleeding woman to touch "the edge of his cloak" (v. 44), and he takes the girl's corpse "by the hand" (v. 54). His mission includes reaching out to outcasts, his presence transcends purity regulations by cleansing the defiled, and he himself is not defiled by uncleanness.
8:40 These two healing stories take place when Jesus "returned" to the western coast of the Lake of Gennesaret.
8:41 synagogue leader. A recognized and respected leader in the community who is in charge of operating the synagogue. **fell at Jesus' feet.** Jairus willingly submits to Jesus' authority.

As Jesus was on his way, the crowds almost crushed him. 43And a woman was there who had been
subject to bleeding[a] for twelve years,[a] but no one could heal her. 44She came up behind him and
touched the edge of his cloak,[b] and immediately her bleeding stopped.

45"Who touched me?" Jesus asked.

When they all denied it, Peter said, "Master,[c] the people are crowding and pressing against you."

46But Jesus said, "Someone touched me;[d] I know that power has gone out from me."[e]

47Then the woman, seeing that she could not go unnoticed, came trembling and fell at his feet. In the
presence of all the people, she told why she had touched him and how she had been instantly healed.
48Then he said to her, "Daughter, your faith has healed you.[f] Go in peace."[g]

49While Jesus was still speaking, someone came from the house of Jairus, the synagogue leader.[h]
"Your daughter is dead," he said. "Don't bother the teacher anymore."

50Hearing this, Jesus said to Jairus, "Don't be afraid; just believe, and she will be healed."

51When he arrived at the house of Jairus, he did not let anyone go in with him except Peter, John and
James,[i] and the child's father and mother. 52Meanwhile, all the people were wailing and mourning[j] for
her. "Stop wailing," Jesus said. "She is not dead but asleep."[k]

53They laughed at him, knowing that she was dead. 54But he took her by the hand and said, "My
child, get up!"[l] 55Her spirit returned, and at once she stood up. Then Jesus told them to give her
something to eat. 56Her parents were astonished, but he ordered them not to tell anyone what had
happened.[m]

Jesus Sends Out the Twelve

9:3-5pp — Mt 10:9-15; Mk 6:8-11
9:7-9pp — Mt 14:1,2; Mk 6:14-16

9 When Jesus had called the Twelve together, he gave them power and authority to drive out all demons[n] and to cure diseases,[o] 2and he sent them out to proclaim the kingdom of God[p] and to heal
the sick. 3He told them: "Take nothing for the journey — no staff, no bag, no bread, no money, no extra
shirt.[q] 4Whatever house you enter, stay there until you leave that town. 5If people do not welcome you,
leave their town and shake the dust off your feet as a testimony against them."[r] 6So they set out and
went from village to village, proclaiming the good news and healing people everywhere.

7Now Herod[s] the tetrarch heard about all that was going on. And he was perplexed because some
were saying that John[t] had been raised from the dead,[u] 8others that Elijah had appeared,[v] and still

8:43 [a]Lev 15:25-30
8:44 [b]Mt 9:20
8:45 [c]Lk 5:5
8:46 [d]Mt 14:36; Mk 3:10 [e]Lk 5:17; 6:19
8:48 [f]Mt 9:22 [g]Ac 15:33
8:49 [h]ver 41
8:51 [i]Mt 4:21
8:52 [j]Lk 23:27 [k]Mt 9:24; Jn 11:11,13
8:54 [l]Lk 7:14
8:56 [m]Mt 8:4
9:1 [n]Mt 10:1 [o]Mt 4:23; Lk 5:17
9:2 [p]Mt 3:2
9:3 [q]Lk 10:4; 22:35
9:5 [r]Mt 10:14
9:7 [s]Mt 14:1 [t]Mt 3:1 [u]ver 19
9:8 [v]Mt 11:14

[a] *43* Many manuscripts *years, and she had spent all she had on doctors*

8:43 bleeding for twelve years. This woman fits the OT description of a woman who "has a discharge of blood for many days at a time other than her monthly period" and who "will be unclean as long as she has the discharge" (Lev 15:25). With this perpetual discharge, she is rendered unclean; thus, she is excluded from the religious and social lives of her people. Implications of the "unclean" status are severe.
8:46 power has gone out from me. Cf. 6:19. This statement should not be understood to mean that Jesus was not in control of his power.
8:47 trembling. The woman knew that an unclean person should not come in contact with others.
8:48 Daughter. Jesus reincorporates her into the people of God (cf. 13:16).
8:51 Peter, John and James. They now appear as the inner circle of Jesus' disciples (cf. 9:28). They were among the first Jesus called (5:1–11), and their giving up everything and following Jesus (5:11) become an example for others (cf. 14:33).
8:52 She is not dead but asleep. She is not permanently dead. She is temporarily dead, so "her spirit" (v. 55) needs to return. **asleep.** A euphemism for "dead" (cf. John 11:11; Acts 7:60; 13:36; 1 Cor 15:6,51; 1 Thess 5:10).
8:55 Her spirit returned. She is alive again. This may allude to Elijah's prayer when he brought a boy back to life: "LORD my God, let this boy's life [or 'spirit'] return to him!" (1 Kgs 17:21).
8:56 Unlike Jesus' earlier command to the Gentile man to testify to God's work (v. 39), in this Jewish context Jesus again "ordered them not to tell anyone what had happened" (cf. 4:41).
9:1–9 *Jesus Sends Out the Twelve.* Jesus commissions the 12 disciples that he had appointed (6:12–16). As Jesus was able to cast out demons (8:26–39) and cure diseases (8:40–56), the 12 disciples now receive power to continue Jesus' ministry by performing the same miracles (v. 1). As Jesus was rejected by his own people (4:14–30; cf. 7:30–35), these disciples will also suffer the same fate (v. 5). Herod's question concerning Jesus' identity (vv. 7–9) anticipates vv. 18–27.
9:2 proclaim ... heal. In word and in deed, Jesus' ministry is "to proclaim the year of the Lord's favor" (4:19).
9:3 Take nothing for the journey. They must learn to rely on God's provision, and this will provide those willing to hear the gospel with a chance to receive them (v. 5).
9:5 shake the dust off your feet. A sign of separation. Jews traditionally performed this act when leaving the land of the Gentiles. Those who reject the gospel are now considered outside the community of God's people, which explains why this act that confers judgment on these people is "a testimony against them."
9:7 Herod the tetrarch. Herod Antipas (see 3:1 and note). The rumor that John had been raised from the dead presupposes that John had already been killed (Mark 6:17–29).
9:8 Jews expected the return of Elijah, as promised in Mal 4:5 (cf. 7:27, quoting Mal 3:1).

9:8 [w] ver 19; Jn 1:21
9:9 [x] Lk 23:8
9:10 [y] Mk 6:30 [z] Mt 11:21
9:11 [a] ver 2; Mt 3:2
9:16 [b] Mt 14:19
9:18 [c] Lk 3:21
9:19 [d] Mt 3:1 [e] ver 7,8

others that one of the prophets of long ago had come back to life.[w] 9But Herod said, "I beheaded John.
Who, then, is this I hear such things about?" And he tried to see him.[x]

Jesus Feeds the Five Thousand

9:10-17pp — Mt 14:13-21; Mk 6:32-44; Jn 6:5-13
9:13-17Ref — 2Ki 4:42-44

10When the apostles[y] returned, they reported to Jesus what they had done. Then he took them
with him and they withdrew by themselves to a town called Bethsaida,[z] 11but the crowds learned
about it and followed him. He welcomed them and spoke to them about the kingdom of God,[a] and healed those who needed healing.

12Late in the afternoon the Twelve came to him and said, "Send the crowd away so they can go to the surrounding villages and countryside and find food and lodging, because we are in a remote place here."

13He replied, "You give them something to eat."

They answered, "We have only five loaves of bread and two fish — unless we go and buy food for all this crowd."
14(About five thousand men were there.)

But he said to his disciples, "Have them sit down in groups
of about fifty each." 15The disciples did so, and everyone sat
down. 16Taking the five loaves and the two fish and looking up to heaven, he gave thanks and broke them.[b] Then he gave them to the disciples to distribute to the people. 17They all ate
and were satisfied, and the disciples picked up twelve basketfuls of broken pieces that were left over.

Aerial view of possible site of New Testament Bethsaida, looking south toward the Sea of Galilee.

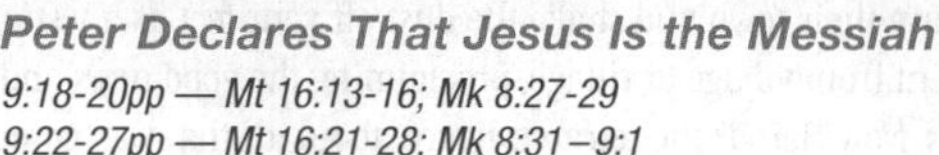

Peter Declares That Jesus Is the Messiah

9:18-20pp — Mt 16:13-16; Mk 8:27-29
9:22-27pp — Mt 16:21-28; Mk 8:31–9:1

18Once when Jesus was praying[c] in private and his disciples were with him, he asked them, "Who do the crowds say I am?"

19They replied, "Some say John the Baptist;[d] others say Elijah; and still others, that one of the prophets of long ago has come back to life."[e]

9:9 The reason why Herod would like to see him is explained in 23:8: "he hoped to see him perform a sign of some sort."
9:10–17 *Jesus Feeds the Five Thousand.* With this miracle that appears in all four Gospels (Matt 14:13–21; Mark 6:30–44; John 6:1–15), Jesus answers Herod's question in v. 9 concerning his identity. As God miraculously fed people during the ministries of Moses (Exod 16) and Elisha (2 Kgs 4:42–44), Jesus provides for the people in the wilderness. But Jesus is not simply "one of the prophets of long ago" (v. 8); he is the Messiah (vv. 18–20) who would die on the cross and be raised from the dead (vv. 21–27).
9:10 Bethsaida. Mark 6:45 says that *after* performing this miracle, Jesus "made his disciples get into the boat and go on ahead of him to Bethsaida." This is not a contradiction. The Bethsaida in Luke likely refers to the town northeast of the Lake of Gennesaret (i.e., the Sea of Galilee; see note on 5:1), while the Bethsaida in Mark refers to the one on the west coast of the lake in the region of Galilee (cf. John 12:21). The Bethsaida here in Luke was the birthplace of Peter, Andrew, and Philip (John 1:44), and it is likely to be identified with the site of et-Tell.
9:14 sit down in groups of about fifty each. Probably to aid in distributing the food. It may allude to how the Israelites were organized in the wilderness (cf. Exod 18:21).
9:16 Taking the … loaves … he gave thanks and broke them. Possibly anticipates the Last Supper account (22:19), though this description may merely reflect first-century meal rituals. The same sequence appears in Act 27:35 when Paul shares a meal with non-Christians.
9:17 twelve basketfuls of broken pieces that were left over. Points to the extent of Jesus' miracle: there was plenty of food available for those present. It also reminds the reader of Elisha's feeding a hundred men with 20 loaves, because they too "had some left over" (2 Kgs 4:44).
9:18–20 *Peter Declares That Jesus Is the Messiah.* This is the climax of Jesus' Galilean ministry. It provides a second answer to Herod's earlier question about Jesus' identity (v. 9; see note on vv. 10–17) and explains the source of the authority behind Jesus' words and deeds.
9:18 was praying in private. Cf. 3:21; 6:12. Other Gospels specify that this takes place in Caesarea Philippi (Matt 16:13; Mark 8:27).
9:19 Different opinions of the crowd parallel Herod's question in vv. 7–9.

[20]“But what about you?” he asked. “Who do you say I am?”
Peter answered, “God’s Messiah.”[f]

Jesus Predicts His Death

[21]Jesus strictly warned them not to tell this to anyone.[g] [22]And he said, “The Son of Man[h] must suffer
many things[i] and be rejected by the elders, the chief priests and the teachers of the law,[j] and he must
be killed[k] and on the third day[l] be raised to life.”[m]
[23]Then he said to them all: “Whoever wants to be my disciple must deny themselves and take up their
cross daily and follow me.[n] [24]For whoever wants to save their life will lose it, but whoever loses their life
for me will save it.[o] [25]What good is it for someone to gain the whole world, and yet lose or forfeit their
very self? [26]Whoever is ashamed of me and my words, the Son of Man will be ashamed of them[p] when
he comes in his glory and in the glory of the Father and of the holy angels.[q]
[27]“Truly I tell you, some who are standing here will not taste death before they see the kingdom of God.”

The Transfiguration

9:28-36pp — Mt 17:1-8; Mk 9:2-8

[28]About eight days after Jesus said this, he took Peter, John and James[r] with him and went up onto
a mountain to pray.[s] [29]As he was praying, the appearance of his face changed, and his clothes became
as bright as a flash of lightning. [30]Two men, Moses and Elijah, appeared in glorious splendor, talking
with Jesus. [31]They spoke about his departure,[a][t] which he was about to bring to fulfillment at Jerusalem.
[32]Peter and his companions were very sleepy,[u] but when they became fully awake, they saw his glory
and the two men standing with him. [33]As the men were leaving Jesus, Peter said to him, “Master,[v] it is

9:20 [f]Jn 1:49; 6:66-69; 11:27
9:21 [g]Mt 16:20; Mk 8:30
9:22 [h]Mt 8:20 [i]Mt 16:21 [j]Mt 27:1,2 [k]Ac 2:23; 3:13 [l]Mt 16:21 [m]Mt 16:21
9:23 [n]Mt 10:38; Lk 14:27
9:24 [o]Jn 12:25
9:26 [p]Mt 10:33; Lk 12:9; 2Ti 2:12 [q]Mt 16:27
9:28 [r]Mt 4:21 [s]Lk 3:21
9:31 [t]2Pe 1:15
9:32 [u]Mt 26:43
9:33 [v]Lk 5:5

[a] *31* Greek *exodos*

9:20 God’s Messiah. Highlights the relationship between Jesus and his Father (cf. “You are the Messiah, the Son of the living God,” Matt 16:16). Jesus is already identified as “the Messiah” in 2:11; Peter’s confession here reaffirms that Jesus is the royal Messiah in the line of David, although he transcends even the status of King David (20:41–44; cf. Ps 110:1) since his kingdom is “not of this world” (John 18:36).

9:21–27 *Jesus Predicts His Death.* The disciples do not yet fully comprehend Jesus’ Messiahship. Many first-century Jews expected the Messiah to be a powerful and glorious warrior who would deliver them from the political oppression of the Gentiles. Peter apparently shares this widespread Jewish view about the Messiah. In this section, Jesus supplements this understanding of the Messiah with the suffering “Son of Man” (v. 22). Jesus must pass through the cross before his glorification (vv. 22,26). This also concerns the disciples since they must deny their own lives when they follow Jesus.

9:21 this. That he is the Messiah (v. 20; cf. Matt 16:20). Jesus prohibits this because they falsely or incompletely understand the meaning of his Messiahship.

9:22 The Son of Man. In light of v. 26 (“comes in his glory”), it may recall the heavenly figure of Dan 7:13–14, but here the focus is on Jesus’ humanity. The two related images that follow qualify this glorious title. **suffer many things.** May point to the suffering servant of Isa 52:13—53:12. **rejected.** May allude to Ps 118:22. **must.** Jesus again uses “must” in reference to his death and resurrection because it is part of God’s plan (see note on 2:49).

9:23 deny themselves. Abandon their own ambitions and goals. **take up their cross.** Imitate Jesus and follow the will of his Father. Discipleship demands a drastic shift in one’s “daily” life to take on the mission of Jesus, even to the point of death. After Jesus’ death, resurrection, and ascension, disciples are called to continue his mission by representing him here on earth.

9:24 This explains v. 23: only those who, like Jesus, are willing to give up their own earthly desires and ambitions can obtain the spiritual blessings that Jesus’ resurrection brings.

9:26 The call to be faithful to Jesus in the context of references to his death and resurrection (v. 22) also appears in later Christian confessions of faith (2 Tim 2:11–12). As Jesus is rejected by many on his way to the cross, those who follow him are called to participate in this act of rejection. **when he comes in his glory.** Alludes again to Dan 7:13–14 (see note on Luke 9:22).

9:27 the kingdom of God. Best understood in this context as Jesus’ death and resurrection. The reign of God has already been introduced in Jesus’ ministry (10:9; 11:20; 16:16; 17:21), although the critical point in the manifestation of this kingdom lies in Jesus’ death and resurrection (cf. 24:44–49).

9:28–36 *The Transfiguration.* This story parallels the sequence in the previous section: Jesus is the glorious Messiah (vv. 30,32), but his death on the cross must precede his full glorification (v. 31). The disciples misunderstand Jesus’ mission, so Peter wants to build shelters, attempting to prolong the glorious scene (v. 33).

9:28 About eight days. An approximation. Mark 9:2 says “after six days.” Luke may be evoking the Jewish Festival of Tabernacles (cf. Lev 23:36), especially since he refers to “three shelters” (v. 33; cf. Lev 23:42). **Peter, John and James.** They again accompany Jesus (cf. 8:51), and Jesus prays before this important event.

9:30 Moses and Elijah. Both had unusual departures from their earthly lives (Deut 34:5–6; 2 Kgs 2:11) and witnessed God’s glory (Exod 24:12–18; 1 Kgs 19:8–18). They both play important roles in the OT Law and Prophets, and figures modeled upon them are expected to appear in the final age (Deut 18:15–18; Mal 4:5). Jesus’ appearance with these two figures points to a decisive revelation of God’s glory.

9:31 departure. See NIV text note. Other than referring to Jesus’ death, this word may also point to how his death will bring about the new exodus event when God will deliver his people again from darkness and the bondage of evil.

9:33 Peter’s request reveals his ignorance concerning Jesus’ mission to the cross.

9:35 [w]Isa 42:1 [x]Mt 3:17
9:36 [y]Mt 17:9
9:41 [z]Dt 32:5
9:44 [a]ver 22
9:45 [b]Mk 9:32
9:46 [c]Lk 22:24
9:47 [d]Mt 9:4
9:48 [e]Mt 10:40 [f]Mk 9:35
9:49 [g]Lk 5:5
9:50 [h]Mt 12:30; Lk 11:23

good for us to be here. Let us put up three shelters—one for you, one for Moses and one for Elijah." (He did not know what he was saying.)

34While he was speaking, a cloud appeared and covered them, and they were afraid as they entered the cloud. 35A voice came from the cloud, saying, "This is my Son, whom I have chosen;[w] listen to him."[x] 36When the voice had spoken, they found that Jesus was alone. The disciples kept this to themselves and did not tell anyone at that time what they had seen.[y]

Jesus Heals a Demon-Possessed Boy

9:37-42,43-45pp — Mt 17:14-18,22,23; Mk 9:14-27,30-32

37The next day, when they came down from the mountain, a large crowd met him. 38A man in the crowd called out, "Teacher, I beg you to look at my son, for he is my only child. 39A spirit seizes him and he suddenly screams; it throws him into convulsions so that he foams at the mouth. It scarcely ever leaves him and is destroying him. 40I begged your disciples to drive it out, but they could not."

41"You unbelieving and perverse generation,"[z] Jesus replied, "how long shall I stay with you and put up with you? Bring your son here."

42Even while the boy was coming, the demon threw him to the ground in a convulsion. But Jesus rebuked the impure spirit, healed the boy and gave him back to his father. 43And they were all amazed at the greatness of God.

Jesus Predicts His Death a Second Time

While everyone was marveling at all that Jesus did, he said to his disciples, 44"Listen carefully to what I am about to tell you: The Son of Man is going to be delivered into the hands of men."[a] 45But they did not understand what this meant. It was hidden from them, so that they did not grasp it,[b] and they were afraid to ask him about it.

46An argument started among the disciples as to which of them would be the greatest.[c] 47Jesus, knowing their thoughts,[d] took a little child and had him stand beside him. 48Then he said to them, "Whoever welcomes this little child in my name welcomes me; and whoever welcomes me welcomes the one who sent me.[e] For it is the one who is least among you all who is the greatest."[f]

49"Master,"[g] said John, "we saw someone driving out demons in your name and we tried to stop him, because he is not one of us."

50"Do not stop him," Jesus said, "for whoever is not against you is for you."[h]

9:34 cloud. Signifies that God is present (Exod 16:10; 24:15–16; 33:9–10; Num 9:15–23) and manifesting his glory (1 Kgs 8:11; 2 Chr 5:14; Ezek 10:4).

9:35 This is my Son. Alludes to Ps 2:7 and 2 Sam 7:14 (cf. Luke 3:22). **whom I have chosen.** Likely alludes to the description of the servant in Isa 42:1, which lies behind "whom I love" in Luke 3:22. Also relevant is Deut 17:15, especially in the context of the discussion of the royal son. **listen to him.** Comes from Deut 18:15 and refers to the call to obey the future prophet like Moses. As the new Moses who establishes God's new covenant with his people, Jesus becomes the fulfillment of the Mosaic law. God's people are therefore called to be obedient to this Jesus who is the decisive and final revelation of God's will.

9:37–43a *Jesus Heals a Demon-Possessed Boy.* This miracle story reveals the unique authority of Jesus and the unbelief of the people. These two themes—Jesus' authority and the people's unbelief—dominate the central section of Luke's Gospel (9:51—19:44).

9:39 A spirit seizes him and he suddenly screams. Reflects the accounts of both Mark ("possessed by a spirit that has robbed him of speech," Mark 9:17) and Matthew ("has seizures and is suffering greatly," Matt 17:15).

9:41 unbelieving and perverse generation. The disciples and the crowd can be compared to Israel's wilderness generation, who were unfaithful to God despite witnessing his mighty acts (cf. Deut 32:4–5,20).

9:43b–50 *Jesus Predicts His Death a Second Time.* As in the previous sections, this section presents the glorious Messiah (v. 43b; cf. v. 20), his suffering (v. 44; cf. vv. 21–27), and the disciples' failure to understand his mission (v. 45; cf. v. 33). The focus shifts to the reason for their ignorance (vv. 46–50).

9:45 they did not understand. The meaning of Jesus' death remains "hidden from them" (cf. 18:34) until the risen Jesus opens their eyes (24:45–47). Both God's sovereignty and human responsibility are emphasized here: because of a consistent pattern of the disciples' failure to comprehend Jesus and his mission, God has kept this from their understanding.

9:46 Jesus is willing to be "rejected" (v. 22; cf. v. 44) by everyone in following God's plan, but the disciples compete to be recognized as "the greatest." This is the clearest sign that the disciples are ignorant of Jesus' mission.

9:48 welcomes me. Takes up their cross and follows Jesus (v. 23). **least among you.** Willing to humble oneself like Jesus did (cf. 18:14).

9:49 he is not one of us. May refer to those who have a relationship with Jesus but are not part of the Twelve.

9:50 A similar statement in 11:23 reaffirms that it is one's relationship with Jesus that is important.

Samaritan Opposition

[51]As the time approached for him to be taken up to heaven,[i] Jesus resolutely set out for Jerusalem.[j]
[52]And he sent messengers on ahead, who went into a Samaritan[k] village to get things ready for him;
[53]but the people there did not welcome him, because he was heading for Jerusalem. [54]When the disciples
James and John[l] saw this, they asked, "Lord, do you want us to call fire down from heaven to destroy
them[a]?"[m] [55]But Jesus turned and rebuked them. [56]Then he and his disciples went to another village.

The Cost of Following Jesus

9:57-60pp — Mt 8:19-22

[57]As they were walking along the road,[n] a man said to him, "I will follow you wherever you go."
[58]Jesus replied, "Foxes have dens and birds have nests, but the Son of Man[o] has no place to lay his head."
[59]He said to another man, "Follow me."[p]
But he replied, "Lord, first let me go and bury my father."
[60]Jesus said to him, "Let the dead bury their own dead, but you go and proclaim the kingdom of God."[q]
[61]Still another said, "I will follow you, Lord; but first let me go back and say goodbye to my family."[r]
[62]Jesus replied, "No one who puts a hand to the plow and looks back is fit for service in the kingdom
of God."

Jesus Sends Out the Seventy-Two

10:4-12pp — Lk 9:3-5
10:13-15,21,22pp — Mt 11:21-23,25-27
10:23,24pp — Mt 13:16,17

10 After this the Lord[s] appointed seventy-two[b] others[t] and sent them two by two[u] ahead of him to
every town and place where he was about to go.[v] [2]He told them, "The harvest is plentiful, but
the workers are few. Ask the Lord of the harvest, therefore, to send out workers into his harvest field.[w]

[a] *54* Some manuscripts *them, just as Elijah did* [b] *1* Some manuscripts *seventy*; also in verse 17

9:51 [i]Mk 16:19 [j]Lk 13:22; 17:11; 18:31; 19:28
9:52 [k]Mt 10:5
9:54 [l]Mt 4:21 [m]2Ki 1:10,12
9:57 [n]ver 51
9:58 [o]Mt 8:20
9:59 [p]Mt 4:19
9:60 [q]Mt 3:2
9:61 [r]1Ki 19:20
10:1 [s]Lk 7:13 [t]Lk 9:1,2, 51,52 [u]Mk 6:7 [v]Mt 10:1
10:2 [w]Mt 9:37,38; Jn 4:35

9:51—19:44 *Journey to Jerusalem.* This lengthy central section, much of which is unique to Luke, collects Jesus' teachings and interactions with both his followers and those who oppose him. Although it is not always clear why Luke arranges the various stories the way he does, several major themes emerge: the rebellious nature of God's people, the prophetic message of repentance, the rejection of Jesus the prophet, the redefinition of God's people, the impending death of Jesus in Jerusalem, and the final judgment of God. As Jesus travels to Jerusalem to suffer on the cross, God's own people become the object of his judgment.

9:51—11:13 *Commission and Reception.* As Jesus begins his journey in the midst of opposition (9:51–56), he warns his disciples (9:57–62) as he sends them out (10:1–24). Through a parable (10:25–37) and teachings (10:38—11:13), Jesus calls his disciples to focus on God and his kingdom while receiving one's neighbors.

9:51–56 *Samaritan Opposition.* Jesus begins his journey from Galilee to Jerusalem (9:51—19:44). Although facing increased opposition from the people, he continues to call people to repent. Just as Jesus' own people reject him at the beginning of his Galilean ministry (4:16–30), so here some reject him. Jesus refuses to cast the final judgment on a Samaritan village (vv. 52–55), which reaffirms that he is committed to those the Jews reject (cf. 10:30–37; 17:11–19).

9:51 the time ... for him to be taken up to heaven. Refers primarily to Jesus' ascension (Acts 1:9–11,22), but the use of the plural Greek noun translated "time" (Greek *tas hēmeras* [the days]) may indicate that Luke is referring to the period of time from Jesus' death to his ascension. **resolutely set out.** The OT prophets often use this phrase (which could be translated, "set his face") in the context of proclaiming judgment against God's people (Isa 50:7; Jer 21:10; Ezek 6:2; 13:17; 20:46).

9:52–53 After the fall of Samaria in 722 BC (2 Kgs 17), Samaria was resettled with people who later came to be known as Samaritans. The relationship between the Judeans and those living in the region of Samaria continued to deteriorate (Ezra 4:1; Neh 13:3,30), and their animosity intensified when the Judean ruler John Hyrcanus destroyed the Samaritan temple on Mount Gerizim in 128 or 127 BC. Jewish pilgrims traveling to Jerusalem would often travel on the east side of the Jordan River to avoid Samaria. See notes on John 4:4,9,20.

9:54 call fire down from heaven. Their request recalls Elijah's call for fire to destroy the messengers of King Ahaziah of Samaria (2 Kgs 1:9–16). **destroy them.** See NIV text note.

9:57–62 *The Cost of Following Jesus.* After this Samaritan village rejects Jesus, he again reminds his disciples of the cost (vv. 57–58) and the commitment required (vv. 59–62) to follow him.

9:59–60 People often practiced a two-stage burial. Shortly after the death of his father, this man should have already completed the first stage by burying his father in a cave. After one year, in the second stage, he would return to the cave to collect his father's bones and place them with those of his dead ancestors. Thus, Jesus said, "Let the dead [the ancestors] bury [receive] their own dead [the one who recently died]." In this context, the man's request most likely refers to the second stage of burial, but Jesus' urgent mission cannot accommodate this delay.

9:61–62 This person's request is similar to Elisha's request after Elijah called him (1 Kgs 19:20a). Elijah reluctantly approved (1 Kgs 19:20b), though Elisha did not delay, but Jesus refuses because his mission is even more urgent than Elijah's.

10:1–24 *Jesus Sends Out the Seventy-Two.* As Jesus sent out the Twelve in 9:1–6, here he sends out the "seventy-two" (or "seventy," see NIV text note on v. 1). Only Luke includes this account, probably to anticipate the mission to a wider circle beyond the confines of Israel (cf. vv. 13–15) and perhaps to remind the readers that Moses appointed seventy-two—or "seventy" plus Eldad and Medad—to share his work (Num 11:16–17,24–26).

10:1 two by two. Likely a model of early Christian missionary practices

10:3 [x]Mt 10:16
10:7 [y]Mt 10:10; 1Co 9:14; 1Ti 5:18
10:8 [z]1Co 10:27
10:9 [a]Mt 3:2; 10:7
10:11 [b]Mt 10:14; Mk 6:11 [c]ver 9
10:12 [d]Mt 10:15 [e]Mt 11:24
10:13 [f]Lk 6:24-26 [g]Rev 11:3
10:15 [h]Mt 4:13
10:16 [i]Mt 10:40; Jn 13:20
10:17 [j]ver 1 [k]Mk 16:17
10:18 [l]Mt 4:10 [m]Isa 14:12; Rev 9:1; 12:8,9
10:19 [n]Mk 16:18; Ac 28:3-5
10:20 [o]Ex 32:32; Ps 69:28; Da 12:1; Php 4:3; Heb 12:23; Rev 13:8; 20:12; 21:27
10:21 [p]1Co 1:26-29
10:22 [q]Mt 28:18 [r]Jn 1:18
10:24 [s]1Pe 1:10-12
10:25 [t]Mt 19:16; Lk 18:18

[3]Go! I am sending you out like lambs among wolves.[x] [4]Do not take a purse or bag or sandals; and do not greet anyone on the road.

[5]"When you enter a house, first say, 'Peace to this house.' [6]If someone who promotes peace is there, your peace will rest on them; if not, it will return to you. [7]Stay there, eating and drinking whatever they give you, for the worker deserves his wages.[y] Do not move around from house to house.

[8]"When you enter a town and are welcomed, eat what is offered to you.[z] [9]Heal the sick who are there and tell them, 'The kingdom of God[a] has come near to you.' [10]But when you enter a town and are not welcomed, go into its streets and say, [11]'Even the dust of your town we wipe from our feet as a warning to you.[b] Yet be sure of this: The kingdom of God has come near.'[c] [12]I tell you, it will be more bearable on that day for Sodom[d] than for that town.[e]

[13]"Woe to you,[f] Chorazin! Woe to you, Bethsaida! For if the miracles that were performed in you had been performed in Tyre and Sidon, they would have repented long ago, sitting in sackcloth[g] and ashes. [14]But it will be more bearable for Tyre and Sidon at the judgment than for you. [15]And you, Capernaum,[h] will you be lifted to the heavens? No, you will go down to Hades.[a]

[16]"Whoever listens to you listens to me; whoever rejects you rejects me; but whoever rejects me rejects him who sent me."[i]

[17]The seventy-two[j] returned with joy and said, "Lord, even the demons submit to us in your name."[k]

[18]He replied, "I saw Satan[l] fall like lightning from heaven.[m] [19]I have given you authority to trample on snakes[n] and scorpions and to overcome all the power of the enemy; nothing will harm you. [20]However, do not rejoice that the spirits submit to you, but rejoice that your names are written in heaven."[o]

[21]At that time Jesus, full of joy through the Holy Spirit, said, "I praise you, Father, Lord of heaven and earth, because you have hidden these things from the wise and learned, and revealed them to little children.[p] Yes, Father, for this is what you were pleased to do.

[22]"All things have been committed to me by my Father.[q] No one knows who the Son is except the Father, and no one knows who the Father is except the Son and those to whom the Son chooses to reveal him."[r]

[23]Then he turned to his disciples and said privately, "Blessed are the eyes that see what you see. [24]For I tell you that many prophets and kings wanted to see what you see but did not see it, and to hear what you hear but did not hear it."[s]

The Parable of the Good Samaritan

10:25-28pp — Mt 22:34-40; Mk 12:28-31

[25]On one occasion an expert in the law stood up to test Jesus. "Teacher," he asked, "what must I do to inherit eternal life?"[t]

[a] *15* That is, the realm of the dead

(cf. Acts 13:2; 15:27,39–40; 17:14; 19:22). This may also reflect the Jewish law requiring "two or three witnesses" to convict someone of a crime (Deut 17:6; 19:15), since the messengers Jesus sends out testify when people reject the gospel (Luke 10:10–12).

10:4 This is comparable to Jesus' instruction to the Twelve, except for the additional command not to bring "sandals" or "greet anyone on the road." This additional command possibly emphasizes that the mission is urgent (cf. 2 Kgs 4:29).

10:6 peace ... will return to you. May mean simply that the greeting of peace is void, or it may carry a stronger sense of condemnation, as in the saying "Your blood be on your own heads!" (Acts 18:6).

10:9 The kingdom of God has come near to you. Through Jesus' presence as well as his ministries of words and deeds (cf. 4:14–44); although it is his death and resurrection that formally ushers in God's kingdom (9:27).

10:11 wipe from our feet. See note on 9:5.

10:12 Sodom. Symbolizes wickedness and God's judgment (Gen 13:13; Deut 29:23; 32:32; Isa 13:19; Jer 49:18; Amos 4:11), and the OT often compares Israel's sins to Sodom's (Isa 1:9–10; 3:9; Jer 23:14; Lam 4:6; Ezek 16:43–58).

10:13 Chorazin ... Bethsaida. Villages in Galilee with a significant Jewish presence. **sitting in sackcloth and ashes.** An expression of mourning (Esth 4:1,3; Jer 6:26) and repentance (Isa 58:5; cf. Dan 9:3).

10:14 Tyre and Sidon. Gentile cities north of Galilee; they often represent idol worship (Isa 23:1–16; Ezek 26–28; Amos 1:9–10). By comparing the Jews to idol worshipers, Jesus highlights that God's own people are wicked.

10:15 This alludes to the fall of Babylon noted in Isa 14:13,15.

10:19 Jesus has power over Satan and his demonic forces. **authority to trample on snakes and scorpions.** Highlights God's power and protection (cf. Ps 91:13).

10:20 Jesus implies two sets of contrast: (1) Disciples should focus on their status before Christ instead of on their own power since it is only in the name of Christ that victory can be achieved (vv. 19,22). (2) Disciples should focus on what happens "in heaven" rather than on their performance on earth.

10:24 see ... hear. Jesus uniquely reveals God, and it benefits his followers. Unlike the outsiders who "though seeing, they may not see; though hearing, they may not understand" (8:10, quoting Isa 6:9), those who follow Jesus can now see and hear the salvation of God (cf. Isa 52:15).

10:25–37 *The Parable of the Good Samaritan.* Most Jews would have known the primary importance of loving God and one's neighbor. This

Modern Bethany.

26 "What is written in the Law?" he replied. "How do you read it?"
27 He answered, " 'Love the Lord your God with all your heart and with all your soul and with all your strength and with all your mind'[a];[u] and, 'Love your neighbor as yourself.'[b]"[v]
28 "You have answered correctly," Jesus replied. "Do this and you will live."[w]
29 But he wanted to justify himself,[x] so he asked Jesus, "And who is my neighbor?"
30 In reply Jesus said: "A man was going down from Jerusalem to Jericho, when he was attacked by
robbers. They stripped him of his clothes, beat him and went away, leaving him half dead. 31 A priest
happened to be going down the same road, and when he saw the man, he passed by on the other side.[y]
32 So too, a Levite, when he came to the place and saw him, passed by on the other side. 33 But a Samaritan,[z] as he traveled, came where the man was; and when he saw him, he took pity on him. 34 He went
to him and bandaged his wounds, pouring on oil and wine. Then he put the man on his own donkey,
brought him to an inn and took care of him. 35 The next day he took out two denarii[c] and gave them
to the innkeeper. 'Look after him,' he said, 'and when I return, I will reimburse you for any extra expense you may have.'
36 "Which of these three do you think was a neighbor to the man who fell into the hands of robbers?"

10:27 [u] Dt 6:5 [v] Lev 19:18; Mt 5:43
10:28 [w] Lev 18:5; Ro 7:10
10:29 [x] Lk 16:15
10:31 [y] Lev 21:1-3
10:33 [z] Mt 10:5

[a] *27* Deut. 6:5 [b] *27* Lev. 19:18 [c] *35* A denarius was the usual daily wage of a day laborer (see Matt. 20:2).

parable defines one's neighbor and thus redefines how to love God. In discussing the various people groups within Jewish society, the audience would have expected Jesus to name these three groups: priests, Levites, and the people (cf. 2 Chr 34:30; 35:2,7; Ezra 2:70; 8:15; Neh 7:73; 11:3); but Jesus surprises the audience by replacing the people with a Samaritan. More important, this Samaritan exemplifies mercy (v. 37). Further, Jesus portrays the one lying on the ground as one who falls among robbers and is stripped, beaten, and abandoned. These descriptions match those applied to Jesus when he dies on the cross (22:63–65; 23:32,39; John 19:1–2,23). Eternal life is defined not simply by acts of kindness but by properly responding to Jesus.

10:27 Love the Lord your God. Luke uses a fourfold description—heart, soul, strength, mind (cf. Mark 12:30)—instead of the threefold description in Deut 6:5 ("heart ... soul ... strength"; cf. Matt 22:37; Mark 12:33) since the Greek for "heart" and "mind" translate the full spectrum of meaning of the Hebrew word for "heart." **Love your neighbor as yourself.** From Lev 19:18, where in its context "neighbor" is understood as referring to "your people."

10:30–32 Jewish law considers a corpse unclean, and some by extension may consider the "half dead" (v. 30) unclean as well, which explains how the priest and Levite respond. A priest serves in the Jerusalem temple (1:5,8; 5:14) and is thus particularly sensitive to such a purity concern (Lev 5:2–6; 21:1–4; Num 5:2; 6:6–8; Ezek 44:25–27). A Levite assists the priests in temple services (Deut 33:8–11; 1 Chr 23:28) and thus shares a similar concern.

10:33–35 Unlike the Samaritan village in 9:51–56, the Samaritan here provides a model response. Significantly, it is this hated foreigner who is commended by Jesus (see note on 9:52–53), and this Samaritan demonstrates the love that is not constrained by ethnic boundaries.

10:36 Jesus reverses the original question ("who is my neighbor?" v. 29) to challenge his audience to examine whether they are acting like a neighbor to those around them. If one defines "neighbor" as the

10:38 [a] Jn 11:1; 12:2
10:39 [b] Jn 11:1; 12:3 [c] Lk 8:35
10:40 [d] Mk 4:38
10:41 [e] Mt 6:25-34; Lk 12:11,22
10:42 [f] Ps 27:4
11:1 [g] Lk 3:21 [h] Jn 13:13
11:2 [i] Mt 3:2
11:4 [j] Mt 18:35; Mk 11:25 [k] Mt 26:41; Jas 1:13

37 The expert in the law replied, "The one who had mercy on him."
Jesus told him, "Go and do likewise."

At the Home of Martha and Mary

38 As Jesus and his disciples were on their way, he came to a village where a woman named Martha[a]
opened her home to him. 39 She had a sister called Mary,[b] who sat at the Lord's feet[c] listening to what
he said. 40 But Martha was distracted by all the preparations that had to be made. She came to him and
asked, "Lord, don't you care[d] that my sister has left me to do the work by myself? Tell her to help me!"
41 "Martha, Martha," the Lord answered, "you are worried[e] and upset about many things, 42 but few
things are needed—or indeed only one.[a][f] Mary has chosen what is better, and it will not be taken
away from her."

Jesus' Teaching on Prayer

11:2-4pp — Mt 6:9-13
11:9-13pp — Mt 7:7-11

11 One day Jesus was praying[g] in a certain place. When he finished, one of his disciples said to
him, "Lord,[h] teach us to pray, just as John taught his disciples."
2 He said to them, "When you pray, say:

"'Father,[b]
hallowed be your name,
your kingdom[i] come.[c]
3 Give us each day our daily bread.
4 Forgive us our sins,
for we also forgive everyone who sins against us.[d][j]
And lead us not into temptation.[e]'"[k]

5 Then Jesus said to them, "Suppose you have a friend, and you go to him at midnight and say,
'Friend, lend me three loaves of bread; 6 a friend of mine on a journey has come to me, and I have no
food to offer him.' 7 And suppose the one inside answers, 'Don't bother me. The door is already locked,
and my children and I are in bed. I can't get up and give you anything.' 8 I tell you, even though he will

[a] 42 Some manuscripts *but only one thing is needed* [b] 2 Some manuscripts *Our Father in heaven* [c] 2 Some manuscripts *come. May your will be done on earth as it is in heaven.* [d] 4 Greek *everyone who is indebted to us* [e] 4 Some manuscripts *temptation, but deliver us from the evil one*

object of one's love, then the Samaritan becomes the blessed one as he receives the one lying on the ground. Significantly, while "neighbor" is often defined as someone within one's own ethnic group (see note on v. 27), to call this Samaritan a "neighbor" is then a challenge to the traditional boundaries.

10:38–42 *At the Home of Martha and Mary.* While the parable of the Good Samaritan deals with "love your neighbor as yourself" (v. 27), this section focuses on "love the Lord your God" (v. 27). Martha is divided among various concerns of this life (vv. 40–41), but Mary focuses on Jesus and his teaching (v. 39).

10:38 village. Bethany (John 11:1), about two miles (about 3 kilometers) from Jerusalem. **Martha.** Sister of Mary and Lazarus.

10:40–41 Martha's problem is not her "preparations" (v. 40) for her guests but her being "distracted" (v. 40) and "worried and upset about many things" (v. 41). The worries of this life prevent the word of God from growing (8:14) and prevent some from seeking the kingdom of God (12:22–34). Transcending cultural perceptions, women are now welcome as students of Jesus.

11:1–13 *Jesus' Teaching on Prayer.* Following the call to focus on the kingdom of God (10:38–42), this section presents Jesus' teaching on kingdom prayer (vv. 1–4). Although Jesus' teaching on prayer is slightly abbreviated compared to Matt 6:9–13, both versions emphasize the centrality of the kingdom in the present age. Following the prayer (vv. 2–4), Jesus uses a parable to urge his disciples to boldly pray for God to provide the Spirit (vv. 5–13).

11:2 hallowed be your name. One's name represents one's standing and reputation. As Israel's disobedience has profaned the name of God, God will sanctify his own name at the end of time (cf. Ezek 36:22–23). This clause, directed toward God, is therefore also a call to believers to be faithful to God. **your kingdom come.** Anticipates the ultimate consummation of God's promises (cf. 19:11) while asking God to continue to extend his reign among his people.

11:3 daily. Can also be translated "tomorrow." "Give us each day our bread for tomorrow" is a plea for God to provide for our future needs. **bread.** Can refer both to daily sustenance and to spiritual nourishment (cf. v. 13) that belongs to the consummated kingdom. This is consistent with Jesus' teaching that believers should not focus simply on "what you will eat" (12:22); instead, believers are called to "seek his kingdom" (12:31), and God will provide for them.

11:4 Forgive us our sins. Linked with the need for us to "forgive everyone who sins against us" (cf. 6:37). As believers, we are to act in a way that acknowledges our indebtedness to God's grace. Neither Matthew's version ("forgive ... as we also have forgiven," Matt 6:12) nor Luke's ("forgive ... for we also forgive") considers human forgiveness to be the basis of God's forgiveness; instead, human forgiveness demonstrates true repentance and allows one to receive God's forgiveness.

not get up and give you the bread because of friendship, yet because of your shameless audacity[a] he
will surely get up and give you as much as you need.[l]
9“So I say to you: Ask and it will be given to you;[m] seek and you will find; knock and the door will be
opened to you. 10For everyone who asks receives; the one who seeks finds; and to the one who knocks,
the door will be opened.
11“Which of you fathers, if your son asks for[b] a fish, will give him a snake instead? 12Or if he asks
for an egg, will give him a scorpion? 13If you then, though you are evil, know how to give good gifts to
your children, how much more will your Father in heaven give the Holy Spirit to those who ask him!”

Jesus and Beelzebul

11:14,15,17-22,24-26pp — Mt 12:22,24-29,43-45
11:17-22pp — Mk 3:23-27

14Jesus was driving out a demon that was mute. When the demon left, the man who had been mute
spoke, and the crowd was amazed.[n] 15But some of them said, “By Beelzebul,[o] the prince of demons, he
is driving out demons.”[p] 16Others tested him by asking for a sign from heaven.[q]
17Jesus knew their thoughts[r] and said to them: “Any kingdom divided against itself will be ruined,
and a house divided against itself will fall. 18If Satan[s] is divided against himself, how can his kingdom
stand? I say this because you claim that I drive out demons by Beelzebul. 19Now if I drive out demons by
Beelzebul, by whom do your followers drive them out? So then, they will be your judges. 20But if I drive
out demons by the finger of God,[t] then the kingdom of God[u] has come upon you.
21“When a strong man, fully armed, guards his own house, his possessions are safe. 22But when
someone stronger attacks and overpowers him, he takes away the armor in which the man trusted and
divides up his plunder.
23“Whoever is not with me is against me, and whoever does not gather with me scatters.[v]
24“When an impure spirit comes out of a person, it goes through arid places seeking rest and does
not find it. Then it says, ‘I will return to the house I left.’ 25When it arrives, it finds the house swept
clean and put in order. 26Then it goes and takes seven other spirits more wicked than itself, and they go
in and live there. And the final condition of that person is worse than the first.”[w]
27As Jesus was saying these things, a woman in the crowd called out, “Blessed is the mother who
gave you birth and nursed you.”[x]
28He replied, “Blessed rather are those who hear the word of God[y] and obey it.”[z]

11:8 [l] Lk 18:1-6
11:9 [m] Mt 7:7
11:14 [n] Mt 9:32,33
11:15 [o] Mk 3:22 [p] Mt 9:34
11:16 [q] Mt 12:38
11:17 [r] Mt 9:4
11:18 [s] Mt 4:10
11:20 [t] Ex 8:19 [u] Mt 3:2
11:23 [v] Mt 12:30; Mk 9:40; Lk 9:50
11:26 [w] 2Pe 2:20
11:27 [x] Lk 23:29
11:28 [y] Heb 4:12 [z] Pr 8:32; Lk 6:47; 8:21; Jn 14:21

[a] 8 Or *yet to preserve his good name* [b] 11 Some manuscripts *for bread, will give him a stone? Or if he asks for*

11:13 Jesus argues from “the lesser to the greater,” drawing on human experience to point to God’s far greater mercy. **Holy Spirit.** Anticipates the Spirit’s descent on God’s people in Acts 2:33 (cf. Luke 24:49; Acts 1:4). Instead of “the Holy Spirit” (here), Matthew’s “good gifts” (Matt 7:11) is probably another way of speaking of spiritual gifts (cf. Rom 1:11; 1 Cor 1:7).

11:14—13:35 *Call to Repentance in the Midst of Opposition.* The opposition to Jesus intensifies as the Jewish religious leaders suggest that demonic power is the source of Jesus’ authority (11:14–28). In response, Jesus directly challenges these leaders on numerous occasions (11:29–32,37–54; 12:1–12; 13:10–21) and calls God’s people to recognize the present moment (12:49–59), repent (11:33–36; 13:1–9,22–35), and live in light of the progression of God’s kingdom (12:13–48).

11:14–28 *Jesus and Beelzebul.* Jesus responds when people challenge the source of his authority to cast out demons. He explains how his power cannot be from the evil one (vv. 17–20), and he illustrates his challenge to Satan’s power with two parables. The first borrows from the exodus narrative as Jesus describes how God delivers his people while depriving his enemies (vv. 21–23; Exod 3:21–22). The second emphasizes not only that the evil forces have to be cast out but that God’s people must also receive his word as they welcome the power of God’s kingdom (vv. 24–28).

11:15 Beelzebul. Satan. This name may be a reference to the pagan god Baal-Zebub (2 Kgs 1:2–3,6,16), or it may refer to the abode of Baal (Hebrew *zĕbûl* means “residence” or “palace”; see note on Matt 10:25).

11:19 your followers. Could be the disciples of the Pharisees since Matt 12:24 identifies Jesus’ accusers as Pharisees. Jesus is assuming for the sake of argument that they can cast out demons. **they will be your judges.** Their followers who claim to have cast out demons would be the first to argue against them since those followers would surely not attribute their power to Beelzebul.

11:20 the finger of God. In the OT, it can refer to God’s presence and his works in history in the context of the assertion of God’s power in the midst of competing powers (Exod 8:19). The parallel in Matt 12:28 has “the Spirit of God.”

11:21 strong man. Satan.

11:22 someone stronger. Jesus. **divides up his plunder.** Jesus claims what rightfully belongs to him. This may allude to the exodus, when the Israelites took back what rightfully belonged to them (Exod 3:22), thus explaining why Jesus would use such violent imagery.

11:24–26 Unlike the Jews, whose work leaves room only for Satan’s more destructive activities (so that “the final condition of that person is worse than the first,” v. 26), Jesus’ ministry directly challenges Satan and replaces Satan’s kingdom with “the kingdom of God” (v. 20).

11:28 those who hear the word of God and obey it. They will be part of God’s victory over the power of Satan. The contrast between the two

11:29 [a]ver 16; Mt 12:38 [b]Jnh 1:17; Mt 16:4
11:31 [c]1Ki 10:1; 2Ch 9:1
11:32 [d]Jnh 3:5
11:33 [e]Mt 5:15; Mk 4:21; Lk 8:16
11:37 [f]Lk 7:36; 14:1
11:38 [g]Mk 7:3,4
11:39 [h]Lk 7:13 [i]Mt 23:25,26; Mk 7:20-23
11:40 [j]Lk 12:20; 1Co 15:36
11:41 [k]Lk 12:33 [l]Ac 10:15
11:42 [m]Lk 18:12 [n]Dt 6:5; Mic 6:8 [o]Mt 23:23

The Sign of Jonah

11:29-32pp — Mt 12:39-42

29 As the crowds increased, Jesus said, "This is a wicked generation. It asks for a sign,[a] but none will
be given it except the sign of Jonah.[b] 30 For as Jonah was a sign to the Ninevites, so also will the Son of
Man be to this generation. 31 The Queen of the South will rise at the judgment with the people of this
generation and condemn them, for she came from the ends of the earth to listen to Solomon's wisdom;[c]
and now something greater than Solomon is here. 32 The men of Nineveh will stand up at the judgment
with this generation and condemn it, for they repented at the preaching of Jonah;[d] and now something
greater than Jonah is here.

The Lamp of the Body

11:34,35pp — Mt 6:22,23

33 "No one lights a lamp and puts it in a place where it will be hidden, or under a bowl. Instead they
put it on its stand, so that those who come in may see the light.[e] 34 Your eye is the lamp of your body.
When your eyes are healthy,[a] your whole body also is full of light. But when they are unhealthy,[b] your
body also is full of darkness. 35 See to it, then, that the light within you is not darkness. 36 Therefore,
if your whole body is full of light, and no part of it dark, it will be just as full of light as when a lamp
shines its light on you."

Woes on the Pharisees and the Experts in the Law

37 When Jesus had finished speaking, a Pharisee invited him to eat with him; so he went in and
reclined at the table.[f] 38 But the Pharisee was surprised when he noticed that Jesus did not first wash
before the meal.[g]

39 Then the Lord[h] said to him, "Now then, you Pharisees clean the outside of the cup and dish, but
inside you are full of greed and wickedness.[i] 40 You foolish people![j] Did not the one who made the outside
make the inside also? 41 But now as for what is inside you — be generous to the poor,[k] and everything
will be clean for you.[l]

42 "Woe to you Pharisees, because you give God a tenth[m] of your mint, rue and all other kinds of
garden herbs, but you neglect justice and the love of God.[n] You should have practiced the latter without
leaving the former undone.[o]

a *34* The Greek for *healthy* here implies *generous*. *b* *34* The Greek for *unhealthy* here implies *stingy*.

blessings brings out a significant theme in Luke: those who are obedient to God are more blessed than those who are related to the Messiah by blood (see notes on 1:39–45).

11:29–32 *The Sign of Jonah.* After the people ask for a sign (v. 16), Jesus says that they will receive only "the sign of Jonah" (v. 29). As Jonah proclaimed judgment, so Jesus proclaims judgment. Unlike Jonah's audience, however, the Jews around Jesus persist in opposing God and his Messiah (v. 32).

11:29 a wicked generation. See notes on 7:31; 9:41. **Jonah.** Can symbolize deliverance (Jonah 2:10; cf. in the Apocrypha, 3 Maccabees 6:8) or judgment (Jonah 1:2; 3:1–4). In this context, which emphasizes this generation's wickedness (vv. 14–26; cf. 10:13–16) and the coming judgment (vv. 31–32,37–54), the "sign of Jonah" points to God's judgment. The richness of this metaphor is reflected in the parallel in Matt 12:40, where the sign can also refer to Jesus' resurrection.

11:31–32 These two examples present two sets of contrast: (1) Since even Gentiles such as the Queen of the South (1 Kgs 10:1–13; 2 Chr 9:1–12) and the people of Nineveh (Jonah 3:1–10) responded to God, Israel's failure to repent deserves even greater condemnation. (2) Since Jesus is "greater than" both Solomon and Jonah, he deserves even greater respect.

11:33–36 *The Lamp of the Body.* People must receive light so that they will no longer be filled with darkness.

11:33 lamp. Represents the word of God embodied in Jesus' life and teachings (8:16; cf. 8:11). The hearers are responsible to properly respond to the light.

11:34–36 "Healthy" eyes allow light to shine into the body and cast out "darkness" because through the witness of Christ's words and deeds, light enters a person. In the same way, people must open their hearts and allow the word of God to cast out the darkness within them.

11:37–54 *Woes on the Pharisees and the Experts in the Law.* When the Pharisees (v. 38) and the experts in the law (v. 45) again judge Jesus in a meal setting (cf. 7:36–43), he critiques their lives and teachings at length. He repeatedly uses the banquet motif to define the community of God's people (5:27–32; 7:34; 14:8–24; 15:2; 19:7). Here Jesus distinguishes himself from the Jewish religious leaders.

11:38 Although the Mosaic regulations do not stipulate washing before meals, "the Pharisees and all the Jews do not eat unless they give their hands a ceremonial washing, holding to the tradition of the elders" (Mark 7:3). By refusing to follow this tradition as a guest, Jesus deliberately provokes a confrontation.

11:39–41 Jesus' criticism of the hypocrisy of the Pharisees reflects the teachings of the prophets (Hos 6:6; cf. Matt 9:13; 12:7).

11:42 Jesus is not criticizing the Pharisees for tithing (cf. Lev 27:30–32; Num 18:21; Deut 14:22–27) but for tithing that which is unimportant while failing to pay attention to what is necessary, as the prophets have repeatedly emphasized: **justice and the love of God.** Cf. Hos 12:6; Amos 5:15; Mic 6:8.

43“Woe to you Pharisees, because you love the most important seats in the synagogues and respectful greetings in the marketplaces.[p]

44“Woe to you, because you are like unmarked graves,[q] which people walk over without knowing it.”

45One of the experts in the law[r] answered him, “Teacher, when you say these things, you insult us also.”

46Jesus replied, “And you experts in the law, woe to you, because you load people down with burdens they can hardly carry, and you yourselves will not lift one finger to help them.[s]

47“Woe to you, because you build tombs for the prophets, and it was your ancestors who killed them. 48So you testify that you approve of what your ancestors did; they killed the prophets, and you build their tombs.[t] 49Because of this, God in his wisdom[u] said, ‘I will send them prophets and apostles, some of whom they will kill and others they will persecute.’[v] 50Therefore this generation will be held responsible for the blood of all the prophets that has been shed since the beginning of the world, 51from the blood of Abel[w] to the blood of Zechariah,[x] who was killed between the altar and the sanctuary. Yes, I tell you, this generation will be held responsible for it all.[y]

52“Woe to you experts in the law, because you have taken away the key to knowledge. You yourselves have not entered, and you have hindered those who were entering.”[z]

53When Jesus went outside, the Pharisees and the teachers of the law began to oppose him fiercely and to besiege him with questions, 54waiting to catch him in something he might say.[a]

Warnings and Encouragements

12:2-9pp — Mt 10:26-33

12 Meanwhile, when a crowd of many thousands had gathered, so that they were trampling on one another, Jesus began to speak first to his disciples, saying: “Be[a] on your guard against the yeast of the Pharisees, which is hypocrisy.[b] 2There is nothing concealed that will not be disclosed, or hidden that will not be made known.[c] 3What you have said in the dark will be heard in the daylight, and what you have whispered in the ear in the inner rooms will be proclaimed from the roofs.

4“I tell you, my friends,[d] do not be afraid of those who kill the body and after that can do no more. 5But I will show you whom you should fear: Fear him who, after your body has been killed, has authority to throw you into hell. Yes, I tell you, fear him.[e] 6Are not five sparrows sold for two pennies? Yet not one of them is forgotten by God. 7Indeed, the very hairs of your head are all numbered.[f] Don’t be afraid; you are worth more than many sparrows.[g]

8“I tell you, whoever publicly acknowledges me before others, the Son of Man will also acknowledge before the angels of God.[h] 9But whoever disowns me before others will be disowned[i] before the angels

11:43 [p] Mt 23:6,7; Mk 12:38-39; Lk 14:7; 20:46
11:44 [q] Mt 23:27
11:45 [r] Mt 22:35
11:46 [s] Mt 23:4
11:48 [t] Mt 23:29-32; Ac 7:51-53
11:49 [u] 1Co 1:24,30; Col 2:3 [v] Mt 23:34
11:51 [w] Ge 4:8 [x] 2Ch 24:20,21 [y] Mt 23:35,36
11:52 [z] Mt 23:13
11:54 [a] Mt 12:10; Mk 12:13
12:1 [b] Mt 16:6,11,12; Mk 8:15
12:2 [c] Mk 4:22; Lk 8:17
12:4 [d] Jn 15:14,15
12:5 [e] Heb 10:31
12:7 [f] Mt 10:30 [g] Mt 12:12
12:8 [h] Lk 15:10
12:9 [i] Mk 8:38; 2Ti 2:12

[a] *1* Or *speak to his disciples, saying: “First of all, be*

11:44 Jews usually whitewashed their tombs because “anyone who touches a human bone or a grave, will be unclean for seven days” (Num 19:16). Ironically, although the Pharisees insist on ritual cleanliness, they are themselves “unmarked graves” that render others unclean.

11:45 experts in the law. See note on 7:30.

11:46 load people down. By adding to the law of Moses, Jewish leaders add a burden to God’s people, a burden that they themselves are not able to bear. Peter later issues a similar criticism against those who insist that one must be circumcised to be saved (Acts 15:10).

11:47 build tombs for the prophets. To exhibit their piety.

11:48 approve of what your ancestors did. By rejecting Jesus the prophet as their ancestors did (cf. Acts 7:52).

11:49 Jesus does not directly quote the OT, though he does reflect the content of several passages (e.g., 1 Kgs 19:10,14; Jer 7:25–26; Ezek 2:3–8).

11:51 Chronologically, Zechariah was not the last OT prophet to be killed, but in the Hebrew arrangement of the OT books, Zechariah’s death is the last murder recorded in the OT canon (2 Chr 24:20–25).

11:52 the key to knowledge. The original intent of the law. In taking away the “key,” these experts “shut the door of the kingdom of heaven” (Matt 23:13).

12:1–12 *Warnings and Encouragements.* Jesus calls his disciples to live in light of the future. They must be alert and faithful to him, even in the midst of persecution.

12:1 yeast of the Pharisees. As a little yeast can permeate a large amount of dough, the hypocrisy of the Pharisees can infect many (cf. 11:44,52).

12:2–3 What is “hidden” or “said” privately will be revealed in the final judgment (cf. 8:16–18; 11:33–36).

12:5 authority to throw you into hell. Only God has this authority (cf. Deut 32:39; 1 Sam 2:6; 2 Kgs 5:7). Those who are persecuted should only fear the one who deserves such fear.

12:6 pennies. Roman coins worth 1/16th of a laborer’s daily wage.

12:7 the very hairs of your head. Points to God’s sovereignty in the midst of persecution. In the OT, “not a hair of his head will fall to the ground” is used in reference to God’s sovereignty (1 Sam 14:45; cf. 2 Sam 14:11b; 1 Kgs 1:52), and a similar use can be found later in this Gospel (21:18).

12:9 whoever disowns me before others will be disowned before the angels of God. Jesus contrasts the present on earth with the future in heaven. Jesus’ disciples must acquire the right perspective to respond to the challenges of this age.

12:10 [j]Mt 8:20 [k]Mt 12:31,32; Mk 3:28-29; 1Jn 5:16
12:11 [l]Mt 10:17,19; Mk 13:11; Lk 21:12,14
12:12 [m]Ex 4:12; Mt 10:20; Mk 13:11; Lk 21:15
12:15 [n]Job 20:20; 31:24; Ps 62:10
12:20 [o]Jer 17:11; Lk 11:40 [p]Job 27:8 [q]Ps 39:6; 49:10
12:21 [r]ver 33
12:24 [s]Job 38:41; Ps 147:9
12:27 [t]1Ki 10:4-7
12:28 [u]Mt 6:30
12:30 [v]Lk 6:36 [w]Mt 6:8
12:31 [x]Mt 3:2 [y]Mt 19:29
12:32 [z]Mt 14:27 [a]Mt 25:34

of God. 10 And everyone who speaks a word against the Son of Man[j] will be forgiven, but anyone who
blasphemes against the Holy Spirit will not be forgiven.[k]
11 "When you are brought before synagogues, rulers and authorities, do not worry about how you
will defend yourselves or what you will say,[l] 12 for the Holy Spirit will teach you at that time what you
should say."[m]

The Parable of the Rich Fool

13 Someone in the crowd said to him, "Teacher, tell my brother to divide the inheritance with me."
14 Jesus replied, "Man, who appointed me a judge or an arbiter between you?" 15 Then he said to
them, "Watch out! Be on your guard against all kinds of greed; life does not consist in an abundance
of possessions."[n]
16 And he told them this parable: "The ground of a certain rich man yielded an abundant harvest.
17 He thought to himself, 'What shall I do? I have no place to store my crops.'
18 "Then he said, 'This is what I'll do. I will tear down my barns and build bigger ones, and there I
will store my surplus grain. 19 And I'll say to myself, "You have plenty of grain laid up for many years.
Take life easy; eat, drink and be merry."'
20 "But God said to him, 'You fool![o] This very night your life will be demanded from you.[p] Then who
will get what you have prepared for yourself?'[q]
21 "This is how it will be with whoever stores up things for themselves but is not rich toward God."[r]

Do Not Worry

12:22-31pp — Mt 6:25-33

22 Then Jesus said to his disciples: "Therefore I tell you, do not worry about your life, what you will
eat; or about your body, what you will wear. 23 For life is more than food, and the body more than
clothes. 24 Consider the ravens: They do not sow or reap, they have no storeroom or barn; yet God feeds
them.[s] And how much more valuable you are than birds! 25 Who of you by worrying can add a single
hour to your life[a]? 26 Since you cannot do this very little thing, why do you worry about the rest?
27 "Consider how the wild flowers grow. They do not labor or spin. Yet I tell you, not even Solomon in
all his splendor[t] was dressed like one of these. 28 If that is how God clothes the grass of the field, which
is here today, and tomorrow is thrown into the fire, how much more will he clothe you—you of little
faith![u] 29 And do not set your heart on what you will eat or drink; do not worry about it. 30 For the pagan
world runs after all such things, and your Father[v] knows that you need them.[w] 31 But seek his kingdom,[x]
and these things will be given to you as well.[y]
32 "Do not be afraid,[z] little flock, for your Father has been pleased to give you the kingdom.[a] 33 Sell

[a] 25 Or *single cubit to your height*

12:10 blasphemes against the Holy Spirit. In light of Mark 3:29, where the one who "blasphemes against the Holy Spirit" attributes Jesus' work to Satan (see Mark 3:22–30; Matt 12:25–37), the contrast here between speaking "against the Son of Man" and blaspheming "against the Holy Spirit" should therefore be understood as the contrast between offending Jesus in particular contexts and generally denying the Holy Spirit's work in Jesus (12:8–9).

12:13–21 *The Parable of the Rich Fool.* Jesus uses familiar themes from OT wisdom literature to express the need for a proper perspective in light of the coming kingdom of God: productivity, wealth, and pleasure are futile (vv. 16–17; cf. Eccl 2:1,5–11); death powerfully reveals the meaning of our present existence (v. 20; cf. Eccl 2:16; 7:2–4); and future judgment is real (vv. 20–21; cf. Eccl 11:8–10).

12:13 Mosaic regulations provide specific instructions concerning inheritance (Num 27:1–11; 36:7–9; Deut 21:15–17). The request for Jesus to mediate this dispute between two brothers apparently involves issues of greed.

12:19 eat, drink and be merry. This can be a sign of God's blessing (cf. Eccl 2:24; 3:13; 5:18; 8:15), but in this context it reflects a lax and irreverent lifestyle (cf. Exod 32:6; 2 Sam 11:11; Isa 22:12–13; Jer 16:8). The underlying point is the uncertainty of life and the need to be alert (see note on 12:35–48).

12:22–34 *Do Not Worry.* Jesus extends the previous discussion on the vanity of wealth and possessions. Our worries reveal the object of our worship, and those seeking the kingdom of God should not be controlled by the worries of this life. "You cannot serve both God and money" (16:13; Matt 6:24).

12:24 ravens. Recalls Ps 147:9 (cf. Job 38:41). Since God cares for these unclean birds (Lev 11:13–15; Deut 14:11–14), how much more must he care for his own people?

12:27 splendor. Characterized the life of Solomon (1 Kgs 3:13; 1 Chr 29:25), but even this human glory fades in comparison to the wild flowers that are cared for by God himself.

12:31 seek his kingdom. To seek God's kingdom is to follow Jesus because Jesus' ministry embodies the presence of this kingdom (cf. 11:20; 17:21). The priority of putting God and his kingdom first is explicitly stated in Matthew: "seek first his kingdom" (Matt 6:33). **these things.** The things "you need" (v. 30). What we need often transcends the material realm (vv. 4–7,13–21).

12:33 Sell your possessions and give to the poor. Leave everything

your possessions and give to the poor.[b] Provide purses for yourselves that will not wear out, a treasure
in heaven[c] that will never fail, where no thief comes near and no moth destroys.[d] 34For where your
treasure is, there your heart will be also.[e]

Watchfulness

12:35,36pp — Mt 25:1-13; Mk 13:33-37
12:39,40; 42-46pp — Mt 24:43-51

35"Be dressed ready for service and keep your lamps burning, 36like servants waiting for their master
to return from a wedding banquet, so that when he comes and knocks they can immediately open the
door for him. 37It will be good for those servants whose master finds them watching when he comes.[f]
Truly I tell you, he will dress himself to serve, will have them recline at the table and will come and wait
on them.[g] 38It will be good for those servants whose master finds them ready, even if he comes in the
middle of the night or toward daybreak. 39But understand this: If the owner of the house had known at
what hour the thief[h] was coming, he would not have let his house be broken into. 40You also must be
ready,[i] because the Son of Man will come at an hour when you do not expect him."
41Peter asked, "Lord, are you telling this parable to us, or to everyone?"
42The Lord[j] answered, "Who then is the faithful and wise manager, whom the master puts in charge
of his servants to give them their food allowance at the proper time? 43It will be good for that servant
whom the master finds doing so when he returns. 44Truly I tell you, he will put him in charge of all his
possessions. 45But suppose the servant says to himself, 'My master is taking a long time in coming,' and
he then begins to beat the other servants, both men and women, and to eat and drink and get drunk.
46The master of that servant will come on a day when he does not expect him and at an hour he is not
aware of.[k] He will cut him to pieces and assign him a place with the unbelievers.
47"The servant who knows the master's will and does not get ready or does not do what the master
wants will be beaten with many blows.[l] 48But the one who does not know and does things deserving
punishment will be beaten with few blows.[m] From everyone who has been given much, much will be
demanded; and from the one who has been entrusted with much, much more will be asked.

Not Peace but Division

12:51-53pp — Mt 10:34-36

49"I have come to bring fire on the earth, and how I wish it were already kindled! 50But I have a
baptism[n] to undergo, and what constraint I am under until it is completed![o] 51Do you think I came to
bring peace on earth? No, I tell you, but division. 52From now on there will be five in one family divided
against each other, three against two and two against three. 53They will be divided, father against son

12:33 [b]Mt 19:21; Ac 2:45 [c]Mt 6:20 [d]Jas 5:2
12:34 [e]Mt 6:21
12:37 [f]Mt 24:42,46; 25:13 [g]Mt 20:28
12:39 [h]Mt 6:19; 1Th 5:2; 2Pe 3:10; Rev 3:3; 16:15
12:40 [i]Mk 13:33; Lk 21:36
12:42 [j]Lk 7:13
12:46 [k]ver 40
12:47 [l]Dt 25:2
12:48 [m]Lev 5:17; Nu 15:27-30
12:50 [n]Mk 10:38 [o]Jn 19:30

and follow Jesus (5:11,28). This echoes the parable of the rich fool (vv. 13–21) by focusing on the futility of accumulating wealth and possessions.

12:35–48 *Watchfulness.* Jesus' three parables urge his followers to prepare for his return. The first two address the need to be alert and ready since his return will be unexpected (vv. 35–38,39–40). The third urges those who are waiting to remain faithful (vv. 41–48).

12:37 master ... will dress himself to serve. Illustrates the teachings of Jesus, who elsewhere encourages his disciples to be humble servants (22:27). Those who wait must also serve faithfully (vv. 41–48). **watching.** Being alert at the end of time (21:36; 1 Thess 5:6; Rev 3:3; 16:15; cf. 1 Cor 16:13).

12:39 thief. An image often used to refer to Jesus' returning when people "do not expect him" (v. 40; Matt 24:44; cf. 1 Thess 5:2,4; 2 Pet 3:10; Rev 3:3; 16:15).

12:42–45 Those who "give them their food allowance at the proper time" (v. 42) behave like subordinates, while the ones who "eat and drink and get drunk" (v. 45) act like they are the master, and they do not expect him to return.

12:46 cut him to pieces. Decisive judgment against God's unfaithful people (cf. Jer 14:17–19). **assign him a place with the unbelievers.** Final judgment when the unfaithful are eternally separated from God (cf. 13:27–28).

12:48 given much ... entrusted with much. Responsible stewardship demands both the recognition of one's gifts as originating from God and the necessity of a proper response to the reception of those gifts.

12:49–53 *Not Peace but Division.* Shifting his attention from the future back to the present, Jesus urges his followers to recognize the critical time in which they live. Repentance is called for as the time of judgment approaches.

12:49 fire. Symbolizes God's judgment (Isa 4:4–5; Jer 21:12; Mal 4:1). John the Baptist used fire to describe an aspect of Jesus' ministry (3:16).

12:50 baptism. Mark 10:38 connects this to the "cup" that Jesus must drink. The "cup" refers to Jesus' giving "his life as a ransom for many" (Mark 10:45).

12:51 peace. See 1:79; 2:14; 7:50; 8:48; 10:5–6; 24:36; Acts 10:36. **division.** Results from God's own people's rejecting this peace (cf. 19:42).

12:52,53 divided. Gabriel promised Zechariah that John the Baptist will "turn the hearts of the parents to their children" (1:17) and so fulfill the prophecy of Mal 4:6. By reversing this description, Jesus announces the arrival of the "great and dreadful day of the Lord" (Mal 4:5), when family members will be divided.

12:53 [p] Mic 7:6; Mt 10:21
12:54 [q] Mt 16:2
12:56 [r] Mt 16:3
12:58 [s] Mt 5:25
12:59 [t] Mt 5:26; Mk 12:42
13:1 [u] Mt 27:2
13:2 [v] Jn 9:2,3
13:4 [w] Jn 9:7,11
13:5 [x] Mt 3:2; Ac 2:38
13:6 [y] Isa 5:2; Jer 8:13; Mt 21:19
13:7 [z] Mt 3:10
13:10 [a] Mt 4:23
13:11 [b] ver 16

and son against father, mother against daughter and daughter against mother, mother-in-law against daughter-in-law and daughter-in-law against mother-in-law."[p]

Interpreting the Times

54He said to the crowd: "When you see a cloud rising in the west, immediately you say, 'It's going to rain,' and it does.[q] 55And when the south wind blows, you say, 'It's going to be hot,' and it is. 56Hypocrites! You know how to interpret the appearance of the earth and the sky. How is it that you don't know how to interpret this present time?[r]

57"Why don't you judge for yourselves what is right? 58As you are going with your adversary to the magistrate, try hard to be reconciled on the way, or your adversary may drag you off to the judge, and the judge turn you over to the officer, and the officer throw you into prison.[s] 59I tell you, you will not get out until you have paid the last penny."[t]

Repent or Perish

13 Now there were some present at that time who told Jesus about the Galileans whose blood Pilate[u] had mixed with their sacrifices. 2Jesus answered, "Do you think that these Galileans were worse sinners than all the other Galileans because they suffered this way?[v] 3I tell you, no! But unless you repent, you too will all perish. 4Or those eighteen who died when the tower in Siloam[w] fell on them — do you think they were more guilty than all the others living in Jerusalem? 5I tell you, no! But unless you repent,[x] you too will all perish."

6Then he told this parable: "A man had a fig tree growing in his vineyard, and he went to look for fruit on it but did not find any.[y] 7So he said to the man who took care of the vineyard, 'For three years now I've been coming to look for fruit on this fig tree and haven't found any. Cut it down![z] Why should it use up the soil?'

8" 'Sir,' the man replied, 'leave it alone for one more year, and I'll dig around it and fertilize it. 9If it bears fruit next year, fine! If not, then cut it down.' "

Jesus Heals a Crippled Woman on the Sabbath

10On a Sabbath Jesus was teaching in one of the synagogues,[a] 11and a woman was there who had been crippled by a spirit for eighteen years.[b] She was bent over and could not straighten up at all.

12:54–59 *Interpreting the Times.* Jesus uses the weather to explain the need for discerning the signs of this critical time.
12:54 rising in the west. In the Holy Land, rain clouds come from the Mediterranean Sea in the west.
12:55 south wind blows. The dry winds come from the desert to the south.
12:56 this present time. The critical time of God's salvation. People who refuse to respond to the gospel will experience God's judgment because they "did not recognize the time of God's coming to [them]" (19:44).
12:57–58 Jesus said, "Do not judge, and you will not be judged" (6:37). Jesus again urges his audience to reconcile with one another so that they will not be judged.
12:59 penny. This penny (Greek *lepton*) is worth even less than one of the pennies (Greek *assariōn*) in v. 6 (see note there). God's judgment is severe and exhaustive.
13:1–9 *Repent or Perish.* Jesus continues to call the people to repent and emphasizes the need to discern the times. Commenting on two events, Jesus reminds his audience that they are not immune to God's judgment (vv. 1–5). He concludes with a parable that explains the impending judgment but allows a glimpse of hope for those who are willing to repent (vv. 6–9).
13:1 Pilate. See note on 3:1. This verse describes an otherwise unknown incident in which Pilate killed Galileans who were apparently offering sacrifices in Jerusalem during one of the major pilgrim festivals. This is consistent with ancient descriptions of Pilate's cruel behavior.
13:2–3 Calamities often appear as God's judging his unfaithful people (Exod 20:5; Prov 10:4–25), but suffering does not always reflect God's wrath (John 9:1–3). Jesus' point is that those who are not affected by recent calamities should not assume that they are innocent and therefore immune from God's judgment.
13:4 those eighteen who died. Another otherwise unknown incident (see note on v. 1). **tower in Siloam.** Presumably a structure near the Pool of Siloam (cf. John 9:7) in the southeastern section of Jerusalem.
13:6 Both the fig tree (Jer 8:13; Hos 9:10; Mic 7:1) and vineyard (Isa 1:8; 3:14; 5:7; Jer 12:10) can refer to God's people. This possible judgment on the vineyard recalls Isa 5:7, where God is disappointed with his own vineyard.
13:7 Cut it down! Ps 105:33 proclaims God's judgment on the enemies of Israel in similar terms. Now Jesus warns of a similar judgment on God's people.
13:8–9 Noting God's mercy in spite of human sinfulness (cf. 9:51–56; 15:1–32; 18:35–43), Jesus urges the people to repent while they still have time (cf. vv. 1–5,31–35; 10:13–16; 11:29–32; 12:13–21).
13:10–17 *Jesus Heals a Crippled Woman on the Sabbath.* By setting free a woman who was "bound" (v. 16), Jesus shows that despite opposition he is committed to his mission to "set the oppressed free" (4:18; cf. Isa 58:6). Luke emphasizes that the Jewish leaders are rejecting Jesus' ministry. They insist on their own Sabbath rules and regulations, forgetting that God made the Sabbath to celebrate his deliverance of his people (Deut 5:12–15). Thus, they are rejecting God's ultimate deliverance brought about by his Son.
13:11 crippled by a spirit. The spiritual and physical are connected.

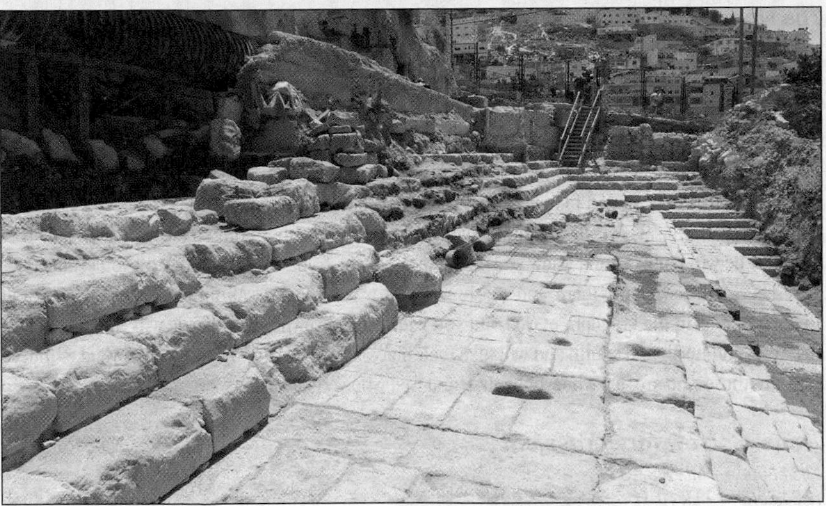

In 2004, steps to the Pool of Siloam were discovered in Jerusalem.
Todd Bolen/www.BiblePlaces.com

12When Jesus saw her, he called her forward and said to her, "Woman, you are set free from your infirmity." 13Then he put his hands on her,[c] and immediately she straightened up and praised God.
14Indignant because Jesus had healed on the Sabbath,[d] the synagogue leader[e] said to the people,
"There are six days for work.[f] So come and be healed on those days, not on the Sabbath."
15The Lord answered him, "You hypocrites! Doesn't each of you on the Sabbath untie your ox or
donkey from the stall and lead it out to give it water?[g] 16Then should not this woman, a daughter of
Abraham,[h] whom Satan[i] has kept bound for eighteen long years, be set free on the Sabbath day from
what bound her?"
17When he said this, all his opponents were humiliated,[j] but the people were delighted with all the
wonderful things he was doing.

13:13 [c]Mk 5:23
13:14 [d]Mt 12:2; Lk 14:3 [e]Mk 5:22 [f]Ex 20:9
13:15 [g]Lk 14:5
13:16 [h]Lk 3:8; 19:9 [i]Mt 4:10
13:17 [j]Isa 66:5
13:18 [k]Mt 3:2 [l]Mt 13:24
13:19 [m]Lk 17:6 [n]Mt 13:32
13:21 [o]1Co 5:6

The Parables of the Mustard Seed and the Yeast

13:18,19pp — Mk 4:30-32
13:18-21pp — Mt 13:31-33

18Then Jesus asked, "What is the kingdom of God[k] like?[l] What shall I compare it to? 19It is like a
mustard seed, which a man took and planted in his garden. It grew and became a tree,[m] and the birds
perched in its branches."[n]
20Again he asked, "What shall I compare the kingdom of God to? 21It is like yeast that a woman took
and mixed into about sixty pounds[a] of flour until it worked all through the dough."[o]

[a] *21* Or about 27 kilograms

People understood that demonic forces are sometimes the cause of illness and disease.

13:12 Woman. See NIV text note on John 2:4.

13:13 immediately. Jesus demonstrates his power by instantly healing a woman who was crippled for 18 years (v. 11; cf. 4:39; 5:25; 8:44,47,55; 18:43).

13:14 Jewish traditions that forbade treating nonemergency medical problems on a Sabbath are extrapolated from Mosaic Sabbath regulations (cf. Exod 20:9–10; Deut 5:13–14).

13:15 ox or donkey. Jesus criticizes the Jews for caring for their animals but neglecting the needs of "a daughter of Abraham" (v. 16).

13:16 a daughter of Abraham. Jesus considers her to be a member of God's restored people. Jesus also identifies a tax collector who has received God's "salvation" as "a son of Abraham" (19:9).

13:18–21 *The Parables of the Mustard Seed and the Yeast.* Despite the opposition to Jesus (cf. vv. 10–17), God's kingdom will continue to grow until it is fulfilled in glory.

13:19 a mustard seed. "The smallest of all seeds on earth" (Mark 4:31) known to Jesus' audience. **tree.** Cf. "the largest of all garden plants" in Mark 4:32.

13:21 This parable further develops the point of the previous one (vv. 18–19). The previous parable contrasts a small beginning with a spectacular ending; this parable continues with the theme of the growth of the kingdom, but it introduces the kingdom's hiddenness to those who have not responded to its gospel. In the eyes of many, the kingdom is invisible (cf. 17:20–21), but it will be revealed fully at the end of time.

13:22 [p] Lk 9:51
13:24 [q] Mt 7:13
13:25 [r] Mt 7:23; 25:10-12
13:27 [s] Mt 7:23; 25:41
13:28 [t] Mt 8:12
13:29 [u] Mt 8:11
13:30 [v] Mt 19:30
13:31 [w] Mt 14:1
13:32 [x] Heb 2:10
13:33 [y] Mt 21:11
13:34 [z] Mt 23:37
13:35 [a] Jer 12:17; 22:5 [b] Ps 118:26; Mt 21:9; Lk 19:38

The Narrow Door

22 Then Jesus went through the towns and villages, teaching as he made his way to Jerusalem.[p]
23 Someone asked him, "Lord, are only a few people going to be saved?"
He said to them, 24 "Make every effort to enter through the narrow door,[q] because many, I tell you,
will try to enter and will not be able to. 25 Once the owner of the house gets up and closes the door, you
will stand outside knocking and pleading, 'Sir, open the door for us.'
"But he will answer, 'I don't know you or where you come from.'[r]
26 "Then you will say, 'We ate and drank with you, and you taught in our streets.'
27 "But he will reply, 'I don't know you or where you come from. Away from me, all you evildoers!'[s]
28 "There will be weeping there, and gnashing of teeth,[t] when you see Abraham, Isaac and Jacob and
all the prophets in the kingdom of God, but you yourselves thrown out. 29 People will come from east
and west[u] and north and south, and will take their places at the feast in the kingdom of God. 30 Indeed
there are those who are last who will be first, and first who will be last."[v]

Jesus' Sorrow for Jerusalem

13:34,35pp — Mt 23:37-39
13:34,35Ref — Lk 19:41

31 At that time some Pharisees came to Jesus and said to him, "Leave this place and go somewhere
else. Herod[w] wants to kill you."
32 He replied, "Go tell that fox, 'I will keep on driving out demons and healing people today and tomorrow, and on the third day I will reach my goal.'[x] 33 In any case, I must press on today and tomorrow
and the next day — for surely no prophet[y] can die outside Jerusalem!
34 "Jerusalem, Jerusalem, you who kill the prophets and stone those sent to you, how often I have
longed to gather your children together, as a hen gathers her chicks under her wings,[z] and you were
not willing. 35 Look, your house is left to you desolate.[a] I tell you, you will not see me again until you
say, 'Blessed is he who comes in the name of the Lord.'[a]"[b]

[a] *35* Psalm 118:26

13:22–30 *The Narrow Door.* Jesus uses various household metaphors to describe how God's people consist only of those who respond to the gospel: an open and shut door (vv. 24–25), a household banquet (vv. 26,29), and the boundaries of the household (vv. 27–28). Those who were excluded will replace those who were once included in this household of God's people.

13:22 he made his way to Jerusalem. Jesus is on his way to the cross (cf. 17:11; 18:31; 19:28,41). This journey gives the Jews further opportunity to repent, even as Jerusalem becomes the symbol of their rejection of the gospel (vv. 31–35).

13:24 narrow door. In a different context Jesus uses this metaphor to warn his followers that they will face difficulties (Matt 7:13–14), but in this context Jesus uses it to urge people to respond properly to him and his gospel before "the owner of the house ... closes the door" (v. 25).

13:26 We ate and drank with you. The Jewish leaders who oppose Jesus can also claim this (11:37–54; cf. 14:1). **taught in our streets.** The crowd also heard what Jesus taught (5:1; 6:1,17; 7:1; 8:1; 9:11; 11:29). Neither action automatically qualifies them as members of God's household.

13:27 This recalls the language of the psalmist who was persecuted by his enemies (Ps 6:8).

13:28 Abraham, Isaac and Jacob. Represent God's people of old (cf. Acts 3:13; 7:32). **thrown out.** Those who are excluded from the kingdom (cf. 20:15).

13:29 People ... from east and west and north and south. The Gentiles who will participate in God's kingdom.

13:30 those who are last. Those considered to be outcasts, such as the Gentiles. **last ... first ... first ... last.** Jesus' life and ministry accomplish a reversal (cf. 2:34–35; 4:22–30; 14:15–24). **first who will be last.** Jews who reject Jesus.

13:31–35 *Jesus' Sorrow for Jerusalem.* Responding to the Pharisees' warning (v. 31), Jesus criticizes not only Herod, who was planning to kill him (vv. 32–33), but also Jerusalem, whose people rejected God and his prophets (vv. 34–35). Jesus thus identifies himself as an obedient, suffering prophet on his way to be rejected by his own people (v. 33).

13:31 Pharisees. See note on 5:17. They warn Jesus that Herod plans to kill him. Since Luke has consistently portrayed them negatively, he may be highlighting their ignorance that God planned for Jesus to suffer on the cross. **Herod.** Antipas (see note on 3:1), who had earlier wondered about Jesus' identity (9:7–9).

13:32 fox. A metaphor for a cunning and destructive person. Cf. Song 2:15 for the image of foxes ruining a vineyard. **third day.** May refer to Jesus' resurrection, but the phrase "today and tomorrow, and on the third day" likely refers to the necessary movement of the plan of God within an indefinite but limited period of time. Verse 33 confirms this.

13:33 today and tomorrow and the next day. See note on v. 32. **no prophet can die outside Jerusalem!** Ironically, God's own people have persecuted the prophets (cf. 11:47–51; Acts 7:52).

13:34 I have longed to gather your children together. Symbolizes God's desire to restore and gather his people in the age of salvation (cf. Ps 106:47; Isa 27:12; 52:12; Jer 31:8). **you were not willing.** Refers to Israel's refusal to accept this salvation. Despite God's offer of salvation, the Jews do not always respond to this offer.

13:35 your house is left to you desolate. Alludes to Jeremiah's prophecy against Jerusalem (Jer 12:7; cf. Jer 22:5). **Blessed is he who comes in the name of the Lord.** This quotation from Ps 118:26 is a positive affirmation in the context of worship of the identity of the Messiah. Only those who recognize Jesus as the promised Davidic Messiah will "see" Jesus again.

Jesus at a Pharisee's House

14:8-10Ref — Pr 25:6,7

14 One Sabbath, when Jesus went to eat in the house of a prominent Pharisee,[c] he was being
carefully watched.[d] [2]There in front of him was a man suffering from abnormal swelling of his
body. [3]Jesus asked the Pharisees and experts in the law,[e] "Is it lawful to heal on the Sabbath or not?"[f]
[4]But they remained silent. So taking hold of the man, he healed him and sent him on his way.
[5]Then he asked them, "If one of you has a child[a] or an ox that falls into a well on the Sabbath day,
will you not immediately pull it out?"[g] [6]And they had nothing to say.
[7]When he noticed how the guests picked the places of honor at the table,[h] he told them this parable:
[8]"When someone invites you to a wedding feast, do not take the place of honor, for a person more distinguished than you may have been invited. [9]If so, the host who invited both of you will come and say to
you, 'Give this person your seat.' Then, humiliated, you will have to take the least important place. [10]But
when you are invited, take the lowest place, so that when your host comes, he will say to you, 'Friend,
move up to a better place.' Then you will be honored in the presence of all the other guests. [11]For all
those who exalt themselves will be humbled, and those who humble themselves will be exalted."[i]
[12]Then Jesus said to his host, "When you give a luncheon or dinner, do not invite your friends, your
brothers or sisters, your relatives, or your rich neighbors; if you do, they may invite you back and so you
will be repaid. [13]But when you give a banquet, invite the poor, the crippled, the lame, the blind,[j] [14]and you
will be blessed. Although they cannot repay you, you will be repaid at the resurrection of the righteous."[k]

The Parable of the Great Banquet

14:16-24Ref — Mt 22:2-14

[15]When one of those at the table with him heard this, he said to Jesus, "Blessed is the one who will
eat at the feast[l] in the kingdom of God."[m]
[16]Jesus replied: "A certain man was preparing a great banquet and invited many guests. [17]At the time
of the banquet he sent his servant to tell those who had been invited, 'Come, for everything is now ready.'
[18]"But they all alike began to make excuses. The first said, 'I have just bought a field, and I must
go and see it. Please excuse me.'

[a] 5 Some manuscripts *donkey*

14:1 [c]Lk 7:36; 11:37 [d]Mt 12:10
14:3 [e]Mt 22:35 [f]Mt 12:2
14:5 [g]Lk 13:15
14:7 [h]Lk 11:43
14:11 [i]Mt 23:12; Lk 18:14
14:13 [j]ver 21
14:14 [k]Ac 24:15
14:15 [l]Isa 25:6; Mt 26:29; Lk 13:29; Rev 19:9 [m]Mt 3:2

14:1 — 19:27 *Identity of God's People.* Jesus continues to call people to repent and follow him (14:25 – 35; 16:1 – 18; 17:1 – 10,20 – 37; 18:1 – 8; 19:11 – 27) as he approaches Jerusalem on his way to the cross (18:31 – 34). God is redefining his people since those who were confident that they were in God's kingdom will not be part of it unless they respond to Jesus and his gospel (14:1 – 24; 15:1 – 32; 16:19 – 31; 17:11 – 19; 18:9 – 30,35 – 43; 19:1 – 10).

14:1 – 14 *Jesus at a Pharisee's House.* In a meal setting, Jesus challenges the authority of the Jewish religious leaders and then uses two illustrations to teach them to humble themselves and care for society's outcasts. These parables illustrate the principle of reversal (see 13:30 and note) and pave the way for the next parable, which discusses how those who do not humble themselves will themselves be excluded from the final banquet (vv. 15 – 24).

14:1 carefully watched. Cf. 6:7.

14:2 abnormal swelling of his body. The condition of dropsy (also known as edema) that often reflects the weakening of one's heart, kidneys, or liver.

14:3 Jewish religious leaders previously accused Jesus of healing on the Sabbath (6:1 – 11; 13:10 – 17). Here Jesus silences them by challenging them on how *they* keep the Sabbath.

14:5 If . . . will you not. Jesus compares healing a chronically ill person with healing in an emergency situation to illustrate that one should not draw an arbitrary line as to what type of healing one may perform on the Sabbath.

14:8 invites. This verb occurs in vv. 8 – 10,12 – 13. It can be translated "call" and can carry the meaning "elect" in Paul's letters (e.g., Rom 8:28 – 30); in the Synoptic Gospels, the focus is on God's "invitation" rather than on the effective call that exerts God's sovereign will.

14:10 Similar advice on humility and propriety can be found in the OT (cf. Prov 25:6 – 7).

14:11 exalt . . . humbled . . . humble . . . exalted. This principle of reversal recalls 13:30 (see note there), but it more explicitly exhorts people to humble themselves. It also recalls Ezekiel's criticism of the religious leaders of his time (Ezek 21:26).

14:13 the poor, the crippled, the lame, the blind. Refers to the description of God's salvation of the oppressed (4:18; 7:22).

14:14 you will be blessed. Cf. the beatitudes of 6:20 – 22. **resurrection of the righteous.** Although the Pharisees believe in resurrection (Acts 23:8), they do not act according to their belief when they treasure the honor of this world. While all will be resurrected (cf. Dan 12:2; John 5:28 – 29), the "resurrection of the righteous" belongs to those who respond to the gospel (20:35 – 36) and are declared righteous on the basis of the atoning death of Christ (Rom 8:1 – 4).

14:15 – 24 *The Parable of the Great Banquet.* Extending the theme of the previous two banquet parables, Jesus portrays the kingdom of God as the great feast. He corrects a misconstrued theology of salvation by clarifying that God will exclude from the final banquet those whom he invites but who refuse to participate in his salvation.

14:15 the feast in the kingdom of God. The anticipated great Messianic wedding banquet (Isa 25:6; Rev 19:9).

14:18 – 20 bought a field . . . bought five yoke of oxen . . . got married.

14:21 [n] ver 13
14:24 [o] Mt 21:43; Ac 13:46
14:26 [p] Mt 10:37; Jn 12:25
14:27 [q] Mt 10:38; Lk 9:23
14:33 [r] Php 3:7,8
14:34 [s] Mk 9:50
14:35 [t] Mt 5:13 [u] Mt 11:15
15:1 [v] Lk 5:29
15:2 [w] Mt 9:11

19 “Another said, ‘I have just bought five yoke of oxen, and I’m on my way to try them out. Please excuse me.’

20 “Still another said, ‘I just got married, so I can’t come.’

21 “The servant came back and reported this to his master. Then the owner of the house became angry and ordered his servant, ‘Go out quickly into the streets and alleys of the town and bring in the poor, the crippled, the blind and the lame.’[n]

22 “ ‘Sir,’ the servant said, ‘what you ordered has been done, but there is still room.’

23 “Then the master told his servant, ‘Go out to the roads and country lanes and compel them to come in, so that my house will be full. 24 I tell you, not one of those who were invited will get a taste of my banquet.’ ”[o]

The Cost of Being a Disciple

25 Large crowds were traveling with Jesus, and turning to them he said: 26 “If anyone comes to me and does not hate father and mother, wife and children, brothers and sisters — yes, even their own life — such a person cannot be my disciple.[p] 27 And whoever does not carry their cross and follow me cannot be my disciple.[q]

28 “Suppose one of you wants to build a tower. Won’t you first sit down and estimate the cost to see if you have enough money to complete it? 29 For if you lay the foundation and are not able to finish it, everyone who sees it will ridicule you, 30 saying, ‘This person began to build and wasn’t able to finish.’

31 “Or suppose a king is about to go to war against another king. Won’t he first sit down and consider whether he is able with ten thousand men to oppose the one coming against him with twenty thousand? 32 If he is not able, he will send a delegation while the other is still a long way off and will ask for terms of peace. 33 In the same way, those of you who do not give up everything you have cannot be my disciples.[r]

34 “Salt is good, but if it loses its saltiness, how can it be made salty again?[s] 35 It is fit neither for the soil nor for the manure pile; it is thrown out.[t]

“Whoever has ears to hear, let them hear.”[u]

The Parable of the Lost Sheep

15:4-7pp — Mt 18:12-14

15 Now the tax collectors[v] and sinners were all gathering around to hear Jesus. 2 But the Pharisees and the teachers of the law muttered, “This man welcomes sinners and eats with them.”[w]

This may remind readers of similar reasons for which ancient Israelites could be excused from military service (Deut 20:5 – 7) since these important activities maintain civic life. If so, Jesus uses them to remind the Jews not to ignore the arrival of the age of salvation by being preoccupied in their daily routine. While these may be excuses not to serve in an army, they cannot excuse one from participating in a banquet.

14:24 those who were invited. The Jews who were not willing to respond to the gospel of God’s Son (see 13:30 and note).

14:25 – 35 *The Cost of Being a Disciple.* Jesus urges those willing to follow him to give up everything (vv. 25 – 33) and be faithful to him (vv. 34 – 35).

14:26 hate father and mother. Can carry a comparative sense, thus, “love me more than father and mother” (Matt 10:37). Moreover, when Gentiles convert to Judaism, they are to be separated from their “father and mother, wife and children, brothers and sisters.” The decision to follow Jesus is nothing short of a conversion experience at which time followers are to abandon their past and reset their priorities.

14:27 carry their cross. Deny themselves (see 9:23 and note).

14:28 estimate the cost. Jesus is not saying that his followers are to evaluate their gifts and resources before following him, since by themselves no one is able to follow him without denying everything and relying entirely on him (vv. 26 – 27,33). To “estimate the cost” is thus to recognize that their resources are limited and therefore be firmly committed to Jesus.

14:31 – 32 Jesus’ followers cannot fight the evil one by themselves. Recognizing their own limitations, they can only rely on one who is greater than themselves.

14:33 Linked with vv. 26 – 27, disciples who recognize the limit of their resources must “give up everything” and follow Jesus.

14:34 Salt. Can fertilize soil (v. 35) and preserve a “manure pile” (v. 35) for future use in the soil. **if it loses its saltiness.** Since genuine, pure salt cannot lose its saltiness, Jesus appears to suggest that those who fail to give up all and follow him cannot be his true disciples. Salt that is diluted with impurities can lead to the loss of its saltiness; if so, Jesus is also calling his followers to follow him with a pure heart. Those who fail to respond to the urgent call to follow Jesus will be “thrown out” (v. 35) and excluded from God’s kingdom (see 13:28 and note).

15:1 – 7 *The Parable of the Lost Sheep.* In Matt 18:10 – 14, a similar parable is addressed to the disciples as Jesus emphasizes God’s concern for everyone within the community of Jesus’ followers, even the least among them. The parable here is the first of three parables in ch. 15 in which Jesus responds to the Jewish religious leaders who criticize him for welcoming “sinners” (v. 2). All three emphasize the love and mercy of God the Father in reaching out to the lost, but the third presents an implied call to those whom God has invited to the great banquet to provide a proper response (vv. 11 – 32).

15:1 – 2 The Jewish religious leaders again criticize Jesus, “a friend of tax collectors and sinners” (7:34), for associating with these marginalized people.

15:2 muttered. In the Greek translation of the OT, this Greek word always applies to the grumbling of the Israelites in the exodus account (Exod 15:24; 16:2; 17:3; Num 14:2; 16:11; Deut 1:27; cf. Josh 9:18b).

3Then Jesus told them this parable:[x] 4"Suppose one of you has a hundred sheep and loses one of
them. Doesn't he leave the ninety-nine in the open country and go after the lost sheep until he finds
it?[y] 5And when he finds it, he joyfully puts it on his shoulders 6and goes home. Then he calls his friends
and neighbors together and says, 'Rejoice with me; I have found my lost sheep.'[z] 7I tell you that in the
same way there will be more rejoicing in heaven over one sinner who repents than over ninety-nine
righteous persons who do not need to repent.[a]

The Parable of the Lost Coin

8"Or suppose a woman has ten silver coins[a] and loses one. Doesn't she light a lamp, sweep the house
and search carefully until she finds it? 9And when she finds it, she calls her friends and neighbors together and says, 'Rejoice with me; I have found my lost coin.'[b] 10In the same way, I tell you, there is
rejoicing in the presence of the angels of God over one sinner who repents."[c]

The Parable of the Lost Son

11Jesus continued: "There was a man who had two sons.[d] 12The younger one said to his father, 'Father, give me my share of the estate.'[e] So he divided his property[f] between them.

13"Not long after that, the younger son got together all he had, set off for a distant country and there
squandered his wealth[g] in wild living. 14After he had spent everything, there was a severe famine in
that whole country, and he began to be in need. 15So he went and hired himself out to a citizen of that
country, who sent him to his fields to feed pigs.[h] 16He longed to fill his stomach with the pods that the
pigs were eating, but no one gave him anything.

17"When he came to his senses, he said, 'How many of my father's hired servants have food to spare,
and here I am starving to death! 18I will set out and go back to my father and say to him: Father, I have
sinned[i] against heaven and against you. 19I am no longer worthy to be called your son; make me like
one of your hired servants.' 20So he got up and went to his father.

"But while he was still a long way off, his father saw him and was filled with compassion for him;
he ran to his son, threw his arms around him and kissed him.[j]

15:3 [x] Mt 13:3
15:4 [y] Ps 23; 119:176; Jer 31:10; Eze 34:11-16; Lk 5:32; 19:10
15:6 [z] ver 9
15:7 [a] ver 10
15:9 [b] ver 6
15:10 [c] ver 7
15:11 [d] Mt 21:28
15:12 [e] Dt 21:17 [f] ver 30
15:13 [g] ver 30; Lk 16:1
15:15 [h] Lev 11:7
15:18 [i] Lev 26:40; Mt 3:2
15:20 [j] Ge 45:14,15; 46:29; Ac 20:37

[a] 8 Greek *ten drachmas,* each worth about a day's wages

Here the Jewish leaders likewise fail to understand and appreciate God's mighty acts among them.

15:4 The shepherd's gathering of his sheep often appears as imagery for God's delivering his own people at the end time (cf. Isa 40:11; Jer 31:10–11; Ezek 34:11–12). The contrast between the 99 sheep in his fold and the lost one highlights God's love for even a single individual.

15:6 Rejoice. Unlike v. 5, which portrays the shepherd's joy, this calls the entire community to celebrate the return of the lost sheep. Jesus responds to those criticizing his mission to the outcasts by emphasizing the need to celebrate God's work in this new age of salvation.

15:7 in heaven. Includes "the angels of God" who are in heaven (v. 10). Instead of participating in this heavenly joy, the Jewish religious leaders complain and refuse to acknowledge the work of God. **righteous persons who do not need to repent.** An ironic note that reveals the self-understanding of the Jewish religious leaders (cf. 5:31–32; 18:11–12).

15:8–10 *The Parable of the Lost Coin.* This reinforces the points made in the note on vv. 1–7: (1) the merciful God does not desire anyone to be lost, and (2) every lost individual is precious in his sight.

15:8 ten silver coins. See NIV text note. This may constitute a significant portion of the woman's savings, especially if she is a widow (the story does not mention her husband).

15:9–10 Jesus again concludes with notes of both earthly and heavenly joy.

15:11–32 *The Parable of the Lost Son.* In the lengthiest of the three parables in this chapter, Jesus extends the discussion by emphasizing the responses of both the younger son and the older son: (1) Unlike sheep and coins, a son can take the initiative to return to his father (vv. 17–20a). Thus, this parable focuses not just on God's mercy but also on the need to repent (cf. vv. 7,10). (2) A significant portion of this parable is devoted to how the older son reacts (vv. 25–32) after his younger brother returns. His anger and refusal to participate in the family banquet (v. 28) parallels the attitude of the Jewish religious leaders, who despise including tax collectors and sinners with God's people. The open-ended call "to celebrate and be glad" (v. 32) becomes a call for these leaders to repent and participate in this banquet with their "younger brother."

15:12 The younger son insults his father with this request. The Mosaic regulations discuss distributing inheritance only after a person's death (Num 27:8–11; 36:7–9), and later Jewish writings explicitly discourage any such discussion before a person's death.

15:13 the younger son got together all he had. Reflects his resolve to leave and be cut off from his father. He is unfaithful to his father ("squandered his wealth") and his people (living among Gentiles in "a distant country"). How one uses wealth reflects the object of one's worship (cf. 16:1–15,19–31).

15:15 pigs. Jews considered pigs unclean (Lev 11:7; Deut 14:8), suggesting that the younger son is living among Gentiles. Later Jewish traditions note that "to feed pigs" is to be cursed.

15:17 When he came to his senses. This can refer to the younger son's repentance, which he carries out by returning to his father. The love of God is expressed in similarly vivid ways in vv. 20,22–23.

15:18 I have sinned against heaven and against you. Unlike Pharaoh's less than sincere confession (Exod 10:16–17), this younger son acts out his confession by returning to this father. **heaven.** Here refers to God.

15:20 ran to his son. An unexpected act that ignores Near Eastern cultural protocol, thus emphasizing the initiative of the father as he welcomes his son. **threw his arms around him and kissed him.** The father shows mercy and love.

PARABLES OF JESUS

PARABLE	MATTHEW	MARK	LUKE
Lamp under a bowl	5:14–15	4:21–22	8:16; 11:33
Wise and foolish builders	7:24–27		6:47–49
New cloth on an old garment	9:16	2:21	5:36
New wine in old wineskins	9:17	2:22	5:37–38
Sower and the soils	13:3–8,18–23	4:3–8,14–20	8:5–8,11–15
Weeds	13:24–30,36–43		
Mustard seed	13:31–32	4:30–32	13:18–19
Yeast	13:33		13:20–21
Hidden treasure	13:44		
Valuable pearl	13:45–46		
Net	13:47–50		
Owner of a house	13:52		
Lost sheep	18:12–14		15:4–7
Unmerciful servant	18:23–34		
Workers in the vineyard	20:1–16		
Two sons	21:28–32		
Tenants	21:33–44	12:1–11	20:9–18
Wedding banquet	22:2–14		
Fig tree	24:32–35	13:28–29	21:29–31
Faithful and wise servant	24:45–51		12:42–48

15:21 [k]Ps 51:4
15:22 [l]Zec 3:4; Rev 6:11 [m]Ge 41:42
15:24 [n]Eph 2:1,5; 5:14; 1Ti 5:6 [o]ver 32
15:28 [p]Jnh 4:1
15:30 [q]ver 12,13 [r]Pr 29:3

21 "The son said to him, 'Father, I have sinned against heaven and against you.[k] I am no longer
worthy to be called your son.'
22 "But the father said to his servants, 'Quick! Bring the best robe[l] and put it on him. Put a ring on
his finger[m] and sandals on his feet. 23 Bring the fattened calf and kill it. Let's have a feast and celebrate.
24 For this son of mine was dead and is alive again;[n] he was lost and is found.' So they began to celebrate.[o]
25 "Meanwhile, the older son was in the field. When he came near the house, he heard music and
dancing. 26 So he called one of the servants and asked him what was going on. 27 'Your brother has
come,' he replied, 'and your father has killed the fattened calf because he has him back safe and sound.'
28 "The older brother became angry[p] and refused to go in. So his father went out and pleaded with
him. 29 But he answered his father, 'Look! All these years I've been slaving for you and never disobeyed
your orders. Yet you never gave me even a young goat so I could celebrate with my friends. 30 But when
this son of yours who has squandered your property[q] with prostitutes[r] comes home, you kill the fattened calf for him!'

15:21 The son is unable to complete his rehearsed speech (vv. 18–19) before his father welcomes him again as a son.
15:22 robe ... ring. The father restores him to his position as a son (cf. Gen 41:42; Esth 3:10; 8:2). **sandals on his feet.** Servants often were barefoot.
15:23 feast and celebrate. The younger son is a member of God's restored people (cf. the banquet parables of 14:7–24). This celebration also echoes the rejoicing over recovering the lost sheep and coin (vv. 3–10).
15:24 The younger son was considered "dead" when he left his father's household and "is alive again" when he returns and is reunited with his family. The life and death metaphor underlines the significance of both his departure and his return. **lost and ... found.** Ties all three parables together (vv. 4,8; cf. v. 27) in expressing the joy when salvation is granted when God reaches out to welcome sinners.
15:28 The older brother became angry and refused to go in. This reaction contrasts with his father's rejoicing (vv. 22–24; cf. vv. 6–7, 9–10). He fails to understand the significance of the moment and insults his father, who hosts the banquet.
15:29 slaving ... never disobeyed. The older son's claims stand for the Jewish religious leaders in v. 2 who claim to be righteous in God's presence (cf. 18:11–12). **a young goat.** Of less value than a fattened calf (v. 23).
15:30 this son of yours. The older son refuses to recognize the younger son as his brother. **squandered your property with prostitutes.** The

PARABLE	MATTHEW	MARK	LUKE
Ten virgins	25:1–13		
Bags of gold (minas)	25:14–30		19:12–27
Sheep and goats	25:31–46		
Growing seed		4:26–29	
Watchful servants		13:35–37	12:35–40
Moneylender			7:41–43
Good Samaritan			10:30–37
Friend in need			11:5–8
Rich fool			12:16–21
Unfruitful fig tree			13:6–9
Lowest seat at the feast			14:7–14
Great banquet			14:16–24
Cost of discipleship			14:28–33
Lost coin			15:8–10
Lost (prodigal) son			15:11–32
Shrewd manager			16:1–8
Rich man and Lazarus			16:19–31
Master and his servant			17:7–10
Persistent widow			18:2–8
Pharisee and tax collector			18:10–14

31"'My son,' the father said, 'you are always with me, and everything I have is yours. 32But we had to celebrate and be glad, because this brother of yours was dead and is alive again; he was lost and is found.'"[s]

15:32 [s] ver 24; Mal 3:17
16:1 [t] Lk 15:13,30

The Parable of the Shrewd Manager

16 Jesus told his disciples: "There was a rich man whose manager was accused of wasting his possessions.[t] 2So he called him in and asked him, 'What is this I hear about you? Give an account
of your management, because you cannot be manager any longer.'
3"The manager said to himself, 'What shall I do now? My master is taking away my job. I'm not
strong enough to dig, and I'm ashamed to beg— 4I know what I'll do so that, when I lose my job here,
people will welcome me into their houses.'
5"So he called in each one of his master's debtors. He asked the first, 'How much do you owe my master?'

older son may intend to evoke the Mosaic regulation against "a stubborn and rebellious son" (Deut 21:18) who deserves to be stoned to death (Deut 21:21).

15:32 had to. They must obey God's salvation plan (see 2:49 and note). This concluding note includes an implicit call for "the Pharisees and the teachers of the law" (v. 2) to join in celebrating the salvation of the lost. Otherwise "not one of those who were invited will get a taste of my banquet" (14:24).

16:1–15 *The Parable of the Shrewd Manager.* A manager in the midst of crisis shrewdly uses his wealth. Jesus' followers must also shrewdly use their wealth and worship God rather than money (v. 13). While the main lesson is clear (one should use wealth shrewdly and by extension gain friendship with God), scholars disagree on how to interpret details in the parable. One problem is that the "dishonest manager" is praised for acting "shrewdly" (v. 8) when he reduces the debt of his master's debtors (vv. 5–7). Suggested possibilities include these: (1) The amount taken off the account is not part of the original debt but is the commission or interest that rightly belongs to the manager. (2) Since the manager earlier shamed his master (v. 1), his distributing his master's wealth may restore his master's status as an honorable benefactor. (3) The manager uses "wealth to gain friends" (v. 9) and thus can form a network that provides for him when he is unemployed.

16:1 wasting. This connects this parable with the previous one, in which the younger son "squandered his wealth" (15:13). This manager was "accused of" committing the same mistake and thus bringing shame to his master.

16:4 welcome me into their houses. To provide him with food or even to allow him to manage their households.

16:8 [u]Ps 17:14 [v]Ps 18:26 [w]Jn 12:36; Eph 5:8; 1Th 5:5
16:9 [x]ver 11,13 [y]Mt 19:21; Lk 12:33
16:10 [z]Mt 25:21,23; Lk 19:17
16:11 [a]ver 9,13
16:13 [b]ver 9,11; Mt 6:24
16:14 [c]1Ti 3:3 [d]Lk 23:35
16:15 [e]Lk 10:29 [f]1Sa 16:7; Rev 2:23
16:16 [g]Mt 11:12,13 [h]Mt 4:23
16:17 [i]Mt 5:18
16:18 [j]Mt 5:31,32; 19:9; Mk 10:11; Ro 7:2,3; 1Co 7:10,11

6 " 'Nine hundred gallons[a] of olive oil,' he replied.
"The manager told him, 'Take your bill, sit down quickly, and make it four hundred and fifty.'
7 "Then he asked the second, 'And how much do you owe?'
" 'A thousand bushels[b] of wheat,' he replied.
"He told him, 'Take your bill and make it eight hundred.'
8 "The master commended the dishonest manager because he had acted shrewdly. For the people of
this world[u] are more shrewd[v] in dealing with their own kind than are the people of the light.[w] 9 I tell
you, use worldly wealth[x] to gain friends for yourselves, so that when it is gone, you will be welcomed
into eternal dwellings.[y]
10 "Whoever can be trusted with very little can also be trusted with much,[z] and whoever is dishonest
with very little will also be dishonest with much. 11 So if you have not been trustworthy in handling
worldly wealth,[a] who will trust you with true riches? 12 And if you have not been trustworthy with someone else's property, who will give you property of your own?
13 "No one can serve two masters. Either you will hate the one and love the other, or you will be devoted to the one and despise the other. You cannot serve both God and money."[b]
14 The Pharisees, who loved money,[c] heard all this and were sneering at Jesus.[d] 15 He said to them,
"You are the ones who justify yourselves[e] in the eyes of others, but God knows your hearts.[f] What people
value highly is detestable in God's sight.

Additional Teachings

16 "The Law and the Prophets were proclaimed until John.[g] Since that time, the good news of the
kingdom of God is being preached,[h] and everyone is forcing their way into it. 17 It is easier for heaven
and earth to disappear than for the least stroke of a pen to drop out of the Law.[i]
18 "Anyone who divorces his wife and marries another woman commits adultery, and the man who
marries a divorced woman commits adultery.[j]

[a] *6* Or about 3,000 liters [b] *7* Or about 30 tons

16:6 Nine hundred gallons of olive oil. About 3,000 liters; equivalent to three years' wages for a day laborer. Reducing the debt by half may take away the commission owed to the manager, but this may also cut into the original debt to appease the debtor (cf. v. 4).
16:7 A thousand bushels of wheat. About 30 tons (27 metric tons); equivalent to eight to ten years' wages for a day laborer.
16:8 The first sentence is probably part of the parable. While not condoning all that the manager has done, the master commends the manager for "shrewdly" planning for his own future. The second sentence is Jesus' own comment on the parable: since even the worldly manager is able to sacrifice his (or his master's) money in times of crisis, how much more should "the people of the light" (cf. John 12:36; Eph 5:8; 1 Thess 5:5) give up all that they have to follow Jesus at this critical moment in the history of salvation.
16:9 use worldly wealth to gain friends for yourselves. In the context of Jesus' own teaching, this may mean "sell your possessions and give to the poor" (12:33a). **so that when it is gone, you will be welcomed into eternal dwellings.** Worldly gains should not be used to satisfy the desires of this world; instead, they should be used for things that are of eternal value (cf. 12:33b). These followers of Jesus will be welcomed either by friends whom they have helped or by God himself, who will reward them for their generosity.
16:10 very little. Wealth in this narrow context. **much.** The "true riches" (v. 11) that matter in view of eternity. True discipleship is reflected not by the amount with which one is entrusted but by the way one uses it.
16:13 hate ... love. One must choose between two masters. Jesus uses similar language to describe what those who follow him must do (see 14:26 and note). **God and money.** God is the center of one's concerns as one lives in view of eternity, and money represents the currency of one's earthly existence.
16:14 Pharisees ... loved money. In Luke's perspective, this is one of the most severe criticisms Jesus can level. In light of v. 13, the Pharisees are accused of hating God.
16:15 the ones who justify yourselves in the eyes of others. Those "who were confident of their own righteousness and looked down on everyone else" (18:9). **What people value highly.** This can refer to wealth (v. 14), but it can also apply to the honor and respect that come with wealth. **detestable.** Often found in OT polemics against idols and false gods (Deut 7:25–26; 1 Kgs 14:24; Ezra 9:11; Isa 44:19); this word reinforces the contrast between God and money in v. 13.
16:16–18 *Additional Teachings.* After directly criticizing the Pharisees, Luke here addresses two areas that touch on how they interpret the law: the relationship between the period of the Law and the Prophets and the new age of God's kingdom (vv. 16–17) and divorce (v. 18).
16:16 The Law and the Prophets. Represent the OT age (cf. Acts 24:14; 28:23). **John.** John the Baptist; he is a transitional figure: he represents the final one of those who serve before Jesus' death and resurrection, but he also proclaims "the good news" (3:18) as he paves the way for Jesus' ministry (cf. 3:1–18; 7:26; Acts 1:22). While not downplaying the continuity between the old and the new, Jesus here focuses on the significant shift as he himself represents the climax of God's work among his people. **forcing their way.** This may refer to the difficulties in entering "the narrow door" (13:24). If it is passive (i.e., "everyone is urged to enter into it"), then this clause parallels the previous one, which also contains a passive verb ("the good news of the kingdom of God is being preached").
16:17 The OT never assumes that heaven and earth will last forever (Job 14:12; Ps 102:25–27; Isa 51:6; Jer 4:23–26), but their existence shows that God continues to be faithful to his creation (Jer 33:25–26). **the Law.** It continues to be significant because Jesus fulfills it (24:44).
16:18 To explain how the law continues to be valid, Jesus evokes the Mosaic regulation on divorce (cf. Deut 24:1–4), but he gives a stricter

The Rich Man and Lazarus

19“There was a rich man who was dressed in purple and fine linen and lived in luxury every day.[k]
20At his gate was laid a beggar[l] named Lazarus, covered with sores 21and longing to eat what fell from
the rich man’s table.[m] Even the dogs came and licked his sores.
22“The time came when the beggar died and the angels carried him to Abraham’s side. The rich
man also died and was buried. 23In Hades, where he was in torment, he looked up and saw Abraham
far away, with Lazarus by his side. 24So he called to him, ‘Father Abraham,[n] have pity on me and send
Lazarus to dip the tip of his finger in water and cool my tongue, because I am in agony in this fire.’[o]
25“But Abraham replied, ‘Son, remember that in your lifetime you received your good things, while
Lazarus received bad things,[p] but now he is comforted here and you are in agony.[q] 26And besides all
this, between us and you a great chasm has been set in place, so that those who want to go from here
to you cannot, nor can anyone cross over from there to us.’
27“He answered, ‘Then I beg you, father, send Lazarus to my family, 28for I have five brothers. Let
him warn them,[r] so that they will not also come to this place of torment.’
29“Abraham replied, ‘They have Moses[s] and the Prophets;[t] let them listen to them.’
30“ ‘No, father Abraham,’[u] he said, ‘but if someone from the dead goes to them, they will repent.’
31“He said to him, ‘If they do not listen to Moses and the Prophets, they will not be convinced even
if someone rises from the dead.’ ”

Sin, Faith, Duty

17 Jesus said to his disciples: “Things that cause people to stumble[v] are bound to come, but woe to
anyone through whom they come.[w] 2It would be better for them to be thrown into the sea with a
millstone tied around their neck than to cause one of these little ones[x] to stumble.[y] 3So watch yourselves.
“If your brother or sister[a] sins against you, rebuke them;[z] and if they repent, forgive them.[a]

16:19 [k]Eze 16:49
16:20 [l]Ac 3:2
16:21 [m]Mt 15:27
16:24 [n]ver 30; Lk 3:8 [o]Mt 5:22
16:25 [p]Ps 17:14 [q]Lk 6:21,24,25
16:28 [r]Ac 2:40; 20:23; 1Th 4:6
16:29 [s]Lk 24:27,44; Jn 5:45-47; Ac 15:21 [t]Lk 4:17; Jn 1:45
16:30 [u]ver 24; Lk 3:8
17:1 [v]Mt 5:29 [w]Mt 18:7
17:2 [x]Mk 10:24; Lk 10:21 [y]Mt 5:29
17:3 [z]Mt 18:15 [a]Eph 4:32; Col 3:13

[a] 3 The Greek word for *brother or sister* (*adelphos*) refers here to a fellow disciple, whether man or woman.

interpretation that prohibits divorce. This not only gets at the true intent of the Mosaic regulations (Matt 19:8) but also depicts Jesus as the law’s authoritative interpreter. He may also have been targeting the many Pharisees (v. 14), who belonged to the school of Hillel; they interpreted the Mosaic regulation very liberally and allowed for various trivial reasons as legitimate bases of divorce. These Pharisees claimed to be faithful to the law, but they deliberately misconstrued it according to their own interests and for their own benefit.

16:19–31 *The Rich Man and Lazarus.* This story extends the previous discussion on wealth (vv. 1–13) as well as the criticism of the Pharisees “who loved money” (v. 14). The lesson is clear: wealth does not guarantee a place in the kingdom of God. While the rich man wrongly relied on his wealth, there is no list of Lazarus’s virtues. The story focuses on the reversal that God himself brought about: “He has filled the hungry with good things but has sent the rich away empty” (1:53).

16:19 dressed in purple and fine linen. The lifestyle of royalty (cf. Prov 31:22). Like those in the time of Noah who were oblivious to the events that were to come (cf. 17:27), the rich man “lived in luxury every day” and failed to recognize God’s impending judgment.

16:20 It is unusual for Jesus to provide the personal name of a character within one of his parables. The meaning of Lazarus (the Greek form of Eleazar) may then be important; it means “whom God has helped.” Note that this is not the Lazarus that Jesus raised from the dead in John 11:38–44.

16:22 Abraham’s side. Likely the prominent place next to Abraham, reclining at the heavenly feast. Jesus previously refers to the kingdom banquet with Abraham (13:28–29) and here emphasizes eating and drinking (vv. 21,24).

16:23 Hades. Here refers to the eternal place of punishment (cf. 10:15; see note on Matt 11:20–24).

16:24 Crying out to father Abraham recalls John the Baptist’s comment in 3:8. The description of Hades recalls Isa 66:24.

16:27–28 While the first part of the story focuses on the principle of reversal, the second part reminds listeners that they must repent while they still can. The rich man requests that Abraham send Lazarus to warn his family without reflecting on the fact that their own Scriptures constantly call people to repent, and that God had already sent Jesus to call people to repent.

16:29 They have Moses and the Prophets. Implications: (1) The Jews already have God’s word, but many of them are neither able nor willing to follow it (cf. Acts 15:10). (2) Since Moses and the Prophets point to Jesus (24:27), the Jews should listen to him. **listen to them.** Parallels the call to listen to Jesus in 9:35 (cf. Deut 18:15).

16:30–31 someone from the dead. Within the story itself this may refer to Lazarus, but in light of the development of Luke’s narrative, this also refers to Jesus and his resurrection. Ironically, while the Jewish leaders (whom the rich man represents) may request one who rises from the dead to preach the gospel to them, they reject the resurrected Jesus and his message (see Acts 4:13–22).

17:1–10 *Sin, Faith, Duty.* Jesus warns the disciples against causing anyone to stumble (vv. 1–4), illustrates the power of faith with the parable of a mustard seed (vv. 5–6), and concludes with another parable on the proper attitude of a servant (vv. 7–10). All three sections teach that Jesus’ followers must see through the eyes of faith rather than be blinded by the concerns of the present age.

17:1 Things that cause people to stumble. Likely the words and deeds of the Jewish leaders (cf. 16:14) who were the objects of Jesus’ woes (11:39–52).

17:2 millstone. A heavy stone used for grinding grain; the imagery also appears in reference to God’s final judgment of the great Babylon (Rev 18:21). **these little ones.** Can refer to those who are young in faith, but can also include any who are deemed insignificant (as Lazarus is in 16:19–31).

17:3 rebuke them. The Mosaic law requires this (Lev 19:17). But Jesus goes further: he urges his disciples to forgive those who repent when they are rebuked.

17:4 [b]Mt 18:21,22
17:5 [c]Mk 6:30 [d]Lk 7:13
17:6 [e]Mt 13:31; 17:20; Lk 13:19 [f]Mt 21:21; Mk 9:23
17:8 [g]Lk 12:37
17:10 [h]1Co 9:16
17:11 [i]Lk 9:51 [j]Lk 9:51, 52; Jn 4:3,4
17:12 [k]Mt 8:2 [l]Lev 13:45,46
17:13 [m]Lk 5:5
17:14 [n]Lev 14:2; Mt 8:4
17:15 [o]Mt 9:8
17:16 [p]Mt 10:5
17:19 [q]Mt 9:22
17:20 [r]Mt 3:2
17:21 [s]ver 23

[4]Even if they sin against you seven times in a day and seven times come back to you saying 'I repent,'
you must forgive them."[b]

[5]The apostles[c] said to the Lord,[d] "Increase our faith!"

[6]He replied, "If you have faith as small as a mustard seed,[e] you can say to this mulberry tree, 'Be
uprooted and planted in the sea,' and it will obey you.[f]

[7]"Suppose one of you has a servant plowing or looking after the sheep. Will he say to the servant
when he comes in from the field, 'Come along now and sit down to eat'? [8]Won't he rather say, 'Prepare
my supper, get yourself ready and wait on me[g] while I eat and drink; after that you may eat and drink'?
[9]Will he thank the servant because he did what he was told to do? [10]So you also, when you have done
everything you were told to do, should say, 'We are unworthy servants; we have only done our duty.'"[h]

Jesus Heals Ten Men With Leprosy

[11]Now on his way to Jerusalem,[i] Jesus traveled along the border between Samaria and Galilee.[j] [12]As
he was going into a village, ten men who had leprosy[a][k] met him. They stood at a distance[l] [13]and called
out in a loud voice, "Jesus, Master,[m] have pity on us!"

[14]When he saw them, he said, "Go, show yourselves to the priests."[n] And as they went, they were
cleansed.

[15]One of them, when he saw he was healed, came back, praising God[o] in a loud voice. [16]He threw
himself at Jesus' feet and thanked him — and he was a Samaritan.[p]

[17]Jesus asked, "Were not all ten cleansed? Where are the other nine? [18]Has no one returned to give
praise to God except this foreigner?" [19]Then he said to him, "Rise and go; your faith has made you well."[q]

The Coming of the Kingdom of God

17:26,27pp — Mt 24:37-39

[20]Once, on being asked by the Pharisees when the kingdom of God would come,[r] Jesus replied, "The
coming of the kingdom of God is not something that can be observed, [21]nor will people say, 'Here it is,'
or 'There it is,'[s] because the kingdom of God is in your midst."[b]

[a] *12* The Greek word traditionally translated *leprosy* was used for various diseases affecting the skin.
[b] *21* Or *is within you*

17:4 seven times ... forgive. Unlimited forgiveness, as highlighted by the more exaggerated "seventy-seven times" in Matt 18:22.

17:5 Increase our faith! The disciples, whom Jesus previously addressed as "you of little faith" (12:28), ask this so that they can follow what Jesus teaches in vv. 1–4.

17:6 a mustard seed. See 13:18–21 and notes. In 13:18–21 the mustard seed describes the kingdom of God, but here it describes personal faith. In Matt 17:20, the "faith as small as a mustard seed" applies to the power of prayer, but here the disciples need faith to forgive others (vv. 3–4).

17:7–10 Jesus addresses the attitude of the disciples. Their duty is to serve God faithfully, recognizing that they are unworthy to serve their master. The Pharisees, in contrast, boast of their acts of piety (18:11–12).

17:11–19 *Jesus Heals Ten Men With Leprosy.* In the midst of Jesus being rejected by the Jewish leaders, this account not only focuses on Jesus the healer but contrasts how Jews and a Samaritan respond to Jesus' mercy. A Gentile leper in the region of Samaria who is healed from a distance responds with praise and thanksgiving. It echoes Elisha's healing of a Gentile (2 Kgs 5:1–19a), which Jesus notes at the beginning of his ministry (4:27).

17:11 on his way to Jerusalem. This reminds the reader of Jesus' conviction to follow the steps of the suffering prophets (9:31,51,53; 13:22,33). **border between Samaria and Galilee.** Luke does not provide an exact location of this event, but it is close to both Jews and Samaritans.

17:12 These lepers likely lived in a village separated from the general population (Lev 13:45–46; Num 5:2–3; cf. 2 Kgs 7:3; 2 Chr 26:21). **They stood at a distance.** Separated from others.

17:14 show yourselves to the priests. Jesus again follows the Mosaic regulations (5:14; cf. Lev 13:9–17; 14:1–20). **they were cleansed.** Cleansed not only physically but also "made clean" ritually, so that they can now rejoin the community of God's people.

17:16 He threw himself at Jesus' feet. Parallels "thanked him" because thanksgiving is an act of worship (Ezra 3:11; Pss 35:18; 100:4). **Samaritan.** The dispute between Jews and Samaritans included disagreement on the proper place of worship (John 4:21–24). Here the other nine lepers were going to the Jerusalem temple to see the priests, while only the Samaritan recognized Jesus as the person who deserved his worship and thanksgiving. By drawing attention to the fate of this Samaritan, Luke again highlights Jesus' inclusion of the marginalized. See notes on John 4:4,9,20.

17:18 foreigner. Greek *allogenēs*; occurs only here in the NT. An inscription that warns Gentiles not to enter the temple proper uses the same word (see photo, p. 1974). This foreigner cannot enter the Jerusalem temple, but he can worship Jesus, the Son of God.

17:19 your faith has made you well. Can also be translated "your faith has healed you," as in other healing miracles (8:48; 18:42). His faith is not simply believing that Jesus can heal the sick but recognizing Jesus' unique status and identity.

17:20–37 *The Coming of the Kingdom of God.* Jesus responds to the Pharisees' question concerning the coming of the kingdom of God (v. 20): the kingdom is present in both his life and ministry (v. 21) and will be fulfilled when he returns (v. 24). People should be prepared for the judgment that will accompany the final arrival of God's kingdom (vv. 26–37).

17:21 the kingdom of God is in your midst. Jesus is present in their midst. Both the manifestation of Jesus' power (11:20) and his fulfillment of ancient promises (4:18–19; cf. Isa 58:6; 61:1–2) should evoke the

[22]Then he said to his disciples, "The time is coming when you will long to see one of the days of
the Son of Man,[t] but you will not see it.[u] [23]People will tell you, 'There he is!' or 'Here he is!' Do not go
running off after them.[v] [24]For the Son of Man in his day[a] will be like the lightning,[w] which flashes and
lights up the sky from one end to the other. [25]But first he must suffer many things[x] and be rejected[y]
by this generation.[z]

[26]"Just as it was in the days of Noah,[a] so also will it be in the days of the Son of Man. [27]People were
eating, drinking, marrying and being given in marriage up to the day Noah entered the ark. Then the
flood came and destroyed them all.

[28]"It was the same in the days of Lot.[b] People were eating and drinking, buying and selling, planting
and building. [29]But the day Lot left Sodom, fire and sulfur rained down from heaven and destroyed
them all.

[30]"It will be just like this on the day the Son of Man is revealed.[c] [31]On that day no one who is on
the housetop, with possessions inside, should go down to get them. Likewise, no one in the field should
go back for anything.[d] [32]Remember Lot's wife![e] [33]Whoever tries to keep their life will lose it, and whoever loses their life will preserve it.[f] [34]I tell you, on that night two people will be in one bed; one will
be taken and the other left. [35]Two women will be grinding grain together; one will be taken and the
other left."[g] [36] [b]

[37]"Where, Lord?" they asked.

He replied, "Where there is a dead body, there the vultures will gather."[h]

The Parable of the Persistent Widow

18 Then Jesus told his disciples a parable to show them that they should always pray and not give
up.[i] [2]He said: "In a certain town there was a judge who neither feared God nor cared what
people thought. [3]And there was a widow in that town who kept coming to him with the plea, 'Grant me
justice[j] against my adversary.'

[4]"For some time he refused. But finally he said to himself, 'Even though I don't fear God or care

17:22 [t] Mt 8:20 [u] Mt 9:15; Lk 5:35
17:23 [v] Mt 24:23; Mk 13:21; Lk 21:8
17:24 [w] Mt 24:27
17:25 [x] Mt 16:21 [y] Lk 9:22; 18:32 [z] Mk 13:30; Lk 21:32
17:26 [a] Ge 7:6-24
17:28 [b] Ge 19:1-28
17:30 [c] Mt 10:23; 16:27; 24:3,27,37,39; 25:31; 1Co 1:7; 1Th 2:19; 2Th 1:7; 2:8; 2Pe 3:4; Rev 1:7
17:31 [d] Mt 24:17,18; Mk 13:15-16
17:32 [e] Ge 19:26
17:33 [f] Jn 12:25
17:35 [g] Mt 24:41
17:37 [h] Mt 24:28
18:1 [i] Isa 40:31; Lk 11:5-8; Ac 1:14; Ro 12:12; Eph 6:18; Col 4:2; 1Th 5:17
18:3 [j] Isa 1:17

[a] *24* Some manuscripts do not have *in his day.* [b] *36* Some manuscripts include here words similar to Matt. 24:40.

reaction noted in the Prophets: "Surely God is with you, and there is no other; there is no other god" (Isa 45:14).

17:22 one of the days of the Son of Man. Jesus' earthly ministry. It contrasts with "his day" (v. 24), when he will return.

17:23 False messiahs "will come in [Jesus'] name, claiming, 'I am he,' and 'The time is near' " (21:8).

17:24 the Son of Man in his day. When "the Son of Man is revealed" (v. 30). False prophets will attempt to convince others that they are the Christ (v. 23), but everyone will witness Jesus' return, like "the lightning, which flashes and lights up the sky" (cf. 2 Thess 1:7; Rev 1:7).

17:25 suffer ... be rejected. Another passion prediction (cf. 9:22,44; 18:31–33). Jesus introduces the next verses, which show that God's people are callous.

17:26–29 Jesus compares the days before his return to the times of Noah (vv. 26–27; cf. Gen 6–7) and Lot (vv. 28–29; cf. Gen 19), when people carried out their normal activities (cf. 16:19), unaware of God's impending judgment.

17:30 the day the Son of Man is revealed. The time of "the coming of the Son of Man" (Matt 24:39). This alludes to the description of the Son of Man in Dan 7:13: "one like a son of man, coming with the clouds of heaven."

17:31–32 The call to escape immediately builds on the lesson of Lot's wife, who "looked back, and ... became a pillar of salt" (Gen 19:26). Jesus' call to those who would follow him reflects this urgency (9:62).

17:33 tries to keep their life. Focuses on earthly existence. **loses their life.** For Christ (cf. 9:24). Jesus is not asking people to leave their normal lives; rather, they are to put Jesus ahead of everything in their lives (14:26).

17:34 night. The Son of Man will return unexpectedly (12:38,40; cf. 1 Thess 5:2). **one will be taken and the other left.** The act is not random but is the result of how people respond to the impending judgment (cf. vv. 26–33). It is not clear whether the one taken is taken for judgment or for salvation, although the stories of Noah (vv. 26–27) and Lot (vv. 28–29) seem to support the latter. The main point, however, is the decisive and final separation of the saved from the condemned that will come when Jesus returns.

17:36 See NIV text note.

17:37 Where, Lord? Asks about God's judgment. **dead body ... vultures will gather.** This may highlight that God's judgment is public. If so, this proverb underscores the point of Jesus' statement in v. 24 concerning the public nature of his return. Matthew 24:27–28 places the proverb side by side with Jesus' statement concerning his return, each reinforcing the other.

18:1–8 *The Parable of the Persistent Widow.* In this parable, Jesus begins with a call to persist in prayer (vv. 1–5) and concludes with God's answer: the manifestation of his justice for his chosen ones (vv. 6–8).

18:1 not give up. Not simply insisting on pursuing one's own wishes but faithfully persevering until the end.

18:3 Widows, who were a marginalized group in ancient societies, are often the object of God's special love and care throughout Luke (2:37; 4:26; 7:12; 21:2–3).

18:4–5 Despite this judge's character (cf. v. 2), he is forced to yield to the widow's requests because of the threat to his own well-being. **eventually come and attack me!** Highlights not the widow's violent character but her insistence on receiving a hearing. The negative portrayal of this "unjust judge" (v. 6) sets up a lesser-to-greater argument: if an evil judge would yield to a poor widow's requests, how much more will God respond to those who continually cry out to him (cf. v. 7).

18:5 [k] Lk 11:8
18:6 [l] Lk 7:13
18:7 [m] Ex 22:23; Ps 88:1; Rev 6:10
18:8 [n] Mt 8:20 [o] Mt 16:27
18:9 [p] Lk 16:15 [q] Isa 65:5
18:10 [r] Ac 3:1
18:11 [s] Mt 6:5; Mk 11:25
18:12 [t] Isa 58:3; Mt 9:14 [u] Mal 3:8; Lk 11:42
18:13 [v] Isa 66:2; Jer 31:19; Lk 23:48 [w] Lk 5:32; 1Ti 1:15
18:14 [x] Mt 23:12; Lk 14:11
18:17 [y] Mt 11:25; 18:3
18:18 [z] Lk 10:25

what people think, 5 yet because this widow keeps bothering me, I will see that she gets justice, so that
she won't eventually come and attack me!' "[k]
6 And the Lord[l] said, "Listen to what the unjust judge says. 7 And will not God bring about justice for his
chosen ones, who cry out[m] to him day and night? Will he keep putting them off? 8 I tell you, he will see
that they get justice, and quickly. However, when the Son of Man[n] comes,[o] will he find faith on the earth?"

The Parable of the Pharisee and the Tax Collector

9 To some who were confident of their own righteousness[p] and looked down on everyone else,[q] Jesus
told this parable: 10 "Two men went up to the temple to pray,[r] one a Pharisee and the other a tax collector.
11 The Pharisee stood by himself[s] and prayed: 'God, I thank you that I am not like other people — robbers,
evildoers, adulterers — or even like this tax collector. 12 I fast[t] twice a week and give a tenth[u] of all I get.'
13 "But the tax collector stood at a distance. He would not even look up to heaven, but beat his breast[v]
and said, 'God, have mercy on me, a sinner.'[w]
14 "I tell you that this man, rather than the other, went home justified before God. For all those who
exalt themselves will be humbled, and those who humble themselves will be exalted."[x]

The Little Children and Jesus

18:15-17pp — Mt 19:13-15; Mk 10:13-16

15 People were also bringing babies to Jesus for him to place his hands on them. When the disciples
saw this, they rebuked them. 16 But Jesus called the children to him and said, "Let the little children
come to me, and do not hinder them, for the kingdom of God belongs to such as these. 17 Truly I tell you,
anyone who will not receive the kingdom of God like a little child[y] will never enter it."

The Rich and the Kingdom of God

18:18-30pp — Mt 19:16-29; Mk 10:17-30

18 A certain ruler asked him, "Good teacher, what must I do to inherit eternal life?"[z]
19 "Why do you call me good?" Jesus answered. "No one is good — except God alone. 20 You know the

---

18:7 Jesus moves beyond the topic of prayer to God's justice. **bring about justice for ... [those] who cry out to him day and night.** Reflects God's promise to his suffering people who await the final manifestation of God's justice (cf. Rev 6:10).
18:8 will he find faith on the earth? The answer is yes, but implicit in this question is that not all will remain faithful to him. Here Jesus shifts the focus from God to his people. Since God will prove faithful to his people, his people must likewise be faithful to the end (cf. 17:30 – 36).
18:9 – 14 *The Parable of the Pharisee and the Tax Collector.* The respected Pharisee boasts of his religiosity while standing at the center of the Jewish cult, whereas the despised tax collector confesses his sins "at a distance" (v. 13). This stark contrast illustrates that true righteousness is granted only to those who humble themselves and rely solely on God's mercy.
18:9 confident of their own righteousness. Recalls a similar criticism offered by Ezekiel (Ezek 33:13; cf. Deut 9:4).
18:11 This Pharisee "looked down on everyone else" (v. 9).
18:12 fast twice a week. Conforms to the Jewish customs of the time, though not required by Mosaic law. **give a tenth of all.** Based on OT regulations that relate to main crops and livestock (cf. Lev 27:30 – 32; Num 18:21 – 26; Deut 14:22 – 27), but the Pharisees extended it to include garden herbs.
18:13 beat his breast. An act of grief and repentance (cf. Isa 32:12; Jer 31:19; Ezek 21:12). **have mercy on me.** Resembles the language of OT prayers of confession and penitence (e.g., Pss 25:11; 51:1 – 3; 65:3).
18:14 justified before God. Acts 13:39 defines justification as being "set free from every sin" through Jesus. Utterly dependent on God rather than on his own righteousness (cf. v. 9), God reckoned him to be righteous through a righteousness that is "revealed" in the gospel (Rom 1:17). **exalt ... humbled ... humble ... exalted.** Luke mentions the principle of reversal again (see 1:52 – 55 and note; see also notes on 1:46 – 56; 6:17 – 26,27 – 36; 13:30; 14:1 – 14; 16:19 – 31).
18:15 – 17 *The Little Children and Jesus.* After affirming that the one who humbled himself is now exalted when justified before God (v. 14), Jesus uses little children to illustrate how one can "receive the kingdom of God" (v. 17).
18:15 babies. Can refer to newborns (2:12,16) or little children (v. 16; cf. Matt 19:13; Mark 10:13).
18:16 – 17 the kingdom of God belongs to such as these. Not because of any particular childhood virtue but because children totally depend on those who care for them. They will "receive the kingdom" not because of their own works but because of the reversal brought about by the arrival of God's salvation, "for it is the one who is least among you all who is the greatest" (9:48). The lowly receive salvation because of their lowly status, but despite their lowly status, God is able to grant them a place in his kingdom.
18:18 – 30 *The Rich and the Kingdom of God.* Unlike the little children of the previous section, the rich man in this parable is "very wealthy" (v. 23) and proud, but he is excluded from God's kingdom (v. 25) because he is not willing to follow Jesus with all his heart. The rich man is a foil to Zacchaeus (19:1 – 10), who demonstrates how a rich man can enter God's kingdom.
18:18 ruler. Perhaps a leader of the Pharisees (14:1), a synagogue ruler (8:41,49), or a Jewish elder (12:58; 23:13,35; 24:20). An expert in the law also asked this question (10:25). **inherit eternal life.** "Enter the kingdom of God" (v. 24) or "be saved" (v. 26).
18:19 Jesus is not denying that he is "good"; rather, Jesus challenges the ruler to see if he actually considers Jesus to be good (i.e., God). The ruler shows that he does not consider Jesus to be God by refusing to follow him (v. 23).
18:20 Jesus' response draws on five of the Ten Commandments (Exod 20:12 – 16; Deut 5:16 – 20).

commandments: 'You shall not commit adultery, you shall not murder, you shall not steal, you shall
not give false testimony, honor your father and mother.'[a]"[a]
[21]"All these I have kept since I was a boy," he said.
[22]When Jesus heard this, he said to him, "You still lack one thing. Sell everything you have and give
to the poor,[b] and you will have treasure in heaven.[c] Then come, follow me."
[23]When he heard this, he became very sad, because he was very wealthy. [24]Jesus looked at him and
said, "How hard it is for the rich to enter the kingdom of God![d] [25]Indeed, it is easier for a camel to go
through the eye of a needle than for someone who is rich to enter the kingdom of God."
[26]Those who heard this asked, "Who then can be saved?"
[27]Jesus replied, "What is impossible with man is possible with God."[e]
[28]Peter said to him, "We have left all we had to follow you!"[f]
[29]"Truly I tell you," Jesus said to them, "no one who has left home or wife or brothers or sisters or
parents or children for the sake of the kingdom of God [30]will fail to receive many times as much in this
age, and in the age to come[g] eternal life."[h]

18:20 [a]Ex 20:12-16; Dt 5:16-20; Ro 13:9
18:22 [b]Ac 2:45 [c]Mt 6:20
18:24 [d]Pr 11:28
18:27 [e]Mt 19:26
18:28 [f]Mt 4:19
18:30 [g]Mt 12:32 [h]Mt 25:46
18:31 [i]Lk 9:51 [j]Ps 22; Isa 53 [k]Mt 8:20
18:32 [l]Lk 23:1
18:33 [m]Mt 16:21 [n]Ac 2:23 [o]Mt 16:21 [p]Mt 16:21
18:34 [q]Mk 9:32; Lk 9:45
18:35 [r]Lk 19:1
18:37 [s]Lk 19:4
18:38 [t]ver 39; Mt 9:27 [u]Mt 17:15; Lk 18:13

Jesus Predicts His Death a Third Time

18:31-33pp — Mt 20:17-19; Mk 10:32-34

[31]Jesus took the Twelve aside and told them, "We are going up to Jerusalem,[i] and everything that
is written by the prophets[j] about the Son of Man[k] will be fulfilled. [32]He will be delivered over to the
Gentiles.[l] They will mock him, insult him and spit on him; [33]they will flog him[m] and kill him.[n] On the
third day[o] he will rise again."[p]
[34]The disciples did not understand any of this. Its meaning was hidden from them, and they did not
know what he was talking about.[q]

A Blind Beggar Receives His Sight

18:35-43pp — Mt 20:29-34; Mk 10:46-52

[35]As Jesus approached Jericho,[r] a blind man was sitting by the roadside begging. [36]When he
heard the crowd going by, he asked what was happening. [37]They told him, "Jesus of Nazareth is
passing by."[s]
[38]He called out, "Jesus, Son of David,[t] have mercy[u] on me!"

[a] *20* Exodus 20:12-16; Deut. 5:16-20

18:22 Sell everything. Alludes to the last of the Ten Commandments, which calls people not to place anything above God: "You shall not covet" (Exod 20:17; Deut 5:21). **follow me.** Implies that Jesus is the one God and demands total devotion since to follow Jesus is to leave all "for the sake of the kingdom of God" (v. 29).

18:25 a camel to go through the eye of a needle. This should most probably be taken as hyperbole rather than as a reference to a small entrance in the city wall of Jerusalem (as some have suggested). It is difficult for wealthy people to abandon all and follow Jesus.

18:27 God's mercy and grace are necessary to save an individual, and God's power can accomplish the impossible (cf. 1:37).

18:29 This expands v. 22 and repeats 14:26. People must follow Jesus "for the sake of the kingdom of God" because Jesus' life, death, and resurrection usher in this kingdom (cf. 17:21).

18:30 many times. The great spiritual blessings one receives when following Jesus.

18:31–34 *Jesus Predicts His Death a Third Time.* Jesus demonstrates what it means to leave everything "for the sake of the kingdom of God" (v. 29). This is the third and last time Jesus directly predicts his own suffering in Luke (cf. 9:22,44–45), although indirect references can also be found earlier in 17:25. These repeated references show that his death is according to the plan of God rather than an accident in history.

18:31 everything that is written by the prophets. Jews often attributed all the OT books to the prophets. Many individual passages concern the Messiah, but Jesus' death and resurrection are the turning point of the entire history of salvation.

18:32–33 mock ... insult ... spit on ... flog ... kill. Jesus will suffer pain and humiliation.

18:33 On the third day he will rise again. Not only the ultimate example of reversal (see v. 14 and note), but also the force behind this reversal since it is because of his resurrection that such reversal is possible.

18:34 did not understand any of this. Cf. 9:45. It was only after Jesus' resurrection that he "opened their minds so they could understand the Scriptures" (24:45) and appreciate the full significance of his death and resurrection.

18:35–43 *A Blind Beggar Receives His Sight.* Unlike the "very wealthy" man (v. 23) who refused to follow Jesus and thus could not inherit eternal life (vv. 18–25), a blind beggar follows Jesus (v. 43), who heals the beggar because of his faith (v. 42).

18:35 approached. This may mean that Jesus was just in the vicinity of Jericho (the Roman city southwest of the ruins of the old city). If so, this aligns with Mark 10:46 (cf. Matt 20:29), which further identifies this blind man as Bartimaeus.

18:38 Luke has already introduced Jesus as a descendant of David (1:32,69; 2:4,11; 3:31), but this blind man is the first in Jesus' public ministry to identify him as the "Son of David." The man may not have understood the full meaning of this title, but Jesus accepts it. "The Messiah is the son of David" (20:41).

18:39 [v] ver 38
18:42 [w] Mt 9:22
18:43 [x] Mt 9:8; Lk 13:17
19:1 [y] Lk 18:35
19:4 [z] 1Ki 10:27; 1Ch 27:28; Isa 9:10 [a] Lk 18:37
19:7 [b] Mt 9:11
19:8 [c] Lk 7:13 [d] Lk 3:12, 13 [e] Ex 22:1; Lev 6:4, 5; Nu 5:7; 2Sa 12:6
19:9 [f] Lk 3:8; 13:16; Ro 4:16; Gal 3:7
19:10 [g] Eze 34:12, 16; Jn 3:17
19:11 [h] Mt 3:2 [i] Lk 17:20; Ac 1:6

39 Those who led the way rebuked him and told him to be quiet, but he shouted all the more, "Son of David, have mercy on me!"[v]

40 Jesus stopped and ordered the man to be brought to him. When he came near, Jesus asked him, 41 "What do you want me to do for you?"

"Lord, I want to see," he replied.

42 Jesus said to him, "Receive your sight; your faith has healed you."[w] 43 Immediately he received his sight and followed Jesus, praising God. When all the people saw it, they also praised God.[x]

Zacchaeus the Tax Collector

19 Jesus entered Jericho[y] and was passing through. 2 A man was there by the name of Zacchaeus; he was a chief tax collector and was wealthy. 3 He wanted to see who Jesus was, but because he was short he could not see over the crowd. 4 So he ran ahead and climbed a sycamore-fig[z] tree to see him, since Jesus was coming that way.[a]

5 When Jesus reached the spot, he looked up and said to him, "Zacchaeus, come down immediately. I must stay at your house today." 6 So he came down at once and welcomed him gladly.

7 All the people saw this and began to mutter, "He has gone to be the guest of a sinner."[b]

8 But Zacchaeus stood up and said to the Lord,[c] "Look, Lord! Here and now I give half of my possessions to the poor, and if I have cheated anybody out of anything,[d] I will pay back four times the amount."[e]

9 Jesus said to him, "Today salvation has come to this house, because this man, too, is a son of Abraham.[f] 10 For the Son of Man came to seek and to save the lost."[g]

The Parable of the Ten Minas

19:12-27Ref — Mt 25:14-30

11 While they were listening to this, he went on to tell them a parable, because he was near Jerusalem and the people thought that the kingdom of God[h] was going to appear at once.[i] 12 He said: "A man of

18:41 The Son of David is "Lord" (20:42; see Ps 110:1), though here it may simply express respect (cf. "Rabbi," Mark 10:51).

18:42 your faith has healed you. This may point beyond merely physical healing (i.e., "your faith has saved you," 7:50), which would explain why the blind man then follows Jesus (v. 43).

18:43 praised God. This parallels how the crowd responds in 7:16.

19:1–10 *Zacchaeus the Tax Collector.* The story of this "wealthy" (v. 2) tax collector shows how a rich man can be saved (cf. 18:24–26). In contrast to the rich man who refuses to give up his wealth to follow Jesus (18:18–25), Zacchaeus, like the tax collector in 18:9–14, confesses that he is a sinner and gives up some of his wealth in order to follow Jesus.

19:2 chief tax collector. In charge of many tax collectors within a district, who paid him commissions on what they collected. Jews despised tax collectors because they worked for the Jews' oppressors (see 3:12 and note), and they especially despised chief tax collectors because their wealth was built on the general population's suffering.

19:4 a sycamore-fig tree. Like an oak tree, it has a short trunk and wide branches that can hold a grown person.

19:5 must. Necessary in the unfolding of God's salvation plan (see 2:49 and note; 9:22; 15:32). **stay at your house.** Jesus "welcomes sinners and eats with them" (15:2). **today.** When God saves an individual or people group (v. 9; 2:11; 4:21; 5:26; 13:32–33; 23:43).

19:7 Many call the tax collector a "sinner" (cf. 5:30; 7:34; 15:1), but in 18:13–14 it is the tax collector who confesses to being a "sinner" and who is "justified before God."

19:8 I give half of my possessions to the poor. This surpasses the tithing requirement. He does not "sell everything … and give to the poor" (18:22) because he needs to repay the people he has cheated. **four times.** May reflect the OT practice of paying back four times what was stolen (Exod 22:1; 2 Sam 12:6). Zacchaeus's voluntary act of giving to the poor and repaying others clearly transcends what is required by the law.

19:9 Today salvation has come to this house. Parallels "I must stay at your house today" (v. 5). Jesus embodies God's salvation. Unlike those who claim Abraham as their father (3:8), Zacchaeus becomes a true "son of Abraham" by receiving Jesus and the salvation he offers.

19:10 to seek and to save. This encapsulates the purpose of Jesus' ministry and reaffirms his mission to "call … sinners to repentance" (5:32). Not only is he able to save, but he also takes initiative in seeking those who need to be saved since he is both a powerful and merciful Savior. **the lost.** Links this to the parables of the lost sheep, coin, and son (ch. 15).

19:11–27 *The Parable of the Ten Minas.* Immediately before Jesus enters Jerusalem, he announces judgment on those who will not welcome him as "king over them" (v. 27). He does not direct this parable against these people simply because they hate him as the subjects hate their king (v. 14); he criticizes them for failing to carry out the mission God entrusted to them (v. 22). He also refers to the time between his death and return (cf. Matt 25:14–30). At the final judgment God will punish those who continue to be unfaithful to him.

19:11 near Jerusalem. Jesus is journeying to Jerusalem to be rejected and killed (13:33). **the people thought that the kingdom of God was going to appear at once.** They misunderstand the goal of this journey. Both the delay of the full arrival of this kingdom and its spiritual rather than military and political nature disappoint Jesus' audience.

19:12 appointed king … return. This "man" may reflect Herod the Great, who was appointed king in 39 BC before he returned to Judea to rule (37–4 BC). After Herod the Great's death, his son Archelaus also traveled to Rome to petition to succeed his father as king. In this context, to be appointed king while away may refer to Jesus' resurrection (22:69; 24:26) since his resurrection is often understood in terms

noble birth went to a distant country to have himself appointed king and then to return. [13]So he called ten of his servants[j] and gave them ten minas.[a] 'Put this money to work,' he said, 'until I come back.'

[14]"But his subjects hated him and sent a delegation after him to say, 'We don't want this man to be our king.'

[15]"He was made king, however, and returned home. Then he sent for the servants to whom he had given the money, in order to find out what they had gained with it.

[16]"The first one came and said, 'Sir, your mina has earned ten more.'

[17]" 'Well done, my good servant!'[k] his master replied. 'Because you have been trustworthy in a very small matter, take charge of ten cities.'[l]

[18]"The second came and said, 'Sir, your mina has earned five more.'

[19]"His master answered, 'You take charge of five cities.'

[20]"Then another servant came and said, 'Sir, here is your mina; I have kept it laid away in a piece of cloth. [21]I was afraid of you, because you are a hard man. You take out what you did not put in and reap what you did not sow.'[m]

[22]"His master replied, 'I will judge you by your own words,[n] you wicked servant! You knew, did you, that I am a hard man, taking out what I did not put in, and reaping what I did not sow?[o] [23]Why then didn't you put my money on deposit, so that when I came back, I could have collected it with interest?'

[24]"Then he said to those standing by, 'Take his mina away from him and give it to the one who has ten minas.'

[25]" 'Sir,' they said, 'he already has ten!'

[26]"He replied, 'I tell you that to everyone who has, more will be given, but as for the one who has nothing, even what they have will be taken away.[p] [27]But those enemies of mine who did not want me to be king over them—bring them here and kill them in front of me.' "

Jesus Comes to Jerusalem as King

19:29-38pp — Mt 21:1-9; Mk 11:1-10
19:35-38pp — Jn 12:12-15

[28]After Jesus had said this, he went on ahead, going up to Jerusalem.[q] [29]As he approached Bethphage and Bethany[r] at the hill called the Mount of Olives,[s] he sent two of his disciples, saying to them, [30]"Go to the village ahead of you, and as you enter it, you will find a colt tied there, which no one has ever ridden. Untie it and bring it here. [31]If anyone asks you, 'Why are you untying it?' say, 'The Lord needs it.' "

[a] *13* A mina was about three months' wages.

19:13 [j]Mk 13:34
19:17 [k]Pr 27:18 [l]Lk 16:10
19:21 [m]Mt 25:24
19:22 [n]2Sa 1:16; Job 15:6 [o]Mt 25:26
19:26 [p]Mt 13:12; 25:29; Lk 8:18
19:28 [q]Mk 10:32; Lk 9:51
19:29 [r]Mt 21:17 [s]Mt 21:1

of enthronement (Acts 2:32–36). A rigid allegorical reading is to be avoided, however, since the next section (vv. 28–44) affirms that Jesus is king now.

19:13 ten minas. See NIV text note.

19:14 his subjects hated him. If v. 12 alludes to Archelaus's petition to be king (see note on v. 12), this verse may allude to the failure of his petition since his own subjects opposed it. Here it is applied to Jesus' rejection by his own people (cf. 4:24; 23:18,23).

19:15 The servants are accountable to their king; they must faithfully manage what he entrusts to them (cf. 12:43,46; 16:2); they do not own his money and therefore must obey his will (cf. 18:22; 19:8).

19:20–21 This servant not only fails to follow the king's will but criticizes the king for being hard and greedy. The responses of this king to his faithful servants (vv. 16–19) are not entirely consistent with the evaluation of this unfaithful servant since a hard and greedy man would not have approved of those who had earned relatively less for him (vv. 18–19).

19:22–23 The servant's action contradicts his own comments about his master (vv. 20–21): if he knew that his master was a hard man, he should have been more diligent in working for his master.

19:26 given ... taken away. Recalls 8:18. **the one who has nothing.** An enemy of Jesus who refuses to acknowledge him as "the king who comes in the name of the Lord" (v. 38; cf. Ps 118:26).

19:27 kill. Cf. 12:46.

19:28–44 *Jesus Comes to Jerusalem as King.* Luke's numerous statements anticipating Jesus' journey to Jerusalem (9:51; 13:22; 18:31) foreshadow this final episode in Jesus' journey from Galilee to Jerusalem that summarizes the journey's main themes: Jesus is the one God sent (v. 38), Jewish religious leaders oppose him (v. 39), and judgment is coming (vv. 43–44). Luke presents these in the context of Jesus' glorious entry into Jerusalem as king (vv. 28–40). This joyous occasion quickly becomes the basis of God's judgment on Jerusalem since the people of Jerusalem refuse to receive their king (vv. 41–44).

19:28 This takes place on the Sunday of Passion Week.

19:29 Bethphage. Its exact location is unclear. **Bethany.** It was "less than two miles [about 3 kilometers] from Jerusalem" (John 11:18). **the Mount of Olives.** Appears in the OT description of the final days (Zech 14:4), and Luke notes it several times in the following chapters (v. 37; 21:37; 22:39).

19:30 village. Probably Bethphage since Jesus is staying in Bethany (cf. Mark 11:11–12). **colt.** Points back to Zechariah's description of the arrival of the final king on a colt (Zech 9:9; cf. Matt 21:5).

19:31 This is the first time Jesus refers to himself as "the Lord," the sovereign one who controls his own destiny even as he enters Jerusalem to suffer at the hands of many.

19:32 [t]Lk 22:13
19:36 [u]2Ki 9:13
19:37 [v]Mt 21:1
19:38 [w]Ps 118:26; Lk 13:35 [x]Lk 2:14
19:39 [y]Mt 21:15,16
19:40 [z]Hab 2:11
19:41 [a]Isa 22:4; Lk 13:34,35
19:43 [b]Isa 29:3; Jer 6:6; Eze 4:2; 26:8; Lk 21:20
19:44 [c]Ps 137:9 [d]Mt 24:2; Mk 13:2; Lk 21:6 [e]1Pe 2:12
19:46 [f]Isa 56:7 [g]Jer 7:11
19:47 [h]Mt 26:55

32 Those who were sent ahead went and found it just as he had told them.[t] 33 As they were untying the
colt, its owners asked them, "Why are you untying the colt?"
34 They replied, "The Lord needs it."
35 They brought it to Jesus, threw their cloaks on the colt and put Jesus on it. 36 As he went along,
people spread their cloaks[u] on the road.
37 When he came near the place where the road goes down the Mount of Olives,[v] the whole crowd of
disciples began joyfully to praise God in loud voices for all the miracles they had seen:

38 "Blessed is the king who comes in the name of the Lord!"[a][w]

"Peace in heaven and glory in the highest!"[x]

39 Some of the Pharisees in the crowd said to Jesus, "Teacher, rebuke your disciples!"[y]
40 "I tell you," he replied, "if they keep quiet, the stones will cry out."[z]
41 As he approached Jerusalem and saw the city, he wept over it[a] 42 and said, "If you, even you, had only
known on this day what would bring you peace—but now it is hidden from your eyes. 43 The days will
come upon you when your enemies will build an embankment against you and encircle you and hem
you in on every side.[b] 44 They will dash you to the ground, you and the children within your walls.[c] They
will not leave one stone on another,[d] because you did not recognize the time of God's coming[e] to you."

Jesus at the Temple

19:45,46pp — Mt 21:12-16; Mk 11:15-18; Jn 2:13-16

45 When Jesus entered the temple courts, he began to drive out those who were selling. 46 "It is written,"
he said to them, "'My house will be a house of prayer'[b];[f] but you have made it 'a den of robbers.'[c]"[g]
47 Every day he was teaching at the temple.[h] But the chief priests, the teachers of the law and the

[a] *38* Psalm 118:26 [b] *46* Isaiah 56:7 [c] *46* Jer. 7:11

19:32 just as he had told them. Reinforces that Jesus is Lord.

19:36 spread their cloaks on the road. This follows ancient rituals for welcoming a king (cf. 2 Kgs 9:13).

19:37 the whole crowd of disciples. Welcomes Jesus even as the Pharisees continue to oppose him (v. 39). **joyfully.** How people should react to the arrival of God's salvation (cf. v. 6; 1:14; 2:10; 6:23; 13:17; 15:5,32). **praise God.** How people should respond to such acts (cf. 2:13,20; Acts 2:47; 3:8–9). These disciples welcome Jesus because of "all the miracles they had seen," but they do not understand why Jesus enters Jerusalem (cf. 20:9–18).

19:38 Blessed … Lord! From a royal coronation psalm: "Blessed is he who comes in the name of the LORD" (Ps 118:26). The addition of the word "king" in Luke's version further highlights the royal connotation of this event (cf. vv. 39–40). **Peace … highest!** Echoes the "great company of the heavenly host" at the beginning of this Gospel (2:13).

19:39 Teacher. The Pharisees refuse to acknowledge Jesus as "the Lord" (v. 34) or "the king" (v. 38).

19:40 stones will cry out. Language of judgment; e.g., Hab 2:11: "the stones of the wall will cry out" as they witness God judging his enemies. In this context, however, this phrase appears as praise in acknowledging Jesus as King.

19:42 what would bring you peace. "God's coming to you" (v. 44). In this Gospel, peace is the result of God's work of salvation (1:79; 2:14,29; 14:32). **hidden from your eyes.** Because the Jewish religious leaders reject Jesus, they can neither see nor understand his work (cf. 8:10; Isa 6:9).

19:43 Jesus uses OT language to describe the fall of Jerusalem in AD 70 (cf. Isa 29:3; Jer 6:6–21; 52:4–5; Ezek 4:1–3).

19:44 They will not leave one stone on another. Recalls an OT judgment against Jerusalem: "Jerusalem will become a heap of rubble" (Mic 3:12).

19:45—24:53 *Death and Vindication of Jesus.* This final section describes the climax of Jesus' life. His dispute with the Jewish religious leaders intensifies as he enters the center of their realm of power (19:45—21:38). As he predicted (see 9:22), these leaders reject and kill him (22:1—23:56), but he rises on the third day and later ascends into the heavens in glory (24:1–53).

19:45—21:38 *Controversy With Jerusalem Leaders.* After entering Jerusalem, Jesus again responds to the Jewish religious leaders who continue to challenge his authority (20:1–8,20–44), and he directly challenges them and accuses them of unfaithfulness to God (19:45–48; 20:9–19,45–47; 21:1–4). This culminates in his prophesying the temple's destruction as one of the signs of the end times (21:5–38).

19:45–48 *Jesus at the Temple.* Luke begins recounting Jesus' final days in and around Jerusalem. This ends the lengthy account of Jesus' journey to Jerusalem, which is necessary partly because "no prophet can die outside Jerusalem" (13:33). This episode also marks the beginning of Jesus' final confrontation with the Jewish religious leaders. Jesus challenges the Jewish leaders for misusing the temple and corrects the people for misunderstanding the Messiah's role. Instead of challenging the Roman rulers when he arrives in Jerusalem, Jesus targets the misconduct of God's own people and thus becomes the object of their anger and persecution.

19:45 temple courts. Likely the court of the Gentiles, where people sold animals for sacrifices. Mark 11:15–16 gives a more detailed account of Jesus' act, but Luke focuses on his words against the religious leaders.

19:46 My house will be a house of prayer. From Isa 56:7: "My house will be called a house of prayer for all nations." Jesus omits "all nations" because he focuses on God's judgment of his people. Including the Gentiles is the focus of Luke's second volume (the book of Acts). **den of robbers.** From Jer 7:11, where Jeremiah accuses God's people of worshiping "other gods you have not known" (Jer 7:9); consequently, God will destroy "the temple you trust in" (Jer 7:14). The Jerusalem temple of Jesus' time will suffer the same fate (cf. vv. 42–44; 21:20–24).

19:47 This begins fulfilling what Jesus predicted in 9:22.

leaders among the people were trying to kill him.[i] 48Yet they could not find any way to do it, because
all the people hung on his words.

The Authority of Jesus Questioned

20:1-8pp — Mt 21:23-27; Mk 11:27-33

20 One day as Jesus was teaching the people in the temple courts[j] and proclaiming the good
news,[k] the chief priests and the teachers of the law, together with the elders, came up to him.
2"Tell us by what authority you are doing these things," they said. "Who gave you this authority?"[l]
3He replied, "I will also ask you a question. Tell me: 4John's baptism[m]—was it from heaven, or of
human origin?"
5They discussed it among themselves and said, "If we say, 'From heaven,' he will ask, 'Why didn't you
believe him?' 6But if we say, 'Of human origin,' all the people[n] will stone us, because they are persuaded
that John was a prophet."[o]
7So they answered, "We don't know where it was from."
8Jesus said, "Neither will I tell you by what authority I am doing these things."

The Parable of the Tenants

20:9-19pp — Mt 21:33-46; Mk 12:1-12

9He went on to tell the people this parable: "A man planted a vineyard,[p] rented it to some farmers
and went away for a long time.[q] 10At harvest time he sent a servant to the tenants so they would give
him some of the fruit of the vineyard. But the tenants beat him and sent him away empty-handed. 11He
sent another servant, but that one also they beat and treated shamefully and sent away empty-handed.
12He sent still a third, and they wounded him and threw him out.
13"Then the owner of the vineyard said, 'What shall I do? I will send my son, whom I love;[r] perhaps
they will respect him.'
14"But when the tenants saw him, they talked the matter over. 'This is the heir,' they said. 'Let's kill
him, and the inheritance will be ours.' 15So they threw him out of the vineyard and killed him.
"What then will the owner of the vineyard do to them? 16He will come and kill those tenants[s] and
give the vineyard to others."

19:47 [i] Mt 12:14; Mk 11:18
20:1 [j] Mt 26:55 [k] Lk 8:1
20:2 [l] Jn 2:18; Ac 4:7; 7:27
20:4 [m] Mk 1:4
20:6 [n] Lk 7:29 [o] Mt 11:9
20:9 [p] Isa 5:1-7 [q] Mt 25:14
20:13 [r] Mt 3:17
20:16 [s] Lk 19:27

20:1–8 *The Authority of Jesus Questioned.* After Jesus exerted his authority by driving out those who were selling in the temple courts (19:45) and teaching in the temple courts (v. 1; 19:47), the Jewish religious leaders again challenge him to identify the source of his authority. By tempting Jesus to claim divine authority for himself, they hope to accuse Jesus of blasphemy, but instead Jesus demonstrates that they have consistently rejected those God sent.
20:1 The series of events in 20:1—21:36 appear to occur on the Tuesday of the final week of Jesus' earthly ministry, but Luke uses "one day" as one example of the "every day" that "he was teaching at the temple" (19:47). Jesus perseveres in the midst of opposition throughout his entire earthly ministry.
20:2 After Jesus challenges the standing of the Jewish religious leaders and as a result damages their monetary profits, a question concerning the source of Jesus' authority reappears (cf. 11:15). The Jewish religious leaders assume that they alone possess divine authority and that all who oppose them are necessarily using an evil force. As the story unfolds, it becomes plain that these Jewish religious leaders themselves are instruments of Satan (22:3–4).
20:3–4 Jesus' response assumes that John the Baptist was popular among the people, although the religious leaders opposed him (cf. 7:29–30). Jesus again affirms John's significant status as a prophet from God (cf. 1:76).
20:7 We don't know. Their ignorance is ironic because it reveals that their own authority is "of human origin" (v. 4). They "don't know how to interpret this present time" (12:56).
20:8 Jesus refuses to answer them because they will not believe him (22:67). He is not denying that he is the Son of God (cf. 22:70), but he refuses to entertain them when they are not truly interested in learning about him and the source of his authority.
20:9–19 *The Parable of the Tenants.* As opposition from the Jewish religious leaders escalates, they wickedly reject John and Jesus, whose authority was "from heaven" (vv. 4–5). But Jesus is not simply another prophet like John; he is God's "son" (v. 13) and thus the proper "heir" (v. 14). Those who reject the "son" and "heir" will be thrown out and killed (vv. 15b–16).
20:9 vineyard. Often represents God's people (Ps 80:8–13; Isa 5:1–2; 27:2–3; Jer 2:21; Hos 10:1). But to "give the vineyard to others" (v. 16) does not fit that analogy here, even though it appears to help us understand the rest of the parable. The vineyard probably refers only to the remnant of God's people—those who are faithful to God despite their wicked counterparts (cf. 2 Kgs 19:30; Isa 3:14; 37:31; Jer 6:9).
20:10 The OT often calls a prophet God's "servant" (cf. 1 Kgs 14:18; 2 Kgs 9:36; Ezra 9:11; Isa 20:3; 44:26; Jer 26:5). Leaders of God's people repeatedly rejected these servants.
20:13 my son, whom I love. Echoes how the heavenly voice identifies Jesus in 3:22. Jesus is the son of the parable, and he accepts his mission on his way to the cross.
20:14 Let's kill him. A clear reference to Jesus' impending death at the hands of the Jewish religious leaders (cf. v. 19). **inheritance.** Can refer to the blessings God's people will inherit at the end of the ages (Isa 49:8). Luke applies it to the blessings that both Jews and Gentiles who respond to the gospel share (Acts 20:32).
20:16 He will come and kill those tenants. This may refer to the fall of Jerusalem in AD 70 (cf. 19:43), but the full force of God's wrath can only

20:17 [t]Ps 118:22; Ac 4:11
20:18 [u]Isa 8:14,15
20:19 [v]Lk 19:47 [w]Mk 11:18
20:20 [x]Mt 12:10 [y]Mt 27:2
20:21 [z]Jn 3:2
20:25 [a]Lk 23:2; Ro 13:7
20:27 [b]Ac 4:1 [c]Ac 23:8; 1Co 15:12

When the people heard this, they said, "God forbid!"
17 Jesus looked directly at them and asked, "Then what is the meaning of that which is written:

"'The stone the builders rejected
has become the cornerstone'[a]?[t]

18 Everyone who falls on that stone will be broken to pieces; anyone on whom it falls will be crushed."[u]
19 The teachers of the law and the chief priests looked for a way to arrest him[v] immediately, because
they knew he had spoken this parable against them. But they were afraid of the people.[w]

Paying Taxes to Caesar

20:20-26pp — Mt 22:15-22; Mk 12:13-17

20 Keeping a close watch on him, they sent spies, who pretended to be sincere. They hoped to catch
Jesus in something he said,[x] so that they might hand him over to the power and authority of the governor.[y] 21 So the spies questioned him: "Teacher, we know that you speak and teach what is right, and
that you do not show partiality but teach the way of God in accordance with the truth.[z] 22 Is it right for
us to pay taxes to Caesar or not?"
23 He saw through their duplicity and said to them, 24 "Show me a denarius. Whose image and inscription are on it?"
"Caesar's," they replied.
25 He said to them, "Then give back to Caesar what is Caesar's,[a] and to God what is God's."
26 They were unable to trap him in what he had said there in public. And astonished by his answer,
they became silent.

The Resurrection and Marriage

20:27-40pp — Mt 22:23-33; Mk 12:18-27

27 Some of the Sadducees,[b] who say there is no resurrection,[c] came to Jesus with a question. 28 "Teacher," they said, "Moses wrote for us that if a man's brother dies and leaves a wife but no children, the

[a] *17* Psalm 118:22

be felt in the final judgment. This is both a promise of impending judgment and a call for God's people to repent in light of this judgment.

20:17 Jesus quotes from Ps 118:22 to depict his own predicament (for other quotations and allusions to Ps 118, see 7:19; 13:35; 19:38). **has become the cornerstone.** Extends the story within the parable by vindicating the Son. Peter later uses this quotation to refer to Jesus' resurrection (Acts 4:10).

20:18 Everyone who falls on that stone will be broken to pieces. Alludes to Isa 8:14–15, and here refers to those who reject Jesus and his gospel. **anyone on whom it falls will be crushed.** Alludes to Dan 2:34 and depicts God's judgment on those who oppose him and his Messiah.

20:20–26 *Paying Taxes to Caesar.* By questioning Jesus on the sensitive issue of paying taxes to the Roman emperor, the Jewish religious leaders again attempt to trap him. If Jesus condones the Roman tax system, the people will turn against him because they consider taxation an instrument of the oppressive Roman rule; if Jesus in any way hints at bypassing the tax system, the leaders will accuse him of insubordination against the Romans. With a profound reply (v. 25), Jesus not only saves himself from their trap but affirms God's sovereign rule without making an explicit political statement against Rome.

20:20 governor. The Roman prefect Pontius Pilate, who oversaw the regions of Judea and Samaria (see note on 3:1). The Jewish religious leaders challenge the source of Jesus' "authority" (v. 2) even as they themselves submit to and cooperate with the human authority of the time.

20:22 Caesar. The term came from the personal name of Gaius Julius Caesar but became the title of the subsequent Roman emperors. At this time Tiberius was emperor (cf. 3:1). The title here refers to Roman imperial power in general.

20:24 denarius. A common Roman coin worth a day's wages for a laborer. In Jesus' time every denarius bore the image of Tiberius and the following inscription: "Tiberius Caesar, Son of the Divine Augustus, Augustus" (i.e., Tiberius Caesar, the august Son of the Divine Augustus). For the Jews, such coins violated the second of the Ten Commandments (Exod 20:4; Deut 5:8).

20:25 Jesus' statement has two layers of meaning. On the surface, by distinguishing between God and Caesar, Jesus separates the religious from the political. But for the Jews, "what is God's" refers to all realms of existence. "Give back to Caesar what is Caesar's" cannot be disputed. But nothing really belongs to Caesar since God alone is the Creator. "Give back … to God what is God's" thus affirms that God is the sovereign ruler of the universe (cf. Acts 4:19–20). Without explicitly challenging the power and authority of Roman imperial rule, Jesus nonetheless affirms God's unique sovereignty.

20:27–40 *The Resurrection and Marriage.* Before Jesus came to Jerusalem, the Pharisees and their scribes were often the ones who opposed him. In Jerusalem, however, most of the leaders of the temple cult were Sadducees. Sadducees, "who say there is no resurrection" (v. 27), challenge Jesus by suggesting that the doctrine of resurrection is irrational. Jesus responds to this theoretical issue but adds an allusion to his own resurrection (cf. vv. 41–44).

20:27 Sadducees. Mostly aristocrats. Politically, they were more inclined than the Pharisees to support Roman rule. Theologically, they rejected the oral traditions that the Pharisees accepted. Focusing primarily on the Pentateuch, the Sadducees also rejected doctrines that the rest of the OT canon develops more explicitly; these include the afterlife and the resurrection of the dead (cf. Acts 23:8). Many cultic

man must marry the widow and raise up offspring for his brother.[d] 29Now there were seven brothers.
The first one married a woman and died childless. 30The second 31and then the third married her, and
in the same way the seven died, leaving no children. 32Finally, the woman died too. 33Now then, at the
resurrection whose wife will she be, since the seven were married to her?"

34Jesus replied, "The people of this age marry and are given in marriage. 35But those who are considered worthy of taking part in the age to come[e] and in the resurrection from the dead will neither
marry nor be given in marriage, 36and they can no longer die; for they are like the angels. They are
God's children,[f] since they are children of the resurrection. 37But in the account of the burning bush,
even Moses showed that the dead rise, for he calls the Lord 'the God of Abraham, and the God of Isaac,
and the God of Jacob.'[a][g] 38He is not the God of the dead, but of the living, for to him all are alive."

39Some of the teachers of the law responded, "Well said, teacher!" 40And no one dared to ask him
any more questions.[h]

Whose Son Is the Messiah?

20:41-47pp — Mt 22:41–23:7; Mk 12:35-40

41Then Jesus said to them, "Why is it said that the Messiah is the son of David?[i] 42David himself declares in the Book of Psalms:

> " 'The Lord said to my Lord:
> "Sit at my right hand
> 43 until I make your enemies
> a footstool for your feet." '[b][j]

44David calls him 'Lord.' How then can he be his son?"

Warning Against the Teachers of the Law

45While all the people were listening, Jesus said to his disciples, 46"Beware of the teachers of the law.
They like to walk around in flowing robes and love to be greeted with respect in the marketplaces and
have the most important seats in the synagogues and the places of honor at banquets.[k] 47They devour
widows' houses and for a show make lengthy prayers. These men will be punished most severely."

20:28 [d] Dt 25:5
20:35 [e] Mt 12:32
20:36 [f] Jn 1:12; 1Jn 3:1-2
20:37 [g] Ex 3:6
20:40 [h] Mt 22:46; Mk 12:34
20:41 [i] Mt 1:1
20:43 [j] Ps 110:1; Mt 22:44
20:46 [k] Lk 11:43

[a] *37* Exodus 3:6 [b] *43* Psalm 110:1

and political leaders who confronted Jesus in Jerusalem belonged to the Sadducee party.

20:28 if a man's brother dies and leaves a wife but no children, the man must marry the widow. Draws from Deut 25:5. **raise up offspring for his brother.** Alludes to Gen 38:8. The purpose of this custom of "levirate marriage" (from the Latin *levir*, "brother-in-law") is that "the first son she bears shall carry on the name of the dead brother so that his name will not be blotted out from Israel" (Deut 25:6).

20:33 This question challenges Jesus (1) whether it is rational to believe in resurrection (Jesus responds in vv. 34–36) and (2) how to properly interpret the Mosaic law (Jesus responds in vv. 37–38).

20:35 neither marry nor be given in marriage. They will acquire a resurrected body that will not decay (cf. Acts 13:33–35), so they do not need to give birth to extend a family's bloodline.

20:36 God's children. Cf. 6:35; 11:2. As such, physical lineage is no longer important, making the question about levirate marriage irrelevant. **children of the resurrection.** They will be a part of the resurrection of the righteous (cf. 14:14).

20:37 account of the burning bush. Exod 3:1—4:17. **Moses showed that the dead rise.** The Pentateuch includes the doctrine of resurrection. **the God of Abraham ... Isaac ... Jacob.** From Exod 3:6. Since God identifies himself to Moses as the God of Abraham, Isaac, and Jacob, the three patriarchs must have survived their own death in some sense.

20:38 to him all are alive. This can have multiple layers of meaning: (1) in his sight, (2) through his power, and (3) for him (cf. Rom 1:4; 6:5).

20:39 Well said, teacher! Those teachers of the law who agree with Jesus are likely Pharisees, who believe in the resurrection of the dead.

20:41–44 *Whose Son Is the Messiah?* Jesus continues to interpret Scripture with authority. By explaining the relationship between the Messiah and his ancestor David, Jesus challenges the teachers of the law on their view of the son of David as inferior to David himself (see note on Matt 22:41–46).

20:41 son of David. The OT often directly and indirectly identifies the Messiah as "the son of David" (e.g., 2 Sam 7:1–29; Ps 89:19–37; Isa 9:6–9; 11:1–10; Jer 23:5–8; Ezek 34:23–24). Jesus' question centers on the unique relationship of the Messiah to his ancestors.

20:42–43 Jesus responds to his own question (v. 41) by quoting from Ps 110:1.

20:42 David himself declares. David wrote Ps 110. **The Lord.** God himself. **my Lord.** By implication the Messiah.

20:44 Lord. How can David's descendant be his "Lord"? The Messiah is David's descendant, he will sit on his ancestor's throne, and his status and authority will surpass King David's. Jesus later applies this psalm to himself (22:69) and thus reveals himself as this Davidic Messiah.

20:45–47 *Warning Against the Teachers of the Law.* Jesus directly criticizes the Jewish religious leaders who seek power and glory for themselves and in doing so neglect the needs of the poor and lowly.

20:46 teachers of the law. Cf. vv. 1,19,39; 19:47; see note on 5:17. **marketplaces ... synagogues ... banquets.** The commercial, religious, and household spheres of life. These teachers were exalting themselves in all areas of life (cf. 11:43; 14:7–11).

20:47 Widows often symbolize the weak and vulnerable (cf. 4:25–26;

21:1 [l]Mt 27:6; Jn 8:20
21:4 [m]2Co 8:12
21:6 [n]Lk 19:44
21:8 [o]Lk 17:23
21:10 [p]2Ch 15:6; Isa 19:2
21:11 [q]Isa 29:6; Joel 2:30

The Widow's Offering

21:1-4pp — Mk 12:41-44

21 As Jesus looked up, he saw the rich putting their gifts into the temple treasury.[l] 2He also saw a
poor widow put in two very small copper coins. 3"Truly I tell you," he said, "this poor widow
has put in more than all the others. 4All these people gave their gifts out of their wealth; but she out of
her poverty put in all she had to live on."[m]

The Destruction of the Temple and Signs of the End Times

21:5-36pp — Mt 24; Mk 13
21:12-17pp — Mt 10:17-22

5Some of his disciples were remarking about how the temple was adorned with beautiful stones and
with gifts dedicated to God. But Jesus said, 6"As for what you see here, the time will come when not one
stone will be left on another;[n] every one of them will be thrown down."

7"Teacher," they asked, "when will these things happen? And what will be the sign that they are
about to take place?"

8He replied: "Watch out that you are not deceived. For many will come in my name, claiming, 'I
am he,' and, 'The time is near.' Do not follow them.[o] 9When you hear of wars and uprisings, do not be
frightened. These things must happen first, but the end will not come right away."

10Then he said to them: "Nation will rise against nation, and kingdom against kingdom.[p] 11There
will be great earthquakes, famines and pestilences in various places, and fearful events and great signs
from heaven.[q]

12"But before all this, they will seize you and persecute you. They will hand you over to synagogues
and put you in prison, and you will be brought before kings and governors, and all on account of my

7:11–17; 18:1–8). **devour widows' houses.** May refer either to deceptively handling the property of a widow's deceased husband or more generally to oppressing the weak and vulnerable members of society. In light of 21:1–4, Jesus may be criticizing how leaders mishandle temple funds that include money offered by someone like poor widows. **for a show make lengthy prayers.** This recalls the proud Pharisee in 18:10–12 and more closely parallels the "hypocrites" and "pagans" in Matt 6:5,7.

21:1–4 *The Widow's Offering.* A poor widow's offering exemplifies how the Jewish religious leaders "devour widows' houses" (20:47). Because they misuse the temple and its funds, judgment is imminent (vv. 5–36). The wider theme of properly using wealth reappears here as Jesus encourages his followers not to "[store] up things for themselves" (12:21; cf. 16:1–15,19–31; 18:18–30; 19:8).

21:1 Rich people probably showing off their wealth and generosity (cf. 20:46). **temple treasury.** A place to collect offerings (Neh 12:44). It was located in the court of women and consisted of 13 receptacles shaped like trumpets (cf. John 8:20).

21:2 two very small copper coins. About 2/100ths of the daily wage of a laborer.

21:4 all she had to live on. Or "the entire life that she has." While the rich give up part of their wealth, this poor widow gave up her entire living. This contrast echoes Jesus' earlier statement in the parable of the rich fool: "life does not consist in an abundance of possessions" (12:15).

21:5–38 *The Destruction of the Temple and Signs of the End Times.* This sermon took place on the Mount of Olives (Matt 24:3; Mark 13:3), and therefore it came to be known as the Olivet discourse. Jesus has already said that Jerusalem will be destroyed (13:34–35; 19:41–44), the Son of Man will return (12:35–48; 17:20–37), and his followers will suffer (9:23–27; 12:4–12). Here he intertwines all three events. He begins with the fall of Jerusalem and the destruction of the temple (vv. 5–6) and then connects it with the signs of the end times (vv. 7–11). But "before all this" (v. 12), his followers will be persecuted (vv. 12–19). He then returns to the destruction of the Jerusalem temple (vv. 20–24) and the signs of the end times (vv. 25–28). He affirms the certainty of the consummation of God's kingdom (vv. 29–33) and calls his disciples to remain alert and faithful (vv. 34–36). By connecting the impending destruction of the Jerusalem temple with the final consummation of history, he situates the persecution of God's people within this final period of history. Although this section focuses on the end times, Jesus repeatedly notes that this end has yet to arrive (vv. 9,12,24). Instead of speculating about the precise date of the end, Jesus' followers must "be always on the watch" (v. 36).

21:5 The remodeling of the Jerusalem temple, which Herod the Great began in AD 19, created a structure that all admired. **beautiful stones.** Possibly the temple's marble blocks, said to be 36 feet (11 meters) long, 18 feet (5.5 meters) wide, and 12 feet (3.7 meters) tall. **gifts dedicated to God.** May be the "finest offerings" (in the Apocrypha, 2 Maccabees 9:16), such as the golden vines with grape clusters "as tall as a man's height" (Josephus, *Wars*, 5.210).

21:6 not one stone will be left on another. Repeats the prophecy of 19:43–44 and is fulfilled in the destruction of the Jerusalem temple in AD 70. The stones in vv. 5–6 may contrast with the stone of 20:17 (cf. Ps 118:22). The rejected Jesus has become the cornerstone, but the beautiful stones of the temple will be nothing but ruins.

21:7 these things. Not limited to the destruction of the temple (v. 6). They include the events leading up to the final days of this age (vv. 25–28).

21:8 I am he. I am the (returning) Messiah. **The time.** The end times when God pronounces his judgment (cf. Dan 7:22).

21:10–11 Jesus again uses images familiar to the Jews in describing the time of judgment (cf. Isa 19:2; 29:6; 51:19; Jer 11:22; 14:12; 32:24; Ezek 6:12; 38:19). These events by themselves are not to be misconstrued as the sign of Jesus' second coming, but they will take place before his return. Matt 24:8 and Mark 13:8 label this period as "the beginning of birth pains" since these chaotic and difficult times will pave the way for the glorious return of Jesus.

21:11 great signs from heaven. Likely those in v. 25.

21:12 This anticipates the experience of the apostles in Luke's second volume (the book of Acts): **seize** (Acts 4:3), **persecute** (Acts 9:4–5), **hand you over to synagogues** (Acts 13:42–46; 14:1–2; 18:5–7), **put you in prison** (Acts 5:18; 8:3; 12:4–5; 16:23–24,37; 26:10), and **be brought before kings and governors** (Acts 9:15; 26:27–30).

name. 13 And so you will bear testimony to me.[r] 14 But make up your mind not to worry beforehand how
you will defend yourselves.[s] 15 For I will give you[t] words and wisdom that none of your adversaries will
be able to resist or contradict. 16 You will be betrayed even by parents, brothers and sisters, relatives and
friends,[u] and they will put some of you to death. 17 Everyone will hate you because of me.[v] 18 But not a
hair of your head will perish.[w] 19 Stand firm, and you will win life.[x]

20 "When you see Jerusalem being surrounded by armies,[y] you will know that its desolation is near.
21 Then let those who are in Judea flee to the mountains, let those in the city get out, and let those in
the country not enter the city.[z] 22 For this is the time of punishment[a] in fulfillment[b] of all that has been
written. 23 How dreadful it will be in those days for pregnant women and nursing mothers! There will
be great distress in the land and wrath against this people. 24 They will fall by the sword and will be
taken as prisoners to all the nations. Jerusalem will be trampled[c] on by the Gentiles until the times of
the Gentiles are fulfilled.

25 "There will be signs in the sun, moon and stars. On the earth, nations will be in anguish and
perplexity at the roaring and tossing of the sea.[d] 26 People will faint from terror, apprehensive of what
is coming on the world, for the heavenly bodies will be shaken.[e] 27 At that time they will see the Son of
Man[f] coming in a cloud[g] with power and great glory. 28 When these things begin to take place, stand up
and lift up your heads, because your redemption is drawing near."[h]

29 He told them this parable: "Look at the fig tree and all the trees. 30 When they sprout leaves, you
can see for yourselves and know that summer is near. 31 Even so, when you see these things happening,
you know that the kingdom of God[i] is near.

32 "Truly I tell you, this generation[j] will certainly not pass away until all these things have happened.
33 Heaven and earth will pass away, but my words will never pass away.[k]

34 "Be careful, or your hearts will be weighed down with carousing, drunkenness and the anxieties
of life,[l] and that day will close on you suddenly[m] like a trap. 35 For it will come on all those who live on

21:13 [r] Php 1:12
21:14 [s] Lk 12:11
21:15 [t] Lk 12:12
21:16 [u] Lk 12:52,53
21:17 [v] Jn 15:21
21:18 [w] Mt 10:30
21:19 [x] Mt 10:22
21:20 [y] Lk 19:43
21:21 [z] Lk 17:31
21:22 [a] Isa 63:4; Da 9:24-27; Hos 9:7 [b] Mt 1:22
21:24 [c] Isa 5:5; 63:18; Da 8:13; Rev 11:2
21:25 [d] 2Pe 3:10,12
21:26 [e] Mt 24:29
21:27 [f] Mt 8:20 [g] Rev 1:7
21:28 [h] Lk 18:7
21:31 [i] Mt 3:2
21:32 [j] Lk 11:50; 17:25
21:33 [k] Mt 5:18
21:34 [l] Mk 4:19 [m] Lk 12:40,46; 1Th 5:2-7

21:15 I will give you words and wisdom. Recalls God's comfort to Moses when he likewise faced the enemies of God's people (Exod 4:12). **none of your adversaries will be able to resist or contradict.** Stephen's ministry fulfills this: "But they [i.e., the Jews] could not stand up against the wisdom the Spirit gave him as he spoke" (Acts 6:10).
21:16 betrayed. As those closest to Jesus betray him (22:1–6,47–62), so the families and friends of his followers will betray them (cf. 18:29–30).
21:18 a hair of your head. Describes God's protection (cf. 12:7). In light of the reference to death in v. 16, this protection is a spiritual and eternal one.
21:20 Jerusalem being surrounded by armies. Jesus has already prophesied this (19:43), but here he links it with the "desolation" in Dan 12:11, where "the abomination that causes desolation" likewise refers to the power that threatens God's temple. This clearly refers to the fall of Jerusalem in AD 70, but other statements in this section are to be fulfilled at the end times (see note on vv. 5–38).
21:21 flee to the mountains. Recalls how prophets describe the end times (Ezek 7:16; Zech 14:5). The call to leave the city is also the call for prophets to leave Babylon: "Come out of her, my people! Run for your lives! Run from the fierce anger of the LORD" (Jer 51:45). Now Jerusalem and the whole region of Judea become the object of God's wrath.
21:22 all that has been written. Includes the messages of the numerous prophets who pronounce "the time of punishment" on God's people with similar language (Ezek 14:21; 16:41; 24:8; Hos 9:7).
21:23 pregnant women and nursing mothers. The calamity will be so severe that even those who are normally considered blessed (i.e., with children) cannot escape this series of disasters (cf. Hos 13:16; Amos 1:13).
21:24 Jerusalem will be trampled. As it once had been (cf. Zech 12:3 [in the Septuagint, the pre-Christian Greek translation of the OT]). **times of the Gentiles.** When Gentiles persecute God's people, although this period may also witness the salvation of the Gentiles (cf. Rom 11:25). **fulfilled.** Suggests that God limits his wrath (cf. Matt 24:22; Mark 13:20).
21:25 signs in the sun, moon and stars. May allude to Joel 2:30–31, which Luke later quotes in Acts 2:20.
21:27 the Son of Man coming in a cloud with power and great glory. Depicts Jesus' return with the language of Dan 7:13–14.
21:28 After a period of suffering, God's faithful people will witness their final "redemption" and join Jesus in his glory in their resurrected bodies (cf. Rom 8:23; 1 Cor 15:52–54).
21:29 Matthew 24:32 and Mark 13:28 mention only the "fig tree," but Luke includes "all the trees" probably to shift the focus from the fig tree's symbolic significance (in reference to Israel) to planting imagery in general that depicts the natural change of seasons (cf. Song 2:11–13).
21:32 this generation. May refer to the many among Jesus' audience who will witness the fall of Jerusalem (vv. 6,20). **all these things.** The events that precede the Son of Man's return. If so, the Greek term for "this generation" (*genea*) does not necessarily refer to the 20 to 30 years of a physical generation since Jesus repeatedly emphasizes the gap between the present moment and his return (vv. 9,12,24). In light of Luke's use of the term elsewhere, "this generation" may refer to the "unbelieving and perverse generation" (9:41) and the "wicked generation" (11:29) like the wilderness generation of Israel's past (cf. Deut 32:4–5,20). Thus, Jesus is not setting a time limit for the end of the present age. Instead, he describes the continually rebellious nature of the Jews who will oppose him and his messengers, even when these things are taking place.
21:34 Be careful. This is the central message of this section. Echoing the earlier descriptions of those occupied by the concerns of the present age (cf. 12:22,29,45; 16:19; 17:27–28), Jesus again calls his disciples to be faithful and alert since the day of Jesus' return will be upon them "suddenly," i.e., unexpectedly (cf. 12:40). For those who are not ready, his return will be "a trap" because it represents the divine judgment from which they cannot escape.
21:35 all those who live on the face of the whole earth. Unlike those who privately claim to be the Messiah (v. 8), Jesus' return will be a

21:36 [n]Mt 26:41
21:37 [o]Mt 26:55
[p]Mk 11:19 [q]Mt 21:1
21:38 [r]Jn 8:2
22:1 [s]Jn 11:55
22:2 [t]Mt 12:14
22:3 [u]Mt 4:10; Jn 13:2
[v]Mt 10:4
22:4 [w]ver 52;
Ac 4:1; 5:24
22:5 [x]Zec 11:12
22:7 [y]Ex 12:18-20;
Dt 16:5-8; Mk 14:12
22:8 [z]Ac 3:1,11;
4:13,19; 8:14

the face of the whole earth. 36Be always on the watch, and pray[n] that you may be able to escape all that
is about to happen, and that you may be able to stand before the Son of Man."
37Each day Jesus was teaching at the temple,[o] and each evening he went out[p] to spend the night
on the hill called the Mount of Olives,[q] 38and all the people came early in the morning to hear him
at the temple.[r]

Judas Agrees to Betray Jesus

22:1,2pp — Mt 26:2-5; Mk 14:1,2,10,11

22 Now the Festival of Unleavened Bread, called the Passover, was approaching,[s] 2and the chief
priests and the teachers of the law were looking for some way to get rid of Jesus,[t] for they were
afraid of the people. 3Then Satan[u] entered Judas, called Iscariot,[v] one of the Twelve. 4And Judas went
to the chief priests and the officers of the temple guard[w] and discussed with them how he might betray
Jesus. 5They were delighted and agreed to give him money.[x] 6He consented, and watched for an opportunity to hand Jesus over to them when no crowd was present.

The Last Supper

22:7-13pp — Mt 26:17-19; Mk 14:12-16
22:17-20pp — Mt 26:26-29; Mk 14:22-25; 1Co 11:23-25
22:21-23pp — Mt 26:21-24; Mk 14:18-21; Jn 13:21-30
22:25-27pp — Mt 20:25-28; Mk 10:42-45
22:33,34pp — Mt 26:33-35; Mk 14:29-31; Jn 13:37,38

7Then came the day of Unleavened Bread on which the Passover lamb had to be sacrificed.[y] 8Jesus
sent Peter and John,[z] saying, "Go and make preparations for us to eat the Passover."
9"Where do you want us to prepare for it?" they asked.
10He replied, "As you enter the city, a man carrying a jar of water will meet you. Follow him to the
house that he enters, 11and say to the owner of the house, 'The Teacher asks: Where is the guest room,
where I may eat the Passover with my disciples?' 12He will show you a large room upstairs, all furnished.
Make preparations there."

public event (cf. 17:24) witnessed by all. This event will be cosmic in scope (cf. vv. 25–27), destroying not just Jerusalem (vv. 6,20).

21:37 spend the night on the hill called the Mount of Olives. Jesus likely spent the night in "Bethphage [or] Bethany at the hill called the Mount of Olives" (19:29). Matthew (21:17) and Mark (11:11–12) both specify that he spent the night in Bethany.

22:1—23:56 *Betrayal and Death of Jesus.* Jesus' last week with his disciples includes betrayal (22:1–6) and denial (22:54–62), even after Jesus explains the meaning of his death (22:7–46). The final events unfold as Jesus is arrested (22:47–53), tried (22:63—23:25), crucified (23:26–49), and buried (23:50–56). This section is characterized by the explicit work of "Satan" (22:3) as "darkness reigns" (22:53). The darkness contrasts with the final section of the Gospel, which recounts Jesus' resurrection and ascension (24:1–53).

22:1–6 *Judas Agrees to Betray Jesus.* Luke begins Jesus' passion account by highlighting significant themes: (1) It takes place during the Passover Festival (v. 1). (2) The Jewish religious leaders reject Jesus (v. 2). (3) One of Jesus' own disciples betrays him (vv. 3–6). (4) Satan is behind those who oppose Jesus (v. 3).

22:1 In OT times, the Passover occurred on the evening of the 14th of Nisan (the first month in the Jewish calendar) to commemorate God's delivering his people from Egypt (Exod 12:3–14; Num 9:1–14). **the Festival of Unleavened Bread.** Occurred in the week that follows Passover, and Israelites were "to eat bread made without yeast" (Exod 12:15). In NT times, Jews often used the designations "Passover" and "Festival of Unleavened Bread" interchangeably.

22:2 chief priests. See note on Matt 2:4. **the teachers of the law.** See note on 5:17. They again join forces "to get rid of Jesus" (cf. 20:1).

22:3 Satan. Or "the devil"; he appears for the first time since leaving Jesus after his temptation "until an opportune time" (4:13). Jesus' ministry directly challenges Satan's power (10:18), and Jesus' death is the climax of that confrontation. John also highlights the role of Satan in Judas's betrayal of Jesus (John 13:2).

22:4 officers of the temple guard. Responsible for maintaining order in the temple area (cf. Acts 5:26) and protecting the chief priests (Acts 4:1; 5:24,26). **betray.** Greek *paradō*; fulfills Jesus' prophecy in 9:44, where the same Greek word is used: "The Son of Man is going to be delivered [*paradidosthai*] into the hands of men."

22:5 money. "Thirty pieces of silver" (Matt 26:15).

22:7–38 *The Last Supper.* This account has three parts: (1) meal preparation (vv. 7–13), (2) the meal itself (vv. 14–23), and (3) Jesus' teaching at the table (vv. 24–38). These correspond to three themes in this section: (1) Despite appearances to the contrary, Jesus is the Lord of history and the one in control. (2) Jesus' death establishes the new covenant between God and his people. (3) God's people must properly respond to the establishment of this new covenant.

22:7 This occurred the afternoon of Thursday, the 14th of Nisan (cf. Matt 26:17; Mark 14:12), before the evening Passover meal (when it was the 15th of Nisan).

22:10 a man carrying a jar of water. This is unusual since a woman would normally draw or carry water.

22:11 guest room. A room within an inn or within a regular residence. During pilgrim festivals when a crowd was expected, many people were willing to rent out their extra rooms to accommodate the pilgrims. Most Jews would share this Passover meal with their family members; Jesus' eating with his disciples may demonstrate the formation of the new family of God (cf. 8:19–21; 11:27–28).

13 They left and found things just as Jesus had told them.[a] So they prepared the Passover.
14 When the hour came, Jesus and his apostles[b] reclined at the table.[c] 15 And he said to them, "I have
eagerly desired to eat this Passover with you before I suffer.[d] 16 For I tell you, I will not eat it again until
it finds fulfillment in the kingdom of God."[e]
17 After taking the cup, he gave thanks and said, "Take this and divide it among you. 18 For I tell you
I will not drink again from the fruit of the vine until the kingdom of God comes."
19 And he took bread, gave thanks and broke it,[f] and gave it to them, saying, "This is my body given
for you; do this in remembrance of me."
20 In the same way, after the supper he took the cup, saying, "This cup is the new covenant[g] in my
blood, which is poured out for you.[a] 21 But the hand of him who is going to betray me is with mine on
the table.[h] 22 The Son of Man[i] will go as it has been decreed.[j] But woe to that man who betrays him!"
23 They began to question among themselves which of them it might be who would do this.
24 A dispute also arose among them as to which of them was considered to be greatest.[k] 25 Jesus said
to them, "The kings of the Gentiles lord it over them; and those who exercise authority over them call
themselves Benefactors. 26 But you are not to be like that. Instead, the greatest among you should be
like the youngest,[l] and the one who rules like the one who serves.[m] 27 For who is greater, the one who
is at the table or the one who serves? Is it not the one who is at the table? But I am among you as one
who serves.[n] 28 You are those who have stood by me in my trials. 29 And I confer on you a kingdom,[o] just
as my Father conferred one on me, 30 so that you may eat and drink at my table in my kingdom[p] and
sit on thrones, judging the twelve tribes of Israel.[q]
31 "Simon, Simon, Satan has asked[r] to sift all of you as wheat.[s] 32 But I have prayed for you,[t] Simon,
that your faith may not fail. And when you have turned back, strengthen your brothers."[u]

22:13 [a] Lk 19:32
22:14 [b] Mk 6:30 [c] Mt 26:20; Mk 14:17,18
22:15 [d] Mt 16:21
22:16 [e] Lk 14:15; Rev 19:9
22:19 [f] Mt 14:19
22:20 [g] Ex 24:8; Isa 42:6; Jer 31:31-34; Zec 9:11; 2Co 3:6; Heb 8:6; 9:15
22:21 [h] Ps 41:9
22:22 [i] Mt 8:20 [j] Ac 2:23; 4:28
22:24 [k] Mk 9:34; Lk 9:46
22:26 [l] 1Pe 5:5 [m] Mk 9:35; Lk 9:48
22:27 [n] Mt 20:28; Lk 12:37
22:29 [o] Mt 25:34; 2Ti 2:12
22:30 [p] Lk 14:15 [q] Mt 19:28
22:31 [r] Job 1:6-12 [s] Am 9:9
22:32 [t] Jn 17:9,15; Ro 8:34 [u] Jn 21:15-17

[a] *19,20* Some manuscripts do not have *given for you . . . poured out for you.*

22:13 just as Jesus had told them. Confirms Jesus' words in vv. 10–12 (cf. 19:32). This paves the way for reading the entire passion narrative. Jesus' death is not outside the Father's plan.
22:15 Jesus connects the meaning of Passover with his own suffering and death. In Jesus' time, Jews considered the Passover to be a sacrifice, which explains why Jesus' blood is poured out to establish the new covenant (v. 20).
22:16 fulfillment in the kingdom of God. Likely the Messianic banquet at the end times, when Jesus' return consummates God's promises to his people (cf. 14:15–16; 1 Cor 11:26). Jesus' death as the unblemished "Passover lamb" (1 Cor 5:7) provides the perfect atoning sacrifice for believers, but it is only when he returns that the full effect of this atoning sacrifice is felt and realized for these believers. The Lord's Supper, which looks back to Jesus' death, therefore also points forward to the greater consummation that is to come.
22:17 the cup. Luke mentions two cups (v. 20); see the textual problem noted in the NIV text note on vv. 19–20. In the Jewish Passover meal, people drink two cups before sharing the lamb and two more cups afterward. The cup referred to here probably refers to the first cup of the meal. The other NT accounts mention only one cup (Matt 26:26–27; Mark 14:22–24; 1 Cor 11:23–26), probably to draw attention to the parallel symbols of the cup ("blood") and the bread ("body").
22:19 bread. "Made without yeast" (Exod 12:8). **This is my body.** This clause is subject to various interpretations, but in the context of the Passover meal in which the redemptive significance of Jesus' death is explained, the verb "is" should be understood in the sense of "signifies" or "represents." **for you.** Jesus' atoning death is substitutionary (cf. Rom 5:6,8; 8:32; 14:15; 1 Cor 15:3; Gal 2:20). **do this in remembrance of me.** Jesus urges the disciples to participate in his death without losing sight of the final consummation of his redemptive work (cf. vv. 16,18).
22:20 After the supper Jesus uses the cup to explain why his death is significant. Shedding his blood inaugurates the "new covenant" (cf. Jer 31:31; Ezek 16:60; 1 Cor 11:25) since "it is the blood that makes atonement for one's life" (Lev 17:11) and a covenant can be made only with blood (cf. Exod 24:8). **poured out for you.** The preposition "for" likely carries the sense of "in the place of" (cf. John 11:50; 2 Cor 5:14; 1 Tim 2:5–6), pointing to Jesus' atoning death as substitutionary (see v. 19 and note; cf. Isa 53:12).
22:22 as it has been decreed. God's sovereign plan must be fulfilled (cf. 9:44; 18:31). **woe to that man who betrays him!** Humans are responsible in the midst of God's unfolding plan.
22:25 Benefactors. Patrons who supported people lower in rank in return for honor and authority. Jesus warns his disciples not to imitate such benefactors, who serve solely to consolidate their own status and power. Unlike the benefactors, "the one who serves" (v. 26) does so without expecting anything in return since the sole purpose is to bring honor to the one they serve.
22:27 as one who serves. This may be a general reference to Jesus' numerous acts of humility (cf. John 13:5), but in this context, where his death is in view (cf. vv. 19–20), he is likely referring to his death as the ultimate example of humble service. Similar remarks in Matthew and Mark make Jesus' atoning death even more explicit: the Son of Man serves "to give his life as a ransom for many" (Mark 10:45; cf. Matt 20:28).
22:28 You ... have stood by me. This becomes a call for the disciples to continue to be faithful to Jesus. **my trials.** Jesus' suffering and rejection.
22:29 Jesus promises a "kingdom," recalling 12:32 and referring to the future consummation of God's plan in history. The disciples will begin to participate in this kingdom when Jesus is enthroned through his resurrection and ascension (Acts 2:34–36).
22:30 sit on thrones, judging the twelve tribes of Israel. Share in the royal Messianic kingdom (cf. Ps 122:4–5). The role of Jesus' disciples shows that God reconstitutes his people; membership in the 12 tribes of Israel is defined no longer by ethnic identity but by a relationship with Jesus.
22:31 sift ... as wheat. Satan's temptation and the division that causes such temptation.
22:32 when you have turned back. Jesus focuses on Peter's repentance and renewal after he denies Jesus.

PASSION WEEK

The Roman road climbed steeply to the crest of the Mount of Olives, affording spectacular views of the Desert of Judea to the east and of Jerusalem across the Kidron Valley to the west.

❶ Arrival in Bethany

FRIDAY (John 12:1)

Jesus arrived in Bethany six days before the Passover to spend some time with his friends, Mary, Martha, and Lazarus. On the following Tuesday evening, while Jesus was still in Bethany, Mary anointed his feet with costly perfume as an act of humility. This tender expression indicated Mary's devotion to Jesus and her willingness to serve him.

❷ Sabbath—day of rest

SATURDAY

Not mentioned in the Gospels.

The Lord spent the Sabbath day in traditional fashion with his friends.

❸ The "Triumphal" Entry

SUNDAY (Matt 21:1–11; Mark 11:1–11; Luke 19:28–44; John 12:12–19)

On the first day of the week Jesus rode into Jerusalem on a donkey, fulfilling an ancient prophecy (Zech 9:9). The crowd welcomed him with the words of Ps 118:25–26, thus ascribing to him a Messianic title as the agent of the Lord, the coming King of Israel.

❹ Clearing of the temple

MONDAY (Matt 21:12–17; Mark 11:15–18; Luke 19:45–48)

Jesus returned to the temple and found the court of the Gentiles full of traders and money changers making a large profit. Jesus drove them out and overturned their benches and tables.

❺ Day of controversy and parables

TUESDAY (Matt 21:23—24:51; Mark 11:27—13:37; Luke 20:1—21:36)

IN JERUSALEM

Jesus evaded the traps set by the priests.

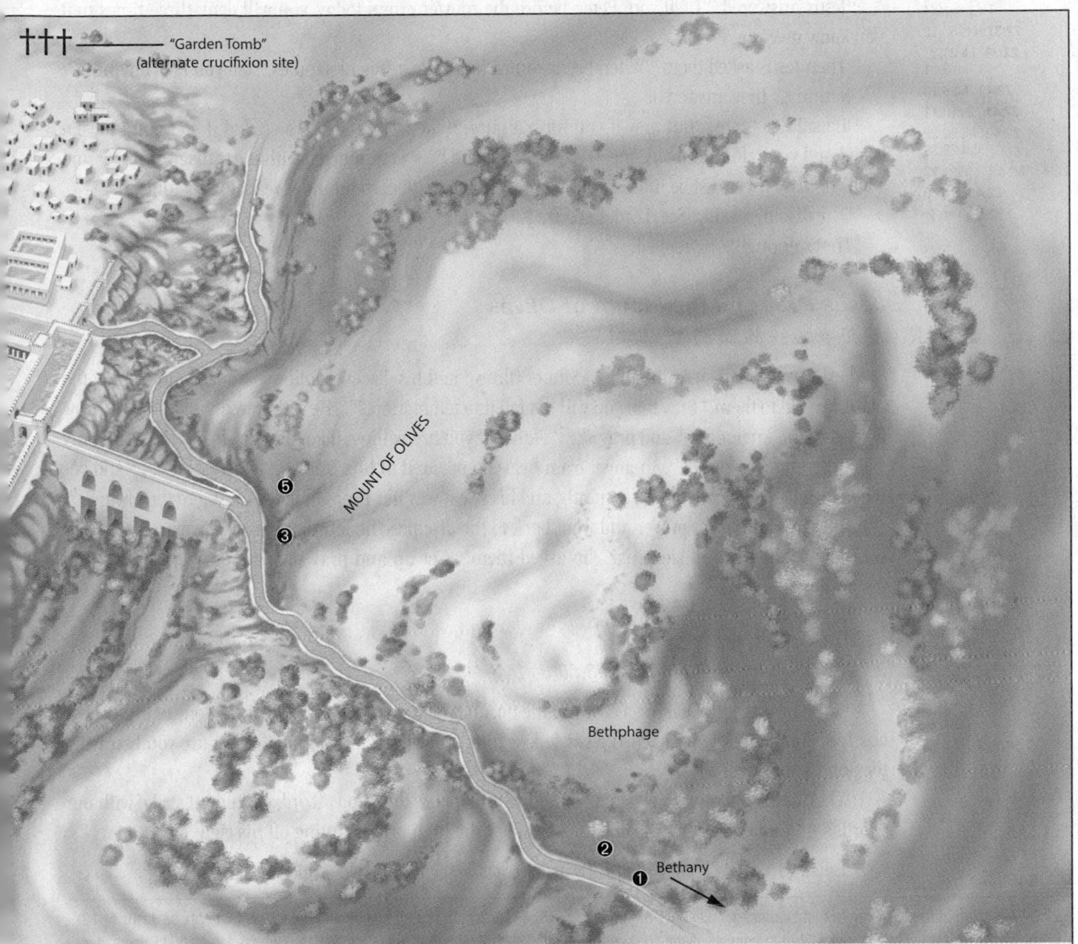

ON THE MOUNT OF OLIVES OVERLOOKING JERUSALEM

(Tuesday afternoon, exact location unknown)

Jesus taught in parables and warned the people against the Pharisees. He predicted the destruction of Herod's great temple and told his disciples about future events, including his own return.

Day of rest

WEDNESDAY

Although the Gospels do not mention this day, the counting of the days (Mark 14:1; John 12:1) seems to indicate that there was another day about which the Gospels record nothing.

❻ Passover, Last Supper

THURSDAY (Matt 26:17–30; Mark 14:12–26; Luke 22:7–23)

In an upper room Jesus prepared both himself and his disciples for his death. He gave the Passover meal a new meaning. The loaf of bread and cup of wine represented his body soon to be sacrificed and his blood soon to be shed. And so he instituted the "Lord's Supper." After singing a hymn they went to Gethsemane, where Jesus prayed in agony, knowing what lay ahead for him.

❼ Crucifixion

FRIDAY (Matt 27; Mark 15; Luke 22:66—23:56; John 18:28—19:37)

Following betrayal, arrest, desertion, false trials, denial, condemnation, beatings, and mockery, Jesus was required to carry his cross to "the place of the skull" (Matt 27:33), where he was crucified with two other prisoners.

❽ In the tomb

Jesus' body was placed in the tomb before 6:00 p.m. Friday evening, when the Sabbath began and all work stopped, and it lay in the tomb throughout the Sabbath.

❾ Resurrection

SUNDAY (Matt 28:1–10; Mark 16:1–8; Luke 24:1–49; John 20)

Early in the morning, women went to the tomb and found that the stone closing the tomb's entrance had been rolled back. An angel told them Jesus was alive and gave them a message. Jesus appeared to Mary Magdalene in the garden, to Peter, to two disciples on the road to Emmaus and later that day to all the disciples but Thomas.

22:33 [v] Jn 11:16
22:35 [w] Mt 10:9,10; Lk 9:3; 10:4
22:37 [x] Isa 53:12
22:39 [y] Lk 21:37 [z] Mt 21:1
22:40 [a] Mt 6:13
22:41 [b] Lk 18:11
22:42 [c] Mt 20:22 [d] Mt 26:39
22:43 [e] Mt 4:11; Mk 1:13
22:46 [f] ver 40
22:49 [g] ver 38

33 But he replied, "Lord, I am ready to go with you to prison and to death."[v]
34 Jesus answered, "I tell you, Peter, before the rooster crows today, you will deny three times that
you know me."
35 Then Jesus asked them, "When I sent you without purse, bag or sandals,[w] did you lack anything?"
"Nothing," they answered.
36 He said to them, "But now if you have a purse, take it, and also a bag; and if you don't have a
sword, sell your cloak and buy one. 37 It is written: 'And he was numbered with the transgressors'[a];[x] and
I tell you that this must be fulfilled in me. Yes, what is written about me is reaching its fulfillment."
38 The disciples said, "See, Lord, here are two swords."
"That's enough!" he replied.

Jesus Prays on the Mount of Olives

22:40-46pp — Mt 26:36-46; Mk 14:32-42

39 Jesus went out as usual[y] to the Mount of Olives,[z] and his disciples followed him. 40 On reaching the
place, he said to them, "Pray that you will not fall into temptation."[a] 41 He withdrew about a stone's throw
beyond them, knelt down[b] and prayed, 42 "Father, if you are willing, take this cup[c] from me; yet not my
will, but yours be done."[d] 43 An angel from heaven appeared to him and strengthened him.[e] 44 And being in anguish, he prayed more earnestly, and his sweat was like drops of blood falling to the ground.[b]
45 When he rose from prayer and went back to the disciples, he found them asleep, exhausted from
sorrow. 46 "Why are you sleeping?" he asked them. "Get up and pray so that you will not fall into
temptation."[f]

Jesus Arrested

22:47-53pp — Mt 26:47-56; Mk 14:43-50; Jn 18:3-11

47 While he was still speaking a crowd came up, and the man who was called Judas, one of the Twelve,
was leading them. He approached Jesus to kiss him, 48 but Jesus asked him, "Judas, are you betraying
the Son of Man with a kiss?"
49 When Jesus' followers saw what was going to happen, they said, "Lord, should we strike with our
swords?"[g] 50 And one of them struck the servant of the high priest, cutting off his right ear.

[a] *37* Isaiah 53:12 [b] *43,44* Many early manuscripts do not have verses 43 and 44.

22:34 The third of the four Roman night watches (midnight–3:00 a.m.) is known as the "crow of the cocks," but in popular usage "before the rooster crows" can refer to any time before daybreak. Jesus foreknows and controls events even in the midst of betrayal and rejection.
22:36 Jesus reverses what he earlier instructed (9:3; 10:4) either because the present crisis is urgent or because he anticipates that the disciples will take lengthy journeys to bring the gospel to foreign lands, where a "sword" may become necessary (the Greek word for "sword" often appears in ancient travel accounts as something a traveler might carry).
22:37 Jesus quotes from Isa 53:12. Like the righteous sufferer in Isa 53, Jesus died vicariously as the righteous servant of God. **fulfilled in me ... reaching its fulfillment.** God sovereignly planned Jesus' death. In light of this divine plan, Jesus' death will lead to both his resurrection and the spread of the gospel (cf. 24:46–47). Therefore Jesus' call to the disciples to prepare themselves (cf. v. 36) looks beyond his own death to the wider fulfillment of God's plan.
22:38 swords. Cannot prevent Jesus from dying on the cross (cf. vv. 49–51).
22:39–46 *Jesus Prays on the Mount of Olives.* Jesus is committed to obeying his Father (v. 42). By twice warning his disciples not to "fall into temptation" (vv. 40,46), Jesus situates the following events within the spiritual battle between God and Satan.
22:39 Mount of Olives. Where Jesus spent the nights during his final week of ministry in the Jerusalem area (21:37). Matt 26:36 identifies it as "Gethsemane," at the foot of the Mount of Olives.
22:40 temptation. Satan is behind the forces that oppose Jesus (4:13) and is here behind those (such as Peter) who fail to stand by Jesus during his trials (cf. vv. 31,54–62).
22:42 cup. Often refers to God's wrath (cf. Ps 75:8; Isa 51:17; Jer 25:15). Here it represents Jesus' death (cf. Matt 20:22–23; Mark 10:38–39) that bears the consequence of God's wrath against those who sin against him (see v. 20 and note).
22:43–44 See NIV text note.
22:44 like drops of blood. May refer to hematidrosis, a rare condition in which a person sweats blood when under extreme stress. But the use of the term "like" indicates that this is to be taken as a simile: Jesus sweats like he is bleeding in this time of agony.
22:45–46 asleep ... sleeping. They failed to comprehend fully the significance of the events unfolding before them.
22:45 sorrow. The disciples knew that Jesus would depart from them (cf. 9:31–32).
22:47–53 *Jesus Arrested.* As Jesus prophesied (v. 21), one of his own betrays him (v. 47), and the power of "darkness" challenges him (v. 53). But his fulfilled prophecies indicate that the power of darkness has no ultimate control over the transpiring events.
22:47–48 Matt 26:48–49 and Mark 14:44–45 describe how Judas arranged to kiss Jesus. Luke focuses on what Jesus asks Judas.
22:50 Unlike earlier references to the "chief priests" (vv. 2,4; 19:47), Luke here introduces the high priest, who plays an important part in Jesus' trial (v. 54). John 18:13,24–25 provide the name of the high

51But Jesus answered, "No more of this!" And he touched the man's ear and healed him.
52Then Jesus said to the chief priests, the officers of the temple guard,[h] and the elders, who had come
for him, "Am I leading a rebellion, that you have come with swords and clubs? 53Every day I was with you
in the temple courts,[i] and you did not lay a hand on me. But this is your hour[j]—when darkness reigns."[k]

Peter Disowns Jesus

22:55-62pp — Mt 26:69-75; Mk 14:66-72; Jn 18:16-18,25-27

54Then seizing him, they led him away and took him into the house of the high priest.[l] Peter followed at a distance.[m] 55And when some there had kindled a fire in the middle of the courtyard and had
sat down together, Peter sat down with them. 56A servant girl saw him seated there in the firelight. She
looked closely at him and said, "This man was with him."
57But he denied it. "Woman, I don't know him," he said.
58A little later someone else saw him and said, "You also are one of them."
"Man, I am not!" Peter replied.
59About an hour later another asserted, "Certainly this fellow was with him, for he is a Galilean."[n]
60Peter replied, "Man, I don't know what you're talking about!" Just as he was speaking, the rooster
crowed. 61The Lord[o] turned and looked straight at Peter. Then Peter remembered the word the Lord
had spoken to him: "Before the rooster crows today, you will disown me three times."[p] 62And he went
outside and wept bitterly.

The Guards Mock Jesus

22:63-65pp — Mt 26:67,68; Mk 14:65; Jn 18:22,23

63The men who were guarding Jesus began mocking and beating him. 64They blindfolded him and
demanded, "Prophesy! Who hit you?" 65And they said many other insulting things to him.[q]

Jesus Before Pilate and Herod

22:67-71pp — Mt 26:63-66; Mk 14:61-63; Jn 18:19-21
23:2,3pp — Mt 27:11-14; Mk 15:2-5; Jn 18:29-37
23:18-25pp — Mt 27:15-26; Mk 15:6-15; Jn 18:39–19:16

66At daybreak the council[r] of the elders of the people, both the chief priests and the teachers of the
law, met together,[s] and Jesus was led before them. 67"If you are the Messiah," they said, "tell us."

22:52 [h] ver 4
22:53 [i] Mt 26:55 [j] Jn 12:27 [k] Mt 8:12; Jn 1:5; 3:20
22:54 [l] Mt 26:57; Mk 14:53 [m] Mt 26:58; Mk 14:54; Jn 18:15
22:59 [n] Lk 23:6
22:61 [o] Lk 7:13 [p] ver 34
22:65 [q] Mt 16:21
22:66 [r] Mt 5:22 [s] Mt 27:1; Mk 15:1

priest (Caiaphas; see Luke 3:2 and note; Acts 4:6), his servant (Malchus), and the disciple who struck the servant (Simon Peter).

22:51 Only Luke mentions that Jesus heals the servant.

22:53 your [plural] hour—when darkness reigns. Satan (see note on v. 3) is the power behind the Jewish religious leaders. Although Satan appears to be in control, Jesus' death and resurrection is the beginning of their demise. The risen Lord's commission to Paul reflects this reversal (Acts 26:17–18).

22:54–62 *Peter Disowns Jesus.* As Jesus prophesied (v. 34), Peter denies him. Peter's experience only strengthens him, and he in turn will "strengthen [his] brothers" (v. 32).

22:54 the high priest. Caiaphas is the current high priest (cf. Matt 26:57), and his house was a gathering place for Jewish religious leaders. John 18:13 also mentions the involvement of his father-in-law, Annas, a former high priest (see Luke 3:2 and note). Jesus' series of trials begins here.

22:59 he is a Galilean. Peter's "accent" gave him away (Matt 26:73; cf. Judg 12:5–6). Although many Galileans would have been present during the Passover Festival, not too many were likely to be in the courtyard of the high priest's house.

22:61 The Lord ... looked straight at Peter. Only Luke mentions this. Jesus was in Caiaphas's house, and he must have looked through the window and caught Peter's eyes. It shows that Jesus accurately predicted Peter's denials (v. 34) and that Jesus has compassion for Peter despite his failure (v. 32).

22:63–65 *The Guards Mock Jesus.* Jesus is a prophet whose own people reject him (cf. 4:24).

22:63 mocking and beating. Fulfills what Jesus predicted in 18:32–33, which fits how the OT sometimes describes the treatment of prophets (cf. Isa 50:6).

22:66—23:25 *Jesus Before Pilate and Herod.* This section contains the four trials of Jesus: (1) before the council of the elders (22:66–71), (2) before Pilate (23:1–6), (3) before Herod (23:7–12), and (4) before Pilate again (23:13–25). It presents Jesus as "the Son of God" (22:70), the "Messiah" (23:2), and "the king of the Jews" (23:3), and reveals that Jesus is innocent even in the eyes of human authorities (23:14–15,20,22). The emphasis on Jesus' identity here points forward to the resurrection account, which shows that Jesus the innocent one (23:4,14) is indeed the risen "Lord" (24:34).

22:66 At daybreak. A formal trial of the Sanhedrin to pass the death sentence could be held only after daylight. To hold a trial on the morning of a feast day is unusual, although it could happen when the circumstances demanded it. **the council of the elders.** Dealt primarily with legal and civic matters within the Jewish community (cf. Acts 5:21; 22:30; 23:1). The high priest presided over this council (cf. Acts 5:21,27), which probably convened in or near his own house. In Jesus' day, it is unclear whether this was an ad hoc committee or a stable body that met regularly.

22:67 Others already identified Jesus as the Messiah (e.g., 2:11,26; 4:41). The Jewish religious leaders test Jesus: if he accepts this title,

22:68 [t] Lk 20:3-8
22:69 [u] Mk 16:19
22:70 [v] Mt 4:3 [w] Mt 27:11; Lk 23:3
23:1 [x] Mt 27:2; Mk 15:1; Jn 18:28
23:2 [y] ver 14 [z] Lk 20:22 [a] Jn 19:12
23:4 [b] ver 14,22,41; Mt 27:23; Jn 18:38; 1Ti 6:13; 2Co 5:21
23:5 [c] Mk 1:14
23:6 [d] Lk 22:59
23:7 [e] Mt 14:1; Lk 3:1
23:8 [f] Lk 9:9
23:9 [g] Mk 14:61
23:11 [h] Mk 15:17-19; Jn 19:2,3
23:12 [i] Ac 4:27
23:14 [j] ver 4
23:16 [k] ver 22; Mt 27:26; Jn 19:1; Ac 16:37; 2Co 11:23,24
23:18 [l] Ac 3:13,14

Jesus answered, "If I tell you, you will not believe me, 68 and if I asked you, you would not answer.[t]
69 But from now on, the Son of Man will be seated at the right hand of the mighty God."[u]
70 They all asked, "Are you then the Son of God?"[v]
He replied, "You say that I am."[w]
71 Then they said, "Why do we need any more testimony? We have heard it from his own lips."

23 Then the whole assembly rose and led him off to Pilate.[x] 2 And they began to accuse him, saying, "We have found this man subverting our nation.[y] He opposes payment of taxes to Caesar[z]
and claims to be Messiah, a king."[a]
3 So Pilate asked Jesus, "Are you the king of the Jews?"
"You have said so," Jesus replied.
4 Then Pilate announced to the chief priests and the crowd, "I find no basis for a charge against
this man."[b]
5 But they insisted, "He stirs up the people all over Judea by his teaching. He started in Galilee[c] and
has come all the way here."
6 On hearing this, Pilate asked if the man was a Galilean.[d] 7 When he learned that Jesus was under
Herod's jurisdiction, he sent him to Herod,[e] who was also in Jerusalem at that time.
8 When Herod saw Jesus, he was greatly pleased, because for a long time he had been wanting to see
him.[f] From what he had heard about him, he hoped to see him perform a sign of some sort. 9 He plied
him with many questions, but Jesus gave him no answer.[g] 10 The chief priests and the teachers of the
law were standing there, vehemently accusing him. 11 Then Herod and his soldiers ridiculed and mocked
him. Dressing him in an elegant robe,[h] they sent him back to Pilate. 12 That day Herod and Pilate became friends[i]—before this they had been enemies.
13 Pilate called together the chief priests, the rulers and the people, 14 and said to them, "You brought
me this man as one who was inciting the people to rebellion. I have examined him in your presence and
have found no basis for your charges against him.[j] 15 Neither has Herod, for he sent him back to us; as you
can see, he has done nothing to deserve death. 16 Therefore, I will punish him[k] and then release him." [17][a]
18 But the whole crowd shouted, "Away with this man! Release Barabbas to us!"[l] 19 (Barabbas had
been thrown into prison for an insurrection in the city, and for murder.)
20 Wanting to release Jesus, Pilate appealed to them again. 21 But they kept shouting, "Crucify him!
Crucify him!"

[a] *17* Some manuscripts include here words similar to Matt. 27:15 and Mark 15:6.

they will accuse him of stirring up the people (23:5); if he does not, it will invalidate his entire ministry.

22:69 Jesus' answer alludes to Ps 110:1 (cf. Dan 7:13–14) and refers to his resurrection and ascension (cf. Acts 2:33–35; 5:31; 7:55–56). He indirectly affirms that he is the Davidic Messiah, and the one who is judged becomes the one who judges.

22:70–71 Jesus' allusion to Ps 110:1 (v. 69) leads the leaders to ask him if he is the Son of God (cf. 1:35; 4:41), especially since the one sitting at the right hand of God is often understood to be God's son (cf. Ps 2:4–7). Because Jesus does not refuse to accept the titles "Messiah" and "Son of God," the leaders consider him a threat to the rule of Caesar (cf. 23:2).

23:1 After the trial before the Jewish council, Jesus is transferred to the Roman prefect Pilate (see 3:1 and note). This fulfills Jesus' prediction that "he will be delivered over to the Gentiles" (18:32).

23:2 Messiah, a king. Although Jesus does claim this (cf. v. 3; 22:67), he is not "subverting [the] nation" by leading a political movement, and he never "opposes payment of taxes to Caesar" (cf. 20:25). The Jewish leaders twist Jesus' words to present him as a political revolutionary before the Roman authorities.

23:3–4 Jesus is "the king of the Jews," but his kingdom is not of this earth (22:69). Pilate correctly concludes that there is "no basis for a charge" against Jesus.

23:5 Judea. The land of the Jews that included lower Galilee. In the time of Jesus it had a significant Jewish presence (cf. 1:5).

23:7 The jurisdiction of Herod Antipas included Galilee and Perea (3:1 and note). Because of the difficult relationship between Pilate and the Jews (13:1), Pilate eagerly sent Jesus to Herod, "who was also in Jerusalem" during the Passover. When Pilate, who usually resided in Caesarea, traveled to Jerusalem for the major pilgrim festivals, he would stay in the palace of Herod the Great, while Herod Antipas would stay in the nearby Hasmonean Palace.

23:8 Herod earlier wanted to see Jesus (9:7–9), though the Pharisees previously alleged that Herod was hoping to get rid of him (13:31).

23:11 Herod and his soldiers dress Jesus in an "elegant robe" to mock his acceptance of the title "king of the Jews" (v. 3; cf. Matt 27:28; Mark 15:18; John 19:2–3).

23:15 he has done nothing to deserve death. Pilate responds to the accusation of the Jews that Jesus is "worthy of death" (Matt 26:66; Mark 14:64).

23:18 Release Barabbas. Because "it was the custom at the festival to release a prisoner whom the people requested" (Mark 15:6; cf. Matt 27:15; John 18:39). Acts 3:14 contrasts Jesus and Barabbas: "You disowned the Holy and Righteous One and asked that a murderer be released to you."

23:21 Crucify him! In Roman times, crucifixion was among the cruelest forms of punishment and was reserved for prisoners and slaves. In the OT, if someone was hung on a pole, it meant they were under God's curse, but the body was only hung on a pole after the criminal was put to death (Deut 21:22–23). In Jesus' time, Jews had the right to sentence a person to death only if that person violated the sanctity of the temple. In

Model of the Herodian palace, a possible location at which Pilate would have stayed during the festival.

[22]For the third time he spoke to them: "Why? What crime has this man committed? I have found in him no grounds for the death penalty. Therefore I will have him punished and then release him."[m]
[23]But with loud shouts they insistently demanded that he be crucified, and their shouts prevailed.
[24]So Pilate decided to grant their demand. [25]He released the man who had been thrown into prison for insurrection and murder, the one they asked for, and surrendered Jesus to their will.

The Crucifixion of Jesus

23:33-43pp — Mt 27:33-44; Mk 15:22-32; Jn 19:17-24

[26]As the soldiers led him away, they seized Simon from Cyrene,[n] who was on his way in from the
country, and put the cross on him and made him carry it behind Jesus.[o] [27]A large number of people
followed him, including women who mourned and wailed[p] for him. [28]Jesus turned and said to them,
"Daughters of Jerusalem, do not weep for me; weep for yourselves and for your children.[q] [29]For the
time will come when you will say, 'Blessed are the childless women, the wombs that never bore and the
breasts that never nursed!'[r] [30]Then

> " 'they will say to the mountains, "Fall on us!"
> and to the hills, "Cover us!" '[a][s]

[a] *30* Hosea 10:8

23:22 [m] ver 16
23:26 [n] Mt 27:32 [o] Mk 15:21; Jn 19:17
23:27 [p] Lk 8:52
23:28 [q] Lk 19:41-44; 21:23,24
23:29 [r] Mt 24:19
23:30 [s] Isa 2:19; Hos 10:8; Rev 6:16

other cases they relied on the power of the Roman magistrates to carry out the death sentence.

23:25 surrendered Jesus to their will. Pilate delivers Jesus to the Jews without realizing that ultimately it is God's will that has prevailed (Acts 2:23).

23:26–43 *The Crucifixion of Jesus.* Despite Jesus' humiliating death, Luke presents him as the Messiah (vv. 35,39), the Chosen One (v. 35), the King of the Jews (v. 38), and a righteous man (v. 47). People respond differently to Jesus' death: Simon of Cyrene (v. 26), the women who followed Jesus (vv. 27,49,55–56), the rulers (v. 35), the soldiers (vv. 36–37), the criminals (vv. 39–43), the centurion (v. 47), the crowd (v. 48), and Joseph (vv. 50–54).

23:26 Simon. "The father of Alexander and Rufus" (Mark 15:21). He may have come to Jerusalem for the Passover Festival (cf. Acts 2:10), though some "Jews of Cyrene" apparently resided permanently in Jerusalem (cf. Acts 6:9). **Cyrene.** A city in North Africa with a large Jewish population. **cross.** The vertical pole was already erected at the place of crucifixion, but the criminal was responsible for carrying the crossbeam to the place of his execution.

23:28 Daughters of Jerusalem. Those who mourn for Jesus. In the OT, this often refers to the city of Jerusalem (cf. Ps 9:14; Jer 6:2,23; Mic 4:8). The irony is clear: instead of weeping for Jesus, they (i.e., the people of Jerusalem) should weep for themselves because of their impending fall (cf. Jer 9:17–19).

23:29 wombs ... breasts. Jesus uses images of barren women for calamities that will fall on Jerusalem (cf. 21:23). Isa 54:1–8 uses similar language for God's reversing the fortunes of his suffering people when they witness his salvation. But because they refuse to accept salvation, Jesus uses the images for the coming judgment.

23:30 Fall on us! Jesus quotes from Hos 10:8, evoking the wider

23:31 [t]Eze 20:47
23:32 [u]Isa 53:12; Mt 27:38; Mk 15:27; Jn 19:18
23:34 [v]Mt 11:25 [w]Mt 5:44 [x]Ps 22:18
23:35 [y]Ps 22:17 [z]Isa 42:1
23:36 [a]Ps 22:7 [b]Ps 69:21; Mt 27:48
23:37 [c]Lk 4:3,9
23:38 [d]Mt 2:2
23:39 [e]ver 35,37
23:41 [f]ver 4
23:42 [g]Mt 16:27
23:43 [h]2Co 12:3,4; Rev 2:7
23:44 [i]Am 8:9
23:45 [j]Ex 26:31-33; Heb 9:3,8 [k]Heb 10:19,20

31 For if people do these things when the tree is green, what will happen when it is dry?"[t]
32 Two other men, both criminals, were also led out with him to be executed.[u] 33 When they came to
the place called the Skull, they crucified him there, along with the criminals—one on his right, the
other on his left. 34 Jesus said, "Father,[v] forgive them, for they do not know what they are doing."[a][w] And
they divided up his clothes by casting lots.[x]
35 The people stood watching, and the rulers even sneered at him.[y] They said, "He saved others; let
him save himself if he is God's Messiah, the Chosen One."[z]
36 The soldiers also came up and mocked him.[a] They offered him wine vinegar[b] 37 and said, "If you
are the king of the Jews,[c] save yourself."
38 There was a written notice above him, which read: THIS IS THE KING OF THE JEWS.[d]
39 One of the criminals who hung there hurled insults at him: "Aren't you the Messiah? Save yourself and us!"[e]
40 But the other criminal rebuked him. "Don't you fear God," he said, "since you are under the same
sentence? 41 We are punished justly, for we are getting what our deeds deserve. But this man has done
nothing wrong."[f]
42 Then he said, "Jesus, remember me when you come into your kingdom.[b]"[g]
43 Jesus answered him, "Truly I tell you, today you will be with me in paradise."[h]

The Death of Jesus

23:44-49pp — Mt 27:45-56; Mk 15:33-41; Jn 19:29-30

44 It was now about noon, and darkness came over the whole land until three in the afternoon,[i]
45 for the sun stopped shining. And the curtain of the temple[j] was torn in two.[k] 46 Jesus called out with

[a] *34* Some early manuscripts do not have this sentence. [b] *42* Some manuscripts *come with your kingly power*

context of Hos 10, in which God would judge idolatrous Israel. As in the time of Hosea, the Jews who reject Jesus will call out to the mountains, "Fall on us!" because they will no longer be able to bear the magnitude of God's judgment.

23:31 when the tree is green. When Jesus and his gospel are present. **when it is dry.** The time of judgment. God's people will suffer much because they rejected Jesus when he proclaimed God's salvation to them.

23:33 place called the Skull. Matthew and Mark refer to this with the Aramaic term "Golgotha" and define it as "the place of the skull" (Matt 27:33; Mark 15:22; cf. John 19:17). The English term Calvary comes from the Latin *Calvaria* (i.e., "the Skull"). The place is probably called the Skull because the Romans used it for executions, though it is also possible that the topographical features resembled a skull. The exact location remains unknown.

23:34 they do not know what they are doing. The apostles repeatedly note this in their preaching (Acts 3:17; 13:27; 14:16; 17:30; 26:9). Jesus becomes the model for his followers by willingly forgiving those who persecuted him (cf. Acts 7:60). **they divided up his clothes by casting lots.** Alludes to the similar fate of the righteous sufferer of Ps 22:18.

23:35 Like v. 34, this quotation alludes to Ps 22: "All who see me mock me ... 'He trusts in the LORD,' they say, 'let the LORD rescue him' " (Ps 22:7–8). Ironically, Jesus saves others precisely by not saving himself. The readers should therefore understand that his death on the cross is not inconsistent with his identity as "God's Messiah" (cf. 9:20) and "the Chosen One" (cf. 9:35).

23:36 offered him wine vinegar. This parallels the fate of the psalmist who was similarly insulted with the offer of vinegar (Ps 69:21).

23:38 written notice. Listed the crime of the person being crucified. John 19:19–20 specifies that the notice "was written in Aramaic, Latin and Greek" with the full title "JESUS OF NAZARETH, THE KING OF THE JEWS."

23:40–42 Only Luke mentions this criminal trusting Jesus after criticizing the other criminal who insulted Jesus (cf. Matt 27:41–44; Mark 15:31–32).

23:42 remember me. "Have mercy on me" or "Deliver me" (cf. Exod 2:24; 6:5; Lev 26:42–45; Ps 105:42).

23:43 today. God's salvation is immediately made available to this criminal (cf. 2:11; 4:21; 5:26; 19:5,9). **paradise.** Depicts the new creation (Isa 51:3; Ezek 28:13; 31:8–9) by reflecting the language of the Garden of Eden (cf. Gen 2:8–10). Jesus' response suggests that the criminal does not have to wait for the fulfillment of Jesus' "kingdom" (v. 42) to experience God's salvation.

23:44–49 *The Death of Jesus.* Jesus' rejection and suffering now culminate in his death on the cross. Darkness coming "over the whole land" (v. 44) shows that the battle between God and Satan is cosmically significant. The "darkness" caused by the stopping of "the sun" (vv. 44–45a) underlines the event's cosmic significance, and the tearing of "the curtain of the temple" (v. 45b) symbolizes its redemptive significance. This portrays Jesus as "a righteous man" (v. 47) even before his resurrection.

23:44 about noon ... until three in the afternoon. The Greek uses the typical Roman way of reckoning time: "about the sixth hour ... until the ninth hour." **darkness.** The manifestation of God's wrath (Jer 13:16; Joel 2:10; Amos 8:9). Here it represents the battle between God and Satan (22:53).

23:45 curtain. Likely the one that divides the Most Holy Place from the Holy Place (Exod 26:33; Lev 21:23; 24:3), although it could also be the one that separates the temple from the outer court (Exod 26:36–37; 38:18; Num 3:26). Tearing it in two can have two layers of meaning: (1) One can now approach God directly through Jesus' atoning death (Heb 9–10). (2) The temple is no longer to be considered as the center of God's presence.

23:46 into your hands I commit my spirit. When Jesus quotes Ps 31:5a, he may also have the second part of the verse in mind: "Deliver me, LORD, my faithful God" (Ps 31:5b). These words reflect his trust in his Father.

a loud voice,[l] "Father, into your hands I commit my spirit."[a m] When he had said this, he breathed
his last.[n]

[47]The centurion, seeing what had happened, praised God[o] and said, "Surely this was a righteous
man." [48]When all the people who had gathered to witness this sight saw what took place, they beat their
breasts[p] and went away. [49]But all those who knew him, including the women who had followed him
from Galilee,[q] stood at a distance,[r] watching these things.

23:46 [l]Mt 27:50 [m]Ps 31:5; 1Pe 2:23 [n]Jn 19:30
23:47 [o]Mt 9:8
23:48 [p]Lk 18:13
23:49 [q]Lk 8:2 [r]Ps 38:11
23:51 [s]Lk 2:25,38
23:54 [t]Mt 27:62
23:55 [u]ver 49
23:56 [v]Mk 16:1; Lk 24:1 [w]Ex 12:16; 20:10

The Burial of Jesus

23:50-56pp — Mt 27:57-61; Mk 15:42-47; Jn 19:38-42

[50]Now there was a man named Joseph, a member of the Council, a good and upright man, [51]who
had not consented to their decision and action. He came from the Judean town of Arimathea, and he
himself was waiting for the kingdom of God.[s] [52]Going to Pilate, he asked for Jesus' body. [53]Then he took
it down, wrapped it in linen cloth and placed it in a tomb cut in the rock, one in which no one had yet
been laid. [54]It was Preparation Day,[t] and the Sabbath was about to begin.

[55]The women who had come with Jesus from Galilee[u] followed Joseph and saw the tomb and how
his body was laid in it. [56]Then they went home and prepared spices and perfumes.[v] But they rested on
the Sabbath in obedience to the commandment.[w]

[a] *46* Psalm 31:5

Inside a kokhim of the Tomb of the Kings in Jerusalem. See illustration, p. 2058.

23:47 this was a righteous man. This can mean "this was an innocent man" (cf. Prov 6:17; Joel 3:19), but it likely carries a fuller sense of being righteous in God's presence. This is consistent with Luke's use of the Greek term elsewhere (cf. v. 50 ["upright"]; 1:6,17; 2:25; 12:57 ["right"]) and would also explain why the centurion "praised God." The claim found in Matt 27:54 and Mark 15:39 further elaborates the meaning of this claim: "Surely he/this man was the Son of God!" This Gentile centurion contrasts with the Jews, who "disowned the Holy and Righteous One" (Acts 3:14).
23:48 beat their breasts. Because of their grief or guilt (cf. 18:13).
23:50–56 *The Burial of Jesus.* This transitional passage describes Jesus' burial and paves the way for discovering the empty tomb. The 12 disciples are absent because they apparently abandoned Jesus, but Joseph and the women honor him with a proper burial, although even they do not anticipate the coming resurrection.
23:50 good and upright man. Like Zechariah and Elizabeth (1:6).
23:51 Arimathea. The exact location remains unknown (cf. Matt 27:57; Mark 15:43; John 19:38). **waiting for the kingdom of God.** Like Simeon (2:25).
23:53 tomb cut in the rock. Reflects the wealth of the owner. **one in which no one had yet been laid.** This explains the later discovery that the tomb was entirely empty when Jesus was raised from the dead (cf. 24:12,24).
23:54 Preparation Day. The day before the Sabbath. **Sabbath was about to begin.** This explains why Jesus was buried in a hurry (cf. Deut 21:22–23) and why the women returned after the Sabbath with proper "spices and perfumes" (v. 56; cf. 24:1).

24:1 [x]Lk 23:56
24:3 [y]ver 23,24
24:4 [z]Jn 20:12
24:6 [a]Mt 17:22,23; Mk 9:30-31; Lk 9:22; 24:44
24:7 [b]Mt 8:20 [c]Mt 16:21
24:8 [d]Jn 2:22
24:10 [e]Lk 8:1-3 [f]Mk 6:30
24:11 [g]Mk 16:11
24:12 [h]Jn 20:3-7 [i]Jn 20:10
24:13 [j]Mk 16:12
24:15 [k]ver 36
24:16 [l]Jn 20:14; 21:4

Jesus Has Risen

24:1-10pp — Mt 28:1-8; Mk 16:1-8; Jn 20:1-8

24 On the first day of the week, very early in the morning, the women took the spices they had
prepared[x] and went to the tomb. 2They found the stone rolled away from the tomb, 3but when
they entered, they did not find the body of the Lord Jesus.[y] 4While they were wondering about this, suddenly two men in clothes that gleamed like lightning[z] stood beside them. 5In their fright the women
bowed down with their faces to the ground, but the men said to them, "Why do you look for the living
among the dead? 6He is not here; he has risen! Remember how he told you, while he was still with you
in Galilee:[a] 7'The Son of Man[b] must be delivered over to the hands of sinners, be crucified and on the
third day be raised again.' "[c] 8Then they remembered his words.[d]

9When they came back from the tomb, they told all these things to the Eleven and to all the others.
10It was Mary Magdalene, Joanna, Mary the mother of James, and the others with them[e] who told this
to the apostles.[f] 11But they did not believe[g] the women, because their words seemed to them like nonsense. 12Peter, however, got up and ran to the tomb. Bending over, he saw the strips of linen lying by
themselves,[h] and he went away,[i] wondering to himself what had happened.

On the Road to Emmaus

13Now that same day two of them were going to a village called Emmaus, about seven miles[a] from
Jerusalem.[j] 14They were talking with each other about everything that had happened. 15As they talked
and discussed these things with each other, Jesus himself came up and walked along with them;[k] 16but
they were kept from recognizing him.[l]

17He asked them, "What are you discussing together as you walk along?"

a *13* Or about 11 kilometers

24:1–53 *Resurrection and Ascension of Jesus.* Luke provides the basis of the early Christian confession: "You killed the author of life, but God raised him from the dead. We are witnesses of this" (Acts 3:15). Luke begins with the discovery of the empty tomb (vv. 1–12); discusses the meaning of Jesus' death and resurrection (vv. 13–35); links his life, death, and resurrection to the disciples' continued mission as his witnesses (vv. 36–49); and ends with Jesus' ascension (vv. 50–53), reserving a more detailed description for the beginning of his second volume (Acts 1:1–11).

24:1–12 *Jesus Has Risen.* Like the other Gospel writers, Luke begins with the loyal women discovering the empty tomb (vv. 1–3). They are surprised (vv. 4–8). But the focus quickly shifts to how stubborn Jesus' disciples and followers are; they neither believe nor understand what they have heard (vv. 9–12). They utterly fail to appreciate this most striking miracle. This ignorance motif paves the way for vv. 13–35, which discuss the meaning and significance of Jesus' death and resurrection.

24:1 first day of the week. Sunday. See note on John 20:1. **very early in the morning.** Sabbath ends Saturday night, and it was then that the women bought spices for Jesus' body (Mark 16:1). When "it was still dark" (John 20:1) Sunday morning, they started out on the way to the tomb. They arrived at the tomb as soon as the sun rose after the Sabbath rest (cf. Matt 28:1; Mark 16:2).

24:2 stone. To block the entrance to the tomb. Pilate ordered the tomb sealed because of Jesus' prediction of his own resurrection (cf. Matt 27:62–66). **rolled away.** By the angel (cf. Matt 28:2).

24:4 two men. "Angels" (v. 23; cf. Matt 28:2,5; John 20:12). Luke provides a more comprehensive account by noting two angels (cf. John 20:12), while Matthew only mentions the one who opened the tomb (Matt 28:2) and Mark simply mentions the presence of a "young man" (Mark 16:5). **clothes that gleamed like lightning.** Likely describes not simply the color of their clothing (bright white) but also their heavenly glory (cf. 9:29; Acts 1:10; 10:30). **stood.** Matt 28:2 and John 20:12 mention sitting, likely describing a different point of the event.

24:6 with you in Galilee. Jesus predicted his death and resurrection during his Galilean ministry (v. 7; cf. 9:22) and to these women, "who had followed him from Galilee" (23:49).

24:9 the Eleven. Assumes that Judas has died (Matt 27:1–10) and highlights that they need to replace him to complete the number 12 (cf. Acts 1:15–26). **all the others.** "All those who knew him" (23:49).

24:10 Mary Magdalene, Joanna, Mary the mother of James. Among those who followed Jesus from Galilee (8:2–3; Mark 15:40). Mary Magdalene is always named first among those who came to the tomb (cf. Matt 28:1; Mark 16:1; John 20:1), and she is the first to encounter the risen Lord (cf. John 20:11–18).

24:12 Peter. John also mentions "the other disciple, the one Jesus loved" (John 20:2; see note on John 13:23). **saw the strips of linen lying by themselves.** With "the cloth that had been wrapped around Jesus' head" (John 20:7). **wondering to himself what had happened.** Peter was aware that something significant had happened (cf. 1:21,63; 2:18).

24:13–35 *On the Road to Emmaus.* Found only in this Gospel, this summarizes Jesus' life and significance: he is Israel's powerful prophet and redeemer; yet his people rejected him and crucified him on the cross; but he rose from the dead on the third day (vv. 19–24). His disciples need to search through the Scriptures to understand the full significance of all that happened concerning him (vv. 25–32). The disciples can only confess, "The Lord has risen" (v. 34) when they understand the significance of Jesus' resurrection within God's redemptive plan.

24:13 two of them. Among those who followed Jesus from Galilee (23:49); one is "Cleopas" (v. 18). **Emmaus.** All we know about the location of this place is that it is "seven miles [about 11 kilometers] from Jerusalem."

24:16 The risen Jesus probably wanted them to understand his life, death, and resurrection within God's wider plan of salvation before they recognized him (cf. vv. 25–27).

They stood still, their faces downcast. 18 One of them, named Cleopas,[m] asked him, "Are you the only
one visiting Jerusalem who does not know the things that have happened there in these days?"
19 "What things?" he asked.
"About Jesus of Nazareth,"[n] they replied. "He was a prophet,[o] powerful in word and deed before God
and all the people. 20 The chief priests and our rulers[p] handed him over to be sentenced to death, and
they crucified him; 21 but we had hoped that he was the one who was going to redeem Israel.[q] And what
is more, it is the third day[r] since all this took place. 22 In addition, some of our women amazed us.[s]
They went to the tomb early this morning 23 but didn't find his body. They came and told us that they
had seen a vision of angels, who said he was alive. 24 Then some of our companions went to the tomb
and found it just as the women had said, but they did not see Jesus."[t]
25 He said to them, "How foolish you are, and how slow to believe all that the prophets have spoken!
26 Did not the Messiah have to suffer these things and then enter his glory?"[u] 27 And beginning with

24:18 [m] Jn 19:25
24:19 [n] Mk 1:24 [o] Mt 21:11
24:20 [p] Lk 23:13
24:21 [q] Lk 1:68; 2:38; 21:28 [r] Mt 16:21
24:22 [s] ver 1-10
24:24 [t] ver 12
24:26 [u] Heb 2:10; 1Pe 1:11

24:19 a prophet, powerful in word and deed. They might have identified Jesus with Moses, who "was powerful in speech and action" (Acts 7:22) and whose own people rejected him (Acts 7:27–28), which Jesus' own people did when they "handed him over to be sentenced to death" (v. 20). To these disciples, Jesus may simply be "one of the prophets of long ago [who] has come back to life" (9:19). They cannot comprehend what the empty tomb means (vv. 22–24).

24:21 we had hoped. They apparently were disappointed that Jesus did not fulfill their expectations. **redeem Israel.** Recalls what Simeon and Anna expected (2:25,38), but what these two disciples here meant is likely the political deliverance of God's people from the hands of the Gentiles.

24:23 vision of angels. May simply highlight that the event was supernatural (cf. 1:22; Acts 26:19).

24:24 some of our companions ... did not see Jesus. Cf. v. 12; suggests they doubted the women's report was reliable.

24:25 foolish. They refused to trust God and his promises (cf. Gal 3:1, 3; 1 Tim 6:9; Titus 3:3): they did not believe the women's report, "all that the prophets have spoken," or Jesus' own teachings (v. 26).

24:26 Cf. v. 26 with 9:22.

24:27 Moses and all the Prophets. Refers to "all the Scriptures." Jesus does not fulfill only the Messianic prophecies contained in the OT; he fulfills the whole Scripture because it points to him as the climax of God's delivering his people. There are several implications: (1) In terms of continuity, Jesus fulfills rather than abrogates the OT Scriptures. (2) In terms of discontinuity, he brings something new as he completes God's redemptive plan as contained in those Scriptures. (3) In terms of interpretation, all Scriptures should be read in light of God's work through Jesus, and these Scriptures in turn explain the significance of Jesus and his mission.

JESUS' RESURRECTION APPEARANCES

APPEARANCE	PLACE	TIME	MATTHEW	MARK	LUKE	JOHN	ACTS	1 COR
The empty tomb	Jerusalem	Resurrection Sunday	28:1–10	16:1–8	24:1–12	20:1–9		
To Mary Magdalene in the garden	Jerusalem	Resurrection Sunday		16:9–11		20:11–18		
To other women	Jerusalem	Resurrection Sunday	28:9–10					
To two people going to Emmaus	Road to Emmaus	Resurrection Sunday		16:12–13	24:13–32			
To Peter	Jerusalem	Resurrection Sunday			24:34			15:5
To the ten disciples in the upper room	Jerusalem	Resurrection Sunday			24:36–43	20:19–25		
To the 11 disciples in the upper room	Jerusalem	Following Sunday		16:14		20:26–31		15:5
To seven disciples fishing	Sea of Galilee	Some time later				21:1–23		
To the 11 disciples on a mountain	Galilee	Some time later	28:16–20	16:15–18				
To more than 500	Unknown	Some time later						15:6
To James	Unknown	Some time later						15:7
To his disciples at his ascension	Mount of Olives	40 days after Jesus' resurrection			24:44–49		1:3–8	
To Paul	Damascus	Several years later					9:1–19 22:3–16 26:9–18	9:1

24:27 [v] Ge 3:15; Nu 21:9; Dt 18:15 [w] Isa 7:14; 9:6; 40:10,11; 53; Eze 34:23; Da 9:24; Mic 7:20; Mal 3:1 [x] Jn 1:45
24:30 [y] Mt 14:19
24:31 [z] ver 16
24:32 [a] Ps 39:3 [b] ver 27,45
24:34 [c] 1Co 15:5
24:35 [d] ver 30,31
24:36 [e] Jn 20:19, 21,26; 14:27
24:37 [f] Mk 6:49
24:39 [g] Jn 20:27; 1Jn 1:1
24:43 [h] Ac 10:41
24:44 [i] Lk 9:45; 18:34 [j] Mt 16:21; Lk 9:22,44; 18:31-33; 22:37 [k] ver 27 [l] Ps 2; 16; 22; 69; 72; 110; 118
24:47 [m] Ac 5:31; 10:43; 13:38 [n] Mt 28:19

Moses[v] and all the Prophets,[w] he explained to them what was said in all the Scriptures concerning himself.[x]

28 As they approached the village to which they were going, Jesus continued on as if he were going farther. 29 But they urged him strongly, "Stay with us, for it is nearly evening; the day is almost over." So he went in to stay with them.

30 When he was at the table with them, he took bread, gave thanks, broke it[y] and began to give it to them. 31 Then their eyes were opened and they recognized him,[z] and he disappeared from their sight. 32 They asked each other, "Were not our hearts burning within us[a] while he talked with us on the road and opened the Scriptures[b] to us?"

33 They got up and returned at once to Jerusalem. There they found the Eleven and those with them, assembled together 34 and saying, "It is true! The Lord has risen and has appeared to Simon."[c] 35 Then the two told what had happened on the way, and how Jesus was recognized by them when he broke the bread.[d]

Jesus Appears to the Disciples

36 While they were still talking about this, Jesus himself stood among them and said to them, "Peace be with you."[e]

37 They were startled and frightened, thinking they saw a ghost.[f] 38 He said to them, "Why are you troubled, and why do doubts rise in your minds? 39 Look at my hands and my feet. It is I myself! Touch me and see;[g] a ghost does not have flesh and bones, as you see I have."

40 When he had said this, he showed them his hands and feet. 41 And while they still did not believe it because of joy and amazement, he asked them, "Do you have anything here to eat?" 42 They gave him a piece of broiled fish, 43 and he took it and ate it in their presence.[h]

44 He said to them, "This is what I told you while I was still with you:[i] Everything must be fulfilled[j] that is written about me in the Law of Moses,[k] the Prophets and the Psalms."[l]

45 Then he opened their minds so they could understand the Scriptures. 46 He told them, "This is what is written: The Messiah will suffer and rise from the dead on the third day, 47 and repentance for the forgiveness of sins will be preached in his name[m] to all nations,[n] beginning at Jerusalem. 48 You are

24:30 took bread, gave thanks, broke it and began to give it to them. Jesus also did this at his last supper with his disciples before he died (22:19; see 9:16).

24:31–32 their eyes were opened ... opened the Scriptures. God opened their eyes so that they could recognize Jesus (cf. vv. 16,35) and understand who he is in light of what the Scriptures promise. While in the past many, including Jesus' own disciples, failed to comprehend and refused to accept him and his mission, God's direct intervention through the Scriptures changes not only minds but hearts.

24:34 appeared to Simon. Jesus did this during the time between Simon Peter's witnessing the empty tomb (v. 12) and this gathering of the disciples (cf. 1 Cor 15:5; see NIV text note there). The following story highlights Peter's role as an important witness to Jesus' resurrection (cf. Acts 2:29–32; 3:13–15).

24:36–49 *Jesus Appears to the Disciples.* As in the earlier account of when Jesus appeared to his disciples (vv. 13–32), the OT is important to understanding Jesus' identity and mission (cf. v. 11), but this account uniquely emphasizes (1) the proof of Jesus' bodily resurrection (vv. 36–43), (2) the connection between the ministry of Jesus and the apostles (vv. 45–48), and (3) Jesus' promising "power from on high" (v. 49). This provides a firm foundation for the book of Acts, the second volume of Luke's writings.

24:37 ghost. A spirit that "does not have flesh and bones" (v. 39; cf. Acts 23:8–9).

24:39 Jesus assumes that the disciples can recognize him by looking at his hands and feet because both had been nailed to the cross when he was crucified. John 20:25 makes this explicit when Thomas asks to "see the nail marks in his hands and put [his] finger where the nails were." This account focuses not only on who Jesus is but also on the physical presence of Jesus' resurrected body.

24:43 ate. Jesus further confirms that he is not simply a spirit but that he also has a physical body that can consume food.

24:44 This echoes v. 27: Jesus fulfills "all the Scriptures." **the Law of Moses, the Prophets and the Psalms.** The three-part Hebrew OT; the Psalms, being the longest book, represents the Writings. This all-encompassing claim points to Jesus as the one in whom all promises are fulfilled, including the redemption of not only his people (1:68) but the Gentiles as well (3:6) and the final restoration of all things (Acts 3:19–21).

24:46 This is what is written. What follows does not exactly quote the OT, but vv. 46–49 allude to Pss 16:8–11; 110:1; Isa 49:6; 53:7–8; 55:3. The entire OT, rather than only individual verses, points to Jesus as the climax of God's redemptive plan.

24:47 repentance for the forgiveness of sins. The prediction of Christ's death and resurrection is not separated from the acts of repentance that it demands (cf. 3:8; Acts 20:21; 26:20). This response will in turn lead to the forgiveness of sins (cf. 7:47–49; Acts 2:38; 5:31; 26:18). **will be preached.** Jesus' death and resurrection connect to the apostles' mission. **to all nations, beginning at Jerusalem.** This is essentially the outline of the book of Acts. This mission is grounded in the OT, and the risen Lord commissions it (Acts 1:8).

24:48–49 As the mission "to all nations" (v. 47) anticipates Jesus' call to go "to the ends of the earth" (Acts 1:8c), so "you are witnesses of these things" (v. 48) anticipates "you will be my witnesses" (Acts 1:8b), and "stay in the city until you have been clothed with power from on high" (v. 49) anticipates "you will receive power when the Holy Spirit comes on you" (Acts 1:8a). That the apostles are "witnesses" fulfills the prophetic call to God's people to be his witnesses (Isa 43:10; 44:8), and the descent of the "power from on high" (v. 49) also fulfills the words of the prophets (Isa 32:15; see Acts 2:4).

witnesses[o] of these things. 49I am going to send you what my Father has promised;[p] but stay in the city
until you have been clothed with power from on high."

The Ascension of Jesus

50When he had led them out to the vicinity of Bethany,[q] he lifted up his hands and blessed them.
51While he was blessing them, he left them and was taken up into heaven.[r] 52Then they worshiped him
and returned to Jerusalem with great joy. 53And they stayed continually at the temple,[s] praising God.

24:48 [o] Ac 1:8; 2:32; 5:32; 13:31; 1Pe 5:1
24:49 [p] Jn 14:16; Ac 1:4
24:50 [q] Mt 21:17
24:51 [r] 2Ki 2:11
24:53 [s] Ac 2:46

24:50–53 *The Ascension of Jesus.* Luke concludes his Gospel with the theme of adoration in response to Jesus' "blessing them" (v. 51): "they worshiped him" (v. 52) and were "praising God" (v. 53). This is how the disciples should have responded to the life, death, and resurrection of Jesus. Acts 1:1–11 presents a more detailed account of Jesus' final moments on earth, and Luke reserves his second volume (the book of Acts) for the fuller significance of Jesus' ascension: "God has made this Jesus, whom you crucified, both Lord and Messiah" (Acts 2:36), and as such he has become the "Lord of all" (Acts 10:36). It is because of the lordship of Christ that "everyone who calls on the name of the Lord will be saved" (Acts 2:21; cf. Joel 2:32).

24:51 left them. But Acts 1:11 notes the promise following Jesus' visible departure: Jesus "will come back in the same way you have seen him go into heaven."

24:52 God is the only proper object of worship (4:8; Acts 24:14). **they worshiped him.** They recognized Jesus as the divine Son of God. **with great joy.** Jesus radically reversed the sadness they felt when they thought he was still dead (cf. v. 17).

24:53 at the temple. Luke begins with experiencing God's grace in the temple (1:8) and ends with the disciples returning to the temple. The early disciples would continue to meet in the temple (Acts 2:46–47; 3:1–10; 5:21,42), although they also realize that God's presence is not limited to this temple (Acts 7:47–50). **praising God.** The only appropriate response to God's mighty acts through his Son, Jesus. In the OT, praising God is a way to recount his mighty deeds for his people (Exod 15:1–18; Deut 32:1–43; 1 Chr 16:8–36; Ps 22:23–31); the disciples would continue to praise him by proclaiming the salvation that he has accomplished through his Son (Acts 2:14–41; 3:11–26; 4:8–17; 10:34–43; 13:16–41). The readers of this Gospel are likewise called to extend this act of worship.

INTRODUCTION TO JOHN

AUTHOR

Like the Gospels according to Matthew, Mark, and Luke, the Fourth Gospel (as John's Gospel is often called) does not explicitly assert its author's name. As far as we can prove, the title "According to John" (still used in certain translations like the KJV) was attached to it as soon as the four Gospels began to circulate together as "the fourfold Gospel." In part, no doubt, this was to distinguish it from the rest of the collection, but it may have served as the title from the beginning.

The most straightforward reading of the evidence for authorship is still the traditional one: it is highly probable that John the son of Zebedee, "the disciple whom Jesus loved" (see note on 13:23), wrote the Fourth Gospel (cf. 21:24 and note). This makes no difference whatsoever to the book's authority (after all, Luke's Gospel does not claim to be by an eyewitness), but it does affect how we think about the book's background and purpose.

PLACE

The Fourth Gospel does not specify where John wrote it. Four places are commonly proposed: Alexandria, Antioch, Palestine, and Ephesus. The traditional view is that John wrote it in Ephesus, and no other location has the support of the church fathers. If John wrote it while residing in Ephesus, then perhaps he prepared it for readers in this general part of the empire while still hoping for the widest possible circulation.

DATE

Almost any date between about AD 55 and 95 is possible. None of the arguments for a more precise date is entirely convincing. But if we must suggest a date for when John wrote the Fourth Gospel, we may very tentatively advance AD 80 – 85. One of many reasons for this is to allow some time between the writing of John's Gospel and the writing of his three letters, which were probably written in the early 90s and which combat an incipient form of Gnosticism and respond in part to a Gnostic misunderstanding of the Fourth Gospel (see Introduction to 1 – 3 John: Gnosticism).

PURPOSE AND ADDRESSEES

The proper place to begin is with John's own purpose statement (20:30 – 31). John presents specific "signs" (20:30) — *sign*ificant displays of power that point beyond themselves to the deeper realities that we can perceive with eyes of faith. John includes the eight "signs," numbering only the first two (see "The Eight Signs of John's Gospel," p. 2141).

Many scholars hold that this Gospel was written to encourage churches connected with John, churches that were feeling the stress of progressive alienation from Jewish synagogues. This is certainly possible. But while John clearly wrote 1 John to encourage Christians (1 John 5:13), the purpose for his Gospel seems to be evangelistic. This impression is confirmed by the solid evidence that the first purpose clause in John 20:31 can be rendered "that you may

THE EIGHT SIGNS OF JOHN'S GOSPEL

SIGN	VERSES
1. Changing water into wine	(2:1 – 11); "the first of the signs" (2:11)
2. Healing an official's son	(4:43 – 54); "the second sign" (4:54)
3. Healing a disabled man at a pool	(5:1 – 15; see "signs" in 6:2)
4. Feeding the 5,000	(6:1 – 14; see "sign" in 6:14 and "signs" in 6:26)
5. Walking on water	(6:16 – 21)
6. Healing a man born blind	(9:1 – 12; see "such signs" in 9:16)
7. Raising Lazarus from the dead	(11:1 – 44; see "signs" in 11:47 and "this sign" in 12:18)
8. Rising from the dead	(20:1 – 31; see "many other signs" in 20:30)

believe that the Messiah, the Son of God, is Jesus." Thus, the fundamental question the Fourth Gospel addresses is not "Who is Jesus?" but "Who is the Messiah, the Son of God?" In its context, the latter is a question of identity, not of kind: that is, the question "Who is the Messiah?" should not here be taken to mean "What kind of Messiah are you talking about?" but "So you claim to know who the Messiah is. Prove it, then: Who is he?"

The Christians of John's day would not have asked that kind of question because they already knew the answer. The most likely people to ask that sort of question would have been Jews and Jewish proselytes who knew what "the Messiah" meant, had some sort of Messianic expectation, and were perhaps in dialogue with Christians and wanted to know more.

In short, not only is John's Gospel evangelistic in its purpose but aims in particular to evangelize Jews outside of the Holy Land as well as Jewish proselytes.

COMPARISON WITH THE SYNOPTIC GOSPELS

Differences

1. John omits many of Jesus' words and works that are characteristic of the Synoptic Gospels (Matthew, Mark, and Luke): narrative parables, exorcisms, the account of the transfiguration, the record of the institution of the Lord's Supper, and many of Jesus' more concise sayings.

2. John omits or barely mentions themes central to the Synoptic Gospels, especially the theme of the kingdom of God.

3. John includes a substantial amount of material not mentioned in the Synoptic Gospels. This includes nearly all the material in John 1 – 5, Jesus' frequent visits to Jerusalem and the events that take place there, the resurrection of Lazarus, Jesus' explicit identification with God (1:1,18; 20:28), and Jesus' series of "I am" statements (e.g., 6:35; 8:12; 10:7,11; 11:25; 14:6; 15:1). John also includes extended dialogues and discourses not found elsewhere in the Gospels.

4. Doubtless some of this can be accounted for by the different geographic focus: John focuses on Jesus' ministry in the south (Judea and Samaria), while the Synoptic Gospels focus on Jesus' ministry in the north (Galilee). But one cannot legitimately reduce all distinctions to questions of geography.

Similarities

It appears likely that John read Mark, Luke, and possibly even Matthew, but we cannot prove that John directly borrowed from the Synoptic Gospels (in the sense that Matthew and Luke likely borrowed from Mark).

1. Parallel incidents include the Spirit's anointing of Jesus as John the Baptist testified (1:32), the contrast between John the Baptist's baptism with water and the Messiah's anticipated baptism with the Spirit (1:33), feeding the 5,000 (6:1 – 15), and Jesus' walking on water (6:16 – 21).

2. Many sayings are at least partially parallel (e.g., 4:35,44; 5:29; 10:14 – 15; 12:39 – 40).

3. More significant yet are the subtle parallels: both John and the Synoptic Gospels describe a Jesus given to colorful metaphors and proverbs, many drawn from the world of nature (e.g., 4:37; 5:19 – 20a; 8:35; 9:4; 10:1 – 18; 11:9 – 10; 12:24; 15:1 – 16; 16:21). All four Gospels depict Jesus with a unique sense of sonship to his heavenly Father; all of them note the distinctive authority Jesus displays in his teaching; all of them show Jesus referring to himself as the Son of Man, a title used neither by nor toward anyone else (John 12:34 is not a real exception).

MIRACLES OF JESUS

HEALING MIRACLES	MATTHEW	MARK	LUKE	JOHN
Man with leprosy	8:2–4	1:40–42	5:12–13	
Roman centurion's servant	8:5–13		7:1–10	
Peter's mother-in-law	8:14–15	1:30–31	4:38–39	
Two men from Gadara	8:28–34	5:1–15	8:27–35	
Paralyzed man	9:2–7	2:3–12	5:18–25	
Woman with bleeding	9:20–22	5:25–29	8:43–48	
Two blind men	9:27–31			
Mute, demon-possessed man	9:32–33			
Man with a shriveled hand	12:10–13	3:1–5	6:6–10	
Blind, mute, demon-possessed man	12:22		11:14	
Canaanite woman's daughter	15:21–28	7:24–30		
Demon-possessed boy	17:14–18	9:17–29	9:38–43	
Two blind men (including Bartimaeus)	20:29–34	10:46–52	18:35–43	
Deaf mute		7:31–37		
Demon-possessed man in synagogue		1:23–26	4:33–35	
Blind man at Bethsaida		8:22–26		
Crippled woman			13:11–13	
Man with abnormal swelling			14:1–4	
Ten men with leprosy			17:11–19	
The high priest's servant			22:50–51	
Official's son at Capernaum				4:46–54
Sick man at pool of Bethesda				5:1–9
Man born blind				9:1–7
MIRACLES SHOWING POWER OVER NATURE				
Calming the storm	8:23–27	4:37–41	8:22–25	
Walking on water	14:25	6:48–51		6:19–21
Feeding the 5,000	14:15–21	6:35–44	9:12–17	6:6–13
Feeding the 4,000	15:32–38	8:1–9		
Coin in fish's mouth	17:24–27			
Fig tree withered	21:18–22	11:12–14,20–25		
Large catch of fish			5:4–11	
Water turned into wine				2:1–11
Another large catch of fish				21:1–11
MIRACLES OF RAISING THE DEAD				
Jairus's daughter	9:18–19,23–25	5:22–24,38–42	8:41–42,49–56	
Widow's son at Nain			7:11–15	
Lazarus				11:1–44

4. Even more impressive are the many places where John and the Synoptic Gospels represent an *interlocking* tradition, i.e., where they mutually reinforce or explain each other without necessarily borrowing from each other.

John explains several events from the Synoptic Gospels. For example, the charge that Jesus had threatened to destroy the temple (Mark 14:58; 15:29) finds its only adequate explanation in John 2:19. Mark gives no reason as to why the Jewish authorities should bother bringing Jesus to Pilate; John provides the reason (18:31–32). Only John explains why Peter can be placed within the high priest's courtyard (18:15–18; cf. Mark 14:54,66–72).

Conversely, numerous features in John are explained by details reported only in the Synoptic Gospels. For instance, in chs. 18–19 the trial plunges so quickly into the Roman court that it is difficult to see just what judicial action the Jews have taken, if any, to precipitate this trial; the Synoptic Gospels provide the answer (see "Jesus' Trials," p. 2055).

CHARACTERISTICS AND THEMES

John has written a subtle book that he expects people to read more than once; new insights then come to light on subsequent readings. John's thought is so wonderfully integrated that attempts to compartmentalize it by itemizing its components are destined in some measure to misrepresent it. Nevertheless, among John's more important contributions are the following:

1. *Enriching perspective.* By telling the same story from another angle, John adds a stereoscopic depth to the picture of Jesus that we might not gain from the Synoptic Gospels alone.

2. *Son of God.* Fundamental to all else that is said of him, Jesus is peculiarly the Son of God, or simply the Son. He is functionally submissive to the Father and does and says only those things the Father gives him to do and say, but he does everything that the Father does (5:19–30). Jesus discloses nothing more and nothing less than the words and deeds of God. See "Sonship," p. 2664.

3. *Cross.* Despite the heavy emphasis on Jesus as the one who reveals his Father, salvation does not come merely by revelation (as in Gnosticism; see Introduction to 1–3 John: Gnosticism). All the movement of the plot is toward the cross and resurrection. The cross is not merely a revelatory moment. It is the victory of the Lamb of God (1:29,36); the life that is given for the world (6:25–58); the death of the shepherd for his sheep (10:11–18); the sacrifice of one man for his nation (11:50–52); and the triumph of the obedient Son, who by his death, resurrection, and ascension gives us life, peace, joy, and the Spirit (chs. 14–16).

4. *Tension between "already" and "not yet."* All the major NT writings display the tension that (1) God's promised "last days" have already arrived in Jesus' ministry, death, resurrection, and exaltation, and (2) the fullness of hope is not yet here but still to come. Different authors display this tension in different ways, and John's distinctive emphasis is bound up with his use of the "present and future" theme (e.g., 2:4; 7:6): Believers have already "crossed over from death to life" (5:24). The hour "is coming and has now come" (4:23; 5:25). Jesus has given his peace, but in this world we will have trouble (16:33). In the wake of Jesus' exaltation and his gift of the Spirit, we can possess eternal life right now, but this is never at the expense of all future hope (5:28–30).

5. *Holy Spirit.* By giving the Spirit, Jesus introduces what is characteristic under the new covenant (3:5–8; 7:37–39). Jesus gives the Spirit, the Advocate, in consequence of his death and exaltation (chs. 14–16). The elements of what came to be called the doctrine of the Trinity find their clearest articulation in John's Gospel.

6. *Use of the Old Testament.* Although John does not cite the OT as frequently as Matthew does, his use of the OT is characterized by an extraordinary number of allusions and above all by his insistence that Jesus, in certain respects, replaces or fulfills revered figures and institutions from the old covenant (e.g., tabernacle, temple, serpent, Passover, vine, Moses). Six passages say that Scripture or some OT writer speaks or writes of Christ, though John does not cite specific passages (1:45; 2:22; 3:10–15; 5:39,45–46; 20:9).

7. *Misunderstandings.* People frequently misunderstand Jesus (see notes on 2:19–22; 4:11–12,31–33; 5:46; 6:28; 7:35–36; 8:19,21–22,33,52–53,57; 10:6; 11:11–14; 12:16; 13:6–10; 14:5; 16:17–19,29–30; 18:11), and John skillfully employs irony concerning this (see notes on 5:12,46; 6:42; 7:3–4,27,35,41,47–48,49; 8:21–22,41,53,54; 10:33; 13:38; 18:28,35; 19:3,22,31). No Gospel better preserves the ways in which Jesus' contemporaries (including his own disciples) misunderstood him until after his exaltation. This is significant for reflecting on the relation between the old and new covenants. See "Covenant," p. 2646.

8. *People of God.* John devotes much attention to the concept of belonging to the people of God. Although there is nothing on church order per se, there is much on the election, life, origin, nature, witness, suffering, fruit-bearing, prayer, love, and unity of God's people.

9. *Vocabulary.* John, in certain respects and on relatively restricted topics, provides greater depth than do the Synoptic Gospels. This is a major reason that John uses a smaller vocabulary than that found in the Synoptic Gospels;

John uses certain words and expressions repeatedly (e.g., believe, love, world, send, Father) to reflect important themes.

10. *God's sovereignty and human responsibility.* John repeatedly explores the complexities that bind together election, faith, and the function of signs. If faith bursts forth in consequence of what is revealed in the signs, then signs legitimately serve as a basis for faith (e.g., 10:38). Yet in contrast, Jesus rebukes people for depending on signs (4:48). In the last analysis, faith turns on sovereign election by the Son (15:16) and on being part of the Father's gift to the Son (6:37–44). This truth is at the heart of a book that is persistently evangelistic.

OUTLINE

I. Prologue: The Word Became Flesh (1:1–18)

II. Jesus' Self-Disclosure in Word and Deed (1:19—10:42)

A. Prelude to Jesus' Public Ministry (1:19–51)
1. John the Baptist Denies Being the Messiah (1:19–28)
2. John Testifies About Jesus (1:29–34)
3. John's Disciples Follow Jesus (1:35–42)
4. Jesus Calls Philip and Nathanael (1:43–51)

B. Early Ministry: Signs, Works, and Words (2:1—4:54)
1. Jesus Changes Water Into Wine (2:1–12)
2. Jesus Clears the Temple Courts (2:13–25)
3. Jesus Teaches Nicodemus (3:1–21)
4. John Testifies Again About Jesus (3:22–36)
5. Jesus Talks With a Samaritan Woman (4:1–26)
6. The Disciples Rejoin Jesus (4:27–38)
7. Many Samaritans Believe (4:39–42)
8. Jesus Heals an Official's Son (4:43–54)

C. Rising Opposition: More Signs, Works, and Words (5:1—8:11)
1. The Healing at the Pool (5:1–15)
2. The Authority of the Son (5:16–30)
3. Testimonies About Jesus (5:31–47)
4. Jesus Feeds the Five Thousand (6:1–15)
5. Jesus Walks on the Water (6:16–24)
6. Jesus the Bread of Life (6:25–59)
7. Many Disciples Desert Jesus (6:60–71)
8. Jesus Goes to the Festival of Tabernacles (7:1–13)
9. Jesus Teaches at the Festival (7:14–24)
10. Division Over Who Jesus Is (7:25–44)
11. Unbelief of the Jewish Leaders (7:45–52)
12. The Woman Caught in Adultery (7:53—8:11)

D. Radical Confrontation: Climactic Signs, Works, and Words (8:12—10:42)
1. Dispute Over Jesus' Testimony (8:12–20)
2. Dispute Over Who Jesus Is (8:21–30)
3. Dispute Over Whose Children Jesus' Opponents Are (8:31–47)
4. Jesus' Claims About Himself (8:48–59)
5. Jesus Heals a Man Born Blind (9:1–12)
6. The Pharisees Investigate the Healing (9:13–34)
7. Spiritual Blindness (9:35–41)
8. The Good Shepherd and His Sheep (10:1–21)
9. Further Conflict Over Jesus' Claims (10:22–42)

III. Transition: Life and Death, King and Suffering Servant (11:1—12:50)

A. The Death and Resurrection of Lazarus (11:1–44)
1. The Death of Lazarus (11:1–16)

2. Jesus Comforts the Sisters of Lazarus (11:17–37)
3. Jesus Raises Lazarus From the Dead (11:38–44)

B. The Judicial Decision to Kill Jesus (11:45–54)

C. Triumph and Impending Death (11:55—12:36)
1. The Setting: The Passover of the Jews (11:55–57)
2. Jesus Anointed at Bethany (12:1–11)
3. Jesus Comes to Jerusalem as King (12:12–19)
4. Jesus Predicts His Death (12:20–36)

D. Theology of Unbelief (12:37–50)

IV. Jesus' Self-Disclosure in His Cross and Exaltation (13:1—20:31)

A. The Last Supper (13:1–30)
1. Jesus Washes His Disciples' Feet (13:1–17)
2. Jesus Predicts His Betrayal (13:18–30)

B. The Farewell Discourse (13:31—16:33)
1. Jesus Predicts Peter's Denial (13:31–38)
2. Jesus Comforts His Disciples (14:1–4)
3. Jesus the Way to the Father (14:5–14)
4. Jesus Promises the Holy Spirit (14:15–31)
5. The Vine and the Branches (15:1–17)
6. The World Hates the Disciples (15:18–25)
7. The Work of the Holy Spirit (15:26—16:15)
8. The Disciples' Grief Will Turn to Joy (16:16–33)

C. The Prayer of Jesus (17:1–26)
1. Jesus Prays to Be Glorified (17:1–5)
2. Jesus Prays for His Disciples (17:6–19)
3. Jesus Prays for All Believers (17:20–26)

D. The Trial and Passion of Jesus (18:1—19:42)
1. Jesus Arrested (18:1–14)
2. Peter's First Denial (18:15–18)
3. The High Priest Questions Jesus (18:19–24)
4. Peter's Second and Third Denials (18:25–27)
5. Jesus Before Pilate (18:28–40)
6. Jesus Sentenced to Be Crucified (19:1–16a)
7. The Crucifixion of Jesus (19:16b–27)
8. The Death of Jesus (19:28–37)
9. The Burial of Jesus (19:38–42)

E. The Resurrection of Jesus (20:1–31)
1. The Empty Tomb (20:1–10)
2. Jesus Appears to Mary Magdalene (20:11–18)
3. Jesus Appears to His Disciples (20:19–23)
4. Jesus Appears to Thomas (20:24–29)
5. The Purpose of John's Gospel (20:30–31)

V. Epilogue (21:1–25)

A. Jesus and the Miraculous Catch of Fish (21:1–14)

B. Jesus Reinstates Peter (21:15–25)

JOHN

1:1 [a]Rev 19:13 [b]Jn 17:5; 1Jn 1:2 [c]Php 2:6
1:2 [d]Ge 1:1
1:3 [e]1Co 8:6; Col 1:16; Heb 1:2
1:4 [f]Jn 5:26; 11:25; 14:6 [g]Jn 8:12
1:5 [h]Jn 3:19
1:6 [i]Mt 3:1
1:7 [j]ver 15,19,32 [k]ver 12
1:9 [l]1Jn 2:8 [m]Isa 49:6
1:10 [n]Heb 1:2
1:12 [o]ver 7

The Word Became Flesh

1 In the beginning was the Word,[a] and the Word was with God,[b] and the Word was God.[c] 2He was
with God in the beginning.[d] 3Through him all things were made; without him nothing was made
that has been made.[e] 4In him was life,[f] and that life was the light[g] of all mankind. 5The light shines in
the darkness, and the darkness has not overcome[a] it.[h]
6There was a man sent from God whose name was John.[i] 7He came as a witness to testify[j] concerning that light, so that through him all might believe.[k] 8He himself was not the light; he came only as
a witness to the light.
9The true light[l] that gives light to everyone[m] was coming into the world. 10He was in the world, and
though the world was made through him,[n] the world did not recognize him. 11He came to that which
was his own, but his own did not receive him. 12Yet to all who did receive him, to those who believed[o]

[a] 5 Or *understood*

1:1–18 *Prologue: The Word Became Flesh.* This foyer into the rest of John's Gospel simultaneously draws the reader in and introduces major themes and thematic words (e.g., life, witness, world, children, glory, truth). It summarizes how the Word became a human being in order to disclose God's glory and grace.
1:1 In the beginning. Prior to creation. This echoes the Bible's opening verse (Gen 1:1). See "Creation," p. 2642. **was.** Already existed. **Word.** God's "Word" in the OT is his powerful self-expression in creation, revelation, and salvation; God's Son, Jesus, personifies that "Word" as God's ultimate self-disclosure. **with God.** The Word is distinct from God the Father and enjoys a personal relationship with him (v. 2). **was God.** God's own peer and God's own self. Jesus is fully God (v. 18; 20:28; Rom 9:5; Titus 2:13; Heb 1:8; 2 Pet 1:1; 1 John 5:20). Here are some of the many elements in the NT that go into what is later called the doctrine of the Trinity.
1:3 Jesus was God's agent in creating all that exists (v. 10; Col 1:16–17; Heb 1:2; Rev 3:14).
1:4 life. The Word's self-existing life, which he dispensed at creation. **light.** Either our essential constitution (i.e., humans are made in the image of God) or the Word's reflection in the universe he created (i.e., what theologians call "general" revelation) or more specific revelation bound up with the Son's coming.
1:5 A masterpiece of planned ambiguity: this may appear to refer exclusively to creation, without moral overtones (Gen 1:2–3), but it anticipates the light-darkness duality that dominates much of the rest of the book. **light.** Revelation bound up not only with creation but also with salvation (3:19–20; 12:36). **darkness.** Evil; not only absence of light (3:19; 8:12; 12:35,46; cf. 1 John 1:5–6; 2:8–9,11). **overcome.** Or "understood" (see NIV text note); translates a Greek verb that could mean either and here probably means both. At creation and in the coming of the Word, the light prevailed; the darkness has not "understood" the light (v. 10).
1:6–8 John the Baptist is a foil for the true light because he is transitory and functions as a witness (v. 15). See Matt 11:11 and note.
1:9 true light that gives light. The Word genuinely and ultimately discloses God to humans. Jesus announced, "I am the light of the world" (8:12). **coming into the world.** Incarnation (v. 14), an act distinct from creation. **world.** For John, it is usually not the universe in general but the created order, especially humans, in rebellion against its Creator (see note on 3:16; cf. v. 10; 7:7; 8:42; 15:18–19; 16:8; 1 John 2:15–17).
1:10–13 There are two reactions to the "true light" (v. 9): reject it and flee lest it expose one's deeds (vv. 10–11; 3:19–20) or receive it (vv. 12–13; 3:21).
1:10 world. See note on v. 9. People are morally responsible to the Word because the Word made them.
1:11 his own ... his own. The first "his own" (neuter in Greek) refers to Jesus' own home or domain, especially the Jewish nation and heritage; the second (masculine in Greek) refers to Jesus' own people (probably Jews; see 4:22).
1:12 receive ... believed. Two ways of describing the same thing, which includes personally welcoming, trusting, and submitting to Jesus. John is introducing a theme of growing importance in his Gospel. **name.** A person's character or even the person himself. **children of God.** Both John and Paul distinguish between the "sonship" of believers and the unique "sonship" of Jesus. In John's Gospel, the believer becomes God's "child," but only Jesus is God's "son." Paul describes both Jesus and believers as God's "sons," but believers are characteristically "sons" by adoption (see note on Rom 8:15). This builds on how the OT frequently calls Israel God's children (e.g., Deut 14:1). See "Sonship," p. 2664.

in his name,[p] he gave the right to become children of God[q]— 13children born not of natural descent,
nor of human decision or a husband's will, but born of God.[r]
14The Word became flesh[s] and made his dwelling among us. We have seen his glory, the glory of the
one and only Son, who came from the Father, full of grace and truth.[t]
15(John testified[u] concerning him. He cried out, saying, "This is the one I spoke about when I said,
'He who comes after me has surpassed me because he was before me.' ")[v] 16Out of his fullness[w] we have
all received grace in place of grace already given. 17For the law was given through Moses;[x] grace and
truth came through Jesus Christ.[y] 18No one has ever seen God,[z] but the one and only Son, who is himself
God and[a][a] is in closest relationship with the Father, has made him known.

John the Baptist Denies Being the Messiah

19Now this was John's testimony when the Jewish leaders[b][b] in Jerusalem sent priests and Levites to
ask him who he was. 20He did not fail to confess, but confessed freely, "I am not the Messiah."[c]
21They asked him, "Then who are you? Are you Elijah?"[d]
He said, "I am not."
"Are you the Prophet?"[e]
He answered, "No."
22Finally they said, "Who are you? Give us an answer to take back to those who sent us. What do
you say about yourself?"
23John replied in the words of Isaiah the prophet, "I am the voice of one calling in the wilderness,[f]
'Make straight the way for the Lord.' "[c][g]

1:12 [p] 1Jn 3:23 [q] Gal 3:26
1:13 [r] Jn 3:6; Jas 1:18; 1Pe 1:23; 1Jn 3:9
1:14 [s] Gal 4:4; Php 2:7,8; 1Ti 3:16; Heb 2:14 [t] Jn 14:6
1:15 [u] ver 7 [v] ver 30; Mt 3:11
1:16 [w] Eph 1:23; Col 1:19
1:17 [x] Jn 7:19 [y] ver 14
1:18 [z] Ex 33:20; Jn 6:46; Col 1:15; 1Ti 6:16 [a] Jn 3:16,18; 1Jn 4:9
1:19 [b] Jn 2:18; 5:10,16; 6:41,52
1:20 [c] Jn 3:28; Lk 3:15,16
1:21 [d] Mt 11:14 [e] Dt 18:15
1:23 [f] Mt 3:1 [g] Isa 40:3

[a] *18* Some manuscripts *but the only Son, who* [b] *19* The Greek term traditionally translated *the Jews* (*hoi Ioudaioi*) refers here and elsewhere in John's Gospel to those Jewish leaders who opposed Jesus; also in 5:10, 15, 16; 7:1, 11, 13; 9:22; 18:14, 28, 36; 19:7, 12, 31, 38; 20:19. [c] *23* Isaiah 40:3

1:13 born of God. Different from being born into a human family. This new birth is an act of God. See 3:3–8 and notes.

1:14 The Word became flesh. God became human. Jesus took on flesh ("incarnation") without ceasing to be God (see Phil 2:6–7). The mere formulation scarcely does justice to this most staggering of assertions. **made his dwelling.** Pitched his tabernacle; lived in his tent. This recalls Israel's "tabernacle" in which God dwelled among his people in the wilderness (Exod 25:8–9; 40:34–35). Now God dwells among his people in a more personal way: in the Word become flesh. See "Temple," p. 2652. **We have seen his glory.** This verse alludes to Exod 33:12—34:28, where God's glory is supremely his goodness (Exod 33:18–19). John and others with eyes of faith saw Jesus display his glory on earth (2:11; Luke 9:32). See "The Glory of God," p. 2640. **one and only Son.** See "Sonship," p. 2664. **full of grace and truth.** Describes Jesus' "glory" and parallels "love and faithfulness" in Exod 34:6 (also in Ps 26:3; Prov 16:6), which describes the nature of the goodness that is God's glory. "Love" (Hebrew *ḥesed*) refers to a gracious covenant love (see "Love and Grace," p. 2684), and "faithfulness" (Hebrew *'ĕmet*), when referring to words, means faithful words, truth. The glory that Moses saw in Exod 33:12—34:28 is the same glory that John saw in the Word made flesh.

1:15 before. In time and rank: as the Word, Jesus existed before John was born, and Jesus is God (see v. 1 and note; see also v. 30).

1:16 fullness. Connects to "full" in v. 14. **grace in place of grace already given.** Grace instead of grace, probably not "grace in addition to grace" or "one blessing after another." Verse 17 gives the reason (see note there).

1:17 Explains the reason for "grace in place of grace" (v. 16): "the law [that] was given through Moses" is an earlier display of grace (what v. 16 calls "grace already given"), and the "grace and truth" (see note on v. 14) that "came through Jesus Christ" replaces the Mosaic law-covenant. Jesus is the climax of God's revelation in the history of salvation (see Matt 5:17–20; 11:13; Heb 1:1–4 and notes). See "Law," p. 2649.

1:18 No one has ever seen God. That is, fully. This alludes to Exod 33:18–20 (see note on Exod 33:20). See also note on v. 14. **who is himself God.** Jesus is God (see v. 1 and note; cf. 2 Cor 4:4; Col 1:15,19; 2:9). **has made him known.** Jesus later says, "Anyone who has seen me has seen the Father" (14:9; cf. 5:37; 6:46). The rest of John's Gospel explains how the Son expounds God to humans.

1:19—10:42 *Jesus' Self-Disclosure in Word and Deed.* In miracles, conversations, and public discourses, some of them tied tightly together (e.g., the feeding of the 5,000 [6:1–15] is tied to the bread of life discourse [6:25–58]), Jesus discloses who he is and why he has come.

1:19–51 *Prelude to Jesus' Public Ministry.* John the Baptist is a "witness" (v. 7) concerning Jesus (vv. 19–34), who gains his first disciples (vv. 35–51).

1:19–28 *John the Baptist Denies Being the Messiah.* First-century Palestine was filled with Messianic expectations, and some people wondered if John was the Messiah.

1:19 Jewish leaders. See NIV text note.

1:20–21 John the Baptist's three denials contrast with Peter's three denials of Jesus (18:15–18,25–27; see 21:15–17 and notes).

1:20 Messiah. A title that means "anointed one." In the OT "anointed one" refers to Israel's king (see, e.g., 2 Sam 1:14; see also 1 Sam 16:1–13), priest (see, e.g., Lev 4:3; see also Exod 29:7), and patriarchs in their role as prophets (see Ps 105:15; see also 1 Kgs 19:16). Jesus is the anointed king, priest, and prophet *par excellence.*

1:21 Elijah. An OT prophet who never died (2 Kgs 2:11). Jesus identified John the Baptist with the promised Elijah of Mal 4:5 (see Matt 11:14; 17:12; Mark 9:13; see also Luke 1:17), but the Gospels never suggest that John the Baptist himself made the connection. Here he refuses to make it, which suggests that he did not detect as much significance in his own ministry as Jesus did. **the Prophet.** One whom many Jews expected based on Deut 18:15,18 (see notes on Deut 18:15,17–18); cf. 6:14; 7:40; Acts 3:22; 7:37.

1:23 John the Baptist applies Isa 40:3 (see note there) to his own ministry (see Matt 3:3; Mark 1:3; Luke 3:4). Isa 40:1–11 comforts

1:27 [h]ver 15,30
1:28 [i]Jn 3:26; 10:40
1:29 [j]ver 36; Isa 53:7; 1Pe 1:19; Rev 5:6
1:30 [k]ver 15,27
1:32 [l]Mt 3:16; Mk 1:10
1:33 [m]Mk 1:4 [n]Mt 3:11; Mk 1:8
1:34 [o]ver 49; Mt 4:3

24 Now the Pharisees who had been sent 25 questioned him, "Why then do you baptize if you are not
the Messiah, nor Elijah, nor the Prophet?"
26 "I baptize with[a] water," John replied, "but among you stands one you do not know. 27 He is the one
who comes after me,[h] the straps of whose sandals I am not worthy to untie."
28 This all happened at Bethany on the other side of the Jordan,[i] where John was baptizing.

John Testifies About Jesus

29 The next day John saw Jesus coming toward him and said, "Look, the Lamb of God,[j] who takes
away the sin of the world! 30 This is the one I meant when I said, 'A man who comes after me has surpassed me because he was before me.'[k] 31 I myself did not know him, but the reason I came baptizing
with water was that he might be revealed to Israel."
32 Then John gave this testimony: "I saw the Spirit come down from heaven as a dove and remain
on him.[l] 33 And I myself did not know him, but the one who sent me to baptize with water[m] told me,
'The man on whom you see the Spirit come down and remain is the one who will baptize with the Holy
Spirit.'[n] 34 I have seen and I testify that this is God's Chosen One."[b][o]

[a] *26* Or *in*; also in verses 31 and 33 (twice) [b] *34* See Isaiah 42:1; many manuscripts *is the Son of God.*

God's exiled people by announcing that God will deliver them out of their captivity in Babylon, and Isa 40:3–5 commands them to ready themselves for the Lord's coming by preparing a way for him. Similarly, John the Baptist's audience must ready themselves for the Messiah's coming by repenting. This connection to Isa 40 suggests that John the Baptist is proclaiming a new exodus in which God will, through Jesus, deliver his people from their bondage to sin (see "Exile and Exodus," p. 2659).

1:24 Pharisees. Religious leaders who were extremely scrupulous about attaining righteousness and keeping God's favor by observing every minute detail of his law as they understood it and by establishing an oral tradition about how to observe it. See notes on Mark 2:16; Luke 5:17.

1:25–27 Some converts to Judaism baptized themselves in their conversion process by a washing ceremony, but John was baptizing people who were Jewish. The Pharisees are asking by whose authority he does so. John affirms that he does indeed baptize people and implies that he does so with God's authority but that he himself is nothing compared with the coming Messiah.

1:27 not worthy to untie. At the time, students were expected to do for their teacher whatever a slave would do—except take off his shoes (cf. 3:30; 13:1–17).

1:28 Bethany. Located east of the Jordan, possibly Batanea (Bashan in the OT); different from the Bethany located west of the Jordan and just south of Jerusalem (see, e.g., 11:1,18).

1:29–34 *John Testifies About Jesus.* John the Baptist publicly witnesses concerning Jesus.

1:29 Lamb of God, who takes away the sin. John the Baptist probably has in mind the apocalyptic warrior-lamb (found in some Jewish texts and picked up in Rev 5:6,12; 7:17; 13:8; 17:14; 19:7,9; 21:22–23; 22:1–3), who would come in terrible judgment of all unrepentant sinners (see Matt 3:12). But John the author, writing after Jesus' sacrificial death and resurrection, could grasp a fuller picture than John the Baptist and also apply this title to Jesus as the sacrificial, substitutionary lamb of Isa 53:7,10 or perhaps as the Passover lamb. See "Sacrifice," p. 2656. **world.** All humans without distinction, not all without exception (see vv. 11–12). The sacrifice is not restricted to ethnic Jews.

1:30 before. See note on v. 15.

1:31–33 John the Baptist apparently had baptized Jesus before he said this (Matt 3:13–17; Mark 1:9–11; Luke 3:21–22).

1:31 did not know him. As the Messiah.

1:32 saw the Spirit come down. This identifies the Messiah to John the Baptist. "God anointed Jesus of Nazareth with the Holy Spirit and power" (Acts 10:38), fulfilling promises such as Isa 11:1–2; 42:1; 61:1. **remain.** Jesus permanently experienced the Spirit's presence and power (unlike Saul; see 1 Sam 16:14; 2 Sam 7:15; cf. Ps 51:11).

1:33 will baptize with the Holy Spirit. The promised age (e.g., Ezek 36:25–26) is dawning.

1:34 Chosen One. See NIV text note.

SITE OF JESUS' BAPTISM (traditional)

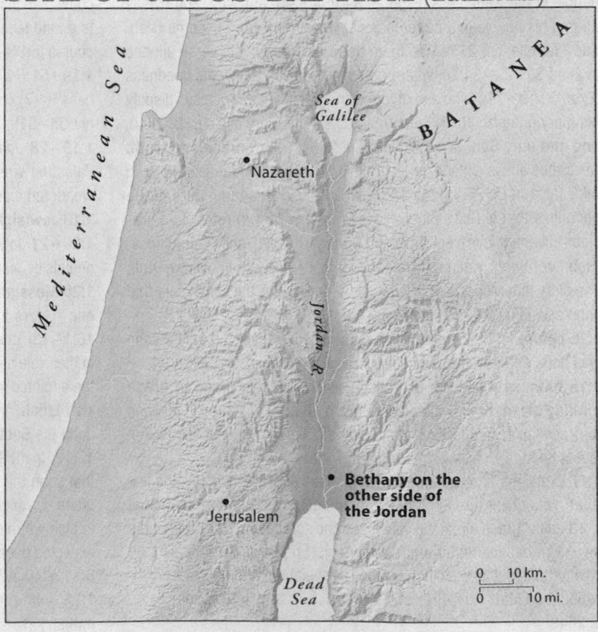

John's Disciples Follow Jesus

1:40-42pp — Mt 4:18-22; Mk 1:16-20; Lk 5:2-11

35The next day John[p] was there again with two of his disciples. 36When he saw Jesus passing by, he
said, "Look, the Lamb of God!"[q]
37When the two disciples heard him say this, they followed Jesus. 38Turning around, Jesus saw them
following and asked, "What do you want?"

They said, "Rabbi"[r] (which means "Teacher"), "where are you staying?"

39"Come," he replied, "and you will see."

So they went and saw where he was staying, and they spent that day with him. It was about four in
the afternoon.

40Andrew, Simon Peter's brother, was one of the two who heard what John had said and who had
followed Jesus. 41The first thing Andrew did was to find his brother Simon and tell him, "We have found
the Messiah" (that is, the Christ).[s] 42And he brought him to Jesus.

Jesus looked at him and said, "You are Simon son of John. You will be called[t] Cephas" (which, when
translated, is Peter[a]).[u]

Jesus Calls Philip and Nathanael

43The next day Jesus decided to leave for Galilee. Finding Philip,[v] he said to him, "Follow me."[w]
44Philip, like Andrew and Peter, was from the town of Bethsaida.[x] 45Philip found Nathanael[y] and
told him, "We have found the one Moses wrote about in the Law,[z] and about whom the prophets also
wrote[a]—Jesus of Nazareth,[b] the son of Joseph."[c]
46"Nazareth! Can anything good come from there?"[d] Nathanael asked.

"Come and see," said Philip.

47When Jesus saw Nathanael approaching, he said of him, "Here truly is an Israelite[e] in whom there
is no deceit."[f]
48"How do you know me?" Nathanael asked.

Jesus answered, "I saw you while you were still under the fig tree before Philip called you."
49Then Nathanael declared, "Rabbi,[g] you are the Son of God;[h] you are the king of Israel."[i]
50Jesus said, "You believe[b] because I told you I saw you under the fig tree. You will see greater things

1:35 [p] Mt 3:1
1:36 [q] ver 29
1:38 [r] ver 49; Mt 23:7
1:41 [s] Jn 4:25
1:42 [t] Ge 17:5,15 [u] Mt 16:18
1:43 [v] Mt 10:3; Jn 6:5-7; 12:21,22; 14:8,9 [w] Mt 4:19
1:44 [x] Mt 11:21; Jn 12:21
1:45 [y] Jn 21:2 [z] Lk 24:27 [a] Lk 24:27 [b] Mt 2:23; Mk 1:24 [c] Lk 3:23
1:46 [d] Jn 7:41,42,52
1:47 [e] Ro 9:4,6 [f] Ps 32:2
1:49 [g] ver 38; Mt 23:7 [h] ver 34; Mt 4:3 [i] Mt 2:2; 27:42; Jn 12:13

[a] *42 Cephas* (Aramaic) and *Peter* (Greek) both mean *rock.* [b] *50* Or *Do you believe . . . ?*

1:35–42 *John's Disciples Follow Jesus.* This occurs before Jesus formally "calls" his disciples in Matt 4:18–22; Mark 1:16–20; Luke 5:1–11.

1:36 Lamb of God. See note on v. 29.

1:41 Andrew is the first recorded person to privately witness about Jesus friend-to-friend, brother-to-brother—the most common and effective Christian testimony. **Messiah ... Christ.** Andrew probably identifies Jesus as the "anointed one." See note on v. 20.

1:42 Cephas ... Peter. See NIV text note. In the Gospels, Peter is impulsive and unstable, not a rock. But in Acts, he gradually becomes a pillar of the early church. See note on Matt 16:18. Jesus knows people thoroughly (see vv. 47–48) and makes them what he calls them to be.

1:43–51 *Jesus Calls Philip and Nathanael.* Although in general Jesus' own people did not receive him (v. 11), some did (v. 12), including Philip and Nathanael.

1:43 Galilee. See notes on Matt 4:15; Mark 1:9.

1:44 Bethsaida. See note on Mark 8:22.

1:45 told him. The foundational principle of Christian expansion: Jesus' new followers bear witness of him to others, who in turn become disciples and repeat the process (see note on v. 41). **the one Moses wrote about in the Law, and about whom the prophets also wrote.** Jesus fulfills the OT (see 5:39; Luke 24:44). **the Law ... the prophets.** Together refer to the entire OT (Matt 5:17). The earliest disciples could not have identified Jesus as the promised Messiah without believing that the OT points to him. See Introduction: Characteristics and Themes, 6. **Joseph.** Jesus' legal but not natural father (see Matt 1:18–25 and notes).

1:46 Nazareth. A small town in Galilee that apparently even fellow Galileans despised (Nathanael was from Cana [21:2], another town in Galilee). Jesus was born in Bethlehem, but because he was raised in Nazareth, he was known as "Jesus of Nazareth" (v. 45) or "Jesus the Nazarene" (Mark 16:6) instead of "Jesus the Bethlehemite," which would have carried royal, Davidic overtones (Mic 5:2).

1:47 no deceit. Without duplicitous motives (unlike Jacob in Gen 27:35–36, to whom Jesus alludes in v. 51). Nathanael examined the claims about Jesus for himself.

1:48 Perhaps Nathanael was meditating and praying in the shade of a fig tree. The point is that Jesus displays supernatural knowledge (see also 2:4; 4:17–18; 6:70; 9:3; 11:4,11; 13:10–11,38).

1:49 Rabbi. See v. 38. **Son of God.** The OT presents Israel as God's son (Exod 4:22–23; Deut 1:31; 32:6; Jer 31:9,20; Hos 11:1), and the NT presents Jesus as the true Israel (see "Sonship," p. 2664). More pertinent here (given the end of v. 49), the OT presents the Davidic king as God's son (2 Sam 7; Ps 2), and the NT presents Jesus as the ultimate king in David's line (e.g., Matt 1:2–17). **king of Israel.** Many Jews tied this title to a political liberator (12:13). Jesus is the promised King, but his kingdom is "not of this world" (18:36). See "The Kingdom of God," p. 2662.

1:50 greater things. Including the miracles in John's Gospel, starting with 2:1–11 and climaxing with Jesus' death, resurrection, and exaltation. The "greater things" the disciples see will confirm that God has appointed Jesus as the Messiah.

1:51 [j]Mt 3:16 [k]Ge 28:12 [l]Mt 8:20
2:1 [m]Jn 4:46; 21:2 [n]Mt 12:46
2:4 [o]Jn 19:26 [p]Mt 8:29 [q]Mt 26:18; Jn 7:6
2:5 [r]Ge 41:55
2:6 [s]Mk 7:3,4; Jn 3:25
2:9 [t]Jn 4:46
2:11 [u]ver 23; Jn 3:2; 4:48; 6:2,14,26,30; 12:37; 20:30 [v]Jn 1:14 [w]Ex 14:31
2:12 [x]Mt 4:13 [y]Mt 12:46
2:13 [z]Jn 11:55 [a]Dt 16:1-6; Lk 2:41

than that." 51 He then added, "Very truly I tell you,[a] you[a] will see 'heaven open,[j] and the angels of God ascending and descending[k] on'[b] the Son of Man."[l]

Jesus Changes Water Into Wine

2 On the third day a wedding took place at Cana in Galilee.[m] Jesus' mother[n] was there, 2 and Jesus and his disciples had also been invited to the wedding. 3 When the wine was gone, Jesus' mother said to him, "They have no more wine."

4 "Woman,[c][o] why do you involve me?"[p] Jesus replied. "My hour[q] has not yet come."

5 His mother said to the servants, "Do whatever he tells you."[r]

6 Nearby stood six stone water jars, the kind used by the Jews for ceremonial washing,[s] each holding from twenty to thirty gallons.[d]

7 Jesus said to the servants, "Fill the jars with water"; so they filled them to the brim.

8 Then he told them, "Now draw some out and take it to the master of the banquet."

They did so, 9 and the master of the banquet tasted the water that had been turned into wine.[t] He did not realize where it had come from, though the servants who had drawn the water knew. Then he called the bridegroom aside 10 and said, "Everyone brings out the choice wine first and then the cheaper wine after the guests have had too much to drink; but you have saved the best till now."

11 What Jesus did here in Cana of Galilee was the first of the signs[u] through which he revealed his glory;[v] and his disciples believed in him.[w]

12 After this he went down to Capernaum[x] with his mother and brothers[y] and his disciples. There they stayed for a few days.

Jesus Clears the Temple Courts

2:14-16pp — Mt 21:12,13; Mk 11:15-17; Lk 19:45,46

13 When it was almost time for the Jewish Passover,[z] Jesus went up to Jerusalem.[a] 14 In the temple courts he found people selling cattle, sheep and doves, and others sitting at tables exchanging money. 15 So he made a whip out of cords, and drove all from the temple courts, both sheep and cattle; he scattered the coins of the money changers and overturned their tables. 16 To those who sold doves he said,

a 51 The Greek is plural. *b 51* Gen. 28:12 *c 4* The Greek for *Woman* does not denote any disrespect.
d 6 Or from about 75 to about 115 liters

1:51 heaven open, and the angels of God ascending and descending. Alludes to Gen 28:12 (see Jacob's dream in Gen 28:10–22). Jesus is the decisive, ultimate connection between heaven and earth. Jacob "called that place Bethel" (Gen 28:19; see Gen 35:15), which means "house of God" (Gen 28:17), because God revealed himself to Jacob there. God is now revealing himself to people not at Bethel but through Jesus, the new Bethel. **Son of Man.** See note on Matt 8:20.

2:1—4:54 *Early Ministry: Signs, Works, and Words.* This conveys what Paul says in 2 Cor 5:17: "The old has gone, the new is here!"

2:1–12 *Jesus Changes Water Into Wine.* This is Jesus' first sign in John's Gospel (see v. 11; see also Introduction: Purpose and Addressees).

2:1 wedding. Celebrations could last an entire week. **Jesus' mother.** Also appears in 19:25–27.

2:3 wine. Not merely grape juice ("too much to drink" in v. 10 refers to becoming intoxicated). Wine in the ancient world was diluted with water to between one-third and one-tenth of its fermented strength. **gone.** Socially embarrassing (especially in a "shame" culture) for the host and groom (cf. vv. 9–10).

2:4 Woman. See NIV text note. **hour.** The appointed time for Jesus' death, resurrection, and exaltation and related events (7:30; 8:20; 12:23,27; 13:1; 16:32; 17:1). Jesus' response to Mary may imply that (1) he detects symbolism, i.e., the wedding symbolizes the consummation of the Messianic age (e.g., Matt 22:1–14; 25:1–13), where wine will flow freely (Isa 25:6; Jer 31:12; Hos 14:7; Joel 3:18; Amos 9:13–14); (2) he is the Messianic bridegroom (John 3:27–30; Mark 2:18–22) who will supply all the "wine" for the Messianic banquet; (3) his mission and its timing must follow the Father's schedule, not human ones.

2:5 Mary trusts Jesus. She is perfectly content to leave the matter in his hands.

2:6–7 The water in the "water jars" used for "ceremonial washing" may represent the old order of Jewish law and custom, which Jesus replaces with something better (see note on v. 4).

2:10 Jesus' wine is superior, as is everything tied to the new, Messianic age Jesus is introducing.

2:11 first of the signs. See Introduction: Purpose and Addressees. **revealed his glory.** See note on 1:14.

2:12 Capernaum. See note on Matt 4:13.

2:13–25 *Jesus Clears the Temple Courts.* This event is probably distinct from Jesus' cleansing the temple at the end of his ministry (Matt 21:12–13; Mark 11:15–17; Luke 19:45–46).

2:13 Passover. See note on Luke 2:41. John mentions at least three Passovers (here; 6:4; 11:55), possibly four (5:1).

2:14 temple courts. The court of the Gentiles (the outermost court), the one part of the temple where Gentiles could come to pray (see photo, p. 1975). **selling cattle, sheep and doves.** For sacrificial worship at the temple. It was convenient to purchase the animals on-site, especially for those who traveled to Jerusalem from afar. **exchanging money.** Converting money to the approved currency for the required temple tax (and charging a percentage for the service).

2:15–16 Jesus is not condemning the merchants for dishonest business practices but for being in the temple area at all and thus excluding the Gentiles from praying there (see note on v. 14). They transformed what should have been a place for worshipful prayer into a noisy market. Jesus may be fulfilling the Messianic expectations of Zech 14:21, where

"Get these out of here! Stop turning my Father's house[b] into a market!" 17His disciples remembered that it is written: "Zeal for your house will consume me."[a][c]

18The Jews then responded to him, "What sign can you show us to prove your authority to do all this?"[d]

19Jesus answered them, "Destroy this temple, and I will raise it again in three days."[e]

20They replied, "It has taken forty-six years to build this temple, and you are going to raise it in three days?" 21But the temple he had spoken of was his body.[f] 22After he was raised from the dead, his disciples recalled what he had said.[g] Then they believed the scripture and the words that Jesus had spoken.

23Now while he was in Jerusalem at the Passover Festival,[h] many people saw the signs he was performing and believed in his name.[b] 24But Jesus would not entrust himself to them, for he knew all people. 25He did not need any testimony about mankind, for he knew what was in each person.[i]

Jesus Teaches Nicodemus

3 Now there was a Pharisee, a man named Nicodemus[j] who was a member of the Jewish ruling council.[k] 2He came to Jesus at night and said, "Rabbi, we know that you are a teacher who has come from God. For no one could perform the signs[l] you are doing if God were not with him."[m]

3Jesus replied, "Very truly I tell you, no one can see the kingdom of God unless they are born again.[c]"[n]

4"How can someone be born when they are old?" Nicodemus asked. "Surely they cannot enter a second time into their mother's womb to be born!"

5Jesus answered, "Very truly I tell you, no one can enter the kingdom of God unless they are born of water and the Spirit.[o] 6Flesh gives birth to flesh, but the Spirit[d] gives birth to spirit.[p] 7You should not

[a] *17* Psalm 69:9 [b] *23* Or *in him* [c] *3* The Greek for *again* also means *from above*; also in verse 7.
[d] *6* Or *but spirit*

2:16 [b] Lk 2:49
2:17 [c] Ps 69:9
2:18 [d] Mt 12:38
2:19 [e] Mt 26:61; 27:40; Mk 14:58; 15:29
2:21 [f] 1Co 6:19
2:22 [g] Lk 24:5-8; Jn 12:16; 14:26
2:23 [h] ver 13
2:25 [i] Mt 9:4; Jn 6:61,64; 13:11
3:1 [j] Jn 7:50; 19:39 [k] Lk 23:13
3:2 [l] Jn 9:16,33 [m] Ac 2:22; 10:38
3:3 [n] Jn 1:13; 1Pe 1:23
3:5 [o] Titus 3:5
3:6 [p] Jn 1:13; 1Co 15:50

"Canaanite" could be translated "merchant" (see NIV text note there), and Mal 3:1,3.

2:17 remembered. John does not clarify here whether this remembering took place while Jesus was cleansing the temple or later on, after his resurrection (as v. 22 mentions). This quotes Ps 69:9, where David endures opposition because he is committed to the temple ("your house"). Jesus is David's greater Son: cleansing the temple shows that he is concerned for rightly worshiping God, and he suffers righteously ("consume" refers to his death).

2:18 Jews. Jewish leaders (see NIV text note on 1:19).

2:19–22 No one understood Jesus' reply at the time (cf. vv. 20,22), and this sheds light on Matt 26:61; 27:40. A temple is the place where God dwells, where humans can meet God. This was a prominent feature of Israel's worship starting with the tabernacle and then the temples built by Solomon, Zerubbabel, and finally Herod. Jesus is the new temple, rendering the previous ones obsolete, since he uniquely manifests God the Father (see notes on 1:14,18). The ultimate, once-for-all-time sacrifice took place in this "temple" when others "destroyed" it, but Jesus rose from the dead in three days. See "Temple," p. 2652.

2:23 believed. Sadly, their faith was spurious, and Jesus knew it (vv. 24–25).

3:1–21 *Jesus Teaches Nicodemus.* It is difficult to know where Jesus' exchange with Nicodemus ends. Verses 16–21 appear to be John's extended comment.

3:1 Pharisee. See note on 1:24. **Nicodemus.** A religious leader and distinguished teacher (v. 10). At this point he is interested in Jesus but not particularly open to the truth: Jesus' signs are the conversation starter but not a trigger for faith (v. 2). Yet later he defends Jesus (7:45–52) and buries his body (19:38–42).

3:2 night. Symbolizes spiritual darkness in 9:4; 11:10; 13:30 (cf. vv. 19–21). Nicodemus's own "night" was darker than he knew. **we.** Nicodemus sees himself speaking for at least some of the Pharisees or Sanhedrin (v. 1) who essentially agreed with him. **a teacher who has come from God.** Simply one mightily endowed with God's power, not the promised Messiah. Nicodemus's statement implies a question: "So who are you?" Like the Jewish leaders who demand a sign in 2:18, Nicodemus presupposes that he can assess any evidence Jesus shares.

3:3 see. Basically synonymous with "enter" in v. 5; includes participation. **kingdom of God.** God's saving reign, which in certain respects has already been inaugurated in the person, works, and message of Jesus. See "The Kingdom of God," p. 2662. **born again.** See NIV text note; synonymous with "become children of God" and "born of God" (1:12–13; cf. Titus 3:5; 1 Pet 1:3,23; 1 John 2:29; 3:9; 4:7; 5:1,4,18). See note on v. 5. This implies a predicament: if Nicodemus, a knowledgeable, gifted, and prestigious religious teacher, cannot enter God's kingdom based on his standing and works, what hope is there for anyone else?

3:4 Nicodemus does not understand what Jesus is talking about, so he is incredulous.

3:5 born of water and the Spirit. Parallel with "born again" (vv. 3,7) and "born of the Spirit" (v. 8), emphasizing a (single) Spirit-produced birth. This makes several interpretations unlikely: (1) that "born of water" refers to natural birth (no ancient sources picture natural birth as "from water," where "water" is the amniotic fluid that breaks before childbirth); (2) that "born of water" refers to Christian baptism (these words would have had no relevance to Nicodemus at the time); (3) that "born of water" refers to John's baptism (also, vv. 9–12 then do not logically follow); (4) that "the Spirit" refers to the Word of God (John's other metaphoric uses of "water" in this Gospel refer to Spirit-produced life [4:14; 7:38–39], not to God's Word). The most plausible interpretation of "born of water and the Spirit" is the purifying and transforming new birth. Since Jesus expects Nicodemus to understand what he means (vv. 7,10), the background to the concept is previous Scripture. Water in the OT often refers to renewal or cleansing, and the most significant OT connection bringing together water and spirit is Ezek 36:25–27, where water cleanses from impurity and the Spirit transforms hearts. So "born of water and the Spirit" signals a new birth that cleanses and transforms.

3:6 Like generates like. Humans physically produce more (spiritually dead) humans. Only God's Spirit can produce spiritual life (1:13).

3:7 You should not be surprised. From his study of the OT, Nicodemus

3:9 [q] Jn 6:52,60
3:10 [r] Lk 2:46
3:11 [s] Jn 1:18; 7:16,17 [t] ver 32
3:13 [u] Pr 30:4; Ac 2:34; Eph 4:8-10 [v] Jn 6:38,42
3:14 [w] Nu 21:8,9 [x] Jn 8:28; 12:32
3:15 [y] ver 16,36
3:16 [z] Ro 5:8; Eph 2:4; 1Jn 4:9,10 [a] ver 36; Jn 6:29,40; 11:25,26
3:17 [b] Jn 6:29,57; 10:36; 11:42; 17:8,21; 20:21 [c] Jn 12:47; 1Jn 4:14
3:18 [d] Jn 5:24

be surprised at my saying, 'You[a] must be born again.' 8 The wind blows wherever it pleases. You hear
its sound, but you cannot tell where it comes from or where it is going. So it is with everyone born of
the Spirit."[b]

9 "How can this be?"[q] Nicodemus asked.

10 "You are Israel's teacher,"[r] said Jesus, "and do you not understand these things? 11 Very truly I tell
you, we speak of what we know,[s] and we testify to what we have seen, but still you people do not accept
our testimony.[t] 12 I have spoken to you of earthly things and you do not believe; how then will you believe if I speak of heavenly things? 13 No one has ever gone into heaven[u] except the one who came from
heaven[v] — the Son of Man.[c] 14 Just as Moses lifted up the snake in the wilderness,[w] so the Son of Man
must be lifted up,[dx] 15 that everyone who believes[y] may have eternal life in him."[e]

16 For God so loved[z] the world that he gave his one and only Son, that whoever believes in him
shall not perish but have eternal life.[a] 17 For God did not send his Son into the world[b] to condemn
the world, but to save the world through him.[c] 18 Whoever believes in him is not condemned,[d] but
whoever does not believe stands condemned already because they have not believed in the name

[a] *7* The Greek is plural. [b] *8* The Greek for *Spirit* is the same as that for *wind*. [c] *13* Some manuscripts *Man, who is in heaven* [d] *14* The Greek for *lifted up* also means *exalted*. [e] *15* Some interpreters end the quotation with verse 21.

should have understood the need for a God-given new birth (see note on v. 5). **You must.** This applies to all people, not just to Nicodemus (see NIV text note).

3:8 The effects of both the "wind" and the "Spirit" (see NIV text note) are unmistakable, but humans can neither control nor fully understand the invisible origin and movement of the wind or the Spirit. As being "born of water and the Spirit" (v. 5) is grounded in Ezek 36:25–27 (see note on v. 5), this may allude to Ezek 37:1–14, where God's Spirit sovereignly gives life to dry bones.

3:10 Israel's teacher. Nicodemus was a recognized master, an established religious authority (such as, e.g., "the Reverend Professor Doctor"). See notes on vv. 5,7.

3:11 we ... we ... we ... we ... our. Jesus ironically imitates the plural that Nicodemus used (see note on v. 2), as if to say, "*We* know one or two things too, *we* do!"

3:12 earthly things. Probably the new birth itself (Jesus had just spoken about that and Nicodemus did not believe), which happens on earth when people are born again. **heavenly things.** Details about God's glorious kingdom, which one can enter only by the new birth.

3:13 No one has ascended to and remained in heaven in such a way as to return to talk about heavenly things (v. 12; cf. Prov 30:4a), but heaven was Jesus' home in the first place.

3:14–15 This connects to what precedes it in two ways: (1) Jesus further explains the new birth. God miraculously granted (physical) life through the bronze "snake in the wilderness" (Num 21:4–9). Similarly, God miraculously gives (spiritual, eternal) life through Jesus, who unlike the snake has life in himself (1:4; 5:26). (2) "Lifted up" combines two notions in John's Gospel: Jesus' being physically raised up on the cross and Jesus' glorious exaltation (8:28; 12:32,34; see NIV text note on 3:14; cf. Isa 52:13). Verse 15 states the purpose: eternal life (see note on v. 15).

3:15 eternal life. Resurrection life of the age to come that believers experience in some measure now (17:3).

3:16–21 This starkly contrasts two groups of people. See "Believers and Unbelievers," this page.

3:16 For. Jesus' being raised up on the cross and his glorious exaltation (see note on vv. 14–15) are grounded in God's love. **so.** In this way. This emphasizes the intensity of God's love. **loved the world.** Not because "the world" is loveable or because we loved God first (1 John 4:9–10,19). God's love is amazing not because the world is so big but because the world is so bad (see note on 1:9). God's love is

BELIEVERS AND UNBELIEVERS

BELIEVERS	UNBELIEVERS
Believe in the Son	Do not believe in the Son
Have eternal life	Shall perish
Are not condemned	Are condemned already
Love light	Love darkness; hate the light
Live by the truth	Do evil

unselfish, costly, and praiseworthy (unlike how sinners selfishly love the world by conforming to it [1 John 2:15–17]). The Bible speaks of God's love in at least five ways: (1) the peculiar love of the Father for the Son (v. 35; 5:20), and of the Son for the Father (14:31); (2) God's providential love over all that he has made (Ps 145:9,13,17); (3) God's saving stance toward his fallen world (v. 16); (4) God's particular, effective, selecting love toward his elect (Eph 5:25); (5) God's love toward his own people conditioned on obedience (15:10). See "Love and Grace," p. 2684. **that ... that.** The first indicates result ("with the result that"); the second indicates purpose ("in order that"). **one and only Son.** Emphasizes the greatness of God's gift. See "Sonship," p. 2664. **whoever believes in him.** That person experiences new birth (vv. 3,5), has "eternal life" (see note on v. 15), and is saved (v. 17); the only alternative is to "perish" in eternal judgment (cf. 10:28), lose one's life (12:25), and be "doomed to destruction" (17:12). See "Wrath," p. 2681.

3:17 not ... to condemn. Jesus came into a world that was already condemned (vv. 18,36); it was not a neutral world in which he would condemn some and save others. He came to save, not condemn (12:47). But saving some entails leaving others in their condemned state; in that derivative sense, Jesus came into the world "for judgment" (9:39). **send.** Jesus was on a mission from his Father (v. 34; 5:36,38; 6:29,57; 7:29; 8:42; 10:36; 11:42; 17:3,8,18,21,23,25; 20:21). **to save the world.** The purpose of the Son's mission.

3:18 Personally trusting Jesus distinguishes those who are not condemned from those who are (14:6).

of God's one and only Son.[e] 19This is the verdict: Light[f] has come into the world, but people loved
darkness instead of light because their deeds were evil. 20Everyone who does evil hates the light,
and will not come into the light for fear that their deeds will be exposed.[g] 21But whoever lives by the
truth comes into the light, so that it may be seen plainly that what they have done has been done
in the sight of God.

John Testifies Again About Jesus

22After this, Jesus and his disciples went out into the Judean countryside, where he spent some
time with them, and baptized.[h] 23Now John also was baptizing at Aenon near Salim, because there
was plenty of water, and people were coming and being baptized. 24(This was before John was put in
prison.)[i] 25An argument developed between some of John's disciples and a certain Jew over the matter
of ceremonial washing.[j] 26They came to John and said to him, "Rabbi,[k] that man who was with you
on the other side of the Jordan—the one you testified[l] about—look, he is baptizing, and everyone
is going to him."

27To this John replied, "A person can receive only what is given them from heaven. 28You yourselves
can testify that I said, 'I am not the Messiah but am sent ahead of him.'[m] 29The bride belongs to the
bridegroom.[n] The friend who attends the bridegroom waits and listens for him, and is full of joy when
he hears the bridegroom's voice. That joy is mine, and it is now complete.[o] 30He must become greater;
I must become less."[a]

31The one who comes from above[p] is above all; the one who is from the earth belongs to the earth,
and speaks as one from the earth.[q] The one who comes from heaven is above all. 32He testifies to what
he has seen and heard,[r] but no one accepts his testimony.[s] 33Whoever has accepted it has certified
that God is truthful. 34For the one whom God has sent[t] speaks the words of God, for God[b] gives the
Spirit[u] without limit. 35The Father loves the Son and has placed everything in his hands.[v] 36Whoever
believes in the Son has eternal life,[w] but whoever rejects the Son will not see life, for God's wrath
remains on them.

3:18 [e] 1Jn 4:9
3:19 [f] Jn 1:4; 8:12
3:20 [g] Eph 5:11,13
3:22 [h] Jn 4:2
3:24 [i] Mt 4:12; 14:3
3:25 [j] Jn 2:6
3:26 [k] Mt 23:7 [l] Jn 1:7
3:28 [m] Jn 1:20,23
3:29 [n] Mt 9:15 [o] Jn 16:24; 17:13; Php 2:2; 1Jn 1:4; 2Jn 12
3:31 [p] ver 13 [q] Jn 8:23; 1Jn 4:5
3:32 [r] Jn 8:26; 15:15 [s] ver 11
3:34 [t] ver 17 [u] Mt 12:18; Lk 4:18; Ac 10:38
3:35 [v] Mt 28:18; Jn 5:20, 22; 17:2
3:36 [w] ver 15; Jn 5:24; 6:47

[a] *30* Some interpreters end the quotation with verse 36. [b] *34* Greek *he*

3:19 verdict. Negative (vv. 19–20) and positive (v. 21). **Light.** The incarnate Word (1:4–5), the holy and pure light of the world (8:12; cf. 1 John 1:5). **darkness ... light.** See note on 1:5. **because their deeds were evil.** The reason unbelievers prefer darkness is fundamentally moral: they love their sin and do not want the light to expose it.
3:21 in the sight of God. Or, "in God" or even "through God": what they have done they have accomplished in union with God, and thus by his enabling.
3:22–36 *John Testifies Again About Jesus.* It is difficult to know where John the Baptist's witness ends. Verses 31–36 appear to be the author's extended comment.
3:22 baptized. Only Jesus' disciples actually baptized (4:2).
3:23 The ministries of John the Baptist and Jesus overlapped.
3:24 John explains that this episode (and probably all of Jesus' Judean ministry in chs. 2–4) occurs earlier than any of Jesus' ministry in the Synoptic Gospels, which start with Jesus' Galilean ministry "after John was put in prison" (Mark 1:14).
3:25–26 Perhaps this debate about Jewish purification rites arises because John the Baptist did not follow certain traditional Jewish practices (cf. 1:25). In any case, it apparently leads some of John's disciples to become envious as Jesus' popularity increases and their master's decreases.
3:27 This proverb implies that God ("heaven") sovereignly gives humans whatever they possess (19:11; 1 Cor 4:7). And God has given John the Baptist a particular role in the history of redemption. Discontent over God's wise gifts betrays unbelief and idolatrous arrogance.
3:28 John meant what he said, and he was entirely content with his God-given role. **sent ahead.** May allude to Mal 3:1.
3:29 This parable of a Judean wedding explains how John the Baptist understands his God-given role. **bridegroom.** Jesus (Rev 21:9), Israel's King and Messiah (Isa 62:4–5; Jer 2:2; Hos 2:16–20). **friend who attends the bridegroom.** John the Baptist (the ancient equivalent of a "best man"). **now complete.** John the Baptist has successfully completed his role (cf. 5:35).
3:30 John the Baptist wholeheartedly embraces his God-given role, which assigns supremacy to Jesus.
3:31 The one who comes from above. Jesus (v. 13; see 1 Cor 15:47). **from above.** Recalls vv. 3,7 (see NIV text note on v. 3). **the one who is from the earth.** John the Baptist, who is finite.
3:32 Repeats Jesus' evaluation in v. 11. **no one.** In general. There are exceptions (v. 33; see 1:11–12).
3:33 God is truthful. Jesus so completely says and does only and all that God says and does (5:19–30; 6:37–40; 8:29) that to believe Jesus is to believe God. Conversely, not to believe Jesus is to call God a liar (12:44–50; 1 John 5:10).
3:34 God gives the Spirit without limit. As opposed to how God gave only the measure of the Spirit required for his anointed servants to complete their tasks at earlier stages of redemptive history. See note on 1:32.
3:35 The Father loves the Son. See 5:20; 10:17; 15:9; 17:23–24,26. **placed everything in his hands.** See Matt 11:27; Luke 10:22.
3:36 believes ... rejects. There are only two possibilities: genuine faith (vv. 15–16; 1:12) or defiant disobedience. **has eternal life.** See note on v. 15. **wrath.** See "Wrath," p. 2681. **remains.** Unbelievers are "condemned already" (v. 18; see note on v. 17).

4:1 [x]Jn 3:22,26
4:3 [y]Jn 3:22
4:5 [z]Ge 33:19; 48:22; Jos 24:32
4:8 [a]ver 5,39
4:9 [b]Mt 10:5; Lk 9:52,53
4:10 [c]Isa 44:3; Jer 2:13; Zec 14:8; Jn 7:37,38; Rev 21:6; 22:1,17
4:12 [d]ver 6
4:14 [e]Jn 6:35 [f]Jn 7:38 [g]Mt 25:46
4:15 [h]Jn 6:34

Jesus Talks With a Samaritan Woman

4 Now Jesus learned that the Pharisees had heard that he was gaining and baptizing more disciples
than John[x]— 2although in fact it was not Jesus who baptized, but his disciples. 3So he left Judea[y]
and went back once more to Galilee.
4Now he had to go through Samaria. 5So he came to a town in Samaria called Sychar, near the plot
of ground Jacob had given to his son Joseph.[z] 6Jacob's well was there, and Jesus, tired as he was from
the journey, sat down by the well. It was about noon.
7When a Samaritan woman came to draw water, Jesus said to her, "Will you give me a drink?" 8(His
disciples had gone into the town[a] to buy food.)
9The Samaritan woman said to him, "You are a Jew and I am a Samaritan[b] woman. How can you
ask me for a drink?" (For Jews do not associate with Samaritans.[a])
10Jesus answered her, "If you knew the gift of God and who it is that asks you for a drink, you would
have asked him and he would have given you living water."[c]
11"Sir," the woman said, "you have nothing to draw with and the well is deep. Where can you get this
living water? 12Are you greater than our father Jacob, who gave us the well[d] and drank from it himself,
as did also his sons and his livestock?"
13Jesus answered, "Everyone who drinks this water will be thirsty again, 14but whoever drinks the
water I give them will never thirst.[e] Indeed, the water I give them will become in them a spring of water[f]
welling up to eternal life."[g]
15The woman said to him, "Sir, give me this water so that I won't get thirsty[h] and have to keep coming here to draw water."
16He told her, "Go, call your husband and come back."
17"I have no husband," she replied.
Jesus said to her, "You are right when you say you have no husband. 18The fact is, you have had
five husbands, and the man you now have is not your husband. What you have just said is quite true."

[a] 9 Or *do not use dishes Samaritans have used*

4:1–26 *Jesus Talks With a Samaritan Woman.* Like the previous chapters (2:6; 3:5), this account includes water symbolism (4:7–15) and dialogue in which Jesus discloses himself as fulfilling OT promises and institutions (see notes on v. 14; 1:45; 2:4,6–7,10,15–16,19–22; 3:5,14–15). Unlike Nicodemus in 3:1–15, the person at the well in ch. 4 is female, Samaritan, not seeking Jesus, uneducated, socially despised, and immoral—but both need Jesus.
4:1–2 See notes on 3:22–24.
4:4 had to go through Samaria. Because it was the most direct route taken by Jewish travelers heading from Judea to Galilee (see map, p. 2155) and it was part of the mission on which God sent Jesus (cf. "had to" in 20:9). Jews despised Samaritans (8:48; Luke 10:33) because they were defiled with Gentile blood and pagan worship practices. When the northern kingdom of Israel and its capital of Samaria (1 Kgs 16:24) was defeated by the Assyrians in 722 BC, the Assyrians deported many Israelites to Assyria and repopulated Israel with foreigners (2 Kgs 17:24–31) who intermarried with the remaining Israelites. The result was Samaritans, whom Jews regarded as ethnic half-breeds. Samaritans had their own version of the Pentateuch and rejected the rest of the OT. See notes on vv. 9,20.
4:5 Sychar. Probably the modern village of Askar, on the shoulder of Mount Ebal and opposite Mount Gerizim. **given.** See Gen 48:22.
4:6 Jacob's well. Not mentioned elsewhere in Scripture; probably associated with Jacob's move to the Shechem area (Gen 33:18–20). It is about a half mile (0.8 kilometers) south of Askar. **tired.** Jesus is fully human (1:14; see 19:28). **about noon.** May indicate that the woman in v. 7 was a social outcast since there is some evidence that women did not normally fetch water during the sun's hottest hours.
4:7 Jesus breaches social custom (v. 9).
4:9 Jews do not associate with Samaritans. The reason the woman is surprised by Jesus' request (see note on v. 4). Many Jews viewed all Samaritans as ritually defiled. The woman did not expect Jesus to talk to her (cf. v. 27), let alone become ritually defiled by drinking from a Samaritan's water pot (see NIV text note). She does not know that Jesus cannot become ritually defiled; he sanctifies what he touches (Matt 8:3).
4:10 Jesus' reply raises at least four questions for the woman: (1) What is "the gift of God"? It is probably eternal life, which only Jesus can give. (2) Who is this man? See vv. 12,19,29. (3) What is "living water"? On a physical level, it is fresh, flowing water from springs as opposed to stagnant cistern water. On a spiritual level, it is "the gift of God," the eternally satisfying life that Jesus provides through the Spirit, who produces spiritual life (see notes on 3:5,6,8,14–15; 7:38; cf. Jer 2:13). (4) How can he get this water without a bucket? See v. 11.
4:11–12 Like Nicodemus in 3:4,9, the woman misunderstands Jesus (see also v. 15).
4:11 deep. Over 100 feet (30 meters) today; probably deeper at that time.
4:12 The question implies a negative answer. The woman thinks that Jesus is a charlatan, but she is twice wrong: (1) Jesus' "living water" does not come from an ordinary well (see note on v. 10). (2) Jesus is far greater than Jacob.
4:13 this water. From the well.
4:14 the water I give them. "Living water" (see v. 10 and note). **never thirst.** For God and eternal life in his presence (see Isa 12:3; 44:3; 49:10; 55:1–3; Rev 7:16). **spring of water welling up to eternal life.** The Spirit, who produces spiritual life and indwells believers (6:63; 7:37–39).
4:15 The woman still does not understand who Jesus is and what "living water" is (see note on vv. 11–12).
4:16–18 Jesus shows the woman that he knows about her sins (cf. 2:24–25) to help her realize that she is thirsty for his living water.
4:17 I have no husband. Technically true if they were deceased or divorced, but she doubtless intends to ward off any further probing of this sensitive area of her life while masking her guilt and pain (3:19–20). Jesus gently exposes the whole truth.

JESUS IN JUDEA AND SAMARIA

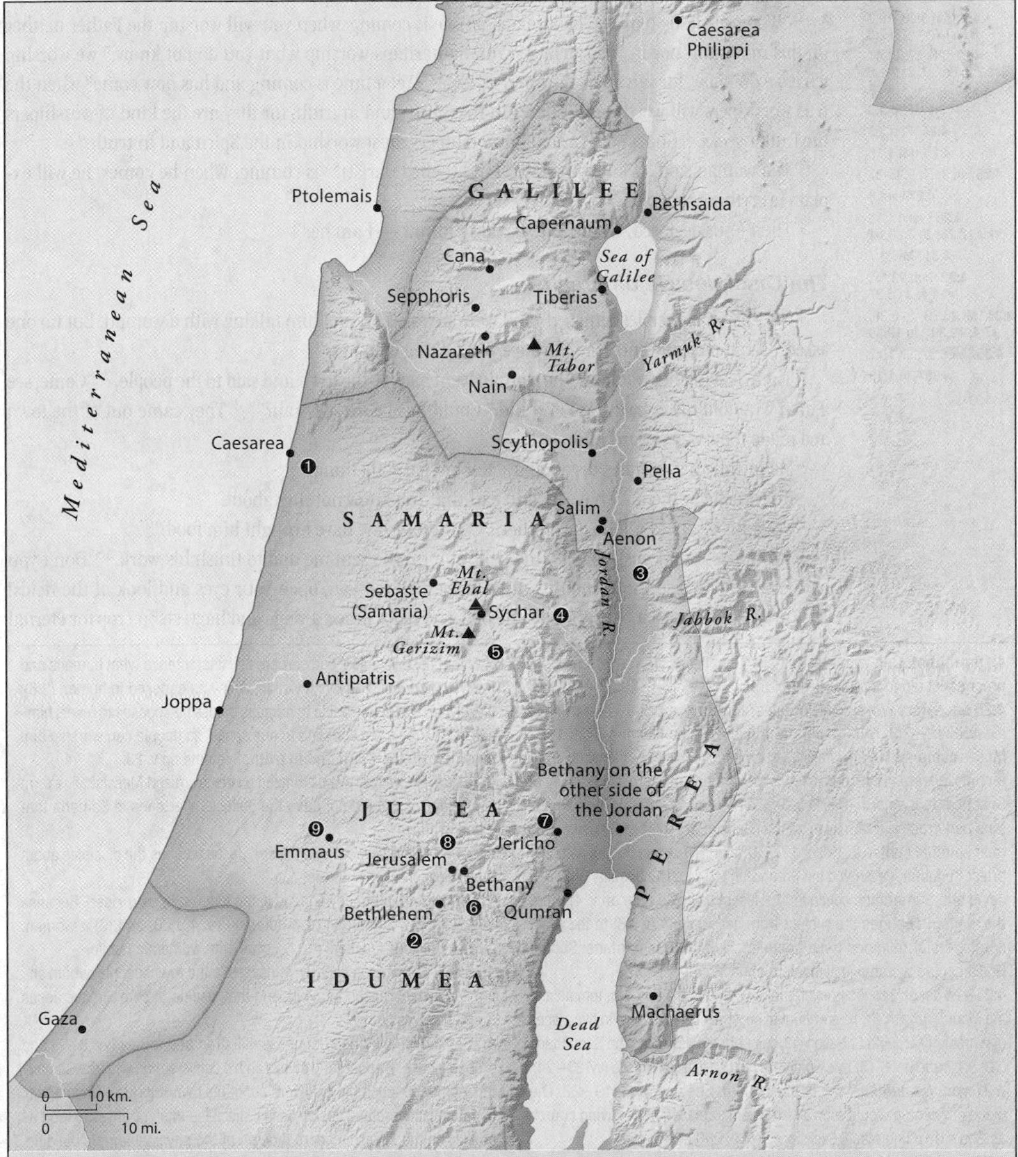

❶ The most important port in the Holy Land in NT times

❷ The birthplace of Jesus (Matt 2:1; Luke 2:4)

❸ John the Baptist baptized here (John 3:23). Aenon was also the probable location of John's ministry.

❹ Jesus talked with a Samaritan woman at Jacob's well (John 4:5).

❺ The mountain referred to by the Samaritan woman at the well as the worship center for the Samaritans (John 4:20–23)

❻ Jesus raised Lazarus from the dead (John 11:43–44). Here at Bethany Jesus was anointed in the house of Simon the Leper (Matt 26:6). It was also the scene of the ascension (Luke 24:50–51).

❼ Jesus healed a blind man at Jericho (Matt 20:29) and called Zacchaeus down from a tree (Luke 19:1). The Good Samaritan helped a traveler en route here (Luke 10:30).

❽ Most important biblical city. Jesus was crucified at Jerusalem as predicted (Matt 16:21; Mark 10:33; Luke 18:31).

❾ The resurrected Jesus appeared to two people walking to Emmaus, and he ate with them there (Luke 24:13).

4:19 [i] Mt 21:11
4:20 [j] Dt 11:29; Jos 8:33 [k] Lk 9:53
4:21 [l] Jn 5:28; 16:2 [m] Mal 1:11; 1Ti 2:8
4:22 [n] 2Ki 17:28-41 [o] Isa 2:3; Ro 3:1,2; 9:4,5
4:23 [p] Jn 5:25; 16:32 [q] Php 3:3
4:24 [r] Php 3:3
4:25 [s] Mt 1:16
4:26 [t] Jn 8:24; 9:35-37
4:27 [u] ver 8
4:29 [v] ver 17,18 [w] Mt 12:23; Jn 7:26,31
4:31 [x] Mt 23:7
4:32 [y] Job 23:12; Mt 4:4; Jn 6:27
4:34 [z] Mt 26:39; Jn 6:38; 17:4; 19:30 [a] Jn 19:30
4:35 [b] Mt 9:37; Lk 10:2
4:36 [c] Ro 1:13

19 “Sir,” the woman said, “I can see that you are a prophet.[i] 20 Our ancestors worshiped on this mountain,[j] but you Jews claim that the place where we must worship is in Jerusalem.”[k]
21 “Woman,” Jesus replied, “believe me, a time is coming[l] when you will worship the Father neither
on this mountain nor in Jerusalem.[m] 22 You Samaritans worship what you do not know;[n] we worship
what we do know, for salvation is from the Jews.[o] 23 Yet a time is coming and has now come[p] when the
true worshipers will worship the Father in the Spirit[q] and in truth, for they are the kind of worshipers
the Father seeks. 24 God is spirit,[r] and his worshipers must worship in the Spirit and in truth.”
25 The woman said, “I know that Messiah” (called Christ)[s] “is coming. When he comes, he will explain everything to us.”
26 Then Jesus declared, “I, the one speaking to you—I am he.”[t]

The Disciples Rejoin Jesus

27 Just then his disciples returned[u] and were surprised to find him talking with a woman. But no one
asked, “What do you want?” or “Why are you talking with her?”
28 Then, leaving her water jar, the woman went back to the town and said to the people, 29 “Come, see
a man who told me everything I ever did.[v] Could this be the Messiah?”[w] 30 They came out of the town
and made their way toward him.
31 Meanwhile his disciples urged him, “Rabbi,[x] eat something.”
32 But he said to them, “I have food to eat[y] that you know nothing about.”
33 Then his disciples said to each other, “Could someone have brought him food?”
34 “My food,” said Jesus, “is to do the will[z] of him who sent me and to finish his work.[a] 35 Don’t you
have a saying, ‘It’s still four months until harvest’? I tell you, open your eyes and look at the fields!
They are ripe for harvest.[b] 36 Even now the one who reaps draws a wage and harvests[c] a crop for eternal

4:19 prophet. One with special insight, not necessarily a full-orbed OT prophet, let alone the Messiah (v. 25).
4:20 ancestors worshiped. Includes Abraham (Gen 12:6–7) and Jacob (Gen 33:19–20). **this mountain.** Mount Gerizim (see map, p. 2155). Moses commanded the Israelites to pronounce the law’s blessings from Mount Gerizim and its curses from Mount Ebal just across the valley of Shechem to the north (Deut 11:29; 27:12–13; Josh 8:33). The Samaritans had erected a temple on Mount Gerizim; it replaced Jerusalem as their spiritual center. In 128 or 127 BC, John Hyrcanus, the Jewish high priest in Judea, destroyed the Samaritan temple. The hostility between Jews and Samaritans continued to Jesus’ day (see note on v. 4). Here the woman changes the subject from her adultery (v. 18) to the most controversial religious issue between Jews and Samaritans: Should God’s people worship in Jerusalem or on Mount Gerizim?
4:21–24 Jesus’ response is threefold: (1) Both the Jerusalem temple and the Mount Gerizim shrine are about to become obsolete as definitive places of worship (v. 21). (2) Salvation springs from the Jews, not the Samaritans (see v. 22 and note). (3) True worship is not tied to a sacred site (vv. 23–24).
4:21 you. Samaritans. **nor in Jerusalem.** See note on 2:19–22. The place of worship would soon be irrelevant, replaced by the living church as God’s dwelling place. See “Temple,” p. 2652.
4:22 worship what you do not know. They had their own version of the Pentateuch and rejected the rest of the OT, so their worship was not characterized by truth and knowledge. **salvation is from the Jews.** God revealed himself in the OT through the Jews (Ps 76:1), and the Savior, the Messiah, comes from them.
4:23 time. “Hour” (see note on 2:4). **has now come.** Before the cross, this period of true worship is already present in the person and ministry of Jesus. See Introduction: Characteristics and Themes, 4. **true worshipers.** Identified not by where they worship but whom and how they worship. **in the Spirit and in truth.** Or “in spirit and truth.” True worship is empowered by “the Spirit of truth” (14:17; 15:26; 16:13) and is in accordance with truth. It can occur only in and through Jesus, who is “the truth” (14:6; see 1:14) and the true temple (see note on 2:19–22).
4:24 God is spirit. “Spirit” characterizes what God is like in the same way that flesh, location, and corporeality characterize what humans and their world are like. God is invisible, divine as opposed to human (3:6), life-giving, and unknowable to humans unless he chooses to reveal himself (1:18). He is not confined to one space, so people can worship him anywhere. **in the Spirit and in truth.** See note on v. 23.
4:26 I am he. Jesus reveals himself as the promised Messiah. The term “Messiah” (v. 25) did not have the political overtones in Samaria that it had in Judea.
4:27–38 *The Disciples Rejoin Jesus.* Jesus teaches the disciples about their mission.
4:27 returned. From buying food in the town (v. 8). **surprised.** Because this was (1) a Samaritan (see notes on vv. 4,9,20) and (2) a woman. Jewish religious teachers rarely spoke with women in public.
4:28–30 The woman eagerly witnesses to the townspeople, whom she previously had reason to avoid, and they decide to come to see Jesus for themselves.
4:31–33 Jesus, though doubtless still tired and thirsty (vv. 6–7) and probably hungry, apparently dwells on his conversation with the Samaritan woman to teach his followers about his own priorities. Once again, people misunderstand Jesus: Jesus’ disciples think of physical food as quickly as the Jewish leaders thought of the physical temple building, Nicodemus thought of physical birth, and the Samaritan woman thought of physical water (see notes on vv. 11–12,15; 2:19–22; 3:4).
4:34 Likely alludes to Deut 8:3, which Jesus exemplifies. Jesus was performing his Father’s will in his exchange with the Samaritan woman, and that was greater sustenance and more satisfying than any food the disciples could offer him. He came to do the Father’s will (5:36; 6:38), and he always did it (8:29). His works were the works of God (9:3–4; 10:25,32,37–38; 14:10), and he successfully completed his mission (17:4; 19:30).
4:35–38 The harvest has already begun in the history of salvation. Jesus himself is engaged in that harvest, which is part of the work the Father gave him to do (v. 34).
4:36 crop. People who become followers of Jesus (e.g., the Samaritans in vv. 39–42). **the sower and the reaper may be glad together.**

life,[d] so that the sower and the reaper may be glad together. 37 Thus the saying 'One sows and another reaps'[e] is true. 38 I sent you to reap what you have not worked for. Others have done the hard work, and you have reaped the benefits of their labor."

Many Samaritans Believe

39 Many of the Samaritans from that town[f] believed in him because of the woman's testimony, "He told me everything I ever did."[g] 40 So when the Samaritans came to him, they urged him to stay with them, and he stayed two days. 41 And because of his words many more became believers.

42 They said to the woman, "We no longer believe just because of what you said; now we have heard for ourselves, and we know that this man really is the Savior of the world."[h]

Jesus Heals an Official's Son

43 After the two days[i] he left for Galilee. 44 (Now Jesus himself had pointed out that a prophet has no honor in his own country.)[j] 45 When he arrived in Galilee, the Galileans welcomed him. They had seen all that he had done in Jerusalem at the Passover Festival,[k] for they also had been there.

46 Once more he visited Cana in Galilee, where he had turned the water into wine.[l] And there was a certain royal official whose son lay sick at Capernaum. 47 When this man heard that Jesus had arrived in Galilee from Judea,[m] he went to him and begged him to come and heal his son, who was close to death.

48 "Unless you people see signs and wonders,"[n] Jesus told him, "you will never believe."

49 The royal official said, "Sir, come down before my child dies."

50 "Go," Jesus replied, "your son will live."

The man took Jesus at his word and departed. 51 While he was still on the way, his servants met him with the news that his boy was living. 52 When he inquired as to the time when his son got better, they said to him, "Yesterday, at one in the afternoon, the fever left him."

53 Then the father realized that this was the exact time at which Jesus had said to him, "Your son will live." So he and his whole household[o] believed.

54 This was the second sign[p] Jesus performed after coming from Judea to Galilee.

The Healing at the Pool

5 Some time later, Jesus went up to Jerusalem for one of the Jewish festivals. 2 Now there is in Jerusalem near the Sheep Gate[q] a pool, which in Aramaic[r] is called Bethesda[a] and which is surrounded by five covered colonnades. 3 Here a great number of disabled people used to lie—the blind, the lame,

[a] 2 Some manuscripts *Bethzatha*; other manuscripts *Bethsaida*

4:36 [d] Mt 25:46
4:37 [e] Job 31:8; Mic 6:15
4:39 [f] ver 5 [g] ver 29
4:42 [h] Lk 2:11; 1Jn 4:14
4:43 [i] ver 40
4:44 [j] Mt 13:57; Lk 4:24
4:45 [k] Jn 2:23
4:46 [l] Jn 2:1-11
4:47 [m] ver 3,54
4:48 [n] Da 4:2,3; Jn 2:11; Ac 2:43; 14:3; Ro 15:19; 2Co 12:12; Heb 2:4
4:53 [o] Ac 11:14
4:54 [p] ver 48; Jn 2:11
5:2 [q] Ne 3:1; 12:39 [r] Jn 19:13,17,20; 20:16; Ac 21:40; 22:2; 26:14

Recalls Amos 9:13, perhaps implying that those coming days have dawned in Jesus' ministry as sowing and reaping coincide.

4:37–38 Verse 37 summarizes v. 38: Jesus sent his disciples to reap what others sowed. John the Baptist is the last in the succession of prophets and others who sowed but did not live long enough to reap (Luke 16:16).

4:39–42 *Many Samaritans Believe.* Many Samaritans believe in Jesus because of (1) the woman's testimony (v. 29) and (2) Jesus' words, which confirm her testimony (vv. 41–42).

4:42 Savior of the world. Jesus is the Savior not just of the Jews but of the Samaritans as well (see vv. 22,23 and notes; 10:16; 11:51–52). Greek gods and Roman emperors were called in various ways "savior of the world," but Jesus is the true Savior. **world.** See notes on 1:9,29; 3:16. Jesus' mission anticipates the church's mission in Acts 1:8: going from Jerusalem (2:13—3:15) to Samaria (4:1–42) to the Gentiles.

4:43–54 *Jesus Heals an Official's Son.* This is Jesus' second sign in John's Gospel (see v. 54; see also Introduction: Purpose and Addressees).

4:44 his own country. Galilee as it represents Jewish land over against Samaritan land (Matt 13:57; Mark 6:4; Luke 4:24).

4:45 welcomed. Their superficial welcome was actually a kind of rejection because they were interested only in Jesus' miracles, not in Jesus as the Messiah and Savior. John has already let his readers know how Jesus viewed that kind of spurious faith that was so dependent on miracles (2:23–25; cf. 6:26).

4:46 royal official. Evidently an officer of Herod Antipas (see notes on Matt 14:1; Luke 3:1,19).

4:47 come. Unlike the centurion of Matt 8:5–13; Luke 7:2–10. Not until after Jesus' miracle does the royal official display any faith that goes beyond desperation (vv. 52–53).

4:48 Jesus detects in the royal official a faith that desires a miraculous cure but that does not truly trust him (see notes on vv. 45,47). Jesus' rebuke addresses the people at large because the royal official exemplifies what is wrong with the Galileans as a whole (1:11).

4:49 come down. See note on v. 47.

4:51–53 The miracle's precise timing strengthens the royal official's faith (v. 50).

4:53 whole household. Cf. Acts 11:14; 16:15,31–34; 18:8.

4:54 second sign. See Introduction: Purpose and Addressees.

5:1—8:11 *Rising Opposition: More Signs, Works, and Words.* This records the shift from people being merely reserved and hesitant about Jesus to people openly and sometimes officially opposing him.

5:1–15 *The Healing at the Pool.* This is another of Jesus' signs (see "signs" in 6:2; see also Introduction: Purpose and Addressees).

5:2 covered colonnades. Walkways with rows of columns supporting the roof and open on the side facing the pool. This site is probably the twin pools near the present-day Saint Anne's Church. There would have been a colonnade on each of the four sides and another between the two pools.

5:8 [s] Mt 9:5,6; Mk 2:11; Lk 5:24
5:9 [t] Jn 9:14
5:10 [u] ver 16 [v] Ne 13:15-22; Jer 17:21; Mt 12:2
5:14 [w] Mk 2:5; Jn 8:11
5:15 [x] Jn 1:19
5:17 [y] Jn 9:4; 14:10
5:18 [z] Jn 7:1 [a] Jn 10:30,33; 19:7
5:19 [b] ver 30; Jn 8:28

the paralyzed. [4] [a] 5One who was there had been an invalid for thirty-eight years. 6When Jesus saw
him lying there and learned that he had been in this condition for a long time, he asked him, "Do you
want to get well?"

7"Sir," the invalid replied, "I have no one to help me into the pool when the water is stirred. While I
am trying to get in, someone else goes down ahead of me."

8Then Jesus said to him, "Get up! Pick up your mat and walk." [s] 9At once the man was cured; he
picked up his mat and walked.

The day on which this took place was a Sabbath, [t] 10and so the Jewish leaders [u] said to the man who
had been healed, "It is the Sabbath; the law forbids you to carry your mat." [v]

11But he replied, "The man who made me well said to me, 'Pick up your mat and walk.' "

12So they asked him, "Who is this fellow who told you to pick it up and walk?"

13The man who was healed had no idea who it was, for Jesus had slipped away into the crowd that
was there.

14Later Jesus found him at the temple and said to him, "See, you are well again. Stop sinning [w] or
something worse may happen to you." 15The man went away and told the Jewish leaders [x] that it was
Jesus who had made him well.

The Authority of the Son

16So, because Jesus was doing these things on the Sabbath, the Jewish leaders began to persecute
him. 17In his defense Jesus said to them, "My Father is always at his work [y] to this very day, and I too am
working." 18For this reason they tried all the more to kill him; [z] not only was he breaking the Sabbath,
but he was even calling God his own Father, making himself equal with God. [a]

19Jesus gave them this answer: "Very truly I tell you, the Son can do nothing by himself; [b] he can do

[a] *3,4* Some manuscripts include here, wholly or in part, *paralyzed—and they waited for the moving of the waters. [4]From time to time an angel of the Lord would come down and stir up the waters. The first one into the pool after each such disturbance would be cured of whatever disease they had.*

5:3–4 See NIV text note, which includes text that does not appear in the oldest and best manuscripts; but v. 7 shows that it matches a popular belief at the time. Intermittent springs that fed the pools may have stirred the water. But how the pool worked is not essential to the story.
5:5 invalid. John does not identify the illness, but based on v. 7, the man is probably paralyzed or lame.
5:6 learned. Or "knew," suggesting supernatural knowledge (cf. 1:47–48; 4:17–18). Jesus compassionately initiates this healing; the person who is disabled did not ask for it.
5:7 See notes on vv. 3–4,5. A charitable reading sees the disabled person as aptly answering Jesus' question (v. 6). But given how John darkly depicts the disabled person (he parries the accusation of the Jewish leaders by blaming Jesus [v. 11], does not even know Jesus' name [v. 13], and reports Jesus to the Jewish leaders [v. 15]), this is likely the grumbling of an imperceptive man who thinks he is answering an obvious question.
5:8–9a Jesus commands the man to do what the man is unable to do, and his powerful word heals the man (cf. vv. 25,28–29). **mat.** Normally made of straw; light enough to be rolled up and easily carried on a healthy person's shoulder.
5:9b on ... a Sabbath. This triggers controversy (vv. 16–17; cf. Mark 2:23—3:6; Luke 13:10–17; 14:1–6).
5:10 the law. Not the OT (where "work" seems to be one's customary employment) but detailed regulations or traditions that the Jewish leaders added when they interpreted the OT.
5:11 The man defends himself by blaming Jesus (see note on v. 7).
5:12 There may be a hint of irony here: when the Jewish leaders hear of the miraculous healing and the formal breach of their code, they are interested only in the breach. They think they see what is important, but in religious matters there are none so blind as those who are always certain that they see (9:39–41).
5:14 at the temple. Somewhere in the temple precincts. **Stop sinning or something worse may happen to you.** Some—but not all (e.g., 9:2–3)—instances of suffering are the direct result of specific sin. **something worse.** May refer to final judgment (see v. 29).
5:15 The man ingratiates himself with the Jewish leaders.
5:16–30 *The Authority of the Son.* Jesus' healing on the Sabbath (vv. 1–15) triggers some opposition that he quickly transforms into a teaching about the nature of his sonship to the Father (see "Sonship," p. 2664). The Father has granted the Son authority to raise the dead (see "Death and Resurrection," p. 2670) and to judge (see "Wrath," p. 2681).
5:17–18 Jesus could have defended himself by distinguishing between the OT and their traditions (see note on v. 10). Instead, he argues that he too is "working": what justifies God's continuous work from creation on also justifies Jesus' continuous work (the Jewish rabbis agreed that God works continuously). Jesus' work includes telling the disabled person to carry his mat, but it also includes the healing itself and all his redemptive activity. In Mark 2:23–28, the disciples can "pick some heads of grain" (Mark 2:23) on the Sabbath since Jesus is "Lord even of the Sabbath" (Mark 2:28); here the disabled person can carry his mat since Jesus' work falls into the same category as his Father's.
5:18 making himself equal with God. The Jewish leaders rightly understand at least part of what Jesus implies (see note on 1:1). Claiming to be God's equal is far more serious than breaking their Sabbath law, so their desire to murder Jesus intensifies. But Jesus is not claiming to be *another* or a *competing* God (vv. 19–30; see 10:33 and note).
5:19 by himself. On his own initiative. The Son cannot act independently of the Father. **can do only what he sees his Father doing.** Their Father-Son relationship is not reciprocal; Scripture never says that the Father does only what he sees the Son doing. They have distinct roles: the Father initiates, sends, commands, commissions, grants; the Son responds, obeys, performs his Father's will, receives authority. The Son

Model of the pool of Bethesda.

only what he sees his Father doing, because whatever the Father does the Son also does. 20For the Father
loves the Son[c] and shows him all he does. Yes, and he will show him even greater works than these,[d] so
that you will be amazed. 21For just as the Father raises the dead and gives them life,[e] even so the Son
gives life[f] to whom he is pleased to give it. 22Moreover, the Father judges no one, but has entrusted all
judgment to the Son,[g] 23that all may honor the Son just as they honor the Father. Whoever does not
honor the Son does not honor the Father, who sent him.[h]

24"Very truly I tell you, whoever hears my word and believes him who sent me has eternal life and
will not be judged[i] but has crossed over from death to life.[j] 25Very truly I tell you, a time is coming and
has now come[k] when the dead will hear[l] the voice of the Son of God and those who hear will live. 26For
as the Father has life in himself, so he has granted the Son also to have life in himself. 27And he has
given him authority to judge[m] because he is the Son of Man.

5:20 [c] Jn 3:35 [d] Jn 14:12
5:21 [e] Ro 4:17; 8:11 [f] Jn 11:25
5:22 [g] ver 27; Jn 9:39; Ac 10:42; 17:31
5:23 [h] Lk 10:16; 1Jn 2:23
5:24 [i] Jn 3:18 [j] 1Jn 3:14
5:25 [k] Jn 4:23 [l] Jn 8:43,47
5:27 [m] ver 22; Ac 10:42; 17:31

is the Father's agent, though much more than an agent. **whatever the Father does the Son also does.** This is why ("because") it is impossible for the Son to act independently and set himself over against the Father as another God. It is also another claim that Jesus is God (see note on 1:1).
5:20 the Father loves the Son and shows him all he does. The Father displays his love for the Son by continuously disclosing to the Son all he does. This explains how ("For") the Son does "whatever the Father does" (v. 19). Thus, the Son is revealing the Father (1:18; 14:9), which depends not on God's love for us but on the Father's and Son's love for each other. **greater works.** Jesus will exercise the authority and prerogatives of God himself by raising the dead and judging (see vv. 21,22 and notes). **these.** Jesus' healing and teaching in vv. 1–20. **so that you will be amazed.** Marveling at Jesus' works may be their first step toward faith (10:38).
5:21 For. This verse illustrates vv. 19–20. **raises the dead.** A prerogative of God alone (Deut 32:39; 1 Sam 2:6; 2 Kgs 5:7). **the Son gives life.** Jesus gives eternal life now (see notes on 3:14–15) and will raise the dead in the future (vv. 25b,28–29; 1 Thess 4:16).
5:22 Moreover. Introduces a further reason for v. 21: the authority to judge on the last day entails the authority to give resurrection life (cf. the connection between vv. 26–27). **judges.** A prerogative of God alone (Gen 18:25; Matt 25:31–33; Acts 10:42; 17:31). One of the rights and responsibilities of the king, whether the king is God or someone in David's line, is to judge impartially and perfectly (see, e.g., Ps 72; Isa 11).
5:23 that. Introduces the purpose of v. 22: the Son is at one with the Father not only in activity (vv. 19–20) but also in honor (cf. Isa 42:8; 48:11). Glorifying the Son also glorifies the Father (12:28; Phil 2:9–11). Therefore, not honoring the Son means not honoring the Father. Jesus is claiming to be no less than God himself, which leaves only three options: (1) Jesus is a liar, (2) Jesus is a lunatic, or (3) Jesus is Lord. Since he makes this claim, it is illogical and unscriptural to consider Jesus to be a good man and/or a great prophet without also honoring him as God.
5:24 hears. Includes believing and obeying. **my word.** Brings either "eternal life" (see note on v. 21; see also 6:63,68) and cleansing (15:3) or judgment (12:48). **believes him who sent me.** Because the Son, in all he says and does, mediates the Father to us (vv. 19–23), placing one's faith in the Son is placing it in the Father. **judged.** Condemned (as in 3:18). Not being condemned is virtually indistinguishable from the doctrine of justification in Paul's letters: the believer does not come to the final judgment but leaves the court already acquitted (see notes on Acts 13:39; Rom 3:24). **has crossed over from death to life.** See Introduction: Characteristics and Themes, 4.
5:25 a time is coming and has now come. See Introduction: Characteristics and Themes, 4. **the dead.** The spiritually dead, i.e., unbelievers. The same resurrection life that comes to the physically dead in the end time is already being manifest in a preliminary way as spiritual life for some of the spiritually dead.
5:26–27 These verses explain how the Son can (1) generate resurrection life by his powerful word and (2) exercise divine judgment (vv. 21–25): the Father authorized him to do both.
5:26 life in himself. The Father is not dependent on anyone else; he is self-existent (Acts 17:25). The Father's granting the Son "life in himself" must be part of the eternal Father-Son relationship; therefore, many theologians tie this to what they call "the eternal generation of the Son."
5:27 because he is the Son of Man. Another reason the Son can exercise divine judgment: he is uniquely qualified to judge because

5:28 [n] Jn 4:21
5:29 [o] Da 12:2; Mt 25:46
5:30 [p] ver 19 [q] Jn 8:16 [r] Mt 26:39; Jn 4:34; 6:38
5:31 [s] Jn 8:14
5:32 [t] ver 37; Jn 8:18
5:33 [u] Jn 1:7
5:34 [v] 1Jn 5:9
5:35 [w] 2Pe 1:19
5:36 [x] 1Jn 5:9 [y] Jn 14:11; 15:24 [z] Jn 3:17; 10:25
5:37 [a] Jn 8:18 [b] Dt 4:12; 1Ti 1:17; Jn 1:18
5:38 [c] 1Jn 2:14 [d] Jn 3:17
5:39 [e] Ro 2:17,18 [f] Lk 24:27,44; Ac 13:27
5:41 [g] ver 44
5:44 [h] Ro 2:29
5:45 [i] Jn 9:28 [j] Ro 2:17
5:46 [k] Ge 3:15; Lk 24:27,44; Ac 26:22
5:47 [l] Lk 16:29,31

28 “Do not be amazed at this, for a time is coming[n] when all who are in their graves will hear his
voice 29 and come out—those who have done what is good will rise to live, and those who have done
what is evil will rise to be condemned.[o] 30 By myself I can do nothing;[p] I judge only as I hear, and my
judgment is just,[q] for I seek not to please myself but him who sent me.[r]

Testimonies About Jesus

31 “If I testify about myself, my testimony is not true.[s] 32 There is another who testifies in my favor,[t]
and I know that his testimony about me is true.

33 “You have sent to John and he has testified[u] to the truth. 34 Not that I accept human testimony;[v]
but I mention it that you may be saved. 35 John was a lamp that burned and gave light,[w] and you chose
for a time to enjoy his light.

36 “I have testimony weightier than that of John.[x] For the works that the Father has given me to finish—the very works that I am doing[y]—testify that the Father has sent me.[z] 37 And the Father who sent
me has himself testified concerning me.[a] You have never heard his voice nor seen his form,[b] 38 nor does
his word dwell in you,[c] for you do not believe the one he sent.[d] 39 You study[*a*] the Scriptures[e] diligently
because you think that in them you have eternal life. These are the very Scriptures that testify about
me,[f] 40 yet you refuse to come to me to have life.

41 “I do not accept glory from human beings,[g] 42 but I know you. I know that you do not have the love
of God in your hearts. 43 I have come in my Father’s name, and you do not accept me; but if someone
else comes in his own name, you will accept him. 44 How can you believe since you accept glory from
one another but do not seek the glory that comes from the only God[*b*]?[h]

45 “But do not think I will accuse you before the Father. Your accuser is Moses,[i] on whom your hopes
are set.[j] 46 If you believed Moses, you would believe me, for he wrote about me.[k] 47 But since you do not
believe what he wrote, how are you going to believe what I say?”[l]

a *39* Or *39Study* *b* *44* Some early manuscripts *the Only One*

he receives a kingdom that entails total dominion (Dan 7:13–14), and he belongs to humanity (Acts 17:31); rejecting his gracious revelation brings judgment.

5:28 this. That Jesus’ voice will call forth all the physically dead on the last day. Jesus provides a foretaste of this authority in the raising of Lazarus (11:1–44).

5:29 done what is good ... done what is evil. This does not mean that Jesus will judge humans on the basis of their good or bad works; in John’s Gospel, doing good means believing in Jesus, and doing evil means rejecting him. Further, good works spring from genuine faith and thus evidence it (see notes on Jas 2:14–26).

5:30 Reiterates vv. 19–20, specifically regarding Jesus’ authority to judge.

5:31–47 *Testimonies About Jesus.* After his central claims about himself, Jesus names several witnesses concerning himself: the Father (vv. 32,37–38), John the Baptist (vv. 33–35), Jesus’ own works (v. 36), and the Scriptures (v. 39), especially Moses (vv. 45–47).

5:31 Jesus is certainly not saying that if he speaks without supporting witness he is necessarily a liar (8:13–14). Rather, the kind of claims he is making cannot possibly be true if he testifies about himself outside the framework he has just established in vv. 19–30 (i.e., everything he says is nothing more and nothing less than what the Father gives him to say). Jesus’ tremendous claims do not depend exclusively on his self-attestation.

5:32 another. The Father (vv. 19–30).

5:33 You have sent. See 1:19. **testified to the truth.** John the Baptist witnessed to the true light (1:6–9,19–34).

5:34 Not that I accept human testimony. Jesus himself did not depend on John the Baptist’s witness to establish who he was in his own mind. Jesus did not need a human testimony since the Father testifies in his favor (v. 32; cf. 1 John 5:9). **that you may be saved.** Jesus mentions John the Baptist’s witness for the sake of his hearers. People are saved by believing in Jesus, and John the Baptist’s witness may help them believe.

5:35 a lamp that burned and gave light. Probably alludes to Ps 132:17. John was “a lamp” but not “the light”: Jesus is “the true light” (1:6–9). **for a time.** Their commitment was no deeper than the superficial belief of those in 2:23–25.

5:36 works. Include all of Jesus’ ministry, including his “signs” and climactic work of redemption accomplished in the cross and resurrection (cf. 9:3–4; 10:25,37–38; 14:11; 17:4). Everything Jesus does simultaneously attests to who he is and who the Father is since all that Jesus does is nothing more and nothing less than what the Father gives him to do (vv. 19–30).

5:37 the Father ... has himself testified. Perhaps a general reference to all of the Father’s revealing work, including Scripture (see vv. 38–39) and at Jesus’ baptism (Matt 3:17).

5:38 for. Introduces the evidence that supports Jesus’ indictment.

5:39–40 Jesus fulfills the OT Scriptures (Matt 5:17–18; 11:13; Luke 24:25–27,45; Heb 1:1–2), so by not believing in Jesus, the Scripture experts show that they have not rightly understood and obeyed the Scriptures. There is nothing intrinsically life-giving about studying the Scriptures if one fails to discern their content and purpose. Jesus—not Scripture itself—imparts life. See Introduction: Characteristics and Themes, 6.

5:41 Unlike Jesus’ opponents (v. 44), Jesus does not depend on human testimony (see notes on vv. 33–40).

5:42 I know you. Cf. 2:24–25. **love of God.** May mean God’s love for them or theirs for God. Probably it is the latter (3:19).

5:43 I have come in my Father’s name. And thus Jesus shares the Father’s authority (vv. 19–30). **you do not accept me.** They would if they truly loved God (1 John 3:23). **if someone else comes in his own name, you will accept him.** Verse 44 explains why they reject Jesus and accept Messianic pretenders (cf. 12:43; Rom 2:28–29).

5:45 Moses. The very one whom they so highly esteem as the mediator of the law they so highly venerate.

5:46 he wrote about me. See note on vv. 39–40. The Jewish leaders wrongly pin their hopes on Moses instead of the one Moses wrote

Jesus Feeds the Five Thousand

6:1-13pp — Mt 14:13-21; Mk 6:32-44; Lk 9:10-17

6 Some time after this, Jesus crossed to the far shore of the Sea of Galilee (that is, the Sea of Tiberias), 2 and a great crowd of people followed him because they saw the signs[m] he had performed by
healing the sick. 3 Then Jesus went up on a mountainside[n] and sat down with his disciples. 4 The Jewish
Passover Festival[o] was near.

5 When Jesus looked up and saw a great crowd coming toward him, he said to Philip,[p] "Where shall
we buy bread for these people to eat?" 6 He asked this only to test him, for he already had in mind what
he was going to do.

7 Philip answered him, "It would take more than half a year's wages[a] to buy enough bread for each
one to have a bite!"

8 Another of his disciples, Andrew, Simon Peter's brother,[q] spoke up, 9 "Here is a boy with five small
barley loaves and two small fish, but how far will they go among so many?"[r]

10 Jesus said, "Have the people sit down." There was plenty of grass in that place, and they sat down
(about five thousand men were there). 11 Jesus then took the loaves, gave thanks,[s] and distributed to
those who were seated as much as they wanted. He did the same with the fish.

12 When they had all had enough to eat, he said to his disciples, "Gather the pieces that are left over.
Let nothing be wasted." 13 So they gathered them and filled twelve baskets with the pieces of the five
barley loaves left over by those who had eaten.

14 After the people saw the sign[t] Jesus performed, they began to say, "Surely this is the Prophet who
is to come into the world."[u] 15 Jesus, knowing that they intended to come and make him king[v] by force,
withdrew again to a mountain by himself.[w]

Jesus Walks on the Water

6:16-21pp — Mt 14:22-33; Mk 6:47-51

16 When evening came, his disciples went down to the lake, 17 where they got into a boat and set off
across the lake for Capernaum. By now it was dark, and Jesus had not yet joined them. 18 A strong wind
was blowing and the waters grew rough. 19 When they had rowed about three or four miles,[b] they saw
Jesus approaching the boat, walking on the water;[x] and they were frightened. 20 But he said to them,

6:2 [m] Jn 2:11
6:3 [n] ver 15
6:4 [o] Jn 2:13; 11:55
6:5 [p] Jn 1:43
6:8 [q] Jn 1:40
6:9 [r] 2Ki 4:43
6:11 [s] ver 23; Mt 14:19
6:14 [t] Jn 2:11 [u] Dt 18:15, 18; Mt 11:3; 21:11
6:15 [v] Jn 18:36 [w] Mt 14:23; Mk 6:46
6:19 [x] Job 9:8

[a] *7* Greek *take two hundred denarii* [b] *19* Or about 5 or 6 kilometers

about, and they do not believe Jesus because they misunderstand and disobey Moses. Ironically, they later publicly execute Jesus by appealing to the law itself (19:7); John is inviting the reader to understand the law in a way that many Jews of Jesus' day did not (see "Law," p. 2649).

6:1–15 *Jesus Feeds the Five Thousand.* This is another of Jesus' signs (see "sign" in v. 14; see also Introduction: Purpose and Addressees). In some ways this account mirrors Num 11, where Moses needs to find meat for the Israelites in the desert. In both accounts one finds a plaintive question (Num 11:13; John 6:5); grumbling (Num 11:1; John 6:41,43); a description of the food, real or metaphoric (Num 11:7–9; John 6:31); mention of the eating of meat/flesh (Num 11:21; John 6:7–9); and the disproportion between the need and the resources God/Jesus supplies (Num 11:22,32; John 6:7–9,13). A further parallel exists between John 6 and Exod 16, where God provides manna and the motif of testing surfaces. Only in John, however, does the miracle point to the discourse in which Jesus himself is the ultimate bread of life (vv. 25–59). See note on Luke 9:10–17.

6:1 Sea of Galilee. See note on Luke 5:1. See map, p. 1936.

6:2 because they saw the signs. Not because they wanted to obey Jesus (cf. 2:23–25; see note on 2:23).

6:3 mountainside. May mean simply "the hill country," east of the lake.

6:4 Passover. Recalls the Israelites' exodus from Egypt (see "Exile and Exodus," p. 2659) and includes slaughtering a lamb (cf. 1:29,36; see "Sacrifice," p. 2656). See note on 2:13.

6:6 Jesus already had his own plan.

6:9 This tiny meal was ludicrously inadequate compared to the need. John mentions it to heighten the miracle.

6:10 about five thousand men. The total number of people, including women and children, may have exceeded 20,000 (see note on Matt 14:21).

6:11 gave thanks. Jesus "blesses" God, i.e., he thanks God; he does not "bless" the food. **as much as they wanted.** A lavish supply.

6:13 twelve. May symbolize that the Lord has enough to supply the needs of the 12 tribes of Israel.

6:14 the Prophet. Refers to the prophet like Moses in Deut 18:15,18. Jesus' providing so much bread to so many people in a wilderness area prompts some to think (rightly) of Moses' role in providing manna, though they focus on Jesus for the wrong reasons (vv. 15,26–27).

6:15 make him king by force. The Passover Festival (v. 4) was a rallying point for nationalistic zeal. If Moses had led the people out of Egyptian slavery, surely the coming prophet like Moses (see note on v. 14) would help them escape Roman servitude (Luke 24:21). The nature of Jesus' unique kingship becomes a major issue in the passion narrative (18:33–39; 19:3,14–15,19).

6:16–24 *Jesus Walks on the Water.* This is another of Jesus' signs (see Introduction: Purpose and Addressees).

6:18 Sudden storms often sweep over the Sea of Galilee.

6:19 three or four miles. This miracle occurs "in the middle of the lake" (Mark 6:47).

6:20 It is I. Jesus calms their fears by identifying himself. The Greek expression clearly alludes to God's self-disclosure in the name "I AM" (Exod 3:14; see Isa 43:10). See note on v. 35.

6:20 [y]Mt 14:27
6:22 [z]ver 2 [a]ver 15-21
6:23 [b]ver 1 [c]ver 11
6:25 [d]Mt 23:7
6:26 [e]ver 24 [f]ver 30; Jn 2:11
6:27 [g]Isa 55:2 [h]ver 54; Mt 25:46; Jn 4:14 [i]Mt 8:20 [j]Ro 4:11; 1Co 9:2; 2Co 1:22; Eph 1:13; 4:30; 2Ti 2:19; Rev 7:3
6:29 [k]1Jn 3:23 [l]Jn 3:17
6:30 [m]Jn 2:11 [n]Mt 12:38
6:31 [o]Nu 11:7-9 [p]Ex 16:4,15; Ne 9:15; Ps 78:24; 105:40
6:33 [q]ver 50
6:34 [r]Jn 4:15
6:35 [s]ver 48,51 [t]Jn 4:14
6:37 [u]ver 39; Jn 17:2,6,9,24

"It is I; don't be afraid."[y] 21 Then they were willing to take him into the boat, and immediately the boat
reached the shore where they were heading.

22 The next day the crowd that had stayed on the opposite shore of the lake[z] realized that only one
boat had been there, and that Jesus had not entered it with his disciples, but that they had gone away
alone.[a] 23 Then some boats from Tiberias[b] landed near the place where the people had eaten the bread
after the Lord had given thanks.[c] 24 Once the crowd realized that neither Jesus nor his disciples were
there, they got into the boats and went to Capernaum in search of Jesus.

Jesus the Bread of Life

25 When they found him on the other side of the lake, they asked him, "Rabbi,[d] when did you get
here?"

26 Jesus answered, "Very truly I tell you, you are looking for me,[e] not because you saw the signs[f] I
performed but because you ate the loaves and had your fill. 27 Do not work for food that spoils, but for
food that endures[g] to eternal life,[h] which the Son of Man[i] will give you. For on him God the Father has
placed his seal[j] of approval."

28 Then they asked him, "What must we do to do the works God requires?"

29 Jesus answered, "The work of God is this: to believe[k] in the one he has sent."[l]

30 So they asked him, "What sign[m] then will you give that we may see it and believe you?[n] What will
you do? 31 Our ancestors ate the manna[o] in the wilderness; as it is written: 'He gave them bread from
heaven to eat.'[a]"[p]

32 Jesus said to them, "Very truly I tell you, it is not Moses who has given you the bread from heaven,
but it is my Father who gives you the true bread from heaven. 33 For the bread of God is the bread that
comes down from heaven[q] and gives life to the world."

34 "Sir," they said, "always give us this bread."[r]

35 Then Jesus declared, "I am the bread of life.[s] Whoever comes to me will never go hungry, and
whoever believes in me will never be thirsty.[t] 36 But as I told you, you have seen me and still you do
not believe. 37 All those the Father gives me[u] will come to me, and whoever comes to me I will never

[a] *31* Exodus 16:4; Neh. 9:15; Psalm 78:24,25

6:21 immediately the boat reached the shore. May suggest another miracle and probably alludes to Ps 107:30.

6:22–24 The crowds seek Jesus for the wrong reason (vv. 26–27).

6:25–59 *Jesus the Bread of Life.* Jesus' feeding 5,000 (vv. 1–15) and walking on the water (vv. 16–24) introduce his "bread of life" discourse: Jesus claims that he himself is the true manna, the living bread that we must eat to satisfy our souls. See note on vv. 1–15.

6:26 not because you saw the signs. Though they see the miraculous sign (v. 14), they fail to see what it truly signifies. Not even Jesus' 12 disciples understand (Mark 6:52). Jesus' "bread of life" discourse explains how this symbol-laden sign points to him.

6:27 work for. Pour one's energy into pursuing; "believe in" (vv. 28–29). **food that spoils.** Physical food. Jesus is rebuking their purely materialistic notions of the kingdom and their seeking a miracle worker who will merely fill their stomachs with bread (see notes on vv. 14,15). **food that endures to eternal life.** Jesus himself (vv. 35,53): because this "food" endures eternally, the life it sustains endures eternally. **which.** Could refer to either "food" or "eternal life." **For.** Introduces the reason that the Son can give this. **placed his seal of approval.** The Father has certified the Son as his own agent, authorizing him as the only one who can give this.

6:28 The crowd misunderstands Jesus (see notes on 4:11–12,31–33; 5:46). They essentially ask, "Tell us what works God requires, and we will perform them." But eternal life is a gift (Eph 2:8–9; Titus 3:5), and faith (v. 29) is the fruit of God's activity (vv. 44,65).

6:29 The work of God. The work God requires; the opposite of what Paul means by "the works of the law" (Rom 3:20; see note there). The idea here is almost indistinguishable from Rom 3:28. **to believe.** Faith.

6:30–31 The crowd seeks another sign, one more spectacular than the miracle of manna (Exod 16), apparently challenging Jesus to prove that he is the Messiah, a greater prophet than Moses (v. 32; see notes on vv. 14,15).

6:31 bread from heaven. See Exod 16:4,15; Neh 9:15; Pss 78:23–24; 105:40.

6:32 true bread. Not manna (vv. 30–31) or physical bread (vv. 5–13, 26–27) but what the Father is now giving: Jesus himself (vv. 35,48,51). Jesus fulfills God's giving manna in the OT by repeating that event at a deeper, climactic level in the history of salvation.

6:33 world. The Israelites received manna in the OT, but this expands the recipients to unbelievers without distinction (see notes on 1:9,29; 3:16).

6:34 Cf. 4:15. The crowd still does not understand who Jesus is and what "true bread" (v. 32) is.

6:35 I am. Apart from the instances where the simple form "I am" occurs in Greek with overtones of the divine name (see note on v. 20), John's Gospel records seven so-called "I am" sayings (see chart, p. 2163). **the bread of life.** Also in v. 48; see vv. 41,51. May mean "the bread that is living" and/or "the bread that gives life." **comes to … believes in.** Synonymous and parallel to "eats" and "drinks"; this establishes what the eating and drinking metaphors mean in vv. 50–58. **never go hungry … never be thirsty.** Jesus spiritually satisfies one's deepest need and desire: to know God (see note on 4:14; see also 17:3; Rev 7:16).

6:36 The crowd sees Jesus only as a miracle worker and potential king (vv. 14–15), not as the Son of God who perfectly expresses the Father's words and deeds (see 5:19–30 and notes).

6:37 All those the Father gives me will come to me. Jesus is not surprised that some do not believe in him (v. 36), nor does their unbelief suggest that Jesus fails to accomplish his mission. Rather, Jesus

JESUS' SEVEN "I AM" SAYINGS IN JOHN

I am the bread of life (6:35,48) and living bread (6:51).
I am the light of the world (8:12).
I am the gate (10:7,9).
I am the good shepherd (10:11,14).
I am the resurrection and the life (11:25).
I am the way and the truth and the life (14:6).
I am the true vine (15:1,5).

drive away. 38For I have come down
from heaven not to do my will but
to do the will of him who sent me.[v]
39And this is the will of him who sent
me, that I shall lose none of all those
he has given me,[w] but raise them up
at the last day.[x] 40For my Father's will
is that everyone who looks to the Son
and believes in him shall have eternal
life,[y] and I will raise them up at the
last day."
41At this the Jews there began to
grumble about him because he said,
"I am the bread that came down from heaven." 42They said, "Is this not Jesus, the son of Joseph,[z] whose
father and mother we know?[a] How can he now say, 'I came down from heaven'?"[b]
43"Stop grumbling among yourselves," Jesus answered. 44"No one can come to me unless the Father
who sent me draws them,[c] and I will raise them up at the last day. 45It is written in the Prophets: 'They
will all be taught by God.'[a][d] Everyone who has heard the Father and learned from him comes to me.
46No one has seen the Father except the one who is from God;[e] only he has seen the Father. 47Very truly
I tell you, the one who believes has eternal life. 48I am the bread of life.[f] 49Your ancestors ate the manna
in the wilderness, yet they died.[g] 50But here is the bread that comes down from heaven,[h] which anyone
may eat and not die. 51I am the living bread that came down from heaven. Whoever eats this bread will
live forever. This bread is my flesh, which I will give for the life of the world."[i]
52Then the Jews began to argue sharply among themselves,[j] "How can this man give us his flesh
to eat?"
53Jesus said to them, "Very truly I tell you, unless you eat the flesh of the Son of Man[k] and drink his
blood, you have no life in you. 54Whoever eats my flesh and drinks my blood has eternal life, and I will

6:38 [v] Jn 4:34; 5:30
6:39 [w] Jn 10:28; 17:12; 18:9 [x] ver 40,44,54
6:40 [y] Jn 3:15,16
6:42 [z] Lk 4:22 [a] Jn 7:27, 28 [b] ver 38,62
6:44 [c] ver 65; Jer 31:3; Jn 12:32
6:45 [d] Isa 54:13; Jer 31:33,34; Heb 8:10,11; 10:16
6:46 [e] Jn 1:18; 5:37; 7:29
6:48 [f] ver 35,51
6:49 [g] ver 31,58
6:50 [h] ver 33
6:51 [i] Heb 10:10
6:52 [j] Jn 7:43; 9:16; 10:19
6:53 [k] Mt 8:20

[a] *45* Isaiah 54:13

is confident that the Father will fully accomplish his saving purposes by enabling specific people to come to Jesus (vv. 39,44,65). **whoever comes.** Because the Father gave them to Jesus. **never drive away.** Certainly keep or preserve (vv. 38–40; 10:28–29).

6:38 For. Introduces the reason Jesus will perfectly preserve all those whom the Father has given him (v. 37): Jesus came to earth to do the Father's will, namely, to lose "none" (v. 39), i.e., no individual, the Father has given him.

6:40 Reiterates vv. 38–39 but describes those the Father has given the Son as those who look to and believe in the Son. God's sovereignty (see notes on vv. 37,38) does not mitigate human responsibility (5:40). This fits with the position that modern philosophy calls "compatibilism" (i.e., God's sovereignty and human responsibility are compatible).

6:41 the Jews there. The synagogue congregation in Capernaum (v. 59) or at least its leaders. **grumble.** Like their ancestors in the wilderness who complained before (Exod 16:2,8–9) and after (Num 11:4–6) God provided manna.

6:42 son of Joseph. They are incensed because Jesus claims a heavenly origin when they think they know his earthly origin (cf. Mark 6:3; Luke 4:22). The irony is twofold: (1) They think they know who Jesus' father is, but they are unaware of Jesus' virginal conception (see Matt 1:18–25 and notes) and true identity, and do not know his Father at all (8:19,55; 15:21; 16:3; 17:25). (2) Jesus knows who their "father" is: the devil (8:42–44).

6:44 The negative counterpart of v. 37a and reiterated in v. 65. **No one can.** Humans are unable to come to Christ on their own initiative. The decisive cause of their "coming" is the Father. **draws.** The Father gives select individuals the desire and ability to come to Christ; e.g., the Father did not draw Judas (vv. 64–65,70–71). **I will raise them up at the last day.** Everyone whom the Father draws comes to Christ because Christ resurrects them (vv. 39–40).

6:45 Jesus explains that the Father draws (v. 44) by teaching or illuminating people (Matt 16:17; cf. Jer 31:31–34; Ezek 36:24–26; 1 Cor 4:6; 1 Thess 4:9; 1 John 2:20,27). This fulfills Isa 54:13 (which Jesus paraphrases) by repeating that OT situation (God's teaching a restored Jerusalem after the Babylonian exile) at a deeper, climactic level in the history of salvation (Jesus' teaching ministry).

6:46 Only Jesus has fully seen the Father (1:18; 3:13; cf. 14:7–9). People are "taught by God" (v. 45) only if they truly "hear" Jesus.

6:47 Cf. 3:15,36.

6:48 I am. See note on v. 35.

6:49–58 The terms "eat," "drink," and "feed on" dominate this passage and are metaphors for believing in Jesus (see note on v. 35).

6:49–50 Jesus contrasts two breads (vv. 30–33): eating manna resulted in dying, and "eating" Jesus, the bread from heaven (see note on v. 32), results in not dying (i.e., eternal life).

6:51 The first two sentences restate vv. 49–50. **flesh.** Recalls 1:14. **I will give for the life of the world.** Jesus implies here that his death will be a vicarious sacrifice (1:29,36). **world.** See notes on 1:9,29; 3:16.

6:52 How. The crowd does not think that Jesus is advocating cannibalism and offering himself, yet they do not understand what Jesus means (see notes on v. 28; 4:11–12,31–33; 5:46).

6:53–54 This repeats the basic theme of vv. 49–51 and adds the metaphor of drinking blood, a scandalous and abhorrent notion to Jews (Lev 19:26). Eating and drinking are metaphors for believing in Jesus (v. 54 closely parallels v. 40; see note on v. 35). Some argue that this refers to the Lord's Supper, but two factors stand against that view: (1) The setting of this passage is during Jesus' ministry before he instituted the Lord's

6:54 [l] ver 39
6:56 [m] Jn 15:4-7; 1Jn 3:24; 4:15
6:57 [n] Jn 3:17
6:58 [o] ver 49-51; Jn 3:36
6:60 [p] ver 66
6:61 [q] Mt 11:6
6:62 [r] Mk 16:19; Jn 3:13; 17:5
6:63 [s] 2Co 3:6
6:64 [t] Jn 2:25
6:65 [u] ver 37,44
6:66 [v] ver 60
6:67 [w] Mt 10:2
6:68 [x] Mt 16:16
6:69 [y] Mk 8:29; Lk 9:20
6:70 [z] Jn 15:16,19 [a] Jn 13:27
7:1 [b] Jn 1:19 [c] Jn 5:18
7:2 [d] Lev 23:34; Dt 16:16
7:3 [e] Mt 12:46

raise them up at the last day.[l] 55 For my flesh is real food and my blood is real drink. 56 Whoever eats my flesh and drinks my blood remains in me, and I in them.[m] 57 Just as the living Father sent me[n] and I live because of the Father, so the one who feeds on me will live because of me. 58 This is the bread that came down from heaven. Your ancestors ate manna and died, but whoever feeds on this bread will live forever."[o] 59 He said this while teaching in the synagogue in Capernaum.

Many Disciples Desert Jesus

60 On hearing it, many of his disciples[p] said, "This is a hard teaching. Who can accept it?"

61 Aware that his disciples were grumbling about this, Jesus said to them, "Does this offend you?[q] 62 Then what if you see the Son of Man ascend to where he was before![r] 63 The Spirit gives life;[s] the flesh counts for nothing. The words I have spoken to you — they are full of the Spirit[a] and life. 64 Yet there are some of you who do not believe." For Jesus had known[t] from the beginning which of them did not believe and who would betray him. 65 He went on to say, "This is why I told you that no one can come to me unless the Father has enabled them."[u]

66 From this time many of his disciples[v] turned back and no longer followed him.

67 "You do not want to leave too, do you?" Jesus asked the Twelve.[w]

68 Simon Peter answered him,[x] "Lord, to whom shall we go? You have the words of eternal life. 69 We have come to believe and to know that you are the Holy One of God."[y]

70 Then Jesus replied, "Have I not chosen you,[z] the Twelve? Yet one of you is a devil!"[a] 71 (He meant Judas, the son of Simon Iscariot, who, though one of the Twelve, was later to betray him.)

Jesus Goes to the Festival of Tabernacles

7 After this, Jesus went around in Galilee. He did not want[b] to go about in Judea because the Jewish leaders[b] there were looking for a way to kill him.[c] 2 But when the Jewish Festival of Tabernacles[d] was near, 3 Jesus' brothers[e] said to him, "Leave Galilee and go to Judea, so that your disciples there may

[a] *63* Or *are Spirit*; or *are spirit* [b] *1* Some manuscripts *not have authority*

Supper. (2) During the first two centuries, whenever Christians clearly speak of the Lord's Supper, they speak of the "body" and "blood" of the Lord, not (as here) the "flesh" and "blood" of the Lord. On the other hand, by the time John's Gospel was circulating, the church had existed for several decades, and the Lord's Supper was celebrated everywhere; therefore, informed Christians who pondered these verses probably could not avoid reflecting on how the elements of the Lord's Supper point back to the historic death of Jesus, calling us again and again to belief in him.

6:56 The reason for v. 55. **remains in me.** The believer identifies with Jesus and continues or perseveres as a believer. **I in them.** Jesus identifies with and blesses the believer. On mutual indwelling, see notes on 15:1–10.

6:57 A compressed form of Jesus' argument in 5:21,24–27. Jesus mediates eternal life.

6:58 manna. See notes on vv. 30–33,41,49–50.

6:59 this. Probably vv. 26–58. **Capernaum.** See v. 24.

6:60–71 *Many Disciples Desert Jesus.* Many of Jesus' disciples turn against him.

6:60 disciples. Different than "the Twelve" (v. 67). Just as there is spurious faith and genuine faith (2:23–25), so there are spurious disciples and genuine disciples (8:31). **hard.** Hard to accept, not hard to understand (v. 61). These "disciples" will not long remain disciples because they find Jesus' teaching unpleasant, especially the language in vv. 49–58.

6:61 grumbling. One of the perennial sins of the Israelites when they wandered in the wilderness and God provided manna. It reflected a wretched lack of faith in God's goodness and ability to provide for his people and was therefore a kind of idolatry (see note on Exod 15:24).

6:62 Jesus just said, "I have come down from heaven" (v. 38). **ascend.** Probably the series of events that began with the cross, where Jesus was glorified (7:39). **where he was before.** Jesus existed before he became human (8:58; 17:5).

6:63 The Spirit gives life; the flesh counts for nothing. Apart from God's Spirit, humans cannot experience eternal life (3:5–8). **The words I have spoken.** One cannot "feed on" (i.e., believe in) Jesus without feeding on his words (v. 68; 5:24). **full of the Spirit and life.** The Spirit generates life through Jesus' words.

6:64 Unbelief does not surprise Jesus (2:23–25). **who would betray him.** Judas (vv. 70–71).

6:65 This. Unbelief (v. 64). Because Jesus knew in advance that many would reject him, he explained that the Father must draw those whom he has given to Jesus and enable them to believe (see vv. 37,44 and notes).

6:66 From this time. May also mean "For this reason." **many of his disciples.** Those who found Jesus' earlier discourse intolerable (v. 60). **turned back and no longer followed him.** Abandoned Jesus decisively, proving that their initial "faith" was not genuine.

6:68 Only Jesus has the words of life (v. 63).

6:69 Holy One. See "Holiness," p. 2676.

6:70 Have I not chosen you … ? Peter's answer (vv. 68–69) appears somewhat pretentious, as if he and his fellow disciples are superior to the fickle "disciples" who have turned away. But ultimately, they did not choose Jesus; Jesus chose them. **Yet one of you is a devil.** Jesus knows (cf. 13:11) that the devil will prompt Judas to betray him (v. 71; 13:2).

7:1–13 *Jesus Goes to the Festival of Tabernacles.* Skepticism and uncertainty regarding Jesus continue, even among members of his own family.

7:1 looking for a way to kill him. See 5:18.

7:2 Festival of Tabernacles. Commemorated God's goodness to the people during the wilderness wanderings and celebrated the completion of the harvest (see note on Lev 23:34).

7:3–4 "Jesus' brothers" (v. 3) most likely refers to the sons of Mary and Joseph, all younger than Jesus. Their request is ironic in three ways: (1) They want Jesus to put on a display, but John's readers

see the works you do. 4No one who wants to become a public figure acts in secret. Since you are doing
these things, show yourself to the world." 5For even his own brothers did not believe in him.[f]
6Therefore Jesus told them, "My time[g] is not yet here; for you any time will do. 7The world cannot
hate you, but it hates me[h] because I testify that its works are evil.[i] 8You go to the festival. I am not[a]
going up to this festival, because my time[j] has not yet fully come." 9After he had said this, he stayed
in Galilee.
10However, after his brothers had left for the festival, he went also, not publicly, but in secret. 11Now
at the festival the Jewish leaders were watching for Jesus[k] and asking, "Where is he?"
12Among the crowds there was widespread whispering about him. Some said, "He is a good man."
Others replied, "No, he deceives the people."[l] 13But no one would say anything publicly about him
for fear of the leaders.[m]

7:5 [f]Mk 3:21
7:6 [g]Mt 26:18
7:7 [h]Jn 15:18,19 [i]Jn 3:19,20
7:8 [j]ver 6
7:11 [k]Jn 11:56
7:12 [l]ver 40,43
7:13 [m]Jn 9:22; 12:42; 19:38
7:14 [n]ver 28; Mt 26:55
7:15 [o]Jn 1:19 [p]Ac 26:24 [q]Mt 13:54

Jesus Teaches at the Festival

14Not until halfway through the festival did Jesus go up to the temple courts and begin to teach.[n] 15The
Jews[o] there were amazed and asked, "How did this man get such learning[p] without having been taught?"[q]

[a] 8 Some manuscripts *not yet*

The fourth-century synagogue at Capernaum, built over the remains of a first-century synagogue.
Barry Beitzel/www.BiblePlaces.com

already know that such a display would pander to corrupt motives (6:14–15,26–31) and would not ensure genuine faith (2:23–25; 4:48). (2) They want Jesus to show himself to "the world" (i.e., everybody at the festival), but the "world" is precisely what cannot receive him without ceasing to be the "world" (see notes on 1:9,29; 3:16). And in one sense, Jesus has no intention of showing himself to the "world" (see 14:22 and note). (3) They want Jesus to put on a display in Jerusalem, and it is in Jerusalem where Jesus later reveals himself most dramatically—not in the spectacular miracles the brothers want but in the ignominy of the cross.

7:5 For. Introduces the reason for the request in vv. 3–4. Jesus' brothers did not perceive what Jesus' signs signified. **did not believe.** Apparently, they did not follow Jesus until after his resurrection (Acts 1:14).

7:6 Therefore. Jesus explains that his brothers' judgment is faulty because they projected onto him what they would have done under similar circumstances (cf. 2:4). **time ... time.** For going up to Jerusalem for this Festival of Tabernacles.

7:7 The world cannot hate you. Because they belong to it and the world loves its own (15:19). **it hates me.** Because Jesus does not belong to it and testifies that what it does is evil (v. 19; 3:19–20; 8:31–59; 9:39–41; 16:8–11; see notes on 1:9,29; 3:16).

7:8–10 I am not going up to this festival ... he went also. The apparent contradiction is superficial: because the Father's appointments regulate his life, Jesus is not at that time (see NIV text note on v. 8) going to the festival in line with when and how his brothers want him to go. He will go when and how the Father sanctions the trip.

7:10 not publicly, but in secret. Exactly the opposite of what Jesus' brothers had in mind (see vv. 3–4 and note). If Jesus went publicly with the other pilgrims at the beginning of the festival, they may have forced a premature "triumphal entry" on him.

7:11 The Jewish leaders are hostile toward Jesus (v. 13).

7:12 The crowds are divided in their opinion of Jesus (see note on 5:23).

7:14–24 *Jesus Teaches at the Festival.* Jesus teaches a crowd that superficially judges him.

7:14 halfway through. See notes on vv. 8–10. Teaching in the temple courts did not foster privacy, but Jesus was concerned not about privacy but about obeying his Father. He went public with teaching, not miracles.

7:15 A rabbi did not train Jesus (cf. Matt 7:28–29).

7:16 [r] Jn 3:11; 14:24
7:17 [s] Ps 25:14; Jn 8:43
7:18 [t] Jn 5:41; 8:50,54
7:19 [u] Jn 1:17 [v] ver 1; Mt 12:14
7:20 [w] Jn 8:48; 10:20
7:22 [x] Lev 12:3 [y] Ge 17:10-14
7:24 [z] Isa 11:3,4; Jn 8:15
7:26 [a] ver 48
7:27 [b] Mt 13:55; Lk 4:22
7:28 [c] ver 14 [d] Jn 8:14 [e] Jn 8:26,42
7:29 [f] Mt 11:27
7:30 [g] ver 32,44; Jn 10:39
7:31 [h] Jn 8:30 [i] Jn 2:11

16 Jesus answered, "My teaching is not my own. It comes from the one who sent me.[r] 17 Anyone who chooses to do the will of God will find out[s] whether my teaching comes from God or whether I speak on my own. 18 Whoever speaks on their own does so to gain personal glory,[t] but he who seeks the glory of the one who sent him is a man of truth; there is nothing false about him. 19 Has not Moses given you the law?[u] Yet not one of you keeps the law. Why are you trying to kill me?"[v]

20 "You are demon-possessed,"[w] the crowd answered. "Who is trying to kill you?"

21 Jesus said to them, "I did one miracle, and you are all amazed. 22 Yet, because Moses gave you circumcision[x] (though actually it did not come from Moses, but from the patriarchs),[y] you circumcise a boy on the Sabbath. 23 Now if a boy can be circumcised on the Sabbath so that the law of Moses may not be broken, why are you angry with me for healing a man's whole body on the Sabbath? 24 Stop judging by mere appearances, but instead judge correctly."[z]

Division Over Who Jesus Is

25 At that point some of the people of Jerusalem began to ask, "Isn't this the man they are trying to kill? 26 Here he is, speaking publicly, and they are not saying a word to him. Have the authorities[a] really concluded that he is the Messiah? 27 But we know where this man is from;[b] when the Messiah comes, no one will know where he is from."

28 Then Jesus, still teaching in the temple courts,[c] cried out, "Yes, you know me, and you know where I am from.[d] I am not here on my own authority, but he who sent me is true.[e] You do not know him, 29 but I know him[f] because I am from him and he sent me."

30 At this they tried to seize him, but no one laid a hand on him,[g] because his hour had not yet come. 31 Still, many in the crowd believed in him.[h] They said, "When the Messiah comes, will he perform more signs[i] than this man?"

32 The Pharisees heard the crowd whispering such things about him. Then the chief priests and the Pharisees sent temple guards to arrest him.

7:16 My teaching is not my own. Rabbis say the same thing. But while they appeal to a long chain of human tradition, Jesus appeals to the Father (5:19–30; 8:28).
7:17 chooses to do the will of God. Commits to doing God's will without setting themselves up as judging God and his ways. Hindrances to faith are fundamentally moral rather than intellectual (3:19–21; see note on 3:19).
7:18 on their own. Their egos are bound up with their witness. **to gain personal glory.** The real reason Jesus' opponents cannot assess him rightly (5:44). **a man of truth.** Jesus is trustworthy and not self-seeking (8:46).
7:19 not one of you keeps the law. See Rom 2:17–29. **trying to kill me.** Evidence that they attempt to break the law (Exod 20:13). See "Law," p. 2649.
7:20 The crowd assumes that Jesus is paranoid, perhaps suffering from delusions of grandeur (cf. 10:20).
7:21 one miracle. The healing at the pool when Jesus was previously in Jerusalem (5:1–15). **amazed.** Not astonishment that leads to praise but marvel that someone would actually tell another to carry their mat on the Sabbath (v. 23; see notes on 5:9b,10).
7:22 it did not come from Moses, but from the patriarchs. God instituted circumcision as a covenant sign while Abraham was still alive (Gen 17:10–14) and later formalized it as part of the Mosaic law (Lev 12:3). Since the Jews have put Moses on a pedestal, John includes this aside to lessen Moses a little and establish that circumcision existed before the Mosaic law and thus takes precedence over it (Gal 3:17). **you circumcise a boy on the Sabbath.** The Jews faced a choice when an infant's eighth day was a Sabbath: either obey the law to circumcise him on the eighth day or obey the law (as they understood it: see notes on 5:9b,10) to observe the Sabbath. They chose to circumcise their sons on the Sabbath, yet they were angry when Jesus healed a "man's whole body" on the Sabbath (v. 23).
7:24 They judge by superficial criteria: they misconstrue Jesus' character based on a fundamentally flawed set of deductions from OT law. **judge correctly.** Requires moral and theological discernment in the context of obedient faith (v. 17).
7:25–44 *Division Over Who Jesus Is.* People are divided whether Jesus is the Messiah.
7:25 Some have naive doubts (vv. 19–20), but some from Jerusalem know that the Jerusalem authorities are trying to kill Jesus (v. 1; 5:16,18).
7:27 They immediately dismiss the possibility that Jesus is the Messiah (v. 26) based on one of three popular notions about the Messiah that this chapter mentions (vv. 31,42). They presuppose that the Messiah would be unknown until he appeared to redeem Israel, but they "know" where Jesus came from: he sprang from Nazareth, and his family home was now in Capernaum. Ironically, they are not as informed about Jesus' true origins as they think (1:1–3,14).
7:28 Jesus exposes their ignorance. **true.** Real; regardless of what they might think of Jesus' origins, the Father is the one who sent him. **You do not know him.** They do not understand the law (5:46) or the God who gave it because they are rejecting the Son (8:19,42).
7:29 See 5:19–30.
7:30 because his hour had not yet come. John tells only why Jesus escaped, not how. **hour.** See note on 2:4.
7:31 Faith based on signs is better than nothing (10:38), but there is no hint that these people develop any deep understanding of the *sign*ificance of the signs and grasp all that the signs show Jesus to be. They are simply impressed by the number of spectacular displays of power they have witnessed.
7:32 temple guards. A temple "police" force, drawn from the Levites, with primary responsibility for maintaining order in the temple area.

ACCUSATIONS LEVELED AGAINST JESUS BY HIS OPPONENTS IN JOHN'S GOSPEL

Galilean, Nazarene	1:46; 7:41,52; 18:5,7; 19:19
Breaking the Sabbath	5:16,18; 9:16
Blaspheming	5:18; 8:59; 10:31,33,39; 19:7 (cf. Lev 24:16)
Deceiving the people	7:12,47
Demon-possessed	7:20; 8:48–52; 10:20–21
Illegitimate birth	8:41
Samaritan (apostate?)	8:48
A sinner	9:16,24–25,31
Madness	10:20
A criminal	18:30
Royal pretender, political threat	19:12; cf. 19:15,21

33 Jesus said, "I am with you for only a short time,[j] and then I am going to the one who sent me.[k]
34 You will look for me, but you will not find me; and where I am, you cannot come."[l]
35 The Jews said to one another, "Where does this man intend to go that we cannot find him? Will
he go where our people live scattered[m] among the Greeks,[n] and teach the Greeks? 36 What did he mean
when he said, 'You will look for me, but you will not find me,' and 'Where I am, you cannot come'?"
37 On the last and greatest day of the festival,[o] Jesus stood and said in a loud voice, "Let anyone who
is thirsty come to me and drink.[p] 38 Whoever believes in me, as Scripture has said,[q] rivers of living water[r]
will flow from within them."[a][s] 39 By this he meant the Spirit,[t] whom those who believed in him were
later to receive.[u] Up to that time the Spirit had not been given, since Jesus had not yet been glorified.[v]
40 On hearing his words, some of the people said, "Surely this man is the Prophet."[w]
41 Others said, "He is the Messiah."
Still others asked, "How can the Messiah come from Galilee?[x] 42 Does not Scripture say that the Messiah will come from David's descendants[y] and from Bethlehem,[z] the town where David lived?" 43 Thus
the people were divided[a] because of Jesus. 44 Some wanted to seize him, but no one laid a hand on him.[b]

[a] *37,38* Or *me. And let anyone drink* 38*who believes in me." As Scripture has said, "Out of him* (or *them*) *will flow rivers of living water."*

7:33 [j] Jn 13:33; 16:16 [k] Jn 16:5,10,17,28
7:34 [l] Jn 8:21; 13:33
7:35 [m] Jas 1:1 [n] Jn 12:20; 1Pe 1:1
7:37 [o] Lev 23:36 [p] Isa 55:1; Rev 22:17
7:38 [q] Isa 58:11 [r] Jn 4:10 [s] Jn 4:14
7:39 [t] Joel 2:28; Ac 2:17, 33 [u] Jn 20:22 [v] Jn 12:23; 13:31,32
7:40 [w] Mt 21:11; Jn 1:21
7:41 [x] ver 52; Jn 1:46
7:42 [y] Mt 1:1 [z] Mic 5:2; Mt 2:5,6; Lk 2:4
7:43 [a] Jn 9:16; 10:19
7:44 [b] ver 30

7:33–34 Jesus speaks of his imminent departure in words that are clear to any reader, especially after reading the entire book at least once. **7:33 short time.** Before the cross. This presupposes the Father's fore-ordained schedule. **7:34 You will look for me, but you will not find me.** They will go on looking for the Messiah, but they will chase an ephemeral wisp because they have rejected the only Messiah there is. **where I am, you cannot come.** Returning to his glory with the Father (13:33; see 17:5). **7:35–36** Once again, people misunderstand Jesus (see Introduction: Characteristics and Themes, 7): the Jews, who think they know all there is to know about Jesus' origins (see v. 27 and note), cannot imagine that Jesus can go where they cannot find him. **7:35 teach the Greeks.** Ironically, after Jesus' ascension, the gospel will spread in Jewish and Gentile circles throughout the Roman Empire and beyond. **7:37–38** See 4:10–14; 6:35. **7:37 festival.** See note on v. 2. This included a well-known water-pouring rite that symbolized the fruitfulness that only rain can bring and anticipated the spiritual "rain" God promised to pour out in the Messianic age (Zech 13:1; 14:16–17). Jesus fulfills what the Festival of Tabernacles anticipated. **Let anyone who is thirsty come to me and drink.** Jesus supplies the drink and quenches thirst (Isa 55:1; Rev 22:17).

7:38 as Scripture has said. Refers generally to a matrix of OT teachings and may allude specifically to Neh 9:15,19–20, where Israel observes the Festival of Tabernacles (Neh 8:5–18) and God's providing manna and water symbolize his giving the law and the Spirit. **rivers of living water will flow from within them.** See NIV text note. The source of the water is Jesus. John explicitly connects the water and the Spirit in v. 39 (see notes on 4:10,14). **7:39 later to receive.** God fully gave the Spirit to permanently indwell all believers after Jesus completed his mission (20:22; Acts 2:1–4). **glorified.** See note on 12:23. **7:40–41 the Prophet ... the Messiah.** Some Jews thought of these as two separate individuals (1:19–21), but Jesus is both. See notes on 1:20; 6:14. **7:41 from Galilee.** Some Jews thought that Jesus was a Galilean and that the Messiah would be a descendant of David (2 Sam 7:12–16; Ps 89:3–4; Isa 9:7) and born in Bethlehem (Mic 5:2; Matt 2:1). They do not realize the irony: Jesus was "a descendant of David" (Rom 1:3; see Matt 2:1,5–6) and born in Bethlehem (Luke 2:4,15). **7:43 divided.** See 9:16; 10:19. **7:44 no one laid a hand on him.** Because his hour had not yet come (see note on 2:4; see also 8:20).

7:46 [c]Mt 7:28
7:47 [d]ver 12
7:48 [e]Jn 12:42
7:50 [f]Jn 3:1; 19:39
7:52 [g]ver 41
8:1 [h]Mt 21:1
8:2 [i]ver 20; Mt 26:55
8:5 [j]Lev 20:10; Dt 22:22
8:6 [k]Mt 22:15,18 [l]Mt 12:10
8:7 [m]Dt 17:7 [n]Ro 2:1,22
8:11 [o]Jn 3:17 [p]Jn 5:14
8:12 [q]Jn 6:35 [r]Jn 1:4; 12:35 [s]Pr 4:18; Mt 5:14

Unbelief of the Jewish Leaders

45 Finally the temple guards went back to the chief priests and the Pharisees, who asked them, "Why didn't you bring him in?"

46 "No one ever spoke the way this man does,"[c] the guards replied.

47 "You mean he has deceived you also?"[d] the Pharisees retorted. 48 "Have any of the rulers or of the Pharisees believed in him?[e] 49 No! But this mob that knows nothing of the law—there is a curse on them."

50 Nicodemus,[f] who had gone to Jesus earlier and who was one of their own number, asked, 51 "Does our law condemn a man without first hearing him to find out what he has been doing?"

52 They replied, "Are you from Galilee, too? Look into it, and you will find that a prophet does not come out of Galilee."[g]

[The earliest manuscripts and many other ancient witnesses do not have John 7:53—8:11. A few manuscripts include these verses, wholly or in part, after John 7:36, John 21:25, Luke 21:38 or Luke 24:53.]

8 *53 Then they all went home, 1 but Jesus went to the Mount of Olives.*[h]
2 At dawn he appeared again in the temple courts, where all the people gathered around him, and he sat down to teach them.[i] *3 The teachers of the law and the Pharisees brought in a woman caught in adultery. They made her stand before the group 4 and said to Jesus, "Teacher, this woman was caught in the act of adultery. 5 In the Law Moses commanded us to stone such women.*[j] *Now what do you say?" 6 They were using this question as a trap,*[k] *in order to have a basis for accusing him.*[l]

But Jesus bent down and started to write on the ground with his finger. 7 When they kept on questioning him, he straightened up and said to them, "Let any one of you who is without sin be the first to throw a stone[m] *at her."*[n] *8 Again he stooped down and wrote on the ground.*

9 At this, those who heard began to go away one at a time, the older ones first, until only Jesus was left, with the woman still standing there. 10 Jesus straightened up and asked her, "Woman, where are they? Has no one condemned you?"

11 "No one, sir," she said.

"Then neither do I condemn you,"[o] *Jesus declared. "Go now and leave your life of sin."*[p]

Dispute Over Jesus' Testimony

12 When Jesus spoke again to the people, he said, "I am[q] the light of the world.[r] Whoever follows me will never walk in darkness, but will have the light of life."[s]

7:45–52 *Unbelief of the Jewish Leaders.* The confrontational exchanges at the Festival of Tabernacles (vv. 14–44) lead to the first organized opposition from the Jewish authorities.

7:45 The Jewish leaders had already authorized an official arrest warrant (v. 32).

7:46 The guards speak truer than they know since Jesus is not merely a human being but the incarnate Word (1:14) whose every word and deed reveals the Father (5:19–30; 8:28–29).

7:47–48 The sneering question from the Pharisees (v. 47) mocks the guards not as police officers who should follow orders, but as Levites (see note on v. 32) who should follow the religious authorities and not be seduced by an imposter who does not deceive the real thinkers. The irony is threefold: (1) The Pharisees imply that no leader believes in Jesus, yet the Pharisee Nicodemus (3:1), "Israel's teacher" (3:10), is about to speak on Jesus' behalf (v. 51; cf. 12:42). (2) The Pharisees require the people to observe their law, but Nicodemus is about to highlight their own disregard for their law in this instance (v. 51; cf. Deut 1:16–17; 19:18). (3) The Jewish leaders boast that they have not been duped, but the substance of their boasting is precisely what has duped them (cf. Matt 11:25; 1 Cor 1:26–31).

7:49 knows nothing. The religious leaders view the common people condescendingly, presuming that they are easily deceived because they are ignorant. John's irony continues to quietly chuckle in the background.

7:51 A procedural point that would work in Jesus' favor. See note on vv. 47–48.

7:52 The Pharisees are frustrated and wrong: Jonah (and possibly Nahum and other prophets) came from Galilee. See note on v. 41.

7:53—8:11 *The Woman Caught in Adultery.* See bracketed and italicized NIV text after v. 52. Although this story probably recounts a real event from Jesus' life, it almost certainly was not originally part of John's Gospel. Modern English versions set it off from the rest of the text because these verses are absent from virtually all early Greek manuscripts we possess.

8:12—10:42 *Radical Confrontation: Climactic Signs, Works, and Words.* Conflict escalates as Jesus debates Jewish leaders (8:12–59), heals a man born blind (ch. 9), presents himself as the good shepherd (10:1–21), and claims to be both the Messiah and Son of God (10:22–42).

8:12–20 *Dispute Over Jesus' Testimony.* This presents themes that the rest of ch. 8 develops: where Jesus comes from (vv. 23,26,29), where Jesus is going (vv. 21–22,28), who the Father is (vv. 26–27,38,54–55), and who Jesus is (vv. 23–26,38,54–55).

8:12 I am. See note on 6:35. **light ... darkness.** See notes on 1:5; 3:19.

[13]The Pharisees challenged him, "Here you are, appearing as your own witness; your testimony is
not valid."[t]
[14]Jesus answered, "Even if I testify on my own behalf, my testimony is valid, for I know where I came
from and where I am going.[u] But you have no idea where I come from[v] or where I am going. [15]You
judge by human standards;[w] I pass judgment on no one.[x] [16]But if I do judge, my decisions are true,
because I am not alone. I stand with the Father, who sent me.[y] [17]In your own Law it is written that the
testimony of two witnesses is true.[z] [18]I am one who testifies for myself; my other witness is the Father,
who sent me."[a]
[19]Then they asked him, "Where is your father?"
"You do not know me or my Father,"[b] Jesus replied. "If you knew me, you would know my Father
also."[c] [20]He spoke these words while teaching[d] in the temple courts near the place where the offerings
were put.[e] Yet no one seized him, because his hour had not yet come.[f]

Dispute Over Who Jesus Is

[21]Once more Jesus said to them, "I am going away, and you will look for me, and you will die[g] in
your sin. Where I go, you cannot come."[h]
[22]This made the Jews ask, "Will he kill himself? Is that why he says, 'Where I go, you cannot
come'?"
[23]But he continued, "You are from below; I am from above. You are of this world; I am not of this
world.[i] [24]I told you that you would die in your sins; if you do not believe that I am he,[j] you will indeed
die in your sins."
[25]"Who are you?" they asked.
"Just what I have been telling you from the beginning," Jesus replied. [26]"I have much to say in
judgment of you. But he who sent me is trustworthy,[k] and what I have heard from him I tell the
world."[l]
[27]They did not understand that he was telling them about his Father. [28]So Jesus said, "When you
have lifted up[a] the Son of Man,[m] then you will know that I am he and that I do nothing on my own but
speak just what the Father has taught me. [29]The one who sent me is with me; he has not left me alone,[n]
for I always do what pleases him."[o] [30]Even as he spoke, many believed in him.[p]

a 28 The Greek for *lifted up* also means *exalted*.

8:13 [t]Jn 5:31
8:14 [u]Jn 13:3; 16:28 [v]Jn 7:28; 9:29
8:15 [w]Jn 7:24 [x]Jn 3:17
8:16 [y]Jn 5:30
8:17 [z]Dt 17:6; Mt 18:16
8:18 [a]Jn 5:37
8:19 [b]Jn 16:3 [c]Jn 14:7; 1Jn 2:23
8:20 [d]Mt 26:55 [e]Mk 12:41 [f]Mt 26:18; Jn 7:30
8:21 [g]Eze 3:18 [h]Jn 7:34; 13:33
8:23 [i]Jn 3:31; 17:14
8:24 [j]Jn 4:26; 13:19
8:26 [k]Jn 7:28 [l]Jn 3:32; 15:15
8:28 [m]Jn 3:14; 5:19; 12:32
8:29 [n]ver 16; Jn 16:32 [o]Jn 4:34; 5:30; 6:38
8:30 [p]Jn 7:31

The light metaphor is steeped in OT allusions (e.g., Exod 13:21–22; Pss 27:1; 119:105). Jesus is the promised light (Isa 9:2; 42:6; 49:6; 60:19–20; cf. Acts 13:47).
8:13–14 See note on 5:31. The Pharisees (mis)understand Jesus' words as if he were interested in nothing more than establishing the legal criteria for acceptable testimony (Deut 19:15). So Jesus goes over the same ground as in 5:19–30,36–37—but he uses slightly different terms.
8:15 judge by human standards. See note on 7:24. **I pass judgment on no one.** The way Jesus' opponents do. Jesus does not judge by superficial criteria. But that does not mean that he does not judge in any sense (v. 26; 5:27; 9:39).
8:16 with the Father. Jesus does not judge alone (5:30).
8:17 your own Law. The Pharisees are appealing to the law of Moses to question Jesus' practice, but Jesus fulfills the law. See "Law," p. 2649.
8:18 I ... the Father. This meets even the law's formal conditions (Deut 17:6; 19:15) because there are two witnesses: Jesus and the Father (see notes on 5:19–30,36).
8:19 Where is your father? Once again, people misunderstand Jesus (see Introduction: Characteristics and Themes, 7): they are apparently thinking of a purely human father, not of Jesus' heavenly Father. **If you knew me, you would know my Father also.** See note on 6:42.
8:20 hour. See note on 2:4.
8:21–30 *Dispute Over Who Jesus Is.* Jesus again explains who he is.
8:21–22 See 7:33–36 and notes. Once again, people misunderstand Jesus (see Introduction: Characteristics and Themes, 7): they think that he is contemplating suicide. This may ironically prophesy Jesus' death, akin to 11:49–50, since Jesus willingly lays down his life (10:18), not in suicide but in submitting to the Father's will.
8:23 The second sentence explains the first: **from below.** Equals "of this world." **from above.** Equals "not of this world." **world.** See notes on 1:9,29; 3:16.
8:24 I told you. See v. 21. **if you do not believe.** The only possibility of escape is genuine faith. **I am he.** See vv. 28,58. This likely alludes to Isa 40–55 (which alludes to Exod 3:13–14), where the Greek phrase repeatedly occurs in the pre-Christian Greek translation of the OT, the Septuagint (e.g., Isa 41:4; 43:10,25; 46:4; 47:8,10; 48:12; 52:6). By applying these words to himself, Jesus claims to be God (see note on 1:1).
8:25 Jesus has consistently witnessed about himself.
8:26 Jesus is not speaking on his own (vv. 28–29; 5:19–30). **trustworthy.** See 7:28 and note.
8:27 They did not understand. See Introduction: Characteristics and Themes, 7.
8:28a lifted up. See NIV text note; see also note on 3:14–15. **then you will know.** The cross reveals who Jesus is. **I am he.** See note on v. 24.
8:28b–29 Restates Jesus' argument in v. 16; 3:34; 5:19–30; 6:38.
8:30 believed. Professed faith, but as in 2:23–25 (cf. 4:45; 5:35; 6:2,26,60,64; 7:3–5), they are spurious believers: they are slaves to

8:31 [q] Jn 15:7; 2Jn 9
8:32 [r] Ro 8:2; Jas 2:12
8:33 [s] ver 37,39; Mt 3:9
8:34 [t] Ro 6:16; 2Pe 2:19
8:35 [u] Gal 4:30
8:37 [v] ver 39,40
8:38 [w] Jn 5:19,30; 14:10,24
8:39 [x] ver 37; Ro 9:7; Gal 3:7
8:40 [y] ver 26
8:41 [z] ver 38,44 [a] Isa 63:16; 64:8
8:42 [b] 1Jn 5:1 [c] Jn 16:27; 17:8 [d] Jn 7:28 [e] Jn 3:17
8:44 [f] 1Jn 3:8 [g] ver 38,41 [h] Ge 3:4
8:45 [i] Jn 18:37
8:47 [j] Jn 18:37; 1Jn 4:6

Dispute Over Whose Children Jesus' Opponents Are

[31]To the Jews who had believed him, Jesus said, "If you hold to my teaching,[q] you are really my disciples. [32]Then you will know the truth, and the truth will set you free."[r]

[33]They answered him, "We are Abraham's descendants[s] and have never been slaves of anyone. How can you say that we shall be set free?"

[34]Jesus replied, "Very truly I tell you, everyone who sins is a slave to sin.[t] [35]Now a slave has no permanent place in the family, but a son belongs to it forever.[u] [36]So if the Son sets you free, you will be free indeed. [37]I know that you are Abraham's descendants. Yet you are looking for a way to kill me,[v] because you have no room for my word. [38]I am telling you what I have seen in the Father's presence,[w] and you are doing what you have heard from your father.[a]"

[39]"Abraham is our father," they answered.

"If you were Abraham's children,"[x] said Jesus, "then you would[b] do what Abraham did. [40]As it is, you are looking for a way to kill me, a man who has told you the truth that I heard from God.[y] Abraham did not do such things. [41]You are doing the works of your own father."[z]

"We are not illegitimate children," they protested. "The only Father we have is God himself."[a]

[42]Jesus said to them, "If God were your Father, you would love me,[b] for I have come here from God.[c] I have not come on my own;[d] God sent me.[e] [43]Why is my language not clear to you? Because you are unable to hear what I say. [44]You belong to your father, the devil,[f] and you want to carry out your father's desires.[g] He was a murderer from the beginning, not holding to the truth, for there is no truth in him. When he lies, he speaks his native language, for he is a liar and the father of lies.[h] [45]Yet because I tell the truth,[i] you do not believe me! [46]Can any of you prove me guilty of sin? If I am telling the truth, why don't you believe me? [47]Whoever belongs to God hears what God says.[j] The reason you do not hear is that you do not belong to God."

[a] *38* Or *presence. Therefore do what you have heard from the Father.* [b] *39* Some early manuscripts *"If you are Abraham's children," said Jesus, "then*

sin (v. 34), indifferent to Jesus' word (v. 37), children of the devil (v. 44), liars (v. 55), and guilty of mob tactics, including attempting to murder the one in whom they professed to believe (v. 59).

8:31–47 *Dispute Over Whose Children Jesus' Opponents Are.* Jesus disabuses the Jews of any sense of privilege that depends on merely physical lineage to Abraham. Their beliefs and actions reveal their spiritual parentage (cf. 1 John 3:10).

8:31 hold to my teaching. "Hold" translates the same Greek word as "remain" in 15:4–7,9–10. A genuine believer perseveres in Jesus' teaching by obeying it and seeking to understand it better (see 2 John 9; cf. Heb 3:14; Jas 2:14–26). Persevering has two results: (1) It establishes genuine faith ("you are really my disciples"). It separates spurious faith from true faith, fickle disciples from committed disciples (see note on v. 30). (2) It is a way to know the liberating "truth" (v. 32; see notes on 1:14; 7:18). This process includes both intellectual assessment and moral commitment (see note on 7:17).

8:32 set you free. From sin, not ignorance (see v. 34 and note).

8:33 By offering the Jews freedom (vv. 31–32), Jesus implies that they are currently slaves, but they misunderstand the nature of their slavery (see Introduction: Characteristics and Themes, 7). **We are Abraham's descendants.** Their sense of inherited privilege is so strong that they can neither acknowledge their own need nor recognize who Jesus is. **have never been slaves of anyone.** There was scarcely a major power the Jews had not served (Egypt, Assyria, Babylon, Greece, Syria, Rome); they are probably talking about spiritual, inward freedom and privilege.

8:34 slave to sin. Jesus makes plain the kind of slavery he has in mind. Only Jesus can liberate one from sin's guilt and power (v. 36; Rom 6:17–18; 8:2; cf. John 3:18; 5:24).

8:35 Slaves are not permanently secure in a family, but sons are. The Jews think of themselves as sons (of Abraham), but in reality they are slaves (to sin).

8:36 if the Son sets you free. True freedom is possible only if Jesus grants it (see note on v. 34). **free indeed.** Having the desire and ability to serve God rather than sin.

8:37 you are Abraham's descendants. Physically (see note on v. 33) but not spiritually (see vv. 39–41; cf. Jer 9:26; Rom 2:28–29; 9:6–8; Gal 4:21–31). The Jews falsely claim Abraham as their spiritual father (see note on vv. 31–47), and Jesus rightly claims God as his. **word.** Translated "teaching" in v. 31.

8:38 your father. Neither God nor Abraham (v. 44).

8:39 what Abraham did. Believed and obeyed God (Gen 15:6; 26:5). Their conduct is diametrically opposed to Abraham's, so their father must be someone else (see v. 44).

8:41 illegitimate. May have been a slander aimed at Jesus (for the irony, see note on 6:42). **The only Father we have is God himself.** An ironic claim in light of 1:12–13; 3:3–8.

8:42 God's children love Jesus, but not all religious people love Jesus.

8:43 language. The actual words. **what I say.** The message. The flaw is not with Jesus' communication but with the audience's spiritual parentage (v. 44).

8:44 the devil. Satan. See note on Job 1:6. **your father's desires.** Include (1) murder and (2) deceit. **from the beginning.** Probably refers to tempting Adam and Eve, who fell and brought death to mankind (Gen 3; Rom 5:12). **liar.** "It is impossible for God to lie" (Heb 6:18). **father of lies.** Beginning with Gen 3:4, contradicting God in Gen 2:17.

8:45 because. Introduces a reason, not a concession ("although"). The devil's children do not love the truth but follow the devil's lies. This explains unbelief; other passages explain belief in a way that removes any grounds for believers to boast (see, e.g., v. 47; 6:37,44–45,65,70).

8:47 Answers Jesus' second question in v. 46. See note on v. 45.

Jesus' Claims About Himself

48The Jews answered him, "Aren't we right in saying that you are a Samaritan[k] and demon-possessed?"[l]
49"I am not possessed by a demon," said Jesus, "but I honor my Father and you dishonor me. 50I am
not seeking glory for myself;[m] but there is one who seeks it, and he is the judge. 51Very truly I tell you,
whoever obeys my word will never see death."[n]
52At this they exclaimed, "Now we know that you are demon-possessed! Abraham died and so did the
prophets, yet you say that whoever obeys your word will never taste death. 53Are you greater than our
father Abraham?[o] He died, and so did the prophets. Who do you think you are?"
54Jesus replied, "If I glorify myself,[p] my glory means nothing. My Father, whom you claim as your
God, is the one who glorifies me.[q] 55Though you do not know him,[r] I know him.[s] If I said I did not, I
would be a liar like you, but I do know him and obey his word.[t] 56Your father Abraham[u] rejoiced at the
thought of seeing my day; he saw it[v] and was glad."
57"You are not yet fifty years old," they said to him, "and you have seen Abraham!"
58"Very truly I tell you," Jesus answered, "before Abraham was born,[w] I am!"[x] 59At this, they picked
up stones to stone him,[y] but Jesus hid himself,[z] slipping away from the temple grounds.

Jesus Heals a Man Born Blind

9 As he went along, he saw a man blind from birth. 2His disciples asked him, "Rabbi,[a] who sinned,[b]
this man[c] or his parents,[d] that he was born blind?"
3"Neither this man nor his parents sinned," said Jesus, "but this happened so that the works of God
might be displayed in him.[e] 4As long as it is day,[f] we must do the works of him who sent me. Night is
coming, when no one can work. 5While I am in the world, I am the light of the world."[g]
6After saying this, he spit[h] on the ground, made some mud with the saliva, and put it on the man's
eyes. 7"Go," he told him, "wash in the Pool of Siloam"[i] (this word means "Sent"). So the man went
and washed, and came home seeing.[j]
8His neighbors and those who had formerly seen him begging asked, "Isn't this the same man who
used to sit and beg?"[k] 9Some claimed that he was.
Others said, "No, he only looks like him."
But he himself insisted, "I am the man."
10"How then were your eyes opened?" they asked.

8:48 [k]Mt 10:5 [l]ver 52; Jn 7:20
8:50 [m]ver 54; Jn 5:41
8:51 [n]Jn 11:26
8:53 [o]Jn 4:12
8:54 [p]ver 50 [q]Jn 16:14; 17:1,5
8:55 [r]ver 19 [s]Jn 7:28,29 [t]Jn 15:10
8:56 [u]ver 37,39 [v]Mt 13:17; Heb 11:13
8:58 [w]Jn 1:2; 17:5,24 [x]Ex 3:14
8:59 [y]Lev 24:16; Jn 10:31; 11:8 [z]Jn 12:36
9:2 [a]Mt 23:7 [b]ver 34; Lk 13:2; Ac 28:4 [c]Eze 18:20 [d]Ex 20:5; Job 21:19
9:3 [e]Jn 11:4
9:4 [f]Jn 11:9; 12:35
9:5 [g]Jn 1:4; 8:12; 12:46
9:6 [h]Mk 7:33; 8:23
9:7 [i]ver 11; 2Ki 5:10; Lk 13:4 [j]Isa 35:5; Jn 11:37
9:8 [k]Ac 3:2,10

8:48–59 *Jesus' Claims About Himself.* No mere human can honestly claim what Jesus does about himself.
8:48 Samaritan. See notes on 4:4,9,20.
8:49 you dishonor me. See 5:23 and note.
8:51 obeys my word. Equivalent to holding to Jesus' teaching (see note on v. 31). **never see death.** Their bodies will die, but they will not because they possess eternal life (5:24; 6:40,47,63,68; 11:25–26).
8:52–53 Once again, people misunderstand Jesus (see Introduction: Characteristics and Themes, 7): the Jews are thinking only of the death of the body (see note on v. 51).
8:52 taste. Experience. Synonymous with "see" in v. 51. See Mark 9:1; Heb 2:9.
8:53 The first question implies a negative answer, but the irony is that Jesus is far greater than Abraham.
8:54 whom you claim as your God. The irony is that they display no knowledge that the Father is profoundly committed to glorifying Jesus. **glorifies me.** In the humiliation of the cross and then Jesus' return to the glory he previously enjoyed with the Father (17:5).
8:55 liar like you. Like their "father" (v. 44).
8:56 Jesus ultimately fulfills all of Abraham's hopes and joys. Jesus is probably not referring to any one occasion but to Abraham's general joy in God's fulfilling his purposes in the Messiah, through whom God would bless all peoples on earth (Gen 12:2–3).
8:57 Once again, people misunderstand Jesus (see Introduction: Characteristics and Themes, 7): the Jews think that Jesus is claiming to be a contemporary of Abraham, who had been dead for 2,000 years. They still do not realize who Jesus claims to be (contrast how they react in v. 59).
8:58 The confrontation's climax. **I am!** Jesus could say "I was" to claim that he existed merely before Abraham, but he is claiming to exist eternally as God. See note on v. 24.
8:59 The Jews attempt to murder Jesus because they rightly understand that he claims to be God but wrongly conclude that he is blaspheming (Lev 24:16). See notes on 1:1; 5:23.
9:1–12 *Jesus Heals a Man Born Blind.* This is another of Jesus' signs (see "such signs" in v. 16; see also Introduction: Purpose and Addressees).
9:1 blind from birth. Heightens the effect of Jesus' miracle and may symbolize how humans are spiritually blind from birth.
9:2 The disciples wrongly (v. 3) assume that there must be a direct cause-and-effect connection between an individual's specific sin and an individual's specific suffering (see note on 5:14).
9:3 The disciples ask what the cause of the man's blindness is (v. 2), and Jesus tells them the purpose ("so that"): to display God's works.
9:4 Night. See notes on 1:5; 3:2,19.
9:5 The "light" (see note on 8:12) shines brightly while Jesus lives out his human life up to the moment of his glorification (cf. 12:35).
9:6 spit. Cf. Mark 7:33; 8:23.
9:7 Pool of Siloam. Archaeologists identified this in 2004. The aqueduct leading into the pool was part of the major water system that King Hezekiah developed (see note on 2 Kgs 20:20). **Sent.** A play on words since Jesus is the one whom God "sent" (see note on 3:17).

9:11 [l] ver 7
9:14 [m] Jn 5:9
9:15 [n] ver 10
9:16 [o] Mt 12:2 [p] Jn 6:52; 7:43; 10:19
9:17 [q] Mt 21:11
9:18 [r] Jn 1:19
9:22 [s] Jn 7:13 [t] ver 34; Lk 6:22 [u] Jn 12:42; 16:2
9:23 [v] ver 21
9:24 [w] Jos 7:19 [x] ver 16
9:27 [y] ver 15
9:28 [z] Jn 5:45
9:29 [a] Jn 8:14
9:31 [b] Ge 18:23-32; Ps 34:15,16; 66:18; 145:19,20; Pr 15:29; Isa 1:15; 59:1,2; Jn 15:7; Jas 5:16-18; 1Jn 5:14,15
9:33 [c] ver 16; Jn 3:2
9:34 [d] ver 2 [e] ver 22,35; Isa 66:5

11 He replied, "The man they call Jesus made some mud and put it on my eyes. He told me to go to Siloam and wash. So I went and washed, and then I could see."[l]

12 "Where is this man?" they asked him.

"I don't know," he said.

The Pharisees Investigate the Healing

13 They brought to the Pharisees the man who had been blind. 14 Now the day on which Jesus had made the mud and opened the man's eyes was a Sabbath.[m] 15 Therefore the Pharisees also asked him how he had received his sight.[n] "He put mud on my eyes," the man replied, "and I washed, and now I see."

16 Some of the Pharisees said, "This man is not from God, for he does not keep the Sabbath."[o]

But others asked, "How can a sinner perform such signs?" So they were divided.[p]

17 Then they turned again to the blind man, "What have you to say about him? It was your eyes he opened."

The man replied, "He is a prophet."[q]

18 They[r] still did not believe that he had been blind and had received his sight until they sent for the man's parents. 19 "Is this your son?" they asked. "Is this the one you say was born blind? How is it that now he can see?"

20 "We know he is our son," the parents answered, "and we know he was born blind. 21 But how he can see now, or who opened his eyes, we don't know. Ask him. He is of age; he will speak for himself." 22 His parents said this because they were afraid of the Jewish leaders,[s] who already had decided that anyone who acknowledged that Jesus was the Messiah would be put out[t] of the synagogue.[u] 23 That was why his parents said, "He is of age; ask him."[v]

24 A second time they summoned the man who had been blind. "Give glory to God by telling the truth,"[w] they said. "We know this man is a sinner."[x]

25 He replied, "Whether he is a sinner or not, I don't know. One thing I do know. I was blind but now I see!"

26 Then they asked him, "What did he do to you? How did he open your eyes?"

27 He answered, "I have told you already[y] and you did not listen. Why do you want to hear it again? Do you want to become his disciples too?"

28 Then they hurled insults at him and said, "You are this fellow's disciple! We are disciples of Moses![z] 29 We know that God spoke to Moses, but as for this fellow, we don't even know where he comes from."[a]

30 The man answered, "Now that is remarkable! You don't know where he comes from, yet he opened my eyes. 31 We know that God does not listen to sinners. He listens to the godly person who does his will.[b] 32 Nobody has ever heard of opening the eyes of a man born blind. 33 If this man were not from God,[c] he could do nothing."

34 To this they replied, "You were steeped in sin at birth;[d] how dare you lecture us!" And they threw him out.[e]

Spiritual Blindness

35 Jesus heard that they had thrown him out, and when he found him, he said, "Do you believe in the Son of Man?"

9:13–34 *The Pharisees Investigate the Healing.* Unlike the disabled person in 5:1–15 (see note on 5:7), the healed man is grateful, quick-witted, and cynical toward religious leaders who will not face facts.
9:13 The healed man's neighbors (v. 8) want advice from their local synagogue leaders about what they should make of the healing.
9:14 Sabbath. Some Pharisees think that Jesus transgressed their oral law regarding the Sabbath on several points (see notes on 5:17–18; 7:22): (1) healing when life was not in danger; (2) kneading (by making mud from spittle); and possibly (3) anointing eyes. For this reason ("therefore," v. 15), they focus on "how" (v. 15) Jesus healed the man.
9:16 divided. Like the crowds earlier (7:40–43).
9:17 prophet. See note on 4:19.
9:21 of age. Probably means old enough to give legal testimony (i.e., at least 13 years old).
9:22–23 Explains why the parents are reticent to answer the final question in v. 19.
9:24 The "truth" the Pharisees want the healed man to confess is that "this man" (contemptuously referring to Jesus) is a sinner.
9:26 What … How. See note on v. 14.
9:27 The man displays cynical wit.
9:28 disciples of Moses. They do not rightly understand Moses because Moses wrote about Jesus (see 1:17; 5:39–40,45,46 and notes).
9:29 we don't even know where he comes from. Jesus' claims (e.g., 8:14) are confusing them (see 7:27 and note).
9:30–33 The man displays increased courage and cynical wit (cf. Isa 29:18; 35:5; 42:7).
9:34 The Pharisees, outraged by what they perceive as ignorant insolence, verbally attack the man instead of evenhandedly evaluating the healing. **steeped in sin at birth.** See vv. 2,3 and notes. **threw him out.** Probably the excommunication his parents feared (vv. 22–23).
9:35–41 *Spiritual Blindness.* When the light shines, God enables some to see, but others who think they see turn away, blinded by the light.

36"Who is he, sir?" the man asked. "Tell me so that I may believe in him."[f]
37Jesus said, "You have now seen him; in fact, he is the one speaking with you."[g]
38Then the man said, "Lord, I believe," and he worshiped him.[h]
39Jesus said,[a] "For judgment[i] I have come into this world,[j] so that the blind will see[k] and those who
see will become blind."[l]
40Some Pharisees who were with him heard him say this and asked, "What? Are we blind too?"[m]
41Jesus said, "If you were blind, you would not be guilty of sin; but now that you claim you can see,
your guilt remains.[n]

The Good Shepherd and His Sheep

10 "Very truly I tell you Pharisees, anyone who does not enter the sheep pen by the gate, but climbs
in by some other way, is a thief and a robber. 2The one who enters by the gate is the shepherd of
the sheep.[o] 3The gatekeeper opens the gate for him, and the sheep listen to his voice.[p] He calls his own
sheep by name and leads them out. 4When he has brought out all his own, he goes on ahead of them,
and his sheep follow him because they know his voice. 5But they will never follow a stranger; in fact,
they will run away from him because they do not recognize a stranger's voice." 6Jesus used this figure
of speech,[q] but the Pharisees did not understand what he was telling them.
7Therefore Jesus said again, "Very truly I tell you, I am the gate for the sheep. 8All who have come
before me[r] are thieves and robbers, but the sheep have not listened to them. 9I am the gate; whoever
enters through me will be saved.[b] They will come in and go out, and find pasture. 10The thief comes
only to steal and kill and destroy; I have come that they may have life, and have it to the full.
11"I am the good shepherd.[s] The good shepherd lays down his life for the sheep.[t] 12The hired hand
is not the shepherd and does not own the sheep. So when he sees the wolf coming, he abandons the
sheep and runs away.[u] Then the wolf attacks the flock and scatters it. 13The man runs away because he
is a hired hand and cares nothing for the sheep.
14"I am the good shepherd;[v] I know my sheep[w] and my sheep know me— 15just as the Father knows

9:36 [f] Ro 10:14
9:37 [g] Jn 4:26
9:38 [h] Mt 28:9
9:39 [i] Jn 5:22 [j] Jn 3:19 [k] Lk 4:18 [l] Mt 13:13
9:40 [m] Ro 2:19
9:41 [n] Jn 15:22,24
10:2 [o] ver 11,14
10:3 [p] ver 4,5,14,16,27
10:6 [q] Jn 16:25
10:8 [r] Jer 23:1,2
10:11 [s] ver 14; Isa 40:11; Eze 34:11-16,23; Heb 13:20; 1Pe 5:4; Rev 7:17 [t] Jn 15:13; 1Jn 3:16
10:12 [u] Zec 11:16,17
10:14 [v] ver 11 [w] ver 27

[a] *38,39* Some early manuscripts do not have *Then the man said . . . 39Jesus said.* [b] *9* Or *kept safe*

9:35 found him. Jesus takes the initiative (cf. 5:14). **believe in.** Place your trust in (not "Do you believe that the Son of Man exists?"). **Son of Man.** Reveals God to man. See 1:51; 3:13–14; 5:27; 6:27,53,62; 8:28.
9:37 See 4:26.
9:38 Contrast 6:36.
9:39 For judgment. See note on 3:17. **so that.** Introduces a purpose ("in order that"). **the blind will see.** Those who are in spiritual darkness and realize it will receive the "light" of revelation (v. 5). **those who see will become blind.** Those who think they see but are really in spiritual darkness inevitably reject the true light. See notes on 1:5; 3:2,19.
9:40 heard him. Apparently Jesus found the healed man in a public place where some Pharisees were able to listen in.
9:41 blind. In spiritual darkness but crying out for illumination (see note on v. 39). **sin.** Particularly unbelief, i.e., rejecting the Son. **claim you can see.** They are satisfied with the light of the law as their received traditions interpret it, but they reject the true light.
10:1–21 *The Good Shepherd and His Sheep.* Jesus uses a Palestinian sheep-farming metaphor (vv. 1–5) and expands three features in it: the gate (vv. 7–10), the shepherd (vv. 11–18), and his own sheep (vv. 26–30). The most important background for this metaphor is Ezek 34, where God berates Israel's false shepherds for fleecing God's sheep rather than guarding, guiding, and nurturing them (cf. Isa 56:11; Jer 23:1–4; Zech 11). God is the ultimate shepherd of his people (Pss 23:1; 80:1; Isa 40:11).
10:1 sheep pen. Probably a large enclosure where several families kept their sheep. **thief ... robber.** Symbolizes the Pharisees, who belittle and expel the sheep (see, e.g., how they treat the healed man in ch. 9).
10:2 shepherd. Symbolizes Jesus (vv. 11,14,16).
10:3 gatekeeper. A hired undershepherd who guards the gate and opens it for the sheep's shepherd (vv. 12–13). **listen to his voice.** Presupposes that several flocks are in the fold (see note on v. 1); the shepherd calls out *his* sheep. **his own.** The sheep belong to the shepherd before he calls them (cf. vv. 26–29; 6:37,39,44,64–65; 17:6,9,24; 18:9). **by name.** Individually. **leads them out.** Jesus calls out his own flock out of the sheep pen of Judaism (see v. 16; cf. Num 27:15–17).
10:4 follow. Pictures the master-disciple relationship. Shepherds led their sheep; they did not drive them.
10:6 did not understand. See Introduction: Characteristics and Themes, 7.
10:7–10 Expands the gate metaphor in vv. 1–5.
10:7 I am. See note on 6:35. **gate.** Symbolizes security and plenty (vv. 9–10). Cf. Ps 118:20.
10:8 All who have come before me. False shepherds (see note on vv. 1–21), including Messianic pretenders who falsely promised the people freedom (e.g., Acts 5:36–37; 21:38). Jesus promises a different kind of freedom (see notes on 8:32,34,36).
10:9 through me. Jesus is the only way his sheep may experience his safe fold and luxurious pasture (14:6).
10:10 life ... to the full. Fat, contented, safe, flourishing sheep symbolize life at its best.
10:11 I am. See note on 6:35. **good shepherd.** In contrast to the hired hand, who cares more about his own well-being (vv. 12–13). **lays down his life.** Willingly (v. 18) risks his life for (e.g., 1 Sam 17:34–37). Shepherds never *intended* to die in this way, but Jesus did (15:13). **for the sheep.** A sacrificial death in their place: the sheep are in mortal danger, and the shepherd dies in order to save his sheep. That is why this shepherd is "good" ("great" in Heb 13:20).
10:14 See note on v. 11. **know ... know.** Experiential mutual knowledge (presupposed in vv. 3–4), which is grounded in the Father and Son's relationship (17:21).

10:15 [x]Mt 11:27
10:16 [y]Isa 56:8 [z]Jn 11:52; Eph 2:11-19 [a]Eze 37:24; 1Pe 2:25
10:17 [b]ver 11,15,18
10:18 [c]Mt 26:53 [d]Jn 15:10; Php 2:8; Heb 5:8
10:19 [e]Jn 7:43; 9:16
10:20 [f]Jn 7:20 [g]Mk 3:21
10:21 [h]Mt 4:24 [i]Ex 4:11; Jn 9:32,33
10:23 [j]Ac 3:11; 5:12
10:24 [k]Jn 1:19 [l]Jn 16:25,29
10:25 [m]Jn 8:58 [n]Jn 5:36
10:26 [o]Jn 8:47
10:27 [p]ver 14 [q]ver 4
10:28 [r]Jn 6:39
10:29 [s]Jn 17:2,6,24 [t]Jn 14:28
10:30 [u]Jn 17:21-23
10:31 [v]Jn 8:59
10:33 [w]Lev 24:16; Jn 5:18
10:34 [x]Jn 8:17; Ro 3:19 [y]Ps 82:6
10:36 [z]Jer 1:5 [a]Jn 6:69 [b]Jn 3:17 [c]Jn 5:17,18
10:37 [d]ver 25; Jn 15:24

me and I know the Father[x]—and I lay down my life for the sheep. 16 I have other sheep[y] that are not of this sheep pen. I must bring them also. They too will listen to my voice, and there shall be one flock[z] and one shepherd.[a] 17 The reason my Father loves me is that I lay down my life[b]—only to take it up again. 18 No one takes it from me, but I lay it down of my own accord.[c] I have authority to lay it down and authority to take it up again. This command I received from my Father."[d]

19 The Jews who heard these words were again divided.[e] 20 Many of them said, "He is demon-possessed[f] and raving mad.[g] Why listen to him?"

21 But others said, "These are not the sayings of a man possessed by a demon.[h] Can a demon open the eyes of the blind?"[i]

Further Conflict Over Jesus' Claims

22 Then came the Festival of Dedication[*a*] at Jerusalem. It was winter, 23 and Jesus was in the temple courts walking in Solomon's Colonnade.[j] 24 The Jews[k] who were there gathered around him, saying, "How long will you keep us in suspense? If you are the Messiah, tell us plainly."[l]

25 Jesus answered, "I did tell you,[m] but you do not believe. The works I do in my Father's name testify about me,[n] 26 but you do not believe because you are not my sheep.[o] 27 My sheep listen to my voice; I know them,[p] and they follow me.[q] 28 I give them eternal life, and they shall never perish; no one will snatch them out of my hand.[r] 29 My Father, who has given them to me,[s] is greater than all[*b*];[t] no one can snatch them out of my Father's hand. 30 I and the Father are one."[u]

31 Again his Jewish opponents picked up stones to stone him,[v] 32 but Jesus said to them, "I have shown you many good works from the Father. For which of these do you stone me?"

33 "We are not stoning you for any good work," they replied, "but for blasphemy, because you, a mere man, claim to be God."[w]

34 Jesus answered them, "Is it not written in your Law,[x] 'I have said you are "gods"'[*c*]?[y] 35 If he called them 'gods,' to whom the word of God came—and Scripture cannot be set aside— 36 what about the one whom the Father set apart[z] as his very own[a] and sent into the world?[b] Why then do you accuse me of blasphemy because I said, 'I am God's Son'?[c] 37 Do not believe me unless I do the works of my Father.[d] 38 But

[*a*] *22* That is, Hanukkah [*b*] *29* Many early manuscripts *What my Father has given me is greater than all* [*c*] *34* Psalm 82:6

10:16 other sheep. Those outside the sheep pen of Judaism, i.e., Samaritans and Gentiles (see note on v. 3; see also 11:51–52; Isa 56:8). God will accomplish his worldwide saving purpose (Rev 5:9). **one flock.** See Eph 2:11–22; see also "People of God," p. 2672.

10:17 only to. Or "in order to."

10:18 Jesus willingly died according to the Father's plan (Acts 2:23; 4:27–28).

10:19–21 See 7:12,40–43; 9:16. See note on 5:23.

10:22–42 *Further Conflict Over Jesus' Claims.* By claiming to be both the Messiah and Son of God, Jesus engenders open opposition. Verses 40–42 close a large inclusio (a literary device where a section of text is bracketed): Jesus' public ministry begins and ends with the witness of John the Baptist (1:19—10:42).

10:22 Festival of Dedication. See NIV text note. Commemorated Judas Maccabeus's rededicating the temple in 165 BC after Antiochus IV Epiphanes profaned it in 167 BC (see "The Time Between the Testaments," p. 1893).

10:23 Solomon's Colonnade. See note on Acts 3:11.

10:24 plainly. The Jews seek an unambiguous statement that would incriminate Jesus, who gives them far more (v. 30; see v. 33).

10:25 I did tell you. All of Jesus' words and deeds pointed in that direction. **works.** See note on 5:36.

10:26 not my sheep. Explains why many do not follow Jesus. This does not reduce their moral responsibility; it indicts them.

10:27 See vv. 3–4,14,16.

10:28 eternal life. See note on 3:15. **perish.** See note on 3:16. **no one will snatch them out of my hand.** Jesus powerfully keeps his sheep from harm (e.g., vv. 1,8,11). Their security rests with the good shepherd, who faithfully fulfills his mission to preserve everyone the Father has given to him (6:37–40).

10:29 greater than all. Therefore, no force or person can sever the relation between the true believer and Jesus. There can be no greater security (Col 3:3).

10:30 one. The Greek is neuter: "one thing," not "one person." Starting with 1:1, the entire book distinguishes between the Father and Son as distinct persons (e.g., the Father sends the Son, and the Son prays to the Father). But they are perfectly unified in essence, will, and action so that what Jesus does, the Father does, and vice versa (see 5:19–30 and notes; see also v. 38).

10:31 stone him. See note on 8:59.

10:33 claim to be God. See notes on 5:18,23. The irony is that Jesus is not a man who makes himself God but is God who became a man (see 1:14 and note).

10:34–36 Jesus quotes Ps 82:6 to question their umbrage: "gods" can refer to others than God himself, so if God called humans "gods" and "sons of the Most High" (i.e., sons of God) in some sense, on what Scriptural basis can the Jews charge that Jesus—whom the Father sent—is necessarily guilty of blasphemy when he says that he is God's Son?

10:35 set aside. Annulled or proved false. Scripture is completely authoritative and reliable.

10:36 set apart as his very own and sent. See note on 3:17; cf. 17:17–19.

10:37–38 Reiterates the argument in v. 25.

10:38 the Father is in me, and I in the Father. Explains v. 30; developed in 14:10–11; 17:21.

if I do them, even though you do not believe me, believe the works, that you may know and understand
that the Father is in me, and I in the Father."[e] 39Again they tried to seize him,[f] but he escaped their grasp.[g]
40Then Jesus went back across the Jordan[h] to the place where John had been baptizing in the early
days. There he stayed, 41and many people came to him. They said, "Though John never performed a
sign,[i] all that John said about this man was true."[j] 42And in that place many believed in Jesus.[k]

The Death of Lazarus

11 Now a man named Lazarus was sick. He was from Bethany,[l] the village of Mary and her sister
Martha.[m] 2(This Mary, whose brother Lazarus now lay sick, was the same one who poured
perfume on the Lord and wiped his feet with her hair.)[n] 3So the sisters sent word to Jesus, "Lord, the
one you love[o] is sick."
4When he heard this, Jesus said, "This sickness will not end in death. No, it is for God's glory[p] so
that God's Son may be glorified through it." 5Now Jesus loved Martha and her sister and Lazarus. 6So
when he heard that Lazarus was sick, he stayed where he was two more days, 7and then he said to his
disciples, "Let us go back to Judea."[q]
8"But Rabbi,"[r] they said, "a short while ago the Jews there tried to stone you,[s] and yet you are going back?"
9Jesus answered, "Are there not twelve hours of daylight? Anyone who walks in the daytime will not
stumble, for they see by this world's light.[t] 10It is when a person walks at night that they stumble, for
they have no light."
11After he had said this, he went on to tell them, "Our friend[u] Lazarus has fallen asleep;[v] but I am
going there to wake him up."
12His disciples replied, "Lord, if he sleeps, he will get better." 13Jesus had been speaking of his death,
but his disciples thought he meant natural sleep.[w]
14So then he told them plainly, "Lazarus is dead, 15and for your sake I am glad I was not there, so
that you may believe. But let us go to him."
16Then Thomas[x] (also known as Didymus[a]) said to the rest of the disciples, "Let us also go, that we
may die with him."

Jesus Comforts the Sisters of Lazarus

17On his arrival, Jesus found that Lazarus had already been in the tomb for four days.[y] 18Now Bethany[z] was less than two miles[b] from Jerusalem, 19and many Jews had come to Martha and Mary to

[a] 16 *Thomas* (Aramaic) and *Didymus* (Greek) both mean *twin*. [b] 18 Or about 3 kilometers

10:38 [e] Jn 14:10,11,20; 17:21
10:39 [f] Jn 7:30 [g] Lk 4:30; Jn 8:59
10:40 [h] Jn 1:28
10:41 [i] Jn 2:11; 3:30 [j] Jn 1:26,27,30,34
10:42 [k] Jn 7:31
11:1 [l] Mt 21:17 [m] Lk 10:38
11:2 [n] Mk 14:3; Lk 7:38; Jn 12:3
11:3 [o] ver 5,36
11:4 [p] ver 40; Jn 9:3
11:7 [q] Jn 10:40
11:8 [r] Mt 23:7 [s] Jn 8:59; 10:31
11:9 [t] Jn 9:4; 12:35
11:11 [u] ver 3 [v] Ac 7:60
11:13 [w] Mt 9:24
11:16 [x] Mt 10:3; Jn 14:5; 20:24-28; 21:2; Ac 1:13
11:17 [y] ver 6,39
11:18 [z] ver 1

10:39 escaped. Because his hour had not yet come (see note on 2:4; cf. 7:30,44; 8:20,59).

10:40 place. Probably Batanea (see note on 1:28).

11:1 — 12:50 *Transition: Life and Death, King and Suffering Servant.* Jesus has claimed to be the bread of life, the water of life, and the light of life. Here he gives life itself (11:25 – 26), anticipating his own life-giving death (12:23 – 24).

11:1 – 44 *The Death and Resurrection of Lazarus.* This foreshadows Jesus' death and resurrection, and it is another of Jesus' signs (see "signs" in v. 47 and "this sign" in 12:18; see also Introduction: Purpose and Addressees).

11:1 – 16 *The Death of Lazarus.* When Jesus hears that Lazarus is sick, he intentionally delays traveling to see Lazarus's family.

11:1 Bethany. See note on 1:28. See photo, p. 2097. **Mary ... Martha.** Also mentioned in Luke 10:38 – 42.

11:2 poured ... wiped. Since John does not record this event until 12:3, he presupposes that his audience has already heard about it.

11:3 the one you love. Hints at Jesus' friendships that the Gospels barely explore (vv. 5,36).

11:4 will not end in death. Ultimately, it will end in resurrection. **for God's glory so that God's Son may be glorified.** Raising Lazarus will reveal God's glory in order to glorify his Son (cf. 9:3; see "The Glory of God," p. 2640).

11:5 loved. What Jesus says in v. 4 is not callous.

11:6 So. Because Jesus loved them (v. 5). Most likely, Jesus is a four-day journey from Bethany (see 10:40; see also note on 1:28) and does not depart until he supernaturally knows that Lazarus has died (see v. 17 and note). Jesus' two-day delay benefits all concerned: himself (vv. 4,25), his disciples (v. 15), Jewish onlookers (v. 45), and Lazarus and his family.

11:8 See 10:31,39.

11:9 – 10 See 9:4; see also notes on 1:5; 3:2,19.

11:11 – 14 Once again, people misunderstand Jesus (see Introduction: Characteristics and Themes, 7).

11:11 wake him up. Jesus will one day wake up his friends who fall "asleep" (vv. 25 – 26).

11:16 Thomas reflects not doubt (cf. 20:24 – 25) but raw devotion and courage, though he misunderstands Jesus' implicit assurance in vv. 9 – 10 and does not comprehend that the disciples cannot possibly share in Jesus' death as the Lamb of God (1:29,36).

11:17 – 37 *Jesus Comforts the Sisters of Lazarus.* Jesus talks to Martha and Mary before going to Lazarus's tomb.

11:17 four days. See note on v. 6. Lazarus was irrevocably dead. If Jesus had left immediately, Lazarus would have been dead for only two days before Jesus arrived — not enough time to offset possible superstitions associated with resuscitations within the first three days of death.

11:18 – 19 Implies that the "many Jews" (v. 19) are from Jerusalem, which suggests that the family is rather prominent.

11:19 [a] ver 31; Job 2:11
11:20 [b] Lk 10:38-42
11:21 [c] ver 32,37
11:22 [d] ver 41,42; Jn 9:31
11:24 [e] Da 12:2; Jn 5:28, 29; Ac 24:15
11:25 [f] Jn 1:4
11:27 [g] Lk 2:11 [h] Mt 16:16 [i] Jn 6:14
11:28 [j] Mt 26:18; Jn 13:13
11:30 [k] ver 20
11:31 [l] ver 19
11:32 [m] ver 21
11:33 [n] ver 38 [o] Jn 12:27
11:35 [p] Lk 19:41
11:36 [q] ver 3
11:37 [r] Jn 9:6,7 [s] ver 21,32
11:38 [t] ver 33 [u] Mt 27:60; Lk 24:2; Jn 20:1
11:39 [v] ver 17
11:40 [w] ver 23-25 [x] ver 4
11:41 [y] Jn 17:1 [z] Mt 11:25

comfort them in the loss of their brother.[a] 20 When Martha heard that Jesus was coming, she went out
to meet him, but Mary stayed at home.[b]
21 "Lord," Martha said to Jesus, "if you had been here, my brother would not have died.[c] 22 But I know
that even now God will give you whatever you ask."[d]
23 Jesus said to her, "Your brother will rise again."
24 Martha answered, "I know he will rise again in the resurrection[e] at the last day."
25 Jesus said to her, "I am the resurrection and the life.[f] The one who believes in me will live, even
though they die; 26 and whoever lives by believing in me will never die. Do you believe this?"
27 "Yes, Lord," she replied, "I believe that you are the Messiah,[g] the Son of God,[h] who is to come into
the world."[i]
28 After she had said this, she went back and called her sister Mary aside. "The Teacher[j] is here," she
said, "and is asking for you." 29 When Mary heard this, she got up quickly and went to him. 30 Now Jesus
had not yet entered the village, but was still at the place where Martha had met him.[k] 31 When the Jews
who had been with Mary in the house, comforting her,[l] noticed how quickly she got up and went out,
they followed her, supposing she was going to the tomb to mourn there.
32 When Mary reached the place where Jesus was and saw him, she fell at his feet and said, "Lord, if
you had been here, my brother would not have died."[m]
33 When Jesus saw her weeping, and the Jews who had come along with her also weeping, he was
deeply moved[n] in spirit and troubled.[o] 34 "Where have you laid him?" he asked.
"Come and see, Lord," they replied.
35 Jesus wept.[p]
36 Then the Jews said, "See how he loved him!"[q]
37 But some of them said, "Could not he who opened the eyes of the blind man[r] have kept this man
from dying?"[s]

Jesus Raises Lazarus From the Dead

38 Jesus, once more deeply moved,[t] came to the tomb. It was a cave with a stone laid across the entrance.[u] 39 "Take away the stone," he said.
"But, Lord," said Martha, the sister of the dead man, "by this time there is a bad odor, for he has
been there four days."[v]
40 Then Jesus said, "Did I not tell you that if you believe,[w] you will see the glory of God?"[x]
41 So they took away the stone. Then Jesus looked up[y] and said, "Father,[z] I thank you that you have

11:21–22 Not a rebuke but words of grief and faith: she remains confident that Jesus would have healed Lazarus had Jesus arrived before Lazarus's death. See note on v. 39.
11:23 Your brother will rise again. A masterpiece of planned ambiguity: Martha thinks that Jesus is referring to the resurrection at the last day (v. 24; see "Death and Resurrection," p. 2670), but Jesus is also promising a more immediate resurrection for Lazarus.
11:25 I am. See note on 6:35. **resurrection ... will live, even though they die.** Jesus has insisted that he alone, under the Father's sanction, will raise the dead on the last day (5:21,25–29; 6:39–40).
11:26 lives ... will never die. See notes on 3:6,14–15; 4:10,14; 5:21,26–27; 6:35,57,63,68; 8:51; 10:9,10; 14:6. **Do you believe this?** Jesus asks Martha if she personally trusts in him as the resurrection and the life.
11:27 Martha recognizes that if Jesus is "the resurrection and the life" (v. 25), then he is God's promised Messiah. John wants all his readers to echo Martha's confession (20:31).
11:32 See note on vv. 21–22.
11:33 weeping. Loud wailing. **the Jews who had come along with her also weeping.** Jewish funeral custom dictated that even a poor family hire at least two flute players and a professional wailing woman, and this family was not poor (see 12:1–5). **deeply moved.** Outraged—not merely emotionally upset because of empathy, grief, or pain but angry—at (1) the sin, sickness, and death in this fallen world that wreaks so much havoc and generates so much sorrow and/or (2) unbelief itself, for the people were grieving like pagans, "like the rest of mankind, who have no hope" (1 Thess 4:13). **in spirit.** Internally, in the core of his being.
11:35 wept. Shed tears (a different word than the loud "weeping" in v. 33)—not because Lazarus was dead (Jesus knew he was about to raise Lazarus from the dead [v. 11]) but because of the same sin that prompted his outrage (see note on v. 33). Grief and compassion without outrage shrink to mere sentiment, while outrage without grief hardens into self-righteous, hot-tempered arrogance.
11:36 The Jews are right that Jesus loved Lazarus, but they are wrong that his tears evidence grief as despairing as their own.
11:37 The Jews are right that Jesus could have kept Lazarus from dying but wrong not to trust him and instead look for displays of power.
11:38–44 *Jesus Raises Lazarus From the Dead.* The story reaches its climax in vv. 43–44.
11:38 deeply moved. See note on v. 33.
11:39 Martha is not anticipating Lazarus's resurrection. **four days.** See notes on vv. 6,17.
11:40 Summarizes what Jesus promised in vv. 23–26. **glory.** See note on v. 4.
11:41 you have heard me. Assumes that Jesus has already asked for Lazarus's life.

heard me. [42]I knew that you always hear me, but I said this for the benefit of the people standing here,[a]
that they may believe that you sent me."[b]

[43]When he had said this, Jesus called in a loud voice, "Lazarus, come out!"[c] [44]The dead man came
out, his hands and feet wrapped with strips of linen,[d] and a cloth around his face.[e]
Jesus said to them, "Take off the grave clothes and let him go."

The Plot to Kill Jesus

[45]Therefore many of the Jews who had come to visit Mary,[f] and had seen what Jesus did,[g] believed in
him.[h] [46]But some of them went to the Pharisees and told them what Jesus had done. [47]Then the chief
priests and the Pharisees[i] called a meeting[j] of the Sanhedrin.[k]
"What are we accomplishing?" they asked. "Here is this man performing many signs.[l] [48]If we let
him go on like this, everyone will believe in him, and then the Romans will come and take away both
our temple and our nation."
[49]Then one of them, named Caiaphas,[m] who was high priest that year,[n] spoke up, "You know nothing at all! [50]You do not realize that it is better for you that one man die for the people than that the
whole nation perish."[o]
[51]He did not say this on his own, but as high priest that year he
prophesied that Jesus would die for the Jewish nation,
[52]and not only for that nation but also for the scattered children of God, to bring them together and
make them one.[p] [53]So from that day on they plotted to take his life.[q]
[54]Therefore Jesus no longer moved about publicly among the people of Judea.[r] Instead he withdrew to a region near the wilderness, to a village
called Ephraim, where he stayed with his disciples.
[55]When it was almost time for the Jewish Passover,[s] many went up from the country to Jerusalem
for their ceremonial cleansing[t] before the Passover.
[56]They kept looking for Jesus,[u] and as they stood in
the temple courts they asked one another, "What do
you think? Isn't he coming to the festival at all?"
[57]But the chief priests and the Pharisees had given
orders that anyone who found out where Jesus was
should report it so that they might arrest him.

The ornate Caiaphas ossuary was discovered in 1990. It is inscribed "Joseph, son of Caiaphas" and held the bones of a sixty-year-old male.
Wikimedia Commons

11:42 [a]Jn 12:30 [b]Jn 3:17
11:43 [c]Lk 7:14
11:44 [d]Jn 19:40 [e]Jn 20:7
11:45 [f]ver 19 [g]Jn 2:23 [h]Ex 14:31; Jn 7:31
11:47 [i]ver 57 [j]Mt 26:3 [k]Mt 5:22 [l]Jn 2:11
11:49 [m]Mt 26:3 [n]ver 51; Jn 18:13,14
11:50 [o]Jn 18:14
11:52 [p]Isa 49:6; Jn 10:16
11:53 [q]Mt 12:14
11:54 [r]Jn 7:1
11:55 [s]Ex 12:13,23,27; Mt 26:1,2; Mk 14:1; Jn 13:1 [t]2Ch 30:17,18
11:56 [u]Jn 7:11

11:42 Jesus crafts his public prayer with the public in mind.
11:43–44 This anticipates the final resurrection (5:25,28–29).
11:45–54 *The Judicial Decision to Kill Jesus.* The story of Lazarus (vv. 1–44) directly leads to the decision to kill Jesus.
11:45 many ... believed. Apparently answers Jesus' prayer in v. 42.
11:47 Sanhedrin. The highest Jewish judicial body in the land. Under Roman authority, it controlled all Jewish internal affairs as the judiciary, legislative, and (through the high priest) executive body. **What are we accomplishing?** The answer to this rhetorical question is "Nothing!"
11:48 They fear that rising popular Messianic expectations could set off an uprising that would result in (1) Rome removing Israel's semi-autonomy and (2) their losing their own positions of power and prestige (see "better for you" in v. 50).
11:49 Caiaphas. See note on Matt 26:3. **You know nothing at all!** "You don't know what you are talking about!"
11:50 better for you. See note on v. 48. Caiaphas is concerned primarily with political expediency. **die for.** As a substitutionary sacrifice (see note on 10:11). Ironically, in AD 70 the nation still perished.
11:51 prophesied. Caiaphas spoke more truth than he knew: when Caiaphas voiced his opinion to the Sanhedrin, God was also speaking, even if Caiaphas and God intended different meanings through the same words (cf. Acts 4:27–28). **die for.** Both Caiaphas and God want Jesus to die as a substitute and a sacrifice: either Jesus dies or the nation dies (see note on 10:11). Yet the distinction between what Caiaphas means and what God means is clear: Jesus dies for the nation not by removing political trouble but by taking away the sins of those who believe in him.
11:52 scattered children of God. Gentile (see 10:16 and note) believers (1:12–13) dispersed throughout the world (1 Pet 1:1). **to.** Introduces the purpose: unity among Jewish and Gentile believers (see Eph 2:11–22).
11:53 plotted. Resolved.
11:54 Jesus' enemies could not force him to the cross (10:18); he would die at the Father's appointed time.
11:55—12:36 *Triumph and Impending Death.* Jesus' "hour" has come.
11:55–57 *The Setting: The Passover of the Jews.* Interest in and debate about Jesus grows among Jews who have traveled to Jerusalem for the Passover.
11:55 Passover. The third (or possibly fourth) one John mentions (see note on 2:13). **ceremonial cleansing.** Ceremonially unclean people could not celebrate the Passover (Num 9:6).

12:1 [v]Jn 11:55 [w]Mt 21:17
12:2 [x]Lk 10:38-42
12:3 [y]Mk 14:3 [z]Jn 11:2
12:4 [a]Mt 10:4
12:6 [b]Jn 13:29
12:7 [c]Jn 19:40
12:8 [d]Dt 15:11
12:9 [e]Jn 11:43,44
12:11 [f]ver 17,18; Jn 11:45 [g]Jn 7:31
12:13 [h]Ps 118:25,26 [i]Jn 1:49
12:15 [j]Zec 9:9
12:16 [k]Mk 9:32 [l]Jn 2:22; 7:39; 14:26

Jesus Anointed at Bethany

12:1-8Ref — Mt 26:6-13; Mk 14:3-9; Lk 7:37-39

12 Six days before the Passover,[v] Jesus came to Bethany,[w] where Lazarus lived, whom Jesus had raised from the dead. 2 Here a dinner was given in Jesus' honor. Martha served,[x] while Lazarus was among those reclining at the table with him. 3 Then Mary took about a pint[a] of pure nard, an expensive perfume;[y] she poured it on Jesus' feet and wiped his feet with her hair.[z] And the house was filled with the fragrance of the perfume.

4 But one of his disciples, Judas Iscariot, who was later to betray him,[a] objected, 5 "Why wasn't this perfume sold and the money given to the poor? It was worth a year's wages.[b]" 6 He did not say this because he cared about the poor but because he was a thief; as keeper of the money bag,[b] he used to help himself to what was put into it.

7 "Leave her alone," Jesus replied. "It was intended that she should save this perfume for the day of my burial.[c] 8 You will always have the poor among you,[c][d] but you will not always have me."

9 Meanwhile a large crowd of Jews found out that Jesus was there and came, not only because of him but also to see Lazarus, whom he had raised from the dead.[e] 10 So the chief priests made plans to kill Lazarus as well, 11 for on account of him[f] many of the Jews were going over to Jesus and believing in him.[g]

Jesus Comes to Jerusalem as King

12:12-15pp — Mt 21:4-9; Mk 11:7-10; Lk 19:35-38

12 The next day the great crowd that had come for the festival heard that Jesus was on his way to Jerusalem. 13 They took palm branches and went out to meet him, shouting,

"Hosanna![d]"

"Blessed is he who comes in the name of the Lord!"[e][h]

"Blessed is the king of Israel!"[i]

14 Jesus found a young donkey and sat on it, as it is written:

15 "Do not be afraid, Daughter Zion;
see, your king is coming,
seated on a donkey's colt."[f][j]

16 At first his disciples did not understand all this.[k] Only after Jesus was glorified[l] did they realize that these things had been written about him and that these things had been done to him.

[a] *3* Or about 0.5 liter [b] *5* Greek *three hundred denarii* [c] *8* See Deut. 15:11. [d] *13* A Hebrew expression meaning "Save!" which became an exclamation of praise [e] *13* Psalm 118:25,26 [f] *15* Zech. 9:9

12:1–11 *Jesus Anointed at Bethany.* Anticipating the death of the true Passover lamb, Mary anoints Jesus, displaying sacrificial love for him — the only kind of any value. For parallel accounts, see Matt 26:6–13; Mark 14:3–9 (Luke 7:36–39 recounts a different event).

12:1 Six days before the Passover. Probably Saturday before Passover, which that year occurred on Thursday evening/Friday.

12:2 Martha served. See Luke 10:38–42.

12:3 expensive. See v. 5. **wiped his feet with her hair.** Displays humble devotion and love.

12:5 Judas's objection is superficially plausible but displays a utilitarianism that pits compassion (concern for the poor) against extravagant, unqualified devotion.

12:6 Judas's personal greed masquerades as altruism.

12:7 Mary kept the perfume rather than sell it and distribute the proceeds to the poor.

12:8 You will always have the poor among you. See Deut 15:11. **you will not always have me.** The anointing points to Jesus' death. Mary's act symbolized more than she knew.

12:10 made plans. Resolved.

12:11 believing. See note on 11:45.

12:12–19 *Jesus Comes to Jerusalem as King.* The "triumphal entry" announces Jesus' kingship, but the ominous signs are already present that this kingship will be unlike any other. See Matt 21:1–11; Mark 11:1–11; Luke 19:28–44 and notes.

12:13 The crowd quotes from Ps 118:25–26. **Hosanna!** See NIV text note. **king of Israel.** Identifies Jesus as the Messiah, whom they understood to be the nation's political deliverer (see notes on 1:20,49; 6:15).

12:14–15 Jesus would have whipped the political aspirations of the vast crowds into insurrectionist frenzy had he entered Jerusalem on a war horse, but he dampens nationalist expectations by coming "lowly and riding on a donkey" (Zech 9:9).

12:15 Daughter Zion. Personifies Jerusalem (2 Kgs 19:21).

12:16 did not understand. See 2:22; see Introduction: Characteristics and Themes, 7. **glorified.** See note on v. 23.

17Now the crowd that was with him[m] when he called Lazarus from the tomb and raised him from
the dead continued to spread the word. 18Many people, because they had heard that he had performed
this sign,[n] went out to meet him. 19So the Pharisees said to one another, "See, this is getting us nowhere.
Look how the whole world has gone after him!"[o]

Jesus Predicts His Death

20Now there were some Greeks[p] among those who went up to worship at the festival. 21They came to
Philip, who was from Bethsaida[q] in Galilee, with a request. "Sir," they said, "we would like to see Jesus."
22Philip went to tell Andrew; Andrew and Philip in turn told Jesus.
23Jesus replied, "The hour has come for the Son of Man to be glorified.[r] 24Very truly I tell you, unless
a kernel of wheat falls to the ground and dies,[s] it remains only a single seed. But if it dies, it produces
many seeds. 25Anyone who loves their life will lose it, while anyone who hates their life in this world
will keep it[t] for eternal life. 26Whoever serves me must follow me; and where I am, my servant also will
be.[u] My Father will honor the one who serves me.
27"Now my soul is troubled,[v] and what shall I say? 'Father,[w] save me from this hour'?[x] No, it was for
this very reason I came to this hour. 28Father, glorify your name!"

Then a voice came from heaven,[y] "I have glorified it, and will glorify it again." 29The crowd that was
there and heard it said it had thundered; others said an angel had spoken to him.
30Jesus said, "This voice was for your benefit,[z] not mine. 31Now is the time for judgment on this
world;[a] now the prince of this world[b] will be driven out. 32And I, when I am lifted up[a] from the
earth,[c] will draw all people to myself."[d] 33He said this to show the kind of death he was going to
die.[e]
34The crowd spoke up, "We have heard from the Law that the Messiah will remain forever,[f] so how
can you say, 'The Son of Man[g] must be lifted up'?[h] Who is this 'Son of Man'?"
35Then Jesus told them, "You are going to have the light[i] just a little while longer. Walk while you
have the light,[j] before darkness overtakes you.[k] Whoever walks in the dark does not know where they

12:17 [m] Jn 11:42
12:18 [n] ver 11
12:19 [o] Jn 11:47,48
12:20 [p] Jn 7:35; Ac 11:20
12:21 [q] Mt 11:21; Jn 1:44
12:23 [r] Jn 13:32; 17:1
12:24 [s] 1Co 15:36
12:25 [t] Mt 10:39; Mk 8:35; Lk 14:26
12:26 [u] Jn 14:3; 17:24; 2Co 5:8; 1Th 4:17
12:27 [v] Mt 26:38,39; Jn 11:33,38; 13:21 [w] Mt 11:25 [x] ver 23
12:28 [y] Mt 3:17
12:30 [z] Jn 11:42
12:31 [a] Jn 16:11 [b] Jn 14:30; 16:11; 2Co 4:4; Eph 2:2; 1Jn 4:4
12:32 [c] ver 34; Jn 3:14; 8:28 [d] Jn 6:44
12:33 [e] Jn 18:32
12:34 [f] Ps 110:4; Isa 9:7; Eze 37:25; Da 7:14 [g] Mt 8:20 [h] Jn 3:14
12:35 [i] ver 46 [j] Eph 5:8 [k] 1Jn 2:11

[a] *32* The Greek for *lifted up* also means *exalted.*

12:19 whole world. Hyperbole.

12:20–36 *Jesus Predicts His Death.* The arrival of some Gentiles (v. 20) triggers Jesus' announcement: his "hour" (v. 23; see note on 2:4) has come.

12:20 Greeks. Gentiles who come from any part of the Greek-speaking world. These are probably God-fearing Gentiles, possibly converts to Judaism.

12:21 see. Converse with (cf. Luke 8:20; 9:9; Acts 28:20). The text does not explain why they make this request or why they approach the disciples instead of Jesus himself.

12:23 hour. See note on 2:4. **has come.** Up to this point, the "hour" has always been future (4:21,23; 7:30; 8:20). **glorified.** Jesus' death and subsequent resurrection and exaltation (cf. vv. 16,28; 7:39; 13:31–32). Jesus' death supremely manifested his glory (see notes on 1:14; 8:54).

12:24 if it dies, it produces many seeds. Illustrates the principle of life through death. Jesus' death generates an abundant harvest (1 Cor 15:36–38).

12:25 See Matt 10:39; Mark 8:35; Luke 14:26. **loves their life.** Idolatrously focuses on oneself. **hates.** The opposite of "loves"; the contrast reflects a Semitic idiom for fundamental preference, not absolute hatred (e.g., Gen 29:31,33). Jesus' followers (see v. 26) sacrificially give up something of value for the sake of something that is of infinitely greater value: Jesus and "eternal life" (see note on 3:15). **world.** See notes on 1:9,29; 3:16.

12:27 Cf. Matt 26:38–39. **troubled.** Also in 11:33; 13:21. **hour.** See note on 2:4.

12:28 I have glorified it. In Jesus' incarnation (see 1:14 and note) and throughout his earthly ministry. **will glorify it again.** In Jesus' death, resurrection, and exaltation (see note on v. 23).

12:29 The crowd hears God's voice but does not properly recognize it.

12:30 your benefit, not mine. Probably a Semitic contrast (see note on v. 25): *more* for the crowd's benefit than for his. Jesus' disciples will benefit from this especially after they live through the period of the cross and urgently try to make sense of it all (cf. 16:12).

12:31 Now ... now. The end times have already begun. It is not that there is nothing reserved for the consummation; rather, Jesus is about to take the decisive step in his death, resurrection, and exaltation. See Introduction: Characteristics and Themes, 4. **judgment.** See notes on 3:17; 5:22–30; 8:15,16; see also "Wrath," p. 2681. **world.** See notes on 1:9,29; 3:16. **prince of this world.** Satan (14:30; 16:11; cf. 2 Cor 4:4; Eph 2:2; 6:12; 1 John 5:19). **driven out.** Decisively defeated through the cross (see v. 33), although it might seem like Satan's triumph. Jesus' death and resurrection fundamentally smash Satan's reign of tyranny (Col 2:14–15; Heb 2:14–15; Rev 12:11).

12:32 lifted up. See note on 3:14–15. **draw.** See note on 6:44. **all people.** All kinds of people, i.e., all people without distinction (i.e., not just Jews but Gentiles too) rather than all people without exception (cf. the "judgment" theme in v. 31; see note there). It is significant that Gentiles were present on this occasion (see notes on v. 20; 10:16; 11:52).

12:34 The crowd makes two (correct) connections: (1) the glorification of the Son of Man (v. 23) and the "lifting up" of Jesus (v. 32) are tied to Jesus' death (see note on 3:14–15). (2) Jesus' self-presentation as the "Son of Man" is a Messianic claim. **Law ... forever.** What OT passage they have in mind is uncertain (cf. Pss 72:17; 89:35–37; Isa 9:7; Ezek 37:25).

12:35,36 light. Jesus (see notes on 1:5,9; 3:19; 8:12; 9:5,35–41).

12:35 just a little while longer. Refers to Jesus' impending death. **before.** Lest.

12:36 [l]Lk 16:8 [m]Jn 8:59
12:37 [n]Jn 2:11
12:38 [o]Isa 53:1; Ro 10:16
12:40 [p]Isa 6:10; Mt 13:13,15
12:41 [q]Isa 6:1-4 [r]Lk 24:27
12:42 [s]ver 11; Jn 7:48 [t]Jn 7:13 [u]Jn 9:22
12:43 [v]Jn 5:44
12:44 [w]Mt 10:40; Jn 5:24
12:45 [x]Jn 14:9
12:46 [y]Jn 1:4; 3:19; 8:12; 9:5
12:47 [z]Jn 3:17
12:48 [a]Jn 5:45
12:49 [b]Jn 14:31
13:1 [c]Jn 11:55 [d]Jn 12:23 [e]Jn 16:28

are going. 36 Believe in the light while you have the light, so that you may become children of light."[l]
When he had finished speaking, Jesus left and hid himself from them.[m]

Belief and Unbelief Among the Jews

37 Even after Jesus had performed so many signs[n] in their presence, they still would not believe in
him. 38 This was to fulfill the word of Isaiah the prophet:

> "Lord, who has believed our message
> and to whom has the arm of the Lord been revealed?"[a][o]

39 For this reason they could not believe, because, as Isaiah says elsewhere:

> 40 "He has blinded their eyes
> and hardened their hearts,
> so they can neither see with their eyes,
> nor understand with their hearts,
> nor turn—and I would heal them."[b][p]

41 Isaiah said this because he saw Jesus' glory[q] and spoke about him.[r]
42 Yet at the same time many even among the leaders believed in him.[s] But because of the Pharisees[t]
they would not openly acknowledge their faith for fear they would be put out of the synagogue;[u] 43 for
they loved human praise more than praise from God.[v]
44 Then Jesus cried out, "Whoever believes in me does not believe in me only, but in the one who
sent me.[w] 45 The one who looks at me is seeing the one who sent me.[x] 46 I have come into the world as
a light,[y] so that no one who believes in me should stay in darkness.
47 "If anyone hears my words but does not keep them, I do not judge that person. For I did not
come to judge the world, but to save the world.[z] 48 There is a judge for the one who rejects me and
does not accept my words; the very words I have spoken will condemn them[a] at the last day. 49 For
I did not speak on my own, but the Father who sent me commanded me[b] to say all that I have spoken. 50 I know that his command leads to eternal life. So whatever I say is just what the Father has
told me to say."

Jesus Washes His Disciples' Feet

13 It was just before the Passover Festival.[c] Jesus knew that the hour had come[d] for him to leave
this world and go to the Father.[e] Having loved his own who were in the world, he loved them
to the end.

[a] *38* Isaiah 53:1 [b] *40* Isaiah 6:10

12:36 children of light. See Eph 5:8; 1 Thess 5:5.

12:37–50 *Theology of Unbelief.* Jesus reveals the nature and inevitability of unbelief as his public ministry draws to a close.

12:37 Cf. Deut 29:3–4. Faith based on signs may be inferior, but it is better than unbelief (2:11; 10:38; 14:11).

12:38–41 The Jews' unbelief fulfills Scripture (see Rom 9–11 and notes). Verse 39 connects their unbelief to the texts cited in v. 38 (Isa 53:1) and v. 40 (Isa 6:10).

12:38 The supreme servant of the Lord is Jesus the Messiah (see Isa 52:13—53:12 and notes). **our message.** Jesus' teaching. **arm of the Lord.** Primarily Jesus' miraculous signs.

12:39 could not believe. See note on v. 40. Cf. 1:13; 6:44.

12:40 blinded … hardened. God's judicial hardening is a holy condemnation of guilty people who are condemned to do and be what they themselves have chosen (see 3:18). This is part of God's ultimate redemptive purposes (see Rom 9:22–33). In Isa 6, God commissions Isaiah, who knows that his preaching will evoke, and in some sense cause, a negative response; in that sense God hardens their hearts (see John 8:45 and note; Rom 9:18). But God's sovereignty is never pitted against human responsibility (v. 37 presumes that humans are responsible).

12:41 Jesus' glory. When Isaiah saw the Lord in Isa 6:1–4, he saw the glory of the preincarnate Christ, who is God (see note on 1:1). **spoke about him.** John may be thinking of Isaiah's exalted suffering servant since both Isaiah passages he cites in vv. 38,40 share the themes of hardening, being lifted up (Isa 6:1; 52:13), glory (Isa 6:3; 52:13), and sin (6:7; 53:12).

12:42 believed. Perhaps spurious faith (v. 43; cf. 2:23–25; 4:45; 5:35; 6:2,26,60,64; 7:3–5; 8:30–31), especially in light of 5:44; at best a weak faith.

12:44–50 John has already introduced most of the themes in these verses. The main point is that God himself stands behind Jesus.

12:44–45 See notes on 5:16–30; 6:37–40; 8:28b–29.

12:46 light … darkness. See notes on 1:5; 3:2,19; 8:12.

12:47–48 judge … save … condemn. See notes on 3:17; 8:15.

12:47 keep them. See note on 8:31.

12:49–50 See notes on 5:16–30; 8:28b–29.

13:1—20:31 *Jesus' Self-Disclosure in His Cross and Exaltation.* Chs. 13–17 explain before the events the significance of Jesus' death, resurrection, and exaltation that take place in chs. 18–20.

13:1–30 *The Last Supper.* Jesus and his disciples eat a Passover

2The evening meal was in progress, and the devil had already prompted Judas, the son of Simon Iscariot, to betray Jesus. 3Jesus knew that the Father had put all things under his power,[f] and that he had
come from God[g] and was returning to God; 4so he got up from the meal, took off his outer clothing,
and wrapped a towel around his waist. 5After that, he poured water into a basin and began to wash his
disciples' feet,[h] drying them with the towel that was wrapped around him.
6He came to Simon Peter, who said to him, "Lord, are you going to wash my feet?"
7Jesus replied, "You do not realize now what I am doing, but later you will understand."[i]
8"No," said Peter, "you shall never wash my feet."
Jesus answered, "Unless I wash you, you have no part with me."
9"Then, Lord," Simon Peter replied, "not just my feet but my hands and my head as well!"
10Jesus answered, "Those who have had a bath need only to wash their feet; their whole body is clean.
And you are clean,[j] though not every one of you." 11For he knew who was going to betray him, and that
was why he said not every one was clean.
12When he had finished washing their feet, he put on his clothes and returned to his place. "Do you
understand what I have done for you?" he asked them. 13"You call me 'Teacher'[k] and 'Lord,'[l] and rightly
so, for that is what I am. 14Now that I, your Lord and Teacher, have washed your feet, you also should
wash one another's feet.[m] 15I have set you an example that you should do as I have done for you.[n] 16Very
truly I tell you, no servant is greater than his master,[o] nor is a messenger greater than the one who sent
him. 17Now that you know these things, you will be blessed if you do them.[p]

Jesus Predicts His Betrayal

18"I am not referring to all of you;[q] I know those I have chosen.[r] But this is to fulfill this passage of
Scripture: 'He who shared my bread[s] has turned[a] against me.'[b][u]

13:3 [f] Mt 28:18 [g] Jn 8:42; 16:27,28,30
13:5 [h] Lk 7:44
13:7 [i] ver 12
13:10 [j] Jn 15:3
13:13 [k] Jn 11:28 [l] Lk 6:46; 1Co 12:3; Php 2:11
13:14 [m] 1Pe 5:5
13:15 [n] Mt 11:29
13:16 [o] Mt 10:24; Lk 6:40; Jn 15:20
13:17 [p] Mt 7:24,25; Lk 11:28; Jas 1:25
13:18 [q] ver 10 [r] Jn 15:16, 19 [s] Mt 26:23 [t] Jn 6:70 [u] Ps 41:9

a 18 Greek *has lifted up his heel* *b 18* Psalm 41:9

meal on Thursday evening (though to develop a consistent chronology of Jesus' last week before his crucifixion has proved challenging to scholars; (see note on 18:28; see also Matt 26:17–29; Mark 14:12–25; Luke 22:7–20).

13:1–17 *Jesus Washes His Disciples' Feet.* Jesus' stunning, humble act (vv. 4–5) displays his love (v. 1), symbolizes spiritual cleansing (vv. 6–10), and models how Jesus' disciples should serve each other (vv. 12–17). His footwashing points to his death on the cross: the exalted Messiah assumes the role of the despised servant to cleanse others.

13:1 Passover. See note on 2:13. **hour had come.** See note on 12:23. **loved his own ... loved them.** The footwashing here anticipates his deep love for "his own" (cf. 15:19) displayed in the cross (cf. 15:13). **world.** See notes on 1:9,29; 3:16. **to the end.** Either (1) utterly or (2) to the very end of his life.

13:2 devil. The plot against Jesus is satanic. **betray.** See vv. 18–30; 18:2–13.

13:3 all things under his power. Some might expect Jesus to use his supreme power and rank to defeat the devil (and Judas) in an immediate and flashy confrontation. Instead, Jesus washes his disciples' feet (including Judas's).

13:4–5 Jesus adopts the dress and duty of the lowliest of menial servants. Doubtless the disciples would have been happy to wash Jesus' feet, but they could not conceive of washing one another's feet let alone their master washing their feet. Jesus is a servant (Mark 10:45; Luke 22:27; Phil 2:7).

13:6–10 All the disciples are extremely embarrassed by Jesus' footwashing, and all but Peter keep silent. Once again, people misunderstand Jesus (see Introduction: Characteristics and Themes, 7): Peter's well-motivated objection is totally ignorant of his Master's course to the cross, the means of the cleansing that this footwashing foreshadows (cf. Matt 16:22–23).

13:7 later. After Jesus' death, resurrection, and exaltation.

13:8 wash ... wash. Peter thinks that Jesus' footwashing is not socially fitting, but for Jesus it symbolizes his washing away a person's sin.

13:9 Unrestrained exuberance (cf. Matt 17:4).

13:10 need only to wash their feet. Some manuscripts read "do not need to wash." The disciples have already "had a bath," so they do not need a complete washing since "their whole body is clean." The footwashing in vv. 9–10 could symbolize either (1) their complete washing (see note on v. 8) or (2) an additional cleansing, the type they constantly need for sins they commit after Jesus has initially and fundamentally cleansed them from their sin (1 John 1:9); people who have taken a bath and are basically clean may need to wash their feet after a short walk on dusty roads, even though another bath is unnecessary. Most English translations support the second option; the alternate reading ("do not need to wash") supports the first. **not every one of you.** Judas is not "clean" (v. 11).

13:14–15 The heart of Jesus' command is humility and helpfulness toward brothers and sisters in Christ (1 Tim 5:10). Cf. vv. 34–35; Gal 5:13.

13:16 Jesus also applies this proverb elsewhere (15:20; Matt 10:24; Luke 6:40).

13:17 these things. Probably vv. 14–15. **do them.** See note on 8:31.

13:18–30 *Jesus Predicts His Betrayal.* Jesus leaves no doubt that he remains in charge of his own destiny, in submission to his Father's will. John has repeatedly warned about the treachery of someone within the ranks of the Twelve (vv. 2,10–11; 6:70–71; 12:4).

13:18 fulfill. See 17:12. Jesus repeats David's experience in Ps 41:9 at a deeper, climactic level in the history of salvation. Because of passages like 2 Sam 7:12–16 and Ps 2, David became a "type," or model, of his greater Son, the promised Messiah. This does not mean that everything that happened to David must find its echo in Jesus, but the NT understands many of the broad themes of his life that way (cf. Ps 16:8–11 in Acts 2:24–28; Ps 45:6–7 in Heb 1:8–9), especially those that focus on his suffering, weakness, betrayal by friends, and discouragement (e.g., Ps 22 in the passion narratives).

13:19 [v]Jn 14:29; 16:4 [w]Jn 8:24
13:20 [x]Mt 10:40; Lk 10:16
13:21 [y]Jn 12:27 [z]Mt 26:21
13:23 [a]Jn 19:26; 20:2; 21:7,20
13:25 [b]Jn 21:20
13:27 [c]Lk 22:3
13:29 [d]Jn 12:6
13:30 [e]Lk 22:53
13:31 [f]Jn 7:39 [g]Jn 14:13; 17:4; 1Pe 4:11
13:32 [h]Jn 17:1
13:33 [i]Jn 7:33,34
13:34 [j]1Jn 2:7-11; 3:11 [k]Lev 19:18; 1Th 4:9; 1Pe 1:22 [l]Jn 15:12; Eph 5:2; 1Jn 4:10,11
13:35 [m]1Jn 3:14; 4:20
13:36 [n]ver 33; Jn 14:2 [o]Jn 21:18,19; 2Pe 1:14
13:38 [p]Jn 18:27

19 "I am telling you now before it happens, so that when it does happen you will believe[v] that I am
who I am.[w] 20 Very truly I tell you, whoever accepts anyone I send accepts me; and whoever accepts me
accepts the one who sent me."[x]
21 After he had said this, Jesus was troubled in spirit[y] and testified, "Very truly I tell you, one of you
is going to betray me."[z]
22 His disciples stared at one another, at a loss to know which of them he meant. 23 One of them, the
disciple whom Jesus loved,[a] was reclining next to him. 24 Simon Peter motioned to this disciple and said,
"Ask him which one he means."
25 Leaning back against Jesus, he asked him, "Lord, who is it?"[b]
26 Jesus answered, "It is the one to whom I will give this piece of bread when I have dipped it in the
dish." Then, dipping the piece of bread, he gave it to Judas, the son of Simon Iscariot. 27 As soon as Judas
took the bread, Satan entered into him.[c]
So Jesus told him, "What you are about to do, do quickly." 28 But no one at the meal understood why
Jesus said this to him. 29 Since Judas had charge of the money,[d] some thought Jesus was telling him to
buy what was needed for the festival, or to give something to the poor. 30 As soon as Judas had taken the
bread, he went out. And it was night.[e]

Jesus Predicts Peter's Denial

13:37,38pp — Mt 26:33-35; Mk 14:29-31; Lk 22:33,34

31 When he was gone, Jesus said, "Now the Son of Man is glorified[f] and God is glorified in him.[g] 32 If
God is glorified in him,[a] God will glorify the Son in himself,[h] and will glorify him at once.
33 "My children, I will be with you only a little longer. You will look for me, and just as I told the Jews,
so I tell you now: Where I am going, you cannot come.[i]
34 "A new command[j] I give you: Love one another.[k] As I have loved you, so you must love one another.[l] 35 By this everyone will know that you are my disciples, if you love one another."[m]
36 Simon Peter asked him, "Lord, where are you going?"
Jesus replied, "Where I am going, you cannot follow now,[n] but you will follow later."[o]
37 Peter asked, "Lord, why can't I follow you now? I will lay down my life for you."
38 Then Jesus answered, "Will you really lay down your life for me? Very truly I tell you, before the
rooster crows, you will disown me three times![p]

[a] *32* Many early manuscripts do not have *If God is glorified in him.*

13:19 so that. Jesus informs his disciples about Judas's impending betrayal of him (cf. 14:29) with the goal of enabling them to see, after the event, that Jesus was neither the pawn of a cheap plot nor a sad victim. Rather, Judas's treachery serves the redemptive purposes of the mission on which the Father sent Jesus (v. 20). Such knowledge will settle the disciples' faith. **I am who I am.** See notes on 6:35; 8:24.
13:20 See Matt 10:40. **anyone I send.** Anticipates 20:21. **me ... the one who sent me.** See 5:19–30 and notes.
13:23 disciple whom Jesus loved. Also in 19:26–27; 20:2–9; 21:7,20–25; probably John, the author of this Gospel (see Introduction: Author). The expression does not mean that Jesus did not love the others; it may be the author's way to avoid giving even the impression of sharing a platform with Jesus. It also testifies to one disciple's profound sense of being loved by Jesus, even as it reminds readers that the author is an eyewitness of the events he recounts.
13:26 Apparently Jesus answers so quietly that the other disciples cannot hear because they do not know why Judas leaves (vv. 28–29).
13:27 entered. Probably signifies thorough possession. **quickly.** Judas may as well get on with his treachery and be done with it. Jesus voluntarily lays down his life (10:18).
13:30 night. Ominous; more than just a time indicator (see note on 3:2). Judas was swallowed up by the most awful darkness (Matt 8:12; 22:13; 25:30) and heading to his own place (Acts 1:25; see notes on John 1:5; 3:19). For Jesus, this was the "hour—when darkness reigns" (Luke 22:53).
13:31—16:33 *The Farewell Discourse.* Jesus explains the significance of his death and exaltation and the role of the promised Holy Spirit, whom Jesus gives to believers after his exaltation.
13:31–38 *Jesus Predicts Peter's Denial.* Jesus tells his disciples that he will soon depart. Then he predicts that Peter will deny him three times.
13:31–32 Now ... at once. Judas's departure puts the machinery of Jesus' arrest, trial, and execution into motion.
13:31 the Son of Man is glorified. See note on 12:23. **God is glorified in him.** Jesus' obedience, sacrificial death, resurrection, and exaltation glorify God.
13:32 himself. Probably the Father.
13:33 just as I told the Jews. See 7:34 and note. **you cannot come.** Now; but they can later (see v. 36). Jesus' tone is different here since he will prepare a place for his followers (14:1–3), who will see him and live (14:19; contrast 8:21).
13:34 new command ... As I have loved you. The standard is no longer how we love ourselves (Lev 19:18; Matt 22:37–40) but how Jesus loves us (see notes on 1 John 2:7–8). Jesus displays his love in footwashing (see vv. 1–17 and notes) and supremely in the cross (see 15:13). Cf. 15:13,17.
13:35 love. A distinguishing mark of Jesus' followers (1 John 4:7–12,19–21).
13:36 See note on 16:5. **later.** See 21:18–19.
13:38 Will you really lay down your life for me? The irony is that (1) Jesus is laying down his life for Peter (10:11,15,17–18) and

Jesus Comforts His Disciples

14 "Do not let your hearts be troubled.[q] You believe in God[a]; believe also in me. 2 My Father's
house has many rooms; if that were not so, would I have told you that I am going there[r] to
prepare a place for you? 3 And if I go and prepare a place for you, I will come back and take you to be
with me that you also may be where I am.[s] 4 You know the way to the place where I am going."

Jesus the Way to the Father

5 Thomas[t] said to him, "Lord, we don't know where you are going, so how can we know the way?"
6 Jesus answered, "I am the way[u] and the truth and the life.[v] No one comes to the Father except
through me. 7 If you really know me, you will know[b] my Father as well.[w] From now on, you do know
him and have seen him."
8 Philip said, "Lord, show us the Father and that will be enough for us."
9 Jesus answered: "Don't you know me, Philip, even after I have been among you such a long time?
Anyone who has seen me has seen the Father.[x] How can you say, 'Show us the Father'? 10 Don't you
believe that I am in the Father, and that the Father is in me?[y] The words I say to you I do not speak
on my own authority.[z] Rather, it is the Father, living in me, who is doing his work. 11 Believe me when
I say that I am in the Father and the Father is in me; or at least believe on the evidence of the works
themselves.[a] 12 Very truly I tell you, whoever believes[b] in me will do the works I have been doing,[c] and
they will do even greater things than these, because I am going to the Father. 13 And I will do whatever
you ask[d] in my name, so that the Father may be glorified in the Son. 14 You may ask me for anything
in my name, and I will do it.

Jesus Promises the Holy Spirit

15 "If you love me, keep my commands.[e] 16 And I will ask the Father, and he will give you another
advocate[f] to help you and be with you forever— 17 the Spirit of truth.[g] The world cannot accept him,[h]

[a] *1* Or *Believe in God* [b] *7* Some manuscripts *If you really knew me, you would know*

14:1 [q] ver 27
14:2 [r] Jn 13:33,36
14:3 [s] Jn 12:26
14:5 [t] Jn 11:16
14:6 [u] Jn 10:9 [v] Jn 11:25
14:7 [w] Jn 8:19
14:9 [x] Jn 12:45; Col 1:15; Heb 1:3
14:10 [y] Jn 10:38 [z] Jn 5:19
14:11 [a] Jn 5:36; 10:38
14:12 [b] Mt 21:21 [c] Lk 10:17
14:13 [d] Mt 7:7
14:15 [e] ver 21,23; Jn 15:10; 1Jn 5:3
14:16 [f] Jn 15:26; 16:7
14:17 [g] Jn 15:26; 16:13; 1Jn 4:6 [h] 1Co 2:14

(2) Peter will lay down his life for Jesus some 30 years later (see 21:18–19 and notes).

14:1–4 *Jesus Comforts His Disciples.* Jesus himself is "troubled" (12:27; 13:21) because he is heading for the agony of the cross, yet he is still the one who comforts others.

14:1 troubled. Because they are confused and afraid that Jesus will imminently depart (13:33,36). **You believe in God.** See NIV text note. Cf. Ps 56:3–4; Isa 26:3–4.

14:2–3 The disciples should not be "troubled" about Jesus' departure because it will benefit them.

14:2 My Father's house. The abode of God; in one sense, the ultimate temple (see Rev 21). **rooms.** Dwelling places. The Son provides more than enough space for every one of his followers to join him (cf. Luke 16:9).

14:3 I will come back. Jesus' second coming (see v. 28; 21:22–23).

14:4 Because they know Jesus. **the way.** Raises the question in v. 5 and anticipates v. 6.

14:5–14 *Jesus the Way to the Father.* Jesus is the only way to the Father, is in the Father, is going to the Father, and answers prayer to glorify the Father.

14:5 Thomas (cf. 11:16; 20:24–25) does not understand that Jesus just spelled out the destination (vv. 2–3).

14:6 Answers the question in v. 5. **I am.** See note on 6:35. **the way.** To God—because Jesus so mediates God's truth and God's life. **the truth.** See notes on 1:14; 3:33. **the life.** Cf. 11:25–26; see notes on 3:14–15; 5:21,26–27; 6:35,63,68; 11:1—12:50. **except through me.** Jesus is the exclusive way to God (Acts 4:12). Those who claim to know God but reject Jesus do not know God (see 5:39–47 and notes). Christianity is not merely one viable religion among many.

14:7 me ... my father. See 5:37–38; 8:19.

14:8 Cf. Exod 33:18.

14:9 such a long time. During Jesus' ministry. **Anyone who has seen me has seen the Father.** See 1:14,18 and notes; 12:45.

14:10 I am in the Father ... the Father is in me. See 10:30 and note. **I do not speak on my own authority.** See 5:19–30 and notes.

14:11 works. See 5:36 and note. The miracles themselves are signs (see Introduction: Purpose and Addressees).

14:12 greater things. Not more works or more spectacular works but works that point to Jesus in the age that Jesus' death, resurrection, and exaltation introduce (cf. the parallel in 5:20 and the similar contrast in Matt 11:11). This promise of greater things anticipates the need for enabling power (vv. 16–17). **because I am going to the Father.** The basis for the "greater things."

14:13–14 I will do whatever you ask ... ask me for anything ... and I will do it. A stunning promise.

14:13 in my name. In accord with Jesus' character and thus for God's glory. This qualifies the prayers Jesus answers (cf. conditions in 15:7; Mark 11:24; 1 John 5:14). **so that.** Introduces the purpose for which Jesus answers our prayers (cf. 7:18; 8:50,54; 12:28).

14:15–31 *Jesus Promises the Holy Spirit.* The Father will give Jesus' followers the Holy Spirit after Jesus departs.

14:15 Also vv. 21a,23a,24a (cf. 15:10,14; 1 John 5:2–3). God's people obey Jesus because they love him. See 15:9–10. Similarly, Jesus obeys the Father (4:34; 6:38; 8:29).

14:16 he will give. Jesus describes this sending in complementary ways (v. 26; 15:26; 16:7), granted the tight cohesion of the Father and Son (5:19–30). **another.** Besides Jesus (1 John 2:1). **advocate.** Greek *paraklētos* (translated "Advocate" in v. 26; 15:26; 16:7), hence some call him the "Paraclete"; a counselor who helps those in trouble with the law.

14:17 Spirit of truth. Also in 15:26; 16:13. He communicates the truth (v. 26; 16:12–15) about Jesus, who is "the truth" (v. 6). See Introduction:

14:18 [i]ver 3,28
14:19 [j]Jn 7:33,34; 16:16 [k]Jn 6:57
14:20 [l]Jn 10:38
14:21 [m]1Jn 5:3 [n]1Jn 2:5
14:22 [o]Lk 6:16; Ac 1:13 [p]Ac 10:41
14:23 [q]ver 15 [r]1Jn 2:24; Rev 3:20
14:24 [s]Jn 7:16
14:26 [t]Jn 15:26; 16:7 [u]Ac 2:33 [v]Jn 16:13; 1Jn 2:20,27 [w]Jn 2:22
14:27 [x]Jn 16:33; Php 4:7; Col 3:15
14:28 [y]ver 2-4,18 [z]Jn 5:18 [a]Jn 10:29; Php 2:6
14:29 [b]Jn 13:19; 16:4
14:30 [c]Jn 12:31
14:31 [d]Jn 10:18; 12:49

because it neither sees him nor knows him. But you know him, for he lives with you and will be[a] in
you. [18]I will not leave you as orphans; I will come to you.[i] [19]Before long, the world will not see me
anymore, but you will see me.[j] Because I live, you also will live.[k] [20]On that day you will realize that I
am in my Father,[l] and you are in me, and I am in you. [21]Whoever has my commands and keeps them
is the one who loves me.[m] The one who loves me will be loved by my Father,[n] and I too will love them
and show myself to them."

[22]Then Judas[o] (not Judas Iscariot) said, "But, Lord, why do you intend to show yourself to us and
not to the world?"[p]

[23]Jesus replied, "Anyone who loves me will obey my teaching.[q] My Father will love them, and we will
come to them and make our home with them.[r] [24]Anyone who does not love me will not obey my teaching. These words you hear are not my own; they belong to the Father who sent me.[s]

[25]"All this I have spoken while still with you. [26]But the Advocate,[t] the Holy Spirit, whom the Father
will send in my name,[u] will teach you all things[v] and will remind you of everything I have said to you.[w]
[27]Peace I leave with you; my peace I give you.[x] I do not give to you as the world gives. Do not let your
hearts be troubled and do not be afraid.

[28]"You heard me say, 'I am going away and I am coming back to you.'[y] If you loved me, you would
be glad that I am going to the Father,[z] for the Father is greater than I.[a] [29]I have told you now before
it happens, so that when it does happen you will believe.[b] [30]I will not say much more to you, for the
prince of this world[c] is coming. He has no hold over me, [31]but he comes so that the world may learn
that I love the Father and do exactly what my Father has commanded me.[d]

"Come now; let us leave.

[a] *17* Some early manuscripts *and is*

Characteristics and Themes, 5. **world.** See notes on 1:9,29; 3:16. **cannot accept him.** See 1 Cor 2:14. **he lives with you and will be in you.** God was "with" believers under the old covenant, not least by dwelling among them in the temple, sometimes appearing in a pillar of cloud or fire, and coming upon individuals by his Spirit. After Jesus' death and resurrection, the Spirit will come upon believers and permanently indwell them (v. 23; 7:39).

14:18 Doubtless the disciples still feel abandoned, so Jesus consoles them (cf. Deut 31:6; Josh 1:5; Heb 13:5). **I will come to you.** Probably after Jesus' resurrection (vv. 19–20; 16:16–30; 20:19,26) but possibly with the gift of the Spirit (vv. 16–17,25–26) or at Jesus' second coming (vv. 3,28).

14:19 I live. Jesus' resurrection.

14:20 On that day you will realize. Jesus' resurrection will radically change how his followers think (cf. 2:22). They will comprehend what he has told them about his relationship with the Father in vv. 7–11. **you are in me, and I am in you.** See 15:1–17 and notes.

14:21 See v. 15 and note. **has.** Grasps with the mind.

14:22 Cf. note on 7:3–4. Judas wrongly assumes that Jesus, as the Messianic King, must now startle the world with undeniable, irresistible power and splendor.

14:23 obey. See v. 15 and note. **make our home with.** Cf. Eph 3:17. This anticipates the consummation, when God will live with his people (Rev 21:3,22). See "Temple," p. 2652.

14:24 The opposite of vv. 15,21a,23a. **not my own.** See 5:19–30 and notes.

14:26 Advocate. See note on v. 16. **the Father will send.** See note on v. 16. **in my name.** As Jesus' emissary, just as Jesus was the Father's emissary (5:43; 10:25). **teach you . . . remind you.** Explains how Jesus' disciples who were with him during his earthly ministry (15:27) come to more accurately and fully understand Jesus' teaching (16:13–15) since they repeatedly fail to understand its significance before his resurrection (2:22; 12:16; 20:9; see Introduction: Characteristics and Themes, 7).

14:27 Peace . . . peace. Reflects the Hebrew *šālôm*, the customary Jewish word of greeting (see 20:19,21,26) and farewell. Peace fundamentally characterizes the Messianic kingdom anticipated in the OT (Num 6:26; Ps 29:11; Isa 9:6; Ezek 37:26; Hag 2:9) and fulfilled in the NT (Acts 10:36; Rom 1:7; 5:1; Eph 2:14–17). The *pax Romana* ("Roman peace") was won and maintained by a brutal sword, and many Jews thought their Messiah would secure peace with an even mightier sword. Instead, the Messiah secured it by suffering and dying (Col 1:20). **as the world gives.** The world promises peace but cannot give genuine peace. **troubled . . . afraid.** For individuals, Jesus' peace secures composure in the midst of trouble and dissolves fear (16:33; Phil 4:7; Col 3:15). See "Shalom," p. 2693.

14:28 You heard me say. See vv. 2–4,12,18–19. **you would be glad.** The disciples have been responding in an emotional, self-centered way rather than rejoicing that Jesus will depart to his own "home" after accomplishing his mission. **the Father is greater than I.** The Father in his undiminished glory is greater than the Son in his incarnate state. That is the primary thought here, for the context shows that Jesus anticipates his departure precisely because it means he will return to that glory (17:5). This does not imply that Jesus is less than fully God because "greater than" does not refer to their being and essence (see notes on 1:1; 5:17–19,23; 8:24; 12:41). Yet "the Father is greater than I" also echoes 3:17; 5:19–30. The difference in roles between the Father and the Son means the Father sends his Son into the world and the Son obeys (v. 31); the Father "shows" him what to do and the Son performs it (5:20). The functional submission of the Son reaches back into eternity.

14:30 prince of this world. See note on 12:31. **coming.** In the person of Judas (13:2,27) and others. **He has no hold over me.** Satan could have a claim on Jesus only if he could justifiably accuse him, and Jesus is sinless.

14:31 The world (like Satan) may think that Jesus is defeated by his death, but Jesus' obedient death vindicates him and displays how deeply he loves the Father (10:17–18). **let us leave.** May mean that they leave the upper room and proceed to Gethsemane (18:1).

The Vine and the Branches

15 "I am the true vine,[e] and my Father is the gardener. [2]He cuts off every branch in me that
bears no fruit, while every branch that does bear fruit he prunes[a] so that it will be even more
fruitful. [3]You are already clean because of the word I have spoken to you.[f] [4]Remain in me, as I also
remain in you.[g] No branch can bear fruit by itself; it must remain in the vine. Neither can you bear
fruit unless you remain in me.

[5]"I am the vine; you are the branches. If you remain in me and I in you, you will bear much fruit;[h]
apart from me you can do nothing. [6]If you do not remain in me, you are like a branch that is thrown
away and withers; such branches are picked up, thrown into the fire and burned.[i] [7]If you remain in me
and my words remain in you, ask whatever you wish, and it will be done for you.[j] [8]This is to my Father's
glory,[k] that you bear much fruit, showing yourselves to be my disciples.[l]

[9]"As the Father has loved me,[m] so have I loved you. Now remain in my love. [10]If you keep my
commands,[n] you will remain in my love, just as I have kept my Father's commands and remain in
his love. [11]I have told you this so that my joy may be in you and that your joy may be complete.[o]
[12]My command is this: Love each other as I have loved you.[p] [13]Greater love has no one than this: to
lay down one's life for one's friends.[q] [14]You are my friends[r] if you do what I command.[s] [15]I no longer call you servants, because a servant does not know his master's business. Instead, I have called
you friends, for everything that I learned from my Father I have made known to you.[t] [16]You did not
choose me, but I chose you and appointed you[u] so that you might go and bear fruit — fruit that will
last — and so that whatever you ask in my name the Father will give you. [17]This is my command:
Love each other.[v]

15:1 [e] Isa 5:1-7
15:3 [f] Jn 13:10; 17:17; Eph 5:26
15:4 [g] Jn 6:56; 1Jn 2:6
15:5 [h] ver 16
15:6 [i] ver 2
15:7 [j] Mt 7:7
15:8 [k] Mt 5:16 [l] Jn 8:31
15:9 [m] Jn 17:23,24,26
15:10 [n] Jn 14:15
15:11 [o] Jn 17:13
15:12 [p] Jn 13:34
15:13 [q] Jn 10:11; Ro 5:7,8
15:14 [r] Lk 12:4 [s] Mt 12:50
15:15 [t] Jn 8:26
15:16 [u] Jn 6:70; 13:18
15:17 [v] ver 12

[a] 2 The Greek for *be prunes* also means *be cleans.*

15:1 – 17 *The Vine and the Branches.* Jesus presents an extended metaphor (vv. 1 – 8) and explains it (vv. 9 – 17). Unlike Jesus' parables with vines and vineyards in the other Gospels (e.g., Matt 20:1 – 16; Mark 12:1 – 12; Luke 13:6 – 9), this comparison centers on a vine, and the vine is Jesus — not Israel. The vine produces its fruit through the branches (believers), imagery that unpacks the mutual indwelling in 14:20: "you are in me, and I am in you."

15:1 I am. See note on 6:35. **the true vine.** The vine frequently symbolizes Israel in the OT as failing to produce fruit (e.g., Ps 80:8 – 16; Isa 5:1 – 7; 27:2 – 6; Jer 2:21; Ezek 15:1 – 8). In contrast to Israel, Jesus is the *true* vine who genuinely and ultimately produces good fruit. **gardener.** Vinedresser (cf. Isa 5:1 – 7).

15:2 Fruitless branches represent professing believers who demonstate that their connection to Jesus is superficial (see v. 6; e.g., Judas in 13:1 – 2,10 – 11,26 – 30; cf. 1 John 2:19; see notes on 2:23; 4:45; 5:35; 6:2,60; 7:5; 8:30), and fruitful branches represent genuine believers (see note on 8:31). The vinedresser ensures increased fruitfulness by removing dead branches ("cuts off") and removing undesired parts from fruitful ones ("prunes").

15:3 You are already clean. In contrast to Judas, an unfruitful branch (see 13:10 – 11).

15:4 Remain in me, as I also remain in you. See notes on vv. 7,9. This command implies that believers are already organically connected to Jesus and are responsible to maintain that vital connection. Believers should do this for three reasons: (1) Fruitfulness is impossible apart from doing so (vv. 4 – 5). (2) Doing so results in fruitfulness (v. 5). (3) Failing to do so results in final judgment (v. 6; see "Wrath," p. 2681).

15:7 my words remain in you. Parallel to "I also remain in you" in v. 4, which implies that Jesus remains in believers when his specific utterances remain in believers (6:63). **ask whatever you wish, and it will be done for you.** When believers internalize Jesus' individual utterances, they will make Scripturally informed requests that God will answer (see 14:13 – 14 and notes).

15:8 This is to my Father's glory. Jesus glorifies his Father through fruitful believers. **showing yourselves to be my disciples.** Cf. 8:31 and note; Col 1:23; 1 John 2:24.

15:9 remain in my love. Parallel to "remain in me" in v. 4 (see note).

15:10 keep my commands. The condition for remaining in Jesus' love (v. 9). Thus, believers remain in Jesus by obeying him (see 14:15 and note; 1 John 2:5; 3:24; 5:2 – 3). **just as I.** Jesus remains in the Father's love by obeying him (4:34; 5:19 – 30; 6:38; 8:29,55; 10:17 – 18; 14:31). The letter of 1 John explores practical tensions that (sinful) believers experience with this ultimate standard.

15:11 so that. Introduces the purpose for which Jesus exhorts believers to remain in him by obeying him (vv. 9 – 10). **my joy may be in you.** Obeying Jesus (see note on v. 10) is not drudgery (see 1 John 1:4; 5:2 – 3). **complete.** Presupposes that human joy in a fallen world will at best be ephemeral, shallow, and incomplete until one experiences God's love in Jesus, the love for which we were created, a mutual love that issues in obedience without reserve.

15:12 See note on 13:34. Love for God is tied to and verified by love for other believers (1 John 4:11 – 21).

15:13 Displayed supremely in Jesus' sacrificial death (10:11,14 – 15, 17 – 18; Rom 5:7 – 8; Eph 5:25; 1 John 3:16).

15:14 my friends. Like Abraham (2 Chr 20:7; Isa 41:8; Jas 2:23) and Moses (Exod 33:11), who were called friends of God. **if you do what I command.** Obedience is not what *makes* believers Jesus' friends but what *characterizes* Jesus' friends.

15:15 no longer. In times past God's people were not as informed of his saving plan as they are now. **servants ... friends.** A king simply tells his servants what to do, but he takes his friends into his confidence, informing them of his motives, plans, and purposes.

15:16 You did not choose me, but I chose you and appointed you. Believers enjoy privileges (vv. 14 – 15) not because they are wiser or better than others but ultimately because Jesus selected them and set them apart. **so that ... so that.** Introduces two purposes for which Jesus "chose" and "appointed" his followers. **fruit.** New converts. **in my name.** See note on 14:13.

15:17 See v. 12 and note on 13:34. This love contrasts with the world's hatred in vv. 18 – 25.

15:18 [w]1Jn 3:13
15:19 [x]ver 16 [y]Jn 17:14
15:20 [z]Jn 13:16 [a]2Ti 3:12
15:21 [b]Mt 10:22 [c]Jn 16:3
15:22 [d]Jn 9:41; Ro 1:20
15:24 [e]Jn 5:36
15:25 [f]Ps 35:19; 69:4
15:26 [g]Jn 14:16 [h]Jn 14:26 [i]Jn 14:17 [j]1Jn 5:7
15:27 [k]Lk 24:48; 1Jn 1:2; 4:14 [l]Lk 1:2
16:1 [m]Jn 15:18-27 [n]Mt 11:6
16:2 [o]Jn 9:22 [p]Isa 66:5; Ac 26:9,10; Rev 6:9
16:3 [q]Jn 15:21; 17:25; 1Jn 3:1
16:4 [r]Jn 13:19
16:5 [s]Jn 7:33 [t]Jn 13:36; 14:5
16:7 [u]Jn 14:16,26; 15:26 [v]Jn 7:39

The World Hates the Disciples

18 “If the world hates you,[w] keep in mind that it hated me first. 19 If you belonged to the world, it would
love you as its own. As it is, you do not belong to the world, but I have chosen you[x] out of the world. That
is why the world hates you.[y] 20 Remember what I told you: ‘A servant is not greater than his master.’[a][z] If
they persecuted me, they will persecute you also.[a] If they obeyed my teaching, they will obey yours also.
21 They will treat you this way because of my name,[b] for they do not know the one who sent me.[c] 22 If I had
not come and spoken to them, they would not be guilty of sin; but now they have no excuse for their sin.[d]
23 Whoever hates me hates my Father as well. 24 If I had not done among them the works no one else did,[e]
they would not be guilty of sin. As it is, they have seen, and yet they have hated both me and my Father.
25 But this is to fulfill what is written in their Law: ‘They hated me without reason.’[b][f]

The Work of the Holy Spirit

26 “When the Advocate[g] comes, whom I will send to you from the Father[h]—the Spirit of truth[i] who
goes out from the Father—he will testify about me.[j] 27 And you also must testify,[k] for you have been
with me from the beginning.[l]

16 “All this[m] I have told you so that you will not fall away.[n] 2 They will put you out of the synagogue;[o] in fact, the time is coming when anyone who kills you will think they are offering a
service to God.[p] 3 They will do such things because they have not known the Father or me.[q] 4 I have told
you this, so that when their time comes you will remember[r] that I warned you about them. I did not
tell you this from the beginning because I was with you, 5 but now I am going to him who sent me.[s]
None of you asks me, ‘Where are you going?’[t] 6 Rather, you are filled with grief because I have said these
things. 7 But very truly I tell you, it is for your good that I am going away. Unless I go away, the Advocate[u]
will not come to you; but if I go, I will send him to you.[v] 8 When he comes, he will prove the world to be

[a] *20* John 13:16 [b] *25* Psalms 35:19; 69:4

15:18–25 *The World Hates the Disciples.* The world hates Jesus' community of love not for sociological reasons but for theological ones.
15:18–19 By warning his disciples in advance, Jesus ensures that they will not be surprised when they experience persecution (1 John 3:13).
15:18 world. See notes on 1:9,29; 3:16. **it hated me first.** See 7:7 and note. After Jesus chooses believers out of the world, they become outcasts to the world.
15:20 A servant is not greater than his master. See 13:16 and note. **If … If.** The argument is probably this: "If they persecuted me (and many of them did), they will persecute you also. If they obeyed my teaching (and some of them did), they will obey yours also."
15:21–24 If they truly knew God, they would recognize who Jesus is; to hate Jesus is to hate the Father (5:37–38; 8:19).
15:21 name. See note on 1:12. People's responses to Jesus' followers depend not on who they are but on who Jesus is.
15:22,24 If I had not … they would not be guilty of sin. The idea is not that if Jesus had not come, the people would be sinless. Rather, if Jesus had not come, they would not be guilty of the weighty sin of directly rejecting and hating Jesus, whose words ("spoken," v. 22) and works ("done … the works no one else did," v. 24) were the clearest light and fullest revelation of the Father (vv. 18,23,24).
15:22 no excuse. Privilege and responsibility go together.
15:25 Their hating Jesus does not jeopardize God's saving plan. It fulfills their very own Scripture (Ps 69:4; cf. Ps 35:19) by repeating David's experience at a deeper, climactic level in the history of salvation: If David could be hated for no reason, how much more the Messiah, David's greater Son? See notes on 2:17; 13:18.
15:26—16:15 *The Work of the Holy Spirit.* The Holy Spirit joins with the disciples in testifying about Jesus to the world (15:26–27). The focus shifts from what causes persecution (15:18–25) to how Jesus' disciples respond to it (16:1–4). The Spirit will continue Jesus' work by convicting the world (16:5–11) and revealing the truth to Jesus' disciples (16:12–15).
15:26–27 testify … testify. The repetition underscores the importance of bearing witness to, or testifying to, the Lord Jesus, almost as if in a court of law.
15:26 Advocate … I will send. See note on 14:16. **Spirit of truth.** See note on 14:17. **goes out.** Rendered "proceeds" in some translations, hence an old doctrinal debate called "the procession of the Spirit": Does the Spirit proceed (1) from only the Father or (2) from both the Father and the Son? Though this passage (and 16:7) specifies the Spirit's mission rather than the nature of his eternal relationship with the Father, the second view is eminently defensible.
15:27 This applies primarily to Jesus' first disciples and derivatively to later Christians.
16:1 All this. See 15:18–27. **so that.** Introduces why Jesus forewarns his followers about persecution (see note on 15:18–19). **fall away.** Cf. 1 John 2:19.
16:2 put you out of the synagogue. Cf. 9:22; 12:42. **think they are offering a service to God.** For example, Saul/Paul (Acts 8:1–3; 26:9–11; Gal 1:13–14; 1 Tim 1:13).
16:3 Cf. 15:18–21.
16:4 so that. See note on v. 1.
16:5 None of you asks me, 'Where are you going?' Peter asked this question in 13:36 (cf. 14:5), so Jesus may be saying, "None of you *right now are asking* me …" Further, Peter's concern was with what would happen to them, not with where Jesus was going; the implied question behind 13:36 seems to be, "Why are you leaving us?"
16:6 filled with grief. Because Jesus announced that he is leaving.
16:7 It is better to live after Jesus' resurrection and exaltation than it is to live during his earthly ministry (see 14:12 and note). The Spirit continues Jesus' ministry worldwide in the age of the new covenant, which the OT anticipates (e.g., Joel 2:28–32; Acts 2). **Advocate.** See note on 14:16. **I will send.** See note on 14:16.
16:8 prove … to be in the wrong. Expose and convict of personal guilt in a way that results in shame and calls for repentance. **world.** See

in the wrong about sin and righteousness and judgment: 9about sin,[w] because people do not believe in
me; 10about righteousness,[x] because I am going to the Father, where you can see me no longer; 11and
about judgment, because the prince of this world[y] now stands condemned.
12"I have much more to say to you, more than you can now bear.[z] 13But when he, the Spirit of truth,[a]
comes, he will guide you into all the truth.[b] He will not speak on his own; he will speak only what he
hears, and he will tell you what is yet to come. 14He will glorify me because it is from me that he will
receive what he will make known to you. 15All that belongs to the Father is mine.[c] That is why I said
the Spirit will receive from me what he will make known to you."

The Disciples' Grief Will Turn to Joy

16Jesus went on to say, "In a little while[d] you will see me no more, and then after a little while you
will see me."[e]
17At this, some of his disciples said to one another, "What does he mean by saying, 'In a little while
you will see me no more, and then after a little while you will see me,'[f] and 'Because I am going to
the Father'?"[g] 18They kept asking, "What does he mean by 'a little while'? We don't understand what
he is saying."
19Jesus saw that they wanted to ask him about this, so he said to them, "Are you asking one another
what I meant when I said, 'In a little while you will see me no more, and then after a little while you
will see me'? 20Very truly I tell you, you will weep and mourn[h] while the world rejoices. You will grieve,
but your grief will turn to joy.[i] 21A woman giving birth to a child has pain[j] because her time has come;
but when her baby is born she forgets the anguish because of her joy that a child is born into the world.
22So with you: Now is your time of grief,[k] but I will see you again[l] and you will rejoice, and no one will
take away your joy. 23In that day you will no longer ask me anything. Very truly I tell you, my Father
will give you whatever you ask in my name.[m] 24Until now you have not asked for anything in my name.
Ask and you will receive, and your joy will be complete.[n]
25"Though I have been speaking figuratively,[o] a time is coming[p] when I will no longer use this kind
of language but will tell you plainly about my Father. 26In that day you will ask in my name.[q] I am not

16:9 [w] Jn 15:22
16:10 [x] Ac 3:14; 7:52; 1Pe 3:18
16:11 [y] Jn 12:31
16:12 [z] Mk 4:33
16:13 [a] Jn 14:17 [b] Jn 14:26
16:15 [c] Jn 17:10
16:16 [d] Jn 7:33 [e] Jn 14:18-24
16:17 [f] ver 16 [g] ver 5
16:20 [h] Lk 23:27 [i] Jn 20:20
16:21 [j] Isa 26:17; 1Th 5:3
16:22 [k] ver 6 [l] ver 16
16:23 [m] Mt 7:7; Jn 15:16
16:24 [n] Jn 3:29; 15:11
16:25 [o] Mt 13:34; Jn 10:6 [p] ver 2
16:26 [q] ver 23,24

---

notes on 1:9,29; 3:16. **sin and righteousness and judgment.** Most likely what the world is guilty of (explained in vv. 9–11; see notes there).
16:9 sin. See note on 9:41; cf. 3:19–21; 8:34. People who believe in Jesus believe what he says about their guilt and turn to him. That is, the Spirit's convicting work graciously helps the world recognize that they are sinners and need a Savior. Through this process they turn to believe in Jesus and thus stop being "the world."
16:10 righteousness. Some hold that this refers to God's righteousness, or even to justification, but these readings do not easily explain why the world is convicted of righteousness. More plausibly, the world is convicted of *its* righteousness, which is entirely false (e.g., displayed by the self-righteousness of many of the Jewish religious leaders throughout John's Gospel).
16:11 judgment. Most plausibly the world's false judging (see 7:24 and note), especially about who Jesus is; less plausibly Satan's defeat (v. 11b) or the condemnation the world is under (3:17–18; 5:24–25), for it is hard to see how the world is convicted of these things. **prince of this world.** See note on 12:31.
16:12–15 See 14:26 and note.
16:13 Spirit of truth. See note on 14:17. **guide you into all the truth.** The Spirit will lead the disciples into all the implications of the truth intrinsically bound up with Jesus (see 14:26 and note). **not speak on his own ... only what he hears.** Just as Jesus never spoke or acted on his own initiative but said and did exactly what the Father gave him to say and do (see 5:19,20 and notes); explained in vv. 14–15. **what is yet to come.** Probably the consequences of Jesus' life, death, resurrection, exaltation, and future coming that the NT presents and preserves.
16:14 He will glorify me. Just as Jesus glorifies the Father (17:4). **make known.** The Spirit discloses Jesus' person and work.
16:15 All that belongs to the Father is mine. Cf. 17:10.
16:16–33 *The Disciples' Grief Will Turn to Joy.* Jesus now unpacks his impending departure, less in terms of the Spirit who will replace him and more in terms of his resurrection and the unbounded joy it will evoke. Yet all of this is couched in fairly hidden language because the disciples have not yet come to terms with Jesus' death, let alone his resurrection.
16:16 In a little while you will see me no more. When Jesus dies (7:33; 13:33). **after a little while you will see me.** When Jesus rises from the dead.
16:17–19 The disciples still have no category to allow them to make sense of a Messiah who would die and rise from the dead (cf. Introduction: Characteristics and Themes, 7).
16:20 weep and mourn. When Jesus is dead. **world.** See notes on 1:9,29; 3:16. **rejoices.** Because they killed Jesus. **turn to joy.** When Jesus rises from the dead (20:20).
16:21 Illustrates the dramatic change from grief to joy in vv. 20,22 (cf. Isa 26:16–21; 66:7–14; Hos 13:13–14).
16:22 I will see you again. When Jesus rises from the dead.
16:23 that day. The last days, the end of the age (e.g., Acts 2:18; 2 Tim 1:12,18). Jesus refers to the period after his resurrection as the end of history (cf. 1 John 2:18). **no longer ask me.** Either (1) they will instead ask the Father in Jesus' name or (2) they will no longer ask Jesus for information about his death, which would be unnecessary after the resurrection. **whatever you ask in my name.** See note on 14:13.
16:24 Ask and you will receive, and your joy will be complete. Cf. 15:7,11.
16:25 figuratively. Enigmatically, cryptically. **a time is coming.** After the resurrection (Luke 24:27; Acts 1:3).
16:26–27 In light of vv. 23–24, Jesus assures his followers that they are not distanced from the Father.
16:26 that day. See note on v. 23. **in my name.** See note on 14:13. **I am**

16:27 [r] Jn 14:21,23
16:28 [s] Jn 13:3
16:29 [t] ver 25
16:32 [u] ver 2,25
[v] Mt 26:31 [w] Jn 8:16,29
16:33 [x] Jn 14:27
[y] Jn 15:18-21 [z] Ro 8:37; 1Jn 4:4
17:1 [a] Jn 11:41
[b] Jn 12:23; 13:31,32
17:2 [c] ver 6,9,24; Da 7:14; Jn 6:37,39
17:3 [d] ver 8,18,21, 23,25; Jn 3:17
17:4 [e] Jn 13:31 [f] Jn 4:34
17:5 [g] Php 2:6 [h] Jn 1:2
17:6 [i] ver 26 [j] ver 2; Jn 6:37,39
17:8 [k] ver 14,26
[l] Jn 16:27 [m] ver 3,18,21, 23,25; Jn 3:17
17:9 [n] Lk 22:32

saying that I will ask the Father on your behalf. 27 No, the Father himself loves you because you have
loved me[r] and have believed that I came from God. 28 I came from the Father and entered the world;
now I am leaving the world and going back to the Father."[s]

29 Then Jesus' disciples said, "Now you are speaking clearly and without figures of speech.[t] 30 Now we
can see that you know all things and that you do not even need to have anyone ask you questions. This
makes us believe that you came from God."

31 "Do you now believe?" Jesus replied. 32 "A time is coming[u] and in fact has come when you will be
scattered,[v] each to your own home. You will leave me all alone. Yet I am not alone, for my Father is
with me.[w]

33 "I have told you these things, so that in me you may have peace.[x] In this world you will have trouble.[y] But take heart! I have overcome[z] the world."

Jesus Prays to Be Glorified

17 After Jesus said this, he looked toward heaven[a] and prayed:

"Father, the hour has come. Glorify your Son, that your Son may glorify you.[b] 2 For you granted
him authority over all people that he might give eternal life to all those you have given him.[c]
3 Now this is eternal life: that they know you, the only true God, and Jesus Christ, whom you have
sent.[d] 4 I have brought you glory[e] on earth by finishing the work you gave me to do.[f] 5 And now,
Father, glorify me in your presence with the glory I had with you[g] before the world began.[h]

Jesus Prays for His Disciples

6 "I have revealed you[a][i] to those whom you gave me[j] out of the world. They were yours; you
gave them to me and they have obeyed your word. 7 Now they know that everything you have given
me comes from you. 8 For I gave them the words you gave me[k] and they accepted them. They knew
with certainty that I came from you,[l] and they believed that you sent me.[m] 9 I pray for them.[n] I

[a] 6 Greek *your name*

not saying that I will ask. Does not contradict Rom 8:34; Heb 7:25; 1 John 2:1. Those passages focus on Jesus' mediatorial role in the plan of redemption: he is the basis on which God accepts Christians. Jesus does not mechanically convey a Christian's prayers to the Father, as if by so doing he restricts a Christian's access to the Father; rather, his role is to provide his disciples with ready access to the Father.

16:28 Summarizes Jesus' earthly mission as the Father's envoy. Like God and his word in Isa 55:11, the Father sends Jesus the Word (see 1:1 and note), Jesus accomplishes the Father's purpose, and Jesus returns to the Father. **entered the world.** Cf. 1:14.

16:29–30 Jesus' followers do not understand that Jesus will speak "plainly" after the resurrection (see v. 25 and note). Misunderstanding is even more pathetic when people think it no longer exists (cf. Introduction: Characteristics and Themes, 7).

16:32 scattered. Cf. Zech 13:7, quoted in Matt 26:31. **alone ... not alone.** Contrasts Jesus' fickle followers with his faithful Father.

16:33 these things. See 13:31—16:32. **so that.** Introduces the purpose of Jesus' farewell discourse. **peace.** See note on 14:27. **trouble.** Distress and persecution. **overcome.** Conquered. Anticipates Jesus' death and resurrection, which made the world's opposition pointless and beggarly because Jesus won the decisive victory and will triumph in the end.

17:1–26 *The Prayer of Jesus.* Jesus' longest recorded prayer.

17:1–5 *Jesus Prays to Be Glorified.* Jesus prays for himself (but is not providing a model of how we pray for ourselves). His one request is that the Father would glorify him (vv. 1,5).

17:1 After Jesus said this. His prayer in vv. 1–26 is thematically connected with 13:31—16:33. **looked toward heaven.** A customary posture in prayer (11:41; Ps 123:1). **hour.** See note on 2:4. **Glorify.** Restore the splendor Jesus had before he took on flesh (v. 5; see notes on 1:14; 8:54; 12:23). This implies that Jesus is God (Isa 42:8; 48:11; see note on 1:1). **your Son may glorify you.** See note on 13:31.

17:2 For. Or "just as." This verse is the grounds for v. 1b. **those you have given him.** See vv. 6,9,12,24; see also 6:37–39,44 and notes.

17:3 eternal life. To have this is to personally know the eternal, only true God and Jesus Christ whom he has sent (see note on 3:15; cf. Jer 31:34; Heb 8:11).

17:4 work. Perhaps only what Jesus has done up to this point but more likely everything Jesus will do, including his death, resurrection, and exaltation (cf. 4:34; 5:36; 19:30).

17:5 Implies that Jesus' preexistence extends into eternity past, before the creation, with the Father and the Son existing in shared glory. See note on v. 1. **before the world began.** Prior to creation (v. 24; see 1:1; 8:58 and notes).

17:6–19 *Jesus Prays for His Disciples.* Jesus prays only for his disciples (not the world) for three reasons: (1) They belong to the Father. (2) They bring him glory. (3) He is about to leave them (vv. 6–11a). Then Jesus asks the Father to protect his disciples (vv. 11b–16) and sanctify them (vv. 17–19).

17:6 revealed. See 1:14,18 and notes; cf. 8:38; 14:7–11; 15:15. **you.** See NIV text note and note on 1:12. **world.** See notes on 1:9,29; 3:16. **obeyed your word.** Evidence that they belong to God (see 8:31,51; 14:15; 15:9–11 and notes).

17:7–8 The disciples at this point may not understand that Jesus must die and rise again or how he fulfills OT motifs such as the temple, Passover lamb, priest, and suffering servant. But they believe that Jesus teaches God's truth. **everything you have given me ... I gave them the words you gave me.** See 3:33–34; 5:19–30; 7:16; 8:28,38,40; 12:49–50.

am not praying for the world, but for those you have given me, for they are yours. 10All I have is
yours, and all you have is mine.[o] And glory has come to me through them. 11I will remain in the
world no longer, but they are still in the world,[p] and I am coming to you.[q] Holy Father, protect
them by the power of[a] your name, the name you gave me, so that they may be one[r] as we are
one.[s] 12While I was with them, I protected them and kept them safe by[b] that name you gave me.
None has been lost[t] except the one doomed to destruction[u] so that Scripture would be fulfilled.
13"I am coming to you now, but I say these things while I am still in the world, so that they may
have the full measure of my joy[v] within them. 14I have given them your word and the world has hated
them,[w] for they are not of the world any more than I am of the world.[x] 15My prayer is not that you take
them out of the world but that you protect them from the evil one.[y] 16They are not of the world, even
as I am not of it.[z] 17Sanctify them by[c] the truth; your word is truth.[a] 18As you sent me into the world,[b]
I have sent them into the world.[c] 19For them I sanctify myself, that they too may be truly sanctified.

Jesus Prays for All Believers

20"My prayer is not for them alone. I pray also for those who will believe in me through their
message, 21that all of them may be one, Father, just as you are in me and I am in you.[d] May they
also be in us so that the world may believe that you have sent me.[e] 22I have given them the glory
that you gave me, that they may be one as we are one[f]— 23I in them and you in me—so that
they may be brought to complete unity. Then the world will know that you sent me[g] and have
loved them[h] even as you have loved me.
24"Father, I want those you have given me to be with me where I am,[i] and to see my glory,[j] the
glory you have given me because you loved me before the creation of the world.[k]
25"Righteous Father, though the world does not know you,[l] I know you, and they know that
you have sent me.[m] 26I have made you[d] known to them,[n] and will continue to make you known
in order that the love you have for me may be in them[o] and that I myself may be in them."

17:10 [o]Jn 16:15
17:11 [p]Jn 13:1 [q]Jn 7:33 [r]ver 21-23 [s]Jn 10:30
17:12 [t]Jn 6:39 [u]Jn 6:70
17:13 [v]Jn 3:29
17:14 [w]Jn 15:19 [x]Jn 8:23
17:15 [y]Mt 5:37
17:16 [z]ver 14
17:17 [a]Jn 15:3
17:18 [b]ver 3,8,21,23,25 [c]Jn 20:21
17:21 [d]Jn 10:38 [e]ver 3, 8,18,23,25; Jn 3:17
17:22 [f]Jn 14:20
17:23 [g]Jn 3:17 [h]Jn 16:27
17:24 [i]Jn 12:26 [j]Jn 1:14 [k]ver 5; Mt 25:34
17:25 [l]Jn 15:21; 16:3 [m]ver 3,8,18,21,23; Jn 3:17; 7:29; 16:27
17:26 [n]ver 6 [o]Jn 15:9

[a] *11* Or *Father, keep them faithful to* [b] *12* Or *kept them faithful to* [c] *17* Or *them to live in accordance with* [d] *26* Greek *your name*

17:11 Holy Father. Combines awe-inspiring transcendence with familial intimacy (cf. Matt 11:25) and prepares the way for vv. 17–19 (see notes there). **protect them by the power of.** See NIV text note. **name.** See note on 1:12. **they may be one.** See note on v. 21. **we are one.** See note on 10:30.

17:12 None has been lost. See 6:38–39 and note on 6:38. **the one doomed to destruction.** Judas Iscariot, whom Jesus knew would betray him (6:64,70–71; 13:2,10–11,18,21–22,26–30). **Scripture.** Probably Ps 41:9 (see 13:18 and note); cf. Acts 1:20, which cites Pss 69:25; 109:8.

17:13 these things. Possibly only ch. 17 but probably also 13:31—16:33. **my joy.** See 15:11 and note.

17:14 Cf. 15:18–25 and notes.

17:15–16 Jesus' followers must remain *in* the world but not be *of* the world.

17:15 Implies that following Jesus while living in the world is perilous. **the evil one.** Satan (Matt 6:13; 1 John 5:18–19).

17:17 Sanctify. Make holy. See "Holiness," p. 2676. **truth; your word.** The means of "sanctification." Jesus is "the truth" (14:6; see notes on 1:14; 3:33; 7:18) and teaches "the truth" (8:31–32), and he supremely mediates God's "word" (v. 6) as "the Word" who became flesh (1:1,14). "The Spirit of truth" (14:17; 15:26; 16:13; see note on 14:17) will guide Jesus' disciples "into all the truth" (16:13; see note there). This revealed "truth" is now embodied in the Bible, the word of God.

17:18 sent me ... sent them. In John's Gospel sanctification is always for a mission. As the Father set apart Jesus and sent him on a mission into the world (10:36; see note on 3:17), Jesus sets apart his followers—who belonged to the world and whom Jesus chose out of the world (15:19)—and sends them on a mission to the world (20:21).

17:19 For them. Cf. 10:11 and note. **I sanctify myself.** Jesus set himself apart to accomplish the mission the Father gave him (cf. 10:36). **that.** Introduces the purpose: that Jesus' followers would be set apart to accomplish the mission Jesus gives them (v. 18). **truly sanctified.** Sanctified by the truth, as in v. 17 (see note there).

17:20–26 *Jesus Prays for All Believers.* Jesus prays that all believers would be one (vv. 20–23) and perfected to see his glory (vv. 24–26).

17:20 Jesus' prayer was not just for his eleven disciples who were with him at the time but for all future believers.

17:21 one. Unified in their common purpose and mission. **just as.** The unity of believers should reflect the unity between the Father and Son (vv. 11,22). **you are in me and I am in you.** See 14:10–11,20 and note on 10:30. **in us.** Probably alludes to the "union" language in the vine metaphor (15:1–17). **so that the world may believe that you have sent me.** The purpose for displaying compelling unity (cf. 13:35).

17:22 I have given them the glory that you gave me. Jesus' "glory" includes his humble incarnation, culminating in his death, resurrection, and exaltation (vv. 5,24; see notes on 1:14; 8:54; 12:23,28). Jesus has revealed God's character, or person, to his followers, who like Jesus reflect God's glory (see 2 Cor 3:18 and note; see also "The Glory of God," p. 2640). **one as we are one.** See note on v. 21.

17:23 See note on v. 21. **brought to complete unity.** Implies that the unity believers have is not yet perfect; they must grow in their unity. **even as you have loved me.** The Father loves believers as extravagantly as he loves his Son.

17:24 glory. In unveiled splendor (see notes on vv. 1,22). **before the creation of the world.** See v. 5; 1:1–2.

17:25 Righteous. Cf. 2 Thess 1:5–6; Rev 15:3; 16:5,7; 19:2. **they.** Believers.

17:26 See NIV text note and note on 1:12. **them.** Believers. **will continue to make you known.** Through the Holy Spirit (chs. 14–16).

18:1 [p]2Sa 15:23 [q]ver 26 [r]Mt 26:36
18:2 [s]Lk 21:37; 22:39
18:3 [t]Ac 1:16 [u]ver 12
18:4 [v]Jn 6:64; 13:1,11 [w]ver 7
18:7 [x]ver 4
18:9 [y]Jn 17:12
18:11 [z]Mt 20:22
18:12 [a]ver 3
18:13 [b]ver 24; Mt 26:3
18:14 [c]Jn 11:49-51
18:15 [d]Mt 26:3 [e]Mt 26:58; Mk 14:54; Lk 22:54

Jesus Arrested

18:3-11pp — Mt 26:47-56; Mk 14:43-50; Lk 22:47-53

18 When he had finished praying, Jesus left with his disciples and crossed the Kidron Valley.[p] On
the other side there was a garden,[q] and he and his disciples went into it.[r]
2 Now Judas, who betrayed him, knew the place, because Jesus had often met there with his disciples.[s] 3 So Judas came to the garden, guiding[t] a detachment of soldiers and some officials from the chief
priests and the Pharisees.[u] They were carrying torches, lanterns and weapons.
4 Jesus, knowing all that was going to happen to him,[v] went out and asked them, "Who is it you want?"[w]
5 "Jesus of Nazareth," they replied.
"I am he," Jesus said. (And Judas the traitor was standing there with them.) 6 When Jesus said, "I am
he," they drew back and fell to the ground.
7 Again he asked them, "Who is it you want?"[x]
"Jesus of Nazareth," they said.
8 Jesus answered, "I told you that I am he. If you are looking for me, then let these men go." 9 This happened so that the words he had spoken would be fulfilled: "I have not lost one of those you gave me."[a][y]
10 Then Simon Peter, who had a sword, drew it and struck the high priest's servant, cutting off his
right ear. (The servant's name was Malchus.)
11 Jesus commanded Peter, "Put your sword away! Shall I not drink the cup[z] the Father has given me?"
12 Then the detachment of soldiers with its commander and the Jewish officials[a] arrested Jesus. They
bound him 13 and brought him first to Annas, who was the father-in-law of Caiaphas,[b] the high priest
that year. 14 Caiaphas was the one who had advised the Jewish leaders that it would be good if one man
died for the people.[c]

Peter's First Denial

18:16-18pp — Mt 26:69,70; Mk 14:66-68; Lk 22:55-57

15 Simon Peter and another disciple were following Jesus. Because this disciple was known to the
high priest,[d] he went with Jesus into the high priest's courtyard,[e] 16 but Peter had to wait outside at the
door. The other disciple, who was known to the high priest, came back, spoke to the servant girl on
duty there and brought Peter in.
17 "You aren't one of this man's disciples too, are you?" she asked Peter.

[a] 9 John 6:39

in order that. Introduces the purpose. Believers are not merely the object of God's love; God's love transforms them so that they love one another as God loves them (see 13:34–35; 15:9–12 and notes). **I myself may be in them.** See 14:20,23; 15:1–17.

18:1—19:42 *The Trial and Passion of Jesus.* Jesus' trial, passion, and resurrection (chs. 18–20) are the climax of John's Gospel. This section emphasizes the nature of Jesus' kingship (see note on 18:31; see also 18:33–37,39; 19:2–3,11–12,14–15,19–22).

18:1–14 *Jesus Arrested.* The Jewish authorities and Roman soldiers arrest Jesus.

18:1 finished praying. Or "said these things," which may refer to 13:31—17:26. **left.** Either the upper room or the city (see 14:31 and note). **Kidron Valley.** East of Jerusalem. **garden.** Gethsemane (Matt 26:36; Mark 14:32).

18:2 often met there with his disciples. See Luke 21:37; 22:39.

18:3 detachment of soldiers. A Roman cohort, normally about 600 men (but not all were necessarily present). They supported the temple officials probably because arresting someone as popular as Jesus could incite a mob.

18:4 knowing all that was going to happen to him. See 10:18 and note.

18:5 I am. See notes on 6:35; 8:24,58.

18:9 See 6:39 and note on 6:38; 10:28 and note; 17:12.

18:10–11 Cf. Matt 26:51–52; Mark 14:47; Luke 22:49–51.

18:11 cup. See note on Matt 26:39. Peter does not understand (see Introduction: Characteristics and Themes, 7) that Jesus, resolved to accomplish the Father's mission, is in the process of laying down his life (10:18).

18:12 Jewish officials. The Jewish authorities. Their highest court was the Sanhedrin, which the high priest presided over. Chs. 18–19 present them as clinging to the minutiae of the law (e.g., v. 28; 19:7) while failing to understand how the law points to Jesus the Messiah (see 5:39–40 and note).

18:13 Annas. Held the office of high priest from AD 6–15 and continued to hold enormous influence afterward. Many Jews resented that a foreign power arbitrarily deposed and appointed high priests, and five of Annas's sons, along with his son-in-law Caiaphas, held the office. Annas was thus the patriarch of a high priestly family, and many still considered him the "real" high priest even though Roman officials considered Caiaphas to be the high priest at the time (see Luke 3:2 and note; see chart/map, pp. 1930–1931).

18:14 See 11:49–51 and notes.

18:15–18 *Peter's First Denial.* Jesus predicted this (13:38). Even his most intimate followers abandoned him (vv. 25–27).

18:15 another disciple. Probably John, "the disciple whom Jesus loved" (see 13:23 and note). **high priest.** Annas (see note on v. 13). **courtyard.** The private atrium connected with Annas's house.

18:17 I am not. Peter begins his descent into shame.

He replied, "I am not."[f]
18 It was cold, and the servants and officials stood around a fire[g] they had made to keep warm. Peter
also was standing with them, warming himself.[h]

The High Priest Questions Jesus

18:19-24pp — Mt 26:59-68; Mk 14:55-65; Lk 22:63-71

19 Meanwhile, the high priest questioned Jesus about his disciples and his teaching.
20 "I have spoken openly to the world," Jesus replied. "I always taught in synagogues[i] or at the temple,[j] where all the Jews come together. I said nothing in secret.[k] 21 Why question me? Ask those who
heard me. Surely they know what I said."
22 When Jesus said this, one of the officials[l] nearby slapped him in the face.[m] "Is this the way you
answer the high priest?" he demanded.
23 "If I said something wrong," Jesus replied, "testify as to what is wrong. But if I spoke the truth, why
did you strike me?"[n] 24 Then Annas sent him bound to Caiaphas[o] the high priest.

Peter's Second and Third Denials

18:25-27pp — Mt 26:71-75; Mk 14:69-72; Lk 22:58-62

25 Meanwhile, Simon Peter was still standing there warming himself.[p] So they asked him, "You aren't
one of his disciples too, are you?"
He denied it, saying, "I am not."[q]
26 One of the high priest's servants, a relative of the man whose ear Peter had cut off,[r] challenged
him, "Didn't I see you with him in the garden?"[s] 27 Again Peter denied it, and at that moment a rooster
began to crow.[t]

Jesus Before Pilate

18:29-40pp — Mt 27:11 18,20-23, Mk 15:2-15; Lk 23:2,3,18-25

28 Then the Jewish leaders took Jesus from Caiaphas to the palace of the Roman governor.[u] By now it
was early morning, and to avoid ceremonial uncleanness they did not enter the palace,[v] because they
wanted to be able to eat the Passover.[w] 29 So Pilate came out to them and asked, "What charges are you
bringing against this man?"
30 "If he were not a criminal," they replied, "we would not have handed him over to you."

18:17 [f] ver 25
18:18 [g] Jn 21:9 [h] Mk 14:54,67
18:20 [i] Mt 4:23 [j] Mt 26:55 [k] Jn 7:26
18:22 [l] ver 3 [m] Mt 16:21; Jn 19:3
18:23 [n] Mt 5:39; Ac 23:2-5
18:24 [o] ver 13; Mt 26:3
18:25 [p] ver 18 [q] ver 17
18:26 [r] ver 10 [s] ver 1
18:27 [t] Jn 13:38
18:28 [u] Mt 27:2; Mk 15:1; Lk 23:1 [v] ver 33; Jn 19:9 [w] Jn 11:55

18:18 cold ... fire ... to keep warm. Confirms that it was nighttime (especially since the days were usually warm during Passover season).

18:19–24 *The High Priest Questions Jesus.* Annas questions Jesus, recognizes that he will get nowhere, and sends him to Caiaphas.

18:19 high priest. Annas (cf. v. 24; see note on v. 13).

18:20 openly. Implies that it should be easy to find witnesses (v. 21). **nothing in secret.** Jesus did not secretly teach his disciples a subversive message that differed from his public one.

18:21 An implicit rebuke to Annas because proper legal procedure at the time was to first interrogate the witnesses, not the defendant, and to hear witnesses for the defendant before witnesses against him.

18:23 Jesus does not back down because he has nothing to apologize for; his response was neither illegal nor inappropriate. He is asking for a fair trial.

18:24 Caiaphas. The reigning high priest and chairman of the Sanhedrin (see notes on v. 13; Matt 26:3). He must legally accuse Jesus in order to bring him before Pilate.

18:25–27 *Peter's Second and Third Denials.* See vv. 15–18 and notes. By interweaving the questionings of Peter and Jesus in ch. 18, John contrasts how Jesus denies nothing and Peter denies everything. But disowning the Master is not the end of Peter's story (see 21:15–19 and notes).

18:25 Meanwhile. Back to v. 18. **they asked him.** Some find it problematic that Matt 26:71 says another girl asked this question, Mark 14:69 says it was the same girl, and Luke 22:58 says that it was a man. But with a group of servants talking around a fire, several would doubtless repeat such a question, which may be what John means by "they."

18:27 a rooster began to crow. Fulfills 13:38.

18:28–40 *Jesus Before Pilate.* Pilate questions the prosecution (vv. 28–32), Jesus (vv. 33–38a), and the Jews (vv. 38b–40).

18:28 palace of the Roman governor. The headquarters in Jerusalem for Pilate (see note on v. 29). The normal headquarters for the Roman governors in this region was in Caesarea, but they resided in Jerusalem during Jewish festivals to be available to quell any disturbance. **to avoid ceremonial uncleanness ... to eat the Passover.** The irony is that the Jewish leaders take elaborate precautions to avoid ritual contamination (a result of entering a Gentile residence) in order to observe the entire seven-day Festival of Passover and Unleavened Bread (2 Chr 30:21; Luke 22:1) at the very time they are manipulating the judicial system to execute the innocent Jesus, who alone is the true Passover lamb (see note on 6:4; cf. 1 Cor 5:7). The challenges of tying the chronology of John's passion narrative to the chronology of the passion narratives of the Synoptics are difficult to resolve because there are so many unknowns. Even the labels used may differ from writer to writer: Does "Passover" refer to one day or does it include the ensuing week, including the Festival of Unleavened Bread (2 Chr 30:21; Luke 22:1)? Does Jesus die just as the Passover lambs are being killed in the temple precincts? In any case, John establishes the theological connection between Jesus and the Passover.

18:29 Pilate. The Roman governor of Judea (see note on Matt 27:2).

18:30 The Jewish leaders are aggressively defiant. They expected Pilate to confirm their judgment and order Jesus' execution — not begin a new trial.

18:32 [x]Mt 20:19; 26:2; Jn 3:14; 8:28; 12:32,33
18:33 [y]ver 28,29; Jn 19:9 [z]Lk 23:3; Mt 2:2
18:36 [a]Mt 3:2 [b]Mt 26:53 [c]Lk 17:21; Jn 6:15
18:37 [d]Jn 3:32 [e]Jn 8:47; 1Jn 4:6
18:38 [f]Lk 23:4; Jn 19:4,6
18:40 [g]Ac 3:14
19:1 [h]Dt 25:3; Isa 50:6; 53:5; Mt 27:26
19:3 [i]Mt 27:29 [j]Jn 18:22
19:4 [k]Jn 18:38

31 Pilate said, "Take him yourselves and judge him by your own law."
"But we have no right to execute anyone," they objected. 32 This took place to fulfill what Jesus had
said about the kind of death he was going to die.[x]
33 Pilate then went back inside the palace,[y] summoned Jesus and asked him, "Are you the king of
the Jews?"[z]
34 "Is that your own idea," Jesus asked, "or did others talk to you about me?"
35 "Am I a Jew?" Pilate replied. "Your own people and chief priests handed you over to me. What is
it you have done?"
36 Jesus said, "My kingdom[a] is not of this world. If it were, my servants would fight to prevent my
arrest by the Jewish leaders.[b] But now my kingdom is from another place."[c]
37 "You are a king, then!" said Pilate.
Jesus answered, "You say that I am a king. In fact, the reason I was born and came into the world is
to testify to the truth.[d] Everyone on the side of truth listens to me."[e]
38 "What is truth?" retorted Pilate. With this he went out again to the Jews gathered there and said,
"I find no basis for a charge against him.[f] 39 But it is your custom for me to release to you one prisoner
at the time of the Passover. Do you want me to release 'the king of the Jews'?"
40 They shouted back, "No, not him! Give us Barabbas!" Now Barabbas had taken part in an uprising.[g]

Jesus Sentenced to Be Crucified

19:1-16pp — Mt 27:27-31; Mk 15:16-20

19 Then Pilate took Jesus and had him flogged.[h] 2 The soldiers twisted together a crown of thorns
and put it on his head. They clothed him in a purple robe 3 and went up to him again and
again, saying, "Hail, king of the Jews!"[i] And they slapped him in the face.[j]
4 Once more Pilate came out and said to the Jews gathered there, "Look, I am bringing him out[k] to

18:31 Pilate does not want to arbitrate an internal religious squabble (v. 35). The Jewish leaders must persuade Pilate that Jesus is guilty of a capital crime, so they use political categories that Pilate understands: they charge that Jesus treasonously claims to be the king of the Jews in opposition to Caesar (see note on 18:1—19:42).

18:32 what Jesus had said. Jesus predicted that he would die by crucifixion, i.e., by being "lifted up" (3:14; 8:28; 12:32–33; cf. Matt 20:19; 26:2). Jewish execution was by stoning (cf. 10:33; Lev 24:16), but Jesus must die by crucifixion, whereby he would bear the curse (Deut 21:22–23; Gal 3:13). The Romans, not the Jews, had to execute Jesus. God ordained the whole process (Acts 2:23; 4:27–28).

18:33 Are you the king of the Jews? Presupposes that the Jewish leaders leveled this charge against Jesus to Pilate (see note on v. 31; cf. Luke 23:2).

18:34 Jesus does not answer with a simple "Yes" or "No" unless Pilate will clarify the nature of kingship he has in mind. Pilate might be asking, "Are you a rebel?" or "Are you the Messianic King?"

18:35 Am I a Jew? An indignant reply, perhaps showing contempt. **What is it you have done?** Pilate is unsatisfied with the Sanhedrin's charges against Jesus and wants to know what is behind their severe animosity. The irony is that while Pilate despises and distrusts the Jewish leaders, he eventually adopts their position.

18:36 My kingdom. Jesus acknowledges that he is a king but describes his "kingdom" to show that he is not a military threat to Rome (see note on v. 31). **world.** See notes on 1:9,29; 3:16. **from another place.** Or "not from here." Jesus' reign does not have its source or origin in this world (see 8:23 and note).

18:37 You are a king. See note on v. 31. **You say.** Implies, "You rightly say." **to testify to the truth.** Jesus qualifies the nature of his kingship by describing the reason for his kingly mission: to reveal God in his Son, who is "the truth" (14:6; see notes on 1:14; 3:33). **listens to me.** Cf. 10:3,16,27. Jesus invites his judge to be his follower.

18:38 What is truth? Probably a curt and cynical question. **no basis for a charge against him.** Also 19:4,6; cf. Luke 23:4,14,22. Pilate understands that Jesus is not a political threat (see notes on vv. 31, 33–37).

18:39 Pilate's verdict should have ended the matter. The text does not specify why he offers to release Jesus (though see Acts 4:27). The specific suggestion that Pilate apply to Jesus the Passover custom of releasing a prisoner was perhaps to help the Jews save face (if he thinks that some of them have dug themselves into a hole and would now like to retreat from their position) or to save his own skin (if he already received private threats like the public one in 19:12) or to embarrass the Jewish leaders before the crowd, whom he thought would support Jesus. **the king of the Jews.** See note on v. 31.

18:40 No, not him! Give us Barabbas! They condemn an innocent man who is not a threat to Rome and choose to release a murderer who participated in an insurrection against Rome (Mark 15:7; Luke 23:19; Acts 3:14). **taken part in an uprising.** A terrorist (from the Roman point of view) or guerrilla (from the Jewish nationalist perspective).

19:1–16a *Jesus Sentenced to Be Crucified.* Pilate attempts to release Jesus but ends up condemning him.

19:1 flogged. Probably the least severe form of Roman flogging because Pilate has not sentenced Jesus to be crucified and because he aims to release Jesus. He thinks that punishing Jesus will satisfy the Jews and perhaps evoke a little sympathy for him (cf. Luke 23:13–16). Jesus received a second flogging after Pilate sentenced him to crucifixion (cf. v. 16) that was probably the most severe form (Matt 27:26; see Mark 15:15; Acts 22:24 and notes).

19:2–3 The soldiers mock Jesus as a "king" (Isa 50:6; 1 Pet 2:22–23). See note on 18:31.

19:2 crown of thorns. A mock royal crown, probably twisted together from the long spikes of the date palm or some other thorny plant. **purple robe.** A mock royal robe.

19:3 Hail, king of the Jews! The irony is that they speak truer than they know (cf. note on 11:51), for Jesus is the true king of Israel (1:49; 3:3,5; 18:36). **slapped.** Cf. 18:22.

19:4 no basis for a charge against him. See note on 18:38.

you to let you know that I find no basis for a charge against him."[l] 5When Jesus came out wearing the crown of thorns and the purple robe,[m] Pilate said to them, "Here is the man!"

6As soon as the chief priests and their officials saw him, they shouted, "Crucify! Crucify!"

But Pilate answered, "You take him and crucify him.[n] As for me, I find no basis for a charge against him."[o]

7The Jewish leaders insisted, "We have a law, and according to that law he must die,[p] because he claimed to be the Son of God."[q]

8When Pilate heard this, he was even more afraid, 9and he went back inside the palace.[r] "Where do you come from?" he asked Jesus, but Jesus gave him no answer.[s] 10"Do you refuse to speak to me?" Pilate said. "Don't you realize I have power either to free you or to crucify you?"

11Jesus answered, "You would have no power over me if it were not given to you from above.[t] Therefore the one who handed me over to you[u] is guilty of a greater sin."

12From then on, Pilate tried to set Jesus free, but the Jewish leaders kept shouting, "If you let this man go, you are no friend of Caesar. Anyone who claims to be a king[v] opposes Caesar."

13When Pilate heard this, he brought Jesus out and sat down on the judge's seat[w] at a place known as the Stone Pavement (which in Aramaic[x] is Gabbatha). 14It was the day of Preparation[y] of the Passover; it was about noon.[z]

"Here is your king,"[a] Pilate said to the Jews.

15But they shouted, "Take him away! Take him away! Crucify him!"

"Shall I crucify your king?" Pilate asked.

"We have no king but Caesar," the chief priests answered.

16Finally Pilate handed him over to them to be crucified.[b]

The Crucifixion of Jesus

19:17-24pp — Mt 27:33-44; Mk 15:22-32; Lk 23:33-43

So the soldiers took charge of Jesus. 17Carrying his own cross,[c] he went out to the place of the Skull[d] (which in Aramaic[e] is called Golgotha). 18There they crucified him, and with him two others[f]—one on each side and Jesus in the middle.

19:4 [l] ver 6; Lk 23:4
19:5 [m] ver 2
19:6 [n] Ac 3:13 [o] ver 4; Lk 23:4
19:7 [p] Lev 24:16 [q] Mt 26:63-66; Jn 5:18; 10:33
19:9 [r] Jn 18:33 [s] Mk 14:61
19:11 [t] Ro 13:1 [u] Jn 18:28-30; Ac 3:13
19:12 [v] Lk 23:2
19:13 [w] Mt 27:19 [x] Jn 5:2
19:14 [y] Mt 27:62 [z] Mk 15:25 [a] ver 19,21
19:16 [b] Mt 27:26; Mk 15:15; Lk 23:25
19:17 [c] Ge 22:6; Lk 14:27; 23:26 [d] Lk 23:33 [e] Jn 5:2
19:18 [f] Lk 23:32

19:5 Pilate presents Jesus to the Jews as a beaten, harmless, pitiful man (see note on v. 1).
19:6 You take him and crucify him. A sarcastic taunt expressing frustration and disgust: "You brought him to me for trial, but you will not accept my judgment." Pilate knows that Rome does not grant the Jews authority to carry out the death penalty in this situation (18:31). **no basis for a charge against him.** See note on 18:38.
19:7 law. Probably Lev 24:16. The Jewish authorities think that Jesus' Messianic pretensions are both religious and political in nature, but they have been emphasizing the political elements to Pilate (see note on 18:31). Now they emphasize the religious elements: they think that Jesus is guilty of blasphemy (see notes on 5:17–18; 8:59; 10:33–36; cf. Mark 14:63–64). A Roman prefect was responsible not only for keeping the peace but for maintaining local law. **Son of God.** See "Sonship," p. 2664.
19:8 even more afraid. Or "more afraid than ever." Pilate was evidently superstitious (cf. Matt 27:19).
19:9 no answer. Cf. Mark 14:61; 15:5. See Isa 53:7.
19:10 Jesus' silence irritates Pilate, who has final judicial authority.
19:11 it. The event of Jesus' betrayal. **from above.** From God, who is sovereign over even the worst evil (Acts 2:23; 4:27–28). On compatibilism, see note on 6:40. **the one who handed me over to you.** Possibly Judas (6:64,70–71; 13:2,10–11,18,21–22,27–30; 18:2–5), probably Caiaphas (see note on Matt 26:1–16; cf. 14:61–64). **greater sin.** Taking the initiative to betray Jesus. Pilate is guilty for his spineless, politically motivated decision in v. 16, but he is less blameworthy because his role is *relatively* passive: he did not engineer and initiate the betrayal that brought Jesus into court.
19:12 From then on. Or "for this reason." **tried to set Jesus free.** Pilate is convinced that Jesus did nothing worthy of death. **no friend of Caesar.** A shrewd political move (see note on 18:31) with an implied threat: the Jewish leaders will ruin Pilate's career by reporting him to Caesar if he does not punish Jesus, who "opposes Caesar." Pilate's status with Caesar may have been precarious at the time, so this threat would concern him. The Jewish leaders pretend to be more loyal to Caesar than Pilate, but Jesus is far less of a threat to Caesar than the Jews are (about 40 years later the Jews unsuccessfully revolt against Rome).
19:14 day of Preparation. Friday, when Jews typically prepared for the Sabbath (v. 31). **Passover.** Can refer to the Passover meal (which Jesus and his disciples already observed on Thursday evening), the day of the Passover meal, or more probably (as here) the entire Passover week. **about noon.** Lit. "about the sixth hour." Mark 15:25 says that Jesus was crucified at "nine in the morning" (lit. "the third hour"). It is possible that Mark's Gospel contains a copyist's error or that John was using Roman time or simply that the times are only approximate since people did not keep precise time. **your king.** See note on v. 3.
19:15 Shall I crucify your king? Mock concern and taunting. **no king but Caesar.** Blasphemy (see "The Kingdom of God," p. 2662).
19:16a to them. I.e., to satisfy the Jews (see Luke 23:24). Roman soldiers crucified Jesus (vv. 16b,23–24; see note on 18:32).
19:16b–27 *The Crucifixion of Jesus.* The Roman soldiers unknowingly fulfill Scripture as they crucify Jesus.
19:16b At this point the Roman soldiers probably administered the terrible flogging (see note on v. 1).
19:17 Carrying his own cross. See notes on Mark 15:21; Luke 23:26. **he went out.** The Mosaic law required that executions take place outside the camp or city (Lev 24:14,23; cf. Heb 13:12). **Golgotha.** See notes on Matt 27:33; Mark 15:22; Luke 23:33.
19:18 There. In public, where all could see him. In the ancient world,

19:19 [g]Mk 1:24 [h]ver 14,21
19:20 [i]Heb 13:12
19:21 [j]ver 14
19:24 [k]ver 28,36,37; Mt 1:22 [l]Ps 22:18
19:25 [m]Mt 27:55,56; Mk 15:40,41; Lk 23:49 [n]Mt 12:46 [o]Lk 24:18
19:26 [p]Mt 12:46 [q]Jn 13:23
19:28 [r]ver 30; Jn 13:1 [s]ver 24,36,37
19:29 [t]Ps 69:21
19:30 [u]Lk 12:50; Jn 17:4
19:31 [v]ver 14,42 [w]Dt 21:23; Jos 8:29; 10:26,27

19 Pilate had a notice prepared and fastened to the cross. It read: JESUS OF NAZARETH,[g] THE KING OF THE
JEWS.[h] 20 Many of the Jews read this sign, for the place where Jesus was crucified was near the city,[i] and
the sign was written in Aramaic, Latin and Greek. 21 The chief priests of the Jews protested to Pilate, "Do
not write 'The King of the Jews,' but that this man claimed to be king of the Jews."[j]

22 Pilate answered, "What I have written, I have written."

23 When the soldiers crucified Jesus, they took his clothes, dividing them into four shares, one for
each of them, with the undergarment remaining. This garment was seamless, woven in one piece from
top to bottom.

24 "Let's not tear it," they said to one another. "Let's decide by lot who will get it."

This happened that the scripture might be fulfilled[k] that said,

> "They divided my clothes among them
> and cast lots for my garment."[a][l]

So this is what the soldiers did.

25 Near the cross[m] of Jesus stood his mother,[n] his mother's sister, Mary the wife of Clopas, and Mary
Magdalene.[o] 26 When Jesus saw his mother[p] there, and the disciple whom he loved[q] standing nearby, he
said to her, "Woman,[b] here is your son," 27 and to the disciple, "Here is your mother." From that time
on, this disciple took her into his home.

The Death of Jesus

19:29,30pp — Mt 27:48,50; Mk 15:36,37; Lk 23:36

28 Later, knowing that everything had now been finished,[r] and so that Scripture would be fulfilled,[s]
Jesus said, "I am thirsty."[t] 29 A jar of wine vinegar[t] was there, so they soaked a sponge in it, put the sponge
on a stalk of the hyssop plant, and lifted it to Jesus' lips. 30 When he had received the drink, Jesus said,
"It is finished."[u] With that, he bowed his head and gave up his spirit.

31 Now it was the day of Preparation,[v] and the next day was to be a special Sabbath. Because the Jewish leaders did not want the bodies left on the crosses[w] during the Sabbath, they asked Pilate to have

[a] 24 Psalm 22:18 [b] 26 The Greek for *Woman* does not denote any disrespect.

this most terrible of punishments is always associated with shame and horror. **crucified.** See note on Matt 27:22. **two others.** Probably guerrilla fighters (see note on 18:40; cf. Isa 53:12; Luke 23:32–33,39–43).
19:19 notice. A placard stating the crime for which someone was executed. **THE KING OF THE JEWS.** Jesus' alleged crime is sedition (see note on 18:31).
19:20 Aramaic. Judea's common language (along with Hebrew). **Latin.** Rome's official language. **Greek.** The Roman Empire's common language. The sign's trilingual inscription may account for the slight differences in wording in the four Gospels (Matt 27:37; Mark 15:26; Luke 23:38).
19:21 See note on 18:31.
19:22 Pilate probably worded the mocking sign as an act of revenge against the Jewish leaders (see note on v. 12). But see note on v. 3.
19:23 took. A customary privilege of executioners. **clothes.** Probably Jesus' outer robe, belt, sandals, and head covering. **four.** The number of soldiers in the execution squad (cf. Acts 12:4). **undergarment.** Tunic, a shirt reaching from the neck to the knees or ankles. **seamless.** Thus too valuable to cut up.
19:24 scripture. Ps 22:18. **fulfilled.** Jesus repeats David's experience in Ps 22 at a deeper, climactic level in the history of salvation (see notes on 13:18; 15:25). Ps 22 refers to the righteous sufferer's thirst (cf. v. 28 with Ps 22:15) and pierced hands and feet (cf. vv. 18,34,37; 20:25–27 with Ps 22:16). Jesus himself drew attention to Ps 22 by quoting Ps 22:1 while on the cross (see Matt 27:46; Mark 15:34 and note).
19:25 Many women were at the cross (Matt 27:55–56; Mark 15:40; Luke 23:49). **Mary Magdalene.** Appears in the crucifixion and resurrection story in all four Gospels, but apart from that appears only in Luke 8:2.
19:26–27 Jesus thoughtfully cares for his mother by entrusting a disciple to look after her.
19:26 disciple whom he loved. Probably John (see note on 13:23). **Woman.** See NIV text note.
19:28–37 *The Death of Jesus.* Jesus' death fulfills Scripture.
19:28 knowing ... so that. Others may unconsciously play their part in God's plan (see Acts 13:29), but Jesus obediently carries out his Father's plan even to this point of painful death (4:34; 8:29; 14:31; 15:10; see notes on 5:19–30). **Scripture.** Possibly Ps 22:15 (see note on v. 24) but probably Ps 69:21, a psalm that John quotes in 2:17 and 15:25 (see notes there) and apparently alludes to in vv. 29–30. **fulfilled.** See note on v. 24.
19:29 wine vinegar. Probably not the "wine mixed with myrrh" that charitable people offered Jesus on the way to the cross to function as a mild sedative and pain reliever (see Mark 15:23 and note). The incident here concerning the wine parallels Matt 27:34; Mark 15:36; Luke 23:36. Far from being a sedative, this thirst-quenching drink would prolong life and therefore prolong pain.
19:30 received the drink. Matthew says that "after tasting it, he refused to drink it" (Matt 27:34), which is simply a more detailed way at arriving at the same conclusion. **It is finished.** Jesus accomplished the mission the Father assigned him up to this point (see 17:4 and note). **gave up.** See 10:18 and note. **spirit.** Cf. Luke 23:46.
19:31 day of Preparation. See note on v. 14. **special Sabbath.** On the most likely chronology, that Sabbath was special because the second day of the Passover festival fell on it, which was also the first day of the Festival of Unleavened Bread. **did not want the bodies left on the crosses during the Sabbath.** The Romans normally left crucified people on the cross until they died (which could take days) and then left their rotting bodies hanging there for vultures to devour. But the Mosaic

the legs broken and the bodies taken down. 32The soldiers therefore came and broke the legs of the first
man who had been crucified with Jesus, and then those of the other.[x] 33But when they came to Jesus
and found that he was already dead, they did not break his legs. 34Instead, one of the soldiers pierced[y]
Jesus' side with a spear, bringing a sudden flow of blood and water.[z] 35The man who saw it[a] has given
testimony, and his testimony is true.[b] He knows that he tells the truth, and he testifies so that you also
may believe. 36These things happened so that the scripture would be fulfilled:[c] "Not one of his bones
will be broken,"[ad] 37and, as another scripture says, "They will look on the one they have pierced."[be]

The Burial of Jesus

19:38-42pp — Mt 27:57-61; Mk 15:42-47; Lk 23:50-56

38Later, Joseph of Arimathea asked Pilate for the body of Jesus. Now Joseph was a disciple of Jesus,
but secretly because he feared the Jewish leaders. With Pilate's permission, he came and took the body
away. 39He was accompanied by Nicodemus,[f] the man who earlier had visited Jesus at night. Nicodemus brought a mixture of myrrh and aloes, about seventy-five pounds.[c] 40Taking Jesus' body, the two
of them wrapped it, with the spices, in strips of linen.[g] This was in accordance with Jewish burial customs.[h] 41At the place where Jesus was crucified, there was a garden, and in the garden a new tomb, in
which no one had ever been laid. 42Because it was the Jewish day of Preparation[i] and since the tomb
was nearby,[j] they laid Jesus there.

The Empty Tomb

20:1-8pp — Mt 28:1-8; Mk 16:1-8; Lk 24:1-10

20 Early on the first day of the week, while it was still dark, Mary Magdalene[k] went to the tomb
and saw that the stone had been removed from the entrance.[l] 2So she came running to Simon
Peter and the other disciple, the one Jesus loved,[m] and said, "They have taken the Lord out of the tomb,
and we don't know where they have put him!"[n]

3So Peter and the other disciple started for the tomb.[o] 4Both were running, but the other disciple
outran Peter and reached the tomb first. 5He bent over and looked in[p] at the strips of linen[q] lying there
but did not go in. 6Then Simon Peter came along behind him and went straight into the tomb. He saw

a 36 Exodus 12:46; Num. 9:12; Psalm 34:20 *b 37* Zech. 12:10 *c 39* Or about 34 kilograms

19:32 [x] ver 18
19:34 [y] Zec 12:10 [z] 1Jn 5:6,8
19:35 [a] Lk 24:48 [b] Jn 15:27; 21:24
19:36 [c] ver 24,28,37; Mt 1:22 [d] Ex 12:46; Nu 9:12; Ps 34:20
19:37 [e] Zec 12:10; Rev 1:7
19:39 [f] Jn 3:1; 7:50
19:40 [g] Lk 24:12; Jn 11:44; 20:5,7 [h] Mt 26:12
19:42 [i] ver 14,31 [j] ver 20,41
20:1 [k] ver 18; Jn 19:25 [l] Mt 27:60,66
20:2 [m] Jn 13:23 [n] ver 13
20:3 [o] Lk 24:12
20:5 [p] ver 11 [q] Jn 19:40

law says not to leave a body hanging on a pole overnight because that would desecrate the land (Deut 21:22–23). On the irony, see note on 18:28. **have the legs broken.** To hasten death because then the victim could not put any weight on their legs; asphyxiation would follow when arm strength failed.

19:33 did not break his legs. See v. 36 and note.

19:34 pierced. Probably to confirm that Jesus is dead (see v. 37 and note). **sudden flow of blood and water.** Evidence that Jesus died and is fully human (see Introduction to 1–3 John: Gnosticism). It also reminds readers of how they are to "drink" Jesus' blood (6:53–56) and thereby receive life from him (see note on 6:53–54).

19:35 man. Probably John (see vv. 26–27 and note on v. 26; see also Introduction: Author). **so that you also may believe.** We appropriate the benefits that flow from Jesus' death by faith (see 20:31).

19:36 These things. The events in vv. 31–33. **scripture.** Probably Exod 12:46 and Num 9:12 (and/or possibly Ps 34:20). Jesus is the Passover lamb slain for his people (1 Cor 5:7; 1 Pet 1:19; see "Sacrifice," p. 2656). As the Passover lamb brought life to the Israelite firstborn males, so Jesus brings eternal life to all for whom he dies. **fulfilled.** See note on v. 24.

19:37 scripture. Zech 12:10 (see note there); also cited in Rev 1:7. **pierced.** See Isa 53:5.

19:38–42 *The Burial of Jesus.* Joseph and Nicodemus bury Jesus.

19:38 Joseph of Arimathea. See Matt 27:57; Mark 15:43 and notes.

19:39 Nicodemus. See 3:1–15; 7:50–52. **myrrh and aloes.** To stifle the smell of putrefaction.

19:41 new tomb. Probably an artificial cave. That Jesus was buried in a rich man's tomb (Matt 27:57) fulfills Isa 53:9.

19:42 day of Preparation. See note on v. 14. **nearby.** Convenient since it was near sunset on Friday evening, when the Sabbath would start and they could not work.

20:1–31 *The Resurrection of Jesus.* John recounts several of Jesus' resurrection appearances and concisely states his Gospel's purpose. The resurrection is another of Jesus' signs (see "many other signs" in v. 30; see also Introduction: Purpose and Addressees).

20:1–10 *The Empty Tomb.* Some of Jesus' followers discover that the tomb is empty (see photo, p. 2135).

20:1 first day of the week. Sunday. All four Gospels say this (Matt 28:1; Mark 16:2; Luke 24:1) rather than "the third day" (1 Cor 15:3–4), despite Jesus' predictions (see 2:19–22 and note; Matt 12:40; 16:21; 17:23; 20:19; 27:63–64). The reason may be to present Jesus' resurrection as the beginning of something new. **Mary Magdalene.** She knows where to go because she saw where Jesus was laid (Mark 15:47).

20:2 the one Jesus loved. Probably John (see note on 13:23). **taken the Lord out of the tomb.** Grave robbery was not uncommon. Mary assumes that Jesus is still dead.

20:6–7 strips of linen lying there ... cloth ... in its place. Evidence that no one simply moved the body. It is unlikely that thieves would have taken the time to remove the cloth, leave behind the expensive linen and even more expensive spices, or leave the cloth in an orderly arrangement.

the strips of linen lying there, 7 as well as the cloth that had been wrapped around Jesus' head.[r] The
cloth was still lying in its place, separate from the linen. 8 Finally the other disciple, who had reached
the tomb first,[s] also went inside. He saw and believed. 9 (They still did not understand from Scripture[t]
that Jesus had to rise from the dead.)[u] 10 Then the disciples went back to where they were staying.

Jesus Appears to Mary Magdalene

11 Now Mary stood outside the tomb crying. As she wept, she bent over to look into the tomb[v] 12 and
saw two angels in white,[w] seated where Jesus' body had been, one at the head and the other at the foot.
13 They asked her, "Woman, why are you crying?"[x]
"They have taken my Lord away," she said, "and I don't know where they have put him."[y] 14 At this,
she turned around and saw Jesus standing there,[z] but she did not realize that it was Jesus.[a]
15 He asked her, "Woman, why are you crying?[b] Who is it you are looking for?"
Thinking he was the gardener, she said, "Sir, if you have carried him away, tell me where you have
put him, and I will get him."
16 Jesus said to her, "Mary."
She turned toward him and cried out in Aramaic,[c] "Rabboni!"[d] (which means "Teacher").
17 Jesus said, "Do not hold on to me, for I have not yet ascended to the Father. Go instead to my
brothers[e] and tell them, 'I am ascending to my Father[f] and your Father, to my God and your God.'"
18 Mary Magdalene[g] went to the disciples[h] with the news: "I have seen the Lord!" And she told them
that he had said these things to her.

Jesus Appears to His Disciples

19 On the evening of that first day of the week, when the disciples were together, with the doors locked
for fear of the Jewish leaders,[i] Jesus came and stood among them and said, "Peace[j] be with you!"[k] 20 After
he said this, he showed them his hands and side.[l] The disciples were overjoyed[m] when they saw the Lord.
21 Again Jesus said, "Peace be with you![n] As the Father has sent me,[o] I am sending you."[p] 22 And with
that he breathed on them and said, "Receive the Holy Spirit.[q] 23 If you forgive anyone's sins, their sins
are forgiven; if you do not forgive them, they are not forgiven."[r]

20:7 [r] Jn 11:44
20:8 [s] ver 4
20:9 [t] Mt 22:29; Jn 2:22 [u] Lk 24:26,46
20:11 [v] ver 5
20:12 [w] Mt 28:2,3; Mk 16:5; Lk 24:4; Ac 5:19
20:13 [x] ver 15 [y] ver 2
20:14 [z] Mt 28:9; Mk 16:9 [a] Lk 24:16; Jn 21:4
20:15 [b] ver 13
20:16 [c] Jn 5:2 [d] Mt 23:7
20:17 [e] Mt 28:10 [f] Jn 7:33
20:18 [g] ver 1 [h] Lk 24:10,22,23
20:19 [i] Jn 7:13 [j] Jn 14:27 [k] ver 21,26; Lk 24:36-39
20:20 [l] Lk 24:39,40; Jn 19:34 [m] Jn 16:20,22
20:21 [n] ver 19 [o] Jn 3:17 [p] Mt 28:19; Jn 17:18
20:22 [q] Jn 7:39; Ac 2:38; 8:15-17; 19:2; Gal 3:2
20:23 [r] Mt 16:19; 18:18

20:7 Contrasts with Lazarus in 11:44. Lazarus was raised to a mortal, "natural body"; Jesus was raised to an immortal, "spiritual body" (1 Cor 15:44).
20:8 saw and believed. With sudden intuition he perceives that the only explanation is that Jesus has risen from the dead. This theme of seeing and believing climaxes in v. 29.
20:9 still did not understand. The disciples did not perceive from OT prophecy "that Jesus had to rise from the dead," so they certainly did not make up a resurrection story to fit a preconceived understanding of OT prophecy. See 2:19–22 and note; Luke 24:25–27,32,44–46. **Scripture.** Either a specific OT text (e.g., Ps 16:10; Isa 53:10–12; Hos 6:2) or the entire OT.
20:11–18 *Jesus Appears to Mary Magdalene.* Mary Magdalene is the first eyewitness to see (and hear and touch) the resurrected Jesus. Jews would not have fabricated this story because a woman could not even testify in court.
20:11 crying. Mary still does not understand the empty tomb's significance (see note on v. 2).
20:12 two angels. See note on Matt 28:2–3. The empty tomb cannot be explained by appealing to grave robbers; God himself has been at work.
20:13 Woman. See NIV text note on 19:26; see also notes on vv. 2,11.
20:14 did not realize that it was Jesus. Perhaps it is not fully light (v. 1), Mary's tears obscure her vision, and/or she turns and sees someone there but then turns immediately back toward the tomb as she speaks (she again turns toward Jesus when she addresses him in v. 16). Cf. 21:4; Luke 24:16.
20:15 Woman. See NIV text note on 19:26. **gardener.** The tomb was in a garden (19:41).
20:16 See 10:3–4. Astonishment and delight instantly swallow up Mary's anguish and despair.
20:17 Do not hold on to me. Or "Stop clinging to me." Mary probably fell to her face and was grasping Jesus by the feet (Matt 28:9). **not yet ascended.** Jesus' ascension is still some time off (Luke 24:51; Acts 1:9–11), so Mary does not have to hang on to him as if he is about to disappear permanently. **my brothers.** Jesus' disciples (v. 18). **ascending.** In the process of ascending. **my Father and your Father.** God is the Father of both Jesus and believers but in different senses (1:12,14,18; cf. Rom 8:15–16; Heb 2:11–12). See "Sonship," p. 2664.
20:19–23 *Jesus Appears to His Disciples.* Although Peter and John have come to terms with the empty tomb (vv. 1–10), now Jesus actually appears to the apostolic band.
20:19–20 See Luke 24:36–41.
20:19 disciples. Probably the Twelve minus Judas and Thomas (v. 24). **locked.** Implies that Jesus miraculously appears among them. **Peace be with you!** See 14:27; 16:33; see also "Shalom," p. 2693.
20:20 hands and side. Parts of his body with scars. **overjoyed.** Jesus turns their grief to joy, just as he promised (see 14:18; 16:20–22 and notes).
20:21 Peace be with you! See note on v. 19. **As the Father has sent me, I am sending you.** See note on 17:18. Central to Jesus' mission was what he accomplished through his death and resurrection (see note on 3:17; see also Introduction: Characteristics and Themes, 3). Jesus' complete obedience to and dependence upon his Father (4:34; 8:29; 14:31; 15:10) is the model for his disciples.
20:22 with that. Ties the commission in v. 21 to Jesus' giving the Spirit. **Receive the Holy Spirit.** Probably symbolizes that the long-promised gift of the Spirit (7:39; 14:17) is now imminent, anticipating what happens 50 days later on the day of Pentecost (Acts 2).
20:23 are forgiven ... are not forgiven. The passive voice implies that God is the one who forgives (or does not forgive) people's sins. God does not grant or withhold forgiveness because the apostles (or we) do so. But through the Holy Spirit (v. 22) the apostles and all believers

Jesus Appears to Thomas

[24]Now Thomas[s] (also known as Didymus[a]), one of the Twelve, was not with the disciples when Jesus
came. [25]So the other disciples told him, "We have seen the Lord!"

But he said to them, "Unless I see the nail marks in his hands and put my finger where the nails
were, and put my hand into his side,[t] I will not believe."[u]

[26]A week later his disciples were in the house again, and Thomas was with them. Though the doors
were locked, Jesus came and stood among them and said, "Peace[v] be with you!"[w] [27]Then he said to
Thomas, "Put your finger here; see my hands. Reach out your hand and put it into my side. Stop
doubting and believe."[x]

[28]Thomas said to him, "My Lord and my God!"

[29]Then Jesus told him, "Because you have seen me, you have believed;[y] blessed are those who have
not seen and yet have believed."[z]

The Purpose of John's Gospel

[30]Jesus performed many other signs[a] in the presence of his disciples, which are not recorded in this
book.[b] [31]But these are written that you may believe[bc] that Jesus is the Messiah, the Son of God,[d] and
that by believing you may have life in his name.[e]

Jesus and the Miraculous Catch of Fish

21 Afterward Jesus appeared again to his disciples,[f] by the Sea of Galilee.[cg] It happened this
way: [2]Simon Peter, Thomas[h] (also known as Didymus[a]), Nathanael[i] from Cana in Galilee,[j]
the sons of Zebedee,[k] and two other disciples were together. [3]"I'm going out to fish," Simon Peter told
them, and they said, "We'll go with you." So they went out and got into the boat, but that night they
caught nothing.[l]

[4]Early in the morning, Jesus stood on the shore, but the disciples did not realize that it was Jesus.[m]

[5]He called out to them, "Friends, haven't you any fish?"

"No," they answered.

[6]He said, "Throw your net on the right side of the boat and you will find some." When they did, they
were unable to haul the net in because of the large number of fish.[n]

[7]Then the disciple whom Jesus loved[o] said to Peter, "It is the Lord!" As soon as Simon Peter heard

[a] *24,2 Thomas* (Aramaic) and *Didymus* (Greek) both mean *twin.* [b] *31* Or *may continue to believe*
[c] *1* Greek *Tiberias*

20:24 [s] Jn 11:16
20:25 [t] ver 20 [u] Mk 16:11
20:26 [v] Jn 14:27 [w] ver 21
20:27 [x] ver 25; Lk 24:40
20:29 [y] Jn 3:15 [z] 1Pe 1:8
20:30 [a] Jn 2:11 [b] Jn 21:25
20:31 [c] Jn 3:15; 19:35 [d] Mt 4:3 [e] Mt 25:46
21:1 [f] Jn 20:19,26 [g] Jn 6:1
21:2 [h] Jn 11:16 [i] Jn 1:45 [j] Jn 2:1 [k] Mt 4:21
21:3 [l] Lk 5:5
21:4 [m] Lk 24:16; Jn 20:14
21:6 [n] Lk 5:4-7
21:7 [o] Jn 13:23

participate in Jesus' saving mission by declaring that God will forgive all those who repent and believe in Jesus and that God will not forgive those who do not repent and believe (see "The Gospel," p. 2686). Cf. Matt 16:19; 18:18–19 and notes.

20:24–29 *Jesus Appears to Thomas.* Jesus appears again to his disciples, and Thomas believes.

20:24 Thomas. See 11:16; 14:5 and notes. **Didymus.** See NIV text note. **when Jesus came.** See vv. 19–23.

20:26 locked. See note on v. 19. **Peace be with you!** See note on v. 19.

20:27 The text does not say whether Thomas touches Jesus; it gives the impression that the sight itself proves sufficient and overcomes Thomas with awe and reverence (v. 28).

20:28 my God. Thomas exclaims and confesses that Jesus is God (see note on 1:1).

20:29 you ... those. The contrast is not that Thomas's faith is inferior to that of other believers, as if faith that is not based in signs is superior (vv. 30–31). Rather, the contrast is between the first generation of believers, like Thomas, who were witnesses to Jesus' resurrection, and all later generations. **not seen and yet have believed.** See 1 Pet 1:8; cf. 2 Cor 5:7.

20:30–31 *The Purpose of John's Gospel.* This is the climax of the book, encapsulating several of the important themes John has developed. See Introduction: Purpose and Addressees.

21:1–25 *Epilogue.* John not only ties up several loose ends (e.g., Peter's restoration to service) but in symbolic ways points to the church's growth and diversity of gifts and callings. He appropriately ends with a tribute to Jesus' greatness (v. 25).

21:1–14 *Jesus and the Miraculous Catch of Fish.* The account not only provides a third narrative resurrection account, complete with eyewitness details, but establishes Jesus' power to draw in fish when his disciples cannot do it on their own. Their roles as fishers of people will have Christ's authority behind them.

21:1 appeared. Or "revealed himself" (cf. 2:11; 17:6). **Sea of Galilee.** See note on Luke 5:1.

21:2 sons of Zebedee. James and John (Matt 4:21; Luke 5:10).

21:3 to fish. Does not imply that these disciples have apostatized or sunk into despair, though ch. 21 does not portray them as displaying the joy, assurance, unity, and sense of mission that they do after receiving the Spirit at Pentecost in Acts 2 (see note on John 20:22). **night.** Favored by fishermen then (cf. Luke 5:5).

21:4 did not realize that it was Jesus. Perhaps because of dim light and their distance from the shore (see note on 20:14; cf. Luke 24:16).

21:6 Cf. Luke 5:4–7.

21:7 disciple whom Jesus loved. Probably John (see note on 13:23). **wrapped his outer garment around him.** To prepare to greet Jesus.

21:9 [p]Jn 18:18 [q]ver 10,13
21:13 [r]ver 9
21:14 [s]Jn 20:19,26
21:15 [t]Mt 26:33,35; Jn 13:37 [u]Lk 12:32
21:16 [v]Mt 2:6; Ac 20:28; 1Pe 5:2,3
21:17 [w]Jn 13:38 [x]Jn 16:30 [y]ver 16
21:19 [z]Jn 12:33; 18:32 [a]2Pe 1:14
21:20 [b]ver 7; Jn 13:23 [c]Jn 13:25
21:22 [d]Mt 16:27; 1Co 4:5; Rev 2:25 [e]ver 19
21:23 [f]Ac 1:16

him say, "It is the Lord," he wrapped his outer garment around him (for he had taken it off) and
jumped into the water. [8]The other disciples followed in the boat, towing the net full of fish, for they
were not far from shore, about a hundred yards.[a] [9]When they landed, they saw a fire[p] of burning coals
there with fish on it,[q] and some bread.

[10]Jesus said to them, "Bring some of the fish you have just caught." [11]So Simon Peter climbed back
into the boat and dragged the net ashore. It was full of large fish, 153, but even with so many the net
was not torn. [12]Jesus said to them, "Come and have breakfast." None of the disciples dared ask him,
"Who are you?" They knew it was the Lord. [13]Jesus came, took the bread and gave it to them, and did
the same with the fish.[r] [14]This was now the third time Jesus appeared to his disciples[s] after he was
raised from the dead.

Jesus Reinstates Peter

[15]When they had finished eating, Jesus said to Simon Peter, "Simon son of John, do you love me
more than these?"

"Yes, Lord," he said, "you know that I love you."[t]

Jesus said, "Feed my lambs."[u]

[16]Again Jesus said, "Simon son of John, do you love me?"

He answered, "Yes, Lord, you know that I love you."

Jesus said, "Take care of my sheep."[v]

[17]The third time he said to him, "Simon son of John, do you love me?"

Peter was hurt because Jesus asked him the third time, "Do you love me?"[w] He said, "Lord, you know
all things;[x] you know that I love you."

Jesus said, "Feed my sheep.[y] [18]Very truly I tell you, when you were younger you dressed yourself and
went where you wanted; but when you are old you will stretch out your hands, and someone else will
dress you and lead you where you do not want to go." [19]Jesus said this to indicate the kind of death[z] by
which Peter would glorify God.[a] Then he said to him, "Follow me!"

[20]Peter turned and saw that the disciple whom Jesus loved[b] was following them. (This was the one
who had leaned back against Jesus at the supper and had said, "Lord, who is going to betray you?")[c]
[21]When Peter saw him, he asked, "Lord, what about him?"

[22]Jesus answered, "If I want him to remain alive until I return,[d] what is that to you? You must follow me."[e] [23]Because of this, the rumor spread among the believers[f] that this disciple would not die.

[a] *8* Or about 90 meters

21:9 fire of burning coals. As in 18:18, where Peter first denied Jesus. **fish ... bread.** Jesus meets their tiredness after a night of toil with a hot breakfast (v. 13). As their risen Lord, he serves them still (cf. 13:4–16).
21:11 153. A miraculous, generous provision (as in 2:1–12; 6:1–15). The many attempts to detect some symbol-laden significance to the number are not convincing. **not torn.** Contrast Luke 5:6.
21:12 Who are you? That is, "Is it *really* you?"
21:13 See note on v. 9.
21:14 third time. Probably enumerates only the appearances reported in this Gospel (20:19–23,26–29). This does not count Jesus' appearance to Mary Magdalene (20:11–18) since that was not an appearance "to his disciples."
21:15–25 *Jesus Reinstates Peter.* Probably written after Peter's martyrdom (more than three decades after the events in ch. 21), this account explains how Peter was restored. The man who denied Christ became a powerful and influential apostle, owing to Jesus' forbearance, forgiveness, and grace.
21:15–17 The Greek text includes four pairs of synonyms with no discernible difference in meaning: (1) **love.** Occurs seven times; the first and third translate *agapaō* and the other five *phileō.* (2) **Feed ... Take care of.** (3) **lambs ... sheep.** (4) **know.** Occurs four times; the fourth translates a different word.
21:15 than these. Probably means "than these other disciples do"—perhaps with some irony (cf. 13:37; Matt 26:33; Mark 14:29).
21:17 third time. Mirrors Peter's recent threefold denial (see 18:15–18,25–27 and notes), inviting Peter to reverse his denials and reaffirm his love for Jesus three times. **Feed my sheep.** Jesus graciously accepts Peter's declaration, restores him to fellowship, and commissions him to service, emphasizing his pastoral role (cf. 1 Pet 5:1–4).
21:18 stretch out your hands. Crucifixion. **dress ... lead.** The "stretching" of crucifixion sometimes occurred when a condemned prisoner was tied to the cross-member and forced to carry their "cross" to the place of execution (cf. 19:17).
21:19 kind of death. Jesus predicts Peter's martyrdom (cf. 12:33; 18:32). **glorify God.** By following Jesus to suffering and death (cf. 12:27–28; 13:31–32; 17:1; 1 Pet 4:14–16). Remarkably, Peter served for three decades with this prediction hanging over him; he most likely died in Rome under the emperor Nero (see Introduction to 1 Peter: Date).
21:20 disciple whom Jesus loved. Probably John (see note on 13:23).
21:22 until I return. Jesus will come again (see notes on Acts 1:11; 1 Cor 15:23–28; 1 Thess 4:13—5:11; Rev 19:11–16). **what is that to you?** Implies that it is none of Peter's business. **You must follow me.** Regardless of what paths Jesus designs for his other followers.
21:23 That John can envisage his own death has a bearing on how

But Jesus did not say that he would not die; he only said, "If I want him to remain alive until I return,
what is that to you?"
[24]This is the disciple who testifies to these things[g] and who wrote them down. We know that his
testimony is true.[h]
[25]Jesus did many other things as well.[i] If every one of them were written down, I suppose that even
the whole world would not have room for the books that would be written.

21:24 [g] Jn 15:27 [h] Jn 19:35
21:25 [i] Jn 20:30

he understands the concept of eternal life elsewhere in this Gospel. He envisages something far more than the mere extension of this life. **21:24 the disciple who … wrote.** The author of this Gospel is "the disciple whom Jesus loved," probably John (see v. 20; see also note on 13:23; Introduction: Author). **these things.** The Gospel of John. **We.** Possibly John and others with him but probably an editorial "we," referring to John himself (see 1:14; 1 John 1:4).

21:25 After identifying himself in v. 24, John concludes by focusing on Jesus. **many other things.** John was selective (see 20:30). **not have room.** If John described all of Jesus' deeds, the world would be a small, inadequate library, for there is far more to know about Jesus—the powerful Creator, incarnate Word, obedient Son, suffering Messiah, and risen Lord—than one could ever write down.

HARMONY OF THE GOSPELS

DATE	EVENT	LOCATION	MATTHEW	MARK	LUKE	JOHN
INTRODUCTIONS TO JESUS CHRIST						
	(1) Luke's introduction				1:1–4	
	(2) Preincarnate Christ					1:1–18
	(3) Genealogy of Jesus Christ		1:1–17		3:23b–38	
BIRTH, INFANCY, AND ADOLESCENCE OF JESUS AND JOHN THE BAPTIST						
7 BC	(1) Announcement of birth of John	Jerusalem (temple)			1:5–25	
7 or 6 BC	(2) Announcement of birth of Jesus to the virgin Mary	Nazareth			1:26–38	
ca. 5 BC	(3) Song of Elizabeth to Mary	Hill country of Judea			1:39–45	
	(4) Mary's song of praise				1:46–56	
5 BC	(5) Birth, infancy, and purpose for future of John the Baptist	Judea			1:57–80	
	(6) Announcement of Jesus' birth to Joseph	Nazareth	1:18–25a			
5–4 BC	(7) Birth of Jesus Christ	Bethlehem	1:25b		2:1–7	
	(8) Proclamation by the angels	Near Bethlehem			2:8–14	
	(9) The visit of homage by shepherds	Bethlehem			2:15–20	
	(10) Jesus' circumcision	Bethlehem			2:21	
4 BC	(11) First temple visit with acknowledgments by Simeon and Anna	Jerusalem			2:22–38	
	(12) Visit of the Magi	Jerusalem & Bethlehem	2:1–12			
	(13) Flight into Egypt and massacre of innocents	Bethlehem, Jerusalem & Egypt	2:13–18			
	(14) From Egypt to Nazareth with Jesus		2:19–23		2:39	
Afterward AD 7–8	(15) Childhood of Jesus	Nazareth			2:40	
	(16) Jesus, 12 years old, visits the temple	Jerusalem			2:41–50	
Afterward	(17) 18-year account of Jesus' adolescence and adulthood	Nazareth			2:51–52	
TRUTHS ABOUT JOHN THE BAPTIST						
ca. AD 25–27	(1) John's ministry begins	Judean Wilderness	3:1	1:1–4	3:1–2	1:19–28
	(2) Man and message		3:2–12	1:2–8	3:3–14	1:20–23
	(3) His picture of Jesus		3:11–12	1:7–8	3:15–18	1:24–27
	(4) His courage		14:4–12		3:19–20	
BEGINNING OF JESUS' MINISTRY						
ca. AD 27	(1) Jesus baptized	Jordan River	3:13–17	1:9–11	3:21–23a	1:29–34
	(2) Jesus tempted	Wilderness	4:1–11	1:12–13	4:1–13	
	(3) Calls first disciples	Beyond Jordan				1:35–51
	(4) The first miracle	Cana in Galilee				2:1–11

DATE	EVENT	LOCATION	MATTHEW	MARK	LUKE	JOHN
BEGINNING OF JESUS' MINISTRY (CONT.)						
AD 27	(5) First stay in Capernaum	(Capernaum is "his" city)				2:12
	(6) First cleansing of the temple	Jerusalem				2:13–22
	(7) Received at Jerusalem	Jerusalem				2:23–25
	(8) Teaches Nicodemus about second birth	Jerusalem				3:1–21
	(9) Co-ministry with John	Judea				3:22–36
	(10) Leaves for Galilee	Judea	4:12	1:14	4:14	4:1–4
	(11) Samaritan woman at Jacob's Well	Samaria (town of Sychar)				4:5–42
	(12) Returns to Galilee			1:15	4:15	4:43–45
THE GALILEAN MINISTRY OF JESUS						
AD 27–29						
AD 27	(1) Healing of the royal official's son	Cana				4:46–54
	(2) Rejected at Nazareth	Nazareth			4:16–30	
	(3) Moved to Capernaum	Capernaum	4:13–17			
	(4) Four become fishers of people	Sea of Galilee	4:18–22	1:16–20	5:1–11	
	(5) Impure spirit driven out on the Sabbath day	Capernaum		1:21–28	4:31–37	
	(6) Peter's mother-in-law cured, plus others	Capernaum	0.14–17	1:29–34	4:38–41	
ca. AD 27	(7) First preaching tour of Galilee	Galilee	4:23–25	1:35–39	4:42–44	
	(8) Leper healed and response recorded	Galilee	8:1–4	1:40–45	5:12–16	
	(9) Paralyzed man healed	Capernaum	9:1–8	2:1–12	5:17–26	
	(10) Matthew's call and reception held	Capernaum	9:9–13	2:13–17	5:27–32	
	(11) Disciples defended via a parable	Capernaum	9:14–17	2:18–22	5:33–39	
AD 28	(12) Goes to Jerusalem for second passover; heals lame man	Jerusalem				5:1–47
	(13) Plucked grain precipitates Sabbath controversy	En route to Galilee	12:1–8	2:23–28	6:1–5	
	(14) Shriveled hand healed causes another Sabbath controversy	Galilee	12:9–14	3:1–6	6:6–11	
	(15) Multitudes healed	Sea of Galilee	12:15–21	3:7–12	6:17–19	
	(16) Twelve apostles selected after a night of prayer	Near Capernaum		3:13–19	6:12–16	
	(17) Sermon on the Mount	Near Capernaum	5:1—7:29		6:20–49	
	(18) Centurion's servant healed	Capernaum	8:5–13		7:1–10	
	(19) Raises widow's son from the dead	Nain			7:11–17	
	(20) Jesus allays John the Baptist's doubts	Galilee	11:2–19		7:18–35	

DATE	EVENT	LOCATION	MATTHEW	MARK	LUKE	JOHN
THE GALILEAN MINISTRY OF JESUS (CONT.)						
AD 28	(21) Woes upon the privileged		11:20–30			
	(22) A sinful woman anoints Jesus	Simon the Pharisee's house, Capernaum			7:36–50	
	(23) Another tour of Galilee	Galilee			8:1–3	
	(24) Jesus accused of blasphemy	Capernaum	12:22–37	3:20–30	11:14–23	
	(25) Jesus' answer to a demand for a sign	Capernaum	12:38–45		11:24–26, 29–36	
	(26) Mother, brothers seek audience	Capernaum	12:46–50	3:31–35	8:19–21	
	(27) Famous parables of sower, seed, weeds, lamp, mustard seed, yeast, treasure, pearl, net, told	By Sea of Galilee	13:1–52	4:1–34	8:4–18	
	(28) Sea made serene	Sea of Galilee	8:23–27	4:35–41	8:22–25	
	(29) Gadarene (Gerasene) demon-possessed men healed	Eastern shore of Galilee	8:28–34	5:1–20	8:26–39	
	(30) Jairus's daughter raised and woman with hemorrhage healed		9:18–26	5:21–43	8:40–56	
	(31) Two blind men's sight restored		9:27–31			
	(32) Mute demon-possessed man healed		9:32–34			
	(33) Nazareth's second rejection of Christ	Nazareth	13:53–58	6:1–6		
	(34) Twelve sent out		9:35—11:1	6:7–13	9:1–6	
	(35) Fearful Herod beheads John the Baptist	Galilee	14:1–12	6:14–29	9:7–9	
Spring AD 29	(36) Return of 12, Jesus withdraws, 5,000 fed	Near Bethsaida	14:13–21	6:30–44	9:10–17	6:1–15
	(37) Walks on the water	Sea of Galilee	14:22–33	6:45–52		6:16–21
	(38) Sick people healed in Gennesaret	Gennesaret	14:34–36	6:53–56		
	(39) Peak of popularity passes in Galilee	Capernaum				6:22—7:1
AD 29	(40) Traditions attacked		15:1–20	7:1–23		
	(41) Aborted retirement in Tyre: Syrophoenician's daughter healed	Tyre	15:21–28	7:24–30		
	(42) Afflicted healed	Decapolis	15:29–31	7:31–37		
	(43) 4,000 fed	Decapolis	15:32–39	8:1–9		
	(44) Pharisees increase attack	Magadan	16:1–4	8:10–13		
	(45) Disciples' carelessness condemned; blind man healed		16:5–12	8:14–26		
	(46) Peter confesses Jesus is the Christ	Near Caesarea Philippi	16:13–20	8:27–30	9:18–21	
	(47) Jesus foretells his death	Caesarea Philippi	16:21–26	8:31–38	9:22–25	

DATE	EVENT	LOCATION	MATTHEW	MARK	LUKE	JOHN
THE GALILEAN MINISTRY OF JESUS (CONT.)						
AD 29	(48) Kingdom promised		16:27–28	9:1	9:26–27	
	(49) The transfiguration	Mountain unnamed	17:1–13	9:2–13	9:28–36	
	(50) Demon-possessed boy healed	Mount of Transfiguration	17:14–21	9:14–29	9:37–42	
	(51) Again tells of death, resurrection	Galilee	17:22–23	9:30–32	9:43–45	
	(52) Taxes paid	Capernaum	17:24–27			
	(53) Disciples contend about greatness; Jesus defines it; also patience, loyalty, forgiveness	Capernaum	18:1–35	9:33–50	9:46–50	
	(54) Jesus rejects his brothers' advice	Galilee				7:2–9
Fall AD 29	(55) Galilee departure and Samaritan rejection		19:1–2		9:51–56	7:10
	(56) Cost of discipleship		8:18–22		9:57–62	
LAST JUDEAN AND PEREAN MINISTRY OF JESUS						
AD 29–30						
Fall AD 29	(1) Festival of Tabernacles	Jerusalem				7:2,11–52
	(2) Forgiveness of woman caught in the act of adultery	Jerusalem				[7:53— 8:11]
AD 29	(3) Christ the light of the world	Jerusalem				8:12
	(4) Pharisees dispute the prophet's words and thus try to destroy him	Jerusalem—temple				8:13–59
	(5) Man born blind healed; following consequences	Jerusalem				9:1–41
	(6) Parable of the Good Shepherd	Jerusalem				10:1–21
	(7) The service of the 72	Probably Judea			10:1–24	
	(8) Expert in the law hears the story of the Good Samaritan	Judea (?)			10:25–37	
	(9) The hospitality of Martha and Mary	Bethany			10:38–42	
	(10) Another lesson on prayer	Judea (?)			11:1–13	
	(11) Accused of connection with Beelzebul				11:14–36	
	(12) Judgment against pharisees and experts in the law				11:37–54	
	(13) Jesus deals with hypocrisy, greed, worry, and watchfulness				12:1–59	
	(14) Repent or perish				13:1–5	
	(15) Barren fig tree				13:6–9	
	(16) Crippled woman healed on Sabbath				13:10–17	
	(17) Parables of mustard seed and yeast	Probably Perea			13:18–21	

DATE	EVENT	LOCATION	MATTHEW	MARK	LUKE	JOHN
LAST JUDEAN AND PEREAN MINISTRY OF JESUS (CONT.)						
Winter AD 29	(18) Festival of Dedication	Jerusalem				10:22–39
	(19) Withdrawal beyond Jordan					10:40–42
	(20) Jesus teaches, with special words about Herod	Perea			13:22–35	
	(21) Meal with a Pharisee ruler; heals man with abnormal swelling; parables of ox, best places at the table, and great banquet				14:1–24	
	(22) Demands of discipleship	Perea			14:25–35	
	(23) Parables of lost sheep, coin, son				15:1–32	
	(24) Parables of shrewd manager, rich man and Lazarus				16:1–31	
	(25) Lessons on forgiveness, duty, influence, faith				17:1–10	
	(26) Resurrection of Lazarus	Perea to Bethany				11:1–44
	(27) Reaction to resurrection of Lazarus: withdrawal of Jesus					11:45–54
AD 30	(28) Begins last journey to Jerusalem via Samaria & Galilee	Samaria, Galilee			17:11	
	(29) Heals ten lepers				17:12–19	
	(30) Lessons on the coming kingdom				17:20–37	
	(31) Parables: persistent widow, Pharisee and tax collector				18:1–14	
	(32) Teaching on divorce		19:3–12	10:1–12		
	(33) Jesus blesses children; objections	Perea	19:13–15	10:13–16	18:15–17	
	(34) Rich ruler	Perea	19:16–30	10:17–31	18:18–30	
	(35) Parable of the workers		20:1–16			
	(36) Foretells death and resurrection	Near Jerusalem	20:17–19	10:32–34	18:31–34	
	(37) Ambition of James and John		20:20–28	10:35–45		
	(38) Blind Bartimaeus and his companion healed	Jericho	20:29–34	10:46–52	18:35–43	
	(39) Interview with Zacchaeus	Jericho			19:1–10	
	(40) Parable of the minas	Jericho			19:11–27	
	(41) Returns to home of Mary and Martha	Bethany				11:55—12:1
	(42) Plot to kill Lazarus	Bethany				12:9–11
JESUS' FINAL WEEK AROUND AND IN JERUSALEM						
Spring AD 30						
Sunday	(1) Triumphal Entry	Bethany, Jerusalem, Bethany	21:1–9	11:1–11	19:28–44	12:12–19
Monday	(2) Fig tree cursed and temple cleansed	Bethany to Jerusalem	21:10–19	11:12–18	19:45–48	

DATE	EVENT	LOCATION	MATTHEW	MARK	LUKE	JOHN
JESUS' FINAL WEEK AROUND AND IN JERUSALEM (CONT.)						
	(3) The necessity of sacrifice	Jerusalem				12:20–50
Tuesday	(4) Withered fig tree testifies	Bethany to Jerusalem	21:20–22	11:19–26		
	(5) Sanhedrin challenges Jesus. He answers by parables: two sons, workers in the vineyard and marriage feast	Jerusalem	21:23—22:14	11:27—12:12	20:1–19	
	(6) Tribute to Caesar	Jerusalem	22:15–22	12:13–17	20:20–26	
	(7) Sadducees question the resurrection	Jerusalem	22:23–33	12:18–27	20:27–40	
	(8) Pharisees question commandments	Jerusalem	22:34–40	12:28–34		
	(9) Jesus and David	Jerusalem	22:41–46	12:35–37	20:41–44	
	(10) Jesus' last sermon	Jerusalem	23:1–39	12:38–40	20:45–47	
	(11) Widow's offering	Jerusalem		12:41–44	21:1–4	
	(12) Jesus tells of the future	Mount of Olives	24:1–51	13:1–37	21:5–36	
	(13) Parables: ten virgins, talents, the day of judgment	Mount of Olives	25:1–46			
	(14) Jesus tells date of crucifixion		26:1–5	14:1–2	22:1–2	
	(15) Anointing by Mary at Simon the Leper's feast	Bethany	26:6–13	14:3–9		12:2–8
	(16) Judas contracts the betrayal		26:14–16	14:10–11	22:3–6	
Thursday	(17) Preparation for the Passover	Jerusalem	26:17–19	14:12–16	22:7–13	
Thursday p.m.	(18) Passover eaten, jealousy rebuked	Jerusalem	26:20	14:17	22:14–16, 24–30	
	(19) Feet washed	Upper Room				13:1–20
	(20) Judas revealed, defects	Upper Room	26:21–25	14:18–21	22:21–23	13:21–30
	(21) Jesus warns about further desertion; cries of loyalty	Upper Room	26:31–35	14:27–31	22:31–38	13:31–38
	(22) The last supper	Upper Room	26:26–29	14:22–25	22:17–20	
	(23) Last speech to the apostles and intercessory prayer	Jerusalem				14:1—17:26
Thursday-Friday	(24) The grief of Gethsemane	Mount of Olives	26:30, 36–46	14:26, 32–42	22:39–46	18:1
Friday	(25) Betrayal, arrest, desertion	Gethsemane	26:47–56	14:43–52	22:47–53	18:2–12
	(26) First examined by Annas	Jerusalem				18:13–14, 19–23
	(27) Trial by Caiaphas and Sanhedrin; following indignities	Jerusalem	26:57, 59–68	14:53, 55–65	22:54a, 63–65	18:24
Friday	(28) Peter's triple denial	Jerusalem	26:58, 69–75	14:54, 66–72	22:54b–62	18:15–18, 25–27
	(29) Condemnation by the Sanhedrin	Jerusalem	27:1	15:1a	22:66–71	
	(30) Suicide of Judas	Jerusalem	27:3–10			
	(31) First appearance before Pilate	Jerusalem	27:2,11–14	15:1b–5	23:1–6	18:28–38

DATE	EVENT	LOCATION	MATTHEW	MARK	LUKE	JOHN
JESUS' FINAL WEEK AROUND AND IN JERUSALEM (CONT.)						
	(32) Jesus before Herod	Jerusalem			23:7–12	
	(33) Second appearance before Pilate	Jerusalem	27:15–26	15:6–15	23:13–25	18:39—19:16a
	(34) Mockery by Roman soldiers	Jerusalem	27:27–30	15:16–19		
	(35) Led to Golgotha	Jerusalem	27:31–34	15:20–23	23:26–32	19:16b–17
	(36) Events of first three hours on cross	Golgotha	27:35–44	15:24–32	23:33–43	19:18–27
Friday	(37) Last three hours on cross	Golgotha	27:45–50	15:33–37	23:44,46	19:28–30
	(38) Events attending Jesus' death		27:51–56	15:38–41	23:45, 47–49	
	(39) Burial of Jesus	Jerusalem	27:57–61	15:42–46	23:50–54	19:31–42
Friday-Saturday	(40) Tomb sealed	Jerusalem	27:62–66			
	(41) Women watch	Jerusalem		15:47	23:55–56	
THE RESURRECTION THROUGH THE ASCENSION						
AD 30						
Dawn of First Day (Sunday, "Lord's Day")	(1) Women visit the tomb	Near Jerusalem	28:1–8	16:1–8	24:1–11	20:1–2
	(2) Peter and John see the empty tomb				24:12	20:3–10
	(3) Jesus' appearance to Mary Magdalene	Jerusalem		[16:9–11]		20:11–18
	(4) Jesus' appearance to the other women	Jerusalem	28:9–10			
	(5) Guards' report of the resurrection		28:11–15			
Sunday Afternoon	(6) Jesus' appearance to two disciples on way to Emmaus			[16:12–13]	24:13–35	
Late Sunday	(7) Jesus' appearance to ten disciples without Thomas	Jerusalem			24:36–43	20:19–25
One Week Later	(8) Appearance to disciples with Thomas	Jerusalem			24:44–49	20:26–31
During 40 Days until Ascension	(9) Jesus' appearance to seven disciples by Sea of Galilee	Galilee				21:1–25
	(10) Great Commission		28:16–20	[16:14–18]		
	(11) The Ascension	Mount Olivet		[16:19–20]	24:50–53	

INTRODUCTION TO

ACTS

THE UNITY OF LUKE-ACTS

There is almost universal agreement that the same author wrote both the third Gospel (Luke) and the book of Acts because: (1) They both address the same individual, Theophilus (1:1; Luke 1:3). (2) Acts refers to the "former book" the author wrote (1:1). (3) The two books share common style and vocabulary. (4) They share common theological themes and emphases.

Not only did the same author write both books, but he probably intended them to be a single two-volume work. When Luke wrote his Gospel, he already had the book of Acts in mind. Evidence for this are key themes that he introduces in the Gospel that do not come to fulfillment until Acts. For example, in Luke 1:32–33, the angel Gabriel announces that Jesus will one day assume the throne of David. While Luke's Gospel presents Jesus' resurrection as vindication that he is the Messiah, it is Peter in Acts 2:30–36 who identifies Jesus' ascension as a Davidic enthronement (and so fulfills Luke 1:32–33). Similarly, in Luke's birth narrative, Simeon announces that Jesus will be a "light for revelation to the Gentiles" (Luke 2:32; alluding to Isa 42:6; 49:6), a prophecy that is not fulfilled until Acts 13:47, where Paul turns to the Gentiles and cites the same OT passages (Isa 42:6; 49:6). Already while writing his Gospel, the author has an eye on events that will be recorded in Acts. Scholars commonly refer to the two-volume work as "Luke-Acts."

AUTHOR

An unbroken tradition of witnesses for Luke's authorship of the third Gospel and Acts can be traced back to the middle of the second century, and there are no statements in the surviving literature of the early church that point to any other author. Considering Luke's relative obscurity in the NT, it is unlikely that a Gospel would have been attributed to him had he not written it.

To this external evidence we can add internal evidence. At certain points in Acts the author speaks in the first person plural ("we"). These "we" sections confirm that the author joined Paul briefly on his second missionary journey from Troas to Philippi (16:10–17) and then rejoined him at Philippi on Paul's return from his third journey (20:5—21:18). He was with Paul at Caesarea after Paul's arrest and accompanied him to Rome (27:1—28:16). Though Paul, of course, had other associates (Barnabas, Mark, Silas, Timothy, Titus, Aristarchus, Demas, Epaphras, etc.), when we place this internal evidence beside the strong and unanimous external testimony, there seems no reason to doubt Luke's authorship.

Luke was a physician (Col 4:14) and a part-time missionary associate of the apostle Paul. Paul refers to him as a "dear friend" (Col 4:14) and co-worker (Phlm 24). In addition to the journeys described above, Luke was with Paul during Paul's second Roman imprisonment and the last days before his martyrdom (2 Tim 4:11). Luke was likely a Gentile since Paul names him in a separate list from his Jewish associates (Col 4:11,14). This helps to explain Luke's intense interest in the gospel's movement from its Jewish roots outward to the Gentile world (see Themes and Theology).

Luke also claims to be a reliable historian, having interviewed eyewitnesses and investigated these events carefully in order to write an orderly account (Luke 1:2–3). The historical details in Acts confirm his skills as a historian: he repeatedly identifies place-names and titles of local and provincial government officials correctly. For example, he refers to Sergius Paulus as *anthypatos* ("proconsul") of Cyprus (13:7) and Publius as the *prōtos* ("the chief official") of Melita/Malta (28:7). City officials are *stratēgoi* ("magistrates") in Philippi (16:20), *politarchai* ("city officials") in Thessalonica (17:6), and *asiarchai* ("officials") in Ephesus (19:31) — all historically accurate designations. Since such names and titles changed frequently, getting them right is impressive evidence for Luke's skills as a historian.

DATE

Scholars debate the date of the composition of Acts, which is closely tied to the date of the third Gospel. There are two main options: the early AD 60s and post-AD 70 (perhaps as late as the 80s or 90s).

In favor of the early 60s, the book ends with Paul still alive in prison in Rome (ca. AD 62; see 28:30–31) and provides no account of his martyrdom (between 64 and 67). The relatively positive attitude toward Roman governmental officials throughout the book also suggests that the severe persecutions under the emperor Nero (AD 64) had not yet begun.

Others who consider that Mark's Gospel was one of Luke's primary sources hold the later date, post-AD 70. If Mark were written in the late 60s on the eve of the Jewish war, as many believe (see Mark 13:14), then Luke must be later — in the 70s, 80s or even 90s. Luke describes the destruction of Jerusalem (AD 70) with greater detail than Mark (Luke 19:43–44; 21:20–24; 23:28–31), possible evidence that he is writing after the fact. In this case, Luke would have had theological reasons for ending his story with Paul still alive in Rome: to demonstrate that the gospel was indeed advancing to "the ends of the earth" (Acts 1:8). Of course Mark's Gospel could have been written earlier, as early as the mid-50s, which would allow Luke to use Mark as a source and still write in the early 60s.

RECIPIENTS, PLACE OF WRITING, DESTINATION

Luke addresses both his Gospel and Acts to a certain "Theophilus" (1:1; Luke 1:3). The name means "one who loves God," and some claim that it refers to those seeking God in general or perhaps all believers. More likely it is an individual since Greek literature attests to the proper name and since Luke refers to him as "most excellent" (Luke 1:3), a title typical for an individual of high social status. There are various suggestions concerning his identity: (1) a questioning unbeliever, (2) a new believer in need of catechism, (3) a government official, perhaps in charge of Paul's trial, or (4) the patron who sponsored the production and circulation of Luke's Gospel. Though these are not all mutually exclusive, the last is the most likely. In the ancient world, the time and expense neces-

POSSIBLE LOCATIONS WHERE LUKE WROTE THE BOOK OF ACTS

sary for producing volumes like Luke and Acts were enormous, and authors commonly dedicated their works to their sponsors.

Although addressed to Theophilus, Luke-Acts clearly addresses a wider audience. This audience is almost certainly believers rather than unbelievers since Luke's purpose seems to be to provide *confirmation* and *assurance* for those who already have faith in Jesus (see Occasion and Purpose). It is also likely that the audience is predominantly Gentile, with a minority of Jews, since this was the makeup of most churches Paul started. This would also help explain Luke's strong emphasis on the legitimacy of the Gentile mission and the church's expansion from its Jewish roots into the Gentile world.

No consensus has been reached on the place of composition of Luke-Acts. Various suggestions include Rome, Antioch in Syria, Achaia, Caesarea, Corinth, and Ephesus. The two most likely places of composition are Antioch and Rome. In the fourth century AD, the early church historian Eusebius claimed that Luke came from Antioch in Syria, and the author of Acts shows special interest in the church's establishment and growth there. Antioch was the first truly mixed Gentile-Jewish church and became the key sending church for Paul and his missionary companions (13:1 – 3; 15:35,40; 18:22 – 23). Some have even suggested that Luke is the same as Lucius, one of the prophets and teachers at Antioch (13:1). Some scholars have suggested Rome as the place of writing because so much of Acts focuses on Rome as Paul's destination. Paul's long incarceration there would have provided the time necessary for Luke to complete his account, and the well-established church at Rome would have been an appropriate audience for defending Christianity in general and the Gentile mission in particular. In the end, however, both Antioch and Rome remain educated guesses.

OCCASION AND PURPOSE

Though the specific destination and audience of Acts is uncertain, Luke's general purpose is clear. He is writing at a time of increasing animosity between the early Christians and their Jewish opponents. Both Jews and Christians are claiming to be the true people of God, and both assert that the Hebrew Scriptures (the OT) relate to them. A look at the major themes of Luke-Acts suggests that these questions are challenging the church: How can Jesus be the Messiah if he suffered and died as a common criminal? Why did the kingdom of God arrive on earth in an unexpected way? How can the church be the people of God if most Jews, God's chosen people, have rejected Jesus and the church is rapidly becoming a Gentile entity? Is the apostle Paul a renegade Jew who has betrayed his Jewish heritage by welcoming "unclean" Gentiles into the people of God without circumcision or keeping the law? Worse yet, is Paul teaching other Jews not to circumcise their children and to reject the traditions of his ancestors?

Luke writes to respond to these and similar charges by confirming the gospel message and the gospel messengers. He seeks to establish the continuity between God's promises to Israel in the OT and their fulfillment in Christ and the church. He writes to show that God's great plan of salvation, prophesied in the OT, has come to fulfillment in the events of Jesus' life, death, resurrection, and ascension, and it continues to unfold in the growth and expansion of the early church. The church, made up of the righteous remnant of Israel and the Gentiles, represents the people of God in the new age of salvation. The miraculous progress of the gospel confirms that this is indeed the work of God.

Luke's overall purpose, then, is to assure his readers of the truth of Christianity and legitimize and defend the church as the authentic people of God. Or as he writes to Theophilus, "so that you may know the certainty of the things you have been taught" (Luke 1:4). Besides this overarching purpose, Luke likely has a variety of subsidiary purposes, including encouraging harmony between Jews and Gentiles in the church and evangelizing unbelievers.

THEMES AND THEOLOGY

This central purpose of Luke-Acts (confirming the gospel) plays out in the key themes in Acts:

1. *The mission and the messengers.* If the Gospel of Luke is about "all that Jesus began to do and to teach" (Acts 1:1), Acts is about what Jesus continues to do through his disciples in the power of the Spirit. The role of the disciples is to be Jesus' "witnesses" (1:8), his representatives. Acts 1:8 represents both the central theme of the book (the unstoppable progress of the gospel) and its general outline: beginning in Jerusalem and moving outward in concentric circles through Judea, Samaria, and to the ends of the earth. The traditional title of the book, "the Acts of the Apostles," fails to reflect accurately the book's contents, since the 12 apostles play a relatively minor role. The main human characters, like Peter, Barnabas, Stephen, Philip, and Paul, play a central role not because of their *status* as apostles but because of their *function* in breaking down barriers to the advance of the gospel. Acts is fundamentally about the mission of the church and the progress of salvation from its Jewish roots to the Gentile world.

Modern Antakya, site of ancient Antioch. This is one of the two most likely sites where Acts was written.

Rick Hess

2. *God's sovereign purpose in salvation history.* Throughout Acts, Luke seeks to show that all that happened — Jesus' coming and the early church's growth and expansion — is part of God's purpose and plan. At the beginning of Acts, Jesus tells the disciples to wait in Jerusalem until they receive "the gift my Father promised" — the Holy Spirit (1:4). A few days later, the Spirit is poured out, and the church is born. In the chapters that follow, God guides and orchestrates everything that happens. Though wicked people put Jesus to death, God raised him from the dead (2:24; 3:15,26; 4:10; 10:40; 13:30,34,37). Acts 5 illustrates this theme: members of the Sanhedrin threaten to kill the apostles for continuing to preach about Jesus. The Pharisee Gamaliel stands up and cautions restraint. If this movement is *not* from God, he says, it will come to nothing. "But if it is from God, you will not be able to stop these men; you will only find yourselves fighting against God" (5:39). His words prove prophetic. Throughout the rest of Acts, the gospel faces incredible odds and constant obstacles yet continues to roll forward. It is unstoppable because nothing can thwart God's sovereign purpose.

3. *Jesus the Messiah and Lord now vindicated and exalted to the right hand of God.* The purpose of God is being fulfilled through Jesus the Messiah, whose life, death, and resurrection fulfill OT promises. Jesus is the culmination of God's plan and the center point of human history. Healing and forgiveness of sins are now available to those who repent and believe in him. The signs and wonders that God did through Jesus confirm that he is the Messiah (2:22). Jesus suffered and died not as a criminal but as the innocent and "Righteous One," the servant of the Lord predicted in the Scriptures (3:14; 7:52; 13:28; Luke 23:4,14 – 15,22,41,47). His death was no tragedy since all along the Scriptures prophesied that the Messiah would suffer and rise again and that through that resurrection, repentance and forgiveness of sins would be preached to all nations (3:18; 17:3; 26:23; Luke 24:26,46 – 47). Jesus' life, death, resurrection, and ascension to the right hand of God has inaugurated the kingdom of God. The Messianic reign has begun (2:34 – 35).

4. *The Holy Spirit as guide, empowering agent, and sign of the new age.* For Luke, the gift of the Holy Spirit marks the dawn of the new age of salvation that Jesus' life, death, and resurrection inaugurate. The book has often been called the "Acts of the Holy Spirit" because the Spirit plays a leading role. During Jesus' public ministry he alone is endowed with the Spirit and performs miracles and exorcisms in the power of the Holy Spirit. In Acts, by virtue of his death, resurrection, and exaltation to the right hand of God, Jesus pours out the Spirit, empowering his disciples for mission (2:1 – 24,33; see Joel 2:28 – 32). Throughout the rest of Acts, the Spirit fills and empowers believers (2:4; 4:8,31; 6:3,5; 7:55; 9:17; 11:24) and guides and directs the progress of the gospel (8:29,39; 10:19 – 20; 11:28; 13:2,9 – 12; 16:6 – 7; 21:4). Receiving the Spirit marks entrance into the people of God (2:38; 8:15,17 – 19; 10:44 – 48; 11:16 – 17; 15:8; 19:2 – 7). The new age of salvation is the age of the Spirit (2:16 – 21; see Joel 2:28 – 32).

5. *The Jewish roots of the gospel and its rejection by many in Israel.* Throughout both Luke and Acts, the author stresses the strong continuity between the old covenant and the new. Salvation comes forth from Israel and goes first to Israel. Luke's Gospel, sometimes called a "Gentile Gospel," is a very Jewish Gospel, beginning and ending in the temple in Jerusalem (Luke 1:8–10; 24:53). The original apostles are all Jews, and they first proclaim the gospel to Israel (Acts 2–5). The early chapters of Acts point to the astonishing success of the church among the Jews. On the day of Pentecost, about 3,000 come to faith in Jesus the Messiah (2:41) and by 4:4 there are more than 5,000 believers. Statements of numerical growth punctuate the narrative that follows (2:47; 5:14; 6:1,7; 9:31; 21:20). Luke's point is that the church and its expansion fulfills God's promises to Israel.

At the same time, the church faces strong opposition from its Jewish opponents, first from the priestly leadership in Jerusalem (4:1–22; 5:17–42; 6:8–15) and then from Jews throughout the empire (9:23; 13:45,50; 14:2,4–5; 17:5,13; 18:12; 20:19; 21:11,27; 22:30; 23:12; 24:9; 25:2,7,15; 28:24–25). How does Luke explain this? His answer appears in Stephen's speech before his execution. Israel's rejection simply continues their rebellious history (7:51–53). The nation has always been rebellious and hard-hearted, rejecting God's messengers (cf. Luke 4:24; 6:23; 11:47–50; 13:33–34). Yet a faithful remnant has been saved and—together with the Gentiles who believe—has become the foundation of the end-time people of God. From Luke's perspective, God has not rejected Israel; a righteous remnant and an unrepentant majority have divided Israel.

6. *The expansion of the gospel and the Gentile mission.* Throughout Acts, when the Jews reject Paul, he turns to the Gentiles (13:46–47; 18:6; 22:21; 26:20; 28:28; cf. Rom 11:11). Although first for the Jews, God's salvation is all along meant for all people everywhere. Luke spends a great deal of space defending the Gentile mission and its leading advocate, the apostle Paul. He seeks to show that Scripture predicts that the Gentiles would accept the gospel and that it is part of God's purpose and plan (10:34–35; 13:47; 15:16–18; Luke 2:32). God himself instigated the Gentile mission (9:15; 10:9–16,34; 11:15–18; 15:7–18; 22:21; 26:17). The major emphases on Paul—his conversion (chs. 9; 22; 26), missionary journeys (chs. 13–20), and arrest and trials (chs. 21–28)—demonstrate that he is not a renegade Jew but is faithful to his Jewish heritage and to the God of his ancestors. All along God intended to include the Gentiles in the end-time people of God.

7. *The innocence of Christianity under Roman law.* This theme is related to the church's place in the larger society. In the midst of the growing suspicion of Christianity by the Roman and other local authorities, Luke seeks to show that God's people can be good citizens and good Christians. Though crucified as a common criminal, Jesus was innocent of the charges against him (3:14; 13:28; Luke 23:4,14–15,22,41,47). Paul and the early Christians

Harbor of Attalia near Perga (Acts 14:25), where Paul stopped on his first missionary journey.

are not troublemakers but rather loyal and peace-loving citizens. The Roman authorities repeatedly find Paul to be innocent (23:29; 24:12–13,20; 25:10,25; 26:31). Christianity is not a new and illegal religion; it fulfills God's promises made long ago.

GENRE

Acts has parallels with a variety of Greek literary forms of its day, including Hellenistic biographies, histories, and even epic literature. Its closest parallels, however, are biblical—the OT and the Gospels.

In line with the biblical story, it is not the Greek idea of fate or destiny that guides events forward; it is the sovereign hand of God. Luke himself places his work in the same category as the Gospels by presenting Acts as the sequel to his own story of Jesus. While the third Gospel tells what Jesus began to do, Acts tells what he continues to do through his church (1:1).

There are also remarkable parallels between the actions of Jesus in Luke's Gospel and those of his followers in Acts. At his martyrdom, Stephen commends his spirit to Jesus (7:59) in the same way Jesus commends his spirit to the Father (Luke 23:46). Both Peter and Paul heal lame men (3:1–8; 14:8–10) just as Jesus makes the lame walk (Luke 7:22). Paul's raising Eutychus (20:9–12) parallels Peter's raising Tabitha (9:40), and both recall similar miracles of Jesus (Luke 7:11–15; 8:49–56). Paul's journey to Jerusalem, where dangers await him (20:22–25; 21:4,11–14), parallels Jesus' journey to Jerusalem in Luke's Gospel (Luke 9–19), which repeatedly predicts his coming suffering (Luke 9:22,44,51; 13:33–34; 18:31–33; 22:22). During his arrest and trial, Paul is repeatedly declared to be innocent (23:9,29; 24:12–13,20; 25:10,19–20,25; 26:31) in the same way Jesus suffers innocently as the "Righteous One" (3:14; 7:52; see Luke 23:4,14–15,22,41,47). Continuity is the key for Luke: (1) between the old and new covenant people of God and (2) between the salvation that Jesus accomplished and that which his representatives now announce.

THE GREEK TEXT OF ACTS

There are four major "families" of NT manuscripts: Alexandrian, Caesarean, Western, and Byzantine. A "family" is a group of related manuscripts that appear to come from a common original. The book of Acts poses one of the most unusual textual issues in the NT since it has come down to us in two versions. The Western text significantly varies from both the Alexandrian and Byzantine text types.

Manuscript D, known as Codex Bezae, is almost one-tenth longer than the Alexandrian text. It is characterized by paraphrase, expansion, explanation, harmonization, and certain theological idiosyncrasies. Sometimes these changes represent incidental details. For example, at 12:10, D adds that Peter and the angel "went down seven steps" from the prison where he had been kept to the street. Other times there are explanatory additions. In 19:9, it notes that Paul preached daily "from eleven o'clock to four" in the lecture hall of Tyrannus. This is a period when Tyrannus would not normally have been holding sessions.

While some of these additions and alterations may represent authentic tradition, the majority appear to be tendentious. A few scholars have argued for the priority of the Western text, but most consider it to be inferior, the result of later expansion by copyists.

OUTLINE

I. The Spirit Empowers the Church for Witness (1:1—2:47)
- A. Jesus Taken Up Into Heaven (1:1–11)
- B. Matthias Chosen to Replace Judas (1:12–26)
- C. The Events on the Day of Pentecost (2:1–47)
  1. The Holy Spirit Comes at Pentecost (2:1–13)
  2. Peter Addresses the Crowd (2:14–41)
  3. The Fellowship of the Believers (2:42–47)

II. The Apostolic Witness in Jerusalem (3:1—5:42)
- A. Healing and Preaching in Jerusalem (3:1—4:31)
  1. Peter Heals a Lame Beggar (3:1–10)
  2. Peter Speaks to the Onlookers (3:11–26)
  3. Peter and John Before the Sanhedrin (4:1–22)
  4. The Believers Pray (4:23–31)

B. Community Life in Jerusalem (4:32—5:16)
1. The Believers Share Their Possessions (4:32–37)
2. Ananias and Sapphira (5:1–11)
3. The Apostles Heal Many (5:12–16)
C. The Apostles Persecuted (5:17–42)

III. The Witness Beyond Jerusalem (6:1—12:24)
A. The Choosing of the Seven (6:1–7)
B. Stephen's Arrest and Martyrdom (6:8—7:60)
1. Stephen Seized (6:8–15)
2. Stephen's Speech to the Sanhedrin (7:1–53)
3. The Stoning of Stephen (7:54—8:1a)
C. The Church Persecuted and Scattered (8:1b–3)
D. Philip's Ministry (8:4–40)
1. Philip in Samaria (8:4–8)
2. Simon the Sorcerer and the Jerusalem Delegation to Samaria (8:9–25)
3. Philip and the Ethiopian (8:26–40)
E. Saul's Conversion and Early Witness (9:1–31)
1. Saul's Conversion (9:1–19a)
2. Saul in Damascus and Jerusalem (9:19b–31)
F. Aeneas and Dorcas (9:32–43)
G. Peter's Ministry to Cornelius and His Household (10:1—11:18)
1. Cornelius Calls for Peter (10:1–8)
2. Peter's Vision (10:9–23a)
3. Peter at Cornelius's House (10:23b–48)
4. Peter Explains His Actions (11:1–18)
H. The Church in Antioch (11:19–30)
I. Peter's Miraculous Escape From Prison (12:1–19a)
J. Herod's Death (12:19b–24)

IV. The Witness to the Ends of the Earth (12:25—28:31)
A. Paul's First Missionary Journey (12:25—14:28)
1. Barnabas and Saul Sent Off (12:25—13:3)
2. On Cyprus (13:4–12)
3. In Pisidian Antioch (13:13–52)
4. In Iconium (14:1–7)
5. In Lystra and Derbe (14:8–20)
6. The Return to Antioch in Syria (14:21–28)
B. The Decision of the Jerusalem Council (15:1–35)
1. The Council at Jerusalem (15:1–21)
2. The Council's Letter to Gentile Believers (15:22–35)
C. Paul's Second Missionary Journey (15:36—18:22)
1. Disagreement Between Paul and Barnabas (15:36–41)
2. Timothy Joins Paul and Silas (16:1–5)
3. Paul's Vision of the Man of Macedonia (16:6–10)
4. Lydia's Conversion in Philippi (16:11–15)
5. Paul and Silas in Prison (16:16–40)
6. In Thessalonica (17:1–9)
7. In Berea (17:10–15)
8. In Athens (17:16–34)
9. In Corinth (18:1–17)
10. Return to Antioch (18:18–22)

D. Paul's Third Missionary Journey (18:23—21:16)
1. Priscilla, Aquila, and Apollos (18:23–28)
2. Paul in Ephesus (19:1–22)
3. The Riot in Ephesus (19:23–41)
4. Through Macedonia and Greece (20:1–6)
5. Eutychus Raised From the Dead at Troas (20:7–12)
6. Paul's Farewell to the Ephesian Elders (20:13–38)
7. On to Jerusalem (21:1–16)

E. Paul's Fourth Journey: Arrest and Journey to Rome (21:17—28:31)
1. Paul's Arrival at Jerusalem (21:17–26)
2. Paul Arrested (21:27–36)
3. Paul Speaks to the Crowd (21:37—22:21)
4. Paul the Roman Citizen (22:22–29)
5. Paul Before the Sanhedrin (22:30—23:11)
6. The Plot to Kill Paul (23:12–22)
7. Paul Transferred to Caesarea (23:23–35)
8. Paul's Trial Before Felix (24:1–27)
9. Paul's Trial Before Festus (25:1–12)
10. Festus Consults King Agrippa (25:13–22)
11. Paul Before Agrippa (25:23—26:32)
12. Paul Sails for Rome (27:1–12)
13. The Storm and the Shipwreck (27:13–44)
14. Paul Ashore on Malta (28:1–10)
15. Paul's Arrival at Rome (28:11–16)
16. Paul Preaches at Rome Under Guard (28:17–31)

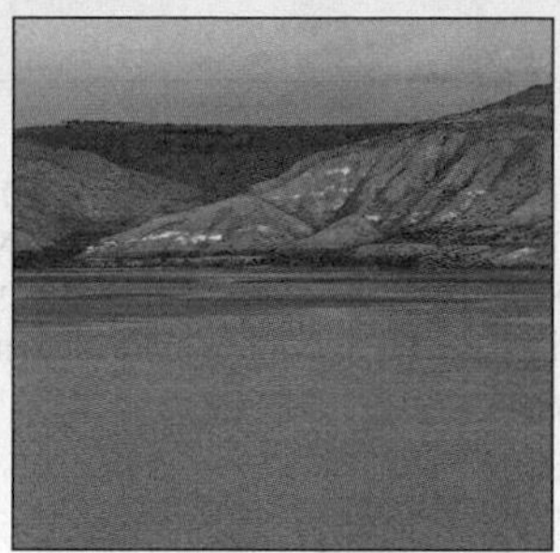

ACTS

Jesus Taken Up Into Heaven

1 In my former book,[a] Theophilus, I wrote about all that Jesus began to do and to teach[b] 2until the
day he was taken up to heaven,[c] after giving instructions[d] through the Holy Spirit to the apostles[e]
he had chosen.[f] 3After his suffering, he presented himself to them and gave many convincing proofs
that he was alive. He appeared to them[g] over a period of forty days and spoke about the kingdom of
God. 4On one occasion, while he was eating with them, he gave them this command: "Do not leave
Jerusalem, but wait for the gift my Father promised, which you have heard me speak about.[h] 5For John
baptized with[a] water, but in a few days you will be baptized with[a] the Holy Spirit."

6Then they gathered around him and asked him, "Lord, are you at this time going to restore[i] the
kingdom to Israel?"

7He said to them: "It is not for you to know the times or dates the Father has set by his own authority.[j] 8But you will receive power when the Holy Spirit comes on you;[k] and you will be my witnesses[l] in
Jerusalem, and in all Judea and Samaria,[m] and to the ends of the earth."[n]

1:1 [a] Lk 1:1-4 [b] Lk 3:23
1:2 [c] ver 9,11; Mk 16:19 [d] Mt 28:19,20 [e] Mk 6:30 [f] Jn 13:18
1:3 [g] Mt 28:17; Lk 24:34, 36; Jn 20:19,26; 21:1, 14; 1Co 15:5-7
1:4 [h] Lk 24:49; Jn 14:16; Ac 2:33
1:6 [i] Mt 17:11
1:7 [j] Mt 24:36
1:8 [k] Ac 2:1-4 [l] Lk 24:48 [m] Ac 8:1-25 [n] Mt 28:19

[a] 5 Or *in*

1:1—2:47 *The Spirit Empowers the Church for Witness.* The first two chapters of Acts may be viewed as introductory and preparatory for the main outline of the book, which is set forth in 1:8: In the power of the Holy Spirit the church as Christ's witnesses will take the gospel to Jerusalem (3:1—5:42), beyond Jerusalem to Judea and Samaria (6:1—12:24) and to the ends of the earth (12:25—28:31). In this section we see the preparation and empowering of the church for this purpose.

1:1–11 *Jesus Taken Up Into Heaven.* Only Luke among the Gospel writers narrates the ascension of Jesus, and he describes it twice, at the end of the Gospel (Luke 24:50–52) and at the beginning of Acts (vv. 2,9–11). It is enormously important for Luke's theology because it demonstrates that Jesus is the Messiah at the right hand of God (2:33; 5:31; 7:55; Luke 22:69; cf. Rom 8:34; Eph 1:20; Col 3:1; Heb 1:3; 8:1; 10:12; 12:2), that Jesus assumes the throne of David (Acts 2:30–33; Luke 1:32–33), and that Jesus has authority to pour out the Holy Spirit, inaugurating the end times (Acts 2:16–21,33; Joel 2:28–32). The Spirit will represent Jesus' presence in the church, guiding and empowering believers throughout Acts.

1:1 Luke alone in the NT begins his two volumes with a formal literary prologue in the style of Greek writers of his day (see note on Luke 1:1–4). **former book.** The Gospel of Luke. **Theophilus.** See Introduction: Recipients, Place of Writing, Destination. While Luke's Gospel is about "all that Jesus began to do and to teach," so Acts recounts what *Jesus continues to do* through his church in the power of the Spirit.

1:3 gave many convincing proofs ... over a period of forty days. Jesus' resurrection is therefore beyond dispute (cf. 1 Cor 15:3–8). His teaching concerned the "kingdom of God," which was also the central theme of his teaching in the Gospel of Luke (the expression occurs 32 times; see Luke 4:43). In its broadest sense, the "kingdom of God" refers to God's sovereign rule over his creation, a rule that Jesus restores by bringing forgiveness of sins and reconciliation through his life, death, and resurrection. Though the phrase "kingdom of God" occurs only six times in Acts (here; 8:12; 14:22; 19:8; 28:23,31), it appears prominently at the beginning and end, framing the entire book.

1:4 Do not leave Jerusalem. Since the disciples are powerless without "the gift my Father promised" (see Luke 24:49; cf. John 14:26)—the Holy Spirit, God's empowering presence. The coming of the Holy Spirit on the day of Pentecost marks the birth of the church and the dawn of the new age of salvation inaugurated by Jesus the Messiah (see note on 2:1–13).

1:5 John the Baptist predicted the Messiah's baptism "with the Holy Spirit" (see Luke 3:15–17; cf. Matt 3:11; Mark 1:8; John 1:33), a prophecy fulfilled (at least in part) at the Pentecost event (2:2–4). While John's baptism with water was one of preparation and repentance (13:24; 19:4; Luke 3:3), Jesus' baptism with the Spirit will inaugurate the new age of salvation and provide empowerment for ministry (see v. 8).

1:6–7 In line with Jewish expectations of their day, the disciples are thinking of the kingdom of Israel in nationalistic terms. While Jesus does not deny the future consummation of the kingdom, the "times or dates" are not to be their concern (cf. Mark 13:32; 1 Thess 5:1). Their role is to complete Jesus' mission (v. 1) by taking the message of salvation to the ends of the earth (v. 8).

1:8 This is both the general outline and central theme of Acts. The gospel will proceed from Jerusalem (chs. 1–7), to Judea and Samaria (chs. 8–12), and to the ends of the earth (chs. 13–28). Thematically, the

1:9 [o]ver 2
1:10 [p]Lk 24:4; Jn 20:12
1:11 [q]Ac 2:7 [r]Mt 16:27
1:12 [s]Lk 24:52 [t]Mt 21:1
1:13 [u]Ac 9:37; 20:8 [v]Mt 10:2-4; Mk 3:16-19; Lk 6:14-16

9After he said this, he was taken up[o] before their very eyes, and a cloud hid him from their sight.
10They were looking intently up into the sky as he was going, when suddenly two men dressed in
white[p] stood beside them. 11"Men of Galilee,"[q] they said, "why do you stand here looking into the sky?
This same Jesus, who has been taken from you into heaven, will come back[r] in the same way you have
seen him go into heaven."

Matthias Chosen to Replace Judas

12Then the apostles returned to Jerusalem[s] from the hill called the Mount of Olives,[t] a Sabbath
day's walk[a] from the city. 13When they arrived, they went upstairs to the room[u] where they were
staying. Those present were Peter, John, James and Andrew; Philip and Thomas, Bartholomew and
Matthew; James son of Alphaeus and Simon the Zealot, and Judas son of James.[v] 14They all joined

[a] *12* That is, about 5/8 mile or about 1 kilometer

disciples' *role* is to be Jesus' "witnesses." Their *power* is the Holy Spirit. Their *task* is to take this message from "Jerusalem . . . to the ends of the earth." This movement is both geographic (from Jerusalem to Rome) and ethnic (from Jews to Gentiles). The movement also continues what started in Luke's Gospel. While the great central section of Luke's Gospel describes Jesus' journey *to Jerusalem* to accomplish God's salvation (Luke 9–19), Acts describes the outward movement *from Jerusalem* to proclaim God's salvation everywhere.

1:9 Luke's second account of the ascension gives greater detail than the first (Luke 24:50–52) and clarifies that it occurred 40 days after the resurrection (v. 3). **cloud.** Commonly indicates the presence of God (Exod 40:34; Luke 9:34–36).

1:10 two men. Angels, as their white garments indicate (cf. Mark 16:5; John 20:12; Rev 4:4).

1:11 in the same way. Jesus' return will be bodily, visible, from heaven, and with the clouds (Luke 21:27; cf. Matt 24:30; 26:64; Mark 13:26; 14:62).

1:12–26 *Matthias Chosen to Replace Judas.* Replacing Judas restores the original number of apostles and emphasizes the importance of apostolic eyewitness testimony to the events of Jesus' life and resurrection (vv. 21–22). According to Peter, the replacement is necessary because of Scriptural precedent (Ps 109:8; see note on v. 20). It is also necessary to restore the number of the 12 tribes of Israel and so identify the apostles with the restored remnant of Israel (cf. Luke 22:28–30).

1:12 Mount of Olives. The hill east of Jerusalem overlooking the temple mount. It has end-times significance in Zech 14:4; the Lord will stand upon it on the day of judgment. **Sabbath day's walk.** See NIV text note. This was the farthest Jews were allowed to walk on the Sabbath without violating the OT law (Exod 20:10). Jewish tradition (not the OT law) identified this as 2,000 cubits (about 0.6 miles or about 1 kilometer).

1:13 room. Sometimes identified as the room of the Last Supper (Luke 22:11) and/or the house of Mary, John Mark's mother (12:12); but this is speculation. **Those present.** Only here does Acts list the names of all the apostles (cf. Luke 6:13–16).

1:14 women. Jesus' female disciples, who supported him financially (Luke 8:2–3) and witnessed the crucifixion, burial, and empty tomb

Looking west over Jerusalem to the Mount of Olives, the site of Jesus' ascension.
Todd Bolen/www.BiblePlaces.com

together constantly in prayer,[w] along with the women[x] and Mary the mother of Jesus, and with his
brothers.[y]
15In those days Peter stood up among the believers (a group numbering about a hundred and
twenty) 16and said, "Brothers and sisters,[a] the Scripture had to be fulfilled[z] in which the Holy Spirit
spoke long ago through David concerning Judas,[a] who served as guide for those who arrested Jesus.
17He was one of our number[b] and shared in our ministry."[c]
18(With the payment[d] he received for his wickedness, Judas bought a field;[e] there he fell headlong,
his body burst open and all his intestines spilled out. 19Everyone in Jerusalem heard about this, so they
called that field in their language Akeldama, that is, Field of Blood.)
20"For," said Peter, "it is written in the Book of Psalms:

"'May his place be deserted;
let there be no one to dwell in it,'[b][f]

and,

"'May another take his place of leadership.'[c][g]

21Therefore it is necessary to choose one of the men who have been with us the whole time the Lord
Jesus was living among us, 22beginning from John's baptism[h] to the time when Jesus was taken up from
us. For one of these must become a witness[i] with us of his resurrection."
23So they nominated two men: Joseph called Barsabbas (also known as Justus) and Matthias. 24Then
they prayed,[j] "Lord, you know everyone's heart.[k] Show us which of these two you have chosen 25to take
over this apostolic ministry, which Judas left to go where he belongs." 26Then they cast lots, and the lot
fell to Matthias; so he was added to the eleven apostles.[l]

a *16* The Greek word for *brothers and sisters* (*adelphoi*) refers here to believers, both men and women, as part of God's family; also in 6:3; 11:29; 12:17; 16:40; 18:18, 27; 21:7, 17; 28:14, 15. *b* *20* Psalm 69:25 *c* *20* Psalm 109:8

1:14 [w]Ac 2:42; 6:4 [x]Lk 23:49,55 [y]Mt 12:46
1:16 [z]ver 20 [a]Jn 13:18
1:17 [b]Jn 6:70,71 [c]ver 25
1:18 [d]Mt 26:14,15 [e]Mt 27:3-10
1:20 [f]Ps 69:25 [g]Ps 109:8
1:22 [h]Mk 1:4 [i]ver 8
1:24 [j]Ac 6:6; 14:23 [k]1Sa 16:7; Jer 17:10; Ac 15:8; Rev 2:23
1:26 [l]Ac 2:14

(Luke 23:49,55; 24:1–11). They probably also include the wives of the apostles (1 Cor 9:5). Luke shows special concern for women throughout his Gospel and Acts. **brothers.** Jesus had four: James, Judas, Joseph, and Simon (Mark 6:3; Luke 8:19). Though they apparently rejected Jesus' Messiahship during his earthly ministry (John 7:5), they are now believers (probably because they saw the risen Christ; 1 Cor 15:7). James becomes a key leader in the Jerusalem church (12:17; 15:13; 21:18; cf. Gal 1:19; 2:9,12; Jas 1:1; Jude 1).

1:15 Peter takes the lead as representative of the apostles, a role he often plays in the Gospels and the early chapters of Acts. As Jesus predicted, Peter will become a foundational "rock" in the early church (Matt 16:18).

1:16 the Holy Spirit spoke ... through David. A clear affirmation of the divine inspiration of the Bible. The Spirit of God communicated his message through the human agency of David.

1:18–19 These verses are Luke's narrative comment (note the parentheses). Matthew gives a somewhat different account, in which Judas hangs himself and the Sanhedrin purchases the field (Matt 27:3–10). The two accounts can be harmonized if we assume the rope broke as Judas tried to hang himself and so he "fell headlong." Another possibility is that "hanged" in Matt 27:5 means Judas committed suicide by impaling himself on a stake. The Sanhedrin may have purchased the field in Judas's name, or perhaps they acquired it from Judas's heirs. People call the field "Akeldama," Aramaic for "Field of Blood," either because Judas died gruesomely or because the purchase was made with blood money.

1:20 Peter combines two OT passages (see NIV text notes) to justify the replacement of Judas. It is not clear whether "it [was] necessary" (v. 21) to replace Judas in order to fulfill prophecy or whether these OT passages simply illustrate a biblical principle of leadership replacement.

1:21–22 Key qualifications to become one of the Twelve include that the person (1) was with Jesus throughout his whole ministry, which began with his baptism by John, and (2) saw the resurrected Lord. The Twelve were to be authoritative eyewitnesses to the story of Jesus (2:42; 6:2; cf. Eph 2:19–20; Rev 21:14). Luke generally uses the term "apostles" in Acts to designate the Twelve (1:2,12,26, etc.), though he twice uses it for Paul and Barnabas (14:4,14). The requirements for this latter broader category of "apostle"—a position that Paul, Barnabas (14:4,14), James (Gal 1:19), and others also occupied—were seeing the resurrected Lord and receiving a direct commission from him (1 Cor 9:1; Gal 1:1). This rules out the possibility of apostles, in this sense, beyond the first generation.

1:23 Joseph called Barsabbas. "Barsabbas" means either "son of the Sabbath," probably because he was born on the Sabbath, or "son of Saba" (a proper name). If the latter, he could be the brother of Judas, also called Barsabbas (15:22).

1:24 they prayed. Just as Jesus prayed before choosing the Twelve (Luke 6:12–13). **you know everyone's heart.** God's knowledge of people's hearts is a common theme in Scripture (1 Sam 16:6–7; 1 Kgs 8:39; 1 Chr 28:9; 2 Chr 6:30; Pss 7:9; 44:21; Jer 11:20; John 2:24–25; Rev 2:23).

1:26 cast lots. A method used in the OT for determining God's will (1 Chr 26:13–16; Neh 11:1; Prov 16:33; cf. Jonah 1:7). It probably meant shaking marked stones in a jar until one fell out. Nowhere else in the NT do the people of God use this method, and we may assume it became obsolete after the Holy Spirit came (ch. 2) since he guides and directs God's servants. Some claim that the apostles made a mistake and should have waited for God to choose Paul as the twelfth apostle, but nothing in the text suggests this. God answers their prayers and chooses Matthias through casting lots. Paul was the Apostle to the Gentiles and so not one of the Twelve, whose particular ministry was to the Jews (Gal 2:8–9).

2:1 [m]Lev 23:15,16; Ac 20:16 [n]Ac 1:14
2:2 [o]Ac 4:31
2:4 [p]Mk 16:17; 1Co 12:10
2:5 [q]Ac 8:2
2:7 [r]ver 12 [s]Ac 1:11
2:9 [t]1Pe 1:1 [u]Ac 18:2 [v]Ac 16:6; Ro 16:5; 1Co 16:19; 2Co 1:8
2:10 [w]Ac 16:6; 18:23 [x]Ac 13:13; 15:38 [y]Mt 27:32
2:13 [z]1Co 14:23

The Holy Spirit Comes at Pentecost

2 When the day of Pentecost[m] came, they were all together[n] in one place. 2 Suddenly a sound like the
blowing of a violent wind came from heaven and filled the whole house where they were sitting.[o]
3 They saw what seemed to be tongues of fire that separated and came to rest on each of them. 4 All of
them were filled with the Holy Spirit and began to speak in other tongues[a][p] as the Spirit enabled them.
5 Now there were staying in Jerusalem God-fearing[q] Jews from every nation under heaven. 6 When
they heard this sound, a crowd came together in bewilderment, because each one heard their own language being spoken. 7 Utterly amazed,[r] they asked: "Aren't all these who are speaking Galileans?[s] 8 Then
how is it that each of us hears them in our native language? 9 Parthians, Medes and Elamites; residents
of Mesopotamia, Judea and Cappadocia,[t] Pontus[u] and Asia,[b][v] 10 Phrygia[w] and Pamphylia,[x] Egypt and
the parts of Libya near Cyrene;[y] visitors from Rome 11 (both Jews and converts to Judaism); Cretans and
Arabs—we hear them declaring the wonders of God in our own tongues!" 12 Amazed and perplexed,
they asked one another, "What does this mean?"
13 Some, however, made fun of them and said, "They have had too much wine."[z]

Peter Addresses the Crowd

14 Then Peter stood up with the Eleven, raised his voice and addressed the crowd: "Fellow Jews and
all of you who live in Jerusalem, let me explain this to you; listen carefully to what I say. 15 These people

[a] *4* Or *languages*; also in verse 11 [b] *9* That is, the Roman province by that name

2:1–47 *The Events on the Day of Pentecost.* The coming of the Spirit (2:1–13) and Peter's speech that follows (2:14–41) mark the beginning of the church, which becomes a fellowship of unity, support, power, and witness (2:42–47).

2:1–13 *The Holy Spirit Comes at Pentecost.* The pouring out of the Spirit at Pentecost marks the inauguration of the new covenant and the promised end-time coming of the Holy Spirit (Joel 2:28–32; cf. Isa 32:15; 44:3–4; Jer 31:33–34; Ezek 36:26–27; 39:29). Though the Spirit was present in the old covenant, new covenant believers permanently possess the Spirit, who uniquely empowers them for witness. The miracle at Pentecost of speaking in other tongues (v. 4) also reverses the events at the tower of Babel (Gen 11:1–9). Just as that event divided people into diverse nations and languages, so now the arrival of God's salvation brings the nations of the world (v. 5) together to form one new people of God.

2:1 Pentecost. Means "fiftieth day"; the start of the Jewish holiday occurred 50 days after Passover. It was also known as the Festival of Weeks (Deut 16:10) and the Festival of Harvest (Exod 23:16).

2:2 violent wind. Appropriately indicates the Holy Spirit since both the Hebrew and Greek words for "Spirit" can also mean "wind" or "breath" (cf. Gen 2:7; Ezek 37:9; John 3:8).

2:3 tongues of fire. Indicates the fire's shape but also points to the speaking in "tongues" that follows (v. 4). Fire often symbolizes God's presence (Exod 3:2). John the Baptist predicted that the Messiah would baptize with "the Holy Spirit and fire" (Luke 3:16), which symbolizes the Spirit's purging and judging role.

2:4 All of them. Probably the 120 followers of Jesus rather than just the Twelve since the whole church is gathered together in the previous episode (1:15) and since the quotation from Joel speaks of both men and women receiving the Spirit (vv. 17–18). **filled with the Holy Spirit.** As Jesus predicted (1:4–5,8; cf. Luke 24:49). **tongues.** Greek *glōssa*; can mean "languages" (see NIV text note). There is much debate whether *glōssolalia* ("speaking in tongues") refers to human languages or an ecstatic (perhaps angelic) prayer language (see notes on 1 Cor 12:8–10; 13:1; 14:2). Here "tongues" refers to human languages (vv. 6,8,11) since this is a miracle of speaking, not hearing. The speakers, not the hearers, have the Holy Spirit. The Spirit comes in a variety of ways, sometimes accompanied by speaking in tongues (10:46; 19:6) and sometimes not (8:17).

2:5 God-fearing Jews. See notes on v. 11; 10:2. **from every nation.** From all over the Jewish Diaspora ("scattering"; see vv. 9–10). They are present in Jerusalem to worship and celebrate at the festival. Many probably came for Passover and stayed through Pentecost. Others became permanent residents.

2:6–8 Though most Jews throughout the Mediterranean understood Greek as a second (trade) language, the miracle is that the believers were speaking in each group's "native language" (v. 8).

2:9–11 The regions named cover much of the Roman Empire and especially where Jews had emigrated.

2:9 Parthians. From the Parthian Empire on the western frontier of the Roman Empire, from the Tigris River to India. **Medes.** Modern-day Kurds from Media, northeast of Mesopotamia. **Elamites.** From Elam, north of the Persian Gulf (part of modern Iran). **Mesopotamia.** Between the Tigris and Euphrates Rivers (modern-day Iraq). **Judea.** The Jewish homeland, including Judea and Galilee. **Cappadocia, Pontus and Asia.** Parts of Asia Minor (modern Turkey).

2:10 Phrygia and Pamphylia. Parts of Asia Minor (modern Turkey). **Egypt.** Had a large Jewish population. Alexandria, Egypt, was a major center of Jewish learning (see Apollos in 18:24). **Libya.** In north Africa, west of Egypt (modern Libya). **Cyrene.** Capital of Cyrenaica, a province in Libya. **Rome.** Capital of the Roman Empire; like Alexandria, it had one of the largest Jewish populations outside of Israel.

2:11 converts to Judaism. Former Gentiles who became full Jews through circumcision (for males) and by obeying the Mosaic law; also called "proselytes." In Acts Luke also mentions "God-fearers," Gentiles who believe in the God of Israel but have not fully converted (see 10:2 and note). **Cretans.** From the island of Crete in the Mediterranean Sea south of Greece (see 27:7,12–13; Titus 1:5). **Arabs.** From the Nabatean kingdom south and east of Judea, sometimes called "Arabia" (Gal 1:17).

2:14–41 *Peter Addresses the Crowd.* Peter assures the crowd that the disciples are not drunk (it's only 9:00 a.m.!) and confirms that this is the end-time outpouring of the Holy Spirit that the prophet Joel predicted. God's end-time salvation has arrived through the life, death, resurrection, and exaltation to God's right hand of Jesus the Messiah (Ps 110:1). We may outline Peter's speech in three parts: (1) Peter interprets the miracle of tongues in the light of Joel 2:28–32 (vv. 14–21); (2) God fulfills his promises through Jesus, the Messiah from David's line (vv. 22–36); and (3) Peter calls the people to repent and be baptized (vv. 37–40). Peter gives sermons that summarize the gospel message in chs. 3; 4; 5; 10. This is the first of almost 30 speeches in Acts.

2:14–16 Peter serves as spokesperson for the apostles. He first says

are not drunk, as you suppose. It's only nine in the morning![a] 16No, this is what was spoken by the prophet Joel:

17" 'In the last days, God says,
I will pour out my Spirit on all people.[b]
Your sons and daughters will prophesy,[c]
your young men will see visions,
your old men will dream dreams.
18Even on my servants, both men and women,
I will pour out my Spirit in those days,
and they will prophesy.[d]
19I will show wonders in the heavens above
and signs on the earth below,
blood and fire and billows of smoke.
20The sun will be turned to darkness
and the moon to blood[e]
before the coming of the great and glorious day of the Lord.
21And everyone who calls
on the name of the Lord will be saved.'[a][f]

22"Fellow Israelites, listen to this: Jesus of Nazareth was a man accredited by God to you by miracles, wonders and signs,[g] which God did among you through him,[h] as you yourselves know. 23This man was handed over to you by God's deliberate plan and foreknowledge;[i] and you, with the help of wicked men,[b] put him to death by nailing him to the cross.[j] 24But God raised him from the dead,[k] freeing him from the agony of death, because it was impossible for death to keep its hold on him.[l] 25David said about him:

" 'I saw the Lord always before me.
Because he is at my right hand,
I will not be shaken.
26Therefore my heart is glad and my tongue rejoices;
my body also will rest in hope,
27because you will not abandon me to the realm of the dead,
you will not let your holy one see decay.[m]
28You have made known to me the paths of life;
you will fill me with joy in your presence.'[c]

2:15 [a] 1Th 5:7
2:17 [b] Isa 44:3; Jn 7:37-39; Ac 10:45 [c] Ac 21:9
2:18 [d] Ac 21:9-12
2:20 [e] Mt 24:29
2:21 [f] Ro 10:13
2:22 [g] Jn 4:48; Ac 10:38 [h] Jn 3:2
2:23 [i] Lk 22:22; Ac 3:18; 4:28 [j] Lk 24:20; Ac 3:13
2:24 [k] ver 32; 1Co 6:14; 2Co 4:14; Eph 1:20; Col 2:12; Heb 13:20; 1Pe 1:21 [l] Jn 20:9
2:27 [m] ver 31; Ac 13:35

[a] *21* Joel 2:28-32 [b] *23* Or *of those not having the law* (that is, Gentiles) [c] *28* Psalm 16:8-11 (see Septuagint)

what this is not: drunkenness. Then he says what it is: the end-time outpouring of the Holy Spirit.

2:17–18 While in the OT the Spirit empowered individuals for ministry, the hallmark of God's final salvation is the outpouring of the Spirit on "all people," regardless of gender ("sons and daughters ... men and women"), age ("young men ... old men"), or social status ("even on my servants"). **prophesy ... prophesy.** We see here the renewal of the prophetic word, which the rabbis believed ceased with the last of the OT prophets.

2:17 In the last days. With these words Peter emphasizes that the Spirit's coming marks the inauguration of the end times (cf. Isa 32:15; 44:3–4; Jer 31:33–34; Ezek 36:26–27; 39:29). Later in the sermon, Peter clarifies that the pouring out of the Spirit is the result of Jesus' resurrection and exaltation (vv. 32–36). His resurrection is the beginning of the end-time resurrection of the dead (1 Cor 15:20; Col 1:18). **last days.** See Isa 2:2; Mic 4:1; Heb 1:1–2; Jas 5:3; 1 Pet 1:20; 1 John 2:18.

2:19–21 The apocalyptic signs in vv. 19–20 probably refer to the still-future consummation of the kingdom, though some argue that they were fulfilled figuratively on the day of Pentecost or literally at the crucifixion. In any case, Peter intentionally continues the quote through Joel 2:32 to reach the phrase "everyone who calls on the name of the Lord will be saved" (v. 21). "The LORD" in Joel 2:32 is the Lord God, and in Peter's sermon "the Lord" is Jesus, which implicitly affirms his deity.

2:22 miracles, wonders and signs. Evidence that Jesus is the Messiah, God's agent of salvation. The miracles the apostles accomplish in Jesus' name similarly confirm the truth of their message (v. 43; 4:30; 5:12; 6:8; 14:3; 15:12).

2:23 Paradoxically, the death of Jesus, though carried out by "wicked men," was all along part of "God's deliberate plan." This is a major theme throughout Acts (3:15; 4:10; 10:39–40; 13:29–30; 17:31). Peter affirms both God's sovereignty over the events of history and human culpability for evil actions. Though this paradox is not easy to explain, similar statements stand beside each other throughout Scripture.

2:24 The NT views the resurrection as God's vindication that Jesus is who he claims to be.

2:25–31 Peter quotes from Ps 16:8–11, where David expresses confidence that God would not abandon him to the grave and then applies it to Jesus (Acts 2:31; cf. 13:35). Since "David died and was buried" and his body decayed, David must have been speaking as a "prophet" of the "resurrection of the Messiah," whose body did not see decay.

2:29 [n]Ac 7:8,9 [o]1Ki 2:10; Ac 13:36 [p]Ne 3:16
2:30 [q]2Sa 7:12; Ps 132:11
2:31 [r]Ps 16:10
2:32 [s]ver 24 [t]Ac 1:8
2:33 [u]Php 2:9 [v]Mk 16:19 [w]Ac 1:4 [x]Jn 7:39; 14:26 [y]Ac 10:45
2:35 [z]Ps 110:1; Mt 22:44
2:36 [a]Lk 2:11
2:37 [b]Lk 3:10,12,14
2:38 [c]Ac 8:12,16,36,38; 22:16 [d]Lk 24:47; Ac 3:19
2:39 [e]Isa 44:3 [f]Ac 10:45; Eph 2:13
2:40 [g]Dt 32:5
2:42 [h]Ac 1:14
2:43 [i]Ac 5:12

29 “Fellow Israelites, I can tell you confidently that the patriarch[n] David died and was buried,[o] and
his tomb is here[p] to this day. 30 But he was a prophet and knew that God had promised him on oath
that he would place one of his descendants on his throne.[q] 31 Seeing what was to come, he spoke of the
resurrection of the Messiah, that he was not abandoned to the realm of the dead, nor did his body see
decay.[r] 32 God has raised this Jesus to life,[s] and we are all witnesses[t] of it. 33 Exalted[u] to the right hand of
God,[v] he has received from the Father[w] the promised Holy Spirit[x] and has poured out[y] what you now
see and hear. 34 For David did not ascend to heaven, and yet he said,

> “ ‘The Lord said to my Lord:
> “Sit at my right hand
> 35 until I make your enemies
> a footstool for your feet.” ’[a][z]

36 “Therefore let all Israel be assured of this: God has made this Jesus, whom you crucified, both
Lord and Messiah.”[a]

37 When the people heard this, they were cut to the heart and said to Peter and the other apostles,
“Brothers, what shall we do?”[b]

38 Peter replied, “Repent and be baptized,[c] every one of you, in the name of Jesus Christ for the forgiveness of your sins.[d] And you will receive the gift of the Holy Spirit. 39 The promise is for you and your
children[e] and for all who are far off[f]—for all whom the Lord our God will call.”

40 With many other words he warned them; and he pleaded with them, “Save yourselves from this
corrupt generation.”[g] 41 Those who accepted his message were baptized, and about three thousand were
added to their number that day.

The Fellowship of the Believers

42 They devoted themselves to the apostles' teaching and to fellowship, to the breaking of bread and to
prayer.[h] 43 Everyone was filled with awe at the many wonders and signs performed by the apostles.[i] 44 All the

[a] *35* Psalm 110:1

2:29 tomb. Both the OT and Jewish tradition speak of the tomb of David in the City of David on the south side of Jerusalem (1 Kgs 2:10; Neh 3:16). **2:30 oath that he would place one of his descendants on his throne.** Alludes to Ps 132:11, which goes back to the promise to David in 2 Sam 7:11–16 that the Messiah from his line will establish an eternal kingdom. **2:33** Jesus' faithfulness to his Messianic role resulted in his exaltation "to the right hand of God" and a return to the glory he had before the incarnation (Phil 2:6–11). The Spirit guided and empowered Jesus during his earthly ministry (Luke 3:21–22; 4:1,14,18), and now Jesus directs the Spirit. **2:34** Peter cites Ps 110:1 as evidence that David predicted not only Jesus' resurrection (vv. 25–31) but also his exaltation (vv. 33–36). David himself did not ascend to heaven but spoke of God ("the Lord") exalting the Messiah ("my Lord") to sit at his right hand (see note on vv. 19–21). The NT cites and alludes to Ps 110 more than any other OT passage since the early church recognized that it predicts the Messiah's vindication. Jesus cites Ps 110:1 in Luke 20:42–43 to show that the Messiah is more than simply the Son of David. Jesus also alludes to this passage at his trial before the Sanhedrin to affirm that after suffering he will be exalted to God's right hand (Luke 22:69). **2:36** Peter says that at Jesus' ascension, God "made this Jesus ... both Lord and Messiah." Though Jesus was born the Messiah-to-be (Luke 2:11) and "anointed" as Messiah ("Anointed One") at his baptism (Luke 3:21–22; 4:18; cf. Acts 4:27; 10:38), God enthroned him as Messiah when he exalted Jesus to his right hand. **Lord and Messiah.** That is, "the Messiah now reigning as Lord of all" (cf. 10:36). **2:38 Repent and be baptized.** Though Peter does not mention faith, he implies it in the terms "repent" and "be baptized." Faith is often mentioned without repentance (16:31; John 3:16). Both are shorthand expressions that imply the other. **be baptized ... for the forgiveness of your sins.** Does not mean that the waters of baptism save. We are saved by grace through faith (Eph 2:8–9). Yet Jesus commands baptism (Matt 28:19), and it outwardly professes the inward transformation that the Spirit accomplishes (1 Pet 3:21). **baptized ... in the name of Jesus.** Another shorthand expression for the fuller Trinitarian formula in Matt 28:19. **gift of the Holy Spirit.** The Holy Spirit himself, who is given to all believers (Rom 8:9–11; 1 Cor 12:13). **2:39 all who are far off.** Points to the outreach to the Gentiles, a leading theme in Acts. **2:40 With many other words.** Peter's sermon was much longer than Luke reproduces. All the speeches in Acts must be brief summaries since each would take only a few minutes to recite. **2:41** Adding 3,000 to the original 120 begins the church's astonishing growth in these early days, which increases to 5,000 by 4:4 (cf. 2:47; 5:14; 6:1,7; 9:31; 21:20). **2:42–47** *The Fellowship of the Believers.* This is the first major summary of the church's activity. Such summaries are common throughout Acts (see 4:32–37; 5:12–16; 6:7; 9:31; 16:1–5; 19:20 and notes). Luke depicts the Jerusalem church as a loving, caring, and supportive community. **2:42 apostles' teaching.** This likely included Jesus' own teaching (Matt 28:20) and stories about him recalled by the apostles (see the qualification for an apostle in 1:21–22). The apostles were the guardians of this material, which was originally passed down orally and eventually put into written form in our Gospels. **fellowship.** Greek *koinōnia*; participating together toward a common goal. **breaking of bread.** Probably a communal meal followed by the Lord's Supper (v. 46). **prayer.** The church's lifeblood (cf. 1:14,24; 4:31; 6:6). **2:43 many wonders and signs.** Confirm that the apostles are continuing the work of Jesus (1:1), whose miracles in the Gospels evidence

Model of the semicircular Nicanor Gate, a possible location for the "Beautiful" gate where the lame man was placed to beg (Acts 3:2).

believers were together and had everything in common.[j] 45 They sold property
and possessions to give to anyone who
had need.[k] 46 Every day they continued
to meet together in the temple courts.[l]
They broke bread[m] in their homes and
ate together with glad and sincere
hearts, 47 praising God and enjoying the
favor of all the people.[n] And the Lord
added to their number[o] daily those who
were being saved.

Peter Heals a Lame Beggar

3 One day Peter and John[p] were going up to the temple[q] at the time
of prayer—at three in the afternoon.[r]
2 Now a man who was lame from
birth[s] was being carried to the temple
gate[t] called Beautiful, where he was
put every day to beg[u] from those going into the temple courts. 3 When he
saw Peter and John about to enter, he
asked them for money. 4 Peter looked
straight at him, as did John. Then Peter said, "Look at us!" 5 So the man
gave them his attention, expecting to
get something from them.
6 Then Peter said, "Silver or gold I
do not have, but what I do have I give you. In the name of Jesus Christ of Nazareth,[v] walk." 7 Taking
him by the right hand, he helped him up, and instantly the man's feet and ankles became strong. 8 He
jumped to his feet and began to walk. Then he went with them into the temple courts, walking and

2:44 [j] Ac 4:32
2:45 [k] Mt 19:21
2:46 [l] Lk 24:53; Ac 5:21, 42 [m] Ac 20:7
2:47 [n] Ro 14:18 [o] ver 41; Ac 5:14
3:1 [p] Lk 22:8 [q] Ac 2:46 [r] Ps 55:17
3:2 [s] Ac 14:8 [t] Lk 16:20 [u] Jn 9:8
3:6 [v] ver 16; Ac 4:10

the dawn of salvation and the in-breaking power of the kingdom of God (Luke 9:2,11; 10:9; 11:20).

2:44–45 had everything in common. They sold property and possessions. Not communalism or communism since this giving is voluntary (5:4) and since people still retain personal possessions like homes (12:12; 17:5) and property (4:37). A better analogy is that the church views itself as a family, and healthy families take care of their own. See 4:32,34–35.

2:46 continued to meet together in the temple courts. Since the temple was the center of Israel's community life. The believers do not view themselves as starting a new religion but as announcing the arrival of Israel's promised salvation.

2:47 praising God. A major theme throughout Luke-Acts (here; 3:8–9; 4:21; 11:18; 13:48; 16:25; 21:20; Luke 2:20; 5:25–26; 7:16; 13:13; 17:15,18; 18:43; 19:37; 24:53). The arrival of God's end-time salvation is a time for joy and praise.

3:1—5:42 *The Apostolic Witness in Jerusalem.* The first major phase of outreach in Acts and the fulfillment of the first part of 1:8 ("in Jerusalem") appears in these three chapters.

3:1—4:31 *Healing and Preaching in Jerusalem.* Chs. 3–4 form a closely connected unit: a healing miracle (3:1–10) and two speeches by Peter, one before a crowd in the temple (3:11–26) and one before the Sanhedrin after he and John are arrested (4:1–22). After their release, the believers gather and pray, thanking God for the privilege of suffering for him (4:23–31). Luke follows with a second summary (4:32–37), parallel in many respects to 2:42–47.

3:1–10 *Peter Heals a Lame Beggar.* This healing miracle is similar to Jesus' miracles in Luke's Gospel (5:17–26; 7:22) as well as Paul's later healing of a man at Lystra (14:8–11).

3:1 Peter and John. Together with James they were part of Jesus' "inner circle" of disciples in the Gospels (Luke 8:51; 9:28; 22:8) and continue to be key leaders in Acts (1:13; 4:1; 8:14; cf. Gal 2:9). **time of prayer.** One of three daily prayer times set out in Jewish tradition: morning, "three in the afternoon," and sunset. The first two coincided with times of daily sacrifice in the temple.

3:2 gate called Beautiful. Though traditionally identified with the Shushan Gate, it more likely refers to the Nicanor Gate, also called the "Corinthian Gate," a magnificent structure made of Corinthian bronze. It was apparently located on the eastern side of the temple courts and led from the court of the Gentiles into the temple proper (nine gates led into the inner courts). Giving alms to the poor was an important sign of piety in Judaism, and the lame man had a prime spot to receive gifts.

3:6 The apostles heal not by their own power but "in the name of Jesus"—through the authority Jesus gave them. Acts reports the continuing work of Jesus through his church (1:1).

3:8 jumped. Comes from the same root as the verb used in the Greek version of Isa 35:6, where "the lame" will "leap like a deer" at the restoration of creation.

3:8 [w]Ac 14:10
3:9 [x]Ac 4:16,21
3:10 [y]ver 2
3:11 [z]Lk 22:8 [a]Jn 10:23; Ac 5:12
3:13 [b]Ac 5:30 [c]Mt 27:2 [d]Lk 23:4
3:14 [e]Mk 1:24; Ac 4:27 [f]Ac 7:52 [g]Mk 15:11; Lk 23:18-25
3:15 [h]Ac 2:24
3:17 [i]Lk 23:34 [j]Ac 13:27
3:18 [k]Ac 2:23 [l]Lk 24:27 [m]Ac 17:2,3; 26:22,23
3:19 [n]Ac 2:38
3:21 [o]Ac 1:11 [p]Mt 17:11

jumping,[w] and praising God. 9When all the people[x] saw him walking and praising God, 10they recognized him as the same man who used to sit begging at the temple gate called Beautiful,[y] and they were
filled with wonder and amazement at what had happened to him.

Peter Speaks to the Onlookers

11While the man held on to Peter and John,[z] all the people were astonished and came running to
them in the place called Solomon's Colonnade.[a] 12When Peter saw this, he said to them: "Fellow Israelites, why does this surprise you? Why do you stare at us as if by our own power or godliness we had
made this man walk? 13The God of Abraham, Isaac and Jacob, the God of our fathers,[b] has glorified his
servant Jesus. You handed him over to be killed, and you disowned him before Pilate,[c] though he had
decided to let him go.[d] 14You disowned the Holy[e] and Righteous One[f] and asked that a murderer be
released to you.[g] 15You killed the author of life, but God raised him from the dead.[h] We are witnesses
of this. 16By faith in the name of Jesus, this man whom you see and know was made strong. It is Jesus'
name and the faith that comes through him that has completely healed him, as you can all see.
17"Now, fellow Israelites, I know that you acted in ignorance,[i] as did your leaders.[j] 18But this is how
God fulfilled what he had foretold[k] through all the prophets,[l] saying that his Messiah would suffer.[m]
19Repent, then, and turn to God, so that your sins may be wiped out,[n] that times of refreshing may
come from the Lord, 20and that he may send the Messiah, who has been appointed for you — even Jesus.
21Heaven must receive him[o] until the time comes for God to restore everything,[p] as he promised long

3:9 praising God. See note on 2:47.
3:11–26 *Peter Speaks to the Onlookers.* This speech follows a common pattern in Acts and has two main parts: the first part connects the man's healing to Jesus' life, death, and resurrection (vv. 12–16), and the second part calls for a response based on who Jesus is and what he has accomplished (vv. 17–26). The speech introduces several important new titles for Jesus: Righteous One (v. 14), Holy One (v. 14), author of life (v. 15), and prophet like Moses (v. 22).
3:11 Solomon's Colonnade. A large porch in the court of the Gentiles on the eastern side of the temple mount. The group has evidently moved outside the inner courts now to accommodate the growing crowd.
3:13–14 glorified his servant Jesus ... Righteous One. Jesus is the suffering servant of Isa 52:13—53:12.
3:13 The God of Abraham, Isaac and Jacob. Grounds the gospel in its OT roots, a common theme throughout Luke-Acts. **Pilate.** On Pilate's attempt to release Jesus, see Luke 23:4,20; John 19:12.
3:14 Holy ... One. A Messianic title (13:35; Mark 1:24; Luke 1:35; 4:34; John 6:69; 1 John 2:20). **murderer.** Barabbas (Luke 23:18–19,25).
3:15 author. Greek *archēgos*; has a variety of possible meanings, including "author/source/origin," "pioneer/founder," or "ruler/prince." It is translated "Prince" in 5:31 and "pioneer" in Heb 2:10; 12:2. Here the sense appears to be "source of (true) life." Contrasting what evil men did and how God reversed it through the resurrection is a common theme throughout Acts (see note on 2:23). **witnesses.** See 1:8.
3:17 Sins of ignorance had less severe consequences in the OT (Num 15:22–31; cf. 17:30; 1 Cor 2:8; 1 Tim 1:13). The people's ignorance was in not recognizing that Jesus truly is the Messiah.
3:18 The Scripture's predicting that the Messiah would suffer is a major theme in Luke-Acts and is part of Luke's defense that Jesus is indeed the Messiah (17:3; 26:22–23; Luke 24:26,46; see note on 17:3). While Isa 53 is certainly in mind (see Acts 8:32–33 and NIV text note on 8:33), other OT texts predicting the Messiah's suffering include Pss 2:1–2 (see Acts 4:25–26 and NIV text note on 4:26); 16:8–11 (see Acts 2:25–28 and NIV text note on 2:28; Acts 13:35 and NIV text note); 118:22 (see Acts 4:11 and NIV text note).
3:19 Repent ... and turn to God. Repentance is turning away from sin. Faith is turning to God for salvation. See 2:38 and note. **times of refreshing.** The blessings and glories of the Messianic age, synonymous with "the time ... for God to restore everything" (v. 21). Though the kingdom of God has been inaugurated through the life, death, and resurrection of Jesus, it is yet to be consummated in the future.
3:21 Heaven must receive him. Jesus' ascension to and reign at the

Solomon's Colonnade was along the eastern side of the outer courts and was where Peter spoke to the people (Acts 3:11).
Todd Bolen/www.BiblePlaces.com

ago through his holy prophets.[q] 22For Moses said, 'The Lord your God will raise up for you a prophet
like me from among your own people; you must listen to everything he tells you.[r] 23Anyone who does
not listen to him will be completely cut off from their people.'[a][s]

24"Indeed, beginning with Samuel, all the prophets[t] who have spoken have foretold these days. 25And
you are heirs[u] of the prophets and of the covenant[v] God made with your fathers. He said to Abraham,
'Through your offspring all peoples on earth will be blessed.'[b][w] 26When God raised up[x] his servant, he
sent him first[y] to you to bless you by turning each of you from your wicked ways."

Peter and John Before the Sanhedrin

4 The priests and the captain of the temple guard[z] and the Sadducees[a] came up to Peter and John
while they were speaking to the people. 2They were greatly disturbed because the apostles were
teaching the people, proclaiming in Jesus the resurrection of the dead.[b] 3They seized Peter and John
and, because it was evening, they put them in jail[c] until the next day. 4But many who heard the message
believed; so the number of men who believed grew[d] to about five thousand.

5The next day the rulers,[e] the elders and the teachers of the law met in Jerusalem. 6Annas the high
priest was there, and so were Caiaphas,[f] John, Alexander and others of the high priest's family. 7They
had Peter and John brought before them and began to question them: "By what power or what name
did you do this?"

8Then Peter, filled with the Holy Spirit, said to them: "Rulers and elders of the people![g] 9If we are
being called to account today for an act of kindness shown to a man who was lame[h] and are being
asked how he was healed, 10then know this, you and all the people of Israel: It is by the name of Jesus
Christ of Nazareth, whom you crucified but whom God raised from the dead,[i] that this man stands
before you healed. 11Jesus is

> " 'the stone you builders rejected,
> which has become the cornerstone.'[c][j]

3:21 [q] Lk 1:70
3:22 [r] Dt 18:15,18; Ac 7:37
3:23 [s] Dt 18:19
3:24 [t] Lk 24:27
3:25 [u] Ac 2:39 [v] Ro 9:4,5 [w] Ge 12:3; 22:18; 26:4; 28:14
3:26 [x] ver 22; Ac 2:24 [y] Ac 13:46; Ro 1:16
4:1 [z] Lk 22:4 [a] Mt 3:7
4:2 [b] Ac 17:18
4:3 [c] Ac 5:18
4:4 [d] Ac 2:41
4:5 [e] Lk 23:13
4:6 [f] Mt 26:3; Lk 3:2
4:8 [g] ver 5; Lk 23:13
4:9 [h] Ac 3:6
4:10 [i] Ac 2:24
4:11 [j] Ps 118:22; Isa 28:16; Mt 21:42

[a] *23* Deut. 18:15,18,19 [b] *25* Gen. 22:18; 26:4 [c] *11* Psalm 118:22

right hand of God (see 2:33,34,36 and notes) represents both his vindication as the Messiah and the interim period between his first coming and second coming.

3:22 Jesus is a prophet like Moses (cf. 7:37), which fulfills Deut 18:15,18 and warns against rejecting the one who speaks for God. Jesus' role as one who is both a prophet and more than a prophet is an important theme in Luke's Gospel (Luke 4:24; 7:16,39; 11:47–52; 13:33; 24:19–21).

3:23 cut off from their people. Lose status as part of the covenant people of God (cf. Lev 23:29).

3:24 all the prophets. See Luke 24:26–27. The Jews viewed Samuel as the first of the major line of Israel's prophets. He also represented the transition from the period of judges to the period of kings (and the beginning of the Davidic dynasty).

3:25 offspring. Singular and ultimately refers to Jesus, a point Paul makes in Gal 3:16 (see note). Though Israel sought to jealously guard God's blessings, the promise to Abraham was that through the Messiah "all peoples on earth will be blessed" (Gen 22:18; cf. Gen 12:3; 26:4; 28:14).

3:26 first to you. As the covenant people of God, Israel had priority in God's plan of salvation made available through the Messiah (13:46; Rom 1:16).

4:1–22 *Peter and John Before the Sanhedrin.* Peter and John's arrest for preaching in the temple marks the beginning of a pattern of persecution against the church that continues throughout Acts. Yet it also provides another opportunity to proclaim the Good News and to demonstrate the unstoppable progress of the gospel of Jesus.

4:1 This action against Peter and John comes from the temple authorities. **priests.** Those on duty at the temple that week (Luke 1:23). **captain.** Second to the high priest in authority over the temple precinct. **temple guard.** A police force that kept order (5:24,26; Luke 22:4,52). The presence of Jewish guards to handle disturbances prevented Gentile Roman soldiers from defiling the temple sanctuary. **Sadducees.** The religious party that dominated the priestly leadership and the Sanhedrin (see notes on v. 5; Matt 3:7; Luke 20:27).

4:2 The Sadducees did not believe in the resurrection, so the preaching about Jesus' resurrection particularly disturbed them (23:6–8; see Luke 20:27 and note).

4:4 Another summary of the remarkable growth of the church (see 2:41; 5:14; 6:7). **men.** Greek *andres*; often means males, so this may mean 5,000 family units—phenomenal growth since the 3,000 who were saved on the day of Pentecost (2:41).

4:5 rulers. Ruling priests. **elders.** Lay leaders. **teachers of the law.** Also called "scribes" (see notes on Matt 2:4; 5:20). These three groups comprise the Sanhedrin, the 71-member Jewish high council (v. 15; see notes on v. 1; Matt 16:21; 26:3; Mark 14:55; John 11:47).

4:6 Annas the high priest. The former high priest (who served from AD 6–15) and father-in-law of Caiaphas, the official high priest (from AD 18–36). The Romans had deposed Annas, but he still carried enormous influence, so Luke rightly refers to him as "high priest" (cf. Luke 3:2; John 18:13,24). **John, Alexander.** Identities uncertain; probably influential members of the high priest's family.

4:8 Peter is "filled with the Holy Spirit," who empowers and guides believers throughout Acts (1:8; 2:4). Jesus promised that the Spirit would give them words to say in such circumstances (Luke 12:11–12).

4:10 This is the third speech in which Peter proclaims that in the resurrection God vindicated Jesus, whom Israel unjustly put to death (2:23–24; 3:15; cf. 10:39–40; 13:29–30; 17:31).

4:11 Peter quotes Ps 118:22 to show that Scripture predicted the vindication of the rejected Messiah. Jesus quoted this same passage after the parable of the wicked tenant farmers, which was directed against these same leaders of Israel (Luke 20:17 parallels; cf. Isa 28:16; 1 Pet 2:7).

4:12 [k]Mt 1:21; Ac 10:43; 1Ti 2:5
4:13 [l]Lk 22:8 [m]Mt 11:25
4:15 [n]Mt 5:22
4:16 [o]Jn 11:47 [p]Ac 3:6-10
4:18 [q]Ac 5:40
4:19 [r]Ac 5:29
4:21 [s]Ac 5:26 [t]Mt 9:8
4:25 [u]Ac 1:16
4:26 [v]Ps 2:1,2; Da 9:25; Lk 4:18; Ac 10:38; Heb 1:9
4:27 [w]Mt 14:1 [x]Mt 27:2; Lk 23:12 [y]ver 30
4:28 [z]Ac 2:23
4:29 [a]ver 13,31; Ac 9:27; 14:3; Php 1:14
4:30 [b]Jn 4:48 [c]ver 27

12 Salvation is found in no one else, for there is no other name under heaven given to mankind by which we must be saved."[k]

13 When they saw the courage of Peter and John[l] and realized that they were unschooled, ordinary men,[m] they were astonished and they took note that these men had been with Jesus. 14 But since they could see the man who had been healed standing there with them, there was nothing they could say. 15 So they ordered them to withdraw from the Sanhedrin[n] and then conferred together. 16 "What are we going to do with these men?"[o] they asked. "Everyone living in Jerusalem knows they have performed a notable sign,[p] and we cannot deny it. 17 But to stop this thing from spreading any further among the people, we must warn them to speak no longer to anyone in this name."

18 Then they called them in again and commanded them not to speak or teach at all in the name of Jesus.[q] 19 But Peter and John replied, "Which is right in God's eyes: to listen to you, or to him?[r] You be the judges! 20 As for us, we cannot help speaking about what we have seen and heard."

21 After further threats they let them go. They could not decide how to punish them, because all the people[s] were praising God[t] for what had happened. 22 For the man who was miraculously healed was over forty years old.

The Believers Pray

23 On their release, Peter and John went back to their own people and reported all that the chief priests and the elders had said to them. 24 When they heard this, they raised their voices together in prayer to God. "Sovereign Lord," they said, "you made the heavens and the earth and the sea, and everything in them. 25 You spoke by the Holy Spirit through the mouth of your servant, our father David:[u]

> " 'Why do the nations rage
> and the peoples plot in vain?
> 26 The kings of the earth rise up
> and the rulers band together
> against the Lord
> and against his anointed one.[a,b][v]

27 Indeed Herod[w] and Pontius Pilate[x] met together with the Gentiles and the people of Israel in this city to conspire against your holy servant Jesus,[y] whom you anointed. 28 They did what your power and will had decided beforehand should happen.[z] 29 Now, Lord, consider their threats and enable your servants to speak your word with great boldness.[a] 30 Stretch out your hand to heal and perform signs and wonders[b] through the name of your holy servant Jesus."[c]

a 26 That is, Messiah or Christ *b* 26 Psalm 2:1,2

4:12 There is no other means of salvation than Jesus the Messiah (Matt 11:27; John 3:18; 14:6; 1 Tim 2:5; 1 John 5:12). Yet this "exclusive" salvation is fully inclusive: available to all who believe (10:43).

4:13 unschooled, ordinary men. The apostles had no formal rabbinic training and were not religious authorities.

4:16–17 Though the leaders recognize the reality of the miracle, they are more interested in protecting their own authority than submitting to God's purpose (cf. Luke 20:5–7).

4:19–20 Peter and John are compelled to obey God rather than any human authority (see note on 5:29).

4:21 In contrast to the apostles, fear of the people rather than fear of God motivates the religious leaders (5:26; cf. Luke 19:47–48; 22:2).

4:23–31 *The Believers Pray.* When Peter and John return to their fellow believers and report what happened, the church turns to God in prayer. Though they have no political power or influence, they have the greatest source of strength in the universe: the awesome Creator, God. The prayer, which interprets Ps 2 as a prophecy of the Messiah spoken by David, has two main parts: acknowledgment of God's sovereign character and saving work through Jesus the Messiah (vv. 24–28), and request for greater boldness and power to serve (vv. 29–30). God then affirms their prayer (v. 31) through external signs (a physical shaking) and internal power ("filled with the Holy Spirit and spoke the word of God boldly").

4:25–28 Ps 2 describes the surrounding nations rebelling against the Davidic king (see Introduction to Ps 2). God enthrones and vindicates his anointed one, warning these nations against rebellion. The believers apply the psalm to the actions of King Herod, Pontius Pilate, the Gentiles (Roman soldiers), and "the people of Israel" (the religious leaders) against Jesus, God's Anointed One (cf. Luke 23). Their evil actions turned out to be exactly what God's "power and will had decided beforehand should happen." Though God did not will their evil actions, his plan all along was to use their evil actions to accomplish his salvation.

4:25 You [God] spoke by the Holy Spirit through the mouth of ... David. A remarkable statement expressing the nature of biblical inspiration.

4:29 The apostles pray not for safety but "to speak your word with great boldness."

31After they prayed, the place where they were meeting was shaken.[d] And they were all filled with the
Holy Spirit and spoke the word of God boldly.[e]

The Believers Share Their Possessions

32All the believers were one in heart and mind. No one claimed that any of their possessions was
their own, but they shared everything they had.[f] 33With great power the apostles continued to testify[g]
to the resurrection[h] of the Lord Jesus. And God's grace was so powerfully at work in them all 34that
there were no needy persons among them. For from time to time those who owned land or houses sold
them,[i] brought the money from the sales 35and put it at the apostles' feet,[j] and it was distributed to
anyone who had need.[k]

36Joseph, a Levite from Cyprus, whom the apostles called Barnabas[l] (which means "son of encouragement"), 37sold a field he owned and brought the money and put it at the apostles' feet.[m]

Ananias and Sapphira

5 Now a man named Ananias, together with his wife Sapphira, also sold a piece of property. 2With
his wife's full knowledge he kept back part of the money for himself, but brought the rest and put
it at the apostles' feet.[n]

3Then Peter said, "Ananias, how is it that Satan[o] has so filled your heart[p] that you have lied to the
Holy Spirit[q] and have kept for yourself some of the money you received for the land? 4Didn't it belong
to you before it was sold? And after it was sold, wasn't the money at your disposal? What made you think
of doing such a thing? You have not lied just to human beings but to God."

5When Ananias heard this, he fell down and died.[r] And great fear[s] seized all who heard what had
happened. 6Then some young men came forward, wrapped up his body,[t] and carried him out and
buried him.

7About three hours later his wife came in, not knowing what had happened. 8Peter asked her, "Tell
me, is this the price you and Ananias got for the land?"

"Yes," she said, "that is the price."[u]

9Peter said to her, "How could you conspire to test the Spirit of the Lord?[v] Listen! The feet of the men
who buried your husband are at the door, and they will carry you out also."

10At that moment she fell down at his feet and died.[w] Then the young men came in and, finding her
dead, carried her out and buried her beside her husband. 11Great fear[x] seized the whole church and all
who heard about these events.

4:31 [d] Ac 2:2 [e] ver 29
4:32 [f] Ac 2:44
4:33 [g] Lk 24:48 [h] Ac 1:22
4:34 [i] Mt 19:21; Ac 2:45
4:35 [j] ver 37; Ac 5:2 [k] Ac 2:45; 6:1
4:36 [l] Ac 9:27; 1Co 9:6
4:37 [m] ver 35; Ac 5:2
5:2 [n] Ac 4:35,37
5:3 [o] Mt 4:10 [p] Jn 13:2, 27 [q] ver 9
5:5 [r] ver 10 [s] ver 11
5:6 [t] Jn 19:40
5:8 [u] ver 2
5:9 [v] ver 3
5:10 [w] ver 5
5:11 [x] ver 5; Ac 19:17

4:31 place … was shaken. Evidence of God's presence and affirmation. **filled with the Holy Spirit.** Cf. 2:4.

4:32—5:16 *Community Life in Jerusalem.* Luke's account of the healing of the lame beggar and its aftermath of persecution (3:1—4:31) is followed by several episodes illustrating the nature of the church as a community of love, unity, purity, and healing.

4:32–37 *The Believers Share Their Possessions.* This is another summary statement of the growth and witness of the church (see 2:42–47 and note). While mentioning the apostles' powerful witness (v. 33), this focuses primarily on the community's unity and generosity with one another (vv. 32–35). The positive example of Barnabas (vv. 36–37) and the negative one of Ananias and Sapphira (5:1–11) illustrate this.

4:32 shared everything. See note on 2:44–45.

4:34 no needy persons among them. The church meets God's requirement in Deut 15:4. Like a family, they are willing to give up personal possessions to meet the needs of one another (v. 35). This is voluntary, not forced or coerced, sharing (5:4; see note on 2:44–45).

4:36 Barnabas … "son of encouragement." Joseph's nickname is well earned. Throughout Acts he is a reconciler and bridge-builder among people and communities (9:27; 11:22–26,30; 13:2; 15:1–2,37). **Levite.** Traditionally, a Levite would not own inherited land in Israel (Num 18:20; Deut 10:9), so where did Barnabas get his property? There are various possibilities: (1) Perhaps Jews did not enforce these OT laws by the first century; (2) Barnabas may have been buying and selling land for business; (3) Barnabas may have inherited land on his wife's side; (4) this land may have been in Cyprus, where the prohibition did not apply. **Cyprus.** Where Barnabas is from, where he and Paul go on their first missionary journey (13:4–6), and where Barnabas and John Mark return after Barnabas separates from Paul (15:39).

5:1–11 *Ananias and Sapphira.* In strong contrast to the positive example of giving that Barnabas sets (4:36–37), Ananias and Sapphira are a negative example, and God judges them severely. Their sin is not the small amount of their gift or the low percentage they give; it is their deception (vv. 4,9). God powerfully preserves his church's purity, something particularly important in these early days. For similar severe punishment for rebellion or deception in the OT, see Lev 10:1–5; Josh 7:16–26.

5:3–4 Peter attributes Ananias's actions to the influence of Satan, the great deceiver (Gen 3:4; John 8:44; Rev 12:9). **lied to the Holy Spirit … lied … to God.** Lying to the Holy Spirit is the same as lying to God, evidence that the Holy Spirit is both God and a person.

5:4 wasn't the money at your disposal? Their sin is not withholding part of the money, which is their right, but conspiring to deceive.

5:11 Great fear. How people ought to react when they encounter God's awesome purity and perfection (v. 5; cf. Isa 6:5; Heb 10:31).

5:12 [y]Ac 2:43 [z]Ac 4:32 [a]Ac 3:11
5:13 [b]Ac 2:47; 4:21
5:15 [c]Ac 19:12
5:16 [d]Mk 16:17
5:17 [e]Ac 15:5 [f]Ac 4:1
5:18 [g]Ac 4:3
5:19 [h]Mt 1:20; Lk 1:11; Ac 8:26; 27:23 [i]Ac 16:26
5:20 [j]Jn 6:63,68
5:21 [k]Ac 4:5,6 [l]ver 27, 34,41; Mt 5:22
5:24 [m]Ac 4:1
5:26 [n]Ac 4:21
5:27 [o]Mt 5:22
5:28 [p]Ac 4:18 [q]Mt 23:35; 27:25; Ac 2:23,36; 3:14,15; 7:52
5:29 [r]Ac 4:19

The Apostles Heal Many

12The apostles performed many signs and wonders[y] among the people. And all the believers used to
meet together[z] in Solomon's Colonnade.[a] 13No one else dared join them, even though they were highly
regarded by the people.[b] 14Nevertheless, more and more men and women believed in the Lord and were
added to their number. 15As a result, people brought the sick into the streets and laid them on beds and
mats so that at least Peter's shadow might fall on some of them as he passed by.[c] 16Crowds gathered
also from the towns around Jerusalem, bringing their sick and those tormented by impure spirits, and
all of them were healed.[d]

The Apostles Persecuted

17Then the high priest and all his associates, who were members of the party[e] of the Sadducees,[f] were
filled with jealousy. 18They arrested the apostles and put them in the public jail.[g] 19But during the night
an angel[h] of the Lord opened the doors of the jail[i] and brought them out. 20"Go, stand in the temple
courts," he said, "and tell the people all about this new life."[j]
21At daybreak they entered the temple courts, as they had been told, and began to teach the people.
When the high priest and his associates[k] arrived, they called together the Sanhedrin[l]—the full
assembly of the elders of Israel—and sent to the jail for the apostles. 22But on arriving at the jail, the
officers did not find them there. So they went back and reported, 23"We found the jail securely locked,
with the guards standing at the doors; but when we opened them, we found no one inside." 24On hearing this report, the captain of the temple guard and the chief priests[m] were at a loss, wondering what
this might lead to.
25Then someone came and said, "Look! The men you put in jail are standing in the temple courts
teaching the people." 26At that, the captain went with his officers and brought the apostles. They did
not use force, because they feared that the people[n] would stone them.
27The apostles were brought in and made to appear before the Sanhedrin[o] to be questioned by the
high priest. 28"We gave you strict orders not to teach in this name,"[p] he said. "Yet you have filled Jerusalem with your teaching and are determined to make us guilty of this man's blood."[q]
29Peter and the other apostles replied: "We must obey God rather than human beings![r] 30The God

---

5:12–16 *The Apostles Heal Many.* This summary illustrates key characteristics of the church: unity, purity, and spiritual authority through the Spirit (see notes on 2:42–47; 4:32–37). The apostles' miracles of healing (vv. 12,15–16) and exorcism (v. 16) recall similar miracles of Jesus, which demonstrate the power and presence of the kingdom of God (Luke 7:20–23; 11:20).

5:12 Solomon's Colonnade. See note on 3:11.

5:13–14 No one else dared join them ... Nevertheless, more and more men and women believed in the Lord and were added to their number. Because of fear and awe (vv. 5,11). This apparent paradox shows that the church's growth is not superficial but comes from those who weigh the cost and are truly committed. Pruning bad growth (like Ananias and Sapphira) produces new, good growth (John 15:1–11). For an account of the church's phenomenal growth, see 2:47; 4:4; 6:1,7; 9:31; 21:20.

5:15 Peter's shadow. Illustrates the people's incredible awe and respect for the apostles. The shadow did not possess magical powers, but, as in the case of the woman who touched Jesus' garment (Mark 5:28; Luke 8:44) and those healed by Paul's handkerchiefs (Acts 19:12), the healing resulted from their faith. On the relationship between faith and healing, see note on Jas 5:15.

5:17–42 *The Apostles Persecuted.* A second round of persecution (see 4:1–22) begins as the Jerusalem leaders arrest all 12 apostles. Their motivation is "jealousy" (v. 17; cf. 13:45; 17:5) because of the apostles' growing influence among the people. The key themes are the remarkable boldness of the apostles in the face of great danger (v. 29), the unstoppable progress of the gospel because God is at work (v. 39), and the privilege and joy of suffering for Christ (v. 41).

5:17 high priest. See note on 4:6. **his associates.** Members of his family and other ruling priests. **Sadducees.** The dominant political party among the priesthood, the Jerusalem aristocracy, and the Sanhedrin. See notes on 4:1,2.

5:19 angel. One similarly releases Peter in 12:6–11. Angels also appear in Acts as messengers from God (1:10–11; 8:26; 10:3–7,22; 11:13–14; 27:23–24); in the case of Herod Agrippa, an angel is an agent of divine judgment (12:23).

5:21–26 The whole scene has an air of comedy about it: with formal pomp and ritual, the elders gather and call for the prisoners only to discover that the jail is locked but no one is inside. After a dramatic pause (v. 24), a messenger announces that the apostles are once again preaching in the temple courts! Jail bars are useless against the unstoppable progress of the gospel—the central theme of Acts.

5:21 Sanhedrin. Led by the high priest, it was the highest leadership council in Israel. It had significant authority over Jewish political, as well as religious, affairs. See note on 4:5.

5:29 We must obey God rather than human beings! While Christians must submit to government authorities (Rom 13:1–7), the exception is when human commands directly contradict God's commands.

5:30–32 Peter summarizes his message at Pentecost (2:22–39): through Jesus' resurrection, exaltation, and the pouring out of the Spirit, God vindicated his Messiah as "Prince and Savior." God intended this to "bring Israel to repentance and forgive their sins."

5:30 Far from shying away from the high priest's accusation (v. 28), Peter boldly accuses the leaders of killing God's Messiah. **hanging him on a cross.** Alludes to Deut 21:23: "anyone who is hung on a pole is under God's curse" (cf. 10:39; 13:29). This passage originally referred to the shame of impalement on a stake without a noble burial, but Christians came to see it as evidence that Jesus became a curse for us by taking the penalty of our sins (see Gal 3:13).

of our ancestors[s] raised Jesus from the dead[t]—whom you killed by hanging him on a cross.[u] 31 God
exalted him to his own right hand[v] as Prince and Savior[w] that he might bring Israel to repentance and
forgive their sins.[x] 32 We are witnesses of these things,[y] and so is the Holy Spirit,[z] whom God has given
to those who obey him."

33 When they heard this, they were furious[a] and wanted to put them to death. 34 But a Pharisee named
Gamaliel,[b] a teacher of the law,[c] who was honored by all the people, stood up in the Sanhedrin and ordered that the men be put outside for a little while. 35 Then he addressed the Sanhedrin: "Men of Israel,
consider carefully what you intend to do to these men. 36 Some time ago Theudas appeared, claiming
to be somebody, and about four hundred men rallied to him. He was killed, all his followers were dispersed, and it all came to nothing. 37 After him, Judas the Galilean appeared in the days of the census[d]
and led a band of people in revolt. He too was killed, and all his followers were scattered. 38 Therefore,
in the present case I advise you: Leave these men alone! Let them go! For if their purpose or activity is
of human origin, it will fail.[e] 39 But if it is from God, you will not be able to stop these men; you will
only find yourselves fighting against God."[f]

40 His speech persuaded them. They called the apostles in and had them flogged.[g] Then they ordered
them not to speak in the name of Jesus, and let them go.

41 The apostles left the Sanhedrin, rejoicing[h] because they had been counted worthy of suffering disgrace for the Name.[i] 42 Day after day, in the temple courts[j] and from house to house, they never stopped
teaching and proclaiming the good news that Jesus is the Messiah.

The Choosing of the Seven

6 In those days when the number of disciples was increasing,[k] the Hellenistic Jews[a][l] among them
complained against the Hebraic Jews because their widows[m] were being overlooked in the daily
distribution of food.[n] 2 So the Twelve gathered all the disciples together and said, "It would not be right
for us to neglect the ministry of the word of God in order to wait on tables. 3 Brothers and sisters,[o]
choose seven men from among you who are known to be full of the Spirit and wisdom. We will turn
this responsibility over to them 4 and will give our attention to prayer[p] and the ministry of the word."

5 This proposal pleased the whole group. They chose Stephen,[q] a man full of faith and of the Holy

5:30 [s]Ac 3:13 [t]Ac 2:24 [u]Ac 10:39; 13:29; Gal 3:13; 1Pe 2:24
5:31 [v]Ac 2:33 [w]Lk 2:11 [x]Mt 1:21; Lk 24:47; Ac 2:38
5:32 [y]Lk 24:48 [z]Jn 15:26
5:33 [a]Ac 2:37; 7:54
5:34 [b]Ac 22:3 [c]Lk 2:46
5:37 [d]Lk 2:1,2
5:38 [e]Mt 15:13
5:39 [f]Pr 21:30; Ac 7:51; 11:17
5:40 [g]Mt 10:17
5:41 [h]Mt 5:12 [i]Jn 15:21
5:42 [j]Ac 2:46
6:1 [k]Ac 2:41 [l]Ac 9:29 [m]Ac 9:39,41 [n]Ac 4:35
6:3 [o]Ac 1:16
6:4 [p]Ac 1:14
6:5 [q]ver 8; Ac 11:19

[a] *1* That is, Jews who had adopted the Greek language and culture

5:34 Though the Sadducees were in the majority in the Sanhedrin, Pharisees also had an influential voice. **Gamaliel.** One of the leading rabbis of his day and Saul's (Paul's) mentor (22:3).

5:36–38 Gamaliel gives the example of two revolutionaries to show that the Christian movement will surely fail if God is not behind it.

5:36 Theudas. An unknown rebel, though the Jewish historian Josephus mentions another man by that name who led a revolt at a later time (AD 44–46).

5:37 Judas the Galilean. Led a tax revolt against the Romans around AD 6. His actions inspired the later Zealot movement that provoked the Jewish war of AD 66–73.

5:39 Ironically, the growth of the church throughout Acts confirms Gamaliel's assertion as the gospel advances unhindered.

5:40 flogged. Likely administered with a leather whip and may have been the maximum 39 lashes (2 Cor 11:24; cf. Deut 25:3). The Jewish Mishnah says to administer one-third of such blows on the chest and two-thirds on the back.

5:41 The apostles consider it a privilege to suffer "for the Name" (the name represents the person) because Jesus suffered so much for them. For joy in the face of suffering, see Matt 5:11–12; Rom 5:3; Col 1:24; Jas 1:2–3; 1 Pet 4:13.

5:42 never stopped. The Sanhedrin's threat has no effect on the apostles, who continue to boldly proclaim the message.

6:1—12:24 *The Witness Beyond Jerusalem.* This second major phase of outreach in Acts represents the fulfillment of the second part of 1:8 ("in all Judea and Samaria"). The martyrdom of Stephen (7:54–60) is the precipitating factor that scatters the Jerusalem believers and impels them to proclaim the gospel beyond the bounds of Jerusalem.

6:1–7 *The Choosing of the Seven.* The first internal conflict in the Jerusalem church that Luke describes involves neglecting Greek-speaking widows when daily distributing food within the Christian community. The apostles stay faithful to their calling to preach the gospel and still resolve the issue by encouraging the community to choose seven men to help distribute the food. The episode illustrates the church's care for its own and also sets the stage for Stephen's arrest and martyrdom (6:8—8:1a), the church's dispersion and expanded witness (8:1b–3), and Philip's evangelistic outreach (8:4–40).

6:1 The church's rapid growth creates growing pains. **Hellenistic Jews.** Greek-speaking Jews who returned to the promised land of Israel after living in the diaspora. See NIV text note. **Hebraic Jews.** Aramaic-speaking Jews. **widows.** Among the most vulnerable members of society; the Bible often singles them out as needing special care (Deut 14:29; Ps 68:5; Isa 10:2; Luke 20:47; 1 Tim 5:3; Jas 1:27).

6:2 The apostles know they must not "neglect the ministry of the word of God" since that is the primary commission Jesus gave them (1:8; 2:42; 4:2; 5:25,42; 6:4).

6:3 full of the Spirit and wisdom. Key qualities for Christian leadership. Stephen is "full of faith and of the Holy Spirit" (v. 5) and "full of God's grace and power" (v. 8). All of these attributes come through the Holy Spirit's presence and power.

6:5 The Seven all have Greek names, indicating that they are from the Hellenistic-Jewish community. It was important to choose Christian leadership from *within* that community to reflect the church's

6:5 [r]Ac 11:24 [s]Ac 8:5-40; 21:8
6:6 [t]Ac 1:24; 8:17; 13:3; 2Ti 1:6 [u]Nu 8:10; Ac 9:17; 1Ti 4:14
6:7 [v]Ac 12:24; 19:20
6:8 [w]Jn 4:48
6:9 [x]Mt 27:32 [y]Ac 15:23, 41; 22:3; 23:34 [z]Ac 2:9
6:10 [a]Lk 21:15
6:11 [b]1Ki 21:10 [c]Mt 26:59-61
6:12 [d]Mt 5:22
6:13 [e]Ac 21:28
6:14 [f]Ac 15:1; 21:21; 26:3; 28:17
6:15 [g]Mt 5:22
7:2 [h]Ac 22:1 [i]Ps 29:3 [j]Ge 11:31; 15:7
7:3 [k]Ge 12:1

Spirit;[r] also Philip,[s] Procorus, Nicanor, Timon, Parmenas, and Nicolas from Antioch, a convert to Judaism. 6 They presented these men to the apostles, who prayed[t] and laid their hands on them.[u]

7 So the word of God spread.[v] The number of disciples in Jerusalem increased rapidly, and a large number of priests became obedient to the faith.

Stephen Seized

8 Now Stephen, a man full of God's grace and power, performed great wonders and signs[w] among the people. 9 Opposition arose, however, from members of the Synagogue of the Freedmen (as it was called) — Jews of Cyrene[x] and Alexandria as well as the provinces of Cilicia[y] and Asia[z] — who began to argue with Stephen. 10 But they could not stand up against the wisdom the Spirit gave him as he spoke.[a]

11 Then they secretly[b] persuaded some men to say, "We have heard Stephen speak blasphemous words against Moses and against God."[c]

12 So they stirred up the people and the elders and the teachers of the law. They seized Stephen and brought him before the Sanhedrin.[d] 13 They produced false witnesses, who testified, "This fellow never stops speaking against this holy place[e] and against the law. 14 For we have heard him say that this Jesus of Nazareth will destroy this place and change the customs Moses handed down to us."[f]

15 All who were sitting in the Sanhedrin[g] looked intently at Stephen, and they saw that his face was like the face of an angel.

Stephen's Speech to the Sanhedrin

7 Then the high priest asked Stephen, "Are these charges true?"

2 To this he replied: "Brothers and fathers,[h] listen to me! The God of glory[i] appeared to our father Abraham while he was still in Mesopotamia, before he lived in Harran.[j] 3 'Leave your country and your people,' God said, 'and go to the land I will show you.'[a][k]

[a] *3* Gen. 12:1

diversity. The narratives that follow concern two of the Seven: Stephen (6:8 — 8:1a) and Philip (8:4 – 40). **convert to Judaism.** A former Gentile who at some point received circumcision and entered the covenant people of Israel.

6:6 The community chose the Seven, but the apostles "laid their hands on them," a sign of affirmation and commissioning (see 13:3 and note).

6:7 Another summary of the church's remarkable growth (2:41,47; 4:4; 5:14; 6:1; 9:31; 12:24; 16:5; 19:20). **a large number of priests.** Remarkably, even those involved in the old covenant's sacrificial system are beginning to recognize that Jesus the Messiah has inaugurated the new covenant.

6:8 — 7:60 *Stephen's Arrest and Martyrdom.* Stephen's martyrdom, the first in Acts, was a great tragedy and crisis for the church. Yet through this event, God propelled the gospel beyond the bounds of Jerusalem and prepared for its expansion to the ends of the earth. Throughout Acts we see the theme that God takes even sinful human actions and accomplishes his purposes through them (3:15; 4:10; 10:39 – 40; 13:29 – 30).

6:8 – 15 *Stephen Seized.* Though chosen as one of the Seven to help distribute food, Stephen is also a gifted evangelist and boldly proclaims the gospel, provoking opposition from the Greek-speaking Jewish community.

6:8 This is the first reference in Acts to someone other than the apostles performing "wonders and signs" (cf. 2:43; 3:7 – 8; 5:12,15 – 16). This displays Stephen's spiritual gifts and filling by the Holy Spirit (see note on v. 3).

6:9 Synagogue of the Freedmen. Evidently made up of freed slaves from various Hellenistic cities and provinces: Cyrene (in north Africa), Alexandria (in Egypt), Cilicia (Paul's home province in south-central Turkey), and Asia (Roman province in western Turkey).

6:13 – 14 this holy place ... this place. The temple. People similarly accused Jesus of threatening the temple (Matt 26:61; Mark 14:58; 15:29), perhaps distorting his prediction of its destruction (Mark 13:2; Luke 21:6; cf. John 2:19). People later make these same accusations against Paul (21:28; 24:6; 25:7 – 8). The temple charge may be related to the Christian claims that Jesus' sacrificial death completes and fulfills the temple's sacrificial system (Heb 10:1 – 4,11 – 14) and that Jesus and his body, the church, represent the new temple of God (Luke 20:17; 1 Cor 3:16; Eph 2:20 – 22).

6:14 change the customs Moses handed down to us. This accusation may come from the Christian claim that salvation comes through faith in Christ rather than by the works of the law (Rom 3:28; Gal 2:16). It may also relate to Jesus' supposed overruling of the OT law (Mark 7:19; Luke 6:5,7; 13:14).

6:15 like the face of an angel. Recalls Moses' face at Mount Sinai (Exod 34:29 – 35) and Jesus' face at the transfiguration (Luke 9:29).

7:1 – 53 *Stephen's Speech to the Sanhedrin.* Stephen's speech is the longest in Acts. It is not really his defense before his accusers but rather summarizes Israel's history and indicts the nation for rejecting the Messiah. The defendant becomes the prosecuting attorney! The speech has two central themes: (1) Israel repeatedly rejected God's messengers, climaxing in their rejecting the Messiah. (2) God is sovereign and majestic, and temples made with human hands cannot contain him. Israel's leadership was trying to put God in a box and control him for their own means. The historical summary in the speech has four main parts: (1) Abraham's call (vv. 2 – 8), (2) the story of Joseph (vv. 9 – 16), (3) Moses and the deliverance from Egypt (vv. 17 – 44), and (4) a summary from the conquest of Canaan to Solomon (vv. 45 – 47).

7:2 – 8 Stephen appropriately starts his speech with God's call of Abraham and his covenant with him, the foundation of Israel's theological self-identity.

7:2 Mesopotamia. From Genesis it is not clear whether Abraham's original call came in Ur (in Mesopotamia) or later in Harran (Gen 12:1; 15:7). Stephen says it was the former.

Replica of the Theodotus inscription found in Jerusalem, written in Greek from early first century AD. The inscription mentions the priest Theodotus, who established a synagogue that is dated to late in the Second Temple period. Members from a similar synagogue were bringing opposition to Stephen in Acts 6:9.

Todd Bolen/www.BiblePlaces.com

4 "So he left the land of the Chaldeans and settled in Harran. After the death of his father, God sent
him to this land where you are now living.[l] 5 He gave him no inheritance here, not even enough ground
to set his foot on. But God promised him that he and his descendants after him would possess the land,[m]
even though at that time Abraham had no child. 6 God spoke to him in this way: 'For four hundred
years your descendants will be strangers in a country not their own, and they will be enslaved and mistreated.[n] 7 But I will punish the nation they serve as slaves,' God said, 'and afterward they will come out
of that country and worship me in this place.'[a][o] 8 Then he gave Abraham the covenant of circumcision.[p]
And Abraham became the father of Isaac and circumcised him eight days after his birth.[q] Later Isaac
became the father of Jacob,[r] and Jacob became the father of the twelve patriarchs.[s]

9 "Because the patriarchs were jealous of Joseph,[t] they sold him as a slave into Egypt.[u] But God was
with him[v] 10 and rescued him from all his troubles. He gave Joseph wisdom and enabled him to gain
the goodwill of Pharaoh king of Egypt. So Pharaoh made him ruler over Egypt and all his palace.[w]

11 "Then a famine struck all Egypt and Canaan, bringing great suffering, and our ancestors could
not find food.[x] 12 When Jacob heard that there was grain in Egypt, he sent our forefathers on their
first visit.[y] 13 On their second visit, Joseph told his brothers who he was,[z] and Pharaoh learned about
Joseph's family. 14 After this, Joseph sent for his father Jacob and his whole family,[a] seventy-five in all.[b]
15 Then Jacob went down to Egypt, where he and our ancestors died.[c] 16 Their bodies were brought back

7:4 [l] Ge 12:5
7:5 [m] Ge 12:7; 17:8; 26:3
7:6 [n] Ex 12:40
7:7 [o] Ex 3:12
7:8 [p] Ge 17:9-14 [q] Ge 21:2-4 [r] Ge 25:26 [s] Ge 29:31-35; 30:5-13, 17-24; 35:16-18,22-26
7:9 [t] Ge 37:4,11 [u] Ge 37:28; Ps 105:17 [v] Ge 39:2,21,23
7:10 [w] Ge 41:37-43
7:11 [x] Ge 41:54
7:12 [y] Ge 42:1,2
7:13 [z] Ge 45:1-4
7:14 [a] Ge 45:9,10 [b] Ge 46:26,27; Ex 1:5; Dt 10:22
7:15 [c] Ge 46:5-7; 49:33; Ex 1:6

[a] 7 Gen. 15:13,14

7:4 After the death of his father. This seems to conflict with the Genesis account, which says Terah was 70 at Abraham's birth (Gen 11:26) and died at age 205 (Gen 11:32). Since Abraham left Harran at age 75 (Gen 12:4), Terah should have lived 60 more years. One possible solution is that Gen 11:26 refers to the birth of Abraham's brother Haran, not Abraham, and that Abraham was born 60 years later. Another possibility is that the Hebrew text is corrupted here and Terah actually died at age 145, a tradition that the Samaritan Pentateuch and the Jewish philosopher Philo record.

7:5 He gave him no inheritance. Although God had promised Abraham that his descendants would inherit the land where he was living (Gen 12:7; 17:8; 26:3), Abraham did not receive it during his lifetime. Abraham trusted God even though he "did not receive the things promised" (Heb 11:13).

7:6 four hundred years. A round number. Exod 12:40–41 has "430 years."

7:8 covenant of circumcision. See Gen 17:10–11.

7:9–16 The second part of Stephen's speech tells the story of Joseph, whose brothers rejected him but whom God exalted over all Egypt. In the same way, Jesus' own people rejected him, but God exalted him.

7:14 seventy-five. Follows the Septuagint, the pre-Christian Greek translation of the OT (Gen 46:27; Exod 1:5). See note on Gen 46:26.

7:16 Stephen apparently abbreviates a series of purchases and burials. Abraham purchased a cave in Hebron where he, Isaac, and Jacob were buried (Gen 23:17–20; 25:9–11; 35:29), while Jacob purchased land from the sons of Hamor at Shechem, where Joseph was later buried (Gen 33:19; Josh 24:32).

7:16 [d]Ge 23:16-20; 33:18,19; 50:13; Jos 24:32
7:17 [e]Ex 1:7; Ps 105:24
7:18 [f]Ex 1:8
7:19 [g]Ex 1:10-22
7:20 [h]Ex 2:2; Heb 11:23
7:21 [i]Ex 2:3-10
7:22 [j]1Ki 4:30; Isa 19:11
7:29 [k]Ex 2:11-15
7:31 [l]Ex 3:1-4
7:32 [m]Ex 3:6
7:33 [n]Ex 3:5; Jos 5:15
7:34 [o]Ex 3:7-10
7:35 [p]ver 27
7:36 [q]Ex 12:41; 33:1 [r]Ex 14:21

to Shechem and placed in the tomb that Abraham had bought from the sons of Hamor at Shechem for
a certain sum of money.[d]
17 “As the time drew near for God to fulfill his promise to Abraham, the number of our people in
Egypt had greatly increased.[e] 18 Then ‘a new king, to whom Joseph meant nothing, came to power in
Egypt.’[a][f] 19 He dealt treacherously with our people and oppressed our ancestors by forcing them to throw
out their newborn babies so that they would die.[g]
20 “At that time Moses was born, and he was no ordinary child.[b] For three months he was cared for by
his family.[h] 21 When he was placed outside, Pharaoh’s daughter took him and brought him up as her own
son.[i] 22 Moses was educated in all the wisdom of the Egyptians[j] and was powerful in speech and action.
23 “When Moses was forty years old, he decided to visit his own people, the Israelites. 24 He saw one of
them being mistreated by an Egyptian, so he went to his defense and avenged him by killing the Egyptian. 25 Moses thought that his own people would realize that God was using him to rescue them, but
they did not. 26 The next day Moses came upon two Israelites who were fighting. He tried to reconcile
them by saying, ‘Men, you are brothers; why do you want to hurt each other?’
27 “But the man who was mistreating
the other pushed Moses aside and said,
‘Who made you ruler and judge over us?
28 Are you thinking of killing me as you
killed the Egyptian yesterday?’[c] 29 When
Moses heard this, he fled to Midian,
where he settled as a foreigner and had
two sons.[k]
30 “After forty years had passed, an angel appeared to Moses in the flames of a
burning bush in the desert near Mount
Sinai. 31 When he saw this, he was amazed
at the sight. As he went over to get a closer
look, he heard the Lord say:[l] 32 ‘I am the
God of your fathers, the God of Abraham,
Isaac and Jacob.’[d] Moses trembled with
fear and did not dare to look.[m]
33 “Then the Lord said to him, ‘Take
off your sandals, for the place where you
are standing is holy ground.[n] 34 I have indeed seen the oppression of my people in
Egypt. I have heard their groaning and
have come down to set them free. Now
come, I will send you back to Egypt.’[e][o]
35 “This is the same Moses they had rejected with the words, ‘Who made you ruler and judge?’[p] He
was sent to be their ruler and deliverer by God himself, through the angel who appeared to him in the
bush. 36 He led them out of Egypt[q] and performed wonders and signs in Egypt, at the Red Sea[r] and for
forty years in the wilderness.

MANY OF THE PLACES MENTIONED IN STEPHEN’S SPEECH

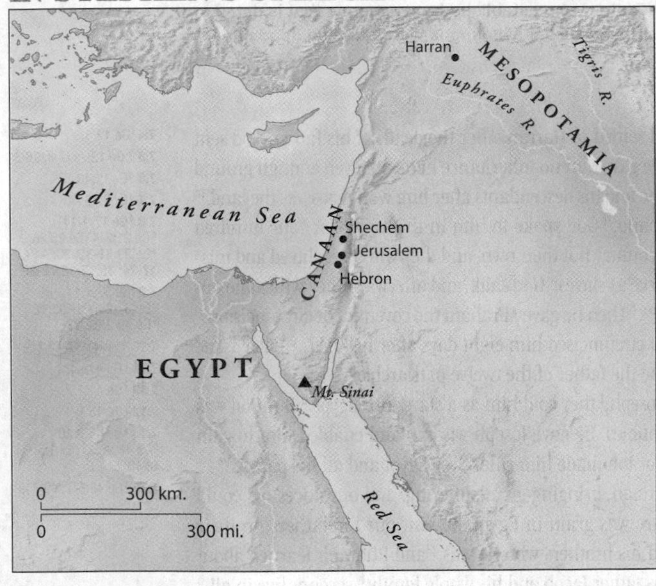

[a] 18 Exodus 1:8 [b] 20 Or *was fair in the sight of God* [c] 28 Exodus 2:14 [d] 32 Exodus 3:6
[e] 34 Exodus 3:5,7,8,10

7:17–44 The third and longest part of Stephen’s speech concerns God’s delivering Israel under Moses and the wilderness period. Its main theme is that Israel stubbornly rejected Moses’ leadership (vv. 23–28,35,39–43). The conclusion of the speech (vv. 51–53) drives this point home by showing how Israel has always rejected God’s messengers and has now rejected the Messiah.

7:22 educated in all the wisdom of the Egyptians. The OT does not mention this, but it was part of Jewish tradition (both Josephus and Philo cite it). **powerful in speech.** See Exod 4:10 and note.

7:23–28 The episode concerning Moses and the Egyptian illustrates how Moses’ people rejected his leadership (vv. 27,35).

7:30 forty years. Moses’ life is divided into three 40-year periods (vv. 23,30,36; cf. Exod 2:15): his early years (vv. 20–22), his exile from Egypt and sojourn in Midian (vv. 23–29), and the events surrounding the exodus and wilderness wanderings (vv. 30–44). These ages are not mentioned in the exodus account. Stephen sometimes draws from Jewish tradition outside the OT.

7:36 Moses’ “wonders and signs” parallel those of Jesus (2:22) and the

37"This is the Moses who told the Israelites, 'God will raise up for you a prophet like me from your
own people.'[a][s] 38He was in the assembly in the wilderness, with the angel[t] who spoke to him on Mount
Sinai, and with our ancestors;[u] and he received living words[v] to pass on to us.[w]
39"But our ancestors refused to obey him. Instead, they rejected him and in their hearts turned back
to Egypt.[x] 40They told Aaron, 'Make us gods who will go before us. As for this fellow Moses who led us out
of Egypt — we don't know what has happened to him!'[b][y] 41That was the time they made an idol in the
form of a calf. They brought sacrifices to it and reveled in what their own hands had made.[z] 42But God
turned away from them[a] and gave them over to the worship of the sun, moon and stars.[b] This agrees
with what is written in the book of the prophets:

"'Did you bring me sacrifices and offerings
forty years in the wilderness, people of Israel?
43You have taken up the tabernacle of Molek
and the star of your god Rephan,
the idols you made to worship.
Therefore I will send you into exile'[c][c] beyond Babylon.

44"Our ancestors had the tabernacle of the covenant law[d] with them in the wilderness. It had been
made as God directed Moses, according to the pattern he had seen.[e] 45After receiving the tabernacle, our
ancestors under Joshua brought it with them when they took the land from the nations God drove out before them.[f] It remained in the land until the time of David, 46who enjoyed God's favor and asked that he
might provide a dwelling place for the God of Jacob.[d][g] 47But it was Solomon who built a house for him.
48"However, the Most High does not live in houses made by human hands.[h] As the prophet says:

49"'Heaven is my throne,
and the earth is my footstool.[i]
What kind of house will you build for me?
says the Lord.
Or where will my resting place be?
50Has not my hand made all these things?'[e][j]

51"You stiff-necked people![k] Your hearts[l] and ears are still uncircumcised. You are just like your ancestors: You always resist the Holy Spirit! 52Was there ever a prophet your ancestors did not persecute?[m] They
even killed those who predicted the coming of the Righteous One. And now you have betrayed and murdered him[n] — 53you who have received the law that was given through angels[o] but have not obeyed it."

a 37 Deut. 18:15 *b 40* Exodus 32:1 *c 43* Amos 5:25-27 (see Septuagint) *d 46* Some early manuscripts *the house of Jacob* *e 50* Isaiah 66:1,2

7:37 [s]Dt 18:15,18; Ac 3:22
7:38 [t]ver 53 [u]Ex 19:17 [v]Dt 32:45-47; Heb 4:12 [w]Ro 3:2
7:39 [x]Nu 14:3,4
7:40 [y]Ex 32:1,23
7:41 [z]Ex 32:4-6; Ps 106:19,20; Rev 9:20
7:42 [a]Jos 24:20; Isa 63:10 [b]Jer 19:13
7:43 [c]Am 5:25-27
7:44 [d]Ex 38:21 [e]Ex 25:8,9,40
7:45 [f]Jos 3:14-17; 18:1; 23:9; 24:18; Ps 44:2
7:46 [g]2Sa 7:8-16; Ps 132:1-5
7:48 [h]1Ki 8:27; 2Ch 2:6
7:49 [i]Mt 5:34,35
7:50 [j]Isa 66:1,2
7:51 [k]Ex 32:9; 33:3,5 [l]Lev 26:41; Dt 10:16; Jer 4:4; 9:26
7:52 [m]2Ch 36:16; Mt 5:12 [n]Ac 3:14; 1Th 2:15
7:53 [o]ver 38; Gal 3:19; Heb 2:2

apostles (2:43; 4:30; 5:12; 6:8; 8:13; 14:3; 15:12; 19:11), confirming that he was God's messenger.
7:37 God will raise up for you a prophet like me. Quotes Deut 18:15, which Peter alludes to in 3:22 (see note).
7:38 The notion that God mediated the law through angels is not in the OT, but it appears in Jewish tradition and elsewhere in the NT (cf. v. 53; Gal 3:19; Heb 2:2).
7:39 they rejected him. A key theme of the speech: Israel rejected God's messengers (see note on vv. 1–53).
7:42 God … gave them over. The same language Paul uses of the degradation that idolatry causes (Rom 1:24,26,28). **book of the prophets.** Refers to the Book of the Twelve, the Minor Prophets, which were identified as a single "book" in the Hebrew Bible.
7:43 Babylon. Amos 5:27 says "Damascus," referring to the Assyrian invasion. Stephen replaces "Damascus" with "Babylon" since the Jews viewed the Babylonian exile as God's great judgment for the nation's idolatry.
7:44 tabernacle of the covenant law. Stephen calls Israel's portable temple in the wilderness this because it contained the tablets of the Ten Commandments: "the tablets of the covenant law" (Exod 25:16,21).
7:45–47 The fourth and last part of Stephen's historical summary moves rapidly from Joshua to Solomon, focusing on the tabernacle and Solomon's temple replacing it.
7:48–53 Stephen's conclusion summarizes his two main themes: (1) a man-made temple cannot contain God (vv. 48–49), and (2) Israel has always rejected God's messengers (v. 52).
7:49–50 Stephen quotes from Isa 66:1–2 to show that the whole universe is God's temple and that no house can be built that can contain him. Solomon himself made this same point at the dedication of the first temple (1 Kgs 8:27).
7:51 stiff-necked … hearts … uncircumcised. In the OT these images commonly describe how Israel stubbornly resisted God. **stiff-necked.** See Exod 32:9; 33:3,5; 34:9; Deut 9:6,13. **hearts … uncircumcised.** See Lev 26:41; Deut 10:16; Jer 4:4; 9:26. Though outwardly circumcised, in their hearts they are no different from the pagans.
7:52 Israel rejected the prophets, culminating in their rejection of Jesus — a common theme in Luke's Gospel (Luke 4:24; 6:22–23; 11:47–51; 13:33–34). **Righteous One.** Alludes to Isa 53:11 ("righteous servant"). See note on 3:13–14.
7:53 law that was given through angels. See note on v. 38.

7:54 [p]Ac 5:33
7:55 [q]Mk 16:19
7:56 [r]Mt 3:16 [s]Mt 8:20
7:58 [t]Lk 4:29 [u]Lev 24:14,16; Dt 13:9 [v]Ac 22:20 [w]Ac 8:1
7:59 [x]Ps 31:5; Lk 23:46
7:60 [y]Ac 9:40 [z]Mt 5:44
8:1 [a]Ac 7:58 [b]Ac 11:19 [c]Ac 9:31
8:3 [d]Ac 7:58 [e]Ac 22:4, 19; 26:10,11; 1Co 15:9; Gal 1:13,23; Php 3:6; 1Ti 1:13
8:4 [f]ver 1 [g]Ac 15:35
8:5 [h]Ac 6:5

The Stoning of Stephen

54 When the members of the Sanhedrin heard this, they were furious[p] and gnashed their teeth at him.
55 But Stephen, full of the Holy Spirit, looked up to heaven and saw the glory of God, and Jesus standing
at the right hand of God.[q] 56 "Look," he said, "I see heaven open[r] and the Son of Man[s] standing at the
right hand of God."

57 At this they covered their ears and, yelling at the top of their voices, they all rushed at him,
58 dragged him out of the city[t] and began to stone him.[u] Meanwhile, the witnesses laid their coats[v] at
the feet of a young man named Saul.[w]

59 While they were stoning him, Stephen prayed, "Lord Jesus, receive my spirit."[x] 60 Then he fell on his
knees[y] and cried out, "Lord, do not hold this sin against them."[z] When he had said this, he fell asleep.

8 And Saul[a] approved of their killing him.

The Church Persecuted and Scattered

On that day a great persecution broke out against the church in Jerusalem, and all except the apostles were scattered[b] throughout Judea and Samaria.[c] 2 Godly men buried Stephen and mourned deeply
for him. 3 But Saul[d] began to destroy the church.[e] Going from house to house, he dragged off both men
and women and put them in prison.

Philip in Samaria

4 Those who had been scattered[f] preached the word wherever they went.[g] 5 Philip[h] went down to a
city in Samaria and proclaimed the Messiah there. 6 When the crowds heard Philip and saw the signs

7:54—8:1a *The Stoning of Stephen.* By challenging the temple and accusing the religious leaders, Stephen provokes the fury of the Sanhedrin, and they drag him outside Jerusalem and stone him to death. But his violent death produces the positive result of scattering the Christians, resulting in the wider proclamation of the gospel.
7:56 Son of Man. On the glorious exaltation of the "Son of Man," see Dan 7:13–14; Luke 22:69. This is the only time in the NT that someone other than Jesus uses the title for Jesus (except when Jesus' words are quoted back to him in John 12:34 and in the exposition of Ps 8 in Heb 2). **standing at the right hand of God.** Why is Jesus standing instead of sitting (2:34; Ps 110:1; Luke 20:42; 22:69; Eph 1:20; Col 3:1; Heb 1:3; 8:1)? He may be standing to receive Stephen into his presence.
7:57–58a There is irony here in that the Jewish leaders act precisely how Stephen accused them of acting in the past (vv. 51–52). It is debated whether the stoning is a mob action or a formal execution carried out by the Sanhedrin. The spontaneous rage expressed in v. 57 suggests mob violence, but the presence of "witnesses" indicates a formal execution. In either case, it is illegal since the Roman authorities retained jurisdiction for capital crimes (John 18:31).
7:58b This is the first mention of Saul (Paul), who becomes the main human character of the second half of Acts (chs. 9; 13–28). It is unclear whether Saul is overseeing the execution or merely a bystander. In either case, he "approved of their killing him" (8:1a; cf. 26:10–11).
7:59 As Jesus prayed for the Father to receive his spirit (Luke 23:46; cf. Ps 31:5), so Stephen prays for the Lord Jesus to receive his. Prayer offered to Jesus is evidence of his deity.
7:60 Like Jesus (Luke 23:34), Stephen asks that his executioners be forgiven. **fell asleep.** A common expression that points to the impermanence of death for believers (13:36; Luke 8:52; John 11:11; 1 Cor 15:6,18,20; 1 Thess 4:14–15; 5:10).
8:1b–3 *The Church Persecuted and Scattered.* Though the apostles were arrested twice and beaten once (4:1–3; 5:40), Stephen's martyrdom marks a new and devastating level of persecution. Yet throughout Acts God uses setbacks to advance his gospel, and the persecution compels the church to take the Good News beyond its Jerusalem enclave.
8:1b all except the apostles. May mean that people persecuted primarily Greek-speaking Jewish Christians (like the Seven in 6:5), whom they viewed as sharing Stephen's radical views on the law and the temple. The apostles also likely felt responsible to stay with their flock in Jerusalem. **Judea and Samaria.** Jesus' commission in 1:8 is beginning to be fulfilled.
8:2 Godly men buried Stephen and mourned deeply for him. Confirms Stephen's righteousness. Jewish tradition allowed burial of executed persons but discouraged lamentation. Their mourning implies defiance and with it a considerable risk of retribution (cf. Nicodemus and Joseph of Arimathea in John 19:38–39).
8:3 Saul began to destroy the church. This is the third mention of Saul in three paragraphs (cf. 7:58; 8:1a) and foreshadows the significant role he will play in the subsequent narrative, when the persecutor becomes the apostle (9:1–19). Saul views Jesus as a false messiah and his followers as heretics. **both men and women.** Saul is bent on totally destroying the church.
8:4–40 *Philip's Ministry.* Like Stephen, Philip was one of the Seven, a servant who met the needs of the Hellenistic widows in the church (6:5). Also like Stephen, Philip is used by God to expand the gospel beyond Jerusalem. God used Stephen's persecution and martyrdom to scatter the believers. God then used Philip to utilize the opportunity afforded by this persecution to proclaim the gospel in Samaria (8:4–8) and to the Ethiopian eunuch (8:26–40).
8:4–8 *Philip in Samaria.* This episode illustrates the gospel's continued expansion despite opposition and its power to break down ethnic and religious barriers. The Jews hated the Samaritans as a half-breed race and as heretics, but for Luke they are examples of outsiders for whom the gospel is good news (cf. Luke 9:52–56; 10:25–37; 17:11–19). Here they function as a mediating people between Jews and Gentiles and thus a natural step in the gospel's gradual spread from Jerusalem to the ends of the earth (1:8).
8:4 The gospel advances despite—even because of—the persecution.
8:5 Philip. Like Stephen, he is one of the Seven (6:3,5), a Hellenistic Jewish Christian. **a city in Samaria.** Some manuscripts read "the city of Samaria," which may refer to the old capital city of Samaria, which Herod the Great rebuilt and renamed Sebaste. But since Luke usually identifies Samaria as a region (1:8; 8:25; 9:31; Luke 9:52), "a city" is more likely. It could have been Sebaste, Shechem (the religious center of Samaria), Neapolis (Nablus), Gitta (Simon Magus's hometown), or somewhere else.
8:6–7 The "signs" Philip performs—healings and exorcisms—replicate

he performed, they all paid close attention to what he said. 7For with shrieks, impure spirits came out
of many,[i] and many who were paralyzed or lame were healed.[j] 8So there was great joy in that city.

Simon the Sorcerer

9Now for some time a man named Simon had practiced sorcery[k] in the city and amazed all the
people of Samaria. He boasted that he was someone great,[l] 10and all the people, both high and low,
gave him their attention and exclaimed, "This man is rightly called the Great Power of God."[m]
11They followed him because he had amazed them for a long time with his sorcery. 12But when
they believed Philip as he proclaimed the good news of the kingdom of God[n] and the name of Jesus
Christ, they were baptized,[o] both men and women. 13Simon
himself believed and was baptized. And he followed Philip
everywhere, astonished by the great signs and miracles[p]
he saw.

14When the apostles in Jerusalem heard that Samaria[q]
had accepted the word of God, they sent Peter and John[r] to
Samaria. 15When they arrived, they prayed for the new believers there that they might receive the Holy Spirit,[s] 16be-
cause the Holy Spirit had not yet come on any of them;[t] they
had simply been baptized in the name of the Lord Jesus.[u]
17Then Peter and John placed their hands on them,[v] and they
received the Holy Spirit.

18When Simon saw that the Spirit was given at the laying
on of the apostles' hands, he offered them money 19and said,
"Give me also this ability so that everyone on whom I lay my
hands may receive the Holy Spirit."

20Peter answered: "May your money perish with you, because you thought you could buy the gift of God with money![w] 21You have no part or share in this ministry, because
your heart is not right[x] before God. 22Repent of this wickedness and pray to the Lord in the hope that he may forgive you
for having such a thought in your heart. 23For I see that you
are full of bitterness and captive to sin."

8:7 [i]Mk 16:17 [j]Mt 4:24
8:9 [k]Ac 13:6 [l]Ac 5:36
8:10 [m]Ac 14:11; 28:6
8:12 [n]Ac 1:3 [o]Ac 2:38
8:13 [p]ver 6; Ac 19:11
8:14 [q]ver 1 [r]Lk 22:8
8:15 [s]Ac 2:38
8:16 [t]Ac 19:2 [u]Mt 28:19; Ac 2:38
8:17 [v]Ac 6:6
8:20 [w]2Ki 5:16; Da 5:17; Mt 10:8; Ac 2:38
8:21 [x]Ps 78:37

PHILIP'S AND PETER'S MISSIONARY JOURNEYS

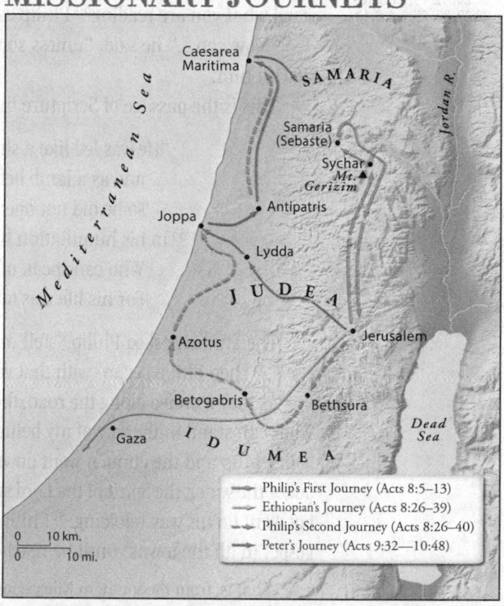

Jesus' miracles and so demonstrate the presence and power of the kingdom of God (Luke 11:20), continuing the story of Jesus that began in Luke's Gospel (Acts 1:1,8).

8:8 Joy and rejoicing are major themes in Luke-Acts (e.g., Acts 5:41; 8:39; 13:52; 16:34; Luke 2:10; 6:23; 10:17,21; 15:6,9–10), the natural response to the arrival of God's great end-time salvation.

8:9–25 *Simon the Sorcerer and the Jerusalem Delegation to Samaria.* This passage narrates two events with reference to the Samaritans: (1) The story of Simon contrasts the authentic power of the kingdom with the impotence and fraudulence of pagan magic (vv. 9–13,18–24). (2) The apostolic delegation from Jerusalem confirms the Samaritans' faith (vv. 14–17). Together these events highlight the key themes of the early church's power and unity.

8:9 Simon. Known in church history as Simon Magus ("the magician"). According to later church tradition, Simon became an arch-heretic and founder of the Simonians, a Gnostic sect. His travels eventually took him to Rome, where he opposed the church there. **practiced sorcery.** Probably as a healer, exorcist, and wonder-worker.

8:10 both high and low. People of all social classes. **Great Power of God.** Likely a claim to deity.

8:12 When confronted with the authentic power of the kingdom of God, Simon's magic seems like cheap parlor tricks, and his followers quickly switch allegiance.

8:13 Simon himself believed. Luke does not say whether this faith is authentic or superficial profession. Simon's obsession with Philip's miracles (v. 13b) and Peter's later words of condemnation (vv. 20–23) both suggest that his faith is not genuine.

8:14 In light of the historical hatred and mistrust between Jews and Samaritans, the Jerusalem church "sent Peter and John to Samaria" as an official delegation to check out the claims of Samaritan conversions.

8:16 had not yet come. The delay of the Holy Spirit is surprising considering that the more common pattern in Acts is an immediate receiving of the Spirit upon belief (2:38; 10:44; Luke himself treats it as unusual here). While some claim that the Samaritans' faith was inadequate or that they *had* received the Spirit, a better explanation is that God delayed giving the Spirit for the sake of Christian unity: (1) to confirm to the Samaritans that they were one with the Jerusalem church and (2) to confirm to the Jerusalem church that the Samaritans were indeed saved. The period of Acts is a time of transition, and the book's purpose is to show the gospel's relentless advance, not to establish normative patterns for church life and polity.

8:18 offered them money. Simon, a professional magician, treats the gift of the Spirit as one more power to acquire and exploit for financial gain.

8:20 May your money perish with you. Salvation is a gift, so we cannot buy or earn it. As in the case of Ananias and Sapphira (5:1–11), pride, greed, and selfishness lead to destruction.

8:21 your heart is not right before God. Implies that Simon's faith was inauthentic and self-serving from the start (see note on v. 13).

8:24 [y]Ex 8:8; Nu 21:7; 1Ki 13:6
8:25 [z]ver 40
8:26 [a]Ac 5:19
8:27 [b]Ps 68:31; 87:4; Zep 3:10 [c]Isa 56:3-5 [d]1Ki 8:41-43; Jn 12:20
8:29 [e]Ac 10:19; 11:12; 13:2; 20:23; 21:11
8:33 [f]Isa 53:7,8
8:35 [g]Mt 5:2 [h]Lk 24:27; Ac 17:2; 18:28; 28:23
8:36 [i]Ac 10:47
8:39 [j]1Ki 18:12; 2Ki 2:16; Eze 3:12,14; 8:3; 11:1,24; 43:5; 2Co 12:2
8:40 [k]ver 25 [l]Ac 10:1, 24; 12:19; 21:8,16; 23:23,33; 25:1,4,6,13

24 Then Simon answered, "Pray to the Lord for me[y] so that nothing you have said may happen
to me."
25 After they had further proclaimed the word of the Lord and testified about Jesus, Peter and John
returned to Jerusalem, preaching the gospel in many Samaritan villages.[z]

Philip and the Ethiopian

26 Now an angel[a] of the Lord said to Philip, "Go south to the road — the desert road — that goes
down from Jerusalem to Gaza." 27 So he started out, and on his way he met an Ethiopian[ab] eunuch,[c]
an important official in charge of all the treasury of the Kandake (which means "queen of the Ethiopians"). This man had gone to Jerusalem to worship,[d] 28 and on his way home was sitting in his chariot
reading the Book of Isaiah the prophet. 29 The Spirit told[e] Philip, "Go to that chariot and stay near it."
30 Then Philip ran up to the chariot and heard the man reading Isaiah the prophet. "Do you understand what you are reading?" Philip asked.
31 "How can I," he said, "unless someone explains it to me?" So he invited Philip to come up and
sit with him.
32 This is the passage of Scripture the eunuch was reading:

"He was led like a sheep to the slaughter,
and as a lamb before its shearer is silent,
so he did not open his mouth.
33 In his humiliation he was deprived of justice.
Who can speak of his descendants?
For his life was taken from the earth."[bf]

34 The eunuch asked Philip, "Tell me, please, who is the prophet talking about, himself or someone
else?" 35 Then Philip began[g] with that very passage of Scripture[h] and told him the good news about Jesus.
36 As they traveled along the road, they came to some water and the eunuch said, "Look, here is water.
What can stand in the way of my being baptized?"[i] [37][c] 38 And he gave orders to stop the chariot. Then
both Philip and the eunuch went down into the water and Philip baptized him. 39 When they came up
out of the water, the Spirit of the Lord suddenly took Philip away,[j] and the eunuch did not see him again,
but went on his way rejoicing. 40 Philip, however, appeared at Azotus and traveled about, preaching the
gospel in all the towns[k] until he reached Caesarea.[l]

a *27* That is, from the southern Nile region *b* *33* Isaiah 53:7,8 (see Septuagint) *c* *37* Some manuscripts include here *Philip said, "If you believe with all your heart, you may." The eunuch answered, "I believe that Jesus Christ is the Son of God."*

8:24 Pray to the Lord for me. It is unclear whether Simon's repentance is authentic or whether he attempts to avoid punishment. If the church traditions about Simon's heresy are accurate (see note on v. 9), his remorse is temporary. But Luke does not say so, and the story ends on an open note.
8:25 Preaching the gospel in "many Samaritan villages" represents the evangelization of greater Samaria, fulfilling the commission of 1:8.
8:26–40 *Philip and the Ethiopian.* This episode highlights two key themes of Acts: (1) the gospel breaks down all social, racial, and ethnic barriers, and (2) God sovereignly guides and empowers his servants. An angel directs Philip to a desert road (v. 26); the Spirit instructs him to approach a chariot (v. 29); the man is reading just the right text of Scripture (v. 32); water is available for baptism (v. 36); the Spirit whisks away Philip for another mission (vv. 39–40). All evidence of God's guiding hand.
8:26 Go south. The Hebrew can also mean "Go at noon." **Gaza.** About 50 miles (about 80 kilometers) southwest of Jerusalem, the last watering stop before the desert leading to Egypt.
8:27 Ethiopian. Not modern Ethiopia but the Nubian Empire (which the OT calls Cush), located in what is today southern Egypt and northern Sudan, between Aswan and Khartoum (see NIV text note). **eunuch.** A castrated male who served in the royal court, often in a position of very high status. This man is the finance minister of the royal court. **Kandake.** A title rather than a name, referring to the queen mother. Since the Ethiopian has "gone to Jerusalem to worship," he is likely a God-fearer, a Gentile who worshiped the true God of Israel. Because of their physical defect, eunuchs were not allowed to participate fully in Israel's religious life (Deut 23:1). But Isa 56:3–5 promises that one day God will give to eunuchs who are faithful "a name better than sons and daughters" (Isa 56:5). Luke may have this promise in mind as he sees all barriers falling before the advancing kingdom of God.
8:28 chariot. Probably not a war chariot but a slow-moving carriage pulled by oxen.
8:30 heard the man reading. In the ancient world, people commonly read aloud.
8:32–33 God's providence is seen again in the man's choice of text since the fourth servant song (Isa 52:13—53:12) is the most important OT passage relating to the Messiah's suffering.
8:37 See NIV text note. A later copyist evidently felt that the story was incomplete without a confession of faith and so added this traditional baptismal formula.
8:39 rejoicing. A major theme in Luke-Acts (see note on v. 8).
8:40 God has been directing every aspect of the story, and the Spirit suddenly takes Philip away. **Azotus.** The OT calls it Ashdod, one of five main Philistine cities, a coastal town 20 miles (32 kilometers) north of

Saul's Conversion

9:1-19pp — Ac 22:3-16; 26:9-18

9 Meanwhile, Saul was still breathing out murderous threats against the Lord's disciples.[m] He went
to the high priest 2and asked him for letters to the synagogues in Damascus, so that if he found any
there who belonged to the Way,[n] whether men or women, he might take them as prisoners to Jerusalem.
3As he neared Damascus on his journey, suddenly a light from heaven flashed around him.[o] 4He fell to
the ground and heard a voice say to him, "Saul, Saul, why do you persecute me?"
5"Who are you, Lord?" Saul asked.
"I am Jesus, whom you are persecuting," he replied. 6"Now get up and go into the city, and you will
be told what you must do."[p]
7The men traveling with Saul stood there speechless; they heard the sound[q] but did not see anyone.[r]
8Saul got up from the ground, but when he opened his eyes he could see nothing. So they led him by
the hand into Damascus. 9For three days he was blind, and did not eat or drink anything.
10In Damascus there was a disciple named Ananias. The
Lord called to him in a vision,[s] "Ananias!"
"Yes, Lord," he answered.
11The Lord told him, "Go to the house of Judas on
Straight Street and ask for a man from Tarsus[t] named Saul,
for he is praying. 12In a vision he has seen a man named
Ananias come and place his hands on[u] him to restore his
sight."
13"Lord," Ananias answered, "I have heard many reports
about this man and all the harm he has done to your holy
people[v] in Jerusalem.[w] 14And he has come here with authority from the chief priests[x] to arrest all who call on your
name."
15But the Lord said to Ananias, "Go! This man is my chosen instrument[y] to proclaim my name to the Gentiles[z] and
their kings[a] and to the people of Israel. 16I will show him how
much he must suffer for my name."[b]
17Then Ananias went to the house and entered it. Placing his hands on[c] Saul, he said, "Brother Saul, the Lord —

9:1 [m]Ac 8:3
9:2 [n]Ac 19:9,23; 22:4; 24:14,22
9:3 [o]1Co 15:8
9:6 [p]ver 16
9:7 [q]Jn 12:29 [r]Da 10:7; Ac 22:9
9:10 [s]Ac 10:3,17,19
9:11 [t]ver 30; Ac 21:39; 22:3
9:12 [u]Mk 5:23
9:13 [v]ver 32; Ro 1:7; 16:2,15 [w]Ac 8:3
9:14 [x]ver 2,21
9:15 [y]Ac 13:2; Ro 1:1; Gal 1:15 [z]Ro 11:13; 15:15,16; Gal 2:7,8; Eph 3:7,8 [a]Ac 25:22, 23; 26:1
9:16 [b]Ac 20:23; 21:11; 2Co 11:23-27
9:17 [c]Ac 6:6

SAUL'S CONVERSION

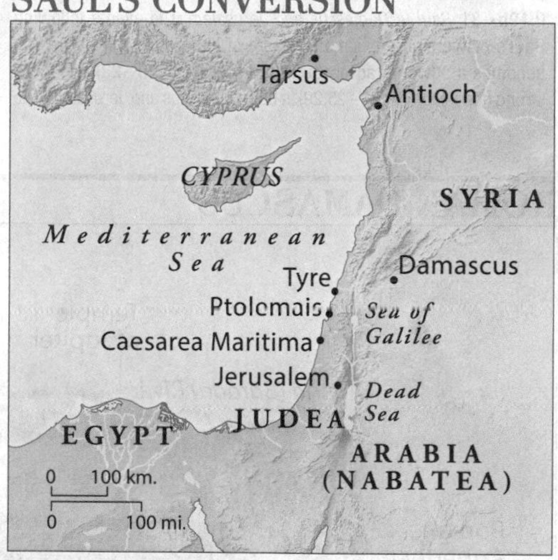

Gaza. Philip, always faithful to his calling, kept "preaching the gospel in all the towns until he reached Caesarea." He appears in Caesarea again in 21:8, some 20 years later.

9:1–31 *Saul's Conversion and Early Witness.* Having introduced Saul (i.e., Paul; see note on 13:9 for the use of the two names) of Tarsus in the account of Stephen's martyrdom (7:58; 8:1a), Luke now narrates Saul's dramatic conversion. This radical transformation from persecutor to apostle is centrally important both for the narrative of Acts and for the history of Christianity. Luke will focus on Paul throughout the second half of Acts (chs. 13–28), using his story to defend the expansion of the gospel to the Gentiles by demonstrating that this "Apostle to the Gentiles" is not a renegade Jew: God himself called and appointed Paul.

9:1–19a *Saul's Conversion.* Saul's conversion is recounted three times by Luke (9:1–19a; 22:1–21; 26:1–29), and it is repeatedly referred to by Paul in his letters (1 Cor 9:1; 15:8; Gal 1:12–17; 1 Tim 1:12). It represents a key turning point in Acts and prepares for the gospel's expansion "to the ends of the earth" (1:8).

9:1 high priest. Caiaphas (see note on 4:6).

9:2 letters. Possibly letters of reference commending Saul's work or extradition requests to return Christians who had fled Jerusalem because of persecution (8:1b). **synagogues.** Jewish centers of worship, education, administration, and community life. There would have been many in Damascus. **Damascus.** A major city with a large Jewish population, located in Syria, 135 miles (217 kilometers) north of Jerusalem (a five- to six-day journey). **the Way.** A common self-designation for the early Christians (cf. 18:25–26; 19:9,23; 22:4; 24:14,22), meaning "God's path" or "the way of salvation" (cf. John 14:6).

9:4 me. Since the disciples represent Jesus (1:8), to persecute them is to persecute him.

9:5 I am Jesus. These words transform Paul's world: he recognizes that the one whose followers he has been persecuting is the Messiah, his Lord.

9:7 they heard the sound. See 22:9.

9:8 Saul's blindness does not seem to be an act of judgment; rather, it symbolizes the spiritual blindness that has characterized his life to this point (v. 18).

9:10 Yes, Lord. The Greek idiom behind this echoes similar calls in the OT (Gen 22:1; 31:11; 1 Sam 3:4–8; Isa 6:8).

9:11 Straight Street. The main east-west thoroughfare of Damascus; it is still visible today and known as Darb el-Mostakim. **Tarsus.** See note on 21:39.

9:14 call on your name. See note on 2:19–21.

9:15 Paul's primary commission is to the Gentiles (22:21; 26:17; Rom 1:13–14), but in each city he goes first to the synagogue (see note on 13:5) and preaches to the people of Israel since the gospel was "first to the Jew, then to the Gentile" (Rom 1:16). For his preaching to kings, see Agrippa (Acts 26:1) and his appeal to Caesar in Rome (25:10–11).

9:19 [d]Ac 11:26 [e]Ac 26:20
9:20 [f]Ac 13:5,14 [g]Mt 4:3
9:21 [h]Ac 8:3 [i]Gal 1:13,23
9:22 [j]Ac 18:5,28

Jesus, who appeared to you on the road as you were coming here — has sent me so that you may see
again and be filled with the Holy Spirit." 18Immediately, something like scales fell from Saul's eyes,
and he could see again. He got up and was baptized, 19and after taking some food, he regained his
strength.

Saul in Damascus and Jerusalem

Saul spent several days with the disciples[d] in Damascus.[e] 20At once he began to preach in the synagogues[f] that Jesus is the Son of God.[g] 21All those who heard him were astonished and asked, "Isn't he
the man who raised havoc in Jerusalem among those who call on this name?[h] And hasn't he come here
to take them as prisoners to the chief priests?"[i] 22Yet Saul grew more and more powerful and baffled
the Jews living in Damascus by proving that Jesus is the Messiah.[j]
23After many days had gone by, there was a conspiracy among the Jews to kill him, 24but Saul learned

9:18 Restoring Saul's sight demonstrates the healing power of the kingdom of God (cf. 3:8; 8:7; Luke 4:18; 7:21–22) and symbolizes his transformation from spiritual darkness to spiritual light.

9:19b–31 *Saul in Damascus and Jerusalem.* The events following Saul's conversion provide a foretaste of his coming ministry as he becomes a powerful advocate for the gospel (vv. 20–22) and faces strong opposition (vv. 23–25,29) in both Damascus and Jerusalem. The prophecy of v. 16 is already beginning to be fulfilled. In Gal 1:17–18, Paul refers to spending time in Arabia (the Nabatean kingdom east of Damascus) during this period.

9:22 grew more and more powerful. The passionate persecutor now becomes an equally passionate defender. His central message is that Jesus is "the Son of God" (v. 20; cf. Rom 1:3–4) and "the Messiah" (v. 22), claims he previously viewed as anathema.

ROMAN DAMASCUS

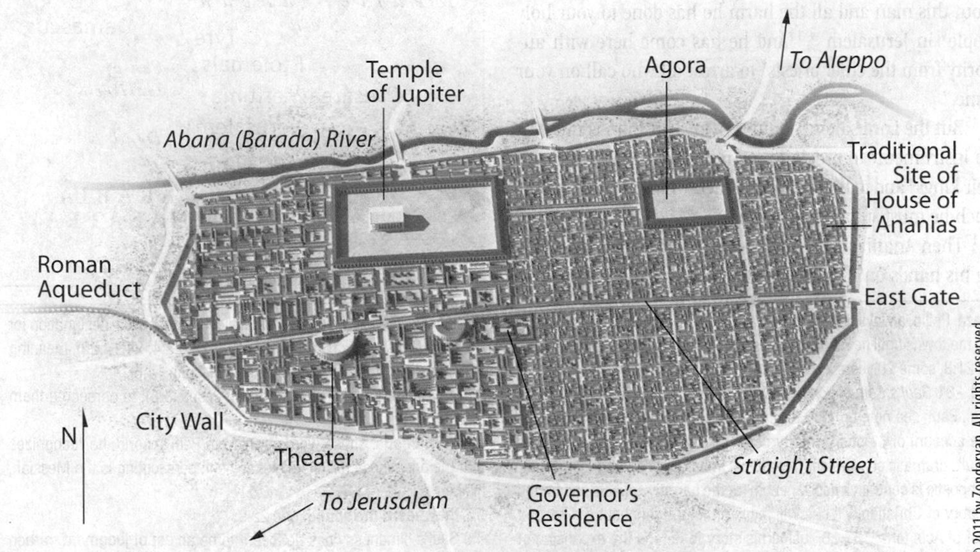

Damascus represented much more to Saul, the strict Pharisee, than any other stop on his campaign of repression. It was the hub of a vast commercial network with far-flung lines of caravan trade reaching into north Syria, Mesopotamia, Anatolia, Persia, and Arabia. If the new "Way" of Christianity flourished in Damascus, it would quickly reach all these places. From the viewpoint of the Sanhedrin and of Saul, the archpersecutor, it had to be stopped in Damascus.

The dominant political figure at the time of Paul's escape from Damascus (2 Cor 11:32–33) was Aretas IV, king of the Nabateans (9 BC–AD 40), though normally the Decapolis cities were attached to the province of Syria and were thus under the influence of Rome.

The city itself was a veritable oasis, situated in a plain watered by the Biblical rivers Abana and Pharpar (see note on 2 Kgs 5:12). Roman architecture overlaid the Hellenistic town plan with a great temple to Jupiter and a mile-long colonnaded street, the "Straight Street" of Acts 9:11. The city gates and a section of the town wall may still be seen today, as well as the lengthy bazaar that runs along the line of the ancient street.

of their plan.[k] Day and night they kept close watch on the city gates in order to kill him. 25 But his followers took him by night and lowered him in a basket through an opening in the wall.[l]
26 When he came to Jerusalem,[m] he tried to join the disciples, but they were all afraid of him, not
believing that he really was a disciple. 27 But Barnabas[n] took him and brought him to the apostles. He
told them how Saul on his journey had seen the Lord and that the Lord had spoken to him,[o] and how
in Damascus he had preached fearlessly in the name of Jesus.[p] 28 So Saul stayed with them and moved
about freely in Jerusalem, speaking boldly in the name of the Lord. 29 He talked and debated with the
Hellenistic Jews,[a][q] but they tried to kill him.[r] 30 When the believers[s] learned of this, they took him down
to Caesarea[t] and sent him off to Tarsus.[u]
31 Then the church throughout Judea, Galilee and Samaria[v] enjoyed a time of peace and was
strengthened. Living in the fear of the Lord and encouraged by the Holy Spirit, it increased in numbers.

Aeneas and Dorcas

32 As Peter traveled about the country, he went to visit the Lord's people[w] who lived in Lydda. 33 There
he found a man named Aeneas, who was paralyzed and had been bedridden for eight years. 34 "Aeneas,"
Peter said to him, "Jesus Christ heals you.[x] Get up and roll up your mat." Immediately Aeneas got up.
35 All those who lived in Lydda and Sharon[y] saw him and turned to the Lord.[z]
36 In Joppa[a] there was a disciple named Tabitha (in Greek her name is Dorcas); she was always doing
good[b] and helping the poor. 37 About that time she became sick and died, and her body was washed and
placed in an upstairs room.[c] 38 Lydda was near Joppa; so when the disciples[d] heard that Peter was in
Lydda, they sent two men to him and urged him, "Please come at once!"
39 Peter went with them, and when he arrived he was taken upstairs to the room. All the widows[e]
stood around him, crying and showing him the robes and other clothing that Dorcas had made while
she was still with them.
40 Peter sent them all out of the room;[f] then he got down on his knees[g] and prayed. Turning toward
the dead woman, he said, "Tabitha, get up." She opened her eyes, and seeing Peter she sat up. 41 He took

9:24 [k] Ac 20:3,19
9:25 [l] 1Sa 19:12; 2Co 11:32,33
9:26 [m] Ac 22:17; 26:20; Gal 1:17,18
9:27 [n] Ac 4:36 [o] ver 3-6 [p] ver 20,22
9:29 [q] Ac 6:1 [r] 2Co 11:26
9:30 [s] Ac 1:16 [t] Ac 8:40 [u] ver 11
9:31 [v] Ac 8:1
9:32 [w] ver 13
9:34 [x] Ac 3:6,16; 4:10
9:35 [y] 1Ch 5:16; 27:29; Isa 33:9; 35:2; 65:10 [z] Ac 11:21
9:36 [a] Jos 19:46; 2Ch 2:16; Ezr 3:7; Jnh 1:3; Ac 10:5 [b] 1Ti 2:10; Titus 3:8
9:37 [c] Ac 1:13
9:38 [d] Ac 11:26
9:39 [e] Ac 6:1
9:40 [f] Mt 9:25 [g] Lk 22:41; Ac 7:60

a 29 That is, Jews who had adopted the Greek language and culture

9:25 lowered him in a basket. Paul refers to this event in 2 Cor 11:32–33, where the opposition comes from the local governor (ethnarch) under King Aretas IV of Nabatea. It is unclear whether the Romans or Nabateans had authority over Damascus at this time. If the Romans, perhaps Paul's Jewish opponents were watching the gates from within while the king's soldiers were hoping to catch Paul as he left the city. Paul may have incurred the king's wrath during his ministry in Arabia (Gal 1:17).
9:26–31 This is probably the visit Paul refers to in Gal 1:18–20 (see notes there). Luke shows that the Jerusalem apostles accept Paul and that the church is unified; Paul shows that he received his essential gospel not from the apostles but from Jesus himself. This explains why Paul emphasizes meeting only Peter ("Cephas") and James, the Lord's brother (Gal 1:18–19), while Luke speaks generally of meeting "the apostles." For the use of "apostles" to refer to those other than the Twelve, see 14:4,14.
9:27 Barnabas. Appears again as a mediator and reconciler (see note on 4:36).
9:29 tried to kill him. Opposition against Paul, like that against Stephen, comes primarily from the Hellenistic Jews, perhaps because Paul focuses his ministry on the Greek-speaking synagogues.
9:30 Approximately ten years will pass from Paul's return to Tarsus until his first missionary journey (13:1–3). He spends this time ministering in Cilicia (the province in which Tarsus was located, Gal 1:21) and then with Barnabas in Antioch, Syria (11:19–30).
9:31 Another summary stressing the church's growth (2:42–47; 4:32–35; 5:12–16; 6:7). **the church.** Used here in the singular (*ekklēsia*) to refer to the whole body of believers. The term can refer to a single house church (Matt 18:17; Rom 16:5; 1 Cor 16:19), the churches in a city or region (Acts 5:11; 8:1b; 1 Cor 1:2; 16:1; 2 Cor 1:1), or all believers worldwide (Matt 16:18; 1 Cor 12:28; Eph 5:25). **enjoyed a time of peace.** Because (1) the church's greatest opponent is now its greatest advocate, and (2) his volatile presence has been removed from Jerusalem. **fear of the Lord.** A sense of awe and reverence at the mighty power of God. Such awe can result in worship (as here) or fear of judgment (see note on 5:11).
9:32–43 *Aeneas and Dorcas.* Following his account of Saul's conversion, Luke returns to the ministry of Peter, last seen in Samaria. The two episodes about Aeneas and Dorcas continue to illustrate that God is confirming the gospel through the apostles' miracles and that the gospel is expanding outward into Judea (1:8).
9:32 Lydda. About 30 miles (48 kilometers) west-northwest of Jerusalem. The OT calls it Lod (1 Chr 8:12).
9:33 The text does not say whether Aeneas is a believer, but it may imply it since Peter is visiting the Christians in Lydda.
9:34 Peter makes it clear that Jesus Christ heals Aeneas. Acts continues Jesus' saving actions (see 1:1 and note). **Get up.** Recalls Jesus' healing the paralyzed man in Luke 5:24–25. **roll up your mat.** Lit. "prepare (for) yourself"; the idiom could mean to take up his bedding or to take nourishment (cf. Luke 8:55).
9:36–43 With the account of the raising of Tabitha/Dorcas from the dead, Luke continues to present the apostles performing miracles reminiscent of Jesus' miracles (see Luke 7:11–17; 8:49–56). The miracles also recall similar OT miracles by the prophets Elijah (1Kgs 17:17–24) and Elisha (2 Kgs 4:32–37).
9:36 Joppa. Judea's primary port, located about 10 miles (about 16 kilometers) northwest of Lydda and 38 miles (61 kilometers) west-northwest of Jerusalem. **Tabitha ... Dorcas.** Tabitha (Aramaic) and Dorcas (Greek) both mean "gazelle."
9:39 widows. Among the most vulnerable members of society, and caring for them was a sign of particular godliness (6:1; Jas 1:27).
9:40 Tabitha, get up. Would have sounded almost identical in Aramaic

her by the hand and helped her to her feet. Then he called for the believers, especially the widows, and presented her to them alive. 42This became known all over Joppa, and many people believed in the Lord. 43Peter stayed in Joppa for some time with a tanner named Simon.[h]

Cornelius Calls for Peter

10 At Caesarea[i] there was a man named Cornelius, a centurion in what was known as the Italian Regiment. 2He and all his family were devout and God-fearing;[j] he gave generously to those in need and prayed to God regularly. 3One day at about three in the afternoon[k] he had a vision.[l] He distinctly saw an angel[m] of God, who came to him and said, "Cornelius!"

4Cornelius stared at him in fear. "What is it, Lord?" he asked.

The angel answered, "Your prayers and gifts to the poor have come up as a memorial offering[n] before God.[o] 5Now send men to Joppa[p] to bring back a man named Simon who is called Peter. 6He is staying with Simon the tanner,[q] whose house is by the sea."

7When the angel who spoke to him had gone, Cornelius called two of his servants and a devout soldier who was one of his attendants. 8He told them everything that had happened and sent them to Joppa.[r]

Peter's Vision

10:9-32Ref — Ac 11:5-14

9About noon the following day as they were on their journey and approaching the city, Peter went up on the roof[s] to pray. 10He became hungry and wanted something to eat, and while the meal was being prepared, he fell into a trance.[t] 11He saw heaven opened and something like a large sheet being let down to earth by its four corners. 12It contained all kinds of four-footed animals, as well as reptiles and birds. 13Then a voice told him, "Get up, Peter. Kill and eat."

14"Surely not, Lord!"[u] Peter replied. "I have never eaten anything impure or unclean."[v]

15The voice spoke to him a second time, "Do not call anything impure that God has made clean."[w]

16This happened three times, and immediately the sheet was taken back to heaven.

9:43 [h]Ac 10:6
10:1 [i]Ac 8:40
10:2 [j]ver 22,35; Ac 13:16,26
10:3 [k]Ac 3:1 [l]Ac 9:10 [m]Ac 5:19
10:4 [n]Mt 26:13 [o]Rev 8:4
10:5 [p]Ac 9:36
10:6 [q]Ac 9:43
10:8 [r]Ac 9:36
10:9 [s]Mt 24:17
10:10 [t]Ac 22:17
10:14 [u]Ac 9:5 [v]Lev 11:4-8,13-20; 20:25; Dt 14:3-20; Eze 4:14
10:15 [w]Mt 15:11; Ro 14:14,17,20; 1Co 10:25; 1Ti 4:3,4; Titus 1:15

to Jesus' words "*Talitha koum*" ("little girl, get up") in Mark 5:41, illustrating the close relationship between the apostles' miracles in Acts and Jesus' miracles in the Gospels (see 1:1 and note). Both evidence the in-breaking power of the kingdom of God.

10:1—11:18 *Peter's Ministry to Cornelius and His Household.* The conversion of the Roman centurion Cornelius (10:1—11:18) is a major development in the narrative of Acts, as God confirms through Peter that Gentiles have the same access as Jews to the salvation available through Jesus Christ (see 10:34–35). This prepares the way for the Jerusalem council's decision (ch. 15) and Luke's detailed account of the missionary journeys of Paul, the Apostle to the Gentiles (chs. 13–28). Central to the Cornelius story is the theme that God, not Peter, orchestrates these events and initiates the mission to the Gentiles. Repetition demonstrates the story's importance: Luke describes Cornelius's vision four times (10:3–6,22,30–32; 11:13–14) and Peter's vision twice (10:9–16; 11:4–10), and Peter recounts the whole episode to the Jerusalem church (11:4–17).

10:1–8 *Cornelius Calls for Peter.* Luke introduces Cornelius as a devout seeker of God, a prime candidate for entrance into the church. Yet as elsewhere in Acts, it is God who initiates the advance of the gospel, this time through a vision given to Cornelius (v. 3).

10:1 Caesarea. Refers to the coastal city of Caesarea Maritima (not to be confused with Caesarea Philippi), the Roman administrative center of Judea. Herod the Great built it on a grand scale ca. 25–13 BC and named it for Caesar Augustus. **centurion.** A commander of about 100 men. They were the backbone of the Roman army. **Italian Regiment.** Regiments had both numbers and names (see the "Imperial Regiment" in 27:1) and were made up of about 600 soldiers. Ten regiments made up a Roman legion (about 6,000 troops).

10:2 God-fearing. Cornelius is a "God-fearer," a Gentile who worships the one true God of Israel but has not fully converted to Judaism as a "proselyte," which entails circumcision and keeping OT dietary laws. These God-fearing Gentiles are among the most receptive to the gospel. **gave generously ... and prayed.** Judaism considered almsgiving and prayer signs of piety. For another pious centurion, see Luke 7:1–10.

10:3 three in the afternoon. One of the traditional times of Jewish prayer (the others were early morning and sunset/evening).

10:4 memorial offering. May be the OT language of sacrifice (Lev 2:2,9,16; cf. Phil 4:18), though it could simply mean "as a constant reminder (of your faithfulness)."

10:5 Joppa. On the Mediterranean coast about 30 miles (about 48 kilometers) south of Caesarea (see 9:36 and note).

10:9–23a *Peter's Vision.* Peter's symbolic vision of "unclean" animals and God's command not to "call anything impure that God has made clean" (v. 15) prepare Peter to meet the Gentile centurion Cornelius and emphasize God's initiative in the church's outreach to the Gentiles.

10:9 up on the roof. Roofs were flat, and people used them for storage and living space—a good place for private prayer.

10:10 hungry. Provides the narrative context for a vision about food.

10:12 four-footed animals ... reptiles and birds. A common threefold division of the animal kingdom (see Gen 1:30; 6:20; Rom 1:23).

10:13–14 Kill and eat ... Surely not, Lord! Peter probably thinks this is a test of his faithfulness and so refuses to eat. In the OT, God declares certain animals "impure or unclean" (see Lev 11) and commands Jews not to eat them.

10:15 The coming of the new covenant age of salvation means both the full inclusion of the Gentiles in the people of God and the fulfillment of OT laws of ritual purity (Mark 7:19; Col 2:16–17). The vision here previews both these things and opens the way for table-fellowship between Jews and Gentiles.

10:16 three times. Confirms its validity.

The harbor at Caesarea Maritima. Caesarea was the headquarters for the Roman forces, and Cornelius was stationed there as a centurion (Acts 10:1).

17 While Peter was wondering about the meaning of the vision, the men sent by Cornelius[x] found out
where Simon's house was and stopped at the gate. 18 They called out, asking if Simon who was known
as Peter was staying there.

19 While Peter was still thinking about the vision, the Spirit said[y] to him, "Simon, three[a] men are
looking for you. 20 So get up and go downstairs. Do not hesitate to go with them, for I have sent them."[z]

21 Peter went down and said to the men, "I'm the one you're looking for. Why have you come?"

22 The men replied, "We have come from Cornelius the centurion. He is a righteous and God-fearing
man,[a] who is respected by all the Jewish people. A holy angel told him to ask you to come to his house so
that he could hear what you have to say."[b] 23 Then Peter invited the men into the house to be his guests.

Peter at Cornelius's House

The next day Peter started out with them, and some of the believers[c] from Joppa went along.[d] 24 The
following day he arrived in Caesarea.[e] Cornelius was expecting them and had called together his relatives and close friends. 25 As Peter entered the house, Cornelius met him and fell at his feet in reverence.
26 But Peter made him get up. "Stand up," he said, "I am only a man myself."[f]

27 While talking with him, Peter went inside and found a large gathering of people. 28 He said to them:
"You are well aware that it is against our law for a Jew to associate with or visit a Gentile.[g] But God has
shown me that I should not call anyone impure or unclean.[h] 29 So when I was sent for, I came without
raising any objection. May I ask why you sent for me?"

10:17 [x]ver 7,8
10:19 [y]Ac 8:29
10:20 [z]Ac 15:7-9
10:22 [a]ver 2 [b]Ac 11:14
10:23 [c]Ac 1:16 [d]ver 45; Ac 11:12
10:24 [e]Ac 8:40
10:26 [f]Ac 14:15; Rev 19:10
10:28 [g]Jn 4:9; 18:28; Ac 11:3 [h]Ac 15:8,9

[a] *19* One early manuscript *two*; other manuscripts do not have the number.

10:23a Peter is already beginning to understand the significance of the vision since Jews would not normally stay under the same roof as an "unclean" Gentile (see v. 28).

10:23b–48 *Peter at Cornelius's House.* Peter's journey to Cornelius's house (vv. 23b–33), his preaching there (vv. 34–43), and the reception of the Spirit by Cornelius and his household (vv. 44–48) mark the first explicit Gentile conversion and reception of the Spirit in the book of Acts. Some people call this episode the "Gentile Pentecost" (see also the "Samaritan Pentecost" in 8:17).

10:23b Peter wisely takes "some of the believers from Joppa"—Jewish Christians ("six brothers" according to 11:12)—as witnesses to whatever happens.

10:25 in reverence. Can mean either "revere" or "worship." Cornelius is probably honoring rather than worshiping Peter, but Peter takes no chances and makes it clear he is "only a man" (v. 26), not a god. Contrast Herod's prideful acceptance of divine acclamation and its result in 12:19b–23.

10:28 God has shown me. Peter repeatedly affirms that he now understands the meaning of the vision (see vv. 34–35,47–48; 11:17). The separation between Jew ("clean") and Gentile ("unclean") is being broken down.

10:34 [i]Dt 10:17; 2Ch 19:7; Job 34:19; Ro 2:11; Gal 2:6; Eph 6:9; Col 3:25; 1Pe 1:17
10:35 [j]Ac 15:9
10:36 [k]Ac 13:32 [l]Lk 2:14 [m]Mt 28:18; Ro 10:12
10:38 [n]Ac 4:26 [o]Mt 4:23 [p]Jn 3:2
10:39 [q]Lk 24:48 [r]Ac 5:30
10:40 [s]Ac 2:24
10:41 [t]Jn 14:17,22 [u]Lk 24:43; Jn 21:13
10:42 [v]Mt 28:19,20 [w]Jn 5:22; Ac 17:31; Ro 14:9; 2Co 5:10; 2Ti 4:1; 1Pe 4:5
10:43 [x]Isa 53:11 [y]Ac 15:9
10:44 [z]Ac 8:15,16; 11:15; 15:8
10:45 [a]ver 23 [b]Ac 2:33, 38 [c]Ac 11:18
10:46 [d]Mk 16:17
10:47 [e]Ac 8:36 [f]Ac 11:17
10:48 [g]Ac 2:38; 8:16
11:1 [h]Ac 1:16
11:2 [i]Ac 10:45
11:3 [j]Ac 10:25,28; Gal 2:12
11:5 [k]Ac 9:10; 10:9-32

[30]Cornelius answered: "Three days ago I was in my house praying at this hour, at three in the afternoon. Suddenly a man in shining clothes stood before me [31]and said, 'Cornelius, God has heard your
prayer and remembered your gifts to the poor. [32]Send to Joppa for Simon who is called Peter. He is a
guest in the home of Simon the tanner, who lives by the sea.' [33]So I sent for you immediately, and it
was good of you to come. Now we are all here in the presence of God to listen to everything the Lord
has commanded you to tell us."

[34]Then Peter began to speak: "I now realize how true it is that God does not show favoritism[i] [35]but accepts from every nation the one who fears him and does what is right.[j] [36]You know the message God sent to
the people of Israel, announcing the good news[k] of peace[l] through Jesus Christ, who is Lord of all.[m] [37]You
know what has happened throughout the province of Judea, beginning in Galilee after the baptism that
John preached— [38]how God anointed[n] Jesus of Nazareth with the Holy Spirit and power, and how he went
around doing good and healing[o] all who were under the power of the devil, because God was with him.[p]

[39]"We are witnesses[q] of everything he did in the country of the Jews and in Jerusalem. They killed him
by hanging him on a cross,[r] [40]but God raised him from the dead[s] on the third day and caused him to be
seen. [41]He was not seen by all the people,[t] but by witnesses whom God had already chosen—by us who
ate[u] and drank with him after he rose from the dead. [42]He commanded us to preach to the people[v] and
to testify that he is the one whom God appointed as judge of the living and the dead.[w] [43]All the prophets
testify about him[x] that everyone[y] who believes in him receives forgiveness of sins through his name."

[44]While Peter was still speaking these words, the Holy Spirit came on[z] all who heard the message.
[45]The circumcised believers who had come with Peter[a] were astonished that the gift of the Holy Spirit
had been poured out[b] even on Gentiles.[c] [46]For they heard them speaking in tongues[a][d] and praising God.

Then Peter said, [47]"Surely no one can stand in the way of their being baptized with water.[e] They have
received the Holy Spirit just as we have."[f] [48]So he ordered that they be baptized in the name of Jesus
Christ.[g] Then they asked Peter to stay with them for a few days.

Peter Explains His Actions

11 The apostles and the believers[h] throughout Judea heard that the Gentiles also had received the
word of God. [2]So when Peter went up to Jerusalem, the circumcised believers[i] criticized him
[3]and said, "You went into the house of uncircumcised men and ate with them."[j]

[4]Starting from the beginning, Peter told them the whole story: [5]"I was in the city of Joppa praying,
and in a trance I saw a vision.[k] I saw something like a large sheet being let down from heaven by its four
corners, and it came down to where I was. [6]I looked into it and saw four-footed animals of the earth,
wild beasts, reptiles and birds. [7]Then I heard a voice telling me, 'Get up, Peter. Kill and eat.'

[8]"I replied, 'Surely not, Lord! Nothing impure or unclean has ever entered my mouth.'

[a] *46* Or *other languages*

10:30 Three days ago. Lit. "from the fourth day until this hour," which is equivalent to "three days ago" (the present day is the fourth day, so the vision was three days previous).

10:36 the people of Israel. The message goes first to them (Rom 1:16–17) and then to all nations. **Lord of all.** Lord of both Jews and Gentiles (1:8; Luke 2:30–32; 24:47).

10:37–42 Peter concisely summarizes the key events of Jesus' ministry as the Gospels record them: (1) the preaching of John the Baptist, (2) Jesus anointed with the Spirit at his baptism, (3) healing and exorcisms in Galilee, (4) journey through Judea to Jerusalem, (5) arrest and crucifixion, (6) resurrection on the third day, (7) resurrection appearances, (8) the Great Commission, and (9) Jesus' future return as judge of all.

10:37 You know. Peter says that they know of these events. The fame of Jesus and John the Baptist has evidently come to the attention of Roman authorities in Caesarea (see Paul's similar statement to Herod Agrippa II in 26:26–27).

10:39–40 They killed him ... but God raised him. Despite the actions of evil men, God sovereignly accomplished his saving purpose through Jesus' death and resurrection. This God-designed reversal is a major theme in Acts (2:23–24; 3:15; 4:10; 13:29–30; 17:31).

10:39 hanging him on a cross. See 5:30 and note.

10:44–46 The presence of the Holy Spirit confirms their salvation and proves that God has initiated and approved the mission to the Gentiles. In Acts "speaking in tongues" (v. 46) is sometimes (but not always) the external evidence of the Spirit's coming (2:4,11; 19:6).

10:47 baptized with water. The external sign of the internal salvation accomplished by the Holy Spirit. **They.** Gentiles. **just as we have.** At Pentecost (ch. 2).

11:1–18 *Peter Explains His Actions.* When Peter returns to Jerusalem, some of the Jewish Christians challenge him for entering the home of an uncircumcised Gentile (vv. 2–3). Peter responds by recounting the Cornelius episode in detail, again demonstrating that Gentiles accepted the gospel because of God's work rather than any human initiative. Repeating the story confirms its importance for Luke.

11:2 circumcised believers. The conservative wing of the Jewish Christians in Jerusalem who believed that Gentiles should become Jews (be circumcised and keep the OT law) in order to be saved. These Jewish Christians are concerned that Peter ate with the Gentiles (v. 3), since table-fellowship demonstrated social acceptance and since contact with Gentiles ceremonially defiled Jews.

9“The voice spoke from heaven a second time, ‘Do not call anything impure that God has made
clean.’[l] 10This happened three times, and then it was all pulled up to heaven again.
11“Right then three men who had been sent to me from Caesarea stopped at the house where I was
staying. 12The Spirit told[m] me to have no hesitation about going with them.[n] These six brothers also
went with me, and we entered the man’s house. 13He told us how he had seen an angel appear in his
house and say, ‘Send to Joppa for Simon who is called Peter. 14He will bring you a message through
which you and all your household[o] will be saved.’
15“As I began to speak, the Holy Spirit came on[p] them as he had come on us at the beginning.[q]
16Then I remembered what the Lord had said: ‘John baptized with[a] water, but you will be baptized with[a]
the Holy Spirit.’[r] 17So if God gave them the same gift he gave us[s] who believed in the Lord Jesus Christ,
who was I to think that I could stand in God’s way?”
18When they heard this, they had no further objections and praised God, saying, “So then, even to
Gentiles God has granted repentance that leads to life.”[t]

The Church in Antioch

19Now those who had been scattered by the persecution that broke out when Stephen was killed[u]
traveled as far as Phoenicia, Cyprus and Antioch,[v] spreading the word only among Jews. 20Some of
them, however, men from Cyprus[w] and Cyrene,[x] went to Antioch and began to speak to Greeks also,
telling them the good news about the Lord Jesus. 21The Lord’s hand was with them,[y] and a great number
of people believed and turned to the Lord.[z]
22News of this reached the church in Jerusalem, and they
sent Barnabas[a] to Antioch. 23When he arrived and saw what
the grace of God had done,[b] he was glad and encouraged
them all to remain true to the Lord with all their hearts.[c]
24He was a good man, full of the Holy Spirit and faith, and a
great number of people were brought to the Lord.[d]
25Then Barnabas went to Tarsus[e] to look for Saul, 26and
when he found him, he brought him to Antioch. So for a
whole year Barnabas and Saul met with the church and
taught great numbers of people. The disciples[f] were called
Christians first[g] at Antioch.
27During this time some prophets[h] came down from

[a] *16* Or *in*

ROMAN EMPERORS

EMPEROR	DATE OF REIGN
Octavian “Augustus”	31 BC–AD 14
Tiberius	14–37
Gaius “Caligula”	37–41
Claudius	41–54
Nero	54–68

11:9 [l]Ac 10:15
11:12 [m]Ac 8:29 [n]Ac 15:9; Ro 3:22
11:14 [o]Jn 4:53; Ac 16:15,31-34; 1Co 1:11,16
11:15 [p]Ac 10:44 [q]Ac 2:4
11:16 [r]Mk 1:8; Ac 1:5
11:17 [s]Ac 10:45,47
11:18 [t]Ro 10:12,13; 2Co 7:10
11:19 [u]Ac 8:1,4 [v]ver 26, 27; Ac 13:1; 18:22; Gal 2:11
11:20 [w]Ac 4:36 [x]Mt 27:32
11:21 [y]Lk 1:66 [z]Ac 2:47
11:22 [a]Ac 4:36
11:23 [b]Ac 13:43; 14:26; 20:24 [c]Ac 14:22
11:24 [d]ver 21; Ac 5:14
11:25 [e]Ac 9:11
11:26 [f]Ac 6:1,2; 13:52 [g]Ac 26:28; 1Pe 4:16
11:27 [h]Ac 13:1; 15:32; 1Co 12:28,29; Eph 4:11

11:17 who was I to . . . stand in God’s way? The central theme of Acts, demonstrated throughout this passage, is that the advance of the gospel is the unstoppable work of God.

11:19–30 *The Church in Antioch.* Luke narrates the founding of the multiethnic church in Antioch, which becomes the launching point for the widespread mission to the Gentiles (13:1–4; 15:40; 18:23). Much of this section is a flashback, picking up from the scattering of believers in 8:1b. Luke probably presents the Cornelius episode first (10:1—11:18) to demonstrate that God initiates the Gentile mission through the apostle Peter, who was highly respected among the Jewish Christians.

11:19 Phoenicia. The narrow country along the Mediterranean coast north of Israel (present-day Lebanon). Its chief cities were Tyre and Sidon. **Cyprus.** An island nation in the northeast Mediterranean about 70 miles (about 112 kilometers) off the coast of Phoenicia. Barnabas was from Cyprus (4:36). **Antioch.** The third largest city in the Roman Empire (behind Rome and Alexandria) with a population of 250,000–500,000 people; located on the Orontes River, 15 miles (24 kilometers) east of the Mediterranean Sea.

11:20 Cyrene. See note on 2:10. **Greeks.** Greek-speaking Gentiles; the same Greek word is used in Rom 1:16; 2:9; 3:9, where it is translated “Gentile(s).”

11:22 As it previously did with the Samaritans (8:14), the Jerusalem church sends a representative to investigate this report. **Barnabas.** He already has a track record as a mediator, a role he plays throughout Acts (4:36–37; 9:27; 11:23–26,30; 13:2; 15:37).

11:25 Luke last mentioned Saul departing for Tarsus after his Jerusalem visit in 9:26–30 (cf. Gal 1:18–19), perhaps six to nine years earlier. He has likely been ministering in and around Tarsus since then.

11:26 Christians. Means “belonging to Christ” or “followers of Christ.” Unbelievers likely first called them this, perhaps in a derogatory sense (see 26:28; 1 Pet 4:16). The name suggests that people are beginning to view them as members of a group distinct from Judaism. Luke generally refers to Christians as “brothers and sisters,” “believers,” “disciples,” or followers of “the Way.”

11:27–30 This visit (AD 47–48) is probably the one Paul refers to in Gal 2:1, about 14 years after his conversion (AD 33). Like Paul’s later collection for the poor in Jerusalem (Rom 15:25–27; 1 Cor 16:1–4; 2 Cor 8–9), this act of compassion demonstrates unity and that the church at Antioch supports the mother church in Jerusalem.

11:27 prophets. Had special Spirit-given gifts to announce a message from the Lord (13:1; 15:32; 19:6; 21:9; Rom 12:6; 1 Cor 12:10; 14:29–37), which sometimes included predicting the future, as in the case of Agabus (v. 28). Agabus appears again in 21:10.

11:28 [i]Ac 21:10 [j]Mt 24:14 [k]Ac 18:2
11:29 [l]ver 26 [m]Ro 15:26; 2Co 9:2 [n]Ac 1:16
11:30 [o]Ac 14:23 [p]Ac 12:25
12:2 [q]Mt 4:21
12:3 [r]Ac 24:27 [s]Ex 12:15; 23:15
12:5 [t]Eph 6:18
12:6 [u]Ac 21:33
12:7 [v]Ac 5:19 [w]Ac 16:26
12:9 [x]Ac 9:10
12:10 [y]Ac 5:19; 16:26

Jerusalem to Antioch. 28 One of them, named Agabus,[i] stood up and
through the Spirit predicted that a severe famine would spread over
the entire Roman world.[j] (This happened during the reign of Claudius.)[k] 29 The disciples,[l] as each one was able, decided to provide
help[m] for the brothers and sisters[n] living in Judea. 30 This they did,
sending their gift to the elders[o] by Barnabas and Saul.[p]

Peter's Miraculous Escape From Prison

12 It was about this time that King Herod arrested some who
belonged to the church, intending to persecute them. 2 He had
James, the brother of John,[q] put to death with the sword. 3 When he saw
that this met with approval among the Jews,[r] he proceeded to seize Peter also. This happened during the Festival of Unleavened Bread.[s]
4 After arresting him, he put him in prison, handing him over to
be guarded by four squads of four soldiers each. Herod intended
to bring him out for public trial after the Passover.

5 So Peter was kept in prison, but the church was earnestly
praying to God for him.[t]

6 The night before Herod was to bring him to trial, Peter was sleeping between two soldiers, bound with two chains,[u] and sentries stood
guard at the entrance. 7 Suddenly an angel[v] of the Lord appeared and
a light shone in the cell. He struck Peter on the side and woke him up.
"Quick, get up!" he said, and the chains fell off Peter's wrists.[w]

8 Then the angel said to him, "Put on your clothes and sandals." And Peter did so. "Wrap your cloak
around you and follow me," the angel told him. 9 Peter followed him out of the prison, but he had no
idea that what the angel was doing was really happening; he thought he was seeing a vision.[x] 10 They
passed the first and second guards and came to the iron gate leading to the city. It opened for them by
itself,[y] and they went through it. When they had walked the length of one street, suddenly the angel
left him.

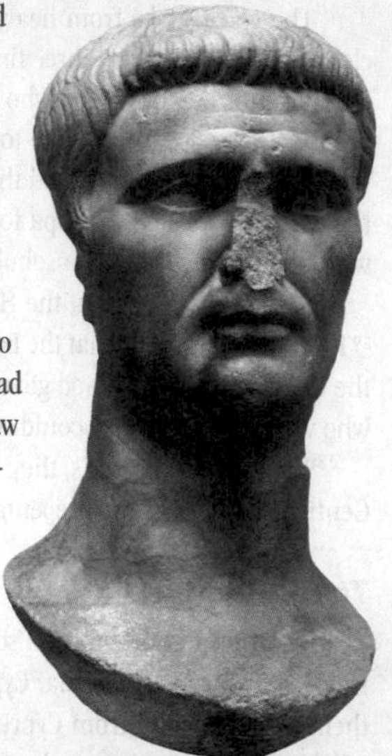

Bust of Claudius, Roman emperor AD 41–54.

11:28 severe famine. Claudius was emperor AD 41–54, and there were many famines throughout the Roman Empire during his reign. **entire Roman world.** There were various regional famines (Rome, Greece, Egypt, etc.) during Claudius's reign, which could be said to have affected the whole empire. One inscription from Asia Minor speaks of one of these famines gripping the whole world. For a similar expression, see Luke 2:1. Luke may be referring to a famine that occurred in Judea around AD 46. If so, ch. 12 in Acts is a flashback since Herod died in AD 44 (12:19–24).

11:30 elders. This is the first time that Luke calls the leaders in the Jerusalem church "elders" (cf. 15:2,4,6,22,23; 16:4; 21:18). For elder leadership in the mission churches, see 14:23; 20:17; 1 Tim 3:1–7 ("overseer"); 5:17; Titus 1:5–9.

12:1–19a *Peter's Miraculous Escape From Prison.* The church faces its greatest crisis yet as King Herod Agrippa I arrests and executes the apostle James. This is the second martyrdom in Acts (see 7:54—8:1a), and James is the first of the 12 apostles to be killed. Pleased with the response of the Jewish leadership, Herod puts Peter in jail to await trial and likely execution. Yet the gospel is unstoppable (5:39), and an angel of the Lord miraculously intervenes to free Peter, surprising even the church that is praying for him.

12:1 King Herod. Agrippa I, son of Aristobulus and grandson of Herod the Great. Raised in Rome, he gained the favor of influential friends (especially the emperors Caligula and Claudius) and over time was granted rule over a Jewish kingdom almost as great as his famous grandfather, including Judea, Samaria, Galilee, the Transjordan, and the Decapolis. He worked hard to curry favor with his Jewish subjects, which explains why he persecuted the church (see chart/map, pp. 1930–1931).

12:2 James. The apostle, son of Zebedee, and "brother of John" (Luke 5:10; 6:14; 8:51; 9:28), not Jesus' half brother James (v. 17). Jesus predicted that James and John would suffer and possibly die (Mark 10:35,39). **put to death with the sword.** Probably beheaded (cf. John the Baptist in Mark 6:24–29; Luke 9:9).

12:3 approval. The Jewish leadership in Jerusalem is suspicious and jealous of the growing Christian movement (5:17), so executing one of its key leaders pleases them. Seeing this positive result, Herod arrests an even more prominent apostle, Peter himself. **Festival of Unleavened Bread.** The week-long festival that immediately follows Passover (Exod 12:1–20; 23:15; 34:18; Deut 16:1–8). This event likely occurred in the spring of AD 43 or 44.

12:4 four squads of four soldiers each. They probably rotated, each squad taking a three-hour watch of the night. One soldier would be chained to Peter on his left, one on his right, and one would be posted at each of the two gates leading out of the jail (vv. 6,10).

12:5 prison. Probably in the Fortress of Antonia, on the northwest corner of the temple mount, though possibly at Herod's palace, west of the temple mount.

12:7–10 An angel previously delivered the apostles from jail (5:17–23; cf. 16:25–26). Peter is groggy and half asleep and must be told what to do each step of the way. This is God's deliverance, not Peter's escape.

12:7 woke him up. Peter's sound sleep could be from exhaustion, but it more likely indicates his confidence in God, whatever the outcome of his trial. Peter is a changed man since the resurrection (2:14–39; 3:11–26; 4:8–13; 5:29–32).

[11]Then Peter came to himself[z] and said, "Now I know without a doubt that the Lord has sent his
angel and rescued me[a] from Herod's clutches and from everything the Jewish people were hoping
would happen."
[12]When this had dawned on him, he went to the house of Mary the mother of John, also called
Mark,[b] where many people had gathered and were praying.[c] [13]Peter knocked at the outer entrance,
and a servant named Rhoda came to answer the door.[d] [14]When she recognized Peter's voice, she was so
overjoyed[e] she ran back without opening it and exclaimed, "Peter is at the door!"

12:11 [z]Lk 15:17 [a]Ps 34:7; Da 3:28; 6:22; 2Co 1:10; 2Pe 2:9
12:12 [b]ver 25; Ac 15:37, 39; Col 4:10; Phm 24; 1Pe 5:13 [c]ver 5
12:13 [d]Jn 18:16,17
12:14 [e]Lk 24:41

12:12 Evidently a house church meets in Mary's home. She is likely a widow since the text does not mention her husband. Her son "John, also called Mark," is Barnabas's cousin. He goes with Paul and Barnabas on their first missionary journey (v. 25; 13:5). Though he alienates Paul as a result of abandoning the group during this mission (13:13; 15:37–39), the two later reconcile (Col 4:10; 2 Tim 4:11; Phlm 24). This Mark is also a later associate of the apostle Peter (1 Pet 5:13) and the author of the second Gospel.

12:13–16 Luke delights in a good story, and there is both humor and irony here: Rhoda in her excitement forgets to open the door, and the church that is praying for Peter refuses to believe that God has delivered him.

PAUL'S LIFE

DATE	EVENT
AD 33	Paul's conversion
33–35	Paul preaches in Damascus
36	Paul's first Jerusalem visit
36–45	Paul's stay in Syria and Cilicia
44	James the apostle dies
44	Herod Agrippa I dies
45–46	Paul's ministry in Antioch
46	Famine in Jerusalem area
46	Paul's second Jerusalem visit (famine relief)
46–47	Paul's first missionary journey
47–48	Paul's stay in Antioch
48	Council at Jerusalem
49–52	Paul's second missionary journey
fall of 50 to spring of 52	Paul's founding visit to Corinth (18 months)
51	Paul began to involve Timothy in ministry
52–57	Paul's third missionary journey (and collects money for Jerusalem believers)
52–55	Paul's stay in Ephesus
summer or fall of 55	Paul's brief "painful" (second) visit to Corinth
Spring of 56	Paul wrote "severe letter" to Corinth (it no longer exists)
Winter 56/57	Paul's "final" visit to Corinth (3 months long)
Spring of 57	Paul travels through Macedonia and Greece after leaving Corinth
Spring 57	Paul returns to Judea
57–59	Paul's imprisonment in Judea (in Caesarea)
60	Paul arrives in Rome
60–62	Paul's first imprisonment in Rome
62–64	Paul's fourth missionary journey
64	Paul's second imprisonment
64–67 (?)	Paul's death in Rome

12:15 [f]Mt 18:10
12:17 [g]Ac 13:16; 19:33; 21:40 [h]Ac 15:13 [i]Ac 1:16
12:19 [j]Ac 16:27 [k]Ac 8:40
12:20 [l]Mt 11:21 [m]1Ki 5:9,11; Eze 27:17

15 "You're out of your mind," they told her. When she kept insisting that it was so, they said, "It must
be his angel."[f]
16 But Peter kept on knocking, and when they opened the door and saw him, they were astonished.
17 Peter motioned with his hand[g] for them to be quiet and described how the Lord had brought him
out of prison. "Tell James[h] and the other brothers and sisters[i] about this," he said, and then he left for
another place.
18 In the morning, there was no small commotion among the soldiers as to what had become of Peter.
19 After Herod had a thorough search made for him and did not find him, he cross-examined the guards
and ordered that they be executed.[j]

Herod's Death

Then Herod went from Judea to Caesarea[k] and stayed there. 20 He had been quarreling with the people of Tyre and Sidon;[l] they now joined together and sought an audience with him. After securing the
support of Blastus, a trusted personal servant of the king, they asked for peace, because they depended
on the king's country for their food supply.[m]
21 On the appointed day Herod, wearing his royal robes, sat on his throne and delivered a public address to the people. 22 They shouted, "This is the voice of a god, not of a man." 23 Immediately, because

Model of the Fortress of Antonia, the probable location of Peter's imprisonment (Acts 12:5).

12:15 his angel. May reflect Jewish belief in a guardian angel for each person (Ps 91:11; Matt 18:10; Heb 1:14) or perhaps they suspect that Peter has been executed and Rhoda has seen his spirit.
12:17 James. Jesus' half brother (see note on 1:14). He has moved into leadership among the elders of the Jerusalem church (15:13–21; 21:18; 1 Cor 15:7; Gal 1:19; 2:9,12; see Introduction to James: Author). The other apostles may be hiding because of Herod's actions. **he left for another place.** Peter likely went to a place of safety away from Herod. This is not a permanent departure, since Peter is back in Jerusalem for the Jerusalem council in 15:7–21.
12:19a executed. Roman law specified that guards who let a prisoner escape were to receive the punishment that the prisoner would have received.
12:19b–24 *Herod's Death.* As judgment for Herod's evil actions against the church and his arrogantly accepting divine worship, an angel of the Lord strikes him down in an act of retribution. No one, no matter how politically or militarily powerful, is a match for the Spirit-empowered progress of the gospel. The Jewish historian Josephus provides a similar account of Herod's death (*Antiquities*, 19.343–352). He notes that the occasion was a festival in honor of Caesar. When Herod appeared in silver robes sparkling in the sun, the people acclaimed him a god. He did not deny it and suddenly experienced violent pains in his belly. He was carried out and into the palace, where he died five days later.
12:20 Tyre and Sidon. Important coastal cities in Phoenicia, north of Israel. They were often dependent on Israel for their grain supply (1 Kgs 5:11; Ezek 27:17). **Blastus.** Nothing else is known about Herod's chamberlain, or personal assistant.
12:23 struck him down. God's dramatic judgment against Herod recalls the severe judgment against Ananias and Sapphira (5:1–11). **eaten by worms.** The Greek word order shows that this is part of the judgment against Herod rather than what happened to his body after death. Though the nature of the disease is unknown (intestinal disease exacerbated by parasites?), it was clearly a painful and gruesome death.

FOUR JAMESES IN THE EARLY CHURCH

James, the father of Judas	• his son, Judas, was one of the 12 apostles (Luke 6:16; Acts 1:13)
James, the son of Alphaeus	• one of the 12 apostles (Luke 6:15; Acts 1:13)
James, the brother of John	• the son of Zebedee (Luke 5:10; 9:28, 54) • one of the 12 apostles (Acts 1:13) • killed by Herod Agrippa (Acts 12:2)
James, the brother of the Lord	• half brother of the Lord Jesus; son of Mary and Joseph (Acts 12:17; 15:13; 21:18; 1 Cor 15:7; Gal 1:19; 2:9, 12; Jas 1:1; Jude 1)

Herod did not give praise to God, an angel of the Lord struck him down,[n] and he was eaten by worms
and died.
[24]But the word of God continued to spread and flourish.[o]

Barnabas and Saul Sent Off

[25]When Barnabas[p] and Saul had finished their mission,[q] they returned from[a] Jerusalem, taking
13 with them John, also called Mark.[r] [1]Now in the church at Antioch[s] there were prophets[t] and
teachers: Barnabas,[u] Simeon called Niger, Lucius of Cyrene, Manaen (who had been brought
up with Herod[v] the tetrarch) and Saul. [2]While they were worshiping the Lord and fasting, the Holy Spirit
said,[w] "Set apart for me Barnabas and Saul for the work[x] to which I have called them."[y] [3]So after they
had fasted and prayed, they placed their hands on them[z] and sent them off.[a]

On Cyprus

[4]The two of them, sent on their way by the Holy Spirit,[b] went down to Seleucia and sailed from there
to Cyprus.[c] [5]When they arrived at Salamis, they proclaimed the word of God in the Jewish synagogues.[d]
John[e] was with them as their helper.
[6]They traveled through the whole island until they came to Paphos. There they met a Jewish sorcerer[f]

12:23 [n] 1Sa 25:38; 2Sa 24:16,17
12:24 [o] Ac 6:7; 19:20
12:25 [p] Ac 4:36 [q] Ac 11:30 [r] ver 12
13:1 [s] Ac 11:19 [t] Ac 11:27 [u] Ac 4:36; 11:22-26 [v] Mt 14:1
13:2 [w] Ac 8:29 [x] Ac 14:26 [y] Ac 22:21
13:3 [z] Ac 6:6 [a] Ac 14:26
13:4 [b] ver 2,3 [c] Ac 4:36
13:5 [d] Ac 9:20 [e] Ac 12:12
13:6 [f] Ac 8:9

[a] 25 Some manuscripts *to*

12:24 For similar summaries of the church's growth, see 2:41,47; 4:4; 5:14; 6:1,7; 9:31; 16:5; 19:20.

12:25—28:31 *The Witness to the Ends of the Earth.* This is the third major phase of outreach in Acts (Jerusalem: 3:1—5:42; Judea and Samaria: 6:1—12:24), one that continues through the rest of the book. Paul's three missionary journeys and his journey under guard to Rome represent for Luke the fulfillment of the third part of Jesus' commission in 1:8 ("to the ends of the earth").

12:25—14:28 *Paul's First Missionary Journey.* Paul's first missionary journey brings the gospel to Cyprus and Galatia (13:1—14:28). Churches are established in Pisidian Antioch, Iconium, Lystra, and Derbe. The success of this mission is summarized in 14:27, where the missionaries report that "God ... had opened a door of faith to the Gentiles." The journey thus represents a major breakthrough in the advance of the gospel to all nations.

12:25—13:3 *Barnabas and Saul Sent Off.* Like so many events in Acts, the first missionary journey is not the work of any human agent, but is initiated and directed by the Spirit of God. See note on 13:2.

12:25 Luke transitions back to the church in Antioch by concluding the account of Paul and Barnabas's famine visit to Jerusalem (11:27–30). **John, also called Mark.** See note on v. 12.

13:1 church at Antioch. The first church with a significant outreach to the Gentiles (11:19–26). They now become the first to launch a major missionary outreach beyond their borders. **prophets and teachers.** The leadership of the church at Antioch. On the spiritual gift of prophecy, see note on 1 Cor 12:1—14:40; see also notes on 1 Cor 12:8–10; 14:1–25,29–35; Eph 2:20; 4:11; see further "Prophets and Prophecy," p. 2668. Prophecy can entail "foretelling" (predicting the future) but is primarily "forthtelling" (proclaiming God's message). The names of these leaders suggest significant ethnic and sociocultural diversity. **Barnabas.** See note on 4:36. **Niger.** Means "black," so Simeon may have been African, or the term could refer to his dark complexion. **Cyrene.** In Libya, north Africa (see note on 2:10). **Manaen.** Evidently raised in the royal court as a childhood friend of "Herod the tetrarch," i.e., Herod Antipas (see Luke 3:1 and note).

13:2 the Holy Spirit said. The Holy Spirit is the guiding force throughout Acts and so calls forth this missionary outreach. This is God's work, not the result of human plans (5:39). The church discerns his will in the context of "worshiping" and "fasting." The message likely came through one of the prophets in the church.

13:3 placed their hands on them. A sign of affirmation, support, and partnership (see 6:6; 1 Tim 5:22; 2 Tim 1:6; Heb 6:2 and notes). It is also common in healing (9:17; 28:8; Luke 4:40; 13:13) and preparing to receive the Spirit (Acts 8:17; 9:17; 19:6).

13:4–12 *On Cyprus.* The missionaries head first to the island of Cyprus, Barnabas's homeland (4:36). There Paul wins a spiritual victory over a sorcerer named Elymas (vv. 6–11) and converts the proconsul of the island, Sergius Paulus (v. 12; see v. 7).

13:4–5 The missionary team travels 16 miles (25 kilometers) from Antioch to the seaport of Seleucia and then crosses over by ship 130 miles (209 kilometers) to Salamis on the eastern coast of Cyprus.

13:5 in the Jewish synagogues. They begin preaching there first, a pattern repeated throughout Acts (v. 14; 9:20; 14:1; 17:1–2,10,17; 18:4; 19:8; see note on 9:15).

13:6 Paphos. About 100 miles (about 160 kilometers) from Salamis, on the island's western coast. It was the seat of Roman government. **Bar-Jesus.** "Son of Jesus/Joshua"; a Jewish magician and "false prophet." Judaism of the first century was often syncretistic, with sorcerers like Bar-Jesus combining pagan and Jewish practices.

13:6 [g] Mt 7:15
13:7 [h] ver 8,12; Ac 19:38
13:8 [i] Ac 8:9 [j] ver 7 [k] Ac 6:7
13:9 [l] Ac 4:8
13:10 [m] Mt 13:38; Jn 8:44 [n] Hos 14:9
13:11 [o] Ex 9:3; 1Sa 5:6,7; Ps 32:4
13:12 [p] ver 7
13:13 [q] ver 6 [r] Ac 12:12
13:14 [s] Ac 14:19,21 [t] Ac 16:13 [u] Ac 9:20
13:15 [v] Ac 15:21
13:16 [w] Ac 12:17
13:17 [x] Ex 6:6,7; Dt 7:6-8
13:18 [y] Dt 1:31 [z] Ac 7:36
13:19 [a] Dt 7:1 [b] Jos 19:51
13:20 [c] Jdg 2:16 [d] 1Sa 3:19,20
13:21 [e] 1Sa 8:5,19 [f] 1Sa 10:1 [g] 1Sa 9:1,2
13:22 [h] 1Sa 15:23,26 [i] 1Sa 16:13; Ps 89:20 [j] 1Sa 13:14

and false prophet[g] named Bar-Jesus, 7 who was an attendant of the proconsul,[h] Sergius Paulus. The proconsul, an intelligent man, sent for Barnabas and Saul because he wanted to hear the word of God. 8 But
Elymas the sorcerer[i] (for that is what his name means) opposed them and tried to turn the proconsul[j]
from the faith.[k] 9 Then Saul, who was also called Paul, filled with the Holy Spirit,[l] looked straight at Elymas and said, 10 "You are a child of the devil[m] and an enemy of everything that is right! You are full of all
kinds of deceit and trickery. Will you never stop perverting the right ways of the Lord?[n] 11 Now the hand of
the Lord is against you.[o] You are going to be blind for a time, not even able to see the light of the sun."

Immediately mist and darkness came over him, and he groped about, seeking someone to lead him
by the hand. 12 When the proconsul[p] saw what had happened, he believed, for he was amazed at the
teaching about the Lord.

In Pisidian Antioch

13 From Paphos,[q] Paul and his companions sailed to Perga in Pamphylia, where John[r] left them to return to Jerusalem. 14 From Perga they went on to Pisidian Antioch.[s] On the Sabbath[t] they entered the synagogue[u] and sat down. 15 After the reading from the Law[v] and the Prophets, the leaders of the synagogue
sent word to them, saying, "Brothers, if you have a word of exhortation for the people, please speak."

16 Standing up, Paul motioned with his hand[w] and said: "Fellow Israelites and you Gentiles who worship God, listen to me! 17 The God of the people of Israel chose our ancestors; he made the people prosper
during their stay in Egypt; with mighty power he led them out of that country;[x] 18 for about forty years
he endured their conduct[a][y] in the wilderness;[z] 19 and he overthrew seven nations in Canaan,[a] giving
their land to his people[b] as their inheritance. 20 All this took about 450 years.

"After this, God gave them judges[c] until the time of Samuel the prophet.[d] 21 Then the people asked
for a king,[e] and he gave them Saul[f] son of Kish, of the tribe of Benjamin,[g] who ruled forty years. 22 After
removing Saul,[h] he made David their king.[i] God testified concerning him: 'I have found David son of
Jesse, a man after my own heart;[j] he will do everything I want him to do.'

[a] *18* Some manuscripts *he cared for them*

13:7 Bar-Jesus is an adviser or attendant to the "proconsul" of the island, Sergius Paulus. **proconsul.** A governor of a Roman senatorial province, under the authority of the Roman Senate. Sergius Paulus hears about Paul and Barnabas and wants to learn about their message.
13:8–11 In a battle of spiritual authority, Paul pronounces judgment over Bar-Jesus and strikes him blind. The scene recalls Peter's authority over the magician Simon Magus (8:9–13,18–24) and Jesus' victories over demonic forces (Luke 4:33–35,41; 6:18; 7:21; 8:32; 9:42; 11:14). This is the first recorded evangelism of a Gentile who is not a God-fearer (see note on 10:2) and thus is unassociated with any synagogue. As with the expansion into Samaria (ch. 8), so here there is a clear demonic/magical challenge thwarted directly by the evangelist. From this point Saul is called Paul (see note on 13:9) and, while continuing to work through Jewish centers in cities, he moves more and more into the Gentile world.
13:9 Saul, who was also called Paul. Paul likely received both his Jewish name (Saul) and Roman name (Paul) at birth, but he begins using the name Paul in his ministry to the Gentiles. **filled with the Holy Spirit.** See 4:8 and note.
13:13–52 *In Pisidian Antioch.* Paul's address at Pisidian Antioch is his first recorded synagogue sermon in Acts; it illustrates the message Paul brought to Jews and God-fearing Gentiles in the synagogues where he preached. The episode also sets the pattern of response that continues throughout Acts. After showing initial interest, the Jews of Pisidian Antioch become jealous and reject the message (vv. 44–45), and Paul turns to the Gentiles (vv. 46–48). This pattern is repeated throughout Acts: many Jews reject the gospel, a remnant of Jews responds favorably, and many Gentiles accept it. Persecution usually follows, forcing the missionaries to move on.
13:13 From Paphos ... to Perga. The three missionaries leave the island of Cyprus and cross to the region of Pamphylia, in present-day south central Turkey, traveling 12 miles (19 kilometers) inland from the coast to Perga. **John left them.** The text does not state the reason; it could have been fatigue, homesickness, fear of the dangerous journey ahead, disillusionment about Paul's leadership, or doubts concerning Paul's message to the Gentiles. Whatever the cause, Paul later claims Mark "deserted" them (15:36–38).
13:14 From Perga ... to Pisidian Antioch. An arduous and dangerous journey 100 miles (160 kilometers) through the Taurus mountain range, where roadside bandits often lay in wait. **Pisidian Antioch.** Seleucus I Nicator named the city; he founded the Seleucid Empire after the death of Alexander the Great and named 16 cities "Antioch" after his father Antiochus. Though located in Phrygia, the city was so named because it bordered Pisidia. In Paul's day it was part of the Roman province of Galatia. **synagogue.** As was their pattern (see note on v. 5), the missionaries went there, where they would find both Jews and God-fearing Gentiles.
13:15 A typical synagogue service would include prayers and a reading from the OT Law and Prophets, followed by a sermon or homily. Either by prearrangement or because they recognize Paul and Barnabas as rabbis, the synagogue leaders invite them to speak.
13:16–43 Paul's message may be divided into three sections, each beginning with a new address to the listeners: (1) he summarizes Israel's history leading up to God's promise to David (vv. 16–25); (2) he argues that Jesus' death and resurrection fulfill that promise (vv. 26–37); and (3) he calls them to respond (vv. 38–41).
13:16 motioned with his hand. Perhaps a call for silence. Paul addresses both key groups present: (1) **Fellow Israelites.** Jews. (2) **you Gentiles who worship God.** God-fearing Gentiles (see note on 10:2).
13:17–23 Paul concisely summarizes Israel's history, emphasizing God's sovereign role in choosing, establishing, and delivering his people. Paul moves quickly to David in order to show that Jesus fulfills God's promise to David of the coming Messiah (2 Sam 7:11b–16; cf. Isa 11).

PAUL'S FIRST MISSIONARY JOURNEY
ca. AD 46–47 (Acts 12:25–14:28)

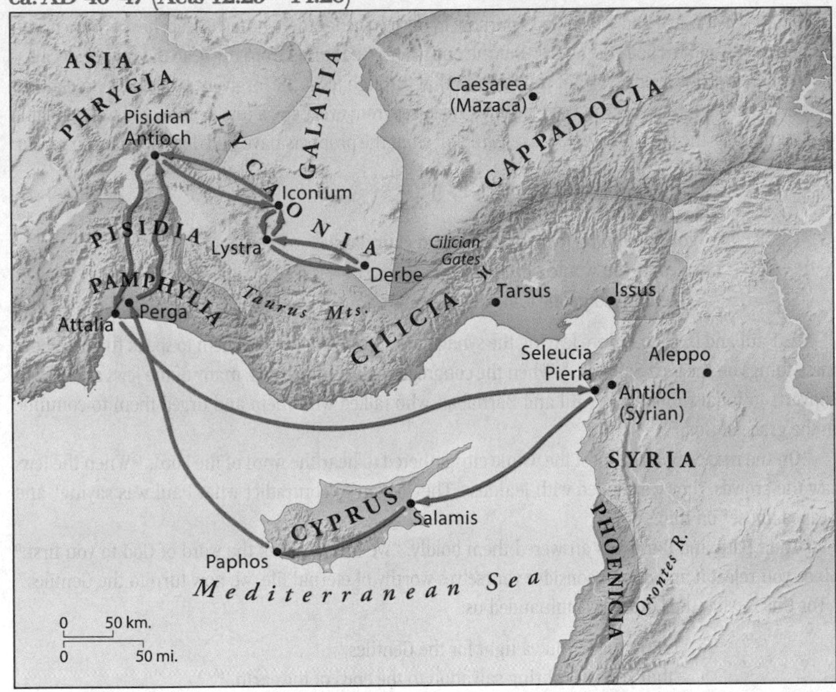

[23]"From this man's descendants[k] God has brought to Israel the Savior[l] Jesus,[m] as he promised.[n]
[24]Before the coming of Jesus, John preached repentance and baptism to all the people of Israel.[o] [25]As
John was completing his work,[p] he said: 'Who do you suppose I am? I am not the one you are looking
for.[q] But there is one coming after me whose sandals I am not worthy to untie.'[r]

[26]"Fellow children of Abraham and you God-fearing Gentiles, it is to us that this message of salvation[s] has been sent. [27]The people of Jerusalem and their rulers did not recognize Jesus,[t] yet in condemning him they fulfilled the words of the prophets[u] that are read every Sabbath. [28]Though they found no
proper ground for a death sentence, they asked Pilate to have him executed.[v] [29]When they had carried
out all that was written about him,[w] they took him down from the cross[x] and laid him in a tomb.[y] [30]But
God raised him from the dead,[z] [31]and for many days he was seen by those who had traveled with him
from Galilee to Jerusalem.[a] They are now his witnesses[b] to our people.

[32]"We tell you the good news:[c] What God promised our ancestors[d] [33]he has fulfilled for us, their
children, by raising up Jesus. As it is written in the second Psalm:

> "'You are my son;
> today I have become your father.'[a][e]

[34]God raised him from the dead so that he will never be subject to decay. As God has said,

> "'I will give you the holy and sure blessings promised to David.'[b][f]

a 33 Psalm 2:7 *b* 34 Isaiah 55:3

13:23 [k]Mt 1:1 [l]Lk 2:11 [m]Mt 1:21 [n]ver 32
13:24 [o]Mk 1:4
13:25 [p]Ac 20:24 [q]Jn 1:20 [r]Mt 3:11; Jn 1:27
13:26 [s]Ac 4:12
13:27 [t]Ac 3:17 [u]Lk 24:27
13:28 [v]Mt 27:20-25; Ac 3:14
13:29 [w]Lk 18:31 [x]Ac 5:30 [y]Lk 23:53
13:30 [z]Mt 28:6; Ac 2:24
13:31 [a]Mt 28:16 [b]Lk 24:48
13:32 [c]Ac 5:42 [d]Ac 26:6; Ro 4:13
13:33 [e]Ps 2:7
13:34 [f]Isa 55:3

13:24–25 The Gospels (Matt 3:1–12; Mark 1:1–8; Luke 3:1–18; John 1:6–8,15–36) and Acts (1:5; 10:37; 11:16) view the coming of John the Baptist and his testimony about Jesus as the beginning of the gospel.

13:27 in condemning him they fulfilled the words of the prophets. This is a key theme in Acts: though wicked people killed Jesus, Scripture all along predicted it as part of God's plan (vv. 29–30; 2:23–24; 3:15; 4:10; 10:39–40; 17:31).

13:31 for many days. The 40 days of 1:3.

13:33 Paul applies Ps 2:7 to Jesus' resurrection, which vindicates Jesus' claim to be the Messiah and Son of God (Rom 1:3–4).

13:34 the holy and sure blessings promised to David. God's covenant

13:35 [g]Ps 16:10; Ac 2:27
13:36 [h]1Ki 2:10; Ac 2:29
13:38 [i]Lk 24:47; Ac 2:38
13:39 [j]Ro 3:28
13:41 [k]Hab 1:5
13:42 [l]ver 14
13:43 [m]Ac 11:23; 14:22
13:45 [n]1Th 2:16 [o]Ac 18:6; 1Pe 4:4; Jude 10
13:46 [p]ver 26; Ac 3:26 [q]Ac 18:6; 22:21; 28:28
13:47 [r]Lk 2:32 [s]Isa 49:6
13:50 [t]1Th 2:16
13:51 [u]Mt 10:14; Ac 18:6 [v]Ac 14:1,19,21; 2Ti 3:11
14:1 [w]Ac 13:51

35 So it is also stated elsewhere:

> " 'You will not let your holy one see decay.'[a][g]

36 "Now when David had served God's purpose in his own generation, he fell asleep; he was buried with his ancestors[h] and his body decayed. 37 But the one whom God raised from the dead did not see decay.

38 "Therefore, my friends, I want you to know that through Jesus the forgiveness of sins is proclaimed to you.[i] 39 Through him everyone who believes is set free from every sin, a justification you were not able to obtain under the law of Moses.[j] 40 Take care that what the prophets have said does not happen to you:

> 41 " 'Look, you scoffers,
> wonder and perish,
> for I am going to do something in your days
> that you would never believe,
> even if someone told you.'[b]"[k]

42 As Paul and Barnabas were leaving the synagogue,[l] the people invited them to speak further about these things on the next Sabbath. 43 When the congregation was dismissed, many of the Jews and devout converts to Judaism followed Paul and Barnabas, who talked with them and urged them to continue in the grace of God.[m]

44 On the next Sabbath almost the whole city gathered to hear the word of the Lord. 45 When the Jews saw the crowds, they were filled with jealousy. They began to contradict what Paul was saying[n] and heaped abuse[o] on him.

46 Then Paul and Barnabas answered them boldly: "We had to speak the word of God to you first.[p] Since you reject it and do not consider yourselves worthy of eternal life, we now turn to the Gentiles.[q] 47 For this is what the Lord has commanded us:

> " 'I have made you[c] a light for the Gentiles,[r]
> that you[c] may bring salvation to the ends of the earth.'[d]"[s]

48 When the Gentiles heard this, they were glad and honored the word of the Lord; and all who were appointed for eternal life believed.

49 The word of the Lord spread through the whole region. 50 But the Jewish leaders incited the God-fearing women of high standing and the leading men of the city. They stirred up persecution against Paul and Barnabas, and expelled them from their region.[t] 51 So they shook the dust off their feet[u] as a warning to them and went to Iconium.[v] 52 And the disciples were filled with joy and with the Holy Spirit.

In Iconium

14 At Iconium[w] Paul and Barnabas went as usual into the Jewish synagogue. There they spoke so effectively that a great number of Jews and Greeks believed. 2 But the Jews who refused to believe stirred up the other Gentiles and poisoned their minds against the brothers. 3 So Paul and Barnabas

[a] *35* Psalm 16:10 (see Septuagint) [b] *41* Hab. 1:5 [c] *47* The Greek is singular. [d] *47* Isaiah 49:6

with David that God would one day raise up from his descendants the Messiah, who would reign forever on David's throne (2 Sam 7:14–16; 1 Chron 17:4–15; Ps 132:11–12; Isa 55:3). Jesus fulfills this promise.

13:35–37 Paul makes the same point from Ps 16:10 that Peter does on the day of Pentecost (2:27): David prophesied not about himself but about the Messiah's resurrection.

13:39 Though "justification" by faith is not a major theme in Acts, this accurately reflects Paul's theology. Justification is God's declaration that a sinner is righteous and their sins are forgiven (v. 38) on the basis of Christ's sacrificial death on the cross.

13:43 devout converts to Judaism. Proselytes, i.e., Gentiles who fully converted to Judaism, including being circumcised and keeping the OT law (2:11; 6:5; Matt 23:15).

13:46 speak the word of God to you first. Paul and Barnabas had to present the gospel first to the Jews since they are God's covenant people to whom God made the promises (Rom 1:16; 9:1–5; 10:1–3).

13:47 light for the Gentiles. Paul applies Isaiah's Messianic prophecy concerning the servant of the Lord (Isa 49:6; cf. Isa 42:6) to himself and the other missionaries since the church carries out the Messiah's mission to the world.

13:48 Salvation entails both God's divine election ("appointed for eternal life") and a human response ("believed").

13:51 shook the dust off their feet. A sign of rejection, leaving the place to God's judgment (Matt 10:14; Mark 6:11; Luke 9:5; 10:11).

14:1–7 *In Iconium.* The pattern set at Pisidian Antioch repeats in Iconium. While the Jews are divided, a number of Gentiles respond positively to the gospel. This division of Israel between a remnant who believe and a majority who do not recurs throughout Acts, climaxing in 28:24.

14:1 Iconium. Located about 90 miles (about 145 kilometers) southeast of Pisidian Antioch; an important agricultural center with flourishing orchards and wool industries. **as usual into the Jewish synagogue.**

spent considerable time there, speaking boldly[x] for the Lord, who confirmed the message of his grace
by enabling them to perform signs and wonders.[y] 4The people of the city were divided; some sided with
the Jews, others with the apostles.[z] 5There was a plot afoot among both Gentiles and Jews, together with
their leaders, to mistreat them and stone them.[a] 6But they found out about it and fled[b] to the Lycaonian
cities of Lystra and Derbe and to the surrounding country, 7where they continued to preach[c] the gospel.[d]

In Lystra and Derbe

8In Lystra there sat a man who was lame. He had been that way from birth[e] and had never walked.
9He listened to Paul as he was speaking. Paul looked directly at him, saw that he had faith to be healed[f]
10and called out, "Stand up on your feet!" At that, the man jumped up and began to walk.[g]
11When the crowd saw what Paul had done, they shouted in the Lycaonian language, "The gods have
come down to us in human form!"[h] 12Barnabas they called Zeus, and Paul they called Hermes because
he was the chief speaker. 13The priest of Zeus, whose temple was just outside the city, brought bulls and
wreaths to the city gates because he and the crowd wanted to offer sacrifices to them.
14But when the apostles Barnabas and Paul heard of this, they tore their clothes[i] and rushed out
into the crowd, shouting: 15"Friends, why are you doing this? We too are only human,[j] like you. We are
bringing you good news,[k] telling you to turn from these worthless things[l] to the living God,[m] who made
the heavens and the earth[n] and the sea and everything in them.[o] 16In the past, he let[p] all nations go
their own way.[q] 17Yet he has not left himself without testimony:[r] He has shown kindness by giving you
rain from heaven and crops in their seasons;[s] he provides you with plenty of food and fills your hearts
with joy." 18Even with these words, they had difficulty keeping the crowd from sacrificing to them.
19Then some Jews[t] came from Antioch and Iconium[u] and won the crowd over. They stoned Paul[v] and
dragged him outside the city, thinking he was dead. 20But after the disciples[w] had gathered around him,
he got up and went back into the city. The next day he and Barnabas left for Derbe.

The Return to Antioch in Syria

21They preached the gospel in that city and won a large number of disciples. Then they returned to
Lystra, Iconium[x] and Antioch, 22strengthening the disciples and encouraging them to remain true to

14:3 [x]Ac 4:29 [y]Jn 4:48; Heb 2:4
14:4 [z]Ac 17:4,5
14:5 [a]ver 19
14:6 [b]Mt 10:23
14:7 [c]Ac 16:10 [d]ver 15,21
14:8 [e]Ac 3:2
14:9 [f]Mt 9:28,29
14:10 [g]Ac 3:8
14:11 [h]Ac 8:10; 28:6
14:14 [i]Mk 14:63
14:15 [j]Ac 10:26; Jas 5:17 [k]ver 7,21; Ac 13:32 [l]1Sa 12:21; 1Co 8:4; 1Th 1:9 [m]Mt 16:16 [n]Ge 1:1; Jer 14:22 [o]Ps 146:6; Rev 14:7
14:16 [p]Ac 17:30 [q]Ps 81:12; Mic 4:5
14:17 [r]Ac 17:27; Ro 1:20 [s]Dt 11:14; Job 5:10; Ps 65:10
14:19 [t]Ac 13:45 [u]Ac 13:51 [v]2Co 11:25; 2Ti 3:11
14:20 [w]ver 22,28; Ac 11:26
14:21 [x]Ac 13:51

Because the gospel is for the Jew first (Rom 1:16) and because Paul and Barnabus find there both Jews and God-fearing Gentiles receptive to their message concerning Jesus the Messiah.

14:3 Because of the opposition (v. 2), Paul and Barnabas remain in Iconium a considerable time in order to strengthen the believers there. **signs and wonders.** Throughout Acts they help confirm the gospel message (see 2:22,43; 4:30; 5:12; 6:8; 8:6,13).

14:4 apostles. Though Luke usually reserves the term for the Twelve (1:2,12, etc.), he uses it of Paul and Barnabas here and in v. 14. See note on 1:21–22.

14:5 Stoning was the most common Jewish means of execution. Though the plot fails in Iconium, it succeeds against Paul in Lystra (v. 19).

14:6 Lystra and Derbe. Cities in Lycaonia, a district east of Pisidia. Both Pisidia and Lycaonia were incorporated in the Roman province of Galatia.

14:8–20 *In Lystra and Derbe.* When Paul heals a lame man in Lystra, the people try to worship Paul and Barnabas as gods. They forcefully reject such worship, pointing to the one true God whose salvation they are proclaiming. Their fortunes dramatically turn as the Jews from Antioch and Iconium provoke the crowds to stone Paul.

14:8–10 Healing the lame man closely parallels Peter's similar miracle in 3:1–8 (cf. 9:33–35). Such healings evidence the arrival of God's end-time salvation (cf. Isa 35:5–6).

14:8 Lystra. A small Roman colony 20 miles (32 kilometers) south of Iconium. Few Jews appear to be there since the text does not mention a synagogue and Paul preaches in the streets.

14:11 Paul and Barnabas spoke Greek, not the local Lycaonian language, so they did not at first understand what was happening.

14:12 Zeus. The king of the Greek pantheon of gods (like the Roman Jupiter). **Hermes.** The messenger of the gods (like the Roman Mercury). Lystra had a temple to Zeus, its patron god. According to a local legend, these same gods, Zeus and Hermes, once descended to this region disguised as humans seeking lodging. Though they asked at a thousand homes, none took them in. Finally, at a humble cottage of straw and reeds, an elderly couple, Philemon and Baucis, freely welcomed them with a banquet. In appreciation, the gods transformed the cottage into a temple and appointed Philemon and Baucis priest and priestess. They then sent a flood to destroy the homes of the inhospitable people who had turned them away (Ovid, *Metamorphoses* 8.626–724). Perhaps the people of Lystra are hoping to gain a similar advantage.

14:14 tore their clothes. A sign of sorrow, dismay, or rage (Gen 37:29,34; Num 14:6; Josh 7:6; Isa 37:1; Mark 14:63).

14:15–17 Paul's message to his pagan listeners differs from his synagogue sermon to Jews and God-fearers in Pisidian Antioch, which focused on the promises to Israel (13:16–41). He points instead to God's role as creator and provider for all people. He gives a similar message to "pagan" Greek philosophers on the Areopagus ("Mars Hill") in Athens (ch. 17).

14:19 Paul refers to this in his "résumé" of sufferings in 2 Cor 11:23–25.

14:20 he got up and went back into the city. Paul's remarkable recovery was probably a miracle, though the incident also points to the apostle's remarkable fortitude and perseverance (2 Cor 11:23–28). **Derbe.** About 60 miles (about 97 kilometers) southeast of Lystra.

14:21–28 *The Return to Antioch in Syria.* Rather than taking the much shorter route eastward through Cilicia to Syria, Paul and Barnabas return to further instruct and strengthen the disciples and to appoint leaders in the churches established during their journey. Returning to Antioch, they

14:22 [y]Ac 11:23; 13:43 [z]Jn 16:33; 1Th 3:3; 2Ti 3:12
14:23 [a]Ac 11:30; Titus 1:5 [b]Ac 13:3 [c]Ac 20:32
14:26 [d]Ac 11:19 [e]Ac 15:40 [f]Ac 13:1,3
14:27 [g]Ac 15:4,12; 21:19 [h]1Co 16:9; 2Co 2:12; Col 4:3; Rev 3:8
15:1 [i]ver 24; Gal 2:12 [j]ver 5; Gal 5:2,3 [k]Ac 6:14
15:2 [l]Gal 2:2 [m]Ac 11:30
15:3 [n]Ac 14:27
15:4 [o]ver 12; Ac 14:27
15:8 [p]Ac 1:24 [q]Ac 10:44,47
15:9 [r]Ac 10:28,34; 11:12 [s]Ac 10:43
15:10 [t]Mt 23:4; Gal 5:1
15:11 [u]Ro 3:24; Eph 2:5-8
15:12 [v]Jn 4:48 [w]Ac 14:27
15:13 [x]Ac 12:17

the faith.[y] "We must go through many hardships[z] to enter the kingdom of God," they said. 23 Paul and
Barnabas appointed elders[a][a] for them in each church and, with prayer and fasting,[b] committed them
to the Lord,[c] in whom they had put their trust. 24 After going through Pisidia, they came into Pamphylia,
25 and when they had preached the word in Perga, they went down to Attalia.
26 From Attalia they sailed back to Antioch,[d] where they had been committed to the grace of God[e] for
the work they had now completed.[f] 27 On arriving there, they gathered the church together and reported
all that God had done through them[g] and how he had opened a door[h] of faith to the Gentiles. 28 And
they stayed there a long time with the disciples.

The Council at Jerusalem

15 Certain people[i] came down from Judea to Antioch and were teaching the believers: "Unless
you are circumcised,[j] according to the custom taught by Moses,[k] you cannot be saved." 2 This
brought Paul and Barnabas into sharp dispute and debate with them. So Paul and Barnabas were
appointed, along with some other believers, to go up to Jerusalem[l] to see the apostles and elders[m]
about this question. 3 The church sent them on their way, and as they traveled through Phoenicia and
Samaria, they told how the Gentiles had been converted.[n] This news made all the believers very glad.
4 When they came to Jerusalem, they were welcomed by the church and the apostles and elders, to whom
they reported everything God had done through them.[o]
5 Then some of the believers who belonged to the party of the Pharisees stood up and said, "The
Gentiles must be circumcised and required to keep the law of Moses."
6 The apostles and elders met to consider this question. 7 After much discussion, Peter got up and addressed them: "Brothers, you know that some time ago God made a choice among you that the Gentiles
might hear from my lips the message of the gospel and believe. 8 God, who knows the heart,[p] showed
that he accepted them by giving the Holy Spirit to them,[q] just as he did to us. 9 He did not discriminate
between us and them,[r] for he purified their hearts by faith.[s] 10 Now then, why do you try to test God by
putting on the necks of Gentiles a yoke[t] that neither we nor our ancestors have been able to bear? 11 No!
We believe it is through the grace[u] of our Lord Jesus that we are saved, just as they are."
12 The whole assembly became silent as they listened to Barnabas and Paul telling about the signs
and wonders[v] God had done among the Gentiles through them.[w] 13 When they finished, James[x] spoke
up. "Brothers," he said, "listen to me. 14 Simon[b] has described to us how God first intervened to choose
a people for his name from the Gentiles. 15 The words of the prophets are in agreement with this, as it
is written:

[a] 23 Or *Barnabas ordained elders*; or *Barnabas had elders elected* [b] 14 Greek *Simeon*, a variant of *Simon*; that is, Peter

then report how God "opened a door of faith to the Gentiles" (v. 27). The church that first reached out to Gentiles (11:19–26) is at the forefront of the Gentile mission.

14:23 appointed elders. Leadership is essential for these new churches. The Greek word used here may refer to direct appointment or to an election by the members (see NIV text note). **elders.** For qualifications, see 1 Tim 3:1–13; Titus 1:5–9.

15:1–35 *The Decision of the Jerusalem Council.* Ch. 15 is the center of the book of Acts in both its position and its theology. The Jerusalem church acknowledges that God saves Gentiles by faith alone, apart from circumcision or keeping the Jewish law (i.e., apart from becoming Jews). The church does, however, encourage Gentile believers to follow certain stipulations in order to maintain peace and fellowship with their Jewish-Christian brothers and sisters.

15:1–21 *The Council at Jerusalem.* The council at Jerusalem sought to resolve the fundamental question of whether Gentiles must first become Jews in order to be saved. The controversy pitted the Judaizers (see note on v. 1) against Paul's gospel of free grace and represented one of the earliest and most significant threats to the unity of the early church. Paul deals with this same issue in his letter to the Galatians, probably written about this same time.

15:1 Certain people. "Judaizers," conservative Jewish Christians who believed that Gentiles must first become Jews in order to be saved. Many Gentiles responded to the gospel in Antioch without being required to keep the law (11:19–26).

15:3–4 The journey from Antioch in Syria to Jerusalem was about 250 miles (about 400 kilometers) and may have taken several weeks. Paul and Barnabas used the journey profitably to share with believers along the way the good news about the Gentiles turning to God.

15:5 some of the believers ... belonged to the party of the Pharisees. It is not surprising that some Pharisees joined the new movement since, unlike their opponents the Sadducees, the Pharisees held in common with Christians certain basic beliefs: a coming Messiah, the afterlife, and the resurrection of the dead.

15:13–21 James, Jesus' half brother (Mark 6:3; Gal 1:19), has by this time assumed a leadership role in the Jerusalem church (12:17; 21:18). While Peter represents the apostles, James represents the elders, the church's leadership council. It is he who pronounces the verdict. James affirms that (1) *God*, not any human being, chose the Gentiles for salvation and (2) the OT prophets predicted that God would save the Gentiles (citing Amos 9:11–12).

[16]"'After this I will return
and rebuild David's fallen tent.
Its ruins I will rebuild,
and I will restore it,
[17]that the rest of mankind may seek the Lord,
even all the Gentiles who bear my name,
says the Lord, who does these things'[a][y] —
[18]things known from long ago.[b]

[19]"It is my judgment, therefore, that we should not make it difficult for the Gentiles who are turning
to God. [20]Instead we should write to them, telling them to abstain from food polluted by idols,[z] from
sexual immorality,[a] from the meat of strangled animals and from blood.[b] [21]For the law of Moses has
been preached in every city from the earliest times and is read in the synagogues on every Sabbath."[c]

The Council's Letter to Gentile Believers

[22]Then the apostles and elders, with the whole church, decided to choose some of their own men and
send them to Antioch with Paul and Barnabas. They chose Judas (called Barsabbas) and Silas,[d] men
who were leaders among the believers. [23]With them they sent the following letter:

The apostles and elders, your brothers,

To the Gentile believers in Antioch,[e] Syria and Cilicia:[f]

Greetings.[g]

[24]We have heard that some went out from us without our authorization and disturbed you, troubling your minds by what they said.[h] [25]So we all agreed to choose some men and send them to you
with our dear friends Barnabas and Paul — [26]men who have risked their lives[i] for the name of our
Lord Jesus Christ. [27]Therefore we are sending Judas and Silas to confirm by word of mouth what we
are writing. [28]It seemed good to the Holy Spirit[j] and to us not to burden you with anything beyond
the following requirements: [29]You are to abstain from food sacrificed to idols, from blood, from
the meat of strangled animals and from sexual immorality.[k] You will do well to avoid these things.

Farewell.

[30]So the men were sent off and went down to Antioch, where they gathered the church together and
delivered the letter. [31]The people read it and were glad for its encouraging message. [32]Judas and Silas,
who themselves were prophets, said much to encourage and strengthen the believers. [33]After spending

15:17 [y]Am 9:11,12
15:20 [z]1Co 8:7-13; 10:14-28; Rev 2:14,20 [a]1Co 10:7,8 [b]ver 29; Ge 9:4; Lev 3:17; Dt 12:16,23
15:21 [c]Ac 13:15; 2Co 3:14,15
15:22 [d]ver 27,32,40
15:23 [e]ver 1 [f]ver 41 [g]Ac 23:25,26; Jas 1:1
15:24 [h]ver 1; Gal 1:7; 5:10
15:26 [i]Ac 9:23-25; 14:19
15:28 [j]Ac 5:32
15:29 [k]ver 20; Ac 21:25

[a] *17* Amos 9:11,12 (see Septuagint) [b] *17,18* Some manuscripts *things'* — / [18]*the Lord's work is known to him from long ago*

15:16 David's fallen tent. The dynasty of David that Jesus, the Davidic Messiah, has restored (2 Sam 7:11b–16; Isa 9:1–7; 11:1–16). While the Hebrew text of Amos 9:11–12 speaks of Israel possessing Edom, James quotes from the Septuagint, the pre-Christian Greek translation of the OT, which refers to the "rest of mankind" seeking the Lord (v. 17). The point in both versions is that the end-time people of God will include Gentiles.

15:20 The four stipulations James sets out are not requirements for salvation, which for both Jews and Gentiles comes through grace by faith alone (vv. 9,11). Rather, they are guidelines that allow Jews and Gentiles to share table-fellowship. There are parallels to each in the guidelines for resident aliens living in Israel in Lev 17–18. **food polluted by idols.** Food offered to a pagan god (see v. 29; 1 Cor 8:7–13). There is no contradiction with Paul's teaching on food sacrificed to idols in 1 Cor 8–10, where he allows eating such food in certain contexts. The principle in both passages is to avoid these practices when it would break fellowship or cause someone else to sin. **sexual immorality.** Perhaps specific kinds of relationships forbidden in the OT law, such as those between close relatives, or general sexual sins common in the pagan world. **meat of strangled animals.** Animals killed without draining the blood. **blood.** The OT forbids eating blood (Gen 9:4; Lev 17:10–12).

15:21 the law of Moses has been preached in every city. This puzzling statement may mean that (1) Jews are present in every city (these practices offend Jews) or (2) these stipulations should not be surprising to Gentile God-fearers, who hear them regularly in the synagogue.

15:22–35 *The Council's Letter to Gentile Believers.* The council's letter repeats James's stipulations (vv. 19–21). It will be delivered not only to the church in Antioch (vv. 30–31) but also to the mission churches started on Paul's first missionary journey (16:4–5).

15:22 Judas (called Barsabbas). Perhaps the brother of Joseph Barsabbas (see note on 1:23). **Silas.** Joins Paul on his second missionary journey (see 16:40).

15:28 James recognizes that the Holy Spirit had led them in their decision, just as the Holy Spirit confirmed that God had accepted the Gentiles (v. 8).

15:33 [l]Mk 5:34; Ac 16:36; 1Co 16:11
15:35 [m]Ac 8:4
15:36 [n]Ac 13:4,13,14, 51; 14:1,6,24,25
15:37 [o]Ac 12:12
15:38 [p]Ac 13:13
15:40 [q]ver 22 [r]Ac 11:23
15:41 [s]ver 23 [t]Ac 6:9 [u]Ac 16:5
16:1 [v]Ac 14:6 [w]Ac 17:14; 18:5; 19:22; Ro 16:21; 1Co 4:17; 2Co 1:1,19; 1Th 3:2,6; 1Ti 1:2,18; 2Ti 1:2,5,6
16:2 [x]ver 40 [y]Ac 13:51
16:3 [z]Gal 2:3
16:4 [a]Ac 11:30 [b]Ac 15:2 [c]Ac 15:28,29
16:5 [d]Ac 9:31; 15:41
16:6 [e]Ac 18:23 [f]Ac 18:23; Gal 1:2; 3:1 [g]Ac 2:9
16:7 [h]Ro 8:9; Gal 4:6
16:8 [i]ver 11; 2Co 2:12; 2Ti 4:13
16:9 [j]Ac 9:10 [k]Ac 20:1,3
16:10 [l]ver 10-17 [m]Ac 14:7

some time there, they were sent off by the believers with the blessing of peace[l] to return to those who
had sent them. [34] *a* 35But Paul and Barnabas remained in Antioch, where they and many others taught
and preached[m] the word of the Lord.

Disagreement Between Paul and Barnabas

36Some time later Paul said to Barnabas, "Let us go back and visit the believers in all the towns[n]
where we preached the word of the Lord and see how they are doing." 37Barnabas wanted to take John,
also called Mark,[o] with them, 38but Paul did not think it wise to take him, because he had deserted
them[p] in Pamphylia and had not continued with them in the work. 39They had such a sharp disagreement that they parted company. Barnabas took Mark and sailed for Cyprus, 40but Paul chose Silas[q]
and left, commended by the believers to the grace of the Lord.[r] 41He went through Syria[s] and Cilicia,[t]
strengthening the churches.[u]

Timothy Joins Paul and Silas

16 Paul came to Derbe and then to Lystra,[v] where a disciple named Timothy[w] lived, whose mother
was Jewish and a believer but whose father was a Greek. 2The believers[x] at Lystra and Iconium[y]
spoke well of him. 3Paul wanted to take him along on the journey, so he circumcised him because of the
Jews who lived in that area, for they all knew that his father was a Greek.[z] 4As they traveled from town
to town, they delivered the decisions reached by the apostles and elders[a] in Jerusalem[b] for the people to
obey.[c] 5So the churches were strengthened[d] in the faith and grew daily in numbers.

Paul's Vision of the Man of Macedonia

6Paul and his companions traveled throughout the region of Phrygia[e] and Galatia,[f] having been
kept by the Holy Spirit from preaching the word in the province of Asia.[g] 7When they came to the border
of Mysia, they tried to enter Bithynia, but the Spirit of Jesus[h] would not allow them to. 8So they passed
by Mysia and went down to Troas.[i] 9During the night Paul had a vision[j] of a man of Macedonia[k] standing and begging him, "Come over to Macedonia and help us." 10After Paul had seen the vision, we[l] got
ready at once to leave for Macedonia, concluding that God had called us to preach the gospel[m] to them.

a 34 Some manuscripts include here *But Silas decided to remain there.*

15:34 See NIV text note. A later scribe likely added this verse because he wondered how Silas could leave in vv. 32–33 but be back in Antioch in v. 40. The better answer is that Silas left and returned.

15:36—18:22 *Paul's Second Missionary Journey.* This is the beginning of what is called Paul's second missionary journey. While his first journey took the gospel to Cyprus and Galatia (ch. 13–14), this second journey goes to Macedonia (northern Greece) and Achaia (southern Greece), his first outreach on the continent of Europe (15:36—18:17). Paul and his associates establish important churches at Philippi, Thessalonica, Berea, and Corinth. Paul also gives his famous Mars Hill address at the Areopagus in Athens.

15:36–41 *Disagreement Between Paul and Barnabas.* This conflict shows that Luke is not afraid to present the early church "warts and all" (cf. 6:1). It is not surprising that Barnabas wants to give John Mark a second chance since he is his cousin and since Barnabas, whose name means "son of encouragement" (4:36), is a natural mediator (9:26–27; 11:22–25,30). Paul is thinking strategically and does not want to risk a second desertion that might jeopardize their mission (13:13; see Gal 2:11–13 for another possible source of tension between Paul and Barnabas). For evidence of Paul's eventual reconciliation with Mark, see note on 12:12. Silas is a good choice since he represents the Jerusalem church and thus lends credibility to the Jerusalem decrees (vv. 22,31–32; 16:4–5). The positive outcome is that one missionary outreach now becomes two. As frequently noted in Acts, God uses apparent setbacks to accomplish his purpose.

16:1–5 *Timothy Joins Paul and Silas.* Paul and Silas return to strengthen the churches established on the first missionary journey. In Lystra, they enlist the help of Timothy, who becomes one of Paul's most trusted associates (1 Cor 4:17; Phil 2:19–22; 1 Tim 1:2).

16:3 circumcised him. Although elsewhere Paul insists that circumcision is not necessary for salvation and that Gentiles who become circumcised are seeking to be saved through the works of the law (Gal 2:3; 5:2), Paul did not compromise his principles by circumcising Timothy. Timothy was half Jewish (his mother was Jewish, v. 1), and so he was viewed as Jewish in the eyes of most Jews. Because Timothy was not circumsized (his father was Greek), Paul was accused of telling Jews not to circumcise their children. Circumcising Timothy was therefore necessary for effective ministry and for maintaining table-fellowship with the Jews.

16:6–10 *Paul's Vision of the Man of Macedonia.* Paul's goal is to travel west to evangelize the Roman province of Asia. But God has other plans and redirects them away from Asia and Bithynia to Macedonia.

16:6–7 the Holy Spirit ... the Spirit of Jesus. Interchangeable expressions. Luke's association of Jesus' Spirit with the Holy Spirit of God suggests that Luke views Jesus as the transcendent Lord, equal with God the Father (cf. Rom 8:9; Gal 4:6; Phil 1:19; 1 Pet 1:11).

16:6 having been kept. Luke does not say how the Holy Spirit directed the missionaries. It could have been through a vision, a dream, a prophecy, or circumstances.

16:8 Troas. A port city 30 miles (49 kilometers) south of ancient Troy. Its harbor provided the main sea access to Macedonia.

16:9 a man of Macedonia. The text does not identify him, but some speculate that it may have been Luke himself, since the author joins the missionary group in the next verse (see note on v. 10).

16:10 we ... us. The first "we" section begins here (see Introduction to Acts: Author), showing that Luke joins the missionary group at this point. The "we" sections confirm that the author joins Paul briefly on

Lydia's Conversion in Philippi

11 From Troas[n] we put out to sea and sailed straight for Samothrace, and the next day we went on to
Neapolis. 12 From there we traveled to Philippi,[o] a Roman colony and the leading city of that district[a]
of Macedonia.[p] And we stayed there several days.
13 On the Sabbath[q] we went outside the city gate to the river, where we expected to find a place of
prayer. We sat down and began to speak to the women who had gathered there. 14 One of those listening
was a woman from the city of Thyatira[r] named Lydia, a dealer in purple cloth. She was a worshiper of
God. The Lord opened her heart[s] to respond to Paul's message. 15 When she and the members of her
household[t] were baptized, she invited us to her home. "If you consider me a believer in the Lord," she
said, "come and stay at my house." And she persuaded us.

Paul and Silas in Prison

16 Once when we were going to the place of prayer,[u] we were met by a female slave who had a spirit[v]
by which she predicted the future. She earned a great deal of money for her owners by fortune-telling.
17 She followed Paul and the rest of us, shouting, "These men are servants of the Most High God,[w] who
are telling you the way to be saved." 18 She kept this up for many days. Finally Paul became so annoyed
that he turned around and said to the spirit, "In the name of Jesus Christ I command you to come out
of her!" At that moment the spirit left her.[x]
19 When her owners realized that their hope of making money[y] was gone, they seized Paul and Silas[z] and dragged[a] them into the marketplace to face the authorities. 20 They brought them before the
magistrates and said, "These men are Jews, and are throwing our city into an uproar[b] 21 by advocating
customs unlawful for us Romans[c] to accept or practice."[d]
22 The crowd joined in the attack against Paul and Silas, and the magistrates ordered them to be
stripped and beaten with rods.[e] 23 After they had been severely flogged, they were thrown into prison,
and the jailer[f] was commanded to guard them carefully. 24 When he received these orders, he put them
in the inner cell and fastened their feet in the stocks.[g]

a 12 The text and meaning of the Greek for *the leading city of that district* are uncertain.

16:11 [n] ver 8
16:12 [o] Ac 20:6; Php 1:1; 1Th 2:2 [p] ver 9
16:13 [q] Ac 13:14
16:14 [r] Rev 1:11 [s] Lk 24:45
16:15 [t] Ac 11:14
16:16 [u] ver 13 [v] Dt 18:11; 1Sa 28:3,7
16:17 [w] Mk 5:7
16:18 [x] Mk 16:17
16:19 [y] ver 16; Ac 19:25, 26 [z] Ac 15:22 [a] Ac 8:3; 17:6; 21:30; Jas 2:6
16:20 [b] Ac 17:6
16:21 [c] ver 12 [d] Est 3:8
16:22 [e] 2Co 11:25; 1Th 2:2
16:23 [f] ver 27,36
16:24 [g] Job 13:27; 33:11; Jer 20:2,3; 29:26

this second missionary journey (vv. 9–40) and rejoins him at Philippi on Paul's return from his third missionary journey (20:1–17). Luke stays with Paul at Caesarea after Paul's arrest and accompanies him to Rome (chs. 20–28).

16:11–40 Luke records three key events of the Philippian ministry: the conversion of Lydia (vv. 11–15), the exorcism of a demon-possessed fortune-telling slave girl (vv. 16–24), and the conversion of the Philippian jailer (vv. 25–40). The church Paul establishes at Philippi will be one of the most supportive of all his churches, a true partner in ministry (Phil 1:5–6; 4:1).

16:11–15 *Lydia's Conversion in Philippi.* Paul's first convert in Philippi is Lydia, a worshiper of God (either a Gentile God-fearer or a Jewish convert) and a business woman who sells purple cloth, a luxury item. Thyatira, her hometown, was famous for its purple goods. It was located in the ancient kingdom of Lydia, so her name may mean "the Lydian woman." She obviously has significant means since she owns a home large enough to accommodate the missionaries and presumably to host a house church.

16:13 There is likely no synagogue in Philippi because of the small Jewish population (a synagogue required ten Jewish men), so the missionaries visit a Jewish "place of prayer" beside the river.

16:14 The Lord opened her heart to respond. It is ultimately the work of the Holy Spirit, not the persuasiveness of the argument, that provokes a response of faith.

16:16–40 *Paul and Silas in Prison.* As so often throughout Acts, a disaster turns to success. Though Paul and Silas are severely beaten and jailed for exorcising a demon from a fortune-telling slave girl, this setback turns to success when the jailer believes the gospel and the fledgling church in Philippi is strengthened.

16:16 a spirit by which she predicted the future. Lit. "a python spirit." The python symbolized the oracle at Delphi in central Greece, where a priestess in a trance-like state represented the god Apollo and predicted the future. The python terminology is sometimes also associated with ventriloquism, since the priestess would speak involuntarily with the voice of the god. Both Greeks and Romans put great stock in divination.

16:17–19 come out … left … was gone. All three verbs reflect one Greek word. Luke makes a play on words by repeating the same word to describe both the demon and the owner's hope of profit as departing. The girl's owners do not care about her well-being but only about losing their profit.

16:17 servants of the Most High God. Like the demons who recognized Jesus in the Gospels (Luke 4:34,41; 8:28), the girl accurately recognizes Paul and his companions. Identifying a spirit's name was sometimes seen as a way to gain authority over it.

16:18 annoyed. Paul likely casts the demon out because it irritates him and disrupts their ministry.

16:20 These men are Jews. The owners are tapping into anti-Semitism common in the Greco-Roman world, especially in a proud Roman colony like Philippi. The charges now concern not financial loss (which would go nowhere with the city officials) but the more serious charges of disturbing the peace and violating Roman customs (v. 21).

16:22 beaten with rods. A Roman method of punishment. Paul says that he received this punishment three times and the Jewish method of "forty lashes minus one" five times (2 Cor 11:24–25). These actions are clearly illegal since Paul and Silas were not given a formal trial or a chance to defend themselves. In 1 Thess 2:2 Paul speaks of being "treated outrageously in Philippi."

16:25 [h]Eph 5:19
16:26 [i]Ac 4:31 [j]Ac 12:10 [k]Ac 12:7
16:27 [l]Ac 12:19
16:30 [m]Ac 2:37
16:31 [n]Ac 11:14
16:33 [o]ver 25
16:34 [p]Ac 11:14
16:36 [q]ver 23,27 [r]Ac 15:33
16:37 [s]Ac 22:25-29
16:38 [t]Ac 22:29
16:39 [u]Mt 8:34
16:40 [v]ver 14 [w]ver 2; Ac 1:16
17:1 [x]ver 11,13; Php 4:16; 1Th 1:1; 2Th 1:1; 2Ti 4:10
17:2 [y]Ac 9:20 [z]Ac 13:14 [a]Ac 8:35
17:3 [b]Lk 24:26; Ac 3:18 [c]Lk 24:46 [d]Ac 9:22; 18:28
17:4 [e]Ac 15:22

25 About midnight Paul and Silas were praying and singing hymns[h] to God, and the other prisoners
were listening to them. 26 Suddenly there was such a violent earthquake that the foundations of the prison
were shaken.[i] At once all the prison doors flew open,[j] and everyone's chains came loose.[k] 27 The jailer
woke up, and when he saw the prison doors open, he drew his sword and was about to kill himself because he thought the prisoners had escaped.[l] 28 But Paul shouted, "Don't harm yourself! We are all here!"

29 The jailer called for lights, rushed in and fell trembling before Paul and Silas. 30 He then brought
them out and asked, "Sirs, what must I do to be saved?"[m]

31 They replied, "Believe in the Lord Jesus, and you will be saved—you and your household."[n]
32 Then they spoke the word of the Lord to him and to all the others in his house. 33 At that hour of the
night[o] the jailer took them and washed their wounds; then immediately he and all his household were
baptized. 34 The jailer brought them into his house and set a meal before them; he[p] was filled with joy
because he had come to believe in God—he and his whole household.

35 When it was daylight, the magistrates sent their officers to the jailer with the order: "Release those
men." 36 The jailer[q] told Paul, "The magistrates have ordered that you and Silas be released. Now you
can leave. Go in peace."[r]

37 But Paul said to the officers: "They beat us publicly without a trial, even though we are Roman
citizens,[s] and threw us into prison. And now do they want to get rid of us quietly? No! Let them come
themselves and escort us out."

38 The officers reported this to the magistrates, and when they heard that Paul and Silas were Roman
citizens, they were alarmed.[t] 39 They came to appease them and escorted them from the prison, requesting them to leave the city.[u] 40 After Paul and Silas came out of the prison, they went to Lydia's house,[v]
where they met with the brothers and sisters[w] and encouraged them. Then they left.

In Thessalonica

17 When Paul and his companions had passed through Amphipolis and Apollonia, they came to
Thessalonica,[x] where there was a Jewish synagogue. 2 As was his custom, Paul went into the
synagogue,[y] and on three Sabbath[z] days he reasoned with them from the Scriptures,[a] 3 explaining and
proving that the Messiah had to suffer[b] and rise from the dead.[c] "This Jesus I am proclaiming to you
is the Messiah,"[d] he said. 4 Some of the Jews were persuaded and joined Paul and Silas,[e] as did a large
number of God-fearing Greeks and quite a few prominent women.

16:25 praying and singing hymns. Paul and Silas illustrate Christian joy and peace in the midst of suffering (Matt 5:11–12; Rom 5:3; Jas 1:2; 1 Pet 1:6; 4:13). Peter slept soundly while in prison (12:6). Here the missionaries sing and praise God.

16:26 Earthquakes are common in this region, though the timing of this one is certainly miraculous.

16:27 Jailers were personally responsible for their prisoners and could be executed for allowing them to escape (see 12:19a and note).

16:30–31 Ironically, the purpose of the earthquake is not to physically save Paul and Silas (who do not leave) but to spiritually save the jailer.

16:30 what must I do to be saved? The jailer's question probably arose after hearing Paul and Silas speaking, singing, and praying about the "salvation" available through Jesus Christ.

16:31 Believe in the Lord Jesus. This is the simple yet profound answer to the desperate cry of the repentant sinner. Salvation comes through believing the gospel (15:7; Mark 1:15; Rom 1:16), the content of which is Jesus Christ (e.g., 8:12; 11:17; 19:4; John 3:16,36; Rom 3:22).

16:32–33 The jailer must have taken Paul and Silas to his home so his whole household could hear the message of salvation. As in the case of Cornelius and his household (10:48), scholars debate whether only those who personally expressed faith in Jesus were baptized or whether infants were included.

16:35 The magistrates evidently deem that a severe beating and night in jail are sufficient punishment for a minor disturbance of the peace.

16:37–38 It was contrary to Roman law to beat Roman citizens without trial, so the magistrates are justifiably alarmed. Paul's insistence on an apology may seem arrogant, but in a first-century culture of honor and shame, public vindication was essential to legitimize Paul and the church he established. The church was founded not by shady Jewish itinerants who slunk out of town but by esteemed Roman citizens. Luke takes pains throughout Acts to show that Christianity is legally innocent (see note on 23:29).

17:1–9 *In Thessalonica.* As in Philippi, Paul establishes an important church in Thessalonica, to which he writes two of his NT letters. Paul preaches in Thessalonica on "three Sabbath days" (v. 2). How long Paul stays in the city after this is not clear, but persecution cuts short his ministry (v. 10; cf. 1 Thess 2:2,17). When he writes 1 Thessalonians, Paul has been deeply concerned about the fate of this young church and is thrilled to hear that they are thriving despite suffering and persecution (1 Thess 2:17—3:10). Perseverance is a major theme in Scripture (Heb 10:32–36; Jas 1:12; 1 Pet 4:16,19).

17:1 Thessalonica. A thriving seaport and capital of the province of Macedonia, located about 100 miles (about 160 kilometers) from Philippi. Unlike Philippi, it had a large Jewish population, so Paul follows his normal pattern of preaching first in the synagogue (vv. 2,10,17; 13:14; 14:1; 18:4).

17:3 the Messiah had to suffer and rise from the dead. This is an important theme in Luke-Acts (3:18; 26:23; Luke 24:26,46; see Introduction to Acts: Occasion and Purpose; Themes and Theology). One of Luke's purposes is to respond to those who claimed that Jesus could not be the Messiah since he suffered and died.

17:4 prominent women. There is literary and inscriptional evidence

5But other Jews were jealous; so they rounded up some bad characters from the marketplace, formed
a mob and started a riot in the city.[f] They rushed to Jason's[g] house in search of Paul and Silas in order
to bring them out to the crowd.[a] 6But when they did not find them, they dragged[h] Jason and some other
believers before the city officials, shouting: "These men who have caused trouble all over the world[i] have
now come here,[j] 7and Jason has welcomed them into his house. They are all defying Caesar's decrees,
saying that there is another king, one called Jesus."[k] 8When they heard this, the crowd and the city
officials were thrown into turmoil. 9Then they made Jason[l] and the others post bond and let them go.

17:5 [f] ver 13; 1Th 2:16 [g] Ro 16:21
17:6 [h] Ac 16:19 [i] Mt 24:14 [j] Ac 16:20
17:7 [k] Lk 23:2; Jn 19:12
17:9 [l] ver 5
17:10 [m] ver 13; Ac 20:4

In Berea

10As soon as it was night, the believers sent Paul and Silas away to Berea.[m] On arriving there, they
went to the Jewish synagogue. 11Now the Berean Jews were of more noble character than those in

[a] 5 Or *the assembly of the people*

that many upper-class women in the Greco-Roman world were interested in Judaism and often became patrons for the synagogue communities (see v. 12; 16:14).

17:5 As at Pisidian Antioch (13:45), Iconium (14:2), and Lystra (14:19), opposition arises in Thessalonica from some Jews who are jealous that Paul's ministry is attracting the support of their influential Gentile supporters (see v. 4 and note).

17:6 Jason. Paul's host at Thessalonica. Perhaps like Aquila and Priscilla, he shared Paul's trade of tent making (18:2–3; 1 Thess 2:9).

17:7 another king. The trumped-up charges against the missionaries include sedition, claiming Jesus is a rival king to Caesar (cf. Luke 23:2–4), and disturbing the peace. The charge of sedition was equivalent to treason and could result in capital punishment.

17:8 city officials. The Greek term *politarchēs* was unknown in Greek literature outside of Acts until it was discovered in 1835 on an inscription in Thessalonica. The use of the title here is evidence of Luke's scrupulous attention to historical detail.

17:10–15 *In Berea.* The Bereans have become famous because, unlike the Jews of Thessalonica who used disreputable men to start a riot, they "examined the Scriptures every day to see if what Paul said was true" (v. 11). While believers today often use this example to encourage fellow believers to read their Bibles as "Bereans," the context here concerns unbelieving Jews who are willing to give Paul's message a legitimate hearing and test his words against the Hebrew Scriptures.

17:10 Berea. About 45 miles (about 72 kilometers) west of Thessalonica (a two- to three-day journey on foot).

17:11 noble. Originally meant "high born," i.e., from an upper-class family. It came to mean "open," "tolerant," or "generous."

PAUL'S SECOND MISSIONARY JOURNEY
ca. AD 49–52 (Acts 15:36–18:22)

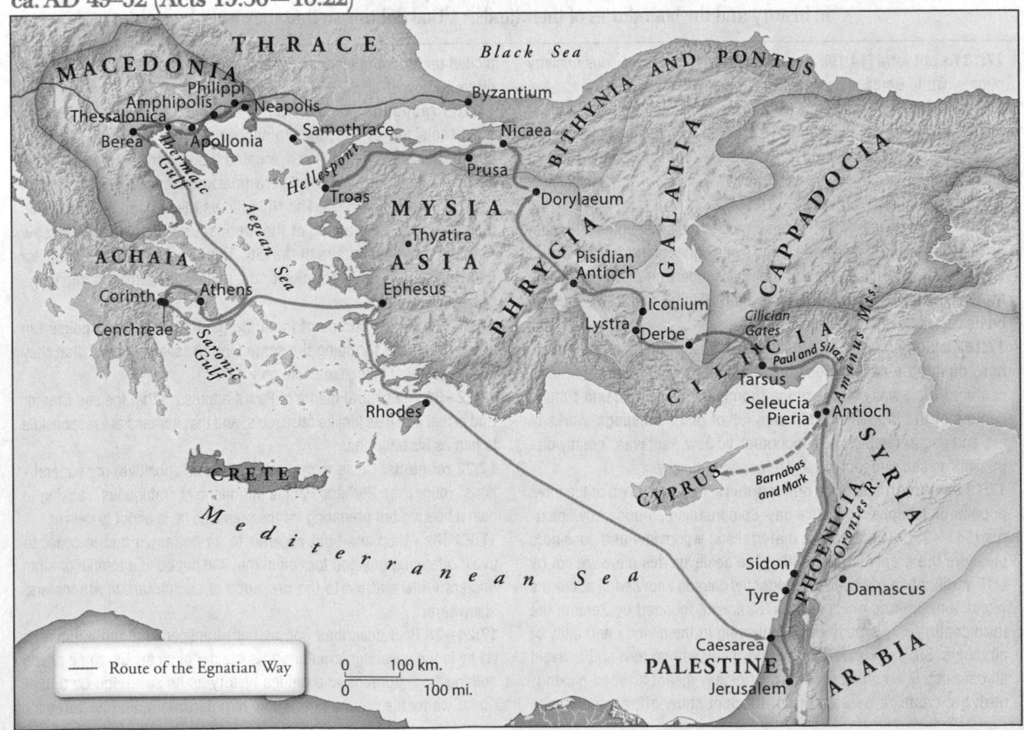

17:11 [n]ver 1 [o]Lk 16:29; Jn 5:39
17:14 [p]Ac 15:22 [q]Ac 16:1
17:15 [r]ver 16,21,22; Ac 18:1; 1Th 3:1 [s]Ac 18:5
17:17 [t]Ac 9:20
17:18 [u]ver 31,32; Ac 4:2
17:19 [v]ver 22 [w]Mk 1:27
17:23 [x]Jn 4:22
17:24 [y]Isa 42:5; Ac 14:15 [z]Dt 10:14; Mt 11:25 [a]Ac 7:48
17:25 [b]Ps 50:10-12; Isa 42:5
17:26 [c]Dt 32:8; Job 12:23

Thessalonica,[n] for they received the message with great eagerness and examined the Scriptures[o] every
day to see if what Paul said was true. 12 As a result, many of them believed, as did also a number of
prominent Greek women and many Greek men.
13 But when the Jews in Thessalonica learned that Paul was preaching the word of God at Berea,
some of them went there too, agitating the crowds and stirring them up. 14 The believers immediately sent Paul to the coast, but Silas[p] and Timothy[q] stayed at Berea. 15 Those who escorted Paul
brought him to Athens[r] and then left with instructions for Silas and Timothy to join him as soon
as possible.[s]

In Athens

16 While Paul was waiting for them in Athens, he was greatly distressed to see that the city was full
of idols. 17 So he reasoned in the synagogue[t] with both Jews and God-fearing Greeks, as well as in the
marketplace day by day with those who happened to be there. 18 A group of Epicurean and Stoic philosophers began to debate with him. Some of them asked, "What is this babbler trying to say?" Others
remarked, "He seems to be advocating foreign gods." They said this because Paul was preaching the
good news about Jesus and the resurrection.[u] 19 Then they took him and brought him to a meeting of
the Areopagus,[v] where they said to him, "May we know what this new teaching[w] is that you are presenting? 20 You are bringing some strange ideas to our ears, and we would like to know what they mean."
21 (All the Athenians and the foreigners who lived there spent their time doing nothing but talking about
and listening to the latest ideas.)
22 Paul then stood up in the meeting of the Areopagus and said: "People of Athens! I see that in every
way you are very religious. 23 For as I walked around and looked carefully at your objects of worship, I
even found an altar with this inscription: TO AN UNKNOWN GOD. So you are ignorant of the very thing you
worship[x]—and this is what I am going to proclaim to you.
24 "The God who made the world and everything in it[y] is the Lord of heaven and earth[z] and does not
live in temples built by human hands.[a] 25 And he is not served by human hands, as if he needed anything. Rather, he himself gives everyone life and breath and everything else.[b] 26 From one man he made
all the nations, that they should inhabit the whole earth; and he marked out their appointed times
in history and the boundaries of their lands.[c] 27 God did this so that they would seek him and perhaps

17:13 As at Lystra (14:19), Jews familiar with Paul's previous ministry pursue him to Berea and create problems there.

17:14–15 Though Paul travels to Athens alone, Timothy and Silas eventually join him there, and from there Paul sends Timothy back to check on the church at Thessalonica (1 Thess 3:1–2). When Timothy returned and reported that the church was thriving, Paul wrote 1 Thessalonians to encourage them (1 Thess 3:6–10).

17:16–34 *In Athens.* While Paul's sermon in the synagogue at Pisidian Antioch illustrates his message to the synagogues of the Jewish dispersion (13:16–41), his address to the philosophers on the Areopagus in Athens illustrates his message to pagan Gentiles (vv. 22–31). For a briefer example, see 14:15–17.

17:16 Though first-century Athens was a shadow of its former greatness during the days of Socrates, Plato, and Aristotle (fifth to fourth century BC), it was still one of the prominent intellectual and cultural centers of the Roman world. It was full of grand buildings, works of art, and pagan temples. As a monotheistic Jew, Paul was "greatly distressed" to see rampant idolatry throughout the city.

17:18 Epicurean and Stoic philosophers. Represent two of the most popular philosophies of Paul's day. Epicureanism, founded by Epicurus (341–270 BC), affirms a materialistic worldview and considers pleasure the greatest good in life. One achieves this pleasure not by self-gratification but by living modestly, gaining knowledge about the world, and limiting one's desires. Stoicism, founded by Zeno in the third century BC, is pantheistic, believing in the divinity and unity of all things. Stoics seek to maintain harmony with nature and to avoid all destructive emotions. **babbler.** Originally meant a "seed-picking" bird, but came to be used of an arrogant show-off, someone who picked up random pieces of useless information and passed himself off as a know-it-all.

17:19 Areopagus. Means "Hill of Ares" or "Mars Hill." Ares was the Greek god of war, the Roman equivalent of Mars. The term could refer to (1) the hill itself, located below and to the west of the Acropolis and south of the Agora (marketplace) or (2) the council that originally met there. The NIV follows the second interpretation by referring to "a meeting of the Areopagus." The council oversaw civic and religious affairs of the city. This is not an official "trial" for Paul, but rather an opportunity for the philosophers to hear and judge this new teaching.

17:21 In this side comment (note the parentheses), Luke pokes fun at the Athenians for being the same kind of "seed-pickers" that they accused Paul of being (see note on v. 18).

17:22–31 The central theme of Paul's address is that the one Creator God is real and true (unlike false idols) and that humans are responsible to him as his offspring.

17:22 religious. Could mean either "devout" (positive) or "superstitious" (negative). Perhaps Paul is intentionally ambiguous, seeking to gain a hearing but preparing for the message he is about to deliver.

17:23 The Athenians built an altar to an unknown god in order to avoid offending any god for whom they did not build a temple or altar. Ancient writers attest to the presence of such altars in Athens and elsewhere.

17:24–28 Paul describes God as both transcendent and immanent: (1) he is the sovereign creator and sustainer of all things, so he needs nothing from humans and guides history as its sovereign Lord; and (2) he wants his creatures to know him personally, and he cares for

reach out for him and find him, though he is not far from any one of us.[d] 28‘For in him we live and
move and have our being.’[ae] As some of your own poets have said, ‘We are his offspring.’[b]
29“Therefore since we are God’s offspring, we should not think that the divine being is like gold or
silver or stone — an image made by human design and skill.[f] 30In the past God overlooked[g] such ignorance,[h] but now he commands all people everywhere to repent.[i] 31For he has set a day when he will
judge[j] the world with justice[k] by the man he has appointed.[l] He has given proof of this to everyone by
raising him from the dead.”[m]
32When they heard about the resurrection of the dead,[n] some of them sneered, but others said, “We
want to hear you again on this subject.” 33At that, Paul left the Council. 34Some of the people became
followers of Paul and believed. Among them was Dionysius, a member of the Areopagus,[o] also a woman
named Damaris, and a number of others.

In Corinth

18 After this, Paul left Athens[p] and went to Corinth.[q] 2There he met a Jew named Aquila, a native
of Pontus, who had recently come from Italy with his wife Priscilla,[r] because Claudius[s] had
ordered all Jews to leave Rome. Paul went to see them, 3and because he was a tentmaker as they were,
he stayed and worked with them.[t] 4Every Sabbath[u] he reasoned in the synagogue, trying to persuade
Jews and Greeks.
5When Silas[v] and Timothy[w] came from Macedonia,[x] Paul devoted himself exclusively to preaching,

17:27 [d]Dt 4:7; Jer 23:23,24; Ac 14:17
17:28 [e]Job 12:10; Da 5:23
17:29 [f]Isa 40:18-20; Ro 1:23
17:30 [g]Ac 14:16; Ro 3:25 [h]ver 23; 1Pe 1:14 [i]Lk 24:47; Titus 2:11,12
17:31 [j]Mt 10:15 [k]Ps 9:8; 96:13; 98:9 [l]Ac 10:42 [m]Ac 2:24
17:32 [n]ver 18,31
17:34 [o]ver 19,22
18:1 [p]Ac 17:15 [q]Ac 19:1; 1Co 1:2; 2Co 1:1,23; 2Ti 4:20
18:2 [r]Ro 16:3; 1Co 16:19; 2Ti 4:19 [s]Ac 11:28
18:3 [t]Ac 20:34; 1Co 4:12; 1Th 2:9; 2Th 3:8
18:4 [u]Ac 13:14
18:5 [v]Ac 15:22 [w]Ac 16:1 [x]Ac 16:9; 17:14,15

[a] *28* From the Cretan philosopher Epimenides [b] *28* From the Cilician Stoic philosopher Aratus

them as his offspring. This teaching refutes both the agnosticism of the Epicureans and the pantheism of the Stoics.

17:28 in him we live and move and have our being. According to early Christian sources, this comes from the Cretan poet Epimenides (ca. 600 BC) in his poem *Cretica*. Some scholars doubt this and think that Paul is summing up general Greek thought. Paul quotes from this same poet in Titus 1:12. **We are his offspring.** Comes from the Stoic poet Aratus (315–240 BC) in his *Phaenomena*. In a real sense, all people, because they are created in God’s image, are his children, though this relationship is fractured and needs to be restored through the salvation available in Jesus Christ.

17:30 overlooked such ignorance. God did not judge people for their idolatry as severely as they deserved when they committed it (Rom 3:25), giving people time to repent (2 Pet 3:9). But the coming of Jesus the Messiah means that God’s full revelation has arrived (2:38; 3:19–21; Luke 3:7–9).

17:31 day when he will judge the world ... given proof. This day is coming, and Jesus is the one “appointed” to enact this judgment (10:40–42; Dan 7:13–14; Matt 25:31–46), as his resurrection confirms (cf. 2:24,32; 13:33–34).

17:32–34 Paul’s teaching on the resurrection of the dead provokes a strong reaction and apparently brings his message to a premature end. Though Greeks were divided on whether the soul exists after death, they uniformly rejected the resurrection of the physical body. The people respond to Paul’s message in three ways: outright rejection (“sneered”), continued interest without commitment (“we want to hear you again”), and belief. Though there is no record of a church established in Athens, “some of the people ... believed,” including at least one “member of the Areopagus,” a man named Dionysius. As far as we know, only men served on the Areopagus, so the woman Damaris may be a visiting dignitary or perhaps a believer from Paul’s earlier ministry in the synagogue or marketplace. Luke shows special interest in how prominent women respond to the gospel (cf. vv. 4,12; 16:14).

18:1–17 *In Corinth.* From Athens, Paul moves on to Corinth, where he spends 18 months (v. 11), the longest in any church except for Ephesus, where he stayed about three years (19:8,10; see note on 18:23—21:16). As major cities in the empire, Corinth and Ephesus become the missionaries’ bases of operation to evangelize the surrounding regions. Paul has a long (and sometimes tempestuous) relationship with the church at Corinth, which suffers from the kinds of problems typical of those who convert from a pagan environment of immorality and idolatry.

18:1 Corinth. The largest city in Greece; a major crossroads of commerce and culture. Located on the narrow isthmus connecting the Peloponnesus with the Greek mainland, it was the major Greek thoroughfare for east-west trade. Ships arriving at one of its two ports, Lechaeum on the east and Cenchreae on the west, would unload their goods to transport them across the isthmus; smaller ships would be placed on rolling carts and dragged across. This was preferable to the long and dangerous journey around the Peloponnesus. As a major urban area, the city was well known for its immorality and idolatry. The verb “to live like a Corinthian” (*korinthiazesthai*) meant to act like a prostitute. Although some statements about the worst of Corinthian debauchery (like 1,000 prostitutes at the temple of Aphrodite) were related to the old city, which the Romans destroyed in 146 BC, Corinth still suffered from the kinds of moral and religious challenges common to major metropolitan areas.

18:2 Aquila ... Priscilla. A Jewish-Christian couple and Paul’s fellow tentmakers who become key partners in his ministry (Rom 16:3; 1 Cor 16:19; 2 Tim 4:19). Priscilla’s name is usually listed first, an unusual practice in Greco-Roman society, indicating her higher social status or greater prominence in the Christian community (or both). **Claudius.** Ruled the Roman Empire AD 41–54. **ordered all Jews to leave Rome.** Corroborated by the Roman historian Suetonius (*Life of Claudius* 25.4), who says that the expulsions resulted from riots instigated by a certain “Chrestus.” Suetonius probably misunderstood conflicts between Jews and Christians over “the Christ” as a conflict involving an individual named Chrestus (a common slave name).

18:3 tentmaker. Or leather worker. Rabbis of Paul’s day were encouraged to practice a trade. Cilicia, Paul’s home province, was known for its goat-skin leather goods. Though only this text specifies his trade, Paul often speaks of working hard to pay his own way so as not to be a burden to others or accused of profiting financially from the gospel (20:34; 1 Cor 4:12; 9:12; 2 Cor 11:7; 1 Thess 2:9).

18:4 reasoned in the synagogue. Paul’s usual custom (see note on 9:15).

18:5 Timothy and Silas evidently brought a financial gift from the churches of Macedonia (2 Cor 11:8–9; Phil 4:14–15) that freed up Paul

18:5 [y]ver 28; Ac 17:3
18:6 [z]Ac 13:45 [a]2Sa 1:16; Eze 18:13; 33:4 [b]Ac 20:26 [c]Ac 13:46
18:7 [d]Ac 16:14
18:8 [e]1Co 1:14 [f]Mk 5:22 [g]Ac 11:14
18:10 [h]Mt 28:20
18:12 [i]ver 27
18:15 [j]Ac 23:29; 25:11,19
18:17 [k]1Co 1:1
18:18 [l]Ac 1:16 [m]Ro 16:1 [n]Nu 6:2,5,18; Ac 21:24
18:19 [o]ver 21,24; 1Co 15:32
18:21 [p]Ro 1:10; 1Co 4:19; Jas 4:15
18:22 [q]Ac 8:40 [r]Ac 11:19

testifying to the Jews that Jesus was the Messiah.[y] 6But when they opposed Paul and became abusive,[z]
he shook out his clothes in protest and said to them, "Your blood be on your own heads![a] I am innocent
of it.[b] From now on I will go to the Gentiles."[c]
7Then Paul left the synagogue and went next door to the house of Titius Justus, a worshiper of God.[d]
8Crispus,[e] the synagogue leader,[f] and his entire household[g] believed in the Lord; and many of the Corinthians who heard Paul believed and were baptized.
9One night the Lord spoke to Paul in a vision: "Do not be afraid; keep on speaking, do not be silent.
10For I am with you,[h] and no one is going to attack and harm you, because I have many people in this
city." 11So Paul stayed in Corinth for a year and a half, teaching them the word of God.
12While Gallio was proconsul of Achaia,[i] the Jews of Corinth made a united attack on Paul and
brought him to the place of judgment. 13"This man," they charged, "is persuading the people to worship God in ways contrary to the law."
14Just as Paul was about to speak, Gallio said to them, "If you Jews were making a complaint
about some misdemeanor or serious crime, it would be reasonable for me to listen to you. 15But
since it involves questions about words and names and your own law[j]—settle the matter yourselves. I will not be a judge of such things." 16So he drove them off. 17Then the crowd there turned
on Sosthenes[k] the synagogue leader and beat him in front of the proconsul; and Gallio showed no
concern whatever.

Priscilla, Aquila and Apollos

18Paul stayed on in Corinth for some time. Then he left the brothers and sisters[l] and sailed for Syria,
accompanied by Priscilla and Aquila. Before he sailed, he had his hair cut off at Cenchreae[m] because
of a vow he had taken.[n] 19They arrived at Ephesus,[o] where Paul left Priscilla and Aquila. He himself
went into the synagogue and reasoned with the Jews. 20When they asked him to spend more time with
them, he declined. 21But as he left, he promised, "I will come back if it is God's will."[p] Then he set sail
from Ephesus. 22When he landed at Caesarea,[q] he went up to Jerusalem and greeted the church and
then went down to Antioch.[r]

to devote himself "exclusively to preaching." For more details on the movements of Paul, Timothy, and Silas during this time, see Introduction to 1 Thessalonians: Paul and the Thessalonian Church.

18:6 From now on. Everywhere he went, Paul preached the gospel first to the Jews and then, when he faced rejection, to the Gentiles (13:46; 19:8–9; 28:28). The gospel is first for the Jews since they received God's promises (Rom 1:16; 3:1; 9:4–5).

18:7 Titius Justus. Probably one of Paul's Gentile converts from the synagogue. Though Jews forced Paul to leave the synagogue, Luke stresses that Paul's ministry to the Jews is still effective since even the synagogue ruler Crispus (v. 8) and his family believe and are baptized. Paul personally baptized Crispus (1 Cor 1:14).

18:9–11 In the face of what becomes a difficult and challenging relationship with this church (see Introduction to 2 Corinthians: Date), as well as strong persecution from without (vv. 12–17), God sends Paul a vision to encourage him (cf. 23:11; 27:23–24).

18:9–10 Do not be afraid ... For I am with you. Echoes God's call of individuals in the OT, like Moses (Exod 3:2–12), Joshua (Josh 1:1–9), Jeremiah (Jer 1:5–10), and the servant of the Lord (Isa 42:1–4). Paul needs this encouragement since he has come to Corinth "in weakness with great fear and trembling" (1 Cor 2:3).

18:10 many people in this city. Whether this indicates God's foreknowledge, his predestination of those in the city of Corinth who will believe, or both, the effect is to provide the apostle with confidence that his preaching will not be in vain.

18:12–17 Paul's trial before Gallio provides important information for dating Paul's ministry. Gallio (v. 12) was proconsul of Achaia ca. AD 51–52, so we know that Paul was at Corinth around AD 50–52. Gallio's decree also has important implications for the legal status of Christianity. By identifying the conflict as an internal Jewish debate ("questions about words and names and your own law," v. 15), Gallio essentially rules that (1) Christianity is a protected religion, like Judaism, under Roman law and (2) Christians are innocent of breaking Roman law. This provides a measure of protection for the Christians in the near future.

18:17 the crowd ... beat him. Perhaps (1) an act of anti-Jewish sentiment sparked by Gallio's claim that the Jews are wasting his time or (2) an angry response by the Jews present against one of their own because either (a) as their spokesman Sosthenes botched the case or (b) Sosthenes was showing sympathy for the Christians. This may be the same Sosthenes Paul mentions in 1 Cor 1:1 as coauthor of the letter and his "brother" in Christ.

18:18–22 *Return to Antioch.* Paul's return to Antioch marks the end of what is called his "second missionary journey" (15:36—18:22), centered on northern Greece (Macedonia) and southern Greece (Achaia). It also transitions to his third missionary journey since his brief visit to Ephesus becomes the prelude to his three-year ministry there (ch. 19).

18:18 Paul's haircut in Cenchreae, the southern (Aegean) port of Corinth, probably signaled the end of a Nazirite vow, a period of special devotion to God (Num 6:1–21). Luke stresses that Paul remained a faithful Jew throughout his life. Christianity is not a new religion; it is Judaism fulfilled.

18:19 Paul left Priscilla and Aquila. To begin the ministry in Ephesus. See note on v. 2. Paul returns after visiting the sending church in Antioch, Syria.

18:22 Caesarea. See note on 10:1. **Jerusalem.** The Greek text does not explicitly name Jerusalem but implies it since Paul "went up" to the church there. Jews always "went up to" Jerusalem since it is located in the hills and (especially) since it is God's holy city and the location of the temple.

[23]After spending some time in Antioch, Paul set out from there and traveled from place to place
throughout the region of Galatia[s] and Phrygia, strengthening all the disciples.[t]
[24]Meanwhile a Jew named Apollos,[u] a native of Alexandria, came to Ephesus. He was a learned man,
with a thorough knowledge of the Scriptures. [25]He had been instructed in the way of the Lord, and he
spoke with great fervor[a][v] and taught about Jesus accurately, though he knew only the baptism of John.[w]
[26]He began to speak boldly in the synagogue. When Priscilla and Aquila heard him, they invited him to
their home and explained to him the way of God more adequately.
[27]When Apollos wanted to go to Achaia,[x] the brothers and sisters[y] encouraged him and wrote to the

18:23 [s]Ac 16:6 [t]Ac 14:22; 15:32,41
18:24 [u]Ac 19:1; 1Co 1:12; 3:5,6,22; 4:6; 16:12; Titus 3:13
18:25 [v]Ro 12:11 [w]Ac 19:3
18:27 [x]ver 12 [y]ver 18

[a] 25 Or *with fervor in the Spirit*

18:23—21:16 *Paul's Third Missionary Journey.* Paul's "third missionary journey" centers in Ephesus, the leading city of the province of Asia. Paul strategically uses Ephesus as a base of operations to reach the entire province of Asia (19:10). His three months in the synagogue (19:8), two years in the hall of Tyrannus (19:10), and a period of time after that (19:22) confirm that Paul is in Ephesus about three years (see 20:31).
18:23–28 *Priscilla, Aquila, and Apollos.* While Paul is returning from his second missionary journey (vv. 18–22) and beginning his third (v. 23), Luke adds a parenthetic comment about Apollos, a powerful speaker and Hellenistic-Jewish Christian from Alexandria, Egypt, whom Priscilla and Aquila further instruct.
18:23 Paul returns to the regions of Galatia and Phrygia in order to strengthen all the disciples in the churches established during his first missionary journey (12:25—14:28). Paul is deeply concerned that his converts are spiritually healthy and continually growing.
18:24 Alexandria. A city in Egypt, known for its education and philosophy, that had a large Jewish population. Apollos's "thorough knowledge of the Scriptures" and his powerful speaking gifts made him a potent advocate for the gospel.
18:25 great fervor. Or "fervent in spirit," an idiom that can mean "with fervor in the Spirit" (see NIV text note). **knew only the baptism of John.** Perhaps Apollos is not yet a follower of Jesus but only a follower of John the Baptist (see notes on 19:4,5). However, since he "taught about Jesus accurately," Apollos is probably a believer but has not yet been fully instructed about Christian baptism (see Matt 28:18–20).
18:26 Priscilla and Aquila. See note on v. 2.
18:27 For Apollos's ministry in Achaia (Corinth), see 1 Cor 1:12; 3:4–6, 22; 4:6. Apollos later returns to Ephesus (1 Cor 16:12).

PAUL'S THIRD MISSIONARY JOURNEY
ca. AD 52–57 (Acts 18:23—21:16)

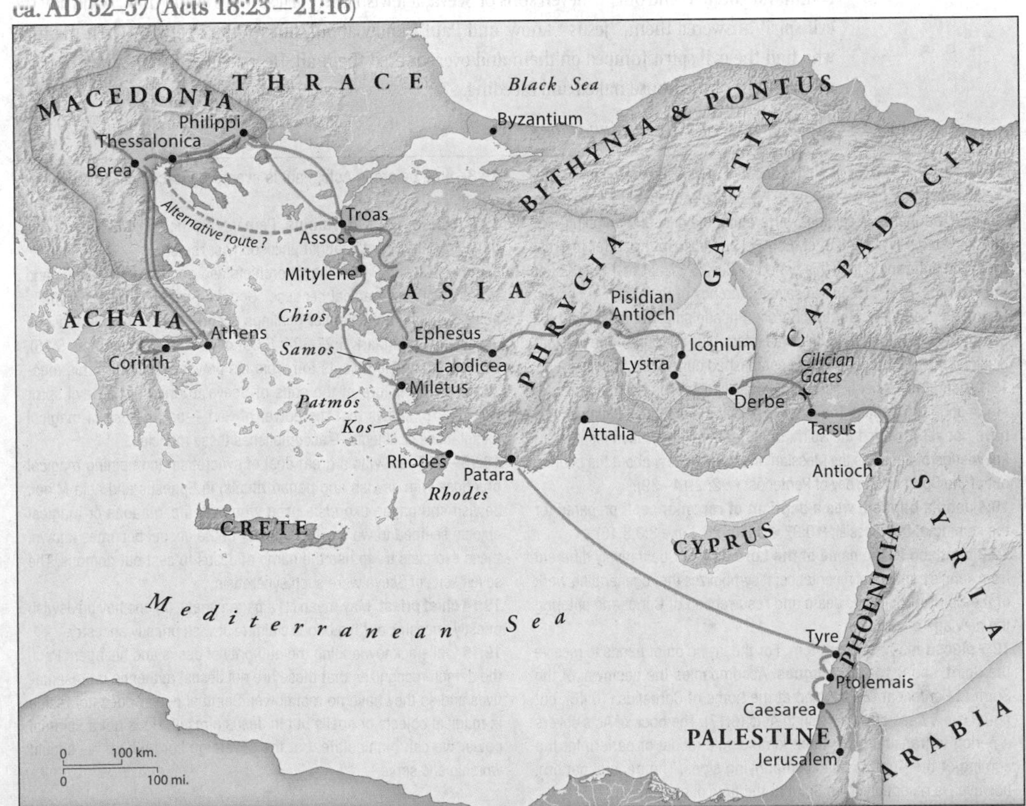

18:28 [z]Ac 17:2 [a]ver 5; Ac 9:22
19:1 [b]Ac 18:1 [c]Ac 18:19
19:4 [d]Jn 1:7; Ac 13:24,25
19:6 [e]Ac 6:6; 8:17 [f]Ac 2:4 [g]Mk 16:17; Ac 10:46
19:8 [h]Ac 9:20 [i]Ac 1:3; 28:23
19:9 [j]Ac 14:4 [k]ver 23; Ac 9:2 [l]ver 30; Ac 11:26
19:10 [m]Ac 20:31 [n]ver 22,26,27
19:11 [o]Ac 8:13
19:12 [p]Ac 5:15
19:13 [q]Mt 12:27 [r]Mk 9:38

disciples there to welcome him. When he arrived, he was a great help to those who by grace had believed. [28]For he vigorously refuted his Jewish opponents in public debate, proving from the Scriptures[z]
that Jesus was the Messiah.[a]

Paul in Ephesus

19 While Apollos was at Corinth,[b] Paul took the road through the interior and arrived at Ephesus.[c] There he found some disciples [2]and asked them, "Did you receive the Holy Spirit when[a]
you believed?"
They answered, "No, we have not even heard that there is a Holy Spirit."
[3]So Paul asked, "Then what baptism did you receive?"
"John's baptism," they replied.
[4]Paul said, "John's baptism was a baptism of repentance. He told the people to believe in the one
coming after him, that is, in Jesus."[d] [5]On hearing this, they were baptized in the name of the Lord Jesus.
[6]When Paul placed his hands on them,[e] the Holy Spirit came on them,[f] and they spoke in tongues[b][g]
and prophesied. [7]There were about twelve men in all.
[8]Paul entered the synagogue[h] and spoke boldly there for three months, arguing persuasively about
the kingdom of God.[i] [9]But some of them[j] became obstinate; they refused to believe and publicly maligned the Way.[k] So Paul left them. He took the disciples[l] with him and had discussions daily in the
lecture hall of Tyrannus. [10]This went on for two years,[m] so that all the Jews and Greeks who lived in the
province of Asia[n] heard the word of the Lord.
[11]God did extraordinary miracles[o] through Paul, [12]so that even handkerchiefs and aprons that
had touched him were taken to the sick, and their illnesses were cured[p] and the evil spirits left them.
[13]Some Jews who went around driving out evil spirits[q] tried to invoke the name of the Lord Jesus over
those who were demon-possessed. They would say, "In the name of the Jesus[r] whom Paul preaches, I
command you to come out." [14]Seven sons of Sceva, a Jewish chief priest, were doing this. [15]One day the
evil spirit answered them, "Jesus I know, and Paul I know about, but who are you?" [16]Then the man
who had the evil spirit jumped on them and overpowered them all. He gave them such a beating that
they ran out of the house naked and bleeding.

[a] 2 Or *after* [b] 6 Or *other languages*

19:1–22 *Paul in Ephesus.* Luke's account of Paul's three-year ministry in Ephesus (see note on 18:23—21:16) is selective and focuses especially on the theme of spiritual warfare and the gospel triumphing over popular magic (vv. 11–20; cf. Eph 6:12). Paul's letters refer to great trials and suffering during this period (1 Cor 15:32; 2 Cor 1:8; cf. 2 Cor 4:9–12; 6:4–10; 11:23). The seven churches of Revelation (Ephesus, Smyrna, Pergamum, Thyatira, Sardis, Philadelphia, Laodicea) and the churches at Hierapolis and Colossae (started by Epaphras, one of Paul's disciples, Col 1:7) probably were established during this period.
19:1 disciples. Either believers in Jesus (like Apollos, 18:25) or followers of John the Baptist. The latter is perhaps more likely because they have not yet received the Spirit. In either case, they have insufficient knowledge of Jesus as the Messiah and do not know about the pouring out of the Spirit on the day of Pentecost (v. 2; 2:14–39).
19:4 John's baptism was a baptism of repentance. It prepared for the coming of the Messiah (10:37; 13:24–25; Luke 3:3,8,16).
19:5 baptized in the name of the Lord Jesus. Qualitatively different from John's baptism of repentance; it symbolizes the regenerating work of the Spirit through the death and resurrection of Christ and entering the new age of salvation.
19:6 placed his hands on them. For the laying on of hands to receive the Spirit, see 8:15–17. **tongues.** Accompanies the bestowal of the Spirit at Pentecost (2:4,11) and at the home of Cornelius (10:46), but not in every case of conversion in Acts (8:17). The book of Acts covers a period of transition, and there is no single model or pattern for the coming of the Spirit or its accompanying signs. The general pattern, however, is reception of the Spirit at the time of conversion.
19:8–9 As before in Acts, Paul is eventually forced out of the synagogue.
19:9 lecture hall of Tyrannus. Perhaps a school in which Tyrannus (meaning "the tyrant") taught philosophy or rhetoric.
19:11–12 Using Paul's "handkerchiefs and aprons" for healings and exorcisms is not magical because "God did [these] extraordinary miracles through Paul." Similar healings occurred when people touched Jesus' clothing (Mark 5:27–34; 6:56) or Peter's shadow (Acts 5:15). God uses tangible objects to reveal his power and confirm his messengers. The failure of the sons of Sceva to drive out an evil spirit (vv. 13–16) shows that the power of God—not the use of magical incantations or objects—accomplishes these miracles.
19:13–14 There was a great deal of syncretism (combining magical practices with Jewish and pagan rituals) in Ephesus and Asia Minor. Jewish and pagan exorcists used whatever incantations or magical objects seemed to work. As the power of the gospel becomes known, these exorcists try to use the name of Jesus to cast out demons. The seven sons of Sceva were such syncretists.
19:14 chief priest. May mean (1) a pagan priest, (2) one having Jewish priestly ancestry, or (3) a bogus claim to Jewish priestly ancestry.
19:15 While acknowledging the authority of Jesus and his agent Paul, the demon recognizes that these are not Jesus' authentic representatives and so they have no real power. Spiritual power does not reside in magical objects or spells but in Jesus himself. He is not a spiritual power we can manipulate, but the sovereign Lord whom we should worship and serve.

17 When this became known to the Jews and Greeks living in Ephesus,[s] they were all seized with fear,[t]
and the name of the Lord Jesus was held in high honor. 18 Many of those who believed now came and
openly confessed what they had done. 19 A number who had practiced sorcery brought their scrolls together and burned them publicly. When they calculated the value of the scrolls, the total came to fifty
thousand drachmas.[a] 20 In this way the word of the Lord spread widely and grew in power.[u]

21 After all this had happened, Paul decided[b] to go to Jerusalem,[v] passing through Macedonia[w] and
Achaia.[x] "After I have been there," he said, "I must visit Rome also."[y] 22 He sent two of his helpers,[z]
Timothy[a] and Erastus,[b] to Macedonia, while he stayed in the province of Asia[c] a little longer.

The Riot in Ephesus

23 About that time there arose a great disturbance about the Way.[d] 24 A silversmith named Demetrius,
who made silver shrines of Artemis, brought in a lot of business for the craftsmen there. 25 He called
them together, along with the workers in related trades, and said: "You know, my friends, that we receive
a good income from this business.[e] 26 And you see and hear how this fellow Paul has convinced and
led astray large numbers of people here in Ephesus[f] and in practically the whole province of Asia. He
says that gods made by human hands are no gods at all.[g] 27 There is danger not only that our trade
will lose its good name, but also that the temple of the great goddess Artemis will be discredited; and
the goddess herself, who is worshiped throughout the province of Asia and the world, will be robbed of
her divine majesty."

28 When they heard this, they were furious and began shouting: "Great is Artemis of the Ephesians!"[h]
29 Soon the whole city was in an uproar. The people seized Gaius[i] and Aristarchus,[j] Paul's traveling
companions from Macedonia,[k] and all of them rushed into the theater together. 30 Paul wanted to appear before the crowd, but the disciples would not let him. 31 Even some of the officials of the province,
friends of Paul, sent him a message begging him not to venture into the theater.

32 The assembly was in confusion: Some were shouting one thing, some another.[l] Most of the people
did not even know why they were there. 33 The Jews in the crowd pushed Alexander to the front, and
they shouted instructions to him. He motioned[m] for silence in order to make a defense before the people. 34 But when they realized he was a Jew, they all shouted in unison for about two hours: "Great is
Artemis of the Ephesians!"

35 The city clerk quieted the crowd and said: "Fellow Ephesians,[n] doesn't all the world know that the

19:17 [s]Ac 18:19 [t]Ac 5:5,11
19:20 [u]Ac 6:7; 12:24
19:21 [v]Ac 20:16,22; Ro 15:25 [w]Ac 16:9 [x]Ac 18:12 [y]Ro 15:24,28
19:22 [z]Ac 13:5 [a]Ac 16:1 [b]Ro 16:23; 2Ti 4:20 [c]ver 10,26,27
19:23 [d]Ac 9:2
19:25 [e]Ac 16:16,19,20
19:26 [f]Ac 18:19 [g]Dt 4:28; Ps 115:4; Isa 44:10-20; Jer 10:3-5; Ac 17:29; 1Co 8:4; Rev 9:20
19:28 [h]Ac 18:19
19:29 [i]Ac 20:4; Ro 16:23; 1Co 1:14 [j]Ac 20:4; 27:2; Col 4:10; Phm 24 [k]Ac 16:9
19:32 [l]Ac 21:34
19:33 [m]Ac 12:17
19:35 [n]Ac 18:19

[a] *19* A drachma was a silver coin worth about a day's wages. [b] *21* Or *decided in the Spirit*

19:19 scrolls. Likely contained magic spells and formulas to ward off evil spirits and disease. Many such documents, known as the Magical Papyri, have been discovered in the sands of Egypt. **fifty thousand drachmas.** See NIV text note. A laborer earned about a drachma per day. Assuming $10 per hour, or $100 per day, this would be about $5 million today.
19:20 spread widely and grew in power. This encapsulates the central theme of the book of Acts: the gospel's progress is unstoppable.
19:21 Luke does not say why Paul decided to go to Jerusalem, but in his letters Paul repeatedly refers to a collection he is taking for the poverty-stricken Christians there (24:17; Rom 15:25–31; 1 Cor 16:1–3; 2 Cor 8–9). For Paul's plans to travel through Macedonia and Achaia, see Introduction to 2 Corinthians: Place of Composition. Paul's journey to Jerusalem, where dangers await him (20:22–25; 21:4,11–14), parallels Jesus' journey to Jerusalem (Luke 9:51; 13:33–34).
19:22 Timothy. See note on 16:1–5. **Erastus.** May be the same individual named in Rom 16:23b; 2 Tim 4:20. Paul identifies him as the city treasurer or director of public works. This may also be the same Erastus named on an inscription excavated at Corinth.
19:23–41 *The Riot in Ephesus.* The theme of spiritual warfare at Ephesus continues as the guild of craftsmen provoke a riot against Paul and his fellow missionaries. The many conversions to faith in Jesus were causing a recession in the idol-making business, so they take action against Paul. Civic life at Ephesus centered on the worship of the goddess Artemis (the Roman Diana), and her magnificent temple was one of the seven wonders of the ancient world. At Ephesus the traditional Greek Artemis, a goddess of the hunt, was merged with the traditional Anatolian fertility goddess Cybele. The many-breasted statue of Artemis stood in the temple at Ephesus, and a week-long festival in the spring, known as the Artemision, attracted thousands of devotees to the city. Worshiping the goddess was a source of enormous civic pride.
19:23 the Way. One of Luke's favorite designations for the early Christian movement (see note on 9:2; cf. v. 9; 18:25–26; 22:4; 24:14,22).
19:24 silver shrines of Artemis. Small replicas of the famous temple of Artemis.
19:25–27 Demetrius focuses first on the Ephesian's economic loss and then appeals to their loyalty to the goddess, who brought fame to Ephesus. Greed and pride are among the strongest (and most dangerous) of human motivations.
19:29 theater. An open-air amphitheater almost 500 feet (150 meters) in diameter that could hold over 20,000 people. It was built on the slopes of Mount Pion and faced west toward the harbor. Evidently Aristarchus and Gaius are not harmed since they become part of the delegation that travels with Paul to Jerusalem (see notes on 20:4; 27:2).
19:33 Alexander. Probably a Jewish representative trying to disassociate the Christians from the Jews and show that the Jews are not responsible for any sacrilege against Artemis. The crowd shouts him down because they recognize him as a Jew who rejects idols.
19:35 city clerk. The city's chief administrative officer (something like a mayor) who presided over the city council and served as liaison to provincial authorities. He calms the crowd with four points (vv. 36–40):

The theater in Ephesus was the location of the riot of the silversmiths (Acts 19:29). The silversmiths were upset that Paul's teachings were hurting their idol-making business.

19:37 [o]Ro 2:22
19:38 [p]Ac 13:7,8,12
20:1 [q]Ac 11:26 [r]Ac 16:9
20:3 [s]ver 19; Ac 9:23, 24; 23:12,15,30; 25:3; 2Co 11:26 [t]Ac 16:9
20:4 [u]Ac 19:29 [v]Ac 17:1 [w]Ac 19:29 [x]Ac 16:1 [y]Eph 6:21; Col 4:7; 2Ti 4:12; Titus 3:12 [z]Ac 21:29; 2Ti 4:20

city of Ephesus is the guardian of the temple of the great Artemis and of her image, which fell from
heaven? 36 Therefore, since these facts are undeniable, you ought to calm down and not do anything
rash. 37 You have brought these men here, though they have neither robbed temples[o] nor blasphemed
our goddess. 38 If, then, Demetrius and his fellow craftsmen have a grievance against anybody, the courts
are open and there are proconsuls.[p] They can press charges. 39 If there is anything further you want to
bring up, it must be settled in a legal assembly. 40 As it is, we are in danger of being charged with rioting
because of what happened today. In that case we would not be able to account for this commotion, since
there is no reason for it." 41 After he had said this, he dismissed the assembly.

Through Macedonia and Greece

20 When the uproar had ended, Paul sent for the disciples[q] and, after encouraging them, said
goodbye and set out for Macedonia.[r] 2 He traveled through that area, speaking many words
of encouragement to the people, and finally arrived in Greece, 3 where he stayed three months. Because some Jews had plotted against him[s] just as he was about to sail for Syria, he decided to go back
through Macedonia.[t] 4 He was accompanied by Sopater son of Pyrrhus from Berea, Aristarchus[u] and
Secundus from Thessalonica,[v] Gaius[w] from Derbe, Timothy[x] also, and Tychicus[y] and Trophimus[z] from

(1) Artemis is too great for these events to threaten her. (2) Paul and the others have not directly blasphemed the goddess or robbed her temple. (3) There are civil courts to handle issues of liability and financial loss. (4) If a violent riot breaks out, the Roman authorities will hold this crowd responsible. This sane and balanced perspective introduces a recurring theme in Acts: Christianity is innocent under Roman law. An important part of Luke's purpose is to demonstrate to the Roman authorities that the Christians who live among them are law-abiding citizens and not enemies of the empire. See Introduction to Acts: Themes and Theology, 7.
her image ... fell from heaven. Perhaps a meteorite kept in the temple that they consider a sacred sign from heaven of Artemis's greatness.
20:1–6 *Through Macedonia and Greece.* Paul travels north from Ephesus to Troas and then across to Macedonia (v. 1), finally coming to Corinth in Achaia (southern Greece). Paul provides the reason for this journey in more detail in 2 Cor 1–7. Paul has been in conflict with the Corinthian church and sent Titus with a letter to try to restore good relations (2 Cor 2:3–4). After missing Titus in Troas, he finally meets him in Macedonia (2 Cor 2:12–13), where Titus reports the good news that the church repented and has reconciled (2 Cor 2:5–11; 7:5–13). From Macedonia Paul writes 2 Corinthians as a letter of reconciliation. He then travels to Corinth, where he spends three months (vv. 2–3). From there he writes Romans, his greatest theological work, to prepare for his visit to the church at Rome (Rom 1:10–13; 15:23–29).
20:3 through Macedonia. Paul takes the land route north because some Jews had plotted against him. Paul is evidently concerned that his enemies would be watching for him at a key transportation hub like the port of Cenchreae and that the small confines of a ship would make him an easy target. He is especially vulnerable since he is carrying a large collection of money for the Jerusalem church (see note on 19:21).
20:4 Traveling with Paul is a delegation from the churches of Galatia (Gaius and Timothy from Derbe; Sopater from Berea), Asia (Tychicus and Trophimus) and Macedonia (Aristarchus and Secundus of Thessalonica). These men are accompanying the collection (1 Cor 16:1–4; 2 Cor 8:18–19).

the province of Asia. 5These men went on ahead and waited for us[a] at Troas.[b] 6But we sailed from Philippi[c] after the Festival of Unleavened Bread, and five days later joined the others at Troas,[d] where we stayed seven days.

Eutychus Raised From the Dead at Troas

7On the first day of the week[e] we came together to break bread. Paul spoke to the people and, because he intended to leave the next day, kept on talking until midnight. 8There were many lamps in the upstairs room[f] where we were meeting. 9Seated in a window was a young man named Eutychus, who was sinking into a deep sleep as Paul talked on and on. When he was sound asleep, he fell to the ground from the third story and was picked up dead. 10Paul went down, threw himself on the young man[g] and put his arms around him. "Don't be alarmed," he said. "He's alive!"[h] 11Then he went upstairs again and broke bread[i] and ate. After talking until daylight, he left. 12The people took the young man home alive and were greatly comforted.

Paul's Farewell to the Ephesian Elders

13We went on ahead to the ship and sailed for Assos, where we were going to take Paul aboard. He had made this arrangement because he was going there on foot. 14When he met us at Assos, we took him aboard and went on to Mitylene. 15The next day we set sail from there and arrived off Chios. The day after that we crossed over to Samos, and on the following day arrived at Miletus.[j] 16Paul had decided to sail past Ephesus[k] to avoid spending time in the province of Asia, for he was in a hurry to reach Jerusalem,[l] if possible, by the day of Pentecost.[m]

17From Miletus, Paul sent to Ephesus for the elders[n] of the church. 18When they arrived, he said to them: "You know how I lived the whole time I was with you,[o] from the first day I came into the province of Asia. 19I served the Lord with great humility and with tears and in the midst of severe testing by the plots of my Jewish opponents.[p] 20You know that I have not hesitated to preach anything[q] that would be helpful to you but have taught you publicly and from house to house. 21I have declared to both Jews[r] and Greeks that they must turn to God in repentance[s] and have faith in our Lord Jesus.[t]

20:5 [a]Ac 16:10 [b]Ac 16:8
20:6 [c]Ac 16:12 [d]Ac 16:8
20:7 [e]1Co 16:2; Rev 1:10
20:8 [f]Ac 1:13
20:10 [g]1Ki 17:21; 2Ki 4:34 [h]Mt 9:23,24
20:11 [i]ver 7
20:15 [j]ver 17; 2Ti 4:20
20:16 [k]Ac 18:19 [l]Ac 19:21 [m]Ac 2:1; 1Co 16:8
20:17 [n]Ac 11:30
20:18 [o]Ac 18:19-21; 19:1-41
20:19 [p]ver 3
20:20 [q]ver 27
20:21 [r]Ac 18:5 [s]Ac 2:38 [t]Ac 24:24; 26:18; Eph 1:15; Col 2:5; Phm 5

20:5–6 Another "we" section of Acts begins here (see note on 16:10). Since the previous "we" section ended in Philippi (16:16–17) and this one begins there, it is possible Luke remained in Philippi doing ministry during the intervening years. Since he is present with Paul on his journey to Jerusalem (vv. 5–16; 21:1–17) and again on his journey to Rome (27:1—28:16), Luke presumably stays with Paul through this whole period until the end of the book.

20:6 Festival of Unleavened Bread. Lasted for a week after Passover, which began on the 15th of Nisan in the Jewish calendar (March–April). This is the spring of AD 57.

20:7–12 *Eutychus Raised From the Dead at Troas.* Paul's raising Eutychus parallels Peter's raising Tabitha (9:40), and the miracles by the apostles in Acts parallel Jesus' miracles in Luke's Gospel (Luke 7:11–15; 8:49–56; cf. John 11:38–44). Paul's throwing himself on the young man also echoes the similar actions of Elijah (1 Kgs 17:19–22) and Elisha (2 Kgs 4:34–35).

20:7 first day of the week. Sunday, the day of worship celebrating the resurrection. This is one of the earliest historical references to the church's meeting on Sunday instead of the Sabbath (i.e., Saturday; cf. 1 Cor 16:2; Rev 1:10). **break bread.** Likely celebrating the Lord's Supper (Luke 22:19), perhaps followed by a communal meal (2:42,46).

20:13–38 *Paul's Farewell to the Ephesian Elders.* Paul's address to the Ephesian elders is the only speech in Acts given to believers. Luke provides three main examples of Paul's messages: (1) to Jews and God-fearers in the synagogue at Pisidian Antioch (13:16–41), (2) to pagan Gentiles on Mars Hill in Athens (17:22–31), and (3) to the church leaders of Ephesus (vv. 17–35). This is a classic exhortation on Christian leadership. Paul doesn't expect to see them again, so he gives a farewell discourse. The closest parallels are Paul's farewell comments in Phil 1:19–30 during his first Roman imprisonment and especially his comments in 2 Timothy during his second imprisonment, when he is facing almost certain execution. Paul's address contains an exhortation to the elders to faithfully shepherd God's flock (vv. 28–31), framed on either side with a description of his own ministry of integrity and faithfulness (vv. 18–27; vv. 32–35).

20:13 Assos. A port city about 20 miles (about 32 kilometers) southeast of Troas. Paul takes the shorter cross-country route across the peninsula while the ship sails around.

20:17 Miletus. A port city about 30 miles (about 48 kilometers) south of Ephesus. Paul fears that traveling to Ephesus would delay him too long to reach Jerusalem by Pentecost (50 days after Passover; see note on v. 6). His many friends in Ephesus would probably want to see him and thus delay his departure.

20:19 humility. One of the most important traits of a Christian leader. Paul often refers to himself as Christ's "servant" (Greek *diakonos*: 1 Cor 3:5–6; 2 Cor 3:6 ["ministers"]; 6:4; 11:23; Eph 3:7; Col 1:23,25; Greek *doulos*: Rom 1:1; Gal 1:10; Phil 1:1; Titus 1:1), and he calls his churches to unity through humility (Eph 4:2; Phil 2:3; Col 3:12). **tears.** Paul is emotionally involved with and intimately concerned for those he serves (v. 31; 2 Cor 2:4; Phil 3:18). Luke does not mention plots and opposition from Paul's Jewish opponents in Ephesus, but they occurred throughout his ministry in Pisidian Antioch, Iconium, Lystra, Thessalonica, Berea, and Corinth.

20:20 publicly. Probably Paul's teaching in the synagogue and then the lecture hall of Tyrannus (19:8–9). **house to house.** House churches, the standard meeting place for believers (cf. 2:46).

20:21 both Jews and Greeks. Paul's inclusive message of salvation is the hallmark of his apostolic ministry (Rom 1:15–16). **repentance … faith in our Lord Jesus.** The essential message of the gospel. This is the Good News of the kingdom Jesus preached (Mark 1:15).

20:22 [u]ver 16
20:23 [v]Ac 21:4 [w]Ac 9:16
20:24 [x]Ac 21:13 [y]2Co 4:1 [z]Gal 1:1; Titus 1:3
20:25 [a]ver 38
20:26 [b]Ac 18:6
20:27 [c]ver 20
20:28 [d]1Pe 5:2
20:29 [e]Mt 7:15 [f]ver 28
20:30 [g]Ac 11:26
20:31 [h]Ac 19:10 [i]ver 19
20:32 [j]Ac 14:23 [k]Eph 1:14; Col 1:12; 3:24; Heb 9:15; 1Pe 1:4 [l]Ac 26:18
20:33 [m]1Sa 12:3; 1Co 9:12; 2Co 7:2; 11:9; 12:14-17
20:34 [n]Ac 18:3
20:36 [o]Lk 22:41; Ac 21:5
20:37 [p]Lk 15:20
20:38 [q]ver 25
21:1 [r]Ac 16:10
21:2 [s]Ac 11:19

22 “And now, compelled by the Spirit, I am going to Jerusalem,[u] not knowing what will happen to me
there. 23 I only know that in every city the Holy Spirit warns me[v] that prison and hardships are facing
me.[w] 24 However, I consider my life worth nothing to me;[x] my only aim is to finish the race and complete the task[y] the Lord Jesus has given me[z]—the task of testifying to the good news of God’s grace.

25 “Now I know that none of you among whom I have gone about preaching the kingdom will ever
see me again.[a] 26 Therefore, I declare to you today that I am innocent of the blood of any of you.[b] 27 For
I have not hesitated to proclaim to you the whole will of God.[c] 28 Keep watch over yourselves and all the
flock of which the Holy Spirit has made you overseers.[d] Be shepherds of the church of God,[*a*] which he
bought with his own blood.[*b*] 29 I know that after I leave, savage wolves[e] will come in among you and
will not spare the flock.[f] 30 Even from your own number men will arise and distort the truth in order to
draw away disciples[g] after them. 31 So be on your guard! Remember that for three years[h] I never stopped
warning each of you night and day with tears.[i]

32 “Now I commit you to God[j] and to the word of his grace, which can build you up and give you an
inheritance[k] among all those who are sanctified.[l] 33 I have not coveted anyone’s silver or gold or clothing.[m] 34 You yourselves know that these hands of mine have supplied my own needs and the needs of
my companions.[n] 35 In everything I did, I showed you that by this kind of hard work we must help the
weak, remembering the words the Lord Jesus himself said: ‘It is more blessed to give than to receive.’ ”

36 When Paul had finished speaking, he knelt down with all of them and prayed.[o] 37 They all wept
as they embraced him and kissed him.[p] 38 What grieved them most was his statement that they would
never see his face again.[q] Then they accompanied him to the ship.

On to Jerusalem

21 After we[r] had torn ourselves away from them, we put out to sea and sailed straight to Kos.
The next day we went to Rhodes and from there to Patara. 2 We found a ship crossing over to
Phoenicia,[s] went on board and set sail. 3 After sighting Cyprus and passing to the south of it, we sailed

a 28 Many manuscripts *of the Lord* *b* 28 Or *with the blood of his own Son.*

20:22–24 The Holy Spirit is both compelling Paul to go to Jerusalem (v. 22; cf. 16:6–7; 19:21) and warning him that prison and hardship await him (v. 23). God never promises Christians an easy life, and Paul often speaks of his willingness to suffer for Christ (2 Cor 4:7–12; 6:4–10; 12:9–10; Phil 1:19–26; 2:17; 3:8; Col 1:24). His only goal is to finish the race, a metaphor Paul uses frequently (v. 24; cf. 1 Cor 9:24–27; Gal 2:2; Phil 2:16; 3:13–14; 2 Tim 4:7).
20:25 none of you … will ever see me again. Paul is describing his expectations, not making a prophetic prediction. Though he did not expect to see the Ephesians again, the Pastoral Letters (1–2 Timothy; Titus) reveal that he was released from his first Roman imprisonment and returned to Ephesus (1 Tim 1:3).
20:26 Paul alludes to the watchman analogy in Ezek 33:1–6, where the watchman at the city gate is innocent if he sounds the trumpet at the approach of the enemy, even if the people do not heed the alarm.
20:27 the whole will of God. Paul did not merely proclaim what pleased his listeners or made him popular. He preached the whole plan of salvation, including a warning of coming judgment and the need to repent (see v. 21 and note).
20:28 shepherds. Church leaders are called “elders” (v. 17; Titus 1:5), “overseers” (Phil 1:1; 1 Tim 3:2; Titus 1:7; sometimes translated “bishops”), and “shepherds” (here)—probably three names for the same office. The term “shepherds” is a common biblical metaphor for leaders, who provide for and protect God’s flock (Jer 23:2; Zech 10:3; 11:4–17; John 21:15–17; 1 Pet 2:25; 5:2). The model leader is the Lord God, who is a shepherd over his people (Ps 23:1; Ezek 34:11–16; 1 Pet 2:25). Jesus is also the Good Shepherd, who gives up his life for the sheep (John 10:11,14–16). **God … bought with his own blood.** Christ sacrificially died on the cross, ransoming us from sin (Mark 10:45). The phrase is unusual since here is the only place the NT refers to God’s blood. Some suggest that it should be translated “with the blood of his own Son [Jesus]” or, alternatively, that “Lord” (as a reference to Christ) should be read in place of “God” (see NIV text notes).
20:29 savage wolves. False teachers who prey on God’s flock (Ezek 22:27; Zeph 3:3; Matt 7:15; Luke 10:3). Although external persecution was the greatest problem for the church of Paul’s day, his expectations were met as the later NT books reveal false teachers increasingly infiltrating the churches (Col 2:8; 1 Tim 4:1–3; 2 Tim 1:15; 2:16–18; 3:1–9; 2 Pet 2:1–22; 1 John 2:18–19; Jude 3–16; Rev 2:2).
20:33–35 Traveling philosophers and teachers in the Greco-Roman world often worked for a fee, exploiting their customers. Paul demonstrated the integrity of his ministry among the Ephesians by working to support himself (cf. 1 Cor 4:12; 9:12,15; 2 Cor 11:7; 12:13; 1 Thess 2:5,9; 2 Thess 3:7–8). This does not mean Christian workers should not be paid. At times Paul received support from his churches (Phil 4:15–16), and both Jesus and Paul said that “the worker deserves his wages” (Luke 10:7; 1 Tim 5:18). What Paul means is that leaders must be people of integrity and transparency. They must not only practice “hard work” (v. 35; cf. 1 Thess 4:11; 2 Thess 3:6–15) but also “help the weak” (v. 35; cf. Rom 15:1; Gal 6:2; Eph 4:28; 1 Thess 5:14).
20:35 It is more blessed to give than to receive. This quotation from Jesus is similar to Luke 6:38, but it does not appear in the NT Gospels. Jesus said and did much more than the Gospels record (John 21:25).
20:37 Paul spent three intense years of ministry with these leaders (19:8,10,22), so his departure is an extremely emotional event.
21:1–16 *On to Jerusalem.* Two key themes mark Paul’s return journey to Jerusalem: (1) An extensive network of churches and believers is developing across the Roman Empire. Everywhere Paul and his associates go, believers meet them and supply hospitality (vv. 4,7,16). (2) Paul receives repeated warnings about the dangers awaiting him in Jerusalem (vv. 4,10–14; cf. 20:22–23). Though Paul’s life is in peril, he pushes forward unconcerned and is ready to die “for the name of the

on to Syria. We landed at Tyre, where our ship was to unload its cargo. 4 We sought out the disciples[t]
there and stayed with them seven days. Through the Spirit[u] they urged Paul not to go on to Jerusalem.
5 When it was time to leave, we left and continued on our way. All of them, including wives and children,
accompanied us out of the city, and there on the beach we knelt to pray.[v] 6 After saying goodbye to each
other, we went aboard the ship, and they returned home.
7 We continued our voyage from Tyre[w] and landed at Ptolemais, where we greeted the brothers and
sisters[x] and stayed with them for a day. 8 Leaving the next day, we reached Caesarea[y] and stayed at the
house of Philip[z] the evangelist,[a] one of the Seven. 9 He had four unmarried daughters who prophesied.[b]
10 After we had been there a number of days, a prophet named Agabus[c] came down from Judea.
11 Coming over to us, he took Paul's belt, tied his own hands and feet with it and said, "The Holy Spirit
says, 'In this way the Jewish leaders in Jerusalem will bind[d] the owner of this belt and will hand him
over to the Gentiles.' "[e]
12 When we heard this, we and the people there pleaded with Paul not to go up to Jerusalem. 13 Then
Paul answered, "Why are you weeping and breaking my heart? I am ready not only to be bound, but
also to die[f] in Jerusalem for the name of the Lord Jesus."[g] 14 When he would not be dissuaded, we gave
up and said, "The Lord's will be done."
15 After this, we started on our way up to Jerusalem. 16 Some of the disciples from Caesarea[h] accompanied us and brought us to the home of Mnason, where we were to stay. He was a man from Cyprus[i]
and one of the early disciples.

Paul's Arrival at Jerusalem

17 When we arrived at Jerusalem, the brothers and sisters received us warmly.[j] 18 The next day Paul
and the rest of us went to see James,[k] and all the elders[l] were present. 19 Paul greeted them and reported
in detail what God had done among the Gentiles[m] through his ministry.[n]
20 When they heard this, they praised God. Then they said to Paul: "You see, brother, how many

21:4 [t] Ac 11:26 [u] ver 11; Ac 20:23
21:5 [v] Ac 20:36
21:7 [w] Ac 12:20 [x] Ac 1:16
21:8 [y] Ac 8:40 [z] Ac 6:5; 8:5-40 [a] Eph 4:11; 2Ti 4:5
21:9 [b] Lk 2:36; Ac 2:17
21:10 [c] Ac 11:28
21:11 [d] ver 33 [e] 1Ki 22:11
21:13 [f] Ac 20:24 [g] Ac 9:16
21:16 [h] Ac 8:40 [i] ver 3,4
21:17 [j] Ac 15:4
21:18 [k] Ac 15:13 [l] Ac 11:30
21:19 [m] Ac 14:27 [n] Ac 1:17

Lord Jesus" (v. 13). This motif parallels Jesus' final journey to Jerusalem in Luke 9–19, which is marked by repeated predictions of his coming suffering (Luke 9:22,44; 13:33–34; 18:31–33). On the collection for the poor that Paul is carrying to Jerusalem, see note on 19:21.

21:1 Kos ... Rhodes. Kos (about 40 miles [about 65 kilometers] south of Miletus) and Rhodes were both islands with main cities also called Kos and Rhodes. **Patara.** The main port of the province of Lycia, where Paul and his co-workers leave the small coastal ship and board a larger seagoing vessel for the 400-mile (650-kilometer) journey to Tyre (see note on v. 3).

21:2 Phoenicia. The coastal nation northwest of Israel (see note on 11:19). At this time Phoenicia was part of the Roman province of Syria (v. 3).

21:3 Cyprus. See note on 11:19. **Tyre.** The most important port of Phoenicia.

21:4 The Spirit's message to these disciples *not* to go to Jerusalem appears to contradict the Spirit's message to Paul compelling him *to* go (20:22). The likely answer is that the Spirit reveals to them—as he does to Agabus (vv. 10–11)—what would happen to Paul in Jerusalem, and on their own initiative they urge Paul not to go.

21:7 Ptolemais. Also known as Akko (Judg 1:31), 25 miles (40 kilometers) south of Tyre and 35 miles (56 kilometers) north of Caesarea (v. 8).

21:8 Philip the evangelist. See 6:5; 8:5–40.

21:9 daughters who prophesied. Women in the early church had this spiritual gift, which Joel prophesied (Joel 2:28) and which was fulfilled on the day of Pentecost (2:17).

21:10–11 Agabus also prophesied about the famine in Judea (11:28). Symbolic actions like Agabus's use of Paul's belt are common among the OT prophets (1 Kgs 11:29–31; Isa 8:1–4; 20:1–6; Jer 13:1–11; 19:1–13; 27:1–22; Hos 1:2). For a NT example, see Jesus' cursing of a fig tree and clearing of the temple, both symbolizing the coming destruction of Jerusalem (Mark 11:12–25). The parallels between Jesus and Paul continue as Agabus predicts that "the Jewish leaders in Jerusalem will ... hand him over to the Gentiles" (v. 11; cf. Matt 20:18–19; Luke 18:32).

21:14 The Lord's will be done. This statement, which recalls Jesus' words in the Garden of Gethsemane (Luke 22:42), could mean (1) that they finally conclude that God *does* want Paul to go to Jerusalem, or (2) that whatever happens to Paul, God will accomplish his divine will. The latter is a major theme of Acts: no matter what the challenges or setbacks, God is guiding events toward his saving purposes (2:23–24; 3:13–15; 4:10; 5:30–31).

21:17—28:31 *Paul's Fourth Journey: Arrest and Journey to Rome.* Paul's "fourth missionary journey" in fact represents his arrest in Jerusalem, two-year imprisonment in Caesarea, appeal to Caesar, journey in custody to Rome, and house arrest there. Although this period is not an intentional outreach planned and implemented by Paul, it is appropriately called a "missionary journey" since (1) Paul continues to take every opportunity to share the gospel, and (2) Luke uses the narrative of Paul's arrest and journey to Rome to show that the gospel continues to advance despite opposition and apparent setbacks. According to Acts, the expansion of the church is unstoppable, since it is the work of God. See note on 28:31.

21:17–26 *Paul's Arrival at Jerusalem.* Paul's arrival in Jerusalem and meeting with James results in an attempt at reconciliation between Paul and some Jewish Christians who are suspicious of his message of salvation by grace apart from the works of the law (vv. 20–25). This is a good example of Paul following his policy expressed in 1 Cor 9: "To those under the law I become like one under the law" (1 Cor 9:20).

21:18 James. Not the apostle James (who was killed in 12:2), but the half brother of Jesus, a leader of the Jerusalem church, and the author of the NT letter of James. See Acts 15:13 and note on 15:13–21; Gal 1:19 and note.

21:20–21 In response to Paul's report of success among the Gentiles (v. 19), the elders report continued success among the Jews, who remained faithful to their Jewish heritage. Yet some opponents are distorting Paul's message of salvation by faith alone, claiming that he encourages Jews not to circumcise their children or keep Jewish customs. This

21:20 [o]Ac 22:3; Ro 10:2; Gal 1:14 [p]Ac 15:1,5
21:21 [q]ver 28 [r]Ac 15:19-21; 1Co 7:18, 19 [s]Ac 6:14
21:23 [t]Ac 18:18
21:24 [u]ver 26; Ac 24:18 [v]Ac 18:18
21:25 [w]Ac 15:20,29
21:26 [x]Nu 6:13-20; Ac 24:18
21:27 [y]Ac 24:18; 26:21
21:28 [z]Mt 24:15; Ac 24:5,6
21:29 [a]Ac 20:4 [b]Ac 18:19
21:30 [c]Ac 26:21 [d]Ac 16:19
21:32 [e]Ac 23:27
21:33 [f]ver 11 [g]Ac 12:6 [h]Ac 20:23; Eph 6:20; 2Ti 2:9
21:34 [i]Ac 19:32 [j]ver 37; Ac 23:10,16,32
21:35 [k]ver 40
21:36 [l]Lk 23:18; Jn 19:15; Ac 22:22
21:37 [m]ver 34

thousands of Jews have believed, and all of them are zealous[o] for the law.[p] 21They have been informed that
you teach all the Jews who live among the Gentiles to turn away from Moses,[q] telling them not to circumcise their children[r] or live according to our customs.[s] 22What shall we do? They will certainly hear that you
have come, 23so do what we tell you. There are four men with us who have made a vow.[t] 24Take these men,
join in their purification rites[u] and pay their expenses, so that they can have their heads shaved.[v] Then everyone will know there is no truth in these reports about you, but that you yourself are living in obedience
to the law. 25As for the Gentile believers, we have written to them our decision that they should abstain from
food sacrificed to idols, from blood, from the meat of strangled animals and from sexual immorality."[w]
26The next day Paul took the men and purified himself along with them. Then he went to the temple to give notice of the date when the days of purification would end and the offering would be made
for each of them.[x]

Paul Arrested

27When the seven days were nearly over, some Jews from the province of Asia saw Paul at the temple.
They stirred up the whole crowd and seized him,[y] 28shouting, "Fellow Israelites, help us! This is the
man who teaches everyone everywhere against our people and our law and this place. And besides, he
has brought Greeks into the temple and defiled this holy place."[z] 29(They had previously seen Trophimus[a] the Ephesian[b] in the city with Paul and assumed that Paul had brought him into the temple.)
30The whole city was aroused, and the people came running from all directions. Seizing Paul,[c] they
dragged him[d] from the temple, and immediately the gates were shut. 31While they were trying to kill
him, news reached the commander of the Roman troops that the whole city of Jerusalem was in an
uproar. 32He at once took some officers and soldiers and ran down to the crowd. When the rioters saw
the commander and his soldiers, they stopped beating Paul.[e]
33The commander came up and arrested him and ordered him to be bound[f] with two[g] chains.[h] Then
he asked who he was and what he had done. 34Some in the crowd shouted one thing and some another,[i]
and since the commander could not get at the truth because of the uproar, he ordered that Paul be
taken into the barracks.[j] 35When Paul reached the steps,[k] the violence of the mob was so great he had
to be carried by the soldiers. 36The crowd that followed kept shouting, "Get rid of him!"[l]

Paul Speaks to the Crowd

22:3-16pp — Ac 9:1-22; 26:9-18

37As the soldiers were about to take Paul into the barracks,[m] he asked the commander, "May I say
something to you?"

accusation is not true. Paul teaches only that such works do not earn salvation, which comes only through Christ's death on the cross.

21:22–23 These men are involved in a Nazirite vow, a time of special dedication to God (see Num 6:1–21 and note). By paying for their expenses, Paul would show that he remains loyal to his Jewish heritage. Paul himself kept a Nazirite vow (18:18) and circumcised Timothy to avoid offending the Jews (16:3). Paul, as a Jew himself, is quite willing to continue to observe certain Jewish practices, but he insists that these acts do not bring salvation (Rom 3:28).

21:25 The elders cite the stipulations of the Jerusalem council (15:23–29) to show the importance of acting in a way that does not cause offense and that encourages fellowship between Jews and Gentiles.

21:27–36 *Paul Arrested.* While Paul is in the temple finishing his support for the Nazirite vow, some of his Jewish opponents from Ephesus recognize him and accuse him of (1) teaching against the Jewish people; (2) teaching against the law, (3) teaching against the temple, and (4) bringing Gentiles beyond the outer court of the Gentiles and into the inner courts. All could have been capital offenses under Jewish law. The second and third accusations likely arose from Paul's teaching that salvation comes from faith in Christ alone, not from keeping the law or offering sacrifices in the temple. (See the similar accusations against Stephen in 6:13.) The fourth accusation is false, but it is prompted when Paul's opponents see Trophimus, a Gentile from Ephesus, with Paul in Jerusalem (v. 29).

21:27 seven days. The days of purification to complete the Nazirite vow (Num 6:9).

21:28 brought Greeks into the temple. Gentiles were forbidden from entering the inner courts of the temple, and signs warned of immediate execution for any who entered. Archaeologists have discovered two of these signs. See photo, p. 1974.

21:29 Trophimus. See 20:4.

21:30 gates. Separating the court of the Gentiles from the inner courts of the temple. The Jews shut the gates to keep the rioting crowds from defiling the inner temple courts and especially to keep out the Roman troops who would arrive shortly.

21:31 The Roman commander (Claudius Lysias, see 23:26) and his troops were garrisoned in the Fortress of Antonia, overlooking the northwest corner of the temple mount. His role was to keep the peace and quell any rebellious crowds in the volatile political and religious atmosphere surrounding the temple.

21:33 two chains. Perhaps (1) for Paul's hands and feet or (2) attached to a soldier on either side.

21:36 Get rid of him! Generally, the same thing the crowds had shouted about Jesus (Luke 23:18).

21:37—22:21 *Paul Speaks to the Crowd.* Paul's message is one of several defenses he gives during his arrest and incarceration, all meant to show his faithfulness to his Jewish heritage, his dramatic conversion

“Do you speak Greek?” he replied. 38 “Aren’t you the Egyptian who started a revolt and led four thousand terrorists out into the wilderness[n] some time ago?”[o]
39 Paul answered, “I am a Jew, from Tarsus[p] in Cilicia,[q] a citizen of no ordinary city. Please let me
speak to the people.”
40 After receiving the commander’s permission, Paul stood on the steps and motioned[r] to the crowd.
22 When they were all silent, he said to them in Aramaic[a]:[s] 1 “Brothers and fathers,[t] listen now
to my defense.”
2 When they heard him speak to them in Aramaic,[u] they became very quiet.
Then Paul said: 3 “I am a Jew,[v] born in Tarsus[w] of Cilicia, but brought up in this city. I studied under[x]
Gamaliel[y] and was thoroughly trained in the law of our ancestors.[z] I was just as zealous[a] for God as any
of you are today. 4 I persecuted[b] the followers of this Way to their death, arresting both men and women
and throwing them into prison,[c] 5 as the high priest and all the Council[d] can themselves testify. I even
obtained letters from them to their associates[e] in Damascus,[f] and went there to bring these people as
prisoners to Jerusalem to be punished.
6 “About noon as I came near Damascus, suddenly a bright light from heaven flashed around me.[g]
7 I fell to the ground and heard a voice say to me, ‘Saul! Saul! Why do you persecute me?’
8 “ ‘Who are you, Lord?’ I asked.
“ ‘I am Jesus of Nazareth, whom you are persecuting,’ he replied. 9 My companions saw the light,[h]
but they did not understand the voice[i] of him who was speaking to me.
10 “ ‘What shall I do, Lord?’ I asked.
“ ‘Get up,’ the Lord said, ‘and go into Damascus. There you will be told all that you have been assigned to do.’[j] 11 My companions led me by the hand into Damascus, because the brilliance of the light
had blinded me.[k]
12 “A man named Ananias came to see me.[l] He was a devout observer of the law and highly respected
by all the Jews living there.[m] 13 He stood beside me and said, ‘Brother Saul, receive your sight!’ And at
that very moment I was able to see him.
14 “Then he said: ‘The God of our ancestors[n] has chosen you to know his will and to see[o] the Righteous One[p] and to hear words from his mouth. 15 You will be his witness[q] to all people of what you have
seen and heard. 16 And now what are you waiting for? Get up, be baptized[r] and wash your sins away,[s]
calling on his name.’[t]

[a] *40* Or possibly *Hebrew*; also in 22:2

21:38 [n] Mt 24:26 [o] Ac 5:36
21:39 [p] Ac 9:11 [q] Ac 22:3
21:40 [r] Ac 12:17 [s] Jn 5:2
22:1 [t] Ac 7:2
22:2 [u] Ac 21:40
22:3 [v] Ac 21:39 [w] Ac 9:11 [x] Lk 10:39 [y] Ac 5:34 [z] Ac 26:5 [a] Ac 21:20
22:4 [b] Ac 8:3 [c] ver 19,20
22:5 [d] Lk 22:66 [e] Ac 13:26 [f] Ac 9:2
22:6 [g] Ac 9:3
22:9 [h] Ac 26:13 [i] Ac 9:7
22:10 [j] Ac 16:30
22:11 [k] Ac 9:8
22:12 [l] Ac 9:17 [m] Ac 10:22
22:14 [n] Ac 3:13 [o] 1Co 9:1; 15:8 [p] Ac 7:52
22:15 [q] Ac 23:11; 26:16
22:16 [r] Ac 2:38 [s] Heb 10:22 [t] Ro 10:13

when he met Jesus the Messiah, and his fulfillment of God’s call to bring salvation to the Gentiles. Paul is not so much defending himself as taking the opportunity to proclaim the gospel. We may divide the message itself (22:3–21) into four parts: he persecuted “the Way” (vv. 3–5; cf. 9:1–2); he met the resurrected Jesus on the road to Damascus (vv. 6–11; cf. 9:3–8); he was healed of blindness and baptized by Ananias (vv. 12–16; cf. 9:9–18); and he had a vision in the temple at Jerusalem (vv. 17–21).

21:38 Egyptian who started a revolt. The Jewish historian Josephus refers to this Egyptian, a false prophet who gained a following of 30,000 and led them to the Mount of Olives, claiming that the walls of Jerusalem would fall down at his command. The Roman governor Felix routed them, but the Egyptian escaped. Josephus’s number (30,000) may exaggerate Luke’s more accurate number of 4,000. **terrorists.** Greek *sikarioi* or “dagger-men.” Josephus refers to them as one of various groups opposed to the Romans. They would use hidden knives to assassinate Romans and their Jewish sympathizers.

21:39 Paul identifies himself as a respected Jew, not a terrorist (v. 38). **Tarsus … no ordinary city.** A major commercial and educational center, it was located 10 miles (16 kilometers) from the Mediterranean on the Cydnus River.

21:40 Aramaic. The NT writers use the same Greek word to refer to the Hebrew and Aramaic languages. While the people of Israel used Hebrew in Jewish synagogues, they commonly spoke Aramaic, so this is probably intended here (see NIV text note). The crowd grows silent (22:2) when they hear Paul speaking in their mother tongue (instead of Greek, the main trade language).

22:3 Tarsus. See note on 21:39. **brought up in this city.** Paul evidently studied in Jerusalem under Gamaliel, one of the most respected rabbis of the first century (see note on 5:34), at an early age (cf. Gal 1:14; Phil 3:4–6).

22:4 persecuted. See 8:1–3; 9:1–2; 26:9–11; 1 Cor 15:9; Gal 1:13; 1 Tim 1:13. **this Way.** See note on 9:2.

22:6–21 Acts recounts Paul’s conversion three times: (1) the event itself described from Luke’s perspective (9:3–22); (2) described from Paul’s perspective to a Jewish audience in Jerusalem (vv. 6–13); and (3) described from Paul’s perspective to a Gentile audience (Festus and Herod Agrippa II, 26:12–18). The repetition shows that this event is important to Luke.

22:6 about noon. The original account of the event in ch. 9 does not mention this.

22:12–16 Paul recounts the events of 9:10–18 from his perspective.

22:12 devout observer of the law. This would have been important to Paul’s Jerusalem audience.

22:14 This encounter with the resurrected Christ is fundamental to Paul’s commission as an apostle (26:16; 1 Cor 9:1; 15:8). **Righteous One.** For Jesus as the “innocent” or “righteous” one, see 3:13–14; Luke 23:47 and notes.

22:16 be baptized and wash your sins away. The water itself does not spiritually cleanse people of their sins; it outwardly symbolizes the Holy Spirit’s inward cleansing. See notes on 2:38; Rom 6:4; Titus 3:5; 1 Pet 3:21.

22:17 [u]Ac 9:26 [v]Ac 10:10
22:19 [w]ver 4; Ac 8:3 [x]Mt 10:17
22:20 [y]Ac 7:57-60; 8:1
22:21 [z]Ac 9:15; 13:46
22:22 [a]Ac 21:36 [b]Ac 25:24
22:23 [c]Ac 7:58 [d]2Sa 16:13
22:24 [e]Ac 21:34 [f]ver 29
22:25 [g]Ac 16:37
22:29 [h]ver 24,25; Ac 16:38
22:30 [i]Ac 23:28 [j]Ac 21:33 [k]Mt 5:22
23:1 [l]Ac 22:30 [m]Ac 22:5 [n]Ac 24:16; 1Co 4:4; 2Co 1:12; 2Ti 1:3; Heb 13:18
23:2 [o]Ac 24:1 [p]Jn 18:22

17"When I returned to Jerusalem[u] and was praying at the temple, I fell into a trance[v] 18and saw the
Lord speaking to me. 'Quick!' he said. 'Leave Jerusalem immediately, because the people here will not
accept your testimony about me.'

19" 'Lord,' I replied, 'these people know that I went from one synagogue to another to imprison[w] and
beat[x] those who believe in you. 20And when the blood of your martyr[a] Stephen was shed, I stood there
giving my approval and guarding the clothes of those who were killing him.'[y]

21"Then the Lord said to me, 'Go; I will send you far away to the Gentiles.' "[z]

Paul the Roman Citizen

22The crowd listened to Paul until he said this. Then they raised their voices and shouted, "Rid the
earth of him![a] He's not fit to live!"[b]

23As they were shouting and throwing off their cloaks[c] and flinging dust into the air,[d] 24the commander
ordered that Paul be taken into the barracks.[e] He directed[f] that he be flogged and interrogated in order to
find out why the people were shouting at him like this. 25As they stretched him out to flog him, Paul said to
the centurion standing there, "Is it legal for you to flog a Roman citizen who hasn't even been found guilty?"[g]

26When the centurion heard this, he went to the commander and reported it. "What are you going
to do?" he asked. "This man is a Roman citizen."

27The commander went to Paul and asked, "Tell me, are you a Roman citizen?"

"Yes, I am," he answered.

28Then the commander said, "I had to pay a lot of money for my citizenship."

"But I was born a citizen," Paul replied.

29Those who were about to interrogate him withdrew immediately. The commander himself was
alarmed when he realized that he had put Paul, a Roman citizen,[h] in chains.

Paul Before the Sanhedrin

30The commander wanted to find out exactly why Paul was being accused by the Jews.[i] So the next
day he released him[j] and ordered the chief priests and all the members of the Sanhedrin[k] to assemble.
Then he brought Paul and had him stand before them.

23 Paul looked straight at the Sanhedrin[l] and said, "My brothers,[m] I have fulfilled my duty to God
in all good conscience[n] to this day." 2At this the high priest Ananias[o] ordered those standing
near Paul to strike him on the mouth.[p] 3Then Paul said to him, "God will strike you, you whitewashed

[a] 20 Or *witness*

22:17–21 Paul's vision takes place during his first visit to Jerusalem after his conversion (9:26–28; Gal 1:17–19).

22:17 praying at the temple. Confirms for the crowd that Paul is not a renegade Jew but is faithful to his Jewish heritage.

22:21 While Paul wanted to stay in Jerusalem and testify to his dramatic conversion (vv. 19–20), God commanded him to leave, commissioning him to go "far away to the Gentiles."

22:22–29 *Paul the Roman Citizen.* When another riot begins to break out, the Romans seize Paul again, take him to the Fortress of Antonia, and hold him in protective custody. Paul is able to avoid a flogging by claiming his Roman citizenship (cf. 16:37).

22:22 Paul's claim that God commissioned him to go to the Gentiles (v. 21) sparks a violent response. This parallels what had happened to Jesus in the synagogue at Nazareth (Luke 4:14–30), where the people of his hometown turned on him for speaking of God's concern for the Gentiles. Though God intended Israel to be a light to the nations, they turned inward and became exclusivist, believing that God loved them and no one else.

22:23 throwing off their cloaks. Perhaps (1) equivalent to tearing their clothing as a sign of sorrow and/or rage at blasphemy (14:14; Matt 26:65; Mark 14:63) or (2) in preparation for stoning him (7:58). **flinging dust into the air.** A sign of rage and/or grief (2 Sam 16:13; Job 2:12) at hearing something offensive or blasphemous.

22:24 flogged. Flogging (Latin *flagellum*) was a cruel and gruesome method of Roman interrogation. It entailed lashing the bare back of the victim with a leather whip embedded with shards of glass or metal. See notes on Matt 27:26; Mark 15:15.

22:25–26 Roman citizens could not be flogged unless convicted. They also had the right to a final appeal before Caesar when accused of a capital offense (25:11–12,21,25; 26:32).

22:27–28 Roman citizenship was a high honor and not granted to everyone. People could gain it by birth, emancipation from slavery, significant service to the Roman Empire, and sometimes purchase (usually involving bribery). Citizenship by birth was viewed as the most noble.

22:28 I had to pay a lot of money for my citizenship. May be sarcastic, meaning that the price of citizenship must be deflated if a lowly Jew like Paul could obtain it.

22:30—23:11 *Paul Before the Sanhedrin.* The commander (Lysias, see 23:26; 24:22) decides that the best way to understand the charges against Paul is to bring him before the Sanhedrin, the Jewish high court. This is a dangerous situation for Paul since this is the same body that condemned Jesus (Luke 22:66–71; 23:18,23).

23:1 I have fulfilled my duty. Translates a Greek word that comes from a root meaning "live as a citizen." Though a Roman citizen, Paul's true citizenship is in God's kingdom (Phil 3:20).

23:2 high priest Ananias. Known for his cruelty, greed, and complicity with the Romans during his time in office (AD 47–59).

23:3 God will strike you. Turns out to be prophetic since Jewish freedom fighters killed Ananias at the outbreak of the Jewish revolt of

wall![q] You sit there to judge me according to the law, yet you yourself violate the law by commanding
that I be struck!"[r]
4Those who were standing near Paul said, "How dare you insult God's high priest!"
5Paul replied, "Brothers, I did not realize that he was the high priest; for it is written: 'Do not speak
evil about the ruler of your people.'[a]"[s]
6Then Paul, knowing that some of them were Sadducees and the others Pharisees, called out in
the Sanhedrin, "My brothers,[t] I am a Pharisee,[u] descended from Pharisees. I stand on trial because
of the hope of the resurrection of the dead."[v] 7When he said this, a dispute broke out between the
Pharisees and the Sadducees, and the assembly was divided. 8(The Sadducees say that there is no
resurrection,[w] and that there are neither angels nor spirits, but the Pharisees believe all these
things.)
9There was a great uproar, and some of the teachers of the law who were Pharisees[x] stood up and
argued vigorously. "We find nothing wrong with this man,"[y] they said. "What if a spirit or an angel
has spoken to him?"[z] 10The dispute became so violent that the commander was afraid Paul would be
torn to pieces by them. He ordered the troops to go down and take him away from them by force and
bring him into the barracks.[a]
11The following night the Lord stood near Paul and said, "Take courage![b] As you have testified about
me in Jerusalem, so you must also testify in Rome."[c]

23:3 [q]Mt 23:27 [r]Lev 19:15; Dt 25:1,2; Jn 7:51
23:5 [s]Ex 22:28
23:6 [t]Ac 22:5 [u]Ac 26:5; Php 3:5 [v]Ac 24:15,21; 26:8
23:8 [w]Mt 22:23
23:9 [x]Mk 2:16 [y]ver 29; Ac 25:25; 26:31 [z]Ac 22:7,17,18
23:10 [a]Ac 21:34
23:11 [b]Ac 18:9 [c]Ac 19:21; 28:23
23:12 [d]ver 14,21,30; Ac 25:3
23:14 [e]ver 12
23:15 [f]ver 1; Ac 22:30
23:16 [g]ver 10; Ac 21:34
23:18 [h]Eph 3:1
23:20 [i]ver 1 [j]ver 14,15
23:21 [k]ver 13 [l]ver 12,14

The Plot to Kill Paul

12The next morning some Jews formed a conspiracy and bound themselves with an oath not to eat
or drink until they had killed Paul.[d] 13More than forty men were involved in this plot. 14They went to
the chief priests and the elders and said, "We have taken a solemn oath not to eat anything until we
have killed Paul.[e] 15Now then, you and the Sanhedrin[f] petition the commander to bring him before
you on the pretext of wanting more accurate information about his case. We are ready to kill him before he gets here."
16But when the son of Paul's sister heard of this plot, he went into the barracks[g] and told Paul.
17Then Paul called one of the centurions and said, "Take this young man to the commander; he has
something to tell him." 18So he took him to the commander.
The centurion said, "Paul, the prisoner,[h] sent for me and asked me to bring this young man to you
because he has something to tell you."
19The commander took the young man by the hand, drew him aside and asked, "What is it you
want to tell me?"
20He said: "Some Jews have agreed to ask you to bring Paul before the Sanhedrin[i] tomorrow on the
pretext of wanting more accurate information about him.[j] 21Don't give in to them, because more than
forty[k] of them are waiting in ambush for him. They have taken an oath not to eat or drink until they
have killed him.[l] They are ready now, waiting for your consent to their request."

[a] 5 Exodus 22:28

AD 66–73. **whitewashed wall.** A metaphor for hypocrisy: something impressive on the outside but corrupt on the inside (Matt 23:27) or a wall painted white to hide its decrepit state (Ezek 13:10–11).

23:4–5 How could Paul not recognize the high priest? Some say because of poor eyesight (see Gal 4:15; 6:11); others say Paul has been away from Jerusalem so long he does not know the high priest. More likely, the statement is sarcastic and ironic: "I didn't recognize him because he is not acting like a high priest." If so, Paul's quoting from Exod 22:28 means that he respects the office but not the man.

23:6 Sadducees. See notes on 4:1,2. **Pharisees.** See notes on 15:5; Matt 3:7. **I am a Pharisee.** See Phil 3:5 and note. Paul's words divide the assembly since Pharisees believe in the resurrection of the dead but Sadducees do not.

23:9 Because Pharisees believe in angels and the supernatural, they are more open to the possibility that Paul has actually seen a vision from God.

23:11 For similar reassuring visions, see 18:9–10; 27:23–24. Before his arrest Paul was making plans to go to Rome (19:21; Rom 1:11–13; 15:23–24,32), and the Lord now confirms that Paul will preach the gospel there (see 28:11–31). The Good News will reach "the ends of the earth" (1:8).

23:12–22 *The Plot to Kill Paul.* A plot to ambush and kill Paul on the way to the Sanhedrin is discovered by Paul's nephew and reported to the commander, who takes immediate action to transfer Paul to Caesarea under the cover of darkness.

23:12 bound ... with an oath. Greek *anathematizō*; it can mean to call down a curse upon themselves if they break the vow. As in the case of Judas's betrayal of Jesus, the Sanhedrin conspires with others against God's messenger.

23:16 This reference to Paul's nephew is all we learn of his relatives from either the book of Acts or Paul's letters. Though born in Tarsus, Paul was educated in Jerusalem (22:3), perhaps while living with his uncle and aunt.

Herod's palace in Caesarea where Paul was kept under guard (Acts 23:35).
© Hanan Isachar/Alamy

[22]The commander dismissed the young man with this warning: "Don't tell anyone that you have reported this to me."

Paul Transferred to Caesarea

[23]Then he called two of his centurions and ordered them, "Get ready a detachment of two hundred soldiers, seventy horsemen and two hundred spearmen[a] to go to Caesarea[m] at nine tonight.[n] [24]Provide horses for Paul so that he may be taken safely to Governor Felix."[o]

[25]He wrote a letter as follows:

[26]Claudius Lysias,

To His Excellency,[p] Governor Felix:

Greetings.[q]

[27]This man was seized by the Jews and they were about to kill him,[r] but I came with my troops and rescued him,[s] for I had learned that he is a Roman citizen.[t] [28]I wanted to know why they were accusing him, so I brought him to their Sanhedrin.[u] [29]I found that the accusation had to do with questions about their law,[v] but there was no charge against him[w] that deserved death or imprisonment. [30]When I was informed[x] of a plot[y] to be carried out against the man, I sent him to you at once. I also ordered his accusers[z] to present to you their case against him.

23:23 [m]Ac 8:40 [n]ver 33 **23:24** [o]ver 26,33; Ac 24:1-3,10; 25:14 **23:26** [p]Lk 1:3; Ac 24:3; 26:25 [q]Ac 15:23 **23:27** [r]Ac 21:32 [s]Ac 21:33 [t]Ac 22:25-29 **23:28** [u]Ac 22:30 **23:29** [v]Ac 18:15; 25:19 [w]ver 9; Ac 26:31 **23:30** [x]ver 20,21 [y]Ac 20:3 [z]ver 35; Ac 24:19; 25:16

a 23 The meaning of the Greek for this word is uncertain.

23:23–35 *Paul Transferred to Caesarea.* The Romans would have likely transferred Paul to the governor's headquarters in Caesarea eventually, but the plot provokes them to transfer Paul immediately by night.
23:23–24 The large contingent of 470 solders, almost half the Jerusalem garrison, provides overwhelming force against any ambush and protects Paul, the Roman citizen.
23:23 spearmen. See NIV text note; it may mean additional horses rather than soldiers.
23:26–30 Claudius Lysias's letter gives a generally reliable account of Paul's arrest. Some think that Claudius Lysias twists the wording of the letter to his advantage by saying that he took Paul into protective custody because he learned about his Roman citizenship, when he actually learned about it while preparing to flog him (22:24–29). But the grammatical point is disputed, and it is possible to understand it to be saying that the commander rescued Paul and then found out he was a Roman citizen, which is in line with what happened.
23:29 no charge against him that deserved death. Paul's innocence is a major theme throughout the account of his arrest and incarceration (v. 9; 24:12–13,20; 25:10,25; 26:31). This parallels Jesus' innocence in both Luke's Gospel and Acts, where others repeatedly declare him to be both innocent (Luke 23:4,14–15,22,41) and "righteous" (Luke 23:47; cf. "the Righteous One" in Acts 3:14; 7:52; 22:14).

31So the soldiers, carrying out their orders, took Paul with them during the night and brought him
as far as Antipatris. 32The next day they let the cavalry[a] go on with him, while they returned to the barracks.[b] 33When the cavalry[c] arrived in Caesarea,[d] they delivered the letter to the governor[e] and handed
Paul over to him. 34The governor read the letter and asked what province he was from. Learning that
he was from Cilicia,[f] 35he said, "I will hear your case when your accusers[g] get here." Then he ordered
that Paul be kept under guard[h] in Herod's palace.

Paul's Trial Before Felix

24 Five days later the high priest Ananias[i] went down to Caesarea with some of the elders and a
lawyer named Tertullus, and they brought their charges[j] against Paul before the governor.[k]
2When Paul was called in, Tertullus presented his case before Felix: "We have enjoyed a long period of
peace under you, and your foresight has brought about reforms in this nation. 3Everywhere and in every way, most excellent[l] Felix, we acknowledge this with profound gratitude. 4But in order not to weary
you further, I would request that you be kind enough to hear us briefly.

5"We have found this man to be a troublemaker, stirring up riots[m] among the Jews[n] all over the
world. He is a ringleader of the Nazarene[o] sect[p] 6and even tried to desecrate the temple;[q] so we seized
him. [7][a] 8By examining him yourself you will be able to learn the truth about all these charges we
are bringing against him."

9The other Jews joined in the accusation,[r] asserting that these things were true.

10When the governor[s] motioned for him to speak, Paul replied: "I know that for a number of years
you have been a judge over this nation; so I gladly make my defense. 11You can easily verify that no
more than twelve days[t] ago I went up to Jerusalem to worship. 12My accusers did not find me arguing
with anyone at the temple,[u] or stirring up a crowd[v] in the synagogues or anywhere else in the city. 13And
they cannot prove to you the charges they are now making against me.[w] 14However, I admit that I worship the God of our ancestors[x] as a follower of the Way,[y] which they call a sect.[z] I believe everything that

23:32 [a]ver 23 [b]Ac 21:34
23:33 [c]ver 23,24 [d]Ac 8:40 [e]ver 26
23:34 [f]Ac 6:9; 21:39
23:35 [g]ver 30; Ac 24:19; 25:16 [h]Ac 24:27
24:1 [i]Ac 23:2 [j]Ac 23:30, 35 [k]Ac 23:24
24:3 [l]Lk 1:3; Ac 23:26; 26:25
24:5 [m]Ac 16:20; 17:6 [n]Ac 21:28 [o]Mk 1:24 [p]ver 14; Ac 26:5; 28:22
24:6 [q]Ac 21:28
24:9 [r]1Th 2:16
24:10 [s]Ac 23:24
24:11 [t]Ac 21:27; ver 1
24:12 [u]Ac 25:8; 28:17 [v]ver 18
24:13 [w]Ac 25:7
24:14 [x]Ac 3:13 [y]Ac 9:2 [z]ver 5

[a] 6-8 Some manuscripts include here *him, and we would have judged him in accordance with our law. 7But the commander Lysias came and took him from us with much violence, 8ordering his accusers to come before you.*

23:31 Antipatris. A Roman military outpost 35 miles (56 kilometers) northwest of Jerusalem, about halfway to Caesarea. The foot soldiers return after getting Paul safely out of Jerusalem (v. 32), where the ambush was to take place.

23:34 governor. Marcus Antonius Felix (vv. 24,26; see note on 24:2a). He asks about Paul's home province to determine if he has jurisdiction in this case. He does since both Judea and Cilicia were under the administrative authority of the legate of Syria, under whom Felix served.

24:1–27 *Paul's Trial Before Felix.* At Paul's conversion God told Ananias that Paul would stand before "Gentiles and their kings" (9:15). This comes to fulfillment as Paul bears witness before two Roman governors, Felix (vv. 1–27) and Festus (25:1–12; 25:23—26:32), and before the Jewish king Agrippa II (25:23—26:32). The first two episodes are formal trials during which Paul defends himself against his Jewish accusers. While Paul is on trial to defend himself, his "defense" (v. 10) becomes an opportunity for him to bear witness to Jesus. On the theme of Paul's innocence throughout this section, see note on 23:29.

24:1 Ananias. See notes on 23:2,3. That the high priest would travel all the way to Caesarea shows how important Paul's case was to the Jewish leadership. **Tertullus.** Perhaps a Jewish lawyer familiar with Roman law or a Gentile lawyer whom the high priest hired to represent the Jewish leaders.

24:2a Felix. Marcus Antonius Felix, procurator of Judea (AD 52–59). He was a former slave who had risen through the ranks with the help of his brother Pallas, also a freed slave. Felix's governorship over Judea was marked by corruption and growing discontent among the Jews. He treated his subjects with general disdain and responded to opposition with brutal oppression. Rome recalled him in AD 59 because of complaints from the Jews. Felix appears in Acts as Paul's protector against Paul's Jewish opponents, but Felix is also shown as corrupt, refusing to free Paul despite the lack of evidence against him. According to Luke, Felix does this to keep the Jewish leaders happy (v. 27) and in hopes of receiving a bribe from Paul (v. 26).

24:2b–3 It was common to offer praise to the judge at the beginning of one's case (known as *capitatio benevolentiae*), but this is mostly false flattery. Though there was a measure of peace because of Felix's violent suppression of dissent, there were few reforms during his governorship. Yet Felix likely welcomed the praise, since the Romans viewed themselves as establishing the great *Pax Romana* ("Roman peace") and as great benefactors for their subject peoples.

24:5–6 Tertullus accuses Paul of three crimes: (1) "stirring up riots" throughout the empire (rebellion or sedition), (2) being a "ringleader of the Nazarene sect," and (3) trying to "desecrate the temple." The first crime is political, the third is religious, and the second is both since unauthorized sects were illegal under Roman law.

24:5 Nazarene sect. Christians were called Nazarenes because they followed Jesus of Nazareth. The name may have been derogatory since Nazareth was such an insignificant place (John 1:46).

24:10–21 Paul's defense answers the three charges: (1) He refutes the charge of sedition (vv. 11–13). (2) He confirms his credentials as a Jew faithful to his God and his heritage (vv. 14–16). (3) He denies that he tried to defile the temple (vv. 17–21). He was at the temple only to offer gifts and offerings; he was ceremonially clean; and he did not start a riot.

24:10 Unlike Tertullus (vv. 2–3), Paul does not pour on the flattery. He simply acknowledges Felix's authority and his gratitude for the opportunity to defend himself.

24:14 [a]Ac 26:6,22; 28:23
24:15 [b]Ac 23:6; 28:20 [c]Da 12:2; Jn 5:28,29
24:16 [d]Ac 23:1
24:17 [e]Ac 11:29,30; Ro 15:25-28,31; 1Co 16:1-4,15; 2Co 8:1-4; Gal 2:10
24:18 [f]Ac 21:26 [g]ver 12
24:19 [h]Ac 23:30
24:21 [i]Ac 23:6
24:23 [j]Ac 23:35 [k]Ac 28:16 [l]Ac 23:16; 27:3
24:24 [m]Ac 20:21
24:25 [n]Gal 5:23; 2Pe 1:6 [o]Ac 10:42
24:27 [p]Ac 25:1,4,9,14 [q]Ac 12:3; 25:9 [r]Ac 23:35; 25:14
25:1 [s]Ac 8:40
25:2 [t]ver 15; Ac 24:1
25:4 [u]Ac 24:23
25:6 [v]ver 17

is in accordance with the Law and that is written in the Prophets,[a] 15and I have the same hope in God
as these men themselves have, that there will be a resurrection[b] of both the righteous and the wicked.[c]
16So I strive always to keep my conscience clear[d] before God and man.
17"After an absence of several years, I came to Jerusalem to bring my people gifts for the poor[e] and
to present offerings. 18I was ceremonially clean[f] when they found me in the temple courts doing this.
There was no crowd with me, nor was I involved in any disturbance.[g] 19But there are some Jews from
the province of Asia, who ought to be here before you and bring charges if they have anything against
me.[h] 20Or these who are here should state what crime they found in me when I stood before the Sanhedrin— 21unless it was this one thing I shouted as I stood in their presence: 'It is concerning the
resurrection of the dead that I am on trial before you today.' "[i]
22Then Felix, who was well acquainted with the Way, adjourned the proceedings. "When Lysias the
commander comes," he said, "I will decide your case." 23He ordered the centurion to keep Paul under
guard[j] but to give him some freedom[k] and permit his friends to take care of his needs.[l]
24Several days later Felix came with his wife Drusilla, who was Jewish. He sent for Paul and listened
to him as he spoke about faith in Christ Jesus.[m] 25As Paul talked about righteousness, self-control[n] and
the judgment[o] to come, Felix was afraid and said, "That's enough for now! You may leave. When I find
it convenient, I will send for you." 26At the same time he was hoping that Paul would offer him a bribe,
so he sent for him frequently and talked with him.
27When two years had passed, Felix was succeeded by Porcius Festus,[p] but because Felix wanted to
grant a favor to the Jews,[q] he left Paul in prison.[r]

Paul's Trial Before Festus

25 Three days after arriving in the province, Festus went up from Caesarea[s] to Jerusalem, 2where
the chief priests and the Jewish leaders appeared before him and presented the charges against
Paul.[t] 3They requested Festus, as a favor to them, to have Paul transferred to Jerusalem, for they were
preparing an ambush to kill him along the way. 4Festus answered, "Paul is being held[u] at Caesarea,
and I myself am going there soon. 5Let some of your leaders come with me, and if the man has done
anything wrong, they can press charges against him there."
6After spending eight or ten days with them, Festus went down to Caesarea. The next day he convened
the court[v] and ordered that Paul be brought before him. 7When Paul came in, the Jews who had come

24:17 gifts for the poor. If these "gifts" refer to the collection Paul brought from the Gentile churches, this is the only reference in Acts to this collection (Rom 15:25–27; 1 Cor 16:1–4; 2 Cor 8–9; see notes on 19:21; 20:3).
24:21 Paul's defense climaxes with the most important theme of his preaching: "the resurrection of the dead."
24:22 In his seven or so years of governing Judea, Felix is "well acquainted with the Way" (i.e., the Christian movement), so he knows that Christians are not violent insurrectionists. He claims that he delays his decision to wait for the Roman commander Lysias, but in reality he delays because keeping Paul in custody gives him a political advantage: he can both please the Jews (v. 27) and hope for a bribe from Paul (v. 26).
24:23 From the relative freedom he gives to Paul, Felix makes it clear he does not view Paul as a dangerous criminal. High-status Roman prisoners were often given such privileges (cf. 28:30–31).
24:24 Drusilla. Felix's third wife, the daughter of Herod Agrippa I. Felix coaxed her to leave her first husband and marry him when she was 16. This morally questionable behavior may be why Paul's talk about "righteousness, self-control and the judgment to come" disturbs Felix and causes him to dismiss Paul (v. 25).
24:26 bribe. Felix may summon Paul often both because he is fascinated with Paul's religious convictions and because he hopes for a bribe. Though bribes were illegal in Roman law, such corruption was common.
24:27 Felix was succeeded. Felix was summoned to Rome in AD 59 when the Jewish leaders made a case against him for mismanagement, especially his poor handling of a conflict between Jews and Syrians in Caesarea. Felix keeps Paul in prison "to grant a favor to the Jews," which might help Felix's chances as he faces their accusations in Rome. **Porcius Festus.** Succeeded Felix and was governor for only about two years (AD 59–62) before dying in office. Little is known about him apart from the Acts account, but he appears to have been a generally competent ruler, maintaining order and ridding the countryside of bandits.
25:1–12 *Paul's Trial Before Festus.* A new and dangerous stage of Paul's imprisonment occurs with his appearance before Festus, the recently appointed governor of Judea. When Paul's Jewish opponents appeal to Festus to return him to Jerusalem for trial, Festus asks if Paul is willing to be tried there. Knowing that such a transfer would likely result in his assassination, Paul exercises his right as a Roman citizen and appeals to Caesar. Festus agrees and events are set in motion that will take Paul to Rome and bring about the climax of Luke's narrative in Acts.
25:1–3 Among Festus's first tasks is introducing himself to the Jewish leadership in Jerusalem. Paul is clearly on their minds, and they immediately request that Festus transfer Paul to Jerusalem for trial. The Jewish leaders hatch a plot against Paul similar to that recounted in 23:12.
25:4–5 Festus wisely chooses to have Paul's trial again in Caesarea, where he has much greater control of the situation than he would have in the volatile atmosphere of Jerusalem.
25:7–8 Paul's response indicates that their "many serious charges" (v. 7) are the same as the earlier ones: breaking the Jewish law, defiling the temple, and provoking revolution against Caesar and Rome (v. 8; see 21:27–36; 24:5–6 and notes). None are true, as Paul stated at his earlier trial (see 24:10–21 and note; cf. 22:3; 23:6).

down from Jerusalem stood around him. They brought many serious charges against him,[w] but they
could not prove them.[x]
8 Then Paul made his defense: "I have done nothing wrong against the Jewish law or against the
temple[y] or against Caesar."
9 Festus, wishing to do the Jews a favor,[z] said to Paul, "Are you willing to go up to Jerusalem and stand
trial before me there on these charges?"[a]
10 Paul answered: "I am now standing before Caesar's court, where I ought to be tried. I have not
done any wrong to the Jews, as you yourself know very well. 11 If, however, I am guilty of doing anything
deserving death, I do not refuse to die. But if the charges brought against me by these Jews are not true,
no one has the right to hand me over to them. I appeal to Caesar!"[b]
12 After Festus had conferred with his council, he declared: "You have appealed to Caesar. To Caesar
you will go!"

Festus Consults King Agrippa

13 A few days later King Agrippa and Bernice arrived at Caesarea[c] to pay their respects to Festus.
14 Since they were spending many days there, Festus discussed Paul's case with the king. He said: "There
is a man here whom Felix left as a prisoner.[d] 15 When I went to Jerusalem, the chief priests and the elders
of the Jews brought charges against him[e] and asked that he be condemned.
16 "I told them that it is not the Roman custom to hand over anyone before they have faced their accusers and have had an opportunity to defend themselves against the charges.[f] 17 When they came here
with me, I did not delay the case, but convened the court the next day and ordered the man to be brought
in.[g] 18 When his accusers got up to speak, they did not charge him with any of the crimes I had expected.
19 Instead, they had some points of dispute[h] with him about their own religion[i] and about a dead man
named Jesus who Paul claimed was alive. 20 I was at a loss how to investigate such matters; so I asked if
he would be willing to go to Jerusalem and stand trial there on these charges.[j] 21 But when Paul made his
appeal to be held over for the Emperor's decision, I ordered him held until I could send him to Caesar."[k]
22 Then Agrippa said to Festus, "I would like to hear this man myself."
He replied, "Tomorrow you will hear him."[l]

Paul Before Agrippa

26:12-18pp — Ac 9:3-8; 22:6-11

23 The next day Agrippa and Bernice[m] came with great pomp and entered the audience room with
the high-ranking military officers and the prominent men of the city. At the command of Festus, Paul

25:7 [w] Mk 15:3; Lk 23:2,10; Ac 24:5,6 [x] Ac 24:13
25:8 [y] Ac 6:13; 24:12; 28:17
25:9 [z] Ac 24:27 [a] ver 20
25:11 [b] ver 21,25; Ac 26:32; 28:19
25:13 [c] Ac 8:40
25:14 [d] Ac 24:27
25:15 [e] ver 2; Ac 24:1
25:16 [f] ver 4,5; Ac 23:30
25:17 [g] ver 6,10
25:19 [h] Ac 18:15; 23:29 [i] Ac 17:22
25:20 [j] ver 9
25:21 [k] ver 11,12
25:22 [l] Ac 9:15
25:23 [m] ver 13; Ac 26:30

25:9 Festus proposes a compromise solution: Paul's trial would occur in Jerusalem (to satisfy the Jews), but he would stand trial before Festus (the Roman court would protect Paul's rights as a citizen).
25:11 I appeal to Caesar! The right of every Roman citizen. Paul knows that he would have little chance for a fair trial in Jerusalem and that his life would be in constant danger (23:12; 25:3). **Caesar.** Originally a family name of Julius Caesar, but became a title for the emperor. The Caesar at this time was Nero, who would later persecute the Christians.
25:12 Festus confers with his "council" (advisers and legal experts) to determine the validity of Paul's appeal to Caesar, and he then grants it. This solves Festus's dilemma to provide justice for Paul or please the Jewish leaders. Festus can say that his hands are tied and that he must send Paul to Rome.
25:13–22 *Festus Consults King Agrippa.* By visiting Caesarea, the Jewish king Agrippa II provides Festus an opportunity to clarify the charges against Paul and so prepare a brief to send with Paul to Rome.
25:13 King Agrippa. Agrippa II, the son of Agrippa I (see note on 12:1) and great-grandson of Herod the Great (see Luke 1:5 and note). Agrippa II was only 17 when his father died, so the Romans placed his father's kingdom under the authority of Roman governors. In the years that followed, Rome gradually gave him authority over a number of (mostly Gentile) cities north and east of Galilee. While the Roman governor ruled Judea, Galilee, and Samaria, Rome gave Agrippa — the Jewish king — authority to appoint the Jerusalem high priest. **Bernice.** Agrippa's sister, with whom he was widely rumored to be having an incestuous affair. Agrippa and Bernice are in Caesarea to "pay their respects" to the new governor.
25:16 Festus presents himself as the defender of Roman justice.
25:18 See note on 23:29.
25:21 Emperor. Greek *sebastos* (also v. 25), which means "revered," "sovereign," or "august one" (i.e., "his majesty"). The title was first given to Caesar "Augustus" but came to be used of other emperors (see note on v. 11). Here it refers to Nero.
25:23 — 26:32 *Paul Before Agrippa.* Paul's final defense before heading to Rome is the longest and most comprehensive of all his speeches after his arrest. It closely parallels his defense before the temple mob (22:1–21): (1) He is faithful to his Jewish heritage (26:4–8). (2) He persecuted the church (26:9–11). (3) On the Damascus road, he encountered Jesus, who commissioned him to preach to the Gentiles (26:12–18). (4) He preached everywhere to Jews and Gentiles alike (26:19–20). (5) Jews arrested him in Jerusalem (26:21). In this speech he highlights the resurrection (26:6–8,23), which is central to his gospel message (1 Cor 15). As elsewhere in his trial, Paul's actions parallel those of Jesus, who appeared before both a Roman governor (Pilate) and a Jewish king (Herod Antipas), and both Pilate and Herod acknowledged that Jesus was innocent (Luke 23:6–15).
25:23 high-ranking military officers. Probably the tribunes over the

25:24 [n]ver 2,3,7 [o]Ac 22:22
25:25 [p]Ac 23:9 [q]ver 11
26:1 [r]Ac 9:15; 25:22
26:3 [s]ver 7; Ac 6:14 [t]Ac 25:19
26:4 [u]Gal 1:13,14; Php 3:5
26:5 [v]Ac 22:3 [w]Ac 23:6; Php 3:5
26:6 [x]Ac 23:6; 24:15; 28:20 [y]Ac 13:32; Ro 15:8
26:7 [z]Jas 1:1 [a]1Th 3:10; 1Ti 5:5 [b]ver 2
26:8 [c]Ac 23:6
26:9 [d]1Ti 1:13 [e]Jn 16:2 [f]Jn 15:21
26:10 [g]Ac 9:13 [h]Ac 8:3; 9:2,14,21 [i]Ac 22:20
26:11 [j]Mt 10:17
26:14 [k]Ac 9:7
26:16 [l]Eze 2:1; Da 10:11 [m]Ac 22:14,15
26:17 [n]Jer 1:8,19 [o]Ac 9:15
26:18 [p]Isa 35:5 [q]Isa 42:7,16; Eph 5:8; Col 1:13; 1Pe 2:9 [r]Lk 24:47; Ac 2:38 [s]Ac 20:21,32

was brought in. 24 Festus said: "King Agrippa, and all who are present with us, you see this man! The whole Jewish community[n] has petitioned me about him in Jerusalem and here in Caesarea, shouting that he ought not to live any longer.[o] 25 I found he had done nothing deserving of death,[p] but because he made his appeal to the Emperor[q] I decided to send him to Rome. 26 But I have nothing definite to write to His Majesty about him. Therefore I have brought him before all of you, and especially before you, King Agrippa, so that as a result of this investigation I may have something to write. 27 For I think it is unreasonable to send a prisoner on to Rome without specifying the charges against him."

26 Then Agrippa said to Paul, "You have permission to speak for yourself."[r]

So Paul motioned with his hand and began his defense: 2 "King Agrippa, I consider myself fortunate to stand before you today as I make my defense against all the accusations of the Jews, 3 and especially so because you are well acquainted with all the Jewish customs[s] and controversies.[t] Therefore, I beg you to listen to me patiently.

4 "The Jewish people all know the way I have lived ever since I was a child,[u] from the beginning of my life in my own country, and also in Jerusalem. 5 They have known me for a long time[v] and can testify, if they are willing, that I conformed to the strictest sect of our religion, living as a Pharisee.[w] 6 And now it is because of my hope[x] in what God has promised our ancestors[y] that I am on trial today. 7 This is the promise our twelve tribes[z] are hoping to see fulfilled as they earnestly serve God day and night.[a] King Agrippa, it is because of this hope that these Jews are accusing me.[b] 8 Why should any of you consider it incredible that God raises the dead?[c]

9 "I too was convinced[d] that I ought to do all that was possible to oppose[e] the name of Jesus of Nazareth.[f] 10 And that is just what I did in Jerusalem. On the authority of the chief priests I put many of the Lord's people[g] in prison,[h] and when they were put to death, I cast my vote against them.[i] 11 Many a time I went from one synagogue to another to have them punished,[j] and I tried to force them to blaspheme. I was so obsessed with persecuting them that I even hunted them down in foreign cities.

12 "On one of these journeys I was going to Damascus with the authority and commission of the chief priests. 13 About noon, King Agrippa, as I was on the road, I saw a light from heaven, brighter than the sun, blazing around me and my companions. 14 We all fell to the ground, and I heard a voice[k] saying to me in Aramaic,[a] 'Saul, Saul, why do you persecute me? It is hard for you to kick against the goads.'

15 "Then I asked, 'Who are you, Lord?'

" 'I am Jesus, whom you are persecuting,' the Lord replied. 16 'Now get up and stand on your feet.[l] I have appeared to you to appoint you as a servant and as a witness of what you have seen and will see of me.[m] 17 I will rescue you[n] from your own people and from the Gentiles.[o] I am sending you to them 18 to open their eyes[p] and turn them from darkness to light,[q] and from the power of Satan to God, so that they may receive forgiveness of sins[r] and a place among those who are sanctified by faith in me.'[s]

[a] *14* Or *Hebrew*

five Roman cohorts (1,000 men each) stationed at Caesarea. **prominent men of the city.** Wealthy citizens and civic leaders. Paul gains the opportunity to preach the gospel before a prestigious audience.

25:25 See note on 23:29.

25:27 Ironically, Festus is seeking charges against Paul to put in his report to Caesar while at the same time acknowledging that Paul is innocent.

26:2 As in his defense before Felix (see notes on 24:2b–3,10), Paul does not pour on the flattery but simply states his gratitude for the opportunity to defend himself before the Jewish king Agrippa.

26:3 well acquainted with all the Jewish customs and controversies. Agrippa II (see note on 25:13), as one who is Jewish but also part of the ruling Roman elite, understands both the theological (Jewish) and legal (Roman) aspects of Paul's case.

26:4–5 As elsewhere in his defenses, Paul begins by affirming that he is faithful to his Jewish heritage (cf. 22:3–5; 24:14–16). For Paul's education in Jerusalem under Gamaliel, see 22:3 and note.

26:5 Pharisee. See 23:6; Phil 3:5 and notes.

26:6–7 Israel's hope was that God would save his people and raise the dead. Paul points to the irony that he is on trial for proclaiming that Jesus has fulfilled that hope.

26:8 Paul defends the resurrection, preparing for the climax of his message in v. 23. Some groups within Judaism, like the Sadducees, denied the resurrection (23:8; see notes on 4:1,2), and Greeks in general rejected a bodily resurrection. Whether or not Agrippa believed in the resurrection, he was closely associated with the Sadducees since he appointed the high priest (see note on 25:13).

26:10 cast my vote against them. Some claim this means Paul must have been a member of the Sanhedrin. But the phrase could simply mean that he supported and approved the decision.

26:12–18 Luke recounts Paul's conversion for a third time (9:1–30; 22:5–21; see note on 9:1–19a). In Paul's retelling, he focuses on the commission Jesus gave him (vv. 16–18).

26:14 Aramaic. See note on 21:40. **It is hard for you to kick against the goads.** A proverb, here meaning "It is hard for you [Paul] to resist God's purpose for your life." A goad is a stick used to prod an animal.

19 "So then, King Agrippa, I was not disobedient to the vision from heaven. 20 First to those in Damascus,[t] then to those in Jerusalem[u] and in all Judea, and then to the Gentiles,[v] I preached that they should repent[w] and turn to God and demonstrate their repentance by their deeds.[x] 21 That is why some Jews seized me[y] in the temple courts and tried to kill me.[z] 22 But God has helped me to this very day; so I stand here and testify to small and great alike. I am saying nothing beyond what the prophets and Moses said would happen[a]— 23 that the Messiah would suffer and, as the first to rise from the dead,[b] would bring the message of light to his own people and to the Gentiles."[c]

24 At this point Festus interrupted Paul's defense. "You are out of your mind,[d] Paul!" he shouted. "Your great learning[e] is driving you insane."

25 "I am not insane, most excellent[f] Festus," Paul replied. "What I am saying is true and reasonable. 26 The king is familiar with these things,[g] and I can speak freely to him. I am convinced that none of this has escaped his notice, because it was not done in a corner. 27 King Agrippa, do you believe the prophets? I know you do."

28 Then Agrippa said to Paul, "Do you think that in such a short time you can persuade me to be a Christian?"[h]

29 Paul replied, "Short time or long—I pray to God that not only you but all who are listening to me today may become what I am, except for these chains."[i]

30 The king rose, and with him the governor and Bernice[j] and those sitting with them. 31 After they left the room, they began saying to one another, "This man is not doing anything that deserves death or imprisonment."[k]

32 Agrippa said to Festus, "This man could have been set free[l] if he had not appealed to Caesar."[m]

Paul Sails for Rome

27 When it was decided that we[n] would sail for Italy,[o] Paul and some other prisoners were handed over to a centurion named Julius, who belonged to the Imperial Regiment.[p] 2 We boarded a ship from Adramyttium about to sail for ports along the coast of the province of Asia,[q] and we put out to sea. Aristarchus,[r] a Macedonian[s] from Thessalonica,[t] was with us.

3 The next day we landed at Sidon;[u] and Julius, in kindness to Paul,[v] allowed him to go to his friends so they might provide for his needs.[w] 4 From there we put out to sea again and passed to the lee of Cyprus because the winds were against us.[x] 5 When we had sailed across the open sea off the coast of Cilicia[y]

26:20 [t]Ac 9:19-25 [u]Ac 9:26-29; 22:17-20 [v]Ac 9:15; 13:46 [w]Ac 3:19 [x]Mt 3:8; Lk 3:8
26:21 [y]Ac 21:27,30 [z]Ac 21:31
26:22 [a]Lk 24:27,44; Ac 10:43; 24:14
26:23 [b]1Co 15:20,23; Col 1:18; Rev 1:5 [c]Lk 2:32
26:24 [d]Jn 10:20; 1Co 4:10 [e]Jn 7:15
26:25 [f]Ac 23:26
26:26 [g]ver 3
26:28 [h]Ac 11:26
26:29 [i]Ac 21:33
26:30 [j]Ac 25:23
26:31 [k]Ac 23:9
26:32 [l]Ac 28:18 [m]Ac 25:11
27:1 [n]Ac 16:10 [o]Ac 18:2; 25:12,25 [p]Ac 10:1
27:2 [q]Ac 2:9 [r]Ac 19:29 [s]Ac 16:9 [t]Ac 17:1
27:3 [u]Mt 11:21 [v]ver 43 [w]Ac 24:23; 28:16
27:4 [x]ver 7
27:5 [y]Ac 6:9

26:20 repent and turn to God. Either (1) "repent" and "turn to God" are synonymous or (2) it means a change of mind ("repent") followed by a change of life direction ("turn to God"). In either case, the change in his converts would be evident in their "deeds" (see Eph 2:8–10; Phil 2:12 and notes).
26:22–23 Two important themes throughout Luke-Acts: (1) The OT Scriptures ("the prophets and Moses") predicted that "the Messiah would suffer" (see note on 3:18). (2) The message of salvation is for all people, regardless of social status ("small and great") or ethnicity ("to his own people ... and to the Gentiles").
26:23 first to rise from the dead. Jesus' resurrection begins the end-time resurrection and guarantees that all believers will rise as he did (see 1 Cor 15:20–23 and notes on 15:20–22; see also Col 1:18; 1 John 3:2 and notes).
26:24 You are out of your mind, Paul! Paul's preaching about the resurrection seems insane to the Gentile Festus (1 Cor 1:23).
26:27 do you believe the prophets? A dilemma for Agrippa: answering "yes" would impress his Jewish subjects but open him up to Paul's further preaching. Instead of answering, Agrippa chides Paul for trying to convert him (v. 28).
26:28 Christian. The second time this title appears in Acts (see 11:26 and note; cf. 1 Pet 4:16).
26:30–32 For Paul's innocence, see note on 23:29.
27:1–12 *Paul Sails for Rome.* This is one of the great accounts of a sea voyage from ancient literature. Luke provides remarkable nautical detail of the journey (vv. 1–12), storm (vv. 13–26), and shipwreck (vv. 27–44). The main theological theme is God's providence: he continues to protect Paul, and the gospel relentlessly moves forward toward its goal of reaching "the ends of the earth" (1:8).
27:1 we. Another "we" section begins here (see note on 16:10). Luke returned with Paul from Philippi to Jerusalem (20:6—21:17) and has evidently been with him throughout his two-year imprisonment in Caesarea. The "we" section continues when Paul arrives in Rome (28:16), implying that Luke stays with him through this entire time of incarceration. **Imperial Regiment.** Roman regiments, or cohorts (approximately 600 men each, though this varied), had both numbers and names (see the "Italian Regiment" in 10:1), and this regiment is identified as "Imperial" or Augustan (Greek *sebastos*, see note on 25:21). Cohorts of auxiliary troops often received this honorary title.
27:2 ship. Probably a small coastal ship rather than the larger ocean-going vessel that would take them to Rome. **Adramyttium.** A port on the northwest coast of Asia Minor. **Aristarchus.** See notes on 19:29; 20:4. He remains with Paul during his Roman imprisonment (Col 4:10; Phlm 24).
27:3 Sidon. About 70 miles (about 113 kilometers) north of Caesarea. **Julius.** The centurion in charge of the prisoners (v. 1). He shows favor to Paul throughout the voyage. **friends.** Believers at Sidon. Small networks of believers have sprung up everywhere (see note on 21:1–16).
27:4 passed to the lee. They sail on the sheltered side of the island (the east side of Cyprus) to avoid the westerly winds.
27:5 Cilicia and Pamphylia ... Lycia. Provinces along the southern part of Asia Minor (modern Turkey). From Sidon to Myra is about 500 miles (about 800 kilometers) and would take about 15 days. **Myra.** A growing port for essential grain shipments from Egypt to Rome.

27:6 [z]Ac 28:11 [a]ver 1
27:7 [b]ver 4 [c]ver 12,13,21
27:9 [d]Lev 16:29-31; 23:27-29; Nu 29:7
27:10 [e]ver 21
27:14 [f]Mk 4:37
27:17 [g]ver 26,39
27:18 [h]ver 19,38; Jnh 1:5
27:21 [i]ver 10 [j]ver 7
27:22 [k]ver 25,36
27:23 [l]Ac 5:19 [m]Ro 1:9 [n]Ac 18:9; 23:11; 2Ti 4:17
27:24 [o]Ac 23:11

and Pamphylia, we landed at Myra in Lycia. [6]There the centurion found an Alexandrian ship[z] sailing
for Italy[a] and put us on board. [7]We made slow headway for many days and had difficulty arriving off
Cnidus. When the wind did not allow us to hold our course,[b] we sailed to the lee of Crete,[c] opposite
Salmone. [8]We moved along the coast with difficulty and came to a place called Fair Havens, near the
town of Lasea.

[9]Much time had been lost, and sailing had already become dangerous because by now it was after
the Day of Atonement.[a][d] So Paul warned them, [10]"Men, I can see that our voyage is going to be disastrous and bring great loss to ship and cargo, and to our own lives also."[e] [11]But the centurion, instead
of listening to what Paul said, followed the advice of the pilot and of the owner of the ship. [12]Since the
harbor was unsuitable to winter in, the majority decided that we should sail on, hoping to reach Phoenix and winter there. This was a harbor in Crete, facing both southwest and northwest.

The Storm

[13]When a gentle south wind began to blow, they saw their opportunity; so they weighed anchor
and sailed along the shore of Crete. [14]Before very long, a wind of hurricane force,[f] called the Northeaster, swept down from the island. [15]The ship was caught by the storm and could not head into
the wind; so we gave way to it and were driven along. [16]As we passed to the lee of a small island
called Cauda, we were hardly able to make the lifeboat secure, [17]so the men hoisted it aboard. Then
they passed ropes under the ship itself to hold it together. Because they were afraid they would run
aground[g] on the sandbars of Syrtis, they lowered the sea anchor[b] and let the ship be driven along.
[18]We took such a violent battering from the storm that the next day they began to throw the cargo
overboard.[h] [19]On the third day, they threw the ship's tackle overboard with their own hands. [20]When
neither sun nor stars appeared for many days and the storm continued raging, we finally gave up
all hope of being saved.

[21]After they had gone a long time without food, Paul stood up before them and said: "Men, you
should have taken my advice[i] not to sail from Crete;[j] then you would have spared yourselves this
damage and loss. [22]But now I urge you to keep up your courage,[k] because not one of you will be
lost; only the ship will be destroyed. [23]Last night an angel[l] of the God to whom I belong and whom
I serve[m] stood beside me[n] [24]and said, 'Do not be afraid, Paul. You must stand trial before Caesar;[o]

[a] *9* That is, Yom Kippur [b] *17* Or *the sails*

27:6 The group transfers to a larger Alexandrian grain ship sailing for Italy.

27:7–8 The wind from the west makes for slow progress, so after reaching Cnidus, the ship turns south to catch the lee (shelter, see note on v. 4) of Crete. Yet they face very slow going along the southern shore of Crete, finally reaching Fair Havens.

27:9 Day of Atonement. Or "the Fast," referring to the Jewish holiday that occurred in late September to mid-October. **Paul warned them.** Because of high winds and storms, sailing in the Mediterranean was considered risky after mid-September and highly dangerous from mid-November onward, so Paul warns against continuing. Paul is a seasoned sea traveler and knows its dangers well (see 2 Cor 11:25–26).

27:12 Since the harbor at Fair Havens is not well protected, the centurion takes the advice of the pilot and the ship's owner to make for Phoenix, just along the southern coast of Crete (v. 11). **Phoenix.** The location is uncertain but is probably associated with Phineka Bay west of Loutro.

27:13–44 *The Storm and the Shipwreck.* Luke's account emphasizes two themes: (1) God providentially protects Paul and his companions. God promised Paul that he would testify in Rome, and no obstacle can thwart God's purpose. (2) Paul is levelheaded and calm in the face of grave danger. He takes charge of the situation, reassuring the other passengers. The attitude of the Roman centurion Julius moves from that of ignoring Paul's advice (v. 11) to that of following his lead and even protecting him from the soldiers' plan to kill the prisoners (vv. 42–43).

27:14 Northeaster. A typhoon-like wind that can occur in the central and western Mediterranean during winter months. The Northeaster blows the ship south, away from Crete and from their destination of Phoenix.

27:16 Cauda. An island known today as Gozzo, 23 miles (37 kilometers) from where they started. Briefly under the shelter of this small island, they can take emergency measures.

27:17 They secure the lifeboat and undergird the hull with cables or ropes to keep it from breaking apart. **sandbars of Syrtis.** Dangerous shoals off the north coast of Africa known as a graveyard for ships. Though these are several hundred miles/kilometers to the south, panic is setting in. **sea anchor.** The Greek here is ambiguous and could refer to lowering a sea anchor to create drag or lowering the main yard (cross piece on the mast) on which they hung the mainsail (see NIV text note). In either case the purpose is to slow the ship.

27:18–19 They cast some of the ship's cargo and tackle overboard to lighten the ship and thus keep it from being swamped. They do not throw out the grain (probably the main cargo) until v. 38. The owner is likely trying to save his investment.

27:21 you should have taken my advice. Paul is not chiding them ("I told you so") but is trying to get a hearing based on his previous sound advice (vv. 9–10).

27:23 Paul's prediction in v. 10 was based on reason and experience, but his assurance now comes from divine revelation.

27:24 God's purpose for Paul is to testify before Caesar (see 23:11), so nothing, not even a deadly storm, can thwart God's plan.

and God has graciously given you the lives of all who sail with you.'[p] 25So keep up your courage,[q]
men, for I have faith in God that it will happen just as he told me.[r] 26Nevertheless, we must run
aground[s] on some island."[t]

The Shipwreck

27On the fourteenth night we were still being driven across the Adriatic[a] Sea, when about midnight
the sailors sensed they were approaching land. 28They took soundings and found that the water was a
hundred and twenty feet[b] deep. A short time later they took soundings again and found it was ninety
feet[c] deep. 29Fearing that we would be dashed against the rocks, they dropped four anchors from the
stern and prayed for daylight. 30In an attempt to escape from the ship, the sailors let the lifeboat[u] down
into the sea, pretending they were going to lower some anchors from the bow. 31Then Paul said to the
centurion and the soldiers, "Unless these men stay with the ship, you cannot be saved."[v] 32So the soldiers cut the ropes that held the lifeboat and let it drift away.
33Just before dawn Paul urged them all to eat. "For the last fourteen days," he said, "you have

27:24 [p]ver 44
27:25 [q]ver 22,36 [r]Ro 4:20,21
27:26 [s]ver 17,39 [t]Ac 28:1
27:30 [u]ver 16
27:31 [v]ver 24

[a] *27* In ancient times the name referred to an area extending well south of Italy. [b] *28* Or about 37 meters
[c] *28* Or about 27 meters

27:27 Adriatic Sea. Today this name refers to the expanse of sea between Italy and Greece; in Paul's day it referred to a much larger area extending south into the middle of the Mediterranean (see NIV text note). **sensed they were approaching land.** Perhaps because the experienced sailors hear breakers or see changes in the sea's movements, patterns, and color.

27:30–32 The sailors expect the boat will be destroyed, so they decide that their best chance is on their own in the lifeboat. Paul warns that without the experienced sailors no one will be saved. He has now earned the respect of the centurion, who responds to his warning (though cutting off the only lifeboat may not have been the best course of action!).

27:33–34 Paul is again the voice of reason and calm.

PAUL'S JOURNEY TO ROME
ca. AD 59–60 (Acts 27:1–28:16)

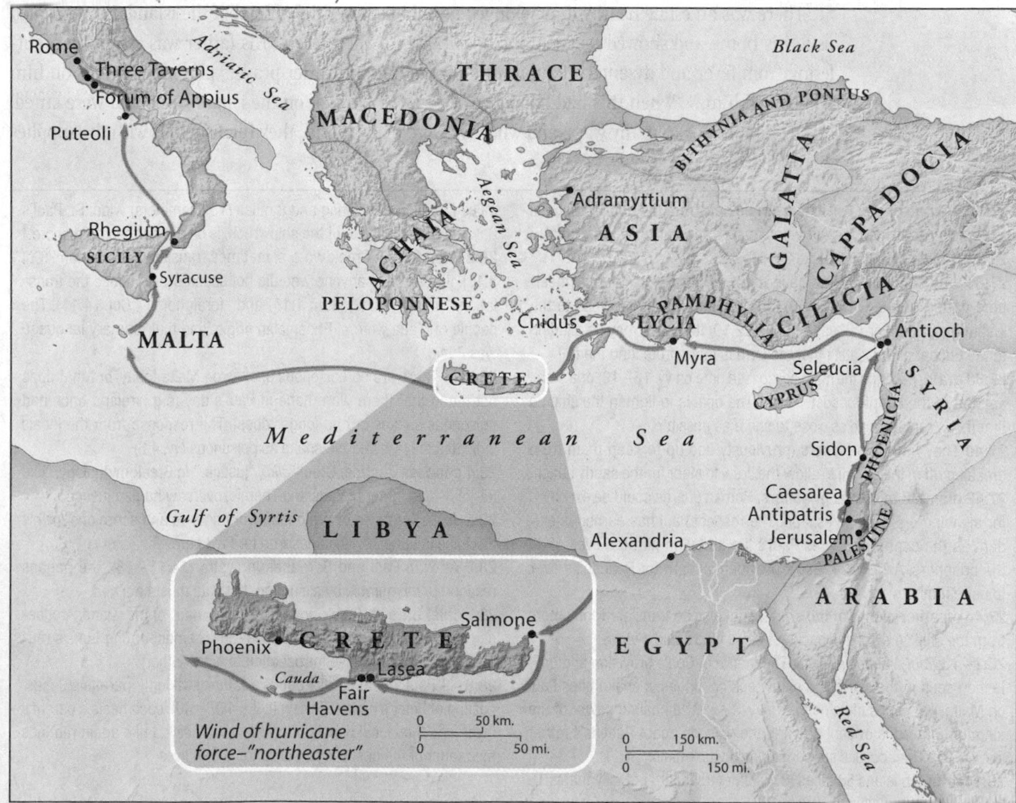

27:34 [w] Mt 10:30
27:35 [x] Mt 14:19
27:36 [y] ver 22,25
27:38 [z] ver 18; Jnh 1:5
27:39 [a] Ac 28:1
27:40 [b] ver 29
27:41 [c] 2Co 11:25
27:43 [d] ver 3
27:44 [e] ver 22,31
28:1 [f] Ac 16:10 [g] Ac 27:26,39
28:4 [h] Mk 16:18 [i] Lk 13:2,4
28:5 [j] Lk 10:19
28:6 [k] Ac 14:11
28:8 [l] Jas 5:14,15 [m] Ac 9:40

been in constant suspense and have gone without food—you haven't eaten anything. 34Now I urge you to take some food. You need it to survive. Not one of you will lose a single hair from his head."[w] 35After he said this, he took some bread and gave thanks to God in front of them all. Then he broke it[x] and began to eat. 36They were all encouraged[y] and ate some food themselves. 37Altogether there were 276 of us on board. 38When they had eaten as much as they wanted, they lightened the ship by throwing the grain into the sea.[z]

39When daylight came, they did not recognize the land, but they saw a bay with a sandy beach,[a] where they decided to run the ship aground if they could. 40Cutting loose the anchors,[b] they left them in the sea and at the same time untied the ropes that held the rudders. Then they hoisted the foresail to the wind and made for the beach. 41But the ship struck a sandbar and ran aground. The bow stuck fast and would not move, and the stern was broken to pieces by the pounding of the surf.[c]

42The soldiers planned to kill the prisoners to prevent any of them from swimming away and escaping. 43But the centurion wanted to spare Paul's life[d] and kept them from carrying out their plan. He ordered those who could swim to jump overboard first and get to land. 44The rest were to get there on planks or on other pieces of the ship. In this way everyone reached land safely.[e]

Paul Ashore on Malta

28 Once safely on shore, we[f] found out that the island[g] was called Malta. 2The islanders showed us unusual kindness. They built a fire and welcomed us all because it was raining and cold. 3Paul gathered a pile of brushwood and, as he put it on the fire, a viper, driven out by the heat, fastened itself on his hand. 4When the islanders saw the snake hanging from his hand,[h] they said to each other, "This man must be a murderer; for though he escaped from the sea, the goddess Justice has not allowed him to live."[i] 5But Paul shook the snake off into the fire and suffered no ill effects.[j] 6The people expected him to swell up or suddenly fall dead; but after waiting a long time and seeing nothing unusual happen to him, they changed their minds and said he was a god.[k]

7There was an estate nearby that belonged to Publius, the chief official of the island. He welcomed us to his home and showed us generous hospitality for three days. 8His father was sick in bed, suffering from fever and dysentery. Paul went in to see him and, after prayer,[l] placed his hands on him and healed him.[m] 9When this had happened, the rest of the sick on the island came and were cured. 10They honored us in many ways; and when we were ready to sail, they furnished us with the supplies we needed.

27:34 Not one of you will lose a single hair from his head. A Semitic expression that means "You won't suffer any harm" (1 Sam 14:45; 2 Sam 14:11; 1 Kgs 1:52; Luke 21:18).

27:35 took some bread and gave thanks ... broke it. A normal mealtime pattern (Luke 9:16; 24:30), but the language is so close to the institution of the Lord's Supper (Luke 22:19) that Luke may be alluding to the Eucharist, indicating that the Lord is there protecting them.

27:38 grain. Perhaps the main cargo (see note on vv. 18–19) or a small amount of food kept for sustenance. The goal is to lighten the ship so that it can run aground as close to shore as possible.

27:40 They untie the rudders (previously tied up to keep them from breaking off in the storm) to allow the crew to steer for the sandy beach.

27:42 planned to kill the prisoners. Roman guards could be executed for allowing prisoners to escape. The respect Paul has earned is evident as the centurion spares Paul's life and with him the lives of all the prisoners. As in v. 24, God's providential care for Paul spills over to benefit others.

27:44 on other pieces of the ship. Might also be translated "on others from the ship" (i.e., on the backs of those who could swim).

28:1–10 *Paul Ashore on Malta.* The theme of God's provision and protection seen in the storm and shipwreck continues: a snake bites Paul on Malta, yet Paul suffers no harm (vv. 3–6). The healing power of the kingdom of God is evident again in the episode about Publius's father (vv. 7–10). The apostles are continuing Jesus' ministry (1:1).

28:1 Malta. An island 58 miles (93 kilometers) south of Sicily that is 18 miles (29 kilometers) long and 8 miles (13 kilometers) wide. St. Paul's Bay, the traditional site of the shipwreck, is on the northeastern shore.

28:2 islanders. A Greek word sometimes translated "barbarian" (Col 3:11). It referred to anyone who did not speak Greek, hence the translations "non-Greeks" (Rom 1:14) and "foreigner" (1 Cor 14:11). The people of Malta were of Phoenician origin, and their primary language was Punic.

28:3–4 There are no poisonous snakes on Malta today, but that does not mean that there were none in Paul's day (e.g., Ireland once had poisonous snakes but no longer does). The response from the locals indicates they viewed the snake as poisonous (vv. 4,6).

28:4 goddess Justice. Greek *dikē*, "justice." In Greek mythology, Dike (di-kay), a daughter of Zeus and Themis, oversaw human justice.

28:5 Jesus' promise of protection from snakes and scorpions for his disciples in Luke 10:19 comes true for Paul here.

28:6 As with Paul and Barnabas in Lystra (14:11–18), the pagans respond to the miracle by assuming that Paul must be a god.

28:7 chief official. Greek *prōtos*, the "first man" of the island. Archaeologists have confirmed this unusual title, demonstrating Luke's reliability as a historian (see Introduction to Acts: Author).

28:8–9 Paul's healing of Publius's father strikingly parallels Jesus' healing of Peter's mother-in-law (Luke 4:38–40): each heals a parent's fever, and then local people bring them their sick. Luke again reminds the reader of the gospel's power to transform lives.

Paul's Arrival at Rome

11After three months we put out to sea in a ship that had wintered in the island — it was an Alexandrian ship[n] with the figurehead of the twin gods Castor and Pollux. 12We put in at Syracuse and stayed
there three days. 13From there we set sail and arrived at Rhegium. The next day the south wind came
up, and on the following day we reached Puteoli. 14There we found some brothers and sisters[o] who
invited us to spend a week with them. And so we came to Rome. 15The brothers and sisters[p] there had
heard that we were coming, and they traveled as far as the Forum of Appius and the Three Taverns to
meet us. At the sight of these people Paul thanked God and was encouraged. 16When we got to Rome,
Paul was allowed to live by himself, with a soldier to guard him.[q]

Paul Preaches at Rome Under Guard

17Three days later he called together the local Jewish leaders.[r] When they had assembled, Paul said
to them: "My brothers,[s] although I have done nothing against our people[t] or against the customs of
our ancestors,[u] I was arrested in Jerusalem and handed over to the Romans. 18They examined me[v] and
wanted to release me,[w] because I was not guilty of any crime deserving death.[x] 19The Jews objected, so
I was compelled to make an appeal to Caesar.[y] I certainly did not intend to bring any charge against
my own people. 20For this reason I have asked to see you and talk with you. It is because of the hope of
Israel[z] that I am bound with this chain."[a]

21They replied, "We have not received any letters from Judea concerning you, and none of our people[b] who have come from there has reported or said anything bad about you. 22But we want to hear
what your views are, for we know that people everywhere are talking against this sect."[c]

23They arranged to meet Paul on a certain day, and came in even larger numbers to the place where
he was staying. He witnessed to them from morning till evening, explaining about the kingdom of God,[d]
and from the Law of Moses and from the Prophets[e] he tried to persuade them about Jesus.[f] 24Some
were convinced by what he said, but others would not believe.[g] 25They disagreed among themselves

28:11 [n]Ac 27:6
28:14 [o]Ac 1:16
28:15 [p]Ac 1:16
28:16 [q]Ac 24:23; 27:3
28:17 [r]Ac 25:2 [s]Ac 22:5 [t]Ac 25:8 [u]Ac 6:14
28:18 [v]Ac 22:24 [w]Ac 26:31,32 [x]Ac 23:9
28:19 [y]Ac 25:11
28:20 [z]Ac 26:6,7 [a]Ac 21:33
28:21 [b]Ac 22:5
28:22 [c]Ac 24:5,14
28:23 [d]Ac 19:8 [e]Ac 8:35 [f]Ac 17:3
28:24 [g]Ac 14:4

28:11–16 *Paul's Arrival at Rome.* As Paul approaches Rome, believers from Puteoli (vv. 13–14) and Rome (v. 15) greet him. It is unclear when Christianity spread to Rome, but the church there likely began in the AD 30s when Jews returned from Jerusalem after the day of Pentecost (2:10). After believers appear at Puteoli and Rome, the Roman church disappears from the narrative. Throughout Acts (see notes on v. 31; 4:1–22; 5:17–42,21–26,39; 11:17; 12:1–19a; 19:20; 21:17—28:31), Luke describes the gospel's unstoppable advance (vv. 30–31) and how the Jews (vv. 17–27) and Gentiles (v. 28) respond to it.
28:11 After three months. After the worst of the winter months. **Alexandrian ship.** Likely another vessel carrying grain from Egypt to Rome. **Castor and Pollux.** In Greek mythology, twin sons of Zeus who protected sailors.
28:12 Syracuse. The capital city of Sicily and a major port on the southeastern coast, 90 miles (145 kilometers) from Malta.
28:13 Rhegium. A port on the southern tip of Italy, 70 miles (113 kilometers) from Syracuse and at the southern entrance to the Strait of Messina. Just north of here supposedly lie the legendary whirlpool of Charybdis and the rock of Scylla. **Puteoli.** Modern Pozzuoli, on the western coast of Italy about 130 miles (about 210 kilometers) southeast of Rome.
28:14 brothers and sisters. Their presence at Puteoli shows that the gospel has already reached not only Rome but also the regions around it. Though Paul has never been to Rome, it is not surprising that a number of believers come out to welcome him. Writing from Corinth to the church in Rome about three years earlier (AD 57), Paul greets many friends and acquaintances in the church there (Rom 16:3–16). **And so we came to Rome.** Seems premature in light of v. 16. It probably means "in this manner we came to Rome," summarizing vv. 13–16.
28:15 Forum of Appius. On the Appian Way, 43 miles (69 kilometers) south of Rome. **Three Taverns.** A common stopping point about 25 miles (40 kilometers) from the city.

28:17–31 *Paul Preaches at Rome Under Guard.* The book of Acts ends with Paul's arrival in Rome and a two-year house arrest there. Though Rome was not "the ends of the earth" (1:8), it was the center of the Roman Empire, so it symbolizes the church's mission to reach the whole world with the Good News. The book ends with its central themes: (1) Israel is divided between those who accept the gospel and the majority who reject it (vv. 24–27). (2) Salvation is offered to the Gentiles (v. 28). (3) The gospel's unstoppable advance (vv. 30–31).
28:17–20 As has been his pattern throughout Acts, Paul preaches to the Jews first (9:15, 20; 13:14,46–47; 14:1; 17:1–3,10,17; 18:4; 19:8; cf. Rom 1:16).
28:17 local Jewish leaders. Likely the elders of the major synagogues of Rome. Though Emperor Claudius expelled the Jews from Rome in AD 49 (see note on 18:2), they quickly returned after Rome lifted the ban, and by this time (about AD 60) Rome again has a large Jewish population. Paul assumes that negative reports about him have reached Rome, so he defends his innocence.
28:20 hope of Israel. The coming of the Messiah and especially the resurrection of the dead that his salvation would bring (23:6; 24:15; 26:6–8,22–23).
28:21–22 Though the Jews of Rome have heard negative reports about Christianity (v. 22), they have not received specific reports about Paul (v. 21), so they want to give him a fair hearing.
28:23 Paul's message is about "the kingdom of God" (see note on 1:3) and how Jesus the Messiah fulfills OT prophecies. **from the Law of Moses and from the Prophets.** The Hebrew Scriptures, i.e., the OT (24:14; Matt 5:17; Luke 16:16; 24:27,44).
28:24 Some were convinced ... but others would not believe. As throughout Acts, Israel is divided (2:41,47; 5:14,17; 6:7; 8:1; 13:43,45; 14:1,4; 17:4–5; 19:8–10).

28:27 [h]Ps 119:70 [i]Isa 6:9,10
28:28 [j]Lk 2:30 [k]Ac 13:46
28:31 [l]ver 23; Mt 4:23

and began to leave after Paul had made this final statement: "The Holy Spirit spoke the truth to your ancestors when he said through Isaiah the prophet:

> 26 " 'Go to this people and say,
> "You will be ever hearing but never understanding;
> you will be ever seeing but never perceiving."
> 27 For this people's heart has become calloused;[h]
> they hardly hear with their ears,
> and they have closed their eyes.
> Otherwise they might see with their eyes,
> hear with their ears,
> understand with their hearts
> and turn, and I would heal them.'[i][a]

28 "Therefore I want you to know that God's salvation[j] has been sent to the Gentiles,[k] and they will
listen!" [29] [b]
30 For two whole years Paul stayed there in his own rented house and welcomed all who came to see
him. 31 He proclaimed the kingdom of God[l] and taught about the Lord Jesus Christ—with all boldness
and without hindrance!

[a] 27 Isaiah 6:9,10 (see Septuagint) [b] 29 Some manuscripts include here *After he said this, the Jews left, arguing vigorously among themselves.*

28:26–27 Quotes Isa 6:9–10, a passage Jesus also cited to explain why Israel rejected the gospel (Matt 13:14–15; Mark 4:12; Luke 8:10; John 12:40; cf. Rom 11:8; 2 Cor 3:14; 4:4).
28:28 As on other occasions, Paul takes the gospel first to the Jews and then turns to the Gentiles (13:46; 18:6; 26:20,23; Rom 1:16).
28:30 The book ends in about AD 62, after Paul had been imprisoned for two years in Rome (see Introduction to Acts: Date). Paul probably wrote his four "Prison Letters" (Ephesians, Philippians, Colossians, and Philemon) during this time (see Introductions to these books). Though Luke does not record anything further about Paul's ministry, Paul was likely released and continued his ministry for several years before being arrested again and executed in Rome, sometime between AD 64 and 67 (see Introductions to 1–2 Timothy; Titus).
28:31 The book of Acts ends with its main theme: the gospel's progress is unstoppable (see notes on vv. 11–16; 4:1–22; 5:17–42,21–26, 39; 11:17; 12:1–19a; 19:20; 21:17—28:31). Though Paul is in chains, the gospel cannot be chained, and despite his house arrest, Paul continues to preach "with all boldness and without hindrance!"

INTRODUCTION TO

THE LETTERS AND REVELATION

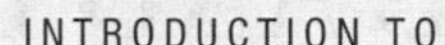

ROMANS

1 CORINTHIANS

2 CORINTHIANS

GALATIANS

EPHESIANS

PHILIPPIANS

COLOSSIANS

1 THESSALONIANS

2 THESSALONIANS

1 TIMOTHY

2 TIMOTHY

TITUS

PHILEMON

HEBREWS

JAMES

1 PETER

2 PETER

1 JOHN

2 JOHN

3 JOHN

JUDE

REVELATION

THE LETTERS AND REVELATION

Douglas J. Moo

Letters occupy an important place in the NT. Of the 27 books of the NT, 21 are letters — 35 percent of the NT. By contrast, no OT book is in the form of a letter, though letters are preserved within those books.

There are many reasons that letters loom so large in the NT, but three deserve mention. First, letters were a very popular method of communication in the NT world (see The Letters: New Testament Letters in Their Ancient Context). Second, the early Christian movement was scattered across a wide area, and letters afforded a natural way for believers to keep in touch with each other. Apostles, who are responsible for at least 19 of the 21 NT letters, traveled widely and used letters as a means of "pastoring" churches from a distance. Third, and related to this second factor, the letter was considered a means of establishing one's personal presence at a distance. When the apostles were unable to assert their authority in person, they used letters as a "stand-in" for their presence (1 Cor 5:4; Col 2:5).

NT letter writers, as we would expect, focus on issues relevant to their audiences. Spread across the eastern Mediterranean world, from modern Turkey to Rome, Christians are thanked for sending gifts (Phil), warned about false teachers (2 Pet, Jude), encouraged in the midst of persecution (1 Pet), and rebuked for dallying with idol worship (1 Cor). Yet these first-century issues are addressed in light of God's revelation of his Son. They have been preserved in our Bibles as enduring witnesses to the truth of the gospel and to the way that truth is to form the lives of God's people.

Classifying the New Testament Letters

The 21 NT letters were written by six different early Christian leaders: 13 letters are attributed to the apostle Paul; two to the apostle Peter; one to James; and one to Jude, "a brother of James" (Jude 1). No specific name is associated with the four remaining letters. The author of Hebrews cannot be identified. The author of 2 and 3 John is identified as "the elder" (2 John 1; 3 John 1), and the similarities in style and content with 1 John make it likely that the same author is responsible for all three. As the titles in our Bibles suggest, John the son of Zebedee, one of the 12 apostles and the author of the fourth Gospel, is probably the writer of these three letters. (These titles indicate the way these letters were viewed in the early church, but the titles were not part of the original NT text.)

Hebrews and the General Letters

Paul wrote 13 of the NT letters. The remaining eight letters defy simple classification. Many Christians in the first centuries of the church thought that Paul wrote Hebrews, so it was included among the Pauline letters. The other seven letters (James, 1 – 2 Pet, 1 – 3 John, Jude) were then categorized as "catholic" (in the sense of "universal") or "general" letters because it was thought that they were written to the church as a whole (see Eusebius, *Ecclesiastical History*, 2:23 – 25). The titles given to these books reflect this way of looking at them: rather than being named according to their destinations or audiences, as in the case of all the Pauline letters and Hebrews, they are named according to their authors.

This traditional way of categorizing the letters does not stand up to scrutiny. Hebrews was almost certainly not written by Paul (see Introduction to Hebrews: Author). Nor is it likely that the remaining seven letters were written to the church "universal." To be sure, none of them is explicitly addressed to a single local church (or group of house churches). But they do have specific audiences in view. The letters of 2 – 3 John explicitly address, respectively, a local church (taking "the lady chosen by God" in this sense [2 John 1]) and a Christian leader (Gaius [3 John 1]). First Peter addresses Christians living in five Roman provinces in northern Asia Minor. Three of the letters, to be sure, have very general addressees. James writes to "the twelve tribes" (Jas 1:1), a reference to the people of God in the era of fulfillment; Peter writes in his second letter to "those who through the righteousness of our God and Savior Jesus Christ have received a faith as precious as ours" (2 Pet 1:1); and Jude writes to "those who have been called, who are loved in God the Father and kept for Jesus Christ" (Jude 1). But the content of these letters shows that the authors are dealing with specific problems that are probably confined to a particular church or group of churches. The same is true of 1 John (which lacks any addressee).

Paul's Letters

Paul, for his part, addresses nine of his letters to particular local churches, three to co-workers in ministry (1 – 2 Tim, Titus), and one primarily to a co-worker and secondarily to two other prominent believers and the church that met in his house (Phlm). Paul's letters have usually been divided into four main groups:

1. Romans, 1 – 2 Corinthians, and Galatians have been labeled the "chief letters" because of their length and theological content.

2. Ephesians, Philippians, Colossians, and Philemon are called the "prison letters" because Paul claims to be "in chains" in each of them.

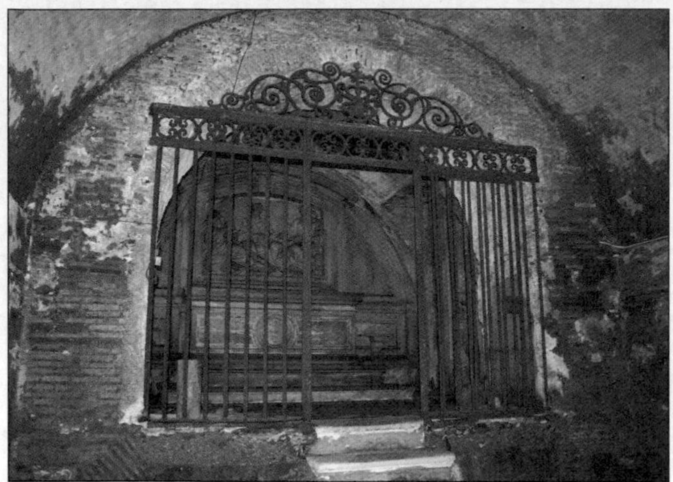

Crypt of Santa Maria in via Lata in Rome. This area was built in the first century, but radically restructured in the third century. It is a possible location for Paul's house arrest.

3. 1 – 2 Timothy and Titus are called the "pastoral letters" because of their common themes and the fact that they are addressed to Paul's co-workers.

4. 1 – 2 Thessalonians comprise the fourth group.

This traditional scheme corresponds generally to the historical circumstances in which the letters were written — with two exceptions. First, while Galatians shares many themes with Romans, it may not come from the same period of time as the other three "chief letters." Second, Philippians stands apart from the other prison letters. The common themes and specific historical references common to Ephesians, Colossians, and Philemon are absent from Philippians. Whether Paul wrote Philippians at a different time during the same imprisonment as the others or during an entirely different imprisonment is not clear.

New Testament Letters in Their Ancient Context

Though letters were used as a means of communication for centuries (e.g., 2 Sam 11:14 – 15; Ezra 4 – 5), in the Greco-Roman world letters became an established and popular method of communication. The NT, as we have seen, reflects this situation. In addition to the 21 canonical letters, the NT refers to at least nine other letters written by and to believers (Acts 15:23; 18:27; 1 Cor 5:9; 7:1; 16:3; 2 Cor 2:3 – 4; Col 4:16 [two different letters are mentioned]; 2 Thess 2:2; note also the seven letters to the churches in Rev 2 – 3).

Introduction and Conclusion

NT letters follow the general pattern of the Greco-Roman letter, although there are differences. The typical Greco-Roman letter was composed of an address and greeting, a body, and a conclusion.

The address and greeting were usually very short, typically taking the form "A to B, greetings." NT letters tend to expand this formula, adding characterizations of the sender (e.g., "James, a servant of God and of the Lord Jesus Christ" [Jas 1:1]) and of the recipients (e.g., "To God's holy people in Colossae, the faithful brothers and sisters in Christ" [Col 1:2]). In Romans, Paul spends six verses introducing himself. On the other hand, some NT letters (Hebrews, 1 John) have no letter opening at all.

In place of the usual "greeting" found in Greco-Roman letters, NT letters often include a "grace wish" (it is found in all the Pauline letters, 1 – 2 Pet, and 2 John). The NT letter writers may be indulging in a bit of wordplay: Greek "greetings" is *chairein*, whereas Greek "grace" is *charis*. Ancient letters also often opened with a "health wish" (see 3 John 2); perhaps the NT penchant for putting a thanksgiving (all the Pauline letters except 2 Cor, Gal, 1 Tim, and Titus) or blessing (2 Cor, Eph, 1 Pet) at the beginning of letters reflects this practice.

The concluding elements in the ancient letter varied considerably, although they typically included a request to greet other people. NT letter closings often include such requests for greetings and in addition, often mention travel plans, the movements and work of other ministry workers, requests for prayer, and benedictions and doxologies.

What is true concerning Paul's teaching about the law in Galatians is true for many, if not most, of the issues discussed in the NT letters.

Body

The formal introduction and conclusion framed the letter body. Naturally, the letter body differed considerably in length and substance, depending on the purpose and audience of the letter.

Some ancient letters were very brief personal notes requesting information or asking someone to perform a specific task. None of the NT letters is this kind of private note. Even the letters written to individuals (1–2 Tim, Titus, 3 John) deal with practical and theological issues affecting other Christians. At the other end of the spectrum, some ancient letters were written for a very general audience and intended for wide distribution (somewhat comparable to our "letter to the editor"). Especially relevant for the NT are letters sent by philosophers to communicate their teachings to a wider audience. Some NT letters tend toward this type (Rom, Eph, 1 John). Yet even these more generally focused letters are written for specific audiences.

While using the popular letter form of their time, the writers adopt the form for their own uses. For instance, many of the NT letters stand out from their contemporary secular models in length. Private letters in the ancient world averaged 87 words in length. Public letters were longer. Two of the most prolific letter writers in the ancient world were the Romans Cicero and Seneca. The former's letters average 295 words; Seneca's, 995. By contrast, the shortest NT letter (2 John) is 219 words, the longest (Romans) is 7,111 words, and they average 2,141 words.

Fourth-century relief of an orator dictating to a scribe. An amanuensis was often used to produce letters in NT times, including those written by Paul (Rom 16:22).

Relief depicting orator dictating to scribe, from Temple of Hercules at Ostia Antica/De Agostini Picture Library/G. Dagli Orti/Bridgeman Images

Writing, Sending, and Receiving New Testament Letters

Communicating by letter writing in the ancient world was a cooperative enterprise. The first-person singular verbs scattered through all the NT letters make clear that one particular individual is largely responsible for each of them. However, Paul frequently includes co-workers when he introduces the writers of his letters: Timothy in Philippians, Colossians, and Philemon; Timothy and Silas in 1–2 Thessalonians; and "all the brothers and sisters with me" in Galatians (1:2). Paul usually mentioned these co-workers because they were with him as he wrote and had significant contact with the believers being addressed. Mentioning other believers (as in the broader group in Gal) may also strengthen Paul's appeal in the letter by reminding the recipients that he was speaking for a wider group of believers.

Producing letters was also a cooperative venture. The parchment on which the words of letters were physically recorded was expensive, and most ancient letter writers dictated their letters to a scribe, or "amanuensis," who was skilled at fitting a lot of words into a very small space. We have one definite reference to such an amanuensis in the NT: "I, Tertius, who wrote down this letter, greet you in the Lord" (Rom 16:22). Tertius recorded the words of Romans as Paul dictated them to him (many interpreters think that 1 Pet 5:12 may also single out Silas as the amanuensis of that letter). The actual "author" of the letter would sometimes add a final, authenticating greeting in his own hand (Gal 6:11; 2 Thess 3:17; Phlm 19). Most of the NT letters were probably produced in this way. Authors who knew and trusted their amanuenses would often entrust that amanuensis with the precise wording of a letter. This may explain some of the variety in style among NT letters with the same author (Paul and Peter). We can assume that NT authors took ownership of their letters by checking them over to make sure that the amanuensis had accurately communicated the author's intentions.

If the writing of a letter was a collective enterprise, so was its delivery. Mail service was basically nonexistent in the ancient world. The only way to get a letter to its destination was to entrust it to a friend or associate who was traveling to the destination of the letter. While never mentioned explicitly in the NT, letter carriers can be identified by language such as we find in Eph 6:21: "Tychicus, the dear brother and faithful servant in the Lord, will tell you everything, so that you also may know how I am and what I am doing." Col 4:7 is similar; see also Phoebe in Rom 16:1–2, Epaphroditus in Phil 2:25–30, and Silas in 1 Pet 5:12 (if he is not the amanuensis; see preceding paragraph). These letter carriers probably also played a significant role in the dissemination of the letter once it reached its destination. They would often be the ones to read the letter to the assembled congregation, adding information and perhaps clarification along the way (see Eph 6:21, quoted above, and also Col 4:7–9).

The Authenticity of New Testament Letters

Many books in the ancient world were written by an anonymous person in the name of a more famous person. A Jewish apocalyptic work from the first century AD, for instance, is attributed to the ancient Israelite scribe Ezra. Many modern scholars identify this phenomenon, called "pseudepigraphy," in the NT letters. It is typical, for instance, to claim that the apostle Paul himself actually wrote only seven of the thirteen letters attributed to him (Rom, 1 – 2 Cor, Gal, Phil, 1 Thess, and Phlm) and that Paul's followers wrote the other six letters in his name. Similar doubt is cast on the authorship of James and 1 – 2 Peter. According to one form of this theory, the authors who wrote in the names of the apostles were not being deceptive but simply using a standard literary device of the time to communicate Christian truth. However, while pseudepigraphy in general was widespread in the ancient world, the writing of letters in someone else's name did not often take place. And when it did, the practice was frowned upon. The church fathers are very clear on this point: they viewed writing a letter in someone else's name as inherently deceptive, and they roundly rejected any letter suspected of being pseudepigraphical. In light of this attitude, we should take the claims about authorship of NT letters at face value.

Interpreting New Testament Letters

Occasion

NT letters are "occasional," i.e., they are written to a particular first-century

SUMMARY OF THE NEW TESTAMENT LETTERS

	LETTER	AUTHOR	RECIPIENTS	PLACE OF WRITING	DATE
	James	James, brother of the Lord	Jewish believers living outside of Israel	Jerusalem	AD 45 – 48 (or 60s)
First Missionary Journey of Paul	Galatians	Paul	Believers in the Roman province of Galatia or believers in the ethnic region of Galatia	Antioch or Ephesus (?)	48 (or 51 – 52 or 54 – 55)
Second Missionary Journey of Paul	1 Thessalonians	Paul	Believers in Thessalonica	Corinth	50 – 51
	2 Thessalonians	Paul	Believers in Thessalonica	Corinth	50 – 51
Third Missionary Journey of Paul	1 Corinthians	Paul	Believers in Corinth	Ephesus	54
	2 Corinthians	Paul	Believers in Corinth	Macedonia	55 – 56
	Romans	Paul	Believers in Rome	Corinth	57
	Ephesians	Paul	Believers in Ephesus (and in nearby cities)	Rome	60 – 61
	Colossians	Paul	Believers in Colossae	Rome	60 – 61
	Philemon	Paul	Philemon, a ministry co-worker in Colossae, and the church that met in his home	Rome	60 – 62
	Philippians	Paul	Believers in Philippi	Rome (or Ephesus?)	60 – 62 (or 54 – 55)
	1 Timothy	Paul	Timothy, a ministry associate working in Ephesus	Macedonia (?)	ca. 60 – 63
	Titus	Paul	Titus, a ministry associate working in Crete	Unknown	62 – 63
	2 Timothy	Paul	Timothy, a ministry associate	Rome	64 – 65 (or 67)
	Hebrews	Unknown	Believers in Rome (?)	Unknown	60s
	1 Peter	The apostle Peter	Believers in northern Asia Minor	Rome (?)	ca. 60 – 63
	2 Peter	The apostle Peter	Believers in northern Asia Minor	Unknown	63 – 65
	Jude	Jude, a brother of James	Unknown	Unknown	Late 50s to late 60s
	1 John	The apostle John	Believers in Ephesus and surrounding regions (?)	Ephesus (?)	Early 90s
	2 John	The apostle John	A church in the region of Ephesus	Ephesus (?)	Early 90s
	3 John	The apostle John	Gaius, a ministry co-worker	Ephesus (?)	Early 90s

audience and therefore naturally deal with issues relevant to that audience. Because the NT letter writers are engaged in helping their recipients understand the significance of Christ's coming and putting into practice the implications of his lordship, the issues the NT deals with are often the same issues Christians face today. But even when those issues are the same, faithfully interpreting the NT letters demands that we take into account the occasional nature of those letters.

Paul's teaching on the significance of the law of Moses in Galatians provides a good example. His teaching on this issue is clearly of enduring relevance, and what he says on this matter must figure importantly in our attempt to understand the place of the law of Moses in the history of salvation and in the life of the church. But we must also recognize that Paul writes to the Galatians about the law of Moses with a particular purpose: to convince them not to follow false teachers who have taken a wrong view about the law. Because Paul is refuting a particular viewpoint, his teaching is inevitably slanted to one side of the issue.

What is true concerning Paul's teaching about the law in Galatians is true for many, if not most, of the issues discussed in the NT letters. Many of these letters were written directly to counter some kind of false teaching, and what the NT letter writers say is tailored to that situation. To read and interpret these letters rightly, then, requires that we understand the situations in which they were written; this information is provided in this study Bible's separate book introductions. At the same time, we must always compare Scripture with Scripture before drawing broad conclusions about what the NT or the Bible says about any particular topic.

Social and Cultural Context

The occasional nature of the NT letters provides another interpretive challenge: recognizing how the first-century social and cultural context might affect our reading. Both the writers and readers of the NT letters often simply assumed this context, but it is sometimes utterly foreign to modern readers. For example, just what were the women in Corinth doing that upset Paul (1 Cor 11:2 – 16)? Were they refusing to wear a veil over their heads? Were they refusing to put their hair up on their heads? And in either case, why would Paul have a problem with it? Only by understanding the culture of that day can we hope to accurately understand what Paul is teaching in this passage. Faithfully reading the NT letters will often, then, require the believer to learn something about the first-century world — an inquiry that the notes on particular passages in this study Bible should assist with.

General Principles

Whatever the particular issue a NT letter deals with, the way in which the author responds to it has much to teach us. We learn not only from the specific instructions the letter writers give but also from the general principles they constantly bring to bear on each issue they confront. Again and again the NT letter writers remind us of the all-encompassing importance of the lordship of Christ and the work of the Holy Spirit. The believer's every thought and action must be subjected to Christ, who as Lord wants to reign over every facet of the believer's life. And it is the Holy Spirit who both empowers and guides this radically Christ-centered new life. When the NT letter writers call on believers to think and act in accord with the person of Christ, they expect believers to respond because God has sent his Spirit into the hearts of his people, producing from within the attitudes and perspectives that will enable them to obey. As "occasional" letters, we must read each NT letter against the background of its particular setting, asking: when was it written? for whom? why? in what circumstances? But at the same time, God himself speaks to us in and through these occasional letters. As canonical Scripture, these letters ultimately address the church of every age and of every place. ■

Statue of woman wearing a chiton and himation, first century AD. It is important to understand the cultural context of Paul's comments on covering the head in worship (1 Cor 11).

Kim Walton, taken at the National Archaeological Museum of Athens

INTRODUCTION TO ROMANS

AUTHOR

The letter to the Romans was written by the apostle Paul (1:1). No co-author is mentioned, although Tertius was the man who served as Paul's scribe, or amanuensis, writing down Paul's words as he dictated them (16:22).

OCCASION, DATE, AND PLACE OF WRITING

Paul gives us considerable information about his situation in 15:14 – 33. He suggests that he has reached an important turning point in his ministry. He speaks of having "fully proclaimed" the gospel "from Jerusalem all the way around to Illyricum" (15:19) — the territory where he planted vibrant churches during his first three missionary journeys. The next focus of his missionary effort is all the way at the other end of the Mediterranean basin: Spain (15:24). Before going to Spain, however, he has two important stops to make. His immediate plans are to travel to Jerusalem in order to deliver to the Jewish Christians there some money from many of the Gentile churches he planted (15:25 – 27). After Jerusalem, Paul hopes to pass through Rome to visit this important center of Christianity and to enlist their support for his new missionary venture (15:23 – 24). When we add to this information to Paul's reference to a woman from Cenchreae (16:1), a city very close to Corinth, the setting of Romans becomes pretty certain: he was writing from Corinth during his three-month stay there toward the end of his third missionary journey

LOCATIONS VISITED BY PAUL

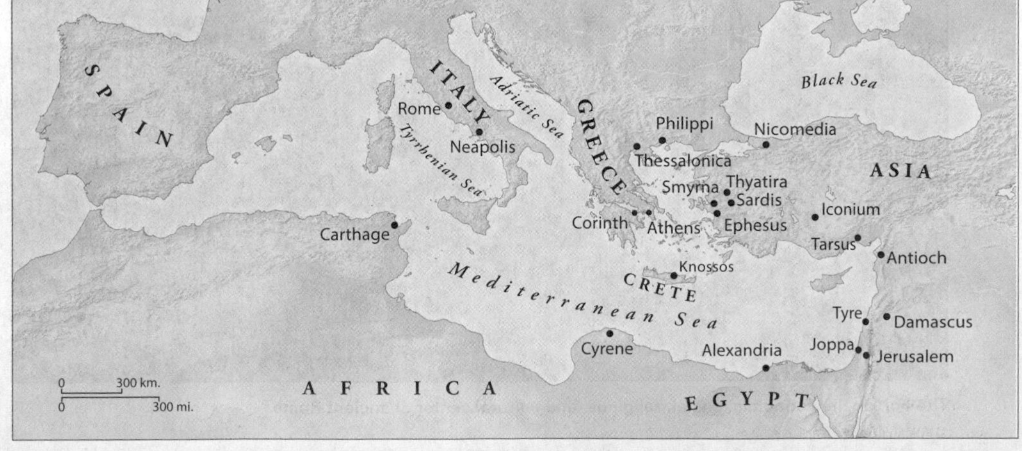

(Acts 20:3–4). The date of this stay was probably AD 57. Romans, then, was the third letter Paul wrote on this missionary journey (after 1 Cor in perhaps AD 54 and 2 Cor in AD 55–56).

RECIPIENTS

Paul writes to all the believers in the city of Rome (1:7). The NT tells us nothing about how Christianity first came to Rome, but a plausible scenario is that Jewish believers who were present in Jerusalem on the day of Pentecost (Acts 2:10 says that "visitors from Rome" were there) brought their new faith back to their home city. The early Christian given the name Ambrosiaster (late fourth century), then, was probably right in claiming in his commentary on Paul's letters that the Romans "embraced the faith of Christ, albeit according to the Jewish rite, without seeing any sign of mighty works or any of the apostles."

Several passages in Romans suggest, however, that most of the Roman Christians were Gentiles when Paul wrote (1:6–7,13; 15:15–16). Some Gentiles were probably attracted to the faith from the beginning, having heard about the message of Jesus as "God-fearers" (Gentiles who attended the synagogue without converting to Judaism). The Gentile element in the Roman church received a significant boost in AD 49 when Claudius expelled all the Jews from Rome (see Acts 18:2). Jewish Christians would have been included in this eviction order, so the Christian movement would have become almost entirely Gentile overnight. By the time Paul wrote the letter to the church in Rome, however, Jews had been allowed back into the city. Thus, Paul's audience included Jewish Christians such as Priscilla and Aquila (16:3–5; cf. Acts 18:2).

PURPOSE

Paul has several purposes in writing to the Romans.

1. Paul hopes to enlist the support of the Roman Christians for his new ministry in Spain (15:24). Spain is a long way from his original "sending" church in Antioch, and he needs a ministry base closer to Spain to provide monetary and logistical support. Paul writes Romans, then, partly to introduce himself to a church that he did not found and has never visited (1:13; 15:22).

2. While Romans is justly famous for its deep theology, Paul is also concerned, as he is in all his letters, to address the situation of his readers. Of course, we must avoid the mistake of thinking that very deep theology might not be of very fundamental practical importance! But 14:1—15:13 reveals that Paul does have an eye on a particular issue in Rome. The believers are divided into two factions, which Paul labels the "weak" in faith and the "strong" in faith

The Forum: the economic, social, religious, and cultural center of ancient Rome.

(15:1). These factions were quarreling over whether Christians must continue to observe certain Jewish practices derived from the law of Moses. Paul hopes to heal this unfortunate division.

3. The conflict between the "weak" and "strong" in Rome was a microcosm of the major theological issue in Paul's day. As the Christian movement became increasingly Gentile over the decades, the relationship between Christianity and its OT and Jewish roots became more and more controversial. Some, mainly Jewish Christians, were arguing for a great deal of continuity: Christians were a Jewish Messianic sect that should continue to observe the law of Moses (this was the view of the "agitators" whom Paul combats in Galatia [Gal 5:12]). Others, mainly Gentile Christians, wondered why they should have anything to do with the OT or the law at all. As Paul writes to the Romans about the division there between these two general positions, he develops a theology of universal significance that seeks a middle position between these views.

MAJOR THEMES

Romans is one of the most important theological documents of all time. Its influence on the course of Christian history and the development of Christian theology is inestimable. It offers several themes:

- fundamental insights into the nature of the human predicament (1:18—3:20);
- God's response to that predicament in the new standing with God offered to all humans through the work of Christ, the utterly gracious character of God's provision, and the consequent requirement of faith as the only way to experience that provision (3:21—4:25);
- security for this life and the future day of judgment that Christians enjoy (5:1—8:39);
- the mysterious and wonderful plan of God to include both Jews and Gentiles in his people (9:1—11:36); and
- the transformed thinking and living that God expects of his redeemed people (12:1—15:13).

Perhaps the single overarching theme of Romans is the gospel, which the letter prominently mentions in both its opening and closing (1:1,2,9,15; 15:16,19) and which is the lead term in Paul's statement of the letter's theme (1:16). The gospel, or Good News, is that God has intervened in our history in order to reestablish his lordship over a created world that has rebelled against him. Paul especially emphasizes that God has offered the opportunity to all human beings, through simple faith in Christ, to be placed in a right standing before God.

Because the division between Jew and Gentile is so important an issue in both Rome and in the broader Christian world, Paul focuses often on the way the gospel includes both groups. On the one hand, the gospel provides for the fulfillment of all God's OT promises to Israel (1:2; 9:1—11:36). On the other hand, the gospel opens the door to Gentiles so that they can become equal participants with faithful Jews in God's new covenant people.

OUTLINE

I. The Letter Opening (1:1–17)
- A. Prescript (1:1–7)
- B. Paul's Longing to Visit Rome (1:8–17)

II. The Heart of the Gospel: Justification by Faith (1:18—4:25)
- A. The Universal Reign of Sin (1:18—3:20)
  - 1. God's Wrath Against Sinful Humanity (1:18–32)
  - 2. Jews Are Accountable to God for Sin (2:1—3:8)
    - a. God's Righteous Judgment (2:1–16)
    - b. The Jews and the Law (2:17–29)
    - c. God's Faithfulness (3:1–8)
  - 3. No One Is Righteous (3:9–20)
- B. Justification by Faith (3:21—4:25)
  - 1. Righteousness Through Faith (3:21–31)
  - 2. Abraham Justified by Faith (4:1–25)

III. The Assurance Provided by the Gospel: The Hope of Salvation (5:1—8:39)
- A. The Hope of Glory (5:1–21)
  - 1. Peace and Hope (5:1–11)
  - 2. Death Through Adam, Life Through Christ (5:12–21)

- B. Freedom From Bondage to Sin (6:1 – 23)
  1. Dead to Sin, Alive in Christ (6:1 – 14)
  2. Slaves to Righteousness (6:15 – 23)
- C. Freedom From Bondage to the Law (7:1 – 25)
  1. Released From the Law, Bound to Christ (7:1 – 6)
  2. The Law and Sin (7:7 – 25)
- D. Assurance of Eternal Life in the Spirit (8:1 – 39)
  1. Life Through the Spirit (8:1 – 17)
  2. Present Suffering and Future Glory (8:18 – 30)
  3. More Than Conquerors (8:31 – 39)

IV. The Defense of the Gospel: The Problem of Israel (9:1 — 11:36)

- A. Paul's Anguish Over Israel (9:1 – 5)
- B. God's Sovereign Choice (9:6 – 29)
- C. Israel's Unbelief (9:30 — 10:21)
- D. The Remnant of Israel (11:1 – 10)
- E. Ingrafted Branches (11:11 – 24)
- F. All Israel Will Be Saved (11:25 – 32)
- G. Doxology (11:33 – 36)

V. The Transforming Power of the Gospel: Christian Conduct (12:1 — 15:13)

- A. A Living Sacrifice (12:1 – 2)
- B. Humble Service in the Body of Christ (12:3 – 8)
- C. Love in Action (12:9 – 21)
- D. Submission to Governing Authorities (13:1 – 7)
- E. Love Fulfills the Law (13:8 – 10)
- F. The Day Is Near (13:11 – 14)
- G. The Weak and the Strong (14:1 — 15:13)
  1. Do Not Judge Each Other (14:1 – 23)
  2. Accept Each Other in Christ (15:1 – 13)

VI. The Letter Closing (15:14 — 16:27)

- A. Paul the Minister to the Gentiles (15:14 – 22)
- B. Paul's Plan to Visit Rome (15:23 – 33)
- C. Personal Greetings (16:1 – 27)

ROMANS

1 Paul, a servant of Christ Jesus, called to be an apostle[a] and set apart[b] for the gospel of God[c]— 2 the
gospel he promised beforehand through his prophets in the Holy Scriptures[d] 3 regarding his Son,
who as to his earthly life[a][e] was a descendant of David, 4 and who through the Spirit of holiness was
appointed the Son of God in power[b] by his resurrection from the dead: Jesus Christ our Lord. 5 Through
him we received grace and apostleship to call all the Gentiles[f] to the obedience that comes from[c] faith[g]
for his name's sake. 6 And you also are among those Gentiles who are called to belong to Jesus Christ.[h]

7 To all in Rome who are loved by God[i] and called to be his holy people:

Grace and peace to you from God our Father and from the Lord Jesus Christ.[j]

1:1 [a] 1Co 1:1 [b] Ac 9:15 [c] 2Co 11:7
1:2 [d] Gal 3:8
1:3 [e] Jn 1:14
1:5 [f] Ac 9:15 [g] Ac 6:7
1:6 [h] Rev 17:14
1:7 [i] Ro 8:39 [j] 1Co 1:3

[a] *3* Or *who according to the flesh* [b] *4* Or *was declared with power to be the Son of God* [c] *5* Or *that is*

1:1–17 *The Letter Opening.* The first section (1:1–17) and last section of Romans (15:14—16:27) provide the literary framework for the letter. The opening includes a salutation (vv. 1–7), a thanksgiving (vv. 8–15), and a statement of the letter's theme (vv. 16–17).

1:1–7 *Prescript.* Ancient letters typically began by briefly identifying the sender and recipients, followed by a greeting (see Acts 15:23: "The apostles and elders, your brothers, To the Gentile believers in Antioch, Syria and Cilicia: Greetings"). Paul elaborates on this simple formula in all his letters but nowhere more so than in Romans—perhaps because he is writing to a church that he has never visited.

1:1 servant. Could also be translated "slave." It stresses that Paul owes allegiance to Christ as his Lord, and it also alludes to the OT "servant of the LORD," a description of important leaders of Israel: Moses (Deut 34:5; Josh 14:7; 2 Kgs 18:12), Joshua (Josh 24:29), Elijah (2 Kgs 10:10) and, especially often, David (e.g., Ps 18 title; see 2 Sam 7:8). **set apart.** Either from the womb of his mother (Gal 1:15; cf. Jer 1:5) or at the time God called him to be an apostle (1 Cor 1:1). **gospel.** "Good News," a key theme in Romans. The language is prominent in the letter's opening (here; vv. 9,15,16) and closing (15:16,19,20; 16:25; see 2:16; 10:15; 11:28). The OT uses "good news" to depict God's intervention on behalf of his people in the last days (Isa 40:9; 52:7 [cited in Rom 10:15]; 61:1; Nah 1:15). But it was also used in Paul's day to refer to the benefits the Roman emperors won for their subjects. Paul's apostolic ministry involves proclaiming that Jesus fulfills OT prophecies of restoration and that Jesus, not the Roman emperor, is the source of our hope and the one who claims our ultimate allegiance.

1:2 through his prophets. An important focus of Romans is the connection between the OT (especially its promises) and the gospel of Christ (3:21; 9:4–6; 11:28; 15:8–12). This verse and 16:26—"made known through the prophetic writings"—bracket the letter as a whole.

1:3 regarding his Son. The Good News is a person: God's Son. **as to his earthly life.** Could also be translated "according to the flesh." Paul uses "flesh" (Greek *sarx*) to denote the state of being human, emphasizing the weakness and susceptibility to sin that typifies what it means to be human after the fall. The word sometimes has the sense of human existence apart from or even in contrast to God (e.g., 8:4–13), but at other times, as here, it refers simply to being human. **descendant of David.** Alludes to Jesus' fulfilling the OT expectation of a "son of David," a king or Messiah, who would liberate and rule God's people (e.g., 2 Sam 7:13–16; Ps 2).

1:4 appointed the Son of God in power. Jesus is eternally God's Son, but his resurrection from the dead enabled him to enter a new phase of existence in which his work on the cross empowers him to save all who believe (see v. 16).

1:5 call all the Gentiles. While committed to preach the gospel to all kinds of people, Paul was called to preach especially to the Gentiles (11:13–14; cf. Gal 2:7). **obedience that comes from faith.** This phrase, also used in 16:26, is another phrase that brackets the argument of Romans (see note on v. 2). Paul may mean that faith is the form that obedience takes in the new era (in other words, "the obedience that is faith"; see 10:16, where Paul says that not all the Israelites "accepted" [translating the same Greek word for "obeyed"] the gospel). But he probably means that faith in Christ naturally leads to a life of dedicated faithfulness to Christ, of obedience to Christ. For Paul, "faith" and "obedience," while always to be distinguished, are inseparable, two sides of the same coin. One cannot have faith in Christ Jesus without acknowledging him as Lord, with all the consequences that follow from that basic commitment.

1:6 called. That is, not "invited," but actually brought into relationship with God by his own sovereign act (what is labeled in theology "the effectual call"; see 8:28).

1:7 his holy people. Greek *hagioi,* meaning "holy ones" or "saints." **holy.** The OT uses this term to describe the Israelites, who were "set apart" to be God's own people (e.g., Lev 20:24,26). The NT often uses this word and related words to denote, not people who are particularly holy in their lifestyle (this is why "saints" can be a misleading English translation), but

1:8 [k]1Co 1:4 [l]Ro 16:19
1:9 [m]2Ti 1:3 [n]Php 1:8
1:10 [o]Ro 15:32
1:11 [p]Ro 15:23
1:13 [q]Ro 15:22,23
1:14 [r]1Co 9:16
1:15 [s]Ro 15:20
1:16 [t]2Ti 1:8 [u]1Co 1:18 [v]Ac 3:26 [w]Ro 2:9,10
1:17 [x]Ro 3:21 [y]Hab 2:4; Gal 3:11; Heb 10:38
1:18 [z]Eph 5:6; Col 3:6

Paul's Longing to Visit Rome

8 First, I thank my God through Jesus Christ for all of you,[k] because your faith is being reported all
over the world.[l] 9 God, whom I serve[m] in my spirit in preaching the gospel of his Son, is my witness[n]
how constantly I remember you 10 in my prayers at all times; and I pray that now at last by God's will
the way may be opened for me to come to you.[o]

11 I long to see you[p] so that I may impart to you some spiritual gift to make you strong— 12 that is,
that you and I may be mutually encouraged by each other's faith. 13 I do not want you to be unaware,
brothers and sisters,[a] that I planned many times to come to you (but have been prevented from doing so
until now)[q] in order that I might have a harvest among you, just as I have had among the other Gentiles.

14 I am obligated[r] both to Greeks and non-Greeks, both to the wise and the foolish. 15 That is why I
am so eager to preach the gospel also to you who are in Rome.[s]

16 For I am not ashamed of the gospel,[t] because it is the power of God[u] that brings salvation to everyone who believes: first to the Jew,[v] then to the Gentile.[w] 17 For in the gospel the righteousness of God
is revealed[x]—a righteousness that is by faith from first to last,[b] just as it is written: "The righteous
will live by faith."[c][y]

God's Wrath Against Sinful Humanity

18 The wrath of God[z] is being revealed from heaven against all the godlessness and wickedness of
people, who suppress the truth by their wickedness, 19 since what may be known about God is plain to

[a] *13* The Greek word for *brothers and sisters* (*adelphoi*) refers here to believers, both men and women, as part of God's family; also in 7:1, 4; 8:12, 29; 10:1; 11:25; 12:1; 15:14, 30; 16:14, 17. [b] *17* Or *is from faith to faith* [c] *17* Hab. 2:4

all those people whom God has called to belong to him (v. 6). Status, not behavior, is in view (see "Holiness," p. 2676).

1:8–17 *Paul's Longing to Visit Rome.* As he usually does in his letters, Paul gives thanks for his readers (vv. 8–15) before announcing the theme of the letter (vv. 16–17).

1:8 thank. Paul's letters usually feature a thanksgiving in the opening section. **all over the world.** That is, across the Roman Empire of Paul's day.

1:11 spiritual gift. Either a particular one that Paul hopes to bestow on the Roman believers (12:6–8) or a spiritual benefit that Paul's ministry in Rome will convey.

1:12 mutually. Writing to a church that he did not establish and has never visited, Paul is appropriately humble.

1:13 prevented. Probably by pressing ministry needs in the eastern Mediterranean, where Paul has been preaching the gospel for over a decade (see 15:19).

1:14 Greeks. The cultured people in Paul's world who often spoke Greek and followed Greek ways of life. **non-Greeks.** Barbarians (Greek *barbaros*).

1:16 salvation. Not only conversion but also ultimate deliverance from sin, death, and judgment (5:9–10; 13:11). **everyone who believes.** Salvation is offered to all people on the same grounds. An important theme in Romans is including Gentiles as equal participants with Jews in God's new covenant (3:23–24,29–30; 4:9–12,16–17; 9:24–26,30–31; 10:4,11–13; 15:8–12). **first to the Jew.** Paul insists that Jews still have a prominent place in God's plan of salvation. God directed his word to them first (3:2) and made irrevocable promises to them (9:4–5; 11:28).

1:17 righteousness of God. A key concept in Romans (3:5,21,22,25,26; 10:3 [twice]; cf. Matt 6:33; 2 Cor 5:21; Jas 1:20). Paul takes this language from the OT, where "righteousness of God" denotes God doing what is right or acting to put things right (e.g., 1 Sam 12:7; Pss 7:9; 145:17; Jer 9:24; 11:20; Mic 6:5; see note on Rom 3:21). In dependence on some key prophetic texts (see especially Isa 46:13; 51:5–8), Paul uses the phrase in the latter sense here. In the OT God promised that he would put right, or vindicate, his people Israel (Deut 32:35,43; Pss 79:10; 135:14; Jer 51:36); now, Paul announces, anyone who believes (v. 16) can experience God's vindication. This vindication is a forensic, or judicial, act that confers on believers the status of "righteousness." While God acts in the gospel of Christ to put people in the right, they experience the benefits of God's activity only when they respond in faith. **by faith from first to last.** Another (less likely) translation would be "from the faith (or faithfulness) of Christ to the faith of believers" (see note on 3:22). **The righteous will live by faith.** Or "the one who is *righteous by faith* will live." See Hab 2:4. Paul develops the idea of being "righteous by faith" in 3:21—4:25 and the idea of "life" in chs. 5–8.

1:18—4:25 *The Heart of the Gospel: Justification by Faith.* The gospel proclaims that human beings, while locked up under sin, can enter into a saving relationship with God through faith in Jesus Christ.

1:18—3:20 *The Universal Reign of Sin.* Before elaborating on "the righteousness of God ... given through faith" (3:21–22) in 3:21—4:25, Paul explains why God has taken the extraordinary step of sending his own Son in human form (1:3) to bring good news to the world (1:2,16): human beings are locked up under sin (3:9). Both Gentiles (1:18–32) and Jews (2:1—3:8) have failed to respond to God's gracious revelation and thus are subject to God's wrath.

1:18–32 *God's Wrath Against Sinful Humanity.* Paul paints a dismal picture of the situation of all human beings (particularly Gentiles) who refuse to worship the true God in order to worship gods of their own making. God reacts (note the threefold "God gave them over" in vv. 24,26,28) by consigning people to the sins they have chosen—an expression of his wrath (v. 18).

1:18 wrath. The inevitable reaction of a holy God against sin in any form. The OT describes outbreaks of God's wrath within history (e.g., Exod 32:10–12; Num 11:1; Jer 21:3–7) and predicts a final outpouring of wrath at the end of history (e.g., Isa 63:1–6; Mic 5:10–15). **is being revealed.** The ultimate manifestation of God's wrath often features in Paul's teaching (2:5), but this refers to the present condition of human beings, who turn away from God's revelation: they stand condemned because of their "godlessness and wickedness."

1:19–23 God has provided in the world he created evidence of his "eternal power and divine nature" (v. 20). This "natural revelation" is available

them, because God has made it plain to them.[a] [20]For since the creation of the world God's invisible
qualities—his eternal power and divine nature—have been clearly seen, being understood from what
has been made,[b] so that people are without excuse.

[21]For although they knew God, they neither glorified him as God nor gave thanks to him, but their
thinking became futile and their foolish hearts were darkened.[c] [22]Although they claimed to be wise,
they became fools[d] [23]and exchanged the glory of the immortal God for images[e] made to look like a
mortal human being and birds and animals and reptiles.

[24]Therefore God gave them over[f] in the sinful desires of their hearts to sexual impurity for the degrading of their bodies with one another.[g] [25]They exchanged the truth about God for a lie,[h] and worshiped and served created things[i] rather than the Creator—who is forever praised.[j] Amen.

[26]Because of this, God gave them over[k] to shameful lusts.[l] Even their women exchanged natural
sexual relations for unnatural ones.[m] [27]In the same way the men also abandoned natural relations
with women and were inflamed with lust for one another. Men committed shameful acts with other
men, and received in themselves the due penalty for their error.[n]

[28]Furthermore, just as they did not think it worthwhile to retain the knowledge of God, so God gave
them over[o] to a depraved mind, so that they do what ought not to be done. [29]They have become filled
with every kind of wickedness, evil, greed and depravity. They are full of envy, murder, strife, deceit and
malice. They are gossips,[p] [30]slanderers, God-haters, insolent, arrogant and boastful; they invent ways
of doing evil; they disobey their parents;[q] [31]they have no understanding, no fidelity, no love,[r] no mercy.
[32]Although they know God's righteous decree that those who do such things deserve death,[s] they not
only continue to do these very things but also approve[t] of those who practice them.

God's Righteous Judgment

2 You, therefore, have no excuse,[u] you who pass judgment on someone else, for at whatever point
you judge another, you are condemning yourself, because you who pass judgment do the same
things.[v] [2]Now we know that God's judgment against those who do such things is based on truth. [3]So

1:19 [a]Ac 14:17
1:20 [b]Ps 19:1-6
1:21 [c]Jer 2:5; Eph 4:17,18
1:22 [d]1Co 1:20,27
1:23 [e]Ps 106:20; Jer 2:11; Ac 17:29
1:24 [f]Eph 4:19 [g]1Pe 4:3
1:25 [h]Isa 44:20 [i]Jer 10:14 [j]Ro 9:5
1:26 [k]ver 24,28 [l]1Th 4:5 [m]Lev 18:22,23
1:27 [n]Lev 18:22; 20:13
1:28 [o]ver 24,26
1:29 [p]2Co 12:20
1:30 [q]2Ti 3:2
1:31 [r]2Ti 3:3
1:32 [s]Ro 6:23 [t]Ps 50:18; Lk 11:48; Ac 8:1; 22:20
2:1 [u]Ro 1:20 [v]2Sa 12:5-7; Mt 7:1,2

to all human beings, but because of sin, people turn away from this evidence of God's existence. Like the people of Israel when they fashioned the golden calf to worship (Exod 32; cf. Jer 2:11), human beings have "exchanged the glory of the immortal God for images made to look like a mortal human being and birds and animals and reptiles" (v. 23). The threefold division of animals alludes to the creation account (Gen 1:28). In the OT idols sometimes took the form of animals, but an idol is anything that a human puts in place of God, and idols take an infinite variety of forms.

1:24,26,28 God gave them over. In response to humans' deciding to put idols in the place of the only God, God hands people over to the consequences of their sin. Following the OT and the pattern of Jewish condemnations of the Gentile world (in the Apocrypha see The Wisdom of Solomon 13–15), Paul singles out sexual sins as particularly clear evidence of this turning away from God.

1:25 worshiped and served created things rather than the Creator. Succinctly describes the fundamental human sin of idolatry.

1:26 Paul again follows OT and Jewish tradition in singling out homosexual relations as an especially clear indication of human sinfulness (see especially Gen 19:1–28; Lev 18:22; 20:13; Deut 23:17–18; in the Apocrypha, see The Wisdom of Solomon 14:24–31; in the OT pseudepigrapha, see Sibylline Oracles 3.594–600). **unnatural ones.** Could also be translated "those that are against nature," where "nature" refers to the created world as God intends it to be (see also "abandoned natural relations" in v. 27). In making humans beings male and female (Gen 1:27; 5:2; cf. Gen 2:24), God manifests his intention for human sexual relations.

1:27 due penalty for their error. When human beings turn from God's intention for them, they appropriately become subject to God's judgment. This judgment can take many different forms, but the ultimate consequence of all sin is "death" (v. 32) or the "wrath of God" (v. 18).

1:28 think it worthwhile ... depraved. Paul uses a play on words to emphasize the equivalence between human sin and God's response: people chose not to "approve" of God, so he condemned them to an "unapproved" mind—that is, a "worthless" way of thinking that does not conform to God's own purposes and values. The many forms of human sin, which Paul illustrates in vv. 28b–31, are rooted in sinful minds. Fundamental to the new life, therefore, is renewing those very minds (12:2).

1:32 they know God's righteous decree. In addition to knowing that God exists and that he is the powerful Creator (v. 20), people also have an inbuilt moral sense that tells them that certain acts deserve God's judgment. **approve.** Approving of sins to which one is not especially prone is in some ways worse than committing the sin itself. Paul may again be reflecting OT ideas and popular Jewish teaching; cf. in the OT pseudepigrapha, Testament of Asher 6:2: "The two-faced are doubly punished because they both practice evil and approve of others who practice it; they imitate the spirits of error and join in the struggle against mankind."

2:1—3:8 *Jews Are Accountable to God for Sin.* Having indicted Gentiles for sinfully rejecting God's revelation, Paul shows that Jews have also turned from the even clearer revelation that God gave them.

2:1–16 *God's Righteous Judgment.* Jews, who typically stand in judgment over Gentiles, are in reality doing "the same things" (vv. 1,3) and are therefore also subject to God's wrath. It is this "doing," or "works," that will be the criterion of judgment for both Jew and Gentile.

2:1 You. Singular in Greek. Paul uses an ancient literary style called the diatribe, in which writers use a fictional dialogue between themselves and the proponent of another viewpoint to instruct and persuade their audience. Paul may be referring to any self-righteous person but is probably referring to Jews who assumed that God's covenant with them meant automatic protection from judgment. **the same things.** Also in v. 3; in addition to the sins in 1:28b–31, perhaps this includes the Jews' idolatrous tendency to prize the law so highly (2:17–24; Phil 3:3–10).

2:2–4 Both the OT (e.g., Jer 7:1–29) and NT (e.g., Matt 3:7–10)

2:4 [w]Ro 9:23; Eph 1:7, 18; 2:7 [x]Ro 11:22 [y]Ro 3:25 [z]Ex 34:6 [a]2Pe 3:9
2:5 [b]Jude 6
2:6 [c]Ps 62:12; Mt 16:27
2:7 [d]ver 10 [e]1Co 15:53,54
2:8 [f]2Th 2:12
2:9 [g]1Pe 4:17
2:10 [h]ver 9
2:11 [i]Ac 10:34
2:12 [j]Ro 3:19; 1Co 9:20,21
2:13 [k]Jas 1:22,23,25
2:14 [l]Ac 10:35
2:16 [m]Ecc 12:14 [n]Ac 10:42 [o]Ro 16:25
2:17 [p]ver 23; Mic 3:11; Ro 9:4

when you, a mere human being, pass judgment on them and yet do the same things, do you think you
will escape God's judgment? [4]Or do you show contempt for the riches[w] of his kindness,[x] forbearance[y]
and patience,[z] not realizing that God's kindness is intended to lead you to repentance?[a]

[5]But because of your stubbornness and your unrepentant heart, you are storing up wrath against
yourself for the day of God's wrath, when his righteous judgment[b] will be revealed. [6]God "will repay
each person according to what they have done."[a][c] [7]To those who by persistence in doing good seek
glory, honor[d] and immortality,[e] he will give eternal life. [8]But for those who are self-seeking and who
reject the truth and follow evil,[f] there will be wrath and anger. [9]There will be trouble and distress
for every human being who does evil: first for the Jew, then for the Gentile;[g] [10]but glory, honor and
peace for everyone who does good: first for the Jew, then for the Gentile.[h] [11]For God does not show
favoritism.[i]

[12]All who sin apart from the law will also perish apart from the law, and all who sin under the law[j]
will be judged by the law. [13]For it is not those who hear the law who are righteous in God's sight, but it
is those who obey[k] the law who will be declared righteous. [14](Indeed, when Gentiles, who do not have
the law, do by nature things required by the law,[l] they are a law for themselves, even though they do
not have the law. [15]They show that the requirements of the law are written on their hearts, their consciences also bearing witness, and their thoughts sometimes accusing them and at other times even
defending them.) [16]This will take place on the day when God judges people's secrets[m] through Jesus
Christ,[n] as my gospel[o] declares.

The Jews and the Law

[17]Now you, if you call yourself a Jew; if you rely on the law and boast in God;[p] [18]if you know his will
and approve of what is superior because you are instructed by the law; [19]if you are convinced that you
are a guide for the blind, a light for those who are in the dark, [20]an instructor of the foolish, a teacher

[a] *6* Psalm 62:12; Prov. 24:12

condemn the tendency of Jews to think that their special relationship with God will shield them from judgment.

2:5 day of God's wrath. While God's wrath is manifested in the present (1:18), it will be decisively and universally revealed on the future day of judgment (Isa 13:13; Zeph 1:15; 1 Thess 1:10).

2:6–11 This is a particularly clear example of "chiasm" (the word comes from the Greek letter *chi*, formed like our *X*), a literary device in which parallel lines correspond in an *X*-pattern such as *a-b-c / c´-b´-a´*:

a God judges everyone the same (v. 6)
  b Life is the reward for doing good (v. 7)
    c Wrath is the penalty for evil (v. 8)
    c´ Wrath for doing evil (v. 9)
  b´ Life for doing good (v. 10)
a´ God shows no favoritism (v. 11)

2:6 Paul quotes the OT (Ps 62:12 or Prov 24:12; see Eccl 12:14; Hos 12:2) to make clear that, for those who are not in Christ, God will judge them according to what they have actually done.

2:7 Paul's claim that people can gain "eternal life" by "doing good" is the first of several similar assertions in this chapter (vv. 10,13,26–27). He may refer to Christians, whose "doing," or "works," will provide critical and necessary evidence of their faith and the transforming power of the Spirit on the day of judgment (2 Cor 5:10; Jas 2:14–26). Or he may refer to people in general, arguing that sincerely and consistently doing good will bring eternal life. But his subsequent argument shows that sin's power prevents every human from living up to this standard (3:9).

2:9 first for the Jew. The precedence of Jews, a recurring theme in the letter (e.g., v. 10; 1:16), involves their privilege in receiving the "words of God" (3:2)—whether the outcome is judgment or salvation.

2:12 law ... law ... law ... law. Refers in Paul's writings basically to the commanding element of the Torah that God gave to his people Israel through Moses at Sinai (1 Cor 9:8–9; see Rom 5:13–14; Gal 3:17). So people who sin "apart from the law" are Gentiles, who did not receive the Mosaic law.

2:13 obey. Jewish teaching stressed the importance of doing the law: "Not the expounding [of the law] is the chief thing, but the doing [of it]" (Mishnah *'Abot* 1:17; see Jas 1:22). **declared righteous.** See note on v. 7.

2:14–15 These "Gentiles" (v. 14) may be Gentile Christians, who, though not having the law "by nature" (i.e., by birth), have the law of God "written on their hearts" (v. 15) in accordance with the prophecy of Jer 31:31–34. Alternatively, they may be non-Christian Gentiles who, while not having *the* law (of Moses), have knowledge of God's general moral will in their consciences and so, like Jews, have a kind of "law" ("a law for themselves," v. 14). By putting vv. 14–15 in parentheses, the NIV leans toward this second view: Paul qualifies the absolute distinction between those who have the law and those who do not in v. 12. Paul uses "defending" (v. 15), not "saving," because only God's grace in the gospel of Christ saves. If Paul is referring to non-Christian Gentiles, he means that their consciences sometimes witness that they have done things that God requires; at the same time, however, their consciences are also "accusing them" (v. 15).

2:16 people's secrets. The hidden things of the heart. "The LORD does not look at the things people look at. People look at the outward appearance, but the LORD looks at the heart" (1 Sam 16:7; cf. Ps 139:1–2; Jer 17:10).

2:17–29 *The Jews and the Law.* Addressing his dialogue partner explicitly for the first time as a "Jew" (see note on v. 1), Paul claims that the Jews' reliance on the law (vv. 17–24) and circumcision (vv. 25–29) are futile because they fail to keep the law.

2:17–20 The list of things that Jews boast in are legitimate sources of pride. God entered into relationship with Israel alone among all the nations, gave them his law, and set them out as a "light" (v. 19) to the nations (e.g., Isa 49:6).

of little children, because you have in the law the embodiment of knowledge and truth— [21]you, then, who teach others, do you not teach yourself? You who preach against stealing, do you steal?[q] [22]You who say that people should not commit adultery, do you commit adultery? You who abhor idols, do you rob temples?[r] [23]You who boast in the law,[s] do you dishonor God by breaking the law? [24]As it is written: "God's name is blasphemed among the Gentiles because of you."[a][t]

The half shekel was used to pay the temple tax, and not paying it may have been considered "robbing" the temple (Rom 2:22). This first-century coin was found at the temple mount in 2008.

Z. Radovan/www.BibleLandPictures.com

[25]Circumcision has value if you observe the law,[u] but if you break the law, you have become as though you had not been circumcised.[v] [26]So then, if those who are not circumcised keep the law's requirements,[w] will they not be regarded as though they were circumcised?[x] [27]The one who is not circumcised physically and yet obeys the law will condemn you[y] who, even though you have the[b] written code and circumcision, are a lawbreaker.

[28]A person is not a Jew who is one only outwardly,[z] nor is circumcision merely outward and physical.[a] [29]No, a person is a Jew who is one inwardly; and circumcision is circumcision of the heart, by the Spirit,[b] not by the written code.[c] Such a person's praise is not from other people, but from God.[d]

God's Faithfulness

3 What advantage, then, is there in being a Jew, or what value is there in circumcision? [2]Much in every way! First of all, the Jews have been entrusted with the very words of God.[e]

[3]What if some were unfaithful?[f] Will their unfaithfulness nullify God's faithfulness?[g] [4]Not at all! Let God be true,[h] and every human being a liar.[i] As it is written:

2:21 [q]Mt 23:3,4
2:22 [r]Ac 19:37
2:23 [s]ver 17
2:24 [t]Isa 52:5; Eze 36:22
2:25 [u]Gal 5:3 [v]Jer 4:4
2:26 [w]Ro 8:4 [x]1Co 7:19
2:27 [y]Mt 12:41,42
2:28 [z]Mt 3:9; Jn 8:39; Ro 9:6,7 [a]Gal 6:15
2:29 [b]Php 3:3; Col 2:11 [c]Ro 7:6 [d]Jn 5:44; 1Co 4:5; 2Co 10:18; 1Th 2:4; 1Pe 3:4
3:2 [e]Dt 4:8; Ps 147:19
3:3 [f]Heb 4:2 [g]2Ti 2:13
3:4 [h]Jn 3:33 [i]Ps 116:11

[a] *24* Isaiah 52:5 (see Septuagint); Ezek. 36:20,22 [b] *27* Or *who, by means of a*

2:21 you, then, who teach others, do you not teach yourself? Although they have the law and teach it to others, the Jews have not consistently obeyed that law (v. 13). Paul is not claiming that all Jews "steal" (here), "commit adultery" (v. 22), and "rob temples" (v. 22). In dependence on OT prophetic denunciations of Israel (e.g., Jer 7:9), Paul cites examples of behavior that starkly contrast with the demands of the law God gave them.

2:24 Paul quotes from Isa 52:5, which refers to the way Israel's exile and oppression by Gentiles have led people to discredit God himself. In an ironic twist, Paul applies it to Jews failing to live up to their covenant obligations.

2:25 Circumcision. God instructed Abraham to circumcise every male in the Israelite household as "the sign of the covenant" (Gen 17:11) that God entered into with Abraham and his descendants (Gen 17:9–14). Circumcision became an important distinguishing mark of the people of Israel, gaining special prominence in the aftermath of the attempt of the pagan king Antiochus IV to stamp out the Jewish religion (167–164 BC). Many Jews in Paul's day lived where they had to struggle to preserve their identity among pagans, so they emphasized outward distinguishing marks of their Jewish faith such as circumcision, dietary rules, and Sabbath observance. **has value if you observe the law.** Again, "doing" is what counts in God's judgment of humans (see note on v. 7).

2:26 not circumcised. Paul again (see note on v. 7) may refer to Christian Gentiles, who "fulfill" the law through faith and the Spirit (v. 29; 8:4). Alternatively, he may simply be giving the flip side of v. 25: just as Jews who disobey the law lose their status as God's people, so Gentiles who obey it are given that status. Whether there are Gentiles who, in fact, do fulfill the law is another question.

2:27,29 the written code. Or "letter" (Greek *gramma*). Refers to the law of Moses, exemplified by the Ten Commandments, "written" in letters on the stone tablets that Moses received from God (7:6; Exod 31:18; cf. especially 2 Cor 3:3).

2:29 circumcision of the heart, by the Spirit, not by the written code. Moses called on Israel to "circumcise [their] hearts" (Deut 10:16; see Jer 4:4), i.e., transform themselves in their inner persons so that they might obey God consistently. Ultimately, however, the human heart is so hard that only God can circumcise his people's hearts. Moses therefore predicted that God would one day do just that (Deut 30:6), and the prophets also stressed that God would one day replace his peoples' "heart[s] of stone" with "heart[s] of flesh" by means of the work of his Spirit (Ezek 36:26–27). These promises are fulfilled in the new covenant inaugurated by Jesus' death and resurrection and marked by the coming of God's Spirit on his people with power (Acts 2:1–41).

3:1–8 *God's Faithfulness.* While Jews and Gentiles are on the same footing with respect to God's ultimate judgment, Jews continue to enjoy the advantage of possessing detailed revelation from God in the OT. Their failure to respond appropriately to that revelation does not cancel God's faithfulness to his promises—including his promise to punish his people for their sin.

3:1 Following the diatribe style (see note on 2:1), Paul uses rhetorical questions to advance his argument. Ch. 2 could suggest that Jews no longer have any "advantage" over Gentiles.

3:2 First of all. Paul breaks off his list of advantages to comment on the implications of Jews being "entrusted with the very words of God." See 9:4–5 for a longer list of Jewish privileges.

3:4 proved right. Paul quotes David's confession of his sin of adultery with Bathsheba (Ps 51:4; see 2 Sam 11) to show that God is "in the right" when he punishes his people for their sin.

3:4 [j]Ps 51:4
3:5 [k]Ro 6:19; Gal 3:15
3:6 [l]Ge 18:25
3:7 [m]ver 4
3:8 [n]Ro 6:1
3:9 [o]ver 19,23; Gal 3:22
3:12 [p]Ps 14:1-3
3:13 [q]Ps 5:9 [r]Ps 140:3
3:14 [s]Ps 10:7
3:18 [t]Ps 36:1
3:19 [u]Jn 10:34 [v]Ro 2:12

"So that you may be proved right when you speak
and prevail when you judge."[a][j]

5 But if our unrighteousness brings out God's righteousness more clearly, what shall we say? That
God is unjust in bringing his wrath on us? (I am using a human argument.)[k] 6 Certainly not! If that
were so, how could God judge the world?[l] 7 Someone might argue, "If my falsehood enhances God's
truthfulness and so increases his glory,[m] why am I still condemned as a sinner?" 8 Why not say—as
some slanderously claim that we say—"Let us do evil that good may result"?[n] Their condemnation
is just!

No One Is Righteous

9 What shall we conclude then? Do we have any advantage? Not at all! For we have already made the
charge that Jews and Gentiles alike are all under the power of sin.[o] 10 As it is written:

"There is no one righteous, not even one;
11 there is no one who understands;
there is no one who seeks God.
12 All have turned away,
they have together become worthless;
there is no one who does good,
not even one."[b][p]
13 "Their throats are open graves;
their tongues practice deceit."[c][q]
"The poison of vipers is on their lips."[d][r]
14 "Their mouths are full of cursing and bitterness."[e][s]
15 "Their feet are swift to shed blood;
16 ruin and misery mark their ways,
17 and the way of peace they do not know."[f]
18 "There is no fear of God before their eyes."[g][t]

19 Now we know that whatever the law says,[u] it says to those who are under the law,[v] so that every
mouth may be silenced and the whole world held accountable to God. 20 Therefore no one will be de-

[a] *4* Psalm 51:4 [b] *12* Psalms 14:1-3; 53:1-3; Eccles. 7:20 [c] *13* Psalm 5:9 [d] *13* Psalm 140:3
[e] *14* Psalm 10:7 (see Septuagint) [f] *17* Isaiah 59:7,8 [g] *18* Psalm 36:1

3:5 God's righteousness. Can refer to God's putting his people "in the right" (see 1:17 and note) but also, as here, to his acting in accordance with his own nature and revelation. God is "in the right," or just, even when he inflicts wrath on his people because, as a holy God, he must punish sinfulness.
3:6 judge the world. See Gen 18:25: "Will not the Judge of all the earth do right?"
3:8 as some slanderously claim. As the "apostle to the Gentiles" (11:13), Paul was thrust into the center of controversy, and false rumors about his teaching were evidently circulating in Rome. **Let us do evil that good may result.** Paul's claim that a person is justified by faith alone sounds to some as if he is opening the door to unrestrained behavior. He simply dismisses this unfounded charge here, but he deals with it in more detail in ch. 6.
3:9–20 *No One Is Righteous.* Paul's indictment of both Gentiles (1:18–32) and Jews (2:1—3:8) climaxes in this summary that portrays both as helpless under sin's power (v. 9) and thus unable to escape from its clutches by their own efforts (v. 20).
3:9 Do we have any advantage? "We" probably refers to Jews. Even though Jews have a certain "advantage" in possessing "the very words of God" (v. 2), they do not have any ultimate advantage over Gentiles when it comes to salvation and damnation. **under the power of sin.** Throughout Romans, Paul refers to sin in the singular to make the point that the many sins people commit stem from a single, basic fact: they are helpless slaves to sin's power. This fundamental human predicament is matched by God's work in Christ to break through sin and liberate humans, who are enslaved to it (3:24; 6:1–23).
3:10–18 Paul uses five quotations from different parts of the OT to underline that sin is universal. It is possible, though by no means certain, that early Christians gathered together this series of references before Paul's ministry began. It echoes a Jewish practice called "pearl-stringing," citing OT texts on a particular theme. The series is framed by quotations using the opening words "there is no" to show that all people, without exception, are caught in sin's power (vv. 10,11,12,18). In between, quotations focus on the evidence of sin in human speaking (vv. 13–14) and general lifestyle (vv. 15–17).
3:19 law. The entire OT. Paul usually uses "law" to refer to the commandments given to Israel at Sinai, but the prominence of this body of legislation for the life of Israel meant that the "law" could also refer to the OT Scriptures as a whole (1 Cor 9:8–9; 14:21,34; Gal 4:21b–22). **those who are under the law.** Jews, to whom God gave the Mosaic law (2:12). **the whole world held accountable to God.** If the OT brands God's own people as sinful, how much more are Gentiles also guilty? See "Law," p. 2649.
3:20 works of the law. Whatever a human being does in obeying God's

clared righteous in God's sight by the works of the law;[w] rather, through the law we become conscious
of our sin.[x]

Righteousness Through Faith

21 But now apart from the law the righteousness of God[y] has been made known, to which the Law
and the Prophets testify.[z] 22 This righteousness is given through faith[a] in[a] Jesus Christ to all who believe.
There is no difference between Jew and Gentile,[b] 23 for all have sinned and fall short of the glory of God,
24 and all are justified freely by his grace[c] through the redemption[d] that came by Christ Jesus. 25 God
presented Christ as a sacrifice of atonement,[b][e] through the shedding of his blood[f]—to be received by
faith. He did this to demonstrate his righteousness, because in his forbearance he had left the sins committed beforehand unpunished[g]— 26 he did it to demonstrate his righteousness at the present time, so
as to be just and the one who justifies those who have faith in Jesus.
27 Where, then, is boasting?[h] It is excluded. Because of what law? The law that requires works? No,

[a] *22* Or *through the faithfulness of* [b] *25* The Greek for *sacrifice of atonement* refers to the atonement cover on the ark of the covenant (see Lev. 16:15,16).

3:20 [w] Ac 13:39; Gal 2:16 [x] Ro 7:7
3:21 [y] Ro 1:17; 9:30 [z] Ac 10:43
3:22 [a] Ro 9:30 [b] Ro 10:12; Gal 3:28; Col 3:11
3:24 [c] Ro 4:16; Eph 2:8 [d] Eph 1:7,14; Col 1:14; Heb 9:12
3:25 [e] 1Jn 4:10 [f] Heb 9:12,14 [g] Ac 17:30
3:27 [h] Ro 2:17,23; 4:2; 1Co 1:29-31; Eph 2:9

law (v. 28; Gal 2:16 [three times]; 3:2,5,10). **through the law.** The law of Moses. But the relationship between "works of the law" and "works" in general elsewhere in Romans (4:2,4,6; 9:12; 11:6) indicates that Paul's claim includes ultimately anything humans do. God's verdict of "righteous" cannot come through human activity of any kind, but only by faith (3:22; 4:1–8).

3:21—4:25 *Justification by Faith.* Paul develops the theme of God's righteousness (3:21–26) announced in 1:17, and he elaborates on why faith is important, first generally (3:27–31) and then with reference to Abraham (4:1–25).

3:21–31 *Righteousness Through Faith.* In one of the most important theological sections in the Bible, Paul explains that (1) God's righteousness involves his completely gracious justification of any person who puts their faith in Christ; (2) this justification is based on Christ's sacrificial death; and (3) the nature of Christ's death enables God to remain just even as he justifies sinful humans. Paul then elaborates on the importance of faith, a key element in vv. 21–26.

3:21 But now. With these two simple words, Paul conveys the incredibly good news that a new era, in which "the righteousness of God has been made known," has begun. **apart from the law ... to which the Law and the Prophets testify.** In a balance typical of Romans, Paul insists that God's new work in Christ breaks new ground in God's plan (it moves beyond the era of the old covenant and its law) but is what God has all along planned to do (the whole OT testifies to it).

3:22 faith in. Could also be translated "the faithfulness of" (see NIV text note), referring to Jesus' obedience to the will of the Father in going to the cross for sinful humanity (5:19; Phil 2:8). But Paul's emphasis throughout this context of human believing (as in the case of Abraham in ch. 4) favors the NIV rendering. In this case, Paul adds the phrase "to all who believe" to emphasize a key point in his argument: as all humans are caught up in sin (v. 23; 1:18—3:20), so God's righteousness is available for all humans, Jew and Gentile alike (1:16).

3:24 all are justified. "All" is not in the Greek text but is carried over from v. 23. Justification is an important Pauline theological teaching. Paul uses the verb for "justify" (Greek *dikaioō*) 25 times, primarily in Romans (15 times) and Galatians (6 times). In addition, many of the occurrences of the related word for "righteousness" (Greek *dikaiosynē*) relate to the doctrine of justification (Paul uses this noun 56 times, 32 times in Romans and 4 times in Galatians). "Justify" language is taken from the world of a court of law and refers to a declaration of status, not to moral transformation. Justification has a negative and a positive side: God no longer holds our sins against us in his judgment (4:8), and he gives us a righteous standing before him. **freely by his grace.** Whatever God does for us is done in grace (4:4–5; 5:1). **grace.** "Grace" is a thread that runs throughout Romans. The display of God's grace in the gospel is rooted in the character of God himself. As 4:4–5 makes clear, no human can ever make a claim on God because of anything they have done (11:5–6). A holy God can never be indebted to his creatures. Whatever he gives us, therefore, he gives "freely" and without compulsion (4:16). Not only is grace needed at the beginning of the Christian life, but believers "stand" in grace (5:2): we live in the realm in which grace "reign[s]" (5:21; see 5:15,17,20). That reign of grace, Paul hastens to clarify, does not absolve us of the need to live righteously before God; rather, it gives us the power to do so (6:1,14–15,17). So interwoven is grace in this new era of salvation that Paul can even speak of his own ministry (1:5; 12:3; 15:15) and the ministry of believers generally (12:6) as a matter of "grace." It is quite appropriate, therefore, that Romans is framed by prayers that God's people might fully experience this grace of God (1:7; 16:20). **redemption.** In Paul's day referred to paying money to secure a slave's freedom. In Christ, God has paid a price to secure the release of every believer from sin's slavery (v. 9). The OT uses "redemption" to refer to the exodus: God intervened to release his people Israel from their slavery in Egypt (Ps 111:9; cf. Ex 6:6; 15:13). Christ's death provides a new, spiritual "exodus" for the people of God.

3:25 sacrifice of atonement. Greek *hilastērion*, which refers to the "atonement cover" in Heb 9:5 and most of its occurrences in the Greek OT. This "atonement cover" was a plate that covered the ark of the covenant law in the inner sanctuary (the Most Holy Place) of the OT tabernacle. It figures prominently in the Day of Atonement ritual (Lev 16:2,13–15) and came to signify the place where God deals with his people's sins. Christ, on the cross, is now the final and definitive "place" where God deals with the sins of his people. As in the OT ritual, Christ's sacrifice is propitiatory; i.e., it functions, among other things, to satisfy God's wrath against sin (1:18; 2:5; 1 John 2:2). **his righteousness.** Perhaps, as in vv. 21–22, God's act of putting people "in the right" or even God's covenant faithfulness. But more likely, it refers to God's own attribute of "justness": God's failure to punish past sins with the wrath they deserved (as in the case of the OT believers) created the perception that God was not being fully just, a problem that Christ's sacrificial death on behalf of all God's people fully answers.

3:26 just and the one who justifies. Succinctly summarizes the two key themes in the paragraph: Christ's sacrificial death enables God to (1) justify sinful people (2) while he remains just.

3:27 law that requires faith. Perhaps the OT law, which, in the broad sense of the Pentateuch, calls for faith (e.g., Gen 15:6; cf. Rom 4); or perhaps, in a play on words, the "law," or "principle," of faith (v. 28) in contrast to the law of Moses that calls for works.

3:28 [i]ver 20,21; Ac 13:39; Eph 2:9
3:29 [j]Ro 9:24
3:30 [k]Gal 3:8
4:2 [l]1Co 1:31
4:3 [m]ver 5,9,22; Ge 15:6; Gal 3:6; Jas 2:23
4:4 [n]Ro 11:6
4:8 [o]Ps 32:1,2; 2Co 5:19
4:9 [p]Ro 3:30 [q]ver 3
4:11 [r]Ge 17:10,11 [s]ver 16,17; Lk 19:9 [t]Ro 3:22

because of the law that requires faith. [28]For we maintain that a person is justified by faith apart from
the works of the law.[i] [29]Or is God the God of Jews only? Is he not the God of Gentiles too? Yes, of Gentiles
too,[j] [30]since there is only one God, who will justify the circumcised by faith and the uncircumcised
through that same faith.[k] [31]Do we, then, nullify the law by this faith? Not at all! Rather, we uphold
the law.

Abraham Justified by Faith

4 What then shall we say that Abraham, our forefather according to the flesh, discovered in this matter? [2]If, in fact, Abraham was justified by works, he had something to boast about—but not before
God.[l] [3]What does Scripture say? "Abraham believed God, and it was credited to him as righteousness."[a][m]
[4]Now to the one who works, wages are not credited as a gift[n] but as an obligation. [5]However, to the
one who does not work but trusts God who justifies the ungodly, their faith is credited as righteousness.
[6]David says the same thing when he speaks of the blessedness of the one to whom God credits righteousness apart from works:

> [7]"Blessed are those
> whose transgressions are forgiven,
> whose sins are covered.
> [8]Blessed is the one
> whose sin the Lord will never count against them."[b][o]

[9]Is this blessedness only for the circumcised, or also for the uncircumcised?[p] We have been saying that Abraham's faith was credited to him as righteousness.[q] [10]Under what circumstances was it
credited? Was it after he was circumcised, or before? It was not after, but before! [11]And he received
circumcision as a sign, a seal of the righteousness that he had by faith while he was still uncircumcised.[r] So then, he is the father[s] of all who believe[t] but have not been circumcised, in order that
righteousness might be credited to them. [12]And he is then also the father of the circumcised who not
only are circumcised but who also follow in the footsteps of the faith that our father Abraham had
before he was circumcised.

[a] *3* Gen. 15:6; also in verse 22 [b] *8* Psalm 32:1,2

3:28 works of the law. See note on v. 20.

3:30 there is only one God. Paul argues that the central Jewish confession in the "oneness" of God, the "Shema" (Deut 6:4; cf. 1 Cor 8:4; Gal 3:20; Jas 2:19), means that Gentiles and Jews have access to this one God—and on the same basis: by faith.

3:31 we uphold the law. Paul's teaching may uphold the law by (1) reasserting its condemning function (vv. 19–20), (2) insisting that the OT testifies to justification by faith (v. 21; see Gen 15:6; cf. Rom 4), or (3) maintaining the need for the law's commands to be fulfilled—by Christ, our representative (v. 25; see 8:4).

4:1–25 *Abraham Justified by Faith.* Paul uses Abraham to elaborate three of the key points he makes about faith generally in 3:27–31: (1) Faith excludes "boasting" (vv. 1–2; cf. 3:27). (2) Faith must be distinguished from works, from the effort to please God by what we do (vv. 3–8; cf. 3:28). (3) Faith brings Gentiles and Jews together into one family of God (vv. 9–17; cf. 3:29–30). Paul concludes by poignantly describing the nature of Abraham's faith (vv. 18–25). A recurring thread in Paul's discussion is the key verse Gen 15:6 (vv. 3,9,22). God's promise to Abraham was a foundational event in God's unfolding plan to create a people for himself and to reassert his sovereignty over all creation (Gen 12–22). Some Jewish interpretations stressed Abraham's fidelity to the law, but Paul focuses on Abraham's faith in response to the promise of God—a faith, to be sure, that issued in works of righteousness (see Heb 11:8–12,17–19; Jas 2:21–23).

4:1–8 Abraham has nothing to boast about before God because his status before God is nothing he earned but is God's gift in response to his faith.

4:1 our forefather according to the flesh. While Abraham was physically ("according to the flesh") the ancestor of the Jewish people, he is, in a spiritual sense, "the father of all who believe" (v. 11).

4:3 Paul quotes Gen 15:6, which describes how God graciously considered Abraham's faith (in response to God's promise [cf. Gen 15:1–5]) to fulfill all that God expected of him. This connection between faith and righteousness is the heart of Paul's argument in 3:21—4:25.

4:5 God who justifies the ungodly. A justly famous claim about the nature of God's justification of sinful humans. God does not justify people who believe they have earned their righteousness, as in the case of an employer who is obliged to pay employees for the work they have done. Rather, God justifies people who are, in themselves, ungodly, illustrating that justification is by grace alone.

4:6–8 Following Jewish methods of citing Scripture, Paul confirms his claim based on "the law" (see 3:27 and note), or the Pentateuch (v. 3, which quotes Gen 15:6), with the Prophets and the Writings—in this case, from Ps 32:1–2. **credits ... count.** Translates the same Greek word rendered "credited" in vv. 3–5, connecting Ps 32:1–2 with Gen 15:6. But more important is the conceptual parallel: righteousness before God and forgiveness of sins are gracious gifts of God.

4:9–12 The argument of this brief paragraph rests on simple chronology: God instituted the rite of circumcision as a "sign of the covenant" (Gen 17:11) at least 13 years (29 years in Jewish tradition) after God accepted Abraham because of his faith (Gal 3:15–18). Abraham, then, is qualified to be the "father of all who believe" (v. 11): both Gentiles

13 It was not through the law that Abraham and his offspring received the promise[u] that he would
be heir of the world,[v] but through the righteousness that comes by faith. 14 For if those who depend on
the law are heirs, faith means nothing and the promise is worthless,[w] 15 because the law brings wrath.[x]
And where there is no law there is no transgression.[y]

16 Therefore, the promise comes by faith, so that it may be by grace[z] and may be guaranteed[a] to all
Abraham's offspring—not only to those who are of the law but also to those who have the faith of
Abraham. He is the father of us all. 17 As it is written: "I have made you a father of many nations."[a][b] He
is our father in the sight of God, in whom he believed—the God who gives life[c] to the dead and calls[d]
into being things that were not.[e]

18 Against all hope, Abraham in hope believed and so became the father of many nations,[f] just
as it had been said to him, "So shall your offspring be."[b][g] 19 Without weakening in his faith, he
faced the fact that his body was as good as dead[h]—since he was about a hundred years old[i]—
and that Sarah's womb was also dead.[j] 20 Yet he did not waver through unbelief regarding the
promise of God, but was strengthened in his faith and gave glory to God,[k] 21 being fully persuaded
that God had power to do what he had promised.[l] 22 This is why "it was credited to him as righteousness."[m] 23 The words "it was credited to him" were written not for him alone, 24 but also for
us,[n] to whom God will credit righteousness—for us who believe in him[o] who raised Jesus our
Lord from the dead.[p] 25 He was delivered over to death for our sins[q] and was raised to life for our
justification.

4:13 [u] Gal 3:16,29 [v] Ge 17:4-6
4:14 [w] Gal 3:18
4:15 [x] Ro 7:7-25; 1Co 15:56; 2Co 3:7; Gal 3:10; Ro 7:12 [y] Ro 3:20; 7:7
4:16 [z] Ro 3:24 [a] Ro 15:8
4:17 [b] Ge 17:5 [c] Jn 5:21 [d] Isa 48:13 [e] 1Co 1:28
4:18 [f] ver 17 [g] Ge 15:5
4:19 [h] Heb 11:11,12 [i] Ge 17:17 [j] Ge 18:11
4:20 [k] Mt 9:8
4:21 [l] Ge 18:14; Heb 11:19
4:22 [m] ver 3
4:24 [n] Ro 15:4; 1Co 9:10; 10:11 [o] Ro 10:9 [p] Ac 2:24
4:25 [q] Isa 53:5,6; Ro 5:6,8

a 17 Gen. 17:5 *b 18* Gen. 15:5

who come to faith without being circumcised and Jews who believe while being circumcised.

4:13–17 Paul continues to use Abraham's experience to make a point that is vital to his overall purpose in Romans: to make clear to the squabbling Gentile and Jewish Christians in Rome (chs. 14–15) that they are united through their common faith in the God who always intended to create people for himself—a people from "many nations" (v. 17).

4:13 not through the law. In Gal 3:15–18, Paul points out that God gave the law of Moses "430 years" (Gal 3:17) after his promise to Abraham. Here Paul focuses on the law's intrinsic inability to bring sinful humans into the state of righteousness. **heir of the world.** The OT focuses on the land of Israel as the "inheritance" that Abraham and his descendants would receive (Gen 12:7; 13:14–15; 15:7,18–21; 17:8; see Exod 32:13). But from the beginning, God promised that Abraham would be the means by which "all peoples on earth [would] be blessed" (Gen 12:3). Later parts of the OT (e.g., Isa 11:10–14; 55:3–5) and some Jewish traditions (in the Apocrypha, see Sirach 44:21; in the OT pseudepigrapha, see Jubilees 19:21; 2 Baruch 14:13; 51:3) stress that God's promise to Abraham and his descendants is universal. Paul, reflecting certain OT texts (e.g., Isa 65:17–25), pushes this universalization further, suggesting that the entire cosmos has replaced the promise of a particular land on this earth (see the language of "new creation" in 2 Cor 5:17; Gal 6:15; see also the "new heaven" and "new earth" of Rev 21:1–5).

4:15 the law brings wrath. Sinful humans cannot fulfill God's good and holy law (7:12). The law cannot liberate sinners from their helplessness but simply confirms that they, indeed, fall far short of God's standard (3:20; 5:20; 7:7–11). **transgression.** Greek *parabasis*; specifically violating a law or commandment that one is formally responsible to obey (2:23; 5:14; Gal 3:19; 1 Tim 2:14). The law, then, brings wrath down on God's people because it formally and in detail spells out their responsibility to honor God—a responsibility that sin prevents them from discharging.

4:16 not only to those who are of the law but also to those who have the faith of Abraham. The reference may be to two groups: Jews in general, who still enjoy the benefits of God's promises (11:1–2,28), and Christians, who share Abraham's faith. But Paul more likely has in view Jewish Christians: those who are "of the law" and who also believe.

4:17 many nations. Gen 17:5 (which Paul quotes here) probably includes Gentiles; Paul certainly applies it this way. **the God who gives life to the dead and calls into being things that were not.** Paul probably intends four related ideas: (1) "Calls into being things that were not" alludes to God's creating all things from nothing (*ex nihilo*; cf. Isa 41:4; 48:13). (2) Jews used the phrase "gives life to the dead" to refer to conversion from paganism (especially in the OT pseudepigrapha, Joseph and Asenath). (3) God gave "life" to the "dead" body of Abraham and the "dead" womb of Sarah in the miraculous birth of Isaac (v. 19). (4) God also gave "life" to the dead body of Jesus by raising him from the dead (v. 24).

4:18–25 Abraham believed "against all hope" (v. 18), i.e., in the face of contrary evidence, and "in hope" (v. 18), i.e., by resting on the hope of God's sure promise. His faith in a God who brings life from the dead is then a paradigm for Christians, who also believe in a God who brought life to the dead body of Jesus.

4:20 he did not waver through unbelief. This claim appears to be in tension with Abraham's laughter when he heard God's promise about having a son (Gen 17:17). Some Jewish and Christian interpreters have interpreted his laughter as a joyful response to God's promise, but the text of Genesis, which in fact makes clear Abraham's failings, does not support this reading. Paul is probably generalizing, referring to the basic course of Abraham's life (see especially the remarkable demonstration of Abraham's faith in Gen 22).

4:24 us who believe in him who raised Jesus our Lord from the dead. Christians, like Abraham, believe in a God who "gives life to the dead" (v. 17). Abraham looked ahead to the ultimate fulfillment of God's promises (Heb 11:13). Christians can look ahead to this consummation with even greater assurance because we also look back at the climactic fulfillment of God's promises in Jesus.

4:25 delivered over to death for our sins. See Isa 53:5–6,8,12. **raised to life for our justification.** As Jesus' own resurrection was his "justification," or vindication (1 Tim 3:16), so we, who are "alive" and "raised with Christ" (Col 2:13; 3:1; see Rom 6:5,8; Eph 2:5–6), are justified with him. The two-part parallel saying in v. 25 may be an early Christian confessional formula.

5:1 [r]Ro 3:28
5:2 [s]Eph 2:18 [t]1Co 15:1 [u]Heb 3:6
5:3 [v]Mt 5:12 [w]Jas 1:2,3
5:5 [x]Php 1:20 [y]Ac 2:33
5:6 [z]Gal 4:4 [a]Ro 4:25
5:8 [b]Jn 15:13; 1Pe 3:18
5:9 [c]Ro 3:25 [d]Ro 1:18
5:10 [e]Ro 11:28; Col 1:21 [f]2Co 5:18,19; Col 1:20,22 [g]Ro 8:34
5:12 [h]ver 15,16,17; 1Co 15:21,22 [i]Ge 2:17; 3:19; Ro 6:23

Peace and Hope

5 Therefore, since we have been justified through faith,[r] we[a] have peace with God through our Lord Jesus Christ, [2]through whom we have gained access[s] by faith into this grace in which we now stand.[t] And we[b] boast in the hope[u] of the glory of God. [3]Not only so, but we[b] also glory in our sufferings,[v] because we know that suffering produces perseverance;[w] [4]perseverance, character; and character, hope. [5]And hope[x] does not put us to shame, because God's love has been poured out into our hearts through the Holy Spirit,[y] who has been given to us.

[6]You see, at just the right time,[z] when we were still powerless, Christ died for the ungodly.[a] [7]Very rarely will anyone die for a righteous person, though for a good person someone might possibly dare to die. [8]But God demonstrates his own love for us in this: While we were still sinners, Christ died for us.[b]

[9]Since we have now been justified by his blood,[c] how much more shall we be saved from God's wrath[d] through him! [10]For if, while we were God's enemies,[e] we were reconciled[f] to him through the death of his Son, how much more, having been reconciled, shall we be saved through his life![g] [11]Not only is this so, but we also boast in God through our Lord Jesus Christ, through whom we have now received reconciliation.

Death Through Adam, Life Through Christ

[12]Therefore, just as sin entered the world through one man,[h] and death through sin,[i] and in this way death came to all people, because all sinned—

[a] *1* Many manuscripts *let us* [b] *2,3* Or *let us*

5:1—8:39 *The Assurance Provided by the Gospel: The Hope of Salvation.* The first half of Romans (chs. 1–8) is sometimes divided between chs. 1–5 ("justification") and chs. 6–8 ("sanctification"), but the sequence of thought makes better sense with the transition occurring between chs. 4 and 5. The first main part (1:18—4:25) focuses on right standing with God ("righteousness," "justification"), and the second main part (chs. 5–8) describes the benefits that those who have attained this right standing enjoy. Paul's argument in chs. 5–8 follows a general chiastic pattern (*a-b-c / c´-b´-a´*):

- *a* Believers can be confident of final glory (5:1–11)
  - *b* Because believers are in Christ rather than in Adam (condemnation) (5:12–21)
    - *c* Believers are set free from the power of sin (6:1–23)
    - *c´* Believers are set free from the binding authority of the law (7:1–25)
  - *b´* Believers are free from condemnation because of the Spirit's work (8:1–17)
- *a´* Therefore, believers can be confident of final glory (8:18–39)

5:1–21 *The Hope of Glory.* Faith joins believers to Jesus Christ, the "second Adam" (see v. 14; 1 Cor 15:21–22,45 and notes; see also note on vv. 12–21), and because of that relationship believers can be certain that they will be saved on the day of judgment.

5:1–11 *Peace and Hope.* Because we have been justified by faith, we enjoy the benefit of peace with God (reconciliation) in the present (vv. 1,11) and have a secure hope that, despite the trials we face in this life (vv. 3–4), God's love and his work for us in Christ and the Spirit will save us from God's wrath on the day of judgment (vv. 5–10) and bring us to glory (v. 2).

5:1 Therefore, since we have been justified through faith. Summarizes the central argument of the first part of the letter (1:18—4:25) and transitions to the second main section (5:1—8:39). **we have.** Makes better sense in this context than "let us have" (see NIV text note). **peace with God.** Not the subjective feeling of the peace *of* God, but the objective state of being at peace *with* God. The enmity that characterizes the relationship between God and his sinful, rebellious creatures is ended for those who are justified by faith (vv. 10–11; Eph 2:16; Col 1:21–22).

5:2 this grace in which we now stand. While God has always acted toward humans in grace, the new era of salvation is especially characterized by an effusion of God's grace (John 1:17). **hope of the glory of God.** The hope that God will glorify us. This future glory that God promises to believers brackets chs. 5–8 (8:18,30). This use of "glory" reflects how the OT uses the Hebrew *kābôd* to depict God's "weighty" nature: his honor, majesty, and overwhelming presence (Deut 28:58; Ps 22:23; Isa 26:15; Ezek 39:13). Sinful humans "fall short" of God's glory (3:23), but in accordance with the prophetic promise (Isa 60:1–2), believers are promised a share in that glory.

5:3–4 The road to glory is strewn with rocks and strange turns. But far from lessening our hope, these "sufferings" (v. 3), in God's providence, become the means of strengthening us and thus deepening our hope.

5:5 put us to shame. In the OT, "shame" sometimes refers to a negative verdict in the judgment of God (e.g., Pss 6:9–10; 25:3; 119:80; Isa 28:16 ["panic"]; 45:16; 45:24; Jer 17:13). Believers need not fear this outcome "because God's love has been poured out into our hearts through the Holy Spirit." Paul is alluding to Joel 2:28–32, which promises an outpouring of God's Spirit (Acts 2:17–21).

5:6 at just the right time. The time God had determined was the appropriate time for him to fulfill his promises (see Gal 4:4: "when the set time had fully come"; cf. Mark 1:15).

5:7 righteous person ... good person. Perhaps the distinction is between an upright, law-abiding person and a person who is good to us.

5:8 God not only enables us, through his Spirit, to feel his love in our hearts (v. 5), but he also powerfully demonstrates his love for us by sending his Son to die on our behalf.

5:9–10 Paul signals the importance of what he says here by saying it twice: God's initial work in justifying sinful people and reconciling them to himself shows that he will surely complete his work by saving those same people from his wrath at the time of his judgment. **shall we be saved ... shall we be saved.** Ultimate deliverance from temptation, sin, and death, as is often found in Paul's letters (1:16; 13:11; 1 Cor 5:5; 2 Cor 1:6; Phil 1:19,28; 2:12; 1 Thess 5:9; 1 Tim 2:15; 4:16; 2 Tim 4:18).

5:12–21 *Death Through Adam, Life Through Christ.* The building block of this passage is comparing ("just as ... so also") Adam and Christ (vv. 12,18,19,21). Each is a key figure in redemptive history, whose acts have ultimate significance for all whom they represent. Adam's

13 To be sure, sin was in the world before the law was given, but sin is not charged against anyone's
account where there is no law.[j] 14 Nevertheless, death reigned from the time of Adam to the time of
Moses, even over those who did not sin by breaking a command, as did Adam, who is a pattern of the
one to come.[k]
15 But the gift is not like the trespass. For if the many died by the trespass of the one man,[l] how much
more did God's grace and the gift that came by the grace of the one man, Jesus Christ,[m] overflow to the
many! 16 Nor can the gift of God be compared with the result of one man's sin: The judgment followed
one sin and brought condemnation, but the gift followed many trespasses and brought justification.
17 For if, by the trespass of the one man, death[n] reigned through that one man, how much more will
those who receive God's abundant provision of grace and of the gift of righteousness reign in life
through the one man, Jesus Christ!
18 Consequently, just as one trespass resulted in condemnation for all people,[o] so also one righteous
act resulted in justification[p] and life for all people. 19 For just as through the disobedience of the one
man[q] the many were made sinners, so also through the obedience[r] of the one man the many will be
made righteous.
20 The law was brought in so that the trespass might increase.[s] But where sin increased, grace increased all the more,[t] 21 so that, just as sin reigned in death,[u] so also grace might reign through righteousness to bring eternal life through Jesus Christ our Lord.

5:13 [j] Ro 4:15
5:14 [k] 1Co 15:22,45
5:15 [l] ver 12,18,19 [m] Ac 15:11
5:17 [n] ver 12
5:18 [o] ver 12 [p] Ro 4:25
5:19 [q] ver 12 [r] Php 2:8
5:20 [s] Ro 7:7,8; Gal 3:19 [t] 1Ti 1:13,14
5:21 [u] ver 12,14

sin, which brought death and condemnation to all humans, is more than made up for by Christ's obedience, which brings righteousness and life to all who receive God's gracious gift.

5:12 This forms a chiasm (see note on 2:6–11):

a Sin enters
b Death results
b´ Death comes to all
a´ Because all sinned

Therefore. Could also be rendered "In order to accomplish this," with "this" referring to vv. 1–11. According to this view, Paul is arguing that our confidence in salvation (vv. 9–10) is based on our belonging to the "second Adam," Jesus Christ (see note on 5:1–21). **sin entered the world through one man.** Paul assumes that his readers know the tragic story of the fall of the original humans (Gen 3). **death through sin.** As God warned Adam and Eve (Gen 2:17), death followed in the wake of sin. The parallel between this verse and v. 18 suggests that "death" refers mainly to spiritual death, or "condemnation"—although physical death, at least in its painful side, may be included as well. **all sinned.** When and how this took place is debated. At first it might seem that Paul means simply that all humans die because all humans, in their own persons, commit sin. But the parallel passages in vv. 18a,19a stress the significance of the "one trespass" by the "one man," Adam. We can reconcile these emphases if we understand that Adam's one sin led to all humans becoming subject to sin's power, leading inevitably to their own sinning. But it is also possible that Paul is viewing Adam as a representative figure, whose own sin is, at the same time, the sin of all human beings. The OT assumes the "corporate" significance of key individuals (e.g., Achan's sin is also the sin of Israel [Josh 7:1,11]; see also Heb 7:9–10).

5:13–14 Paul does not finish the sentence he began in v. 12 (the dash at the end of v. 12 indicates this break). He turns aside from his main argument to deal with a related matter. He may simply be emphasizing that death is universal: even people who lived before God gave the Mosaic law were subject to death. But Paul may be providing evidence for the "representative" reading of v. 12: even people who did not directly violate a commandment (as Adam did in the Garden of Eden and the Israelites did after God gave the law) suffered the penalty of death, and only their participation in Adam's sin can finally explain this.

5:14 pattern. Greek *typos*, from which we get the word "typology." Adam is a "type" of Christ, "the one to come." God has designed the history of salvation in such a way that OT events, persons, and places foreshadow NT events, persons, and places. The way Adam represents humans points ahead to the way Christ represents believers.

5:15–16 In one sense Adam's sin and Christ's obedience are comparable. But in another sense they are very different: God is at work in his grace through Christ, so Christ's act of obedience more than cancels the long history of human sins and their consequences.

5:15 many ... one. "Many" contrasts with "one." Only context indicates whether "many" includes everyone. Paul clearly teaches that all humans are bound up with Adam's sin and death, so "many died" must mean "all died." But Paul also clearly teaches that only believers fully benefit from Christ's work, so "the many" who experience the grace of Christ cannot be universal.

5:17 those who receive. Read in isolation from the rest of Scripture, vv. 18–19 could suggest that just as all humans have been condemned in Adam, so all humans will have eternal life in Christ. But this verse qualifies that universalism (i.e., that "all people" will be saved) by emphasizing *receiving* the gift: only those who respond in faith (3:21—4:25) eternally benefit from Christ's act of obedience. Both Adam and Jesus are representatives of humans: Adam represents all, Jesus represents all who receive God's gift.

5:18 one righteous act. Christ's obedience to the Father's will in going to the cross. **justification and life for all people.** See note on v. 17. Paul might mean that Christ has in principle made it possible for all human beings to experience justification and life (cf. "those who receive," v. 17). But he might be referring simply to "all people" who are in Christ in contrast to "all people" who are in Adam.

5:19 made sinners. Or possibly "considered to be sinners" (e.g., "condemned," as in the parallel v. 18). **made righteous.** Not transformed into people who act righteously, but considered to be righteous in the judicial sense (see note on 3:24).

5:20 so that the trespass might increase. One of the reasons that God gave the Mosaic law was to reveal the extent of human sin and the need for new measures to deal with that sin. By multiplying commandments, the law provides many more opportunities for disobeying God (see 3:20; 4:15; 7:7–12; Gal 3:19).

5:21 While vv. 12–21 are very important verses about "original sin," they focus on (as the last clause makes clear) the incredibly powerful effects of Christ's "one righteous act" (v. 18). **through righteousness.** As a result of being justified. Believers, who belong to Christ, can be sure that God's grace reigns over them: their present state of right standing before God will certainly result in eternal life.

6:1 [v] ver 15; Ro 3:5,8
6:2 [w] Col 3:3,5; 1Pe 2:24
6:3 [x] Mt 28:19
6:4 [y] Col 2:12 [z] Ro 7:6; Gal 6:15; Eph 4:22-24; Col 3:10
6:5 [a] 2Co 4:10; Php 3:10,11
6:6 [b] Eph 4:22; Col 3:9 [c] Gal 2:20; Col 2:12,20 [d] Ro 7:24
6:9 [e] Ac 2:24 [f] Rev 1:18
6:10 [g] ver 2
6:11 [h] ver 2
6:13 [i] ver 16,19; Ro 7:5 [j] Ro 12:1; 1Pe 2:24
6:14 [k] Gal 5:18 [l] Ro 3:24

Dead to Sin, Alive in Christ

6 What shall we say, then? Shall we go on sinning so that grace may increase?[v] 2By no means! We
are those who have died to sin;[w] how can we live in it any longer? 3Or don't you know that all of us
who were baptized[x] into Christ Jesus were baptized into his death? 4We were therefore buried with him
through baptism into death in order that, just as Christ was raised from the dead[y] through the glory of
the Father, we too may live a new life.[z]
5For if we have been united with him in a death like his, we will certainly also be united with him in
a resurrection like his.[a] 6For we know that our old self[b] was crucified with him[c] so that the body ruled
by sin[d] might be done away with,[a] that we should no longer be slaves to sin— 7because anyone who
has died has been set free from sin.
8Now if we died with Christ, we believe that we will also live with him. 9For we know that since Christ
was raised from the dead,[e] he cannot die again; death no longer has mastery over him.[f] 10The death he
died, he died to sin[g] once for all; but the life he lives, he lives to God.
11In the same way, count yourselves dead to sin[h] but alive to God in Christ Jesus. 12Therefore do not
let sin reign in your mortal body so that you obey its evil desires. 13Do not offer any part of yourself to
sin as an instrument of wickedness,[i] but rather offer yourselves to God as those who have been brought
from death to life; and offer every part of yourself to him as an instrument of righteousness.[j] 14For sin
shall no longer be your master, because you are not under the law,[k] but under grace.[l]

[a] 6 Or *be rendered powerless*

6:1–23 *Freedom From Bondage to Sin.* Those who are justified by faith can have confidence that God will vindicate them in his future judgment (ch. 5). But they also can have confidence that God has provided, in Christ, for what they need to live faithful and fruitful lives for God in the present. For God not only liberates sinners from the penalty of sin ("justification"; cf. 3:21—4:25, see note on 3:24) but also frees them from the power of sin (v. 6).

6:1–14 *Dead to Sin, Alive in Christ.* Believers, who are united to Christ, participate in his victory over sin and the new life his resurrection inaugurated.

6:1 Shall we go on sinning ...? The immediate occasion for Paul's rhetorical question is 5:20: "where sin increased, grace increased all the more." But this same question naturally arises from Paul's broader teaching about the gospel: if people are justified by faith alone, are they free to live any way they want?

6:2 By no means! Paul rejects any such implication with his strongest negative (Greek *mē genoito*, a formula typical of the diatribe style Paul is using [see note on 2:1]). **died to sin.** Not removed entirely from sin's influence but set free from its absolute power (vv. 6,14,18,22).

6:4 baptism. Could refer to "baptism" (i.e., "immersion") in the Spirit (perhaps, e.g., 1 Cor 12:13) but probably refers to the widespread early Christian practice of water baptism. This may suggest that baptism has the symbolic value of picturing the believer's death to sin (entering the water) and rising again to new life (coming up from the water). Or baptism may function here as shorthand for the conversion experience since the NT closely associates water baptism with conversion (Acts 2:38; 1 Pet 3:21). In any case, Paul is clear that faith, not baptism, is what effects the transfer from the old life to the new. **glory of the Father.** God's glory is often closely associated with his power (Ps 145:11; Col 1:11; 1 Pet 4:11). **we too may live a new life.** As our identification with Christ's death in baptism sets us free from sin's power, so our identification with Christ in his resurrection (vv. 5,8) enables us to live according to God's will and the Spirit's direction (7:6).

6:6 our old self. Or "our old man." The masculine rendering has the virtue of bringing out more clearly the connection between this verse and Adam, who is called "the man" throughout 5:12–21. The "old man" is a way of describing humans in their natural state, represented by Adam, *the* "old man," and therefore dominated by sin and death. See also Eph 4:22; Col 3:9. **was crucified with him.** As God deems all people to be "in Adam" (prior to conversion), so he deems believers to be "in Christ." In our relationship to him, we participate in his death, burial, and resurrection and all the benefits those central redemptive events secured. See also Gal 2:20. **body ruled by sin.** Humans in their preregenerate state, dominated by sin's power. **might be done away with.** Not destroyed but "rendered powerless" (see NIV text note); the old self no longer dictates how a believer lives.

6:7 set free. Or "justified." But the unusual Pauline use of the preposition "from" after "set free" suggests he is referring to liberation rather than justification (but see Acts 13:38).

6:8 we will also live with him. The reference may be to the spiritual life we now enjoy in and with Christ (v. 11; Eph 2:5–6; Col 2:13) or to the future physical resurrection (2 Cor 4:14; Phil 3:21; 1 Thess 4:17; 2 Tim 2:11). See also v. 5.

6:10 he died to sin. Although Christ was sinless and never succumbed to sin's power (2 Cor 5:21; Heb 4:15), his full identification with human beings in the incarnation meant that sin's power affected him. He therefore had to "die" to it. This provides a crucial step in the logic of this section: Christ died to sin (v. 10), and believers died with Christ (v. 6); therefore, believers died to sin (v. 2).

6:11–13 Our participation in Christ's death and resurrection puts us in a decisively new relationship to sin and to God. But we also need to live out this new relationship by thinking about ourselves in a new way (v. 11) and by acting in accordance with our new status (vv. 12–13).

6:14 sin shall no longer be your master. Succinctly summarizes what this section teaches in the form of a promise. **under the law.** Might mean "under the condemnation pronounced by the law" but more likely refers to the general state of being bound to the authority of the Mosaic law (v. 15; 1 Cor 9:20; Gal 3:23; 4:4–5,21; 5:18). So the contrast ("not under the law, but under grace") is probably salvation-historical—between the Mosaic law that was central to the old covenant and the grace that reigns with new power in the new covenant (see John 1:17). Paul is not, of course, saying that there is no "law" in the new covenant era (1 Cor 7:19; 9:20–22; Gal 6:2) nor is he saying that there was no grace in the old covenant. But as much as the law of Moses was a gracious gift to Israel, it did not provide the power to conquer sin's power. So the prophets looked to a time when God would act in a new way to transform the human heart (Ezek 36:25–27). It is Christ's new covenant work that provides this power.

Slaves to Righteousness

[15]What then? Shall we sin because we are not under the law
but under grace? By no means! [16]Don't you know that when
you offer yourselves to someone as obedient slaves, you are
slaves of the one you obey—whether you are slaves to
sin,[m] which leads to death,[n] or to obedience, which leads
to righteousness? [17]But thanks be to God[o] that, though
you used to be slaves to sin, you have come to obey
from your heart the pattern of teaching[p] that has now
claimed your allegiance. [18]You have been set free from
sin[q] and have become slaves to righteousness.

[19]I am using an example from everyday life[r] because of your human limitations. Just as you used to
offer yourselves as slaves to impurity and to ever-increasing wickedness, so now offer yourselves as slaves
to righteousness[s] leading to holiness. [20]When you were
slaves to sin,[t] you were free from the control of righteousness. [21]What benefit did you reap at that time from the
things you are now ashamed of? Those things result in
death![u] [22]But now that you have been set free from sin[v]
and have become slaves of God,[w] the benefit you reap
leads to holiness, and the result is eternal life. [23]For the
wages of sin is death,[x] but the gift of God is eternal life[y]
in[a] Christ Jesus our Lord.

Roman relief of a slave being freed. In Rom 6:16–18, Paul likens sin to slavery and notes that believers have been set free from sin and have become slaves to righteousness.

Roman civilization, Relief portraying slave being freed/De Agostini Picture Library/A. Dagli Orti/Bridgeman Images

6:16 [m]Jn 8:34; 2Pe 2:19 [n]ver 23
6:17 [o]Ro 1:8; 2Co 2:14 [p]2Ti 1:13
6:18 [q]ver 7,22; Ro 8:2
6:19 [r]Ro 3:5 [s]ver 13
6:20 [t]ver 16
6:21 [u]ver 23
6:22 [v]ver 18 [w]1Co 7:22; 1Pe 2:16
6:23 [x]Ge 2:17; Ro 5:12; Gal 6:7,8; Jas 1:15 [y]Mt 25:46
7:1 [z]Ro 1:13

Released From the Law, Bound to Christ

7 Do you not know, brothers and sisters[z]—for I am speaking to those who know the law—that the
law has authority over someone only as long as that person lives? [2]For example, by law a married
woman is bound to her husband as long as he is alive, but if her husband dies, she is released from the

[a] 23 Or *through*

6:15–23 *Slaves to Righteousness.* Paul uses another rhetorical question, similar to the one in v. 1, to reinforce his teaching from vv. 1–14. The focus shifts from the negative (free from sin) to the positive (slaves of God).
6:16 obedience, which leads to righteousness. In the first part of Romans, Paul uses "righteousness" to refer to "right standing" before God. But in 6:15–23, Paul contrasts "righteousness" with "sin" (vv. 18,20) and "impurity" (v. 19), revealing that he is using the word in another of its biblical senses: behavior that conforms to God's standard.
6:17 slaves to sin. As he does throughout Romans, Paul refers to "sin" (singular) as a power that exerts its influence over people. The many sins people commit are a symptom of the ruling authority of the sinful impulse within fallen human beings. **pattern of teaching that has now claimed your allegiance.** The Greek (using *typos*) suggests that the gospel stamps a new set of standards on the hearts of people who respond to the gospel. New covenant obedience stems from transformed hearts (see the promise of Jer 31:31–34; Heb 8:9–12).
6:19 human limitations. Greek *sarx* ("flesh"). Paul could mean that our sinful tendency makes it necessary for him to remind us of God's holy standards. But it is more likely that he refers to our difficulty in understanding the things of God, requiring him to use analogies "from everyday life" (such as slavery) to make his point. **holiness.** Could also be translated "sanctification." God himself sanctifies all those who believe in Jesus: they become "holy," or "saints," members of God's own people (e.g., 1:7). But sanctification is also a process of becoming increasingly obedient to the will of God (1 Thess 4:3); believers need to engage in this lifelong pursuit of holiness if they expect to enjoy eternal life (v. 22; see Heb 12:14: "without holiness no one will see the Lord").
7:1–25 *Freedom From Bondage to the Law.* Paul now develops the idea of not being "under the law" (6:14,15), insisting that believers must be set free from the binding authority of the law of Moses in order to enjoy new life in Christ (vv. 1–6). The possibility that this teaching (and other teachings about the law in Romans) might be interpreted as disparaging the law leads Paul to assert emphatically that the law is "holy, righteous and good" (v. 12). Nevertheless, sin has used God's good law to bring death (vv. 7–11), a startling development that Paul explains further in vv. 13–25.
7:1–6 *Released From the Law, Bound to Christ.* After reminding his readers of a common truth (v. 1) and illustrating it (vv. 2–3), Paul makes his central point (v. 4) and explains it (vv. 5–6).
7:1 the law. Probably, as throughout ch. 7, the law of Moses. Since God gave this law specifically to Jews, "those who know the law" may refer to Jewish Christians. But many, if not most, of the Gentile Christians in Rome were probably former "God-fearers": Gentiles who had not converted to Judaism but who were interested in Judaism, attending the synagogue and coming to know the law of Moses in that setting.
7:2 For example. Paul illustrates the principle of v. 1 in vv. 2–3 with reference to the marriage relationship. This is not an allegory in which the various details stand for some spiritual entity. Since this is an illustration with one purpose, we must be careful about reading significance into the details. It would probably be wrong, for instance, to draw any conclusions from it about biblical grounds for divorce and remarriage.

7:2 [a]1Co 7:39
7:4 [b]Ro 8:2; Gal 2:19 [c]Col 1:22
7:5 [d]Ro 7:7-11 [e]Ro 6:13
7:6 [f]Ro 2:29; 2Co 3:6
7:7 [g]Ro 3:20; 4:15 [h]Ex 20:17; Dt 5:21
7:8 [i]ver 11 [j]Ro 4:15; 1Co 15:56
7:10 [k]Lev 18:5; Lk 10:26-28; Ro 10:5; Gal 3:12
7:11 [l]Ge 3:13
7:12 [m]1Ti 1:8

law that binds her to him.[a] 3So then, if she has sexual relations with another man while her husband
is still alive, she is called an adulteress. But if her husband dies, she is released from that law and is not
an adulteress if she marries another man.

4So, my brothers and sisters, you also died to the law[b] through the body of Christ,[c] that you might
belong to another, to him who was raised from the dead, in order that we might bear fruit for God.
5For when we were in the realm of the flesh,[a] the sinful passions aroused by the law[d] were at work in
us,[e] so that we bore fruit for death. 6But now, by dying to what once bound us, we have been released
from the law so that we serve in the new way of the Spirit, and not in the old way of the written code.[f]

The Law and Sin

7What shall we say, then? Is the law sinful? Certainly not! Nevertheless, I would not have known what
sin was had it not been for the law.[g] For I would not have known what coveting really was if the law
had not said, "You shall not covet."[b][h] 8But sin, seizing the opportunity afforded by the commandment,[i]
produced in me every kind of coveting. For apart from the law, sin was dead.[j] 9Once I was alive apart
from the law; but when the commandment came, sin sprang to life and I died. 10I found that the very
commandment that was intended to bring life[k] actually brought death. 11For sin, seizing the opportunity afforded by the commandment, deceived me,[l] and through the commandment put me to death.
12So then, the law is holy, and the commandment is holy, righteous and good.[m]

13Did that which is good, then, become death to me? By no means! Nevertheless, in order that sin

a 5 In contexts like this, the Greek word for *flesh* (*sarx*) refers to the sinful state of human beings, often presented as a power in opposition to the Spirit. *b* 7 Exodus 20:17; Deut. 5:21

7:4 you also died to the law. As with the phrase "under the law" in 6:14,15, Paul might have in mind the condemning power of the law. But he may, more broadly, refer to the binding authority of the law of Moses. To be bound to that law means to be bound still to the old covenant, which was unable to set its adherents free from sin's power. One must therefore be separated from that law and its covenant in order to "belong to another," namely, Christ, in whose resurrection power we participate (6:4–5,8).
7:5 realm of the flesh. Greek *sarx*, a key motif in this part of Romans (see also vv. 18,25 [see NIV text notes]; 8:3 [three times],4,5 [twice],6,7, 8,9,12 [twice],13). Paul uses the word *sarx* to refer to "natural" human existence apart from God (see note on 1:3). He pictures unbelievers as living in a realm dominated by this power. **sinful passions aroused by the law.** A startling claim that Paul explains in vv. 7–11.
7:6 But now. As Paul often does, he contrasts the old realm, dominated by the flesh, sin, and death, with the new realm believers now live in. **what once bound us.** The law of Moses (see v. 4). **Spirit ... written code.** Paul contrasts the new covenant gift of the Spirit and the law of Moses, pictured in terms of the Ten Commandments, carved on stone (2:29; 2 Cor 3:3,6–7).
7:7–25 *The Law and Sin.* Verses 7–12 are framed by the issue of the nature of the law: it is not "sinful" (v. 7a); rather, it is "holy, righteous and good" (v. 12). But while the law is not itself sinful, Paul reiterates that sin has used it to bring death (vv. 7b–11).

Verses 13–25 respond to a question that vv. 7–12 naturally raise: how could God's good law become the occasion for sin and death? Paul's answer focuses on human inability: God gives his good law to people who are already captive to the power of sin; therefore, they cannot obey the law that God has given them, and death results. The spiritual status of the person whom Paul describes in these verses is debated. Noting that Paul apparently refers to himself using the present tense ("I am," "I do," "I want," etc.) and that the person "delight[s] in God's law" (v. 22), many interpreters think Paul is describing his own experience as a Christian. Others, however, think that Paul is describing his past experience as a Jew under the law. They point to language that appears to contradict what Paul says in Romans about Christians: "sold as a slave to sin" (v. 14) versus "set free from sin" (6:18,22); "a prisoner of the law of sin" (7:23) versus "free from the law of sin" (8:2). Whatever specific situation Paul has in view, his teaching in this passage stands: humans are unable to obey God's law and cannot therefore find salvation through it.
7:7 Is the law sinful? The question naturally arises from the claim of v. 5 ("sinful passions aroused by the law") and the earlier series of negative comments on the law (v. 4; 3:20; 4:15; 5:20; 6:14–15). **I ... I.** From this point to the end of the chapter, Paul uses the first-person singular ("I," "me"). He is undoubtedly reflecting on (1) his own experience, but in keeping with first-century Jewish ways of thinking, his own experience is bound up with (2) his solidarity as a human being with Adam and his sin and with (3) his own people Israel. These three foci mingle in this passage. In this verse Paul is thinking of his own life but also of the experience of Israel as a whole: it was through the law that the Israelites became "conscious of [their] sin" (3:20).
7:8,11 the opportunity. The Greek word has the sense of a bridgehead, a position seized in enemy territory that becomes a base of operations. The law's series of specific "dos" and "don'ts" stimulated in Paul and other Jews the desire to rebel against God and his rules.
7:8 sin was dead. Sin exists in every human since Adam, but the law has enabled sin to become especially powerful.
7:9 Once I was alive apart from the law. Paul may be reflecting on (1) his own state of relative "innocence" in childhood or before he came truly to understand what the law was requiring of him; (2) his solidarity with Adam, who was, indeed, "alive" before he disobeyed God's commandment about the tree of the knowledge of good and evil (Gen 2:17; 3:1–7); or (3) his solidarity with the Israelites, who experienced a kind of "death" (v. 10) when God's law came and branded them clearly as sinners (3:20; 4:15; 5:13–14).
7:10 the very commandment that was intended to bring life. Probably a generalization, representing the Mosaic law, which promised life for those who faithfully followed its precepts (Lev 18:5; Deut 30:15–20).
7:11 deceived me. Possibly alludes to Eve's response to God in Gen 3:13: "The serpent deceived me, and I ate."
7:13 Did that which is good ... become death to me? As he so often does in Romans, Paul uses a question arising from his previous teaching to move his argument along. How could the "good" law (v. 12) be the occasion of death?

might be recognized as sin, it used what is good to bring about my death, so that through the commandment sin might become utterly sinful.
14We know that the law is spiritual; but I am unspiritual,[n] sold[o] as a slave to sin. 15I do not understand what I do. For what I want to do I do not do, but what I hate I do.[p] 16And if I do what I do not
want to do, I agree that the law is good.[q] 17As it is, it is no longer I myself who do it, but it is sin living
in me.[r] 18For I know that good itself does not dwell in me, that is, in my sinful nature.[a][s] For I have the
desire to do what is good, but I cannot carry it out. 19For I do not do the good I want to do, but the evil
I do not want to do—this I keep on doing.[t] 20Now if I do what I do not want to do, it is no longer I who
do it, but it is sin living in me that does it.[u]
21So I find this law at work:[v] Although I want to do good, evil is right there with me. 22For in my inner being[w] I delight in God's law;[x] 23but I see another law at work in me, waging war[y] against the law
of my mind and making me a prisoner of the law of sin at work within me. 24What a wretched man I
am! Who will rescue me from this body that is subject to death?[z] 25Thanks be to God, who delivers me
through Jesus Christ our Lord!
So then, I myself in my mind am a slave to God's law, but in my sinful nature[b] a slave to the law of sin.

Life Through the Spirit

8 Therefore, there is now no condemnation[a] for those who are in Christ Jesus,[b] 2because through
Christ Jesus the law of the Spirit who gives life[c] has set you[c] free[d] from the law of sin[e] and death.
3For what the law was powerless[f] to do because it was weakened by the flesh,[d] God did by sending his

[a] *18* Or *my flesh* [b] *25* Or *in the flesh* [c] *2* The Greek is singular; some manuscripts *me* [d] *3* In contexts like this, the Greek word for *flesh* (*sarx*) refers to the sinful state of human beings, often presented as a power in opposition to the Spirit; also in verses 4-13.

7:14 [n] 1Co 3:1 [o] 1Ki 21:20,25; 2Ki 17:17
7:15 [p] ver 19; Gal 5:17
7:16 [q] ver 12
7:17 [r] ver 20
7:18 [s] ver 25
7:19 [t] ver 15
7:20 [u] ver 17
7:21 [v] ver 23,25
7:22 [w] Eph 3:16 [x] Ps 1:2
7:23 [y] Gal 5:17; Jas 4:1; 1Pe 2:11
7:24 [z] Ro 6:6; 8:2
8:1 [a] ver 34 [b] ver 39; Ro 16:3
8:2 [c] 1Co 15:45 [d] Ro 6:18 [e] Ro 7:4
8:3 [f] Ac 13:39; Heb 7:18

7:14 law. The law of Moses. What Paul says in these verses about the law of Moses applies to any law, or commandment, or even the promptings of the conscience (see 2:14–15)—anything that brings us face-to-face with the will of God for us. **but.** Paul announces at the outset the basic tension of the passage: the law is "spiritual" (here), "good" (v. 16), something to "delight in" (v. 22)—it is "God's law" (vv. 22,25); but the human being is "unspiritual, sold as a slave to sin" (here), "wretched" (v. 24), "a slave to the law of sin" (v. 25; cf. v. 23)—a person in whom "good ... does not dwell" (v. 18). See "Law," p. 2649.
7:15–20 Paul vividly portrays the frustration of the human condition. The very best people seek to obey God, but they find themselves unable to do so consistently. What this reveals, Paul concludes, is that people are subject to some kind of sinful power: "sin living in me" (vv. 17,20), "my sinful nature" (v. 18). Paul is not suggesting that people are not responsible for their actions. Rather, he is reminding us that human beings are fatally bent away from God and toward sin by virtue of their involvement in Adam's sin (5:12–21).
7:21 this law. Perhaps the law of Moses; but more likely Paul is using "law" in the sense of "principle."
7:22 my inner being. Paul uses this same language elsewhere with reference to believers (2 Cor 4:16; Eph 3:16), but it was also used widely among Greek authors to depict the Godward, immortal side of the human being. Christians, of course, delight in God's law, but so did faithful Jews.
7:23 the law of my mind ... the law of sin. These phrases could refer to contrasting sides of the same law of Moses. This law is "God's law" (v. 22) that the person approves of and seeks to do and that, at the same time, sin has used to bring death (vv. 7–11). It may be more likely, however, that the second phrase uses a play on words: fighting against the law of God is another "law," or "power": sin (see 8:2).
7:24 What a wretched man I am! The cry from the heart of every person who sincerely seeks to obey God but finds themselves unable to meet his demands. **this body that is subject to death.** Either the physical body that is doomed to die (8:10) or the human person generally, which is under sentence of spiritual death because of sin (vv. 5,9–11,13).
7:25 Thanks be to God ...! This cry of victory comes before a final restatement of the struggle, which might suggest that Paul speaks in this section as a Christian, conscious of his deliverance through Christ but also aware of his continuing struggle with sin. On the other hand, the thanksgiving could be an interjection of Paul the Christian into a passage that describes the defeat that he experienced as a Jew trying to live up to the demands of the law of Moses.
8:1–39 *Assurance of Eternal Life in the Spirit.* Paul begins by restating the basic point he has made in ch. 5: Christians, who belong to Christ Jesus, no longer fear the "condemnation" that those who are "in Adam" must inevitably experience (5:16,18). The confidence in ultimate salvation crops up repeatedly in ch. 8 (vv. 6,10–11,17–18,29–30,31–39). The ministry of the Spirit, a key motif (ch. 8 mentions the Spirit 18 times), is an important source of this confidence. But the Spirit also gives the believer the power to please God in this life (vv. 4–9,12–13,26–27).
8:1–17 *Life Through the Spirit.* The Spirit brings life to people who are dead because of sin (7:5,7–11,24). Applying the benefits of Christ's death on our behalf (v. 3), the Spirit gives us life now by liberating us from the power of sin and death (v. 2), and he is also instrumental in giving us life in the future, when our bodies are raised from the dead (v. 11). The Spirit conquers the flesh, setting believers on a new path that conforms to the will of God (vv. 4–9). Yet believers must not be inactive: they must put into effect the power of the Spirit if they expect to experience eternal life (vv. 12–13). And by the Spirit's power, believers become children of God, with all the benefits the status of "adoption" (v. 15) brings them, both now and in the future (vv. 14–17).
8:1 Therefore. The joyful proclamation of "no condemnation" rests on our incorporation into Christ and the benefits of his death (5:12–21). This is the central point of all of chs. 5–8, which Paul here restates in light of the believer's new relationship to sin (ch. 6) and the law (ch. 7; cf. 8:2).
8:2 law of the Spirit. Probably the "power" of the Spirit. **law of sin and death.** Either the Mosaic law, which sin has used to bring death (7:7–11) or, as in the first part of the verse, the "power" of sin that brings death (7:23).
8:3 what the law was powerless to do. Succinctly summarizes the

8:3 [g] Php 2:7 [h] Heb 2:14,17
8:4 [i] Gal 5:16
8:5 [j] Gal 5:19-21 [k] Gal 5:22-25
8:6 [l] Gal 6:8
8:7 [m] Jas 4:4
8:9 [n] 1Co 6:19; Gal 4:6 [o] Jn 14:17; 1Jn 4:13
8:10 [p] Gal 2:20; Eph 3:17; Col 1:27
8:11 [q] Ac 2:24 [r] Jn 5:21
8:13 [s] Gal 6:8
8:14 [t] Gal 5:18 [u] Jn 1:12; Rev 21:7
8:15 [v] 2Ti 1:7; Heb 2:15 [w] Mk 14:36; Gal 4:5,6
8:16 [x] Eph 1:13
8:17 [y] Ac 20:32; Gal 4:7 [z] 1Pe 4:13
8:18 [a] 2Co 4:17; 1Pe 4:13

own Son in the likeness of sinful flesh[g] to be a sin offering.[a][h] And so he condemned sin in the flesh, 4 in
order that the righteous requirement of the law might be fully met in us, who do not live according to
the flesh but according to the Spirit.[i]

5 Those who live according to the flesh have their minds set on what the flesh desires;[j] but those who
live in accordance with the Spirit have their minds set on what the Spirit desires.[k] 6 The mind governed
by the flesh is death, but the mind governed by the Spirit is life[l] and peace. 7 The mind governed by the
flesh is hostile to God;[m] it does not submit to God's law, nor can it do so. 8 Those who are in the realm
of the flesh cannot please God.

9 You, however, are not in the realm of the flesh but are in the realm of the Spirit, if indeed the Spirit
of God lives in you.[n] And if anyone does not have the Spirit of Christ,[o] they do not belong to Christ.
10 But if Christ is in you,[p] then even though your body is subject to death because of sin, the Spirit gives
life[b] because of righteousness. 11 And if the Spirit of him who raised Jesus from the dead[q] is living in
you, he who raised Christ from the dead will also give life to your mortal bodies[r] because of[c] his Spirit
who lives in you.

12 Therefore, brothers and sisters, we have an obligation—but it is not to the flesh, to live according to it. 13 For if you live according to the flesh, you will die; but if by the Spirit you put to death the
misdeeds of the body, you will live.[s]

14 For those who are led by the Spirit of God[t] are the children of God.[u] 15 The Spirit you received does
not make you slaves, so that you live in fear again;[v] rather, the Spirit you received brought about your
adoption to sonship.[d] And by him we cry, *"Abba,*[e] Father."[w] 16 The Spirit himself testifies with our spirit[x]
that we are God's children. 17 Now if we are children, then we are heirs[y]—heirs of God and co-heirs
with Christ, if indeed we share in his sufferings in order that we may also share in his glory.[z]

Present Suffering and Future Glory

18 I consider that our present sufferings are not worth comparing with the glory that will be revealed
in us.[a] 19 For the creation waits in eager expectation for the children of God to be revealed. 20 For the

[a] *3* Or *flesh, for sin* [b] *10* Or *you, your body is dead because of sin, yet your spirit is alive* [c] *11* Some manuscripts *bodies through* [d] *15* The Greek word for *adoption to sonship* is a term referring to the full legal standing of an adopted male heir in Roman culture; also in verse 23. [e] *15* Aramaic for *father*

argument of 7:7–25: the law, though God's good gift to his people, cannot liberate people from sin's enslaving power ("the flesh"). **likeness of sinful flesh.** Christ became truly human, taking on "flesh" (John 1:14). But "likeness" suggests that the flesh he took on was not exactly like our "sinful flesh": he was not guilty of sin "in Adam" as we are. **sin offering.** The Greek here ("concerning sin"; see NIV text note) could mean simply that Christ's death was related to sin. But the Septuagint, the pre-Christian Greek translation of the OT, uses this Greek phrase to refer to the "sin offering" in Ps 40:6–8 (see also Heb 10:6,8; 13:11). **so he condemned sin in the flesh.** Christ entered the realm of the flesh, where sin seems to hold sway, to conquer the power of sin. Sin is "condemned" so that believers are not (v. 1).

8:4 the righteous requirement of the law might be fully met in us. May refer to the Spirit's enabling believers to conform to the demands of God's law. Or Paul might mean that because Christ has fulfilled the law in our place, God considers all who are "in Christ" to have fulfilled the law.

8:5–9 "The flesh" is Paul's way of describing the bias toward sin that affects all human life (vv. 7,8; see the note on 7:5). But believers are "not in the realm of the flesh" (v. 9); this bias toward sin no longer controls them. Rather, "the Spirit of God lives in [them]" (v. 9) and creates in them a new way of thinking (vv. 5–6) and living (v. 4).

8:9–11 Paul switches quickly from "the Spirit of God lives in you" (v. 9) to "the Spirit of Christ" (v. 9) to "Christ is in you" (v. 10) to "the Spirit ... is living in you" (v. 11). The NT does not explicitly teach the doctrine of the Trinity (that God is one God existing in three Persons), but passages such as this clearly imply it.

8:12–13 These verses are often connected to the following paragraph (vv. 14–17), but more likely they conclude vv. 1–11: the life that the Spirit creates for us is worked out as believers respond to the work of the Spirit by actively using his power to conquer sin.

8:14 In the OT, God calls Israel (sometimes also called "Ephraim") his "son" (Exod 4:22; Jer 31:9,20), and Israelites accordingly call God "Father" (Jer 3:19). So by naming believers "the children of God," Paul is identifying them as the people of God, destined for "life" (v. 10).

8:15 adoption to sonship. Greek *huiothesia*; refers to the Greco-Roman practice of adoption, which guaranteed to adopted children all the rights and privileges of natural children (v. 23; 9:4; Gal 4:5; Eph 1:5). See "Sonship," p. 2664. While already adopted into God's family, many of the benefits of that status will be given only when God's work of redemption is finished (see v. 23). ***Abba.*** An Aramaic word for "Father" often used in intimate family settings. Jesus addressed God with this word (Mark 14:36), and believers adopted into God's family enjoy the same kind of intimate relationship with God.

8:16 testifies with our spirit. God's Spirit enables believers to experience their new life in their inner beings.

8:17 if indeed we share in his sufferings. Only those who fully identify with Christ in this life, entering into the sufferings that always accompany a godly lifestyle, will be able to share also in the glory that Christ already enjoys.

8:18–30 *Present Suffering and Future Glory.* This passage is framed by promises of the glory to which believers are destined (vv. 18,30). Like the created world, believers long for their ultimate redemption (vv. 19–23), waiting for it in hope (vv. 24–25). Believers can persevere in this hope because they recognize that the Spirit is helping them to pray rightly (vv. 26–27) and because God is at work on their behalf (vv. 28–30).

creation was subjected to frustration, not by its own choice, but by the will of the one who subjected
it,[b] in hope 21 that[a] the creation itself will be liberated from its bondage to decay[c] and brought into the
freedom and glory of the children of God.

22 We know that the whole creation has been groaning[d] as in the pains of childbirth right up to the
present time. 23 Not only so, but we ourselves, who have the firstfruits of the Spirit,[e] groan[f] inwardly as
we wait eagerly[g] for our adoption to sonship, the redemption of our bodies. 24 For in this hope we were
saved.[h] But hope that is seen is no hope at all. Who hopes for what they already have? 25 But if we hope
for what we do not yet have, we wait for it patiently.

26 In the same way, the Spirit helps us in our weakness. We do not know what we ought to pray for, but
the Spirit himself intercedes for us[i] through wordless groans. 27 And he who searches our hearts[j] knows
the mind of the Spirit, because the Spirit intercedes for God's people in accordance with the will of God.

28 And we know that in all things God works for the good of those who love him, who[b] have been
called[k] according to his purpose. 29 For those God foreknew[l] he also predestined[m] to be conformed to
the image of his Son,[n] that he might be the firstborn among many brothers and sisters. 30 And those
he predestined,[o] he also called; those he called, he also justified;[p] those he justified, he also glorified.[q]

More Than Conquerors

31 What, then, shall we say in response to these things?[r] If God is for us, who can be against us?[s] 32 He
who did not spare his own Son,[t] but gave him up for us all—how will he not also, along with him,
graciously give us all things? 33 Who will bring any charge[u] against those whom God has chosen? It is

8:20 [b] Ge 3:17-19
8:21 [c] Ac 3:21; 2Pe 3:13; Rev 21:1
8:22 [d] Jer 12:4
8:23 [e] 2Co 5:5 [f] 2Co 5:2, 4 [g] Gal 5:5
8:24 [h] 1Th 5:8
8:26 [i] Eph 6:18
8:27 [j] Rev 2:23
8:28 [k] 1Co 1:9; 2Ti 1:9
8:29 [l] Ro 11:2 [m] Eph 1:5,11 [n] 1Co 15:49; 2Co 3:18; Php 3:21; 1Jn 3:2
8:30 [o] Eph 1:5,11 [p] 1Co 6:11 [q] Ro 9:23
8:31 [r] Ro 4:1 [s] Ps 118:6
8:32 [t] Jn 3:16; Ro 4:25; 5:8
8:33 [u] Isa 50:8,9

[a] *20,21* Or *subjected it in hope.* *21For* [b] *28* Or *that all things work together for good to those who love God, who*; or *that in all things God works together with those who love him to bring about what is good—with those who*

8:18 our present sufferings. As in the related text in 5:3–4, Paul is frank about the reality of Christian suffering. As Paul and Barnabas warned the new believers in the province of Galatia, "We must go through many hardships to enter the kingdom of God" (Acts 14:22).
8:19 creation. The "subhuman" creation. Following OT examples (e.g., Ps 65:12–13; Isa 24:4; Jer 4:28; 12:4), Paul personifies the created world.
8:20 the one who subjected it. God, who cursed "the ground" in response to Adam's original sin (Gen 3:17). See "Creation," p. 2642.
8:21 the creation itself will be liberated. While the created world will be thoroughly renovated (2 Pet 3:7–13), it will not be destroyed. The "new heaven and a new earth" (Rev 21:1) will be a renewing of this world, not a replacement (cf. Col 1:20; Rev 21:5).
8:22 groaning as in the pains of childbirth. Combines suffering with hope and a joyful outcome (see also Matt 24:8; Mark 13:8; John 16:20–22).
8:23 firstfruits of the Spirit. In the OT, "firstfruits" describes the first and best part of a crop that is to be offered to God (e.g., Exod 23:19; Lev 2:12). Similarly, God gives the Spirit to believers as the down payment on the many other blessings that he promises to bestow on his heirs, his adopted children (v. 17; see 2 Cor 1:22; 5:5; Eph 1:14). **groan inwardly.** Not audible groans, but a way of connoting the frustrated longing for ultimate deliverance (Exod 3:7). **adoption to sonship, the redemption of our bodies.** Illustrates the typical NT tension between the "already" and the "not yet": while already given the status of God's adopted children (v. 15), believers do not yet possess all the benefits of that adoption, such as resurrected, renewed bodies.
8:26 the Spirit himself intercedes. The Spirit makes up for our helplessness when we do not know what to pray for; unknown to us, he brings before God the prayer that perfectly matches God's will for us. **wordless groans.** The Spirit, along with creation (v. 22) and believers (v. 23), "groans." These groans may be "wordless" because they do not take the form of normal human language or, more likely, because they are unspoken.
8:28 in all things God works for the good. A second reason—in addition to the Spirit's intercession (vv. 26–27)—that believers can "wait ... patiently" (v. 25) for their ultimate redemption: they can be confident that God works in all the circumstances of their lives to accomplish his good purpose for them. This is one of the great promises of Scripture. "The good" is not necessarily what believers might think is good but is what God deems will be best to assist their growth into the image of Christ (v. 29) and bring them to final glory (v. 30). **called.** God's "effectual" calling, whereby he powerfully draws sinners into relationship with him (1:6–7).
8:29–30 This sequence (or "chain") of God's acts on behalf of believers explains the "purpose" (v. 28) that God has for his people. The believer's confidence for the present time, as well as for future glory, is rooted in God's sovereign determination to call them into relationship with him, preserve them in that relationship, and vindicate them on the last day.
8:29 foreknew. Perhaps "knew ahead of time" (see Acts 26:5; 2 Pet 3:17, where the same Greek word is used): God "foreknew" who would believe in him and so predestined them. But "know" probably has the biblical sense of "enter into relationship with" (see Gen 18:19; Jer 1:5; Amos 3:2, where the same Hebrew word is translated "chosen," "knew," and "chosen," respectively): God chose to initiate a relationship with people "before the creation of the world" (Eph 1:4; cf. Rom 11:2; Acts 2:23; 1 Pet 1:2,20) and on that basis "predestined" them.
8:30 glorified. The final link in the "chain" of God's gracious acts on our behalf (see note on vv. 29–30) and the focus of Paul's concern. Having done all these other things for us, we can be utterly confident that God will complete his work by bringing us to glory.
8:31–39 *More Than Conquerors.* A moving hymnic response to the confidence that believers can have for the judgment to come (5:1—8:30). God is "for us" (v. 31), tirelessly working on our behalf (vv. 31–34) and showering his love upon us (vv. 35–39).
8:31 these things. The many promises found in 5:1—8:30. **who can be against us?** Satan may continue to battle against us and people may oppose us, but nothing can ever successfully separate the believer from God.
8:32 The logic here is similar to 5:9–10: since God has done the difficult thing (sending his Son to die for us), we can depend on him to give us all other things, especially what is necessary to bring us to final glory.

8:34 [v]Ro 5:6-8 [w]Mk 16:19 [x]Heb 7:25; 9:24; 1Jn 2:1
8:35 [y]1Co 4:11
8:36 [z]Ps 44:22; 2Co 4:11
8:37 [a]1Co 15:57 [b]Gal 2:20; Rev 1:5; 3:9
8:38 [c]Eph 1:21; 1Pe 3:22
8:39 [d]Ro 5:8
9:1 [e]2Co 11:10; Gal 1:20; 1Ti 2:7 [f]Ro 1:9
9:3 [g]Ex 32:32 [h]1Co 12:3; 16:22 [i]Ro 11:14
9:4 [j]Ex 4:22 [k]Ge 17:2; Ac 3:25; Eph 2:12 [l]Ps 147:19 [m]Heb 9:1 [n]Ac 13:32
9:5 [o]Mt 1:1-16 [p]Jn 1:1 [q]Ro 1:25
9:6 [r]Ro 2:28,29; Gal 6:16

God who justifies. 34 Who then is the one who condemns? No one. Christ Jesus who died[v]—more than
that, who was raised to life—is at the right hand of God[w] and is also interceding for us.[x] 35 Who shall
separate us from the love of Christ? Shall trouble or hardship or persecution or famine or nakedness
or danger or sword?[y] 36 As it is written:

"For your sake we face death all day long;
we are considered as sheep to be slaughtered."[a][z]

37 No, in all these things we are more than conquerors[a] through him who loved us.[b] 38 For I am convinced that neither death nor life, neither angels nor demons,[b] neither the present nor the future, nor
any powers,[c] 39 neither height nor depth, nor anything else in all creation, will be able to separate us
from the love of God[d] that is in Christ Jesus our Lord.

Paul's Anguish Over Israel

9 I speak the truth in Christ—I am not lying,[e] my conscience confirms[f] it through the Holy Spirit— 2 I have great sorrow and unceasing anguish in my heart. 3 For I could wish that I myself[g]
were cursed[h] and cut off from Christ for the sake of my people, those of my own race,[i] 4 the people of
Israel. Theirs is the adoption to sonship;[j] theirs the divine glory, the covenants,[k] the receiving of the
law,[l] the temple worship[m] and the promises.[n] 5 Theirs are the patriarchs, and from them is traced the
human ancestry of the Messiah,[o] who is God over all,[p] forever praised![c][q] Amen.

God's Sovereign Choice

6 It is not as though God's word had failed. For not all who are descended from Israel are Israel.[r]
7 Nor because they are his descendants are they all Abraham's children. On the contrary, "It is through

[a] *36* Psalm 44:22 [b] *38* Or *nor heavenly rulers* [c] *5* Or *Messiah, who is over all. God be forever praised!* Or *Messiah. God who is over all be forever praised!*

8:34 Who then is the one who condemns? Paul alludes to a similar expression of confidence in God's deliverance in Isa 50:7–9.

8:35 trouble or hardship or persecution or famine or nakedness or danger or sword. Paul had experienced firsthand God's faithfulness in the midst of such trials (2 Cor 11:23–27).

8:39 neither height nor depth. Perhaps refers to spiritual powers, but more likely is simply a figurative way of referring to everything in the created world (Eph 3:18).

9:1—11:36 *The Defense of the Gospel: The Problem of Israel.* Paul tackles one of the most pressing theological problems of his day: how to reconcile God's promises to Israel with Israel's failure to believe the Good News about Jesus the Messiah (9:1–5). Paul writes to the Roman Christians at a time when Gentiles are increasingly dominating the church both in Rome and in the wider Mediterranean world (see Introduction: Recipients; Purpose, 3). This situation is seemingly difficult to reconcile with God's OT promises addressed (at least mainly) to Israel. Paul's response is clear: "It is not as though God's word had failed" (9:6). Paul defends this claim in a four-stage argument. (1) God's promise had never embraced all Jews but only those whom God had chosen—whether Jews or Gentiles (9:6b–29). (2) Israel's predicament is a result of their failure to believe in Christ (9:30—10:21). (3) God's continuing faithfulness to his promises to Israel is seen in the present time in the many Jews (like Paul) who have responded to the gospel (11:1–10). (4) That faithfulness will be seen in the future when God saves "all Israel" (11:26; see 11:11–32). The question discussed in these chapters is vital to the truth of the gospel that Paul presents in Romans, for the gospel retains its power only so long as it culminates God's one plan of salvation (1:2; 3:21).

9:1–5 *Paul's Anguish Over Israel.* The central issue in chs. 9–11 is the tension between Israel's predicament (vv. 1–3) and God's promises (vv. 4–5).

9:3 my people. The Jews. Paul's deep and sincere sorrow for the Jews stems from most of them failing to believe the Good News about Jesus. Like Moses (Exod 32:30–32), Paul goes so far as to offer his own life on behalf of his fellow Jews—an offer he knows cannot be accepted.

9:4 people of Israel. In chs. 1–8, Paul refers to "Jews" as a way of connoting national identity. His shift to "Israel" and "Israelites" in chs. 9–11 emphasizes their covenant standing with God (vv. 6,27,31; 10:1,16,19,21; 11:2,7,11,25,26). **adoption to sonship.** This same status is given to believers in Christ (8:15,23). While God's adoption of Christians secures their salvation, Israel's "sonship" means that the people received God's blessing and promises (Exod 4:22; Jer 3:19; 31:9–10; Hos 11:1). **covenants.** In addition to the foundational covenant that God entered into with Israel at Sinai (e.g., Deut 5:2–3), the OT mentions several other covenants: with Abraham (Gen 17), Phinehas (Num 25:12–13), and David (2 Sam 23:5), and the "new covenant" (Jer 31:31–34). See also "the covenants of the promise" in Eph 2:12 and "Covenant," p. 2646.

9:5 Messiah, who is God over all, forever praised! The punctuation (which is not part of the original manuscripts) is debated (see NIV text note). But referring to the Messiah's "human ancestry" leads us to expect a contrasting reference to his divine status. This would then be one of a handful of NT texts that explicitly call Jesus "God" (John 1:1,18; 20:28; Titus 2:13; Heb 1:8; 2 Pet 1:1). **Messiah.** Greek *christos*; translates a Hebrew word that means "anointed one." The OT uses this language to refer to kings and, by extension, the coming ruler who would deliver Israel from sin and oppression (Ps 2:2; Isa 61:1; Dan 9:25–27 [perhaps]). English translations usually carry over the Greek word into English ("Christ"), but in places where it focuses attention on the OT and Jewish background, the NIV picks up the original Hebrew word (rendered "Messiah").

9:6–29 *God's Sovereign Choice.* Verse 6a states the thesis of chs. 9–11: God will be faithful to his word (i.e., in this context, his OT promises to Israel). The first stage in Paul's argument for this thesis unfolds in vv. 6b–29. Paul shows from the OT that God never intended for his promise to Israel to apply to all ethnic Israelites but only to those people whom God chose from within Israel (vv. 6b–13) and even from outside

THE TWO ISRAELS IN ROMANS 9:6

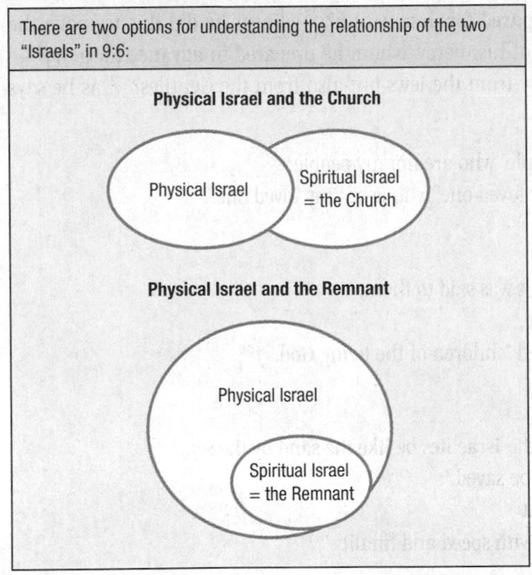

Isaac that your offspring will be reckoned."[as] 8In other words, it is not the
children by physical descent who are
God's children,[t] but it is the children of
the promise who are regarded as Abraham's offspring. 9For this was how the
promise was stated: "At the appointed
time I will return, and Sarah will have
a son."[bu]

10Not only that, but Rebekah's children were conceived at the same time
by our father Isaac.[v] 11Yet, before the
twins were born or had done anything
good or bad—in order that God's purpose[w] in election might stand: 12not by
works but by him who calls—she was
told, "The older will serve the younger."[cx] 13Just as it is written: "Jacob I
loved, but Esau I hated."[dy]

14What then shall we say? Is God unjust? Not at all![z] 15For he says to Moses,

> "I will have mercy on whom I have mercy,
> and I will have compassion on whom I have compassion."[ea]

16It does not, therefore, depend on human desire or effort, but on God's mercy.[b] 17For Scripture says
to Pharaoh: "I raised you up for this very purpose, that I might display my power in you and that my
name might be proclaimed in all the earth."[fc] 18Therefore God has mercy on whom he wants to have
mercy, and he hardens whom he wants to harden.[d]

19One of you will say to me:[e] "Then why does God still blame us? For who is able to resist his will?"[f]
20But who are you, a human being, to talk back to God? "Shall what is formed say to the one who

9:7 [s] Ge 21:12; Heb 11:18
9:8 [t] Ro 8:14
9:9 [u] Ge 18:10,14
9:10 [v] Ge 25:21
9:11 [w] Ro 8:28
9:12 [x] Ge 25:23
9:13 [y] Mal 1:2,3
9:14 [z] 2Ch 19:7
9:15 [a] Ex 33:19
9:16 [b] Eph 2:8
9:17 [c] Ex 9:16
9:18 [d] Ex 4:21
9:19 [e] Ro 11:19 [f] 2Ch 20:6; Da 4:35

[a] *7* Gen. 21:12 [b] *9* Gen. 18:10,14 [c] *12* Gen. 25:23 [d] *13* Mal. 1:2,3 [e] *15* Exodus 33:19
[f] *17* Exodus 9:16

Israel (vv. 24–29). Paul interrupts this argument to defend God's election (vv. 14–23).

9:6 are Israel. Perhaps all the people of God, both Jew and Gentile (see Gal 6:16 and note), but probably the elect from within physical Israel (vv. 7–13). True, "spiritual" Israel, to whom God's promises apply, is not identical to physical Israel (see "The Two Israels in Romans 9:6," this page).

9:7 Abraham's children. Since the people of Israel were descended from Abraham, they were known as Abraham's "descendants" (2 Chr 20:7; Ps 105:6; Isa 41:8; Jer 33:26) or "children" (Acts 13:26). Paul quotes the OT to show how God selected only some of Abraham's physical descendants to belong to Abraham's true, spiritual descendants (see also Gal 3:7). **through Isaac.** As Gen 21:12 indicates, God chose Abraham's son Isaac, not his other son Ishmael (Gen 16; 17:18–21; see Gal 4:21–31), to continue the line of promise.

9:10–12 The next patriarchal generation illustrates even more clearly that God chooses without regard to any human characteristics or virtues: Esau and Jacob were born to the same parents at the same time (they were twins), yet God chose one and not the other. Indeed, he even chose the younger (Jacob) of the two (Gen 25:23).

9:13 Jacob I loved, but Esau I hated. The sense is "Jacob I chose, but Esau I rejected" (see Luke 14:26 and note). The words are taken from Mal 1:2–3 and refer to the nations of Israel and Edom. It is possible that Paul applies the words in that sense here, referring to the way God has used different nations in accomplishing his purposes. But the context makes it more likely that he applies the text to personal election.

9:14 Is God unjust? A natural question arising from v. 13.

9:15 God is sovereign, bestowing his mercy on whom he chooses.

9:17 I raised you up for this very purpose. God made Pharaoh ruler of Egypt at the time of the exodus for his own purposes (Exod 9:16). Pharaoh's repeated refusal to let Israel go stimulated God to perform a series of signs and wonders, which caused God's "name" to become widely known (see note on Exod 9:16).

9:18 hardens whom he wants to harden. The exodus narrative describes Pharaoh as hardening his own heart (e.g., Exod 8:15,32; 9:34) as well as God acting to harden Pharaoh's heart (Exod 7:3; 9:12; 14:4,17; see Exod 4:21 and note). Paul refers to these latter texts to make a point about the sovereignty of God in both salvation (having mercy) and condemnation. Of course, Paul also insists that human beings justly earn their condemnation (1:21; see the emphasis on Israel's unbelief in 9:30—10:21).

9:19 Then why does God still blame us? Another question (cf. v. 14) in response to Paul's stress on God's sovereignty.

9:20–21 The references are to Isa 29:16; 45:9 and to the widespread OT comparison between God and the potter (e.g., Job 10:9; 38:14; Isa 64:8; Jer 18:1–6). God has the right to treat his human creatures as he chooses. Paul does not intend to deny human responsibility; as his repeated emphasis on the importance of faith reveals, human decisions

9:20 [g]Isa 64:8 [h]Isa 29:16
9:21 [i]2Ti 2:20
9:22 [j]Ro 2:4
9:23 [k]Ro 2:4 [l]Ro 8:30
9:24 [m]Ro 8:28 [n]Ro 3:29
9:25 [o]Hos 2:23; 1Pe 2:10
9:26 [p]Hos 1:10
9:27 [q]Ge 22:17; Hos 1:10 [r]Ro 11:5
9:28 [s]Isa 10:22,23
9:29 [t]Jas 5:4 [u]Isa 1:9; Dt 29:23; Isa 13:19; Jer 50:40
9:30 [v]Ro 1:17; 10:6; Gal 2:16; Php 3:9; Heb 11:7
9:31 [w]Isa 51:1; Ro 10:2, 3 [x]Gal 5:4
9:32 [y]1Pe 2:8

formed it,[g] 'Why did you make me like this?' "[a][h] 21 Does not the potter have the right to make out of the
same lump of clay some pottery for special purposes and some for common use?[i]
22 What if God, although choosing to show his wrath and make his power known, bore with great
patience[j] the objects of his wrath — prepared for destruction? 23 What if he did this to make the
riches of his glory[k] known to the objects of his mercy, whom he prepared in advance for glory[l] —
24 even us, whom he also called,[m] not only from the Jews but also from the Gentiles?[n] 25 As he says
in Hosea:

> "I will call them 'my people' who are not my people;
> and I will call her 'my loved one' who is not my loved one,"[b][o]

26 and,

> "In the very place where it was said to them,
> 'You are not my people,'
> there they will be called 'children of the living God.' "[c][p]

27 Isaiah cries out concerning Israel:

> "Though the number of the Israelites be like the sand by the sea,[q]
> only the remnant will be saved.[r]
> 28 For the Lord will carry out
> his sentence on earth with speed and finality."[d][s]

29 It is just as Isaiah said previously:

> "Unless the Lord Almighty[t]
> had left us descendants,
> we would have become like Sodom,
> we would have been like Gomorrah."[e][u]

Israel's Unbelief

30 What then shall we say? That the Gentiles, who did not pursue righteousness, have obtained it, a
righteousness that is by faith;[v] 31 but the people of Israel, who pursued the law as the way of righteousness,[w] have not attained their goal.[x] 32 Why not? Because they pursued it not by faith but as if it were by
works. They stumbled over the stumbling stone.[y] 33 As it is written:

a 20 Isaiah 29:16; 45:9 *b 25* Hosea 2:23 *c 26* Hosea 1:10 *d 28* Isaiah 10:22,23 (see Septuagint) *e 29* Isaiah 1:9

---

are significant. But God's sovereignty over all things, including salvation and eternal condemnation, is a foundational theme of the Bible. We must affirm both God's sovereignty and human responsibility without denying one or the other.

9:22 objects of his wrath. People who have earned God's wrath by their sin and so are destined for condemnation. **destruction.** Not annihilation but the ultimate "undoing" of humans in hell.

9:23 objects of his mercy. People whom God has chosen to benefit from his grace and enjoy his glory (cf. 5:2; 8:18,30).

9:24–29 Including Gentiles in the people of God is a persistent theme in Romans (e.g., 1:16). Paul illustrates in chiastic order (*a-b / b´-a´*):

- *a* God calls people from the Jews (v. 24b)
  - *b* God calls people from the Gentiles (v. 24c)
  - *b´* The OT confirms that God calls people from the Gentiles (vv. 25–26)
- *a´* The OT confirms that God calls people from the Jews (vv. 27–29)

The "not my people" of Hosea (Hos 1:10; 2:23) are the northern tribes of Israel. Paul, reading this prophecy in light of the Abrahamic promises, understands this phrase to include Gentiles as well (vv. 25–26; see 4:16–17). On the other hand, Isaiah (Isa 1:9; 10:22–23) speaks words of both warning and promise to Israel (vv. 27–29). Many Israelites had been unfaithful to God's covenant, leaving only a "remnant" to be saved (v. 27). But God commits himself to preserve this remnant in faithfulness to his promises to Israel (see 11:1–10).

9:30 — 10:21 *Israel's Unbelief.* The unexpected turn in salvation history — with many Gentiles and comparatively few Jews becoming saved — can be explained from the standpoint of God's election (9:6–29) or from the standpoint of human belief and unbelief (9:30 — 10:21). Gentiles have chosen to submit to God's righteousness in faith, while Israel, as a whole, has not.

9:30 a righteousness that is by faith. Right standing with God is available only through faith (3:21 — 4:25; see note on 3:21–31).

9:31 law as the way of righteousness. The people of Israel have, generally, not found right standing with God because they viewed the law of Moses, and the works it demands, as a way of attaining that right standing.

9:32 stumbling stone. Christ, the one whom God puts in everyone's path. People either build on him in faith or stumble over him to their ruin.

9:33 Paul quotes Isa 8:14; 28:16, which 1 Pet 2:4–8 also brings together (cf. Ps 118:22 in Mark 12:10 and parallels; see notes on Mark 12:10; 1 Pet 2:4–10).

> "See, I lay in Zion a stone that causes people to stumble
> and a rock that makes them fall,
> and the one who believes in him will never be put to shame."[a][z]

10 Brothers and sisters, my heart's desire and prayer to God for the Israelites is that they may be
saved. [2]For I can testify about them that they are zealous[a] for God, but their zeal is not based
on knowledge. [3]Since they did not know the righteousness of God and sought to establish their own,
they did not submit to God's righteousness.[b] [4]Christ is the culmination of the law[c] so that there may be
righteousness for everyone who believes.[d]

[5]Moses writes this about the righteousness that is by the law: "The person who does these things
will live by them."[b][e] [6]But the righteousness that is by faith[f] says: "Do not say in your heart, 'Who will
ascend into heaven?' "[c][g] (that is, to bring Christ down) [7]"or 'Who will descend into the deep?' "[d] (that
is, to bring Christ up from the dead). [8]But what does it say? "The word is near you; it is in your mouth
and in your heart,"[e][h] that is, the message concerning faith that we proclaim: [9]If you declare[i] with
your mouth, "Jesus is Lord," and believe in your heart that God raised him from the dead,[j] you will be
saved. [10]For it is with your heart that you believe and are justified, and it is with your mouth that you
profess your faith and are saved. [11]As Scripture says, "Anyone who believes in him will never be put to
shame."[f][k] [12]For there is no difference between Jew and Gentile[l]—the same Lord is Lord of all[m] and
richly blesses all who call on him, [13]for, "Everyone who calls on the name of the Lord[n] will be saved."[g][o]

[14]How, then, can they call on the one they have not believed in? And how can they believe in the
one of whom they have not heard? And how can they hear without someone preaching to them? [15]And
how can anyone preach unless they are sent? As it is written: "How beautiful are the feet of those who
bring good news!"[h][p]

[16]But not all the Israelites accepted the good news. For Isaiah says, "Lord, who has believed our message?"[i][q] [17]Consequently, faith comes from hearing the message,[r] and the message is heard through the
word about Christ.[s] [18]But I ask: Did they not hear? Of course they did:

9:33 [z]Isa 28:16; Ro 10:11
10:2 [a]Ac 21:20
10:3 [b]Ro 1:17
10:4 [c]Gal 3:24; Ro 7:1-4 [d]Ro 3:22
10:5 [e]Lev 18:5; Ne 9:29; Eze 20:11,13,21; Ro 7:10
10:6 [f]Ro 9:30 [g]Dt 30:12
10:8 [h]Dt 30:14
10:9 [i]Mt 10:32; Lk 12:8 [j]Ac 2:24
10:11 [k]Isa 28:16; Ro 9:33
10:12 [l]Ro 3:22,29 [m]Ac 10:36
10:13 [n]Ac 2:21 [o]Joel 2:32
10:15 [p]Isa 52:7; Na 1:15
10:16 [q]Isa 53:1; Jn 12:38
10:17 [r]Gal 3:2,5 [s]Col 3:16

[a] *33* Isaiah 8:14; 28:16 [b] *5* Lev. 18:5 [c] *6* Deut. 30:12 [d] *7* Deut. 30:13 [e] *8* Deut. 30:14
[f] *11* Isaiah 28:16 (see Septuagint) [g] *13* Joel 2:32 [h] *15* Isaiah 52:7 [i] *16* Isaiah 53:1

10:2 their zeal is not based on knowledge. Paul's fellow Jews display a commendable dedication to God, but it is not directed by true insight into the purposes of God. The Gospels repeatedly touch on this issue, as Jews fail to understand that God is revealing himself in Jesus (Matt 12:22–37; John 9:13–41).

10:3 sought to establish their own. Like Paul in his pre-Christian days (Phil 3:6), many Jews viewed their commitment to the law as a basis for their right standing before God. They failed to understand that God has made available his own way of putting them right before him in Christ (9:31–32; 10:5).

10:4 culmination. Greek *telos*; combines the ideas of "end" and "goal." Like the finish line in a race, Christ was what the law all along was directed toward; and now that Israel has reached the finish line (the coming of Christ), the race (the law) has ended. The law no longer governs the people of God in the way that it did before Christ (6:14–15; 7:4–6; Gal 3:23–25). **everyone who believes.** Gentiles as well as Jews (vv. 11–13).

10:5 The person who does these things will live by them. The promise of Lev 18:5 (see note there) summarized a key element of the Mosaic law (see also Ezek 20:11,13,21): the "life" of God's covenant promise would be achieved through obeying the law's commandments. Of course, the Pentateuch as a whole makes clear that faith was always the basis for a relationship with God (Gen 15:6).

10:6–8 Paul quotes language from Deut 30:12–14 to characterize "the righteousness that is by faith" (v. 6), which contrasts with "the righteousness that is by the law" (v. 5). The grace that characterized God's gift of his law in the old economy is now decisively displayed in Christ. Just as Moses made God's requirements accessible to the people of Israel, so Christ, who has come down from heaven and been raised from the dead, is accessible to all people by faith.

10:9 mouth ... heart. Paul takes up the words he quotes in v. 8 (taken from Deut 30:14). Paul's desire to reflect these terms means that we should be careful not to invest public confession of Christ with more significance than the rest of Scripture warrants. **Jesus is Lord.** A fundamental affirmation of Christian faith (1 Cor 12:3).

10:11 Paul returns to the language of Isa 28:16 (9:32–33).

10:12 there is no difference between Jew and Gentile. Jesus is Lord of both Jew and Gentile, and both have equal access to this Lord by the same means: faith (v. 4).

10:13 name of the Lord. "The LORD" in Joel 2:32 (from which Paul quotes) is Yahweh, the name that the OT uses over 6,000 times to depict the God of Israel. For Paul, however, this Lord is clearly Jesus (see v. 9). By applying to Christ an OT text that refers to Yahweh, Paul associates Christ with God himself.

10:14 they ... they ... they ... they ... they ... them. Perhaps Israelites in particular (see v. 2), but more likely all people, as in vv. 12–13. Paul lays out the steps necessary for people to call "on the name of the Lord" (v. 13), but in reverse order: preachers are sent, the preachers proclaim the message, people hear the message, and those who hear believe. Paul suggests in vv. 16–21 that God has completed the first three of these steps for Israel: the problem, then, is their failure to believe.

10:15 How beautiful are the feet of those who bring good news! Paul quotes Isa 52:7, which refers to those who announce the good news that the exiled people of Israel will be able to return to their own land. Paul applies the verse to Christian preachers, who proclaim the ultimate "good news" about God's intervention on behalf of all people in Christ (1:16).

10:18 Paul is not claiming that Ps 19:4 (which he quotes here) refers directly to the preaching of the gospel. Rather, he uses the language of

10:18 [t]Ps 19:4; Mt 24:14; Col 1:6,23; 1Th 1:8
10:19 [u]Ro 11:11,14 [v]Dt 32:21
10:20 [w]Isa 65:1; Ro 9:30
10:21 [x]Isa 65:2
11:1 [y]1Sa 12:22; Jer 31:37 [z]2Co 11:22 [a]Php 3:5
11:2 [b]Ro 8:29
11:3 [c]1Ki 19:10,14
11:4 [d]1Ki 19:18
11:5 [e]Ro 9:27
11:6 [f]Ro 4:4
11:7 [g]Ro 9:31 [h]ver 25; Ro 9:18
11:8 [i]Mt 13:13-15 [j]Dt 29:4; Isa 29:10
11:10 [k]Ps 69:22,23

"Their voice has gone out into all the earth,
their words to the ends of the world."[a][t]

19 Again I ask: Did Israel not understand? First, Moses says,

"I will make you envious[u] by those who are not a nation;
I will make you angry by a nation that has no understanding."[b][v]

20 And Isaiah boldly says,

"I was found by those who did not seek me;
I revealed myself to those who did not ask for me."[c][w]

21 But concerning Israel he says,

"All day long I have held out my hands
to a disobedient and obstinate people."[d][x]

The Remnant of Israel

11 I ask then: Did God reject his people? By no means![y] I am an Israelite myself, a descendant of
Abraham,[z] from the tribe of Benjamin.[a] 2 God did not reject his people, whom he foreknew.[b]
Don't you know what Scripture says in the passage about Elijah — how he appealed to God against
Israel: 3 "Lord, they have killed your prophets and torn down your altars; I am the only one left, and
they are trying to kill me"[e]?[c] 4 And what was God's answer to him? "I have reserved for myself seven
thousand who have not bowed the knee to Baal."[f][d] 5 So too, at the present time there is a remnant[e]
chosen by grace. 6 And if by grace, then it cannot be based on works;[f] if it were, grace would no longer be grace.

7 What then? What the people of Israel sought so earnestly they did not obtain.[g] The elect among
them did, but the others were hardened,[h] 8 as it is written:

"God gave them a spirit of stupor,
eyes that could not see
and ears that could not hear,[i]
to this very day."[g][j]

9 And David says:

"May their table become a snare and a trap,
a stumbling block and a retribution for them.
10 May their eyes be darkened so they cannot see,
and their backs be bent forever."[h][k]

[a] *18* Psalm 19:4 [b] *19* Deut. 32:21 [c] *20* Isaiah 65:1 [d] *21* Isaiah 65:2 [e] *3* 1 Kings 19:10,14 [f] *4* 1 Kings 19:18 [g] *8* Deut. 29:4; Isaiah 29:10 [h] *10* Psalm 69:22,23

the psalm (which is about God's revelation in nature) to describe the widespread availability of the gospel (see Col 1:23).
10:19 Did Israel not understand? By quoting from Deut 32:21 in v. 19 and Isa 65:1–2 in vv. 20–21, Paul justifies his implicit claim that Israel has, indeed, understood. In Deut 32:21, God made Israel "envious" to punish them for idolatry.
10:20 those who did not seek me. Gentiles. Both Moses and Isaiah, then, contrast faithless Israel (v. 21) with Gentiles whom God is using positively in his purposes. This contrast harks back to the beginning of this section (9:30–31). Nevertheless, the section ends on a note of hope (v. 21), a note that ch. 11 repeatedly sounds: God still holds out his hands to his people Israel.
11:1–10 *The Remnant of Israel.* The focus on a "remnant" (v. 5) in this section shows that Paul returns to a theme he first broached in 9:27. The existence of a remnant of true believers reveals God's continuing faithfulness to his promise to Israel (vv. 1–2).
11:1 Paul traces his ancestry to Benjamin, one of the 12 patriarchs (Gen 35:23–26; see Phil 3:5)—a mark of true Jewishness.
11:2 foreknew. Chose beforehand (see note on 8:29).
11:5 a remnant. The key point in this section. As in the time of Elijah, there is hope in the midst of widespread apostasy: God is preserving for himself faithful Jews who, like Paul, have responded in faith to the Good News.
11:6 if by grace, then it cannot be based on works. Echoes earlier teaching (4:4–5). Entrance into the remnant comes as a gift from God, not from human works of any kind.
11:7 What the people of Israel sought so earnestly. Right standing with God (9:31). **hardened.** Though the Greek verb is a different one, the idea here is the same as in 9:18 (see note there). As the OT quotations of Deut 29:4; Isa 29:10; Ps 69:22–23 show (respectively in vv. 8–10), this hardening, while not unrelated to human unbelief, is an act of God (see Isa 6:8–10; Mark 4:12).

Ingrafted Branches

11 Again I ask: Did they stumble so as to fall beyond recovery? Not at all![l] Rather, because of their
transgression, salvation has come to the Gentiles[m] to make Israel envious.[n] 12 But if their transgression
means riches for the world, and their loss means riches for the Gentiles,[o] how much greater riches will
their full inclusion bring!

13 I am talking to you Gentiles. Inasmuch as I am the apostle to the Gentiles,[p] I take pride in my
ministry 14 in the hope that I may somehow arouse my own people to envy[q] and save[r] some of them.
15 For if their rejection brought reconciliation[s] to the world, what will their acceptance be but life from
the dead?[t] 16 If the part of the dough offered as firstfruits[u] is holy, then the whole batch is holy; if the
root is holy, so are the branches.

17 If some of the branches have been broken off,[v] and you, though a wild olive shoot, have been
grafted in among the others[w] and now share in the nourishing sap from the olive root, 18 do not
consider yourself to be superior to those other branches. If you do, consider this: You do not support
the root, but the root supports you.[x] 19 You will say then, "Branches were broken off so that I could
be grafted in." 20 Granted. But they were broken off because of unbelief, and you stand by faith.[y] Do
not be arrogant,[z] but tremble.[a] 21 For if God did not spare the natural branches, he will not spare
you either.

11:11 [l]ver 1 [m]Ac 13:46 [n]Ro 10:19
11:12 [o]ver 25
11:13 [p]Ac 9:15
11:14 [q]ver 11; Ro 10:19 [r]1Co 1:21; 1Ti 2:4; Titus 3:5
11:15 [s]Ro 5:10 [t]Lk 15:24,32
11:16 [u]Lev 23:10,17; Nu 15:18-21
11:17 [v]Jer 11:16; Jn 15:2 [w]Ac 2:39; Eph 2:11-13
11:18 [x]Jn 4:22
11:20 [y]1Co 10:12; 2Co 1:24 [z]Ro 12:16; 1Ti 6:17 [a]1Pe 1:17

11:11–24 *Ingrafted Branches.* God's "hardening" of many Jews (v. 7) does not mean that he has given up on Israel. His plan still includes Jews.
11:11 their transgression. Most Jews refused to believe in Christ. **to make Israel envious.** God designed the salvation that Gentiles enjoy to stimulate Jews to repent (10:19).
11:12 riches for the world. The spiritual benefits bestowed on Gentiles who believe. **greater riches.** The extensive blessings that arrive at the culmination of the ages. **full inclusion.** Or "fullness," or "completeness"; probably the fulfillment of God's purposes for Israel when he saves many of them (vv. 25–26).
11:13 the apostle to the Gentiles. See 1:5; 15:16,18; Acts 9:15; 22:21; 26:17–18; Gal 1:16; 2:7,9; Eph 3:1,6,8; 1 Thess 2:15–16; 1 Tim 2:7; 2 Tim 4:17. Paul does not want the Gentile Christians in Rome to think that his focus on Gentiles implies that he has abandoned all hope for Israel.
11:15 their rejection. Either the Jews' rejecting God or, more likely (vv. 7–10), God's rejecting (many) Jews. **their acceptance.** God's accepting Jews into his kingdom (see 14:3; 15:7), in contrast to "their rejection." **life from the dead.** Either renewal to spiritual life (cf. 6:13; Paul may see the "full inclusion" of Jews [v. 12] as taking place over the course of the church age as Jews come to Christ) or the resurrection from the dead in the last day (God's "acceptance" of many Jews may be associated with the end times when the dead are physically raised).
11:16 dough offered as firstfruits. See Num 15:17–21. Offering the "first portion" of the harvested grain to the Lord consecrated the whole batch. **root.** The patriarchs (in the Apocrypha, see 1 Enoch 93:5; see also Philo, *Heir,* 279; Jubilees 21:24). **branches.** Jewish people. While all Jews are set apart as God's people in a general sense (3:1; 9:4–5; 11:1–2,28), only God's election, activated by faith, enables Jews (as well as Gentiles) to be saved.
11:17 some of the branches have been broken off. Some Jews have been cut off from true Israel because of God's hardening and their unbelief (see "their transgression" in vv. 11,12 and "their rejection" in v. 15). **wild olive shoot.** A Gentile, who does not naturally belong to the olive tree.
11:18 do not consider yourself to be superior. Throughout vv. 11–32 Paul has Gentile Christians especially in view (v. 13). Because so many Gentiles have come to Christ and make up so large a part of the church, they are beginning to look down on their Jewish brothers and sisters.
11:20 tremble. Or "fear." Believers must never presume the security God promises them in Christ. They remain within the people of God only as long as they persist in faith.

THE PATTERN OF GOD'S SAVING PLAN FOR ALL PEOPLE: JEWS AND GENTILES IN ROMANS 11

v. 11: because of their (the Jews) transgression → salvation has come to the Gentiles → to make Israel envious
v. 12: their (the Jews) transgression → riches for the world their loss → riches for the Gentiles their full inclusion → greater riches
v. 15: their (the Jews) rejection → reconciliation to the world their acceptance → life from the dead
vv. 17–23: some of the branches have been broken off → you (Gentiles), though a wild olive shoot, have been grafted in → God is able to graft them in again
vv. 25–26: Israel has experienced a hardening in part → until the full number of the Gentiles has come in → and in this way all Israel will be saved
vv. 30–31: as a result of their (the Jews) disobedience → you who were at one time disobedient to God have now received mercy, and as a result of God's mercy to you → they too may now receive mercy

11:22 [b]Ro 2:4 [c]1Co 15:2; Heb 3:6 [d]Jn 15:2
11:23 [e]2Co 3:16
11:25 [f]Ro 1:13 [g]Ro 16:25 [h]Ro 12:16 [i]ver 7; Ro 9:18 [j]Lk 21:24
11:27 [k]Isa 27:9; Heb 8:10,12
11:28 [l]Ro 5:10 [m]Dt 7:8; 10:15; Ro 9:5
11:29 [n]Ro 8:28 [o]Heb 7:21
11:30 [p]Eph 2:2
11:32 [q]Ro 3:9
11:33 [r]Ro 2:4 [s]Ps 92:5 [t]Job 11:7
11:34 [u]Isa 40:13,14; Job 15:8; 36:22; 1Co 2:16
11:35 [v]Job 35:7

22 Consider therefore the kindness[b] and sternness of God: sternness to those who fell, but kindness
to you, provided that you continue[c] in his kindness. Otherwise, you also will be cut off.[d] 23 And if they
do not persist in unbelief, they will be grafted in, for God is able to graft them in again.[e] 24 After all,
if you were cut out of an olive tree that is wild by nature, and contrary to nature were grafted into a
cultivated olive tree, how much more readily will these, the natural branches, be grafted into their
own olive tree!

All Israel Will Be Saved

25 I do not want you to be ignorant[f] of this mystery,[g] brothers and sisters, so that you may not be
conceited:[h] Israel has experienced a hardening[i] in part until the full number of the Gentiles has come
in,[j] 26 and in this way[a] all Israel will be saved. As it is written:

"The deliverer will come from Zion;
he will turn godlessness away from Jacob.
27 And this is[b] my covenant with them
when I take away their sins."[c][k]

28 As far as the gospel is concerned, they are enemies[l] for your sake; but as far as election is concerned, they are loved on account of the patriarchs,[m] 29 for God's gifts and his call[n] are irrevocable.[o]
30 Just as you who were at one time disobedient[p] to God have now received mercy as a result of their
disobedience, 31 so they too have now become disobedient in order that they too may now[d] receive mercy
as a result of God's mercy to you. 32 For God has bound everyone over to disobedience[q] so that he may
have mercy on them all.

Doxology

33 Oh, the depth of the riches[r] of the wisdom and[e] knowledge of God![s]
How unsearchable his judgments,
and his paths beyond tracing out![t]
34 "Who has known the mind of the Lord?
Or who has been his counselor?"[f][u]
35 "Who has ever given to God,
that God should repay them?"[g][v]

[a] 26 Or *and so* [b] 27 Or *will be* [c] 27 Isaiah 59:20,21; 27:9 (see Septuagint); Jer. 31:33,34
[d] 31 Some manuscripts do not have *now.* [e] 33 Or *riches and the wisdom and the* [f] 34 Isaiah 40:13
[g] 35 Job 41:11

11:22 provided that you continue. Only believers who persevere in faith will be saved from God's wrath on the day of judgment. Some theologians think that verses like this reveal that genuine believers can fail to persevere and so not be saved in the end. Others, however, insist that God himself, by his Spirit, maintains believers in the faith.
11:24 contrary to nature. Perhaps alludes to God's grace, which transforms sinful people into God's holy people. But more likely it simply notes that grafting a wild olive branch into a cultivated olive tree is an unusual procedure. See "The Pattern of God's Saving Plan for All People: Jews and Gentiles in Romans 11," p. 2313.
11:25–32 *All Israel Will Be Saved.* God is faithful to his promises to Israel (vv. 1–2) not only by preserving a remnant of Jewish believers now but also by acting to save "all Israel" (v. 26) in the future.
11:25 mystery. A word Paul uses for an element in God's plan that the OT does not clearly reveal (16:25; 1 Cor 2:1,7; 4:1; 13:2; 14:2; 15:51; Eph 1:9; 3:3,4,9; 5:32; 6:19; Col 1:26,27; 2:2; 4:3; 2 Thess 2:7 ["secret"]; 1 Tim 3:9 ["deep truths"],16). *This* mystery is the process by which God is using Israel's "hardening" and the salvation of Gentiles to save all Israel (vv. 25b–26a). **until the full number of the Gentiles has come in.** Probably when all elect Gentiles come into God's kingdom.
11:26 all Israel will be saved. "All Israel" need not mean every single Israelite. The OT uses this expression for a significant or representative number of Israelites (e.g., Josh 7:25; 2 Sam 16:22; Dan 9:11; cf. also Mishnah *Sanhedrin* 10:1). There are three main ways to explain this promise about one of the important results of God's providential work in history: (1) God saves all his elect people, both Jews and Gentiles, as they respond in faith to God's grace throughout history. "Israel" would then refer to the church (see Gal 6:16 and note for this possibility). (2) God saves all elect Jews as they respond in faith to God's grace throughout history. (3) God will save a significant number of Jews at the end of history. Whichever of these Paul has in mind, the salvation will be—as it always is since the coming of Christ into the world—through faith in Christ (10:9–13). **The deliverer will come from Zion.** Either Jesus' first or second coming.
11:28 they are enemies for your sake. God is using the Jewish people's estrangement from him to bring salvation to Gentiles (v. 11). **they are loved.** The striking juxtaposition of "enemies" and "loved" sums up the heart of Paul's teaching about the Jewish people in this chapter.
11:32 all. Not every single person, but every kind of person—Jew and Gentile alike.
11:33–36 *Doxology.* Paul fittingly concludes his sweeping description of God's plan of salvation with a doxology that expresses wonder and awe at what God is doing.
11:33–35 No one can fully comprehend God, who has no counselors or creditors.

36 For from him and through him and for him are all things.[w]
To him be the glory forever! Amen.[x]

A Living Sacrifice

12 Therefore, I urge you,[y] brothers and sisters, in view of God's mercy, to offer your bodies as a living sacrifice,[z] holy and pleasing to God—this is your true and proper worship. 2 Do not conform[a] to the pattern of this world,[b] but be transformed by the renewing of your mind.[c] Then you will be able to test and approve what God's will is[d]—his good, pleasing and perfect will.

Humble Service in the Body of Christ

3 For by the grace given me[e] I say to every one of you: Do not think of yourself more highly than you ought, but rather think of yourself with sober judgment, in accordance with the faith God has distributed to each of you. 4 For just as each of us has one body with many members, and these members do not all have the same function,[f] 5 so in Christ we, though many, form one body,[g] and each member belongs to all the others. 6 We have different gifts,[h] according to the grace given to each of us. If your gift is prophesying, then prophesy in accordance with your[a] faith;[i] 7 if it is serving, then serve; if it is teaching, then teach;[j] 8 if it is to encourage, then give encouragement;[k] if it is giving, then give generously;[l] if it is to lead,[b] do it diligently; if it is to show mercy, do it cheerfully.

Love in Action

9 Love must be sincere.[m] Hate what is evil; cling to what is good. 10 Be devoted to one another in love.[n] Honor one another above yourselves.[o] 11 Never be lacking in zeal, but keep your spiritual fervor,[p] serving the Lord. 12 Be joyful in hope,[q] patient in affliction,[r] faithful in prayer. 13 Share with the Lord's people who are in need. Practice hospitality.[s]

14 Bless those who persecute you;[t] bless and do not curse. 15 Rejoice with those who rejoice; mourn with those who mourn.[u] 16 Live in harmony with one another.[v] Do not be proud, but be willing to associate with people of low position.[c] Do not be conceited.[w]

[a] 6 Or *the* [b] 8 Or *to provide for others* [c] 16 Or *willing to do menial work*

11:36 [w] 1Co 8:6; Col 1:16; Heb 2:10 [x] Ro 16:27
12:1 [y] Eph 4:1 [z] Ro 6:13, 16, 19; 1Pe 2:5
12:2 [a] 1Pe 1:14 [b] 1Jn 2:15 [c] Eph 4:23 [d] Eph 5:17
12:3 [e] Ro 15:15; Gal 2:9; Eph 4:7
12:4 [f] 1Co 12:12-14; Eph 4:16
12:5 [g] 1Co 10:17
12:6 [h] 1Co 7:7; 12:4, 8-10 [i] 1Pe 4:10, 11
12:7 [j] Eph 4:11
12:8 [k] Ac 15:32 [l] 2Co 9:5-13
12:9 [m] 1Ti 1:5
12:10 [n] Heb 13:1 [o] Php 2:3
12:11 [p] Ac 18:25
12:12 [q] Ro 5:2 [r] Heb 10:32, 36
12:13 [s] 1Ti 3:2
12:14 [t] Mt 5:44
12:15 [u] Job 30:25
12:16 [v] Ro 15:5 [w] Jer 45:5; Ro 11:25

11:36 from … through … for. God is the source, means, and goal of all things.

12:1—15:13 *The Transforming Power of the Gospel: Christian Conduct.* The last major section of the body of Romans sets forth general principles and some specific applications of the gospel. The gospel provides not only salvation from God's wrath but also the power to live changed lives. Christ cannot be our Savior without also being our Lord.

12:1–2 *A Living Sacrifice.* This is a basic but comprehensive call to respond to God's multifaceted "mercy" (v. 1; the word is plural in the Greek). This call to transformed living is the heading for all that follows.

12:1 bodies. Not just the physical body but the whole person, with a view to our engaging the world around us. **living.** God's grace in Christ has made Christians spiritually alive (6:13). **true and proper worship.** The worship appropriate for thinking creatures who recognize all that God has done for them. This worship is not confined to the Sunday morning worship service; it embraces the whole of life.

12:2 pattern of this world. This present evil "age" (Greek *aiōn*; see Luke 16:8; 1 Cor 2:6,8; 3:18; Gal 1:4; Eph 2:2; 1 Tim 6:17; 2 Tim 4:10) has its own pattern of thinking and living that redeemed believers must avoid. **renewing of your mind.** The work of God's Spirit within must reprogram the "depraved mind" (1:28) that characterizes this world (see Eph 4:23).

12:3–8 *Humble Service in the Body of Christ.* Those who are being transformed through the renewing of their minds will refrain from thinking too highly of themselves, recognizing the gifts of others.

12:3 the faith God has distributed to each of you. Either the varying degrees of faith God has given to each believer or the Christian faith that all believers hold in common.

12:4–6 one body … different gifts. See 1 Cor 12.

12:6 gifts … grace. The Greek words are similar, suggesting that the gifts believers use to edify the community are the product of God's grace. **prophesying.** See note on 1 Cor 12:8–10.

12:7 serving. Any form of service to Christ and his people. **teaching.** See note on 1 Cor 12:28.

12:8 lead. The Greek word could also mean "give aid to."

12:9–21 *Love in Action.* In a rapid-fire series of commands, Paul urges believers to demonstrate "sincere" love (v. 9) to both fellow believers (vv. 10,13,15–16) and unbelievers (vv. 14,17–21).

12:9 Love. Not a directionless emotion, but a moral orientation toward kingdom values.

12:10 Honor one another above yourselves. The Lord Jesus himself models this attitude (Phil 2:3–7).

12:11 but keep your spiritual fervor. An alternative translation is "be set on fire by the Spirit."

12:12 joyful … patient … faithful. The three commands are related: focusing on the certain hope for glory that we have in Christ enables us to handle affliction with patience (see especially 5:5), and prayer taps into this distinctly countercultural mindset (1 Thess 5:16–18).

12:14 Paul's instructions in chs. 12–13 often reflect the teaching of Jesus. The parallel is very clear here (Matt 5:44; Luke 6:27–28).

12:16 Do not be proud. While broadly applicable, this manifestation of sincere love might apply specifically to the situation of the Roman Christians, especially the Gentile ones (v. 3; 11:18,25; 14:3,10,13). **be willing to associate with people of low position.** The NIV text note gives an alternate interpretation, taking the Greek for "people of low position" to refer to the low position itself.

12:17 [x]Pr 20:22 [y]2Co 8:21
12:18 [z]Mk 9:50; Ro 14:19
12:19 [a]Lev 19:18; Pr 20:22; 24:29 [b]Dt 32:35
12:20 [c]Pr 25:21,22; Mt 5:44; Lk 6:27
13:1 [d]Titus 3:1; 1Pe 2:13,14 [e]Da 2:21; Jn 19:11
13:3 [f]1Pe 2:14
13:4 [g]1Th 4:6
13:7 [h]Mt 17:25; 22:17,21; Lk 23:2

17 Do not repay anyone evil for evil.[x] Be careful to do what is right in the eyes of everyone.[y] 18 If it is possible, as far as it depends on you, live at peace with everyone.[z] 19 Do not take revenge,[a] my dear friends, but leave room for God's wrath, for it is written: "It is mine to avenge; I will repay,"[a][b] says the Lord. 20 On the contrary:

> "If your enemy is hungry, feed him;
> if he is thirsty, give him something to drink.
> In doing this, you will heap burning coals on his head."[b][c]

21 Do not be overcome by evil, but overcome evil with good.

Submission to Governing Authorities

13 Let everyone be subject to the governing authorities,[d] for there is no authority except that which God has established.[e] The authorities that exist have been established by God. 2 Consequently, whoever rebels against the authority is rebelling against what God has instituted, and those who do so will bring judgment on themselves. 3 For rulers hold no terror for those who do right, but for those who do wrong. Do you want to be free from fear of the one in authority? Then do what is right and you will be commended.[f] 4 For the one in authority is God's servant for your good. But if you do wrong, be afraid, for rulers do not bear the sword for no reason. They are God's servants, agents of wrath to bring punishment on the wrongdoer.[g] 5 Therefore, it is necessary to submit to the authorities, not only because of possible punishment but also as a matter of conscience.

6 This is also why you pay taxes, for the authorities are God's servants, who give their full time to governing. 7 Give to everyone what you owe them: If you owe taxes, pay taxes;[h] if revenue, then revenue; if respect, then respect; if honor, then honor.

a 19 Deut. 32:35 *b 20* Prov. 25:21,22

12:17 Do not repay anyone evil for evil. Another possible reference to the teaching of Jesus (Matt 5:39–42,44–45; cf. 1 Thess 5:15; 1 Pet 3:9). **do what is right in the eyes of everyone.** The explicit qualification "if it is possible" in v. 18 is implicit here also. Christians cannot (and should not) please everyone, but they should make "the teaching about God our Savior attractive" (Titus 2:10) by the way they love people inside and outside the church.

12:18 live at peace with everyone. See Matt 5:9; Jas 3:18.

12:19 leave room for God's wrath. Recognizing that God will judge all people in absolute equity means that believers should feel no compulsion to right all wrongs themselves.

12:20 you will heap burning coals on his head. Paul might mean that our kindness to enemies deepens the seriousness of their sin and so brings greater judgment upon them ("burning" and "fire" are frequent metaphors for judgment in the OT). But Paul more likely means that our kindness might result in their repentance (see Prov 25:21–22, from which Paul quotes; see also note on Prov 25:22).

12:21 evil ... good. The exposition of the many dimensions of love ends where it began (v. 9).

13:1–7 *Submission to Governing Authorities.* Paul turns his attention to governing authorities because they are God's "agents of wrath" (v. 4), charged with judging evil in this world (12:19). Believers, because they are committed to Christ as Lord, may be tempted to ignore or even stand against secular rulers, but believers must recognize the place of government in God's providential ordering of the world (vv. 1,5).

13:1 be subject. Or "be submissive." To submit means to recognize one's place under someone else in a hierarchy that God himself established (1 Cor 14:32,34; Eph 5:21; Col 3:18; Titus 2:5,9; 3:1; 1 Pet 3:1,5). So submission will usually result in obeying the "authority" placed over us. But crowning all hierarchies is God, so our submitting to secular rulers must always take place in light of our allegiance to our ultimate authority: God (see Acts 4:18–20). **governing authorities.** In Paul's day, these "authorities" would have included everyone from the Roman emperor down to local bureaucrats. **God has established ... established by God.** The Bible consistently recognizes that God's sovereignty extends to secular rulers (e.g., 1 Sam 12:8; Prov 8:15–16; Isa 41:2–4; 45:1–7; Jer 21:7,10; 27:5–6; Dan 2:21,37–38; 4:17).

13:2 judgment. Either the punishment inflicted by secular rulers or, perhaps more likely, God's judgment.

13:3 Paul describes secular rulers as they should function, not as they always do function. He knows from firsthand experience and from the long history of his own people that rulers do not always reward good and punish evil.

13:4 your good. For both individual believers and society as a whole. **sword.** A symbol of the force that the Roman Empire used to enforce order. Paul clearly acknowledges that government has the right to use force to punish wrongdoing; whether this force includes capital punishment is debated.

13:5 Paul succinctly summarizes his two points in vv. 1b–4: believers submit to rulers out of fear of being punished for wrongdoing (vv. 3–4) and because they recognize that God has appointed those rulers (vv. 1b–2). On this reading, "conscience" refers to a sense of right and wrong (2:15; 9:1). But it can also refer to the painful knowledge of a wrong that one has committed. If this is the meaning here, then Paul warns believers that they will have a sense of wrongdoing if they do not submit to the authorities.

13:6 The issue of paying taxes may reflect the influence of Jesus' teaching; he delivered his famous maxim "Give back to Caesar what is Caesar's, and to God what is God's" (Matt 22:21) in the midst of a discussion about taxes. It is also possible that Paul has an eye on the Roman Christians since secular historians mention a "tax revolt" in Rome at about the time Paul writes Romans.

Love Fulfills the Law

[8]Let no debt remain outstanding, except the continuing debt to love one another, for whoever loves
others has fulfilled the law.[i] [9]The commandments, "You shall not commit adultery," "You shall not
murder," "You shall not steal," "You shall not covet,"[a] and whatever other command there may be,
are summed up in this one command: "Love your neighbor as yourself."[b][k] [10]Love does no harm to a
neighbor. Therefore love is the fulfillment of the law.[l]

The Day Is Near

[11]And do this, understanding the present time: The hour has already come[m] for you to wake up from
your slumber,[n] because our salvation is nearer now than when we first believed. [12]The night is nearly
over; the day is almost here.[o] So let us put aside the deeds of darkness[p] and put on the armor[q] of light.
[13]Let us behave decently, as in the daytime, not in carousing and drunkenness, not in sexual immorality
and debauchery, not in dissension and jealousy.[r] [14]Rather, clothe yourselves with the Lord Jesus Christ,[s]
and do not think about how to gratify the desires of the flesh.[c]

The Weak and the Strong

14 Accept the one whose faith is weak,[t] without quarreling over disputable matters. [2]One person's
faith allows them to eat anything, but another, whose faith is weak, eats only vegetables. [3]The
one who eats everything must not treat with contempt[u] the one who does not, and the one who does

[a] *9* Exodus 20:13-15,17; Deut. 5:17-19,21 [b] *9* Lev. 19:18 [c] *14* In contexts like this, the Greek word for *flesh* (*sarx*) refers to the sinful state of human beings, often presented as a power in opposition to the Spirit.

13:8 [i]ver 10; Jn 13:34; Gal 5:14; Col 3:14
13:9 [j]Ex 20:13-15,17; Dt 5:17-19,21 [k]Lev 19:18; Mt 19:19
13:10 [l]ver 8; Mt 22:39,40
13:11 [m]1Co 7:29-31; 10:11 [n]Eph 5:14; 1Th 5:5,6
13:12 [o]1Jn 2:8 [p]Eph 5:11 [q]Eph 6:11,13
13:13 [r]Gal 5:20,21
13:14 [s]Gal 3:27; 5:16; Eph 4:24
14:1 [t]Ro 15:1; 1Co 8:9-12
14:3 [u]Lk 18:9

13:8–10 *Love Fulfills the Law.* Paul returns to the key Christian virtue of love (12:9–21).

13:8 Let no debt remain outstanding. Not "never incur a debt" but "make sure that you pay debts you incur on time." **continuing debt.** There is one debt Christians will never discharge: the debt to love. As often in the NT, the focus is on the obligation Christians have toward "one another" (fellow believers; cf. Gal 6:10). But believers are also called to love all people (12:9–21).

13:9 The commandments. Paul cites, respectively, the seventh, sixth, eighth, and tenth commandments from the Decalogue (Exod 20:13–17; Deut 5:17–21). This sequence is also found in some manuscripts of the Septuagint (the pre-Christian Greek translation of the OT) and in other Jewish writings. **Love your neighbor as yourself.** Paul once again echoes Jesus (Matt 22:34–40), who, when asked what is the greatest commandment in the law, cited the command to love God from Deut 6:5 and this command to love one's neighbor from Lev 19:18. As Jesus teaches so memorably in the parable of the Good Samaritan, the "neighbor" whom we must love is anyone the Lord puts in our path (Luke 10:25–37).

13:10 love is the fulfillment of the law. See also v. 8. Genuine love for others inevitably leads us to obey all the other commandments that set forth our obligations to other humans.

13:11–14 *The Day Is Near.* Paul frames his call to a distinctly Christian lifestyle with reminders of the nature of the time in which believers live: rescued from this evil age (see 12:2 and note); living in "the daytime" (v. 13), the time when God's plan has come to fulfillment; and looking ahead to the day when our salvation will be complete (v. 11).

13:11 this. Everything Paul commands in 12:1—13:10. **our salvation is nearer now.** Paul often uses the language of "salvation" to refer to the ultimate completion of God's work in our lives—a work that will not be finished until Christ returns and transforms our bodies so that we can enjoy the eternal kingdom of God (see 5:9–10 and note).

13:12 "Night" (and "darkness") and "day" (and "light") were ways of referring, respectively, to evil and good behavior in Paul's day (and ours). But "day" also alludes to the OT predictions about the day of the Lord, when God intervenes to save his people and judge their enemies (e.g., Isa 27; Jer 30:8–9; Joel 2:32; 3:18; Obad 15–17; cf. 1 Cor 3:13; 5:5; 2 Cor 6:2; Phil 1:6,10; 2:16; 1 Thess 5:2–8; 2 Thess 2:2–3; 2 Tim 1:12,18; 4:8). In keeping with NT teaching elsewhere, that day, when Christ returns to fully redeem his people, is imminent (1 Cor 7:29; Phil 4:5; Jas 5:9; 1 Pet 4:7; 1 John 2:18; see note on Amos 2:16).

13:13 daytime. Or simply "day," probably referring to the inaugurated "day of the Lord" (see note on v. 12).

13:14 clothe yourselves. See also Gal 3:27. Paul often uses the imagery of putting on clothes to urge believers to adopt the new way of life in Christ (v. 12; Eph 4:24; 6:11,14; Col 3:10,12; 1 Thess 5:8). The imagery may come from the early Christian baptism ritual in which new converts would put on a new set of clothes to symbolize their transition to a new existence.

14:1—15:13 *The Weak and the Strong.* Christians in Rome were divided over whether believers needed to continue to observe certain traditional Jewish practices derived from the law of Moses. Paul labels the Christian who thinks that believers should continue to observe those Jewish practices as "one whose faith is weak" (14:1); Paul labels those who do not believe that these practices are necessary as the "strong" (15:1). Paul urges them to live in peace with each other, respecting the opinions of believers they might differ with on this issue. While dealing with a first-century problem, Paul's advice is timeless. He gives believers guidelines on how to get along when they disagree about issues that are not central to the faith. See also the somewhat parallel passage in 1 Cor 8:1—11:1.

14:1–23 *Do Not Judge Each Other.* Paul addresses both the "weak" and the "strong," but he focuses special attention on the need for the strong to give up their rights to avoid creating spiritual problems for the weak.

14:1 the one whose faith is weak. A person who is not convinced that their faith in Christ gives them liberty to engage in certain kinds of behavior.

14:2 eats only vegetables. Refrains from eating meat (see v. 6). While the Mosaic law does not forbid meat, many Jews living in pagan environments would refrain from eating meat because of fears that it might have some association with pagan religion (Dan 1:3–16).

14:3 God has accepted them. Paul refrains from correcting either the "strong" or the "weak," showing that he views the issue dividing them as belonging to the *adiaphora*—practices that Scripture neither requires nor prohibits.

14:3 [v]Col 2:16
14:4 [w]Jas 4:12
14:5 [x]Gal 4:10
14:6 [y]Mt 14:19; 1Co 10:30,31; 1Ti 4:3,4
14:7 [z]2Co 5:15; Gal 2:20
14:8 [a]Php 1:20
14:9 [b]Rev 1:18 [c]2Co 5:15
14:10 [d]2Co 5:10
14:11 [e]Isa 45:23; Php 2:10,11
14:12 [f]Mt 12:36; 1Pe 4:5
14:13 [g]Mt 7:1
14:14 [h]Ac 10:15 [i]1Co 8:7
14:15 [j]Eph 5:2 [k]1Co 8:11
14:16 [l]1Co 10:30
14:17 [m]1Co 8:8 [n]Ro 15:13
14:18 [o]2Co 8:21
14:19 [p]Ps 34:14; Ro 12:18; Heb 12:14 [q]Ro 15:2; 2Co 12:19
14:20 [r]ver 15

not eat everything must not judge[v] the one who does, for God has accepted them. [4]Who are you to judge
someone else's servant?[w] To their own master, servants stand or fall. And they will stand, for the Lord
is able to make them stand.
[5]One person considers one day more sacred than another;[x] another considers every day alike. Each
of them should be fully convinced in their own mind. [6]Whoever regards one day as special does so to
the Lord. Whoever eats meat does so to the Lord, for they give thanks to God;[y] and whoever abstains
does so to the Lord and gives thanks to God. [7]For none of us lives for ourselves alone,[z] and none of us
dies for ourselves alone. [8]If we live, we live for the Lord; and if we die, we die for the Lord. So, whether
we live or die, we belong to the Lord.[a] [9]For this very reason, Christ died and returned to life[b] so that he
might be the Lord of both the dead and the living.[c]
[10]You, then, why do you judge your brother or sister[*a*]? Or why do you treat them with contempt? For
we will all stand before God's judgment seat.[d] [11]It is written:

"'As surely as I live,' says the Lord,
'every knee will bow before me;
every tongue will acknowledge God.'"[*b*e]

[12]So then, each of us will give an account of ourselves to God.[f]
[13]Therefore let us stop passing judgment[g] on one another. Instead, make up your mind not to put
any stumbling block or obstacle in the way of a brother or sister. [14]I am convinced, being fully persuaded in the Lord Jesus, that nothing is unclean in itself.[h] But if anyone regards something as unclean,
then for that person it is unclean.[i] [15]If your brother or sister is distressed because of what you eat, you
are no longer acting in love.[j] Do not by your eating destroy someone for whom Christ died.[k] [16]There-
fore do not let what you know is good be spoken of as evil.[l] [17]For the kingdom of God is not a matter
of eating and drinking,[m] but of righteousness, peace and joy in the Holy Spirit,[n] [18]because anyone who
serves Christ in this way is pleasing to God and receives human approval.[o]
[19]Let us therefore make every effort to do what leads to peace[p] and to mutual edification.[q] [20]Do not
destroy the work of God for the sake of food.[r] All food is clean, but it is wrong for a person to eat any-

[*a*] *10* The Greek word for ***brother or sister*** (*adelphos*) refers here to a believer, whether man or woman, as part of God's family; also in verses 13, 15 and 21. [*b*] *11* Isaiah 45:23

14:5 one day more sacred than another. Probably Jewish ceremonial days as well as the Sabbath. See also Gal 4:10; Col 2:16. **fully convinced in their own mind.** A principle that runs through this passage (vv. 14,16,22–23). Paul does not want a person to be forced to do something that their conscience is telling them not to do (1 Cor 8:7, 10,12).

14:6 does so to the Lord. Again, Paul views both the "weak" and the "strong" as sincere believers acting out of good motives.

14:7–9 Christ's death and resurrection establishes his lordship, which extends to every part of the believer's life.

14:10 You, then, why do you judge your brother or sister? Addressed to the "weak" believer who judges the "strong" believer for ignoring standard Jewish piety (v. 3). **why do you treat them with contempt?** Addressed to the "strong" believer who views with disdain and condescension the "weak" believer's insistence on clinging to certain rules. **we will all stand before God's judgment seat.** It is God, not our fellow believers, to whom each Christian is ultimately answerable. We should not let other believers force us to violate our conscience, nor should we presume to stand in the place of God by judging fellow believers.

14:13 The two parts of this verse bridge the two parts of ch. 14: the first summarizes vv. 1–12, and the second introduces the key idea of vv. 14–23. **stumbling block or obstacle.** Originally referred to, respectively, as (1) a physical object that might cause one to trip and fall and (2) a trap or snare. The Bible widely uses both words to refer to matters that might cause a believer to stray from their commitment to God (v. 20; cf. Exod 23:33; Josh 23:13; Ps 106:36; Isa 8:14; Matt 18:7; 1 Cor 8:9; 1 John 2:10).

14:14 nothing is unclean in itself. Following the lead of Jesus, who "declared all foods clean" (Mark 7:19), Paul is convinced that Christians no longer need to view any food as forbidden (Acts 10:15,28; 1 Tim 4:4; Titus 1:15). **for that person it is unclean.** Pious Jews who had been taught since birth that faithfulness to God required them to avoid certain foods would not easily have lost this scruple when they became believers. As he does throughout this passage, Paul recognizes the seriousness of violating one's conscience (vv. 5,23; cf. 1 Cor 8:4–7).

14:15 distressed because of what you eat. Addressed to the "strong" in faith. The concern is that the "strong" believer's eating might put pressure on the "weak" believer to eat also, which would violate the "weak" believer's conscience and thus cause them spiritual harm. **you are no longer acting in love.** All believers should be motivated in their behavior not by their own rights but by the central Christian virtue of love for others (12:9; 13:8–10). **destroy someone for whom Christ died.** Bring ultimate spiritual ruin on a person for whom Christ gave his life. It is not clear whether Paul views this as a real possibility or whether he uses very strong language to motivate believers to act in a loving way toward each other.

14:16 what you know is good. The freedom in Christ to eat any food or treat every day the same.

14:17 righteousness. Either one's righteous status before God (4:3; 5:17) or behavior that meets God's standard (e.g., 6:16,18).

14:20 the work of God. Perhaps the individual believer, "for whom Christ died" (v. 15), but more likely the Christian community. **All food is clean.** See note on v. 14.

thing that causes someone else to stumble.[s] 21It is better not to eat meat or drink wine or to do anything
else that will cause your brother or sister to fall.[t]
22So whatever you believe about these things keep between yourself and God. Blessed is the one who
does not condemn[u] himself by what he approves. 23But whoever has doubts[v] is condemned if they eat,
because their eating is not from faith; and everything that does not come from faith is sin.[a]

15 We who are strong ought to bear with the failings of the weak[w] and not to please ourselves.
2Each of us should please our neighbors for their good,[x] to build them up.[y] 3For even Christ
did not please himself[z] but, as it is written: "The insults of those who insult you have fallen on me."[b][a]
4For everything that was written in the past was written to teach us,[b] so that through the endurance
taught in the Scriptures and the encouragement they provide we might have hope.
5May the God who gives endurance and encouragement give you the same attitude of mind[c] toward
each other that Christ Jesus had, 6so that with one mind and one voice you may glorify the God and
Father[d] of our Lord Jesus Christ.
7Accept one another,[e] then, just as Christ accepted you, in order to bring praise to God. 8For I tell you
that Christ has become a servant of the Jews[c][f] on behalf of God's truth, so that the promises[g] made to
the patriarchs might be confirmed 9and, moreover, that the Gentiles[h] might glorify God[i] for his mercy.
As it is written:

> "Therefore I will praise you among the Gentiles;
> I will sing the praises of your name."[d][j]

10Again, it says,

> "Rejoice, you Gentiles, with his people."[e][k]

11And again,

> "Praise the Lord, all you Gentiles;
> let all the peoples extol him."[f][l]

12And again, Isaiah says,

14:20 [s] 1Co 8:9-12
14:21 [t] 1Co 8:13
14:22 [u] 1Jn 3:21
14:23 [v] ver 5
15:1 [w] Ro 14:1; Gal 6:1,2; 1Th 5:14
15:2 [x] 1Co 10:33 [y] Ro 14:19
15:3 [z] 2Co 8:9 [a] Ps 69:9
15:4 [b] Ro 4:23,24
15:5 [c] Ro 12:16; 1Co 1:10
15:6 [d] Rev 1:6
15:7 [e] Ro 14:1
15:8 [f] Mt 15:24; Ac 3:25, 26 [g] 2Co 1:20
15:9 [h] Ro 3:29 [i] Mt 9:8 [j] 2Sa 22:50; Ps 18:49
15:10 [k] Dt 32:43
15:11 [l] Ps 117:1

[a] *23* Some manuscripts place 16:25-27 here; others after 15:33. [b] *3* Psalm 69:9 [c] *8* Greek *circumcision*
[d] *9* 2 Samuel 22:50; Psalm 18:49 [e] *10* Deut. 32:43 [f] *11* Psalm 117:1

14:21 drink wine. Perhaps simply another matter that illustrates Paul's general point, but probably another of the issues (along with eating meat and observing special days) that divided the "strong" and the "weak." Jews often abstained from wine to avoid possible ritual contamination (Dan 1:3–16).
14:22 keep between yourself and God. The "strong" believer does not need to give up their liberty, but they must be willing to avoid practicing their liberty in situations that might cause spiritual harm to others.
14:23 from faith … from faith. What one's faith convinces a person they can or cannot do (see note on v. 1).
15:1–13 *Accept Each Other in Christ.* Paul concludes his plea for unity among the Roman Christians by exhorting the "strong" (vv. 1–4), summarizing his key concern (vv. 5–7), and rehearsing the theological point that underlies his exhortation: the equality of Jew and Gentile in the new covenant people of God (vv. 8–13).
15:1 We who are strong. Those who are convinced that their faith gives them liberty to eat anything (14:2), treat every day alike (14:5), and drink wine (14:21). Even though he is a Jewish Christian, Paul aligns himself with the "strong" (14:14). **bear with the failings of the weak.** See Gal 6:2.
15:2 neighbors. Alludes to the love command of Lev 19:18, quoted in Rom 13:9 (see note).
15:3 Christ did not please himself. Christ went to the cross at the will of the Father, sacrificing himself for the sake of others (Mark 14:36; 2 Cor 8:9; Phil 2:6–7). **The insults of those who insult you have fallen on me.** A quotation from Psalms, from which NT authors frequently draw to describe Christ's passion (Matt 27:34; Mark 15:35–36; Luke 23:36; John 15:25; 19:28 and note). Here Paul refers to how Christ (the "me" of Ps 69:9) on the cross suffered for doing the Father's will.
15:4 everything that was written in the past was written to teach us. A fundamental principle in the Christian understanding of the Bible. What God caused to be written in the OT has ultimate relevance to Christians, who experience the fulfillment of the OT promises (see 1 Cor 10:6,11; 2 Tim 3:16–17). Of course the many different kinds of material in the OT relate to Christians in different ways.
15:5 the same attitude of mind toward each other that Christ Jesus had. A mindset that puts the interests of others ahead of our own (Phil 2:4–7).
15:7 Accept one another. Not grudgingly accept into our fellowship believers we disagree with but welcome them warmly as true brothers and sisters.
15:8 a servant of the Jews. Christ focused his earthly mission on his fellow Jews (Matt 15:24). Israel, as Paul also insists, has a certain priority in God's plan by virtue of being chosen as God's OT people (1:16; 3:1–2; 11:1–2,28).
15:9–12 This series of OT quotations (see NIV text notes) focuses on the participation of Gentiles in the worship of the God of Israel. By choosing OT texts that focus on praising God and rejoicing in him, Paul reinforces the concern of v. 6.
15:9 that the Gentiles might glorify God. Summarizes a keynote in the theology of Romans: God faithfully fulfills his promises to his people Israel while at the same time accomplishing his purpose to integrate Gentiles fully into the people of God (see especially 11:11–32).
15:12 in him the Gentiles will hope. Isa 11:10 (which Paul is quoting)

15:12 [m]Rev 5:5 [n]Isa 11:10; Mt 12:21
15:13 [o]Ro 14:17 [p]ver 19; 1Co 2:4; 1Th 1:5
15:14 [q]Eph 5:9 [r]2Pe 1:12
15:15 [s]Ro 12:3
15:16 [t]Ac 9:15; Ro 11:13 [u]Ro 1:1 [v]Isa 66:20
15:17 [w]Php 3:3 [x]Heb 2:17
15:18 [y]Ac 15:12; 21:19; Ro 1:5 [z]Ro 16:26
15:19 [a]Jn 4:48; Ac 19:11 [b]ver 13 [c]Ac 22:17-21
15:20 [d]2Co 10:15,16
15:21 [e]Isa 52:15
15:22 [f]Ro 1:13
15:23 [g]Ac 19:21; Ro 1:10,11
15:24 [h]ver 28

"The Root of Jesse[m] will spring up,
one who will arise to rule over the nations;
in him the Gentiles will hope."[a][n]

13 May the God of hope fill you with all joy and peace[o] as you trust in him, so that you may overflow
with hope by the power of the Holy Spirit.[p]

Paul the Minister to the Gentiles

14 I myself am convinced, my brothers and sisters, that you yourselves are full of goodness,[q] filled
with knowledge[r] and competent to instruct one another. 15 Yet I have written you quite boldly on some
points to remind you of them again, because of the grace God gave me[s] 16 to be a minister of Christ Jesus
to the Gentiles.[t] He gave me the priestly duty of proclaiming the gospel of God,[u] so that the Gentiles
might become an offering[v] acceptable to God, sanctified by the Holy Spirit.
17 Therefore I glory in Christ Jesus[w] in my service to God.[x] 18 I will not venture to speak of anything
except what Christ has accomplished through me in leading the Gentiles[y] to obey God[z] by what I have
said and done— 19 by the power of signs and wonders,[a] through the power of the Spirit of God.[b] So
from Jerusalem[c] all the way around to Illyricum, I have fully proclaimed the gospel of Christ. 20 It has
always been my ambition to preach the gospel where Christ was not known, so that I would not be
building on someone else's foundation.[d] 21 Rather, as it is written:

"Those who were not told about him will see,
and those who have not heard will understand."[b][e]

22 This is why I have often been hindered from coming to you.[f]

Paul's Plan to Visit Rome

23 But now that there is no more place for me to work in these regions, and since I have been longing for many years to visit you,[g] 24 I plan to do so when I go to Spain.[h] I hope to see you while passing
through and to have you assist me on my journey there, after I have enjoyed your company for a

a 12 Isaiah 11:10 (see Septuagint) *b 21* Isaiah 52:15 (see Septuagint)

reads "the nations will rally to him." The difference is a matter of wording only; Paul, as usual, is using the Septuagint (the pre-Christian Greek translation of the OT).
15:14—16:27 *The Letter Closing.* This includes many of the standard elements in such closings: the author's travel plans (15:14–29), a request for prayer (15:30–33), a reference to ministry associates (16:1–2,21–23), greetings (16:3–16), and a doxology (16:25–27). Each of these elements is much longer in Romans than in most of the other NT letters.
15:14–22 *Paul the Minister to the Gentiles.* Paul reminds the Romans of his past ministry.
15:14 As he does in the letter opening (1:8–12), Paul reveals a deft diplomatic touch by speaking so highly of believers who live in a city he has never visited.
15:16 a minister of Christ Jesus to the Gentiles. Paul's authority to write "quite boldly" (v. 15) to the Roman Christians is based on God's own appointment of him to be "the apostle to the Gentiles" (see 11:13 and note; cf. Gal 1:15–16). **the Gentiles might become an offering acceptable to God.** Describing his apostolic ministry in priestly terminology, Paul identifies the offering he makes: the Gentiles themselves. Paul may have in mind the prophecy of Isa 66:19–20, which speaks of declaring God's glory "among the nations" and of bringing people from "all the nations" to Jerusalem as an "offering to the LORD."
15:19 signs and wonders. Paul's ministry was accompanied by authenticating miracles (Acts 14:8–10; 16:16–18; 19:11–12; 20:9–12; 28:8–9; 2 Cor 12:12), much as God revealed his power through the "signs and wonders" at the time of the exodus (Exod 7:3; see also Exod 11:9–10). **from Jerusalem all the way around to Illyricum.** For the ministry of Paul in Jerusalem, see Acts 9:28–29. The NT never refers to a ministry of Paul in Illyricum, a Roman province in the region of modern-day Croatia, Bosnia, Serbia, and Albania. But Paul might mean that he ministered "as far as the border of" Illyricum (e.g., in Macedonia and Greece). Paul's Greek suggests the idea of an arc, and an arc drawn from Jerusalem to Illyricum would touch on the regions in the eastern Mediterranean where Paul planted churches. **I have fully proclaimed the gospel.** In key cities throughout this region, Paul planted vibrant churches that can carry on the work of evangelism in their own locales.
15:20–21 Paul is convinced that God has called him to a ministry of pioneer church planting, a ministry he thinks is foreshadowed by Isaiah's prophecy about the servant of the Lord (Isa 52:15); Paul applies language from Isaiah's "servant" texts to himself elsewhere (1:1; Gal 1:15–16; Eph 3:7; Col 1:23).
15:23–33 *Paul's Plan to Visit Rome.* Paul shifts his focus to his present situation and his future plans.
15:23 no more place for me to work in these regions. Paul has completed his ministry of initial church planting.
15:24 Spain. The entire Iberian Peninsula in Paul's day (i.e., the territory now associated with the countries of Spain and Portugal), which had become a Roman province only recently. Paul might have chosen to preach in Spain because he identified it with places such as Tarshish or "the distant islands" in OT prophecy (e.g., Isa 66:19). **assist me on my journey there.** Spain was a long way from Paul's "sending church" (Antioch), and he needed financial and logistical help from a church closer to his new ministry area.

while. [25]Now, however, I am on my way to Jerusalem[i] in the service[j] of the Lord's people there. [26]For
Macedonia[k] and Achaia[l] were pleased to make a contribution for the poor among the Lord's people in
Jerusalem. [27]They were pleased to do it, and indeed they owe it to them. For if the Gentiles have shared
in the Jews' spiritual blessings, they owe it to the Jews to share with them their material blessings.[m]
[28]So after I have completed this task and have made sure that they have received this contribution, I
will go to Spain and visit you on the way. [29]I know that when I come to you,[n] I will come in the full
measure of the blessing of Christ.

[30]I urge you, brothers and sisters, by our Lord Jesus Christ and by the love of the Spirit,[o] to join me
in my struggle by praying to God for me.[p] [31]Pray that I may be kept safe[q] from the unbelievers in Judea and that the contribution I take to Jerusalem may be favorably received by the Lord's people there,
[32]so that I may come to you[r] with joy, by God's will,[s] and in your company be refreshed.[t] [33]The God of
peace[u] be with you all. Amen.

15:25 [i]Ac 19:21 [j]Ac 24:17
15:26 [k]Ac 16:9; 2Co 8:1 [l]Ac 18:12
15:27 [m]1Co 9:11
15:29 [n]Ro 1:10,11
15:30 [o]Gal 5:22 [p]2Co 1:11; Col 4:12
15:31 [q]2Th 3:2
15:32 [r]Ro 1:10,13 [s]Ac 18:21 [t]1Co 16:18
15:33 [u]Ro 16:20; 2Co 13:11; Php 4:9; 1Th 5:23; Heb 13:20
16:1 [v]2Co 3:1 [w]Ac 18:18
16:2 [x]Php 2:29
16:3 [y]Ac 18:2 [z]ver 7,9,10
16:5 [a]1Co 16:19; Col 4:15; Phm 2 [b]1Co 16:15

Personal Greetings

16 I commend[v] to you our sister Phoebe, a deacon[a,b] of the church in Cenchreae.[w] [2]I ask you to
receive her in the Lord[x] in a way worthy of his people and to give her any help she may need
from you, for she has been the benefactor of many people, including me.

[3]Greet Priscilla[c] and Aquila,[y] my co-workers in Christ Jesus.[z] [4]They risked their lives for me. Not only
I but all the churches of the Gentiles are grateful to them.
[5]Greet also the church that meets at their house.[a]
Greet my dear friend Epenetus, who was the first convert[b] to Christ in the province of Asia.

[a] *1* Or *servant* [b] *1* The word *deacon* refers here to a Christian designated to serve with the overseers/elders of the church in a variety of ways; similarly in Phil. 1:1 and 1 Tim. 3:8,12. [c] *3* Greek *Prisca*, a variant of *Priscilla*

15:25 the service of the Lord's people there. The "collection" for impoverished Jewish believers in Jerusalem. Paul mentions this important project in all three letters written on his third missionary journey (here; 1 Cor 16:1–2; 2 Cor 8–9).
15:26 Macedonia and Achaia. Christians living in these Roman provinces, which included the cities of Philippi, Thessalonica, Berea, Athens, and Corinth. **the poor among the Lord's people in Jerusalem.** Several severe famines afflicted Jerusalem and its surrounding territory in Paul's lifetime (Acts 11:27–28 refers to a famine affecting the entire Roman Empire).
15:27 the Jews' spiritual blessings. The ancestors of the Jews were the original recipients of the promises. Gentiles enjoy the blessings God promised his people only by being included in the one people of God (11:17–24). See "The Pattern of God's Saving Plan for All People: Jews and Gentiles in Romans 11," p. 2313.
15:31 Pray that I may be kept safe from the unbelievers in Judea. Paul's bold turn to the Gentiles in his preaching of the gospel was very contentious among Jews, especially in the Jewish homeland of Judea. He was right to be worried about his reception; when he arrived in Jerusalem, Jews misconstrued his actions in the temple and rioted against him (Acts 21:27–32). **favorably received.** Paul viewed the collection not only as a work of charity but also as a way to ease the developing tension between Jews and Gentiles in the church of his day. Getting Gentiles to give money to their Jewish brothers and sisters and getting the Jewish believers to accept it was a practical way of binding the two groups together.
16:1–27 *Personal Greetings.* Paul had been engaged in missionary work for 25 years when he wrote Romans. He had developed relationships with believers scattered all across the eastern Mediterranean world.
16:1–2 Phoebe was a prominent Christian who was planning to travel to Rome. Paul probably took the opportunity of her planned trip to entrust her with the delivery of his letter to the Roman Christians.
16:1 deacon. Greek *diakonos*; could also be translated "servant" (see NIV text note). But calling Phoebe a *diakonos* "of the church" suggests that she holds some kind of official position. Her apparent wealth (she was a "benefactor" [v. 2]) fits well with the office of deacon, which apparently focused on financially and logistically supporting the church (1 Tim 3:11 may mention female deacons [see note]; on "deacons," see also Phil 1:1; 1 Tim 3:8–10). **Cenchreae.** A port about six miles (nine kilometers) from Corinth, where Paul is apparently located as he writes this letter (Acts 20:2–3).
16:2 benefactor. The "patron," an important figure in the Greco-Roman world who used their money and influence to support various causes. Phoebe used her worldly advantages to help many believers, including Paul himself.
16:3–16 Although Paul has never visited Rome, he has encountered many of the Christians who live there in the course of his ministry in the eastern Mediterranean. The names of people in the ancient world often signaled their ethnic origin or social status. The 26 names in these verses reveal that the Roman Christian community was very diverse, with men and women, Jews and Gentiles, and people from both the upper and lower classes (Gal 3:28).
16:3 Priscilla and Aquila. Paul first met them in Corinth during his second missionary journey (Acts 18:2). They were apparently natives of Rome who, along with other Jews and Jewish Christians, had been forced to leave Rome when the emperor Claudius expelled all the Jews from the city (probably in AD 49). They not only shared Paul's passion for Christian ministry but were also in the same leather-working trade as Paul.
16:4 risked their lives for me. The NT does not record this incident, but the last part of this verse implies that it was widely known.
16:5 church that meets at their house. Christians in Paul's day did not have dedicated church buildings; they met in private homes. This list of greetings may refer to at least two other such "house churches" (see vv. 14,15). **province of Asia.** The Roman province located in western Asia Minor (see note on 2 Tim 1:15).

16:7 [c]ver 11,21
16:9 [d]ver 3
16:11 [e]ver 7,21
16:15 [f]ver 2 [g]ver 14
16:16 [h]1Co 16:20; 2Co 13:12; 1Th 5:26
16:17 [i]Gal 1:8,9; 1Ti 1:3; 6:3 [j]2Th 3:6,14; 2Jn 10
16:18 [k]Php 3:19 [l]Col 2:4
16:19 [m]Ro 1:8 [n]Mt 10:16; 1Co 14:20
16:20 [o]Ro 15:33 [p]Ge 3:15 [q]1Th 5:28
16:21 [r]Ac 16:1 [s]Ac 13:1 [t]Ac 17:5 [u]ver 7,11

6 Greet Mary, who worked very hard for you.
7 Greet Andronicus and Junia, my fellow Jews[c] who have been in prison with me. They are outstanding among[a] the apostles, and they were in Christ before I was.
8 Greet Ampliatus, my dear friend in the Lord.
9 Greet Urbanus, our co-worker in Christ,[d] and my dear friend Stachys.
10 Greet Apelles, whose fidelity to Christ has stood the test.
Greet those who belong to the household of Aristobulus.
11 Greet Herodion, my fellow Jew.[e]
Greet those in the household of Narcissus who are in the Lord.
12 Greet Tryphena and Tryphosa, those women who work hard in the Lord.
Greet my dear friend Persis, another woman who has worked very hard in the Lord.
13 Greet Rufus, chosen in the Lord, and his mother, who has been a mother to me, too.
14 Greet Asyncritus, Phlegon, Hermes, Patrobas, Hermas and the other brothers and sisters with them.
15 Greet Philologus, Julia, Nereus and his sister, and Olympas and all the Lord's people[f] who are with them.[g]
16 Greet one another with a holy kiss.[h]
All the churches of Christ send greetings.

17 I urge you, brothers and sisters, to watch out for those who cause divisions and put obstacles in
your way that are contrary to the teaching you have learned.[i] Keep away from them.[j] 18 For such people
are not serving our Lord Christ, but their own appetites.[k] By smooth talk and flattery they deceive[l] the
minds of naive people. 19 Everyone has heard[m] about your obedience, so I rejoice because of you; but I
want you to be wise about what is good, and innocent about what is evil.[n]

20 The God of peace[o] will soon crush[p] Satan under your feet.
The grace of our Lord Jesus be with you.[q]

21 Timothy,[r] my co-worker, sends his greetings to you, as do Lucius,[s] Jason[t] and Sosipater, my fellow
Jews.[u]
22 I, Tertius, who wrote down this letter, greet you in the Lord.

[a] 7 Or *are esteemed by*

16:6 Mary. The NT mentions six persons with this name. This Mary is otherwise unknown. Paul commends her for dedicated service of Christ (see also v. 12).

16:7 Andronicus and Junia. Probably a husband-and-wife missionary team. While the Greek word for "Junia" could denote either a woman or a man, it probably here denotes a woman. **in prison with me.** This imprisonment cannot be identified; Paul alludes to many imprisonments (2 Cor 11:23) not recorded in Acts or his letters. **outstanding among the apostles.** Or "esteemed by the apostles" (see NIV text note). In any case, the word "apostle" may not refer to the authoritative position that Paul and "the Twelve" occupied (e.g., 1:1; Luke 6:13). The Greek word here was also used in the sense of "accredited messenger," "representative," or "missionary" (1 Cor 9:5; 2 Cor 8:23; Phil 2:25).

16:8–10 Ampliatus ... Urbanus ... Stachys ... Apelles. Common slave names. They may have been either slaves or "freedmen," former slaves who had gained their freedom.

16:10 Aristobulus. Probably the brother of Herod Agrippa I (ruled Palestine from AD 41–44). Aristobulus was dead at the time Paul wrote Romans (see chart/map, pp. 1930–1931), so the "household" of Aristobulus refers to slaves who served the family that still went by his name.

16:12 Tryphena and Tryphosa. Siblings were often given similar sounding names in the ancient world, so these women were probably sisters, perhaps even twins.

16:13 Rufus. Perhaps the son of Simon of Cyrene, who carried Christ's cross on the way to his execution (Mark 15:21).

16:14–15 None of these people are otherwise known to us. Their names suggest that they were slaves or freedmen (see note on vv. 8–10).

16:16 holy kiss. A common greeting in the ancient world generally and among Jews in particular (1 Cor 16:20; 2 Cor 13:12; 1 Thess 5:26; 1 Pet 5:14).

16:17–19 A warning about false teachers is unusual in NT letter closings—especially in this case since the letter does not explicitly mention false teaching anywhere else. Paul's description of the teachers is too general to enable us to identify who they were or what they were teaching.

16:18 appetites. Or "bellies," a vivid way of indicating their preoccupation with satisfying their own bodily comforts (cf. Phil 3:19). **naive people.** "Innocence" about doing evil is a good thing (v. 19), but innocence that involves ignorance about Christian doctrine is dangerous.

16:19 wise about what is good, and innocent about what is evil. Christians should have the wisdom to discern the good they should be doing, and they should be unacquainted with doing what is evil.

16:20 The God of peace will soon crush Satan under your feet. A startling juxtaposition, reminding us that the "peace" (Hebrew *šālôm*) that God intends to establish involves an ultimate victory over evil. Paul alludes to the first promise of redemption given in the Garden of Eden: God promised that Eve's offspring would "crush" Satan's "head" (Gen 3:15).

16:21 Timothy. One of Paul's closest ministry associates; he joined Paul on his second missionary journey (Acts 16:1–3) and was with Paul in Corinth as he wrote this letter to the Romans (Acts 20:3–4). **Jason.** Perhaps the same Jason with whom Paul stayed during his ministry in Thessalonica (Acts 17:5–9).

16:22 wrote down this letter. It was customary in Paul's day for people to dictate their letters to trained scribes (amanuenses).

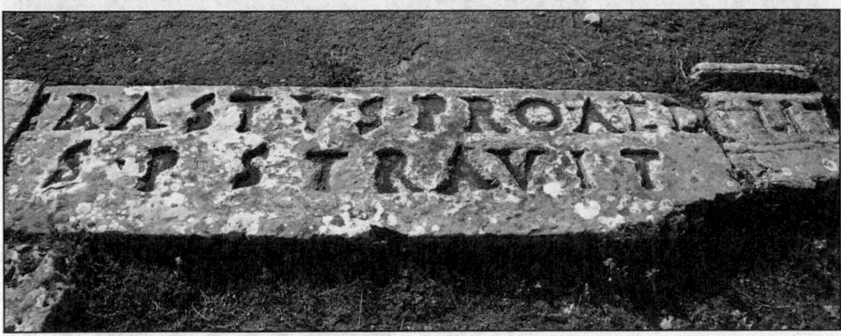

A Latin inscription in Corinth dating to the mid-first century AD mentions an "Erastus," probably the same Erastus mentioned by Paul (see Rom 16:23 and note). The inscription reads: "Erastus, in return for his aedileship, laid [this pavement] at his own expense."

www.HolyLandPhotos.org

23 Gaius, whose hospitality I and the whole church here enjoy, sends you his greetings.
Erastus,[v] who is the city's director of public works, and our brother Quartus send you their greetings. [24][a]

25 Now to him who is able[w] to establish you in accordance with my gospel,[x] the message I proclaim
about Jesus Christ, in keeping with the revelation of the mystery[y] hidden for long ages past, 26 but now
revealed and made known through the prophetic writings by the command of the eternal God, so that
all the Gentiles might come to the obedience that comes from[b] faith— 27 to the only wise God be glory
forever through Jesus Christ! Amen.[z]

16:23 [v]Ac 19:22
16:25 [w]Eph 3:20 [x]Ro 2:16 [y]Eph 1:9; Col 1:26,27
16:27 [z]Ro 11:36

[a] 24 Some manuscripts include here *May the grace of our Lord Jesus Christ be with all of you. Amen.*
[b] 26 Or *that is*

16:23 Gaius. Perhaps the Gaius mentioned in 1 Cor 1:14. This Gaius may also have been known as Titius Justus, whom Acts 18:7 identifies as the person with whom Paul stayed in Corinth. **Erastus ... the city's director of public works.** The Greek word rendered "director of public works" probably corresponds to the Latin *aedile.* An inscription discovered on an ancient block of stone in Corinth probably refers to this same Erastus: "Erastus, in return for his aedileship, laid [this pavement] at his own expense." Acts 19:22; 2 Tim 4:20 also mention an Erastus, but the name was common enough that it is uncertain whether they refer to the same man.

16:25–27 Some manuscripts of Romans omit this doxology or put it in a different place in the letter. But the doxology is found in most manuscripts and is probably original.

16:25 mystery. Certain aspects of God's fulfillment of his plan that were not clear before Christ came (see note on 11:25).

16:26 prophetic writings. The entire OT, viewed in terms of its anticipation of the fulfillment of God's purposes. The phrase corresponds to "through his prophets in the Holy Scriptures" at the beginning of the letter (1:2). **all the Gentiles.** Paul often associates the "mystery" (v. 25) with including Gentiles in the people of God (Eph 3:6; Col 1:26–27). **obedience that comes from faith.** Another phrase that echoes the beginning of the letter (1:5).

INTRODUCTION TO 1 CORINTHIANS

Paul wrote the letter we know as 1 Corinthians to the Christians in Corinth probably in AD 54, three years after he established the church (the fall of 50 to the spring of 52). Paul set out from Antioch in Syria in the spring of 49, after the Jerusalem council concluded, to engage in missionary ministry in the province of Asia, a plan that God did not allow to be carried out. When the new goal of preaching the gospel in the province of Bithynia also proved elusive, Paul accepted God's guidance and crossed over to Europe (Acts 15:40 — 16:10). After establishing churches in the province of Macedonia, including Philippi, Thessalonica, and Berea (16:11 — 17:15), Paul moved south into the province of Achaia, where he founded churches in Athens (17:16 – 34) and Corinth (18:1 – 18).

THE CITY OF CORINTH

Corinth was situated in a strategic position about six miles (ten kilometers) west of the isthmus on the junction of the routes linking the Peloponnese and Attica. The city flourished from about 725 BC and first struck coins about 600 BC. Since it led the resistance against Rome, Corinth was destroyed in 146 BC by the Roman consul Lucius Mummius. The city remained virtually deserted for a century. In 44 BC Julius Caesar reestablished the city as a Roman colony (*Colonia Laus Iulia Corinthus*), settling 3,000 freed slaves and army veterans there. The colony was intended to safeguard Roman control of the trade between Rome and the eastern Mediterranean. Corinth flourished soon after it was reestablished. Many of the destroyed buildings were restored, including the temple of Apollo, the temple of Asclepius, the South Stoa, the Fountain of Peirene, the Fountain of Glauke, and the theater; new buildings were erected with a distinctly Roman architecture. By 27 BC Corinth was the administrative center of the senatorial province of Achaia. The famous Isthmian Games were returned to Corinthian control in AD 50. It is estimated that Roman Corinth had

LOCATION OF CORINTH

about 80,000 inhabitants; if we include the inhabitants of the towns and villages belonging to the territory of Corinth, that number would grow to 100,000. To understand the society and culture of Corinth in the first century, one needs to analyze Roman rather than (classical) Greek culture: the majority of inscriptions dating to the first century were written in Latin. The most important deities were Aphrodite and Poseidon. The Latin-speaking elite were active in the imperial cult. The deities Demeter and Kore/Persephone were popular among the poorer population, as were Isis and Sarapis. The presence of Jews is attested by Luke's account in Acts 18 as well as by a second- or third-century lintel with the inscription "synagogue of the Hebrews."

PAUL AND THE PROBLEMS OF THE CHURCH IN CORINTH

In 52–55, while establishing a new center of missionary work in Ephesus, the capital of the province of Asia, Paul received news about problems in the Corinthian church. He first responded by writing a letter about how the church should treat Christians living sexually immoral lives (see 1 Cor 5:9); this letter has not been preserved. Paul evidently heard of further problems in Corinth, prompting him to send his co-worker Timothy, who was to remind the Corinthians of apostolic life and teaching (4:17). Further news from Corinth prompted Paul to write the letter we call 1 Corinthians. The news about Corinth came from at least two sources: (1) a letter some Corinthian believers wrote to Paul (7:1) and (2) verbal information given to Paul by people from the household of a certain Chloe (1:11; cf. 5:1).

The multiplicity and variety of themes that Paul discusses in 1 Corinthians does not mean that he simply addresses various problems of the Christians in Corinth of which he has been made aware. Paul argues with a basic coherence and unity. The problems in the Corinthian church derive from contemporary cultural values of Greco-Roman society that some of the Corinthian believers never abandoned or to which they returned after Paul left the city. They include concerns with superior rhetoric, competitively evaluating orators (the church's missionaries and pastors), purely pragmatic behavior regarding sexuality, social status expressed in dress codes, ranking spiritual gifts, and dominating church meetings.

The themes that Paul discusses in 1 Corinthians can be divided into two main areas: conflict within the congregation and compromises with the non-Christian, hedonistic values of Greco-Roman society. Five themes are connected with congregational conflict: church leaders (1:10—4:21), lawsuits (6:1–11), the Lord's Supper (11:17–34), spiritual gifts (chs. 12–14), and Stephanas and Apollos (16:12–18). Seven themes are associated with cultural compromise: incest (5:1–13), sexual immorality (6:12–20), marriage (7:1–24), the unmarried (7:25–40), dining in pagan temples (8:1—11:1), head coverings (11:2–16), and resurrection (15:1–58).

What connects all these subjects is the gospel: God forgives and saves people through Jesus Christ, the crucified and risen Savior and Lord—a fundamental reality that directly affects the life of the church and individual believers. God's power as revealed in Jesus' death and resurrection powerfully moves Jews and Gentiles, rich and poor, educated and uneducated (1:26–29) to believe the gospel (2:1–5); and the gospel powerfully transforms Christians so they can resist the lure and convenience of "worldly" traditions and the values of contemporary society (3:1; 5:10–11; 6:9–11; 15:32–34) and live lives of "righteousness, holiness and redemption" (1:30).

Paul addresses ethical questions by clarifying the relevant theological parameters, focusing on the person and work of Jesus Christ. Thus, in addition to revealing Paul's position on specific ethical matters, 1 Corinthians provides fundamental insight into Paul's theology and its application to specific questions of everyday behavior and lifestyle.

FOCUS ON JESUS CHRIST

Paul consistently focuses on Jesus' death on the cross and its consequences. (The only exceptions are his discussions regarding head coverings [11:2–16] and the gifts of the Spirit [chs. 12–14].) Paul demonstrates the futility of divisions and rivalry in the church by emphasizing that the center of the gospel is "Christ crucified" (1:23): Jesus, the crucified Messiah, is a stumbling block to Jews and foolishness to Greeks but "the power of God and the wisdom of God" (1:24; see 1:30; 2:1–2) for those whom God has called. The one and only foundation of the church is thus Jesus Christ (3:11; see 4:15). The missionaries and pastors of the church should not be judged "until the Lord comes" (4:5), at which time the Lord will expose the motivations of each Christian worker. When Paul addresses a case of incest in the church, he speaks of "Christ, our Passover lamb" (5:7). In his critique of believers who initiate lawsuits against other believers, he reminds the Corinthian Christians that they were washed, sanctified, and justified "in the name of the Lord Jesus Christ and by the Spirit of our God" (6:11). Paul clarifies that one of the reasons believers must not have sexual relations with prostitutes is that they "were bought at a price" (6:20), which refers to Christ's death on the cross. Paul repeats this when discussing changing one's social status: "you were bought at a price" (7:23). When discussing

Ruins of the Temple of Apollo at Corinth.

whether Christians can participate in banquets held in pagan temples and eat food that has been sacrificed to idols, Paul repeatedly refers to Jesus' death. He reminds Christians that Jesus Christ is the mediator of creation, God's own agent in creation, the one who caused all things to come into being; Jesus is Lord as God is Lord (8:6). Paul exhorts believers to avoid behavior that would destroy a fellow believer "for whom Christ died" (8:11), and Paul demonstrates the incompatibility of dining in pagan temples and participating in the Lord's Supper by pointing out that in the Lord's Supper, Christians enjoy and celebrate "participation in the blood of Christ … [and] the body of Christ" (10:16). As regards the neglect of poor Christians by rich Christians during the meetings of the congregation, Paul extensively narrates the tradition of the Lord's Supper with its remembrance of Jesus giving his body and his blood (11:24–25), reminding the believers that as they "proclaim the Lord's death" (11:26) in their meetings, they must be willing to share with others as Jesus shared, indeed sacrificed, his life. Finally, Paul's discussion of the resurrection of the body is prefaced by an extensive reference to the gospel tradition that all Christians receive and believe: "Christ died for our sins according to the Scriptures [and] … was raised on the third day according to the Scriptures" (15:3–4).

OUTLINE

I. Introduction (1:1–9)

II. Divisions in the Church (1:10—4:21)

A. A Church Divided Over Leaders (1:10–17)
B. Christ Crucified Is God's Power and Wisdom (1:18—2:5)
C. God's Wisdom Revealed by the Spirit (2:6–16)
D. The Church and Its Leaders (3:1–23)
E. The Nature of True Apostleship (4:1–13)
F. Paul's Appeal and Warning (4:14–21)

III. Ethical Confusion in the Church (5:1—6:20)

A. Dealing With a Case of Incest (5:1–13)
B. Lawsuits Among Believers (6:1–11)
C. Sexual Immorality (6:12–20)

IV. Issues Related to Lifestyle (7:1—11:1)
- A. Marriage and Celibacy (7:1–40)
  1. Concerning Married Life (7:1–16)
  2. Concerning Change of Status (7:17–24)
  3. Concerning the Unmarried (7:25–40)
- B. Food Sacrificed to Idols and Participation in Banquets (8:1—11:1)
  1. Concerning Food Sacrificed to Idols (8:1–13)
  2. Illustration: Paul's Own Behavior (9:1–27)
     - a. Paul's Rights as an Apostle (9:1–18)
     - b. Paul's Use of His Freedom (9:19–23)
     - c. The Need for Self-Discipline (9:24–27)
  3. Warnings From Israel's History (10:1–13)
  4. Idol Feasts and the Lord's Supper (10:14–22)
  5. The Believer's Freedom (10:23—11:1)

V. Issues Related to Behavior in Church Meetings (11:2—14:40)
- A. On Covering the Head in Worship (11:2–16)
- B. Correcting an Abuse of the Lord's Supper (11:17–34)
- C. The Gifts of the Spirit (12:1—14:40)
  1. Concerning Spiritual Gifts (12:1–11)
  2. Unity and Diversity in the Body (12:12–31a)
  3. Love Is Indispensable (12:31b—13:13)
  4. Intelligibility in Worship (14:1–25)
  5. Good Order in Worship (14:26–40)

VI. Resurrection (15:1–58)
- A. The Resurrection of Christ (15:1–11)
- B. The Resurrection of the Dead (15:12–34)
- C. The Resurrection Body (15:35–58)

VII. Concluding Matters (16:1–24)
- A. The Collection for the Lord's People (16:1–4)
- B. Personal Requests (16:5–18)
- C. Final Greetings (16:19–24)

1 CORINTHIANS

1:1 [a]Ro 1:1; Eph 1:1 [b]2Co 1:1 [c]Ac 18:17
1:2 [d]Ac 18:1 [e]Ro 1:7
1:3 [f]Ro 1:7
1:4 [g]Ro 1:8
1:5 [h]2Co 9:11 [i]2Co 8:7
1:6 [j]Rev 1:2
1:7 [k]Php 3:20; Titus 2:13; 2Pe 3:12
1:8 [l]1Th 3:13
1:9 [m]Isa 49:7; 1Th 5:24 [n]1Jn 1:3

1 Paul, called to be an apostle[a] of Christ Jesus by the will of God,[b] and our brother Sosthenes,[c]

2 To the church of God in Corinth,[d] to those sanctified in Christ Jesus and called[e] to be his holy people,
together with all those everywhere who call on the name of our Lord Jesus Christ—their Lord and ours:

3 Grace and peace to you from God our Father and the Lord Jesus Christ.[f]

Thanksgiving

4 I always thank my God for you[g] because of his grace given you in Christ Jesus. 5 For in him you have been
enriched[h] in every way—with all kinds of speech and with all knowledge[i]— 6 God thus confirming our testimony[j] about Christ among you. 7 Therefore you do not lack any spiritual gift as you eagerly wait for our Lord
Jesus Christ to be revealed.[k] 8 He will also keep you firm to the end, so that you will be blameless[l] on the day of
our Lord Jesus Christ. 9 God is faithful,[m] who has called you into fellowship with his Son, Jesus Christ our Lord.[n]

A Church Divided Over Leaders

10 I appeal to you, brothers and sisters,[a] in the name of our Lord Jesus Christ, that all of you agree
with one another in what you say and that there be no divisions among you, but that you be perfectly

[a] *10* The Greek word for *brothers and sisters* (*adelphoi*) refers here to believers, both men and women, as part of God's family; also in verses 11 and 26; and in 2:1; 3:1; 4:6; 6:8; 7:24, 29; 10:1; 11:33; 12:1; 14:6, 20, 26, 39; 15:1, 6, 50, 58; 16:15, 20.

1:1–9 *Introduction.* Following the traditional format of letter openings, Paul mentions himself as the author/sender of the letter (v. 1) and identifies the recipients (v. 2) before greeting the believers in Corinth (v. 3) and expressing thanks to God (vv. 4–9). Though Paul founded the church (4:15; 9:2), when he thinks of the church, he gives thanks to God because the church is not his work but God's work (3:5–17), the result of God granting grace to sinners (2 Cor 4:15) in Christ Jesus, i.e., through the death and resurrection of Jesus, Israel's Messiah (2:2; 15:3–7). The Corinthian believers have received God's grace, and God has given them riches of speech, knowledge, and spiritual gifts—gifts that Paul addresses in the letter. Paul emphasizes that Christians need to continue depending on God.

1:1 called. Occurred when Paul was traveling to Damascus, where he planned to arrest, interrogate, and punish Christians (Acts 9:1–19). Paul is a missionary not because he volunteered but because he responded to God's will.

1:2 sanctified ... holy people. Paul's description may sound surprising in view of the problems in the Corinthian church; however, for Paul, these attributes are not qualities that result from the (transformed) behavior of the believers but are theological assertions: the congregation is "the church of God," i.e., an assembly God himself brought into existence (1 Thess 1:4; 2:12; 4:7); their status of being "sanctified" ("made holy"; the verb *hagiazō* has the same Greek root as the adjective *hagios* ["holy"]) is due to God's purifying action in Jesus Christ, and as a result, their sins have been forgiven, enabling them to serve God; they are "holy" because of the initiative of God, who "called" them (cf. Exod 19:6; Lev 19:2; Deut 7:6); and they are people who trust in Jesus as Messiah and Lord.

1:5 in every way. The riches God has given the Corinthian believers are not restricted, because they express God's grace (v. 4) and result from Christ's work ("in him"). **speech ... knowledge.** Communication and spiritual insight, two areas that the Corinthians evidently value more than others; they involve rhetorical abilities, prayer, teaching, words of wisdom, words of knowledge, speaking in unlearned languages, and prophecy.

1:6 testimony about Christ. The gospel preached to them. God is using the spiritual riches he gave to the Corinthian church to strengthen the believers in understanding and in applying the gospel.

1:8–9 Believers place their confidence not in their spiritual riches but in Jesus Christ and in God's faithfulness.

1:8 keep you firm. Or strengthen you. **the end ... the day.** When Jesus returns (5:5; 2 Cor 1:14; Phil 1:10; 1 Thess 5:2). As a result of Jesus' work in the lives of the believers, they will be "blameless" (i.e., irreproachable) on the day of judgment, because they have responded to the call of God (1:2; see note).

1:9 faithful. God's promise of perseverance until the end is trustworthy. **fellowship.** Believers participate in the sonship of Jesus, who is the firstborn among a large family (Rom 8:29) and with whom believers have been crucified and will be raised from the dead (Rom 6:6,8; Col 2:20; 3:1).

1:10—4:21 *Divisions in the Church.* The first problem Paul tackles.

united in mind and thought. [11]My brothers and sisters, some from Chloe's household have informed me
that there are quarrels among you. [12]What I mean is this: One of you says, "I follow Paul";[o] another, "I
follow Apollos";[p] another, "I follow Cephas[a]";[q] still another, "I follow Christ."
[13]Is Christ divided? Was Paul crucified for you? Were you baptized in the name of Paul?[r] [14]I thank
God that I did not baptize any of you except Crispus[s] and Gaius,[t] [15]so no one can say that you were baptized in my name. [16](Yes, I also baptized the household of Stephanas;[u] beyond that, I don't remember
if I baptized anyone else.) [17]For Christ did not send me to baptize,[v] but to preach the gospel — not with
wisdom[w] and eloquence, lest the cross of Christ be emptied of its power.

1:12 [o]1Co 3:4,22 [p]Ac 18:24 [q]Jn 1:42
1:13 [r]Mt 28:19
1:14 [s]Ac 18:8; Ro 16:23 [t]Ac 19:29
1:16 [u]1Co 16:15
1:17 [v]Jn 4:2 [w]1Co 2:1,4,13
1:18 [x]2Co 2:15 [y]Ro 1:16
1:19 [z]Isa 29:14

Christ Crucified Is God's Power and Wisdom

[18]For the message of the cross is foolishness to those who are perishing,[x] but to us who are being
saved it is the power of God.[y] [19]For it is written:

> "I will destroy the wisdom of the wise;
> the intelligence of the intelligent I will frustrate."[b][z]

[a] *12* That is, Peter [b] *19* Isaiah 29:14

1:10–17 *A Church Divided Over Leaders.* This introduction to 1:10—4:21 reveals two related problems: (1) There are divisions in the church that have led to proclamations of loyalty to one or another of the missionaries and leaders of the church (Paul, Apollos, Cephas). (2) Some people in the church do not place the proclamation of Jesus the crucified Messiah at the center of their understanding of the gospel. The divisions were based on the rhetorical refinement and argumentative brilliance ("wisdom and eloquence," v. 17) of the church's preachers, teachers, and missionaries (cf. 2:1,4,13).

1:10,11 brothers and sisters. Reminds the Corinthians that they are one single family and is the basis for the exhortation to unity: a harmoniously functioning family. Paul's appeal is based not on his personal opinion but on the presence of the Lord Jesus Christ in the congregation.

1:10 in the name of our Lord Jesus Christ. Suggests Jesus' presence in the apostle's admonition. **divisions.** Dissension resulting from conflicting objectives, convictions, or emphases. **perfectly united in mind and thought.** United in the same mind and in the same conviction. The believers must work for the same cause — the gospel — by restoring unity and common theological judgment.

1:11 Chloe's household. People associated with Chloe, perhaps slaves or other associates. We do not know whether Chloe, a woman who lived in Corinth, was a believer. **quarrels.** Rivalries producing discord; the reason for the divisions in the church.

1:12 Paul, Apollos, and Cephas (i.e., Peter; see 15:5; John 1:42) were missionaries and teachers. Paul founded the church (3:6,10; 9:2; Acts 18:1–18), and Apollos taught in Corinth after Paul left the city (3:6–9). Paul's positive statements about Apollos (3:4–6,22; 4:6) do not reveal any division between Paul and Apollos. Peter was the first teacher, and one of the most important teachers, of the church (Acts 2; 9–10). He was known in Corinth (3:22; 9:5; 15:5), but we do not know whether he visited there. **I follow Christ.** Probably does not refer to a "Christ party" but ironically and dramatically escalates the Corinthians' party slogans. Attempts to find theological differences between Paul, Apollos, and Peter on which the Corinthians may have based their distinct "party affiliation" have not led to a consensus. Paul's subsequent discussion indicates that the divisions were based on the Corinthians' evaluations of their teachers' rhetorical competence.

1:13 Three rhetorical questions reveal that it is absurd to proclaim loyalty to individual teachers, because (1) there is only one Messiah; (2) Paul was not crucified and thus is the basis of no one's salvation; and (3) believers are baptized in the name of Jesus Christ — not in the name of Paul (Acts 2:38; 8:16; 10:48; 19:5; see Matt 28:19).

1:14–16 Paul apparently avoided baptizing new converts, leaving this task to his co-workers. This does not mean that Paul regarded baptism as unimportant (Eph 4:4–6). In a society in which loyalty to patrons was common and supremely important, Paul wanted to avoid the danger inherent in baptism that might lead people to assume that they had a special relationship with the teacher who baptized them. Missionaries do not bind people to themselves; people who come to faith in Jesus are bound to Jesus, which is why Jesus' name is invoked when people are baptized. Paul recalls baptizing only a limited number of people in Corinth.

1:17 The task of preaching the gospel has priority over baptizing new converts, for baptism cannot effectively convey salvation. **wisdom and eloquence.** Greek *sophia* and *logos*, terms used in first-century Greek and Roman literature to describe rhetoric, the study and practice of the most effective means of persuasion in public oratory. The issue was primarily the form (rather than the content) of the proclamation. When Paul preached the Good News of Jesus Christ, he was concerned not with rhetorical brilliance and argumentative competence but with the cross of Christ (see 2:2). It is not possible to speak eloquently about a person executed by crucifixion, a slow and horrible death meant to bring the utmost shame on the crucified person. The power of persuasion in Christian proclamation is not rhetorical brilliance but the message of Jesus' death on the cross, by which the power of God (1:18; 2:5) effectively leads people to faith in Jesus as the crucified Messiah. **emptied of its power.** The effect of Jesus' death on the cross is rendered void if it is removed from its central place in Christian preaching.

1:18—2:5 *Christ Crucified Is God's Power and Wisdom.* Paul describes the gospel (1:18–25), the church (1:26–31), and his missionary proclamation (2:1–5) as focused on Jesus, the crucified Messiah and Savior.

1:18 The proclamation of a crucified savior is nonsense to unbelievers: no orator in antiquity ever spoke eloquently about a man dying on a cross. For believers the news of the crucified Savior is "the power of God," because God is at work in proclaiming this message. God himself persuades sinners to come to faith in Jesus and thus be saved as the news of Jesus, the crucified Savior, is proclaimed.

1:19 Paul proves the assertion of v. 18 with Scripture (here), experience (v. 20), and history (v. 21). The quotation of Isa 29:14 confirms that what God achieved through Jesus' death on the cross transcends human comprehension. The Corinthians' fixation on rhetorical brilliance is reminiscent of the people described in Isa 29:13: they gave superficial lip service to God, but their hearts were far from him.

1:20 [a]Isa 19:11,12 [b]Job 12:17; Ro 1:22
1:22 [c]Mt 12:38
1:23 [d]Lk 2:34; Gal 5:11 [e]1Co 2:14
1:24 [f]Ro 8:28 [g]ver 30; Col 2:3
1:25 [h]ver 18 [i]2Co 13:4
1:27 [j]Jas 2:5 [k]ver 20
1:28 [l]Ro 4:17
1:29 [m]Eph 2:9
1:30 [n]Jer 23:5,6; 2Co 5:21 [o]Ro 3:24; Eph 1:7,14
1:31 [p]Jer 9:23,24; 2Co 10:17
2:1 [q]1Co 1:17
2:2 [r]Gal 6:14; 1Co 1:23
2:3 [s]Ac 18:1-18

20 Where is the wise person?[a] Where is the teacher of the law? Where is the philosopher of this age?
Has not God made foolish[b] the wisdom of the world? 21 For since in the wisdom of God the world through
its wisdom did not know him, God was pleased through the foolishness of what was preached to save
those who believe. 22 Jews demand signs[c] and Greeks look for wisdom, 23 but we preach Christ crucified:
a stumbling block[d] to Jews and foolishness[e] to Gentiles, 24 but to those whom God has called,[f] both Jews
and Greeks, Christ the power of God and the wisdom of God.[g] 25 For the foolishness[h] of God is wiser than
human wisdom, and the weakness[i] of God is stronger than human strength.

26 Brothers and sisters, think of what you were when you were called. Not many of you were wise by
human standards; not many were influential; not many were of noble birth. 27 But God chose[j] the foolish[k] things of the world to shame the wise; God chose the weak things of the world to shame the strong.
28 God chose the lowly things of this world and the despised things — and the things that are not[l] — to
nullify the things that are, 29 so that no one may boast before him.[m] 30 It is because of him that you are
in Christ Jesus, who has become for us wisdom from God — that is, our righteousness,[n] holiness and
redemption.[o] 31 Therefore, as it is written: "Let the one who boasts boast in the Lord."[a][p]

2 And so it was with me, brothers and sisters. When I came to you, I did not come with eloquence or
human wisdom[q] as I proclaimed to you the testimony about God.[b] 2 For I resolved to know nothing
while I was with you except Jesus Christ and him crucified.[r] 3 I came to you[s] in weakness with great fear

[a] *31* Jer. 9:24 [b] *1* Some manuscripts *proclaimed to you God's mystery*

1:20 The proof from experience, carried out with four rhetorical questions, alludes to the Septuagint translation (the pre-Christian Greek translation of the OT) of Isa 33:18. **wise person.** Includes the Jewish intellectual ("the teacher of the law") and the Greek/Roman intellectual ("the philosopher"). God vastly surpasses their intellectual prowess. Their (human) wisdom has been revealed to be "foolish": they have not recognized God's action in and through Jesus Christ.
1:21 The proof from history: God saved people through the preaching of Jesus, the crucified Messiah. **the foolishness of what was preached.** The Jewish teacher of the law and the Greek philosopher despise the message of the cross as nonsense, not understanding that it is an act of God's power to save fallen humankind, who in God's judgment are destined to perish (v. 18).
1:22–24 Jews will be convinced that the crucified Jesus is the Messiah only by "signs" (v. 22; see Matt 12:38–39; Mark 8:11–13; Luke 11:16,29–32; John 2:18–22; 6:30), whether cosmic manifestations or some social or political action that would prove that Jesus, who was executed by crucifixion, is indeed the promised Savior. Because no such sign is given, the message of a crucified savior is a "stumbling block" (v. 23; see Rom 9:32–33; 11:9; 1 Pet 2:8), a message that causes offense and revulsion resulting in opposition, disapproval, and hostility. Gentiles will be convinced that Jesus is the Savior only if there are persuasive arguments ("wisdom," v. 22) that induce them to believe. Because there are no such arguments, they regard the message of a crucified savior as "foolishness" (v. 23), utter nonsense and absurd folly. But God has called some Jews and Greeks to acknowledge and accept Jesus as "the power of God" (v. 24; i.e., God's power to forgive sins) and "the wisdom of God" (v. 24; i.e., God's mastery of the problem of sin).
1:25 the foolishness of God. Many Jews and Greeks think the message of God forgiving sins through Jesus' death on the cross is nonsense. **human wisdom.** The wisdom of the teacher of the law and of the philosopher (v. 20). **the weakness of God.** The perceived weakness of a message that speaks of a man hanging on a cross. **stronger.** The message of Jesus' death on the cross is stronger than anything human strength can accomplish because Jesus saves sinners.
1:26 The nature of the church corresponds to the message of a crucified savior (vv. 26–31). The believers in the Corinthian church were living proof that salvation does not depend on philosophical arguments and brilliant rhetoric. Most Corinthian Christians did not belong to the upper class. **called.** When God convinced them of the truth of the gospel. **wise.** Part of the educated elite. **influential.** The power brokers and officeholders in the city. **of noble birth.** Members of aristocratic families. See 1 Sam 2:1–10; Luke 1:46–55.
1:27–28 Most believers in Corinth belonged to the class of people the educated elite regarded as "foolish" (uneducated and intellectually incompetent), "weak" (without power and influence), "lowly" (not of noble birth and thus insignificant), "despised" (treated as being without merit or worth), and "things that are not" (nonentities). God chose precisely these kinds of people to come to faith in Jesus and receive the riches of his grace (vv. 4–5). Thus, God shamed and nullified the wise: he passed over the educated elite, who will be helpless on the day of judgment (see vv. 7–8).
1:30 because of him. On account of the power of God, who chose the Corinthian believers to come to faith in Jesus and accept Jesus as the "wisdom from God" who saves through his death on the cross. Since "wisdom" was such an important but misunderstood term for the Corinthians, Paul carefully defines it in terms of the effects of God's action in Jesus' death: (1) **righteousness.** God's justifying sinners (see 2 Cor 5:21; Rom 1:17; 3:21–22,25–26; 5:17–21; 10:3–10; Gal 2:21; 3:21; Phil 3:9). (2) **holiness.** That is, sanctification, God's purifying and transforming work that turns sinners into God's "holy people" (1:2). (3) **redemption.** God's liberating rebellious sinners by forgiving their sins.
1:31 boast. Take pride in (Phil 3:3; see Gal 6:14, where "boast" is used with regard to the cross). The quotation of Jer 9:24 confirms that the identity of the believer is fundamentally linked with the Lord Jesus Christ, not with a teacher of the church.
2:1 eloquence. Rhetorical competence. **human wisdom.** Clever argumentation; "human" clarifies that "wisdom" here does not refer to God's wisdom (1:24). The text emphasizes the attitude of superiority (*kath' hyperochēn*) that Paul renounces as a missionary.
2:2 I resolved. Paul shows that he judges the categories of traditional Greco-Roman rhetoric as "nothing" (see 1:17 and note). **crucified.** When Paul proclaims Jesus Christ, he always preaches about Jesus' death on the cross.
2:3–4 Paul's demeanor as a missionary was the exact opposite of the ideal Greco-Roman orator.
2:3 weakness. Note the physical difficulties that beset Paul's life (2 Cor 12:7; Gal 4:13–15). **fear and trembling.** Not psychological handicaps. Rather, Paul refuses to use himself as proof for the credibility of his message: he does not seek to impress his listeners by a powerful appearance (*ēthos* in Greek rhetoric); he does not overwhelm his audience with a persuasive presentation (*pathos* in Greek rhetoric); he does not use

and trembling. [4]My message and my preaching were not with wise and persuasive words, but with a demonstration of the Spirit's power,[t] [5]so that your faith might not rest on human wisdom, but on God's power.[u]

God's Wisdom Revealed by the Spirit

[6]We do, however, speak a message of wisdom among the mature,[v] but not the wisdom of this age[w]
or of the rulers of this age, who are coming to nothing. [7]No, we declare God's wisdom, a mystery that
has been hidden and that God destined for our glory before time began. [8]None of the rulers of this age
understood it, for if they had, they would not have crucified the Lord of glory.[x] [9]However, as it is written:

"What no eye has seen,
what no ear has heard,
and what no human mind has conceived"[a] —
the things God has prepared for those who love him —[y]

[10]these are the things God has revealed[z] to us by his Spirit.[a]
The Spirit searches all things, even the deep things of God. [11]For who knows a person's thoughts[b]
except their own spirit[c] within them? In the same way no one knows the thoughts of God except the
Spirit of God. [12]What we have received is not the spirit[d] of the world,[e] but the Spirit who is from God, so
that we may understand what God has freely given us. [13]This is what we speak, not in words taught us
by human wisdom[f] but in words taught by the Spirit, explaining spiritual realities with Spirit-taught
words.[b] [14]The person without the Spirit does not accept the things that come from the Spirit of God but
considers them foolishness,[g] and cannot understand them because they are discerned only through the
Spirit. [15]The person with the Spirit makes judgments about all things, but such a person is not subject
to merely human judgments, [16]for,

[a] *9* Isaiah 64:4 [b] *13* Or *Spirit, interpreting spiritual truths to those who are spiritual*

2:4 [t] Ro 15:19
2:5 [u] 2Co 4:7; 6:7
2:6 [v] Eph 4:13; Php 3:15; Heb 5:14 [w] 1Co 1:20
2:8 [x] Ac 7:2; Jas 2:1
2:9 [y] Isa 64:4; 65:17
2:10 [z] Mt 13:11; Eph 3:3,5 [a] Jn 14:26
2:11 [b] Jer 17:9 [c] Pr 20:27
2:12 [d] Ro 8:15 [e] 1Co 1:20,27
2:13 [f] 1Co 1:17
2:14 [g] 1Co 1:18

"wise and persuasive words" (v. 4) in a brilliantly arranged argument (*logos* in Greek rhetoric). He renounces the traditional rhetorical means of persuasion because he knows that Jews and Greeks will accept the proclamation of Jesus only as a result of "a demonstration of the Spirit's power" (v. 4), i.e., if and when the powerful Spirit of God convinces people of the truth of the gospel. Paul does not disparage learning and eloquence as such, as his speech before the Areopagus council demonstrates (Acts 17:22–31), but he excludes it from determining the content of the gospel and from assessing the credibility of the preacher.

2:5 Paul's renunciation of persuasion by rhetoric ensures that faith is grounded in "God's power," not in human cleverness. God himself—not Paul—demonstrates the truth of the gospel.

2:6–16 *God's Wisdom Revealed by the Spirit.* Paul describes his proclamation of the gospel as the message of wisdom among the mature (vv. 6–12) and as the message of the apostles as taught by the Spirit (vv. 13–16).

2:6 the mature. Those who have come to faith in Jesus Christ (1:18,21,24). **the wisdom of this age.** All wisdom that is not God's wisdom; purely human wisdom (1:19,20; 2:5,13). **the rulers of this age.** Political and social elites.

2:7 God's wisdom. A crucified savior. The salvation of sinners through Jesus' death on the cross is a "mystery": it is "hidden" for Jews who regard this message as a "stumbling block" (1:23) and for Greeks who regard it as "foolishness" (1:23). **mystery.** Knowledge that people cannot understand unless God graciously reveals it to them. Here the "mystery" is related to the "scandalous" and "foolish" message that Jesus' death on the cross is the climax of God's plan of salvation. For other contexts, see 15:51; Rom 11:25; Eph 3:4–6; 5:32; Col 2:2. God destined before the creation of the world that sinners are saved on account of Jesus' death on the cross.

2:8 the rulers of this age. The elites of Jewish and Greco-Roman society, in particular the Jewish leaders in Jerusalem and the Roman prefect Pilate. They have not understood that Jesus' death on the cross was a demonstration of God's wisdom. Had they grasped the significance of Jesus as "the Lord of glory" (see the expression "the God of glory" in Ps 29:3; see also Acts 7:2; Eph 1:17), they would not have crucified Jesus.

2:9 Isa 64:4 proves that neither human perception nor human reason can perceive the wisdom of God that is revealed in Jesus' death on the cross. God helps "those who love him," i.e., believers, to understand that wisdom.

2:10 the things. The significance of Jesus. **by his Spirit.** Supernaturally rather than by human rhetoric or clever argumentation. **the deep things of God.** God's mind; the mystery of God's inscrutable plan of salvation centered on Jesus as the crucified Messiah and Savior. Only God's Spirit knows that.

2:12 the spirit of the world. The merely human capacity for knowledge, which people have as sinners. **the Spirit who is from God.** The Holy Spirit, who reveals God's mind to believers. **understand what God has freely given.** Grasp the significance of the crucified Jesus in God's plan of salvation as the wisdom of God (1:21,24,30; 2:6–7) and the mystery of God (2:1,7). This is what Paul proclaims, and Christians understand the gospel because they have received God's Spirit (Rom 8:14–16). This message is not the result of human wisdom; God's Spirit reveals it.

2:13 spiritual realities. The reality revealed by the Holy Spirit and proclaimed by the apostles.

2:14 Unbelievers regard the message of Jesus and of salvation on account of his death on the cross as "foolishness" (1:18,23) because they have not received God's Spirit and thus cannot possibly understand God's mind (vv. 10–11). **The person without the Spirit.** A person with merely physical life (contrast v. 13).

2:15 The person with the Spirit. A person who has received the Spirit of God. **all things.** The "spiritual realities" of v. 13. Believers understand the message of Jesus, the crucified Messiah and Savior, which secular people regard as foolishness. **merely human judgments.** Evaluations of the Christian message based on merely human standards. Christians, who have received God's Spirit and understand the gospel of Jesus Christ as God's wisdom, do not have to be concerned about the merely human judgments that ridicule Jesus' death.

2:16 Paul quotes Isa 40:13 to confirm that nobody can understand

2:16 [h]Isa 40:13 [i]Jn 15:15
3:1 [j]1Co 2:15 [k]Ro 7:14; 1Co 2:14 [l]Heb 5:13
3:2 [m]Heb 5:12-14; 1Pe 2:2 [n]Jn 16:12
3:3 [o]1Co 1:11; Gal 5:20
3:4 [p]1Co 1:12
3:6 [q]Ac 18:4-11
3:8 [r]Ps 62:12
3:9 [s]2Co 6:1 [t]Isa 61:3 [u]Eph 2:20-22; 1Pe 2:5
3:10 [v]Ro 12:3 [w]Ro 15:20
3:11 [x]Isa 28:16; Eph 2:20

"Who has known the mind of the Lord
so as to instruct him?"[a][h]

But we have the mind of Christ.[i]

The Church and Its Leaders

3 Brothers and sisters, I could not address you as people who live by the Spirit[j] but as people who
are still worldly[k]—mere infants[l] in Christ. [2]I gave you milk, not solid food,[m] for you were not yet
ready for it.[n] Indeed, you are still not ready. [3]You are still worldly. For since there is jealousy and quarreling[o] among you, are you not worldly? Are you not acting like mere humans? [4]For when one says, "I
follow Paul," and another, "I follow Apollos,"[p] are you not mere human beings?

[5]What, after all, is Apollos? And what is Paul? Only servants, through whom you came to believe—
as the Lord has assigned to each his task. [6]I planted the seed,[q] Apollos watered it, but God has been
making it grow. [7]So neither the one who plants nor the one who waters is anything, but only God, who
makes things grow. [8]The one who plants and the one who waters have one purpose, and they will each
be rewarded according to their own labor.[r] [9]For we are co-workers in God's service;[s] you are God's
field,[t] God's building.[u]

[10]By the grace God has given me,[v] I laid a foundation[w] as a wise builder, and someone else is building on it. But each one should build with care. [11]For no one can lay any foundation other than the
one already laid, which is Jesus Christ.[x] [12]If anyone builds on this foundation using gold, silver, costly

[a] *16* Isaiah 40:13

God's mind and wisdom unless God's Spirit grants insight into God's plans. **the mind of Christ.** "The Spirit who is from God" (v. 12) reveals the deep truths of God's wisdom that helps sinners understand the significance of Jesus' death as the climax of God's plan of salvation (see vv. 10–13).

3:1–23 *The Church and Its Leaders.* The Corinthian believers are controlled by secular standards when they speak about missionaries and pastors (vv. 1–4). Apostles and teachers are servants and field workers whose ministries totally depend upon God's work (vv. 5–9). Paul and other teachers are responsible to build up the church (vv. 10–15), which is God's temple (vv. 16–17). False wisdom and self-praise are foolish (vv. 18–23).

3:1 worldly. Material, belonging to the physical realm, human; the secular traditions of Greco-Roman society that continue to control the values and lifestyle of the Corinthian Christians. **mere infants.** Small children who have no legal standing and who are weak and immature, needing the protection and support of parents.

3:2 milk. Paul gave them the basic message of the gospel, while they have fixated on rhetorical brilliance. **solid food.** The message of Jesus' death on the cross fully expounded. If they want to belong to the mature (2:6), they must change their perspective from worldly values to spiritual insight (2:7–16).

3:3 quarreling. Christians engaging in rivalry about the superiority of missionaries and teachers, which demonstrates their worldly perspective. **like mere humans.** They are acting like unconverted people, those who show no evidence that they have received God's Spirit (2:15).

3:4 These party slogans represent secular behavior that conforms to the human values of society.

3:5 Paul denounces the party slogans by asking questions that downgrade the importance of the church's teachers such as Apollos and Paul. **Only servants.** People don't quarrel about servants. **the Lord has assigned to each his task.** Each is responsible to the Lord, not to the Corinthian critics.

3:6–7 Paul views the church as a "field" (v. 9). He uses agricultural metaphors ("planted" and "watered") to describe how the church's missionary (Paul) and teacher (Apollos) ministered. Paul was a pioneer missionary, preaching the gospel where it had not been preached before. Apollos taught the new converts in the church that Paul had established. God makes both plants and churches grow (v. 7). Christians should not quarrel about what the Lord accomplishes through Paul, Apollos, or Peter, because neither the church planter nor the pastor or teacher is "anything" (v. 7); by themselves they are nothing (see 2 Cor 3:5; 6:10). It is absurd to quarrel about the superiority of teachers in the church, because only God matters.

3:8 Another reason to end the declarations of loyalty to teachers is the common "purpose" of apostles and teachers: they are all the Lord's servants; they work toward the same harvest; they all preach and teach the gospel; their individual ministries complement each other. God—not critics in the church—will reward the apostles and teachers (see 3:15–17; 4:4–5) when they stand before his throne (see 2 Cor 11:15; Matt 16:27; Rom 2:6; 2 Tim 4:14; 1 Pet 1:17; Rev 2:23; 20:12–13). **own labor.** Each individual is fulfilling God's commission. Their reward, described as a prize (9:24) and a victor's crown (9:25; see also 2 Tim 4:8), is praise from God (4:5); bringing pleasure to God (2 Cor 5:9); receiving glory, honor, and peace from God (Rom 2:10; see Rom 8:17–18); and being awarded righteousness by God (2 Tim 4:8).

3:9 co-workers in God's service. The genitive of possession ("co-workers belonging to God") establishes that declaring loyalty to apostles and teachers is absurd. The church is compared not only to a field (see v. 6) but also to a building, specifically a temple (see v. 16). **God's.** The church belongs to God, not to apostles or teachers.

3:10 Expanding the metaphor of the church as a building, Paul explains his responsibilities and the responsibilities of other teachers in the church. **foundation.** Paul is not speaking of a private home but of a monumental building—such as a temple (v. 16) or a large colonnaded hall—that needs a solid foundation. **wise builder.** Greek *architektōn.* Alternative translations might be "expert builder" (GNT) or "skilled master builder" (NRSV). As the pioneer missionary in Corinth, Paul established the church. Some see here a reference to Bezalel's building of the tabernacle (Exod 31:2–4).

3:11 foundation. The gospel of Jesus, the crucified Messiah and Savior. No other foundation can support the "building" of the church as God's "temple" (v. 16). A different gospel is no gospel at all (Gal 1:6–7).

3:12 Paul lists materials according to their costliness; he mentions neither rocks nor bricks, the most common building materials. **gold, silver, costly stones.** Not building materials but materials used to

stones, wood, hay or straw, [13]their work will be shown for what it is,[y] because the Day[z] will bring it to light. It will be revealed with fire, and the fire will test the quality of each person's work. [14]If what has been built survives, the builder will receive a reward. [15]If it is burned up, the builder will suffer loss but yet will be saved—even though only as one escaping through the flames.[a]

[16]Don't you know that you yourselves are God's temple[b] and that God's Spirit dwells in your midst? [17]If anyone destroys God's temple, God will destroy that person; for God's temple is sacred, and you together are that temple.

[18]Do not deceive yourselves. If any of you think you are wise[c] by the standards of this age, you should become "fools" so that you may become wise. [19]For the wisdom of this world is foolishness[d] in God's sight. As it is written: "He catches the wise in their craftiness"[a],[e] [20]and again, "The Lord knows that the thoughts of the wise are futile."[b][f] [21]So then, no more boasting about human leaders![g] All things are yours,[h] [22]whether Paul or Apollos or Cephas[c][i] or the world or life or death or the present or the future[j]—all are yours, [23]and you are of Christ,[k] and Christ is of God.

The Nature of True Apostleship

4 This, then, is how you ought to regard us: as servants of Christ and as those entrusted[l] with the mysteries[m] God has revealed. [2]Now it is required that those who have been given a trust must prove faithful. [3]I care very little if I am judged by you or by any human court; indeed, I do not even judge myself. [4]My conscience is clear, but that does not make me innocent.[n] It is the Lord who judges me. [5]Therefore judge nothing[o] before the appointed time; wait until the Lord comes. He will bring to

a 19 Job 5:13 *b 20* Psalm 94:11 *c 22* That is, Peter

3:13 [y] 1Co 4:5 [z] 2Th 1:7-10
3:15 [a] Jude 23
3:16 [b] 1Co 6:19; 2Co 6:16
3:18 [c] Isa 5:21; 1Co 8:2
3:19 [d] 1Co 1:20,27 [e] Job 5:13
3:20 [f] Ps 94:11
3:21 [g] 1Co 4:6 [h] Ro 8:32
3:22 [i] 1Co 1:12 [j] Ro 8:38
3:23 [k] 1Co 15:23; 2Co 10:7; Gal 3:29
4:1 [l] 1Co 9:17; Titus 1:7 [m] Ro 16:25
4:4 [n] Ro 2:13
4:5 [o] Mt 7:1,2; Ro 2:1

decorate a finished building. **wood, hay or straw.** Essential, cheap building materials: wood for the roof, windows, and door frames; hay and straw for plasterwork. Paul is not comparing a building made of gold, silver, or costly stones (such never existed) with a building made of wood, hay, or straw. He is comparing a building built on a solid foundation with one built in complete disregard of the existing foundation. The former will survive a catastrophic event, while the latter will likely collapse.

3:13 the Day. The day of judgment (see 1:8; 5:5; 2 Cor 1:14; Rom 13:12; Phil 1:6,10; 2:16; 1 Thess 5:2; 2 Thess 2:2), a catastrophic event that will demonstrate whether the builders (the teachers of the church) built on the right foundation. **fire.** Often linked with judgment (see Mal 3:2–3). The fire here does not punish (Jude 7; Rev 18:8; 19:20; 21:8), destroy (Matt 3:10; 13:40,42,50; Heb 10:27), or purify (1 Pet 1:7); it manifests the quality of the teachers' work with regard to the (up)building of the church on the foundation of the gospel.

3:14–15 reward ... loss. The positive and negative results of God's examining the work of the church's teachers (v. 8). "Loss" is at least the painful experience of not receiving God's praise and of a lack of the joy that comes from people coming to faith in Jesus, the crucified Messiah and Savior (1 Thess 2:19–20). This "loss" does not affect the personal salvation of Christian teachers who ignore the foundation of the gospel.

3:15 escaping. Such teachers will just scrape through.

3:16 Don't you know. Implies that the Corinthians had been taught this already. **God's temple.** The "building" (v. 9) that the church represents; the place where God is present (Eph 2:21–22). **dwells.** God's Spirit mediates God's presence. Here Paul speaks of the community of Corinthian Christians as God's temple; in 6:19 he speaks of the individual Christian as a temple of the Holy Spirit.

3:17 Rivalries about apostles and teachers disregard the "foundation" (v. 11) that has been laid for the building (the church). Certain Christians in the church destroy the church through the promotion of rivalries; they destroy God's temple, which is a sacrilege God will not allow to happen. There will be consequences on the day of judgment (v. 15).

3:19–20 Paul confirms the dichotomy between God (and his wisdom) and human beings (and their secular values) by quoting Job 5:13 and Ps 94:11. Human thinking that dispenses with God and his revelation is futile.

3:21–23 Christians must not boast about human leaders (1:29). Such boasting reflects secular values and is futile and foolish.

3:21 All things are yours. Repeated at the end of v. 22; contrasts declaring loyalty to other people (Paul, Apollos, Cephas), inevitably a narrow heritage, with the heritage belonging to *all* believers in Jesus Christ. All believers are God's people and will inherit the earth or "all things" (6:2; 7:31; Dan 7:13–14; 12:1–3; Matt 5:3,5; Rom 8:28). Quarreling about apostles and teachers is absurd since the world, life, death, the present, and the future belong to the church of Jesus Christ.

3:23 you are of Christ. The church belongs to Christ (1:30). **Christ is of God.** Jesus is God's Messiah and is in union with the Father (John 10:30). If Christ belongs to God, so do believers. Believers do not belong to missionaries or teachers.

4:1–13 *The Nature of True Apostleship.* Paul clarifies how Christians should view the apostles and teachers of the church (vv. 1–5), and he specifies the true indicators of an apostle (vv. 6–13).

4:1 servants of Christ. Apostles, pastors, and teachers assist Christ as his subordinates. **those entrusted with.** Or "stewards" of. **mysteries.** The truths of God's plan of salvation centered on Jesus, the crucified Messiah and Savior (2:7). A steward, who might be a slave, manages the estate or household of a master or patron. As servants and stewards, apostles and teachers work for God and Christ, not for themselves and their own prestige or advantage.

4:2 those who have been given a trust. Stewards (see v. 1 and note). **prove faithful.** The key criterion in evaluating stewards. Stewards must be faithful to the gospel of Jesus, the crucified Messiah and Savior (1:18—2:5; 3:10–11).

4:3–4 Paul uses himself as an example of how to properly evaluate a teacher of the church. He is independent of human evaluation, whether the Corinthians' judgment or his own.

4:4 the Lord who judges. Paul does not care about other evaluations, because no human verdict preempts the judgment of Jesus Christ.

4:5 appointed time. When Christ returns; the day of judgment. **the motives of the heart.** The intentions of people that are hidden from view to others. See 1 Sam 16:7; 1 Kgs 8:39; 1 Chr 28:9; Ps 139:23–24;

4:5 [p]Ro 2:29
4:6 [q]1Co 1:19,31; 3:19,20 [r]1Co 1:12
4:7 [s]Jn 3:27; Ro 12:3,6
4:8 [t]Rev 3:17,18
4:9 [u]Ro 8:36 [v]Heb 10:33
4:10 [w]1Co 1:18; Ac 17:18 [x]1Co 3:18 [y]1Co 2:3
4:11 [z]Ro 8:35; 2Co 11:23-27
4:12 [a]Ac 18:3 [b]1Pe 3:9
4:13 [c]La 3:45
4:14 [d]1Th 2:11
4:15 [e]1Co 9:12, 14,18,23
4:16 [f]1Co 11:1; Php 3:17; 1Th 1:6; 2Th 3:7,9

light what is hidden in darkness and will expose the motives of the heart. At that time each will receive
their praise from God.[p]

[6]Now, brothers and sisters, I have applied these things to myself and Apollos for your benefit, so that
you may learn from us the meaning of the saying, "Do not go beyond what is written."[q] Then you will
not be puffed up in being a follower of one of us over against the other.[r] [7]For who makes you different
from anyone else? What do you have that you did not receive?[s] And if you did receive it, why do you
boast as though you did not?

[8]Already you have all you want! Already you have become rich![t] You have begun to reign—and that
without us! How I wish that you really had begun to reign so that we also might reign with you! [9]For it
seems to me that God has put us apostles on display at the end of the procession, like those condemned
to die[u] in the arena. We have been made a spectacle[v] to the whole universe, to angels as well as to human beings. [10]We are fools for Christ,[w] but you are so wise in Christ![x] We are weak, but you are strong![y]
You are honored, we are dishonored! [11]To this very hour we go hungry and thirsty, we are in rags, we
are brutally treated, we are homeless.[z] [12]We work hard with our own hands.[a] When we are cursed, we
bless;[b] when we are persecuted, we endure it; [13]when we are slandered, we answer kindly. We have become the scum of the earth, the garbage[c] of the world—right up to this moment.

Paul's Appeal and Warning

[14]I am writing this not to shame you but to warn you as my dear children.[d] [15]Even if you had ten
thousand guardians in Christ, you do not have many fathers, for in Christ Jesus I became your father
through the gospel.[e] [16]Therefore I urge you to imitate me.[f] [17]For this reason I have sent to you Timothy,

Prov 16:2; Luke 16:15; Heb 4:12–13. Jesus will evaluate the apostles' work and their motives when he returns. **praise from God.** The positive evaluation of the apostles' work by God on the day of judgment. Each teacher who has been faithful to the gospel (4:2) will be praised by God, whether or not the Corinthian critics praise them.

4:6 saying. May refer to (1) the statements in Scripture Paul quoted in his critique of the Corinthian quarrels about apostles and teachers (see 1:19,31; 2:16; 3:19–20), (2) Paul's statements in the letter up to this point, or (3) a general maxim. Authentic faith is centered on Jesus, the crucified Messiah and Savior, and rejects any behavior that pits one apostle against another on the basis of secular values about rhetoric.

4:7 The three questions invite self-critique: (1) The Corinthian critics are human beings who accord superiority to individual apostles and teachers, which is irrelevant in view of God's judgment (vv. 4–5). (2) The Corinthians do not have any riches they have not received (1:5). (3) Gifts exalt the giver, not the recipients. Christians who acknowledge that their abilities are from God will be humble, not arrogant.

4:8 The three statements about the Corinthians are ironic. The way they view themselves sharply contrasts with the thankfulness and humility implied in v. 7. **have begun to reign.** They think they are already participating fully in Christ's reign, or they regard themselves as "rulers" over the apostles due to their rhetorical education and their social status. Paul wants them to see how poor and dependent they really are.

4:9–13 Paul describes how the apostles live.

4:9 at the end. Or "as last of all." **procession.** The practice of victorious Roman generals staging a triumphal procession in the city of Rome, with captives of war bringing up the rear. The Greek text does not specifically refer to a procession: "condemned to die in the arena" speaks of people who have been condemned to be executed and are presented to the people of the city in the theater (Greek *Theatron*). Paul emphasizes that as traveling preachers, the apostles have no power base in any city. They are foreigners with few rights and no prestige. They have the same status as slaves, criminals, and prisoners of war who are condemned to die in the arena. They are regarded as pitiful and doomed because they preach Jesus as the crucified Messiah and Savior of the world.

4:10 Three antithetical statements contrast how the Corinthians view themselves with how they view the apostles. **fools.** Because the apostles preach the "foolishness" of the cross (1:18,23). **weak.** Because the apostles do not belong to the elites of the cities in which they preach the gospel. **dishonored.** Because the apostles have no prominent status in society and are ridiculed and persecuted on account of the message they proclaim.

4:11–13 Paul describes his suffering as a missionary with key elements. See 9:6; 2 Cor 11:7–10,24–27; 12:14; Acts 14:19; 23:2; Phil 4:12; cf. Matt 10:11–14,17. He relates how he and the other apostles reacted to suffering in three antithetical statements. Even though they are cursed (Acts 16:20–21; 17:5–8; 18:12–13), persecuted (Acts 13:50–51; 14:5–6,19; 16:23–24; 17:5–9,13–14; 18:12–16), and slandered, they bless, endure, and answer kindly (Matt 5:44; Luke 6:28; Rom 12:14; 1 Pet 2:23; 3:9).

4:13 scum … garbage. Dirt or refuse. The apostles are regarded as dirty, loathsome people who should be eliminated.

4:14–21 *Paul's Appeal and Warning.* Paul admonishes them as their father.

4:14–15 Paul explains his ironic, sarcastic, provocative admonition in vv. 6–13 in terms of his fatherly concern for them. Although his previous statement may have indeed shamed the Corinthians, it was not his purpose to cause them pain and embarrassment or make them look unworthy.

4:14 children. People who have come to faith through Paul's preaching and whom he loves.

4:15 guardians. People—in antiquity, often slaves—who are responsible for others who need guidance (e.g., children) (Gal 3:24). The authority of a father is superior to that of a guardian, who works for the father.

4:16 imitate me. As Paul focused on Jesus, the crucified Messiah and Savior (1:18—2:5), and as he depended on God, who alone makes the church grow (3:5–17), so the Corinthian Christians are to make sure that Jesus Christ is the center of their faith and that they completely depend on him.

4:17 Timothy. He is evidently already on the way to Corinth. **son.** Timothy came to faith through Paul's preaching. Paul recruited him as a coworker (Acts 16:1–3), and Timothy served faithfully.

my son[g] whom I love, who is faithful in the Lord. He will remind you of my way of life in Christ Jesus,
which agrees with what I teach everywhere in every church.[h]
18Some of you have become arrogant, as if I were not coming to you. 19But I will come to you very
soon,[i] if the Lord is willing,[j] and then I will find out not only how these arrogant people are talking,
but what power they have. 20For the kingdom of God is not a matter of talk but of power. 21What do you
prefer? Shall I come to you with a rod of discipline,[k] or shall I come in love and with a gentle spirit?

Dealing With a Case of Incest

5 It is actually reported that there is sexual immorality among you, and of a kind that even pagans
do not tolerate: A man is sleeping with his father's wife.[l] 2And you are proud! Shouldn't you rather
have gone into mourning[m] and have put out of your fellowship the man who has been doing this? 3For
my part, even though I am not physically present, I am with you in spirit.[n] As one who is present with
you in this way, I have already passed judgment in the name of our Lord Jesus[o] on the one who has
been doing this. 4So when you are assembled and I am with you in spirit, and the power of our Lord
Jesus is present, 5hand this man over[p] to Satan for the destruction of the flesh,[a,b] so that his spirit may
be saved on the day of the Lord.
6Your boasting is not good.[q] Don't you know that a little yeast[r] leavens the whole batch of dough?[s]
7Get rid of the old yeast, so that you may be a new unleavened batch — as you really are. For Christ, our
Passover lamb, has been sacrificed.[t] 8Therefore let us keep the Festival, not with the old bread leavened
with malice and wickedness, but with the unleavened bread[u] of sincerity and truth.
9I wrote to you in my letter not to associate[v] with sexually immoral people — 10not at all meaning
the people of this world[w] who are immoral, or the greedy and swindlers, or idolaters. In that case you

4:17 [g] 1Ti 1:2 [h] 1Co 7:17
4:19 [i] 2Co 1:15,16 [j] Ac 18:21
4:21 [k] 2Co 1:23; 13:2,10
5:1 [l] Lev 18:8; Dt 22:30
5:2 [m] 2Co 7:7-11
5:3 [n] Col 2:5 [o] 2Th 3:6
5:5 [p] 1Ti 1:20
5:6 [q] Jas 4:16 [r] Mt 16:6, 12 [s] Gal 5:9
5:7 [t] Mk 14:12; 1Pe 1:19
5:8 [u] Ex 12:14,15; Dt 16:3
5:9 [v] Eph 5:11; 2Th 3:6,14
5:10 [w] 1Co 10:27

[a] 5 In contexts like this, the Greek word for *flesh* (*sarx*) refers to the sinful state of human beings, often presented as a power in opposition to the Spirit. [b] 5 Or *of his body*

4:19 power. When Paul comes to Corinth, he will be less interested in what his critics have to say about his preaching and more interested in whether or not they have the power connected with the kingdom of God that Paul proclaims when he preaches the gospel of Jesus, the crucified Messiah and Savior.

4:20 kingdom of God. The reign of God in the lives of his people (see note on Matt 3:2), which is the power of the new birth (John 3:3–8).

4:21 rod of discipline. The stick with which children were punished for misbehavior is used as a metaphor for church discipline (5:3–5).

5:1—6:20 *Ethical Confusion in the Church.* Paul deals with a case of incest (5:1–13), lawsuits among believers (6:1–11), and sexual immorality (6:12–20).

5:1–13 *Dealing With a Case of Incest.* Paul gives his verdict in the case of a church member's incestuous behavior (vv. 1–5) on the basis of the church's purity (vv. 6–8) since believers must not be sexually immoral (vv. 9–13).

5:1 among you. In the church. **that even pagans do not tolerate.** Roman incest laws strictly prohibited intimate relations between relatives to the third degree and between a stepson and stepmother and between a stepdaughter and stepfather; the punishment was losing property, being exiled on an island, and losing social status. **his father's wife.** Presumably his stepmother. Such a sexual relationship is prohibited (Lev 18:8; Deut 22:30).

5:2 The Corinthians were proud of this church member's flagrant sin. Perhaps the man had a high social status and the church was proud to have him as a member and did not dare to challenge him.

5:5 hand this man over to Satan. Exclude him from the church and consign him to the world controlled by Satan and his destructive forces; cf. removing yeast (vv. 6–8) and the warning not to associate with Christians who are sexually immoral (vv. 9–11). **the destruction of the flesh.** If "flesh" is interpreted in terms of the physical body of the sinner, the phrase can be understood as a curse announcing the death of the sinner (Lev 20:11; Acts 5:1–11) or as a curse announcing bodily harm (Job 2:4). If "flesh" is interpreted in terms of the sinful nature, which is more plausible in the light of 3:1, Paul asserts that the sinner must "destroy," or totally renounce, his incestuous relationship. **his spirit.** He himself. **the day of the Lord.** The day of judgment.

5:6 yeast. "Leaven" is an alternative translation. It is fermented dough that starts the fermentation process in a new batch of dough. The analogy of fermented dough is usually used negatively (Gal 5:9; also Matt 16:6; Mark 8:15; Luke 12:1), but the analogy is used positively in Matt 13:33. Tolerating a church member's incest (or any other sinful behavior, see v. 11) is dangerous: the sin, if tolerated, can spread to other church members and affect the entire church.

5:7 The reference to yeast in v. 6 prompts Paul to speak of the Festival of Passover, which reminded the Jews of the exodus from Egypt, a time when the Israelites had to eat unleavened bread (Exod 12:14–20). Before the Israelites celebrated Passover prior to the exodus from Egypt, they had to remove all old yeast from their houses (Exod 13:3–10; 23:15; Deut 16:3–8). In an allegorical interpretation, Paul exhorts the Corinthians to remove the sinner ("the old yeast") so that the church can be the true people ("a new unleavened batch") who experience God's rescue mission; as believers in Jesus Christ, they have already been made holy (1:2; 6:11). **our Passover lamb.** The blood of the Passover lamb protected the Israelites from destruction (Exod 12:23).When Jesus died on the cross, he died as "the Lamb of God, who takes away the sin of the world" (John 1:29). John ties Jesus' death on the cross to the slaughter of the Passover lambs (see John 19:31,42).

5:9 in my letter. Paul had written a previous letter to the Corinthian Christians before writing this letter (1 Corinthians). The previous letter has not been found.

5:10 not at all meaning. Paul clarifies that he is not calling for a radical termination of all relationships with unbelievers. Here, exclusion and separation applies to fellow believers (v. 11). **this world.** Outside the Christian community is the world controlled by Satan, "the god of this age" (2 Cor 4:4).

5:11 [x]1Co 10:7,14
5:12 [y]Mk 4:11 [z]ver 3-5; 1Co 6:1-4
5:13 [a]Dt 13:5
6:1 [b]Mt 18:17
6:2 [c]Mt 19:28; Lk 22:30
6:5 [d]1Co 4:14 [e]Ac 1:15
6:6 [f]2Co 6:14,15
6:7 [g]Mt 5:39,40
6:8 [h]1Th 4:6
6:9 [i]Gal 5:21 [j]1Co 15:33; Jas 1:16
6:11 [k]Eph 2:2 [l]Ac 22:16 [m]1Co 1:2

would have to leave this world. [11]But now I am writing to you that you must not associate with anyone
who claims to be a brother or sister[a] but is sexually immoral or greedy, an idolater[x] or slanderer, a
drunkard or swindler. Do not even eat with such people.

[12]What business is it of mine to judge those outside[y] the church? Are you not to judge those inside?[z]
[13]God will judge those outside. "Expel the wicked person from among you."[b][a]

Lawsuits Among Believers

6 If any of you has a dispute with another, do you dare to take it before the ungodly for judgment
instead of before the Lord's people?[b] [2]Or do you not know that the Lord's people will judge the
world?[c] And if you are to judge the world, are you not competent to judge trivial cases? [3]Do you
not know that we will judge angels? How much more the things of this life! [4]Therefore, if you have
disputes about such matters, do you ask for a ruling from those whose way of life is scorned in the
church? [5]I say this to shame you.[d] Is it possible that there is nobody among you wise enough to judge
a dispute between believers?[e] [6]But instead, one brother takes another to court — and this in front
of unbelievers![f]

[7]The very fact that you have lawsuits among you means you have been completely defeated already. Why not rather be wronged? Why not rather be cheated?[g] [8]Instead, you yourselves cheat and
do wrong, and you do this to your brothers and sisters.[h] [9]Or do you not know that wrongdoers will
not inherit the kingdom of God?[i] Do not be deceived:[j] Neither the sexually immoral nor idolaters
nor adulterers nor men who have sex with men[c] [10]nor thieves nor the greedy nor drunkards nor
slanderers nor swindlers will inherit the kingdom of God. [11]And that is what some of you were.[k] But
you were washed,[l] you were sanctified,[m] you were justified in the name of the Lord Jesus Christ and
by the Spirit of our God.

[a] *11* The Greek word for *brother or sister* (*adelphos*) refers here to a believer, whether man or woman, as part of God's family; also in 8:11, 13. [b] *13* Deut. 13:5; 17:7; 19:19; 21:21; 22:21,24; 24:7 [c] *9* The words *men who have sex with men* translate two Greek words that refer to the passive and active participants in homosexual acts.

5:11 you must not associate. Christians must not associate with people who claim to be Christians but who live like pagans. Continuing in fellowship with Christians who refuse to repent of reprehensible sins may suggest to unbelievers that the church approves of immoral conduct. See 2 Thess 2:6,14–15.

5:12 those outside the church. Unbelievers, whom "God will judge" (v. 13). Believers are responsible to judge the behavior of fellow believers, not that of unbelievers.

5:13 Paul's final exhortation quotes Deuteronomy (see NIV text note). The church's responsibility is the same as Israel's: God's people must remove from the community people who deliberately and consistently disregard God's law.

6:1–11 *Lawsuits Among Believers.* Paul addresses Christians who take disputes with other Christians about petty cases to the local courts (v. 1). He argues that the church community should be able to settle such disputes (vv. 2–6) and that Christians should be willing to renounce their rights (vv. 7–11).

6:1 dispute. A legal dispute with another Christian; some Christians initiated lawsuits against fellow Christians. **the ungodly.** Pagan judges often rendered unrighteous verdicts on account of bribes or a friendship with one of the plaintiffs. In Corinth, civil cases were decided by two magistrates who were elected for one year as the officers of record with jurisdiction in the city. Since only members of the upper class had access to the courts, those initiating lawsuits were members of the elite who apparently were willing to treat fellow Christians as (legal) enemies. The contrast between "the ungodly" and "the Lord's people" is deliberate: Paul has no sympathy for Christians who appeal to people who are unrighteous to make decisions in their favor rather than consult with fellow Christians, who are holy (1:2).

6:2–3 Since God's holy people will judge the world and the angels (Dan 7:22; Matt 19:28; Luke 22:30; Rev 20:4), they should be able to judge trivial cases (legal actions about petty matters between believers).

6:4 those whose way of life is scorned in the church. People who have no standing in the community of God's holy people.

6:5 I say this to shame you. Strong language in a culture in which personal honor was supremely important, especially for members of the cultural elite. The following rhetorical question formulates a demand: the church should be able to find members who are able to settle disputes between believers.

6:6 brother. Underlines the absurdity of the situation: brothers fight against brothers in public, in courts of law, before unbelieving judges.

6:7 completely defeated already. Because believers are dragging fellow believers before pagan judges, they have lost the integrity of their status as holy people. **wronged.** Suffer injustice. **cheated.** Defrauded, suggesting that the dispute is financial or about some other material matter. See 13:5; Matt 5:39–40; Rom 12:17–21.

6:9–10 These "vices" describe wrong behavior — wrong for Christians (and Jews). Most people in Greco-Roman society regarded most of these practices as acceptable.

6:9 inherit the kingdom of God. Enter God's new world in the future consummation (see Gal 5:21; Eph 5:5). **Do not be deceived.** Underlines the permanent need for self-examination. **sexually immoral.** Includes sexual relations with prostitutes, adultery, and homosexuality.

6:10 greedy. Greed influences business practices. **drunkards.** Drunkenness was common at banquets.

6:11 some of you were. But. Most of the Corinthian believers came from pagan backgrounds and had practiced the vices listed in vv. 9–10. But they now behave differently because God has transformed their lives. **washed.** God removed the dirt of their transgressions and forgave their sins. **sanctified.** God removed their unholiness and declared them holy on account of Jesus' atoning death on the cross (1:2), with the result that their community is God's temple, the place of the presence of the holy God. **justified.** God removed their guilt and declared them righteous, a status granted on account of the work of the Lord Jesus

The *bema* at Corinth. The Greek word "bema" usually refers to a tribunal from which judgment and other official public business was conducted. Paul urges believers to resolve disputes among themselves rather than bringing them to the ungodly for judgment (1 Cor 6:1–11).

Sexual Immorality

12"I have the right to do anything," you say—but not everything is beneficial.[n] "I have the right
to do anything"—but I will not be mastered by anything. 13You say, "Food for the stomach and the
stomach for food, and God will destroy them both."[o] The body, however, is not meant for sexual immorality but for the Lord, and the Lord for the body. 14By his power God raised the Lord from the dead,
and he will raise us also.[p] 15Do you not know that your bodies are members of Christ himself?[q] Shall
I then take the members of Christ and unite them with a prostitute? Never! 16Do you not know that he
who unites himself with a prostitute is one with her in body? For it is said, "The two will become one
flesh."[a r] 17But whoever is united with the Lord is one with him in spirit.[b s]

6:12 [n] 1Co 10:23
6:13 [o] Col 2:22
6:14 [p] Ro 6:5; Eph 1:19,20
6:15 [q] Ro 12:5
6:16 [r] Ge 2:24; Mt 19:5; Eph 5:31
6:17 [s] Jn 17:21-23; Gal 2:20

[a] *16* Gen. 2:24 [b] *17* Or *in the Spirit*

Christ and a status that leads to a changed life on account of the effective presence of the Holy Spirit.

6:12–20 *Sexual Immorality.* Some of the Corinthian believers continued their preconversion practice of engaging in sexual relations with prostitutes. Paul corrects their false understanding of Christian freedom (vv. 12–14). Having sexual relations with prostitutes offends Christ (v. 15), one's own body (vv. 16–18), and the Holy Spirit (vv. 19–20).

6:12 "I have the right to do anything." A slogan of some Corinthians (thus the quotation marks and the concluding words "you say"). **beneficial.** Edifying to the church (10:23,33); the criterion for what is allowed. Christian behavior should benefit others (7:35: 10:33; 12:7).

6:13 "Food for the stomach and the stomach for food ..." How the Corinthians justified their hedonistic lifestyle (thus the quotation marks): sexual relations with prostitutes is as natural as eating and drinking. **not meant for sexual immorality but for the Lord.** Food and the stomach fulfill their God-given roles only when they interact in accordance with their intended relationship to each other, and the human body (which is alive due to food and the stomach) fulfills its proper role only when it acts in accordance with its relationship to the Lord. Jesus Christ is the Lord of believers: they belong to him, and they do what he commands; therefore, sexual immorality is unacceptable.

6:14 The past resurrection of Jesus and the future resurrection of believers is the logical basis for Paul's argument against engaging in sexual relations with prostitutes. Believers, who are "sanctified in Christ Jesus and called to be his holy people" (1:2) and who are God's temple (3:16–17), must live holy lives in the present because they will be raised in the future to new life in the presence of the holy God. A body destined for resurrection must not be degraded by immoral practices.

6:15 bodies are members of Christ. The physical bodies of believers are inseparably connected with Christ (ch. 12). The Lord Jesus Christ "owns" not only the values and thoughts of Christians but also their bodies (see vv. 19b–20), so they must not unite their bodies with prostitutes. Greco-Roman practice, in contrast, was to accept and practice prostitution as a matter of course. (There are over 50 synonyms for the word *prostitute* in Latin.)

6:16 unites himself. A close association, a permanent attachment. **one ... one flesh.** A sexual relationship establishes a one-flesh unity in the sense of Gen 2:24, which Jesus quotes when he prohibits divorce (Matt 19:6; Mark 10:7–8) and which Paul quotes when he emphasizes the unity of Christ and the church (Eph 5:31–32). The fact that Paul discusses an ongoing sexual relationship (note the term "unites," formulated as a present tense participle) does not mean that he would condone "one-time" sexual encounters (see note on v. 14).

6:18 [t]2Co 12:21; 1Th 4:3,4; Heb 13:4 [u]Ro 6:12
6:19 [v]Jn 2:21 [w]Ro 14:7,8
6:20 [x]Ac 20:28; 1Co 7:23; 1Pe 1:18,19; Rev 5:9
7:1 [y]ver 8,26
7:3 [z]Ex 21:10; 1Pe 3:7
7:5 [a]Ex 19:15; 1Sa 21:4, 5 [b]Mt 4:10 [c]1Th 3:5
7:6 [d]2Co 8:8
7:7 [e]ver 8; 1Co 9:5 [f]Mt 19:11,12; Ro 12:6; 1Co 12:4,11
7:8 [g]ver 1,26
7:9 [h]1Ti 5:14

18Flee from sexual immorality.[t] All other sins a person commits are outside the body, but whoever
sins sexually, sins against their own body.[u] 19Do you not know that your bodies are temples[v] of the Holy
Spirit, who is in you, whom you have received from God? You are not your own;[w] 20you were bought at
a price.[x] Therefore honor God with your bodies.

Concerning Married Life

7 Now for the matters you wrote about: "It is good for a man not to have sexual relations with a
woman."[y] 2But since sexual immorality is occurring, each man should have sexual relations
with his own wife, and each woman with her own husband. 3The husband should fulfill his marital
duty to his wife,[z] and likewise the wife to her husband. 4The wife does not have authority over her
own body but yields it to her husband. In the same way, the husband does not have authority over his
own body but yields it to his wife. 5Do not deprive each other except perhaps by mutual consent and
for a time,[a] so that you may devote yourselves to prayer. Then come together again so that Satan[b] will
not tempt you[c] because of your lack of self-control. 6I say this as a concession, not as a command.[d]
7I wish that all of you were as I am.[e] But each of you has your own gift from God; one has this gift,
another has that.[f]

8Now to the unmarried[a] and the widows I say: It is good for them to stay unmarried, as I do.[g]
9But if they cannot control themselves, they should marry,[h] for it is better to marry than to burn
with passion.

10To the married I give this command (not I, but the Lord): A wife must not separate from her

[a] 8 Or *widowers*

6:18 Since sexual intercourse with a prostitute constitutes a one-flesh unity and since Christians are linked with Christ in a one-Spirit unity, Christians must renounce all sexual immorality. **against their own body.** While other sins may also involve the body, sexual sins directly attack the body since they involve the physical union of two bodies.

6:19 your bodies are temples. The physical body of each individual believer is a place where God is present (see note on 3:16). The place where the Holy Spirit is at home must not be a place that is joined to prostitutes. **You are not your own.** Believers do not belong to themselves and must not decide on their own—independent of the Lord and the Holy Spirit—how they should live.

6:20 bought at a price. The reason that believers do not belong to themselves (v. 19b). This image of a "cash payment purchase" refers to Jesus' death on the cross. It refers to redeeming a slave through a cash payment (7:23) that Christ paid (Gal 3:13; 4:5) with his blood (1 Pet 1:18–19; Rev 5:9). **Therefore.** The logical and necessary conclusion is that believers should honor God with their entire existence, including their bodies.

7:1—11:1 *Issues Related to Lifestyle.* This section addresses marriage and celibacy (7:1–40) as well as food sacrificed to idols and participating in banquets (8:1—11:1).

7:1–40 *Marriage and Celibacy.* Since some Corinthian Christians argued for sexual abstinence, Paul addresses marriage and celibacy.

7:1–16 *Concerning Married Life.* Paul addresses sexuality in marriage (vv. 1–7), marriage and celibacy for the unmarried and for widows (vv. 8–9), and divorce for married Christians (vv. 10–16).

7:1 matters you wrote about. Besides oral information (1:10–11), Paul had received written communication from some Corinthian believers about problems in the church (8:1; 12:1; 16:1). **"It is good for a man not to have sexual relations with a woman."** A motto of some Corinthian believers, not Paul's conviction.

7:2 Married couples should have intimate relations in order to avoid sexual immorality. While this is not the main reason for being married (as a Jewish Scripture expert, Paul would refer to Gen 1:26–28; 2:4–25 in a discussion about the reason for marriage), it is an important one: since most human beings will have sexual relations, they must follow God's order at creation that places sexual relations within the context of the union of one man and one woman.

7:3 marital duty. Encompasses many different elements but certainly includes sexual intercourse. Both the wife and the husband have marital duties.

7:4 The wife does not have authority ... the husband does not have authority. Married Christians do not follow the principle of self-determination and self-gratification, because they do not have exclusive authority over their own bodies (unlike people engaging in sexual immorality, who seek only their own satisfaction). As regards sexual relations, there is complete equality between the husband and the wife.

7:5 deprive each other. Abstain from sexual intercourse. **so that Satan will not tempt you.** Married couples should have intimate relations so that they will not be tempted to have sexual encounters outside the marriage, which is what Satan would want them to do.

7:6 not as a command. Married Christian couples do not *have* to refrain from intercourse in order to pray. Paul formulates a concession, not a command.

7:7 as I am. Unmarried, which Paul prefers to being married (see vv. 8–9,25–40). **own gift.** Not everybody has the gift of staying single (cf. Matt 19:12). Some regard singleness as a gift of the Spirit (sometimes with reference to 12:31, where Paul does not have celibacy in mind, however).

7:8 stay unmarried. Paul's advice is probably connected with the "present crisis" (v. 26) in which everyday life is more difficult for married people. Paul emphasizes again that this is not advice that every Christian can or should follow: single believers and widows certainly should marry if they "burn with passion" (v. 9). People must not fulfill sexual desires outside of marriage.

7:10 command (not I, but the Lord). Paul cites Jesus' prohibition of divorce (see Matt 5:32; 19:9; Mark 10:11; Luke 16:18). **A wife must not separate.** Suggests that the impetus to abandon all sexual relations (v. 1) may have come from the married women in the church, who would find pregnancy during the "present crisis" (v. 26) especially difficult.

husband.[i] 11But if she does, she must remain unmarried or else be reconciled to her husband. And a
husband must not divorce his wife.
12To the rest I say this (I, not the Lord):[j] If any brother has a wife who is not a believer and she is
willing to live with him, he must not divorce her. 13And if a woman has a husband who is not a believer
and he is willing to live with her, she must not divorce him. 14For the unbelieving husband has been
sanctified through his wife, and the unbelieving wife has been sanctified through her believing husband. Otherwise your children would be unclean, but as it is, they are holy.[k]
15But if the unbeliever leaves, let it be so. The brother or the sister is not bound in such circumstances; God has called us to live in peace.[l] 16How do you know, wife, whether you will save[m] your
husband?[n] Or, how do you know, husband, whether you will save your wife?

Concerning Change of Status

17Nevertheless, each person should live as a believer in whatever situation the Lord has assigned to
them, just as God has called them.[o] This is the rule I lay down in all the churches.[p] 18Was a man already
circumcised when he was called? He should not become uncircumcised. Was a man uncircumcised
when he was called? He should not be circumcised.[q] 19Circumcision is nothing and uncircumcision is
nothing.[r] Keeping God's commands is what counts. 20Each person should remain in the situation they
were in when God called them.[s]
21Were you a slave when you were called? Don't let it trouble you — although if you can gain your
freedom, do so. 22For the one who was a slave when called to faith in the Lord is the Lord's freed person;[t] similarly, the one who was free when called is Christ's slave.[u] 23You were bought at a price;[v] do
not become slaves of human beings. 24Brothers and sisters, each person, as responsible to God, should
remain in the situation they were in when God called them.[w]

7:10 [i] Mal 2:14-16; Mt 5:32; 19:3-9; Mk 10:11; Lk 16:18
7:12 [j] ver 6,10; 2Co 11:17
7:14 [k] Mal 2:15
7:15 [l] Ro 14:19; 1Co 14:33
7:16 [m] Ro 11:14 [n] 1Pe 3:1
7:17 [o] Ro 12:3 [p] 1Co 4:17; 14:33; 2Co 8:18; 11:28
7:18 [q] Ac 15:1,2
7:19 [r] Ro 2:25-27; Gal 5:6; 6:15; Col 3:11
7:20 [s] ver 24
7:22 [t] Jn 8:32,36; Phm 16 [u] Eph 6:6
7:23 [v] 1Co 6:20
7:24 [w] ver 20

7:11 But if she does. Not an exception to the rule but refers to a Christian woman who has already divorced her husband. There are only two options for a divorced woman: (1) remain unmarried or (2) reconcile with her husband. **a husband must not divorce his wife.** Just as a woman must not divorce her husband; again Paul formulates no exception.

7:12 I, not the Lord. Paul comments on the origin, not the authority, of the following point. **who is not a believer.** A Christian who is married to a non-Christian may not divorce, because of the Lord's command in vv. 10–11. A Christian in such a marriage can rest assured that the non-Christian spouse does not cause the Christian partner to become impure.

7:14 sanctified. Does not refer to sanctifying or saving faith in Jesus Christ, because the unbelieving partner continues to remain a pagan (v. 16); Paul is probably referring to the sphere of the Holy Spirit into which the non-Christian spouse is brought: the Spirit's power neutralizes the harmful consequences of the pagan lifestyle of the non-Christian spouse.

7:15 let it be so. When a non-Christian spouse divorces a Christian spouse, the Christian cannot do anything about it. **not bound in such circumstances.** It is often suggested that this allows a deserted Christian spouse to remarry since the Christian is not "bound" to the marriage that has been dissolved. This interpretation is not plausible: (1) In v. 11 Paul prohibits remarriage in cases where divorce has taken place. (2) The Greek verb does not mean "bound"; it means "enslaved" or "under bondage." (3) The thrust of the context is maintaining marriage. (4) Paul speaks of "freedom" for a new marriage only in cases when the spouse has died (v. 39; Rom 7:1–3). If a non-Christian spouse leaves the marriage, the Christian spouse is not responsible for the divorce. Christian spouses may not initiate divorce from non-Christian spouses on religious grounds. **God has called us to live in peace.** Another argument for remaining married to a non-Christian.

7:16 Christian spouses may be able to save their non-Christian partners.

7:17–24 *Concerning Change of Status.* Christians should live confidently for the Lord in the specific situation where the Lord has placed them (vv. 17,20,24). This serves a dual purpose: married Christians should stay married (vv. 1–16), and unmarried Christians should stay unmarried (vv. 25–40). Paul gives several examples to illustrate this principle.

7:18–20 The first example of the principle of v. 17 (see preceding note) is Jewish Christians ("circumcised," v. 18) and Gentile Christians ("uncircumcised," v. 18). Jews should not seek to reverse circumcision (a procedure, called epispasm, that some Diaspora Jews carried out), and Gentiles should not seek to be circumcised, succumbing to the pressure of Jewish Christians who make such a demand (Acts 15:1–5; Gal 5:1–3).

7:19 Circumcision is nothing. Reflects Paul's understanding of the significance of Jesus' death and resurrection, which inaugurated the new creation (Gal 5:2,6; 6:15). Ethnicity has become irrelevant to the question of who is or is not accepted among God's covenant people (Gal 3:28; Eph 2:11–18; 3:6; Col 3:11). **God's commands.** Revealed in Scripture and in the apostles' teachings.

7:21–24 The second example (see note on vv. 18–20) of the principle of v. 17 (see note on vv. 17–24) is Christians who are slaves and Christians who are freeborn. If Christian slaves have the opportunity to become free, they should become free. Slaves in the Roman Empire could be set free by their owners, e.g., as a reward for years of hard work or as a result of payment offered by the slave; manumission was selective, however; there were no guarantees. The freedmen, i.e., the slaves who were manumitted, acquired the family name of their former master if the latter was a Roman citizen; they continued to provide benefits to their "patron."

7:22 the Lord's freed person. Because Christians who are slaves belong to the Lord, they are freed from sin's penalty and power (Rom 3:24; 6:7,14–15,18,22; 8:2,21). **Christ's slave.** Believers whose social status is that of a freeborn person are not "free" in the sense that they alone determine how they live; rather, they belong to Christ, whose commands they obey.

7:25 [x] ver 6; 2Co 8:8
[y] 2Co 4:1; 1Ti 1:13,16
7:26 [z] ver 1,8
7:29 [a] ver 31; Ro 13:11,12
7:31 [b] 1Jn 2:17
7:32 [c] 1Ti 5:5
7:34 [d] Lk 2:37
7:35 [e] Ps 86:11
7:36 [f] ver 28
7:38 [g] Heb 13:4

Concerning the Unmarried

25 Now about virgins: I have no command from the Lord,[x] but I give a judgment as one who by the
Lord's mercy[y] is trustworthy. 26 Because of the present crisis, I think that it is good for a man to remain
as he is.[z] 27 Are you pledged to a woman? Do not seek to be released. Are you free from such a commitment? Do not look for a wife. 28 But if you do marry, you have not sinned; and if a virgin marries, she
has not sinned. But those who marry will face many troubles in this life, and I want to spare you this.

29 What I mean, brothers and sisters, is that the time is short.[a] From now on those who have wives
should live as if they do not; 30 those who mourn, as if they did not; those who are happy, as if they were
not; those who buy something, as if it were not theirs to keep; 31 those who use the things of the world,
as if not engrossed in them. For this world in its present form is passing away.[b]

32 I would like you to be free from concern. An unmarried man is concerned about the Lord's affairs[c] — how he can please the Lord. 33 But a married man is concerned about the affairs of this
world — how he can please his wife — 34 and his interests are divided. An unmarried woman or virgin
is concerned about the Lord's affairs: Her aim is to be devoted to the Lord in both body and spirit.[d] But
a married woman is concerned about the affairs of this world — how she can please her husband. 35 I
am saying this for your own good, not to restrict you, but that you may live in a right way in undivided[e]
devotion to the Lord.

36 If anyone is worried that he might not be acting honorably toward the virgin he is engaged to,
and if his passions are too strong[a] and he feels he ought to marry, he should do as he wants. He is not
sinning.[f] They should get married. 37 But the man who has settled the matter in his own mind, who is
under no compulsion but has control over his own will, and who has made up his mind not to marry
the virgin — this man also does the right thing. 38 So then, he who marries the virgin does right,[g] but
he who does not marry her does better.[b]

[a] *36* Or *if she is getting beyond the usual age for marriage* [b] *36-38* Or *[36] If anyone thinks he is not treating his daughter properly, and if she is getting along in years* (or *if her passions are too strong*), *and he feels she ought to marry, he should do as he wants. He is not sinning. He should let her get married. [37] But the man who has settled the matter in his own mind, who is under no compulsion but has control over his own will, and who has made up his mind to keep the virgin unmarried — this man also does the right thing. [38] So then, he who gives his virgin in marriage does right, but he who does not give her in marriage does better.*

7:25–40 *Concerning the Unmarried.* Paul gives unmarried, sometimes engaged, Christians the advice not to marry (vv. 25–28). The main reasons: "the present crisis" (v. 26) and the "many troubles in this life" (v. 28). Paul explains his advice to stay unmarried (vv. 29–31) by referencing Jesus' anticipated return and then further explains his advice (vv. 32–35). He then repeats what he said in vv. 26–28 concerning unmarried (possibly engaged) Christians (vv. 36–38) before applying his advice to widows (vv. 39–40).

7:25 virgins. Young, unmarried women. **I have no command from the Lord, but I give a judgment.** Paul's instructions about virgins, unmarried men, and widows represent his personal advice, not an authoritative command from Jesus as in the case of believers who are married (vv. 10–11). While Paul regards the advice he gives as the preferable course of action, he does not issue a command.

7:26 the present crisis. The reason Paul prefers staying unmarried and probably the reason some of the Corinthians wanted to abandon sexual relations within marriage (v. 1). It may be connected with the famine of AD 51/52, which caused severe food shortages in Greece. Some Christians may have interpreted such a time of distress in the context of Jesus' warning concerning pregnant women in the time before the end (Matt 24:19; Mark 13:17; Luke 21:23). In vv. 29–31 Paul refers to the time before Jesus' return, implying that Jesus may return very soon. It is easier for single people to live through a period of crisis and distress than for married couples to do so, because married couples have to care for each other and their children. Paul's recommendation to stay unmarried does not apply to all times and all situations.

7:27–31 Paul reiterates what he wrote in vv. 10–11: a married Christian must not seek a divorce, and an unmarried Christian should not seek to get married — although if Christians do marry, they do not sin. Paul advises single Christians not to marry, because married people will face "many troubles" (v. 28; triggered by the "present crisis," v. 26) and because "the time is short" (v. 29). Jesus will return soon. Paul does not say how close the time of Jesus' return is, but he seems to allow for the possibility that it could be during his and the Corinthians' lifetime.

7:31 this world in its present form is passing away. The world will come to an end (see "the last hour" in 1 John 2:18; cf. Rom 13:11). Since Christians always live in anticipation of Jesus' return, the attachments and activities of their everyday lives must not control them, whether they are married or not.

7:32–35 It is preferable to stay unmarried because unmarried Christians can focus more consistently on "the Lord's affairs" (v. 32), particularly edifying the church (3:10–14; 14:12) and preaching the gospel beyond Corinth in the entire province (2 Cor 1:1). Married Christians must be "concerned about the affairs of this world" (v. 33), supporting their spouse and children.

7:34 his interests are divided. Not critiquing married life but realistically viewing the priorities of married people.

7:36 If anyone. Some interpret this phrase as referring to fathers who have unmarried daughters. However, there is no evidence that a father could insist on his daughter remaining unmarried. Also, the phrase "if his passions are too strong" most plausibly provides the subject for the beginning of the sentence. It is thus preferable to interpret "anyone" in terms of a Christian who is engaged to a virgin. Paul's advice for engaged Christians follows his previous counsel: they can marry, although it is better to stay unmarried.

[39]A woman is bound to her husband as long as he lives.[h] But if her husband dies, she is free to marry
anyone she wishes, but he must belong to the Lord.[i] [40]In my judgment,[j] she is happier if she stays as
she is — and I think that I too have the Spirit of God.

Concerning Food Sacrificed to Idols

8 Now about food sacrificed to idols:[k] We know that "We all possess knowledge."[l] But knowledge puffs
up while love builds up. [2]Those who think they know something[m] do not yet know as they ought
to know.[n] [3]But whoever loves God is known by God.[a][o]
[4]So then, about eating food sacrificed to idols:[p] We know that "An idol is nothing at all in the world"[q]
and that "There is no God but one."[r] [5]For even if there are so-called gods,[s] whether in heaven or on
earth (as indeed there are many "gods" and many "lords"), [6]yet for us there is but one God, the Father,[t]
from whom all things came[u] and for whom we live; and there is but one Lord,[v] Jesus Christ, through
whom all things came[w] and through whom we live.
[7]But not everyone possesses this knowledge. Some people are still so accustomed to idols that when
they eat sacrificial food they think of it as having been sacrificed to a god, and since their conscience
is weak,[x] it is defiled. [8]But food does not bring us near to God;[y] we are no worse if we do not eat, and
no better if we do.
[9]Be careful, however, that the exercise of your rights does not become a stumbling block[z] to the
weak.[a] [10]For if someone with a weak conscience sees you, with all your knowledge, eating in an idol's
temple, won't that person be emboldened to eat what is sacrificed to idols? [11]So this weak brother or
sister, for whom Christ died, is destroyed[b] by your knowledge. [12]When you sin against them[c] in this way
and wound their weak conscience, you sin against Christ. [13]Therefore, if what I eat causes my brother
or sister to fall into sin, I will never eat meat again, so that I will not cause them to fall.[d]

[a] *2,3* An early manuscript and another ancient witness *think they have knowledge do not yet know as they ought to know. [3]But whoever loves truly knows.*

7:39 [h]Ro 7:2,3 [i]2Co 6:14
7:40 [j]ver 25
8:1 [k]Ac 15:20 [l]Ro 15:14
8:2 [m]1Co 3:18 [n]1Co 13:8,9,12; 1Ti 6:4
8:3 [o]Ro 8:29; Gal 4:9
8:4 [p]ver 1,7,10 [q]1Co 10:19 [r]Dt 6:4; Eph 4:6
8:5 [s]2Th 2:4
8:6 [t]Mal 2:10 [u]Ro 11:36 [v]Eph 4:5 [w]Jn 1:3
8:7 [x]Ro 14:14; 1Co 10:28
8:8 [y]Ro 14:17
8:9 [z]Gal 5:13 [a]Ro 14:1
8:11 [b]Ro 14:15,20
8:12 [c]Mt 18:6
8:13 [d]Ro 14:21

7:39–40 Paul applies the principle of vv. 25–28 to widows in the church. A married woman is bound to her husband as long as the husband lives; she cannot divorce him. If her husband dies, she may remarry only if her second husband is a Christian ("he must belong to the Lord," v. 39), or she may remain unmarried, which Paul prefers in view of the "present crisis" (v. 26).

8:1—11:1 *Food Sacrificed to Idols and Participation in Banquets.* The Corinthian Christians compromised with the secular values and lifestyles of their contemporary society in other areas: visiting pagan temples, participating in pagan banquets, and eating food that was known to have been sacrificed to idols. Paul urges them not to compromise their faith or the faith of fellow Christians.

8:1–13 *Concerning Food Sacrificed to Idols.* Paul argues from the more general principle of true knowledge and love among Christians (vv. 1–6) and the danger that visiting pagan temples poses for fellow Christians (vv. 7–13).

8:1 "We all possess knowledge." A slogan of Corinthian Christians (thus the quotation marks). Knowledge is important and belongs to the gifts of God's Spirit (12:8). **puffs up.** It leads some Corinthians to an exaggerated self-confidence.

8:2 do not yet know. Paul counters that they do not yet have the necessary knowledge that loving God, which is the basic relationship with God (v. 3), entails a love that "builds up" (v. 1). True love is not "puffed up" because it is not self-seeking (13:4–5).

8:4 "An idol is nothing at all in the world." A slogan (thus the quotation marks) of Corinthian Christians that Paul acknowledges is true. **An idol.** A cult image that represents an alleged transcendent being (12:2; Acts 7:41; Rev 9:20); in the biblical tradition, the term frequently means "fabricated deity," a product of human imagination that has no reality (see, e.g., Exod 20:4; Lev 19:4). **nothing at all in the world.** It does not represent a real god and has no power (Ps 115:4; Isa 41:21–29; 44:9–17). **"There is no God but one."** Christians agree with the confession of God's people in Deut 6:4 (see, e.g., 1 Kgs 8:60; Isa 43:10; 44:6; 45:5–6).

8:5 so-called gods. Pagans treat idols as deities by worshiping them through sacrifices, processions, and hymns.

8:6 us. Christians. **one God.** The Creator of the universe and the Father of his people (Deut 6:4). Paul expands the confession of Jewish monotheism: there is "but one God, the Father," and there is "but one Lord, Jesus Christ," who is the mediator of creation and salvation (John 1:3; Col 1:16; Heb 1:2).

8:7 Some people. Newly converted pagans who have been sacrificing and eating in the local temples. **their conscience is weak.** Because they do not yet have firm convictions regarding the significance of pagan temples and sacrifices to pagan deities. If Christians who know that idols are "nothing" (v. 4) eat in pagan temples, they send the message that they accept the reality or existence of these pagan gods.

8:9 your rights. The rights of Corinthian Christians to eat "in an idol's temple" (v. 10). Between the temple of Asclepius and the Lerna Fountain in Corinth, dining rooms have been discovered that were in use in the Roman period. Christians may have been invited by their pagan friends to dine in pagan temples. **stumbling block.** The metaphor of a stone that causes people to stumble. The cause for offense was not the subjective indignation of some Christians regarding "weak" Christians who should be taught to become stronger so that they will share the "knowledge" (v. 10) of those who dine in pagan temples. Rather, it describes new Christians who will be "destroyed" (v. 11) if they return to pagan temples and eat there, returning to the traditional pagan views of gods, temples, and food sacrificed in the local temples, abandoning their Christian faith.

8:13 causes ... to fall into sin. Seduces a fellow Christian to sin, in this case by eating in a pagan temple and tacitly acknowledging the reality of the god worshiped there. Christians who love fellow Christians (vv. 1–3) refrain from eating any food that may cause a fellow Christian to commit a sin and abandon the faith (v. 11).

9:1 [e]2Co 12:12 [f]1Co 15:8 [g]1Co 3:6; 4:15
9:2 [h]2Co 3:2,3
9:4 [i]1Th 2:6
9:5 [j]1Co 7:7,8 [k]Mt 12:46
9:6 [l]Ac 4:36
9:7 [m]Dt 20:6; Pr 27:18
9:9 [n]Dt 25:4; 1Ti 5:18 [o]Dt 22:1-4
9:10 [p]Ro 4:23,24 [q]2Ti 2:6
9:11 [r]Ro 15:27
9:12 [s]Ac 18:3 [t]2Co 11:7-12
9:13 [u]Lev 6:16,26; Dt 18:1
9:14 [v]Mt 10:10; 1Ti 5:18
9:15 [w]Ac 18:3 [x]2Co 11:9,10
9:16 [y]Ro 1:14; Ac 9:15
9:17 [z]1Co 3:8,14 [a]Gal 2:7; Col 1:25
9:18 [b]2Co 11:7; 12:13

Paul's Rights as an Apostle

9 Am I not free? Am I not an apostle?[e] Have I not seen Jesus our Lord?[f] Are you not the result of my work in the Lord?[g] [2]Even though I may not be an apostle to others, surely I am to you! For you are the seal[h] of my apostleship in the Lord.

[3]This is my defense to those who sit in judgment on me. [4]Don't we have the right to food and drink?[i] [5]Don't we have the right to take a believing wife[j] along with us, as do the other apostles and the Lord's brothers[k] and Cephas[a]? [6]Or is it only I and Barnabas[l] who lack the right to not work for a living?

[7]Who serves as a soldier at his own expense? Who plants a vineyard[m] and does not eat its grapes? Who tends a flock and does not drink the milk? [8]Do I say this merely on human authority? Doesn't the Law say the same thing? [9]For it is written in the Law of Moses: "Do not muzzle an ox while it is treading out the grain."[b][n] Is it about oxen that God is concerned?[o] [10]Surely he says this for us, doesn't he? Yes, this was written for us,[p] because whoever plows and threshes should be able to do so in the hope of sharing in the harvest.[q] [11]If we have sown spiritual seed among you, is it too much if we reap a material harvest from you?[r] [12]If others have this right of support from you, shouldn't we have it all the more?

But we did not use this right.[s] On the contrary, we put up with anything rather than hinder[t] the gospel of Christ.

[13]Don't you know that those who serve in the temple get their food from the temple, and that those who serve at the altar share in what is offered on the altar?[u] [14]In the same way, the Lord has commanded that those who preach the gospel should receive their living from the gospel.[v]

[15]But I have not used any of these rights.[w] And I am not writing this in the hope that you will do such things for me, for I would rather die than allow anyone to deprive me of this boast.[x] [16]For when I preach the gospel, I cannot boast, since I am compelled to preach.[y] Woe to me if I do not preach the gospel! [17]If I preach voluntarily, I have a reward;[z] if not voluntarily, I am simply discharging the trust committed to me.[a] [18]What then is my reward? Just this: that in preaching the gospel I may offer it free of charge,[b] and so not make full use of my rights as a preacher of the gospel.

[a] *5* That is, Peter [b] *9* Deut. 25:4

9:1–27 *Illustration: Paul's Own Behavior.* Paul uses the example of his own behavior to argue his point: he has rights on which he could insist, but he relinquishes such rights for the sake of the gospel. This illustrates the proper relationship between freedom and love.

9:1–18 *Paul's Rights as an Apostle.* Paul describes his authority as an apostle (vv. 1–2), his behavior as a missionary (vv. 3–6), and his rights as an apostle (vv. 7–14) to demonstrate that he has relinquished his rights (vv. 15–18).

9:1–2 Paul begins his discussion of personal rights and how they are related to the way Christians act by reviewing his apostolic authority.

9:1 Am I not free? Paul's freedom *not* to eat food sacrificed to idols in the local temples (8:13). Christians are free to act, *not* in their own self-interest, but in the interests of fellow Christians (9:19; 10:29). The next three rhetorical questions in v. 1 underline Paul's apostolic authority: he is an apostle, he has seen the Lord (15:8; cf. Acts 1:22; 9:3–6; Gal 1:11–19), and he has established the church in Corinth.

9:3 defense. Suggests that Corinthian Christians criticized not only Paul's rhetorical oratory (1:10–17) but also his decision not to accept financial support from them. Because itinerant orators were supported financially by local patrons, Corinthian Christians who belonged to the cultural elite evidently criticized Paul for not accepting their money.

9:4–5 Since Paul is an apostle, he has the "right" to financial and material support, not only for himself but also, potentially (7:8), for a wife he might take along on his travels.

9:5 the other apostles. Jesus' 12 disciples (among them "Cephas," i.e., Peter) but also a wider circle of envoys or missionaries who had seen the risen Jesus Christ (vv. 1–2; see 15:6) and received the commission to preach the gospel (e.g., Barnabas). **the Lord's brothers.** Jesus' earthly brothers: James, Josephus, Simon, and Judas (see Matt 13:55; Mark 6:3). Julius Africanus relates about AD 225 that Jesus' relatives, based in the Galilean towns of Nazareth and Kokhaba, traveled around preaching the gospel.

9:7–11 Paul asks rhetorical questions to argue that he has the right of support; he uses examples from the military, agriculture, and animal husbandry. "The Law," i.e., Scripture, confirms that the apostles have the right to material support (Deut 25:4). Paul argues from the lesser to the greater: if God is concerned about an ox that treads out the grain (v. 9), he is surely more concerned about envoys who preach his gospel.

9:12 Even though Paul has the right to material support, he has relinquished it. He accepts financial support from churches he has established (2 Cor 11:8–9; Phil 4:10–19), and he solicits material support for other Christians, in particular, support for the poor believers in Jerusalem (16:1–4; 2 Cor 8–9). But he refuses to make a living from people to whom he preaches the gospel. Paul willingly puts up with anything that this decision entails, including dishonor, hunger, thirst, ragged clothes, and work with his own hands (4:10–12). Accepting material support from people in a city in which he has just arrived as a missionary could easily lead them to falsely assess his motives (1 Thess 2:3–6) and thus "hinder the gospel of Christ."

9:13 those who serve in the temple. Priests and Levites who serve in the temple in Jerusalem and make a living from the work they do (Lev 6:16–18; Num 18:8–20; Deut 18:1–5). Even cult personnel in pagan temples received portions of sacrifices and other donations from the people.

9:14 the Lord has commanded. Alludes to what Jesus says in Matt 10:9–10; Luke 10:7. **those who preach the gospel.** Missionaries, pastors, teachers, evangelists. **receive their living from the gospel.** Receive financial support as they preach the gospel.

9:15 this boast. Paul was proud that he preached the gospel without receiving financial support from Corinthian patrons.

9:18 free of charge. Preaching the gospel without demanding or expecting payment from the people whom he seeks to reach with the gospel.

Paul's Use of His Freedom

19Though I am free[c] and belong to no one, I have made myself a slave to everyone,[d] to win as many as possible.[e] 20To the Jews I became like a Jew, to win the Jews.[f] To those under the law I became like one under the law (though I myself am not under the law), so as to win those under the law. 21To those not having the law I became like one not having the law[g] (though I am not free from God's law but am under Christ's law), so as to win those not having the law. 22To the weak I became weak, to win the weak. I have become all things to all people[h] so that by all possible means I might save some.[i] 23I do all this for the sake of the gospel, that I may share in its blessings.

The Need for Self-Discipline

24Do you not know that in a race all the runners run, but only one gets the prize? Run[j] in such a way as to get the prize. 25Everyone who competes in the games goes into strict training. They do it to get a crown that will not last, but we do it to get a crown that will last forever.[k] 26Therefore I do not run like someone running aimlessly; I do not fight like a boxer beating the air. 27No, I strike a blow to my body[l] and make it my slave so that after I have preached to others, I myself will not be disqualified for the prize.

Warnings From Israel's History

10 For I do not want you to be ignorant of the fact, brothers and sisters, that our ancestors were all under the cloud[m] and that they all passed through the sea.[n] 2They were all baptized into Moses in the cloud and in the sea. 3They all ate the same spiritual food 4and drank the same spiritual drink;

9:19 [c] ver 1 [d] Gal 5:13 [e] Mt 18:15; 1Pe 3:1
9:20 [f] Ac 16:3; 21:20-26; Ro 11:14
9:21 [g] Ro 2:12,14
9:22 [h] 1Co 10:33 [i] Ro 11:14
9:24 [j] Gal 2:2; 2Ti 4:7; Heb 12:1
9:25 [k] Jas 1:12; Rev 2:10
9:27 [l] Ro 8:13
10:1 [m] Ex 13:21 [n] Ex 14:22,29

9:19–23 *Paul's Use of His Freedom.* Paul's relinquishing his rights (vv. 1–18) is a basis for his admonition that the Corinthian Christians should relinquish rights that they claim to have.

9:19 slave to everyone. Only someone who is "free" can make himself a "slave"; Paul speaks not of legal dependence on "everyone" but of his way of life as a missionary being determined by the way his listeners live. **win.** To bring to faith in Jesus and save from God's judgment, a goal that would be compromised if the people whom he seeks to win were to pay for his expenses. See notes on vv. 20–22.

9:20 Paul illustrates in vv. 20–22 his goal of winning as many people as possible for Christ with three examples that describe how missionaries contextualize. When he proclaims the gospel to the Jews, he lives "like a Jew": he keeps commandments that he does not have to keep as a believer in Jesus (e.g., food laws, the circumcision of Timothy [Acts 16:3], and purification rites in the Jerusalem temple [Acts 21:20–26]). **not under the law.** Not required to keep all the law's commandments, many of which Jesus fulfilled (e.g., laws about sacrifices, purity laws, food laws), since Jesus atoned for sins and bestows holiness.

9:21 those not having the law. From a Jewish perspective, all Gentiles. **though I am not free from God's law.** That Paul lives like a Gentile does not mean that he engages in sinful behavior that characterizes Gentile lifestyles (6:9–10). **Christ's law.** Paul follows the law, which has been modified as a result of the coming of Jesus, Israel's Messiah and Savior of the world, and his death on the cross that atones for sins. The prohibition of idolatry, the first of the Ten Commandments, continues to be binding for Paul and all believers, as he will argue in 10:1–22.

9:22 the weak. Those who do not belong to the local elites; those without education, influence, or social standing (1:26–28)—not only those with a weak conscience. **all things to all people so that by all possible means I might save some.** Summarizes Paul's approach to missionary work. He preaches the gospel to all people, excluding no ethnic, religious, or social group. He adapts to the culture of each group without reserving privileges for himself.

9:24–27 *The Need for Self-Discipline.* Paul uses athletic metaphors to picture the Christian life as rigorous, requiring self-discipline and perseverance.

9:24–25 Runners who compete in games go into strict training: they exercise self-control when they train for a competition. Athletes who competed in the games in Olympia had to swear an oath confirming that they had abstained from wine, meat, and sexual intercourse in the previous ten months. Runners focus on winning the prize, which in the games in Olympia and in Isthmia was a crown, a wreath made of foliage (in the games in Isthmia, controlled by the city of Corinth, the wreath was made of celery). See 2 Tim 4:8; Jas 1:12; 1 Pet 5:4; Rev 2:10. The goal of winning determines an athlete's lifestyle.

9:25 crown that will last forever. Eternal life in an imperishable new body (15:42,50,53–54). Christians must avoid anything that could jeopardize reaching the goal. Self-control is part of the fruit of the Spirit (Gal 5:23).

9:26–27 Paul applies the athletic analogies of a runner and a boxer to himself. As a gospel preacher, he is focused on reaching the goal and winning the prize and thus is characterized by self-control. He does not allow the desires and urges of his body to control his behavior.

10:1–13 *Warnings From Israel's History.* Paul argues with another example: when the people of Israel compromised with idolatry, it led to God's judgment.

10:1 the cloud. The pillar of cloud that accompanied the people of Israel during the exodus from Egypt (Exod 13:21–22; 14:24; see Ps 105:39). **passed through the sea.** Crossed the Red Sea (Exod 14:21–22; see Ps 78:13).

10:2 baptized into Moses. Figurative use of the Greek word *baptizō*, the basic meaning of which is "immerse." Paul speaks of the Israelites' incorporation into, or affiliation with, Moses, whom God appointed as Israel's leader and whom they were to obey.

10:3 spiritual food. The miracle of the quail and the manna (Exod 16:1–16; Num 11:4–34).

10:4 spiritual drink. The miracle of the water from the rock (Exod 17:1–7; Num 20:7–11). The two miracles are interpreted typologically in terms of the salvation provided by God through Jesus Christ. **the spiritual rock that accompanied them.** Jewish tradition deduced, from the reference to the rock at the beginning (Exod 17:1–7) and at the end (Num 20:2–13) of the desert journey, that the rock followed ("accompanied") the people of Israel. When Paul speaks of a "spiritual" rock, he indicates that he does not think of the physical rock in the

10:4 [o]Ex 17:6; Nu 20:11; Ps 78:15
10:5 [p]Nu 14:29; Heb 3:17
10:7 [q]ver 14 [r]Ex 32:4,6,19
10:8 [s]Nu 25:1-9
10:9 [t]Nu 21:5,6
10:10 [u]Nu 16:41 [v]Nu 16:49 [w]Ex 12:23
10:11 [x]Ro 13:11
10:12 [y]Ro 11:20
10:13 [z]1Co 1:9 [a]2Pe 2:9
10:16 [b]Mt 26:26-28
10:17 [c]Ro 12:5; 1Co 12:27
10:18 [d]Lev 7:6,14,15

for they drank from the spiritual rock[o] that accompanied them, and that rock was Christ. 5 Nevertheless, God was not pleased with most of them; their bodies were scattered in the wilderness.[p]

6 Now these things occurred as examples to keep us from setting our hearts on evil things as they did. 7 Do not be idolaters,[q] as some of them were; as it is written: "The people sat down to eat and drink and got up to indulge in revelry."[a r] 8 We should not commit sexual immorality, as some of them did—and in one day twenty-three thousand of them died.[s] 9 We should not test Christ,[b] as some of them did—and were killed by snakes.[t] 10 And do not grumble, as some of them did[u]—and were killed[v] by the destroying angel.[w]

11 These things happened to them as examples and were written down as warnings for us, on whom the culmination of the ages has come.[x] 12 So, if you think you are standing firm,[y] be careful that you don't fall! 13 No temptation[c] has overtaken you except what is common to mankind. And God is faithful;[z] he will not let you be tempted[c] beyond what you can bear.[a] But when you are tempted,[c] he will also provide a way out so that you can endure it.

Idol Feasts and the Lord's Supper

14 Therefore, my dear friends, flee from idolatry. 15 I speak to sensible people; judge for yourselves what I say. 16 Is not the cup of thanksgiving for which we give thanks a participation in the blood of Christ? And is not the bread that we break a participation in the body of Christ?[b] 17 Because there is one loaf, we, who are many, are one body,[c] for we all share the one loaf.

18 Consider the people of Israel: Do not those who eat the sacrifices[d] participate in the altar? 19 Do I

[a] *7* Exodus 32:6 [b] *9* Some manuscripts *test the Lord* [c] *13* The Greek for *temptation* and *tempted* can also mean *testing* and *tested.*

desert that gave water. **that rock was Christ.** The rock is interpreted symbolically: the gifts of salvation that God provides for his people are given through Christ. Just as Paul transferred the term "Lord" from God to Jesus Christ (e.g., 1:2), so he transfers the term "rock" from God (e.g., Deut 32:4,15,30–31) to Jesus. Since he described Jesus as mediator of creation in 8:6, he may also be thinking of the preexistent Christ. Paul's main point is the early history of Israel: though sustained by God's grace, the Israelites were destroyed in the desert due to their idolatry.

10:5 Despite the experience of redemption from Egypt and the miracles in the desert, "God was not pleased with most of [the Israelites]," with the result that he sent judgment. With only two exceptions (Caleb and Joshua, Num 14:24–35), none of the adult Israelites who had been rescued from Egypt entered the promised land; they all died in the desert.

10:6–11 Paul applies the events in Israel's early history to the Corinthian Christians (v. 6). Paul alludes to four episodes from the exodus story when he exhorts them not to be idolaters (v. 7), not to be sexually immoral (v. 8), not to put Christ to the test (v. 9), and not to complain (v. 10).

10:6 these things. Events connected with the generation of Israelites who perished in the desert. **evil things.** Eating food sacrificed to idols and participating in banquets held in local temples, which some Corinthians insist is their right (vv. 14,18,20–21; 8:1,4).

10:7 Do not be idolaters. Israel committed idolatry when they had Aaron produce a golden calf. Paul's quotation of Exod 32:6 alludes to the episode of the golden calf (Exod 32:5–6,17–19). Paul's major concern in chs. 8–10 is that eating food sacrificed to idols and participating in banquets held in pagan temples is idolatry. **revelry.** See note on Exod 32:6.

10:8 not commit sexual immorality. Israelite men indulged in idolatry and sexual immorality with Moabite women, resulting in the death of thousands of Israelites (see Num 25:1–9, where v. 2 refers to eating the sacrificial meat offered to the gods; see also Paul's warnings in 5:1–13; 6:12–20; 7:2–5). Num 25:9 mentions 24,000 dead; Paul refers to 23,000 dead. Perhaps Paul alludes not only to Num 25:9 but also to the episode of the golden calf in Exod 32:28, where 3,000 Israelites are killed: he may have taken the figure 3,000 from Exod 32:28 and combined it with the figure 20,000 from the Septuagint version (the pre-Christian Greek translation of the OT) of Num 25:9 (which has "4,000 and 20,000") in order to point to the connection between the punishment for immorality in Num 25 with the punishment for idolatry in Exod 32.

10:9 test Christ. Israel complained about the manna God had given them (Num 21:5); as judgment, snakes killed many of them (Num 21:6). But those who looked at the bronze snake on a pole lived (Num 21:8–9). Paul again sees Christ as being spiritually present with Israel during the desert wanderings.

10:10 grumble. Israel repeatedly complained in the desert (Exod 17:1–7; Num 11; 14; 16).

10:11 examples ... warnings. The Corinthian Christians must make sure they do not repeat Israel's mistakes. **culmination of the ages.** Jesus' coming fulfilled God's promises and marked the beginning of the last days (Heb 9:26; see 2 Cor 5:1–5; 1 Thess 5:4–8; Heb 1:2; 1 Pet 1:20).

10:14–22 *Idol Feasts and the Lord's Supper.* Christians must not participate in banquets held in pagan temples.

10:14 The main concern is the need to avoid idolatry at all costs (see vv. 6–7). **my dear friends.** Underlines the warning's significance.

10:16 cup of thanksgiving. The cup of wine at a Jewish feast over which someone spoke a blessing; in the Passover meal this was the third cup. Here it describes the cup over which someone prayed with praise and thanksgiving at the beginning of the meals in the Christian congregation, when the Lord's Supper was celebrated. **blood of Christ.** Jesus' death, which atoned for our sins (11:23–25; Rom 6:4–5). **bread that we break.** Breaking and eating bread when celebrating the Lord's Supper. **body of Christ.** Jesus' death; his body was "broken" when he died at the cross.

10:17 one loaf ... one body. Underlines the unity of the community of believers, which Paul regards as Christ's body (see 12:12,27; Eph 1:22–23). **many.** All believers observing the Lord's Supper.

10:18–20 Participating in the Lord's Supper is incompatible with eating in pagan temples, because banquets that take place in pagan temples are connected with the worship of false gods, with demons. Jewish people ("the people of Israel," v. 18) offer sacrifices in the temple in Jerusalem and thus "participate in the altar" (v. 18) when they eat a portion of the sacrifice "in the presence of the LORD" (Deut 14:23,26). Eating food that is sacrificed on an altar is an expression of one's affiliation with the god to whom the altar is dedicated. Paul applies this truth to "food sacrificed to an idol" (v. 19). While it is true that an idol is not "anything" (v. 19), i.e., is nothing, this does not mean that pagan sacrifices are offered to "nothing" or that Christians may eat food sacrificed to idols.

mean then that food sacrificed to an idol is anything, or that an idol is anything?[e] 20No, but the sacrifices
of pagans are offered to demons,[f] not to God, and I do not want you to be participants with demons. 21You
cannot drink the cup of the Lord and the cup of demons too; you cannot have a part in both the Lord's
table and the table of demons.[g] 22Are we trying to arouse the Lord's jealousy?[h] Are we stronger than he?[i]

The Believer's Freedom

23"I have the right to do anything," you say—but not everything is beneficial.[j] "I have the right
to do anything"—but not everything is constructive. 24No one should seek their own good, but the
good of others.[k]

25Eat anything sold in the meat market without raising questions of conscience,[l] 26for, "The earth
is the Lord's, and everything in it."[a][m]

27If an unbeliever invites you to a meal and you want to go, eat whatever is put before you[n] without
raising questions of conscience. 28But if someone says to you, "This has been offered in sacrifice," then do
not eat it, both for the sake of the one who told you and for the sake of conscience.[o] 29I am referring to the
other person's conscience, not yours. For why is my freedom[p] being judged by another's conscience? 30If
I take part in the meal with thankfulness, why am I denounced because of something I thank God for?[q]

31So whether you eat or drink or whatever you do, do it all for the glory of God.[r] 32Do not cause
anyone to stumble,[s] whether Jews, Greeks or the church of God[t]— 33even as I try to please everyone
in every way.[u] For I am not seeking my own good but the good of many, so that they may be saved.[v]

11 1Follow my example,[w] as I follow the example of Christ.

On Covering the Head in Worship

2I praise you[x] for remembering me in everything[y] and for holding to the traditions just as I passed
them on to you.[z] 3But I want you to realize that the head of every man is Christ,[a] and the head of the
woman is man,[b][b] and the head of Christ is God.[c] 4Every man who prays or prophesies with his head

10:19 [e]1Co 8:4
10:20 [f]Dt 32:17; Ps 106:37; Rev 9:20
10:21 [g]2Co 6:15,16
10:22 [h]Dt 32:16,21 [i]Ecc 6:10; Isa 45:9
10:23 [j]1Co 6:12
10:24 [k]ver 33; Ro 15:1,2; 1Co 13:5; Php 2:4,21
10:25 [l]Ac 10:15; 1Co 8:7
10:26 [m]Ps 24:1
10:27 [n]Lk 10:7
10:28 [o]1Co 8:7,10-12
10:29 [p]Ro 14:16; 1Co 9:1,19
10:30 [q]Ro 14:6
10:31 [r]Col 3:17; 1Pe 4:11
10:32 [s]Ac 24:16 [t]Ac 20:28
10:33 [u]Ro 15:2; 1Co 9:22 [v]Ro 11:14
11:1 [w]1Co 4:16
11:2 [x]ver 17,22 [y]1Co 4:17 [z]1Co 15:2,3; 2Th 2:15
11:3 [a]Eph 1:22 [b]Ge 3:16; Eph 5:23 [c]1Co 3:23

[a] *26* Psalm 24:1 [b] *3* Or *of the wife is her husband*

Rather, sacrifices offered in pagan temples are "offered to demons" (v. 20). On the one hand, pagan gods are "nothing" (8:4); on the other hand, they are "demons" (vv. 20,21; cf. Deut 32:17; Pss 96:5; 106:37; Isa 65:3; demons [i.e., evil spirits] are Satan's angels according to Matt 25:41; cf. Eph 2:2). People who sacrifice on pagan altars and eat that food affiliate with demons (are "participants with demons," v. 20).

10:21–22 Participating in the Lord's Supper excludes participating in banquets held in pagan temples, where the food and drink that is served has been dedicated to a pagan god (i.e., to a demon). Christians must not dine in pagan temples.

10:23—11:1 *The Believer's Freedom.* Believers may eat meat bought in the market or offered at private dinners to which they have been invited as long as they do not know that the food was previously offered as a sacrifice in a pagan temple.

10:23 "I have the right to do anything." A slogan of Corinthian Christians—one that Paul decisively refutes (cf. 8:9; 9:1,4,12,15). A Christian's freedom is limited by how their actions affect other Christians.

10:25–26 When Christians buy meat in the market, they do not have to ask whether the meat came from a local temple, where it would have been offered to idols. Since the earth belongs to the Lord (the quotation in v. 26 is from Ps 24:1), Christians can eat any food that is sold in the market.

10:27–30 When Christians are invited to dine in a private home, they can eat the meat on the menu. There is one exception to this rule: if someone says that the meat was offered in a local temple, then a Christian present must not eat it for the sake of "the other person's conscience" (most plausibly the conscience of the person who pointed out where the meat came from, v. 29). If a non-Christian person sees a Christian eating meat that comes from a local temple, they might conclude that the Christian acknowledges the "holiness" of the meat and thus the reality of the local god.

10:31—11:1 What Christians do should always be motivated by their desire to glorify God. The glory of the holy God nullifies the slogan "I have the right to do anything" (10:23). Not everything is permitted. Whatever contradicts God's glory is prohibited. Christians must seek to avoid causing non-Christians and Christians to stumble. This principle governs Paul's behavior: he seeks not his own advantage but the good of others so that unbelievers may be saved.

11:2—14:40 *Issues Related to Behavior in Church Meetings.* Paul addresses head coverings (11:2–16), the Lord's Supper (11:17–34), and spiritual gifts (chs. 12–14).

11:2–16 *On Covering the Head in Worship.* Paul admonishes Christian men not to wear head coverings and Christian women to wear them (vv. 2–6). He discusses the relationship between husband and wife (vv. 7–12) and appeals to discernment (vv. 13–16). In Roman society (and thus in the city of Corinth), men pulled their togas over their heads when they officiated in religious cults, thus signaling their elevated social status; married women wore head coverings, often a thin head scarf, in public to signal that they were married and to symbolize their chastity and virtue.

11:2 traditions. Probably the Christian teachings in Corinth and other churches (11:23; 15:3; Rom 6:17; 2 Thess 2:15; 3:6).

11:3 head. Figuratively, what is most prominent, preeminent. Every person has a relationship to another person who has a preeminent status: for men (and women) this is Jesus Christ; for wives it is their husband; for Christ it is God the Father. The first pair references only men because the following discussion (vv. 4–16) gives separate directions for men and women. Paul is concerned about the proper relationship between husbands and wives in the church, not between men and women more generally.

11:4 with his head covered. In Roman society, men covered their heads with their togas when they officiated in religious cults; only

11:5 [d]Ac 21:9 [e]Dt 21:12
11:7 [f]Ge 1:26; Jas 3:9
11:8 [g]Ge 2:21-23; 1Ti 2:13
11:9 [h]Ge 2:18
11:12 [i]Ro 11:36
11:16 [j]1Co 7:17
11:17 [k]ver 2,22
11:18 [l]1Co 1:10-12; 3:3

covered dishonors his head. 5But every woman who prays or prophesies[d] with her head uncovered
dishonors her head—it is the same as having her head shaved.[e] 6For if a woman does not cover her
head, she might as well have her hair cut off; but if it is a disgrace for a woman to have her hair cut off
or her head shaved, then she should cover her head.

7A man ought not to cover his head,[a] since he is the image[f] and glory of God; but woman is the glory of
man. 8For man did not come from woman, but woman from man;[g] 9neither was man created for woman,
but woman for man.[h] 10It is for this reason that a woman ought to have authority over her own[b] head, because of the angels. 11Nevertheless, in the Lord woman is not independent of man, nor is man independent
of woman. 12For as woman came from man, so also man is born of woman. But everything comes from God.[i]

13Judge for yourselves: Is it proper for a woman to pray to God with her head uncovered? 14Does not
the very nature of things teach you that if a man has long hair, it is a disgrace to him, 15but that if a
woman has long hair, it is her glory? For long hair is given to her as a covering. 16If anyone wants to be
contentious about this, we have no other practice—nor do the churches of God.[j]

Correcting an Abuse of the Lord's Supper

11:23-25pp — Mt 26:26-28; Mk 14:22-24; Lk 22:17-20

17In the following directives I have no praise for you,[k] for your meetings do more harm than good.
18In the first place, I hear that when you come together as a church, there are divisions[l] among you,

[a] 4-7 Or *4Every man who prays or prophesies with long hair dishonors his head. 5But every woman who prays or prophesies with no covering of hair dishonors her head—she is just like one of the "shorn women." 6If a woman has no covering, let her be for now with short hair; but since it is a disgrace for a woman to have her hair shorn or shaved, she should grow it again. 7A man ought not to have long hair*
[b] 10 Or *have a sign of authority on her*

members of the social elite occupied priestly offices. **dishonors his head.** A Christian man who participates in the church's worship meetings with his head covered (thus signaling that he is a member of the social elite of the city) dishonors Christ, who is his "head," i.e., who is preeminent and to whom he is responsible. Such a man draws attention to himself rather than to Christ.

11:5 A Christian woman who participates in the church's worship meetings, which were open to the public, with her head uncovered "dishonors her head," i.e., her husband, to whom she is responsible. She brings shame on her husband by her appearance; that she is without a head covering may suggest to observers that she withdraws from her marriage, claims independence from her husband, and insults her husband's honor. Paul tells Christian wives to behave as married wives do in Roman culture: a Christian Corinthian wife is to show respect for her husband by wearing the traditional head covering. A wife's respect for her husband (and vice versa) is expressed in different ways in different cultures.

11:7–10 The argument from creation underlines the exhortation that wives must not bring shame on their husbands.

11:7 man ... is the image and glory of God. Refers to Gen 1:26–27 and emphasizes man's function as God's representative in creation. As "the image ... of God," he is "the glory of God": he reflects God's glory in creation (Ps 8:6–7). **but woman is the glory of man.** In the context of Gen 2:21–23, Paul focuses on the temporal sequence of the creation of Adam and Eve: the man was created first and reflects the glory of God; the woman was created second and reflects the glory of the man. This does not reduce the value of women. Paul is discussing here not the nature of males and females but the relationship between a husband and his wife. Since the woman is, from man's perspective, "bone of my bones and flesh of my flesh" (Gen 2:23), she shares the man's image-of-God status.

11:8–9 The issue is not differences in nature or quality but the temporal sequence of God's creating man and woman (Gen 2:21–23). God created the woman *from* man (chronological priority) and *for* man (function allocation). In Roman society, wives were often considerably younger than their husbands, a fact that would have made it easy for Paul's readers in Corinth to follow his argument.

11:10 authority. Probably the woman's "power," or control, over her own head. **over her own head.** Behaves in such a manner that she manifestly accepts her role as her husband's wife. A married woman should take care not to be lured into behavioral patterns that compromise her husband's priority in marriage, as set by God's order of creation. That would happen if she appeared in public without the traditional head scarf. **angels.** Some see a reference to the invisible heavenly beings as guardians of the created order, as present when Christians pray and prophesy, as interested in all aspects of the salvation and lives of Christians, as participating in the last judgment. Others understand the Greek term *angeloi* in terms of its frequent meaning of "messenger" (e.g., Matt 11:10; Luke 9:52): when non-Christians who are contemplating a visit to the church's assemblies send messengers in order to receive a report about what the Christians do, they would be very disturbed if they found that married women were behaving as if they were not married.

11:11 Husbands and wives are not independent entities; they depend on each other.

11:12 everything. Includes the creational differences between men and women, husbands and wives. **comes from God.** These differences continue to have validity since they come from God (i.e., God ordained them). The coequal status of husbands and wives as God's creation and as married people who depend on each other does not nullify the wife's obligation to honor her husband.

11:13–16 Paul closes his exhortation to the Christian women in Corinth who shamed their husbands by appearing in public without the traditional head covering by appealing to cultural propriety and decency (v. 13), nature (vv. 14–15), and the practice of other Christian churches (v. 16).

11:17–34 *Correcting an Abuse of the Lord's Supper.* Paul admonishes rich Corinthian Christians who are behaving selfishly during the regular church meals. He critiques their behavior (vv. 17–22) on the basis of the tradition of the Lord's Supper (vv. 23–26), from which he draws conclusions for solving the problem (vv. 27–34).

11:18 divisions. Cf. 1:10–13. It seems that it is well-to-do Christians

and to some extent I believe it. 19 No doubt there have to be differences among you to show which of
you have God's approval.[m] 20 So then, when you come together, it is not the Lord's Supper you eat, 21 for
when you are eating, some of you go ahead with your own private suppers.[n] As a result, one person remains hungry and another gets drunk. 22 Don't you have homes to eat and drink in? Or do you despise
the church of God[o] by humiliating those who have nothing?[p] What shall I say to you? Shall I praise
you?[q] Certainly not in this matter!

23 For I received from the Lord[r] what I also passed on to you:[s] The Lord Jesus, on the night he was
betrayed, took bread, 24 and when he had given thanks, he broke it and said, "This is my body, which
is for you; do this in remembrance of me." 25 In the same way, after supper he took the cup, saying,
"This cup is the new covenant[t] in my blood;[u] do this, whenever you drink it, in remembrance of me."
26 For whenever you eat this bread and drink this cup, you proclaim the Lord's death until he comes.

27 So then, whoever eats the bread or drinks the cup of the Lord in an unworthy manner will be guilty
of sinning against the body and blood of the Lord.[v] 28 Everyone ought to examine themselves[w] before
they eat of the bread and drink from the cup. 29 For those who eat and drink without discerning the body
of Christ eat and drink judgment on themselves. 30 That is why many among you are weak and sick,
and a number of you have fallen asleep. 31 But if we were more discerning with regard to ourselves, we
would not come under such judgment.[x] 32 Nevertheless, when we are judged in this way by the Lord, we
are being disciplined[y] so that we will not be finally condemned with the world.

11:19 [m] 1Jn 2:19
11:21 [n] 2Pe 2:13; Jude 12
11:22 [o] 1Co 10:32 [p] Jas 2:6 [q] ver 2,17
11:23 [r] Gal 1:12 [s] 1Co 15:3
11:25 [t] Lk 22:20 [u] 1Co 10:16
11:27 [v] Heb 10:29
11:28 [w] 2Co 13:5
11:31 [x] Ps 32:5; 1Jn 1:9
11:32 [y] Ps 94:12; Heb 12:7-10; Rev 3:19

who are causing most of the problems: they divide the church (1) with party slogans based on secular values of rhetoric and (2) by underlining the difference between poor and more affluent Christians by their behavior during common meals.

11:19 The events in the church reveal who the authentic Christians are. This is the only positive result of the divisions in the Corinthian church.

11:21 when you are eating. The church members regularly shared meals. In accordance with Greco-Roman practice, they ate the main meal of the day in the late afternoon. It consisted of appetizers (in the case of the well-to-do), the main course (multiple dishes), and dessert. **go ahead.** Probably "partake" or "consume" (cf. v. 21b). More affluent believers ate their fill without taking care of the poor believers who were hungry. The church's meals were evidently organized as "potluck" dinners, so everyone brought some food. The problem was that the wealthier believers did not share with the poor believers. **private suppers.** The problem that prompted Paul's intervention.

11:22 The rhetorical questions are meant to shame the rich believers responsible for the damage: they should (1) eat their lavish meals at home, (2) not despise the church of God by humiliating the poor, and (3) not expect Paul's approval of their present behavior.

11:23–26 Jesus' last meal with his disciples, which is the basis for the church's celebration of the Lord's Supper, underlines that the rich Corinthian Christians need to change their behavior. See Matt 26:26–29; Mark 14:22–25; Luke 22:17–20.

11:23 on the night he was betrayed. The Corinthian Christians had received teaching in which the details of Jesus' arrest, trial, and death were recounted. **betrayed.** The action of Judas Iscariot (see Matt 26:14–16,25,47–50 and parallels). The Greek verb can also be translated "handed over": Paul could assert that God initiated the events that led to Jesus' death (Rom 4:25; 8:32). The phrase "handed over" would then refer not only to Judas but also to (1) the Jewish leaders who initiated trial proceedings against Jesus and condemned him on account of blasphemy and (2) Pilate, who condemned Jesus to death because of a claim to kingship. This verse alludes to Isa 53:12.

11:24 This. The bread that Jesus had just broken into pieces symbolizes Jesus giving his body to die on the cross. Receiving the bread in the celebration of the Lord's Supper signifies participating in the effects of the self-sacrifice of Jesus, whose death atones for sin. **do this in remembrance of me.** A call to repeat Jesus' action of breaking bread and remembering his death. Regularly remembering the significance of Jesus' death is a fundamental activity of Christians.

11:25 after supper. The meal occurred after what Jesus said about the bread (v. 24) and before what he said about the cup (here). What Christian churches today celebrate in a single ceremony was originally connected with a real meal during which participants broke the bread at the beginning of the meal and drank the cup of blessing at the end of the meal. **cup.** Of wine; it symbolizes Jesus' death ("blood"), which inaugurated the "new covenant" that God had promised (Jer 31:31–34; see 2 Cor 3:6; Heb 8:8; 9:15; 12:24). See Exod 24:8, where God's covenant with the people of Israel was sealed with the sprinkling of blood; see also Exod 24:11, where Israel's leaders share a meal in God's presence immediately after the sealing of the covenant. As Passover eventually led to the covenant at Sinai, Jesus' last supper with his disciples initiated the events that led to his death and resurrection and the inauguration of the new covenant.

11:27 unworthy manner. Without love and regard for the poor in the congregation. **guilty of sinning.** During these meals some Corinthian Christians ate full meals in the presence of poor Christians who were hungry. They sinned not only against the poor Christians but, more important, "against the body and blood of the Lord," i.e., against Jesus, who gave himself for others in his death on the cross.

11:28 examine themselves. Examine their behavior during the meals of the congregation—meals at which Christians from different social backgrounds ate together—especially their behavior concerning the poor. A more general application refers to self-examination regarding any unconfessed sin before partaking in the Lord's Supper.

11:29 discerning the body of Christ. Both the physical body of Jesus and the church as Christ's body (12:13). When Christians celebrate the Lord's Supper, which they did in Corinth in connection with meals, they must realize that the reason for being a Christian and for being the church (Christ's body) is Jesus' death. When well-to-do Christians take this connection seriously, they will not overlook the poorer believers but will care for them as Jesus cared for sinners by giving himself to death on the cross. **eat and drink judgment on themselves.** Probably a reference not to the final judgment but to present divine judgment, as in v. 30. Christians who show no regard for the poor in the church and who, more generally, do not stop sinful behavior will be judged by God.

11:30 Some Corinthian Christians had fallen ill, and some had even died, because of this specific sin. This underlines the seriousness of Paul's warning regarding God's judgment in v. 29. Not all illnesses are the result of sin, but sinful actions *can* lead to sickness and death.

11:34 [z]ver 21 [a]ver 22 [b]1Co 4:19
12:1 [c]Ro 1:11; 1Co 14:1,37
12:2 [d]Eph 2:11,12; 1Pe 4:3 [e]Ps 115:5; Jer 10:5; Hab 2:18,19; 1Th 1:9
12:3 [f]Ro 9:3 [g]Jn 13:13 [h]1Jn 4:2,3
12:4 [i]Ro 12:4-8; Eph 4:11; Heb 2:4
12:6 [j]Eph 4:6
12:7 [k]Eph 4:12
12:8 [l]1Co 2:6 [m]2Co 8:7
12:9 [n]Mt 17:19,20; 2Co 4:13 [o]ver 28,30
12:10 [p]Gal 3:5 [q]1Jn 4:1 [r]Mk 16:17
12:11 [s]ver 4
12:12 [t]Ro 12:5 [u]ver 27
12:13 [v]Eph 2:18

33So then, my brothers and sisters, when you gather to eat, you should all eat together. 34Anyone who
is hungry[z] should eat something at home,[a] so that when you meet together it may not result in judgment.
And when I come[b] I will give further directions.

Concerning Spiritual Gifts

12 Now about the gifts of the Spirit,[c] brothers and sisters, I do not want you to be uninformed.
2You know that when you were pagans,[d] somehow or other you were influenced and led astray
to mute idols.[e] 3Therefore I want you to know that no one who is speaking by the Spirit of God says,
"Jesus be cursed,"[f] and no one can say, "Jesus is Lord,"[g] except by the Holy Spirit.[h]
4There are different kinds of gifts, but the same Spirit[i] distributes them. 5There are different kinds
of service, but the same Lord. 6There are different kinds of working, but in all of them and in everyone
it is the same God[j] at work.
7Now to each one the manifestation of the Spirit is given for the common good.[k] 8To one there is
given through the Spirit a message of wisdom,[l] to another a message of knowledge[m] by means of the
same Spirit, 9to another faith[n] by the same Spirit, to another gifts of healing[o] by that one Spirit, 10to another miraculous powers,[p] to another prophecy, to another distinguishing between spirits,[q] to another
speaking in different kinds of tongues,[a][r] and to still another the interpretation of tongues.[a] 11All these
are the work of one and the same Spirit,[s] and he distributes them to each one, just as he determines.

Unity and Diversity in the Body

12Just as a body, though one, has many parts, but all its many parts form one body,[t] so it is with
Christ.[u] 13For we were all baptized by[b] one Spirit[v] so as to form one body—whether Jews or Gentiles,

[a] *10* Or *languages*; also in verse 28 [b] *13* Or *with*; or *in*

11:33–34 Paul concludes with specific advice.
11:33 all eat together. Receive one another; share the food they each bring. If a church member is hungry and cannot wait for the meal in the church, they should eat at home. When they eat together in the church, they must accept one another and share with one another in order to avoid God's judgment.
12:1—14:40 *The Gifts of the Spirit.* There are also divisions in the church in connection with the use of spiritual gifts, particularly the gift of prophecy and the gift of speaking in an unlearned language. Paul argues more generally from the nature of the church, which is one body consisting of many members (12:1–31), describes self-giving love as the norm for Christian behavior (13:1–13), and directs them regarding how to use the gift of prophecy and the gift of languages in congregational meetings (14:1–40).
12:1–11 *Concerning Spiritual Gifts.* Different gifts function diversely in the church.
12:1 gifts of the Spirit. The Greek here and in 14:1 can also be translated "spiritual gifts," where the Greek adjective (translated "spiritual") is plural. Cf. 2:13, where "spiritual realities" and "Spirit-taught words" (i.e., "spiritual words") use the same plural adjective in the Greek.
12:2–3 Paul describes the religious experiences of pagans, non-Christian Jews, and Christians.
12:2 led astray. The pagan population was regularly "led" in processions through the city to the pagan temples. **mute idols.** Local gods, who cannot speak.
12:3 Jesus be cursed. Jews who did not believe that Jesus was the Messiah thought he was cursed by God, applying Deut 21:23 to Jesus' crucifixion. **Jesus is Lord.** Christians confess Jesus as Lord: they accept that Jesus, a crucified Jew, is Lord; they accept this "by the Holy Spirit," i.e., as a result of the power of the Spirit of God, who causes Jews and Gentiles to abandon their verdicts concerning Jesus and his death (1:22–23) and accept Jesus and his death as the wisdom of God (2:1–5).
12:4–6 The gifts of the Spirit all have the same origin: the triune God. They are given by the Spirit, the Lord Jesus, and God the Father. There is a diversity of gifts, a diversity of purposes for the gifts, and a diversity of activities linked with the gifts.
12:7 manifestation of the Spirit. Each particular gift of the Spirit. **for the common good.** The general purpose of all spiritual gifts is to benefit all Christians in the local congregation.
12:8–10 Paul lists the following gifts of the Spirit: (1) **message of wisdom.** Properly explaining what God has revealed about Jesus' death on the cross (2:6–16). (2) **message of knowledge.** Providing the proper theological rationale for decisions concerning Christian living (see chs. 8–10). (3) **faith.** Trusting God with an inexplicable confidence in a specific situation for a specific outcome for which there is no divine promise. (This is not referring to saving faith.) (4) **gifts of healing.** Healing various illnesses. (5) **miraculous powers.** Probably (in the context of the previous gift) driving out demons and overcoming pagan bondage. (6) **prophecy.** Receiving and communicating spontaneous and usually verbal revelation that one understands as revealed truth and communicates to the church with divine authority, whether that authority is said to be of God, Jesus Christ, or the Holy Spirit, often in the sense of applying the truth of the gospel to specific situations (see 14:3,29; e.g., Acts 11:28; 13:1–2; 14:1–5; 21:10–11). (7) **distinguishing between spirits.** Examining the authenticity of prophetic messages (see 14:29; 1Thess 5:20–21). This is necessary because evil spirits can inspire false prophecies (1 John 4:1). (8) **different kinds of tongues.** The Greek term *glōssa*, translated "tongues," refers in the context of speech to "language"; this is the supernatural gift of speaking in unlearned human languages (e.g., the events at Pentecost in Acts 2:4–11). The reference to "tongues [languages] . . . of angels" in 13:1 leaves open the possibility that non-human utterances are in view as well. (9) **interpretation of tongues.** Translating a spoken, unlearned language.
12:11 Whatever gifts believers have received, they all come from the same Spirit, who sovereignly distributes them all. There is no reason for Christians to feel superior because they have a particular gift.
12:12–31a *Unity and Diversity in the Body.* Some Corinthian Christians believed that the use of their particular gift in church meetings was more important than the use of other gifts. The church must not allow a particular gift to destroy the church's unity.
12:12 body. The human body, with its "many parts," illustrates that it

slave or free[w] — and we were all given the one Spirit to drink.[x] 14Even so the body is not made up of
one part but of many.
15Now if the foot should say, "Because I am not a hand, I do not belong to the body," it would not
for that reason stop being part of the body. 16And if the ear should say, "Because I am not an eye, I do
not belong to the body," it would not for that reason stop being part of the body. 17If the whole body
were an eye, where would the sense of hearing be? If the whole body were an ear, where would the
sense of smell be? 18But in fact God has placed[y] the parts in the body, every one of them, just as he
wanted them to be.[z] 19If they were all one part, where would the body be? 20As it is, there are many
parts, but one body.[a]
21The eye cannot say to the hand, "I don't need you!" And the head cannot say to the feet, "I don't
need you!" 22On the contrary, those parts of the body that seem to be weaker are indispensable, 23and
the parts that we think are less honorable we treat with special honor. And the parts that are unpresentable are treated with special modesty, 24while our presentable parts need no special treatment. But God
has put the body together, giving greater honor to the parts that lacked it, 25so that there should be no
division in the body, but that its parts should have equal concern for each other. 26If one part suffers,
every part suffers with it; if one part is honored, every part rejoices with it.
27Now you are the body of Christ,[b] and each one of you is a part of it.[c] 28And God has placed in the
church[d] first of all apostles,[e] second prophets, third teachers, then miracles, then gifts of healing,[f] of
helping, of guidance,[g] and of different kinds of tongues.[h] 29Are all apostles? Are all prophets? Are all
teachers? Do all work miracles? 30Do all have gifts of healing? Do all speak in tongues[a]?[i] Do all interpret? 31Now eagerly desire[j] the greater gifts.

[a] 30 Or *other languages*

12:13 [w] Gal 3:28; Col 3:11 [x] Jn 7:37-39
12:18 [y] ver 28 [z] ver 11
12:20 [a] ver 12,14
12:27 [b] Eph 1:23; 4:12; Col 1:18,24 [c] Ro 12:5
12:28 [d] 1Co 10:32 [e] Eph 4:11 [f] ver 9 [g] Ro 12:6-8 [h] ver 10
12:30 [i] ver 10
12:31 [j] 1Co 14:1,39

is necessary to preserve the church's unity despite its diverse spiritual gifts. **many parts.** As the human body is one entity with many members, so the church (the "body of Christ," v. 27) is one entity with many members.
12:13 baptized by one Spirit. Followers of Jesus have been incorporated by one and the same Spirit into one single body (i.e., the church; v. 27). Some interpret this in terms of a reference to water baptism. **Jews or Gentiles, slave or free.** In the church there are no ethnic, cultural, or social distinctions that divide people: God gives his Spirit to all people who come to faith.
12:14 but of many. Diverse gifts of the Spirit: as the human body has many different parts, so the one church has people with many different gifts.
12:15–16 The idea of a body part self-sufficient and disassociated from the body is absurd and grotesque.
12:17–18 It is absurd for a lone eye or a single ear to be the entire body. The rhetorical questions underline the obvious truth that the various members and organs of the body depend upon one another; they have different God-assigned tasks within one single body. The church must not accept the elevation of one particular gift over others.
12:21 Paul has discussed the disassociation of a body part from the body and declared the absolute value of each body part (vv. 15–19). Here he discusses the disassociation of a body part from other body parts. The claim of an eye to be able to function independently of the hand is as ridiculous as the claim of a head to be independent of the feet.
12:22–26 The members of the human body are indisputably unified.
12:22–24 weaker ... less honorable .... unpresentable ... the parts that lacked [honor]. Probably genitals; they are "indispensable" (v. 22), treated "with special honor" (v. 23) and "special modesty" (v. 23), and given "greater honor" (i.e., procreation, v. 24). God sovereignly arranged the diverse functions of the members of the human body. Applied to the church, this means that Christians who are regarded as having less important functions in the congregation are actually indispensable. God has "put the body together" (v. 24), i.e., arranged the various members of the human body and divided the labor. When all the body parts fulfill their functions and are mutually concerned for each other, there is no division in the body.
12:27–31 Paul applies the metaphor of the body to the congregation. The "body of Christ" (v. 27) is the local congregation of believers in Corinth. They are a single entity created by Jesus Christ. As a human body consists of individual body parts, so the church consists of individual believers, which means that every single believer is a part of the body of Christ. Each local congregation is the body of Christ, as is the universal church (Eph 1:22–23; 4:4,12; Col 1:24).
12:28 As God has created the various body parts, so God has appointed people with specific gifts, tasks, and functions in the church. This list of spiritual gifts is different from the list in vv. 8–10 (see note there), which suggests that there is not a fixed, "closed" list of spiritual gifts. See also Rom 12:6–8; Eph 4:11. Paul does not rank the gifts, although the reference to apostles, prophets, and teachers as "first," "second," and "third" indicates their foundational importance for the church (Acts 1:21–22; Eph 2:20). **helping.** The ministry to the poor and sick (Acts 6:1–6; 20:35; 1 Tim 6:2). **guidance.** Administrative and organizational gifts: keeping order (including in the church services, which is the context of chs. 12–14) and guiding the church through crises.
12:29–30 The rhetorical questions, which expect a negative answer, emphasize the individuality and equality of the individual members of the church and their God-given gifts, tasks, and functions. Christians have different gifts, no one has all gifts, and no gift has been given to all.
12:31a greater. While the Spirit's gifts are equal in essence, some are greater in function because they more clearly and consistently edify the church (see chs. 13–14). The measurement of a spiritual gift's value is not how a Christian benefits from their own gift but how that gift benefits the congregation as a whole.
12:31b—13:13 *Love Is Indispensable.* The norm for using the Spirit's gifts in the church is love. Paul affirms love's superiority over all the gifts of the Spirit (13:1–3), describes love's nature (13:4–7), and celebrates love's eternal permanence (13:8–13). The Greek term *agapē*, translated "love," is a general word for warm regard, esteem, affection; in many NT passages it has the sense of selfless concern for the welfare of others (John 3:16; Eph 5:25).

13:1 [k]ver 8
13:2 [l]1Co 14:2
[m]1Co 12:9 [n]Mt 17:20; 21:21
13:3 [o]Mt 6:2 [p]Da 3:28
13:4 [q]1Th 5:14
13:5 [r]1Co 10:24
13:6 [s]2Th 2:12 [t]2Jn 4; 3Jn 3,4
13:8 [u]ver 2 [v]ver 1
13:9 [w]ver 12; 1Co 8:2
13:10 [x]Php 3:12
13:12 [y]Ge 32:30; 2Co 5:7; 1Jn 3:2
[z]1Co 8:3
13:13 [a]Gal 5:5,6
[b]1Co 16:14

Love Is Indispensable

And yet I will show you the most excellent way.

13 If I speak in the tongues[a][k] of men or of angels, but do not have love, I am only a resounding
gong or a clanging cymbal. 2If I have the gift of prophecy and can fathom all mysteries[l] and
all knowledge, and if I have a faith[m] that can move mountains,[n] but do not have love, I am nothing.
3If I give all I possess to the poor[o] and give over my body to hardship that I may boast,[b][p] but do not
have love, I gain nothing.
4Love is patient,[q] love is kind. It does not envy, it does not boast, it is not proud. 5It does not dishonor others, it is not self-seeking,[r] it is not easily angered, it keeps no record of wrongs. 6Love does
not delight in evil[s] but rejoices with the truth.[t] 7It always protects, always trusts, always hopes, always
perseveres.
8Love never fails. But where there are prophecies,[u] they will cease; where there are tongues,[v] they
will be stilled; where there is knowledge, it will pass away. 9For we know in part[w] and we prophesy in
part, 10but when completeness comes,[x] what is in part disappears. 11When I was a child, I talked like a
child, I thought like a child, I reasoned like a child. When I became a man, I put the ways of childhood
behind me. 12For now we see only a reflection as in a mirror; then we shall see face to face.[y] Now I know
in part; then I shall know fully, even as I am fully known.[z]
13And now these three remain: faith, hope and love.[a] But the greatest of these is love.[b]

[a] *1* Or *languages* [b] *3* Some manuscripts *body to the flames*

12:31b the most excellent way. The love that ch. 13 describes. This behavior builds up the church and prepares its members to see God "face to face" (13:12). Chs. 12–14 emphasize that without love, spiritual gifts are worthless.

13:1 The ability to speak miraculously in "the tongues of men" (unlearned human languages) or "of angels" is mere noise that communicates no meaning if it is done without love. **resounding gong.** Probably metal vessels such as large bronze vases that were used in Greek theaters to help project the music and the voices of the actors. **clanging cymbal.** A metal basin banged against another metal basin, producing a shrill sound.

13:2 all mysteries and all knowledge. Paul uses hyperbole to express the fact that even if a person could know and understand everything, it would be useless without love. **move mountains.** Accomplish something humanly impossible (Isa 54:10; Matt 17:20; Mark 11:22–23). **I am nothing.** Without love, even the Christian who has the most effective faith contributes nothing to the edification of the church.

13:3 give over my body to hardship. The Greek text can be rendered "give over my body to be burned," an example of supreme self-sacrifice (see Dan 3:19–23; Heb 11:34) that includes the willingness to die for the sake of the gospel. Love that builds up the church is more important than the sacrifice of all possessions and even one's body. Love is a matter of not only actions but also motivation.

13:4–7 Paul describes the nature of love with two positive statements, then eight negative ones (the last element has a positive counterpart), and then four positive ones. The preponderance of negative statements can be linked with the problems in the Corinthian church that Paul addresses in this letter. All qualities of love are qualities of God the Father and Jesus Christ: the Christian should live as Jesus lived.

13:4 patient. The fruit of the Spirit (Gal 5:22) that constrains wrath, endures provocation, and preserves peace. **kind.** The fruit of the Spirit that gives friendly, merciful, helpful attention to others. **not envy.** Renounces negative, self-centered feelings with regard to the gifts or achievements of others. **not boast.** Does not heap praise on oneself or brag about one's own gifts. **not proud.** Does not have an exaggerated view of oneself.

13:5 not dishonor others. Acting contrary to the conventions of decent behavior, i.e., in a disgraceful and indecent manner. **not self-seeking.** Not narcissistically fixating on oneself and one's own advantage. **not easily angered.** Refusing to become irritated and provoked to wrath. **keeps no record of wrongs.** Does not remember the wrongdoings of other people; does not refuse to fully forgive others.

13:7 always trusts. Believes all things. This does not mean that Christians are gullible, believing anyone or anything. Trust is faith in God and Jesus Christ; it is faith that becomes effective through love (Gal 5:6). There is no crisis, no sin, no problem in the church that can shatter faith in God.

13:8 never fails. Love does not end, because it will never cease to be a reality—unlike the gifts of prophecy, tongues (speaking in unlearned languages) and knowledge. Prophecies, tongues, and knowledge will cease, because they provide only partial insights (v. 9) and will be unnecessary when the perfection of God's new world arrives with Jesus' return (v. 12).

13:9 in part. In a fragmentary, incomplete, imperfect manner. Exercising the God-given gifts of wisdom and prophecy provides only partial knowledge, so one should not boast that these gifts are superior to others, which destroys the congregation's unity.

13:10 completeness. Or "the perfect" or "the time of perfection"; the time that comes after the present time (cf. 15:24). When God's new world arrives, the world in which we will see God "face to face" (v. 12), everything that is partial will disappear.

13:11–12 Two analogies compare the present time of this world with the future time of God's new world: (1) A child who grows up to become a man compares the present time of partial maturity with the complete maturity of the future in God's kingdom. (2) A mirror, made of polished bronze in antiquity, gives only an imperfect reflection. Our present experience of the gifts of God's Spirit are imperfect, only reflections of the glorious reality of God, which Christians will personally see in God's new world. See Rev 7:17; 21:3–4.

13:13 faith, hope and love. Mentioned together in 1 Thess 1:3; 5:8; see also Rom 5:1–5; Gal 5:5–6; Eph 4:2–5; Col 1:4–5; Titus 2:2; Heb 6:10–12; 10:22–24; 1 Pet 1:3–9. Even in the future perfection of God's kingdom, Christians will depend on God (faith) and focus on God (hope) as their love for God is consummated. **the greatest of these is love.** Love is greater than all spiritual gifts because "God is love" (1 John 4:8), has given his love to all believers (Rom 5:5), and has commanded all believers to love one another (8:1; John 13:34–35; Rom 13:10; Gal 5:6; Eph 4:16; 5:2).

Intelligibility in Worship

14 Follow the way of love[c] and eagerly desire[d] gifts of the Spirit,[e] especially prophecy. 2For anyone who speaks in a tongue[a][f] does not speak to people but to God. Indeed, no one understands them; they utter mysteries[g] by the Spirit. 3But the one who prophesies speaks to people for their
strengthening,[h] encouraging and comfort. 4Anyone who speaks in a tongue[i] edifies themselves, but the
one who prophesies[j] edifies the church. 5I would like every one of you to speak in tongues,[b] but I would
rather have you prophesy.[k] The one who prophesies is greater than the one who speaks in tongues,[b]
unless someone interprets, so that the church may be edified.

6Now, brothers and sisters, if I come to you and speak in tongues, what good will I be to you, unless I
bring you some revelation[l] or knowledge or prophecy or word of instruction?[m] 7Even in the case of lifeless things that make sounds, such as the pipe or harp, how will anyone know what tune is being played
unless there is a distinction in the notes? 8Again, if the trumpet does not sound a clear call, who will get
ready for battle?[n] 9So it is with you. Unless you speak intelligible words with your tongue, how will anyone know what you are saying? You will just be speaking into the air. 10Undoubtedly there are all sorts
of languages in the world, yet none of them is without meaning. 11If then I do not grasp the meaning
of what someone is saying, I am a foreigner to the speaker, and the speaker is a foreigner to me. 12So
it is with you. Since you are eager for gifts of the Spirit, try to excel in those that build up the church.

13For this reason the one who speaks in a tongue should pray that they may interpret what they say.
14For if I pray in a tongue, my spirit prays, but my mind is unfruitful. 15So what shall I do? I will pray
with my spirit, but I will also pray with my understanding; I will sing[o] with my spirit, but I will also sing
with my understanding. 16Otherwise when you are praising God in the Spirit, how can someone else,
who is now put in the position of an inquirer,[c] say "Amen"[p] to your thanksgiving,[q] since they do not
know what you are saying? 17You are giving thanks well enough, but no one else is edified.

[a] *2* Or *in another language*; also in verses 4, 13, 14, 19, 26 and 27 [b] *5* Or *in other languages*; also in verses 6, 18, 22, 23 and 39 [c] *16* The Greek word for *inquirer* is a technical term for someone not fully initiated into a religion; also in verses 23 and 24.

14:1 [c]1Co 16:14 [d]ver 39; 1Co 12:31 [e]1Co 12:1
14:2 [f]Mk 16:17 [g]1Co 13:2
14:3 [h]ver 4,5,12,17,26; Ro 14:19
14:4 [i]Mk 16:17 [j]1Co 13:2
14:5 [k]Nu 11:29
14:6 [l]ver 26; Eph 1:17 [m]Ro 6:17
14:8 [n]Nu 10:9; Jer 4:19
14:15 [o]Eph 5:19; Col 3:16
14:16 [p]Dt 27:15-26; 1Ch 16:36; Ne 8:6; Ps 106:48; Rev 5:14; 7:12 [q]1Co 11:24

14:1–25 *Intelligibility in Worship.* Edification (vv. 1–5) and intelligibility (vv. 6–19) are criteria for using the gifts of the Spirit, particularly the gifts of prophecy and speaking in tongues, in the church's meetings. Prophecy is superior to speaking in unlearned languages (vv. 20–25).

14:1 the way of love. The description in ch. 13. Christians who love the church seek to edify it, not gain personal advantage or prestige. **gifts of the Spirit.** See note on 12:1.

14:2 tongue. An unlearned language that hearers can understand only when it is translated. **to God.** Speaking in an unlearned language addresses God and is thus a form of prayer—unlike prophecy and preaching, both of which address people. **no one understands.** Since other Christians do not understand the language in which a Christian with this particular gift prays, they do not understand what is being said. **mysteries.** Probably the mode of communication: because nobody understands the language, what is being said remains a mystery.

14:3 Christians who have the gift of prophecy and convey a prophecy in the church's meetings speak to people: they address people directly in intelligible speech and thus edify them.

14:4 edifies themselves. They are not necessarily selfish, but they do not edify the church. The person who speaks in an unlearned language is edified, but no one else is. A person who prophesies "edifies the church": all believers who listen are edified.

14:5 Because all Christians understand prophecy but not an unknown language, the believer who prophesies is "greater than" the believer who speaks in a miraculous, unlearned language "unless someone interprets"—the words spoken in tongues are translated either by someone present who knows the language or by the Spirit's miraculous intervention—in which case the words then become intelligible for the entire congregation. **so that the church may be edified.** The criterion for using the gifts of the Spirit in the church's meetings.

14:6–8 Both Paul's ministry in Corinth and musical instruments illustrate the principle of intelligibility during the church's meetings.

14:7 pipe or harp. The Greek instruments *aulos* (a pipe of reed, wood, or bone) and *kithara* (a stringed instrument). **distinction in the notes.** If only one note is repeated, there is no tune that can be recognized.

14:8 trumpet. An instrument made of metal and capable of producing six notes. It was used in military contexts, festivals, and sacrifices.

14:9–11 The rule of intelligibility applies to all contributions in the church's meetings. Understanding requires intelligible words (v. 9); all human languages have meaning (v. 10); and hearing an unintelligible language turns listeners into foreigners who do not understand what is being said (v. 11).

14:12 So it is with you. The principle applies to the Corinthian church. While it is wonderful to be enthusiastic regarding the gifts of the Spirit, the church should strive to have an abundance of those gifts that are intelligible for everyone present and thus edify the church.

14:13–17 If the gift of tongues is used in the church's meetings, it must be translated in order to be intelligible.

14:13 Christians with the gift of speaking in tongues "should pray" that others might be able to translate their words into the language of the believers who are present, so they can understand.

14:14–15 When believers address God in an unlearned language, their human spirit is involved but not their mind, because they do not understand what they say. When the mind is involved, the believer speaks with understanding, and then the people who hear benefit from what is being said.

14:16 in the Spirit. Or "with your spirit," i.e., praising God with an unlearned language that God's Spirit has inspired. **inquirer.** See the NIV text note. The Greek term (*idiōtēs*) describes a person who has no professional knowledge, a layperson who is unskilled or inexperienced in some activity or area of knowledge. Those who are not familiar with

14:20 [r]Eph 4:14; Heb 5:12,13; 1Pe 2:2 [s]Ro 16:19
14:21 [t]Jn 10:34 [u]Isa 28:11,12
14:22 [v]ver 1
14:23 [w]Ac 2:13
14:25 [x]Isa 45:14; Zec 8:23
14:26 [y]1Co 12:7-10 [z]Eph 5:19 [a]ver 6 [b]Ro 14:19
14:29 [c]1Co 12:10
14:32 [d]1Jn 4:1
14:33 [e]ver 40 [f]Ac 9:13

18 I thank God that I speak in tongues more than all of you. 19 But in the church I would rather speak
five intelligible words to instruct others than ten thousand words in a tongue.
20 Brothers and sisters, stop thinking like children.[r] In regard to evil be infants,[s] but in your thinking
be adults. 21 In the Law[t] it is written:

> "With other tongues
> and through the lips of foreigners
> I will speak to this people,
> but even then they will not listen to me,[u]
> says the Lord."[a]

22 Tongues, then, are a sign, not for believers but for unbelievers; prophecy,[v] however, is not for unbelievers but for believers. 23 So if the whole church comes together and everyone speaks in tongues,
and inquirers or unbelievers come in, will they not say that you are out of your mind?[w] 24 But if an
unbeliever or an inquirer comes in while everyone is prophesying, they are convicted of sin and are
brought under judgment by all, 25 as the secrets of their hearts are laid bare. So they will fall down and
worship God, exclaiming, "God is really among you!"[x]

Good Order in Worship

26 What then shall we say, brothers and sisters? When you come together, each of you[y] has a hymn,[z]
or a word of instruction,[a] a revelation, a tongue or an interpretation. Everything must be done so that
the church may be built up.[b] 27 If anyone speaks in a tongue, two—or at the most three—should
speak, one at a time, and someone must interpret. 28 If there is no interpreter, the speaker should keep
quiet in the church and speak to himself and to God.
29 Two or three prophets should speak, and the others should weigh carefully what is said.[c] 30 And
if a revelation comes to someone who is sitting down, the first speaker should stop. 31 For you can all
prophesy in turn so that everyone may be instructed and encouraged. 32 The spirits of prophets are
subject to the control of prophets.[d] 33 For God is not a God of disorder[e] but of peace—as in all the
congregations of the Lord's people.[f]
34 Women[b] should remain silent in the churches. They are not allowed to speak, but must be in

[a] *21* Isaiah 28:11,12 [b] *33,34* Or *peace. As in all the congregations of the Lord's people,* [34]*women*

the spoken language cannot respond affirmatively ("Amen") to what is being said and are therefore not edified.

14:18–19 Paul himself has the gift of speaking in tongues, but he seems to practice it privately: in the church and in his public ministry, he speaks intelligible words.

14:20 like children. The Corinthian Christians need to change their childish attitude regarding the gift of tongues. **be adults.** Mature Christians do not vilify understanding nor do they focus on self-edification. Rather, in the church's meetings they build up others and advance others' understanding of the gospel.

14:21 Paul quotes Isa 28:11–12 to underline that speaking in unlearned languages will not lead to the conversion of non-Christians. The people of Israel were unwilling to listen to God even when God resorted to the unusual measure of speaking to them through "foreigners" (the Assyrians) who spoke a foreign language.

14:22–23 The gift of unlearned languages is indeed a "sign" (v. 22)—not for Christians, who know that believers are praising God with this gift, but for non-Christians, who think the Christians are out of their minds, which may harden non-Christians in their unbelief.

14:24–25 Prophecy is superior to an untranslated language because non-Christians who attend the meetings of the church will be convicted of sin when they hear words of prophecy and are driven to acknowledge God's presence in the congregation.

14:26–40 *Good Order in Worship.* Paul gives rules for the church meetings (vv. 26–35) and concludes with a final exhortation (vv. 36–40).

14:26 Elements of the Corinthian church's meetings included hymns, instruction, revelation (prophecy), and prayer in an unlearned language or interpretation. This is not a comprehensive list of what can be done in the weekly meeting of the church. **hymn.** A song of praise or a psalm, which includes the OT psalms; translated as "psalms" in the phrase "psalms, hymns, and songs" (Eph 5:19; Col 3:16). **instruction.** The teachings of the apostles (cf. Acts 2:42, which also mentions fellowship, communal meals, and prayers) that explain the OT Scriptures, the words of Jesus, and Jesus' death and resurrection.

14:27–28 Rules for speaking in unlearned languages in the meetings of the local church: (1) only two or three people with the gift of speaking unlearned languages may speak in a worship service; (2) they must speak one at a time; (3) someone must interpret what is spoken; (4) if no translator is present, those who have the gift of unlearned languages must be quiet and pray quietly or at home. These rules clearly indicate that speaking in tongues is not an ecstatic event in which the speakers cannot control themselves.

14:29–35 Rules for prophesying in the meetings of the local church: (1) only two or three people with the gift of prophecy may speak in a worship service; (2) people in the church who have the gift of "distinguishing between spirits" (12:10), i.e., discerning the origin of the prophecy, must examine the prophecy; (3) those who have the gift of prophecy must speak in turn, without interrupting the previous speaker (because prophecy is not an ecstatic event in which the speakers cannot control themselves and because God is a God of order and peace); (4) women must "remain silent" (v. 34; see note).

14:34 remain silent. Evidently when others examine a spoken prophecy.

submission,[g] as the law[h] says. 35If they want to inquire about something, they should ask their own
husbands at home; for it is disgraceful for a woman to speak in the church.[a]
36Or did the word of God originate with you? Or are you the only people it has reached? 37If anyone
thinks they are a prophet[i] or otherwise gifted by the Spirit, let them acknowledge that what I am writing
to you is the Lord's command.[j] 38But if anyone ignores this, they will themselves be ignored.[b]
39Therefore, my brothers and sisters, be eager[k] to prophesy, and do not forbid speaking in tongues.
40But everything should be done in a fitting and orderly[l] way.

The Resurrection of Christ

15 Now, brothers and sisters, I want to remind you of the gospel[m] I preached to you, which you
received and on which you have taken your stand. 2By this gospel you are saved,[n] if you hold
firmly[o] to the word I preached to you. Otherwise, you have believed in vain.
3For what I received[p] I passed on to you[q] as of first importance[c]: that Christ died for our sins[r] according to the Scriptures,[s] 4that he was buried, that he was raised[t] on the third day[u] according to the
Scriptures,[v] 5and that he appeared to Cephas,[d][w] and then to the Twelve.[x] 6After that, he appeared to
more than five hundred of the brothers and sisters at the same time, most of whom are still living,
though some have fallen asleep. 7Then he appeared to James, then to all the apostles,[y] 8and last of all
he appeared to me also,[z] as to one abnormally born.

14:34 [g] 1Ti 2:11,12 [h] Ge 3:16
14:37 [i] 2Co 10:7 [j] 1Jn 4:6
14:39 [k] 1Co 12:31
14:40 [l] ver 33
15:1 [m] Ro 2:16
15:2 [n] Ro 1:16 [o] Ro 11:22
15:3 [p] Gal 1:12 [q] 1Co 11:23 [r] Isa 53:5; 1Pe 2:24 [s] Lk 24:27; Ac 26:22,23
15:4 [t] Ac 2:24 [u] Mt 16:21 [v] Ac 2:25,30,31
15:5 [w] Lk 24:34 [x] Mk 16:14
15:7 [y] Lk 24:33,36,37; Ac 1:3,4
15:8 [z] Ac 9:3-6,17; 1Co 9:1

[a] *34,35* In a few manuscripts these verses come after verse 40. [b] *38* Some manuscripts *But anyone who is ignorant of this will be ignorant* [c] *3* Or *you at the first* [d] *5* That is, Peter

Paul is not issuing a general command for women to be silent: they pray and prophesy in the assemblies of the church (11:5). Paul is addressing married women (v. 35) who might want to be involved in the evaluation of their husband's prophecy or who disrupt the service by speaking with their husbands. **in submission.** Married women are to honor their husbands and avoid any contribution in the worship service that brings disgrace upon their husbands, e.g., evaluating their husband's prophecy (which is the context of vv. 34–35) as false—a verdict that should be left to others to pronounce. **as the law says.** Paul seems to appeal in general terms to woman's creation from man in Gen 2.

14:35 inquire about something. Ask questions about the prophecy that (presumably) the husband proclaimed and that other members in the church evaluated.

14:37–38 Paul's apostolic authority confirms that what he writes is the Lord's command and that the church in Corinth must obey it.

14:39 Therefore. Paul summarizes and concludes his discussion about how to use spiritual gifts. **be eager to prophesy.** This gift edifies the church (see vv. 1,4). **do not forbid speaking in tongues.** Paul is not abolishing the gift of speaking in an unlearned language; he is correcting its improper use.

14:40 Paul appeals to norms of general decency: it is inappropriate to use a foreign language in the presence of people who cannot understand that language or to allow two or three people to speak simultaneously. Paul appeals to the norm of "order" given in vv. 26–33.

15:1–58 *Resurrection.* Paul responds to doubts about the resurrection of the body when Jesus returns: the resurrection of the dead is fundamental to the gospel (vv. 1–34), and the future resurrection of the dead involves transforming the human body (vv. 35–58). This underscores the importance of the body, a foundational truth that should motivate believers to "stop sinning" (v. 34).

15:1–11 *The Resurrection of Jesus Christ.* The foundation of Paul's discussion of the resurrection of the dead is Jesus' resurrection, confirmed by witnesses who saw Jesus alive after his crucifixion. The historical certainty of Jesus' resurrection is the first step in the argument for the certainty of the bodily resurrection of believers.

15:1–2 The resurrection of Jesus belongs to the teaching tradition of the gospel that Paul has received and passed on to the Corinthian believers. Without Jesus' resurrection from the dead, the gospel is not good news, since sinners would not be saved. The Christian faith serves no purpose (is "in vain") without Jesus' resurrection and thus provides no salvation; if one translates the Greek as "without due consideration," Paul says that people who think of themselves as Christians have an incoherent faith if they do not accept Jesus' resurrection as a historical fact.

15:3–5 Paul teaches "what [he] received" (v. 3), i.e., the message of Jesus' death and resurrection that the other apostles also teach. What follows in vv. 3–5 is the fundamental Christian confession that Paul passes on to the churches he establishes.

15:3 Christ died for our sins. Jesus, Israel's Messiah, died instead of us (who are sinners) and thus for our benefit. **according to the Scriptures.** Isa 52:13—53:12 (and passages such as Isa 40:1–11; Jer 31:31–34; Ezek 36–37; Dan 9; Hos 6:2) and the tradition of the righteous man who suffers (Pss 10:17–18; 16:8–11; 37:32; 41:9; 42:5; 140:8, all of which are alluded to in the passion narratives in the Gospels).

15:4 buried. Confirms that Jesus died. **raised.** After Jesus' death on the cross (1:23; 2:2,8), he was raised from the dead.

15:5 appeared. Confirms that Jesus rose again. His resurrection is a historical event: it happened "on the third day" (v. 4), and he appeared to Cephas (Peter) and the rest of the Twelve. **Cephas.** That is, Peter, also called Simon. Jesus appeared to Peter in Luke 24:34. **the Twelve.** Mentioned as a group, even though Judas Iscariot was no longer with them; Matthias, who replaced Judas (Acts 1:26), may have been present. Jesus appeared to them in Luke 24:36–43; John 20:19–23.

15:6–7 Further proof that Jesus' resurrection is an objective reality: over 500 people simultaneously saw Jesus after his resurrection (perhaps the appearance of Matt 28:16–20). Most of these witnesses to Jesus' resurrection were still alive at the time Paul wrote to the Corinthians, which means that people could ask these witnesses about their encounter with the risen Jesus.

15:6 fallen asleep. Died.

15:7 James. Jesus' brother. He had serious doubts about Jesus' ministry (Mark 3:21) but seems to have become a disciple when Jesus appeared to him after the crucifixion, an encounter not reported in the Gospels or Acts. James became the leader of the Jerusalem church (Acts 12:17; 15:13; 21:18; Gal 1:19; 2:9).

15:8 last of all. Paul's encounter with the risen Jesus is last in the series of Jesus' resurrection appearances. **one abnormally born.** Not a birth defect but an untimely birth or miscarriage; when Paul encountered Jesus while traveling to Damascus (Acts 9:1–9), he was like a stillborn

15:9 [a]Eph 3:8; 1Ti 1:15 [b]Ac 8:3
15:10 [c]Ro 12:3 [d]2Co 11:23 [e]Php 2:13
15:12 [f]Ac 17:32; 23:8; 2Ti 2:18
15:14 [g]1Th 4:14
15:15 [h]Ac 2:24
15:17 [i]Ro 4:25
15:19 [j]1Co 4:9
15:20 [k]1Pe 1:3 [l]ver 23; Ac 26:23; Rev 1:5 [m]ver 6,18
15:21 [n]Ro 5:12
15:22 [o]Ro 5:14-18
15:23 [p]ver 20 [q]ver 52
15:24 [r]Da 7:14,27 [s]Ro 8:38
15:25 [t]Ps 110:1; Mt 22:44
15:26 [u]2Ti 1:10; Rev 20:14; 21:4
15:27 [v]Ps 8:6 [w]Mt 28:18
15:28 [x]Php 3:21 [y]1Co 3:23

9 For I am the least of the apostles[a] and do not even deserve to be called an apostle, because I persecuted[b] the church of God. 10 But by the grace of God I am what I am, and his grace to me[c] was not
without effect. No, I worked harder than all of them[d]—yet not I, but the grace of God that was with
me.[e] 11 Whether, then, it is I or they, this is what we preach, and this is what you believed.

The Resurrection of the Dead

12 But if it is preached that Christ has been raised from the dead, how can some of you say that there
is no resurrection of the dead?[f] 13 If there is no resurrection of the dead, then not even Christ has been
raised. 14 And if Christ has not been raised,[g] our preaching is useless and so is your faith. 15 More than
that, we are then found to be false witnesses about God, for we have testified about God that he raised
Christ from the dead.[h] But he did not raise him if in fact the dead are not raised. 16 For if the dead are
not raised, then Christ has not been raised either. 17 And if Christ has not been raised, your faith is futile;
you are still in your sins.[i] 18 Then those also who have fallen asleep in Christ are lost. 19 If only for this
life we have hope in Christ, we are of all people most to be pitied.[j]

20 But Christ has indeed been raised from the dead,[k] the firstfruits[l] of those who have fallen asleep.[m]
21 For since death came through a man,[n] the resurrection of the dead comes also through a man. 22 For
as in Adam all die, so in Christ all will be made alive.[o] 23 But each in turn: Christ, the firstfruits;[p] then,
when he comes,[q] those who belong to him. 24 Then the end will come, when he hands over the kingdom[r]
to God the Father after he has destroyed all dominion, authority and power.[s] 25 For he must reign until
he has put all his enemies under his feet.[t] 26 The last enemy to be destroyed is death.[u] 27 For he "has put
everything under his feet."[a][v] Now when it says that "everything" has been put under him, it is clear that
this does not include God himself, who put everything under Christ.[w] 28 When he has done this, then the
Son himself will be made subject to him who put everything under him,[x] so that God may be all in all.[y]

[a] *27* Psalm 8:6

infant, incapable of (spiritual) life, unworthy to meet Jesus because he had persecuted Jesus' followers (Acts 8:1–3; 9:1,13; Gal 1:13).

15:10 The "grace of God"—not some personal decision—completely transformed Paul's life. **harder than all of them.** Paul worked hard to spread the gospel after his conversion. He does not set himself up over the other apostles but emphasizes that he is an unworthy apostle (v. 9) and that God's grace made his missionary work effective (2:4–5; 3:7–8). "Harder" probably refers to his constant missionary travels, which allowed him to cover a wider territory than that of the other apostles.

15:11 The gospel that Paul proclaims to the Corinthians agrees with what the other apostles proclaim.

15:12–34 *The Resurrection of the Dead.* Jesus' resurrection is foundational for the faith of Christians because if Jesus was not raised from the dead, there are significant consequences for the gospel (vv. 12–19), the resurrection of Christians (vv. 20–28), and how Christians live (vv. 29–34).

15:12 some of you say that there is no resurrection of the dead. This statement formulates the problem that Paul addresses in this section. Both Paul and much Greco-Roman thought held that the soul is immortal, and some of the Corinthians, thinking in Greco-Roman categories, denied the resurrection *of the body*. But they seem to have accepted Jesus' resurrection (v. 4) as being similar to the so-called resurrections of many Greek heroes.

15:13–19 Paul spells out the implications of a denial of bodily resurrection: (1) Christ has not been raised from the dead (vv. 13,16); (2) the apostolic preaching is useless (v. 14); (3) faith is useless (vv. 14,17); (4) the apostles are falsely testifying about God (v. 15); (5) the sins of Christians have not been forgiven (v. 17); (6) the Christians who have died are lost forever (v. 18); and (7) Christians are the most pitiful people because they base their lives on a lie (v. 19).

15:20 firstfruits. The first portion of the harvest. In the OT, firstfruits and firstborn animals had to be sacrificed to God (Exod 23:19; 34:19; Lev 2:12; 23:9–14; Deut 12:6,11). The firstfruits belong to God and anticipate the full harvest. Jesus is the firstfruits of those who have died in the sense that his resurrection signals the beginning of the new creation promised in Isa 43:18–19; 65:17; 66:22; Jesus is the "firstborn from the dead" (Rev 1:5). Jesus' resurrection from the dead marks the beginning of the general resurrection of the dead.

15:21–22 Comparing Adam and Christ explains how Christ is the "firstfruits" from the dead (v. 20). **death came through a man ... in Adam all die.** Adam's sin, which was punished by death and excluded him from God's presence (Gen 2:17; 3:1–24), brought death to all his descendants (Rom 5:15–18). **the resurrection of the dead comes also through a man ... in Christ all will be made alive.** Jesus' resurrection establishes the reality of the future resurrection of all believers. As Adam represented the human race, his sin affecting all his descendants, so Jesus Christ represents the new "race," his death and resurrection affecting all who believe in him. For Jesus as the "second" or "last" Adam, see v. 45; Rom 5:12–21.

15:23–28 The events at the end of history argue for a bodily resurrection: Christ was raised from the dead first, and his followers will be raised from the dead when he returns (v. 23); Christ's return brings the end of the present world as he finally eliminates all powers that oppose God (v. 24); Jesus' present rule lasts until he has subjected all enemies to God's rule (v. 25, alluding to Ps 110:1); then death, the believers' last enemy, will be destroyed (vv. 26–27, which quotes Ps 8:6) and Christ's victory will result in God's victory (v. 28). The "kingdom" (v. 24) and Christ's reign (v. 25) is Christ's rule over history as mediator and sustainer of creation (Col 1:15–17), over the church as his body (Col 1:18), and over the individual lives of his people. Note that Jesus said the kingdom of God had dawned in and through his ministry (Luke 17:21). Some relate Christ's reign to the millennium (1,000 years) mentioned in Rev 20:1–6.

15:28 the Son himself will be made subject. The subordination of the Son to the Father is not one of divinity or dignity but one of function: God the Father is supreme, not subject to anyone; Jesus the Son, fully divine, carries out the Father's will; the Spirit (not mentioned here) communicates the reality of God's presence, truth, and salvation.

29Now if there is no resurrection, what will those do who are baptized for the dead? If the dead are not
raised at all, why are people baptized for them? 30And as for us, why do we endanger ourselves every hour?[z]
31I face death every day[a] — yes, just as surely as I boast about you in Christ Jesus our Lord. 32If I fought
wild beasts[b] in Ephesus[c] with no more than human hopes, what have I gained? If the dead are not raised,

> "Let us eat and drink,
> for tomorrow we die."[a][d]

33Do not be misled: "Bad company corrupts good character."[b] 34Come back to your senses as you ought,
and stop sinning; for there are some who are ignorant of God — I say this to your shame.

The Resurrection Body

35But someone will ask,[e] "How are the dead raised? With what kind of body will they come?"[f] 36How foolish![g] What you sow does not come to life unless it dies.[h] 37When you sow, you do not plant the body that will
be, but just a seed, perhaps of wheat or of something else. 38But God gives it a body as he has determined, and
to each kind of seed he gives its own body.[i] 39Not all flesh is the same: People have one kind of flesh, animals
have another, birds another and fish another. 40There are also heavenly bodies and there are earthly bodies;
but the splendor of the heavenly bodies is one kind, and the splendor of the earthly bodies is another. 41The
sun has one kind of splendor, the moon another and the stars another; and star differs from star in splendor.
42So will it be[j] with the resurrection of the dead. The body that is sown is perishable, it is raised imperishable; 43it is sown in dishonor, it is raised in glory;[k] it is sown in weakness, it is raised in power;
44it is sown a natural body, it is raised a spiritual body.[l]

If there is a natural body, there is also a spiritual body. 45So it is written: "The first man Adam
became a living being"[c];[m] the last Adam,[n] a life-giving spirit.[o] 46The spiritual did not come first, but
the natural, and after that the spiritual. 47The first man was of the dust of the earth;[p] the second man

a *32* Isaiah 22:13 *b* *33* From the Greek poet Menander *c* *45* Gen. 2:7

15:30 [z]2Co 11:26
15:31 [a]Ro 8:36
15:32 [b]2Co 1:8 [c]Ac 18:19 [d]Isa 22:13; Lk 12:19
15:35 [e]Ro 9:19 [f]Eze 37:3
15:36 [g]Lk 11:40 [h]Jn 12:24
15:38 [i]Ge 1:11
15:42 [j]Da 12:3; Mt 13:43
15:43 [k]Php 3:21; Col 3:4
15:44 [l]ver 50
15:45 [m]Ge 2:7 [n]Ro 5:14 [o]Jn 5:21; Ro 8:2
15:47 [p]Ge 2:7; 3:19

15:29 baptized for the dead. This phrase is most plausibly understood as referring to Christian water baptism, described in a manner that adapts to the context: if there is no resurrection from the dead, it makes no sense for new Christians (who were spiritually "dead" before their conversion) to undergo baptism if faith and baptism have no effect on what happens after death. Christians who deny a future resurrection of the body render baptism, which connects the "dead" sinner with the crucified and risen Lord Jesus Christ, meaningless. Others interpret the phrase as referring to a vicarious baptism on behalf of deceased people, a practice that would have been unique to the Corinthian church.
15:30–32 If there is no bodily resurrection, then Paul and the other apostles are meaninglessly putting their lives in danger.
15:32 fought wild beasts. Probably a life-threatening situation in Ephesus (Acts 19:23–31; cf. Rom 16:3–4). **"Let us eat and drink, for tomorrow we die."** If there is no bodily resurrection, one might as well follow this hedonistic motto, which quotes Isa 22:13 (cf. the Latin motto *carpe diem*, "seize the day").
15:33 Do not be misled. Paul spends so much time discussing bodily resurrection because it is a serious mistake to think that the believers' future is not affected by their present behavior. **"Bad company corrupts good character."** The quotation is usually said to derive from a lost comedy by the Greek poet Menander; Socrates suggests that the saying goes back to the Greek tragedian Euripides. For Paul, the "bad company" are the people who claim that there is no resurrection (v. 12).
15:34 Paul admonishes the Corinthians with two further exhortations: (1) return to a sound theological and ethical position and practice, and (2) stop engaging in a sinful lifestyle. **stop sinning.** This admonition establishes the foundational nature of Paul's discussion of bodily resurrection: Christians who look forward to the resurrection of their bodies do not take sin lightly but do everything they can to avoid it.
15:35–58 *The Resurrection Body.* Resurrection transforms the human body (vv. 35–49) and guarantees victory over death (vv. 50–58).
15:35 Paul has shown that the dead *will* be raised and now he explains *how* they will be raised (i.e., "with what kind of body").
15:36–38 Transformation happens in nature. Seed that is sown dies in the ground before the plants grow out of the ground. Farmers do not sow plants; they sow seed, and God transforms the seed into plants.
15:39–41 The polarity between the heavenly and earthly realms is not an insurmountable problem for a bodily resurrection. Some bodies are "heavenly" (i.e., extraterrestrial or celestial), such as the sun, moon, and stars; some bodies are "earthly" (i.e., terrestrial), such as humans, animals, birds, and fish.
15:42–44 Paul applies the analogy of heavenly and earthly bodies (vv. 39–41) to the resurrection from the dead and explains the meaning of the seed and the different bodies that God creates (vv. 36–38). Human bodies are mortal, dishonorable, weak, and natural; resurrection bodies will be immortal, glorious, empowered by God's power, and spiritual. God, who creates plants from seeds and who has demonstrated his creative power in the diversity of the bodies (forms) of human beings, animals, and stars will create new bodies for believers when they are raised from the dead.
15:44 natural body. The earthly body of human beings, created by God but temporal. **spiritual body.** The new resurrection body of the believer, having a supernatural origin, created by God's Spirit and thus eternal.
15:45 Paul confirms his argument by quoting Gen 2:7. **last Adam.** Jesus, the goal of God's creation and the Savior of the world. **life-giving spirit.** Jesus represents God's powerful and transforming presence that creates new life and raises people from the dead.
15:46 natural. The present existence, which derives from Adam's creation, is characterized by "nature," i.e., by a physical body (v. 44). **spiritual.** The future existence, which derives from Jesus' resurrection, is characterized by "Spirit," i.e., by God's presence.
15:47 first man … dust. Adam came from the dust of the earth (Gen 2:7). **second man … heaven.** Jesus, the "last Adam" in contrast to the

15:47 [q]Jn 3:13,31
15:48 [r]Php 3:20,21
15:49 [s]Ge 5:3 [t]Ro 8:29
15:50 [u]Jn 3:3,5
15:51 [v]1Co 13:2 [w]Php 3:21
15:52 [x]Mt 24:31 [y]Jn 5:25
15:53 [z]2Co 5:2,4
15:54 [a]Isa 25:8; Rev 20:14
15:55 [b]Hos 13:14
15:56 [c]Ro 5:12 [d]Ro 4:15
15:57 [e]2Co 2:14 [f]Ro 8:37
15:58 [g]1Co 16:10
16:1 [h]Ac 24:17 [i]Ac 9:13 [j]Ac 16:6
16:2 [k]Ac 20:7 [l]2Co 9:4,5

is of heaven.[q] [48]As was the earthly man, so are those who are of the earth; and as is the heavenly man,
so also are those who are of heaven.[r] [49]And just as we have borne the image of the earthly man,[s] so
shall we[a] bear the image of the heavenly man.[t]

[50]I declare to you, brothers and sisters, that flesh and blood[u] cannot inherit the kingdom of God, nor
does the perishable inherit the imperishable. [51]Listen, I tell you a mystery:[v] We will not all sleep, but
we will all be changed[w]— [52]in a flash, in the twinkling of an eye, at the last trumpet. For the trumpet
will sound,[x] the dead[y] will be raised imperishable, and we will be changed. [53]For the perishable must
clothe itself with the imperishable,[z] and the mortal with immortality. [54]When the perishable has been
clothed with the imperishable, and the mortal with immortality, then the saying that is written will
come true: "Death has been swallowed up in victory."[b][a]

> [55]"Where, O death, is your victory?
> Where, O death, is your sting?"[c][b]

[56]The sting of death is sin,[c] and the power of sin is the law.[d] [57]But thanks be to God![e] He gives us the
victory through our Lord Jesus Christ.[f]

[58]Therefore, my dear brothers and sisters, stand firm. Let nothing move you. Always give yourselves
fully to the work of the Lord,[g] because you know that your labor in the Lord is not in vain.

The Collection for the Lord's People

16 Now about the collection[h] for the Lord's people:[i] Do what I told the Galatian[j] churches to
do. [2]On the first day of every week,[k] each one of you should set aside a sum of money in
keeping with your income, saving it up, so that when I come no collections will have to be made.[l]

[a] *49* Some early manuscripts *so let us* [b] *54* Isaiah 25:8 [c] *55* Hosea 13:14

"first Adam" (v. 45), came from heaven and thus is characterized by imperishability, glory, and power (vv. 42–44).

15:48–49 The contrast between Adam and Jesus applies to those who belong to Adam and Jesus, which explains why it is significant that both the "first" man and "second" man represent humankind.

15:48 As was the earthly man, so are those who are of the earth. As Adam was formed from the dust of the earth and thus was transient, dishonorable, and powerless, so are the people whom Adam represents. **as is the heavenly man, so also are those who are of heaven.** As Jesus came from heaven, so the people whom Jesus represents will be characterized by a heavenly body; they will have resurrection bodies like Jesus' resurrection body.

15:49 we have borne the image of the earthly man. As Adam's descendants, the bodies of Christians have the form of the man created from the dust of the earth: they are mortal, transient, weak. **so shall we bear the image of the heavenly man.** As followers of Christ, the bodies of Christians will be transformed into heavenly, spiritual bodies that, as Paul has argued, will be physical bodies at the same time.

15:50–58 Victory over death is triumphantly certain because of the resurrection.

15:50 People with human and thus mortal bodies ("flesh and blood") cannot live in the new world of God's imperishable and immortal kingdom.

15:51 mystery. That all believers, including those who are alive at the time of Jesus' return, will enter the perfection of God's new world through the transformation of their bodies. **We will not all sleep.** Not all human beings will die before the end of the present world arrives.

15:52 last trumpet. Announces the Lord's coming (Isa 27:13; Joel 2:1; Zeph 1:16; Zech 9:14; Matt 24:31; 1 Thess 4:16; Rev 8:2—11:10). When Christ returns, the dead will be raised and the living transformed.

15:53–56 God will transform both dead and living mortal, human bodies into imperishable, immortal bodies. This fulfills Isa 25:8; Hos 13:14. Jesus' resurrection defeats once and for all the fatal power that death had over humans; it breaks the power of death since God carried out the death sentence (the just and necessary punishment for sin) when Jesus died on the cross instead of and for the benefit of sinners.

15:56 sting of death. Adam's sin introduced death into the world, which is now the fate of all human beings (Rom 5:12–21). **the power of sin is the law.** The presence of sin forces the law to pronounce the death sentence; it is only Jesus' vicarious death on the cross that atones for sin.

15:57 Christians thank God for the victory over death that he accomplished through Christ's death and resurrection. God defeated death and will totally eliminate it, and Christians will live in his presence with transformed bodies.

15:58 Paul concludes with three exhortations: (1) **stand firm.** Christians must not abandon the hope that the dead will be raised with new bodies, and they must not abandon the gospel of the crucified and risen Jesus Christ (vv. 1–2). (2) **Let nothing move you.** Christians must resist being moved away from the gospel and the hope of resurrection. (3) **Always give yourselves fully.** Christians must completely devote themselves to the Lord's work by building up the church (3:13–15; 9:1; 16:10), a task that is never futile.

16:1–24 *Concluding Matters.* Paul concludes his letter.

16:1–4 *The Collection for the Lord's People.* Paul gives directions regarding the collection for the Jerusalem church that he is collecting from the churches he has established.

16:1 the collection. Paul is collecting money "for the Lord's people," i.e., the believers in Jerusalem (2 Cor 8–9; Rom 15:26; Gal 2:10). The Jerusalem believers may have become impoverished as a result of a famine (Acts 11:28).

16:2 the first day of every week. Sunday, the day after the day of rest (the Sabbath). "Week" implies that Paul uses the Jewish calendar (the Hellenistic and Roman world did not know a "week" as such). Some churches met on the first day of the week (Acts 20:7). "The Lord's Day" (Rev 1:10) also refers to the first day of the week; it was the day on which Jesus was raised from the dead (see note on Rev 1:10). Christian teachers writing at the end of the first century confirm the practice of Christians meeting on Sundays. **each one.** Both well-to-do and poor Christians can contribute something to the collection. **set aside.** Contribute regularly to the collection. **in keeping with your income.** The criterion for the amount Christians should give. Paul does not suggest a specific amount, such as

3Then, when I arrive, I will give letters of introduction to the men you approve[m] and send them with your gift to Jerusalem. 4If it seems advisable for me to go also, they will accompany me.

Personal Requests

5After I go through Macedonia, I will come to you[n]—for I will be going through Macedonia.[o] 6Perhaps I will stay with you for a while, or even spend the winter, so that you can help me on my journey,[p] wherever I go. 7For I do not want to see you now and make only a passing visit; I hope to spend some time with you, if the Lord permits.[q] 8But I will stay on at Ephesus[r] until Pentecost,[s] 9because a great door for effective work has opened to me,[t] and there are many who oppose me.

10When Timothy[u] comes, see to it that he has nothing to fear while he is with you, for he is carrying on the work of the Lord,[v] just as I am. 11No one, then, should treat him with contempt.[w] Send him on his way in peace[x] so that he may return to me. I am expecting him along with the brothers.

12Now about our brother Apollos:[y] I strongly urged him to go to you with the brothers. He was quite unwilling to go now, but he will go when he has the opportunity.

13Be on your guard; stand firm[z] in the faith; be courageous; be strong.[a] 14Do everything in love.[b]

15You know that the household of Stephanas[c] were the first converts[d] in Achaia,[e] and they have devoted themselves to the service of the Lord's people. I urge you, brothers and sisters, 16to submit[f] to such people and to everyone who joins in the work and labors at it. 17I was glad when Stephanas, Fortunatus and Achaicus arrived, because they have supplied what was lacking from you.[g] 18For they refreshed[h] my spirit and yours also. Such men deserve recognition.[i]

Final Greetings

19The churches in the province of Asia send you greetings. Aquila and Priscilla[a][j] greet you warmly in the Lord, and so does the church that meets at their house.[k] 20All the brothers and sisters here send you greetings. Greet one another with a holy kiss.[l]

21I, Paul, write this greeting in my own hand.[m]

22If anyone does not love the Lord,[n] let that person be cursed![o] Come, Lord[b]![p]

23The grace of the Lord Jesus be with you.[q]

24My love to all of you in Christ Jesus. Amen.[c]

16:3 [m]2Co 8:18,19
16:5 [n]1Co 4:19 [o]Ac 19:21
16:6 [p]Ro 15:24
16:7 [q]Ac 18:21
16:8 [r]Ac 18:19 [s]Ac 2:1
16:9 [t]Ac 14:27
16:10 [u]Ac 16:1 [v]1Co 15:58
16:11 [w]1Ti 4:12 [x]Ac 15:33
16:12 [y]Ac 18:24; 1Co 1:12
16:13 [z]Gal 5:1; Php 1:27; 1Th 3:8; 2Th 2:15 [a]Eph 6:10
16:14 [b]1Co 14:1
16:15 [c]1Co 1:16 [d]Ro 16:5 [e]Ac 18:12
16:16 [f]Heb 13:17
16:17 [g]2Co 11:9; Php 2:30
16:18 [h]Phm 7 [i]Php 2:29
16:19 [j]Ac 18:2 [k]Ro 16:5
16:20 [l]Ro 16:16
16:21 [m]Gal 6:11; Col 4:18
16:22 [n]Eph 6:24 [o]Ro 9:3 [p]Rev 22:20
16:23 [q]Ro 16:20

a *19* Greek *Prisca*, a variant of *Priscilla* *b* *22* The Greek for *Come, Lord* reproduces an Aramaic expression (*Marana tha*) used by early Christians. *c* *24* Some manuscripts do not have *Amen*.

the tithes of the OT; he respects the different economic situations of the believers, who are free to decide how much they will give.

16:3–4 This explains how Paul plans to transfer the funds to Jerusalem. See Rom 15:25–26.

16:5–18 *Personal Requests.* Paul shares travel plans (vv. 5–12) and final exhortations (vv. 13–18).

16:5–7 When Paul leaves Ephesus, he plans to visit the churches in Macedonia before he comes to Corinth.

16:7 if the Lord permits. Our plans are in the Lord's hands. In this case, circumstances forced Paul to change his plans (2 Cor 1:15–16): he traveled to Corinth for a short visit (probably in the summer or fall of AD 55; see 2 Cor 2:13; 7:5–6) before he left for Macedonia (AD 55–56), and he reached Corinth for the promised longer visit in the winter of AD 56/57, two years after he wrote this letter.

16:8 until Pentecost. In the Jewish calendar, Pentecost is the 50th day after Passover. Paul wants to finish his missionary work in Ephesus by mid-June.

16:9 a great door. A wonderful opportunity for spreading the gospel in Ephesus and the entire province of Asia (Acts 19:10). **oppose.** Opposition may arise even when God blesses a missionary's ministry. It is impossible to know whether this opposition refers to the early stages of the opposition of the guild of the silversmiths in Ephesus (Acts 19:23–40).

16:10 Timothy. Paul sent Timothy to Macedonia (Acts 19:22) and then on to Corinth (1 Cor 4:17). **that he has nothing to fear.** Perhaps Timothy was prone to be timid (1 Tim 4:12; 2 Tim 1:7); Paul wants the Corinthians to treat Timothy with kindness.

16:12 Apollos. See 1:12; 3:4–9,22; 4:6. Apollos may have insisted on staying in Ephesus in connection with the "great door" (v. 9) that God had opened in Ephesus.

16:13–14 The problems that Paul addresses in this letter will be solved if the Corinthian Christians obey these five commands.

16:13 Be on your guard. Fits Paul's repeated reference to the final judgment (1:8; 3:13; 5:5; 7:16; see Rom 13:11–14; 1 Thess 5:6).

16:14 Do everything in love. Reminds readers of ch. 13.

16:19–24 *Final Greetings.* Paul's final greetings include a final warning (v. 22).

16:20 holy kiss. Demonstrates love among family members (see 2 Cor 13:12; Rom 16:16); there was no corresponding practice in Greco-Roman religious cults.

16:21 in my own hand. Paul signs the letter that he had dictated to a secretary, perhaps to authenticate the letter (2 Thess 3:17) or to send a personal greeting (Col 4:18; see Gal 6:11; Phlm 19).

16:22 let that person be cursed! Warning that God will curse the people who refuse to love the Lord. **Come, Lord!** Translates two Aramaic words (which Paul writes in Greek letters) that early Christians used when praying for Jesus' return (Rev 22:20).

16:23 grace ... be with you. Promise of God's grace. God's covenant with his people presents blessings and curses (Lev 26; Deut 27–28). God's grace commits his people to do his will.

16:24 Paul ends his letter to the Corinthian believers, whom he had to admonish repeatedly and severely for serious misbehavior, on the high note of love.

INTRODUCTION TO 2 CORINTHIANS

AUTHOR

The author twice identifies himself as Paul (1:1; 10:1), and the letter reflects Paul's usual style of writing Greek. The letter also refers to many of Paul's distinctive doctrines, such as justification by grace through faith, the Christian life as being lived "in Christ" and by the power of the Spirit, and Christian suffering as sharing in Christ's suffering. Moreover, it is unlikely that a writer seeking to imitate Paul would portray him as an apostle in danger of losing his authority at Corinth or as a pastor struggling to preserve the infant church there from apostasy. People sometimes question whether Paul wrote some of the letters traditionally attributed to him (such as 1–2 Timothy and Titus), but this is not the case with 2 Corinthians.

DATE

Paul's relationship to his converts at Corinth is complex. It seems that he visited the city of Corinth on three occasions: (1) his founding visit of 18 months (from the fall of AD 50 to the spring of 52; Acts 18:1–8); (2) a brief visit (the summer or fall of 55; 2:1; 12:21; 13:2; not mentioned in Acts) that proved "painful" (2:1) both to him and to the Corinthians; (3) a final visit of three months (the winter of 56/57; Acts 20:2b–3a), during which time he wrote Romans.

Moreover, it appears that he wrote at least four letters to his friends at Corinth: (1) a letter previous to that of 1 Corinthians (1 Cor 5:9–11), which no longer exists; (2) 1 Corinthians, which Paul probably wrote in AD 54 and was presumably delivered by the delegation mentioned in 1 Cor 16:12; (3) a severe letter (2:3–4,9; 7:8,12), which Paul probably sent in the spring of 56 and also no longer exists; (4) 2 Corinthians, which was sent in 56 or 57, although Paul probably wrote it in stages. When we remember the relentless demands and pressures of Paul's pastoral service (11:28), it seems likely that he composed all of his letters, apart from Philemon, over a considerable period, perhaps days or even weeks or months.

So then, we may speak of three visits (founding, "painful," and final) and four letters ("previous," 1 Corinthians, "severe," 2 Corinthians).

CORINTH AND THE AEGEAN

PLACE OF COMPOSITION

Several references within 2 Corinthians suggest that Paul was in the province of Macedonia when writing (2:13; 7:5; 8:1; 9:2–4). Of special significance is the present tense in

9:2: "I have been boasting about it [the Corinthians' eagerness to help] to the Macedonians." This is confirmed by Greek manuscripts that note in the subscription to the letter that Paul wrote it "from Philippi," a Macedonian city.

OCCASION AND PURPOSE

Two events prompted Paul to write this letter. First, his pastoral assistant Titus arrived (7:6–16) with welcome news that the majority of the Corinthians to whom Paul wrote the "severe letter" had responded favorably. Second, fresh, disturbing news arrived that some of Paul's vocal opponents had said and done things that harmfully affected the believers.

Paul wrote with three main purposes: (1) to express his great relief and delight that the Corinthians reacted positively to his "severe letter" that Titus had delivered and reinforced (2:9,12–14; 7:5–16); (2) to encourage the Corinthians to complete the collection they promised to take for believers at Jerusalem before his next visit (8:6–7,10–11; 9:3–5); (3) to prepare them for his imminent visit through self-examination and self-judgment (12:14; 13:1,5,11). In essence, Paul had one overriding aim: to pave the way for his planned third visit so it would be free of embarrassment and everyone would enjoy it.

Was Paul's final visit to Corinth a pleasant one? Apparently it was, for during this three-month stay in "Greece" (primarily Corinth; Acts 20:2–3), Paul wrote or completed his letter to the Romans, which gives no hint of trouble at Corinth. Moreover, Rom 15:26–27 indicates that the Corinthians completed their collection for needy fellow believers in Jerusalem. And the very preservation of 2 Corinthians (presumably at Corinth) argues that Paul's visit was successful.

STRUCTURE

There are three clearly distinguishable sections in 2 Corinthians: (1) chs. 1–7 explain Paul's recent conduct toward the Corinthians (1:1—2:11) and describe his apostolic ministry (2:12—7:16); (2) chs. 8–9 call the Corinthian church to complete their collection for the poor believers in Jerusalem; (3) chs. 10–13 vigorously defend how Paul exercised and will exercise his apostolic authority. The first section is basically explanation; the second, encouragement; and the third, defense; or, use the technical terms, apologetic, hortatory, and polemical.

THEMES

An English phrase such as "I must rejoice" (cf. 6:10; 7:4,7,9,13,16) sums up the distinctive tone of chs. 1–9, while its major theme is comfort in the midst of affliction (1:3–7; 7:4,6–7,13). On the other hand, "I must go on boasting" (12:1; cf. 10:8,13,16–17; 11:18,21,30; 12:5–6,9) sums up the tone of chs. 10–13, and it chiefly emphasizes strength in the midst of weakness (11:23–33; 12:5,9–10; 13:4). Paul liked to express truth through paradox, so in addition to the two paradoxes just mentioned, he speaks of life in the midst of death (4:10–12; 5:4; 6:9), spiritual renewal in the midst of physical weakeness (4:16), joy in the midst of sorrow (6:10), and generosity in the midst of poverty (6:10; 8:2).

UNITY

At 10:1 there is such a sudden and unexpected change of tone that some scholars propose that the letter is made up of two separate letters (chs. 1–9 and chs. 10–13) and that Paul wrote chs. 10–13 either before or after chs. 1–9. There are, however, several compelling reasons for believing that Paul sent the letter as a single document, even if he wrote it over a period of time, during which the situation at Corinth changed for the worse:

1. All the contents of the letter can be related to a single, unifying purpose in writing, namely, to prepare the way for Paul's imminent third visit to Corinth (9:3–5; 10:2,11; 12:14,20–21; 13:1–2,10) by removing any obstacles that might prevent that visit from pleasing and benefiting everyone.

2. The entire letter is an "apology" in the sense that it defends Paul against various complaints or charges that at least some of the Corinthians and the intruders from Judea made (1:12–13,17; 5:11–13; 8:13–15; 10:1,10; 11:6; 13:6). Paul asks, "Have you been thinking all along that we have been defending ourselves to you?" (12:19). What Paul writes in 1 Cor 9 about defending his apostolic rights (1 Cor 9:4–12) could equally apply to 2 Corinthians as a whole: "This is my defense to those who sit in judgment on me" (1 Cor 9:3).

3. Several expressions in chs. 10–13 seem to echo or refer back to similar statements in chs. 1–9. For example, "We have been speaking in the sight of God as those in Christ" (12:19) echoes "in Christ we speak before God [with sincerity]" (2:17), where the Greek phrase is identical and is found nowhere else in Paul's letters.

View from the Acrocorinth toward the Gulf of Corinth.

4. We can explain the abrupt change of tone at 10:1 by suggesting that at the end of ch. 9 there was an interval of some length in Paul's dictation. During that time, Paul received news of a worsening situation at Corinth that prompted him to defend his apostolic authority and sternly warn about his forthcoming visit (chs. 10–13).

5. With regard to the alternative views that see 2 Corinthians as a composite document, it is difficult to think of circumstances that might have led to a combination of two separate letters, one without a normal ending and another without a regular beginning such as Paul's other letters would lead us to expect. Also, there is no manuscript evidence that supports the division of the letter into two or more parts.

THEOLOGICAL VALUE

Traditionally, Paul's two letters to Timothy and his one letter to Titus are called the "Pastoral Letters." But 2 Corinthians has a strong claim to be regarded as the supreme pastoral letter because it witnesses so vividly to the "daily ... pressure" (11:28) of Paul's anxious concern for the Corinthian believers. "Who is weak, and I do not feel weak? Who is led into sin, and I do not inwardly burn?" (11:29). Paul, the matchless pastor, penned a profound, though brief, autobiography. In this letter we have beautiful examples of the tenderness of a spiritual shepherd sensitive to the needs of his flock (1:24; 2:6–7; 6:1; 10:2; 13:5,10); the pleading of a spiritual father jealous for his children's affection, purity, and unity (6:11–13; 11:2–3; 13:11); and the fears of a spiritual mentor as he confronts the persistent sin of his charges (12:20–21; 13:2,10).

This letter also includes classic discussions about the meaning of Christian suffering (1:3–11; 4:7–18; 6:3–10; 12:1–10), the proper exercise of Christian discipline (2:5–11; 7:8–13; 13:1–4), the role of a minister of the new covenant (2:14–17; 4:1–5; 5:16–21; 11:28–29; 12:14–15), the relation between the old and new covenants (3:7–18), the theology of death and resurrection (4:7—5:10), the nature and means of reconciliation (5:18–21), and the principles and practice of Christian stewardship (8:1—9:15).

OUTLINE

I. Paul's Explanation of His Conduct (1:1—2:11)
- A. Salutation (1:1–2)
- B. Praise to the God of All Comfort (1:3–11)
  - 1. A Doxology Celebrating Divine Comfort (1:3–7)
  - 2. Deliverance From Affliction (1:8–11)
- C. Paul's Change of Plans (1:12—2:4)
  - 1. Characteristics of His Conduct (1:12–14)
  - 2. Charge of Fickleness Answered (1:15–22)
  - 3. A Canceled, Possibly Painful Visit (1:23—2:4)
- D. Forgiveness for the Offender (2:5–11)

II. Paul's Explanation of His Apostolic Ministry (2:12—7:16)
- A. Ministers of the New Covenant (2:12—3:6)
  - 1. Restlessness at Troas (2:12–13)
  - 2. The Privilege of Apostolic Service (2:14–17)
  - 3. The Results of the Ministry (3:1–3)
  - 4. Competence for Service (3:4–6)
- B. The Greater Glory of the New Covenant (3:7–18)
  - 1. Lesser and Greater Glory (3:7–11)
  - 2. Veiling and Unveiling (3:12–18)
- C. Present Weakness and Resurrection Life (4:1–18)
  - 1. The Light Brought by the Gospel (4:1–6)
  - 2. The Trials and Rewards of Apostolic Service (4:7–15)
  - 3. Glory Through Suffering (4:16–18)
- D. Awaiting the New Body (5:1–10)
- E. The Ministry of Reconciliation (5:11—6:2)
  - 1. Motivation for Service (5:11–15)
  - 2. The Messengers of Reconciliation (5:16—6:2)
- F. Paul's Hardships (6:3–13)
- G. Warning Against Idolatry (6:14—7:1)
- H. Paul's Joy Over the Church's Repentance (7:2–16)

III. Paul's Summons to Complete the Collection for Believers in Jerusalem (8:1—9:15)
- A. The Collection for the Lord's People (8:1–15)
  - 1. The Generosity of the Macedonians (8:1–6)
  - 2. A Plea for Liberal Giving (8:7–12)
  - 3. The Aim of Equality (8:13–15)
- B. Titus Sent to Receive the Collection (8:16—9:5)
  - 1. The Delegates and Their Credentials (8:16–24)
  - 2. The Need for Readiness (9:1–5)
- C. Generosity Encouraged (9:6–15)

IV. Paul's Defense of His Apostolic Authority (10:1—13:14)
- A. Paul's Defense of His Ministry (10:1–18)
  - 1. The Potency of Apostolic Authority (10:1–11)
  - 2. Legitimate Spheres of Activity and Boasting (10:12–18)
- B. Paul and the False Apostles (11:1–15)
- C. Paul Boasts About His Sufferings (11:16–33)
- D. Paul's Vision and His Thorn (12:1–10)
- E. Paul's Concern for the Corinthians (12:11–21)
- F. Final Warnings (13:1–10)
- G. Final Greetings (13:11–14)

2 CORINTHIANS

1:1 [a]1Co 1:1; Eph 1:1; Col 1:1; 2Ti 1:1 [b]1Co 10:32 [c]Ac 18:12
1:2 [d]Ro 1:7
1:3 [e]Eph 1:3; 1Pe 1:3
1:4 [f]2Co 7:6,7,13
1:5 [g]2Co 4:10; Col 1:24
1:6 [h]2Co 4:15
1:7 [i]Ro 8:17
1:8 [j]1Co 15:32

1 Paul, an apostle of Christ Jesus by the will of God,[a] and Timothy our brother,

To the church of God[b] in Corinth, together with all his holy people throughout Achaia:[c]

[2]Grace and peace to you from God our Father and the Lord Jesus Christ.[d]

Praise to the God of All Comfort

[3]Praise be to the God and Father of our Lord Jesus Christ,[e] the Father of compassion and the God of all comfort, [4]who comforts us[f] in all our troubles, so that we can comfort those in any trouble with the comfort we ourselves receive from God. [5]For just as we share abundantly in the sufferings of Christ,[g] so also our comfort abounds through Christ. [6]If we are distressed, it is for your comfort and salvation;[h] if we are comforted, it is for your comfort, which produces in you patient endurance of the same sufferings we suffer. [7]And our hope for you is firm, because we know that just as you share in our sufferings,[i] so also you share in our comfort.

[8]We do not want you to be uninformed, brothers and sisters,[a] about the troubles we experienced[j]

[a] 8 The Greek word for *brothers and sisters* (*adelphoi*) refers here to believers, both men and women, as part of God's family; also in 8:1; 13:11.

1:1—2:11 *Paul's Explanation of His Conduct.* The appropriateness of Paul's conduct toward the Corinthians had been questioned, so he feels compelled to explain his pastoral motives and the reasons for his seemingly fickle behavior.

1:1–2 *Salutation.* Following the letter-writing customs of his time, Paul names the authors and recipients of his letter (cf. Acts 23:26).

1:1 apostle. Means "one who is sent." Although Paul was not one of the original 12 apostles Christ chose (Mark 3:14–19), he claimed equality with them as an apostle (1 Cor 15:9; Gal 2:8) on the basis of the special revelation of Christ that God gave him at his conversion (1 Cor 9:1; Gal 1:15–16). **his holy people.** Christians are God's secure possession and have been given a right standing before him. The expression can also be translated "the holy ones," "God's people," or "those who are consecrated to God."

1:2 Grace. God's unsought, unbought, and unmerited favor. Paul refers to God's grace at the beginning and end of all his letters. **God our Father and the Lord Jesus Christ.** Together they form a single source of divine grace and peace; this implies the deity of Christ.

1:3–11 *Praise to the God of All Comfort.* Usually Paul follows his salutation by thanking God for his converts and summarizing what he prays for them (e.g., Phil 1:3–11). Here, however, because of his distressing experience in Asia (vv. 8–10) and the depression he recently experienced (2:12–13; 7:5–6), he focuses on his own circumstances and requests prayer for himself (v. 11). This section contains a theology of Christian suffering: (1) patiently enduring suffering deepens our appreciation of God's character (vv. 3–4); (2) suffering drives us to trust God alone (v. 9); (3) suffering brings identification with Christ (v. 5); (4) to experience God's comfort in the midst of our own suffering encourages and equips us to bring his comfort to those undergoing any type of suffering (vv. 4,6).

1:3–7 *A Doxology Celebrating Divine Comfort.* Throughout this letter God's comfort is his consoling, strengthening, and refreshing of believers in the midst of adversity.

1:3 God's compassion is limitless (Ps 145:9; Lam 3:22; Mic 7:19) and his comfort never-failing (Isa 40:1; 51:3,12; 66:13).

1:4 us ... our ... we ... we ourselves. When Paul uses these words, he often means himself (as here) but sometimes includes his co-workers, his addressees, fellow Jews, all Christians, or people in general. The context usually shows which he means.

1:5 the sufferings of Christ. Cannot refer to the atoning work of Christ that Paul regards as completed (Rom 5:8–11; 6:10) but probably include all the sufferings, whether physical or spiritual, that those in Christ (2 Cor 5:17; 12:2) experience as they serve Christ (cf. 4:10–12). They are *Christ's* sufferings because they imitate his sufferings and because Christ continues to identify himself with his afflicted church (Acts 9:4–5).

1:8–11 *Deliverance From Affliction.* Whatever the nature of Paul's devastating experience in Asia (possibly an attack of his "thorn," 12:7), it was equivalent to dying, and God's gracious rescue was equivalent to being raised from death (1:8–9). Paul is forced to give up his self-reliance and adopt a new guiding principle for his life: "our competence comes from God" (3:5). This shattering encounter with death prompts

in the province of Asia. We were under great pressure, far beyond our ability to endure, so that we despaired of life itself. [9]Indeed, we felt we had received the sentence of death. But this happened that we
might not rely on ourselves but on God,[k] who raises the dead. [10]He has delivered us from such a deadly
peril,[l] and he will deliver us again. On him we have set our hope that he will continue to deliver us,
[11]as you help us by your prayers.[m] Then many will give thanks[n] on our behalf for the gracious favor
granted us in answer to the prayers of many.

Paul's Change of Plans

[12]Now this is our boast: Our conscience[o] testifies that we have conducted ourselves in the world, and
especially in our relations with you, with integrity[a] and godly sincerity.[p] We have done so, relying not
on worldly wisdom[q] but on God's grace. [13]For we do not write you anything you cannot read or understand. And I hope that, [14]as you have understood us in part, you will come to understand fully that you
can boast of us just as we will boast of you in the day of the Lord Jesus.[r]

[15]Because I was confident of this, I wanted to visit you[s] first so that you might benefit twice.[t] [16]I
wanted to visit you on my way[u] to Macedonia and to come back to you from Macedonia, and then to
have you send me on my way to Judea. [17]Was I fickle when I intended to do this? Or do I make my plans
in a worldly manner[v] so that in the same breath I say both "Yes, yes" and "No, no"?

[18]But as surely as God is faithful,[w] our message to you is not "Yes" and "No." [19]For the Son of God,
Jesus Christ, who was preached among you by us—by me and Silas[b] and Timothy—was not "Yes"
and "No," but in him it has always[x] been "Yes." [20]For no matter how many promises[y] God has made,
they are "Yes" in Christ. And so through him the "Amen"[z] is spoken by us to the glory of God. [21]Now it
is God who makes both us and you stand firm in Christ. He anointed[a] us, [22]set his seal of ownership on
us, and put his Spirit in our hearts as a deposit, guaranteeing what is to come.[b]

[23]I call God as my witness[c]—and I stake my life on it—that it was in order to spare you[d] that I did
not return to Corinth. [24]Not that we lord it over[e] your faith, but we work with you for your joy, because
it is by faith you stand firm.[f]

2 [1]So I made up my mind that I would not make another painful visit
to you.[g] [2]For if I grieve you,[h] who is left to make me glad but you whom I have grieved? [3]I wrote as
I did,[i] so that when I came I would not be distressed[j] by those who should have made me rejoice. I had

1:9 [k]Jer 17:5,7
1:10 [l]Ro 15:31
1:11 [m]Ro 15:30; Php 1:19 [n]2Co 4:15
1:12 [o]Ac 23:1 [p]2Co 2:17 [q]1Co 2:1,4,13
1:14 [r]1Co 1:8
1:15 [s]1Co 4:19 [t]Ro 1:11, 13; 15:29
1:16 [u]1Co 16:5-7
1:17 [v]2Co 10:2,3
1:18 [w]1Co 1:9
1:19 [x]Heb 13:8
1:20 [y]Ro 15:8 [z]1Co 14:16
1:21 [a]1Jn 2:20,27
1:22 [b]2Co 5:5
1:23 [c]Ro 1:9; Gal 1:20 [d]1Co 4:21; 2Co 2:1,3; 13:2,10
1:24 [e]1Pe 5:3 [f]Ro 11:20; 1Co 15:1
2:1 [g]2Co 1:23
2:2 [h]2Co 7:8
2:3 [i]2Co 7:8,12 [j]2Co 12:21

[a] *12* Many manuscripts *holiness* [b] *19* Greek *Silvanus*, a variant of *Silas*

him to ponder more deeply than before the nature and consequences of the believer's death (5:1–10).

1:11 gracious favor. God would again deliver Paul from death so he could continue his ministry (cf. Phil 1:22–25).

1:12—2:4 *Paul's Change of Plans.* Paul's "Plan A" was to travel from Ephesus to Macedonia to Corinth and possibly to Jerusalem (1 Cor 16:2–8). His "Plan B" is Ephesus to Corinth to Macedonia to Corinth to (now definitely) Judea (2 Cor 1:15–16). His actual itinerary seems to have been Ephesus to Corinth (the "painful visit," 2:1) to Ephesus to Troas (2:12–13) to Macedonia (7:5; the place of writing) to Corinth (Acts 20:2–3). Paul seemed to say "yes, no, yes" to Plan A and "yes, no" to Plan B. This was ammunition for his opponents' attack. In this section Paul vigorously maintains that in all his dealings with the Corinthians he has been reliable and straightforward.

1:12–14 *Characteristics of His Conduct.* In defending his trustworthiness, Paul appeals to the Corinthians' firsthand knowledge (Acts 18:11) of his "integrity and godly sincerity" (v. 12).

1:13 When Paul wrote anything to the Corinthians, there was never a need, he claims, to "read between the lines"; his meaning was clear.

1:14 They need to understand Paul better but they already had reason to be proud of him.

1:15–22 *Charge of Fickleness Answered.* Paul responds to the charge of being unreliable and purely human in his planning (v. 17) by pointing to the unambiguous and positive gospel message he and others had preached at Corinth that was "not 'Yes' and 'No'" but "always ... 'Yes'" (vv. 18–19), for all God's promises (cf. Rom 1:2) are "Yes" or "Amen" (i.e., "this is true") in Christ (v. 20). Moreover, God was constantly producing stability not fickleness in Paul and the Corinthians, who were his secure possession, sealed and indwelt by the Spirit (vv. 21–22).

1:21–22 God ... Christ ... Spirit. The text is Trinitarian.

1:22 a deposit, guaranteeing what is to come. Captures both senses of the Greek word *arrabōn*: "installment" and "pledge." See note on 5:5.

1:23—2:4 *A Canceled, Possibly Painful Visit.* After the Corinthians received the letter known as 1 Corinthians, their situation apparently grew worse when agitators from Judea arrived. Paul was forced to make a brief visit (Ephesus to Corinth to Ephesus) that turned out to be "painful" (2:1). Now, writing from Macedonia, he tells his converts at Corinth that he had decided at Ephesus after that first "painful visit" not to pay them what might have been a second mutually distressing visit. Instead he visited them by a letter (2:3–4; cf. 7:8,12) that itself proved difficult to write and is usually called the "severe letter" (see Introduction: Date).

1:23 I call God as my witness—and I stake my life on it. Paul is so sure of his own truthfulness on this delicate point about his motivation that he says, in effect, "Let God destroy me if I am lying." His change of plans had been motivated by his love and concern for his converts.

1:24 we work with you. True pastoral care aims not to dominate or intimidate but to promote "progress and joy in the faith" (Phil 1:25).

2:1 painful visit. It is unlikely that this was Paul's initial visit to Corinth (Acts 18:1–18), which for the Corinthians was anything but painful.

2:3 [k]2Co 8:22; Gal 5:10
2:4 [l]2Co 7:8,12
2:5 [m]1Co 5:1,2
2:6 [n]1Co 5:4,5
2:7 [o]Gal 6:1; Eph 4:32
2:9 [p]2Co 10:6
2:11 [q]Mt 4:10 [r]Lk 22:31; 2Co 4:4; 1Pe 5:8,9
2:12 [s]Ac 16:8 [t]Ro 1:1 [u]Ac 14:27
2:13 [v]2Co 7:5 [w]2Co 7:6, 13; 12:18
2:14 [x]Ro 6:17 [y]Eph 5:2; Php 4:18

confidence[k] in all of you, that you would all share my joy. 4 For I wrote you[l] out of great distress and anguish of heart and with many tears, not to grieve you but to let you know the depth of my love for you.

Forgiveness for the Offender

5 If anyone has caused grief,[m] he has not so much grieved me as he has grieved all of you to some
extent — not to put it too severely. 6 The punishment[n] inflicted on him by the majority is sufficient.
7 Now instead, you ought to forgive and comfort him,[o] so that he will not be overwhelmed by excessive
sorrow. 8 I urge you, therefore, to reaffirm your love for him. 9 Another reason I wrote you was to see if
you would stand the test and be obedient in everything.[p] 10 Anyone you forgive, I also forgive. And what
I have forgiven — if there was anything to forgive — I have forgiven in the sight of Christ for your sake,
11 in order that Satan[q] might not outwit us. For we are not unaware of his schemes.[r]

Ministers of the New Covenant

12 Now when I went to Troas[s] to preach the gospel of Christ[t] and found that the Lord had opened a
door[u] for me, 13 I still had no peace of mind,[v] because I did not find my brother Titus[w] there. So I said
goodbye to them and went on to Macedonia.

14 But thanks be to God,[x] who always leads us as captives in Christ's triumphal procession and uses
us to spread the aroma[y] of the knowledge of him everywhere. 15 For we are to God the pleasing aroma

2:4 While Paul undoubtedly wrote parts of 1 Cor "out of great distress and anguish of heart," this is hardly true of that letter as a whole. Paul is referring to a stern letter that does not exist any longer; he wrote it after the "painful visit" (2:1) and sent it with Titus, who later reported to Paul on its success (7:6–7). Paul's main aim in writing the "severe letter" was not to inflict pain on or "grieve" the Corinthians but to convince them how intense his affection is for them. **not to ... but to.** The antithesis reflects a Semitic idiom that expresses a comparison ("not so much X, as Y" or "not primarily X, but Y") as a bold contrast ("not X, but Y"). Thus, "I desire mercy, not sacrifice" (Hos 6:6) means "My desire is primarily for mercy, rather than sacrifice." See also 2 Cor 2:5; 7:12. Here Paul is not rejecting pain or grief as a God-given means of repentance. Love and the infliction of pain are not incompatible. God can use love-inflicted pain to produce a "repentance that leads to salvation and leaves no regret" (7:10).

2:5–11 *Forgiveness for the Offender.* After Paul's brief painful visit to Corinth, apparently someone there publicly insulted or opposed Paul or his representative. Whatever the precise offense, it clearly involved Paul since he personally offers forgiveness (v. 10). At first the congregation had not rallied to Paul's defense, but stung by his "severe letter" that demanded the person be punished, the majority inflicted some unspecified penalty on the man. Now the apostle calls for the church to end the penalty and reaffirm their love toward this man.

2:11 that Satan might not outwit us. If the church withheld forgiveness when the man was repentant, they would be playing into the hands of Satan, who cunningly tries to create disunity within the church. The NT teaches that some offenses are serious enough to warrant corporate church discipline, such as open, unrepentant immorality (1 Cor 5:1–11), actively spreading false teaching (Rom 16:17), or divisiveness (Titus 3:10). In such cases there are six stages in successful discipline: (1) The identification of the wrongdoing (2 Cor 2:5), which implies an offending party and sometimes an injured party (7:12). (2) The punishment, which the majority or full assembly administer (v. 6). (3) Pain or grief (vv. 5,7), which the wrongdoer suffers (v. 7) and in a different sense the whole congregation feels (v. 5). (4) Repentance (implied in v. 6), which is the outcome of "godly sorrow" (7:9–10). (5) Forgiveness (vv. 7,10), which the whole congregation and the offended party grant. (6) Affirmation (v. 8), which involves publicly reinstating and restoring the wrongdoer to full fellowship within the congregation.

2:12—7:16 *Paul's Explanation of His Apostolic Ministry.* This is the longest segment of the letter and includes a major digression (2:14—7:4) that itself contains a minor one (6:14—7:1); 7:5 picks up the travel narrative left at 2:13, and 7:2 looks back to 6:13. This major digression describes four aspects of Paul's apostolic ministry: grandeur and superiority (2:14—4:6); suffering and glory (4:7—5:10); essence and exercise (5:11—6:10); and openness and consolation (6:11—7:4).

2:12—3:6 *Ministers of the New Covenant.* Paul focuses on the exalted role of those entrusted with spreading the knowledge of Christ, a task that calls for divine empowerment.

2:12–13 *Restlessness at Troas.* Paul had arranged to meet Titus at Troas after Titus delivered the "severe letter" to Corinth. Although the Lord provided Paul with special opportunities for preaching at Troas, Paul lacked "peace of mind" (v. 13) and surprisingly (1 Cor 9:16) cut short his evangelism there and left for Macedonia, probably the city of Philippi. He was remarkably restless because he was concerned for Titus's safety in traveling (2 Cor 7:6b–7a; 11:26) and especially because his uncertainty and fears were growing (7:5b) regarding the situation at Corinth because Titus had not arrived.

2:14–17 *The Privilege of Apostolic Service.* Paul begins a massive digression (2:14—7:4; see note on 2:12—7:16), remembering his happy reunion with Titus in Macedonia.

2:14 leads us as captives in Christ's triumphal procession. Titus had brought very encouraging news from Corinth (7:5–16), so Paul likens God's triumph at Corinth to the victory procession of a Roman general. Captives from the conquered territory were chained in front of the general's chariot while the victorious soldiers followed, shouting, "Hail, triumphant one!" Paul sees himself and his fellow apostles not as excited soldiers who share in their general's victory pageant but as willing, joyful captives who count it a privilege to be part of God's triumph. The only other NT use of this Greek verb that means "lead in triumphal procession" is in Col 2:15, where the defeated powers and authorities are unwilling captives driven before God's triumphal chariot.

2:15–16 aroma. Perfumes were sometimes sprinkled or incense burned along the processional route. As faithful preachers of the good news about Christ, the apostles themselves formed "the pleasing aroma of Christ" (v. 15) rising up to God as a sweet fragrance. Irrespective of the human response to the gospel that brings life or brings death, its proclamation delights God's heart because it centers on the Son, whom he loves.

2:15 are being saved. Paul can speak of salvation in three tenses: past (Eph 2:5–8; Titus 3:4–5), present (here; 1 Cor 1:18), and future (Rom 5:9; 8:23; 1 Thess 1:10).

of Christ among those who are being saved and those who are perishing.[z] 16To the one we are an aroma
that brings death;[a] to the other, an aroma that brings life. And who is equal to such a task?[b] 17Unlike
so many, we do not peddle the word of God for profit.[c] On the contrary, in Christ we speak before God
with sincerity,[d] as those sent from God.[e]

3 Are we beginning to commend ourselves[f] again? Or do we need, like some people, letters of recommendation[g] to you or from you? 2You yourselves are our letter, written on our hearts, known and
read by everyone.[h] 3You show that you are a letter from Christ, the result of our ministry, written not
with ink but with the Spirit of the living God, not on tablets of stone[i] but on tablets of human hearts.[j]
4Such confidence[k] we have through Christ before God. 5Not that we are competent in ourselves to
claim anything for ourselves, but our competence comes from God.[l] 6He has made us competent as
ministers of a new covenant[m]—not of the letter but of the Spirit; for the letter kills, but the Spirit
gives life.[n]

The Greater Glory of the New Covenant

7Now if the ministry that brought death, which was engraved in letters on stone, came with glory, so
that the Israelites could not look steadily at the face of Moses because of its glory,[o] transitory though it
was, 8will not the ministry of the Spirit be even more glorious? 9If the ministry that brought condemnation[p] was glorious, how much more glorious is the ministry that brings righteousness![q] 10For what
was glorious has no glory now in comparison with the surpassing glory. 11And if what was transitory
came with glory, how much greater is the glory of that which lasts!
12Therefore, since we have such a hope, we are very bold.[r] 13We are not like Moses, who would put
a veil over his face[s] to prevent the Israelites from seeing the end of what was passing away. 14But their
minds were made dull,[t] for to this day the same veil remains when the old covenant[u] is read.[v] It has
not been removed, because only in Christ is it taken away. 15Even to this day when Moses is read, a veil
covers their hearts. 16But whenever anyone turns to the Lord,[w] the veil is taken away.[x] 17Now the Lord

2:15 [z] 1Co 1:18
2:16 [a] Lk 2:34 [b] 2Co 3:5,6
2:17 [c] 2Co 4:2 [d] 1Co 5:8 [e] 2Co 1:12
3:1 [f] 2Co 5:12; 12:11 [g] Ac 18:27
3:2 [h] 1Co 9:2
3:3 [i] Ex 24:12 [j] Pr 3:3; Jer 31:33; Eze 11:19
3:4 [k] Eph 3:12
3:5 [l] 1Co 15:10
3:6 [m] Lk 22:20 [n] Jn 6:63
3:7 [o] Ex 34:29-35
3:9 [p] ver 7 [q] Ro 1:17; 3:21,22
3:12 [r] Eph 6:19
3:13 [s] ver 7; Ex 34:33
3:14 [t] Ro 11:7,8 [u] Ac 13:15 [v] ver 6
3:16 [w] Ro 11:23 [x] Ex 34:34

2:17 peddle the word of God. The false teachers who had infiltrated the Corinthian church had converted preaching into a means of personal gain.

3:1–3 *The Results of the Ministry.* Paul's opponents apparently came to Corinth with letters of recommendation from Judea and demanded that he should produce his letters to prove he was not an impostor. Paul's response: "You yourselves are our letter" (v. 2). The Corinthians themselves, as believers in Christ, are Paul's eloquent testimonial that proves his apostolic status and authority. Christ, through the Spirit, authored this letter, and Paul was the scribe (an inference from "the result of our ministry," v. 3). It was not recorded in ink on papyrus nor engraved on lifeless tablets of stone (Exod 31:18; 32:15–16) but was indelibly inscribed on living tablets: sensitive human hearts (Jer 31:33; Ezek 11:19; 36:26–27).

3:4–6 *Competence for Service.* Paul disowns any qualification to claim credit for what was, in reality, God's work. His qualification and his competence for the work of the ministry were not through natural ability or personal initiative but by divine enabling (1 Cor 15:9–10). God gifted and motivated Paul to be an agent of a "new covenant" (v. 6; cf. 1 Cor 11:25; Jer 31:31–34; Mark 14:24) at his Damascus call, when he became Christ's "chosen instrument" and was filled with the Spirit (Acts 9:15,17–19). The basis of the old covenant between Yahweh and Israel was a lifeless written code or letter, "the Book of the Covenant" (Exod 24:7), which pronounced a sentence of death (Rom 7:9–11; Gal 3:10). The basis of the new covenant between God and the church is a dynamic, pervasive Spirit who transforms lives (Rom 7:6; 8:3–4). Where the letter or written law is powerless, the Spirit is powerful, producing holy lives and enabling people to meet "the righteous requirement of the law" (Rom 8:4).

3:7–18 *The Greater Glory of the New Covenant.* Both covenants were accompanied by glory, but so superior was the glory of the new covenant that the glory of the old faded into insignificance by comparison. This section has two parts: (1) vv. 7–11 comment on Exod 34:29–30, and the crucial terms are "glory" and "glorious"; (2) vv. 12–18 comment on Exod 34:33–35, and the pivotal terms are "bold" and "veil."

3:7–11 *Lesser and Greater Glory.* When Moses came down from Mount Sinai with the two tablets on which God wrote the Ten Commandments (Exod 34:29–30), his face shone so brightly that "the Israelites could not look steadily at [him]" (v. 7). If glory like this attended the giving of the law under the administration that brought death and condemned people, "how much more glorious is the ministry [of the Spirit] that brings righteousness!" (v. 9). If the sun is up, the moon no longer seems bright. The new covenant has "surpassing glory" (v. 10) since it more adequately reveals God's character.

3:12–18 *Veiling and Unveiling.* Moses used to veil or mask his face after he had come out of the "tent of meeting" and spoken to the people (Exod 33:7,9; 34:33). Paul assumes that Moses put on the veil not so much to prevent the Israelites from being dazzled by its brightness (cf. Exod 34:30) as to prevent them from gazing in amazement until his face totally lost its reflected glory. Moses knew that someday the newly established order at Mount Sinai was going to pass away. But the Jews of Moses' time failed to understand that, and right down to Paul's day a veil over Jewish hearts kept them from believing (vv. 14–15). Now that veil was lifted only as they came to be "in Christ" (v. 14) by turning "to the Lord" (v. 16).

3:16 the Lord. In the present era, "the LORD" (i.e., Yahweh) of Exod 34:34, to whom the unbeliever must turn, is the life-giving Spirit (v. 6).

3:17 the Lord is the Spirit. Paul is not identifying the risen Lord Jesus with the Holy Spirit. God the Father, the Lord Jesus, and the Holy Spirit are distinct persons although they all share the same nature. **freedom.** The Spirit gives believers freedom of access into God's presence without fear, as well as freedom from bondage to sin, to death, and to the law as a means of acquiring righteousness.

3:17 [y] Isa 61:1,2 [z] Jn 8:32
3:18 [a] 1Co 13:12 [b] 2Co 4:4,6 [c] Ro 8:29
4:1 [d] 1Co 7:25
4:2 [e] 1Co 4:5 [f] 2Co 2:17 [g] 2Co 5:11
4:3 [h] 2Co 2:12 [i] 2Co 3:14 [j] 1Co 1:18
4:4 [k] Jn 12:31 [l] 2Co 3:14
4:5 [m] 1Co 1:13 [n] 1Co 9:19
4:6 [o] Ge 1:3 [p] 2Pe 1:19
4:7 [q] Job 4:19; 2Co 5:1 [r] 1Co 2:5
4:8 [s] 2Co 7:5
4:9 [t] Jn 15:20 [u] Heb 13:5 [v] Ps 37:24
4:10 [w] Ro 6:5
4:11 [x] Ro 8:36
4:12 [y] 2Co 13:9
4:13 [z] Ps 116:10
4:14 [a] 1Th 4:14 [b] Eph 5:27
4:15 [c] 2Co 1:11
4:16 [d] Ro 7:22

is the Spirit,[y] and where the Spirit of the Lord is, there is freedom.[z] 18 And we all, who with unveiled
faces contemplate[a][a] the Lord's glory,[b] are being transformed into his image[c] with ever-increasing glory,
which comes from the Lord, who is the Spirit.

Present Weakness and Resurrection Life

4 Therefore, since through God's mercy[d] we have this ministry, we do not lose heart. 2 Rather, we have
renounced secret and shameful ways;[e] we do not use deception, nor do we distort the word of God.[f]
On the contrary, by setting forth the truth plainly we commend ourselves to everyone's conscience[g] in
the sight of God. 3 And even if our gospel[h] is veiled,[i] it is veiled to those who are perishing.[j] 4 The god[k]
of this age has blinded[l] the minds of unbelievers, so that they cannot see the light of the gospel that
displays the glory of Christ, who is the image of God. 5 For what we preach is not ourselves,[m] but Jesus
Christ as Lord, and ourselves as your servants[n] for Jesus' sake. 6 For God, who said, "Let light shine out
of darkness,"[b][o] made his light shine in our hearts[p] to give us the light of the knowledge of God's glory
displayed in the face of Christ.
7 But we have this treasure in jars of clay[q] to show that this all-surpassing power is from God[r] and
not from us. 8 We are hard pressed on every side,[s] but not crushed; perplexed, but not in despair; 9 persecuted,[t] but not abandoned;[u] struck down, but not destroyed.[v] 10 We always carry around in our body
the death of Jesus, so that the life of Jesus may also be revealed in our body.[w] 11 For we who are alive
are always being given over to death for Jesus' sake,[x] so that his life may also be revealed in our mortal
body. 12 So then, death is at work in us, but life is at work in you.[y]
13 It is written: "I believed; therefore I have spoken."[c][z] Since we have that same spirit of[d] faith, we also
believe and therefore speak, 14 because we know that the one who raised the Lord Jesus from the dead will
also raise us with Jesus[a] and present us with you to himself.[b] 15 All this is for your benefit, so that the grace
that is reaching more and more people may cause thanksgiving[c] to overflow to the glory of God.
16 Therefore we do not lose heart. Though outwardly we are wasting away, yet inwardly[d] we are being

[a] *18* Or *reflect* [b] *6* Gen. 1:3 [c] *13* Psalm 116:10 (see Septuagint) [d] *13* Or *Spirit-given*

3:18 Here Paul draws his conclusion regarding the superiority of the new covenant. Under the new economy, (1) not one man alone but all believers see and then reflect "the Lord's glory"; (2) unlike the Jews, who still read the law with veiled hearts (vv. 14–15), Christians see the glory of Yahweh (which is Christ) "with unveiled faces" in the mirror of the gospel; (3) glory is displayed inwardly in the character, not outwardly on the face; (4) far from waxing and waning, this glory progressively increases until the believer gains through resurrection a "glorious body" like Christ's (Phil 3:21).

4:1–18 *Present Weakness and Resurrection Life.* This chapter contains five main themes: light shining in the midst of darkness (vv. 3–6), power in the midst of weakness (vv. 7–9), life in the midst of death (vv. 10–12), faith leading to speech (vv. 13–14), and glory through suffering (vv. 16–18). Antitheses and paradoxes are common in Paul's letters.

4:1–6 *The Light Brought by the Gospel.* Although unbelievers remain blind to the light of the gospel, God has caused that light to illuminate the hearts of believers.

4:2 Paul renounced the "secret and shameful ways" of the false teachers at Corinth that were totally foreign to a Christian minister's conduct.

4:3 it is veiled to those who are perishing. The gospel is veiled to them not because of the gospel itself (it brings enlightenment, v. 4b) nor because Paul is its agent but because Satan blinds their minds to its truth (v. 4a).

4:4 god of this age. Satan rules over the present age (John 12:31; 1 John 5:19), which has made him its god. Satan is not the god of the age to come. **Christ, who is the image of God.** Christ visibly and perfectly represents or expresses the unseen God (John 1:18; Col 1:15).

4:5 Jesus Christ as Lord. Acknowledgment of Jesus as Lord leads naturally and inevitably to lowly and unquestioning service to one's fellow believers. To confess "Jesus is Lord" (1 Cor 12:3; Rom 10:9) involves saying to other Christians, "I am your slave, for Jesus' sake." **your servants.** Paul sees himself related to his converts not as a spiritual overlord (1:24) but as a willing slave as well as a concerned father (1 Cor 4:15).

4:6 In the second creation, as in the first, God disperses darkness and creates light. In the first creation, it was a personal word: "Let there be light" (Gen 1:3); in the second, it is a personal act: "God … made his light shine in our hearts."

4:7–15 *The Trials and Rewards of Apostolic Service.* This section includes the second of five lists of Paul's hardships found in his letters to Corinth (vv. 8–9; 6:4–10; 11:23–28; 12:10; 1 Cor 4:9–13).

4:7 this treasure. The gospel. **jars of clay.** The people to whom God entrusts the gospel (1 Thess 2:4). Although clay jars had little value or beauty in themselves, they could contain priceless treasure. Paul is not disparaging the physical body but contrasting the relative insignificance and unattractiveness of the bearers of the gospel light with the inestimable worth and beauty of the gospel itself.

4:10–11 "The death [or dying] of Jesus" (v. 10) that Paul carries around in his body is his "always being given over to death for Jesus' sake" (v. 11). He constantly faces hazards: "I face death every day" (1 Cor 15:31).

4:12 Paul is basically saying, "I am always exposed to physical death for your sake (v. 15); you have spiritual life as a result." The link between his experience and theirs is the divine comfort that he receives in the midst of his afflictions and then could dispense to the Corinthians (1:4).

4:13–14 Paul patiently endures trials (vv. 8–12) because he shared the psalmist's conviction that faith cannot remain silent (Ps 116:10) and he knows that Christ's resurrection guarantees the resurrection of believers.

4:16–18 *Glory Through Suffering.* "Therefore we do not lose heart" (v. 16) looks back to vv. 1,14–15. Paul gives several reasons for refusing to be discouraged in spite of overwhelming difficulties: (1) he was commissioned by God as a minister of a new and superior covenant (v. 1); (2) he will share Christ's triumphant resurrection from the dead

renewed[e] day by day. 17 For our light and momentary troubles are achieving for us an eternal glory that
far outweighs them all.[f] 18 So we fix our eyes not on what is seen, but on what is unseen,[g] since what is
seen is temporary, but what is unseen is eternal.

Awaiting the New Body

5 For we know that if the earthly[h] tent[i] we live in is destroyed, we have a building from God, an eternal
house in heaven, not built by human hands. 2 Meanwhile we groan,[j] longing to be clothed instead with
our heavenly dwelling,[k] 3 because when we are clothed, we will not be found naked. 4 For while we are in this
tent, we groan and are burdened, because we do not wish to be unclothed but to be clothed instead with our
heavenly dwelling,[l] so that what is mortal may be swallowed up by life. 5 Now the one who has fashioned
us for this very purpose is God, who has given us the Spirit as a deposit, guaranteeing what is to come.[m]

6 Therefore we are always confident and know that as long as we are at home in the body we are
away from the Lord. 7 For we live by faith, not by sight.[n] 8 We are confident, I say, and would prefer to be
away from the body and at home with the Lord.[o] 9 So we make it our goal to please him,[p] whether we
are at home in the body or away from it. 10 For we must all appear before the judgment seat of Christ, so
that each of us may receive what is due us[q] for the things done while in the body, whether good or bad.

The Ministry of Reconciliation

11 Since, then, we know what it is to fear the Lord,[r] we try to persuade others. What we are is plain to
God, and I hope it is also plain to your conscience.[s] 12 We are not trying to commend ourselves to you

4:16 [e] Col 3:10
4:17 [f] Ro 8:18; 1Pe 1:6,7
4:18 [g] Ro 8:24; Heb 11:1
5:1 [h] 1Co 15:47 [i] 2Pe 1:13,14
5:2 [j] ver 4; Ro 8:23 [k] 1Co 15:53,54
5:4 [l] 1Co 15:53,54
5:5 [m] Ro 8:23; 2Co 1:22
5:7 [n] 1Co 13:12
5:8 [o] Php 1:23
5:9 [p] Ro 14:18
5:10 [q] Mt 16:27; Ro 14:10; Eph 6:8
5:11 [r] Heb 10:31; Jude 23 [s] 2Co 4:2

(v. 14); (3) his immediate task is to promote the Corinthians' spiritual welfare and the glory of God (v. 15). Now he adds another reason: he will receive "an eternal glory" (v. 17) that is out of all proportion to his "light and momentary troubles" (v. 17; cf. Rom 8:18).

4:16 wasting away ... being renewed. Matching the progressive weakening of Paul's physical powers is the daily renewal of his inner person (cf. Eph 3:16) that is part of the progressive transformation of all believers into the image of Christ (2 Cor 3:18), a process resurrection will accelerate and complete (4:14).

4:17 far outweighs. Since it is actually the troubles that produce the glory (here regarded as a substantial entity), the greater the affliction Paul suffered, the greater the glory these troubles produced for him. When viewed in the light of eternity, present "troubles" seem "light and momentary."

4:18 seen ... unseen. The contrast is not exactly between visible and invisible realities, but is between what mortals can now see and what they cannot yet see, between the "already" and the "not yet" (cf. 1 Cor 13:12; Rom 8:24–25). Paul is certainly not rejecting interest in the visible world. Rather, his affections are set on the realm above (Col 3:1–2), on lasting realities as yet unseen, on "the hope stored up ... in heaven" (Col 1:5; cf. 1 Pet 1:4).

5:1–10 *Awaiting the New Body.* Paul's dramatic encounter with death (1:8–11), constant suffering (4:8–12; 11:23–29), and progressive physical weakness (4:16) prompt him to reflect on the nature of death for Christians. He specifies three sources of divine comfort available to believers who face death: (1) they will certainly possess a heavenly body (vv. 1–2); (2) they presently possess the Spirit as God's pledge of a resurrection transformation (vv. 4–5); and (3) death means departing into Christ's immediate presence (v. 8).

5:1 As a leatherworker whose trade includes making and repairing tents (Acts 18:3), Paul naturally compares his present body to an "earthly tent." He calls his future body a "building" that God supplies and a "house" destined to last forever "in heaven ... our heavenly dwelling" (vv. 2,4). He also calls it "a spiritual body" (1 Cor 15:44), which perfectly responds to the resurrected human spirit or to the Holy Spirit and is perfectly suited to heaven.

5:2–4 groan ... groan ... burdened. Paul is frustrated with the limitations and disabilities of existence on earth, a feeling that is prompted by his intense longing for his perfect heavenly embodiment (cf. Rom 8:19–23; Phil 3:20–21).

5:3–4 naked ... unclothed. It seems that some Corinthians want to be permanently disembodied in the life to come, a view Paul here strongly rejects. But some commentators believe these terms refer to the state between death and resurrection, when believers are waiting for their resurrection bodies.

5:5 a deposit, guaranteeing what is to come. Greek *arrabōn.* This rich commercial term has two meanings: (1) a pledge or guarantee that differs in kind from the final payment but makes it obligatory; (2) a first installment of a purchase, a down payment or deposit, that requires further payments.

5:7–8 Living "by faith" becomes living "by sight" when we exchange temporary residence in our "earthly tent" (v. 1) for permanent residence "with the Lord" (v. 8), a perfected form of the intimate fellowship with Christ that the believer experiences on earth.

5:9 we make it our goal to please him. Believers seek the Master's constant approval because of their destiny with him (v. 8) and because they are accountable to him (v. 10).

5:10 For Paul, God's justifying us on the basis of faith and recompensing us in accordance with works are complementary ideas. "The judgment seat of Christ" determines not status but reward. Christians are already delivered from "the works of the law" (Rom 3:28), or the law that requires works, through justifying faith, and they are presently committed to "work produced by faith" (1 Thess 1:3), which Christ will assess and reward at his tribunal.

5:11—6:2 *The Ministry of Reconciliation.* God reconciles sinners on the basis of Christ's atoning death, which appeases his holy displeasure against their sin, removes the enmity between them and him, and restores their relationship with him (cf. Rom 5:10–11; Col 1:20–22). God entrusts to Paul and his fellow evangelists the task of announcing this divine act and appealing for a human response: "Be reconciled to God" (5:20). Reconciliation is integral to Paul's (and the NT's) central theme of God the Father's salvation through Christ and the Spirit. In that salvation, God justifies sinners and thereby reconciles and adopts them as his sons and daughters.

5:11–15 *Motivation for Service.* Paul's awareness of his accountability to Christ (v. 10) and Christ's shining example of self-sacrificing devotion (v. 14) motivate him in all his service.

5:11 Paul tries to "persuade others" about the truth of the gospel, his pure motives (cf. 1:12), and his sound apostolic credentials and conduct (cf. 3:1–6; 4:1–6).

A cast from a portion of the Ara Pacis altar on display in the Vatican Museum. Men are wearing togas with tunics under them. Paul awaits his new body, longing to be clothed instead with his heavenly dwelling (2 Cor 5:2–4).
Kim Walton, taken at the Vatican Museum

5:12 [t]2Co 3:1 [u]2Co 1:14
5:13 [v]2Co 11:1,16,17
5:14 [w]Gal 2:20
5:15 [x]Ro 14:7-9
5:16 [y]2Co 11:18
5:17 [z]Gal 6:15
[a]Isa 65:17; Rev 21:4,5
5:18 [b]Ro 5:10; Col 1:20
5:19 [c]Ro 4:8
5:20 [d]2Co 6:1; Eph 6:20

again,[t] but are giving you an opportunity to take pride in us,[u] so that you can answer those who take
pride in what is seen rather than in what is in the heart. 13If we are "out of our mind,"[v] as some say,
it is for God; if we are in our right mind, it is for you. 14For Christ's love compels us, because we are
convinced that one died for all, and therefore all died.[w] 15And he died for all, that those who live should
no longer live for themselves[x] but for him who died for them and was raised again.

16So from now on we regard no one from a worldly[y] point of view. Though we once regarded Christ
in this way, we do so no longer. 17Therefore, if anyone is in Christ, the new creation[z] has come:[a] The
old has gone, the new is here![a] 18All this is from God, who reconciled us to himself through Christ[b] and
gave us the ministry of reconciliation: 19that God was reconciling the world to himself in Christ, not
counting people's sins against them.[c] And he has committed to us the message of reconciliation. 20We
are therefore Christ's ambassadors,[d] as though God were making his appeal through us. We implore

[a] 17 Or *Christ, that person is a new creation.*

5:13 Apparently Paul's critics accused him of being "out of [his] mind," perhaps because his teaching seemed difficult to understand (cf. Acts 26:24) or because he worked so tirelessly.

5:14–15 all … all … all. These probably refer to all people without distinction, while "those who live" (v. 15) are those who are "alive to God in Christ Jesus" (Rom 6:11). **all died.** In the death of Christ, all underwent the death deservedly theirs because of sin. The scope of redemption is universal since God's offer of salvation excludes no one, but the application of redemption is limited since not all people appropriate the benefits afforded by this universally offered salvation. Some, however, restrict the three cases of "all" to Christians. In this view, Paul is saying Christ died for all those who through faith embrace God's provision of salvation. They will see the "all" here as the same as the second "many" in Rom 5:15,19.

5:16—6:2 *The Messengers of Reconciliation.* Although only God brought about reconciliation (5:18), he appeals to people through his co-workers, who are Christ's ambassadors, to be reconciled to him (5:20).

5:16 Before his conversion Paul regarded Jesus "from a worldly point of view" as a false messiah whose followers needed to be destroyed (Acts 9:1–2; 26:9–11). Since his conversion, he views people not primarily in terms of ethnicity but according to their relation to Jesus the Messiah. The Jew-Gentile division is now less important for him than the believer-unbeliever distinction (Rom 2:28–29; 10:12–13; Gal 3:28; Eph 2:11–22).

5:17 the new creation has come. When "anyone" comes to be "in Christ" by faith, this signals the restoration and fulfillment of God's purposes in creation (cf. Rom 8:19–23; Eph 2:10). Or it may mean there is a "new" act of "creation" on God's part when he makes his light shine in the believer's heart (2 Cor 4:6). The translation given in the NIV text note—"that person is a new creation"—refers to the radical reorientation of life that comes through regeneration. When a person becomes a Christian, God totally restructures their life, altering its whole fabric—thinking, feeling, willing, and acting. In this "new creation," however understood, one set of conditions or relationships has passed out of existence and a new set has come to stay.

5:19 God was reconciling the world to himself in Christ. In the person and through the work of Christ, God "was reconciling the world" of human beings "to himself." It is also possible to translate this clause as "God was in Christ, reconciling the world to himself"; i.e., it was only because all God's fullness dwelt in Christ (Col 1:19; 2:9) that God accomplished reconciliation. See "Creation," p. 2642.

you on Christ's behalf: Be reconciled to God. 21God made him who had no sin[e] to be sin[a] for us, so that
in him we might become the righteousness of God.[f]

6 As God's co-workers[g] we urge you not to receive God's grace in vain. 2For he says,

> "In the time of my favor I heard you,
> and in the day of salvation I helped you."[b][h]

I tell you, now is the time of God's favor, now is the day of salvation.

Paul's Hardships

3We put no stumbling block in anyone's path,[i] so that our ministry will not be discredited. 4Rather, as
servants of God we commend ourselves in every way: in great endurance; in troubles, hardships and distresses; 5in beatings, imprisonments[j] and riots; in hard work, sleepless nights and hunger;[k] 6in purity,
understanding, patience and kindness; in the Holy Spirit[l] and in sincere love; 7in truthful speech[m] and
in the power of God; with weapons of righteousness[n] in the right hand and in the left; 8through glory
and dishonor,[o] bad report and good report; genuine, yet regarded as impostors;[p] 9known, yet regarded
as unknown; dying,[q] and yet we live on;[r] beaten, and yet not killed; 10sorrowful, yet always rejoicing;[s]
poor, yet making many rich;[t] having nothing, and yet possessing everything.[u]

11We have spoken freely to you, Corinthians, and opened wide our hearts to you.[v] 12We are not withholding our affection from you, but you are withholding yours from us. 13As a fair exchange—I speak
as to my children[w]—open wide your hearts also.

Warning Against Idolatry

14Do not be yoked together[x] with unbelievers. For what do righteousness and wickedness have in
common? Or what fellowship can light have with darkness?[y] 15What harmony is there between Christ

[a] *21* Or *be a sin offering* [b] *2* Isaiah 49:8

5:21 [e] Heb 4:15; 1Pe 2:22,24; 1Jn 3:5 [f] Ro 1:17
6:1 [g] 1Co 3:9; 2Co 5:20
6:2 [h] Isa 49:8
6:3 [i] Ro 14:13,20; 1Co 9:12; 10:32
6:5 [j] 2Co 11:23-25 [k] 1Co 4:11
6:6 [l] 1Th 1:5
6:7 [m] 2Co 4:2 [n] 2Co 10:4; Eph 6:10-18
6:8 [o] 1Co 4:10 [p] Mt 27:63
6:9 [q] Ro 8:36 [r] 2Co 1:8-10; 4:10,11
6:10 [s] 2Co 7:4 [t] 2Co 8:9 [u] Ro 8:32; 1Co 3:21
6:11 [v] 2Co 7:3
6:13 [w] 1Co 4:14
6:14 [x] 1Co 5:9,10 [y] Eph 5:7,11; 1Jn 1:6

5:21 God made him ... to be sin. Paul wants to say more than that Christ was made a sin offering but less than that Christ became a sinner. God treated Christ as if he were a sinner, and Christ became the object of God's wrath and bore the penalty of sin in our place. The Son's firm resolution to go to Jerusalem to suffer (Mark 8:31; Luke 9:51) matched the Father's set purpose not to spare his own Son but to give him up for us all (Rom 8:32). **him who had no sin.** Christ "had no sin" both inwardly and outwardly (cf. Heb 4:15; 7:26; 1 Pet 2:22; 1 John 3:5). He was without any acquaintance with sin that might have come through his ever having a sinful attitude or doing a sinful act. **righteousness of God.** Being "in Christ" ("in him") makes believers righteous before God; they "become the righteousness of God" (cf. Rom 5:19). This does not mean believers become as righteous as God inherently is; unlike us, he does not and cannot sin. Rather, believers are given a new and permanent right standing in the divine court, "the righteousness that comes from God on the basis of faith" (Phil 3:9).

6:1 not to receive God's grace in vain. Paul exhorts the Corinthians not to show by their lives that they received God's grace to no purpose or to spurn God's grace that was always being offered to them.

6:3–13 *Paul's Hardships.* It seems that various charges had been made against Paul due to the success of his ministry and human jealousy. By listing his hardships (cf. 4:8–12; 11:23–29; 12:10), he was providing the Corinthians with material they could use in defending him (5:12) and validating his credentials as an ambassador of Christ (5:20) and as a suffering and therefore true apostle. Also, 6:4–10 prepares for his passionate request to the Corinthians for openness and warm mutual relations (vv. 11–13). How could they, in their relative comfort, not be moved by his catalog of afflictions to deeper affection for their spiritual father?

6:3 Paul was concerned that no minister of reconciliation (5:18) be guilty of dishonest or inconsistent conduct and that no evidence be given to adversaries who wished to discredit the gospel. On the contrary, every Christian's life should be the gospel's most eloquent advertisement.

6:4–10 In this catalog of hardships and triumphs, Paul first mentions outward circumstances, such as general trials, sufferings inflicted by others, and self-inflicted hardships (vv. 4b–5), then inward qualities (v. 6), spiritual equipment (v. 7), and finally the extremes and tensions of apostolic life and ministry (vv. 8–10).

6:6 in the Holy Spirit. In the middle of a catalog of moral virtues, this possibly means "by the gifts of the Holy Spirit."

6:11–13 Corinthians. Paul addresses his audience by name only when his emotions are deeply stirred (cf. Gal 3:1; Phil 4:15). While he desires warm and open family relationships with his converts, he is very aware that affection can only be given, not taken.

6:14—7:1 *Warning Against Idolatry.* This call to holiness of life forms a minor digression, for 7:2 repeats the request of 6:13. The apparent abruptness of 6:14 may be explained by Paul's coming to the point immediately, since both Paul and the Corinthians know that some or many of them have an uneasy conscience about their continuing pagan associations. He sets out "the truth plainly" (4:2), "speaking the truth in love" (Eph 4:15).

6:14–16 This is not an injunction against all association with unbelievers (cf. 1 Cor 5:9–10; 10:27). Paul actually encouraged the Christian spouse of an unbeliever to maintain the relationship as long as possible (1 Cor 7:12–16). Rather, Paul prohibits forming close attachments with non-Christians that might compromise their faith. Examples include contracting marriages between believers and unbelievers (cf. Deut 7:1–3), initiating frivolous litigation before unbelieving officials in cases involving believers (1 Cor 6:1–8), and flirting with idolatry by sharing meals at idol shrines or continuing to attend ceremonies in pagan temples or maintaining membership in some local pagan cult.

6:14 Do not be yoked together with unbelievers. Paul is content to state a general principle that needs specific application under the Holy Spirit's guidance. Each of Paul's five rhetorical questions (vv. 14–16) assumes a strong negative answer: "None whatever!" Intimate relationships or fellowship between believers and unbelievers are incongruous (1 Cor 10:21). See note on vv. 14–16.

6:15 Belial. Means "worthlessness" or "destruction," but here it is a name for the devil.

6:15 [z]Ac 5:14
6:16 [a]1Co 3:16
[b]Lev 26:12; Jer 32:38; Eze 37:27
6:17 [c]Rev 18:4
[d]Isa 52:11
6:18 [e]Isa 43:6
7:1 [f]2Co 6:17,18
7:2 [g]2Co 6:12,13
7:3 [h]2Co 6:11,12
7:4 [i]2Co 6:10
7:5 [j]2Co 2:13 [k]2Co 4:8
[l]Dt 32:25
7:6 [m]2Co 1:3,4 [n]ver 13; 2Co 2:13

and Belial[a]? Or what does a believer[z] have in common with an unbeliever? 16What agreement is there
between the temple of God and idols? For we are the temple[a] of the living God. As God has said:

> "I will live with them
> and walk among them,
> and I will be their God,
> and they will be my people."[b][b]

17Therefore,

> "Come out from them[c]
> and be separate,
> says the Lord.
> Touch no unclean thing,
> and I will receive you."[c][d]

18And,

> "I will be a Father to you,
> and you will be my sons and daughters,[e]
> says the Lord Almighty."[d]

7 Therefore, since we have these promises,[f] dear friends, let us purify ourselves from everything that
contaminates body and spirit, perfecting holiness out of reverence for God.

Paul's Joy Over the Church's Repentance

2Make room for us in your hearts.[g] We have wronged no one, we have corrupted no one, we have
exploited no one. 3I do not say this to condemn you; I have said before that you have such a place in
our hearts[h] that we would live or die with you. 4I have spoken to you with great frankness; I take great
pride in you. I am greatly encouraged; in all our troubles my joy knows no bounds.[i]
5For when we came into Macedonia,[j] we had no rest, but we were harassed at every turn[k]—conflicts
on the outside, fears within.[l] 6But God, who comforts the downcast,[m] comforted us by the coming of
Titus,[n] 7and not only by his coming but also by the comfort you had given him. He told us about your
longing for me, your deep sorrow, your ardent concern for me, so that my joy was greater than ever.

a *15* Greek *Beliar*, a variant of *Belial* *b* *16* Lev. 26:12; Jer. 32:38; Ezek. 37:27 *c* *17* Isaiah 52:11; Ezek. 20:34,41 *d* *18* 2 Samuel 7:14; 7:8

6:16 we are the temple of the living God. Here "we" refers to the whole body of Christ, the total Christian community (cf. 1 Cor 3:16–17), "a dwelling in which God lives by his Spirit" (Eph 2:22). Paul expresses the complementary truth in 1 Cor 6:19: believers' bodies are "temples of the Holy Spirit."

6:17 separate. In keeping with the promise of his presence and protection (v. 16), God demands that his people be pure and separate from evil. Isa 52:11 calls for God's people to "depart" (i.e., separate) from Babylon, with its pagan idolatry. Paul calls believers to separate from unbelievers (2 Cor 6:14), with their pagan way of life. The passage is not dealing with possible grounds for separating from other believers.

7:1 these promises. The chain of OT quotations in 6:16–18 (see NIV text notes) stress the privilege of being the dwelling place of God (6:16) and the benefits of obeying the divine will (6:17–18). Having these promises, Christians must avoid every possible source of defilement in their whole personality, outwardly and inwardly, "body and spirit." If they do this, they will be bringing their holiness nearer to completion "out of reverence for God." Only at the second advent do believers become "blameless and holy" (1 Thess 3:13; cf. Phil 3:12–14).

7:2–16 *Paul's Joy Over the Church's Repentance.* When Titus, Paul's emissary to Corinth, arrived safely in Macedonia with news of the Corinthians' positive reaction to the "severe letter" (see Introduction: Date; Occasion and Purpose), Paul felt immense relief, comfort, and joy (vv. 4,6–7,9,13,16). Paul returns in v. 5 to his travel narrative that was suspended at 2:13 (2:14—7:4 is the longest digression in all Paul's letters).

7:2 wronged no one. Evidently Paul had been charged with wronging, corrupting, and exploiting some people at Corinth. As before (cf. 4:2; 5:11; 6:3; 1 Cor 4:4), he can do no more in reply than insist that the charges are groundless, appealing to his clear conscience and the Corinthians' knowledge of his conduct.

7:5–7 As at Troas earlier (2:13), Paul was restless when he arrived in Macedonia because he was anxious about how the Corinthians received Titus, about Titus's safety in travel, and about how the Corinthians would respond to his "severe letter." In addition to these "fears within" (v. 5), there were also now "conflicts on the outside" (v. 5), perhaps violent quarreling that focused on Paul or persistent opposition. It seems to Paul that from a human point of view his whole future as an apostle to the Gentiles is in the balance.

7:6 God, who comforts the downcast. This is one of several timeless affirmations about God's character and actions in this letter (cf. 1:3–4,9; 13:11). Here God comforts the dejected apostle in three ways: (1) by Titus's safe arrival (here), (2) by Titus's positive experience at Corinth (v. 7), and (3) by the reassuring news Titus brought about the Corinthians' attitude toward Paul (v. 7). No Scriptural verse better sums up Paul's feelings expressed in vv. 5–7 than Ps 94:19: "When anxiety was great within me, your [the Lord's] consolation brought me joy."

8 Even if I caused you sorrow by my letter,[o] I do not regret it. Though I did regret it—I see that my
letter hurt you, but only for a little while— 9 yet now I am happy, not because you were made sorry,
but because your sorrow led you to repentance. For you became sorrowful as God intended and so were
not harmed in any way by us. 10 Godly sorrow brings repentance that leads to salvation[p] and leaves no
regret, but worldly sorrow brings death. 11 See what this godly sorrow has produced in you: what earnestness, what eagerness to clear yourselves, what indignation, what alarm, what longing, what concern,[q] what readiness to see justice done. At every point you have proved yourselves to be innocent in
this matter. 12 So even though I wrote to you,[r] it was neither on account of the one who did the wrong[s]
nor on account of the injured party, but rather that before God you could see for yourselves how devoted
to us you are. 13 By all this we are encouraged.

In addition to our own encouragement, we were especially delighted to see how happy Titus[t] was,
because his spirit has been refreshed by all of you. 14 I had boasted to him about you,[u] and you have
not embarrassed me. But just as everything we said to you was true, so our boasting about you to Titus[v] has proved to be true as well. 15 And his affection for you is all the greater when he remembers
that you were all obedient,[w] receiving him with fear and trembling.[x] 16 I am glad I can have complete
confidence in you.[y]

The Collection for the Lord's People

8 And now, brothers and sisters, we want you to know about the grace that God has given the Macedonian[z] churches. 2 In the midst of a very severe trial, their overflowing joy and their extreme
poverty welled up in rich generosity. 3 For I testify that they gave as much as they were able,[a] and even
beyond their ability. Entirely on their own, 4 they urgently pleaded with us for the privilege of sharing
in this service[b] to the Lord's people.[c] 5 And they exceeded our expectations: They gave themselves first
of all to the Lord, and then by the will of God also to us. 6 So we urged[d] Titus,[e] just as he had earlier
made a beginning, to bring also to completion[f] this act of grace on your part. 7 But since you excel in

7:8 [o] 2Co 2:2,4
7:10 [p] Ac 11:18
7:11 [q] ver 7
7:12 [r] ver 8; 2Co 2:3,9 [s] 1Co 5:1,2
7:13 [t] ver 6; 2Co 2:13
7:14 [u] ver 4 [v] ver 6
7:15 [w] 2Co 2:9 [x] Php 2:12
7:16 [y] 2Co 2:3
8:1 [z] Ac 16:9
8:3 [a] 1Co 16:2
8:4 [b] Ac 24:17 [c] Ro 15:25; 2Co 9:1
8:6 [d] ver 17; 2Co 12:18 [e] ver 16,23 [f] ver 10,11

7:10 Godly sorrow ... worldly sorrow. There are two ways to react to pain or sorrow: (1) Sorrow borne God's way ("godly sorrow," or sorrow as God intended) always produces a change of heart, and this repentance "leads to salvation" (both present spiritual vitality and future eternal life) and therefore gives no cause for regret. (2) Sorrow borne in a worldly way ("worldly sorrow") does not lead to repentance but has the deadly effect of producing resentment or bitterness. What makes suffering remedial is not actually experiencing it but reacting to it: a "godly" or positive reaction brings spiritual benefit, both now and in the hereafter, whereas a "worldly" or negative reaction causes serious harm.
7:12 As it is stated, Paul's sole purpose in writing the "severe letter" was that the Corinthians would recognize "before God" how devoted to their spiritual father they really were. **neither ... nor ... but.** Not a contrast but a comparison: "not so much this or this as that" (see note on 2:4). So the purpose of the "severe letter" was also to punish the guilty party ("the one who did the wrong," the man who had publicly insulted or opposed Paul or his representative) and vindicate "the injured party" (Paul himself or his representative).
8:1—9:15 *Paul's Summons to Complete the Collection for Believers in Jerusalem.* From AD 52–57, a considerable proportion of Paul's time and energy was devoted to organizing a collection among his Gentile churches for "the poor among the Lord's people in Jerusalem" (Rom 15:26) who had material needs. Paul's aim in chs. 8–9 is not simply to have the Christians in Corinth finalize their contribution to this collection (8:6,11) and do so before he arrives (9:4–5), but to have them contribute generously. Of the three main sections in these two chapters (8:1–15; 8:16—9:5; 9:6–15), the first and third focus on this "generosity" (8:2; 9:11,13)—its need (8:1–15) and its results (9:6–15).

Chs. 8–9 highlight several characteristics of genuine Christian stewardship. It is voluntary, not enforced (8:3; 9:5,7); generous, not parsimonious (8:2; 9:6,13); enthusiastic, not grudging (8:4,11–12; 9:7); deliberate, not haphazard (9:7); and sensible, not reckless (8:11–13).

8:1–15 *The Collection for the Lord's People.* There were several reasons for the continuing poverty in Jerusalem: (1) After their conversion to Christ, many Jews in Jerusalem would have been ostracized socially and economically. (2) The experiment in community sharing (described in Acts 2:44–45; 4:32,34–35) may have aggravated, though it did not cause, their poverty. (3) Persistent food shortages in Judea because of overpopulation culminated in the famine of AD 46 (Acts 11:27–30). (4) As the mother church of Christendom, the Jerusalem church had to support a proportionately large number of teachers and probably had to provide hospitality for frequent Christian visitors to the holy city. (5) Jews in Judea were subject to crippling twofold taxation—Jewish and Roman—which in the first century may have been as much as 40 percent.
8:1–6 *The Generosity of the Macedonians.* Tactfully, Paul begins with an example, not a plea. Although the Macedonian churches (such as those at Philippi, Thessalonica, and Berea) were at that time facing "a very severe trial" (v. 2) involving persecution (cf. 1 Thess 1:6; 2:14), they had contributed extremely generously (see note on 8:2).
8:2 This verse might be translated: "Their [the Macedonians'] exuberant joy and rock-bottom poverty combined to overflow in lavish generosity." Just as material prosperity may conceal spiritual poverty, as in the case of the Laodiceans (Rev 3:14–22), so also material poverty may cloak spiritual wealth, as in the case of the Macedonians. **rich generosity.** Paul makes three points concerning the Macedonians: (1) They gave far more generously than their slender means and adverse circumstances really permitted them to do (v. 3). (2) Acting on their own initiative (v. 3c), they "urgently pleaded [with Paul] for the privilege" (v. 4) of participating in the project. (3) They "exceeded [Paul's] expectations" (v. 5) by not restricting their contribution to financial aid. They realized that serving Christ involves serving his servants and that serving them is, in reality, serving Christ.
8:7–12 *A Plea for Liberal Giving.* Paul has encouraged the Corinthians

8:7 [g] 2Co 9:8 [h] 1Co 1:5
8:8 [i] 1Co 7:6
8:9 [j] 2Co 13:14 [k] Mt 20:28; Php 2:6-8
8:10 [l] 1Co 7:25,40 [m] 1Co 16:2,3; 2Co 9:2
8:11 [n] 2Co 9:2
8:12 [o] Mk 12:43,44; Lk 21:3
8:14 [p] 2Co 9:12
8:15 [q] Ex 16:18
8:16 [r] 2Co 2:14 [s] Rev 17:17 [t] 2Co 2:13
8:17 [u] ver 6
8:18 [v] 2Co 12:18 [w] 1Co 7:17 [x] 2Co 2:12
8:19 [y] 1Co 16:3,4

everything[g] — in faith, in speech, in knowledge,[h] in complete earnestness and in the love we have kindled in you[a] — see that you also excel in this grace of giving.
[8]I am not commanding you,[i] but I want to test the sincerity of your love by comparing it with the
earnestness of others. [9]For you know the grace of our Lord Jesus Christ,[j] that though he was rich, yet
for your sake he became poor,[k] so that you through his poverty might become rich.
[10]And here is my judgment[l] about what is best for you in this matter. Last year you were the first not
only to give but also to have the desire to do so.[m] [11]Now finish the work, so that your eager willingness[n]
to do it may be matched by your completion of it, according to your means. [12]For if the willingness
is there, the gift is acceptable according to what one has,[o] not according to what one does not have.
[13]Our desire is not that others might be relieved while you are hard pressed, but that there might be
equality. [14]At the present time your plenty will supply what they need,[p] so that in turn their plenty will
supply what you need. The goal is equality, [15]as it is written: "The one who gathered much did not have
too much, and the one who gathered little did not have too little."[b][q]

Titus Sent to Receive the Collection

[16]Thanks be to God,[r] who put into the heart[s] of Titus[t] the same concern I have for you. [17]For Titus
not only welcomed our appeal, but he is coming to you with much enthusiasm and on his own initiative.[u] [18]And we are sending along with him the brother[v] who is praised by all the churches[w] for his
service to the gospel.[x] [19]What is more, he was chosen by the churches to accompany us[y] as we carry the

[a] 7 Some manuscripts *and in your love for us* [b] 15 Exodus 16:18

to complete their contribution by appealing to the example of the Macedonians (vv. 1–5) and the Corinthians' own promising beginning (v. 6). Now he appeals to their desire for spiritual excellence (v. 7), the eagerness of the Macedonians (v. 8), the supreme example of Christ (v. 9), and finally their need to match their eager willingness to contribute with a successful completion of their giving (vv. 10–12).

8:9 became poor. By becoming "flesh" (John 1:14), that is, by his incarnation, which followed his preincarnate setting aside of his heavenly glory (cf. Phil 2:6–8), Christ went from wealth to poverty. The glory of heavenly existence is true wealth, and the lowliness of earthly existence is by comparison poverty. **through his poverty.** "As a consequence of his poverty," not "by means of his poverty." Christians are enriched not exactly or solely by means of Christ's poverty (i.e., his incarnation) but by his death as the climax of his entire incarnate life of obeying God. Paul would have been the first to insist that the cross is central (e.g., Rom 5:8–10; Gal 6:14; Col 1:20,22) and to observe that Calvary complements Bethlehem. The incarnation became a saving event through the crucifixion. However, if poverty here sums up Jesus' incarnation, life, death, and resurrection, the difficulty disappears. Unlike the Macedonians, who gave when they were extremely poor (v. 2), Christ gave when he was incalculably rich. In their present circumstances, the Corinthians fell somewhere between these extremes.

8:11 according to your means. Provided one willingly gives a gift, God accepts it in relation to whatever they have at their disposal, not in relation to what they do not have (v. 12). God assesses the value of a monetary gift not in terms of the actual amount one gives but by comparing what one gives with one's total financial resources. This is the lesson of the widow's offering (Mark 12:41–44). Paul here advocates giving in proportion to one's means, not giving by any particular percentage.

8:13–15 *The Aim of Equality.* Verse 13 encourages a sharing of financial burdens that may lead to an equality in the supply of the necessities of life. Then v. 14 speaks of mutual sacrifice that will maintain that equality. Paul is not predicting economic plenty in Jerusalem and economic need in Corinth. With the uncertain economic conditions in the first century, it was not inconceivable for the Jerusalem Christians someday to become the donors of financial aid and the Corinthian Christians to become the recipients.

8:15 Paul now illustrates this principle of sharing from the account of God providing manna to the Israelites in the wilderness (Exod 16:13–36). While some gathered more than others because of differences in age and energy, God met the needs of all. In the process of measuring the manna after they collected it, there was a miraculous equalizing to one omer each, with neither surplus nor deficiency. Any imbalance that hoarding might have caused was ruled out because on the second day unused manna putrefied (Exod 16:20). But Paul's illustration also contrasts the enforced equality that the Israelites miraculously experienced in the wilderness with the voluntary equality that Christians themselves must create in the church.

8:16—9:5 *Titus Sent to Receive the Collection.* Chs. 8–9 are basically Paul's urgent call to the Corinthians to fulfill their intent (8:11; 9:2) and promise (9:5) to contribute to his collection for destitute believers within the Jerusalem church. Here Paul describes his plan to fulfill their intent and promise. He is about to dispatch a three-man delegation to Corinth; they will arrive before he does and oversee the completion of the collection so that they can avoid pressured giving when Paul arrives.

8:16–24 *The Delegates and Their Credentials.* This amounts to Paul's "letter of recommendation" (cf. 3:1–3; 3 John 12) to the church of Corinth. He gives the credentials of Titus (his personal delegate) and the two unnamed Christian brothers (appointees probably of the Macedonian churches), and he encourages the Corinthians to welcome them warmly.

8:16 Although Titus's affection for the Corinthians naturally developed as a result of his positive interaction with them (7:13–15; 8:6), Paul could trace Titus's keen interest in the welfare of the Corinthians to the providential working of God. Nothing could be more reassuring to the Corinthians than knowing that Paul and Titus's devotion and concern for them reflected God's own affection for them.

8:19 to honor the Lord himself. That is, to promote the glory of the Lord God. Paul had many motives for organizing the collection, but this is the dominant one: the success of the project would prompt people to praise God (9:11–13). Other motives were: (1) to give evidence of his "eagerness to help" (here) brothers and sisters in the mother church to demonstrate brotherly love (Rom 12:13; 13:8; Gal 6:10) and the unity of Jew and Gentile in Christ (Gal 3:28; Eph 2:11–22); (2) to help effect an equal provision of the necessities of life (vv. 13–15); (3) to dramatize in material terms the spiritual indebtedness of Gentile believers to the church at Jerusalem (Rom 15:19,27); and (4) to fulfill an implied promise (Gal 2:10).

offering, which we administer in order to honor the Lord himself and to show our eagerness to help.[z]
20 We want to avoid any criticism of the way we administer this liberal gift. 21 For we are taking pains to
do what is right, not only in the eyes of the Lord but also in the eyes of man.[a]

22 In addition, we are sending with them our brother who has often proved to us in many ways that
he is zealous, and now even more so because of his great confidence in you. 23 As for Titus, he is my
partner[b] and co-worker[c] among you; as for our brothers,[d] they are representatives of the churches and
an honor to Christ. 24 Therefore show these men the proof of your love and the reason for our pride in
you,[e] so that the churches can see it.

9 There is no need[f] for me to write to you about this service to the Lord's people.[g] 2 For I know your
eagerness to help, and I have been boasting[h] about it to the Macedonians, telling them that since
last year[i] you in Achaia[j] were ready to give; and your enthusiasm has stirred most of them to action.
3 But I am sending the brothers in order that our boasting about you in this matter should not prove
hollow, but that you may be ready, as I said you would be.[k] 4 For if any Macedonians[l] come with me
and find you unprepared, we—not to say anything about you—would be ashamed of having been
so confident. 5 So I thought it necessary to urge the brothers to visit you in advance and finish the arrangements for the generous gift you had promised. Then it will be ready as a generous gift,[m] not as
one grudgingly given.[n]

Generosity Encouraged

6 Remember this: Whoever sows sparingly will also reap sparingly, and whoever sows generously
will also reap generously.[o] 7 Each of you should give what you have decided in your heart to give,[p]
not reluctantly or under compulsion,[q] for God loves a cheerful giver.[r] 8 And God is able[s] to bless you
abundantly, so that in all things at all times, having all that you need,[t] you will abound in every good
work. 9 As it is written:

> "They have freely scattered their gifts to the poor;
> their righteousness endures forever."[a][u]

[a] 9 Psalm 112:9

8:19 [z] ver 11,12
8:21 [a] Ro 12:17; 14:18
8:23 [b] Phm 17 [c] Php 2:25 [d] ver 18,22
8:24 [e] 2Co 7:4,14; 9:2
9:1 [f] 1Th 4:9 [g] 2Co 8:4
9:2 [h] 2Co 7:4,14 [i] 2Co 8:10 [j] Ac 18:12
9:3 [k] 1Co 16:2
9:4 [l] Ro 15:26
9:5 [m] Php 4:17 [n] 2Co 12:17,18
9:6 [o] Pr 11:24,25; 22:9; Gal 6:7,9
9:7 [p] Ex 25:2; 2Co 8:12 [q] Dt 15:10 [r] Ro 12:8
9:8 [s] Eph 3:20 [t] Php 4:19
9:9 [u] Ps 112:9

8:20–21 Paul learned from experience that he must anticipate the suspicions or accusations of his detractors and take the necessary precautions (cf. 11:9,12). As the prime mover behind the Jerusalem collection that he expected to be sizable ("liberal," v. 20), he was open to malicious charges that the whole project was designed to bribe the Jerusalem church to support his ministry or that he was quietly retaining a commission for his services as the gift's administrator. This explains, for example, why he was originally uncertain whether he would accompany the churches' delegates to Jerusalem (1 Cor 16:3–4; but cf. 2 Cor 1:16; Rom 15:25), why he insisted that the Corinthians appoint their own accredited representatives (1 Cor 16:3), and why he sent to Corinth two delegates along with his personal representative, Titus, before he himself arrived (vv. 18–19,22–23).

8:21 Paul probably has in mind Prov 3:4, which, in the Septuagint (the pre-Christian Greek translation of the OT) that he usually quotes, reads: "Give consideration to what is honorable before both the Lord and people."

9:1–5 *The Need for Readiness.* It might seem strange that Paul can hold up first the Macedonians as a model for the Corinthians to follow (8:1–5) and then the Corinthians as an example for the Macedonians to follow (v. 2). We must carefully distinguish between the Corinthians' ready desire to give and their actual readiness in having completed the collection. It was the Corinthians' "enthusiasm" to participate in the collection (v. 2), not their "completion" of it (8:11), that "stirred most of [the Macedonians'] to action" (v. 2). On the other hand, because the Macedonians successfully completed (8:1–5) what they enthusiastically commenced under the stimulus of the Corinthian example, their exemplary action formed one ground for Paul's appeal to the Corinthians to complete their contribution (8:6,10–11).

Paul's main reason for writing 2 Corinthians was to prepare the way for his forthcoming visit (12:14; 13:1–2) in order to ensure it would be enjoyable and profitable for everyone. He wanted to avoid two unfortunate but possible outcomes: (1) that his repeated and confident boast to the Macedonians about the Corinthians' "eagerness to help" (v. 2) and their expected readiness on arrival should turn out to be without foundation (v. 3); (2) that if delegates from the Macedonian churches (not to be confused with the two companions of Titus) arrived in Corinth with Paul, the Corinthians would still be unprepared and this would be acutely embarrassing for him—not to mention for the Corinthians themselves (v. 4). To make sure neither of these predicaments arose, Paul decided to send the three-man delegation on ahead to Corinth to supervise the final arrangements for the collection there (v. 5).

9:6–15 *Generosity Encouraged.* Having spoken of the need for generosity (8:1–15), Paul explains the twofold result of generosity: (1) The "cheerful giver" (v. 7) who sows generously will also generously reap both the spiritual grace and material prosperity that God provides ("God is able to bless you abundantly," v. 8), permitting them constantly to give spiritual and material benefits to others ("you will abound in every good work," v. 8). (2) Because generous giving is an evidence of God's grace (v. 14; cf. 8:1–4), it prompts "many expressions of thanks to God" (v. 12; see vv. 11b–13).

9:7 Giving should result from inward resolve, not an impulsive or casual decision. We should give cheerfully, "not reluctantly" (as though giving involved a painful loss) or "under compulsion" (because there seems to be no alternative or because of exerted pressure).

9:8 As regularly as generous giving depletes the resources of the cheerful giver, God's grace replenishes what is needed. This gives such a person a complete sufficiency ("all that you need") that comes from depending on an all-sufficient God.

9:10 [v]Isa 55:10 [w]Hos 10:12
9:11 [x]1Co 1:5 [y]2Co 1:11
9:12 [z]2Co 8:14 [a]2Co 1:11
9:13 [b]2Co 8:4 [c]Mt 9:8 [d]2Co 2:12
9:15 [e]2Co 2:14 [f]Ro 5:15,16
10:1 [g]Mt 11:29 [h]Gal 5:2
10:2 [i]1Co 4:21; 2Co 13:2,10
10:4 [j]2Co 6:7 [k]1Co 2:5 [l]Jer 1:10; 2Co 13:10
10:5 [m]Isa 2:11,12; 1Co 1:19 [n]2Co 9:13
10:6 [o]2Co 2:9; 7:15
10:7 [p]Jn 7:24 [q]1Co 1:12; 3:23; 14:37 [r]2Co 11:23

10 Now he who supplies seed to the sower and bread for food[v] will also supply and increase your store of
seed and will enlarge the harvest of your righteousness.[w] 11 You will be enriched[x] in every way so that
you can be generous on every occasion, and through us your generosity will result in thanksgiving to
God.[y]

12 This service that you perform is not only supplying the needs[z] of the Lord's people but is also overflowing in many expressions of thanks to God.[a] 13 Because of the service[b] by which you have proved
yourselves, others will praise God[c] for the obedience that accompanies your confession of the gospel of
Christ,[d] and for your generosity in sharing with them and with everyone else. 14 And in their prayers for
you their hearts will go out to you, because of the surpassing grace God has given you. 15 Thanks be to
God[e] for his indescribable gift![f]

Paul's Defense of His Ministry

10 By the humility and gentleness[g] of Christ, I appeal to you — I, Paul,[h] who am "timid" when
face to face with you, but "bold" toward you when away! 2 I beg you that when I come I may
not have to be as bold[i] as I expect to be toward some people who think that we live by the standards
of this world. 3 For though we live in the world, we do not wage war as the world does. 4 The weapons
we fight with[j] are not the weapons of the world. On the contrary, they have divine power[k] to demolish
strongholds.[l] 5 We demolish arguments and every pretension that sets itself up against the knowledge of
God,[m] and we take captive every thought to make it obedient[n] to Christ. 6 And we will be ready to punish
every act of disobedience, once your obedience is complete.[o]

7 You are judging by appearances.[a][p] If anyone is confident that they belong to Christ,[q] they should
consider again that we belong to Christ just as much as they do.[r] 8 So even if I boast somewhat freely

[a] 7 Or *Look at the obvious facts*

9:10 seed. Paul argues from God's bounty in nature to his even greater liberality in grace. If God supplies humans with the seed needed to produce a harvest of grain and thus food (cf. Isa 55:10), he certainly will supply and multiply all the resources ("your store of seed") needed to produce a full harvest of good deeds ("your righteousness").

9:12 The overflow of giving to the needy is praise offered to God. Paul did not place these two purposes of the collection (human relief and divine praise) on an equal footing. **is not only ... but is also.** "Not only" here has the nuance of "not merely," which indicates that the historical purpose is secondary to the theological aim.

9:15 The doxology is a final appeal to the lofty grandeur of divine giving (cf. vv. 8,10–11; 8:9). **indescribable gift.** This may refer to "the surpassing grace" (v. 14) that God imparts, but the primary reference is to the Father's gift (Greek *charis*) of his Son (cf. Rom 8:32). This key word *charis* occurs ten times in chs. 8–9, and the NIV appropriately renders it in a variety of ways: (1) *grace*, referring either to God's lavishly displayed generosity (8:9; also 9:8, "bless") or to God's enablement, especially his enabling them to participate worthily in the collection (v. 14; 8:1); (2) *privilege*, used of the honor and opportunity of participating in the offering (8:4); (3) *act of grace* or *offering*, denoting that the collection itself expresses and proves goodwill (8:6,19); (4) *grace of giving*, referring to grace as a virtuous act of sharing or as gracious help (8:7); (5) *thanks* (v. 15; 8:16).

10:1 — 13:14 *Paul's Defense of His Apostolic Authority.* An abrupt change of tone marks the transition from ch. 9 to ch. 10. Some indefinite time after Paul wrote chs. 1–9, he received distressing news of further problems at Corinth that prompted him to write chs. 10–13 and then send off all 13 chapters as a single letter (see Introduction: Unity). Perhaps the intruders from Judea had become more open and aggressive in their efforts to discredit Paul, and the Corinthians in general may have become more receptive to their teaching and more open to their influence. Throughout 10:1 — 11:15 there is a strong undercurrent of direct or indirect charges against Paul's rivals: they are not submissive to Christ; they lack authority from the Lord; they have no God-assigned sphere of operation in Corinth, yet they boast of their success there; they preach a different gospel; they are a financial burden on the Corinthians; and far from being apostles of Christ and agents of righteousness (as they claim), they are Satan's deputies and deceitful operators.

10:1 – 18 *Paul's Defense of His Ministry.* Paul's opponents were aware that if his converts could be persuaded that he was not a genuine apostle, they would see that his ministry lacked a proper basis and then cease to believe his teaching. So in defense of his ministry, Paul has no option but to boast "somewhat freely" about his apostolic authority (v. 8) and defend Corinth as his legitimate pastoral territory (vv. 13–18).

10:1 – 11 *The Potency of Apostolic Authority.* Paul wished to avoid a display of boldness on his forthcoming visit. Yet he was totally ready to exercise his apostolic authority, whatever the outcome, if the Corinthians did not reject his opponents and mend their ways (cf. 12:20–21; 13:11; 1 Cor 4:21).

10:2 Here and throughout chs. 10–13, Paul identifies the views of certain unnamed people (e.g., vv. 7,10–12; 11:4,12–13,15,20–23; 13:2), whether Paul's rivals or their supporters at Corinth, who formed a distinctive group. He does this to alert the whole church (cf. 12:19; 13:11–13) to the danger of becoming spiritually infected (cf. 11:2–3).

10:3 – 4 wage war ... weapons. Christians can wage a successful campaign in the spiritual realm only when they abandon human resources and totally rely on spiritual weapons such as the Spirit's power, Scripture, faith, and prayer. These are very effective in God's service for demolishing "strongholds" (v. 4) where evil is entrenched and from which the gospel is attacked.

10:6 Paul expresses two important principles: (1) Unless a church as a whole is willing to recognize and support spiritual discipline, that discipline will remain largely ineffective. (2) Obeying Christ (v. 5) involves submitting to his appointed representatives ("your obedience" means their obedience to Christ and Paul).

10:8 Paul's authority comes from God (cf. 3:5–6; 13:10), and he uses it for the common good (cf. 1 Cor 12:7). But Paul does not reject "tearing ... down" as a legitimate intermediate technique for shaping his converts' conduct (cf. v. 2; 13:2,10). Though punishment is sometimes a prerequisite for "building ... up," it can never be the ultimate goal of pastoral ministry, which always aims to build up (cf. Jer 31:28; Ezek 36:26).

about the authority the Lord gave us for building you up rather than tearing you down,[s] I will not be
ashamed of it. 9I do not want to seem to be trying to frighten you with my letters. 10For some say, "His
letters are weighty and forceful, but in person he is unimpressive[t] and his speaking amounts to nothing."[u] 11Such people should realize that what we are in our letters when we are absent, we will be in
our actions when we are present.

12We do not dare to classify or compare ourselves with some who commend themselves.[v] When they
measure themselves by themselves and compare themselves with themselves, they are not wise. 13We,
however, will not boast beyond proper limits, but will confine our boasting to the sphere of service God
himself has assigned to us,[w] a sphere that also includes you. 14We are not going too far in our boasting, as would be the case if we had not come to you, for we did get as far as you[x] with the gospel of
Christ.[y] 15Neither do we go beyond our limits by boasting of work done by others.[z] Our hope is that, as
your faith continues to grow,[a] our sphere of activity among you will greatly expand, 16so that we can
preach the gospel in the regions beyond you.[b] For we do not want to boast about work already done in
someone else's territory. 17But, "Let the one who boasts boast in the Lord."[a][c] 18For it is not the one who
commends himself[d] who is approved, but the one whom the Lord commends.[e]

Paul and the False Apostles

11 I hope you will put up with[f] me in a little foolishness.[g] Yes, please put up with me! 2I am jealous for you with a godly jealousy. I promised you to one husband,[h] to Christ, so that I might
present you[i] as a pure virgin to him. 3But I am afraid that just as Eve was deceived by the serpent's
cunning,[j] your minds may somehow be led astray from your sincere and pure devotion to Christ. 4For
if someone comes to you and preaches a Jesus other than the Jesus we preached,[k] or if you receive a
different spirit[l] from the Spirit you received, or a different gospel[m] from the one you accepted, you put
up with it easily enough.

5I do not think I am in the least inferior to those "super-apostles."[b][n] 6I may indeed be untrained as

10:8 [s]2Co 13:10
10:10 [t]1Co 2:3; Gal 4:13, 14 [u]1Co 1:17
10:12 [v]2Co 3:1
10:13 [w]ver 15,16
10:14 [x]1Co 3:6 [y]2Co 2:12
10:15 [z]Ro 15:20 [a]2Th 1:3
10:16 [b]Ac 19:21
10:17 [c]Jer 9:24; 1Co 1:31
10:18 [d]ver 12 [e]Ro 2:29; 1Co 4:5
11:1 [f]ver 4,19,20; Mt 17:17 [g]ver 16,17,21; 2Co 5:13
11:2 [h]Hos 2:19; Eph 5:26,27 [i]2Co 4:14
11:3 [j]Ge 3:1-6,13; Jn 8:44; 1Ti 2:14; Rev 12:9
11:4 [k]1Co 3:11 [l]Ro 8:15 [m]Gal 1:6-9
11:5 [n]2Co 12:11; Gal 2:6

[a] 17 Jer. 9:24 [b] 5 Or *to the most eminent apostles*

10:9–11 Paul reminds those who made unfavorable comparisons between "Paul the bold" (what they believed to be his boldness by a "forceful" letter at a distance) and "Paul the timid" (his "unimpressive" presence and feeble speaking ability when face to face [cf. v. 1]) that when he arrives he will act with the same bold authority as in his letters.

10:12–18 *Legitimate Spheres of Activity and Boasting.* Behind Paul's continuing self-defense in this section lies an indirect attack on the intruders. He makes two indirect charges: (1) The false apostles trespassed on his assigned territory at Corinth, defying the apostolic agreement of Gal 2:1–10 that God distinctively assigned Paul to preach Christ throughout the Gentile world (Gal 2:7–9; Eph 3:1–6). When God created a Christian community at Corinth as a result of Paul's pioneering evangelism, Corinth became his legitimate domain of activity. (2) By their unrestrained self-commendation (v. 12), Paul's opponents falsely claimed credit for his work.

10:13 The presence of Paul's rivals at Corinth was not a technical breach of any apostolic "treaty," but it repudiated the spirit of this "gentlemen's agreement" about the apostolic division of labor (Gal 2:1–10), for his rivals were in Corinth not to aid Paul (as Apollos had been, 1 Cor 3:5–6) but to supplant him. This improper invasion of Paul's rightful mission field (v. 14) was probably one of the "act[s] of disobedience" (v. 6) he planned to punish on his next visit. **sphere of service.** Greek *kanōn*, which basically refers to a rod or rule used as a measure or as a test of straightness. In this passage it means "sphere of service" (here), "sphere of activity" (v. 15), "territory" (v. 16), or domain.

10:16 regions beyond you. The western Mediterranean, where Christ's name was not yet known (cf. Rom 15:20), and Spain in particular (Rom 15:24,28).

10:17 boasts. Jeremiah 9:23–24 contrasts improper boasting (boasting of one's own wisdom, strength, and riches) and proper boasting (boasting about understanding and knowing the Lord, who exercises kindness, justice, and righteousness on earth). For Christians, only boasting "in the Lord" is legitimate—boasting about who Jesus Christ is and what he has done for them (Gal 6:14) or through them (Rom 15:18; cf. Acts14:27).

11:1–15 *Paul and the False Apostles.* Before unmasking the false apostles and describing who they really are (vv. 13–15), Paul pleads with the Corinthians to put up with him in a little foolish boasting (vv. 1–6) and defends his financial independence from them (vv. 7–12).

11:1 Paul firmly stated that self-praise was inappropriate and worthless (3:1; 5:12; 10:12). But since his adversaries were indulging in self-praise (5:12; 10:7,12–18) and the Corinthians seemed largely sympathetic, he reluctantly feels compelled to use his opponents' methods in order to win the Corinthians' attention, gain a fair hearing (v. 18; 12:11), and win them back to their former affections (v. 3; 6:11–13).

11:2–3 With a jealousy like God's own jealousy (e.g., Hos 2:19–20; 4:12; 6:4; 11:8), Paul is jealous for his converts' "sincere and pure devotion to Christ" (v. 3) in the interval between their conversion (when he "promised" [v. 2], or betrothed, them to Christ) and their glorification (when he would present them "as a pure virgin" (v. 2) to their heavenly bridegroom, Christ).

11:3 deceived. False apostles are Satan's agents (v. 15), capable of repeating at Corinth what Satan achieved in the Garden of Eden (Gen 3:13; 1 Tim 2:14): deception by cunning.

11:4 Jesus … the Spirit … [the] gospel. These three elements stand or fall together, for "a Jesus other than the Jesus [Paul] preached" inevitably means both a different spirit, since the Spirit is the Spirit of Jesus Christ (Rom 8:9; Phil 1:19), and a different gospel, since the gospel is about Jesus Christ (2 Cor 2:12; 9:13; 10:14).

11:5 those "super-apostles." Some regard this as Paul's sarcastic description of the "false apostles" of v. 13. Others think the phrase is how Paul's opponents describe the Jerusalem apostles and how Paul

11:6 [o]1Co 1:17 [p]Eph 3:4
11:7 [q]2Co 12:13 [r]1Co 9:18
11:8 [s]Php 4:15,18
11:9 [t]2Co 12:13,14,16
11:10 [u]Ro 9:1 [v]Ac 18:12 [w]1Co 9:15
11:11 [x]2Co 12:15
11:13 [y]2Pe 2:1 [z]Titus 1:10 [a]Rev 2:2
11:15 [b]Php 3:19
11:16 [c]ver 1
11:17 [d]1Co 7:12,25
11:18 [e]Php 3:3,4
11:19 [f]1Co 4:10
11:20 [g]Gal 2:4
11:21 [h]2Co 10:1,10 [i]Php 3:4
11:22 [j]Php 3:5 [k]Ro 9:4
11:23 [l]1Co 15:10 [m]Ac 16:23; 2Co 6:4,5
11:24 [n]Dt 25:3
11:25 [o]Ac 16:22 [p]Ac 14:19
11:26 [q]Ac 9:23; 14:5 [r]Ac 21:31 [s]Gal 2:4
11:27 [t]1Co 4:11,12; 2Co 6:5

a speaker,[o] but I do have knowledge.[p] We have made this perfectly clear to you in every way. 7Was it a sin[q] for me to lower myself in order to elevate you by preaching the gospel of God to you free of charge?[r] 8I robbed other churches by receiving support from them[s] so as to serve you. 9And when I was with you and needed something, I was not a burden to anyone, for the brothers who came from Macedonia supplied what I needed. I have kept myself from being a burden to you[t] in any way, and will continue to do so. 10As surely as the truth of Christ is in me,[u] nobody in the regions of Achaia[v] will stop this boasting[w] of mine. 11Why? Because I do not love you? God knows I do![x]

12And I will keep on doing what I am doing in order to cut the ground from under those who want an opportunity to be considered equal with us in the things they boast about. 13For such people are false apostles,[y] deceitful[z] workers, masquerading as apostles of Christ.[a] 14And no wonder, for Satan himself masquerades as an angel of light. 15It is not surprising, then, if his servants also masquerade as servants of righteousness. Their end will be what their actions deserve.[b]

Paul Boasts About His Sufferings

16I repeat: Let no one take me for a fool.[c] But if you do, then tolerate me just as you would a fool, so that I may do a little boasting. 17In this self-confident boasting I am not talking as the Lord would,[d] but as a fool. 18Since many are boasting in the way the world does, I too will boast.[e] 19You gladly put up with fools since you are so wise![f] 20In fact, you even put up with anyone who enslaves you[g] or exploits you or takes advantage of you or puts on airs or slaps you in the face. 21To my shame I admit that we were too weak[h] for that!

Whatever anyone else dares to boast about—I am speaking as a fool—I also dare to boast about.[i] 22Are they Hebrews? So am I.[j] Are they Israelites? So am I.[k] Are they Abraham's descendants? So am I. 23Are they servants of Christ? (I am out of my mind to talk like this.) I am more. I have worked much harder,[l] been in prison more frequently,[m] been flogged more severely, and been exposed to death again and again. 24Five times I received from the Jews the forty lashes[n] minus one. 25Three times I was beaten with rods,[o] once I was pelted with stones,[p] three times I was shipwrecked, I spent a night and a day in the open sea, 26I have been constantly on the move. I have been in danger from rivers, in danger from bandits, in danger from my fellow Jews,[q] in danger from Gentiles; in danger in the city,[r] in danger in the country, in danger at sea; and in danger from false believers.[s] 27I have labored and toiled and have often gone without sleep; I have known hunger and thirst and have often gone without food;[t] I have been cold and naked. 28Besides everything else, I face daily the pressure of my concern for all the churches. 29Who is weak, and I do not feel weak? Who is led into sin, and I do not inwardly burn?

---

quotes them (cf. 12:11). Still others believe it is the apostle's ironic description of the exalted view of the Twelve held by the false apostles.

11:7–12 Paul's rivals apparently interpreted his refusing to accept support from the Corinthians as evidence that he is not a true apostle (cf. 1 Cor 9:3–18). It was Paul's policy not to accept financial support from churches he was currently serving, but he sometimes accepted gifts from distant fellow believers (vv. 8–9; Phil 4:16) or as he was leaving a region (2 Cor 1:16; 1 Cor 16:6; Rom 15:24) to enable him to pursue evangelistic or pastoral opportunities, not as a payment for services rendered. Paul was committed to maintaining this policy so that his envious rivals could not boast, as he could, about preaching his message "free of charge" (v. 7; cf. 1 Cor 9:18).

11:13–15 Like their principal, the arch-deceiver (John 8:44), whose habit was to masquerade "as an angel of light" (v. 14), Paul's adversaries relied on disguise and deceit to carry out their schemes (cf. v. 20; 2:11).What was false was not simply their claim to apostleship but also their message (cf. v. 4).

11:16–33 *Paul Boasts About His Sufferings.* From 11:16—12:13 Paul boasts about things that are not fit for boasting and answers fools according to their folly (Prov 26:5). But he sees that not all will recognize that he is play-acting in his "self-confident boasting" (vv. 16–17).

11:19–21a Paul is scathingly ironic (cf. 12:13), but with a positive purpose (cf. 12:19).

11:21b–29 This is an extended comparison between Paul and his rivals at Corinth. The two key expressions are (1) "I also" or "So am I" (vv. 21b–22), pointing to Paul's equality with his rivals in certain limited respects (bold boasting, v. 21b; lineage, citizenship, and heritage, v. 22), and (2) "I am more" (v. 23), pointing to Paul's vast superiority in service and suffering (vv. 23–29). Paul's list of "accomplishments" recounts not triumphs but apparent defeats and relates not to strengths but to weaknesses (v. 30; 12:5,9–10). Lowliness and weakness as seen in Christian service give the clearest evidence that Paul is a genuine apostle.

11:23–25 Luke's account in Acts records only one of Paul's imprisonments before Acts 20 (when 2 Corinthians was written)—that at Philippi—and only one of his three (Roman) beatings with rods, also at Philippi (Acts 16:22–40). Nor does Acts tell us about the five whippings in Jewish synagogal courts, the other two beatings at the hands of Gentiles, the three shipwrecks (Acts 27:13–44 describes a later shipwreck), or the day and night in the open sea. The narrative of Acts is clearly selective. The Jewish floggings show that by practice Paul was a Jew, attending the synagogue and being subject to its discipline.

11:28 concern. None of Paul's afflictions mentioned in vv. 23–27 were continuous, but his crowning trial and privilege is unceasing: the daily pressure of his anxious concern for all the churches (cf. Acts 20:18–21,28–31). Yet Paul was not violating the teaching of Jesus about anxiety (Matt 6:25–34). Paul's concern arose from seeking first the kingdom of God; he was grappling realistically with present, not future, problems; and he had no anxiety about the relatively trivial

30 If I must boast, I will boast of the things that show my weakness.[u] 31 The God and Father of the Lord
Jesus, who is to be praised forever,[v] knows that I am not lying. 32 In Damascus the governor under King
Aretas had the city of the Damascenes guarded in order to arrest me.[w] 33 But I was lowered in a basket
from a window in the wall and slipped through his hands.[x]

Paul's Vision and His Thorn

12 I must go on boasting.[y] Although there is nothing to be gained, I will go on to visions and revelations[z] from the Lord. 2 I know a man in Christ who fourteen years ago was caught up[a] to the
third heaven.[b] Whether it was in the body or out of the body I do not know—God knows.[c] 3 And I know
that this man—whether in the body or apart from the body I do not know, but God knows— 4 was
caught up to paradise[d] and heard inexpressible things, things that no one is permitted to tell. 5 I will
boast about a man like that, but I will not boast about myself, except about my weaknesses. 6 Even if I
should choose to boast, I would not be a fool,[e] because I would be speaking the truth. But I refrain, so
no one will think more of me than is warranted by what I do or say, 7 or because of these surpassingly
great revelations. Therefore, in order to keep me from becoming conceited, I was given a thorn in my
flesh,[f] a messenger of Satan, to torment me. 8 Three times I pleaded with the Lord to take it away from
me.[g] 9 But he said to me, "My grace is sufficient for you, for my power[h] is made perfect in weakness."

11:30 [u] 1Co 2:3
11:31 [v] Ro 9:5
11:32 [w] Ac 9:24
11:33 [x] Ac 9:25
12:1 [y] 2Co 11:16,30 [z] ver 7
12:2 [a] Ac 8:39 [b] Eph 4:10 [c] 2Co 11:11
12:4 [d] Lk 23:43; Rev 2:7
12:6 [e] 2Co 11:16
12:7 [f] Nu 33:55
12:8 [g] Mt 26:39,44
12:9 [h] Php 4:13

matters of food and clothing (cf. v. 27). As a faithful "undershepherd," he shared the constant burden of the Chief Shepherd with regard to all the sheep (cf. 1 Pet 5:2–4).

11:31 God ... knows. Lest anyone should dismiss the description of his afflictions, the enmity of King Aretas (v. 32), and Paul's ascent into paradise as wild exaggerations (12:2–4), Paul appeals to the divine omniscience (cf. vv. 10–11; 1:18; Rom 9:1; Gal 1:20; 1 Tim 2:7). Invoking God like this as a witness to his truthfulness does not, of course, fall under Christ's ban on unnecessary or frivolous swearing (Matt 5:33–37; Jas 5:12).

11:32 King Aretas. Aretas IV, the father-in-law of Herod Antipas, ruled over the kingdom of the Nabatean Arabs from about 9 BC–AD 40. Nabatea (the "Arabia" of Gal 1:17) stretched east and south of the Jordan River.

11:33 Luke's account of Paul's escape from Damascus (Acts 9:23–25) reveals that the Jews were watching the gates in order to kill Paul; Paul explains here that "the governor under King Aretas" (v. 32) had the city guarded to arrest him. Damascus was probably under Roman rule at this time, and the governor may have been head of a semi-autonomous colony of Nabateans in Damascus. If so, there was a coalition of Jews (Luke's account) and Nabateans (Paul's account) acting through the Nabatean governor to arrest or kill Paul. It is highly ironic that the man who had set out for Damascus in a daylight advance against his foes (Acts 9:1–2; 22:6) now turned his back on Damascus in a nocturnal retreat from his foes.

12:1–10 *Paul's Vision and His Thorn.* By insisting that their teachers should display their credentials ("I must go on boasting," v. 1), the Corinthians were forcing Paul to break a 14-year silence (v. 2) and boast about a vision the Lord had given him.

12:2–4 a man ... caught up to paradise. The "man in Christ" is undoubtedly Paul himself for several reasons: (1) He knew the exact time in the distant past when the revelation took place (v. 2) and that its content was beyond words, even if it had been permissible to try to communicate it (v. 4). (2) The revelation was directly related to a "thorn" (v. 7) that the Lord gave to Paul himself. (3) The reference to a lack of awareness as to whether or not the man was in the body (vv. 2–3) points to a personal experience. (4) For Paul to relate a remarkable experience that happened to some Christian unknown to the Corinthians but known to Paul would have been irrelevant. The scene of the vision was "paradise" (v. 4), the dwelling place of the righteous dead that is located within "the third [highest] heaven" (v. 2), the abode of God. The first heaven is the earth's atmosphere and the second heaven is the space beyond, with its constellations, below the third heaven. One reason the Lord gave the vision was to strengthen Paul for future service and sufferings (Acts 9:16; Rom 8:18). Glimpses the NT does give of the coming glory aim to strengthen faith and promote holiness (cf. 2 Pet 3:10–14; 1 John 3:2–3), not satisfy curiosity.

12:5 Paul distinguishes between "a man like that" and himself because he is embarrassed at needing to boast at all (vv. 1,11) and wishes to avoid suggesting that he is in any sense a special kind of Christian (the initiative was God's). Also he wants to dispel any idea that the experience adds to his personal status or importance.

12:7 thorn. God gave the "thorn"—"I was given" is a "theological passive"—for a beneficial purpose (preventing spiritual pride), and Paul asked the Lord to take it away (v. 8). Suggestions about the nature of this thorn fall into three categories: (1) spiritual or psychological anxiety (such as anguish over Israel's stubborn unbelief); (2) opposition to his ministry or message; and (3) a recurring and tormenting physical malady (the most probable option). Precisely because we do not know the nature of the affliction or disability, those to whom God gives any "thorn" can share Paul's experience of divinely sufficient grace (v. 9). As well as being a gift from God, the thorn is, surprisingly, "a messenger of Satan," perhaps because it brings Paul within the shadow of death (cf. 1:8–9) or hinders the advance of the gospel, either by arousing the contempt of the hearers (cf. Gal 4:13–14) or by so weakening Paul that travel plans are frustrated or must be abandoned.

12:8 The "thorn" (v. 7) proved so tormenting to Paul that on three separate occasions he "pleaded with the Lord" (Jesus; see v. 9) to remove it. In the NT, formal or liturgical prayer is usually offered through Christ to the Father in the power of the Spirit (Eph 2:18), but on occasion an individual (Acts 7:59–60; 9:10–17; 22:16,19) or a group (1 Cor 1:2; 16:22; Acts 1:24; 9:21; Rev 22:20) invokes the Lord Jesus directly.

12:9–10 The thorn remains, but so too does Paul's recollection of the divine reply. In the midst of the distressing weakness inflicted at various times by his ailment, the supporting grace of Christ (13:14) is adequate, precisely because divine power finds its full scope and strength only in human weakness, i.e., when Christians acknowledge that they cannot serve Christ effectively apart from his empowering (cf. Eph 3:16; Phil 4:13). But it is not simply that weakness is a prerequisite for power. Both weakness and power existed simultaneously in Paul's life (vv. 9b,10b; cf. 4:10–11), as they did in Christ's ministry and death. Indeed, the cross of Christ is the supreme example of "power ... in weakness" (v. 9).

12:10 [i]2Co 6:4 [j]Ro 5:3; 2Th 1:4 [k]2Co 13:4
12:11 [l]2Co 11:1 [m]2Co 11:5 [n]1Co 15:9,10
12:12 [o]Jn 4:48
12:13 [p]1Co 9:12,18 [q]2Co 11:7
12:14 [r]2Co 13:1 [s]1Co 4:14,15 [t]Pr 19:14
12:15 [u]Php 2:17; 1Th 2:8
12:16 [v]2Co 11:9
12:18 [w]2Co 8:6,16 [x]2Co 8:18
12:19 [y]Ro 9:1 [z]2Co 10:8
12:20 [a]2Co 2:1-4 [b]1Co 4:21 [c]1Co 1:11; 3:3 [d]Gal 5:20 [e]Ro 1:29 [f]1Co 14:33
12:21 [g]2Co 2:1,4 [h]2Co 13:2
13:1 [i]2Co 12:14 [j]Dt 19:15; Mt 18:16
13:2 [k]2Co 1:23 [l]2Co 12:21

Therefore I will boast all the more gladly about my weaknesses, so that Christ's power may rest on me. 10 That is why, for Christ's sake, I delight in weaknesses, in insults, in hardships,[i] in persecutions,[j] in difficulties. For when I am weak, then I am strong.[k]

Paul's Concern for the Corinthians

11 I have made a fool of myself,[l] but you drove me to it. I ought to have been commended by you, for I am not in the least inferior to the "super-apostles,"[a][m] even though I am nothing.[n] 12 I persevered in demonstrating among you the marks of a true apostle, including signs, wonders and miracles.[o] 13 How were you inferior to the other churches, except that I was never a burden to you?[p] Forgive me this wrong![q]

14 Now I am ready to visit you for the third time,[r] and I will not be a burden to you, because what I want is not your possessions but you. After all, children should not have to save up for their parents,[s] but parents for their children.[t] 15 So I will very gladly spend for you everything I have and expend myself as well.[u] If I love you more, will you love me less? 16 Be that as it may, I have not been a burden to you.[v] Yet, crafty fellow that I am, I caught you by trickery! 17 Did I exploit you through any of the men I sent to you? 18 I urged[w] Titus to go to you and I sent our brother[x] with him. Titus did not exploit you, did he? Did we not walk in the same footsteps by the same Spirit?

19 Have you been thinking all along that we have been defending ourselves to you? We have been speaking in the sight of God[y] as those in Christ; and everything we do, dear friends, is for your strengthening.[z] 20 For I am afraid that when I come[a] I may not find you as I want you to be, and you may not find me as you want me to be.[b] I fear that there may be discord,[c] jealousy, fits of rage, selfish ambition,[d] slander, gossip,[e] arrogance and disorder.[f] 21 I am afraid that when I come again my God will humble me before you, and I will be grieved[g] over many who have sinned earlier[h] and have not repented of the impurity, sexual sin and debauchery in which they have indulged.

Final Warnings

13 This will be my third visit to you.[i] "Every matter must be established by the testimony of two or three witnesses."[b][j] 2 I already gave you a warning when I was with you the second time. I now repeat it while absent: On my return I will not spare[k] those who sinned earlier[l] or any of the others,

[a] *11* Or *the most eminent apostles* [b] *1* Deut. 19:15

12:11–21 *Paul's Concern for the Corinthians.* As Paul thought about his forthcoming third visit (v. 14), he was fearful that the visit might lead to mutual disappointment and embarrassment (v. 20a), that sin might continue to be rampant in the church (v. 20b), and that he might again be humiliated and grieved because of certain unrepentant Corinthians (v. 21).

12:11 even though I am nothing. Paul may be ironically citing his opponents' opinion of him, or he may be seriously disavowing any personal merit that might have made him worthy of apostleship (cf. 1 Cor 15:8–10).

12:12 signs, wonders and miracles. These do not describe three types of miracles but miracles in general considered from three aspects: they authenticate the message ("signs"), arouse awe ("wonders"), and display divine power (mighty deeds). Other marks of apostleship include faithfulness to the apostolic message (11:4) and conduct that is in agreement with the example of Christ (10:1; 13:14).

12:14 As the Corinthians' spiritual father (6:13), Paul had no designs on their possessions or money; what he did want to ensure was their spiritual well-being ("I want … you"). The concept that Paul appeals to—that "children should not have to save up for their parents, but parents for their children"—is not universally applicable. Paul defended the right of apostles to be supported by their spiritual children (1 Cor 9:3–14); he himself had received financial support from some of his converts (2 Cor 11:8–9; Phil 4:15–16). And later he insists that it is a Christian obligation and pleasing to God to provide for one's relatives, including parents and grandparents (1 Tim 5:4,8).

12:15 I will very gladly spend for you. Far from coveting the Corinthians' possessions (v. 14), Paul plans to use all of his own resources to achieve their highest good; he would spare neither property nor energy to win their exclusive devotion to Christ (cf. 11:2–3; Acts 20:24). Yet he looks for "a fair exchange" (6:13): "If I love you more, will you love me less?"

12:19 It is to God, not to the Corinthians, that Paul is ultimately accountable (cf. 5:10; 1 Cor 4:3–5; Rom 14:10), so that self-defense before others is never his primary concern. His aim in all his relations with the Corinthians—especially his letters—is not personal vindication but "strengthening" and stabilizing their individual and corporate faith and enriching them.

13:1–10 *Final Warnings.* Verses 1–4 state what Paul assumes the Corinthians would not want him to be on his third visit—someone who administers punishment. Then he issues a plea for self-examination (vv. 5–10) that he hopes will lead to a change of attitude and behavior before he arrives so that he "may not have to be harsh in [his] use of authority" (v. 10).

13:1–2 On the basis of the fears expressed in 12:20–21, Paul issues two direct warnings. Perhaps the threatened punishment is handing the wrongdoers "over to Satan for the destruction of the flesh" (1 Cor 5:5), i.e., illness leading to death, unless there is repentance (cf. 1 Cor 11:30).

13:1 two or three witnesses. Cf. Deut 19:15. These are probably Paul's three visits to Corinth, two actual (the founding and "painful" visits) and one promised. On the testimony of these three witnesses, justice would certainly fall on the dissidents at Corinth. Paul is saying, "Sufficient warning has been given; punishment is imminent."

13:2 those who sinned earlier. The immoral persons of 12:21b who did not repent during Paul's "painful visit" and were evidently still indulging in sexual sins. **any of the others.** Probably those Corinthians who need

3since you are demanding proof that Christ is speaking through me.[m] He is not weak in dealing with
you, but is powerful among you. 4For to be sure, he was crucified in weakness,[n] yet he lives by God's
power.[o] Likewise, we are weak[p] in him, yet by God's power we will live with him in our dealing with you.
5Examine yourselves[q] to see whether you are in the faith; test yourselves.[r] Do you not realize that
Christ Jesus is in you[s] — unless, of course, you fail the test? 6And I trust that you will discover that we
have not failed the test. 7Now we pray to God that you will not do anything wrong — not so that people
will see that we have stood the test but so that you will do what is right even though we may seem to
have failed. 8For we cannot do anything against the truth, but only for the truth. 9We are glad whenever
we are weak but you are strong; and our prayer is that you may be fully restored.[t] 10This is why I write
these things when I am absent, that when I come I may not have to be harsh in my use of authority —
the authority the Lord gave me for building you up, not for tearing you down.[u]

13:3 [m] Mt 10:20; 1Co 5:4
13:4 [n] Php 2:7,8; 1Pe 3:18 [o] Ro 1:4; 6:4 [p] ver 9
13:5 [q] 1Co 11:28 [r] Jn 6:6 [s] Ro 8:10
13:9 [t] ver 11
13:10 [u] 2Co 10:8
13:11 [v] 1Th 4:1; 2Th 3:1 [w] Mk 9:50 [x] Ro 15:33; Eph 6:23
13:12 [y] Ro 16:16
13:13 [z] Php 4:22
13:14 [a] Ro 16:20; 2Co 8:9 [b] Ro 5:5; Jude 21 [c] Php 2:1

Final Greetings

11Finally, brothers and sisters,[v] rejoice! Strive for full restoration, encourage one another, be of one
mind, live in peace.[w] And the God of love and peace[x] will be with you.
12Greet one another with a holy kiss.[y] 13All God's people here send their greetings.[z]
14May the grace of the Lord Jesus Christ,[a] and the love of God,[b] and the fellowship of the Holy Spirit[c]
be with you all.

a warning for the sake of deterrence. So these two groups embrace the whole church, just as 12:20–21 does.
13:4 in weakness. An alternative translation is "because of weakness." The "weakness" is not physical frailty or moral impotence but rather the "weakness" of non-retaliation or non-aggressiveness before people and the "weakness" of obeying God. People who are weak in human estimation because they seek to do God's will are supremely strong. But that "weakness" of Christ is past. Now he lives a resurrection life sustained "by God's power," "the Spirit of holiness" (Rom 1:4). As a result of his union with Christ ("in him") through faith, Paul shared the "weakness" of Christ's passion. But in his dealing with the Corinthians, he would be fully alive ("we will live"), along with Christ ("with him"), "by God's power."
13:5 Examine ... test. Rather than "demanding proof" (v. 3) that Christ is speaking through Paul, the Corinthians should "examine" and "test" themselves to find out whether they are continuing to be true to the faith. Although he adds an ironic aside or hypothetical modification ("unless, of course, you fail the test"), Paul does not believe the majority of Corinthians are counterfeit. But possibly some of them must be exposed as falsely professing Christians.
13:8 Paul does not need to exercise his apostolic authority where "truth" (i.e., authentic Christian conduct) already exists, but he is able and willing, if necessary, to decisively reestablish "truth," i.e., work toward restoring the Corinthians to wholeness (v. 9b) in attitude and behavior.
13:10 building you up, not ... tearing you down. If destruction proves to be a necessary prelude to the positive task of construction, Paul would reluctantly undertake it — and with the same authority (cf. 10:8). In Paul's eyes, a disposition of meekness (cf. 10:1) and a display of power (cf. v. 2; 10:2) are not incompatible (cf. Num 12:3; 16:15–33).
13:11–14 *Final Greetings.* Paul closes his letter with exhortations (vv. 11–12), greetings (v. 13), and a benediction (v. 14).
13:11 full restoration. Would include heeding Paul's call for a break with all idolatry (6:14 — 7:1), showing warm hospitality to the three delegates (8:24), contributing generously and promptly to the Jerusalem relief fund (chs. 8–9), and having a changed attitude toward Paul himself (chs. 10–13).
13:12 holy kiss. Expressed love (1 Pet 5:14) as well as union and fellowship within the one family of God; it was a sign of mutual forgiveness and reconciliation that they sometimes exchanged before celebrating the Lord's Supper (cf. 1 Cor 16:20b,22; Matt 5:23–24). It also demonstrated Christian liberty — transcending divisions based on gender, race, and status — for male and female, Jew and Greek, and slave and free exchanged the kiss (cf. Gal 3:28).
13:14 grace ... love ... fellowship. Paul wishes that his converts would always be fortified by the grace Christ imparts, by the love God the Father supplies, and by their common participation in the life, power, and gifts of the Holy Spirit. This benediction, commonly used at the end of Christian worship, is noteworthy for the unusual order of Son-Father-Spirit, whereas we normally refer to "Father, Son, and Holy Spirit." Paul's order reflects Christian experience: we come to Christ and so encounter God and then receive his Spirit.

INTRODUCTION TO GALATIANS

AUTHOR

The letter to the Galatians was written by the apostle Paul (1:1). Unlike several of Paul's other letters (e.g., 1 Thess 1:1), he does not mention a co-sender who might have served as a coauthor. Paul tells us more about himself and his past in Galatians than in any of his other letters (2 Cor 11:21 — 12:10; Phil 3:4 – 11), and a number of themes that we especially associate with the apostle Paul appear in this letter (e.g., justification by faith, freedom from the law, the conflict between the flesh and the Spirit, the fruit of the Spirit), as do treasured verses of his personal testimony (2:20; 6:14).

DATE

The year in which Paul wrote this letter is disputed. At the center of the debate is Gal 2:1 – 10, where Paul describes a meeting in Jerusalem in which the leaders of the Jerusalem church validated his (law-free) gospel. Differences between his account in 2:1 – 10 and the account of a meeting in Acts 15:4 – 29 have convinced many interpreters that these are different occasions; the meeting referred to in Galatians is then thought to have taken place during Paul and Barnabas's trip to Jerusalem mentioned in Acts 11:29 – 30. Other interpreters doubt that Gal 2 and Acts 15 can refer to different meetings, highlighting the similarities between the accounts and attributing differences to the different emphases of the two writers.

If the incident referred to in 2:1 – 10 took place at the time of Acts 11:29 – 30, then the absence in Galatians of any reference to the meeting of Acts 15 (a meeting of importance for the subject matter of the letter) presumably means that it was written before that meeting took place (around AD 48). In that case, Galatians is Paul's earliest letter still in existence — and likely the earliest known Christian text.

If 2:1 – 10 describes the same meeting as Acts 15, then the letter could have been written at any subsequent date. In neither case can we know for certain where Paul was when he wrote the letter, though Antioch is a plausible suggestion for the first interpretation (cf. Acts 14:26 – 28) and Ephesus for the second (cf. Acts 19:1,8 – 10).

GALATIA

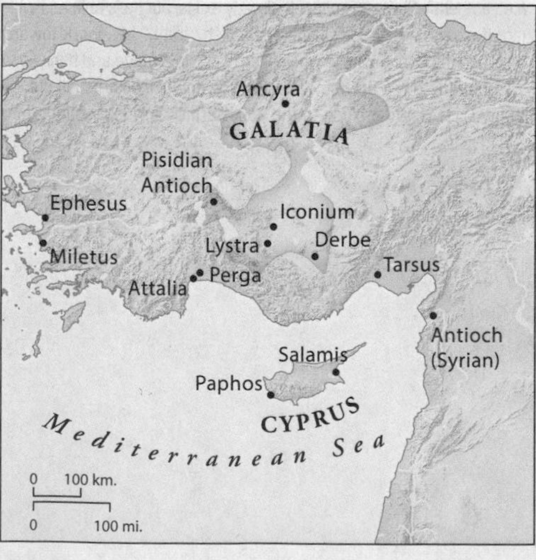

RECIPIENTS

The letter was written "to the churches in Galatia" (1:2), to people identified as "Galatians" (3:1). In Paul's day Galatia was a Roman province in the central region of what is now Turkey. Since it included various southern cities mentioned in Acts 13 – 14 as evangelized by Paul and Barnabas (Pisidian Antioch, Iconium, Lystra, and Derbe), many interpreters think the letter was written to believers in these cities (this view is called the "South Galatian hypothesis"). The inhabitants of these cities were not, however, ethnically Galatian; ethnic Galatians were found farther north, in the area of the city of Ancyra. For that reason, other interpreters think the letter was sent to believers in the northern region (this view is called the "North Galatian hypothesis") even though Acts never mentions Paul's missionary activity in that area (unless Acts 16:6 and 18:23 are so understood). Since the narrative of Acts is not an exhaustive account of all Paul did, the North Galatian hypothesis is possible, but the South Galatian hypothesis seems more likely.

After Paul (and probably Barnabas) evangelized the Galatians, missionaries of a different sort visited them. These opponents of Paul believed that Jesus was the Messiah promised to the Jews, but they saw the coming of the Jewish Messiah as no reason to doubt that God's people were still the Jews or that God's will for their lives was still to be found in the Mosaic law. In their view, believing in Jesus as the Messiah was a first step if Gentiles were to be saved, but it needed to be followed by circumcision and a commitment to observe the law of Moses. Aware that what they were saying departed from the message of Paul, they appear to have suggested Paul was no true apostle — at least not an apostle on a level with those (like Peter and John) who had accompanied Jesus throughout his ministry. Paul, they apparently contended, received his message secondhand through what others told him about Christ, and he got the message wrong. To address the issues and counter the danger posed by these teachers, Paul wrote his letter to the Galatians.

OVERVIEW

The undercutting of his apostleship requires Paul to begin his letter by insisting that he received both his apostleship and his message not from human sources but through a revelation from Jesus Christ himself (1:1,11 – 12,15 – 16). His contacts with the Jerusalem apostles were limited — he did not receive his message from them (1:16 – 24) — but the leaders of the Jerusalem church approved his apostleship and message (2:1 – 10).

Basilica of St. Paul in Pisidian Antioch, built in the fourth century AD. Paul preached one of his sermons in the synagogue at Antioch (Acts 13:13–43), in South Galatia.

www.HolyLandPhotos.org

Paul then turns to the issue of law observance. Granted, the law prescribes a path to righteousness and life by obeying its commands (3:12), but since human beings transgress these commands (3:10) and live "under the control of sin" (3:22), neither righteousness nor life is attainable through the law (2:21; 3:21). Christ, in dying, took upon himself the law's curse on transgressors (3:13), so that those rightly subject to that curse might be delivered from it and live a new life, apart from the law, empowered by the Spirit (4:5; 5:18). This does not make the law a bad thing, but it does mean that God never intended the law to provide the path to life (3:21); its purpose is more limited (3:19–24), and God intended the covenant to which it belonged to apply only for the period from Moses until the coming of Christ (3:17–19). For the Galatians to be circumcised would thus mean binding themselves to a covenant that required fully observing its commands (5:3) and cutting themselves off from Christ and his grace (5:4).

Believers, though not "under the law" (5:18), are nonetheless to "walk by the Spirit" (5:16). As they do so, God's Spirit within them will produce fruit that no law condemns (5:22–23) and a love that represents the true fulfillment of God's law (5:14).

THEMES

Important themes in this letter include the nature of Paul's apostleship and the origin of his gospel (1:1—2:10); justification (by faith, not by works of the law [2:11—3:14; see note on 2:16]); the nature and role of the law (3:10–25); the freedom of the believer (4:21—5:1,13); the gift of the Spirit (3:2–5,14 [see note on 3:2]; 4:6–7); the ongoing struggle between the flesh and the Spirit in the life of the believer (5:16–17); and Christian ethics (as focused on love, 5:14; as walking in the Spirit, 5:16; and as producing the Spirit's fruit, 5:22–23).

OUTLINE

- **I. Introduction (1:1–10)**
  - A. Salutation (1:1–5)
  - B. No Other Gospel (1:6–10)
- **II. The Origin and Defense of Paul's Gospel (1:11—2:21)**
  - A. Paul Called by God (1:11–24)
  - B. Paul Accepted by the Apostles (2:1–10)
  - C. Paul Opposes Cephas (2:11–21)
- **III. Law and Gospel (3:1—4:31)**
  - A. Faith or Works of the Law (3:1–14)
  - B. The Law and the Promise (3:15–22)
  - C. Children of God (3:23—4:7)
  - D. Paul's Concern for the Galatians (4:8–20)
  - E. Hagar and Sarah (4:21–31)
- **IV. Instructions in Christian Living (5:1—6:10)**
  - A. Freedom in Christ (5:1–12)
  - B. Life by the Spirit (5:13–26)
  - C. Doing Good to All (6:1–10)
- **V. Conclusion: Not Circumcision but the New Creation (6:11–18)**

GALATIANS

1 Paul, an apostle — sent not from men nor by a man, but by Jesus Christ[a] and God the Father, who raised him from the dead[b] — 2 and all the brothers and sisters[a] with me,[c]

To the churches in Galatia:[d]

3 Grace and peace to you from God our Father and the Lord Jesus Christ,[e] 4 who gave himself for our sins[f] to rescue us from the present evil age, according to the will of our God and Father,[g] 5 to whom be glory for ever and ever. Amen.[h]

No Other Gospel

6 I am astonished that you are so quickly deserting the one who called[i] you to live in the grace of Christ and are turning to a different gospel[j] — 7 which is really no gospel at all. Evidently some people

[a] 2 The Greek word for *brothers and sisters* (*adelphoi*) refers here to believers, both men and women, as part of God's family; also in verse 11; and in 3:15; 4:12, 28, 31; 5:11, 13; 6:1, 18.

1:1 [a] Ac 9:15 [b] Ac 2:24
1:2 [c] Php 4:21 [d] Ac 16:6; 1Co 16:1
1:3 [e] Ro 1:7
1:4 [f] Mt 20:28; Ro 4:25; Gal 2:20 [g] Php 4:20
1:5 [h] Ro 11:36
1:6 [i] Gal 5:8 [j] 2Co 11:4

1:1–10 *Introduction.* Paul passes quickly from an opening greeting and benediction to an expression of his concern over the Galatians' attraction to a false gospel.
1:1–5 *Salutation.* Paul begins his opening greeting and benediction with an unusual emphasis on the divine origin of his apostleship.
1:1 apostle. A delegate entrusted with a mission, carrying the authority of the sender. The same word is translated "messenger" (John 13:16; Phil 2:25) and "representatives" (2 Cor 8:23). Jesus himself is referred to as an "apostle," i.e., one sent on a mission by God (Heb 3:1). Paul does not confine the circle of "apostles" of Jesus Christ to the 12 who accompanied Jesus during his earthly ministry; he includes those (like himself, Barnabas, and Silas) who had seen the (risen) Lord and been commissioned by him (1 Cor 9:1,5–6). While Paul was concerned for the salvation of his own (Jewish) people, his apostolic commission was "to the Gentiles" (Rom 11:13; cf. Gal 2:7; Acts 22:21; Rom 1:5; 15:16). **sent not from men nor by a man.** A human neither sent Paul on a mission nor delivered his (divine) commission. Rather, "Jesus Christ and God the Father" commissioned him. This chapter distinguishes Jesus from human beings and associates him with God the Father (vv. 1,10,12). Since Paul's commission (cf. 1 Thess 2:4) and message (Gal 1:11–12) were divine in origin, he is not proposing that the Galatians should follow *his* interpretation of the gospel rather than that of his opponents; he is saying the gospel he preaches is the gospel of God (Rom 1:1; 1 Thess 2:2) and must be heeded as such. **God the Father.** Since God is the source of every human being's life, he may rightly be spoken of as the Father of all (Acts 17:28–29). But when Paul speaks of God as Father, he generally means either the "Father of our Lord Jesus Christ" (Rom 15:6) or the Father of all those "adopted" into God's family because of their faith in Christ (Gal 3:26; 4:4–7; Rom 8:15–16). **who raised him from the dead.** Distinctive of, and decisive for, the Christian understanding of God is not the notion of God as Father, but the conviction that God was at work in the death and resurrection of Jesus Christ to save humans.
1:2 all the brothers and sisters. Paul mentions these unnamed fellow Christians perhaps to indicate that they share the concerns he expresses in the letter. **churches in Galatia.** Paul intends the letter to circulate among Christian assemblies within a large geographic area (see Introduction: Recipients).
1:3 Grace and peace. This is a standard greeting (or blessing) at the start of Paul's letters, but it is no empty formula. The Galatians need to learn that they owe their part in God's new creation solely to God's grace and that they are to live by God's grace (cf. v. 6). They will then enjoy spiritual well-being (God's "peace"). **God our Father and the Lord Jesus Christ.** Both are the source of divine blessing. As frequently in Paul's writings, "God" denotes the deity of the Father; "Lord," the deity of the Son (see 1 Cor 8:6).
1:4 gave himself. Christ's death was a voluntary self-sacrifice (2:20; Matt 20:28; John 10:17–18; Heb 9:26). **for our sins.** See Matt 1:21; 1 Cor 15:3; 1 Pet 2:24. We need Christ to rescue us because we sin — both obvious "willful sins" (Ps 19:13) and those so everyday that we hardly think of them as sins (Ps 19:12; Matt 5:22,28; Luke 10:30–32); all sins reflect our failure to love God as we should. **present evil age.** The world and everyone in it belong to God (Ps 24:1), and his rule is both universal and eternal (Pss 103:19; 145:13). But the present age is "evil" inasmuch as God's rule goes widely unacknowledged while people (wittingly or not) give their allegiance to the powers of evil (cf. 2 Cor 4:4). Though believers have been rescued from the "dominion of darkness" and have entered "the kingdom of the Son [God] loves" (Col 1:13), the values and mindset of a world that has turned against God remain a temptation and source of danger (Rom 12:2; Jas 4:4; 1 John 2:15).
1:6–10 *No Other Gospel.* Paul's opponents appear as Christians who proclaim the gospel. But theirs is a "different gospel" (v. 6) that is not

1:7 [k]Ac 15:24; Gal 5:10
1:8 [l]2Co 11:4 [m]Ro 9:3
1:9 [n]Ro 16:17
1:10 [o]Ro 2:29; 1Th 2:4
1:11 [p]1Co 15:1
1:12 [q]ver 1 [r]ver 16
1:13 [s]Ac 26:4,5 [t]Ac 8:3
1:14 [u]Mt 15:2
1:15 [v]Isa 49:1,5; Jer 1:5 [w]Ac 9:15
1:16 [x]Gal 2:9 [y]Mt 16:17
1:18 [z]Ac 9:22,23 [a]Ac 9:26,27

are throwing you into confusion[k] and are trying to pervert the gospel of Christ. 8 But even if we or an
angel from heaven should preach a gospel other than the one we preached to you,[l] let them be under
God's curse![m] 9 As we have already said, so now I say again: If anybody is preaching to you a gospel other
than what you accepted,[n] let them be under God's curse!

10 Am I now trying to win the approval of human beings, or of God? Or am I trying to please people?[o]
If I were still trying to please people, I would not be a servant of Christ.

Paul Called by God

11 I want you to know, brothers and sisters,[p] that the gospel I preached is not of human origin. 12 I did
not receive it from any man,[q] nor was I taught it; rather, I received it by revelation[r] from Jesus Christ.

13 For you have heard of my previous way of life in Judaism,[s] how intensely I persecuted the church
of God and tried to destroy it.[t] 14 I was advancing in Judaism beyond many of my own age among my
people and was extremely zealous for the traditions of my fathers.[u] 15 But when God, who set me apart
from my mother's womb[v] and called me[w] by his grace, was pleased 16 to reveal his Son in me so that I
might preach him among the Gentiles,[x] my immediate response was not to consult any human being.[y]
17 I did not go up to Jerusalem to see those who were apostles before I was, but I went into Arabia. Later
I returned to Damascus.

18 Then after three years,[z] I went up to Jerusalem[a] to get acquainted with Cephas[*a*] and stayed with

[*a*] *18* That is, Peter

good news at all. The gospel (which Paul already proclaimed to the Galatians) is the ultimate standard of truth, not the one who proclaims it.

1:6 I am astonished. Without pausing (as in other letters) to give God thanks for the faith of those to whom he is writing, Paul expresses immediately his concerns. **the one who called you.** God uses the (human) proclamation of the gospel to "call" hearers to himself (2 Cor 5:19–20; 2 Thess 2:14). Those who hear the gospel aright receive it not as the words of a human being but as the word of God (1 Thess 2:13). The moment of their coming to faith is thus the time of their "calling" (cf. 1 Cor 1:26; 7:20). **to live in the grace of Christ.** Grace is a sphere within which one may live: the sphere in which one experiences God's favor, though without having earned it (cf. Rom 5:2). Such favor is necessarily linked to Christ, the mediator between God and humankind (1 Tim 2:5); to cut oneself off from Christ is to cut oneself off from grace (Gal 5:4).

1:7 some people. Presumably from outside Galatia since "you" refers to the Galatian believers.

1:8 under God's curse. Should even Paul or an angel from heaven pervert the gospel, they are subject to God's curse on those who offend others' faith (cf. Matt 18:6).

1:10 trying to please people. The desire to please others keeps many people from believing in Christ (John 5:44); it is incompatible with serving him (cf. Matt 6:1).

1:11—2:21 *The Origin and Defense of Paul's Gospel.* Paul cites the divine origin of his apostleship (1:11–24), the acceptance of his message by the "pillars" among the apostles (2:9; see 2:1–10), and his defense of the gospel in Antioch (2:11–14) before explaining why justification must be by faith, apart from the "works of the law" (2:16; see 2:15–21).

1:11–24 *Paul Called by God.* Paul's message is the product of a direct revelation of Jesus Christ. Even after this revelation, Paul's contact with other apostles was too limited for him to have received his message from them.

1:13 my previous way of life in Judaism. Paul's preconversion devotion to Judaism shows that God has transformed his life. But since the Galatians are, in effect, being tempted to embrace Judaism without Christ, Paul's personal testimony—that he knows that way of life well but has abandoned it to serve Christ—should encourage them to resist the temptation. Paul is not denying his Jewish ethnicity (Rom 11:1). The covenant inaugurated at Mount Sinai and centered on the Mosaic law reached its intended end with the coming of Christ (Gal 3:19–24). Thus, "Judaism" here means living under the laws of an obsolete covenant (cf. Phil 3:4–9). **the church of God.** "Church" is not used to refer to the Israelite community in the OT (see "assembly" in Acts 7:38) but of the community of believers in the NT (Matt 16:18; Eph 1:22; Col 1:18).

1:14 traditions of my fathers. Perhaps (nonbiblical) Pharisaic traditions, since Pharisees were well known for adhering to traditional observances not prescribed in Scripture (Matt 15:1–9) and since Paul sprang from Pharisee stock (Phil 3:5). But Jews could speak of the laws of Moses in this way as well.

1:15 from my mother's womb. Means "from the day I was born." The expression recalls Isa 49:1; Paul too is a servant "called" into God's service in God's eternal plan.

1:16 to reveal his Son in me. May mean either that (1) God revealed to Paul that Jesus is God's Son or (2) God chose to use Paul to reveal that truth to others, specifically "Gentiles" (Rom 11:13–14). **not to consult any human being.** Paul did not need humans to confirm or supplement what God had revealed to him.

1:17 went into Arabia. Paul does not indicate the purpose of his going to Arabia, the Nabatean kingdom of King Aretas (see 2 Cor 11:32 and note). Paul may have engaged in mission activity there. But he mentions where he was at this time only to rule out the idea that he was in Jerusalem receiving instruction from the apostles. **returned to Damascus.** God revealed himself to Paul (called Saul in Acts 9) on his way to Damascus, where he was baptized.

1:18–20 Paul did not derive his gospel from church leaders in Jerusalem.

1:18 three years. Since a "year" could mean any part of a year (e.g., December of one year; January of another), "three years" can mean any period of time from roughly 14 months to a full three years. **Cephas.** The name Jesus gave "Simon son of Jonah" (Matt 16:17), also called "Simon son of John" (John 1:42; 21:15–17). Its Greek equivalent is Peter (John 1:42). The purpose of Paul's visit to Jerusalem was limited (to get to know Peter), and it did not take place until "three years" after his conversion. He was there for only 15 days, and he did not meet any other apostles (but see note on Gal 1:19).

A Roman cardo at Tarsus. Paul was from Tarsus (part of Cilicia) and traveled there on other occasions (Gal 1:21).

Cheryl Dunn for Talbot Bible Lands

him fifteen days. 19 I saw none of the other apostles—only James,[b] the Lord's brother. 20 I assure you
before God that what I am writing you is no lie.[c]
21 Then I went to Syria and Cilicia.[d] 22 I was personally unknown to the churches of Judea[e] that are
in Christ. 23 They only heard the report: "The man who formerly persecuted us is now preaching the
faith[f] he once tried to destroy." 24 And they praised God[g] because of me.

Paul Accepted by the Apostles

2 Then after fourteen years, I went up again to Jerusalem,[h] this time with Barnabas. I took Titus
along also. 2 I went in response to a revelation and, meeting privately with those esteemed as leaders, I presented to them the gospel that I preach among the Gentiles.[i] I wanted to be sure I was not running and had not been running my race[j] in vain. 3 Yet not even Titus,[k] who was with me, was compelled
to be circumcised, even though he was a Greek.[l] 4 This matter arose because some false believers[m] had

1:19 [b] Mt 13:55
1:20 [c] Ro 9:1
1:21 [d] Ac 6:9
1:22 [e] 1Th 2:14
1:23 [f] Ac 6:7
1:24 [g] Mt 9:8
2:1 [h] Ac 15:2
2:2 [i] Ac 15:4, 12 [j] 1Co 9:24; Php 2:16
2:3 [k] 2Co 2:13 [l] Ac 16:3; 1Co 9:21
2:4 [m] 2Co 11:26

1:19 none of the other apostles—only James. This translation may suggest that Paul did not regard James as an apostle. It is also possible to understand the verse as saying that James was the only other apostle whom Paul saw at this time. **James, the Lord's brother.** Cf. Matt 13:55. He was apparently not among Jesus' followers during his earthly ministry (John 7:5); but the risen Lord appeared to him (1 Cor 15:7), and he later took on a leadership role among the Jerusalem believers (see note on Acts 15:13–21). It is natural to assume, though nowhere is it explicitly stated, that Jas 1:1 refers to the same person.
1:20 I assure you. Paul rests the truth of his gospel on his not receiving it from human beings, so he solemnly promises that he is telling the truth about his limited contacts with Jerusalem.
1:21 Syria. Included Antioch. **Cilicia.** Included Tarsus. See Acts 9:30; 11:25–26 (see map, p. 2247).
1:22 personally unknown. During this period Paul also kept a distance from believers in Judea (including Jerusalem). He was known to them only by the report of his remarkable conversion.
2:1–10 *Paul Accepted by the Apostles.* Paul did not return to Jerusalem for many years. When he did, the church leaders recognized his apostleship and acknowledged the truth of his message.
2:1 after fourteen years. May mean anything from a little more than 12 years to a full 14 years (see note on 1:18). This time period may date from Paul's conversion or from his previous visit to Jerusalem. **Barnabas.** For Paul's partnership with Barnabas, see Acts 11:25–26; 13:1—15:39. **Titus.** A trusted co-worker of Paul (2 Cor 2:13; 7:6, 13–15; Titus 1:4). The issue whether Gentile believers should be circumcised could not be discussed simply in the abstract because Titus was in their midst: Was he to be welcomed as a brother in Christ or told that he needed to be circumcised?
2:2 revelation. Paul offers no particulars about how he received this divine guidance. A prophet in the Antioch church may have communicated it. **privately.** The mention of "false believers" in v. 4 raises the question whether these people intruded on the private meeting of v. 2, whether their position was simply discussed at that private meeting, or whether the private meeting of v. 2 preceded more public events described in the following verses. **running ... in vain.** Confident that he received his gospel by a revelation from Jesus, Paul does not mean to suggest doubt about its truth. But his evangelizing efforts would surely be undermined if he was not supported by the leaders of the Jerusalem church, and the unity of the church would be compromised.
2:4 false believers. Or "false brothers." As those who believed that Jesus is the Messiah, they appeared to be "believers." As those who insisted that Gentile believers must submit to the Mosaic law, Paul regards them as "false." **make us slaves.** To submit to the law of Moses

2:4 [n]Jude 4 [o]Ac 15:1; Gal 5:1,13
2:5 [p]ver 14
2:6 [q]Gal 6:3 [r]Ac 10:34
2:7 [s]1Th 2:4; 1Ti 1:11 [t]Ac 9:15 [u]ver 9,11,14
2:8 [v]Ac 1:25
2:9 [w]ver 7,11,14 [x]1Ti 3:15 [y]Ac 4:36 [z]Ro 12:3
2:10 [a]Ac 24:17
2:11 [b]ver 7,9,14 [c]Ac 11:19
2:12 [d]Ac 11:3 [e]Ac 11:2
2:13 [f]ver 1; Ac 4:36
2:14 [g]ver 5 [h]ver 7,9,11 [i]Ac 10:28
2:15 [j]Php 3:4,5 [k]1Sa 15:18

infiltrated our ranks to spy on[n] the freedom[o] we have in Christ Jesus and to make us slaves. 5We did not
give in to them for a moment, so that the truth of the gospel[p] might be preserved for you.
6As for those who were held in high esteem[q]—whatever they were makes no difference to me; God
does not show favoritism[r]—they added nothing to my message. 7On the contrary, they recognized that
I had been entrusted with the task[s] of preaching the gospel to the uncircumcised,[a][t] just as Peter[u] had
been to the circumcised.[b] 8For God, who was at work in Peter as an apostle[v] to the circumcised, was
also at work in me as an apostle to the Gentiles. 9James, Cephas[c][w] and John, those esteemed as pillars,[x]
gave me and Barnabas[y] the right hand of fellowship when they recognized the grace given to me.[z]
They agreed that we should go to the Gentiles, and they to the circumcised. 10All they asked was that we
should continue to remember the poor,[a] the very thing I had been eager to do all along.

Paul Opposes Cephas

11When Cephas[b] came to Antioch,[c] I opposed him to his face, because he stood condemned. 12For
before certain men came from James, he used to eat with the Gentiles.[d] But when they arrived, he began
to draw back and separate himself from the Gentiles because he was afraid of those who belonged to
the circumcision group.[e] 13The other Jews joined him in his hypocrisy, so that by their hypocrisy even
Barnabas[f] was led astray.
14When I saw that they were not acting in line with the truth of the gospel,[g] I said to Cephas[h] in front
of them all, "You are a Jew, yet you live like a Gentile and not like a Jew.[i] How is it, then, that you force
Gentiles to follow Jewish customs?
15"We who are Jews by birth[j] and not sinful Gentiles[k] 16know that a person is not justified by the

[a] *7* That is, Gentiles [b] *7* That is, Jews; also in verses 8 and 9 [c] *9* That is, Peter; also in verses 11 and 14

is to be cut off from Christ (5:4); the Mosaic law's path to righteousness and life (through obedience to its commands [3:12]) leads those who take it into slavery to sin (3:22; 4:21—5:1) and liability to the law's curse (3:10). Christ offers freedom from both (2:4; 3:13; 5:1). Paul wants those tempted to turn to the law to grasp the implications of its service.

2:6 whatever they were. May allude to the Jerusalem apostles' following Jesus during his earthly ministry. **added nothing.** They saw nothing defective in the gospel as Paul preached it.

2:7 entrusted with the task of preaching the gospel. Cf. 1 Thess 2:4. Paul's divine commissioning is apparent because God is clearly "at work" (v. 8) in his ministry.

2:9 esteemed as pillars. Peter, together with James and John, the sons of Zebedee, had made up an inner circle around Jesus within the wider circle of the Twelve (Mark 5:37; 9:2; 14:33). Herod Agrippa killed James son of Zebedee (Acts 12:1–2), but the James of this verse (as also in 1:19) is the "brother of the Lord." Their closeness to Jesus contributed to the esteem in which others held them. To regard them as "pillars" of the community may suggest that the community itself was seen as the temple of God (1 Cor 3:16; Eph 2:21). **gave ... the right hand of fellowship.** Acknowledged that Paul and Barnabas were partners in the same ministry. **we should go to the Gentiles, and they to the circumcised.** While they all proclaimed the same message (1 Cor 15:9–11), Paul and Barnabas focused on outreach to the Gentiles, whereas James, Cephas, and John focused on the Jews.

2:10 the poor. The impoverished members of the church in Jerusalem (Rom 15:26). Paul (with Barnabas) had already shown concern for their need (Acts 11:29–30), and the collection that he would later gather from his Gentile churches (Rom 15:25–27; 2 Cor 8–9) expresses the same concern.

2:11–21 *Paul Opposes Cephas.* Paul and the Jerusalem leaders had agreed that Gentile believers were not to be circumcised. Nothing in that agreement prevented Jewish believers, however, from continuing to observe the Mosaic law. Paul himself allowed those whose sense of right and wrong had been shaped by their upbringing under the law and whose faith was weak to continue its observance, since to do otherwise would violate their conscience (Rom 14:1—15:4). The problem that arose in Antioch (Gal 2:11–13) was presumably not anticipated at the Jerusalem meeting: How could Jewish believers anxious to maintain their law observance share common meals with Gentile believers who ate an unrestricted diet? Initially impressed by the demonstration of unity shown in Antioch, Peter joined in meals eaten by Jewish and Gentile believers together; later, under pressure from representatives of James, he withdrew from such meals. For Paul, such conduct betrayed the truth of the gospel. Paul introduces his response to Peter in v. 14. But what he then says to Peter has relevance for the Galatians as well, and at some point in the verses that follow (certainly by 3:1, but perhaps earlier), his response to Peter gives way to what he wants to say directly to the Galatians.

2:11 stood condemned. Peter's actions were wrong in God's eyes, however they were regarded by human beings.

2:12–13 We do not know what the men from James said to Peter to influence his behavior (and that of Barnabas and other Jewish believers). Is the point that (1) the apparent indifference toward the law shown by Jews who ate with Gentiles jeopardized unity among Jewish believers, whose number included devotees of the law ("the circumcision group"); (2) Jewish believers who flaunted their freedom from the law were in danger of persecution from non-Christian Jews; or (3) those whose mission was directed to Jews (like Peter, James, and John) would jeopardize the success of their outreach if word were to spread that they had eaten with Gentiles? Paul has no interest in uncovering the thinking of those who compromised the truth of the gospel. They showed their "hypocrisy" by acting inconsistently with the unity that Jewish and Gentile believers share in Christ.

2:14 in front of them all. Peter's public departure from "the truth of the gospel" required public correction. **live like a Gentile.** Peter had broken Jewish food laws by eating with Gentile believers. **force Gentiles to follow Jewish customs.** By ceasing to have fellowship with Gentile believers in order to maintain Jewish practices, Peter conveyed the message that Jewish practices were important, perhaps crucial, even for Christians.

2:15 sinful Gentiles. Jews regarded the Gentile world en masse as sinful because of their idolatry and consequent widespread immorality.

2:16 The issue whether Gentile believers should be circumcised and

works of the law, but by faith in Jesus Christ.[l] So we, too, have put our faith in Christ Jesus that we may
be justified by faith in[a] Christ and not by the works of the law, because by the works of the law no one
will be justified.
17 "But if, in seeking to be justified in Christ, we Jews find ourselves also among the sinners,[m] doesn't
that mean that Christ promotes sin? Absolutely not![n] 18 If I rebuild what I destroyed, then I really would
be a lawbreaker.
19 "For through the law I died to the law[o] so that I might live for God.[p] 20 I have been crucified with
Christ[q] and I no longer live, but Christ lives in me.[r] The life I now live in the body, I live by faith in the
Son of God,[s] who loved me[t] and gave himself for me.[u] 21 I do not set aside the grace of God, for if righteousness could be gained through the law,[v] Christ died for nothing!"[b]

Faith or Works of the Law

3 You foolish Galatians! Who has bewitched you?[w] Before your very eyes Jesus Christ was clearly
portrayed as crucified.[x] 2 I would like to learn just one thing from you: Did you receive the Spirit
by the works of the law, or by believing what you heard?[y] 3 Are you so foolish? After beginning by means

2:16 [l] Ac 13:39; Ro 9:30
2:17 [m] ver 15 [n] Gal 3:21
2:19 [o] Ro 7:4 [p] Ro 6:10, 11,14; 2Co 5:15
2:20 [q] Ro 6:6 [r] 1Pe 4:2 [s] Mt 4:3 [t] Ro 8:37 [u] Gal 1:4
2:21 [v] Gal 3:21
3:1 [w] Gal 5:7 [x] 1Co 1:23
3:2 [y] Ro 10:17

[a] *16* Or *but through the faithfulness of . . . justified on the basis of the faithfulness of* [b] *21* Some interpreters end the quotation after verse 14.

obey the law of Moses can only be resolved when a more fundamental question has been considered: How can anyone, Jew or Gentile, be found righteous in God's eyes (as any must be who would belong to God's people)? When Jews (like Peter and Paul) put their faith in Jesus Christ, this clearly implies that their law observance is not sufficient; they, no less than "sinful Gentiles" (v. 15), are sinners. **justified.** Declared (not *made*) righteous, found righteous, acquitted. Such declarations are typically made by judges, whom God commands to "declare righteous" those who *are* righteous (i.e., acquit the innocent) and "condemn" the guilty (Deut 25:1, cf. Isa 5:23). But those whom God declares righteous in Gal 2:16 are *not* themselves righteous, but sinners (see notes on vv. 15,17; see also Rom 4:5; 5:8–9); it is only because God has provided Christ as the atonement for their sins that he can remain righteous himself while declaring unrighteous people to be righteous (Rom 3:24–26). **faith in.** Can also be translated "the faithfulness [i.e., obedience] of," which would mean that sinners can be justified only because Christ was "obedient to death—even death on a cross" (Phil 2:8; cf. Rom 5:19). But "faith in" is preferable because in this context Christ's faithfulness is not under discussion; Paul's point is that God attributes righteousness to the one who believes (Gal 3:6; Rom 4:3,22–24). **faith.** Means the faith of believers when Paul contrasts "faith" with "works," the "works of the law," or "the law" as paths to righteousness (Rom 3:20–22; 4:2–3,5; 9:31–33; 10:5–9 [the "faith" of v. 6 is the believer's; see vv. 8–9]). **by the works of the law.** Jews and Gentiles alike are required to do what is "good" (Rom 2:6–7,9–10). Jews encounter the requirement in the "works" demanded by the written law; Gentiles, in the law "written on their hearts" (Rom 2:14–15). To say that no one can be justified "by the works of the law" is thus equivalent to saying that no one can be justified by doing good. **no one.** Paul is paraphrasing Ps 143:2 ("no one living is righteous before [God]") and changes "no one living" to "no flesh" (in the Greek) to underline human frailty and sinfulness and the enormous chasm that separates "flesh" from God, who is spirit (cf. 2 Chr 32:8). Paul applies the universal truth of Ps 143:2 to the specific point at issue: not even those who strive to be righteous by observing the law's commands attain their goal (Rom 9:31).

2:17 Christ promotes sin? An argument that might be raised against justification by faith. If Jewish believers in Christ use their faith as an excuse for breaking the law by eating with Gentiles, then faith in Christ is an excuse for sin, and Christ promotes sin.

2:18 rebuild what I destroyed. Submit to the law once more. By placing their faith in Christ, believers die to the law (vv. 19–20; Rom 7:6), and since the dead are no longer subject to the law, they cannot be accused of breaking it (Rom 7:1–6).

2:19 through the law. Christ died "through the law" when he took upon himself the law's curse and condemnation of transgressors (3:10,13); Paul saw Christ's death as entailing the death of his own old way of life as well. **to the law.** The law and its condemnation no longer have authority over Paul (Rom 7:1–6). **so that I might live for God.** Paul, a former zealot of the law, never wrote anything more astonishing than this claim that he had to "die" to the law in order to live for God. But he needed to be delivered from the law that condemned him as a sinner if he was to be free to serve God "in the new way of the Spirit, and not in the old way of the written code" (Rom 7:6).

2:20 crucified with Christ. Christ's crucifixion represents the condemnation of fallen humanity in its rebellion against God (cf. Rom 8:3). Paul's "baptism into [Christ's] death" (Rom 6:4) means the end of his own life under sin: he "died to sin" (Rom 6:2). **Christ lives in me.** Baptism represents not only a death (with Christ) to the old way of life but also a rising (with Christ) to a new one (Rom 6:1–11; cf. Gal 3:27). Christ continues to live within believers by his Spirit (Rom 8:9–10).

2:21 The drastic remedy that God deemed necessary to provide for sin—the death of his Son—proves that by no lesser means can human beings be found righteous. It follows, then, that "righteousness" cannot be "gained through the law," but only through "the grace of God."

3:1—4:31 *Law and Gospel.* Paul discusses what it means to be "under the law" (4:21) and why justification is necessarily by faith.

3:1–14 *Faith or Works of the Law.* Paul proves that faith is the God-ordained path to righteousness and life by appealing to (1) the Galatians' own experience (vv. 1–5), (2) the example of Abraham (vv. 6–9), and (3) what Scripture says about the different natures and effects of the law and faith (vv. 10–14).

3:1 You foolish Galatians! Who has bewitched you? Paul is astonished (cf. 1:6) that the Galatians could foolishly consider law observance as necessary in view of the blessings they already enjoy. He implies that the deception affecting them must be more than human. **Jesus Christ was clearly portrayed as crucified.** As in Corinth (1 Cor 2:2), "Jesus Christ and him crucified" was the focus of Paul's message in Galatia.

3:2 receive the Spirit. In OT times, the Spirit of God came upon individual people at certain times to enable them to perform crucial tasks with divine ability (e.g., Exod 31:1–5; Num 24:2–3; Judg 3:10); ideally, however, all God's people would possess God's Spirit (Num 11:29), and God promised that, at a future time of blessing, this would happen (Ezek 36:27; Joel 2:28–29). Jesus repeated the promise (John 14:16–17; Acts 1:4–5), and Peter announced its fulfillment on the day of Pentecost (Acts 2:16–21). Other blessings of the new age inaugurated by Christ's resurrection await his return, but the Spirit has already been given "as

3:5 [z] 1Co 12:10
3:6 [a] Ge 15:6; Ro 4:3
3:7 [b] ver 9
3:8 [c] Ge 12:3; Ac 3:25
3:9 [d] ver 7; Ro 4:16
3:10 [e] Dt 27:26; Jer 11:3
3:11 [f] Hab 2:4; Gal 2:16; Heb 10:38
3:12 [g] Lev 18:5; Ro 10:5
3:13 [h] Gal 4:5 [i] Dt 21:23; Ac 5:30
3:14 [j] Ro 4:9,16 [k] ver 2; Joel 2:28; Ac 2:33

of the Spirit, are you now trying to finish by means of the flesh?[a] 4 Have you experienced[b] so much in
vain — if it really was in vain? 5 So again I ask, does God give you his Spirit and work miracles[z] among
you by the works of the law, or by your believing what you heard? 6 So also Abraham "believed God, and
it was credited to him as righteousness."[c][a]
7 Understand, then, that those who have faith[b] are children of Abraham. 8 Scripture foresaw that God
would justify the Gentiles by faith, and announced the gospel in advance to Abraham: "All nations will be
blessed through you."[d][c] 9 So those who rely on faith[d] are blessed along with Abraham, the man of faith.
10 For all who rely on the works of the law are under a curse, as it is written: "Cursed is everyone who
does not continue to do everything written in the Book of the Law."[e][e] 11 Clearly no one who relies on the
law is justified before God, because "the righteous will live by faith."[f][f] 12 The law is not based on faith;
on the contrary, it says, "The person who does these things will live by them."[g][g] 13 Christ redeemed us
from the curse of the law[h] by becoming a curse for us, for it is written: "Cursed is everyone who is hung
on a pole."[h][i] 14 He redeemed us in order that the blessing given to Abraham might come to the Gentiles
through Christ Jesus,[j] so that by faith we might receive the promise of the Spirit.[k]

The Law and the Promise

15 Brothers and sisters, let me take an example from everyday life. Just as no one can set aside or add
to a human covenant that has been duly established, so it is in this case. 16 The promises were spoken

[a] *3* In contexts like this, the Greek word for *flesh* (*sarx*) refers to the sinful state of human beings, often presented as a power in opposition to the Spirit. [b] *4* Or *suffered* [c] *6* Gen. 15:6 [d] *8* Gen. 12:3; 18:18; 22:18 [e] *10* Deut. 27:26 [f] *11* Hab. 2:4 [g] *12* Lev. 18:5 [h] *13* Deut. 21:23

a deposit, guaranteeing what is to come" (2 Cor 1:22). As in Acts (see 2:4; 10:44–46; 19:6), the initial coming of the Spirit upon the Galatians when they believed the gospel message was marked by unmistakable signs of his presence (Gal 3:5). Paul finds it incredible that the Galatians, having "experienced so much" (v. 4) without "the works of the law," could now imagine that they needed to observe its prescriptions, which were intended rather to serve as a "guardian" (v. 24) of Israel in the "flesh" until Christ came and the Spirit was given. **believing what you heard.** Faith, evoked by the gospel message (Rom 10:17) and the power of the Spirit (1 Cor 2:4–5), recognizes that message as the word of God (1 Thess 2:13) and responds to it as the call of God (Gal 1:6).

3:3 by means of the flesh. "Flesh" is sometimes used in a neutral sense of the embodied life of human beings (cf. 2:20, where "in the body" is literally "in the flesh"); most frequently in Paul's writings it refers to the sinful nature, in rebellion against God, found in all the descendants of Adam (cf. Rom 5:19; 8:5–8). The law, given to human beings in the flesh to remind them of their responsibilities before God, exacerbated their rebellion (Rom 7:7–13). In turning to the law, the Galatians were abandoning the Spirit-led service of God characteristic of the new age and returning to the old way of life (cf. Rom 7:5–6).

3:4 experienced. In the context, this rendering seems most fitting, but "suffered" is also possible.

3:6 believed God. Abraham too responded to the word of God with faith, and he — though sinful like all human beings — was credited with righteousness because of his faith (Gen 15:6; Rom 4:2–5).

3:7 children of Abraham. Abraham is the forefather of God's people (Abraham's "seed"); he and they alike are the recipients of God's promises (Gen 12:2–3; 17:4–8; 22:17–18). But Abraham's true "seed" is made up not of those merely physically descended from him (cf. Matt 3:9; Rom 9:6–9) but of those — Jews and Gentiles alike (Rom 4:11–12) — who live by faith as he did (John 8:39). God declares them (as he declared Abraham) righteous (Rom 4:22–24). In this way Abraham becomes the "father of many nations" (Rom 4:17) — as promised (Gen 17:5).

3:8 God's promise that he would bless Gentiles (though sinful, see 2:15) through Abraham, in effect "announced the gospel" of God's grace "in advance."

3:10 under a curse. The law promised a blessing and life to those who obeyed its commandments, a curse and death to those who disobeyed (Deut 11:26–28; 30:19–20). But sinners (all human beings!) do not — and cannot — obey the law (Rom 8:7–8), so only the law's curse came into effect (cf. 2 Cor 3:7,9). Some interpreters think that Paul refers specifically to those who believe they can be righteous through their own works.

3:11 the righteous will live by faith. By an alternative rendering, "The one who is righteous through faith shall live." Paul's quotation comes from Hab 2:4. If (as Hab 2:4 indicates) righteousness comes from faith (see NIV text note on Hab 2:4), then it cannot come from the law, which operates on a different principle (see Gal 3:12 and note).

3:12 The law is not based on faith. The same contrast between the righteousness of faith and the righteousness based on law is found in Rom 10:5–9; Phil 3:9. The righteousness based on law requires observance of its commands — a requirement that sinners cannot meet. It is very different from the principle that righteousness is credited to those whose deeds are not righteous but who respond to the gospel with faith (Rom 4:5; Eph 2:8–9).

3:13 Christ redeemed us from the curse of the law. Some interpreters think "us" refers to Jews, since they were the law's subjects (Rom 2:12). But since God has placed in the hearts of Gentiles an awareness of the moral requirements of the Mosaic law (Rom 2:14–15), and neither Gentiles nor Jews have fulfilled them, the curse may be said to rest on Jewish and Gentile sinners alike. The crucified Christ bore the curse pronounced on all transgressors.

3:14 redeemed us ... by faith. Redemption from the law's curse and justification by faith are preconditions for receiving God's blessing. **promise.** For the promised blessing of the Spirit, see note on 3:2.

3:15–22 *The Law and the Promise.* The law given to Moses could not alter the promise God had already given to Abraham. It served a different purpose.

3:15 human covenant. The Greek word Paul uses can refer to a last will or testament, but in Scripture it is commonly used of the covenants God made with his people. Paul regards God's promise to Abraham as such a covenant and insists that it cannot be set aside by the (later) law of Moses.

3:16 seeds ... seed. Scripture uses the singular "seed" where a plural (e.g., "children") would have been possible. God's promise to Abraham

to Abraham and to his seed.[l] Scripture does not say "and to seeds," meaning many people, but "and to
your seed,"[a] meaning one person, who is Christ. 17What I mean is this: The law, introduced 430 years[m]
later, does not set aside the covenant previously established by God and thus do away with the promise.
18For if the inheritance depends on the law, then it no longer depends on the promise;[n] but God in his
grace gave it to Abraham through a promise.

19Why, then, was the law given at all? It was added because of transgressions[o] until the Seed[p] to
whom the promise referred had come. The law was given through angels[q] and entrusted to a mediator.[r]
20A mediator,[s] however, implies more than one party; but God is one.

21Is the law, therefore, opposed to the promises of God? Absolutely not![t] For if a law had been given
that could impart life, then righteousness would certainly have come by the law.[u] 22But Scripture has
locked up everything under the control of sin,[v] so that what was promised, being given through faith
in Jesus Christ, might be given to those who believe.

Children of God

23Before the coming of this faith,[b] we were held in custody[w] under the law, locked up until the faith
that was to come would be revealed. 24So the law was our guardian until Christ came[x] that we might be
justified by faith.[y] 25Now that this faith has come, we are no longer under a guardian.

26So in Christ Jesus you are all children of God[z] through faith, 27for all of you who were baptized
into Christ[a] have clothed yourselves with Christ.[b] 28There is neither Jew nor Gentile, neither slave nor
free,[c] nor is there male and female, for you are all one in Christ Jesus.[d] 29If you belong to Christ,[e] then
you are Abraham's seed, and heirs according to the promise.[f]

4 What I am saying is that as long as an heir is underage, he is no different from a slave, although
he owns the whole estate. 2The heir is subject to guardians and trustees until the time set by his
father. 3So also, when we were underage, we were in slavery[g] under the elemental spiritual forces[c] of
the world.[h] 4But when the set time had fully come,[i] God sent his Son, born of a woman,[j] born under

3:16 [l]Lk 1:55; Ro 4:13,16
3:17 [m]Ge 15:13,14; Ex 12:40
3:18 [n]Ro 4:14
3:19 [o]Ro 5:20 [p]ver 16 [q]Ac 7:53 [r]Ex 20:19
3:20 [s]Heb 8:6; 9:15; 12:24
3:21 [t]Gal 2:17 [u]Gal 2:21
3:22 [v]Ro 3:9-19; 11:32
3:23 [w]Ro 11:32
3:24 [x]Ro 10:4 [y]Gal 2:16
3:26 [z]Ro 8:14
3:27 [a]Mt 28:19; Ro 6:3 [b]Ro 13:14
3:28 [c]Col 3:11 [d]Jn 10:16; 17:11; Eph 2:14,15
3:29 [e]1Co 3:23 [f]ver 16
4:3 [g]Gal 2:4 [h]Col 2:8,20
4:4 [i]Mk 1:15; Eph 1:10 [j]Jn 1:14

[a] *16* Gen. 12:7; 13:15; 24:7 [b] *22,23* Or *through the faithfulness of Jesus . . . 23Before faith came*
[c] *3* Or *under the basic principles*

(Gen 13:15; 17:8; 24:7) finds its unique fulfillment in Christ—though (as Gal 3:29 adds) it includes those who belong to Christ.

3:17 430 years. See Exod 12:40. Paul's point is that the law came much later than God's promise to Abraham and cannot set his promise aside.

3:18 if the inheritance depends on the law. That is, on human observance of the law. The inheritance would thus no longer depend solely on God's promise and grace. In that sense, law and promise (or grace) are exclusive alternatives.

3:19 Why, then, was the law given at all? God must have had a purpose in giving the law, though Paul only hints at that purpose before underlining that the law (and the Mosaic covenant to which it belonged) was an interim measure intended to last only from Moses until the coming of Christ, "the Seed" promised to Abraham. **because of transgressions.** May suggest that fear of the punishments prescribed by the law served to prevent some transgressions from taking place; more likely Paul's point is that the law, in spelling out God's requirements, revealed the rebellion against God implicit in its transgression (Rom 7:7–11) and thus how "utterly sinful" sin really is (Rom 7:13; cf. Rom 5:20). **given through angels.** See Acts 7:38,53; Heb 2:2.

3:20 mediator ... implies more than one party. Both Israel and God had obligations under the covenant mediated by Moses: God would bless Israel if they obeyed his commandments (an unfulfilled condition). But the promise God gave to Abraham was one-sided in its obligation: God made a commitment, and he would fulfill it.

3:21 if a law had been given that could impart life. A law telling sinners (who are spiritually dead) what they ought to do cannot give them life.

3:22 Scripture has locked up. "Scripture" here may simply mean "the law": though the law's commandments are "holy, righteous and good" (Rom 7:12), they are inevitably broken by those hostile to the divine Lawgiver. Hence the giving of the law led to slavery under sin. Alternatively, "Scripture" may refer to texts (like those cited in Rom 3:10–18) that speak of humanity's enslavement to sin. **faith in Jesus Christ.** As in 2:16 (see note there), some interpreters translate this "faithfulness of Jesus Christ."

3:23—4:7 *Children of God.* Faith in Jesus Christ brings the blessings enjoyed by God's children to those previously enslaved by the law.

3:23 Before the coming of this faith. Abraham, David, and other OT people of God were justified by faith (Rom 4:1–8), but the forgiveness they enjoyed, like that of believers in every age, depended on Christ's atoning death for their sins (Rom 3:25). In that sense, the righteousness of faith first came into effect with the work of Christ.

3:24 guardian. Greek *paidagōgos*, a slave charged with attending on and supervising the conduct of a boy until he reached the age of maturity. Paul sees the Mosaic law as exercising a similarly confining role for a limited period of time.

3:27 Those "baptized into Christ" (Rom 6:1–11; 1 Cor 12:13), God's Son, share in the joys of his sonship. **clothed yourselves with Christ.** See Rom 13:14; Eph 4:24; Col 3:10.

3:28 all one in Christ Jesus. Distinctions based on race, class, and gender characterize life in the old age; since this age is "passing away" (1 Cor 7:31) but has not yet passed away, its distinctions are still in evidence (1 Cor 7:17–24; 11:2–16; Eph 5:21—6:9). But in Christ Jesus, all are equally embraced and on the same terms (1 Cor 12:13; Col 3:11).

4:3 under the elemental spiritual forces of the world. See Col 2:8,20; see also 2 Cor 4:4; Eph 2:2; 6:12. Powers of evil prevail in this age and dominate the lives of sinful human beings. The law of God, which can only condemn the sin of its subjects, is also an enslaving force. From all such slavery, Christ brings deliverance.

4:4 the set time. See v. 2. Christ came at the time the Father set for those subject to "guardians" (the elemental spiritual forces of v. 3,

4:4 [k]Lk 2:27
4:5 [l]Jn 1:12
4:6 [m]Ro 5:5 [n]Ro 8:15,16
4:7 [o]Ro 8:17
4:8 [p]1Co 1:21; Eph 2:12; 1Th 4:5 [q]2Ch 13:9; Isa 37:19
4:9 [r]1Co 8:3 [s]ver 3 [t]Col 2:20
4:10 [u]Ro 14:5
4:11 [v]1Th 3:5
4:12 [w]Gal 6:18
4:13 [x]1Co 2:3
4:14 [y]Mt 10:40
4:16 [z]Am 5:10
4:18 [a]ver 13,14
4:19 [b]1Co 4:15 [c]Eph 4:13
4:22 [d]Ge 16:15 [e]Ge 21:2
4:23 [f]Ro 9:7,8 [g]Ge 18:10-14; Heb 11:11

the law,[k] 5 to redeem those under the law, that we might receive adoption[l] to sonship.[a] 6 Because you are
his sons, God sent the Spirit of his Son into our hearts,[m] the Spirit who calls out, *"Abba,*[b] Father."[n] 7 So
you are no longer a slave, but God's child; and since you are his child, God has made you also an heir.[o]

Paul's Concern for the Galatians

8 Formerly, when you did not know God,[p] you were slaves to those who by nature are not gods.[q] 9 But
now that you know God—or rather are known by God[r]—how is it that you are turning back to those
weak and miserable forces[c]? Do you wish to be enslaved[s] by them all over again?[t] 10 You are observing
special days and months and seasons and years![u] 11 I fear for you, that somehow I have wasted my
efforts on you.[v]

12 I plead with you, brothers and sisters,[w] become like me, for I became like you. You did me no
wrong. 13 As you know, it was because of an illness[x] that I first preached the gospel to you, 14 and even
though my illness was a trial to you, you did not treat me with contempt or scorn. Instead, you welcomed me as if I were an angel of God, as if I were Christ Jesus himself.[y] 15 Where, then, is your blessing
of me now? I can testify that, if you could have done so, you would have torn out your eyes and given
them to me. 16 Have I now become your enemy by telling you the truth?[z]

17 Those people are zealous to win you over, but for no good. What they want is to alienate you from
us, so that you may have zeal for them. 18 It is fine to be zealous, provided the purpose is good, and to
be so always, not just when I am with you.[a] 19 My dear children,[b] for whom I am again in the pains of
childbirth until Christ is formed in you,[c] 20 how I wish I could be with you now and change my tone,
because I am perplexed about you!

Hagar and Sarah

21 Tell me, you who want to be under the law, are you not aware of what the law says? 22 For it is
written that Abraham had two sons, one by the slave woman[d] and the other by the free woman.[e] 23 His
son by the slave woman was born according to the flesh,[f] but his son by the free woman was born as
the result of a divine promise.[g]

24 These things are being taken figuratively: The women represent two covenants. One covenant is

a 5 The Greek word for *adoption to sonship* is a legal term referring to the full legal standing of an adopted male heir in Roman culture. *b* 6 Aramaic for *Father* *c* 9 Or *principles*

together with the law) to enter into the privileges of his adopted children. **born of a woman, born under the law.** Christ shared the condition of those he would redeem. In taking upon himself the law's curse on transgressors (3:10,13), he set believers free from its condemning regime to enjoy the blessings of God's children.

4:6 *Abba*, Father. Jesus' own distinctive way of addressing God (Mark 14:36) is taken over by those who enjoy through him a child's relationship with God. The Spirit of God enables them to speak to God in this way (cf. 1 Cor 12:3; see also Rom 8:15–16).

4:7 heir. See 3:14,29. Those who are God's children "inherit" all God's blessings through their union with his Son (cf. 3:26–27; Eph 1:3).

4:8–20 *Paul's Concern for the Galatians.* Paul draws on memories of the good relationship he has enjoyed with the Galatians in appealing to them not to submit to the law.

4:9 now that you know God—or rather are known by God. "Now that you know God" might wrongly suggest that the Galatians themselves had taken the initiative in coming to know God. **turning back to those weak and miserable forces.** As in v. 3, Paul links slavery under the law with captivity under the evil powers that dominate sinners: to turn to the law is to return to such slavery.

4:10 special days. Treating certain times as more sacred than others was typical both of Jewish law and pagan religions. It is not an essential feature of Christian faith (Rom 14:5; Col 2:16–17).

4:12 I became like you. Paul's missionary strategy was to become like those to whom he brought the gospel (1 Cor 9:19–23).

4:13,14 illness. Paul leaves the nature of the illness undefined (as he does with the affliction of 2 Cor 12:7–9).

4:15 your blessing of me. The words "of me" are supplied by the translator; alternatively, read simply "your blessing." Paul may be asking what has happened to the blessedness the Galatians themselves experienced when they first received Paul and the gospel.

4:18 Paul implies a contrast between his own lasting concern for the Galatians' well-being and the desire shown by his opponents for the esteem of the Galatians when they are with them.

4:19 pains of childbirth. Cf. 1 Thess 2:7–8.

4:21–31 *Hagar and Sarah.* To submit to the law is to become a slave like Hagar; but God calls us to enjoy freedom like Sarah. Though God had promised Abraham offspring as numerous as "the dust of the earth" (Gen 13:16), Abraham and Sarah remained without children. Abraham turned to Hagar, his wife's Egyptian slave, and had a son (Ishmael) by her (Gen 16:1–16). At the appointed time, however, Abraham and Sarah had a son (Isaac) in fulfillment of God's promise (Gen 21:1–3).

4:21 under the law ... the law says. The books of Moses (Genesis–Deuteronomy) contain the commandments given to Israel on Mount Sinai (referred to here in the expression "under the law"), and for that reason they are often themselves referred to simply as "the law" (here "what the law says").

4:23 according to the flesh. Nothing distinguished the birth of Ishmael from any other human being. **result of a divine promise.** Isaac's birth to parents long past the age when it was humanly possible fulfilled God's promise (Gen 13:15–16; 17:19; 18:10; Rom 4:18–21; Heb 11:11–12).

4:24 figuratively. The NT frequently finds foreshadowings of NT realities in OT figures, stories, and institutions. See, e.g., Rom 5:14; 1 Cor 5:7; 10:1–11; Col 2:11,16–17; 1 Pet 3:20–21; and especially the letter to the Hebrews.

from Mount Sinai and bears children who are to be slaves: This is Hagar. 25Now Hagar stands for Mount Sinai in Arabia and corresponds to the present city of Jerusalem, because she is in slavery with her children. 26But the Jerusalem that is above[h] is free, and she is our mother. 27For it is written:

> "Be glad, barren woman,
>   you who never bore a child;
> shout for joy and cry aloud,
>   you who were never in labor;
> because more are the children of the desolate woman
>   than of her who has a husband."[a][i]

28Now you, brothers and sisters, like Isaac, are children of promise. 29At that time the son born according to the flesh[j] persecuted the son born by the power of the Spirit.[k] It is the same now. 30But what does Scripture say? "Get rid of the slave woman and her son, for the slave woman's son will never share in the inheritance with the free woman's son."[b][l] 31Therefore, brothers and sisters, we are not children of the slave woman, but of the free woman.

Freedom in Christ

5 It is for freedom that Christ has set us free.[m] Stand firm,[n] then, and do not let yourselves be burdened again by a yoke of slavery.[o]

2Mark my words! I, Paul, tell you that if you let yourselves be circumcised,[p] Christ will be of no value to you at all. 3Again I declare to every man who lets himself be circumcised that he is obligated to obey the whole law.[q] 4You who are trying to be justified by the law have been alienated from Christ; you have fallen away from grace.[r] 5For through the Spirit we eagerly await by faith the righteousness for which we hope.[s] 6For in Christ Jesus neither circumcision nor uncircumcision has any value.[t] The only thing that counts is faith expressing itself through love.[u]

7You were running a good race.[v] Who cut in on you[w] to keep you from obeying the truth? 8That

4:26 [h] Heb 12:22; Rev 3:12
4:27 [i] Isa 54:1
4:29 [j] ver 23 [k] Ge 21:9
4:30 [l] Ge 21:10
5:1 [m] Jn 8:32 [n] 1Co 16:13 [o] Ac 15:10; Gal 2:4
5:2 [p] Ac 15:1
5:3 [q] Gal 3:10
5:4 [r] Heb 12:15; 2Pe 3:17
5:5 [s] Ro 8:23,24
5:6 [t] 1Co 7:19 [u] 1Th 1:3
5:7 [v] 1Co 9:24 [w] Gal 3:1

[a] *27* Isaiah 54:1 [b] *30* Gen. 21:10

4:25 Hagar stands for Mount Sinai ... she is in slavery with her children. Hagar, who gave birth in the normal human way, stands for all those who see themselves as children of Abraham because of their normal, human descent from him. Her slavery corresponds to the slavery (to sin and the law) they experience. **present city of Jerusalem.** Inhabited largely by physical descendants of Abraham who live under the covenant of Mount Sinai.
4:26 Jerusalem that is above. The spiritual and eternal home of all who are righteous by faith (Rev 21:2; cf. Phil 3:20–21).
4:27 it is written. Isa 54:1, speaking of the coming habitation of now desolate Jerusalem, enunciates the principle that God can bring abundant blessing where, humanly speaking, none is forthcoming. That principle, already at work in the birth of Isaac to barren Sarah, found expression in Paul's day when Gentile believers became part of the people of God.
4:28 like Isaac. Isaac became a child of Abraham only through the fulfillment of a divine promise. In that respect, he stands for all those who by faith become heirs of the promise God gave to Abraham (3:29). And they share in the freedom (in their case, from the law and its condemnation) of Sarah, Isaac's mother (4:26,31).
4:29 persecuted. The tradition that Ishmael persecuted Isaac grew out of the interpretation of Gen 21:9. **the same now.** For persecution in Paul's day, see 5:11; 6:12; 1 Thess 2:14–16.
4:30 Get rid. See Gen 21:10. Paul implies that the Galatian churches should drive out those who pervert the gospel.
5:1—6:10 *Instructions in Christian Living.* Paul insists again that believers are not to return to slavery under the law but are to live by the Spirit (5:1–26); then he outlines the principles by which they are to live (6:1–10).
5:1–12 *Freedom in Christ.* Paul makes a final appeal to the Galatians not to be circumcised, warning of the consequences of such an action and wondering again how they can have been persuaded to think otherwise.
5:2 Christ will be of no value. Those who now become circumcised forfeit the benefit of Christ's redemption since circumcision marks the beginning of a life submitted to the law. Christ came to redeem those who were under the law (4:4–5).
5:3 obligated to obey the whole law. Obedience to the law represented Israel's obligation under the covenant they entered into at Mount Sinai. Were the Galatians to become circumcised, they would be entering a life under the terms of that covenant, bound to obey all its laws and regulations.
5:4 alienated from Christ ... fallen away from grace. Since sinners cannot gain righteousness on the terms prescribed by the law, Christ came to atone for their sins and open the door to righteousness by God's grace through faith. One cannot, however, enjoy righteousness as a gift of God's grace through faith while embarking on the very different path prescribed by the law.
5:5 the righteousness for which we hope. Those with faith in Christ look forward to the day when God will declare them righteous—in Christ—at the last judgment. That declaration is anticipated already in those who respond to the gospel message with faith (Rom 5:1), and it is reaffirmed at the last judgment for those whose faith has proved genuine (1 Cor 15:2; Col 1:22–23).
5:6 The distinction between circumcision and uncircumcision was vital under the Mosaic covenant but makes no difference "in Christ Jesus" (3:28). **faith ... love.** Decisive now, for Jew and Gentile alike, is the true faith that finds expression in love.

5:8 [x]Ro 8:28; Gal 1:6
5:9 [y]1Co 5:6
5:10 [z]2Co 2:3 [a]Php 3:15 [b]Gal 1:7
5:11 [c]Gal 4:29; 6:12 [d]1Co 1:23
5:12 [e]ver 10
5:13 [f]1Co 8:9; 1Pe 2:16 [g]1Co 9:19; Eph 5:21
5:14 [h]Lev 19:18; Mt 22:39
5:16 [i]Ro 8:2,4-6,9,14 [j]ver 24
5:17 [k]Ro 8:5-8 [l]Ro 7:15-23
5:18 [m]Ro 6:14; 1Ti 1:9
5:19 [n]1Co 6:18
5:21 [o]Ro 13:13
5:22 [p]Mt 7:16-20; Eph 5:9 [q]Col 3:12-15
5:23 [r]Ac 24:25
5:24 [s]Ro 6:6 [t]ver 16,17
5:26 [u]Php 2:3

kind of persuasion does not come from the one who calls you.[x] 9 "A little yeast works through the
whole batch of dough."[y] 10 I am confident[z] in the Lord that you will take no other view.[a] The one who
is throwing you into confusion,[b] whoever that may be, will have to pay the penalty. 11 Brothers and
sisters, if I am still preaching circumcision, why am I still being persecuted?[c] In that case the offense[d]
of the cross has been abolished. 12 As for those agitators,[e] I wish they would go the whole way and
emasculate themselves!

Life by the Spirit

13 You, my brothers and sisters, were called to be free. But do not use your freedom to indulge the
flesh[a],[f] rather, serve one another[g] humbly in love. 14 For the entire law is fulfilled in keeping this one
command: "Love your neighbor as yourself."[b][h] 15 If you bite and devour each other, watch out or you
will be destroyed by each other.

16 So I say, walk by the Spirit,[i] and you will not gratify the desires of the flesh.[j] 17 For the flesh desires
what is contrary to the Spirit, and the Spirit what is contrary to the flesh.[k] They are in conflict with
each other, so that you are not to do whatever[c] you want.[l] 18 But if you are led by the Spirit, you are
not under the law.[m]

19 The acts of the flesh are obvious: sexual immorality,[n] impurity and debauchery; 20 idolatry and
witchcraft; hatred, discord, jealousy, fits of rage, selfish ambition, dissensions, factions 21 and envy;
drunkenness, orgies, and the like.[o] I warn you, as I did before, that those who live like this will not
inherit the kingdom of God.

22 But the fruit[p] of the Spirit is love,[q] joy, peace, forbearance, kindness, goodness, faithfulness, 23 gentleness and self-control.[r] Against such things there is no law. 24 Those who belong to Christ Jesus have
crucified the flesh[s] with its passions and desires.[t] 25 Since we live by the Spirit, let us keep in step with
the Spirit. 26 Let us not become conceited,[u] provoking and envying each other.

[a] *13* In contexts like this, the Greek word for *flesh* (*sarx*) refers to the sinful state of human beings, often presented as a power in opposition to the Spirit; also in verses 16, 17, 19 and 24; and in 6:8. [b] *14* Lev. 19:18 [c] *17* Or *you do not do what*

5:8 the one who calls you. God (1:6; 1 Thess 2:12).

5:9 yeast ... batch of dough. Tolerating a false gospel ("yeast") affects the whole community ("batch of dough").

5:11 why am I still being persecuted? Non-Christian Jews would hardly oppose those who promoted a Jewish lifestyle (starting with circumcision). They persecuted Paul for preaching that the Messiah's mission ended on a cross ("the offense of the cross"; cf. 1 Cor 1:23) that marked the end of the law's regime; Romans opposed Paul because of the turmoil aroused by his mission. Paul's practice of avoiding unnecessary offense by accommodating his own way of life to that of those with whom he lived (1 Cor 9:19–23; cf. Acts 16:1–3) may have led to the rumor that he was "still preaching circumcision."

5:12 emasculate. Various pagan cults practiced castration. Paul implies that circumcision brings one no closer to God than such pagan practices.

5:13–26 *Life by the Spirit.* The alternative to life under the law is not a life in which the flesh expresses itself without restraint, but one directed and empowered by God's Spirit.

5:13 freedom. Liberty from the Mosaic law that comes with faith in Christ. **indulge the flesh.** Gratify one's rebellious human nature. Christian liberty is not license to sin but freedom to serve one another in love.

5:14 the entire law is fulfilled. The law was imposed on rebellious human beings; its practical effect was to exacerbate their rebelliousness (Rom 7:7–13). Paradoxically, it is those who are "not under the law" but "led by the Spirit" (Gal 5:18) who are enabled to show the love that was the goal of all the law's commandments. See Rom 8:4; 13:8–10.

5:16–21 The presence of God's Spirit in the lives of believers, a mark of the new age inaugurated by Christ's resurrection, both guides them and enables them to obey God's will (see note on 3:2; cf. Ezek 36:27; Rom 8:4,13–14); they are no longer subject to the regulations and sanctions of the Mosaic covenant ("not under the law," Gal 5:18). But until Christ's return, the old age, which is resistant to God, coexists with the new; the Spirit that marks the new age is at war with the "flesh" that marks the old (see note on 3:3), and the believer must resist the sinful desires of the "flesh" ("whatever you want," 5:17; cf. v. 24; Rom 8:13) through the power of the Spirit. Examples of the deeds prompted by the desires of the flesh include indulging sinful bodily cravings, worshiping false gods, illegitimately attempting to harness supernatural powers for one's own ends, and other acts expressing the flesh's self-centeredness (vv. 19–21).

5:21 not inherit the kingdom of God. Those tempted to indulge the flesh are reminded that no one who lives to gratify its desires can have a place in God's kingdom, where God's will is done. Similar warnings are found in Rom 8:13; 1 Cor 6:9–11; Eph 5:5.

5:22–23 fruit of the Spirit. As a fruit-bearing tree naturally grows fruit, so a life controlled by God's Spirit naturally and inevitably expresses the virtues of love, joy, peace, etc. **Against such things there is no law.** While no law can command or bring about such virtues, no rightful law will condemn the deeds to which they lead. As in v. 14, the goal of the law is reached not by the self-inspired efforts of those "under the law" (v. 18) but by a life directed and empowered by God's Spirit.

5:24 crucified the flesh. Cf. 2:20; 6:14; Rom 6:2–7. To turn to Christ in faith is necessarily to turn away from the God-resisting life of the flesh. In that sense repentance is inherent in the very nature of faith.

5:25 live by the Spirit. Believers owe their new life to the Spirit (cf. John 3:5–6).

Doing Good to All

6 Brothers and sisters, if someone is caught in a sin, you who live by the Spirit[v] should restore that
person gently. But watch yourselves, or you also may be tempted. 2 Carry each other's burdens,
and in this way you will fulfill the law of Christ.[w] 3 If anyone thinks they are something[x] when they
are not, they deceive themselves. 4 Each one should test their own actions. Then they can take pride
in themselves alone, without comparing themselves to someone else, 5 for each one should carry their
own load. 6 Nevertheless, the one who receives instruction in the word should share all good things
with their instructor.[y]
7 Do not be deceived:[z] God cannot be mocked. A man reaps what he sows.[a] 8 Whoever sows to please
their flesh, from the flesh will reap destruction;[b] whoever sows to please the Spirit, from the Spirit will
reap eternal life.[c] 9 Let us not become weary in doing good,[d] for at the proper time we will reap a harvest if we do not give up.[e] 10 Therefore, as we have opportunity, let us do good[f] to all people, especially
to those who belong to the family[g] of believers.

Not Circumcision but the New Creation

11 See what large letters I use as I write to you with my own hand![h]
12 Those who want to impress people by means of the flesh are trying to compel you to be circumcised.[i] The only reason they do this is to avoid being persecuted[j] for the cross of Christ. 13 Not even those
who are circumcised keep the law,[k] yet they want you to be circumcised that they may boast about your
circumcision in the flesh.[l] 14 May I never boast except in the cross of our Lord Jesus Christ, through
which[a] the world has been crucified to me, and I to the world.[m] 15 Neither circumcision nor uncircumcision means anything;[n] what counts is the new creation.[o] 16 Peace and mercy to all who follow this
rule — to[b] the Israel of God.
17 From now on, let no one cause me trouble, for I bear on my body the marks[p] of Jesus.
18 The grace of our Lord Jesus Christ[q] be with your spirit,[r] brothers and sisters. Amen.

a 14 Or *whom* *b* 16 Or *rule and to*

6:1 [v] 1Co 2:15
6:2 [w] Ro 15:1; Jas 2:8
6:3 [x] Ro 12:3; 1Co 8:2
6:6 [y] 1Co 9:11,14
6:7 [z] 1Co 6:9 [a] 2Co 9:6
6:8 [b] Job 4:8; Hos 8:7 [c] Jas 3:18
6:9 [d] 1Co 15:58 [e] Rev 2:10
6:10 [f] Pr 3:27 [g] Eph 2:19
6:11 [h] 1Co 16:21
6:12 [i] Ac 15:1 [j] Gal 5:11
6:13 [k] Ro 2:25 [l] Php 3:3
6:14 [m] Ro 6:2,6
6:15 [n] 1Co 7:19 [o] 2Co 5:17
6:17 [p] Isa 44:5; 2Co 1:5
6:18 [q] Ro 16:20 [r] 2Ti 4:22

6:1–10 *Doing Good to All.* Paul concludes his ethical instructions by encouraging the Galatian believers to support each other.

6:1 caught in a sin. By succumbing to temptation. Such temptations remain the experience of believers throughout this life; prayer and vigilance are required to resist them (Matt 6:13; 1 Pet 5:7). **restore.** Through gentle correction and a willingness to forgive (Luke 17:3; Eph 4:32; 2 Tim 4:2).

6:2 Carry each other's burdens. Give support to the weak and afflicted. That in the end believers are accountable for their own lives (v. 5) does not mean that they are not to care for the needs of others. **the law of Christ.** Probably the love commandment is specifically in view (John 13:34), though the phrase may refer in a general way to Jesus' ethical teaching and example, or even to his interpretation of Mosaic law (Matt 5:17–48; 22:34–40, etc.).

6:4 test their own actions. Mutual concern should not lead to mutual competition or to insidious comparisons of one's own imagined spiritual maturity with that perceived in others.

6:6 all good things. Material goods. Though these are never commensurate with spiritual goods, it remains appropriate for the recipients of spiritual goods to express their gratitude by contributing to the material needs of those who bless them (Luke 10:7; Rom 15:27; 1 Cor 9:11,14; Phil 4:14–19).

6:7 A man reaps what he sows. One "reaps" in the age to come ("destruction" or "eternal life," v. 8) what one "sows" in this life (living to gratify the sinful flesh or living to please the Spirit). As in 5:21, Paul is warning those who profess faith that their profession must be matched by, and their faith expressed in, appropriate deeds (see 5:6).

6:9 we will reap. In the age to come. Cf. 1 Cor 15:58. The certain hope of the believer should motivate persistence in well-doing.

6:10 to all ... to the family of believers. Like Jesus, Paul exhorts believers not only to "love *one another*" (John 13:34) but to reach out to others as well (Matt 5:43–48).

6:11–18 *Conclusion: Not Circumcision but the New Creation.* Paul closes the letter by returning to the crisis at hand: circumcision belongs to the old order; it has no place in God's new creation.

6:11 large letters. Presumably for emphasis, though some (taking 4:15 in a literal sense) suggest that Paul suffered from poor eyesight. Though a secretary had presumably written the letter to this point at Paul's dictation (Rom 16:22), Paul writes the conclusion with his own hand (1 Cor 16:21; Col 4:18; 2 Thess 3:17).

6:12 avoid being persecuted. See note on 5:11.

6:14 never boast except in the cross. Crucifixion was regarded as the shameful end of a misdirected life. That the Messiah's redemptive work should lead to a cross was offensive to Jews and utter foolishness to Gentiles (1 Cor 1:18–25). For Paul, however, it made effective "the power of God that brings salvation to everyone who believes" (Rom 1:16) and as such was the object of his pride and joy. **the world has been crucified to me, and I to the world.** The world that had crucified Christ could hold no attraction for one who loved and followed Christ.

6:15 new creation. Cf. 2 Cor 5:17; see note there. As in Gal 3:28, distinctions significant in the old creation are of no importance in the new.

6:16 follow this rule. Realize that distinctions regarding circumcision (v. 15) are irrelevant in God's new creation. **the Israel of God.** On the interpretation that lies behind the NIV text, Paul identifies such people as God's (spiritual) Israel (cf. Phil 3:3). On the interpretation that lies behind the NIV text note, Paul extends the blessing to include ethnic Israel, which, though unbelieving now, is destined for God's salvation (Rom 11:25–26).

6:17 marks of Jesus. As slaves bore the brand mark of their owner, so the marks of Paul's suffering identify him as Christ's slave (cf. 2 Cor 11:23–29).

INTRODUCTION TO EPHESIANS

AUTHOR

Ephesians is the quintessential Pauline document, summing up many important themes of Paul's letters and of his ministry as the Apostle to the Gentiles. The letter claims to be written by Paul himself (1:1; 3:1). Nevertheless, the unusual linguistic style and verbal similarity with many parts of Colossians lead some to suggest that Ephesians is pseudonymous, written by an imitator who relied on Colossians. The NT (2 Thess 2:2; 3:17; see Introduction to 2 Thessalonians: Author) and the early church fathers, however, rejected pseudonymity. The literary relationship between Ephesians and Colossians is better explained on the assumption that Paul composed both works at the same time and that he modified the themes of each letter for different readers facing different circumstances.

DATE, PLACE OF COMPOSITION, AND DESTINATION

Paul wrote Ephesians probably in AD 60 – 61 during his Roman imprisonment. The destination of the letter is debated. The phrase "in Ephesus" (1:1) is lacking in some early manuscripts, suggesting that the letter is written not *specifically* "to God's holy people in Ephesus" (1:1), but *broadly* to "God's holy people" in southwestern Asia Minor. This conclusion is consistent with the impersonal nature of the letter. Eph 1:15 and 3:2 imply that Paul and his readers only heard reports of each other. The letter also lacks personal greetings (cf. Rom 16; Col 4:10 – 17) that would be present if it were addressed primarily to the believers in Ephesus since Paul spent three years there (Acts 19:8,10; 20:31) and knew the elders well (Acts 20:17 – 38). So Ephesians is probably a circular letter Paul sent to Gentile believers in the churches of southwestern Asia Minor. It was eventually connected with Ephesus because of the importance of that city and because it was one of the cities to which Paul sent the letter.

EPHESUS AND NEARBY CITIES

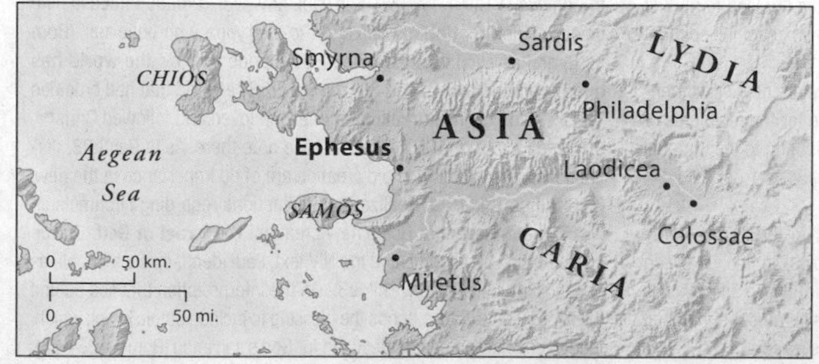

CITY OF EPHESUS

With an estimated population of 200,0000 – 250,000, Ephesus was called the "mother city" of Asia. Economically, Ephesus was the largest trading center in western Asia Minor. Located on the mouth of the Cayster River, which emptied into the Aegean Sea, Ephesus had a harbor (now silted up) that provided access to major shipping routes. In addition, Ephesus was situated at the intersection of major land routes.

Religiously, Ephesus had the honor of being the "guardian of the temple of the great Artemis and of her image, which fell from heaven" (Acts 19:35). The temple of Artemis (the Roman goddess Diana) was one of the seven wonders of the ancient world, and the influence of the Artemis cult pervaded every facet of life in the city. Artemis was considered the guardian of the city, her temple served as the primary banking institution of the city, her image graced the coinage, and festivals and games were held in her honor. The worship of Artemis was not restricted to Ephesus. Demetrius, a silversmith in Ephesus, claimed that Artemis was "worshiped throughout the province of Asia and the world" (Acts 19:27).

Paul preached in Ephesus over a period of three years with the result that "all the Jews and Greeks who lived in the province of Asia heard the word of the Lord" (Acts 19:10; cf. 19:26). He also did extraordinary miracles and cast out demons (Acts 19:11–16). Many believed in the Lord and those who formerly practiced sorcery burned their scrolls, the value of which totaled "fifty thousand drachmas" (Acts 19:19). Opposition arose and Paul narrowly escaped a huge mob in the theater (Acts 19:23–41). The theater still stands today and could possibly seat 25,000 people. For other civic structures familiar to Paul, see the following map. The location of the "lecture hall of Tyrannus" (Acts 19:9) is unknown.

EPHESUS IN THE TIME OF PAUL

The Roman province of Asia with its many splendid cities was one of the jewels on a belt of Roman lands encircling the Mediterranean.

Located on the most direct sea and land routes to the eastern provinces of the empire, Ephesus was an emporium that had few equals anywhere in the world. Certainly no city in Asia was more famous or more populous. It ranked with Rome, Corinth, Antioch, and Alexandria among the foremost urban centers of the empire.

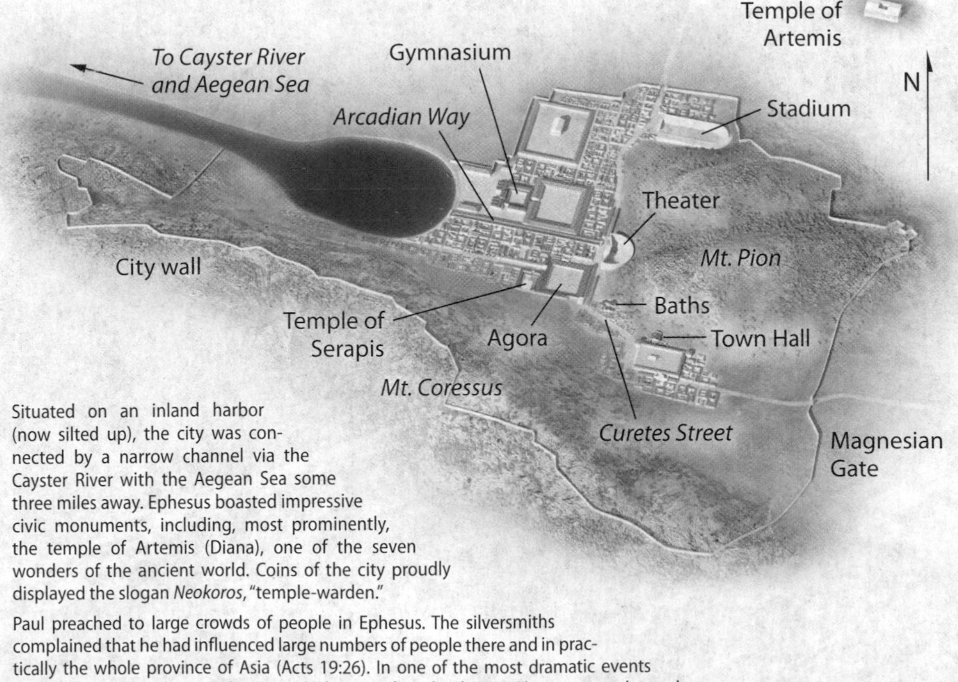

Situated on an inland harbor (now silted up), the city was connected by a narrow channel via the Cayster River with the Aegean Sea some three miles away. Ephesus boasted impressive civic monuments, including, most prominently, the temple of Artemis (Diana), one of the seven wonders of the ancient world. Coins of the city proudly displayed the slogan *Neokoros*, "temple-warden."

Paul preached to large crowds of people in Ephesus. The silversmiths complained that he had influenced large numbers of people there and in practically the whole province of Asia (Acts 19:26). In one of the most dramatic events recorded in the NT, the apostle escaped a huge mob in the theater. This structure, located on the slope of Mount Pion at the end of the Arcadian Way, could seat 25,000 people.

Other places doubtless familiar to the apostle were the Commercial Agora, the Magnesian Gate, the Town Hall, and Curetes Street.

OCCASION AND PURPOSE

Ephesians is the least situational of all Paul's letters because it does not explicitly address any specific problem. But as a circular letter, it is a manifesto for the church, describing its essence and identity: who it is, how it came about, how it must conduct itself, and what its mission is within the larger framework of Christ's cosmic rule. As such, Ephesians develops a major theme in Colossians: cosmic reconciliation in Christ. Although not explicitly stated, this theme of reconciliation presupposes that the cosmos did not remain in the condition in which God created it. The unity and harmony of creation was ruptured (Rom 8:18 – 22) and needed a reconciliation or new creation to recover the original state. Although Colossians and Ephesians share this common narrative of alienation and reconciliation, there are differences. Colossians emphasizes Christ's role in both creation and reconciliation; Ephesians emphasizes reconciliation. Colossians emphasizes the reconciliation of the cosmos and humanity to God; Ephesians carries this theme but also emphasizes the reconciliation between Jews and Gentiles. Moreover, Ephesians draws out the implications for how this reconciled humanity, the church comprising Jews and Gentiles, must understand its identity and function within God's grand vision of cosmic peace and unity in Christ.

GENRE AND STRUCTURE

Ephesians follows the standard pattern of a Hellenistic letter with an opening (1:1 – 2), body (1:3 — 6:20), and closing (6:21 – 24). The body of the letter broadly divides into two parts: doctrinal (1:3 — 3:21) and ethical (4:1 — 6:20).

THEMES

Unity

The two parts of the letter's body (1:3 — 3:21 and 4:1 — 6:20) support the letter's central message: peace and unity in Christ. Chs. 1 – 3 present the foundational story of how the church must understand its identity within God's vision of cosmic unity in Christ. God chose the church before the creation of the world (1:4) and made known to it his plan of uniting all things in Christ (1:9 – 10). Central to this plan is the unity of the church, a unity in which vertical rec-

Aerial view of the theater and the commercial agora of Ephesus.

Barry Beitzel/www.BiblePlaces.com

onciliation to God (2:1–10) forms the basis of horizontal reconciliation between Jews and Gentiles (2:11–22). Paul elaborates further on this union of Jews and Gentiles into one body (3:1–13): the church's function is to proclaim the reality and wisdom of God's cosmic plan of reconciliation to the "rulers and authorities in the heavenly realms" (3:10). Paul prays that his readers will comprehend the love of Christ and love one another (3:14–21) so they can live out the unity they have in Christ.

Chs. 4–6 exhort the church to conduct itself in light of its calling within God's plan of peace and unity in Christ. Believers are to maintain the church's unity (4:1–16) by embracing the corporate ethos of their new identity (4:17—5:20), establishing household unity (5:21—6:9), and standing together against a common enemy (6:10–20).

Christ

Ephesians, like Colossians, presents a cosmic Christ. Christ brings all of history to completion (1:10). He is seated at the right hand of God, exalted above all spiritual powers, and is the authoritative head over everything (1:20–22). He possesses "boundless riches" (3:8), and he freely gives gifts to the church (4:7–11). While focusing on Christ's resurrection, exaltation, and enthronement, Ephesians also speaks of his death on the cross as the basis for redemption and reconciliation (1:7; 2:13,16; 5:2,25). Ephesians, like Colossians, uses the phrase "in Christ" more than Paul's other letters. This expression is probably rooted in Paul's understanding of Christ as a corporate figure. As Adam determines the fate of all who belong to him, Christ also determines the fate of those who exercise faith and are "in him" (see Rom 5:12–21; 1 Cor 15:22). Thus, those who are "in Christ" are united with him and participate in his death, resurrection, and new life. They have a new identity that necessitates reorienting one's entire existence (2 Cor 5:14–17). In Ephesians and Colossians, Paul expands the use of this language to a cosmic scale such that the creation and redemption of the cosmos is also said to be "in Christ" (Eph 1:9–10; 3:11; Col 1:16–17). Despite the overlapping occurrences of this expression between the two letters, Ephesians differs by using it more significantly to denote the basis on and the sphere in which believers have fellowship not only with God but also with one another. Vertically, Christ connects God and the church; horizontally, Christ connects all believers, even those who come from diverse socioeconomic backgrounds.

Church

Although "church" generally denotes a local assembly or congregation in Paul's earlier letters (Rom 16:5; 1 Cor 1:2; Gal 1:2; 1 Thess 1:1), the term in Ephesians always has a wider reference and designates the universal church to which all true believers belong.

Paul describes the church using several metaphors:

A body. Organically, the church is a body whose head is Christ (5:23). As a body, the different members of the church are dependent on one another (4:12–16) and exemplify the necessity of unity in diversity. As the body of Christ, the church depends on Christ for its growth (4:16) and submits to his headship (5:24). This introduction of Christ as the head of the church is a distinctive contribution of Ephesians (and Colossians).

A temple. Architecturally, the church is a holy temple filled with the presence of God and built on the foundation of the apostles and prophets, with Christ Jesus himself as the chief cornerstone (2:20–22).

A commonwealth. Politically, the church is a commonwealth that embodies the reconciliation of two former hostile ethnic groups (2:11–22) and that battles evil spiritual powers (6:10–20).

A household. From the perspective of social structures, the church is a household unit in which God is the Father (1:3,17; 2:18; 3:14; 4:6; 5:20; 6:23) and believers are adopted as his children through Jesus Christ (1:5; 2:19).

A bride. Drawing on the OT depiction of Israel as the bride of Yahweh, the church is also portrayed as the bride of Christ (5:23–32). He cares, feeds, and sanctifies the church in order that he might present it to himself as radiant, "without stain or wrinkle or any other blemish" (5:27). As his wife, the church submits to Christ.

Trinity

Unlike the Gospel of John, Ephesians does not contain any explicit Trinitarian language stating that the Father, Son, and Holy Spirit (or the Father and Son) are one. Nevertheless, it uses suggestive Trinitarian language (1:17; 2:18,22; 3:14–17; 5:18–20), highlights the collective work of the Trinity in effecting reconciliation (1:3–14), and bases the unity of the church on one Spirit, one Lord, and one God and Father (4:4–6). Early church fathers, such as Ignatius, adopted such Trinitarian language as the basis for the unity of the Trinity, and they used the unity of the Trinity as the basis for the unity of the church.

OUTLINE

I. Letter Opening (1:1–2)

II. Calling of the Church Within Christ's Cosmic Reconciliation (1:3—3:21)

A. Praise for Spiritual Blessings in Christ (1:3–14)
B. Thanksgiving and Prayer (1:15–23)
C. Made Alive in Christ (2:1–10)
D. Jew and Gentile Reconciled Through Christ (2:11–22)
E. God's Marvelous Plan for the Gentiles (3:1–13)
F. A Prayer for the Ephesians (3:14–21)

III. Conduct of the Church Within Christ's Cosmic Reconciliation (4:1—6:20)

A. Unity and Maturity in the Body of Christ (4:1–16)
B. Instructions for Christian Living (4:17—5:20)
C. Instructions for Christian Households (5:21—6:9)
D. The Armor of God (6:10–20)

IV. Final Greetings (6:21–24)

EPHESIANS

1 Paul, an apostle[a] of Christ Jesus by the will of God,[b]

To God's holy people in Ephesus,[a] the faithful[c] in Christ Jesus:

[2]Grace and peace to you from God our Father and the Lord Jesus Christ.[d]

1:1 [a] 1Co 1:1 [b] 2Co 1:1 [c] Col 1:2
1:2 [d] Ro 1:7
1:3 [e] 2Co 1:3 [f] Eph 2:6; 3:10; 6:12

Praise for Spiritual Blessings in Christ

[3]Praise be to the God and Father of our Lord Jesus Christ,[e] who has blessed us in the heavenly realms[f]
with every spiritual blessing in Christ. [4]For he chose us in him before the creation of the world to be

[a] *1* Some early manuscripts do not have *in Ephesus.*

1:1–2 *Letter Opening.* The opening of Ephesians, as in other Pauline letters, contains the names of the sender and recipients, and a greeting. **1:1 apostle.** See note on 4:11. **God's holy people.** Paul regularly calls his readers this (Rom 1:7; 1 Cor 1:2; 2 Cor 1:1; Phil 1:1) not because they are pious but because they believe in the definitive cleansing of sins made possible by Christ (Acts 13:38–39). By faith, Christ, through his death, has made them holy (Eph 5:25–27; cf. Acts 15:9), i.e., set them apart to be God's people of the new covenant. Nevertheless, believers must also reflect the holiness of the God who called them (v. 4; see "Holiness," p. 2676). By appropriating a term that was used for God's covenantal people in the OT (Exod 19:6; 22:31), Paul reminds his Gentile readers that they stand within the stream of God's redemptive history. **in Ephesus.** See Introduction: Date, Place of Composition, and Destination.
1:3—3:21 *Calling of the Church Within Christ's Cosmic Reconciliation.* Paul unfolds for his readers God's eternal plan to unify all things in Christ (see Introduction: Occasion and Purpose; Themes [Unity]), and explains how the church is to understand its call and identity—who it is, how it came about, and what its mission is within this plan.
1:3–14 *Praise for Spiritual Blessings in Christ.* Appearing as one long sentence in the original Greek, this section is often called a "doxology." Here, Paul praises God for his spiritual blessings in Christ (v. 3). These blessings are based on the work of the triune God: election and adoption by the Father (vv. 4–6), redemption in Christ (vv. 7–12), and sealing in the Spirit (vv. 13–14). Each of these three subsections concludes with a similar refrain that praises God's glory (vv. 6,12,14). This entire section presents a grand sweep of God's saving purposes. It begins with our election from "before the creation of the world" (v. 4) and climaxes with the pronouncement of God's will to bring unity to the cosmos under Christ (v. 10).
1:3 heavenly realms. Where not only God and the ascended Christ reside but also the evil spiritual powers reside (1:20–21; 6:12; cf. 3:10). The heavenly realms in Ephesians must be understood from Paul's eschatological perspective of two ages: "the present age" and "the one to come" (v. 21; cf. Matt 12:32). We currently live in the overlap of these two ages. The age to come has been inaugurated by the exaltation and enthronement of Christ to God's "right hand … far above all rule and authority" (vv. 20–21). The present age nevertheless continues until the final consummation of the age to come when Christ returns. As the heavenly realms are still part of the "present evil age" (Gal 1:4; cf. Eph 5:16), evil powers continue to be active in the heavenly realms until the final consummation, when they will be completely eradicated (1 Cor 15:24–26). Through our union with Christ, believers who are physically on earth also presently reside with Christ in the heavenly realms (Eph 2:6). Believers consequently share in every blessing that belongs to and comes from the heavenly realms. At the same time, our battle is not against "flesh and blood," but against the powers that war against God in these realms (6:12). **every spiritual blessing.** Verses 4–14 specify the contents of these blessings, which cover the whole scope of God's saving work in Christ. This includes our election, adoption to sonship, redemption, forgiveness, and sealing. These blessings are spiritual not so much in the sense that they are non-physical but in the sense that the Spirit of God graciously gives them. **in Christ.** Paul highlights Christ's centrality in vv. 3–14 by repeatedly noting that God's plan of reconciliation is accomplished and its blessings made available "in Christ" (vv. 3,9,12,13), "in him" (vv. 4,7,11,13), and "in the One he loves" (v. 6). See Introduction: Themes (Christ).
1:4 he chose us. In vv. 3–14 Paul emphasizes God's eternal decision to grant salvation to believers in the following ways: "he chose us" (v. 4), "he predestined us" (v. 5), and "we were also chosen, having been predestined" (v. 11). Since this divine election of believers occurred "before the creation of the world" (v. 4), it is based solely on God's gracious decision and not on any human merit (cf. God's choosing Israel to be his treasured possession in Deut 7:6–8, or God's choosing of Jacob over Esau before they "were born or had done anything good or bad" in Rom 9:11). See also John 5:21; 6:37,39,44; 15:16; 17:6; Rom 8:29–30; 9:6–26; 11:5,7,28; Col 3:12; 1 Thess 1:4; 2 Thess 2:13; Titus 1:1; 1 Pet 1:1; 2:9; Rev 17:8. **to be holy and blameless.** The goal, not the basis, of God's election is ethical purity. See note on v. 1.

1:4 [g]Eph 5:27; Col 1:22 [h]Eph 4:2,15,16
1:5 [i]Ro 8:29,30 [j]1Co 1:21
1:6 [k]Mt 3:17
1:7 [l]Ro 3:24
1:9 [m]Ro 16:25
1:10 [n]Gal 4:4 [o]Col 1:20
1:11 [p]Eph 3:11; Heb 6:17
1:12 [q]ver 6,14
1:13 [r]Col 1:5 [s]Eph 4:30
1:14 [t]Ac 20:32
1:15 [u]Col 1:4
1:16 [v]Ro 1:8

holy and blameless[g] in his sight. In love[h] 5 he[a] predestined[i] us for adoption to sonship[b] through Jesus
Christ, in accordance with his pleasure[j] and will— 6 to the praise of his glorious grace, which he has
freely given us in the One he loves.[k] 7 In him we have redemption[l] through his blood, the forgiveness
of sins, in accordance with the riches of God's grace 8 that he lavished on us. With all wisdom and understanding, 9 he[c] made known to us the mystery[m] of his will according to his good pleasure, which he
purposed in Christ, 10 to be put into effect when the times reach their fulfillment[n]—to bring unity to
all things in heaven and on earth under Christ.[o]

11 In him we were also chosen,[d] having been predestined according to the plan of him who works
out everything in conformity with the purpose[p] of his will, 12 in order that we, who were the first to put
our hope in Christ, might be for the praise of his glory.[q] 13 And you also were included in Christ when
you heard the message of truth,[r] the gospel of your salvation. When you believed, you were marked in
him with a seal,[s] the promised Holy Spirit, 14 who is a deposit guaranteeing our inheritance[t] until the
redemption of those who are God's possession—to the praise of his glory.

Thanksgiving and Prayer

15 For this reason, ever since I heard about your faith in the Lord Jesus and your love for all God's
people,[u] 16 I have not stopped giving thanks for you,[v] remembering you in my prayers. 17 I keep asking

[a] *4,5* Or *sight in love. 5He* [b] *5* The Greek word for *adoption to sonship* is a legal term referring to the full legal standing of an adopted male heir in Roman culture. [c] *8,9* Or *us with all wisdom and understanding. 9And he* [d] *11* Or *were made heirs*

1:5 predestined. Predetermined. See note on v. 4. **adoption to sonship.** In the Roman world, sons were adopted to carry on the family name and maintain property ownership. The adopted son was no longer responsible to his natural father but was only responsible to his new adoptive father. Similarly, all believers, male and female, who receive the Spirit that brings about adoption (Rom 8:15,23) acquire a new status with its accompanying privileges and responsibilities. We are no longer obligated to our old father, the devil (John 8:38,44).

1:6 to the praise. Our election and redemption is ultimately for God's glory. See vv. 12,14. **the One he loves.** Echoes what the Father pronounced at Jesus' baptism and transfiguration (Matt 3:17; 17:5).

1:7 we have. A present reality. **redemption.** Denotes releasing someone from imprisonment or slavery through paying a ransom. Just as God delivered Israel from slavery in Egypt (Deut 7:8), Christ also procured the release of believers from captivity to evil, death, and the "curse of the law" (Gal 3:13) by his sacrificial death ("through his blood"; cf. Eph 2:13; Heb 9:15; 1 Pet 1:18–19). Redemption not only cancels God's just judgment against our acts of disobedience ("forgiveness of sins"; cf. Col 1:14) but it also frees us from the spiritual forces that formerly bound us (Eph 2:1–3). See also 1:14; 4:30; Rom 3:24; Titus 2:14.

1:9 mystery. The mystery religions of Paul's day use "mystery" (Greek *mystērion*) to refer to an esoteric truth that is known only to its initiates. Paul, however, uses it to refer to a divine reality that was once hidden but is now revealed by God to his people (3:3–5,9; Rom 16:25–26; Col 1:26). The most significant references to Paul's use of "mystery" occur in Ephesians and Colossians. Both letters maintain that the central focus of God's mystery is the fulfillment of his plan of salvation in Christ; Ephesians, however, highlights the uniting of all things in Christ. See notes on v. 10; 3:3–6; 5:32; 6:19.

1:10 bring unity. Greek *anakephalaioō*. A significant term that conveys three emphases in this context: (1) Christ is the head or ruler (v. 22), (2) Christ "sums up" or brings things into a coherent and meaningful whole, and (3) Christ restores harmony to a universe that has come into chaos because of sin (Col 1:20). In essence, the content of the "mystery" (Eph 1:9) is God's will to sum up and unify all creation, both the animate and inanimate, under Christ's headship.

1:11 we. Probably refers to Paul and Jewish believers. The "we" contrasts with "you" (Gentile believers) in v. 13, and this we-you contrast anticipates the Jew-Gentile issue in ch. 2. **chosen.** Jewish believers in Christ "were made heirs" (see NIV text note), or more specifically, God claimed them as his inheritance and possession in much the same way that he claimed Israel as his possession and heritage in the OT (Exod 19:5; Deut 4:20; 9:29; 32:9). **predestined.** See note on v. 4. **works out everything in conformity with the purpose of his will.** Emphasizes God's providence and sovereignty. Everything that happens results from God's will in some way, and everything that God planned will certainly come to pass (Dan 4:35; Rom 11:36). At the same time, God never does evil and Scripture never blames God for evil or sin (Job 1:21–22; Rom 5:12). Humans are still responsible for their actions (Eccl 7:29; Rom 9:19–20). They should do right and not grieve the Spirit (Eph 4:30).

1:12 first to put our hope in Christ. Paul affirms the salvation-historical priority of the Jews (John 4:22).

1:13 you. The majority of Paul's readers were probably Gentile. See note on v. 11. **marked ... with a seal.** In Paul's day, a seal indicated ownership and protection. The seal used to mark believers as God's people (Ezek 9:4–6; Rev 7:1–8; 9:4) and to preserve them until they attain their final "redemption" (Eph 1:14) is the Holy Spirit whom God promised (Ezek 36:26–27; Joel 2:28–29). Being marked with this seal does not refer to some second blessing or subsequent action; it refers to receiving the Spirit "when" Gentiles believe the gospel.

1:14 deposit guaranteeing. As the down payment or first installment, the Holy Spirit not only guarantees but also gives us a foretaste of the glorious life to come. **our.** Probably Jewish and Gentile believers. **inheritance.** While the OT tribes of Israel were allotted land for their inheritance, NT believers have a share in the kingdom of God. See Col 1:12; Heb 9:15; 1 Pet 1:4; cf. Eph 5:5. **until the redemption.** Although redemption has a present aspect (see Eph 1:7, which refers to release from the penalty and power of sin), there is nevertheless a future aspect—a time when believers will be released from the presence of sin and their bodies will be transformed. See 4:30; Rom 8:23; 2 Cor 1:22; 5:5; 1 Pet 1:5.

1:15–23 *Thanksgiving and Prayer.* Paul thanks God for what he is doing in the lives of his readers (vv. 15–16) and prays that the blessings God has given in vv. 3–14 will be fully realized in their lives (vv. 17–23). Specifically, Paul prays that they will have a deeper understanding of God's plan of salvation and their place within this cosmic plan. Like vv. 3–14, this section comprises one long sentence in Greek.

1:15 ever since I heard. See Introduction: Date, Place of Composition, and Destination.

that the God of our Lord Jesus Christ, the glorious Father,[w] may give you the Spirit[a] of wisdom[x] and
revelation, so that you may know him better. 18I pray that the eyes of your heart may be enlightened[y] in
order that you may know the hope to which he has called you, the riches of his glorious inheritance in
his holy people, 19and his incomparably great power for us who believe. That power[z] is the same as the
mighty strength[a] 20he exerted when he raised Christ from the dead[b] and seated him at his right hand
in the heavenly realms, 21far above all rule and authority, power and dominion, and every name[c] that
is invoked, not only in the present age but also in the one to come. 22And God placed all things under
his feet[d] and appointed him to be head[e] over everything for the church, 23which is his body, the fullness
of him who fills everything in every way.

1:17 [w]Jn 20:17 [x]Col 1:9
1:18 [y]Ac 26:18; 2Co 4:6
1:19 [z]Col 1:29 [a]Eph 6:10
1:20 [b]Ac 2:24
1:21 [c]Php 2:9,10
1:22 [d]Mt 28:18 [e]Eph 4:15; 5:23
2:1 [f]ver 5; Col 2:13
2:2 [g]Col 3:7 [h]Jn 12:31; Eph 6:12 [i]Eph 5:6
2:3 [j]Gal 5:16

Made Alive in Christ

2 As for you, you were dead in your transgressions and sins,[f] 2in which you used to live[g] when you followed the ways of this world and of the ruler of the kingdom of the air,[h] the spirit who is now at work
in those who are disobedient.[i] 3All of us also lived among them at one time, gratifying the cravings of our
flesh[b][j] and following its desires and thoughts. Like the rest, we were by nature deserving of wrath. 4But

[a] *17* Or *a spirit* [b] *3* In contexts like this, the Greek word for *flesh* (*sarx*) refers to the sinful state of human beings, often presented as a power in opposition to the Spirit.

1:17 Spirit of wisdom and revelation. Paul prays that the Holy Spirit, whom they had already received, might impart "wisdom and revelation." This request is not for esoteric wisdom or new revelation but for a deeper understanding of God—of his will and saving purposes as revealed in Christ (1 Cor 2:6–16).

1:18–19 eyes of your heart may be enlightened. The "heart" refers to the center of one's mind, will, and spirit. In essence, Paul prays that they will receive spiritual insight regarding three blessings that are theirs: (1) **hope.** The certain expectation for a glorious future (Rom 5:2–5; Col 1:27) with a cosmos that is united under Christ (Eph 1:9–10); not a hopeful wish, but a confident expectation of what is to come since it is ultimately grounded on God's faithfulness. See also 4:4. (2) **riches of his glorious inheritance.** Probably not the believer's inheritance (v. 14), but God's inheritance comprising Jewish and Gentile believers. We are his treasured possession (see note on v. 11). (3) **incomparably great power ... mighty strength.** Paul uses multiple terms to emphasize the greatness of God's power that is presently available to believers.

1:18 called. See note on 4:1.

1:20 right hand. The position of supreme honor and divine power (cf. Ps 110:1).

1:21 far above all rule ... every name that is invoked. Christ is above every supernatural being, including the evil powers (4:8; Col 2:15; 1 Pet 3:19–22). Many worshiped the goddess Artemis (Acts 19:23–41) as the Queen of Heaven, but Christ sovereignly rules the cosmos. **present age ... the one to come.** See note on v. 3.

1:22 placed all things under his feet. Paul quotes Ps 8:6, which itself recalls Gen 1:26–28. Both Paul and Heb 2:6–9 apply this psalm to Christ; Christ is the last Adam, who restores dominion over creation. **head.** Greek *kephalē*, generally implies authority. Christ is the preeminent and authoritative ruler over all things. See note on 4:16.

1:23 Paul highlights the significance of the church in God's redemptive plan by using two terms to describe the church's relationship to Christ: (1) **his body.** Shows the organic unity between Christ and his bride, the church, in much the same way that "one flesh" describes the union between man and wife in marriage. See 5:28–32. (2) **fullness.** The church is the central locus of Christ's rule and presence in the cosmos. See notes on 3:19; 4:13; 5:18. **fills.** Christ pervades everything with his sovereign rule. See note on 4:10.

2:1–10 *Made Alive in Christ.* Paul wrote earlier of God's plan to unite all things under the headship of Christ (1:10). He now explains how God will accomplish his purposes, beginning with the reconciliation of individuals to God. This section contrasts the believers' sinful past (vv. 1–3) with their present salvation in Christ (vv. 4–7) and affirms the grace of God as the basis of this salvation (vv. 8–10). The presence of a "we-you" contrast continues the theme of 1:11–14 (see note on 1:11). Both Jews and Gentiles are in the same predicament without Christ, and both share the same privileges in Christ. Paul's description of the salvation of believers is thoroughly God-centered. God initiates our salvation, his love and mercy motivate it, and his grace grounds it. Ultimately, the display of God's grace is the purpose of our salvation.

2:1 dead. Before God's action, everybody who is born is spiritually dead and alienated from the God who is life and gives life. There is no way that we can respond positively to the gospel. **in your transgressions and sins.** The Greek construction not only denotes the cause of our pitiful condition (cf. Gen 2–3; Rom 6:23) but also emphasizes our position outside Christ. Instead of being "in Christ" (Eph 2:6,7,10), we were "in ... transgressions and sins." The two plural synonyms "transgressions and sins" highlight the severity and variety of our deliberate and willful rebellion against God's holiness and righteousness.

2:2 Before introducing the grace of God, Paul further shows our plight in vv. 2–3. **live.** Or "walk" (see note on v. 10). **this world.** Unbelievers are oriented to life in this "present evil age" (Gal 1:4) rather than in the "one to come" (Eph 1:21). **ruler.** Satan. **the air.** Part of the heavenly realms that is the abode of evil spirits (see note on 1:3). **spirit ... at work in those who are disobedient.** Satan influences unbelievers, those who reject the authority of God.

2:3 us ... our ... we. Paul switches to first person plural pronouns, indicating that Jewish believers prior to their conversion were in the same predicament as his Gentile readers. Belonging to the covenant people of Israel does not automatically assure acceptance by God. Neither possession of the law nor physical circumcision has any benefit unless the law is obeyed (Rom 2:1—3:8). **flesh.** The unregenerate state of human beings; our natural propensity to oppose God's will and the Spirit (Gal 5:16–21). **by nature.** As descendants of Adam, we inherit his guilt and deserve God's anger and judgment (Rom 5:12–21). **wrath.** God's wrath is not a mechanistic process of cause and effect but is a personal manifestation of his perfect holiness. Unlike the capricious and vindictive spite of many Greco-Roman deities, God's wrath is the necessary and appropriate response to creatures who reject their Creator and spurn his mercy (John 3:36). God metes out his wrath in the present (Rom 1:18) and will do so climactically in the future (Rom 2:5; 1 Thess 1:10). See "Wrath," p. 2681.

2:4 But. Introduces the contrasting situation that solely God's action brings about. **great love.** God's wrath does not contradict his love. God in his perfection displays his wrath against us because we have offended him; but God in his perfection loves us because he is a loving

2:5 [k]ver 1 [l]ver 8; Ac 15:11
2:6 [m]Eph 1:20 [n]Eph 1:3
2:7 [o]Titus 3:4
2:8 [p]ver 5
2:9 [q]2Ti 1:9 [r]1Co 1:29
2:10 [s]Eph 4:24 [t]Titus 2:14
2:11 [u]Col 2:11
2:12 [v]Gal 3:17 [w]1Th 4:13
2:13 [x]ver 17; Ac 2:39 [y]Col 1:20
2:14 [z]1Co 12:13

because of his great love for us, God, who is rich in mercy, [5]made us alive with Christ even when we were
dead in transgressions[k]—it is by grace you have been saved.[l] [6]And God raised us up with Christ and seated
us with him[m] in the heavenly realms[n] in Christ Jesus, [7]in order that in the coming ages he might show the
incomparable riches of his grace, expressed in his kindness[o] to us in Christ Jesus. [8]For it is by grace you
have been saved,[p] through faith—and this is not from yourselves, it is the gift of God— [9]not by works,[q]
so that no one can boast.[r] [10]For we are God's handiwork, created[s] in Christ Jesus to do good works,[t] which
God prepared in advance for us to do.

Jew and Gentile Reconciled Through Christ

[11]Therefore, remember that formerly you who are Gentiles by birth and called "uncircumcised"
by those who call themselves "the circumcision" (which is done in the body by human hands)[u]—
[12]remember that at that time you were separate from Christ, excluded from citizenship in Israel and
foreigners to the covenants of the promise,[v] without hope[w] and without God in the world. [13]But now in
Christ Jesus you who once were far away have been brought near[x] by the blood of Christ.[y]
[14]For he himself is our peace, who has made the two groups one[z] and has destroyed the barrier, the

God. God's wrath and love are simultaneously displayed on the cross. **rich in mercy.** God's compassion toward us stems from his great love rather than any good we do.

2:5–6 you have been saved ... in Christ Jesus. In these verses, Paul emphasizes aspects of our salvation that are a present reality. Due to our union "with Christ," God has accomplished three events spiritually for believers that he did for Christ: (1) **made us alive.** We possess a living relationship with God (Rom 6:1–11). (2) **raised us up.** We presently experience spiritual resurrection life. The resurrection of our physical bodies will occur when Christ returns. (3) **seated us.** Being seated with Christ, we share in his victory over the demonic powers (1:20–21) and are no longer obligated to follow the world, the devil, and the flesh (vv. 1–3). **with him.** Although seated with Christ, we are not seated at God's right hand. That exalted position is reserved for Christ alone.

2:5 grace. See note on v. 8.

2:7 show ... his grace. The climactic purpose of God's act of salvation in vv. 4–6 is to demonstrate his grace for all eternity.

2:8 by grace you have been saved. This phrase first occurs in v. 5 and is repeated here for emphasis. Grace is the basis and cause of our salvation (Rom 3:24; 11:6; Titus 3:7). It is God's unmerited favor toward those who have transgressed his commandments and deserve his wrath. We could not help ourselves because "we were dead" (Eph 2:5). See "Love and Grace," p. 2684. **through faith.** Faith, itself a gift of God, is the human response by which we receive God's salvation. It is a confident trust in God whereby we refuse to justify ourselves based on our achievements but gratefully receive what God has already accomplished in Christ (see Rom 3:21–31). **this.** The process of salvation by grace through faith. **not from yourselves.** Human effort can never contribute to our salvation. **the gift of God.** Salvation, including our faith (Phil 1:29), is God's initiative and activity; it is entirely "the gift of God" (cf. Titus 3:5).

2:9 works. Any human effort; equivalent to "works of the law" (Rom 3:20,28) in a Jewish context. **boast.** God's salvation excludes any human boasting (1 Cor 1:26–31). We should instead boast in the Lord (2 Cor 10:17; Gal 6:14)—in his glory (Eph 1:3–14), grace (2:7), and wisdom (3:10).

2:10 handiwork. The Greek word can connote the skillful work of a craftsman. **created.** The transformation of believers from death to life is so radical that it is considered a new act of creation (4:24; 2 Cor 5:17). The scope of this new creation is more than the individual. It also includes the community of faith (vv. 14–16; Gal 6:15), and, together, the new creation of the individual and the community anticipates that of the cosmos (Eph 1:10; Rom 8:18–25). See notes on Eph 2:15; 4:24; see also "Creation," p. 2642. **for us to do.** Or "that we should walk in them." The occurrence of the Greek for "walk" here and in v. 2 contrasts our former and present lifestyles. Instead of "walking" in "transgressions and sins" (v. 1), God has created us anew to "walk" in "good works." These good works are not the basis of but the evidence of God's new creative work in us.

2:11–22 *Jew and Gentile Reconciled Through Christ.* Paul now draws out the implication of vv. 1–10. As Jewish and Gentile believers are individually reconciled to God in Christ, these formerly hostile peoples are also reconciled with one another in Christ. Paul proceeds by explaining the nature (vv. 11–13), means (vv. 14–18), and consequences (vv. 19–22) of this reconciliation between Jews and Gentiles.

2:11 Therefore. Suggests that horizontal reconciliation (vv. 11–22) depends on vertical reconciliation (vv. 1–10). **remember.** Remembering God's deliverance in the past is more than mere recall of facts; rather, it should lead us to praise and obey God in the present (cf. the appeal to Israel to recall their slavery in Egypt; see Exod 13:3; Deut 5:15). **formerly.** As in vv. 1–10, Paul employs a "formerly-now" structure in vv. 11–22, contrasting his Gentile readers' past exclusion from the privileges given to Israel with their present inclusion as the people of God (see "People of God," p. 2672). **"uncircumcised."** A Jewish ethnic slur for Gentiles. **"the circumcision."** Although other people practiced circumcision, it became the defining mark of Jewish identification since it was the physical sign of the Abrahamic covenant. **done in the body by human hands.** Expresses the limitations of physical circumcision in contrast to heart circumcision (Deut 30:6; Rom 2:29; Col 2:11).

2:12 Christ. The Messiah and king of Israel. **foreigners to the covenants of the promise.** Gentiles were excluded from the covenants that promised salvation to Israel (see "Covenant," p. 2646). **without hope.** No expectation of receiving salvation (cf. 1 Thess 4:13).

2:13 But now. Contrast: Gentiles who *once* were "far away" have *now* been "brought near" through Christ's sacrificial death. Although rabbinic literature uses "brought near" to describe proselytes to Judaism, the present context refers to Gentiles having access to God without conversion to Judaism.

2:14 he himself is our peace. Christ not only brings peace and reconciliation (Col 1:20) but is the embodiment and personification of peace (Isa 9:6; Mic 5:5). The focus here is the peace between Jewish and Gentile believers ("two groups"); however, Eph 2:16–18 shows that the vertical peace that believers have with God is foundational for this horizontal peace. This horizontal peace is not just the absence of hostility; it involves mutual acceptance and love (4:16,32). **the barrier, the dividing wall of hostility.** May refer to the railing in the Jewish temple that separated the court of Gentiles from the inner courts (see photo, p. 1975) with a sign prohibiting Gentiles from entering on pain of death. Nevertheless, the fundamental reason for this barrier is the Mosaic law with its holiness code that separated Israel from the other nations and caused hostility between Jews and Gentiles.

dividing wall of hostility, 15 by setting aside in his flesh[a] the law with its commands and regulations.[b] His
purpose was to create in himself one[c] new humanity out of the two, thus making peace, 16 and in one
body to reconcile both of them to God through the cross,[d] by which he put to death their hostility. 17 He
came and preached peace to you who were far away and peace to those who were near.[e] 18 For through
him we both have access[f] to the Father[g] by one Spirit.[h]
19 Consequently, you are no longer foreigners and strangers,[i] but fellow citizens[j] with God's people
and also members of his household,[k] 20 built on the foundation[l] of the apostles and prophets, with Christ
Jesus himself as the chief cornerstone.[m] 21 In him the whole building is joined together and rises to
become a holy temple[n] in the Lord. 22 And in him you too are being built together to become a dwelling
in which God lives by his Spirit.

God's Marvelous Plan for the Gentiles

3 For this reason I, Paul, the prisoner[o] of Christ Jesus for the sake of you Gentiles—
2 Surely you have heard about the administration of God's grace that was given to me[p] for you,
3 that is, the mystery[q] made known to me by revelation,[r] as I have already written briefly. 4 In reading
this, then, you will be able to understand my insight[s] into the mystery of Christ, 5 which was not made
known to people in other generations as it has now been revealed by the Spirit to God's holy apostles
and prophets.[t] 6 This mystery is that through the gospel the Gentiles are heirs[u] together with Israel,
members together of one body,[v] and sharers together in the promise in Christ Jesus.

2:15 [a] Col 1:21,22 [b] Col 2:14 [c] Gal 3:28
2:16 [d] Col 1:20,22
2:17 [e] Ps 148:14; Isa 57:19
2:18 [f] Eph 3:12 [g] Col 1:12 [h] 1Co 12:13
2:19 [i] ver 12 [j] Php 3:20 [k] Gal 6:10
2:20 [l] Mt 16:18; Rev 21:14 [m] 1Pe 2:4-8
2:21 [n] 1Co 3:16,17
3:1 [o] Ac 23:18; Eph 4:1
3:2 [p] Col 1:25
3:3 [q] Ro 16:25 [r] 1Co 2:10
3:4 [s] 2Co 11:6
3:5 [t] Ro 16:26
3:6 [u] Gal 3:29 [v] Eph 2:15,16

2:15 setting aside ... the law. Christ sets aside the old covenant with its Mosaic law and replaces it with a new covenant for all believers. Consequently, the Mosaic law cannot serve as a barrier between Jewish and Gentile believers. Although new covenant believers are not under the Mosaic law, they are under "Christ's law" (1 Cor 9:21; cf. Matt 5:17; Rom 3:31; Gal 6:2). See "Law," p. 2649. **his flesh.** Christ's physical death. **create ... one new humanity.** As a new creation, this new humanity comprising all believers is distinct from Jews and Gentiles (1 Cor 10:32). It is a community in which Jews and Gentiles are united in peace. See notes on Eph 2:10; 4:24.

2:16 reconcile. Bring two estranged parties into a peaceful relationship (Rom 5:10–11; 2 Cor 5:19; Col 1:22). Christ not only reconciles Jewish and Gentile believers "in one body" (the church), he also reconciles "both of them to God." The cross destroys not only the "hostility" between Jewish and Gentile believers but also the hostility between humanity and God.

2:17 preached peace ... far away and ... near. Using the language of Isa 52:7; 57:19, Paul affirms that Jesus preached peace to those "far" (Gentiles) and "near" (Jews).

2:19 Consequently. The reconciliation described in vv. 19–22 is dependent upon what Christ accomplished through his death described in vv. 14–18. **foreigners and strangers.** Generally looked upon with contempt and suspicion in the ancient world. **fellow citizens.** Instead of their disenfranchised status, Gentile believers now share in the rights and privileges of God's people.

2:20 foundation of the apostles and prophets. In 1 Cor 3:10–17, Christ is the foundation upon which the apostles build. Here, Paul employs a different imagery. The foundation is now the apostles and prophets of the first-century church because they are the first to proclaim the gospel. The message they preach are the very words of God, revealed to them by the Spirit (Eph 3:5). In this imagery, Christ is the "chief cornerstone"—the first stone to be laid and the stone that determines the placement of the foundation and all other subsequent stones. **apostles and prophets.** Can refer to (1) NT apostles and OT prophets, (2) NT apostles who also prophesy, or (3) NT apostles and NT prophets. There are difficulties with the first two options. In 3:5 this same phrase refers to people in the NT era. In 4:11 (and 1 Cor 12:28–29), Paul distinguishes apostles from prophets, viewing them as two separate groups. Thus, the last option is preferable.

2:21–22 holy temple ... being built together. Paul metaphorically describes the church, Christ's body, as a temple. Christ's physical body is the ultimate fulfillment of all that the physical temple in Jerusalem was meant to be (John 2:19–21). At the same time, as Jewish and Gentile believers are incorporated into Christ's body, they are "being built together" (Eph 2:22) as "living stones" (1 Pet 2:5) into God's temple (1 Cor 3:16–17; 2 Cor 6:16). This new multiethnic temple, the church, is the fulfillment of Isa 56:3–8; 66:18–20. **in the Lord.** Existing in the Lord, this temple is not a physical building. **dwelling in which God lives.** Just as the presence of God in OT times filled first the tabernacle and then later the temple, so also God now dwells in the church "by his Spirit" (see notes on 3:19; 5:18; see also "Temple," p. 2652).

3:1–13 *God's Marvelous Plan for the Gentiles.* Paul explains God's plan for the Gentiles via two moves. He first explains the mystery of Christ (vv. 2–6), focusing on its revelation (vv. 3–5) and content (v. 6). He then expands on his ministry of the gospel (vv. 7–13), highlighting the purpose of proclaiming the wisdom of God to the spiritual powers through the church (v. 10).

3:1 For this reason. Because of the inclusion of Gentiles in salvation history (2:11–22, especially vv. 19–22). **prisoner of Christ Jesus.** Paul is a prisoner of Rome for the sake of Christ (4:1; Phil 1:13). After this verse, Paul breaks off his thought only to resume it in v. 14.

3:2 Surely you have heard. The church in Ephesus would have been aware of Paul's ministry given his long stay there; however, other churches would not have known much about it if Ephesians was a circular letter (see Introduction: Date, Place of Composition, and Destination). **administration of God's grace.** The apostolic commission that was given to Paul by an act of grace (see v. 7 and note). As the word "administration" (Greek *oikonomia*) can mean "management of a household," Paul's task is to execute God's plan of including Gentiles within God's "household" (Greek *oikeios*, 2:19).

3:3 mystery. See notes on 1:9,10; 3:4,6; 5:32. **by revelation.** Primarily in the Damascus road experience (Gal 1:12,15–16). **I have already written briefly.** May refer to 1:9–10; 2:11–22.

3:4 mystery of Christ. The mystery is about Christ and the role that he plays in uniting believers.

3:5 not made known. See note on v. 6. **apostles and prophets.** See note on 2:20.

3:6 This mystery is that. The content of the mystery mentioned in vv. 3–4 is now declared. **together ... together ... together.** Repetition of this word emphasizes the unique aspect of the mystery that was not

3:7 [w] 1Co 3:5 [x] Eph 1:19
3:8 [y] 1Co 15:9
3:9 [z] Ro 16:25
3:10 [a] 1Co 2:7 [b] 1Pe 1:12 [c] Eph 1:21
3:12 [d] Eph 2:18 [e] Heb 4:16
3:14 [f] Php 2:10
3:16 [g] Col 1:11 [h] Ro 7:22
3:17 [i] Jn 14:23 [j] Col 1:23
3:18 [k] Job 11:8,9
3:19 [l] Col 2:10 [m] Eph 1:23
3:20 [n] Ro 16:25
3:21 [o] Ro 11:36

7 I became a servant of this gospel[w] by the gift of God's grace given me through the working of his
power.[x] 8 Although I am less than the least of all the Lord's people,[y] this grace was given me: to preach
to the Gentiles the boundless riches of Christ, 9 and to make plain to everyone the administration of
this mystery,[z] which for ages past was kept hidden in God, who created all things. 10 His intent was
that now, through the church, the manifold wisdom of God[a] should be made known[b] to the rulers
and authorities[c] in the heavenly realms, 11 according to his eternal purpose that he accomplished in
Christ Jesus our Lord. 12 In him and through faith in him we may approach God[d] with freedom and
confidence.[e] 13 I ask you, therefore, not to be discouraged because of my sufferings for you, which are
your glory.

A Prayer for the Ephesians

14 For this reason I kneel[f] before the Father, 15 from whom every family[*a*] in heaven and on earth
derives its name. 16 I pray that out of his glorious riches he may strengthen you with power[g] through
his Spirit in your inner being,[h] 17 so that Christ may dwell in your hearts[i] through faith. And I pray that
you, being rooted[j] and established in love, 18 may have power, together with all the Lord's holy people, to
grasp how wide and long and high and deep[k] is the love of Christ, 19 and to know this love that surpasses
knowledge—that you may be filled[l] to the measure of all the fullness of God.[m]

20 Now to him who is able[n] to do immeasurably more than all we ask or imagine, according to his
power that is at work within us, 21 to him be glory in the church and in Christ Jesus throughout all
generations, for ever and ever! Amen.[o]

a *15* The Greek for *family* (*patria*) is derived from the Greek for *father* (*pater*).

previously known: Gentiles mutually and equally share in God's blessings with Jews in the church. Although the OT declared God's intention to bless Gentiles (Gen 12:3), the manner and extent to which God would accomplish his saving purposes by incorporating both Jews and Gentiles on equal footing into one body in Christ was not made known until the NT era.

3:7 by the gift of God's grace given me. Paul is an apostle because he was gifted by Christ. This gift for ministry, including other gifts mentioned in 4:11, arises from God's grace (Rom 12:6). Since not all believers have the same gift, this grace is a special endowment, given "as Christ apportioned it" (4:7; cf. 1 Cor 12:11), and goes beyond the grace by which each believer is saved.

3:8 less than the least. True humility. Paul is acutely aware of his unworthiness (cf. 1 Cor 15:9; 1 Tim 1:15) since he persecuted Christ and the church (Acts 9:4; Phil 3:6). Nevertheless, he is amazed that God in his abundant grace would use someone such as him.

3:10 now. In contrast to "ages past" (v. 9). **through the church.** Given God's incredible work of reconciling two hostile groups into one organic body, the church is the perfect means to display God's wisdom. Insofar as the church exists as a spiritually united multiethnic community, it accomplishes this task. **rulers and authorities in the heavenly realms.** Can refer to good or evil spiritual powers. Beholding God's wisdom as displayed through the church leads good angels to glorify God since they "long to look" into God's redemptive plan (1 Pet 1:12). Evil powers, on the other hand, are reminded that God's plan of uniting all things under Christ (Eph 1:9–10) has decisively begun and that their final defeat is imminent (1 Cor 15:24).

3:11 according to his eternal purpose. Since the redemption that God "purposed in Christ" (1:9) originated in eternity past, the display of God's wisdom through the church is not a hastily devised plan in response to Israel's failure.

3:12 See Heb 4:16; 10:19–22 and notes.

3:13 your glory. Paul's apostolic sufferings mediate salvation to others (2 Cor 1:6; 4:12), enabling them to experience "glory"—a glory they participate in now as God's treasured possession ("inheritance," Eph 1:18; see note on 1:18–19) but a glory that will be fully realized in the last day (Rom 8:17–18,30; Phil 3:21). See 2 Tim 2:10.

3:14–21 *A Prayer for the Ephesians.* Paul's prayer has three parts: address (vv. 14–15), appeals (vv. 16–19), and adoration (vv. 20–21). In the appeals, Paul prays for power, love, and spiritual maturity—elements the church needs to fulfill (1) its role in displaying the wisdom of God to the spiritual powers (v. 10) and (2) its calling to be God's redeemed community in the world (4:1).

3:14–15 For this reason. Resumes the thought of v. 1. **I kneel.** Expresses deep worship and reverence since most people in Paul's day stood to pray (Mark 11:25; Luke 18:11,13). **Father ... family.** The Greek for "family" (*patria*) is derived from the Greek for "father" (*patēr*; see NIV text note on v. 15), reinforcing the headship of a father over a family. By addressing God as the "Father" who names (i.e., defines the identity of) every group of angelic beings ("in heaven") and humanity ("on earth"), Paul affirms God's greatness (cf. Ps 147:4; Isa 40:26). God brings into existence and exercises dominion over all creation.

3:16 inner being. Not the "new self" of 4:24, but the seat of one's consciousness and moral being. It is equivalent to heart (v. 17) or mind (4:23). See notes on Rom 7:22; 2 Cor 4:16.

3:17 dwell. Not Christ's initial dwelling at the moment of salvation but his controlling presence over our attitudes and conduct as we continually trust him. **hearts.** The center of one's being (see notes on v. 16; 1:18–19).

3:18 Cf. Rom 8:35–39.

3:19 know. Not just intellectual knowledge, but also experiential knowledge. **surpasses knowledge.** Not unknowable, but so great that it can never be fully known. **filled ... fullness of God.** Just as the presence and glory of God filled the temple in the OT (1 Kgs 8:10–11), so also Paul prays that God would fill the church to the full measure of himself—his presence, moral excellence, power, and love. See notes on 1:23; 2:21–22; 4:13; 5:18.

3:21 to him be glory. Paul ends the first part of his letter on the same tone of praise with which he began it, reminding us that the final goal of salvation in history is the eternal glorification of God. **in the church and in Christ Jesus.** God is glorified in the church as it displays his power and love, and God is glorified in Christ because his death brought the church into existence. See "The Glory of God," p. 2640.

Unity and Maturity in the Body of Christ

4 As a prisoner[p] for the Lord, then, I urge you to live a life worthy[q] of the calling you have received.
2Be completely humble and gentle; be patient, bearing with one another[r] in love.[s] 3Make every
effort to keep the unity[t] of the Spirit through the bond of peace. 4There is one body and one Spirit,[u] just
as you were called to one hope when you were called; 5one Lord, one faith, one baptism; 6one God and
Father of all, who is over all and through all and in all.[v]
7But to each one of us[w] grace has been given[x] as Christ apportioned it. 8This is why it[a] says:

> "When he ascended on high,
> he took many captives[y]
> and gave gifts to his people."[b][z]

9(What does "he ascended" mean except that he also descended to the lower, earthly regions[c]? 10He
who descended is the very one who ascended higher than all the heavens, in order to fill the whole
universe.) 11So Christ himself gave the apostles,[a] the prophets, the evangelists,[b] the pastors and teachers, 12to equip his people for works of service, so that the body of Christ[c] may be built up 13until we all
reach unity[d] in the faith and in the knowledge of the Son of God and become mature,[e] attaining to the
whole measure of the fullness of Christ.

a 8 Or *God* *b* 8 Psalm 68:18 *c* 9 Or *the depths of the earth*

4:1 [p] Eph 3:1 [q] Php 1:27; Col 1:10
4:2 [r] Col 3:12,13 [s] Eph 1:4
4:3 [t] Col 3:14
4:4 [u] 1Co 12:13
4:6 [v] Ro 11:36
4:7 [w] 1Co 12:7,11 [x] Ro 12:3
4:8 [y] Col 2:15 [z] Ps 68:18
4:11 [a] 1Co 12:28 [b] Ac 21:8
4:12 [c] 1Co 12:27
4:13 [d] ver 3,5 [e] Col 1:28

4:1—6:20 *Conduct of the Church Within Christ's Cosmic Reconciliation.* On the basis of what God has accomplished (1:3—3:21), Paul instructs his readers how to live out their calling.

4:1–16 *Unity and Maturity in the Body of Christ.* Paul stresses the importance of maintaining unity (vv. 1–6) and of using diverse gifts to attain maturity in the church (vv. 7–16). This passage (especially v. 1) sets the stage for what follows since subsequent passages detail what it means for believers to live worthy of their calling and to maintain the unity of the Spirit in the community (4:17—5:20) and in the household (5:21—6:9).

4:1 prisoner. See note on 3:1. **then.** Marks the transition between the doctrinal and ethical sections (chs. 1–3 and 4–6, respectively); the ethical instructions depend on what God has done in Christ for humanity. **calling.** Described in chs. 1–3 and includes the blessings of salvation, the one new humanity comprising Jews and Gentiles, and their participation in God's plan for cosmic unity (3:10,21).

4:3 keep the unity of the Spirit. The Spirit creates unity, and believers are responsible to maintain ("keep") it. See note on v. 13. **bond of peace.** Peace is the bond that binds them together.

4:4 There is. In vv. 4–6, Paul gives seven confessional statements of oneness that provide the basis for the unity in vv. 1–3. Although declaratory, these statements also implicitly exhort the community to unity. **one body.** Paul's primary concern in this section is the church (2:14–16). **one Spirit.** Recalls 2:18. **one hope.** The corporate hope of the community. See note on 1:18–19.

4:5 one Lord. The early church affirmed that Jesus is Lord on the basis of his resurrection and exaltation. **one faith.** The common set of core Christian beliefs. **one baptism.** The initiatory rite of water baptism and the spiritual union with Christ that the rite symbolizes (see note on Rom 6:4).

4:6 one God and Father of all ... over all and through all and in all. Confession of God's transcendence, sovereignty, and omnipresence.

4:7 to each one of us. Christ has given every member of the body gifts as he deems fit (cf. Rom 12:6; 1 Cor 12:11). **grace.** See note on 3:7.

4:8 Ps 68:18 describes God's triumphal ascension to his throne after defeating his enemies. Paul applies this to Christ's triumphal ascension (Eph 1:20–22). **captives.** The spiritual powers Christ conquered by the cross (Col 2:15). **gave gifts.** In Ps 68:18, God "received gifts." Paul probably adapts this psalm to show that Christ, as the ultimate victor, is able to give gifts (the leaders of v. 11) to the church. It is also possible that Paul, in order to more accurately bring out the meaning of Ps 68, uses a different textual tradition than that found in the current OT. Syriac and Aramaic translations of Ps 68:18 attest to this textual tradition as they also have "gave gifts."

4:9 ascended ... descended. Christ's ascent into the heavens presupposes his descent to earth in his incarnation. The passage probably does not refer to Christ's descent into Hades.

4:10 fill. Just as God "[fills] heaven and earth" with his sovereign rule (Jer 23:24; cf. Eph 4:6), so also Christ fills all things with his mighty rule (1:20–23).

4:11 Christ himself gave. The ultimate significance of Ps 68:18 is found in the exalted Christ giving spiritual gifts or gifted people to the church. The list here is not comprehensive (cf. Rom 12:6–8; 1 Cor 12:8–10,28–30; 1 Pet 4:10–11). **apostles.** Those commissioned by Christ to proclaim his message and establish the church. Qualifications for the initial group of apostles are found in Acts 1:21–22. Paul was commissioned as an apostle when Christ appeared to him on the Damascus road (Acts 9:1–19; 22:6–21; 26:12–23; 1 Cor 15:8–9). See also notes on Mark 6:30; Rom 1:1; 1 Cor 1:1. **prophets.** Those who communicate a message from God that is appropriate to the situation facing the church (Acts 11:27–28; 1 Cor 14:3). See also notes on Eph 2:20; 1 Cor 12:8–10. **evangelists.** Greek *euangelistēs*, related to "gospel" (Greek *euaggelion*), those who preach the gospel. See Acts 21:8; 2 Tim 4:5. **pastors.** Or "shepherds"; used figuratively of leaders who "shepherd" their people (2 Sam 5:2, Jer 3:15; Zech 10:3). **teachers.** There is debate whether "the pastors and teachers" refers to individuals who have two gifts (i.e., "the pastor-teacher") or to two separate groups of gifted people (i.e., "the pastors and the teachers"). The Greek construction suggests that the two gifts are related since teaching is an essential part of pastoral ministry (cf. 1 Tim 3:2).

4:12 to equip his people. Christ gifts leaders (v. 11) so that they can train believers to exercise their own respective gifts (v. 7) for ministry rather than do *all* the work for them. **so that the body of Christ may be built up.** Spiritual gifts are ultimately for the edification of the church, not for self-aggrandizement (1 Cor 12:7; 1 Pet 4:10).

4:13 unity. Recalls the ideal of vv. 1–6. Unity is more than having a loving or tolerant attitude. It is uniting around the core Christian beliefs of the faith and the knowledge of the Son of God (cf. v. 5; 1 Tim 3:9; Jude 3; see "apostles' teaching" in Acts 2:42). **become mature.** Or "to a mature man." Contrasts with "infants" in v. 14. Apart from the obvious difference in maturity levels indicated by their ages, the *singular* "man" also contrasts with the *plural* "infants" and emphasizes the importance of corporate unity (v. 15). **fullness of Christ.** The standard

4:14 [f] 1Co 14:20 [g] Jas 1:6 [h] Eph 6:11
4:15 [i] Eph 1:22
4:16 [j] Col 2:19
4:17 [k] Ro 1:21
4:18 [l] Ro 1:21 [m] Eph 2:12 [n] 2Co 3:14
4:19 [o] 1Ti 4:2 [p] Ro 1:24 [q] Col 3:5
4:22 [r] 1Pe 2:1 [s] Ro 6:6
4:23 [t] Col 3:10
4:24 [u] Ro 6:4 [v] Eph 2:10
4:25 [w] Zec 8:16 [x] Ro 12:5

14 Then we will no longer be infants,[f] tossed back and forth by the waves,[g] and blown here and there
by every wind of teaching and by the cunning and craftiness of people in their deceitful scheming.[h]
15 Instead, speaking the truth in love, we will grow to become in every respect the mature body of him
who is the head,[i] that is, Christ. 16 From him the whole body, joined and held together by every supporting ligament, grows[j] and builds itself up in love, as each part does its work.

Instructions for Christian Living

17 So I tell you this, and insist on it in the Lord, that you must no longer live as the Gentiles do, in the
futility of their thinking.[k] 18 They are darkened in their understanding[l] and separated from the life of
God[m] because of the ignorance that is in them due to the hardening of their hearts.[n] 19 Having lost all
sensitivity,[o] they have given themselves over[p] to sensuality[q] so as to indulge in every kind of impurity,
and they are full of greed.

20 That, however, is not the way of life you learned 21 when you heard about Christ and were taught in
him in accordance with the truth that is in Jesus. 22 You were taught, with regard to your former way of life,
to put off[r] your old self,[s] which is being corrupted by its deceitful desires; 23 to be made new in the attitude
of your minds;[t] 24 and to put on the new self,[u] created to be like God in true righteousness and holiness.[v]

25 Therefore each of you must put off falsehood and speak truthfully[w] to your neighbor, for we are
all members of one body.[x] 26 "In your anger do not sin"[a]: Do not let the sun go down while you are still

[a] *26* Psalm 4:4 (see Septuagint)

of maturity to which the church aspires is Christ in all his perfection. See notes on 1:23; 3:19; 5:18.

4:14 infants. Contrasts with "become mature" in v. 13 (see note there). **tossed.** Immaturity leads to instability and susceptibility to every kind of false teaching (cf. Acts 20:29–30; 1 Tim 1:3–4; 6:3–5; 1 John 4:1–2).

4:15 speaking the truth. The truth of the gospel (v. 21; 1:13) must be proclaimed "in love," not with a combative attitude. **grow to become ... the head.** Restatement of v. 13 using the imagery of Christ as head of the body. **mature body.** This translation brings out Paul's emphasis on corporate maturity—the growth of the church.

4:16 Paul continues to use the imagery of the body to describe church growth. **From him.** Christ, as head of the body, is the source of sustenance for the church (cf. Col 2:19). **together ... every ... each.** Shows the necessity of each member utilizing the gifts that Christ has given them (see v. 7 and note) for the corporate growth of the body. **love.** Its repetition (see vv. 2,15) emphasizes its importance for maturity and unity.

4:17—5:20 *Instructions for Christian Living.* Paul instructs believers how to "live a life worthy of [their] calling" (4:1) in the community of faith. They must live according to the new self rather than the old (4:17–24). Paul clarifies this with specific instructions about the new and old life (4:25—5:2) and by distinguishing between believers and unbelievers with the metaphor of light and darkness (5:3–14). He finally exhorts believers to live a wise and Spirit-filled life (5:15–20).

4:17 as the Gentiles do. Paul's predominantly Gentile readers are to abandon their former lifestyle. **thinking.** Greek *nous*; indicates both cognitive and moral perception. The mindset of those who do not acknowledge God is empty and meaningless (cf. Eccl 1:2; Rom 1:21).

4:18 darkened in their understanding. Continues the theme of a futile reasoning process and contrasts with the enlightened hearts of believers (1:18). **due to the hardening of their hearts.** Their willful "ignorance" of God and his demands does not negate their culpability because it stems from their stubborn and obstinate hearts (Rom 1:18–23).

4:19 they have given themselves over. This does not contradict the divine judgment "God gave them over" of Rom 1:24,26,28 since God gave them over to the "sensuality" that they gladly chose. **indulge in every kind of impurity ... full of greed.** Unbelieving Gentiles may not assess their own moral behavior as negatively as Paul does. Paul's argument, however, is that any lifestyle that is not centered on the revealed will of the Creator is ultimately meaningless, falling short of the holiness that God demands. This indictment must be seen from God's perspective, not that of believers.

4:21 truth that is in Jesus. The truth that Jesus taught and embodied during his earthly ministry.

4:22 put off. Believers must make a fundamental break with their past. **old self.** Contrasts with "new self" in v. 24. The "old self" is the preconversion unregenerate person who is ruled by sin and lives under the dominion of this present evil age.

4:23 See notes on Rom 12:2; Col 3:9b–10.

4:24 put on. Believers have already "put off" (v. 22) the old and "put on" the new at their conversion (note the past action in the parallel in Col 3:9; cf. Rom 6:6). The exhortation here to "put off" and "put on" does not mean to repeat continually the original putting off and putting on but means to live out its significance in light of who believers now are in Christ. **new self.** Related to the "new humanity" of 2:15 since both are "created" by God and both terms are based on the same Greek words *kainos anthrōpos* (or "new man"). While 2:15 emphasizes the corporate aspect of this new self as one humanity comprising Jewish and Gentile believers, this verse focuses on the individual aspect of this "new self," who in contrast to the "old self," is the individual who lives in the life of the age to come and who is part of the new creation. The change from the old to the new speaks not of a change in nature but of a change in relationship. The "old self" is what believers were "in Adam"; the "new self" is what believers are "in Christ" (1 Cor 15:22).

4:25 Therefore. In 4:25—5:2, Paul provides specific instructions about the old and new life based on the truths outlined in 4:17–24. **speak truthfully to your neighbor.** See Zech 8:16; Col 3:9. **neighbor.** Probably means other believers in this context.

4:26–27 In your anger do not sin. Or "Be angry and do not sin," an exact quotation from the Greek translation of Ps 4:4 (see NIV text note there). Some take "be angry" as a command to righteous indignation, in contrast to the unrighteous anger of v. 31. However, the prohibition "do not sin" and the next two prohibitions ("Do not let the sun ... and do not give the devil") suggest that the context admonishes one not to sin *whenever* anger is present; whether the anger is justified is not in view. Believers must deal with anger quickly lest they give Satan an opportunity to bring about greater evil.

angry, 27 and do not give the devil a foothold. 28 Anyone who has been stealing must steal no longer, but
must work,[y] doing something useful with their own hands,[z] that they may have something to share
with those in need.[a]
29 Do not let any unwholesome talk come out of your mouths,[b] but only what is helpful for building
others up according to their needs, that it may benefit those who listen. 30 And do not grieve the Holy
Spirit of God,[c] with whom you were sealed for the day of redemption.[d] 31 Get rid of all bitterness, rage
and anger, brawling and slander, along with every form of malice.[e] 32 Be kind and compassionate to
5 one another, forgiving each other, just as in Christ God forgave you.[f] 1 Follow God's example,[g]
therefore, as dearly loved children 2 and walk in the way of love, just as Christ loved us and gave
himself up for us[h] as a fragrant offering and sacrifice to God.[i]
3 But among you there must not be even a hint of sexual immorality, or of any kind of impurity, or
of greed,[j] because these are improper for God's holy people. 4 Nor should there be obscenity, foolish talk
or coarse joking, which are out of place, but rather thanksgiving.[k] 5 For of this you can be sure: No immoral, impure or greedy person—such a person is an idolater[l]—has any inheritance in the kingdom
of Christ and of God.[a][m] 6 Let no one deceive you with empty words, for because of such things God's
wrath[n] comes on those who are disobedient. 7 Therefore do not be partners with them.
8 For you were once[o] darkness, but now you are light in the Lord. Live as children of light[p] 9 (for the
fruit[q] of the light consists in all goodness, righteousness and truth) 10 and find out what pleases the Lord.
11 Have nothing to do with the fruitless deeds of darkness, but rather expose them. 12 It is shameful even to

[a] 5 Or *kingdom of the Messiah and God*

4:28 [y] Ac 20:35 [z] 1Th 4:11 [a] Lk 3:11
4:29 [b] Col 3:8
4:30 [c] 1Th 5:19 [d] Ro 8:23
4:31 [e] Col 3:8
4:32 [f] Mt 6:14,15
5:1 [g] Lk 6:36
5:2 [h] Gal 1:4 [i] 2Co 2:15; Heb 7:27
5:3 [j] Col 3:5
5:4 [k] ver 20
5:5 [l] Col 3:5 [m] 1Co 6:9
5:6 [n] Ro 1:18
5:8 [o] Eph 2:2 [p] Lk 16:8
5:9 [q] Gal 5:22

4:28 must work. Paul elsewhere advocates work as a means to provide for one's own needs (2 Thess 3:6–12). Here the motivation for work is not individual profit but philanthropic support of "those in need"—especially those within the church (Gal 6:10).
4:29 unwholesome talk. Includes obscenity, slander, gossip, and abusive language. Such speech not only "defiles" the person (Matt 15:11) but also harms the community.
4:30 grieve the Holy Spirit. Paul warns his readers not to repeat the mistake of the Israelites who "rebelled and grieved" the Holy Spirit in the wilderness (Isa 63:10). Sin, especially those sins mentioned in Eph 4:25–31, destroys the unity of the community, thereby bringing sorrow to the Holy Spirit, who produced that unity (v. 3). **grieve.** Shows that the Spirit is a person, not just an impersonal force, since only a person can be grieved. **sealed.** See note on 1:13. God owns and protects believers and will finally possess them in the "day of redemption"—the day Christ returns (see note on 1:14; cf. 1 Pet 1:5).
4:31 all. Every kind of. **rage ... anger.** Greek *thymos ... orgē*; virtually synonymous terms.
4:32 just as. God's forgiveness of our sins is the standard and the basis by which we forgive other believers. See Hos 3:1; Col 3:13.
5:1–2 therefore. Verses 1–2 summarize 4:25–32 with a concluding exhortation to imitate God. **walk in the way of love.** One specific example of imitating God. **just as.** Christ's sacrificial love for us (Gal 2:20) as demonstrated on the cross is the reason and pattern by which we are to love others (Eph 5:25; John 13:34). **fragrant.** Indicating an offering pleasing to God (Gen 8:21; Exod 29:18,25,41; Lev 1:9,13,17; 17:6; Num 28:13). Its use here shows that Christ's sacrificial offering for our sins was truly acceptable to God (Heb 7:27).
5:3 sexual immorality. Greek *porneia*; refers broadly to all illicit sexual acts outside marriage, such as premarital sex, sex with prostitutes, homosexual activity, incest, and adultery. See 1 Thess 4:3–8. **greed.** All forms of excessive desire, including sexual lust.
5:4 thanksgiving. An acknowledgment of our dependence on God and our grateful response to God's gift of redemption, recognizing that he is the source of every blessing. Such an attitude corrects the self-serving focus found in the preceding vices of sexual immorality, greed, and obscene speech. See v. 20; 1 Thess 5:18.
5:5 immoral, impure or greedy. Recalls v. 3. **idolater.** A greedy person values possessions more than God, thereby committing idolatry (Col 3:5). **has any.** Paul is referring not to believers who might fall into such sin but to those who persistently and unrepentantly give themselves over to such a lifestyle. See 1 Cor 6:9–10; 15:50; Gal 5:21. **inheritance.** See 1:14 and note. **the kingdom of Christ and of God.** A unique phrase. Christ presently rules from the right hand of God (1:20), and he will one day hand his kingdom ("the kingdom of the Son," Col 1:13) to God the Father "after he has destroyed all dominion, authority and power" (1 Cor 15:24). The phrase may therefore refer to both the present and future aspects of the divine kingdom—the one kingdom that is ruled by Christ and God.
5:6 deceive you. Believers should not be misled, thinking that such a lifestyle (vv. 3–5) has no consequences. **God's wrath.** See note on 2:3.
5:7 be partners. Although we have normal social relationships with unbelievers, we must not participate in their sinful lifestyle. See note on 2 Cor 6:14.
5:8 For. Believers must reject the sinful lifestyle of vv. 3–5 because they have undergone a fundamental identity change from "darkness" to "light" when they came to the one who is light (v. 14; John 8:12; Acts 26:18; 1 Pet 2:9). **Live as children of light.** See Isa 2:5; 1 Thess 5:5–8; 1 John 1:5–7.
5:9 fruit of the light. The ethical actions of those who live in God's light (Matt 7:16–20; Gal 5:22–23; Phil 1:11).
5:10 find out. The general principles contained in Scripture may not directly address certain situations in the lives of believers. Nevertheless, as Scripture is consulted, the Holy Spirit enables and enlightens them to discern "what pleases the Lord." See Rom 12:2.
5:11 Have nothing to do with. See v. 7; 1 Tim 5:22. **fruitless deeds of darkness.** Contrasts with "fruit of the light" (v. 9). **expose them.** Not only have believers been illumined by the light, but they are now also the means to bring that light to "deeds of darkness" (cf. Matt 5:14–16). Believers expose these deeds either verbally or through their lifestyle. By not participating in such actions, they show these deeds to be the evil that they are.
5:12 the disobedient. Debatable whether this refers to unbelievers or disobedient believers, but the language of "the dead" in v. 14 suggests unbelievers (but see note on v. 13).

5:13 [r]Jn 3:20,21 **5:14** [s]Ro 13:11 [t]Jn 5:25 [u]Isa 60:1 **5:16** [v]Col 4:5 [w]Eph 6:13 **5:17** [x]Ro 12:2; 1Th 4:3 **5:18** [y]Pr 20:1 [z]Lk 1:15 **5:19** [a]Ac 16:25; Col 3:16 **5:20** [b]Ps 34:1 **5:21** [c]Gal 5:13 **5:22** [d]Ge 3:16; 1Pe 3:1, 5,6 [e]Eph 6:5

mention what the disobedient do in secret. [13]But everything exposed by the light[r] becomes visible — and
everything that is illuminated becomes a light. [14]This is why it is said:

> "Wake up, sleeper,[s]
> rise from the dead,[t]
> and Christ will shine on you."[u]

[15]Be very careful, then, how you live — not as unwise but as wise, [16]making the most of every opportunity,[v] because the days are evil.[w] [17]Therefore do not be foolish, but understand what the Lord's will is.[x]
[18]Do not get drunk on wine,[y] which leads to debauchery. Instead, be filled with the Spirit,[z] [19]speaking to
one another with psalms, hymns, and songs from the Spirit.[a] Sing and make music from your heart to
the Lord, [20]always giving thanks[b] to God the Father for everything, in the name of our Lord Jesus Christ.

Instructions for Christian Households

5:22 – 6:9pp — Col 3:18 – 4:1

[21]Submit to one another[c] out of reverence for Christ.
[22]Wives, submit yourselves to your own husbands[d] as you do to the Lord.[e] [23]For the husband is the

5:13 everything ... visible. God's light inevitably shows the true character of one's deeds. **becomes a light.** Light not only exposes the sins of unbelievers but also transforms unbelievers so that they can become "children of light" (v. 8). If we take "the disobedient" in v. 12 to refer to believers rather than unbelievers, we would interpret vv. 13 – 14 not as a summons to evangelism but as a summons to discipleship; believers are to rouse themselves from their spiritual slumber so that they can again, with the aid of the Spirit, produce "fruit of the light" (v. 9).
5:14 it is said. Probably means that what follows is an early Christian hymn, possibly based on Isa 26:19 and 60:1 – 2. **sleeper ... dead.** Images of the sinner (cf. 2:1). The hymn calls unbelievers to come to Christ and receive his life-giving light. See note on v. 13.
5:15 unwise ... wise. The distinction between unwise and wise living is rooted in OT wisdom literature, where the fear of the Lord is the beginning of wisdom (Job 28:28; Prov 1:7; 9:10). Wisdom is obeying God's revealed will (Deut 4:5 – 6; Pss 19:7; 119:98; Matt 7:24; Jas 3:13 – 17).
5:16 making the most of every opportunity. To do good works (2:10). See Col 4:5. **the days are evil.** This present age is controlled by the devil (2:2; 2 Cor 4:4). See note on 1:3.
5:17 understand. Goes beyond cognitive comprehension to applied knowledge (cf. Prov 2:1 – 9). **what the Lord's will is.** In Ephesians, it centers not so much on personal guidance for our immediate future but on God's saving plan to unify all things under the headship of Christ (1:9 – 10) and on our behavior in light of this grand vision of redemption.
5:18 Do not get drunk on wine ... be filled with the Spirit. Paul uses the present tense of these verbs to denote not a onetime experience but a consistent pattern of life that believers should cultivate. In essence, Paul wants believers not to come under the influence of wine but to allow the Spirit to take full control of their lives. The former "leads to debauchery" (cf. Prov 23:29 – 35; Rom 13:13); the latter leads to a life characterized by a series of participles in the Greek: speaking, singing, making music (v. 19), giving thanks (v. 20), and submitting (v. 21). **filled.** Greek *plēroō.* Paul's exhortation recalls earlier passages about being filled to the whole measure of the "fullness [Greek *plērōma*] of God" (3:19) and the "fullness [Greek *plērōma*] of Christ" (4:13). Together they present a picture of the church being filled with the presence of the triune God in much the same way as the OT temple was filled with the presence of God (see 2:21 – 22; 3:19 and notes).
5:19 speaking. The focus here is not to praise God but to "teach and admonish one another" (Col 3:16). **psalms, hymns, and songs.** Probably synonymous terms, indicating the use of every appropriate form that the Spirit prompts. **Sing and make music ... to the Lord.** Joyful worship of Christ.
5:20 in the name. On the basis of who Christ is and what he has done.
5:21 — 6:9 *Instructions for Christian Households.* After instructing believers how to live worthy of their calling within the community of faith (4:17 — 5:20), Paul instructs them how to live within the household. The link between these two sections is 5:21; the submission called for in the household instructions depends on being "filled with the Spirit" (5:18; see note there). These instructions primarily differ from traditional Greco-Roman codes by presenting Christ as the true head of the family. The order within these codes reflects how the Christian household should work out Christ's unity over all things (1:10). See Col 3:18 — 4:1; 1 Pet 2:18 — 3:7; cf. 1 Tim 2:8 – 15; 5:1 – 2; 6:1 – 2; Titus 2:1 – 10.
5:21 Submit to one another. There are two interpretations for how this relates to what follows: (1) This is a general exhortation to submit to those to whom you are obligated, and Paul specifies the particular ways in which this general command is worked out in the following household instructions (5:22 — 6:9). The command is not fully reciprocal since the household code does not command husbands, fathers, and masters to submit to their wives, children, and slaves. (2) This exhortation is fully reciprocal. Thus, even those in authority "submit" to their subordinates in some sense as they discharge the responsibilities called for in the household code. The first view is more likely since it understands submission in its normal meaning of accepting one's place within a hierarchical structure. But regardless of interpretation, Paul addresses both parties of the various household relationships, seeking to promote harmonious relationships based on mutual respect and concern for the good of the other. **reverence for Christ.** The motivation for submission. Just as the fear of Yahweh was the guiding principle for wise living and relationships within the covenant community in the OT, the fear of or reverential obligation to Christ is now the principle for the new community of faith.
5:22 submit. Frequently synonymous with "obey" (cf. 1 Pet 3:5 – 6). Nevertheless, submission recognizes a divinely ordered set of relationships, and submission to another human is conditioned on the submission that one ultimately owes to God. Moreover, submission does not imply inferiority (cf. Gal 3:28) but a difference in role since Christ functionally submits to the Father (1 Cor 15:28). **as you do to the Lord.** The motivation for a wife's submitting voluntarily to her husband. As the wife submits to her husband, she is also submitting to the Lord.
5:23 For. The wife submits because the husband-wife relationship mirrors the Christ-church relationship: as Christ sacrificially (as its "Savior") leads his church, so husbands lead in the marriage relationship. **head.** See notes on 1:22; 1 Cor 11:3.

head of the wife as Christ is the head of the church,[f] his body, of which he is the Savior. [24]Now as the
church submits to Christ, so also wives should submit to their husbands in everything.
[25]Husbands, love your wives,[g] just as Christ loved the church and gave himself up for her[h] [26]to make
her holy, cleansing[a] her by the washing[i] with water through the word, [27]and to present her to himself
as a radiant church, without stain or wrinkle or any other blemish, but holy and blameless.[j] [28]In this
same way, husbands ought to love their wives[k] as their own bodies. He who loves his wife loves himself.
[29]After all, no one ever hated their own body, but they feed and care for their body, just as Christ does the
church— [30]for we are members of his body.[l] [31]"For this reason a man will leave his father and mother
and be united to his wife, and the two will become one flesh."[b m] [32]This is a profound mystery—but I
am talking about Christ and the church. [33]However, each one of you also must love his wife[n] as he loves
himself, and the wife must respect her husband.

6 Children, obey your parents in the Lord, for this is right.[o] [2]"Honor your father and mother"—
which is the first commandment with a promise— [3]"so that it may go well with you and that
you may enjoy long life on the earth."[c p]
[4]Fathers,[d] do not exasperate your children;[q] instead, bring them up in the training and instruction
of the Lord.[r]
[5]Slaves, obey your earthly masters with respect[s] and fear, and with sincerity of heart,[t] just as you
would obey Christ.[u] [6]Obey them not only to win their favor when their eye is on you, but as slaves of
Christ, doing the will of God from your heart. [7]Serve wholeheartedly, as if you were serving the Lord,
not people,[v] [8]because you know that the Lord will reward each one for whatever good they do,[w] whether
they are slave or free.

5:23 [f] 1Co 11:3; Eph 1:22
5:25 [g] Col 3:19 [h] ver 2
5:26 [i] Ac 22:16
5:27 [j] Eph 1:4; Col 1:22
5:28 [k] ver 25
5:30 [l] 1Co 12:27
5:31 [m] Ge 2:24; Mt 19:5; 1Co 6:16
5:33 [n] ver 25
6:1 [o] Col 3:20
6:3 [p] Ex 20:12
6:4 [q] Col 3:21 [r] Ge 18:19; Dt 6:7
6:5 [s] 1Ti 6:1 [t] Col 3:22 [u] Eph 5:22
6:7 [v] Col 3:23
6:8 [w] Col 3:24

[a] *26* Or *having cleansed* [b] *31* Gen. 2:24 [c] *3* Deut. 5:16 [d] *4* Or *Parents*

5:24 submit ... in everything. In every area of life except in matters that are contrary to God's commands (Acts 5:29). Paul presents an ideal picture of Christian marriage: just as the church submits to Christ for her benefit, so the wife submits to her husband, presupposing a relationship in which the husband loves her and has her best interests in view. Each party serves the other unselfishly.

5:25 Husbands. Paul shows that marriage is not a one-sided submission but a reciprocal relationship. The instructions given to husbands are three times longer than those given to wives. **love.** Not just an emotional response but an act of the will that is explained by what follows. **as Christ.** Husbands must follow Christ's example, lovingly sacrificing their own interests for the wife's good.

5:26 make her holy. There are two senses in which Christ sanctifies the church: (1) Christ sets apart the church to be his bride; she belongs to him only. (2) Christ purifies the church of her sin. He not only brings forgiveness of sins but also effects a life of holiness in the church (cf. v. 27). See note on 1:1. **washing with water.** May refer to water baptism or the bridal bath (cf. Ezek 16:9). But regardless of interpretation, it is clear that Christ spiritually cleanses his bride, the church (Rev 19:7; 21:9), "through the word" of the gospel (cf. John 15:3; 17:17; Jas 1:18; 1 Pet 1:23). Other passages that speak of cleansing, washing, and water include John 3:5; Titus 3:5; Heb 10:22; 1 Pet 3:21.

5:27 holy and blameless. See note on 1:4.

5:28–31 as their own bodies ... loves himself ... their own body. Based on the quotation in v. 31 of Gen 2:24. If the husband and wife "become one flesh," then the husband's love for his wife is akin to loving one who is part of himself.

5:32 mystery. See notes on 1:9,10; 3:3–6; 6:19. **but I am talking about.** The imagery of the church as the bride of Christ draws upon the OT imagery of Israel as the bride of Yahweh (Isa 54:5; 62:5; Jer 31:32). Paul goes further in Eph 5:31 by quoting Gen 2:24 to show that Christ and the church are one body (see v. 30). The union of man (Adam in Gen 2) and wife in marriage prefigures and points to the reality of the union between Christ, the last Adam, and his bride, the church. This is a "profound mystery" because no one could have understood Gen 2:24 this way apart from God's revelation (cf. Dan 2:18–19,30). The union of Christ and the church finds its ultimate consummation in the wedding of the Lamb and the new Jerusalem (Rev 19:7–8; 21:2,9).

5:33 However. Concluding summary of vv. 22–32.

6:1 Children. May refer to adult children, but v. 4 suggests that younger children are in view—those who are still growing up and dependent on their parents. **obey your parents.** See Prov 6:20; 30:17; Rom 1:30; Col 3:20; 2 Tim 3:2. **in the Lord.** In fellowship with and in obedience to the Lord.

6:2–3 Honor. Obeying one's parents is a form of honoring them. **promise.** Just as the original command in Deut 5:16 (see Exod 20:12) came with the promise of a full life in the land of Canaan, so also the command in the new covenant comes with a general promise of well-being ("go well with you ... enjoy long life") in this present earthly life. There will be exceptions, but the general principle holds true.

6:4 do not exasperate. Parents (see NIV text note), especially fathers, should not be unnecessarily harsh or domineering (Col 3:21). **of the Lord.** That comes from or is prescribed by the Lord. As the Lord's agents, parents are to raise their children according to his mandate. See 4:20–21.

6:5 Slaves. Paul does not critique the institution of slavery, nor does he condone and provide a theological basis for it. Rather, he provides practical ways of dealing with the realities of his day, helping believers negotiate the tension between being "free" in Christ (Col 3:11) yet obligated to serve an earthly master. The ultimate lordship of Christ relativizes the slave-master relationship, transforming individuals who will then influence society. Although Paul does not seek to abolish slavery, he nevertheless instructs believers elsewhere not to become slaves, and he encourages slaves who are able to obtain freedom to do so (1 Cor 7:21,23; see Introduction to Philemon: Occasion and Purpose). While acknowledging substantive differences with the ancient world, we can cautiously apply the general principles from this passage to our various socioeconomic authority structures, such as the workplace, prison, and the military.

6:8 the Lord will reward. Although earthly masters may not reward their slaves, slaves will receive a reward for their good deeds when they stand before the judgment seat of Christ (Matt 16:27; 1 Cor 3:8,14; 2 Cor 5:10). Paul does not specify the content of the reward here;

6:9 [x]Job 31:13,14
6:10 [y]1Co 16:13 [z]Eph 1:19
6:11 [a]Ro 13:12
6:12 [b]Eph 1:21 [c]Ro 8:38 [d]Eph 1:3
6:14 [e]Isa 11:5 [f]Isa 59:17
6:15 [g]Isa 52:7
6:16 [h]1Jn 5:4
6:17 [i]Isa 59:17 [j]Heb 4:12
6:18 [k]Lk 18:1 [l]Mt 26:41; Php 1:4
6:19 [m]1Th 5:25

9And masters, treat your slaves in the same way. Do not threaten them, since you know that he who
is both their Master and yours[x] is in heaven, and there is no favoritism with him.

The Armor of God

10Finally, be strong in the Lord[y] and in his mighty power.[z] 11Put on the full armor of God,[a] so that
you can take your stand against the devil's schemes. 12For our struggle is not against flesh and blood,
but against the rulers, against the authorities,[b] against the powers[c] of this dark world and against the
spiritual forces of evil in the heavenly realms.[d] 13Therefore put on the full armor of God, so that when
the day of evil comes, you may be able to stand your
ground, and after you have done everything, to
stand. 14Stand firm then, with the belt of truth
buckled around your waist,[e] with the breastplate of righteousness in place,[f] 15and with
your feet fitted with the readiness that comes
from the gospel of peace.[g] 16In addition to all
this, take up the shield of faith,[h] with which
you can extinguish all the flaming arrows of
the evil one. 17Take the helmet of salvation[i]
and the sword of the Spirit, which is the word
of God.[j]

18And pray in the Spirit on all occasions[k]
with all kinds of prayers and requests.[l] With
this in mind, be alert and always keep on
praying for all the Lord's people. 19Pray also
for me,[m] that whenever I speak, words may be

First-century relief of Roman soldiers in their armor (belt, breastplate, boots, shield, and sword). Paul compares the armor of a soldier with the armor of God in Eph 6:10–17.
Kim Walton, taken at the Altes Museum, Berlin

Col 3:24 identifies it as the eternal inheritance that God has prepared for believers.
6:9 masters. In antiquity they had the power of life and death over their slaves. But Paul advocates reciprocal attitudes. **in the same way.** With the integrity and dedication of one who is similarly governed by a heavenly master. **no favoritism.** See Deut 10:17; Acts 10:34; Rom 2:11.
6:10–20 *The Armor of God.* Paul concludes the exhortation section of the letter (chs. 4–6) by describing the spiritual battle against evil in the heavenly realms. This passage has three sections: be strong in the Lord (vv. 10–13), stand firm with the armor (vv. 14–17), and pray constantly (vv. 18–20).
6:10 be strong. Relying not on our own inadequate strength but on God's "mighty power" (cf. 1:19).
6:11 Put on. Recalls 4:24 (see note there), suggesting that putting on the "new self" is fundamentally the same as putting on God's armor. **the full armor of God.** The means by which we are to "be strong in the Lord" (v. 10). Although the armor imagery might cause his Gentile readers to recall armor worn by Roman soldiers, Paul primarily draws on OT passages that describe the armor of Yahweh (Isa 59:17) and his Messiah (Isa 11:4–5). See note on Eph 6:13. **the devil's schemes.** The devil is singled out as the primary enemy, the leader of the opposing army described in v. 12.
6:12 not against flesh and blood. The Christian life is a spiritual battle in which the ultimate opposition to the gospel stems from evil spiritual powers (cf. 1:21; 3:10 and notes). These powers can operate through humans (4:14,27) and institutions, but they cannot be reduced solely to these manifestations. **rulers ... forces of evil.** These various terms show the diversity and comprehensiveness of the enemy's power, reminding us that the battle cannot be fought merely with human resources.
6:13 full armor of God. We are able to stand only by putting on the full armor, which is comprised of the belt, breastplate, shoes, shield, helmet, and sword. These metaphorically represent truth, righteousness, the gospel, faith, salvation, and the word of God. Since the devil attacks individual believers and the corporate church (especially its unity), the armor represents resources that protect not only the individual but also the unity of the church. **stand.** Occurs four times in vv. 11–14. Christ has already won the decisive victory (1:20–22; 4:8; Col 2:15). Nevertheless, the consummation of cosmic harmony is still future. Paul does not call believers to invade the domain of evil; he calls them only to "stand," maintaining what Christ has already won.
6:14 truth. Appropriate the truth of the gospel (1:13; 4:21) and be truthful with others (4:15,25; 5:9). **righteousness.** Hold fast to God's gift of justifying righteousness (Rom 3:22; 4:24; cf. Eph 1:7; 2:16), and do right and practice justice toward others (4:24; 5:9; 6:1).
6:15 readiness. Be ready for battle by appropriating the gospel, with its focus on peace vertically with God (2:1–10) and horizontally with other people (2:11–22).
6:16 shield. The Roman shield, made of wooden planks and covered with leather, could be soaked in water so as to extinguish flame-tipped arrows. **faith.** Trust steadfastly in God's resources (1:19–20; 3:17), and hold firm to the community's common set of beliefs (4:5,13). See 1 Pet 5:8–9. **flaming arrows.** Examples include demonic attacks, temptations, and rage (4:26–27) that confront individuals, and false teachings and divisions that threaten the community's unity.
6:17 salvation. Appropriate the salvation that God has already accomplished for believers in Christ (2:5–6). **sword of the Spirit.** A weapon for self-defense and offense. Its power and effectiveness come from the Spirit (Heb 4:12). **the word of God.** The gospel (1:13).
6:18 pray. Prayer is not another piece of armor but is the way believers appropriate God's armor and stand firm. **in the Spirit.** Inspired and guided by the Spirit, who himself provides access to God (2:18).
6:19 Pray also for me. Leaders should be willing to ask for prayer. **mystery of the gospel.** The gospel is the mystery that has been revealed and is now to be proclaimed publicly. See notes on 1:9,10; 3:3–6.

given me so that I will fearlessly[n] make known the mystery of the gospel, [20]for which I am an ambassador[o] in chains.[p] Pray that I may declare it fearlessly, as I should.

6:19 [n]Ac 4:29; 2Co 3:12
6:20 [o]2Co 5:20 [p]Ac 21:33
6:21 [q]Ac 20:4
6:22 [r]Col 4:7-9
6:23 [s]Gal 6:16; 1Pe 5:14

Final Greetings

[21]Tychicus,[q] the dear brother and faithful servant in the Lord, will tell you everything, so that you
also may know how I am and what I am doing. [22]I am sending him to you for this very purpose, that
you may know how we are,[r] and that he may encourage you.

[23]Peace[s] to the brothers and sisters,[a] and love with faith from God the Father and the Lord Jesus
Christ. [24]Grace to all who love our Lord Jesus Christ with an undying love.[b]

[a] *23* The Greek word for *brothers and sisters* (*adelphoi*) refers here to believers, both men and women, as part of God's family. [b] *24* Or *Grace and immortality to all who love our Lord Jesus Christ.*

6:21–24 *Final Greetings.* This conclusion illustrates the theme of unity and love that Paul advocates in the letter. Despite his imprisonment, Paul's concern is for the welfare of his readers.

6:21–22 These two verses echo Col 4:7–8, suggesting that Paul wrote both Ephesians and Colossians around the same time and that Tychicus carried both letters to the churches in Asia Minor.

INTRODUCTION TO PHILIPPIANS

AUTHOR

Paul claims to be the author of this letter (1:1), and there has been no serious dispute about this claim.

ADDRESSEES

Paul first visited the Roman colony of Philippi on his second missionary journey (Acts 16:12) in the early 50s. The first converts were Lydia and her household (Acts 16:14 – 15), the jailer and his household (Acts 16:33 – 34), and others (Acts 16:40). The letter also names Epaphroditus (2:25) and Euodia and Syntyche (4:2). There were probably many more, though it is impossible to know how many.

DATE AND PLACE OF COMPOSITION

We do not know for certain when or where Paul wrote the letter to the Philippians. Conclusions depend largely upon which imprisonment 1:13 refers to and upon what "palace guard" (1:13) and "Caesar's household" (4:22) mean. Paul might have been in prison in Ephesus about AD 55, though this is not based on strong evidence; he certainly was in prison in Caesarea about AD 57 – 59 (Acts 24:22 – 27) and in prison in Rome about AD 60 – 62 (Acts 28:15 – 31). The reference to "Caesar's household" does not rule out Caesarea, but Rome is more likely. Paul, therefore, probably wrote Philippians from Rome about AD 60 – 62, while Nero was emperor, and so the church was about ten years old when he composed this letter.

In the book of Philippians, Paul speaks of "being poured out like a drink offering." See 2:17 and note.

Greek civilization, red-figure pottery, Kylix by Douris depicting youth near an altar/De Agostini Picture Library/G. Nimatallah/Bridgeman Images

OCCASION AND PURPOSE

One of Paul's main impulses for writing is to acknowledge the gifts from the Philippians (4:10 – 19). He also urges two individuals to be reconciled to one another, and he encourages the Philippians to remain faithful to the Lord (4:1 – 3). He reassures them about his circumstances and his plans to send Timothy in the future (chs. 1 – 2), and he warns of false teachers (ch. 3). Paul has the opportunity to write, which might not otherwise have arisen, because he is sending Epaphroditus back to Philippi (2:25).

PHILIPPI AND SURROUNDING AREAS

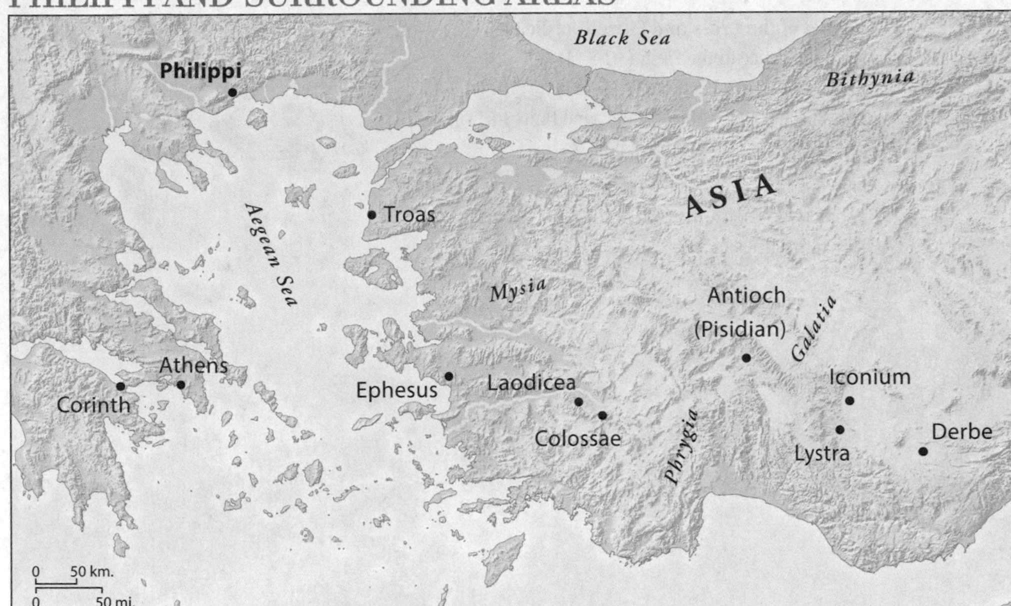

THEOLOGY AND THEMES

Theologically, the most significant passage is the so-called hymn of Christ (2:5 – 11). Whether a hymn or not, it is one of the most exalted statements about Christ in the NT. With John 1:1 – 18, it sets out Christ's divinity and preexistence: John 1 adds the detail that Christ is cocreator with the Father; Phil 2 has a point not mentioned in John 1; namely, that Christ is to be worshiped (2:10 – 11). Phil 2 also sets out, in remarkably dense form, that this supremely divine person descends to a humiliating death on the cross for our salvation.

Phil 2:6 – 11 is thus a brief account of the gospel, a theme prominent in other parts of Philippians (the word "gospel" appears 10 times: 1:5,7,12,14,16,27 [twice]; 2:22; 4:3,15; cf. also "the word of life" [2:16]). Paul also gives unity and the humility needed to foster such unity considerable attention (1:27 — 2:4). He stresses that justification is freely given by the words of God, through faith in Christ not the law (3:9). The letter is not primarily doctrinal; it also focuses on knowing Christ (3:8 – 11); "joy" (1:4,25; 2:2,29; 4:1) and "gladness/rejoicing" (1:18 [twice]; 2:17 – 18 [4 times]; 3:1; 4:4 [twice]; 4:10) are prominent, appearing 15 times in this short letter.

OUTLINE

I. Introduction (1:1 – 11)
- A. Opening Greeting (1:1 – 2)
- B. Thanksgiving (1:3 – 8)
- C. Prayer (1:9 – 11)

II. Paul's Chains Advance the Gospel (1:12 – 26)
- A. The Results of Paul's Imprisonment (1:12 – 14)
- B. Paul's Rivals (1:15 – 18)
- C. Paul's Confidence in Death and Life (1:19 – 26)

III. Unity and Humility (1:27 — 2:18)
- A. Life Worthy of the Gospel (1:27 – 30)
- B. Imitating Christ's Humility (2:1 – 11)
- C. Do Everything Without Grumbling (2:12 – 18)

IV. Timothy and Epaphroditus (2:19 – 30)

V. Enemies of the Cross and Citizens of Heaven (3:1 — 4:3)

- A. No Confidence in the Flesh (3:1 – 14)
- B. Following Paul's Example (3:15 – 21)
- C. Closing Appeal for Steadfastness and Unity (4:1 – 3)

VI. Conclusions (4:4 – 23)

- A. Final Exhortations (4:4 – 9)
- B. Thanks for Their Gifts (4:10 – 20)
- C. Final Greetings (4:21 – 23)

PHILIPPIANS

1 Paul and Timothy,[a] servants of Christ Jesus,

To all God's holy people[b] in Christ Jesus at Philippi,[c] together with the overseers[d] and deacons[a]:[e]

2 Grace and peace to you from God our Father and the Lord Jesus Christ.[f]

Thanksgiving and Prayer

3 I thank my God every time I remember you.[g] 4 In all my prayers for all of you, I always pray[h]
with joy 5 because of your partnership[i] in the gospel from the first day[j] until now, 6 being confident of this, that he who began a good work in you will carry it on to completion until the day of
Christ Jesus.[k]

7 It is right[l] for me to feel this way about all of you, since I have you in my heart[m] and, whether I am
in chains[n] or defending[o] and confirming the gospel, all of you share in God's grace with me. 8 God can
testify[p] how I long for all of you with the affection of Christ Jesus.

1:1 [a] Ac 16:1; 2Co 1:1 [b] Ac 9:13 [c] Ac 16:12 [d] 1Ti 3:1 [e] 1Ti 3:8
1:2 [f] Ro 1:7
1:3 [g] Ro 1:8
1:4 [h] Ro 1:10
1:5 [i] Ac 2:42; Php 4:15 [j] Ac 16:12-40
1:6 [k] ver 10; 1Co 1:8
1:7 [l] 2Pe 1:13 [m] 2Co 7:3 [n] ver 13,14,17; Ac 21:33 [o] ver 16
1:8 [p] Ro 1:9

[a] *1* The word *deacons* refers here to Christians designated to serve with the overseers/elders of the church in a variety of ways; similarly in Romans 16:1 and 1 Tim. 3:8,12.

1:1–11 *Introduction.* This opening, consisting of a greeting (vv. 1–2), thanksgiving (vv. 3–8), and prayer (vv. 9–11), is similar to the openings of other letters of Paul (cf. 1 Cor 1:1–9; Col 1:1–14; Phlm 1–7).
1:1–2 *Opening Greeting.* As in most ancient letters, the authors and recipients are both mentioned at the beginning.
1:1 Paul and Timothy. Paul often co-authored letters with Timothy. The son of a Jewish mother and Greek father (Acts 16:1), Timothy was from Lystra, and after Paul visited there on his second missionary journey, he took Timothy along as a co-worker (Phil 2:19–24). **Christ Jesus.** See notes on 2:6–11. **God's holy people.** As people who belong to God and are incorporated into his service, they are set apart from the world for him. The OT uses the phrase "holy people" of Israel (e.g., Exod 22:31), so it is striking that Paul can freely apply it to what was probably a predominantly Gentile congregation in Philippi. As Paul emphasizes in ch. 3, those who believe in Christ and are incorporated into him now share in the privileges God bestowed on Israel in the OT. **holy.** Christ's death has made Christians holy (Eph 5:25–26). **in Christ Jesus at Philippi.** Expresses the double location of believers: (1) they are in Christ, no longer in Adam but members of Christ's body, and (2) they belong to the Roman colony of Philippi (see Introduction: Addressees). **overseers.** Synonymous with "elders," men responsible for the spiritual direction of and preaching in the congregation (1 Tim 3:1–7). **deacons.** Responsible for affairs in the church of a more practical nature. The role has its origin in the difficult situation in Acts 6:1–6, where believers select "deacons" to distribute the food to widows. This is no lowly task, however, for those appointed in Acts 6 were "known to be full of the Spirit and wisdom" (Acts 6:3); deacons must display traits of mature godliness (1 Tim 3:8–10,12–13).
1:2 Adapting elements from Jewish and Greek letter writing, Paul prays for the Philippians to receive "grace" (God's work in them to accomplish what they cannot do on their own) and "peace" (experiencing the blessings of being reconciled to God).
1:3–8 *Thanksgiving.* Paul expresses his great love for the Philippians, as is evident from the joy (v. 4), confidence (v. 6), and affection (v. 8) with which he thanks God for them.
1:4 with joy. Paul expresses the emotions that accompany his prayers, first mentioning joy.
1:5 partnership. Paul rejoices that the Philippians join in the work of the gospel, which includes financially supporting him (4:15). **from the first day.** When they first accepted the gospel (cf. 4:15).
1:6 being confident. A second emotion (after joy in v. 4) that remembering the Philippians prompts. Paul's confidence in God's sovereignty leads not to inactivity but to prayer for what he knows God will do. Paul is convinced that prayers are a means God uses to accomplish his purposes. **work in you.** Paul knows that the Philippians' perseverance in the faith and the gospel fruit that they bear are the work of God himself (2:12–13). **the day of Christ Jesus.** God's faithful work in them endures right up until the day on which Jesus returns.
1:7 defending. Implies that Paul is responding to challenges from those who are not Christians. **confirming.** Suggests that Paul is further grounding believers in the truth.
1:8 After his expressions of "joy" (v. 4) and "confidence" (v. 6), Paul confesses to feeling overwhelming "affection" for the Philippians.

1:9 [q] 1Th 3:12
1:10 [r] ver 6; 1Co 1:8
1:11 [s] Jas 3:18
1:13 [t] ver 7,14,17
1:14 [u] ver 7,13,17
1:16 [v] ver 7,12
1:17 [w] Php 2:3
[x] ver 7,13,14
1:19 [y] 2Co 1:11 [z] Ac 16:7
1:20 [a] Ro 8:19 [b] ver 14
[c] 1Co 6:20 [d] Ro 14:8
1:21 [e] Gal 2:20
1:23 [f] 2Ti 4:6 [g] Jn 12:26; 2Co 5:8

9 And this is my prayer: that your love[q] may abound more and more in knowledge and depth of insight, 10 so that you may be able to discern what is best and may be pure and blameless for the day of Christ,[r] 11 filled with the fruit of righteousness[s] that comes through Jesus Christ—to the glory and praise of God.

Paul's Chains Advance the Gospel

12 Now I want you to know, brothers and sisters,[a] that what has happened to me has actually served to advance the gospel. 13 As a result, it has become clear throughout the whole palace guard[b] and to everyone else that I am in chains[t] for Christ. 14 And because of my chains,[u] most of the brothers and sisters have become confident in the Lord and dare all the more to proclaim the gospel without fear.

15 It is true that some preach Christ out of envy and rivalry, but others out of goodwill. 16 The latter do so out of love, knowing that I am put here for the defense of the gospel.[v] 17 The former preach Christ out of selfish ambition,[w] not sincerely, supposing that they can stir up trouble for me while I am in chains.[x] 18 But what does it matter? The important thing is that in every way, whether from false motives or true, Christ is preached. And because of this I rejoice.

Yes, and I will continue to rejoice, 19 for I know that through your prayers[y] and God's provision of the Spirit of Jesus Christ[z] what has happened to me will turn out for my deliverance.[c] 20 I eagerly expect[a] and hope that I will in no way be ashamed, but will have sufficient courage[b] so that now as always Christ will be exalted in my body,[c] whether by life or by death.[d] 21 For to me, to live is Christ[e] and to die is gain. 22 If I am to go on living in the body, this will mean fruitful labor for me. Yet what shall I choose? I do not know! 23 I am torn between the two: I desire to depart[f] and be with Christ,[g] which is better by far; 24 but it is more necessary for you that I remain in the body. 25 Convinced of this, I know that I will remain, and I will continue with all of you for your progress and joy in the faith, 26 so that through my being with you again your boasting in Christ Jesus will abound on account of me.

a 12 The Greek word for *brothers and sisters* (*adelphoi*) refers here to believers, both men and women, as part of God's family; also in verse 14; and in 3:1, 13, 17; 4:1, 8, 21. *b* 13 Or *whole palace* *c* 19 Or *vindication*; or *salvation*

1:9–11 *Prayer.* Paul prays that in view of the return of Christ, the Philippians would abound in the fruit of the gospel in the present.

1:9 knowledge and depth of insight. The mind is important in this letter, but not out of any intellectualism: Paul desires their unity and humility, i.e., that they be "of one mind" with each other (2:2) and "have the same mindset as Christ Jesus" (2:5). Paul prays that they outgrow a naive love that is marked by acting in an unChristlike manner to each other and outsiders, and that they develop an informed love that is discerning (v. 10). Cf. Paul's emotions in vv. 4,6,8.

1:10 pure and blameless for the day of Christ. Paul sees the work of Christ as presenting the church "holy and blameless" (Eph 5:27; see Col 1:22), and Paul's own ministry as sharing in this work: Paul also sees himself as presenting the church to Christ (2 Cor 11:2; Col 1:28). Through prayer Paul participates in this work so that it will be complete on the final day. Paul wants the Philippians even now to aspire to be pure and blameless rather than settle for a halfhearted faith.

1:11 righteousness. Here, godly action rather than justification.

1:12–26 *Paul's Chains Advance the Gospel.* Paul's situation of being "in chains for Christ" (v. 13) is worsened by those who are making trouble for him (v. 17). Despite this, Paul rejoices at the spread of the good news.

1:12–14 *The Results of Paul's Imprisonment.* Paul's situation has led to the advance of the gospel in two ways here: in his own preaching of the gospel to the palace guard (v. 13) and in the way his imprisonment has spurred others on to greater boldness (v. 14).

1:13 the whole palace guard and to everyone else. The imperial household and staff. Paul's first reason for rejoicing is that he has the opportunity to preach to those around him. **in chains for Christ.** Accusations by the high priest Ananias led to Paul's imprisonment first under Felix (Acts 24) and then under Festus (Acts 25), after which he was taken and placed under house arrest in Rome (Acts 28:16).

1:14 Paul's second reason for rejoicing (see note on v. 13) is that this restriction on his ministry ("my chains") has emboldened other believers.

1:15–18 *Paul's Rivals.* Even Christians who set themselves against Paul do not discourage him.

1:15,18 some preach Christ out of envy and rivalry . . . But what does it matter? Paul's third reason for rejoicing (see notes on vv. 13–14) is that even those making trouble for him still preach the gospel and are advancing his cause.

1:19–26 *Paul's Confidence in Death and Life.* Paul continues to rejoice further: despite his conviction that he will remain alive for the benefit of the Philippians, he would be equally happy if he were to be taken home to be with the Lord.

1:19 my deliverance. Probably release from imprisonment, as vv. 25–26 and especially 2:24 clarify.

1:20 no way be ashamed. Cf. Paul's "boasting" (see v. 26 and note). **my body.** The vehicle for Paul's gospel ministry (cf. filling up the sufferings of Christ "in my flesh" [Col 1:24]). **or by death.** Probably hypothetical because he is convinced that he will be released (vv. 19,25–26).

1:21 to die is gain. Paul's remarkable perspective here is explained in v. 23, where he looks forward to being "with Christ, which is better by far."

1:23 to depart and be with Christ. Paul here refers to what will happen to him when he dies. Before the final "day of Christ Jesus" (v. 6), those who die go to joyful fellowship with Christ (cf. Luke 23:43). Believers do not cease to exist at death in order to be re-created again from scratch later; rather, they go to be with Christ spiritually, which is "better by far" than being beset by sin and suffering. But that is still not God's final purpose: ultimately, at the final resurrection of all believers, God will restore fellowship between believers and Christ that is both physical and undisturbed by the effects of the fall.

1:24–25 Paul feels sure that it is God's will for him to "remain in the body" (v. 24) because of the Philippians' need for Paul, who will then continue to minister to them for their "progress and joy in the faith" (v. 25).

1:26 my being with you again. See note on vv. 24–25. **boasting.** Not negative, which it usually is in English; it goes back to Jer 9:23–24.

Life Worthy of the Gospel

27 Whatever happens, conduct yourselves in a manner worthy[h] of the gospel of Christ. Then, whether
I come and see you or only hear about you in my absence, I will know that you stand firm[i] in the one
Spirit,[a] striving together[j] as one for the faith of the gospel 28 without being frightened in any way by
those who oppose you. This is a sign to them that they will be destroyed, but that you will be saved—
and that by God. 29 For it has been granted to you[k] on behalf of Christ not only to believe in him, but
also to suffer[l] for him, 30 since you are going through the same struggle[m] you saw[n] I had, and now
hear[o] that I still have.

Imitating Christ's Humility

2 Therefore if you have any encouragement from being united with Christ, if any comfort from his
love, if any common sharing in the Spirit,[p] if any tenderness and compassion,[q] 2 then make my
joy complete[r] by being like-minded,[s] having the same love, being one[t] in spirit and of one mind. 3 Do
nothing out of selfish ambition or vain conceit.[u] Rather, in humility value others above yourselves,[v]
4 not looking to your own interests but each of you to the interests of the others.
5 In your relationships with one another, have the same mindset as Christ Jesus:[w]

> 6 Who, being in very nature[b] God,[x]
> did not consider equality with God[y] something to be used to his own
> advantage;
> 7 rather, he made himself nothing
> by taking the very nature[c] of a servant,[z]
> being made in human likeness.[a]
> 8 And being found in appearance as a man,
> he humbled himself

[a] 27 Or *in one spirit* [b] 6 Or *in the form of* [c] 7 Or *the form*

1:27 [h] Eph 4:1 [i] 1Co 16:13 [j] Jude 3
1:29 [k] Mt 5:11,12 [l] Ac 14:22
1:30 [m] Col 2:1; 1Th 2:2 [n] Ac 16:19-40 [o] ver 13
2:1 [p] 2Co 13:14 [q] Col 3:12
2:2 [r] Jn 3:29 [s] Php 4:2 [t] Ro 12:16
2:3 [u] Gal 5:26 [v] Ro 12:10; 1Pe 5:5
2:5 [w] Mt 11:29
2:6 [x] Jn 1:1 [y] Jn 5:18
2:7 [z] Mt 20:28 [a] Jn 1:14; Heb 2:17

First, it means having confidence that Jesus has saved us and will save us from judgment. The opposite of boasting is shame, and God promises that "the one who trusts in him will never be put to shame" (1 Pet 2:6; see Isa 28:16 [in the Septuagint, the pre-Christian Greek translation of the OT]; Rom 9:33; 10:11). Second, in common with our English usage, it is vocal: it is not only an inner confidence but also an eagerness to preach the good news (cf. Gal 6:14).

1:27—2:18 *Unity and Humility.* The call to live out the gospel requires united service (1:27–30), and that harmony can only be achieved by imitating Christ's humility (2:1–11), by avoiding grumbling, and by not acting like non-Christians (2:12–18).

1:27–30 *Life Worthy of the Gospel.* Paul explains that this worthy living consists in standing united, refusing to be afraid of opponents, and being willing to suffer for the gospel.

1:28 This is a sign to them. The courage of Christians in the face of opposition declares to the "enemies of the cross" (3:18) that believers are confident of their salvation and that God will recompense these enemies for their persecution.

1:29 granted ... to suffer for him. Suffering for Christ is not accidental, nor does God merely tolerate it in his providence. It is a gift from God (cf. 1 Pet 2:21) and is participation in the sufferings of Christ (3:10).

2:1–11 *Imitating Christ's Humility.* After giving the reasons for unity in vv. 1–4, it is notable that the great account of Christ's death and glorification in vv. 6–11 is primarily given as motivation for the Philippians to be humble.

2:1–4 The letter to the Philippians is cheerful compared to Galatians (in which Paul is contending for the gospel in a desperate situation) or 1 Corinthians (in which Paul is addressing a number of serious problems, though less severe than that of the Galatian crisis). Nevertheless, there is a problem of unity that seems to be focused around two women, Euodia and Syntyche, who perhaps have their own groups of supporters within the church (4:2). The first half of ch. 2 (vv. 1–11) emphasizes the need for unity that comes about through imitating Christ's humility.

2:1 Paul presupposes four convictions and kinds of feeling in the Philippian congregation, each introduced by "if any."

2:2–4 Based on what Paul assumes in v. 1, he exhorts the Philippians to have a particular "mind" (v. 2) and be united in "love" and "spirit" (v. 2). Paul is interested in their thoughts and the actions that arise out of those thoughts.

2:5 For believers, humility is not just a pragmatic strategy for a united congregation; it is conformity to the "mindset" of Christ Jesus.

2:6 in very nature. Or "in the form of" (not appearance in contrast to reality but form that reflects reality). Before the incarnation that v. 7 describes, Christ was truly divine (as he remained; see v. 10) and preexistent (John 17:5). **equality with God.** Christ is not inferior to God (John 5:18; 10:30). Just as all humans are equal in being despite legitimate authority in human relationships (e.g., children submit to their parents), so it is with the Father and Christ: they are equal even though the Son submits to the Father (John 5:30).

2:7–8 likeness ... appearance. Jesus was not in "human likeness" without really being human; he, without ceasing to be God, clothed himself in real humanity: "God sent his Son, born of a woman" (Gal 4:4), and there is "one mediator between God and mankind, the man Christ Jesus" (1 Tim 2:5).

2:7 he made himself nothing by taking the very nature of a servant. Again presupposes the preexistence of Christ (see note on v. 6). In the incarnation Christ did not cease to be God as if he changed from the form of God into something else. Some church fathers thus emphasized "taking": hence the Son can remain God while also being a man. He added humanity to himself rather than transforming himself into a human.

2:8 Paul's primary purpose for describing Jesus' death is to show the Philippians their model to follow. They should live in "humility" (v. 3) because Christ "humbled himself." He considered others better than himself not in the sense of thinking that the Philippians were of higher

2:8 [b] Mt 26:39; Jn 10:18; Heb 5:8
2:9 [c] Ac 2:33; Heb 2:9 [d] Eph 1:20,21
2:10 [e] Ro 14:11 [f] Mt 28:18
2:11 [g] Jn 13:13
2:12 [h] 2Co 7:15
2:13 [i] Ezr 1:5
2:14 [j] 1Co 10:10; 1Pe 4:9
2:15 [k] Mt 5:45,48; Eph 5:1 [l] Ac 2:40

by becoming obedient to death[b] —
even death on a cross!

9 Therefore God exalted him[c] to the highest place
and gave him the name that is above every name,[d]
10 that at the name of Jesus every knee should bow,[e]
in heaven and on earth and under the earth,[f]
11 and every tongue acknowledge that Jesus Christ is Lord,[g]
to the glory of God the Father.

Do Everything Without Grumbling

12 Therefore, my dear friends, as you have always obeyed — not only in my presence, but now much
more in my absence — continue to work out your salvation with fear and trembling,[h] 13 for it is God
who works in you[i] to will and to act in order to fulfill his good purpose.
14 Do everything without grumbling[j] or arguing, 15 so that you may become blameless and pure,
"children of God[k] without fault in a warped and crooked generation."[a][l] Then you will shine among

[a] *15* Deut. 32:5

value than himself but by adopting the position of servant for their good. Christ's humble death was not an end in itself: he became "obedient to death" for us and for our salvation. Elsewhere in Paul's letters (and the rest of the NT), the cross is God's appointed means of salvation: the gospel is the proclamation of Christ's death in our place, whereby he took the penalty "for our sins" (1 Cor 15:3–4; cf. Rom 4:25; Gal 1:4). This is the gospel Paul is so focused on in Philippians, the gospel that inspires such passion and produces such joy in its advance (1:12). **even death on a cross!** Christ's crucifixion is the most humiliating low point in contrast to what precedes ("being in very nature God," v. 6) and what follows ("exalted him to the highest place," v. 9). A century before Paul, the Roman politician and philosopher Cicero called crucifixion the "most cruel and disgusting punishment," and Paul's contemporary, the philosopher Seneca, stated that anyone facing crucifixion would prefer to die before going to the cross.

2:9 Therefore. Not "nevertheless." In response to Christ's acting in accordance with his Father's will and dying for sins, the Father vindicates the Son by raising and exalting him. **exalted ... to the highest place.** Resurrection is a necessary but not a sufficient reversal of Christ's situation in death. He also will be restored to the right hand of God in glory (Rom 8:34). Paul uses a very rare Greek word here, which the Greek translation of Ps 97:9 used of the Lord: "you *are exalted far above* all gods." **the name that is above every name.** "Lord." Although Paul occasionally calls Jesus "God" (Rom 9:5; Titus 2:13), his tendency is to call the Father "God" and Jesus "Lord," which is also a divine title. In translations going back to the Greek version of the OT in Paul's day, "Lord" was the word used as a substitute for the untranslatable personal name "Yahweh." As Lord, Jesus shares in the divine identity, being cocreator with the Father (1 Cor 8:6), the saving Lord of Joel 2:32 (cf. Rom 10:9–13), and the object of worship in vv. 10–11. This is not a name or title given to Jesus for the first time: he was divine before the incarnation (v. 6). But although there were fleeting recognitions of his deity during his earthly ministry (e.g., Matt 14:33), Jesus was not customarily known and addressed then as "the Lord," as Paul now customarily calls him (15 times in Philippians alone).

2:10–11 at the name of Jesus every knee should bow ... and every tongue acknowledge that Jesus Christ is Lord. Along with v. 6, this is another indication that Christ is divine. God states in Isa 45:23, "By myself I have sworn, my mouth has uttered in all integrity a word that will not be revoked: Before me every knee will bow; by me every tongue will swear." That verse and the whole surrounding passage uncompromisingly insist that there is one God and no other (Isa 45:5–7,14,18,21–22). Remarkably, Paul borrows the language in Isaiah of how God alone is to be worshiped and uses it to talk of the worship that Jesus is to receive (cf. Rev 4–5). There is only one God, but Christ — with the Father and the Spirit — is included in the being of the one God.

2:10 in heaven and on earth and under the earth. Paul is not necessarily distinguishing between three kinds of knees (heavenly, earthly, and subterranean). He emphasizes the whole created sphere, material and spiritual (cf. Rev 5:3,13). If one draws out the statement's implications, then "in heaven" means that even angels worship Jesus (Heb 1:4,6); "on earth" focuses primarily on human beings but also includes the whole creation (as Ps 148:7–13 expresses poetically); and "under the earth" perhaps alludes to Satan and the evil powers, who even from the Abyss (cf. Luke 8:31; Rev 20:3) will be forced to concede Jesus' lordship.

2:11 to the glory of God the Father. Having affirmed that Christ is divine (vv. 6,10), Paul still distinguishes between Christ and the Father. Theologians in the early church after the NT time spoke of the Father and the Son as one in being but distinct persons, drawing in part on the words of Paul and especially John. Paul is similarly saying that Jesus is "in very nature God" (v. 6) and deserves worship like the Father (v. 10). At the same time, Paul makes clear here that Christ and the Father are distinct and that the glory of the Father is ultimate and the worship of Christ penultimate. This balance in Paul's writings mirrors John's Gospel, where Jesus says both "I and the Father are one" (John 10:30) and "the Father is greater than I" (John 14:28).

2:12–18 *Do Everything Without Grumbling.* In contrast to grumbling, Paul exhorts the Philippians to work out their salvation (v. 12), to hold fast to the word of life (v. 16), and to rejoice (v. 18).

2:12–13 Our actions as Christians are not part-God and part-us; rather, we can act because God is acting in us.

2:12 to work out your salvation. Paul places a responsibility on the Philippians that sounds almost uncharacteristic of him. But Paul can put the point so strongly because our "working out" comes from the work of God: "for it is God who works in you" (v. 13), both in our *minds* to formulate our thoughts and plans ("to will," v. 13) and in what we actually do ("to act," v. 13). Christian obedience is being "led by the Spirit" (Rom 8:14; Gal 5:18), such that Paul described his ministry as "not I, but the grace of God that was with me" (1 Cor 15:10). The Philippians should continue obediently, just as God's faithfulness means that Christians will persevere (1:6).

2:15 blameless and pure. Not sinless perfection but a status of being irreproachable before the world as well as approved as faithful by God. **children of God without fault in a warped and crooked generation.** Paul refers to Moses' song (Deut 32:5), also a free-standing hymn in

them like stars in the sky [16]as you hold firmly to the word of life. And then I will be able to boast on the day of Christ that I did not run or labor in vain.[m] [17]But even if I am being poured out like a drink offering[n] on the sacrifice[o] and service coming from your faith, I am glad and rejoice with all of you. [18]So you too should be glad and rejoice with me.

Timothy and Epaphroditus

[19]I hope in the Lord Jesus to send Timothy to you soon,[p] that I also may be cheered when I receive news about you. [20]I have no one else like him,[q] who will show genuine concern for your welfare. [21]For everyone looks out for their own interests,[r] not those of Jesus Christ. [22]But you know that Timothy has proved himself, because as a son with his father[s] he has served with me in the work of the gospel. [23]I hope, therefore, to send him as soon as I see how things go with me.[t] [24]And I am confident[u] in the Lord that I myself will come soon.

[25]But I think it is necessary to send back to you Epaphroditus, my brother, co-worker[v] and fellow soldier,[w] who is also your messenger, whom you sent to take care of my needs.[x] [26]For he longs for all of you[y] and is distressed because you heard he was ill. [27]Indeed he was ill, and almost died. But God had mercy on him, and not on him only but also on me, to spare me sorrow upon sorrow. [28]Therefore I am all the more eager to send him, so that when you see him again you may be glad and I may have less anxiety. [29]So then, welcome him in the Lord with great joy, and honor people like him,[z] [30]because he almost died for the work of Christ. He risked his life to make up for the help you yourselves could not give me.[a]

No Confidence in the Flesh

3 Further, my brothers and sisters, rejoice in the Lord! It is no trouble for me to write the same things to you again, and it is a safeguard for you. [2]Watch out for those dogs,[b] those evildoers,

2:16 [m] 1Th 2:19
2:17 [n] 2Ti 4:6 [o] Ro 15:16
2:19 [p] ver 23
2:20 [q] 1Co 16:10
2:21 [r] 1Co 10:24; 13:5
2:22 [s] 1Co 4:17; 1Ti 1:2
2:23 [t] ver 19
2:24 [u] Php 1:25
2:25 [v] Php 4:3 [w] Phm 2 [x] Php 4:18
2:26 [y] Php 1:8
2:29 [z] 1Co 16:18; 1Ti 5:17
2:30 [a] 1Co 16:17
3:2 [b] Ps 22:16,20

Paul's day. It contrasts the crookedness of the people with God's rock-like faithfulness (Deut 32:4), expressing that the people are no longer God's children because of their wickedness. Paul says that God has now fulfilled his promises, however, and made people his children again (cf. Rom 9:25–26, where God changes "not my people" into "my people" so that they are then his "children"; cf. also "adoption" in Rom 8:23; Eph 1:5).

2:16 Paul looks forward to seeing the fruits of his labors when on the final day the Philippians are present with him before the Lord. **word of life.** The gospel (as in 1:14), not Scripture as a whole.

2:17 poured out like a drink offering on the sacrifice and service. Drink offerings were an integral part of the OT sacrificial system, and the image would also be partially comprehensible to Gentiles unfamiliar with the OT because these "libations" were also offerings in Greek religion. Here, as in the OT daily offerings (Exod 29:40–41) or harvest offerings (Lev 23), the drink offering accompanies a "sacrifice." Paul's being "poured out" also draws attention to his suffering (cf. 2 Tim 4:6). **I am glad and rejoice.** Paul has set out his reasons for rejoicing in 1:12–20, and nothing—not even his "chains" (1:13–14,17) and the suffering in his being "poured out"—can rob him of his joy in Christ.

2:19–30 *Timothy and Epaphroditus.* Paul describes two individuals who model Christian life and ministry. The characteristics of these two apostolic delegates hark back to Paul's instruction in vv. 1–4.

2:19 Cf. 1 Thess 3:2–6.

2:20–21 Paul wants to send Timothy not just so Paul can hear news about them but so that they can see him model the behavior Paul commends in vv. 3–4.

2:24 See note on 1:19.

2:25 send back to you Epaphroditus. Paul's letters were delivered by members of his circle as there was no public mail system. In this case Epaphroditus, a less frequent companion of Paul than Timothy (Epaphroditus is not mentioned in Acts), is taking the letter. The Philippians sent Epaphroditus with gifts for Paul (4:18), and now Paul is sending Epaphroditus back. **my brother, co-worker and fellow soldier.** This sequence is a crescendo: fellow Christian, fellow Christian working together with Paul for the gospel, and fellow Christian fighting and struggling hard with Paul for the gospel. **your messenger.** As Paul implies by declaring that he would send *back* Epaphroditus, this companion of Paul was a member of the Philippian church. He had brought the gifts for the support of Paul's ministry (4:18).

2:27,30 almost died. Epaphroditus became ill somehow in the course of his ministry, probably on his journey bringing aid from the Philippians to Paul (4:18).

3:1—4:3 *Enemies of the Cross and Citizens of Heaven.* Paul here contrasts the mindset of false believers with the Christian's confidence—i.e., confidence that is in Christ (3:7–11), in "the righteousness that comes from God" (3:9), and in the hope of being with Christ in the future (3:14)—to "confidence in the flesh" (3:3)—i.e., confidence in Jewish privilege and achievement (3:2–6) or in Roman civic status (see note on 3:20).

3:1–14 *No Confidence in the Flesh.* Here Paul contrasts his previous confidence with his present righteousness from God through Christ.

3:1 Cf. 1 Cor 15:1–5.

3:2 dogs. In the Jewish and early Christian world, dogs were not "man's best friend" but were seen as disgusting animals—like the proverbial dog that "returns to its vomit" (Prov 26:11; 2 Pet 2:22). "Dogs" could be used, as Paul does here, as a metaphor for "evildoers": "Dogs surround me, a pack of villains encircles me" (Ps 22:16). Jesus himself contrasts the "children" of Israel with Gentile "dogs" (Matt 15:26). This is particularly relevant here since the "evildoers" claim to be the true children of Israel by enforcing the Mosaic law on Gentile Christians. Paul is stating that it is actually the other way around: those who claim to be true Israelites are in fact pagan "dogs" and "evildoers." **mutilators of the flesh.** These false teachers are enforcing circumcision, which was right and proper under the old covenant for Abraham's children, the Israelites. But as Paul argues at greater length in Galatians, Gentiles do not have to become Jews in order to follow Jesus and worship the one true God. They are acceptable to God as Gentiles. They are heirs of Abraham because they share in Abraham's faith, but they do not need to be incorporated *physically* into Abraham's family (Rom 4).

3:3 [c]Ro 2:28,29; Gal 6:15; Col 2:11
3:5 [d]Lk 1:59 [e]2Co 11:22 [f]Ro 11:1 [g]Ac 23:6
3:6 [h]Ac 8:3 [i]Ro 10:5
3:7 [j]Mt 13:44; Lk 14:33
3:8 [k]Eph 4:13; 2Pe 1:2
3:9 [l]Ro 10:5

those mutilators of the flesh. [3]For it is we who are the circumcision,[c] we who serve God by his Spirit,
who boast in Christ Jesus, and who put no confidence in the flesh— [4]though I myself have reasons
for such confidence.

If someone else thinks they have reasons to put confidence in the flesh, I have more: [5]circumcised[d]
on the eighth day, of the people of Israel,[e] of the tribe of Benjamin,[f] a Hebrew of Hebrews; in regard
to the law, a Pharisee;[g] [6]as for zeal, persecuting the church;[h] as for righteousness based on the law,[i]
faultless.

[7]But whatever were gains to me I now consider loss[j] for the sake of Christ. [8]What is more, I consider
everything a loss because of the surpassing worth of knowing[k] Christ Jesus my Lord, for whose sake I
have lost all things. I consider them garbage, that I may gain Christ [9]and be found in him, not having
a righteousness of my own that comes from the law,[l] but that which is through faith in[a] Christ—the

[a] 9 Or *through the faithfulness of*

3:3 For. Paul lists four reasons (in the four "who" phrases) why Christians, not these false teachers, are the true members of the people of God. (1) **it is we who are the circumcision.** Circumcision is the removal of a piece of the foreskin, normally when a baby is eight days old (v. 5; Gen 17:12). Paul does not reject the image of circumcision but understands its true meaning: it is not incorporation into physical Israel but is God's bringing someone into his people, the church. Circumcision was never meant merely to symbolize a national identity; it was also a commitment to righteousness. God condemned the Israelites for being uncircumcised in their hearts even though they were physically circumcised (Jer 9:25–26), but after all the curses of the covenant, he promised, "The Lord your God will circumcise your hearts and the hearts of your descendants, so that you may love him with all your heart and with all your soul, and live" (Deut 30:6). (2) **we who serve God by his Spirit.** Service to God is no longer focused on sacrifices and the temple in Jerusalem; true worship is initiated by the Holy Spirit (John 4:23–24) and is about the whole of life (Rom 12:1). The Spirit lives within us so that our bodies are "temples of the Holy Spirit" (1 Cor 6:19). Serving God is therefore about living our whole lives for God's glory. (3) **who boast in Christ Jesus.** See note on 1:26. (4) **who put no confidence in the flesh.** The opposite of boasting in Christ. Paul, following Jer 9:23–24, rules out boasting in any privilege or prowess such as "the law" (Rom 2:23), people (1 Cor 3:21), or "works" (Eph 2:9).

3:4–6 Paul's hypothetical "boast" (cf. 2 Cor 11:18–30) consists of *seven* characteristics, a kind of "fleshly perfection." These are privileges given to him (v. 5) as well as his own achievements (v. 6).

3:5 circumcised on the eighth day. Circumcision was essential for Israelites (Gen 17:10–14). Unlike some Jews who did not practice circumcision (according to Philo of Alexandria, a contemporary of Paul), Paul's parents were careful to have him circumcised on the day God appointed (Gen 17:12). **people of Israel.** God chose Israel to be his own people, his "treasured possession" if they obeyed (Exod 19:5), a "kingdom of priests and a holy nation" (Exod 19:6), and God's "inheritance" (Deut 9:29). Israel alone had this status among all the nations of the world. Some Jewish writings even assert that God created the world for the sake of Israel. **tribe of Benjamin.** Benjamin was the youngest of Jacob's 12 sons. He was born to Jacob's favorite wife, Rachel (Gen 35:16–18). After the conquest of the promised land, the territory apportioned to the tribe of Benjamin included not only Jericho but also what later became Jerusalem (Josh 18:21–28). **Hebrew of Hebrews.** Paul was a Hebrew not only by nationality but also by education: he could speak Hebrew. Most first-century Jews probably spoke only Greek and/or Aramaic. Paul was educated in Jerusalem in the school of Rabbi Gamaliel I (Acts 22:3), one of the leading teachers of the day, whose interpretations of the law are often cited in the Mishnah and Talmud. **in regard to the law, a Pharisee.** As a Pharisee, Paul followed the law according to the interpretation of that particular school of thought as opposed to how others, such as the Sadducees or Essenes, read it. In the first century, "Pharisee" did not mean "hypocrite," nor were the Pharisees the harshest party. (In Acts 26:5, "strictest" means "most accurate" rather than "most restrictive.") Pharisaism, as the first-century Jewish historian Josephus describes it, favored older teachers and ancestral tradition, extended purity laws, and (unlike the Sadducees, Mark 12:18; Acts 23:8; see note on Acts 15:5) affirmed the resurrection and final judgment. It was the most respected school of thought among most Jews.

3:6 as for zeal, persecuting the church. Cf. Acts 9:1–2; Gal 1:13–14. For a zealous Pharisee, for the Messiah to be cursed by the law in crucifixion (Gal 3:13) was anathema. Similarly, a human being—especially one who piqued the authorities as Jesus did—claiming to be equal with God was blasphemy (Mark 2:5–7; John 5:18). **as for righteousness based on the law, faultless.** Paul claims not sinlessness but a very high level of comprehensive obedience to the law: there was no public sin for which he could be blamed.

3:7 gains ... loss. Paul speaks in financial language: he previously placed the items in vv. 5–6 on the "profit" side of the balance sheet. They had previously been reasons why he had "put confidence in the flesh" (v. 4b). But Paul states that he now considers none of these things as profitable because the only worthwhile thing is Christ. Christ is the all-encompassing gift who cannot be supplemented and with whom nothing can compete.

3:8 I consider everything a loss. Paul generalizes even beyond the items in vv. 5–6. For example, he also lost his career (Gal 1:14–16) and his connections (Acts 9:1–2,14), but these he can cheerfully give up now that he follows Christ. **knowing Christ.** Paul is a disciple with a deep personal relationship with Jesus. As one who knows Christ (see also v. 10), he sees the worthlessness of what he previously relied upon. **garbage.** Can be translated "trash" or "dung."

3:9 found in him. Being "in Christ" contrasts with being "in Judaism" (Gal 1:13–14) or "under the law" (Rom 3:19). **a righteousness of my own that comes from the law.** If Paul had obeyed the law fully, he would be righteous by that law: "And if we are careful to obey all this law before the Lord our God, as he has commanded us, that will be our righteousness" (Deut 6:25). As becomes clear already in Deuteronomy, however, Israel will not obey the law, and indeed—as a stiff-necked people—they cannot (Deut 29:4; cf. 30:1–3). The law cannot provide true righteousness before God because (1) people are incapable of obeying: the human condition is too weak to obey (Rom 8:3), but more than that, it is actually hostile and rebellious toward God (Rom 8:7), and (2) Christ has come, so the law cannot be the route to salvation: "if righteousness could be gained through the law, Christ died for nothing!" (Gal 2:21). **through faith in Christ.** We receive righteousness from God through trusting the Son. Trusting in Christ is similar to boasting in Christ (v. 3), calling on the name of the Lord (Rom 10:13), and hoping in Christ (1 Thess 1:3). **righteousness that comes from God.** God does not save people as a reward for obeying the law. God gives this *gift* of righteousness freely, by

righteousness that comes from God on the basis of faith.[m] 10I want to know Christ—yes, to know the
power of his resurrection and participation in his sufferings,[n] becoming like him in his death,[o] 11and
so, somehow, attaining to the resurrection[p] from the dead.
12Not that I have already obtained all this, or have already arrived at my goal,[q] but I press on to take
hold[r] of that for which Christ Jesus took hold of me.[s] 13Brothers and sisters, I do not consider myself
yet to have taken hold of it. But one thing I do: Forgetting what is behind[t] and straining toward what
is ahead, 14I press on[u] toward the goal to win the prize for which God has called[v] me heavenward in
Christ Jesus.

Following Paul's Example

15All of us, then, who are mature[w] should take such a view of things.[x]
And if on some point you think differently, that too God will make clear
to you. 16Only let us live up to what we have already attained.
17Join together in following my example,[y] brothers
and sisters, and just as you have us as a model, keep
your eyes on those who live as we do. 18For, as I have
often told you before and now tell you again even with
tears,[z] many live as enemies of the cross of Christ.[a]
19Their destiny is destruction, their god is their stomach,[b]
and their glory is in their shame.[c] Their mind is set on
earthly things.[d] 20But our citizenship[e] is in heaven.[f]
And we eagerly await a Savior from there, the Lord
Jesus Christ,[g] 21who, by the power[h] that enables him to
bring everything under his control, will transform our
lowly bodies[i] so that they will be like his glorious body.[j]

Roman heelbone and nail of a crucified man. Crucifixion was a brutal and humiliating form of execution, but Paul emphasizes that Jesus was "obedient to death—even death on a cross!" (Phil 2:8).

Kim Walton, taken at the Israel Museum, Jerusalem

3:9 [m]Ro 9:30
3:10 [n]Ro 8:17 [o]Ro 6:3-5
3:11 [p]Rev 20:5,6
3:12 [q]1Co 13:10 [r]1Ti 6:12 [s]Ac 9:5,6
3:13 [t]Lk 9:62
3:14 [u]Heb 6:1 [v]Ro 8:28
3:15 [w]1Co 2:6 [x]Gal 5:10
3:17 [y]1Co 4:16; 1Pe 5:3
3:18 [z]Ac 20:31 [a]Gal 6:12
3:19 [b]Ro 16:18 [c]Ro 6:21 [d]Ro 8:5,6
3:20 [e]Eph 2:19 [f]Col 3:1 [g]1Co 1:7
3:21 [h]Eph 1:19 [i]1Co 15:43-53 [j]Col 3:4

his own decision rather than in response to anything we have done. **on the basis of faith.** Faith is not the foundation of our righteousness from God; it is the means of receiving the gracious gift of righteousness. Faith is accepting what God holds out to us in Christ, namely, the righteousness that comes to us through Christ's death on the cross for our sins.

3:10–11 The death and resurrection of Christ are unrepeatable, unique events for our salvation (cf. 1 Cor 15:3–4), but they are also events in which we share. To "know Christ" is to participate "in his sufferings" (v. 10), because those who identify with him will receive the same treatment that he did (John 15:18–21). But in the Bible the suffering of God's people is never final. Joseph is thrown into a pit but ends his career as vice-regent of Egypt (Gen 37:24; 41:40–44). Israel experiences exile, but exile is followed by restoration. All this foreshadows Christ: his suffering was followed by his resurrection (cf. note on 2:9). This side of the first Easter, the life of the Christian looks *back* to Christ and reflects his suffering and resurrection. As "co-heirs with Christ," we are to "share in his sufferings in order that we may also share in his glory" (Rom 8:17). Compare also the believer's symbolic sharing of Christ's death and resurrection in baptism (Rom 6:3–4).

3:12–13 Although in one sense new life has already come because we have the Spirit living within us, the resurrection lies in the future as a hope to come.

3:14 heavenward. Cf. v. 20. This might suggest to us a disembodied, merely spiritual reality, but Paul has just talked not about our spirits rising out of our bodies but "resurrection from the dead" (v. 11). See note on v. 21.

3:15–21 *Following Paul's Example.* The Philippians are to imitate both Paul's mindset (vv. 15–16) and actions (v. 17), in contrast to those who are fatally bad examples (vv. 18–19).

3:15–16 Paul's apostolic ministry is to teach the truth. Like the other apostles, he was commissioned by Christ for a unique role in carrying out the purposes of God (Eph 3:2–5; 2 Pet 3:2; Jude 17; cf. Rev 21:14).

3:17 my example. Verses 15–16 focus on instruction, but this verse emphasizes Paul's apostolic display of Christlike living for the Philippians to imitate (cf. 1 Cor 11:1). **those who live as we do.** Paul ensures that the Philippians have models in addition to himself, partly perhaps because of his own absence but also because Christians need more than one example. A single model cannot fully display all facets of following Christ and may have personal weaknesses or eccentricities that will not be apparent as such unless there is someone else to whom the model can be compared.

3:18 enemies of the cross of Christ. The need for strong Christian models is heightened by the constant presence of those modeling a lifestyle opposed to the gospel. These "enemies" are different from those who undermine Paul in 1:17; they are more like the "dogs" of 3:2.

3:20 But our citizenship is in heaven. There is an explicit contrast here between "us," Christians whose citizenship is in heaven, and those whose minds are "set on earthly things" (v. 19). There is also an implied contrast with the Roman citizenship that the Philippians enjoyed: they were grafted into an ancient Roman family line that is celebrated in a number of first-century inscriptions from the city, and they received a number of taxation privileges. As a mere earthly matter, they cannot put their confidence in Roman citizenship (cf. v. 3; see Acts 16:37), since they are citizens of heaven. **we eagerly await.** Christians anticipate Christ's return and the bodily resurrection (Rom 8:23).

3:21 his glorious body. Can be explained from the Gospels, especially Luke and John, which describe Jesus' body as *physical* but also glorious and not limited by being material. The risen Lord could be touched (Luke 24:39; John 20:27), and he could eat (Luke 24:42–43). On the other hand, he was also mysteriously unrecognizable (Luke 24:16; John 20:15) and could pass into a locked room (John 20:26); rather than being a constant physical presence with the disciples as he was before the crucifixion, he appeared, disappeared, and reappeared over 40 days (Luke 24:31; John 21:14; Acts 1:3).

4:1 [k]Php 1:8 [l]1Co 16:13; Php 1:27
4:2 [m]Php 2:2
4:4 [n]Ro 12:12; Php 3:1
4:5 [o]Heb 10:37; Jas 5:8,9
4:6 [p]Mt 6:25-34 [q]Eph 6:18
4:7 [r]Isa 26:3; Jn 14:27; Col 3:15
4:9 [s]Php 3:17 [t]Ro 15:33
4:10 [u]2Co 11:9
4:11 [v]1Ti 6:6,8
4:12 [w]1Co 4:11 [x]2Co 11:9
4:13 [y]2Co 12:9
4:14 [z]Php 1:7
4:15 [a]Php 1:5 [b]2Co 11:8,9
4:16 [c]Ac 17:1

Closing Appeal for Steadfastness and Unity

4 Therefore, my brothers and sisters, you whom I love and long for,[k] my joy and crown, stand firm[l] in the Lord in this way, dear friends!

2 I plead with Euodia and I plead with Syntyche to be of the same mind[m] in the Lord. 3 Yes, and I ask you, my true companion, help these women since they have contended at my side in the cause of the gospel, along with Clement and the rest of my co-workers, whose names are in the book of life.

Final Exhortations

4 Rejoice in the Lord always. I will say it again: Rejoice![n] 5 Let your gentleness be evident to all. The Lord is near.[o] 6 Do not be anxious about anything,[p] but in every situation, by prayer and petition, with thanksgiving, present your requests to God.[q] 7 And the peace of God,[r] which transcends all understanding, will guard your hearts and your minds in Christ Jesus.

8 Finally, brothers and sisters, whatever is true, whatever is noble, whatever is right, whatever is pure, whatever is lovely, whatever is admirable — if anything is excellent or praiseworthy — think about such things. 9 Whatever you have learned or received or heard from me, or seen in me — put it into practice.[s] And the God of peace[t] will be with you.

Thanks for Their Gifts

10 I rejoiced greatly in the Lord that at last you renewed your concern for me.[u] Indeed, you were concerned, but you had no opportunity to show it. 11 I am not saying this because I am in need, for I have learned to be content[v] whatever the circumstances. 12 I know what it is to be in need, and I know what it is to have plenty. I have learned the secret of being content in any and every situation, whether well fed or hungry,[w] whether living in plenty or in want.[x] 13 I can do all this through him who gives me strength.[y]

14 Yet it was good of you to share[z] in my troubles. 15 Moreover, as you Philippians know, in the early days[a] of your acquaintance with the gospel, when I set out from Macedonia, not one church shared with me in the matter of giving and receiving, except you only;[b] 16 for even when I was in Thessalonica,[c]

4:1–3 *Closing Appeal for Steadfastness and Unity.* This gets to the heart of Paul's point in Philippians: continue to remain faithful to the Lord, and be united.

4:2 be of the same mind. Echoes the very same phrase in 2:2 ("being like-minded").

4:3 companion. The Greek word here is rare, so some scholars think this refers to a person, "Syzygus." But that name is also rare. **they have contended at my side.** A number of Paul's co-workers were women (Rom 16 names some of them). **the book of life.** Here and in Revelation it is a list of those who will receive eternal life. In Revelation it is associated with predestination, because the names have been written there "from the creation of the world" (Rev 17:8), as Ps 139:16 already suggests.

4:4–23 *Conclusions.* This concluding section is far from being Paul's way of simply wrapping up his letter. It is highly significant, for it consists of crucial exhortations to focus on God's will (vv. 4–9), Paul's thanks for the Philippians' gifts (vv. 10–20), as well as a greeting and final blessing (vv. 21–23).

4:4–9 *Final Exhortations.* Paul here encourages the Philippians to rejoice and to pray (vv. 4–6) so that God will establish peace in their hearts (v. 7), and to focus on and practice what they have learned from Paul (vv. 8–9) so that God will be with them (v. 9).

4:4 Rejoice in the Lord always. Because true joy does not depend on circumstances but on the presence of the Lord with us, we can have permanent joy. This joy is not a continuous smile but a satisfaction in what the Lord has done and in his presence with us.

4:5 The Lord is near. The Lord Jesus is close to us, and his return is also near. Paul does not necessarily think that Jesus' return is imminent. "Nearness" is, of course, a relative concept: "near" in time might mean very different things according to whether the speaker is an astronomer, a historian, a geologist, or a three-year-old child (cf. 2 Pet 3:8–9): the essential point is that the Lord's return is the next event to take place in salvation history. This nearness of the Lord is the basis for what Paul says in v. 6.

4:6 Do not be anxious about anything, but ... present your requests to God. Prayer is the antidote to worry. The nearness of the Lord (v. 5) grounds both: because the Lord is close to us, we do not need to be anxious, and we can also pray because he is close to us (Ps 34:15).

4:7 And the peace of God ... will guard your hearts. The result of prayer is God's gift of peace, namely, the secure confidence that God is sovereign and loving.

4:9 Paul returns to the theme of 3:15–17.

4:10–20 *Thanks for Their Gifts.* Paul acknowledges the gifts given to support his ministry. Without directly thanking the Philippians, he rejoices in their gifts (v. 10) and says it was good of them to give those gifts (v. 14).

4:10 at last. Paul is relieved that the Philippians have "renewed [their] concern" for him. He is not rebuking them. Because of the vagaries of communication in the ancient world, the Philippians may not have known where Paul was and therefore unable to get a gift to him: they "had no opportunity to show" their concern.

4:13 I can do all this through him who gives me strength. In context, "this" is perhaps being content in every situation (v. 12), but God's empowering presence is essential to all aspects of Christian life and ministry.

4:15 when I set out from Macedonia. The best fit for this event is probably on the return leg of Paul's third missionary journey (Acts 20:6).

4:16 Thessalonica. Another Macedonian town, about 100 miles (160 kilometers) away (about a three-day journey), with Amphipolis and Apollonia evenly spaced between Philippi and Thessalonica (cf. Acts 17:1; see illustration, p. 2448).

you sent me aid more than once when I was in need.[d] [17]Not that I desire your gifts; what I desire is that
more be credited to your account.[e] [18]I have received full payment and have more than enough. I am
amply supplied, now that I have received from Epaphroditus[f] the gifts you sent. They are a fragrant[g]
offering, an acceptable sacrifice, pleasing to God. [19]And my God will meet all your needs[h] according to
the riches of his glory[i] in Christ Jesus.

[20]To our God and Father[j] be glory for ever and ever. Amen.[k]

4:16 [d] 1Th 2:9
4:17 [e] 1Co 9:11,12
4:18 [f] Php 2:25 [g] 2Co 2:14
4:19 [h] Ps 23:1; 2Co 9:8 [i] Ro 2:4
4:20 [j] Gal 1:4 [k] Ro 11:36
4:21 [l] Gal 1:2
4:22 [m] Ac 9:13
4:23 [n] Ro 16:20

Final Greetings

[21]Greet all God's people in Christ Jesus. The brothers and sisters who are with me[l] send greetings.
[22]All God's people[m] here send you greetings, especially those who belong to Caesar's household.
[23]The grace of the Lord Jesus Christ[n] be with your spirit. Amen.[a]

[a] 23 Some manuscripts do not have *Amen*.

4:17 Perhaps one reason that Paul is rejoicing at their gifts rather than thanking them is that he desires that God bless them as a result.

4:18 Epaphroditus. Paul describes him in 2:25 as "your messenger, whom you sent to take care of my needs." At the time of writing, he is still with Paul, and now Paul is sending him back to the Philippians, presumably with this letter. **fragrant offering.** Most naturally connotes the use of incense in the OT sacrificial system (e.g., Exod 30:7), though animal sacrifices could also produce an aroma; Paul calls Christ's death for us a fragrant offering in Eph 5:2. **acceptable sacrifice.** Conveys a different image that usually, though not always, involved slaughtering an animal.

4:19 In the light of the gifts of the Philippians to Paul, he draws attention to God's generosity and magnificent "riches," which God will lavish upon the Ephesians.

4:20 This is not just a rhetorical flourish; it reflects Paul's ultimate concern for God's supreme excellence and the creation's recognition of it. God's glory is his own aim (Eph 1:4–6) and the aim of Christ's work; it is also Paul's aim (Phil 1:20; Rom 5:2b; 11:36) and of Christian discipleship as a whole (1 Cor 10:31).

4:21–23 *Final Greetings.* These verses consist of both an instruction (v. 21a), greetings proper (vv. 21b–22), and a closing prayer (v. 23).

4:21 Greet all God's people. This statement is a little puzzling: did the letter go first to the leaders mentioned in 1:1? Or does it imply that because of people's circumstances the believers would not all have been free to attend the meeting where the letter was read aloud (there being no Sunday "day off" in Roman culture)? In a church beset with divisions, Paul is not taking a side but is again urging unity. **who are with me.** Paul probably distinguishes here between "the brothers and sisters" who are temporarily visiting him and the members of the churches in Rome ("all God's people here" in v. 22).

4:22 Caesar's household. The phrase is a conventional one, referring not so much to the family but to the court, consisting both of menial servants as well as influential functionaries.

4:23 A final prayer, not just a conventional "signing off."

INTRODUCTION TO COLOSSIANS

AUTHOR

Colossians, along with Ephesians, Philemon, and Philippians, belongs to the cluster of letters commonly known as the Prison Letters. It is normally linked together with Philemon since both letters mention Epaphras, who appears to have founded the church in Colossae (1:7; 4:12 – 13; Phlm 23), as well as Mark, Aristarchus, Demas, and Luke (4:10, 14; Phlm 23). Paul's authorship of Philemon is undisputed, but his authorship of Colossians is debated. Some argue that differences in vocabulary, style, and theology point to a later imitator who, writing under Paul's name, concocted the fiction of sending the letter to Laodicea (4:16) to explain how it appeared in that city. Explanations as to why someone would carry out such a ruse are unsatisfactory. Nothing in Colossians is inconsistent with Paul's theology as found in the undisputed letters, and Colossians can be said to develop his theology to apply to a different situation. The unfamiliar vocabulary occurs in the section dealing with the "philosophy" (2:8). Stylistic differences can be explained if Paul composed the letter with the help of a secretary or authorized his associate Timothy to flesh out the general line of thought. Many had never met Paul in person (2:1), which may explain the letter's more formal tone.

DATE AND PLACE OF COMPOSITION

Paul did not say where he was imprisoned (4:3,10,18; cf. 1:24). Rome is the traditional view. Travel between Rome and the East was not difficult. It would have allowed for an interchange of communication. It is probable that Aristarchus, Paul's fellow prisoner (4:10), accompanied Paul to Rome (Acts 27:2). Luke (Col 4:14) was also with Paul in Rome (Acts 28:14; 2 Tim 4:11). Ephesus' proximity to Colossae makes it another candidate. If Ephesians was also written around the same time, why would Paul write to the Ephesians from Ephesus? Paul's Roman imprisonment still seems to be the best option, and the date of the letter's composition was probably AD 60 – 61.

DESTINATION

Colossae was situated on the southern bank in the upper Lycus River Valley in Phrygia, about 110 miles (177 kilometers) east of Ephesus. Its neighboring cities, Laodicea (10 miles [16 kilometers] to the west) and Hierapolis (12 miles [19 kilometers] to the northwest on the opposite side of the river), far surpassed it in importance. An earthquake severely damaged the area in AD 60. Laodicea recovered, but Colossae may have been completely destroyed. The site has not been excavated, and primary evidence about the city is sparse.

OCCASION AND PURPOSE

Paul writes to buttress the Colossians' faith. It is not teetering on the brink of extinction or trapped in error, but an outside "philosophy" (2:8) disparages the Colossians' hope in Christ and threatens their assurance. The "philosophy" (2:8,16 – 23) is not a Christian heresy, but no single identification of the error is convincing (e.g., Essenism, Jewish mysticism, Judaism, Cynic philosophy, mystery cults, Middle Platonism, or syncretistic folk religion). The most one can say is that the error devalues Christ's supremacy and the adequacy of salvation through him. It promotes mystical experiences, additional spiritual agents, and a regimen of ritual or ascetic observances to achieve well-being. The congregation needs encouragement (2:2; 4:8) about the certainty of their faith to give them full assurance and a thankful spirit for what God has done for them (1:12; 2:7; 3:15,17; 4:2).

LOCATION OF COLOSSAE

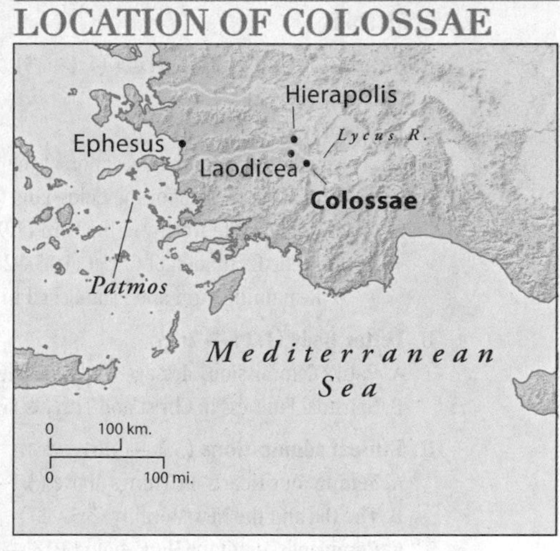

Against this threat, Paul argues for the all-sufficiency of Christ. Christ is preeminent as the one in whom, through whom, and for whom all things were created (1:16) and through whom all things will be reconciled (1:20). He is head of the church (1:18) and head over every power and authority (2:10). Paul answers the error by asserting three truths: (1) all the fullness of the Deity dwells in Christ, (2) believers are complete in Christ, and (3) Christ has authority over all angelic beings and cosmic powers (2:9 – 15). Consequently, no other mediators are needed for salvation, and nothing more needs to be done for believers to become full members of the community of God's holy people (1:12), to be delivered more fully from their sins, to be protected more completely from evil forces, or to be more strongly assured of eternal hope.

Being saved by Christ and living in Christ have direct bearing upon how believers should behave (3:1 – 17). Paul emphasizes the lordship of Christ over all aspects of life. Christians are in Christ, and Christ is in them. Right belief should lead to right practice. The ethical exhortations in the letter are expressed in paradoxes. They are living, yet at the same time they are dead to sin (3:3). They are equal in Christ, yet they may occupy roles that subordinate them to others (3:11,18 — 4:1).

The unexcavated tell at Colossae. A tell is a mound of ancient ruins including several layers built one over another through time.

Clinton E. Arnold

OUTLINE

I. Salutation and Thanksgiving (1:1 – 23)
- A. Salutation (1:1 – 2)
- B. Thanksgiving (1:3 – 23)
  - 1. Thanksgiving for the Reception of the Gospel in Colossae and the Whole World (1:3 – 8)
  - 2. Paul's Intercession for the Colossians (1:9 – 23)
    - a. Living a Life Worthy of the Lord (1:9 – 14)
    - b. Poetic Exaltation of Christ (1:15 – 20)
    - c. Remaining Firm and Established in the Faith (1:21 – 23)

II. Letter Body (1:24 — 2:23)
- A. Paul's Commission, Message, and Struggle (1:24 — 2:5)
- B. Spiritual Fullness in Christ and Threats From a Philosophy (2:6 – 23)

III. Ethical Admonitions (3:1 — 4:6)
- A. Setting Your Hearts on Things Above (3:1 – 4)
- B. The Old and the New Morality (3:5 – 17)
- C. Commands About the Household (3:18 — 4:1)
- D. Exhortation to Unflagging Prayer and Wise Behavior (4:2 – 6)

IV. Final Greetings (4:7 – 18)

COLOSSIANS

1 Paul, an apostle[a] of Christ Jesus by the will of God,[b] and Timothy our brother,

[2]To God's holy people in Colossae, the faithful brothers and sisters[a] in Christ:

Grace[c] and peace to you from God our Father.[bd]

1:1 [a]1Co 1:1 [b]2Co 1:1
1:2 [c]Col 4:18 [d]Ro 1:7
1:3 [e]Ro 1:8
1:4 [f]Gal 5:6 [g]Eph 1:15
1:5 [h]1Th 5:8; Titus 1:2 [i]1Pe 1:4
1:6 [j]Jn 15:16 [k]Ro 10:18

Thanksgiving and Prayer

[3]We always thank God,[e] the Father of our Lord Jesus Christ, when we pray for you, [4]because we have
heard of your faith in Christ Jesus and of the love[f] you have for all God's people[g]—[5]the faith and
love that spring from the hope[h] stored up for you in heaven[i] and about which you have already heard
in the true message of the gospel [6]that has come to you. In the same way, the gospel is bearing fruit[j]
and growing throughout the whole world[k]—just as it has been doing among you since the day you

[a] 2 The Greek word for *brothers and sisters* (*adelphoi*) refers here to believers, both men and women, as part of God's family; also in 4:15. [b] 2 Some manuscripts *Father and the Lord Jesus Christ*

1:1–23 *Salutation and Thanksgiving.* The first two sections, Paul's customary salutation (vv. 1–2) and his prayer of thanksgiving (vv. 3–23), help set the agenda for the letter.
1:1–2 *Salutation.* Paul transforms traditional greetings into a theological affirmation of God's free, unmerited favor on them and their resulting peace, or reconciliation, with God.
1:1 an apostle ... by the will of God. Paul is called by God (Acts 9:15), and God empowers him. Paul understands that he was set apart by God from his mother's womb to preach the gospel to the Gentiles (Rom 11:13; Gal 1:15–16; 2:7). His authority is not increased by the use of the title "apostle" (here) just as it is not reduced when he omits it (1 Thess 1:1; 2 Thess 1:1) or substitutes "servant" (Phil 1:1) or "prisoner" (Phlm 1). He is a "fellow servant" (Col 1:7; 4:7) who carries out a commission God gave him for them (vv. 24–25), not a domineering master over them. **Timothy.** Also co-sent 2 Corinthians, Philippians, 1–2 Thessalonians, and Philemon. Timothy was spoken well of by believers in Lystra and Iconium, and Paul took Timothy with him from there on his missionary journeys (Acts 16:1–3). Paul praises him as one who served with him like a son with a father (Phil 2:20–22). Later, Timothy was also imprisoned for the gospel (Heb 13:23).
1:2 holy. Set apart to be God's own people in the world with their commitments owed solely to God, an idea that is reinforced by the adjective "faithful." **in Christ.** More important than being "in Colossae." Faith in Christ creates a spiritual kinship in him that supersedes blood ties. For a formerly devout Jew to call Gentiles, many of whom he has never met, "brothers and sisters," reveals one of the drastic consequences of the gospel—it sweeps away all racial prejudices that isolate people from one another.
1:3–23 *Thanksgiving.* Beginning and ending with the key ideas of faith, hope, and hearing, this thanksgiving is a prayer to be read aloud in Christian worship; it thereby becomes a witness of Christian faith and a means of Christian instruction.
1:3–8 *Thanksgiving for the Reception of the Gospel in Colossae and the Whole World.* Paul begins and ends by mentioning the church's "faith" (faithfulness) and "love" (vv. 4–5,7–8). Paul shifts from focusing on the gospel's effect in the church (vv. 3–5) to the gospel's growth in the whole world (v. 6), and then Paul recaps how the Colossians received the gospel from Epaphras (v. 7). Paul gives them a global perspective of how God's work is accomplishing his purposes throughout the world.
1:3 always ... pray. Paul continuously prayed for his churches. An important facet of communal faith is that when one cannot pray, others pray on one's behalf. Paul introduces God not abstractly as some universal divine force but as the one who acted in history in the life, death, and resurrection of Jesus Christ. Jesus expressed his unique relationship to God as "Father" in his own teaching and prayers (Matt 11:25–27).
1:4–5 faith ... love ... hope. Central to the Christian life and mentioned frequently by Paul (Rom 5:1–5; 1 Cor 13:13; Gal 5:5–6; Eph 4:2–5; 1 Thess 1:3; 5:8). **hope.** The glorious future that Christ has established for Christians in the heavenly realm beyond this earthly existence (3:4,24). It is the ground of their faith and love, which are expressed in actions, not simply feelings. **the true message of the gospel.** Implies that they have been exposed to a false message that offers false hope.
1:6 bearing fruit. Evidence for the truth of the gospel is its fruitfulness in the lives of believers. **growing.** The gospel continues to grow because it speaks to the universal condition of all people regardless of their cultural, ethnic, or socioeconomic background.

1:7 [l]Phm 23 [m]Col 4:7
1:8 [n]Ro 15:30
1:9 [o]Eph 1:15 [p]Eph 5:17 [q]Eph 1:17
1:10 [r]Eph 4:1
1:11 [s]Eph 3:16 [t]Eph 4:2
1:12 [u]Eph 5:20 [v]Ac 20:32
1:13 [w]Ac 26:18 [x]Eph 6:12; 2Pe 1:11 [y]Mt 3:17
1:14 [z]Ro 3:24 [a]Eph 1:7
1:15 [b]2Co 4:4 [c]Jn 1:18
1:16 [d]Jn 1:3

heard it and truly understood God's grace. 7 You learned it from Epaphras,[l] our dear fellow servant,[a]
who is a faithful minister[m] of Christ on our[b] behalf, 8 and who also told us of your love in the Spirit.[n]
9 For this reason, since the day we heard about you,[o] we have not stopped praying for you. We continually ask God to fill you with the knowledge of his will[p] through all the wisdom and understanding that
the Spirit gives,[c][q] 10 so that you may live a life worthy[r] of the Lord and please him in every way: bearing
fruit in every good work, growing in the knowledge of God, 11 being strengthened with all power[s] according to his glorious might so that you may have great endurance and patience,[t] 12 and giving joyful
thanks to the Father,[u] who has qualified you[d] to share in the inheritance[v] of his holy people in the
kingdom of light. 13 For he has rescued us from the dominion of darkness[w] and brought us into the
kingdom[x] of the Son he loves,[y] 14 in whom we have redemption,[z] the forgiveness of sins.[a]

The Supremacy of the Son of God

15 The Son is the image[b] of the invisible God,[c] the firstborn over all creation. 16 For in him all things
were created:[d] things in heaven and on earth, visible and invisible, whether thrones or powers or rulers

[a] 7 Or *slave* [b] 7 Some manuscripts *your* [c] 9 Or *all spiritual wisdom and understanding*
[d] 12 Some manuscripts *us*

1:7 Epaphras. Probably one of the residents of Asia who heard Paul's preaching in Ephesus and became a Christian (Acts 19:10). He became the founding evangelist of all three churches in the Lycus Valley: Colossae, Laodicea, and Hierapolis (Col 4:13). As Paul's beloved fellow servant of Christ, he was a reliable source of the gospel.
1:9–23 *Paul's Intercession for the Colossians.* In this letter Paul presents his teaching in the context of prayer. Pleasing God is the chief human obligation (Rom 8:8; 12:1–2; 1 Cor 7:32; 2 Cor 5:9; Eph 5:10; Phil 4:18).
1:9–14 *Living a Life Worthy of the Lord.* Paul describes four elements of a life that is worthy of and fully pleasing to the Lord: bearing fruit, growing in knowledge of God, being strengthened for endurance and patience, and giving joyful thanks. These fundamentals will fend off the harmful pressures from false teachers.
1:9 knowledge ... wisdom ... understanding. One is not saved by being filled with such knowledge, but spiritual crises are worsened by its absence. Christians are expected to grow beyond fundamentals (Heb 5:12,14) and mastery of basic facts to greater insight in divine truth. Maturing wisdom leads to transformed relationships with God and with others and provides a safeguard against false teaching.
1:10 bearing fruit in every good work. Assumes that Christians, as God's new creation, will live by new standards according to the final restoration of creation's goodness and abandon conduct that characterizes the old humanity (cf. 3:5–9). Paul expects not only that they will know good from evil but also that their transformed lives will yield fruitful, not futile, effects. **growing in the knowledge of God.** Can also be rendered "growing *by* the knowledge of God," expressing the means by which they grow. Understanding how God's purposes for the universe are being accomplished through Christ and his death is crucial for understanding how one is to live.
1:11 strengthened with all power. The same glorious power that raised Jesus from the dead also strengthens Christians so that they might have both "endurance" and "patience" in difficult times and circumstances. Endurance, patience, and "joyful thanks" (v. 12) guard Christians from the lure of false teaching and draw others to the Christian faith.
1:12 inheritance. Formerly was exclusively Israel's, but now extends to Gentile believers who become co-heirs with Jewish believers. The response to God's initiative unleashes thanks with joy, since they recognize that salvation comes as a divine gift they did not and could not earn. **kingdom of light.** It has penetrated the world's darkness and delivered believers from the bondage of the dark powers (Eph 6:12). As a result, Christians are to walk as "children of light" and bear "the fruit of the light" (Eph 5:8–9).
1:13–14 dominion of darkness. Blinds humans from seeing the truth of their condition and how they might be saved from it. Those who live under its power do evil (Rom 13:12; Eph 5:11–12). Some Colossian Christians may have worried that they were still prisoners of the sinister powers that ruled the present realm and that they needed to be delivered through means other than Christ. Paul assures them that God has liberated Christians from every power (Eph 6:12) and has resettled them in the Lord (Eph 5:8). **redemption.** Recalls God's rescue of Israel from slavery in Egypt (Exod 6:6–8); God has redeemed Christians from the far more potent power of the evil one.
1:15–20 *Poetic Exaltation of Christ.* Paul interjects poetic praise of Christ that affirms that Christ is not simply one of many spiritual powers but is preeminent over all. Many think that vv. 15–20 are an early Christian hymn that Paul quotes and adapts to his argument. The first stanza acclaims Jesus as the preexistent agent and regent of creation (vv. 15–18a); the second esteems him as the reconciler of creation (vv. 18b–20). Christ's reconciling work on the cross affects every part of the created cosmos—things in heaven and on earth (vv. 16,20). "The church" (v. 18a) is where one sees and experiences the reconciliation of all things on earth. In Christ, the Colossians have received all the benefits of Christ's death, and their salvation is complete.

Paul applies to Christ what the OT says of God as the Creator (Pss 96:5; 146:5–6; Isa 40:12–31). Jesus not only makes God known but is also part of the divine identity.
1:15 image. A reflection that shares the reality it reveals. In Christ, vague notions about the unseen God (Heb 11:27) become distinct (John 1:18). Christ is *the* image, not simply *an* image. He displays divine mercy and love, divine power that works in weakness, and the divine mystery that will reconcile all creation through the cross. The Colossians do not need any supplementary visions to understand God more fully (Col 2:18), and their new self "is being renewed in knowledge in the image of its Creator" (3:10). Christ alone bridges the gulf between heaven and earth, and humans do not need a ladder of intermediate beings to intercede to God for them. **firstborn over all creation.** A metaphor referring to Jesus' preeminence (Ps 89:27). He is not the first created being with primacy *within* creation; he has primacy *over* all creation.
1:16 thrones or powers or rulers or authorities. Various forms of invisible and visible spiritual powers that humans experience (Rom 8:38–39). They only hold their seats of power in trust (1 Cor 8:5–6; Phil 2:9–11). Those who are in Christ do not need to revere, fear, or appease these potentates. Christians have come to fullness (Col 2:10) by being in the one who is the guardian over all things. **for him.** Reminds readers that Christ was not only at the beginning of creation when things

or authorities;[e] all things have been created through him and for him.[f] 17 He is before all things,[g] and
in him all things hold together. 18 And he is the head[h] of the body, the church; he is the beginning and
the firstborn from among the dead,[i] so that in everything he might have the supremacy. 19 For God was
pleased[j] to have all his fullness[k] dwell in him, 20 and through him to reconcile[l] to himself all things,
whether things on earth or things in heaven,[m] by making peace through his blood,[n] shed on the cross.
21 Once you were alienated from God and were enemies[o] in your minds[p] because of[a] your evil behavior. 22 But now he has reconciled you by Christ's physical body[q] through death to present you holy in his
sight, without blemish and free from accusation[r] — 23 if you continue in your faith, established[s] and
firm, and do not move from the hope[t] held out in the gospel. This is the gospel that you heard and that
has been proclaimed to every creature under heaven,[u] and of which I, Paul, have become a servant.[v]

Paul's Labor for the Church

24 Now I rejoice in what I am suffering for you, and I fill up in my flesh what is still lacking in regard
to Christ's afflictions,[w] for the sake of his body, which is the church. 25 I have become its servant[x] by the
commission God gave me[y] to present to you the word of God in its fullness — 26 the mystery[z] that has

1:16 [e] Eph 1:20,21 [f] Ro 11:36
1:17 [g] Jn 1:2
1:18 [h] Eph 1:22 [i] Ac 26:23; Rev 1:5
1:19 [j] Eph 1:5 [k] Jn 1:16
1:20 [l] 2Co 5:18 [m] Eph 1:10 [n] Eph 2:13
1:21 [o] Ro 5:10 [p] Eph 2:3
1:22 [q] Ro 7:4 [r] Eph 5:27
1:23 [s] Eph 3:17 [t] ver 5 [u] Ro 10:18 [v] ver 25; 1Co 3:5
1:24 [w] 2Co 1:5
1:25 [x] ver 23 [y] Eph 3:2
1:26 [z] Ro 16:25

[a] *21* Or *minds, as shown by*

were created "through him" (cf. John 1:3; 1 Cor 8:6), but he also reigns at the end as the goal of creation.

1:17 before all things. A reference to Christ's preexistence before creation. Christ is the key who unlocks the meaning and purpose of the universe and of what God has done, is doing, and will do. If Christ sustains the whole universe, then he can sustain believers.

1:18 head. Refers to Christ's supremacy over the church. Christ is the supreme ruler of the cosmos (even angels worship him, Heb 1:6), and he is present as the head of the church. The head not only directs and governs the body but also gives it life and strength (Col 2:19). The church exists not to satisfy itself or to ensure its institutional survival but to fulfill the purposes of its head. **firstborn from among the dead.** Christ's resurrection (1 Cor 15:20; Rev 1:5). He was the first to be raised from the dead never to die again, and his resurrection ensures the resurrection of those who follow him.

1:19 was pleased. Expresses the sovereignty and mystery of God's will. **dwell in him.** God in all his fullness chose to dwell in Christ alone (2:9; John 1:14) and in no one or nothing else, such as the temple (cf. Ps 68:16). Christ perfectly exhibits God's Spirit, word, wisdom, and glory.

1:20 reconcile … all things. Everything was created through Christ, but the created universe is fallen and needs reconciliation to God. That reconciliation was achieved within history through Christ alone, who took on the flesh of his creation and endured the agonizing suffering of the cross (2:14–15). This does not refer to universal salvation; Christ's enemies are vanquished (2:15; 1 Cor 15:24–26). **blood, shed on the cross.** The climax of the poetic praise. God turned murder and an instrument of death into an atoning sacrifice that brings life and peace.

1:21–23 *Remaining Firm and Established in the Faith.* Paul addresses the past, present, and future for believers: their former plight ("once," v. 21), their rescue ("now," v. 22), and their responsibility to guard their future hope ("if," v. 23). All creation still awaits the consummation when it will be drawn into complete harmony with the Father. If believers are to be presented as holy, blameless, and above reproach, they must continue to be stable and steadfast in the faith.

1:21 alienated. Implies isolation, loneliness, and hostility (Eph 4:18). It is caused by sinful actions that generate a never-ending cycle of sinful actions that separate humans from God and others.

1:22 holy. Believers cannot make themselves acceptable to God by their own efforts, but Christ's reconciliation works in them to transform them so that they will stand blameless before God in the last judgment.

1:23 continue. The Colossians cannot take their new status in Christ for granted and be nonchalant about the responsibility it incurs. If they allow themselves to be dislodged from their foundation in the gospel that they had heard and received from Epaphras, they will lose their hope. **every creature under heaven.** May be an exaggeration (cf. Acts 2:5) that makes a point about the universality of the gospel.

1:24—2:23 *Letter Body.* Paul updates the recipients about his missionary endeavors and his commitment to them. Key themes are: Paul is suffering on behalf of Christ and the church (1:24); God commissioned Paul as his servant (1:25,28; 2:2,4); Paul proclaims the mystery of God (1:26; 2:2); and Paul toils and struggles for the word of God (1:29; 2:1).

Paul sums up the message of the letter (2:6–7). Christ should define the believer's entire life. The opponents, with their persuasive words and legal strictures, would undermine that allegiance. Paul issues three warnings: (1) do not be taken captive by the deceptive "philosophy" (2:8); (2) do not accept the censure of these detractors (2:16); and (3) do not be charmed by their worship of angels (2:18). He argues against the false philosophy (2:8–15) and parodies its specific practices (2:16–23). The Colossians have been rescued once (1:13), but unless they beware, they may be recaptured by the powers of darkness through this hollow philosophy. If they grasp the full scope of God's triumph in Christ, they will see the futility of the philosophy's legalistic demands that threaten to undermine their faith.

1:24—2:5 *Paul's Commission, Message, and Struggle.* Paul focuses on his apostolic commission and sheds light on his conception of that commission.

1:24 suffering. Its reality and necessity (Acts 9:15–16; 2 Cor 11:23–27) are not changed by Christ's lordship over all creation (Col 1:15). Paul does not view suffering for Christ as a problem. If Christians share in dying and rising with Christ (3:1,3–4), they also share in Christ's sufferings (Rom 8:17; 2 Cor 1:5–6). Paul firmly believes in the solidarity of Christians with Christ and with one another (1 Cor 12:26; 2 Cor 7:3–4). **fill up in my flesh.** Paul's physical suffering as a member of Christ's body and as an apostle extends Christ's vocation of suffering for the world. **what is still lacking in regard to Christ's afflictions.** Perhaps a measure of afflictions that had to be completed before Christ would return in glory (Rev 6:9–11). Or "what is still lacking" may refer to Christ's physical absence (cf. 1 Cor 16:17; Phil 2:30). Paul does not imply that his sufferings somehow make up for some deficiency in Christ's atoning death.

1:25 servant by the commission God gave me. God commissioned Paul to preach the gospel in all its richness (1 Cor 1:17; 9:16).

1:26 mystery. God's redemptive purpose for creation and how it will be carried out (v. 27; 2:2; 4:3; Rom 16:25; 1 Cor 2:7; Eph 3:4–6,9). It is a truth that human minds cannot discover on their own; God must reveal it. Christ is the center of the mystery. Humans cannot know God in all his fullness apart from Christ, nor can they know God's purposes apart from Christ.

1:27 [a]Mt 13:11
1:28 [b]Col 3:16 [c]1Co 2:6, 7 [d]Eph 5:27
1:29 [e]1Co 15:10 [f]Col 2:1 [g]Eph 1:19
2:1 [h]Col 1:29; 4:12 [i]Rev 1:11
2:2 [j]Col 4:8
2:3 [k]Ro 11:33; 1Co 1:24,30
2:4 [l]Ro 16:18
2:5 [m]1Th 2:17 [n]1Co 14:40 [o]1Pe 5:9
2:6 [p]Col 1:10
2:7 [q]Eph 3:17
2:8 [r]1Ti 6:20 [s]Gal 4:3

been kept hidden for ages and generations, but is now disclosed to the Lord's people. 27 To them God
has chosen to make known[a] among the Gentiles the glorious riches of this mystery, which is Christ in
you, the hope of glory.
28 He is the one we proclaim, admonishing[b] and teaching everyone with all wisdom,[c] so that we may
present everyone fully mature[d] in Christ. 29 To this end I strenuously[e] contend[f] with all the energy Christ
so powerfully works in me.[g]

2 I want you to know how hard I am contending[h] for you and for those at Laodicea,[i] and for all
who have not met me personally. 2 My goal is that they may be encouraged in heart[j] and united
in love, so that they may have the full riches of complete understanding, in order that they may know
the mystery of God, namely, Christ, 3 in whom are hidden all the treasures of wisdom and knowledge.[k]
4 I tell you this so that no one may deceive you by fine-sounding arguments.[l] 5 For though I am absent
from you in body, I am present with you in spirit[m] and delight to see how disciplined[n] you are and how
firm[o] your faith in Christ is.

Spiritual Fullness in Christ

6 So then, just as you received Christ Jesus as Lord,[p] continue to live your lives in him, 7 rooted[q] and
built up in him, strengthened in the faith as you were taught, and overflowing with thankfulness.
8 See to it that no one takes you captive through hollow and deceptive philosophy,[r] which depends on
human tradition and the elemental spiritual forces[a] of this world[s] rather than on Christ.

[a] 8 Or *the basic principles*; also in verse 20

1:27 This "mystery" (v. 26) involves God's saving Gentiles, to whom God appointed Paul to proclaim the gospel (Rom 11:13; 15:15–16; Gal 1:16). It is defined here as "Christ in you." Being fully bonded with Christ means that believers will experience the final glory (Rom 5:2).
1:28 everyone … everyone. Repeated to emphasize the gospel's universality. Since the gospel is proclaimed to all, it is not targeted to only the spiritually or intellectually elite. The gospel grows throughout the whole world so that everyone may become fully mature, i.e., entirely focused on and directed by Christ.
1:29 I strenuously contend. Paul provides the exertion but Christ provides the power in Paul's ministry (Phil 2:12–13).
2:1 all who have not met me personally. The universal gospel requires that an apostle struggle in his ministry not only for those he knows personally but also for those he has never met.
2:2 Paul lists three goals of his apostolic contending. (1) **encouraged in heart.** The heart was considered to be the center of one's will and reasoning and not merely that of one's emotions. (2) **united in love.** Love is both a unifying force (3:14) and an atmosphere in which one lives. (3) **complete understanding.** This experience will lead them to grasp with full assurance God's larger purpose for the world in Christ.
2:3 hidden … treasures. Christ unlocks access to stores of divine truth, "the deep things of God" (1 Cor 2:10). These hidden treasures—wisdom and knowledge, how to gain life and how to live—are now made available to all.
2:4 deceive you. All spiritual wisdom is to be found in Christ alone. Any who claim to offer the secret to life outside of Christ only hoodwink themselves and others.
2:5 disciplined … firm. Military metaphors. The Colossians' faith means that they march in good order in a close, unyielding phalanx that gives Paul confidence that they will resist the false teaching.
2:6–23 *Spiritual Fullness in Christ and Threats From a Philosophy.* Paul establishes the all-sufficiency of Christ (vv. 9–15). His argument provides the theological underpinning for the direct rebuttal of the opponents (vv. 16–23). This direct polemic is the key passage for identifying the error threatening the Colossians.
2:6 as you received. When one receives Jesus Christ as Lord, one also receives the obligation to live a certain way. Receiving Christ also implies receiving the traditions about Christ—what he did and taught and what it means—and this tradition, rather than human tradition (v. 8), provides the guidelines for the Christian life. **continue to live.** Christians do not need to add—and should not add—other guidelines for living a life pleasing to the Lord (1:10). The implication is that Christians must look to Christ alone.
2:7 rooted … built up … strengthened. These participles are in the passive voice, which implies that someone has done these things for them, namely God. The Christian faith is not a do-it-yourself religion. Christians are bound to the Lord by their faith and are bound to be obedient to him and to live with thanksgiving. **thankfulness.** Christians with a thankful spirit respond to what God has done in Christ and are mindful that their lives depend entirely upon God, not themselves. A thankful spirit also wards off false teaching.
2:8 philosophy. Paul does not dismiss the importance of critical thinking and sound learning in the modern discipline of philosophy. In Paul's day, *philosophy* was a broad term that could describe various factions, movements, or opinions; some Hellenistic Jewish writers presented Judaism to the Hellenistic world as a "philosophy." **depends on human tradition.** What makes this "philosophy" worthless is that it derives from human speculation in this present evil age and does not transmit divine wisdom. All Christ-less teaching, no matter how high-sounding, is hollow at its core. **the elemental spiritual forces of this world.** Cf. v. 20; Gal 4:3,9. This phrase could refer to the four physical elements: fire, water, earth, and air. Or the word "elemental" could be used for something arranged in regular order, like the alphabet, and could refer to basic principles, or ABCs, of some area of study. The key expression is "of this world." Paul views the world as alienated from God and needing redemption and reconciliation. The translation assumes that Paul refers to personalized spiritual forces that were thought to have influence over day-to-day existence. He does not dismiss these powers as primitive myths. They exist and compete for human reverence and loyalty, but they are weak and temporary, a shadow of reality (Col 2:17). They enslave those who follow their dictates (Gal 4:3) and deflect them from a true knowledge of God. Since Christ has triumphed over them (Col 2:14; Gal 4:5), Christians do not need to fear or revere them.

9For in Christ all the fullness of the Deity lives in bodily form, 10and in Christ you have been brought
to fullness. He is the head[t] over every power and authority. 11In him you were also circumcised[u] with a
circumcision not performed by human hands. Your whole self ruled by the flesh[a][v] was put off when you
were circumcised by[b] Christ, 12having been buried with him in baptism, in which you were also raised
with him[w] through your faith in the working of God, who raised him from the dead.[x]
13When you were dead in your sins[y] and in the uncircumcision of your flesh, God made you[c] alive
with Christ. He forgave us all our sins, 14having canceled the charge of our legal indebtedness,[z] which
stood against us and condemned us; he has taken it away, nailing it to the cross.[a] 15And having disarmed the powers and authorities,[b] he made a public spectacle of them, triumphing over them[c] by
the cross.[d]

Freedom From Human Rules

16Therefore do not let anyone judge you[d] by what you eat or drink,[e] or with regard to a religious
festival,[f] a New Moon celebration[g] or a Sabbath day.[h] 17These are a shadow of the things that were to
come;[i] the reality, however, is found in Christ. 18Do not let anyone who delights in false humility[j] and
the worship of angels disqualify you.[k] Such a person also goes into great detail about what they have
seen; they are puffed up with idle notions by their unspiritual mind. 19They have lost connection with

2:10 [t]Eph 1:22
2:11 [u]Ro 2:29; Php 3:3 [v]Gal 5:24
2:12 [w]Ro 6:5 [x]Ac 2:24
2:13 [y]Eph 2:1,5
2:14 [z]Eph 2:15 [a]1Pe 2:24
2:15 [b]Eph 6:12 [c]Lk 10:18
2:16 [d]Ro 14:3,4 [e]Ro 14:17 [f]Ro 14:5 [g]1Ch 23:31 [h]Gal 4:10
2:17 [i]Heb 8:5
2:18 [j]ver 23 [k]Php 3:14

a 11 In contexts like this, the Greek word for *flesh* (*sarx*) refers to the sinful state of human beings, often presented as a power in opposition to the Spirit; also in verse 13. *b 11* Or *put off in the circumcision of* *c 13* Some manuscripts *us* *d 15* Or *them in him*

2:9 Deity. Christ's nature is divine. God was pleased now to abide in the body of the living Christ and not to dwell in a sacred building like the temple as was true in the past (Ps 68:16).
2:10 fullness. Paul again asserts Christ's matchlessness. God has definitively revealed himself in Christ (1:15,19). Christ is the all-sufficient fullness of life and salvation for Christians, and the only way humans can find fulfillment is in Christ. Paul counters the deceptive philosophy: Since Christ is "the head over every power and authority," why should anyone imagine fullness could be provided by some junior power?
2:11–12 circumcision ... baptism. Paul uses these vivid metaphors from Jewish initiation rites to underscore what Christ's death and resurrection achieved for believers. Christian conversion requires more than spiritual cosmetic surgery. **flesh.** Human nature that sin has corrupted and enslaved; a power sphere opposed to the Spirit (Gal 5:17). **circumcised by Christ.** Pictures a major spiritual "operation" in which Christ cuts off "the body ruled by sin" (Rom 6:6) and our solidarity with the old Adam (Rom 5:12–14; 1 Cor 15:22). Christ cuts off believers' sinful compulsions when they submit to him. **baptism.** More than simply a rite marking the believer's entry into the church, it is the watery grave for the flesh that is dead in its trespasses (Rom 6:4) and the birthplace of the new creation in Christ. It symbolically reenacts Christ's death and resurrection and represents the whole experience of conversion. It marks the Christian's death to sin, total surrender to God, and solidarity with Christ by being buried and raised with him. **faith in the working of God.** Trust that God indeed raised Christ from the dead and inaugurated the new age that dismantles the reign of sin and death.
2:13 dead in your sins ... alive with Christ. Sin brings death. Forgiveness and life come only from being made alive with Christ.
2:14 the charge of our legal indebtedness. Paul uses the metaphor of a legal bond or certificate of debt (an IOU) in which humans promise to obey what they know to be God's will (cf. Rom 1:32). It becomes our death warrant when we fail to obey (cf. Rom 3:23) because we cannot possibly repay the debt. But God blotted out the list of debts and destroyed all the incriminating evidence against us when Christ was nailed on the cross in our place. Christ took away the burden of our guilt. Believers receive the verdict of his righteousness.
2:15 disarmed. In the crucifixion God paradoxically did to the powers what they did to Christ when they dragged him through Jerusalem, stripped him naked, treated him with contempt, and nailed the charges against him on the cross. God stripped the "powers and authorities" of their power and exposed their weakness. Christ's victory on the cross brings freedom from the tyranny of these alien forces. **triumphing over them by the cross.** Roman generals celebrated their victories by marching through the streets of Rome exhibiting the spoils of war and parading their captives. Paul's metaphor of the victory parade (2 Cor 2:14; Eph 4:8) imagines the cross as the chariot in which Christ rode as a triumphant general. Paul may envision Christ's vanquished foes trailing behind him in humiliating defeat.
2:16 eat ... drink ... religious festival ... celebration ... Sabbath day. The opponents impose food laws and the observance of sacred days as part of their criteria for judging the Colossians' spiritual merit. No one can invalidate their standing in Christ when they do not defer to these dictated stipulations that derive from "human tradition and the elemental spiritual forces of this world" (v. 8) rather than from Christ.
2:17 a shadow. Paul contrasts appearance and reality. NT writers viewed the OT and its laws as promises belonging to the old era that culminated with the coming of Christ (cf. Heb 10:1). Paul warns the Colossians not to retreat to this shadow-world when they have been made eligible "to share in the inheritance of [God's] holy people in the kingdom of light" (Col 1:12).
2:18 false humility ... puffed up. The opponents, as self-appointed religious referees, arrogantly declare the Colossians unfit because they fail to measure up on issues related to ascetic practices (v. 23), angel worship, and visions. **worship of angels.** Either they aspire to enter heaven to worship as the angels do, or they worship angels, entreating them to protect them from evil. **what they have seen.** They may engage in ascetic practices to help trigger visions, which they recount in detail to glorify themselves. They are obsessed with their own private religious rapture that serves only to inflate their egos.
2:19 lost connection. Disconnected from "the head" (Christ, v. 10; 1:18), the parts of the body cannot grow but will wither and die. Those who promote the false philosophy are not mature, as they boast, but are spiritually malnourished and perishing because they do not depend on Christ. Trying to ascend to heavenly realms through one's own efforts—through asceticism and visions—is hopeless. One has access to the divine realm only by being united with Christ, who ascended to heaven (Eph 4:8–10) and sits at God's right hand (Col 3:1; Rom 8:34; Eph 1:20).

2:19 [l]Eph 1:22 [m]Eph 4:16
2:20 [n]Gal 4:3,9 [o]ver 14,16
2:22 [p]1Co 6:13 [q]Isa 29:13; Mt 15:9; Titus 1:14
3:2 [r]Php 3:19,20
3:3 [s]Ro 6:2; 2Co 5:14
3:4 [t]1Co 1:7 [u]1Pe 1:13; 1Jn 3:2
3:5 [v]Eph 5:3 [w]Eph 5:5
3:6 [x]Ro 1:18
3:7 [y]Eph 2:2
3:8 [z]Eph 4:22 [a]Eph 4:31 [b]Eph 4:29
3:9 [c]Eph 4:22,25

the head,[l] from whom the whole body, supported and held together by its ligaments and sinews, grows
as God causes it to grow.[m]
20 Since you died with Christ to the elemental spiritual forces of this world,[n] why, as though you still
belonged to the world, do you submit to its rules:[o] 21 "Do not handle! Do not taste! Do not touch!"?
22 These rules, which have to do with things that are all destined to perish[p] with use, are based on merely
human commands and teachings.[q] 23 Such regulations indeed have an appearance of wisdom, with
their self-imposed worship, their false humility and their harsh treatment of the body, but they lack
any value in restraining sensual indulgence.

Living as Those Made Alive in Christ

3 Since, then, you have been raised with Christ, set your hearts on things above, where Christ is,
seated at the right hand of God. 2 Set your minds on things above, not on earthly things.[r] 3 For you
died,[s] and your life is now hidden with Christ in God. 4 When Christ, who is your[a] life, appears,[t] then
you also will appear with him in glory.[u]
5 Put to death, therefore, whatever belongs to your earthly nature: sexual immorality, impurity, lust,
evil desires and greed,[v] which is idolatry.[w] 6 Because of these, the wrath of God[x] is coming.[b] 7 You used to
walk in these ways, in the life you once lived.[y] 8 But now you must also rid yourselves[z] of all such things
as these: anger, rage, malice, slander,[a] and filthy language from your lips.[b] 9 Do not lie to each other,[c]
since you have taken off your old self with its practices 10 and have put on the new self, which is being

[a] 4 Some manuscripts *our* [b] 6 Some early manuscripts *coming on those who are disobedient*

2:20 The taboos of the philosophy depend on superstitions about "the elemental spiritual forces of this world" (v. 8; see note there) and on pointless human "rules" (v. 22). Since the Colossians have died with Christ, they have been set free from the bondage these things create. Christ alone must rule them, not delusions about how to satisfy God and placate evil forces.
2:21 Do not handle! Do not taste! Do not touch! Mocks the way the false teachers approach life. They have taken Jewish rules about purity to an exaggerated extreme. Paul echoes Jesus' teaching that what defiles a person comes from within (Mark 7:14–23).
2:22 human commands and teachings. Paul's teaching parallels Jesus' criticism of the Pharisees for focusing on human tradition and ignoring God's command (Mark 7:1–8). These rules concern the things of this world and are destined to pass away.
2:23 appearance of wisdom ... lack any value in restraining sensual indulgence. The false teaching poses as wisdom because of its strict moralizing, rigorous self-denial, and severe self-mortification. But it offers no cure for "sensual indulgence" since it does not get to the core of the problem: the sinful impulse that bedevils fallen humanity. The sinful nature can be transformed only by putting it to death in Christ.
3:1—4:6 *Ethical Admonitions.* Paul explains how being dead to the elemental spiritual forces of this world and being destined for glory pertains to Christian living. Believers are not called to escape the world but to obey God within it. The transcendent realm where Christ reigns is to set the priorities for their lives. Believers are called to obey because they have already been saved and created anew, and they are to exalt God's work in the world.
3:1–4 *Setting Your Hearts on Things Above.* This transitional paragraph reaffirms previous theological arguments and lays the foundation for the following ethical admonitions.
3:1–2 Paul develops the ethical implications of being "raised with Christ," which complements "since you died with Christ" (2:20). Being "raised with Christ" is the source of power for living the new life (Rom 6:1–14). God's irresistible power overcomes the irresistible compulsion to sin. Christ's exaltation "above" means that believers, who are joined to Christ, should set their hearts and minds "on things above."
3:3 you died. A reminder of what Paul said in 2:20; they died to the elemental spirits, so those forces have no power over them (cf. Rom 6:2; 7:5–6; Gal 2:19–20). **hidden with Christ.** A believer's true status remains concealed to others who do not have Christian insight. Believers already belong to the higher world where Christ reigns, and they do not need to resort to baseless observances to access that sphere or to seek safety from the powers of this world. **hidden.** May also refer to their security; they are hidden in a safe place (Pss 27:5; 31:20; Isa 49:2).
3:4 God is gradually transforming believers into the image of Christ now (2 Cor 4:16–18) and will fully transform them at the end (1 John 3:2; cf. Rom 8:29).
3:5–17 *The Old and the New Morality.* Paul explains the vices of the old morality that need to be abandoned (vv. 5–9), the new creation (vv. 10–11), the virtues of the new morality that need to be practiced (vv. 12–14), and the new worship (vv. 15–17).
3:5 therefore. Paul elaborates on the new way of thinking (vv. 1–4) with specific instructions. The imperatives correlate with the indicatives: you are, now be. It means that they are to unite with the transforming divine power working within them. One is either dead *in* sin (2:13) or dead *to* sin (Rom 6:11). The old nature is not renewed or reformed; it is "put to death." Believers are to eradicate any persisting marks of the old life: its values, customs, and practices. These are summarized as "idolatry," putting something else before God (e.g., sex, money, power) and wanting more and more of these things.
3:6 wrath of God. The consequences of God's "wrath" are already at work punishing sin (Rom 1:18–32). At the final judgment, God's holy wrath will rip off the disguise that made these sins so alluring and bar the persistently disobedient from God's kingdom (Eph 5:5–6). See "Wrath," p. 2681.
3:7 walk. A Hebraism that refers to moral behavior. The Colossians are to root out anger, control their language, and speak the truth (vv. 8–9).
3:9–10 taken off ... put on. The Colossians are to do more than simply reform their ways. Their whole nature has been exchanged—from an old self to a new self—and they are to live accordingly (Eph 4:20–25; cf. Gal 3:27). This renewing is an ongoing process (2 Cor 4:16). Those who are being renewed in "the image of [their] Creator" will produce Christlike conduct because that is the natural effect of their new nature.

renewed[d] in knowledge in the image of its Creator.[e] 11Here there is no Gentile or Jew,[f] circumcised or
uncircumcised,[g] barbarian, Scythian, slave or free,[h] but Christ is all,[i] and is in all.
12Therefore, as God's chosen people, holy and dearly loved, clothe yourselves with compassion, kindness, humility,[j] gentleness and patience.[k] 13Bear with each other[l] and forgive one another if any of you
has a grievance against someone. Forgive as the Lord forgave you.[m] 14And over all these virtues put on
love,[n] which binds them all together in perfect unity.[o]
15Let the peace of Christ[p] rule in your hearts, since as members of one body you were called to peace.
And be thankful. 16Let the message of Christ[q] dwell among you richly as you teach and admonish one
another with all wisdom[r] through psalms, hymns, and songs from the Spirit, singing to God with gratitude in your hearts.[s] 17And whatever you do,[t] whether in word or deed, do it all in the name of the Lord
Jesus, giving thanks[u] to God the Father through him.

3:10 [d]Ro 12:2; Eph 4:23 [e]Eph 2:10
3:11 [f]Ro 10:12 [g]1Co 7:19 [h]Gal 3:28 [i]Eph 1:23
3:12 [j]Php 2:3 [k]2Co 6:6; Gal 5:22,23
3:13 [l]Eph 4:2 [m]Eph 4:32
3:14 [n]1Co 13:1-13 [o]Eph 4:3
3:15 [p]Jn 14:27
3:16 [q]Ro 10:17 [r]Col 1:28 [s]Eph 5:19
3:17 [t]1Co 10:31 [u]Eph 5:20
3:18 [v]Eph 5:22

Instructions for Christian Households

3:18–4:1pp — Eph 5:22–6:9

18Wives, submit yourselves to your husbands,[v] as is fitting in the Lord.
19Husbands, love your wives and do not be harsh with them.
20Children, obey your parents in everything, for this pleases the Lord.
21Fathers,[a] do not embitter your children, or they will become discouraged.
22Slaves, obey your earthly masters in everything; and do it, not only when their eye is on you and
to curry their favor, but with sincerity of heart and reverence for the Lord. 23Whatever you do, work at

[a] *21* Or *Parents*

3:11 barbarian. One who did not speak Greek and was assumed to be uncivilized (Rom 1:14). **Scythian.** Perceived as savage and ruthless. **Christ is all, and is in all.** The gospel breaks down walls of race, tribe, nationality, and class. Regeneration through Christ creates a new humanity that is the church.

3:12–13 God's chosen people must reflect godly qualities in their lives. Paul outlines the new morality that is to replace their former life. The list is similar to the fruit of the Spirit (Gal 5:22–23).

3:12 humility. A Christlike attitude of putting the interests of others ahead of one's own (Phil 2:3–8).

3:13 Forgive as the Lord forgave you. Jesus emphasized that receiving forgiveness from God obliges one to forgive others (Matt 6:12,14; 18:21–35).

3:14 love. The all-inclusive commandment (Matt 5:43–48; Mark 12:28–33; Rom 13:8–10; 1 Cor 13:1–13) and foundation of the other virtues.

3:15 peace of Christ. It rules where the message of Christ dwells (v. 16); the church should display harmony and thankfulness as a result.

3:16 message of Christ. The reliable and profound teaching about Christ that is the heart of corporate worship. **teach and admonish.** Conveys the message about Christ with warnings about the hazards of drifting from its truth (1:28) through singing praise (Eph 5:19). **psalms.** May derive from Scripture (1 Cor 14:26). **hymns.** May be praise of God and Christ (Acts 16:25; Heb 2:12). **songs from the Spirit.** May be spur-of-the-moment compositions prompted by the Spirit (Rev 5:9; 14:3; 15:3). "Wisdom" and "gratitude" should characterize worship.

3:18—4:1 *Commands About the Household.* Life in the new age begins at home, where anger often surfaces and gratitude often evaporates. This section affirms that the family is one of the primary contexts for faith formation and for living out one's faith. Paul addresses three pairs in the household (wives and husbands, children and parents, and slaves and masters) and insists that the more powerful of the pair show concern for the less powerful. Husbands must treat wives with love, parents must treat children with understanding, and masters must treat slaves as human beings deserving justice. The motivation for the behavior is distinctively Christian. Christ's lordship (Paul mentions "the Lord" six times) imposes itself over all aspects of our lives and leads to gentle submission, love, service, obedience, and conscientious work.

3:18–19 Wives ... Husbands. The basic unit of the household.

3:18 submit yourselves. Christian wives are voluntarily to put themselves under the authority of their husbands by treating their submission as part of the service they owe to Christ. Cultural conventions must be examined through the prism of Christ to determine if they are "fitting" or unfitting for a Christian. Elsewhere, Paul assumes that Christian marriage entails deference to the needs of the spouse in different situations (1 Cor 7:2–5). All Christians are expected to engage in submissive service to God (Jas 4:7) and to others (1 Pet 4:10).

3:19 love. No other code on marriage relationships in the ancient world required husbands to love their wives. Love, exemplified by Christ's sacrificial love (Eph 5:25–27), is willing to pay the supreme cost and cherish the beloved even when the beloved is unworthy of that love (1 Cor 13:4–8a). **do not be harsh with them.** Balances the positive command to love. Harshness may be triggered in the husband by some perceived failure of his wife, but it does not cancel the husband's obligation to overcome resentment and love his wife.

3:20 parents. Paul addresses committed Christian parents and assumes they have the best interests of their children at heart and would not demand anything improper. Paul emphasizes that children are to please the Lord and not simply their parents.

3:21 Parents should inspire Christian values and faith in their children. Coercive dominance on the one hand or a complete lack of discipline on the other can destroy children. Children can become "discouraged" by being unnecessarily provoked, nagged, or belittled, or by being ignored and neglected.

3:22 Slaves ... masters. Paul's instruction contrasts with ancient contemporary parallels that advise masters only on how best to handle slaves. Slaves were regarded as equivalent to animate tools. To give them moral duties, as Paul does, treats them as human beings and affirms that being in Christ bestows on them a new status (v. 11).

3:23 as working for the Lord. The problems between the slave Onesimus and his master Philemon may have raised Paul's sensitivity to the things that slaves might do to arouse anger. Obeying as a slave is transformed into obeying Christ. Work becomes something done for a

3:24 [w]Ac 20:32
3:25 [x]Ac 10:34
4:2 [y]Lk 18:1
4:3 [z]Ac 14:27 [a]Eph 6:19,20
4:5 [b]Eph 5:15 [c]Mk 4:11 [d]Eph 5:16
4:6 [e]Eph 4:29 [f]Mk 9:50 [g]1Pe 3:15
4:7 [h]Ac 20:4 [i]Eph 6:21,22
4:8 [j]Eph 6:21,22
4:9 [k]Phm 10
4:10 [l]Ac 19:29 [m]Ac 4:36

it with all your heart, as working for the Lord, not for human masters, [24]since you know that you will
receive an inheritance[w] from the Lord as a reward. It is the Lord Christ you are serving. [25]Anyone who
does wrong will be repaid for their wrongs, and there is no favoritism.[x]

4 Masters, provide your slaves with what is right and fair, because you know that you also have a
Master in heaven.

Further Instructions

[2]Devote yourselves to prayer,[y] being watchful and thankful. [3]And pray for us, too, that God may open
a door[z] for our message, so that we may proclaim the mystery of Christ, for which I am in chains.[a]
[4]Pray that I may proclaim it clearly, as I should. [5]Be wise[b] in the way you act toward outsiders;[c] make
the most of every opportunity.[d] [6]Let your conversation be always full of grace,[e] seasoned with salt,[f] so
that you may know how to answer everyone.[g]

Final Greetings

[7]Tychicus[h] will tell you all the news about me. He is a dear brother, a faithful minister and fellow
servant[a][i] in the Lord. [8]I am sending him to you for the express purpose that you may know about our[b]
circumstances and that he may encourage your hearts.[j] [9]He is coming with Onesimus,[k] our faithful and
dear brother, who is one of you. They will tell you everything that is happening here.
[10]My fellow prisoner Aristarchus[l] sends you his greetings, as does Mark, the cousin of Barnabas.[m]
(You have received instructions about him; if he comes to you, welcome him.) [11]Jesus, who is called

[a] *7* Or *slave*; also in verse 12 [b] *8* Some manuscripts *that he may know about your*

greater Master. Nothing justifies Christians returning evil for evil or even halfhearted service for evil. Dependability and service should characterize all Christians (Mark 10:44; Luke 17:7–10). They should serve Christ and serve others as Christ did, who himself took the form of a servent (Mark 10:45; Phil 2:7).

3:24 you will receive an inheritance. Slaves could not inherit according to the ancient world's laws, but the Lord of the universe promises them an "inheritance." They have been bought with a price (1 Cor 6:20) and now belong to a new Master, who holds them dear.

3:25 Anyone. All Christians will be held responsible for their actions and cannot plead special circumstances to justify any misconduct. God will be the one who judges offenders, whether they are slaves or masters.

4:1 Paul places everything in a cosmic perspective. He reminds masters that they have "a Master in heaven" who owns them as well as their slaves. Most wealthy masters would have considered it odd to be told to treat a slave, who was regarded as a piece of property, fairly and with justice.

4:2–6 *Exhortation to Unflagging Prayer and Wise Behavior.* This concluding exhortation gives directions about being diligent in prayer and graciously proclaiming the gospel to others. Paul seeks an open door to spread the gospel and urges them to seize opportunities to defend the gospel effectively.

4:2 Devote yourselves to prayer. Recalls the description of the first disciples after the resurrection (Acts 1:14; 2:42; 6:4). **watchful.** Praying with resolute persistence (Rom 12:12; 1 Thess 5:17), not being caught off guard by a time of trial (Mark 14:38).

4:3 pray for us, too. Paul does not ask them to pray for anything that will bring any personal advantage to him. He asks not that he be released from his chains but that he and his co-workers have more opportunities to evangelize (2 Thess 3:1–2). **for which I am in chains.** He plans to keep on doing the same things that brought him to prison: proclaiming "the mystery of Christ," God's purpose to save humanity, Jew and Gentile, through Christ. God's power opens doors even when the proclaimer might be in chains.

4:5 Be wise. Paul is concerned that Christians, a minority in a hostile environment, engage others effectively in proclaiming the gospel. The most effective missionaries can be ordinary Christians who demonstrate Christ's teaching in their lives as they intermingle with others. **make the most of every opportunity.** The time is short, and Christians should not squander opportunities to evangelize others.

4:6 full of grace. Either divine grace or pleasant graciousness that should be the mark of casual conversation with others. Christians should not needlessly antagonize outsiders (cf. 1 Pet 3:15–16). **seasoned with salt.** May be a metaphor for wisdom in answering challenges, or may refer to winsome speech that is not insipid or boring but appealing to others.

4:7–18 *Final Greetings.* The final section introduces the bearers of the letter, Tychicus and Onesimus (vv. 7–9), shares greetings from the associates with Paul (vv. 10–14), greets other Christians in the area (vv. 15–17), and closes with Paul's final blessing written in his own handwriting (v. 18).

4:7–9 Maintaining the network of partnerships with churches in different areas required a lot of costly and dangerous coming and going. The letter serves as a substitute for Paul's presence, but these messengers do more than transport a letter and impart news. They represent Paul to the community and extend his ministry to them in person. The news about Paul is not vital to knowing the mystery of Christ, and Paul does not give details about his situation.

4:7 Tychicus. A native of Asia (Acts 20:4) and probably one of the companions who traveled with Paul to Jerusalem with the collection.

4:9 Onesimus. Paul identifies him simply as a Christian (a "faithful and dear brother"), not as Philemon's slave (Phlm 16), which hints at how being in Christ transforms one's status.

4:10 Paul's co-workers offer him assistance and hearten his spirits during the dark days of his confinement as he awaits the final decision about his case. **Aristarchus.** A Macedonian from Thessalonica who traveled with Paul to Jerusalem and then to Rome (Acts 19:29; 20:4; 27:2; Phlm 24). **Mark.** Presumably John, also called Mark (Acts 12:12,25; 13:5,13; 15:36–41; see 2 Tim 4:11; Phlm 24; 1 Pet 5:13), whose stature is bolstered when identified as "the cousin of Barnabas" (Acts 11:25–26; 14:3,14; 15:12; Gal 2:9).

4:11 Jesus, who is called Justus. Jews with Semitic names favored a second Greek or Latin name. **Jews.** Translates the phrase "of the circumcision" (see NIV text note). These Jewish believers willingly forfeited

Justus, also sends greetings. These are the only Jews[a] among my co-workers for the kingdom of God,
and they have proved a comfort to me. 12 Epaphras,[n] who is one of you and a servant of Christ Jesus,
sends greetings. He is always wrestling in prayer for you,[o] that you may stand firm in all the will of God,
mature[p] and fully assured. 13 I vouch for him that he is working hard for you and for those at Laodicea[q]
and Hierapolis. 14 Our dear friend Luke,[r] the doctor, and Demas[s] send greetings. 15 Give my greetings to
the brothers and sisters at Laodicea, and to Nympha and the church in her house.[t]

16 After this letter has been read to you, see that it is also read[u] in the church of the Laodiceans and
that you in turn read the letter from Laodicea.

17 Tell Archippus:[v] "See to it that you complete the ministry you have received in the Lord."[w]

18 I, Paul, write this greeting in my own hand.[x] Remember[y] my chains. Grace be with you.[z]

4:12 [n] Col 1:7; Phm 23 [o] Ro 15:30 [p] 1Co 2:6
4:13 [q] Col 2:1
4:14 [r] 2Ti 4:11; Phm 24 [s] 2Ti 4:10
4:15 [t] Ro 16:5
4:16 [u] 2Th 3:14
4:17 [v] Phm 2 [w] 2Ti 4:5
4:18 [x] 1Co 16:21 [y] Heb 13:3 [z] 1Ti 6:21; 2Ti 4:22; Titus 3:15; Heb 13:25

[a] 11 Greek *only ones of the circumcision group*

their religious entitlements for the sake of the gospel. Neither Jew nor Greek, circumcised nor uncircumcised (3:11) have special status over others under God's grace.

4:12 wrestling. Greek *agōnizomai.* Paul uses this Greek word in 1:29 ("strenuously contend") to refer to the struggle of his missionary labor. See also 1 Cor 9:25 ("competes in the games"); 1 Tim 6:12 ("fight"); 2 Tim 4:7 ("fought"). A noun form of this Greek word in Luke 22:44 ("anguish") describes how Christ prayed in Gethsemane.

4:14 Luke. May have become a devoted co-worker after joining Paul in a professional capacity when Paul suffered the serious malady he mentions in Gal 4:13–14. The first "we" passage in Acts occurs about this time (Acts 16:10). **Demas.** Paul does not commend him, perhaps a hint of his future failure (2 Tim 4:10).

4:15 Nympha. Presumably a wealthy woman who opened her home and her resources for the church. **the church in her house.** Churches did not have separate buildings; they met at homes large enough to accommodate the group.

4:16 also read. Paul assumes that other churches will read his letter. **the letter from Laodicea.** May refer to Ephesians, which Paul wrote to churches in the surrounding area as a circular letter without greetings or advice tailored to a specific setting (see Introduction to Ephesians: Date, Place of Composition, and Destination"). If that is not the case, the "letter from Laodicea" was somehow lost to us.

4:17 Tell Archippus. It is likely that this is a positive encouragement to Archippus rather than a warning to him to complete a ministry that Paul does not specify and we cannot know. Paul's charge to Timothy is similar (2 Tim 4:5). Paul addresses the charge to the community, which means they share responsibility in helping this minister fulfill his assignment.

4:18 in my own hand. Writing was a far more laborious process than it is now, and Paul customarily dictated his letters (Rom 16:22). **Remember my chains.** Paul is glad to suffer for Christ (1:24), but he depends on their prayer support (cf. Phil 1:19). The letter begins (Col 1:2) and ends with "grace."

INTRODUCTION TO

1 THESSALONIANS

CITY OF THESSALONICA

There are four unique features of the city of Thessalonica that are important for understanding Paul's letters to this place:

1. *A Strategic Location.* Thessalonica enjoys the best natural harbor in the Aegean Sea. The city was located at a juncture of the Via Egnatia (a major east-west Roman highway) and a road north to the Danube. These two geographic features caused Thessalonica to become the most populous (100,000 people) and important (provincial capital) city in Macedonia.

2. *A Favored Status.* As a reward for siding with the victorious Octavian in the Roman civil wars, Thessalonica was granted the designation "free city." This favored status resulted in more autonomy over local matters, the right to mint its own coins, tax concessions, and freedom from military occupation.

3. *A Unique Political Structure.* As a free city, Thessalonica was allowed to keep its traditional city institutions. The lowest level involved the "citizen assembly" ("crowd" in Acts 17:5), and the highest level involved the city council, made up of unique officers called "politarchs" ("city officials" in Acts 17:6,8).

4. *A Religiously Pluralistic Setting.* Archaeological and inscriptional evidence indicates the presence of various Greco-Roman deities, such as Dionysus, Asclepius, Aphrodite, Demeter, and Zeus. The Egyptian gods Isis and Serapis were also popular, as was the imperial cult with its worship of the Roman Empire. The city also housed a large Jewish synagogue consisting of "a large number of God-fearing Greeks and quite a few prominent women" (Acts 17:4). Most of the Thessalonian church had participated in these various cults before they "turned to God from idols" (1 Thess 1:9).

LETTER TO THESSALONICA

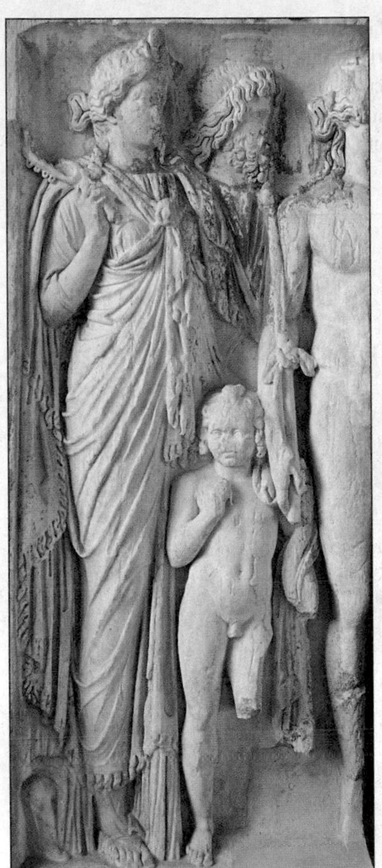

Second-century relief of a few Greco-Roman deities: Isis, Sarapis, Harpocrates, and Dionysos. Thessalonica had a religiously pluralistic setting.
Wikimedia Commons

PAUL AND THE THESSALONIAN CHURCH

Paul's two letters to the Thessalonians should be read in light of the various events connected with the apostle's ministry to these believers:

1. Paul, along with Silas and Timothy, departed from Philippi, traveled 90 miles (145 kilometers) along the Via Egnatia, and arrived four or five days later in Thessalonica (2:1 – 2; Acts 17:1).

2. Paul preached for three Sabbaths in the synagogue; converts included some Jews and even more Gentiles, including women from leading families (Acts 17:2 – 4).

3. During the week, Paul supported himself by working as a tentmaker (Acts 18:3), thereby not only providing the new Christians with an example of self-sufficient work (1 Thess 2:9; 2 Thess 3:7 – 10) but avoiding potential charges that his ministry was selfishly motivated (1 Thess 2:1 – 12).

4. Paul's missionary success aroused opposition. The Jews acted first (they "drove us out," 2:15) and with the help of "bad characters from the marketplace" started a city riot against the apostle, accusing him of disturbing the peace and violating Caesar's decrees (Acts 17:5 – 8).

5. Paul, Silas, and Timothy left Thessalonica to protect the believers and traveled west for two days to Berea (Acts 17:10). But Jews from Thessalonica followed the apostle to Berea and forced him to leave town. Some believers escorted Paul to Athens, likely by sea.

6. Silas and Timothy joined Paul in Athens a short time later only to be sent back to Macedonia: Timothy to Thessalonica (3:1 – 5) and Silas possibly to Philippi. Paul tried but was prevented from revisiting Thessalonica (2:17 – 18).

7. Paul traveled from Athens to begin an 18-month ministry in Corinth, where Timothy and Silas rejoined him from Macedonia (Acts 18:5). Timothy gave Paul a largely positive report about the Thessalonian church (1 Thess 3:6 – 10) but shared four concerns (see Introdution: Purposes) that caused the apostle to write 1 Thessalonians from Corinth in AD 50 – 51.

8. A short time later Paul received an alarming report from Thessalonica concerning a false claim that "the day of the Lord has already come" (2 Thess 2:2) and informing him that the problem of idle believers had become worse (2 Thess 3:6 – 15). To respond to these two problems, Paul wrote 2 Thessalonians.

AUTHOR, DATE, AND PLACE OF WRITING

Although Silas and Timothy are listed as co-senders, Paul is the letter's primary author (note the use of the singular "I" in 2:18; 3:5; 5:27). Pauline authorship is supported by both internal and external evidence: the letter exhibits features typical of the apostle's writing style, and the early church writers all affirm Paul as the author, with testimonies beginning as early as AD 140 (Marcion). The apostle wrote the letter in AD 50 – 51 during his 18-month ministry in Corinth. Support for this date comes from the Delphic Inscription, a letter from Emperor Claudius found in Delphi that dates Gallio's governorship of Achaia to AD 51 – 52 and thus places Paul in Corinth at the same time (see note on Acts 18:12 – 17). Except for the possibility of an early date for Galatians (AD 48), 1 Thessalonians is Paul's earliest canonical letter.

PURPOSES

After Paul sent Timothy back to Thessalonica (3:1 – 5), Timothy returned to the apostle with a largely positive report about the Thessalonian church (3:6). Yet Timothy also informed Paul about four concerns that caused the apostle to write 1 Thessalonians:

1. *Paul's Integrity.* Non-Christians in Thessalonica accused Paul of impure, selfish motives, causing the apostle in the first half of the letter to defend his ministry and that of his co-workers, Silas and Timothy (2:1—3:10).

2. *Persecution.* Paul encourages his readers who were being persecuted for their new faith (2:14; 3:1–5).

3. *Proper Moral Conduct.* Paul exhorts his readers to live a holy life (4:1–12; 5:12–22).

4. *Christ's Return.* Paul comforts his readers about the fate of both deceased (4:13–18) and living (5:1–11) believers at Christ's return.

OUTLINE

I. Opening (1:1)

II. Thanksgiving for the Thessalonians' Faith (1:2–10)

III. Defense of Past Ministry and Present Absence (2:1—3:10)

- A. Defense of Past Ministry in Thessalonica (2:1–16)
- B. Defense of Present Absence From Thessalonica (2:17—3:10)

IV. Transitional Prayers (3:11–13)

V. Exhortations to the Thessalonians (4:1—5:22)

- A. Pleasing God in Sexual Conduct and Love for Others (4:1–12)
- B. Comfort Concerning Deceased Christians at Christ's Return (4:13–18)
- C. Comfort Concerning Living Christians at Christ's Return (5:1–11)
- D. Exhortations on Congregational Life and Worship (5:12–22)

VI. Closing (5:23–28)

1 THESSALONIANS

1 Paul, Silas[a] and Timothy,[a]

To the church of the Thessalonians[b] in God the Father and the Lord Jesus Christ:

Grace and peace to you.[c]

1:1 [a]Ac 16:1; 2Th 1:1 [b]Ac 17:1 [c]Ro 1:7
1:2 [d]Ro 1:8
1:3 [e]2Th 1:11
1:5 [f]2Th 2:14

Thanksgiving for the Thessalonians' Faith

2We always thank God for all of you[d] and continually mention you in our prayers. 3We remember
before our God and Father your work produced by faith,[e] your labor prompted by love, and your endurance inspired by hope in our Lord Jesus Christ.
4For we know, brothers and sisters[b] loved by God, that he has chosen you, 5because our gospel[f]

[a] *1* Greek *Silvanus*, a variant of *Silas* [b] *4* The Greek word for *brothers and sisters* (*adelphoi*) refers here to believers, both men and women, as part of God's family; also in 2:1, 9, 14, 17; 3:7; 4:1, 10, 13; 5:1, 4, 12, 14, 25, 27.

1:1 *Opening.* Paul follows his typical pattern of beginning his letters with an opening that consists of three elements: sender, recipient, and greeting. He does not adapt this opening in any significant way as in some of his other letters (Rom 1:1–7; 1 Cor 1:1–3; Gal 1:1–5), reflecting the good relationship he enjoys with the Thessalonian church.
1:1 Silas. See note on Acts 15:22. **Timothy.** See Introduction to 1 Timothy: Recipient. Including Silas and Timothy as co-senders gives extra authority to Paul's letter since it shows the Thessalonians that the apostle is well-informed from the recently returned Timothy (3:6) about their situation and that all three leaders agree on the letter's contents. **church.** Used in the Septuagint (the pre-Christian Greek translation of the OT that was commonly used by the earliest Christians, including Paul) to refer to Israel as God's covenant people. By identifying his readers as "the church," Paul reflects his understanding of the predominantly Gentile church of Thessalonica as now belonging to the people of God. **in.** This begins the prepositional phrase that emphasizes the primary role of the divine: the existence of the Thessalonian church is ultimately due not to the work of the three missionaries but to the Father and Christ. **Grace and peace.** See notes on Gal 1:3; Phlm 3.
1:2–10 *Thanksgiving for the Thessalonians' Faith.* Paul typically includes a thanksgiving between the letter opening and the beginning of the letter body. The apostle uses the thanksgiving to (1) reestablish his relationship with his readers, (2) implicitly exhort them to live up to the praise that he brings to God for them, and (3) foreshadow key issues he addresses in the rest of the letter. Paul enjoys a warm relationship with the Thessalonian believers and is thankful for their exemplary life (vv. 6–7), evangelistic activity (v. 8), and conversion (v. 9)—events that originate ultimately from God's electing them (vv. 4–5).
1:3 We remember. The first or "immediate" reason for giving thanks (cf. note on v. 4) focuses on the activity of the Thessalonian believers: their faith, hope, and love. Paul frequently uses this triad (5:8; Rom 5:1–5; 1 Cor 13:13; Gal 5:5–6; Eph 4:2–5; Col 1:4–5), varying the order so that the emphasized virtue occurs in the climactic final position. **work produced by faith.** Faith naturally leads to action (2 Thess 1:11; Rom 1:5; 16:26; Gal 5:6; Eph 2:8–10; Jas 2:14–26). **labor prompted by love.** Christian deeds that stem from love. **endurance inspired by hope in our Lord Jesus Christ.** Not a feeble and general wish that things will turn out right in the end but a confident and specific belief that Christ will return from heaven to save believers from the coming judgment (v. 10). By emphasizing this end-time hope, Paul foreshadows his discussion of Christ's second coming in 4:13–18 and 5:1–11.
1:4 For we know. The second or "ultimate" reason for giving thanks (cf. note on v. 3) focuses on the activity of God: his election of the Thessalonians. **brothers and sisters.** In Paul's two brief letters to the Thessalonians, he addresses his readers with this phrase 21 times, thereby testifying to the warm relationship that the apostle shared with them. **loved by God.** Paul takes language originally applied to Israel (e.g., Deut 32:15 [in the Septuagint, the pre-Christian Greek translation of the OT]; 33:12; Pss 60:5; 108:6; Isa 44:2; Jer 11:15; 12:7) and reapplies it to the predominantly Gentile congregation of Thessalonica, reflecting his conviction that the church—made up of *both* Jewish and Gentile Christians—now constitutes the renewed Israel of God. **chosen.** Although this is its only occurrence in the letter, the rest of the correspondence evokes the theme of divine election with the language of God "calling" and "appointing" (2:12; 4:7; 5:9,24). Paul nowhere explains this language, which implies that the subject was an integral part of his mission-founding preaching in Thessalonica such that his readers well understand what he references. Paul's thanksgiving for the Thessalonians is ultimately grounded not in their human achievement but in God's divine work in their lives.
1:5 our gospel came to you. Paul defends the genuineness of his past preaching ministry in Thessalonica by contrasting his "words" with his "power" (1 Cor 2:1–5; 4:19–20), the latter term likely referring to

1:6 [g]1Co 4:16 [h]Ac 17:5-10 [i]Ac 13:52
1:8 [j]Ro 1:8; 10:18
1:9 [k]1Co 12:2; Gal 4:8
1:10 [l]Ac 2:24 [m]Ro 5:9
2:1 [n]1Th 1:5,9
2:2 [o]Ac 16:22; Php 1:30
2:3 [p]2Co 2:17
2:4 [q]Gal 2:7 [r]Gal 1:10
2:5 [s]Ac 20:33 [t]Ro 1:9

came to you not simply with words but also with power, with the Holy Spirit and deep conviction. You know how we lived among you for your sake. 6You became imitators of us[g] and of the Lord, for you welcomed the message in the midst of severe suffering[h] with the joy given by the Holy Spirit.[i] 7And so you became a model to all the believers in Macedonia and Achaia. 8The Lord's message rang out from you not only in Macedonia and Achaia—your faith in God has become known everywhere.[j] Therefore we do not need to say anything about it, 9for they themselves report what kind of reception you gave us. They tell how you turned to God from idols[k] to serve the living and true God, 10and to wait for his Son from heaven, whom he raised from the dead[l]—Jesus, who rescues us from the coming wrath.[m]

Paul's Ministry in Thessalonica

2 You know, brothers and sisters, that our visit to you[n] was not without results. 2We had previously suffered[o] and been treated outrageously in Philippi, as you know, but with the help of our God we dared to tell you his gospel in the face of strong opposition. 3For the appeal we make does not spring from error or impure motives,[p] nor are we trying to trick you. 4On the contrary, we speak as those approved by God to be entrusted with the gospel.[q] We are not trying to please people[r] but God, who tests our hearts. 5You know we never used flattery, nor did we put on a mask to cover up greed[s]—God is our witness.[t] 6We were not looking for praise from people, not from you or anyone else, even though

miracles (Acts 14:3; 15:12; Rom 15:18–19; 2 Cor 12:12). The apostle then qualifies this power with a reference both to "the Holy Spirit," the divine source of these miracles, and to "deep conviction," the consequence of this Spirit-given power, namely, the boldness with which Paul preached. **You know how we lived.** Paul further defends himself by appealing to his readers' firsthand knowledge of how sincerely he acted in their midst. This foreshadows Paul's defense of his integrity in 2:1—3:10.

1:6 imitators of us and of the Lord. The theme of imitation occurs frequently in Paul's letters, as he presents a variety of examples whom his readers should emulate: himself (here; 2 Thess 3:7,9; 1 Cor 4:16; 11:1; Phil 3:17), God (Eph 5:1), Christ (here; 1 Cor 11:1; Phil 2:5–11), Timothy (Phil 2:19–23), Epaphroditus (Phil 2:25–30), and the churches of Judea (2:14). The call to imitate Paul is rooted not in Paul's own authority but in his imitation of Christ, since his words in 1 Cor 11:1 ("Follow my example, as I follow the example of Christ") are a fuller expression of what we find here. **severe suffering.** See 2:14 and events recorded in Acts 17:5–14. Not physical persecution but social harassment, since there is no evidence that Christians anywhere during the 50s suffered from organized opposition or physical oppression. Many sources do indicate, however, the offense and even disgust that non-Christian neighbors felt when converts to Christianity refused to take part in common social and cultic activities.

1:7 Macedonia and Achaia. The northern and southern provinces into which Greece was then divided.

1:8 rang out. A rare verb from which the English word *echo* derives. Paul presents an image of an ongoing sound—either the evangelistic activity or, more likely, news of the readers' newfound faith—that emanates from Thessalonica and reverberates throughout the hills and valleys of Macedonia, Achaia, and beyond.

1:9 turned to God from idols. The majority of the Thessalonian believers were Gentiles who previously worshiped various pagan deities (see Introduction: City of Thessalonica). **living and true God.** Both terms are common descriptions of God in the OT (Exod 34:6 [in the Septuagint, the pre-Christian Greek translation of the OT]; Num 14:21,28; Deut 32:40; 2 Chr 15:3; Pss 42:2; 86:15 [in the Septuagint]; Isa 65:16) and are used here to contrast him with the dead and false gods that the Christians in Thessalonica formerly worshiped.

1:10 wait for his Son from heaven. Foreshadows 4:13–18. **raised from the dead.** Anticipates the argument of 4:14, where Christ's resurrection is Paul's first reason why the Thessalonians can have hope for their deceased fellow believers at Christ's return. **rescues us from the coming wrath.** Foreshadows 5:1–11, especially 5:9. God's wrath is a necessary and just response to human sin. Although this wrath is a current reality for those who live in sin (Rom 1:18,24,26,28), it awaits its future completion (1 Thess 5:9; Rom 5:9; Col 3:6), just as salvation is already present but will not be fully experienced until the last day (Rom 5:21; 6:22).

2:1—3:10 *Defense of Past Ministry and Present Absence.* Paul spends the opening half of the letter defending his past conduct and motives during his mission-founding visit (2:1–16) as well as his failure to return (2:17—3:10). He does this in the opening half of the letter to ensure that his readers will trust him and thus obey his exhortations in the closing half of the letter (4:1—5:22).

2:1–16 *Defense of Past Ministry in Thessalonica.* Paul's opponents come from *outside* the church: unbelieving citizens in Thessalonica ("your own people," v. 14) accused him of being insincere, interested only in winning praise and money from others. So Paul presents several arguments that defend his integrity and that of his co-workers, Silas and Timothy, during their past ministry in Thessalonica.

2:1 You know. The first of several appeals to the firsthand knowledge the Thessalonians have about Paul and his integrity (vv. 2,5,9–12). **our visit.** The key subject that vv. 1–16 address. Paul acted sincerely during his mission-founding visit in Thessalonica. **without results.** The Greek word *kenos* in this context is better translated "insincere." Paul is defending his honest motives during his past visit, not the successful results of that visit.

2:2 treated outrageously in Philippi. See Acts 16:19–39. **dared to tell.** Paul's willingness to preach despite experiencing "strong opposition" in both Philippi and Thessalonica is powerful proof of the genuineness of his motives.

2:3 error ... impure motives ... trick. Paul denies these three charges made against him by non-Christian citizens in Thessalonica. The word "trick" (Greek *dolos*) originally referred to catching fish by means of bait, so it developed the metaphoric meaning of deceit, cunning, or treachery.

2:4 Paul appeals to God, who "tests" (and so also approves) the genuineness of his speech.

2:5 This is the first of two appeals to God as "witness" (see also v. 10). God alone can attest to Paul's motives.

2:6 our authority. Apostles were entitled to be supported by the churches to whom they were ministering (2 Thess 3:9; 1 Cor 9:3–14; 2 Cor 11:7–11). Paul sometimes did not take advantage of this right in order to avoid charges that his ministry was selfishly motivated.

as apostles[u] of Christ we could have asserted our authority. 7 Instead, we were like young children[a]
among you.
Just as a nursing mother cares for her children,[v] 8 so we cared for you. Because we loved you so
much, we were delighted to share with you not only the gospel of God but our lives as well.[w] 9 Surely
you remember, brothers and sisters, our toil and hardship; we worked[x] night and day in order not to be
a burden to anyone[y] while we preached the gospel of God to you. 10 You are witnesses,[z] and so is God,
of how holy,[a] righteous and blameless we were among you who believed. 11 For you know that we dealt
with each of you as a father deals with his own children,[b] 12 encouraging, comforting and urging you
to live lives worthy[c] of God, who calls you into his kingdom and glory.
13 And we also thank God continually[d] because, when you received the word of God,[e] which you heard
from us, you accepted it not as a human word, but as it actually is, the word of God, which is indeed at
work in you who believe. 14 For you, brothers and sisters, became imitators of God's churches in Judea,[f]
which are in Christ Jesus: You suffered from your own people[g] the same things those churches suffered
from the Jews 15 who killed the Lord Jesus[h] and the prophets[i] and also drove us out. They displease God and
are hostile to everyone 16 in their effort to keep us from speaking to the Gentiles[j] so that they may be saved.
In this way they always heap up their sins to the limit.[k] The wrath of God has come upon them at last.[b]

2:6 [u] 1Co 9:1,2
2:7 [v] ver 11
2:8 [w] 2Co 12:15; 1Jn 3:16
2:9 [x] Ac 18:3 [y] 2Th 3:8
2:10 [z] 1Th 1:5 [a] 2Co 1:12
2:11 [b] ver 7; 1Co 4:14
2:12 [c] Eph 4:1
2:13 [d] 1Th 1:2 [e] Heb 4:12
2:14 [f] Gal 1:22 [g] Ac 17:5; 2Th 1:4
2:15 [h] Ac 2:23 [i] Mt 5:12
2:16 [j] Ac 13:45,50 [k] Mt 23:32
2:17 [l] 1Co 5:3; Col 2:5 [m] 1Th 3:10
2:18 [n] Mt 4:10 [o] Ro 1:13; 15:22

Paul's Longing to See the Thessalonians

17 But, brothers and sisters, when we were orphaned by being separated from you for a short time (in
person, not in thought),[l] out of our intense longing we made every effort to see you.[m] 18 For we wanted
to come to you—certainly I, Paul, did, again and again—but Satan[n] blocked our way.[o] 19 For what

[a] 7 Some manuscripts *were gentle* [b] 16 Or *them fully*

2:7 young children. The NIV follows the more ancient and reliable manuscripts that have the Greek word *nēpioi* ("infants, young children") rather than other manuscripts that have the similar sounding Greek word *ēpioi*, meaning "gentle" (see NIV text note). This is the first of three family metaphors that Paul uses along with "nursing mother" (v. 7b) and "father" (v. 11). This metaphor highlights Paul's integrity. Unlike the wandering philosopher-teachers of that day who were interested only in "looking for praise from people" (v. 6a) and who "used flattery" as a "mask to cover up greed" (v. 5), Paul and his fellow missionaries acted as innocently as infants. **nursing mother.** Instead of the common word for "mother," Paul uses the specialized term meaning "wet nurse"—someone who suckles children. This second family metaphor stresses Paul's sincere love for his readers: he acted among them as lovingly as a nursing mother.
2:9 we worked night and day. Paul, along with Silas and Timothy, worked with their "hands" (Acts 20:34; 1 Cor 4:12), probably as tentmakers (Acts 18:3). Such work not only effectively rebutted the charge that Paul preached only for money but also provided a positive example to some in the Thessalonian church who were lazy and refused to work (1 Thess 4:11b; 5:14; 2 Thess 3:6–15).
2:10 witnesses. Paul continues to defend himself in this passage, invoking yet again both his readers (vv. 1,2,5,11) and God (see v. 5) as witnesses of his integrity. **holy, righteous and blameless.** The significance of these three terms lies not in their distinctive meanings (they are virtually synonymous) but in their number, as they emphasize the irreproachable character of Paul's conduct "among you who believed."
2:11 father. Paul's third family metaphor emphasizes how he instructed his readers (see v. 7 and note). In the Greco-Roman world, the father was responsible to educate and train his children.
2:12 calls. Paul's letter evokes the theme of God's election throughout (1:4 and note; 3:3b; 4:7; 5:9,24).
2:13 not as a human word, but ... of God. Paul views himself and his co-workers as those through whom God is speaking an authoritative message.
2:14 Jews. Paul's harsh words in vv. 14–16 stem from his frustration with fellow Jews who have threatened the Gentile mission. He does not have in view all Jews but only those who in some way were involved in the itemized list of events.
2:15 drove us out. Agrees with Acts 17:5–10, which describes how local Jews instigated the riot against Paul that led to his forced departure from the city.
2:16 wrath of God has come upon them. It is difficult to determine with certainty to what this refers, though Paul's readers would have readily understood it. It may refer to one of the national disasters that the Jews suffered, such as famine in AD 46 (Acts 11:28), banishment from Rome in AD 49 (Acts 18:2), or the riot and resulting massacre of thousands in Jerusalem in AD 49. Less likely, "the wrath of God" could refer to a future event (1:10; 5:9) spoken of as already present either because it has already begun to be fulfilled or because it is so certain to happen.
2:17—3:10 *Defense of Present Absence From Thessalonica.* Non-Christians in the city used Paul's inability to return to Thessalonica to cast further doubt on the genuineness of his motives (2:14). So Paul is concerned about two things: first, he reassures the church of his continued love for them (2:17–20) and second, he ensures that their new faith remains strong despite persecution from their fellow citizens (3:1–5). He concludes by bringing these two concerns together in Timothy's good report about them (3:6–10).
2:17 orphaned. Paul continues his family metaphors (see vv. 7,11 and notes) by comparing himself to a child who has been orphaned from his parents—so deep were his feelings of anguish over being separated from his Thessalonian converts.
2:18 Satan. From the Hebrew meaning "accuser," it is the term Paul uses most often to refer to a personal, evil, spiritual being whose purposes are opposed to God and his people (2 Thess 2:9; Rom 16:20; 1 Cor 5:5; 7:5; 2 Cor 2:11; 11:14; 12:7; 1 Tim 1:20; 5:15). Paul elsewhere refers to this figure as "the tempter" (3:5), "the devil" (Eph 4:27; 6:11; 1 Tim 3:6–7; 2 Tim. 2:26), "Belial" (2 Cor 6:15), "the serpent" (2 Cor 11:3), and "the evil one" (2 Thess 3:3; Eph 6:16). **blocked.** The military practice of cutting up a road so that a pursuing army cannot pass it.
2:19 crown. Not a royal tiara but a laurel wreath given to victorious athletes. Such wreaths would soon deteriorate, unlike the imperishable

2:19 [p]Php 4:1 [q]2Co 1:14 [r]Mt 16:27; 1Th 3:13
2:20 [s]2Co 1:14
3:1 [t]ver 5 [u]Ac 17:15
3:3 [v]Ac 9:16; 14:22
3:4 [w]1Th 2:14
3:5 [x]ver 1 [y]Mt 4:3 [z]Gal 2:2; Php 2:16
3:6 [a]Ac 18:5 [b]1Th 1:3
3:8 [c]1Co 16:13
3:9 [d]1Th 1:2
3:10 [e]2Ti 1:3 [f]1Th 2:17
3:12 [g]1Th 4:9,10
3:13 [h]1Co 1:8 [i]1Th 2:19

is our hope, our joy, or the crown[p] in which we will glory[q] in the presence of our Lord Jesus when he
comes?[r] Is it not you? [20]Indeed, you are our glory[s] and joy.

3 So when we could stand it no longer,[t] we thought it best to be left by ourselves in Athens.[u] [2]We sent
Timothy, who is our brother and co-worker in God's service in spreading the gospel of Christ, to
strengthen and encourage you in your faith, [3]so that no one would be unsettled by these trials. For you
know quite well that we are destined for them.[v] [4]In fact, when we were with you, we kept telling you
that we would be persecuted. And it turned out that way, as you well know.[w] [5]For this reason, when I
could stand it no longer,[x] I sent to find out about your faith. I was afraid that in some way the tempter[y]
had tempted you and that our labors might have been in vain.[z]

Timothy's Encouraging Report

[6]But Timothy has just now come to us from you[a] and has brought good news about your faith and
love.[b] He has told us that you always have pleasant memories of us and that you long to see us, just
as we also long to see you. [7]Therefore, brothers and sisters, in all our distress and persecution we were
encouraged about you because of your faith. [8]For now we really live, since you are standing firm[c] in
the Lord. [9]How can we thank God enough for you[d] in return for all the joy we have in the presence
of our God because of you? [10]Night and day we pray[e] most earnestly that we may see you again[f] and
supply what is lacking in your faith.
[11]Now may our God and Father himself and our Lord Jesus clear the way for us to come to you. [12]May
the Lord make your love increase and overflow for each other[g] and for everyone else, just as ours does
for you. [13]May he strengthen your hearts so that you will be blameless[h] and holy in the presence of our
God and Father when our Lord Jesus comes[i] with all his holy ones.

crown given to believers (1 Cor 9:25; 1 Pet 5:4). **when he comes.** Paul joyfully anticipates presenting to Jesus at his second coming his victorious converts as proof that Paul has faithfully carried out his apostolic calling (Phil 4:1).

3:1 stand it no longer. An uncommon verb (also in v. 5) that refers to substances that do not allow themselves to be penetrated by water, air, light, fire, or anything else. Paul evokes an image in which he is so full of emotion for the Thessalonians that he can no longer stop his deep affection for them from leaking out. **left by ourselves in Athens.** Silas and Timothy rejoin Paul in Athens from Berea (Acts 17:15) but are sent back to Macedonia: Timothy to Thessalonica (vv. 1–5) and Silas perhaps to Philippi.

3:2 co-worker in God's service. A strikingly lofty title used to stress Timothy's credentials; although Paul could not return to Thessalonica personally, he sent Timothy, who is no mere junior apostle but a co-worker of Paul and even of God. **to strengthen ... you in your faith.** Paul sent Timothy back to Thessalonica specifically to strengthen their faith in the midst of opposition from their fellow citizens (cf. 2:14).

3:3 trials. The hostility aimed at the Thessalonian converts for their new faith (see also 2:2,14–15; 2 Thess 1:4–7; Acts 17:5–7,13; 2 Cor 8:1–2). **destined.** The Christian faith inevitably evokes opposition—a common conviction for Paul (Rom 5:3; 8:17; 2 Cor 4:7–12; 6:3–10; Phil 1:29; 2 Tim 3:12).

3:4 During his mission-founding visit, Paul repeatedly (the verb form expresses the idea of repetition: "we kept telling you") warned the Thessalonians that they would be persecuted for their faith, and his prophetic words came true. This prophecy-fulfillment argument ("I told you this would happen, and it did") reestablishes the credibility of Paul and his message.

3:5 stand it no longer. See note on v. 1. **tempter.** The evil spiritual being whom Paul identifies as "Satan" in 2:18 (see note there). Paul interprets historical events that prevent his return to Thessalonica and the afflictions that his readers endure from their fellow citizens as ultimately part of the spiritual battle between the kingdom of God and the kingdom of evil (cf. Eph 6:12).

3:6 come to us. Timothy rejoins Paul, who has moved on from Athens to Corinth (Acts 18:1–8), where he writes 1 Thessalonians. **brought good news.** Paul's verb choice (Greek *euangelizō*) is noteworthy, since elsewhere in his writings (20 occurrences) this word always refers to preaching the gospel. Paul was so thankful for Timothy's positive report about the Thessalonians that it was to the apostle like hearing the good news of the gospel. Paul mentions the two specific concerns at work in the first half of the letter (2:1—3:10): (1) **faith.** What Paul sent Timothy to "strengthen" (3:2) and "find out about" (3:5); afflictions from their fellow citizens are testing their ongoing faith in Christ. (2) **love.** Their ongoing love for Paul, despite the attacks against his integrity and his inability to return to them.

3:10 Although Timothy's report about the Thessalonians' faith and love was very positive, he also shared with Paul some areas of concern. So Paul prays that God will allow him to return to the church and "supply what is lacking." Since Satan prevents Paul from going back (2:18) and doing this in person, the apostle does it instead by means of a letter: the second half of this letter (4:1—5:22) takes up those matters where their faith is "lacking."

3:11–13 *Transitional Prayers.* Paul skillfully moves from the first half of the letter (2:1—3:10) to the second half (4:1—5:22) by means of two prayers. The first prayer (3:11) looks *backward* to Paul's defensive concern over his inability to return to the Thessalonians (2:17—3:10). The second prayer (vv. 12–13) looks *ahead* to three concerns that Paul is about to address: holiness in sexual conduct (4:3–8), love for others (4:9–12), and Christ's return (4:13—5:11).

3:11 God ... and our Lord Jesus. These two subjects occur with a singular verb, suggesting that Paul views these two as essentially a unit and so hints at the full deity of Jesus. **clear the way.** This request looks backward to the metaphor of 2:18 (see note). Paul prays that God and Jesus will remove the obstacles that Satan is using to block his path back to the Thessalonian church.

3:12 make your love increase and overflow. Foreshadows the discussion of love for others in 4:9–12.

3:13 so that you will be blameless and holy ... with all his holy ones. Foreshadows the discussion of holiness in sexual conduct in 4:3–8. **when our Lord Jesus comes.** Foreshadows the discussion of

Living to Please God

4 As for other matters, brothers and sisters,[j] we instructed you how to live in order to please God,[k] as
in fact you are living. Now we ask you and urge you in the Lord Jesus to do this more and more.
[2]For you know what instructions we gave you by the authority of the Lord Jesus.
[3]It is God's will that you should be sanctified: that you should avoid sexual immorality;[l] [4]that each of
you should learn to control your own body[a][m] in a way that is holy and honorable, [5]not in passionate lust[n]
like the pagans,[o] who do not know God; [6]and that in this matter no one should wrong or take advantage
of a brother or sister.[b][p] The Lord will punish all those who commit such sins,[q] as we told you and warned
you before. [7]For God did not call us to be impure, but to live a holy life.[r] [8]Therefore, anyone who rejects this
instruction does not reject a human being but God, the very God who gives you his Holy Spirit.[s]
[9]Now about your love for one another[t] we do not need to write to you,[u] for you yourselves have been
taught by God to love each other.[v] [10]And in fact, you do love all of God's family throughout Macedonia.[w]
Yet we urge you, brothers and sisters, to do so more and more,[x] [11]and to make it your ambition to lead
a quiet life: You should mind your own business and work with your hands,[y] just as we told you, [12]so
that your daily life may win the respect of outsiders[z] and so that you will not be dependent on anybody.

4:1 [j]2Co 13:11 [k]2Co 5:9
4:3 [l]1Co 6:18
4:4 [m]1Co 7:2,9
4:5 [n]Ro 1:26 [o]Eph 4:17
4:6 [p]1Co 6:8 [q]Heb 13:4
4:7 [r]Lev 11:44; 1Pe 1:15
4:8 [s]Ro 5:5; Gal 4:6
4:9 [t]Ro 12:10 [u]1Th 5:1 [v]Jn 13:34
4:10 [w]1Th 1:7 [x]1Th 3:12
4:11 [y]Eph 4:28; 2Th 3:10-12
4:12 [z]Mk 4:11

[a] *4* Or *learn to live with your own wife*; or *learn to acquire a wife* [b] *6* The Greek word for *brother or sister* (*adelphos*) refers here to a believer, whether man or woman, as part of God's family.

Christ's return in 4:13—5:11. **holy ones.** Either angels or, more likely, believers who have died and will return with Jesus (4:14).

4:1—5:22 *Exhortations to the Thessalonians.* In the first half of the letter (2:1—3:10) Paul has been defending his integrity and so reestablishing the confidence of his readers. This renewed trust in the apostle not only encourages the Thessalonians in the midst of their persecution but also ensures that they will obey the moral instructions he will now give them in the second half of the letter (4:1—5:22), in which Paul seeks to "supply what is lacking in your faith" (3:10; see note there).

4:1–12 *Pleasing God in Sexual Conduct and Love for Others.* After opening with a general appeal to increase conduct that is pleasing to God (4:1–2), Paul addresses the specific issues of holiness in sexual conduct (4:3–8) and love for others within the church community (4:9–12).

4:1 live. One of Paul's favorite words to describe the Christian life (32 occurrences). **please God.** The notion of pleasing God as the goal of human conduct stems from the OT (Num 23:27; 1 Kgs 14:13; Job 34:9; Pss 19:14; 69:31; Prov 15:26; 16:7; Mal 3:4) and is another of Paul's favorite terms for right behavior (1 Thess 2:4,15; Rom 8:8; 1 Cor 7:32–34; 2 Cor 5:9; Gal 1:10; Eph 6:6; Col 1:10; 3:22). **as in fact you are living ... do this more and more.** Although the Thessalonians have made progress in living a God-pleasing Christian life, Paul desires even further growth. **we ask you and urge you.** Paul resorts to "commanding" his readers only if the situation is serious and requires it (2 Thess 3:6). Normally, he employs softer, more user-friendly language of "asking" or "urging" (here; 4:10b; 5:12,14; 2 Thess 2:1; Rom 12:1–2; 15:30–32; 16:17; 1 Cor 1:10; 4:16; 16:15–16; 2 Cor 10:1–2; Phil 4:2 [twice]; Phlm 9–12 [twice]). Yet even then (as here) he speaks in an authoritative manner ("in the Lord Jesus") that indicates his appeal must be obeyed (see note on v. 2).

4:2 instructions. Something one must obey; this word was used for military commands or orders that civil magistrates issued.

4:3 sanctified. Can also be translated "holiness," a key word in vv. 3–8 that occurs in various forms four times (vv. 3,4,7,8). Holiness is an important OT concept that conveys the notion of "separation"—the need for God's covenant people to "come out" and be "distinct" from the surrounding peoples (Exod 19:5–6; Lev 20:23–26; Deut 26:18–19). Holiness, therefore, is the boundary marker that separates God's people from all other nations, whether in sexual conduct or any other area of life (see "Holiness," p. 2676). It is significant that Paul takes this standard of holiness, which had previously been the exclusive calling of Israel, and applies it to the predominantly Gentile church in Thessalonica. **sexual immorality.** The Greek term refers broadly to all kinds of sexual misconduct, including both premarital and extramarital sex, as well as homosexual activity. Paul forbids any sexual act that is done outside the bounds of heterosexual marriage (Eph 5:3).

4:4 body. The Greek *skeuos* can also be translated "vessel," as in a household dish, but has here a metaphoric meaning. The two main possibilities are that it refers figuratively to either a "wife" (see NIV text note) or one's own "body." A more narrow view of the second option is that Paul refers euphemistically to a particular part of one's body, namely, the sex organ. The apostle's main point in this verse is that believers need to develop self-control in regard to their sexual desires and conduct.

4:5 like the pagans. The Greco-Roman world's attitude toward sexual conduct was very tolerant in many sectors of society—an attitude that the majority of the Thessalonian believers, as former pagans, also had before their conversion (1:9).

4:6a wrong or take advantage. Sexual sin harms not only those who engage in it but also others: e.g., adultery harms a spouse, premarital sex harms a future spouse or fellow believers who are negatively impacted by knowledge of such sinful conduct.

4:6b–8 Paul gives three reasons why believers must live a holy life with regard to their sexual conduct, and each reason involves a different time period and person of the Trinity: (1) the future coming of the Lord Jesus Christ to "punish all those who commit such sins" (v. 6); (2) the past electing action of God, who "calls us ... to live a holy life" (v. 7); and (3) the present working of the Holy Spirit, whom "God gives" to empower believers to live a holy life (v. 8).

4:9 love for one another. Paul shifts the topic to brotherly and sisterly love (vv. 9–12). **taught by God.** Paul alludes to how Isaiah describes the Messianic age as a time when God will live so intimately among his people through his Spirit that they will no longer need human teachers but will be "taught by the LORD" (Isa 54:13; cf. Isa 2:3; Jer 31:33–34; Mic 4:1–3; John 6:45; 1 John 2:27). Paul once again (see notes on 1:1,4) takes "new covenant" language originally describing Israel and applies it to the predominantly Gentile church of Thessalonica.

4:11–12 work with your hands ... not be dependent on anybody. Some in the Thessalonian church were not working but were living off the generosity of fellow church members. Paul first warned against such idle conduct during his mission-founding visit. He next addresses the problem both here and in 5:14. The problem, however, becomes worse, and so he takes it up for the third time at much greater length in 2 Thess 3:6–15.

The remains of a first-century bath next door to a brothel in Thessalonica. Paul urges believers to live holy lives, not ones of passionate lust (1 Thess 4:5).

Todd Bolen/www.BiblePlaces.com

4:13 [a] Eph 2:12
4:14 [b] 1Co 15:18
4:15 [c] 1Co 15:52
4:16 [d] Mt 24:31 [e] 1Co 15:23; 2Th 2:1
4:17 [f] 1Co 15:52

Believers Who Have Died

13 Brothers and sisters, we do not want you to be uninformed about those who sleep in death, so that
you do not grieve like the rest of mankind, who have no hope.[a] 14 For we believe that Jesus died and
rose again, and so we believe that God will bring with Jesus those who have fallen asleep in him.[b] 15 According to the Lord's word, we tell you that we who are still alive, who are left until the coming of the
Lord, will certainly not precede those who have fallen asleep.[c] 16 For the Lord himself will come down
from heaven, with a loud command, with the voice of the archangel and with the trumpet call of God,[d]
and the dead in Christ will rise first.[e] 17 After that, we who are still alive and are left[f] will be caught up

4:13–18 *Comfort Concerning Deceased Christians at Christ's Return.* The Thessalonian church was grieving over fellow believers who died before Christ's return, fearing these deceased members would miss out or be disadvantaged at Jesus' second coming compared to believers who were still alive on that day. After introducing the problem (v. 13), Paul responds by appealing first to Jesus' resurrection (v. 14) and then to Jesus' words (vv. 15–17) before concluding with an encouraging exhortation (v. 18).

4:13 sleep. This euphemism for death is common in biblical texts and antiquity, so it does not support the notion of "soul sleep"—the idea that the soul exists in a nonconscious state of "sleeping" between death and resurrection. **no hope.** The ancient Greek poet Theocritus concisely captures the widespread sense of hopelessness in the Greco-Roman world concerning life after death: "Hopes are for the living; the dead have no hope" (*Idyll* 4.42).

4:14 Jesus died and rose again. The first reason that the Thessalonian church can have hope for their fellow believers who have died is grounded in Jesus' resurrection, which in Paul's theology guarantees that God will resurrect believers (Rom 8:11; 1 Cor 6:14; 15:12–23; 2 Cor 4:14; Col 1:18) so that they will be alive and participate fully in Christ's glorious return.

4:15 Lord's word. The second reason for hope is grounded in Jesus' words, which may refer to a saying of Jesus not recorded in the Gospels (John 21:25), a paraphrase of Jesus' end-time teaching (Matt 24; Mark 13), a general summary of Jesus' teaching, or a teaching revealed to Paul on the Damascus road or elsewhere. Paul is giving not merely his opinion but an authoritative teaching of the Lord Jesus himself. Jesus' words emphasize that living believers "will certainly not precede those who have fallen asleep." All believers—the deceased-but-now-resurrected ones (1 Thess 4:14,16) and the living-but-now-transformed ones (1 Cor 15:51–52)—will share equally in the glorious "coming of the Lord." Paul employs yet again (1 Thess 2:19; 3:13) a term (Greek *parousia*) commonly used to describe the coming of an emperor, general or other dignitary into a city with great pomp and celebration (see v. 17 and note).

4:16 with a loud command, with the voice of the archangel and with the trumpet call of God. These three phrases suggest that Christ's return will be a public event that is heard and witnessed by all people, not just believers. **dead in Christ will rise first.** Paul continues to comfort his readers, stressing that their deceased loved ones will rise first—even before the ascension of living believers (see v. 17 and note)—and thus not miss out on Christ's return.

4:17 caught up. The only explicit reference in the Bible to the "rapture" (from the Latin translation of the Greek verb used here). Paul envisions

together with them in the clouds[g] to meet the Lord in the air. And so we will be with the Lord[h] forever.
18Therefore encourage one another with these words.

The Day of the Lord

5 Now, brothers and sisters, about times and dates[i] we do not need to write to you,[j] 2for you know
very well that the day of the Lord[k] will come like a thief in the night.[l] 3While people are saying,
"Peace and safety," destruction will come on them suddenly, as labor pains on a pregnant woman, and
they will not escape.

4But you, brothers and sisters, are not in darkness[m] so that this day should surprise you like a thief.
5You are all children of the light and children of the day. We do not belong to the night or to the darkness. 6So then, let us not be like others, who are asleep,[n] but let us be awake and sober. 7For those who
sleep, sleep at night, and those who get drunk, get drunk at night.[o] 8But since we belong to the day, let
us be sober, putting on faith and love as a breastplate,[p] and the hope of salvation[q] as a helmet.[r] 9For
God did not appoint us to suffer wrath but to receive salvation through our Lord Jesus Christ.[s] 10He died
for us so that, whether we are awake or asleep, we may live together with him.[t] 11Therefore encourage
one another and build each other up, just as in fact you are doing.

4:17 [g]Ac 1:9; Rev 11:12 [h]Jn 12:26
5:1 [i]Ac 1:7 [j]1Th 4:9
5:2 [k]1Co 1:8 [l]2Pe 3:10
5:4 [m]Ac 26:18; 1Jn 2:8
5:6 [n]Ro 13:11
5:7 [o]Ac 2:15; 2Pe 2:13
5:8 [p]Eph 6:14 [q]Ro 8:24 [r]Eph 6:17
5:9 [s]2Th 2:13,14
5:10 [t]2Co 5:15

the church being "raptured," joined to Christ at his return. **together with them.** Paul's concern is not to predict but to pastor, as he stresses (the word order in Greek is emphatic) yet again that both living and deceased believers in Thessalonica will participate equally in Christ's glorious return. **meet.** Greek *apantēsis*; refers to a delegation party meeting an arriving dignitary outside of town to bestow honor on that visitor by escorting him back to their city. This practice of sending a delegation party to meet and escort an important visitor on the final leg of their journey is found in the only two other NT occurrences of this Greek term (Matt 25:6; Acts 28:15). Paul's word choice, therefore, implies that the church, once it has been "raptured" to Christ in the air, escorts him to earth.

4:18 encourage. Paul's primary purpose in discussing Christ's return in vv. 13–18 is not to predict the future but to comfort the grieving Thessalonian church (cf. 5:11; 2 Thess 2:16–17).

5:1–11 *Comfort Concerning Living Christians at Christ's Return.* Whereas 4:13–18 deal with the fate of *deceased* Christians at Christ's return, these verses deal with the fate of *living* Christians at the same end-time event. The Thessalonian Christians were apparently not merely curious about the timing of Christ's return but worried about their own fate on that day because Paul (1) twice reassures his readers of who they already are (vv. 5,8), (2) reminds them that "God did not appoint us to suffer wrath" (v. 9), and (3) exhorts them to "encourage one another and build each other up" (v. 11).

5:1–2 times and dates. A fixed expression referring to the timing of eschatological events (see Acts 1:7). **we do not need to write to you, for you know very well.** Paul taught the Thessalonian church repeatedly about these end-time events during his mission-founding visit (see note on 2 Thess 2:5). His readers thus know enough about these things that they need not fear "the day of the Lord" (v. 2). In the OT this expression refers to a future time when God will come to both punish the wicked and vindicate his people, though it more commonly stresses judgment (Jer 46:10; Ezek 30:2–3; Joel 1:15; 2:1,11,31; Amos 5:18–20; Obad 15; Zeph 1:14–18; Zech 14:1–21). Since both this judgment and deliverance will take place at Christ's return, the "day of the Lord" is another way of referring to Jesus' "coming" (Greek *parousia*; 1 Thess 2:19; 3:13; 4:15). **like a thief in the night.** This metaphor originates in Jesus' teaching (Matt 24:43; Luke 12:39), which other NT writers also use (2 Pet 3:10; Rev 3:3; 16:15). Paul uses this metaphor to emphasize both the unexpectedness of the day's arrival and its threatening character as a time of judgment for those unprepared. But the Thessalonians "know very well" about this (v. 2), so they are prepared for the day's coming and will experience not judgment but vindication.

5:3 Peace and safety. Paul is alluding not to OT warnings against false claims of peace (Jer 6:14; Ezek 13:10; Mic 3:5) but to Roman propaganda. Coins, monuments, official inscriptions, and writings vigorously promoted the ideas of "Roman peace" (*Pax Romana*) and to a lesser extent "safety." **destruction will come on them ... they will not escape.** Destruction refers not to annihilation but to being shut out from the presence and glory of the Lord (see note on 2 Thess 1:9). The negative "not" is emphatic: they will *certainly* not escape. A sober warning for all those who trust in the political power of Rome instead of God.

5:4–5 But you. Paul comforts his readers by stressing their unique status: they are "children of the light" (v. 5). A Hebrew idiom, to be "children of" a specific quality meant to be characterized by that quality. Christians do not merely live in the light but are characterized by the light. As such their status differs dramatically from those outside the Christian community who foolishly look to the Roman Empire for peace and security and who will be surprised by the judgment they receive at Christ's return.

5:6 So then, let us. Based on the readers' status (vv. 4–5), Paul sets forth commands for moral behavior. **be awake and sober.** Metaphors for living in a vigilant and sober-minded way in anticipation of Christ's return.

5:8 breastplate ... helmet. The imagery originates from Isa 59:17, which portrays God as a warrior wearing armor. Paul uses this military image to describe a variety of virtues with which Christians should arm themselves in their spiritual battle (cf. Rom 13:12; 2 Cor 6:7; Eph 6:10–17). The three virtues that he exhorts the Thessalonians to put on consist of the familiar triad of faith, love, and hope (see note on 1:3).

5:9 For. Links this verse to the preceding commands of vv. 6–8, providing the reason the Thessalonians should "be awake and sober" (v. 6) concerning the day of the Lord. **God did not appoint.** The ultimate destiny of the Thessalonian believers rests not in their own work but in God's. Paul assumes that his readers understand this theme of the divine initiative, which appears throughout the letter (v. 24; 1:4; 2:12; 3:3; 4:7), so he never explains it. He comforts his readers by claiming that God has "appointed," or chosen, them not "to suffer wrath but to receive salvation."

5:10 awake or asleep. Living or dead. Paul skillfully combines the concern of 5:1–11 (fate of living believers at Christ's return) with 4:13–18 (fate of deceased believers at Christ's return).

5:11 encourage. Paul's primary purpose here, as in his other discussions on the end times (see notes on 4:18; 2 Thess 2:1–17), is not to predict but to pastor.

5:12 [u] 1Ti 5:17; Heb 13:17
5:13 [v] Mk 9:50
5:14 [w] 2Th 3:6,7,11 [x] Ro 14:1
5:15 [y] 1Pe 3:9 [z] Gal 6:10; Eph 4:32
5:16 [a] Php 4:4
5:19 [b] Eph 4:30
5:20 [c] 1Co 14:1-40
5:21 [d] 1Co 14:29; 1Jn 4:1
5:23 [e] Ro 15:33
5:24 [f] 1Co 1:9
5:25 [g] Eph 6:19
5:26 [h] Ro 16:16
5:27 [i] Col 4:16
5:28 [j] Ro 16:20

Final Instructions

12Now we ask you, brothers and sisters, to acknowledge those who work hard among you, who care
for you in the Lord[u] and who admonish you. 13Hold them in the highest regard in love because of their
work. Live in peace with each other.[v] 14And we urge you, brothers and sisters, warn those who are idle[w]
and disruptive, encourage the disheartened, help the weak,[x] be patient with everyone. 15Make sure
that nobody pays back wrong for wrong,[y] but always strive to do what is good for each other[z] and for
everyone else.

16Rejoice always,[a] 17pray continually, 18give thanks in all circumstances; for this is God's will for
you in Christ Jesus.

19Do not quench the Spirit.[b] 20Do not treat prophecies[c] with contempt 21but test them all;[d] hold on
to what is good, 22reject every kind of evil.

23May God himself, the God of peace,[e] sanctify you through and through. May your whole spirit,
soul and body be kept blameless at the coming of our Lord Jesus Christ. 24The one who calls you is
faithful,[f] and he will do it.

25Brothers and sisters, pray for us.[g] 26Greet all God's people with a holy kiss.[h] 27I charge you before
the Lord to have this letter read to all the brothers and sisters.[i]

28The grace of our Lord Jesus Christ be with you.[j]

5:12–22 *Exhortations on Congregational Life and Worship.* Paul deals with four issues specifically connected to the church situation in Thessalonica: respecting congregational leaders (vv. 12–13); ministering to troubled congregational members (vv. 14–15); doing God's will in congregational worship (vv. 16–18); and testing prophecy (vv. 19–22).
5:12 we ask. See note on 4:1. **acknowledge.** Not merely recognize them as leaders but honor and respect them (v. 13). **those who work hard … who care for … who admonish.** Describes not three groups but one—congregational leaders, likely elders (Acts 14:23), who have at least three distinct functions. The verb used to describe the second function (Greek *proistēmi*) conveys both the notion of *authority* ("to rule") and *concern* ("to care for"). This linking of exercising authority and providing care is a characteristic feature of leadership in the NT: the one who leads is to be like the one who serves (Luke 22:26).
5:13 Live in peace. This command hints at some tension within the Thessalonian congregation (see note on v. 26), likely between the leaders and the "idle and disruptive" (v. 14).
5:14 you, brothers and sisters. Paul addresses the subsequent exhortations not just to the congregational leaders but to the whole church: *all* Christians must minister to troubled members. **idle and disruptive.** Translates one Greek word: *ataktos.* It has two meanings: the broad sense is "disorderly, insubordinate," and the narrow sense is "idle, lazy." Some in the church are refusing to work and are thus also disobeying Paul's teaching and example of self-sufficient employment (see 4:11; 2 Thess 3:6–15). **disheartened.** Perhaps those who were shaken by persecution (2:14; 3:1–5) or those grieving the fate of deceased believers at Christ's return (4:13–18). **weak.** Perhaps those excessively anxious about their own status on the day of the Lord (vv. 1–11).
5:15 nobody pays back wrong for wrong. The principle of non-retaliation (Rom 12:17). **each other … everyone else.** Christians must do good—not just to fellow believers ("each other") but also to nonbelievers ("everyone else"; see Gal 6:10).
5:16–18 Rejoice … pray … give thanks. These three commands are likely linked in Paul's mind to the working of the Holy Spirit: joy (1:6; Rom 14:17; Gal 5:22), prayer (Rom 8:26–27; 1 Cor 14:15; Eph 6:18; Phil 1:19), and thanksgiving (1 Cor 14:16). If so, they transition to his exhortations about the Spirit and Spirit-inspirited prophecy in the context of worship (vv. 19–22).
5:19–22 Paul structures the five commands into two parts: two negative commands warn against cynically rejecting Spirit-inspired prophecy (vv. 19–20), and three positive commands warn against gullibly accepting prophecy (vv. 21–22). Paul may be anticipating the problem that he later must address: an untested prophecy claiming that "the day of the Lord has come" (2 Thess 2:2). **test.** Paul does not here give criteria for testing prophecy, but elsewhere he provides the general standard that it should be for "the common good" (1 Cor 12:7) and should build up the church (1 Cor 14:3–5). Prophecy must also agree with apostolic teaching (2 Thess 2:2; 1 John 4:1–6) as it has been recorded in the Bible.
5:23–28 *Closing.* Paul skillfully adapts the epistolary conventions commonly found at the end of his letters so that this closing relates more directly to the major concerns taken up previously in the body of the letter.
5:23–24 May God himself. Instead of the simple formula "May the God of peace be with you" (cf. Rom 15:33; 2 Cor 13:11; Phil 4:9b), Paul greatly expands this peace benediction so that it echoes three major concerns addressed earlier in the letter: (1) The prayer for God to "sanctify you" and for the Thessalonians to be "kept blameless" (v. 23) recalls the concern about proper moral conduct in general and holiness in particular (4:1–12). (2) "The coming of our Lord Jesus Christ" (v. 23) echoes the concern about Christ's return (4:13—5:11). (3) The reassurance that "the one who calls you is faithful, and he will do it" (v. 24) recalls the language of calling and the divine initiative (v. 9; 1:4; 2:12; 3:3; 4:7)—language that comforts the Thessalonians in the midst of persecution. **your whole spirit, soul and body.** A rhetorical way to refer to the whole person (Matt 10:28; Mark 12:30; 1 Cor 7:34; cf. Heb 4:12); Paul is not asserting that humans have three parts.
5:26 holy kiss. The greeting kiss in the ancient world expressed not merely friendship but also reconciliation and unity (Gen 33:4; 45:15; 2 Sam 14:33; Luke 15:20). Paul's command, therefore, may have in view internal tension in the church (see note on v. 13) and challenges the Thessalonians to remove any hostility.
5:27 I charge. Paul typically dictates his letter to a secretary but closes the letter in his own hand (2 Thess 3:17; 1 Cor 16:21; Gal 6:11; Col 4:18; Phlm 19). He uses here a very strong verb that causes someone to swear an oath to do something. Paul's strident tone is likely aimed not at the overall congregation with whom he was quite pleased but at those in the church who are "idle and disruptive" (v. 14) and who proved to be an ongoing problem (2 Thess 3:6–15).
5:28 grace. The grace benediction here, along with the preceding peace benediction of v. 23, frames the letter closing (vv. 23–28) and balances in a chiastic, or inverted, fashion the opening greeting of "Grace and peace" in 1:1.

INTRODUCTION TO

2 THESSALONIANS

THESSALONICA: THE CITY AND THE CHURCH

See Introduction to 1 Thessalonians.

AUTHOR

The letter claims to be written by "Paul, Silas and Timothy," although the shift to the first-person singular (2:5; 3:17) makes it clear that Paul is the main author. Some have questioned whether Paul wrote 2 Thessalonians for at least four reasons: (1) Its tone is cold and authoritarian compared to 1 Thessalonians. (2) The eschatology of 2:1–17 differs from 1 Thess 5:1–11. (3) It sounds like a pseudonymous author wrote 2:2 and 3:17. (4) The lexical and literary similarities with 1 Thessalonians are too great to be authentically Pauline but stem from literary dependence by a different author.

An evaluation of these objections, however, shows that they are overstated and unconvincing. (1) Paul restricts his harsher language for unbelievers who are persecuting the church and believers who continue to live in idleness;

View looking northwest at the excavations of the forum/agora of Thessalonica.

www.HolyLandPhotos.org

THESSALONICA IN THE TIME OF PAUL

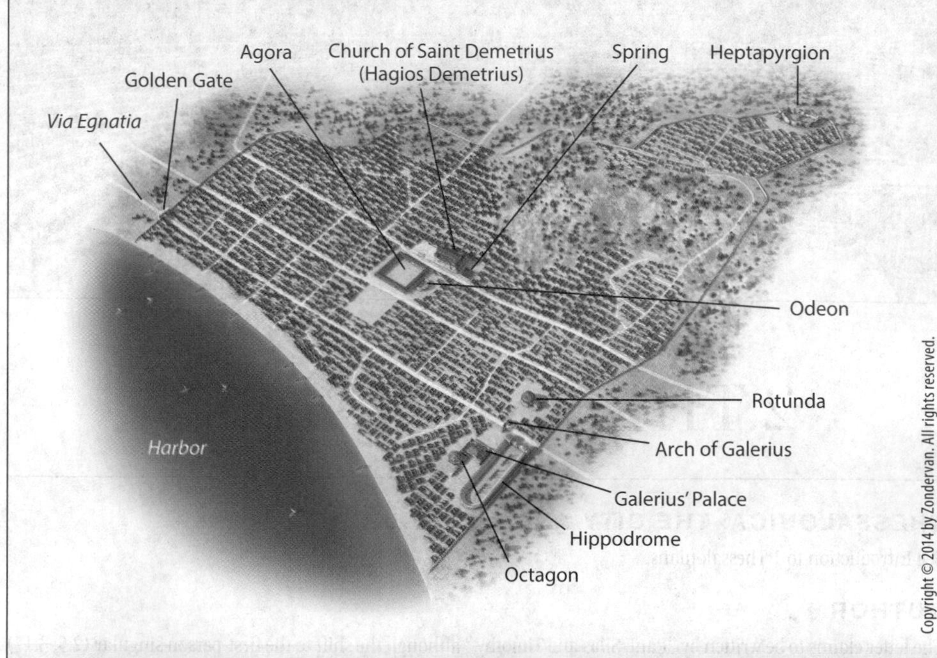

Thessalonica (modern Thessaloniki) was founded ca. 315 BC. It remained an important trade city and became the oldest community of Jews in Europe. When Paul and Silas came to Thessalonica they had to flee an angry Jewish group. He would remember how the church at Philippi aided him (Phil 4:16).

he affectionately addresses the majority of the church. (2) There are many similarities in how both letters describe the day of the Lord (e.g., that day involves surprise and judgment for unbelievers but anticipation and vindication for believers), and the differences involve not contradictions but clarifications that reflect the specific concern Paul addresses. (3) In 2:2 and 3:17, Paul naturally responds to the possibility of a forged letter circulating in his name. (4) The similarities in vocabulary and form between the two letters are great enough to conclude that the same author wrote both but not so great that we should view 2 Thessalonians as a Pauline forger's slavish imitation. There are no compelling reasons, therefore, to reject the universal judgment of the early church, which accepted that Paul wrote 2 Thessalonians.

SITUATION OF 2 THESSALONIANS

The close similarities to 1 Thessalonians suggest that Paul wrote this second letter shortly after the first: in AD 50 – 51 from Corinth. Paul received a report (3:11) that three issues raised in 1 Thessalonians continued to be a problem: (1) fellow citizens were persecuting the church (1 Thess 1:6; 2:14; 3:1 – 5); (2) a false claim about the day of the Lord frightened the readers about their status at that end-time event (1 Thess 5:1 – 11); and (3) the problem of idle church members became worse (1 Thess 4:11 – 12; 5:14).

PURPOSES

1. Commend the church for enduring persecution (1:3 – 12).
2. Comfort the church, which was frightened by a false claim about the day of the Lord (2:1 – 17).
3. Instruct the church how to deal with its idle members (3:1 – 15).

OUTLINE

I. Opening (1:1–2)

II. Thanksgiving and Prayer (1:3–12)
- A. Commendation for Spiritual Growth in the Face of Persecution (1:3–4)
- B. Comfort Concerning the Just Judgment of God (1:5–10)
- C. Challenge: Prayer for God to Work in the Thessalonians' Lives (1:11–12)

III. Comfort Concerning the Day of the Lord (2:1–17)
- A. Crisis: Fear Over Claim That "The Day of the Lord Has Already Come" (2:1–2)
- B. Correction: Events That Must Precede the Day of the Lord (2:3–12)
- C. Comfort: God Ensures the Salvation of the Thessalonians (2:13–14)
- D. Command: Stand Firm by Holding Fast to Paul's Teachings (2:15)
- E. Concluding Prayer: Prayer That God Will Comfort the Thessalonians (2:16–17)

IV. Exhortations Concerning Idle Church Members (3:1–15)
- A. General: The Lord's Work in Paul's Ministry and the Thessalonian Church (3:1–5)
- B. Specific: Discipline the Idlers (3:6–15)

V. Closing (3:16–18)

2 THESSALONIANS

1:1 [a]Ac 16:1; 1Th 1:1
1:2 [b]Ro 1:7
1:3 [c]1Th 3:12
1:4 [d]2Co 7:14 [e]1Th 1:3 [f]1Th 2:14
1:5 [g]Php 1:28
1:6 [h]Col 3:25; Rev 6:10

1 Paul, Silas[a] and Timothy,[a]

To the church of the Thessalonians in God our Father and the Lord Jesus Christ:

[2]Grace and peace to you from God the Father and the Lord Jesus Christ.[b]

Thanksgiving and Prayer

[3]We ought always to thank God for you, brothers and sisters,[b] and rightly so, because your faith is growing more and more, and the love all of you have for one another is increasing.[c] [4]Therefore, among God's
churches we boast[d] about your perseverance and faith[e] in all the persecutions and trials you are enduring.[f]
[5]All this is evidence[g] that God's judgment is right, and as a result you will be counted worthy of the
kingdom of God, for which you are suffering. [6]God is just: He will pay back trouble to those who trouble
you[h] [7]and give relief to you who are troubled, and to us as well. This will happen when the Lord Jesus is

[a] *1* Greek *Silvanus*, a variant of *Silas* [b] *3* The Greek word for *brothers and sisters* (*adelphoi*) refers here to believers, both men and women, as part of God's family; also in 2:1, 13, 15; 3:1, 6, 13.

1:1–2 *Opening.* This is very similar to the opening of 1 Thessalonians (see notes on 1 Thess 1:1).
1:1,2 in/from God our/the Father and the Lord Jesus Christ. In both phrases God and Jesus function as the double object of the single preposition "in"/"from." Paul, though steeped in Jewish monotheism, without comment connects Jesus so closely with God that he not only implies that Jesus is God but also takes for granted that his readers affirm it.
1:1 our Father. God has adopted the Thessalonians as his children (Rom 8:14–17; Gal 3:26; 4:4–7), so they constitute his family.
1:3–12 *Thanksgiving and Prayer.* Paul typically adds prior to the body of the letter a thanksgiving that serves three functions (see note on 1 Thess 1:2–10). These functions are at work throughout the thanksgiving of vv. 3–12, which falls structurally into three sections: commendation (vv. 3–4), comfort (vv. 5–10), and challenge (vv. 11–12).
1:3–4 *Commendation for Spiritual Growth in the Face of Persecution.* Paul commends the Thessalonians for their remarkable spiritual growth despite experiencing strong opposition.
1:3 ought. Paul does not view thanksgiving as an onerous obligation but rather acknowledges the need to thank God. Paul knows that it is God—not his own apostolic labor or the labor of the Thessalonians—who is responsible for the church's remarkable spiritual growth in the face of persecution. This God-centered theology parallels Paul's thanksgiving in the first letter, which is ultimately grounded in God's work of election (1 Thess 1:4). **faith.** In Christ. **love.** For each other. Paul was particularly concerned about their faith and love in his previous letter (see note on 1 Thess 3:6).
1:4 boast. The Thessalonians' spiritual growth despite being persecuted is so remarkable that Paul boasts about them to other Christians in Macedonia, Achaia, and elsewhere (1 Thess 1:8). **persecutions and trials.** See note on 1 Thess 1:6. Their suffering started at their conversion (1 Thess 1:6; 2:2; Acts 17:5–7), continued during Paul's absence and Timothy's later visit (1 Thess 3:1–5), and had not ceased when Paul wrote 2 Thessalonians.
1:5–10 *Comfort Concerning the Just Judgment of God.* Paul comforts the Thessalonians about God's just judgment, which will involve punishing those persecuting church members and rewarding those being persecuted.
1:5 evidence. Given in vv. 6–10. **God's judgment is right.** This is seen in how God will (1) punish the persecutors and (2) reward the persecuted. Paul first presents this double truth in brief (vv. 6–7a) and then repeats it in the same order at greater length: the punishment of the persecutors is described in vv. 7b–9 and the reward of the persecuted in v. 10.
1:6 He will pay back. The principle of divine retribution, the *lex talionis* ("an eye for an eye, a tooth for a tooth"), is often associated in the OT with the day of the Lord. This principle is not appropriate for human conduct (Matt 5:38–48; Rom 12:17–21), since a person may act vindictively. Such a danger, however, does not exist in divine conduct, since "God's judgment is right" (v. 5). Paul uses this principle to comfort his readers by pointing them to the future judgment when God will justly punish their persecutors and vindicate their faith.
1:7 Whereas the primary actor in vv. 5–7a is God and his just judgment, this shifts in vv. 7b–10 to the Lord Jesus, who carries out this just judgment. **revealed.** Stresses the revelatory aspect of Christ's return: that Jesus the Judge will come to carry out God's just judgment is currently hidden from those persecuting the Thessalonians, but the believers in Thessalonica know this truth. This enables them to endure persecution until Jesus "is revealed from heaven," when these hidden things will finally become manifest to all.

revealed from heaven in blazing fire with his powerful angels.[i] 8 He will punish those who do not know
God[j] and do not obey the gospel of our Lord Jesus.[k] 9 They will be punished with everlasting destruction[l]
and shut out from the presence of the Lord and from the glory of his might[m] 10 on the day[n] he comes to
be glorified[o] in his holy people and to be marveled at among all those who have believed. This includes
you, because you believed our testimony to you.[p]

11 With this in mind, we constantly pray for you, that our God may make you worthy[q] of his calling,
and that by his power he may bring to fruition your every desire for goodness and your every deed
prompted by faith.[r] 12 We pray this so that the name of our Lord Jesus may be glorified in you,[s] and you
in him, according to the grace of our God and the Lord Jesus Christ.[a]

1:7 [i] 1Th 4:16; Jude 14
1:8 [j] Gal 4:8 [k] Ro 2:8
1:9 [l] Php 3:19; 2Pe 3:7 [m] 2Th 2:8
1:10 [n] 1Co 3:13 [o] Jn 17:10 [p] 1Co 1:6
1:11 [q] ver 5 [r] 1Th 1:3
1:12 [s] Php 2:9-11
2:1 [t] Mk 13:27; 1Th 4:15-17
2:2 [u] 2Th 3:17 [v] 1Co 1:8
2:3 [w] Eph 5:6-8

The Man of Lawlessness

2 Concerning the coming of our Lord Jesus Christ and our being gathered to him,[t] we ask you,
brothers and sisters, 2 not to become easily unsettled or alarmed by the teaching allegedly from
us—whether by a prophecy or by word of mouth or by letter[u]—asserting that the day of the Lord[v] has
already come. 3 Don't let anyone deceive you[w] in any way, for that day will not come until the rebellion

[a] *12* Or *God and Lord, Jesus Christ*

1:8 This judgment will apply not just to those persecuting the Thessalonian Christians but more broadly to "those who do not know God and do not obey the gospel." This refers not to two distinct groups (e.g., Gentiles and Jews) but to one, since this involves a parallel description of those whom God will justly punish for failing both to acknowledge him and to respond with obedience to the gospel.
1:9 everlasting destruction. Paul has in view not the annihilation of unbelievers but their unending punishment. This is suggested by three factors: this is the teaching of Jesus (Matt 5:29–30; 12:32; 18:8–9; 25:41,46; Luke 16:23–25) with which Paul would have been familiar; the eternal punishment of the wicked was a common idea in the apostle's Jewish heritage; and the parallel phrases in this verse ("shut out from the presence of the Lord and from the glory of his might") presuppose the ongoing existence of the wicked rather than their annihilation.
1:10 glorified ... marveled at. OT allusions (Pss 89:7 and 68:35, respectively) in which Paul takes references to God and applies them to Jesus, reflecting his high view of Christ expressed throughout 1–2 Thessalonians. **in his holy people.** In contrast to the fate of unbelievers, who will be "shut out from the presence of the Lord" (v. 9), believers will experience Christ's glorification (see v. 12). **This includes you.** Paul's readers belong to those whom God will reward at Christ's coming; Paul thus reassures those who were unduly anxious about their own status on the day of the Lord (see note on 1 Thess 5:1–11).
1:11–12 *Challenge: Prayer for God to Work in the Thessalonians' Lives.* Paul challenges the Thessalonians to live up to the standard of conduct he spells out in his prayer for them.
1:11–12 we constantly pray ... We pray. Paul sometimes ends his thanksgiving with a prayer report (Rom 1:10; Phil 1:9–11; Col 1:9–14) summarizing what he prays for his readers. He comforts his persecuted readers by stressing God's initiative in their salvation: "Our God" is the one who will make them worthy of "his calling" and who "by his power" will complete their every good desire and deed. God will thus ensure that "the name of our Lord Jesus may be glorified in you, and you in him." The Thessalonian believers are again (see note on 2 Thess 1:10) comforted with the promise that their faith will be vindicated by being personally present in the end-time glorification of Christ ("in you"), and they will also themselves be glorified ("and you in him").
2:1–17 *Comfort Concerning the Day of the Lord.* The first major topic of the letter concerns a false claim about the day of the Lord that caused the Thessalonian church to become greatly alarmed. Paul's purpose is not to *predict* the future but to *pastor* his readers by giving them a word of comfort about this end-time event.
2:1–2 *Crisis: Fear Over the Claim That "The Day of the Lord Has Already Come."* Someone has falsely claimed that the day of the Lord has already come, thereby causing the young church to fear that they might not avoid the wrath of God connected with the day of judgment.
2:1 our being gathered to him. The immediate reference is to the comforting concept of how all believers, both deceased and living, will be gathered to Jesus at his return (1 Thess 4:16–17; 5:10). But this idea goes back to the OT hope in the gathering of the scattered exiles to their own land on the day of the Lord (e.g., Ps 106:47; Isa 11:10–12; 27:13; 43:4–7; Jer 31:8; Joel 3:1–2).
2:2 alarmed. Jesus issued the identical command (Mark 13:7). Paul is not merely satisfying his readers' curiosity about the end times but providing desperately needed pastoral comfort to a church frightened about the day of the Lord and unsure about their salvation on that day—a fear that also lies behind 1 Thess 5:1–11 (see notes there). **prophecy ... word of mouth ... letter.** Paul seemingly suspects that the source of the false claim about the day of the Lord was the first member of the triad: a prophecy (see second note on v. 15). **has already come.** Asserting that the day is actually present, not that it is imminent (as in the KJV: "is at hand"). The Thessalonians may have viewed the day of the Lord as consisting of several events of which Christ's coming was just one part. Although the claim is false, the Thessalonian church—already apprehensive about the day of the Lord (1 Thess 5:1–11)—became alarmed. Fear is often irrational and contagious.
2:3–12 *Correction: Events That Must Precede the Day of the Lord.* Paul corrects the false claim by reminding the Thessalonians that the day of the Lord will not take place until certain clearly defined events take place first.
2:3 Two events must precede the day of the Lord: (1) **the rebellion.** It is not Christians who rebel against God (Paul expects his readers to persevere in the faith to the end; see vv. 13–14; 1:3–4,10–12; 1 Thess 1:3,6; 2:14; 3:6–8; 5:4,9) but the rest of humanity. This rebellion will be primarily religious in nature, but any rebellion against God will naturally also involve a revolt against the general laws and morals of society. (2) **the man of lawlessness is revealed.** He is not Satan, as v. 9 makes clear, but is typically identified with the antichrist (1 John 2:18,22; 4:3; 2 John 7). This figure's description in vv. 3b–4 has striking similarities to OT texts (Isa 14:12–14; Ezek 28:2; Dan 6:7) and events from the Second Temple period (Antiochus IV desecrating the Jerusalem temple in 167 BC, Roman general Pompey entering the Jerusalem temple in 63 BC, and Roman emperor Caligula seeking to set up a statue of himself in the Jerusalem temple in AD 40). Paul employs a familiar theme to portray the supreme evil character of the coming lawless one.

2:3 [x]Da 7:25; 8:25; 11:36; Rev 13:5,6
2:4 [y]1Co 8:5 [z]Isa 14:13,14; Eze 28:2
2:8 [a]Isa 11:4; Rev 19:15
2:9 [b]Mt 24:24; Jn 4:48
2:10 [c]1Co 1:18
2:11 [d]Ro 1:28
2:12 [e]Ro 1:32
2:13 [f]Eph 1:4 [g]1Th 5:9 [h]1Pe 1:2
2:15 [i]1Co 16:13 [j]1Co 11:2

occurs and the man of lawlessness[a] is revealed,[x] the man doomed to
destruction. 4He will oppose and will exalt himself over everything
that is called God[y] or is worshiped, so that he sets himself up in
God's temple, proclaiming himself to be God.[z]
5Don't you remember that when I was with you I used to tell
you these things? 6And now you know what is holding him back,
so that he may be revealed at the proper time. 7For the secret power
of lawlessness is already at work; but the one who now holds it back
will continue to do so till he is taken out of the way. 8And then the lawless one will be revealed, whom the Lord Jesus will overthrow with the
breath of his mouth[a] and destroy by the splendor of his coming. 9The
coming of the lawless one will be in accordance with how Satan works.
He will use all sorts of displays of power through signs and wonders[b]
that serve the lie, 10and all the ways that wickedness deceives those
who are perishing.[c] They perish because they refused to love the truth
and so be saved. 11For this reason God sends them[d] a powerful delusion so that they will believe the lie
12and so that all will be condemned who have not believed the truth but have delighted in wickedness.[e]

Roman emperor Caligula, AD 37–41.
Kim Walton, taken at the National Archaeological Museum of Athens

Stand Firm

13But we ought always to thank God for you, brothers and sisters loved by the Lord, because God chose
you as firstfruits[b][f] to be saved[g] through the sanctifying work of the Spirit[h] and through belief in the truth.
14He called you to this through our gospel, that you might share in the glory of our Lord Jesus Christ.
15So then, brothers and sisters, stand firm[i] and hold fast to the teachings[c] we passed on to you,[j]
whether by word of mouth or by letter.

[a] *3* Some manuscripts *sin* [b] *13* Some manuscripts *because from the beginning God chose you* [c] *15* Or *traditions*

2:4 God's temple. Almost certainly the historic temple of Jerusalem (see Matt 24:15 and note), not the heavenly temple or the church. But Paul likely uses this sanctuary metaphorically by picking up the well-known theme of desecration by foreign kings. If so, this says more about the character of the man of lawlessness than where he will appear.
2:5 I used to tell. This verb highlights the repeated nature of the action: Paul delivered several sermons about events connected with the day of the Lord during his visit to Thessalonica.
2:6–7 what. Neuter (i.e., the *thing*). **secret power of lawlessness.** A rebellion against God and his will that is hidden and unobservable to unbelievers but revealed by God to believers and so readily known to them. **already at work.** Distinct from a future rebellion that will precede the day of the Lord (v. 3). **the one.** Masculine. This complicates the already difficult task of identifying the "restrainer." See "Who is the Restrainer?" p. 2453.
2:8 overthrow with the breath of his mouth. Paul interrupts the description of the lawless one to describe this evil figure's ultimate demise by Jesus, thereby comforting his readers. This imagery from Isa 11:4 emphasizes not the *ease* with which the returning Christ will "destroy" (the Greek conveys the stronger act of destruction rather than a mere overthrow) the man of lawlessness but the *power* of his breath as a potent and fearful weapon of war.
2:9 coming. Greek *parousia*, the same word used of Christ's coming. Satan enables the man of lawlessness to perform counterfeit signs and wonders (Matt 24:24).
2:10–12 Paul shifts from describing the lawless one to his deceived followers "who are perishing" (v. 10). This message of their judgment ultimately comforts the Thessalonian church since it vindicates their faith and demonstrates that God is just (1:5–10). **they refused to love the truth ... have not believed the truth.** The blame for their destructive end rests on themselves because they rejected the truth of the gospel message that Paul preached. **For this reason.** God's action does not cause people to reject the truth but is a consequence of their previous rejection. **God sends them.** Paul elsewhere similarly speaks of God giving sinners over to their own sin (Rom 1:24,26,28; 11:8; 2 Tim 4:4). The apostle's words here are difficult, yet his purpose is not to give a theological explanation of God's role in the judgment of sinners but to comfort the persecuted Christians in Thessalonica.
2:13–17 It is crucial to connect these verses with the preceding ones. If one reads only up to v. 12, the passage ends with judging unbelievers. But if one reads all the way to v. 17, the passage closes with comforting the Thessalonian believers.
2:13–14 *Comfort: God Ensures the Salvation of the Thessalonians.* Paul comforts the Thessalonians with a thanksgiving about God's election that guarantees they will not receive judgment on the day of the Lord but salvation.
2:13 ought. See note on 1:3. **loved by the Lord ... God chose ... sanctifying work of the Spirit.** All three persons of the Trinity are involved: the Son loves, the Father elects, and the Spirit makes holy. **firstfruits.** In the OT, this refers to the first produce or animal that one offers to God. God chose the Thessalonian church as the first (of many others whom God has also chosen) fruit at the great end-time harvest. **saved ... through belief in the truth.** Contrast the unbelievers who "refused to love the truth and so be saved" (v. 10).
2:14 called. The theme of election or God's initiative in the readers' salvation is important in both letters (v. 13; 1 Thess 1:4; 2:12; 3:3b; 4:7; 5:9,24). **glory.** The ultimate goal of God's redemptive work in believers' lives is not their justification but their glorification (Rom 8:30).
2:15 *Command: Stand Firm by Holding Fast to Paul's Teachings.* Paul corrects the crisis that has arisen from a *new* assertion about the day of the Lord by commanding the Thessalonians to hold fast to those traditions which he *previously* taught them.
2:15 stand firm. A fitting antidote to the problem of being "unsettled" (v. 2). **hold fast to the teachings.** Clarifies how the Thessalonians are

16May our Lord Jesus Christ himself and God our Father, who loved us[k] and by his grace gave us
eternal encouragement and good hope, 17encourage[l] your hearts and strengthen[m] you in every good
deed and word.

Request for Prayer

3 As for other matters, brothers and sisters,[n] pray for us[o] that the message of the Lord[p] may spread
rapidly and be honored, just as it was with you. 2And pray that we may be delivered from wicked
and evil people,[q] for not everyone has faith. 3But the Lord is faithful,[r] and he will strengthen you and
protect you from the evil one.[s] 4We have confidence[t] in the Lord that you are doing and will continue to
do the things we command. 5May the Lord direct your hearts[u] into God's love and Christ's perseverance.

Warning Against Idleness

6In the name of the Lord Jesus Christ,[v] we command you, brothers and sisters, to keep away from[w]
every believer who is idle and disruptive[x] and does not live according to the teaching[a] you received

2:16 [k]Jn 3:16
2:17 [l]1Th 3:2 [m]2Th 3:3
3:1 [n]1Th 4:1 [o]1Th 5:25 [p]1Th 1:8
3:2 [q]Ro 15:31
3:3 [r]1Co 1:9 [s]Mt 5:37
3:4 [t]2Co 2:3
3:5 [u]1Ch 29:18
3:6 [v]1Co 5:4 [w]Ro 16:17 [x]ver 7,11

[a] 6 Or *tradition*

to stand firm: by holding fast to the teachings that Paul personally gave them, either orally ("by word of mouth") or in written form ("by letter"). Significant by its omission is the third possible means of transmission: "by a prophecy" (v. 2), which Paul likely considers to be the source of the false claim about the day of the Lord.

2:16–17 *Concluding Prayer: Prayer That God Will Comfort the Thessalonians.* Paul concludes with a prayer that emphasizes his intention throughout the passage to comfort the Thessalonians.

2:16–17 encouragement … encourage. Paul's prayer includes a double reference to encouragement, which reflects his overall goal to comfort the persecuted and frightened Thessalonian church.

3:1–15 *Exhortations Concerning Idle Church Members.* The second major topic of the letter concerns idle church members. Paul issues various exhortations: general ones (vv. 1–5), which are preparatory for the specific ones (vv. 6–15) that deal with idle believers.

3:1–5 *General: The Lord's Work in Paul's Ministry and the Thessalonian Church.* Paul's general exhortations, though covering disparate topics, are joined together by their common function of preparing the readers to obey the specific exhortations about disciplining believers who are living idly (vv. 6–15).

3:1 spread rapidly. Or "runs"; combined with "be honored," this suggests that Paul depicts the "message" (gospel) as a victorious runner in the athletic games who justly receives honor. **just as it was with you.** Paul commends his readers and so makes them predisposed to obey the specific exhortations of vv. 6–15.

3:2–3 A clever contrast: Paul prays to be rescued from "wicked and evil people" because "not everyone has faith," but he reassures his readers that "the Lord is faithful" and so will protect them "from the evil one." In this way Christ's faithfulness is sharply contrasted with people's lack of faith.

3:4 We have confidence. An expression frequently used in letters of Paul's day to persuade readers to comply with the writer's request and so live up to the confidence the writer has in them. Yet Paul's confidence is grounded not in the Thessalonians' native talents but in the Lord, who is "faithful" (v. 3). **you are doing and will continue to do.** Not a generic affirmation of the Thessalonians, but as in the previous letter (cf. 1 Thess 4:1,10; 5:11), an acknowledgment of a specific thing the church is doing well: working and not being guilty of idleness. This additional commendation (see note on 2 Thess 3:1) further induces the readers to obey the upcoming exhortations in vv. 6–15. **things we command.** Refers not *back* to the command to remember Paul in prayer (v. 1) but *ahead* to instructions about working and disciplining the idlers (vv. 6–15), where the key verb "command" occurs three more times (vv. 6,10 [NIV "rule"],12).

3:5 Elsewhere Paul similarly uses a prayer to close his discussion and transition to the following topic (2:16–17; 1 Thess 3:11–13; Rom 15:5–6,13). **God's love and Christ's perseverance.** If the Thessalonians remember how God loves them (cf. 2:16) and how Christ endured for them, they will readily obey the commands given to them by Paul.

3:6–15 *Specific: Discipline the Idlers.* Paul frames his specific exhortations with opening (v. 6) and closing commands (vv. 13–15) to avoid those who are idle. Between these framing commands he sandwiches

WHO IS THE RESTRAINER?

Many proposals attempt to solve the "riddle of the restrainer"—to identify the thing and person that Paul refers to in both impersonal (2 Thess 2:6) and personal (2 Thess 2:7) terms:

1. The Roman Empire and the Roman emperor
2. The principle of law and order and the political leaders in general
3. The proclamation of the gospel and Paul
4. The presence of the church and the Holy Spirit
5. The power of evil and Satan
6. The false prophecy and the false prophet
7. The activity and person of the archangel Michael

The last proposal, though not widely held, is strongly supported by allusions to Dan 10–12. Michael, the patron angel of God's people, is said to withstand (restrain?) the evil angels (Dan 10:13,20–21) and so protect God's people. Paul's reference to the restrainer being removed ("taken out of the way," 2 Thess 2:7) likely originates from Dan 12:1a, where Michael and his restraining force is removed, thereby ushering in a period of unparalleled distress for God's people (2 Thess 2:3–4,8a; Dan 12:1b) that is then followed by their vindication and their enemies' punishment (2 Thess 2:8b–14; Dan 12:1c–3).

3:6 [y] 1Co 11:2
3:7 [z] 1Co 4:16
3:8 [a] Ac 18:3; Eph 4:28
3:9 [b] 1Co 9:4-14 [c] ver 7
3:10 [d] 1Th 3:4 [e] 1Th 4:11
3:11 [f] ver 6,7; 1Ti 5:13
3:12 [g] 1Th 4:1 [h] 1Th 4:11; Eph 4:28
3:13 [i] Gal 6:9
3:14 [j] ver 6
3:15 [k] Gal 6:1; 1Th 5:14
3:16 [l] Ro 15:33 [m] Ru 2:4
3:17 [n] 1Co 16:21
3:18 [o] Ro 16:20

from us.[y] 7 For you yourselves know how you ought to follow our example.[z] We were not idle when
we were with you, 8 nor did we eat anyone's food without paying for it. On the contrary, we worked[a]
night and day, laboring and toiling so that we would not be a burden to any of you. 9 We did this, not
because we do not have the right to such help,[b] but in order to offer ourselves as a model for you to
imitate.[c] 10 For even when we were with you,[d] we gave you this rule: "The one who is unwilling to
work[e] shall not eat."

11 We hear that some among you are idle and disruptive. They are not busy; they are busybodies.[f]
12 Such people we command and urge in the Lord Jesus Christ[g] to settle down and earn the food they
eat.[h] 13 And as for you, brothers and sisters, never tire of doing what is good.[i]

14 Take special note of anyone who does not obey our instruction in this letter. Do not associate with
them,[j] in order that they may feel ashamed. 15 Yet do not regard them as an enemy, but warn them as
you would a fellow believer.[k]

Final Greetings

16 Now may the Lord of peace[l] himself give you peace at all times and in every way. The Lord be with
all of you.[m]

17 I, Paul, write this greeting in my own hand,[n] which is the distinguishing mark in all my letters.
This is how I write.

18 The grace of our Lord Jesus Christ be with you all.[o]

appeals to both his example (vv. 7–9) and his teaching (v. 10) and to the application of this double appeal to the specific situation in Thessalonica (vv. 11–12).

3:6 command. The problem of some believers living idly became worse, so Paul switches from the softer language of "urge" (1 Thess 5:14) to the stronger "command" (here and also in v. 12). **keep away.** This verb, along with "do not associate with" in v. 14, refers to social ostracism or excommunication: exclusion from corporate worship and the meal that was part of the Lord's Supper celebration (1 Cor 5:11; 11:17–34). Such exclusion would be devastating for the idle in Thessalonica, who lived in a communal culture in which honor and shame were powerful forces controlling social behavior. **idle and disruptive.** Translates one Greek word whose root (*atakt-*) occurs three times in this passage (vv. 6,7,11). See note on 1 Thess 5:14. Paul never states *why* some were living in idleness. One possibility is that the Thessalonians' excitement over the imminent return of Jesus caused them to abandon ordinary earthly activities as not worthwhile. Another possibility is that some were merely lazy and took advantage of the generosity of wealthier believers and then used their free time to meddle in the affairs of others (v. 11; 1 Thess 4:11).

3:7 For. Paul grounds his command to discipline by appealing firstly to his example of self-sufficient work (see note on v. 10).

3:8 eat ... food. A Hebraism (Gen 3:19; 2 Sam 9:7; Ps 41:9; Ezek 12:18–19; Amos 7:12) that refers to providing primarily food but also housing, clothes, or any daily need. **we worked night and day.** See note on 1 Thess 2:9.

3:9 not because we do not have the right. As an apostle, Paul had the right to demand that churches provide him with housing and food (1 Cor 9:3–7). But he refused this right as part of his missionary strategy: to provide an example of self-sufficient work for his converts to follow, to avoid becoming a financial burden (2 Thess 3:8; 1 Thess 2:9), and to rebut any charge that his ministry was selfishly motivated (1 Thess 2:1–12).

3:10 For. Paul grounds his command to discipline by appealing secondly to his teaching about self-sufficient work (see note on v. 7). **we gave you this rule.** Contextually, the Greek emphasizes the repetitive nature of Paul's teaching: "we were repeatedly commanding you." **unwilling to work.** Those who rebelliously refuse to work, not those who cannot work because of infirmity or unemployment.

3:11–12 Paul applies his example (vv. 7–9) and previous teaching (v. 10) about self-sufficient work directly to the idlers within the Thessalonian church.

3:11 busy ... busybodies. This translation nicely captures Paul's clever wordplay: instead of being "busy" (Greek *ergazomenous*) with their work, the idlers are "busybodies" (Greek *periergazomenous*), spending their free time meddling in others' affairs and so causing unrest (see also 1 Thess 4:11).

3:13–15 This second command to "not associate with" (v. 14) the idlers parallels the first command of v. 6, thereby framing the whole discussion of vv. 6–15.

3:13 never tire of doing what is good. The church, although disciplining believers who refuse to work, must diligently help believers who are genuinely in need (Gal 6:10; Eph 4:28; 1 Tim 5:3–8; Titus 3:14).

3:14 feel ashamed. The goal of discipline is not to punish but to restore: the offending believer will feel ashamed and then hopefully repent and be restored (see 1 Cor 5:5).

3:15 not ... as an enemy, but ... as ... a fellow believer. Discipline must be done in a loving manner (cf. Gal 6:1), never harshly.

3:16–18 *Closing.* Paul makes subtle changes to the epistolary conventions typically found in his letter closings so that this ending relates more directly to issues raised in the body of the letter.

3:16 peace ... peace. Looks back to Paul's exhortations concerning the rebellious idle members and the resulting internal tension.

3:17 in my own hand. Paul takes over from his secretary and writes the closing greeting himself—an "autograph" (see note on 1 Thess 5:27). **distinguishing mark.** Although the function of Paul's autograph may be to authenticate the letter as genuine (cf. 2:2), it more likely conveys his presence and authority, especially for the idlers whom he fears will not obey his exhortations (3:14a).

3:18 all. This addition to the grace benediction (elsewhere in Paul's letters only in 2 Cor 13:13; Eph 6:24; Titus 3:15) stems from the apostle's desire to include all members, including the idlers (see also 2 Thess 3:16b).

INTRODUCTION TO
1 TIMOTHY

AUTHOR

The first word of the letter follows the custom of the day by naming its author: "Paul" (1:1). Acts 16 tells of the beginning of his association with Timothy, whom Acts mentions elsewhere (Acts 17:14–15; 18:5; 19:22; 20:4). Paul names Timothy in all of his letters except Galatians, Ephesians, and Titus. The pair worked in close and fruitful connection for well over a decade, and 1 Timothy was likely written near the end of that era.

In the last two centuries some scholars have doubted Paul's authorship of 1 Timothy (along with 2 Timothy and Titus; see Introduction: Author of those letters). Some allege that the words and style of 1 Timothy are different from that of other known Pauline letters. They claim that 1 Timothy does not fit into the historical order of Paul's life, or they assert that the setting, which the author of 1 Timothy assumes and many of the letter's details, are fictitious.

Others question the factual basis and wisdom of this skepticism. How did the church for some 1,800 years fail to detect a so-called forgery? Available evidence suggests that early Christians rejected letters falsely claiming to be apostolic; their commonsense policy was an application of 2 Thess 2:2.

Any claim made in a biblical document can be doubted, including Paul's authorship of 1 Timothy. Yet plausible responses have been advanced to answer skeptical queries. Perhaps most important, the strong autobiographical tone (beginning with the first word) underlying much that is found in 1 Timothy justifies optimism that the apostle Paul was its author, whether directly or with the assistance of a scribe. The study notes on this letter's features and teachings assume that the letter originated with Paul.

RECIPIENT

As the opening words indicate (1:2), Paul writes to Timothy, a native of Lystra (in modern Turkey). Perhaps it was there that Paul led Timothy to Christian faith, as the apostle calls him his "true son in the faith" (1:2; see note there). Timothy was called "a disciple" and was admired by fellow believers when Paul called him to join him and Silas on his second missionary journey (Acts 16:1–2). Since Timothy's mother was Jewish (Acts 16:1; his father was not), it was both ethical and expedient to have him circumcised to avoid offending Jewish sensibilities while engaging in missionary work among them (Acts 16:3).

Timothy was party to the evangelization of Macedonia and Achaia (Acts 17:14–15; 18:5) and was present for much of Paul's Ephesian ministry (Acts 19:22). He was with Paul on travels between various sites of Paul's church-planting activity, accompanying him, e.g., from Ephesus north to Macedonia and then back southward to Asia Minor on Paul's return to Jerusalem with a monetary collection for the Judean churches (Acts 20:1–6). Timothy was with Paul in the Roman imprisonment from which Paul wrote the Prison Letters (Phil 1:1; Col 1:1; Phlm 1).

Timothy's association with Paul continued after the apostle's release (following Acts 28). At Paul's direction Timothy became a resident in Ephesus and served in a central church leadership role (1 Tim 1:3) that was similar to that of Titus (Titus 1:5). At the end of Paul's second Roman imprisonment, Paul asked Timothy to visit him (2 Tim 4:9,21).

Timothy himself experienced imprisonment and release (Heb 13:23). While Timothy was not an apostle in the sense that Paul and others were, the events he witnessed and the teaching he received from the apostolic generation mark him as a key leader and as a primary bridge between the apostolic and subsequent periods.

DATE, PLACE OF COMPOSITION, AND DESTINATION

There are no definite clues indicating when Paul wrote 1 Timothy, but little in this letter hinges on knowing the exact year it was written. Paul did not involve Timothy in his work until ca. AD 51, so 1 Timothy must have been written after that. A few have proposed that Paul wrote it shortly after he wrote 1 Corinthians. During this time Paul traveled into Macedonia (1 Cor 16:5; cf. 1 Tim 1:3). Others trace the letter to the time after Paul's first Roman imprisonment (ca. AD 60–62) and subsequent release. There is no reason why Paul could not have struck out for Macedonia then, too, and that time frame seems the most plausible. Paul writes regarding Timothy's pastoral oversight of churches in and around Ephesus (1 Tim 1:3).

Acts 19 portrays Ephesus as robustly venerating the occult and broadly opposing the gospel's progress. A few years later Paul foresaw trouble there arising in the form of treacherous leaders who would pervert the truth and subvert the churches by forming enclaves of disciples who would affirm aberrant teachings (Acts 20:29–30). 1 Timothy warns against just such tendencies and developments. It also urges Timothy to vigilance and to the grueling, exacting labor of ministry practiced by Paul himself (Acts 20:31,35).

CHALLENGES

Contemporary scholarship continues to scrutinize 1 Timothy's authorship, its historical and social setting, its overall teaching in conjunction (and sometimes in contrast) with 2 Timothy and Titus, its doctrines of Christ and salvation, its relation to known Pauline letters, and its implications for topics like ethics, ministry, and the doctrine of the church generally. Other perennial issues include Paul's teaching on women in ministry (2:9–15) and the opponents about whom Paul warns Timothy from start (1:3) to finish (6:20–21).

PURPOSE

This letter is not a formal treatise with a single explicit thesis. The tone and substance are both friendly and profoundly pastoral. We can infer that Paul writes to keep Timothy stable and confident in his current location, to exhort him to battle valiantly for gospel truth in keeping with his calling (1:18), to preserve decorum in public worship (ch. 2), and to select good pastors and deacons (3:1–13). In general, Paul aims to give Timothy counsel and tools that will promote godly conduct among members of "God's household" (3:15), the church. Paul also deals with more specific and local aims, like dealing with end-times circumstances (ch. 4) and caring properly for widows, the elderly, and slaves (5:1—6:2a).

LOCATION OF EPHESUS

GENRE

1 Timothy is undoubtedly a letter, as indicated by its opening and closing. It is written not to a group but to Timothy personally, whom Paul addresses by name three times (1:2,18; 6:20). In the Greek there are some 41 second-person singular verb forms and 14 second-person singular pronouns. Grammatically and rhetorically, this is a missive from one named individual to another. While the form is a conventional Hellenistic letter, an unusual and highly significant feature is the author's claim to be "an apostle of Christ Jesus by the command of God our Savior and of

Looking down Curetes street toward the Library of Celsus in Ephesus. Timothy had pastoral oversight of the churches in and around Ephesus (1 Tim 1:3).

Christ Jesus our hope" (1:1). For Christian readers, this lends a divine dimension and authority to the discourse that transcend any conventional genre.

Paul wrote with a particular situation in mind, but the letter is by no means limited in its implications to the person and situation Paul addressed. Paul customarily wrote while conscious of his apostolic status and the authority of his teaching for "all those everywhere who call on the name of our Lord Jesus Christ" (1 Cor 1:2; see 1 Cor 4:17; 7:17). Paul urges Timothy to affirm doctrines and practices that were universal among early Christian congregations. God's people have hallowed these same doctrines and practices in all generations since.

CANONICITY

The "canon" is the collection of writings found in the Bible. Early Christian writings like 1 and 2 Clement, Ignatius, and Polycarp quote from, allude to, or reverberate in 1 Timothy. Writers from later generations like Irenaeus, Athenagoras, Clement of Alexandria, Tertullian, and Eusebius clearly regarded 1 Timothy (along with 2 Timothy and Titus) as Pauline and, in that sense, canonical. Writers who seem to have ignored or looked askance at 1 Timothy (e.g., Tatian, Marcion) were not widely received and regarded in their day. In general, including 1 Timothy in modern Bibles reflects the most widespread ancient conviction that it is as much a Pauline production as his other 12 letters in the canon.

THEMES AND THEOLOGY

While statistics alone do not tell everything, the dozen most frequently repeated significant words in 1 Timothy (with their number of occurrences) are God (22), faith (19), Christ (15), Jesus (14), faithful (11), person (10), woman or wife (9), teaching (8), godliness (8), word (8), widow (8), and truth (6). Paul is preoccupied with God, Jesus the Christ, and their implications for confessing Christians with regard to their everyday lives and their relations with others. Paul also models a mentoring tie to Timothy, impressing on him the high standards required for church leaders (3:1–3). It is important to avoid needlessly contentious or combative behavior (1:4; 4:3,7; 6:4–5). However, at times conflict is unavoidable. Money should be used in godly ways (6:5–10,17–19). Fidelity to apostolic doctrine and the gospel is nonnegotiable (1:10b–11; 2:5–7; 4:6,11,16). Pastoral leadership, like all Christian expression and action, should be suffused with love (1:5; 4:12; 6:11).

OUTLINE

I. Paul's Greeting (1:1 – 2)

II. Rallying Timothy's Resolve (1:3 – 20)

A. Timothy Charged to Oppose False Teachers (1:3 – 11)
B. The Lord's Grace to Paul (1:12 – 17)
C. The Charge to Timothy Renewed (1:18 – 20)

III. Order in Church and Life (2:1 — 6:2a)

A. Instructions on Worship (2:1 – 15)
B. Qualifications for Overseers and Deacons (3:1 – 13)
C. Reasons for Paul's Instructions (3:14 — 4:16)
D. Widows, Elders, and Slaves (5:1 — 6:2a)

IV. Final Clarification and Exhortation (6:2b – 21)

A. False Teachers and the Love of Money (6:2b – 10)
B. Final Charge to Timothy (6:11 – 21)

1 TIMOTHY

1 Paul, an apostle of Christ Jesus by the command of God[a] our Savior and of Christ Jesus our hope,[b]

2 To Timothy[c] my true son[d] in the faith:

Grace, mercy and peace from God the Father and Christ Jesus our Lord.

1:1 [a]Titus 1:3 [b]Col 1:27
1:2 [c]Ac 16:1 [d]2Ti 1:2; Titus 1:4
1:3 [e]Ac 18:19 [f]Gal 1:6,7
1:4 [g]1Ti 4:7; Titus 1:14 [h]1Ti 6:4
1:5 [i]2Ti 2:22 [j]2Ti 1:5

Timothy Charged to Oppose False Teachers

3 As I urged you when I went into Macedonia, stay there in Ephesus[e] so that you may command certain people not to teach false doctrines[f] any longer 4 or to devote themselves to myths[g] and endless genealogies. Such things promote controversial speculations[h] rather than advancing God's work—which is
by faith. 5 The goal of this command is love, which comes from a pure heart[i] and a good conscience and
a sincere faith.[j] 6 Some have departed from these and have turned to meaningless talk. 7 They want to be
teachers of the law, but they do not know what they are talking about or what they so confidently affirm.

1:1–2 *Paul's Greeting.* Paul uses the standard letter form but stretches it to refer to God and Christ and to pronounce blessing on Timothy.
1:1 apostle. Paul did not volunteer to be an apostle; the Father and Son commanded it. **God our Savior.** Occurs five times in the OT and six times in the NT, mainly in the Pastoral Letters (2:3; Titus 1:3; 2:10; 3:4; Jude 25). In both the OT and NT, God is a protector and rescuer. For Christ as Savior, see 2 Tim 1:10 and note. Paul represents not only primarily himself in what he writes but also Christ Jesus. **our hope.** Jesus Christ (Col 1:27; Titus 2:13; Heb 6:18–19; 1 John 3:3). **hope.** Not vague optimism but assured expectation of what God will do. Challenging ministry settings and Christian living generally call for such "hope" (cf. 1 Tim 4:10; 5:5; 6:17), one of three great aspects of the saving knowledge of God (cf. 1 Cor 13:13).
1:2 true son in the faith. Paul calls Timothy his "son" because of Paul's role in Timothy's entrance into and progress in "the faith" (Acts 16:1–3). Timothy is "true" in the sense that his confession over the years has proven steadfast; Paul can trust him fully. **Grace, mercy and peace.** "Grace" and "peace" are part of Paul's greetings in all his letters; here and in 2 Timothy 1:2 he adds "mercy" (cf. 2 John 3; Jude 2). Certain circumstances may call for an explicit sense that God is present and bestowing his favor.
1:3–20 *Rallying Timothy's Resolve.* Timothy faces daunting challenges, like pastors in all places and times. Paul deftly combines exhortation, encouragement, instruction, and testimony to stabilize his young friend and give him confidence.
1:3–11 *Timothy Charged to Oppose False Teachers.* These verses (1) describe the challenges Timothy faces and (2) contain the response Paul counsels.
1:3 As I urged you. This letter follows up on earlier counsel; it is not a new subject between Paul and Timothy. **Macedonia.** Where churches like those in Philippi, Thessalonica, and Berea were located. Paul may have wished to visit them or to plant new churches elsewhere in that region. **Ephesus.** The leading city of the Roman province of Asia (now western Turkey). Timothy may have seen reason to depart, but Paul urges him to stay to offset false teachers and their "false doctrines."
1:4 myths. Traditional stories, often legendary; they were prominent in pagan religion. **endless genealogies.** Lists of ancestors. They played an important role among Jewish sects. Either myths, genealogies, or both could have been factors here. Undue attention to them resulted in preoccupation with "controversial speculations." But churches should be "advancing God's work," not quarreling and dreaming. **work.** Refers to God's plan of salvation as it unfolds in human history according to his plan and aims (cf. 1 Cor 9:17; Eph 1:10; 3:2,9; Col 1:25). It resembles what Jesus meant by "kingdom of God" (e.g., Matt 12:28). Becoming part of God's work occurs "by faith," a familiar Pauline theme.
1:5 Paul writes with a particular goal for Timothy and the churches. **command.** The Greek word here links to a similar Greek word in v. 3 and is a prominent motif of the whole letter (v. 18; 4:11; 5:7; 6:13,17). It is frequent in Paul's other letters (1 Cor 7:10; 11:17; 1 Thess 4:2,11; 2 Thess 3:4,6,10,12). **love.** Just as Jesus commanded love in the two great commandments (Matt 22:37–40), Paul urges it as the central focus of church life. This is more than generic human affection; it comes from a "pure heart and a good conscience and a sincere faith" growing out of the gospel's transforming work. **heart.** Inner disposition, including the will. **conscience.** Awareness of right and wrong. **faith.** Personal trust.
1:6 Some. Like the "certain people" in v. 3, this is vague. They have rejected what Paul holds central. Perhaps the exact membership of the contrarian groups and the extent of their divergence were unclear. Paul's concern is to halt harmful drift, not to engineer personal attacks. **meaningless talk.** Echoes the "controversial speculations" of v. 4 (cf. Titus 1:10, where "the circumcision group" is a problem). God's power lies in "the kingdom of God," not in mere "talk" (1 Cor 4:20).
1:7 teachers of the law. May point to Jewish identity or influence

1:8 [k]Ro 7:12
1:9 [l]Gal 3:19
1:10 [m]2Ti 4:3; Titus 1:9
1:11 [n]Gal 2:7
1:12 [o]Php 4:13
1:13 [p]Ac 8:3 [q]Ac 26:9
1:14 [r]Ro 5:20 [s]2Ti 1:13
1:15 [t]1Ti 3:1; 2Ti 2:11; Titus 3:8
1:16 [u]ver 13
1:17 [v]Rev 15:3 [w]Col 1:15 [x]Ro 11:36

[8]We know that the law is good[k] if one uses it properly. [9]We also know that the law is made not for the righteous but for lawbreakers and rebels,[l] the ungodly and sinful, the unholy and irreligious, for those who kill their fathers or mothers, for murderers, [10]for the sexually immoral, for those practicing homosexuality, for slave traders and liars and perjurers — and for whatever else is contrary to the sound doctrine[m] [11]that conforms to the gospel concerning the glory of the blessed God, which he entrusted to me.[n]

The Lord's Grace to Paul

[12]I thank Christ Jesus our Lord, who has given me strength,[o] that he considered me trustworthy, appointing me to his service. [13]Even though I was once a blasphemer and a persecutor[p] and a violent man, I was shown mercy because I acted in ignorance and unbelief.[q] [14]The grace of our Lord was poured out on me abundantly,[r] along with the faith and love that are in Christ Jesus.[s]

[15]Here is a trustworthy saying[t] that deserves full acceptance: Christ Jesus came into the world to save sinners — of whom I am the worst. [16]But for that very reason I was shown mercy[u] so that in me, the worst of sinners, Christ Jesus might display his immense patience as an example for those who would believe in him and receive eternal life. [17]Now to the King[v] eternal, immortal, invisible,[w] the only God, be honor and glory for ever and ever. Amen.[x]

(the identical Greek word occurs in Luke 5:17; Acts 5:34). Since Paul writes "want to be," they might not have the knowledge or ability, just the ambition. If moralism or ceremonial ritual replaces salvation through faith in Christ, that is bad enough, but even on their own subject matter, these teachers are in over their heads, not knowing "what they are talking about." Both Jesus (Matt 23:8) and James (Jas 3:1) warn about presuming to teach. Yet God gifts pastoral leaders with teaching capacities and gives them to the church (1 Cor 12:28; Eph 4:11). Paul himself was a "teacher" (2:7), but a teacher "of this gospel" (2 Tim 1:11), not a teacher of speculations that divert attention away from the gospel.

1:8 We know. A common Pauline rhetorical convention, especially in Rom and 1–2 Cor. Paul reviews a basic teaching of which Timothy might lose sight. **the law is good.** Also Paul's teaching in Rom 7–8. Paul himself referred to and drew from the OT extensively (as did Jesus). But the law needs to be used "properly," as vv. 8–11 explain. Paul employs deft wordplay with the words "law" (Greek *nomos*) and "properly" (Greek *nomimōs*).

1:9 the law is made not for the righteous. The righteous are "justified through faith" (Rom 5:1), not by meritorious obedience to the law. The false teachers may have been obscuring or denying this. But even if obeying "the law" is not the means of salvation, it still does speak directly and forcefully to those who flagrantly violate it. In vv. 9–10 Paul lists behaviors that God's law condemns, and he has in mind especially the OT books of Moses (Gen–Deut). Many have noted that the violations correspond broadly to the sweep of the Ten Commandments. God's holy character and desire for human flourishing as expressed in the Decalogue (i.e., the Ten Commandments) do not waver, then or now.

1:10 those practicing homosexuality. Greek *arsenokoitēs*. The same Greek word is used in 1 Cor 6:9, where it is translated "men who have sex with men." **whatever else.** Paul is not being exhaustive; he is probably simply naming selected issues that he knows Timothy faces at Ephesus. These issues remain pressing for churches everywhere today. **doctrine.** See note on 4:2.

1:11 conforms to the gospel ... entrusted to me. This is the key to dealing rightly with God's law. The false teachers evidently set forth some other key. **the glory of the blessed God.** Conveyed via "the gospel" message, which cleanses and enlightens those who accept their condemnation by the law, repent, and trust in Christ — like Paul had done decades before writing this letter.

1:12–17 *The Lord's Grace to Paul.* Paul employs gracious but shrewd diplomacy with Timothy. By describing his own despicable offenses yet deliverance, Paul tacitly calls Timothy to recognize afresh the sole sufficiency of divine grace in Christ as the source of strength for Timothy's trials and labors.

1:12 strength. The inner dynamic of Christ living through Paul (cf. Gal 2:20). Paul attributes his insight and vigor solely and emphatically to the one who died and rose and appeared to him on the Damascus road (Acts 9), where Christ called Paul "to his service." **considered me trustworthy.** Corresponds to Paul's teaching (e.g., in Romans) that through faith God reckons the ungodly to be worthy of God's trust and valuable in his service.

1:13 I was shown mercy. Despite Paul's own flagrant law-breaking. He needed God's mercy in light of his willful "ignorance and unbelief," which in times past led Paul to persecute the church (Gal 1:13). Paul's teaching on law and grace was not theory but his own personal experience. Because he can smell the brimstone, so to speak, of the judgment his evil richly deserved, he vehemently insists on the "sound doctrine" (v. 10) that mediates forgiveness and new life.

1:14 grace of our Lord. God's grace in his saving work through Christ Jesus, which makes the unrighteous into the people of God, rescued Paul from his rebelliousness (see Titus 2:11 and note). This grace "was poured out ... abundantly" on Paul, along with "the faith and love" he displays and urges on Timothy (cf. v. 5). Paul's testimony to "grace" has the effect of repudiating the teachers of the law (v. 7).

1:15 trustworthy saying. Timothy can fully affirm and bank on this (see similar expressions in 3:1; 4:9; 2 Tim 2:11; Titus 1:9; 3:8; these were truths widely affirmed in the early Christian churches). **Christ Jesus came ... to save sinners.** Paul echoes Jesus' explicit teaching that he came to call sinners, not the righteous (Matt 9:13; Mark 2:17; Luke 5:32; 15:7). **came into the world.** Implicitly affirms the incarnation. **to save sinners.** Confirms what the angel told Joseph about Jesus' destiny and the reason for (meaning of) his name (Matt 1:21). **I am the worst.** Means not that Paul continues to live rebelliously but that due to his close walk with God, he is conscious of divine holiness (cf. Isa 6:5) despite his former evil deeds (v. 13).

1:16 mercy ... patience. Just as God chose Israel for no merit or cause on their part (Deut 9:4–5), he showed mercy to Paul despite his heinous error. If Paul could be saved, anyone could. This owed nothing to Paul but everything to Christ Jesus and his "immense patience." Paul becomes an example for others who might believe in Christ Jesus and receive eternal life (cf. 6:12; Rom 2:7; 5:21; 6:22–23; Gal 6:8; Titus 1:2; 3:7). Timothy should take heart given Paul's turnaround.

1:17 King ... only God. Recalling God's patience and gift of eternal life (see v. 16 and note) moves Paul to exalt the King, who is likewise the "only God" in his matchless attributes (cf. 6:15).

The Charge to Timothy Renewed

18Timothy, my son, I am giving you this command in keeping with the prophecies once made
about you,[y] so that by recalling them you may fight the battle well,[z] 19holding on to faith and a
good conscience, which some have rejected and so have suffered shipwreck with regard to the faith.[a]
20Among them are Hymenaeus[b] and Alexander,[c] whom I have handed over to Satan[d] to be taught not
to blaspheme.

Instructions on Worship

2 I urge, then, first of all, that petitions, prayers, intercession and thanksgiving be made for all
people— 2for kings and all those in authority,[e] that we may live peaceful and quiet lives in all
godliness and holiness. 3This is good, and pleases God our Savior, 4who wants[f] all people[g] to be saved
and to come to a knowledge of the truth.[h] 5For there is one God[i] and one mediator[j] between God and
mankind, the man Christ Jesus, 6who gave himself as a ransom for all people. This has now been witnessed to[k] at the proper time.[l] 7And for this purpose I was appointed a herald and an apostle—I am
telling the truth, I am not lying—and a true and faithful teacher[m] of the Gentiles.[n]

1:18 [y] 1Ti 4:14 [z] 2Ti 2:3
1:19 [a] 1Ti 6:21
1:20 [b] 2Ti 2:17 [c] 2Ti 4:14 [d] 1Co 5:5
2:2 [e] Ezr 6:10; Ro 13:1
2:4 [f] Eze 18:23,32 [g] Titus 2:11 [h] 2Ti 2:25
2:5 [i] Ro 3:29,30 [j] Gal 3:20
2:6 [k] 1Co 1:6 [l] 1Ti 6:15
2:7 [m] 2Ti 1:11 [n] Ac 9:15; Eph 3:7,8

1:18–20 *The Charge to Timothy Renewed.* Paul reminds Timothy of his heritage and points him toward his duty. He also mentions two trouble-makers with whom Paul is already dealing (v. 20), perhaps to assure Timothy that Paul is toiling alongside him in the struggles he faces.

1:18 command. Timothy should stay in Ephesus (vv. 3,5; see note on v. 5). **prophecies.** Uttered concerning Timothy when he was set apart for his ministry (4:14; see Acts 16:1–3). Prophecy occurs at other junctures in the early church too (Acts 13:1–3); God revealed his unfolding will through godly leaders. Recalling these prophecies will fortify Timothy to fight the battle he faces. **battle.** Paul uses military metaphors repeatedly in appealing to Timothy (see also 6:12; 2 Tim 2:3; 4:7).

1:19 faith and a good conscience. Two of Timothy's main weapons in "the battle" (v. 18) to which he is called. **some.** May refer to the troublemakers at Ephesus. They have forfeited the "good conscience," the awareness of right and wrong, that is to some extent innate but that is enhanced by accepting apostolic doctrine. The result is calamity in terms of "the faith" that Paul and Timothy uphold. **suffered shipwreck.** Abandoned their earlier confession, perhaps because it was never real (cf. 1 John 2:19). **the faith.** In the first part of the verse it refers to personal trust, but it can also, as it does at the end of the verse, denote the body of teaching that mediates saving knowledge of God through Christ (see note on 3:9).

1:20 Paul names two prominent examples of those who "have suffered shipwreck" (v. 19): **Hymenaeus.** Perhaps the same Hymenaeus of 2 Tim 2:17–18. If so, he is guilty of falsely teaching about the resurrection and subverting people's trust in Christ. In every generation there seem to be figures who reinterpret Christian teaching by attaching foreign meanings to its central concepts. **Alexander.** A very common name; nothing more is known of this Alexander. It is not certain that he is the Alexander mentioned in 2 Tim 4:14. **handed over to Satan.** Paul hands the troublemakers to Satan (cf. 1 Cor 5:3–5) in the hope that they will learn their lesson and get back on track. Paul intends to restore, not get revenge. He probably has in mind putting them out of the church, where they will be more exposed to the blandishments and snares of the devil and learn "not to blaspheme" (i.e., they will cease misrepresenting God by their false teaching).

2:1—6:2a *Order in Church and Life.* Pressures at Ephesus could have led to church chaos. Paul reminds Timothy of practices, qualities, principles, and policies that will enable Timothy's pastoral administration to proceed "in a fitting and orderly way" (1 Cor 14:40).

2:1–15 *Instructions on Worship.* The language of this chapter envisions both personal and especially corporate worship (the two can hardly be completely separated). Key concerns include prayer, lives of integrity, God's saving will in Jesus' mediatorial work, the legitimacy of Paul's apostleship (which detractors continually disputed), and the deportment in worship that honors God most highly.

2:1 prayers. In its various forms and aims, prayer is the cornerstone of worship. If people do not believe enough in God to address him in clear, coherent speech, other worship exercises (praise, confession, Scripture reading, proclamation) are unlikely to be fruitful. Prayer should be made "for all people"—not just for believers, but for everyone else too. Jesus stressed that this included even enemies (Luke 6:27–28).

2:2 kings and all those in authority. This is not all that the church should pray for, but it is a salient example. In a political and social atmosphere of "peaceful and quiet lives," there is freedom to pursue activities consistent with God's will for his people, like rearing children in the Lord, serving the community's needy, and taking the gospel out into the world. **godliness.** Greek *eusebeia*; it is a repeated ideal in 1 Timothy (3:16; 4:7,8; 6:3,5,6,11).

2:3 Praying as directed in v. 2 is "good," benefiting the person who prays and bringing results that are pleasing to "God our Savior" (see 1:1 and note).

2:4 all people. May mean "all kinds of people" (cf. v. 1 and note). **come to a knowledge of the truth.** To affirm saving trust in the gospel message (see note on Titus 1:14). What God "wants" may be hindered by lack of human faith.

2:5 For. Indicates that vv. 5–6 will explain v. 4. **one God.** God's uniqueness is an axiom of the OT and early Christian belief (Deut 6:4; Gal 3:20). The Roman world was awash in gods and religions, just as today most deny that the God and Christ found in Scripture are the only means to be saved. But in fact "there is one God" and only "one mediator." **one mediator.** Jesus "mediates," or serves as the bridge, between the invisible God and people who seek God (John 1:18; 1 Pet 3:18). Most people prefer to deal with (their natural notions of) God directly rather than humbly access him through Christ Jesus alone.

2:6 ransom. Jesus paid the necessary price to set people free. **all people.** God does not play favorites (Rom 2:11); he welcomes all nationalities, social classes, and personality types. This means not that everyone will be saved but that Christ has done what is needed for all people who call on him to receive the new life he promised. **witnessed to.** People proclaimed Jesus' saving work in the apostolic era (Gal 4:4–5). Even apart from human preaching, Christ's self-giving testifies to God's goodness (vv. 3–4).

2:7 this purpose. The saving message "witnessed to" in v. 6 (see note). **herald.** One who announces. **apostle.** One who passes along faithfully what has been entrusted to him. Paul may be addressing charges that his ministry is bogus. **truth.** See note on Titus 1:14. **Gentiles.** In general, believers around Ephesus were Gentiles.

2:8 [o]Ps 134:2; Lk 24:50
2:9 [p]1Pe 3:3
2:11 [q]1Co 14:34
2:13 [r]Ge 2:7,22; 1Co 11:8
2:14 [s]Ge 3:1-6,13; 2Co 11:3

8 Therefore I want the men everywhere to pray, lifting up holy hands[o] without anger or disputing.
9 I also want the women to dress modestly, with decency and propriety, adorning themselves, not with
elaborate hairstyles or gold or pearls or expensive clothes,[p] 10 but with good deeds, appropriate for
women who profess to worship God.
11 A woman[a] should learn in quietness and full submission.[q] 12 I do not permit a woman to teach
or to assume authority over a man;[b] she must be quiet. 13 For Adam was formed first, then Eve.[r]
14 And Adam was not the one deceived; it was the woman who was deceived and became a sinner.[s]

[a] *11* Or *wife*; also in verse 12 [b] *12* Or *over her husband*

2:8–15 These verses have raised much controversy in recent decades and deserve special comment. Paul seems to hold that despite creational oneness (Gen 1:27; 1 Cor 11:11–12), Adam's origin differs from Eve's (Gen 2:15–25; 1 Cor 11:8–9). Their progeny who come into personal fellowship with God through faith in his Son glorify him in his kingdom and church in ways that are equally important but not always identical.

There are three general approaches to vv. 8–15. (1) Some feel that Paul's views on women in this section are patriarchal, wrong, and do not reflect God's will. (2) Others agree that Paul has a patriarchal outlook, but they accept that his counsel was binding for the church of his time. Yet they hold that since some in the West now affirm a postpatriarchal or egalitarian view of marriage and society, Paul's teaching must give way to current relational and social convictions. A variation of this view is that there were unique circumstances at Ephesus, and the teaching of vv. 8–15 is not binding in those cultures in which social circumstances have changed. (3) Still others, including most Christians through almost all of church history, have understood Paul's teaching to be that in general men are called to certain leadership responsibilities in the church that women under most circumstances are not. This means not that men are more capable or gifted than women but that God has distinct expectations for women and for men, expectations consistent with differences he bestowed on them in creation. He calls them to flourish by enhancing their lives through faith in Christ within these blessed differences. The following study notes are most consistent with view 3.

2:8 Paul returns to the theme of prayer he began in v. 1. **everywhere.** Can be translated "in every place"; Paul may have in mind each household church where believers would congregate. **anger or disputing.** Inclinations of men that poison worship. Paul says much more about male offenses elsewhere in this letter.

2:9 elaborate hairstyles or gold or pearls or expensive clothes. This is not a blanket prohibition of all jewelry and fine clothing but a warning against seductive, prideful, or ostentatious self-display. Peter gives similar counsel and points to the example of righteous OT women (1 Pet 3:3–6). The issue is not *whether* women should seek to display beauty but *how* they do so: "good deeds" (v. 10) glorify God and confer dignity and true beauty on worshiping women who practice them.

2:11 Paul seems to be envisioning the portion of worship activity that focuses on Scripture reading and interpretation (4:13). **should learn.** A "disciple" is a "learner," and women are called to discipleship as much as men. **in quietness and full submission.** The disposition modeled by Lazarus's sister Mary (Luke 10:39). The reason for this reference to women is unclear—surely men (except for speaking leaders) were expected to listen and be receptive too (1 Cor 14:29–33,40). Were some, like Martha, "distracted by all the preparations that had to be made" (Luke 10:40)? This is certainly a possibility in the setting of house churches. Were some Ephesian women disruptive with whispering or inattention? Did some, not sharing their husbands' faith, verbally challenge Scripture reading or preaching? Paul's counsel stands even if we cannot pinpoint exactly what occasioned it.

2:12 permit. When the NT uses this word, it always refers to what a figure in authority allows (or prohibits). As an apostle (see v. 7), Paul fits this description. The first-person form ("I do not") makes sense as Paul pens these personal reminders to his younger associate. **teach ... assume authority.** Teaching (Greek *didsakein*) and oversight (Greek *authentein*, to exercise oversight) are two major domains of pastoral leadership (4:11; cf. 2 Tim 4:2; Col 1:28; 1 Thess 4:2; Heb 13:17; 1 Pet 5:2–3). Paul is not thinking of two separate, unrelated activities but of the worship setting in which the congregation's overseers (3:1–7) exercise leadership by what they teach and urge on God's people. In other settings women may very well play prominent roles (Acts 18:26; Rom 16:1–2). Paul is not addressing women's roles in every circumstance of daily church life or roles in other social settings like business or government or everyday life outside the church. **must be quiet.** Even in worship, Paul does not teach that women "must be quiet" at all times; 1 Cor 11:5 assumes that women prayed and prophesied in the assembly. (The Greek word translated "quiet" also occurs in v. 2, where it applies to the lives of men and women alike.) It is reasonable to assume women sang (Eph 5:19; Col 3:16; Jas 5:13). Yet there are no clear examples in the NT of women serving as overseers (3:1) in apostolic churches. The counsel of this verse reflects that precedent and, as far as our evidence goes, the universal policy in early Christian generations and beyond.

2:13 For. Indicates that this verse helps explain Paul's counsel in previous verses. He appeals to Gen 2–3. **formed.** The same Greek word appears in the Septuagint (the pre-Christian Greek translation of the OT) in Gen 2:7,8. Some hold that this appeal to Scripture makes Paul's teaching universal and permanent. Adam's priority—he was "formed first," which predates the fall—has a bearing on how men and women in the church should continue to serve and interrelate. Others place less weight on "For" and hold that Paul is addressing a situation specific to Ephesus; they do not see here a basis for conforming women's church activities today to what Paul teaches in this passage.

2:14 Adam was not ... deceived. Recalls that the serpent "deceived" Eve (2 Cor 11:3). Adam followed consciously and willfully. As the one "formed first" (see v. 13 and note), he bears primary responsibility (Rom 5:12: "sin entered the world through one man"). Paul's conclusion

Fayum mummy portrait, AD 60. Paul encourages women to dress modestly and adorn themselves with good deeds rather than gold and pearls (1 Tim 2:9).

Kim Walton, taken at the Altes Museum, Berlin

15 But women[a] will be saved through childbearing — if they continue in faith, love[t] and holiness
with propriety.

Qualifications for Overseers and Deacons

3 Here is a trustworthy saying:[u] Whoever aspires to be an overseer[v] desires a noble task. 2 Now the
overseer is to be above reproach,[w] faithful to his wife, temperate, self-controlled, respectable, hospitable,[x] able to teach,[y] 3 not given to drunkenness, not violent but gentle, not quarrelsome,[z] not a lover
of money.[a] 4 He must manage his own family well and see that his children obey him, and he must do
so in a manner worthy of full[b] respect.[b] 5 (If anyone does not know how to manage his own family, how
can he take care of God's church?)[c] 6 He must not be a recent convert, or he may become conceited[d]
and fall under the same judgment as the devil. 7 He must also have a good reputation with outsiders, so
that he will not fall into disgrace and into the devil's trap.[e]
8 In the same way, deacons[c][f] are to be worthy of respect, sincere, not indulging in much wine,[g] and not
pursuing dishonest gain. 9 They must keep hold of the deep truths of the faith with a clear conscience.[h]
10 They must first be tested; and then if there is nothing against them, let them serve as deacons.
11 In the same way, the women[d] are to be worthy of respect, not malicious talkers[i] but temperate and
trustworthy in everything.

[a] *15* Greek *she* [b] *4* Or *him with proper* [c] *8* The word *deacons* refers here to Christians designated to serve with the overseers/elders of the church in a variety of ways; similarly in verse 12; and in Romans 16:1 and Phil. 1:1. [d] *11* Possibly deacons' wives or women who are deacons

2:15 [t] 1Ti 1:14
3:1 [u] 1Ti 1:15 [v] Ac 20:28
3:2 [w] Titus 1:6-8 [x] Ro 12:13 [y] 2Ti 2:24
3:3 [z] 2Ti 2:24 [a] Heb 13:5; 1Pe 5:2
3:4 [b] Titus 1:6
3:5 [c] 1Co 10:32
3:6 [d] 1Ti 6:4
3:7 [e] 2Ti 2:26
3:8 [f] Php 1:1 [g] Titus 2:3
3:9 [h] 1Ti 1:19
3:11 [i] 2Ti 3:3; Titus 2:3

seems to be that what happened in Eden has a bearing on the church order he expects Timothy to maintain.

2:15 saved through childbearing. Some think this alludes to the birth of the Christ-child (the incarnation was necessary for there to be a cross and a resurrection). Others argue that Paul refers to women's health and safety in childbirth. **childbearing.** Could refer to Christ-honoring motherhood, which may be confirmed by Paul's desire that women abide in "faith, love and holiness." These are qualities that should adorn all women (vv. 9–10). See 5:14 for a fuller list of ways for married women to honor God. Paul elsewhere affirms singleness (1 Cor 7:8); marriage and childbearing are not expected of all women. **propriety.** The same Greek word occurs in v. 9 and carries the idea of self-discipline and wise deportment.

3:1–13 *Qualifications for Overseers and Deacons.* Timothy's task in Ephesus is not only direct congregational care but also helping identify and appoint overseers along with others charged with congregational service (deacons). This section sketches some necessary traits for both offices. The point is not to furnish a full job description but to remind of character markers and the Christian maturity required for effective church leadership.

3:1 trustworthy saying. See 1:15 and note. **overseer.** In Greco-Roman society the word described a civic or religious leader. The equivalent term in Jewish contexts (e.g., the synagogue) was "elder." Paul calls the church "elders" at Ephesus "overseers" (Acts 20:17,28). Their task is to be "shepherds of the church of God" (Acts 20:28), which in context is clearly a pastoral role. They were to teach and preach (1:3; 5:17), exercise management (vv. 4–5; 5:17), and, as all of 1 Timothy shows, protect the church from false doctrine and unholy living. **a noble task.** Pastoral leadership is an honorable pursuit.

3:2 is to be. The Greek word *dei* implies moral and perhaps divine necessity; in other places (e.g., vv. 7,15; 5:13) it is translated with words like "must" or "ought." **above reproach.** Even Jesus was criticized, and he said his followers would be too. Paul means free from justified charges of corruption or incompetence. **faithful to his wife.** Loving her as Christ loved the church (Eph 5:25) and not committing acts of infidelity. All of the other traits in this verse were lived out to perfection by Jesus, whose life in the Gospels furnishes hints at how aspiring overseers should live.

3:3 Excessive alcohol consumption, combativeness, and greed disqualify someone from pastoral appointment, because they show that the person is not "above reproach ... temperate, self-controlled, [and] respectable," which v. 2 calls for.

3:4 manage his own family well. A leader who is not a catalyst for orderly godliness within his own home and family does not inspire the confidence needed to teach and guide other households making up a particular congregation ("God's church," v. 5). More than formal, academic, or professional qualifications are vital. A man's marriage and parental skills are open books for assessing pastoral readiness.

3:6 conceited. Describes people whose convictions and behavior defy apostolic norms (cf. 6:4; 2 Tim 3:4). **same judgment as the devil.** Implies God's direct disapproval; translated in a slightly different way, it could also mean to be "handed over to Satan" as in 1:20 (see note).

3:7 good reputation with outsiders. Leadership assessment is not a purely in-house matter. People from outside the congregation and the faith may shed light on a candidate's qualities. **with outsiders.** Implies that people in the church will have connection with unbelievers (cf. 1 Cor 5:9–10). **devil's trap.** Perhaps the sense of condemnation that Satan loves to stir up with his accusations.

3:8 In the same way. Like overseers, deacons were held to stringent standards. Several of the qualities listed appear in previous verses, though deacons are not required to be able to teach. (Yet note Stephen's speaking gift in Acts 7:2–53). While the Greek word translated "deacons" simply means "those who serve," deacons held office alongside overseers (Phil 1:1). They may have focused on areas of service that would free up overseers to devote more time to prayer and teaching or preaching (Acts 6:1–6).

3:9 deep truths. Translates the Greek word *mystērion* (1 Cor 2:7; 4:1; 15:51; Eph 3:3,4,9; Col 1:26–27; 2:2–3; 4:3 and notes), a word Paul uses to describe God's formerly hidden but now revealed plan (see Rom 16:25–26 and notes) to bring salvation through Christ. **truths.** See note on Titus 1:14. Whereas overseers must be "able to teach" (v. 2), deacons must show they have fully grasped "the faith" and uphold it in an exemplary fashion. **the faith.** Refers here to apostolic teaching, as it does at the end of 1:19 (see note; see also 4:1,6; 6:10,12,21; 2 Tim 4:7; Titus 1:13).

3:10 be tested. Diaconal service is not a testing ground or low-level office for novices. A period of testing and careful assessment should precede appointment.

3:11 women. Some think this refers to female "deacons." It could also be translated "wives," referring to deacons' wives (see NIV text note).

3:12 [j] ver 4
3:15 [k] ver 5; Eph 2:21
3:16 [l] Ro 16:25 [m] Jn 1:14 [n] Col 1:23 [o] Mk 16:19
4:1 [p] Jn 16:13 [q] 2Ti 3:1 [r] 2Th 2:3
4:2 [s] Eph 4:19
4:3 [t] Heb 13:4

12 A deacon must be faithful to his wife and must manage his children and his household well.[j]
13 Those who have served well gain an excellent standing and great assurance in their faith in Christ
Jesus.

Reasons for Paul's Instructions

14 Although I hope to come to you soon, I am writing you these instructions so that, 15 if I am delayed,
you will know how people ought to conduct themselves in God's household, which is the church[k] of
the living God, the pillar and foundation of the truth. 16 Beyond all question, the mystery[l] from which
true godliness springs is great:

> He appeared in the flesh,[m]
> was vindicated by the Spirit,[a]
> was seen by angels,
> was preached among the nations,[n]
> was believed on in the world,
> was taken up in glory.[o]

4 The Spirit[p] clearly says that in later times[q] some will abandon the faith and follow deceiving spirits[r] and things taught by demons. 2 Such teachings come through hypocritical liars, whose consciences have been seared as with a hot iron.[s] 3 They forbid people to marry[t] and order them to abstain

[a] 16 Or *vindicated in spirit*

Because (male) deacons are mentioned again in v. 12, it is less likely that v. 11 refers to a separate order of women deacons (but see Rom 16:1 and note, and NIV text note). It may well include overseers' wives too, given how vv. 4–5 emphasize a quality household atmosphere. **temperate.** A quality also required for overseers (v. 2) and the older men of the church (Titus 2:2).

3:12 Applies to deacons the same expectations Paul gave for overseers (see vv. 2,4 and notes).

3:13 served well. Paul wants Timothy to promote excellence in ministry, not mediocrity. **assurance.** A significant factor is faithful (and often arduous) service for Christ Jesus. Labor for Christ confirms faith in him. Confidence grows through observing the gospel at work changing lives and building the church.

3:14—4:16 *Reasons for Paul's Instructions.* Through the remainder of ch. 3, Paul takes a step back from the dense directions he has been formulating. He summarizes his reason for treating the particular topics he has stated thus far. In conclusion he exults in aspects of Christ's excellence. In ch. 4 Paul first alerts Timothy that he will likely encounter sinister figures who are destructively influencing believers (vv. 1–5). Rather than stir up personal antagonism against them, Paul dissects the error of their ways. He also exhorts Timothy to be pastorally intense (vv. 6–16). He gives tips that will optimize Timothy's pastoral work and, by extension, the work of those he appoints and oversees. At points Paul underscores how critical his instructions are and how vital it is that Timothy diligently follow them.

3:14–15 Paul hopes to come to Ephesus soon; apparently his trip to Macedonia (1:3) was not planned to be a lengthy one.

3:15 ought. See note on v. 2 ("is to be"). It is not just expedient but imperative in God's sight that his people live in harmony with his revealed will. **God's household.** The church is not just another human organization. As family members make up a domestic household, the church consists of households among which Christ dwells (Matt 18:20). Paul uses "household" (Greek *oikos*) or related words to describe the church and its ministry (1 Cor 3:1; Gal 6:10; Eph 2:19; see 1 Pet 4:17; cf. vv. 4–5,12; 5:4,8,14). **pillar.** The church upholds the truth entrusted to it. **foundation.** The church is the functional basis for the reception and spread of the saving gospel message and all the other wisdom and riches of insight God has revealed. As the temple in OT times signified God's saving presence emanating into all the world, the church (singly and corporately) embodies God's active will in all the world (cf. Eph 3:10–11). **truth.** See note on Titus 1:14.

3:16 mystery. See note on v. 9. Here Paul refers to things formerly hidden but now made visible by God's revelatory activity, described in a luminous six-line composite portrait. This activity centers on (1) Christ's incarnation; (2) Christ's resurrection, which confirmed his identity as the Son of God (Rom 1:4); (3) the angelic recognition at Christ's resurrection (Matt 28:2) and ascension (Acts 1:10); (4) the expansive proclamation as Christ's followers preach throughout the world; (5) Christ's transformative presence in far-flung believing communities as the gospel message goes forth; and (6) Christ's glorious triumph, dramatized in the ascension (see Luke 24:50–53; Acts 1:9–11 and notes). There is not, then, strict chronological order to the sequence. Many see poetic or hymnic features in the verse. **godliness.** Its essence is Christ's work, received by faith (see note on 2:2).

4:1 Spirit clearly says. Paul could be paraphrasing what he sensed the Spirit to be saying. Or this could point to the pronouncements of others with prophetic gifts. Jesus taught of dangers as the end approaches (e.g., Matt 24–25). **later times.** Both present and future: these "times" began in some sense with Jesus' resurrection (some would say at Pentecost), which signaled the arrival of the age to come. Paul and Timothy were already living in these days (see 2 Tim 3:1), so Timothy must be ready to deal with some people abandoning the faith in that present time as well as in the future. People will run after "deceiving spirits" and demonic teachings.

4:2 teachings. The Greek is sometimes translated "doctrine" or "instruction"; it appears eight times in 1 Timothy (1:10; 4:1,6,13,16; 5:17; 6:1,3). It is a major pastoral concern and responsibility, so when false views surface, pastoral action is called for. **liars.** People who speak untruths; they speak things taught by "deceiving spirits and ... demons" (v. 1). Their hypocrisy lies in their evident claim to speak truth when their "consciences [are] seared as with a hot iron." This means their sense of true and false, of right and wrong, is withered and hardened as if cauterized.

4:3 Two examples of people whom Timothy should watch out for; they: (1) **forbid people to marry.** Perhaps abstention from marriage or from sexual relations in marriage; or perhaps the error of sexual freedom even outside of marriage on the basis that grace is sufficient to cover all sins (Rom 6:1,15). (2) **abstain from certain foods.** Unfounded dietary

from certain foods,[u] which God created[v] to be received with thanksgiving[w] by those who believe and
who know the truth. 4For everything God created is good,[x] and nothing is to be rejected if it is received
with thanksgiving, 5because it is consecrated by the word of God and prayer.

6If you point these things out to the brothers and sisters,[a] you will be a good minister of Christ Jesus,
nourished on the truths of the faith[y] and of the good teaching that you have followed. 7Have nothing
to do with godless myths and old wives' tales;[z] rather, train yourself to be godly. 8For physical training
is of some value, but godliness has value for all things,[a] holding promise for both the present life[b] and
the life to come. 9This is a trustworthy saying[c] that deserves full acceptance. 10That is why we labor and
strive, because we have put our hope in the living God, who is the Savior of all people, and especially
of those who believe.

11Command and teach these things.[d] 12Don't let anyone look down on you because you are young,
but set an example[e] for the believers in speech, in conduct, in love, in faith[f] and in purity. 13Until I
come, devote yourself to the public reading of Scripture, to preaching and to teaching. 14Do not neglect
your gift, which was given you through prophecy[g] when the body of elders laid their hands on you.[h]

4:3 [u] Col 2:16 [v] Ge 1:29 [w] Ro 14:6
4:4 [x] Ro 14:14-18
4:6 [y] 1Ti 1:10
4:7 [z] 2Ti 2:16
4:8 [a] 1Ti 6:6 [b] Ps 37:9, 11; Mk 10:29,30
4:9 [c] 1Ti 1:15
4:11 [d] 1Ti 5:7; 6:2
4:12 [e] Titus 2:7; 1Pe 5:3 [f] 1Ti 1:14
4:14 [g] 1Ti 1:18 [h] Ac 6:6; 2Ti 1:6

[a] 6 The Greek word for *brothers and sisters* (*adelphoi*) refers here to believers, both men and women, as part of God's family.

restrictions. This might refer to views that only certain foods or drink were allowed for believers (Rom 14:2,17). Marriage and food are things "God created" (Gen 1–2, especially Gen 1:12,21,25,31) and are generally lawful for all, including "those who believe and who know the truth." Elsewhere Paul discusses debates about food, some rooted in Jewish dietary practices (Rom 14; 1 Cor 8–10). Both dietary and sexual restrictions may have arisen at Colossae (Col 2:20–23). But salvation comes through Jesus' work, not by merit achieved through ascetic self-denial. **truth.** See note on Titus 1:14.

4:4 good. God's creation "was very good" (Gen 1:31) until sin entered the world. Even then, OT feasts (Gen 21:8; Deut 33:19; Ps 36:8) and Jesus' example of attending a wedding (John 2:1–12) and banquets (e.g., Luke 15:2) warn against a purely negative approach to life's lawful enjoyments. **nothing is to be rejected.** Affirms sexual and dietary practices acceptable in God's sight. Paul is not setting aside biblical teaching elsewhere calling for holiness and restraint in these domains. Believers may not, e.g., safely fornicate or eat to obesity as long as they do so "with thanksgiving."

4:5 word of God. Scripture; it supports marriage and enjoying food (v. 3). **prayer.** Whether public in the church, private, or before meals, it is a parallel means by which God's good gifts are "consecrated."

4:6 these things. Refers at least to the preceding paragraph (see also v. 11; cf. v. 15; 3:14; 5:7; 6:2b). **minister.** Servant; the same Greek word refers to "deacons" in 3:8,12. Pastoral leadership is not dictatorial. Christ became a "servant" (Rom 15:8), and Apollos and Paul were "servants" (1 Cor 3:5). **nourished.** For Timothy to flourish in shepherding the church, he himself must be properly "nourished on the truths of the faith and of the good teaching." It is vital that he internalize and pass along Paul's counsel. **truths.** See note on Titus 1:14.

4:7 Have nothing to do with. Some arguments are fruitless, and some opponents intractable (cf. 2 Tim 2:23; Titus 3:10). Paul warns against vacuous myths and fables, pseudocertainties to be found in every social setting. **train.** Pursue like an athlete in training. **godly.** See note on 2:2.

4:8 some value. Could also mean "value for a little while" (the same Greek phrase in Jas 4:14 is translated "for a little while"), i.e., for the present age. We should not underestimate the physical toughness of someone like Paul, who walked thousands of miles/kilometers on his journeys and endured extreme physical deprivation over decades (2 Cor 11:23–27). Timothy would have trekked his share of miles/kilometers alongside Paul. The point is not to denigrate fitness but to contrast its (temporal) utility with the eternal worth of "godliness" (see note on 2:2).

4:9 trustworthy saying. See 1:15 (and note); 3:1; 2 Tim 2:11; Titus 3:8. It underscores the importance of v. 8 and perhaps also the elements conducive to godliness found in vv. 6–7.

4:10 The disciplined pursuit of godliness (see preceding verses) is why Paul and Timothy "labor and strive." Placing full personal trust and "hope in the living God" confers life purpose, focus, and drive: "We love because he first loved us" (1 John 4:19). **Savior of all people, and especially of those who believe.** See 2:4; Gal 6:10; 1 John 2:2 and notes. God is provider and preserver (a meaning of "savior") of all people (and animals too; e.g., Ps 36:6; Jonah 4:11). God gives sun and rain to all (Matt 5:45; Acts 14:17). He reveals his being and grandeur to all (Rom 1:20). This does not mean that none are lost or condemned by God in the end; it means that God's mercy and kindness are made evident to all persons.

4:11 Command. See note on 1:5. Though this letter maintains a collegial tone, Timothy is under divine constraint (v. 14). **teach.** Exhorting God's people and teaching them (see note on v. 2) are core pastoral duties (see note on 2:12), since at the heart of making disciples is instruction (Matt 28:19–20).

4:12 young. Timothy was minimally well into his 20s and possibly 30 or more. But that could still be regarded as youthful by those who were older, especially if they did not welcome aspects of Timothy's instruction, style, or background. (Timothy, from Lystra, was a provincial; residents of Ephesus could have viewed themselves as cultural sophisticates by comparison.) **set an example.** As is true for overseers (3:1–7), Timothy needs to live out the force of his convictions in daily, practical, and relational ways, not merely formally or officially.

4:13 Until I come. Paul plans a visit soon (3:14). This may explain why some of his instructions are not more detailed: he can clarify in the near future in person. **Scripture.** Primarily what we call the OT. Some of what became NT documents could also be in view (see 5:18 and NIV text note; see also 2 Pet 3:15–16). Regular and extended public Scripture reading was a formative heritage from OT and synagogue practice. Private copies of Scripture were rare due to cost, and many people could not read. Reading, hearing, and remembering (Ps 119:11) would reinforce Christian identity in contrast with deceivers. **preaching.** Scripture-based exhortation (Acts 13:15; Rom 15:4–5; 1 Cor 14:3; Heb 13:22). **teaching.** See notes on vv. 2,11.

4:14 gift ... given you. As Paul had a distinctive apostolic gift of divine grace given to him (Rom 12:3; Gal 2:9; Eph 3:7; more broadly see 1 Cor 14:18–19), so did Timothy. This is a work of the Holy Spirit, who gifts all believers so they may serve one another and glorify God (Rom 12:6–8; 1 Cor 12; 1 Pet 4:10–11). When Timothy was set apart for his ministry (cf. Acts 13:1–2), someone present prophesied, perhaps confirming Timothy's "gift" and calling. **laid their hands on.** See 2 Tim 1:6; Acts 6:6; Heb 6:1–2; this gesture expressed divine approval as well as congregational endorsement.

5:1 [i]Titus 2:2 [j]Lev 19:32 [k]Titus 2:6
5:3 [l]ver 5,16
5:4 [m]Eph 6:1,2 [n]1Ti 2:3
5:5 [o]ver 3,16 [p]1Co 7:34; 1Pe 3:5 [q]Lk 2:37
5:6 [r]Lk 15:24
5:7 [s]1Ti 4:11
5:8 [t]2Pe 2:1; Jude 4; Titus 1:16
5:10 [u]Ac 9:36; 1Ti 6:18; 1Pe 2:12 [v]Lk 7:44 [w]ver 16

15 Be diligent in these matters; give yourself wholly to them, so that everyone may see your progress.
16 Watch your life and doctrine closely. Persevere in them, because if you do, you will save both yourself
and your hearers.

Widows, Elders and Slaves

5 Do not rebuke an older man[i] harshly,[j] but exhort him as if he were your father. Treat younger
men[k] as brothers, 2 older women as mothers, and younger women as sisters, with absolute purity.
3 Give proper recognition to those widows who are really in need.[l] 4 But if a widow has children or
grandchildren, these should learn first of all to put their religion into practice by caring for their own
family and so repaying their parents and grandparents,[m] for this is pleasing to God.[n] 5 The widow who
is really in need[o] and left all alone puts her hope in God[p] and continues night and day to pray[q] and to
ask God for help. 6 But the widow who lives for pleasure is dead even while she lives.[r] 7 Give the people
these instructions,[s] so that no one may be open to blame. 8 Anyone who does not provide for their relatives, and especially for their own household, has denied[t] the faith and is worse than an unbeliever.

9 No widow may be put on the list of widows unless she is over sixty, has been faithful to her husband, 10 and is well known for her good deeds,[u] such as bringing up children, showing hospitality,
washing the feet[v] of the Lord's people, helping those in trouble[w] and devoting herself to all kinds of
good deeds.

11 As for younger widows, do not put them on such a list. For when their sensual desires overcome
their dedication to Christ, they want to marry. 12 Thus they bring judgment on themselves, because they

4:15 Be diligent. Paul stresses the high level of engagement required. Pastoral labor is not a leisure activity or hobby. Sloth or indifference to the task would suck the credibility out of all that Paul is commanding Timothy to teach and do. **progress.** The Greek word (*prokopē*) occurs only two other times in the NT: Paul uses it to refer to the gospel's "advance" (Phil 1:12) and to the Philippians' growth and joy in the faith (Phil 1:25).

4:16 Watch ... Persevere. Ministry has many pitfalls, some of which Paul has mentioned, so Timothy must "be diligent" (v. 15). Paul also held himself to this standard (1 Cor 9:27). For God's use of some humans in saving others, see Rom 11:14; 1 Cor 7:16; 9:22. Timothy's steadfastness will directly benefit his "hearers" and validate his own confession and calling.

5:1—6:2a *Widows, Elders, and Slaves.* Paul moves from matters that affect Timothy and the whole church to directions for pastoral care of specific subgroups. The care of God's household (see 3:15 and note) extends especially to those who are often undervalued (1 Cor 12:22), such as widows (1 Tim 5:3–16) and slaves (6:1–2a), and those who may not easily get along with each other (like the young and old; see 5:1–2).

5:1 To command respect it is wise to show respect. **Do not rebuke.** Applies to all four kinds of people mentioned in vv. 1–2. **exhort.** A way of steering and encouraging people. This task will be more fruitful if the pastor approaches older men like a father, not a subordinate, and if he treats peers as brothers. In the household of God (see 3:15 and note), it should be natural to regard others as family members.

5:2 women. Like men, they are members of God's household with claims on their pastor's attention, care, and instruction. Timothy should not ignore, patronize, or exploit them. **purity.** Note the same word in 4:12; it does not exist in isolation in the pastor's inner life. Timothy's heart and motivations must be clean, like they would be if he were dealing with his own "sisters."

5:3 recognition. Both respect (v. 2) and material support. **widows.** God is "a defender of widows" (Ps 68:5). Their care was an early church concern from the start (Acts 6:1) and part of "pure and faultless" religion (Jas 1:27). Widows at that time were vulnerable due to the longer life spans of women than those of men (true also today) and the absence of pensions and other social safety nets. **really in need.** Having no one but the church to render care (v. 4).

5:4 caring for their own family. The "religion" of Paul and Timothy was "first of all" to be lived out among "family" (3:4–5,12). Children owe no less to their "parents and grandparents," who gave them life. **pleasing to God.** A repeated Pauline concern (2:3; Rom 12:1; Eph 5:10).

5:5 widow who ... puts her hope in God. Paul commends them like Jesus did (Mark 12:43; cf. Luke 2:37). Widows may attract unusual blessing (Luke 4:26) and contribute powerfully to aspects of congregational service. But to offer church aid, Timothy must verify that they are absorbed in prayer and the pursuit of God. **really in need.** See note on v. 3.

5:6 lives for pleasure. See Jas 5:5. The sorrows of widowhood are not a license to self-indulgence. **dead even while she lives.** Like the "lost" son of Luke 15:24, who was physically alive but spiritually dead. See also v. 15.

5:7 Give ... instructions. Paul wants Timothy to be forceful. The same verb of command occurs in 1:3; 4:11; 6:13,17.

5:8 provide for their relatives. Church ties and relations do not nullify the links of family; "honor your father and your mother" (Exod 20:12) still applies, and this has implications for extended family. This is especially true for relatives under the same roof (of "their own household"). **denied the faith.** Faith is a matter not only of what we say but also of what we do. **the faith.** See 3:9 and note. **worse than an unbeliever.** Paul may be saying that many unbelievers care for family members, or he may be saying that professing faith but not caring for family is worse than the sin of unbelief.

5:9 list of widows. The church must care for widows. Apparently at Ephesus the church kept a list of those whom they cared for. Yet Paul upholds personal responsibility (v. 16). Along with a formal age requirement ("over sixty"), a widow receiving church support must have lived in marital fidelity and must exemplify Christlike service to others (v. 10).

5:10 washing the feet. See John 13:14; Jesus performed this menial task, an act of hospitality necessitated by dusty roads and the customary footwear (sandals).

5:11 Timothy should treat "younger women as sisters" (v. 2). But if they are widowed and want church support, they are not to be added to the "list" (see v. 9 and note) because they may want to marry again.

5:12 first pledge. Perhaps a vow taken to consecrate their widowhood; subsequent marriage would break that vow. It could also be translated "former faith" (ESV). In that case, Paul refers to a widow who turns her back on God, perhaps by marrying an unbeliever. This could lead to grave outcomes (v. 15).

have broken their first pledge. [13]Besides, they get into the habit of being idle and going about from
house to house. And not only do they become idlers, but also busybodies[x] who talk nonsense, saying
things they ought not to. [14]So I counsel younger widows to marry,[y] to have children, to manage their
homes and to give the enemy no opportunity for slander.[z] [15]Some have in fact already turned away to
follow Satan.[a]

[16]If any woman who is a believer has widows in her care, she should continue to help them and
not let the church be burdened with them, so that the church can help those widows who are really
in need.[b]

[17]The elders[c] who direct the affairs of the church well are worthy of double honor,[d] especially those
whose work is preaching and teaching. [18]For Scripture says, "Do not muzzle an ox while it is treading out
the grain,"[ae] and "The worker deserves his wages."[bf] [19]Do not entertain an accusation against an elder[g]
unless it is brought by two or three witnesses.[h] [20]But those elders who are sinning you are to reprove[i] before everyone, so that the others may take warning.[j] [21]I charge you, in the sight of God and Christ Jesus[k]
and the elect angels, to keep these instructions without partiality, and to do nothing out of favoritism.

[22]Do not be hasty in the laying on of hands,[l] and do not share in the sins of others.[m] Keep yourself pure.

[23]Stop drinking only water, and use a little wine[n] because of your stomach and your frequent
illnesses.

[24]The sins of some are obvious, reaching the place of judgment ahead of them; the sins of others trail
behind them. [25]In the same way, good deeds are obvious, and even those that are not obvious cannot
remain hidden forever.

6 All who are under the yoke of slavery should consider their masters worthy of full respect,[o] so that
God's name and our teaching may not be slandered.[p] [2]Those who have believing masters should
not show them disrespect just because they are fellow believers.[q] Instead, they should serve them even

5:13 [x]2Th 3:11
5:14 [y]1Co 7:9 [z]1Ti 6:1
5:15 [a]Mt 4:10
5:16 [b]ver 3-5
5:17 [c]Ac 11:30 [d]Php 2:29; 1Th 5:12
5:18 [e]Dt 25:4; 1Co 9:7-9 [f]Lk 10:7; Lev 19:13; Dt 24:14,15; Mt 10:10; 1Co 9:14
5:19 [g]Ac 11:30 [h]Mt 18:16
5:20 [i]2Ti 4:2; Titus 1:13 [j]Dt 13:11
5:21 [k]1Ti 6:13; 2Ti 4:1
5:22 [l]Ac 6:6 [m]Eph 5:11
5:23 [n]1Ti 3:8
6:1 [o]Eph 6:5; Titus 2:9; 1Pe 2:18 [p]Titus 2:5,8
6:2 [q]Phm 16

[a] *18* Deut. 25:4 [b] *18* Luke 10:7

5:13 In contrast to the virtuous widow (vv. 5,9–10), these women have too much time on their hands and undermine congregational aims with idleness and gossip. Such behavior was disallowed for all in the church (2 Thess 3:11–12).
5:14 counsel. Translated "want" elsewhere in the Pastoral Letters (e.g., 2:8; Titus 3:8); it is more than mere personal advice. Paul lists ways that married women can glorify God; these duties may shed light on what Paul summarizes with one term ("childbearing") in 2:15. **manage their homes.** Women assumed responsibility in household oversight (see Titus 2:5 and note). **the enemy.** The Greek word most often refers to human, not demonic, detractors; the same Greek word is used in Luke 13:17 ("opponents"); 21:15 ("adversaries"); 1 Cor 16:9 ("who oppose"); Gal 5:17 ("in conflict"); Phil 1:28 ("who oppose"). But the devil may be in view in light of v. 15 (2 Thess 2:4).
5:15 turned away. This is a problem confronting Timothy in other connections too (1:6; 2 Tim 4:4). **follow Satan.** They go back on their earlier "dedication to Christ" (v. 11) and "pledge" (v. 12).
5:16 This assumes that some women in the church were caring for widows by their own initiative. This is preferable to having the entire local assembly "burdened." Circumstances of those "really in need" vary and have to be assessed accordingly; it is important that the church be free to address true hardship cases (vv. 9–10).
5:17 elders. Pastoral leaders (Titus 1:5). They have oversight responsibilities (hence the label of "overseer" in 3:1); some excel at "preaching and teaching." **worthy.** Could refer to the respect God gives, the congregation gives, or both. **double honor.** Might be figurative but could also refer to wages; congregations should not be stingy in their support for paid staff.
5:18 Scripture. In Paul's era this meant primarily the OT, which continues to be important to Christians. **Do not muzzle an ox.** Paul applies the same verse (Deut 25:4) in 1 Cor 9:9 (see note on 1 Cor 9:7–11). **The worker deserves his wages.** This "Scripture" appears to quote Jesus from Luke 10:7. If so, it indicates that portions of what we call the NT were viewed in the early church as just as authoritative as the OT (see also 2 Pet 3:16 and note).
5:19 two or three witnesses. Echoes the teaching of Moses (Deut 19:15), Jesus (Matt 18:16), and Paul elsewhere (2 Cor 13:1). The Western legal system largely incorporates this principle.
5:20 reprove ... so that the others may take warning. An example of church discipline for deterrent effect. Of course, one must first establish proof of sin (v. 19). Leaders are held to a high and public standard.
5:21 I charge you. Church discipline (v. 20) is never easy. Nor is it easy for disciplinary measures to be orderly, fair, and impartial. Timothy must not skirt these duties, so Paul invokes "God and Christ Jesus and the elect angels" (not Satan and other fallen angels) to underscore his words.
5:22 Do not be hasty. People must be tested before leading a congregation (3:8). **laying on of hands.** Recognized God's selection of people for his service (2 Tim 1:6; Acts 6:6; 13:3). **Keep yourself pure.** May be a restatement of earlier counsel (v. 2; 1:5; 4:12). Or it may warn Timothy against the taint of promoting an unworthy man to church leadership.
5:23 Paul's instructions about leaders in the church includes counsel for the leader to whom he writes. **use a little wine.** Could have a sterilizing effect on impure water. Despite Timothy's high standing as Paul's aide and church overseer, like Paul (2 Cor 12:7) he endured "frequent illnesses" that God did not see fit to take away (cf. Trophimus in 2 Tim 4:20).
5:24–25 Both "sins" and "good deeds" will eventually work their way into the open (Prov 5:21; 15:3; Matt 10:26). Paul confirms in Timothy a sense of ethical urgency, both for his sake and for leaders under his supervision. For there is "judgment ahead."
6:1 Paul's attention shifts to the slave-master relationship. If slaves can gain free status, that is good (1 Cor 7:21). But until such time, their full respect of masters will enhance Christian witness.
6:2b–21 *Final Clarification and Exhortation.* Ephesus was a thriving

6:2 [r] 1Ti 4:11
6:3 [s] 1Ti 1:3 [t] 1Ti 1:10
6:4 [u] 2Ti 2:14
6:5 [v] Titus 1:15
6:6 [w] Php 4:11; Heb 13:5 [x] 1Ti 4:8
6:7 [y] Job 1:21; Ecc 5:15
6:8 [z] Heb 13:5
6:9 [a] Pr 15:27 [b] 1Ti 3:7
6:10 [c] 1Ti 3:3 [d] Jas 5:19
6:11 [e] 2Ti 3:17 [f] 2Ti 2:22
6:12 [g] 1Co 9:25,26; 1Ti 1:18 [h] Php 3:12
6:13 [i] Jn 18:33-37 [j] 1Ti 5:21
6:15 [k] 1Ti 1:11

better because their masters are dear to them as fellow believers and are devoted to the welfare[a] of
their slaves.

False Teachers and the Love of Money

These are the things you are to teach and insist on.[r] 3If anyone teaches otherwise[s] and does not
agree to the sound instruction[t] of our Lord Jesus Christ and to godly teaching, 4they are conceited and
understand nothing. They have an unhealthy interest in controversies and quarrels about words[u] that
result in envy, strife, malicious talk, evil suspicions 5and constant friction between people of corrupt
mind, who have been robbed of the truth[v] and who think that godliness is a means to financial gain.
6But godliness with contentment[w] is great gain.[x] 7For we brought nothing into the world, and we
can take nothing out of it.[y] 8But if we have food and clothing, we will be content with that.[z] 9Those
who want to get rich[a] fall into temptation and a trap[b] and into many foolish and harmful desires that
plunge people into ruin and destruction. 10For the love of money[c] is a root of all kinds of evil. Some
people, eager for money, have wandered from the faith[d] and pierced themselves with many griefs.

Final Charge to Timothy

11But you, man of God,[e] flee from all this, and pursue righteousness, godliness, faith, love,[f] endurance and gentleness. 12Fight the good fight[g] of the faith. Take hold of[h] the eternal life to which you
were called when you made your good confession in the presence of many witnesses. 13In the sight of
God, who gives life to everything, and of Christ Jesus, who while testifying before Pontius Pilate[i] made
the good confession, I charge you[j] 14to keep this command without spot or blame until the appearing
of our Lord Jesus Christ, 15which God will bring about in his own time — God, the blessed[k] and only

[a] 2 Or *and benefit from the service*

commercial and cultural center. Worldly prosperity and principles dominated the minds of many who came into the church. Paul concludes his letter with special attention to prominent threats to Christian integrity. Central is a grand vision of God (vv. 15–16) and his grace (v. 21; cf. 1:2,14).

6:2b–10 *False Teachers and the Love of Money.* Paul offers perspective on opponents of his teaching, along with insight into the danger of linking the pursuit of God with financial gain. Of the eight times that the Greek word *eusebeia* ("godliness") occurs in 1 Timothy (see note on 2:2), three of those times are in this section (vv. 3,5,6).

6:2b These … things. Paul's counsel in previous verses. **insist on.** Apostolic teaching may be hard to accept and unpopular to advocate, but it is vital for the church's existence and mission. Timothy must not back down.

6:3 teaches otherwise. The same Greek word is translated "teach false doctrines" in 1:3. This is a primary concern of the entire letter. Paul views what he writes and its implications as expressing Christ's own "instruction." **godly.** See note on 2:2.

6:4 Gospel instruction aims at unity and love. Unsound doctrine yields ugly results with verbal strife at the center.

6:5 robbed of the truth. On "truth" see note on Titus 1:14. The Greek construction could suggest that these people are self-corrupted. In any case their error is evident from their focus on monetary gain. Like Jesus (e.g., Matt 6:19), Paul taught and modeled primarily the pursuit of faith and the true knowledge of God, not getting rich. **godliness.** See note on 2:2.

6:6 godliness. See note on 2:2. **contentment.** Fellowship with Christ bestows an inner "contentment" that greed can never render (Phil 4:12).

6:7 brought nothing into the world. Not only a common sense observation but also the clear teaching of the OT (Job 1:21; Ps 49:17; Eccl 5:15). It is easy to forget that what ultimately, truly matters in this world is what matters in the world to come.

6:8 See Phil 4:11–12. **food and clothing.** Jesus in his temptations (Matt 4:1–11), Paul in his trials (2 Cor 11:23–27), and God's people in their lives of faith (Heb 11:37–38) sometimes lacked even these basics. This is also true today of many persecuted Christians worldwide. Christians with little still have enough to be content.

6:9 Wealth itself is not a sin (see vv. 17–18 and notes). But wealth becomes a problem when the desire to get rich lures the gullible away from God and "into ruin."

6:10 love of money. The word *order* in Greek stresses the heinous nature of "money love." Like the false doctrine used to justify it, it leads away from "the faith" and causes "many griefs."

6:11–21 *Final Charge to Timothy.* Thus far Paul has oscillated between counseling Timothy and instructing those Timothy leads and serves. Most of the closing verses pertain to Timothy directly.

6:11 man of God. Draws on OT language (Deut 33:1; 1 Sam 9:6) to underscore Timothy's integrity and responsibility. This Greek term appears elsewhere in the NT only in 2 Tim 3:17 ("servant of God"; see note there). **all this.** The ills and evils like those warned against in vv. 4–5,9–10. But the point is not simply to "flee"; it is to "pursue" the qualities and actions that life in Christ makes possible. **godliness.** See note on 2:2.

6:12 fight. Paul likens faithful living to a vigorous and sometimes perilous engagement with enemy forces. **the faith.** Divinely revealed teaching (see note on 3:9). **good confession.** May refer to Timothy's baptism or when he was set apart for gospel service.

6:13 I charge you. Five other times in 1 Timothy, Paul tells Timothy to "charge" or "command" others (v. 17; 1:3; 4:11; 5:7 ["Give … instructions"], 21). But Timothy too is under divine command. Christ's "good confession" is the basis for Timothy's (v. 12).

6:14 this command. Paul's charge beginning in v. 11, though it does not exclude all Paul has written in the letter regarding teaching and caring for the church. **appearing of our Lord Jesus Christ.** Christ's "appearing" (2 Tim 1:10; 4:1,8; 2 Thess 2:8; Titus 2:13) lends urgency to life and gives incentive for readiness.

6:15–16 Paul's vision of God's grandeur is second to none in Scripture. He stresses God's transcendence, uniqueness, omnipotence, eternality, and excellence. Basic to Paul's ethics is his acute perception of God.

6:15 in his own time. Creation (Gen 1:1) and the incarnation (Gal 4:4) occurred on God's timetable. So will Christ's return (v. 14).

Ruler,[l] the King of kings and Lord of lords,[m] 16 who alone is immortal[n] and who lives in unapproachable
light, whom no one has seen or can see.[o] To him be honor and might forever. Amen.

17 Command those who are rich in this present world not to be arrogant nor to put their hope in
wealth,[p] which is so uncertain, but to put their hope in God,[q] who richly provides us with everything
for our enjoyment.[r] 18 Command them to do good, to be rich in good deeds,[s] and to be generous and
willing to share.[t] 19 In this way they will lay up treasure for themselves[u] as a firm foundation for the
coming age, so that they may take hold of the life that is truly life.

20 Timothy, guard what has been entrusted[v] to your care. Turn away from godless chatter[w] and the
opposing ideas of what is falsely called knowledge, 21 which some have professed and in so doing have
departed from the faith.[x]

Grace be with you all.[y]

6:15 [l] 1Ti 1:17 [m] Rev 17:14; 19:16
6:16 [n] 1Ti 1:17 [o] Jn 1:18
6:17 [p] Lk 12:20,21 [q] 1Ti 4:10 [r] Ac 14:17
6:18 [s] 1Ti 5:10 [t] Ro 12:8,13
6:19 [u] Mt 6:20
6:20 [v] 2Ti 1:12,14 [w] 2Ti 2:16
6:21 [x] 2Ti 2:18 [y] Col 4:18

6:16 whom no one has seen. God the Father in his full heavenly glory (John 1:18). All things earthly and human pale by comparison. Biblical passages that speak of seeing God (e.g., Exod 24:11; 33:11; Isa 6:1) refer to preliminary glimpses of his glory (Exod 33:18–23).

6:17 Command those who are rich. It seems that wealthy persons posed a challenge to Timothy's oversight. "Life does not consist in an abundance of possessions" (Luke 12:15), yet God "richly provides" for the sake of human "enjoyment." Paul's teaching is not ascetic. What God provides may not be wealth.

6:18 be generous and willing to share. Believers should place wealth at God's disposal as a means of extending his kingdom by meeting human needs.

6:19 lay up treasure. May mean to confirm their salvation, to assure heavenly treasure (Matt 6:20; 19:21), or both. **truly life.** Human existence at the purely material level falls short of God's design. Present life is noble when lived as preparation for "the coming age."

6:20 Timothy. Could be translated "O Timothy!" to convey depth of feeling. As in v. 11 ("you, man of God") and 1:18, Paul sounds a dramatic note of personal appeal; these are the only three nouns of direct address in the letter. **guard.** For the sake of the flock, pastoral leaders must often guard against elements hostile to God and his people. **what has been entrusted.** Refers to the gospel message; see 2 Tim 1:13–14 and notes. **knowledge.** Translates the Greek word *gnōsis*. In the second century, "gnostic" systems arose that borrowed and twisted Christian belief. But Gnosticism in this more developed sense arose well after Paul's lifetime.

6:21 departed. See 1:6; 2 Tim 2:18. The letter ends on the same note it begins: with concern about departures from normative Christian teaching. **you all.** See also 2 Tim 4:22 and note. Paul writes to Timothy but addresses him here as a member of the community he has been called to serve. He may also expect Timothy to read this letter to the entire Ephesian congregation.

INTRODUCTION TO 2 TIMOTHY

AUTHOR

Paul names himself as author in the first word (1:1). Personal allusions throughout (see 1:4–6,15–18; 2:1–2, 22–26; 3:14–15; 4:2,5,9–22) give the impression that this is the apostle Paul, who chose Timothy as his co-worker (Acts 16:1–5).

In the past 200 years, a tradition of doubting Pauline authorship has arisen (see Introduction to 1 Timothy: Author). But there are reasonable replies to skeptical queries. 2 Timothy has strong claim to authenticity whether we think in terms of its ties with other Pauline letters or its place in early Christian history. Calls to reject Paul's authorship lack a compelling foundation.

DATE, PLACE OF COMPOSITION, AND DESTINATION

There is evidence that Paul's first Roman imprisonment (Acts 28) ended in his release around AD 62 and was followed by a fourth missionary journey. It is most likely that during this ministry Paul wrote 1 Timothy and Titus. As Paul writes 2 Timothy, he knows his time of "departure is near" (4:6). He is "chained like a criminal" (2:9) and undergoing trial, the outcome of which could be "the lion's mouth" (4:17). He was evidently arrested a second time by Roman authorities (under Nero, who reigned AD 54–68) and writes or dictates 2 Timothy from jail. He has been accused of a crime punishable by death. Yet he is confident that "the Lord will rescue [him]" and "bring [him] safely to [God's] heavenly kingdom" (4:18). His physical circumstances seem hopeless, but he has not lost spiritual hope. Paul writes this second letter to Timothy from Roman imprisonment around AD 64–67.

PURPOSE AND RECIPIENT

This letter, clearly addressed to Timothy (1:2; see Introduction to 1 Timothy: Recipient), serves several purposes. (1) The final verse (4:22) may imply ("you all") that the letter will be read to the entire Ephesian congregation; this means that 2 Timothy was a message not to Timothy alone but to a much wider circle of believers to whom Paul wished to reach out. (2) Paul is concerned for the integrity of the gospel message in an adverse age (1:14; 3:14; 4:2) and writes to reinforce Timothy's commitment to it. (3) Paul writes to confirm his wish for Timothy to visit him as soon as possible (4:9; see 1:4). Paul experiences the pangs of human loneliness. Many have deserted him, including Phygelus, Hermogenes, and Demas (1:15; 4:10). Co-workers like Crescens, Titus, and Tychicus have left for ministry elsewhere (4:10,12). His only companion is Luke (4:11). He needs Mark (4:11) but especially Timothy, whom he regards as a son (1:2; Phil 2:22) and who has for years shared closely in Paul's labors (Rom 16:21; 1 Cor 4:17; Phil 2:20). 2 Timothy is Paul's plea for Timothy to "come to me quickly" (4:9). (4) In the interim, he knows that Timothy needs encouragement. Paul steels Timothy for his duties by appealing to God's grace, Christ's enabling, his (Paul's) own example, and the enemy's folly. What Paul tells Timothy, Timothy must pass on to the people of the Ephesian church (2:2,14). (5) The final chapter dignifies Timothy in his trials by issuing an ennobling charge to persevere for the sake of his eventual crown of righteousness as a gospel servant (4:1–8).

GENRE

2 Timothy is a letter from an apostle to a younger co-worker and, by extension, to the churches among which this co-worker serves (see Introduction to 1 Timothy: Genre; see note on 1 Tim 6:21). The imminence of the author's death adds the air of a last will and testament.

CANONICITY

As in the case of 1 Timothy and Titus (see Introduction to 1 Timothy: Canonicity), there is evidence that 2 Timothy was known and cited as a Pauline writing by around AD 100. This helps account for the fairly uniform high regard that the letter has received throughout church history (until recent times in some circles).

View of a menorah carved on one of the marble steps of the Celsus Library. This seven-branched lampstand is the only archaeological indication of the presence of Jews at Ephesus.
www.HolyLandPhotos.org

THEMES AND THEOLOGY

The five nouns occurring most frequently in 2 Timothy are Lord (16), God (13), Jesus (13), Christ (13), and faith (9). This points to the centrality of the doctrines of God and of Christ in this letter, as well as the need for personal active faith. Based upon that bedrock, Paul offers deep insight into martyrdom (4:6–8), the unchangeable essence of the grace of the gospel that is to be passed on faithfully (2:1–3) until the Lord returns (1:12,18; 4:1,8), and the suffering that often attends discipleship (1:8,12; 2:2,9,12; 3:11–12). Like Jesus, Paul found opposition to the gospel all around, and 2 Timothy gives hope that just as ancient forces arrayed against the Christian message did not prevail (2:14–18; 3:1–9; 4:3–4), so too the church today can go about its mission with confidence on the basis of the "sound teaching" that it lives out and guards "with the help of the Holy Spirit" (1:13–14).

OUTLINE

I. Greeting and Reasons for Writing (1:1–18)
- A. Greeting (1:1–2)
- B. Thanksgiving (1:3–5)
- C. Appeal for Loyalty to Paul and the Gospel (1:6–14)
- D. Examples of Disloyalty and Loyalty (1:15–18)

II. Priorities for Timothy (2:1—3:9)
- A. The Appeal Renewed (2:1–13)
- B. Dealing With False Teachers (2:14—3:9)

III. Concluding Reminders, Instructions, and Greetings (3:10—4:22)
- A. A Final Charge to Timothy (3:10—4:8)
- B. Personal Remarks (4:9–18)
- C. Final Greetings (4:19–22)

2 TIMOTHY

1:1 [a]2Co 1:1 [b]Eph 3:6; 1Ti 6:19
1:2 [c]Ac 16:1 [d]1Ti 1:2
1:3 [e]Ro 1:8 [f]Ro 1:10
1:4 [g]Ac 20:37 [h]2Ti 4:9
1:5 [i]1Ti 1:5 [j]Ac 16:1
1:6 [k]1Ti 4:14
1:7 [l]Ro 8:15
1:8 [m]Mk 8:38; Ro 1:16 [n]Eph 3:1

1 Paul, an apostle of Christ Jesus by the will of God,[a] in keeping with the promise of life that is in
Christ Jesus,[b]

2 To Timothy,[c] my dear son:[d]

Grace, mercy and peace from God the Father and Christ Jesus our Lord.

Thanksgiving

3 I thank God,[e] whom I serve, as my ancestors did, with a clear conscience, as night and day I constantly remember you in my prayers.[f] 4 Recalling your tears,[g] I long to see you,[h] so that I may be filled
with joy. 5 I am reminded of your sincere faith,[i] which first lived in your grandmother Lois and in your
mother Eunice[j] and, I am persuaded, now lives in you also.

Appeal for Loyalty to Paul and the Gospel

6 For this reason I remind you to fan into flame the gift of God, which is in you through the laying on of my hands.[k] 7 For the Spirit God gave us does not make us timid,[l] but gives us power, love
and self-discipline. 8 So do not be ashamed[m] of the testimony about our Lord or of me his prisoner.[n]

1:1–18 *Greeting and Reasons for Writing.* Though "chained like a criminal" (2:9), Paul writes calmly and warmly to connect with his faithful co-worker, stir up his passion for pastoral labor (1:6), and admonish him to steadfastness and diligence (1:13–14).

1:1–2 *Greeting.* This is how letters started in NT times. The language—terms like "apostle," "Christ Jesus," "grace," and "peace"—help mark this letter as apostolic in origin and revelatory in substance. Another important factor is the identity of the author using this language. Paul had met Christ (Acts 9:1–19; 22:1–21; 26:9–23), been granted access to heavenly glories (2 Cor 12:1–7), and suffered extensively for Christ's sake (e.g., 2 Cor 11:16–33), which he will mention later in this letter (e.g., v. 8; 2:3; 3:12). His experience lends gravity to his words, just as his ties to Timothy (see Introduction: Purpose and Recipient) would have helped the greeting convey warmth.

1:1 the promise of life. May have been vivid to Paul as he faced death (4:6).

1:2 Paul's words are identical to 1 Tim 1:2, except there Paul calls Timothy not "my dear son" but rather "my true son in the faith." Paul refers to Timothy's "sincere faith" in v. 5.

1:3–5 *Thanksgiving.* Like the greeting, this is a literary convention. Paul reminds Timothy of his family heritage in the faith along with Paul's affection as a personal friend and co-worker.

1:3 ancestors. Paul refers to his Jewish heritage. Yet as an "apostle to the Gentiles" (Rom 11:13; Gal 2:8), he is aware that those who receive Christ become "children of Abraham" by faith (Gal 3:7). They become part of the family, or household, of God (1 Tim 3:15).

1:4 tears. An unknown event. Word may have reached Paul of grief or other calamity in Timothy's life. **joy.** Paul frequently mentions joy in his other letters but only here in the Pastoral Letters.

1:5 sincere. Occurs four times in Paul's letters, referring to faith (here and 1 Tim 1:5) or love (Rom 12:9; 2 Cor 6:6). **grandmother ... mother.** Timothy's father was apparently not a believer, though his mother (of Jewish descent) was (Acts 16:1). Timothy's faith could be traced to his grandmother and mother (3:15).

1:6–14 *Appeal for Loyalty to Paul and the Gospel.* Paul must have received word that Timothy was facing steep challenges. He writes to urge Timothy to stand his ground.

1:6 fan into flame the gift of God. Either the Holy Spirit himself or the spiritual gifts he bestows (see 1 Tim 4:14 and note). Timothy needs this to overcome timidity (v. 7) and join Paul in suffering (v. 8). The Spirit enables for ministry, but his gifts call for reception and intentional response (Eph 5:18; 1 Thess 5:19). **laying on of my hands.** In the OT this was a sign of dedication to the Lord's service (e.g., Num 8:10; 27:18).

1:7 Only the Spirit can equip Timothy with these essential qualities. **timid.** Using a related Greek word, Jesus rebuked his disciples for cowardice (Matt 8:26; Mark 4:40; see Rev 21:8). The fruit of the Spirit includes love (Gal 5:22), which displaces fear (1 John 4:18), and self-control (Gal 5:23). God's presence bestows courage (Prov 28:1; Acts 4:31).

1:8 testimony. Most likely the particulars of the gospel message. **me his prisoner.** To support Paul might bring unwanted attention to

Rather, join with me in suffering for the gospel,[o] by the power of God. 9He has saved us and called[p]
us to a holy life — not because of anything we have done but because of his own purpose and grace.
This grace was given us in Christ Jesus before the beginning of time, 10but it has now been revealed[q]
through the appearing of our Savior, Christ Jesus, who has destroyed death[r] and has brought life
and immortality to light through the gospel. 11And of this gospel I was appointed a herald and an
apostle and a teacher.[s] 12That is why I am suffering as I am. Yet this is no cause for shame, because
I know whom I have believed, and am convinced that he is able to guard[t] what I have entrusted to
him until that day.[u]

13What you heard from me, keep[v] as the pattern of sound teaching, with faith and love in Christ
Jesus.[w] 14Guard the good deposit that was entrusted to you — guard it with the help of the Holy Spirit
who lives in us.[x]

Examples of Disloyalty and Loyalty

15You know that everyone in the province of Asia has deserted me,[y] including Phygelus and
Hermogenes.

16May the Lord show mercy to the household of Onesiphorus,[z] because he often refreshed me and
was not ashamed of my chains. 17On the contrary, when he was in Rome, he searched hard for me until
he found me. 18May the Lord grant that he will find mercy from the Lord on that day! You know very
well in how many ways he helped me[a] in Ephesus.

The Appeal Renewed

2 You then, my son, be strong[b] in the grace that is in Christ Jesus. 2And the things you have heard
me say[c] in the presence of many witnesses[d] entrust to reliable people who will also be qualified to
teach others. 3Join with me in suffering, like a good soldier[e] of Christ Jesus. 4No one serving as a soldier

1:8 [o] 2Ti 2:3,9; 4:5
1:9 [p] Ro 8:28
1:10 [q] Eph 1:9 [r] 1Co 15:26,54
1:11 [s] 1Ti 2:7
1:12 [t] 1Ti 6:20 [u] ver 18
1:13 [v] Titus 1:9 [w] 1Ti 1:14
1:14 [x] Ro 8:9
1:15 [y] 2Ti 4:10,11,16
1:16 [z] 2Ti 4:19
1:18 [a] Heb 6:10
2:1 [b] Eph 6:10
2:2 [c] 2Ti 1:13 [d] 1Ti 6:12
2:3 [e] 1Ti 1:18

Timothy. Paul had been imprisoned frequently over the years (Acts 16:25; 23:18; 2 Cor 11:23) and wrote four other letters while in chains (Ephesians, Philippians, Colossians, Philemon). **suffering.** Since ministering involves suffering, it is tempting to be slack. **power of God.** An effect of the Spirit (v. 7).

1:9 to a holy life. Could also be translated "with a holy calling." God's call (Rom 8:30) is saving, life-changing, and undeserved. **grace.** Salvation is by grace through faith (Eph 2:8–9; see Titus 2:11 and note) and not a reward for good works (Rom 3:28; Titus 3:5). **before ... time.** Prior to birth (Gal 1:15) and even creation itself (Eph 1:4; 1 Pet 1:20; Rev 13:8). God is at work long before we are aware.

1:10 appearing. See note on 1 Tim 6:14. **our Savior.** Often refers to God (see 1 Tim 1:1 and note), but Christ Jesus fills the same role (Titus 1:4; 3:6). **destroyed death.** See 1 Cor 15:26,54–57; Heb 2:14–15. **through the gospel.** Recalls Rom 1:16–17, where the gospel, the power of God, reveals God's righteousness through faith with life-changing effect. Here God's "grace" (v. 9) is "revealed through the appearing of our Savior, Christ Jesus, who ... brought life and immortality ... through the gospel."

1:11 Though Timothy was not an "apostle" like Paul, his duties were similar as a pastoral teacher (4:2) and an "evangelist" (4:5). Paul is trying to rally Timothy to Paul's level of courage and fidelity.

1:12 suffering. Paul's gospel ministry (v. 11) drew opposition, just as it did for his followers (3:12; Phil 1:29; 1 Thess 2:4; 2 Thess 1:5). **I know whom.** Paul's knowledge of God was not just a concept or theory but interpersonal communion. **able to guard.** Paul is convinced of God's faithfulness (2 Thess 3:3). **entrusted.** Could be either what Paul has placed in God's hands (his daily existence and eternal destiny) or what God has entrusted to Paul (the gospel message, especially to the Gentiles). **that day.** See v. 18; see also notes on 4:8; Amos 2:16. God will vindicate Paul at the final judgment (1 Cor 3:13; 2 Cor 5:10), whatever opposition to him the gospel message may spawn.

1:13 What you heard from me. Timothy had been Paul's ministry partner for over a decade. **pattern of sound teaching.** See Rom 6:17. This is more than information; it is enlivened "with faith and love in Christ Jesus," which could describe either how Timothy should "keep" Paul's teaching or how he had heard and received it over the years.

1:14 Guard. The same word is used of God's protection in v. 12 (see note). **the good deposit.** The gospel message he received. **entrusted.** See 2:2; 1 Tim 6:20. **with the help of.** The Spirit is the decisive agent in what Timothy cannot accomplish on his own. **Spirit who lives in us.** In the same way that faith (see v. 5) and the word about Christ (Col 3:16) are alive in believers, God himself by the Spirit indwells his people. He is "in" each one personally and connects them corporately to Christ, making the many into one (1 Cor 12:13–14).

1:15–18 *Examples of Disloyalty and Loyalty.* After seeking to rally Timothy in the previous section, Paul concedes that he faces challenges, too. Yet there are consolations like Onesiphorus, for whom Paul expresses praise and asks God's mercy.

1:15 everyone. Paul likely overstates to express his sorrow over the apparent loss of support for Christ. **province of Asia.** Not the Far East but the region around Ephesus, in the western part of modern Turkey (see map, p. 2456). **deserted me.** Ministers today may recast or abandon the core gospel message because of various pressures, but this is nothing new: many in Paul's own lifetime "deserted" or at least despised him and the other apostles (1 Cor 4:9–13; 2 Cor 4:7–12; 1 John 2:19).

1:16 Roman prisoners relied on help from relatives or friends. **Onesiphorus.** He rose to the occasion despite Paul's "chains." For Paul as a prisoner, see 1:8 and note.

1:17 searched hard. Onesiphorus was determined to find the obscure site where Paul was confined.

1:18 that day. See note on v. 12. **he helped me.** May refer to Onesiphorus's help during Paul's three-year ministry in Ephesus (Acts 19–20).

2:1 — 3:9 *Priorities for Timothy.* Paul has known and worked with Timothy for some 15 years. He is able to put his finger on issues most pertinent and constructive for Timothy's continued growth in ministry.

2:1–13 *The Appeal Renewed.* Paul resumes the theme of exhortation. He draws on practical examples (vv. 3–6), on the suffering of Jesus and

2:5 [f]1Co 9:25
2:8 [g]Ac 2:24 [h]Mt 1:1 [i]Ro 2:16
2:9 [j]Ac 9:16
2:10 [k]Col 1:24 [l]2Co 4:17
2:11 [m]Ro 6:2-11
2:12 [n]Ro 8:17; 1Pe 4:13 [o]Mt 10:33
2:13 [p]Nu 23:19; Ro 3:3

gets entangled in civilian affairs, but rather tries to please his commanding officer. 5 Similarly, anyone
who competes as an athlete does not receive the victor's crown[f] except by competing according to the
rules. 6 The hardworking farmer should be the first to receive a share of the crops. 7 Reflect on what I
am saying, for the Lord will give you insight into all this.

8 Remember Jesus Christ, raised from the dead,[g] descended from David.[h] This is my gospel,[i] 9 for
which I am suffering[j] even to the point of being chained like a criminal. But God's word is not chained.
10 Therefore I endure everything[k] for the sake of the elect, that they too may obtain the salvation that
is in Christ Jesus, with eternal glory.[l]

11 Here is a trustworthy saying:

If we died with him,
we will also live with him;[m]
12 if we endure,
we will also reign with him.[n]
If we disown him,
he will also disown us;[o]
13 if we are faithless,
he remains faithful,[p]
for he cannot disown himself.

Paul (vv. 8–10), and on a saying that had become popular by that time in the early church (vv. 11–13).

2:1 You then. See note on 3:10. **be strong.** Could refer to the strengthening effect of the Spirit (1:7,14), who bestows God's "grace ... in Christ Jesus" (see note on Titus 2:11).

2:2 things. Elements of the gospel Paul taught and preached. **many witnesses.** Paul's ministry was bold and public, not timid (cf. 1:7) and concealed. Timothy should stand tall. **entrust ... teach.** Echoes Jesus' directives in Matt 28:18–20 that his followers be disciples in order to make disciples. **reliable.** The Greek word (*pistois*) conveys the idea of integrity in matters of faith and Christian obedience. **will also be qualified.** Future tense; they must first receive instruction.

2:3 Join with me in suffering. Repeats 1:8; see also 2:9; 4:5. Following Christ exposes believers to persecution (3:12). **good soldier.** One who is loyal and ready to lay down his life; like a disciple. Verses 4–6 give practical examples of hardship (a soldier, an athlete, a farmer).

2:4 his commanding officer. Christ. Paul calls on Timothy to shun distractions and pay intense attention to Christ.

2:5 anyone who competes as an athlete. Paul depicts the Christian life for "anyone" as being not a leisure or spectator activity but as fierce competition. Rigorous training is necessary; the "victor's crown" is the goal. Timothy cannot be content with a casual approach to serving Christ. For Paul's example in pursuing the "crown," see 1 Cor 9:24–27. **the rules.** One who follows Christ must be willing to suffer. Without that Timothy will not obtain the goal set for believers (4:8).

2:6 The hardworking farmer. He reaps a harvest; so too the long-suffering and unselfish believer realizes the blessing of suffering for Jesus' sake. Some see other benefits in view, like salvation or God's material provision or a harvest of converts.

2:7 the Lord will give you insight. Timothy must ponder prayerfully to benefit from the wisdom of what Paul has written and to be strong in "the grace that is in Christ Jesus" (v. 1).

2:8 Remember Jesus Christ. Death did not defeat Jesus, so his follower Timothy need not fear. **Jesus Christ.** Used by Paul six times in the Pastoral Letters (here; 1 Tim 6:3,14; Titus 1:1; 2:13; 3:6). More commonly (two dozen times) he uses "Christ Jesus." **Christ.** The meaning ("anointed one") connects Jesus with David, Israel's ancient anointed king, mentioned later in the verse. **raised.** Christ's resurrection declares his deity (Rom 1:4). **descended from David.** David was a regal and powerful conquering warrior and king. Victory is in Jesus' earthly bloodline, despite the suffering that ended his life. As ruler over all, including death, Christ receives the kingdom promised to his forebear (2 Sam 7:1–16) and administers its benefits to all nations.

2:9 I am suffering. Paul is not asking Timothy (v. 3) to do something that Paul does not do himself. **criminal.** The same Greek word occurs elsewhere in the NT only in Luke's account of Jesus' crucifixion as he hung between two "criminals" (Luke 23:32,33,39). **God's word is not chained.** It remains mobile, spreading "rapidly" (2 Thess 3:1) and enduring forever (1 Pet 1:23–25).

2:10 endure everything. For a list of what Paul faced and overcame, see 2 Cor 11:23—12:10. **for the sake of the elect.** The vindication of the gospel fulfills God's promises to all his people in all times. The fact that God "elects" (chooses) those who believe (Deut 7:6; Jer 3:14; John 15:16; Rom 9:11; 11:7; 2 Pet 1:10) works together with the offer of salvation to all (John 3:16; Rom 9:33; 1 Pet 2:6).

2:11 trustworthy saying. See note on 1 Tim 1:15. Paul continues to urge Timothy to remember Jesus (v. 8) so he will be enabled to suffer if necessary (v. 3). **died with him.** See Gal 2:20. God united with Christ on the cross all who did or would believe in him (Rom 6:6). **live with him.** May refer to future glory in the wake of present suffering (Rom 8:17–18). It also serves to encourage Timothy in bearing suffering in this life.

2:12 reign with him. Enjoy fellowship with Christ in the age to come (Rev 5:10; 22:5). **he will also disown us.** God knows and keeps his own (v. 19). But those who show by their beliefs and actions that Christ is not their Lord cannot expect God's approval, in this age or the next (Matt 7:21–23).

2:13 he remains faithful. Paul could speak from the experience of opposing Christ but then receiving God's grace, faith, and love (1 Tim 1:13–14). See Deut 7:9; Ps 31:5; 1 Cor 1:9; 10:13; 2 Cor 1:18. Human unbelief does not nullify God's utter and eternal faithfulness (Rom 3:3–4). **cannot disown himself.** God's character is unchanging (Mal 3:6; Heb 13:8). This may be a warning for Timothy not to weaken. Or it may be a reminder of God's abundant grace and love toward any who turn to him in repentance and faith (1 John 1:9).

Dealing With False Teachers

14 Keep reminding God's people of these things. Warn them before God against quarreling about words;[q]
it is of no value, and only ruins those who listen. 15 Do your best to present yourself to God as one approved,
a worker who does not need to be ashamed and who correctly handles the word of truth.[r] 16 Avoid godless
chatter,[s] because those who indulge in it will become more and more ungodly. 17 Their teaching will spread
like gangrene. Among them are Hymenaeus[t] and Philetus, 18 who have departed from the truth. They say
that the resurrection has already taken place, and they destroy the faith of some.[u] 19 Nevertheless, God's
solid foundation stands firm,[v] sealed with this inscription: "The Lord knows those who are his,"[w] and,
"Everyone who confesses the name of the Lord[x] must turn away from wickedness."
20 In a large house there are articles not only of gold and silver, but also of wood and clay; some are
for special purposes and some for common use.[y] 21 Those who cleanse themselves from the latter will be
instruments for special purposes, made holy, useful to the Master and prepared to do any good work.[z]
22 Flee the evil desires of youth and pursue righteousness, faith, love[a] and peace, along with those who
call on the Lord out of a pure heart.[b] 23 Don't have anything to do with foolish and stupid arguments,
because you know they produce quarrels. 24 And the Lord's servant must not be quarrelsome but must be
kind to everyone, able to teach, not resentful.[c] 25 Opponents must be gently instructed, in the hope that
God will grant them repentance leading them to a knowledge of the truth,[d] 26 and that they will come to
their senses and escape from the trap of the devil,[e] who has taken them captive to do his will.

3 But mark this: There will be terrible times in the last days.[f] 2 People will be lovers of themselves, lovers of money,[g] boastful, proud,[h] abusive, disobedient to their parents,[i] ungrateful, unholy, 3 without
love, unforgiving, slanderous, without self-control, brutal, not lovers of the good, 4 treacherous, rash,

2:14 [q] 1Ti 6:4
2:15 [r] Eph 1:13; Jas 1:18
2:16 [s] Titus 3:9
2:17 [t] 1Ti 1:20
2:18 [u] 1Ti 1:19
2:19 [v] Isa 28:16 [w] Jn 10:14 [x] 1Co 1:2
2:20 [y] Ro 9:21
2:21 [z] 2Ti 3:17
2:22 [a] 1Ti 1:14; 6:11 [b] 1Ti 1:5
2:24 [c] 1Ti 3:2,3
2:25 [d] 1Ti 2:4
2:26 [e] 1Ti 3:7
3:1 [f] 1Ti 4:1
3:2 [g] 1Ti 3:3 [h] Ro 1:30 [i] Ro 1:30

2:14—3:9 *Dealing With False Teachers.* Thus far Paul has been reminding Timothy of his calling and resources. Now the spotlight swings to Timothy's mandate of "reminding God's people" (v. 14) of these matters in the face of false teachers and the havoc they cause.
2:14 before God. Indicates the gravity of Timothy's responsibility. God is observing Timothy's leadership and people's response. **quarreling about words.** See 1 Tim 6:4. Paul warns against meaningless argument. Yet there are times when it is right and necessary to assert exactly what words do and do not mean (Matt 22:31–32). Sometimes disobedience to God must be honestly opposed (Gal 2:11). Debate and decision regarding matters of faith and practice have always been unavoidable in the life of the church (Acts 15:1–21).
2:15 Do your best. Exercise utmost effort without delay (4:9,21; Titus 3:12). **correctly handles.** Interprets in a straightforward way, not in a way that is shifty or shady. **word of truth.** Scripture and the teaching it upholds. **truth.** See note on Titus 1:14.
2:16 godless chatter. See 1 Tim 6:20. **indulge.** Some delight in devious disputation.
2:17 gangrene. The Greek word could refer to various spreading diseases and underscores the repulsive nature of this particular "godless chatter" (v. 16). Substandard teaching is an infectious pox. In contrast, true teaching is "sound" (1:13; 4:3; 1 Tim 1:10; Titus 1:9; 2:1), a word from the medical field meaning "healthy." **Hymenaeus.** See 1 Tim 1:20; apparently earlier disciplinary measures were unsuccessful.
2:18 truth. See note on Titus 1:14. **the resurrection.** Christ's resurrection has already occurred (v. 8), with great benefit to believers, but believers still await a final and glorious bodily resurrection in the age to come (1 Cor 15:51–57). The false teachers viewed "resurrection" as a new spiritual awareness or state of the soul that had already taken place. They did not think Christians would receive new bodies after death like Jesus did. This contradicted the teachings of both Jesus (Matt 22:23–33) and Paul (1 Cor 15).
2:19 God is in control even amid deviation from his ways. **foundation.** May refer to the church, consisting of all whom "the Lord knows" (Num 16:5; Nah 1:7; John 10:14,17) and who accordingly "turn away from wickedness," implying a radical departure from it. Or the "foundation" could be God (or Christ) himself, his promises, and his saving works (1 Cor 3:11; Eph 2:20).
2:20 large house. Paul uses a metaphor to describe how people should conduct themselves in the church, "God's household" (1 Tim 3:15). **gold ... silver ... wood ... clay.** There is diversity in the body of Christ (1 Cor 12).
2:21 cleanse themselves. Those who follow Christ and "turn away from wickedness" (v. 19) are "made holy." They are primed for action "useful to the Master." **Master.** Refers to God in his total control and oversight (Luke 2:29; Acts 4:24; 2 Pet 2:1; Jude 4; Rev 6:10). The same word is used for slave-masters (e.g., 1 Tim 6:1–2; Titus 2:9).
2:22 Flee ... pursue. Christ liberates from evil (Rom 6:18) and substitutes pursuit of "righteousness, faith, love and peace," and other qualities instead (Phil 4:8–9). **evil desires of youth.** Could include lust but may also refer to immature timidity (1:7), self-dependence rather than trust in the Spirit (1:14), and willingness to engage in fruitless debate (2:14,16). **along with.** Forsaking evil and seeking good is not a solitary mission but a project in which believers uphold each other.
2:23 Vain disputation leading to quarrels is to be shunned (cf. vv. 14,16).
2:24 servant. Greek *doulos,* the word for "slave." Paul calls himself a "servant of God" (Titus 1:1). All believers are called to be servants of God and "slaves to righteousness" (Rom 6:19), but here the term may refer to Timothy's pastoral responsibility. As an example of the "flee ... pursue" command in v. 22, Timothy must flee the urge to be "quarrelsome" and instead exercise pastoral care that is kind, instructive, and not resentful even in the face of provocations.
2:25 repentance leading ... to a knowledge of the truth. Without repentance, which only God can grant, saving knowledge will be blocked. **truth.** See note on Titus 1:14.
2:26 escape. They are presently ensnared. **captive.** Captured alive. **his will.** Satan is a being who seeks to recruit support for his agenda. In contrast, believers daily pray and desire, "your will be done" (Matt 6:10).
3:1 last days. Not only future times, when things will worsen (Matt 24:21–31), but also the present. These "days," also called "later times" (1 Tim 4:1 and note), began with Christ's coming (Heb 1:1–2), intensified with Christ's resurrection and the Spirit's powerful arrival (Acts 2:17), and continue until his return.
3:2–5 Paul lists some 19 qualities of the evildoers whose presence

3:4 [j]1Ti 3:6
3:6 [k]Jude 4
3:8 [l]Ex 7:11 [m]Ac 13:8 [n]1Ti 6:5
3:9 [o]Ex 7:12
3:10 [p]1Ti 4:6
3:11 [q]Ac 13:14,50 [r]2Co 11:23-27 [s]Ps 34:19
3:12 [t]Ac 14:22
3:13 [u]2Ti 2:16
3:14 [v]2Ti 1:13
3:15 [w]2Ti 1:5 [x]Jn 5:39 [y]Ps 119:98,99
3:16 [z]2Pe 1:20,21 [a]Ro 4:23,24

conceited,[j] lovers of pleasure rather than lovers of God— 5having a form of godliness but denying its
power. Have nothing to do with such people.
6They are the kind who worm their way[k] into homes and gain control over gullible women, who are
loaded down with sins and are swayed by all kinds of evil desires, 7always learning but never able to
come to a knowledge of the truth. 8Just as Jannes and Jambres opposed Moses,[l] so also these teachers
oppose[m] the truth. They are men of depraved minds,[n] who, as far as the faith is concerned, are rejected.
9But they will not get very far because, as in the case of those men,[o] their folly will be clear to everyone.

A Final Charge to Timothy

10You, however, know all about my teaching,[p] my way of life, my purpose, faith, patience, love,
endurance, 11persecutions, sufferings—what kinds of things happened to me in Antioch,[q] Iconium
and Lystra, the persecutions I endured.[r] Yet the Lord rescued me from all of them.[s] 12In fact, everyone
who wants to live a godly life in Christ Jesus will be persecuted,[t] 13while evildoers and impostors will go
from bad to worse,[u] deceiving and being deceived. 14But as for you, continue in what you have learned
and have become convinced of, because you know those from whom you learned it,[v] 15and how from
infancy[w] you have known the Holy Scriptures,[x] which are able to make you wise[y] for salvation through
faith in Christ Jesus. 16All Scripture is God-breathed[z] and is useful for teaching,[a] rebuking, correcting

bears out that "terrible times" (v. 1) are at hand. For similar lists of evil deeds, see 1 Tim 1:8–11; Matt 15:17–20; Rom 1:29–31; 1 Cor 5:9–11; 1 Pet 4:3–4; Rev 21:8; 22:15. English cannot convey fully the colorful, artful, and finally, harrowing word picture Paul paints.

3:4 lovers of pleasure. Partially summarizes their wickedness. Whereas God calls people to love him and "have no other gods before [him]" (Exod 20:3), these evildoers enthrone their own warped self-gratification.

3:5 a form. Their "godliness" is in reality a sham. **Have nothing to do with.** Likely means exclusion from the congregation's activities. **such people.** "Opponents" are targets of correction, and Timothy should seek their repentance (2:25). But in the case of those whose behavior remains mired in the pattern described in 3:2–4, action is necessary for the sake of the integrity of the church's witness and the protection of its members and message.

3:6–7 Subverting "homes" destabilizes the entire church. **loaded down ... swayed ... always learning.** Describes the women, not those who victimize them. To learn is a mark of a disciple (a word that means "learner") of Jesus, but falsity always distances one from God's "truth" (see note on Titus 1:14). This is why Titus (like 1–2 Timothy) stresses sound (healthy, true) teaching.

3:8 Jannes and Jambres. Two of Pharaoh's sorcerer-priests who opposed Moses (Exod 7:11–12), according to Jewish tradition (their names do not appear in the OT). As they opposed God's saving work then, Timothy's opponents "oppose the truth" now. **truth.** See note on Titus 1:14.

3:9 Paul urges confidence, perhaps based on God's victory over Pharaoh through Moses, perhaps based on Christ's supremacy (1:12).

3:10—4:22 *Concluding Reminders, Instructions, and Greetings.* In eloquent and often poignant appeals, Paul exhorts and instructs Timothy, urging him to visit Paul soon (4:21). Paul's death could be imminent (4:6), yet "the lion's mouth" (4:17) pales compared with Paul's unshakable conviction that God will bring him "safely to his heavenly kingdom" (4:18).

3:10—4:8 *A Final Charge to Timothy.* Paul now reminds Timothy that what the gospel minister stands for has unimpeachable validity, particularly in the form of the Scriptures (3:10–17). On that basis, he admonishes Timothy (4:1–5). Calling to mind his often embattled life of service, Paul assures Timothy that the bruising life of honest ministry is well worth it in the end (4:6–8).

3:10 You. Emphatic; occurs when Paul seeks to rivet Timothy's attention (v. 14; 2:1; 4:5; see 1 Tim 6:11; Titus 2:1). Timothy should not be intimidated by the opponents and problems mentioned in previous verses. He should rather ponder and pursue Paul's teaching and example.

3:11 Antioch, Iconium and Lystra. See Acts 13:13—14:23, which describes when the gospel came to the region of Timothy's upbringing, resulting in his eventual enlistment as Paul's co-worker (Acts 16:1–5). **the Lord rescued me.** This does not mean deliverance from all harm, for Paul was stoned and left for dead (Acts 14:19–20) and experienced much opposition during this time. It means rather that the Lord kept him from death and empowered him for continued ministry. As God upholds Paul, he can likewise strengthen Timothy in his demanding situation.

3:12 everyone ... will be persecuted. Echoes Jesus' promise that following him means taking up one's cross (Matt 10:38; 16:24). See also Paul's conclusion from over a decade earlier (Acts 14:22), perhaps uttered in Timothy's hearing. Christian living in Paul's time attracted opposition resulting in persecution. Physical suffering may lessen when a society accepts the Bible's values. But in much of the world through most of history, Jesus' promises of persecution (John 15:18–21; 16:33; cf. 2 Tim 2:3) have found fulfillment. These words currently are verified daily in many locations of the church.

3:13 evildoers and imposters. They will prosper with seeming impunity (a situation already foreshadowed in OT times: Job 12:6; Pss 37:1,7; 92:7; Hab 1:13; Mal 3:15; see Job 21:7–15; Ps 73:3–12). Paul is conceding that things may seem grim if not hopeless to Timothy.

3:14 But as for you. See note on v. 10. **those from whom you learned it.** Not just Paul but also home influences (1:5) and doubtless others in the church. We also learn from others' trials in the faith, so that God can enable us to survive and even thrive.

3:15 from infancy. Timothy had a godly upbringing (see 1:5 and note) and would have learned the OT writings both at home and in the synagogue from about age five (see commands to teach children in Deut 6:7; Pss 71:17; 78:5–6). **able to make you wise for salvation.** Scripture works powerfully in the heart when combined with "faith in Christ Jesus."

3:16 All Scripture. In Paul's time the OT, but also the NT as it was being composed. The Bible both contains and is, in whole and in part, God's Word. **God-breathed.** Sometimes translated "inspired." The Greek word means given by the work of God's Spirit (see 2 Pet 1:20–21 and note). "The Holy Spirit spoke" in the writings of OT leaders and writers like David (Acts 1:16; see Acts 4:25). By extension this applies to NT writings as well (see 2 Pet 3:15–16 and note on 3:16). God has chosen to reveal himself not only in nature (Ps 8:1,3; Rom 1:20) and human moral awareness (Rom 2:15) but also supremely by spoken and written human language. This is the doctrine of inspiration. This doctrine

and training in righteousness, 17so that the servant of God[a][b] may be thoroughly equipped for every
good work.[c]

4 In the presence of God and of Christ Jesus, who will judge the living and the dead,[d] and in view of
his appearing and his kingdom, I give you this charge:[e] 2Preach[f] the word;[g] be prepared in season
and out of season; correct, rebuke[h] and encourage—with great patience and careful instruction. 3For
the time will come when people will not put up with sound doctrine.[i] Instead, to suit their own desires,
they will gather around them a great number of teachers to say what their itching ears want to hear.
4They will turn their ears away from the truth and turn aside to myths.[j] 5But you, keep your head in all
situations, endure hardship,[k] do the work of an evangelist,[l] discharge all the duties of your ministry.

6For I am already being poured out like a drink offering,[m] and the time for my departure is near.[n]
7I have fought the good fight,[o] I have finished the race,[p] I have kept the faith. 8Now there is in store
for me[q] the crown of righteousness, which the Lord, the righteous Judge, will award to me on that
day[r]—and not only to me, but also to all who have longed for his appearing.

Personal Remarks

9Do your best to come to me quickly, 10for Demas,[s] because he loved this world,[t] has deserted me
and has gone to Thessalonica. Crescens has gone to Galatia,[u] and Titus to Dalmatia. 11Only Luke[v] is

3:17 [b] 1Ti 6:11 [c] 2Ti 2:21
4:1 [d] Ac 10:42 [e] 1Ti 5:21
4:2 [f] 1Ti 4:13 [g] Gal 6:6 [h] 1Ti 5:20; Titus 1:13; 2:15
4:3 [i] 1Ti 1:10
4:4 [j] 1Ti 1:4
4:5 [k] 2Ti 1:8 [l] Ac 21:8
4:6 [m] Php 2:17 [n] Php 1:23
4:7 [o] 1Ti 1:18 [p] 1Co 9:24
4:8 [q] Col 1:5 [r] 2Ti 1:12
4:10 [s] Col 4:14 [t] 1Jn 2:15 [u] Ac 16:6
4:11 [v] Col 4:14

[a] *17* Or *that you, a man of God,*

---

does not downplay human action in Scripture's authorship but affirms Scripture's ultimate origin in God, who gave it. This makes it "useful for teaching" and related pastoral purposes, because it provides coherent, consistent, and reliable testimony to Christ (Luke 24:27,44; John 5:39–40; 1 Cor 15:3–4).

3:17 servant of God. Or "man of God" (see 1 Tim 6:11 and note, the only other place in the NT the Greek term appears). The phrase is used over 60 times in the Septuagint (the pre-Christian Greek translation of the OT) to refer to figures including Moses, Samuel, Shemaiah, Elijah, Elisha, several unnamed prophets, and David. Like Timothy, these men were called to leadership through prophetic gifting (1:6; 1 Tim 1:18; 4:14). The expression would be meaningful to Timothy with his OT knowledge (v. 15), though it has application to all who know Christ (v. 15) and recognize the God who gives Scripture (v. 16). **thoroughly equipped.** Effective and faithful service thrives on secure Scriptural equipping.

4:1 appearing. See note on 1 Tim 6:14. The return of Christ is an important incentive for godly living. **his kingdom.** Both his present and his coming reign. **charge.** The Greek word is used only four times in Paul's letters (here; 2:14 ["warn"]; 1 Tim 5:21; 1 Thess 4:6 ["warned"]), always connoting strong warning. The gravity of Paul's urging is clear also in his calling as witnesses both God and Christ Jesus.

4:2 in season and out of season. At all times, when it is easy and productive and when it is not. Timothy may have been tempted to be silent in the face of opposition. Paul's directives describe the main activities of his own ministry. In reminding Timothy to "correct" and to give "careful instruction," Paul affirms two main roles of pastoral responsibility (see note on 1 Tim 2:12).

4:3 the time. As in 3:1 (see note), Paul speaks of a future that in some respects has already arrived and is still with us today. **not put up with.** People will resist what they need most. **sound doctrine.** See note on 2:17. **own desires.** See 3:4 ("lovers of pleasure"). Raw self-gratification replaces finding gratification in God.

4:4 turn their ears away from the truth. This is fatal when salvation comes through hearing (Deut 6:4; Rom 10:17; Gal 3:2,5; 1 Thess 2:13). Jesus insists that "whoever has ears" had better hear (Matt 11:15; Mark 4:9; Luke 14:35b; see Mark 4:23), not shop for a more favorable message elsewhere. In the OT, prophets who pleased their listeners were usually false prophets (Jer 6:14; 8:11; Ezek 13:10,16; Mic 3:5). **truth.** See note on Titus 1:14.

4:5 But you. See note on 3:10. **keep your head.** Stay focused and sober at times others might sleep or fall idle. Paul exhorts with the same Greek word, translated "sober," in 1 Thess 5:6,8.

4:6 drink offering. Paul likens his life to a sacrifice (Rom 12:1) poured out in dedication to the Lord (Phil 2:17). These offerings were part of both OT (Num 15:1–12; 28:7) and Greco-Roman religious observance. As he passes from the scene, it is vital that co-workers like Timothy be in place to carry on what Paul and other apostles have begun (2:2).

4:7 Paul's example can guide Timothy. Whereas the English word order stresses "I," the original Greek stresses "the good fight ... the race ... [and] the faith." **fought.** Like the soldier mentioned earlier (2:3–4), Paul has battled for Christ's cause. He has matched the intensity of athletes in competition (2:5). **kept the faith.** See note on 1 Tim 3:9. Paul has not allowed the "deposit" (1:14; see note) of Christian truth to be watered down or adulterated.

4:8 crown of righteousness. A wreath (Greek *stephanos*, not the kingly *diadēma*) was awarded for first place in a race (v. 7), like a gold medal today. This crown may be understood in three ways: (1) the reward for a righteous life, (2) a reward consisting of righteousness, or (3) a reward bestowed justly by "the righteous Judge." **award to me.** See 1 Cor 3:14; Col 3:24. It "will last forever" (1 Cor 9:25). **that day.** A time of final reckoning, for good or ill. See 1:12,18; see also note on 1:12. Jesus spoke of "that day" over a dozen times, both as judgment (Luke 21:34) and as a joyful time of reward (Luke 6:23) and reunion with Christ (Matt 26:29). **also to all.** Victors' crowns are not only for apostles but also for Timothy and all other believers. **appearing.** See note on 1 Tim 6:14; it serves as a primary motivator and goal.

4:9–18 *Personal Remarks.* In addition to asking Timothy to come soon, Paul shares news about associates whom they have in common (vv. 9–15). He also comments on his trial process underway (vv. 16–18).

4:9 come. See also v. 13. Paul needs supplies and companionship as many have abandoned him (v. 16; 1:15).

4:10 Demas. Only a few years before, he was a loyal co-worker (Col 4:14; Phlm 24). **world.** Could be translated "the present age," in contrast to the age or world to come, of which Paul is acutely aware (vv. 6–8). **Crescens.** Mentioned only here in Scripture. **Titus.** He (2 Cor 7:6,13; 8:6,16–17,23; 12:18; Gal 2:1; Titus 1:4) and Paul had worked together in other settings but are currently separated.

4:11 Luke. Paul's co-worker and a physician (Col 4:14). **Mark.** He and Paul have reconciled after a falling out years earlier (Acts 15:37–39).

4:11 [w]2Ti 1:15 [x]Ac 12:12
4:12 [y]Ac 20:4
4:14 [z]Ac 19:33 [a]Ro 12:19
4:16 [b]Ac 7:60
4:17 [c]Ac 23:11 [d]Ac 9:15
4:18 [e]Ps 121:7 [f]Ro 11:36
4:19 [g]Ac 18:2
4:20 [h]Ac 19:22 [i]Ac 20:4
4:21 [j]ver 9
4:22 [k]Gal 6:18; Phm 25 [l]Col 4:18

with me.[w] Get Mark[x] and bring him with you, because he is helpful to me in my ministry. 12I sent Tychicus[y] to Ephesus. 13When you come, bring the cloak that I left with Carpus at Troas, and my scrolls,
especially the parchments.
14Alexander[z] the metalworker did me a great deal of harm. The Lord will repay him for what he
has done.[a] 15You too should be on your guard against him, because he strongly opposed our message.
16At my first defense, no one came to my support, but everyone deserted me. May it not be held
against them.[b] 17But the Lord stood at my side[c] and gave me strength, so that through me the message might be fully proclaimed and all the Gentiles might hear it.[d] And I was delivered from the lion's
mouth. 18The Lord will rescue me from every evil attack[e] and will bring me safely to his heavenly
kingdom. To him be glory for ever and ever. Amen.[f]

Final Greetings

19Greet Priscilla[a] and Aquila[g] and the household of Onesiphorus. 20Erastus[h] stayed in Corinth, and
I left Trophimus[i] sick in Miletus. 21Do your best to get here before winter.[j] Eubulus greets you, and so
do Pudens, Linus, Claudia and all the brothers and sisters.[b]
22The Lord be with your spirit.[k] Grace be with you all.[l]

a 19 Greek *Prisca,* a variant of *Priscilla* *b 21* The Greek word for *brothers and sisters* (*adelphoi*) refers here to believers, both men and women, as part of God's family.

4:12 Tychicus. Long a co-worker of Paul (Titus 3:12) and courier of two earlier letters—Ephesians (Eph 6:21) and Colossians (Col 4:7)—Paul wrote while in prison (see note on 1:8).
4:13 When you come. Timothy would pass through Troas in traveling from Ephesus to Rome. **cloak.** A heavy garment like a blanket with a hole in it to fit over the head. Paul needed it with winter coming (v. 21). **Carpus.** A Roman name; he is likely a Gentile convert. **scrolls … parchments.** Could be Paul's own notes and records. They could also include portions of OT Scriptures and what later would become NT Scriptures. Paul remained a reader and thinker devoted to the ministry of the Word until the end.
4:14 Alexander. Perhaps mentioned also in 1 Tim 1:20 and therefore someone probably expelled from the church (see note on 1 Tim 1:20). Alexander may have lived in Troas (v. 13) and posed a threat to Timothy when he stopped by there, as he had done "a great deal of harm" to Paul.
4:15 opposed. The same word used of Jannes and Jambres and false teachers in 3:8.
4:16 first defense. Perhaps a pretrial arraignment. Since Paul is still captive, the outcome must have been unfavorable. Like Jesus in his extremity (Luke 23:34), Paul forgives those whose support flagged under pressure. To stand alongside a man accused of a capital offense might have been risky; Paul understands this reluctance. He still counted friends around him (v. 21).
4:17 When people proved fickle, "the Lord stood" with Paul so he could uphold the "message."
4:18 The Lord will rescue me. To the end, Paul is confident of the Lord's rescue (see note on 3:11) and entrance into the "heavenly kingdom." This leads him to ascribe eternal glory to God. **Amen.** Confirms Paul's assurance and invites Timothy to join him in praise.
4:19–22 *Final Greetings.* Paul passes along greetings from himself and others. He underscores his need for Timothy to visit him soon and concludes with final blessings.
4:19 Priscilla and Aquila. Longtime co-workers of Paul apparently serving with or near Timothy. **Onesiphorus.** See 1:16.
4:20 Erastus. A co-worker of Paul (Acts 19:22) who held public office in Corinth (Rom 16:23). **Trophimus.** An Ephesian who worked with Paul earlier (Acts 20:4; 21:29).
4:21 get here. See v. 9. Paul's strong faith in God did not reduce his sense of dependence on fellow believers. **before winter.** Sea lanes were closed from around early November until early March due to storms. If Timothy did not arrive soon, Paul might not survive long enough to see him. **Eubulus … Pudens, Linus, Claudia.** None of these names is mentioned elsewhere in the NT. Why these friends did not support Paul at his trial (v. 16) is unclear.
4:22 your. Singular, referring to Timothy. **you all.** Plural, evidently addressing Timothy's fellow leaders or perhaps his congregation (see 1 Tim 6:21 and note). Paul's final word to Timothy confirms that Timothy does not stand before God or his congregation alone but as a member of the body of Christ.

INTRODUCTION TO
TITUS

AUTHOR

The first word of the letter names "Paul, a servant of God and an apostle of Jesus Christ" (1:1), as its author. This locates the letter among a dozen other NT documents with similar openings. Titus is Paul's associate (2 Cor 8:23; Gal 2:1,3; 2 Tim 4:10). While doubts about Paul's authorship of Titus have been expressed (see Introductions to 1 and 2 Timothy: Author), there is nothing in the setting, language, teaching, or underlying theology of this letter sufficient to prevent accepting the first word's testimony.

DATE, PLACE OF COMPOSITION, AND DESTINATION

Titus is a pastoral leader whom Paul assigned to put things in order on the island of Crete (1:5). He and Paul worked together for well over a decade (see note on 2 Tim 4:10). Paul writes perhaps in the early AD 60s after release from his first imprisonment. He appears to be on a mission as he writes; the precise location is unknown, but he plans to arrive in Nicopolis soon (3:12). Nicopolis was on the west coast of the province of Epirus in central Greece.

PURPOSE

It is not known just how or when the faith was established in Crete. But at the time Paul writes, it seems local gatherings of believers (probably house churches) have reached a point where they require more formal and established leaders (as in Acts 14:23). The letter furnishes guidance for this process. In addition to upright leadership (1:5–9), Paul is concerned that both sexes, all ages, and all social classes live out the gospel (2:1–10). Titus must refute leaders who mislead (1:10–16), avoiding useless controversy and exercising church discipline where required (3:9–11). He needs to make progress in these tasks soon enough to join Paul before winter (3:12).

GENRE

Titus is a letter from an apostle to a trusted co-worker and, by extension, to the churches he has been called to stabilize via leadership development (see Introduction to 1 Timothy: Genre). While Paul's words are particularly relevant to the original recipients, they retain appeal and indeed authority for followers of Christ today, for the apostolic faith was not only for then and there but continues in the church until the end of the age (Matt 28:20).

TITUS'S MINISTRY ON THE ISLAND OF CRETE

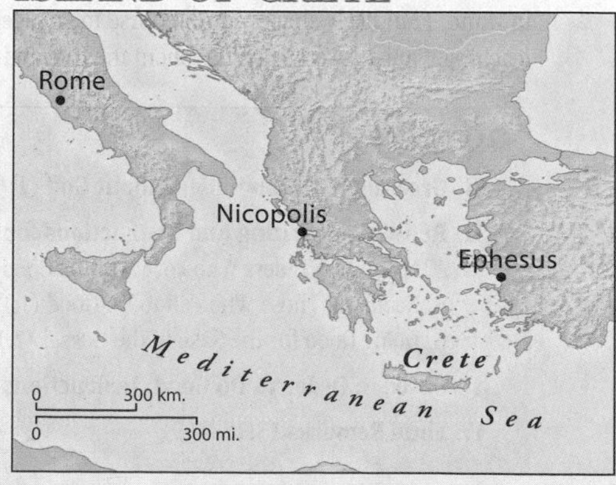

The harbor at Phoenix, Crete.
Richard Rigsby

CANONICITY

As in the case of 1 – 2 Timothy, there is evidence that Titus was known and cited as a Pauline writing by the early second century (see Introductions to 1 – 2 Timothy: Canonicity). This helps account for the fairly uniform high regard that the letter has received throughout church history (until recent times in some circles).

THEMES AND THEOLOGY

The nouns occurring most frequently in Titus (with their number of occurrences) are *God* (13), *work* (as in "good works"; 8), *faith* (6), and *Savior* (6). Christ is presented in elevated (but not exaggerated) terms. His earthly appearance showed him to be Savior, just like God the Father (1:4; 2:10). His future appearance is "the blessed hope" wrapped up in the revelation of "our great God and Savior, Jesus Christ" (2:13). Titus 2:13 is one of several NT verses that explicitly identifies Jesus as God (see also John 1:1,18; 20:28; Rom 9:5; Heb 1:8; 2 Pet 1:1; 1 John 5:20).

Christ's divinity is not an abstract truth, however glorious, but a transformative witness that impels followers to good works ("what is good"; 1:8; 2:7,14; 3:1,8,14). False followers identify themselves in part by lack of such actions (1:16). Paul's many ethical promptings are therefore calls for believers to show in real life the gospel they profess. For Paul, saving faith (1:1,4,13; 2:2; 3:8,15) is shown not least in its actions.

The message of Titus takes shape against a unique social background. Cretan culture was widely regarded as disorderly and rife with dishonesty. The prominent mythical god Zeus allegedly was born and died on Crete, earning divine status by his generosity to humans. Some passages in Titus take on sharper meaning when this myth is borne in mind; Paul likely shapes his discourse to engage Cretan convictions, for these may have challenged Christian teaching. Paul drew on teachings about the true and living God, not a mythical one.

OUTLINE

I. Greeting With Reminders About God (1:1 – 4)

II. Reason for Writing and Instructions for Titus (1:5 — 2:15)

A. Appointing Elders Who Love What Is Good (1:5 – 9)
B. Rebuking Those Who Fail to Do Good (1:10 – 16)
C. Doing Good for the Sake of the Gospel (2:1 – 15)

III. Saved in Order to Do Good: Instructions for the Church (3:1 – 11)

IV. Final Remarks (3:12 – 15)

TITUS

1 Paul, a servant of God[a] and an apostle of Jesus Christ to further the faith of God's elect and their
knowledge of the truth[b] that leads to godliness— 2in the hope of eternal life,[c] which God, who
does not lie, promised before the beginning of time,[d] 3and which now at his appointed season[e] he has
brought to light[f] through the preaching entrusted to me[g] by the command of God our Savior,[h]

4To Titus,[i] my true son in our common faith:

Grace and peace from God the Father and Christ Jesus our Savior.

1:1 [a]Ro 1:1 [b]1Ti 2:4
1:2 [c]2Ti 1:1 [d]2Ti 1:9
1:3 [e]1Ti 2:6 [f]2Ti 1:10 [g]1Ti 1:11 [h]Lk 1:47
1:4 [i]2Co 2:13
1:5 [j]Ac 27:7 [k]Ac 11:30
1:6 [l]1Ti 3:2

Appointing Elders Who Love What Is Good

1:6-8Ref — 1Ti 3:2-4

5The reason I left you in Crete[j] was that you might put in order what was left unfinished and appoint[a] elders[k] in every town, as I directed you. 6An elder must be blameless,[l] faithful to his wife, a man whose children

[a] 5 Or *ordain*

1:1–4 *Greeting With Reminders About God.* It was usual to begin a letter with the author's name and then the name of the letter's recipient. What is unusual is the rich series of remarks found between "Paul" (v. 1) and "Titus" (v. 4). Among Paul's letters, only the greeting of Romans is comparable. Paul begins this letter with an abundance of information about God and his saving work. Some think he does this to underscore the true God's distance from Cretan conceptions of Zeus and other pagan deities.
1:1 servant of God. Greek *doulos*, a word often translated "slave" (see 2 Tim 2:24 and note). Paul, like others before him—including Moses (Ps 105:26), David (2 Sam 7:4,8) and other prophets (e.g., Amos 3:7)—served God faithfully and received revelation from God. To be God's "servant" is not demeaning but ennobling (Mark 10:45). **God's elect.** See 2 Tim 2:10 and note. **truth.** See note on 1:14.
1:2–3 the hope of eternal life ... brought to light through the preaching. When people hear and accept that hope, it becomes theirs.
1:2 hope. Proven assurance, not groundless optimism. **does not lie.** Unlike the often devious and fallible gods of traditional Cretan belief. Discussions about the truthfulness of the Bible often cite these words since Scripture is God-breathed (see 2 Tim 3:16 and note) and would therefore not make false statements.
1:3 command of God. This is also why Paul is an apostle (see 1 Tim 1:1 and note).
1:4 true son. Suggests that Titus is considerably younger and faithfully passing along what Paul taught him. **Savior.** In the book of Titus, God the Father is called Savior three times (here; 2:10; 3:4; see also 1 Tim 1:1 and note; 2:3; 4:10 and note), with Jesus also called Savior three times (here; 2:13; 3:6; see 2 Tim 1:10). Given the OT conviction that God, who is one (Deut 6:4), is the only Savior (Isa 43:11; 45:21), Paul is likely viewing the Son as divine like the Father.

1:5—2:15 *Reason for Writing and Instructions for Titus.* A working lead pastor (or overseer, bishop) needs guidelines for his central task of leadership training. Paul reminds Titus why he left him in Crete and what he faces there. Since Titus does not minister to "people" in the abstract, Paul sets forth age- and gender-specific guidelines. Finally, he points to God's mighty grace (2:11) that is the basis for the Christian's "blessed hope" (2:13).
1:5–9 *Appointing Elders Who Love What Is Good.* Titus has served alongside Paul for years, so these instructions can be concise rather than comprehensive. Paul reminds Titus of the key ways in which candidates for elder (a term used for pastors; Acts 20:17,28; 1 Pet 5:1–3) must be men of quality. They must also be adept and faithful defenders of apostolic doctrine. Much in vv. 6–9 is paralleled in 1 Tim 3:1–7 (see notes). Differences may be due to the contrasting circumstances in Crete and Ephesus.
1:5 Paul reminds Titus of his mission in Crete. **unfinished.** The work had been begun but awaited completion. **elders in every town.** May imply a plurality of pastoral leaders for a congregation rather than just one (Acts 14:23).
1:6 blameless. Repeated in v. 7. This means the leader's life should measure up to standards described in this passage. Even faithful disciples may be maligned unjustly (Matt 5:11). Any accusations need to be confirmed (1 Tim 5:19). **faithful to his wife.** Refers to a dedicated, Christ-centered, monogamous marriage, with the husband loving his wife as Christ loved the church (see Eph 5:25–33; 1 Tim 3:2 and notes). **children believe.** A leader in God's household (see 1 Tim 3:15 and note) should be able to nurture faith in his own. If the meaning is "children are trustworthy" (see NIV text note), the concern is for character and behavior that reflect reverence for God and respect for parents.

1:7 [m]1Ti 3:1 [n]1Co 4:1 [o]1Ti 3:3,8
1:8 [p]1Ti 3:2 [q]2Ti 3:3
1:9 [r]1Ti 1:19 [s]1Ti 1:10
1:10 [t]1Ti 1:6 [u]Ac 11:2
1:11 [v]2Ti 3:6
1:12 [w]Ac 17:28 [x]Ac 2:11
1:13 [y]2Co 13:10 [z]Titus 2:2
1:14 [a]1Ti 1:4 [b]Col 2:22
1:15 [c]Ro 14:14,23
1:16 [d]1Jn 2:4
2:1 [e]1Ti 1:10
2:2 [f]Titus 1:13

believe[a] and are not open to the charge of being wild and disobedient. 7 Since an overseer[m] manages God's
household,[n] he must be blameless—not overbearing, not quick-tempered, not given to drunkenness, not
violent, not pursuing dishonest gain.[o] 8 Rather, he must be hospitable,[p] one who loves what is good,[q] who
is self-controlled, upright, holy and disciplined. 9 He must hold firmly[r] to the trustworthy message as it has
been taught, so that he can encourage others by sound doctrine[s] and refute those who oppose it.

Rebuking Those Who Fail to Do Good

10 For there are many rebellious people, full of meaningless talk[t] and deception, especially those of
the circumcision group.[u] 11 They must be silenced, because they are disrupting whole households[v] by
teaching things they ought not to teach—and that for the sake of dishonest gain. 12 One of Crete's
own prophets[w] has said it: "Cretans[x] are always liars, evil brutes, lazy gluttons."[b] 13 This saying is true.
Therefore rebuke[y] them sharply, so that they will be sound in the faith[z] 14 and will pay no attention
to Jewish myths[a] or to the merely human commands[b] of those who reject the truth. 15 To the pure, all
things are pure, but to those who are corrupted and do not believe, nothing is pure.[c] In fact, both their
minds and consciences are corrupted. 16 They claim to know God, but by their actions they deny him.[d]
They are detestable, disobedient and unfit for doing anything good.

Doing Good for the Sake of the Gospel

2 You, however, must teach what is appropriate to sound doctrine.[e] 2 Teach the older men to be temperate, worthy of respect, self-controlled, and sound in faith,[f] in love and in endurance.
3 Likewise, teach the older women to be reverent in the way they live, not to be slanderers or addicted

[a] *6* Or *children are trustworthy* [b] *12* From the Cretan philosopher Epimenides

1:7 overseer. Parallel with "elder" in v. 5. The terms can be interchanged (cf. Acts 20:17,28; 1 Pet 5:1–2). "Elder" may stress experience and mature wisdom; "overseer" may point to administrative and leadership responsibilities (see note on 1 Tim 3:1). **manages.** Along with teaching (1 Tim 3:2), a major task of the pastor is oversight (see 1 Tim 2:12 and note). **God's household.** See 1 Tim 3:15 and note. A congregation, consisting largely of families, makes up "God's household" in a local community. **blameless.** As in v. 6, a summary of the traits Paul goes on to list. The repetition of "not" five times may shed light on qualities sadly prevalent among Cretan leadership candidates.

1:8 loves what is good. Otherwise the prospects for church members *doing* "what is good" (2:7,14; 3:1,8,14) will be dim. Leaders must set the example. **self-controlled.** This was lacking among some in Crete (vv. 10–14). Paul commends the need for it repeatedly (2:2,5,6,12).

1:9 trustworthy message. See 1 Tim 1:15 and note; likely refers to the core gospel message. **as it has been taught**. Innovation in the sense of new and contrary assertions would signify departure from the faith. **sound doctrine.** See 2:1; 2 Tim 4:3; cf. 1 Tim 1:10; 2 Tim 2:17 and note. Could also be translated "healthy teaching"; the welfare of the flock depends on the quality of what its shepherd feeds it.

1:10–16 *Rebuking Those Who Fail to Do Good.* Apparently churches on Crete were troubled by "rebellious people" (v. 10) who stirred up dissensions. Their error was twofold: (1) they upheld Jewish practices (like circumcision, v. 10) and "myths" (v. 14; see 1 Tim 1:4 and note) in damaging ways, and (2) they spread false teaching to disrupt and get money (v. 11). Paul reminds Titus of the character and the gravity of their activity and his responsibility in limiting their harmful influence.

1:10 circumcision group. There is a long history of conflict with this quarter in the early church (Acts 15:1). While Jesus affirmed that "salvation is from the Jews" (John 4:22), he also challenged Jewish understanding of many of their practices, like certain practices on the Sabbath (John 5:18; 7:23; 9:16) and food laws (Mark 7:19). Apostolic leaders like Peter (Acts 10–11) and Paul (Rom 2:28–29; 1 Cor 7:19; Gal 5:6; 6:15), along with Barnabas, James, and others (Acts 15:1–21), were led by God to see that circumcision was not required for Gentiles to be saved. To teach otherwise was to question whether Christ alone was sufficient for salvation. Titus was ministering in a largely Gentile region. A "group" championing circumcision would be running counter to the gospel message as it applied to Gentiles.

1:11 must be silenced. Sometimes conflicts cannot be resolved; sources of error must be removed. This is after discussion and reasoned examination of views (3:10).

1:12 Paul finds common ground between (1) a characterization made by several past writers (Epimenides, Polybius, Cicero) about Cretan behavior and (2) the unruly teachers "disrupting whole households" (v. 11) in the churches. Paul appears to quote a sixth-century BC native of Crete named Epimenides (he quotes other pagan sayings in Acts 17:28 [see NIV text note]; 1 Cor 15:33 [see NIV text note]). The point is not that every Cretan is like this but that decadence and dishonesty are a threat to the churches Titus oversees because they are deeply embedded in the everyday life of the surrounding culture.

1:13 the faith. See note on 1 Tim 3:9.

1:14 merely human commands. In contrast to Paul's teaching and the broader gospel message, which came into the world through prophets, apostles, and ultimately Christ himself. **reject the truth.** "Truth" is a prominent concern in the Pastoral Letters. In some cases, as here, people reject, turn away from, distort, or simply miss the truth (1 Tim 6:5; 2 Tim 2:18; 3:7–8; 4:4). More often Paul uses "truth" to refer to the message about Christ that saves (1 Tim 2:4; 3:9,15; 4:3,6; 2 Tim 2:15,25) and "leads to godliness" (Titus 1:1).

1:15 all things are pure. Believers do not need "human commands" (v. 14; these possibly involved Jewish food laws, as in 1 Tim 4:3 [see note]) to cleanse them because Jesus has done that by his sacrificial death for them. **nothing is pure.** Recalls Jesus' dealing with religious leaders whom he accused of outward religiosity but inward corruption (Luke 11:38–41). Freedom to enjoy the good things God has created (see 1 Tim. 4:4 and note) comes through a right relationship with the Creator through faith in Christ. But this is a point that the Cretan adversaries apparently miss.

1:16 by their actions they deny him. Jesus asked, "Why do you call me, 'Lord, Lord,' and do not do what I say?" (Luke 6:46; Matt 23:3).

2:1–15 *Doing Good for the Sake of the Gospel.* There are ways to honor

to much wine,[g] but to teach what is good. 4 Then they can urge the younger women to love their husbands and children, 5 to be self-controlled and pure, to be busy at home, to be kind, and to be subject to
their husbands,[h] so that no one will malign the word of God.[i]
6 Similarly, encourage the young men[j] to be self-controlled. 7 In everything set them an example[k] by doing
what is good. In your teaching show integrity, seriousness 8 and soundness of speech that cannot be condemned, so that those who oppose you may be ashamed because they have nothing bad to say about us.[l]
9 Teach slaves to be subject to their masters in everything,[m] to try to please them, not to talk back to
them, 10 and not to steal from them, but to show that they can be fully trusted, so that in every way they
will make the teaching about God our Savior attractive.[n]
11 For the grace of God has appeared that offers salvation to all people.[o] 12 It teaches us to say "No" to
ungodliness and worldly passions,[p] and to live self-controlled, upright and godly lives[q] in this present
age, 13 while we wait for the blessed hope — the appearing of the glory of our great God and Savior, Jesus
Christ,[r] 14 who gave himself for us to redeem us from all wickedness and to purify for himself a people
that are his very own,[s] eager to do what is good.[t]
15 These, then, are the things you should teach. Encourage and rebuke with all authority. Do not let
anyone despise you.

2:3 [g] 1Ti 3:8
2:5 [h] Eph 5:22 [i] 1Ti 6:1
2:6 [j] 1Ti 5:1
2:7 [k] 1Ti 4:12
2:8 [l] 1Pe 2:12
2:9 [m] Eph 6:5
2:10 [n] Mt 5:16
2:11 [o] 1Ti 2:4
2:12 [p] Titus 3:3 [q] 2Ti 3:12
2:13 [r] 2Pe 1:1
2:14 [s] Ex 19:5 [t] Eph 2:10
3:1 [u] Ro 13:1 [v] 2Ti 2:21
3:2 [w] Eph 4:31; 2Ti 2:24

Saved in Order to Do Good

3 Remind the people to be subject to rulers and authorities,[u] to be obedient, to be ready to do
whatever is good,[v] 2 to slander no one,[w] to be peaceable and considerate, and always to be gentle
toward everyone.

God from within every station in life — regardless of age, gender, or situation. Paul goes beyond describing who needs to do what; he lays out the theological foundations of the ethics he outlines (vv. 11–14).

2:1 You, however. In contrast to the false teachers. Along with oversight (1:7), a pastor's chief duty is to "teach," for Christians are by definition disciples ("learners"). **sound doctrine.** See note on 2 Tim 2:17.

2:2 self-controlled. Cretans had a reputation for wildness. Paul calls for self-control not only for older men but also for overseers (1:8), younger women (v. 5), younger men (v. 6), and indeed everyone in the church (v. 12).

2:3 older women. Their deportment is key to the health of congregations. They are responsible to "teach," particularly "the younger women" (v. 4).

2:4–5 The Cretan social order did not always encourage marital fidelity nor even the basics of maternal commitment to offspring. The "older women" (v. 3) could help the "younger women" (v. 4) answer the high calling of nurturing households that truly serve God's aims.

2:5 self-controlled. See note on v. 2. **busy at home.** This rare Greek word *oikourgos* can also be translated "good managers of the household" (NRSV). This is a command not to stay cooped up at home but to exercise managerial gifts and skills for the family's sake. This does not rule out working outside the home (see Prov 31:16,18,24) but confirms responsibility for domestic oversight. **subject to their husbands.** See Eph 5:22; Col 3:18; 1 Pet 3:1. A husband's Christlike love for his wife (Eph 5:25) should prevent this from being harsh or onerous.

2:6 Similarly. Both genders and all age groups have particular responsibilities in the household of faith. **young men.** From mid-teens to around age 40. **self-controlled.** See note on v. 2.

2:7 set them an example. Christian leaders are player-coaches, not theoreticians who place burdens on people but "are not willing to lift a finger to move them" (Matt 23:4).

2:8 The church serves the Lord and not the world. Yet it must be conscious of what "those who oppose" the church say and think about the church (see also v. 10). **nothing bad to say.** As an elder should "have a good reputation with outsiders" (1 Tim 3:7), so should congregations, where this is possible (Rom 12:18).

2:9 slaves. Part of the Roman social and economic order. They were commonly mistreated and sometimes treated as subhuman. But the gospel message saved all who accepted it, and among these were many in this social class. Both slaves and their owners were responsible to regard each other as fellow Christians, not as adversaries (see Eph 6:5–9; see also note on Eph 6:5).

2:10 God our Savior. See 1 Tim 1:1 and note. As in v. 8, the way believers, including slaves, live must reflect the attractiveness of the gospel's teaching.

2:11 For. This verse and those following give the doctrinal basis for the behavior called for in previous verses. **grace of God.** God's saving grace in Jesus' incarnation, atonement, resurrection, and more amounts to the offer of "salvation to all people." **grace.** Appears in the Pastoral Letters over a dozen times, about half of those in greetings or farewells. But often, as here, the use is theologically significant. It sums up the reality and effect of God's unmerited favor made possible by Christ's sinless self-sacrifice. The fruit of this grace saved OT people of faith who awaited the fulfillment of God's promise to send a savior (John 5:46; 8:56; 12:41; Heb 11:39–40). Paul attributed his conversion from violence and blaspheming to grace (1 Tim 1:14). Salvation (or justification; Titus 3:7) and holy living are "not because of anything we have done but because of [God's] own purpose and grace" conferred "before the beginning of time" (2 Tim 1:9). There is a "grace ... in Christ Jesus" that enables the believer to be strong (2 Tim 2:1).

2:12 God's grace in the gospel (v. 11) does not merely save from sin. It "teaches" (like a parent instructs a child, with nurture, encouragement, information, and, when needed, discipline) the inner person and transforms the outward life. **self-controlled.** See note on v. 2.

2:13 wait. Not in idleness but "like servants waiting for their master to return" (Luke 12:36), which implies fervent readiness. **blessed hope.** The confident expectation of Christ's second coming and the glory that will bring. **our great God and Savior, Jesus Christ.** See 1 Tim 1:1 and note. This translation affirms Jesus' divinity on par with that of God himself.

2:14 gave himself. Died on the cross. **redeem.** This means liberation from lives of "wickedness" (1 Pet 1:18). **to purify for himself a people.** God is holy and transforms people so they may enjoy fellowship with him and serve him effectively. **eager to do what is good.** See Introduction: Themes and Theology.

3:1–11 *Saved in Order to Do Good: Instructions for the Church.* God's saving work (v. 5) has direct implications for the way in which believers behave in the world. They should be devoted to doing the right and best

3:4 [x]Eph 2:7 [y]Titus 2:11
3:5 [z]Eph 2:9 [a]Ro 12:2
3:6 [b]Ro 5:5
3:7 [c]Ro 3:24 [d]Ro 8:17 [e]Ro 8:24 [f]Titus 1:2
3:8 [g]1Ti 1:15 [h]Titus 2:14
3:9 [i]1Ti 1:4; 2Ti 2:14
3:10 [j]Ro 16:17
3:12 [k]Ac 20:4 [l]2Ti 4:9,21
3:13 [m]Ac 18:24
3:14 [n]ver 8
3:15 [o]1Ti 1:2 [p]Col 4:18

3 At one time we too were foolish, disobedient, deceived and enslaved by all kinds of passions and
pleasures. We lived in malice and envy, being hated and hating one another. 4 But when the kindness[x]
and love of God our Savior appeared,[y] 5 he saved us, not because of righteous things we had done,[z]
but because of his mercy. He saved us through the washing of rebirth and renewal[a] by the Holy Spirit,
6 whom he poured out on us[b] generously through Jesus Christ our Savior, 7 so that, having been justified
by his grace,[c] we might become heirs[d] having the hope[e] of eternal life.[f] 8 This is a trustworthy saying.[g]
And I want you to stress these things, so that those who have trusted in God may be careful to devote
themselves to doing what is good.[h] These things are excellent and profitable for everyone.

9 But avoid foolish controversies and genealogies and arguments and quarrels[i] about the law, because these are unprofitable and useless. 10 Warn a divisive person once, and then warn them a second
time. After that, have nothing to do with them.[j] 11 You may be sure that such people are warped and
sinful; they are self-condemned.

Final Remarks

12 As soon as I send Artemas or Tychicus[k] to you, do your best to come to me at Nicopolis, because I
have decided to winter there.[l] 13 Do everything you can to help Zenas the lawyer and Apollos[m] on their
way and see that they have everything they need. 14 Our people must learn to devote themselves to doing
what is good,[n] in order to provide for urgent needs and not live unproductive lives.

15 Everyone with me sends you greetings. Greet those who love us in the faith.[o]

Grace be with you all.[p]

---

thing in every situation (vv. 1–2,8). This includes pursuing peaceable relations with others if that is possible (vv. 9–11).

3:1 be subject ... be obedient. Cretans had a reputation for lack of restraint. This command implies that "rulers and authorities" are not commanding rebellion against God but fulfilling their God-ordained duties (see Rom 13:1–7). But sometimes to obey God it is necessary to go against what authorities dictate (see Dan 6 and note on 6:10; Acts 4:18–20; 5:29 and note).

3:2 Echoes Jesus' "blessed are the peacemakers" (Matt 5:9). **toward everyone.** Not just toward friends or others in the church (Matt 5:46–47).

3:3 we too. However bad the Cretans might be (1:12), Paul knows that he and all believers are by nature and past deeds no better.

3:4 appeared. See 2:11 and note. The incarnation manifested "kindness and love" despite the sorry state of all people as described in vv. 1–3.

3:5 Encapsulates a vast amount of teaching on Christian salvation. Salvation is not because of human merit but because of divine "mercy." **washing of rebirth.** God's regeneration of the human heart (John 3:3–8) resulting in changed living. Baptism is a recognition of and catalyst for this divine saving work. **renewal by the Holy Spirit.** See 1 Cor 12:13 and note. God by his Spirit (Luke 3:16; Rom 8:1–2) sets revolutionary changes in motion when the "disobedient" (v. 3) come to faith.

3:6 poured out. This Greek word appears in Joel 2:28,29 (Joel 3:1 in the Septuagint, the pre-Christian Greek translation of the OT), which the Pentecost account quotes (Acts 2:17–18; see also Acts 2:33). It is the language of abundant overflow.

3:7 justified by his grace. Summarizes a central Pauline teaching found in Romans, Galatians, and elsewhere. See note on 2:11. **heirs.** Implies adoption (see Rom 8:14–17).

3:8 stress these things. It is not only the "practical" directives of ch. 2 that matter but also their theological foundation in ch. 3. **for everyone.** They ("these things") benefit not only those in the church but also those in the world, to whom God calls the church to witness.

3:9 Probably describes the sorts of challenges and provocations that Titus faced in the church. There is a time for "opponents [to be] gently instructed" (2 Tim 2:25) and a time when those opponents are beyond the aid of dialogue and instruction (v. 10).

3:10 divisive person. Someone who absolutely will not abide by the Christian message and apostolic doctrine. **nothing to do with.** Probably indicates what was later called excommunication: these people were not welcome at the Lord's table until they repented and were restored (see 1 Cor 5:11–13; 2 Thess 3:14–15; 1 Tim 1:20 and notes). Jesus gave instructions for dealing with people who condemn themselves by refusing to come to terms with their transgression (Matt 18:15–17). Redemptive exclusion may bring about honest reform.

3:11 self-condemned. They might blame Titus or Paul or the church, but their woes are the result of their own stubborn views.

3:12–15 *Final Remarks.* Paul personally instructs Titus and confirms his letter's main thrust (v. 14). He also gives traditional, though stylized, greetings and final good wishes.

3:12 Artemas or Tychicus. Will apparently replace Titus so he can join Paul at Nicopolis.

3:13 Zenas ... Apollos. Members of Paul's ministry circle. They may have carried this letter to Titus from Paul. **lawyer.** If Zenas was Jewish, this term implies expertise in OT laws and traditions. **Apollos.** Though a common name, this is likely the same Alexandrian church leader with whom Paul had associated at Corinth and Ephesus in earlier years (Acts 18:24; 19:1; 1 Cor 1:12; 3:4–6,22; 4:6; 16:12).

3:14 doing what is good. For the sixth and final time in this letter (see also 1:8; 2:7,14; 3:1,8), Paul exhorts Titus to promote "doing" the things gospel belief calls for. Mere assent is not saving faith.

3:15 love ... faith. Combined with Paul's blessing of "grace," he closes with mention of three of the gospel's greatest gifts. **you all.** As with the last verses of 1 and 2 Timothy (see notes on 1 Tim 6:21; 2 Tim 4:22), this confirms that Titus does not stand before God or his congregation alone but as a member of the body of Christ. It may also imply that this letter was to be read to the entire church.

INTRODUCTION TO PHILEMON

AUTHOR, DATE, AND PLACE OF WRITING

Paul is the undisputed author of the letter. He could have composed it during his Roman imprisonment (AD 60 – 62) or earlier during an Ephesian imprisonment (AD 52 – 55) that Acts does not mention (see Introduction to Colossians: Date and Place of Composition).

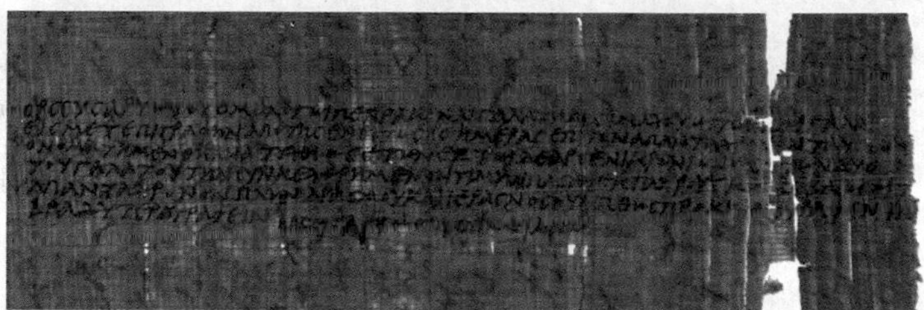

First-century papyrus document recording the purchase of two slaves. Paul makes a plea for Philemon's slave, Onesimus (vv. 8 – 20).

Image digitally reproduced with the permission of the Papyrology Collection, Graduate Library, University of Michigan

OCCASION AND PURPOSE

The reader enters into the middle of this saga without being provided the backstory. The traditional interpretation of the letter views it as Paul's request for Philemon to welcome back Philemon's slave Onesimus (see note on Eph 6:5). If Onesimus were a runaway slave (the traditional interpretation), Paul mentions it only obliquely to curb Philemon's anger and perhaps to conceal it from the authorities. Another interpretation suggests that Onesimus was not a fugitive but had committed some misdeed and sought out Paul to intercede for him with his master. One thing is clear: meeting Paul in prison resulted in Onesimus becoming a Christian.

Paul wants to awaken Philemon's generous Christian spirit so that he will receive Onesimus as his brother in Christ out of love (v. 9). Paul also expects Onesimus to act out of love. Onesimus returns to Philemon with Paul's ringing endorsement but with no guarantee that Philemon will honor it. Like the lost (prodigal) son returning home, he can only confess and cast himself on the mercy of his master. We do not know the outcome of this appeal, but the inclusion of this short and intimate letter in the canon suggests that it was successful. It reveals how the Christian faith breaks down what seems to be insurmountable social walls (Gal 3:28; Col 3:11).

OUTLINE

I. **Paul's Greeting (1 – 3)**

II. **Paul's Prayer and Thanksgiving (4 – 7)**

III. **Paul's Appeal (8 – 22)**

IV. **Paul's Final Greeting and Blessing of Grace (23 – 25)**

PHILEMON

1 [a]ver 9,23; Eph 3:1 [b]2Co 1:1 [c]Php 2:25
2 [d]Col 4:17 [e]Php 2:25 [f]Ro 16:5
4 [g]Ro 1:8
5 [h]Eph 1:15; Col 1:4
7 [i]2Co 7:4,13 [j]ver 20

1 Paul, a prisoner[a] of Christ Jesus, and Timothy our brother,[b]

To Philemon our dear friend and fellow worker[c] — 2 also to Apphia our sister and Archippus[d] our
fellow soldier[e] — and to the church that meets in your home:[f]

3 Grace and peace to you[a] from God our Father and the Lord Jesus Christ.

Thanksgiving and Prayer

4 I always thank my God[g] as I remember you in my prayers, 5 because I hear about your love for all
his holy people[h] and your faith in the Lord Jesus. 6 I pray that your partnership with us in the faith may
be effective in deepening your understanding of every good thing we share for the sake of Christ. 7 Your
love has given me great joy and encouragement,[i] because you, brother, have refreshed[j] the hearts of
the Lord's people.

Paul's Plea for Onesimus

8 Therefore, although in Christ I could be bold and order you to do what you ought to do, 9 yet I
prefer to appeal to you on the basis of love. It is as none other than Paul — an old man and now

[a] 3 The Greek is plural; also in verses 22 and 25; elsewhere in this letter "you" is singular.

1–3 *Paul's Greeting.* Paul's brief letter to Philemon follows the standard letter form found throughout antiquity: name of the writer, names of the addressees, and a greeting.
1 a prisoner of Christ Jesus. Paul identifies himself as such only here in a salutation. It may mean that he belongs to Christ Jesus. In that case, he was Christ's captive long before he became a captive of Rome. It may also mean that he is a prisoner for the sake of Christ or because of his service for Christ. Mentioning his imprisonment could only arouse Philemon's sympathy for his "dear friend" and spur him to grant Paul a favor. As Paul's "fellow worker," however, the issue encompasses their work for Christ.
2 Apphia. Probably Philemon's wife. Since wives were charged with running household affairs, she would have a stake in the matter concerning their slave. **Archippus.** Either a member of Philemon's household or a distinguished member of the church. The special mention of his ministry in Col 4:17 suggests that he is a church leader. **fellow soldier.** The image evokes ideas of discipline, dedication, and willingness to risk one's life in the gospel campaign (Phil 2:25). **to the church that meets in your home.** The early Christians did not have special buildings for their church services but met in the homes of Christians (Rom 16:3–5,23; 1 Cor 16:19; Col 4:15). Philemon is wealthy enough to have a church meet in his house and to offer aid to other Christians. Paul addresses the entire church since Christians act out of a communal context. He permits Philemon to decide for himself what he will do, but he expects Philemon to consider its impact on the whole church.
3 Grace and peace. Philemon has experienced grace from God through Jesus Christ, and peace has come through Christ's death (Rom 5:1; Eph 2:14–17). Grace brings the forgiveness of sin, and peace brings reconciliation with God and others (see note on Gal 1:3). Paul places Jesus Christ on the same level with God the Father as the source of grace and peace, and Paul expects Philemon to extend the same grace and reconciliation he has received from Christ to a fellow Christian who has wronged him.
4–7 *Paul's Prayer and Thanksgiving.* Before Paul makes his appeal, he graciously and tactfully expresses his thanksgiving for Philemon (vv. 4–5) and describes how he prays for him (vv. 6–7). This thanksgiving previews themes in the letter: love (v. 9), sharing or partnership (v. 17), doing good (v. 14), heart (vv. 12,20), and refreshing (v. 20). Because of Philemon's Christian love and partnership with him in the gospel, Paul hopes that he will do a good deed and refresh Paul's heart.
4 remember you in my prayers. Implies more than simply calling persons to mind; he also appeals to God on their behalf.
5–6 love ... faith. Paul highlights Philemon's love and faith rather than the church's (cf. Col 1:4). One's love toward others and faith in God should be evidence of Christ's reconcilation of the world to God.
7 refreshed the hearts of the Lord's people. "Hearts" is figurative language for the emotions of pity and love (see vv. 12,20; see also Ps 7:9 and note). Philemon's generosity prepares for Paul's request that Philemon now refresh Paul's heart. This request makes a play on words since Paul describes Onesimus as his "very heart" in v. 12.
8–22 *Paul's Appeal.* Paul identifies Onesimus as the object of his appeal

also a prisoner[k] of Christ Jesus— [10]that I appeal to you for my son[l] Onesimus,[a m] who became my
son while I was in chains. [11]Formerly he was useless to you, but now he has become useful both to
you and to me.
[12]I am sending him—who is my very heart—back to you. [13]I would have liked to keep him with
me so that he could take your place in helping
me while I am in chains for the gospel. [14]But I
did not want to do anything without your consent, so that any favor you do would not seem
forced[n] but would be voluntary. [15]Perhaps the
reason he was separated from you for a little
while was that you might have him back forever— [16]no longer as a slave, but better than
a slave, as a dear brother.[o] He is very dear to me
but even dearer to you, both as a fellow man
and as a brother in the Lord.
[17]So if you consider me a partner,[p] welcome him as you would welcome me. [18]If he
has done you any wrong or owes you anything,
charge it to me. [19]I, Paul, am writing this
with my own hand. I will pay it back—not
to mention that you owe me your very self.

9 [k]ver 1,23
10 [l]1Co 4:15 [m]Col 4:9
14 [n]2Co 9:7; 1Pe 5:2
16 [o]Mt 23:8; 1Ti 6:2
17 [p]2Co 8:23

Roman slave serving his master.

[a] *10 Onesimus* means *useful.*

and gently brings up how Onesimus had injured Philemon without going into any details (vv. 8–12). The first half of the petition begins and ends with an appeal to love (v. 9). The second half states what he wants Philemon to do and connects Onesimus's waywardness to divine providence. Paul requests that Philemon receive Onesimus back, not as a slave, but as a brother in Christ (vv. 15–16), and Paul buttresses his entreaty with a pledge to pay any damages Philemon might have suffered (vv. 17–20).

Forgiving slaves for serious wrongs was extremely rare in Greco-Roman culture, but Christians live by a higher standard. Paul hints at the more forceful pressure he could apply in getting Philemon to do what is right (vv. 8–9,13–14), but he avoids demands and threats. Instead, he appeals to Philemon's love (v. 9), his sympathy (vv. 9,13), their personal bond (vv. 17,19), and the mutual duties binding on those in a spiritual family (vv. 10,16,20). He leaves the final decision to Philemon to do what is "fitting in the Lord" (Col 3:18).

8–9 Paul does not apply authoritarian pressure as an apostle. That would yield only grudging compliance.

9 old man. Suggests that Paul is in the final stage of a normal lifespan. He is identified as a "young man" in Acts 7:58 when he supported the stoning of Stephen, and that was some 30 years prior to this time. That the younger should defer to an older member of a family (Lev 19:32) encourages Paul to make his delicate request.

10 my son. Onesimus has become precious to the imprisoned Paul. **became my son.** Translates a Greek verb that means "to give birth"; refers to Onesimus's conversion (1 Cor 4:15).

11 useless ... useful. Onesimus means "useful," and Paul makes a pun on his name. Masters gave slaves names that expressed their hope for them. Onesimus was not useful before because he was without Christ. Now that he is in Christ, he has become truly useful—not just in some physical sense but in a spiritual sense.

12 If Onesimus was a fugitive slave, he could be subject to a variety of disciplinary actions meted out at his master's discretion, from flogging to branding to manacles to execution. Paul hopes to avert such retribution by identifying Onesimus as his "very heart." He emphasizes how dear this "son" (v. 10) has become to him in Christ.

13 Paul's need for someone to assist him as a prisoner is greater than any need Philemon might have of his slave. He wants to keep Onesimus with him, but he wants Philemon to make the decision himself (2 Cor 9:7). In sending back Onesimus, Paul demonstrates the kind of unselfish love that he wants Philemon to show in response.

14 favor. Paul does not specify what he would have Philemon do: Keep Onesimus as his slave and send him back to serve Paul? Set Onesimus free and allow him to return as a freedman with greater independence to serve Paul and the gospel?

15 he was separated from you. Paul de-emphasizes the reason behind Onesimus's absence by using the passive voice, which encourages Philemon to see God as the agent and to attribute the absence to God's mysterious purposes. God intended this separation for good (Gen 50:20) so that they might be united forever.

16 no longer as a slave. Christians are no longer to regard others according to human categories (2 Cor 5:16). As brothers and sisters in Christ, Christians share a bond that transcends the legal master-slave relationship (Gal 3:28; Col 3:11). They become slaves to one another through love (Gal 5:13), and that tie lasts beyond death. When a master is expected to treat a slave as a brother in Christ and as the representative of the apostle Paul (Phlm 17), the institution of slavery is subverted. One can serve Christ as a slave of some earthly master, but Paul does not regard it as a desirable state (1 Cor 7:21).

17 as you would welcome me. Paul asks that Philemon accept Onesimus as Paul's emissary. Theirs is not a business partnership but a spiritual alliance.

18 charge it to me. Paul makes no excuses for Onesimus. He takes for granted that Onesimus committed some offense, but he does not name it to avoid rubbing salt in the wound. Whatever it was, it cost Philemon financially and brought dishonor to him. Paul removes a barrier to forgiveness with his promise to repay any damages from theft or loss of services.

19 with my own hand. Paul took the stylus from the secretary's hand to write this promissory note that legally assumes the debt. His offer models what Christ did for us on a far greater scale. Paul takes upon himself the charge of Onesimus's legal indebtedness so that Philemon

20 [q] ver 7
21 [r] 2Co 2:3
22 [s] Php 1:25; 2:24 [t] 2Co 1:11
23 [u] Col 1:7
24 [v] Ac 12:12 [w] Ac 19:29 [x] Col 4:14
25 [y] 2Ti 4:22

20 I do wish, brother, that I may have some benefit from you in the Lord; refresh[q] my heart in Christ.
21 Confident[r] of your obedience, I write to you, knowing that you will do even more than I ask.
22 And one thing more: Prepare a guest room for me, because I hope to be[s] restored to you in answer
to your prayers.[t]

23 Epaphras,[u] my fellow prisoner in Christ Jesus, sends you greetings. 24 And so do Mark,[v] Aristarchus,[w] Demas[x] and Luke, my fellow workers.
25 The grace of the Lord Jesus Christ be with your spirit.[y]

might forgive him (cf. Col 2:14). **you owe me your very self.** One last moving reason for Philemon to grant Paul's request: Paul reminds Philemon either that he was converted under Paul's ministry or that Paul brought the gospel to his area.

20 benefit. Greek *oninēmi*, another play on the name Onesimus. **in the Lord.** Paul is interested not in how he might benefit materially but in how the work of the Lord benefits.

21 Paul exudes confidence that Philemon will grant his request, not because Philemon is a good man, but because he is in the Lord. The Lord creates obedience. **even more.** May allude to freeing Onesimus, not just forgiving him.

22 Prepare a guest room. This is the only direct command in the letter. Hospitality was vital to traveling missionaries. **answer to your prayers.** Paul's own release.

23–25 *Paul's Final Greeting and Blessing of Grace.* Paul ends the letter with a greeting from his co-workers and another salutation.

23–24 Almost the same list of co-workers appears in Col 4:10–14 with more details.

25 grace. Brackets this letter. Paul expects Philemon to extend the same grace to Onesimus that the "Lord Jesus Christ" extended to him (v. 3). **your spirit.** Plural; Paul expects the spirit of the whole church to be infused with divine graciousness.

INTRODUCTION TO HEBREWS

Hebrews is profound, distinctive, rewarding, and puzzling. Its impassioned and polished argument for the superiority of Christ captures the imagination even in a quick reading, and its theological depths continue to reward faithful reflection over a lifetime of study.

AUTHOR

Hebrews includes no explicit claim of authorship. The writer certainly knew the readers and vice versa (5:11 – 12; 6:10; 10:32 – 34; 13:23 – 24), but identifying information was lost as the book was widely circulated. Patristic tradition about its author was divided early on. The Eastern church thought the ideas were from Paul but that the writer was one of his associates. The Western church did not accept it as Pauline until widespread use in the East convinced them that it must be apostolic, and they eventually concluded Paul was the author. However, this was called into question from the Reformation forward, and very few scholars accept it as Pauline today. The Greek style and its characteristic themes are quite different from Paul's, and at least one verse presents nearly insuperable difficulties (2:3 indicates the author received the gospel indirectly; cf. Gal 1:11 – 17). From the small group of first-century Christians known to the later church, other potential authors have been suggested across the centuries with varying degrees of plausibility

LOCATIONS IN HEBREWS

(e.g., Luke, Barnabas, Clement of Rome, Apollos, Priscilla, Silas, Epaphras, Timothy). The evidence for these is so thin that they are little more than guesses, particularly since we have no writing sample from most of them to base comparisons on. And it is a mistake to assume that the author must be someone already familiar to us. It is best to acknowledge that we do not know who the author is.

DATE

As with other features of the book's original situation, the date of composition is uncertain. The original readers were second-generation Christians (2:3–4), and some time had passed since their conversion (5:12), enough time for prior experiences of suffering to be a fading memory (10:32–34). It seems that persecution against them had not meant loss of life (12:4). But none of these factors lends much clarity to its dating. A bit more definitive is the lack of any mention of Jerusalem's destruction and the end of the temple's priestly ritual, which occurred in AD 70 (see note on 8:4 for the relevance of present-tense usage). In view of the book's argument for Christ's superiority to the Mosaic order, this silence makes it difficult to think it was written after AD 70. A date in the mid-60s seems most likely.

PLACE OF COMPOSITION AND DESTINATION

Hebrews gives no indication of the location or circumstances of its author, except that he hoped to return to the readers quite soon (13:19,23). Many have understood the original readers' location to be the area around Jerusalem or somewhere in Syria-Palestine, assuming that attention to the priesthood and sacrificial ritual would be more relevant to readers closer to Jerusalem. But Hebrews actually never mentions the temple itself (Solomon's or Herod's). Its descriptions always pertain to the tabernacle and its service as stipulated in the OT (see note on 8:4). The author pursues this line of argument not because of the readers' location near the temple but to remind them of God's final sacrifice for sin accomplished by Christ (see Occasion and Purpose). The location of the original readers is indicated rather clearly in 13:24: former residents of Italy (companions of the writer, wherever he is) send their greetings to the readers, presumably in Italy, the area around Rome (see note on 13:24 for mention of an alternative view).

OCCASION AND PURPOSE

Although the title "To the Hebrews" was used in the second century AD and reflects the book's recipients, it was not part of the original work and likely arose from a genuine insight into the major content of the book (extensive treatment of OT priestly themes to show the superiority of Christ) and its central exhortation based on that content (the readers must not turn away from Christ—presumably back to Judaism). The author never explicitly warns against returning to Judaism, and his exhortations could be taken more generally (i.e., not forsaking Christ or the true God by reverting to paganism). But the author is not explicit about a pagan background either, and there would be less reason to pursue the detailed argument he presents based on the promises and institutions of the OT for an audience

Remains of Jerusalem's Temple Mount.
© Radek Sturgolewski/Shutterstock

that had no prior loyalty to them. His insistence that the readers maintain faith in Christ because of that which God has done in Christ strongly implies that they were tempted to return to that prior system. The only modification of this early view would be that the ethnic background of the readers could certainly have been broader than "Hebrews" only. Gentiles in the first-century Mediterranean world were often drawn to the synagogue and its ancient roots in the OT; from there they sometimes converted to Christianity. Informed loyalty to the OT, such as Hebrews assumes, was not limited to ethnic Jewish converts.

GENRE AND STRUCTURE

Hebrews has traditionally been labeled a letter, but the main part of it does not read that way. It ends like a letter (see the epistolary features in 13:20 – 25) but begins more like a theological treatise or essay. The author himself describes the book as "my word of exhortation" (13:22), which clarifies things quite a bit. In Acts 13:15 the same phrase describes a synagogue sermon and a message of encouragement and challenge based on Scripture. This matches what we find in Hebrews as a whole: theological and practical exposition of OT passages urging the readers to remain faithful to Christ. It is carefully crafted and rhetorically powerful, mixing interpretation of several central OT passages (Pss 8; 95; 110; Jer 31) — with a variety of others cited in support — along with five sections of intense appeal, based on the exposition, for the readers to endure in their faith (Heb 2:1 – 4; 3:6 — 4:13; 5:11 — 6:20; 10:19 – 39; 12:14 – 29). The other indication that the book is composed to be a sermon is the consistent use of "say" or "speak" instead of "write" when the author refers to his work (2:5; 5:11; 6:9; 8:1; 11:32). Even though he has of necessity sent it to them in written form and he clearly has specific recipients in mind (5:12; 6:9 – 10; 10:32 – 34), its genre is sermonic through and through. Since it is now in written form, the study notes that follow refer to the recipients as "readers" rather than "hearers."

Differing schemes have been suggested for outlining the argument of Hebrews. The Outline shows Hebrews arranged in a symmetrical pattern that is centered on a long section of crucial exposition at the heart of the book — Christ's high priestly ministry (5:11 — 10:39) — and bracketed by the strongest passages of exhortation. Two main sections prepare the way for this central exposition (1:5 — 2:18; 3:1 — 5:10) and two wind down the argument (11:1 — 12:12; 12:14 — 13:21). The transition into each main section is signaled by key words at the end of the previous unit that announce the topic of the section to follow (see notes on 1:4; 2:17,18; 5:10; 10:35 – 39; 12:12 – 13).

CANONICITY

Early opinion about who wrote Hebrews was mixed (see Author), and this naturally affected its early acknowledgment as canonical. It is not listed in the Muratorian Canon (late second century in the West), but the Eastern church widely accepted it. It is included in an early and important papyrus manuscript (P46) with eight of Paul's letters

(ca. AD 200). Hesitation about its canonicity eventually faded in the West based on its evident orthodoxy and widespread use in the East.

THEMES AND ARGUMENT

One of the most important contributions of Hebrews is its balance of continuity and advance in relating the OT and NT to each other. The same God who spoke in former times has now revealed himself fully and finally in his Son (1:1 – 2). Hebrews argues for the superiority of Christ and his saving work and supports its argument from OT Scripture, viewed as God's revelation by the Spirit (3:7; 9:8; 10:15). The author often does this by quoting an OT passage and then explaining a few key words to draw out their theological meaning in context (2:8 – 9; 8:13; 10:8 – 10).

A distinctive dimension of Hebrew's balance of continuity and advance in God's redemptive plan is how it traces the relationship of OT to NT by means of pattern and escalation. The OT presents God-intended patterns, or types (9:8 – 10), to foreshadow in incomplete ways (10:1) certain NT parallels that are true in a heightened or ultimate sense (a "how much more" fulfillment). Hebrews has typologies of covenant and sacrifice (8:6; 9:1 – 14,18 – 23), of judgment and deliverance (2:1 – 4; 3:6 — 4:11; 10:28 – 29; 12:25), and of sonship and priesthood (1:5 – 13; 2:5 – 18; 5:1 – 10; 7:11 – 28). In many of these the OT type is true only metaphorically or in a manner of speaking, while the NT counterpart has come to be so in profound reality (see notes on 1:5,8 – 9; 7:3,9 – 10; 9:13 – 14). Of course, this does not diminish the experience of OT believers, who by God's grace respond with faith and obedience to the provision God made for them, a provision whose core reality still lay ahead.

The central theme of Hebrews is that Jesus Christ as exalted Son and high priest is God's final revelation and provides full cleansing from sin and open access to God — the reality that the OT anticipated but was never meant to accomplish. This view of the exalted Christ is the focal point at which the major theological themes of Hebrews converge: its teachings on who Christ is, all that he has accomplished for human salvation, and how God's prior revelation to Israel and his restoration of all things will be fulfilled through Christ. Based on these themes, the central argument of Hebrews is that Christians can and must hold firmly to their faith in Christ's high priestly work in spite of adversity.

OUTLINE

I. Prologue: The Son as God's Final Revelation (1:1 – 4)

II. The Son as Superior to Angels (1:5 — 2:18)
- A. The Son as Exalted Royal Messiah (1:5 – 14)
- B. Warning: Pay Careful Attention to the Gospel (2:1 – 4)
- C. Jesus and the Destiny of Mankind (2:5 – 18)

III. The Son as Merciful and Faithful High Priest (3:1 — 5:10)
- A. Jesus and Moses (3:1 – 6)
- B. Warning: Respond to God's Word With Enduring Faith (3:7 — 4:13)
- C. Jesus Our Compassionate High Priest (4:14 — 5:10)

IV. Central Exposition: The Son's Melchizedekian Priesthood (5:11 — 10:39)
- A. Introductory Exhortation: Moving Toward Maturity (5:11 — 6:20)
- B. Christ as Priest in Melchizedek's Order (7:1 – 28)
- C. Christ as Heavenly High Priest of a Better Covenant (8:1 – 13)
- D. Christ's Priestly Service in the Heavenly Sanctuary (9:1 – 28)
- E. Conclusion of the Exposition: Contrast of the Old and New Sacrifices (10:1 – 18)
- F. Concluding Exhortation: Draw Near Through Christ in Enduring Faith (10:19 – 39)

V. The Need for Faith and Endurance in the Struggle (11:1 — 12:13)
- A. Examples of God-Pleasing Faith (11:1 – 40)
- B. Endure Suffering as Fatherly Discipline (12:1 – 13)

VI. Final Warning and Instructions About Community Life (12:14 — 13:21)
- A. Final Warning: Do Not Refuse God's Gracious Word Through Jesus (12:14 – 29)
- B. Instructions About Community Life (13:1 – 21)

VII. Epilogue: Epistolary Closing (13:22 – 25)

HEBREWS

God's Final Word: His Son

1 In the past God spoke[a] to our ancestors through the prophets[b] at many times and in various ways,[c]
2but in these last days he has spoken to us by his Son, whom he appointed heir[d] of all things, and
through whom[e] also he made the universe. 3The Son is the radiance of God's glory[f] and the exact representation of his being, sustaining all things[g] by his powerful word. After he had provided purification
for sins,[h] he sat down at the right hand of the Majesty in heaven.[i] 4So he became as much superior to
the angels as the name he has inherited is superior to theirs.[j]

1:1 [a] Jn 9:29; Heb 2:2,3 [b] Ac 2:30 [c] Nu 12:6,8
1:2 [d] Ps 2:8 [e] Jn 1:3
1:3 [f] Jn 1:14 [g] Col 1:17 [h] Heb 7:27 [i] Mk 16:19
1:4 [j] Eph 1:21; Php 2:9,10

1:1–4 *Prologue: The Son as God's Final Revelation.* These bold and polished lines prepare the way for the main themes of the book. They fall into two parts: (1) the initial contrastive statement about how God has spoken (vv. 1–2a) and (2) seven brief descriptions of the Son (vv. 2b–4). The pivot point is the phrase "by his Son" (v. 2a).

1:1–2a One of the main themes of Hebrews is the shift from old to new in God's revelation. While there are contrasts here, there is also significant continuity: the same God "spoke" in the past and now "has spoken" decisively in the Son. God's revelation in former times points forward to what has now been revealed in the person and work of his Son.

1:2a in these last days. The decisive shift has come in God's dealings with humankind. In Jesus Christ, God has inaugurated the long-awaited time of fulfillment that the OT anticipates in various ways (9:26). **by his Son.** Culminates vv. 1–2a and launches the seven descriptions of vv. 2b–4. The father-son imagery shows why Jesus is perfectly suited to reveal God: Who better to reflect God and his ways than one who completely shares the divine nature?

1:2b–4 Seven descriptions sketch out particular traits of the Son to show why God's revelation culminates in the Son. These are arranged not chronologically but thematically in a ring structure that begins and ends with Christ's exaltation to the position of greatest authority with God in heaven.

1:2b appointed heir of all things. Inheritance naturally connects to sonship, but in this case it refers to the Messianic authority God gave the Son in his resurrection and exaltation (Pss 2:6–8; 89:26–27; Acts 2:33–36; Rom 1:3–4). **through whom also he made the universe.** This moves back in time from the exaltation to the Son's more fundamental qualifications as the revealer of God. The Son is the one through whom God created all things (John 1:3,10; 1 Cor 8:6; Col 1:16), confirming his personal existence prior to the creation of the world—and in this context his right to become the "heir of all things."

1:3 The Son's inheritance is based on his eternal participation in the divine nature. **the radiance of God's glory and the exact representation of his being.** These two images—God's glory shining forth in the Son and the imprint of God's essence seen in the Son—portray the Son's eternal *being*, not just his *function*, as fully divine. This asserts that the Son *is* God (v. 8), which forms the ultimate ground for his decisive role in revelation and redemption as seen throughout Hebrews. **sustaining all things by his powerful word.** The Son upholds the universe and carries it forward to its God-ordained purpose (Isa 46:3–4,9–10; Col 1:17). The Son's shared authority in fulfilling God's intent for creation mirrors God's sovereign authority in creating: he spoke and it was done (Heb 11:3; Gen 1; Ps 33:6–11). **provided purification for sins.** The central section of Hebrews (chs. 7–10) extensively develops this. Here it provides the right frame for again highlighting the Son's exalted position in God's presence (vv. 3–4). **sat down at the right hand of the Majesty in heaven.** This again focuses on exaltation, alluding to Ps 110:1, a central OT text for early Christianity; the NT cites or alludes to it over 15 times, including 5 times in Hebrews (here; v. 13; 8:1; 10:12–13; 12:2). Christ took his seat at God's right hand in heaven following his "purification for sins," which plays a major role in the theology of Hebrews, especially in connection with Jesus' appointment as high priest, as Ps 110:4 declares (cited 10 times in Hebrews [5:6,10; 6:20; 7:3,11,15,17,21,24,28]). **the Majesty.** A divine attribute used as an appellation for God (used also in 8:1; cf. 12:2; Mark 14:62 and parallels).

1:4 became ... superior to the angels. The final description focuses on the Son's exaltation and builds a bridge to the next section (vv. 5–14). "*Became* ... superior" (italics added) calls attention to the honored position the Father gave the Son as a result of his suffering and death (2:9–10). The seven descriptions present a threefold sense in which Jesus is "Son," emphasizing his exalted Sonship at the beginning and end but also tracing his eternal Sonship (vv. 2c–3b) and his earthly Sonship (v. 3c), which form the indispensable background for his exaltation. His superiority to angels is significant in Hebrews for two reasons: (1) it sets up the lesser-to-greater argument of 2:1–4 by comparing the law through angels to the gospel through the Lord Jesus; (2) it underlines the greater authority the Father gave the Son now and in the future (vv. 5–14; 2:5) by comparing it to the role of angels in expressing God's rule in the present age (see NIV text note on Deut 32:8; see also Dan 10:20–21; Eph 1:20–21; Phil 2:9–10; 1 Pet 3:22). **the name he has inherited.** "Son." This title is in v. 5 at the beginning and end, respectively, of two OT quotations. Jesus was God's "Son" from all eternity but not in the sense of a royal, exalted Son (as in vv. 4–5).

1:5 [k]Ps 2:7 [l]2Sa 7:14
1:6 [m]Heb 10:5 [n]Dt 32:43 (LXX and DSS); Ps 97:7
1:7 [o]Ps 104:4
1:9 [p]Php 2:9 [q]Isa 61:1,3

The Son Superior to Angels

5 For to which of the angels did God ever say,

"You are my Son;
today I have become your Father"[a]?[k]

Or again,

"I will be his Father,
and he will be my Son"[b]?[l]

6 And again, when God brings his firstborn into the world,[m] he says,

"Let all God's angels worship him."[c][n]

7 In speaking of the angels he says,

"He makes his angels spirits,
and his servants flames of fire."[d][o]

8 But about the Son he says,

"Your throne, O God, will last for ever and ever;
a scepter of justice will be the scepter of your kingdom.
9 You have loved righteousness and hated wickedness;
therefore God, your God, has set you above your companions[p]
by anointing you with the oil[q] of joy."[e]

[a] 5 Psalm 2:7 [b] 5 2 Samuel 7:14; 1 Chron. 17:13 [c] 6 Deut. 32:43 (see Dead Sea Scrolls and Septuagint)
[d] 7 Psalm 104:4 [e] 9 Psalm 45:6,7

1:5—2:18 *The Son as Superior to Angels.* The book begins with two sections of exposition (1:5–14; 2:5–18) sandwiching a brief initial warning (2:1–4). Here, as well as in the prologue (1:1–4), the author shows his full agreement with wider Christian teaching, especially pointing to Christ's eternal preexistence (1:1–3), his exaltation (1:13), and his incarnation (2:10–18). This provides a foundation of familiar concepts early in the book before moving into distinctive ideas (e.g., Christ's high priesthood in 2:17).

1:5–14 *The Son as Exalted Royal Messiah.* The first exposition traces seven OT quotations explicitly declaring the Son's superiority to angels. Almost identical phrases introduce the first and last quotations (vv. 5,13). The quotations contrast the royal, eternal authority of the Son with the subordinate, transitory role of angels.

1:5 The exposition begins with Ps 2:7 and 2 Sam 7:14, which in their OT contexts refer to a king in the line of David whom God metaphorically identifies as his "Son." Ps 2 describes installing such a king on Zion, anointed to be God's vice-regent over the nations (Ps 2:1–6) with a further promise that God will subordinate all the earth to him (Ps 2:8–12). God speaks of this royal installation in highly figurative terms: **You are my Son; today I have become your Father.** From Ps 2:7b. In the OT context this "sonship" does not speak of divine essence but of a king anointed to rule on God's behalf as vice-regent on earth. 2 Sam 7 uses the same metaphor to describe God's choice to extend David's rule in the person of Solomon and a series of kings in David's lineage. **I will be his Father, and he will be my Son.** From 2 Sam 7:14a; see also 1 Chr 17:13. Reading these texts typologically (as is common in Hebrews; see Introduction: Themes and Argument), the author understands these verses to refer ultimately to God's installing Jesus in his royal status as Davidic Messiah (Matt 1:1; Mark 12:35–37; 14:62; Luke 1:32–33; 2:11; Acts 2:34–36; 13:32–37; Rom 1:3; 2 Tim 2:8). He rules already at God's right hand in heaven (but has not yet come to the culmination of his rule on earth in the end times [2:5,8–9]).

1:6 when God brings his firstborn into the world. This is debated. It could refer to the incarnation, but this was when the Son assumed a status "lower than the angels" (2:9). It is possibly the second coming of Christ (9:28); interpreting "again" with "brings" may show this. But "again" goes more smoothly with "says" (presenting a further quotation, as in v. 5; 2:13; 4:5; 10:30). In addition, the theme of vv. 5–14 and the reference to this "world" in 2:5 ("the world to come, about which we are speaking") make it more likely that this is the time of Christ's exaltation. When God seated the Son at his right hand, he thereby brought him into the "world to come" that already exists in heaven, where the heavenly court worships him. In early Jewish and Christian thought, God will establish this "world to come" on earth when he renews all things in the end times (in the pseudepigrapha see 4 Ezra 7:26; 8:52; 10:54; 13:36; 2 Baruch 4:3–6; see also notes on 2:5; 4:9; 11:10,16; 12:22–24; 13:14). **firstborn.** A title for Jesus drawn from Ps 89:27, continuing the image of the ultimate Davidic king as God's privileged Son, the legal heir and authoritative representative of God's rule (Col 1:15). **Let all God's angels worship him.** A quotation from the Septuagint (the pre-Christian Greek translation of the OT) of Deut 32:43 (see NIV text note), which in Deuteronomy is a call to worship Yahweh. Here it is applied to the Son, who also deserves worship as God (cf. v. 3; John 5:23).

1:7 spirits ... flames of fire. A few lines from Ps 104:4 speak about angels and (in contrast to what v. 8 says about the Son) suggest their fleeting, transitory character as well as their subordinate role (v. 14).

1:8–9 The fifth quotation is drawn from Ps 45:6–7 and reinforces the Son's identity as divine but also declares the enduring and righteous reign in which God has anointed him to serve. Ps 45 celebrates a royal wedding in Jerusalem and gives exaggerated praise to the human king, seen metaphorically as God because the king represents God's rule on earth. Likewise the psalm commends the permanence and justness of the earthly king's rule in ideal and overstated terms. But these descriptions in typological escalation are profoundly true of Jesus as King (see Introduction: Themes and Argument). Jesus is truly God (John 1:1,18; 20:28; Rom 9:5; Titus 2:13; 2 Pet 1:1) and has "loved righteousness and hated wickedness" not just in a manner of speaking but in reality.

[10]He also says,

"In the beginning, Lord, you laid the foundations of the earth,
and the heavens are the work of your hands.
[11]They will perish, but you remain;
they will all wear out like a garment.[r]
[12]You will roll them up like a robe;
like a garment they will be changed.
But you remain the same,[s]
and your years will never end."[a][t]

[13]To which of the angels did God ever say,

"Sit at my right hand
until I make your enemies
a footstool[u] for your feet"[b]?[v]

[14]Are not all angels ministering spirits[w] sent to serve those who will inherit salvation?[x]

Warning to Pay Attention

2 We must pay the most careful attention, therefore, to what we have heard, so that we do not drift
away. [2]For since the message spoken[y] through angels[z] was binding, and every violation and disobedience received its just punishment,[a] [3]how shall we escape if we ignore so great a salvation?[b] This
salvation, which was first announced by the Lord,[c] was confirmed to us by those who heard him.[d] [4]God
also testified to it by signs, wonders and various miracles,[e] and by gifts of the Holy Spirit[f] distributed
according to his will.[g]

1:11 [r]Isa 34:4
1:12 [s]Heb 13:8 [t]Ps 102:25-27
1:13 [u]Jos 10:24; Heb 10:13 [v]Ps 110:1
1:14 [w]Ps 103:20 [x]Heb 5:9
2:2 [y]Heb 1:1 [z]Dt 33:2; Ac 7:53 [a]Heb 10:28
2:3 [b]Heb 10:29 [c]Heb 1:2 [d]Lk 1:2
2:4 [e]Jn 4:48 [f]1Co 12:4 [g]Eph 1:5

a *12* Psalm 102:25-27 *b* *13* Psalm 110:1

1:10–12 The sixth quotation comes from Ps 102:25–27, which reinforces the theme of the Son's permanent existence. Because the Son "in the beginning" is the Creator of the heavens and earth (see also vv. 2c–3b), he will "remain the same" (v. 12; see 13:8) when all of creation changes (12:26–27), and his "years will never end" (v. 12). The Son's eternal existence is foundational to his abiding priesthood and its effects, an important theme later in the sermon (7:3,16, 24–25).
1:13 The seventh quotation comes from Ps 110:1 and closes out the series. Verse 3 alludes to this verse, which appears numerous times throughout the NT. Jesus applies it to himself (Mark 12:35–37; 14:62 and parallels); and Peter (Acts 2:33–36; 1 Pet 3:22), Paul (Rom 8:34; 1 Cor 15:25; Eph 1:20; Col 3:1), and John (Rev 3:21) likewise cite it in reference to Christ. It expresses a central theme in the theology of Hebrews (see notes on 8:1; 10:12,13; 12:2). In its OT context, Ps 110:1 speaks figuratively of the special relationship with the Lord that an earthly king in Jerusalem enjoyed and the pledge to extend his rule, manifesting God's kingship over the earth. The psalm's reference to being seated in heaven is a metaphor for how the king represents and expresses the Lord's rule on earth: it is as though the king were sharing directly in God's rule from heaven as his earthly vice-regent. But in the typology of the Bible, what is true of David or an earthly king in OT days foreshadows what is true now of Christ, who intensifies the pattern. Christ, like those earthly kings, is David's anointed descendant, enjoying a special relationship with God, elevated to a heavenly position to exert the rule of God himself on earth. **until I make your enemies a footstool for your feet.** Prepares for what is explicit in 2:8–9: the Son's rule, while already inaugurated, has not yet come to its complete fulfillment.
1:14 ministering spirits sent to serve. This reinforces the contrast between angels who "serve" (vv. 6–7) and the Son who reigns. **will inherit salvation.** Hebrews speaks of Christian "salvation" as something primarily future (9:28) that will have eternal effects (5:9; 7:25). But it also describes central aspects of this salvation as already true in the past or present (4:3; 6:9–10,18–19; 9:15; 10:14; 12:22,28).
2:1–4 *Warning: Pay Careful Attention to the Gospel.* This initial warning is brief and moderate compared to the ones that come later (3:7—4:13; 5:11—6:20; 10:19–39; 12:14–29). It is a comparison from the lesser to the greater (a pattern, or typology, of judgment): if God justly punished people for violating the Mosaic commands, then he will certainly punish people for neglecting the gospel of Christ (see 10:28–29; 12:25). This comparison is grounded in God's full and final revelation in the Son, who is superior to angels (1:1–14).
2:1 pay the most careful attention. The author is concerned that the readers not "drift away" or "ignore" (v. 3) the message of God's great salvation through Christ. They were lethargic and needed to hold fast to their confession of faith.
2:2 message spoken through angels. Based on the implications of a few OT texts (Deut 33:2–4; Ps 68:17–18), Jewish tradition spoke of God's giving the law to Moses on Sinai through angels (in the pseudepigrapha see Jubilees 1:27,29; see also Josephus, *Antiquities*, 15.136; reflected also in Acts 7:38,53; Gal 3:19; not explicit in Exod 19–20).
2:3 how shall we escape if we ignore so great a salvation? Unavoidable consequences come to those who neglect God's revelation through Christ. This message was "first announced by the Lord" as Jesus preached God's salvation in his earthly ministry. Hebrews mentions various details about Jesus' earthly life—more than any other NT book outside of the Gospels themselves (e.g., vv. 10–18; 4:15–16; 5:7–8; 7:14; 10:10; 12:2–3; 13:12). **us.** The author and original readers. **confirmed ... by those who heard him.** The apostles and eyewitnesses proclaimed the message to the next generation of Christians (4:2; 13:7). The author apparently includes himself among that later generation (see Introduction: Author for implications regarding the book's author and date). God added his own confirmation to the apostolic preaching by means of "signs, wonders and various miracles, and by gifts of the Holy Spirit" that witnessed to its divine origin (v. 4).

2:6 [h] Job 7:17
2:8 [i] Ps 8:4-6; 1Co 15:25

Jesus Made Fully Human

[5] It is not to angels that he has subjected the world to come, about which we are speaking. [6] But there
is a place where someone has testified:

> "What is mankind that you are mindful of them,
> a son of man that you care for him?[h]
> [7] You made them a little[a] lower than the angels;
> you crowned them with glory and honor
> [8] and put everything under their feet."[b,c][i]

In putting everything under them,[d] God left nothing that is not subject to them.[d] Yet at present we do
not see everything subject to them.[d] [9] But we do see Jesus, who was made lower than the angels for a

[a] 7 Or *them for a little while* [b] 6-8 Psalm 8:4-6 [c] 7,8 Or [7] *You made him a little lower than the angels;/ you crowned him with glory and honor/* [8] *and put everything under his feet."* [d] 8 Or *him*

2:5–18 *Jesus and the Destiny of Mankind.* The author quotes Ps 8:4–6 and explains its fulfillment in Jesus' incarnation, suffering, and exaltation. He introduces and quotes the psalm (vv. 5–8a), briefly explains specific phrases from it (vv. 8b–9), and reflects on its theological meaning as fulfilled in Christ (vv. 10–18). Jesus shared fully in our humanity and experienced death for all of us so that we can share fully in his glorious victory over death and the devil.

2:5 not to angels. An understatement intended to imply its positive counterpart (i.e., to Christ instead). This literary device is used frequently in Hebrews (e.g., v. 11; 4:15; 6:10; 7:20; 13:17). **the world to come, about which we are speaking.** The author mentioned this "world" in 1:6 (and in the larger topic of Jesus' exaltation to heaven as the Davidic royal Messiah in 1:5–14). It is a "world to come," a realm subjected to the Son already in heaven but yet to come on earth (cf. vv. 8–9; 6:5; 13:14). The early Jewish and Christian view was that the Messiah's future reign is already established in heaven but will come to earth in the end times (see notes on 11:10,16; 12:22–24; 13:14). Verse 8 shows that God "subjected the world to come" to the Son.

2:6a a place where someone has testified. The specific passage (Ps 8:4–6) is not identified because it is well-known. Ps 8 appears frequently in early Jewish literature and in the NT (Matt 21:16; Rom 1:20; 1 Cor 15:27; Eph 1:22). Not identifying it specifically arises also from a sentiment that all Scripture is from God, so the exact location is less important.

2:6b–8a This quotes Ps 8:4–6 directly from the Septuagint (the pre-Christian Greek translation of the OT) to show that the exalted role for mankind that God intended at creation (Gen 1:26–28) will come to fulfillment through Jesus Christ, who shared in our humanity.

2:6b What is mankind that you are mindful of them ...? Ps 8 celebrates the Lord's majestic glory, reflecting on God's magnificent creation of the heavens and the earth. In comparison, human beings seem insignificant. **a son of man that you care for him?** This line is synonymously parallel with the previous one, and "a son of man" in the context of Ps 8 refers to "any human being." It thus continues the exclamation about mankind's lowly condition: Why would the magnificent Lord care for such creatures? In the context of Hebrews, this is the foundational sense seen in the verse. But the phrase "a son of man," in light of Jesus' frequent use of it to refer to himself, suggests also the connection to the Messianic title rooted in Dan 7:13–14: Jesus is a "son of man" to whom the Ancient of Days will give dominion over all the world's kingdoms. This complements the interpretation of Ps 8 that vv. 8–9 give. With great delicacy of style, the author allows this point to carry itself without belaboring it.

2:7–8a The psalmist looks back to Gen 1:26–28 and marvels at God's grace in forming humans in his image ("made them a little lower than the angels," v. 7) as the glory of his creative work ("crowned them with glory and honor," v. 7) and giving them dominion over the rest of creation ("put everything under their feet," v. 8a). The pronoun "them" in these lines could refer specifically to Jesus (see alternative rendering in NIV text note on vv. 7–8) instead of humans, but it is more likely that Hebrews begins with a reference to humans and shows how Jesus will restore God's design for mankind. The wording of Ps 8:5a in v. 7a follows the Septuagint (the pre-Christian Greek translation of the OT: "angels," Greek *angeloi*) rather than the other possible sense of the Hebrew ("god," Hebrew *ʾĕlōhîm*). The Hebrew term *ʾĕlōhîm* occasionally means "heavenly beings, angels" (e.g., Ps 82:1,6, where the NIV renders it "gods"), and the Greek translators probably chose "angels" out of reverence, i.e., to avoid speaking too familiarly of God. To refer to heavenly beings reflects an exalted position for humans without expressing something that may seem to denigrate God himself. The Septuagint (the pre-Christian Greek translation of the OT), however, shows more clearly the superiority of the Son to angels, the larger theme of 1:5—2:18.

2:8b In putting everything under them, God left nothing that is not subject to them. In good interpretive fashion, the author ponders the full sense of key words from the psalm: "everything" means that nothing in creation can be left "not subject" to mankind. In the larger context of Ps 8 (especially its allusion to Gen 1 and God's creation of all things), these words reflect the greater theological sense of the OT text. The psalm declares God's intent that humans would reflect his image by exerting dominion over creation. **Yet at present we do not see everything subject to them.** The psalm expresses a noble vision, one that is true in regard to God's design but not true in actuality at its time of writing. Humans after the fall (Gen 3) are more dominated than they are dominion-bearers, especially in regard to the power of evil and death (v. 14).

2:9 But we do see Jesus. The larger vision of Ps 8 is fulfilled in the incarnation, death, resurrection, and exaltation of Jesus according to God's gracious plan for mankind's salvation. This is the first occurrence in Hebrews of the personal name "Jesus." Previously the author has called him "Son" (1:2,3,5,8). Key phrases from Ps 8 trace how Jesus fulfills the psalm's vision: **made lower than the angels for a little while.** Jesus left behind heaven's glory to become human. In the psalm "a little" (Ps 8:5) refers to rank; here it implies span of time (see alternative rendering in NIV text note on v. 7), since Jesus has now been exalted above the angels again (1:5–14). **now crowned with glory and honor.** What the psalm declares to be true of humans only in a provisional, ideal way has already been fulfilled profoundly and completely in the exaltation of Christ to God's right hand. Jesus has become "the pioneer" of salvation (v. 10) and will restore the God-given destiny of all mankind. **he suffered death, so that by the grace of God he might taste death for everyone.** Restoring humans to God's original intent required cleansing from sin (1:3) that could be provided only by sacrificial death (chs. 8–10). This restoration is rooted in God's

little while, now crowned with glory and honor[j] because he suffered death,[k] so that by the grace of God
he might taste death for everyone.[l]
[10]In bringing many sons and daughters to glory, it was fitting that God, for whom and through
whom everything exists,[m] should make the pioneer of their salvation perfect through what he suffered.[n]
[11]Both the one who makes people holy and those who are made holy[o] are of the same family. So Jesus
is not ashamed to call them brothers and sisters.[a][p] [12]He says,

"I will declare your name to my brothers and sisters;
in the assembly I will sing your praises."[b][q]

[13]And again,

"I will put my trust in him."[c][r]

And again he says,

"Here am I, and the children God has given me."[d][s]

[14]Since the children have flesh and blood, he too shared in their humanity[t] so that by his death he
might break the power[u] of him who holds the power of death—that is, the devil[v]— [15]and free those
who all their lives were held in slavery by their fear[w] of death. [16]For surely it is not angels he helps, but
Abraham's descendants. [17]For this reason he had to be made like them,[e][x] fully human in every way, in
order that he might become a merciful[y] and faithful high priest[z] in service to God,[a] and that he might
make atonement for the sins of the people. [18]Because he himself suffered when he was tempted, he is
able to help those who are being tempted.[b]

2:9 [j]Ac 2:33; 3:13; Php 2:9 [k]Php 2:7-9 [l]Jn 3:16; 2Co 5:15
2:10 [m]Ro 11:36 [n]Lk 24:26; Heb 7:28
2:11 [o]Heb 10:10 [p]Mt 28:10; Jn 20:17
2:12 [q]Ps 22:22
2:13 [r]Isa 8:17 [s]Isa 8:18; Jn 10:29
2:14 [t]Jn 1:14 [u]1Co 15:54-57; 2Ti 1:10 [v]1Jn 3:8
2:15 [w]2Ti 1:7
2:17 [x]Php 2:7 [y]Heb 5:2 [z]Heb 4:14,15; 7:26,28 [a]Heb 5:1
2:18 [b]Heb 4:15

[a] *11* The Greek word for *brothers and sisters* (*adelphoi*) refers here to believers, both men and women, as part of God's family; also in verse 12; and in 3:1, 12; 10:19; 13:22. [b] *12* Psalm 22:22 [c] *13* Isaiah 8:17 [d] *13* Isaiah 8:18 [e] *17* Or *like his brothers*

costly grace (already implicit in Ps 8) in providing salvation through the death of his Son.

2:10 In bringing many sons and daughters to glory, it was fitting. God is at work in Christ to restore humans to the "glory" he intended for them at creation (Rom 8:18–30). The image of "bringing" or leading his people to glory hints at an exodus motif that is important in ch. 3 (see 6:20). Jesus as our "forerunner" (6:20) precedes us to heavenly glory. **pioneer.** This title carries nuances of "initiator, leader," one who is in solidarity with others—the Greek word is used a number of times in the Septuagint (the pre-Christian Greek translation of the OT) of the head of a tribe or family—and leads them through to a new situation. The Greek word is used four times in the NT, always of Christ in his role as Savior (here; 12:2; Acts 3:15 ["author"]; 5:31 ["Prince"]). **perfect.** Perfection—both of Jesus (here; 5:9; 7:28) and of Christians (7:11,19; 9:11; 10:1,14; 12:23)—is a unique and important theme in Hebrews. **through what he suffered.** Jesus was made "perfect" by the pathway of weakness, suffering, and death that God called him to follow in accomplishing our salvation (5:8–9; 7:28; 10:14). This does not mean that he changed from sinful to sinless (4:15; 7:26–28; 9:14); rather, it denotes his becoming fully qualified to act as our high priest, in the sense that he demonstrated his full obedience to God despite temptation and that he identified with humans fully in their weakness to sympathize with them in high priestly intercession (vv. 17–18; 4:15–16; 5:7–10; 7:25–26).

2:11 makes people holy. A general description of Jesus' sanctifying work (cf. 10:10,14; 13:12) that captures his full identification with humans to provide redemption. Those who benefit and the one who provides the benefit are "of the same family" (or "of one"), referring probably to their shared humanity (a reflection arising from how Ps 8 describes mankind); this is picked up again in vv. 14,17.

2:12–13 Two OT quotations confirm Jesus' solidarity with those he came to save ("my brothers and sisters" [v. 12] and "the children God has given me" [v. 13]). The wider context of each OT passage carries profound Messianic significance: Ps 22:22 (quoted in v. 12) follows prophecies about Jesus' suffering on the cross (Ps 22:1,6–8,16–18; see Mark 15:24,29,34; John 19:24). Isa 8:17–18 (quoted in v. 13) speak about the prophet's "trust" in the Lord despite others in Israel who "stumble" in their faith (Isa 8:14; see Rom 9:33; 1 Pet 2:8).

2:14 he too shared in their humanity. One of the most explicit theological reflections in the NT on Jesus' incarnation and its necessity (v. 17a). In fulfilling the God-given destiny of humans (Ps 8), Jesus entered into our physical, earthly existence ("flesh and blood") to provide deliverance for us "by his death" (see v. 9). **him who holds the power of death.** An allusion to Gen 3. Falling into sin and death at the serpent's instigation marred the God-given dignity of humans. The devil gained a limited power over mankind through his ability to incite sin that leads to death (John 8:44; Rom 5:20–21; 6:20–23; 2 Tim 2:26; 1 John 3:8). Jesus' death and resurrection provides complete victory over death and the devil (see 1 Cor 15:20–28,54–55, especially 1 Cor 15:27, where Ps 8:6 is quoted).

2:16 Abraham's descendants. A tie to the larger narrative of God's redemption: God chose one person and nation to be the channel through which he would bless all the nations of the world (6:13–18; 11:8–19; Gen 12:1–3). **descendants.** Includes not Israel alone but all those who share Abraham's faith (Rom 4:16; Gal 3:7,29).

2:17 a merciful and faithful high priest in service to God. Because of who Jesus is (fully divine and fully human), he is able to provide the ultimate sacrifice for sin, following the pattern of the OT priestly order but surpassing and fulfilling it. **make atonement.** Sacrifice required to satisfy God's anger against sin (vv. 9,14–15; 10:30–31; 12:29). Jesus' high priestly ministry is the major theme of the central section of Hebrews; the first exposition (1:5—2:18) gives a foundation for this theme, which vv. 17–18 explicitly introduce.

2:18 able to help those who are being tempted. Jesus gained empathy for humans through his own experience of temptation and suffering in faithfulness to God. This is an important theme in Hebrews (vv. 9–10; 4:15–16; 5:7–9; 7:25).

3:1 [c]Heb 2:11 [d]Heb 4:14 [e]Heb 2:17
3:2 [f]Nu 12:7
3:5 [g]Ex 14:31 [h]ver 2; Nu 12:7
3:6 [i]Heb 1:2 [j]1Co 3:16 [k]Ro 11:22 [l]Ro 5:2
3:7 [m]Heb 9:8

Jesus Greater Than Moses

3 Therefore, holy brothers and sisters,[c] who share in the heavenly calling, fix your thoughts on
Jesus, whom we acknowledge[d] as our apostle and high priest.[e] 2He was faithful to the one who
appointed him, just as Moses was faithful in all God's house.[f] 3Jesus has been found worthy of greater
honor than Moses, just as the builder of a house has greater honor than the house itself. 4For every
house is built by someone, but God is the builder of everything. 5"Moses was faithful as a servant[g] in all
God's house,"[a][h] bearing witness to what would be spoken by God in the future. 6But Christ is faithful
as the Son[i] over God's house. And we are his house,[j] if indeed we hold firmly[k] to our confidence and
the hope[l] in which we glory.

Warning Against Unbelief

7So, as the Holy Spirit says:[m]

> "Today, if you hear his voice,
> 8 do not harden your hearts

[a] 5 Num. 12:7

3:1—5:10 *The Son as Merciful and Faithful High Priest.* This new section develops the two key points of 2:17 in reverse order: (1) the Son is a faithful high priest (warning: respond to him with enduring faith [3:1—4:13]); and (2) the Son is a merciful high priest (encouragement: seek his help in temptation [4:14—5:10]).
3:1–6 *Jesus and Moses.* Moses was a "faithful" servant (vv. 2,5), but Jesus is a greater "faithful" servant (vv. 2,6; cf. 2:17; Num 12:1–9).
3:2 Moses was faithful in all God's house. The author commends Moses by quoting from Num 12:7 (v. 5), where God rebukes rebellion against Moses as the leader and revealer (to whom God speaks "face to face," Num 12:8). **house.** God's "house" in vv. 2–6 refers to God's "household," the community of God's people.
3:3 Jesus has been found worthy of greater honor than Moses. Based on Jesus' role in creation and new creation. **the builder of a house.** Suggests Jesus' work as Savior, building God's redeemed community through his sacrificial death (v. 6; 2:10).
3:4 God is the builder of everything. God the Father is the ultimate source of all things, physical and spiritual. As elsewhere, the author thinks of the Father acting through the Son in both creation (1:2,10) and new creation (2:9; 9:14; 10:9–10).
3:5–6 Key words drawn from Num 12:7 trace the comparison with Christ again: Moses was "faithful as a servant" as he led in God's "house," i.e., among God's people. But Christ has proven "faithful as the Son over God's house."
3:5 bearing witness to what would be spoken by God in the future. The law given through Moses foreshadows the reality that has come in Christ (1:1–2).
3:6 if indeed we hold firmly to our confidence. The original readers had publicly confessed faith in Jesus, so the author can address them as "holy brothers and sisters, who share in the heavenly calling" (v. 1). But the evidence that they are genuinely part of God's household is their enduring faith (v. 14; 4:14; 10:23; cf. 1 John 2:19). This does not describe what *will* be true if they hold firm; it tells what is *already* true of them ("we are his house"), and maintaining their hope demonstrates this relationship. It does not *make* it true; it *provides evidence* of what is the case (v. 14). On the other hand, the exhortations that follow in 3:7—4:13 warn against a faith that gives up when tested.
3:7—4:13 *Warning: Respond to God's Word With Enduring Faith.* Based on the parallels between Moses and Christ in 3:1–6, this section sets out a typology of judgment using Israel's wilderness generation as a warning not to turn away from the message of the gospel. It incorporates ideas drawn from several OT passages (Gen 2; Num 14; Ps 95).
3:7–11 This extended quotation from Ps 95:7b–11 refers to Israel's unbelief and God's rejecting them in the wilderness (Num 14). The wider theme of Ps 95 is God's rule as the great King due to his rights as the Creator (Ps 95:3–6), a connection important to the exposition about God's own rest in 4:1–11. Israel's wilderness generation is a common paradigm, or typology, of sin and unbelief (e.g., Num 32:7–11; Deut 1:19–35; Ps 106:24–26; 1 Cor 10:1–13; Jude 5–7).
3:7a the Holy Spirit says. Hebrews shares with ancient Judaism and early Christianity the conviction that Scripture is written under the influence of God's Spirit (Mark 12:36; Acts 4:25; 2 Tim 3:16; 2 Pet 1:20–21), so God speaks in Scripture, even to generations subsequent to its time of writing (vv. 13,15; 4:7). But Hebrews does not lose sight of the original human situation with its specific time and place (and its relevance for interpretation, 4:7–9).
3:7b–9 The quoted psalm begins with a call to worship God as the great King (Ps 95:1–6) and then warns not to "harden your hearts" when "you hear his voice" (in the form perhaps of God's word being

JERUSALEM AND SINAI

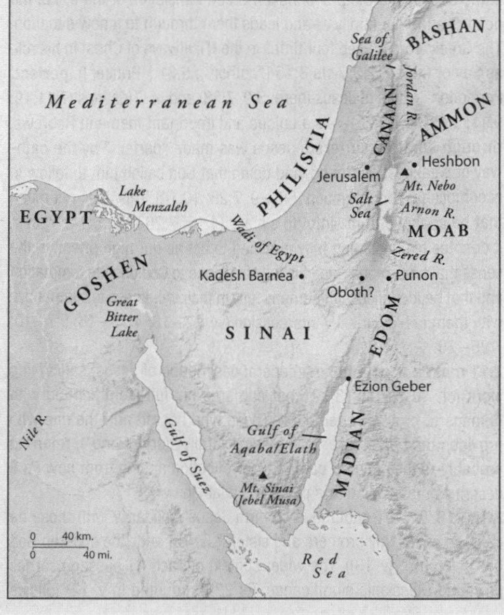

as you did in the rebellion,
during the time of testing in the wilderness,
9 where your ancestors tested and tried me,
though for forty years they saw what I did.[n]
10 That is why I was angry with that generation;
I said, 'Their hearts are always going astray,
and they have not known my ways.'
11 So I declared on oath in my anger,
'They shall never enter my rest.' "[a][p]

12 See to it, brothers and sisters, that none of you has a sinful, unbelieving heart that turns away
from the living God. 13 But encourage one another daily,[q] as long as it is called "Today," so that none of
you may be hardened by sin's deceitfulness.[r] 14 We have come to share in Christ, if indeed we hold[s] our
original conviction firmly to the very end. 15 As has just been said:

"Today, if you hear his voice,
do not harden your hearts
as you did in the rebellion."[b][t]

16 Who were they who heard and rebelled? Were they not all those Moses led out of Egypt?[u]
17 And with whom was he angry for forty years? Was it not with those who sinned, whose bodies
perished in the wilderness?[v] 18 And to whom did God swear that they would never enter his rest[w]
if not to those who disobeyed?[x] 19 So we see that they were not able to enter, because of their
unbelief.[y]

[a] *11* Psalm 95:7-11 [b] *15* Psalm 95:7,8

3:9 [n] Ac 7:36
3:11 [o] Heb 4:3,5 [p] Ps 95:7-11
3:13 [q] Heb 10:24,25 [r] Eph 4:22
3:14 [s] ver 6
3:15 [t] ver 7,8; Ps 95:7,8
3:16 [u] Nu 14:2
3:17 [v] Nu 14:29; Ps 106:26
3:18 [w] Nu 14:20-23 [x] Heb 4:6
3:19 [y] Jn 3:36

read in worship). The psalmist cites the wilderness generation as an example to avoid: "the rebellion ... the time of testing in the wilderness, where your ancestors tested and tried [God]." This is a slightly broader summary of Israel's resistance to God in the wilderness than Num 14 records, alluding to passages like Exod 17:7; Num 20:13,24; Deut 33:8. The Septuagint (the pre-Christian Greek translation of the OT) translates the place-names in the Hebrew text of Ps 95:8 ("Meribah" and "Massah"; see NIV text notes on Ps 95:8) as abstract nouns ("quarreling" and "testing"); Hebrews follows this sense in v. 9.

3:10–11 God "was angry with that generation" for their waywardness, and he pronounced a solemn judgment on them: they would never enter his rest.

3:11 They shall never enter my rest. Num 14:20–35 records God's decisive oath of judgment against that whole generation, but the psalmist summarizes what they lost with the word "rest" (Ps 95:11). **rest.** In the context of the Pentateuch and the conquest, "rest" meant refreshment and prosperity in the land God promised them, God's presence in their midst, and security from their enemies all around (Exod 33:14; Deut 3:18–20; 12:9–10; 25:19; Josh 1:13,15; 21:44; 23:1). Psalm 95, however, shows that the entrance into the promised land could not have been entrance into the ultimate rest of God. In the context of Ps 95 and the later OT, "rest" meant that they continued to enjoy God's blessings in the land or anticipated that God would restore those blessings under a future Davidic king (2 Sam 7:1,11; 1 Kgs 8:56; Ps 132:8–18; Isa 11:10–16; 14:1–3; 32:17–18; Ezek 34:15). These blessings are rooted in God's promises to Abraham (Gen 12:1–3; 15:17–21; 17:7–8) and David (2 Sam 7:4–17; Ps 89:3–4,19–37). For the sense of "rest" for the readers of Hebrews, see 4:6–9.

3:12–13 Avoiding stubborn unbelief comes from a finely tuned balance of individual responsibility ("that none of you has a sinful, unbelieving heart ... that none of you may be hardened") and community concern ("see to it, brothers and sisters ... encourage one another daily"). Community support helps to overcome myopic individualism that cannot see its true condition ("hardened by sin's deceitfulness"), but even within the community of God's people, some individuals can resist to the point that their heart "turns away from the living God." Turning away means willfully rejecting, withdrawing from a religious loyalty one previously held or seemed to hold (Luke 8:13; 1 Tim 4:1). And the stakes are high: rejecting the only true and "living God" in stubborn unbelief. Encouragement is a daily need because while we have a present opportunity to respond to God's word ("as long as it is called 'Today' "), we must do so with enduring faith.

3:14 hold our original conviction firmly to the very end. Enduring in faith strengthens believers against the dangers just mentioned (vv. 12–13) since it gives evidence of what is already true of us: "We have come to share in Christ," i.e., we have benefited from his high priestly work (v. 1; 2:10–18). This "sharing" is not something that will come about only in the future; it has already come to be the case. Holding firmly to faith in God (vv. 12–13,19) despite day-by-day struggles does not *qualify* us for this status now or in the future; it *reflects* a status already gained. So this verse is not so much exhorting or admonishing (i.e., "we must endure in faith or we will not share in Christ") as it is defining (i.e., "those who have come to share in Christ are the ones who will endure in faith"). The author indicates elsewhere that to "share in Christ" brings also the inward and outward resources that enable us to hold firm in faith (cf. 7:25; 9:13–15; 13:20–21).

3:15 Today, if you hear his voice. Reinforces the urgency from Ps 95 of responding in faith when God speaks.

3:16–18 A series of rhetorical questions reveals what went wrong for the wilderness generation (Num 14:1–35). They had a clear opportunity to believe God's word because God gave them full exposure to his power and promise, but they "disobeyed" (Heb 3:18) and were judged.

3:19 unbelief. The obvious lesson from the sad example of the wilderness generation is the need for enduring faith.

4:1 [z]Heb 12:15
4:2 [a]1Th 2:13
4:3 [b]Ps 95:11; Heb 3:11
4:4 [c]Ge 2:2,3; Ex 20:11
4:5 [d]Ps 95:11
4:6 [e]Heb 3:18
4:7 [f]Ps 95:7,8; Heb 3:7,8,15
4:8 [g]Jos 22:4 [h]Heb 1:1

A Sabbath-Rest for the People of God

4 Therefore, since the promise of entering his rest still stands, let us be careful that none of you be
found to have fallen short of it.[z] 2For we also have had the good news proclaimed to us, just as they
did; but the message they heard was of no value to them, because they did not share the faith of those
who obeyed.[a][a] 3Now we who have believed enter that rest, just as God has said,

> "So I declared on oath in my anger,
> 'They shall never enter my rest.' "[b][b]

And yet his works have been finished since the creation of the world. 4For somewhere he has spoken
about the seventh day in these words: "On the seventh day God rested from all his works."[c][c] 5And again
in the passage above he says, "They shall never enter my rest."[d]

6Therefore since it still remains for some to enter that rest, and since those who formerly had the
good news proclaimed to them did not go in because of their disobedience,[e] 7God again set a certain
day, calling it "Today." This he did when a long time later he spoke through David, as in the passage
already quoted:

> "Today, if you hear his voice,
> do not harden your hearts."[d][f]

8For if Joshua had given them rest,[g] God would not have spoken[h] later about another day. 9There remains, then, a Sabbath-rest for the people of God; 10for anyone who enters God's rest also rests from

[a] *2* Some manuscripts *because those who heard did not combine it with faith* [b] *3* Psalm 95:11; also in verse 5 [c] *4* Gen. 2:2 [d] *7* Psalm 95:7,8

4:1–11 These further exhortations are based on Num 14 and Ps 95, but they focus on the mention of "rest" in Ps 95:11 and expand the biblical-theological base to include Gen 2.

4:1–2 "The promise of entering [God's] rest still stands" (v. 1a) because Num 14 and Ps 95 set up a pattern that finds its greater fulfillment in "the good news proclaimed to us" (v. 2a). The "message" that the wilderness generation "heard" (v. 2b) was God's promise to bring them into the promised land (Num 14:7–9), but the overwhelming portion of the people "did not share the faith of those who obeyed" (v. 2c; i.e., Joshua and Caleb). Now a more profound "good news" has come through a greater messenger than Moses (3:1–6), and so they must have greater concern for individuals among them to ensure "that none of [them] be found to have fallen short of it" (v. 1b). Verses 3–11 clarify the heightened sense of the "rest" now offered and how people enter it.

4:3 we who have believed enter that rest. Since the original readers have responded in faith to "the good news proclaimed to [them]" (v. 2a; see 2:1–4; 13:7), the author reassures them. This and v. 11 suggest that the "rest" has both a present and a future dimension to it: those who have believed "enter" it now (see v. 10) but also must "make every effort to enter that rest" in the future (v. 11). **just as God has said.** The writer again quotes the "rest" that Ps 95:11 mentions (vv. 3b,5) and reaches back to Gen 2 for its origin and definition (just as ch. 2 looked back through Ps 8 to Gen 1). **my rest.** God's rest from his creative work (Gen 2:2, quoted in v. 4). God has continued to enjoy rest "since the creation of the world," but the fall shattered mankind's participation in that blessing, security, and relief from labor. The wilderness generation later mirrored mankind's original rebellion, a pattern that Ps 95 and Heb 4:11 warn against.

4:6–8 These verses trace the pattern of God's rest—and mankind's opportunity to share in preliminary forms of it—from Gen 2:2 to Num 14 (they "did not go in, because of their disobedience") and then to Ps 95. The theological point Hebrews sees in Ps 95 (quoted again in v. 7) comes from the situation of the human author through whom God speaks in Scripture (see note on v. 7).

4:7 God again set a certain day ... when a long time later he spoke through David. Verse 8 confirms that "God would not have spoken" as he did "later" in Ps 95 if the "rest" had consisted merely in entering Canaan under Joshua. The blessing that Num 14 and Ps 95 offer previewed the ultimate rest inaugurated through the gospel and consummated in God's future restoration of his creation.

4:9 remains ... a Sabbath-rest. Repeats the point of vv. 1,6, using the same verb (opportunity for rest "still stands" or "remains") but a different noun. **Sabbath-rest.** Refers to the same experience of God-given blessing, security, and relief from struggle as in vv. 1,6 ("rest"), but it uses the imagery of Sabbath-celebration or joyful observance in worship (from the verb that means "to celebrate the Sabbath"; Exod 16:30; Lev 23:32; 26:34–35). This also connects the concept of "rest" with that of an eschatological "Sabbath," when God restores his people and the fallen creation to his original intent for them. The complete fulfillment of rest will come in the new creation (Isa 65:17; 66:22; Rev 21:1–4). Connections between "rest" and God's renewal of all things commonly occur in Judaism and early Christianity (in the pseudepigrapha see 1 Enoch 72:1; Jubilees 1:29; 4:26; Testament of Levi 18:9; Testament of Dan 5:12; 4 Ezra 7:75; 8:52; 10:54; 13:36; in the Apostolic Fathers, see Acts of Barnabas 15:1–9). This sense for "rest" in Heb 4 is even more likely since these texts associate eschatological rest with other eschatological concepts found in Hebrews: the age to come (1:6 and note; 2:5); the lasting city to come (11:10,16; 12:22; 13:14); and Zion, the heavenly Jerusalem (12:22). This will be the ultimate fulfillment of God's rest for his people, which Num 14 and Ps 95 prefigure.

4:10 The prospect of enjoying fullness of rest in the future is a motivation for the readers. **anyone who enters God's rest also rests from their works.** Or "the one who has entered ... has rested," viewing future deliverance from struggle and persecution as though it were already done. **their works.** Not human efforts to gain salvation but godly exertions against sin and worldly opposition. However, the future blessing of relief from trouble and danger does not mean inactivity or boredom. We will be in God's presence, joyfully engaged in serving, worshiping, and communing with him forever (Rev 21:1–4; 22:1–5; see note on v. 9).

their works,[a] just as God did from his.[i] 11Let us, therefore, make every effort to enter that rest, so that
no one will perish by following their example of disobedience.[j]
12For the word of God[k] is alive and active.[l] Sharper than any double-edged sword,[m] it penetrates
even to dividing soul and spirit, joints and marrow; it judges the thoughts and attitudes of the heart.[n]
13Nothing in all creation is hidden from God's sight.[o] Everything is uncovered and laid bare before the
eyes of him to whom we must give account.

Jesus the Great High Priest

14Therefore, since we have a great high priest who has ascended into heaven,[b][p] Jesus the Son of God,
let us hold firmly to the faith we profess.[q] 15For we do not have a high priest who is unable to empathize
with our weaknesses, but we have one who has been tempted in every way, just as we are[r] — yet he did
not sin.[s] 16Let us then approach God's throne of grace with confidence, so that we may receive mercy
and find grace to help us in our time of need.

5 Every high priest is selected from among the people and is appointed to represent the people in
matters related to God, to offer gifts and sacrifices[t] for sins.[u] 2He is able to deal gently with those
who are ignorant and are going astray,[v] since he himself is subject to weakness.[w] 3This is why he has
to offer sacrifices for his own sins, as well as for the sins of the people.[x] 4And no one takes this honor
on himself, but he receives it when called by God, just as Aaron was.[y]
5In the same way, Christ did not take on himself the glory[z] of becoming a high priest. But God said[a]
to him,

4:10 [i] ver 4
4:11 [j] Heb 3:18
4:12 [k] 1Pe 1:23 [l] Jer 23:29 [m] Eph 6:17; Rev 1:16 [n] 1Co 14:24,25
4:13 [o] Ps 33:13-15
4:14 [p] Heb 6:20 [q] Heb 3:1
4:15 [r] Heb 2:18 [s] 2Co 5:21
5:1 [t] Heb 8:3 [u] Heb 7:27
5:2 [v] Heb 2:18 [w] Heb 7:28
5:3 [x] Heb 7:27; 9:7
5:4 [y] Ex 28:1
5:5 [z] Jn 8:54 [a] Heb 1:1

[a] *10* Or *labor* [b] *14* Greek *has gone through the heavens*

4:11 make every effort to enter. The blessedness of God's rest in the future (v. 10) is the basis for exhorting the readers to exert themselves now as they face trials of faith. This asks not for works of merit to gain entrance but for the kind of concentrated attention (both individual and corporate) that leads toward enduring faith in the gospel that the author called for earlier (vv. 1–2; 3:6,12–14). No one should mimic the wilderness generation's "example" (the word used here, meaning "model, pattern," supports a typological reading of 3:6—4:11; 8:5; 9:23; see notes on 3:7—4:13; 3:7–11).
4:12–13 These two verses go together (v. 12 begins and v. 13 ends with the same Greek word, translated "word" and "account"). They tell why we need concentrated effort (v. 11) and conclude the whole section beginning at 3:1 on the need to respond faithfully when we hear God's message (vv. 2,7; 3:7,15).
4:12 the word of God is alive and active. Because it comes from God, who sees and knows all, it has penetrating authority to judge "the thoughts and attitudes of the heart." Outward appearance will not suffice when we "must give account" to God (v. 13).
4:14—5:10 *Jesus Our Compassionate High Priest.* Some regard 4:14 as the beginning of a major unit of the book that runs to 7:28 or even to 10:25. But it seems better to see the theme continuing with the second part of the large topic that 2:17 introduces (see note on 3:1—5:10): the Son is a merciful high priest so we should seek his help in temptation (4:14—5:10). Several phrases here link back to key terms in 2:17–18 and 3:1 to signal this shift. See Introduction: Outline.
4:14 great high priest. See 2:17; 3:1. **ascended into heaven.** There in the presence of God (cf. his "throne of grace" in v. 16), Jesus intercedes for us (7:25–26; 9:24), which encourages us to "hold firmly to the faith we profess" (the emphasis of 3:1—4:13). **Son.** See the note on 1:4 for the threefold sense of "Son" in Hebrews (see also 5:5–9).
4:15 Jesus is compassionate toward us in "our weaknesses." **we do not have a high priest who is unable to empathize.** This expresses the idea negatively to reinforce the positive sense. His compassion for us is based on hard-earned human experience: he "has been tempted in every way, just as we are" (this links to several key words in 2:17–18 and connects to the larger theme of Jesus' full humanity in 2:5–18). The only way he was not like us is indicated in the final phrase of v. 15: **he did not sin.** Jesus' sinless life is a frequent theme in Hebrews (5:3; 7:26–27; 9:14) and the whole NT (John 8:46; 2 Cor 5:21; 1 Pet 2:22; 1 John 3:5).
4:16 approach. Come before God in worship, communion, and prayer. This is a common theme in Hebrews (7:25; 10:1,22; 11:6; 12:18,22). **throne.** Because it is characterized by "grace," we can draw near "with confidence" to "receive mercy and find grace to help us in our time of need" ("mercy" and "help" are two further links to 2:17–18).
5:1–10 Having emphasized Jesus as merciful high priest (2:17), the author sets up the typology of priesthood that he will pursue in chs. 7–10. He does this by tracing three points of comparison between the Aaronic priesthood (vv. 1–4) and Jesus as the ultimate high priest (vv. 5–10), continuing to pay special attention to the compassion of the high priest toward his people.
5:1 The first characteristic seen in "every high priest" of the old order is his *function* in mediating between God and humans: he represents "the people in matters related to God," especially in offering "gifts and sacrifices for [their] sins." Because of this, he is "selected from among the people" so that he can identify with them fully (2:11–18; 4:15).
5:2 deal gently. The second high priestly characteristic is *compassion* toward his people. **ignorant and ... going astray.** This implies the OT distinction between defiant sins and sins done in ignorance or error (Lev 4–5; Num 15:22–31). See also 9:7; 10:26. This alludes to the difference in Hebrews between common human failings (for which God's mercy is always available through Christ, 2:17–18; 4:15–16) and defiant rejection of Christ's sacrifice (for which there is no forgiveness, 6:6; 10:26–29). **subject to weakness.** A mild reference to the high priest's human sinfulness (4:15), as evidenced by the obligation to offer "sacrifices for his own sins, as well as for the sins of the people" (v. 3; see 9:7; Lev 16:6,11). Later in Hebrews (7:27) the high priest's offering for his personal sins becomes a point of contrast with Christ, who was sinless (4:15).
5:4 The third high priestly characteristic is *divine calling* to the office. Self-appointment is not valid. One must be "called by God" to this service, "just as Aaron was." In all of his reflection on the former priestly order, the author affirms that God ordained it to serve his purpose.
5:5–10 This marks the shift in the extended comparison (see notes on vv. 1,2,4), showing how Christ fulfills the same characteristics, but

5:5 [b]Ps 2:7
5:6 [c]Ps 110:4; Heb 7:17,21
5:7 [d]Mt 27:46,50 [e]Mk 14:36
5:8 [f]Php 2:8
5:9 [g]Heb 2:10
5:10 [h]ver 5 [i]ver 6
5:12 [j]Heb 6:1 [k]1Co 3:2; 1Pe 2:2
5:13 [l]1Co 14:20
5:14 [m]1Co 2:6 [n]Isa 7:15

"You are my Son;
today I have become your Father."[a][b]

6And he says in another place,

"You are a priest forever,
in the order of Melchizedek."[b][c]

7During the days of Jesus' life on earth, he offered up prayers and petitions with fervent cries and
tears[d] to the one who could save him from death, and he was heard because of his reverent submission.[e] 8Son though he was, he learned obedience from what he suffered[f] 9and, once made perfect,[g] he
became the source of eternal salvation for all who obey him 10and was designated by God to be high
priest[h] in the order of Melchizedek.[i]

Warning Against Falling Away

6:4-6Ref — Heb 10:26-31

11We have much to say about this, but it is hard to make it clear to you because you no longer try
to understand. 12In fact, though by this time you ought to be teachers, you need someone to teach you
the elementary truths[j] of God's word all over again. You need milk, not solid food![k] 13Anyone who lives
on milk, being still an infant,[l] is not acquainted with the teaching about righteousness. 14But solid
food is for the mature,[m] who by constant use have trained themselves to distinguish good from evil.[n]

a 5 Psalm 2:7 *b* 6 Psalm 110:4

in reverse order: divine calling (vv. 5–6), compassion (vv. 7–8), and function (vv. 9–10).

5:5–6 Christ did not appoint himself. God *called* him to "the glory of becoming a high priest." Two OT quotations affirm God's summons; both are phrased as direct personal address from God ("You" is singular). Ps 2:7 (quoted in v. 5) repeats God's appointment of Christ as King or royal "Son" in the line of David (see note on 1:5 and NT texts cited there), reestablishing the earlier picture of Jesus in his exaltation to God's right hand (1:5–14). Ps 110:4 (quoted in v. 6) adds a unique insight: Jesus' presence at God's right hand in heaven (see Ps 110:1 and note on Heb 1:13) is theologically significant for his high priestly work (chs. 7–10 explain this). The most relevant points for this passage are that God appointed Jesus and that Jesus' priesthood differs from the Aaronic priesthood. This is the first of ten times that Hebrews quotes or alludes to Ps 110:4 (vv. 6,10; 6:20; 7:3,11,15,17,21,24,28); the text is not mentioned anywhere else in the NT.

5:6 in the order of Melchizedek. See notes on 7:1–3; Gen 14:18; Ps 110:4.

5:7 During the days of Jesus' life on earth. His whole earthly life is likely in view but with special attention to the agony at Gethsemane (e.g., his prayer to be saved "from death" and his "reverent submission"). God delivered him from death (cf. 13:20) because he submitted to the Father's will instead of his own (Matt 26:36–46). **prayers and petitions with fervent cries and tears.** This vivid description of Jesus' experience of human weakness and utter dependence on God the Father reinforces his *compassion* as high priest.

5:8 Son though he was. Jesus' uniqueness as high priest is grounded in his relation with God the Father as the divine Son (v. 5; 4:14), but this did not exempt him from suffering even to death in accomplishing God's saving purpose. **he learned obedience from what he suffered.** The verbs "learned" and "suffered" form an aphorism with a rhyming play on words in the Greek: "*emathen, epathen,*" similar to our "no pain, no gain." This does not mean "he learned to obey" after moral failure (4:15; 7:26–27; 9:14); rather, he learned through hard experience all that obedience entails, so he became a high priest sympathetic to our human weaknesses (2:17–18; 4:14–16).

5:9 once made perfect. This again traces the connection between Jesus' suffering and his full qualification to become high priest (2:10,17; 7:28). **the source of eternal salvation.** This mirrors what v. 1 lays down as the first characteristic of a high priest: his all-important *function* to offer sacrifices to deliver the people from sin and its consequences (see note on v. 1). In Christ's case, the pattern is fulfilled in the ultimate way: providing "eternal salvation," which previews key points that chs. 7–10 develop.

5:10 high priest in the order of Melchizedek. This second allusion to Ps 110:4 (see note on vv. 5–6) announces the themes the author develops in his central exposition of Jesus' high priesthood "in the order of Melchizedek" in chs. 7–10. The author slows down to insert a strong warning to give attention to this instruction (5:11—6:20a) before resuming the topic in 6:20b—7:1.

5:11—10:39 *Central Exposition: The Son's Melchizedekian Priesthood.* This major unit in the sermon explains how Jesus' priesthood in Melchizedek's order fulfills God's saving work. It is the reality that the OT priesthood and ritual foreshadowed. Sections urging continued faith in Christ introduce (5:11—6:20) and conclude (10:19–39) the exposition.

5:11—6:20 *Introductory Exhortation: Moving Toward Maturity.* This introduction has three parts (which the concluding section in 10:19–39 mirrors): it exhorts readers to move to maturity by heeding the coming exposition (5:11—6:3), severely warns them against falling away (6:4–8), and reassuringly calls them to enduring faith based on God's faithfulness (6:9–20).

5:11 no longer try. The original readers have become lazy or dull of hearing (the Greek is translated "lazy" in 6:12). They have neglected the gospel (2:1–4).

5:12 The evidence of their lethargy (v. 11) is stunted growth or retrogression in spiritual maturity. **by this time.** They are not recent converts, but they need a refresher course on "the elementary truths of God's word," i.e., basic Christian teachings (e.g., 6:1–2) about what God said through his Son and through Scripture (Acts 7:38; Rom 3:2; 1 Pet 4:11). **milk, not solid food!** The contrast illustrates the difference between a spiritual "infant" (v. 13) and a "mature" (v. 14) Christian (see note on v. 14).

5:13 not acquainted with. Unskilled, inexperienced, undiscerning. The contrasting positive trait is "trained … to distinguish good from evil" (v. 14).

5:14 mature. Translates the Greek word (with its cognates) often rendered "perfect" in Hebrews (v. 9; 2:10; 7:28; see 10:14; 11:40; 12:23). It means to be "finished, complete, in full or final form" and so here

6 Therefore let us move beyond[o] the elementary teachings[p] about Christ and be taken forward to
maturity, not laying again the foundation of repentance from acts that lead to death,[a][q] and of
faith in God, 2 instruction about cleansing rites,[b][r] the laying on of hands,[s] the resurrection of the dead,[t]
and eternal judgment. 3 And God permitting,[u] we will do so.
4 It is impossible for those who have once been enlightened,[v] who have tasted the heavenly gift,[w]
who have shared in the Holy Spirit,[x] 5 who have tasted the goodness of the word of God and the powers
of the coming age 6 and who have fallen[c] away, to be brought back to repentance.[y] To their loss they
are crucifying the Son of God all over again and subjecting him to public disgrace. 7 Land that drinks
in the rain often falling on it and that produces a crop useful to those for whom it is farmed receives
the blessing of God. 8 But land that produces thorns and thistles is worthless and is in danger of being
cursed.[z] In the end it will be burned.

[a] *1* Or *from useless rituals* [b] *2* Or *about baptisms* [c] *6* Or *age,* [6]*if they fall*

6:1 [o] Php 3:12-14 [p] Heb 5:12 [q] Heb 9:14
6:2 [r] Jn 3:25 [s] Ac 6:6 [t] Ac 17:18,32
6:3 [u] Ac 18:21
6:4 [v] Heb 10:32 [w] Eph 2:8 [x] Gal 3:2
6:6 [y] 2Pe 2:21; 1Jn 5:16
6:8 [z] Ge 3:17,18; Isa 5:6

"fully developed, mature" (the related Greek word is translated "maturity" in 6:1).

6:1 The primary exhortation of this section (5:11—6:3) is to move forward to Christian "maturity" (the passive sense "be taken forward" [NIV rendering] is not as likely a rendering of the Greek). The accompanying instructions—"move beyond the elementary teachings" and "not laying again the foundation" (both in the sense of "build on this foundation; don't be stuck at the starting point")—support this central appeal. The author specifies several areas of "elementary teachings" in v. 2.

6:2 cleansing rites. This could refer to Christian baptism, but why the plural? The Greek word occurs in 9:10 of Jewish "ceremonial washings," so this could be the sense here. But in this context "baptisms" probably refers to instruction about Christian baptism as distinct from other cleansing rituals. **laying on of hands.** Symbolizes the Spirit's presence either for healing (Luke 13:13; Acts 9:17), blessing (Mark 10:16), reception into the church (Acts 8:17; 19:6), or as a call to special ministry (Acts 6:6; 13:3; 1 Tim 4:14; 5:22; 2 Tim 1:6); it is hard to specify which of these is in view here. The author cites these fundamental teachings not to devalue them but to urge the readers not to stall at step one. The further instruction in chs. 7–10 will provide a deeper grasp of what is central: the sacrifice of Christ for human redemption (similar to Paul's teaching for the "mature" in 1 Cor 1–2).

6:3 God permitting. Acknowledges dependence on God for success. **we will do so.** The writer intends to spur them toward maturity (what v. 1 calls for).

6:4–8 After words of exhortation (5:11—6:3, where the pronouns "we" and "you" predominate), the author moves to a strong warning (vv. 4–8, phrased less directly by using "they"). These severe words ("impossible ... to be brought back to repentance" [vv. 4,6] and "in the end it will be burned" [v. 8]) present great difficulties for interpretation as well as pastoral care that are not easy to resolve. Several closely related (and at times competing) elements in these verses must be taken into account. The most common interpretations are: (1) these are genuine Christians who turn away from Christ and suffer eternal judgment; (2) these are lethargic Christians who come under divine discipline for failing to advance to maturity; and (3) these are people who participate in the Christian community but have turned away from Christ, showing that their faith never was genuine.

6:4a It is impossible. Verses 4–6 comprise one sentence in the original Greek stating the impossibility of returning certain people (described in five phrases following "those who," vv. 4b–6a) to repentance and the reasons it cannot be done (v. 6b). Bringing such people back to repentance is unattainable because of the attitude toward Christ that the rest of v. 6 describes (see notes on vv. 6:4b–6a,6b). Since Christ's sacrifice is God's full and final provision for sin, those who arrogantly reject it can find no other opportunity for turning to God (10:26–27). This is strong language; however, in practical terms, someone who is repentant and desires restoration to Christ thereby shows that he or she is not in the irretrievable condition these verses describe. A repentant heart will always be welcomed.

6:4b–6a Five descriptions follow in these verses. Do they refer to genuine Christian experience or to something very close (a positive exposure to Christ and the gospel) but not quite the full reality of conversion? Parallel uses in Hebrews of some of the key words of vv. 4–6 seem to favor the former view; e.g., these all seem to describe genuine Christian experience: have "been enlightened" (v. 4b; cf. 10:32), "have tasted" (v. 4c; cf. 2:9); "have shared" (v. 4d; cf. 3:1,14); have experienced "the goodness of the word of God and the powers of the coming age" (v. 5; cf. 2:2–4). On the other hand, these may not be definitive and do not employ some of the key terms Hebrews uses elsewhere to describe people Christ redeemed: "made holy," i.e., sanctified (2:11; 10:10,14; see note on 10:29); "made perfect" (10:14; 11:40; 12:23); "saved"/"save"/"salvation" (v. 9; 5:9; 7:25; 9:28). In some passages of the NT, experiences like vv. 4b–6a refer to an exposure to the gospel and the Spirit's miracles that leads to a preliminary positive response but not full Christian conversion (Matt 7:21–23; Luke 8:4–15; John 8:30–47; Acts 8:13–24). The final description (those "who have fallen away" [v. 6a]) is probably parallel to the other four rather than a condition ("if they fall away" [see NIV text note]). The verb has a general sense of "trespass, offend, fall away (from a standard)," and the verbs in the rest of v. 6 clarify the specific and serious nature of this "fall." This is not a matter of everyday sin or occasional failings but a serious "fall," parallel to 3:12 ("turns away from the living God") or 10:29 (arrogantly rejecting the value of Christ's sacrifice), mirroring how the wilderness generation decisively rejected Moses and the Lord (Num 14). This final description ("have fallen away") should cause us to look at the first four descriptions (vv. 4b–5) more carefully. The propositions about Christians in the earlier warning passage (3:6,14) indicate that enduring faith is the evidence of truly having "come to share in Christ" (3:14) or of being "his house" (3:6). Those who do not hold on to faith in Christ show that their experience was superficial rather than genuine. Describing them in ways that mirror genuine conversion so closely (vv. 4b–5) heightens the sense of outrage that someone could turn away from such blessings.

6:6b crucifying the Son of God all over again and subjecting him to public disgrace. Specifies the serious offense of one who has "fallen away" (v. 6a): it is having the attitude that Christ deserved to die a shameful, criminal's death and thereby denying the importance of his high priestly sacrifice (10:29; Matt 27:39–44).

6:7–8 An agricultural example illustrates the spiritual truths of vv. 4–6 (cf. similar metaphors in Matt 7:16–20; 13:3–23). The positive illustration (v. 7) builds toward the negative climax (v. 8), which alludes to God's judgment on human sin in Gen 3:17–18 ("thorns and thistles" and "cursed" land).

6:8 In the end it will be burned. Someone who rejects God's abundant spiritual provision faces severe judgment (10:26–31; 12:25–29).

6:9 [a]1Co 10:14 **6:10** [b]Mt 10:40,42; 25:40; 1Th 1:3 **6:11** [c]Heb 3:6 **6:12** [d]Heb 13:7 [e]2Th 1:4; Jas 1:3; Rev 13:10 [f]Heb 10:36 **6:13** [g]Ge 22:16; Lk 1:73 **6:14** [h]Ge 22:17 **6:15** [i]Ge 21:5 **6:16** [j]Ex 22:11 **6:17** [k]Ps 110:4 [l]Heb 11:9 **6:18** [m]Nu 23:19; Titus 1:2 [n]Heb 3:6 **6:19** [o]Lev 16:2; Heb 9:2,3,7 **6:20** [p]Heb 4:14 [q]Heb 2:17 [r]Heb 5:6 **7:1** [s]Mk 5:7 [t]Ge 14:18-20

9 Even though we speak like this, dear friends,[a] we are convinced of better things in your case—the
things that have to do with salvation. 10 God is not unjust; he will not forget your work and the love you
have shown him as you have helped his people and continue to help them.[b] 11 We want each of you to show
this same diligence to the very end, so that what you hope[c] for may be fully realized. 12 We do not want you
to become lazy, but to imitate[d] those who through faith and patience[e] inherit what has been promised.[f]

The Certainty of God's Promise

13 When God made his promise to Abraham, since there was no one greater for him to swear by, he
swore by himself,[g] 14 saying, "I will surely bless you and give you many descendants."[a][h] 15 And so after
waiting patiently, Abraham received what was promised.[i]

16 People swear by someone greater than themselves, and the oath confirms what is said and puts
an end to all argument.[j] 17 Because God wanted to make the unchanging[k] nature of his purpose very
clear to the heirs of what was promised,[l] he confirmed it with an oath. 18 God did this so that, by two
unchangeable things in which it is impossible for God to lie,[m] we who have fled to take hold of the
hope[n] set before us may be greatly encouraged. 19 We have this hope as an anchor for the soul, firm and
secure. It enters the inner sanctuary behind the curtain,[o] 20 where our forerunner, Jesus, has entered on
our behalf.[p] He has become a high priest[q] forever, in the order of Melchizedek.[r]

Melchizedek the Priest

7 This Melchizedek was king of Salem and priest of God Most High.[s] He met Abraham returning from
the defeat of the kings and blessed him,[t] 2 and Abraham gave him a tenth of everything. First, the
name Melchizedek means "king of righteousness"; then also, "king of Salem" means "king of peace."

[a] *14* Gen. 22:17

6:9–10 After his severe warning (vv. 4–8), the author reassures his readers and again appeals for enduring faith (vv. 9–12).

6:9 convinced of better things ... that have to do with salvation. He expects that their Christian experience is genuine and will not lead to the rejection and judgment he describes in vv. 6,8. The basis for this (v. 10 begins with a Greek conjunction "for," which the NIV does not translate) is the evidence of authentic Christian transformation in their lives: "work" and "love" (v. 10; cf. 10:32–34; 13:21; Phil 1:6; 1 Thess 1:3; Jas 2:14–17; 1 John 3:14–20). The author understands that such conduct is a genuine work of God, and he knows that God is absolutely reliable to carry his work through to the end (3:6,14; 7:25; 9:14–15).

6:11 show this same diligence to the very end. Because of their current malaise (2:1–3; 5:11–12), the readers must revive their spiritual energy and not be "lazy" (v. 12; see note on 5:11). They need enduring faith, in contrast to turning away from Christ's sacrifice (v. 6).

6:12 imitate those who through faith and patience inherit what has been promised. Repeats the author's characteristic appeal (3:12–14; 10:23,35–39; 12:1–3) and introduces Abraham as the cardinal example of such faith (vv. 13–20).

6:13–15 While Abraham is a commendable example (v. 15 repeats key words from v. 12; see 11:8–19), these verses (vv. 13–18) focus on God's fidelity far more than on Abraham's persevering faith. Referring to God's oath (v. 13) emphasizes how absolutely reliable God's promise is and anticipates ch. 7's elaboration of Jesus' priesthood that God gave him by oath according to Ps 110:4 (quoted in 7:17,21; see notes on 7:20,21). Gen 22:17 (quoted in v. 14) highlights God as the agent (reflecting a Semitic emphatic expression, "in blessing I will bless you, and in multiplying I will multiply you").

6:16 People swear by someone greater than themselves. A general principle about how oaths operate in everyday life.

6:17 heirs. God's promise to Abraham included a larger group of beneficiaries than Abraham alone.

6:18 two unchangeable things. (1) His confirming *oath* (v. 17) added to (2) his completely reliable *promise* (v. 17)—reliable because "it is impossible for God to lie." God gave his iron-clad pledge to Abraham about his purpose to bless him and through him to bless the whole world (Gen 12:1–2; 22:17–18; Acts 3:25; Rom 4:16–17; Gal 3:6–9,16). God intended it to give great encouragement also to all those who would "take hold" by faith "of the hope set before" them through Christ, Abraham's greater descendant.

6:19 Hope is "an anchor for the soul, firm and secure" in the midst of struggles, because it is based on God's unchanging purpose: to accomplish our salvation through Christ. **enters the inner sanctuary behind the curtain.** Hope gives us access, through prayer and worship, to the very presence of God in heaven (4:14–16; 10:20–22), pictured here according to the typology of entry into the Most Holy Place, which 9:11–28 develops.

6:20 our forerunner. Jesus opened the way for believers also to enter into God's glorious presence (2:10; 4:3; 12:1–2,22). An important subtheme in Hebrews is our pilgrimage amid suffering in this world to arrive at the glory of the world to come, our true home (10:34; 11:13–16; 13:13–14). Reference to Christ's entering God's presence leads back again to his eternal priesthood "in the order of Melchizedek" (5:6,10), which the introductory exhortation (5:11—6:20) briefly set aside.

7:1–28 *Christ as Priest in Melchizedek's Order.* The central exposition of Christ's high priesthood (7:1—10:18) begins with an explanation of the nature of his priesthood in the order of Melchizedek (vv. 1–10, based on Gen 14:17–20) and moves to the theological significance of such a priesthood (vv. 11–28, based on Ps 110:4).

7:1–3 The author is guided by a pertinent question: If Jesus is a priest like Melchizedek (Ps 110:4, just alluded to in 6:20 and earlier in 5:10), what sort of priest would he be? In good interpretive fashion, the author goes to Gen 14 (the only other OT text to mention Melchizedek) to find answers. The author handles the text typologically (not allegorically), as he does elsewhere in Hebrews. Melchizedek appears in Gen 14 as a genuinely human, historical figure (not a myth, angel, or theophany) who interacts with Abraham after the patriarch rescued Lot from four eastern kings. The author notes what the text says and does not say about Melchizedek and reads it along with Ps 110:4 as imperfectly foreshadowing what Jesus' priestly service ultimately fulfills.

7:1 Melchizedek was king of Salem. According to the sense of his

3Without father or mother, without genealogy,[u] without beginning of days or end of life, resembling the
Son of God,[v] he remains a priest forever.
4Just think how great he was: Even the patriarch[w] Abraham gave him a tenth of the plunder![x] 5Now
the law requires the descendants of Levi who become priests to collect a tenth from the people[y] — that
is, from their fellow Israelites — even though they also are descended from Abraham. 6This man, however, did not trace his descent from Levi, yet he collected a tenth from Abraham and blessed[z] him who
had the promises.[a] 7And without doubt the lesser is blessed by the greater. 8In the one case, the tenth is
collected by people who die; but in the other case, by him who is declared to be living.[b] 9One might even
say that Levi, who collects the tenth, paid the tenth through Abraham, 10because when Melchizedek met
Abraham, Levi was still in the body of his ancestor.

Jesus Like Melchizedek

11If perfection could have been attained through the Levitical priesthood — and indeed the law
given to the people[c] established that priesthood — why was there still need for another priest to come,[d]
one in the order of Melchizedek,[e] not in the order of Aaron? 12For when the priesthood is changed, the
law must be changed also. 13He of whom these things are said belonged to a different tribe,[f] and no
one from that tribe has ever served at the altar.[g] 14For it is clear that our Lord descended from Judah,[h]
and in regard to that tribe Moses said nothing about priests. 15And what we have said is even more
clear if another priest like Melchizedek appears, 16one who has become a priest not on the basis of a
regulation as to his ancestry but on the basis of the power of an indestructible life. 17For it is declared:

> "You are a priest forever,
> in the order of Melchizedek."[a][i]

18The former regulation is set aside because it was weak and useless[j] 19(for the law made nothing
perfect),[k] and a better hope is introduced, by which we draw near to God.[l]

a 17 Psalm 110:4

7:3 [u]ver 6 [v]Mt 4:3
7:4 [w]Ac 2:29 [x]Ge 14:20
7:5 [y]Nu 18:21,26
7:6 [z]Ge 14:19,20 [a]Ro 4:13
7:8 [b]Heb 5:6; 6:20
7:11 [c]ver 18,19; Heb 8:7 [d]Heb 10:1 [e]ver 17
7:13 [f]ver 11 [g]ver 14
7:14 [h]Isa 11:1; Mt 1:3; Lk 3:33
7:17 [i]Ps 110:4; ver 21; Heb 5:6
7:18 [j]Ro 8:3
7:19 [k]Ac 13:39; Ro 3:20; Heb 9:9 [l]Heb 4:16

name and title, Melchizedek (Hebrew for "my king is righteousness") was a royal figure characterized by righteousness and peace (traits also associated with the future Davidic Messiah, Isa 9:6–7; Jer 33:15–16). **priest of God most High.** Melchizedek was a priest as well as a king and functioned as a priest toward Abraham. His royal and priestly roles are both important as foreshadowings of Jesus, but the priestly role is central here in ch. 7.

7:3 Without father or mother, without genealogy, without beginning of days or end of life. Because Gen 14 does not indicate Melchizedek's origin or demise, he represents a priesthood that is eternal ("remains a priest forever"). In Genesis, where genealogies are common, the silence about an important figure's ancestry is striking. **resembling the Son of God.** Melchizedek prefigures superficially what has come to be true of Jesus in profound reality (see Introduction: Themes and Argument).

7:4–7 Melchizedek's concrete historical interactions (vv. 1b–2a) with the "patriarch Abraham" (v. 4) — who represents his descendants, the Levitical priests — reveal Melchizedek's greatness and that his priesthood is superior to the Levitical order. First of all, Abraham "gave him a tenth of the plunder" (v. 4). According to the law (inextricably connected to the Levitical order of priests [vv. 11–12,16,19,28]), "the descendants of Levi who become priests" are privileged to "collect a tenth from … their fellow Israelites" (v. 5). Melchizedek showed that he was superior to Abraham and his priestly descendants of the old order when he "collected a tenth from Abraham" (v. 6) and also when he "blessed" Abraham (v. 6), since "without doubt the lesser is blessed by the greater" (v. 7; see Gen 1:22,28; 48:9; Num 6:22–27).

7:8 people who die. The former priests were mortal, but Jesus "lives forever" (v. 24), a contrast previewing the ideas of vv. 16,23–25. Jesus is the true counterpart of Melchizedek, who only superficially was "declared to be living" (v. 8), since Gen 14 does not record his beginning or end.

7:9–10 "One might even say" (v. 9) means "so to speak" or "in a manner of speaking"; the author overtly signals that his reading of Gen 14 is typological, or representative, rather than strictly literal (see Introduction: Themes and Argument). Since a father can be seen to act for his descendants, "when Melchizedek met Abraham" (v. 10) in Gen 14, Levi and his priestly descendants were, "one might even say," also there "in the body of his ancestor" (v. 10), and they "paid the tenth through Abraham" (v. 9), symbolizing the greatness of Melchizedek's priesthood.

7:11–12 The author turns again to Ps 110:4 to reflect on its theological implications: Why would God speak through the psalmist about "another priest to come, one in the order of Melchizedek, not in the order of Aaron" at a time when the Levitical priesthood was operative? It shows the limited nature of that priestly order and of the "law" that "established" it: it could not attain "perfection" (i.e., provide full redemption from sin and communion with God [v. 19; 9:9; 10:1,14; 11:40; 12:23]). God intended to change both the "priesthood" and the "law."

7:13 He of whom these things are said. The words of Ps 110:4 refer ultimately to Jesus. He "descended from Judah" (v. 14), not Levi, and the Mosaic law did not permit anyone from that tribe to serve as a priest. This is evidence that a change was needed (v. 12).

7:15 even more clear. Further evidence adding to what vv. 13–14 say. **another priest like Melchizedek.** Jesus as the eternal "Son of God" (v. 3) could truly be "a priest forever," as Ps 110:4 says (quoted in v. 17).

7:16 on the basis of a regulation as to his ancestry. Or "according to a law of fleshly commandment"; refers to the Mosaic stipulations about the Levitical priesthood, as in vv. 11–12,14,18–19. **the power of an indestructible life.** Inherent in Jesus' nature as God (1:4,10–12). This is the fundamental basis for his eternally effective high priestly service. This verse anticipates the stronger contrast of vv. 23–25.

7:18–19 This states more strongly what vv. 11–12 say about the law (it would be "changed" because of its provisional nature): it "is set aside"

7:21 [m] 1Sa 15:29 [n] Ps 110:4
7:22 [o] Heb 8:6
7:24 [p] ver 28
7:25 [q] ver 19 [r] Ro 8:34

20 And it was not without an oath! Others became priests without any oath, 21 but he became a priest
with an oath when God said to him:

> "The Lord has sworn
> and will not change his mind:[m]
> 'You are a priest forever.'"[a][n]

22 Because of this oath, Jesus has become the guarantor of a better covenant.[o]
23 Now there have been many of those priests, since death prevented them from continuing in office;
24 but because Jesus lives forever, he has a permanent priesthood.[p] 25 Therefore he is able to save completely[b] those who come to God[q] through him, because he always lives to intercede for them.[r]

[a] *21* Psalm 110:4 [b] *25* Or *forever*

(v. 18; see 8:13) "because it was weak and useless" (v. 18) in regard to accomplishing full redemption (cf. v. 11). The reason is that "the law made nothing perfect" (v. 19; cf. v. 11; 10:1).

7:20 not without an oath. The author refers to the first clause in Ps 110:4 (quoted in v. 21, the only time this clause is cited in the NT; v. 28 alludes to it).

7:21 The Lord has sworn and will not change his mind. This underscores another superior feature of Jesus' priesthood: his appointment comes from God's irrevocable oath (cf. 6:16–18).

7:22 the guarantor of a better covenant. God's solemn appointment and Jesus' priestly sacrifice (9:15; 13:20) ensure the complete effectiveness of a new arrangement for human salvation. This is the first of 17 times that "covenant" occurs in Hebrews, anticipating chs. 8–9.

7:23–24 The first instance of a one-versus-many contrast between Jesus and the older order of priests, implying that their service was ineffective (vv. 27–28; 10:1–4,10–14; see "Contrasts of Levitical Priesthood and Jesus' Priesthood in Hebrews," this page). This specifies a more important contrast: their mortality versus Jesus' "permanent priesthood" (v. 24)—"permanent" because he "lives forever" (v. 24). Jesus' eternal, divine Sonship is the foundation for his superior high priesthood (vv. 3,16; 1:4,10–12; 5:5–9).

7:25 Therefore. The all-important consequence of Jesus' unending, "indestructible" life" (v. 16; cf. "permanent priesthood" in v. 24) is his limitless ability "to save completely." **completely.** In this context probably has a temporal sense: "for all time" or "forever" (see NIV text note; see also "always" in the next clause). The ones he saves forever are "those who come to God through him," which in Hebrews commonly describes the people who gain access to God for worship, prayer, and communion through Jesus' high priestly ministry (4:16; 10:22; 11:6). Jesus can save them for all time "because he always lives to intercede for them." This refers to what his presence at God's right hand represents: constantly appealing to God for saving mercy and enabling grace based on his sacrifice of himself (2:17–18; 4:14–16; 9:24; Rom 8:27,34). This is why Jesus' *ability* ("he is able") "to save completely [forever]" is actual (he can and does save forever), not potential (he can save forever, but he may not). Some take "those

CONTRASTS OF LEVITICAL PRIESTHOOD AND JESUS' PRIESTHOOD IN HEBREWS

LEVITICAL PRIESTS AND HIGH PRIESTS	VERSES IN HEBREWS	JESUS AS HIGH PRIEST
Limited access to God: only the high priest only once a year	4:14–16; 7:19; 9:7–8; 10:19–22	Provides full access to God through Christ for all Christians
Weak, sinful; offered sacrifices first for their own sins	5:2–3; 7:26–28	Holy, blameless; sacrificed for others
Aaronic ancestry	5:4–6; 7:11,14,16	Order of Melchizedek; power of an indestructible life
Appointed by the law, not by God's oath	5:5–6; 7:20–22,28	Appointed by God's oath, after the law
Ineffectual; unable to perfect those who draw near	5:9; 7:11,18–19,25; 9:9,12; 10:1–4,10–18	Saves completely; makes perfect forever
Connected with old covenant/law	7:11–12,22,28; 8:4,6–7	Connected with new covenant
Many priests	7:23–24	One priest
Temporary service due to mortality	7:23–25	Permanent service; he lives forever
Offered animal sacrifices	7:27; 9:11–14,25–26; 10:4,10	Offered himself
Sacrifices repeated daily, yearly; reminder of sins	7:27; 9:25–26,28; 10:1–4,10–12	Sacrificed once for all; sins cleansed once for all
Standing	8:1; 10:11–12	Seated
Prototype and foreshadowing	8:2,5; 9:11,23–24; 10:1	The true reality; the coming of good things
Entered the earthly, man-made sanctuary	8:5; 9:1,11–12,23–24	Entered the heavenly presence of God
External; ceremonial cleansing; guilt of sin remains	9:9–10,13–14; 10:2,22	Internal; cleansing of the conscience

26 Such a high priest truly meets our need — one who is holy, blameless, pure, set apart from sinners,[s] exalted above the heavens.[t] 27 Unlike the other high priests, he does not need to offer sacrifices[u]
day after day, first for his own sins,[v] and then for the sins of the people. He sacrificed for their sins once
for all[w] when he offered himself.[x] 28 For the law appoints as high priests men in all their weakness;[y] but
the oath, which came after the law, appointed the Son,[z] who has been made perfect[a] forever.

7:26 [s]2Co 5:21 [t]Heb 4:14
7:27 [u]Heb 5:1 [v]Heb 5:3 [w]Heb 9:12,26,28 [x]Eph 5:2; Heb 9:14,28
7:28 [y]Heb 5:2 [z]Heb 1:2 [a]Heb 2:10
8:1 [b]Heb 2:17
8:2 [c]Heb 9:11,24
8:3 [d]Heb 5:1 [e]Heb 9:14
8:4 [f]Heb 5:1
8:5 [g]Heb 9:23 [h]Col 2:17; Heb 10:1 [i]Heb 11:7; 12:25

The High Priest of a New Covenant

8 Now the main point of what we are saying is this: We do have such a high priest,[b] who sat down at
the right hand of the throne of the
Majesty in heaven, 2 and who serves in
the sanctuary, the true tabernacle[c] set up
by the Lord, not by a mere human being.
3 Every high priest is appointed to offer both gifts and sacrifices,[d] and so it
was necessary for this one also to have
something to offer.[e] 4 If he were on earth,
he would not be a priest, for there are
already priests who offer the gifts prescribed by the law.[f] 5 They serve at a
sanctuary that is a copy[g] and shadow[h] of
what is in heaven. This is why Moses was
warned[i] when he was about to build the
tabernacle: "See to it that you make everything according to the pattern shown

Reconstruction of the altar of burnt offering at Herod's Temple. Unlike other priests, Jesus "does not need to offer sacrifices day after day" (Heb 7:27).
Leen Ritmeyer

who come to God through him" as a contingency: if they turn back, he cannot save. But the last clause of v. 25 precludes their turning back (9:14–15; 10:12–14; 13:20–21; see notes on 3:14; 6:9–10).
7:26–27 One final quality in vv. 26–28 sets Jesus off as superior to the old covenant high priests: he is "holy, blameless, pure, set apart from sinners" (v. 26; see 4:15; 9:14) in contrast to their "weakness" (v. 28) and their need to offer sacrifices "first for [their] own sins, and then for the sins of the people" (v. 27; cf. 5:2–3; 9:7). That Jesus is "exalted above the heavens" (v. 26) prepares the way for the topic of chs. 9–10: he is the heavenly high priest of a new order. In addition to his complete holiness, in which he is "unlike the other high priests" (v. 27), Jesus "does not need to offer sacrifices day after day" (v. 27). His single sacrifice is completely effective: "once for all ... he offered himself" (v. 27; cf. vv. 23–24). The phrase "once for all" denotes "once for all time, never to be repeated," not "once for all people."
7:28 This concluding verse reinforces two earlier contrasts: (1) priestly appointment rooted in "the law" versus God's "oath" (in Ps 110:4), "which came after the law" (vv. 11,16,20–22); (2) the appointment of "men in all their weakness" (i.e., sinful, mortal, and ineffective [vv. 18,23,27; 5:2–3]) versus "the Son, who has been made perfect forever" (i.e., holy, eternal, and completely effective [vv. 2–3,16,24–25; see 2:10; 5:9]). Hebrews contrasts the Levitical priesthood with Jesus' high priestly service in multiple ways (see "Contrasts of Levitical Priesthood and Jesus' Priesthood in Hebrews," p. 2506).
8:1–13 *Christ as Heavenly High Priest of a Better Covenant.* Christ's superior ministry in the heavenly sanctuary shows that he mediates a superior covenant with superior promises (vv. 1–6). This leads to a lengthy citation of Jer 31:31–34, specifying the superior promises of the new covenant (vv. 7–13).
8:1 Now the main point of what we are saying is this. This sermonic feature clarifies the exposition's focus. **sat down at the right hand.** Ps 110 takes center stage in this exposition of Jesus' high priestly ministry. **Majesty.** See note on 1:3. The one who is priest of a superior order (Ps 110:4, as ch. 7 expounds) is seated in God's presence in heaven (Ps 110:1; see 1:3,13; 10:12–13; 12:2). Chs. 8–10 work out the implications of this in multiple ways.
8:2 the sanctuary, the true tabernacle. The place of worship where Jesus ministers is "in heaven" (v. 1), in the very presence of God. The "throne" of God (v. 1) is located in the "sanctuary," the heavenly temple (1 Sam 4:4; Ps 11:4; Isa 6:1–4; 37:16). The author continues to trace a typology of priesthood and sacrifice to show how Jesus' atoning death fulfills in the ultimate way what the Mosaic forms foreshadowed. **true.** Describes the NT fulfillment, the profound reality that the OT type could picture only in provisional ways (9:24; John 6:32). Ch. 9 develops the tabernacle pattern in full.
8:3 something to offer. Noting the sanctuary where Jesus serves (v. 2) leads to the offering he had to make as high priest, which is developed in 9:11–28.
8:4 on earth. Jesus was not a priest in the earthly, Mosaic order of priests, because he was not qualified for it (7:13–14) and because it already had enough priests. **offer.** Some take this present-tense verb to describe ongoing ministry in the temple in Jerusalem prior to its destruction in AD 70, and they cite it as evidence for dating Hebrews before AD 70. But Hebrews consistently refers not to serving in the *temple* in any era but to the OT regulations and rituals of the *tabernacle*. Hebrews regularly uses the present tense to describe the tabernacle rituals (in the Greek of v. 5; 7:28; 9:6–9,13,25; 10:1,8; 13:10–11) in the sense of a "literary" present, preserved in written form and therefore true at whatever time someone reads it. See Introduction: Date.
8:5 copy and shadow .... pattern. These words present the patterned relationship between Israel's earthly tabernacle and the heavenly sanctuary where Jesus now serves. God showed Moses a "pattern" (Greek *typos*, "type") to guide the layout and construction of the wilderness tabernacle (Exod 25:40). The Mosaic tabernacle in turn became a "prototype" or "outline" (a better sense of the Greek than "copy"; it consistently means not "copy" but "example," something to be copied;

8:5 [l]Ex 25:40
8:6 [k]Lk 22:20 [l]Heb 7:22
8:7 [m]Heb 7:11,18
8:8 [n]Jer 31:31
8:9 [o]Ex 19:5,6
8:10 [p]2Co 3:3; Heb 10:16 [q]Zec 8:8
8:11 [r]Isa 54:13; Jn 6:45

you on the mountain."[a][j] 6 But in fact the ministry Jesus has received is as superior to theirs as the
covenant[k] of which he is mediator[l] is superior to the old one, since the new covenant is established on
better promises.

7 For if there had been nothing wrong with that first covenant, no place would have been sought for
another.[m] 8 But God found fault with the people and said[b]:

"The days are coming, declares the Lord,
when I will make a new covenant[n]
with the people of Israel
and with the people of Judah.
9 It will not be like the covenant
I made with their ancestors[o]
when I took them by the hand
to lead them out of Egypt,
because they did not remain faithful to my covenant,
and I turned away from them,
declares the Lord.
10 This is the covenant I will establish with the people of Israel
after that time, declares the Lord.
I will put my laws in their minds
and write them on their hearts.[p]
I will be their God,
and they will be my people.[q]
11 No longer will they teach their neighbor,
or say to one another, 'Know the Lord,'
because they will all know me,[r]
from the least of them to the greatest.

[a] 5 Exodus 25:40 [b] 8 Some manuscripts may be translated *fault and said to the people.*

4:11; 9:23). It was a "shadow" of the heavenly sanctuary in the sense that it foreshadowed or prefigured the place where Jesus now serves as heavenly high priest (8:1–2). This does not reflect platonic cosmology or Hellenistic dualism, where earthly "shadows" that are illusory and evil reflect the heavenly "forms" that are real and good. Instead it is a feature of biblical expectation and fulfillment, where what exists on earth mirrors, in a preliminary way, what already exists in heaven and anticipates its full establishment on earth in the future (1:6; 2:5; 4:9).

8:6 superior. Jesus' heavenly service is superior to that of the Levitical priests (this culminates the contrast that vv. 2–5 trace), and the new covenant is superior to the Mosaic one (vv. 7,13; 9:15–22; cf. 13:20) because it is "established on better promises" (specified in vv. 8–12; 10:15–18). **mediator.** This may mean simply "guarantor," one who ensures that the covenant is carried out (see use of the related Greek verb in 6:17, where it is translated "confirmed"; see a similar concept in 7:22, which is expressed by a different Greek word and translated "guarantor"). But it can also mean "intermediary," one who establishes common ground between two parties. In Hebrews "mediator" seems to carry a combination of these two senses (see note on 9:15). Jesus' sacrificial death brought the new covenant and its promises into effect (9:15; 12:24; 13:20; Luke 22:20; 1 Cor 11:25).

8:7 The superiority of the later covenant finds support in the OT. Why would Jer 31 speak of a "new" covenant (Jer 31:31) if the former one met the need? **another.** The OT text implies that something was actually "wrong with that first covenant" (see v. 8a and note), but what was "wrong" was that it was limited in its intent and effectiveness (7:11,19; 9:9; 10:1).

8:8a God found fault with the people. The NIV alludes to the *people's* infidelity to the old covenant (v. 9), and that makes good sense. But a more likely reading of the Greek text is "God found fault and said to the people" (see NIV text note). This alternative rendering would reinforce the point of v. 7: the *covenant itself* was "faulty" or limited ("nothing wrong" in v. 7 and "found fault" in v. 8 share the same Greek root). Verse 13 may also support this idea. The old covenant was not evil but incomplete and provisional; God never intended it to be final (1:1–2; Rom 7:12; 10:4; 1 Tim 1:8).

8:8b–12 The Scriptural support for the God-intended limitation of the old covenant is Jer 31:31–34 (see note there). (This is the longest OT citation in the NT.) Hebrews allows the words to carry their clear sense but signals their larger significance with theological comments before and after the quotation (vv. 8a,13). Later the author reinforces some of the "better promises" (v. 6; see 10:15–18).

8:8b new covenant. Verse 13 pays special attention to the historical circumstances within God's redemptive plan: the promise of a future "new covenant" came at a time when the former covenant was still in force.

8:9 It will not be like the covenant. Jeremiah speaks of the two covenants as separate, though related (the new does not renew the old), and this is how Hebrews takes them (vv. 6–7). **did not remain faithful.** Human inability to obey the commands of the former covenant was certainly one of the former covenant's limitations. God intended to remedy this under the new covenant. See "Covenant," p. 2646.

8:10 minds and … hearts. Internalizing God's demands and inward renewal to enable obedience are cardinal features of the new covenant (10:16; see 9:13–14; 10:19–22; 13:20–21; Ezek 36:25–27; 2 Cor 3–4).

8:11 they will all know me. Personal relationship with and true fidelity to God are closely related promises. To "know" God in this sense is to recognize his authority and obey his will.

> 12For I will forgive their wickedness
> and will remember their sins no more.[s][t][a]

13By calling this covenant "new," he has made the first one obsolete;[u] and what is obsolete and outdated will soon disappear.

Worship in the Earthly Tabernacle

9 Now the first covenant had regulations for worship and also an earthly sanctuary.[v] 2A tabernacle[w] was set up. In its first room were the lampstand[x] and the table[y] with its consecrated bread;[z] this was called the Holy Place. 3Behind the second curtain was a room called the Most Holy Place,[a] 4which had the golden altar of incense[b] and the gold-covered ark of the covenant.[c] This ark contained the gold jar of manna,[d] Aaron's staff that had budded,[e] and the stone tablets of the covenant. 5Above the ark were the cherubim of the Glory,[f] overshadowing the atonement cover. But we cannot discuss these things in detail now.

6When everything had been arranged like this, the priests entered regularly[g] into the outer room to carry on their ministry. 7But only the high priest entered[h] the inner room, and that only once a year,[i] and never without blood, which he offered for himself[j] and for the sins the people had committed in ignorance. 8The Holy Spirit was showing[k] by this that the way[l] into the Most Holy Place had not yet been disclosed as long as the first tabernacle was still functioning. 9This is an illustration for the present time, indicating that the gifts and sacrifices being offered[m] were not able to clear the conscience of the

8:12 [s]Heb 10:17 [t]Ro 11:27
8:13 [u]2Co 5:17
9:1 [v]Ex 25:8
9:2 [w]Ex 25:8,9 [x]Ex 25:31-39 [y]Ex 25:23-29 [z]Lev 24:5-8
9:3 [a]Ex 26:31-33
9:4 [b]Ex 30:1-5 [c]Ex 25:10-22 [d]Ex 16:32,33 [e]Nu 17:10
9:5 [f]Ex 25:17-19
9:6 [g]Nu 28:3
9:7 [h]Lev 16:11-19 [i]Lev 16:34 [j]Heb 5:2,3
9:8 [k]Heb 3:7 [l]Jn 14:6; Heb 10:19,20
9:9 [m]Heb 5:1

[a] *12* Jer. 31:31-34

8:12 remember their sins no more. The new covenant emphatically promises full and eternal forgiveness, which the Mosaic order could not accomplish but Jesus has provided in full (10:1–4,11–14,17–18). **8:13 new.** Indicates a provisional character for the former covenant (the Mosaic covenant [Exod 19:5–6; 24:3–8; 2Cor 3:6,14; Gal 4:24], not the Abrahamic one [Gen 12:1–3; Rom 4:16–17; Gal 3:7–9,16–18]). Its time was limited, and God's declaration through Jeremiah made that clear. As elsewhere, the author pays careful attention to the theological sense of Scripture in its specific historical context (2:8–9; 4:7–8; 7:11; 10:8–10). **will soon disappear.** The temporal reference point for "soon" is more likely Jeremiah's day rather than the time when Hebrews was written (just as for "the days are coming" in v. 8). The decisive change came when Christ inaugurated the new covenant by his death on the cross.

9:1–28 *Christ's Priestly Service in the Heavenly Sanctuary.* The ritual of the earthly tabernacle (vv. 1–10) foreshadows Christ's sacrifice and its significance (vv. 11–28).

9:1 This previews vv. 2–10 in reverse order: the layout of the OT sanctuary (vv. 2–5) and its worship ritual (vv. 6–10).

9:2 its first room. The tabernacle's outer chamber, "the Holy Place." Its furnishings were a lampstand (Exod 25:31; 39:37; Lev 24:4) and a table (Exod 25:23; 39:36) on which the priests regularly placed loaves of consecrated bread (Exod 25:30; 39:36; Lev 24:5–9). These are listed without description in order to highlight the glory of the second chamber (vv. 3–5).

9:3 the second curtain. The ornate drape separating the outer room from the inner one (Exod 26:33), "the Most Holy Place."

9:4 The author gives more attention to the sacred furnishings of the inner chamber. **golden altar of incense.** Probably located just outside the inner chamber (although there is some ambiguity about this; Exod 30:6; 40:26–27); its function connected it more closely to the Most Holy Place. The smoke of its incense filled the inner chamber during the Day of Atonement ritual (Lev 16:13). **the gold-covered ark of the covenant.** The wooden box was lined with gold inside and out (Exod 25:10–16) and contained important reminders of God's provision for his people: a jar of manna, Aaron's staff, and the tablets of the covenant (Exod 16:32–34; Num 17:8–11).

9:5 cherubim of the Glory. Impressive statues of winged creatures associated with God's presence (Gen 3:24; Exod 25:17–22; Lev 16:2; Num 7:89; Ezek 10:1–22). **atonement cover.** The Greek word used here denotes "place of atonement" or "means of atonement" (translated "sacrifice of atonement" in Rom 3:25). Here it is the slab of pure gold traditionally called the "mercy seat," which was placed on top of the ark (Exod 25:17–22), where the sacrificial blood was sprinkled on the Day of Atonement (Lev 16:14–15; see 2:17).

9:6–7 A brief contrast of the daily ritual of the "outer room" and the yearly ritual of the "inner room" (Exod 30:10; Lev 16). It focuses on the restricted access to the inner room ("only the high priest ... only once a year, and never without blood").

9:7 sins ... committed in ignorance. The OT distinction between defiant sins and sins done in error or ignorance (Lev 4–5; Num 15:22–31) seems to lie behind this wording, but the author does not develop it here (see notes on 5:2; 10:26–27).

9:8 The Holy Spirit was showing. The ritual arrangements laid out in Scripture, understood now in their full significance, indicate these things. **the Most Holy Place.** This could be the true heavenly sanctuary (vv. 11–12; 8:1–2), but in this context it is more likely the inner room of the earthly tabernacle just described (vv. 3–5, 7). **the first tabernacle.** This may refer to the entire OT tabernacle, looking ahead to the contrast with "the greater and more perfect tabernacle" (v. 11) Christ entered (v. 12). But in light of vv. 2,6, where "the first tent" denotes the outer portion of the earthly tabernacle, that is the more likely sense here as well. The existence of the outer room symbolizes the limited access to God that the OT ritual provided (v. 7). **still functioning.** This may be understood as "still had validity" (or "to have standing" in the sense of legal or cultic validity; 10:9 uses the related Greek verb translated "establish" in referring to the new priestly order).

9:9 This is an illustration for the present time. The imperfect features of the old order point forward to the fulfillment now true in Christ (the Greek word translated "illustration" is the same word translated "parable" in Matt 13:18; here it is used of a symbol or type). **clear the conscience.** Or "perfect the conscience" (v. 14; 7:11,19; 10:1; on perfection, see v. 14; 10:2,22). The OT offerings could not provide full forgiveness of sins, but Christ's sacrifice of himself (v. 14) clears the human conscience of guilt that impedes full communion with God.

9:10 [n]Lev 11:2-23 [o]Col 2:16 [p]Heb 7:16
9:11 [q]Heb 2:17 [r]Heb 10:1 [s]Heb 8:2
9:12 [t]Heb 10:4 [u]ver 24 [v]Heb 7:27
9:13 [w]Nu 19:9,17,18
9:14 [x]1Pe 3:18 [y]Titus 2:14; Heb 10:2,22 [z]Heb 6:1
9:15 [a]1Ti 2:5 [b]Heb 7:22
9:18 [c]Ex 24:6-8

worshiper. 10They are only a matter of food[n] and drink[o] and various ceremonial washings — external
regulations[p] applying until the time of the new order.

The Blood of Christ

11But when Christ came as high priest[q] of the good things that are now already here,[a][r] he went
through the greater and more perfect tabernacle[s] that is not made with human hands, that is to say, is
not a part of this creation. 12He did not enter by means of the blood of goats and calves;[t] but he entered
the Most Holy Place[u] once for all[v] by his own blood, thus obtaining[b] eternal redemption. 13The blood
of goats and bulls and the ashes of a heifer[w] sprinkled on those who are ceremonially unclean sanctify
them so that they are outwardly clean. 14How much more, then, will the blood of Christ, who through
the eternal Spirit[x] offered himself unblemished to God, cleanse our consciences[y] from acts that lead to
death,[c][z] so that we may serve the living God!

15For this reason Christ is the mediator[a] of a new covenant, that those who are called may receive
the promised eternal inheritance — now that he has died as a ransom to set them free from the sins
committed under the first covenant.[b]

16In the case of a will,[d] it is necessary to prove the death of the one who made it, 17because a will is
in force only when somebody has died; it never takes effect while the one who made it is living. 18This
is why even the first covenant was not put into effect without blood.[c] 19When Moses had proclaimed

[a] *11* Some early manuscripts *are to come* [b] *12* Or *blood, having obtained* [c] *14* Or *from useless rituals* [d] *16* Same Greek word as *covenant*; also in verse 17

9:10 external regulations. See the contrast of the outward versus the inward as related to the new covenant in vv. 13–14; 8:10. The OT offerings pointed forward to "the time of the new order" (i.e., the new covenant, priest, sacrifice, and full forgiveness and access) now present in Christ (v. 26; 1:2; 10:1).

9:11 In contrast to the old order (vv. 6–10), "Christ came as high priest of the good things that are now already here" (see similar phrasing in 10:1). In following the pattern God set forth in the OT ritual, Christ entered not the earthly tabernacle ("made with human hands ... a part of this creation") but "the greater and more perfect tabernacle" in heaven (cf. v. 24; 4:14; 8:1–5).

9:12 the blood of goats and calves. The provisional offerings of the old order on the Day of Atonement (Lev 16:14–16; cf. v. 7; 10:1–4). **the Most Holy Place.** The culmination of Christ's high priestly service was entering into God's presence in heaven (v. 24; 6:19–20; 8:1). **by his own blood.** He offered himself once for all time (vv. 26–28; 7:27) as the ultimate, eternally effective sacrifice for sin (10:12–14). **eternal redemption.** Lasting deliverance from sin. **redemption.** Denotes a payment to set someone free or, as here, the release itself (Luke 1:68; 2:38). See a compound of this word in v. 15: "a ransom to set them free" from sins.

9:13–14 This lesser-to-greater argument (a single sentence in the original Greek) picks up the contrast of inward versus outward cleansing from sin (vv. 9–10). Various animal sacrifices of the old order (Lev 16; Num 19) served their God-given purpose to "sanctify" (a literary present; see note on 8:4) in a limited way, but this is a matter of ceremonial, or outward, cleansing, not the true purification people needed (10:1–2). The greater accomplishment of Christ's superior sacrifice (which profoundly heightens the typology; see Introduction: Themes and Argument) is the inward cleansing of "our consciences" from sinful ways "so that we may serve the living God" ("serve" implies worshipful devotion; 10:2; 12:28). This inward transformation leading to obedience alludes to the promises of the new covenant (v. 15; 8:10–12; 10:16–17).

9:14 through the eternal Spirit. The Holy Spirit empowered Christ for all aspects of his ministry (Isa 42:1; 61:1; Matt 3:16). Reference here to all three persons of the Trinity reinforces how Christ's sacrifice embodied the full divine plan for human redemption.

9:15 mediator of a new covenant. Christ's sacrificial death is the basis for God's promised new covenant (7:22; 8:6; 12:24; Luke 22:20; 1 Cor 11:25). **mediator.** Some understand this to mean simply "guarantor," not "intermediary," since the covenant itself is not a mutual agreement between equal parties who need an arbiter to negotiate their differences. Christ is not a mediator in this sense. But in light of Moses' role in inaugurating the former covenant (vv. 15,18–21), it is likely that Christ is seen as "intermediary," as well as "guarantor" (cf. 7:22), of the new covenant. Moses was understood as God's agent in establishing the covenant and in interceding between God and his people (Exod 20:19; 32:31–32; 34:3–9; Num 14:19–20; Deut 5:5,24–27; Gal 3:19–20). Christ fulfills these roles in a greater way under the new covenant (v. 24; 2:17–18; 4:14–16; 7:25; 1 Tim 2:5–6). **those who are called.** The people God has summoned to be the beneficiaries of the covenant promises (cf. 3:1; 11:8). **eternal inheritance.** The lasting benefits God promised through the new covenant (8:8–13), phrased in the imagery of a bequest granted through a will (see vv. 16–17). **ransom to set them free.** Christ's death was a payment that delivers or redeems people from slavery (v. 12; Rom 3:24; Eph 1:7; cf. Exod 6:6; Deut 7:8), in this case from bondage to sin and guilt.

9:16–17 The same Greek word translated "will" in v. 16 is translated "covenant" in v. 15 (see NIV text note on v. 16). One view of vv. 16–17 maintains that "covenant" is the sense intended throughout these verses (vv. 15–20) and the connection with death in vv. 16b–17 alludes to the sacrifice of animals, which put such covenants into effect (Exod 24:5–8). In contrast, the NIV translation "will" understands vv. 16–17 as a play on words introduced by "inheritance" in v. 15. The biblical word "covenant" (Greek *diathēkē* in the Septuagint [the pre-Christian Greek translation of the OT] and in the NT) was commonly used in secular Greek of a "last will and testament," a one-sided stipulation of benefits distributed at death. In normal human practice the inheritance comes "only when somebody has died." In secular Greek a related word (*synthēkē*) was used for a contract between equal parties. Because the biblical covenants were essentially God's pledge to bless his people, the Greek Bible consistently uses the word "testamentary declaration" (*diathēkē*) for the covenants' expression of the divine purpose. On either reading these verses point out that Christ's death put the new covenant into effect (vv. 12–15,26–28).

9:18 What is true of normal human practice (vv. 16–17) is also seen in the pattern of God's institution of the old order through Moses: it required (sacrificial) death ("blood").

9:19–20 blood ... sprinkled ... blood of the covenant. The inauguration of the Sinai covenant (Exod 24:3–8) confirms v. 18. Details from

every command of the law to all the people, he took the blood of calves, together with water, scarlet
wool and branches of hyssop, and sprinkled the scroll and all the people.[d] 20 He said, "This is the blood
of the covenant, which God has commanded you to keep."[a][e] 21 In the same way, he sprinkled with the
blood both the tabernacle and everything used in its ceremonies. 22 In fact, the law requires that nearly
everything be cleansed with blood,[f] and without the shedding of blood there is no forgiveness.[g]
23 It was necessary, then, for the copies[h] of the heavenly things to be purified with these sacrifices,
but the heavenly things themselves with better sacrifices than these. 24 For Christ did not enter a sanctuary made with human hands that was only a copy of the true one;[i] he entered heaven itself, now to
appear for us in God's presence. 25 Nor did he enter heaven to offer himself again and again, the way
the high priest enters the Most Holy Place[j] every year with blood that is not his own.[k] 26 Otherwise Christ
would have had to suffer many times since the creation of the world.[l] But he has appeared once for
all[m] at the culmination of the ages to do away with sin by the sacrifice of himself. 27 Just as people are
destined to die once,[n] and after that to face judgment,[o] 28 so Christ was sacrificed once to take away the
sins of many; and he will appear a second time,[p] not to bear sin,[q] but to bring salvation to those who
are waiting for him.[r]

Christ's Sacrifice Once for All

10 The law is only a shadow[s] of the good things[t] that are coming — not the realities themselves.[u]
For this reason it can never, by the same sacrifices repeated endlessly year after year, make
perfect[v] those who draw near to worship. 2 Otherwise, would they not have stopped being offered? For
the worshipers would have been cleansed once for all, and would no longer have felt guilty for their
sins. 3 But those sacrifices are an annual reminder of sins.[w] 4 It is impossible for the blood of bulls and
goats[x] to take away sins.

9:19 [d] Ex 24:6-8
9:20 [e] Ex 24:8; Mt 26:28
9:22 [f] Lev 8:15 [g] Lev 17:11
9:23 [h] Heb 8:5
9:24 [i] Heb 8:2
9:25 [j] Heb 10:19 [k] ver 7,8
9:26 [l] Heb 4:3 [m] Heb 7:27
9:27 [n] Ge 3:19 [o] 2Co 5:10
9:28 [p] Titus 2:13 [q] 1Pe 2:24 [r] 1Co 1:7
10:1 [s] Heb 8:5 [t] Heb 9:11 [u] Heb 9:23 [v] Heb 7:19
10:3 [w] Heb 9:7
10:4 [x] Heb 9:12,13

[a] *20* Exodus 24:8

related sprinkling rituals fill out the description (Lev 14:14–16,49–52; Num 19:4,17–18).

9:21–22 Moses also sprinkled blood to dedicate "both the tabernacle and everything used in its ceremonies" (Exod 40:9–15; Lev 8:10–24; 16:14–20). More broadly, according to "the law ... nearly everything [is] cleansed with blood, and without the shedding of blood [i.e., sacrificial death; Lev 4:7–34; 8:15; 17:11] there is no forgiveness." Removing sin's guilt was provisional under the old order (10:3–4) but full and final under Christ's new covenant sacrifice (10:17–18).

9:23 copies. A better sense is "examples" or "prototypes" (see note on 8:5). **purified ... with better sacrifices than these.** The earthly sanctuary was a holy place, but its association with a sinful people required its cleansing on the Day of Atonement (Lev 16:14–20). The heavenly sanctuary likewise had to be made pure by Christ's offering of himself to deal with human sin and provide access to God for God's people (4:16; 10:19–22).

9:24 The full typological significance of Christ's priestly work is that "he entered" the "true" sanctuary, "heaven itself, now to appear for us in God's presence" (see vv. 11–12; 8:1–2). Being seated at God's right hand signifies that Christ fully accomplished God's work of salvation (v. 26; 1:3; 2:9–10; 6:19–20; 10:11–14). **copy.** Translates a different Greek word than that used in v. 23; 8:5 (see notes). Here it is "antitype," what mirrors the heavenly "pattern" or "type" that God showed Moses [8:5b; Exod 25:40]).

9:25 offer himself again and again ... every year. Another instance of the one-versus-many contrast between Jesus and the old priestly order (7:23–24), except Jesus' service was fully effective. **blood that is not his own.** This prepares the way for the difference between sacrificing unwilling animals and Jesus' voluntarily offering of himself (v. 26; 10:4–10).

9:26 A strongly worded contrast displays the full significance of Christ's sacrifice for human salvation: "many times since the creation of the world" versus "once for all at the culmination of the ages" (cf. v. 10; Matt 13:39; 1 Pet 1:20). Jesus' incarnation, death, and exaltation mark the decisive start of God's fulfillment (1:1–2), and Christ will fully consummate it when he returns to earth (v. 28).

9:27–28 The universal experience of fallen humanity (2:14) is death (decisively final and thus unrepeatable) and then certain "judgment." Likewise, Christ in his true humanity died once as a sacrifice.

9:28 take away the sins of many. An allusion to Isa 53:12; as God's eternal Son, Christ's offering of himself brought widespread benefit. **appear a second time.** Christ's return to earth (Acts 1:11; 1 Thess 2:19; 1 John 3:2) will consummate the saving work that his sacrifice for sin has initiated (cf. 1:14; Rom 8:18–23). **waiting for him.** This Greek verb implies eager expectation (1 Cor 1:7; Phil 3:20–21; Titus 2:13).

10:1–18 *Conclusion of the Exposition: Contrast of the Old and New Sacrifices.* The central exposition of Christ's high priesthood (7:1—10:18) concludes with a four-part contrast of the Mosaic order with Christ: (1) the law is imperfect with its repeated offerings (vv. 1–4); (2) Christ's offering replaces the law's sacrifices (vv. 5–10); (3) Christ is a seated priest who replaces the standing priests (vv. 11–14); and (4) the new covenant completely provides for sin (vv. 15–18).

10:1 shadow ... realities. God intended the whole Mosaic system to point ahead to how Christ profoundly fulfills it (8:5; 9:8–10,23–24). God did not intend the law to bring perfection (v. 14; 7:11,18–19; 9:9). **repeated endlessly year after year.** Such sacrifices must be ineffective (vv. 11–12; 7:27; 9:25).

10:2 felt guilty for their sins. Or "had consciousness of sin" (9:9,14).

10:3 Instead of dealing decisively with sin, the law's offerings were a constant "reminder" of human sinfulness (cf. Rom 3:20; 4:15; 5:20; 7:7–12).

10:4 bulls and goats. The animal offerings of the Mosaic system provided ritual, outward purification (9:13), not the full, inward cleansing humans need (7:18–19; 9:14). Christ's effective sacrifice suggests two reasons animal sacrifice is insufficient: (1) the incarnate Christ identified fully with humans (v. 5; 2:10–18), and (2) his self-surrender to God accomplished what involuntary offerings could never do (vv. 5–10).

10:5 [y]Heb 1:6 [z]1Pe 2:24
10:7 [a]Jer 36:2 [b]Ps 40:6-8
10:8 [c]ver 5,6; Mk 12:33
10:9 [d]ver 7
10:10 [e]Jn 17:19 [f]Heb 2:14; 1Pe 2:24 [g]Heb 7:27
10:11 [h]Heb 5:1 [i]ver 1,4
10:13 [j]Heb 1:13
10:14 [k]ver 1
10:15 [l]Heb 3:7
10:16 [m]Jer 31:33; Heb 8:10
10:17 [n]Heb 8:12

5 Therefore, when Christ came into the world,[y] he said:

> "Sacrifice and offering you did not desire,
> but a body you prepared for me;[z]
> 6 with burnt offerings and sin offerings
> you were not pleased.
> 7 Then I said, 'Here I am—it is written about me in the scroll[a]—
> I have come to do your will, my God.' "[a][b]

8 First he said, "Sacrifices and offerings, burnt offerings and sin offerings you did not desire, nor were
you pleased with them"[c]—though they were offered in accordance with the law. 9 Then he said, "Here
I am, I have come to do your will."[d] He sets aside the first to establish the second. 10 And by that will, we
have been made holy[e] through the sacrifice of the body[f] of Jesus Christ once for all.[g]

11 Day after day every priest stands and performs his religious duties; again and again he offers the
same sacrifices,[h] which can never take away sins.[i] 12 But when this priest had offered for all time one
sacrifice for sins, he sat down at the right hand of God, 13 and since that time he waits for his enemies to
be made his footstool.[j] 14 For by one sacrifice he has made perfect[k] forever those who are being made holy.

15 The Holy Spirit also testifies[l] to us about this. First he says:

> 16 "This is the covenant I will make with them
> after that time, says the Lord.
> I will put my laws in their hearts,
> and I will write them on their minds."[b][m]

17 Then he adds:

> "Their sins and lawless acts
> I will remember no more."[c][n]

18 And where these have been forgiven, sacrifice for sin is no longer necessary.

[a] *7* Psalm 40:6-8 (see Septuagint) [b] *16* Jer. 31:33 [c] *17* Jer. 31:34

10:5–7 Because a better sacrifice was needed, Christ did God's will by coming to provide it (cf. v. 10). David's devotion to God in Ps 40:6–8 expresses typologically the attitude of David's greater Son at the time of his incarnation. David asks what thanks he can offer for the Lord's wondrous deliverance (Ps 40:1–5) and responds by contrasting ritual sacrifice with fervent commitment to obey God (Ps 40:6–8)—the latter delights God more than the former (a common OT theme; see 1 Sam 15:22; Ps 51:16–17; Isa 1:10–17; Jer 7:21–26; Hos 6:6; Amos 5:21–24; Mic 6:6–8).

10:5 a body you prepared for me. Hebrews cites a Greek translation of Ps 40:6b, which differs from the Hebrew ("my ears you have opened"). But both express the larger sense: "you have prepared me to act in obedience." Using "body" makes clear the point of v. 10 (the sacrifice of Jesus' body).

10:7 in the scroll. The OT itself reveals what God expected of kings (e.g., Deut 17:18–20), and David commits himself to obey it.

10:8 First he said. To interpret the psalm, the author groups key words thematically: first the nouns ("Sacrifices and offerings, burnt offerings and sin offerings"), then the verbs ("you did not desire, nor were you pleased with them"). He notes their connection with "the law" to set up the contrast in v. 9.

10:9 I have come to do your will. The contrast between the law's ritual and wholehearted commitment to serve God's purpose is clear. The larger significance of this for salvation history is that "he sets aside the first" (the law with its priestly system) "to establish the second" (Christ's new covenant with its sacrifice). **sets aside.** Parallel in sense to 7:18 and stronger than "changed" in 7:12; the new covenant removes (not revises) the law (8:7–8a,13).

10:10 by that will, we have been made holy. Christ's action was not his alone in isolation; he fulfilled God's redemptive plan in setting us apart by his sacrificial death (v. 14; 2:9–11).

10:11 Day after day ... again and again ... the same sacrifices. Citing again the endless repetition of OT sacrifices to the same effect (vv. 1–3): they "can never take away sins" (see note on v. 12).

10:12 offered for all time one sacrifice for sins. By his decisive offering, Christ accomplished all that human sin required. **sat down.** Implied already as part of the main point in 8:1, the author makes another point: in the old order "every priest stands" (v. 11; see Deut 10:8; 18:5,7), but Christ "sat down" in God's presence (1:3; 8:1; Ps 110:1).

10:13 he waits for his enemies to be made his footstool. Cf. 1:13; Ps 110:1. What remains is for God to consummate his redemptive plan by triumphing over every enemy (2:8–9,14–15; 9:26–28; 1 Cor 15:23–28).

10:14 made perfect forever. By his single sacrifice Christ decisively accomplished what was needed for us to draw near to God. **being made holy.** This is what God continues to work out in our lives now and will fully accomplish in the future based on Christ's work (v. 10). See also 4:3,11; 9:15; 12:22,28.

10:15–18 Verse 1 mentions the law's provisional nature, and here the author returns to God's pledging a new covenant in Jer 31 through "the Holy Spirit" (v. 15) speaking in Scripture. God promised (v. 16) to "put [his] laws in their hearts" (an important theme in Hebrews: vv. 19–22; 8:10; 9:13–14; 13:20–21). The new covenant also promised complete forgiveness (vv. 17–18; cf. 8:12b; also an important theme in Hebrews: vv. 4,11–12; 1:3; 2:17; 9:26).

10:17 I will remember no more. Contrasts with "an annual reminder of sins" (v. 3).

10:18 sacrifice for sin is no longer necessary. Contrasts with the repeated offerings (vv. 1–2,11).

A Call to Persevere in Faith

19 Therefore, brothers and sisters, since we have confidence to enter the Most Holy Place[o] by the blood
of Jesus, 20 by a new and living way[p] opened for us through the curtain,[q] that is, his body, 21 and since
we have a great priest[r] over the house of God, 22 let us draw near to God[s] with a sincere heart and with
the full assurance that faith brings, having our hearts sprinkled to cleanse us from a guilty conscience[t]
and having our bodies washed with pure water. 23 Let us hold unswervingly to the hope[u] we profess, for
he who promised is faithful.[v] 24 And let us consider how we may spur one another on toward love and
good deeds, 25 not giving up meeting together,[w] as some are in the habit of doing, but encouraging one
another[x] — and all the more as you see the Day approaching.
26 If we deliberately keep on sinning[y] after we have received the knowledge of the truth, no sacrifice
for sins is left, 27 but only a fearful expectation of judgment and of raging fire[z] that will consume the

10:19 [o]Eph 2:18; Heb 9:8,12,25
10:20 [p]Heb 9:8 [q]Heb 9:3
10:21 [r]Heb 2:17
10:22 [s]Heb 7:19 [t]Eze 36:25; Heb 9:14
10:23 [u]Heb 3:6 [v]1Co 1:9
10:25 [w]Ac 2:42 [x]Heb 3:13
10:26 [y]Nu 15:30; 2Pe 2:20
10:27 [z]Isa 26:11; 2Th 1:7; Heb 9:27

10:19–39 *Concluding Exhortation: Draw Near Through Christ in Enduring Faith.* To balance the three-part introduction (see note on 5:11 — 6:20) to his central exposition, the author gives a three-part concluding exhortation: he urges his readers to draw near and continue in faith and obedience (vv. 19–25), severely warns against willfully rejecting God's Son (vv. 26–31), and reassuringly calls them to endurance and faith (vv. 32–39). **10:19 confidence to enter the Most Holy Place.** The three exhortations in vv. 22–24 are grounded first in how Christians may freely access God's presence through Jesus' sacrifice ("by the blood of Jesus").

10:20 through the curtain, that is, his body. "The curtain" refers symbolically to the barrier that previously restricted access to the Most Holy Place in the OT tabernacle (6:19; 9:3,7–8). The curtain is here identified with Jesus' "body," using two possible meanings of "through" in a play on words. The author first uses its spatial sense ("through the curtain") and then implies its instrumental sense ("that is, [through] his body") to capture forcefully that Jesus' sacrifice opened this access for us (cf. v. 10).

Reconstruction of the curtain in Herod's temple. Hebrews states that we have "a new and living way opened for us through the curtain" (Heb 10:20), referring to when the curtain tore in two at Jesus' death.

10:21 a great priest. The second basis (see note on v. 19) for the exhortations in vv. 22–24 is Jesus' high priestly ministry for us, a distinctive theme in Hebrews, which 2:17–18 introduces and chs. 7–10 explain from Scripture. Jesus' high priestly work encourages us to draw near and hold fast to faith in him.

10:22 let us draw near. The first of three parallel exhortations in vv. 22–24. Christians can experience this privileged approach to God in worship, prayer, and communion with inward genuineness and full confidence because of Christ's new covenant sacrifice (8:10–12; 9:13–14). **hearts sprinkled to cleanse us from a guilty conscience.** The inward purification Christ's new covenant brings (Ezek 36:25–27; see notes on 9:13–14). **having our bodies washed.** An allusion to baptism and the cleansing from sin that comes at conversion (6:2; Eph 5:26; Titus 3:5).

10:23 hold unswervingly to the hope we profess. Enduring faith is the characteristic appeal of Hebrews (see v. 36; 3:6; 4:14; 6:11–12,18). Hope is bolstered because God "who promised is faithful" (6:13–20).

10:24 spur one another on. Healthy Christianity is not just maintaining the status quo but also actively pursuing Christian virtue and service (vv. 32–34; 6:10). **love.** Completes the triad of faith (v. 22), hope (v. 23), and love (here) in vv. 22–24.

10:25 not giving up meeting together ... but encouraging one another. The final two phrases tell how we can carry out the three exhortations, especially the final one (v. 24), emphasizing how much the individual Christian needs the support of the whole community (3:12–13; 13:7,17). **giving up meeting together.** Abandoning church gatherings (perhaps due to persecution; vv. 32–34; 12:3–4; 13:3) is a troubling precursor (like 2:1,3; 5:11; 12:12–13) but not full apostasy (v. 29; 3:12; 6:6). **the Day approaching.** The nearness of Christ's coming further motivates Christians to grow in godliness (vv. 36–37; 9:28; Matt 24:42; 1 Cor 3:13; 1 Thess 5:2).

10:26–27 These verses describe someone who "deliberately" (i.e., willfully, defiantly) sins by repudiating Christ. In two other places (5:2; 9:7; see notes) Hebrews alludes to the OT distinction between defiant sins and sins committed in ignorance or error (Lev 4–5; Num 15:22–31). The defiant sin of Num 15:30–31 seems to lie behind this reference. Here "sinning" is mentioned generally in v. 26 and then defined specifically in v. 29 as arrogantly rejecting Christ. The same pattern occurs in 6:6: "fallen away" is general, and the latter part of the verse describes repudiating Christ. So this does not refer to Christians falling prey to everyday temptations and failings; Hebrews encourages us to seek God's mercy and grace in such cases (2:18; 4:15–16; 12:1–6). **no sacrifice for sins is left, but only a fearful expectation of judgment.** This reinforces that "sinning" (v. 26) refers to repudiating Christ. Since Jesus' sacrifice is God's full and final provision for human salvation (chs. 7–10), "no sacrifice for sins is left" for someone who rejects its value. "Fearful ... judgment" is the tragic fate for such a person (vv. 28–31).

10:28 [a] Dt 17:6,7; Heb 2:2
10:29 [b] Heb 6:6 [c] Mt 26:28 [d] Eph 4:30; Heb 6:4 [e] Heb 2:3
10:30 [f] Dt 32:35; Ro 12:19 [g] Dt 32:36
10:31 [h] Mt 16:16
10:32 [i] Heb 6:4 [j] Php 1:29,30
10:33 [k] 1Co 4:9 [l] Php 4:14; 1Th 2:14
10:34 [m] Heb 13:3 [n] Heb 11:16
10:36 [o] Lk 21:19; Heb 12:1
10:37 [p] Mt 11:3 [q] Rev 22:20
10:38 [r] Ro 1:17; Gal 3:11

enemies of God. 28 Anyone who rejected the law of Moses died without mercy on the testimony of two or
three witnesses.[a] 29 How much more severely do you think someone deserves to be punished who has
trampled the Son of God underfoot,[b] who has treated as an unholy thing the blood of the covenant[c]
that sanctified them, and who has insulted the Spirit[d] of grace?[e] 30 For we know him who said, "It is
mine to avenge; I will repay,"[a][f] and again, "The Lord will judge his people."[b][g] 31 It is a dreadful thing
to fall into the hands of the living God.[h]

32 Remember those earlier days after you had received the light,[i] when you endured in a great conflict
full of suffering.[j] 33 Sometimes you were publicly exposed to insult and persecution;[k] at other times you
stood side by side with those who were so treated.[l] 34 You suffered along with those in prison[m] and joyfully accepted the confiscation of your property, because you knew that you yourselves had better and
lasting possessions.[n] 35 So do not throw away your confidence; it will be richly rewarded.

36 You need to persevere[o] so that when you have done the will of God, you will receive what he has
promised. 37 For,

> "In just a little while,
> he who is coming[p] will come
> and will not delay."[c][q]

38 And,

> "But my righteous[d] one will live by faith.[r]
> And I take no pleasure
> in the one who shrinks back."[e]

39 But we do not belong to those who shrink back and are destroyed, but to those who have faith and
are saved.

[a] *30* Deut. 32:35 [b] *30* Deut. 32:36; Psalm 135:14 [c] *37* Isaiah 26:20; Hab. 2:3 [d] *38* Some early manuscripts *But the righteous* [e] *38* Hab. 2:4 (see Septuagint)

10:29 How much more. Administrating justice under the old covenant (e.g., Deut 17:2–7) is the basis for a lesser-to-greater argument, a typology of judgment (as in 2:1–4; 12:25). The heightening in the typology (see Introduction: Themes and Argument) shows that repudiating Christ brings a profoundly more severe judgment than physical death (v. 28). This renders unlikely the view that Hebrews warns against some kind of temporal, physical discipline for such rejection. Eternal, spiritual judgment is in view (6:8–9; 12:25–29). This verse defines the "sinning" with "knowledge" in v. 26 as arrogantly rejecting Jesus' sacrifice (see 6:6). Three phrases assume a prior exposure to Christian teaching about who Jesus is and what his death means: (1) **trampled the Son of God underfoot.** Exposure to Jesus has led to disdain instead of reverence. (2) **treated as an unholy thing the blood of the covenant.** Profanely regarding Jesus' death as something of no value. **that sanctified them.** Heightens the sense of tragedy that someone who has identified with a community professing Christ's sacrifice as its foundational truth would repudiate such a holy thing. (3) **insulted the Spirit of grace.** Disrespected the one who was present in the sacrifice (9:14) and the subsequent preaching about it (2:4).

10:30–31 Two quotations from Deut 32:35–36 (cf. Rom 12:19) show that judgment for someone who rejects Christ is sobering because the Lord will repay such insults and judge those who sin, even those among his own community. Punishment at "the hands of the living God" is a "dreadful thing" (translated "fearful" in v. 27).

10:32 Remember those earlier days. After a severe warning, the author reminds the readers of their past record (6:10): they "endured in a great conflict full of suffering." Endurance is what they still need in their current circumstances (v. 36).

10:33–34 They or Christians dear to them had endured a range of official and unofficial persecution, social ostracism, imprisonment for the faith (13:3), and loss of property. In all this their consolation was the "better and lasting possessions" they had in Christ (11:10,16,26,35; 12:28; 13:14).

10:35 do not throw away your confidence. The basis for this command is their prior conduct (vv. 32–34). **confidence.** A synonym for faith in Hebrews (v. 19; 3:6; 4:14). Maintaining such faith "will be richly rewarded." (Reward appears in the significant description of faith in 11:6 [see 11:26].)

10:36 You need to persevere. Or "you have need of endurance" (the same Greek root as that translated "endured" in v. 32). This introduces part of the next major section's topic: faith and endurance (11:1—12:13). **you will receive what he has promised.** This hope for the future can sustain our fidelity to God. Examples of doing "the will of God" despite present difficulties include Christ (vv. 7,9–10) and Abraham (6:12,15).

10:37–38 Two OT quotations support the call for enduring faith.

10:37 In just a little while. A few words from Isa 26:20 draw upon the urgency of its context ("the Lord is coming" in judgment, Isa 26:21) to reinforce the same idea as Hab 2:3 (v. 37). **he ... will come and will not delay.** These words from Hab 2:3 refer to Christ's return (9:28; Jas 5:8; 2 Pet 3:4,9).

10:38 These words from Hab 2:4 contrast two responses to Christ's return. **live by faith.** This call for enduring faith is characteristic of Hebrews (see note on v. 23). **shrinks back.** Retreating into unbelief due to fear or apathy is what Hebrews warns against (2:1–3; 3:12; 4:11; 11:23–27).

10:39 The author's positive expectation about the readers concludes this section of reassurance (vv. 32–39; similar to 6:9–10,18–20). But he makes clear the stark consequences that Hab 2:4 imply: "destroyed" (eternal condemnation and loss, as in Matt 7:13; Phil 1:28; 2 Pet 2:3) versus "saved" (Luke 17:33; 1 Thess 5:9). Two occurrences of the word "faith" (here; v. 38) introduce the other part of the next major section's topic (see note on v. 36).

Faith in Action

11 Now faith is confidence in what we hope for and assurance about what we do not see.[s] 2 This is
what the ancients were commended for.[t]
3 By faith we understand that the universe was formed at God's command,[u] so that what is seen was
not made out of what was visible.
4 By faith Abel brought God a better offering than Cain did. By faith he was commended as righteous,
when God spoke well of his offerings.[v] And by faith Abel still speaks, even though he is dead.[w]
5 By faith Enoch was taken from this life, so that he did not experience death: "He could not be found,
because God had taken him away."[a][x] For before he was taken, he was commended as one who pleased
God. 6 And without faith it is impossible to please God, because anyone who comes to him[y] must believe
that he exists and that he rewards those who earnestly seek him.
7 By faith Noah, when warned about things not yet seen, in holy fear built an ark[z] to save his family.[a]
By his faith he condemned the world and became heir of the righteousness that is in keeping with faith.
8 By faith Abraham, when called to go to a place he would later receive as his inheritance,[b] obeyed
and went,[c] even though he did not know where he was going. 9 By faith he made his home in the promised land[d] like a stranger in a foreign country; he lived in tents,[e] as did Isaac and Jacob, who were heirs
with him of the same promise.[f] 10 For he was looking forward to the city[g] with foundations,[h] whose
architect and builder is God. 11 And by faith even Sarah, who was past childbearing age,[i] was enabled to
bear children[j] because she[b] considered him faithful who had made the promise. 12 And so from this one

11:1 [s]Ro 8:24; 2Co 4:18
11:2 [t]ver 4,39
11:3 [u]Ge 1; Jn 1:3; 2Pe 3:5
11:4 [v]Ge 4:4; 1Jn 3:12 [w]Heb 12:24
11:5 [x]Ge 5:21-24
11:6 [y]Heb 7:19
11:7 [z]Ge 6:13-22 [a]1Pe 3:20
11:8 [b]Ge 12:7 [c]Ge 12:1-4; Ac 7:2-4
11:9 [d]Ac 7:5 [e]Ge 12:8; 18:1,9 [f]Heb 6:17
11:10 [g]Heb 12:22; 13:14 [h]Rev 21:2,14
11:11 [i]Ge 17:17-19; 18:11-14 [j]Ge 21:2

[a] *5* Gen. 5:24 [b] *11* Or *By faith Abraham, even though he was too old to have children—and Sarah herself was not able to conceive—was enabled to become a father because he*

11:1—12:13 *The Need for Faith and Endurance in the Struggle.* Two major units follow the central exposition (5:11—10:39) before the brief epilogue that concludes Hebrews. This unit develops in reverse order the two topics that 10:36–39 introduce: the need for faith (11:1–40) and endurance (12:1–13).

11:1–40 *Examples of God-Pleasing Faith.* Examples of faith from Israel's history illustrate what faith is (v. 1) and show that God commends it (vv. 2,4–6,39). "Faith" occurs 24 times in the Greek text of ch. 11. Lists of examples such as this appear elsewhere in early Jewish literature (in the Apocrypha see Wisdom of Solomon 10–11; Sirach 44–50; 1 Maccabees 2).

11:1 This description of "faith" focuses on an inward attitude (confident "assurance": a firm, steady conviction) about what is not present but that which we confidently expect ("what we hope for ... what we do not see"). Faith is spiritual perception—an insight into the unseen—to sense God at work (vv. 3,27) despite obstacles and to obey his word courageously. The following examples repeatedly illustrate such faith.

11:2 commended. A major theme of ch. 11: The Greek word also occurs three times in vv. 4–5—where God "commended" (or "spoke well" of) Abel and Enoch—and once in v. 39.

11:3 The first example comes from the very beginning of the OT—not a person but what we "by faith" should "understand" about creation: it "was formed at God's command" ("and God said" in Gen 1; see Ps 33:6,9). **what is seen was not made out of what was visible.** This fills in the implied point: we can be assured "about what we do not see" (v. 1b) when God is at work in the situation.

11:4 spoke well of. God "commended" (same word as in v. 2; see note there) Abel's "offerings," given in faith (Gen 4:4–5), and "even though he is dead," Abel still bears witness to the life of faith (alluding to Gen 4:10; cf. Heb 12:24).

11:5 This verse quotes Gen 5:24b. The Septuagint (the pre-Christian Greek translation of the OT) of Gen 5:24a says that Enoch "pleased God" (see note on v. 6).

11:6 without faith it is impossible to please God. The broader principle that Enoch exemplifies (see note on v. 5). The essence of faith is believing that God "exists" (see vv. 1,27: he is the all-important "unseen" for faith). **rewards.** A related Greek word is used in 10:35. God blesses those who, like Enoch, "seek him" (cf. Pss 9:10; 34:5,10).

11:7 things not yet seen. See v. 1 and note. Noah believed God's warning about coming judgment and responded to it reverently. **condemned the world.** Noah's righteous conduct (Gen 6:9; 7:1; see Ezek 14:14,20; 2 Pet 2:5) was a witness to his wicked generation about God's existence and human accountability to God (cf. v. 6). **heir of the righteousness that is in keeping with faith.** Noah's faith in God illustrates Hab 2:4 (quoted in Heb 10:38) and the inheritance that faith brings (vv. 8–9; 6:12; 9:15).

11:8–10 Abraham obeyed God's call (Gen 12:1–4) to go out to an "inheritance" (v. 8) as yet unseen (v. 1). His faith in God is the outstanding example for believers of all coming generations (6:12–15; Rom 4:3,16; Gal 3:6–9).

11:9 like a stranger in a foreign country. Ironically, Abraham was never able to make the "promised land" his own but lived as a foreigner (v. 13) and not permanently but "in tents" (v. 9; cf. v. 10).

11:10 looking forward to. Confidently expecting. **city with foundations.** Abraham's permanent dwelling that God will establish (see notes on v. 16; 12:22–23; 13:14; cf. Jewish parallel in the OT pseudepigrapha, 4 Ezra 10:27,42–44).

11:11 Sarah. The translation given in the NIV text (taking Sarah as the subject) has strong evidence in its favor. Making Abraham the subject, as in the alternative in the NIV text note, requires taking the words about Sarah ("past childbearing age") as parenthetical, an awkward construction. However, the NIV text note seems more likely in this difficult verse. The decisive phrase is "enabled to bear children" or "enabled to become a father." This Greek idiom consistently refers to the male, not the female, role in procreation. In this alternative reading the verse continues to focus on Abraham's faith and refers to Sarah's age, along with Abraham's, as part of the challenge to faith: "even though he was too old to have children—and Sarah herself was not able to conceive" (see NIV text note). **considered him faithful who had made the promise.** Reflects a frequent theme in Hebrews: God keeps his promises, so we can trust him (6:12–13,17–18; 10:23; Rom 4:20–21).

11:12 descendants as numerous as the stars. God fulfilled his promise to Abraham (v. 11; see Gen 12:2; 15:5; 22:17).

11:12 [k]Ro 4:19 [l]Ge 22:17
11:13 [m]ver 39 [n]Mt 13:17 [o]Ge 23:4; Ps 39:12; 1Pe 1:17
11:15 [p]Ge 24:6-8
11:16 [q]2Ti 4:18 [r]Mk 8:38 [s]Ex 3:6,15 [t]Heb 13:14
11:17 [u]Ge 22:1-10; Jas 2:21
11:18 [v]Ge 21:12; Ro 9:7
11:19 [w]Ro 4:21
11:20 [x]Ge 27:27-29, 39,40
11:21 [y]Ge 48:1,8-22
11:22 [z]Ge 50:24,25; Ex 13:19
11:23 [a]Ex 2:2 [b]Ex 1:16,22
11:24 [c]Ex 2:10,11
11:25 [d]ver 37
11:26 [e]Heb 13:13 [f]Heb 10:35
11:27 [g]Ex 12:50,51
11:28 [h]Ex 12:21-23

man, and he as good as dead,[k] came descendants as numerous as the stars in the sky and as countless
as the sand on the seashore.[l]
13 All these people were still living by faith when they died. They did not receive the things promised;[m]
they only saw them and welcomed them from a distance,[n] admitting that they were foreigners and
strangers on earth.[o] 14 People who say such things show that they are looking for a country of their own.
15 If they had been thinking of the country they had left, they would have had opportunity to return.[p]
16 Instead, they were longing for a better country — a heavenly one.[q] Therefore God is not ashamed[r] to
be called their God,[s] for he has prepared a city[t] for them.
17 By faith Abraham, when God tested him, offered Isaac as a sacrifice.[u] He who had embraced the
promises was about to sacrifice his one and only son, 18 even though God had said to him, "It is through
Isaac that your offspring will be reckoned."[a][v] 19 Abraham reasoned that God could even raise the dead,[w]
and so in a manner of speaking he did receive Isaac back from death.
20 By faith Isaac blessed Jacob and Esau in regard to their future.[x]
21 By faith Jacob, when he was dying, blessed each of Joseph's sons,[y] and worshiped as he leaned on
the top of his staff.
22 By faith Joseph, when his end was near, spoke about the exodus of the Israelites from Egypt and
gave instructions concerning the burial of his bones.[z]
23 By faith Moses' parents hid him for three months after he was born,[a] because they saw he was no
ordinary child, and they were not afraid of the king's edict.[b]
24 By faith Moses, when he had grown up, refused to be known as the son of Pharaoh's daughter.[c]
25 He chose to be mistreated[d] along with the people of God rather than to enjoy the fleeting pleasures
of sin. 26 He regarded disgrace[e] for the sake of Christ as of greater value than the treasures of Egypt,
because he was looking ahead to his reward.[f] 27 By faith he left Egypt,[g] not fearing the king's anger; he
persevered because he saw him who is invisible. 28 By faith he kept the Passover and the application of
blood, so that the destroyer of the firstborn would not touch the firstborn of Israel.[h]

a 18 Gen. 21:12

11:13 All these people. Abraham, Sarah, Isaac, and Jacob. **did not receive the things promised.** They died without seeing the fulfillment of God's promises to them (cf. vv. 36–39). **saw … from a distance.** With the eyes of faith (v. 1); this may also refer to the Jewish tradition that God showed the heavenly Jerusalem to Abraham and later to Moses (in the pseudepigrapha see 2 Baruch 4:4–5). **foreigners and strangers.** Abraham's words when he buried Sarah (Gen 23:4).

11:14 looking for a country of their own. They longed for a homeland as they lived like "strangers" (v. 13) in the land God promised but had not yet delivered to them (vv. 9,13; Gen 12:1–3). This is a type or symbol of the greater fulfillment pledged to Abraham. When Abraham's descendants occupied that land later, it did not exhaust God's promises (see notes on 4:6–9).

11:16 their God. God repeatedly calls himself the God of Abraham, Isaac, and Jacob (e.g., Exod 3:6,15–16; 4:5). **prepared a city for them.** The greater fulfillment is the heavenly Jerusalem (see note on 4:9; cf. v. 10; 12:22; 13:14; Rev 21:1–2,10).

11:17–18 Faith withstands the perplexing tests of life, as Gen 22 recounts (Jas 2:21). Abraham had "embraced" (v. 17) God's promise that Isaac was the son through whom blessing would come (as the quotation from Gen 21:12 confirms).

11:17 one and only son. Isaac had a unique status that Ishmael did not share (cf. John 3:16; 1 John 4:9).

11:19 God could even raise the dead. Abraham's way through this challenge was to rely more deeply on the life-giving power of God (similar to Rom 4:17), and God rewarded his faith. **in a manner of speaking.** Translates the Greek phrase "in a symbol" (cf. 9:9 ["illustration"]). Abraham received Isaac back from near death, foreshadowing Jesus' resurrection from the real death he suffered for us (2:9,14–15; 13:20).

11:20–22 This records the remaining patriarchal generations in Genesis as also acting in faith. They expected God's *future* blessing and deliverance (v. 1).

11:21 top of his staff. See note on Gen 47:31.

11:23 Moses' parents, who hid him in spite of the king's edict, illustrate the risks of courageous faith. **he was no ordinary child.** Picks up a detail from the story in Exod 2:2 ("he was a fine child") about his handsome, refined appearance. In addition to the motive to protect any child, they acted because of this sign of God's special favor on Moses (Acts 7:20; in Jewish tradition see Philo, *Life of Moses* 1.9; Josephus, *Antiquities*, 2.228–231).

11:24–26 The adult Moses likewise accepted the more difficult path in fidelity to God. Moses had only a limited grasp of Israel's future, but he chose to suffer "with the people of God" (v. 25) and so experienced "disgrace for the sake of Christ" (v. 26). Israel as a whole suffered at the hands of those who resisted God's saving purpose through his Messiah (Pss 2:1–2; 89:50–51). This mirrors the readers' dilemma over their loyalty to Christ (10:32–33; 13:12–13).

11:26 treasures of Egypt. Egypt was widely known for its great wealth. **looking ahead to his reward.** Illustrates vv. 1,6.

11:27 he left Egypt. Moses departed for Midian (Exod 2:15). **not fearing the king's anger.** "Moses was afraid" (Exod 2:14), but he overcame his fear and left for an uncertain future (cf. Abraham, v. 8) rather than try to rebuild his life in Egypt. **he persevered because he saw him who is invisible.** Greek usage suggests that this more likely means "he continually, so to speak, looked on him who is invisible." The spiritual perception that God was at work in all his earthly circumstances (cf. vv. 1,6) sustained Moses.

11:28–29 The author briefly summarizes two central events of Moses' faithful leadership in bringing Israel out of Egypt: the Passover (Exod 12) and crossing the Red Sea (Exod 14). The people followed God's commands and counted on his presence in the face of daunting circumstances.

29 By faith the people passed through the Red Sea as on dry land; but when the Egyptians tried to do
so, they were drowned.[i]
30 By faith the walls of Jericho fell, after the army had marched around them for seven days.[j]
31 By faith the prostitute Rahab, because she welcomed the spies, was not killed with those who were
disobedient.[a][k]
32 And what more shall I say? I do not have time to tell about Gideon, Barak,[l] Samson and Jephthah,
about David[m] and Samuel[n] and the prophets, 33 who through faith conquered kingdoms,[o] administered
justice, and gained what was promised; who shut the mouths of lions,[p] 34 quenched the fury of the
flames, and escaped the edge of the sword; whose weakness was turned to strength;[q] and who became
powerful in battle and routed foreign armies.[r] 35 Women received back their dead, raised to life again.[s]
There were others who were tortured, refusing to be released so that they might gain an even better
resurrection. 36 Some faced jeers and flogging,[t] and even chains and imprisonment.[u] 37 They were put to
death by stoning;[b][v] they were sawed in two; they were killed by the sword.[w] They went about in sheepskins and goatskins,[x] destitute, persecuted and mistreated— 38 the world was not worthy of them. They
wandered in deserts and mountains, living in caves[y] and in holes in the ground.
39 These were all commended[z] for their faith, yet none of them received what had been promised,[a]
40 since God had planned something better for us so that only together with us would they be made perfect.
12 Therefore, since we are surrounded by such a great cloud of witnesses, let us throw off everything that hinders and the sin that so easily entangles. And let us run[b] with perseverance[c]
the race marked out for us, 2 fixing our eyes on Jesus, the pioneer and perfecter of faith. For the joy set

11:29 [i] Ex 14:21-31
11:30 [j] Jos 6:12-20
11:31 [k] Jos 2:1,9-14; 6:22-25; Jas 2:25
11:32 [l] Jdg 4-5 [m] 1Sa 16:1,13 [n] 1Sa 1:20
11:33 [o] 2Sa 7:11; 8:1-3 [p] Da 6:22
11:34 [q] 2Ki 20:7 [r] Jdg 15:8
11:35 [s] 1Ki 17:22,23
11:36 [t] Jer 20:2 [u] Ge 39:20
11:37 [v] 2Ch 24:21 [w] 1Ki 19:10 [x] 2Ki 1:8
11:38 [y] 1Ki 18:4
11:39 [z] ver 2,4 [a] ver 13
12:1 [b] 1Co 9:24 [c] Heb 10:36

[a] *31* Or *unbelieving*   [b] *37* Some early manuscripts *stoning; they were put to the test;*

11:30–31 Two events of the conquest (Josh 2:1–23; 6:1–5,15–25) also illustrate bold faith in the living God.

11:32 what more shall I say? I do not have time to tell about. Another sign of the sermonic nature of Hebrews (see note on 8:1). The Greek expression behind "tell about" is masculine, reflecting a male author. Compressing his examples even more, the author cites without description a series of OT figures, some of whom are rather surprising to find as examples of faith. **Gideon, Barak, Samson and Jephthah.** Several of these judges of Israel had a mixed legacy, but they acted in faith at critical times in serving God's purpose (cf. v. 34b; Judg 4–8; 11–16). None of the people mentioned in ch. 11 were faultless, but they evidenced true faith in notable ways. **David.** Exemplified faith in his courageous actions (1 Sam 17:37,45–47) and expressed faith in his praise to God (e.g., Pss 31:1–15; 34:8; 37:3–7). **Samuel and the prophets.** Samuel was included among Israel's prophets (1 Sam 3:20–21; Acts 3:24; 13:20) and responded in faith from an early age and throughout his long service to Israel (1 Sam 3:10; 12:19–25).

11:33–35a This quickly surveys a number of notable successes of people of faith, some quite general and some more specific, from the OT.

11:33 conquered kingdoms, administered justice. The people just named (v. 32), as well as others, defeated foreign invaders or extended the rule of Israel (Judg 4:23–24; 8:12; 2 Sam 8:1–14; 12:26–31) and judged the nation's affairs (Judg 4:4–5; 1 Sam 7:15–17; 2 Sam 8:15; 1 Kgs 3:9–12; 10:9). **gained what was promised.** Israel lived in the land God pledged to give them (Josh 23:14; 24:8,13; 1 Kgs 5:4). **shut the mouths of lions.** Notably Daniel (Dan 6:22); perhaps also Samson (Judg 14:5–6) and David (1 Sam 17:34–37).

11:34 quenched the fury of the flames. Daniel's three friends (Dan 3:26–27). **escaped the edge of the sword.** For example, David (1 Sam 17), Elijah (1 Kgs 19), Elisha (2 Kgs 6:31), and Jeremiah (Jer 26:7–24).

11:35a received back their dead. For example, the sons restored to physical life in 1 Kgs 17:17–24; 2 Kgs 4:18–37.

11:35b–38 A change from the successes to the suffering of people of faith. These are more general examples, although a few correlate with some OT or later Jewish experiences of the faithful.

11:35b gain an even better resurrection. Perhaps the Jewish martyrs during the Maccabean period who anticipated resurrection to eternal life (in the Apocrypha see 2 Maccabees 6–7).

11:37 put to death by stoning. For example, Zechariah (2 Chr 24:20–21) and also various prophets (Matt 23:37), including Jeremiah according to tradition. **sawed in two.** Isaiah's fate according to tradition. True faith does not always lead to victory in this life (cf. v. 13). Those who pleased God often suffered and were mistreated. Instead of experiencing deliverance, they endured heart-wrenching difficulties and opposition; "the world was not worthy" of such people (v. 38; cf. vv. 9,13–16). But they exemplify nonetheless the principle of confident hope in the unseen God and his future blessing (v. 1).

11:39 commended for their faith. Again signals this chapter's theme: God was pleased with their faith (cf. vv. 2,4–5). **none of them received what had been promised.** This statement is more definitive than the similar idea in v. 13, since this refers to the fulfillment v. 40 describes. Even the promises they did see fulfilled (vv. 11,17,33) were only foretastes of the greater promise now accomplished in Christ.

11:40 be made perfect. Complete purification from sin so we can draw near to God (cf. 9:14; 10:1–2,14). Believers of former generations have now entered into this perfection with us through Christ (12:23).

12:1–13 *Endure Suffering as Fatherly Discipline.* The author picks up the second of two closely related topics introduced in 10:35–39.

12:1–3 This part of the new section is a hinge between 11:1–40 (faith) and vv. 1–13 (endurance). It could easily be taken as concluding the previous unit. But Greek words meaning "endure" or "persevere" occur three times in vv. 1–3 to signal a new section (v. 7).

12:1 surrounded by such a great cloud of witnesses. The people of faith just surveyed in ch. 11. In a play on the Greek word for "witness"—meaning "commended" by God in 11:2,4 ("spoke well" of),5,39—this now sees these people as testifying as to or commending to us the life of faith. Their examples urge us to "run with perseverance the race marked out for us." Faith and endurance, or "perseverance," are closely related traits that God's people must maintain even in temptation and adversity (cf. 3:6,12–14,19; 4:1–3,11,14; 10:23,35–39). The athletic imagery lends itself to the call to set aside anything that "entangles" or "hinders" us from enduring.

12:2 Jesus is the ultimate "witness" to spur us to faith and endurance.

12:2 [d]Php 2:8,9 [e]Heb 13:13
12:3 [f]Gal 6:9
12:4 [g]Heb 10:32-34
12:6 [h]Ps 94:12; Rev 3:19 [i]Pr 3:11,12
12:7 [j]Dt 8:5
12:8 [k]1Pe 5:9
12:9 [l]Nu 16:22 [m]Isa 38:16
12:10 [n]2Pe 1:4
12:11 [o]Isa 32:17; Jas 3:17,18
12:12 [p]Isa 35:3
12:13 [q]Pr 4:26 [r]Gal 6:1

before him he endured the cross,[d] scorning its shame,[e] and sat down at the right hand of the throne
of God. 3 Consider him who endured such opposition from sinners, so that you will not grow weary[f]
and lose heart.

God Disciplines His Children

4 In your struggle against sin, you have not yet resisted to the point of shedding your blood.[g] 5 And
have you completely forgotten this word of encouragement that addresses you as a father addresses
his son? It says,

> "My son, do not make light of the Lord's discipline,
> and do not lose heart when he rebukes you,
> 6 because the Lord disciplines the one he loves,[h]
> and he chastens everyone he accepts as his son."[a][i]

7 Endure hardship as discipline; God is treating you as his children.[j] For what children are not disciplined by their father? 8 If you are not disciplined — and everyone undergoes discipline[k] — then you
are not legitimate, not true sons and daughters at all. 9 Moreover, we have all had human fathers who
disciplined us and we respected them for it. How much more should we submit to the Father of spirits[l]
and live![m] 10 They disciplined us for a little while as they thought best; but God disciplines us for our good,
in order that we may share in his holiness.[n] 11 No discipline seems pleasant at the time, but painful. Later
on, however, it produces a harvest of righteousness and peace[o] for those who have been trained by it.
12 Therefore, strengthen your feeble arms and weak knees.[p] 13 "Make level paths for your feet,"[b][q] so
that the lame may not be disabled, but rather healed.[r]

[a] *5,6* Prov. 3:11,12 (see Septuagint) [b] *13* Prov. 4:26

fixing our eyes on. Jesus is the object, as well as model, of faith for Christians (cf. "consider him" [v. 3]). His sacrifice for us is of central importance in Hebrews. **pioneer.** See note on 2:10. By Jesus' saving work he initiated and completed this pathway of faith for us (10:14; 11:40). **For the joy set before him.** "For" could mean "instead of," referring to heavenly or earthly blessing he gave up to go to the cross. But the other occurrence of this Greek preposition in Hebrews means "for the sake of" (see "for" in v. 16), and the latter part of this verse makes it more likely that Jesus anticipated the "joy" of his exaltation. **scorning its shame.** Crucifixion was a humiliating form of execution (6:6; 10:29; 13:12–13; Phil 2:8–9; cf. Isa 53:8–12), but Jesus disregarded this in doing God's will. **sat down at the right hand.** God exalted Jesus after his humiliation (Phil 2:8–9). The final of five allusions to Ps 110:1 in Hebrews.

12:3 Consider him. Reflecting on Jesus' example shows the value of endurance. The faithful are not exempt from opposition in this world (John 15:18–20; Acts 14:22; 1 Pet 2:21), but faithful suffering is the pathway to glory and blessing. **grow weary and lose heart.** Weakness and discouragement in our adversities (v. 4) is what we must guard against (6:11–12; Gal 6:9; Rev 2:3). **lose heart.** Anticipates the quotation in v. 5.

12:4 struggle against sin. Their adversities, while difficult (v. 12), had been minimal compared to what Jesus endured. **sin.** Here seems to mean not personal failings (as v. 1) but external evil rising up against Christians (e.g., "sinners" in v. 3). **shedding ... blood.** The original readers had suffered ostracism, seizure of property, and imprisonments (10:32–34) but not physical injury or death.

12:5 word of encouragement. Through Solomon's words in Prov 3:11–12 (quoted here in vv. 5b–6) God speaks to us as his children. **the Lord's discipline.** See note on v. 7. Verse 6 reminds us that God's discipline and even his chastening (the Greek word denotes punishing or whipping) are evidence of his fatherly love.

12:7–8 Applies the Scripture quoted in vv. 5b–6.

12:7 Endure hardship. By accepting it as God's "discipline" for "his children" (the theme of vv. 1–13). This is how a loving father treats his genuine children. **discipline.** Not limited to punishment for wrongdoing, although that cannot be excluded entirely. It is training toward maturity based on orderly instruction and correction when needed (Acts 7:22; 22:3; Eph 6:4; 2 Tim 3:16; Titus 2:12). It is positive, directing us down right paths of conduct and testing us to bring greater strength and maturity. It is also negative, rebuking and correcting us when we go astray. God uses our struggles and suffering — whether innocent or deserved — to train us in holiness (v. 10).

12:9–10 This lesser-to-greater argument expands the general principle about parenting in vv. 7–8. If we have respectfully accepted imperfect training from our human fathers, we should certainly yield to God's discipline.

12:9 Father of spirits. Refers to God as the ultimate source of life, the one who "gives breath to all living things" (Num 16:22; 27:16).

12:10 share in his holiness. The focus here is holy conduct, rooted in the sanctifying work Christ has already accomplished and anticipating its consummation in the future (v. 14; 1 Pet 1:15–16; cf. v. 23; 10:10,14; 1 Thess 5:23).

12:11 The immediate process of training is unwelcome (it is not pleasant, see v. 2: Jesus endured, anticipating the joy that lay ahead). **a harvest of righteousness and peace.** The ultimate product of discipline encourages us to endure (v. 14; Jas 3:18).

12:12–13 Concluding his exposition of Prov 3:11–12, the author urges his readers to renewed effort in their struggles: "strengthen your feeble arms and weak knees" (drawing from Isa 35:3) and "make level paths for your feet" (drawing from Prov 4:26–27). To "make level paths" means to "choose the straight way; stay obedient." In times of difficulty a fresh perspective on the problems (vv. 5–7) and renewed resolve to endure faithfully will lead to spiritual healing rather than further weakness. References to "paths" (v. 13) and "peace" (v. 11) introduce the topic for the final section of Hebrews. The allusion to "peace" (v. 11) is strengthened by the Septuagint translation (the pre-Christian Greek translation of the OT) of Prov 4:27, which contains a longer verse than the Hebrew, adding a promise (not quoted here but seemingly in mind) that the Lord "will direct your pathways in peace."

Warning and Encouragement

14 Make every effort to live in peace with everyone[s] and to be holy;[t] without holiness no one will see
the Lord.[u] 15 See to it that no one falls short of the grace of God[v] and that no bitter root grows up to
cause trouble and defile many. 16 See that no one is sexually immoral, or is godless like Esau, who for
a single meal sold his inheritance rights as the oldest son.[w] 17 Afterward, as you know, when he wanted
to inherit this blessing, he was rejected. Even though he sought the blessing with tears,[x] he could not
change what he had done.

The Mountain of Fear and the Mountain of Joy

18 You have not come to a mountain that can be touched and that is burning with fire; to darkness,
gloom and storm;[y] 19 to a trumpet blast[z] or to such a voice speaking words that those who heard it
begged that no further word be spoken to them,[a] 20 because they could not bear what was commanded:
"If even an animal touches the mountain, it must be stoned to death."[a][b] 21 The sight was so terrifying
that Moses said, "I am trembling with fear."[b]
22 But you have come to Mount Zion, to the city[c] of the living God, the heavenly Jerusalem.[d] You
have come to thousands upon thousands of angels in joyful assembly, 23 to the church of the firstborn,
whose names are written in heaven.[e] You have come to God, the Judge of all,[f] to the spirits of the righteous made perfect,[g] 24 to Jesus the mediator of a new covenant, and to the sprinkled blood that speaks
a better word than the blood of Abel.[h]
25 See to it that you do not refuse him who speaks. If they did not escape when they refused him who

12:14 [s] Ro 14:19 [t] Ro 6:22 [u] Mt 5:8
12:15 [v] Gal 5:4; Heb 3:12
12:16 [w] Ge 25:29-34
12:17 [x] Ge 27:30-40
12:18 [y] Ex 19:12-22; Dt 4:11
12:19 [z] Ex 20:18 [a] Ex 20:19; Dt 5:5,25
12:20 [b] Ex 19:12,13
12:22 [c] Heb 11:10 [d] Gal 4:26
12:23 [e] Lk 10:20 [f] Ps 94:2 [g] Php 3:12
12:24 [h] Ge 4:10; Heb 11:4

[a] *20* Exodus 19:12,13 [b] *21* See Deut. 9:19.

12:14—13:21 *Final Warning and Instructions About Community Life.* The boundaries of this final unit before the epilogue are debatable. The unit of 12:14—13:21 is suggested by the references to "peace" (12:14; 13:20) that bracket it.

12:14–29 *Final Warning: Do Not Refuse God's Gracious Word Through Jesus.* The final warning passage in Hebrews comes in three segments: the author commands his readers not to fall short of God's grace as Esau did (vv. 14–17), reminds them of the astonishing benefits that have come in the change from the old covenant to the new (vv. 18–24), and warns them not to refuse God's word but thankfully worship him (vv. 25–29).

12:14 Make every effort. The author calls for renewed focus (as in 2:1; 4:11; 6:1; 10:24–25) on "peace" and "holiness." The context of vv. 10b–13 shows that God produces these in us through Christ (see 2:11; 10:10,14; 13:12); he enables us to choose wise pathways (3:14; 7:25; 8:10; 9:13–15; 13:20–21). Only those who are holy in this way "will see the Lord" (i.e., commune with him in the new heaven and new earth, Ps 17:15; Matt 5:8; Rev 22:4).

12:15 As a community (cf. 3:12–13; 10:24–25) the readers must ensure that "no one falls short" of what God's "grace" has provided in Christ (2:9; 4:1). Such a person could tragically lead others astray as well. **bitter root.** Alludes to Deut 29:18, referring to someone who stubbornly turns away from the Lord and influences others toward idolatry.

12:16 sexually immoral, or is godless like Esau. Not "sexually immoral" in the literal sense, but as Deut 29:18 suggests; Esau became idolatrous under the influence of his foreign wives (Gen 26:34–35; Exod 34:14–16). **godless.** Profane; having no respect for holy things. Esau treated "his inheritance rights as the oldest son" as something of no value (Gen 25:30–34).

12:17 wanted to inherit this blessing. Esau later regretted losing his privilege as the oldest son, but it was too late to change things (Gen 27:34–41). **he sought the blessing with tears.** Or "he sought it with tears." Some translations take "it" to refer to repentance (i.e., "change what he had done," as in the NIV text). The focus on blessing is preferable since the strong emphasis of Gen 27 is Esau's desire for Isaac's blessing, not for any change of heart about the true God.

12:18–24 The benefits of the old covenant contrast with those of the new (the old covenant is symbolized by Mount Sinai; the new, by Mount Zion, i.e., Jerusalem [Gal 4:24–26]). This contrast supports the call to not turn away from God's grace in Christ (vv. 14–17).

12:18–21 These verses describe Israel's terrifying experience at the foot of Mount Sinai (Exod 19).

12:20 what was commanded. The command (quoting from Exod 19:12–13) seemed unbearably strict and threatening. **touches the mountain.** A detail that reflects the old covenant's restricted access to God's presence (cf. 9:7–10).

12:21 trembling with fear. Even Moses, who was allowed to approach God, was terrified when he descended from God's presence (Deut 9:19).

12:22–24 This mentions destinations and connections that Christians have already reached through Jesus' new covenant sacrifice. But we will enter into them more fully in the future.

12:22–23 "Mount Zion" represents "the city of the living God, the heavenly Jerusalem," existing already in heaven but yet to be established (11:10,16; 13:14) as part of the new heaven and new earth in the culmination of God's redemption (Isa 65:17–18; 66:22; Rev 21:1–2,10). Through Jesus the heavenly high priest, Christians now have access into God's presence there (4:14–16; 6:19–20; 10:19–22). They have already joined in worship with countless "angels in joyful assembly" (see note on 4:9) and with "the church of the firstborn" ("firstborn" is plural, i.e., humans who are privileged sons and daughters due to the work of Jesus the firstborn Son [1:6; 2:10–17; Rom 8:29; Col 1:18; Rev 1:5]).

12:23 whose names are written in heaven. See Isa 4:3; Dan 12:1; Luke 10:20; Phil 4:3; Rev 21:27. **God, the Judge of all.** Heightens the awesome picture of their destination. **spirits of the righteous made perfect.** Seems to refer to the same group as "the church of the firstborn," now pictured as having met God's judgment through Jesus the perfected high priest (7:28), whose sacrifice has perfected them forever (10:14).

12:24 Jesus the mediator of a new covenant. The contrasts conclude by explicitly citing the new covenant and "the sprinkled blood" that inaugurated it (9:18–26). **mediator.** See notes on 8:6; 9:15. **blood.** Jesus' blood "speaks a better word than the blood of Abel" (11:4; Gen 4:10), because it is an invitation to forgiveness, not a cry for vengeance.

12:25 do not refuse him who speaks. This strong warning to not reject God's word in the gospel (cf. 2:3; 3:15; 4:2,12; 6:6; 10:29) uses imagery

Jebel Musa, the traditional location of Mount Sinai.

© Igor Rogozhnikov/Shutterstock

12:25 [i]Heb 8:5; 11:7 [j]Heb 2:2,3
12:26 [k]Ex 19:18 [l]Hag 2:6
12:27 [m]1Co 7:31; 2Pe 3:10
12:28 [n]Da 2:44 [o]Heb 13:15
12:29 [p]Dt 4:24
13:1 [q]Ro 12:10; 1Pe 1:22
13:2 [r]Mt 25:35 [s]Ge 18:1-33
13:3 [t]Mt 25:36; Col 4:18

warned[i] them on earth, how much less will we, if we turn away from him who warns us from heaven?[j]
26At that time his voice shook the earth,[k] but now he has promised, "Once more I will shake not only
the earth but also the heavens."[a][l] 27The words "once more" indicate the removing of what can be
shaken[m]—that is, created things—so that what cannot be shaken may remain.
28Therefore, since we are receiving a kingdom that cannot be shaken,[n] let us be thankful, and so
worship God acceptably with reverence and awe,[o] 29for our "God is a consuming fire."[b][p]

Concluding Exhortations

13 Keep on loving one another as brothers and sisters.[q] 2Do not forget to show hospitality to
strangers,[r] for by so doing some people have shown hospitality to angels without knowing it.[s]
3Continue to remember those in prison[t] as if you were together with them in prison, and those who are
mistreated as if you yourselves were suffering.

[a] *26* Haggai 2:6 [b] *29* Deut. 4:24

drawn from the contrasts of vv. 18–24. Another lesser-to-greater comparison reinforces the urgency (2:1–4; 10:28–29): severe and sure consequences will come for any who refuse "him who warns us from heaven."
12:26 Words quoting Hag 2:6 specify the warning "from heaven" (v. 25). The OT and later Jewish tradition commonly understood the shaking of the earth at Sinai (Exod 19:18) as a pattern of future judgment (Judg 5:4–6; Pss 18:7; 68:7–8; Isa 13:13; 64:2–4; Jer 10:10; cf. from the pseudepigrapha 1 Enoch 60:1–6; 2 Baruch 32:1–6), and this is the case in Hag 2:6–7,21 and here. **not only the earth but also the heavens.** The pattern intensifies.
12:27 "once more." The author pays close attention to the wording of Hag 2:6 to note a further intensification of the judgment to come: "once more" indicates not further shaking but "the removing of what can be shaken—that is, created things—so that what cannot be shaken may remain." Identifying "created things" as transitory over against what will "remain" is not a cosmological dualism (what is earthly is evil and temporary versus what is heavenly is good and lasting). Removal does not denote destruction but transformation (7:12; 11:5) to something better and lasting in regard to salvation. The shakable things denote all that must be subjected to God's judgment (4:13) leading to restoration and renewal, including his creation and redeemed people (v. 28; 2:5–18).
12:28 a kingdom that cannot be shaken. Alludes to Dan 7:18, the vision of God's holy people who receive a kingdom forever in connection with the Son of Man to whom God grants everlasting dominion. This has already begun ("we are receiving a kingdom"), but it is not yet fully realized (2:8–9; see note on 4:3). Such a hope calls for us to "be thankful" and "worship God acceptably with reverence and awe." **acceptably.** Could be rendered "in a way that pleases" God (anticipating 13:15–16,21).
12:29 consuming fire. Quoting Deut 4:24, this affirms the reverence due to God because of his jealous anger against those who desert the true God for idols.
13:1–21 *Instructions About Community Life.* The last chapter of Hebrews clearly has a different tone. But its connections to the preceding chapters are strong: (1) it continues the call to worship God in word and deed (12:28); (2) it specifies the pathways of life we should choose (12:11–13); and (3) it alludes to various central themes from the body of the sermon (see notes on vv. 7,8,10,11,14,20).
13:1–6 This passage moves rapidly through general instructions for Christian living that constitute the right pathways for life (12:11–13).
13:1 loving one another. Mutual affection and service within the church must continue (6:10; 10:24).
13:2 hospitality to strangers. An important expression of love among Christians. **hospitality to angels without knowing it.** Refers to Abraham's (and perhaps others') welcome of strangers who unexpectedly proved to be most worthy (Gen 18,19; Judg 6,13).
13:3 those in prison. First-century prisoners usually had to rely on

4Marriage should be honored by all, and the marriage bed kept pure, for God will judge the adulterer
and all the sexually immoral.[u] 5Keep your lives free from the love of money and be content with what
you have,[v] because God has said,

> "Never will I leave you;
> never will I forsake you."[a][w]

6So we say with confidence,

> "The Lord is my helper; I will not be afraid.
> What can mere mortals do to me?"[b]

7Remember your leaders,[x] who spoke the word of God to you. Consider the outcome of their way of
life and imitate[y] their faith. 8Jesus Christ is the same yesterday and today and forever.[z]
9Do not be carried away by all kinds of strange teachings.[a] It is good for our hearts to be strengthened[b] by grace, not by eating ceremonial foods,[c] which is of no benefit to those who do so. 10We have
an altar from which those who minister at the tabernacle have no right to eat.[d]
11The high priest carries the blood of animals into the Most Holy Place as a sin offering, but the
bodies are burned outside the camp.[e] 12And so Jesus also suffered outside the city gate[f] to make the
people holy through his own blood. 13Let us, then, go to him outside the camp, bearing the disgrace
he bore.[g] 14For here we do not have an enduring city, but we are looking for the city that is to come.[h]
15Through Jesus, therefore, let us continually offer to God a sacrifice[i] of praise—the fruit of lips[j]
that openly profess his name. 16And do not forget to do good and to share with others,[k] for with such
sacrifices[l] God is pleased.

a 5 Deut. 31:6 *b* 6 Psalm 118:6,7

13:4 [u] 1Co 6:9
13:5 [v] Php 4:11 [w] Dt 31:6, 8; Jos 1:5
13:7 [x] ver 17,24 [y] Heb 6:12
13:8 [z] Heb 1:12
13:9 [a] Eph 4:14 [b] Col 2:7 [c] Col 2:16
13:10 [d] 1Co 9:13; 10:18
13:11 [e] Ex 29:14; Lev 16:27
13:12 [f] Jn 19:17
13:13 [g] Heb 11:26
13:14 [h] Php 3:20; Heb 12:22
13:15 [i] 1Pe 2:5 [j] Hos 14:2
13:16 [k] Ro 12:13 [l] Php 4:18

outside help for basic necessities, and Christian service to "the least of these" certainly included prisoners, especially other believers (Matt 25:34–40). **as if you were together with them.** The original readers had established a good record of identifying with the suffering and imprisoned (10:33–34). **mistreated.** See 11:37.

13:4 Marriage should be honored. Marriage must be valued as God's design (Gen 2:24; Matt 19:4–6; Eph 5:22–33). **the marriage bed kept pure.** Sexual fidelity within marriage is God's command (Exod 20:14; Matt 5:27–28). Neither relaxed societal standards nor inflamed personal passion can forestall one's ultimate accountability to God for sexual sin (1 Thess 4:3–8). **sexually immoral.** A term broader than "adulterer"; it refers to unlawful sexual activity of various kinds (John 8:4; 1 Cor 5:1,9–10; 6:9,18; 1 Thess 4:3).

13:5–6 Two OT quotations confirm God's unfailing help to keep us from financial fear (Deut 31:6,8; Ps 118:6–7).

13:5 free from the love of money ... be content. Themes frequently treated together in NT instruction (Luke 12:15; Phil 4:11; 1 Tim 3:3; 6:6–8). The readers previously modeled this (10:34) and should continue to do so.

13:7–19 A new section of instruction about following Jesus in community life (vv. 7–19). This begins and ends with the proper response to church leaders (vv. 7,17–19).

13:7 Remember your leaders. Not "recall the deceased who formerly led you," but "keep in mind your leaders living or dead." **spoke the word of God.** Evangelized and instructed (2:1–4); their faithful ministry of "the word of God" is the ground of their authority in the church. **outcome of their way of life.** The product or effect of their godly conduct.

13:8 Jesus Christ is the same. This is a significant Christological declaration on its own, but it links to the final phrase of v. 7: the one your leaders have proclaimed and trusted through all of life is worthy of your trust as well. He is the unchanging one (1:12; 7:24–25).

13:9 strange teachings. Doctrines that contrast with the single, unchanging focus on Christ that their leaders inculcated (vv. 7–8). **strange.** Not bizarre but foreign, i.e., from outside the community. **hearts ... strengthened by grace.** Alludes to the new covenant's inward transformation (vv. 20–21; 8:10; 9:14–15). **ceremonial foods.** These outside teachings seem to call for Judaistic dietary practices related to OT priestly ritual (cf. Lev 6:26; 7:31–32). The author's brief response connects to the argument of the earlier chapters: these practices afford "no benefit" to those who partake of them (7:19; 9:9–10; 10:1).

13:10 We have an altar. In contrast to the Levitical system, Christians benefit from Christ's eternally effective sacrifice.

13:11 bodies are burned outside the camp. The blood of a bull and a goat was sprinkled on the atonement cover in the Day of Atonement ritual (9:7,25; Lev 16:14–15), but their carcasses were unclean and had to be disposed of outside the wilderness encampment (Lev 16:27).

13:12 Jesus also suffered outside the city gate. Jesus' crucifixion outside Jerusalem (Mark 15:20–22; John 19:20) culminated the rejection and shame he experienced for us (12:2; Ps 22:6; Isa 53:3–4).

13:13 bearing the disgrace he bore. Following Jesus completely may bring rejection and reproach from society (10:33–34; 11:26).

13:14 here we do not have an enduring city. Another theme from earlier chapters (11:10,16; 12:22) confirms our status as outsiders in this world but heirs of what will be far better (10:34; 11:13).

13:15 sacrifice of praise. The Septuagint (the pre-Christian Greek translation of the OT) phrase for "thank offering" in a number of OT passages (Lev 7:12–13; 2 Chr 29:31; Pss 50:14,23; 107:22; 116:17). The OT sacrificial system has been set aside, but our grateful worship should still overflow to God (12:28). **the fruit of lips that openly profess his name.** "Fruit of lips" is also an OT phrase for expressing praise to God (Isa 57:19 ["creating praise on their lips"]; Hos 14:2). God's people of all generations have offered heartfelt worship to our gracious God, but our heightened blessings in Christ should prompt greater thanksgiving.

13:16 to do good and to share with others. Further priestly service for us to offer to God. **share.** Probably means to show generosity or liberality, as in 2 Cor 8:4; 9:13. With such worship "God is pleased" (v. 21; 11:5–6; cf. 12:28).

13:17 [m] Isa 62:6; Ac 20:28
13:18 [n] 1Th 5:25 [o] Ac 23:1
13:19 [p] Phm 22
13:20 [q] Ro 15:33 [r] Isa 55:3; Eze 37:26; Zec 9:11 [s] Ac 2:24 [t] Jn 10:11
13:21 [u] Php 2:13 [v] 1Jn 3:22 [w] Ro 11:36
13:22 [x] 1Pe 5:12
13:23 [y] Ac 16:1
13:24 [z] ver 7,17 [a] Ac 18:2
13:25 [b] Col 4:18

17 Have confidence in your leaders and submit to their authority, because they keep watch over you[m]
as those who must give an account. Do this so that their work will be a joy, not a burden, for that would
be of no benefit to you.
18 Pray for us.[n] We are sure that we have a clear conscience[o] and desire to live honorably in every
way. 19 I particularly urge you to pray so that I may be restored to you soon.[p]

Benediction and Final Greetings

20 Now may the God of peace,[q] who through the blood of the eternal covenant[r] brought back from
the dead[s] our Lord Jesus, that great Shepherd of the sheep,[t] 21 equip you with everything good for doing
his will, and may he work in us[u] what is pleasing to him,[v] through Jesus Christ, to whom be glory for
ever and ever. Amen.[w]

22 Brothers and sisters, I urge you to bear with my word of exhortation, for in fact I have written to
you quite briefly.[x]
23 I want you to know that our brother Timothy[y] has been released. If he arrives soon, I will come
with him to see you.
24 Greet all your leaders[z] and all the Lord's people. Those from Italy[a] send you their greetings.
25 Grace be with you all.[b]

13:17 Have confidence in your leaders and submit to their authority. In the light of threats to their faith (vv. 9–13), the author urges the readers to faithfully follow their faithful leaders. Instead of "have confidence in," some translations say "obey" (see the same Greek verb in Rom 2:8 ["follow"]; Gal 5:7; Jas 3:3). **they keep watch.** The leaders' authority is grounded in faithfully ministering God's word (v. 7) and being accountable to God for shepherding the flock (Acts 20:28; 1 Cor 3:10; 4:5; Jas 3:3) under "Jesus, that great Shepherd of the sheep" (v. 20). Yielding to such leaders so that their work can be "a joy, not a burden" is best for all concerned.

13:18 clear conscience. The author is one of their faithful leaders, and this sermon reflects his role in teaching and exhorting them as a pastor.

13:19 be restored to you soon. There is no indication of the author's circumstances, but he desires to be with them as soon as possible (cf. v. 23).

13:20 A benedictory prayer to the God who brings "peace" (cf. 12:11–14) closes this section about community life (vv. 1–21). **blood of the eternal covenant.** Alludes to Jesus' new covenant sacrifice of himself (Jer 32:40 and Ezek 37:26 describe the promised new covenant as "everlasting"). **brought back from the dead.** This is the only time Hebrews explicitly refers to Jesus' resurrection (cf. 5:7), but the frequent mentions of his exaltation imply it. **great Shepherd of the sheep.** Jesus in his unending concern for us (v. 8) provides the utmost pastoral care (v. 17; 7:25; Ps 23; Isa 40:11; Ezek 34:11–16,23; 37:24; John 10:11,14; 1 Pet 2:25; 5:4).

13:21 equip you with everything good for doing his will ... work in us what is pleasing to him. The author prays that God will fulfill what he pledged in the new covenant (v. 20): to enable them to obey "his will" by transforming them inwardly (8:10; 9:13–14; 10:16,19–22).

13:22–25 *Epilogue: Epistolary Closing.* A few personal comments, travel details, and final greetings wrap up the book in a way more typical of epistles (i.e., letters).

13:22 my word of exhortation. The author modestly requests that the readers listen patiently to the work just completed. This self-description of the work is the main evidence for seeing Hebrews as a sermon in written form (see Introduction: Genre and Structure). The same key words occur in Acts 13:15 of the sermon Paul was invited to give in the synagogue in Pisidian Antioch.

13:23 our brother Timothy. The author and readers of Hebrews clearly knew this Timothy well, and the author hopes Timothy will come with him to see them, perhaps soon. Many think this Timothy is the well-known associate of Paul (Acts 16:1; mentioned in 10 of Paul's 13 letters), but the name Timothy was fairly common in the first-century world. If Hebrews comes from the circles of Paul, this could be the Timothy Paul knew. But we cannot be sure this is that Timothy.

13:24 Those from Italy. This most likely indicates people now elsewhere who once lived near Rome (Acts 18:2) and who pass on their greetings to the readers there. Some take it to mean the author is writing from Rome. But the phrase is not "those *in* Italy" or "send you their greetings from Italy." See Introduction: Place of Composition and Destination.

13:25 This final wish for them (exactly like Titus 3:15) is appropriate in view of the book's emphasis on God's grace through Christ (v. 9; 2:9; 4:16; 12:15).

INTRODUCTION TO
JAMES

AUTHOR

The writer of this letter calls himself simply "James, a servant of God and of the Lord Jesus Christ" (1:1). Of the four men with this name in the NT, only two are prominent enough to identify themselves so simply: James, the brother of John and son of Zebedee, who was one of the 12 original apostles (Mark 1:19), and James, "the Lord's brother" (Gal 1:19), who was the leader of the early Jerusalem church (Acts 15:13; 21:18; Gal 2:9). The apostle James died at too early a date (AD 44; see Acts 12:2) to have written the letter, so this leaves James, the Lord's brother, as the letter's author. Although the matter is often contested, James was probably one of the younger brothers of Jesus (Matt 13:55)

JEWISH DIASPORA

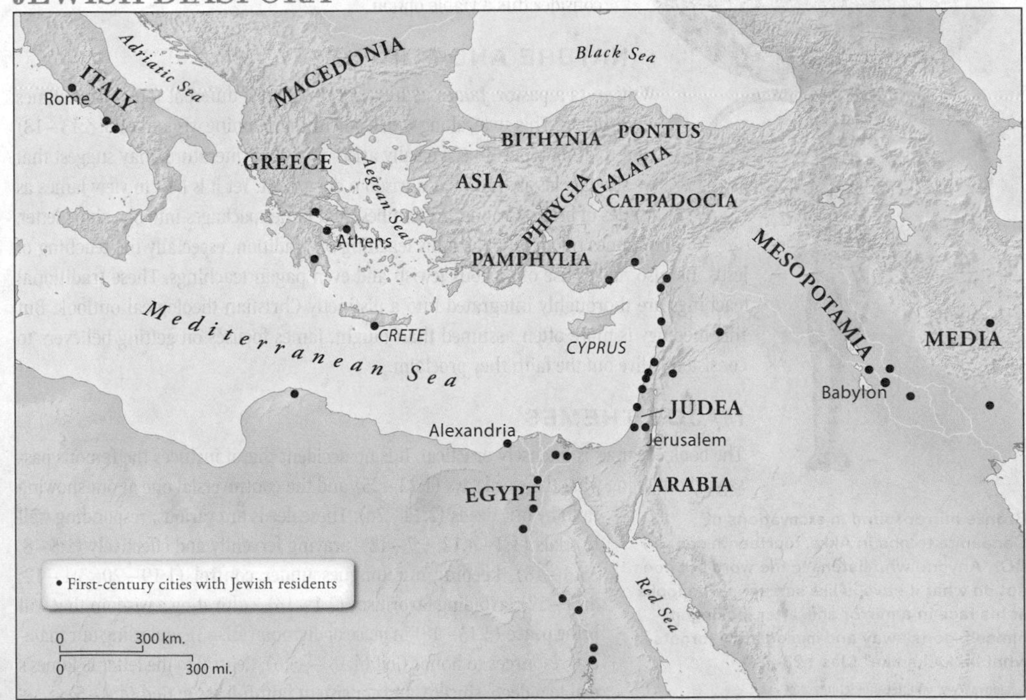

born to Joseph and Mary after Jesus' birth. He was not a disciple during Jesus' earthly ministry (John 7:5) and was perhaps converted when the resurrected Jesus appeared to him (1 Cor 15:7). James's wise leadership of the Jerusalem church and the good name he maintained even among Jews earned him the title "James the Just," according to Jewish and Christian traditions.

RECIPIENTS AND OCCASION

The letter is addressed to "the twelve tribes scattered among the nations" (1:1). This address has led to the tradition of classifying James as a "general" letter, with the whole Christian church in view. But James gives every indication of addressing a specific group of people.

"Twelve tribes" identifies these people as belonging to the people of God of the last days — the entire church, Gentiles and Jews alike (1 Pet 1:1), the Israel (or people of God) of the era of fulfillment. The prophets looked forward to the day when the scattered tribes of Israel would be reunited (Isa 11:11 – 12; 49:6; Jer 31:8 – 14; Ezek 37:21 – 22; 47:13; Zech 10:6 – 12). The NT teaches that God has accomplished this re-gathering through the work of Jesus (Matt 19:28; Rev 7:5 – 8).

The letter's content, however, strongly suggests that James's audience is limited to Jewish Christians. "Scattered among the nations" (1:1) shows that these believers were living outside the boundaries of Israel (cf. John 7:35; Acts 2:5). They may have been the Jewish Christians who were forced to flee Israel because of the persecution that arose after Stephen's death (Acts 11:19). These Jewish Christians would have experienced the trials that befall most refugees, trials to which James frequently refers (1:2 – 4,12; 2:5 – 7; cf. 5:1 – 11). Moreover, if these Jewish Christians came mainly from Jerusalem, it makes perfect sense that their former spiritual leader, James, would send them a letter to encourage them in their trials and exhort them to continue living faithful Christian lives in their new circumstances.

DATE

If the above sketch of the circumstances that gave rise to the letter is correct, then James wrote in the mid to late 40s. It would be the first NT book written. But our information about the letter is sparse enough to encourage caution. Many scholars date the letter in the 60s, and we can consider this a viable option.

NATURE AND PURPOSE

Writing as a pastor, James addresses a number of different topics, sometimes quite briefly. This style, along with explicitly mentioning wisdom (1:5; 3:13 – 18) and treating topics that typically arise in wisdom literature, may suggest that we should classify James as a wisdom document. Yet it is best to view James as a series of brief sermons, or homilies, that James packages into one short letter.

Notably, James frequently bases his teaching on tradition, especially the teaching of Jesus. He also makes use of various Jewish and even pagan teachings. These traditional teachings are thoroughly integrated into a distinctly Christian theological outlook. But this theology is more often assumed than taught. James focuses on getting believers to consistently live out the faith they proclaim.

MAJOR THEMES

The book of James is intensely practical. It is no accident that it includes the famous passage about doing what the word says (1:22 – 25) and the controversial one about showing faith by our deeds (2:14 – 26). These deeds are various: responding well to trials (1:2 – 4,12; 5:7 – 12), praying fervently and effectively (1:5 – 8; 5:13 – 18), keeping our tongues under control (1:19 – 20; 3:1 – 12; 4:11 – 12), avoiding favoritism (2:1 – 13), cultivating a wisdom that will bring peace (3:13 – 18) in place of division (4:1 – 3), and using our material resources to honor God (4:13 — 5:6). Central to the letter is James's call to a deep, sincere, and consistent faithfulness to God (4:4 – 5).

Bronze mirror found in excavations of Canaanite tombs in Akko, fourteenth century BC. "Anyone who listens to the word but does not do what it says is like someone who looks at his face in a mirror and, after looking at himself, goes away and immediately forgets what he looks like" (Jas 1:23–24).

Z. Radovan/www.BibleLandPictures.com

OUTLINE

I. Address and Greeting (1:1)

II. Trials and Temptations (1:2 – 18)
- A. Overcoming Trials (1:2 – 12)
- B. The Source of Temptation (1:13 – 18)

III. Putting the Word Into Practice (1:19 — 2:26)
- A. Listening and Doing (1:19 – 27)
- B. Favoritism Forbidden (2:1 – 13)
- C. Faith and Deeds (2:14 – 26)

IV. Words and Wisdom (3:1 — 4:12)
- A. Taming the Tongue (3:1 – 12)
- B. Two Kinds of Wisdom (3:13 – 18)
- C. Submit Yourselves to God (4:1 – 12)

V. A Christian Perspective on the World (4:13 — 5:12)
- A. Boasting About Tomorrow (4:13 – 17)
- B. Warning to Rich Oppressors (5:1 – 6)
- C. Patience in Suffering (5:7 – 12)

VI. The Prayer of Faith (5:13 – 20)

JAMES

1:1 [a]Ac 15:13 [b]Titus 1:1 [c]Ac 26:7 [d]Dt 32:26; Jn 7:35; 1Pe 1:1
1:2 [e]Mt 5:12; 1Pe 1:6
1:5 [f]1Ki 3:9,10; Pr 2:3-6 [g]Mt 7:7
1:6 [h]Mk 11:24
1:8 [i]Jas 4:8
1:10 [j]1Co 7:31; 1Pe 1:24
1:11 [k]Ps 102:4,11 [l]Isa 40:6-8

1 James,[a] a servant of God[b] and of the Lord Jesus Christ,

To the twelve tribes[c] scattered[d] among the nations:

Greetings.

Trials and Temptations

2 Consider it pure joy, my brothers and sisters,[a] whenever you face trials of many kinds,[e] 3 because you know that the testing of your faith produces perseverance. 4 Let perseverance finish its work so that you may be mature and complete, not lacking anything. 5 If any of you lacks wisdom, you should ask God,[f] who gives generously to all without finding fault, and it will be given to you.[g] 6 But when you ask, you must believe and not doubt,[h] because the one who doubts is like a wave of the sea, blown and tossed by the wind. 7 That person should not expect to receive anything from the Lord. 8 Such a person is double-minded[i] and unstable in all they do.

9 Believers in humble circumstances ought to take pride in their high position. 10 But the rich should take pride in their humiliation — since they will pass away like a wild flower.[j] 11 For the sun rises with scorching heat and withers[k] the plant; its blossom falls and its beauty is destroyed.[l] In the same way, the rich will fade away even while they go about their business.

[a] *2* The Greek word for *brothers and sisters* (*adelphoi*) refers here to believers, both men and women, as part of God's family; also in verses 16 and 19; and in 2:1, 5, 14; 3:10, 12; 4:11; 5:7, 9, 10, 12, 19.

1:1 *Address and Greeting.* The letter of James begins as NT letters usually do, with an identification of the sender and the recipients and a greeting.
1:1 James. See Introduction: Author. **twelve tribes scattered among the nations.** See Introduction: Recipients and Occasion.
1:2–18 *Trials and Temptations.* James moves quickly from one issue to another as he emphasizes that Christians must stand firm in the midst of trials (vv. 2–4,12; cf. vv. 13–15).
1:2–12 *Overcoming Trials.* James frames this passage with an exhortation (vv. 2–3) and a promise (v. 12) that put trials in perspective.
1:2 As elsewhere in James, this exhortation may derive from Jesus himself (Matt 5:11–12). **joy.** Greek *charan*; it forges a literary link with v. 1, where "greetings" translates *chairein.* **trials of many kinds.** The difficulties of life, ranging from persecution (2:6–7) to physical illness (5:14) and financial hardship (1:9). Such hardships are a normal part of the Christian life.
1:3 because you know. Joy in trials is possible when believers consider how God works through those trials to build them up spiritually (cf. Rom 5:3–4; 1 Pet 1:6–7).
1:4–5 lacking ... lacks. Another example of James linking words (see note on v. 2).
1:5 wisdom. Gives people the capacity to understand the world in light of God's Word and purposes; believers need it to rejoice in trials. Wisdom is an important theme in James: although mentioned explicitly elsewhere only in 3:13–18, it is tied into some of James's other themes (e.g., the tongue), and wisdom writings influence James's style. **generously.** Or "single-mindedly," in the sense that God's single, undivided intent is to give us those gifts we need to please him. Such "single-mindedness" is a fundamental theme in James (v. 8; 4:4–10).
1:8 double-minded. James is not saying that our prayers will be answered only if we have a perfect faith that never entertains any kind of doubt. He condemns the believer who is trying to serve two masters at the same time (cf. Matt 6:24).
1:9 humble circumstances. Poverty and powerlessness in society, the "trial" that seems to have been the most difficult for James's readers (v. 27; 2:1–7,15–16; 5:1–6). **high position.** The spiritual "exaltation" they enjoy in Christ (4:10; 1 Pet 5:6).
1:10 the rich. Either rich Christians, who should focus not on their wealth but on their identification with Christ, who "humbled himself" (Phil 2:8; cf. Jas 4:10), or rich non-Christians, in which case James's exhortation to them to "take pride in their humiliation" is ironic. **pass away like a wild flower.** Familiar biblical imagery for transience (Job 14:2; Ps 103:15–16; Isa 40:6–7; 1 Pet 1:24), referring either to the impermanent wealth of rich Christians or to the ultimate judgment of rich non-Christians.

12 Blessed is the one who perseveres under trial because, having stood the test, that person will receive
the crown of life[m] that the Lord has promised to those who love him.[n]
13 When tempted, no one should say, "God is tempting me." For God cannot be tempted by evil, nor
does he tempt anyone; 14 but each person is tempted when they are dragged away by their own evil desire and enticed. 15 Then, after desire has conceived, it gives birth to sin;[o] and sin, when it is full-grown,
gives birth to death.[p]
16 Don't be deceived,[q] my dear brothers and sisters.[r] 17 Every good and perfect gift is from above,[s]
coming down from the Father of the heavenly lights, who does not change[t] like shifting shadows.
18 He chose to give us birth[u] through the word of truth, that we might be a kind of firstfruits[v] of all
he created.

Listening and Doing

19 My dear brothers and sisters, take note of this: Everyone should be quick to listen, slow to speak[w]
and slow to become angry, 20 because human anger does not produce the righteousness that God desires.
21 Therefore, get rid of[x] all moral filth and the evil that is so prevalent and humbly accept the word
planted in you,[y] which can save you.
22 Do not merely listen to the word, and so deceive yourselves. Do what it says. 23 Anyone who listens
to the word but does not do what it says is like someone who looks at his face in a mirror 24 and, after
looking at himself, goes away and immediately forgets what he looks like. 25 But whoever looks intently
into the perfect law that gives freedom,[z] and continues in it — not forgetting what they have heard, but
doing it — they will be blessed in what they do.[a]
26 Those who consider themselves religious and yet do not keep a tight rein on their tongues[b] deceive themselves, and their religion is worthless. 27 Religion that God our Father accepts as pure and
faultless is this: to look after[c] orphans and widows[d] in their distress and to keep oneself from being
polluted by the world.[e]

1:12 [m] 1Co 9:25 [n] Jas 2:5
1:15 [o] Job 15:35; Ps 7:14 [p] Ro 6:23
1:16 [q] 1Co 6:9 [r] ver 19
1:17 [s] Jn 3:27 [t] Nu 23:19; Mal 3:6
1:18 [u] Jn 1:13 [v] Eph 1:12; Rev 14:4
1:19 [w] Pr 10:19
1:21 [x] Eph 4:22 [y] Eph 1:13
1:25 [z] Jas 2:12 [a] Jn 13:17
1:26 [b] Ps 34:13; 1Pe 3:10
1:27 [c] Mt 25:36 [d] Isa 1:17,23 [e] Ro 12:2

1:12 perseveres under trial. A return to the theme at the beginning of this section (vv. 2–4). **crown of life.** The crown that consists of eternal life (cf. Rev 2:10). **crown.** The wreath placed on the head of a victorious athlete or military leader (1 Cor 9:25; 2 Tim 4:8).

1:13–18 *The Source of Temptation.* James warns about the consequences of giving in to one's own sinful desire, and encourages his readers by reminding them of God's good gift of the new birth.

1:13–14 tempted ... tempting ... cannot be tempted ... tempt ... tempted. Another wordplay: the Greek word for "trials" (v. 2) and "trial" (v. 12) shares the same root as the Greek for these words.

1:13 no one should say, "God is tempting me." God brings trials into his people's lives (e.g., Gen 22), but he never desires that believers fall to temptation. **God cannot be tempted by evil.** Because he is perfectly holy, God has nothing in his nature that is open to evil. By becoming fully human, Jesus was capable of being tempted (Matt 4:1–11), but he never yielded to that temptation (Heb 4:15).

1:14 their own evil desire. Temptation comes not from God but from within each person who, until their body is redeemed, has a bent toward evil.

1:15 gives birth to sin. Temptation is not itself sin; people often sin when they open themselves to temptation.

1:17 Every good and perfect gift. Far from enticing people to evil (v. 13), God showers blessings on his people. **Father of the heavenly lights.** The Creator of the universe and all the planets and stars that we see in the heavens above us (Ps 136:7–9).

1:18 give us birth. Spiritual birth, i.e., regeneration (John 3:3,5,7). **through the word of truth.** The gospel, "the power of God that brings salvation" (Rom 1:16; see 2 Cor 6:7; Eph 1:13; Col 1:5; 2 Tim 2:15). **firstfruits of all he created.** The spiritual birth of believers is the first stage in God's cosmic plan to remake the entire universe.

1:19—2:26 *Putting the Word Into Practice.* This section of the letter focuses on the power of God's Word and the need for believers to respond to it in obedience.

1:19–27 *Listening and Doing.* A general exhortation about talking and listening merges quickly into an important plea *to do* and not just *listen to* the Word of God.

1:19 James echoes popular wisdom teaching about the importance of careful listening and the danger of anger that leads to hasty and regrettable words (Prov 10:19; 15:1; 17:27–28).

1:20 righteousness that God desires. Behavior that pleases God. Anger produces sinful acts such as unwise speech (vv. 19,26; 3:1–12) and violence (4:2–3; Matt 5:21–26).

1:21 word planted in you. Reflects the "new covenant" prophecy of Jer 31:31–34, where God promises his people, "I will put my law in their minds and write it on their hearts." **save.** Since James is writing to believers, the salvation here must refer to ultimate deliverance from sin and death in the last day (Rom 5:9–10; 13:14).

1:22 deceive yourselves. The deception is to think that they are destined for final salvation when they really are not.

1:25 perfect law that gives freedom. The Mosaic law is perfected in Christ, who brought the law to its true fulfillment (see notes on Matt 5:17; Rom 10:4). The "law" believers stand under is the "royal law" (2:8), the teaching of Jesus (and the apostles) about the true meaning and application of the law. The law brought bondage to humans, who were prevented by sin from fulfilling the law (Gal 3:22–24). But the law is written on the hearts of new covenant believers, setting them free from that bondage. James makes an important point about the unity of God's Word, which is both the means of our new birth and salvation (vv. 18,21) and a "law" that directs Christian conduct. God's Word is both "gospel" and "law," and Christians cannot rejoice in their liberation through the gospel if they do not at the same time seek, by divine enablement (v. 21), to live under God's "royal" law.

1:27 orphans and widows. Represent all people who find themselves powerless and vulnerable in this world. God is himself "a father to the fatherless, a defender of widows" (Ps 68:5; see Exod 22:22–24) and expects his people to imitate his concern (Isa 1:10–17).

2:1 [f]1Co 2:8 [g]Lev 19:15
2:4 [h]Jn 7:24
2:5 [i]Jas 1:16,19 [j]1Co 1:26-28 [k]Lk 12:21 [l]Jas 1:12
2:6 [m]1Co 11:22 [n]Ac 8:3
2:8 [o]Lev 19:18
2:9 [p]ver 1 [q]Dt 1:17
2:10 [r]Mt 5:19; Gal 3:10
2:11 [s]Ex 20:14; Dt 5:18 [t]Ex 20:13; Dt 5:17
2:12 [u]Jas 1:25
2:13 [v]Mt 5:7; 18:32-35
2:14 [w]Mt 7:26; Jas 1:22-25

Favoritism Forbidden

2 My brothers and sisters, believers in our glorious[f] Lord Jesus Christ must not show favoritism.[g]
[2]Suppose a man comes into your meeting wearing a gold ring and fine clothes, and a poor man
in filthy old clothes also comes in. [3]If you show special attention to the man wearing fine clothes and
say, "Here's a good seat for you," but say to the poor man, "You stand there" or "Sit on the floor by my
feet," [4]have you not discriminated among yourselves and become judges[h] with evil thoughts?
[5]Listen, my dear brothers and sisters:[i] Has not God chosen those who are poor in the eyes of the
world[j] to be rich in faith[k] and to inherit the kingdom he prom-
ised those who love him?[l] [6]But you have dishonored the poor.[m]
Is it not the rich who are exploiting you? Are they not the ones
who are dragging you into court?[n] [7]Are they not the ones who
are blaspheming the noble name of him to whom you belong?
[8]If you really keep the royal law found in Scripture, "Love
your neighbor as yourself,"[a][o] you are doing right. [9]But if you
show favoritism,[p] you sin and are convicted by the law as lawbreakers.[q] [10]For whoever keeps the whole law and yet stumbles
at just one point is guilty of breaking all of it.[r] [11]For he who
said, "You shall not commit adultery,"[b][s] also said, "You shall
not murder."[c][t] If you do not commit adultery but do commit
murder, you have become a lawbreaker.
[12]Speak and act as those who are going to be judged by the
law that gives freedom,[u] [13]because judgment without mercy
will be shown to anyone who has not been merciful.[v] Mercy
triumphs over judgment.

Portrait of a youth in a gold wreath, Fayum mummy portrait, Romano-Egyptian, early second century. James urges believers not to show favoritism to a man wearing "a gold ring and fine clothes" (Jas 2:2).

Faith and Deeds

[14]What good is it, my brothers and sisters, if someone claims
to have faith but has no deeds?[w] Can such faith save them?
[15]Suppose a brother or a sister is without clothes and daily

[a] *8* Lev. 19:18 [b] *11* Exodus 20:14; Deut. 5:18 [c] *11* Exodus 20:13; Deut. 5:17

2:1–13 *Favoritism Forbidden.* James condemns favoritism in the church, a striking example of failing to "do" the Word of God.
2:1 glorious Lord Jesus Christ. James implicitly compares the glory that belongs to Christ alone with the "glory" that believers are giving to powerful, wealthy humans. **favoritism.** Judging people on the basis of their external appearance (see Rom 2:11; Eph 6:9; Col 3:25). Favoritism is prohibited in Lev 19:15, which is only three verses removed from the "love" command (Lev 19:18) that James quotes in v. 8.
2:2 meeting. Translates the Greek word from which we get "synagogue," probably reflecting the early date and Jewish atmosphere shared by James and his readers. Believers were probably meeting in house churches. **gold ring.** A symbol of an upper-class Roman.
2:4 become judges. James might be referring to specific situations when believers sat in judgment over other believers, but he more likely is labeling discrimination against the poor in regular church meetings as judgmental.
2:5–13 Favoritism to the rich is wrong because (1) it contrasts with the attitude of God, who chooses poor people to belong to his kingdom (v. 5); (2) those very rich people are the ones persecuting the church (vv. 6–7); and (3) it violates the "royal law" of love (see v. 8 and note). So God condemns people guilty of it (vv. 8–13).
2:5 chosen those who are poor. God is especially concerned for the poor (Exod 23:11; 1 Sam 2:8; Ps 12:5; Luke 6:20; 1 Cor 1:26–28). **inherit the kingdom.** The kingdom of God was inaugurated when Jesus first came to earth (Matt 12:28), and believers, who enter it now by faith, anticipate being part of its final glorious manifestation (2 Pet 1:11).
2:6 dragging you into court. Rich unbelievers are using their power and influence to persecute believers, probably because they oppose the teaching about Jesus as Messiah and Lord.
2:7 noble name. See v. 1.
2:8 royal law. The law may be called "royal" because it refers to the "love" command, the supreme command in the OT (see Matt 22:34–40; Rom 13:8–10; Gal 5:13–14). But James probably refers to the entire OT law as "royal" in the sense that it is now, as summarized in the love command, the law for the kingdom that Jesus has inaugurated (see note on v. 5). Since many topics from the immediate context of Lev 19:18 come up in James, he may be focusing on this part of the OT law in particular.
2:10 guilty of breaking all of it. God's law reflects the person of God himself (v. 11); to break any of its commands, therefore, is to fall short of God's will.
2:12 those who are going to be judged. Believers who have been brought into relationship with God by faith must still face a day of judgment to come (4:11–12; 5:9). They confront this day with assurance rooted in their relationship to Christ, but they must also take seriously the scrutiny that their actions in this life will receive on that day (Rom 14:10–12; 2 Cor 5:10). **law that gives freedom.** See note on 1:25.
2:13 Mercy triumphs over judgment. People who display mercy toward others will not have to worry on the day of judgment (Matt 18:21–25).
2:14–26 *Faith and Deeds.* James reinforces the importance of Christian behavior in light of the coming day of judgment by insisting that "deeds," or works, are the inevitable outcome of true faith.
2:14 faith ... such faith. In Greek, "such faith" is simply "the faith," but

Pre AD 70 synagogue at Gamla. The Greek word behind "meeting" (Jas 2:2) is the origin of the English word "synagogue."

food.[x] 16If one of you says to them, "Go in peace; keep warm and well fed," but does nothing about
their physical needs, what good is it?[y] 17In the same way, faith by itself, if it is not accompanied by
action, is dead.

18But someone will say, "You have faith; I have deeds."

Show me your faith without deeds,[z] and I will show you my faith by my deeds.[a] 19You believe that
there is one God.[b] Good! Even the demons believe that[c] — and shudder.

20You foolish person, do you want evidence that faith without deeds is useless[a]?[d] 21Was not our father Abraham considered righteous for what he did when he offered his son Isaac on the altar?[e] 22You
see that his faith and his actions were working together,[f] and his faith was made complete by what he
did.[g] 23And the scripture was fulfilled that says, "Abraham believed God, and it was credited to him as

2:15 [x] Mt 25:35,36
2:16 [y] 1Jn 3:17,18
2:18 [z] Ro 3:28 [a] Jas 3:13
2:19 [b] Dt 6:4 [c] Mt 8:29; Lk 4:34
2:20 [d] ver 17,26
2:21 [e] Ge 22:9,12
2:22 [f] Heb 11:17 [g] 1Th 1:3

[a] *20* Some early manuscripts *dead*

the article points back to the earlier mention of faith — the kind of faith that "has no deeds." That kind of faith is not true biblical faith. Having genuine faith means also having God's Spirit residing within us, a spiritual condition that cannot help but produce deeds pleasing to God (Gal 5:6). **save.** Deliver from God's wrath on the day of judgment, as usually in James (1:21; 4:12; 5:20; in 5:15 the same Greek word probably refers to physical healing ["make ... well"]).

2:17 faith ... is dead. This is the counterfeit faith of v. 14.

2:18 You have faith; I have deeds. James quotes a dialogue partner to make his point. This person may be claiming that it is unreasonable to expect every believer to possess both faith and deeds. **show you my faith by my deeds.** Only when people "do" the Word (1:22) can other people see evidence of the faith that Christians claim to have.

2:19 there is one God. The basic Jewish confession drawn from Deut 6:4 (see note). **Even the demons believe that.** The kind of purely intellectual "faith" (v. 18) that demons have is far from the biblical faith that trusts God and results in obedience to him.

2:20 You foolish person. An ancient argumentative style, called the diatribe, which uses a hypothetical question-and-answer format to convey the author's ideas. **faith without deeds is useless.** A recurrent refrain in the section (vv. 17,26).

2:21 considered righteous. See note on v. 24. **offered his son Isaac on the altar.** See Gen 22.

2:22 his faith. James does not minimize the significance of Abraham's faith; indeed, he takes Abraham's faith for granted throughout vv. 21 – 26. James's concern is to test the reality of faith by looking at the evidence that true faith produces. **his faith was made complete.** Doing and believing are two separate but intimately connected activities. Addressing people who were severing the connection between them, James insists that deeds of obedience to God are always the result, or fulfillment, of faith.

2:23 scripture was fulfilled. James follows Jewish teaching by connecting the declaration of Abraham's righteous status before God in Gen 15:6 with his faithful response when God "tested" him by asking him to sacrifice his son: "Was not Abraham found faithful when tested, and it was reckoned to him as righteousness?" (1 Maccabees 2:52 in the Apocrypha [NRSV]). Paul quotes Gen 15:6 to demonstrate that Abraham's faith came first and that God considered it the full measure of the "righteousness" he was looking for (Rom 4:3; Gal 3:6). James argues that Abraham's faith highlighted in Gen 15:6 resulted in acts of obedience that demonstrated the reality of his faith. **God's friend.** Genesis does not call Abraham this, but see 2 Chr 20:7 and Isa 41:8

2:23 [h]Ge 15:6; Ro 4:3 [i]2Ch 20:7; Isa 41:8
2:25 [j]Heb 11:31
2:26 [k]ver 17,20
3:2 [l]1Ki 8:46; Jas 2:10 [m]1Pe 3:10 [n]Mt 12:37 [o]Jas 1:26
3:3 [p]Ps 32:9
3:5 [q]Ps 12:3,4
3:6 [r]Pr 16:27 [s]Mt 15:11,18,19
3:8 [t]Ps 140:3; Ro 3:13
3:9 [u]Ge 1:26,27; 1Co 11:7

righteousness,"[a][h] and he was called God's friend.[i] 24 You see that a person is considered righteous by
what they do and not by faith alone.
25 In the same way, was not even Rahab the prostitute considered righteous for what she did when
she gave lodging to the spies and sent them off in a different direction?[j] 26 As the body without the spirit
is dead, so faith without deeds is dead.[k]

Taming the Tongue

3 Not many of you should become teachers, my fellow believers, because you know that we who teach
will be judged more strictly. 2 We all stumble[l] in many ways. Anyone who is never at fault in what
they say[m] is perfect,[n] able to keep their whole body in check.[o]
3 When we put bits into the mouths of horses to make them obey us, we can turn the whole animal.[p]
4 Or take ships as an example. Although they are so large and are driven by strong winds, they are
steered by a very small rudder wherever the pilot wants to go. 5 Likewise, the tongue is a small part of
the body, but it makes great boasts.[q] Consider what a great forest is set on fire by a small spark. 6 The
tongue also is a fire,[r] a world of evil among the parts of the body. It corrupts the whole body,[s] sets the
whole course of one's life on fire, and is itself set on fire by hell.
7 All kinds of animals, birds, reptiles and sea creatures are being tamed and have been tamed by
mankind, 8 but no human being can tame the tongue. It is a restless evil, full of deadly poison.[t]
9 With the tongue we praise our Lord and Father, and with it we curse human beings, who have been
made in God's likeness.[u] 10 Out of the same mouth come praise and cursing. My brothers and sisters,

[a] *23* Gen. 15:6

(and Jewish tradition: OT pseudepigrapha, Jubilees 19:9; 30:20; Philo, *Abraham* 273).

2:24 This sentence is the basic theological point of the section, framed by parallel illustrations of the patriarch (v. 21) and prostitute (v. 25). **considered righteous.** Could also be translated "justified" (Greek *dikaioō*; also in vv. 21,25). James's insistence that a person is not "justified" by faith alone appears to conflict with Paul's teaching as found, e.g., in Rom 3:28: "For we maintain that a person is justified by faith apart from the works of the law." Both authors stress the importance of faith, but Paul seems to say that works are not involved in justification at all, while James seems to say that works *must* be involved. There are three main approaches to resolving this apparent contradiction. (1) Paul may be denying that a person can be justified by only certain kinds of works (such as adherence to characteristic Jewish practices); James insists that another kind of works, "good works," are needed for justification. This view assumes an unlikely meaning of "works of the law" in Rom 3:20 (see note there). (2) Paul may be insisting that a person is *declared* righteous by faith alone, while James insists that a person *demonstrates* that they are righteous only by faith and works together (v. 18). In other words, James and Paul would be using the word *dikaioō* ("justify," "declare righteous") with different meanings. (3) Paul may be denying that justification can be *based on* human works, while James is insisting that justification will *take into account* human works. On this view, both Paul and James are using the verb "justify" (Greek *dikaioō*) to refer to God's judicial verdict that a person is "right" before him. Paul insists that this divine verdict is a product of God's grace alone and is therefore something humans can experience only by faith alone (Rom 4:4–5). James does not disagree but reminds us that "faith alone" does not mean "a faith that is alone." True faith is always accompanied by works (as Paul himself insists; Gal 5:6). Those works, the necessary evidence of faith, will be taken into account when God confirms his verdict of justification at the end of our lives.

2:25 Rahab the prostitute. See Josh 2; cf. 6:25; Heb 11:31.

3:1—4:12 *Words and Wisdom.* The importance and challenge of controlling our speech frame this section (3:1–12; 4:11–12). "Wisdom that comes from heaven" (3:17) enables believers to tame the tongue and avoid quarrelling (3:13—4:3). Central to this section and to the letter as a whole is James's call for a wholehearted and consistent commitment to God (4:4–10).

3:1–12 *Taming the Tongue.* James elaborates on his earlier point that people who are truly "religious" will "keep a tight rein on their tongues" (1:26). Our words are powerful, and it is difficult to keep them under control.

3:1 Not many of you should become teachers. The rabbi, or teacher, was an honored figure among the Jews, and perhaps some Christians were attracted to the prestige the position would bring them. James does not intend to dissuade those who are gifted and called from pursuing this ministry, but would-be teachers must consider that they "will be judged more strictly." The significance of their ministry means that the Lord will scrutinize them especially carefully (Matt 5:19; Acts 20:26–27).

3:2 perfect. Because the tongue is so difficult to control (vv. 5–8), the person who never sins in their speech must be perfect in every way.

3:3–5 The three images that James uses in these verses—bits and horses, rudders and ships, sparks and forest fires—occur together in ancient literature (e.g., Philo, *Allegorical Interpretation* 3.223–224), and some of them even illustrate the power of speech (Plutarch, *de garrulitate* 10). The tongue has power that is quite out of proportion with its size relative to other parts of the human body.

3:6 world of evil. Our tongues reveal what is in our hearts (Matt 15:18), so they manifest all the worldliness that characterizes humans. **whole course of one's life.** James makes contact with his readers by using a semitechnical phrase from current philosophy: "the wheel of existence."

3:8 no human being. Emphatic. James might be implying that human beings, by their own resources, cannot tame the tongue; a task so difficult requires divine aid.

3:9 made in God's likeness. God created human beings in his "likeness," or "image" (Gen 1:26). That image, while marred because of the fall into sin, has not been eradicated. Human beings possess inherent worth because they continue to manifest that "image."

3:10–12 James again touches on one of his key concerns: Christians failing to respond to God completely and consistently. It is just as incongruous for a Christian, whose heart God's Spirit has transformed, to utter false and demeaning words as it is for a fig tree to bear olives; a grapevine, figs; or a salt spring, fresh water. James may again be reflecting the teaching of Jesus (see Matt 15:18–19).

this should not be. 11Can both fresh water and salt water flow from the same spring? 12My brothers and
sisters, can a fig tree bear olives, or a grapevine bear figs?[v] Neither can a salt spring produce fresh water.

Two Kinds of Wisdom

13Who is wise and understanding among you? Let them show it[w] by their good life, by deeds done
in the humility that comes from wisdom. 14But if you harbor bitter envy and selfish ambition[x] in your
hearts, do not boast about it or deny the truth.[y] 15Such "wisdom" does not come down from heaven[z]
but is earthly, unspiritual, demonic.[a] 16For where you have envy and selfish ambition, there you find
disorder and every evil practice.

17But the wisdom that comes from heaven[b] is first of all pure; then peace-loving, considerate, submissive, full of mercy[c] and good fruit, impartial and sincere.[d] 18Peacemakers who sow in peace reap
a harvest of righteousness.[e]

Submit Yourselves to God

4 What causes fights and quarrels[f] among you? Don't they come from your desires that battle[g]
within you? 2You desire but do not have, so you kill. You covet but you cannot get what you want,
so you quarrel and fight. You do not have because you do not ask God. 3When you ask, you do not
receive,[h] because you ask with wrong motives,[i] that you may spend what you get on your pleasures.

4You adulterous people,[a] don't you know that friendship with the world[j] means enmity against
God?[k] Therefore, anyone who chooses to be a friend of the world becomes an enemy of God.[l] 5Or do you
think Scripture says without reason that he jealously longs for the spirit he has caused to dwell in us[b]?
6But he gives us more grace. That is why Scripture says:

[a] *4* An allusion to covenant unfaithfulness; see Hosea 3:1. [b] *5* Or *that the spirit he caused to dwell in us envies intensely;* or *that the Spirit he caused to dwell in us longs jealously*

3:12 [v] Mt 7:16
3:13 [w] Jas 2:18
3:14 [x] ver 16 [y] Jas 5:19
3:15 [z] Jas 1:17 [a] 1Ti 4:1
3:17 [b] 1Co 2:6 [c] Lk 6:36 [d] Ro 12:9
3:18 [e] Pr 11:18; Isa 32:17
4:1 [f] Titus 3:9 [g] Ro 7:23
4:3 [h] Ps 18:41 [i] 1Jn 3:22; 5:14
4:4 [j] Jas 1:27 [k] 1Jn 2:15 [l] Jn 15:19

3:13–18 *Two Kinds of Wisdom.* A common concern joins this section and the next paragraph (4:1–3): disunity within the church. True biblical wisdom manifests itself in virtues that foster peace rather than division.

3:13 wise and understanding. Perhaps referring especially to the teachers (v. 1). **show it by their good life.** People with intellectual gifts are too often characterized by pride in their own ideas that makes them difficult to get along with. The wisdom all believers should seek above all else (Prov 4:5–9; 8:10–11), by contrast, is inseparably connected to a godly lifestyle.

3:14 selfish ambition. Translates a Greek word that Aristotle used to describe the political factions that were convulsing Athens in his day (*Politics* 5.3.1302b; cf. Rom 2:8; 2 Cor 12:20; Gal 5:20; Phil 1:17; 2:3). **do not boast about it.** Do not brag about having wisdom when you are filled with selfishness. **the truth.** The "truth" of Christianity is something we must not simply understand but live (5:19; 1 John 1:6; 2 John 4) and obey (Gal 5:7; 1 Pet 1:22). When believers do not live in accordance with the gospel they profess, they in effect deny that truth (2 Pet 2:2).

3:15 unspiritual. The Greek word refers to being caught up in the life of this world in contrast to the realm of God and his kingdom (1 Cor 2:14; 15:44,46; Jude 19).

3:16 selfish ambition. See note on v. 14.

3:17–18 James focuses on virtues that will foster harmony among Christians. The list of virtues that characterizes true wisdom is similar, in structure at least, to the list of the "fruit of the Spirit" in Gal 5:22–23. Ultimately, the Spirit produces these virtues.

3:18 harvest of righteousness. The harvest, or "fruit," that peacemakers produce is community-wide conduct that pleases God (1:20): unity in place of disunity, concern for others in place of selfishness. Jesus pronounced a blessing on "peacemakers" (Matt 5:9).

4:1–12 *Submit Yourselves to God.* James continues to rebuke his readers for their quarrelsome attitudes (vv. 1–3) and then, expressing the heart of his concern in this letter, exhorts his readers to give themselves wholly to God (vv. 4–10). He concludes with yet another rebuke regarding speech (vv. 11–12).

4:1 fights and quarrels. The stress brought upon the believers by persecution (1:2–4; 2:6–7) may have exacerbated their infighting (5:9). **desires that battle within you.** James again spotlights inner dividedness as a basic issue (vv. 4–5; 1:10–11; 3:9–11).

4:2 kill. May refer to the physical violence to which zealous Jews in James's day were resorting to defend the faith. More likely, however, James wants to turn his readers away from their argumentative attitudes by reminding them of the ultimate expression of unbridled passion and selfishness. The Jewish writing *Testament of Simeon* describes how "envy" (3:14,16) led Simeon and his brothers to attempt to murder their brother Joseph (Gen 37:11,20).

4:3 ask with wrong motives. God promises to give his people the wisdom they need to live faithful and other-oriented lives (1:5). But believers must ask with sincere faith (1:6–8), not with the desire to elevate themselves or satisfy themselves on pleasures.

4:4 You adulterous people. The form of the Greek word this translates is feminine. Picking up widespread OT imagery, James compares God's people to God's bride or spouse (e.g., Isa 54:5–6) and, as often in the OT, rebukes them for unfaithfulness (e.g., Hos 2:5–7; see also Isa 57:3; Jer 3:20; Ezek 16:38; 23:45).

4:5 Scripture. James probably has in mind the general OT teaching about God's jealousy for his people (Exod 20:5). **he jealously longs for the spirit he has caused to dwell in us.** Could also be translated "the spirit he caused to dwell in us envies intensely" (see the first alternative in the NIV text note), in which case the Scripture would be OT teaching about the human propensity for envy (e.g., Prov 14:30). **the spirit.** Either the spirit that God placed in all human beings in creation (Gen 2:7) or the Holy Spirit who now indwells believers. If the latter is correct, then the Spirit could be either the subject of the sentence (see the second alternative in the NIV text note) or the object.

4:6 more grace. James's focus here might be on (1) the grace that

4:6 [m]Ps 138:6; Pr 3:34; Mt 23:12
4:7 [n]Eph 4:27; 1Pe 5:6-9
4:8 [o]2Ch 15:2 [p]Isa 1:16 [q]Jas 1:8
4:9 [r]Lk 6:25
4:11 [s]1Pe 2:1 [t]Mt 7:1 [u]Jas 1:22
4:12 [v]Mt 10:28 [w]Ro 14:4
4:13 [x]Pr 27:1
4:14 [y]Job 7:7; Ps 102:3
4:15 [z]Ac 18:21
4:16 [a]1Co 5:6
4:17 [b]Lk 12:47; Jn 9:41
5:1 [c]Lk 6:24
5:2 [d]Job 13:28; Mt 6:19,20
5:3 [e]ver 7,8
5:4 [f]Lev 19:13

"God opposes the proud
but shows favor to the humble."[a][m]

[7]Submit yourselves, then, to God. Resist the devil,[n] and he will flee from you. [8]Come near to God and
he will come near to you.[o] Wash your hands,[p] you sinners, and purify your hearts, you double-minded.[q]
[9]Grieve, mourn and wail. Change your laughter to mourning and your joy to gloom.[r] [10]Humble yourselves before the Lord, and he will lift you up.

[11]Brothers and sisters, do not slander one another.[s] Anyone who speaks against a brother or sister[b]
or judges them[t] speaks against the law and judges it. When you judge the law, you are not keeping it,[u]
but sitting in judgment on it. [12]There is only one Lawgiver and Judge, the one who is able to save and
destroy.[v] But you—who are you to judge your neighbor?[w]

Boasting About Tomorrow

[13]Now listen, you who say, "Today or tomorrow we will go to this or that city, spend a year there, carry
on business and make money."[x] [14]Why, you do not even know what will happen tomorrow. What is your
life? You are a mist that appears for a little while and then vanishes.[y] [15]Instead, you ought to say, "If it is
the Lord's will,[z] we will live and do this or that." [16]As it is, you boast in your arrogant schemes. All such
boasting is evil.[a] [17]If anyone, then, knows the good they ought to do and doesn't do it, it is sin for them.[b]

Warning to Rich Oppressors

5 Now listen, you rich people,[c] weep and wail because of the misery that is coming on you. [2]Your
wealth has rotted, and moths have eaten your clothes.[d] [3]Your gold and silver are corroded. Their
corrosion will testify against you and eat your flesh like fire. You have hoarded wealth in the last days.[e]
[4]Look! The wages you failed to pay the workers[f] who mowed your fields are crying out against you. The

[a] *6* Prov. 3:34 [b] *11* The Greek word for *brother or sister* (*adelphos*) refers here to a believer, whether man or woman, as part of God's family.

enables believers to fully meet the awesome demand that we be wholly devoted to our jealous God or (2) the grace that can overcome our strong human tendency to sinful envy. **favor to the humble.** Believers need humility in order to experience the full benefits of God's grace (1 Pet 5:5).

4:7 Resist the devil, and he will flee from you. The exhortation and promise parallel 1 Pet 5:8–9, which may suggest that James is tapping into widespread early Christian teaching.

4:8 Wash your hands. An allusion to the OT priests who washed their hands before they ministered in the tabernacle (Exod 30:17–21). **and purify your hearts.** Ps 24:4 also brings together "clean hands and a pure heart." **double-minded.** A key concern of James (1:8).

4:9 Grieve, mourn and wail. James uses language from the OT prophets to exhort his readers to repent sincerely for sin (e.g., Joel 2:12; cf. 1 Cor 5:2). **joy to gloom.** James is not denying that believers should "rejoice in the Lord always" (Phil 4:4). He rebukes the false joy of believers who fail to take their sin seriously.

4:10 Humble yourselves. This exhortation parallels the call to "submit yourselves ... to God" (v. 7) that began this series of commands. **lift you up.** See 1:9; Matt 23:12; Luke 14:11; 1 Pet 5:6.

4:11–12 These verses return to the issue of community dissension (3:13—4:3).

4:11 do not slander one another. James again brings up the problem of sinful speech (1:26; 3:1–12). **speaks against the law and judges it.** Believers who criticize each other ignore the law and, in effect, think they are superior to it. James probably refers again to the "royal law" (see 2:8 and note) since Lev 19:16 (just two verses away from the love command of Lev 19:18) prohibits slander.

4:12 neighbor. Again (see note on v. 11) connotes the love command.

4:13—5:12 *A Christian Perspective on the World.* The general theme that binds together 4:13–17 and 5:1–12 is the importance of allowing God and his values to shape Christian attitudes toward business and wealth.

4:13–17 *Boasting About Tomorrow.* James rebukes the arrogance that too often characterizes people involved in business, which is closely related to his more pointed rebuke of the rich in 5:1–6.

4:13 you who say. Probably believers (see v. 15).

4:14 mist. Cf. Job 7:7,9,16; Ps 39:5–6. James's rebuke may again reflect the teaching of Jesus, who told a parable about a foolish rich man who made plans to earn more money while failing to reckon with the brevity of his own life (Luke 12:15–21).

4:15 If it is the Lord's will. Whether verbalized or not, this sense of living within God's will for all of life is basic to authentic Christian living.

4:17 Sin is not only doing what God forbids (sins of "commission"); it is also failing to do what God asks us to do (sins of "omission").

5:1–6 *Warning to Rich Oppressors.* James uses the same form of address in both 4:13 and 5:1, indicating that these two paragraphs are related: both rebuke worldly arrogance and selfishness associated with wealth. But while 4:13–17 urges believers to repent, 5:1–6 condemns ungodly rich people since James pronounces doom with no hint that they can repent.

5:1 weep and wail. Typical descriptions of how evil people react to judgment in the day of the Lord (Isa 13:6; 15:3; Amos 8:3).

5:2 These rich people have not followed Jesus' exhortation, "Sell your possessions and give to the poor. Provide purses for yourselves that will not wear out, a treasure in heaven that will never fail, where no thief comes near and no moth destroys" (Luke 12:33).

5:3 in the last days. The selfishness of the rich is all the worse since the Lord has already come to inaugurate the last days (Acts 2:17; 2 Tim 3:1; Heb 1:2; 2 Pet 3:3; Jude 18; see "The Consummation," p. 2695).

5:4 wages you failed to pay the workers. Promptly paying workers was especially important in a society in which people lived "hand to mouth," using daily wages to buy the necessities of life. James may once again have the "royal law" in view (see 2:8 and note): in the context of the love command (Lev 19:18), the Lord warns his people, "Do

cries[g] of the harvesters have reached the ears of the Lord Almighty.[h] 5You have lived on earth in luxury
and self-indulgence. You have fattened yourselves[i] in the day of slaughter.[a][j] 6You have condemned and
murdered the innocent one,[k] who was not opposing you.

Patience in Suffering

7Be patient, then, brothers and sisters, until the Lord's coming. See how the farmer waits for the
land to yield its valuable crop, patiently waiting for the autumn and spring rains.[l] 8You too, be patient
and stand firm, because the Lord's coming is near.[m] 9Don't grumble against one another, brothers and
sisters,[n] or you will be judged. The Judge[o] is standing at the door![p]

10Brothers and sisters, as an example of patience in the face of suffering, take the prophets[q] who
spoke in the name of the Lord. 11As you know, we count as blessed[r] those who have persevered. You
have heard of Job's perseverance[s] and have seen what the Lord finally brought about.[t] The Lord is full
of compassion and mercy.[u]

12Above all, my brothers and sisters, do not swear—not by heaven or by earth or by anything else.
All you need to say is a simple "Yes" or "No." Otherwise you will be condemned.[v]

The Prayer of Faith

13Is anyone among you in trouble? Let them pray.[w] Is anyone happy? Let them sing songs of praise.[x]
14Is anyone among you sick? Let them call the elders of the church to pray over them and anoint them
with oil[y] in the name of the Lord. 15And the prayer offered in faith will make the sick person well; the

5:4 [g]Dt 24:15 [h]Ro 9:29
5:5 [i]Am 6:1 [j]Jer 12:3; 25:34
5:6 [k]Heb 10:38
5:7 [l]Dt 11:14; Jer 5:24
5:8 [m]Ro 13:11; 1Pe 4:7
5:9 [n]Jas 4:11 [o]1Co 4:5; 1Pe 4:5 [p]Mt 24:33
5:10 [q]Mt 5:12
5:11 [r]Mt 5:10 [s]Job 1:21, 22; 2:10 [t]Job 42:10, 12-17 [u]Nu 14:18
5:12 [v]Mt 5:34-37
5:13 [w]Ps 50:15 [x]Col 3:16
5:14 [y]Mk 6:13

[a] 5 Or *yourselves as in a day of feasting*

not hold back the wages of a hired worker overnight" (Lev 19:13b; cf. Deut 24:14–15; Mal 3:5). **crying out against you.** Cf. Gen 4:10.

5:5 fattened yourselves. Vividly condemns the rich for selfishly using their resources on themselves and failing to share them with others (Ezek 16:49). **day of slaughter.** The judgment associated with the day of the Lord (Isa 30:25; Ezek 7:14–23; Rev 19:17–21). Now that "the last days" have dawned (v. 3), judgment is imminent (vv. 7–9). Yet these wicked rich people pursue their selfish lifestyle, fattening themselves like cattle unaware that they are about to be slaughtered.

5:6 the innocent one. Perhaps Jesus, *the* "innocent," or "righteous," one but probably a paradigmatic righteous person. The OT and Jewish writings regularly condemn rich people for exploiting and indirectly killing the poor (in the Apocrypha [NRSV] see Sirach 34:26–27: "to take away a neighbor's living is to commit murder; to deprive an employee of wages is to shed blood"; see also 2:5–7; Pss 10:8–9; 37:32; Amos 2:6; 5:12; Mic 2:2,6–9; 3:1–3,9–12; 6:9–16).

5:7–12 *Patience in Suffering.* Having warned selfish rich people about the judgment they can expect on the day when the Lord returns (vv. 1–6), James now instructs the people of God about how they must live in light of that coming day. The movement from judging those who oppress the poor to encouraging the righteous to wait patiently for God to vindicate them follows the sequence of Ps 37.

5:7 coming. Greek *parousia.* At Christ's second coming, he will deliver the people of God and judge both their enemies and unbelievers (Matt 24:3—25:46; 1 Thess 4:13—5:11; 2 Thess 1:5–10; 2:1–12). **autumn and spring rains.** A good harvest in Israel depended on rain—either to soften the ground before sowing in the autumn or to water the crops prior to the harvest in the spring. The OT consistently uses this imagery to refer to the Lord's faithfulness (Deut 11:14; Jer 5:24; Hos 6:3; Joel 2:23; Zech 10:1).

5:8–9 near ... standing at the door. The NT consistently views Christ's second coming as imminent (Rom 13:12; Heb 10:25; 1 Pet 4:7; Rev 22:20; cf. Mark 1:15). Now that Jesus' first coming has inaugurated the "last days" (v. 3), the next event in salvation history will be Christ's return in glory. So every generation of Christians looks expectantly yet patiently for that day to dawn (Titus 2:13).

5:9 Don't grumble against one another. The pressure of difficult circumstances can lead believers to take their problems out on each other.

5:10 take the prophets. Cf. Matt 5:12; 23:31; Acts 7:52.

5:11 we count as blessed those who have persevered. James returns to a theme from the beginning of his letter (1:2–4,12). **Job's perseverance.** Job had plenty of questions to bring before God, but he stubbornly persisted in his faithfulness to God (Job 1:21; 2:10; 16:19–21; 19:25–27). **what the Lord finally brought about.** A difficult Greek phrase; can also be translated "the end [or goal] of the Lord." The NIV takes it to refer to the blessings that God showers on Job at the end of the book (Job 42:10–17). The phrase could also refer to the "goal" of a virtuous and patient character that the Lord had in view in Job's sufferings.

5:12 Prohibiting swearing and exhorting believers to let their simple word be enough are clear reiterations of Jesus' teaching (Matt 5:33–37). **swear.** Refers to taking oaths, or vows, as a guarantee that a person will follow through on what they promised. Whether Jesus and James prohibit all such oaths or simply ones that might deceive is debated.

5:13–20 *The Prayer of Faith.* As in many NT letters, the closing refers to prayer—in this case prayer for those who are sick. The letter concludes, appropriately, by calling believers to intervene on behalf of brothers and sisters who might be straying from the path of righteousness.

5:14 elders of the church. The spiritual leaders of the Christian community (Acts 11:30; 14:23; 15:2; 20:17; 1 Tim 5:17; Titus 1:5). **anoint them with oil.** Oil was thought to have medicinal value in the ancient world (Luke 10:34), so James might be encouraging the elders to combine prayer with appropriate medical procedures. But anointing with oil more often symbolized setting apart someone for the Lord's special attention (Exod 28:41; 40:15); kings and priests were appointed by being anointed (e.g., 2 Kgs 9:12; Ps 45:7)—hence the association of "the Anointed One" (Messiah) with kingship. Probably, then, the anointing is a way of assuring the sick person that they are being brought before the Lord for his merciful consideration (cf. Mark 6:13). The Roman Catholic Church has found the sacrament of extreme unction promulgated in this text. But the anointing in this passage is intended not to bring spiritual comfort to those who are dying (the focus of the Roman Catholic sacrament) or who are severely ill, but to set apart the sick person with a view to their being physically healed.

5:15 in faith. An important qualification: only those prayers for healing

5:16 [z]Mt 3:6 [a]1Pe 2:24 [b]Jn 9:31
5:17 [c]Ac 14:15 [d]1Ki 17:1; Lk 4:25
5:18 [e]1Ki 18:41-45
5:19 [f]Jas 3:14 [g]Mt 18:15
5:20 [h]Ro 11:14 [i]1Pe 4:8

Lord will raise them up. If they have sinned, they will be forgiven. [16]Therefore confess your sins[z] to
each other and pray for each other so that you may be healed.[a] The prayer of a righteous person is
powerful and effective.[b]

[17]Elijah was a human being, even as we are.[c] He prayed earnestly that it would not rain, and it did
not rain on the land for three and a half years.[d] [18]Again he prayed, and the heavens gave rain, and the
earth produced its crops.[e]

[19]My brothers and sisters, if one of you should wander from the truth[f] and someone should bring
that person back,[g] [20]remember this: Whoever turns a sinner from the error of their way will save[h] them
from death and cover over a multitude of sins.[i]

---

accompanied by genuine faith will be effective, and only where the Lord wills that healing will he inspire such faith. **sick person.** Since this Greek word could also be translated "one who is weary" (as in Heb 12:3), some think vv. 14–16 refer to a person who is spiritually depressed rather than one who is physically ill. But many of the words James uses in these verses occur in the stories of Jesus' healings in the Gospels. **If they have sinned.** Illness or physical incapacity is not by any means always the result of sin (John 9:1–3), but God does sometimes use physical problems to discipline his children (1 Cor 11:30). So confessing sin is sometimes part of the healing process.

5:17 James cites Elijah not in his role as a prophet, specially chosen by God, but as a "human being, even as we are." He was a righteous person (v. 16) whom God heard (1 Kgs 17:1; 18:41–46).

5:20 save them from death. Restored sinners who had been wandering from the truth (v. 19) will experience ultimate spiritual salvation (see note on 2:14). **cover over a multitude of sins.** The sins that are "covered" could also be the sins of the person who has wandered (v. 19), but it might be instead (or also) the sins of the person who has intervened on their behalf (Prov 10:12).

INTRODUCTION TO
1 PETER

The letter of 1 Peter highlights two important topics: (1) what Jesus accomplished by his undeserved suffering and (2) what this means for the life of a Christian. The death of Jesus is presented as the atonement that reconciles sinners to God (2:21 – 25; 3:18), and his resurrection is shown to be God's merciful offer of new birth into an eternal inheritance (1:3 – 4). Christ's ascension was a proclamation of his victory over even the most depraved evil and demonstrates that all "angels, authorities and powers [are] in submission to him" (3:22).

Those who have accepted God's offer of reconciliation and new birth through Christ can live out their faith with the sure confidence that sin and evil will not have the final say. This means both that sin and evil within the believer can be overcome and that the one who follows Christ will not be destroyed by whatever sin and evil may come against them. The believer's willingness to suffer insult and mockery rather than falling into sin follows the example set by Jesus himself (2:21 – 23) and is a powerful testimony to the reality of God's transforming grace.

Peter calls his readers to understand rightly who Jesus is and what he has done, and to live confidently in that faith, for the letter he has written testifies to "the true grace of God" (5:12).

AUTHOR

This letter identifies the apostle Peter as its author (1:1). Modern scholarship has offered various reasons why an anonymous author may have written this letter using the apostle Peter's name as a pseudonym: (1) The quality of the Greek is too good for a Galilean fisherman to have written. (2) The hierarchy of church leadership is developed beyond that of Peter's lifetime. (3) The letter depends on Paul's letters to the Romans and Ephesians. (4) Christianity, and the subsequent persecution of Christians, did not spread to the areas where the addressees resided until decades after Peter's death.

These reasons are not compelling because: (1) The Greek of 1 Peter shows signs that the author's native language was Semitic, and in any case the author may have used a scribe. (2) The only church leadership position mentioned in 1 Peter is that of elder (5:1,5), and elders were appointed in churches from the very earliest times of the church (e.g., Acts 11:30; 14:23). (3) The similarities to Paul's letters, and perhaps even to some of Paul's expressions, would be expected if both authors shared a common understanding of the significance of the life, death, resurrection, and ascension of Jesus. (4) Christianity may have spread more quickly to the geographic regions mentioned in this letter than scholars have previously believed. Rather than evangelists bringing the gospel to these places, people who had become Christians elsewhere may have moved to these regions through colonization, or perhaps migrating people brought the faith with them. Furthermore, the letter describes persecution in the form of social ostracism and harassment from people reacting to the lifestyle of Christians (1:6; 2:18; 4:3 – 4,14) rather than the official state-sponsored persecution that is known to have happened later in the early second century.

Although authors did use pseudonyms for certain types of writing in the ancient world, the form of 1 Peter is that of personal correspondence, and pseudonymity was not acceptable in that form. Furthermore, the ancient church rejected later attempts to forge well-intentioned letters in the name of the apostles. All considered, there is no compelling reason to reject Peter's authorship of this letter.

PROVINCES ADDRESSED IN 1 PETER

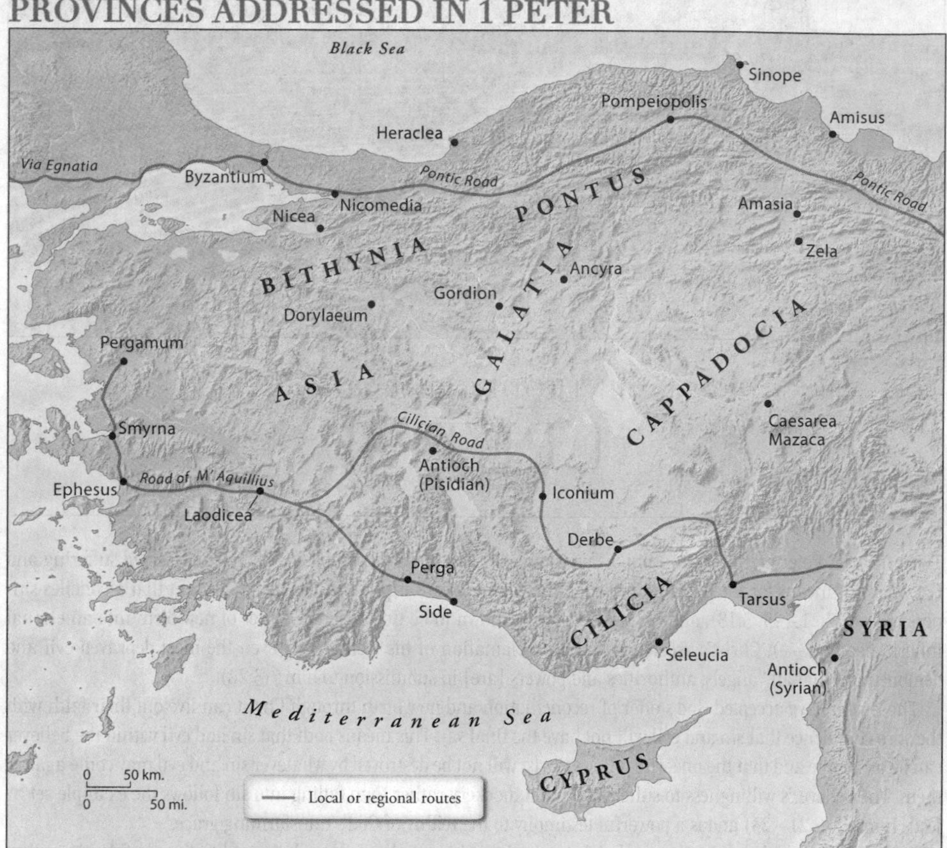

DATE

If the apostle Peter wrote the letter, he must have written it before AD 64–68, when Emperor Nero's persecution of Christians in Rome ended Peter's life. The letter could have been written as early as the 40s or early 50s if Peter himself evangelized the regions mentioned in the letter after he left Jerusalem "for another place" (Acts 12:17). If, however, Peter was in fact aware of Paul's later letters, then 1 Peter would date no earlier than AD 60. History, however, has not preserved the date the Christian gospel came to this area, so we know only that Peter's letter to them would have followed at some later time before his death.

PLACE OF COMPOSITION AND DESTINATION

Although the NT does not mention that Peter went to Rome, there is early, strong, and uncontested Christian tradition that he resided there for a number of years, perhaps even a couple of decades. Interpreters have traditionally understood "Babylon" in 5:13 to be a veiled reference to the city of Rome as the place from which Peter wrote.

Peter wrote "to God's elect, exiles scattered throughout the [Roman] provinces of Pontus, Galatia, Cappadocia, Asia and Bithynia" (1:1; cf. Acts 2:9–11), a vast region located in much of what is now northern and western Turkey, which was known as Asia Minor when this letter was written. Rather than write to the church at a particular location, as the apostle Paul did, Peter wrote to Christians he describes as scattered exiles (i.e., in the Diaspora). Did Peter mean this to refer to their historically true situation or was this purely metaphoric? Traditionally interpreters have taken this as a metaphor referring to people who are temporarily living on earth but whose true home is in heaven. Although this is true of believers through all history, Peter must have had a certain original audience in mind who may have actually been displaced people. He may have then used their situation to explain the reality that all Christians become foreigners to this world when they are born anew into God's kingdom and live by values that make them foreigners in their own society.

If Peter had evangelized this area himself, it seems odd that his letter does not include any personal greetings or refer to individuals by name. Apparently, the readers knew Mark (5:13), which suggests personal contact. This raises the questions of how Peter knew them, why he apparently had spiritual responsibility for them, and whether he had only a general knowledge of their situation as Christians within a society that was hostile to Christian beliefs. If Peter did not have a personal relationship with the original readers, one must ask why they considered him an apostolic authority over them, unless perhaps they had come to know him as an apostle elsewhere, such as in Jerusalem, Antioch, or Rome.

OCCASION AND PURPOSE

Because the precise date of this letter is unknown and little is known about the Christians of northern Asia Minor until the early second century, the specific occasion of this letter is uncertain. If the address to the "exiles" scattered across northern Asia Minor reflects a historical situation — as opposed to expressing a metaphoric understanding of earthly life as an exile away from the believer's heavenly home — then perhaps some recent migration of Christians to those provinces may have raised the need for apostolic instruction about life in their new social setting.

Peter's immediate purpose in writing is clear: The letter is an apostolic exhortation to stand firm in the faith despite the difficult situation challenging the faith and endurance of the Christian believers, something that was apparently widespread across northern Asia Minor. Peter writes to help his readers see their new identity as part of the great covenant people of God. This connects them both to the people of ancient Israel (e.g., 2:8–10) and to believers throughout the Roman Empire at the time Peter wrote the letter (5:9). He writes further to explain why, as Christians, they have become the target of slander and social ostracism (1:6; 2:18; 4:3–4,14). Their suffering does not mean they were wrong to follow Christ. Rather, suffering for their faith confirms their identity in Christ. As they conform their lives to the example of Jesus, they should not be surprised to receive the same hostile reaction that he did. Peter then instructs his readers how to live as faithful Christians within a difficult social situation by accepting suffering as part of their calling (2:21) and living as winsome witnesses to the gospel by blessing those who insult and oppose them (3:9; cf. 2:11–15; 3:1,7).

GENRE AND STRUCTURE

The form of 1 Peter is a personal letter, and it follows the conventions of Hellenistic letters of that time: an opening statement identifying the author and original recipients, greetings, the body of the letter, and closing greetings. Because Peter mentions "scattered" in the salutation (1:1) and "Babylon" in the closing (5:13), he may have been thinking of it as a Diaspora letter, a distinctively Jewish form in which a recognized spiritual authority instructed his readers about how to live as God's holy people scattered to places that did not welcome their faith.

THEMES AND THEOLOGY

The letter has two major themes: (1) Peter wants his readers to believe rightly about Jesus Christ, specifically what has been accomplished by Jesus' death, resurrection, and ascension. (2) Peter wants his readers to live in a way that reflects their understanding of who they are because of what Jesus has accomplished for them. Because of Jesus' suffering and vindication, believers have been reborn as God's children (1:14,23) into an eternal hope (1:3) that will be fully realized when Jesus returns (1:13). What Jesus has done is the foundation of what those who follow him are to become. By coming to Christ, the living cornerstone of God's house, we are "living stones" being built into a spiritual temple in which God's presence dwells on earth (2:4–5). Once we were not a people, but now we are the chosen people of God, called to be a royal priesthood, a holy nation, and God's special possession (2:9–10).

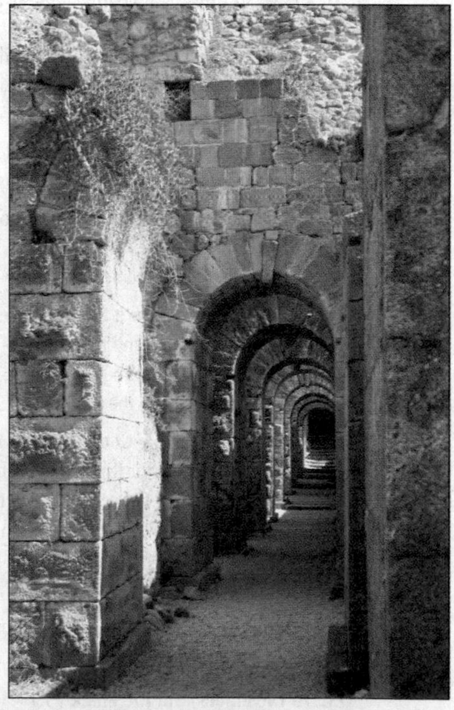

Peter portrays the Christian community as a spiritual house in which each believer takes their place (1 Pet 2:4–5).

The heart of Peter's teaching about Jesus Christ in 2:21–25 is based on the suffering servant passage in Isa 52:13—53:12. Jesus atones for the sin of others through his suffering on the cross, and he is also the victorious Savior who ascends to heaven with all authority (3:18–22). Jesus was willing to suffer to accomplish the Father's plan of salvation, and his costly obedience to God's will is the example Christians are to follow whenever they encounter insults, mockery, and other forms of opposition to their faith (3:9,17). Like Jesus, Christians must choose to suffer rather than to sin. But Jesus' suffering is not the end of his story, and it is just the beginning of ours. His death brings us to God (3:18), his resurrection gives us new birth (1:3), and his ascension assures us that even the powers of hell cannot destroy us (3:22).

Because of all that Jesus has accomplished, those who put their faith in him have a new identity with God as their Father. There is probably no more sweeping description of Christian identity than that of new birth, for it implies that a person is no longer defined by the situation into which they were physically born. But because of this new identity, Christians become foreigners and exiles in this world, called to live by the values of the heavenly Father rather than by those of the society into which they were physically born. Peter wants his readers to live as winsome witnesses to God's redemptive work in all that they do (2:12–17). But because the most basic unit of Greco-Roman society was the household, Peter gives special instructions to slaves, wives, and husbands about how to live out their Christian faith within the household in ways that will not bring shame upon the gospel (2:18—3:7).

CANONICITY

Christian writers from the late first century knew the letter of 1 Peter. Early Christian writers considered it authoritative even before there was a formal canon. Its place in the biblical canon of the universal Christian church has never been disputed.

OUTLINE

I. Salutation (1:1–2)

II. Praise to God for a Living Hope (1:3–12)
- A. Peter's Doxology (1:3–5)
- B. Suffering as Part of the Christian Life (1:6–9)
- C. The Privilege of Living in the Christian Era (1:10–12)

III. Be Holy (1:13—2:3)
- A. Be Children of the Father (1:13–21)
- B. Become What You Are (1:22—2:3)

IV. The Living Stone and a Chosen People (2:4–10)
- A. The Father's House (2:4–8)
- B. Now You Are the People of God (2:9–10)

V. Living Godly Lives in a Pagan Society (2:11—3:7)
- A. Live as Foreigners and Exiles (2:11–12)
- B. Submit to Even Pagan Authority (2:13–17)
- C. Living for Christ in the Household (2:18—3:7)

VI. Suffering for Doing Good (3:8–22)
- A. Christian Virtues for Righteous Living (3:8–12)
- B. Righteous Living Deflects Harm (3:13–17)
- C. Christ's Victory Over Unjust Suffering (3:18–22)

VII. Living for God (4:1–11)
- A. Living Out Christ's Victory (4:1–6)
- B. Living in Light of the End of All Things (4:7–11)

VIII. Suffering for Being a Christian (4:12–19)

IX. To the Elders and the Flock (5:1–11)

X. Final Greetings (5:12–14)

1 PETER

1 Peter, an apostle of Jesus Christ,[a]

To God's elect,[b] exiles scattered throughout the provinces of Pontus, Galatia, Cappadocia, Asia and
Bithynia,[c] 2 who have been chosen according to the foreknowledge[d] of God the Father, through the sanctifying work of the Spirit,[e] to be obedient to Jesus Christ and sprinkled with his blood:[f]

Grace and peace be yours in abundance.

Praise to God for a Living Hope

3 Praise be to the God and Father of our Lord Jesus Christ![g] In his great mercy[h] he has given us new
birth into a living hope through the resurrection of Jesus Christ from the dead,[i] 4 and into an inheritance that can never perish, spoil or fade. This inheritance is kept in heaven for you,[j] 5 who through

1:1 [a] 2Pe 1:1 [b] Mt 24:22 [c] Ac 16:7
1:2 [d] Ro 8:29 [e] 2Th 2:13 [f] Heb 10:22; 12:24
1:3 [g] 2Co 1:3; Eph 1:3 [h] Titus 3:5; Jas 1:18 [i] 1Co 15:20
1:4 [j] Col 1:5

1:1–2 *Salutation.* The book, in the form of a letter, begins with the author's name and addresses the original readers of the letter. This was the conventional form of personal correspondence in the Greco-Roman world. Here, however, Peter enriches the greeting with deep Christian content. The people to whom Peter writes are God's elect (i.e., chosen) exiles who are scattered across the five Roman provinces listed. Some from this area were present in Jerusalem on the day of Pentecost when Peter preached (Acts 2:9–11). All Christians, however, become spiritual exiles in this world because their new life as God's children is shaped by principles and values that earthly societies do not necessarily share.

Israel is designated as God's chosen people in the OT (Deut 4:37; 7:6–8; Ps 106:5; Isa 43:20–21; 45:4), but Peter identifies his Christian readers as God's chosen people, showing the continuity of God's work from OT into NT times. Since Peter is addressing primarily Gentile Christians, he implicitly claims that the church of Jesus Christ is the new Israel, made up of both Jewish and Gentile believers in Christ. "Scattered" (Greek *diaspora*) makes the same claim. Although the term was used to describe the scattering of the Jews in the OT (Deut 28:25; 30:4; Neh 1:9; Ps 147:2; Isa 49:6; Jer 41:17; cf. John 7:35; Jas 1:1), Peter sees a parallel in the church being literally scattered throughout the world.

1:1 Peter, an apostle of Jesus Christ. The letter's claimed author. The name Peter in its Greek form means "rock" and is the nickname Jesus gave to Simon when Simon Peter was the first of Jesus' disciples to recognize Jesus as "the Messiah, the Son of the living God" (Matt 16:16; cf. Mark 8:29; Luke 9:20). See 2 Pet 1:1.

1:2 chosen according to the foreknowledge of God the Father, through the sanctifying work of the Spirit, to be obedient to Jesus Christ. All three persons of the Godhead are involved in the redemption of God's chosen people. Using covenant language (cf. Exod 24; Mark 14:24), Peter describes his readers as those who have been chosen (1) by God's foreknowledge, (2) through the sanctifying work of the Holy Spirit, and (3) for obedience to the covenant sealed by Jesus' blood. God, according to his foreknowledge, not only has chosen the elect (Rom 8:29; Eph 1:4) but also chose Christ before the creation of the world to be the sacrificial lamb (vv. 19–20). The election of believers is achieved through the work of the Holy Spirit, who draws people to faith in Christ, seals their salvation, and empowers them to live godly lives. The Spirit does not call people to some generic spirituality; he calls them to enter into and live within the covenant that was sealed by Jesus' blood.

1:3–12 *Praise to God for a Living Hope.* Peter begins his letter with praise to God, for redemption began in the Father's love and mercy for fallen humanity. In the several verses that follow, Peter lists the blessings that have come to those who have put their faith in Jesus Christ.

1:3–5 *Peter's Doxology.* Peter begins with a doxology of praise for what God has done by raising Jesus Christ from the dead, through which God gives Christians new birth into an eternal inheritance.

1:3 new birth. A sweeping concept alluding to the identity, citizenship, socioeconomic class, and innate potential that people receive at birth. New birth implies that Christians have a new identity and character that redefines their relationship with God and with society. Peter looks to what God has already done by raising Jesus from the dead (v. 3), to the present preservation of those who are God's (v. 5), and to the future inheritance when salvation is fully revealed (v. 5).

1:4 kept in heaven for you. This inheritance is guarded in heaven, and as such it is untouched by troubles in this life.

1:5 who through faith are shielded by God's power. God himself not only keeps this inheritance but also guards those for whom he has prepared salvation.

1:5 [k]Jn 10:28
1:6 [l]Ro 5:2 [m]1Pe 5:10 [n]Jas 1:2
1:7 [o]Jas 1:3 [p]Job 23:10; Ps 66:10; Pr 17:3 [q]Ro 2:7
1:8 [r]Jn 20:29
1:9 [s]Ro 6:22
1:10 [t]Mt 26:24 [u]Mt 13:17
1:11 [v]2Pe 1:21
1:12 [w]ver 25
1:14 [x]Ro 12:2

faith are shielded by God's power[k] until the coming of the salvation that is ready to be revealed in the
last time. 6In all this you greatly rejoice,[l] though now for a little while[m] you may have had to suffer
grief in all kinds of trials.[n] 7These have come so that the proven genuineness[o] of your faith — of greater
worth than gold, which perishes even though refined by fire[p] — may result in praise, glory and honor
when Jesus Christ is revealed.[q] 8Though you have not seen him, you love him; and even though you do
not see him now, you believe in him[r] and are filled with an inexpressible and glorious joy, 9for you are
receiving the end result of your faith, the salvation of your souls.[s]

10Concerning this salvation, the prophets, who spoke[t] of the grace that was to come to you, searched
intently and with the greatest care,[u] 11trying to find out the time and circumstances to which the Spirit
of Christ[v] in them was pointing when he predicted the sufferings of the Messiah and the glories that
would follow. 12It was revealed to them that they were not serving themselves but you, when they spoke
of the things that have now been told you by those who have preached the gospel to you[w] by the Holy
Spirit sent from heaven. Even angels long to look into these things.

Be Holy

13Therefore, with minds that are alert and fully sober, set your hope on the grace to be brought to
you when Jesus Christ is revealed at his coming. 14As obedient children, do not conform[x] to the evil

1:6–9 *Suffering as Part of the Christian Life.* Some people believe that it is God's responsibility to prevent bad things from happening, and often this expectation is disappointed. Embracing the Christian faith does not provide an insurance policy against the suffering that is common to human existence. The profession of faith in Christ may in some situations cause suffering. And there is one form of suffering that God expects of his people — when suffering is necessary to avoid sinning.

1:6 suffer grief in all kinds of trials. Because of their new birth, Christian believers are to have different values, allegiances, and privileges — these bring great joy but also may cause believers to experience hardship within their society.

1:7 the proven genuineness of your faith. When Peter's readers suffer without sinning, their faith, like gold, is purified as it is tested. Suffering because one believes in Christ proves the genuineness of one's faith and the certainty of one's salvation, which is the reason for joy. **may result in praise, glory and honor when Jesus Christ is revealed.** For Peter, conversion is an event that has already happened in the lives of his readers, but their full salvation is a future event not fully realized until Jesus returns.

1:9 the salvation of your souls. Does not exclude the body, but refers to the whole person.

1:10–12 *The Privilege of Living in the Christian Era.* Jesus Christ as the giver of eternal life is God's fullest and final revelation of himself. This means that for most of human history, people who turned to God, such as the prophets, had only intriguing hints of what God would one day fully reveal. Although there is much wonder about the second coming of Christ, God has fully revealed all that we need to know of him for this life. God's redemption of humankind is even of great interest to the angels. To live in this era with full access to the gospel is indeed a profound privilege!

1:10 prophets ... searched intently. Even though the prophets were inspired, they were not omniscient, and there is much that we now know that they wished to know.

1:11 the Spirit of Christ. Christianity was not a new, upstart religion but rather the culmination of God's plan from the beginning of time. For it was the Spirit of Christ who inspired the prophets of the OT, such as Isaiah (e.g., Isa 52:13 — 53:12), when they foresaw "the sufferings of the Messiah and the glories that would follow." The suffering of the Messiah is a theme that runs through the Bible (e.g., Ps 22; Zech 9:9–10; 13:7; Matt 16:21–27; 17:22–23; 20:18–19; Luke 24:26,46; John 2:19; Acts 3:17–21; Phil 2:5–11; 1 Tim 3:16; cf. Luke 9:26; 21:27), and it is the most prominent point about Jesus Christ in this letter (vv. 18–21; 3:17–22; 4:12–16; 5:1,4,9–10). Those who follow in the footsteps of Christ (2:21) should also expect to suffer for their obedience to God, but after suffering, they will enter into glory as Jesus did. Any present suffering becomes more bearable knowing the certainty of the hope that lies ahead (3:21–22).

1:12 things that have now been told you by those who have preached the gospel to you by the Holy Spirit sent from heaven. The apostle Peter was present on the day of Pentecost when the Holy Spirit descended on the infant church (Acts 2:1,32–33). Since that time Christians enjoy a privileged position, because we who have received the gospel have knowledge of the very things the ancient prophets searched intently to understand. The prophecies of old were written to confirm the gospel once God had sent his Son. The sufferings and glories of Christ are of great interest even to the angels. Although Peter's readers were being ostracized by their society because of the gospel, they nevertheless enjoyed, as do all Christians since, a very privileged status in comparison to the prophets and angels.

1:13 — 2:3 *Be Holy.* Because Christians have been given new birth into a new life, we must change the way we think and live to reflect the character of our divine Father. The old way of life is useless (1:18) and our new life was purchased with the precious blood of Jesus (1:19). Because that which people believe about the future determines how they live in the present, Peter exhorts his readers to set their minds on the grace that is yet to come (1:13), to live holy lives (1:15), and to love one another deeply (1:22) as they rid themselves of the attitudes and behaviors that destroy the bonds of community (2:1–3).

1:13–21 *Be Children of the Father.* There is an old saying: "Like father, like son." Because Christians have been born again of God the Father, Peter exhorts them to be obedient children who bear a family resemblance to God.

1:13 with minds that are alert. The Greek is "gird the loins of your mind." In the idiom of that time, a man had to gather up his long garments so he could work or run unhindered (cf. Heb 12:1). In order to live rightly, Christians must learn to think differently than in the past when they did not know Christ. This is the first of a long series of exhortations that extends through 5:11.

1:14 As obedient children. Peter continues the theme of the new birth by referring to those who have been given new birth as children of God the Father (cf. Matt 6:9). According to the NT, while all people are God's creatures, only those who come to faith in Christ are considered his children.

desires you had when you lived in ignorance.[y] 15 But just as he who called you is holy, so be holy in all
you do;[z] 16 for it is written: "Be holy, because I am holy."[a][a]
17 Since you call on a Father who judges each person's work impartially,[b] live out your time as foreigners here in reverent fear.[c] 18 For you know that it was not with perishable things such as silver or
gold that you were redeemed[d] from the empty way of life handed down to you from your ancestors,
19 but with the precious blood of Christ, a lamb[e] without blemish or defect.[f] 20 He was chosen before the
creation of the world,[g] but was revealed in these last times[h] for your sake. 21 Through him you believe
in God,[i] who raised him from the dead and glorified him, and so your faith and hope are in God.
22 Now that you have purified[j] yourselves by obeying the truth so that you have sincere love for each
other, love one another deeply,[k] from the heart.[b] 23 For you have been born again,[l] not of perishable
seed, but of imperishable, through the living and enduring word of God.[m] 24 For,

> "All people are like grass,
> and all their glory is like the flowers of the field;
> the grass withers and the flowers fall,
> 25 but the word of the Lord endures forever."[c][n]

And this is the word that was preached to you.

2 Therefore, rid yourselves[o] of all malice and all deceit, hypocrisy, envy, and slander[p] of every kind.
2 Like newborn babies, crave pure spiritual milk,[q] so that by it you may grow up[r] in your salvation,
3 now that you have tasted that the Lord is good.[s]

The Living Stone and a Chosen People

4 As you come to him, the living Stone[t]—rejected by humans but chosen by God and precious
to him— 5 you also, like living stones, are being built[u] into a spiritual house[d][v] to be a holy

1:14 [y] Eph 4:18
1:15 [z] 2Co 7:1; 1Th 4:7
1:16 [a] Lev 11:44,45
1:17 [b] Ac 10:34 [c] Heb 12:28
1:18 [d] Mt 20:28; 1Co 6:20
1:19 [e] Jn 1:29 [f] Ex 12:5
1:20 [g] Eph 1:4 [h] Heb 9:26
1:21 [i] Ro 4:24
1:22 [j] Jas 4:8 [k] Jn 13:34; Heb 13:1
1:23 [l] Jn 1:13 [m] Heb 4:12
1:25 [n] Isa 40:6-8
2:1 [o] Eph 4:22 [p] Jas 4:11
2:2 [q] 1Co 3:2 [r] Eph 4:15,16
2:3 [s] Heb 6:5
2:4 [t] ver 7
2:5 [u] 1Co 3:9 [v] 1Ti 3:15

[a] *16* Lev. 11:44,45; 19:2 [b] *22* Some early manuscripts *from a pure heart* [c] *25* Isaiah 40:6-8 (see Septuagint) [d] *5* Or *into a temple of the Spirit*

1:15–16 Be holy ... because I am holy. A way of saying that children of God should bear a family likeness to the character of their heavenly Father (Lev 11:44–45; 19:2; 20:7). God's character was revealed in the OT as the basis of human morality and ethics (Exod 20:1–17; Deut 5:1–22). But the fullest and final revelation of God's character is seen in Jesus Christ (John 1:18; Col 1:15; Heb 1:3). Christians are not expected to be like God in his deity but are to strive for human righteousness as demonstrated by Jesus. This call to holiness means that Christians will set themselves apart from the customs and values of their unbelieving society to live by the character and teachings of Jesus, no longer allowing their previous unbelief to define them.

1:17 a Father who judges each person's work impartially. A caution against thinking that God will overlook the sin of his children when they continue to live as the world lives without reverent fear of him. **reverent fear.** Proper respect for and deference to God, which is necessary for godly living.

1:18–19 you were redeemed ... with the precious blood of Christ. In the Bible, redemption refers to freedom gained by payment of a penalty or ransom (see, e.g., Exod 13:13; 21:30). The OT sacrifices foreshadowed the ultimate and true sacrifice of the Son of God, who redeems believers from the curse of the law, which is death (Gal 3:13), and from all wickedness (Titus 2:14). Our redemption was purchased not with money, but with Jesus' blood, i.e., by his death (Matt 20:28; Mark 10:45; John 1:29; 1 Cor 5:7; Eph 1:7; Heb 9:15; Rev 5:9).

1:20 He was chosen. God planned for redemption even before he created the world. He knew ahead of time that Christ's death would redeem his people just as God foreknew those who would be redeemed by it (see v. 2 and note). **last times.** See Acts 2:17; 1 Tim 4:1; 2 Tim 3:1; Heb 1:1–2; 1 John 2:18. **for your sake.** Christ did not come into the world for his own pleasure or self-interest (Matt 20:28; Mark 10:45); he came for the sake of the lost and fallen human race.

1:22—2:3 *Become What You Are.* Because a Christian is someone who has been born of God the Father and has the Holy Spirit within, Peter expects a transformation of character that is expressed in love for others. Such love is expressed by putting off all the things that damage our relationships with others.

1:22 you have purified yourselves ... you have sincere love. Obeying the truth of the gospel of Jesus Christ requires a moral transformation that means believers are to love each other sincerely (John 13:34–35; Rom 12:9; 1 Thess 4:9–10). This does not denote emotional sentimentality, but entails relating to each other in ways that honor God.

1:23 perishable seed ... imperishable. The conception of the new life that believers enjoy through the word of God, which is living and enduring. Human fathers conceive life that is mortal and will die, but because God is eternal, the life that he conceives is imperishable and eternal.

2:1 Therefore, rid yourselves. Because the Christian's new life is to reflect the character of the heavenly Father, believers must end "all malice and all deceit, hypocrisy, envy, and slander"—things that are the opposite of sincere love.

2:2 Like newborn babies, crave pure spiritual milk. Instead of continuing in old vices, Christians are to crave what nourishes spiritual growth for themselves and others.

2:3 now that you have tasted. An allusion to Ps 34:8, which also speaks of the Lord delivering the righteous in their sufferings. Cf. 3:10–12; Ps 34:12–13.

2:4–10 *The Living Stone and a Chosen People.* After describing the new birth and the moral transformation of character necessary to sustain the new life in Christ, Peter presents an image of a spiritual house, or temple, with Jesus Christ as the foundational cornerstone into which believers are being built. Peter takes the stone imagery from the OT (Ps 118:22–23; Isa 8:14–15; 28:16), applies it to Jesus (cf. 1:11), and uses terms that previously described the OT people of God to refer to Christians (v. 9).

2:4–8 *The Father's House.* The Greek word translated "house" provides

2:5 [w] Isa 61:6 [x] Php 4:18; Heb 13:15
2:6 [y] Eph 2:20 [z] Isa 28:16
2:7 [a] 2Co 2:16 [b] Ps 118:22
2:8 [c] Isa 8:14; 1Co 1:23 [d] Ro 9:22
2:9 [e] Dt 10:15 [f] Isa 62:12

priesthood,[w] offering spiritual sacrifices acceptable to God through Jesus Christ.[x] 6 For in Scripture
it says:

> "See, I lay a stone in Zion,
> a chosen and precious cornerstone,[y]
> and the one who trusts in him
> will never be put to shame."[az]

7 Now to you who believe, this stone is precious. But to those who do not believe,[a]

> "The stone the builders rejected
> has become the cornerstone,"[bb]

8 and,

> "A stone that causes people to stumble
> and a rock that makes them fall."[cc]

They stumble because they disobey the message—which is also what they were destined for.[d]
9 But you are a chosen people,[e] a royal priesthood, a holy nation,[f] God's special possession, that you

[a] 6 Isaiah 28:16 [b] 7 Psalm 118:22 [c] 8 Isaiah 8:14

a wonderful play on words. It can refer to a physical building or (in reference to a deity) a temple, as well as a household or family. Christian believers constitute the family of God by virtue of their new birth (1:3). Peter refers to "living stones" (see v. 5 and note) to evoke the image of a building in which God dwells, with each believer taking their place in it.
2:4 the living Stone. The resurrected Christ, who is himself alive forevermore and the giver of life to those who believe that he is the Son of God who atoned for sin.
2:5 living stones ... being built into a spiritual house. An image of Christian believers taking their places in God's great project of redemption. The placement of the living stones with the living Stone shows the close relationship between believers and Jesus Christ and their shared nature as human beings. The living stones are not isolated, heaped in a pile, or scattered across a field; each stone takes its place in the design of the Father's spiritual house. As living stones within a spiritual house, believers are unified, each is significant, and each has a purpose. The Holy Spirit, who has given life to the living stones, also indwells the spiritual house. The OT temple is the background for this metaphor, for the temple was the place of God's presence and of proper worship.

First Peter refers to Jesus as the cornerstone (1 Pet 2:6).

Animals were sacrificed in the OT temple, but in this spiritual house, believers form a priesthood that offers "spiritual sacrifices acceptable to God" (cf. Rom 12:1). **priesthood.** The priesthood of all believers is not a reference to ecclesial authority. Rather, believers are to (1) reflect the holiness of God and that of their high priest (1:15; Heb 7:26; 10:10), (2) offer spiritual sacrifices (here; Rom 12:1; Heb 13:15; the NT also refers to offerings that include money or material goods [Phil 4:18; Heb 13:16]), (3) intercede for others before God (Rom 12:12; 15:30–31; Eph 6:18; Col 4:2; 1 Thess 5:17; 1 Tim 2:1; Jas 5:16; Rev 5:8; 8:3–4), and (4) represent God to others (2:12; Acts 13:47; Rom 15:9,16).
2:6 a chosen and precious cornerstone. Christ (Matt 21:42; Mark 12:10; Luke 20:17; Acts 4:11). The cornerstone was the most important stone in an ancient building, it was the first stone to be set in the foundation, and all other blocks were plumbed to it. Believers take their place in God's spiritual house by squaring their lives to the plans and purposes of Christ.
2:7 The stone the builders rejected has become the cornerstone. Quotes Ps 118:22 to show that Christ is rejected by many who mistakenly think they are building for God, and as a result of their rejection, they stumble and fall. See note on v. 8.
2:8 they were destined for. Some read this to mean that although stumbling is inevitable because of disbelief, God does not cause people to disbelieve. Others argue that God does cause people to disbelieve. What is clear is that disbelieving the gospel message leads to a downfall.
2:9–10 *Now You Are the People of God.* Those who have put their faith in Christ have the privilege of being counted among the people of God. Peter refers to Christians in words that previously described only God's chosen nation of ancient Israel.
2:9 a chosen people, a royal priesthood, a holy nation, God's special possession. Peter continues to describe his Christian readers in terms the OT uses only for the ancient nation of Israel. "Chosen," "royal," and "holy" describe collectively the nature of the relationship between Christian believers and God. **a chosen people.** See Isa 43:10,20–21; see also Eph 1:4 and note. All who believe in Christ—whether Jew or Gentile, regardless of nationality or ethnicity—make up the chosen people. **a royal priesthood, a holy nation, God's special possession.** See Exod 19:5–6. As God's royal priesthood, all Christians are to be holy and set apart for the Lord's service as priests were expected to be in the ancient world. Regardless of one's nationality by birth, Christians, by new birth, form a new nation in the world that is set apart for God (Mark

may declare the praises of him who called you out of darkness into his wonderful light.[g] [10]Once you
were not a people, but now you are the people of God;[h] once you had not received mercy, but now you
have received mercy.

Living Godly Lives in a Pagan Society

[11]Dear friends, I urge you, as foreigners and exiles, to abstain from sinful desires,[i] which wage war
against your soul.[j] [12]Live such good lives among the pagans that, though they accuse you of doing
wrong, they may see your good deeds[k] and glorify God[l] on the day he visits us.
[13]Submit yourselves for the Lord's sake to every human authority:[m] whether to the emperor, as the
supreme authority, [14]or to governors, who are sent by him to punish those who do wrong[n] and to commend those who do right.[o] [15]For it is God's will[p] that by doing good you should silence the ignorant talk
of foolish people.[q] [16]Live as free people,[r] but do not use your freedom as a cover-up for evil; live as God's
slaves.[s] [17]Show proper respect to everyone, love the family of believers,[t] fear God, honor the emperor.[u]
[18]Slaves, in reverent fear of God submit yourselves to your masters,[v] not only to those who are good
and considerate,[w] but also to those who are harsh. [19]For it is commendable if someone bears up under
the pain of unjust suffering because they are conscious of God.[x] [20]But how is it to your credit if you
receive a beating for doing wrong and endure it? But if you suffer for doing good and you endure it,
this is commendable before God.[y] [21]To this[z] you were called, because Christ suffered for you, leaving
you an example,[a] that you should follow in his steps.

2:9 [g]Ac 26:18
2:10 [h]Hos 1:9,10
2:11 [i]Gal 5:16 [j]Jas 4:1
2:12 [k]Php 2:15; 1Pe 3:16 [l]Mt 5:16; 9:8
2:13 [m]Ro 13:1
2:14 [n]Ro 13:4 [o]Ro 13:3
2:15 [p]1Pe 3:17 [q]ver 12
2:16 [r]Jn 8:32 [s]Ro 6:22
2:17 [t]Ro 12:10 [u]Ro 13:7
2:18 [v]Eph 6:5 [w]Jas 3:17
2:19 [x]1Pe 3:14,17
2:20 [y]1Pe 3:17
2:21 [z]Ac 14:22 [a]Mt 16:24

12:17). This holy nation is "God's special possession" in a way that the rest of humankind is not (Deut 4:20; 7:6; 14:2; Isa 43:20–21; Mal 3:17). Christians are set apart to declare the praises of God in a world that rejects him, and they are in some times and places despised for it.
2:10 now you are the people … now you have received mercy. See Hos 1:6,9; 2:1,23; Rom 9:25–26. A distinctive characteristic of God's people is that they have accepted the mercy God offers in Christ.
2:11—3:7 *Living Godly Lives in a Pagan Society.* After describing the new identity of his Christian readers, Peter exhorts them to be faithful and winsome witnesses to the truth of the gospel by living in ways that do not unnecessarily offend the ethical and moral expectations of their society.
2:11–12 *Live as Foreigners and Exiles.* Peter is concerned that Christians live in a way that will not bring unnecessary suspicions about the gospel. He wants pagan neighbors to recognize his readers as good people as far as possible without disobeying the Lord.
2:11 foreigners and exiles. They typically abstained from participating in the customs and practices of their host culture, and they had neither the privileges nor the responsibilities of citizens. This phrase suggests that Christians should abstain from the customs and practices of unbelievers and live instead by values and practices of the holy nation.
2:12 see your good deeds. By God's common grace, not all Christian practices and values are the opposite of social expectations. When Christians do good deeds, unbelievers understand better the transforming grace of the gospel (3:16). **on the day he visits us.** See Luke 19:44. May refer to the future day of judgment when Christ returns or to the day when God visits a person through an encounter with the gospel. In either case, the winsome witness of Christians may influence unbelievers to repent and believe.
2:13–17 *Submit to Even Pagan Authority.* Peter's readers were to think of themselves as foreigners in their society, but that didn't mean they could disrespect and disobey the authorities who governed it. Peter's concern here is primarily for the witness and well-being of the infant church.
2:13 Peter exhorts his readers to submit to the authorities "for the Lord's sake" so that any talk of following Christ as treasonous or socially disruptive might be silenced. How we live as Christians influences what others think of God and Christianity.
2:16 Live as free people … live as God's slaves. People freed by the gospel freely submit to the authority of earthly institutions as long as such submission does not conflict with God's authority. Genuine freedom is freedom from the tyranny of sin (John 8:36; Acts 13:39).
2:17 Show proper respect to everyone. Implies that every person is due respect as a bearer of God's image, but expressing respect should be done in a way appropriate for Christians. **honor the emperor.** At this time the Roman emperor may have been the cruel and godless Nero, who ruled AD 54–68. Tradition says the apostle Peter was executed by Nero.
2:18—3:7 *Living for Christ in the Household.* After giving instructions about how Christians are to submit to their wider society, Peter continues to discuss how Christians are to live as winsome witnesses among the unbelievers in their households. Greco-Roman culture considered the family household to be the foundational unit of society and civilization. New religions were often suspected of having a corrupting influence on the family. Peter wants Christians to live within their households in ways that do not provoke unnecessary accusations against Christianity. At the same time, the gospel subverts the expectations of social order even within the household. Peter addresses both the slave and the wife as responsible moral agents, granting them more dignity and standing than was typically given in the Greco-Roman world. Jesus' endurance in obedience to God despite undeserved suffering is the example for all Christian relationships.
2:18 Slaves … submit yourselves to your masters. By addressing Christian slaves directly as free moral agents, Peter dignifies the most vulnerable members of Greco-Roman society. In general, all Christian believers in the Greco-Roman world lost social status because of their faith in Christ, and so slaves, since they had the least social status and power of all, were fitting models for all. Even the most socially prominent believer must live as a slave to God, obeying him in every aspect of life, even at the risk of lost social standing.
2:19 bears up under the pain of unjust suffering. Slaves who had come to faith in Christ were in a difficult situation because slaves were expected to participate in the religion of their masters. Even though they may have been in a situation of unjust suffering, Christian slaves were to submit to their masters, except where doing so would violate their faith in Christ. **conscious of God.** A Christian's relationship with God should motivate all that they do (v. 13; Eph 6:7–8.)
2:21 To this you were called. Unjust suffering because of faith in Christ is part of the Christian's calling. **Christ suffered for you.** The Son of God became the suffering servant (i.e., slave) of Isa 52:13—53:12 in

2:22 [b]Isa 53:9
2:23 [c]Isa 53:7 [d]Lk 23:46
2:24 [e]Heb 9:28 [f]Ro 6:2 [g]Isa 53:5; Heb 12:13; Jas 5:16
2:25 [h]Isa 53:6 [i]Jn 10:11
3:1 [j]1Pe 2:18 [k]Eph 5:22 [l]1Co 7:16; 9:19
3:3 [m]Isa 3:18-23; 1Ti 2:9
3:4 [n]Ro 7:22
3:5 [o]1Ti 5:5
3:6 [p]Ge 18:12
3:7 [q]Eph 5:25-33
3:8 [r]Ro 12:10 [s]1Pe 5:5
3:9 [t]Ro 12:17 [u]1Pe 2:23 [v]1Pe 2:21 [w]Heb 6:14

22 "He committed no sin,
and no deceit was found in his mouth."[a][b]

23 When they hurled their insults at him, he did not retaliate; when he suffered, he made no threats.[c]
Instead, he entrusted himself[d] to him who judges justly. 24 "He himself bore our sins"[e] in his body
on the cross, so that we might die to sins[f] and live for righteousness; "by his wounds you have been
healed."[g] 25 For "you were like sheep going astray,"[b][h] but now you have returned to the Shepherd[i] and
Overseer of your souls.

3 Wives, in the same way submit yourselves[j] to your own husbands[k] so that, if any of them do not
believe the word, they may be won over[l] without words by the behavior of their wives, 2 when they
see the purity and reverence of your lives. 3 Your beauty should not come from outward adornment, such
as elaborate hairstyles and the wearing of gold jewelry or fine clothes.[m] 4 Rather, it should be that of
your inner self,[n] the unfading beauty of a gentle and quiet spirit, which is of great worth in God's sight.
5 For this is the way the holy women of the past who put their hope in God[o] used to adorn themselves.
They submitted themselves to their own husbands, 6 like Sarah, who obeyed Abraham and called him
her lord.[p] You are her daughters if you do what is right and do not give way to fear.
7 Husbands,[q] in the same way be considerate as you live with your wives, and treat them with respect
as the weaker partner and as heirs with you of the gracious gift of life, so that nothing will hinder
your prayers.

Suffering for Doing Good

8 Finally, all of you, be like-minded, be sympathetic, love one another,[r] be compassionate and humble.[s] 9 Do not repay evil with evil[t] or insult with insult.[u] On the contrary, repay evil with blessing, because
to this[v] you were called so that you may inherit a blessing.[w] 10 For,

[a] *22* Isaiah 53:9 [b] *24,25* Isaiah 53:4,5,6 (see Septuagint)

order to accomplish the Father's purposes. Christ's willingness to suffer rather than disobey God is the example for all Christians. Vicarious atonement does not mean that because Jesus suffered, his followers don't have to. **follow in his steps.** The footsteps of Jesus lead through suffering and death, but they don't stop at the grave. They lead us on to eternal glory with God.

2:22–25 These verses quote and allude to the suffering servant of Isa 52:13—53:12, a prophecy of Jesus' suffering. Christ is the ultimate example of suffering for doing good. He was sinless but nevertheless suffered insults, wounds, and death. Jesus' redemptive death cannot be repeated or imitated, but his example of entrusting himself to God rather than retaliating is an example Peter wants his readers to follow when they suffer unjustly.

2:24 in his body on the cross. Atonement for our sins was achieved by Jesus' suffering and death on the cross, not by his teachings or even his miracles (3:18). **that we might die to sins.** The purpose of Jesus' atoning death is that we might stop sinning, not that we might continue to sin with a false sense of well-being.

2:25 like sheep going astray ... you have returned to the Shepherd. The image of people in need of God as sheep who need a shepherd arises here in connection with the wandering sheep of Isa 53:6 (cf. Ps 23:1; John 10:11,14; Heb 13:20). Jesus' request of Peter to care for his sheep in their final conversation (John 21:15–17) no doubt made a lasting impression on Peter's thinking.

3:1 Wives, in the same way. Peter dignifies women by directly addressing wives and acknowledging them as free moral agents. As all believers are to submit to authority in reverent fear of God (2:13–17), a wife's submission is motivated by her relationship to God. **submit yourselves to your own husbands.** Christian wives should submit even to unbelieving husbands unless doing so would violate obedience to Christ (Gen 3:16; 1 Cor 11:3; Eph 5:22–24; Col 3:18; Titus 2:5). In Greco-Roman society, wives were expected to follow the religion of their husbands. But Peter subverts that expectation by instructing wives on how their unbelieving husbands "may be won over without words."

3:3 elaborate hairstyles and the wearing of gold jewelry or fine clothes. See 1 Tim 2:9. Peter does not forbid wearing fine clothing, jewelry, and going to the salon, but a Christian woman must recognize that the true source of her beauty in God's sight is her inner spirit. In Greco-Roman society, extreme coiffures and excessive jewelry were stylish. Now, as then, Christ transforms a woman's self-image from what society tells her is beautiful to what is beautiful in God's sight.

3:7 Husbands, in the same way. While Peter's words to Christian husbands are brief, they were subversive in first-century society. Rather than lording it over his wife, a husband must be "considerate," living with her in reverent fear of God (2:17–18). This entails treating her with respect and acknowledging her as a spiritual equal. **weaker partner.** This refers primarily to a woman's physical weakness relative to a man's strength, not her moral character or mental capacity. A Christian man who lives in reverent fear of God will not beat or otherwise abuse a woman into submission. **heirs with you of the gracious gift of life.** Women and men share equally in the saving grace of God (Gal 3:28). **so that nothing will hinder your prayers.** A Christian man's relationship with God is hindered if he fails to live with his wife in a godly way.

3:8–22 *Suffering for Doing Good.* Almost everyone suffers at some point in life, and many eventually ask, "Why me?" Suffering that one brings on oneself is understandable (4:15), but it is spiritually confusing when innocent and even righteous people suffer (see the book of Job). Peter addresses a particular kind of suffering that is unique to Christians who, through either the misunderstanding or malice of others, become targets of various forms of persecution because of their faith in Christ.

3:8–12 *Christian Virtues for Righteous Living.* Christian character must consist of virtues that build and sustain community, even when the wider society does not value those virtues. This is true especially in times and places where the dominant society is suspicious of or hostile to the Christian faith and Christians therefore become the victims of

"Whoever would love life
and see good days
must keep their tongue from evil
and their lips from deceitful speech.
11 They must turn from evil and do good;
they must seek peace and pursue it.
12 For the eyes of the Lord are on the righteous
and his ears are attentive to their prayer,
but the face of the Lord is against those who do evil."[a][x]

13 Who is going to harm you if you are eager to do good?[y] 14 But even if you should suffer for what
is right, you are blessed.[z] "Do not fear their threats[b]; do not be frightened."[c][a] 15 But in your hearts revere Christ as Lord. Always be prepared to give an answer[b] to everyone who asks you to give the reason
for the hope that you have. But do this with gentleness and respect, 16 keeping a clear conscience,[c] so
that those who speak maliciously against your good behavior in Christ may be ashamed of their slander.[d] 17 For it is better, if it is God's will,[e] to suffer for doing good[f] than for doing evil. 18 For Christ also
suffered once for sins,[g] the righteous for the unrighteous, to bring you to God. He was put to death in
the body[h] but made alive in the Spirit.[i] 19 After being made alive,[d] he went and made proclamation to
the imprisoned spirits[j] — 20 to those who were disobedient long ago when God waited patiently in the
days of Noah while the ark was being built.[k] In it only a few people, eight in all, were saved[l] through
water, 21 and this water symbolizes baptism that now saves you[m] also — not the removal of dirt from
the body but the pledge of a clear conscience toward God.[e] It saves you by the resurrection of Jesus

3:12 [x] Ps 34:12-16
3:13 [y] Pr 16:7
3:14 [z] 1Pe 2:19,20; 4:15,16 [a] Isa 8:12,13
3:15 [b] Col 4:6
3:16 [c] Heb 13:18 [d] 1Pe 2:12,15
3:17 [e] 1Pe 2:15 [f] 1Pe 2:20
3:18 [g] 1Pe 2:21 [h] Col 1:22; 1Pe 4:1 [i] 1Pe 4:6
3:19 [j] 1Pe 4:6
3:20 [k] Ge 6:3,5,13,14 [l] Heb 11:7
3:21 [m] Titus 3:5

[a] *12* Psalm 34:12-16 [b] *14* Or *fear what they fear* [c] *14* Isaiah 8:12 [d] *18,19* Or *but made alive in the spirit, 19 in which also* [e] *21* Or *but an appeal to God for a clear conscience*

undeserved insult and evil, as they were at the time Peter wrote this letter.

3:8 be like-minded, be sympathetic, love one another, be compassionate and humble. Peter mentions five qualities that are hallmarks of a healthy Christian community, and each quality is necessary to preserve Christian community. Like-minded people share religious beliefs and ethical practices, which produce cohesion within a group. Right beliefs about Jesus Christ and the ethical system that flows from those beliefs are foundational for Christianity as a whole and for healthy local churches. Some societies value understanding, love, compassion, and humility differently than others. For instance, first-century Roman society disdained humility as an expression of weakness. But Jesus Christ humbled himself to serve others — even to death — not because he was weak, but precisely because he is the most exalted and powerful human being. Christians should do likewise, even when such values conflict with social expectations.

3:9 evil with evil or insult with insult. When someone is the target of evil or insult, perhaps the most natural reaction is to retaliate. Certain religious groups even approve such retaliation. A Christian not only refrains from retaliating in kind but repays evil and insult with blessing. Just as God extends grace to a rebellious world that does not deserve it, Christians are to respond graciously even to those who oppose them (2:23; Rom 12:17 – 21).

3:13 – 17 *Righteous Living Deflects Harm.* Peter apparently sees enough common ground between the values of society in first-century Asia Minor and those of the Christian life that he can exhort his readers to do good with the expectation that they will not suffer for it. The potential of suffering for one's Christian faith is not necessarily a universal and inevitable reality of living for Christ.

3:16 ashamed of their slander. Baseless slander will ultimately be shown to be untrue, and the believer's loving attitude shows the opponent's attitude toward the Christian to be wrong.

3:17 if it is God's will. God does not take pleasure when his people suffer, but it is his will that they do what is right, even if suffering is the result.

3:18 – 22 *Christ's Victory Over Unjust Suffering.* Christ has defeated the power of evil by submitting to it in his death on the cross and then conquering it by the power of his resurrection and ascension. In the end he will destroy all who persist in evil without repentance. Therefore, it is ultimately better to suffer for doing good than to be destroyed as one who practices evil. The unjust suffering that Christians experience is not the final word since Christ has vindicated them.

3:18 put to death in the body. That is, in the realm of this life. **but made alive in the Spirit.** When Christ was raised from the grave, he inaugurated a new state of human existence, the realm of the Spirit that lies beyond this life. However, the benefits of eternal life can be enjoyed to some extent even now.

3:19 – 20a These difficult verses have been understood in three very different ways. Traditionally they have been used to support the idea that Jesus descended into hell on the Saturday between his crucifixion and resurrection — when his body was dead but his spirit remained alive (v. 18). At that time he preached either to the souls of people who were disobedient in the days of Noah or to fallen angels who had incited humans to such evil that God sent the flood at the time of Noah to destroy it (Gen 6:1 – 7). A second view is that the preincarnate Christ preached through Noah to the wicked generation destroyed by the flood. A third view is that Christ's resurrection and ascension were the proclamation of victory over the most extreme powers of evil the earth has ever known, which these "imprisoned spirits" represent. With Jesus' victory over death, their condemnation was sealed.

3:20b only a few people ... were saved. The Noahic flood was the most severe judgment the earth has known because of the severe evil of the time. Yet in his mercy, God did not destroy the human race completely. The entire human race deserves to perish in sin, but God will save those who accept his mercy.

3:21 this water symbolizes baptism that now saves you. Baptism saves only in the sense that it represents what Christ has achieved. The waters of the Noahic flood symbolize baptism, and baptism is the sign and seal of salvation "by the resurrection of Jesus Christ" (see Rom 6:4). **the pledge of a clear conscience.** Baptism is not merely a religious

3:21 [n]1Pe 1:3
3:22 [o]Mk 16:19 [p]Ro 8:38
4:2 [q]Ro 6:2
4:3 [r]Eph 2:2
4:4 [s]1Pe 3:16
4:5 [t]Ac 10:42; 2Ti 4:1
4:6 [u]1Pe 3:19
4:7 [v]Ro 13:11
4:8 [w]1Pe 1:22 [x]Pr 10:12
4:9 [y]Php 2:14
4:10 [z]Ro 12:6,7 [a]1Co 4:2
4:11 [b]Eph 6:10 [c]1Co 10:31
4:12 [d]1Pe 1:6,7

Christ,[n] [22]who has gone into heaven and is at God's right hand[o] — with angels, authorities and powers
in submission to him.[p]

Living for God

4 Therefore, since Christ suffered in his body, arm yourselves also with the same attitude, because
whoever suffers in the body is done with sin. [2]As a result, they do not live the rest of their earthly
lives for evil human desires,[q] but rather for the will of God. [3]For you have spent enough time in the
past[r] doing what pagans choose to do — living in debauchery, lust, drunkenness, orgies, carousing
and detestable idolatry. [4]They are surprised that you do not join them in their reckless, wild living, and
they heap abuse on you.[s] [5]But they will have to give account to him who is ready to judge the living
and the dead.[t] [6]For this is the reason the gospel was preached even to those who are now dead,[u] so that
they might be judged according to human standards in regard to the body, but live according to God
in regard to the spirit.

[7]The end of all things is near.[v] Therefore be alert and of sober mind so that you may pray. [8]Above
all, love each other deeply,[w] because love covers over a multitude of sins.[x] [9]Offer hospitality to one another without grumbling.[y] [10]Each of you should use whatever gift you have received to serve others,[z]
as faithful[a] stewards of God's grace in its various forms. [11]If anyone speaks, they should do so as one
who speaks the very words of God. If anyone serves, they should do so with the strength God provides,[b]
so that in all things God may be praised[c] through Jesus Christ. To him be the glory and the power for
ever and ever. Amen.

Suffering for Being a Christian

[12]Dear friends, do not be surprised at the fiery ordeal that has come on you[d] to test you, as though
something strange were happening to you. [13]But rejoice inasmuch as you participate in the sufferings

ritual that washes the body; it is one's pledge to God to live righteously from that time on, which results in a clear conscience before him. Peter reminds his readers of the pledge of their baptism at a time when they are facing suffering because of Christ and are tempted to turn away from the Lord.

4:1 – 11 *Living for God.* Christians, especially those living in societies that are not or are no longer based on the Judeo-Christian tradition, must decide if they will meet God's expectations or society's. Peter suggests that at least some of the time one can do both (2:12), but the more society is implicitly hostile to the gospel, the more distinct and countercultural Christian lifestyle decisions become. Previous to their commitment to Christ, Peter's readers had spent their time living as their pagan society expected. Out of faithfulness to Christ, they now have ceased doing such things and consequently are suffering insults, misunderstanding, and various forms of ostracism (v. 4; 3:14). A Christian's refusal to live as they formerly had implicitly indicts those who continue in those practices.

4:1 – 6 *Living Out Christ's Victory.* Having explained in 3:18 – 22 that Jesus himself suffered unjustly while being obedient to God, even to death, Peter now exhorts Christians to arm themselves with that same resolve, so that they too might live victoriously. Although unbelieving family and friends might condemn a Christian's obedience to God, Peter reassures Christians that it is God's judgment, not human condemnation, that will vindicate the believer. Therefore, the Christian has joy and peace that comes only from being right with the Creator and Judge of all.

4:1 The only way Christians can live victoriously in society is to arm themselves "with the same attitude" as Christ, who resolved to obey God rather than sin — even if it meant suffering, "because whoever suffers in the body is done with sin." Peter's readers face the choice of either taking the path of least resistance (going along with the values, norms, and practices their society accepts and expects) or obeying God and suffering ostracism and judgment from unbelieving family and friends who criticize and condemn them (v. 4). Willingly suffering in this way, even as Christ suffered rejection, demonstrates that the believer has resolved to be done with sin.

4:6 preached even to those who are now dead. Some think this means there is an opportunity for conversion after death, but Heb 9:27 speaks against that possibility. Others interpret the "dead" as those who are spiritually dead but physically alive. But in the immediate context of v. 5, "the dead" forms half of an expression that refers to the whole human race. In the first century many believed that death removed a person from the judgment of the gods, which was operative only during one's earthly life. Peter exposes this kind of thinking to be false. *Because* God will judge people after physical death (v. 5), the gospel message of God's forgiveness for sins that was preached to those who are now dead — whether or not they became believers — is still in effect. Death does not invalidate either the promises or the warnings of the gospel of Jesus Christ. God is the judge of both the living and the dead.

4:7 – 11 *Living in Light of the End of All Things.* What a person believes about the future determines how they will live today. Peter reshapes his readers' self-understanding by explaining that they must decide how to live now in light of the end. The sure hope of a meaningful and just future provides confidence for the Christian believer to live each day with that future in mind.

4:7 The end ... is near. In the end, God the Father delegates judgment to the resurrected Christ (John 5:27; Acts 17:31). Because the resurrection of Jesus has already happened, the coming judgment is "near" in the sense that it is the next event in God's plan of redemption. As people come to faith in Christ now, God is realizing his plan in this final stage, which will culminate in the return of Christ and the end of earthly history. **Therefore.** This knowledge should influence the way Christians think and act now.

4:12 – 19 *Suffering for Being a Christian.* In his final thoughts about suffering, Peter makes four points: (1) Suffering for being a Christian should not come as a surprise. Because evil and sinful people targeted Jesus, those who follow in Jesus' footsteps should not be surprised

of Christ, so that you may be overjoyed when his glory is revealed.[e] [14]If you are insulted because of the name of Christ, you are blessed,[f] for the Spirit of glory and of God rests on you. [15]If you suffer, it should not be as a murderer or thief or any other kind of criminal, or even as a meddler. [16]However, if you suffer as a Christian, do not be ashamed, but praise God that you bear that name.[g] [17]For it is time for judgment to begin with God's household;[h] and if it begins with us, what will the outcome be for those who do not obey the gospel of God?[i] [18]And,

> "If it is hard for the righteous to be saved,
> what will become of the ungodly and the sinner?"[a][j]

[19]So then, those who suffer according to God's will should commit themselves to their faithful Creator and continue to do good.

To the Elders and the Flock

5 To the elders among you, I appeal as a fellow elder[k] and a witness[l] of Christ's sufferings who also will share in the glory to be revealed:[m] [2]Be shepherds of God's flock[n] that is under your care, watching over them — not because you must, but because you are willing, as God wants you to be; not pursuing dishonest gain,[o] but eager to serve; [3]not lording it over[p] those entrusted to you, but being examples[q] to the flock. [4]And when the Chief Shepherd appears, you will receive the crown of glory[r] that will never fade away.

[5]In the same way, you who are younger, submit yourselves[s] to your elders. All of you, clothe yourselves with humility toward one another, because,

> "God opposes the proud
> but shows favor to the humble."[b][t]

[6]Humble yourselves, therefore, under God's mighty hand, that he may lift you up in due time.[u] [7]Cast all your anxiety on him[v] because he cares for you.[w]

4:13 [e] Ro 8:17
4:14 [f] Mt 5:11
4:16 [g] Ac 5:41
4:17 [h] Jer 25:29 [i] 2Th 1:8
4:18 [j] Pr 11:31; Lk 23:31
5:1 [k] Ac 11:30 [l] Lk 24:48 [m] 1Pe 1:5,7; Rev 1:9
5:2 [n] Jn 21:16 [o] 1Ti 3:3
5:3 [p] Eze 34:4 [q] Php 3:17
5:4 [r] 1Co 9:25
5:5 [s] Eph 5:21 [t] Pr 3:34; Jas 4:6
5:6 [u] Jas 4:10
5:7 [v] Ps 37:5; Mt 6:25 [w] Heb 13:5

a 18 Prov. 11:31 (see Septuagint) *b 5* Prov. 3:34

to find themselves targets of similar opposition (v. 12). (2) Suffering because of Christ is a blessing because it confirms one will also enjoy all that Jesus has achieved (vv. 13–14). (3) In response to any suffering that may come because of faith in Christ, Christians should trust God by continuing to live righteously as an expression of their abiding trust (v. 19). Suffering should not be used as an excuse to sin. (4) God is sovereign over even our suffering and gives relief in his good time (v. 19; 5:10).

4:15 If you suffer, it should not be as a murderer ... or even as a meddler. There is suffering that comes from following Christ and suffering that comes from one's own bad behavior. There is no honor or glory in suffering because one has committed evil, even if that evil is simply being inappropriately involved in another's business ("a meddler"). Being a Christian never gives a person license to do evil (3:10–12). There is no right way to do the wrong thing.

4:16 do not be ashamed. Christians should not be ashamed if they suffer for their faith in Christ because "it is time for judgment to begin with God's household" (v. 17 and note; Jer 25:29; Ezek 9:5–6; Amos 3:2; Zech 13:9; Mal 3:1–5).

4:17 judgment. Here refers to the act of judging, not to condemnation. Suffering for Christ is a purifying judgment of God's people because those who are truly believers will suffer for their faith rather than for their sin, and therefore they will be found to belong to God. Those unwilling to stand with Christ when tested by suffering belong to "those who do not obey the gospel of God," who will be both judged and condemned. **God's household.** Greek "house of God"; it referred to the temple in the OT, but now Christians collectively are his temple (2:4–5).

4:19 suffer according to God's will. See note on 3:17.

5:1–11 *To the Elders and the Flock.* Peter's final instructions to his readers encourage them to preserve Christian unity and identity by standing fast in the true grace of God. Despite the believer's current suffering, God will set all things right in the end.

5:1 elders. Those spiritually responsible for the church. The early Christian church continued this structure of leadership from the Jewish synagogue, and "elder" is the most common title for church leadership in the NT. In the first century, elders were typically older believers who were respected and had standing in the community (1 Tim 3:1–7). The author refers to himself here as a "fellow elder," which does not mean that he could not have been an apostle (1:1), for the apostles were certainly considered elders of the church at large in whatever Christian community they resided.

5:2 Be shepherds of God's flock. The church needs this type of shepherd-leadership to survive in times of persecution. Responsible church structure and order is important for seeing the church through the fiery ordeal of testing.

5:4 when the Chief Shepherd appears. Jesus Christ is the Chief Shepherd under whom the elders shepherd the flock. Ps 23 begins with the comforting statement "The Lord is my shepherd." The NT uses the shepherd metaphor to refer to Jesus (2:25; John 10:11,14; Heb 13:20; Rev 7:17; see Matt 2:6; 9:36; 26:31; John 10:16). After his resurrection, Jesus' parting words to Peter were to shepherd the Lord's flock (John 21:15–17). Here Peter passes on that instruction to the elders, who are responsible for the church's spiritual well-being. **the crown of glory.** In that culture, athletes who persevered to victory wore wreath-like crowns. Such crowns were typically made of laurel. The crown for elders who persevere will be the imperishable glory they will receive when the Lord returns.

5:6 Humble yourselves. See Luke 14:11.

5:7 Cast all your anxiety. This may be the way in which Christians can humble themselves (v. 6).

Jesus is the Chief Shepherd (1 Pet 5:4).

Z. Radovan/www.BibleLandPictures.com

5:8 [x] Job 1:7
5:9 [y] Jas 4:7 [z] Col 2:5 [a] Ac 14:22
5:10 [b] 2Co 4:17 [c] 2Th 2:17
5:11 [d] Ro 11:36
5:12 [e] 2Co 1:19 [f] Heb 13:22
5:13 [g] Ac 12:12
5:14 [h] Ro 16:16 [i] Eph 6:23

8 Be alert and of sober mind. Your enemy the devil prowls around[x] like a roaring lion looking for
someone to devour. 9 Resist him,[y] standing firm in the faith,[z] because you know that the family of believers throughout the world is undergoing the same kind of sufferings.[a]
10 And the God of all grace, who called you to his eternal glory[b] in Christ, after you have suffered a
little while, will himself restore you and make you strong,[c] firm and steadfast. 11 To him be the power
for ever and ever. Amen.[d]

Final Greetings

12 With the help of Silas,[a][e] whom I regard as a faithful brother, I have written to you briefly,[f] encouraging you and testifying that this is the true grace of God. Stand fast in it.
13 She who is in Babylon, chosen together with you, sends you her greetings, and so does my son
Mark.[g] 14 Greet one another with a kiss of love.[h]

Peace[i] to all of you who are in Christ.

[a] 12 Greek *Silvanus*, a variant of *Silas*

5:9 believers throughout the world. Peter encourages his readers by telling them they are not alone in their persecution and suffering. Other believers are facing the same things.

5:12–14 *Final Greetings.* Many letters of that time ended with personal greetings and closing remarks, such as are found here. Peter adds a major theological point: what he has written is the true grace of God in which Christians must stand (v. 12).

5:12 With the help of Silas. Silas was likely Paul's courier who delivered the letter to its original recipients, and Silas may have also assisted Peter as a scribe, writing the letter under Peter's direction. Acts mentions Silas many times as an associate of the apostle Paul (Acts 15:22, 27,32,40; 16:19,22,25,29,36,38,40; 17:4–5,10,14–15; 18:5) and Timothy (2 Cor 1:19; 1 Thess 1:1). **encouraging you and testifying ... the true grace of God.** The letter exhorts its readers to begin to or continue to live faithfully for Jesus Christ, and it also provides the theological basis in which a life of obedience must be grounded. This letter sets forth the true grace that God offers through Jesus Christ. Because there is no other source of grace, forgiveness, and eternal life, Peter exhorts his readers to stand fast in it.

5:13 She who is in Babylon. Likely the Christian community in the location from which Peter writes. "Babylon" is probably a veiled reference to Rome (see Introduction: Place of Composition and Destination; Genre and Structure). **my son Mark.** Perhaps John Mark, son of a woman named Mary (Acts 12:12), cousin of Barnabas (Col 4:10), and perhaps the spiritual son of Peter. Like Silas, Mark was also associated with the apostle Paul (Acts 12:25; 15:37–39; 2 Tim 4:11; Phlm 24). Because of Peter's long and apparently close association with Mark, many consider Peter's story of Jesus to be derived from the Gospel of Mark.

5:14 kiss of love. See 1 Cor 16:20. This gesture of mutual love and respect was apparently a practice of the early church that had been carried over from the synagogue. **Peace.** Only those who are in Christ through faith in his atonement have the peace needed to live well in this life, for it is a peace that flows from a right relationship with God and with others.

INTRODUCTION TO
2 PETER

This letter is both positive and negative. It encourages readers to grow in the grace and knowledge of Christ, and it warns against false teaching that hinders that growth.

AUTHOR

"Simon Peter, a servant and apostle of Jesus Christ" (1:1), claims to have written this letter — a claim bolstered by the author's reminiscences about witnessing Jesus' transfiguration (1:13 – 18; cf. Matt 17:1 – 8). Despite these claims, many scholars deny that the apostle Peter wrote this letter. They argue that the letter is pseudonymous, a "falsely named" book, i.e., a book written by someone else using Peter's name. Scholars reject Peter's authorship for six main reasons, but none of these reasons is conclusive:

1. The author uses language and concepts drawn from the Hellenistic world. However, (a) there is nothing in the letter that Peter, after many years of ministry in the Greek world, could not have written; (b) Peter may have deliberately chosen to write in this style because of the needs of his readers; and (c) the more commonplace Greek of 1 Peter may be the result of the help of an amanuensis (a trained scribe), perhaps Silas (1 Pet 5:12).

2. The author combats the second-century heresy called Gnosticism. This, however, is not clear. Nothing the false teachers were propagating was unknown in the first-century church.

3. The author calls Paul's letters Scripture (3:15 – 16), something allegedly not possible in Peter's lifetime. However, other NT texts suggest that the words of the Lord and certain NT books were being regarded as Scriptural from an early period (see, e.g., 1 Tim 5:18).

4. The author refers to apostolic tradition (3:2,16), which betrays a late date when there was a fixed ecclesiastical authority. But nothing in 2 Peter suggests any kind of ecclesiastical organization or hierarchy.

5. The early church doubted whether 2 Peter is Scripture. This is true, but many Christians accepted the book from the beginning. People probably had doubts because the book was not widely used and because so many Petrine forgeries were circulating.

6. The letter is a "testament": a person wrote in the name of a great hero of the faith after that hero's death. However, even if 2 Peter contains some elements of the "testament," the book claims to be a letter, and we should evaluate it as such.

We are left with the choice of accepting the letter's claim or viewing it as a forgery that does not deserve to be included in the Bible. Since the arguments against Peter's authorship are not convincing, we conclude that the letter was written by the apostle and that it deserves its long-held place in Scripture.

DATE AND PLACE

Peter likely wrote this letter shortly before AD 65, the date when, according to reliable early tradition, Nero martyred him while persecuting Christians in Rome. Peter possibly wrote from Rome, and he sensed that the time to fulfill the Lord's prophecy about his death was near (cf. 1:13 – 14; John 21:18 – 19). Identifying the false teachers he refers to

LOCATIONS IN 2 PETER

would help us pin down the date and circumstances of the letter, but we do not have enough evidence; Peter is more interested in condemning the false teaching than describing it.

ADDRESSEES

Peter addresses his letter "to those who through the righteousness of our God and Savior Jesus Christ have received a faith as precious as ours" (1:1). This lack of specificity led Christians in the past to classify 2 Peter as a "general," or "catholic," letter addressed the church worldwide. But the letter suggests a definite audience since a specific false teaching threatens the readers, who have apparently received, or are aware of, at least two of Paul's letters (3:15). Peter appears to allude to 1 Peter by calling this "my second letter to you" (3:1). Since 1 Peter was written to Gentiles, we can conclude that 2 Peter was also. By using religious language familiar to his readers, Peter contextualizes the gospel to meet their needs.

PURPOSE

Peter's purpose is to encourage his readers to mature in how they understand and practice God's grace in Christ (3:18) in the face of a false teaching that threatens to stunt their growth. For this reason, negative descriptions of false teachers and warnings about them dominate the letter.

RELATION TO JUDE

2 Peter and Jude denounce false teachers with very similar language (cf. 2:1,3 – 4,6,10 – 11,13,17; 3:3 with Jude 4,6 – 9,12,18). Since the order is similar and since the Bible does not use many of these words and expressions elsewhere, some kind of relationship probably exists between the two letters. Two options are most likely: (1) Peter borrowed from Jude or (2) Jude borrowed from Peter. But we do not know who borrowed from whom.

Both 2 Peter and Jude describe the false teachers too generally for us to precisely identify them. The letters probably address the same general false teaching, though only Peter mentions that the false teachers are skeptical that Christ will return (but the "scoffers" in Jude 18 may parallel that skepticism).

THEMES

1. *The seriousness of error.* Theological and moral error go hand in hand, and both are serious matters that Peter condemns (2:4,9,12 – 13,17,20 – 21).

2. *The day of the Lord.* This world is destined to be destroyed by fire (3:7 – 13; cf. Isa 30:30; 66:15 – 16; Nah 1:6; Zeph 1:18; 3:8) and transformed into "a new heaven and a new earth" (3:13).

3. *Memory.* Christians must remember — not merely intellectually, but in a transformative way — the teaching they have already received (1:12 – 15; 3:1,5,8).

OUTLINE

I. Greeting (1:1 – 2)
II. Confirming One's Calling and Election (1:3 – 11)
III. Prophecy of Scripture (1:12 – 21)
IV. False Teachers and Their Destruction (2:1 – 22)
V. The Day of the Lord (3:1 – 18)

2 PETER

1:1 [a]Ro 1:1 [b]1Pe 1:1 [c]Ro 3:21-26 [d]Titus 2:13
1:2 [e]Php 3:8
1:3 [f]1Pe 1:5 [g]1Th 2:12
1:4 [h]2Co 7:1 [i]Eph 4:24; Heb 12:10; 1Jn 3:2 [j]2Pe 2:18-20
1:5 [k]Col 2:3
1:6 [l]Ac 24:25 [m]ver 3
1:7 [n]1Th 3:12
1:8 [o]Jn 15:2; Titus 3:14
1:9 [p]1Jn 2:11 [q]Eph 5:26

1 Simon Peter, a servant[a] and apostle of Jesus Christ,[b]

To those who through the righteousness[c] of our God and Savior Jesus Christ[d] have received a faith
as precious as ours:

2 Grace and peace be yours in abundance through the knowledge of God and of Jesus our Lord.[e]

Confirming One's Calling and Election

3 His divine power[f] has given us everything we need for a godly life through our knowledge of him
who called us[g] by his own glory and goodness. 4 Through these he has given us his very great and precious promises,[h] so that through them you may participate in the divine nature,[i] having escaped the
corruption in the world caused by evil desires.[j]
5 For this very reason, make every effort to add to your faith goodness; and to goodness, knowledge;[k]
6 and to knowledge, self-control;[l] and to self-control, perseverance; and to perseverance, godliness;[m]
7 and to godliness, mutual affection; and to mutual affection, love.[n] 8 For if you possess these qualities
in increasing measure, they will keep you from being ineffective and unproductive[o] in your knowledge
of our Lord Jesus Christ. 9 But whoever does not have them is nearsighted and blind,[p] forgetting that
they have been cleansed from their past sins.[q]

1:1–2 *Greeting.* Peter's greeting—which mentions faith, grace, peace, and knowledge—sets the stage for the letter's purpose: to encourage his readers to "grow in the grace and knowledge of ... Christ" (3:18) in the face of false teaching.
1:1 Simon. The author's Jewish name. **Peter.** His Greek name. **our God and Savior Jesus Christ.** The construction in Greek explicitly identifies Jesus as God (Titus 2:13; cf. John 1:1; 20:28; Rom 9:5; Heb 1:8; 1 John 5:20). **faith.** A gift from God (Eph 2:8) rooted in Jesus' saving righteousness. **ours.** Probably Peter and other Christians; the readers, mostly Gentile Christians, have an equal standing before God in the new covenant community of Christians.
1:2 knowledge. An intimate, informed relationship resulting from conversion and growth (cf. vv. 3,5,8; 2:20–21; 3:18).
1:3–11 *Confirming One's Calling and Election.* Because God has given Christians all they need to become spiritually mature (vv. 3–4), they must actively pursue spiritual maturity (vv. 5–9) if they expect to receive a rich welcome into God's eternal kingdom (vv. 10–11).
1:3 godly life. How God expects Christians to behave. Throughout this letter, Peter stresses the importance of living out the values of God's kingdom. He begins by reminding his readers that God is powerfully at work to enable them to live such a life. **called.** Effectively summoned (see notes on Rom 1:6; 8:28; Gal 1:6; Eph 4:1). **glory.** Unique excellence; see "The Glory of God," p. 2640. **goodness.** Moral perfection.
1:4 Through these. Christ fulfills God's "promises" (probably ones in the OT about how God would save and bless his people through the Messiah) by his glory and goodness (see note on v. 3). **participate in the divine nature.** Share God's holy character, especially qualities that help Christians resist sin.
1:5–7 This stair-step structure (add goodness to faith, knowledge to goodness, etc.) was a common literary device that emphasizes the items but not the sequence (e.g., goodness does not necessarily precede knowledge). But "faith" (the list's first item) is a Christian's foundational gift (cf. v. 1), and "love" (the final item) is the supreme virtue that holds the rest together (1 Cor 13; Col 3:14).
1:5 goodness. Moral excellence; virtue. **knowledge.** Discerning God's will and living accordingly (cf. note on v. 2).
1:6 self-control. Avoiding temptations, especially sexual ones. **perseverance.** Endurance, especially through trials such as illness, broken relationships, financial pressures, and persecution. **godliness.** Pleasing God in every phase of life.
1:7 mutual affection. Love expressed among fellow Christians.
1:8–9 The issue is not merely whether Christians possess the virtues of vv. 5–7 (all Christians do to some degree) but whether they are continually growing in them. In contrast, spurious Christians, who claim that Christ has cleansed them but have shut their eyes to the truth, lack these virtues (cf. the false teachers in ch. 2, especially 2:20–22).

10Therefore, my brothers and sisters,[a] make every effort to confirm your calling and election. For
if you do these things, you will never stumble,[r] 11and you will receive a rich welcome into the eternal
kingdom of our Lord and Savior Jesus Christ.

Prophecy of Scripture

12So I will always remind you of these things,[s] even though you know them and are firmly established
in the truth you now have. 13I think it is right to refresh your memory as long as I live in the tent of this
body,[t] 14because I know that I will soon put it aside,[u] as our Lord Jesus Christ has made clear to me.[v] 15And
I will make every effort to see that after my departure[w] you will always be able to remember these things.
16For we did not follow cleverly devised stories when we told you about the coming of our Lord Jesus
Christ in power, but we were eyewitnesses of his majesty.[x] 17He received honor and glory from God the
Father when the voice came to him from the Majestic Glory, saying, "This is my Son, whom I love; with
him I am well pleased."[b][y] 18We ourselves heard this voice that came from heaven when we were with
him on the sacred mountain.[z]
19We also have the prophetic message as something completely reliable, and you will do well to pay
attention to it, as to a light[a] shining in a dark place, until the day dawns and the morning star[b] rises in
your hearts. 20Above all, you must understand that no prophecy of Scripture came about by the prophet's own interpretation of things. 21For prophecy never had its origin in the human will, but prophets,
though human, spoke from God[c] as they were carried along by the Holy Spirit.[d]

False Teachers and Their Destruction

2 But there were also false prophets[e] among the people, just as there will be false teachers among
you.[f] They will secretly introduce destructive heresies, even denying the sovereign Lord[g] who
bought them[h]—bringing swift destruction on themselves. 2Many will follow their depraved conduct

[a] *10* The Greek word for *brothers and sisters* (*adelphoi*) refers here to believers, both men and women, as part of God's family. [b] *17* Matt. 17:5; Mark 9:7; Luke 9:35

1:10 [r] 2Pe 3:17
1:12 [s] Php 3:1; 1Jn 2:21
1:13 [t] 2Co 5:1,4
1:14 [u] 2Ti 4:6 [v] Jn 21:18,19
1:15 [w] Lk 9:31
1:16 [x] Mt 17:1-8
1:17 [y] Mt 3:17
1:18 [z] Mt 17:6
1:19 [a] Ps 119:105 [b] Rev 22:16
1:21 [c] 2Ti 3:16 [d] 2Sa 23:2; Ac 1:16; 1Pe 1:11
2:1 [e] Dt 13:1-3 [f] 1Ti 4:1 [g] Jude 4 [h] 1Co 6:20

1:10–11 Striving for spiritual maturity is not optional for Christians.
1:10 confirm. Christians validate that God called and elected them by cultivating the virtues of vv. 5–7. **stumble.** Probably apostatize, i.e., forsake God (cf. Jude 24).
1:11 receive a rich welcome. Enter into the blessing of the life to come.
1:12–21 *Prophecy of Scripture.* Peter writes as if on his deathbed, reminding his readers one last time of the truth they must embrace (vv. 12–15). Christians can have absolute confidence that Jesus will come again: at Jesus' transfiguration Peter and other apostles glimpsed Jesus' future glory (vv. 16–18), and the prophets—who are utterly reliable because the Spirit speaks through them—confirm the same truth (vv. 19–21). See "Prophets and Prophecy," p. 2668.
1:12 So. Connects vv. 3–11 and vv. 12–15: because their ultimate reward depends on earnestly striving for godliness, Peter continues to "remind [them] of these things" (v. 15). **you know them and are firmly established.** Peter commends his readers for their spiritual maturity.
1:13 tent of this body. Cf. 2 Cor 5:1,4.
1:14 Peter knows that he will die soon. Perhaps Jesus communicated this to him in a vision, but Peter is more likely referring to Jesus' prophecy that Peter would die by crucifixion as a martyr (John 21:18–19).
1:15 Peter hopes that he will have an enduring ministry to his readers (probably through what he writes in this letter).
1:16 For. Connects vv. 12–15 and vv. 16–21: the readers must remember that Christ will return in power (see "The Consummation," p. 2695). Peter returns to this theme in 3:1–13, so it frames ch. 2. **we.** Occurs five times in vv. 16–18 and refers to Peter and the other apostles (in contrast to the first-person singulars in vv. 12–15). **cleverly devised stories.** Cf. 2:3; false teachers (ch. 2) viewed Christ's return as a fable (3:3–4). **eyewitnesses of his majesty.** Peter, James, and John witnessed Jesus' transfiguration, which prefigured his return by revealing him as the glorious King (see NIV text note on v. 17; see also Matt 17:1–8; Mark 9:2–8; Luke 9:28–36).
1:17 Majestic Glory. God the Father.
1:19 prophetic message. Probably the OT. **light.** Cf. Ps 119:105. **day.** The day of the Lord, i.e., when God saves his people and judges his enemies (see note on Amos 2:16). **morning star.** Cf. Num 24:17; Rev 22:16. The night-day (dark-light) contrast refers to Jesus' return (cf. Rom 13:12; 1 Thess 5:4–9).
1:20–21 Whereas 2 Tim 3:16 (see note) presents the *nature* of Scripture's inspiration, this passage presents the *method*: the human authors of Scripture did not think up what they wrote on their own (contrast "cleverly devised stories" [v. 16] and "fabricated stories" [2:3]); God is the origin of what they prophesied. Humans used their own words ("prophets, though human, spoke"), and those words were just what God wanted them to use ("from God as they were carried along by the Holy Spirit").
2:1–22 *False Teachers and Their Destruction.* Peter denounces false teachers in four stages (vv. 1–3,4–10a,10b–16,17–22). See "Wrath," p. 2681.
2:1–3 Peter introduces and describes false teachers: They are subversive (see "secretly," v. 1), immoral (see "depraved conduct" (v. 2), which probably refers to sexual sin), avaricious (see "greed" (v. 3), i.e., they commercialize Christianity [cf. vv. 14–15; 2 Cor 2:17]), and dishonest (see "false," v. 1; "fabricated," v. 3). Their false teaching is "destructive" (v. 1) and will result in their own "destruction" (v. 3).
2:1 there were. In OT times. **there will be false teachers.** Cf. Matt 24:4–5,11,24; Mark 13:22; Acts 20:29–31; 2 Tim 3:1–6. **denying.** Cf. Titus 1:16; Jude 4. **bought.** May mean (1) Christ's death paid the penalty for the sins of the false teachers (although God did not apply that payment to them because they rejected Christ as Savior); (2) Christ's death only appeared to pay the penalty for their sins because they initially appeared to know Christ (vv. 15,20–22; cf. Heb 10:29; 1 John 2:19); or (3) God (or Christ) owned these ungrateful false teachers (alluding to Deut 32:6).
2:2 False teachers mislead many and thus defame the Christian way of life ("the way of truth"; cf. vv. 15,21).

2:3 [i]2Co 2:17; 1Th 2:5
2:4 [j]Jude 6; Rev 20:1,2
2:5 [k]2Pe 3:6 [l]Heb 11:7; 1Pe 3:20
2:6 [m]Ge 19:24,25 [n]Nu 26:10; Jude 7
2:7 [o]Ge 19:16 [p]2Pe 3:17
2:9 [q]1Co 10:13
2:10 [r]2Pe 3:3 [s]Jude 8
2:11 [t]Jude 9

and will bring the way of truth into disrepute. 3 In their greed these teachers will exploit you[i] with fabricated stories. Their condemnation has long been hanging over them, and their destruction has not been sleeping.

4 For if God did not spare angels when they sinned, but sent them to hell,[a] putting them in chains of darkness[b] to be held for judgment;[j] 5 if he did not spare the ancient world[k] when he brought the flood on its ungodly people, but protected Noah, a preacher of righteousness, and seven others;[l] 6 if he condemned the cities of Sodom and Gomorrah by burning them to ashes,[m] and made them an example[n] of what is going to happen to the ungodly; 7 and if he rescued Lot,[o] a righteous man, who was distressed by the depraved conduct of the lawless[p] 8 (for that righteous man, living among them day after day, was tormented in his righteous soul by the lawless deeds he saw and heard) — 9 if this is so, then the Lord knows how to rescue the godly from trials[q] and to hold the unrighteous for punishment on the day of judgment. 10 This is especially true of those who follow the corrupt desire[r] of the flesh[c] and despise authority.

Bold and arrogant, they are not afraid to heap abuse on celestial beings;[s] 11 yet even angels, although they are stronger and more powerful, do not heap abuse on such beings when bringing judgment on them from[d] the Lord.[t] 12 But these people blaspheme in matters they do not understand. They are like

SODOM AND GOMORRAH

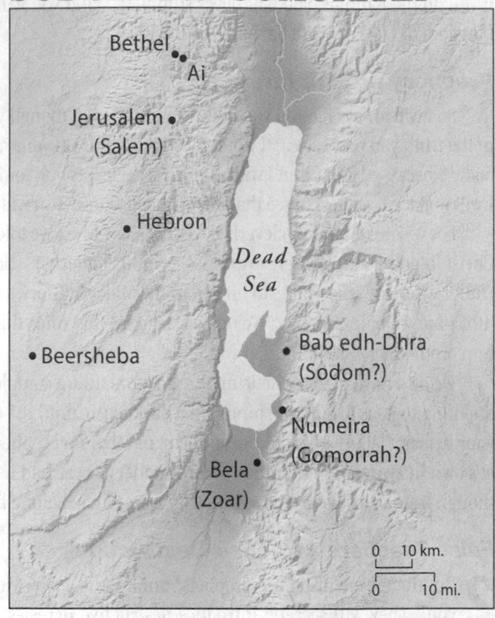

[a] *4* Greek *Tartarus* [b] *4* Some manuscripts *in gloomy dungeons* [c] *10* In contexts like this, the Greek word for *flesh* (*sarx*) refers to the sinful state of human beings, often presented as a power in opposition to the Spirit; also in verse 18. [d] *11* Many manuscripts *beings in the presence of*

2:4–10a Three examples (vv. 4–8) show that God will rescue the godly and judge the ungodly (vv. 9–10a). (Cf. Luke 17:26–29, where Jesus pairs examples 2 and 3.)
2:4 Example 1 (see note on vv. 4–10a): God judged sinful angels. Jewish tradition understands "the sons of God" in Gen 6:1–4 as angels who had intercourse with women and whom God therefore judged (1 Enoch 6–19; cf. Jude 6). Or, less likely, this may refer to the fall of Satan and the evil angels before Adam and Eve fell (cf. Rev 12:7–9). **hell.** Tartarus (see NIV text note), a term Jewish writers borrowed from Greek mythology, is a temporary holding place ("held for judgment"), not a place of final punishment. **chains of darkness.** A common way the ancient world described the underworld; probably a metaphor for punishment.
2:5 Example 2 (see note on vv. 4–10a): God judged the ancient world with a flood and rescued Noah and his family (Gen 6–8). **ungodly.** See Gen 6:5,11–12. **preacher.** The OT does not call Noah this, but intertestamental Jewish writings do. **seven others.** Noah's wife, his three sons, and their wives (Gen 6:18; 7:7,13; cf. 1 Pet 3:20); the godly may be few, but God protects them.
2:6–8 Example 3 (see note on vv. 4–10a): God judged Sodom and Gomorrah with sulfur and rescued Lot (Gen 19).
2:7 righteous man. While far from perfect, Lot demonstrated a fundamental commitment to God by receiving and attempting to protect the angelic visitors and by obediently fleeing the city. He was among the "righteous" people Abraham prayed for in Gen 18 (in the Apocrypha see also Wisdom of Solomon 10:6; 19:17). Lot was "rescued" because of his relation to the Lord, which was demonstrated by the differences between his behavior and that of the other people in Sodom and Gomorrah. Peter's readers can maintain their "secure position" in Christ (3:17) by similarly separating themselves from the false teachers.
2:9 if this is so, then. Although these words have no explicit counterpart in the Greek, they are necessary to summarize the four "if" clauses in vv. 4–7 and set up the "then" clause beginning in v. 9. If God has acted in the past as these "if" clauses indicate, "then" God will rescue the godly from "trials" (challenges to faith that Christians experience) and judge the ungodly. In particular, God will vindicate Peter's readers, who face false teachers who "follow the corrupt desire of the flesh and despise authority" (v. 10a; see note).
2:10a follow the corrupt desire of the flesh. Are sexually immoral. **despise authority.** Are arrogant.
2:10b–16 Peter describes the false prophets as arrogant, sensual, and greedy. This focuses more on how they live than on what they teach; false teaching and evil living often go together (cf. 1 Tim 6:3–10).
2:10b celestial beings. Probably evil angels (demons) in contrast to "angels" (v. 11; cf. Jude 8–10). The astounding arrogance of the false teachers is ignorant and irrational.

unreasoning animals, creatures of instinct, born only to be caught and destroyed, and like animals
they too will perish.[u]
[13]They will be paid back with harm for the harm they have done. Their idea of pleasure is to carouse in broad daylight.[v] They are blots and blemishes, reveling in their pleasures while they feast with
you.[a][w] [14]With eyes full of adultery, they never stop sinning; they seduce[x] the unstable; they are experts
in greed[y] — an accursed brood![z] [15]They have left the straight way and wandered off to follow the way
of Balaam[a] son of Bezer,[b] who loved the wages of wickedness. [16]But he was rebuked for his wrongdoing by a donkey — an animal without speech — who spoke with a human voice and restrained the
prophet's madness.[b]
[17]These people are springs without water[c] and mists driven by a storm. Blackest darkness is reserved
for them.[d] [18]For they mouth empty, boastful words[e] and, by appealing to the lustful desires of the flesh,
they entice people who are just escaping from those who live in error. [19]They promise them freedom,
while they themselves are slaves of depravity — for "people are slaves to whatever has mastered them."[f]
[20]If they have escaped the corruption of the world by knowing[g] our Lord and Savior Jesus Christ and
are again entangled in it and are overcome, they are worse off at the end than they were at the beginning.[h] [21]It would have been better for them not to have known the way of righteousness, than to
have known it and then to turn their backs on the sacred command that was passed on to them.[i] [22]Of
them the proverbs are true: "A dog returns to its vomit,"[c][j] and, "A sow that is washed returns to her
wallowing in the mud."

2:12 [u]Jude 10
2:13 [v]Ro 13:13 [w]1Co 11:20,21; Jude 12
2:14 [x]ver 18 [y]ver 3 [z]Eph 2:3
2:15 [a]Nu 22:4-20; Jude 11
2:16 [b]Nu 22:21-30
2:17 [c]Jude 12 [d]Jude 13
2:18 [e]Jude 16
2:19 [f]Jn 8:34; Ro 6:16
2:20 [g]2Pe 1:2 [h]Mt 12:45
2:21 [i]Heb 6:4-6
2:22 [j]Pr 26:11
3:1 [k]2Pe 1:13

The Day of the Lord

3 Dear friends, this is now my second letter to you. I have written both of them as reminders[k] to
stimulate you to wholesome thinking. [2]I want you to recall the words spoken in the past by the
holy prophets and the command given by our Lord and Savior through your apostles.

[a] *13* Some manuscripts *in their love feasts* [b] *15* Greek *Bosor* [c] *22* Prov. 26:11

2:13 carouse in broad daylight. Cf. Isa 5:11. **reveling in their pleasures while they feast with you.** Some early Christians ate fellowship meals in connection with the Lord's Supper (implied in 1 Cor 11:17–34), and these adulterous and greedy false teachers apparently used those meals for sensual self-indulgence.
2:14 adultery. Or "an adulteress." The false teachers looked at every woman as a potential sexual partner (cf. Matt 5:28).
2:15 Balaam. See Num 22–24. He is a prominent negative example in Scripture (Num 31:16; Deut 23:4–5; Josh 13:22; 24:9–10; Neh 13:1–2; Mic 6:5; Jude 11; Rev 2:14). **loved the wages of wickedness.** The OT hints that greed motivated Balaam's prophetic ministry (he wanted the money Balak offered him), and Jewish tradition developed this theme (cf. 1 Tim 6:3–10).
2:17–22 Peter again describes and condemns the false prophets.
2:17 The false teachers promised spiritual vitality but did not deliver it. Two metaphors depict that what they taught was hollow and therefore disillusioning (cf. Prov 25:14; Jude 12): (1) **springs without water.** Freshwater springs were essential in the dry Mediterranean climate; long stretches of land had little water. (2) **mists driven by a storm.** Storm clouds that seem to forecast life-giving rain may actually turn into hazy mists that dissipate and become the harbinger of dry weather. The Bible often connects water with wisdom and blessing (e.g., Ps 1:3–4; Prov 13:14; Jer 14:3; Rev 7:17; 21:6; 22:1).
2:18 For. Connects v. 17 with vv. 18–19, which explain how false teachers disillusioned and harmed people with their teaching (v. 17a) and why the darkness of hell is reserved for them (v. 17b). **entice people who are just escaping from those who live in error.** The false teachers cleverly lured new converts who were in the process of distancing themselves from the values and lifestyle of their pagan society. The false teachers enticed new converts in two ways: (1) **mouth empty, boastful words.** They spoke showy, persuasive, arrogant words that were actually futile and frustrating (cf. v. 10). (2) **appealing to the lustful desires of the flesh.** They appealed to the sinful sensual desires of the new converts by promising the hypocritical illusion of "freedom" (v. 19) from moral restraint, especially regarding sex (cf. Rom 6:16; 1 Cor 6:12–13; Gal 5:13; 1 Pet 2:16).
2:20–21 they ... they ... them. Possibly the new converts (see note on v. 18), but probably the false teachers. The false teachers knew the truth and initially seemed to be Christians, but they deliberately rejected the truth; so they are more accountable for their sin (cf. Luke 12:47–48) and unlikely to consider the truth again. Willfully turning back from the truth brings terrible consequences. Christians must persevere.
2:21 sacred command that was passed on to them. The totality of Christian instruction traditionally taught to converts (cf. Rom 6:17; 2 Tim 1:14).
2:22 A dog returns to its vomit. The false teachers demonstrate that their fundamental nature has remained unchanged: the unclean return to the unclean. Similarly, those who renounce the Christian faith return to their evil way of life. The test of authenticity is perseverance. **dog.** Seen not as a friendly family pet but as a wild, filthy beast (Prov 26:11; Phil 3:2). **A sow that is washed returns to her wallowing in the mud.** This proverb may come from a popular book of sayings from around 500 BC that says, "My son, you have been to me like the pig who went into the hot bath with people of quality, and when it came out of the hot bath, it saw a filthy hole and went down and wallowed in it" (Ahiqar 8:18).
3:1–18 *The Day of the Lord.* Returning to a topic first introduced in 1:16–21, Peter encourages his readers to remember the teaching of the Lord and the prophets, who clearly predicted the Lord's coming and the day of judgment (vv. 1–13). The false teachers deny this coming intervention, deliberately forgetting that God has directly intervened before in creation and the flood. Peter closes with a final exhortation and doxology (vv. 14–18).
3:1–2 Peter urges his readers to remember the truth.
3:1 second letter. The first was probably 1 Peter.
3:2 holy prophets. The OT prophets; they predicted that God would

3:3 [l] 1Ti 4:1 [m] 2Pe 2:10; Jude 18
3:4 [n] Isa 5:19; Eze 12:22; Mt 24:48 [o] Mk 10:6
3:5 [p] Ge 1:6,9; Heb 11:3 [q] Ps 24:2
3:6 [r] Ge 7:21,22
3:7 [s] ver 10,12; 2Th 1:7
3:8 [t] Ps 90:4
3:9 [u] Hab 2:3; Heb 10:37 [v] Ro 2:4 [w] 1Ti 2:4
3:10 [x] Lk 12:39; 1Th 5:2 [y] Mt 24:35; Rev 21:1
3:12 [z] 1Co 1:7 [a] Ps 50:3 [b] ver 10
3:13 [c] Isa 65:17; 66:22; Rev 21:1

3 Above all, you must understand that in the last days[l] scoffers will come, scoffing and following their
own evil desires.[m] 4 They will say, "Where is this 'coming' he promised?[n] Ever since our ancestors died,
everything goes on as it has since the beginning of creation."[o] 5 But they deliberately forget that long ago
by God's word[p] the heavens came into being and the earth was formed out of water and by water.[q] 6 By
these waters also the world of that time was deluged and destroyed.[r] 7 By the same word the present heavens and earth are reserved for fire,[s] being kept for the day of judgment and destruction of the ungodly.

8 But do not forget this one thing, dear friends: With the Lord a day is like a thousand years, and
a thousand years are like a day.[t] 9 The Lord is not slow in keeping his promise,[u] as some understand
slowness. Instead he is patient[v] with you, not wanting anyone to perish, but everyone to come to
repentance.[w]

10 But the day of the Lord will come like a thief.[x] The heavens will disappear with a roar; the elements
will be destroyed by fire, and the earth and everything done in it will be laid bare.[a][y]

11 Since everything will be destroyed in this way, what kind of people ought you to be? You ought
to live holy and godly lives 12 as you look forward[z] to the day of God and speed its coming.[b][a] That day
will bring about the destruction of the heavens by fire, and the elements will melt in the heat.[b] 13 But
in keeping with his promise we are looking forward to a new heaven and a new earth,[c] where righteousness dwells.

[a] *10* Some manuscripts *be burned up* [b] *12* Or *as you wait eagerly for the day of God to come*

bring his plan to its climax through an earth-shaking event at the end of history (see note on Amos 2:16). **apostles.** They pass on Jesus' basic moral requirement ("command") to be holy (cf. 1 Pet 1:15–16; Matt 5:48). Peter places the OT prophets and NT apostles on an equal plane.

3:3 last days. The period from Jesus' first coming to his second coming (Acts 2:17–18; Heb 1:1–2). This does not merely predict future events; Peter describes his current situation (cf. Acts 20:29–30; 1 Tim 4:1; 1 John 2:18). **scoffers ... scoffing.** Dismissing and mocking the truth of Jesus' second coming rather than arguing with evidence and logic (cf. Prov 1:22; 9:7–8; 13:1). The false teachers foolishly follow "their own evil desires," claiming that Jesus is not returning ("coming," v. 4) and therefore will not judge them.

3:4 everything goes on as it has. They asserted that things had not changed and never would (even though God promised to intervene in history).

3:5–7 The scoffers "deliberately forget" (v. 5)—either willfully ignore or fail to notice—that everything has *not* gone on "as it has since the beginning of creation" (v. 4). God made the world, so he can certainly destroy it. The flood—using the very water God created in the beginning (Gen 1:2,6–10)—"deluged and destroyed" (v. 6) the earth (Gen 6–8). God spoke this universe into existence with his "word" (v. 5; cf. Gen 1; Pss 33:6; 148:5; Heb 11:3), and by that "same word" (v. 7) he will destroy "the present heavens and earth" (v. 7; see note on v. 10) and judge and destroy "the ungodly" (v. 7), including the false teachers. They will cease to exist in this world and will experience the final and terrible separation from God involved in condemnation (see "Wrath," p. 2681).

These three events (creation, flood, and final judgment) are connected: (1) the flood bridges creation (occurring at the beginning of human history; see "Creation," p. 2642) and final judgment (occurring at the end of human history; see "The Consummation," p. 2695); (2) "water" connects creation and the flood; and (3) worldwide destruction connects the flood and final judgment (which Melito of Sardis, a second-century theologian, referred to as "a flood of water" and "a flood of fire"). The rest of ch. 3 is consistent with the flood theme of salvation through judgment (see vv. 9,15); the promise of future judgment incites non-Christians to trust Christ and gives hope to suffering Christians.

3:8 a day is like a thousand years. Peter adapts Ps 90:4: the eternal God does not view time the way we do. He follows his own timetable, and Jesus will return right on schedule.

3:9 not slow. What seems to us like a delay ("slowness"; cf. Hab 2:3) is evidence of God's kind patience (cf. Rom 2:4). **anyone.** Either (1) all humans without exception or (2) Peter's readers, Christians (1:1; see "with you, not wanting anyone" [here] and "dear friends" [vv. 1,8,14,17]) whom the false teachers influenced. If the first, then some view this as an example of what God desires as distinct from what God decrees (see note on 1 Tim 2:4).

3:10 like a thief. Sudden and unexpected (cf. Matt 24:43; Luke 12:39; 1 Thess 5:2). **elements.** Perhaps (1) the sun, moon, and stars (cf. Isa 34:4) but probably (2) the basic components of the physical universe (the next phrase focuses on "the earth"). **destroyed by fire.** Cf. vv. 7,12. Fire is an image of God's judgment associated with the day of the Lord (Isa 30:30; 66:15–16; Nah 1:6; Zeph 1:18; 3:8). On the day of judgment, all things will be manifest ("laid bare") before God for his scrutinizing assessment. **laid bare.** There is a debate whether God will replace or transform the earth at the end of history, and some argue that this verse supports the replacement view because some manuscripts read "burned up" instead of "laid bare" (see NIV text note). While this alternative reading ("burned up") is unlikely, vv. 11–12 use the terms "destroyed" and "melt." But other passages seem to indicate that God will renovate the earth (e.g., Rom 8:18–22). Rev 21 seems to suggest both replacement (Rev 21:1) and transformation (Rev 21:5). The tension exists because the Bible describes what is beyond our experience with language and analogies drawn from our own world; those analogies fall short of matching the reality and capture only part of the full picture. What is clear, however, is that God's destruction of this present universe at the end of history does not mean that the material world ends. The shift from the present heavens and earth to the new heaven and earth (see notes on vv. 11–13) involves both continuity and discontinuity.

3:11–13 Peter does not discuss the end times to satisfy our curiosity. His purpose is practical: in light of this future destruction when Jesus returns, we should "live holy and godly lives" (v. 11) now (cf. 1:3,6–7; 1 Pet 1:15–16).

3:12 look forward. See note on v. 13. **speed its coming.** Hasten the end (from a human perspective) by repenting (cf. Acts 3:19–20; but see NIV text note). **elements will melt in the heat.** See note on v. 10; cf. Mic 1:3–4.

3:13 looking forward. Cf. vv. 12,14. Christians expectantly anticipate that God will vindicate himself and his people and re-create "a new heaven and a new earth" (cf. Isa 65:17; 66:22; Rev 21).

14 So then, dear friends, since you are looking forward to this, make every effort to be found spotless,
blameless[d] and at peace with him. 15 Bear in mind that our Lord's patience[e] means salvation,[f] just as
our dear brother Paul also wrote you with the wisdom that God gave him.[g] 16 He writes the same way
in all his letters, speaking in them of these matters. His letters contain some things that are hard to
understand, which ignorant and unstable[h] people distort, as they do the other Scriptures,[i] to their own
destruction.
17 Therefore, dear friends, since you have been forewarned, be on your guard[j] so that you may not
be carried away by the error[k] of the lawless and fall from your secure position.[l] 18 But grow in the grace
and knowledge of our Lord and Savior Jesus Christ.[m] To him be glory both now and forever! Amen.

3:14 [d] 1Th 3:13
3:15 [e] Ro 2:4 [f] ver 9 [g] Eph 3:3
3:16 [h] 2Pe 2:14 [i] ver 2
3:17 [j] 1Co 10:12 [k] 2Pe 2:18 [l] Rev 2:5
3:18 [m] 2Pe 1:11

3:14 looking forward. See note on v. 13. Christians who are considering the end times must strive ("make every effort"; cf. 1:5–11) to be holy ("spotless, blameless")—like Christ (1 Pet 1:19) and unlike the false teachers (2:13).
3:15 our dear brother Paul. Although Paul rebuked Peter for actions he thought were incompatible with the gospel of free grace (Gal 2:11–14), these two apostles agreed about the essentials of the gospel message (cf. Acts 11:2–18; 15:7–11). According to tradition, both apostles were martyred in Rome in the mid-60s AD.
3:16 all his letters. Peter probably knew of all but one or two of Paul's letters by this time. **other Scriptures.** Peter equates Paul's letters with the God-breathed and authoritative OT Scriptures.
3:17–18 Peter concludes with two commands that summarize the letter: (1) **be on your guard.** The purpose of the letter is to protect them from the false teachers. (2) **grow.** See 1:5–11 and notes (cf. 1 Pet 2:2; Col 1:10).
3:18 in. Or "by means of." **grace and knowledge.** Frames the letter (cf. 1:2). **To him be glory both now and forever! Amen.** Only two other NT letters end with a doxology: Rom 16:25–27 and Jude 24–25. Only two other NT doxologies praise Christ: 2 Tim 4:18 and Rev 1:5–6 (cf. Rom 9:5). See "The Glory of God," p. 2640.

INTRODUCTION TO 1 – 3 JOHN

AUTHOR

The authors of the letters of John do not identify themselves by name. First John is entirely anonymous, and the author of 2 and 3 John describes himself simply as "the elder" (2 John 1; 3 John 1). However, a strong case can be made for identifying the author of all three letters as "the disciple whom Jesus loved" (John 13:23; 21:7,20; cf. 19:26), who in turn may be identified as John, the son of Zebedee (Mark 1:19 – 20), the apostle and author of the Gospel of John. Supporting evidence for this identification includes: (1) the beloved disciple may, based on evidence within the Gospel of John and by a process of elimination, be identified as the apostle John; (2) both the author of John's Gospel and the author of 1 John were eyewitnesses of Jesus' ministry (1:1 – 3); (3) words and ideas in 1, 2, 3 John resemble those found in John's Gospel (e.g., life and death, light and darkness, love and hate, truth and lies); (4) early church fathers, including, e.g., Irenaeus, Dionysius of Alexandria, and Tertullian, ascribe the authorship of both John's Gospel and 1 John unequivocally to John the disciple and apostle of the Lord.

DATE AND PLACE OF COMPOSITION

The letters of John were probably written from Ephesus, where, according to early church tradition, the apostle spent his last days. They may be dated to the early 90s as they appear to have been produced after the Gospel of John and build upon concepts and themes found in the Gospel that is believed to have been written around AD 80 – 85.

DESTINATION

The location of the addressees of 1, 2, 3 John is not indicated in the letters themselves. However, as John spent his later years in Ephesus in the Roman province of Asia, his letters were probably addressed to believers living in that region. 1 John is a circular letter intended for a number of associated churches. 2 John is addressed to one of these churches. 3 John is addressed to one individual (Gaius) in another of the churches.

OCCASION AND PURPOSE

These letters provide a snapshot of life in these churches. They reflect an unhappy time in the life of the Christian community to which John addressed them, a time of dispute involving both theological and behavioral concerns. It seems that sometime after the writing of John's Gospel, difficulties arose within this community. Some of the members espoused beliefs about the person and work of Christ that were unacceptable, denying that Jesus was the Christ, the Son of God, come in the flesh (1 John 4:2 – 3) and denying also, it would appear, that his death was necessary to provide for forgiveness of sins (1 John 5:6 – 7). A sharp disagreement arose, and those who embraced these views seceded from the community (1 John 2:19).

The secessionists were not content to keep their beliefs to themselves. Some of them became itinerant preachers who circulated among the churches and propagated their beliefs (1 John 2:26; 4:1 – 3; 2 John 7). This created confusion among those who remained loyal to the gospel as proclaimed by the eyewitnesses at the beginning. As a result some began to question whether they really knew God, were experiencing eternal life, and were in the truth. 1 John was written to bolster their assurance by providing criteria they could use to evaluate the spurious claims of the secessionists and with which they could reassure themselves (1 John 1:5—2:2; 2:3–11; 3:7–10,14–15; 4:4–8,13–15; 5:13,18–20). This letter appears to have been sent as a circular letter to the churches affected by the teaching of the secessionists.

As a follow-up to this circular letter, John wrote two other letters. He sent the first, 2 John, to one of the churches involved (to the "lady chosen by God and to her children") to warn members about the secessionists and their heretical teaching (2 John 7–8). He urged the readers not to help these teachers by providing them with hospitality. To do so would be to participate in their "wicked work" (2 John 11).

The secessionist teachers were not the only ones traveling around among these churches. There were also people of good standing who had gone from John's church "for the sake of the Name" (3 John 7). These people needed hospitality in Christian homes as they traveled about. John wrote the second of the follow-up letters, 3 John, to an individual named Gaius. He commended Gaius for providing hospitality to traveling preachers of good standing (3 John 5–6) and informed him of the actions of Diotrephes, who lived in the same town but refused to provide this hospitality and who was at loggerheads with John (3 John 9–10). It is not clear whether his refusal was doctrinally based (i.e., he agreed with the secessionists against John) or due to personal conflict (i.e., he rejected John's authority).

John's "communities" were likely small gatherings of Christians in house churches. This artist's rendering shows the earliest Christian church building known (early third century), from Dura-Europos, Syria.

Reconstruction by Dan Warner & Animator Derrick McKenzie

We do not know what happened to the secessionist movement. It may have developed into the sort of second-century Gnosticism we know through the writings of Irenaeus, or it may have simply died out. We do know that the position adopted in the letters of John won the day since they found their way into the NT canon.

GNOSTICISM

Gnosticism is a term used to designate a variety of beliefs, fundamental to which was a dualistic view of reality. The spiritual world was regarded as good, while the material world, including human bodies, was regarded as evil. Gnostic views are found reflected in various literary sources, including the works of early church fathers who rejected such Gnostic teaching, as well as Coptic writings, the Nag Hammadi library, and the Hermetic and Manichean literature.

According to some of these texts, sparks of divinity from the spiritual world were imprisoned in the bodies of certain spiritual individuals. Seeing their plight, God sent a redeemer to provide knowledge (*gnōsis*) concerning their true origin and to enable them to escape imprisonment in their bodies. This knowledge would also enable their spirits to pass unharmed through the planetary spheres so as to return to their original state, reunited with God. Because Gnostics regarded human bodies—part of the material world—as evil, some adopted ascetic practices treating the body harshly, while others indulged in promiscuity, believing what was done in the body did not affect their spiritual lives and their salvation.

It is possible that some of the secessionists were influenced by incipient Gnostic beliefs. Believing the material world is evil, they denied that Jesus is the Christ come in the flesh, i.e., they denied his true humanity (1 John 4:1–3). Some claimed that Christ only "seemed" to be human (Docetism), and others claimed that the Christ spirit descended upon Jesus at his baptism and departed before his crucifixion because it was impossible for Christ as a spiritual being to experience suffering (Cerinthianism). It is also possible that the sinful behavior John accuses the secessionists of practicing (1 John 3:6,10) may stem from the belief that what one does in the body does not affect one's spirit or one's salvation.

Traditional burial site of John at Ephesus.
Wikimedia Commons

While the letters of John are often regarded as a response to an early form of Gnosticism, caution needs to be exercised, especially when comparing the heretical beliefs that John opposes with developed forms of Gnosticism emanating from the second to the fifth centuries.

THEOLOGICAL THEMES

Theological Themes in 1 John

Many important theological themes emerge in 1 John. The most important of these is the nature of God. God is revealed as the Father of Jesus Christ (1:2–3; 2:22–24; 4:14). God is light and in him there is no darkness (1:5). God is love (4:8,16b), and this love was revealed in the sending of his Son as the atoning sacrifice for our sins (4:9–10). God lavishes his love upon believers by making them his children (3:1).

Also important is what John writes about the person and work of Jesus Christ. He is the Son of God come in the flesh, and to deny this is to deny God the Father also (2:22–23; 4:2–3; 5:10–12). Jesus gave himself to be the atoning sacrifice for our sins so that if we confess our sins, God forgives us and cleanses us from all unrighteousness (1:9; 2:12). Having given himself as the atoning sacrifice, Jesus now acts as our advocate with the Father if we sin (2:1). He was revealed to destroy the devil's work (3:8), and he protects us from the evil one (5:18).

A crucial part of John's attempt to reassure his readers is his insistence upon the fact that they have an anointing from God, the Holy Spirit, whom they have received from God and who teaches them what they need to know so that they do not need to give heed to the false teachings of the secessionists (2:27).

Those who believe in Christ have passed from death to life (3:14), having been born of God and having received eternal life (2:25; 5:11). Those who have been born of God do what is right (2:29), love one another (4:7; 5:1), overcome the world (5:4), and do not succumb to sinful behavior, being protected by Christ so that the evil one does not touch them (5:18). Christ gives them understanding so that they may know the One who is true, God the Father (5:20).

Another significant theme is assurance. Assurance is grounded in God's testimony to his Son (5:9–13). Believers may have confidence on the day of judgment when they live godly lives (2:28—3:3; 4:16–21), and obey the command to show love to their fellow believers in practical ways (2:3 – 6; 3:14); this in turn leads to confidence in prayer (3:21 – 22; 5:14).

Theological Themes in 2 John

This brief letter reinforces themes found in 1 John (obedience to the command to love and the importance of confessing that Christ came in the flesh). One new matter introduced in 2 John is a warning against aiding and abetting false teachers by providing them with hospitality. In the Greco-Roman world of the day, providing hospitality involved becoming guarantor for one's guests' bona fides, which therefore made those who provided hospitality for unworthy recipients partakers in their "wicked work" (v. 11).

Theological Themes in 3 John

Hospitality is also an important issue in this letter. Those who provide hospitality for traveling missionaries who preach the truth are commended and "work together for the truth" (v. 8; see vv. 5 – 8). Another matter that emerges is the need to exercise discipline in the church, in particular to deal with one who spreads "malicious nonsense" (v. 10), refuses to provide hospitality, and prevents other church members from doing so (vv. 9 – 10).

OUTLINE OF 1 JOHN

The way 1 John is structured is unusual in that it does not follow a linear plan moving logically from one subject to the next. Instead it revisits the same subjects over and over, each time amplifying them further in what has been called a spiraling structure. This is so because 1 John does not seek to prove anything, but rather by repetition seeks to increase the readers' adherence to known truths of the gospel in face of the threat posed by the secessionists' teachings.

OUTLINE

I. The Incarnation of the Word of Life (1:1 – 4)

II. Light and Darkness, Sin and Forgiveness (1:5 — 2:2)

III. Love and Hatred for Fellow Believers (2:3 – 11)

IV. Reasons for Writing (2:12 – 14)

V. On Not Loving the World (2:15 – 17)

VI. Warning Against Denying the Son (2:18 – 27)

VII. God's Children and Sin (2:28 — 3:10)

VIII. More on Love and Hatred (3:11 – 24)

IX. On Denying the Incarnation (4:1 – 6)

X. God's Love and Ours (4:7 – 21)

XI. Faith in the Incarnate Son of God (5:1 – 12)

XII. Concluding Affirmations (5:13 – 21)

1 JOHN

1:1 [a] Jn 1:2 [b] Jn 1:14; 2Pe 1:16 [c] Jn 20:27
1:2 [d] Jn 1:1-4; 1Ti 3:16
1:3 [e] 1Co 1:9
1:4 [f] 1Jn 2:1 [g] Jn 3:29
1:5 [h] 1Jn 3:11
1:6 [i] 2Co 6:14 [j] Jn 3:19-21
1:7 [k] Heb 9:14; Rev 1:5
1:8 [l] Pr 20:9; Jas 3:2 [m] 1Jn 2:4

The Incarnation of the Word of Life

1 That which was from the beginning,[a] which we have heard, which we have seen with our eyes,[b]
which we have looked at and our hands have touched[c] — this we proclaim concerning the Word
of life. 2 The life appeared;[d] we have seen it and testify to it, and we proclaim to you the eternal life,
which was with the Father and has appeared to us. 3 We proclaim to you what we have seen and heard,
so that you also may have fellowship with us. And our fellowship is with the Father and with his Son,
Jesus Christ.[e] 4 We write this[f] to make our*a* joy complete.[g]

Light and Darkness, Sin and Forgiveness

5 This is the message we have heard[h] from him and declare to you: God is light; in him there is no
darkness at all. 6 If we claim to have fellowship with him and yet walk in the darkness,[i] we lie and do
not live out the truth.[j] 7 But if we walk in the light, as he is in the light, we have fellowship with one
another, and the blood of Jesus, his Son, purifies us from all*b* sin.[k]
8 If we claim to be without sin,[l] we deceive ourselves and the truth is not in us.[m] 9 If we confess our

a 4 Some manuscripts *your* *b* 7 Or *every*

1:1–4 *The Incarnation of the Word of Life.* To strengthen his readers' commitment to what they already know, John begins by reminding them of the origins of the gospel, the message concerning "the Word of life" (v. 1), which constitutes the basis of the fellowship in which he wants them to continue. **1:1 That which was from the beginning.** While this phrase is reminiscent of both Gen 1:1 ("In the beginning God created the heavens and the earth") and John 1:1 ("In the beginning was the Word"), here it refers primarily to the incarnation of "the Word of life" in the person of the historical Jesus. However, its resonance with John 1:1 probably implies an identification of the Word of life incarnate in Jesus with the Word who was with God before the foundation of the world. **we.** John and the other eyewitnesses. Their testimony was based upon the historical flesh-and-blood reality of Jesus' life and ministry on earth. **heard … seen … looked at … touched.** This is the language of sense perception and underlines the fact that John was an eyewitness of the Word of life. Other ancient literature consistently uses this sort of language for actual sense perception. It is not, as some claim, a merely metaphoric expression that does not imply firsthand testimony.
1:2 The life appeared; we have seen it. The Word of life was incarnate in Jesus Christ as well as being proclaimed as a message. As God has life in himself so too Jesus has life in himself (John 1:4; 11:25; 14:6), and he has the power to grant life to whomever he will (John 5:21). **eternal life, which was with the Father.** Refers to the preexistent Word of life and is reminiscent of John 1:1 ("the Word was with God").
1:3 have fellowship with us. "Us" refers to the eyewitnesses rather than the secessionists (see Introduction: Occasion and Purpose; Gnosticism). **our fellowship is with the Father.** This is not the case for those who turn away from the true message of the Word of life, such as the secessionists.
1:4 our joy. "Our" is a better reading than "your" (see NIV text note), being consistent with statements in 2 John 4 and 3 John 4, where John says hearing that his children are walking in the truth gives *him* great joy (cf. Phil 2:2).
1:5—2:2 *Light and Darkness, Sin and Forgiveness.* John defines the content of his message (1:5) and then draws out its ethical implications to deal with the secessionists' false claims of having fellowship with God (while in fact they are walking in darkness) and their claim not to have sinned. He contrasts this with the experience of those who walk in the light (1:6—2:2).
1:5 light. Refers to what is true, good, and holy. **darkness.** Refers to what is false and evil.
1:6 If we claim. A reference to the secessionists. **walk in the darkness.** Denotes a life characterized by wickedness and ignorance and an unwillingness to be open toward God and his revelation in Christ lest one's sinful behavior be exposed (cf. John 3:19–21).
1:7 walk in the light. Denotes a life characterized by truth and holiness and a willingness to be open to God and his revelation, resulting in fellowship with one another and with God. **the blood of Jesus.** His atoning death on the cross. **purifies us from all sin.** Removes the stain of sins committed, making us acceptable to God, closely related to forgiveness (cf. v. 9).
1:8 without sin. Or "do not have sin." To "have sin" means to be guilty of sinful acts (cf. John 9:41; 15:22,24; 19:11). Those who seceded from the community were not claiming to have a sinless nature but probably claiming that they had not actually sinned since coming to know God.
1:9 confess our sins. Honest acknowledgment of one's sins is a pre-

sins, he is faithful and just and will forgive us our sins[n] and purify us from all unrighteousness. 10 If we
claim we have not sinned, we make him out to be a liar[o] and his word is not in us.[p]

2 My dear children,[q] I write this to you so that you will not sin. But if anybody does sin, we have an
advocate[r] with the Father—Jesus Christ, the Righteous One. 2 He is the atoning sacrifice for our
sins,[s] and not only for ours but also for the sins of the whole world.

Love and Hatred for Fellow Believers

3 We know that we have come to know him if we keep his commands.[t] 4 Whoever says, "I know him,"
but does not do what he commands is a liar, and the truth is not in that person.[u] 5 But if anyone obeys
his word,[v] love for God[a] is truly made complete in them.[w] This is how we know we are in him: 6 Whoever
claims to live in him must live as Jesus did.[x]

7 Dear friends, I am not writing you a new command but an old one, which you have had since the
beginning.[y] This old command is the message you have heard. 8 Yet I am writing you a new command;[z] its
truth is seen in him and in you, because the darkness is passing[a] and the true light[b] is already shining.[c]

9 Anyone who claims to be in the light but hates a brother or sister[b] is still in the darkness. 10 Anyone

1:9 [n] Ps 32:5; 51:2
1:10 [o] 1Jn 5:10 [p] 1Jn 2:14
2:1 [q] ver 12,13,28 [r] Ro 8:34; Heb 7:25
2:2 [s] Ro 3:25
2:3 [t] Jn 14:15
2:4 [u] 1Jn 1:6,8
2:5 [v] Jn 14:21,23 [w] 1Jn 4:12
2:6 [x] Mt 11:29; 1Pe 2:21
2:7 [y] 1Jn 3:11,23; 2Jn 5,6
2:8 [z] Jn 13:34 [a] Ro 13:12 [b] Jn 1:9 [c] Eph 5:8; 1Th 5:5

[a] *5* Or *word, God's love* [b] *9* The Greek word for *brother or sister* (*adelphos*) refers here to a believer, whether man or woman, as part of God's family; also in verse 11; and in 3:15, 17; 4:20; 5:16.

requisite for forgiveness. **faithful and just and will forgive us our sins.** God is faithful to his promises when he forgives his people (cf. Exod 34:6–7), and he is also just when doing so because he sent his Son to be the atoning sacrifice for sins (1 John 2:2; 4:10, cf. Rom 3:25–26). When God forgives people, he no longer holds their sins against them; he cancels their "debt" (cf. Matt 6:12; 18:21–35). **purify us from all unrighteousness.** Removes the defilement our sins produce, thus removing the impediment to fellowship with God.

1:10 If we claim we have not sinned. Basically restates what is found in v. 8 but indicates that such a claim involves more than self-deception. It implies also that God is a liar because he regards all people as sinners, for otherwise he would not have sent his Son to be the atoning sacrifice for our sins (2:2; 4:10).

2:1 My dear children. Reflects John's affection for his readers, his age, and the senior position he occupies in relation to them. **if anybody does sin.** John recognizes that believers do sin, something the secessionists deny. **we have an advocate.** Jesus speaks on our behalf in the presence of his Father when we sin (cf. 1 Tim 2:5; Heb 8:1). He pleads our case on the basis of his death, by which forgiveness of sins was made possible.

2:2 atoning sacrifice. Translates a Greek word found in only two places in the NT (here and 4:10) and six times in the Greek OT; in every case but one, it relates to the removal of guilt occasioned by sin, and in most places this is effected through sacrifice. It carries the meanings of both expiation (removing guilt and purifying sinners) and propitiation (appeasing God's anger toward sinners). Here it carries the idea of propitiation since we need an advocate with the Father because of our sins. This must not be confused with pagan notions of propitiation in which humans seek to propitiate capricious deities, for it was God himself who provided his Son to be the atoning sacrifice for our sins (see note on Rom 3:25). **the whole world.** This has been interpreted as the entire world in its breadth and sweep (cf. John 12:19; Rom 1:8), and therefore not limited to one particular group but of worldwide application—for all nations (cf. Gen 12:3; John 1:29). In the present context it means the unbelieving world. Christ's atoning sacrifice was made not only for "our" sins (i.e., believers' sins) but also for the sins of the unbelieving world (cf. 4:14; John 1:29). This does not mean that all people's sins are automatically forgiven even if they do not believe, for John says that "whoever does not have the Son of God does not have life" (1 John 5:12) and that having the Son involves believing in him (5:12–13). Perhaps we may say Jesus' death was sufficient to deal with the sins of the whole world, but it becomes effective only when people believe.

2:3–11 *Love and Hatred for Fellow Believers.* John focuses on the secessionists' claim to know God while not keeping his commands. In particular John commands believers to love one another. True believers have the assurance of knowing God when they obey his commands.

2:3 We know that we have come to know him. John provides several tests believers may apply to themselves and so be assured of salvation (cf. v. 5; 1:7; 3:14; 4:13; 5:2). Here the test is that of obedience. **if we keep his commands.** John was not thinking of believers' obedience to the Mosaic law. In 3:22–23 he refers to believers obeying God's "commands" and then adds "and this is his command: to believe in the name of his Son, Jesus Christ, and to love one another as he commanded us." In biblical terms, belief in Christ and obedience to his commands go hand in hand. **keep his commands.** Does not mean that believers will never disobey (cf. 1:8–9) but that their lives are characterized by obedience.

2:4 the truth is not in that person. In contrast to those who keep God's commands and may thus be sure they know God, the secessionists who claim to know him while disobeying his commands show they are liars.

2:5 love for God is truly made complete. Our love for God completes its work in us when we obey his command to love one another.

2:6 live as Jesus did. Those who claim to live in God must keep God's commands to them as Jesus obeyed God's commands to him.

2:7 not ... a new command but an old one. The old command is to love one another. It was old for John's readers because they'd had it "since the beginning," i.e., since they first believed. It was "the message [they had] heard" when it was handed on to them alongside the gospel.

2:8 I am writing you a new command. The resolution to the apparent contradiction between this verse and the previous one is found in John 13:34, where Jesus says, "A new command I give you: Love one another." The "newness" of Jesus' command was that his disciples should love one another as he had loved them—expressed in his laying down his life for them. But the ministry of Jesus was long past, so his "new command" was now something "old" for John and his readers. **its truth is seen in him and in you.** The love command was actualized in both the life of Jesus and the lives of John's readers. **darkness.** The realm in which sinful behavior predominates. **the true light.** With Jesus Christ, the true light came into the world and the darkness could not overcome it (cf. John 1:4–5,9; 8:12; 9:5; 12:35–36,46).

2:9 Anyone. What John says is of general application, but refers here in particular it to the secessionists. **hates a brother or sister.** John writes in black-and-white terms, not implying they hated all brothers and sisters, for surely they did not hate one another. **in the darkness.**

2:10 [d]1Jn 3:14
2:11 [e]Jn 12:35
2:13 [f]ver 14
2:14 [g]Eph 6:10 [h]Jn 5:38; 1Jn 1:10 [i]ver 13
2:15 [j]Ro 12:2 [k]Jas 4:4
2:16 [l]Ro 13:14 [m]Pr 27:20
2:17 [n]1Co 7:31
2:18 [o]ver 22; 1Jn 4:3; 2Jn 7 [p]1Jn 4:1
2:19 [q]Ac 20:30

who loves their brother and sister[a] lives in the light,[d] and there is nothing in them to make them stumble. [11]But anyone who hates a brother or sister is in the darkness and walks around in the darkness.
They do not know where they are going, because the darkness has blinded them.[e]

Reasons for Writing

[12]I am writing to you, dear children,
because your sins have been forgiven on account of his name.
[13]I am writing to you, fathers,
because you know him who is from the beginning.
I am writing to you, young men,
because you have overcome the evil one.[f]

[14]I write to you, dear children,
because you know the Father.
I write to you, fathers,
because you know him who is from the beginning.
I write to you, young men,
because you are strong,[g]
and the word of God lives in you,[h]
and you have overcome the evil one.[i]

On Not Loving the World

[15]Do not love the world or anything in the world.[j] If anyone loves the world, love for the Father[b] is
not in them.[k] [16]For everything in the world—the lust of the flesh,[l] the lust of the eyes,[m] and the pride
of life—comes not from the Father but from the world. [17]The world and its desires pass away,[n] but
whoever does the will of God lives forever.

Warnings Against Denying the Son

[18]Dear children, this is the last hour; and as you have heard that the antichrist is coming,[o] even now
many antichrists have come.[p] This is how we know it is the last hour. [19]They went out from us,[q] but

[a] *10* The Greek word for *brother and sister* (*adelphos*) refers here to a believer, whether man or woman, as part of God's family; also in 3:10; 4:20, 21. [b] *15* Or *world, the Father's love*

Those who hate are in the realm where sinful behavior predominates (vv. 8–9,11; 1:6).

2:10 lives in the light. Denotes a way of life characterized by truth and holiness and willingness to be open to God and his revelation (cf. John 3:21). **stumble**. Fall into sin. People who hate fellow believers walk in darkness, and their own sinful behavior—in this case their hatred—blinds them (cf. John 12:35).

2:12–14 *Reasons for Writing.* As well as providing tests his readers may use to expose false claims to know God, John writes to assure them that he is confident about their standing as true believers.

2:12,14 children. Refers here to all John's readers as elsewhere in the letter (cf. vv. 1,18,28; 3:7,18; 4:4; 5:21). They fall into two groups: "young men," denoting those of a lesser age (cf. 1 Tim 5:1; 1 Pet 5:5) and "fathers," denoting those of advanced years (cf. 1 Tim 5:1).

2:12 your sins have been forgiven. John has spoken already about forgiveness for those who confess their sins (1:9), something that clearly applies to all believers.

2:13 him who is from the beginning. The Word, Jesus Christ. **the beginning.** Refers not to the beginning of time but to the time when the Word became incarnate in Jesus Christ (see 1:1). **you have overcome the evil one.** References to "the evil one" in 1 John all refer to the devil. The "young men" have overcome him by resisting his attempts to subvert their faith through the false teaching of the secessionists.

2:14 the word of God lives in you. The message Jesus proclaimed and embodies remains in them.

2:15–17 *On Not Loving the World.* John exhorts his readers not to love the world and highlights the positive alternative: doing the will of God and thus living forever.

2:15 the world. Not the people of the world nor the created order, but worldly attitudes or values opposed to God. **anything in the world.** The constituent elements that make up the world are described in v. 16. **love for the Father is not in them.** If people love the world, they do not love the Father. There is no middle ground (cf. Eph. 2:1–3; Col 1:13; Jas 4:4).

2:16 the lust of the flesh. A general category. The following are subcategories: **the lust of the eyes.** Sinful cravings that are activated by what people see. **the pride of life.** Includes being puffed up in pride because of one's material possessions. The word translated "life" (Greek *bios*) can mean life, livelihood, living, property, and possessions. Here it means possessions (its predominant use in the NT).

2:17 does the will of God. The opposite of all that is involved in loving the world (v. 16). It includes believing in the Son and loving fellow believers (3:23). **lives forever.** Jesus promised believers that they will live, even though they die, and that they will live forever (John 6:51,58; 8:51; 10:28; 11:25–26).

2:18–27 *Warning Against Denying the Son.* John urges his readers to remain faithful to the message they have heard from the beginning because there are many antichrists who are seeking to deceive them. The passage has two sections: vv. 18–19 speaks of the coming of antichrists and identifies them as the secessionists, and vv. 20–27 warns

they did not really belong to us. For if they had belonged to us, they would have remained with us; but
their going showed that none of them belonged to us.[r]
20But you have an anointing[s] from the Holy One,[t] and all of you know the truth.[a][u] 21I do not write to
you because you do not know the truth, but because you do know it[v] and because no lie comes from the
truth. 22Who is the liar? It is whoever denies that Jesus is the Christ. Such a person is the antichrist—
denying the Father and the Son.[w] 23No one who denies the Son has the Father; whoever acknowledges
the Son has the Father also.[x]
24As for you, see that what you have heard from the beginning remains in you. If it does, you also
will remain in the Son and in the Father.[y] 25And this is what he promised us—eternal life.
26I am writing these things to you about those who are trying to lead you astray.[z] 27As for you, the
anointing[a] you received from him remains in you, and you do not need anyone to teach you. But as
his anointing teaches you about all things and as that anointing is real, not counterfeit—just as it
has taught you, remain in him.

God's Children and Sin

28And now, dear children,[b] continue in him, so that when he appears[c] we may be confident[d] and
unashamed before him at his coming.[e]
29If you know that he is righteous,[f] you know that everyone who does what is right has been born
of him.

3 See what great love[g] the Father has lavished on us, that we should be called children of God![h] And
that is what we are! The reason the world does not know us is that it did not know him.[i] 2Dear
friends, now we are children of God, and what we will be has not yet been made known. But we know
that when Christ appears,[b] we shall be like him,[j] for we shall see him as he is.[k] 3All who have this hope
in him purify themselves,[l] just as he is pure.

2:19 [r] 1Co 11:19
2:20 [s] 2Co 1:21 [t] Mk 1:24 [u] Jn 14:26
2:21 [v] 2Pe 1:12; Jude 5
2:22 [w] 2Jn 7
2:23 [x] Jn 8:19; 1Jn 4:15
2:24 [y] Jn 14:23
2:26 [z] 2Jn 7
2:27 [a] ver 20
2:28 [b] ver 1 [c] 1Jn 3:2 [d] 1Jn 4:17 [e] 1Th 2:19
2:29 [f] 1Jn 3:7
3:1 [g] Jn 3:16 [h] Jn 1:12 [i] Jn 16:3
3:2 [j] Ro 8:29; 2Pe 1:4 [k] 2Co 3:18
3:3 [l] 2Co 7:1; 2Pe 3:13,14

[a] *20* Some manuscripts *and you know all things* [b] *2* Or *when it is made known*

about the secessionists' attempt to deceive them and arms his readers against the secessionists' deception.

2:18 the last hour. Also called "the last days" and "the last times," it is the period that began with the first coming of Jesus and ends with his second coming (cf. Acts 2:17; Heb 1:2; 1 Pet 1:20). **antichrist ... antichrists.** The coming of an antichrist figure was part of early Christian teaching. It distinguished between the great antichrist figure that would appear near the end of the age (cf. 2 Thess 2:3–5; Rev 13:1–6) and lesser antichrist figures whose influence was already being felt (as in this verse). Both the antichrist and the antichrists that precede him aim to deceive people (cf. Matt 24:4–5,11,24). Only 1 John identifies the former members of a Christian community as antichrists; elsewhere in the NT they attack the church from without. John describes them as liars (1 John 2:4,22) and deceivers (2 John 7) who deny the incarnation (1 John 4:1–3; 2 John 7).

2:19 They went out from us, but they did not really belong to us. Their secession showed they had never really been true members of the Christian community.

2:20 have an anointing. In the OT, priests, kings, and the Messiah are anointed as a sign of their appointment (Exod 28:41; 1 Sam 16:13; Isa 61:1). The anointing John's readers have received is that of the Holy Spirit, whom they received when they first believed. As a result of his ministry, they already "know the truth." **the Holy One.** A reference to Jesus Christ (cf. John 6:69).

2:22 denies that Jesus is the Christ. Here, for the first time, John identifies the false teaching of those who left the community. Combining this with other statements in 1 John (cf. 4:2–3,15; 5:1,6–8), it becomes clear that their aberrant Christology involved a denial that Jesus Christ is the Messiah, God's Son, come in the flesh, whose death was real and vicarious.

2:23 No one who denies the Son has the Father. By denying the Son (see v. 22 and note), they show they do not have the Father either.

2:24 what you have heard from the beginning. The gospel message.

2:25 what he promised us—eternal life. While this is something promised for the future, it is also a present possession for believers (5:13).

2:27 you do not need anyone to teach you. John is not denying the importance of human teachers (cf. Matt 28:20; 1 Cor 12:28; Eph 4:11; Col 3:16; 1 Tim 4:11; 2 Tim 2:2,24), for he himself teaches in this letter. He assures his readers that they do not need to be taught by the secessionists (who may have claimed their own special anointing) because "the anointing ... teaches you about all things." **all things.** Not everything that can possibly be known, but all that they need to know about the true nature of Christ. The Holy Spirit continues to teach believers, helping them understand the Scriptures and how to apply them to their lives.

2:28—3:10 *God's Children and Sin.* John distinguishes the children of God from the children of the devil in terms of doing or not doing what is right, with a parenthetical passage (3:1–3) highlighting the greatness of God's love for believers.

2:28 continue in him. Remain in Christ, following the teaching they heard from the beginning. **confident.** John equates this with being unashamed. **his coming.** Christ's second coming.

2:29 everyone who does what is right has been born of him. The corollary is that those who do not do what is right—no matter what claims they make to a special anointing—have not been born of God (cf. John 1:11–12; 3:1–15).

3:1,2 children of God. People become God's children when they believe in Christ (John 1:12).

3:2 when Christ appears, we shall be like him. At his second coming, Christ will "transform our lowly bodies so that they will be like his glorious body" (Phil 3:21), no longer subject to death or decay (cf. Rom 8:29; 1 Cor 15:49).

3:3 purify themselves, just as he is pure. Moral purity is meant, which is confirmed by v. 5: "He appeared so that he might take away our sins.

3:4 [m] 1Jn 5:17
3:5 [n] 2Co 5:21
3:6 [o] ver 9 [p] 3Jn 11 [q] 1Jn 2:4
3:7 [r] 1Jn 2:1 [s] 1Jn 2:26 [t] 1Jn 2:29
3:8 [u] Jn 8:44
3:9 [v] Jn 1:13 [w] 1Jn 5:18 [x] 1Pe 1:23
3:10 [y] 1Jn 4:8
3:11 [z] 1Jn 1:5 [a] Jn 13:34, 35; 2Jn 5
3:12 [b] Ge 4:8
3:13 [c] Jn 15:18, 19; 17:14
3:14 [d] Jn 5:24 [e] 1Jn 2:9
3:15 [f] Mt 5:21, 22; Jn 8:44 [g] Gal 5:20, 21
3:16 [h] Jn 15:13
3:17 [i] Dt 15:7, 8 [j] 1Jn 4:20
3:18 [k] 1Jn 2:1 [l] Eze 33:31; Ro 12:9

4 Everyone who sins breaks the law; in fact, sin is lawlessness.[m] 5 But you know that he appeared so that he might take away our sins. And in him is no sin.[n] 6 No one who lives in him keeps on sinning.[o] No one who continues to sin has either seen him[p] or known him.[q]

7 Dear children,[r] do not let anyone lead you astray.[s] The one who does what is right is righteous, just as he is righteous.[t] 8 The one who does what is sinful is of the devil,[u] because the devil has been sinning from the beginning. The reason the Son of God appeared was to destroy the devil's work. 9 No one who is born of God[v] will continue to sin,[w] because God's seed[x] remains in them; they cannot go on sinning, because they have been born of God. 10 This is how we know who the children of God are and who the children of the devil are: Anyone who does not do what is right is not God's child, nor is anyone who does not love[y] their brother and sister.

More on Love and Hatred

11 For this is the message you heard[z] from the beginning: We should love one another.[a] 12 Do not be like Cain, who belonged to the evil one and murdered his brother.[b] And why did he murder him? Because his own actions were evil and his brother's were righteous. 13 Do not be surprised, my brothers and sisters,[a] if the world hates you.[c] 14 We know that we have passed from death to life,[d] because we love each other. Anyone who does not love remains in death.[e] 15 Anyone who hates a brother or sister is a murderer,[f] and you know that no murderer has eternal life residing in him.[g]

16 This is how we know what love is: Jesus Christ laid down his life for us. And we ought to lay down our lives for our brothers and sisters.[h] 17 If anyone has material possessions and sees a brother or sister in need but has no pity on them,[i] how can the love of God be in that person?[j] 18 Dear children,[k] let us not love with words or speech but with actions and in truth.[l]

19 This is how we know that we belong to the truth and how we set our hearts at rest in his presence:

[a] *13* The Greek word for *brothers and sisters* (*adelphoi*) refers here to believers, both men and women, as part of God's family; also in verse 16.

And in him is no sin." Our hope of being like Christ when he appears must express itself in an effort to purify ourselves to be like him now.

3:4 John returns to the main theme of 2:28—3:10, the connection between knowing God and doing "what is right" (cf. vv. 7,10). **breaks the law.** Or "commits lawlessness." The Greek word translated "lawlessness" is *anomia*. In the NT it never means transgression of the law. It is used in association with false prophets (Matt 7:23) and evildoers (2 Cor 6:14; 2 Thess 2:3,7) who oppose God.

3:5 he appeared so that he might take away our sins. Christ took away our sins by offering himself as an atoning sacrifice (2:2; 4:10), thereby making it possible for God to be faithful and just when he forgives our sins (1:9).

3:6 No one who lives in him keeps on sinning. The claim that one can remain in Christ while continuing to indulge in sinful behavior is ridiculous, if not blasphemous, for "in him is no sin" (v. 5). See note on v. 9.

3:8 the devil has been sinning from the beginning. This is an allusion to Genesis 3, where the devil tempts the first couple to disobey God (cf. John 8:44). **destroy the devil's work.** The devil seeks to turn people aside from doing God's will, causing them to sin, so that he may accuse them before God and demand judgment upon them. By his death Jesus atoned for human sin, thus removing the basis of the devil's accusation and so destroying his work.

3:9 God's seed. A daring metaphor employing the word "seed" (Greek *sperma*) to depict the Spirit's work in believers. Unlike the children of the devil (in this case the secessionists), the children of God do not go on sinning because the Spirit dwells within them. There is an apparent contradiction in 1 John concerning sin in the believer's life: those who claim not to have sinned are liars (1:10); those born of God do not and cannot sin (3:6,9). A possible resolution is that, in context, 3:4 defines the latter sin as "lawlessness" (Greek *anomia*). In the NT this word refers not to breaking the law but to rebelling against God (like the devil's rebellion). If this is the case, John is saying that those who claim to know God and yet sin in this way certainly do not know God and are, in fact, in league with the devil. This is the sin that those born of God do not and cannot commit. It is possible for believers to sin in other ways, as 1:8—2:1 indicates.

3:11–24 *More on Love and Hatred.* John reminds his readers of Christ's command that his followers should love one another, stressing that genuine love for fellow believers is an important mark of those who "belong to the truth" (v. 19).

3:12 Do not be like Cain. This alludes to Gen 4:1–16, which recounts Cain's murder of Abel because Abel's offering was accepted by the Lord while Cain's was not (cf. Heb 11:4). (It may be inferred from Gen 4:7 that the Lord did not accept Cain's offering because Cain was an evildoer, for before he murdered his brother, the Lord said to him, "If you do what is right, will you not be accepted?")

3:14 We know … because we love. Those who love their fellow believers may assure themselves that they have passed from death to life. **passed from death to life.** In John 5:24 the same expression is synonymous with escaping judgment and obtaining eternal life.

3:15 Anyone who hates … is a murderer. An allusion to Cain, who murdered his brother (v. 12); it agrees with Jesus' teaching (Matt 5:21–22). **eternal life.** It is not just an unending extension of life as we know it; rather, it is "having" the Son. Eternal life is in the Son, and those who believe in him have eternal life because he dwells within them and gives them life (cf. John 5:21,26).

3:16 we ought to lay down our lives. Thus, following Christ's example (cf. John 10:17–18), something John applies in a down-to-earth fashion (cf. 1 John 3:17).

3:17 the love of God. Either God's love poured into believers' hearts (cf. Rom 5:5) or believers' love for God expressed in helping those in need. Both are part of John's teaching concerning the love of God (cf. 1 John 4:19–20).

3:19–22 This passage has been interpreted in terms of believers' assurance in two ways: (1) If our consciences condemn us, God is kinder than our consciences, and if they do not condemn us, we have confi-

20 If our hearts condemn us, we know that God is greater than our hearts, and he knows everything.
21 Dear friends, if our hearts do not condemn us, we have confidence before God[m] 22 and receive from
him anything we ask,[n] because we keep his commands and do what pleases him.[o] 23 And this is his
command: to believe[p] in the name of his Son, Jesus Christ, and to love one another as he commanded
us.[q] 24 The one who keeps God's commands lives in him,[r] and he in them. And this is how we know that
he lives in us: We know it by the Spirit he gave us.[s]

On Denying the Incarnation

4 Dear friends, do not believe every spirit, but test the spirits to see whether they are from God, because many false prophets have gone out into the world.[t] 2 This is how you can recognize the Spirit
of God: Every spirit that acknowledges that Jesus Christ has come in the flesh[u] is from God,[v] 3 but every
spirit that does not acknowledge Jesus is not from God. This is the spirit of the antichrist,[w] which you
have heard is coming and even now is already in the world.
4 You, dear children, are from God and have overcome them, because the one who is in you[x] is greater
than the one who is in the world.[y] 5 They are from the world[z] and therefore speak from the viewpoint
of the world, and the world listens to them. 6 We are from God, and whoever knows God listens to us;
but whoever is not from God does not listen to us.[a] This is how we recognize the Spirit[a] of truth[b] and
the spirit of falsehood.

God's Love and Ours

7 Dear friends, let us love one another,[c] for love comes from God. Everyone who loves has been born
of God and knows God.[d] 8 Whoever does not love does not know God, because God is love.[e] 9 This is how
God showed his love among us: He sent his one and only Son into the world that we might live through
him.[f] 10 This is love: not that we loved God, but that he loved us[g] and sent his Son as an atoning sacrifice
for our sins.[h] 11 Dear friends, since God so loved us,[i] we also ought to love one another. 12 No one has ever
seen God;[j] but if we love one another, God lives in us and his love is made complete in us.[k]

[a] 6 Or *spirit*

3:21 [m] 1Jn 5:14
3:22 [n] Mt 7:7 [o] Jn 8:29
3:23 [p] Jn 6:29 [q] Jn 13:34
3:24 [r] 1Jn 2:6 [s] 1Jn 4:13
4:1 [t] 2Pe 2:1; 1Jn 2:18
4:2 [u] Jn 1:14; 1Jn 2:23 [v] 1Co 12:3
4:3 [w] 1Jn 2:22; 2Jn 7
4:4 [x] Ro 8:31 [y] Jn 12:31
4:5 [z] Jn 15:19
4:6 [a] Jn 8:47 [b] Jn 14:17
4:7 [c] 1Jn 3:11 [d] 1Jn 2:4
4:8 [e] ver 7,16
4:9 [f] Jn 3:16,17; 1Jn 5:11
4:10 [g] Ro 5:8,10 [h] 1Jn 2:2
4:11 [i] Jn 3:16
4:12 [j] Jn 1:18; 1Ti 6:16 [k] 1Jn 2:5

dence that God will hear our prayers. (2) If our consciences condemn us, God is more rigorous than our consciences, but if they do not condemn us, then we have confidence that God will hear our prayers. Alternatively the passage may be interpreted in light of Deut 15:7–9, which warns the Israelites about hardness of heart toward needy people. John insists our mean-spirited hearts must be persuaded to make the sacrifice because we will not escape God's notice. If we do respond generously, we experience confidence in prayer.

3:23 this is his command. There are two parts to the command: believe in Christ and love one another. The love command is inseparable from the gospel message (cf. 2:7; 3:11). Believing in Jesus involves obedience, including obedience to his command that we love one another.

3:24 lives in him, and he in them. The concept of mutual indwelling is a frequent theme in John's Gospel (John 14:20; 15:4–7; 17:22–23) and is found four times in 1 John (here; 4:13,15,16). Believers can be assured that God lives in them and they in him because God has given them the Spirit, suggesting that the Spirit effects this mutual indwelling.

4:1–6 *On Denying the Incarnation.* John counsels his readers to "test the spirits" (v. 1) since the secessionists, whom he identifies as false prophets, deny that Jesus Christ has come in the flesh.

4:1 test the spirits. Involves discerning whether people are moved by the Holy Spirit or by an evil spirit. **false prophets.** These *appear* to be genuine but lead people away from the truth by their false teaching (cf. Matt 7:15; 24:11,24; Mark 13:22; 2 Pet 2:1). **gone out into the world.** This is an allusion to those who left the community, the secessionists, who deny the incarnation (cf. v. 2; 2:18–19,22), and it implies that their affinity is now with the unbelieving world, not the Christian community.

4:2–3 acknowledges that Jesus Christ has come in the flesh ... does not acknowledge Jesus. The spirits are tested concerning their acknowledgment or denial of Jesus' incarnation. By their denial of the incarnation, the secessionists show they are not from God but activated by the spirit of antichrist (see note on 2:18).

4:4 have overcome them. Rejected the heretical teaching of the antichrists (i.e., the secessionists). **the one who is in you.** The Holy Spirit. **the one who is in the world.** The spirit of antichrist, the devil (cf. John 12:31), who is active in the inhabited earth. The spiritual security of believers rests ultimately upon the Spirit's work within them, and there is no power greater than the Spirit of God that can destroy his work. This is a firm basis of Christian assurance.

4:5 They are from the world. The secessionists, who by rejecting the gospel have thrown their lot in with the world. **speak from the viewpoint of the world, and the world listens to them.** Heretical teaching, shaped by worldly categories, is more plausible to many unbelievers than the truth of the gospel.

4:7–21 *God's Love and Ours.* John again urges his readers to love one another, especially since God has shown his love for them in sending his only Son so that they might live through him.

4:7 Everyone who loves. True love for other believers is evidence that a person knows God.

4:8 God is love. Love is not God's only attribute. He is spirit (John 4:24), light (1 John 1:5), faithful and just (1:9), and good (Luke 18:19). Love existed between the Father and the Son before the creation of the world (John 17:24).

4:10 sent his Son as an atoning sacrifice for our sins. See note on 2:2. God's loving nature was revealed in sending his Son to die for sins so that people might have life through him (4:9).

4:11 since God so loved us. Such an expression of God's love should motivate us to love one another.

4:12 No one has ever seen God. The invisibility of God is an

4:13 [l] 1Jn 3:24
4:14 [m] Jn 15:27 [n] Jn 3:17
4:15 [o] Ro 10:9
4:16 [p] ver 8 [q] 1Jn 3:24
4:17 [r] 1Jn 2:5
4:18 [s] Ro 8:15
4:19 [t] ver 10
4:20 [u] 1Jn 2:9 [v] 1Jn 2:4 [w] 1Jn 3:17 [x] ver 12
4:21 [y] Mt 5:43
5:1 [z] 1Jn 2:22 [a] Jn 1:13; 1Jn 2:23 [b] Jn 8:42
5:3 [c] Jn 14:15; 2Jn 6 [d] Mt 11:30
5:4 [e] Jn 16:33

13 This is how we know that we live in him and he in us: He has given us of his Spirit.[l] 14 And we have
seen and testify[m] that the Father has sent his Son to be the Savior of the world.[n] 15 If anyone acknowledges that Jesus is the Son of God,[o] God lives in them and they in God. 16 And so we know and rely on
the love God has for us.

God is love.[p] Whoever lives in love lives in God, and God in them.[q] 17 This is how love is made complete[r] among us so that we will have confidence on the day of judgment: In this world we are like Jesus.
18 There is no fear in love. But perfect love drives out fear,[s] because fear has to do with punishment. The
one who fears is not made perfect in love.

19 We love because he first loved us.[t] 20 Whoever claims to love God yet hates a brother or sister[u] is
a liar.[v] For whoever does not love their brother and sister, whom they have seen,[w] cannot love God,
whom they have not seen.[x] 21 And he has given us this command: Anyone who loves God must also love
their brother and sister.[y]

Faith in the Incarnate Son of God

5 Everyone who believes that Jesus is the Christ[z] is born of God,[a] and everyone who loves the father
loves his child as well.[b] 2 This is how we know that we love the children of God: by loving God and
carrying out his commands. 3 In fact, this is love for God: to keep his commands.[c] And his commands
are not burdensome,[d] 4 for everyone born of God overcomes[e] the world. This is the victory that has
overcome the world, even our faith. 5 Who is it that overcomes the world? Only the one who believes
that Jesus is the Son of God.

---

important theme in John's Gospel (cf. John 1:18; 5:37; 6:46). Believers who love one another demonstrate that the unseen God lives in them, despite what the secessionists might say to the contrary. **his love is made complete in us.** The love of God we experience as a result of his living in us completes its work in us when we show love to one another.

4:14 Savior of the world. This phrase is found elsewhere in the NT only in John 4:42, where the Samaritan villagers respond to the testimony of the woman who encountered Jesus at the well of Sychar, saying, "We no longer believe just because of what you said; now we have heard for ourselves, and we know that this man really is the Savior of the world." In that context it means that Jesus is the Savior of Samaritans as well as Jews. Here, however, it is a response to secessionist denials that Jesus needed to be recognized as Savior at all—that his atoning death for sin was necessary.

4:15 God lives in them and they in God. See note on 3:24.

4:16 God is love. See note on 4:8. **Whoever lives in love lives in God.** This is intended to bolster the confidence of the readers. Unlike the secessionists, they do love one another. This is evidence that God lives in them and they in God.

4:17 love is made complete among us. This is the third of four references (here; vv. 12,18; 2:5) to love being made complete. Here God's love completes its work in us when we face the day of judgment without fear (cf. 2:28). **In this world we are like Jesus.** In the Greek this statement is preceded by a word translated "because," indicating that it provides a reason why we can face judgment without fear. In the context of vv. 7–21, whose overall theme is love for one another, we may say believers who love one another in the same way as Jesus loved his disciples when he was in the world show that they live in God and therefore need have no fear of his judgment.

4:18 perfect love drives out fear. When believers love God because he first loved them (v. 19), their fear is driven out. Love for God and fear of his judgment cannot coexist (cf. Rom 8:15). **The one who fears is not made perfect in love.** When the realization of God's love penetrates our minds and spirits, we are made perfect in love and fear of judgment is removed.

4:20 Whoever claims to love God. An allusion to the secessionists who claim to love God but "hate" other believers, thus showing themselves to be liars. Again John expresses himself in black-and-white terms. He underlines this with an argument from the lesser to the greater: "whoever does not love their brother and sister, whom they have seen, cannot love God, whom they have not seen." On the invisibility of God, see note on v. 12. Claims to know the unseen God must be validated by loving fellow believers, who can be seen. A true experience of God is such that it cannot exist without manifesting itself in love for his people. God is loving and those born of God are loving as well, and those who do not love do not know God (cf. vv. 7–8).

5:1–12 *Faith in the Incarnate Son of God.* Only those who believe that Jesus is the Christ are born of God, and they show they have been born of God by loving the children of God and obeying his commands (cf. 3:23). Believing in Christ involves believing in his incarnation and accepting God's testimony concerning his Son.

5:1 born of God. See John 1:12–13; 3:1–15, where being born of God is distinguished from natural birth. It is a birth that God initiates through his Spirit, and it takes place in conjunction with faith in Christ. **everyone who loves the father loves his child.** This may have been a general proverb that John applies to make the point that all those who love God are marked by their love for his children, their fellow believers.

5:2 This is how we know that we love the children of God. John reverses the approach adopted earlier in which love for one another is evidence that one loves God (4:7–8,20). One cannot love God and keep his commands without loving the children of God, and one cannot love the children of God without loving God and keeping his commands (cf. 3.23).

5:3 love for God. Love for God is expressed by obeying his commands (cf. John 14:15,21), and this includes loving fellow believers. **his commands are not burdensome.** While God's commands are demanding, they are not burdensome for believers (cf. Matt 11:28–30), because having been born of God, they have a desire to please him.

5:4,5 overcomes the world. Those who have been born of God are enabled to overcome the worldly tendency to satisfy their own sinful cravings (cf. 2:15–17) and to resist the pressure that comes from those of the world, in this case from the secessionists.

5:4 This is the victory ... our faith. By maintaining their faith that Jesus is the Son of God, John's readers will be able to resist the false teaching of the secessionists.

6This is the one who came by water and blood[f] — Jesus Christ. He did not come by water only, but by
water and blood. And it is the Spirit who testifies, because the Spirit is the truth.[g] 7For there are three[h]
that testify: 8the[a] Spirit, the water and the blood; and the three are in agreement. 9We accept human
testimony,[i] but God's testimony is greater because it is the testimony of God,[j] which he has given about
his Son. 10Whoever believes in the Son of God accepts this testimony.[k] Whoever does not believe God has
made him out to be a liar,[l] because they have not believed the testimony God has given about his Son.
11And this is the testimony: God has given us eternal life, and this life is in his Son.[m] 12Whoever has the
Son has life; whoever does not have the Son of God does not have life.[n]

Concluding Affirmations

13I write these things to you who believe in the name of the Son of God[o] so that you may know that
you have eternal life.[p] 14This is the confidence[q] we have in approaching God: that if we ask anything
according to his will, he hears us.[r] 15And if we know that he hears us — whatever we ask — we know[s]
that we have what we asked of him.

16If you see any brother or sister commit a sin that does not lead to death, you should pray and God
will give them life.[t] I refer to those whose sin does not lead to death. There is a sin that leads to death.[u]
I am not saying that you should pray about that.[v] 17All wrongdoing is sin,[w] and there is sin that does
not lead to death.[x]

18We know that anyone born of God does not continue to sin; the One who was born of God keeps

5:6 [f] Jn 19:34 [g] Jn 14:17
5:7 [h] Mt 18:16
5:9 [i] Jn 5:34 [j] Mt 3:16, 17; Jn 8:17, 18
5:10 [k] Ro 8:16; Gal 4:6 [l] Jn 3:33
5:11 [m] Jn 1:4; 1Jn 2:25
5:12 [n] Jn 3:15, 16, 36
5:13 [o] 1Jn 3:23 [p] Jn 20:31; 1Jn 1:1, 2
5:14 [q] 1Jn 3:21 [r] Mt 7:7
5:15 [s] ver 18, 19, 20
5:16 [t] Jas 5:15 [u] Heb 6:4-6; 10:26 [v] Jer 7:16
5:17 [w] 1Jn 3:4 [x] 1Jn 2:1

[a] 7,8 Late manuscripts of the Vulgate *testify in heaven: the Father, the Word and the Holy Spirit, and these three are one. 8And there are three that testify on earth: the* (not found in any Greek manuscript before the fourteenth century)

5:6 He did not come by water only, but by water and blood. This is a difficult text to interpret. Jesus' coming "by water" may refer to his baptism in water by John the Baptist and the accompanying endowment with the Spirit he experienced, which marked the commencement of his public ministry (cf. Luke 3:21–22; John 1:29–34). Jesus' coming "by ... blood" refers to his death on the cross as the atoning sacrifice for our sins (cf. 1 John 1:7; 2:2). Apparently the secessionists agreed that Jesus came "by water" (a reference to his baptism when he was anointed with the Spirit) but denied that he came by blood (that he died on the cross to make atonement for sins).
5:7 there are three that testify. In both the OT and NT important issues were decided with the testimony of two or three witnesses (Deut 17:6; 19:15; John 8:17; 2 Cor 13:1; 1 Tim 5:19; Heb 10:28). The three witnesses are identified in v. 8 (see note there).
5:8 the Spirit. He testifies to the truth about Jesus (cf. John 15:26), the truth that John's readers heard from the beginning (cf. 1 John 2:24–27). **the water and the blood.** It is more difficult to say how these make up the second and third witnesses (see 5:7 and note). Normally one *person* gives witness concerning another. However, in John's Gospel, when people will not accept Jesus' testimony about himself, he points them to his works, for these bear silent witness to the truth (cf. John 5:36; 10:25). Here John may be saying that alongside the Spirit's witness concerning Jesus there stands the silent witness of Jesus' baptism ("the water") and his atoning sacrifice ("the blood"). In judicial cases it was vital that the testimony of witnesses should agree. John builds his case by affirming that all three witnesses concur in their testimony that Jesus is the Messiah, the Son of God. The NIV text note on 5:8 records a longer version of this verse, but it is found only in a few late Greek manuscripts dating from the fourteenth to the eighteenth centuries, and it is not regarded as part of the authentic text.
5:11 has given us eternal life. A present possession of believers (cf. John 3:16,36).
5:12 Whoever has the Son has life. To have the Son is closely related to believing in the Son (cf. 5:13). It is only through faith in Christ that we may have life (cf. John 14:6).
5:13–21 *Concluding Affirmations.* John wrote to reassure his readers concerning their possession of eternal life. He explains what this means regarding prayer, reassures them that they are no longer under the power of the evil one, and reminds them that they have been given knowledge of the truth in Jesus Christ.
5:13 I write these things ... so that you may know that you have eternal life. John wrote this letter to bolster his readers' assurance (cf. 2:12–14) and to counteract the effects of the secessionists' false teaching. For believers' assurance, see also 2:3; 3:14 and notes.
5:14 if we ask anything according to his will, he hears us. Earlier John linked believers' confidence in prayer with pleasing God by keeping his commands (3:21–22). Here he links it with asking according to God's will. To pray effectively, believers' requests need to be in accordance with the teaching of Scripture concerning what pleases God.
5:15 we have what we asked of him. This is generally true, but experience shows that believers may not always receive what they ask of God, even when what they request seems to be in accordance with Scripture. Elsewhere Scripture stresses the need for faith (Matt 21:22; Jas 1:6), patience (Luke 18:1–8), godly living (Ps 66:18; 1 Pet 3:12), and a recognition that God knows best (cf. Luke 22:42; Rom 8:28; 1 Pet 4:19).
5:16 If you see any brother of sister commit a sin. Suggests that the sin is observable, not some internal attitude. **a sin that does not lead to death.** A sin that believers commit and for which forgiveness has been secured by the atoning sacrifice of Christ (cf. 1:9; 2:1–2). **give them life.** Probably resurrection life, implying that they will not miss out on what God has promised that they will have on the last day. **a sin that leads to death.** Probably the sin of the secessionists: they denied that Jesus is the Christ come in the flesh, rejected the significance of his atoning death, disobeyed God's commands, and showed no love for true believers. By persistence in these things, people place themselves outside the sphere of forgiveness so that their sins become sins unto death.
5:18,19,20 We know. These verses highlight three important truths that believers know.
5:18 the One who was born of God. Refers here to Jesus, the Son of God.

5:18 [y]Jn 14:30
5:19 [z]1Jn 4:6 [a]Gal 1:4
5:20 [b]Lk 24:45
[c]Jn 17:3 [d]ver 11
5:21 [e]1Co 10:14;
1Th 1:9

them safe, and the evil one cannot harm them.[y] [19]We know that we are children of God,[z] and that the
whole world is under the control of the evil one.[a] [20]We know also that the Son of God has come and
has given us understanding,[b] so that we may know him who is true.[c] And we are in him who is true by
being in his Son Jesus Christ. He is the true God and eternal life.[d]
[21]Dear children, keep yourselves from idols.[e]

5:20 him who is true. Refers to God the Father. **the true God and eternal life.** Refers to either God the Father or Jesus. If it refers to the Father, then John emphasizes that the Father is the true God and the source of eternal life, a noncontroversial statement (cf. John 17:3; 1 Thess 1:9). If it refers to Jesus, then John strikingly calls Jesus "the true God" (cf. John 1:1).

5:21 keep yourselves from idols. This could mean either to refuse to be involved in pagan worship or to refuse to accept the secessionists' false teaching about Christ, which would be tantamount to idolatry.

2 JOHN

Stone relief from Isthmia depicting a victorious athlete with his crowns. "Watch out that you do not lose what we have worked for, but that you may be rewarded fully" (2 John 8).

Cheryl Dunn for Talbot Bible Lands

1 The elder,[a]
To the lady chosen by God[b] and to her children,
whom I love in the truth—and not I only, but also all
who know the truth[c]— 2 because of the truth,[d] which
lives in us[e] and will be with us forever:

3 Grace, mercy and peace from God the Father and
from Jesus Christ,[f] the Father's Son, will be with us in
truth and love.

4 It has given me great joy to find some of your children walking in the truth,[g] just as the Father commanded us. 5 And now, dear lady, I am not writing you
a new command but one we have had from the beginning.[h] I ask that we love one another. 6 And this is love:[i]
that we walk in obedience to his commands. As you
have heard from the beginning, his command is that
you walk in love.

7 I say this because many deceivers, who do not acknowledge Jesus Christ[j] as coming in the flesh, have
gone out into the world.[k] Any such person is the deceiver and the antichrist.[l] 8 Watch out that you do not
lose what we[*a*] have worked for, but that you may be
rewarded fully.[m] 9 Anyone who runs ahead and does
not continue in the teaching of Christ does not have

1 [a] 3Jn 1 [b] Ro 16:13 [c] Jn 8:32
2 [d] 2Pe 1:12 [e] 1Jn 1:8
3 [f] Ro 1:7
4 [g] 3Jn 3,4
5 [h] 1Jn 2:7; 3:11
6 [i] 1Jn 2:5
7 [j] 1Jn 2:22; 4:2,3 [k] 1Jn 4:1 [l] 1Jn 2:18
8 [m] 1Co 3:8

a 8 Some manuscripts *you*

1 The elder. See Introduction: Author. **the lady chosen by God and … her children.** Probably refers to a local church and its members rather than an individual Christian woman and her children (cf. v. 13).
2 the truth. The truth of the gospel internalized by believers, or possibly Christ himself, who embodies truth (cf. John 14:6) and "lives in us and will be with us forever."
4 some of your children walking in the truth. John had apparently encountered members of the church who were living in accordance with the truth of the gospel in a way that was pleasing to God. It may have been from them that he received news that prompted him to write this letter.
5–6 new command … from the beginning. See notes on 1 John 2:7–8.
7 many deceivers … have gone out into the world. The secessionists, who had gone out from the Christian community, were seeking to deceive those who remained in it (see Introduction: Occasion and Purpose). **do not acknowledge Jesus Christ as coming in the flesh.** The secessionists denied Jesus' true humanity. **is the deceiver and the antichrist.** Implies that these deceivers were doing the work of "the deceiver," "the antichrist" (see notes on 1 John 2:18–27; 2:18–19), by seeking to lead people away from the true Christ.
8 we. John and his associates. **rewarded fully.** Receive the reward of eternal life.
9 runs ahead. To run after new and spurious teaching, leaving behind the gospel truth heard from faithful witnesses. **has both the Father and the Son.** See John 14:21,23.

9 [n] 1Jn 2:23
10 [o] Ro 16:17
11 [p] 1Ti 5:22
12 [q] 3Jn 13,14
13 [r] ver 1

God; whoever continues in the teaching has both the Father and the Son.[n] 10 If anyone comes to you
and does not bring this teaching, do not take them into your house or welcome them.[o] 11 Anyone who
welcomes them shares[p] in their wicked work.

12 I have much to write to you, but I do not want to use paper and ink. Instead, I hope to visit you
and talk with you face to face,[q] so that our joy may be complete.

13 The children of your sister, who is chosen by God,[r] send their greetings.

10 do not take them into your house. This may be understood in two ways: (1) They should not provide hospitality in their homes, which in the ancient world included guaranteeing their guests were worthy of acceptance by the rest of the community, something that could not be done if the guests were deceivers. (2) They should not receive heretical preachers in the assembly of the house church (see illustration, p. 2559), implying they should not give them opportunity to propagate their false teaching. All this does not mean that believers should not provide hospitality for strangers (cf. Heb 13:2) or that they should separate themselves from unbelievers (cf. 1 Cor 5:9–10); it is the false teachers that John had in mind. **welcome.** To greet such a person in the way early Christians did (cf. 1 Cor 1:3), which implied recognizing their Christian standing—a standing the secessionists no longer had.

11 shares in their wicked work. If believers provided hospitality for false teachers, they would share responsibility for the effects of the teachers' false teaching.

12 I do not want to use paper and ink. Instead, I hope to visit you. Typical of the friendly letter tradition of the first-century Mediterranean world.

13 The children of your sister. Most likely the members of John's local church rather than the children of a particular Christian woman (cf. v. 1; see note there).

3 JOHN

1The elder,[a]

To my dear friend Gaius, whom I love in the truth.

2Dear friend, I pray that you may enjoy good health and that all may go well with you, even as your
soul is getting along well. 3It gave me great joy when some believers[b] came and testified about your
faithfulness to the truth, telling how you continue to walk in it.[c] 4I have no greater joy than to hear
that my children[d] are walking in the truth.
5Dear friend, you are faithful in what you are doing for the brothers and sisters,[a] even though they
are strangers to you.[e] 6They have told the church about your love. Please send them on their way in a
manner that honors God. 7It was for the sake of the Name[f] that they went out, receiving no help from
the pagans.[g] 8We ought therefore to show hospitality to such people so that we may work together for
the truth.
9I wrote to the church, but Diotrephes, who loves to be first, will not welcome us. 10So when I come,[h]
I will call attention to what he is doing, spreading malicious nonsense about us. Not satisfied with that,
he even refuses to welcome other believers.[i] He also stops those who want to do so and puts them out
of the church.[j]
11Dear friend, do not imitate what is evil but what is good.[k] Anyone who does what is good is from

1 [a]2Jn 1
3 [b]ver 5,10 [c]2Jn 4
4 [d]1Co 4:15; 1Jn 2:1
5 [e]Ro 12:13; Heb 13:2
7 [f]Jn 15:21 [g]Ac 20:33,35
10 [h]2Jn 12 [i]ver 5 [j]Jn 9:22,34
11 [k]Ps 37:27

[a] 5 The Greek word for *brothers and sisters* (*adelphoi*) refers here to believers, both men and women, as part of God's family.

---

1 The elder. See Introduction: Author. **Gaius.** People with this common Roman name are referred to in Acts 19:29; 20:4; Rom 16:23; 1 Cor 1:14; but it is uncertain if any of them are the Gaius addressed here. **whom I love in the truth.** Either an idiom meaning "whom I truly love" or a statement meaning "whom I love as one who, like me, is in the truth," i.e., as one who remains faithful to the gospel.
2 good health ... all may go well with you. Wishes for recipients' good health are common in ancient Greek letters, reinforced here with John's affirmation that this is his prayer for Gaius. **even as your soul is getting along well.** Evidence that Gaius is faithful to the truth of the gospel.
4 my children. While John's readers are children of God (cf. 1 John 3:1–2,10; 5:2; see note on 1 John 3:1,2), they are also John's children, perhaps because they are his converts or because he acts as their spiritual father (cf. 1 Tim 1:2,18; Titus 1:4; Phlm 10).
5 what you are doing. Providing hospitality to faithful itinerant preachers. See note on 2 John 10.
6 They have told the church. When people received hospitality it was incumbent upon them to report positively about their hosts to their own community, as these preachers did when they told their church about Gaius's love. **send them on their way.** A technical term for providing material support (cf. Rom 15:24; 1 Cor 16:6,11; 2 Cor 1:16; Titus 3:13).
7 for the sake of the Name. For the sake of Christ. Paul uses the same expression in Rom 1:5, where it clearly refers to Christ (cf. Acts 5:41; 9:16; 15:26; 21:13).
8 We ought therefore to show hospitality to such people. John provides three reasons why Gaius ought to do so: (1) These preachers had gone out "for the sake of the Name" (v. 7). (2) These preachers depended on the Christian community for hospitality because they received no help from the pagans (v. 7). (3) By so doing Gaius will be working together with these preachers for the truth of the gospel (here).
9 I wrote to the church. A previous letter asking that hospitality be provided for faithful preachers. **Diotrephes.** We know little about him except what may be gleaned from this letter. **who loves to be first.** One who loves prominence and to exercise authority in the church (a tendency that sadly was found even among Jesus' disciples, cf. Mark 10:35–37). **will not welcome us.** Probably means that Diotrephes rejected John's request to provide hospitality and so did not welcome those John commended (cf. v. 10).
10 when I come, I will call attention to what he is doing. John will publicly expose and rebuke Diotrephes for "spreading malicious nonsense about [John and those John commended]." John must show that he did not accept the shame that Diotrephes had heaped upon him.
11 do ... what is good. A general exhortation to do good (cf. Rom 12:21; Gal 6:10) and in particular to provide appropriate hospitality. **do not**

11 [l]1Jn 2:29 [m]1Jn 3:6,9,10
12 [n]1Ti 3:7 [o]Jn 21:24
14 [p]2Jn 12 [q]Jn 10:3

God.[l] Anyone who does what is evil has not seen God.[m] 12 Demetrius is well spoken of by everyone[n]—
and even by the truth itself. We also speak well of him, and you know that our testimony is true.[o]
13 I have much to write you, but I do not want to do so with pen and ink. 14 I hope to see you soon,
and we will talk face to face.[p]

Peace to you. The friends here send their greetings. Greet the friends there by name.[q]

imitate what is evil. Probably an exhortation not to follow Diotrephes' bad example in regard to hospitality or his shameful "politics."
12 Demetrius. The only other reference to a Demetrius in the NT is to the silversmith of Ephesus (Acts 19:24,38); we do not know if this is the same person. The fact that Demetrius is commended at the end of the letter suggests that he was the courier who conveyed it to Gaius (cf. Col 4:7–9; 1 Pet 5:12). By his commendation of Demetrius, John implies Gaius should provide Demetrius with hospitality. **well spoken of ... by the truth itself.** Could mean either that Jesus, as the truth (cf. John 14:6), bears testimony to Demetrius (perhaps through the testimony of "everyone") or that Demetrius's commitment to the truth of the gospel speaks well of him.
13 See note on 2 John 12.
14 friends. An unusual but attractive expression to describe believers, dependent perhaps upon Jesus' description of his disciples as his "friends" (John 15:13–15). With the possible exceptions of Acts 19:31 and 27:3, such a designation is found only here in the NT.

INTRODUCTION TO JUDE

AUTHOR

The author is "Jude, a servant of Jesus Christ and a brother of James" (v. 1). This James is almost certainly the man who became a prominent leader in the early church (Acts 15:13 – 21; 21:18; Gal 2:9) and wrote the NT letter of James. Since this James was also "the Lord's brother" (Gal 1:19; see Matt 13:55; Mark 6:3), the Jude of v. 1 is "Judas," the brother of Jesus mentioned in the Gospels (Matt 13:55; Mark 6:3). The witness of the early church confirms this conclusion, and arguments to the contrary are weak.

DATE AND PLACE

The letter cannot be dated after about AD 90, the latest we can realistically expect even a younger brother of Jesus to have lived. Jude and 2 Peter describe similar false teaching, suggesting that they were written at about the same time. We date 2 Peter to 63 – 65, so we should probably date Jude in the mid to late 60s. Nothing certain can be determined about the place of writing; we don't know whether Jude stayed in Palestine all his life.

ADDRESSEES

Although people traditionally categorize the letter as a "general" one, Jude wrote to a definite church or group of churches. The readers were probably Jewish Christians, perhaps living in the midst of a Gentile culture.

PURPOSE

Jude writes because false teachers "have secretly slipped in among" his readers (v. 4). He condemns the false teachers for their wicked lifestyle: they are sexually immoral (vv. 4,8), scornful of authority (vv. 8 – 10), and selfish (v. 12). They are "grumblers and faultfinders" who "follow their own evil desires" and "boast about themselves and flatter others for their own advantage" (v. 16).

RELATION TO 2 PETER

See Introduction to 2 Peter: Relation to Jude.

KEY ISSUES

1. *False teaching.* Although people do not like to dwell on the negative, it is important to understand the following concerning

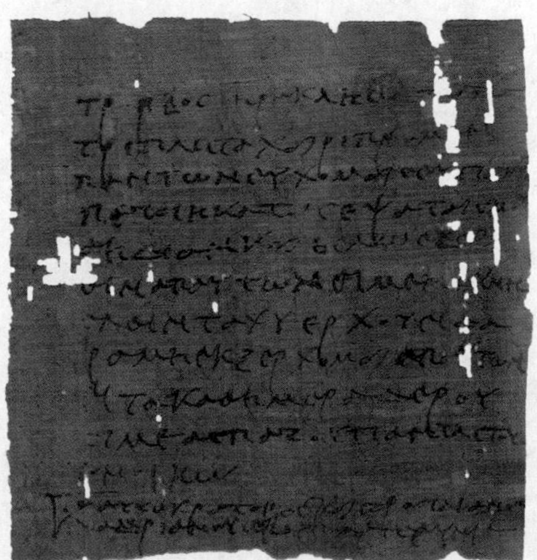

Greek letter on papyrus, AD 127. Jude was also a Greek letter written just a few decades earlier.

Image digitally reproduced with the permission of the Papyrology Collection, Graduate Library, University of Michigan, P.Mich.inv. 1637

false teachers: (a) they exist, (b) their teaching can be both attractive and dangerous, and (c) their condemnation is certain. Jude makes these points by associating the false teachers with sinners, rebels, and heretics in the OT and in Jewish tradition. We can expect people in every generation to defect from truth and morality. Today the church must guard vigilantly against the temptation to welcome heresy in the name of "tolerance."

2. *Canon.* In addition to several possible allusions, Jude refers to two stories not taught in the Bible: the story of Michael's dispute with the devil over Moses' body in v. 9 (apparently from The Assumption of Moses, OT pseudepigrapha) and the prophecy of Enoch in vv. 14–15 (from 1 Enoch 1:9, a Jewish writing from the OT pseudepigrapha). Some wrongly conclude from this that the standard set of OT books (i.e., the OT "canon") was not fixed in Jude's day. Yet Jude cites neither of these books as "Scripture," nor does he use traditional formulas to introduce them. He implies nothing about his view of the books in which the stories are found. He may cite them simply because they are well-known to his audience.

OUTLINE

I. Greeting (1–2)

II. The Sin and Doom of Ungodly People (3–16)

III. A Call to Persevere (17–23)

IV. Doxology (24–25)

JUDE

1 [1]Jude,[a] a servant of Jesus Christ and a brother of James,

To those who have been called,[b] who are loved in God the Father and kept for[a] Jesus Christ:[c]

2 [2]Mercy, peace and love be yours in abundance.[d]

1 [a]Mt 13:55; Ac 1:13 [b]Ro 1:6,7 [c]Jn 17:12
2 [d]2Pe 1:2
3 [e]Titus 1:4 [f]1Ti 6:12
4 [g]Gal 2:4 [h]Titus 1:16; 2Pe 2:1

The Sin and Doom of Ungodly People

3 [3]Dear friends, although I was very eager to write to you about the salvation we share,[e] I felt compelled to write and urge you to contend[f] for the faith that was once for all entrusted to God's holy peo-
4 ple. [4]For certain individuals whose condemnation was written about[b] long ago have secretly slipped in
among you.[g] They are ungodly people, who pervert the grace of our God into a license for immorality
and deny Jesus Christ our only Sovereign and Lord.[h]
5 [5]Though you already know all this, I want to remind you that the Lord[c] at one time delivered his

[a] *1* Or *by*; or *in* [b] *4* Or *individuals who were marked out for condemnation* [c] *5* Some early manuscripts *Jesus*

1–2 *Greeting.* By addressing his readers as "those who have been called," Jude sets them apart from the false teachers who have "secretly slipped in among" them (v. 4) and against whom his readers must "contend" (v. 3).
1 Jude. See Introduction: Author. **servant.** Slave or bondservant—an honorable and authoritative position when representing Christ (cf. Rom 1:1; 2 Pet 1:1). This relationship is similar to OT figures like Moses, Joshua, David, and Elijah, who were called servants of the Lord (Deut 34:5; Josh 24:29; 2 Sam 7:5,8; 2 Kgs 10:10). **called.** Effectively summoned (see notes on Rom 1:6; 8:28; Gal 1:6; Eph 4:1). **kept.** Preserved spiritually intact (cf. John 6:37–40; 17:11–12; 1 Thess 5:23; 1 Pet 1:3–5; 1 John 5:18). God's keeping (also v. 24) gives Christians assurance in the context of false teaching.
2 This is the only greeting in a NT letter that does not mention "grace" (though God's "mercy" and grace are related since both express his goodness), and it is the only one that mentions "love." See "Love and Grace," p. 2684.
3–16 *The Sin and Doom of Ungodly People.* Jude is writing because false teachers have infiltrated the church (vv. 3–4). He exposes and condemns the false teachers in three stages (vv. 5–10,11–13,14–16) by identifying them with notorious sinners from the OT and from other Jewish writings. See "Wrath," p. 2681.
3 Jude would rather write a positive letter about "the salvation we share," but like a good shepherd he focuses on the wolves that are threatening the flock. **contend.** Exert intense effort. This word was applied to athletic contests, such as wrestling matches (the same Greek word is translated "competes" in 1 Cor 9:25); the ancient world was as keen about sports as ours is, so an athletic image was natural. **the faith.** The content of Christian belief as handed down from Christ and his apostles (e.g., Christ's atoning death in the place of sinners, Christ's resurrection, salvation by grace through faith, Christ's second coming, and—especially in Jude's situation—the holy lifestyle that flows from God's grace in Christ). **once for all.** A decisively unique occurrence. The essentials of the Christian faith are nonnegotiable.
4 For. Introduces the reason that Jude "felt compelled" to change the subject of his letter (v. 3). **certain individuals.** False teachers (cf. Matt 7:15; 2 Pet 2). **condemnation.** Cf. 2 Pet 2:3–9,12–13,17. **secretly slipped in.** Sneaked in stealthily; crept in unnoticed. Jude's readers must "contend" (v. 3) with false teachers within the church. **ungodly.** Unrighteous (cf. 2 Pet 2:9; 3:7). Jude's letter focuses not on their false doctrine but on their wicked lifestyle. **pervert.** Change. The false teachers turn something good ("the grace of our God") into something perverse ("a license for immorality")—a constant temptation for Christians (cf. Rom 6). **deny.** Repudiate or disown, probably by their wicked lifestyle.
5–7 Jude compares the false teachers to three examples of notorious OT sinners whom God judged.
5 Example 1 (see note on vv. 5–7): God judged unbelieving Israel in the wilderness. **the Lord.** Possibly the preexistent Jesus (see NIV text note; cf. 1 Cor 10:4) but probably God the Father. **delivered.** God rescued his people from Egyptian slavery (Exod 6–14). **destroyed those who did not believe.** God sentenced the unbelieving generation of Israelites (except Joshua and Caleb) to wander in the wilderness until they died; they were not allowed to enter the promised land (Num 14:29–30; Deut 1:32–36; 2:15). Jude implicitly warns his readers, "Don't think that because God has decisively rescued you from your sins that you can presume on his grace and mercy." See "Exile and Exodus," p. 2659, though here Jude appeals to the exodus primarily to make a moral lesson (as in 1 Cor 10:1–13; Heb 3:7–13).

5 [i]Nu 14:29; Ps 106:26
6 [j]2Pe 2:4,9
7 [k]Dt 29:23 [l]2Pe 2:6
8 [m]2Pe 2:10
9 [n]Da 10:13,21 [o]Zec 3:2
10 [p]2Pe 2:12
11 [q]Ge 4:3-8; 1Jn 3:12 [r]2Pe 2:15 [s]Nu 16:1-3,31-35
12 [t]2Pe 2:13; 1Co 11:20-22 [u]Pr 25:14; 2Pe 2:17 [v]Eph 4:14 [w]Mt 15:13
13 [x]Isa 57:20 [y]Php 3:19 [z]2Pe 2:17
14 [a]Ge 5:18,21-24

people out of Egypt, but later destroyed those who did not believe.[i] 6 And the angels who did not keep
their positions of authority but abandoned their proper dwelling—these he has kept in darkness,
bound with everlasting chains for judgment on the great Day.[j] 7 In a similar way, Sodom and Gomorrah
and the surrounding towns[k] gave themselves up to sexual immorality and perversion. They serve as an
example of those who suffer the punishment of eternal fire.[l]
8 In the very same way, on the strength of their dreams these ungodly people pollute their own bodies,
reject authority and heap abuse on celestial beings.[m] 9 But even the archangel Michael,[n] when he was
disputing with the devil about the body of Moses, did not himself dare to condemn him for slander but
said, "The Lord rebuke you!"[a][o] 10 Yet these people slander whatever they do not understand, and the very
things they do understand by instinct—as irrational animals do—will destroy them.[p]
11 Woe to them! They have taken the way of Cain;[q] they have rushed for profit into Balaam's error;[r]
they have been destroyed in Korah's rebellion.[s]
12 These people are blemishes at your love feasts,[t] eating with you without the slightest qualm—
shepherds who feed only themselves. They are clouds without rain,[u] blown along by the wind;[v] autumn
trees, without fruit and uprooted[w]—twice dead. 13 They are wild waves of the sea,[x] foaming up their
shame;[y] wandering stars, for whom blackest darkness has been reserved forever.[z]
14 Enoch,[a] the seventh from Adam, prophesied about them: "See, the Lord is coming with thousands

[a] 9 Jude is alluding to the Jewish *Testament of Moses* (approximately the first century A.D.).

6 Example 2 (see note on vv. 5–7): God judged rebellious angels (probably alludes to Gen 6:1–4; see note on 2 Pet 2:4). **keep ... kept.** Contrast how God "keeps" (the Greek word is translated "reserved" in v. 13) these angels who did not "keep" their assigned positions with how God keeps Christians (see note on v. 1), who must keep themselves (see note on vv. 20–21).

7 Example 3 (see note on vv. 5–7): God judged Sodom and Gomorrah (Gen 19; see map, p. 2554). **surrounding towns.** Includes Admah and Zeboyim (Deut 29:23). **perversion.** Probably homosexuality (cf. Gen 19:5–10). **serve as an example.** Writers contemporary to Jude witnessed that the area where God destroyed those cities had sulfurous odors, smoke, and a terribly desolate appearance (cf. Gen 19:24–28); that judgment foreshadows worse judgment: **the punishment of eternal fire.** Hell lasts forever (v. 13; Matt 25:41,46; Rev 14:10–11; 20:10).

8 Jude applies the three examples in vv. 5–7 to three ways the false teachers are sinning: (1) They "pollute their own bodies." This parallels examples 2 and 3: the rebellious angels and the Sodomites defiled themselves by their sexual perversions (see notes on vv. 6,7). (2) They "reject authority" (specifically, Christ's lordship). This parallels examples 1, 2, and 3: unbelieving Israel in the wilderness, the rebellious angels, and the Sodomites all "rejected authority" by refusing to follow the Lord's directives (see notes on vv. 5–7). (3) They "heap abuse on celestial beings" (angels; contrast Michael's behavior in v. 9; cf. 2 Pet 2:10). This parallels example 3: the Sodomites disrespected angels who were visiting Lot (see note on v. 7). The false teachers apparently based their immoral behavior on visions they claimed to receive (i.e., "on the strength of their dreams").

9 archangel. The highest rank of angel in Jewish tradition (cf. 1 Thess 4:16). **Michael.** Mentioned four other times in the Bible: Dan 10:13,21; 12:1; Rev 12:7. **disputing with the devil about the body of Moses.** See NIV text note; the story seems to be from The Testament of Moses (OT pseudepigrapha) and is loosely based on Zech 3:1–2. We have no way of knowing what status Jude accorded this story. He may have viewed it as (1) an incident that actually took place or (2) simply a well-known tradition that he can cite to illustrate his point—similar to a contemporary preacher citing an incident in *The Chronicles of Narnia.* Quoting or alluding to nonbiblical works does not suggest that those works are God-breathed, especially when the biblical author does not refer to those works as "Scripture" (vv. 14–15; cf. Paul's quoting of nonbiblical works in Acts 17:28; 1 Cor 15:33; Titus 1:12). See Introduction: Key Issues.

10 Jude returns to the third way that the false teachers sin (see note on v. 8): they slander what they don't even understand. **by instinct—as irrational animals.** Cf. 2 Pet 2:12. Their sexual sins are out of control; they have no moral compass.

11 Jude again compares the false teachers to three examples of notorious OT sinners whom God judged (cf. vv. 5–7): (1) **the way of Cain.** See Gen 4; Heb 11:4; 1 John 3:12. Cain was the first murderer, and in Jewish tradition he became a classic example of an ungodly skeptic who incited others to sin. (2) **Balaam's error.** See note on 2 Pet 2:15. (3) **Korah's rebellion.** See Num 16:1–35; 26:9–10; Ps 106:16–18.

12–13 Jude applies the three examples in v. 11 to how the false teachers are sinning. He describes them with six metaphors: (1) **blemishes at your love feasts.** See note on 2 Pet 2:13. "Blemishes" translates a Greek word that occurs only here in the NT; it could also be translated "hidden reefs," rocky hazards below the surface of the water that destroy ships; this pictures the false teachers as lying in wait to destroy Christians. (2) **shepherds who feed only themselves.** Those who lead God's people are shepherds, and their job is to unselfishly take care of the flock by knowing, feeding, leading, and protecting them (see 2 Sam 5:2; Jer 23:1–2; Ezek 34:2,8,10; Matt 9:36; Acts 20:28; 1 Pet 5:1–3). The ultimate good shepherd is Jesus (John 10:1–18,27–30; Heb 13:20; 1 Pet 5:4; cf. Ps 23). (3) **clouds without rain.** See note on 2 Pet 2:17. (4) **autumn trees, without fruit and uprooted.** Cf. Matt 7:15–20; 15:13; Luke 13:6–9. (5) **wild waves of the sea.** The sea represents chaos or evil (see Ps 107:25–30; Isa 57:20; Ezek 28:8), standing for the entire fallen order; that is why there is no longer any sea in the new heaven and new earth (Rev 21:1). (6) **wandering stars.** This is one way ancient people referred to the planets, which seemed to move across the sky in irregular patterns. The analogy is that the false teachers were unstable. Whether by chance or not, the final four images (clouds, trees, waves, stars/planets) correspond to the typical ancient division of the earth's four "regions": air, earth, sea, and the heavens.

13 shame. Shameful deeds. **blackest darkness.** An image of hell. **has been reserved.** See note on v. 6. **forever.** Their punishment lasts forever (see note on v. 7).

14 Enoch. An early descendant of Adam (Gen 5:18–24; 1 Chr 1:3; Luke 3:37). Enoch is a fascinating character (Gen 5:24; Heb 11:5; cf. 2 Kgs 2:1–12), and at least two Jewish books of apocalyptic visions written between the OT and NT were written in his name: 1 and 2 Enoch. Here Jude quotes from 1 Enoch 1:9 (see NIV text note; see also Introduction: Key Issues; see further note on v. 9) to underscore that God will judge the false teachers who have crept in among Jude's readers.

upon thousands of his holy ones[b] [15]to judge[c] everyone, and to convict all of them of all the ungodly acts
they have committed in their ungodliness, and of all the defiant words ungodly sinners have spoken
against him."[a][d] [16]These people are grumblers and faultfinders; they follow their own evil desires; they
boast[e] about themselves and flatter others for their own advantage.

14 [b]Dt 33:2; Da 7:10
15 [c]2Pe 2:6-9 [d]1Ti 1:9
16 [e]2Pe 2:18
17 [f]2Pe 3:2
18 [g]1Ti 4:1 [h]2Pe 2:1
19 [i]1Co 2:14,15
20 [j]Col 2:7 [k]Eph 6:18
21 [l]Titus 2:13; 2Pe 3:12
23 [m]Am 4:11; Zec 3:2-5 [n]Rev 3:4
24 [o]Ro 16:25 [p]2Co 4:14 [q]Col 1:22
25 [r]Jn 5:44; 1Ti 1:17 [s]Heb 13:8 [t]Ro 11:36

A Call to Persevere

[17]But, dear friends, remember what the apostles of our Lord Jesus Christ foretold.[f] [18]They said to you,
"In the last times[g] there will be scoffers who will follow their own ungodly desires."[h] [19]These are the
people who divide you, who follow mere natural instincts and do not have the Spirit.[i]
[20]But you, dear friends, by building yourselves up[j] in your most holy faith
and praying in the Holy Spirit,[k] [21]keep yourselves in God's love as you wait[l]
for the mercy of our Lord Jesus Christ to bring you to eternal life.
[22]Be merciful to those who doubt; [23]save others by snatching them from the fire;[m] to others show mercy, mixed with
fear—hating even the clothing stained by corrupted
flesh.[b][n]

Doxology

[24]To him who is able[o] to keep you from stumbling
and to present you before his glorious presence[p] without
fault[q] and with great joy— [25]to the only God[r] our Savior
be glory, majesty, power and authority, through Jesus Christ our Lord,
before all ages, now and forevermore![s] Amen.[t]

[a] *14,15* From the Jewish *First Book of Enoch* (approximately the first century B.C.) [b] *22,23* The Greek manuscripts of these verses vary at several points.

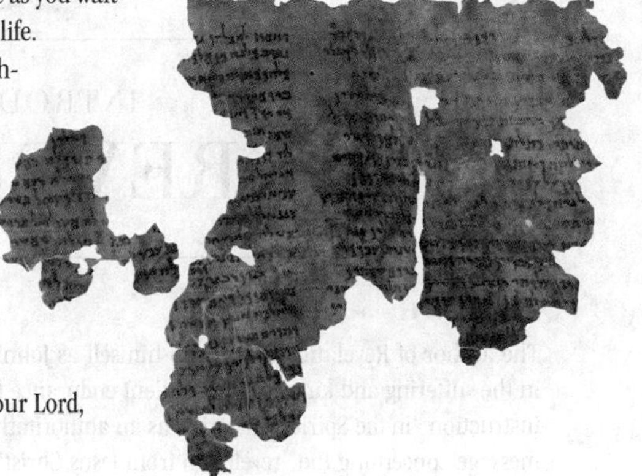

Dead Sea Scroll of 1 Enoch. Jude 14–15 quotes this book.
Courtesy of the Israel Antiquities Authority; Photographer: Shai Halevi

16 grumblers and faultfinders. Like the Israelites in the wilderness (Exod 15:24; 16:2,7–12; 17:3; Num 14:2,27–29,36; 17:5,10; Deut 1:27; Ps 106:25; 1 Cor 10:10). Grumbling and complaining are divisive sins that God judges (Phil 2:14–15; Jas 5:9; cf. Titus 3:10–11). **follow their own evil desires.** Such as sexual lust and greed (cf. vv. 8,10–11; 2 Pet 2:12,18; 3:3). **boast about themselves.** Cf. 2 Pet 2:18. **flatter others for their own advantage.** Perhaps the false teachers were currying favor with the rich while ignoring the poor.

17–23 *A Call to Persevere.* Jude's readers must respond to the false teachers in three ways: (1) They must remember that the apostles predicted that these scoffers would arise (vv. 17–19). God knows what is happening, and he is in control. (2) They must keep themselves in God's love (vv. 20–21). (3) They must reach out to those affected by the false teaching (vv. 22–23).

17–19 Cf. Acts 20:29–31; 1 Tim 4:1–3; 2 Tim 3:1–9; 2 Pet 2:1 (Matt 24:4–5,11,24; Mark 13:22). Jude possibly derives the wording of the quotation in v. 18 from 2 Pet 3:3 (see Introduction to 2 Peter: Relation to Jude).

18 last times. The last days (see note on 2 Pet 3:3).

19 divide. False teachers are inherently divisive. **follow mere natural instincts.** Cf. vv. 10,16; 2 Pet 2:12; 3:3. **do not have the Spirit.** Genuine Christians "have the Spirit" (cf. Rom 8:8–10; 1 Cor 2:14–15).

20–21 God "keeps" Christians (cf. vv. 1,24; see Rom 8:28–39), and they must also "keep" themselves "in God's love" (cf. John 15:9–10). They must do this in three ways: (1) By **building yourselves up in your most holy faith.** Growing doctrinally strong; engaging in a building process of personal and corporate development "in" (either "by means of" or "on the foundation of") the content of Christian belief (see note on v. 3). The "building" imagery for developing the Christian community probably comes from the idea that the Christian church forms God's new temple (see "Temple," p. 2652). (2) By **praying in the Holy Spirit.** Stimulated, guided, and infused by the Spirit (cf. Rom 8:26–27; Eph 6:18). (3) By **wait[ing] for the mercy ... to bring you to eternal life.** Expectantly anticipating and living in light of God's future deliverance (cf. 2 Pet 3:11–14).

22–23 Jude's readers must reach out to those in their community who were affected by the false teaching. The text seems to distinguish three different groups: (1) **Be merciful to those who doubt.** Some were in the early stages of wavering in their commitment to the faith as a result of the false teachers. (2) **save others by snatching them from the fire.** Some were becoming so persuaded by the false teachers that they were in imminent danger of condemnation. (3) **to others show mercy.** This third group probably consists of those who followed the false teachers (or perhaps the false teachers themselves). One way to show mercy is to pray for them (cf. Matt 5:44). **mixed with fear—hating even the clothing stained by corrupted flesh.** Christians must be extremely cautious when showing mercy to false teachers and their followers because their sins can be enticing (cf. Zech 3:1–4; Rev 3:4).

24–25 *Doxology.* Church leaders frequently use this doxology as a liturgical form of dismissal at the end of church services, primarily because it is one of the most beautiful doxologies in the NT.

24 keep. God preserves Christians in his love (see notes on vv. 1,6). **stumbling.** Falling away (e.g., by following the false teachers) and experiencing God's final judgment. **present you ... without fault.** Cf. 2 Cor 4:14; Eph 5:27; Col 1:22. **without fault.** Originally applied to perfect sacrifices (cf. Heb 9:14; 1 Pet 1:19). Based on our own power, we can never appear "without fault" before God, but God supplies through Jesus Christ the moral purity we lack in ourselves.

25 only God. Cf. 1 Tim 1:17. **our Savior.** Jesus is our Savior in that he secures salvation for us, and God is our Savior in that he plans and initiates the process. Cf. 1 Tim 1:1; 2:3; Titus 1:3; 2:10; 3:4. **glory, majesty, power and authority.** Cf. 1 Pet 4:11; Rev 1:6; 4:11; 5:12–13; 7:12; 19:1.

INTRODUCTION TO REVELATION

AUTHOR

The author of Revelation introduces himself as John (1:4), God's "servant" (1:1), "your brother and companion in the suffering and kingdom and patient endurance that are ours in Jesus" (1:9). John receives divine visions and instruction "in the Spirit" and writes as an authoritative prophet in the tradition of the OT prophets (1:10–11). His message concerning the "revelation from Jesus Christ" (1:1) is "trustworthy and true" (21:5; 22:6), and we should read, hear, and heed it (1:3).

John is evidently a Jewish Christian leader who is saturated in the Scriptures and who is known to the seven churches in Asia Minor (1:4). He writes from exile on Patmos (see 1:9 and note). Despite some differences in literary style and theological emphasis between Revelation and the fourth Gospel (differences first noted by Dionysius in the third century), early witnesses such as Justin, Irenaeus, and Polycarp correctly understand that John the apostle wrote both books.

The island of Patmos where John was exiled and where he wrote the book of Revelation.

RECIPIENTS

John writes Revelation to seven historical churches located in the Roman province of Asia, in modern Turkey (1:4,11; 22:16). The order in which he addresses these churches is the order a messenger from Patmos would travel as he made his way around Asia Minor on a circular route (see map, this page). Through John's prophetic pen, the risen Christ addresses the specific circumstances of these first-century churches as they face persecution, false teaching, and spiritual complacency and compromise (chs. 2–3). Two factors suggest that these seven churches represent the universal church. First, each message includes the refrain "Whoever has ears, let them hear what the Spirit says to the *churches*" (2:7,11,17,29; 3:6,13,22; emphasis added; cf. 22:16). Second, John writes to only seven churches, though many others existed in Asia Minor. Elsewhere the number seven symbolizes wholeness or fullness (see "Sevens in Revelation," p. 2582). Thus, John addresses seven historical churches and, by extension, the universal church, so that believers in every place and time should heed the book's testimony concerning the climax of prophecy. As the Muratorian Fragment (ca. AD 170) asserts, "John ... though he writes to seven churches, nevertheless speaks to all" (lines 57–60).

DATE

Ancient and modern interpreters have typically dated Revelation to the reigns of Nero (AD 54–68) or Domitian (81–96). Those preferring an earlier date (68–69) appeal particularly to 17:10 and identify the five "fallen" kings as Julius Caesar, Augustus, Tiberius, Caligula, and Claudius and the one who "is" as Nero. They often interpret 11:1–2 as predicting that Rome will destroy the temple in AD 70 and take 13:3 as referring to a popular legend about Nero's return that circulated after his death.

Most interpreters date Revelation to AD 95–96, following Irenaeus's statement that John received his vision "towards the end of Domitian's reign" (*Against Heresies*, 5.30.3). John addresses Christians in Asia Minor who were facing pressure to participate in Roman religious practices, particularly emperor worship (13:4,15–16). According to the Roman historian Suetonius (ca. AD 69–122), Domitian insisted on being called "our lord and god" (*Life of Domitian*, 13), and each of Revelation's seven cities became official centers for emperor worship by the late first and early second centuries. The testimony of the early church and the situation reflected in the book suggest that John most likely wrote Revelation in AD 95–96 (see notes on 2:13; 13:1,14).

GENRE

Many readers struggle with or misinterpret Revelation because they misunderstand its literary genre. The initial verses indicate that this work belongs to three kinds of ancient literature: *apocalypse*, *prophecy*, and *epistle*, each of which is important for considering the sort of book Revelation is and how we should interpret it.

THE SEVEN CHURCHES OF REVELATION

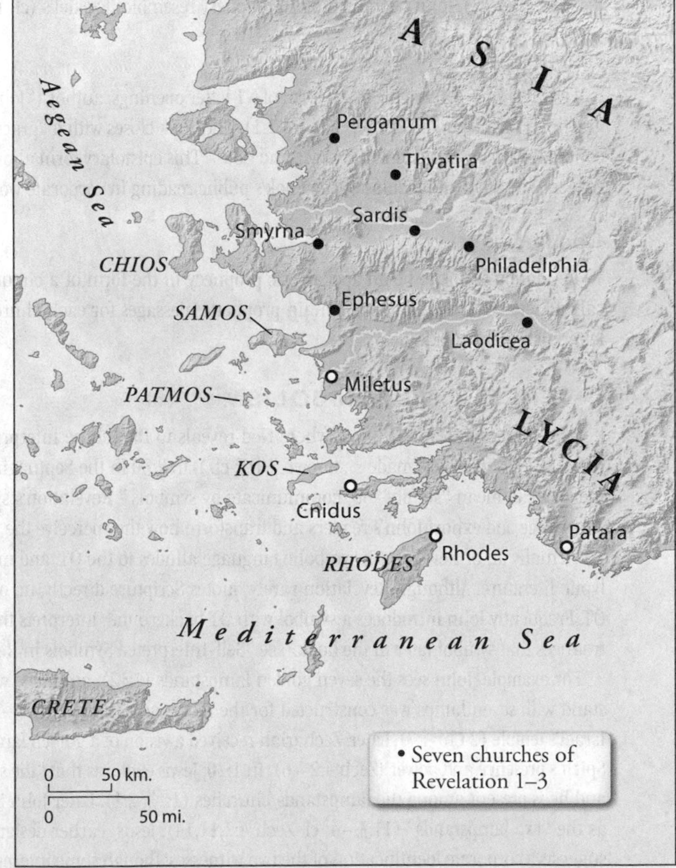

SEVENS IN REVELATION

blessings	1:3; 14:13; 16:15; 19:9; 20:6; 22:7,14
angels	1:20; 8:2,6; 15:1,6–8; 16:1; 17:1; 21:9
churches	1:4,11,20
spirits (of God)	1:4; 3:1; 4:5; 5:6
(golden) lampstands	1:12,20; 2:1
stars	1:16,20; 2:1; 3:1
blazing lamps	4:5
seals	5:1,5; 6:1
horns and eyes	5:6
trumpets	8:2,6
thunders	10:3–4
heads	12:3; 13:1; 17:3,7,9
plagues	15:1,6,8; 21:9
bowls (of wrath)	15:7; 16:1; 17:1; 21:9
hills, kings	17:9–10

Apocalypse

The opening phrase, "the revelation [Greek *apokalypsis*] from Jesus Christ," suggests that Revelation shares characteristics of Jewish and Christian writings that scholars call *apocalypses*. Apocalypses feature revelatory visions within a narrative framework; utilize symbolic, figurative, and metaphoric language; and interpret present, earthly circumstances in light of supernatural, heavenly realities and the future. Like portions of Isaiah, Ezekiel, and especially Daniel and unlike some extrabiblical Jewish apocalypses, John's apocalyptic visions are a vehicle for revealing God's ultimate purposes in judgment and salvation.

Prophecy

Additionally, Revelation is a book of prophecy intended for public reading during Christian worship (1:3; cf. 22:7,10,18–19). Revelation is the climax of all the prophecies in the Bible. John announces that Jesus has fulfilled, is fulfilling, and will one day consummate all earlier prophecies by triumphing as the suffering, conquering King (10:7; 22:6). Like true OT prophets (1 Kgs 18:12; Ezek 3:12; 37:1), John receives divine revelation "in the Spirit" (1:10–11; 4:2; 17:3; 21:10) and writes what he sees and hears (1:10–11,19; Jer 30:2; Hab 2:2). John's commission to prophesy resembles Ezekiel's (cf. 10:9–11 with Ezek 2:8—3:3).

Epistle

Finally, 1:4–6 follows the usual form of NT letter openings: author ("John"), recipients ("to the seven churches"), greeting ("grace and peace"; cf. 1 Thess 1:1). The book closes with a "grace" benediction virtually identical to those concluding many NT letters (see 22:21 and note). This epistolary form allowed John to address Revelation to his first readers' situation and facilitated the book's public reading in corporate worship.

Conclusion

Revelation seems to be an apocalyptic prophecy in the form of a circular letter. While chs. 2–3 are commonly called "letters," these chapters contain prophetic messages for each church that are included within one circular letter distributed to all.

INTERPRETING SYMBOLISM

Rev 1:1 alludes to Dan 2:28–30, where God reveals to Daniel the interpretation of Nebuchadnezzar's dream. The Greek word *sēmainō* ("made ... known," 1:1; cf. Dan 2:30 in the Septuagint, the pre-Christian Greek translation of the OT) can mean "signify" or "communicate by symbols." Revelation's symbolic visions function like parables to encourage and exhort John's readers and transform how they perceive the world.

Virtually all of Revelation's symbolic language alludes to the OT, and many symbols also occur in Jewish apocalyptic literature. Although Revelation rarely quotes Scripture directly, no other NT book is more saturated with the OT. Frequently John introduces a symbol with OT background, interprets that symbol for the readers, and then reintroduces that symbol later in the book (see "Self-Interpreted Symbols in Revelation," p. 2583).

For example, John sees the seven golden lampstands (1:12), an image with rich OT associations. A golden lampstand with seven lamps was constructed for the tabernacle (Exod 25:31–40), and then ten lampstands were set in Israel's temple (2 Chr 4:7). Later, Zechariah received a vision of a golden lampstand, highlighting Israel's need for the Spirit's presence and power (Zech 4:2–6). In 1:20, Jesus explains that "the seven lampstands are the seven churches" and he is present among the lampstands/churches (1:13; 2:1). Later John identifies the "two [prophetic] witnesses" as the "two lampstands" (11:3–4; cf. Zech 4:2,11,14). Jesus' earlier designation of lampstands as churches (1:20) suggests a corporate identification of the two witnesses, though some interpret these figures as future individuals (see

SELF-INTERPRETED SYMBOLS IN REVELATION

REFERENCE	SYMBOL	REVELATION'S INTERPRETATION
1:20	seven stars	angels
1:20	seven lampstands	churches
4:5	seven lamps	God's spirits
5:6	Lamb's seven horns, eyes	God's spirits
5:8	golden bowls	prayers of God's people
7:13–14	white-robed multitude	believers out of the great tribulation
11:4	two olive trees, lampstands	witnesses
14:3–4	the 144,000	undefiled followers of the Lamb
17:9–10	beast's seven heads	hills (Rome), kings
19:8	fine linen	righteous acts of God's people
20:5	thousand-year reign	first resurrection
20:14	lake of fire	second death

notes on 11:3,4). Further, the association between lampstands and witnesses in 11:3–4 sheds light on 2:5: removing Ephesus' lampstand may mean losing its identity as a church witnessing to Christ.

Images of Roman imperial power and pagan religion on coins, murals, statues, and temples regularly confronted John's first readers. Sometimes Revelation recalls these popular Roman images and then prophetically recasts and critiques them. For example, the goddess Roma personified Rome's vast power and was sometimes portrayed as a virtuous woman clothed in battle attire and reclining on Rome's seven hills (cf. 17:9). John's vision in ch. 17 transforms the dignified Roma into a debauched, bloodthirsty prostitute. The name "Babylon the Great" (17:5) associates Rome with Babylon, the violent, idolatrous nation that persecuted Israel and received God's judgment (see note on 14:8). John's satirical presentation moves readers to resist the temptation to compromise loyalty to Jesus for the pleasure and peace the world promises.

THEOLOGY

In Revelation, the one true God—the Creator, Sovereign, and Judge—has begun to execute and will consummate his end-time purposes to save his people and judge evil through Jesus, the slain Lamb, exalted Son of Man, and returning King. The opening salutation in 1:4–5 is implicitly Trinitarian, as John wishes grace and peace from God the Father, the divine Spirit, and Jesus (see note on 1:4).

The heavenly vision in 4:8–11 succinctly summarizes how Revelation portrays God the Father (cf. 1:6) as the one seated on the throne, signifying that God sovereignly rules without rivals (4:9; cf. Isa 6:1; Dan 4:34; 7:9). The living creatures declare that God is holy (three times), almighty, and eternal (4:8; cf. Isa 6:3), and the elders worship him as the Creator and Sustainer of all (4:11; cf. Job 40:10).

John's vision in 5:5–14 is similarly foundational for how the book presents Jesus as Israel's promised King (cf. Gen 49:9–10; Isa 11:1) who triumphs as the slain Lamb (5:5–6). The Lamb saves, forgives, and redeems God's people (1:5; 5:9; 7:10) and will return as the conquering King (19:11–16; 22:7). The Lamb shares God's throne (3:21; 22:1,3) and thus executes God's purposes in judgment and redemption (5:8; 6:1,16; 7:10). Further, Jesus shares God's name as "the Alpha and the Omega" (22:13; cf. 1:8 and note) and is worshiped together with God (5:13).

Revelation's theological message is that God sovereignly rules now and will defeat evil, vindicate his suffering church, and consummate his kingdom.

PURPOSE

Revelation's theological message *challenges* readers to repent of and resist worldly compromise, spiritual complacency, and false teaching (cf. 2:14–16,20–23; 3:2–3,15–19). It also *encourages* and *strengthens* believers to hold fast to their testimony about Jesus, steadfastly endure trials, and resiliently hope in God's present and future reign (1:9; 2:10; 3:11; 12:17; 14:12; 22:7).

INTERPRETIVE APPROACHES

There are five major approaches to interpreting Revelation.

Preterist

Preterists hold that Revelation describes events that would "soon take place" for John and his first-century readers. For preterists, Babylon's destruction (14:8) may refer to judgment on apostate Israel when Rome destroyed Jerusalem (AD 70) or on Rome when the empire fell in the fifth century. Some preterists allow for future fulfillment of some texts in the second coming of Christ, the final judgment, the resurrection, and the new heavens and new earth.

Futurist

Futurists typically interpret chs. 4 – 22 as referring to historical events in the distant future for John and the churches of Asia Minor, including a final crisis period followed by Jesus' return to establish his kingdom on earth, judge evil, and usher in the new creation. Not all futurists agree as to how Revelation portrays the unfolding of future events. *Dispensational futurists* interpret chs. 6 – 19 as a prophecy of a literal seven-year tribulation after the church's rapture. After the tribulation, God will fulfill his promises to bless Israel during a one-thousand-year period that does not directly pertain to the church (20:1 – 6). *Historical premillennialists* espouse a modified or moderate futurist position and hold that the church will pass through the final tribulation and will share in Christ's future earthly rule during the millennium (see Millennial Views). Many futurist interpreters affirm key elements of preterism or idealism.

Historicist

Historicists interpret 6:1 — 20:6 as a prophetic outline of the major historical developments from John's day (6:1) until Jesus' return (19:11), often focusing on Western church history. There are many versions of historicism, though Protestant interpreters have sometimes connected the antichrist and Babylon to the Roman papacy. Few today follow a historicist interpretation of Revelation, though this approach has been very common at other points in church history.

Idealist

For idealists, Revelation symbolically depicts the ongoing conflict between the forces of God and of Satan throughout the church age. Idealists are reticent to identify John's symbols with particular past or future historical events, though many idealists affirm that Jesus will return to establish his eternal kingdom in the new creation.

Eclecticism or Mixed View

Many readers argue for a mixed approach that combines key insights from futurism, preterism, and idealism. Preterists are probably correct that the whole book, not simply chs. 1 – 3, addresses the circumstances and concerns of John's first-century readers. Idealists rightly affirm that Revelation has ongoing relevance throughout history and that John's symbolic visions may have multiple fulfillments. Futurists correctly stress that Jesus will return to judge evil, save God's people, and establish God's everlasting kingdom.

Amid these many interpretive approaches, Revelation's central message is clear: God sovereignly rules history and will complete his plans to judge and save through Jesus, the slain Lamb and returning King.

MILLENNIAL VIEWS

The "millennium" is the thousand-year period in 20:1 – 6. From earliest times, orthodox Christian interpreters have been divided over the nature and timing of the millennium relative to Jesus' second coming. In *premillennialism*, Jesus returns *before* his thousand-year reign on earth. In *postmillennialism*, Jesus returns *after* an earthly golden age. In *amillennialism*, the millennium is a *symbolic* time frame between Jesus' ascension and his return, when deceased believers reign with Christ in heaven.

Premillennialism

Premillennialists believe that Jesus will return *before* (pre-) the millennium to defeat and destroy the beast and false prophet (19:11 – 21). Then Satan will be "bound" for a thousand years (20:2), during which time some believers (martyrs and perhaps others) will receive resurrection bodies and will reign with Christ on the earth over the descendants of those surviving the battle of Armageddon (20:4; cf. 16:16). In this view, Satan will be released after the thousand years to deceive the nations and assemble an army for battle; he will then be finally defeated and judged (20:7–10). Many premillennialists interpret the millennium to be precisely one thousand years, though some hold that the millennium symbolizes a long period of time.

Postmillennialism

Most historicist and preterist interpreters affirm *postmillennialism* and believe Jesus will return *after* (post-) a literal or symbolic millennium. Most modern postmillennialists (like amillennialists) understand a symbolic thousand-year period to be coextensive with the church age, while others understand the millennium to come at the end of the church age after the church's gospel proclamation brings about the nations' conversion and a golden age of God's blessing. Then Satan will be temporarily released for a final assault on the church (20:7–9), after which Jesus returns to defeat his enemies (20:10; cf. 19:11–21).

Amillennialism

Idealists and some preterists and historicists view the millennium as a *symbolic* time frame between Jesus' ascension and his return when deceased believers reign *in heaven* with Jesus. Amillennialism is sometimes called "inaugurated" or "realized millennialism" to clarify the nature and timing of the millennium. Amillennialists believe that Satan was bound through Jesus' death and resurrection and is prevented from deceiving the nations and hindering the gospel's spread during the church age (20:2–3; cf. Matt 12:28–29; John 12:31–32). At the end of this age, Satan will be released for a final onslaught against the church (20:7–9). Then Christ will return to judge his enemies, vindicate his people, and usher in the new creation.

STRUCTURE

Revelation has a clearly defined introduction (1:1–8) and conclusion (22:6–21) that share many verbal and thematic links (see "Links Between Revelation's Introduction and Conclusion," this page).

The main body (1:9—22:5) is difficult to structure with precision. Some interpreters view 1:19 as indicating a threefold outline for the book: "what you have seen" (ch. 1), "what is now" (chs. 2–3), and "what will take place later" (chs. 4–22). Others make no attempt to outline the book on this basis, maintaining that there is a mixture of "now" and "later" throughout Revelation. Other readers argue that Revelation is structured in seven parallel sections or cycles: (1) Christ in the midst of the lampstands (1:1—3:22); (2) the vision of heaven and the seven seals (4:1—8:1); (3) the seven trumpets (8:2—11:19); (4) the persecuting dragon (12:1—14:20); (5) the seven bowls (15:1—16:21); (6) the fall of Babylon (17:1—19:21); the great consummation (20:1—22:21).

Revelation includes four series of sevens: churches (2:1—3:22), seals (6:1—8:1), trumpets (8:2—11:19), and plagues or bowls (15:1—16:21). John's four visions "in the Spirit" (1:10; 4:2; 17:3; 21:10) serve as additional structural markers. John's opening vision of Christ (1:9–20) is foundational for the messages to the churches (chs. 2–3). Likewise, John's throne-room vision (chs. 4–5) initiates three judgment cycles: seven seals (6:1—8:1; cf. 5:5), trumpets (8:6—11:19; cf. 8:2), and bowls (15:1—16:21; cf. 5:8).

LINKS BETWEEN REVELATION'S INTRODUCTION AND CONCLUSION

REVELATION 1:1–8	REVELATION 22:6–8
God sent his angel (v. 1)	The Lord sent his angel (v. 6)
John "testifies to everything he saw" (v. 2)	John "heard and saw these things" (v. 8)
"show . . . what must soon take place" (v. 1)	"show . . . the things that must soon take place" (v. 6)
"Blessed is the one who reads aloud the words of this prophecy" (v. 3)	"Blessed is the one who keeps the words of the prophecy" (v. 7)
"Look, he is coming with the clouds" (v. 7)	"Look, I am coming soon!" (v. 7)

OUTLINE

I. Introduction (1:1–8)

A. Prologue (1:1–3)

B. Greetings and Doxology (1:4–8)

II. Body (1:9—22:5)

A. Christ in the Midst of the Lampstands (1:9—3:22)

1. John's Vision of Christ (1:9–20)
2. Prophetic Messages to the Seven Churches (2:1—3:22)
   a. To the Church in Ephesus (2:1–7)
   b. To the Church in Smyrna (2:8–11)
   c. To the Church in Pergamum (2:12–17)
   d. To the Church in Thyatira (2:18–29)
   e. To the Church in Sardis (3:1–6)
   f. To the Church in Philadelphia (3:7–13)
   g. To the Church in Laodicea (3:14–22)

B. The Heavenly Throne Room and the Seals (4:1—8:5)

1. The Throne in Heaven (4:1–11)
2. The Scroll and the Lamb (5:1–14)
3. The Seals (6:1–17)
4. 144,000 Sealed (7:1–8)
5. The Great Multitude in White Robes (7:9–17)
6. The Seventh Seal and the Golden Censer (8:1–5)

C. The Seven Trumpets (8:6—11:19)

1. The Trumpets (8:6—9:21)
2. The Angel and the Little Scroll (10:1–11)
3. The Two Witnesses (11:1–14)
4. The Seventh Trumpet (11:15–19)

D. The Cosmic Conflict Between the Dragon and the Lamb (12:1—14:20)

1. The Woman and the Dragon (12:1–17)
2. The Beast out of the Sea (13:1–10)
3. The Beast out of the Earth (13:11–18)
4. The Lamb and the 144,000 (14:1–5)
5. The Three Angels (14:6–13)
6. Harvesting the Earth and Trampling the Winepress (14:14–20)

E. The Seven Bowls (15:1—16:21)

1. Seven Angels With Seven Plagues (15:1–8)
2. The Seven Bowls of God's Wrath (16:1–21)

F. Destruction of Babylon, the Prostitute (17:1—19:10)

1. Babylon, the Prostitute on the Beast (17:1–18)
2. Lament Over Fallen Babylon (18:1–3)
3. Warning to Escape Babylon's Judgment (18:4–8)
4. Threefold Woe Over Babylon's Fall (18:9–20)
5. The Finality of Babylon's Doom (18:21–24)
6. Threefold Hallelujah Over Babylon's Fall (19:1–10)

G. The Final Victory, Judgment, and Restoration (19:11—21:8)

1. The Heavenly Warrior Defeats the Beast (19:11–21)
2. The Thousand Years (20:1–6)
3. The Judgment of Satan (20:7–10)
4. The Judgment of the Dead (20:11–15)
5. A New Heaven and a New Earth (21:1–8)

H. The New Jerusalem and God's Glorious Presence (21:9—22:5)
   1. The New Jerusalem, the Bride of the Lamb (21:9–27)
   2. Eden Restored (22:1–5)

III. Conclusion (22:6–21)

A. John and the Angel (22:6–11)

B. Epilogue: Invitation and Warning (22:12–21)

REVELATION

1:1 [a]Rev 22:16
1:2 [b]1Co 1:6; Rev 12:17
1:3 [c]Lk 11:28
1:4 [d]Rev 3:1; 4:5
1:5 [e]Rev 3:14 [f]Col 1:18 [g]Rev 17:14
1:6 [h]1Pe 2:5 [i]Ro 11:36

Prologue

1 The revelation from Jesus Christ, which God gave him to show his servants what must soon take
place. He made it known by sending his angel[a] to his servant John, 2who testifies to everything he
saw — that is, the word of God and the testimony of Jesus Christ.[b] 3Blessed is the one who reads aloud
the words of this prophecy, and blessed are those who hear it and take to heart what is written in it,[c]
because the time is near.

Greetings and Doxology

4John,

To the seven churches in the province of Asia:

Grace and peace to you from him who is, and who was, and who is to come, and from the seven
spirits[a][d] before his throne, 5and from Jesus Christ, who is the faithful witness,[e] the firstborn from the
dead,[f] and the ruler of the kings of the earth.[g]

To him who loves us and has freed us from our sins by his blood, 6and has made us to be a kingdom and priests[h] to serve his God and Father — to him be glory and power for ever and ever! Amen.[i]

[a] *4* That is, the sevenfold Spirit

1:1 – 8 *Introduction.* These verses establish the book's divine origin (v. 1), John's prophetic credentials (vv. 1 – 2), and the first readers' identity (v. 4), and promise divine blessing for those who read and keep these words (v. 3).
1:1 – 3 *Prologue.* "The revelation from Jesus Christ" (v. 1) reaches the church by a three-stage process: (1) God gave it to Jesus, (2) who sent his angel to John, (3) who writes to believers ("his servants," v. 1). This book is identified as "revelation" (v. 1), "prophecy" (v. 3), and Christian Scripture ("the word of God and the testimony of Jesus Christ," v. 2).
1:1 The revelation from Jesus Christ. Book summary or title. It may mean revelation *from* Jesus, revelation *about* Jesus, or both (cf. 1 Cor 1:7; Gal 1:12; 1 Pet 1:7,13). Here it emphasizes that Jesus discloses unseen, divine realities. **what must soon take place.** Alludes to Dan 2:28 – 30; cf. v. 19; 22:6; see Introduction: Interpreting Symbolism. **angel.** In Revelation and other apocalyptic literature, angels mediate God's Word and execute God's purposes (8:2; 10:8 – 10; 22:16; Dan 8:15 – 17; 9:21 – 22). **John.** See Introduction: Author.
1:3 Blessed. Revelation's first beatitude promises God's favor to those who read, hear, and rightly respond to John's prophetic testimony (see "Seven Blessings in Revelation," p. 2589; see also Ps 1:1; Matt 5:3 – 11). **because.** Introduces the reason that virtuous readers are blessed: God's revealed purposes will soon be fulfilled (cf. v. 1; 22:10).
1:4 – 8 *Greetings and Doxology.* John's circular letter to seven Asian churches begins with an introduction and theological greeting typical of other NT letters (vv. 4 – 6; see Introduction: Genre). Then he prophetically announces Jesus' imminent coming (vv. 7 – 8).
1:4 seven churches. See Introduction: Recipients; cf. v. 11. **Grace and peace.** Standard Christian blessing (cf. Rom 1:7), here rooted in the triune God (see Introduction: Theology). **is ... was ... is to come.** Recalls God's self-disclosure as "I AM" in Exod 3:14; cf. v. 8; 4:8; 11:17. **seven spirits.** See NIV text note. Probably alludes to Isa 11:2 (in the Septuagint, the pre-Christian Greek translation of the OT) and denotes the perfect work of God's Spirit (3:1; 4:5; 5:6).
1:5 faithful witness. Cf. 3:14; Isa 55:4. Jesus bore witness unto death (cf. John 18:37; 1 Tim 6:13); believers like John (vv. 2,9), Antipas (2:13), and others "follow the Lamb" (14:4) and must testify amidst suffering (6:9; 11:3; 12:11; 17:6). **firstborn ... ruler.** Jesus' resurrection establishes him as the exalted Davidic king (Ps 89:27; cf. Ps 2:6 – 9) and anticipates believers' future resurrection (cf. 1 Cor 15:20). Jesus — not Caesar — is the supreme ruler, worthy of worship and total allegiance (11:15; 12:10; 17:14; 19:6). **To him.** Introduces a doxology that celebrates Jesus' unsurpassed love for his people (cf. Rom 8:35 – 39) and his atoning death as the slain Lamb (5:8 – 9).
1:6 kingdom and priests. Describes the church's vocation in light of Israel's calling to be a "kingdom of priests" (Exod 19:6; cf. 5:10; 20:6; Isa 61:6; 1 Pet 2:9).

[7]"Look, he is coming with the clouds,"[a][j]
and "every eye will see him,
even those who pierced him";
and all peoples on earth "will mourn[k] because of him."[b]
So shall it be! Amen.

[8]"I am the Alpha and the Omega,"[l] says the Lord God, "who is, and who was, and who is to come,
the Almighty."[m]

John's Vision of Christ

[9]I, John, your brother and companion in the suffering[n] and kingdom and patient endurance[o] that
are ours in Jesus, was on the island of Patmos because of
the word of God and the testimony of Jesus. [10]On the Lord's
Day I was in the Spirit,[p] and I heard behind me a loud voice
like a trumpet,[q] [11]which said: "Write on a scroll what you
see and send it to the seven churches:[r] to Ephesus, Smyrna,
Pergamum, Thyatira, Sardis,[s] Philadelphia and Laodicea."
[12]I turned around to see the voice that was speaking to
me. And when I turned I saw seven golden lampstands,[t] [13]and
among the lampstands was someone like a son of man,[c][u]
dressed in a robe reaching down to his feet and with a golden
sash around his chest.[v] [14]The hair on his head was white like
wool, as white as snow, and his eyes were like blazing fire.[w]
[15]His feet were like bronze glowing in a furnace,[x] and his
voice was like the sound of rushing waters.[y] [16]In his right

[a] *7* Daniel 7:13 [b] *7* Zech. 12:10 [c] *13* See Daniel 7:13.

1:7 [j]Da 7:13 [k]Zec 12:10
1:8 [l]Rev 21:6 [m]Rev 4:8
1:9 [n]Php 4:14 [o]2Ti 2:12
1:10 [p]Rev 4:2 [q]Rev 4:1
1:11 [r]ver 4,20 [s]Rev 3:1
1:12 [t]Ex 25:31-40; Zec 4:2
1:13 [u]Eze 1:26; Da 7:13; 10:16 [v]Da 10:5; Rev 15:6
1:14 [w]Da 7:9; 10:6; Rev 19:12
1:15 [x]Da 10:6 [y]Eze 43:2; Rev 14:2

SEVEN BLESSINGS IN REVELATION

BLESSED IS/ARE ...	REFERENCE
The one who reads, hears, and takes to heart this prophecy	1:3
The dead who die in the Lord	14:13
The one who stays awake and remains clothed	16:15
Those invited to the wedding supper of the Lamb	19:9
Those who share in the first resurrection	20:6
The one who keeps the words of the prophecy	22:7
Those who wash their robes	22:14

1:7 he is coming. Jesus' second coming is a major theme in Revelation (16:15; 22:7,12,20). **with the clouds.** Alludes to Dan 7:13 and recalls Jesus' teaching (Matt 16:27; 24:30; Mark 14:62). **those who pierced him.** Alludes to Zech 12:10. These prophecies find initial fulfillment in Jesus' crucifixion (John 19:34,37) and heavenly exaltation (Acts 7:55–56) but also anticipate Jesus' glorious return (Matt 24:30). **all peoples on earth "will mourn ..."** Refers either to sorrowful repentance from sins (Zech 12:10) or lamentation over divine judgment (cf. 18:9).
1:8 Alpha ... Omega. The first and last letters of the Greek alphabet; equivalent to "the Beginning and the End" (21:6) and "the First and the Last" (v. 17; cf. Isa 44:6). These titles emphasize that God and Christ are eternally and totally sovereign over history (cf. 22:13). **who is ... was ... is to come.** See note on v. 4. **Almighty.** Title emphasizing God's absolute power and control (cf. 4:8; 11:17; see Introduction: Theology).
1:9—22:5 *Body.* The central section of this prophetic letter includes a series of visions concerning the present and future kingdom of God and the Lamb. John's initial vision of Christ (1:9–20) prepares for the messages to the seven churches (chs. 2–3). Then the throne-room vision initiates three cycles of divine judgment, beginning with the seven seals (4:1—8:5). Between the seven trumpets (8:6—11:19) and seven bowls (15:1—16:21), John presents the basic conflict between God and Satan for the nations' allegiance and adoration (12:1—14:20). The body concludes with visions detailing Babylon's punishment (17:1—19:10); God's final victory, judgment, and restoration (19:11—21:8); and his enduring presence with his people in the new Jerusalem (21:9—22:5).
1:9—3:22 *Christ in the Midst of the Lampstands.* John hears and sees the risen Son of Man, who is present with and ruling over the churches (1:10–20). This vision expands upon 1:1–2 and introduces the seven prophetic messages in chs. 2–3.
1:9–20 *John's Vision of Christ.* John recounts his situation in exile (v. 9), his vision of Jesus (vv. 10,12–18), and his commission to write (vv. 11,19–20).
1:9 brother and companion. John identifies with his readers in their present suffering and future glory, modeled on Jesus' own experience (v. 5; cf. 1 Pet 2:21). **suffering.** Expected for believers (cf. 2:9–10; 7:14), who share already in God's "kingdom" and hope for its future fullness (11:15; cf. Acts 14:22). **patient endurance.** Entails waiting on the Lord and overcoming evil amid suffering (cf. 13:10; 14:12). **Patmos.** See map, p. 2581. Because of his faithful testimony about Jesus, John was exiled to this small, rocky, volcanic island in the Aegean Sea, 37 miles (60 kilometers) southwest of Miletus (Acts 20:15).
1:10 Lord's Day. Sunday, "the first day of the week" (Matt 28:1), the day Jesus rose. The majority of Christ's followers see this passage as evidence that already in the first century this day was set aside for worship and fellowship (Acts 20:7; 1 Cor 16:2). **in the Spirit.** Indicates a prophetic vision (4:2; 17:3; 21:10; Ezek 2:2; 3:12) and introduces Revelation's next major section (see Introduction: Structure).
1:11 Write ... what you see. Like some OT prophets (v. 19; Isa 30:8; Jer 36:2; Hab 2:2). **seven churches.** See Introduction: Recipients; cf. v. 4.
1:12 seven golden lampstands. Explained in v. 20. See Introduction: Interpreting Symbolism.
1:13 son of man. Alludes to Dan 7:13; see v. 7. Jesus frequently referred to himself as the Son of Man (Matt 26:64; John 1:51). **robe ... golden sash.** Suggests a king's authority (Isa 22:21), a high priest's purity (Exod 28:4; 29:5–9), or both.
1:14 hair ... white like wool. Symbolizes the perfect wisdom of the Ancient of Days (Dan 7:9), which Jesus also possesses. **eyes ... like blazing fire.** Suggests penetrating, divine insight (2:18; 19:12; Dan 10:6).
1:15 feet ... like bronze. Recalls Dan 10:6, symbolizing glory, stability, and security (cf. 2:18). **voice ... rushing waters.** Alludes to Ezek 1:24; 43:2. Jesus speaks with the awe-inspiring, authoritative divine voice (v. 10).
1:16 he held seven stars. Symbolizes complete power and control (cf.

1:16 [z]Rev 2:1; 3:1 [a]Isa 49:2; Heb 4:12; Rev 2:12,16
1:17 [b]Eze 1:28; Da 8:17, 18 [c]Isa 41:4; 44:6; 48:12; Rev 22:13
1:18 [d]Ro 6:9 [e]Rev 4:9, 10 [f]Rev 20:1
1:20 [g]Zec 4:2 [h]ver 4,11 [i]Mt 5:14,15
2:1 [j]Rev 1:16 [k]Rev 1:12,13
2:2 [l]Rev 3:1,8,15 [m]1Jn 4:1 [n]2Co 11:13
2:3 [o]Jn 15:21

hand he held seven stars,[z] and coming out of his mouth was a sharp, double-edged sword.[a] His face was like the sun shining in all its brilliance.

17 When I saw him, I fell at his feet[b] as though dead. Then he placed his right hand on me and said: "Do not be afraid. I am the First and the Last.[c] 18 I am the Living One; I was dead,[d] and now look, I am alive for ever and ever![e] And I hold the keys of death and Hades.[f]

19 "Write, therefore, what you have seen, what is now and what will take place later. 20 The mystery of the seven stars that you saw in my right hand and of the seven golden lampstands[g] is this: The seven stars are the angels[a] of the seven churches,[h] and the seven lampstands are the seven churches.[i]

STRUCTURE OF MESSAGES TO THE CHURCHES IN REVELATION 2–3

(1) Command to write to the church's angel	All
(2) Christ's self-description	All
(3) Christ's knowledge of the churches	All
(4) Christ's commendation	Ephesus, Smyrna, Pergamum, Thyatira, Philadelphia
(5) Christ's rebuke	Ephesus, Pergamum, Thyatira, Sardis, Laodicea
(6) Exhortation to repent or persevere	All
(7) Summons to hear the Spirit's message	All
(8) Promise for victors	All

To the Church in Ephesus

2 "To the angel[b] of the church in Ephesus write:

These are the words of him who holds the seven stars in his right hand[j] and walks among the seven golden lampstands.[k] 2 I know your deeds,[l] your hard work and your perseverance. I know that you cannot tolerate wicked people, that you have tested[m] those who claim to be apostles but are not, and have found them false.[n] 3 You have persevered and have endured hardships for my name,[o] and have not grown weary.

[a] *20* Or *messengers* [b] *1* Or *messenger*; also in verses 8, 12 and 18

v. 20; 2:1; 3:1). **sword.** Alludes to Isa 11:4; 49:2. Christ will execute judgment on the nations (19:15) and on false teaching and immorality within the church (2:12,16). **face ... like the sun.** Pictures divine glory and light (cf. 21:23; Ps 84:11; Isa 60:19), applied to Jesus here and at the transfiguration (Matt 17:2).

1:17 I fell at his feet. A common response to a prophetic vision (cf. Ezek 1:28; Dan 8:17–18; 10:7–9); appropriate reverence toward the exalted Christ (cf. Matt 17:6) but not toward angelic messengers (19:10; 22:8–9). **the First and the Last.** Alludes to God's self-description in Isa 41:4; 44:6; 48:12; similar to "the Alpha and the Omega" in v. 8; cf. 2:8; 22:13.

1:18 Living One. The risen Christ lives forever like God (4:9–10; cf. Dan 4:34). **keys.** Convey power or control over something (3:7; 9:1; 20:1; Isa 22:22; Matt 16:19): Christ has complete authority over the cosmic forces of "death and Hades" now and will abolish them forever (20:13–14; 1 Cor 15:54–57; Heb 2:14–15).

1:19 Write. See note on v. 11. **therefore.** Because of Christ's resurrection and authority over death. **seen ... now ... later.** Recalls Dan 2:28–29,45 (cf. Rev 1:1); Isa 48:3–6. May recall vv. 4,8: God is the one "who is, and who was, and who is to come." Many futurists interpret this threefold division as indicating the book's outline (see Introduction: Structure).

1:20 mystery. A divine secret previously hidden but now disclosed (10:7; 17:5,7; cf. Dan 2:47; Rom 16:25–26). Here Christ interprets two symbols from the previous vision (vv. 12,16). **stars ... angels.** May refer to (1) heavenly angels, (2) earthly messengers/ministers (see NIV text note), or (3) personifications of each church's identity. In v. 1 and elsewhere in Revelation, the Greek term *angelos* denotes heavenly beings. **lampstands.** Symbolize the churches' light-bearing role (cf. 2:1,5; 11:4; Matt 5:14–16; see Introduction: Interpreting Symbolism).

2:1 — 3:22 *Prophetic Messages to the Seven Churches.* The risen Christ addresses each of the churches that 1:11 introduces. These prophetic messages or edicts follow a common literary structure (see "Structure of Messages to the Churches," this page). Christ highlights features of his earlier self-revelation (1:12–16) relevant to the church's situation. He asserts his detailed knowledge of the church ("I know," 2:2,9,13,19; 3:1,8,15), then commends (for five churches), rebukes (for five churches), and exhorts believers to repent or persevere amidst adversity. Finally, Christ calls everyone to hear the Spirit's message to the churches and promises life and blessing in the new Jerusalem to victorious, persevering believers. These messages directly addressed the struggles of seven first-century churches, but together they present a unified message relevant for all churches.

2:1–7 *To the Church in Ephesus.* Christ commends believers in Ephesus for doing good works, persevering, and rejecting false teaching but summons them to repent of letting their love for Jesus fade, which threatens their very identity as a church.

2:1 angel. See note on 1:20; cf. vv. 8,12,18; 3:1,7,14. **Ephesus.** The fourth largest city in the Roman Empire and a major center for commerce, political administration, and religion, and home to the massive temple of Artemis (Acts 19:27,35; Eph 1:1). See Introduction to Ephesians: City of Ephesus. **him.** Jesus. **stars.** Angels (1:16). **lampstands.** Churches (1:12–13,20).

2:2 I know your deeds. Commendation, as in v. 19; 3:8. **hard work.** Cf. "labor" in 14:13. **perseverance.** Cf. v. 19; "patient endurance" in 1:9. The same three Greek words occur in 1 Thess 1:3 ("work ... labor ... endurance"). **claim to be apostles.** Cf. 2 Cor 11:13.

[4]Yet I hold this against you: You have forsaken the love
you had at first.[p] [5]Consider how far you have fallen! Repent[q] and do the things you did at first. If you do not repent, I will come to you and remove your lampstand[r] from
its place. [6]But you have this in your favor: You hate the
practices of the Nicolaitans,[s] which I also hate.

[7]Whoever has ears, let them hear[t] what the Spirit says
to the churches. To the one who is victorious, I will give
the right to eat from the tree of life,[u] which is in the paradise[v] of God.

Ephesus' patron goddess Artemis was frequently represented by a date palm, seen here on an Ephesian coin. Whereas Jesus gives "the right to eat from the tree of life" (Rev 2:7).

To the Church in Smyrna

[8]"To the angel of the church in Smyrna[w] write:

These are the words of him who is the First and the Last,[x] who died and came to life again.[y]
[9]I know your afflictions and your poverty—yet you are rich![z] I know about the slander of those
who say they are Jews and are not,[a] but are a synagogue of Satan.[b] [10]Do not be afraid of what
you are about to suffer. I tell you, the devil will put some of you in prison to test you,[c] and you
will suffer persecution for ten days.[d] Be faithful,[e] even to the point of death, and I will give you
life as your victor's crown.

[11]Whoever has ears, let them hear what the Spirit says to the churches. The one who is victorious will not be hurt at all by the second death.[f]

To the Church in Pergamum

[12]"To the angel of the church in Pergamum[g] write:

These are the words of him who has the sharp, double-edged sword.[h] [13]I know where you
live—where Satan has his throne. Yet you remain true to my name. You did not renounce your

2:4 [p]Mt 24:12
2:5 [q]ver 16,22 [r]Rev 1:20
2:6 [s]ver 15
2:7 [t]Mt 11:15; Rev 3:6, 13,22 [u]Ge 2:9; Rev 22:2, 14,19 [v]Lk 23:43
2:8 [w]Rev 1:11 [x]Rev 1:17 [y]Rev 1:18
2:9 [z]Jas 2:5 [a]Rev 3:9 [b]Mt 4:10
2:10 [c]Rev 3:10 [d]Da 1:12, 14 [e]ver 13
2:11 [f]Rev 20:6,14; 21:8
2:12 [g]Rev 1:11 [h]Rev 1:16

2:4 I hold this against you. Introduces Christ's rebuke (vv. 14,20). **love you had at first.** Love for Jesus (Eph 6:24) and/or one another (Eph 5:2).
2:5 Consider ... Repent ... do the things you did at first. Jesus exhorts the church to seriously consider their situation and change their mind, heart, and actions. **remove your lampstand.** If the Ephesians do not repent, they will lose their identity as a church.
2:6 Nicolaitans. A heretical sect whose name means "victory people." They apparently promoted false teaching, idolatry, and immorality like Balaam (v. 14) and Jezebel (v. 20), and the Ephesian church opposed their practices, while some in Pergamum did not (v. 15).
2:7 Whoever has ears, let them hear. Echoes similar exhortations in the Gospels (Matt 11:15; Mark 4:9) and the Prophets (Isa 6:9–10; Ezek 3:27) to hear and respond to God's Word. **what the Spirit says.** See note on 14:13. **the one who is victorious.** Believers share in Jesus' victory (5:5; 17:14) and must faithfully bear witness to Jesus (12:11,17) and maintain hope of their promised inheritance (21:7). **tree of life.** Symbolizes eternal life in fellowship with God, fellowship that was lost after humanity's exile from Eden (Gen 2:9; 3:22–24) but is restored in the new creation (22:2,14,19; see "Paradise Restored," p. 2626).
2:8–11 *To the Church in Smyrna.* Jesus praises and encourages the suffering, faithful church at Smyrna.
2:8 Smyrna. A harbor city (modern-day Izmir) 35 miles (56 kilometers) north of Ephesus (see map, p. 2581), Smyrna was renowned for its beauty, civic pride, and claim to be Homer's birthplace. The city was an important center of emperor worship and home to a temple to the goddess Roma. **the First and the Last.** See note on 1:17. **died and came to life again.** Thus, Jesus comforts and secures suffering believers. The city itself had "died" (600 BC) and been magnificently restored (290 BC).
2:9 afflictions. Cf. v. 10 ("suffer persecution"). Includes economic hardship, verbal abuse, and marginalization, likely because they refused to participate in idolatrous trade guilds. **your poverty—yet you are rich!** This church is materially poor yet spiritually prosperous—the antithesis of Laodicea (3:17). Cf. 2 Cor 8:2,9; Jas 2:5. **synagogue of Satan.** Smyrna's large, influential Jewish population persecuted Christians, possibly slandering them in Roman court, thereby aligning with Satan against God's purposes (cf. 3:9; John 8:44–47; Acts 13:10).
2:10 ten days. An intense, brief period of persecution and testing (cf. Dan 1:12,14). **life as your victor's crown.** Athletic imagery fitting for Smyrna and Philadelphia (3:11), famed for their games. Jesus promises honor, victory, and life to maligned believers facing potential death (cf. 2 Tim 4:6–8; Jas 1:12).
2:11 second death. The lake of fire, eternal death (20:6,14; 21:8).
2:12–17 *To the Church in Pergamum.* Jesus commends Pergamum for remaining true amid persecution, but they must repent of doctrinal and moral compromise.
2:12 Pergamum. A magnificent city of 100,000 located 70 miles (113 kilometers) north of Smyrna and 16.5 miles (26.5 kilometers) inland (see map, p. 2581). Pergamum was an important intellectual city with a library holding 200,000 volumes; it was Asia's leading religious center, the foremost city for emperor worship, and home to a 40-foot-high (12 meters) altar to Zeus (king of the gods). **sword.** See note on 1:16. Symbolizes Jesus' ultimate authority to exercise judgment, confronting Roman officials who misused their "right of the sword" to persecute Christians (v. 13) and warning the church to turn from idolatrous compromise (vv. 14,16).
2:13 where Satan has his throne. May refer to the altar of Zeus or the pagan shrine to Asklepios, the god of medicine (symbolized by a serpent); most likely designates the prominent practice of emperor worship

The theater at Pergamum.

2:13 [i]Rev 14:12 [j]ver 9,24
2:14 [k]ver 20 [l]2Pe 2:15 [m]1Co 6:13
2:15 [n]ver 6
2:16 [o]2Th 2:8; Rev 1:16
2:17 [p]Jn 6:49,50 [q]Isa 62:2 [r]Rev 19:12
2:18 [s]Rev 1:11 [t]Rev 1:14,15
2:19 [u]ver 2
2:20 [v]1Ki 16:31; 21:25; 2Ki 9:7

faith in me,[i] not even in the days of Antipas, my faithful witness, who was put to death in your
city — where Satan lives.[j]

14Nevertheless, I have a few things against you:[k] There are some among you who hold to the
teaching of Balaam,[l] who taught Balak to entice the Israelites to sin so that they ate food sacrificed to idols and committed sexual immorality.[m] 15Likewise, you also have those who hold to the
teaching of the Nicolaitans.[n] 16Repent therefore! Otherwise, I will soon come to you and will fight
against them with the sword of my mouth.[o]

17Whoever has ears, let them hear what the Spirit says to the churches. To the one who is victorious, I will give some of the hidden manna.[p] I will also give that person a white stone with a
new name[q] written on it, known only to the one who receives it.[r]

To the Church in Thyatira

18"To the angel of the church in Thyatira[s] write:

These are the words of the Son of God, whose eyes are like blazing fire and whose feet are like
burnished bronze.[t] 19I know your deeds,[u] your love and faith, your service and perseverance, and
that you are now doing more than you did at first.

20Nevertheless, I have this against you: You tolerate that woman Jezebel,[v] who calls herself a

in Pergamum. **Antipas.** The first martyr of Asia, a "faithful witness" (Greek *martys*) unto death like Jesus (1:5; 3:14) and Stephen (Acts 22:20). Christians who refused to show political and religious loyalty to Rome through emperor worship were marginalized and persecuted.
2:14 Balaam. The Gentile prophet who blessed Israel when Balak asked him to curse them (Num 22–24); he advised Balak to use Moabite women to seduce Israel into sexual immorality and idolatry (Num 25:1–2; 31:16; cf. Jude 11).
2:15 Nicolaitans. See note on v. 6.
2:16 Repent. The church must turn away from immorality and false teaching to avoid imminent judgment (v. 5; 3:3,19).
2:17 hidden manna. Recalls Exod 16:32–34, where the Lord commands Moses to preserve an omer of manna for future generations. Jesus, the "living bread" from heaven (John 6:51), promises everlasting food (cf. 19:9) to this church tempted by idolatrous Roman feasts (v. 14). **white stone.** White symbolizes purity and victory (see note on 3:5) and recalls the description of manna in Exod 16:31. White stones were associated with acquittal in court and admission to special feasts for athletic victors or members of a guild; here they may suggest entrance to the Messianic feast. **new name.** In the new creation, victorious believers who remain true to Jesus' name (v. 13) will receive an enduring identity and status in relationship with God (Isa 62:2; 65:15).
2:18–29 *To the Church in Thyatira.* Jesus praises Thyatiran believers for their love and faith but rebukes them for tolerating heresy and immorality. The least important of the seven churches receives the longest, most challenging prophetic message.
2:18 Thyatira. A commercial town about 40 miles (64 kilometers) southeast of Pergamum (see map, p. 2581) known for its many influential trade guilds, each with a patron deity. Lydia was "a dealer in purple cloth" from Thyatira (Acts 16:14). **Son of God.** A common NT title (Mark 1:1) that occurs only here in Revelation. Jesus, not Apollo (son of Zeus), is the true divine Son worthy of worship. **eyes … feet.** See notes on 1:14,15. **bronze.** One of Thyatira's major industries.
2:19 love and faith. Essential Christian virtues (cf. 1 Thess 1:3). **doing more than you did at first.** Contrast with Ephesus (vv. 4–5).
2:20 Jezebel. A false prophet who deceived church members by lead-

prophet. By her teaching she misleads my servants into sexual immorality and the eating of food sacrificed to idols. 21I have given her time[w] to repent of her immorality, but she is unwilling.[x] 22So I will
cast her on a bed of suffering, and I will make those who commit adultery[y] with her suffer intensely,
unless they repent of her ways. 23I will strike her children dead. Then all the churches will know
that I am he who searches hearts and minds,[z] and I will repay each of you according to your deeds.
24Now I say to the rest of you in Thyatira, to you who do not hold to her teaching and have
not learned Satan's so-called deep secrets, 'I will not impose any other burden on you,[a] 25except
to hold on to what you have[b] until I come.'
26To the one who is victorious and does my will to the end, I will give authority over the
nations[c]— 27that one 'will rule them with an iron scepter[d] and will dash them to pieces like pottery'[ae]—just as I have received authority from my Father. 28I will also give that one the morning
star.[f] 29Whoever has ears, let them hear[g] what the Spirit says to the churches.

2:21 [w]Ro 2:4 [x]Rev 9:20
2:22 [y]Rev 17:2; 18:9
2:23 [z]1Sa 16:7; Jer 11:20; Ac 1:24; Ro 8:27
2:24 [a]Ac 15:28
2:25 [b]Rev 3:11
2:26 [c]Ps 2:8; Rev 3:21
2:27 [d]Rev 12:5 [e]Isa 30:14; Jer 19:11
2:28 [f]Rev 22:16
2:29 [g]ver 7
3:1 [h]Rev 1:4 [i]Rev 1:16 [j]Rev 2:2 [k]1Ti 5:6

To the Church in Sardis

3 "To the angel[b] of the church in Sardis write:

These are the words of him who holds the seven spirits[ch] of God and the seven stars.[i] I know
your deeds;[j] you have a reputation of being alive, but you are dead.[k] 2Wake up! Strengthen what

[a] *27* Psalm 2:9 [b] *1* Or *messenger*; also in verses 7 and 14 [c] *1* That is, the sevenfold Spirit

ing them into moral and religious compromise. Her symbolic name alludes to King Ahab's wife, who promoted unprecedented Baal worship, sorcery, and evil in Israel (1 Kgs 16:31–32; 21:25–26). **sexual immorality ... food sacrificed to idols.** Gentile Christians faced pressure to participate in these practices associated with pagan temple worship and guild feasts. Cf. v. 14; Acts 15:29; 1 Cor 8:1.

2:22–23 Physical judgment is imminent for Jezebel and her unrepentant followers. Cf. 1 Cor 11:29–30.

2:23 he who searches hearts and minds. Recalls the Lord's self-description in Jer 17:10. **repay each of you according to your deeds.** Based on Jesus' penetrating divine insight. See 20:12 and note; see also note on 20:11–15.

2:24 Satan's so-called deep secrets. Like early Gnostics (see Introduction to 1 John: Gnosticism), the false teachers may have claimed esoteric insight into "the deep things of God" (1 Cor 2:10b) or advocated that believers' superior "knowledge" allowed them to continue to participate in pagan idolatry (cf. 1 Cor 8:4). Such deep "knowledge" is satanic (cf. v. 9). **any other burden.** Cf. Acts 15:28–29.

2:26 Jesus, the Messianic king, shares his authority, victory, and kingdom rule with believers (1:6; 3:21; 20:4; cf. Matt 28:18).

2:27 iron scepter. Cites Ps 2:9. See note on 12:5.

2:28 morning star. Christ (22:16). Balaam identified a star and scepter as Messianic symbols (Num 24:17).

3:1–6 *To the Church in Sardis.* Sardis believers are spiritually complacent and deceived by their reputation. They must stir to action, repent, and embrace a new identity and way of life.

3:1 Sardis. Located approximately 35 miles (56 kilometers) southeast of Thyatira (see map, p. 2581). Sardis had a glorious past and a large Jewish population in the first century. Sardis and Philadelphia were devastated by an earthquake in AD 17 and rebuilt with Roman aid. **seven spirits.** See notes on 1:4; 5:6. Sardis needs the Spirit's life-giving power that Jesus alone can give. **seven stars.** Identified as angels in 1:20 (see note there). Christ's self-identification here is similar to 2:1 (Ephesus). **I know your deeds.** Highlights the church's weakness (as in v. 15), not its strength (as in v. 8; 2:2,19). **reputation.** Translates a word rendered "people" in v. 4 and "name" in v. 5 (twice), playing on the city's proud reputation. **dead.** Their true spiritual condition.

3:2 Wake up! Sardis had a reputation as an impregnable military stronghold, but in 546 and 214 BC it was defeated because watchmen were not vigilant. The church must awake from *spiritual*

CHRIST'S SELF-DESCRIPTION AND EVALUATION OF THE SEVEN CHURCHES

CHURCH	CHRIST'S SELF-DESCRIPTION	CHRIST'S EVALUATION
Ephesus (2:1–7)	holds the seven stars, walks among the lampstands	*Mixed:* Sound doctrine and endurance; lost first love
Smyrna (2:8–11)	the First and the Last, who died and came to life again	*Positive:* Afflicted and poor but spiritually rich
Pergamum (2:12–17)	has the sharp two-edged sword	*Mixed:* Endurance through persecution; tolerates false teaching
Thyatira (2:18–29)	has eyes like blazing fire, feet like burnished bronze	*Mixed:* Commendable deeds and perseverance; tolerates false teaching
Sardis (3:1–6)	has the seven spirits of God and the seven stars	*Negative:* unfinished deeds, spiritually asleep
Philadelphia (3:7–13)	holy and true, holds the key of David	*Positive:* Persecuted and weak, but faithful to Christ's name
Laodicea (3:14–22)	the Amen, the faithful and true witness, the ruler of God's creation	*Negative:* lukewarm, spiritually blind and wretched

Remains of the Temple of Artemis at Sardis.

3:3 [l] Rev 2:5 [m] 2Pe 3:10
3:4 [n] Jude 23 [o] Rev 4:4; 6:11; 7:9,13,14
3:5 [p] Rev 20:12 [q] Mt 10:32
3:6 [r] Rev 2:7
3:7 [s] Rev 1:11 [t] 1Jn 5:20 [u] Isa 22:22; Mt 16:19
3:8 [v] Ac 14:27 [w] Rev 2:13

remains and is about to die, for I have found your deeds unfinished in the sight of my God.
3 Remember, therefore, what you have received and heard; hold it fast, and repent.[l] But if you do not wake up, I will come like a thief,[m] and you will not know at what time I will come to you.

4 Yet you have a few people in Sardis who have not soiled their clothes.[n] They will walk with me, dressed in white,[o] for they are worthy.
5 The one who is victorious will, like them, be dressed in white. I will never blot out the name of that person from the book of life,[p] but will acknowledge that name before my Father[q] and his angels.
6 Whoever has ears, let them hear[r] what the Spirit says to the churches.

To the Church in Philadelphia

7 "To the angel of the church in Philadelphia[s] write:

These are the words of him who is holy and true,[t] who holds the key of David.[u] What he opens no one can shut, and what he shuts no one can open.
8 I know your deeds. See, I have placed before you an open door[v] that no one can shut. I know that you have little strength, yet you have kept my word and have not denied my name.[w]
9 I will make those who are of the synagogue of

slumber. **unfinished.** Like the city's uncompleted, worthless temple to Artemis.

3:3 Remember … repent. Cf. 2:5. **come like a thief.** The NT often uses this analogy for Jesus' second coming (16:15; Matt 24:42–44; Luke 12:39; 1 Thess 5:2; 2 Pet 3:10). Here Jesus warns that he will come like a thief in judgment if the church refuses to repent.

3:4 Sardis was famous for its textile industry, but most in the church had "soiled" or defiled spiritual garments (cf. 14:4; Jude 23).

3:5 The one who is victorious. See note on 2:7. **white.** Contrasts with soiled clothes. People wore white garments for festivals, sacred ceremonies, and Roman celebrations; here they signify purity, cleansing, and end-time victory (v. 18; 7:9; 19:14; Isa 61:10). **book of life.** The heavenly register listing the names of true believers, who are ultimately protected from Satan's spiritual deception (13:8; 17:8; 20:12; 21:27; Dan 12:1; Luke 10:20). **acknowledge … before my Father.** Alludes to Matt 10:32 (cf. Luke 12:8).

3:7–13 *To the Church in Philadelphia.* Like Smyrna, Philadelphia has remained faithful to Jesus' word and name amid Jewish persecution and receives praise and reassurance.

3:7 Philadelphia. An important commercial city (modern Alashehir, Turkey) 30 miles (48 kilometers) southeast of Sardis (see map, p. 2581), strategically located along trade routes and home to temples to Zeus and the emperor. Following the devastating earthquake of AD 17, Philadelphia (meaning "brotherly love") was temporarily renamed Neocaesarea (meaning "Caesar's new city") out of gratitude for the emperor's aid. **holy and true.** A divine title (6:10) here applied to Jesus. **key of David … opens … shuts.** Alludes to Isa 22:22. The Jews probably excluded Philadelphian Christians from the synagogue (cf. v. 9), but Christ stresses his supreme authority to "open" and "shut" the doors of the kingdom (cf. Matt 16:19).

3:8 I know your deeds. Commendation, as in 2:2,19. **open door.** An opportunity for ministry (Col 4:3) or more likely, access to God's kingdom as in v. 7 (Acts 14:27). **little strength … kept my word.** This persecuted church lacked power and influence but remained faithful. **have not denied my name.** Alludes to Matt 10:32–33; cf. 2:13.

3:9 synagogue of Satan. See note on 2:9. **fall down at your feet.** Jesus' followers will be vindicated before their Jewish persecutors,

Satan,[x] who claim to be Jews though they are not, but are liars—I will make them come and fall
down at your feet[y] and acknowledge that I have loved you.[z] 10 Since you have kept my command
to endure patiently, I will also keep you[a] from the hour of trial that is going to come on the whole
world to test[b] the inhabitants of the earth.[c]

11 I am coming soon. Hold on to what you have,[d] so that no one will take your crown.[e] 12 The
one who is victorious I will make a pillar[f] in the temple of my God. Never again will they leave it. I
will write on them the name of my God[g] and the name of the city of my God, the new Jerusalem,[h]
which is coming down out of heaven from my God; and I will also write on them my new name.
13 Whoever has ears, let them hear what the Spirit says to the churches.

To the Church in Laodicea

14 "To the angel of the church in Laodicea write:

These are the words of the Amen, the faithful and true witness, the ruler of God's creation.[i] 15 I
know your deeds, that you are neither cold nor hot.[j] I wish you were either one or the other! 16 So,
because you are lukewarm—neither hot nor cold—I am about to spit you out of my mouth.
17 You say, 'I am rich; I have acquired wealth and do not need a thing.'[k] But you do not realize
that you are wretched, pitiful, poor, blind and naked. 18 I counsel you to buy from me gold refined
in the fire, so you can become rich; and white clothes to wear, so you can cover your shameful
nakedness;[l] and salve to put on your eyes, so you can see.

19 Those whom I love I rebuke and discipline.[m] So be earnest and repent.[n] 20 Here I am! I stand
at the door[o] and knock. If anyone hears my voice and opens the door,[p] I will come in[q] and eat
with that person, and they with me.

21 To the one who is victorious, I will give the right to sit with me on my throne,[r] just as I was
victorious[s] and sat down with my Father on his throne. 22 Whoever has ears, let them hear[t] what
the Spirit says to the churches."

3:9 [x] Rev 2:9 [y] Isa 49:23 [z] Isa 43:4
3:10 [a] 2Pe 2:9 [b] Rev 2:10 [c] Rev 6:10; 17:8
3:11 [d] Rev 2:25 [e] Rev 2:10
3:12 [f] Gal 2:9 [g] Rev 14:1; 22:4 [h] Rev 21:2,10
3:14 [i] Col 1:16,18
3:15 [j] Ro 12:11
3:17 [k] Hos 12:8; 1Co 4:8
3:18 [l] Rev 16:15
3:19 [m] Pr 3:12; Heb 12:5,6 [n] Rev 2:5
3:20 [o] Mt 24:33 [p] Lk 12:36 [q] Jn 14:23
3:21 [r] Mt 19:28 [s] Rev 5:5
3:22 [t] Rev 2:7

which ironically fulfills OT prophecies that Gentile oppressors would bow down before Israel (Isa 49:23; 60:14).

3:10 keep you from. This Greek phrase can mean either "keep you from undergoing" or "keep you through." The parallel expression in John 17:15 refers to spiritual protection. **hour of trial.** The time of testing and tribulation before God's kingdom comes in its fullness (Dan 12:1–2). **whole world.** Either the entire inhabited earth (cf. 12:9; 16:14) or the inhabitants of the Roman Empire (Luke 2:1; Acts 11:28). **to test.** The purpose of this trial. **the inhabitants of the earth.** Unbelievers who worship the beast, persecute believers, and deserve divine judgment (6:10; 13:8).

3:11 I am coming soon. The risen Christ will come in glory at the end (1:7; 22:7,12,20), but he also comes now to his churches to judge and save (cf. 2:5,16,25). **crown.** See note on 2:10.

3:12 pillar in the temple. Contrasts with pagan temples felled by the earthquake (see note on v. 7) and perhaps with the Jerusalem temple destroyed in AD 70. Victorious believers will never be excluded from God's presence in the new Jerusalem (21:2–4). For the church as God's temple, see note on 2 Cor 6:16. **name of my God ... new Jerusalem ... my new name.** Philadelphia had taken on Caesar's name after the city's destruction (see note on v. 7), but Jesus promises them a new identity (cf. 2:17; 14:1; 22:4) and citizenship in a glorious, eternal city (21:2; Phil 3:20; Heb 11:10,16; 12:22).

3:14–22 *To the Church in Laodicea.* Jesus does not commend Laodicea at all but sternly rebukes them for being spiritually complacent (like Sardis), satisfied with their wealth and material comfort but blind to their true state before God.

3:14 Laodicea. A prosperous center for banking, medicine, and textile industries located about 45 miles (72 kilometers) southeast of Philadelphia (see map, p. 2581). Laodicea's chief deities were Zeus and Men Karou, god of healing and patron of the city's famous medical school. Epaphras likely evangelized Laodicea and nearby Colossae and Hierapolis (Col 4:13). **faithful and true witness.** See note on 1:5. Jesus' faithfulness contrasts with the church's unfaithful witness. **ruler.** Translates a Greek word that can also mean "beginning" (John 1:1). Jesus is both (1:5; 22:13).

3:15–16 cold nor hot ... lukewarm. Colossae, located 10 miles (16 kilometers) east of Laodicea, had plentiful *cold*, pure drinking water, while the *hot* springs of Hierapolis, located 6 miles (9.5 kilometers) north of Laodicea, were famed for their healing power. Laodicea lacked its own water supply, and its solution was inadequate: water flowing in by aqueduct arrived *tepid* and contaminated by minerals. Jesus rebukes the complacent church for not offering life or healing to its community.

3:17 I am rich. Recalls Israel's boast in Hos 12:8 and Laodicea's decision to decline imperial assistance and fund its own rebuilding after the earthquake in AD 60. The church boasted of its self-sufficiency and overlooked its need for God's help.

3:18 gold ... white clothes ... salve. The church's spiritual destitution contrasts with the city's reputation for banking, fine wool, and medicine. They must "buy" from Jesus true spiritual resources (cf. Isa 55:1–3).

3:19 I love ... discipline. Alludes to Prov 3:11–12; cf. Heb 12:5–6.

3:20 stand ... knock. Suggests the return of a lover (Song 5:2) or master (Luke 12:36). Jesus addresses complacent church members, not primarily individuals outside the church. **come in and eat.** In the ancient world, a meal invitation to an estranged person opened the way for reconciliation. Jesus offers to accept and renew intimate fellowship with those who repent, anticipating the final Messianic banquet (19:9).

3:21 sit with me on my throne. Jesus shares his Father's throne as Messianic king and judge (22:3; Ps 110:1; Heb 1:3; see Introduction: Theology), and believers share in his reign (5:10; 20:4; 22:5; 2 Tim 2:12; cf. Matt 19:28).

Ruins of ancient Laodicea.

Clinton E. Arnold

4:1 [u]Rev 1:10 [v]Rev 11:12 [w]Rev 1:19
4:2 [x]Rev 1:10 [y]Isa 6:1; Eze 1:26-28; Da 7:9
4:3 [z]Eze 1:28
4:4 [a]Rev 11:16 [b]Rev 3:4,5
4:5 [c]Rev 8:5; 16:18 [d]Zec 4:2 [e]Rev 1:4
4:6 [f]Rev 15:2 [g]Eze 1:5
4:7 [h]Eze 1:10; 10:14
4:8 [i]Isa 6:2

The Throne in Heaven

4 After this I looked, and there before me was a door standing open in heaven. And the voice I had
first heard speaking to me like a trumpet[u] said, "Come up here,[v] and I will show you what must
take place after this."[w] 2At once I was in the Spirit,[x] and there before me was a throne in heaven[y] with
someone sitting on it. 3And the one who sat there had the appearance of jasper and ruby. A rainbow[z]
that shone like an emerald encircled the throne. 4Surrounding the throne were twenty-four other
thrones, and seated on them were twenty-four elders.[a] They were dressed in white[b] and had crowns of
gold on their heads. 5From the throne came flashes of lightning, rumblings and peals of thunder.[c] In
front of the throne, seven lamps[d] were blazing. These are the seven spirits[a][e] of God. 6Also in front of
the throne there was what looked like a sea of glass,[f] clear as crystal.

In the center, around the throne, were four living creatures,[g] and they were covered with eyes, in
front and in back. 7The first living creature was like a lion, the second was like an ox, the third had a
face like a man, the fourth was like a flying eagle.[h] 8Each of the four living creatures had six wings[i] and
was covered with eyes all around, even under its wings. Day and night they never stop saying:

[a] 5 That is, the sevenfold Spirit

4:1—8:5 *The Heavenly Throne Room and the Seals.* John's second vision "in the Spirit" (4:2; cf. 1:10) directs readers to God's heavenly throne room (ch. 4), where the living creatures and elders declare that Jesus, the slain Lamb, is "worthy" to execute God's plan of judgment and redemption (5:9). The sealed scroll symbolizes this plan (5:1), and Jesus opens it in 6:1—8:5.

4:1–11 *The Throne in Heaven.* John sees the Lord God Almighty enthroned in heaven, receiving unending praise as the holy, eternal creator and ruler of all.

4:1 door standing open in heaven. Similar to other biblical visions (Ezek 1:1; Matt 3:16; Acts 10:11) and Jewish apocalyptic writings. Cf. 19:11 ("heaven standing open"). **Come up here.** Cf. 11:12. **what must take place after this.** See note on 1:19.

4:2 in the Spirit. See note on 1:10. **throne.** Represents God's authority to rule and judge (3:21); contrasts with the thrones of Satan (2:13) and the beast (13:2).

4:3 jasper ... ruby ... emerald. Precious stones signifying God's glory and radiance (21:11,18–20). **rainbow.** Recalls God's covenant promise in Gen 9:13–17 and Ezekiel's vision of divine glory (Ezek 1:28).

4:4 twenty-four elders. May designate the whole company of God's people in heaven but most likely refers to an exalted order or to angels who continually worship and serve God around his throne (vv. 10–11; 5:8; 11:16; 19:4). Their number probably reflects Israel's 12 tribes together with the 12 apostles (cf. 21:12; Matt 19:28), though it also parallels the orders of OT priests who served God in the temple (1 Chr 24:4–19) **white.** Symbolizes purity and holiness (see note on 3:5). **crowns of gold.** Represents royal status; cf. v. 10.

4:5 lightning, rumblings ... thunder. Recalls God's majestic presence in Exod 19:16; 20:18. See note on 8:5. **seven lamps.** Alludes to Ezek 1:13; signifies God's presence. **seven spirits.** See note on 1:4.

4:6 sea of glass. May recall the vault separating the waters in Gen 1:7, on which rests God's exalted throne (Ps 104:3; Ezek 1:22,26; 10:1); cf. Rev 15:2. **clear as crystal.** Ancient glass was semi-opaque; this heavenly sea perfectly reflects and radiates God's perfect holiness. Cf. 21:1; Ezek 1:22. **four living creatures.** Heavenly angels nearest the throne who lead in worship (v. 8; 5:14) and initiate God's judgment (6:1). These beings represent all created life and ever live to worship and glorify God, who "lives" forever (vv. 9–10). John's depiction combines allusions to Isa 6:2–3; Ezek 1:5–14 (see "OT Background for the Living Creatures," p. 2597).

4:7 lion ... ox ... man ... eagle. Represent the noblest, strongest, wisest, and swiftest created beings.

4:8 six wings. Used by the seraphim in Isa 6:2 to cover their eyes and feet and to fly. **eyes all around.** Represent alertness and knowledge

"Holy, holy, holy
is the Lord God Almighty,'[a][j]
who was, and is, and is to come."[k]

[9]Whenever the living creatures give glory, honor and thanks to him who sits on the throne[l] and who
lives for ever and ever, [10]the twenty-four elders[m] fall down before him[n] who sits on the throne[o] and
worship him who lives for ever and ever. They lay their crowns before the throne and say:

[11]"You are worthy, our Lord and God,
to receive glory and honor and power,[p]
for you created all things,
and by your will they were created
and have their being."[q]

The Scroll and the Lamb

5 Then I saw in the right hand of him who sat on the throne[r] a scroll with writing on both sides[s] and
sealed[t] with seven seals. [2]And I saw a mighty angel proclaiming in a loud voice, "Who is worthy to
break the seals and open the scroll?" [3]But no one in heaven or on earth or under the earth could open
the scroll or even look inside it. [4]I wept and wept because no one was found who was worthy to open
the scroll or look inside. [5]Then one of the elders said to me, "Do not weep! See, the Lion[u] of the tribe of
Judah, the Root of David,[v] has triumphed. He is able to open the scroll and its seven seals."
[6]Then I saw a Lamb,[w] looking as if it had been slain, standing at the center of the throne, encircled

4:8 [j]Isa 6:3; Rev 1:8 [k]Rev 1:4
4:9 [l]Ps 47:8
4:10 [m]ver 4 [n]Rev 5:8,14 [o]ver 2
4:11 [p]Rev 5:12 [q]Rev 10:6
5:1 [r]ver 7,13 [s]Eze 2:9,10 [t]Isa 29:11; Da 12:4
5:5 [u]Ge 49:9 [v]Isa 11:1,10; Ro 15:12; Rev 22:16
5:6 [w]Jn 1:29

[a] 8 Isaiah 6:3

(cf. Ezek 1:18; 10:12). **Holy, holy, holy.** Recalls Isa 6:3; see Introduction: Theology. **was ... is ... is to come.** See note on 1:4.
4:10 lay their crowns. Submit to God's supreme authority (cf. 21:24).
4:11 glory and honor and power. Praise for God (cf. 7:12) and the Lamb (cf. 5:12–13). **for.** Introduces a reason to praise God: he is the all-powerful Creator (cf. 10:6; Ps 148:5; Rom 1:25).
5:1–14 *The Scroll and the Lamb.* After setting the heavenly stage (ch. 4), John presents the drama of the slain Lamb taking God's sealed scroll and receiving honor and praise.
5:1 scroll ... sealed with seven seals. Modeled after the double-sided scroll containing "words of lament and mourning and woe" in Ezek 2:9–10 and the sealed books in Isa 29:11; Dan 12:4. A wax seal indicated that important ancient documents were authentic and unaltered, and the number seven indicates fullness or completion (see Introduction: Sevens in Revelation). This scroll contains God's consummate plan of judgment and redemption, which Jesus alone reveals and executes.
5:2 Introduces the problem of the heavenly drama: a "worthy" mediator is needed to "open the scroll" and reveal God's secret plan.
5:4 wept. John laments like the OT prophets (Isa 22:4; Jer 9:1).
5:5 Lion of the tribe of Judah. Alludes to Judah's prophesied kingship (Gen 49:9–10). **Root of David.** Recalls the ideal king in David's line prophesied in Isa 11:1–4; he would execute perfect justice and slay the wicked.
5:6 Lamb. Israel's Messianic king has conquered through sacrifice, not military prowess. Revelation's favorite symbol for Jesus is the lamb, which may combine three OT backgrounds: the Passover lamb (Exod 12:3–6; cf. John 1:29), the slaughtered servant (Isa 53:7; cf. Acts 8:32), and the suffering prophet (Jer 11:19; cf. Luke 11:50). **seven horns.** Symbolizes royal power and strength (cf. Dan 7:24; 8:21–22). Seven signifies completion and perfection (see Introduction). **seven eyes ... seven spirits.** The Lamb executes God's plan with complete knowledge (cf. Zech 4:10), endowed by the fullness of God's Spirit (see note on 1:4; cf. Isa 11:2; John 3:34).

OLD TESTAMENT BACKGROUND FOR THE LIVING CREATURES

REVELATION 4	ISAIAH 6	EZEKIEL 1
Around the throne (v. 6)	The Lord on a throne (v. 1)	
Four living creatures (v. 6)		Four living creatures (v. 5)
Living creatures like a lion, ox, man, and eagle (v. 7)		Each has a human, lion, ox, and eagle face (v. 10)
Living creatures have six wings (v. 8)	Seraphim have six wings (v. 2)	
Living creatures covered with eyes all around (v. 8)		Wheels ... full of eyes all around (vv. 17–18; cf. Ezek 10:12)
Holy, holy, holy ... (v. 8)	Holy, holy, holy ... (v. 3)	

5:6 [x]Zec 4:10
5:7 [y]ver 1
5:8 [z]Rev 14:2 [a]Ps 141:2
5:9 [b]Ps 40:3 [c]Rev 4:11 [d]Heb 9:12 [e]1Co 6:20
5:10 [f]1Pe 2:5
5:11 [g]Da 7:10; Heb 12:22
5:12 [h]Rev 4:11
5:13 [i]ver 3; Php 2:10 [j]Rev 6:16 [k]1Ch 29:11
5:14 [l]Rev 4:9 [m]Rev 4:10; 19:4
6:1 [n]Rev 5:6 [o]Rev 5:1 [p]Rev 4:6,7 [q]Rev 14:2; 19:6
6:2 [r]Zec 6:3; Rev 19:11 [s]Zec 6:11; Rev 14:14 [t]Ps 45:4
6:3 [u]Rev 4:7
6:4 [v]Zec 6:2 [w]Mt 10:34
6:5 [x]Rev 4:7

by the four living creatures and the elders. The Lamb had seven horns and seven eyes,[x] which are the
seven spirits[a] of God sent out into all the earth. 7He went and took the scroll from the right hand of him
who sat on the throne.[y] 8And when he had taken it, the four living creatures and the twenty-four elders
fell down before the Lamb. Each one had a harp[z] and they were holding golden bowls full of incense,
which are the prayers[a] of God's people. 9And they sang a new song, saying:[b]

> "You are worthy[c] to take the scroll
> and to open its seals,
> because you were slain,
> and with your blood[d] you purchased[e] for God
> persons from every tribe and language and people and nation.
> 10You have made them to be a kingdom and priests[f] to serve our God,
> and they will reign[b] on the earth."

11Then I looked and heard the voice of many angels, numbering thousands upon thousands, and
ten thousand times ten thousand.[g] They encircled the throne and the living creatures and the elders.
12In a loud voice they were saying:

> "Worthy is the Lamb, who was slain,
> to receive power and wealth and wisdom and strength
> and honor and glory and praise!"[h]

13Then I heard every creature in heaven and on earth and under the earth[i] and on the sea, and all
that is in them, saying:

> "To him who sits on the throne and to the Lamb[j]
> be praise and honor and glory and power,
> for ever and ever!"[k]

14The four living creatures said, "Amen,"[l] and the elders fell down and worshiped.[m]

The Seals

6 I watched as the Lamb[n] opened the first of the seven seals.[o] Then I heard one of the four living
creatures[p] say in a voice like thunder,[q] "Come!" 2I looked, and there before me was a white horse![r]
Its rider held a bow, and he was given a crown,[s] and he rode out as a conqueror bent on conquest.[t]
3When the Lamb opened the second seal, I heard the second living creature[u] say, "Come!" 4Then
another horse came out, a fiery red one.[v] Its rider was given power to take peace from the earth[w] and
to make people kill each other. To him was given a large sword.
5When the Lamb opened the third seal, I heard the third living creature[x] say, "Come!" I looked, and

[a] *6* That is, the sevenfold Spirit [b] *10* Some manuscripts *they reign*

5:8 living creatures. See notes on 4:6–8. **twenty-four elders.** See note on 4:4. **harp.** Accompanies joyous temple worship (14:2; 15:2; 2 Chr 9:11; Ps 43:4). **incense.** Symbolizes "the prayers of God's people" (Ps 141:2; Luke 1:10), which God dramatically answers in 6:9–11; 8:3–5; 15:7–8.

5:9 new song. Worship celebrating God's saving actions (14:3; Pss 96:1–2; 144:9–10). **You are worthy.** Answers the question in v. 2 and echoes praise to God in 4:11 (cf. v. 12). **because you were slain.** Jesus' sacrificial death is the basis of his worthiness. **purchased.** Commercial metaphor for emancipating slaves (cf. 14:3–4; 1 Cor 7:23). **every tribe and language and people and nation.** God's universal people transcend ethnic, linguistic, cultural, and national boundaries (7:9; Dan 7:14); contrast the nations' false worship in 13:3–8; Dan 3:4–5.

5:10 kingdom and priests. See note on 1:6.

5:12 Both the Lamb and God (7:12) receive sevenfold praise.

5:13 every creature in heaven and on earth. Echoes v. 3; anticipates the Lord Jesus' universal acclamation in Phil 2:11.

6:1–17 *The Seals.* The Lamb progressively opens the scroll's seven seals, initiating judgments on the earth (the four horsemen, vv. 1–8) and cosmic judgments (vv. 9–17; 8:1). These seals are variously understood. Many interpreters stress the first-century relevance of the seals, trumpets, and bowls. Some identify the first seal with the beginning of a future "great tribulation" (7:14), while others understand these judgment cycles to have relevance throughout the church age until Christ's return (see Introduction: Interpretive Approaches).

6:1 living creatures. See notes on 4:6–8. **Come!** Cf. vv. 3,5,7; 22:17,20.

6:2–8 The four colored horses allude to Zech 1:8–10; 6:1–8.

6:2 white horse. Symbolizes conquest. **rider.** Not Christ as in 19:11. **bow ... crown.** Represent military and political power that is "bent on conquest."

6:4 horse ... fiery red. Represents bloodshed from violence (cf. Zech 1:8; 6:2). **take peace ... make people kill.** Desire for conquest leads to war and great strife.

6:5 black horse. Symbolizes mourning from famine caused by war (cf. 2 Kgs 6:24–33; Zech 6:2). **scales.** Symbolize commerce.

there before me was a black horse![y] Its rider was holding a pair of scales in his hand. 6 Then I heard
what sounded like a voice among the four living creatures,[z] saying, "Two pounds[a] of wheat for a day's
wages,[b] and six pounds[c] of barley for a day's wages,[b] and do not damage[a] the oil and the wine!"
7 When the Lamb opened the fourth seal, I heard the voice of the fourth living creature[b] say, "Come!"
8 I looked, and there before me was a pale horse![c] Its rider was named Death, and Hades[d] was following
close behind him. They were given power over a fourth of the earth to kill by sword, famine and plague,
and by the wild beasts of the earth.[e]
9 When he opened the fifth seal, I saw under the altar[f] the souls of those who had been slain[g] because
of the word of God and the testimony they had maintained. 10 They called out in a loud voice, "How
long,[h] Sovereign Lord, holy and true,[i] until you judge the inhabitants of the earth and avenge our
blood?"[j] 11 Then each of them was given a white robe,[k] and they were told to wait a little longer, until
the full number of their fellow servants, their brothers and sisters,[d] were killed just as they had been.[l]
12 I watched as he opened the sixth seal. There was a great earthquake.[m] The sun turned black[n] like
sackcloth made of goat hair, the whole moon turned blood red, 13 and the stars in the sky fell to earth,[o]
as figs drop from a fig tree[p] when shaken by a strong wind. 14 The heavens receded like a scroll being
rolled up, and every mountain and island was removed from its place.[q]
15 Then the kings of the earth, the princes, the generals, the rich, the mighty, and everyone else, both
slave and free, hid in caves and among the rocks of the mountains.[r] 16 They called to the mountains and
the rocks, "Fall on us[s] and hide us[e] from the face of him who sits on the throne and from the wrath of
the Lamb! 17 For the great day[t] of their[f] wrath has come, and who can withstand it?"[u]

144,000 Sealed

7 After this I saw four angels standing at the four corners of the earth, holding back the four winds[v]
of the earth to prevent any wind from blowing on the land or on the sea or on any tree. 2 Then I
saw another angel coming up from the east, having the seal of the living God. He called out in a loud
voice to the four angels who had been given power to harm the land and the sea: 3 "Do not harm[w] the

6:5 [y] Zec 6:2
6:6 [z] Rev 4:6,7 [a] Rev 9:4
6:7 [b] Rev 4:7
6:8 [c] Zec 6:3 [d] Hos 13:14 [e] Jer 15:2,3; Eze 5:12,17
6:9 [f] Rev 14:18; 16:7 [g] Rev 20:4
6:10 [h] Zec 1:12 [i] Rev 3:7 [j] Rev 19:2
6:11 [k] Rev 3:4 [l] Heb 11:40
6:12 [m] Rev 16:18 [n] Mt 24:29
6:13 [o] Mt 24:29; Rev 8:10; 9:1 [p] Isa 34:4
6:14 [q] Jer 4:24; Rev 16:20
6:15 [r] Isa 2:10,19,21
6:16 [s] Hos 10:8; Lk 23:30
6:17 [t] Zep 1:14,15; Rev 16:14 [u] Ps 76:7
7:1 [v] Da 7:2
7:3 [w] Rev 6:6

[a] *6* Or about 1 kilogram [b] *6* Greek *a denarius* [c] *6* Or about 3 kilograms [d] *11* The Greek word for *brothers and sisters* (*adelphoi*) refers here to believers, both men and women, as part of God's family; also in 12:10; 19:10. [e] *16* See Hosea 10:8. [f] *17* Some manuscripts *his*

6:6 wheat ... barley. Primary food staples in the Roman Empire and in Israel (Deut 8:8). The famine prices are inflated 8 to 16 times the normal rate. **do not damage the oil and the wine!** Sets limits on the rider's destruction. Olive trees and vines are not immediately impacted by drought, suggesting a limited shortage rather than a severe famine as in Joel 1:10–11. In AD 92, Domitian ordered half of Asia Minor's vineyards to be destroyed to increase grain production, which caused such outrage that Domitian repealed the edict.
6:8 Death ... Hades. Fearsome satanic forces over which Christ has ultimate authority (see note on 1:18; cf. Hos 13:14). **fourth of the earth.** Severe, yet restrained, judgment. The trumpets ("a third of the earth," 8:7) and the bowls ("the earth," 16:1) intensify the destruction. **sword, famine and plague ... wild beasts.** God's "four dreadful judgments" against Israel (Ezek 14:21; cf. Deut 32:24–26; Jer 24:10).
6:9 under the altar. OT sacrificial imagery recalling the altar of incense or the altar of burnt offering (Lev 4:7). **those who had been slain.** Christian martyrs (20:4), who were "slain" like the Lamb and God's prophets (5:9; 18:24). Like John (1:9), they suffered for their faithful "testimony."
6:10 A prayer for divine justice and vindication (cf. Ps 79:4–6,10) that is answered in 16:5; 19:2.
6:11 white robe. See notes on 3:4,5; 7:9. **wait.** The Greek word is translated "rest" in 14:13b. **full number.** The total number of martyrs that God ordained (a concept that occurs in Jewish apocalyptic writings).
6:12–13 Imagery that depicts the day of the Lord (Isa 13:9–13; Joel 2:10,31; Matt 24:29; see note on Amos 2:16).
6:12 great earthquake. Associated with God's presence and judgment in Isa 29:6; Ezek 38:19. Cf. 11:13; 16:18.
6:14 heavens ... rolled up. Alludes to Isa 34:4. **every mountain and island was removed.** See note on 16:20.
6:15 God's judgment will terrify all unrepentant humanity, regardless of social, political, or economic status (cf. Isa 2:19–21).
6:16 Fall on us. Alludes to Hos 10:8 (cf. Luke 23:30). Those who do not acknowledge the Lamb as worthy will face his "wrath" as righteous judge (Ps 2:12).
6:17 great day of their wrath. Prophesied day of the Lord (cf. Isa 13:9; Joel 2:11; see note on Amos 2:16). **withstand.** The Greek word is translated "standing" in 7:9. Sinners cannot withstand God's wrath (cf. Ps 1:5–6), but John sees the redeemed multitude standing before God's throne (7:9).
7:1–8 *144,000 Sealed.* Between the sixth and seventh seals, John sees two related visions of believers protected from God's terrifying judgment standing in his presence. Interpreters differ on the identity of the 144,000 from Israel's tribes (vv. 4–8), the great multitude from all nations (vv. 9–10), and the relationship between these visions. Some identify the 144,000 as ethnic Jews saved during the future tribulation, who evangelize the great multitude. Others understand both visions as designating Christian martyrs or the complete church from every nation (14:1–4).
7:1 four winds. Agents of divine judgment (Jer 49:36); likely refers to the four horsemen in 6:1–8 (Zech 6:1–5).
7:2 seal. Symbolizes God's ownership (2 Tim 2:19) and protection of his people from coming judgments (Ezek 9:4–6).
7:3 on the foreheads. Alludes to Ezek 9:4; contrasts with the mark of the beast (13:16). God's name is written on believers' foreheads in 14:1; 22:4.

7:3 [x]Eze 9:4; Rev 22:4
7:4 [y]Rev 9:16 [z]Rev 14:1,3
7:9 [a]Rev 5:9 [b]ver 15
7:10 [c]Ps 3:8; Rev 12:10; 19:1
7:11 [d]Rev 4:4 [e]Rev 4:6 [f]Rev 4:10
7:12 [g]Rev 5:12-14

land or the sea or the trees until we put a seal on the foreheads[x] of the servants of our God." 4Then I
heard the number[y] of those who were sealed: 144,000[z] from all the tribes of Israel.

5 From the tribe of Judah 12,000 were sealed,
from the tribe of Reuben 12,000,
from the tribe of Gad 12,000,
6 from the tribe of Asher 12,000,
from the tribe of Naphtali 12,000,
from the tribe of Manasseh 12,000,
7 from the tribe of Simeon 12,000,
from the tribe of Levi 12,000,
from the tribe of Issachar 12,000,
8 from the tribe of Zebulun 12,000,
from the tribe of Joseph 12,000,
from the tribe of Benjamin 12,000.

The Great Multitude in White Robes

9After this I looked, and there before me was a great multitude that no one could count, from
every nation, tribe, people and language,[a] standing before the throne[b] and before the Lamb. They
were wearing white robes and were holding palm branches in their hands. 10And they cried out in a
loud voice:

"Salvation belongs to our God,[c]
who sits on the throne,
and to the Lamb."

11All the angels were standing around the throne and around the elders[d] and the four living creatures.[e] They fell down on their faces[f] before the throne and worshiped God, 12saying:

"Amen!
Praise and glory
and wisdom and thanks and honor
and power and strength
be to our God for ever and ever.
Amen!"[g]

13Then one of the elders asked me, "These in white robes—who are they, and where did they come from?"
14I answered, "Sir, you know."

MULTIPLES OF TWELVE IN REVELATION

144,000 sealed believers (12,000 x 12)	7:4–8; 14:1,3
12 stars in the woman's crown	12:1 (cf. Gen 37:9)
12 gates/pearls in the new Jerusalem	21:12,21
12 angels	21:12
12 tribes of Israel	21:12
12 foundations for the city's walls	21:14
12 apostles	21:14
12 crops of fruit from the tree of life	22:2

7:4 144,000. See note on vv. 1–8. May refer to the literal number of Jewish believers; probably indicates the perfect number (12 x 12 x 1,000) of the redeemed (cf. 14:1–4) given Revelation's frequent use of 12 to symbolize completion (see "Multiples of Twelve in Revelation," this page). Verses 4–8 may echo the census in Num 1–2, numbering Israel's military force, though the tribe of Levi was excluded (Num 1:49). In this interpretation, John hears the census of God's end-time army warring against spiritual foes through faithful witness (cf. 12:11).
7:5–6 Judah. Jacob's fourth son (Gen 35:23) but here listed first as the tribe of Israel's king (5:5; Gen 49:8–10). **Reuben.** Jacob's first son, like Judah, a son of Leah. **Gad … Asher … Naphtali.** Sons from the servants Bilhah and Zilpah appear ahead of the other sons of Leah and Rachel. **Manasseh.** Joseph's firstborn, replacing Dan, a tribe notorious for idolatry (Judg 18:29–30; 1 Kgs 12:29–30; Amos 8:14).
7:9–17 *The Great Multitude in White Robes.* John's vision of the multiethnic throng of worshipers *standing* in God's presence answers the question of 6:17 (see note there ["withstand"]). The first vision stresses God's protection (vv. 1–8); the second, God's salvation (vv. 9–17).
7:9 After this I looked. In 5:5–6, John hears OT Messianic promises (Lion of Judah, Root of David) and then sees a surprising NT fulfillment (slain Lamb); likewise here John's vision reinterprets nationalistic expectation with God's promise to multiply Abraham's descendants and bless all nations in him (Gen 22:18; 26:4). **great multitude.** Explained in v. 14; cf. 19:1,6. **from every nation, tribe, people and language.** See note on 5:9. **standing.** See note on 6:17 ["withstand"]. **white robes.** Symbolize cleansing from defilement (v. 14; cf. Dan 12:10) as well as purity and end-time victory (3:4–5). **palm branches.** Recall the Festival of Tabernacles, which commemorated Israel's exodus and anticipated future redemption (Lev 23:40–43; Zech 14:16; cf. John 12:13).
7:10 Salvation. Cf. 12:10; 19:1; Exod 15:2; Ps 3:8.
7:11–12 Resembles 5:11–13.
7:14 Identifies those in white robes (vv. 9,13). **great tribulation.** Alludes to Dan 12:1 (cf. Matt 24:21). Variously interpreted as an intense persecution,

And he said, "These are they who have come out of the great tribulation; they have washed their
robes[h] and made them white in the blood of the Lamb.[i] 15 Therefore,

"they are before the throne of God[j]
and serve him[k] day and night in his temple;[l]
and he who sits on the throne
will shelter them with his presence.[m]
16 'Never again will they hunger;
never again will they thirst.
The sun will not beat down on them,'[a]
nor any scorching heat.[n]
17 For the Lamb at the center of the throne
will be their shepherd;[o]
'he will lead them to springs of living water.'[a]
'And God will wipe away every tear from their eyes.'[b]"[p]

The Seventh Seal and the Golden Censer

8 When he opened the seventh seal,[q] there was silence in heaven for about half an hour.
2 And I saw the seven angels[r] who stand before God, and seven trumpets were given to them.
3 Another angel,[s] who had a golden censer, came and stood at the altar. He was given much incense
to offer, with the prayers of all God's people,[t] on the golden altar[u] in front of the throne. 4 The smoke
of the incense, together with the prayers of God's people, went up before God[v] from the angel's hand.
5 Then the angel took the censer, filled it with fire from the altar,[w] and hurled it on the earth; and there
came peals of thunder,[x] rumblings, flashes of lightning and an earthquake.[y]

The Trumpets

6 Then the seven angels who had the seven trumpets[z] prepared to sound them.
7 The first angel sounded his trumpet, and there came hail and fire[a] mixed with blood, and it was
hurled down on the earth. A third[b] of the earth was burned up, a third of the trees were burned up, and
all the green grass was burned up.[c]
8 The second angel sounded his trumpet, and something like a huge mountain,[d] all ablaze, was

7:14 [h] Rev 22:14 [i] Heb 9:14; 1Jn 1:7
7:15 [j] ver 9 [k] Rev 22:3 [l] Rev 11:19 [m] Isa 4:5,6; Rev 21:3
7:16 [n] Isa 49:10
7:17 [o] Ps 23:1; Jn 10:11 [p] Isa 25:8; Rev 21:4
8:1 [q] Rev 6:1
8:2 [r] ver 6-13; Rev 9:1, 13; 11:15
8:3 [s] Rev 7:2 [t] Rev 5:8 [u] Ex 30:1-6; Heb 9:4; Rev 9:13
8:4 [v] Ps 141:2
8:5 [w] Lev 16:12,13 [x] Rev 4:5 [y] Rev 6:12
8:6 [z] ver 2
8:7 [a] Eze 38:22 [b] ver 7-12; Rev 9:15,18; 12:4 [c] Rev 9:4
8:8 [d] Jer 51:25

[a] *16,17* Isaiah 49:10 [b] *17* Isaiah 25:8

the final period of hostility before Christ's return, or persecution throughout the church age. The Greek phrase also occurs in 2:22 ("suffer intensely"); Matt 24:21 ("great distress"); Acts 7:11 ("great suffering"). **washed … white.** Recalls OT promises of cleansing from sin (Ps 51:7; Isa 1:18), accomplished by the Lamb's sacrificial death (1 John 1:7; cf. 22:14).

7:15 serve him day and night in his temple. Continuous priestly worship (cf. 3:12; 22:3).

7:16 Never … hunger … thirst. Alludes to Isa 49:10; fulfilled in 21:6; 22:2.

7:17 Lamb … shepherd. Jesus the divine Shepherd-Lamb leads his people to abundant life (cf. Ps 23:1–2; Ezek 34:11–16; John 10:11). **wipe away every tear.** Alludes to Isa 25:8; see note on 21:4.

8:1–5 *The Seventh Seal and the Golden Censer.* This section concludes the seals (v. 1; cf. 6:1–17), prepares for the trumpets (v. 2), and links these divine judgments to the effective prayers of God's people (vv. 3–5).

8:1 seventh seal. The seals cycle resumes after the interlude in ch. 7, and the seven-sealed scroll is fully opened (see note on 5:1). **silence in heaven.** Dramatic pause in the unceasing heavenly praise (4:8); the angels and redeemed anticipate God's further acts of judgment (cf. Hab 2:20; Zeph 1:7; Zech 2:13).

8:2 seven trumpets. See note on v. 6; introduces the next judgment cycle (8:6—11:19).

8:3 golden censer. Firepan used by priests to burn spices in temple worship (Lev 16:12; 1 Kgs 7:50). **altar.** See note on 6:9.

8:4 incense … prayers. See note on 5:8. God hears and answers the martyrs' petitions for justice and vindication (cf. 6:9–11).

8:5 peals of thunder, rumblings, flashes of lightning and an earthquake. Alludes to the Sinai theophany (Exod 19:16–20; cf. Rev 4:5). A storm theophany also concludes the cycles of trumpets (11:19) and bowls (16:18).

8:6—11:19 *The Seven Trumpets.* The seven angels introduced in 8:2 now sound their trumpets, initiating a second cycle of divine judgments (cf. 6:1–17). These judgments lead to heavenly praise (11:15–18).

8:6—9:21 *The Trumpets.* The trumpets demonstrate God's righteous judgment on idolatry (cf. 16:5,7). This judgment cycle may recall earlier plagues on Egypt.

8:6 seven trumpets. Introduced in v. 2. This scene recalls Josh 6:2–5, where seven priests blow trumpets before Jericho's destruction. In Scripture, trumpets summon the community for worship or battle (Lev 23:24; Num 10:1–10) and announce the Lord's glorious presence in revelation (Exod 19:16), judgment (Joel 2:1), and salvation (1 Thess 4:16).

8:7 hail … fire … blood. Modeled after the seventh plague on Egypt (Exod 9:22–25; cf. Pss 78:47; 105:32; Ezek 38:22). **A third of the earth.** Escalation from 6:8 ("a fourth"). Judgment is not limited to one nation as in the exodus. **trees … grass.** Devastating destruction of the natural world follows the sealing of God's servants (7:3; cf. Exod 9:25–26).

8:8 huge mountain, all ablaze. May recall first-century volcanic

8:8 [e]ver 7 [f]Rev 16:3
8:9 [g]ver 7
8:10 [h]Isa 14:12; Rev 6:13; 9:1 [i]Rev 14:7; 16:4
8:11 [j]ver 7 [k]Jer 9:15; 23:15
8:12 [l]ver 7 [m]Ex 10:21-23; Rev 6:12,13
8:13 [n]Rev 14:6; 19:17 [o]Rev 9:12; 11:14
9:1 [p]Rev 8:10 [q]ver 2,11; Lk 8:31
9:2 [r]Ge 19:28; Ex 19:18 [s]Joel 2:2,10
9:3 [t]Ex 10:12-15 [u]ver 5,10
9:4 [v]Rev 6:6 [w]Rev 8:7 [x]Rev 7:2,3
9:5 [y]ver 10 [z]ver 3
9:6 [a]Job 3:21; Jer 8:3; Rev 6:16
9:7 [b]Joel 2:4 [c]Da 7:8
9:8 [d]Joel 1:6
9:9 [e]Joel 2:5
9:10 [f]ver 3,5,19
9:11 [g]ver 1,2
9:12 [h]Rev 8:13
9:13 [i]Ex 30:1-3 [j]Rev 8:3

thrown into the sea. A third[e] of the sea turned into blood,[f] 9 a third[g] of the living creatures in the sea
died, and a third of the ships were destroyed.

10 The third angel sounded his trumpet, and a great star, blazing like a torch, fell from the sky[h] on a
third of the rivers and on the springs of water[i]— 11 the name of the star is Wormwood.[a] A third[j] of the
waters turned bitter, and many people died from the waters that had become bitter.[k]

12 The fourth angel sounded his trumpet, and a third of the sun was struck, a third of the moon,
and a third of the stars, so that a third[l] of them turned dark.[m] A third of the day was without light, and
also a third of the night.

13 As I watched, I heard an eagle that was flying in midair[n] call out in a loud voice: "Woe! Woe! Woe[o] to
the inhabitants of the earth, because of the trumpet blasts about to be sounded by the other three angels!"

9 The fifth angel sounded his trumpet, and I saw a star that had fallen from the sky to the earth.[p]
The star was given the key to the shaft of the Abyss.[q] 2 When he opened the Abyss, smoke rose from
it like the smoke from a gigantic furnace.[r] The sun and sky were darkened[s] by the smoke from the
Abyss. 3 And out of the smoke locusts[t] came down on the earth and were given power like that of scorpions[u] of the earth. 4 They were told not to harm[v] the grass of the earth or any plant or tree,[w] but only
those people who did not have the seal of God on their foreheads.[x] 5 They were not allowed to kill them
but only to torture them for five months.[y] And the agony they suffered was like that of the sting of a
scorpion[z] when it strikes. 6 During those days people will seek death but will not find it; they will long
to die, but death will elude them.[a]

7 The locusts looked like horses prepared for battle.[b] On their heads they wore something like crowns
of gold, and their faces resembled human faces.[c] 8 Their hair was like women's hair, and their teeth
were like lions' teeth.[d] 9 They had breastplates like breastplates of iron, and the sound of their wings
was like the thundering of many horses and chariots rushing into battle.[e] 10 They had tails with sting-
ers, like scorpions, and in their tails they had power to torment people for five months.[f] 11 They had as
king over them the angel of the Abyss,[g] whose name in Hebrew is Abaddon and in Greek is Apollyon
(that is, Destroyer).

12 The first woe is past; two other woes are yet to come.[h]

13 The sixth angel sounded his trumpet, and I heard a voice coming from the four horns[i] of the
golden altar that is before God.[j] 14 It said to the sixth angel who had the trumpet, "Release the four

[a] *11* Wormwood is a bitter substance.

eruptions, such as Mount Vesuvius (AD 79), and Jer 51:25, where God promises to make Babylon "a burned-out mountain." **sea turned into blood.** Alludes to Exod 7:20–21; cf. Rev 16:3.

8:9 a third … died. Limited destruction recalls God's promise in Gen 8:21; contrast the total loss of life in Rev 16:3. **ships.** Rome depended on the sea for food and commerce; the sea captains lament Babylon's ruin in 18:17–19.

8:10 great star … fell. For falling stars, see 6:13; 9:1; Isa 14:12. Readers in Asia Minor may have linked this star with the "great Artemis … which fell from heaven" (Acts 19:35).

8:11 Wormwood. A bitter-tasting shrub (see NIV text note), which symbolizes sorrow (Prov 5:3–4) and judgment (Jer 9:15; 23:15). **waters … bitter.** Recalls the first Egyptian plague (Exod 7:20–21) and the bitter water at Marah (Exod 15:23); contrasts with "springs of living water" (7:17).

8:12 sun … moon … stars … turned dark. Alludes to Exod 10:21–23; Matt 24:29; the darkness is partial, not total, covering "a third of the day." Darkness symbolizes the primordial world (Gen 1:2), evil (Luke 22:53; John 1:5), and final destruction (Isa 13:10; Ezek 32:7; Joel 2:10). The beast and its kingdom will be "plunged into darkness" (16:10).

8:13 Woe! The final three "trumpet blasts" bring imminent, intensified judgment against unrepentant humanity (cf. 6:15–17).

9:1 star … fallen. Cf. 8:10. May represent a fallen angel (possibly Satan, 12:9; Luke 10:18) or a divine agent carrying out God's will (20:1). **key.** See notes on 1:18; 20:1. **Abyss.** The realm of the wicked dead and demons (vv. 2,11; 11:7; see note on Luke 8:31).

9:3 locusts. Recalls Exod 10:12–15 (see "Parallels Between Bowls, Trumpets, and Exodus Plagues," p. 2613) and covenant curses against Israel (Deut 28:38; 2 Chr 7:13; Joel 1:4). **scorpions.** Described in v. 10; symbolize demonic forces in Luke 10:19.

9:4 Locusts always devour vegetation (Exod 10:15; Joel 1:4), but here they are "told not to harm the grass" (contrast 8:7) and instead torture only unbelievers not protected by "the seal of God" (see note on 7:2).

9:5 not allowed to kill. Divinely imposed limitation (v. 10).

9:7–9 John describes the demonic locusts symbolically as swift (like "horses," v. 7; cf. Joel 2:4), ferocious (having "lions' teeth," v. 8; cf. Joel 1:6), intelligent ("human faces," v. 7; cf. Dan 7:8), and armed for battle with "breastplates" and "chariots" (v. 9; cf. Joel 2:5).

9:11 angel of the Abyss. Variously identified as Satan, the antichrist, personified destruction, or the angel of death. **Abaddon.** Hebrew for destruction, often linked with death (Job 26:6; 28:22; Prov 15:11 and NIV text notes). **Apollyon.** May suggest a reference to Apollo, the Greek god of pestilence, often symbolized by the locust. Domitian considered himself Apollo incarnate, so this may be a further presentation of emperor worship as demonic.

9:12 first woe. See note on 8:13.

9:13 golden altar. Recalls 6:9 (see note there); 8:3; suggests this destructive judgment comes in response to the martyrs' prayers (6:10).

9:14 four angels. Either the four angels introduced in 7:1 or, more likely, the four winds previously restrained (see note on 7:1) but now unleashed for destruction. **Euphrates.** The longest river in western Asia and the northeastern border of the promised land (Gen 15:18; Josh 1:4) and the Roman Empire. Recalls OT prophecies of foes from the north

VICE LISTS IN REVELATION

9:20–21	21:8	22:15
did not repent	the cowardly ... unbelieving	
worshiping demons ... idols	idolaters	idolaters
murders	murderers	murderers
magic arts	those practicing magic arts	those practicing magic arts
sexual immorality	sexually immoral	sexually immoral
thefts		
	vile	dogs
	all liars	everyone who loves and practices falsehood

angels who are bound at the great river Euphrates."[k] 15 And the four angels who had been kept ready for this very hour and day and month and year were released to kill a third of mankind.[l] 16 The number of the mounted troops was twice ten thousand times ten thousand. I heard their number.[m]

17 The horses and riders I saw in my vision looked like this: Their breastplates were fiery red, dark blue, and yellow as sulfur. The heads of the horses resembled the heads of lions, and out of their mouths[n] came fire, smoke and sulfur.[o] 18 A third of mankind was killed[p] by the three plagues of fire, smoke and sulfur[q] that came out of their mouths. 19 The power of the horses was in their mouths and in their tails; for their tails were like snakes, having heads with which they inflict injury.

20 The rest of mankind who were not killed by these plagues still did not repent of the work of their hands;[r] they did not stop worshiping demons,[s] and idols of gold, silver, bronze, stone and wood — idols that cannot see or hear or walk.[t] 21 Nor did they repent[u] of their murders, their magic arts,[v] their sexual immorality[w] or their thefts.

9:14 [k] Rev 16:12
9:15 [l] ver 18
9:16 [m] Rev 5:11; 7:4
9:17 [n] Rev 11:5 [o] ver 18
9:18 [p] ver 15 [q] ver 17
9:20 [r] Dt 31:29 [s] 1Co 10:20 [t] Ps 115:4-7; 135:15-17; Da 5:23
9:21 [u] Rev 2:21 [v] Rev 18:23 [w] Rev 17:2,5
10:1 [x] Rev 5:2 [y] Mt 17:2; Rev 1:16 [z] Rev 1:15
10:3 [a] Rev 4:5
10:4 [b] Da 8:26; 12:4,9; Rev 22:10

The Angel and the Little Scroll

10 Then I saw another mighty angel[x] coming down from heaven. He was robed in a cloud, with a rainbow above his head; his face was like the sun,[y] and his legs were like fiery pillars.[z] 2 He was holding a little scroll, which lay open in his hand. He planted his right foot on the sea and his left foot on the land, 3 and he gave a loud shout like the roar of a lion. When he shouted, the voices of the seven thunders[a] spoke. 4 And when the seven thunders spoke, I was about to write; but I heard a voice from heaven say, "Seal up what the seven thunders have said and do not write it down."[b]

(cf. Isa 8:7–8; Jer 1:14–15) and prepares for the sixth bowl judgment (16:12–16).
9:15 kill a third of mankind. Escalation of the fifth trumpet from torture (v. 5) to death; cf. v. 18.
9:16 twice ten thousand times ten thousand. 200 million cavalry, 1,000 times the size of Rome's formidable army.
9:17 breastplates ... horses ... lions. Parallels the locusts' description in vv. 7–9. **fire, smoke and sulfur.** Recalls the destruction of Sodom and Gomorrah (Gen 19:24,28; cf. Deut 29:22–23; Luke 17:29) and anticipates God's eternal judgment on those who side with Satan, the beast, and Babylon (14:10–11; 18:9; 20:10; 21:8).
9:19 snakes. Recalls the judgment against Israel in the wilderness (Num 21:6–7; cf. 1 Cor 10:9) and suggests demonic power associated with "that ancient serpent ... Satan" (12:9; cf. Gen 3:1).
9:20 still did not repent. Unbelieving humanity responds to the plagues with continued hostility toward God. Cf. Pharaoh's hard-hearted response to divine judgments on Egypt (Exod 4:21; 14:4). Cf. 16:9,11. **worshiping demons ... idols of gold.** Recalls how the OT describes the material and spiritual essence of idols (Deut 4:28; 32:16–17; Ps 115:4–7).
9:21 These evil deeds are linked with idolatry (v. 20; cf. Jer 7:5–11) and deserve eternal punishment (21:8; 22:15; see "Vice Lists in Revelation," this page).
10:1–11 *The Angel and the Little Scroll.* The interlude (10:1—11:14) between the sixth and seventh trumpets parallels the earlier parenthesis between the final two seals (ch. 7). Ch. 10 recounts a vision of a mighty angel (vv. 1–7) and John's prophetic commissioning (vv. 8–11), emphasizing that God authorizes and will imminently fulfill John's message.
10:1 another mighty angel. May refer to Christ or a great angel as in 5:2; 18:21. **cloud ... rainbow ... sun ... fiery pillars.** Majestic description using terms elsewhere applied to God (4:3; Exod 13:21) and the Son of Man (1:7,16; 14:14; Matt 17:2).
10:2 little scroll ... open. Alludes to Ezek 2:9–10; see v. 9 and note. May refer to the scroll that the Lamb opened in 6:1—8:1 or to a different scroll. **foot on the sea ... land.** Represents dominion over all creation (cf. vv. 5–6); the devil also exercises authority over the earth and sea for a short time (12:12–13).
10:3 roar of a lion. Emphasizes the speaker's divine authority. The Lord roars like a lion in Hos 11:10; Amos 1:2; 3:8.
10:4 Seal up. John does not disclose what precisely the seven thunders said. Cf. Dan 8:26; 12:4,9; contrast Rev 22:10. **do not write.** Contrast 1:19.

10:5 [c]Da 12:7
10:6 [d]Rev 4:11; 14:7 [e]Rev 16:17
10:7 [f]Ro 16:25
10:8 [g]ver 4
10:9 [h]Jer 15:16; Eze 2:8-3:3
10:11 [i]Eze 37:4,9
11:1 [j]Eze 40:3; Rev 21:15
11:2 [k]Eze 40:17,20 [l]Lk 21:24 [m]Rev 21:2 [n]Da 7:25; Rev 13:5
11:3 [o]Rev 1:5 [p]Ge 37:34
11:4 [q]Ps 52:8; Jer 11:16; Zec 4:3,11 [r]Zec 4:14
11:5 [s]2Ki 1:10; Jer 5:14 [t]Nu 16:29,35

5 Then the angel I had seen standing on the sea and on the land raised his right hand to heaven.[c]
6 And he swore by him who lives for ever and ever, who created the heavens and all that is in them, the
earth and all that is in it, and the sea and all that is in it,[d] and said, "There will be no more delay![e]
7 But in the days when the seventh angel is about to sound his trumpet, the mystery[f] of God will be accomplished, just as he announced to his servants the prophets."

8 Then the voice that I had heard from heaven[g] spoke to me once more: "Go, take the scroll that lies
open in the hand of the angel who is standing on the sea and on the land."

9 So I went to the angel and asked him to give me the little scroll. He said to me, "Take it and eat it.
It will turn your stomach sour, but 'in your mouth it will be as sweet as honey.'[a][h] 10 I took the little
scroll from the angel's hand and ate it. It tasted as sweet as honey in my mouth, but when I had eaten
it, my stomach turned sour. 11 Then I was told, "You must prophesy[i] again about many peoples, nations,
languages and kings."

The Two Witnesses

11 I was given a reed like a measuring rod[j] and was told, "Go and measure the temple of God and
the altar, with its worshipers. 2 But exclude the outer court;[k] do not measure it, because it has
been given to the Gentiles.[l] They will trample on the holy city[m] for 42 months.[n] 3 And I will appoint my
two witnesses,[o] and they will prophesy for 1,260 days, clothed in sackcloth."[p] 4 They are "the two olive
trees"[q] and the two lampstands, and "they stand before the Lord of the earth."[b][r] 5 If anyone tries to
harm them, fire comes from their mouths and devours their enemies.[s] This is how anyone who wants
to harm them must die.[t] 6 They have power to shut up the heavens so that it will not rain during the

[a] *9* Ezek. 3:3 [b] *4* See Zech. 4:3,11,14.

10:5–6 raised his right hand ... swore. Angelic oath based on the Creator God's supreme authority (cf. Dan 12:7).

10:6 no more delay! Emphasizes that God will soon accomplish his purposes (cf. Dan 12:9; Hab 2:3) to vindicate his suffering people (cf. 6:10–11).

10:7 mystery. See note on 1:20. **just as he announced.** John's prophecy (cf. v. 11; 1:3) discloses that God will fulfill earlier biblical prophecy (cf. 17:17; Amos 3:7).

10:8 take. To announce its contents (5:7).

10:9 Take ... eat. John's symbolic commissioning as a prophet, patterned after Ezek 2:8—3:3. **sour.** Because John prophesies bitter judgment (Ezek 2:10; 3:14) and continued suffering for God's people (cf. 6:9–11). **sweet.** Because it is God's true, revealed word (Jer 15:16).

10:10 John obeys his commission, internalizes God's word, and makes it known (v. 11).

10:11 prophesy again. Reiterates John's prophetic calling (cf. 1:19). **many peoples.** Stresses the universal scope of John's witness, recalling Jeremiah's calling as "a prophet to the nations" who is given authority "over nations and kingdoms" (Jer 1:5,10). The nations must worship God and the Lamb (5:9; 7:9–10; 15:4; 21:24); those who ally with Babylon will face divine wrath (11:18; 14:8–10).

11:1–14 *The Two Witnesses.* After God renews John's prophetic commission (10:8–11), John symbolically describes how God spiritually protects his suffering people (vv. 1–2) and vindicates the "two witnesses" (v. 3) after they prophesy and experience persecution (vv. 3–12). Interpreters throughout church history have debated whether these witnesses refer to individual prophets or symbolize the church (see notes on vv. 3,4).

11:1 measuring rod. Alludes to Ezek 40:3; cf. Rev 21:15; Zech 2:1–2. Measuring signifies that God protects and owns his people. **temple of God.** Elsewhere "temple" designates the heavenly temple (v. 19; 7:15), God's presence in the new Jerusalem (21:22), or the church (see note on 3:12; cf. 1 Cor 3:16–17). Alternatively, many preterists read vv. 1–2 as predicting the Jerusalem temple's destruction in AD 70 (see Introduction: Date). Many dispensationalists understand v. 1 to refer to a future temple rebuilt during the great tribulation. **altar.** The place of sacrifice. May refer to literal Jewish sacrifice before AD 70 or during the future tribulation, or to spiritual worship by the church (cf. Rom 12:1; Heb 13:10,13–14). **worshipers.** Variously interpreted as ethnic Jews in the first century (preterists), believing Jews in the future tribulation (dispensationalists), or a figurative reference to individual believers in the church (idealists and some modified futurists).

11:2 outer court. The court of the Gentiles. **Gentiles ... will trample on the holy city.** May refer to Rome destroying the Jerusalem temple (cf. Luke 21:24) or unbelievers persecuting God's people, heirs of the "new Jerusalem" (21:2). **42 months.** Equivalent to 1,260 days (v. 3; 12:6) and "a time, times and half a time" (12:14; cf. Dan 7:25; 12:7). May denote a literal time period at the end of the future tribulation or a symbolic time of the church's witness that is characterized by physical suffering and spiritual preservation. Cf. vv. 3–4.

11:3 my two witnesses. Modeled after Moses and Elijah (see note on v. 5). Variously interpreted as individual prophets at history's end, the witnessing church in its suffering and triumph, or individual prophets who represent the church. **1,260 days.** Same as 42 months in v. 2 (see note there). **sackcloth.** Symbolizes mourning over sin and judgment and possibly a message of repentance (cf. Dan 9:3; Jonah 3:5–8; Matt 11:21).

11:4 two olive trees ... two lampstands. Alludes to Zech 4:2–14, where the gold lampstand represents Israel, and two olive trees probably symbolize Joshua and Zerubbabel, who were empowered by God and "anointed" (Zech 4:14) for rebuilding Israel's temple. John's opening Son of Man vision introduces seven lampstands and interprets this symbol as churches (1:20; see Introduction: Interpreting Symbolism). The change from seven to two lampstands may reflect the number of faithful churches in chs. 2–3 (Smyrna and Philadelphia) and/or the number of witnesses needed to establish a charge (Deut 19:15). Some interpreters identify the two witnesses as future individuals who bring revival and renewed temple worship in Israel, like Joshua and Zerubbabel.

11:5 fire comes from their mouths. Recalls Jer 5:14, where the prophet's word of judgment is likened to devouring fire. In 2 Kgs 1:9–12, consuming fire from heaven validates Elijah as a man of God.

11:6 shut up the heavens. Recalls the drought Elijah announced (1 Kgs

OLD TESTAMENT BACKGROUND FOR THE TWO WITNESSES IN REVELATION 11

REVELATION 11	OT BACKGROUND
"my two witnesses" (v. 3)	"testimony of two ... witnesses" (Deut 19:15)
"1,260 days" (v. 3; cf. 11:2; 12:6,14)	"time, times and half a time" (Dan 7:25)
"two olive trees" (v. 4)	"two olive trees" (Zech 4:3,11)
"two lampstands" (v. 4; cf. 1:20)	"gold lampstand" (Zech 4:2)
"fire comes from their mouths" (v. 5)	"fire fell from heaven" (2 Kgs 1:10); "words in your mouth a fire" (Jer 5:14)
"shut up the heavens ... not rain" (v. 6)	"neither dew nor rain ... except at my word" (1 Kgs 17:1; cf. Luke 4:25)
"turn the waters into blood" (v. 6)	"water ... into blood" (Exod 7:17)
"beast ... will attack them" (v. 7; cf. 13:5,7)	"fourth beast ... horn was waging war against the holy people" (Dan 7:19,21)
"breath of life ... entered them, and they stood" (v. 11)	"breath entered them; they came to life and stood up" (Ezek 37:10)

time they are prophesying; and they have power to turn the waters into blood[u] and to strike the earth
with every kind of plague as often as they want.
[7]Now when they have finished their testimony, the beast[v] that comes up from the Abyss will attack
them,[w] and overpower and kill them. [8]Their bodies will lie in the public square of the great city—
which is figuratively called Sodom[x] and Egypt—where also their Lord was crucified.[y] [9]For three and a
half days some from every people, tribe, language and nation will gaze on their bodies and refuse them
burial.[z] [10]The inhabitants of the earth[a] will gloat over them and will celebrate by sending each other
gifts,[b] because these two prophets had tormented those who live on the earth.
[11]But after the three and a half days the breath[a] of life from God entered them,[c] and they stood on
their feet, and terror struck those who saw them. [12]Then they heard a loud voice from heaven saying
to them, "Come up here."[d] And they went up to heaven in a cloud,[e] while their enemies looked on.
[13]At that very hour there was a severe earthquake[f] and a tenth of the city collapsed. Seven thousand people were killed in the earthquake, and the survivors were terrified and gave glory[g] to the God of heaven.[h]
[14]The second woe has passed; the third woe is coming soon.[i]

a 11 Or *Spirit* (see Ezek. 37:5,14)

11:6 [u]Ex 7:17,19
11:7 [v]Rev 13:1-4 [w]Da 7:21
11:8 [x]Isa 1:9 [y]Heb 13:12
11:9 [z]Ps 79:2,3
11:10 [a]Rev 3:10 [b]Est 9:19,22
11:11 [c]Eze 37:5, 9,10,14
11:12 [d]Rev 4:1 [e]2Ki 2:11; Ac 1:9
11:13 [f]Rev 6:12 [g]Rev 14:7 [h]Rev 16:11
11:14 [i]Rev 8:13

17:1; cf. Luke 4:25; Jas 5:17). **waters into blood.** Recalls the exodus plague (Exod 7:17) and the second trumpet (see 8:8 and note).
11:7 beast ... from the Abyss. Revelation's first reference to this major opponent of God's people (17:8); equivalent to the beast "coming out of the sea" (13:1; cf. Dan 7:3). **attack ... overpower.** The same Greek phrase occurs in 13:7: "power to wage war against God's holy people and to conquer them" (cf. Dan 7:21).
11:8 great city. Babylon (18:10), which the original readers would likely associate with Rome; contrasts with "the holy city" (v. 2; see "A Tale of Two Cities in Revelation," p. 2615). **Sodom.** Proverbial for an immoral, debased society deserving God's judgment (cf. Gen 18:20; 19:24; 2 Pet 2:6). **Egypt.** Symbolizes enslaving and oppressing God's people (Exod 20:2). **where also their Lord was crucified.** Recalls Jerusalem (Luke 13:33–34). Jesus' witnesses follow their suffering master (cf. 1:9; John 15:18–20). Revelation emphasizes the great city's ungodly nature and heritage, not its geographic location.
11:9 three and a half days. Cf. v. 11; recalls the cryptic half week in Dan 9:27. **every people ... nation.** Universal unredeemed humanity who worship the beast and persecute God's people (13:7–8; 17:15). Contrasts with the universal worship of Jesus in 5:9 (see note there). **refuse them burial.** Treated with utter indignity and contempt (cf. Ps 79:1–4).
11:10 two prophets. Designates the two witnesses (v. 3); recalls John's call to prophesy about nations (10:11).
11:11 breath of life ... entered ... they stood. Alludes to Ezek 37:5,10, which depicts Israel's revival after exile as life after death. If the two witnesses symbolize the church (see notes on vv. 3,4), this describes the church's vindication in resurrection at the end of the age (cf. 1 Cor 15:20–23). Alternatively, this predicts the vindication of only the individual witnesses.
11:12 "Come up here." And they went up to heaven. Recalls John's prophetic commission (4:1), as well as Jesus' ascension (Acts 1:9,11).
11:13 severe earthquake. Alludes to Ezek 38:19; anticipates the earthquake accompanying Babylon's destruction (16:18–19). **a tenth of the city.** Limited judgment; contrast with 16:19. **terrified ... gave glory.** The multitude either acknowledge God's power while persisting in unbelief (cf. 6:15–17; 16:21) or respond with reverent fear and repentance (14:7; 15:4).
11:14 second woe ... third woe. Recalls 8:13; 9:12; prepares for the seventh trumpet in v. 15.

11:15 [j]Rev 10:7 [k]Rev 16:17; 19:1 [l]Rev 12:10 [m]Da 2:44; 7:14,27
11:16 [n]Rev 4:4
11:17 [o]Rev 1:8 [p]Rev 19:6
11:18 [q]Ps 2:1 [r]Rev 10:7 [s]Rev 19:5
11:19 [t]Rev 15:5,8 [u]Rev 16:21
12:2 [v]Gal 4:19
12:3 [w]Da 7:7,20; Rev 13:1 [x]Rev 19:12
12:4 [y]Rev 8:7

The Seventh Trumpet

15The seventh angel sounded his trumpet,[j] and there were loud voices[k] in heaven, which said:

"The kingdom of the world has become
the kingdom of our Lord and of his Messiah,[l]
and he will reign for ever and ever."[m]

16And the twenty-four elders,[n] who were seated on their thrones before God, fell on their faces and
worshiped God, 17saying:

"We give thanks to you, Lord God Almighty,[o]
the One who is and who was,
because you have taken your great power
and have begun to reign.[p]
18The nations were angry,[q]
and your wrath has come.
The time has come for judging the dead,
and for rewarding your servants the prophets[r]
and your people who revere your name,
both great and small[s] —
and for destroying those who destroy the earth."

19Then God's temple[t] in heaven was opened, and within his temple was seen the ark of his covenant.
And there came flashes of lightning, rumblings, peals of thunder, an earthquake and a severe hailstorm.[u]

The Woman and the Dragon

12 A great sign appeared in heaven: a woman clothed with the sun, with the moon under her feet
and a crown of twelve stars on her head. 2She was pregnant and cried out in pain[v] as she was
about to give birth. 3Then another sign appeared in heaven: an enormous red dragon with seven heads
and ten horns[w] and seven crowns[x] on its heads. 4Its tail swept a third[y] of the stars out of the sky and flung

11:15–19 *The Seventh Trumpet.* This does not describe but proclaims the "third woe" (v. 14) as worshipers celebrate that God will reign forever and judge his enemies.

11:15 seventh angel sounded his trumpet. Completes the cycle of seven trumpets (cf. 8:7). **loud voices.** Recalls worship in 5:12; 7:10. **the kingdom of our Lord and of his Messiah.** God's kingdom is inextricably bound to the Messiah, Jesus (cf. Ps 2:1–2), who reigns in heaven following his ascension (1:5; Acts 2:33–36) and will return to consummate his kingdom (19:6,11,16). **reign for ever.** Fulfills the OT expectation that God will reign forever through the Davidic king (Isa 9:7; Dan 2:44; Mic 4:7; cf. Luke 1:33). The redeemed will participate in this eternal reign (22:5).

11:16 elders. See note on 4:4.

11:17 Lord God Almighty. See note on 1:8. **who is ... was.** Recalls the divine title in 1:4 (see note there) but omits the final phrase "who is to come" because God's coming reign is realized.

11:18 nations were angry. Recalls Exod 15:14; Ps 2:1. **your wrath.** See notes on 6:16,17. **judging the dead.** See note on 20:12. **rewarding.** Cf. 22:12; Matt 5:12. **your servants the prophets.** Designates (1) OT prophets (10:7; cf. Amos 3:7), (2) Christian prophets like John (1:1), or (3) believers (synonymous with "your people") who fear and serve God (19:5; 22:3) and prophesy (v. 3; cf. Num 11:29; Joel 2:28; Acts 2:17).

11:19 God's temple in heaven. Where God's glorious presence is (v. 1; 3:12; 7:15; 21:22); served as a pattern for Israel's tabernacle and temple (Exod 25:40; see Heb 8:5 and note). **ark.** See note on Exod 25:10–22. Located in the temple's inner sanctuary (1 Kgs 6:19), the place of atonement (Lev 16:2); represents God's holy presence and covenant of mercy. **lightning ... earthquake.** See note on 8:5 (cf. 4:5). **hailstorm.** Recalls the first trumpet (8:7; cf. Exod 9:22–25) and parallels the seventh bowl (16:18,21).

12:1—14:20 *The Cosmic Conflict Between the Dragon and the Lamb.* Between the cycles of trumpet and bowl judgments, a dramatic sequence of visions presents the fundamental contest between the forces of God and Satan (the "dragon," 12:3) for the nations' allegiance and worship. The dragon, beast, and false prophet persecute God's people, but God promises to spiritually protect and gloriously vindicate them. So God exhorts them to steadfastly endure.

12:1–17 *The Woman and the Dragon.* Many interpreters view the dramatic conflict between God and Satan in ch. 12 as the heart of Revelation. Verses 1–6 establish the conflict between two heavenly "signs": the woman (God's people, vv. 1,4,6) and her Messianic child (vv. 4–5) versus the dragon, representing Satan (v. 3). Then vv. 7–12 describe the war in heaven, which results in the dragon being hurled to earth (v. 9). Finally, vv. 13–17 describe the war on earth between the dragon and God's people, whom God protects.

12:1 great sign. Contrasts with v. 3 ("another sign"); these signs introduce the key conflict between the woman and the dragon, which recalls Gen 3:15. **woman.** The faithful people of God, from whom the Messianic son comes (v. 5). **sun ... moon ... twelve stars.** Recalls Joseph's dream in Gen 37:9.

12:3 another sign. See note on v. 1. **dragon.** Recalls OT descriptions of the sea monster Leviathan, representing chaos and God's enemies (Ps 74:13–14; Isa 27:1; Ezek 29:3); identified as Satan in v. 9 (see note there; cf. 20:2). **seven heads and ten horns and seven crowns.** Represents the dragon's great power and claim to sovereignty; copies the depiction of Christ (5:6; 19:12). John describes the "beast" using similar imagery (13:1; 17:3,9–10,12).

12:4 stars. May designate angels aligned with Satan in the original war in heaven (cf. v. 9) or diabolical persecution of God's people (cf. Dan

them to the earth.[z] The dragon stood in front of the woman who was about to give birth, so that it might
devour her child[a] the moment he was born. 5She gave birth to a son, a male child, who "will rule all the
nations with an iron scepter."[a][b] And her child was snatched up to God and to his throne. 6The woman fled
into the wilderness to a place prepared for her by God, where she might be taken care of for 1,260 days.[c]

7Then war broke out in heaven. Michael and his angels fought against the dragon,[d] and the dragon
and his angels fought back. 8But he was not strong enough, and they lost their place in heaven. 9The
great dragon was hurled down — that ancient serpent[e] called the devil,[f] or Satan, who leads the whole
world astray.[g] He was hurled to the earth,[h] and his angels with him.

10Then I heard a loud voice in heaven[i] say:

"Now have come the salvation and the power
and the kingdom of our God,
and the authority of his Messiah.
For the accuser of our brothers and sisters,[j]
who accuses them before our God day and night,
has been hurled down.
11They triumphed over him
by the blood of the Lamb[k]
and by the word of their testimony;[l]
they did not love their lives so much
as to shrink from death.[m]
12Therefore rejoice, you heavens[n]
and you who dwell in them!
But woe[o] to the earth and the sea,[p]
because the devil has gone down to you!
He is filled with fury,
because he knows that his time is short."

13When the dragon[q] saw that he had been hurled to the earth, he pursued the woman who had given
birth to the male child.[r] 14The woman was given the two wings of a great eagle,[s] so that she might fly
to the place prepared for her in the wilderness, where she would be taken care of for a time, times and
half a time,[t] out of the serpent's reach. 15Then from his mouth the serpent spewed water like a river, to
overtake the woman and sweep her away with the torrent. 16But the earth helped the woman by opening

12:4 [z] Da 8:10 [a] Mt 2:16
12:5 [b] Ps 2:9; Rev 2:27
12:6 [c] Rev 11:2
12:7 [d] ver 3
12:9 [e] Ge 3:1-7 [f] Mt 25:41 [g] Rev 20:3,8, 10 [h] Lk 10:18; Jn 12:31
12:10 [i] Rev 11:15 [j] Job 1:9-11; Zec 3:1
12:11 [k] Rev 7:14 [l] Rev 6:9 [m] Lk 14:26
12:12 [n] Ps 96:11; Isa 49:13; Rev 18:20 [o] Rev 8:13 [p] Rev 10:6
12:13 [q] ver 3 [r] ver 5
12:14 [s] Ex 19:4 [t] Da 7:25

[a] 5 Psalm 2:9

8:10). **devour her child.** Recalls the rivalry between the serpent and Eve's child in Gen 3:15.

12:5 male child … iron scepter. Jesus is Israel's promised royal Messiah in David's line; cites Ps 2:9; cf. Rev 2:27; 19:15.

12:6 wilderness. A place of divine protection and provision (v. 14). May recall Israel's exodus (Exod 16:32) and promised restoration after exile (Isa 40:3; Matt 3:3). **1,260 days.** The period of persecution (see 11:2 and note ["42 months"]; 13:5–7), proclamation (11:3), and protection (here) for God's people.

12:7 war … in heaven. Expands on vv. 3–4. **Michael.** The archangel (Jude 9), the heavenly prince who protects God's people (Dan 12:1), frequently mentioned in Jewish apocalyptic literature.

12:8 not strong enough. In Dan 7:21, the "horn was waging war against the holy people and defeating them" (cf. Rev 11:7); here the dragon is overpowered.

12:9 hurled down. Likely refers to Satan's defeat through Jesus' death and resurrection (John 12:31; Col 2:15). Alternatively, this may designate Satan's primordial fall or the heavenly events accompanying the end-time tribulation on earth. **ancient serpent … devil … Satan.** Alludes to Gen 3:1–15, which describes the serpent's deception of Eve (cf. 2 Cor 11:3). False teachers (2:20) and the false prophet (13:14; 19:20) are agents of Satan's deception. Cf. 20:3,8.

12:10 voice in heaven. Interprets John's vision in vv. 7–9. **salvation … power … kingdom.** Recalls earlier hymns to God and the Lamb (4:11; 5:12–13; 7:10; 11:15). **For the accuser … hurled down.** Satan's fall motivates praise; he can no longer accuse or condemn believers (cf. Rom 8:33–34).

12:11 triumphed. Recalls earlier promises to the victorious (see note on 2:7; cf. 21:7). The beast's triumph over God's people will be short-lived (11:7; 13:7). **blood … word.** Believers' ultimate victory comes through Jesus' death (1:5) and their witness, which motivates patient endurance and hope for suffering Christians (see note on 1:9; see also Introduction: Purpose). **they did not love their lives.** Cf. 2:10,13; 6:9; Luke 14:26.

12:12 Cf. 18:20. The heavens and earth "rejoice" together when God's kingdom is established (Ps 96:10–11; Isa 44:23), but here the devil's expulsion from heaven brings "woe to the earth and the sea." See 13:1. **his time is short.** Satan is "filled with fury" because his demise is sure and imminent.

12:13 Expands on v. 6.

12:14 eagle. Symbolizes divine protection and deliverance at the exodus (Exod 19:4) and the second exodus from exile (Isa 40:31). **time, times and half a time.** Alludes to Dan 7:25; 12:7; equivalent to 1,260 days (v. 6), or 42 months (11:2; see note there).

12:15 from his mouth … water. Symbolizes persecution and deceit (cf. Ps 144:7–8).

12:16 earth … swallowing. May recall the judgments on Egypt (Exod 15:12) and on Korah's followers (Num 16:30–33).

12:17 [u] Rev 11:7 [v] Ge 3:15 [w] Rev 14:12 [x] Rev 1:2
13:1 [y] Da 7:1-6; Rev 15:2 [z] Rev 12:3 [a] Da 11:36; Rev 17:3
13:2 [b] Da 7:6 [c] Da 7:5 [d] Da 7:4 [e] Rev 16:10
13:3 [f] ver 12,14 [g] Rev 17:8
13:4 [h] Ex 15:11
13:5 [i] Da 7:8,11,20,25; 11:36; 2Th 2:4 [j] Rev 11:2
13:6 [k] Rev 12:12
13:7 [l] Da 7:21; Rev 11:7 [m] Rev 5:9
13:8 [n] Rev 3:10 [o] Rev 3:5; 20:12 [p] Mt 25:34
13:9 [q] Rev 2:7
13:10 [r] Jer 15:2; 43:11 [s] Heb 6:12 [t] Rev 14:12

its mouth and swallowing the river that the dragon had spewed out of his mouth. [17]Then the dragon
was enraged at the woman and went off to wage war[u] against the rest of her offspring[v]—those who
keep God's commands[w] and hold fast their testimony about Jesus.[x]

The Beast out of the Sea

13 The dragon[a] stood on the shore of the sea. And I saw a beast coming out of the sea.[y] It had
ten horns and seven heads,[z] with ten crowns on its horns, and on each head a blasphemous
name.[a] [2]The beast I saw resembled a leopard,[b] but had feet like those of a bear[c] and a mouth like that
of a lion.[d] The dragon gave the beast his power and his throne and great authority.[e] [3]One of the heads
of the beast seemed to have had a fatal wound, but the fatal wound had been healed.[f] The whole world
was filled with wonder[g] and followed the beast. [4]People worshiped the dragon because he had given
authority to the beast, and they also worshiped the beast and asked, "Who is like[h] the beast? Who can
wage war against it?"

[5]The beast was given a mouth to utter proud words and blasphemies[i] and to exercise its authority for
forty-two months.[j] [6]It opened its mouth to blaspheme God, and to slander his name and his dwelling
place and those who live in heaven.[k] [7]It was given power to wage war[l] against God's holy people and to
conquer them. And it was given authority over every tribe, people, language and nation.[m] [8]All inhabitants of the earth[n] will worship the beast—all whose names have not been written in the Lamb's book
of life,[o] the Lamb who was slain from the creation of the world.[bp]

[9]Whoever has ears, let them hear.[q]

> [10]"If anyone is to go into captivity,
> into captivity they will go.
> If anyone is to be killed[c] with the sword,
> with the sword they will be killed."[dr]

This calls for patient endurance and faithfulness[s] on the part of God's people.[t]

[a] *1* Some manuscripts *And I* [b] *8* Or *written from the creation of the world in the book of life belonging to the Lamb who was slain* [c] *10* Some manuscripts *anyone kills* [d] *10* Jer. 15:2

12:17 her offspring. Believers, in contrast with the male child (vv. 5,13). **those who keep God's commands.** Cf. 14:12; 1 John 3:24. **testimony.** Cf. 1:2,9; 19:10; 20:4.

13:1–10 *The Beast out of the Sea.* John describes a powerful, proud beast that carries out the dragon's will and is permitted for a limited time to oppose God, persecute God's people, and receive the nations' worship. John's vision recalls Daniel's prophecy of four beasts representing four great kings or kingdoms (see note on Dan 7:17). Interpreters have identified the beast with various past or future antichrist individuals or empires. John's readers may have associated the beast with the false worship and oppression authorized by Rome and its emperors (cf. 17:7–10; see Introduction: Interpreting Symbolism).

13:1 beast coming out of the sea. Alludes to Dan 7:2–3; recalls the Abyss in Rev 11:7. **sea.** Symbolizes the realm of evil and chaos (12:12; 20:13; 21:1; see note on Dan 7:2–3). **ten horns.** Represents political and military power or "kings" (17:12; cf. Dan 7:24). Recalls the description of the dragon in 12:3 and the fourth beast in Dan 7:7. **seven heads.** The sum of the four beasts' heads in Dan 7:2–7; represents the completeness of the beast's oppressive power. Interpreted as "seven hills" in 17:9 (see note there). The beast takes on the dragon's image (12:3), a satanic imitation of the Messianic child (12:5). **blasphemous name.** Cf. 17:3. May reflect the divine titles that Emperor Domitian assumed (see notes on 2:13; 9:11; see also Introduction: Date).

13:2 leopard ... bear ... lion. Combines the attributes of the four beasts from Dan 7:3–8, the ultimate kingdom opposed to God and his people. **dragon gave ... power ... throne ... authority.** Satan usurps the sovereign right of God and Jesus to "give authority" (2:26; see 6:8; 9:3; cf. John 17:2). For Satan's throne, cf. 2:13; 16:10.

13:3 fatal wound ... healed. Counterfeit imitation of Jesus' death and resurrection (1:18; 5:6).

13:4 worshiped the dragon ... and ... the beast. Likely refers to idolatrous emperor worship, which John holds to be satanic (see notes on 2:12,13). **Who is like the beast?** Parodies OT confessions of the Lord's incomparability (Exod 15:11; Ps 113:5). **Who can wage war against it?** Ironically recalls 12:7–8, where Michael and the angels overpower the dragon.

13:5 utter proud words and blasphemies ... forty-two months. Recalls Daniel's prophecy of the king who "will speak against the Most High and oppress his holy people" for "a time, times and half a time" (Dan 7:25), equivalent to 42 months (see note on 11:2).

13:6 dwelling place. Likely refers not to a physical temple but to God's people "who live in heaven" (11:1; 21:3).

13:7 given power. Implies that the beast's ultimate opposition to God's people is under God's sovereign control. **wage war ... conquer.** Alludes to Dan 7:21; see note on 11:7. **every tribe, people, language and nation.** Recalls the universal idolatrous worship directed toward Nebuchadnezzar's golden image (Dan 3:7) and contrasts with the multiethnic heavenly worship of God and the Lamb (5:9; 7:9; cf. Dan 7:14).

13:8 book of life. See note on 3:5. **slain from the creation of the world.** Jesus' redemptive death is God's original plan (1 Pet 1:19–20). See NIV text note for an alternative reading.

13:9 hear. See note on 2:7.

13:10 captivity ... sword. OT punishments on unfaithful Israel (Jer 15:2; 43:11; cf. Lev 26:25; Deut 28:41), here suffered by faithful believers who are called to "patient endurance and faithfulness." See note on 1:9; cf. 14:12.

The Beast out of the Earth

11 Then I saw a second beast, coming out of the earth. It had two horns like a lamb, but it spoke like a dragon. 12 It exercised all the authority[u] of the first beast on its behalf,[v] and made the earth and its inhabitants worship the first beast,[w] whose fatal wound had been healed.[x] 13 And it performed great signs,[y] even causing fire to come down from heaven[z] to the earth in full view of the people. 14 Because of the signs[a] it was given power to perform on behalf of the first beast, it deceived[b] the inhabitants of the earth. It ordered them to set up an image in honor of the beast who was wounded by the sword and yet lived. 15 The second beast was given power to give breath to the image of the first beast, so that the image could speak and cause all who refused to worship the image to be killed.[c] 16 It also forced all people, great and small,[d] rich and poor, free and slave, to receive a mark on their right hands or on their foreheads,[e] 17 so that they could not buy or sell unless they had the mark,[f] which is the name of the beast or the number of its name.[g]

18 This calls for wisdom.[h] Let the person who has insight calculate the number of the beast, for it is the number of a man.[a][i] That number is 666.

The Lamb and the 144,000

14 Then I looked, and there before me was the Lamb,[j] standing on Mount Zion,[k] and with him 144,000[l] who had his name and his Father's name[m] written on their foreheads. 2 And I heard a sound from heaven like the roar of rushing waters[n] and like a loud peal of thunder. The sound I heard

[a] 18 Or *is humanity's number*

13:12 [u] ver 4 [v] ver 14 [w] Rev 14:9,11 [x] ver 3
13:13 [y] Mt 24:24 [z] 1Ki 18:38; Rev 20:9
13:14 [a] 2Th 2:9,10 [b] Rev 12:9
13:15 [c] Da 3:3-6
13:16 [d] Rev 19:5 [e] Rev 14:9
13:17 [f] Rev 14:9 [g] Rev 14:11; 15:2
13:18 [h] Rev 17:9 [i] Rev 15:2; 21:17
14:1 [j] Rev 5:6 [k] Ps 2:6 [l] Rev 7:4 [m] Rev 3:12
14:2 [n] Rev 1:15

13:11–18 *The Beast out of the Earth.* A second beast, called the false prophet in 16:13, joins with the first beast and the dragon to form an idolatrous counterfeit of the divine Trinity (cf. 1:4–5). Some futurists identify this beast as a future religious leader who complements an antichrist political leader. Some preterists associate the false prophet with the priests who promoted emperor worship in the seven cities of Asia Minor to which John writes (chs. 2–3).
13:11 second beast. Recalls the beast from the sea (v. 1; Dan 7:2–3), though it is "coming out of the earth" like the "four kings" in Dan 7:17. Later the second beast is called "the false prophet," joining the dragon and beast to form a false trinity (16:13; 20:10). **lamb ... dragon.** Diabolical imitation of Jesus the Lamb (5:6); recalls the evil ruler ("ram") in Dan 8:3 and Jesus' warning against false prophets in Matt 7:15.
13:12 authority. From the first beast, who receives authority from the dragon (v. 2). **worship the first beast.** Cf. v. 4. Likely reflects the public displays of worship and loyalty to the Roman emperor expected in Asian Minor (see Introduction: Date).
13:13 great signs. Deceptive works typical of false teachers and prophets (Exod 7:11; Deut 13:1–3; Matt 24:24; 2 Cor 11:13–15; 2 Thess 2:9). **fire.** Recalls Elijah (1 Kgs 18:38; 2 Kgs 1:10); ironically anticipates God's judgment on Satan's army (20:9).
13:14 image. Recalls the massive gold image that Nebuchadnezzar erected in Babylon (Dan 3:1) and the numerous shrines honoring Roman emperors in John's day. A prominent temple at Ephesus featured a statue of the emperor probably 16–23 feet (5–7 meters) high.
13:15 refused to worship ... killed. Recalls Nebuchadnezzar's decree (Dan 3:4–6) and persecution of Jews under Antiochus IV Epiphanes (167–164 BC). Pliny the Younger wrote to the emperor Trajan (AD 98–117) that people charged with being Christians were summoned under threat of execution to pray to Roman gods, make offerings to the emperor's statue, and revile Christ's name.
13:16 mark. Demonstrates absolute loyalty and perhaps ownership. There is no neutrality: one has either the beast's mark or God's seal (7:3–4; 14:1). It may reflect the ancient practice of branding or tattooing disobedient slaves, soldiers, and loyal adherents to certain pagan cults.
13:17 not buy or sell. Economics and religion were closely intertwined in first-century Asia Minor (Acts 19:23–27), and Christians faced economic pressure to show loyalty to Rome and participate in local trade guilds (see 2:9 and note). **mark ... name of the beast.** Contrasts with believers who have God's name written on their foreheads (14:1; 22:4).
13:18 wisdom. True spiritual understanding allows one to understand the beast's falsehood and resist its deception. Cf. 17:9. **666.** Throughout church history, this enigmatic number has generated countless interpretations and speculations. The number 666 may signify the deficiency of creatures or the false trinity of the devil, beast, and false prophet in contrast to divine completeness symbolized by sevens (see Introduction: Sevens in Revelation). Alternatively, many interpreters appeal to the ancient practice of gematria, a system which assigns letters numerical values. The reference could be to "Nero Caesar," whose name if written in Hebrew characters adds up to 666.
14:1–5 *The Lamb and the 144,000.* This vision highlights the moral purity and spiritual protection of believers redeemed by the Lamb (cf. 7:1–14) and contrasts with the previous vision of the suffering and struggle of God's people (13:1–18).
14:1 Lamb. Jesus. **Mount Zion.** Heavenly Jerusalem (cf. 21:22–26; Ps 2:6; Heb 12:22). **144,000.** Recalls 7:4 (see note there). It may refer to (1) martyrs, (2) believers in the final tribulation, or, more likely, (3) the totality of God's redeemed people (cf. Jer 2:3; Jas 1:18), whom Jesus separates from the unredeemed in the last harvest (vv. 14–20; Matt 13:36–43). **his name ... on their foreheads.** Believers are marked as God's possession and given a new identity and security in Christ (cf. 3:12; 7:3; 22:4); contrasts with the mark of the beast (13:16–17).
14:2 rushing waters ... thunder. Deafening, joyful praise by the heavenly multitude (19:6). **harpists.** See note on 5:8; cf. 15:2.

Massive Roman emperor statue found at Ephesian temple. Only a head and arm were found, but the entire statue was probably 16–23 feet (5–7 meters) high.
Kim Walton, taken at the Ephesus Museum

14:2 [o]Rev 5:8
14:3 [p]Rev 5:9 [q]ver 1
14:4 [r]2Co 11:2; Rev 3:4 [s]Rev 5:9 [t]Jas 1:18
14:5 [u]Ps 32:2; Zep 3:13 [v]Eph 5:27
14:6 [w]Rev 8:13 [x]Rev 3:10 [y]Rev 13:7
14:7 [z]Rev 15:4 [a]Rev 11:13 [b]Rev 8:10
14:8 [c]Isa 21:9; Jer 51:8 [d]Rev 17:2,4; 18:3,9
14:9 [e]Rev 13:14
14:10 [f]Isa 51:17; Jer 25:15 [g]Rev 18:6
14:11 [h]Isa 34:10; Rev 19:3
14:12 [i]Rev 13:10
14:13 [j]1Co 15:18; 1Th 4:16
14:14 [k]Da 7:13; Rev 1:13 [l]Rev 6:2

was like that of harpists playing their harps.[o] 3And they sang a new song[p] before the throne and before
the four living creatures and the elders. No one could learn the song except the 144,000[q] who had been
redeemed from the earth. 4These are those who did not defile themselves with women, for they remained virgins.[r] They follow the Lamb wherever he goes. They were purchased from among mankind[s]
and offered as firstfruits[t] to God and the Lamb. 5No lie was found in their mouths;[u] they are blameless.[v]

The Three Angels

6Then I saw another angel flying in midair,[w] and he had the eternal gospel to proclaim to those who
live on the earth[x] — to every nation, tribe, language and people.[y] 7He said in a loud voice, "Fear God[z]
and give him glory,[a] because the hour of his judgment has come. Worship him who made the heavens,
the earth, the sea and the springs of water."[b]
8A second angel followed and said, " 'Fallen! Fallen is Babylon the Great,'[ac] which made all the nations drink the maddening wine of her adulteries."[d]
9A third angel followed them and said in a loud voice: "If anyone worships the beast and its image[e]
and receives its mark on their forehead or on their hand, 10they, too, will drink the wine of God's fury,[f]
which has been poured full strength into the cup of his wrath.[g] They will be tormented with burning
sulfur in the presence of the holy angels and of the Lamb. 11And the smoke of their torment will rise for
ever and ever.[h] There will be no rest day or night for those who worship the beast and its image, or for
anyone who receives the mark of its name." 12This calls for patient endurance on the part of the people
of God[i] who keep his commands and remain faithful to Jesus.
13Then I heard a voice from heaven say, "Write this: Blessed are the dead who die in the Lord[j] from now on."
"Yes," says the Spirit, "they will rest from their labor, for their deeds will follow them."

Harvesting the Earth and Trampling the Winepress

14I looked, and there before me was a white cloud, and seated on the cloud was one like a son of
man[bk] with a crown[l] of gold on his head and a sharp sickle in his hand. 15Then another angel came

[a] *8* Isaiah 21:9 [b] *14* See Daniel 7:13.

14:3 new song. See note on 5:9. **living creatures.** See notes on 4:6–8. **elders.** See note on 4:4. **redeemed.** Translated "purchased" in v. 4; 5:9.
14:4 those who did not defile themselves ... virgins. Signifies spiritual, ritual, and moral purity of faithful believers (cf. 3:4). Combines two images: Israel's holy and chaste warriors (1 Sam 21:5; cf. 19:14) and the church as Christ's pure bride (19:7–8; 2 Cor 11:2; Eph 5:27). **follow the Lamb.** Recalls Jesus' teaching that disciples must adhere to his teaching and example, which entails endurance of suffering and hostility (Mark 8:34–36; John 10:3–4; 1 Pet 2:21). **firstfruits.** Initial crops that were offered to God in anticipation of the full harvest (Exod 23:19; Lev 23:9–14). Firstfruits language is applied metaphorically to initial converts in a region (the Greek word for "firstfruits" is translated "first convert" in Rom 16:5 and "first converts" in 1 Cor 16:15), to Jesus' resurrection (1 Cor 15:20,23), and to believers' present experience of the Spirit (Rom 8:23).
14:5 No lie. Ethical blamelessness; alludes to Zeph 3:13; cf. Isa 53:9.
14:6–13 *The Three Angels.* Three angels proclaim the hour of divine judgment, Babylon's fall, and the unceasing torment of the beast's worshipers, which contrast with the blessing and glorious rest that awaits those who remain faithful to Jesus.
14:6 eternal gospel. Proclamation of God's eternal purpose concerning judgment and salvation; explained in v. 7. **every nation, tribe, language and people.** See notes on 5:9; 13:7.
14:7 Fear God and give him glory. Cf. 15:4. **Worship.** True praise to the sovereign Creator, who executes righteous judgment; contrasts with false worship of the beast (v. 11; 13:8,12,15).
14:8 Fallen! Fallen is Babylon the Great. Initial announcement of Babylon's divine judgment (cf. 16:19; 17:5; 18:2); alludes to Isa 21:9. Babylon was the arch-oppressor of God's people, destroying Solomon's temple and taking Israel into exile (2 Kgs 25:1–28; Dan 1:1–2). Babylon, or "Babel" (see NIV text note on Gen 11:9), was the site of ancient humanity's proud idolatry that led to confusing languages and scattering peoples (Gen 11:1–9). For John's first readers, "Babylon the Great" likely represented Rome, which like ancient Babylon, destroyed the Jerusalem temple, persecuted God's people (17:6), and engaged in flagrant idolatry and immorality (17:4–5). Some interpreters argue that Babylon refers to the state-sponsored, economic-religious system in the final generation. But Babylon may more generally symbolize the world's idolatrous, seductive, political economy, the archetypal pagan city, which Rome embodied in the first century. See Introduction: Interpreting Symbolism. **maddening wine.** Symbolizes Babylon's deceptive economic, political, and religious influence over the nations (cf. 17:2; 18:3; Jer 51:7).
14:9 worships the beast ... receives its mark. See 13:12,16 and notes.
14:10 wine of God's fury. The final unleashing of divine wrath on Babylon and the wicked (cf. 16:19; Ps 75:8; Jer 25:15; 51:7). **tormented with burning sulfur.** The wicked share the eternal destiny of the devil, beast, and false prophet (20:10; cf. Ps 11:6); recalls Sodom's destruction (Gen 19:24; Luke 17:29).
14:11 smoke ... for ever. Alludes to Isa 34:10 (of Edom); cf. 19:3 (of Babylon). **no rest.** Idolaters' unending anguish contrasts with the ceaseless praise in heaven (4:8).
14:12 patient endurance. See note on 1:9; cf. 13:10.
14:13 Write. See note on 1:11. **Blessed.** Revelation's second promise of blessing to faithful believers (see note on 1:3). **die in the Lord.** Cf. 1 Thess 4:16. **says the Spirit.** The one who addresses the churches (2:7) and inspires prophecy (19:10) here speaks directly (22:17), confirming the exhortation and promise in vv. 12–13. **they will rest.** The martyrs "wait a little longer" (6:11) before entering the eternal "Sabbath-rest" for God's people (Heb 4:9–10).
14:14–20 *Harvesting the Earth and Trampling the Winepress.* John sees

out of the temple and called in a loud voice to him who was sitting on the cloud, "Take your sickle[m] and
reap, because the time to reap has come, for the harvest[n] of the earth is ripe." 16 So he who was seated
on the cloud swung his sickle over the earth, and the earth was harvested.
17 Another angel came out of the temple in heaven, and he too had a sharp sickle. 18 Still another
angel, who had charge of the fire, came from the altar and called in a loud voice to him who had the
sharp sickle, "Take your sharp sickle and gather the clusters of grapes from the earth's vine, because
its grapes are ripe." 19 The angel swung his sickle on the earth, gathered its grapes and threw them into
the great winepress of God's wrath.[o] 20 They were trampled in the winepress[p] outside the city,[q] and blood
flowed out of the press, rising as high as the horses' bridles for a distance of 1,600 stadia.[a]

14:15 [m]Joel 3:13 [n]Jer 51:33
14:19 [o]Rev 19:15
14:20 [p]Isa 63:3 [q]Heb 13:12; Rev 11:8
15:1 [r]Rev 12:1,3 [s]Rev 16:1 [t]Lev 26:21
15:2 [u]Rev 4:6 [v]Rev 13:14
15:3 [w]Ex 15:1; Dt 32:4 [x]Ps 111:2 [y]Ps 145:17
15:4 [z]Jer 10:7 [a]Isa 66:23

Seven Angels With Seven Plagues

15 I saw in heaven another great and marvelous sign:[r] seven angels[s] with the seven last
plagues[t]—last, because with them God's wrath is completed. 2 And I saw what looked like
a sea of glass[u] glowing with fire and, standing beside the sea, those who had been victorious over the
beast and its image[v] and over the number of its name. They held harps given them by God 3 and sang
the song of God's servant Moses[w] and of the Lamb:

"Great and marvelous are your deeds,[x]
 Lord God Almighty.
Just and true are your ways,[y]
 King of the nations.[b]
4 Who will not fear you, Lord,[z]
 and bring glory to your name?
For you alone are holy.
All nations will come
 and worship before you,[a]
for your righteous acts have been revealed."[c]

[a] *20* That is, about 180 miles or about 300 kilometers [b] *3* Some manuscripts *ages* [c] *3,4* Phrases in this song are drawn from Psalm 111:2,3; Deut. 32:4; Jer. 10:7; Psalms 86:9; 98:2.

Jesus, the exalted Son of Man, and an angel from God's temple holding sharp sickles for the end-time harvest (cf. Joel 3:11–13). Verses 14–16 probably depict the gathering of God's people by Jesus (cf. v. 4), while vv. 17–20 describe the terrible judgment of the wicked.

14:14 cloud ... son of man. Alludes to Dan 7:13; Matt 24:30; 26:64; see notes on 1:7,13. The risen Jesus sits enthroned as heavenly king and judge. **crown of gold.** Symbolizes Jesus' end-time victory and regal authority (cf. 19:11–16; see notes on 2:10; 4:4). **sickle.** Represents God's judgment in the last harvest (cf. Joel 3:11–13; Mark 4:26–29).

14:15 the harvest of the earth is ripe. Many scholars interpret this harvest as divine judgment on the wicked as in vv. 18–19 and Joel 3:13, though this harvest may refer to the gathering of God's people, called "firstfruits" in v. 4 (see note there) and "the wheat" in Matt 13:30.

14:17 The second harvest (cf. vv. 14–16), to gather and crush grapes in the winepress (v. 18).

14:18 fire ... altar. Recalls 8:3,5.

14:19 winepress. In the ancient world, grapes were placed in troughs and trampled before collecting juice for fermentation, a vivid OT image for God's crushing the wicked nations in furious "wrath" (cf. 19:15; Isa 63:1–6).

14:20 outside the city. Probably Jerusalem, the site of the final end-time battle (Zech 14:1–4; cf. 20:9); recalls Jesus' suffering "outside the city gate" (Heb 13:12). Cf. "the holy city" (11:2) and "the great city" (11:8). Everything impure, shameful, and deceitful is kept "outside" the new Jerusalem (21:27; 22:15). **1,600 stadia.** See NIV text note; approximately the length of the Holy Land from north to south and the square of 40, symbolizing complete, worldwide judgment.

15:1—16:21 *The Seven Bowls.* Seven angels pour out a final series of judgments on the earth's inhabitants, which recall and consummate the earlier seals (6:1–17) and trumpets (8:6—11:19). The "seven last plagues" (15:1) or "bowls of God's wrath" (16:1) demonstrate God's justice in punishing unrepentant humanity (16:9–11,21) and vindicating his persecuted people (16:6).

15:1–8 *Seven Angels With Seven Plagues.* Verses 2–4 conclude ch. 14's focus on God's vindicating his people; vv. 1,5–8 introduce the angels authorized to carry out the final series of judgments in ch. 16.

15:1 another ... sign. Recalls 12:1,3. **seven angels.** Responsible for carrying out the bowl judgments (v. 6; 16:1; cf. 8:6). **seven last plagues.** Introduces the bowl judgments in 16:1–21; cf. 21:9). **God's wrath is completed.** See notes on 6:16,17; cf. 14:10; 16:1.

15:2–3 held harps ... sang. Recalls the 144,000 (14:2–3) and the 24 elders (5:8–9).

15:2 sea of glass. From God's throne room (4:6). **those who had been victorious.** See note on 12:11.

15:3–4 Alludes to Jer 10:7 (cf. Exod 15:14,18), which celebrates God's uniqueness as powerful Creator and eternal King (Jer 10:10,12) in contrast to the nations' worthless idols (Jer 10:8–9,11).

15:3 song of ... Moses and of the Lamb. Celebrates God's salvation of Israel at the exodus (Exod 15:1–18; cf. Deut 31:30—32:43) and the new-exodus redemption of people from all nations accomplished by the blood of the Lamb (5:9). **deeds.** God's glorious acts of salvation and judgment, reflected particularly in the exodus (Exod 15:11; cf. Ps 111:2–4). **Just and true are your ways.** Recalls Moses' song in Deut 32:4.

15:4 holy. Cf. 4:8. **All nations will come and worship.** Alludes to Ps 86:9. The Almighty, not the beast, is the true sovereign who will duly receive worldwide worship (cf. 7:9–10; contrast 13:8,14).

15:5 [b]Rev 11:19 [c]Nu 1:50
15:6 [d]Rev 14:15 [e]ver 1 [f]Rev 1:13
15:7 [g]Rev 4:6
15:8 [h]Isa 6:4 [i]Ex 40:34, 35; 1Ki 8:10,11; 2Ch 5:13,14
16:1 [j]Rev 15:1
16:2 [k]Rev 8:7 [l]Ex 9:9-11 [m]Rev 13:15-17
16:3 [n]Ex 7:17-21; Rev 8:8,9
16:4 [o]Rev 8:10 [p]Ex 7:17-21
16:5 [q]Rev 15:3 [r]Rev 15:4 [s]Rev 1:4
16:6 [t]Isa 49:26; Rev 17:6
16:7 [u]Rev 6:9 [v]Rev 15:3; 19:2
16:8 [w]Rev 8:12 [x]Rev 14:18
16:9 [y]ver 11,21 [z]Rev 2:21 [a]Rev 11:13
16:10 [b]Rev 13:2

5After this I looked, and I saw in heaven the temple[b]—that is, the tabernacle of the covenant
law[c]—and it was opened. 6Out of the temple[d] came the seven angels with the seven plagues.[e]
They were dressed in clean, shining linen and wore golden sashes around their chests.[f] 7Then one
of the four living creatures[g] gave to the seven angels seven golden bowls filled with the wrath of
God, who lives for ever and ever. 8And the temple was filled with smoke[h] from the glory of God and
from his power, and no one could enter the temple[i] until the seven plagues of the seven angels were
completed.

The Seven Bowls of God's Wrath

16 Then I heard a loud voice from the temple saying to the seven angels,[j] "Go, pour out the seven
bowls of God's wrath on the earth."

2The first angel went and poured out his bowl on the land,[k] and ugly, festering sores[l] broke out on
the people who had the mark of the beast and worshiped its image.[m]
3The second angel poured out his bowl on the sea, and it turned into blood like that of a dead person,
and every living thing in the sea died.[n]
4The third angel poured out his bowl on the rivers and springs of water,[o] and they became blood.[p]
5Then I heard the angel in charge of the waters say:

"You are just in these judgments,[q] O Holy One,[r]
you who are and who were;[s]
6for they have shed the blood of your holy people and your prophets,
and you have given them blood to drink[t] as they deserve."

7And I heard the altar[u] respond:

"Yes, Lord God Almighty,
true and just are your judgments."[v]

8The fourth angel[w] poured out his bowl on the sun, and the sun was allowed to scorch people with
fire.[x] 9They were seared by the intense heat and they cursed the name of God,[y] who had control over
these plagues, but they refused to repent[z] and glorify him.[a]
10The fifth angel poured out his bowl on the throne of the beast,[b] and its kingdom was plunged into

15:5 temple ... opened. See note on 11:19.
15:6 seven angels. Introduced in v. 1; they pour out God's wrath on the earth in ch. 16. **clean, shining linen.** Suggests priestly duties (cf. Lev 16:4; Dan 10:5). **golden sashes.** Resemble the Son of Man's attire (1:13; cf. Dan 10:5).
15:7 living creatures. See notes on 4:6–8. **golden bowls ... wrath of God.** Recalls the bowls that hold the prayers of God's people who cry out for vindication (see note on 5:8; cf. 6:9–10; 8:3–5).
15:8 smoke. Symbolizes God's glorious presence in his sanctuary (Exod 40:34–35; 1 Kgs 8:10–11; Isa 6:1,4).
16:1–21 *The Seven Bowls of God's Wrath.* The bowl judgments parallel the seven trumpets (8:6—11:19) and may recall the plagues on Egypt at the exodus (see "Parallels Between Bowls, Trumpets, and Exodus Plagues," p. 2613). This final series of judgments totally destroys those who conspire against God with the dragon, beast, and false prophet.
16:1 seven angels. See note on 15:1. **bowls.** See note on 15:7.
16:2 on the land. Parallels v. 1; 8:5 ("on the earth"). **sores.** May recall the sixth Egyptian plague (Exod 9:8–12) and covenant curses against Israel (Deut 28:27,35). **mark.** See note on 13:16.
16:3 on the sea. Cf. 8:8. **blood.** Parallels the second trumpet (8:8–9); may recall the first plague (Exod 7:20–21). **every living thing ... died.** Total destruction contrasts with 8:9 ("a third ... died").
16:4 rivers ... springs. Recalls the third trumpet (8:10). **blood.** Cf. vv. 3,6.
16:5 judgments. Demonstrate God's justice and holiness and motivate heavenly worship (cf. 15:3–4; 19:1–2). **you who are ... were.** See note on 11:17.
16:6 for. Introduces the reason God's judgments are just (vv. 5,7) and recalls the martyrs' appeals for God to judge persecutors and avenge their blood (6:10; cf. 18:20; 19:2; Deut 32:43; 2 Kgs 9:7; Ps 79:10,12; Isa 49:26).
16:7 true and just. Cf. 15:3; 19:2.
16:8 sun. Recalls the fourth trumpet (8:12). **allowed to scorch.** Contrast 7:16, where God promises to protect the redeemed from the sun's "scorching heat" (cf. Ps 121:6; Isa 49:10). **fire.** Recalls 9:17–18; the same judgment that befalls Babylon (17:16; 18:8).
16:9 cursed. Cf. vv. 11,21; translated "blaspheme" in 13:6. The unredeemed respond to divine judgment by participating in the beast's blasphemy and slander, while the angels and redeemed praise God for his justice (vv. 5–7; 15:3–4). **control over these plagues.** God is completely sovereign in judgment and salvation (cf. 12:10). **refused to repent.** Cf. v. 11. See note on 9:20.
16:10 poured out his bowl on the throne of the beast. Directly judges the beast's sovereignty. Recalls 13:2 ("the dragon gave the beast ... his throne") and parallels 2:13 (Satan's throne). **darkness.** Recalls the fifth trumpet (9:2) and the ninth plague (Exod 10:21–23). Darkness accompanies the day of the Lord (Joel 2:1–2; Amos 5:20; Matt 24:29; see note on Amos 2:16) and characterizes the eternal judgment of the wicked (Matt 8:12; 25:30; 2 Pet 2:17). **agony.** Cf. Luke 16:24.

darkness.[c] People gnawed their tongues in agony 11and cursed[d] the God of heaven[e] because of their
pains and their sores,[f] but they refused to repent of what they had done.[g]
12The sixth angel poured out his bowl on the great river Euphrates,[h] and its water was dried up to
prepare the way for the kings from the East.[i] 13Then I saw three impure spirits that looked like frogs;
they came out of the mouth of the dragon,[j] out of the mouth of the beast[k] and out of the mouth of the
false prophet.[l] 14They are demonic spirits[m] that perform signs, and they go out to the kings of the whole
world, to gather them for the battle[n] on the great day of God Almighty.

15"Look, I come like a thief! Blessed is the one who stays awake[o] and remains clothed, so as not
to go naked and be shamefully exposed."

16Then they gathered the kings together to the place that in Hebrew[p] is called Armageddon.[q]

16:10 [c] Rev 9:2
16:11 [d] ver 9,21 [e] Rev 11:13 [f] ver 2 [g] Rev 2:21
16:12 [h] Rev 9:14 [i] Isa 41:2
16:13 [j] Rev 12:3 [k] Rev 13:1 [l] Rev 19:20
16:14 [m] 1Ti 4:1 [n] Rev 17:14
16:15 [o] Lk 12:37
16:16 [p] Rev 9:11 [q] 2Ki 23:29,30

16:11 cursed the God of heaven. Divine judgments further harden the beast's followers in their hostility toward God (cf. v. 9).
16:12 sixth angel poured out his bowl. A summary statement explained in vv. 13–14,16. **Euphrates.** See note on 9:14. **water ... dried up.** Recalls God's promises to judge Babylon and restore his people (Isa 11:15; 44:27–28; Jer 50:38; 51:36). **kings from the East.** May symbolize Israel's ancient enemies from the north and east (Assyria and Babylon) or refer to the feared Parthians east of the Roman Empire (cf. Acts 2:9).
16:13 impure ... frogs. Frogs are unclean creatures (Lev 11:9–11), always associated in Scripture with the destructive judgment on Egypt (Exod 8:2–13; Pss 78:45; 105:30). **dragon ... beast ... false prophet.** The false trinity, the great opponents of God's people and the Lamb (see note on 13:11). "False prophet" specifies the identity and activity of the "second beast" of 13:11–17. God's people are repeatedly warned of prophets who are not authorized by God yet promote false teaching and deceptive prophecies among the covenant community (Deut 13:1–2; Jer 14:14; Lam 2:14; Matt 7:15; 2 Pet 2:1; 1 John 4:1–3). Jesus rebukes the churches in Pergamum and Thyatira for tolerating false teachers and prophets (2:14–15,20).
16:14 demonic spirits ... signs. Cf. 13:13–14; 19:20. Recalls the counterfeit signs by Pharaoh's magicians (Exod 8:7), as well as Jesus' warning concerning the "great signs and wonders" by false messiahs and prophets (Matt 24:24). **kings of the whole world.** Includes "the kings from the East" (v. 12) and all earthly political authorities (cf. 19:18–19) who participate in false worship, immorality, and persecution of God's people (v. 6; 17:2; 18:3). Those who do not acknowledge Jesus as the preeminent ruler (cf. 1:5; 17:14) will incur his wrath (vv. 15–17; cf. Ps 2:10–12). **gather them for the battle.** The purpose of the false trinity's deception: assemble an army to war against God's forces (cf. v. 16; 19:19; 20:8) as in the earlier war in heaven (12:7–9). **great day.** See note on 6:17.
16:15 Look, I come like a thief! Christ interjects to urge believers to remain spiritually vigilant in view of his second coming (cf. 3:3). **Blessed.** Third promise of blessing to faithful believers (see note on 1:3). **awake ... clothed.** Recalls Jesus' rebukes of Sardis (3:2–3) and Laodicea (3:17–18) for their spiritual complacency and danger.
16:16 they gathered. Resumes the narration from v. 14; recalls Ps 2:2. **Armageddon.** "Mount Megiddo" in Hebrew. Megiddo, also called the Plain of Megiddo (2 Chr 35:22; Zech 12:11), was an ancient city that Solomon fortified (1 Kgs 9:15). Megiddo was strategically located along the main highway from Egypt to Syria in the Jezreel Valley and was the site of key battles (Judg 5:19–21; 2 Kgs 23:29). Some read this as a literal reference to the site of the final battle, while others interpret Armageddon as a symbol of the final conflict between God and the forces of evil.

PARALLELS BETWEEN BOWLS, TRUMPETS, AND EXODUS PLAGUES

BOWLS	TRUMPETS	EXODUS PLAGUES
1st Bowl (16:2): on land (Greek *gē*); festering sores	**1st Trumpet** (8:7): on earth (Greek *gē*); third of land burned up	**6th Plague** (Exod 9:8–12): dust over land; festering boils
2nd Bowl (16:3): on sea; sea to blood; all sea creatures die	**2nd Trumpet** (8:8–9): on sea; sea to blood; third of sea creatures die	**1st Plague** (Exod 7:20–21): Nile to blood; fish die
3rd Bowl (16:4): on rivers and springs; blood	**3rd Trumpet** (8:10–11): on rivers and springs; turn bitter	**1st Plague** (Exod 7:20–21): Nile to blood
4th Bowl (16:8–9): on sun; people scorched	**4th Trumpet** (8:12): on sun, moon, and stars; third of sun, moon, and stars turn dark	**9th Plague** (Exod 10:21–23): darkness
5th Bowl (16:10–11): on the throne of the beast; darkness; people in *agony*	**5th Trumpet** (9:1–11): the Abyss opened; darkness; locusts *torment* people	**8th and 9th Plagues** (Exod 10:12–15,21–23): locusts; darkness
6th Bowl (16:12–14): on Euphrates; river dried up; deceptive demonic spirits like frogs	**6th Trumpet** (9:13–21): four angels released at the Euphrates; third of people killed	**2nd Plague** (Exod 8:2–7): frogs from the Nile River; magicians' secret arts
7th Bowl (16:17–21): into the air; lightning, rumblings, thunder, severe earthquake, huge hailstones	**7th Trumpet** (11:15–19): lightning, rumblings, thunder, earthquake, severe hailstorm	**7th Plague** (Exod 9:22–25): thunder, hail, lightning

EUPHRATES RIVER

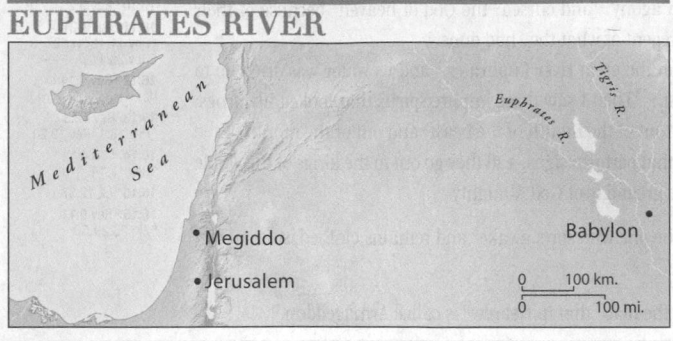

17 The seventh angel poured out
his bowl into the air,[r] and out of the
temple[s] came a loud voice[t] from the
throne, saying, "It is done!"[u] 18 Then
there came flashes of lightning, rumblings, peals of thunder[v] and a severe
earthquake.[w] No earthquake like it
has ever occurred since mankind has
been on earth,[x] so tremendous was the
quake. 19 The great city[y] split into three
parts, and the cities of the nations collapsed. God remembered[z] Babylon the
Great[a] and gave her the cup filled with
the wine of the fury of his wrath.[b] 20 Every island fled away and the mountains could not be found.[c]
21 From the sky huge hailstones,[d] each weighing about a hundred pounds,[a] fell on people. And they
cursed God on account of the plague of hail,[e] because the plague was so terrible.

Babylon, the Prostitute on the Beast

17 One of the seven angels[f] who had the seven bowls[g] came and said to me, "Come, I will show
you the punishment[h] of the great prostitute,[i] who sits by many waters.[j] 2 With her the kings of
the earth committed adultery, and the inhabitants of the earth were intoxicated with the wine of her
adulteries."[k]
3 Then the angel carried me away in the Spirit into a wilderness.[l] There I saw a woman sitting on a
scarlet beast that was covered with blasphemous names[m] and had seven heads and ten horns.[n] 4 The
woman was dressed in purple and scarlet, and was glittering with gold, precious stones and pearls.[o]
She held a golden cup[p] in her hand, filled with abominable things and the filth of her adulteries. 5 The
name written on her forehead was a mystery:

[a] *21* Or about 45 kilograms

16:17 [r] Eph 2:2 [s] Rev 14:15 [t] Rev 11:15 [u] Rev 21:6
16:18 [v] Rev 4:5 [w] Rev 6:12 [x] Da 12:1
16:19 [y] Rev 17:18 [z] Rev 18:5 [a] Rev 14:8 [b] Rev 14:10
16:20 [c] Rev 6:14
16:21 [d] Rev 11:19 [e] Ex 9:23-25
17:1 [f] Rev 15:1 [g] Rev 21:9 [h] Rev 16:19 [i] Rev 19:2 [j] Jer 51:13
17:2 [k] Rev 14:8; 18:3
17:3 [l] Rev 12:6,14 [m] Rev 13:1 [n] Rev 12:3
17:4 [o] Rev 18:16 [p] Jer 51:7; Rev 18:6

16:17 It is done! Repeated in 21:6. God has accomplished his plan (10:7), established his kingdom (11:15), and completed his wrath (15:1,8).
16:18 lightning ... thunder. See note on 8:5 (cf. 11:19). **No earthquake like it.** Unprecedented catastrophe; recalls 6:12–14.
16:19 great city. "Babylon the Great" symbolizes proud, idolatrous human civilization opposed to God, which Rome embodied for Revelation's first readers (17:18; 18:21; see note on 14:8). **split into three parts.** Explains the effects of the earthquake in v. 18. **cities ... collapsed.** The final judgment levels all the political, economic, and social centers that Babylon's idolatry corrupted. **cup ... wrath.** See note on 14:10.
16:20 Parallels 6:14; 20:11. Conclusively destroying the world prepares for the new heaven and new earth (21:1).
16:21 huge hailstones ... fell on people. Recalls and intensifies the earlier trumpet judgments (8:7; 11:19; cf. Exod 9:22–25; Josh 10:11). **cursed.** See note on v. 9.
17:1—19:10 *Destruction of Babylon, the Prostitute.* John receives a vision of Babylon's demise (cf. 14:8–10; 16:19), which prompts earthly lamentation (18:9–19) and heavenly rejoicing (18:20; 19:1–10). Babylon, the "great prostitute" (17:1) and "great city" (17:18), contrasts with the new Jerusalem, the bride of Christ (see "A Tale of Two Cities in Revelation," p. 2615). Interpreters have variously identified Babylon as Rome, the Roman Catholic Church, or the dominant state-sponsored, economic-religious system throughout the ages or in the final generation. John's first readers likely understood Babylon as representing Rome, though this interpretation may be combined with some amillennial or futurist readings (see Introduction: Interpreting Symbolism; see also note on 14:8).
17:1–18 *Babylon, the Prostitute on the Beast.* One of the angels involved in the previous bowl judgments now shows John a vision of Babylon's punishment, which expands upon the seventh bowl (especially 16:19). After being transported "in the Spirit" (v. 3; cf. 1:10), John beholds the prostitute's opulence and abominations (vv. 3–6), then he receives the heavenly interpretation of this symbolic vision (vv. 7–18). For an explanation of Babylon, see note on 14:8.
17:1 angels ... bowls. The agents of God's judgment in ch. 16; 21:9. **Come, I will show you the punishment of the great prostitute.** Introduces the theme of ch. 17 and contrasts with 21:9 ("Come, I will show you the bride"). Verse 18 interprets this prostitute as "the great city," which likely denotes Rome (cf. 11:18; 16:19). **many waters.** Alludes to Babylon's description in Jer 51:13; explained in v. 15 (see note there).
17:2 kings ... committed adultery. Repeated in 18:3,9. Signifies Babylon's corrupting influence, seducing the nations into idolatry and immorality, likely through the empty promise of political power and especially economic gain (cf. 18:2–19). **wine.** See note on 14:8.
17:3 in the Spirit. Introduces a new prophetic vision (1:10; 4:2; 21:10; see Introduction: Structure). **wilderness.** Connotes divine protection and provision in 12:6,14; here the wilderness is a solitary place of deprivation and hardship where John receives revelation about prosperous Babylon's future desolation (cf. 18:2; Isa 21:9). **woman.** The "great prostitute" (v. 1) and "the great city" (v. 18). **scarlet.** Represents wealth (see note on v. 4) and recalls the dragon's red color (12:3). **beast.** See note on 13:1. **ten horns.** See note on 13:1.
17:4 purple and scarlet ... gold, precious stones and pearls. Lavish clothing and jewelry symbolizing great power and wealth, which typified Rome's prosperous commerce (18:12,16). **golden cup.** Recalls Jer 51:7.
17:5 mystery. Interpreted in v. 7; see note on 1:20.

A TALE OF TWO CITIES IN REVELATION

BABYLON THE GREAT	THE NEW JERUSALEM
The great prostitute (17:1)	The wife of the Lamb (21:9)
The great city of earth (17:18)	The holy city from heaven (21:2,10)
Purple and scarlet clothing represents wealth (17:4)	White fine linen represents purity (19:8)
Sinful deeds (18:5–6)	Righteous deeds (19:8)
Gold, jewels, and pearls through corrupt commerce (17:4; 18:12,16)	Heavenly jewels, gold, and pearls reflect God's glory (21:11,18,21)
Kings commit immorality and weep (18:9)	Kings bring glory into the city (21:24)
A haunt for everything unclean (18:2)	Nothing unclean will enter (21:27)
The nations deceived (18:23)	The nations healed (22:2)
Woe and destruction (18:10)	Blessing and life (22:14)
Call to come out (18:4)	Call to enter (22:14)

BABYLON THE GREAT[q]
THE MOTHER OF PROSTITUTES
AND OF THE ABOMINATIONS OF THE EARTH.

6 I saw that the woman was drunk with the blood of God's holy people,[r] the blood of those who bore
testimony to Jesus.
When I saw her, I was greatly astonished. 7 Then the angel said to me: "Why are you astonished? I
will explain to you the mystery[s] of the woman and of the beast she rides, which has the seven heads and
ten horns.[t] 8 The beast, which you saw, once was, now is not, and yet will come up out of the Abyss and
go to its destruction.[u] The inhabitants of the earth[v] whose names have not been written in the book of
life[w] from the creation of the world will be astonished[x] when they see the beast, because it once was,
now is not, and yet will come.
9 "This calls for a mind with wisdom.[y] The seven heads are seven hills on which the woman sits.
10 They are also seven kings. Five have fallen, one is, the other has not yet come; but when he does come,
he must remain for only a little while. 11 The beast who once was, and now is not,[z] is an eighth king. He
belongs to the seven and is going to his destruction.
12 "The ten horns[a] you saw are ten kings who have not yet received a kingdom, but who for one
hour[b] will receive authority as kings along with the beast. 13 They have one purpose and will give their
power and authority to the beast.[c] 14 They will wage war[d] against the Lamb, but the Lamb will triumph

17:5 [q] Rev 14:8
17:6 [r] Rev 18:24
17:7 [s] ver 5 [t] ver 3
17:8 [u] Rev 13:10 [v] Rev 3:10 [w] Rev 13:8 [x] Rev 13:3
17:9 [y] Rev 13:18
17:11 [z] ver 8
17:12 [a] Rev 12:3 [b] Rev 18:10,17,19
17:13 [c] ver 17
17:14 [d] Rev 16:14

17:6 blood of God's holy people. Babylon persecutes those who oppose her idolatry, immorality, and luxury (cf. 6:9; 16:6; 18:24; 19:2). **greatly astonished.** Similar to Daniel's response to the revelation concerning the king of Babylon's humiliation (Dan 4:19).
17:7 The angel interprets John's symbolic vision of the woman (v. 18), the beast (vv. 8,11), and its heads and horns (vv. 9–10,12–14).
17:8 The beast, which you saw. Interprets John's vision of the scarlet beast (v. 3; cf. vv. 7,11). **was, now is not, and yet will come up.** Ironically echoes the description of God (1:4,8) and the Lamb (1:18; 2:8); recalls 13:3,12 where the beast's fatal wound is healed. **out of the Abyss.** Cf. 11:7; 13:1 (the sea). The beast's coming culminates in defeat and eternal "destruction" (cf. v. 11; 20:10). **book of life.** See note on 3:5.
17:9 wisdom. See note on 13:18. **seven heads.** Interprets John's vision in v. 3; see notes on 12:3; 13:1. **seven hills.** Explains "seven heads"; ancient writers like Pliny and Virgil commonly referred to Rome as the city on seven hills.
17:10 seven kings. May denote seven Roman emperors or world empires or the fullness of power that Rome or worldly kingdoms exercised. **one is.** The sixth king may refer to Nero (AD 54–68), Vespasian (AD 69–79), the Roman Empire, or the beast as the culmination of the world's kingdoms.
17:11 eighth king. Variously identified as a Roman emperor such as Nero or Domitian, a future antichrist, or a fuller embodiment of Satanic power. **destruction.** The same fate as the beast from the Abyss (v. 8).
17:12 ten horns ... ten kings. Interprets "the mystery" of the beast's horns in v. 7; alludes to Dan 7:24. May designate the ten provincial governors of Rome, Rome's client kings from conquered territories, or the symbolic power of "the kings of the earth" (v. 18; cf. 16:14). **one hour.** A very short time (Matt 20:12; 26:40); anticipates Babylon's ruin "in one hour" (18:10,17,19).
17:13 one purpose. See note on v. 17.
17:14 wage war ... the Lamb will triumph. Reverses 13:7 (cf. Dan 7:21–22). **King of kings.** A title sometimes used for earthly sovereigns (Ezra 7:12; Dan 2:37); applied ultimately to God and Jesus (cf. 19:16; Dan 2:47; 4:37; 1 Tim 6:15).

17:14 [e]1Ti 6:15; Rev 19:16 [f]Mt 22:14
17:15 [g]Isa 8:7 [h]Rev 13:7
17:16 [i]Rev 18:17,19 [j]Eze 16:37,39 [k]Rev 19:18 [l]Rev 18:8
17:17 [m]Rev 10:7
17:18 [n]Rev 16:19
18:1 [o]Rev 17:1 [p]Rev 10:1 [q]Eze 43:2
18:2 [r]Rev 14:8 [s]Isa 13:21,22; Jer 50:39
18:3 [t]Rev 14:8 [u]Rev 17:2 [v]Eze 27:9-25 [w]ver 7,9
18:4 [x]Isa 48:20; Jer 50:8; 2Co 6:17
18:5 [y]Jer 51:9 [z]Rev 16:19
18:6 [a]Ps 137:8; Jer 50:15,29 [b]Rev 14:10; 16:19

over them because he is Lord of lords and King of kings[e]—and with him will be his called, chosen[f]
and faithful followers."

15 Then the angel said to me, "The waters[g] you saw, where the prostitute sits, are peoples, multitudes,
nations and languages.[h] 16 The beast and the ten horns you saw will hate the prostitute. They will bring
her to ruin[i] and leave her naked;[j] they will eat her flesh[k] and burn her with fire.[l] 17 For God has put it into
their hearts to accomplish his purpose by agreeing to hand over to the beast their royal authority, until
God's words are fulfilled.[m] 18 The woman you saw is the great city[n] that rules over the kings of the earth."

Lament Over Fallen Babylon

18 After this I saw another angel[o] coming down from heaven.[p] He had great authority, and the
earth was illuminated by his splendor.[q] 2 With a mighty voice he shouted:

"'Fallen! Fallen is Babylon the Great!'[a][r]
She has become a dwelling for demons
and a haunt for every impure spirit,
a haunt for every unclean bird,
a haunt for every unclean and detestable animal.[s]
3 For all the nations have drunk
the maddening wine of her adulteries.[t]
The kings of the earth committed adultery with her,[u]
and the merchants of the earth grew rich[v] from her excessive
luxuries."[w]

Warning to Escape Babylon's Judgment

4 Then I heard another voice from heaven say:

"'Come out of her, my people,'[b][x]
so that you will not share in her sins,
so that you will not receive any of her plagues;
5 for her sins are piled up to heaven,[y]
and God has remembered[z] her crimes.
6 Give back to her as she has given;
pay her back[a] double for what she has done.
Pour her a double portion from her own cup.[b]

a 2 Isaiah 21:9 *b* 4 Jer. 51:45

17:15 waters ... peoples. Interprets the symbol in v. 1 (cf. Jer 51:13). Like the beast (13:7), Babylon exercises authority over unredeemed humanity (cf. v. 18).
17:16 Evil will turn against evil as the beast and its "ten horns" (cf. v. 3; see note on 13:1) will destroy "the prostitute" Babylon, the idolatrous economic system that supports them and whose demise they will mourn in 18:9–10. They despise, shamefully expose, and burn Babylon (cf. Isa 47:1–14), which also recalls the judgment against apostate Israel (cf. Ezek 16:35–42; 23:28–30).
17:17 his purpose. Ironically, by serving the beast, the kings carry out God's sovereign design (cf. v. 13). **fulfilled.** Cf. 10:7.
17:18 woman ... great city. The prostitute Babylon (v. 1) refers to the world's idolatrous, immoral economic and cultural system, which Rome embodied for John's first readers (see notes on 11:8; 14:8).
18:1–3 *Lament Over Fallen Babylon.* John's vision in ch. 18 dramatically expands on earlier references to Babylon's demise (14:8; 17:16) and draws repeatedly on OT prophecies against Tyre (Ezek 26–27) and Babylon (particularly Isa 13; 21; Jer 50–51). Here a glorious angel announces Babylon's fall (reiterating 14:8) and the basis of her judgment.
18:1 another angel. Cf. 10:1; 20:1. **splendor.** Alludes to Ezek 43:2; cf. 21:23 (of God's glory).
18:2 Fallen! See note on 14:8. What Babylon "has become" recalls prophecies of her absolute desolation (Isa 13:19–22; Jer 51:37).
18:3 maddening wine. See note on 14:8. **kings ... committed adultery.** See note on 17:2. Kings lament Babylon's fall in vv. 9–10. **merchants ... grew rich.** Recalls the lament concerning Tyre (Ezek 27:12,27). Merchants mourn Babylon in vv. 11–17.
18:4–8 *Warning to Escape Babylon's Judgment.* Following the announcement of Babylon's fall (vv. 1–3), a heavenly voice summons God's people to "come out" of Babylon (v. 4) and stresses God's certain and severe judgment on the world's political and economic system for its immorality and hubris.
18:4 Come out of her, my people. Alludes to Jer 51:45 (cf. Isa 48:20; 52:11). God does not call believers to withdraw from pagan society but calls them to avoid moral compromise as his holy people (cf. 2 Cor 6:17; 1 Pet 2:9–12), an acute concern for several churches John addresses (see 2:20–21; 3:15–18).
18:5 for. Introduces the reason for the exhortation in v. 4; alludes to Jer 51:9.
18:6 Give back to her as she has given. Babylon's punishment fits her crime (cf. Ps 137:8; Jer 50:29; 51:24). **pay her back double.** A just penalty highlighting the gravity of Babylon's sin (cf. Isa 40:2; Jer 16:18).

7 Give her as much torment and grief
as the glory and luxury she gave herself.[c]
In her heart she boasts,
'I sit enthroned as queen.
I am not a widow;[a]
I will never mourn.'[d]
8 Therefore in one day[e] her plagues will overtake her:
death, mourning and famine.
She will be consumed by fire,[f]
for mighty is the Lord God who judges her.

Threefold Woe Over Babylon's Fall

9 "When the kings of the earth who committed adultery with her[g] and shared her luxury see the
smoke of her burning,[h] they will weep and mourn over her.[i] 10 Terrified at her torment, they will stand
far off[j] and cry:

" 'Woe! Woe to you, great city,[k]
you mighty city of Babylon!
In one hour[l] your doom has come!'

11 "The merchants[m] of the earth will weep and mourn over her because no one buys their cargoes
anymore[n]— 12 cargoes of gold, silver, precious stones and pearls; fine linen, purple, silk and scarlet
cloth; every sort of citron wood, and articles of every kind made of ivory, costly wood, bronze, iron
and marble;[o] 13 cargoes of cinnamon and spice, of incense, myrrh and frankincense, of wine and
olive oil, of fine flour and wheat; cattle and sheep; horses and carriages; and human beings sold
as slaves.[p]
14 "They will say, 'The fruit you longed for is gone from you. All your luxury and splendor have vanished, never to be recovered.' 15 The merchants who sold these things and gained their wealth from her[q]
will stand far off, terrified at her torment. They will weep and mourn[r] 16 and cry out:

" 'Woe! Woe to you, great city,
dressed in fine linen, purple and scarlet,
and glittering with gold, precious stones and pearls![s]
17 In one hour[t] such great wealth has been brought to ruin!'[u]

"Every sea captain, and all who travel by ship, the sailors, and all who earn their living from the sea,[v]
will stand far off. 18 When they see the smoke of her burning, they will exclaim, 'Was there ever a city
like this great city?'[w] 19 They will throw dust on their heads,[x] and with weeping and mourning cry out:

[a] 7 See Isaiah 47:7,8.

18:7 [c] Eze 28:2-8 [d] Isa 47:7,8; Zep 2:15
18:8 [e] ver 10; Isa 47:9; Jer 50:31,32 [f] Rev 17:16
18:9 [g] Rev 17:2,4 [h] ver 18; Rev 19:3 [i] Eze 26:17,18
18:10 [j] ver 15,17 [k] ver 16,19 [l] Rev 17:12
18:11 [m] Eze 27:27 [n] ver 3
18:12 [o] Rev 17:4
18:13 [p] Eze 27:13; 1Ti 1:10
18:15 [q] ver 3 [r] Eze 27:31
18:16 [s] Rev 17:4
18:17 [t] ver 10 [u] Rev 17:16 [v] Eze 27:28-30
18:18 [w] Eze 27:32; Rev 13:4
18:19 [x] Jos 7:6; Eze 27:30

18:7 queen ... not a widow. Recalls Babylon's boast in Isa 47:7–8 as well as Laodicea's proud self-reliance (3:17).
18:8 in one day. Swift judgment; alludes to Isa 47:9. **fire.** Cf. 17:16. **for mighty is the Lord God.** God's sovereign power is the ultimate basis for Babylon's demise.
18:9–20 *Threefold Woe Over Babylon's Fall.* The earth's kings (vv. 9–10), merchants (vv. 11–17a), and sea captains (vv. 17–19) bitterly lament Babylon's judgment, which signals their own economic demise. In contrast, God's people rejoice at their vindication (v. 20; cf. 19:1–5). This section closely resembles the prophecy against Tyre in Ezek 26–27 (see "OT Allusions in Revelation 18," p. 2618).
18:9 kings. See note on 17:2; cf. Ps 2:2; Ezek 27:33. **mourn.** Kings lament the fall of Babylon, the source of their power and luxury.
18:10 Terrified at her torment. Parallels v. 15; recalls v. 7; 14:11. **In one hour.** Swift judgment (cf. v. 17); recalls the kings' brief reign ("one hour" in 17:12; see note there).
18:11–17 A second group mourns Babylon's demise. See note on v. 3.
18:11 no one buys their cargoes. The selfish, economic motivation for the merchants' mourning; their wealth derives from Babylon's corrupt commercial system (cf. vv. 3,15).
18:12–13 These commodities recall the remarkable trade of Tyre in Ezek 27:13–22 (see "OT Allusions in Revelation 18," p. 2618). Earlier John saw Babylon the prostitute dressed in purple, scarlet, gold, precious stones, and pearls (see 17:4 and note); such luxurious jewelry, clothing, furnishings, spices, and food—along with the horses and human slaves supporting such lavish living—recall Rome's incredible commercial system, material abundance, and oppression in John's day (cf. v. 16).
18:16 While the kings lament Babylon's lost power (v. 10), the merchants mourn her lost wealth and luxury, from which they themselves profited (vv. 11–13; cf. Ezek 27:7; 28:13).
18:17 In one hour. See note on v. 10; cf. v. 19. **brought to ruin!** Alludes to Ezek 26:19; cf. 17:16; 18:19. **Every sea captain.** Babylon's fall (like Tyre's in Ezek 27) also devastates the seafaring agents who transported the merchants' luxurious cargo (vv. 11–13).
18:18 smoke. See note on 14:11; cf. v. 9; 19:3.
18:19 throw dust on their heads. Mourning (cf. Josh 7:6; Lam 2:10;

18:19 [y]Rev 17:16
18:20 [z]Jer 51:48; Rev 12:12 [a]Rev 19:2
18:21 [b]Rev 5:2 [c]Jer 51:63
18:22 [d]Isa 24:8; Eze 26:13

"'Woe! Woe to you, great city,
where all who had ships on the sea
became rich through her wealth!
In one hour she has been brought to ruin!'[y]

20 "Rejoice over her, you heavens![z]
Rejoice, you people of God!
Rejoice, apostles and prophets!
For God has judged her
with the judgment she imposed on you."[a]

The Finality of Babylon's Doom

21 Then a mighty angel[b] picked up a boulder the size of a large millstone and threw it into the sea,[c]
and said:

"With such violence
the great city of Babylon will be thrown down,
never to be found again.
22 The music of harpists and musicians, pipers and trumpeters,
will never be heard in you again.[d]

Ezek 27:30). The seafarers, like the kings and merchants, epitomize "worldly sorrow" that "brings death" rather than "godly sorrow" that "brings repentance" (2 Cor 7:10).
18:20 Rejoice … Rejoice … Rejoice. Contrasts with the three earthly groups who mourn Babylon in vv. 9–19 (cf. 12:12) and signals the proper response to answered prayers (5:8; 6:10; 8:3–4). Cf. Jer 51:48. **God has judged her.** Reverses Babylon's unjust persecution of God's people (v. 24; cf. Dan 7:21–22) and motivates heavenly rejoicing (cf. 19:2).
18:21–24 *The Finality of Babylon's Doom.* Babylon's lavish prosperity and violent persecution of God's people will end in fitting divine judgment, which prompts heavenly worship (v. 20; 19:1–3).
18:21 boulder … into the sea. This parabolic action recalls Jer 51:63–64 and signifies Babylon's irreversible, climactic judgment. Cf. Ezek 26:12, 21 (of Tyre).
18:22–23 music … will never be heard in you again. Reverses the earlier celebration over the death of God's witnesses (11:10); recalls

OLD TESTAMENT ALLUSIONS IN REVELATION 18

LAMENT OVER BABYLON (REVELATION 18)	LAMENT OVER TYRE (EZEKIEL 26–27)
The "kings of the earth" who shared Babylon's luxury mourn (18:9)	Tyre "enriched the kings of the earth" (27:33)
"gold, silver" (18:12)	"silver … gold" (27:12,22)
"precious stones and pearls" (18:12)	"turquoise" (27:16)
"fine linen, purple" (18:12)	"purple fabric … fine linen" (27:16)
"costly wood" (18:12)	"ebony … cassia" (27:15,19; cf. 26:12)
"ivory … bronze, iron" (18:12)	"bronze … ivory … wrought iron" (27:13,15,19)
"cinnamon and spice" (18:13)	"the finest of all kinds of spices" (27:22)
"wine and olive oil" (18:13)	"olive oil … wine" (27:17,18)
"cattle and sheep" (18:13)	"lambs, rams and goats" (27:21)
"horses and carriages" (18:13)	"chariot horses, cavalry horses" (27:14)
"human beings sold as slaves" (18:13)	"traded human beings" (27:13)
Babylon's wealth "brought to ruin" (Greek *erēmoō*, 18:17)	Tyre made "desolate" (Greek *erēmoō*, 26:19)
"Was there ever a city like this great city?" (18:18)	"How you are destroyed, city of renown" (26:17; cf. 27:32)
Sea captains, travelers, sailors "throw dust on their heads" and weep and mourn (18:17–19)	Mariners, sailors, shipwrights mourn bitterly and "sprinkle dust on their heads" (27:27–30)
"all who had ships on the sea became rich through her wealth" (18:19)	"all the ships of the sea and their sailors came … to trade" (27:9)
"never to be found again" (18:21)	"you will never again be found" (26:21)
"the music of harpists … will never be heard in you again" (18:22)	"the music of your harps will be heard no more" (26:13)

No worker of any trade
will ever be found in you again.
The sound of a millstone
will never be heard in you again.[e]
23 The light of a lamp
will never shine in you again.
The voice of bridegroom and bride
will never be heard in you again.[f]
Your merchants were the world's important people.[g]
By your magic spell[h] all the nations were led astray.
24 In her was found the blood of prophets and of God's holy people,[i]
of all who have been slaughtered on the earth."[j]

Threefold Hallelujah Over Babylon's Fall

19 After this I heard what sounded like the roar of a great multitude[k] in heaven shouting:

"Hallelujah!
Salvation[l] and glory and power[m] belong to our God,
2 for true and just are his judgments.
He has condemned the great prostitute
who corrupted the earth by her adulteries.
He has avenged on her the blood of his servants."[n]

3 And again they shouted:

"Hallelujah!
The smoke from her goes up for ever and ever."[o]

4 The twenty-four elders[p] and the four living creatures[q] fell down[r] and worshiped God, who was
seated on the throne. And they cried:

"Amen, Hallelujah!"

5 Then a voice came from the throne, saying:

"Praise our God,
all you his servants,[s]
you who fear him,
both great and small!"[t]

6 Then I heard what sounded like a great multitude,[u] like the roar of rushing waters and like loud
peals of thunder, shouting:

"Hallelujah!
For our Lord God Almighty reigns.
7 Let us rejoice and be glad
and give him glory!

18:22 [e] Jer 25:10
18:23 [f] Jer 7:34; 16:9; 25:10 [g] Isa 23:8 [h] Na 3:4
18:24 [i] Rev 16:6; 17:6 [j] Jer 51:49
19:1 [k] Rev 11:15 [l] Rev 7:10 [m] Rev 4:11
19:2 [n] Dt 32:43; Rev 6:10
19:3 [o] Isa 34:10; Rev 14:11
19:4 [p] Rev 4:4 [q] Rev 4:6 [r] Rev 5:14
19:5 [s] Ps 134:1 [t] Rev 11:18; 20:12
19:6 [u] Rev 11:15

the devastation in Isa 24:8 (of the earth) and Ezek 26:13 (of Tyre). **millstone ... lamp ... bridegroom and bride.** Alludes to Jer 25:10. **your magic spell.** Recalls divine judgment on Nineveh in Nah 3:4. Cf. 9:21 and note.
18:24 blood. See notes on 16:6; 17:6; 19:2.
19:1–10 *Threefold Hallelujah Over Babylon's Fall.* The heavenly multitude rejoices over the great prostitute's demise (vv. 1–5) and the church's introduction as Christ's bride (vv. 6–10).
19:1 great multitude in heaven shouting. Heavenly praise from believers from every nation (v. 6; 7:9) contrasts with earthly lament over fallen Babylon (18:9–19). **Hallelujah!** A common OT expression meaning "Praise the LORD" (Pss 104:35; 113:1); used in the NT only here and vv. 3,4,6. **Salvation ... glory ... power.** Cf. 4:11; 5:13; 7:10; 12:10.
19:2 God's "judgments" on Babylon demonstrate his truth and justice and motivate worship (cf. 15:4; 16:7; 18:20; Deut 32:4). **avenged.** God answers the martyrs' prayers for vindication (6:10).
19:3 smoke. See note on 14:11; cf. 18:9,18.
19:4 elders. See note on 4:4. **living creatures.** See notes on 4:6–8. **fell down and worshiped God.** Cf. 4:10; 5:14; 7:11; 11:16.
19:5 Praise our God. Equivalent to "Hallelujah" (see note on v. 1).
19:6 multitude. See note on v. 1. **reigns.** See note on 11:15; cf. 11:17.
19:7 God has condemned Babylon the harlot (v. 2), and now the

19:7 [v]Mt 22:2; 25:10; Eph 5:32 [w]Rev 21:2,9
19:8 [x]Rev 15:4
19:9 [y]ver 10 [z]Rev 1:19 [a]Lk 14:15 [b]Rev 21:5; 22:6
19:10 [c]Rev 22:8 [d]Ac 10:25,26; Rev 22:9 [e]Rev 12:17
19:11 [f]Rev 6:2 [g]Rev 3:14 [h]Isa 11:4
19:12 [i]Rev 1:14 [j]Rev 6:2 [k]Rev 2:17
19:13 [l]Isa 63:2,3 [m]Jn 1:1
19:14 [n]ver 8
19:15 [o]Rev 1:16 [p]Isa 11:4; 2Th 2:8 [q]Ps 2:9; Rev 2:27 [r]Rev 14:20
19:16 [s]ver 12 [t]Rev 17:14
19:17 [u]ver 21 [v]Rev 8:13 [w]Eze 39:17

For the wedding of the Lamb[v] has come,
and his bride[w] has made herself ready.
8 Fine linen, bright and clean,
was given her to wear."
(Fine linen stands for the righteous acts[x] of God's holy people.)

9 Then the angel said to me,[y] "Write this:[z] Blessed are those who are invited to the wedding supper of the Lamb!"[a] And he added, "These are the true words of God."[b]
10 At this I fell at his feet to worship him.[c] But he said to me, "Don't do that! I am a fellow servant with you and with your brothers and sisters who hold to the testimony of Jesus. Worship God![d] For it is the Spirit of prophecy who bears testimony to Jesus."[e]

The Heavenly Warrior Defeats the Beast

11 I saw heaven standing open and there before me was a white horse, whose rider[f] is called Faithful and True.[g] With justice he judges and wages war.[h] 12 His eyes are like blazing fire,[i] and on his head are many crowns.[j] He has a name written on him that no one knows but he himself.[k] 13 He is dressed in a robe dipped in blood,[l] and his name is the Word of God.[m] 14 The armies of heaven were following him, riding on white horses and dressed in fine linen,[n] white and clean. 15 Coming out of his mouth is a sharp sword[o] with which to strike down[p] the nations. "He will rule them with an iron scepter."[a][q] He treads the winepress[r] of the fury of the wrath of God Almighty. 16 On his robe and on his thigh he has this name written:[s]

KING OF KINGS AND LORD OF LORDS.[t]

17 And I saw an angel standing in the sun, who cried in a loud voice to all the birds[u] flying in midair,[v] "Come,[w] gather together for the great supper of God, 18 so that you may eat the flesh of

[a] *15* Psalm 2:9

worshipers rejoice because the multitude introduces "the wedding of the Lamb" and his chaste "bride," drawing upon Isa 61:10—62:5. John later identifies the bride as the new Jerusalem, God's people (21:2–3; cf. 2 Cor 11:2; Eph 5:25–27).

19:8 Fine linen, bright and clean. The bride's radiant garments signify enduring moral purity (cf. Isa 61:10; Eph 5:27), while the harlot's purple and scarlet clothes represent her fleeting wealth (see note on 17:4). **was given.** God sovereignly and graciously initiates redemption. **Fine linen ... righteous acts.** Believers' righteous deeds do not merit salvation but serve as a fitting, necessary response to and evidence of God's "righteous acts" (15:4; cf. Eph 2:8–10; Phil 2:12–13; Titus 2:14), which motivate praise to God (vv. 6–7).

19:9 Write this. See note on 1:11. **Blessed.** Revelation's fourth of seven blessings (see note on 1:3). **those who are invited.** Individual members of the church, the bride (v. 7). **wedding supper of the Lamb.** Equivalent to "the feast in the kingdom of God" (Luke 14:15), where believers from every nation will gather to celebrate God's work of final salvation and restoration (Isa 25:6–9; Luke 13:29). **These are the true words of God.** Affirms the veracity of vv. 7–9; cf. 21:5; 22:6.

19:10 Worship God! Only God and the Lamb are worthy of heavenly and earthly worship (cf. 5:8–14); such veneration is improper for angelic and human messengers (22:8–9; Acts 10:25–26). **For it is the Spirit of prophecy who bears testimony to Jesus.** Explains how both angels and those having the testimony of Jesus are God's fellow servants.

19:11—21:8 *The Final Victory, Judgment, and Restoration.* The open heaven (19:11) introduces the book's second-to-last vision sequence. It opens with Jesus' gloriously return as the conquering King (19:11–16) to judge the beast, false prophet, and Satan with their allied armies (19:20–21; 20:9–10), and it concludes with the bride-city, the new Jerusalem, coming down from heaven (21:1–8). Satan's inaugurated judgment and believers' reign with Christ "for a thousand years" (20:2,6) either follow (for premillennialists) or precede (for amillennialists and postmillennialists) Jesus' second coming (see notes on 20:1–6; see also Introduction: Millennial Views).

19:11–21 *The Heavenly Warrior Defeats the Beast.* Jesus returns as the heavenly King to vindicate his followers and decisively judge God's enemies (17:14).

19:11 I saw heaven standing open. Introduces a vision and a new major literary unit (cf. 4:1). **white horse.** The warhorse of the victorious King Jesus; contrasts with 6:2 (see note there). **Faithful and True.** Jesus the warrior Messiah is "the faithful and true witness" (3:14) who embodies God's faithfulness and sure judgments (cf. 16:7; 22:6). **he judges.** Jesus executes God's final judgment (cf. Isa 11:4; John 5:27; Acts 17:31).

19:12 eyes. See note on 1:14. **many crowns.** Symbolize his supreme regal authority (cf. v. 16; Isa 62:3) in contrast with the illegitimate sovereignty of the dragon and the beast (12:3; 13:1). **name.** Some facet of Jesus' divine identity is hidden from created beings; recalls the "new name" God promised Israel (Isa 62:2; cf. Isa 65:15) and believers (2:17), on whom Christ will write his "new name" (3:12).

19:13 blood. May refer to Christ's atoning blood (7:14); probably refers to the blood of his defeated enemies (14:19–20), alluding to Isa 63:2–3. **Word of God.** Jesus, "the Word," is God's ultimate self-disclosure in John 1:1; here Christ embodies God's authoritative Word by proclaiming and executing judgment on the nations (v. 15).

19:14 armies of heaven. Possibly angels; most likely believers who "follow the Lamb" in present suffering (14:4) and future victory (17:14). **fine linen.** See note on v. 8.

19:15 sharp sword. Represents proclaiming judgment on God's enemies, realized in v. 21; cf. 1:16; Isa 11:4; 49:2. **iron scepter.** Alludes to Ps 2:9; see note on 12:5. **treads the winepress.** Jesus executes God's wrath on unbelieving nations (see note on 14:19).

19:16 KING OF KINGS. See note on 17:14.

19:17 angel ... cried. Cf. 18:1–2. **Come, gather together for the**

THE USE OF EZEKIEL 38–39 IN REVELATION 19–20

FINAL BATTLE(S) (REVELATION 19–20)	PROPHECY AGAINST GOG (EZEKIEL 38–39)
Birds called to "gather" (Greek *synachthēte*) for the great supper (19:17)	Birds and wild animals called to "come together" (Greek *synachthēte*) for the sacrifice (39:17)
"eat the flesh of kings, generals, and the mighty, of horses and their riders" (19:18)	"eat the flesh of mighty men … princes … horses and riders" (39:18,20)
"Gog and Magog" (20:8)	"Gog … Magog" (38:2)
Deceived nations gathered for battle (20:8)	Many nations against Israel (38:9,15)
Innumerable army like "sand" (20:8)	Innumerable army like a "cloud" (38:9,16)
"fire came down from heaven" (20:9)	"fire on Magog" (39:6; cf. 38:22)

kings, generals, and the mighty, of horses and their riders, and the flesh of all people,[x] free and
slave, great and small."
19Then I saw the beast and the kings of the earth[y] and their armies gathered together to wage war
against the rider on the horse and his army. 20But the beast was captured, and with it the false prophet[z]
who had performed the signs on its behalf.[a] With these signs he had deluded those who had received
the mark of the beast and worshiped its image. The two of them were thrown alive into the fiery lake[b]
of burning sulfur.[c] 21The rest were killed with the sword[d] coming out of the mouth of the rider on the
horse,[e] and all the birds[f] gorged themselves on their flesh.

19:18 [x]Eze 39:18-20
19:19 [y]Rev 16:14,16
19:20 [z]Rev 16:13 [a]Rev 13:12 [b]Da 7:11; Rev 20:10,14,15; 21:8 [c]Rev 14:10
19:21 [d]ver 15 [e]ver 11,19 [f]ver 17
20:1 [g]Rev 10:1 [h]Rev 1:18
20:2 [i]Rev 12:9 [j]2Pe 2:4
20:3 [k]Da 6:17 [l]Rev 12:9
20:4 [m]Da 7:9 [n]Rev 6:9

The Thousand Years

20 And I saw an angel coming down out of heaven,[g] having the key[h] to the Abyss and holding in
his hand a great chain. 2He seized the dragon, that ancient serpent, who is the devil, or Satan,[i]
and bound him for a thousand years.[j] 3He threw him into the Abyss, and locked and sealed[k] it over
him, to keep him from deceiving the nations[l] anymore until the thousand years were ended. After that,
he must be set free for a short time.
4I saw thrones[m] on which were seated those who had been given authority to judge. And I saw the
souls of those who had been beheaded[n] because of their testimony about Jesus and because of the word

great supper of God. Contrasts with the invitation to the great Messianic banquet (v. 9).
19:18 eat the flesh of kings. Recalls the graphic prophetic curse against Gog (Ezek 39:4,17–20; cf. Rev 20:8).
19:19 gathered together to wage war. See notes on 16:14,16.
19:20 beast … false prophet. See 13:13–17. **fiery lake of burning sulfur.** God's enemies experience everlasting punishment, "the second death" (20:14; cf. Dan 7:11).
19:21 The rest were killed. King Jesus totally destroys the armies gathered against him (cf. Ps 2:12). **sword.** See v. 15 and note. **birds gorged themselves.** The shameful judgment that vv. 17–18 announce.
20:1–6 *The Thousand Years.* Interpreters have long debated this important and difficult passage, which presents the inaugurated judgment of Satan and the priestly reign of deceased, vindicated believers. See Introduction: Millennial Views.
20:1 And I saw. Frequently introduces a new vision (cf. vv. 4,12; 19:11,17,19). Premillennialists hold that the vision in vv. 1–6 describes events that will follow Jesus' return (19:11), while amillennialists hold that it parallels the earlier vision in 19:11–16. **angel coming down.** Cf. 10:1; 18:1. **key to the Abyss.** Represents complete authority over the realm of the dead, which belongs to the risen Christ (1:18; 3:7; 9:1).
20:2 seized … bound. Typical language for arrest and imprisonment (cf. Matt 14:3); alludes to Isa 24:21–22; 27:1. Interpreters disagree about whether Satan's binding is *past* (at Jesus' death and resurrection) or *future* (preceding a golden age) and whether it entails a complete or partial cessation of Satan's earthly activity (see Introduction: Millennial Views). **dragon … Satan.** See notes on 12:3,9. **thousand years.** Called the "millennium" (from the Latin *mille*, "thousand," and *annus*, "year"), mentioned six times in vv. 2–7 (see Introduction: Millennial Views).
20:3 He threw him into the Abyss, and locked and sealed it. Satan's preliminary judgment recalls 12:9 (hurled to earth from heaven). **to keep him from deceiving the nations.** The purpose of Satan's binding, allowing the gospel's spread among the nations during the present church age or a future millennium. **set free for a short time.** Satan's final rebellion (vv. 7–9).
20:4 thrones. Thrones in Revelation typically designate places of heavenly authority under God's supreme rule (4:4; 11:16). Amillennialists hold that vv. 4–6 offer heavenly perspective on the events in vv. 1–3, which fulfill Dan 7:9,22. Premillennialists argue that "an angel coming down out of heaven" (v. 1) and the mention of "the nations" (v. 3) suggest that these "thrones" are on earth during the millennium (cf. v. 1). **those who had been beheaded.** Martyrs (6:9), who represent the faithful church. **came to life.** "The first resurrection" in v. 5. Premillennialists argue that this refers to physical, earthly resurrection, given previous usage of the Greek verb *zaō* in 2:8 (of Christ) and 13:14 (of the beast). For amillennialists, "the first resurrection" (v. 5) denotes the present spiritual life of deceased believers in heaven prior to the future general resurrection (cf. John 5:24–25; 2 Cor 5:1–8; Phil 1:23). **reigned with Christ.** Cf. v. 6; 5:10; 22:5.

20:4 [o]Rev 13:12 [p]Rev 13:16
20:5 [q]Lk 14:14; Php 3:11
20:6 [r]Rev 14:13 [s]Rev 2:11 [t]Rev 1:6 [u]ver 4
20:7 [v]ver 2
20:8 [w]ver 3,10 [x]Eze 38:2; 39:1 [y]Rev 16:14 [z]Heb 11:12
20:9 [a]Eze 38:9,16 [b]Eze 38:22; 39:6
20:10 [c]Rev 19:20 [d]Rev 14:10,11
20:11 [e]Rev 4:2
20:12 [f]Da 7:10 [g]Rev 3:5 [h]Jer 17:10; Mt 16:27; Rev 2:23
20:13 [i]Rev 6:8 [j]Isa 26:19
20:14 [k]1Co 15:26
20:15 [l]ver 12
21:1 [m]Isa 65:17; 2Pe 3:13
21:2 [n]Heb 11:10; 12:22; Rev 3:12

of God. They[a] had not worshiped the beast[o] or its image and had not received its mark on their foreheads or their hands.[p] They came to life and reigned with Christ a thousand years. 5(The rest of the
dead did not come to life until the thousand years were ended.) This is the first resurrection.[q] 6Blessed[r]
and holy are those who share in the first resurrection. The second death[s] has no power over them, but
they will be priests[t] of God and of Christ and will reign with him[u] for a thousand years.

The Judgment of Satan

7When the thousand years are over,[v] Satan will be released from his prison 8and will go out to deceive the nations[w] in the four corners of the earth — Gog and Magog[x] — and to gather them for battle.[y]
In number they are like the sand on the seashore.[z] 9They marched across the breadth of the earth and
surrounded[a] the camp of God's people, the city he loves. But fire came down from heaven[b] and devoured
them. 10And the devil, who deceived them,[c] was thrown into the lake of burning sulfur, where the beast
and the false prophet had been thrown. They will be tormented day and night for ever and ever.[d]

The Judgment of the Dead

11Then I saw a great white throne[e] and him who was seated on it. The earth and the heavens fled from
his presence, and there was no place for them. 12And I saw the dead, great and small, standing before the
throne, and books were opened.[f] Another book was opened, which is the book of life.[g] The dead were judged
according to what they had done[h] as recorded in the books. 13The sea gave up the dead that were in it,
and death and Hades[i] gave up the dead[j] that were in them, and each person was judged according to what
they had done. 14Then death[k] and Hades were thrown into the lake of fire. The lake of fire is the second
death. 15Anyone whose name was not found written in the book of life[l] was thrown into the lake of fire.

A New Heaven and a New Earth

21 Then I saw "a new heaven and a new earth,"[b][m] for the first heaven and the first earth had
passed away, and there was no longer any sea. 2I saw the Holy City, the new Jerusalem,
coming down out of heaven from God,[n] prepared as a bride beautifully dressed for her husband.

[a] 4 Or *God; I also saw those who* [b] 1 Isaiah 65:17

20:5 The rest of the dead. Unbelievers raised for eternal judgment (John 5:29). **first resurrection.** See note on v. 4 ("came to life"); contrasts with "second death" (vv. 6,14; see note on v. 6).
20:6 Blessed. See note on 1:3. **second death.** Eternal punishment (see note on 2:11). **priests ... reign.** See note on 1:6.
20:7–10 *The Judgment of Satan.* At the close of the thousand years, the devil is released, deceives and gathers the nations for battle against God's people, and is climactically defeated and judged by God. Like 19:17–21, this passage alludes to the prophecy against Gog in Ezek 38–39 (see "The Use of Ezekiel 38–39 in Revelation 19–20," p. 2621).
20:7 When the thousand years are over. Resumes v. 2.
20:8 to deceive. Recalls v. 3; 12:9. **Gog and Magog.** Alludes to Ezek 38:2—39:16, a prophecy of northern enemies conspiring with other nations against restored Israel. **battle.** For amillennialists, this is the same battle that 16:13–16 and 19:17–21 present; for premillennialists, this is a separate, later battle.
20:9 the city he loves. Jerusalem (cf. Pss 78:68; 87:2). Some interpreters identify the city as restored earthly Jerusalem during the millennium. More likely, the beloved city is equivalent to "the camp" of God's people (Exod 16:13; 33:7) and describes the oppressed, pilgrim community of believers who will inherit the new Jerusalem (3:12). **fire.** Decisive divine judgment; alludes to Ezek 38:22; 39:6.
20:10 lake of burning sulfur. The second death, eternal torment (cf. v. 14; 19:20).
20:11–15 *The Judgment of the Dead.* At history's end, God will execute perfect justice based on the heavenly records of people's deeds and will abolish the old cosmos to prepare for the glorious new creation (21:1–8; cf. 2 Pet 3:10–13).
20:11 great white throne. Represents the holiness and purity of God, the sovereign judge (4:2–3; Ps 11:4; Dan 7:9). **The earth and the heavens fled.** Recalls 6:14; 16:20; the destruction and passing away of the cosmos make way for "a new heaven and a new earth" (21:1).
20:12 the dead, great and small, standing before the throne. The final judgment of the righteous and wicked; cf. 11:18; 14:14–20. **books were opened.** Alludes to Dan 7:10. **book of life.** See note on 3:5.
20:13 sea ... death and Hades. Personify the realm of evil and disorder (cf. 1:18; 13:1). God justly rewards or punishes each person according to what they have done (v. 12; 22:12; Ps 62:12; Matt 16:27; Rom 2:6–11).
20:14 second death. Eternal, conscious torment (Isa 66:24; Mark 9:47–48), from which believers are delivered (2:11).
20:15 Unbelievers whose names are not "found written in the book of life" will experience everlasting punishment, reserved for the devil (v. 10), his followers (19:20; 21:8) and his realm of death and Hades (v. 14).
21:1–8 *A New Heaven and a New Earth.* This transition passage concludes the sequence of visions of divine judgment and restoration that 19:11 begins, and it introduces the new Jerusalem, new creation, and God's enduring presence with his people, rich biblical-theological themes that 21:9—22:5 develops further. Following John's vision of the new heaven and new earth (vv. 1–2), a series of heavenly voices confirm its significance (vv. 3–6). The section concludes with a challenge urging John's readers to inherit the promises by persevering faith and to avoid cowardice, unbelief, and immorality resulting in eternal destruction (vv. 7–8).
21:1 a new heaven and a new earth. A glorious new creation; alludes to Isa 65:17; 66:22. See note on 2 Pet 3:10. **the first ... passed away.** Cf. 20:11. **sea.** See note on 13:1. Cf. 20:13.
21:2 Holy City, the new Jerusalem. The everlasting heavenly city represents God's redeemed people (cf. vv. 10,19; Isa 52:1; Heb 12:22–24); contrasts with fallen Babylon the Great (18:2–3). **bride.** See note on 19:7.

3And I heard a loud voice from the throne saying, "Look! God's dwelling place is now among the
people, and he will dwell with them. They will be his people, and God himself will be with them
and be their God.[o] 4'He will wipe every tear from their eyes.[p] There will be no more death'[a][q] or
mourning or crying or pain,[r] for the old order of things has passed away."
5He who was seated on the throne[s] said, "I am making everything new!" Then he said, "Write this
down, for these words are trustworthy and true."[t]
6He said to me: "It is done.[u] I am the Alpha and the Omega,[v] the Beginning and the End. To the
thirsty I will give water without cost from the spring of the water of life.[w] 7Those who are victorious
will inherit all this, and I will be their God and they will be my children. 8But the cowardly, the unbelieving, the vile, the murderers, the sexually immoral, those who practice magic arts, the idolaters
and all liars[x] — they will be consigned to the fiery lake of burning sulfur. This is the second death."[y]

The New Jerusalem, the Bride of the Lamb

9One of the seven angels who had the seven bowls full of the seven last plagues[z] came and said to
me, "Come, I will show you the bride,[a] the wife of the Lamb." 10And he carried me away[b] in the Spirit[c]

21:3 [o] 2Co 6:16
21:4 [p] Rev 7:17 [q] 1Co 15:26; Rev 20:14 [r] Isa 35:10; 65:19
21:5 [s] Rev 4:9; 20:11 [t] Rev 19:9
21:6 [u] Rev 16:17 [v] Rev 1:8; 22:13 [w] Jn 4:10
21:8 [x] 1Co 6:9 [y] Rev 2:11
21:9 [z] Rev 15:1,6,7 [a] Rev 19:7
21:10 [b] Rev 17:3 [c] Rev 1:10

a *4* Isaiah 25:8

21:3 God's dwelling place is now among the people. Enduring fellowship between God and his people, which was lost in Eden (Gen 3:8,24), anticipated by the OT tabernacle (Exod 25:8) and temple (2 Chr 6:18), promised by the prophets (Ezek 40–48), and made possible through Jesus' incarnation (Matt 1:23; John 1:14). The new Jerusalem is presented as a glorious temple-city, fulfilling OT prophecies and patterns of God's dwelling with his people. See "The New Jerusalem and Ezekiel's Temple," this page; see also "Temple," p. 2652. **They will be his people, and God himself will ... be their God.** Restored, intimate covenantal relationship (cf. Lev 26:11–12; Jer 32:38; Ezek 37:27; 2 Cor 6:16).
21:4 He will wipe every tear ... no more death. Alludes to Isa 25:8; cf. 7:17; Isa 35:10. God will bring perfect comfort (Matt 5:4) and remove the source of sorrow: the curse and brokenness of the "old order" of sin.
21:5 I am making everything new! Alludes to Isa 43:19; reiterates vv. 1,4. **Write.** See note on 1:11. **trustworthy and true.** Reiterated in 22:6.
21:6 Alpha ... Omega. See note on 1:8. **To the thirsty I will give water without cost.** God fully satisfies and provides for his people in the new creation (cf. 7:16; Isa 49:10; 55:1). See John 4:10,14; 7:37 and notes.
21:7 Those who are victorious. Recalls promises to persevering believers in the seven churches (see note on 2:7; see also "Promised Inheritance for Victorious Believers," p. 2624). **I will be their God.** See note on v. 3.
21:8 The longest of three vice lists in Revelation (see "Vice Lists in Revelation," p. 2603); summarizes the unbelief, immorality, and idolatry of those consigned to eternal punishment and contrasts with "victorious" believers (v. 7), who persevere and inherit eternal blessings. **second death.** See note on 20:14.
21:9—22:5 *The New Jerusalem and God's Glorious Presence.* Revelation's last major section expands on themes that 21:1–8 introduces, and it brings God's redemptive purposes for his people and his world to their climax.
21:9–27 *The New Jerusalem, the Bride of the Lamb.* The new Jerusalem is the glorious alternative to Babylon, earth's great city destined for destruction. Believers should identify with and live for the new Jerusalem (vv. 1–3,7; 3:12) and "come out" of Babylon (18:4). This everlasting temple-city is a place that also represents God's people, the believing community, and fulfills Ezekiel's prophecy of the end-time temple (see "The New Jerusalem and Ezekiel's Temple," this page) and the prophecy of Zion's redemption in Isa 60. See "Temple," p. 2652, and "People of God," p. 2672.
21:9 seven angels. Cf. 15:1; 17:1. **Come, I will show you.** Recalls 17:1; John's vision of Jerusalem the bride deliberately contrasts with the prostitute Babylon (see "A Tale of Two Cities in Revelation," p. 2615). **bride.** God's redeemed people, portrayed as the new Jerusalem (see notes on v. 2; 19:7).
21:10 he carried me away in the Spirit. A structural marker introducing a new vision of the new Jerusalem, contrasted with Babylon (cf.

THE NEW JERUSALEM AND EZEKIEL'S TEMPLE

	REVELATION 21–22	EZEKIEL 40–48
God's dwelling among his people	21:3	43:7; 48:35
Carried in the Spirit, mountain location	21:10	40:2
God's glory	21:11,23	43:2,5
Twelve gates with names of Israel's tribes	21:12	48:31–34
"measuring rod"	21:15 (golden)	40:3
Symmetry	21:16 (city is cubic: 12,000 stadia in length, width, and height)	45:2 (sanctuary is 500 cubits square)
Water of life	22:1 (from God's throne)	47:1 (from under temple's threshold)
Tree(s)	22:2 (tree of life on each side of river yields fruit; leaves for healing)	47:12 (fruit trees on both banks of river; leaves for healing)

21:11 [d]Rev 15:8; 22:5 [e]Rev 4:6
21:12 [f]Eze 48:30-34
21:15 [g]Rev 11:1
21:18 [h]ver 11 [i]ver 21
21:19 [j]Isa 54:11,12
21:20 [k]Rev 4:3
21:21 [l]ver 18
21:22 [m]Jn 4:21,23 [n]Rev 1:8 [o]Rev 5:6
21:23 [p]Isa 24:23; 60:19, 20; Rev 22:5

to a mountain great and high, and showed me the Holy City, Jerusalem, coming down out of heaven
from God. 11It shone with the glory of God,[d] and its brilliance was like that of a very precious jewel, like
a jasper, clear as crystal.[e] 12It had a great, high wall with twelve gates, and with twelve angels at the
gates. On the gates were written the names of the twelve tribes of Israel.[f] 13There were three gates on
the east, three on the north, three on the south and three on the west. 14The wall of the city had twelve
foundations, and on them were the names of the twelve apostles of the Lamb.

15The angel who talked with me had a measuring rod[g] of gold to measure the city, its gates and its
walls. 16The city was laid out like a square, as long as it was wide. He measured the city with the rod
and found it to be 12,000 stadia[a] in length, and as wide and high as it is long. 17The angel measured
the wall using human measurement, and it was 144 cubits[b] thick.[c] 18The wall was made of jasper,[h]
and the city of pure gold, as pure as glass.[i] 19The foundations of the city walls were decorated with every
kind of precious stone.[j] The first foundation was jasper, the second sapphire, the third agate, the fourth
emerald, 20the fifth onyx, the sixth ruby,[k] the seventh chrysolite, the eighth beryl, the ninth topaz, the
tenth turquoise, the eleventh jacinth, and the twelfth amethyst.[d] 21The twelve gates were twelve pearls,
each gate made of a single pearl. The great street of the city was of gold, as pure as transparent glass.[l]

22I did not see a temple[m] in the city, because the Lord God Almighty[n] and the Lamb[o] are its temple.
23The city does not need the sun or the moon to shine on it, for the glory of God gives it light,[p] and the
Lamb is its lamp. 24The nations will walk by its light, and the kings of the earth will bring their splen-

[a] *16* That is, about 1,400 miles or about 2,200 kilometers [b] *17* That is, about 200 feet or about 65 meters
[c] *17* Or *high* [d] *20* The precise identification of some of these precious stones is uncertain.

17:3; see Introduction: Structure). **mountain.** Contrasts with the wilderness setting in 17:3; alludes to Ezek 40:2. **Holy City.** See note on v. 2.
21:11 glory. The awesome, radiant presence of God himself adorns the new Jerusalem; cf. 15:8; 21:23; Isa 60:1; Ezek 43:5. See "The Glory of God," p. 2640. **jasper ... crystal.** Recalls John's initial throne room vision (4:2,6).
21:12 great, high wall. Described in vv. 14,17–18. **twelve gates ... twelve tribes.** Alludes to Ezek 48:30–34; described in v. 21.
21:14 twelve foundations ... twelve apostles. Combines the 12 founding leaders of the church (Acts 1:21–22,26; cf. Eph 2:20) with Israel's 12 tribes (v. 12) to emphasize the unity and continuity of God's redeemed people.
21:15 measure the city. Recalls 11:1, where John is instructed to measure the temple and its worshipers. Here an angel measures "the city, its gates and its walls" (see notes on vv. 16,17; cf. Ezek 40:3; 42:16–19), signifying God's guaranteed presence and protection of the new Jerusalem.
21:16 square. Cf. Ezek 45:2. **12,000 stadia.** See NIV text note; recalls the symbolic number of the redeemed, a multiple of 12 (see 7:4 and note). **wide ... high ... long.** The new Jerusalem is a perfect golden cube, a massive Most Holy Place (cf. 1 Kgs 6:20).
21:17 144 cubits. See NIV text note. The height of the walls and the city's dimensions (v. 16) are all multiples of 12, symbolizing completion (see "Multiples of Twelve in Revelation," p. 2600).
21:18 pure gold. Consistently associated with the tabernacle and temple furnishings (Exod 25:11; 2 Chr 3:4). **pure as glass.** The city's gold is clear to perfectly reflect God's glory (v. 23; 22:5).
21:19–21 The 12 stones substantially correspond to those adorning the high priest's breastplate, which represented Israel's 12 tribes (Exod 28:17–21). They also recall Eden's description in Ezek 28:13–14 and restored Jerusalem in Isa 54:11–12. The new Jerusalem's enduring beauty contrasts with Babylon's fleeting luxury (17:4; 18:16; see "A Tale of Two Cities in Revelation," p. 2615).
21:22 the Lord God Almighty and the Lamb are its temple. Clarifies v. 3. God and Jesus fill the new creation with their glorious presence, superseding the former glory of Israel's temple (cf. Jer 3:16–17; Hab 2:9). See "Temple," p. 2652.
21:23 the glory of God gives it light. Alludes to Isa 60:19; cf. Rev 22:5.
21:24 nations ... kings ... will bring their splendor. Recalls Isa 60:3,5,11.

PROMISED INHERITANCE FOR VICTORIOUS BELIEVERS

END-TIME BLESSING	OT BACKGROUND	PROMISES TO THE SEVEN CHURCHES IN REVELATION	NEW CREATION FULFILLMENT IN REVELATION
Access to the tree of life	Gen 2:9	2:7	22:2,14,19
Hidden manna, entrance to the Messianic feast	Exod 16:31–34; Isa 25:6	2:17	19:9
Ruling over nations with Christ	Ps 2:8–9	2:26–27; cf. 3:21	22:5; cf. 1:6
Given the morning star (Christ)	Num 24:17	2:28	22:16
Clothed with pure garments	Isa 52:1; 61:10	3:5	19:7–8; 21:2
Written in the book of life	Dan 12:1	3:5	21:27
Inclusion in God's temple	Isa 56:5	3:12	21:22–27
New identity and citizenship	Isa 62:2; 65:15	3:12	21:2,10; 22:4

dor into it.[q] 25 On no day will its gates ever be shut,[r] for there will be no night there.[s] 26 The glory and
honor of the nations will be brought into it. 27 Nothing impure will ever enter it, nor will anyone who
does what is shameful or deceitful,[t] but only those whose names are written in the Lamb's book of life.

Eden Restored

22 Then the angel showed me the river of the water of life, as clear as crystal,[u] flowing[v] from the
throne of God and of the Lamb 2 down the middle of the great street of the city. On each side
of the river stood the tree of life,[w] bearing twelve crops of fruit, yielding its fruit every month. And the
leaves of the tree are for the healing of the nations.[x] 3 No longer will there be any curse.[y] The throne of
God and of the Lamb will be in the city, and his servants will serve him.[z] 4 They will see his face,[a] and
his name will be on their foreheads.[b] 5 There will be no more night.[c] They will not need the light of a
lamp or the light of the sun, for the Lord God will give them light.[d] And they will reign for ever and ever.[e]

John and the Angel

6 The angel said to me,[f] "These words are trustworthy and true.[g] The Lord, the God who inspires the
prophets,[h] sent his angel[i] to show his servants the things that must soon take place."

7 "Look, I am coming soon![j] Blessed[k] is the one who keeps the words of the prophecy written in this scroll."

8 I, John, am the one who heard and saw these things.[l] And when I had heard and seen them, I fell
down to worship at the feet[m] of the angel who had been showing them to me. 9 But he said to me, "Don't
do that! I am a fellow servant with you and with your fellow prophets and with all who keep the words
of this scroll.[n] Worship God!"[o]

10 Then he told me, "Do not seal up[p] the words of the prophecy of this scroll, because the time is
near.[q] 11 Let the one who does wrong continue to do wrong; let the vile person continue to be vile; let the
one who does right continue to do right; and let the holy person continue to be holy."[r]

21:24 [q] Isa 60:3,5
21:25 [r] Isa 60:11 [s] Zec 14:7; Rev 22:5
21:27 [t] Isa 52:1; Joel 3:17; Rev 22:14,15
22:1 [u] Rev 4:6 [v] Eze 47:1; Zec 14:8
22:2 [w] Rev 2:7 [x] Eze 47:12
22:3 [y] Zec 14:11 [z] Rev 7:15
22:4 [a] Mt 5:8 [b] Rev 14:1
22:5 [c] Rev 21:25 [d] Rev 21:23 [e] Da 7:27; Rev 20:4
22:6 [f] Rev 1:1 [g] Rev 19:9; 21:5 [h] Heb 12:9 [i] ver 16
22:7 [j] Rev 3:11 [k] Rev 1:3
22:8 [l] Rev 1:1 [m] Rev 19:10
22:9 [n] ver 10,18,19 [o] Rev 19:10
22:10 [p] Da 8:26; Rev 10:4 [q] Rev 1:3
22:11 [r] Eze 3:27; Da 12:10

21:25 On no day will its gates ever be shut. Alludes to Isa 60:11. Closed gates protected cities from enemies at night; the perpetually open gates signal unending security and the welcome of the nations (v. 26).

21:27 Nothing impure. God's eternal city is holy—without moral or ritual defilement. **book of life.** See note on 3:5.

22:1–5 *Eden Restored.* John concludes his vision of the glorious new Jerusalem by highlighting the everlasting drink and food that believers will enjoy (vv. 1–2) and their restored fellowship with God and enduring vocation as priests and kings (vv. 3–5). The new Jerusalem represents a new and greater Eden, free of sin and curse, where God's people will serve him forever (see "Paradise Restored," p. 2626).

22:1 river of the water of life. Recalls Eden (Gen 2:10); fulfills Ezek 47:1; Zech 14:8. **clear as crystal.** See note on 4:6. **from the throne.** God and the Lamb satisfy and sustain believers forever (cf. v. 17; 7:17; Isa 55:1; John 4:10) in contrast to Babylon, whose wine makes the nations drunk (14:8).

22:2 On each side of the river. Alludes to Ezek 47:12. This location may suggest that "the tree of life" refers not to one tree but to a kind of tree filling the new Jerusalem, restoring and exceeding Eden's blessing (Gen 2:9; 3:22–24). **tree of life.** The food of unending life in God's presence; recalls the promise to victors in 2:7 (see note there; see also "Promised Inheritance for Victorious Believers," p. 2624); cf. vv. 14,19. **leaves ... for the healing of the nations.** Again recalls Ezek 47:12; includes total spiritual and physical restoration (cf. v. 3; 7:14–18; 21:4–5).

22:3 No longer ... any curse. Explains the healing in v. 2. The curse on the earth and humanity's exclusion from paradise because of sin will be reversed (Gen 3:17–19,22–24; Zech 14:11). **throne of God and of the Lamb.** See note on 3:21; see also Introduction: Theology. **his servants will serve him.** Priestly service in God's temple-city (7:15; Isa 61:6).

22:4 They will see his face. Moses beheld God's glory but not his face (Exod 33:20,23). Jesus' disciples saw his divine glory (John 1:14; 14:7), and believers by the Spirit "contemplate the Lord's glory [and] are being transformed into his image" (2 Cor 3:18). In the new Jerusalem God's people, freed from sin, finally will be able to behold God's face (cf. Matt 5:8; 1 John 3:2). **his name ... on their foreheads.** See note on 14:1.

22:5 Concludes this climactic vision by reiterating the end of "night" (21:25; Zech 14:7), the glorious "light" of God's presence (21:23; Isa 60:19–20), and believers' unending "reign" (5:10; 20:4; Dan 7:27).

22:6–21 *Conclusion.* John urges readers to heed and hold fast to his divinely inspired message to experience blessing, not judgment, when Jesus returns as King and Judge.

22:6–11 *John and the Angel.* The angel affirms this book's veracity, reliability, and blessing and summons John and readers to worship God alone and prepare for Jesus' imminent coming.

22:6 trustworthy and true. Cf. 21:5; echoes Dan 2:45. **The Lord, the God who inspires the prophets.** Alludes to Num 27:16; cf. 1 Cor 14:32. **his servants.** All believers (cf. vv. 3,9; 19:5). **things that must soon take place.** See note on 1:1.

22:7 Look, I am coming soon! Jesus speaks directly (cf. v. 16; 16:15) and clarifies that "the things" in v. 6 include his imminent return (vv. 12,20). **Blessed.** Sixth blessing formula (see note on 1:3). **keeps the words.** Faithfully obeys God's true revelation (2:26; 14:12). **prophecy written in this scroll.** Summarizes the book's content (vv. 10,18,19; 1:3; see Introduction: Genre).

22:8–9 fell down to worship ... Worship God! John's action and the angel's response parallel 19:10 (see note there).

22:8 I, John ... heard and saw. Reiterates 1:1–2,9.

22:9 your fellow prophets. Probably designates a circle of Christian prophets such as John (cf. v. 6; 1 Cor 12:28); may refer to all faithful believers with the prophetic Spirit (cf. 11:3–4; Num 11:29; Acts 2:17). **Worship God!** Revelation's summary exhortation (19:10).

22:10 Do not seal up. Jesus reveals and climactically fulfills OT prophecies previously sealed until the end (Dan 12:4; cf. 5:1–10; Dan 8:26; 12:9). **because the time is near.** The reason for the previous command; reiterates 1:3 (see note there).

22:11 Summarizes the stark ethical alternatives readers face in view of

PARADISE RESTORED

EDEN (GENESIS 2–3)	NEW JERUSALEM (REVELATION 21–22)
A garden to inhabit and cultivate (2:8–9)	An established, glorious city (21:10)
River from Eden (2:10)	River of the water of life from God's throne (22:1)
Gold and onyx nearby (2:11–12)	Golden streets; walls have every precious stone (21:19–21)
Call to rule and serve (1:26; 2:15)	Serve as kings and priests (22:3,5)
One man and woman (2:22–24)	Believers from all nations (22:2)
Unclean serpent deceives and brings shame (3:1)	Nothing impure, shameful, or deceitful (21:27)
Exile from God's presence (3:23–24)	God's presence endures forever (21:3,23)
Lost access to the tree of life (3:22–24)	Eternal access for food and healing throughout the city (22:2,14)

22:12 [s] ver 7,20 [t] Isa 40:10
22:13 [u] Rev 1:8 [v] Rev 1:17 [w] Rev 21:6
22:14 [x] Rev 2:7 [y] Rev 21:12 [z] Rev 21:27
22:15 [a] 1Co 6:9,10; Gal 5:19-21; Col 3:5,6 [b] Php 3:2
22:16 [c] Rev 1:1 [d] Rev 1:4 [e] Rev 5:5 [f] 2Pe 1:19; Rev 2:28
22:17 [g] Rev 2:7
22:18 [h] Dt 4:2; Pr 30:6 [i] Rev 15:6-16:21
22:19 [j] Dt 4:2
22:20 [k] Rev 1:2 [l] 1Co 16:22
22:21 [m] Ro 16:20

Epilogue: Invitation and Warning

12 “Look, I am coming soon![s] My reward is with me,[t] and I will give to each person according to what
they have done. 13 I am the Alpha and the Omega,[u] the First and the Last,[v] the Beginning and the End.[w]
14 “Blessed are those who wash their robes, that they may have the right to the tree of life[x] and may
go through the gates[y] into the city.[z] 15 Outside[a] are the dogs,[b] those who practice magic arts, the sexually
immoral, the murderers, the idolaters and everyone who loves and practices falsehood.

16 “I, Jesus,[c] have sent my angel to give you[a] this testimony for the churches.[d] I am the Root[e] and
the Offspring of David, and the bright Morning Star.”[f]

17 The Spirit[g] and the bride say, “Come!” And let the one who hears say, “Come!” Let the one who is
thirsty come; and let the one who wishes take the free gift of the water of life.

18 I warn everyone who hears the words of the prophecy of this scroll: If anyone adds anything to
them,[h] God will add to that person the plagues described in this scroll.[i] 19 And if anyone takes words
away[j] from this scroll of prophecy, God will take away from that person any share in the tree of life and
in the Holy City, which are described in this scroll.

20 He who testifies to these things[k] says, “Yes, I am coming soon.”

Amen. Come, Lord Jesus.[l]

21 The grace of the Lord Jesus be with God's people.[m] Amen.

[a] *16* The Greek is plural.

Jesus' imminent return (vv. 10,12); cf. Ezek 3:27; Dan 12:10. The exhortations for unbelievers to continue to do wrong and to be vile may be ironic or may summon the faithful to respond positively to the prophetic word even if others do not.

22:12–21 *Epilogue: Invitation and Warning.* Jesus, the Davidic Messiah and sovereign Lord over history, is coming soon to reward faithful believers and punish wrongdoers.

22:12 coming soon! See note on v. 7. **My reward is with me.** Alludes to Yahweh's promise to come as Savior and King in Isa 40:10; 62:11.

22:13 Alpha ... Omega. Divine title (see note on 1:8) here applied to Jesus, who is sovereign over history and has authority to reward the faithful and punish the wicked “according to what they have done” (v. 12).

22:14 Blessed. Revelation's final beatitude (see note on 1:3). **those who wash their robes.** Recalls 7:14 (see note there). Those cleansed by Jesus' blood gain access to “the tree of life” in the new Jerusalem (cf. v. 2; 2:7), reversing the banishment of Gen 3:24.

22:15 In contrast, God excludes the wicked from the new Jerusalem and punishes them “outside.” See note on 21:8; see also “Vice Lists in Revelation,” p. 2603. **dogs.** Symbolizes false teachers (Phil 3:2) and unbelievers unworthy of holy things (cf. Matt 7:6).

22:16 I, Jesus, have sent my angel. Parallels 1:1–2. **you.** See NIV text note; may refer to John and other Christian prophets; most likely addresses “the churches” as in 1:4. **Root ... Offspring of David.** Recalls 5:5 (see note there). **Morning Star.** Interprets the promise in 2:28; alludes to Num 24:17.

22:17 Come! ... Come! ... come. Alludes to Isa 55:1 and summons “the one who is thirsty” to receive and relish the “free gift” of everlasting life with God (21:6).

22:18–19 The dual warning alludes to OT prohibitions against advancing false teaching and idolatry among God's people (Deut 4:2; 12:32), significant concerns for John's readers (cf. 2:14–15,20). The warning here specifically concerns the book of Revelation.

22:18 plagues. Recalls the “seven plagues” (15:6) and warning of covenant curses in Deut 28:59; 29:19–20.

22:19 tree of life ... Holy City. Cf. vv. 2,14; 2:7.

22:20 Yes, I am coming soon. Reiterates the promise of vv. 7,12 for emphasis. **Come, Lord Jesus.** Fitting prayer for believers eager for Jesus' return (cf. 1 Cor 16:22).

22:21 grace ... be with God's people. Typical closing prayer for NT letters (see Introduction: Genre [Epistle]); expresses John's desire that God's grace would enable the church to understand and obey Revelation's message (cf. 1:4).

TABLE OF WEIGHTS AND MEASURES

	Biblical Unit	Approximate American Equivalent	Approximate Metric Equivalent
Weights	talent (60 minas)	75 pounds	34 kilograms
	mina (50 shekels)	$1\frac{1}{4}$ pounds	560 grams
	shekel (2 bekas)	$\frac{2}{5}$ ounce	11.5 grams
	pim ($\frac{2}{3}$ shekel)	$\frac{1}{4}$ ounce	7.8 grams
	beka (10 gerahs)	$\frac{1}{5}$ ounce	5.7 grams
	gerah	$\frac{1}{50}$ ounce	0.6 gram
	daric	$\frac{1}{3}$ ounce	8.4 grams
Length	cubit	18 inches	45 centimeters
	span	9 inches	23 centimeters
	handbreadth	3 inches	7.5 centimeters
	stadion (pl. stadia)	600 feet	183 meters
Capacity			
Dry Measure	cor [homer] (10 ephahs)	6 bushels	220 liters
	lethek (5 ephahs)	3 bushels	110 liters
	ephah (10 omers)	$\frac{3}{5}$ bushel	22 liters
	seah ($\frac{1}{3}$ ephah)	7 quarts	7.5 liters
	omer ($\frac{1}{10}$ ephah)	2 quarts	2 liters
	cab ($\frac{1}{18}$ ephah)	1 quart	1 liter
Liquid Measure	bath (1 ephah)	6 gallons	22 liters
	hin ($\frac{1}{6}$ bath)	1 gallon	3.8 liters
	log ($\frac{1}{72}$ bath)	$\frac{1}{3}$ quart	0.3 liter

The figures of the table are calculated on the basis of a shekel equaling 11.5 grams, a cubit equaling 18 inches and an ephah equaling 22 liters. The quart referred to is either a dry quart (slightly larger than a liter) or a liquid quart (slightly smaller than a liter), whichever is applicable. The ton referred to in the footnotes is the American ton of 2,000 pounds. These weights are calculated relative to the particular commodity involved. Accordingly, the same measure of capacity in the text may be converted into different weights in the footnotes.

This table is based upon the best available information, but it is not intended to be mathematically precise; like the measurement equivalents in the footnotes, it merely gives approximate amounts and distances. Weights and measures differed somewhat at various times and places in the ancient world. There is uncertainty particularly about the ephah and the bath; further discoveries may shed more light on these units of capacity.

ARTICLES

THE STORY OF THE BIBLE: HOW THE GOOD NEWS ABOUT JESUS IS CENTRAL

Timothy Keller

In *After Virtue*, Alasdair MacIntyre famously illustrates that stories are necessary if we are to assign meaning to anything. He imagines standing at a bus stop when a young man he does not know comes up to him and says, "The name of the common wild duck is *Histrionicus histrionicus histrionicus*." He knows what the sentence literally conveys, but he has no idea what the young man's statement and action mean. The only way to know that is to know the story into which the incident fits. Perhaps, alas, the young man is mentally ill. That sad life story would explain it all. Or what if yesterday someone had approached the young man in the library and asked him the Latin word for the wild duck, and today the young man mistakes the man at the bus stop for that person in the library. That trivial story would explain it as well. Or perhaps the young man is a foreign spy "waiting at a prearranged rendezvous and uttering the ill-chosen code sentence which will identify him to his contact." That dramatic story would make sense of the incident too. But without a story, there's no meaning.

The title of this article includes an all-important assumption: the Bible is not just a diverse assortment of stories and materials; it altogether comprises a master narrative. This is not to say that the Bible is written like a novel with a tight, simple plotline — not at all. It contains many individual stories and a lot of nonnarrative material. But just as J. R. R. Tolkien produced thousands of pages of narratives, poetry, articles, maps, and even lexicons over the course of decades in order to tell one very sweeping story, so God, the author of every part of the Bible, is also telling one overarching story about the real world he created. There is a basic plotline to which all the parts relate and which makes sense of all the pieces.

The Bible begins with God making the world "very good" (Gen 1:31) — without the corruption, decay, and death that now dominate the world (Rom 8:20 – 21). In the world he placed human beings as his masterpiece, made in his image to reflect his own glory (Gen 1:27). We were created to adore and serve God and to love others. If we had chosen to live like that, we would have enjoyed a completely happy life and a perfect world. But instead, we wanted God to serve us and do what we wanted because we made our will the sovereign measure of all things. Instead of living for God and loving our neighbor, we turned away to live self-centered lives (Gen 3:1 – 7). Because our relationship with God has been broken, all other relationships — with other human beings, with our very selves, and with the created world — are also ruptured (Gen 3:8 – 19). The result is spiritual, psychological, social, and physical decay and breakdown. "Things fall apart; the centre cannot hold; / Mere anarchy is loosed upon the world" (William Butler Yeats, "The Second Coming") — that describes the world under sin now.

How did God respond? Did he respond with wrath toward the human race or with love? The answer is yes — to both (Rom 1:18; John 3:16). God insists on truth, demands that we do right, and threatens to punish all disobedience and evil. Nonetheless, he pursues the human race in love, declaring his intention to save and not allow all to perish in their sin. The Lord calls a people to himself in order to create a new human society — people who know his holy character and his law, his love, and his grace. This community began as an extended family (Gen 12:1 – 8) out of which God created an entire nation: the people of Israel, whom God delivered from slavery and established under Moses. With this people God made a covenant in which he promised to be their loving God and they promised to be his faithful people (Exod 19:1 – 8). But the history of this covenant relationship is one of almost unrelieved failure of the people to be what God called them to be.

All stories have plot "tension" and, in the most gripping narratives, it is intense. It comes from the clash of seemingly intractable forces in the struggle to restore things. And here we can see why the Bible is indeed a story. Through two-thirds of the Bible, the part we call the OT, an increasingly urgent, apparently insolvable problem drives the narrative forward. God is a God of holiness and is therefore implacably opposed to evil, injustice, and wrong, and yet he is a God of infinite love. He enters into a relationship with a people who are fatally self-centered. Will he bring down the curse he says must fall on sin and cut off his people, or will he forgive and love his people regardless of their sin? If he does either one *or* the other, sin and evil win! But it seems impossible to do both. Is the covenant relationship he established with his people conditional (so that failure is punished) or unconditional (so that the covenant is maintained despite the people's failure)?

Again, the answer is yes — to both. This resolution is

largely hidden from the reader through the OT, though Isaiah comes closest to unveiling it. The glorious King who *brings* God's judgment in the first part of Isaiah is also the suffering servant who *bears* God's judgment in the second part. It is Jesus. And in the NT, Jesus Christ, the Son of God, comes as our substitute — living the life we should have lived and dying the death we should have died, in our place. By living a perfect life, he earns God's blessing for obedience; by dying on the cross, he takes the curse for disobedience (Gal 3:10 – 14). When we believe in him, he receives the punishment we deserve, and we receive eternal life as a gift (2 Cor 5:21). And he does this in order to not only pardon our guilt but also to eventually free us from all sin and give us glorious new bodies and even a perfect, renewed world (Rom 8:18 – 39).

The best and most compelling stories have high stakes and astonishing, unexpected resolutions. If that is the case, there has never been a greater story than this. The stakes are literally cosmic: everyone and everything is at stake. It seems impossible that God could be true to himself — fully good and loving, fully righteous and just — and still save us. It seems impossible that after all we have done there should be any hope. But victory is achieved through one man's infinite sacrifice on the cross, where God both punishes sin fully yet provides free salvation, where he is revealed as both just and justifier of those who believe (Rom 3:26). Jesus stands as the ultimate protagonist, the hero of heroes.

Because the Bible's basic plotline is the tension between God's justice and his grace and because it is all resolved in the person and work of Jesus Christ, Jesus could tell his followers after the resurrection that the OT — "the Law of Moses, the Prophets and the Psalms" (Luke 24:44) — is really all about him (Luke 24:27,45). Paul says that all God's promises throughout the Scripture find their fulfillment only in Christ (2 Cor 1:20). So everything in the Bible — all its themes and patterns, main images and major figures — points to Jesus.

The Bible, then, is not a collection of Aesop-like fables, fictional stories that give us insights on how to find God and live right. Rather, it is both true history and a unified story about how God came to find us in the person of Jesus Christ, who lived and died in our place so we could be saved by grace through faith and live with him forever in a remade world, the Garden-City of God (Rev 21 – 22). From this basic plot there emerge profound insights, principles, and directives on how to live. But the Bible is not primarily about us and what we should do. It is first and foremost about Jesus and what he has done.

This is the Greatest Story not merely because of its infinitely high stakes and the endless wonder of its resolution but also because of its transforming power. How different is the Bible's story from the dominant one told in the Western world today — that we are accidents, here for no purpose other than what we create for ourselves, living in a world that is marked by one operative principle: the survival of the strong over the weak. Just as MacIntyre's response to the incident at the bus stop will be completely determined by what he discovers the story to be about, how we respond to suffering, death, sex, money, and power will be profoundly influenced by whether we understand and believe the story of the Bible about Jesus — or not.

THE BIBLE AND THEOLOGY

D. A. Carson

It has been said that the Bible is like a body of water in which a child may wade and an elephant may swim. The youngest Christian can read the Bible with profit, for the Bible's basic message is simple (see "The Story of the Bible: How the Good News About Jesus Is Central," p. 2631, and "The Gospel," p. 2686). But we can never exhaust its depth. After decades of intense study, the most senior Bible scholars find that they have barely scratched the surface. Although we cannot know anything with the perfection of God's knowledge (his knowledge is absolutely exhaustive!), yet because God has disclosed things, we can know those things truly.

Trying to make sense of parts of the Bible and of the Bible as a whole can be challenging. What kind of study should be involved when any serious reader of the Bible tries to make sense of the Bible as a whole? Appropriate study involves several basic interdependent disciplines, of which five are mentioned here: careful reading, biblical theology (BT), historical theology (HT), systematic theology (ST), and pastoral theology (PT). What follows looks at each of these individually and shows how they interrelate and how they are more than merely intellectual exercises.

CAREFUL READING

"Exegesis" is the word often used for careful reading. Exegesis answers the questions, What does this text actually say? and, What did the author mean by what he said? We discover this by applying sound principles of interpretation to the Bible.

Fundamental to reading the Bible well is good reading. Good readers pay careful attention to words and their meanings and to the ways sentences, paragraphs, and longer units are put together. They observe that the Bible is a book that includes many different styles of literature—stories, laws, proverbs, poetry, prophecy, history, parables, letters, apocalyptic, and much more. Good readers follow the flow of texts. For example, while it is always worth meditating on individual words and phrases, the most important factor in determining what a word means is how the author uses that word in a specific context.

One of the best signs of good exegesis is asking thoughtful questions that drive us to "listen" attentively to what the Bible says. As we read the text again and again, these questions are progressively honed, sharpened, corrected, or discarded.

BIBLICAL THEOLOGY

BT answers the question, How has God revealed his word historically and organically? BT studies the theology of individual biblical books (e.g., Isaiah, the Gospel of John), of select collections within the Bible (e.g., the Pentateuch, wisdom literature, the Gospels, Paul's letters, John's writings), and then traces out themes as they develop across time within the canon (e.g., the way in which the theme of the temple develops, in several directions, to fill out a "whole Bible" theology of the temple). At least four priorities are essential:

1. *Read the Bible progressively as a historically developing collection of documents.* God did not provide his people with all of the Bible at once. There is a progression to his revelation, and to read the whole back into some early part may seriously distort that part by obscuring its true significance in the flow of redemptive history. This requires not only organizing the Bible's historical material into its chronological sequence but also trying to understand the theological nature of the sequence.

2. *Presuppose that the Bible is coherent.* The Bible has many human authors but one divine Author, and he never contradicts himself. BT uncovers and articulates the unity of all the biblical texts taken together.

3. *Work inductively from the text—from individual books and from themes that run through the Bible as a whole.* Although readers can never entirely divorce themselves from their own backgrounds, students of BT recognize that their subject matter is *exclusively* the Bible. They therefore try to use categories and pursue agendas that the text itself sets.

4. *Make theological connections within the entire Bible that the Bible itself authorizes.* One way to do this is to trace the trajectory of themes straight through the Bible. (That's what the following articles in this study Bible do.)

BT often focuses on the turning points in the Bible's storyline (see "A Biblical-Theological Overview of the Bible," p. 2637), and its most pivotal concern is tied to how the NT uses the OT, observing how later Scripture writers refer to earlier ones.

HISTORICAL THEOLOGY

HT answers the questions, How have people in the past understood the Bible? What have Christians thought about exegesis and theology? and, more specifically, How has Christian doctrine developed over the centuries, especially in response to false teachings? HT is concerned primarily with opinions in periods earlier than our own. But we may also include under this heading the importance of reading the Bible globally—that is, finding out how believers in some other parts of the world read the text. That does not mean that they (or we!) are necessarily right; rather, it means that we recognize that all of us have a great deal to learn.

Carefully studying the history of interpretation is one of the greatest helps in freeing us from unwitting slavery to our biases. It induces humility, clears our minds of unwarranted assumptions, exposes faulty interpretations that others have long since (and rightly) dismissed, and reminds us that responsibly interpreting the Bible must never be a solitary task.

The study notes in this study Bible are informed by HT and reflect such knowledge when they present viable alternative ways to interpret texts. But the study notes focus primarily on exegesis and BT.

SYSTEMATIC THEOLOGY

ST answers the question, What does the whole Bible teach about certain topics? or put another way, What is true about God and his universe?

At the risk of stating the obvious, ST is systematic: it is organized on principles of logic, order, and need. ST is systemic: it is concerned with how the whole Bible logically coheres in systems of thought. It often organizes truth under headings such as the doctrines of God (theology proper), the Bible (bibliology), humans (anthropology), sin (hamartiology), Christ (Christology), the Holy Spirit (Pneumatology), salvation (soteriology), the church (ecclesiology), and the end times (eschatology). ST is generally framed so as to interact with and address the contemporary world. Even systematic theologians who cherish the narrative of Scripture and make much of the varied ways the Bible addresses its readers end up with highly ordered structures, sometimes calling them "theodramas."

The Bible's unity makes ST not only possible but necessary. The biblical data must control ST; however ST must in turn challenge alternative worldviews. Sometimes it is especially important not to "go beyond what is written," for some Christian truths include within their sweep substantial areas of unknown things. For instance, there are important things we do not know about Jesus' incarnation, about the Trinity, and about God's sovereignty and human responsibility. To pretend we know more than we do generates shoddy ST that can prove misleading and dangerous. A large part of orthodoxy resides in listening carefully and humbly to all of Scripture and then properly relating passage with passage, truth with truth.

Everyone holds to some sort of ST. The quality of ST is based on its foundational data, constructive methods, principles for excluding certain information, appropriately expressive language, and logical, accurate conclusions.

PASTORAL THEOLOGY

PT answers the question, How should humans respond to God's revelation? Sometimes that is spelled out by Scripture itself; other times it builds on inferences of what Scripture says. PT practically applies the other four disciplines — so much so that the other disciplines are in danger of being sterile and even dishonoring to God unless tied in some sense to the responses God rightly demands of us. PT may well address such diverse domains as culture, ethics, evangelism, marriage and family, money, the cure of souls, politics, worship, and much more.

LITERARY STRUCTURES

Before we reflect on the way these various approaches to theology interact with one another, something must be said about the literary structures of the Bible. Just as the Bible is not cast as a systematic theology, with separate topical chapters on "God," "Human Beings," "Sin," and so on, so also it is not cast as a series of books that march in tight order through history, each book taking up the story where the previous book stopped.

Some of the different literary genres — i.e., kinds of writing — that make up the Bible are introduced in articles such as "Introduction to the Historical Books," "Introduction to the Wisdom and Lyrical Books," and "Introduction to the Letters." When we look more closely, we find in the pages of the Bible literary genres as diverse as genealogies, parables, laments, confessions, psalms of praise, divine utterances from God, beatitudes, discourse, narrative, government documents and decrees, and even a fable. (A fable is a story without human characters but where animals or trees or other objects represent human beings. See Judg 9:7 – 15).

God displays his providential wisdom in providing us with a Bible made up of all these literary genres, and more. The diversity constitutes a great advantage, for each genre has a slightly different way of appealing to us, of making its impact on us. Together they do even more than instruct our minds: they fire our imaginations, prompt us to meditate, call up mental pictures, invite us to memorize, appeal to our emotions, shame us when our thoughts or actions are tawdry and unworthy, and make our spirits leap for joy. So while we work through the ways in which exegesis is (for example) tied to BT and to ST, we must always remember that God in his perfect wisdom gave us the fundamental texts, the books of the Bible, in spectacularly diverse forms. Nothing about Bible study is boring or mechanical. Here we come into contact with the instructing, evocative, creative, incredibly rich mind of God.

INTERRELATIONSHIPS

Some might think it convenient if we could order these disciplines along a straight line: Exegesis→BT→[HT]→ST→PT. (The brackets around HT suggest that HT directly contributes to the development from BT to ST and PT but is not itself a part of that line.) But this neat paradigm is naive because no exegesis is ever done in a vacuum. Before we ever start doing exegesis, we already have a ST-framework that influences our exegesis. So are we locked into a hermeneutical circle? See "Hermeneutical Circle," this page.

No; there is a better way. We might diagram it like this. See "Feedback Loop," this page.

In other words, there are always feedback loops — information loops that go back and reshape how one does any exegesis or theology. The loops should not take over the final voice, but they shape the process whether one likes it or not. It is absurd to deny that one's ST does not affect one's exegesis. But the line of final control is the straight line from exegesis right through BT and HT to ST and PT. The final authority is the Bible and the Bible alone.

HERMENEUTICAL CIRCLE

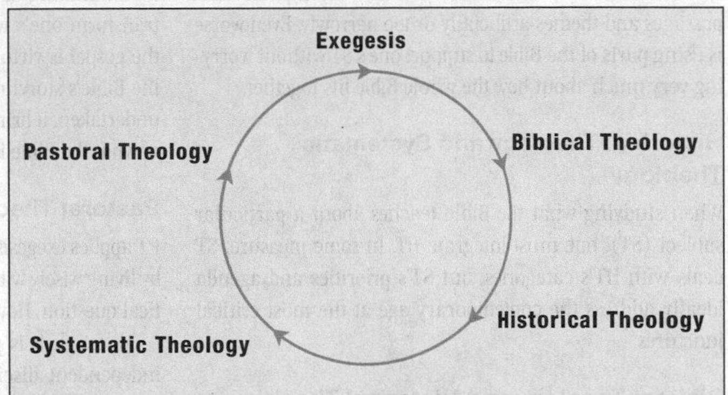

Exegesis and Biblical Theology

BT mediates how exegesis influences ST, partly because it helps one remember that there is promise and fulfillment, type and antitype, development, organic growth, anticipation and consummation (see "A Biblical-Theological Overview of the Bible," p. 2637). The overlap between exegesis and BT is the most striking among the theological disciplines: both are concerned to understand texts, and BT is impossible without exegesis. Exegesis tends to focus on analysis and BT on synthesis. BT reflects on the results of exegesis in the light of individual books and in the developing stream of the narrative of the whole Bible. Exegesis controls BT, and BT influences exegesis.

Exegesis and Historical Theology

The ancient creeds and the history of exegesis and of theology are invaluable, but they do not have the ultimate authority of the Bible itself. Nevertheless, without HT exegesis is likely to degenerate into obscure debates far too tightly tethered to twenty-first-century agendas. Responsible exegesis wrestles with earlier Christian exegesis and theology.

It is possible, however, to become so expert in secondary opinions that one never ponders the text of the Bible itself. Reading the history of interpretation must never usurp the place of reading the Bible.

Exegesis and Systematic Theology

Some think that their exegesis neutrally and objectively discovers the text's meaning and that they build their ST on such discoveries. In reality, ST profoundly influences one's exegesis. Without realizing it, many people develop their own lists of favorite passages of the Bible that then become their controlling grid for interpreting the rest of the Bible; to a large degree this accounts for conflicting exegesis among Christians. This problem may develop in at least two ways.

1. A church tradition may unwittingly overemphasize certain biblical truths at the expense of others, subordinating or even explaining away passages that do not easily "fit" the slightly distorted structure that results. For example, how one understands justification in Galatians may control how one understands justification everywhere else in the NT.

2. A church tradition may self-consciously adopt a certain

FEEDBACK LOOP

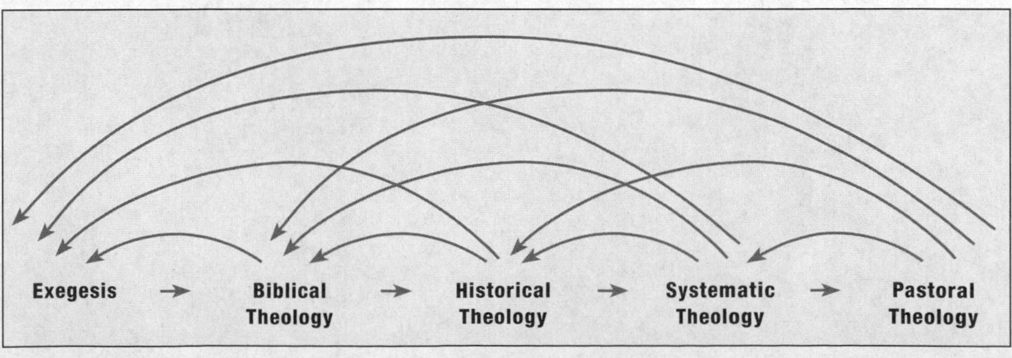

structure by which to integrate all the books of the Bible with the result that they automatically classify and explain some passages and themes artificially or too narrowly. Even worse is using parts of the Bible to support one's ST without worrying very much about how the whole Bible fits together.

Historical Theology and Systematic Theology

When studying what the Bible teaches about a particular subject (ST), one must integrate HT. In some measure, ST deals with HT's categories, but ST's priorities and agenda ideally address the contemporary age at the most critical junctures.

Biblical Theology and Historical Theology

Both BT and HT are aware of the passage of time in their respective disciplines: BT focuses on the time during which the biblical documents were written and collected, while HT focuses on the study of the Bible from the time it was completed. Otherwise put, BT focuses on the Bible, while HT focuses on what significant figures have believed about the Bible. BT functions best when interacting with HT.

Biblical Theology and Systematic Theology

BT is historical and organic; ST is relatively ahistorical and universal. Unlike BT, which is deeply committed to working inductively from the biblical text so that the text itself sets the agenda, ST may (legitimately) be at a second or third or fourth order removed from Scripture as it engages, say, philosophical and scientific questions that the biblical texts themselves do not directly raise. But ST is the most comprehensive of the various theological disciplines.

Exegesis and BT have an advantage over ST because the Bible aligns more immediately with their agendas. ST has an advantage over exegesis and BT because it drives hard toward holistic integration.

ST tends to be a little further removed from the biblical text than does BT, but ST is a little closer to cultural engagement. In some ways, BT is a kind of bridge-discipline between exegesis and ST because it overlaps with them, enabling them to hear each other a little better. In some ways, ST is a culminating discipline because it attempts to form and transform one's worldview. BT is important today because the gospel is virtually incoherent unless people understand the Bible's storyline. ST is important today because, rightly undertaken, it brings clarity and depth to our understanding of what the Bible is about.

Pastoral Theology and the Other Disciplines

PT applies exegesis, BT, HT, and ST to help people glorify God by living wisely with a biblical worldview. It answers the practical question, How then should we live?

Although it is possible to treat pastoral theology as an independent discipline, it is wiser to recognize that the Bible was never given to stir up *merely* or *exclusively* intellectual questions. It was given to transform people's lives; it was given to be practical. The notion of impractical theology — theological study that is unconcerned with repentance, faith, obedience, conformity to Christ, and joy in the Lord — hovers somewhere between the ridiculous and the blasphemous.

We may so quickly pursue "what the Bible means to me" (greatly emphasizing "to me") that we completely ignore the distance between ourselves and the text and compromise the Bible's historical specificity and thus the nature of God's revelation. It is far better to read each part of the Scripture, think it through on its own terms, discern its contribution to the whole Bible, and ask how such truth applies to us and our church and society.

Since God created the universe, we are accountable to him, and he has authoritatively spoken in the Bible. Even if we earnestly try to understand God's gracious self-disclosure on its own terms, that is insufficient if we do not respond to God as he has disclosed himself. Interpreters are inseparable from the interpretive process, and our attitude toward the text is important. Desiring merely to master the text is not enough; we must desire to be mastered by it. For one day we will give an account to the one who says, "These are the ones I look on with favor: those who are humble and contrite in spirit, and who tremble at my word" (Isa 66:2).

A BIBLICAL-THEOLOGICAL OVERVIEW OF THE BIBLE

D. A. Carson

In "The Bible and Theology," p. 2633, we observed how biblical theology is related to other disciplines, including careful reading, systematic theology, historical theology, and pastoral theology. Biblical theology studies the theology of individual biblical books (e.g., Isaiah, the Gospel of John) and of select collections within the Bible (e.g., the Pentateuch, wisdom literature, the Gospels, Paul's letters, John's writings), carefully thinking through their place in the Bible's developing story. It also traces out themes as they develop across time within the canon.

THE PRACTICE OF BIBLICAL THEOLOGY

As currently practiced, biblical theology wears one or more of three "faces":

1. *Face One.* Here one seeks to understand, e.g., the theology of Jeremiah, of Luke-Acts, of the Pentateuch, or of Hebrews. Textbooks abound with the words "Theology of the New Testament" in the title. In most cases these are books with discrete chapters devoted to the distinctive theological emphases of each book or corpus in the NT. The best of these chapters locate the biblical book or corpus within the Bible's entire narrative, not just within the narrative of the NT, and thus they are rightly considered biblical-theological studies.

2. *Face Two.* Alternatively, one may trace certain themes running through the entire Bible, carefully observing how the passage of time enlarges and enriches them. Many of the ensuing articles in this study Bible are devoted to that kind of biblical theology. For example, the study of how the theme of the temple develops across time within the Bible not only generates insight on that theme but also enables us to see more clearly how the entire Bible holds together.

3. *Face Three.* Some writers have recently studied a particular biblical book, then carefully noted how that book uses earlier biblical material, and then examined how later biblical books cite or allude to that book. For example, one might study the theology of the book of Daniel, paying close attention to the ways in which Daniel picks up themes and specific passages from earlier OT material, and then study how Daniel is cited and used in the rest of the Bible. This is another way of saying that even though biblical theology sometimes focuses initially on one book of the Bible or on one theme running through the Bible, sooner or later it is interested in understanding how the Bible holds together, how in God's providence it develops across time to become what we hold in our hands today.

What is striking about all these faces of biblical theology is that they keep one eye focused on the passage of time—i.e., on where any biblical document or theme is located in what is often called "salvation history" (the history of redemption). God did not choose to disclose everything in one moment of spectacular revelation. Rather, he chose to disclose himself and his purposes progressively, through events and words spread across many centuries, climaxing in his Son, Jesus Christ.

WHAT IS SALVATION HISTORY?

Although the word "history" sometimes refers to what has taken place, it more commonly refers to the story or account of what has taken place. No human account of what has taken place can ever be exhaustive: we simply do not and cannot know enough. For example, a history of the Roman Empire cannot possibly tell us everything that took place within the Roman Empire during the centuries the empire existed. Any history of the Roman Empire will necessarily be selective. A history will be judged as excellent or poor on the basis of how representative it is, how the parts are made to cohere, how evidence has been handled, and the like. However the history is organized, it involves sequence (keeping an eye on time), cause and effect, trends, and evaluation of significance.

Salvation history is thus the history of salvation—i.e., the history of events that focus on the salvation of human beings and issues involving the new heaven and the new earth. Even when the focus narrows to one man, Abraham, and his descendants, that man is given the promise that in him and in his seed all the nations of the earth will be blessed (Gen 12:3). Biblical Christianity is not an abstract or timeless philosophy (though of course it involves abstractions): at least in part, it is the account of what God has done, of the events and explanations he has brought about in order to save lost human beings. (Even what "salvation" means, what it means to be "saved," is disclosed in this history.) From this, four things follow:

1. Salvation history is part of world history. It may tell of some events that other historians are not interested in, but it so describes real events that it necessarily overlaps with other histories. The Bible tells of some events bound up with Tiglath-Pileser (2 Kgs 15:29), Nebuchadnezzar (Jer 39), and

Pilate (Matt 27:11 – 26), but we also know of these men from sources with no connection to the Bible.

2. Salvation history is real history. It depicts events that really did take place. This may seem a rather obvious thing to say, but it has to be said, because some theologians have argued that salvation history — biblical history — is often not historical. Sometimes, they say, it relates things as if they really did take place even though they did not take place. The importance of these "events" that never happened, it is argued, lies in their aesthetics, their important themes, or their ability to stir the imagination. But salvation history is real history.

3. Salvation history includes not only events caused by other events that take place in the natural world but also events caused directly by God. Sometimes, of course, God works in providential ways *through* the natural order. For example, although biblical authors know about the water cycle — water evaporates from oceans and seas to form clouds that send their precipitation back to earth to run in rivulets and streams and rivers back to the sea (Eccl 1:7) — they generally prefer to say that God sends the rain (e.g., Matt 5:45). Thus, God works through the natural order. But when God raises Jesus from the dead, there is nothing natural about God's action: this is the direct intervention of God, displaying his might in contravention of nature. Nevertheless, Jesus' resurrection *happened*; it took place *in history*. This must be strongly asserted against those who say that genuinely "historical" events are those that have natural causes. Such a stance rules out what the Bible makes obvious: God can and does directly intervene in history beyond his providential reign that utilizes natural causes. Salvation history includes events like Jesus' resurrection, events that take place but that are caused directly by God.

4. Although the Bible contains a good deal of salvation history, it contains things other than salvation history. For example, it includes wisdom literature, lament, law, prophecy, and much more. But even these disparate kinds of literature that make up the Bible are written at discrete points along the Bible's story line. In other words, salvation history provides the backbone to which all the parts of the Bible are connected.

THE SHAPE OF SALVATION HISTORY

One might summarize salvation history in four words: creation, fall, redemption, consummation. That is the entire story, painted with the broadest brush. Then again, one might add in, after the fall, a number of other turning points: the call of Abraham and the beginning of the Abrahamic covenant, the exodus and the giving of the law, entrance into the promised land, the establishment of the Davidic dynasty, the exile and the end of the exile. Under redemption, one might break down the category into constituent parts: the incarnation, Jesus' atoning death, Jesus' resurrection, and the descent of the Spirit at Pentecost.

Of course, one might then further refine the details of this history. For example, one might specify David's seven-year rule in Hebron over two tribes before he captures Jerusalem, makes it his capital, and simultaneously becomes king over the twelve tribes. In discussing the Davidic dynasty, one might list the various monarchs and what they did for good or ill. One might describe the tabernacle and its function as stipulated in the law of Moses, then trace its history until it is displaced by the temple built by Solomon, observing further the destruction of the temple under Nebuchadnezzar in 586 BC, and the building of another temple under the ministry of prophets like Haggai. Likewise, one might expand the discussion of the exile to distinguish the onset of the exile of Israel in 722 BC by the Assyrians from the onset of the exile of Judah in 586 BC by the Babylonians. The distinction between these two dates is of more than antiquarian interest; e.g., the prophets build on the fact that Israel is taken off to captivity long before her "sister" Judah to argue that Judah ought to learn some lessons from the wretched experience of Israel, while in fact she learns nothing and seems committed to duplicating all Israel's sins, with far less excuse (e.g., Jer 3:6 — 4:31). And so far nothing has been said of the salvation-historical contributions of, e.g., Ruth, Esther, Daniel, and Nehemiah.

All these historical details, many of them significant historical turning points, make up the history of redemption. And all of them, rightly configured, draw lines toward the greatest turning point of all in salvation history: the birth, ministry, death, resurrection, and ascension of Jesus the Messiah.

THE SIGNIFICANCE OF SALVATION HISTORY

Five things might usefully be mentioned.

1. The story line of the Bible, the sweep of salvation history, provides the framework on which so much else in the Bible depends. For example, it would be impossible to trace such themes as the tabernacle/temple, the priestly ministry, the Davidic dynasty, and the Messianic hope apart from the salvation-historical framework in which these themes are embedded. Thus, the discipline of biblical theology is grounded on an appropriate grasp of salvation history.

2. The Bible's salvation history largely establishes the direction of its movement. To return for a moment to the simplest outline of salvation history: we begin with *creation*, with God as the Creator and all that he makes declared to be good; we move to the *fall*, which establishes the nature of the problem throughout the rest of the story; we arrive at *redemption*, which is God's answer to the horrible defiance of human rebellion and guilt, turning as it does on the cross and resurrection of Jesus; and we finally reach the *consummation*, when in the wake of redemption God finally brings

to pass all his purposes, secured in Christ and now brought to completion. Salvation-history is cohesive and discloses God's purposes in the direction in which the narrative unfolds.

3. The trajectories that run through and are part of the history of redemption gradually point to the future and become predictive voices. For example, the promise of a Davidic dynasty (2 Sam 7:11b – 16), a promise made about 1,000 years before Jesus, a dynasty that endures forever, is fleshed out in Ps 2, given new and rich associations in the eighth-century BC prophecies of Isaiah (Isa 9), and provided with further images in the sixth-century BC ministry of Ezekiel (Ezek 34). Once this trajectory is established, thoughtful readers look along this trajectory and cannot fail to discern ways in which the depictions of Davidic kings point forward to the ultimate Davidic king. Similar things can be said of many other trajectories that run through salvation history. For example, the theme of the exodus is picked up and developed in the return of the people to the promised land after the exile and culminates in the new exodus theme in the NT (see "Exile and Exodus," p. 2659).

4. Very often these trajectories (or "typologies," as they are often called) in the history of redemption become intertwined to form rich tapestries. For example, although it is possible to follow the themes of tabernacle/temple, Jerusalem, and the Davidic dynasty as separate trajectories (these are teased out in various articles in this study Bible), they come together in 2 Sam 6 – 7: the ark is brought to Jerusalem and the groundwork is laid for the temple, David's dynasty is established, and Jerusalem, now the capital of Israel, is becoming the city of the great King. From this point forward these themes repeatedly wrap around each other, so that mention of one often pulls in one or both of the others. The destruction of Jerusalem at the onset of the Babylonian exile means the destruction of the temple and the suspension of the Davidic monarchy. Eventually Jesus is hailed as the Messianic King as he rides into Jerusalem (Matt 21:1 – 11), cleans out the temple (Matt 21:12 – 17), and is crucified as the king who reigns from the cross (Matt 27:27 – 37), providing the atonement long anticipated by the rites in the temple (Heb 9:1 — 10:4) and pointing the way forward to the Jerusalem that is above (Gal 4:26; Heb 12:22).

5. Above all, salvation history provides the locus in which God has disclosed himself in events and in the words that explain them. As salvation history is the framework of the Bible's story line, so it is the locus of the revelation of the living God, the Lord of history.

THE GLORY OF GOD

James M. Hamilton Jr.

What is the glory of God? The answer is as infinite as God's glory itself, so the question can never be answered exhaustively. Some key aspects of God's glory, however, can be summarized as follows: the glory of God is the weight of the majestic goodness of who God is and the resulting name, or reputation, that he gains from revealing himself as Creator, Sustainer, Judge, and Redeemer, perfect in justice and mercy, loving-kindness and truth (cf. Exod 34:6–8). God's glory elicits praise.

CREATION

God created the world as a place where he would be known, served, praised, and worshiped — a place where his glory would be both manifest and enjoyed. In this respect, God created the world as a cosmic temple. What God set out to accomplish at the beginning is what he will bring to pass at the end of all things (cf. Rev 21:15 — 22:5). The cosmos is a stunning and fabulous temple, brimming with God's wisdom and creativity. In a sacred garden spot in his cosmic temple, God placed an image of himself. This image was made not of wood or stone or gold or silver but of flesh and blood. Human beings, like the cosmic temple of the universe, radiate God's glory. The human body is an engineering masterpiece; childbirth is a miraculous mystery; and the mercy and justice that humans can display as they relate to one another is simultaneously light and heavy, acute and broad, high and deep, reflecting the very glory of the One whose image they bear. The image of the real God is not like the idolatrous man-made images that neither see nor hear nor eat nor smell but is a living being capable of rational thought, relational engagement, and creative development. God endowed his image-bearers with the capacity to use all their powers in the mysterious and elevating worship of the One who made them, sustains them, and created them for himself.

FALL

God created the world as a theater of his glory, and in the theater he put an image of himself made to enjoy his glory. Moreover, this image of God was to exercise dominion over the world and bring it into subjection (Gen 1:26–28). Rather than covering the dry lands with the glory of the Lord as the waters cover the sea, however, the image-bearer was tempted, sinned, and consequently cast out of the garden of God's presence (Gen 3:6–7,23). Even this, however, did not take God by surprise. The omniscient Creator knew all that would come to pass in the world he created, and he went forward with the project. We can observe that the sin Adam chose to commit opened up previously impossible prospects. With Adam guilty, God now has an opportunity to display the wonder of his mercy, to demonstrate his power to overcome volitional evil, and to show his love by accomplishing salvation. God set mercy and salvation in motion even as he spoke judgment on the sinners, thereby displaying the unique glory of his ability to save and show kindness, love, and mercy even as he keeps his word and upholds righteousness by doing justice (Gen 3:14–19, especially 3:15).

REDEMPTION PROMISED

God did not give up on his original purpose to cover the dry lands with his glory, and there is a clear line from Adam to Abraham (Gen 5:1–32; 11:10–26), and then from Abraham to the nation of Israel (Gen 12:1–3; 26:1–4; 28:1–4; 48:15–16; 49:1–27). The nation was identified as God's "firstborn son" at the exodus from Egypt (Exod 4:22–23), and God showed his glory over Pharaoh at the exodus (e.g., Exod 9:16; 14:4,17), planting Israel in the promised land (Exod 15:17) so they could take up the task Adam forsook (cf. Gen 1:28 and Josh 18:1). Even when judging Israel's sin, God reiterated his purpose: "the glory of Yahweh will fill all the earth" (Num 14:21, author's translation). In the tabernacle and later the temple, God gave to Israel a symbol of the cosmos on a small scale. When his glory filled both (Exod 40:34; 1 Kgs 8:10–11), God gave Israel a preview of the way his glory will one day fill the world, God's cosmic temple. Once the Davidic king was established over Israel, he was identified as God's "son" (2 Sam 7:14; Ps 2:7) and invited to ask God for the nations as his heritage (Ps 2:8). If God's anointed king would heed Deut 17:18–20 and rule on the basis of God's Torah, he would bring the nations around them into subjection, and they too would be ruled by God's good law and enjoy his glory (Deut 2:10–12; cf. Ps 67). As Israel's king reigned with God's wisdom, all the lands would enjoy the dominion of Yahweh's vice-regent (cf. Ps 72:8–17). God's glory would fill the earth (Ps 72:19). But like Adam, the nation and king were tempted, sinned, and cast out of the land of God's presence.

From the writings of Israel's prophets, psalmists, and sages, we receive kaleidoscopic snapshots of what God intends to accomplish. God's name is majestic in all the earth (Ps 8:1), and he makes his praise strong from weak things, like children and infants (Ps 8:2). Yahweh gave dominion over all he made to the son of man (Ps 8:4–8), and the son of man declaring these things in Ps 8 happens to be David, the anointed king of Israel (Ps 8 superscription). The heavens are proclaiming God's glory (Ps 19:1), and all the nations will glorify his name (Ps 86:9). Jerusalem will be the highest mountain on the earth; from there God's Torah will go forth (Isa 2:1–4). The whole earth is full of God's glory (Isa 6:3), and when the promised king from the line of Jesse arises to reign, fully endowed with God's Spirit (Isa 11:1–2), "the earth will be filled with the knowledge of the LORD as the waters cover the sea" (Isa 11:9; cf. Hab 2:14). Justice will be done. The wicked will be crushed (Ps 72:4). Those who trust God will be delivered (Isa 26:3–4). All war will end (e.g., Ps 46:9; Isa 2:4). The curse on the land will be removed (Ps 72:3). The land of Zion will be like Eden, like Yahweh's garden (Isa 51:3). The enmity between the seed of the woman and the serpent will be gone (Isa 11:8). The Spirit will be poured out on all flesh (Joel 2:28–32). Yahweh's anointed king will exercise dominion "from the River to the ends of the earth" (Ps 72:8; Zech 9:10). The serpent's head will be crushed (Gen 3:15; Ps 74:13–14; Isa 27:1). The wicked will lick the dust like their father the devil (Gen 3:14; Ps 72:9). The nations will be blessed in the seed of Abraham (Gen 12:3; Ps 72:17). And all the earth will be filled with Yahweh's glory (Ps 72:18–19).

REDEMPTION ACCOMPLISHED

To consummate his purposes (Eph 1:9–10), God sent Jesus, the servant who would be exalted and glorified (Isa 52:13; cf. John 12:23). The humility and obedience of Jesus display God's glory in what looks to the world like weakness, and this is in keeping with the way God uses the weak things of the world to shame the strong (1 Cor 1:18–31), showing his glory by reversing expectations. God promised to make a great nation of a man with a barren wife (Gen 11:30; 12:1–3). God chose "the fewest of all peoples" to be his own (Deut 7:7). When God decisively answered Satan's pride and rebellion, he sent his Son as a helpless baby born to a peasant girl in questionable circumstances. Praise ordained from the mouths of children and infants indeed (Ps 8:2). God silenced the dragon's roar with the infant's cry (Rev 12:1–12). Not only did God show his foolishness and weakness to be wiser and stronger than that of men, he achieved victory by what looked like defeat. Christ died on the cross. In the paradox of the ages, the humiliation of Christ won him the name above every name (Phil 2:5–11). At the cross Jesus was glorified and glorified the Father (John 12:23,28; 13:31–32). God's wrath was poured out, and the full weight of God's justice was visited on Jesus the Messiah as he died on the cross. Simultaneously, God showed his great love for his people in his willingness to sacrifice his beloved Son, accomplishing the extravagant plan of redemption. At the cross, then, God was glorified for his justice and his mercy (cf. Exod 34:6–7), while Jesus was glorified by his unique ability to satisfy God's wrath and accomplish the redemption of God's people. And Paul asserts that God did this to display his righteous and merciful glory as the just justifier of believers (Rom 3:25–26).

God is now saving his people to the praise of his glory and grace (Eph 1:6,12,14). He is displaying his manifold wisdom through the church to the spiritual authorities in heavenly places (Eph 3:10). Paul ascribes glory to God in the church and in Christ forever (Eph 3:20–21). The redemption of God's people will culminate in the appearance of Christ in glory, dealing out retribution to his enemies and saving those who hope in him (2 Thess 1:5–12).

Across the Scriptures God's people recognize and respond to God's own concern for his glory. Moses (Exod 32:12), Joshua (Josh 7:9), David (2 Sam 7:25–26), Solomon (1 Kgs 8:43,60), Asa (2 Chr 14:11), Jehoshaphat (2 Chr 20:9), Elijah (1 Kgs 18:36–37), Hezekiah (2 Kgs 19:19), Jeremiah (Jer 14:7,21), the psalmists (Pss 25:11; 31:3; 79:9; 109:21), and Daniel (Dan 9:16–19) — they all appeal to God's concern for his own glory as they pray to him. A host of doxologies in the NT ascribe glory to God and his Messiah (Luke 1:68; Rom 1:25; 9:5; 11:33–36; 16:25–27; 2 Cor 1:3; 11:31; Gal 1:4–5; Eph 1:3; 3:20–21; Phil 4:20; 1 Tim 1:17; 6:15–16; 2 Tim 4:18; Heb 13:20–21; 1 Pet 1:3; 4:11; 5:11; 2 Pet 3:18; Jude 24–25; Rev 1:5–6). From the book of Revelation, it appears that God's redeemed people will sing his praise forever (e.g., Rev 5:9–14; 7:9–12; 15:2–4; 19:1–3).

DOES GOD SEEK HIS OWN GLORY?

Is it right for God to seek his own glory? What higher end could he seek? If he put something else before himself, would he not be an idolater breaking the first commandment? Is it unloving for God to seek his own glory (cf. 1 Cor 13:5)? On the contrary, if God is the first and best of beings, if humans were made to show forth and enjoy God's glory, and if loving others entails wanting what is best for them and what will give them most joy, then it would be unloving for God to do anything other than seek his own glory. God is righteous and loving to seek his own glory so that people can celebrate his great name and relish him forever and ever, amen.

CREATION

Henri A. G. Blocher

Luther once dubbed the first chapter of Genesis "the foundation of the whole Scripture." He discerned that the truth it expounds of God's creation presupposes everything the Bible tells. The pride of place the passage enjoys in the Bible, by God's providential design, fittingly symbolizes that role. The Bible addresses the topic of creation, however, in other passages in various ways.

RECONNOITERING BIBLICAL DATA

Genesis 1–3

The sober and majestic prologue through which one enters the biblical library (Gen 1:1—2:3) condenses major themes of a theology of creation. Among these is the *goodness* of God's work (Gen 1:31). This provides the basis for the story of the fall in Gen 3: evil is *not* part of creation; it is an intruder. At the same time (and time is emphasized), the opening chapters show history unfolding in the wake of the initial creation, in the context of the created order. They also introduce the motif of de-creation (the flood).

Prophets

The prophetic books do not focus on creation, but they do refer to it. God's power as displayed in the universe shows his ability to carry out threats and promises (Amos 4:13; 5:8–9; 9:5–6; Zech 12:1). The Lord as Creator contrasts with the petty "gods" of the nations (Jer 10:11; cf. Isa 40–48; see Acts 17:24). More specifically, salvation is a "new creation" (especially Isa 40–66); the "new exodus" will be so radical that it will beget new heavens and a new earth (Isa 51:9–16).

Psalms

The Psalms celebrate the Lord as the Creator, the object of trust and praise—some of them closely akin to the Genesis chapters (Pss 8; 104). God's handiwork reveals his character, his glory (Ps 19:1–6, the counterpart of God's revelation in his law, vv. 7–10). It testifies to his might and wisdom as well as to his loving care (Pss 36:6–9; 147). The psalmists insist on the stability God grants the world (e.g., Ps 93:1), though it is a mere perishable image of the Lord's immutability (Ps 102:25–27).

Wisdom

The Wisdom books are strongly interested in creation. The book of Job aims at casting down human arrogance, reminding creatures of dust of the awful mystery of God's works—how unfathomable his intelligence and untraceable his ways (Job 38–41)! God promises precious fruit to those who inquire into his works of creation, provided they do so with a humble, teachable spirit and in the fear of the Lord. By wisdom and understanding, God set the heavens, the earth, and the deeps in place (Prov 3:19–20), so that observing creatures can make one wiser (Prov 6:6–8), although one must access wisdom first through the word of the Teacher (e.g., Eccl 11:1–6; 12:11). The concordance between the wisdom embedded in the structures of reality and the wisdom taught in Scripture, both proceeding from God, is the key to the efficacy of wisdom. Since wisdom agrees both with God's word and with the world he has made, it reflects reality itself, and so leads to success, life, and happiness.

Prov 8:22–31 boldly develops the role of wisdom in creation. Wisdom personified introduces herself as the Lord's child, begotten from eternity, and the craftsman by his side when the Lord founded the earth. This poetic but evocative description of wisdom's role in creation prompts reflection on the very nature of God. The theme was richly elaborated in Judaism, especially in the deep Apocryphal book called The Wisdom of Solomon (first century BC). Echoes of it in the NT suggest that the development was part of God's revelatory design (e.g., 1 Cor 1:30–31; 2:6–16; Col 1:9; 2:2–3).

New Testament

The "new creation" theme is prominent in Paul's epistles and in Revelation. The catastrophic damage done to the old creation by the fall is now already being overturned by the new creation, which itself will be brought to perfection and completion at the end of the age (Rev 21). The major advance relates to the role of Jesus Christ: the NT presents him not only as both the agent of the new creation and the new Adam but also as the agent of the *first* creation, cocreator with the Father. He is Wisdom come in person, come in the flesh. In his not-yet-incarnate state, he shared in the work of creation: through him all things were made, whether earthly or heavenly. Three passages draw on the Wisdom tradition (springing from Prov 8) and apply its insights to Christ: (1) John 1:1–10 parallels Gen 1, (2) Col 1:15–20 (cf. 1 Cor 8:6) poetically evokes the work of the preincarnate Christ ("the firstborn over all creation," Col 1:15) and the incarnate Christ ("the firstborn from among the dead," Col 1:18), and (3) Heb 1:2 (cf. Heb 3:3–4) is a crowning revelation. Paul uses the doctrine of creation as theological grounds for doing away with clean/unclean categories in things such as foods (1 Tim 4:3–4).

THE MEANING OF CREATION

The meaning of creation is bound up with an array of interpretive challenges. The data just surveyed are found in a variety of literary genres, and more than half are couched in the language of poetry. A cautious, tactful reading avoids projecting on to the text modern questions, interests, or would-be certainties — unless our questions enjoy enough of a kinship with a passage's scope and intention. Certainly, while we may not ignore extrabiblical evidence, we should place greater weight on parallels and developments within the Bible itself — on the "analogy of faith."

The Hebrew verb translated "to create" (*bara'*) is used only for a divine work, but "to make" is found as its parallel (already in Gen 1). Creation is one mode of origination: after the analogy of workers who make things to exist that did not exist before. Other words enrich our understanding of God's work: form or fashion (Gen 2:7–8,19; Zech 12:1); organize or arrange; lay the foundations (e.g., of a building; the world is God's temple, Ps 29:9; this is one of the many parallels between the "foundation" of Eden and the "foundation" of the tabernacle); acquire or beget (Gen 14:19); and terms for specific elements such as stretch, fix, and plant. The NT vocabulary is less rich and the verb "to create" less tightly defined, but the NT terms do not otherwise paint a contradictory.

Is there something specific about this mode of creation? Tradition says that it is made *from nothing*. Scripture does not use those very words, although Rom 4:17 comes close. God speaks of the created order as coming *from himself* — "from whom all things" (1 Cor 8:6) — not in the sense of an emanation of his being, for God *chose* to create all things, he did not simply radiate them or emanate them as an inevitable function of his being (Acts 17:25; 1 Cor 12:18). The idea rules out any second principle in the constitution of reality, any preexistent matter. The invisible source of all visible creatures is the power of the living God (Heb 11:3). This agrees with the use of *bara'*: even when "matter" is present (as it is in the new creation), the emphasis is on newness (Isa 48:6–7; 65:17). Cf. the same emphasis on newness in the dreadful judgment of Num 16:30: "But if the LORD brings about something totally new" (or "if the LORD creates a creation").

Taken together, the teachings of Scripture lead to defining "creation" by a *non-symmetrical* structure. That God creates all things rules out dualism, even the faintest trace of a particle of being that would not proceed from God. That the distinction between Creator and creature cannot be erased rules out pantheism. The world totally depends on God, yet God is absolutely independent of it. Such a pattern is unique. People talk loosely of the "myths of creation" found in the ancient Near East, as if they share much common ground with Genesis because they exhibit curiosity about origins, but creation strict and pure is found only in the Bible. This nonsymmetrical structure between God and the creation is repeated in the dominant biblical depictions of *covenant*, where again the two partners are not in a symmetrical relationship. Structurally, creation and covenant go together.

What does creation confer? The Bible does not promote a concept of "being" in some abstract philosophical sense, but it has its own interest in being. The creative commands God utters in the six days use various words for the creation of earthly creatures, but we read "let there *be*" for the heavenly ones (Gen 1:3,6,14). A few verses expressly focus on the gift of being, of existence (Isa 66:2; John 1:3; Heb 11:3; Rev 4:11). The God Who Is (Ex 3:14; Rev 1:4,8) opposes and exposes rival gods as nonentities, entities without any real being. Creation also institutes orderly *form*: we move from chaos to cosmos, and thus to beauty. This is the function of separation and order, and it is accomplished by the *word*: the sword of the Word cuts through confusion and establishes identities which may, then, be related (Gen 1; Col 1:17). Creation infuses *life*, implying fruitfulness and growth. This is the locus of blessing and belongs to the *Spirit*, the divine Breath who hovered over the primeval waters (Gen 1:2). The blessing of life implies growth. Therefore, creation opens the possibility of a meaningful history flowing from the gift of life — it brings a task and therefore a calling, an implicit promise and therefore a hope (Gen 1:28).

The calling and the promise are first and foremost for humankind: God's image, which God erects in the universe that is his temple. The meaning of creation is concentrated in that paradoxical creature, earthly and yet a little lower than God (*'ĕlōhîm*; Ps 8:5). Humankind is to represent God for the earth, and represent the earth for God.

FROM CREATION TO NEW CREATION

The sequence is well known. History follows, but in dramatic change. Human disobedience brings creation under the bondage of decay. But God does not abandon his covenant-partner. The good news of redemption (freedom recovered through a ransom payment) is told in terms of a *new creation*.

The new creation is not "another" creation, somewhere else, "from nothing." It is the renewal of the "old" creation, washed clean (as after the flood), reformed and made alive; otherwise it would not mean salvation. It is called "creation" because it requires (at least) as much power, wisdom, and love as God's first work.

This implies that humankind's betrayal disfigured but did not abolish creation. God granted the world a grace of preservation. A substantial portion of his creational gifts was maintained — for which many psalms praise him indeed. This entails consequences for ethics: the normative structures established in creation remain in force; redemption may transpose some but does not make them null and void.

New creation means *restoration*: undoing the damage (1 John 3:8). Yet, mysteriously, it also implies a *plus*. Paradise regained is a more glorious paradise! From the garden to the city and the multitude (Rev 7:9; 21:2)! From the fine agreement of heaven and earth to their intimate union in the Lamb's wedding (Rev 21)!

How has this transition come about? The Lamb is the Lord! The new Adam is from heaven: the Wisdom who was with God, through whom all things were made and remade.

SIN

Kevin DeYoung

Sin is another name for that hideous rebellion, that God-defiance, that wretched opposition to the Creator that crouches at the door of every fallen human heart. Sin is both a condition, inherited from Adam (Rom 5:12 – 21), and an action — manifesting itself in thought, word, and deed — that when full-grown gives birth to death (Jas 1:15). In simplest terms, sin is lawlessness (1 John 3:4). It means we have broken God's commands and have fallen short of his glory (Rom 3:23). But sin goes deeper than merely missing the mark. Sin is idolatry (Col 3:5; 1 John 5:21). It is worshiping false gods, whether these deities are overt and physical or more subtle and internal. Sin can also be considered adultery, a spiritual whoring after other lovers and other sources of satisfaction and meaning (Ezek 16:15 – 42). Sin is pollution (Jas 1:27). Sin is pervasive (Rom 3:9 – 20). And sin is *the* problem in the universe. The redemptive story of the Bible does not make sense without it.

SIN INFILTRATES THE GARDEN

In the beginning God created the heavens and the earth — the land, the sky, the sea; the birds, the fish, the animals; the sun, the moon, the stars; a man and a woman. He created all this, and it was "very good" (Gen 1:31).

And sometime later everything good started to come undone.

We know very little about the first sin, except that it manifested itself in an angelic rebellion. Jude 6 explains that some angels "did not keep their positions of authority but abandoned their proper dwelling — these [the Lord] has kept in darkness, bound with everlasting chains for judgment on the great Day." 1 Tim 3:6 suggests that the fall of the devil was the result of pride (see Ezek 28:11 – 19 for another possible allusion). However it happened, Satan ("the adversary") fell. It's important to note that sin originated in the world of spirits, not in the world of human beings. Moreover, it is critical to see that these spirits did not sin by some external power or temptation, but in and by themselves. The devil's sin came out of the devil's own self-twisted arrogance and deception (John 8:44).

While the angelic rebellion is merely hinted at in Scripture, human rebellion is put front and center. Tempted by a speaking serpent — a slithering embodiment of Satan (Rev 12:9) — Eve partakes of the forbidden fruit, with Adam joining in at her side (Gen 3:6). Immediately, they both realize their nakedness and experience shame in God's presence for the first time (Gen 3:7). As a result of Adam's failure to pass the test of the probationary tree, God curses the woman, the man, the serpent, and the ground. The NT later uses this episode to unpack the doctrine of original sin. Because of Adam's transgression, the entire human race has inherited both guilt and corruption (Rom 5:12 – 21). As our federal head, Adam's sin has been imputed to us, and we bear the consequences as those who have participated "in Adam" (1 Cor 15:22) in his rebellion. Consequently, we are by nature dead in transgressions, disobedient, and deserving wrath (Eph 2:1 – 3).

After Adam, and east of Eden, nothing is the way it is supposed to be, especially for the sons and daughters of Adam.

SIN CONTINUES TO SPREAD

At the end of Gen 3, the Lord God banishes Adam and Eve from the garden and bars them from entering again. Although there is already the promise of an offspring-mediator who will crush the head of the serpent (Gen 3:15), the mood of the biblical narrative gets worse before it gets better. Sin continues to spread not merely by imitation but also as an expression of humankind's innate rebellion against God. So Gen 4 introduces us to the first murderer (Cain) and the first polygamist (Lamech). By the time we get to Gen 6, the wickedness of the human race has become so great "that every inclination of the thoughts of the human heart was only evil all the time" (Gen 6:5). God wipes out the earth with a flood and reboots a kind of Creation 2.0.

But sin is just as widespread in the new postflood world. Noah gets drunk, leading his son Ham to sin by seeing his father's nakedness (Gen 9:20 – 27). As Noah's descendants multiply, so does their wickedness, culminating in plans for a self-congratulatory and self-aggrandizing tower of Babel (Gen 11:4).

Even after God calls Abram to be a great nation and the divine conduit of blessing to the nations, wickedness persists. God blesses the patriarchs and their families, but it is despite their perfidy, not because of their perfection. Abraham and Isaac lie about their wives; Sarah laughs at God's promise; Lot's wife turns into a pillar of salt; Jacob shows himself to be a conniving manipulator (and his mother, Rachel, is not much better). Laban is a cheat; Joseph is boastful; his brothers are jealous enslavers; Simeon and Levi slaughter the Shechemites; Reuben sleeps with his father's concubine; Judah sleeps with his daughter-in-law. And this is the good side of the family tree! Sin is clearly the problem, and human beings are clearly *not* the solution.

The implicit assumption — if not the explicit teaching — on every page of the Bible is that the whole world is caught in the grip of sin, both Jews and Gentiles (Rom 3:9), those under the law and those without the law (Rom 2:12–15), the nations that worship the God of Israel and the nations that don't (Amos 1–2). Most fundamentally and most foundationally, what's wrong with the world is that God's imagebearers do not love, reverence, worship, and obey the one true God as they ought.

SIN SHOWS ITS MANY COLORS

From Gen 3 until Rev 21, the story of God's people is, at least in part, the story of sin. But while sin is universal, the biblical language for sin is not univocal. In the Pentateuch sin is breaking the covenant. It is a breach of the legal stipulations given to Moses and to which Israel professed allegiance. But sin is also everyone doing as they see fit (Judg 21:25). Sin is the stupidity of forsaking God and being satisfied with broken cisterns (Jer 2:13). Sin is the breakdown of shalom and the sad triumph of evil over good. Wisdom literature often describes sin as foolishness and vanity. In Kings and Chronicles, sin is forgetting God and refusing to humble oneself before him. In the Prophets, sin is often hypocrisy. Elsewhere in the OT, sin manifests itself as strident injustice or perfunctory obedience (e.g., rending your garments instead of your heart). And on other occasions it represents a failure to love God with all your heart and to love your neighbors as yourself. Sin is the villain with a thousand faces.

And all of those faces oppose God. We must never forget that sin frequently has a horizontal dimension. But just as important, we must remember that sin *always* has a vertical dimension. There are no innocent transgressions. There are no victimless crimes. Every sin, no matter how private or quiet, is an affront to the holiness and benevolence of God. David, in his adultery and murder, may have sinned against Bathsheba, Uriah, Joab, his army, his family, and the whole nation of Israel, but in the deepest sense it was still right for him to say to God, "Against you, you only, have I sinned" (Ps 51:4). No matter how heinous our infractions against others, God still remains the most offended party whenever we sin.

SIN GETS CONFRONTED

Thankfully, the story of sin in the Bible is not the story of unchecked evil and wickedness. Though he may prowl around like a roaring lion seeking someone to devour (1 Pet 5:8), the devil, as a created being, has always been subservient to the Creator. Satan cannot operate apart from God's permission (Job 1:12) and plan (1 Sam 16:14–16). And the divine plan has always been for the downfall of sin and the devil (Gen 3:15). Satan's rage we can endure, for lo, his doom is sure. One little word—the Word of the gospel—shall fell him.

More precisely (to speak with the story line of Scripture), we might say the Word made flesh shall fell him. The incarnation was a frontal assault on the devil. Not only does Jesus begin his mission as the second Adam by resisting Satan's temptation where the first Adam failed (Luke 4:1–13), he also actively makes the exorcism of demons a touchstone of his ministry (Mark 1:39). Even when the crowds and the disciples do not recognize Jesus' true identity, the demons know who he is and cower in fear (Mark 1:24; 3:11; 5:7; Jas 2:19). They know that Satan is about to fall like lightning (Luke 10:18) and the ruler of the world is about to be decisively judged (John 16:11).

Of course, Jesus' confrontation with Satan was also a confrontation with sin. Even before he was born, it was understood that Jesus would save his people from their sins (Matt 1:21). Jesus' miracles impressed the crowds, but what absolutely shocked them was his daring presumption to forgive sins (Mark 2:7). Jesus addressed numerous problems in his ministry—hunger, disability, poverty, fear, demon possession, even death—but the one problem underlying them all, the one that had bedeviled God's people throughout their whole sordid history, was the problem of sin. This is the problem Jesus came to confront. And in the end, it is the one he triumphantly conquered.

SIN GETS CONQUERED

Sin cannot be without consequences. Whether this means plagues on Egypt, captivity in Babylon, fire and sulfur on Sodom, a flood on the earth, or expulsion from the garden, God is a God of justice, and in the end every trespass and every trespasser must face consequences. This principle holds true after death as well as in life.

One way God conquers sin is to throw death and the devil into the lake of fire (Rev 20:10), along with all those whose names are not written in the book of life (Rev 20:15). The eternal punishment of the wicked in hell not only vindicates God's honor and upholds divine justice, it also exposes the utter sinfulness of sin. God would be less than God and sin would be something less than sin if the Lord allowed our treacherous disobedience to go unnoticed and unchecked. If there is any axiom the Bible assumes from start to finish—from the Garden of Eden to the heavenly city, from before Adam to after death, from the OT to the NT—it is that sin must be paid for.

But of course, hell is not the only way sin, death, and the devil can be finally and decisively judged. Hell is but a minor theme next to the soaring melody of the cross. On top of Golgotha we see most clearly the reversal of the curse as the reviled Son of God becomes the curse for us (Gal 3:13). Here Jesus drinks the cup of God's wrath (Mark 14:36). Here Christ lays down his life as a ransom for many (Mark 10:45). Here at the cross we see not the abandonment of justice but the complete fulfillment of it. Jesus overcomes sin by becoming sin for us. Jesus conquers the God-defiant wretchedness of sin by divine satisfaction through divine self-substitution.

COVENANT

Paul R. Williamson

Covenant is one of the most important theological ideas in biblical theology. It is reflected in the traditional labels Old and New *Testaments*, i.e., *covenants*. The concept exists at significant points in the Bible's storyline and is the theological glue that binds promise to fulfillment. So the biblical history of salvation and the unfolding of God's covenants are almost synonymous.

Although the Bible does not explicitly mention a covenant until Gen 6:18 (when God announces that he intends to establish a covenant with Noah), many believe that God made a covenant with Adam (cf. Hos 6:7; see NIV text note there). They refer to this covenant with Adam as "the covenant of works" or a "covenant with creation." Others, however, while not denying that God had a relationship with Adam involving mutual obligations, distinguish this from a covenant, which involves additional formalizing elements such as a sworn and/or enacted oath. Understanding covenant in the more formal sense, the first divine-human covenant is the one God established in the days of Noah (cf. Isa 54:9). That covenant affirms God's commitment to creation after the flood.

However, while the concept of a covenant may not appear until after the flood, the major divine-human covenants (Noahic, Abrahamic, Mosaic, Davidic, and the new covenant) all support and advance God's creative (and redemptive) goal. Each covenant provides further divine assurance that God will realize his purpose for creation in general and humanity in particular by fully establishing his kingdom on earth.

THE UNIVERSAL COVENANT (WITH NOAH AND ALL CREATION)

While God announces his covenant with Noah and all creation prior to the flood (Gen 6:18), he establishes it after the deluge subsides (Gen 8:20 — 9:17). The first mention of this covenant simply highlights God's plan to preserve Noah and the others in the ark (Gen 6:18). God's covenant with Noah reaffirms his original creational intent that the flood had "disrupted." So he solemnly promises that a suspension of the natural order will never again interrupt (Gen 8:21 – 22; 9:11 – 15) the fulfillment of humanity's creational mandate (cf. Gen 1:26 – 30; 9:1 – 7). Moreover, the additional commands (Gen 9:4 – 6) emphasize the value of human life in particular, which further highlights the primary rationale for this covenant: preserving life on earth without further divine interruption. It is at least implicit from the scope of this covenant that God's redemptive goal will ultimately encompass the whole creation. That global emphasis in Gen 1 – 11 is not lost in the subsequent chapters of Genesis and beyond, despite their narrowing focus.

THE ABRAHAMIC COVENANT(S)

The promises encompassed by the patriarchal covenants (those God established with Abraham, Isaac, and Jacob) are recorded in Gen 12:1 – 3. The essence of these divine promises is that God would bless Abraham in two ways: (1) God would make him into a great nation and so make his name great, and (2) through him God would mediate blessing to others (i.e., all peoples on earth). Significantly, each of these two aspects are subsequently ratified by covenant: (1) the national dimension of God's promise is the focus of Gen 15, where God establishes (or "cuts") "a covenant with Abram" (Gen 15:18); (2) the international dimension of the promise is apparently ignored in Gen 15, but it is alluded to in Gen 17 (cf. vv. 4 – 6,16), where God announces an "everlasting covenant" (Gen 17:7), the so-called "covenant of circumcision" (Acts 7:8). While many hold that the latter simply elaborates or enhances the covenant already established back in Gen 15, the different circumstances and emphases at very least suggest that this is a significant second stage in God's covenant history with Abraham. Indeed, if Gen 17 is read in conjunction with Gen 22 (see below), these chapters arguably present a second covenant — one that is distinct from, but related to, the earlier covenant established in Gen 15.

The first of these covenants (Gen 15) formally ratified God's promise to make Abraham into a "great nation" (Gen 12:2), thus the primary focus is on how God will work out his creative goal in Abraham's biological "offspring," subsequently identified as the sons of Jacob (Israel).

This, however, was only the preliminary stage in God's unfolding plan of redemption. The second stage relates to how Abraham, through that great nation descended from him, would mediate blessing to "all peoples on earth" (Gen 12:3). This seems to be the main focus in Gen 17 and 22.

Even though the promise of nationhood is not altogether absent in Gen 17 (cf. v. 8), stress is placed on "nations," "kings," and a perpetual divine-human relationship with Abraham's offspring (Gen 17:4 – 8,16 – 21). Significantly, particular focus is placed on Isaac (Gen 17:21; cf. Gen 21:12) as the one through whom this covenant will be perpetuated, highlighting what was at stake in the divine test of Gen 22. There Abraham's obedient faith (Gen 22:16b,18b) met the demands of Gen 17:1 (cf. Gen 18:19; 26:5), thus prompting God to ratify the promises of Gen 17 (cf. Gen 22:17 – 18a; 26:4) by a solemn oath (Gen 22:16a; cf. 26:3).

Thus understood, two distinct covenants were established between God and Abraham. The first (Gen 15) guaranteed God's promise to make Abraham into a "great nation." The second (anticipated in Gen 17 and ratified by divine oath in Gen 22) affirmed God's promise to bless all nations through Abraham and his "offspring."

THE MOSAIC COVENANT

God established the Mosaic covenant just after a significant development anticipated in Gen 15 had taken place: the emancipation of Abraham's descendants from oppression in a foreign land (cf. Gen 15:13–14; Exod 19:4–6; 20:2). The focus at Sinai is less on what Abraham's descendants must do in order to inherit the land and more on how they must conduct themselves within the land as the unique nation that God intended them to be. In order to be God's "treasured possession," "kingdom of priests," and "holy nation" (Exod 19:5–6), Israel must keep God's covenant by submitting to its requirements (i.e., the stipulations set forth in Exod 20–23). By adhering to these and the subsequent covenant obligations given at Sinai, Israel would be manifestly different from other nations and thus reflect God's wisdom and greatness to surrounding peoples (cf. Deut 4:6–8).

By such means, Abraham's descendants would not only follow in the footsteps of their ancestor (cf. Gen 26:5) but also facilitate the fulfillment of God's promises (Gen 18:19). Thus, like Abraham, Israel must "walk before [God] faithfully and be blameless" (Gen 17:1). Failing to do so would undermine the very reason for Israel's existence, a lesson that the golden calf incident so graphically illustrates (Exod 32–34). Although God reestablished the covenant (Exod 34), this was an act of grace rather than justice (Exod 34:6–7). Moreover, by reissuing the same covenant obligations at the end of this incident, God demonstrated that Israel's responsibility had not changed.

Israel had to obey God in order to fulfill his purpose for delivering them from Egypt and subsequently giving them the promised land: they were to be his priestly kingdom and holy nation. By reflecting God's holiness (Lev 19:2), Israel would showcase true theocracy and thus serve as God's witnesses to a watching world. Moreover, since human rebellion threatened to jeopardize God's ultimate objective (i.e., blessing all nations through Abraham's "offspring"), the Mosaic covenant also encompassed the means by which the divine-human relationship between Yahweh and Israel could be maintained: sacrificial worship, particularly on the Day of Atonement (Lev 16), would ritually atone for Israel's sin and symbolically express God's forgiveness. Therefore, just as the Noahic covenant guaranteed the preservation of human life on earth, so the Mosaic covenant guaranteed the preservation of Israel, Abraham's great nation, in the land. Such was crucial for the next stage in fulfilling God's promises: establishing a royal line through which Abraham's ultimate "seed" and covenant heir would eventually come (cf. Gal 3:16).

THE DAVIDIC COVENANT

After Sinai, the next major covenantal development comes with Nathan's message to David (2 Sam 7; 1 Chr 17). David intends to build a "house" (i.e., temple) for God, but God promises to build a "house" (i.e., dynasty) for David. Neither 2 Sam 7 nor 1 Chr 17 explicitly describes God's promise as a "covenant," but several other texts do (cf. 2 Sam 23:5; 2 Chr 7:18; 13:5; Ps 89:3; Jer 33:21).

The Davidic covenant continues the trajectory of both the Mosaic and Abrahamic covenants. God's plans for David and Israel are clearly intertwined (cf. 2 Sam 7:8–11,23–26). Moreover, significant parallels link David to Abraham:

- God promises both a great name (Gen 12:2; 2 Sam 7:9).
- In the future both will conquer their enemies (Gen 22:17; 2 Sam 7:11; cf. Ps 89:23);
- Both have a special divine-human relationship (Gen 17:7–8; 2 Sam 7:24; cf. Ps 89:26).
- A special line of "offspring" perpetuates both of their names (Gen 21:12; 2 Sam 7:12–16).
- The descendants of both must keep God's laws (Gen 18:19; 2 Sam 7:14; cf. Pss 89:30–32; 132:12).
- The offspring of both would mediate international blessing (Gen 22:18; Ps 72:17).

The Davidic covenant thus identifies more precisely the lineage of the "offspring" who will mediate international blessing: he will be a royal descendant of Abraham through David.

This covenant therefore introduces a subtle but significant shift in focus. With the great nation promised to Abraham now firmly established (2 Sam 7:1), attention zooms in on his royal progeny (cf. Gen 17:6,16). This royal line, already traced explicitly in Genesis (cf. Gen 35:11; 49:10; see also Gen 38; Ruth 4:18–22), culminates in an individual, conquering "offspring" who fulfills the promise of Gen 22:18 and the hope expressed in Ps 72:17.

THE NEW COVENANT

Persistent failure to live according to God's covenant requirements led to inevitable disaster for both the nation and its monarchy, culminating in judgment: the destroyed temple and Babylonian exile. This might have spelled the end had God's plans for Israel not been crucial for fulfilling his covenant promises. The exile of the nation and the demise of the monarchy had to be overcome for God's creation plan to be realized. Covenant history thus continued through the prospect of a "new covenant"—one that would be both continuous and discontinuous with those of the past.

Though referred to explicitly as a "new covenant" only once in the OT (Jer 31:31), several passages, both in Jeremiah and elsewhere, allude to it. In Isaiah this everlasting covenant of peace is closely associated with the servant figure (Isa 42:6; 49:8; 54:10; 55:3; 61:8). It is inclusive in that it incorporates even foreigners and eunuchs (Isa 56:3) but also exclusive in that it is confined to those who "hold fast to" its obligations (Isa 56:5–6; cf. 56:1–2).

While Jeremiah and Ezekiel use different terminology to describe it, both anticipate a fundamental change taking place in the covenant community: Jeremiah speaks of internalizing the Torah (Jer 31:33), whereas Ezekiel speaks of spiritual surgery and radical transformation (Ezek 36:26–27). For both prophets, this inner renewal would result in the ideal divine-human relationship, which this and earlier covenants express in terms of the covenant formula "I will be their God, and they will be my people." In this new covenant, all the hopes and expectations of previous covenants will attain climactic fulfillment and eschatological expression.

It is unsurprising, therefore, that the New *Testament* ("covenant") declares that all God's covenant promises are realized in and through Jesus (cf. Luke 1:54–55,69–75; 2 Cor 1:20), the long-awaited Davidic Messiah (Matt 1:17–18; 2:4–6; 16:16; 21:9; Luke 2:11; John 7:42 Acts 2:22–36). As the ultimate offspring of Abraham (Matt 1:1; Gal 3:16) and royal offspring of David (Matt 1:1; Luke 1:27,32–33; 2:4; Rom 1:3; 2 Tim 2:8; Rev 5:5; 22:16), Jesus also fulfills the role of Isaiah's servant (Acts 3:18; 4:27–28; 8:32–35)—not only in redeeming Israel (Luke 2:38; Acts 3:25–26; Heb 9:12,15) but also by mediating God's blessing to an international community of faith (Acts 10:1—11:18; 15:1–29; Rom 1:2–6; 3:22–24; 4:16–18; 15:8–12; Gal 3:7–14,29).

According to the NT Gospels and letters, the new covenant was ratified through Jesus' sacrificial death on the cross (cf. Matt 26:28; Mark 14:24; Luke 22:20; 1 Cor 11:25). In the inaugural Lord's Supper, Jesus alludes to both the forgiveness linked by Jeremiah to the new covenant (Matt 26:28; cf. Jer 31:34) and the blood associated with the establishment of the old (i.e., Mosaic) covenant (Luke 22:20; cf. Exod 24:8). Accordingly, the NT emphasizes the forgiveness of sins, something only fully attainable under the new covenant (Acts 13:39; cf. Heb 10:4), as the primary benefit of Jesus' death (e.g., Luke 1:77; 24:46–47; Acts 2:38; 10:43; 13:38; 26:18; Rom 3:24–25; Eph 1:7; Col 1:14; Heb 9:12,28; 1 John 1:7; Rev 1:5; 7:14; 12:10–11).

Thus, according to both Paul and the writer of Hebrews, the new covenant is far superior to the old (i.e., the Mosaic covenant). Such is already implicit in the use of the adjective "new" in 1 Cor 11:25 (cf. Luke 22:20), which clearly alludes to Jeremiah's negative contrast (Jer 31:31–32). Paul is even more pointed, however, in 2 Cor 3, where he explicitly contrasts the new and the old covenants, highlighting the vast inferiority of the old in comparison with the surpassing glory and permanence of the new. A similar, negative comparison is also made by his "figurative" contrast between Hagar and Sarah in Gal 4:21–31.

Analogous conclusions are drawn by the author of Hebrews. Having noted the superiority of the new covenant in Heb 7:22, the writer elaborates his point through an extended comment on Jer 31:31–34, which forms a literary bracket around much of the argument in Heb 8–10 (cf. 8:9–12; 10:16–17). Not only does Jesus exercise a permanent, perfect, and heavenly priesthood (Heb 7:23—8:6), but the covenant of which he is mediator "is established on better promises" (Heb 8:6b), explained in terms of an "eternal redemption" (Heb 9:12) and "eternal inheritance" (Heb 9:15) secured through the blood of Christ (Heb 9:11—10:18), later described as "the blood of the eternal covenant" (Heb 13:20). Like Paul, therefore, the contrast is not between something bad and something good, but between something good (but temporal) and something better (because, unlike the old covenant, the new is unbreakable and eternal).

While these new covenant realities are in many respects already present (cf. Heb 9:11), it is nevertheless true that the best is still to come. Just as Israel's restoration hopes were not exhausted in repatriation after the Babylonian exile, neither were they fully realized in the first coming of their Messiah. While in Jesus—the promised "seed" of Abraham (Gal 3:16), the anticipated prophet like Moses (Acts 3:22–23; cf. Deut 18:15; Matt 17:5), King David's greater son (Matt 22:41–46), and the mediator of the new covenant (Heb 8:6)—God's covenant promises for both Israel and the nations have come to fruition, the ultimate expression of God's creative and redemptive goal awaits fulfillment in the eschatological reality of the new creation. Only then will the hope expressed in the age-old covenant formula be most fully experienced (Rev 21:3), for "the throne of God and of the Lamb will be in the city, and his servants will serve him ... And they will reign for ever and ever" (Rev 22:3,5).

LAW

T. D. Alexander

The English term "law" is most commonly understood to denote either a system of rules or a particular rule that regulates human behavior within a country or community. While this understanding of law occurs in the Bible, the word "law" is also used in other ways. "Law" frequently translates the Greek and Hebrew words *nomos* and *torah*, respectively. To complicate the picture, *torah* denotes different things in different OT contexts. It would often make better sense to translate *torah* as "instruction." So the term "law" in the Bible covers a range of quite different things.

GOD AS LAWGIVER AND JUDGE

Central to the biblical understanding of God is the idea that as the creator of everything, he alone determines what is morally right and wrong. God holds people accountable when they either disobey his specific instructions or undertake actions that are counter to his ordering of creation. When Adam and Eve eat the forbidden fruit, they disregard an instruction specific to them. When Cain kills Abel, he acts in a manner that is contrary to God's standards and values. In both cases, those involved are accountable for their actions and duly punished. God is the sole and ultimate arbiter of justice.

When Adam and Eve rebel against God, they reject God as law-giver, preferring to set their own moral standards; they seek to become autonomous, determining their own laws. Furthermore, as a direct consequence of rebelling against God, human nature became perverted. People inevitably fail to live by their own standards, not to mention those of God. Against this background the overall biblical account of redemption centers on how people, as lawbreakers, can be made right with God and how their perverse behavior can be made to conform to what God requires. In the telling of this story, the concept of law figures in a variety of ways.

Throughout the book of Genesis people are held responsible for their immoral actions. This implies that they have some sense of right and wrong, although the text of Genesis only occasionally alludes to the existence of God's laws or regulations (Gen 9:3 – 6; 26:5).

While the account of the Israelites' exodus from Egypt briefly refers to decrees and statutes that God imposed on the people at different times (Exod 12:49; 13:9; 16:4,28; 18:16,20), the first recorded, substantial listing of God's moral values applied to human life comes in the context of the covenant God made at Mount Sinai. Importantly, this covenant comes after God redeemed the people from slavery in Egypt and delivered the firstborn from death. God's salvation precedes the "law," so people do not earn salvation by keeping it. However, having been redeemed by God, the Israelites are expected to live holy lives by keeping the covenant obligations.

THE OBLIGATIONS OF THE SINAI COVENANT

By entering into this covenant, sometimes called the Mosaic covenant, the Israelites willingly agree to fulfill various obligations that God placed on them. Primary among these is a set of broad principles called the Ten Commandments (Exod 20:1 – 17). To these broad principles are added other items that fall under a number of distinctive categories (Exod 20:22 — 23:33). This material may possibly comprise the document known as the Book of the Covenant (Exod 24:7). Supplementing the broad principles of the Ten Commandments are sample case laws designed to help people resolve disputes; these laws describe particular scenarios and appropriate penalties (Exod 21:1 — 22:20). The Book of the Covenant also contains a section concerning moral imperatives that demand a standard of morality that goes beyond that which human law courts may regulate (Exod 22:21 — 23:9). Another section sets out instructions relating to periods of rest associated with the concept of the Sabbath and annual festivals (Exod 23:10 – 19). It gives particular attention to the Sabbath because God designated it as the sign of the covenant (Exod 31:12 – 17); to disregard the Sabbath is to dismiss the importance of the covenant relationship with God. In conjunction with the Ten Commandments, all of this material seeks to shape the behavior of the Israelites, enabling them to be God's holy people. Fundamentally, however, obeying these obligations does not create the covenant relationship with God because he has already redeemed the people.

REGULATIONS FOR A HOLY PEOPLE

The sealing of the covenant at Mount Sinai prepares the way for God to come and dwell in the midst of the Israelite camp. To facilitate this, God instructs Moses to manufacture a special tent, the tabernacle, that will function as God's temporary earthly dwelling place. Additionally, God appoints and consecrates some Israelites as priests to serve within the tabernacle. Since God's presence makes the tent exceptionally holy, he gives various instructions to prevent the Israelites from defiling the tabernacle (by making it ritually unclean) and to remedy such defilement when it occurs. These concerns are reflected in the wide range of areas covered by the instructions in Leviticus such as offering different types of sacrifices, categorizing food as clean and unclean, designating various bodily ailments and conditions as unclean, and giving guidelines for acceptable moral behavior. A constant theme throughout all of this material is God's demand for the Israelites to be holy as he is holy (Lev 11:44–45). In this context holiness is associated with wholeness and life. If the Israelites are to live close to God without being put to death due to their sinful nature, they too must be holy. Ultimately, to be holy is to be perfect like God.

COVENANT RENEWAL AND THE LAW OF MOSES

Following the death of the adult generation that left Egypt, the Israelites renew the covenant initiated at Mount Sinai before they enter the promised land. While this is a renewal of the Sinai covenant and is grounded in what occurred at Mount Sinai, Moses sets out afresh the obligations that the people must fulfill. In this new presentation of the covenant obligations, known as the *torah* (instruction) of Moses, he warns the Israelites that God will judge them based on whether they obey or disobey his *torah*. To underline its importance, all that Moses says is recorded in a document, later called "the Book of the Law [*torah*] of Moses" (e.g., Josh 8:31; 23:6; 2 Kgs 14:6; cf. Deut 28:61; 29:21; 30:10; 31:26). While this "Book of the Law" contains God's "commands" and "decrees" (Deut 30:10), it also includes instructions for building altars and lists of blessings and curses (Josh 8:31,34). Although the precise extent of his book is unclear, it probably consisted of the material now recorded in Deut 5:1—28:68. In this context the "law" (*torah*) is much more than a system of rules. Within the rest of the OT, this *torah* of Moses figures prominently in two important and contrasting ways.

First, some passages in the OT view the *torah* positively as a source of joy for those who delight in its contents (Ps 19:7–10). God will bless those who meditate on it and live by its instruction (e.g., Josh 1:7–8; Pss 1:2–3; 94:12; 119:1). Kings, in particular, were expected to "follow carefully all the words of this law" (Deut 17:19) by reading daily the *torah* of Moses. In light of this, the failure of most Israelite and Judean kings to obey the teaching of the Book of the Law contrasts with Jesus' readiness to quote from Deuteronomy when Satan tempted him (Matt 4:1–11). As heir to the Davidic throne, Jesus lives by the *torah* of Moses.

Second, the "Book of the Law of Moses" becomes the standard by which God judges the actions of the people, especially the kings. Solomon is condemned for disregarding the instructions in Deut 17:16–17, which prohibit a king from amassing wealth, taking foreign wives, and buying horses from Egypt (1 Kgs 10:23,28; 11:1–4). Eventually, the Assyrians and Babylonians decimate the kingdoms of Israel and Judah, respectively, because they flouted the obligations set out in the Book of the Law. As Deut 28:64–68 predicts, God punishes them with exile because they failed to live according to the law.

After the Babylonian exile, renewed attention is given to fulfilling the instructions found within the "Book of the Law." The book of Nehemiah highlights how Ezra read the "Book of the Law of Moses" to the people of Judah over a number of days (Neh 8:1—9:3). This emphasis on conformity to the law continued to influence the religious outlook of the people in the centuries that followed. Such was the prominence given to the "Law of Moses" that by the second century BC the designation "Law" came to be applied to the first five books of the OT. This development complicates the picture, for the "Law of Moses" was subsequently understood to include everything that was said in the books of Genesis through Deuteronomy. By the first century, adherence to the Law played a major part in shaping much of Jewish life.

JESUS AND THE LAW

Against this background, the Gospels contain many passages that directly or indirectly address how Jesus views the law. Jesus is frequently at odds with the different Jewish religious groups regarding how people should keep the law. Two main trends are evident.

First, Jesus criticizes especially how others interpret the OT law in ways that lessen its moral demands. Other religious teachers focus on the minimum level of righteousness that the law requires, but Jesus sees it as pointing toward perfection, something that the Ten Commandments and the moral imperatives found within the Book of the Covenant imply. For Jesus the OT law does not simply draw a line between behavior that is legal and illegal, as his contemporaries suppose. Rather, it is a signpost pointing to the perfection of God. For this reason, Jesus rejects a legalistic approach of interpreting the OT law (cf. Matt 5:21–48). He seeks from his followers a righteousness that surpasses that of the Pharisees and the teachers of the law (Matt 5:20); he encourages his listeners to "be perfect ... as your heavenly Father is perfect" (Matt 5:48), echoing the OT demand for holy living, for holiness is associated with moral wholeness.

Second, Jesus criticizes strongly those who adopt a hypocritical stance concerning the law. He openly condemns the Pharisees for emphasizing lesser aspects of the law while ignoring the most important aspects (Mark 7:1–23). Additionally, their attitude toward ritual cleanliness exposes a key failure to appreciate fully the true cause of human uncleanness. For Jesus, the Pharisees and others too often use the law either to avoid caring for those in distress or on the margins of Jewish society or as a reason to condemn anyone who shows compassion and love to such people. The self-righteous attitude of the Pharisees, based on their misinterpretation of the law, is repugnant to Jesus.

While Jesus is adamant that he has not come to dismiss

what the Law or the Prophets say, but rather has come to fulfill OT expectations (Matt 5:17), he anticipates that his death and resurrection will inaugurate new developments. Among these are the making of a new covenant in place of the Sinai covenant, the inclusion of Gentiles within the community of God's people, and the replacement of the Jerusalem temple with a very different type of temple. These changes directly impact how Jesus' future followers view the OT law and its bearing on Christian living.

With the making of a new covenant, Jesus' followers would no longer be under an obligation to keep the Sabbath, the sign of the Sinai covenant (Gal 4:8–10; Col 2:16; Heb 8:7–13). When Gentiles become part of God's people, the distinction between clean and unclean foods, which was intended to remind the Israelites of their calling to be a holy people, would no longer be relevant (Acts 11:1–18). With the creation of the church as a new temple, the detailed regulations relating to the old temple become redundant. No longer would there be any need for the Levitical priesthood and the sacrificial system that was introduced when the tabernacle was first erected (e.g., Heb 7:18–19; 8:1–6).

In these ways and others, an important transition occurs following the death and resurrection of Jesus and the coming of the Holy Spirit on believers. Not surprisingly, many Jewish-born followers of Jesus struggled to adjust to such dramatic changes. This was made all the more difficult since the early church continued to value the OT law as both a guide to moral perfection and a source of information for understanding how God has worked out his plan in Jesus (e.g., Heb 10:1). In discerning how the OT law should be understood and applied in the light of the new covenant inaugurated by Jesus, Christians should be guided by the teaching of Jesus and the apostles to whom he delegated authority.

PAUL AND THE LAW

Some of the issues Paul addresses in his letters reflect the transition from an OT understanding of the people of God established through the covenant at Mount Sinai to a NT faith based on Jesus' sacrificial death. While some of Paul's opponents vehemently argue that Christians must observe the law (*torah*), Paul insists that Gentile believers are not obligated to keep all aspects of OT instructions and regulations. Paul comes to this conclusion because the Sinai covenant has been replaced by a new covenant that embraces Gentiles as well as Jews. Yet, although Paul no longer sees himself as being "under the law" like other Jews (1 Cor 9:20), he does not see himself as being without any law, for he is "under Christ's law" (1 Cor 9:21). In the light of all that Paul has to say, it seems reasonable to conclude that Christ's law affirms the moral standards reflected in the OT law.

Paul emphasizes that "God would justify the Gentiles by faith" (Gal 3:8) rather than by "works of the law" (Gal 3:5). As supporting evidence he points to how God considered Abraham righteous because he "believed God" (Gal 3:6, referring to Gen 15:6). Paul also argues that God's promise of blessing for Gentiles is associated with faith (Gal 3:8–9,14), but "all who rely on the works of the law are under a curse" because it is not possible to obey fully "everything written in the Book of the Law" (Gal 3:10). While Paul has no desire to disparage the law's importance, he insists that it cannot "impart life" (Gal 3:21). Life comes only through faith in Jesus Christ, who fulfills God's promise of blessing for the Gentiles. God's promise to Abraham occurred 430 years before he made the covenant at Mount Sinai, so it takes precedence over the Sinai covenant and its obligations.

Although the law of Moses had an important function in the nation of Israel, it became redundant with Christ's coming and the inclusion of the Gentiles (Gal 3:23–25). (In his letter to the Romans, Paul expresses comparable sentiments.) While Paul dismisses the observance of the law of Moses as necessary for salvation, he nonetheless views the law as good, being a witness to the righteousness that Christians should display in their lives: "For the entire law is fulfilled in keeping this one command: 'Love your neighbor as yourself'" (Gal 5:14).

The issue of whether Gentile Christians must be circumcised and whether they must observe the law was a central concern at the council of Jerusalem, which Paul attended (Acts 15:1–5). Peter describes the demands of the law of Moses as "a yoke that neither we nor our ancestors have been able to bear" (Acts 15:10); he then adds, "It is through the grace of our Lord Jesus that we are saved" (Acts 15:11). The council decided that they "should not make it difficult for the Gentiles" but should only require them "to abstain from food polluted by idols, from sexual immorality, from the meat of strangled animals and from blood" (Acts 15:19–20). The council thus signals that Gentiles do not need to be circumcised or keep the law of Moses in order to be fully righteous before God.

CONCLUSION

The term "law" does not refer to a single entity in the two testaments but may denote a variety of things depending on the context. Although both testaments affirm that God is the true source of moral guidance, not all of God's instructions are universal requirements for all time. Appreciating both the continuity and discontinuity between the testaments is vital for understanding the law's role in shaping the life of God's people. Both testaments affirm the need to be holy as God is holy, but the practical implications of this differ in a variety of ways as we move from the OT theocracy of Israel to the NT church. A biblical-theological perspective helpfully explains why the early church did or did not implement different aspects of the OT law and how modern Christians should approach the diverse materials that are subsumed under the general heading of "law."

TEMPLE

T. D. Alexander

The concept of temple permeates the whole Bible. The temple functions as the palace of the divine King, where God is present in a unique way. It is associated with various earthly locations throughout the Bible's story: the Garden of Eden, the tabernacle, the Jerusalem temple, Jesus Christ, the church, and the new Jerusalem. Shared features connect these different "temple" manifestations, with the movement from one to another being related closely to the outworking of God's redemption of humanity. There is also a heavenly temple, upon which some of these other temples are modeled (Heb 8:5).

In the overall scheme of biblical history, God creates the earth in order to dwell there with those he creates. At the outset God commissions Adam and Eve to begin populating the earth with people who will build and inhabit a holy city. What begins in the Garden of Eden will eventually result in the new Jerusalem. Although Adam and Eve's betrayal of God delays (with tragic consequences) the project, through various phases God will eventually bring it to completion. Throughout this whole process the concept of temple figures prominently.

THE GARDEN OF EDEN

While it may not appear immediately obvious, the Garden of Eden exhibits features in keeping with a divine sanctuary. Placed within this sacred location, Adam is instructed to serve and guard it (Gen 2:15; the NIV translation "to work it and take care of it" might more helpfully be rendered "to serve it and guard it"), just as the Levites and priests are later required to "serve" and "guard" the tabernacle sanctuary (Num 3:7–8; 8:26; 18:4–7). Tragically, however, when confronted by the scheming serpent, Adam and Eve fail to fulfill this duty. Consequently, God expels the human couple from Eden and hands their role as guardians over to the cherubim stationed at the garden's entrance (Gen 3:24).

One important consequence of Adam and Eve's exile from Eden is their loss of intimacy with God. Defiled by their sin, they can no longer serve within a holy sanctuary. Against this background the rest of the Bible's story centers on restoring holy status to sinful people and repairing the fractured relationship between God and humanity. Later earthly sanctuaries provide, to differing degrees, an opportunity for God and people to come together.

From Adam and Eve's expulsion through to the exodus of the Israelites from Egypt, no earthly sanctuary exists. As Jacob's dream at Bethel reveals, God dwells in heaven (Gen 28:12–13), occasionally coming down to the earth to make himself known (e.g. Gen 18:1,20–21). During the period of the patriarchs, altars function as temporary "sanctuaries," anticipating a time when God will reside permanently on the earth (e.g., Gen 22:1–19).

THE TABERNACLE

After rescuing the Israelites from slavery in Egypt, God enters into a special covenant relationship with them at Mount Sinai. This prepares the way for constructing a portable sanctuary where God resides among the people. Although God chooses to live in a tent like the Israelites, his abode differs significantly. To reflect the royal nature of its occupant, it is made extensively of gold and richly colored fabrics. Consistent with its use as a dwelling, the tabernacle is furnished with household items: a chest, a table for food, and a lampstand. God's presence, however, is not confined to the tabernacle, for he is viewed as sitting on his heavenly throne. The "ark of the covenant," which sat within the Most Holy Place, functioned as the footstool of the heavenly throne (1 Chr 28:2). Heaven and earth were joined within the tabernacle.

The tabernacle was known as the "tent of meeting" because Moses conversed with God there (e.g., Exod 27:21; 28:43; 29:4; 40:1; Lev 1:1; 3:2; Num 1:1; 2:2), replacing an earlier tent that temporarily fulfilled a similar purpose (Exod 33:7–11). The tabernacle was also called the "sanctuary" or holy place (e.g., Exod 25:8; Lev 12:4)—with the inner room of the tent being "the Most Holy Place" (e.g., Exod 26:33–34; Lev 16:2). God's presence made it holy. Only the high priest was permitted to enter the Most Holy Place—and then only once a year on the Day of Atonement.

THE JERUSALEM TEMPLE

Eventually the tabernacle was replaced by a magnificent temple, built by King Solomon in Jerusalem. After Solomon's dedicatory prayer, the glory of the Lord filled the new sanctuary (1 Kgs 8:10–11; 2 Chr 7:1–2) as it had previously filled the tabernacle (Exod 40:34–35). Due to God's special relationship with King David, David's dynasty is closely associated with future developments regarding God's earthly temple. For centuries to follow, the Jerusalem temple became the principal location for worshiping God as pilgrims journeyed there to sing for joy to the living God (Ps 84:1–4; cf. Ps 122:1–9).

Since temples in the ancient Near East were often viewed as miniatures of the cosmos, the Jerusalem temple (and the tabernacle before it) may well have influenced Israelite ideas regarding cosmology (e.g., Job 38:4–7; Pss 75:3; 104:2–3). Moreover, as models of the earth, the tabernacle and temple probably signaled a future time when the whole world would become God's dwelling place.

God's presence within the temple distinguished Jerusalem from all other cities (see "The City of God," p. 2666). Eventually, however, the corruption of its rulers and citizens caused God to punish them by having the Babylonians sack Jerusalem and destroy the temple in 587/586 BC. The prophet Ezekiel gives particular attention to how God abandons his dwelling place (Ezek 9:3; 11:23), highlighting how the sins of the people defiled the temple. Although God's reluctant departure from the Jerusalem sanctuary is clearly explicable, Ezekiel looks beyond this to a time when God will live in a transformed city (Ezek 40–48). While the subsequent overthrow of the Babylonians by the Persians in 539 BC eventually results in the temple being rebuilt in Jerusalem, the outcome falls short of all that the prophets anticipated. Something greater was yet to occur, which would also involve the restoration of the Davidic monarchy.

JESUS CHRIST

As heir to the Davidic dynasty, Jesus' coming inaugurates a new stage in the outworking of God's redemptive plan. When John writes, "The Word became flesh and made his dwelling among us" (John 1:14), he compares Jesus' body to the OT tabernacle. When Jesus remarks, "Destroy this temple, and I will raise it again in three days," John interprets this as referring to Jesus' body (John 2:19–21). The idea that Jesus' body was a temple fits well with the belief that "in Christ all the fullness of the Deity lives in bodily form" (Col 2:9).

Apart from Jesus being a temple himself, the Gospels also present him as both cleansing the Jerusalem temple as the heir to the Davidic dynasty and predicting its future destruction. Through the sacrificial atonement achieved by his death on the cross, Jesus restores to a holy status those who trust in him (Heb 10:10), without which they would not be able to serve within God's temple. Furthermore, as a perfect high priest, Jesus enters the heavenly temple (Heb 4:14; 9:24).

THE CHURCH

Anticipated by the incarnation of Jesus Christ, the church becomes the new temple of God, extending God's presence throughout the earth (1 Cor 3:16–17; 2 Cor 6:16). Beginning with the outpouring of the Holy Spirit at Pentecost, God's dwelling place on earth becomes a multiethnic community of people. The Jerusalem temple is replaced by a very different kind of divine sanctuary made of living stones (1 Pet 2:4–5), Jesus Christ himself being both the prototype and the cornerstone of this temple (Eph 2:20–21). The church is a temple that is both in use and under construction (Eph 2:21), the followers of Jesus Christ being variously equipped by the Holy Spirit as temple builders (1 Cor 3:10). While the majority of NT references to the Holy Spirit dwelling within believers refer to believers corporately as God's temple, 1 Cor 6:19–20 is usually interpreted as implying that each individual Christian is a temple.

THE NEW JERUSALEM

While the creation of the church is important in expanding God's reign throughout the earth, fulfilling God's plans for the whole earth involves creating the new Jerusalem (Rev 21–22). The new Jerusalem brings to fulfillment what began in Eden; both share common features (e.g., the tree of life). John's vision reveals a city of enormous dimensions that is shaped as a golden cube, reminiscent of the Most Holy Place within the Jerusalem temple, also shaped as a cube and plated with gold. Although John explicitly states that there is no temple within the city, he goes on to say, "The Lord God Almighty and the Lamb are its temple" (Rev 21:22). This suggests that the whole city is a Most Holy Place. In this holy city no barriers exist between God and the human population; as priestly royals, every human inhabitant is able to see God's face (Rev 22:4–5).

CONCLUSION

The concept of temple binds together the different phases that occur as events move from the Garden of Eden to the anticipated creation of the new Jerusalem. While the temple's form changes dramatically as God's presence and glory gradually fill the whole earth, a consistent pattern runs throughout, creating a sense of unity.

PRIEST

Dana M. Harris

THE FUNCTION OF BIBLICAL PRIESTS

The essential concerns of a biblical priest involved maintaining holiness and mediating between God and humans. Priests facilitated Israel's service to and worship of the Lord in the context of its covenantal relationship with God.

THE LEVITICAL PRIESTHOOD

After God's paradigmatic work of deliverance, the exodus, God led his people to Sinai and identified them as a kingdom of priests and a holy nation (Exod 19:4 – 6). That the entire nation was understood in priestly terms indicates that Israel was called to mediate God's holiness to the surrounding nations. This priestly designation was an integral part of the covenant that bound Israel to the Lord and facilitated access to his presence (Exod 20 – 24). Aaron and his sons were further set apart as priests for the nation (Exod 28 – 29; Lev 8). Later, when Aaron led the people in idolatrous worship, the Levites alone joined Moses in avenging the Lord's honor (Exod 32:25 – 29). God then commanded Moses to set the Levites apart to assist Aaron and his sons in their priestly duties (Num 3:5 – 9; 8:5 – 26). Thus, there arose two priestly offices: priests and Levites.

Although both priests and Levites were part of the tribe of Levi, priests had to descend directly from Aaron (Num 3:10), whereas Levites did not. Furthermore, the high priest had to descend from Aaron's son Eleazar (Num 20:25 – 28). Priests had to be ceremonially pure (Lev 21:1 – 4,7 – 8) and free from defect (Lev 21:16 – 23; cf. Lev 10:6; 21:5 – 6). This purity reflected God's own holiness and kept the tabernacle from defilement. The high priest alone offered the sin offering on the Day of Atonement (Lev 16) and entered the Most Holy Place. The greater degree of holiness associated with the high priest was indicated by his elaborate garments (Exod 28) and special anointing (Exod 29:7 – 9).

Levites belonged to the Lord in a unique way (Num 3:5 – 13,44 – 45), being set apart to transport the tabernacle (Num 1:47 – 53), including the ark of the covenant — the locus of God's holy presence. Several functions of the Levites physically portrayed important spiritual truths. First, following the plague on the Egyptian firstborn males, God set apart every Israelite firstborn male for himself; however, when the Lord set the Levites apart from the rest of Israel, they functioned as a substitute for the firstborn males of other tribes (Num 3:11 – 13), thereby visually depicting how one person could act representatively, or as a substitute, for another.

Second, during the wilderness wandering, Moses, Aaron, and their descendants camped at the eastern entrance of the tabernacle (Num 3:38), while the Levites' camps surrounded the tabernacle on the west, south, and north (Num 3:23,29,35). Thus, the Levites provided a physical buffer between holy (God's presence in the tabernacle) and profane or unclean (Num 1:53; cf. Lev 10:8 – 11), thereby indicating the increasing degrees of holiness as one approached God's presence (see "Holiness," p. 2676; see also Introduction to Leviticus: Major Theological Themes [Holiness and Purity]).

Finally, although the Levites received specially designated cities (Num 35:1 – 8; Josh 21:1 – 42), they did not receive land allotments as did the other tribes. Instead, the Lord himself was their inheritance (Num 18:20 – 24; Deut 18:1 – 2), thereby signifying that the true inheritance was not ultimately the land itself, but the Giver of the land.

THE MONARCHICAL AND EXILIC PERIODS

When David made Solomon king, he assigned the Levites to supervise the temple's construction (1 Chr 23:1 – 4) and designated both priests and Levites as temple officials, judges, gatekeepers, or musicians (1 Chr 23:1 — 26:28; cf. 1 Chr 6:31 – 47). Because the priest Zadok remained faithful to David, unlike Abiathar (1 Kgs 1:1 – 8), the Zadokites are singled out in Ezekiel's vision of the restored temple (Ezek 44:15 – 16).

The prophets show that the divine judgment leading to exile was partially due to priestly corruption and defilement (Jer 2:5 – 8; 5:31; Lam 4:13; Ezek 22:26; Hos 4:6 – 9; Zeph 3:4; Mal 3:1 – 4). Indeed Josiah's reform included removing pagan priests from Judah (2 Kgs 23:1 – 20) and reaffirming the Levitical priesthood (2 Chr 35:10 – 14). When the temple was rebuilt after the exile, priests and Levites offered the Passover lamb (Ezra 6:19 – 21), taught the Law (Neh 8:7 – 8), and assisted in the covenant renewal (Neh 9:38).

THE PRIESTHOOD AND JESUS

During Jesus' time, priests (such as Zechariah, Luke 1:5 – 23) continued their temple duties. Yet Jesus' clearing of the temple (John 2:13 – 17; cf. Matt 21:12 – 13; Mark 11:15 – 17) demonstrated God's judgment on the temple, which had become corrupt and abusive. The high priest was often politically appointed and cooperated with Rome, although, as the ruler of the Sanhedrin (the Jewish council), he wielded significant power. Priestly opposition to Jesus (especially by the high priest) arose partly from the faulty conviction that the temple and priesthood were permanent, rather than provisional until the ultimate fulfillment of their purposes in the Lord's Anointed. Jesus made this clear in his interactions with the "chief priests" (priests of high rank), teachers of the law, and elders (Matt 16:21; 21:23 – 27; Mark 8:31; 11:27 – 33; Luke 9:22; 20:1 – 8; John 11:45 – 57), and in a parable directed against them (Matt 21:33 – 46; Luke 20:9 – 19). This opposition culminated in Jesus' trial before the Sanhedrin, the high priest Caiaphas (Matthew 26:57 – 68; Mark 14:53 – 65), and Caiaphas's father-in-law Annas (John 18:12 – 24). This opposition extended to the early church (Acts 4:1 – 22; 5:17 – 42; 6:8 — 7:58), even though a number of priests did come to faith (Acts 6:7).

Although Jesus did not perform priestly duties (Matt 8:1 – 4; Mark 1:40 – 44; Luke 5:12 – 14; 17:11 – 14; cf. Heb 7:13), he revealed a priestly self-understanding when he declared the standard of true cleanness (Matt 15:1 – 11; Mark 7:1 – 23; cf. Lev 10:10 – 11; Acts 10:9 – 16,28), interpreted the law (Matt 5:17 – 48; Luke 24:27), and revealed the true intent of the Sabbath (Matt 12:1 – 13; Mark 2:23 — 3:6; Luke 6:1 – 11; 13:10 – 17; cf. John 5:16 – 18). Thus, in Jesus, God's purposes for the priesthood are fulfilled. Furthermore, Jesus understood that the sacrifice he offered for sin was his own (sinless) life (Mark 10:45; Luke 22:19 – 20; cf. John 1:29).

Hebrews uniquely presents Jesus as the true high priest. Detailed comparisons between Jesus and the Levitical priesthood show the anticipatory nature and inherent limitations of the Levitical order, including repeated sacrifices (Heb 10:3), the high priest's own sin (Heb 7:27), and the high priest's eventual death (Heb 7:23). Unlike Levitical high priests, Jesus is appointed as Son (Heb 5:5) by divine oath (Heb 7:20 – 22). Moreover, Jesus is a priest of an entirely different kind: "in the order of Melchizedek" (Heb 5:6,10; 6:20; 7:11,17). The author of Hebrews draws several important conclusions from the account of Melchizedek, a priest of God most high, in Gen 14:17 – 20. In the ancient world, genealogy was usually an essential basis for selecting priests (although in some places high priests or priestesses were chosen by lot). Thus, an individual with no recorded genealogy who performed a priestly role by blessing Abraham is quite remarkable. Moreover, by giving Melchizedek a tithe, Abraham acknowledged Melchizedek as a legitimate priest. But Melchizedek was also a king. Although these offices were distinct throughout Israel's history, Ps 110 designates one who is both king and eternal priest in the order of Melchizedek. For this reason, the author of Hebrews understood Melchizedek as pointing typologically to Christ (Heb 7), the perfect priest and king, although this OT figure himself was neither angelic nor messianic.

The presence of another priesthood confirmed the provisional nature of the Levitical one (Heb 7:11 – 19). Because Jesus' priesthood rests upon the "power of an indestructible life" (Heb 7:16), it is eternal. As the eternal, perfect high priest, Jesus always intercedes for believers (Heb 7:24 – 25; cf. Heb 9:24; Rom 8:34; 1 John 2:1) in the true, heavenly sanctuary. As the priest and mediator of the new, eternal covenant, sins are remembered no more and God's laws are written on believers' hearts and minds (Heb 8:1 – 13; 9:15; 13:20).

Moreover, Jesus' perfect sacrifice (Heb 5:8 – 9; 10:1 – 18) perfectly atones (Heb 2:17) because he is the sinless Son of God (Heb 7:26), who is also fully human (Heb 2:11 – 18). His fully efficacious sacrifice (Heb 9:26,28; 10:12; 1 John 2:2) accomplished what animal sacrifices could not, namely, a cleansed conscience and access to God's presence (Heb 9:14; cf. Eph 2:18; Jude 24 – 25). Unlike Levitical high priests, Jesus had no need to sacrifice for his own sins (Heb 7:27) or to enter the sanctuary repeatedly (Heb 9:25 – 26). Instead, he entered the heavenly Most Holy Place once for all by means of his own blood (Heb 9:12). Having completed his work of purification, he sits exalted at the right hand of God (Heb 1:3) as the great high priest over God's house (Heb 10:21).

BELIEVERS AS PRIESTS

God's intention for humanity is perfect fellowship with him in his holy realm. He entrusted the privilege of tending and extending his realm throughout the earth to Adam and Eve — a privilege that Gen 1 – 2 depicts in both royal and priestly terms. Their rebellion necessitated expulsion from God's holy realm, which also resulted in a loss of their holy, priestly status. God's redemptive plan, however, is outlined in the Abrahamic promises (Gen 12:1 – 3) and is further articulated at Sinai with Israel as "a kingdom of priests and a holy nation" (Exod 19:6). Thus, his plan has always involved a restoration of the holy status originally intended for humanity.

In the NT, titles applied to Israel at Sinai are applied to believers (1 Pet 2:9 – 10; Rev 1:6; 5:10), both Jews and Gentiles. Moreover, just as Israel was set apart and spared by the blood of the Passover lamb in Egypt (Exod 12:21 – 23), so also believers are made holy by the shed blood of the Lamb (cf. 1 Pet 1:18 – 19). The apostle Peter describes a new temple built upon Jesus Christ, the cornerstone, with believers as "living stones" who offer spiritual sacrifices (1 Pet 2:4 – 5) — their very lives (Rom 12:1 – 2) and thanksgiving (Heb 13:15 – 16). As priests, believers declare God's praises to the world, fulfilling what Isaiah foresaw (Isa 66:19 – 21; cf. Isa 61:6; Rom 15:16). Priestly service ultimately involves worshiping the living God now (Heb 9:14) and forever before his throne (Rev 7:9 – 17; 20:6).

SACRIFICE

Jay A. Sklar

Sacrifices were a regular part of life in ancient Israel. People offered them not only at regular annual festivals (Lev 16; 23) but also throughout the year in response to sin (Lev 4 – 5) or for answered prayer (Ps 66:13 – 16; 107:19,22). As a result, almost every OT book mentions or alludes to sacrifice.

There were four main types of animal sacrifice: burnt offerings, fellowship (or "peace") offerings, sin (or "purification") offerings, and guilt (or "reparation") offerings. (For details on these offerings and their different functions, see Lev 1 – 5 and notes.) This article describes the general functions of sacrifice, the related concepts of atonement and blood, and the Passover sacrifice in particular. While the focus will be on the description of these things in the OT, attention will also be paid to the ways in which NT authors use them to explain Jesus' sacrifice on our behalf.

THE REASONS FOR SACRIFICE

Generally speaking, Israelites presented sacrifices for one of three reasons: to praise and thank the Lord, to emphasize their requests to the Lord, and to atone for sin and impurity.

First, they brought sacrifices to praise and thank the Lord. The idea was straightforward: in response to God's goodness, it was appropriate to honor him by giving him something costly. "Then they cried to the LORD in their trouble, and he saved them from their distress … Let them sacrifice thank offerings and tell of his works with songs of joy" (Ps 107:19,22).

These sacrifices of praise were especially common ways for Israelites to fulfill a vow, i.e., a promise to carry out a certain task when the Lord answered their prayer (see Num 30:1 – 16 and notes). By making such a promise, the Israelites were not only emphasizing the seriousness of their prayer but also ensuring that they would thank the Lord appropriately when God answered their prayer. (Since thankfulness vanishes so quickly, this was a helpful safeguard!) Significantly, Israelites fulfilled sacrificial vows at the temple so that they could publicly praise the Lord for what he had done. "I will come to your temple with burnt offerings and fulfill my vows to you … Come and hear, all you who fear God; let me tell you what he has done for me" (Ps 66:13,16; see Ps 116:14,17 – 18; cf. 1 Sam 1:11 with 1 Sam 1:24 — 2:10).

Naturally, it is not only ancient Israelites that should give such costly sacrifices in response to the Lord's goodness. Paul picks up on the same idea when he exhorts Christians, "Therefore, I urge you, brothers and sisters, in view of God's mercy, to offer your bodies as a living sacrifice, holy and pleasing to God — this is your true and proper worship" (Rom 12:1). God's mercies in Jesus are so great (Rom 9 – 11) that the only appropriate response is wholehearted devotion to him.

Second, Israelites presented sacrifices to emphasize their requests to the Lord. It was like putting an exclamation point on their prayers. For example, when the Israelites were threatened in battle, the prophet Samuel "took a suckling lamb and sacrificed it as a whole burnt offering to the LORD. He cried out to the LORD on Israel's behalf, and the LORD answered him" (1 Sam 7:9; see 1 Sam 13:8 – 12; Ps 20:1 – 3). By making such sacrifices, the Israelites were proclaiming that they desperately needed the Lord and his help.

Third, Israelites presented sacrifices to atone for sin and impurity. This took place during annual events for the community, such as the Day of Atonement (see The Day of Atonement [Yom Kippur], p. 2657), and also throughout the year as individuals brought sacrifices to make atonement (Lev 4 – 5). But what exactly is atonement?

ATONEMENT

In the most basic sense, to make atonement is to repair and restore the relationship with the Lord that sin or impurity has broken. In a more specific sense, sacrificial atonement operates according to two different but complementary pictures: ransom and cleansing.

Atonement as Ransom

Many today think of a "ransom" as a payment that delivers an innocent party from a guilty party, as when the family of a kidnapped person pays money to the kidnappers. In ancient Israel, however, it was just the opposite: the guilty party gave a ransom payment to the innocent party in order to be delivered from a just penalty. If, e.g., a man did not guard his aggressive ox properly and it killed someone, he would hope to give a ransom to the victim's family in order to avoid being put to death for his wrongdoing (Exod 21:28 – 30). The ransom payment would serve to deliver the guilty from punishment and appease the innocent party, thus restoring peace to the relationship. Significantly, the guilty party did not have an automatic right to make a ransom payment; it was entirely up to the innocent party — the one who had been wronged — whether to allow this way of escape. To do so was to show sheer grace to the person who deserved far worse.

This is one of the main pictures by which atonement operates in the Bible. The Hebrew word *kipper* ("to make atonement") is directly related to the Hebrew word *kōper* ("ransom"). And Lev 17:11, the central verse on sacrificial atonement, makes clear that sacrifices served as a ransom payment. It was a payment that the Lord, the wronged party, graciously allowed his sinful people to present in order for them to escape a far worse penalty (see Blood, this page). Significantly, Jesus summarizes his own mission with the language of ransom: "For even the Son of Man did not come to be served, but to serve, and to give his life as a ransom for many" (Mark 10:45). His sacrifice ransoms sinners from the just penalty their sins deserve.

Atonement as Cleansing

A second picture of sacrificial atonement is cleansing. "Wash away all my iniquity," the psalmist prays, "and cleanse me from my sin" (Ps 51:2). We identify with these words. Sin often leaves us feeling dirty, as though our heart or soul is unclean. Atonement removes the stain of sin from the sinner. Indeed, the great Day of Atonement ceremony affirms this: "On this day atonement will be made for you, to cleanse you. Then, before the LORD, you will be clean from all your sins" (Lev 16:30).

As stated above, ransom and cleansing are complementary pictures of atonement. The person who is ransomed from a due penalty by sacrifice is at the same time cleansed of sin, while the person who is cleansed of sin by sacrifice is at the same time ransomed from a due penalty. The text sometimes emphasizes one of these more than the other, which is why some verses describe Jesus' sacrificial death as a ransom for sinners (e.g., Mark 10:45) and others as what cleanses us from sin (e.g., 1 John 1:9). But both pictures of atonement work together; they are two sides of the same coin.

Atonement as the Lord's Gracious Gift

Whether the text emphasizes sacrificial atonement as ransom or cleansing, it is evident that such atonement is the Lord's gracious gift to us. He makes this clear in Lev 17:11. The Lord says, in this translation, "For the life of the body is in the blood, and I, I have given it to you to make atonement for your lives on the altar ..." The word "I" occurs twice and is the Lord's way of emphasizing that *he himself* is the one who allows sacrifice to atone for his sinful people. This is an important reversal of how we normally think about sacrifice, namely, as something *we* provide to God. This verse turns that idea completely upside down: God provides the sacrifice for us!

The NT takes this one step further. While the Lord allowed sacrifices to atone for sin in the OT, the people still had to bring their own sacrifices. In the NT, the Lord not only allows a sacrifice to atone for sin but *he himself* provides the sacrifice for his sinful people. "But God demonstrates his own love for us in this: While we were still sinners, Christ died for us" (Rom 5:8). The party sinned against has paid the penalty on the sinner's behalf. This is indeed amazing grace!

BLOOD

Lev 17:11 also identifies the central role that blood plays in sacrificial atonement. It closely associates the animal's blood with the animal's life: "For the life of a creature is in the blood." This association is very natural since a body that loses its blood quickly becomes lifeless. It is indeed why we can speak of "lifeblood." Significantly, sacrifices can atone because the animal's lifeblood is offered: "It is the blood that makes atonement" by means of the life in the blood (Lev 17:11b; see NIV text note).

In terms of the ransom picture of atonement, the animal's lifeblood served as the ransom payment. It was a gracious application of the "life for life" principle of justice (Exod 21:23). When people forfeited their own lifeblood because of sin, they were able to be ransomed by the lifeblood of a blameless substitute — an animal — who took their place (see also important Jewish commentators such as Rashi or Ibn Ezra on Lev 17:11). This same understanding is also central to explaining the sacrificial death of Jesus, who died as a blameless substitute in our place so we might be forgiven (Rom 5:6,8; 1 Pet 1:18 – 19; 3:18; cf. Isa 53).

In terms of the cleansing picture of atonement, lifeblood was the most powerful cleansing agent available in ancient Israel. The reason for this is nowhere explained. What is clear, however, is that sacrificial lifeblood was central to cleansing the Israelites' sins and impurities and thereby atoning for them (Lev 16:15 – 19). The NT applies this to the far greater sacrifice of Jesus, whose "blood ... purifies us from all sin" (1 John 1:7; cf. Heb 9:14). It is only those who "have washed their robes and made them white in the blood of the Lamb" who are truly clean (Rev 7:14).

It is certainly true that the Lord at times allowed atonement for his people's sins without a sacrifice being made. This was usually in the context of corporate sin and happened only after the work of a mediator on the people's behalf (e.g., Exod 32:11 – 14; Num 14:13 – 20; 16:22,45 – 48; cf. 1 Tim 2:5 – 6 for Jesus as both necessary mediator and sacrifice). But as the above shows, the Lord typically emphasized the centrality of sacrifice in order for atonement to occur (see Rom 3:21 – 26). This is especially clear from the importance of sacrifice on one of the highest and holiest days of the Israelites' year: the Day of Atonement.

THE DAY OF ATONEMENT (YOM KIPPUR)

Lev 16 most fully describes the Day of Atonement. As its name implies, its purpose was to make atonement for the Israelites' sins and impurities. Three rites formed the heart of the ceremony, each making atonement in its own way. First, Aaron took the blood of sin offerings and went into the Most Holy Place — the very throne room of the Lord — and sprinkled the blood around, in this way cleansing the Lord's home from the defilement caused by the sins and impurities of the Israelites, including those of Aaron himself and his family (Lev 16:11 – 19). Next, Aaron confessed all of his and the people's sins and placed them on the head of the scapegoat, which then bore the lethal burden of these sins and carried them far away, never to be seen again (Lev 16:20 – 22; cf. Isa 53:8,10). Finally, Aaron presented burnt offerings to underscore the atonement being made (Lev 16:23 – 24). Taken together, these rites fully atoned for the Israelites; their sins and impurities no longer remained; the slate was completely clean (cf. Ps 103:12). The holy God who is offended by sin and impurity is also the compassionate and gracious God who delights to cleanse and forgive it (cf. Lev 16:21 with Exod 34:6b – 7a; see also Mic 7:19; 1 John 1:9).

It was, of course, necessary for the Israelites to accompany these rites with repentance (Lev 16:29,31; cf. Ps 51:17). The Lord is not interested in his people's ability to perform rituals but in whether they embrace him from the heart (cf. Isa 1:10 – 17). As with a wedding, a ritual is an empty event if the participants are not fully committed to one another.

The NT describes the day of Jesus' crucifixion as the ultimate Day of Atonement: Jesus entered into the heavenly throne room itself to atone for sin (Heb 9:24). Unlike Aaron, Jesus was a perfect high priest and did not need to atone for himself (Heb 7:27). What is more, because Jesus was perfect, he was able to offer himself as an atoning sacrifice for the sins of others (Heb 9:12,14,28; 10:19 – 22; cf. Isa 53:11 – 12). Indeed, animal sacrifices were only a temporary measure, a picture that looked forward to Jesus' far greater sacrifice that would atone for sin fully and finally (Heb 7:26 – 27; 9:25 — 10:10). If Israelite believers felt the burden of their sin lifted because of Aaron's ministry on the Day of Atonement, how much more the Christian because of Jesus' sacrifice on the cross!

PASSOVER

A discussion of sacrifice would not be complete without mention of the Passover sacrifice, first described in Exod 12:1 – 14. That occasion was the final blow on Egypt, in which the Lord passed through the land and killed all the Egyptian firstborn (Exod 11:4 – 5). In order to prepare, each Israelite family killed a lamb without defect, placed its blood on their doorframes, and roasted and ate the meat that very night (Exod 12:1 – 10). When the Lord passed through the land, the blood on the doorframe served as a sign that his covenant children were in that house, and he passed over it without executing his justice there (Exod 12:12 – 13,26 – 27). But in the rest of the land the plague was so devastating that it finally prompted Pharaoh to release the Israelites from slavery and let them leave Egypt (Exod 12:31 – 34). From that point on, the Israelites celebrated the Passover every year to remember that the Lord both delivered their firstborn from judgment and led the nation up from the land of slavery (Exod 12:25 – 27,42).

The NT writers use the Passover to explain the death of Jesus, who was crucified at the same general time as the Passover (Matt 26:17; 27:15 – 26). He is "our Passover lamb" (1 Cor 5:7). It is a fitting metaphor since Jesus' sacrifice also delivers us from the Lord's judgment (1 Thess 1:10) and leads us out of sin's slavery into adoption as the Lord's children (John 1:12; Eph 1:5; cf. Exod 4:22). It is during the communion meal, instituted by Jesus at the Passover meal (Luke 22:1 – 23), that Christians remember and proclaim, "Jesus, you are the mighty Savior, the sacrificial Lamb of God who takes away the sin of the world!" (cf. Isa 53:5 – 12; John 1:29).

EXILE AND EXODUS

Thomas Richard Wood

Although the terms "exodus" and "exile" refer primarily to two historical events in the life of the nation of Israel, their theological significance in the storyline of Scripture far exceeds both the Hebrew slaves' dramatic departure from Egypt under Moses and the plight of those carried off in the Assyrian and Babylonian deportations. Exile, more broadly, signals a broken relationship between God and his people. Exodus, on the other hand, promises to restore Israel's relationship with Yahweh and return her to the land of her forefathers. Consequently, Israel's story sounds very much like the story of humanity, a story that begins with the expulsion of Adam and Eve from the Garden of Eden and is not resolved until the resurrection of God's people and the final regathering of believers at the second coming of Christ. To truly appreciate the theological significance of Israel's exile and exodus, one must encounter these events as the Bible has presented them — couched in the larger context of the human story of creation, fall, redemption, and resurrection.

HUMANITY'S EXILE FROM PARADISE

Above all, the biblical notion of exile refers to the banishment of the sinner from the presence of God. Fully realized, it leaves us in bondage to sin and death, unable to free ourselves from their dominion. Our only hope of deliverance lies in God's intervention.

Exile Begins

As a consequence of Adam and Eve's willful decision to distrust the goodness of their Creator, "the LORD God banished [them] from the Garden of Eden" (Gen 3:23). The garden represents the place where humanity had access to God's presence and where God's blessings freely flowed from his hand. Prior to their fall, Adam and Eve lived in harmony with one another, the creation around them, and the One who created them. The introduction of sin into this environment greatly injured each of these relationships, leaving Adam estranged from his wife, the land, and his Maker. The curse of death tainted all aspects of human interaction.

Exile Continues

The story of exile continues in Gen 4. Soon after Cain killed Abel, God pronounces additional curses under which he must live. Cain's response is telling: "Today you are driving me from the land, and I will be hidden from your presence" (Gen 4:14). Even though Adam and Eve had lost the privilege of walking with the Lord in the garden, God would graciously show himself from time to time to their offspring. With the murder of his brother, Cain experienced a whole new level of alienation — a life entirely hidden from God's face. Yahweh also banished him from the very ground that he had worked so effectively, forcing him to become "a restless wanderer on the earth" (Gen 4:3,11 – 12). Like his father before him, Cain's expulsion from the "land" reflected a deeper problem. Whatever relationship he might have had with his Creator was now broken. The story of humankind becoming more and more alienated from the purposes of God is a theme repeated in the accounts of Lamech (Gen 4:19 – 24), the flood (Gen 6 – 8), and the tower of Babel (Gen 11:1 – 9). By the time the descendants of Abraham find themselves enslaved in Egypt, exile has become an outward manifestation of an internal spiritual condition.

ISRAEL'S FIRST EXILE AND EXODUS

The biblical authors further flesh out the repercussions of Adam and Eve's alienation from God, the garden, and each other when they recount the tumultuous history of Israel.

"Exile" in Egypt

From a strictly chronological standpoint, Israel's exodus from Egypt predates the Assyrian and Babylonian exiles. Nevertheless, it is fair to refer to Israel's time of bondage in Egypt as her "first exile." Later biblical writers speak of Israel's forced captivity in Assyria and Babylon as a *return* to Egypt (Deut 28:63 – 68; Ezek 19:4; Hos 8:13; 9:3; 11:5; Zech 10:9 – 10), which further leads them to depict a future regathering as a *second* exodus (Isa 11:11,15 – 16; 14:1 – 2; 62:11 – 12; Ezek 20:32 – 38; Hos 2:14 – 15; 11:11; Zech 10:8 – 12). The author of Genesis concurs: "Then the LORD said to [Abraham], 'Know for certain that for four hundred years your descendants will be strangers in a country not their own and that they will be enslaved and mistreated there' " (Gen 15:13). Though he does not use the Hebrew word for "exile" to describe the dire circumstances of Abraham's descendants in Egypt, the combination of "strangers," "enslaved," and "mistreated" invokes the same connotation. They may not have gone down into Egypt as exiles, but captives they became nonetheless.

Exodus From Egypt

God's successive unleashing of ten plagues upon the land of Egypt ultimately brought about his people's freedom. With each new affliction Pharaoh was temporarily forced to acknowledge the reality and power of Israel's God. Still, he did not capitulate to Moses' request to "let [God's] people go" (Exod 10:3) until he experienced the loss of his firstborn son during the final plague. Meanwhile the Israelites were spared such a calamity not because they were innocent and undeserving of the same fate as the Egyptians but because they had adhered to the instructions of Moses and applied the blood of a lamb to their doorposts. The death angel therefore passed over them as he exacted God's judgment on all others. Hence, the blood of the Passover lamb redeems Israel from her bondage while turning away the penalty (death) that her sins deserved.

Another integral part of the exodus narrative is the Lord's renewed presence with Israel as dramatically demonstrated in the pillar of cloud leading them by day and the pillar of fire guiding them by night. Moreover, when Yahweh instructs Moses to build a tabernacle where the Lord's glory will reside and to situate it in the center of the camp, he is announcing his intention to take up permanent residence with his people. All that remained for their exodus to be complete was for Israel to take possession of the promised land. Instead the nation grumbled against Moses, revealing their unbelieving hearts. As a result the Lord let them perish in the wilderness, exiled from the divine blessings awaiting them on the other side of the Jordan. Even though a more faithful generation of Israelites would eventually enter the land (completing the exodus), subsequent generations would turn away after the gods of the Canaanites. Such rebellion brought upon Israel "exilic-like" conditions in greater and lesser degrees throughout her history. Finally, when her idolatry grew intolerable, God expelled his people from the land, drove them from his presence, and thrust them into the total darkness of exile again (Isa 8:22).

ISRAEL'S SECOND EXILE AND EXODUS

Long before Israel had ever heard of Shalmaneser, king of Assyria, or Nebuchadnezzar, king of Babylon, Moses had warned them that if they turned away from Yahweh to worship idols, they would eventually be uprooted from the land (Deut 29:28), scattered over all of the earth (Deut 28:64), and dispersed among the nations (Deut 30:1). Still he left them with hope: "When you and your children return to the LORD your God and obey him with all your heart and with all your soul ... then the LORD your God will restore your fortunes and have compassion on you and gather you again from all the nations where he scattered you ... and bring you back ... to the land that belonged to your ancestors" (Deut 30:2–5).

Exile Again

Israel's northern and southern kingdoms suffered a second exile in 722 and 586 BC, respectively. The books of Kings and Chronicles describe in detail what led to the downfall of Samaria and Jerusalem. It was not the overwhelming strength of the Assyrian and Babylonian Empires but rather Israel's and Judah's unfaithfulness to Yahweh that brought about their demise. These so-called world powers were mere lapdogs summoned by their master's whistle in order to enact God's judgment on his people (Isa 5:26). God's presence in the form of the *shekinah* glory had already departed from the temple, as well as the holy city (Ezek 10:4,18–22; 11:22–24), when Nebuchadnezzar laid siege against Jerusalem. The nation's fate was sealed. With the royal line of David seemingly extinguished, the temple in ruin, and Israel's survivors taken in chains to faraway lands, the prophetic words of Hosea rang true: "You are not my people, and I am not your God" (Hos 1:9). Finally, the Israelites were forced to face the reality that they had no more standing in the eyes of Yahweh than the Gentiles had. Only the promise of a future restoration could sustain them in their time of tribulation (Hos 2:23).

The Second Exodus

While in Babylon Israel's true spiritual problem became apparent. Daniel, Ezra, and Nehemiah all recognized that it was their ancestors' disregard for the law of God and their unwillingness to heed the words of the prophets that led to their exile. Hence they cried out to Yahweh, offering up prayers of repentance and petitioning him to restore his people, his sanctuary, and his holy city (Ezra 9:6–7; Neh 1:5–11; Dan 9:4–19). In response to Daniel's prayer, and in accordance with the prophecy of Jeremiah, "the LORD moved the heart of Cyrus king of Persia to make a proclamation" (Ezra 1:1) that the survivors of Israel were free to return to Jerusalem and begin rebuilding the temple (Ezra 1:2–4). Soon after the edict was published, a paltry number of Israelites made the journey back to the promised land under the leadership of Sheshbazzar and Zerubbabel. In the next several decades, other migrations of dispossessed Jews arrived in Jerusalem. By the time of Nehemiah, Israel's second exodus seemed to have stalled. Although the temple and the city's walls had been rebuilt and a remnant of God's people had returned to the land, the regathered community looked little like the promised restoration spoken of by the prophets. The returnees continued to suffer under foreign subjugation, the glory of the Lord had seemingly not returned to the temple, a Davidic king did not sit on the throne, and the vast majority of Israelites remained among the Gentile nations. More important, the promise of a new heart and a new spirit associated with a new covenant had not materialized in the lives of the chosen people. Despite signs of Yahweh's renewed favor toward those who had returned to Jerusalem, the surviving remnant continued to disregard his decrees in significant ways (Mal 1:6–14; 2:10–16; 3:7–8). Consequently they missed the opportunity for greater restoration and a new outpouring of God's blessing (Hag 2:15–19; Zech 8:9–19; Mal 3:10–12).

HUMANITY'S EXODUS FROM EXILE

As the Bible story unfolds, it becomes increasingly clear that the Israelites' inability to remain faithful to God was because they had inherited the same sinful nature that has plagued all of humanity since the fall of Adam. Their exile from the land and captivity among the nations exposed a deeper problem: their bondage to sin and death. For God to save his people from this plight, he would have to send a deliverer with divine attributes, one who could change the human heart and conquer death itself.

A New Exodus

Four hundred years after Malachi penned his final warning to Israel, the promised son of David arrived on the scene with the task of regathering the people of God to himself. Although the nation was feeling the heavy hand of Roman occupation at the time, Israel's Messiah turned his attention toward the real cause of the people's suffering. Jesus had come to set the captives free from the power of sin and death (Matt 1:21; Luke 4:18–19; Rom 8:2; Heb 9:14–15) and to reopen a way into the very presence of God (Matt 27:51; Heb 10:19–22). In order to do so he willingly shared in the plight of those he came to save (Phil 2:6–8) and laid down his life in such a way as to cover their sins and avert the judgment of God rightfully directed toward Jew and Gentile alike (1 John 2:2). In his death on the cross, the Son of God became "our Passover lamb" (1 Cor 5:7).

With Jesus "exiled" from God (Mark 15:34), land (Matt 8:20), and others (Matt 26:31), only a new, greater exodus (i.e., resurrection, both spiritual and physical) could deliver him from the horrific death that separated him from his Father, his inheritance, and his beloved disciples. In other words, the long-awaited Messiah was not simply a new Moses sent to rescue Israel from the latest calamity that had befallen them. Rather, he is the corporate head of a new people with a new heart and offers a new kind of exodus while being the very first to participate in it. As the only perfectly obedient Israelite (Heb 4:15; 5:8) — a faithful remnant of one — Jesus (not the unbelieving nation) is the sole heir of all of the covenantal promises made to Abraham, Israel, and David (Heb 1:2; cf. Matt 21:38; 28:18; Acts 2:29–33). Life everlasting, a land flowing with milk and honey, a posterity as numerous as the stars, a perpetual reign over all creation, and uninhibited access to the Father's presence all belong exclusively to him. Others could join this new exodus and become joint heirs with Abraham's "seed" (Gal 3:16–20,29), but not without embracing him as their Savior and Messiah (Acts 3:22–26; Rom 8:17; Gal 3:26 — 4:7; Eph 2:11–13; 3:6).

Exodus Accomplished

As people from every nation, tribe, and tongue accepted Jesus as the divine solution of their exilic-like predicament, the curses placed on Adam and Eve in Gen 3 began to lose their power over them. The process of restoration had begun — an ongoing process that addressed humanity's bondage to sin and death, their broken relationships with one another, and their banishment from God's presence. For the Christian, "the law of the Spirit who gives life has set [them] free from the law of sin and death" (Rom 8:2). Jesus, our peace, has made Jew and Gentile one in Christ, destroying "the barrier, the dividing wall of hostility" between them (Eph 2:14). The children of God "have confidence to enter the Most Holy Place ... by a new and living way opened for [them] through the curtain" (Heb 10:19–20; cf. Heb 4:16). For though they were at one time "without hope and without God," "separate from Christ," even "far away" (i.e., exiled), they have now been "brought near by the blood of Christ" (Eph 2:12–13).

Nevertheless, the followers of Christ still consider themselves to be "foreigners and exiles" (1 Pet 2:11) — "strangers" on this earth "longing for a better country" (Heb 11:13,16) — whose "citizenship is in heaven" (Phil 3:20). The sting of death may have been vanquished (1 Cor 15:55), but the reality of dying remains very much an "enemy" with which to be reckoned (1 Cor 15:25–26). And finally, though Jesus' disciples have been set free from the power of sin, they still have an obligation to live by the Spirit and put to death the misdeeds of the body (Rom 8:12–13). They are no longer dead in their sins, but they are presently engaged in a great struggle against sin's last stronghold, the "flesh." The final exodus of the people of God may have begun with the resurrection of Jesus, but its consummation awaits his second coming, when "at the last trumpet," "in the twinkling of an eye," "the dead will be raised imperishable," the living faithful will be clothed with immortality (1 Cor 15:51–54), and the angels "will gather [the Lord's] elect from the four winds, from one end of the heavens to the other" (Matt 24:31), and all "will be caught up together ... in the clouds to meet the Lord in the air" (1 Thess 4:17). What an end to the new exodus that will be!

THE KINGDOM OF GOD

T. D. Alexander

From beginning to end the Bible proclaims God's eternal sovereignty over all things. He reigns supreme as both creator and sustainer of all that exists. Yet, unexpectedly, the Bible also recounts in detail how Adam and Eve rejected God's authority as universal king with disastrous consequences for the history of humanity. Life on earth becomes chaotic as another replaces God's rule.

From this catastrophic beginning, the Bible reveals how God gradually and patiently reestablishes his reign over the whole earth by redeeming humanity and subduing his opponents. As the NT makes evidently clear, pivotal to this process is Jesus Christ, whose death, resurrection, and ascension is central to extending God's reign throughout the earth. Those who acknowledge Jesus as king become members of the kingdom of God. While the kingdom is already present and growing on the earth, the Bible anticipates a time when Jesus will return in glory as universal king to reward the righteous and punish the wicked. When this happens, God's reign will extend unchallenged throughout a renewed earth.

GOD'S RULE REJECTED

To appreciate Jesus Christ's role in reestablishing God's sovereignty over the earth, we must begin with the opening chapters of Genesis. As the climax to his ordering of creation, God authorizes humanity to exercise dominion on his behalf over all other earthly creatures (Gen 1:26 – 28). To this end God makes human beings in his image and commissions them as his vice-regents to govern the earth.

Although God instructs the first human couple to rule over all the animals, they succumb to the sinister temptation of the "serpent" and betray God (Gen 3:1 – 7). By heeding this strange creature rather than the Creator, they submit to its authority. Consequently, the "serpent" gains dominion over human beings and everything God placed under their rule. This single act of rebellion against God's sovereignty profoundly influences the rest of human history. While Genesis reveals little about the identity of the "serpent," apart from stressing its exceptionally astute nature, Scripture elsewhere identifies the "serpent" as the devil, or Satan (Rev 12:9; 20:2). By manipulating Adam and Eve, Satan becomes the "prince of this world" (John 16:11), usurping God's position as king.

The resulting expulsion of Adam and Eve from the Garden of Eden confirms the end of their special status as God's vice-regents. Exiled from God's presence and with their original nature now corrupted, human beings experience the tragic consequences of being alienated from their Creator and the rest of creation. As the opening chapters of Genesis disclose, human violence soon pollutes God's good creation as people misuse their capacity to rule (Gen 6:5,11 – 13).

RESTORING GOD'S RULE ON THE EARTH

While humanity's rebellion against God has tragic consequences, God does not abandon them to their fate. In a process spanning generations, God embarks on a mission to rescue wayward people from the power of evil and death. This mission of restoration lies at the heart of the whole biblical story, and there are many aspects to it. One essential component is God's providing a human king who will successfully fulfill the vice-regent role originally delegated to Adam and Eve.

Beginning in Genesis, the OT anticipates the coming of an extraordinary king who will bring God's blessing to the nations of the earth. In due course, with the creation of the nation of Israel, God makes David king when the prophet Samuel anoints him with oil (1 Sam 16:1 – 13). David becomes the founder of a unique dynasty.

When David as king of Israel captures Jerusalem and subsequently transports to it the ark of the covenant (the footstool of the heavenly throne of God), a partial convergence of David's kingdom and God's kingdom occurs (2 Sam 6 – 7). Confirmation of this comes when David's son Solomon constructs a splendid temple, or palace, for God in Jerusalem (1 Kgs 5 – 8). With this the palace of the heavenly king stands close to the palace of the Davidic king. As temple-builder the king plays a special role in establishing God's reign on earth. However, as Ps 2 reveals, nations and peoples stand in opposition to both God and his anointed king. Nevertheless, the expectation existed that a future Davidic king would restore God's rule over all the earth, bringing justice and peace (Ps 72). This hope surfaces in prophetic passages that anticipate a future Messianic age (e.g., Isa 2:2 – 4; 9:2 – 7; 11:1 – 12).

Because David's successors failed to remain faithful to God, the OT story moves from the heyday of David's reign to the sacking of Jerusalem and the destruction of the temple by the Babylonians in 587/586 BC. Although this is a major setback to establishing God's reign on the earth, the hope lived on that God would one day subdue the whole earth. This is illustrated most graphically in Nebuchadnezzar's dream of a large statue of gold, silver, bronze, iron, and clay that a rock destroys. Daniel interprets the dream: "In the time of those kings, the God of heaven will set up a kingdom that will never be destroyed, nor will it be left to another people. It will crush all those kingdoms and bring them to an end, but it will itself endure forever" (Dan 2:44).

JESUS AS THE DAVIDIC KING

The OT hopes associated with the Davidic monarchy gave rise to the concept of a messiah. The noun "messiah" derives from the Hebrew term for an "anointed one." While it originally applied to anyone who was anointed with oil for a special purpose, in the NT the word "Messiah" takes on a special significance (its Greek equivalent is *christos*). When the Gospels speak of Jesus as the Messiah, or Christ, they view him as fulfilling the OT expectations involving the Davidic dynasty.

Of all the Gospel writers, Matthew most fully develops Jesus' links with the Davidic dynasty. From Matthew's initial genealogy to his concluding observation about Jesus having all authority in heaven and on earth, he consistently emphasizes Jesus' royal nature. Jesus, however, is no ordinary king.

In spite of displaying exceptional powers over nature, Jesus deliberately shuns establishing God's reign by military power. In fact, as Matthew graphically reveals, the self-giving, sacrificial death of the king creates God's kingdom. Turning everything upside down, Jesus dies on the cross in order to end Satan's rule over the earth and loose human beings from Satan's control. Jesus' death opens the way for releasing those who are enslaved to evil (Matt 12:25–29).

In light of his mission, Jesus (like John the Baptist) proclaims the coming of the "kingdom of heaven" (or "kingdom of God") and urges his listeners to become part of it by repenting (Matt 4:17; cf. Matt 3:2) and believing the good news (Mark 1:15). Through a series of parables, Jesus provides important insights into the nature of the kingdom (Matt 13). The kingdom will grow gradually, starting as something exceptionally small but eventually reaching great size. During this growing phase, the devil will actively seek to hinder the kingdom's expansion. Those who become members of the kingdom will face persecution from both Satan and those who knowingly or unknowingly side with Satan. Even Jesus himself is tempted and must resist Satan's offer of universal kingship (Matt 4:8–9).

Since the coming of the kingdom does not immediately end all evil, Jesus reveals that at the end of the growing phase, he will return as universal judge to separate the righteous and the wicked. At this time, with the destruction of everything evil, God's kingdom will become all that it was meant to be from the beginning.

Highlighting the challenge of kingdom membership, Jesus reminds his listeners that not everyone who initially responds positively will remain submissive to his authority as king. Some will claim kingdom membership, but their actions will reveal otherwise (Matt 7:15–23). While Jesus underlines the tragic consequences of not being within the kingdom, he also speaks positively about the benefits of kingdom membership. To be within the kingdom is worth everything a person possesses (Matt 13:44–46).

Jesus discloses that national boundaries do not delineate the kingdom he has come to establish. Rather, God's kingdom exists wherever people acknowledge him as king. Jesus' followers must pray constantly for the coming of God's kingdom on earth and make disciples throughout the whole world (Matt 28:19–20).

KINGDOMS IN CONFLICT

Although Christ's sacrificial death on the cross ensures Satan's ultimate defeat, the evil one continues to resist the expansion of God's kingdom on the earth. In this ongoing spiritual conflict, the enemies are not "flesh and blood," but "the powers of this dark world" and "the spiritual forces of evil in the heavenly realms" (Eph 6:12). Christians must therefore equip themselves with appropriate armor (Eph 6:13–17).

As God's chosen Messiah, Jesus comes as the king of peace. He deliberately rejects using power or violence to establish his authority over the earth, and instead willingly permits his enemies to execute him as a common criminal. For Jesus the path to creating God's kingdom on the earth is through suffering and death. Yet by laying down his life, Jesus is exalted to rule over all (Phil 2:7–11). As God's true vice-regent, Jesus differs radically from all other human kings. Ultimately, however, he will reign over all, death being the last enemy to be destroyed (1 Cor 15:24–26).

Unfortunately, the history of the church reveals that Christ's followers have not always clearly grasped that they cannot establish the kingdom of God through force. Regrettably, professing Christians have occasionally taken up arms in the name of Christ, believing that this was God's will. To do so, however, models God's kingdom on those established by aggressive humans. The Bible emphasizes that people cannot be forced to submit to God's rule but must be persuaded in love.

This world is divided between those who welcome and those who oppose establishing God's kingdom on the earth. For the present, Christian believers must persevere in the face of opposition, realizing that the conflict between good and evil will one day end when Jesus returns in glory. Till then, our mission is to proclaim the good news of the kingdom, ever praying, "Our Father in heaven, hallowed be your name, your kingdom come, your will be done, on earth as it is in heaven" (Matt 6:9–10).

SONSHIP

D. A. Carson

When the Bible uses "son" metaphorically to refer to someone other than a biological son, the range of its usage is rather large. The high point is Jesus the Son of God; Christians too, both men and women, are called sons (NIV "children") of God. The paths toward the full range of the biblical usage of "son" are rich and diverse.

OVERTONES OF SONSHIP

Sonship in the Ancient World

In addition to the many instances in the Bible where sonship is entirely natural and biological (e.g., Gen 22:2; Ruth 4:13,17; 1 Sam 16:18; Ezek 18:14; Matt 10:37; Luke 15:11), sonship is often metaphoric. The root of these metaphoric uses lies in the way sons achieved their identity. In the Western world today, only about 5 percent of sons end up doing the same work their fathers did; in the ancient world, the overwhelming majority of sons took up the same vocation as that of their fathers. The sons of farmers became farmers, the sons of fishermen became fishermen — and in both cases the sons learned their trade from their fathers, not at a college or in an apprenticeship with someone outside the family. These realities established their identity. That is why Jesus can be identified as "the carpenter's son" (Matt 13:55) and, presumably after the death of his (apparent) father Joseph, as himself "the carpenter" (Mark 6:3).

These social realities generate many of the sonship metaphors in the Bible. Jesus says that the peacemakers "will be called children [sons] of God" (Matt 5:9): he presupposes that God is the supreme peacemaker, and insofar as human beings make peace, they are acting like God; so that on that axis, at least, they can be called sons of God. Similarly, those who love their enemies are "children [sons] of God" (Luke 6:35). Biologically, of course, Abraham is the ancestor of all Israelites, but because faith characterized so much of his life, he is, more important, "the father of all who believe" (Rom 4:11), and believers are "the children [sons] of Abraham" (Gal 3:7). Biologically, the Judeans of Jesus' day are Abraham's descendants, but Jesus is prepared to challenge their claim to Abraham as their father on the grounds that they are not acting like Abraham (John 8:39–41). Their actions — their lies about who Jesus is and their efforts to kill him — demonstrate that their real "father" is the devil himself (John 8:44). In this metaphoric usage, paternity — who one's father is — is established not by genes but by conduct.

The Range of "Sons"

Understandably, in the original languages there are many metaphoric uses of the expression "sons of [something]" that are translated into simpler expressions in English because English does not use "sons of [something]" in the same way. Translators rightly render "son of a murderer" as "murderer" (2 Kgs 6:32). The "son of a bow" is rendered "arrows" (Job 41:28). A "son of might" is a "fighter" (2 Sam 17:10); the "sons of wise men" are "wise counselors" (Isa 19:11). These and many more examples show us the patterns of thought that make some uses of "son(s) of God" easier to understand.

SON(S) OF GOD

The uses of this expression are diverse. The Bible designates Adam as "the son of God" (Luke 3:37): human beings were made in the image of God (Gen 1:27), designed to reflect God in all ways appropriate to their status. As soon as someone in the line of David becomes king, he is declared to be God's "son" (2 Sam 7:14; Ps 2:7; cf. Ps 89:19–29). Even when a Davidic king reigns unjustly, he does not thereby cease being God's "son" (e.g., Ezek 21:10), for the category of "sonship" discloses how he *ought* to be like God.

Collectively, God calls the people of Israel his "son" (Exod 4:22–23), whether they are properly reflecting him or not. The Bible uses the plural expression "sons of God" to refer to angels (see NIV text notes on Job 1:6; 2:1; 38:7; see also Pss 29:1; 89:6, though the NIV renders the expression as "heavenly beings"), including the fallen angel called Satan (Job 1:6; 2:1). The collective "children [sons] of God" frequently refers to God's covenant people, whether under the terms of the old covenant (e.g., Deut 14:1; Isa 43:6; Jer 3:19) or the new (e.g., Rom 8:14; Phil 2:15; 1 John 3:1). This Father-child relationship is in view not only when the Bible calls believers children, but also when believers refer to God as Father (e.g., Mal 2:10) or, in the NT, address him as Father (e.g., Matt 6:9).

One other facet of the Bible's usage of "children [son(s)] of God" as applied to believers must be underscored. The final vision of the Bible ratchets up the intensity or perfection of many expressions introduced much earlier in the Bible — and it does the same for sonship. For example, "God's dwelling place is now among the people ... They will be his people, and God himself will be with them and be their God" (Rev 21:3). When similar words are said to the Israelites in the wake of the giving of the law at Sinai, God's dwelling place is tied to the tabernacle (Exod 25:8) and later the temple (1 Kgs 8:13), and God will be with them, manifesting himself to them as they traverse the wilderness (Exod 29:44–45; Num 1:51). When similar words are connected with the promise of a new covenant (Jer 31:31–34), the focus is no longer on the tabernacle and priestly system but on the inward transformation characteristic of the new covenant. In Rev 21, in the context of a new heaven and a new earth, within the walls of the new Jerusalem, God's presence with his people entails perfection: no more sin, no more of sin's miserable entailments, and no need of tabernacle or temple because the entire city is the Most Holy Place (Rev 21:22; see "Temple," p. 2652). In exactly the same way, this vision in Rev 21 ratchets up the significance of "son": "he who is victorious will inherit all this, and I will be his God and he will be *my son*" (Rev 21:7, author's paraphrase) — and in this context the son, the believer, is utterly sinless (contrast the sins of those who are not sons, v. 8), perfectly reflecting the heavenly Father so far as God's image-bearers can.

JESUS THE SON OF GOD

The Bible applies the title "Son of God" to Jesus in several distinctive ways — and this is where the trajectories of biblical themes running throughout the Bible come together.

The True Israel

Just as Israel is depicted as God's son — a frequently failing son — so Jesus recapitulates key episodes in Israel's life to disclose himself as the Son who does not fail. "Out of Egypt I called my son" (Hos 11:1) pictures the exodus, but Jesus too is "called" out of Egypt (Matt 2:15). Israel was tested and tempted during 40 years in the wilderness and frequently failed; Jesus is tested and tempted during 40 days and nights in the wilderness — the devil casts doubts on whether Jesus really is "the Son of God" — but this Son proves utterly loyal (Matt 4:1 – 11).

The True Davidic King

As is true with other kings in David's line, when Solomon ascends to the throne, God declares, "I will be his father, and he will be my son" (2 Sam 7:14; cf. Ps 2:7). That same passage, however, promises to David (ca. 1000 BC) an unending dynasty (2 Sam 7:16). God progressively discloses how this will be fulfilled. Less than three centuries later, the prophet Isaiah foresees a king "on David's throne" whose "government and peace" will never end and who will be called "Wonderful Counselor, Mighty God, Everlasting Father, Prince of Peace" (Isa 9:6 – 7). Other passages closely identify this coming Davidic king, sometimes designated "Messiah" (see "The Kingdom of God: Jesus as the Davidic King," p. 2663), with God the supreme Shepherd (e.g., Ezek 34:1 – 24). Jesus the Son of God insists that he has received from his Father the command to be the ideal good shepherd (John 10:1 – 18). Mark's Gospel begins by announcing "Jesus the Messiah [almost certainly referring to the Davidic king], the Son of God" (Mark 1:1), and this is confirmed almost immediately at the baptism of Jesus, "You are my Son, whom I love" (Mark 1:11). When Mark's Gospel draws to a close and the centurion who witnesses Jesus' death exclaims, "Surely this man was the Son of God!" (Mark 15:39), whatever pagan notions the centurion presupposes by the expression, Mark's readers recognize that Jesus is, at very least, the promised Davidic king, the Messiah. Jesus supremely enters into this kingly role by his resurrection from the dead (Rom 1:3 – 4). When Heb 1:5 ties Jesus to the promise of 2 Sam 7:14, it is not confusing Jesus with Solomon but connecting him through this verse with the trajectory of Davidic kings that finds its promise and culmination in him. This makes him superior to the angels, for only he reigns perfectly in the name of his heavenly Father.

The Unique Son, One With the Father

NT writers find diverse ways to distinguish Jesus' sonship from ours. For example, in Paul's writings, believers become sons/children of God by adoption; the same thing is never said of Jesus. But it is John who repeatedly insists that Jesus is the "one and only Son" (e.g., John 1:18; 3:16) and then explains more fully what he means. While human beings may be "sons/children of God" because along one axis or another we act like God (making peace, loving our enemies, reigning in David's line), only Jesus is the perfect Son of God because "*whatever* the Father does the Son also does" (John 5:19, emphasis added). For example, as the Word of God, Jesus the Son has created everything (John 1:3); like the Father, the Son raises the dead and "gives life to whom he is pleased to give it" (John 5:21). Small wonder that God is determined that all should honor the Son "just as they honor the Father" (John 5:23), which can certainly not be said of other "sons/children of God." Jesus the Son is not only the one through whom God "made the universe" (Heb 1:2), but he is "the radiance of God's glory and the exact representation of his being, sustaining all things by his powerful word" (Heb 1:3).

Intertwinings

The different ways in which the Bible applies "Son of God" to Jesus do not always follow independent trajectories through the Bible. Frequently they intertwine. For example, while Matt 1 – 4 emphasizes that Jesus as the Son of God is the new Israel, in the midst of this passage are the words "This is my Son, whom I love" (3:17), almost certainly picking up the Davidic/kingly use of sonship that was also implicit in the initial genealogy (ch. 1). Again, while Heb 1:5 – 13 focuses on the Davidic/kingly theme of sonship, the preceding verses display Jesus as the unique Son who is one with his Father (Heb 1:1 – 4). These and other numerous instances of intertwined uses of "Son of God" applied to Jesus demonstrate that the diverse uses, rather than entirely separate uses, "cross-pollinate" one another to generate a theologically rich notion of Jesus the Son of God.

THE CITY OF GOD

T. D. Alexander

Two acts of God's creation frame the books of the Bible: Genesis opens by describing how God created the heavens and the earth, and Revelation concludes by anticipating the creation of a new heaven and a new earth. While the beginning and the end undoubtedly resemble each other, an important difference exists between the first creation and the new creation. Whereas the opening chapters of Genesis focus on a garden with two human inhabitants, the concluding chapters of Revelation describe an enormous, populated city. Resplendent in glory, the new Jerusalem completes what God began when he created the earth. From beginning to end, Scripture is especially interested in constructing a holy city upon the earth, where God and humanity will reside in intimate harmony.

THE HOLY CITY PROJECT

Although it may not be immediately apparent to modern readers, Genesis begins by anticipating the formation of a city that will be inhabited by both God and people. To this end, God delegates authority to people to rule on the earth as his vice-regents, working through them to fulfill his purpose. In line with this, God commands them, "Be fruitful and increase in number; fill the earth and subdue it" (Gen 1:28). Behind these commands lies the expectation that the ever-growing human population will live in community in or around a city in which God will dwell.

Adam and Eve's disobedience in Gen 3 throws everything into chaos. By succumbing to the serpent's temptations, the human couple betrays their Creator and fails to exercise dominion over their cunning opponent. Their God-given authority to rule over the earth is usurped by the serpent, and they themselves become subject to God's enemy. Consequently God punishes them for their disobedience, stripping them of their viceroy status and expelling them from Eden.

THE GODLESS CITY OF BABEL (BABYLON)

Tasked with constructing God's holy city on the earth, rebellious humanity builds an alternative city, traditionally known as Babel (the Hebrew name for Babylon). Although the Gen 11 report of the building of Babel/Babylon is exceptionally brief, the city described there casts a long shadow over the whole Bible. Babel/Babylon is the archetypal godless city. While Adam and Eve aspired to become like God (Gen 3:5), the inhabitants of Babel/Babylon seek to establish themselves as supreme not only on earth but in heaven as well (Gen 11:4). Uniting to make a name for themselves, they attempt to build a tower that will enable them to access and control heaven. Babel/Babylon typifies two contrasting aspects of human existence: (1) the capacity to achieve great things and (2) the arrogance of those who have turned away from God.

Although God intervenes to halt the Babel/Babylon project by scattering the city's inhabitants throughout the earth, the human ambition to construct an alternative, godless city remains. Babel/Babylon typifies every social enterprise that seeks to exalt the creature over the Creator. From Genesis to Revelation, Babel/Babylon features prominently as the symbol of humanity's attempt to govern themselves without reference to and in defiance of God.

THE HOLY CITY ANTICIPATED

The short description of the building of Babel/Babylon precedes the much longer account of Abraham's life. God's promise to make Abraham's name great (Gen 12:2) echoes the aspiration of the people of Babel/Babylon (Gen 11:4). God's providing a particular land for Abraham and his descendants appears to deliberately respond to the city builders' scattering over the whole earth.

In tune with the overall movement in the book of Genesis, the author of Hebrews links the patriarchs (Abraham, Isaac, and Jacob) with God's construction of a unique city. Heb 11:10–16 commends Abraham's faith because he looked forward to "a better country — a heavenly one" (v. 16), "the city with foundations, whose architect and builder is God" (v. 10). Exhorting his readers to have a similar hope, the author of Hebrews expects that both he and his readers will join with others, including the patriarchs, in receiving what God promised (Heb 11:39–40). Describing it as "the city of the living God, the heavenly Jerusalem" (Heb 12:22), he later states, "For here we do not have an enduring city, but we are looking for the city that is to come" (Heb 13:14). The future experience of all believers involves a city.

A "city that is to come" (Heb 13:14) recalls John's vision in Rev 21–22. John sees "the Holy City, the new Jerusalem, coming down out of heaven from God, prepared as a bride beautifully dressed for her husband" (Rev 21:2). He then describes in detail the enormous size and splendor of the city; not only does it fill the entire earth, but it is constructed largely of gold. This unique city is the goal toward which everything in creation is moving; it brings to completion what God began in Gen 1.

THE HOLY CITY FORESEEN IN JERUSALEM

In light of the new Jerusalem, it is hardly surprising that the city of Jerusalem figures prominently within the OT story. From the call of Abraham to the settling of the Israelites in the land of Canaan, the narrative moves toward a momentary climax after King David captures Jerusalem, also known as Zion (2 Sam 5:6 – 10). When the ark of the covenant, the footstool of God's throne, is subsequently brought to Jerusalem, the city becomes the capital of God's kingdom on earth (2 Sam 6). Jerusalem's status as God's special city is further enhanced when Solomon builds a magnificent temple there (1 Kgs 5 – 8). As the interim holy city where God lives with his people, Jerusalem takes on a unique status. Loved by God and chosen as his place of residence, Jerusalem becomes an object of praise due to God's presence (e.g., Ps 48).

While establishing Jerusalem as a holy city marks an important step toward fulfilling God's plan for the earth, God subsequently abandons the city because its immoral inhabitants defiled it (cf. Ezek 8 – 11). This occurs some centuries after the construction of the temple by Solomon when Jerusalem is captured by the Babylonians in 586 BC following a long and horrific siege. The Babylonians sack Jerusalem, demolishing its walls and temple, before taking into captivity some of the population, including the Davidic king (2 Kgs 25).

Although establishing ancient Jerusalem as a holy city is clearly linked to God's creation plan, this was never perceived as permanently fulfilling all that God intended. It merely anticipated something greater to come. As Isaiah reveals in detail, the morally corrupt Jerusalem of OT times will in the future be replaced by a radically transformed Jerusalem, to which the nations will come in peace (e.g., Isa 2:2 – 5; 60:15 – 20; 65:17 – 25). While the hope of a new Jerusalem is prominent in Isaiah, it features also in other OT prophetic books (e.g., Ezek 20:40 – 44; Zeph 3:14 – 20; Zech 1:14 – 17).

THE CHALLENGE OF BABYLON

In the light of God's creation plan to establish his holy city on the earth, the destruction of Jerusalem by the Babylonians is highly ironic. Babylon appears to win the day, reducing to ashes Jerusalem and all that it stood for. God's plan to build his city on the earth appears to receive a major setback.

But this is not the end of the story. Looking beyond the exile, the book of Isaiah contrasts a disgraced Babylon, sitting in dust (Isa 47), with a renewed Jerusalem, shouting for joy and knowing salvation (Isa 54). In a similar vein, Daniel foresees a time when the kingdom of God will destroy the mighty kingdom of Babylon (Dan 2). The name Babylon, however, continues to symbolize humans resisting the establishment of God's holy city on the earth. In Rev 17 – 18, Babylon symbolizes God-defying human enterprise. As the Bible repeatedly highlights, humans continually resist the construction of God's holy city upon the earth. Recognizing how present-day Babylon opposes God, the book of Revelation exhorts Christians to live here and now as citizens of the future new Jerusalem.

THE NEW JERUSALEM

While we do not need to take everything in John's vision of the new Jerusalem literally, it likely anticipates the future existence of a redeemed humanity living together in harmony on a real earth. This expectation lines up with how Paul emphasizes bodily resurrection (1 Cor 15:3 – 58). There is good reason to believe that our existence in the world to come will not be entirely dissimilar to what we experience now, but without the negative impact of evil, sin, and death (Rev 21:1 – 8, 27).

Apart from the architecture's grandeur and splendor, John's vision of the city highlights other significant things. People drawn from many nations will inhabit the city and intimately experience God's presence by seeing his face (Rev 22:4). This intimacy between God and humanity is unique in the Bible. For this reason, the whole city will be a holy temple; every inhabitant will be a priest. Every citizen, without exception, will not only serve and worship God but also reign with him (Rev 22:5).

PROPHETS AND PROPHECY

Sam Storms

IN THE OLD TESTAMENT

A prophet's primary function in the OT was to serve as God's representative or ambassador by communicating God's word to his people. True prophets never spoke on their own authority or shared their personal opinions, but rather delivered the message that God himself gave them. Several texts make this explicit. God promised Moses, "Now go; I will help you speak and will teach you what to say" (Exod 4:12). God assured Moses, "I will raise up for [my people] a prophet like you ... and I will put my words in his mouth. He will tell them everything I command him" (Deut 18:18). The Lord said to Jeremiah, "I have put my words in your mouth" (Jer 1:9). God commissioned Ezekiel by saying, "You must speak my words to them" (Ezek 2:7). And many of the OT prophetic books begin with the words, "The word of the LORD that came to ..." (Hos 1:1; Joel 1:1; Mic 1:1; Zeph 1:1; cf. Jonah 1:1). Amos claimed, "This is what the LORD says" (Amos 1:3).

Prophetic ministry was not restricted to men. In the OT, Miriam, the sister of Moses, is called a "prophet" (Exod 15:20), as are Deborah (Judg 4:4) and Huldah (2 Kgs 22:14–20). We occasionally read of groups, or bands, of prophets ministering in Israel (1 Sam 10:5; 1 Kgs 18:4), referred to as "the company of the prophets" (2 Kgs 2:3,5,7; 4:38). The Bible does not explain how the word of the Lord came to a prophet, although in addition to the audible and internal voice of God there are a number of instances in which the Lord revealed his will through visions (1 Sam 3:1,15; 2 Sam 7:17; Isa 1:1; Ezek 11:24) or dreams (Num 12:6).

The divine inspiration and authority of the OT prophetic voice is nowhere more clearly affirmed than in 2 Pet 1:20–21. Peter declares that "no prophecy of Scripture came about by the prophet's own interpretation of things. For prophecy never had its origin in the human will, but prophets, though human, spoke from God as they were carried along by the Holy Spirit."

Those who claimed to speak for God were held to a strict standard of judgment. Even should an alleged prophet perform a sign or wonder or predict the future accurately, if he says, "Let us follow other gods ... and let us worship them" (Deut 13:2), he is to be rejected (Deut 13:3). Likewise, if the word he speaks "does not take place or come true, that is a message the LORD has not spoken" (Deut 18:22; see Jer 14:14; 23:21,32; 28:15; Ezek 13:6). The punishment for speaking falsely in God's name was death (Deut 18:20).

After Samuel anointed Saul and throughout the time of Israel's monarchy, prophets largely advised the king, delivering words of warning, divine guidance, and encouragement. Nathan's well-known rebuke of David for his adulterous relationship with Bathsheba and his complicity in the death of her husband is a case in point (2 Sam 12:1–14).

In the eighth century BC, the focus of the prophet's message turned more to the people at large. It would be a mistake to think of prophets in the OT as only predicting the future. Their primary role was to make known the holiness of God and the covenant obligations, to denounce injustice, idolatry, and empty ritualism, and to call God's covenant people, Israel, to repentance and faithfulness. In the period leading up to the exile and Judah's deportation to Babylon in the sixth century BC, the prophets often delivered messages denouncing rampant social injustice and the oppression of the poor. In the postexilic period, the prophets turn their attention more specifically to the promise of national renewal and the spiritual blessings that come with trusting God and obeying his will.

Being a mouthpiece for the word of the Lord was often a dangerous calling. People frequently mocked, rejected, persecuted, and even killed God's prophets (2 Chr 36:16; Jer 11:21; 18:18; 20:2,7–10). Stephen, the first martyr of the new covenant, pointedly asked, "Was there ever a prophet your ancestors did not persecute?" (Acts 7:52).

IN THE NEW TESTAMENT

Although it would go beyond the evidence to declare that all prophecy ceased in the life of Israel around 400 BC only to reappear in conjunction with the incarnation of Christ, there can be no doubt but that the voice of the Lord was rarely heard during what we call the intertestamental period. The most prominent prophetic voice in the NT, aside from Jesus himself, was John the Baptist (Matt 11:9; Luke 1:76). On the day of Pentecost, Peter declared that unlike the more limited exercise of prophecy during the time of the old covenant, God would henceforth pour out his Spirit "on all people" (Acts 2:17). Peter said the result would be a fulfillment of God words: "Your sons and daughters will prophesy, your young men will see visions, your old men will dream dreams. Even on my servants, both men and women, I will pour out my Spirit in those days, and they will prophesy" (Acts 2:17–18).

Prophetic ministry in the early church was widespread and diverse. A band of prophets traveled from Jerusalem to Antioch, and one of them, Agabus, "stood up and through the Spirit predicted that a severe famine would spread over the entire Roman world" (Acts 11:28). Prophets were active in the church at Antioch (Acts 13:1), Tyre (Acts 21:4), and Caesarea, where the four daughters of Philip prophesied (Acts 21:8–9). Prophecy, one of the gifts of the Spirit designed for edifying the body of Christ, was also utilized in the churches at Rome (Rom 12:6), Corinth (1 Cor 12:7–11; 14:1–40), Ephesus (Eph 2:20; 4:11; see Acts 19:1–7; 1 Tim 1:18), and Thessalonica (1 Thess 5:19–22).

The extent to which prophecy in the new covenant differs from its exercise under the old covenant is disputed. Many contend that prophecy under both covenants functioned in essentially the same way. Thus, the NT prophet received inspired words from God, and what he declared was equal in authority to the words, say, of Isaiah or Amos. The words of the prophets thus served to lay the foundation of the church by articulating the theological truths and ethical principles binding on the universal body of Christ (Eph 2:20). According to this view, to embrace contemporary prophecy may undermine the finality and sufficiency of Scripture; therefore, the gift of prophecy likely ceased with the death of the last apostle or on the inspiration of the last canonical book.

Others insist that whereas in the old covenant a failure to speak with complete accuracy brought the alleged "prophet" into judgment (Deut 13:2; 18:20–22), with the new covenant and the distribution of the Spirit among all God's people, certain changes came into play. Although God is the inspirational source of all prophetic revelation, its communication by individual prophets is not in all cases protected from error or human admixture. Thus, it must be judged or weighed to determine what is "good" and what is "evil" (1 Thess 5:21–22). According to this view, the gift of prophecy is still potentially available to the church until the return of Christ and is no threat to the finality of the biblical canon.

In 1 Cor 14, Paul encourages everyone to pursue the gift of prophecy (v. 1). The primary purpose of prophetic ministry is to strengthen, encourage, and comfort believers (v. 3). In other words, "the one who prophesies edifies the church" (v. 4). Prophecy may also bring conviction of sin to unbelievers who happen to be visiting the gathering of God's people, as "the secrets of their hearts are laid bare" (vv. 24–25).

Paul envisions prophetic utterances teaching others (1 Cor 14:31) and even serving as the means by which certain spiritual gifts are identified and imparted (1 Tim 4:14). Luke describes situations in which prophecy serves to provide divine direction for ministry (Acts 13:1–3) as well as to issue warnings to God's people (Acts 21:4,10–14).

In any particular church meeting, "two or three prophets should speak, and the others should weigh carefully what is said" (1 Cor 14:29). The most likely interpretation of the controversial passage concerning the silence of women in 1 Cor 14:33b–35 is that women may prophesy (see Acts 2:17–18; 21:9; 1 Cor 11:5) but may not publicly judge the prophetic words of men in the congregation. Prophets were always to be in control of their speech (1 Cor 14:32) as an expression of God's desire for peace (1 Cor 14:33). And as important as this ministry is in the body of Christ, even those claiming to be prophets must be subject to the final authority of the apostles (1 Cor 14:36–38).

Some have mistakenly equated NT prophecy with preaching, but Paul declares that all prophecy is based on a revelation (1 Cor 14:30; cf. 1 Cor 13:2). The NT's use of the noun "revelation" or the verb "to reveal" actually reflects a wide range of meaning and need not be taken as referring to the sort of authoritative revelation that would undermine the finality of the canon. Rather, the apostle likely has in view the sort of divine disclosure or unveiling in which the Spirit makes known something previously hidden (e.g., Matt 11:27; 16:17; 1 Cor 2:10; Gal 1:6; Eph 1:17; Phil 3:15). Thus, prophecy is not based on a hunch, supposition, an inference, educated guess, or even sanctified wisdom. Prophecy is the human report of a divine revelation. This is what distinguishes prophecy from teaching. Teaching is always grounded in an inspired text of Scripture. Prophecy, on the other hand, is always based on a spontaneous revelation. Thus, Paul clearly distinguishes between coming to the corporate meeting of the church with a "word of instruction" and coming with a "revelation" (1 Cor 14:26).

As helpful as prophecy is to the church, Christians are not to gullibly embrace all who claim to speak on behalf of God. Rather, the church must "test the spirits to see whether they are from God, because many false prophets have gone out into the world" (1 John 4:1). Here John is concerned with whether the "prophet" affirms the incarnation of God the Son in the person of Jesus Christ (1 John 4:2–3; 2 John 7–11). This may be, at least in part, what John has in mind when he writes that "it is the Spirit of prophecy who bears testimony to Jesus." (Rev 19:10). In other words, all true prophecy bears witness to Jesus Christ. Prophetic revelation is not only rooted in the gospel of the life, death, and resurrection of Jesus; its ultimate aim or primary focus is also to bear witness to the person of the incarnate Christ. Prophecy, therefore, is fundamentally Christ-centered.

DEATH AND RESURRECTION

Philip S. Johnston

The resurrection of Christ is central to Christian faith (1 Cor 15), part of the radical newness of the gospel. Paul writes that "our Savior, Christ Jesus ... brought life and immortality *to light* through the gospel" (2 Tim 1:10, emphasis added)—so before then the afterlife was an unknown quantity, in the shadows rather than the light. This is the key to a biblical theology of death and resurrection, affirming both the light shed by the gospel and the relative ignorance of earlier times (see Mark 9:10).

DEATH

God punished the first human sin with death. But humans were not created immortal since they had to eat from the tree of life to live forever and since the death sentence was fulfilled by their banishment from that tree (Gen 3:22–23). Sin is strongly linked to substitutionary animal death in the Levitical sacrifices but rarely to human death elsewhere in the OT (e.g., Ps 90:7–10), though the link is made extensively in the NT (e.g., Rom 5:12; 6:23; 1 Cor 15:21). Christ's resurrection potently responds to death as punishment for sin.

Hos 13:14 envisages God ransoming Israel from the power of death, which Paul sees accomplished in Christ's resurrection (1 Cor 15:55,57). God will "destroy the shroud" and "swallow up death forever" (Isa 25:7–8), and the NT cites this in relation to Christ's victory (1 Cor 15:54,57; also Rev 21:4). For the Christian, death may be the last enemy, but it is also a glorious transition.

In the OT the above themes are rare, however, and death is generally presented as the natural end of life. Sometimes death is peaceful (e.g., Abraham, Gen 25:8), sometimes abrupt (e.g., Nabal, 1 Sam 25:38), but usually it is recorded without comment (e.g., Samuel, 1 Sam 25:1). The NT echoes the theme of peaceful death in describing the believer's death as "sleep" (e.g., 1 Cor 15:51). However, the NT seldom portrays death as simply the end of life, partly because there are so few accounts of death, but mainly because of the new, distinctively Christian understanding of it.

THE DEAD

The Old Testament

Strikingly, the OT shows very little interest in the dead, and it mostly envisages one fate: the underworld. This is a realm of sleepy, shadowy existence in the depths of the earth. The most common term for the underworld is *sheol*, occurring 66 times and usually translated "realm of the dead" or "grave." Two texts briefly describe it: the mighty king of Babylon becomes as weak as those he had conquered (Isa 14:9–11), and different armies lie separately in a vast cavern (Ezek 32:17–32). These descriptions are similar to those of contemporary cultures, but the disinterest in the dead is unique to Israel. For them, the Lord was God of the living, faith was for this life, and what followed was relatively unimportant.

While the underworld is the only fate described, it is envisaged mostly for the wicked rather than the righteous, and this is explicit in Ps 49:14–15. There are only four instances of righteous people fearing the underworld; but they all suffer extreme misfortune and probably interpret their current state and future fate as divine punishment. For instance, Jacob fears descent to the grave when separated from his favorite sons (Gen 37:35; 42:38; see Job 14:13; Ps 88:3; Isa 38:10). But years later, when his family is happily reunited, his death is recorded without mentioning the underworld (repeatedly from Gen 46:30 to 50:16). Only two texts seem to indicate that everyone goes to this place, and these occur in the somber contexts of divine punishment (Ps 89:48) and human futility (Eccl 9:10). The OT writers clearly view the underworld negatively.

Alongside this general picture, there are rare glimpses of a more positive afterlife. God "took" Enoch (Gen 5:24), and Elijah ascended to heaven in a fiery chariot (2 Kgs 2:11). However, these instances are unique; godly psalmists and prophets do not generally pray for a similar fate. A few OT passages envisage some form of continued communion with God beyond death, but this is ill-defined and unlocated (Pss 16:10; 49:15; 73:24). In Acts 2, Peter quotes Ps 16, though as prophetic of Christ rather than as personal to the psalmist. Job's defiant wish in Job 19:25–27 may refer to the afterlife, but the severe textual difficulties in this passage make this uncertain.

Later Jewish Thought

Intertestamental Jewish literature displays a spectrum of views on the dead. In the Apocrypha, the traditional Ecclesiasticus (17:28–30) echoes the OT's general perspective, while the Hellenistic Wisdom of Solomon affirms that "the souls of the righteous are in the hands of God" until "the time of their visitation," i.e., resurrection (3:1–8). In the pseudepigraphal book of 1 Enoch the dead are in several separate groups in Hades awaiting judgment (ch. 22); in some texts the wicked will be punished with torment forever, as an eternal spectacle for the righteous (22:11; 27:3), and in others they will be "destroyed forever" (91:19).

The New Testament

The NT gives less attention to the presurrection state of

the dead. Jesus' story in Luke 16 reflects one strand of Jewish belief: the nameless rich man is in Hades, while Lazarus is apparently in heaven (carried to Abraham's side by angels, though still visible to the rich man).

In his early letters, Paul seems to expect the imminent return of Christ and focuses on the resurrection body (1 Cor 15; 1 Thess 4). Later he anticipates the present "earthly tent" being replaced with "our heavenly dwelling" to avoid being "naked" (2 Cor 5:1–4), i.e., in a disembodied intermediate state. Yet elsewhere Paul seems to ignore the state of believers between death and resurrection: he speaks of being immediately in Christ's presence (Phil 1:23) or being brought safely to the heavenly kingdom (2 Tim 4:18) without further detail.

There are a few references in later NT books to the ungodly dead awaiting judgment (2 Pet 3:7; Jude 6–7). After his death Christ "made proclamation to the imprisoned spirits," proclaiming their judgment (1 Pet 3:19).

RESURRECTION

The Old Testament

A few prophetic passages present resurrection as an image for national restoration after the exile (Ezek 37:11–14; Hos 6:1–2). Two texts go further and propose individual resurrection: God's people (but not the wicked) will awake (Isa 26:19), and multitudes (but not necessarily everyone) will awake to everlasting life or contempt (Dan 12:2). These texts apply the ancient belief that God *can* raise the dead (e.g., 1 Sam 2:6) to situations where he *will* do so to vindicate his people. But they are at the edge of OT theology since the rest of the OT retains the traditional view of death outlined above.

Later Jewish Thought

In the mid-second-century BC persecutions, martyrs were bolstered by a growing belief in the physical resurrection with restored and rejuvenated bodies, though for their tormentor Antiochus "there will be no resurrection to life" (2 Maccabees 7:14, in the Apocrypha). A little later another text affirms a total resurrection: after the patriarchs, "all men will rise, some to glory and some to disgrace" (see the pseudepigraphal Testament of Benjamin 10:8).

By NT times, belief in resurrection was common among many Jews, including Pharisees (Acts 23:8). This resurrection was envisaged as God's restoration of Israel in a transformed physical world, not an ethereal heavenly realm. However, some Jewish groups, like the Qumran community, were less sure (there is only one fleeting reference, in 4Q521.ii.12). The Sadducees denied resurrection altogether (Acts 23:8), ostensibly because it is not mentioned in the Torah, but also because such belief encouraged insurrection and martyrdom, which in turn threatened their establishment position.

Gospels and Acts

In Luke 20:27–38 and its parallels, Jesus categorically opposes the Sadducees' trick question regarding multiple marriages and describes a resurrection state in which marriage is superfluous and death unknown. He then freshly interprets Exod 3:6: Israel's God is the God of the living, so his relationship with the patriarchs is not broken by death and the dead must therefore rise. Elsewhere Jesus could speak of "the resurrection of the righteous" (Luke 14:14), but his teaching on final judgment clearly implies universal resurrection (Matt 25:31–46).

Jesus repeatedly tells his disciples of his forthcoming death and resurrection (e.g., Mark 8:31). John typically focuses on the implication of these events: Jesus himself is the resurrection and life, which implies resurrection and eternal life for all believers (John 11:25–26). From Pentecost onward, the center of apostolic preaching is Jesus' resurrection, vindicating him as Messiah and necessitating repentance and faith (e.g., Acts 2:24–36).

The Letters and Revelation

For Paul, Christ's resurrection is the foundation of Christian life and hope, as carefully explained in 1 Cor 15: Jesus' resurrection happened; Christians universally believe it; death came through Adam and resurrection through Christ; this profoundly affects our lifestyle; the perishable "soul-animated" (*psychikon*) body will be raised an imperishable "spirit-animated" (*pneumatikon*) one; and so death itself is "swallowed up in victory" (1 Cor 15:54). Christ's resurrection is thus the prototype of Christian experience.

1 Peter echoes Pauline themes in grounding its opening doxology on Christ's resurrection (1 Pet 1:3) and in contrasting the perishable and the imperishable (1 Pet 1:23). Hebrews similarly lists resurrection as a basic tenet of faith (Heb 6:1–2). Revelation, for all its apocalyptic imagery and eschatological focus, speaks only cryptically of a "first resurrection" of martyrs to a millennial reign with Christ (Rev 20:5–6). Different terminology is used for the final judgment: the sea, death, and Hades "give up" their dead to stand before God's throne (Rev 20:12–13). Here death and the realm of the dead are not just defeated but are forced to surrender all their captives and are finally destroyed. The God of life ultimately triumphs.

PEOPLE OF GOD

Moisés Silva

Among significant theological concepts, few are as fundamental and comprehensive in scope as the biblical teaching on the people of God. With its roots reaching back to the creation narrative, this doctrine takes form in the calling of Abraham and becomes the central focus of OT history. That calling of Abraham included the promise of blessing for all nations (Gen 12:3). But the nation of Israel, as God's people, suffered judgment. Christ came to fulfill God's promises to Abraham and thus reconstitute God's people from all the nations of the earth.

OVERTURE

The first 11 chapters of Genesis provide the theological underpinnings for our understanding of redemptive history, that is, the working out of God's plan of salvation. The Bible simply states as undeniable truth without argumentation that God is the all-powerful Creator of the heavens and the earth (Gen 1:1; cf. Ps 14:1). It repeatedly emphasizes the *goodness* of God's creation (Gen 1:4,10,12,18,21,25); *all* that God had made was "very good" (Gen 1:31).

The highlight of God's good creation occurs when God makes human beings in his image so that they, as his people, might rule the rest of the created order under his authority (Gen 1:26 – 28). Intrinsic to that assignment is the mandate to populate the earth (Gen 1:28 – 30). The entrance of sin into the world (Gen 3) means that both God's people and the created order more generally are placed under a curse, and Gen 4 – 11 describes the progress of sin as an almost unstoppable force. Although it may appear that God's purposes have been thwarted, God immediately begins the process of reconstituting his people, partly through merciful judgments that prevent ultimate condemnation (the expulsion from Eden, Gen 3:22 – 24; the flood, Gen 6 – 8; the destruction of Babel, Gen 11:1 – 9) and partly through preserving a faithful line (Seth, Enosh, and those who called on the name of the Lord, Gen 4:25 – 26; Noah, Gen 5:28 – 29).

PROMISE

Once Noah's descendants scatter "over the face of the whole earth" (Gen 11:9), God realizes his purposes by focusing on one individual. The call of Abram (Abraham) takes a form that is remarkably specific in character and astonishingly universal in scope: Abram must leave his family and travel to a foreign land, where God will make him into a great nation; and through this process *all* other human groups will be blessed (Gen 12:1 – 3). Genesis describes God's special relationship with Abraham and his descendants in terms that echo through the centuries: "I will establish my covenant as an everlasting covenant between me and you and your descendants after you for the generations to come, to be your God and the God of your descendants after you" (Gen 17:7). This promise is tied to the land of Canaan (which God covenants to secure for his people, Gen 17:8), and it comes with the obligation that Abraham and his descendants remain faithful to the covenant (Gen 17:1,9).

NATION

It takes four long centuries (cf. Gen 15:13), but after many twists and turns, God redeems Abraham's descendants from Egyptian slavery, brings them to Mount Sinai, and tells them, "Now if you obey me fully and keep my covenant, then out of all nations you will be my treasured possession. Although the whole earth is mine, you will be for me a kingdom of priests and a holy nation" (Exod 19:5 – 6). Integral to this event are the giving of the law (the covenant obligations, Exod 20 – 24) and the construction of a tent (the tabernacle) for God to dwell among his people (Exod 25 – 40).

Because the people do not trust God (Num 13 – 14), they do not possess the land of Canaan for a whole generation, but eventually God plants them there as a vine: "You cleared the ground for it, and it took root and filled the land. The mountains were covered with its shade, the mighty cedars with its branches" (Ps 80:9 – 10).

During the chaotic period of the judges, however, the Israelites fall into a cycle of sin, punishment, repentance, deliverance, and once again sin (Judg 2:10 – 19). Because there is no king, people act without restraint (Judg 17:6; 21:25).

Because the people desire political stability and international recognition, they ask for a monarchy in Israel, and God grants the request (1 Sam 8). Although their first king, Saul, proves unfaithful (1 Sam 15), the monarchy crystallizes the relationship between God and Israel as similar to that between a king and his people (cf. Pss 10:16; 24:7 – 10; 84:3; 89:18; 95:3; Isa 6:5; 43:15; Jer 46:18; Zech 14:16 – 17). David and Solomon, moreover, prefigure a King to come who would "endure as long as the sun, as long as the moon, through all generations," one through whom all nations would be blessed (Ps 72:5,17).

At David's initiative but during Solomon's reign, Israel builds a magnificent temple in Jerusalem. As had been the case with the wilderness tent (the tabernacle), God fills the temple with the glory of his presence, signifying that he chooses to dwell there in the midst of his people (1 Kgs 8:10 – 12). Sadly, the subsequent centuries see a precipitous decline in the spiritual condition of the Israelites, to such an extent that God judges them by destroying Jerusalem and its temple and exiling them from the very land that he had promised to them as his people. "Your vine is cut down, it is burned with fire; at your rebuke your people perish" (Ps 80:16).

Eventually, groups of Jewish exiles return to the land, but they have no king and are subject to foreign domination. And although they rebuild the temple, the Bible does not say that God filled it with the glory of his presence. It is as though the Lord no longer dwells with his people. "Will you be angry with us forever?… Will you not revive us again, that your people may rejoice in you?" (Ps 85:5–6).

FULFILLMENT

In spite of all the blessings and successes that God's people of faith enjoyed in OT times (Heb 11:1–38), "none of them received what had been promised" (Heb 11:39). That waits until the King, David's son, makes his appearance (Matt 1:1; 21:9). Through him and his works the kingdom of God breaks through (Matt 12:28). He is the one who "will save his people from their sins" (Matt 1:21). He is the Son of God, who "made his dwelling" (or "pitched his tent") among his people and manifested the divine glory (John 1:14).

By choosing 12 apostles (Luke 6:13), Jesus reconstitutes the people of God. But this newly formed nation is no longer identified with a political entity or an ethnic group. After all, his own do not welcome him (John 1:11), so the kingdom of God is taken away from them "and given to a people who will produce its fruit" (Matt 21:43; cf. Acts 15:14).

It now becomes clearer than ever that the true Jew is not the one who is a Jew "only outwardly" with "physical" marks; a true Jew is the one who is a Jew "inwardly … of the heart," through the operation of the Holy Spirit (Rom 2:28–29). And Abraham's true descendants, to whom God made the promise, consist of those who follow in the footsteps of Abraham's faith; indeed, Abraham is "the father of all who believe" (Rom 4:11), whether Jews or Gentiles (Rom 4:9–17). Therefore, even though the nation of Israel as a whole does not receive the King, God's word of promise to his people has not failed. "For not all who are descended from Israel are Israel. Nor because they are his descendants are they all Abraham's children … In other words, it is not the children by physical descent who are God's children, but it is the children of the promise who are regarded as Abraham's offspring" (Rom 9:6–8).

Thus, Peter can apply to believing Gentiles the words that had described the nation of Israel at Sinai: "You are a chosen people, a royal priesthood, a holy nation, God's special possession, that you may declare the praises of him who called you out of darkness into his wonderful light" (1 Pet 2:9; cf. Exod 19:5–6; Titus 2:14; Rev 5:9–10). And Peter further says, "Once you were not a people, but now you are the people of God; once you had not received mercy, but now you have received mercy" (1 Pet 2:10, alluding to Hos 1:8–10; 2:23).

God's people are the "elect" or "chosen ones" (Matt 24:22; Luke 18:7; Rom 8:33; Col 3:12; Titus 1:1; 1 Pet 1:1), the ones God has "called" (Rom 1:6; 8:28–30; 1 Cor 1:24; Jude 1), the "holy ones" (Greek *hagioi* occurs numerous times and is usually translated by the NIV as "holy people," "God's people," and the like; e.g., Acts 9:13; 26:10; Rom 1:7; 8:27; 1 Cor 6:1–2; 2 Cor 8:4; Eph 1:15; Heb 6:10; Rev 5:8). They themselves are now God's temple, and thus the Lord makes his dwelling in them — in Christians individually (1 Cor 6:19) and in believers collectively as God's temple (1 Cor 3:16–17; 2 Cor 6:16; cf. John 14:23; Rom 8:9–11). Thus, the promise is truly fulfilled: "I will live with them and walk among them, and I will be their God, and they will be my people" (2 Cor 6:16b, citing Lev 26:12; cf. Jer 31:33; 32:38; Ezek 37:27; Zech 8:8; Heb 8:10).

DENOUEMENT

Those who have placed their trust in David's royal son receive the promised Spirit, who marks them with a seal, indicating that they belong to God (Gal 3:14; Eph 1:13). Yet this gift is but "a deposit guaranteeing our inheritance until the redemption of those who are God's possession — to the praise of his glory" (Eph 1:14). Though already seated in the heavenly realms in Christ Jesus (Eph 2:6) and enjoying "the firstfruits of the Spirit" (Rom 8:23a), God's people still live in the present evil age (e.g., Rom 12:2; 1 Cor 1:20; Gal 1:4); thus we "groan inwardly as we wait eagerly for our adoption to sonship, the redemption of our bodies" (Rom 8:23b).

The day is coming, however, when "the Lamb will triumph over [his enemies] because he is Lord of lords and King of kings — and with him will be his called, chosen and faithful followers" (Rev 17:14). Then "the old order of things" will pass away (Rev 21:4). We will see "a new heaven and a new earth" as well as "the Holy City, the new Jerusalem, coming down out of heaven from God" (Rev 21:1–2), but there will not be "a temple in the city, because the Lord God Almighty and the Lamb are its temple" (Rev 21:22). Instead, we will hear "a loud voice from the throne saying, 'Look! God's dwelling place is now among the people, and he will dwell with them. They will be his people, and God himself will be with them and be their God'" (Rev 21:3).

WISDOM

Daniel J. Estes

Wisdom in the Bible may begin with a combination of God-given skills and moral faithfulness, but it ends in Jesus Christ.

CONCEPT OF WISDOM

The Hebrew term used for wisdom refers to skill in a variety of endeavors, including crafts such as tailoring (Exod 28:3), trading (Ezek 28:4), navigation (Ps 107:23–30), and divine enabling for constructing the tabernacle (Exod 31:1–11) and temple (1 Kgs 7:13–14). In the moral sense, wisdom is skill in living according to God's way (Prov 2:6). More broadly, wisdom is a way of viewing the world that begins with Yahweh as the creator of the entire universe who ordered it by his purpose (Prov 3:19–20; 8:22–31). Because Yahweh is omniscient, there is recognizable design in his world, and because he is righteous, there is a moral order that structures his world. Wisdom scrutinizes life, observing patterns and from them deriving lessons for life in Yahweh's world (Prov 6:6–11; 24:30–34). These lessons were passed on as tradition to the next generation (Prov 4:1–9). Wisdom teachers crafted their lessons into artful and memorable language (Eccl 12:9–11).

The wisdom teacher describes two antithetical ways: the way of wisdom and the way of folly (Ps 1; Prov 9). Jesus echoes these terms as he contrasts the narrow way leading to life with the broad way leading to destruction (Matt 7:13–14). Those who choose the path of wisdom follow the moral order that Yahweh has prescribed, but those who choose the path of folly are unable or unwilling to follow his way. Wisdom is expressed in righteous actions, attitudes, and values that please Yahweh. Folly is expressed by wicked behavior that deviates from Yahweh's will (Prov 4:18–19). Wisdom leads to a life of blessing, but folly results in death (Prov 8:35–36).

At the heart of wisdom is character formation, because the purpose of wisdom is to guide humans into life that is truly good as Yahweh evaluates it. This life is marked by wise choices (Prov 9:6) and commitments (Prov 4:7) because wisdom insists on radically reorienting life so that pursuing wisdom becomes the primary value (Prov 3:13–15).

CORE OF WISDOM

Central to the concept of wisdom in the Bible is the fear of Yahweh, which is the beginning of wisdom (Prov 9:10). Proverbs cites this expression 18 times, and the prominent occurrences frame the book (Prov 1:7; 31:30). Similar language occurs in Job 28:28 and Eccl 12:13 as well as in two of the wisdom psalms (Pss 34:11; 111:10).

OT wisdom literature emphasizes the fear of Yahweh. This corresponds closely to the law, which exhorts the people of Israel to fear Yahweh (Deut 10:12). It also occurs in the historical literature (Josh 24:14), and the prophets frequently reaffirm it as they call the nation back to faithfully submit to Yahweh their God (Isa 11:2–3; Mal 3:5).

The fear of Yahweh is both the starting point for wisdom (Prov 9:10) and its final goal (Prov 2:5). Wisdom, then, is the ethical principle that guides humans along their entire path toward genuine life. The Hebrew term for "fear" has a range of meaning that includes both (1) overwhelming awe that prompts humans to tremble before God in dread and (2) reverence that turns them toward God in joyful obedience. Fear is the appropriate humble and dependent stance for humans before Yahweh, the creator and sovereign of the universe.

When humans fear the Lord, they embrace what he desires and avoid what he disapproves because they reverence who he is. Because Yahweh is holy, those who fear the Lord hate evil (Prov 8:13). Wisdom, then, does not just provide secular, pragmatic advice about how to become successful in life; it presents the wise life as grounded ultimately in one's relationship with Yahweh.

Just as Yahweh's order permeates the creation, so his moral character is the paradigm for ethics in his universe. Wise living assimilates the values embodied in Yahweh himself, for his character is the ultimate moral standard by which all behavior must be measured, as both the OT (Lev 19:2) and NT (Matt 5:48) affirm. By contrast, sin entered into human experience when Adam and Eve disobeyed the command of Yahweh and chose to act autonomously, wrongly supposing that eating from the tree of the knowledge of good and evil would make them wise (Gen 3:6).

COMPLEXITY OF WISDOM

The wisdom sayings featured most prominently in Prov 10–31 are often called "practical wisdom." By observing common patterns in life that Yahweh embedded in the world, practical wisdom teaches how life typically works by synthesizing from experience general principles for living. By this means, practical wisdom demonstrates how wisdom leads to life, while folly leads to death (Prov 26:27; 28:10; Ps 7:14–16) — an approach to wisdom commonly called "retribution theology." The book of Proverbs for the most part demonstrates a strong correlation between one's acts and the consequences one receives (cf. Deut 30:15–20), but it also hints that the principle of retribution should not be pressed into a rigid, mechanical formula because sometimes the righteous are poor and the wicked are wealthy (Prov 15:16; 16:8,19; 28:6). Wisdom teaches that as a rule the righteous path leads to life, but it also recognizes that Yahweh may overrule the best human plans (Prov 20:24).

The practical wisdom that predominates in Proverbs is complemented by the books of Job and Ecclesiastes, often called "speculative wisdom." Speculative wisdom focuses on those situations in which the general pattern of retribution does not explain some aspects of life as people actually experience it. Two of the wisdom psalms ask why good things happen to bad people, in apparent dissonance with the retribution principle (Pss 49; 73).

The book of Job asks why adversity afflicts an exemplary person whom Yahweh himself describes as "blameless and upright" (Job 1:8; 2:3) and why the wicked often prosper (Job 21). Job and his friends all begin by assuming the validity of the retribution principle. Only when Yahweh speaks at the end of the book does it become evident that his rule cannot be reduced into the tidy formula of rigid retribution theology (Job 38–41). Yahweh's ways are higher than human ways, and his thoughts transcend human thoughts (Job 42:1–6; cf. Isa 55:8–9), so his purpose eludes human comprehension. Yahweh's wisdom includes aspects that remain mysterious to the finite human mind, so the wise person trusts Yahweh, even without understanding how he governs his world. Despite their most diligent efforts, humans cannot find ultimate wisdom (Job 28:1–14) because only God knows the way to it (Job 28:23–28).

CULMINATION OF WISDOM

Proverbs, Job, and Ecclesiastes are so dominated by wisdom themes that they are customarily called "wisdom literature." However, from this epicenter wisdom features reverberate throughout the entire Bible.

In the Pentateuch, Joseph (Gen 41:39) and Moses (Exod 7:10–12), with their wisdom from Yahweh, surpass the sages of Egypt. Moses equates keeping Yahweh's commandments with Israel's wisdom in the sight of the nations (Deut 4:5–6), a juxtaposition of divine instruction and wisdom that the similarities between Deut 6:4–9 and Prov 3:1–12 imply and that Eccl 12:13 explicitly states: "Fear God and keep his commandments, for this is the whole duty of all mankind."

The historical books feature wise women (2 Sam 14:1–20; 20:14–22) and describe Solomon as the paragon of wisdom (1 Kgs 3:9–14). Daniel excels among the wise men of Babylon (Dan 1–6) but unswervingly retains his commitment to Yahweh's law despite intense pressure to compromise. The prophets Jeremiah and Habakkuk echo Job in their anguished complaints about the ascendancy of evil in the world Yahweh governs.

Wisdom also occurs extensively in the psalms. Pss 1, 34, 37, 111, and 119 reflect the emphases of practical wisdom, and Pss 39, 49, 73, and 127 echo the themes of speculative wisdom.

The language of wisdom that permeates the OT continues into the NT, where it finds its incarnation and fulfillment in Christ. The letter of James echoes Proverbs, as James directs those who lack wisdom to ask God, who gives it generously to those who ask in faith (Jas 1:5–8). James also differentiates genuine wisdom that comes from God from deficient earthly "wisdom" (Jas 3:13–18). Throughout his brief letter, James contrasts righteous, wise behaviors with those that are wicked and foolish.

The Gospels repeatedly present Jesus as a wise teacher. Using wisdom sayings, riddles, and parables (Matt 13:10–13), Jesus astounds the people with his teaching (Mark 1:22). He surpasses the wisdom of Solomon (Matt 12:42).

In his letters, Paul explains in theological terms that God's wisdom is ultimately incarnated in Christ. He is the wisdom of God (1 Cor 1:24,30) and the goal of creation and history (Eph 1:10). As the embodiment of divine wisdom, Christ stands over against the folly of human speculations that diverge from him (Col 2:1–8).

HOLINESS

Andrew David Naselli

Holiness is woven through the Bible's storyline. The holy God created holy people who became unholy. He later selected Israel as his holy people, but they repeatedly failed to be holy. Jesus, who embodies holiness, made his people holy, so Christians are holy and must strive to live in a holy manner, however imperfectly, until God consummates his plan to make his people holy.

HOLINESS PERSONIFIED: GOD

Many people equate holiness with taboos. The Bible equates it fundamentally with God.

What Is Holiness?

"Holiness" is commonly defined as being separate or set apart. God is holy in that he is set apart from everything that is not God, and God's people must be holy by being set apart from sin. So holiness, according to this definition, is separateness that entails moral purity. But that does not sufficiently describe the essence of holiness or distinguish different senses in which people and things can be holy. There is a sense in which only God is holy and another sense in which others can be holy.

God Is Holy

In its most focused usage, "holy" is an adjective uniquely associated with God. "Holy, holy, holy is the Lord Almighty" (Isa 6:3; cf. Rev 4:8). Surely this loses something if rendered "Separate, separate, separate" or "Moral, moral, moral." Saying "God is holy" is like saying "God is uniquely God" or "God alone is God": the word "holy" in such a context becomes almost an adjective for God. That God swears by his holiness (Ps 89:35; Amos 4:2) is equivalent to saying that he swears "by himself" (Amos 6:8). God is supremely and exclusively God. He has no rivals. As uniquely excellent, he is his own category: "There is no one holy like the Lord; there is no one besides you" (1 Sam 2:2; cf. Exod 15:11; Ps 77:13; Isa 40:25). The Bible calls God "the Holy One" over 50 times and calls the Spirit of God "the Holy Spirit" over 90 times.

People and Objects Are Holy in Relation to God

God alone is innately holy (Rev 15:4). His name is holy (Isa 57:15). Yet the use of the word "holy" stretches out in widening circles to apply to people and things. If human beings or things are holy, they are holy only derivatively — not because they are divine or moral but because God restricts them for his special use. In a broad sense, everything belongs to God, but in a more narrow sense, some things and people belong exclusively to God in a special way. For example, heaven — God's dwelling place — is holy (Deut 26:15), and God refers to angels as his "holy ones" (Ps 89:5 – 7) and "the holy angels" (Mark 8:38).

HOLINESS LOST: HUMANS

Adam and Eve were the crown of God's good creation, and they walked with God in the sanctuary of Eden. But the sinless couple sinned and lost their holiness, so God expelled them from his presence (Gen 1 – 3; Eccl 7:29). (See "Creation," p. 2642, and "Sin," p. 2644.) The story of the Bible is, from one perspective, about how God is working to restore to an even greater degree the holiness that our first parents forfeited.

HOLINESS ESTABLISHED AND PRACTICED: ISRAEL

God later selected Israel to become his holy people as he dwelt among them. The OT calls God "the Holy One of Israel" over 30 times.

Israel Was Holy

Following the exodus of God's people from Egypt, Israel became a holy nation because God was uniquely present with them. Israel was God's special people: "You are a people holy to the Lord your God. The Lord your God has chosen you out of all the peoples on the face of the earth to be his people, his treasured possession" (Deut 7:6; cf. Exod 19:4 – 6; Deut 14:2).

In the OT, holiness is usually associated with God's special presence in theophanies (see note on Deut 4:24) or at Israel's tabernacle and temple. God's holiness radiated outward from the Most Holy Place, making everything associated with it holy: the building and courtyard (Lev 16:15 – 16; Ps 79:1); the furniture and utensils (Exod 30:26 – 29; Num 4:14 – 15); the priests and their clothing (Exod 29:21; Lev 21:6 – 8); the sacrifices, offerings, and tithed crops (Lev 27:30; Num 18:17); and the oil, incense, and censers (Exod 30:25,34 – 37; Num 16:37). (See "Priest," p. 2654, and "Sacrifice," p. 2656.)

Israel Was Responsible to Be Holy

God commanded Israel, "You are to be my holy people" (Exod 22:31). "Be holy, because I am holy" (Lev 11:44 – 45; cf. Lev 19:2; 20:7; 21:8). "You are to be holy to me because I, the Lord, am holy, and I have set you apart from the nations to be my own" (Lev 20:26).

Israel was responsible to regard God as holy (Isa 8:13) by obeying his commands regarding rituals and morality (Num 15:40; Deut 28:9; cf. Num 20:12). They were to keep God's Sabbaths holy (Exod 20:8–11), and the priests were to "distinguish between the holy and the common, between the unclean and the clean" (Lev 10:10). Uncleanness, which is linked to imperfection and death, is the opposite of holiness, which is linked to wholeness and life. God's instructions about cleanness and uncleanness covered all spheres of life, including diet, purification after childbirth, skin diseases, infections, and bodily discharges, and they reminded the people of their holy calling (Lev 11–15).

But because Israel continually profaned their holy God, who judges unholy people (2 Kgs 17:7–23; 2 Chr 36:15–16), God graciously met the need of sinful humans with a holy Savior.

HOLINESS EMBODIED AND ACCOMPLISHED: JESUS

Jesus Is Holy

"Who can stand in the presence of the LORD, this holy God?" (1 Sam 6:20). Only one can stand on his own merits: Jesus. He is "holy and true" (Rev 3:7; 6:10). Jesus is the one whom "the Father set apart as his very own" (John 10:36). The angel Gabriel announced to Mary, "The holy one to be born will be called the Son of God" (Luke 1:35). An unclean demon recognized Jesus as "the Holy One of God" (Luke 4:34). Jesus made unclean people clean by touching them, and he never became unclean because he is inherently holy. Peter called Jesus "the Holy One of God" (John 6:69), "the Holy and Righteous One" (Acts 3:14), and God's "holy servant" (Acts 4:27,30).

Jesus Makes People Holy

Jesus is both the Holy One and "the one who makes people holy" (Heb 2:11). He is "our righteousness, holiness and redemption" (1 Cor 1:30). His perfect life and sacrificial death satisfied God's holy wrath against sinners: "We have been made holy through the sacrifice of the body of Jesus Christ once for all" (Heb 10:10). "Jesus also suffered outside the city gate to make the people holy through his own blood" (Heb 13:12).

To serve in God's presence, OT priests were made holy by a consecration ritual involving atonement, purification, and eating a special meal. These same elements also underlie the Passover ritual, by which God consecrated Israel as a holy nation. This pattern continues in the NT: Jesus brings about a new exodus that consecrates believers as holy. God is uniquely present with the church, composed of both Jewish and Gentile Christians, because it is "a holy temple in the Lord" (Eph 2:21; cf. 1 Cor 3:17). God has chosen Christians to be "a holy priesthood"; they are "a chosen people, a royal priesthood, a holy nation, God's special possession" (1 Pet 2:5,9). (See "Exile and Exodus," p. 2659, and "Temple," p. 2652.)

HOLINESS APPLIED AND PRACTICED: CHRISTIANS

Many theologians sharply distinguish justification from sanctification. ("Sanctify" means to make holy.) Justification is the instantaneous, completed act in which God declares a believing sinner to be righteous, and sanctification is the progressive, incomplete, lifelong maturing process in which a Christian is gradually made more holy. Those are valid and important systematic categories, but the latter category can confuse people because the NT letters present three tenses of sanctification: past, present, and future. A Christian can say, "I am sanctified. I am being sanctified. And I will be sanctified."

- Past. Definitive or positional sanctification occurs when God sets people apart for himself at the moment they become Christians.
- Present. Progressive sanctification is what many Christians today refer to as sanctification (see above).
- Future. Ultimate sanctification corresponds to glorification. This happens when God sets his people apart from sin's presence and possibility.

Christians Are Holy

When the Bible refers to Christians as "holy" or "sanctified," it usually refers, not to progressive sanctification, but to definitive or positional sanctification (e.g., Rom 1:7; Eph 1:1; 5:3; Col 1:2,12; 3:12; 2 Thess 1:10; Heb 2:11; Jude 3; Rev 13:7). In this sense, every Christian is a saint; every Christian is holy; every Christian is sanctified. For example, Paul addresses the church at Corinth as "those sanctified in Christ Jesus and called to be his holy people" (1 Cor 1:2; cf. 1 Cor 6:11). They were already "sanctified" even though they were failing to be holy in several areas.

Christians Are Responsible to Be Holy

God commands Christians, "Just as he who called you is holy, so be holy in all you do; for it is written: 'Be holy, because I am holy'" (1 Pet 1:15–16, quoting Lev 11:44–45). Christians must worship God by offering their "bodies as a living sacrifice, holy and pleasing to God" (Rom 12:1). Since Christians belong exclusively to God, they must reflect God's moral character with "holy and godly lives" (2 Pet 3:11; cf. Rom 6:19,22; 2 Cor 7:1). "It is God's will that you should be sanctified: that you should avoid sexual immorality; that each of you should learn to control your own body in a way that is holy and honorable ... For God did not call us to be impure, but to live a holy life" (1 Thess 4:3–4,7). "Make every effort to live in peace with everyone and to be holy; without holiness no one will see the Lord" (Heb 12:14).

HOLINESS CONSUMMATED: GLORY

Paul prayed, "May he strengthen your hearts so that you will be blameless and holy in the presence of our God and Father when our Lord Jesus comes with all his holy ones" (1 Thess 3:13; cf. 1 Thess 5:23). A day is coming when Christians will fully become what they already are positionally. The OT anticipates the time when all of God's people "will be called the Holy People, the Redeemed of the LORD" (Isa 62:12). Before God created the world, he chose his people in Christ "to be holy and blameless in his sight" (Eph 1:4; cf. Eph 5:27). With pure hearts God's people will "worship the LORD in the splendor of his holiness" (1 Chr 16:29; Pss 29:2; 96:9) like never before, joining the heavenly hosts who "never stop saying: 'Holy, holy, holy is the Lord God Almighty,' who was, and is, and is to come" (Rev 4:8). (See "Worship," p. 2689, and "The Consummation," p. 2695.)

JUSTICE

Brian S. Rosner

The theme of justice in the Bible reveals God's loving and upright character, our own failure to act justly, the means by which we can be justified, and the need for God's people to love justice.

In the OT the terms for judge, justice, and (civil) laws all derive from the same root. Thus, justice is closely related to and administered as an ideal legal standard. Yet the concept of justice in the Bible covers more than punishing wrongdoing. It includes treating all people not only with fairness but also with protection and care. God calls all people to seek justice for those most vulnerable to suffering injustice. The Bible regularly pairs justice with acting righteously and behaving with mercy, love, kindness, and compassion. For example, "*Administer true justice*; show mercy and compassion to one another. Do not oppress the widow or the fatherless, the foreigner or the poor" (Zech 7:9 – 10, emphasis added).

THE GOD OF JUSTICE

Justice is rooted in God's character and creation. "He is the Rock, his works are perfect, and all his ways are just. A faithful God who does no wrong, upright and just is he" (Deut 32:4). "The LORD is righteous, he loves justice" (Ps 11:7). "The Maker of heaven and earth ... upholds the cause of the oppressed and ... loves the righteous" (Ps 146:6 – 8). God's character includes a zeal for justice that leads him to love tenderly those who are socially powerless (Ps 10:14 – 18). "The LORD Almighty will be exalted by his justice" (Isa 5:16).

JUSTICE AND GOD'S PEOPLE

The nation of Israel must keep God's "righteous decrees and laws" (Deut 4:8) so that all the nations of the world will look enviously at the justice and right ordering of their society and be attracted to God's wisdom (Deut 4:6 – 8). In particular, as God's representatives, judges must acquit the innocent, condemn the guilty, and expose false accusations and bribery (2 Chr 19:5 – 7). They are not to distort justice by favoring either the poor or the rich (Exod 23:3; Lev 19:15). God also charges kings to act justly and instructs them to look after the weak and defenseless. The psalmist prays, "Endow the king with your justice, O God ... May he judge your people in righteousness, your afflicted ones with justice" (Ps 72:1 – 2).

Throughout the OT, God's people must "learn to do right [and] seek justice" (Isa 1:17). When Job confronts his accusers, he insists, "I put on righteousness as my clothing; justice was my robe and my turban. I was eyes to the blind and feet to the lame. I was a father to the needy; I took up the case of the stranger" (Job 29:14 – 16). Similarly, the prophets rail against injustice and insist that the right worship of God cannot exist without loving justice. Amos threatens judgment on "those who oppress the innocent and take bribes and deprive the poor of justice in the courts" (Amos 5:12). "What does the LORD require of you? To act justly and to love mercy and to walk humbly with your God" (Mic 6:8).

Jesus' teaching and ministry continues to underscore the central place of justice. Mary prophesies that Jesus will fill the poor but send the rich away empty (Luke 1:53). When John the Baptist's disciples ask Jesus if he is the Messiah, he points as evidence to his care for the downtrodden, including the blind, lame, deaf, those with leprosy, and the poor (Matt 11:4 – 5). Echoing the OT prophets, Jesus accused the Pharisees of concentrating on religious observance while neglecting "justice and the love of God" (Luke 11:42). For Jesus, a lack of concern for the poor is not a minor oversight but reveals that a person is at odds with God. In the parable of the sheep and the goats, the true sheep of Jesus are those who have a heart for the hungry, the stranger, the poor, the sick, and the imprisoned (Matt 25:35 – 36).

The letter of James confronts injustice, especially exploitation of the poor. James challenges those who have been justified to make justice a mark of their lives. It also recommends waiting patiently for the Judge to bring justice and reverse fortunes: "Be patient, then, brothers and sisters, until the Lord's coming ... The Judge is standing at the door!" (Jas 5:7,9). Bringing these two threads together, the letter directs the new community of faith to allow the hoped-for justice of the kingdom of God to permeate their lives in the present by caring for those in need (Jas 1:27; 2:14 – 26).

Amos calls believers to "let justice roll on like a river, righteousness like a never-failing stream!" (Amos 5:24).

JUSTICE AND GOD'S GOODNESS

The theme of justice raises two formidable problems. The first is the need to defend God's justice and goodness in the light of injustice. How can a just God tolerate evil? The Bible addresses this concern in several places, most pointedly in Habakkuk and Job.

Habakkuk complains to God that his people are ignoring his demand for justice, and he wonders why God allows the unjust to continue in their wickedness: "Why do you make me look at injustice? Why do you tolerate wrongdoing? Destruction and violence are before me; there is strife, and conflict abounds. Therefore the law is paralyzed, and justice never prevails" (Hab 1:3 – 4). Habakkuk asks how God's justice can reconcile with his experience of the world. God's answer is that he has appointed "the Babylonians, that ruthless and impetuous people" (Hab 1:6), to punish his rebellious children by taking them into exile.

Not surprisingly, this raises another moral dilemma for the prophet: Babylon is even more wicked than Judah (Hab 1:13)! How could God use such a vile tool, those who are "a law to themselves" (Hab 1:7)? God assures Habakkuk that he will eventually judge the Babylonians. In the meantime, the just must wait patiently, remain loyal to God, and trust God to show himself as just. In the words of Hab 2:4, a verse the NT quotes three times (Rom 1:17; Gal 3:11; Heb 10:38), "the righteous person will live by his faithfulness."

While Habakkuk asks why the unjust seem to go unpunished, Job asks why a righteous person should suffer. Job is a just and honorable man, but Satan, the accuser, wagers with God that Job's faith is motivated by self-interest. To prove that Job is trustworthy, God allows Satan to take away all of Job's possessions and children and strike him with a severe disease. Job's so-called friends assume that God punishes only the wicked, and they counsel Job to repent: "Who, being innocent, has ever perished?... Those who plow evil and those who sow trouble reap it" (Job 4:7–8).

The book of Job does not address all unjust suffering. Ultimately, Job receives an answer that reduces him to silence. God assures him that there is an order to the world, even if it is at times imperceptible. God's sovereignty and mercy are impressed on him, and Job perseveres in faith. With Job's restoration in mind, Jas 5:11 cites him as a model of endurance: "You have heard of Job's perseverance and have seen what the Lord finally brought about. The Lord is full of compassion and mercy." In one sense the experience of Job points to another righteous sufferer, the suffering servant of Isaiah (Isa 42:1–9; 49:1–7; 50:4–9; 53:1–12), a figure the NT identifies as Jesus.

JUSTICE AND THE DAY OF JUDGMENT

Habakkuk and Job voice the Bible's concern to defend God's justice and goodness, but a second problem is more personal: if God is just, how can you and I stand before him on the day of judgment? Both the OT and NT agree: "no one living is righteous before [God]" (Ps 143:2) and "there is no one righteous, not even one" (Rom 3:10).

The only exception to this sweeping verdict is Jesus Christ. In Luke's account of the crucifixion, the centurion at the cross concludes, "Surely this was a righteous [just] man" (Luke 23:47). Acts repeats this conclusion. Peter accuses the Jewish crowds, saying, "You disowned the Holy and Righteous One and asked that a murderer [i.e., Barabbas] be released to you" (Acts 3:14; cf. Acts 7:52). Ananias states that God chose Paul on the road to Damascus "to see the Righteous One and to hear words from his mouth" (Acts 22:14). Jesus' just and righteous character connects him with Isaiah's suffering servant, who brings salvation: "he was pierced for our transgressions, he was crushed for our iniquities" (Isa 53:5).

The gospel offers us a right standing before God on the basis of Jesus' dying in our place: "For Christ... suffered once for sins, the righteous for the unrighteous, to bring you to God" (1 Pet 3:18). Rom 3:25–26 explains, "God presented Christ as a sacrifice of atonement, through the shedding of his blood — to be received by faith ... He did it to demonstrate his righteousness at the present time, so as to be just and the one who justifies those who have faith in Jesus." The only means of our justification is confessing our failure to live justly and trusting in the death and resurrection of Christ.

The Bible reveals the God of justice, who demands justice from his creatures. It also gives full voice to human cries against injustice and proclaims that God determines to restore justice to the whole earth.

WRATH

Christopher W. Morgan

The story line and message of the Bible is that God is on a gracious mission to save a people and cosmos for his glory (Eph 1:3 – 14; 2:7; 3:10 – 11). A major theme in this story is human sin, and a significant subtheme is sin's fitting consequence: the wrath of God.

WRATH ENTERS

The Bible teaches that the eternal God exists in all his perfection. He is indivisible and yet appropriately characterized by intrinsic and eternal attributes such as holiness, love, goodness, justice, knowledge, power, and so forth. This means, e.g., that God has always been and always will be loving. But unlike love and other intrinsic attributes, the wrath of God was occasioned by historical events. Indeed, as his personal, active, and settled anger toward and opposition to sin, God's wrath is an extension of his holiness and justice. Thus, wrath can only be rightly understood as the odious nature of sin is perceived; sin is fundamentally against God, a foolish and damning mutiny against him. (See "Sin," p. 2644.)

Whether presented as wrath, fury, displeasure, judgment, vengeance, or indignation, God's wrath first takes stage in the biblical story when sin enters. This does not mean that God's wrath should be viewed as something external to him or as a depersonalized and inevitable process of cause and effect in a moral universe. Instead, God's wrath is his holy revulsion against all that is unholy, his righteous judgment against unrighteousness, his firm response to covenant unfaithfulness, his good opposition to the cosmic treason of sin.

These truths about wrath are best understood through the biblical narrative, which begins with God creating everything in a way that pleases him and benefits his creatures (Gen 1 – 2). The goodness of God and his creation are highlighted by the creation account's refrain, "And God saw that it was good" (Gen 1:4,10,12,18,21,25,31). God creates humanity in his image, distinguishing them from the rest of creation and establishing a Creator-creature distinction. Adam and Eve are blessed with an unhindered relationship with God, intimate enjoyment of each other as a human couple, and delegated authority over creation.

Living in God's holy presence requires obeying his will. But rather than submitting to and finding their pleasure in God, Adam and Eve rebel, wanting ultimate autonomy (Gen 3:6). The couple immediately feels shame (Gen 3:7), estrangement from God (Gen 3:8 – 10), and fear (Gen 3:10). They are also alienated from each other: the woman blames the serpent, and the man blames the woman and even God (Gen 3:12 – 13)!

In response, God rightfully pronounces judgments on the serpent (Gen 3:14 – 15), Eve (Gen 3:16), and Adam (Gen 3:17 – 19), resulting in pain, sorrow, relational disharmony, and antagonism with the creation. Even worse, the couple is banished from Eden and thus God's glorious presence (Gen 3:22 – 24). God's prior warning, "For when you eat from it you will certainly die" (Gen 2:17), becomes reality in God's statement, "And to dust you will return" (Gen 3:19).

Unfortunately, though sin enters the garden, it does not remain there. Adam's sin, while personal and historical, is also corporate and cosmic, plunging all humanity into sin (Rom 5:12 – 21) and resulting in a creation that longs for freedom (Rom 8:18 – 23). In Adam, all humans sin, are guilty before God, and die (Rom 5:12 – 21); they not only are dead in sin, enslaved to sin, and living in sin, but are also by nature children of wrath (Eph 2:1 – 3) and under the present and future condemnation that comes from suppressing God's gracious self-revelation (Rom 1:18; 2:5 – 8). Humans are presently guilty and are now under God's wrath (John 3:18,36, Rom 1:18 – 24; 2:5 – 8; 3:9 – 20; 5:5 – 21).

WRATH CONTINUES

The next episode in the biblical story reveals that sin persists, as Cain murders Abel and God curses him with banishment (Gen 4:8 – 16). Then Gen 5 lists the descendants of Adam, and after each one it adds the disheartening refrain, "And then he died" (e.g., vv. 5,8,11). What a contrast to the previous refrain of Gen 1: "And God saw that it was good"! But awareness of death did not keep humans from rebelling against their Creator. Humanity's wickedness was enormous and an affront to God, who judges with the flood, sparing Noah (Gen 6 – 9). Persistent in their quest for autonomy, humans build a tower as a monument to their pride, and God responds by scattering them (Gen 11). These introductory chapters to the Bible (Gen 1 – 11) typify what follows. Humans continue in their revolt, God judges accordingly, and yet he still saves a people.

God's wrath is further displayed throughout the biblical story and at key points. It is sometimes directed at his enemies, such as his judgment of Sodom and Gomorrah (Gen 19) and his judgment of the Egyptians through the plagues and destruction of Pharaoh's army (Exod 7 – 15). God's wrath is also directed at his own people. For example, God demonstrates his wrath at Moses' request for someone else to deliver the people of Israel from slavery (Exod 4:14); at the mistreatment of a foreigner, widow, or orphan (Exod 22:21 – 24); and at the idolatrous worship of the golden calf, when God's "fierce anger" is said to "burn" against the people (Exod 32:10–14; cf. Deut 9:13–21). Moses mediates on behalf of the people, and God spares them (Exod 32:14). Unfortunately, God's people continue to sin, and his wrath follows. Examples abound but include God's anger with and judgment on the wandering Israelites who complained about their situation (Num 11), on those who worshiped the Baal of Peor (Num 25:3–4), on the generation who refused to seize the promised land (Num 32:1–15; Deut 9:22–29), on the sin of Achan and corresponding judgment on Israel (Josh 7:1; 22:20), on pagan nations who opposed God and his people (Isa 13–23), and even on the nation of Israel, which resulted in exile (2 Kgs 18–25; Zech 1:1–7). But in the midst of many of these passages, God's grace still emerges: God answers the prayers of his leaders (Exod 4; 32); he provides a mediator to turn back his wrath from the people of Israel (cf. Num 25:1–13); he uses examples of past wrath and warnings of future wrath to urge his people to obey in the present (cf. Deut 9:7; Ps 95:11; Isa 59:18; Heb 3:11; 4:3); and he even brings salvation through judgment (cf. Gen 3:15; 6:1–18; 7:22–23; 19:29; Exod 15:1–18). Even more, God is described as "slow to anger" and "abounding in love and faithfulness" toward his covenant people (Exod 34:6–7; cf. Num 14:18; Neh 9:17; Pss 78:38; 103:8; Nah 1:3), reacting not only as a just judge but also at times like a wounded lover (Hos 11:1–11). Indeed, sometimes his wrath toward his people lasts only "a moment" (Ps 30:5; cf. Isa 54:1–10).

WRATH PROPITIATED

Although the biblical narrative reveals that God's wrath is directed toward sin and sinners, Jesus voluntarily saves us from divine wrath by bearing this wrath for us (Rom 3:21–26; 5:6–11). He drinks the cup of wrath (Matt 26:39–42), dies as a substitute (Rom 3:25–26; 1 Pet 3:18), and offers himself as a sacrifice for us (Heb 9–10). Through Christ's saving work, the Son who merits blessing receives our curse, and believing and repentant sinners who deserve God's wrath receive mercy (Gal 3:13).

Displaying Trinitarian unity, the loving Father demonstrates his love toward us by sending his unique Son into the world to bear his wrath for us. John states it profoundly: "God is love. This is how God showed his love among us: He sent his one and only Son into the world that we might live through him. This is love: not that we loved God, but that he loved us and sent his Son as an atoning sacrifice for our sins" (1 John 4:8–10; cf. John 3:16–18). God's wrath on our sin is the occasion for Christ's saving work, and his love is the motive of his saving work. Thus, propitiation—Christ's loving, atoning self-sacrifice that satisfies God's wrath on our sin and reconciles us to God (cf. Rom 3:25; Heb 2:17; 1 John 2:2; 4:10)—does not pit the wrathful Father against the loving Son (as some allege); rather, it underscores that the cross both supremely showcases God's love and perfectly satisfies God's wrath. As such, salvation is both unto life and from sin (and its fitting penalty, wrath).

Rom 3:25–26 especially underlines this reality: "God presented Christ as a sacrifice of atonement, through the shedding of his blood—to be received by faith … He did it to demonstrate his righteousness at the present time, so as to be just and the one who justifies those who have faith in Jesus." The Father presents the Son's atoning sacrifice as the basis of the justification of those who have faith in Christ (cf. Heb 9–10). This justification is needed because all people are presently under the wrath of God and stand condemned as guilty before him (Rom 1:18–24; 3:9–20). Thus, Jesus' work on the cross addresses the fundamental problem of our human condition: we are sinners, guilty before God, and under his wrath.

WRATH TO COME

As previously noted, the wrath of God presently rests on all those outside of Christ (John 3:18,36), is currently being revealed against ungodliness (Rom 1:18), and is related to the existing state of condemnation that characterizes the universal human condition (Rom 5:12–21; Eph 2:3). But the wrath of God is not only present, it is also future (Rom 2:5–8; 5:6–11; Col 3:6; 1 Thess 1:10; 5:9; Rev 6:16–17; 14:9–11). It is depicted as coming—it is tied to the final judgment and related to the day of the Lord—and as culminating in hell.

The present and future aspects of God's wrath reflect the progressive nature of salvation history. There is an "already and not yet" or an "inaugurated eschatology" (see "The Consummation: New Testament Fulfillment," p. 2695) of sin and wrath, just as there is of the kingdom, salvation, the church, etc. God's wrath presently abides on sinners, and hell is the final and intensified unleashing of that wrath. Sinners are condemned already and await the ultimate condemnation. They are spiritually dead and await the second death. Unbelievers are currently alienated from God and will be finally excluded from his presence. In some sense, the descriptions of coming wrath in hell are culminations and extensions of the current state of sin of every unbeliever. The descriptions also serve to urge repentance and faith in Christ now.

The biblical story sometimes presents the coming wrath as tragic, as it is awful that people rebel against God and persistently spurn the Savior. As previously noted, God is "slow to anger" and "abounding in love and faithfulness" (Exod 34:6–7), and he does not take pleasure in the punishment of the wicked, just as he does not find pleasure in the existence of sin (Ezek 18:23). Jesus likewise grieved and wept over human lostness, sin, and the impending judgment (Matt 23:37; Luke 19:41; 23:34). The apostle Paul also shared this perspective, earnestly longing and praying for the conversion of his lost fellow Israelites, even to the point of being willing to undergo God's wrath on their behalf (Rom 9:1–5; 10:1).

Yet God's coming wrath is also victorious, being linked to his righteous judgment and the day of Yahweh, "the day of God's wrath" (Rom 2:5). As such, the coming wrath answers (not raises) ultimate questions related to the justice of God. Through the coming wrath, judgment, and hell, God's ultimate victory is displayed over evil, and his righteousness is vindicated (Rev 6:16–17; 11:18; 14:6–20; 15:1—16:21; 19:11–21). There is a "comfort" to wrath and hell. That God will one day avenge his people points to his covenant faithfulness and urges patience, hope, perseverance, and worship (Rom 9:22–23; 12:19; 2 Thess. 1:5–11; Jas 5:1–11; Rev 11:15–19; 15:3–4; 16:5–7; 19:1–10). God will judge everyone, the weak and the powerful (Rev 20:11–15). He and his people will win in the end, and he will ensure that justice prevails. Through his righteous judgment and ultimate victory, God will glorify himself, displaying his greatness and receiving the worship he is due.

LOVE AND GRACE

Graham A. Cole

The God of biblical revelation is no impersonal absolute. The living God is the God of love and grace. But what do such terms mean? We are most familiar with turning to a dictionary and getting equivalent words. It is the genius of Scripture, however, that big terms such as "love" and "grace" are embodied in stories as well as in direct affirmations. In particular it is Jesus Christ and his story that provides the lens through which to view what the big biblical ideas are about. The Scriptures aren't interested in mere abstractions. So the biblical concepts of love and grace may be present in the text even if the actual words aren't.

LOVE

What does divine love look like? Moses found out on Mount Sinai when God appeared and declared his name and nature. In the ancient Near East, to declare one's "name" was to state who one really was. This is the God who is "abounding in love" (Exod 34:6). Israel had just experienced that love when God had set them free from Pharaoh's grip. This is love that chooses, keeps promises, rescues, and covenants (Deut 7:7 – 9). God's love for his people called for an answering love on Israel's part. God commanded Israel, "Love the Lord your God with all your heart and with all your soul and with all your strength" (Deut 6:5). In context that was a call to loyalty to God and a call away from loyalty to idols. Israel over and over again failed the loyalty test. In the face of this, the depths of God's love are seen in the prophet Hosea. He is to love a faithless woman and in so doing mirror the love God has for his faithless people: "Go, show your love to your wife again, though she is loved by another man and is an adulteress. Love her as the Lord loves the Israelites, though they turn to other gods" (Hos 3:1). We can see in Hosea how the divine love pursues the unlovely. Divine love is other-person-centered. Unsurprisingly, then, this same God calls his people to love their neighbors (Lev 19:18).

This love is manifested in action, as the story of Jesus exemplifies. Jesus embodies the divine love in his coming and his cross. As John 3:16 famously affirms, "For God so loved the world that he gave his one and only Son." Paul elaborates, "God demonstrates his own love for us in this: While we were still sinners, Christ died for us" (Rom 5:8). John adds to this testimony: "This is how God showed his love among us: He sent his one and only Son into the world that we might live through him" (1 John 4:9). As in the OT, in the NT practical consequences follow. Jesus exhibits a new paradigm for loving others (John 13:1 – 17). This love serves. This love shows hospitality. This love washes the feet of others. We are to love like that. Love is the new commandment (John 13:34). It is new because it is informed by the story of Christ.

This newness carries over into the Christian household: "Husbands, love your wives, just as Christ loved the church and gave himself up for her" (Eph 5:25). This love is self-sacrificial. For Paul such love constitutes "the most excellent way" (1 Cor 12:31). The Corinthian church, with all its problems, needed to hear that. Even gifts given by the Spirit to the church are futile without love (1 Cor 13:1 – 2). Not even amazing faith profits without love (1 Cor 13:2). Martyrdom or spectacular generosity is in vain without love (1 Cor 13:3). Love is patient, kind, does not envy or boast, is not proud or rude or self-seeking (1 Cor 13: 4 – 5). It is not easily angered, does not keep a record of wrongdoing, and does not delight in evil (1 Cor 13: 5 – 6). Positively, it rejoices in the truth, always protects, always trusts, always hopes, always perseveres (1 Cor 13:6 – 7). This kind of love never fails (1 Cor 13:8). This love is not manufactured by us; it is a fruit of the Spirit of Christ living within us (Gal 5:22). These virtues are the characteristics of Christ himself.

As in the OT, the NT presents no mere duty-ethic. This love is an answering love to the divine love as experienced in Christ: "We love because he first loved us" (1 John 4:19). This love cannot possibly claim to love God while hating other believers (1 John 4:20). Some things — like knowledge and prophecy — fade away (1 Cor 13:8). But love remains (1 Cor 13:13). It never fades.

GRACE

What does grace look like? Divine grace is the undeserved favor of a superior bestowed on an inferior. The Israelites experienced God's grace when he delivered them from Egyptian oppression. God proclaims to Moses on Mount Sinai, "The Lord, the Lord, the compassionate and gracious God" (Exod 34:6). In its form, the covenant that God enters into with Israel on Mount Sinai (the Mosaic covenant) is very much like a particular kind of ancient Near Eastern treaty (a suzerainty treaty). This form of treaty occurs when a superior (a suzerain) enters into a relationship with an inferior (a vassal). Significantly in Israel's case, the covenant is established after the magnificent act of grace that saved Israel from Pharaoh. An ancient form of relationship is given stunningly new content. The exodus event also shows that when God acts graciously, it means salvation for some (Israel) but very often judgment for others (Egypt and its gods, as in Exod 12:12 – 13). In Israel, to be blessed by God is to experience his grace as in the Aaronic blessing: "The LORD make his face shine on you and be gracious to you" (Num 6:25). Many of the prayers in the book of Psalms acknowledge that divine grace is a favor to be sought rather than a right to be expected: "Turn to me and be gracious to me, for I am lonely and afflicted" (Ps 25:16).

God's grace is dramatically on display in the story of Jonah and Nineveh. God called the prophet to proclaim judgment on Nineveh, Israel's hated foe. But Jonah fled. He fled, not because he was afraid for himself, but because he knew the divine character as revealed to Moses on Mount Sinai. He was well aware that the living God is a gracious God. He feared that if the Ninevites repented, God would not judge them, and that's indeed what happened. He laments, "I knew that you are a gracious and compassionate God" (Jonah 4:2). God did what Jonah had feared. He showed grace. In fact the message of warning became the divine vehicle through which a loving God brought about a change of heart on the part of the Ninevites (cf. Jer 18:7–8). Ironically, Jonah is thankful when *he* receives divine grace (Jonah 2:2–9) but not when the Ninevites do. There is a temptation to look for grace for ourselves but only judgment for others.

In Jesus the divine grace comes into view in the most personal of ways, as John points out in his prologue (John 1:17). Paul encapsulates that grace when he encourages the Corinthians to give generously to help the Jerusalem Christians: "For you know the grace of our Lord Jesus Christ, that though he was rich, yet for your sake he became poor, so that you through his poverty might become rich" (2 Cor 8:9). By coming among humankind and dying on the cross, Jesus Christ did what he was not obliged to do, and he did so not for his own sake but for ours, undeserving though we are.

Indeed, Paul summarizes the gospel in terms of grace. He reminds the Ephesian elders that in his three-year ministry among them he testified "to the good news of God's grace," and he commits them "to God and to the word of his grace" (Acts 20:24,32). The canon of Scripture closes on the note of expectation and grace: "Come, Lord Jesus. The grace of the Lord Jesus be with God's people" (Rev 22:20–21). The nature of this undeserved favor removes any grounds for our boasting before God about our meritorious works. As Paul tells the Ephesians, "It is by grace you have been saved, through faith—and this not from yourselves, it is the gift of God—not by works, so that no one can boast" (Eph 2:8–9). This divine grace is gloriously rich and found in Christ (Eph 1:6–8). Paul tells the Roman Christians a similar truth as he contrasts Adam and Christ. Adam's sin brought death and condemnation, but the gift of justification (the great acquittal before the divine court) comes "by the grace of the one man, Jesus Christ" and "overflow[s] to the many" (Rom 5:15).

Likewise, Peter tells the Jerusalem council that whether a person is a Jew or a Gentile (non-Jew), the way of salvation is the same: "We believe it is through the grace of our Lord Jesus that we [Jews] are saved, just as they [Gentiles] are" (Acts 15:11).

Even though the accent on grace in Scripture focuses repeatedly on God or Christ as the gracious one, those who have received such grace must be gracious themselves. This graciousness must show itself especially in Christian generosity (2 Cor 8:9) and speech: "Let your conversation be always full of grace" (Col 4:6). Unsurprisingly, such gracious speech characterized Jesus himself (Luke 4:22).

LOVE AND GRACE DISTINGUISHED

Grace and love occur together in the Bible. We deserve neither God's love nor his grace. They both express God's goodness, as Moses learned on Mount Sinai (Exod 33:18—34:7). Paul tells Titus, "The grace of God has appeared that offers salvation to all people" (Titus 2:11), and then Paul writes, "When the kindness and love of God our Savior appeared, he saved us" (Titus 3:4–5).

Yet love and grace must be distinguished. Paul's benediction on the Corinthians illustrates this distinction: "May the grace of the Lord Jesus Christ, and the love of God, and the fellowship of the Holy Spirit be with you all" (2 Cor 13:14). (Often when Paul writes of God, he has God the Father in view, as in this benediction. Another example is Eph 1:3.) The love of God the Father is seen in the provision of Christ that we might become God's friends: reconciled through Christ's death on the cross and no longer estranged (2 Cor 5:14–21). The grace of Christ is revealed in his giving up his riches by becoming a man and dying so that we might become rich (2 Cor 8:9). Church leader Irenaeus (*Against Heresies*) rightly said in the second century, "[Jesus] became what we are that we might become what he is." Such is grace. Such is love.

THE GOSPEL

Greg D. Gilbert

The word "gospel" derives from the Anglo-Saxon term "god-spell," meaning "good tidings" or "good news." The Greek word *euangelion* ("gospel") and its verbal cognate *euangelizomai* ("evangelize" or "speak good news") together occur more than 130 times in the NT. Whether used in a military, imperial, or religious sense, a "gospel" was always a *message* of good news. It was proclaimed with words, had a definite content, and expected a response from those who heard it.

The gospel that Jesus and his earliest followers proclaimed was no different. It was a well-defined message of good news: Jesus the Messianic King had come to establish God's kingdom on earth and forgive sinful people through his own substitutionary life, death, and resurrection, thereby qualifying them to inherit God's kingdom if they would turn from their sin and rely on him to save them.

BACKGROUND OF THE WORD "GOSPEL"

Neither Jesus nor the apostles coined the word "gospel." It was commonly used as part of the Roman system of emperor worship, in which it referred to the announcement of the "good news" of a royal heir's birth or coming of age or especially of a new emperor's accession to the throne. While the use of "gospel" in the NT to announce the arrival of the Messianic King may have been to some degree a challenge to Roman imperial power, the background to Christians' use of the word is to be found, not primarily in an anti-imperial polemic, but rather in OT prophecies.

The Septuagint, the pre-Christian Greek translation of the OT, often uses the words *euangelion* and *euangelizomai* to translate words deriving from the Hebrew root *bsr*. Usually, *bsr* refers to bringing a message of good news, such as the birth of a child (Jer 20:15), the choice of a king (1 Kgs 1:42), a military victory (e.g., 1 Sam 31:9; 2 Sam 4:10; 18:19,20; Ps 68:11), or deliverance from foreign powers (e.g., Ps 96:2; Nah 1:15; but cf. 1 Sam 4:17, where the news is not good but still momentous). Sometimes, however, the word takes on a greater significance: when referring to God's spiritual salvation of his people.

THE GOSPEL ACCORDING TO ISAIAH

The most important passages in the OT for understanding the background to the NT usage of "gospel" occur in Isa 40–66. In two crucial texts (Isa 40:9; 52:7), a messenger bringing "good news" announces that God is coming to Jerusalem as a victorious king to deliver his people from Babylon's oppression. In both of these passages, the message of the "evangelizer" is that despite the apparent power of the enemy, it is God alone who rules: "Here is your God!" (Isa 40:9) and "Your God reigns!" (Isa 52:7), they declare. The deliverance God accomplishes for his people, however, is wholly undeserved; they are a sinful people (Isa 46:12; 48:1), and God saves them only by his grace. Because there is no righteousness in the people themselves, God promises that he will clothe them in a righteousness that is not their own (Isa 61:10–11) when they come to him in faith and repentance (Isa 55:1,7). But God does not graciously redeem his people at the expense of justice. His people's sins still cry out for judgment, and the Lord who loves justice (Isa 61:8) will not allow the penalty to go unpaid. But here is also where his mercy is most greatly magnified, for God determines that the punishment for his people's sin will be executed, not on them, but on a divine servant-king appointed to be their substitute (Isa 52:13—53:12; see Isa 11:2; 52:13; and 61:1 for the identification of this servant and king, as well as his divine nature). This servant-king will be pierced for their transgressions and crushed for their iniquities, and because of his wounds, they will be healed (Isa 53:5). He will "bear [God's people's] iniquities," make an "offering for sin," and through his suffering "justify many" (Isa 53:10–11). Although this servant-king will be "cut off from the land of the living" (Isa 53:8), have his life "poured out ... unto death" (Isa 53:12), and be "assigned a grave with the wicked" (Isa 53:9), yet "after he has suffered, he will see the light of life and be satisfied" (Isa 53:11). Moreover, after accomplishing the salvation of his people by dying in their place, the risen Savior-King will "reign on David's throne and over his kingdom," ruling "with justice and righteousness from that time on and forever" (Isa 9:7).

This announcement of undeserved, substitutionary salvation is the "gospel," which the Spirit of God anoints the servant to preach to "the poor" (61:1). The "poor" are not primarily the *materially* poor but the *spiritually* poor, those who realize that they have no hope of salvation apart from the servant's substitutionary work in their place. They buy, eat, and drink from God's grace even though they have no money with which to do so (55:1–2).

THE GOSPEL FULFILLED BY JESUS

The Announcement of the Kingdom

The servant's words in Isa 61 are of particular interest because Jesus opened his own ministry with this text, declaring to his audience in Nazareth that his appearance fulfilled what Isaiah prophesied (Luke 4:16–21). The essence of Jesus' preaching through the first stage of his public ministry is stated in his announcement, "The time has come … The kingdom of God has come near. Repent and believe the good news!" (Mark 1:14–15). In other words, the good news Jesus announced is that just as Isaiah prophesied, God has acted now to inaugurate his long-awaited kingdom on earth, and he has done so in the person of his chosen Messiah-King, none other than Jesus himself.

It is clear from Jesus' reading of Isa 61 and its surrounding context, however, that it is not the mere establishment of God's kingdom that constitutes the good news. It is that the spiritually poor, captive, blind, and oppressed (i.e., those who have no claim on the kingdom by right) can enter it by God's grace and the work of the servant-king standing in their place. Jesus' healing miracles thus illustrate that God saves the spiritually hopeless: the blind receive sight (Matt 9:27–31), the lame walk (Mark 2:1–12), and the dead live (Matt 9:18–26; Luke 7:11–15; John 11:1–44; see Matt 11:2–6).

Most important, the good news Jesus proclaimed is that the guilty can be forgiven of their sins (e.g., Mark 2:5,10; Luke 7:48–50). This was the ultimate mission of Isaiah's kingly suffering servant (Isa 53:4–6,10–12; 61:1–3), and it was also the purpose announced by the angel before Jesus' birth: "He will save his people from their sins" (Matt 1:21; see Luke 19:10). The apostle Paul explains that this forgiveness is necessary because it qualifies people "to share in the inheritance of [God's] holy people in the kingdom of light" and to be "rescued … from the dominion of darkness and brought … into the kingdom of the Son he loves," i.e., Jesus (Col 1:11–14). Without forgiveness, by contrast, one can expect only God's wrath, judgment, and fury (Rom 2:5,8).

The Message of the Cross

For this reason, the crucifixion and resurrection of Jesus stand at the center of the Christian gospel message. Thus, the gospel Paul preached was this: "that Christ died for our sins according to the Scriptures, that he was buried, that he was raised on the third day according to the Scriptures, and that he appeared to Cephas [Peter], and then to the Twelve" (1 Cor 15:3–5). Paul recognized, of course, that Jesus' resurrection was critical to the good news of salvation: "If Christ has not been raised, our preaching is useless and … your faith is futile; you are still in your sins" (1 Cor 15:14,17). But since Christ was indeed raised, Paul emphasized the cross as the very center of the gospel message, even equating "the gospel" with "the message of the cross" and "Christ crucified" (1 Cor 1:17–18,23). Among the churches he planted, Paul said that he "resolved to know nothing while [he] was with [them] except Jesus Christ and him crucified" (1 Cor 2:2).

Paul focused on the cross because Jesus' death is the event through which God provided atonement for the sins of his people. Throughout his public ministry, Jesus repeatedly foretold his death and resurrection, and he explained their purpose as well. By dying on the cross, he was giving his life "as a ransom for many" (Mark 10:45) and pouring out his blood "for the forgiveness of sins" (Matt 26:28). By willingly laying down his life by dying on the cross, Jesus was accomplishing the salvation that God promised in the OT and that the Jewish sacrificial system illustrated. By dying in his people's place and paying the penalty for their sin, Jesus became a "sacrifice of atonement" for them (Rom 3:25), took upon himself the wrath of God that they deserved (1 Pet 3:18), and thereby qualified them to be welcomed into God's presence and kingdom (Col 1:12–13). As a miraculous illustration of this, when Jesus died, the curtain of the temple, which symbolized that God exiled humans from his presence, was torn in two from top to bottom (Matt 27:51; Mark 15:38; Luke 23:45). Jesus had not just inaugurated the kingdom; he had also won forgiveness for the sin that separated people from God.

The Call for a Response

The Christian gospel always calls for and expects a response from those who hear it. Thus, Jesus himself preached, "Repent and believe the good news!" (Mark 1:15). Paul declared to everyone to whom he preached, "Turn to God in repentance and have faith in our Lord Jesus" (Acts 20:21). Through faith, sinners receive Jesus' sacrifice of atonement on their behalf and are thereby justified—i.e., declared to be righteous—in God's sight (Rom 3:21–26). At its essence, therefore, to have faith in Jesus is to trust God as completely as Abraham did, "fully persuaded that God had power to do what he had promised" (Rom 4:21). Faith is to trust Jesus, to believe in him, to rely on him alone for salvation.

Of course, faith in Jesus does not abrogate the necessity of turning away from sin to follow him; quite to the contrary, genuine faith in Jesus implies such repentance (Rom 6:1–6). To claim faith while refusing to repent is to identify oneself as a false professor of the faith, one who has the appearance of godliness without truly knowing its power (2 Tim 3:5–7; Heb 6:1–9; 1 John 2:19). Those who truly love and trust Jesus as savior and king will turn away from sin, keep his commandments, and follow him even at the cost of life itself (Matt 16:24; John 14:15,21,23; 1 John 5:3).

The Gospel As Paul Proclaimed It

Of the 76 occurrences of "gospel" in the NT, 60 of them are in the writings of Paul, which makes him a crucial witness to how the earliest Christians understood the content of the gospel message. According to Paul himself, his gospel message was not a corruption of, or even a development of, the one

Jesus preached, nor had he received it from or been taught it by any human being (Gal 1:11 – 12). On the contrary, Paul insisted that he had "received [the gospel] by revelation from Jesus Christ" himself (Gal 1:12; see 1 Cor 15:3), and therefore it was not subject to human judgment but rather carried in itself all divine authority (Gal 1:15 – 17; see Gal 1:1).

In Paul's writings we see the content of the Christian gospel given full form. Human beings, because of their sin, deserve God's wrath and judgment (Rom 1:18). No form of moral self-reformation or law-keeping can rescue them; indeed "by the works of the law no one will be justified" (Gal 2:16), since the law serves only to make sinners "conscious of [their] sin" (Rom 3:20) and thereby renders sin "utterly sinful" (Rom 7:13). What sinners need is "not ... a righteousness of [their] own that comes from the law" (Phil 3:9; see Rom 3:21) but rather "the righteousness that comes from God" (Phil 3:9) that is "apart from the law" (Rom 3:21). That righteousness comes from Jesus, who suffered in the place of sinners "as a sacrifice of atonement" (Rom 3:25) and thereby "redeemed us from the curse of the law by becoming a curse for us" (Gal 3:13). Standing as their representative substitute, Jesus is himself his people's righteousness (1 Cor 1:30), and as such, he secures for them before God a righteous status without regard to their works (Rom 4:6). Sinners appropriate all this — atonement for sin and righteousness before God — by faith. Just as righteousness was credited to Abraham through his faith in God's promise (Gen 15:6; Rom 4:3), so also in the same way "God will credit righteousness [to us] who believe in him who raised Jesus our Lord from the dead. He was delivered over to death for our sins and was raised to life for our justification" (Rom 4:24 – 25).

CONCLUSION

The Christian gospel of the NT was thus a well-defined message of good news: Jesus the Messiah had come to live, die, and rise again in the place of sinners so that all who repent of their sins and believe in him will not suffer God's wrath but rather be forgiven and saved. This was the message the earliest Christians preached. In his sermon at Pentecost, Peter announced Jesus' atoning death and resurrection and then explained what people should do in response: "Repent and be baptized, every one of you, in the name of Jesus Christ for the forgiveness of your sins" (Acts 2:38). In another sermon, Peter again announced the good news of Jesus' substitutionary atonement for sin: "This is how God fulfilled what he had foretold through all the prophets, saying that his Messiah would suffer. Repent, then, and turn to God, so that your sins may be wiped out" (Acts 3:18 – 19). Similarly, when he preached the gospel to Cornelius and his family, Peter said, "We are witnesses of everything he did in the country of the Jews and in Jerusalem. They killed him by hanging him on a cross, but God raised him from the dead on the third day and caused him to be seen ... All the prophets testify about him that everyone who believes in him receives forgiveness of sins through his name" (Acts 10:39 – 40,43). Paul proclaimed the same message in Acts 13:38 – 39: "Therefore, my friends, I want you to know that through Jesus the forgiveness of sins is proclaimed to you. Through him everyone who believes is set free from every sin, a justification you were not able to obtain under the law of Moses." In each proclamation of the gospel, the message is clear: through the death and resurrection of Jesus the Messiah-King, there is righteousness, forgiveness of sin, and the inheritance of God's kingdom for any sinner who will repent and trust in him.

WORSHIP

David G. Peterson

Worship is a dominant theme from Genesis to Revelation because the God who created all things and redeemed us in Christ is worthy to receive all honor, praise, service, and respect (e.g., Gen 12:7–8; 14:19–20; Exod 15:1–18,21; Rev 4:11; 5:9–10,12). However, since certain expressions of worship are unacceptable to God (Gen 4:3–5; Isa 1:10–17; Heb 12:28–29; Rev 9:20–21; 13:1–18), it is important for us to know what pleases God and how he wants us to respond to him. What he has revealed in Scripture must control and direct our worship.

Three groups of words throughout the Bible convey aspects of what we commonly call "worship." NT writers use these and related terms in a transformed way to show how Jesus has fulfilled for us the pattern of worship given to Israel.

WORSHIP AS HOMAGE OR GRATEFUL SUBMISSION TO GOD

The most common word for "worship" literally means "bend over" or "bow down." It describes a gesture of respect or submission to human beings, to God, or to idols (Gen 18:2; Exod 18:7; 20:4–6). Combined with other gesture-words, this term came to be used for the *attitude* of homage that the gesture represented.

Sometimes people expressed homage to God with prayer or praise (Gen 24:26–27,52; Exod 34:8–9) and sometimes with silent acceptance or submission (Exod 4:31; Judg 7:15). The book of Psalms contains many different expressions of worship, including lament, repentance, prayers for vindication, songs of thanksgiving, and praise. Bending over before the Lord as a gesture of homage or grateful submission became associated with sacrifice and public praise in Israel. In such contexts it could be a formal way of expressing devotion to or dependence on God (Deut 26:1–11; 1 Chr 29:20–21; 2 Chr 7:3–4; 29:28–30; Neh 8:6; Ps 95:1–7). But the gesture was meaningful only if it was motivated by a genuine desire to acknowledge God's majesty and holiness and to live under his rule.

The NT uses this terminology to show that Jesus Christ is worthy of the homage and devotion due to the Lord God of Israel (Matt 14:33; 28:9,17; Luke 24:52; John 9:38; Heb 1:6; Rev 5:8–14). "Bending over to the Lord" now means responding with repentance and faith to the person and work of the Lord Jesus Christ (Acts 2:36–39; 10:36–43; cf. Rom 10:9–13). Such worship involves praying to him (Acts 7:59–60; 1 Cor 16:22; 1 Thess 3:11), calling on his name (1 Cor 1:2; Heb 13:15), and obeying him.

In John 4:20–24, a Samaritan woman inquires about the appropriate *place* to worship God, leading Jesus to speak more fundamentally about the *way* to worship acceptably. The Father is seeking "true worshipers" who "will worship the Father in the Spirit and in truth." This fulfills the pattern of worship that God gave Israel under the Mosaic law. New covenant worship involves acknowledging Jesus as the one who finally and fully reveals the truth about the Father and his purpose for Israel and the nations (John 8:45; 12:32; 14:6; 18:37). It also involves responding to the Spirit he gives to transform hearts and lives (John 3:5–8; 7:37–39; cf. John 4:13–14).

WORSHIP AS SERVICE TO GOD

Another group of biblical terms often translated "worship" literally means "serve" or "service." The people of Israel were saved from slavery in Egypt so that they could serve the Lord (Exod 3:12; 4:23; 8:1). The parallel expressions "offer sacrifices to the LORD" (Exod 3:18; 5:3,8,17; 8:8,25–29) and "hold a festival" (Exod 5:1) indicate that some form of ritual service was immediately in view. God later instituted through Moses a complex system of sacrifices and ceremonies so that Israel could serve God as his holy people (Exod 19:5–6). (See "Covenant," p. 2646; "Law," p. 2649; "Temple," p. 2652; "Priest," p. 2654; and "Sacrifice," p. 2656.)

For example, the Passover was a particular "service" to be observed in remembrance of the Lord's saving work at the time of the exodus (Exod 12:25–27; 13:5). The ministry of priests and Levites was a specialized form of service to God. But God required a lifestyle of total allegiance from his people as a whole: service was meant to be expressed in everyday obedience (Deut 10:12–13; Josh 22:5; 24:14–24). God strictly forbade bowing down and serving aspects of the creation or other gods; every temptation to idolatry and unfaithfulness was to be removed (Deut 4:19,28; 5:8–9; 7:4,16).

The sacrificial system was given to Israel to enable cleansing from sin, consecration to God's service, and expressions of gratitude to God (Lev 1–7). The NT describes Jesus' death as "a sacrifice of atonement, through the shedding of his blood—to be received through faith" (Rom 3:25; cf. Heb 2:17; 1 John 2:2). Only by this sacrifice can the wrath of God be averted (Rom 1:18–28; 2:5). (See "Wrath," p. 2681.) As in OT teaching, it is God who provides the means of forgiveness, cleansing, and sanctification (1 Cor 6:11). Christ's unique sacrifice secures for believers all the blessings of the new covenant and enables them to serve him wholeheartedly with consciences cleansed from sin (Heb 9:11–14; 10:11–22; 12:28–29).

In response to what God has done for us in Christ, we are to present our bodies to him as "a living sacrifice, holy and pleasing to God" (Rom 12:1; cf. Rom 6:13,16). Christ's obedience makes possible a new obedience for the people of God. Those who have been brought from death to life belong to God as a "living sacrifice." This is "your true and proper worship" (Rom 12:1), or as an alternate translation, "your understanding service." Acceptable worship is the service rendered by those who truly understand the gospel and want to live out its implications in every sphere of life (Rom 12:2–21).

The service rendered to God in everyday obedience is also the focus of Heb 12:28–29. The motivation and power for such service is the cleansing that comes from the finished work of Christ (Heb 9:28) and the hope that his work sets before us (Heb 12:28). Gratitude expressed in service is evidence that people grasp and appreciate the grace of God. However, acceptable worship should also be characterized by "reverence and awe" (Heb 12:28) because of the holiness and righteousness of God. Heb 13:1–16 shows what this means in practical terms.

In particular, Christians are to offer to God through Jesus "a sacrifice of praise — the fruit of lips that openly profess his name" (Heb 13:15). This could involve celebrating Christ as Savior and Lord in personal or corporate acts of praise, but the immediate context exhorts believers to acknowledge Christ *in the world* in the face of opposition and suffering (Heb 13:12–14). In its widest sense, this sacrifice of praise will be rendered by those who confess Jesus "outside the camp" (Heb 13:13) in various forms of public testimony or evangelism. Allied to this, we are not to forget to do good and to share with others, "for with such sacrifices God is pleased" (Heb 13:16; cf. Jas 1:27).

WORSHIP AS REVERENCE OR RESPECT FOR GOD

A third group of terms sometimes describes worship. Words meaning fear, reverence, or respect for God indicate the need to keep his commandments (Deut 5:29; 6:2,24; Eccl 12:13), obey his voice (1 Sam 12:14; Hag 1:12), walk in his ways (Deut 8:6; 10:12; 2 Chr 6:31), turn from evil (Job 1:1,8; 2:3; 28:28; Prov 3:7), and serve him (Deut 6:13; 10:20; Josh 24:14; Jonah 1:9). Sacrifice and other rituals expressed reverence for God, but faithfulness and obedience to the covenant demands of God in every sphere of life also distinguished true from false religion (Exod 18:21; Ps 25:14; Mal 3:16; 4:2).

The NT indicates that humanity's failure to fear God and show him proper respect brings his wrath (Rom 1:18–25; Rev 14:6–7). Only by being "redeemed ... with the precious blood of Christ" can we be set free to serve God "in reverent fear" (1 Pet 1:17–21; cf. Heb 12:28–29).

WORSHIP AND CONGREGATIONAL GATHERINGS

Worship in the OT sometimes had a corporate expression, and this was meant to encourage God's people to serve him faithfully in their individual lives (Isa 1:10–17; Jer 7:1–29). The NT rarely applies the specific word "worship" to Christian meetings (but see Acts 13:2; 1 Cor 14:25). Nevertheless, prayer, praise, and submission to God's will were central to congregational gatherings (Acts 2:42–47; 4:23–37; Eph 5:18–20; Col 3:16–17). Moreover, the link between ministry to others and service to God is obvious in the way Paul uses worship terminology in a transformed way (Rom 1:9; 15:16,27; 2 Cor 9:12–13; Phil 4:18). The NT is not prescriptive about the way we conduct our meetings, but it certainly provides guidelines and examples of Christians engaging with God together.

Paul regularly uses the terminology of edification, rather than worship, to indicate the purpose and function of Christian gatherings (1 Cor 14:3–5,12,17,26; Eph 4:11–16; 1 Thess 5:11). This imagery portrays the founding, maintaining, and advancing of the church as God's "building" or holy "temple" (1 Cor 3:10–17; Eph 2:19–22). While all ministry responds to God's grace and does not in any sense cultivate his favor, serving others is an aspect of our service or self-giving to God. Moreover, edification is the exalted Christ's work in our midst through the gifts and ministries that he empowers and directs by his Spirit (Eph 2:20–22; 4:7–16). Our task is to apply the truth of God in love to one another.

It may be best to speak of congregational worship as a particular expression of the total life-response that is the worship described in the new covenant. In the giving and receiving of various ministries, we may encounter God and submit ourselves to him afresh in praise and obedience, repentance, and faith (Heb 10:24–25). Singing to God is an important aspect of corporate worship, but it is not the supreme or only way of expressing devotion to God. Ministry exercised for the building up of the body of Christ in teaching, exhorting, and praying is a significant way of worshiping and glorifying God.

MISSION

Andreas J. Köstenberger

The entire Bible traces the journey from the original creation to the new creation, from humanity's rebellion against the Creator to God's provision of redemption in the person and work of the Lord Jesus Christ. The story of the Bible is therefore also the story of God's mission to bring sinful humanity back to himself and to restore it to its original state of living in communion with him.

CREATION, THE FALL, AND THE HISTORY OF ISRAEL

Creation and the Fall

As the one who is eternal and the source of all life, God is shown in the Bible to be on a mission, grounded in creation. As the Creator, God made humanity in his image and placed the first man and woman on this earth as his representatives, charging them to populate the earth and manage it for him. By obeying God's command, God's viceregents on earth would take his presence to the ends of the earth, extending his rule (Gen 1:26 – 31).

When Adam and Eve transgressed the boundaries set by their Creator and rebelled against him, the redemptive component of God's mission was revealed. No longer did humans enjoy direct communion with God; they now needed to be liberated from sin and reconciled with their Creator. The story of God's salvation is the account of his quest to reclaim a people who will take his presence to the ends of the earth once again. A ray of hope arose when God promised that Eve's offspring would overcome the curse (Gen 3:15). The prospect of restoring all creation rested on God's faithfulness to his promise.

The Flood, the Tower of Babel, and the Call of Abraham

Again God's mission was potentially thwarted almost immediately. In keeping with the creation mandate, humans began to multiply and fill the earth. But rather than take God's presence to the ends of the earth, they plunged into evil (Gen 6:1 – 4). God condemned their rebellion through a universal flood and renewed his promise of a new creation to Noah and his family (Gen 6:5 — 9:19). At the tower of Babel, God scattered humanity in judgment (Gen 11:1 – 9) but then called Abraham so that all the peoples of the earth would be blessed through him and his descendants (Gen 12:1 – 3). God entered into an unconditional covenant with Abraham that was predicated on faith and had universal, worldwide implications (Gen 15:1 – 18; Rom 4:16 – 17; Gal 3:6 – 9,26 – 29). God's covenant with Abraham is thus the framework for his dealings with humans during the remainder of biblical history, culminating in the new covenant instituted by Abraham's ultimate offspring, the Lord Jesus Christ (Gal 3:16).

The Growth of Israel Into a Nation, the Exodus, and the Giving of the Law

Faithful to his promise, God made the children of Abraham into a great nation. In a series of mighty acts of deliverance, he rescued his people from bondage in Egypt by the hand of Moses (the exodus). As a nation that God formed and set apart to be holy (see "Holiness," p. 2676), Israel displayed God's character to all the nations, mediating God's presence and blessings to them and summoning them to participate in the renewal of all things by worshiping God alone (Exod 19:5 – 6). God also gave his people the law, which reflects his righteous character. Obeying the law brought God's blessing, while disobeying it resulted in his judgment.

The Monarchy, the Davidic Dynasty, and the Exile

After 40 years of wandering in the wilderness, Moses died, and his successor, Joshua, led Israel into the promised land. God focused the earliest promise of an offspring (Gen 3:15) on a son of King David, whose dynasty would establish an eternal kingdom. During the reign of David's son Solomon, various promises to Abraham and David were fulfilled: the promised land was conquered, Israel became a great nation, and the Jerusalem temple was built (1 Kgs 6 – 8; cf. Deut 12:5 – 11). In his prayer of dedication, Solomon articulates a vision that demonstrates mission as a key part of the priestly/cultic dimension of the OT as well as the covenant/legal dimension (1 Kgs 8:41 – 43,59 – 60; 2 Chr 6:32 – 33). Yet Solomon, and a long string of monarchs in the divided kingdom after him, fell into idolatry, and God scattered first the northern kingdom of Israel and then the southern kingdom of Judah across the nations (the exile). Later, by the edict of the Persian king Cyrus, a remnant returned, rebuilding the temple, the city, and its walls under the leadership of men such as Ezra and Nehemiah. But the nation never recovered its former Solomonic glory.

Jonah, the End-Time Pilgrimage of the Nations, and the Servant of the Lord

During the period of the divided kingdom, the prophet Jonah went reluctantly to preach to the people of Nineveh. But rather than representing a model missionary, he serves as an example of Israel's lack of concern for the spiritual well-being of the other nations. Nevertheless, some OT prophets envision Jerusalem as the site of the end-time pilgrimage of the nations (Isa 2:2–4; 60:1—62:12; Mic 4:1–5), and the enthronement psalms feature Zion as the center of the worship of God (Pss 48; 93; 96–97; 99). Some apocalyptic passages also depict Zion as the center of the new creation (Isa 35:1–10; 65:17–18). Isaiah presents the servant of the Lord as one who would suffer vicariously and subsequently be exalted by God (Isa 52:13—53:12). The servant's ministry would include both Israel and the nations as the means of fulfilling God's promise to Abraham.

THE COMING OF THE MESSIAH, THE CHURCH'S MISSION, AND THE FINAL CONSUMMATION

Jesus the Messiah, Savior, and Lord

All four Gospels present Jesus of Nazareth as the fulfillment of OT Messianic promises and expectations. Matthew casts Jesus as the son of Abraham and David (Matt 1:1) and as Immanuel, "God with us" (Matt 1:23; cf. Matt 28:20). Throughout his Gospel, Matthew shows that Jesus fulfilled OT Messianic predictions in virtually every detail of his life and ministry. Mark presents Jesus as the powerful Son of God (Mark 1:1) who died giving his life as a "ransom for many" (Mark 10:45). Luke traces Jesus' ancestry back all the way to Adam (Luke 3:23,38) and casts Jesus as the compassionate healer and friend of sinners (e.g., Luke 19:7). John presents selected Messianic signs of Jesus as proof that Jesus is the Messianic Son of God (John 20:30–31).

The Gospels concur that Jesus limited the scope of his mission to Israel while occasionally ministering to Gentiles, often at their initiative. Yet the people of Israel rejected Jesus' Messianic claims, leading to his crucifixion. At the same time, Jesus predicted a worldwide extension of his ministry, instructing his disciples that the gospel must first be proclaimed to all nations before the end will come (Matt 24:14; Mark 13:10). Subsequent to his resurrection, Jesus charged his followers to go into all the world and disciple the nations (Matt 28:18–20; cf. Luke 24:46–48; John 20:21). The Gospels also agree that Jesus' death is universally significant, extending salvation to Gentiles as well as Jews (e.g., John 3:16).

The Early Church and Paul

The book of Acts narrates how, after Jesus ascended, God gave the Spirit to all believers and how the early church went about its mission. In keeping with Jesus' command, believers served as witnesses, first in Jerusalem and Judea, and then also in Samaria and all the way to the ends of the earth (Acts 1:8). In a major paradigm shift, God's people no longer displayed their faith in God merely to attract outsiders; they actively went to reach out to unbelievers everywhere. This stands in contrast to OT Israel as well as Second Temple Judaism, neither of which can accurately be described as a missionary religion (the prophet Jonah's ministry to Nineveh notwithstanding).

Key events in the history of the early church include Peter's Pentecost sermon (Acts 2), Stephen's martyrdom (Acts 7), Paul's conversion (Acts 9), Peter's vision prompting his mission to Cornelius (Acts 10), Saul and Barnabas's mission from Antioch to the Gentiles (Acts 13), and the Jerusalem council (Acts 15). In its outreach to the Gentiles, the early church actively moves in fulfillment of the Abrahamic promise (Gen 12:1–3) and in obedience to Jesus' commission of his followers to go into all the world to make disciples (Matt 28:18–20). Nothing could hinder the progress of the gospel from Jerusalem to Rome, the empire's capital (Acts 28:31).

From the time of Paul's conversion on the road to Damascus, the gospel became the singular focus of his life. In a major paradigm shift, Paul realized that if Jesus was the crucified and exalted Messiah, the divine curse fell on Jesus for the sake of others "in order that the blessing given to Abraham might come to the Gentiles through Christ Jesus" (Gal 3:13–14). God entrusted Paul with God's "mystery," the end-time revelation that now Jews and Gentiles alike are gathered together into one body, the church (Rom 16:25–26; Eph 2:1—3:13; Col 1:25–27). While Paul's ministry was directed primarily to Gentiles, he taught that a future remains for ethnic Israel in God's redemptive purposes (Rom 9–11).

The Rest of the New Testament, Including Revelation

Mission is less prominent in the General Letters, or at least the missionary connection is generally less direct. Documents such as Jude, 2 Peter, and 1–3 John call believers to defend against heresy the "faith that was once for all entrusted to God's holy people" (Jude 3). The author of Hebrews contends that now that Jesus has come, there is no turning back to the OT system. This has important implications for the Jews who can no longer trust in the sacrificial system but must believe in Jesus' vicarious once-for-all sacrifice on the cross in order to be saved. Peter describes believers as exiles and foreigners in this world (1 Pet 1:1,17; 2:11) and calls them to view suffering from an eternal perspective (1 Pet 1:3–6). This addresses the dimension of mission as the church's witness to the truth by living God-honoring, spiritually set-apart lives in the midst of the unbelieving world and, if necessary, witness by martyrdom.

The book of Revelation, finally, shows people from every nation gathered in heaven to worship God and Jesus, "the Lamb" (Rev 4:10–11; 5:6–9). This fulfills God's covenants with Abraham and David and completes the journey from the original creation to the new creation, where redeemed humanity will live forever in the presence of God and where, in keeping with the prophetic vision, he will be their God and they will be his people (Rev 21:3).

SHALOM

Timothy Keller

Jesus says, "Peace I leave with you; my peace I give you. I do not give to you as the world gives. Do not let your hearts be troubled and do not be afraid" (John 14:27). When Jesus meets his disciples after the resurrection, he continually says to them, "Peace" (John 20:19,21,26). Under these circumstances it is obvious that the term "peace" is extraordinarily full of meaning. What is this peace Jesus gives us? In order to understand Jesus' words, we must reflect on the many facets of the crucial Hebrew term *shalom*, which lies behind the English word "peace."

Shalom is one of the key words and images for salvation in the Bible. The Hebrew word refers most commonly to a person being uninjured and safe, whole and sound. In the NT, *shalom* is revealed as the reconciliation of all things to God through the work of Christ: "God was pleased ... through [Christ] to reconcile to himself all things, whether things on earth or things in heaven, by making peace through [Christ's] blood, shed on the cross" (Col 1:19–20). *Shalom* experienced is multidimensional, complete well-being — physical, psychological, social, and spiritual; it flows from all of one's relationships being put right — with God, with(in) oneself, and with others.

SHALOM WITH GOD

Most fundamentally, *shalom* means reconciliation with God. God can give us peace with himself or remove it (Ps 85:8; Jer 16:5). Because Phinehas turned away God's wrath on sin, he and his family are given a "covenant of [*shalom*]" with God (Num 25:12). One of the offerings under the Mosaic covenant is the *shelamim* offering — the peace, or fellowship, offering — the only one of the Levitical sacrifices in which the offerer receives back some of the meal to eat. Sin disrupts *shalom*. When anything heals the rupture and closes the gap between us and God, there should be a celebration, a joyful meal in God's presence.

SHALOM WITH OTHERS

Shalom also means peace with others, peace between parties. It means the end of hostilities and war (Deut 20:12; Judg 21:13). The wise woman of Abel Beth Maakah maintained her city's *shalom*, its peacefulness, by averting a siege and war (2 Sam 20:14–22). But *shalom* does not mean only reconciliation between warring factions or nations (1 Kgs 5:12). It also refers to socially just relationships between individuals and classes. Jeremiah insists that unless there is an end to oppression, greed, and violence in social relationships, there can be no *shalom*, however much the false prophets say the word (Jer 6:1–9,14; cf. Jer 8:11).

SHALOM WITH(IN) ONESELF

Shalom consists of not only outward peacefulness — peace between parties — but also peace within. Those who trust in the Lord have inner security; therefore, they can sleep well (Ps 4:8). God gives "perfect peace" (or *shalom-shalom*) — i.e., profound psychological and emotional peace — to those who steadfastly set their minds on him (Isa 26:3). The result of righteousness before God is "peace; its effect will be quietness and confidence forever" (Isa 32:17).

THE PRINCE OF SHALOM: JESUS

Shalom Prophesied

Shalom becomes an especially prominent theme in the prophetic literature. The prophets explain the invasions and exile — the loss of *shalom* — as a curse on Israel for breaking the covenant and as punishment for their disobedience (Isa 48:18; Jer 14:13–16; Mic 3:4–5,9–12). But they also point into the future to a coming time of complete *shalom*, not only for Israel but also for the whole world (Isa 11:1–9; Zech 9:9–10). Only God can create *shalom* (Isa 45:7), and this gift will come through the work of the Messiah, the Prince of *shalom* (Isa 9:6–7). Therefore, *shalom* is perhaps the most basic characteristic of the future kingdom of God, a time when the Lord himself comes to heal all that is wrong with the world.

When the angels tell the shepherds about the birth of Christ, they call him the one who will at last bring peace on earth (Luke 2:14). Jesus is the Prince of *shalom* who will bring in God's kingdom of peace that the prophets foretold (Rom 14:17; 1 Cor 14:33). The gospel of Jesus is "the gospel of peace" (Eph 6:15; cf. Acts 10:36; Eph 2:17).

Shalom Accomplished

Jesus first of all reconciles us to God. He is the ultimate Phinehas who turns away the wrath of God and brings his family into a covenant of peace. But he does so by taking on himself the curse of sin so that all who are united to him by faith receive his blessing of peace (Gal 3:10–13). "The wicked are like the tossing sea, which cannot rest ... 'There is no peace ... for the wicked' " (Isa 57:20–21). But on the cross, God the Father treats Jesus as the wicked deserve to be treated (2 Cor 5:21). Jesus cries out as he loses his fellowship with the Father and experiences unimaginable inner agony (Matt 27:46). He experiences infinite pain so that we can know endless peace (John 14:27).

Shalom Experienced

God is reconciling *all things* to himself through Christ (Col 1:20), and although he has not yet put everything right (Rom 8:19–23), those who believe the gospel enter into and experience this reconciliation.

This peace is first of all peace *with* God through justification by faith (Rom 5:1–2). There was a barrier between God and humanity, but Jesus paid the debt and now there is peace. This peace cannot increase or decrease. Though in ourselves we are actually "ungodly," in Christ we are justified and accepted (Rom 4:5).

Jesus also brings us the peace *of* God—peace within. The peace of God garrisons our hearts against anxiety, difficulties, and sorrows (Phil 4:4–7). It is possible to have a peace so deep that we can be content in any circumstance, even in times of great difficulty (Phil 4:12–13). The peace of Christ is so closely related to joy (John 15:11; Rom 15:13) that we might say that joy is God's peace and reconciliation lived out. The God of peace sanctifies us, growing us into Christlike character and maturity (1 Thess 5:23; cf. Gal 5:22).

Finally, Jesus brings us peace with other human beings. Our peace with and from God gives us the resources to maintain unity and love with others through continual forgiveness and patience (Col 3:13–15). Christ *is* our peace, and by his death on the cross he removes even the high racial and cultural barriers that divide us (Eph 2:11–22).

PEOPLE OF SHALOM: CHRISTIANS

The concept of *shalom* can shape how believers think about their life in this world. They are here to be men and women of peace. What does that mean?

When all the parts of your body are rightly related to each other, you experience health and physical *shalom*. When you experience a season of mental well-being, it is because the things your emotions want are those of which your conscience and reason approve. Your inner faculties are rightly related to each other, and you experience psychological *shalom*—joy and fulfillment. When people share their resources with each other and work together so that shared public services work, the environment is safe and beautiful, the schools educate, the businesses flourish, and poverty and hunger are minimal, then that community is experiencing social *shalom*.

The great disaster of sin, however, means that there is precious little of these forms of *shalom* in the world, and even where it occurs for a while, it soon breaks down. Christians in their daily work and life in their neighborhoods can and should find a thousand ways to maintain or repair physical, psychological, and social/cultural *shalom*. How can we do that? Strengthening *shalom* means sacrificially giving your time, goods, power, and resources to all the various needs of your neighbors.

However, we know the ultimate solution to the world's loss of *shalom*. In the Garden of Eden, Adam and Eve walked with God and served him. All things were marked by *shalom*. Their bodies were completely healthy and their hearts were without sin. All their relationships were perfect because their relationship with God was perfect. All that ended, however, when they turned away from God, rejecting his rule and kingdom. If the fountain of all our problems is the loss of "spiritual *shalom*," i.e., a right relationship with God, then the most fundamental thing we can do about the misery of this world is to say to others,

> God was reconciling the world to himself in Christ, not counting people's sins against them. And he has committed to us the message of reconciliation. We are therefore Christ's ambassadors, as though God were making his appeal through us. We implore you on Christ's behalf: Be reconciled to God. God made him who had no sin to be sin for us, so that in him we might become the righteousness of God (2 Cor 5:19–21).

THE CONSUMMATION

Douglas J. Moo

"I am making everything new!" proclaims the one seated on the throne (Rev 21:5). The story of the Bible is the story of the way our sovereign and loving God is "making everything new." The sin of the first man, Adam, not only brought death to every human (Rom 5:12 – 21) but also subjected the entire creation to "frustration" and "bondage to decay" (Rom 8:20 – 21). God's grand reclamation project extends to every part of the universe that sin has damaged. The cross of Christ provides the basis for this universal "reconciliation" as God works to bring everything in creation back under his sovereign rule (Col 1:20). Human beings, the crown of God's creation, are the special objects of God's reconciling work in Christ. But the plan of God will result, in the end, in nothing less than "a new heaven and a new earth" (Rev 21:1).

OLD TESTAMENT PROMISE

God's plan to remedy the dire consequences of sin begins to take form with his promise to Abram (Gen 12:1 – 3). The promise is both particular and universal: Abram would become "a great nation," and "all peoples on earth" would be blessed through him. The story of how God fulfills this promise focuses on the particular. Through successive generations of Abraham's descendants, God forms "a great nation." That nation, Israel, is birthed through the exodus from Egypt, and God's giving of the law at Sinai provides direction and structure. Yet even as Israel stands poised to enter their new land, Moses hints that the people will fail to obey God's direction and be exiled from their land (Deut 28:15 – 68; 29:20 – 28; 30:15 – 18). Yet exile will not end Israel's story, for in his mercy God promises to restore his people to their land and to the blessing he originally promised (Deut 30:1 – 10). And so unfolds the sad story of Israel's persistent unfaithfulness and the amazing story of God's persistent faithfulness. Israel is finally exiled because of its sin, and God brings his people back from exile to their land again. Yet the return from exile falls far short of the glorious future that God promised Israel through the prophets (e.g., Isa 60). And so the OT story ends on the note of renewed hope for God to intervene in the future and fulfill his promises.

Those promises often focus on Israel's settling securely in their land and prospering (e.g., Ezek 34:11 – 31). But the universal dimensions of the original promise to Abraham are by no means forgotten. The blessings promised to Israel and mediated through Israel's ideal king (see Ps 72:17) would be extended to the Gentiles. Indeed, God's promise will ultimately encompass nothing less than a new heaven and new earth (Isa 65:17 – 25; 66:22 – 24).

NEW TESTAMENT FULFILLMENT

"For no matter how many promises God has made, they are 'Yes' in Christ" (2 Cor 1:20). Paul and the other early Christians rejoiced to live in the era when God had fulfilled so many of these promises. The "last days" that the prophets predicted had dawned with the coming of Christ and the pouring out of the Spirit (Acts 2:14 – 21; 1 Cor 10:11; Heb 1:2). In a typological and spiritual reenactment of the exodus, God had "redeemed" his people, liberating them from the ultimate enemy: sin and death (Rom 3:24; 1 Pet 1:18). But God's people are now defined not by ethnic origin but by faith in Christ, so believing Jews and Gentiles together enjoy the fulfillment of God's promises (Eph 2:11 – 18). And the new covenant people of God not only rejoice in promises fulfilled but also keenly anticipate promises yet to be fulfilled.

NT eschatology is therefore marked by a tension between the "already" of promises fulfilled and the "not yet" of promises yet to be fulfilled. Jesus' teaching about the kingdom reveals this tension: his power over Satan, revealed in his exorcisms, displays the kingdom's presence (Matt 12:28), but he instructs his disciples to pray, "Your kingdom come" (Matt 6:10; Luke 11:2). Likewise, while celebrating believers' "adoption to sonship," Paul claims that believers "groan" in the present, awaiting "our adoption to sonship, the redemption of our bodies" (Rom 8:15,23). This two-stage fulfillment (called "inaugurated eschatology") is a fundamental structure of NT theology and, by extension, biblical theology.

Therefore, as believers look back to and rest on the many promises already fulfilled in Christ's first coming to earth, so they also eagerly anticipate the complete fulfillment of all God's promises when Christ comes back again. The NT refers to Christ's second coming with many words, but especially prominent is the word *parousia* ("presence," "coming"). Jesus himself speaks of his *parousia* in the Olivet discourse (Matt 24:3,27,37,39). While some interpreters think that Jesus is referring to his "coming" to judge Jerusalem in AD 70, Jesus is probably referring to his "return" to gather his own people (Matt 24:31) and judge his enemies (Matt 25:31 – 46). Paul speaks of Jesus' *parousia* both as the "blessed hope" for God's people for which they long (Titus 2:13; cf. 2 Pet 3:12 – 13) and as the time God judges his enemies (2 Thess 1:5 – 10). This dual focus picks up the two sides of "the day of the Lord" as the prophets present it (e.g., Isa 13:6 – 13; 19:16 – 25). Paul hints that this "day" has already dawned (Rom 13:11 – 14), yet he focuses on the "day" associated with Christ's return in glory.

The NT typically presents the *parousia* as imminent

(1 Thess 4:15; Jas 5:7–8; 1 Pet 4:7). Since Christ's first coming inaugurated the "last days," the next item on God's agenda is consummating his redemptive plan. That consummation, associated with Christ's return, can take place at any time. God has determined the time of this final act in the drama of redemption, but no human — not even Jesus himself — knows "that day or hour" (Matt 24:36). Believers live in expectation of that day, "watching" for it by conforming their lives to Christ's image so that they can appear before him without shame (1 Thess 5:4–11; 1 John 2:28).

Since "flesh and blood cannot inherit the kingdom of God," believers must have their bodies "changed" when Christ returns to usher them into God's eternal kingdom (1 Cor 15:50–52). Believers who are living will be transformed and taken up to "meet the Lord in the air" (1 Thess 4:17), while believers who have died will have their bodies raised and transformed (1 Cor 15:52; 1 Thess 4:16). Indeed, all humans will participate in the final resurrection (John 5:28–30; Rev 20:5–6). Believers will be raised "imperishable" (1 Cor 15:52), destined for eternal fellowship with God in the new Jerusalem (Rev 21:2—22:5). Unbelievers, on the other hand, will rise only "to be condemned" (John 5:29; cf. Rev 20:5–6,11–15). The unbelieving dead are consigned to "hell" (*gehenna*), where they experience unending punishment (Matt 25:46) or "destruction" (e.g., Phil 3:19; 2 Thess 1:9), which refers not to "annihilation" but to "undoing."

Many Christians believe that the resurrection of believers and the resurrection of unbelievers will be separated by a period of time — the "thousand years" or "millennium" (Rev 20:1–6) — during which Christians reign with Christ on this earth. This "premillennial" view (Christ returns *before* the millennium) is countered by two other views, "postmillennialism" and "amillennialism," each of which holds (in different forms) that the "thousand years" refers to all or part of the church age. Christians also debate the more minor issue of the relationship of a final period of intense "tribulation" (predicted in some NT passages) to the rapture (see 1 Thess 4:13–18 and notes). Whether believers are physically removed from the earth before the rapture begins ("pretribulationism"), are physically removed from the earth before the infliction of God's wrath during the tribulation (the "pre-wrath" view), or are left on earth during these events ("posttribulationism"), the NT is clear that (1) believers, by whatever means, will be spared God's wrath (1 Thess 5:9) and (2) believers will experience significant "tribulation" in this life (e.g., Acts 14:22).

The NT focuses on the fate of humans at the consummation. But the consummation ultimately includes more than humans. The OT often pictures the consummation in terms of the return of Israel to a prosperous and secure land. Some Christian interpreters think that the NT implicitly endorses this view of the future, suggesting that it will be during a millennial period after Christ's return when these promises to Israel will be fulfilled. While Rom 11:25–27 may, indeed, suggest a spiritual future for some ethnic Israelites, other NT texts (e.g., Rom 4:13) suggest that the OT promise of the land is "universalized," finding its consummation in "a new heaven and a new earth" (Rev 21:1). History ends, not with the annihilation of humans or the universe but with the eternal existence of humans in resurrected bodies and with believers joyfully inhabiting the new heaven and new earth (Rev 21:1) that Isaiah predicted (Isa 65:17; 66:22). This new heaven and new earth, since it is the place where God himself dwells (Rev 21:3), is appropriately also simply "heaven" (Col 1:5). The new heaven and new earth is "new" in the sense that it involves a thorough renovation of the present universe (2 Pet 3:10–12), a renovation that frees the very universe to be what God first intended it to be (Rom 8:19–22). Nevertheless, by climaxing his prophecy with the image of a city, the "new Jerusalem," John implies that this renovated universe is particularly focused on the intimate eternal fellowship of God with his people (Rev 21:1–4).

CONCORDANCE

CONCORDANCE

The NIV Concordance, created by John R. Kohlenberger III, has been developed specifically for use with the New International Version (NIV). Like all concordances, it is a special index that contains an alphabetical listing of words used in the Bible text.

This concordance contains 4,795 word entries, with nearly 36,000 Scripture references. Each word entry is followed by significant Scripture references in which that particular word is found, as well as by a brief excerpt from the surrounding context. In the context, the entry word is abbreviated by its first letter in bold print. Other forms of the entry word and related words indexed in this concordance are in parentheses.

This concordance also contains 339 biographical entries for significant people in the Bible. The descriptive phrases replace the brief context surrounding each occurrence of the name. In those instances where more than one Bible character has the same name, that name is placed under one block entry, and each person is given a number (1), (2), etc.

Two entry words are marked with a dagger (†). LORD† and LORD'S† list occurrences of the proper name of God, *Yahweh*, spelled "LORD" and "LORD's" in the NIV. These entries are distinguished from LORD and LORD's, which list occurrences of the title "Lord" and "Lord's."

There are 1,312 entries that list every appearance of that word in the NIV. When this occurs, the entry is marked with an asterisk (*).

This concordance is a valuable tool for Bible study. While one of its key purposes is to help the reader find forgotten references to familiar verses, it can also be used to do word studies and to locate and trace biblical themes. Whenever you find a significant context, be sure to read at least the whole verse in the NIV to discover its fuller meaning in its larger context.

AARON

Genealogy of (Ex 6:16–20; Jos 21:4, 10; 1Ch 6:3–15).

Priesthood of (Ex 28:1; Nu 17; Heb 5:1 4; 7), garments (Ex 28; 39), consecration (Ex 29), ordination (Lev 8).

Spokesman for Moses (Ex 4:14–16, 27–31; 7:1–2). Supported Moses' hands in battle (Ex 17:8–13). Built golden calf (Ex 32; Dt 9:20). Talked against Moses (Nu 12). Priesthood opposed (Nu 16); staff budded (Nu 17). Forbidden to enter land (Nu 20:1–12). Death (Nu 20:22–29; 33:38–39).

ABADDON*

Rev 9: 11 whose name in Hebrew is **A**

ABANDON (ABANDONED)

Dt 4: 31 he will not **a** or destroy you
1Ki 6: 13 and will not **a** my people Israel."
Ne 9: 19 compassion you did not **a** them
9: 31 not put an end to them or **a** them,
Ps 16: 10 because you will not **a** me
Ac 2: 27 because you will not **a** me
1Ti 4: 1 in later times some will **a** the faith

ABANDONED (ABANDON)

Ge 24: 27 who has not **a** his kindness
2Co 4: 9 persecuted, but not **a**;

ABBA*

Mk 14: 36 "**A**, Father," he said,
Ro 8: 15 by him we cry, "**A**, Father."
Gal 4: 6 the Spirit who calls out, "**A**,

ABEDNEGO

Deported to Babylon with Daniel (Da 1:1–6). Name changed from Azariah (Da 1:7). Refused defilement by food (Da 1:8–20). Refused idol worship (Da 3:1–12); saved from furnace (Da 3:13–30).

ABEL

Second son of Adam (Ge 4:2). Offered proper sacrifice (Ge 4:4; Heb 11:4). Murdered by Cain (Ge 4:8; Mt 23:35; Lk 11:51; 1Jn 3:12).

ABHOR

Lev 26: 30 of your idols, and I will **a** you.
Ps 26: 5 I **a** the assembly of evildoers
139: 21 **a** those who are in rebellion against
Am 6: 8 "I **a** the pride of Jacob and detest
Ro 2: 22 You who **a** idols, do you rob

ABIATHAR

High priest in days of Saul and David (1Sa 22; 2Sa 15; 1Ki 1–2; Mk 2:26). Escaped Saul's slaughter of priests (1Sa 22:18–23). Supported David in Absalom's revolt (2Sa 15:24–29). Supported Adonijah (1Ki 1:7–42); deposed by Solomon (1Ki 2:22–35; cf. 1Sa 2:31–35).

ABIGAIL

1. Sister of David (1Ch 2:16–17).

2. Wife of Nabal (1Sa 25:30); pled for his life with David (1Sa 25:14–35). Became David's wife after Nabal's death (1Sa 25:36–42); bore him Kileab (2Sa 3:3) also known as Daniel (1Ch 3:1).

ABIHU

Son of Aaron (Ex 6:23; 24:1, 9); killed for offering unauthorized fire (Lev 10; Nu 3:2–4; 1Ch 24:1–2).

ABIJAH

1. Second son of Samuel (1Ch 6:28); a corrupt judge (1Sa 8:1–5).

2. An Aaronic priest (1Ch 24:10; Lk 1:5).

3. Son of Jeroboam I of Israel; died as prophesied by Ahijah (1Ki 14:1–18).

4. Son of Rehoboam; king of Judah who fought Jeroboam I attempting to reunite the kingdom (1Ki 14:31—15:8; 2Ch 12:16—14:1; Mt 1:7).

ABILITY (ABLE)

Ex 35: 34 tribe of Dan, the **a** to teach others.
Dt 8: 18 for it is he who gives you the **a**
Ezr 2: 69 According to their **a** they gave
Mt 25: 15 one bag, each according to his **a**.
2Co 1: 8 far beyond our **a** to endure,
8: 3 were able, and even beyond their **a**.

ABIMELEK

1. King of Gerar who took Abraham's wife Sarah, believing her to be his sister (Ge 20). Later made a covenant with Abraham (Ge 21:22–33).

2. King of Gerar who took Isaac's wife Rebekah, believing her to be his sister (Ge 26:1–11). Later made a covenant with Isaac (Ge 26:12–31).

3. Son of Gideon (Jdg 8:31). Attempted to make himself king (Jdg 9).

ABISHAG*

Shunammite virgin; attendant of David in his old age (1Ki 1:1–15; 2:17–22).

ABISHAI

Son of Zeruiah, David's sister (1Sa 26:6; 1Ch 2:16). One of David's chief warriors (1Ch 11:15–21): against Edom (1Ch 18:12–13), Ammon (2Sa 10), Absalom (2Sa 18), Sheba (2Sa 20). Wanted to kill Saul (1Sa 26), killed Abner (2Sa 2:18–27; 3:22–39), wanted to kill Shimei (2Sa 16:5–13; 19:16–23).

ABLE (ABILITY ENABLE ENABLED ENABLES ENABLING)

Nu 14: 16 'The LORD was not **a** to bring
1Ch 29: 14 that we should be **a** to give as
2Ch 2: 6 who is **a** to build a temple for him,
Pr 17: 16 they are not **a** to understand it?
Eze 7: 19 gold will not be **a** to deliver them
Da 3: 17 the God we serve is **a** to deliver us
4: 37 walk in pride he is **a** to humble.
Mt 9: 28 you believe that I am **a** to do this?"
Lk 13: 24 try to enter and will not be **a** to.
14: 30 to build and wasn't **a** to finish.'
21: 15 your adversaries will be **a** to resist
21: 36 pray that you may be **a** to escape
21: 36 you may be **a** to stand before
Ac 5: 39 will not be **a** to stop these men;
11: 29 as each one was **a**,
Ro 8: 39 will be **a** to separate us
14: 4 the Lord is **a** to make them stand.
16: 25 to him who is **a** to establish you
2Co 9: 8 God is **a** to bless you abundantly,
Eph 3: 20 him who is **a** to do immeasurably
6: 13 may be **a** to stand your ground,
1Ti 3: 2 respectable, hospitable, **a** to teach,
2Ti 1: 12 that he is **a** to guard what I have
2: 24 be kind to everyone, **a** to teach,
3: 15 which are **a** to make you wise
Heb 2: 18 he is **a** to help those who are being
7: 25 he is **a** to save completely
Jas 3: 2 **a** to keep their whole body in check.
Jude : 24 To him who is **a** to keep you
Rev 5: 5 He is **a** to open the scroll and its

ABNER

Cousin of Saul and commander of his army (1Sa 14:50; 17:55–57; 26). Made Ish-Bosheth king after Saul (2Sa 2:8–10), but later defected to David (2Sa 3:6–21). Killed Asahel (2Sa 2:18–32), for which he was killed by Joab and Abishai (2Sa 3:22–39).

ABOLISH* (ABOLISHED)
Da 11: 31 and will **a** the daily sacrifice.
Hos 2: 18 and battle I will **a** from the land,
Mt 5: 17 think that I have come to **a** the Law
5: 17 I have not come to **a** them

ABOLISHED* (ABOLISH)
Da 12: 11 time that the daily sacrifice is **a**
Gal 5: 11 the offense of the cross has been **a**.

ABOMINATION*
Da 9: 27 set up an **a** that causes desolation,
11: 31 set up the **a** that causes desolation.
12: 11 the **a** that causes desolation is set
Mt 24: 15 in the holy place 'the **a** that causes
Mk 13: 14 "When you see 'the **a** that causes

ABOUND (ABOUNDING ABOUNDS)
2Co 9: 8 you will **a** in every good work.
Php 1: 9 your love may **a** more and more

ABOUNDING* (ABOUND)
Ex 34: 6 to anger, **a** in love and faithfulness,
Nu 14: 18 **a** in love and forgiving sin
Dt 33: 23 "Naphtali is **a** with the favor
Ne 9: 17 slow to anger and **a** in love.
Ps 86: 5 **a** in love to all who call to you.
86: 15 to anger, **a** in love and faithfulness.
103: 8 gracious, slow to anger, **a** in love.
Joel 2: 13 slow to anger and **a** in love, and he
Jnh 4: 2 slow to anger and **a** in love, a God

ABOUNDS (ABOUND)
2Co 1: 5 also our comfort **a** through Christ.

ABRAHAM

Abram, son of Terah (Ge 11:26–27), husband of Sarah (Ge 11:29).

Covenant relation with the LORD (Ge 12:1–3; 13:14–17; 15; 17; 22:15–18; Ex 2:24; Ne 9:8; Ps 105; Mic 7:20; Lk 1:68–75; Ro 4; Heb 6:13–15).

Called from Ur, via Harran, to Canaan (Ge 12:1; Ac 7:2–4; Heb 11:8–10). Moved to Egypt, nearly lost Sarah to Pharoah (Ge 12:10–20). Divided the land with Lot; settled in Hebron (Ge 13). Saved Lot from four kings (Ge 14:1–16); blessed by Melchizedek (Ge 14:17–20; Heb 7:1–20). Declared righteous by faith (Ge 15:6; Ro 4:3; Gal 3:6–9). Fathered Ishmael by Hagar (Ge 16).

Name changed from Abram (Ge 17:5; Ne 9:7). Circumcised (Ge 17; Ro 4:9–12). Entertained three visitors (Ge 18); promised a son by Sarah (Ge 18:9–15; 17:16). Questioned destruction of Sodom and Gomorrah (Ge 18:16–33). Moved to Gerar; nearly lost Sarah to Abimelek (Ge 20). Fathered Isaac by Sarah (Ge 21:1–7; Ac 7:8; Heb 11:11–12); sent away Hagar and Ishmael (Ge 21:8–21; Gal 4:22–30). Covenant with Abimelek (Ge 21:22–32). Tested by offering Isaac (Ge 22; Heb 11:17–19; Jas 2:21–24). Sarah died; bought field of Ephron for burial (Ge 23). Secured wife for Isaac (Ge 24). Fathered children by Keturah (Ge 25:1–6; 1Ch 1:32–33). Death (Ge 25:7–11).

Called servant of God (Ge 26:24), friend of God (2Ch 20:7; Isa 41:8; Jas 2:23), prophet (Ge 20:7), father of Israel (Ex 3:15; Isa 51:2; Mt 3:9; Jn 8:39–58).

ABSALOM

Son of David by Maakah (2Sa 3:3; 1Ch 3:2). Killed Amnon for rape of his sister Tamar; banished by David (2Sa 13). Returned to Jerusalem; received by David (2Sa 14). Rebelled against David; siezed kingdom (2Sa 15–17). Killed (2Sa 18).

ABSENT
Col 2: 5 For though I am **a** from you

ABSOLUTE*
1Ti 5: 2 women as sisters, with **a** purity.

ABSTAIN (ABSTAINS)
Ex 19: 15 **A** from sexual relations."
Nu 6: 3 they must **a** from wine and other
Ac 15: 20 them to **a** from food polluted
1Pe 2: 11 and exiles, to **a** from sinful desires,

ABSTAINS* (ABSTAIN)
Ro 14: 6 and whoever **a** does so to the Lord

ABUNDANCE (ABUNDANT)
Ge 41: 29 great **a** are coming throughout
Job 36: 31 the nations and provides food in **a**.
Ps 66: 12 but you brought us to a place of **a**.
Ecc 5: 12 rich, their **a** permits them no sleep.
Isa 66: 11 and delight in her overflowing **a**."
Jer 2: 22 and use an **a** of cleansing powder,
Mt 13: 12 more, and they will have an **a**.
25: 29 more, and they will have an **a**.
Lk 12: 15 not consist in an **a** of possessions."
1Pe 1: 2 Grace and peace be yours in **a**.
2Pe 1: 2 yours in **a** through the knowledge
Jude : 2 peace and love be yours in **a**.

ABUNDANT (ABUNDANCE)
Dt 28: 11 will grant you **a** prosperity—
32: 2 grass, like **a** rain on tender plants.
Job 36: 28 and **a** showers fall on mankind.
Ps 68: 9 You gave **a** showers, O God;
78: 15 gave them water as **a** as the seas;
132: 15 I will bless her with **a** provisions;
145: 7 They celebrate your **a** goodness
Pr 12: 11 work their land will have **a** food,
28: 19 work their land will have **a** food,
Jer 33: 9 will tremble at the **a** prosperity
Ro 5: 17 who receive God's **a** provision

ABUSE (ABUSIVE)
2Pe 2: 10 afraid to heap **a** on celestial beings;
2: 11 do not heap **a** on such beings

ABUSIVE (ABUSE)
2Ti 3: 2 proud, **a**, disobedient to their

ABYSS*
Lk 8: 31 not to order them to go into the **A**.
Rev 9: 1 given the key to the shaft of the **A**.
9: 2 he opened the **A**, smoke rose
9: 2 darkened by the smoke from the **A**.
9: 11 king over them the angel of the **A**,
11: 7 up from the **A** will attack them,
17: 8 will come up out of the **A** and go
20: 1 having the key to the **A** and
20: 3 He threw him into the **A**,

ACCEPT (ACCEPTABLE ACCEPTANCE ACCEPTED ACCEPTS)
Ex 23: 8 not **a** a bribe, for a bribe blinds
Dt 16: 19 Do not **a** a bribe, for a bribe blinds
Job 42: 8 and I will **a** his prayer and not deal
Pr 10: 8 The wise in heart **a** commands,
19: 20 Listen to advice and **a** discipline,
Ro 15: 7 **A** one another, then, just as Christ
Jas 1: 21 humbly **a** the word planted in you,

ACCEPTABLE (ACCEPT)
Pr 21: 3 just is more **a** to the LORD than

ACCEPTANCE* (ACCEPT)
Ro 11: 15 what will their **a** be but life
1Ti 1: 15 saying that deserves full **a**:
4: 9 saying that deserves full **a**.

ACCEPTED (ACCEPT)
Ge 4: 7 do what is right, will you not be **a**?
Job 42: 9 and the LORD **a** Job's prayer.
Lk 4: 24 "no prophet is **a** in his hometown.
Gal 1: 9 you a gospel other than what you **a**,

ACCEPTS (ACCEPT)
Ps 6: 9 the LORD **a** my prayer.
Jn 13: 20 whoever **a** me **a** the one who sent

ACCESS*
Est 1: 14 who had special **a** to the king
Ro 5: 2 through whom we have gained **a**
Eph 2: 18 through him we both have **a**

ACCOMPANIED (ACCOMPANY)
1Co 10: 4 from the spiritual rock that **a** them,
Jas 2: 17 if it is not **a** by action, is dead.

ACCOMPANIES (ACCOMPANY)
2Co 9: 13 obedience that **a** your confession

ACCOMPANY (ACCOMPANIED ACCOMPANIES)
Dt 28: 2 **a** you if you obey the LORD your
Mk 16: 17 *signs will **a** those who believe:*

ACCOMPLISH
Ecc 2: 2 And what does pleasure **a**?"
Isa 44: 28 and what will **a** all that I please;
55: 11 but will **a** what I desire and achieve

ACCORD
Nu 24: 13 not do anything of my own **a**,
Jn 10: 18 me, but I lay it down of my own **a**.

ACCOUNT (ACCOUNTABLE)
Ge 2: 4 This is the **a** of the heavens
5: 1 This is the written **a** of Adam's
6: 9 This is the **a** of Noah and his
10: 1 This is the **a** of Shem,
11: 10 This is the **a** of Shem's family line.
11: 27 This is the **a** of Terah's family line.
25: 12 This is the **a** of the family line
25: 19 This is the **a** of the family line
36: 1 This is the **a** of the family line
36: 9 This is the **a** of the family line
37: 2 This is the **a** of Jacob's family line.
Mt 12: 36 will have to give **a** on the day
Lk 16: 2 Give an **a** of your management,
Ro 14: 12 of us will give an **a** of ourselves
Heb 4: 13 of him to whom we must give **a**.

ACCOUNTABLE* (ACCOUNT)
Eze 3: 18 I will hold you **a** for their blood.
3: 20 I will hold you **a** for their blood.
33: 6 I will hold the watchman **a** for
33: 8 I will hold you **a** for their blood.
34: 10 and will hold them **a** for my flock.
Da 6: 2 The satraps were made **a** to them
Jnh 1: 14 Do not hold us **a** for killing
Ro 3: 19 and the whole world held **a** to God.

ACCURATE
Dt 25: 15 You must have **a** and honest
Pr 11: 1 but **a** weights find favor with him.

ACCURSED (CURSE)
2Pe 2: 14 are experts in greed—an **a** brood!

ACCUSATION (ACCUSE)
1Ti 5: 19 not entertain an **a** against an elder

ACCUSE (ACCUSATION ACCUSER ACCUSES ACCUSING)
Pr 3: 30 Do not **a** anyone for no reason—
Lk 3: 14 money and don't **a** people falsely—

ACCUSER* (ACCUSE)
Job 31: 35 let my **a** put his indictment
Ps 109: 6 let an **a** stand at his right hand.
Isa 50: 8 Who is my **a**? Let him confront
Jn 5: 45 Your **a** is Moses, on whom your
Rev 12: 10 the **a** of our brothers and sisters,

ACCUSES* (ACCUSE)
Job 40: 2 Let him who **a** God answer him!"
Isa 54: 17 will refute every tongue that **a** you.
Rev 12: 10 who **a** them before our God day

ACCUSING (ACCUSE)
Ro 2: 15 their thoughts sometimes **a** them

ACHAN*

Sin at Jericho caused defeat at Ai; stoned (Jos 7; 22:20; 1Ch 2:7 ["Achar"]).

ACHE*
Pr 14: 13 Even in laughter the heart may **a**,

ACHIEVE
Ps 45: 4 your right hand **a** awesome deeds.
Isa 55: 11 **a** the purpose for which I sent it.

ACHISH

King of Gath before whom David feigned insanity (1Sa 21:10–15). Later "ally" of David (2Sa 27–29).

ACKNOWLEDGE (ACKNOWLEDGED ACKNOWLEDGES)
Jer 3: 13 Only **a** your guilt—
Hos 6: 3 Let us **a** the LORD; let us press
Mt 10: 32 also **a** before my Father in heaven.
Lk 12: 8 also **a** before the angels of God.
Jn 12: 42 they would not openly **a** their faith
Ro 14: 11 every tongue will **a** God.'"
Php 2: 11 every tongue **a** that Jesus Christ is
1Th 5: 12 **a** those who work hard among you,
Heb 3: 1 whom we **a** as our apostle and high
1Jn 4: 3 spirit that does not **a** Jesus is not

ACKNOWLEDGED (ACKNOWLEDGE)
Lk 7: 29 words, **a** that God's way was right,

ACKNOWLEDGES* (ACKNOWLEDGE)
Ps 91: 14 will protect him, for he **a** my name.
Mt 10: 32 "Whoever **a** me before others,
Lk 12: 8 you, whoever publicly **a** me before

1Jn 2: 23 whoever **a** the Son has the Father
4: 2 Every spirit that **a** that Jesus Christ
4: 15 If anyone **a** that Jesus is the Son

ACQUIRES*
Pr 18: 15 of the discerning **a** knowledge,

ACQUIT (ACQUITTING)
Ex 23: 7 to death, for I will not **a** the guilty.

ACQUITTING* (ACQUIT)
Dt 25: 1 **a** the innocent and condemning
Pr 17: 15 **A** the guilty and condemning

ACT (ACTION ACTIONS ACTIVE ACTIVITY ACTS)
1Ki 2: 2 "So be strong, **a** like a man,
Ps 106: 3 Blessed are those who **a** justly,
119:126 It is time for you to **a**, LORD;

ACTION (ACT)
2Co 9: 2 has stirred most of them to **a**,
Jas 2: 17 if it is not accompanied by **a**,

ACTIONS (ACT)
Gal 6: 4 Each one should test their own **a**.
Titus 1: 16 God, but by their **a** they deny him.

ACTIVE* (ACT)
Heb 4: 12 For the word of God is alive and **a**.

ACTIVITY (ACT)
Ecc 3: 1 for every **a** under the heavens:
3: 17 for there will be a time for every **a**,

ACTS (ACT)
1Ch 16: 9 tell of all his wonderful **a**.
Ps 40: 9 I proclaim your saving **a** in the
71: 15 of your saving **a** all day long—
71: 16 come and proclaim your mighty **a**,
71: 24 tell of your righteous **a** all day long,
105: 2 tell of all his wonderful **a**.
106: 2 Who can proclaim the mighty **a**
145: 4 they tell of your mighty **a**.
145: 12 people may know of your mighty **a**
150: 2 Praise him for his **a** of power;
Isa 64: 6 all our righteous **a** are like filthy

ADAM
1. First man (Ge 1:26—2:23; Ro 5:14, 45; 1Ti 2:13). Sin of (Ge 3; Hos 6:7; Ro 5:12–21). Children of (Ge 4:1—5:5). Death of (Ge 5:5; Ro 5:12–21; 1Co 15:22).
2. City (Jos 3:16).

ADD (ADDED)
Dt 4: 2 Do not **a** to what I command you
12: 32 do not **a** to it or take away from it.
Pr 1: 5 wise listen and **a** to their learning,
9: 9 and they will **a** to their learning.
30: 6 Do not **a** to his words, or he will
Mt 6: 27 you by worrying **a** a single hour
Lk 12: 25 by worrying can **a** a single hour
Rev 22: 18 them, God will **a** to that person

ADDED (ADD)
Ecc 3: 14 nothing can be **a** to it and nothing
Ac 2: 47 the Lord **a** to their number daily
Gal 3: 19 It was **a** because of transgressions

ADDICTED*
Titus 2: 3 to be slanderers or **a** to much wine,

ADMINISTRATION*
Eph 3: 2 heard about the **a** of God's grace
3: 9 to everyone the **a** of this mystery,

ADMIRABLE*
Php 4: 8 whatever is lovely, whatever is **a**—

ADMONISH* (ADMONISHING)
Col 3: 16 and **a** one another with all wisdom
1Th 5: 12 for you in the Lord and who **a** you.

ADMONISHING* (ADMONISH)
Col 1: 28 **a** and teaching everyone with all

ADONIJAH
1. Son of David by Haggith (2Sa 3:4; 1Ch 3:2). Attempted to be king after David; killed by Solomon's order (1Ki 1–2).
2. Levite; teacher of the Law (2Ch 17:8).

ADOPTION*
Gal 4: 5 that we might receive **a** to sonship.
Eph 1: 5 he predestined us for **a** to sonship
Ro 8: 15 brought about your **a** to sonship.
8: 23 wait eagerly for our **a** to sonship,
9: 4 Theirs is the **a** to sonship;

ADORE*
SS 1: 4 How right they are to **a** you!

ADORN (ADORNMENT ADORNS)
1Pe 3: 5 hope in God used to **a** themselves.

ADORNMENT* (ADORN)
1Pe 3: 3 should not come from outward **a**,

ADORNS* (ADORN)
Ps 93: 5 holiness **a** your house for endless
Pr 15: 2 tongue of the wise **a** knowledge,
Isa 61: 10 as a bridegroom **a** his head like
61: 10 as a bride **a** herself with her jewels.

ADULTERER* (ADULTERY)
Lev 20: 10 both the **a** and the adulteress are
Job 24: 15 The eye of the **a** watches for dusk;
Heb 13: 4 for God will judge the **a** and all

ADULTERERS (ADULTERY)
1Co 6: 9 nor idolaters nor **a** nor men who

ADULTERESS (ADULTERY)
Hos 3: 1 loved by another man and is an **a**.

ADULTERIES (ADULTERY)
Jer 3: 8 sent her away because of all her **a**.

ADULTEROUS (ADULTERY)
Mk 8: 38 and my words in this **a** and sinful
Jas 4: 4 You **a** people, don't you know

ADULTERY (ADULTERER ADULTERERS ADULTERESS ADULTERIES ADULTEROUS)
Ex 20: 14 "You shall not commit **a**.
Dt 5: 18 "You shall not commit **a**.
Mt 5: 27 was said, 'You shall not commit **a**.'
5: 28 lustfully has already committed **a**
5: 32 makes her the victim of **a**,
5: 32 a divorced woman commits **a**.
15: 19 murder, **a**, sexual immorality, theft,
19: 9 another woman commits **a**."
19: 18 you shall not commit **a**, you shall
Mk 10: 11 woman commits **a** against her.
10: 12 another man, she commits **a**."
10: 19 you shall not commit **a**, you shall
Lk 16: 18 marries another woman commits **a**,
18: 20 'You shall not commit **a**, you shall
Jn 8: 4 *a woman caught in the act of* ***a***.
Rev 18: 3 of the earth committed **a** with her,

ADULTS*
1Co 14: 20 infants, but in your thinking be **a**.

ADVANCE (ADVANCED)
Ps 18: 29 your help I can **a** against a troop;
Php 1: 12 has actually served to **a** the gospel.

ADVANCED (ADVANCE)
Job 32: 7 **a** years should teach wisdom.'

ADVANTAGE
Ex 22: 22 "Do not take **a** of the widow
Dt 24: 14 Do not take **a** of a hired worker
Ro 3: 1 What **a**, then, is there in being
2Co 11: 20 or exploits you or takes **a** of you
1Th 4: 6 should wrong or take **a** of a brother

ADVERSITY*
Pr 17: 17 a brother is born for a time of **a**.
Isa 30: 20 the Lord gives you the bread of **a**

ADVICE (ADVISERS)
1Ki 12: 8 Rehoboam rejected the **a** the elders
12: 14 he followed the **a** of the young men
2Ch 10: 8 Rehoboam rejected the **a** the elders
Pr 12: 5 but the **a** of the wicked is deceitful.
12: 15 to them, but the wise listen to **a**.
19: 20 Listen to **a** and accept discipline,
20: 18 Plans are established by seeking **a**;
27: 9 springs from their heartfelt **a**.

ADVISERS (ADVICE)
Pr 11: 14 but victory is won through many **a**.

ADVOCATE*
Job 16: 19 is in heaven; my **a** is on high.
Jn 14: 16 he will give you another **a** to help
14: 26 But the **A**, the Holy Spirit,
15: 26 "When the **A** comes, whom I will
16: 7 away, the **A** will not come to you;
1Jn 2: 1 sin, we have an **a** with the Father—

AFFECTION
2Pe 1: 7 mutual **a**; and to mutual **a**, love.

AFFLICTED (AFFLICTION)
Job 2: 7 **a** Job with painful sores
36: 6 alive but gives the **a** their rights.
Ps 9: 12 does not ignore the cries of the **a**.
9: 18 the hope of the **a** will never perish.
73: 14 All day long I have been **a**,
119: 67 Before I was **a** I went astray,
119: 71 me to be **a** so that I might learn
119: 75 that in faithfulness you have **a** me.
Isa 49: 13 have compassion on his **a** ones.
53: 4 by God, stricken by him, and **a**.
53: 7 He was oppressed and **a**, yet he did
Na 1: 12 Although I have **a** you, Judah,

AFFLICTION (AFFLICTED AFFLICTIONS)
Dt 16: 3 the bread of **a**, because you left
Ps 107: 41 he lifted the needy out of their **a**
Isa 30: 20 of adversity and the water of **a**,
48: 10 have tested you in the furnace of **a**.
La 3: 33 For he does not willingly bring **a**
Ro 12: 12 patient in **a**, faithful in prayer.

AFFLICTIONS (AFFLICTION)
Col 1: 24 still lacking in regard to Christ's **a**,

AFRAID (FEAR)
Ge 3: 10 and I was **a** because I was naked;
26: 24 Do not be **a**, for I am with you;
Ex 2: 14 Then Moses was **a** and thought,
3: 6 because he was **a** to look at God.
Dt 1: 21 Do not be **a**; do not be
1: 29 be terrified; do not be **a** of them.
20: 1 than yours, do not be **a** of them,
20: 3 Do not be fainthearted or **a**;
2Ki 25: 24 "Do not be **a** of the Babylonian
1Ch 13: 12 David was **a** of God that day
Ps 27: 1 of my life—of whom shall I be **a**?
56: 3 I am **a**, I put my trust in you.
56: 4 in God I trust and am not **a**.
Pr 3: 24 you lie down, you will not be **a**;
Isa 10: 24 Zion, do not be **a** of the Assyrians,
12: 2 I will trust and not be **a**.
44: 8 Do not tremble, do not be **a**.
Jer 1: 8 Do not be **a** of them, for I am
Mt 8: 26 of little faith, why are you so **a**?"
10: 28 Do not be **a** of those who kill
10: 28 be **a** of the One who can destroy
10: 31 So don't be **a**; you are worth more
Mk 5: 36 said, Jesus told him, "Don't be **a**;
Lk 9: 34 and they were **a** as they entered
Jn 14: 27 hearts be troubled and do not be **a**.
Ac 27: 24 and said, 'Do not be **a**, Paul.
Heb 13: 6 Lord is my helper; I will not be **a**.

AGAG (AGAGITE)
King of Amalekites not killed by Saul (1Sa 15).

AGAGITE (AGAG)
Est 8: 3 to the evil plan of Haman the **A**,

AGED (AGES)
Job 12: 12 Is not wisdom found among the **a**?
Pr 17: 6 children are a crown to the **a**,
Pr 30: 17 that scorns an **a** mother, will be

AGES (AGED)
Pr 8: 23 I was formed long **a** ago, at the
Ro 16: 25 the mystery hidden for long **a** past,
Eph 2: 7 in the coming **a** he might show
3: 9 for **a** past was kept hidden in God,
Col 1: 26 that has been kept hidden for **a**

AGONY
Lk 16: 24 because I am in **a** in this fire.'
Rev 16: 10 People gnawed their tongues in **a**

AGREE (AGREEMENT AGREES)
Mt 18: 19 earth **a** about anything they ask for,
Ro 7: 16 want to do, I **a** that the law is good.

AGREEMENT (AGREE)
2Co 6: 16 What **a** is there between the temple

AGREES* (AGREE)
Ac 7: 42 This **a** with what is written
1Co 4: 17 Jesus, which **a** with what I teach

AGRIPPA*
Descendant of Herod; king before whom Paul pled his case in Caesarea (Ac 25:13—26:32).

AHAB
1. Son of Omri; king of Israel (1Ki 16:28—22:40), husband of Jezebel (1Ki 16:31).

Promoted Baal worship (1Ki 16:31–33); opposed by Elijah (1Ki 17:1; 18; 21), a prophet (1Ki 20:35–43), Micaiah (1Ki 22:1–28). Defeated Ben-Hadad (1Ki 20). Killed for failing to kill Ben-Hadad and for murder of Naboth (1Ki 20:35—21:40).

2. A false prophet (Jer 29:21–22).

AHAZ

1. Son of Jotham; king of Judah, (2Ki 16; 2Ch 28). Idolatry of (2Ki 16:3–4, 10–18; 2Ch 28:1–4, 22–25). Defeated by Aram and Israel (2Ki 16:5–6; 2Ch 28:5–15). Sought help from Assyria rather than the LORD (2Ki 16:7–9; 2Ch 28:16–21; Isa 7).

2. Benjamite, descendant of Saul (1Ch 8:35–36).

AHAZIAH

1. Son of Ahab; king of Israel (1Ki 22:51–2Ki 1:18; 2Ch 20:35–37). Made an unsuccessful alliance with Jehoshaphat of Judah (2Ch 20:35–37). Died for seeking Baal rather than the LORD (2Ki 1).

2. Son of Jehoram; king of Judah (2Ki 8:25–29; 9:14–29), also called Jehoahaz (2Ch 21:17—22:9; 25:23). Killed by Jehu while visiting Joram (2Ki 9:14–29; 2Ch 22:1–9).

AHIJAH

1Sa 14: 18 Saul said to **A**, "Bring the ark
1Ki 14: 2 **A** the prophet is there—the one

AHIMELEK

1. Priest who helped David in his flight from Saul (1Sa 21–22).

2. One of David's warriors (1Sa 26:6).

AHITHOPHEL

One of David's counselors who sided with Absalom (2Sa 15:12, 31–37; 1Ch 27:33–34); committed suicide when his advice was ignored (2Sa 16:15—17:23).

AI

Jos 7: 4 they were routed by the men of **A**,
8: 28 So Joshua burned **A** and made it

AID

Isa 38: 14 Lord, come to my **a**!"
Php 4: 16 you sent me **a** more than once

AIM

1Co 7: 34 Her **a** is to be devoted to the Lord

AIR

1Co 9: 26 not fight like a boxer beating the **a**.
14: 9 You will just be speaking into the **a**.
Eph 2: 2 the ruler of the kingdom of the **a**,
1Th 4: 17 clouds to meet the Lord in the **a**.

ALABASTER*

Mt 26: 7 him with an **a** jar of very expensive
Mk 14: 3 a woman came with an **a** jar of
Lk 7: 37 so she came there with an **a** jar

ALARM (ALARMED)

2Co 7: 11 indignation, what **a**, what longing,

ALARMED (ALARM)

Mk 13: 7 and rumors of wars, do not be **a**.
2Th 2: 2 or **a** by the teaching allegedly

ALERT*

Jos 8: 4 far from it. All of you be on the **a**.
Ps 17: 11 me, with eyes **a**, to throw me
Isa 21: 7 on camels, let him be **a**, fully **a**."
Mk 13: 33 Be **a**! You do not know
Eph 6: 18 be **a** and always keep on praying
1Pe 1: 13 with minds that are **a** and fully
4: 7 Therefore be **a** and of sober mind
5: 8 Be **a** and of sober mind.

ALIENATED*

Job 19: 13 "He has **a** my family from me;
Gal 5: 4 the law have been **a** from Christ;
Col 1: 21 Once you were **a** from God

ALIVE (LIVE)

1Sa 2: 6 LORD brings death and makes **a**;
Lk 24: 23 vision of angels, who said he was **a**.
Ac 1: 3 convincing proofs that he was **a**.
Ro 6: 11 to sin but **a** to God in Christ Jesus.
1Co 15: 22 die, so in Christ all will be made **a**.
Eph 2: 5 made us **a** with Christ even
Heb 4: 12 the word of God is **a** and active.

ALMIGHTY (MIGHT)

Ge 17: 1 to him and said, "I am God **A**;
Ex 6: 3 to Isaac and to Jacob as God **A**,
Ru 1: 20 because the **A** has made my life
Job 11: 7 Can you probe the limits of the **A**?
33: 4 the breath of the **A** gives me life.
Ps 89: 8 Who is like you, LORD God **A**?
91: 1 will rest in the shadow of the **A**.
Isa 6: 3 "Holy, holy, holy is the LORD **A**;
45: 13 or reward, says the LORD **A**."
47: 4 the LORD **A** is his name—
48: 2 the LORD **A** is his name:
51: 15 the LORD **A** is his name.
54: 5 the LORD **A** is his name—
Am 5: 14 the LORD God **A** will be with you,
5: 15 the LORD God **A** will have mercy
Rev 4: 8 holy is the Lord God **A**,' who was,
19: 6 For our Lord God **A** reigns.

ALPHA*

Rev 1: 8 "I am the **A** and the Omega,"
21: 6 I am the **A** and the Omega,
22: 13 the **A** and the Omega, the First

ALTAR

Ge 8: 20 Noah built an **a** to the LORD and,
12: 7 So he built an **a** there
13: 18 There he built an **a** to the LORD.
22: 9 his son Isaac and laid him on the **a**,
26: 25 Isaac built an **a** there and called
35: 1 and build an **a** there to God,
Ex 17: 15 Moses built an **a** and called it
27: 1 "Build an **a** of acacia wood,
30: 1 "Make an **a** of acacia wood
37: 25 They made the **a** of incense
Dt 27: 5 Build there an **a** to the LORD your
Jos 8: 30 on Mount Ebal an **a** to the LORD,
22: 10 Manasseh built an imposing **a**
Jdg 6: 24 So Gideon built an **a** to the LORD
21: 4 the next day the people built an **a**
1Sa 7: 17 he built an **a** there to the LORD.
14: 35 Then Saul built an **a** to the LORD;
2Sa 24: 25 David built an **a** to the LORD
1Ki 12: 33 went up to the **a** to make offerings.
13: 2 he cried out against the **a**: "**A**, **a**!
16: 32 He set up an **a** for Baal
18: 30 he repaired the **a** of the LORD,
2Ki 16: 11 So Uriah the priest built an **a**
1Ch 21: 26 David built an **a** to the LORD
2Ch 4: 1 a bronze **a** twenty cubits long,
4: 19 the golden **a**; the tables
15: 8 He repaired the **a** of the LORD
32: 12 'You must worship before one **a**
33: 16 he restored the **a** of the LORD
Ezr 3: 2 began to build the **a** of the God
Isa 6: 6 had taken with tongs from the **a**.
Eze 40: 47 the **a** was in front of the temple.
Mt 5: 23 if you are offering your gift at the **a**
Ac 17: 23 worship, I even found an **a**
Heb 13: 10 We have an **a** from which those
Rev 6: 9 I saw under the **a** the souls of those

ALTER*

Ps 89: 34 or **a** what my lips have uttered.

ALWAYS

Dt 15: 11 There will **a** be poor people
Ps 16: 8 I keep my eyes **a** on the LORD.
51: 3 and my sin is **a** before me.
119: 98 Your commands are **a** with me
Pr 23: 7 person who is **a** thinking
Mt 26: 11 The poor you will **a** have with you, but you will not **a** have me.
28: 20 And surely I am with you **a**,
Mk 14: 7 The poor you will **a** have with you,
Jn 12: 8 You will **a** have the poor among
1Co 13: 7 It **a** protects, **a** trusts, **a** hopes,
Php 4: 4 Rejoice in the Lord **a**. I will say it
1Pe 3: 15 **A** be prepared to give an answer

AMALEKITES

Ex 17: 8 The **A** came and attacked
1Sa 15: 2 'I will punish the **A** for what they

AMASA

Nephew of David (1Ch 2:17). Commander of Absalom's forces (2Sa 17:24–27). Returned to David (2Sa 19:13). Killed by Joab (2Sa 20:4–13).

AMASSES*

Pr 28: 8 or profit from the poor **a** it for

AMAZED

Mt 7: 28 the crowds were **a** at his teaching,
Mk 6: 6 He was **a** at their lack of faith.
10: 24 The disciples were **a** at his words.
Ac 2: 7 Utterly **a**, they asked:
13: 12 for he was **a** at the teaching

AMAZIAH

1. Son of Joash; king of Judah (2Ki 14; 2Ch 25). Defeated Edom (2Ki 14:7; 2Ch 25:5–13); defeated by Israel for worshiping Edom's gods (2Ki 14:8–14; 2Ch 25:14–24).

2. Idolatrous priest who opposed Amos (Am 7:10–17).

AMBASSADOR* (AMBASSADORS)

Eph 6: 20 for which I am an **a** in chains.

AMBASSADORS (AMBASSADOR)

2Co 5: 20 We are therefore Christ's **a**,

AMBITION*

Ro 15: 20 It has always been my **a** to preach
2Co 12: 20 fits of rage, selfish **a**, slander,
Gal 5: 20 fits of rage, selfish **a**, dissensions,
Php 1: 17 preach Christ out of selfish **a**,
2: 3 Do nothing out of selfish **a** or vain
1Th 4: 11 make it your **a** to lead a quiet life:
Jas 3: 14 envy and selfish **a** in your hearts,
3: 16 where you have envy and selfish **a**,

AMENDS

Pr 14: 9 Fools mock at making **a** for sin,

AMNON

Firstborn of David (2Sa 3:2; 1Ch 3:1). Killed by Absalom for raping his sister Tamar (2Sa 13).

AMON

1. Son of Manasseh; king of Judah (2Ki 21:18–26; 1Ch 3:14; 2Ch 33:21–25).

2. Ruler of Samaria under Ahab (1Ki 22:26; 2Ch 18:25).

AMOS

1. Prophet from Tekoa (Am 1:1; 7:10–17).

2. Ancestor of Jesus (Lk 3:25).

ANAK (ANAKITES)

Nu 13: 28 even saw descendants of **A** there.

ANAKITES (ANAK)

Dt 1: 28 We even saw the **A** there.'"
2: 10 and numerous, and as tall as the **A**.
9: 2 "Who can stand up against the **A**?"

ANANIAS

1. Husband of Sapphira; died for lying to God (Ac 5:1–11).

2. Disciple who baptized Saul (Ac 9:10–19).

3. High priest at Paul's arrest (Ac 22:30—24:1).

ANCESTORS (ANCESTRY)

1Ki 19: 4 I am no better than my **a**."
Jn 4: 20 Our **a** worshiped on this mountain,
Heb 1: 1 to our **a** through the prophets
1Pe 1: 18 handed down to you from your **a**,

ANCESTRY (ANCESTORS)

Ro 9: 5 them is traced the human **a**

ANCHOR

Heb 6: 19 We have this hope as an **a**

ANCIENT

Da 7: 9 and the **A** of Days took his seat.
7: 13 He approached the **A** of Days
7: 22 until the **A** of Days came

ANDREW*

Apostle; brother of Simon Peter (Mt 4:18; 10:2; Mk 1:16–18, 29; 3:18; 13:3; Lk 6:14; Jn 1:35–44; 6:8–9; 12:22; Ac 1:13).

ANGEL (ANGELS ARCHANGEL)

Ge 16: 7 The **a** of the LORD found Hagar
22: 11 the **a** of the LORD called
Ex 23: 20 I am sending an **a** ahead of you
Nu 22: 23 the donkey saw the **a** of the LORD
Jdg 2: 1 The **a** of the LORD went
6: 22 I have seen the **a** of the LORD
13: 15 said to the **a** of the LORD,
2Sa 24: 16 When the **a** stretched out his hand

1Ki 19: 7 The **a** of the LORD came back
2Ki 19: 35 That night the **a** of the LORD went
Ps 34: 7 The **a** of the LORD encamps
Hos 12: 4 He struggled with the **a**
Mt 2: 13 **a** of the Lord appeared to Joseph
28: 2 for an **a** of the Lord came down
Lk 1: 26 God sent the **a** Gabriel to
2: 9 An **a** of the Lord appeared to them,
22: 43 An **a** from heaven appeared to him
Ac 6: 15 his face was like the face of an **a**.
12: 7 Suddenly an **a** of the Lord
2Co 11: 14 Satan himself masquerades as an **a**
Gal 1: 8 or an **a** from heaven should preach

ANGELS (ANGEL)
Ps 8: 5 made them a little lower than the **a**
91: 11 command his **a** concerning you
Mt 4: 6 command his **a** concerning you,
13: 39 of the age, and the harvesters are **a**.
13: 49 The **a** will come and separate
18: 10 that their **a** in heaven always see
25: 41 prepared for the devil and his **a**.
Lk 4: 10 command his **a** concerning you
20: 36 for they are like the **a**.
1Co 6: 3 you not know that we will judge **a**?
13: 1 in the tongues of men or of **a**,
Col 2: 18 the worship of **a** disqualify you.
Heb 1: 4 the **a** as the name he has inherited
1: 6 "Let all God's **a** worship him."
1: 7 "He makes his **a** spirits, and his
1: 14 Are not all **a** ministering spirits
2: 7 them a little lower than the **a**;
2: 9 who was made lower than the **a**
13: 2 hospitality to **a** without knowing it.
1Pe 1: 12 Even **a** long to look into these
2Pe 2: 4 if God did not spare **a** when they
Jude : 6 And the **a** who did not keep their

ANGER (ANGERED ANGRY)
Ex 15: 7 You unleashed your burning **a**;
22: 24 My **a** will be aroused, and I will kill
32: 10 that my **a** may burn against them
32: 11 "why should your **a** burn against
32: 12 Turn from your fierce **a**;
32: 19 his **a** burned and he threw
34: 6 slow to **a**, abounding in love
Lev 26: 28 my **a** I will be hostile toward you,
Nu 14: 18 'The LORD is slow to **a**,
25: 11 has turned my **a** away
32: 10 The LORD's **a** was aroused
32: 13 The LORD's **a** burned against
Dt 9: 19 I feared the **a** and wrath
29: 28 In furious **a** and in great wrath
Jdg 14: 19 Burning with **a**, he returned to his
2Sa 12: 5 burned with **a** against the man
2Ki 22: 13 Great is the LORD's **a** that burns
Ne 9: 17 slow to **a** and abounding in love.
Ps 30: 5 For his **a** lasts only a moment,
78: 38 Time after time he restrained his **a**
86: 15 slow to **a**, abounding in love
90: 7 We are consumed by your **a**
103: 8 slow to **a**, abounding in love.
Pr 15: 1 wrath, but a harsh word stirs up **a**.
30: 33 so stirring up **a** produces strife."
Jnh 4: 2 slow to **a** and abounding in love,
Eph 4: 26 "In your **a** do not sin": Do not let
Jas 1: 20 because human **a** does not produce

ANGERED (ANGER)
Pr 22: 24 do not associate with one easily **a**,
1Co 13: 5 it is not easily **a**, it keeps no record

ANGRY (ANGER)
Ps 2: 12 he will be **a** and your way will lead
95: 10 For forty years I was **a**
Pr 29: 22 An **a** person stirs up conflict,
Mt 5: 22 that anyone who is **a** with a brother
Jas 1: 19 to speak and slow to become **a**,

ANGUISH
Jer 4: 19 Oh, my **a**, my **a**! I writhe in pain.
Zep 1: 15 a day of distress and **a**, a day
Lk 21: 25 nations will be in **a** and perplexity
22: 44 And being in **a**, he prayed more
Ro 9: 2 and unceasing **a** in my heart.

ANIMALS
Ge 1: 24 the wild **a**, each according to its
7: 16 The **a** going in were male
Dt 14: 4 These are the **a** you may eat:
Job 12: 7 "But ask the **a**, and they will teach
Isa 43: 20 The wild **a** honor me, the jackals

ANNOUNCE (ANNOUNCED)
Mt 6: 2 needy, do not **a** it with trumpets,

ANNOUNCED (ANNOUNCE)
Isa 48: 5 before they happened I **a** them
Gal 3: 8 faith, and **a** the gospel in advance

ANNOYANCE*
Pr 12: 16 Fools show their **a** at once,

ANNUAL*
Ex 30: 10 This **a** atonement must be made
Jdg 21: 19 there is the **a** festival of the LORD
1Sa 1: 21 offer the **a** sacrifice to the LORD
2: 19 her husband to offer the **a** sacrifice.
20: 6 an **a** sacrifice is being made
2Ch 8: 13 Moons and the three **a** festivals—
Heb 10: 3 those sacrifices are an **a** reminder

ANOINT (ANOINTED ANOINTING)
Ex 30: 26 use it to **a** the tent of meeting,
30: 30 "**A** Aaron and his sons
1Sa 9: 16 **A** him ruler over my people Israel;
15: 1 to **a** you king over his people Israel;
2Ki 9: 3 I **a** you king over Israel.'
Ps 23: 5 You **a** my head with oil;
Da 9: 24 and to **a** the Most Holy Place.
Jas 5: 14 **a** them with oil in the name

ANOINTED (ANOINT)
1Ch 16: 22 "Do not touch my **a** ones;
Ps 105: 15 "Do not touch my **a** ones;
Isa 61: 1 because the LORD has **a** me
Da 9: 26 the **A** One will be put to death
Lk 4: 18 because he has **a** me to proclaim
Ac 10: 38 how God **a** Jesus of Nazareth

ANOINTING (ANOINT)
Lev 8: 12 He poured some of the **a** oil
1Ch 29: 22 **a** him before the LORD to be ruler
Ps 45: 7 your companions by **a** you
Heb 1: 9 your companions by **a** you
1Jn 2: 20 you have an **a** from the Holy One,
2: 27 as his **a** teaches you about all things

ANT* (ANTS)
Pr 6: 6 Go to the **a**, you sluggard;

ANTICHRIST* (ANTICHRISTS)
1Jn 2: 18 have heard that the **a** is coming,
2: 22 Such a person is the **a**—
4: 3 This is the spirit of the **a**, which
2Jn : 7 person is the deceiver and the **a**.

ANTICHRISTS* (ANTICHRIST)
1Jn 2: 18 even now many **a** have come.

ANTIOCH
Ac 11: 26 were called Christians first at **A**.

ANTS* (ANT)
Pr 30: 25 **A** are creatures of little strength,

ANXIETIES* (ANXIOUS)
Lk 21: 34 drunkenness and the **a** of life,

ANXIETY (ANXIOUS)
Pr 12: 25 **A** weighs down the heart, but
1Pe 5: 7 Cast all your **a** on him because he

ANXIOUS (ANXIETIES ANXIETY)
Php 4: 6 Do not be **a** about anything,

APOLLOS*
Christian from Alexandria, learned in the Scriptures; instructed by Aquila and Priscilla (Ac 18:24–28). Ministered at Corinth (Ac 19:1; 1Co 1:12; 3:4–22; 4:6; 16:42; Titus 3:13).

APOLLYON*
Rev 9: 11 Abaddon and in Greek is **A** (that

APOSTLE (APOSTLES APOSTLES')
Ro 11: 13 Inasmuch as I am the **a**
1Co 9: 1 Am I not an **a**? Have I not seen
2Co 12: 12 among you the marks of a true **a**,
Gal 2: 8 in Peter as an **a** to the circumcised,
2: 8 work in me as an **a** to the Gentiles.
1Ti 2: 7 was appointed a herald and an **a**—
2Ti 1: 11 a herald and an **a** and a teacher.
Heb 3: 1 whom we acknowledge as our **a**

APOSTLES (APOSTLE)
See also Andrew, Bartholomew, James, John, Judas, Matthew, Matthias, Nathanael, Paul, Peter, Philip, Simon, Thaddaeus, Thomas.
Lk 11: 49 'I will send them prophets and **a**,
Ac 1: 26 so he was added to the eleven **a**.
2: 43 and signs performed by the **a**.
1Co 12: 28 placed in the church first of all **a**,
15: 9 For I am the least of the **a** and do
2Co 11: 13 For such people are false **a**,
11: 13 masquerading as **a** of Christ.
Eph 2: 20 built on the foundation of the **a**
4: 11 So Christ himself gave the **a**,
Rev 21: 14 names of the twelve **a** of the Lamb.

APOSTLES' (APOSTLE)
Ac 5: 2 the rest and put it at the **a** feet.
8: 18 at the laying on of the **a** hands,

APPEAL
Ac 25: 11 me over to them. I **a** to Caesar!"
Phm : 9 yet I prefer to **a** to you on the basis

APPEAR (APPEARANCE APPEARANCES APPEARED APPEARING APPEARS)
Ge 1: 9 to one place, and let dry ground **a**."
Lev 16: 2 For I will **a** in the cloud over
Mt 24: 30 will **a** the sign of the Son of Man
Mk 13: 22 false prophets will **a** and perform
Lk 19: 11 of God was going to **a** at once.
2Co 5: 10 we must all **a** before the judgment
Col 3: 4 you also will **a** with him in glory.
Heb 9: 24 now to **a** for us in God's presence.
9: 28 and he will **a** a second time,

APPEARANCE (APPEAR)
1Sa 16: 7 People look at the outward **a**,
Isa 52: 14 his **a** was so disfigured beyond
53: 2 in his **a** that we should desire him.

APPEARANCES* (APPEAR)
Jn 7: 24 Stop judging by mere **a**, but instead
2Co 10: 7 You are judging by **a**. If anyone is

APPEARED (APPEAR)
Nu 14: 10 the glory of the LORD **a** at the tent
Mt 1: 20 an angel of the Lord **a** to him
Lk 2: 9 An angel of the Lord **a** to them,
1Co 15: 5 and that he **a** to Cephas,
Heb 9: 26 But he has **a** once for all

APPEARING (APPEAR)
1Ti 6: 14 blame until the **a** of our Lord Jesus
2Ti 1: 10 now been revealed through the **a**
4: 8 to all who have longed for his **a**.
Titus 2: 13 the **a** of the glory of our great God

APPEARS (APPEAR)
Mal 3: 2 Who can stand when he **a**?
Col 3: 4 who is your life, **a**, then you
1Pe 5: 4 And when the Chief Shepherd **a**,
1Jn 3: 2 But we know that when Christ **a**,

APPETITE
Pr 13: 2 but the unfaithful have an **a**
13: 4 A sluggard's **a** is never filled,
16: 26 The **a** of laborers works for them;
Ecc 6: 7 yet their **a** is never satisfied.
Jer 50: 19 their **a** will be satisfied on the hills

APPLES
Pr 25: 11 Like **a** of gold in settings of silver is

APPLY (APPLYING)
Pr 22: 17 **a** your heart to what I teach,
23: 12 **A** your heart to instruction and

APPLYING (APPLY)
Pr 2: 2 **a** your heart to understanding—

APPOINT (APPOINTED)
Ps 61: 7 **a** your love and faithfulness
1Th 5: 9 God did not **a** us to suffer wrath
Titus 1: 5 and **a** elders in every town, as I

APPOINTED (APPOINT)
Dt 1: 15 **a** them to have authority over you—
Da 11: 27 an end will still come at the **a** time.
Hab 2: 3 For the revelation awaits an **a** time;
Lk 1: 20 will come true at their **a** time."
Jn 15: 16 you and **a** you so that you might go
Ro 9: 9 "At the **a** time I will return,

APPROACH (APPROACHING)
Ex 24: 2 but Moses alone is to **a** the LORD;
Eph 3: 12 in him we may **a** God with freedom
Heb 4: 16 then **a** God's throne of grace

APPROACHING (APPROACH)
Heb 10: 25 all the more as you see the Day **a**.
1Jn 5: 14 is the confidence we have in **a** God:

APPROPRIATE
Ecc 5: 18 that it is **a** for a person to eat,
1Ti 2: 10 deeds, **a** for women who profess
APPROVAL (APPROVE)
Jdg 18: 6 Your journey has the LORD's **a**."
Jn 6: 27 the Father has placed his seal of **a**."
Ro 14: 18 to God and receives human **a**.
1Co 11: 19 to show which of you have God's **a**.
Gal 1: 10 trying to win the **a** of human beings,
APPROVE (APPROVAL APPROVED APPROVES)
Ro 2: 18 **a** of what is superior because you
12: 2 to test and **a** what God's will is—
APPROVED* (APPROVE)
2Co 10: 18 who commends himself who is **a**,
1Th 2: 4 we speak as those **a** by God to be
2Ti 2: 15 to present yourself to God as one **a**,
APPROVES* (APPROVE)
Ro 14: 22 not condemn himself by what he **a**.
APT*
Pr 15: 23 finds joy in giving an **a** reply—
AQUILA*
Husband of Priscilla; co-worker with Paul, instructor of Apollos (Ac 18; Ro 16:3; 1Co 16:19; 2Ti 4:19).
ARABIA
Gal 1: 17 before I was, but I went into **A**.
4: 25 Hagar stands for Mount Sinai in **A**
ARARAT
Ge 8: 4 to rest on the mountains of **A**.
ARAUNAH
2Sa 24: 16 threshing floor of **A** the Jebusite.
ARBITER*
Lk 12: 14 me a judge or an **a** between you?"
ARCHANGEL* (ANGEL)
1Th 4: 16 with the voice of the **a**
Jude : 9 But even the **a** Michael, when he
ARCHER
Pr 26: 10 Like an **a** who wounds at random
ARCHIPPUS*
Col 4: 17 Tell **A**: "See to it that you complete
Phm : 2 sister and **A** our fellow soldier—
ARCHITECT*
Heb 11: 10 whose **a** and builder is God.
AREOPAGUS*
Ac 17: 19 brought him to a meeting of the **A**,
17: 22 stood up in the meeting of the **A**
17: 34 a member of the **A**, also a woman
ARGUE (ARGUMENT ARGUMENTS)
Job 13: 3 and to **a** my case with God.
13: 8 Will you **a** the case for God?
ARGUMENT (ARGUE)
Heb 6: 16 is said and puts an end to all **a**.
ARGUMENTS (ARGUE)
Isa 41: 21 "Set forth your **a**," says Jacob's
Col 2: 4 deceive you by fine-sounding **a**.
2Ti 2: 23 to do with foolish and stupid **a**,
Titus 3: 9 and genealogies and **a** and quarrels
ARK
Ge 6: 14 So make yourself an **a** of cypress
Ex 25: 10 "Have them make an **a** of acacia
25: 21 and put in the **a** the tablets of
Dt 10: 5 put the tablets in the **a** I had made,
1Sa 4: 11 The **a** of God was captured,
7: 2 The **a** remained at Kiriath Jearim
2Sa 6: 17 They brought the **a** of the LORD
1Ki 8: 9 the **a** except the two stone tablets
1Ch 13: 9 out his hand to steady the **a**,
2Ch 35: 3 "Put the sacred **a** in the temple
Heb 9: 4 the gold-covered **a** of the covenant.
9: 4 This **a** contained the gold jar
11: 7 in holy fear built an **a** to save his
Rev 11: 19 within his temple was seen the **a**
ARM (ARMY)
Nu 11: 23 "Is the LORD's **a** too short?
Dt 4: 34 hand and an outstretched **a**,
7: 19 mighty hand and outstretched **a**,
Ps 44: 3 nor did their **a** bring them victory;
98: 1 his holy **a** have worked salvation
Jer 27: 5 outstretched **a** I made the earth
1Pe 4: 1 **a** yourselves also with the same

ARMAGEDDON*
Rev 16: 16 place that in Hebrew is called **A**.
ARMIES (ARMY)
1Sa 17: 26 he should defy the **a** of the living
Rev 19: 14 The **a** of heaven were following
ARMOR (ARMY)
1Ki 20: 11 his **a** should not boast like one who
Ps 35: 2 Take up shield and **a**;
Jer 46: 4 Polish your spears, put on your **a**!
Ro 13: 12 darkness and put on the **a** of light.
Eph 6: 11 Put on the full **a** of God, so that
6: 13 Therefore put on the full **a** of God,
ARMS (ARMY)
Dt 33: 27 underneath are the everlasting **a**.
Ps 18: 32 It is God who **a** me with strength
Pr 31: 17 her **a** are strong for her tasks.
31: 20 She opens her **a** to the poor
Isa 40: 11 He gathers the lambs in his **a**
Mk 10: 16 And he took the children in his **a**,
Heb 12: 12 strengthen your feeble **a** and weak
ARMY (ARM ARMIES ARMOR ARMS)
Ps 33: 16 king is saved by the size of his **a**;
Joel 2: 2 a large and mighty **a** comes,
2: 5 like a mighty **a** drawn up for battle.
2: 11 thunders at the head of his **a**;
Rev 19: 19 the rider on the horse and his **a**.
AROMA
Ge 8: 21 The LORD smelled the pleasing **a**
Ex 29: 18 a pleasing **a**, a food offering
Lev 3: 16 as a food offering, a pleasing **a**.
2Co 2: 14 us to spread the **a** of the knowledge
2: 15 the pleasing **a** of Christ among
2: 16 an **a** that brings death; to the other, an **a** that brings life.
AROUSE (AROUSED)
Ro 11: 14 I may somehow **a** my own people
AROUSED (AROUSE)
Ps 78: 58 they **a** his jealousy with their idols.
ARRAYED*
Ps 110: 3 **A** in holy splendor, your young
Isa 61: 10 **a** me in a robe of his righteousness,
ARREST
Mt 10: 19 But when they **a** you, do not worry
ARROGANCE (ARROGANT)
1Sa 2: 3 or let your mouth speak such **a**,
Pr 8: 13 I hate pride and **a**, evil behavior
Mk 7: 22 lewdness, envy, slander, **a** and folly.
2Co 12: 20 slander, gossip, **a** and disorder.
ARROGANT (ARROGANCE)
Ps 5: 5 The **a** cannot stand in your
119: 78 May the **a** be put to shame
Pr 21: 24 The proud and **a** person—
Ro 1: 30 God-haters, insolent, **a** and
11: 20 Do not be **a**, but tremble.
1Ti 6: 17 this present world not to be **a** nor
ARROW (ARROWS)
Ps 91: 5 of night, nor the **a** that flies by day,
Pr 25: 18 or a sharp **a** is one who gives false
ARROWS (ARROW)
Ps 64: 3 and aim cruel words like deadly **a**.
64: 7 God will shoot them with his **a**;
127: 4 Like **a** in the hands of a warrior are
Pr 26: 18 Like a maniac shooting flaming **a**
Eph 6: 16 can extinguish all the flaming **a**
ARTAXERXES
King of Persia; allowed rebuilding of temple under Ezra (Ezr 4; 7), and of walls of Jerusalem under his cupbearer Nehemiah (Ne 2; 5:14; 13:6).
ARTEMIS
Ac 19: 28 "Great is **A** of the Ephesians!"
ASA
King of Judah (1Ki 15:8–24; 1Ch 3:10; 2Ch 14–16). Godly reformer (2Ch 15); in later years defeated Israel with help of Aram, not the LORD (1Ki 15:16–22; 2Ch 16).
ASAHEL
1. Nephew of David, one of his warriors (2Sa 23:24; 1Ch 2:16; 11:26; 27:7). Killed by Abner (2Sa 2); avenged by Joab (2Sa 3:22–39).
2. Levite; teacher (2Ch 17:8).

ASAPH
1. Recorder to Hezekiah (2Ki 18:18, 37; Isa 36:3, 22).
2. Levitical musician (1Ch 6:39; 15:17–19; 16:4–7, 37). Sons of (1Ch 25; 2Ch 5:12; 20:14; 29:13; 35:15; Ezr 2:41; 3:10; Ne 7:44; 11:17; 12:27–47). Psalms of (2Ch 29:30; Ps 50; 73–83).
ASCEND* (ASCENDED ASCENDING)
Dt 30: 12 "Who will **a** into heaven to get it
Ps 24: 3 Who may **a** the mountain
Isa 14: 13 your heart, "I will **a** to the heavens;
14: 14 will **a** above the tops of the clouds;
Jn 6: 62 of Man **a** to where he was before!
Ac 2: 34 For David did not **a** to heaven,
Ro 10: 6 heart, 'Who will **a** into heaven?'"
ASCENDED (ASCEND)
Ps 68: 18 When you **a** on high, you took
Eph 4: 8 "When he **a** on high, he took many
ASCENDING (ASCEND)
Ge 28: 12 and the angels of God were **a**
Jn 1: 51 angels of God **a** and descending
ASCRIBE*
1Ch 16: 28 **A** to the LORD, all you families
16: 28 **a** to the LORD glory and strength.
16: 29 **A** to the LORD the glory due his
Job 36: 3 I will **a** justice to my Maker.
Ps 29: 1 **A** to the LORD, you heavenly
29: 1 **a** to the LORD glory and strength.
29: 2 **A** to the LORD the glory due his
96: 7 **A** to the LORD, all you families
96: 7 **a** to the LORD glory and strength.
96: 8 **A** to the LORD the glory due his
ASHAMED (SHAME)
Mk 8: 38 If anyone is **a** of me and my words
8: 38 the Son of Man will be **a** of them
Lk 9: 26 Whoever is **a** of me and my words,
9: 26 the Son of Man will be **a** of them
Ro 1: 16 For I am not **a** of the gospel,
2Ti 1: 8 So do not be **a** of the testimony
2: 15 worker who does not need to be **a**
ASHER
Son of Jacob by Zilpah (Ge 30:13; 35:26; 46:17; Ex 1:4; 1Ch 2:2). Tribe of blessed (Ge 49:20; Dt 33:24–25), numbered (Nu 1:40–41; 26:44–47), allotted land (Jos 10:24–31; Eze 48:2), failed to fully possess (Jdg 1:31–32), failed to support Deborah (Jdg 5:17), supported Gideon (Jdg 6:35; 7:23) and David (1Ch 12:36), 12,000 from (Rev 7:6).
ASHERAH (ASHERAHS)
Ex 34: 13 stones and cut down their **A** poles.
1Ki 18: 19 the four hundred prophets of **A**,
ASHERAHS* (ASHERAH)
Jdg 3: 7 and served the Baals and the **A**.
ASHES
Job 42: 6 myself and repent in dust and **a**."
Mt 11: 21 long ago in sackcloth and **a**.
ASHTORETHS
Jdg 2: 13 him and served Baal and the **A**.
1Sa 7: 4 put away their Baals and **A**,
ASLEEP (SLEEP)
1Co 15: 18 who have fallen **a** in Christ are lost.
ASPIRES*
1Ti 3: 1 Whoever **a** to be an overseer
ASSEMBLY
Ps 1: 5 sinners in the **a** of the righteous.
35: 18 will give you thanks in the great **a**;
82: 1 God presides in the great **a**;
149: 1 praise in the **a** of his faithful
ASSIGNED
1Ki 7: 14 and did all the work **a** to him.
Mk 13: 34 each with their **a** task, and tells
1Co 3: 5 as the Lord has **a** to each his task.
7: 17 whatever situation the Lord has **a**
2Co 10: 13 of service God himself has **a** to us,
ASSOCIATE
Pr 22: 24 do not **a** with one easily angered,
Jn 4: 9 Jews do not **a** with Samaritans.)
Ac 10: 28 against our law for a Jew to **a**
Ro 12: 16 be willing to **a** with people of low
1Co 5: 9 in my letter not to **a** with sexually

1Co 5: 11 you must not **a** with anyone who
2Th 3: 14 Do not **a** with them, in order

ASSURANCE (ASSURED)
Heb 10: 22 and with the full **a** that faith brings,

ASSURED (ASSURANCE)
Col 4: 12 the will of God, mature and fully **a**.

ASTRAY
Ps 119: 67 Before I was afflicted I went **a**,
Pr 10: 17 ignores correction leads others **a**.
20: 1 whoever is led **a** by them is not
Isa 53: 6 have gone **a**, each of us has turned
Jer 50: 6 their shepherds have led them **a**
1Pe 2: 25 For "you were like sheep going **a**,"
1Jn 3: 7 do not let anyone lead you **a**.

ASTROLOGERS
Isa 47: 13 Let your **a** come forward,
Da 2: 2 **a** to tell him what he had dreamed.

ATE (EAT)
Ge 3: 6 wisdom, she took some and **a** it.
27: 25 Jacob brought it to him and he **a**;
2Sa 9: 11 So Mephibosheth **a** at David's table
Ps 78: 25 Human beings **a** the bread
Jer 15: 16 When your words came, I **a** them;
Eze 3: 3 So I **a** it, and it tasted as sweet as
Mt 14: 20 They all **a** and were satisfied,
15: 37 They all **a** and were satisfied.
Mk 6: 42 They all **a** and were satisfied,
Lk 9: 17 They all **a** and were satisfied,

ATHALIAH
Granddaughter of Omri; wife of Jehoram and mother of Ahaziah; encouraged their evil ways (2Ki 8:18, 27; 2Ch 22:2). At death of Ahaziah she made herself queen, killing all his sons but Joash (2Ki 11:1–3; 2Ch 22:10–12); killed six years later when Joash was revealed (2Ki 11:4–16; 2Ch 23:1–15).

ATHLETE*
2Ti 2: 5 competes as an **a** does not receive

ATONE* (ATONEMENT)
Ex 30: 15 to the LORD to **a** for your lives.
2Ch 29: 24 for a sin offering to **a** for all Israel,
Da 9: 24 an end to sin, to **a** for wickedness,

ATONED* (ATONEMENT)
Dt 21: 8 Then the bloodshed will be **a** for,
1Sa 3: 14 of Eli's house will never be **a**
Pr 16: 6 love and faithfulness sin is **a** for;
Isa 6: 7 is taken away and your sin **a** for."
22: 14 day this sin will not be **a** for,"
27: 9 will Jacob's guilt be **a** for, and this

ATONEMENT (ATONE ATONED)
Ex 25: 17 "Make an **a** cover of pure gold—
30: 10 Once a year Aaron shall make **a**
Lev 17: 11 blood that makes **a** for one's life.
23: 27 this seventh month is the Day of **A**.
Nu 25: 13 God and made **a** for the Israelites."
Ro 3: 25 presented Christ as a sacrifice of **a**,
Heb 2: 17 that he might make **a** for the sins

ATTACK
Ps 109: 3 they **a** me without cause.

ATTAINED
Php 3: 16 live up to what we have already **a**.
Heb 7: 11 could have been **a** through

ATTENTION (ATTENTIVE)
Pr 4: 1 pay **a** and gain understanding.
4: 20 My son, pay **a** to what I say;
5: 1 My son, pay **a** to my wisdom,
7: 24 listen to me; pay **a** to what I say.
21: 11 by paying **a** to the wise they get
22: 17 Pay **a** and turn your ear
Ecc 7: 21 Do not pay **a** to every word people
Isa 42: 20 many things, but you pay no **a**;
Titus 1: 14 and will pay no **a** to Jewish myths
Heb 2: 1 We must pay the most careful **a**,

ATTENTIVE (ATTENTION)
Ne 1: 11 your ear be **a** to the prayer of this
1Pe 3: 12 and his ears are **a** to their prayer,

ATTITUDE (ATTITUDES)
Eph 4: 23 made new in the **a** of your minds;
1Pe 4: 1 yourselves also with the same **a**,

ATTITUDES* (ATTITUDE)
Heb 4: 12 the thoughts and **a** of the heart.

ATTRACTIVE
Titus 2: 10 teaching about God our Savior **a**.

AUDIENCE
Pr 29: 26 Many seek an **a** with a ruler, but it

AUTHORITIES (AUTHORITY)
Ro 13: 1 be subject to the governing **a**,
13: 5 it is necessary to submit to the **a**,
13: 6 for the **a** are God's servants,
Eph 3: 10 and **a** in the heavenly realms,
6: 12 against the **a**, against the powers
Col 1: 16 thrones or powers or rulers or **a**;
2: 15 having disarmed the powers and **a**,
Titus 3: 1 to be subject to rulers and **a**,
1Pe 3: 22 **a** and powers in submission to

AUTHORITY (AUTHORITIES)
Mt 7: 29 he taught as one who had **a**,
9: 6 the Son of Man has **a** on earth
28: 18 "All **a** in heaven and on earth has
Mk 1: 22 he taught them as one who had **a**,
2: 10 the Son of Man has **a** on earth
Lk 4: 32 teaching, because his words had **a**.
5: 24 the Son of Man has **a** on earth
Jn 10: 18 I have **a** to lay it down and **a** to take
Ac 1: 7 the Father has set by his own **a**.
Ro 7: 1 the law has **a** over someone only as
13: 1 for there is no **a** except
13: 2 rebels against the **a** is rebelling
1Co 11: 10 ought to have **a** over her own head,
15: 24 all dominion, **a** and power.
1Ti 2: 2 for kings and all those in **a**, that we
2: 12 to teach or to assume **a** over a man;
Titus 2: 15 Encourage and rebuke with all **a**.
Heb 13: 17 your leaders and submit to their **a**,
1Pe 2: 13 the Lord's sake to every human **a**:

AUTUMN*
Dt 11: 14 its season, both **a** and spring rains,
Ps 84: 6 the **a** rains also cover it with pools.
Jer 5: 24 who gives **a** and spring rains
Joel 2: 23 has given you the **a** rains because
2: 23 showers, both **a** and spring rains,
Jas 5: 7 crop, patiently waiting for the **a**
Jude : 12 **a** trees, without fruit and uprooted

AVENGE (VENGEANCE)
Lev 26: 25 on you to **a** the breaking
Dt 32: 35 It is mine to **a**; I will repay.
32: 43 for he will **a** the blood of his
Ro 12: 19 "It is mine to **a**; I will repay,"
Heb 10: 30 him who said, "It is mine to **a**;
Rev 6: 10 of the earth and **a** our blood?"

AVENGER (VENGEANCE)
Nu 35: 27 the **a** of blood may kill the accused
Jos 20: 3 protection from the **a** of blood.
Ps 8: 2 to silence the foe and the **a**.

AVENGES (VENGEANCE)
Ps 94: 1 The LORD is a God who **a**. O God who **a**, shine forth.

AVENGING* (VENGEANCE)
1Sa 25: 26 and from **a** yourself with your own
25: 33 from **a** myself with my own hands.
Na 1: 2 The LORD is a jealous and **a** God;

AVOID (AVOIDED AVOIDS)
Pr 4: 15 **A** it, do not travel on it; turn from
15: 12 correction, so they **a** the wise.
20: 3 It is to one's honor to **a** strife,
20: 19 so **a** anyone who talks too much.
Ecc 7: 18 fears God will **a** all extremes.
1Th 4: 3 you should **a** sexual immorality;
2Ti 2: 16 **A** godless chatter, because those
Titus 3: 9 But **a** foolish controversies

AVOIDED* (AVOID)
Pr 16: 6 the fear of the LORD evil is **a**.

AVOIDS* (AVOID)
Pr 16: 17 The highway of the upright **a** evil;

AWAITS (WAIT)
Pr 15: 10 Stern discipline **a** anyone who
28: 22 are unaware that poverty **a** them.

AWAKE (WAKE)
Ps 17: 15 when I **a**, I will be satisfied
Pr 6: 22 when you **a**, they will speak to you.
1Th 5: 6 asleep, but let us be **a** and sober.

AWARD*
2Ti 4: 8 Judge, will **a** to me on that day—

AWARE
Ex 34: 29 he was not **a** that his face was
Mt 24: 50 him and at an hour he is not **a** of.
Lk 12: 46 him and at an hour he is not **a** of.

AWE* (AWESOME OVERAWED)
Jos 4: 14 they stood in **a** of him all the days
4: 14 as they had stood in **a** of Moses.
1Sa 12: 18 So all the people stood in **a**
1Ki 3: 28 they held the king in **a**, because
Job 25: 2 "Dominion and **a** belong to God;
Ps 65: 8 The whole earth is filled with **a**
119:120 I stand in **a** of your laws.
Isa 29: 23 will stand in **a** of the God of Israel.
Jer 2: 19 your God and have no **a** of me,"
33: 9 they will be in **a** and will tremble
Hab 3: 2 I stand in **a** of your deeds, LORD.
Mal 2: 5 me and stood in **a** of my name.
Mt 9: 8 saw this, they were filled with **a**;
Lk 1: 65 the neighbors were filled with **a**,
5: 26 They were filled with **a** and said,
7: 16 They were all filled with **a**
Ac 2: 43 Everyone was filled with **a**
Heb 12: 28 acceptably with reverence and **a**,

AWESOME* (AWE)
Ge 28: 17 and said, "How **a** is this place!
Ex 15: 11 majestic in holiness, **a** in glory,
34: 10 among will see how **a** is the work
Dt 4: 34 or by great and **a** deeds, like all
7: 21 is among you, is a great and **a** God.
10: 17 God, mighty and **a**, who shows no
10: 21 **a** wonders you saw with your own
28: 58 revere this glorious and **a** name—
34: 12 performed the **a** deeds that Moses
Jdg 13: 6 looked like an angel of God, very **a**.
2Sa 7: 23 **a** wonders by driving out nations
1Ch 17: 21 **a** wonders by driving out nations
Ne 1: 5 the great and **a** God, who keeps his
4: 14 who is great and **a**, and fight
9: 32 God, mighty and **a**, who keeps his
Job 10: 16 again display your **a** power against
37: 22 God comes in **a** majesty.
Ps 45: 4 your right hand achieve **a** deeds.
47: 2 For the LORD Most High is **a**,
65: 5 answer us with **a** and righteous
66: 3 to God, "How **a** are your deeds!
66: 5 has done, his **a** deeds for mankind!
68: 35 You, God, are **a** in your sanctuary;
89: 7 he is more **a** than all who surround
99: 3 praise your great and **a** name—
106: 22 Ham and **a** deeds by the Red Sea.
111: 9 holy and **a** is his name.
145: 6 tell of the power of your **a** works—
Isa 64: 3 you did **a** things that we did not
Eze 1: 18 Their rims were high and **a**, and all
1: 22 vault, sparkling like crystal, and **a**.
Da 2: 31 dazzling statue, **a** in appearance.
9: 4 the great and **a** God, who keeps his
Zep 2: 11 The LORD will be **a** to them

AX
Mt 3: 10 The **a** is already at the root
Lk 3: 9 The **a** is already at the root

BAAL
Jdg 6: 25 Tear down your father's altar to **B**
1Ki 16: 32 set up an altar for **B** in the temple
18: 25 Elijah said to the prophets of **B**,
19: 18 knees have not bowed down to **B**
2Ki 10: 28 So Jehu destroyed **B** worship
Jer 19: 5 in the fire as offerings to **B**—
Ro 11: 4 have not bowed the knee to **B**."

BAASHA
King of Israel (1Ki 15:16—16:7; 2Ch 16:1–6).

BABBLER* (BABBLING)
Ac 17: 18 "What is this **b** trying to say?"

BABBLING* (BABBLER)
Mt 6: 7 do not keep on **b** like pagans,

BABIES* (BABY)
Ge 25: 22 The **b** jostled each other within
Ex 2: 6 "This is one of the Hebrew **b**,"
Lk 18: 15 bringing **b** to Jesus for him to place
Ac 7: 19 their newborn **b** so that they would
1Pe 2: 2 Like newborn **b**, crave pure

BABY* (BABIES BABY'S)
Ex 1: 16 you see that the **b** is a boy, kill him;

Ex 2: 6 She opened it and saw the **b**.
2: 7 women to nurse the **b** for you?"
2: 9 "Take this **b** and nurse him for me,
2: 9 the woman took the **b** and nursed
1Ki 3: 17 I had a **b** while she was there
3: 18 was born, this woman also had a **b**.
3: 26 my lord, give her the living **b**!
3: 27 "Give the living **b** to the first
Isa 49: 15 "Can a mother forget the **b** at her
Lk 1: 41 greeting, the **b** leaped in her womb,
1: 44 the **b** in my womb leaped for joy.
1: 57 time for Elizabeth to have her **b**,
2: 6 the time came for the **b** to be born,
2: 12 You will find a **b** wrapped in cloths
2: 16 and the **b**, who was lying
Jn 16: 21 **b** is born she forgets the anguish

BABY'S* (BABY)
Ex 2: 8 the girl went and got the **b** mother.

BABYLON
Ps 137: 1 By the rivers of **B** we sat and wept
Jer 29: 10 seventy years are completed for **B**,
51: 37 **B** will be a heap of ruins, a haunt
Rev 14: 8 'Fallen is **B** the Great,' which made
17: 5 on her forehead was a mystery: B

BACKS
2Pe 2: 21 their **b** on the sacred command

BACKSLIDING* (BACKSLIDINGS)
Jer 2: 19 your **b** will rebuke you.
3: 22 I will cure you of **b**."
15: 6 "You keep on **b**. So I will reach
Eze 37: 23 save them from all their sinful **b**,

BACKSLIDINGS* (BACKSLIDING)
Jer 5: 6 rebellion is great and their **b** many.

BALAAM
Prophet who attempted to curse Israel (Nu 22–24; Dt 23:4–5; 2Pe 2:15; Jude 11). Killed in Israel's vengeance on Midianites (Nu 31:8; Jos 13:22).

BALAK
Moabite king who hired Balaam to curse Israel (Nu 22–24; Jos 24:9).

BALM
Jer 8: 22 Is there no **b** in Gilead? Is there no

BANISH (BANISHED)
Jer 25: 10 will **b** from them the sounds of joy

BANISHED (BANISH)
Dt 30: 4 have been **b** to the most distant

BANNER
Ex 17: 15 and called it The LORD is my **B**.
SS 2: 4 hall, and let his **b** over me be love.
Isa 11: 10 of Jesse will stand as a **b**

BANQUET
SS 2: 4 Let him lead me to the **b** hall,
Lk 14: 13 But when you give a **b**,

BAPTISM* (BAPTIZE)
Mt 21: 25 John's **b**—where did it come from?
Mk 1: 4 preaching a **b** of repentance
10: 38 with the **b** I am baptized with?"
10: 39 with the **b** I am baptized with,
11: 30 John's **b**—was it from heaven,
Lk 3: 3 preaching a **b** of repentance
12: 50 But I have a **b** to undergo, and
20: 4 John's **b**—was it from heaven,
Ac 1: 22 beginning from John's **b** to the
10: 37 after the **b** that John preached—
13: 24 and **b** to all the people of Israel.
18: 25 though he knew only the **b** of John.
19: 3 "Then what **b** did you receive?"
19: 3 "John's **b**," they replied.
19: 4 "John's **b** was a **b** of repentance.
Ro 6: 4 with him through **b** into death
Eph 4: 5 one Lord, one faith, one **b**;
Col 2: 12 having been buried with him in **b**,
1Pe 3: 21 this water symbolizes **b** that now

BAPTIZE* (BAPTISM BAPTIZED BAPTIZING)
Mt 3: 11 "I **b** you with water for repentance.
3: 11 He will **b** you with the Holy Spirit
Mk 1: 8 I **b** you with water, but he will **b** you with the Holy Spirit
Lk 3: 16 them all, "I **b** you with water.
3: 16 He will **b** you with the Holy Spirit
Jn 1: 25 you **b** if you are not the Messiah,
1: 26 "I **b** with water," John replied,
1: 33 one who sent me to **b** with water
1: 33 remain is the one who will **b**
1Co 1: 14 that I did not **b** any of you except
1: 17 For Christ did not send me to **b**,

BAPTIZED* (BAPTIZE)
Mt 3: 6 they were **b** by him in the Jordan
3: 13 to the Jordan to be **b** by John.
3: 14 "I need to be **b** by you, and do you
3: 16 As soon as Jesus was **b**, he went
Mk 1: 5 they were **b** by him in the Jordan
1: 9 and was **b** by John in the Jordan.
10: 38 or be **b** with the baptism I am **b** with?"
10: 39 be **b** with the baptism I am **b** with,
16: 16 *believes and is **b** will be saved,*
Lk 3: 7 crowds coming out to be **b** by him,
3: 12 Even tax collectors came to be **b**.
3: 21 When all the people were being **b**, Jesus was **b** too.
7: 29 because they had been **b** by John.
7: 30 because they had not been **b**
Jn 3: 22 spent some time with them, and **b**.
3: 23 people were coming and being **b**.
4: 2 in fact it was not Jesus who **b**,
Ac 1: 5 For John **b** with water, but in a few days you will be **b**
2: 38 "Repent and be **b**, every one
2: 41 who accepted his message were **b**,
8: 12 they were **b**, both men and women.
8: 13 Simon himself believed and was **b**.
8: 16 had simply been **b** in the name
8: 36 stand in the way of my being **b**?"
8: 38 into the water and Philip **b** him.
9: 18 He got up and was **b**,
10: 47 the way of their being **b** with water.
10: 48 ordered that they be **b** in the name
11: 16 'John **b** with water, but you will be **b** with the Holy Spirit.'
16: 15 members of her household were **b**,
16: 33 he and all his household were **b**.
18: 8 heard Paul believed and were **b**.
19: 5 were **b** in the name of the Lord
22: 16 up, be **b** and wash your sins away,
Ro 6: 3 us who were **b** into Christ Jesus were **b** into his death?
1Co 1: 13 Were you **b** in the name of Paul?
1: 15 say that you were **b** in my name.
1: 16 also **b** the household of Stephanas;
1: 16 don't remember if I **b** anyone else.)
10: 2 They were all **b** into Moses
12: 13 we were all **b** by one Spirit so as
15: 29 those do who are **b** for the dead?
15: 29 at all, why are people **b** for them?
Gal 3: 27 of you who were **b** into Christ have

BAPTIZING* (BAPTIZE)
Mt 3: 7 coming to where he was **b**, he said
28: 19 **b** them in the name of the Father
Jn 1: 28 of the Jordan, where John was **b**.
1: 31 the reason I came **b** with water was
3: 23 also was **b** at Aenon near Salim,
3: 26 he is **b**, and everyone is going
4: 1 and **b** more disciples than John—
10: 40 the place where John had been **b**

BAR-JESUS*
Ac 13: 6 and false prophet named **B**,

BARABBAS
Mt 27: 26 Then he released **B** to them.

BARAK*
Judge who fought with Deborah against Canaanites (Jdg 4–5; 1Sa 12:11; Heb 11:32).

BARBARIAN*
Col 3: 11 circumcised or uncircumcised, **b**,

BARBS*
Nu 33: 55 remain will become **b** in your eyes

BARE
Hos 2: 3 make her as **b** as on the day she
Heb 4: 13 and laid **b** before the eyes of him

BARNABAS*
Disciple, originally Joseph (Ac 4:36), prophet (Ac 13:1), apostle (Ac 14:14). Brought Paul to apostles (Ac 9:27), Antioch (Ac 11:22–30; Gal 2:1–13), on the first missionary journey (Ac 13–14). Together at Jerusalem Council, they separated over John Mark (Ac 15). Later co-workers (1Co 9:6; Col 4:10).

BARREN
Isa 54: 1 "Sing, **b** woman, you who never
Gal 4: 27 "Be glad, **b** woman, you who never

BARTHOLOMEW*
Apostle (Mt 10:3; Mk 3:18; Lk 6:14; Ac 1:13). Possibly also known as Nathanael (Jn 1:45–49; 21:2).

BARUCH
Jeremiah's secretary (Jer 32:12–16; 36; 43:1–6; 45:1–2).

BARZILLAI
1. Gileadite who aided David during Absalom's revolt (2Sa 17:27; 19:31–39).
2. Son-in-law of 1. (Ezr 2:61; Ne 7:63).

BASHAN
Jos 22: 7 Moses had given land in **B**,
Ps 22: 12 strong bulls of **B** encircle me.

BASIN
Ex 30: 18 "Make a bronze **b**, with its bronze

BASKET
Ex 2: 3 she got a papyrus **b** for him
Ac 9: 25 him in a **b** through an opening
2Co 11: 33 was lowered in a **b** from a window

BATCH*
Ro 11: 16 is holy, then the whole **b** is holy;
1Co 5: 6 a little yeast leavens the whole **b**
5: 7 you may be a new unleavened **b**—
Gal 5: 9 yeast works through the whole **b**

BATH (BATHING)
Jn 13: 10 "Those who have had a **b** need

BATHING (BATH)
2Sa 11: 2 From the roof he saw a woman **b**.

BATHSHEBA*
Wife of Uriah who committed adultery with and became wife of David (2Sa 11), mother of Solomon (2Sa 12:24; 1Ki 1–2; 1Ch 3:5; Ps 51:T).

BATTLE (BATTLES)
1Sa 17: 47 for the **b** is the LORD's, and he
2Ch 20: 15 For the **b** is not yours, but God's.
Ps 24: 8 mighty, the LORD mighty in **b**.
Ecc 9: 11 to the swift or the **b** to the strong,
Isa 31: 4 come down to do **b** on Mount Zion
Eze 13: 5 will stand firm in the **b** on the day
Rev 16: 14 them for the **b** on the great day
20: 8 and to gather them for **b**.

BATTLES* (BATTLE)
1Sa 8: 20 go out before us and fight our **b**."
18: 17 and fight the **b** of the LORD."
25: 28 because you fight the LORD's **b**,
2Ch 32: 8 God to help us and to fight our **b**."

BEAR (BEARING BEARS BIRTH BIRTHRIGHT BORE BORN CHILDBEARING CHILDBIRTH FIRSTBORN NEWBORN REBIRTH)
Ge 4: 13 punishment is more than I can **b**.
Ps 38: 4 me like a burden too heavy to **b**.
Isa 11: 7 The cow will feed with the **b**,
53: 11 many, and he will **b** their iniquities.
Da 7: 5 beast, which looked like a **b**.
Mt 7: 18 A good tree cannot **b** bad fruit,
7: 18 and a bad tree cannot **b** good fruit.
Lk 21: 13 And so you will **b** testimony to me.
Jn 15: 2 branch that does **b** fruit he prunes
15: 8 that you **b** much fruit,
15: 16 so that you might go and **b** fruit—
Ro 7: 4 that we might **b** fruit for God.
15: 1 We who are strong ought to **b**
1Co 10: 13 tempted beyond what you can **b**.
Col 3: 13 **B** with each other and forgive one

BEARD
Lev 19: 27 head or clip off the edges of your **b**.
Isa 50: 6 to those who pulled out my **b**;

BEARING (BEAR)
Eph 4: 2 patient, **b** with one another in love.
Col 1: 10 **b** fruit in every good work,
Heb 13: 13 the camp, **b** the disgrace he bore.

BEARS (BEAR)
1Ki 8: 43 house I have built **b** your Name.
Ps 68: 19 Savior, who daily **b** our burdens.

BEAST (BEASTS)
Rev 13: 18 calculate the number of the **b**, for it
16: 2 people who had the mark of the **b**
19: 20 had received the mark of the **b**

BEASTS (BEAST)
Da 7: 3 Four great **b**, each different
1Co 15: 32 If I fought wild **b** in Ephesus

BEAT (BEATEN BEATING BEATINGS)
Isa 2: 4 They will **b** their swords
Joel 3: 10 **B** your plowshares into swords
Mic 4: 3 They will **b** their swords

BEATEN (BEAT)
Lk 12: 47 do what the master wants will be **b**
12: 48 deserving punishment will be **b**
2Co 11: 25 Three times I was **b** with rods,

BEATING (BEAT)
1Co 9: 26 I do not fight like a boxer **b** the air.
1Pe 2: 20 if you receive a **b** for doing wrong

BEATINGS (BEAT)
Pr 19: 29 and **b** for the backs of fools.

BEAUTIFUL* (BEAUTY)
Ge 6: 2 the daughters of humans were **b**,
12: 11 "I know what a **b** woman you are.
12: 14 saw that Sarai was a very **b** woman.
24: 16 The woman was very **b**, a virgin;
26: 7 of Rebekah, because she is **b**."
29: 17 had a lovely figure and was **b**.
49: 21 is a doe set free that bears **b** fawns.
Nu 24: 5 "How **b** are your tents, Jacob,
Dt 21: 11 among the captives a **b** woman
Jos 7: 21 I saw in the plunder a **b** robe
1Sa 25: 3 was an intelligent and **b** woman,
2Sa 11: 2 The woman was very **b**,
13: 1 the **b** sister of Absalom son
14: 27 Tamar, and she became a **b** woman
1Ki 1: 3 Israel for a **b** young woman
1: 4 The woman was very **b**;
Est 2: 2 search be made for **b** young virgins
2: 3 bring all these **b** young women
2: 7 had a lovely figure and was **b**.
Job 42: 15 there found women as **b** as Job's
Ps 48: 2 **B** in its loftiness, the joy
Pr 11: 22 snout is a **b** woman who shows no
24: 4 are filled with rare and **b** treasures.
Ecc 3: 11 He has made everything **b** in its
SS 1: 8 do not know, most **b** of women,
1: 10 Your cheeks are **b** with earrings,
1: 15 How **b** you are, my darling!
1: 15 Oh, how **b**! Your eyes are doves.
2: 10 my darling, my **b** one,
2: 13 my **b** one, come with me."
4: 1 How **b** you are, my darling!
4: 1 Oh, how **b**! Your eyes behind your
4: 7 You are altogether **b**, my darling;
5: 9 than others, most **b** of women?
6: 1 beloved gone, most **b** of women?
6: 4 You are as **b** as Tirzah, my darling,
7: 1 How **b** your sandaled feet,
7: 6 How **b** you are and how pleasing,
Isa 4: 2 the Branch of the LORD will be **b**
28: 5 a **b** wreath for the remnant of his
52: 7 How **b** on the mountains are the
Jer 3: 19 land, the most **b** inheritance of any
6: 2 Daughter Zion, so **b** and delicate.
11: 16 olive tree with fruit **b** in form.
46: 20 "Egypt is a **b** heifer, but a gadfly is
Eze 7: 20 They took pride in their **b** jewelry
16: 12 ears and a **b** crown on your head.
16: 13 You became very **b** and rose to be
20: 6 and honey, the most **b** of all lands.
20: 15 honey, the most **b** of all lands—
23: 42 sister and **b** crowns on their heads.
27: 24 they traded with you **b** garments,
31: 3 with **b** branches overshadowing
31: 9 made it **b** with abundant branches,
33: 32 who sings love songs with a **b** voice
Da 4: 12 Its leaves were **b**, its fruit abundant,
4: 21 with **b** leaves and abundant fruit,
8: 9 to the east and toward the **B** Land.
11: 16 will establish himself in the **B** Land
Da 11: 41 He will also invade the **B** Land.
11: 45 the seas at the **b** holy mountain.
Zec 9: 17 How attractive and **b** they will be!
Mt 23: 27 which look **b** on the outside
26: 10 She has done a **b** thing to me.
Mk 14: 6 She has done a **b** thing to me.
Lk 21: 5 temple was adorned with **b** stones
Ac 3: 2 carried to the temple gate called **B**,
3: 10 begging at the temple gate called **B**,
Ro 10: 15 "How **b** are the feet of those who

BEAUTY* (BEAUTIFUL)
Est 1: 11 order to display her **b** to the people
2: 3 let **b** treatments be given to them.
2: 9 provided her with her **b** treatments
2: 12 months of **b** treatments prescribed
Ps 27: 4 to gaze on the **b** of the LORD
45: 11 the king be enthralled by your **b**;
50: 2 Zion, perfect in **b**, God shines
Pr 6: 25 not lust in your heart after her **b**
31: 30 is deceptive, and **b** is fleeting;
Isa 3: 24 instead of **b**, branding.
28: 1 his glorious **b**, set on the head
28: 4 his glorious **b**, set on the head
33: 17 Your eyes will see the king in his **b**
53: 2 He had no **b** or majesty to attract
61: 3 them a crown of **b** instead of ashes,
La 2: 15 that was called the perfection of **b**,
Eze 16: 14 the nations on account of your **b**,
16: 14 given you made your **b** perfect,
16: 15 you trusted in your **b** and used
16: 15 passed by and your **b** became his.
16: 16 to him, and he possessed your **b**.
16: 25 lofty shrines and degraded your **b**,
27: 3 say, Tyre, "I am perfect in **b**."
27: 4 your builders brought your **b**
27: 11 they brought your **b** to perfection.
28: 7 draw their swords against your **b**
28: 12 full of wisdom and perfect in **b**.
28: 17 proud on account of your **b**,
31: 7 It was majestic in **b**, with its
31: 8 garden of God could match its **b**.
Jas 1: 11 blossom falls and its **b** is destroyed.
1Pe 3: 3 Your **b** should not come
3: 4 unfading **b** of a gentle and quiet

BED (SICKBED)
Isa 28: 20 The **b** is too short to stretch out on,
Lk 11: 7 and my children and I are in **b**.
17: 34 night two people will be in one **b**;
Heb 13: 4 and the marriage **b** kept pure,

BEELZEBUL*
Mt 10: 25 of the house has been called **B**,
12: 24 said, "It is only by **B**, the prince
12: 27 And if I drive out demons by **B**,
Mk 3: 22 said, "He is possessed by **B**!
Lk 11: 15 said, "By **B**, the prince of demons,
11: 18 claim that I drive out demons by **B**.
11: 19 Now if I drive out demons by **B**,

BEER
Pr 20: 1 Wine is a mocker and **b** a brawler;

BEERSHEBA
Ge 21: 14 and wandered in the Desert of **B**.
Jdg 20: 1 all Israel from Dan to **B**
1Sa 3: 20 Dan to **B** recognized that Samuel
2Sa 3: 10 Israel and Judah from Dan to **B**."
17: 11 Let all Israel, from Dan to **B**—
24: 2 the tribes of Israel from Dan to **B**
24: 15 of the people from Dan to **B** died.
1Ki 4: 25 from Dan to **B**, lived in safety,
1Ch 21: 2 count the Israelites from **B** to Dan.
2Ch 30: 5 throughout Israel, from **B** to Dan,

BEGGING
Ps 37: 25 forsaken or their children **b** bread.
Ac 16: 9 of Macedonia standing and **b** him,

BEGINNING
Ge 1: 1 In the **b** God created the heavens
Ps 102: 25 In the **b** you laid the foundations
111: 10 of the LORD is the **b** of wisdom;
Pr 1: 7 the LORD is the **b** of knowledge,
4: 7 The **b** of wisdom is this:
9: 10 of the LORD is the **b** of wisdom,
Ecc 3: 11 fathom what God has done from **b**
Isa 40: 21 it not been told you from the **b**?
46: 10 I make known the end from the **b**,
Mt 24: 8 All these are the **b** of birth pains.
Lk 1: 3 investigated everything from the **b**,
Jn 1: 1 In the **b** was the Word,
1Jn 1: 1 That which was from the **b**,
Rev 21: 6 and the Omega, the **B** and the End.
22: 13 and the Last, the **B** and the End.

BEHAVE (BEHAVIOR)
Ro 13: 13 us **b** decently, as in the daytime,

BEHAVIOR (BEHAVE)
Pr 1: 3 receiving instruction in prudent **b**,
1Pe 3: 1 words by the **b** of their wives,
3: 16 maliciously against your good **b**

BEHEMOTH*
Job 40: 15 "Look at **B**, which I made along

BELIEVE (BELIEVED BELIEVER BELIEVERS BELIEVES BELIEVING)
Ex 4: 1 "What if they do not **b** me or listen
1Ki 10: 7 I did not **b** these things until I
2Ch 9: 6 But I did not **b** what they said until
Ps 78: 32 of his wonders, they did not **b**.
Pr 14: 15 The simple **b** anything,
Hab 1: 5 in your days that you would not **b**,
Mt 18: 6 those who **b** in me—
21: 22 If you **b**, you will receive whatever
27: 42 the cross, and we will **b** in him.
Mk 1: 15 Repent and **b** the good news!"
5: 36 told him, "Don't be afraid; just **b**."
9: 24 the boy's father exclaimed, "I do **b**;
9: 42 those who **b** in me—
11: 24 prayer, **b** that you have received it,
15: 32 the cross, that we may see and **b**."
16: 16 *does not* **b** *will be condemned.*
16: 17 *will accompany those who* **b**:
Lk 8: 12 that they may not **b** and be saved.
8: 13 They **b** for a while, but in the time
8: 50 just **b**, and she will be healed."
22: 67 "If I tell you, you will not **b** me,
24: 25 how slow to **b** all that the prophets
Jn 1: 7 so that through him all might **b**.
3: 18 does not **b** stands condemned
4: 42 "We no longer **b** just because
5: 38 for you do not **b** the one he sent.
5: 46 you would **b** me, for he wrote
6: 29 to **b** in the one he has sent."
6: 69 We have come to **b** and to know
7: 5 even his own brothers did not **b**
8: 24 if you do not **b** that I am he,
9: 35 "Do you **b** in the Son of Man?"
9: 36 "Tell me so that I may **b** in him."
9: 38 "Lord, I **b**," and he worshiped him.
10: 26 you do not **b** because you are not
10: 37 Do not **b** me unless I do the works
10: 38 even though you do not **b** me,
11: 27 "I **b** that you are the Messiah,
11: 40 "Did I not tell you that if you **b**,
12: 36 **B** in the light while you have the
12: 37 they still would not **b** in him.
12: 39 For this reason they could not **b**,
12: 44 in me does not **b** in me only,
13: 19 it does happen you will **b** that I am
14: 1 You **b** in God; **b** also in me.
14: 10 Don't you **b** that I am in the Father,
14: 11 **B** me when I say that I am
14: 11 or at least **b** on the evidence
16: 30 This makes us **b** that you came
16: 31 "Do you now **b**?" Jesus replied.
17: 21 the world may **b** that you have sent
19: 35 he testifies so that you also may **b**.
20: 27 into my side. Stop doubting and **b**."
20: 31 may **b** that Jesus is the Messiah,
Ac 16: 31 They replied, "**B** in the Lord Jesus,
19: 4 He told the people to **b** in the one
24: 14 I **b** everything that is in accordance
26: 27 Agrippa, do you **b** the prophets?
Ro 3: 22 faith in Jesus Christ to all who **b**.
4: 11 he is the father of all who **b**
10: 9 **b** in your heart that God raised
10: 10 For it is with your heart that you **b**
10: 14 how can they **b** in the one of whom
1Co 1: 21 was preached to save those who **b**.
Gal 3: 22 might be given to those who **b**.
Php 1: 29 of Christ not only to **b** in him,
1Th 4: 14 For we **b** that Jesus died and rose
2Th 2: 11 delusion so that they will **b** the lie

1Ti 4: 10 and especially of those who **b**.
Titus 1: 6 a man whose children **b** and are
Heb 11: 6 comes to him must **b** that he exists
Jas 1: 6 you ask, you must **b** and not doubt,
2: 19 You **b** that there is one God. Good! Even the demons **b** that—
1Pe 2: 7 Now to you who **b**, this stone is
1Jn 3: 23 to **b** in the name of his Son,
4: 1 Dear friends, do not **b** every spirit,
5: 13 things to you who **b** in the name

BELIEVED (BELIEVE)
Ge 15: 6 Abram **b** the LORD, and he
Ex 4: 31 and they **b**. And when they heard
Isa 53: 1 Who has **b** our message
Jnh 3: 5 The Ninevites **b** God. A fast was
Lk 1: 45 Blessed is she who has **b**
Jn 1: 12 those who **b** in his name, he gave
2: 11 and his disciples **b** in him.
2: 22 Then they **b** the scripture
3: 18 already because they have not **b**
5: 46 If you **b** Moses, you would believe
7: 31 Still, many in the crowd **b** in him.
7: 39 whom those who **b** in him were
8: 30 Even as he spoke, many **b** in him.
11: 45 had seen what Jesus did, **b** in him.
12: 38 who has **b** our message
20: 8 also went inside. He saw and **b**.
20: 29 you have seen me, you have **b**;
20: 29 who have not seen and yet have **b**."
Ac 13: 48 were appointed for eternal life **b**.
19: 2 the Holy Spirit when you **b**?"
Ro 4: 3 "Abraham **b** God, and it was
10: 14 call on the one they have not **b** in?
10: 16 "Lord, who has **b** our message?"
1Co 15: 2 Otherwise, you have **b** in vain.
Gal 3: 6 So also Abraham "**b** God, and it
2Th 2: 12 who have not **b** the truth
1Ti 3: 16 the nations, was **b** on in the world,
2Ti 1: 12 because I know whom I have **b**,
Jas 2: 23 that says, "Abraham **b** God, and it

BELIEVER* (BELIEVE)
1Ki 18: 3 (Obadiah was a devout **b**
Ac 16: 1 a **b** but whose father was a Greek.
16: 15 you consider me a **b** in the Lord,"
1Co 7: 12 brother has a wife who is not a **b**
7: 13 has a husband who is not a **b** and
7: 17 each person should live as a **b** in
2Co 6: 15 what does a **b** have in common
2Th 3: 15 warn them as you would a fellow **b**.
1Ti 5: 16 any woman who is a **b** has widows
2Th 3: 6 keep away from every **b** who is idle

BELIEVERS (BELIEVE)
Jn 4: 41 of his words many more became **b**.
Ac 1: 15 up among the **b** (a group numbering
2: 44 All the **b** were together and had
4: 32 All the **b** were one in heart
5: 12 all the **b** used to meet together
9: 41 Then he called for the **b**,
10: 45 The circumcised **b** who had come
11: 2 the circumcised **b** criticized him
15: 2 along with some other **b**, to go
15: 5 some of the **b** who belonged
15: 23 To the Gentile **b** in Antioch,
15: 32 to encourage and strengthen the **b**.
21: 25 As for the Gentile **b**, we have
1Co 6: 5 to judge a dispute between **b**?
14: 22 a sign, not for **b** but for unbelievers;
14: 22 is not for unbelievers but for **b**.
2Co 11: 26 and in danger from false **b**.
Gal 2: 4 because some false **b** had infiltrated
6: 10 those who belong to the family of **b**.
1Th 1: 7 a model to all the **b** in Macedonia
1Ti 4: 12 set an example for the **b** in speech,
6: 2 masters are dear to them as fellow **b**
Jas 2: 1 **b** in our glorious Lord Jesus Christ
1Pe 2: 17 love the family of **b**, fear God,
3Jn : 10 he even refuses to welcome other **b**.

BELIEVES* (BELIEVE)
Mk 9: 23 is possible for one who **b**."
11: 23 **b** that what they say will happen,
16: 16 *Whoever* **b** *and is baptized*
Jn 3: 15 everyone who **b** may have eternal
3: 16 whoever **b** in him shall not perish
Jn 3: 18 Whoever **b** in him is not
3: 36 Whoever **b** in the Son has eternal
5: 24 **b** him who sent me has eternal life
6: 35 and whoever **b** in me will never be
6: 40 and **b** in him shall have eternal life,
6: 47 you, the one who **b** has eternal life.
7: 38 Whoever **b** in me, as Scripture has
11: 25 The one who **b** in me will live,
12: 44 "Whoever **b** in me does not believe
12: 46 that no one who **b** in me should stay
14: 12 whoever **b** in me will do the works I
Ac 10: 43 that everyone who **b** in him receives
13: 39 him everyone who **b** is set free
Ro 1: 16 brings salvation to everyone who **b**:
9: 33 the one who **b** in him will never be
10: 4 righteousness for everyone who **b**.
10: 11 "Anyone who **b** in him will never
1Jn 5: 1 Everyone who **b** that Jesus is
5: 5 Only the one who **b** that Jesus is
5: 10 Whoever **b** in the Son of God

BELIEVING* (BELIEVE)
Jn 11: 26 whoever lives by **b** in me will never
12: 11 going over to Jesus and **b** in him.
20: 31 by **b** you may have life in his name.
Ac 9: 26 not **b** that he really was a disciple.
1Co 7: 14 sanctified through her **b** husband.
9: 5 have the right to take a **b** wife along
Gal 3: 2 of the law, or by **b** what you heard?
3: 5 law, or by your **b** what you heard?
1Ti 6: 2 Those who have **b** masters should

BELLY
Ge 3: 14 You will crawl on your **b** and you
Da 2: 32 of silver, its **b** and thighs of bronze,
Mt 12: 40 three nights in the **b** of a huge fish,

BELONG (BELONGS)
Ge 40: 8 "Do not interpretations **b** to God?
Lev 25: 55 for the Israelites **b** to me as servants.
Dt 10: 14 LORD your God **b** the heavens,
29: 29 The secret things **b** to the LORD
29: 29 but the things revealed **b** to us
Job 12: 13 "To God **b** wisdom and power;
12: 16 To him **b** strength and insight;
25: 2 "Dominion and awe **b** to God;
Ps 47: 9 for the kings of the earth **b** to God;
95: 4 and the mountain peaks **b** to him.
115: 16 The highest heavens **b**
Jer 5: 10 for these people do not **b**
Jn 8: 44 You **b** to your father, the devil,
15: 19 As it is, you do not **b** to the world,
Ro 1: 6 those Gentiles who are called to **b**
7: 4 that you might **b** to another, to him
8: 9 of Christ, they do not **b** to Christ.
14: 8 we live or die, we **b** to the Lord.
1Co 7: 39 wishes, but he must **b** to the Lord.
15: 23 when he comes, those who **b** to him.
Gal 3: 29 If you **b** to Christ, then you are
5: 24 Those who **b** to Christ Jesus have
1Th 5: 5 We do not **b** to the night
5: 8 But since we **b** to the day, let us be
1Jn 3: 19 how we know that we **b** to the truth

BELONGS (BELONG)
Lev 27: 30 from the trees, **b** to the LORD;
Dt 1: 17 of anyone, for judgment **b** to God.
Job 41: 11 Everything under heaven **b** to me.
Ps 22: 28 for dominion **b** to the LORD
89: 18 Indeed, our shield **b** to the LORD,
111: 10 To him **b** eternal praise.
Eze 18: 4 For everyone **b** to me, the parent as
Jn 8: 47 Whoever **b** to God hears what God
Ro 12: 5 and each member **b** to all the others.
Rev 7: 10 "Salvation **b** to our God, who sits

BELOVED* (LOVE)
Dt 33: 12 "Let the **b** of the LORD rest
SS 1: 13 My **b** is to me a sachet of myrrh
1: 14 My **b** is to me a cluster of henna
1: 16 How handsome you are, my **b**!
2: 3 the forest is my **b** among the young
2: 8 Listen! My **b**! Look!
2: 9 My **b** is like a gazelle or a young
2: 10 My **b** spoke and said to me, "Arise,
2: 16 My **b** is mine and I am his;
2: 17 my **b**, and be like a gazelle or like
4: 16 Let my **b** come into his garden
5: 2 My **b** is knocking: "Open to me,
SS 5: 4 My **b** thrust his hand through
5: 5 I arose to open for my **b**, and my
5: 6 I opened for my **b**, but my **b** had
5: 8 if you find my **b**, what will you tell
5: 9 How is your **b** better than others,
5: 9 How is your **b** better than others,
5: 10 My **b** is radiant and ruddy,
5: 16 This is my **b**, this is my friend,
6: 1 Where has your **b** gone,
6: 1 Which way did your **b** turn,
6: 2 My **b** has gone down to his garden,
6: 3 am my beloved's and my **b** is mine;
7: 9 May the wine go straight to my **b**,
7: 10 I belong to my **b**, and his desire is
7: 11 my **b**, let us go to the countryside,
7: 13 that I have stored up for you, my **b**.
8: 5 the wilderness leaning on her **b**?
8: 14 my **b**, and be like a gazelle or like
Jer 11: 15 "What is my **b** doing in my temple

BELOVED'S* (LOVE)
SS 6: 3 I am my **b** and my beloved is mine;

BELSHAZZAR
King of Babylon in days of Daniel (Da 5).

BELT
Ex 12: 11 with your cloak tucked into your **b**,
1Ki 18: 46 tucking his cloak into his **b**, he ran
2Ki 4: 29 "Tuck your cloak into your **b**,
9: 1 "Tuck your cloak into your **b**,
Isa 11: 5 Righteousness will be his **b**
Eph 6: 14 the **b** of truth buckled around your

BENEFICIAL* (BENEFIT)
1Co 6: 12 but not everything is **b**.
10: 23 but not everything is **b**.

BENEFIT (BENEFICIAL BENEFITS)
Job 22: 2 "Can a man be of **b** to God?
22: 2 Can even a wise person **b** him?
Isa 38: 17 my **b** that I suffered such anguish.
Ro 6: 22 the **b** you reap leads to holiness,
2Co 4: 15 All this is for your **b**,

BENEFITS (BENEFIT)
Ps 103: 2 my soul, and forget not all his **b**—
Jn 4: 38 and you have reaped the **b** of their

BENJAMIN
Twelfth son of Jacob by Rachel (Ge 35:16–24; 46:19–21; 1Ch 2:2). Jacob refused to send him to Egypt, but relented (Ge 42–45). Tribe of blessed (Ge 49:27; Dt 33:12), numbered (Nu 1:37; 26:41), allotted land (Jos 18:11–28; Eze 48:23), failed to fully possess (Jdg 1:21), nearly obliterated (Jdg 20–21), sided with Ish-Bosheth (2Sa 2), but turned to David (1Ch 12:2, 29). 12,000 from (Rev 7:8).

BEREAN*
Ac 17: 11 Now the **B** Jews were of more noble

BESTOWS
Ps 84: 11 the LORD **b** favor and honor;

BETHANY
Mk 11: 1 and **B** at the Mount of Olives,

BETHEL
Ge 28: 19 He called that place **B**,

BETHLEHEM
Ru 1: 19 went on until they came to **B**.
1Sa 16: 1 I am sending you to Jesse of **B**.
2Sa 23: 15 from the well near the gate of **B**!"
Mic 5: 2 "But you, **B** Ephrathah, though you
Mt 2: 1 After Jesus was born in **B** in Judea,
2: 6 "'But you, **B**, in the land

BETHPHAGE
Mt 21: 1 came to **B** on the Mount of Olives,

BETHSAIDA
Jn 12: 21 Philip, who was from **B** in Galilee,

BETRAY (BETRAYED BETRAYS)
Ps 89: 33 nor will I ever **b** my faithfulness.
Pr 25: 9 do not **b** another's confidence,
Mt 10: 21 "Brother will **b** brother to death,
26: 21 I tell you, one of you will **b** me."

BETRAYED (BETRAY)
Mt 27: 4 said, "for I have **b** innocent blood."

BETRAYS (BETRAY)
Pr 11: 13 A gossip **b** a confidence,
20: 19 A gossip **b** a confidence;

BEULAH*
Isa 62: 4 called Hephzibah, and your land **B**;

BEWITCHED*
Gal 3: 1 Who has **b** you? Before your very

BEZALEL
Judahite craftsman in charge of building the tabernacle (Ex 31:1–11; 35:30—39:31).

BIDDING*
Ps 103: 20 you mighty ones who do his **b**,
148: 8 clouds, stormy winds that do his **b**,

BILDAD
One of Job's friends (Job 8; 18; 25).

BILHAH
Servant of Rachel, mother of Jacob's sons Dan and Naphtali (Ge 30:1–7; 35:25; 46:23–25).

BIND (BINDS BOUND)
Dt 6: 8 and **b** them on your foreheads.
Pr 3: 3 **b** them around your neck,
6: 21 **B** them always on your heart;
7: 3 **B** them on your fingers;
Isa 61: 1 He has sent me to **b**
Mt 16: 19 whatever you **b** on earth will be

BINDS (BIND)
Ps 147: 3 and **b** up their wounds.
Isa 30: 26 when the LORD **b** up the bruises
Ro 7: 2 from the law that **b** her to him.

BIRD (BIRDS)
Pr 27: 8 Like a **b** that flees its nest is anyone
Ecc 10: 20 a **b** on the wing may report what

BIRDS (BIRD)
Mt 8: 20 "Foxes have dens and **b** have nests,
Lk 9: 58 "Foxes have dens and **b** have nests,

BIRTH (BEAR)
Dt 32: 18 forgot the God who gave you **b**.
Ps 51: 5 Surely I was sinful at **b**,
58: 3 Even from **b** the wicked go astray;
Isa 26: 18 in labor, but we gave **b** to wind.
Mt 1: 18 This is how the **b** of Jesus
24: 8 these are the beginning of **b** pains.
Jn 3: 6 Flesh gives **b** to flesh, but the Spirit gives **b** to spirit.
1Pe 1: 3 great mercy he has given us new **b**

BIRTHRIGHT (BEAR)
Ge 25: 34 and left. So Esau despised his **b**.

BITTEN
Nu 21: 8 anyone who is **b** can look at it

BITTER (BITTERNESS EMBITTER)
Ex 12: 8 along with **b** herbs, and bread
Pr 27: 7 hungry even what is **b** tastes sweet.

BITTERNESS (BITTER)
Pr 14: 10 Each heart knows its own **b**,
17: 25 and **b** to the mother who bore him.
Ro 3: 14 mouths are full of cursing and **b**."
Eph 4: 31 Get rid of all **b**, rage and anger,

BLACK
Zec 6: 6 the **b** horses is going toward
Rev 6: 5 and there before me was a **b** horse!

BLAMELESS* (BLAMELESSLY)
Ge 6: 9 **b** among the people of his time,
17: 1 walk before me faithfully and be **b**.
Dt 18: 13 You must be **b** before the LORD
2Sa 22: 24 I have been **b** before him and have
22: 26 to the **b** you show yourself **b**,
Job 1: 1 This man was **b** and upright;
1: 8 is **b** and upright, a man who fears
2: 3 is **b** and upright, a man who fears
4: 6 and your **b** ways your hope?
8: 20 God does not reject one who is **b**
9: 20 if I were **b**, it would pronounce me
9: 21 "Although I am **b**, I have no
9: 22 say, 'He destroys both the **b**
12: 4 though righteous and **b**!
22: 3 would he gain if your ways were **b**?
31: 6 and he will know that I am **b**—
Ps 15: 2 The one whose walk is **b**, who does
18: 23 I have been **b** before him and have
18: 25 to the **b** you show yourself **b**,
19: 13 Then I will be **b**, innocent of great
26: 1 me, LORD, for I have led a **b** life;
26: 11 I lead a **b** life; deliver me and be
37: 18 The **b** spend their days under
Ps 37: 37 Consider the **b**, observe the
50: 23 to the **b** I will show my salvation."
84: 11 from those whose walk is **b**.
101: 2 I will be careful to lead a **b** life—
101: 2 affairs of my house with a **b** heart.
101: 6 one whose walk is **b** will minister
119: 1 are those whose ways are **b**,
Pr 2: 7 is a shield to those whose walk is **b**,
2: 21 land, and the **b** will remain in it;
10: 29 of the LORD is a refuge for the **b**,
11: 5 of the **b** makes their paths straight,
11: 20 delights in those whose ways are **b**.
19: 1 the poor whose walk is **b** than
20: 7 The righteous lead **b** lives;
28: 6 poor whose walk is **b** than the rich
28: 10 trap, but the **b** will receive a good
28: 18 one whose walk is **b** is kept safe,
Eze 28: 15 You were **b** in your ways
1Co 1: 8 so that you will be **b** on the day
Eph 1: 4 world to be holy and **b** in his sight.
5: 27 any other blemish, but holy and **b**.
Php 1: 10 be pure and **b** for the day of Christ,
2: 15 that you may become **b** and pure,
1Th 2: 10 and **b** we were among you who
3: 13 your hearts so that you will be **b**
5: 23 body be kept **b** at the coming of
Titus 1: 6 An elder must be **b**, faithful to his
1: 7 God's household, he must be **b**—
Heb 7: 26 one who is holy, **b**, pure, set apart
2Pe 3: 14 spotless, **b** and at peace with him.
Rev 14: 5 found in their mouths; they are **b**.

BLAMELESSLY* (BLAMELESS)
Lk 1: 6 Lord's commands and decrees **b**.

BLASPHEME* (BLASPHEMED BLASPHEMER BLASPHEMES BLASPHEMIES BLASPHEMING BLASPHEMOUS BLASPHEMY)
Ex 22: 28 "Do not **b** God or curse the ruler
Lev 24: 16 when they **b** the Name they are
Ac 26: 11 and I tried to force them to **b**.
1Ti 1: 20 over to Satan to be taught not to **b**.
2Pe 2: 12 these people **b** in matters they do
Rev 13: 6 It opened its mouth to **b** God,

BLASPHEMED* (BLASPHEME)
Lev 24: 11 of the Israelite woman **b** the Name
1Sa 3: 13 his sons **b** God, and he failed
2Ki 19: 6 of the king of Assyria have **b** me.
19: 22 is it you have ridiculed and **b**?
Isa 37: 6 of the king of Assyria have **b** me.
37: 23 is it you have ridiculed and **b**?
52: 5 day long my name is constantly **b**.
Eze 20: 27 also your ancestors **b** me by being
Ac 19: 37 robbed temples nor **b** our goddess.
Ro 2: 24 "God's name is **b** among

BLASPHEMER* (BLASPHEME)
Lev 24: 14 "Take the **b** outside the camp.
24: 23 they took the **b** outside the camp
1Ti 1: 13 Even though I was once a **b**

BLASPHEMES* (BLASPHEME)
Lev 24: 16 anyone who **b** the name
Nu 15: 30 **b** the LORD and must be cut off
Mk 3: 29 whoever **b** against the Holy Spirit
Lk 12: 10 but anyone who **b** against the Holy

BLASPHEMIES* (BLASPHEME)
Ne 9: 18 or when they committed awful **b**.
9: 26 they committed awful **b**.
Rev 13: 5 mouth to utter proud words and **b**

BLASPHEMING* (BLASPHEME)
Mt 9: 3 to themselves, "This fellow is **b**!"
Mk 2: 7 He's **b**! Who can forgive sins
Jas 2: 7 the ones who are **b** the noble name

BLASPHEMOUS* (BLASPHEME)
Ac 6: 11 Stephen speak **b** words against
Rev 13: 1 horns, and on each head a **b** name.
17: 3 that was covered with **b** names

BLASPHEMY* (BLASPHEME)
Mt 12: 31 but **b** against the Spirit will not be
12: 31 but **b** against the Spirit will not be
26: 65 clothes and said, "He has spoken **b**!
26: 65 Look, now you have heard the **b**.
Mk 14: 64 "You have heard the **b**.
Lk 5: 21 "Who is this fellow who speaks **b**?
Jn 10: 33 replied, "but for **b**, because you,
10: 36 you accuse me of **b** because I said,

BLAST*
Ex 15: 8 By the **b** of your nostrils the waters
19: 13 sounds a long **b** may they approach
19: 16 and a very loud trumpet **b**.
Nu 10: 5 When a trumpet **b** is sounded,
10: 6 At the sounding of a second **b**,
10: 6 The **b** will be the signal for setting
10: 9 you, sound a **b** on the trumpets.
Jos 6: 5 you hear them sound a long **b**
6: 16 the priests sounded the trumpet **b**,
2Sa 22: 16 at the **b** of breath from his nostrils.
Job 4: 9 At the **b** of his anger they are no
39: 25 At the **b** of the trumpet it snorts,
Ps 18: 15 the **b** of breath from your nostrils.
98: 6 and the **b** of the ram's horn—
147: 17 Who can withstand his icy **b**?
Isa 27: 8 with his fierce **b** he drives her out,
Eze 22: 20 furnace to be melted with a fiery **b**,
Am 2: 2 war cries and the **b** of the trumpet.
Heb 12: 19 to a trumpet **b** or to such a voice

BLEATING*
1Sa 15: 14 then is this **b** of sheep in my ears?

BLEMISH* (BLEMISHES)
Lev 22: 21 it must be without defect or **b** to be
Nu 19: 2 you a red heifer without defect or **b**
2Sa 14: 25 of his foot there was no **b** in him.
Eph 5: 27 stain or wrinkle or any other **b**,
Col 1: 22 in his sight, without **b** and free
1Pe 1: 19 Christ, a lamb without **b** or defect.

BLEMISHES* (BLEMISH)
2Pe 2: 13 They are blots and **b**,
Jude : 12 These people are **b** at your love

BLESS (BLESSED BLESSES BLESSING BLESSINGS)
Ge 12: 3 I will **b** those who **b** you,
32: 26 not let you go unless you **b** me."
Dt 7: 13 He will love you and **b** you
33: 11 **B** all his skills, LORD, and be
Ps 72: 15 pray for him and **b** him all day
Ro 12: 14 **B** those who persecute you;

BLESSED (BLESS)
Ge 1: 22 God **b** them and said, "Be fruitful
2: 3 Then God **b** the seventh day
22: 18 all nations on earth will be **b**,
Nu 24: 9 "May those who bless you be **b**
1Ch 17: 27 LORD, have **b** it, and it will be **b**
Ps 1: 1 **B** is the one who does not walk
2: 12 **B** are all who take refuge in him.
32: 2 **B** is the one whose sin the LORD
33: 12 **B** is the nation whose God is
40: 4 **B** is the one who trusts
41: 1 **B** are those who have regard
84: 5 **B** are those whose strength is
89: 15 **B** are those who have learned
94: 12 **B** is the one you discipline, LORD,
106: 3 **B** are those who act justly,
112: 1 **B** are those who fear the LORD,
118: 26 **B** is he who comes in the name
119: 1 **B** are those whose ways are
119: 2 **B** are those who keep his statutes
127: 5 **B** is the man whose quiver is full
Pr 3: 13 **B** are those who find wisdom,
8: 34 **B** are those who listen to me,
28: 20 A faithful person will be richly **b**,
29: 18 **b** is the one who heeds wisdom's
31: 28 Her children arise and call her **b**;
Isa 30: 18 **B** are all who wait for him!
Mal 3: 12 all the nations will call you **b**,
3: 15 But now we call the arrogant **b**.
Mt 5: 3 "**B** are the poor in spirit, for theirs
5: 4 **B** are those who mourn, for they
5: 5 **B** are the meek, for they will
5: 6 **B** are those who hunger and thirst
5: 7 **B** are the merciful, for they will be
5: 8 **B** are the pure in heart, for they
5: 9 **B** are the peacemakers, for they
5: 10 **B** are those who are persecuted
5: 11 "**B** are you when people insult you,
Lk 1: 48 on all generations will call me **b**,
Jn 12: 13 "**B** is he who comes in the name
12: 13 "**B** is the king of Israel!"
Ac 20: 35 'It is more **b** to give than
Titus 2: 13 while we wait for the **b** hope—
Jas 1: 12 **B** is the one who perseveres under

Rev 1: 3 **B** is the one who reads aloud
1: 3 **b** are those who hear it and take
22: 7 **B** is the one who keeps the words
22: 14 "**B** are those who wash their robes,

BLESSES (BLESS)
Ps 29: 11 the LORD **b** his people with peace.
Ro 10: 12 all and richly **b** all who call on him,

BLESSING (BLESS)
Ge 27: 4 I may give you my **b** before I die."
Dt 23: 5 turned the curse into a **b** for you,
33: 1 This is the **b** that Moses the man
Pr 10: 22 The **b** of the LORD brings wealth,
Eze 34: 26 there will be showers of **b**.
Gal 4: 15 Where, then, is your **b** of me now?

BLESSINGS (BLESS)
Dt 11: 29 proclaim on Mount Gerizim the **b**,
Jos 8: 34 of the law—the **b** and the curses—
Pr 10: 6 **B** crown the head of the righteous,
Ro 15: 27 have shared in the Jews' spiritual **b**,
15: 27 share with them their material **b**.

BLIND (BLINDED)
Mt 15: 14 Leave them; they are **b** guides.
15: 14 If the **b** lead the **b**, both will fall
23: 16 "Woe to you, **b** guides! You say,
Mk 10: 46 were leaving the city, a **b** man,
Lk 6: 39 "Can the **b** lead the **b**?
Jn 9: 25 I do know. I was **b** but now I see!"

BLINDED (BLIND)
Jn 12: 40 "He has **b** their eyes and hardened
2Co 4: 4 god of this age has **b** the minds

BLOOD (BLOODSHED BLOODTHIRSTY)
Ge 4: 10 Your brother's **b** cries out to me
9: 6 "Whoever sheds human **b**, by humans shall their **b** be shed;
Ex 12: 13 when I see the **b**, I will pass over
24: 8 "This is the **b** of the covenant
Lev 16: 15 and take its **b** behind the curtain
17: 11 the life of a creature is in the **b**,
17: 11 it is the **b** that makes atonement
Dt 12: 23 be sure you do not eat the **b**, because the **b** is the life,
Ps 59: 2 me from those who are after my **b**.
72: 14 for precious is their **b** in his sight.
Pr 6: 17 hands that shed innocent **b**,
Isa 1: 11 I have no pleasure in the **b** of bulls
Mt 26: 28 This is my **b** of the covenant,
27: 24 "I am innocent of this man's **b**,"
Mk 14: 24 "This is my **b** of the covenant,
Lk 22: 44 his sweat was like drops of **b** falling
Jn 6: 53 of the Son of Man and drink his **b**,
Ac 15: 20 of strangled animals and from **b**.
20: 26 that I am innocent of the **b** of any
Ro 3: 25 through the shedding of his **b**—
5: 9 have now been justified by his **b**,
1Co 11: 25 cup is the new covenant in my **b**;
Eph 1: 7 we have redemption through his **b**,
2: 13 brought near by the **b** of Christ.
Col 1: 20 by making peace through his **b**,
Heb 9: 7 a year, and never without **b**,
9: 12 Place once for all by his own **b**,
9: 20 said, "This is the **b** of the covenant,
9: 22 everything be cleansed with **b**,
12: 24 speaks a better word than the **b**
1Pe 1: 19 but with the precious **b** of Christ,
1Jn 1: 7 and the **b** of Jesus, his Son,
Rev 1: 5 has freed us from our sins by his **b**,
5: 9 with your **b** you purchased for God
7: 14 them white in the **b** of the Lamb.
12: 11 over him by the **b** of the Lamb
19: 13 He is dressed in a robe dipped in **b**,

BLOODSHED (BLOOD)
Jer 48: 10 who keeps their sword from **b**!
Eze 35: 6 I will give you over to **b** and it
Hab 2: 12 to him who builds a city with **b**

BLOODTHIRSTY* (BLOOD)
Ps 5: 6 The **b** and deceitful you, LORD,
26: 9 my life with those who are **b**,
55: 23 the **b** and deceitful will not live
139: 19 Away from me, you who are **b**!
Pr 29: 10 The **b** hate a person of integrity

BLOSSOM
Isa 35: 1 the wilderness will rejoice and **b**.

BLOT (BLOTS)
Ex 32: 32 **b** me out of the book you have
Ps 51: 1 to your great compassion **b** out my
Rev 3: 5 I will never **b** out the name

BLOTS* (BLOT)
Isa 43: 25 "I, even I, am he who **b** out your
2Pe 2: 13 They are **b** and blemishes, reveling

BLOWN
Eph 4: 14 and **b** here and there by every wind
Jas 1: 6 the sea, **b** and tossed by the wind.
Jude : 12 without rain, **b** along by the wind;

BLUSH
Jer 6: 15 they do not even know how to **b**.

BOAST (BOASTING)
1Ki 20: 11 his armor should not **b** like one
Ps 44: 8 In God we make our **b** all day long,
Pr 27: 1 Do not **b** about tomorrow, for you
Isa 45: 25 and will make their **b** in him.
Jer 9: 23 or the strong **b** of their strength
9: 24 let the one who boasts **b** about this:
Ro 2: 17 if you rely on the law and **b** in God;
2: 23 You who **b** in the law, do you
5: 2 And we **b** in the hope of the glory
1Co 1: 31 "Let the one who boasts **b**
2Co 10: 17 "Let the one who boasts **b**
11: 30 If I must **b**, I will **b** of the things
Gal 6: 14 May I never **b** except in the cross
Eph 2: 9 not by works, so that no one can **b**.
Php 3: 3 by his Spirit, who **b** in Christ Jesus,
Jas 4: 16 is, you **b** in your arrogant schemes.

BOASTING (BOAST)
Php 1: 26 you again your **b** in Christ Jesus

BOAZ
Wealthy Bethlehemite who showed favor to Ruth (Ru 2), married her (Ru 4). Ancestor of David (Ru 4:18–22; 1Ch 2:12–15), Jesus (Mt 1:5–16; Lk 3:23–32).

BODIES (BODY)
Isa 26: 19 will live, LORD; their **b** will rise—
Ro 12: 1 to offer your **b** as a living sacrifice,
1Co 6: 15 not know that your **b** are members
6: 19 not know that your **b** are temples
6: 20 Therefore honor God with your **b**.
Eph 5: 28 to love their wives as their own **b**.

BODILY (BODY)
Col 2: 9 of the Deity lives in **b** form,

BODY (BODIES BODILY EMBODIMENT)
Zec 13: 6 are these wounds on your **b**?'
Mt 10: 28 be afraid of those who kill the **b**
10: 28 can destroy both soul and **b** in hell.
26: 26 "Take and eat; this is my **b**."
Mk 14: 22 saying, "Take it; this is my **b**."
Lk 22: 19 "This is my **b** given for you;
Jn 13: 10 their whole **b** is clean.
Ro 12: 4 us has one **b** with many members,
1Co 11: 24 "This is my **b**, which is for you;
12: 12 but all its many parts form one **b**,
12: 13 by one Spirit so as to form one **b**—
12: 24 But God has put the **b** together,
15: 44 it is sown a natural **b**, it is raised a spiritual **b**.
Eph 1: 23 which is his **b**, the fullness of him
4: 25 for we are all members of one **b**.
5: 30 for we are members of his **b**.
Php 1: 20 Christ will be exalted in my **b**,
Col 1: 24 for the sake of his **b**, which is

BOLD (BOLDNESS)
Pr 21: 29 The wicked put up a **b** front,
28: 1 but the righteous are as **b** as a lion.

BOLDNESS* (BOLD)
Ac 4: 29 to speak your word with great **b**.
28: 31 with all **b** and without hindrance!

BONDAGE
Ezr 9: 9 God has not forsaken us in our **b**.

BONES
Ge 2: 23 "This is now bone of my **b**
Ps 22: 14 water, and all my **b** are out of joint.
22: 17 All my **b** are on display;
Eze 37: 1 middle of a valley; it was full of **b**.
Jn 19: 36 "Not one of his **b** will be broken,"

BOOK (BOOKS)
Ex 32: 33 against me I will blot out of my **b**.
Jos 1: 8 Keep this **B** of the Law always
2Ki 22: 8 "I have found the **B** of the Law
2Ch 34: 15 "I have found the **B** of the Law
Ne 8: 8 They read from the **B** of the Law
Ps 69: 28 they be blotted out of the **b** of life
Da 12: 1 name is found written in the **b**—
Jn 20: 30 which are not recorded in this **b**.
Php 4: 3 whose names are in the **b** of life.
Rev 3: 5 of that person from the **b** of life,
20: 12 Another **b** was opened, which is the **b** of life.
20: 15 written in the **b** of life was thrown
21: 27 are written in the Lamb's **b** of life.

BOOKS* (BOOK)
Ecc 12: 12 Of making many **b** there is no end,
Da 7: 10 was seated, and the **b** were opened.
Jn 21: 25 for the **b** that would be written.
Rev 20: 12 the throne, and **b** were opened.
20: 12 they had done as recorded in the **b**.

BORE (BEAR)
Isa 53: 4 up our pain and **b** our suffering,
53: 12 For he **b** the sin of many, and made
Mt 8: 17 our infirmities and **b** our diseases."
1Pe 2: 24 "He himself **b** our sins" in his body

BORN (BEAR)
Ecc 3: 2 a time to be **b** and a time to die,
Isa 9: 6 For to us a child is **b**, to us a son is
66: 8 Can a country be **b** in a day
Lk 2: 11 a Savior has been **b** to you;
Jn 3: 3 of God unless they are **b** again."
3: 4 into their mother's womb to be **b**!"
3: 5 of God unless they are **b** of water
3: 7 my saying, 'You must be **b** again.'
3: 8 it is with everyone **b** of the Spirit."
1Pe 1: 23 For you have been **b** again,
1Jn 3: 9 because they have been **b** of God.
4: 7 Everyone who loves has been **b**
5: 1 that Jesus is the Christ is **b** of God,
5: 4 everyone **b** of God overcomes
5: 18 anyone **b** of God does not continue
5: 18 the One who was **b** of God keeps

BORROWER
Pr 22: 7 and the **b** is slave to the lender.

BOTHER (BOTHERING)
Lk 11: 7 one inside answers, 'Don't **b** me.

BOTHERING (BOTHER)
Lk 18: 5 yet because this widow keeps **b** me,

BOUGHT (BUY)
Ac 20: 28 which he **b** with his own blood.
1Co 6: 20 you were **b** at a price.
7: 23 You were **b** at a price;
2Pe 2: 1 the sovereign Lord who **b** them—

BOUND (BIND)
Isa 56: 3 Let no foreigner who is **b**
Mt 16: 19 bind on earth will be **b** in heaven,
18: 18 bind on earth will be **b** in heaven,
Ro 7: 2 by law a married woman is **b** to her
1Co 7: 39 A woman is **b** to her husband as
Jude : 6 **b** with everlasting chains
Rev 20: 2 and **b** him for a thousand years.

BOUNDARY (BOUNDS)
Nu 34: 3 Your southern **b** will start in the
Pr 23: 10 Do not move an ancient **b** stone
Hos 5: 10 are like those who move **b** stones.

BOUNDLESS
Eph 3: 8 the Gentiles the **b** riches of Christ,

BOUNDS (BOUNDARY)
2Co 7: 4 all our troubles my joy knows no **b**.

BOUNTY*
Ge 49: 26 than the **b** of the age-old hills.
Dt 28: 12 storehouse of his **b**, to send rain
1Ki 10: 13 he had given her out of his royal **b**.
Ps 65: 11 You crown the year with your **b**,
68: 10 settled in it, and from your **b**, God,
Jer 31: 12 will rejoice in the **b** of the LORD—
31: 14 people will be filled with my **b**,"

BOW (BOWED BOWS)
Dt 5: 9 You shall not **b** down to them
1Ki 22: 34 But someone drew his **b** at random

Ps 5: 7 in reverence I **b** down toward your
44: 6 I put no trust in my **b**, my sword
95: 6 Come, let us **b** down in worship,
138: 2 I will **b** down toward your holy
Isa 44: 19 Shall I **b** down to a block
45: 23 Before me every knee will **b**;
Ro 14: 11 Lord, 'every knee will **b** before me;
Php 2: 10 name of Jesus every knee should **b**,

BOWED (BOW)
Ps 145: 14 fall and lifts up all who are **b** down.
146: 8 lifts up those who are **b** down,

BOWS (BOW)
Isa 44: 15 he makes an idol and **b** down to it.
44: 17 he **b** down to it and worships.

BOY (BOY'S BOYS)
Ge 21: 17 God heard the **b** crying,
22: 12 "Do not lay a hand on the **b**,"
Jdg 13: 5 by a razor because the **b** is to be
1Sa 2: 11 the **b** ministered before the LORD
3: 8 that the LORD was calling the **b**.
Isa 7: 16 for before the **b** knows enough
Mt 17: 18 it came out of the **b**, and he was
Lk 2: 43 home, the **b** Jesus stayed behind

BOY'S (BOY)
1Ki 17: 22 and the **b** life returned to him,
2Ki 4: 34 on him, the **b** body grew warm.

BOYS (BOY)
Ge 25: 24 there were twin **b** in her womb.
Ex 1: 18 Why have you let the **b** live?"

BRACE*
Job 38: 3 **B** yourself like a man; I will
40: 7 "**B** yourself like a man; I will
Na 2: 1 watch the road, **b** yourselves,

BRAG*
Am 4: 5 **b** about your freewill offerings—

BRANCH (BRANCHES)
Isa 4: 2 that day the **B** of the LORD will be
Jer 23: 5 raise up for David a righteous **B**,
33: 15 I will make a righteous **B** sprout
Zec 3: 8 going to bring my servant, the **B**.
6: 12 is the man whose name is the **B**,
Jn 15: 2 cuts off every **b** in me that bears

BRANCHES (BRANCH)
Jn 15: 5 "I am the vine; you are the **b**.
Ro 11: 21 if God did not spare the natural **b**,

BRAVE
2Sa 2: 7 then, be strong and **b**, for Saul your
13: 28 you this order? Be strong and **b**."

BREACH (BREAK)
Ps 106: 23 stood in the **b** before him to keep

BREACHING (BREAK)
Pr 17: 14 Starting a quarrel is like **b** a dam;

BREAD
Ex 12: 8 herbs, and **b** made without yeast.
23: 15 the Festival of Unleavened **B**;
25: 30 Put the **b** of the Presence on this
Dt 8: 3 that man does not live on **b** alone
Ps 78: 25 Human beings ate the **b** of angels;
Pr 30: 8 riches, but give me only my daily **b**.
Isa 55: 2 spend money on what is not **b**,
Mt 4: 3 God, tell these stones to become **b**."
4: 4 'Man shall not live on **b** alone,
6: 11 Give us today our daily **b**.
26: 26 Jesus took **b**, and when he had
Mk 14: 22 Jesus took **b**, and when he had
Lk 4: 3 God, tell this stone to become **b**."
4: 4 'Man shall not live on **b** alone.'"
9: 13 "We have only five loaves of **b**
11: 3 Give us each day our daily **b**.
22: 19 And he took **b**, gave thanks
Jn 6: 33 the **b** of God is the **b** that comes
6: 35 Jesus declared, "I am the **b** of life.
6: 41 "I am the **b** that came down
6: 48 I am the **b** of life.
6: 51 I am the living **b** that came down
6: 51 Whoever eats this **b** will live
6: 51 This **b** is my flesh, which I will
21: 13 took the **b** and gave it to them,
1Co 10: 16 And is not the **b** that we break
11: 23 the night he was betrayed, took **b**,
11: 26 For whenever you eat this **b**

BREAK (BREACH BREACHING BREAKERS BREAKING BREAKS BROKE BROKEN BROKENNESS)
Nu 30: 2 must not **b** his word but must do
Jdg 2: 1 'I will never **b** my covenant
Ps 2: 9 You will **b** them with a rod of iron;
Pr 25: 15 and a gentle tongue can **b** a bone.
Isa 42: 3 A bruised reed he will not **b**,
Mt 12: 20 A bruised reed he will not **b**,
Ac 20: 7 week we came together to **b** bread.
1Co 10: 16 the bread that we **b** a participation
Rev 5: 2 "Who is worthy to **b** the seals

BREAKERS* (BREAK)
Ps 42: 7 waves and **b** have swept over me.
93: 4 mightier than the **b** of the sea—
Jnh 2: 3 your waves and **b** swept over me.

BREAKING (BREAK)
Jos 9: 20 fall on us for **b** the oath we swore
Eze 16: 59 my oath by **b** the covenant.
17: 18 the oath by **b** the covenant.
Ac 2: 42 to the **b** of bread and to prayer.
Jas 2: 10 just one point is guilty of **b** all of it.

BREAKS (BREAK)
Jer 23: 29 "and like a hammer that **b** a rock
1Jn 3: 4 Everyone who sins **b** the law;

BREASTPIECE (BREASTPLATE)
Ex 28: 15 a **b** for making decisions—

BREASTPLATE* (BREASTPIECE)
2Ch 18: 33 hit the king of Israel between the **b**
Isa 59: 17 He put on righteousness as his **b**,
Eph 6: 14 the **b** of righteousness in place,
1Th 5: 8 putting on faith and love as a **b**,

BREASTS
La 4: 3 Even jackals offer their **b** to nurse

BREATH (BREATHED GOD-BREATHED)
Ge 2: 7 into his nostrils the **b** of life,

BREATHED (BREATH)
Ge 2: 7 **b** into his nostrils the breath of life,
Mk 15: 37 With a loud cry, Jesus **b** his last.
Jn 20: 22 with that he **b** on them and said,

BRIBE
Ex 23: 8 "Do not accept a **b**, for a **b** blinds
Dt 16: 19 Do not accept a **b**, for a **b** blinds
27: 25 "Cursed is anyone who accepts a **b**
Pr 6: 35 he will refuse a **b**, however great it

BRIDE
Isa 62: 5 as a bridegroom rejoices over his **b**,
Rev 19: 7 and his **b** has made herself ready.
21: 2 prepared as a **b** beautifully dressed
21: 9 I will show you the **b**, the wife
22: 17 The Spirit and the **b** say, "Come!"

BRIDEGROOM
Ps 19: 5 It is like a **b** coming out of his
Mt 25: 1 lamps and went out to meet the **b**.
25: 5 The **b** was a long time in coming,

BRIGHTENS* (BRIGHTNESS)
Pr 16: 15 When a king's face **b**, it means life;
Ecc 8: 1 A person's wisdom **b** their face

BRIGHTER (BRIGHTNESS)
Pr 4: 18 shining ever **b** till the full light

BRIGHTNESS* (BRIGHTENS BRIGHTER)
2Sa 22: 13 Out of the **b** of his presence bolts
23: 4 the **b** after rain that brings grass
Ps 18: 12 Out of the **b** of his presence clouds
Isa 59: 9 for **b**, but we walk in deep
60: 3 and kings to the **b** of your dawn.
60: 19 nor will the **b** of the moon shine
Da 12: 3 who are wise will shine like the **b**
Am 5: 20 pitch-dark, without a ray of **b**?

BRILLIANCE* (BRILLIANT)
Ac 22: 11 because the **b** of the light had
Rev 1: 16 was like the sun shining in all its **b**.
21: 11 **b** was like that of a very precious

BRILLIANT* (BRILLIANCE)
Ecc 9: 11 or wealth to the **b** or favor
Eze 1: 4 and surrounded by **b** light.
1: 27 and **b** light surrounded him.

BRITTLE*
Da 2: 42 will be partly strong and partly **b**.

BROAD
Mt 7: 13 gate and **b** is the road that leads

BROKE (BREAK)
Mt 26: 26 he **b** it and gave it to his disciples,
Mk 14: 22 he **b** it and gave it to his disciples,
Ac 2: 46 They **b** bread in their homes and
20: 11 he went upstairs again and **b** bread
1Co 11: 24 had given thanks, he **b** it and said,

BROKEN (BREAK)
1Sa 2: 10 who oppose the LORD will be **b**.
Ps 34: 20 bones, not one of them will be **b**.
51: 17 My sacrifice, O God, is a **b** spirit;
Ecc 4: 12 of three strands is not quickly **b**.
Lk 20: 18 on that stone will be **b** to pieces;
Jn 7: 23 that the law of Moses may not be **b**,
19: 36 "Not one of his bones will be **b**,"
Ro 11: 20 they were **b** off because of unbelief,

BROKENHEARTED* (HEART)
Ps 34: 18 The LORD is close to the **b**
109: 16 the poor and the needy and the **b**.
147: 3 He heals the **b** and binds up their
Isa 61: 1 He has sent me to bind up the **b**,

BROKENNESS* (BREAK)
Isa 65: 14 of heart and wail in **b** of spirit.

BRONZE
Ex 27: 2 piece, and overlay the altar with **b**.
30: 18 "Make a **b** basin, with its **b** stand,
Nu 21: 9 Moses made a **b** snake and put it
Da 2: 32 of silver, its belly and thighs of **b**,
10: 6 legs like the gleam of burnished **b**,
Rev 1: 15 His feet were like **b** glowing
2: 18 whose feet are like burnished **b**.

BROTHER (BROTHER'S BROTHERLY BROTHERS)
Pr 17: 17 a **b** is born for a time of adversity.
18: 24 a friend who sticks closer than a **b**.
Mt 18: 15 "If your **b** or sister sins,
Mk 3: 35 Whoever does God's will is my **b**
Lk 17: 3 "If your **b** or sister sins against you,
Ro 14: 13 obstacle in the way of a **b** or sister.
14: 15 If your **b** or sister is distressed
14: 21 anything else that will cause your **b**
1Co 7: 15 The **b** or the sister is not bound
8: 13 if what I eat causes my **b** or sister
Phm : 16 but better than a slave, as a dear **b**.
Jas 2: 15 Suppose a **b** or a sister is without
4: 11 Anyone who speaks against a **b**
1Jn 2: 9 but hates a **b** or sister is still
2: 10 who loves their **b** and sister lives
3: 10 does not love their **b** and sister.
3: 15 hates a **b** or sister is a murderer,
3: 17 sees a **b** or sister in need but has
4: 20 claims to love God yet hates a **b**
4: 20 For whoever does not love their **b**
5: 16 If you see any **b** or sister commit

BROTHER'S (BROTHER)
Ge 4: 9 "Am I my **b** keeper?"

BROTHERS (BROTHER)
Mt 12: 49 "Here are my mother and my **b**.
19: 29 everyone who has left houses or **b**
25: 40 did for one of the least of these **b**
Mk 3: 33 "Who are my mother and my **b**?"
10: 29 "no one who has left home or **b**
Lk 21: 16 even by parents, **b** and sisters,
22: 32 turned back, strengthen your **b**."
Jn 7: 5 For even his own **b** did not believe
1Th 4: 10 urge you, **b** and sisters, to do so
2Th 3: 6 we command you, **b** and sisters,
Heb 2: 11 Jesus is not ashamed to call them **b**
13: 1 Keep on loving one another as **b**
Rev 12: 10 the accuser of our **b** and sisters,

BROW
Ge 3: 19 your **b** you will eat your food until

BRUISED (BRUISES)
Isa 42: 3 A **b** reed he will not break,
Mt 12: 20 A **b** reed he will not break,

BRUISES* (BRUISED)
Pr 23: 29 Who has needless **b**? Who has
Isa 30: 26 LORD binds up the **b** of his people

BRUTAL (BRUTE)
2Ti 3: 3 without self-control, **b**, not lovers

BRUTE* (BRUTAL)
Ps 73: 22 I was a **b** beast before you.
Pr 30: 2 Surely I am only a **b**, not a man;
BUBBLING*
Isa 35: 7 pool, the thirsty ground **b** springs.
BUCKET*
Isa 40: 15 the nations are like a drop in a **b**;
BUCKLED*
Eph 6: 14 belt of truth **b** around your waist,
BUD (BUDDED)
Isa 27: 6 Israel will **b** and blossom and fill
BUDDED (BUD)
Heb 9: 4 Aaron's staff that had **b**,
BUILD (BUILDER BUILDERS BUILDING BUILDS BUILT REBUILD REBUILT)
2Sa 7: 5 Are you the one to **b** me a house
1Ki 6: 1 he began to **b** the temple
Ecc 3: 3 time to tear down and a time to **b**,
Mt 16: 18 on this rock I will **b** my church,
Ac 20: 32 which can **b** you up and give you
Ro 15: 2 for their good, to **b** them up.
1Co 3: 10 But each one should **b** with care.
14: 12 excel in those that **b** up the church.
1Th 5: 11 one another and **b** each other up,
BUILDER (BUILD)
Isa 62: 5 so will your **B** marry you;
1Co 3: 10 I laid a foundation as a wise **b**,
Heb 3: 3 just as the **b** of a house has greater
3: 4 but God is the **b** of everything.
11: 10 whose architect and **b** is God.
BUILDERS (BUILD)
Ps 118: 22 The stone the **b** rejected has
Mt 21: 42 "'The stone the **b** rejected has
Mk 12: 10 "'The stone the **b** rejected has
Lk 20: 17 "'The stone the **b** rejected has
Ac 4: 11 is "'the stone you **b** rejected,
1Pe 2: 7 "The stone the **b** rejected has
BUILDING (BUILD)
Ezr 3: 8 to supervise the **b** of the house
Ne 4: 17 who were **b** the wall.
Ro 15: 20 I would not be **b** on someone else's
1Co 3: 9 you are God's field, God's **b**.
2Co 5: destroyed, we have a **b** from God,
10: 8 authority the Lord gave us for **b**
13: 10 the Lord gave me for **b** you up,
Eph 2: 21 him the whole **b** is joined together
4: 29 only what is helpful for **b** others
Jude : 20 by **b** yourselves up in your most
BUILDS (BUILD)
Ps 127: 1 Unless the LORD **b** the house,
Pr 14: 1 The wise woman **b** her house,
1Co 3: 12 If anyone **b** on this foundation
8: 1 puffs up while love **b** up.
Eph 4: 16 grows and **b** itself up in love,
BUILT (BUILD)
1Ki 6: 14 So Solomon **b** the temple
Mt 7: 24 is like a wise man who **b** his house
Lk 6: 49 is like a man who **b** a house
Ac 17: 24 live in temples **b** by human hands.
1Co 3: 14 If what has been **b** survives,
14: 26 so that the church may be **b** up.
2Co 5: 1 in heaven, not **b** by human hands.
Eph 2: 20 **b** on the foundation of the apostles
4: 12 that the body of Christ may be **b**
Col 2: 7 rooted and **b** up in him,
1Pe 2: 5 are being **b** into a spiritual house
BULL (BULLS)
Lev 4: 3 LORD a young **b** without defect as
BULLS (BULL)
1Ki 7: 25 The Sea stood on twelve **b**,
Heb 10: 4 It is impossible for the blood of **b**
BURDEN (BURDENED BURDENS BURDENSOME)
Ps 38: 4 overwhelmed me like a **b** too heavy
Ecc 1: 13 What a heavy **b** God has laid
Mt 11: 30 my yoke is easy and my **b** is light."
Ac 15: 28 to us not to **b** you with anything
2Co 11: 9 kept myself from being a **b** to you
12: 14 and I will not be a **b** to you,
1Th 2: 9 be a **b** to anyone while we preached
2Th 3: 8 so that we would not be a **b** to any
Heb 13: 17 joy, not a **b**, for that would be of no

BURDENED* (BURDEN)
Isa 43: 23 I have not **b** you with grain
43: 24 But you have **b** me with your sins
Mic 6: 3 How have I **b** you? Answer me.
Mt 11: 28 all you who are weary and **b**, and I
2Co 5: 4 we groan and are **b**, because we do
Gal 5: 1 do not let yourselves be **b** again
1Ti 5: 16 not let the church be **b** with them,
BURDENS (BURDEN)
Ps 68: 19 our Savior, who daily bears our **b**.
Lk 11: 46 down with **b** they can hardly carry,
Gal 6: 2 Carry each other's **b**, and in this
BURDENSOME (BURDEN)
1Jn 5: 3 And his commands are not **b**,
BURIED (BURY)
Ru 1: 17 die I will die, and there I will be **b**.
Ro 6: 4 We were therefore **b** with him
1Co 15: 4 that he was **b**, that he was raised
Col 2: 12 been **b** with him in baptism,
BURN (BURNING BURNT)
Dt 7: 5 poles and **b** their idols in the fire.
Ps 79: 5 long will your jealousy **b** like fire?
1Co 7: 9 to marry than to **b** with passion.
BURNING (BURN)
Ex 27: 20 so that the lamps may be kept **b**.
Lev 6: 9 the fire must be kept **b** on the altar.
Ps 18: 28 You, LORD, keep my lamp **b**;
Pr 25: 22 you will heap **b** coals on his head,
Ro 12: 20 you will heap **b** coals on his head."
Rev 19: 20 alive into the fiery lake of **b** sulfur.
BURNISHED*
1Ki 7: 45 of the LORD were of **b** bronze.
Eze 1: 7 of a calf and gleamed like **b** bronze.
Da 10: 6 and legs like the gleam of **b** bronze,
Rev 2: 18 and whose feet are like **b** bronze.
BURNT (BURN)
Ge 8: 20 he sacrificed **b** offerings on it.
22: 2 Sacrifice him there as a **b** offering
Ex 10: 25 **b** offerings to present to the LORD
18: 12 brought a **b** offering and other
40: 6 "Place the altar of **b** offering
Lev 1: 3 the offering is a **b** offering
Jos 8: 31 offered to the LORD **b** offerings
Jdg 6: 26 the second bull as a **b** offering."
13: 16 But if you prepare a **b** offering,
1Ki 3: 4 offered a thousand **b** offerings
9: 25 year Solomon sacrificed **b** offerings
10: 5 and the **b** offerings he made
Ezr 3: 2 Israel to sacrifice **b** offerings on it,
Eze 43: 18 for sacrificing **b** offerings
BURST
Ps 98: 4 **b** into jubilant song with music;
Isa 44: 23 **B** into song, you mountains,
49: 13 **b** into song, you mountains!
52: 9 **B** into songs of joy together,
54: 1 **b** into song, shout for joy, you who
55: 12 hills will **b** into song before you,
BURY (BURIED)
Mt 8: 22 and let the dead **b** their own dead."
Lk 9: 60 "Let the dead **b** their own dead,
BUSH
Ex 3: 2 in flames of fire from within a **b**.
3: 2 though the **b** was on fire it did not
Mk 12: 26 in the account of the burning **b**,
Lk 20: 37 in the account of the burning **b**,
Ac 7: 35 who appeared to him in the **b**.
BUSINESS
Ecc 4: 8 too is meaningless—a miserable **b**!
Da 8: 27 got up and went about the king's **b**.
1Co 5: 12 What **b** is it of mine to judge those
1Th 4: 11 You should mind your own **b**
Jas 1: 11 even while they go about their **b**.
BUSY*
1Ki 18: 27 deep in thought, or **b**, or traveling.
20: 40 While your servant was **b** here
Hag 1: 9 of you is **b** with your own house.
2Th 3: 11 are not **b**; they are busybodies.
Titus 2: 5 pure, to be **b** at home, to be kind,
BUSYBODIES*
2Th 3: 11 They are not busy; they are **b**.
1Ti 5: 13 but also **b** who talk nonsense,

BUY (BOUGHT BUYS)
Pr 23: 23 **B** the truth and do not sell it—
Isa 55: 1 have no money, come, **b** and eat!
Rev 13: 17 so that they could not **b** or sell
BUYS (BUY)
Pr 31: 16 She considers a field and **b** it;
BYWORD (WORD)
1Ki 9: 7 a **b** and an object of ridicule
Ps 44: 14 made us a **b** among the nations;
Joel 2: 17 of scorn, a **b** among the nations.
CAESAR
Mt 22: 21 give back to **C** what is Caesar's,
CAIN
Firstborn of Adam (Ge 4:1), murdered brother Abel (Ge 4:1–16; 1Jn 3:12).
CALAMITIES (CALAMITY)
Dt 31: 17 disasters and **c** will come on them,
31: 21 disasters and **c** come on them,
CALAMITY (CALAMITIES)
Pr 22: 8 Whoever sows injustice reaps **c**,
CALEB
Judahite who spied out Canaan (Nu 13:6); allowed to enter land because of faith (Nu 13:30—14:38; Dt 1:36). Possessed Hebron (Jos 14:6—15:19).
CALF
Ex 32: 4 into an idol cast in the shape of a **c**,
Pr 15: 17 love than a fattened **c** with hatred.
Lk 15: 23 Bring the fattened **c** and kill it.
Ac 7: 41 made an idol in the form of a **c**.
CALL (CALLED CALLING CALLS)
Ex 3: 15 the name you shall **c** me
1Ki 18: 24 you **c** on the name of your god,
18: 24 will **c** on the name of the LORD.
2Ki 5: 11 **c** on the name of the LORD his
Ps 116: 13 and **c** on the name of the LORD.
116: 17 and **c** on the name of the LORD.
145: 18 LORD is near to all who **c** on him,
Pr 31: 28 children arise and **c** her blessed;
Isa 5: 20 Woe to those who **c** evil good
55: 6 **c** on him while he is near.
65: 24 Before they **c** I will answer;
Jer 33: 3 '**C** to me and I will answer you
Zep 3: 9 all of them may **c** on the name
Zec 13: 9 They will **c** on my name and I will
Mt 9: 13 I have not come to **c** the righteous,
Mk 2: 17 I have not come to **c** the righteous,
Lk 5: 32 I have not come to **c** the righteous,
Ac 2: 39 all whom the Lord our God will **c**."
9: 14 to arrest all who **c** on your name."
9: 21 in Jerusalem among those who **c**
Ro 10: 12 richly blesses all who **c** on him,
11: 29 gifts and his **c** are irrevocable.
1Co 1: 2 all those everywhere who **c**
1Th 4: 7 For God did not **c** us to be impure,
2Ti 2: 22 with those who **c** on the Lord
CALLED (CALL)
Ge 2: 23 she shall be **c** 'woman,' for she was
12: 8 and **c** on the name of the LORD.
21: 33 and there he **c** on the name
26: 25 and **c** on the name of the LORD.
1Sa 3: 5 and said, "Here I am; you **c** me."
2Ch 7: 14 my people, who are **c** by my name,
Ps 34: 6 This poor man **c**, and the LORD
116: 4 I **c** on the name of the LORD:
Isa 56: 7 for my house will be **c** a house
La 3: 55 I **c** on your name, LORD,
Hos 11: 1 him, and out of Egypt I **c** my son.
Mt 1: 16 of Jesus who is **c** the Messiah.
2: 15 "Out of Egypt I **c** my son."
21: 13 "'My house will be **c** a house
Mk 11: 17 'My house will be **c** a house
Lk 1: 32 will be **c** the Son of the Most High.
1: 35 be born will be **c** the Son of God.
Ro 1: 1 **c** to be an apostle and set apart
1: 6 among those Gentiles who are **c**
1: 7 by God and **c** to be his holy people:
8: 28 who have been **c** according to his
8: 30 those he predestined, he also **c**;
those he **c**, he also justified;
1Co 1: 1 **c** to be an apostle of Christ Jesus
1: 2 Jesus and **c** to be his holy people,

1Co 1: 24 but to those whom God has **c**,
1: 26 of what you were when you were **c**.
7: 15 God has **c** us to live in peace.
7: 17 to them, just as God has **c** them.
Gal 1: 6 deserting the one who **c** you
1: 15 womb and **c** me by his grace,
5: 13 and sisters, were **c** to be free.
Eph 1: 18 the hope to which he has **c** you,
4: 4 just as you were **c** to one hope
Col 3: 15 of one body you were **c** to peace.
2Th 2: 14 **c** you to this through our gospel,
1Ti 6: 12 you were **c** when you made your
2Ti 1: 9 saved us and **c** us to a holy life—
Heb 9: 15 that those who are **c** may receive
1Pe 1: 15 But just as he who **c** you is holy,
2: 9 the praises of him who **c** you
3: 9 to this you were **c** so that you may
5: 10 who **c** you to his eternal glory
2Pe 1: 3 of him who **c** us by his own glory
Jude : 1 To those who have been **c**, who are

CALLING (CALL)
Isa 40: 3 A voice of one **c**:
Mt 3: 3 "A voice of one **c** in the wilderness,
Mk 1: 3 "a voice of one **c** in the wilderness,
10: 49 On your feet! He's **c** you."
Lk 3: 4 "A voice of one **c** in the wilderness,
Jn 1: 23 voice of one **c** in the wilderness,
Ac 22: 16 your sins away, **c** on his name.'
Eph 4: 1 worthy of the **c** you have received.
2Th 1: 11 may make you worthy of his **c**,
2Pe 1: 10 every effort to confirm your **c**

CALLOUS* (CALLOUSED)
Ps 17: 10 They close up their **c** hearts,
73: 7 From their **c** hearts comes iniquity;
119: 70 Their hearts are **c** and unfeeling,

CALLOUSED* (CALLOUS)
Isa 6: 10 Make the heart of this people **c**;
Mt 13: 15 this people's heart has become **c**;
Ac 28: 27 this people's heart has become **c**;

CALLS (CALL)
Ps 147: 4 the stars and **c** them each by name.
Isa 40: 26 and **c** forth each of them by name.
Joel 2: 32 everyone who **c** on the name
Mt 22: 43 by the Spirit, **c** him 'Lord'?
Jn 10: 3 He **c** his own sheep by name
Ac 2: 21 everyone who **c** on the name
Ro 10: 13 "Everyone who **c** on the name
1Th 2: 12 who **c** you into his kingdom
5: 24 The one who **c** you is faithful,

CALM (CALMS)
Ps 107: 30 They were glad when it grew **c**,
Pr 29: 11 but the wise bring **c** in the end.
Isa 7: 4 careful, keep **c** and don't be afraid.
Eze 16: 42 I will be **c** and no longer angry.

CALMS* (CALM)
Pr 15: 18 one who is patient **c** a quarrel.

CAMEL
Mt 19: 24 easier for a **c** to go through the eye
23: 24 strain out a gnat but swallow a **c**.
Mk 10: 25 easier for a **c** to go through the eye
Lk 18: 25 easier for a **c** to go through the eye

CAMP (ENCAMPS)
Heb 13: 13 go to him outside the **c**,

CANAAN (CANAANITE CANAANITES)
Ge 10: 15 **C** was the father of Sidon his
Lev 14: 34 "When you enter the land of **C**,
25: 38 of Egypt to give you the land of **C**
Nu 13: 2 some men to explore the land of **C**,
33: 51 'When you cross the Jordan into **C**,
Jdg 4: 2 into the hands of Jabin king of **C**,
1Ch 16: 18 **C** as the portion you will inherit."
Ps 105: 11 **C** as the portion you will inherit."
Ac 13: 19 he overthrew seven nations in **C**,

CANAANITE (CANAAN)
Ge 10: 18 Later the **C** clans scattered
28: 1 "Do not marry a **C** woman.
Jos 5: 1 the **C** kings along the coast heard
Jdg 1: 32 lived among the **C** inhabitants

CANAANITES (CANAAN)
Ex 33: 2 before you and drive out the **C**,

CANCEL (CANCELED)
Dt 15: 1 every seven years you must **c** debts.

CANCELED* (CANCEL)
Mt 18: 27 on him, **c** the debt and let him go.
18: 32 'I **c** all that debt of yours because
Col 2: 14 having **c** the charge of our legal

CANDLESTICKS See LAMPSTANDS

CANOPY*
2Sa 22: 12 made darkness his **c** around him—
2Ki 16: 18 He took away the Sabbath **c**
Ps 18: 11 his covering, his **c** around him—
Isa 4: 5 everything the glory will be a **c**.
40: 22 stretches out the heavens like a **c**,
Jer 43: 10 he will spread his royal **c**

CAPERNAUM
Mt 4: 13 he went and lived in **C**, which was
Jn 6: 59 teaching in the synagogue in **C**.

CAPITAL
Dt 21: 22 someone guilty of a **c** offense is put

CAPSTONE* (STONE)
Zec 4: 7 he will bring out the **c** to shouts
4: 10 rejoice when they see the chosen **c**

CAPTIVATE* (CAPTIVE)
Pr 6: 25 or let her **c** you with her eyes.

CAPTIVE (CAPTIVATE CAPTIVES CAPTIVITY CAPTURED)
Ac 8: 23 are full of bitterness and **c** to sin."
2Co 10: 5 we take **c** every thought to make it
Col 2: 8 no one takes you **c** through hollow
2Ti 2: 26 has taken them **c** to do his will.

CAPTIVES (CAPTIVE)
Ps 68: 18 on high, you took many **c**;
Isa 61: 1 to proclaim freedom for the **c**
Eph 4: 8 he took many **c** and gave gifts to

CAPTIVITY (CAPTIVE)
Dt 28: 41 them, because they will go into **c**.
2Ki 25: 21 So Judah went into **c**,
Jer 30: 3 Judah back from **c** and restore
52: 27 So Judah went into **c**,
Eze 29: 14 I will bring them back from **c**

CAPTURED (CAPTIVE)
1Sa 4: 11 The ark of God was **c**, and Eli's two
2Sa 5: 7 David **c** the fortress of Zion—
2Ki 17: 6 the king of Assyria **c** Samaria

CARCASS
Jdg 14: 9 taken the honey from the lion's **c**.
Mt 24: 28 Wherever there is a **c**,

CARE (CAREFUL CAREFULLY CARES CARING)
Ps 8: 4 human beings that you **c** for them?
43: 3 me your light and your faithful **c**,
65: 9 You **c** for the land and water it;
144: 3 human beings that you **c** for them,
Pr 12: 10 The righteous **c** for the needs
29: 7 The righteous **c** about justice
Mk 5: 26 suffered a great deal under the **c**
Lk 10: 34 him to an inn and took **c** of him.
18: 4 fear God or **c** what people think,
Jn 21: 16 Jesus said, "Take **c** of my sheep."
1Co 3: 10 But each one should build with **c**.
Eph 5: 29 but they feed and **c** for their body,
1Ti 3: 5 family, how can he take **c** of God's
6: 20 what has been entrusted to your **c**.
Heb 2: 6 a son of man that you **c** for him?
1Pe 5: 2 of God's flock that is under your **c**,

CAREFUL* (CARE)
Ge 31: 24 "Be **c** not to say anything to Jacob,
31: 29 'Be **c** not to say anything to Jacob,
Ex 19: 12 'Be **c** that you do not approach
23: 13 "Be **c** to do everything I have said
34: 12 Be **c** not to make a treaty with
34: 15 "Be **c** not to make a treaty
Lev 18: 4 laws and be **c** to follow my decrees.
25: 18 decrees and be **c** to obey my laws,
26: 3 and are **c** to obey my commands,
Dt 2: 4 will be afraid of you, but be very **c**.
4: 9 Only be **c**, and watch yourselves
4: 23 Be **c** not to forget the covenant
5: 32 So be **c** to do what the LORD your
6: 3 be **c** to obey so that it may go well
6: 12 be **c** that you do not forget
6: 25 we are **c** to obey all this law before
7: 12 laws and are **c** to follow them,
8: 1 Be **c** to follow every command
Dt 8: 11 Be **c** that you do not forget
11: 16 Be **c**, or you will be enticed to turn
12: 1 laws you must be **c** to follow
12: 13 Be **c** not to sacrifice your burnt
12: 19 Be **c** not to neglect the Levites as
12: 28 Be **c** to obey all these regulations I
12: 30 **c** not to be ensnared by inquiring
15: 5 are **c** to follow all these commands
15: 9 Be **c** not to harbor this wicked
17: 10 Be **c** to do everything they instruct
24: 8 be very **c** to do exactly as
Jos 1: 7 Be **c** to obey all the law my servant
1: 8 that you may be **c** to do everything
22: 5 very **c** to keep the commandment
23: 6 be **c** to obey all that is written
23: 11 So be very **c** to love the LORD
1Ki 8: 25 if only your descendants are **c** in all
2Ki 10: 31 Yet Jehu was not **c** to keep the law
17: 37 You must always be **c** to keep
21: 8 only they will be **c** to do everything
1Ch 22: 13 if you are **c** to observe the decrees
28: 8 Be **c** to follow all the commands
2Ch 6: 16 if only your descendants are **c** in all
33: 8 only they will be **c** to do everything
Ezr 4: 22 Be **c** not to neglect this matter.
Job 36: 18 Be **c** that no one entices you
Ps 45: 10 daughter, and pay **c** attention:
101: 2 I will be **c** to lead a blameless life—
Pr 4: 26 Give **c** thought to the paths for
13: 24 one who loves their children is **c**
21: 28 a **c** listener will testify successfully.
27: 23 give **c** attention to your herds;
Isa 7: 4 him, 'Be **c**, keep calm and don't be
Jer 17: 21 Be **c** not to carry a load
17: 24 But if you are **c** to obey me,
22: 4 For if you are **c** to carry out these
Eze 11: 20 decrees and be **c** to keep my laws.
18: 19 has been **c** to keep all my decrees,
20: 19 decrees and be **c** to keep my laws.
20: 21 they were not **c** to keep my laws,
36: 27 decrees and be **c** to keep my laws.
37: 24 laws and be **c** to keep my decrees.
Hag 1: 5 "Give **c** thought to your ways.
1: 7 "Give **c** thought to your ways.
2: 15 "'Now give **c** thought to this
2: 18 give **c** thought to the day
2: 18 temple was laid. Give **c** thought:
Mt 6: 1 "Be **c** not to practice your
16: 6 "Be **c**," Jesus said to them.
23: 3 So you must be **c** to do everything
Mk 8: 15 "Be **c**," Jesus warned them.
Lk 21: 34 "Be **c**, or your hearts will be
Ro 12: 17 Be **c** to do what is right in the eyes
1Co 8: 9 Be **c**, however, that the exercise
10: 12 firm, be **c** that you don't fall!
Eph 5: 15 Be very **c**, then, how you live—
2Ti 4: 2 great patience and **c** instruction.
Titus 3: 8 God may be **c** to devote themselves
Heb 2: 1 We must pay the most **c** attention,
4: 1 be **c** that none of you be found

CAREFULLY (CARE)
Pr 12: 26 righteous choose their friends **c**,
Mt 2: 8 "Go and search **c** for the child.

CARES* (CARE)
Dt 11: 12 a land the LORD your God **c** for;
Job 39: 16 **c** not that her labor was in vain,
Ps 55: 22 Cast your **c** on the LORD and he
142: 4 no one **c** for my life.
Ecc 5: 3 comes when there are many **c**,
Jer 12: 11 because there is no one who **c**.
30: 17 outcast, Zion for whom no one **c**.'
Na 1: 7 He **c** for those who trust in him,
Jn 10: 13 hand and **c** nothing for the sheep.
1Th 2: 7 Just as a nursing mother **c** for her
1Pe 5: 7 on him because he **c** for you.

CARING* (CARE)
1Ti 5: 4 practice by **c** for their own family

CAROUSING*
Lk 21: 34 will be weighed down with **c**,
Ro 13: 13 daytime, not in **c** and drunkenness,
1Pe 4: 3 orgies, **c** and detestable idolatry.

CARPENTER (CARPENTER'S)
Mk 6: 3 Isn't this the **c**? Isn't this Mary's

CARPENTER'S* (CARPENTER)
Mt 13: 55 "Isn't this the c son?
CARRIED (CARRY)
Ex 19: 4 and how I c you on eagles' wings
Dt 1: 31 how the LORD your God c you,
Isa 63: 9 up and c them all the days of old.
Heb 13: 9 Do not be c away by all kinds
2Pe 1: 21 God as they were c along
3: 17 you may not be c away by the error
CARRIES (CARRY)
Dt 32: 11 to catch them and c them aloft.
Isa 40: 11 arms and c them close to his heart;
CARRY (CARRIED CARRIES CARRYING)
Lev 16: 22 The goat will c on itself all their
26: 15 and fail to c out all my commands
Isa 46: 4 I have made you and I will c you;
Lk 14: 27 whoever does not c their cross
Gal 6: 2 C each other's burdens, and in this
6: 5 each one should c their own load.
CARRYING (CARRY)
Jn 19: 17 C his own cross, he went
1Jn 5: 2 God and c out his commands.
CARVED
Nu 33: 52 Destroy all their c images and their
CASE
Pr 22: 23 for the LORD will take up their c
23: 11 he will take up their c against you.
CAST (CASTING)
Lev 16: 8 He is to c lots for the two goats—
Ps 22: 18 them and c lots for my garment.
55: 22 C your cares on the LORD and he
Pr 16: 33 The lot is c into the lap, but its
Jn 19: 24 them and c lots for my garment."
1Pe 5: 7 C all your anxiety on him because
CASTING (CAST)
Pr 18: 18 C the lot settles disputes and keeps
Mt 27: 35 divided up his clothes by c lots.
CATCH (CATCHES CAUGHT)
Lk 5: 4 and let down the nets for a c."
CATCHES (CATCH)
Job 5: 13 He c the wise in their craftiness,
1Co 3: 19 "He c the wise in their craftiness";
CATTLE
Ps 50: 10 and the c on a thousand hills.
CAUGHT (CATCH)
Ge 22: 13 in a thicket he saw a ram c by its
2Co 12: 2 who fourteen years ago was c up
1Th 4: 17 are left will be c up together
CAUSE (CAUSES)
Ps 7: 16 The trouble they c recoils on them;
25: 3 who are treacherous without c.
Ps 82: 3 uphold the c of the poor
Pr 24: 28 against your neighbor without c—
Ecc 8: 3 Do not stand up for a bad c, for he
Mt 18: 7 the things that c people to stumble!
Ro 14: 21 that will c your brother or sister
1Co 10: 32 Do not c anyone to stumble,
CAUSES (CAUSE)
Isa 8: 14 he will be a stone that c people
Mt 5: 29 If your right eye c you to stumble,
5: 30 if your right hand c you to stumble,
18: 6 "If anyone c one of these little
18: 8 hand or your foot c you to stumble,
Ro 14: 20 eat anything that c someone else
1Co 8: 13 if what I eat c my brother or sister
1Pe 2: 8 "A stone that c people to stumble
CEASE
Ps 46: 9 He makes wars c to the ends
CELEBRATE*
Ex 10: 9 because we are to c a festival
12: 14 to come you shall c it as a festival
12: 17 "C the Festival of Unleavened
12: 17 C this day as a lasting ordinance
12: 47 community of Israel must c it.
12: 48 c the LORD's Passover must have
23: 14 times a year you are to c a festival
23: 15 "C the Festival of Unleavened
23: 16 "C the Festival of Harvest
23: 16 "C the Festival of Ingathering
34: 18 "C the Festival of Unleavened
34: 22 "C the Festival of Weeks
Lev 23: 39 c the festival to the LORD
23: 41 C this as a festival to the LORD
23: 41 c it in the seventh month.
Nu 9: 2 "Have the Israelites c the Passover
9: 3 C it at the appointed time,
9: 4 told the Israelites to c the Passover,
9: 6 of them could not c the Passover
9: 10 are still to c the LORD's Passover,
9: 12 When they c the Passover,
9: 13 on a journey fails to c the Passover,
9: 14 also to c the LORD's Passover
29: 12 C a festival to the LORD for seven
Dt 16: 1 c the Passover of the LORD your
16: 10 Then c the Festival of Weeks
16: 13 C the Festival of Tabernacles
16: 15 For seven days c the festival
Jdg 16: 23 to Dagon their god and to c,
2Sa 6: 21 I will c before the LORD.
2Ki 23: 21 "C the Passover to the LORD
2Ch 30: 1 and c the Passover to the LORD,
30: 2 decided to c the Passover
30: 3 They had not been able to c it
30: 5 and c the Passover to the LORD,
30: 13 in Jerusalem to c the Festival
30: 23 to c the festival seven more days;
Ne 8: 12 of food and to c with great joy,
12: 27 to c joyfully the dedication
Est 9: 21 them c annually the fourteenth
Ps 2: 11 fear and c his rule with trembling.
89: 16 they c your righteousness.
145: 7 They c your abundant goodness
Isa 30: 29 on the night you c a holy festival;
Hos 5: 7 they c their New Moon feasts,
Na 1: 15 C your festivals, Judah, and fulfill
Zec 14: 16 to c the Festival of Tabernacles.
14: 18 up to c the Festival of Tabernacles.
14: 19 up to c the Festival of Tabernacles.
Mt 26: 18 I am going to c the Passover
Lk 15: 23 and kill it. Let's have a feast and c.
15: 24 and is found.' So they began to c.
15: 29 me even a young goat so I could c
15: 32 But we had to c and be glad,
Rev 11: 10 will c by sending each other gifts,
CELESTIAL*
2Pe 2: 10 afraid to heap abuse on c beings;
Jude : 8 and heap abuse on c beings.
CENSER (CENSERS)
Lev 16: 12 is to take a c full of burning coals
Rev 8: 3 had a golden c, came and stood
CENSERS (CENSER)
Nu 16: 6 followers are to do this: Take c
CENTURION
Mt 8: 5 Capernaum, a c came to him,
27: 54 When the c and those with him
Mk 15: 39 And when the c, who stood there
Lk 7: 3 The c heard of Jesus and sent some
23: 47 The c, seeing what had happened,
Ac 10: 1 c in what was known as the Italian
27: 1 handed over to a c named Julius,
CEPHAS* (PETER)
Jn 1: 42 You will be called C" (which,
1Co 1: 12 another, "I follow C";
3: 22 Paul or Apollos or C or the world
9: 5 and the Lord's brothers and C?
Gal 2: 9 James, C and John, those esteemed
CEREMONIAL* (CEREMONY)
Lev 14: 2 at the time of their c cleansing,
15: 13 off seven days for his c cleansing;
Mk 7: 3 they give their hands a c washing,
Jn 2: 6 used by the Jews for c washing,
3: 25 Jew over the matter of c washing.
11: 55 for their c cleansing before
18: 28 to avoid c uncleanness they did not
Heb 9: 10 drink and various c washings—
13: 9 not by eating c foods, which is of
CEREMONIALLY* (CEREMONY)
Lev 4: 12 outside the camp to a place c clean,
5: 2 touch anything c unclean (whether
6: 11 the camp to a place that is c clean.
7: 19 touches anything c unclean must
7: 19 meat, anyone c clean may eat it.
10: 14 Eat them in a c clean place;
11: 4 it is c unclean for you.
Lev 12: 2 to a son will be c unclean for seven
12: 7 she will be c clean from her flow
13: 3 shall pronounce them c unclean.
14: 8 then they will be c clean.
15: 28 and after that she will be c clean.
15: 33 with a woman who is c unclean.
17: 15 they will be c unclean till evening;
21: 1 must not make himself c unclean
22: 3 of your descendants is c unclean
27: 11 they vowed is a c unclean animal—
Nu 5: 2 who is c unclean because of a dead
6: 7 not make themselves c unclean
8: 6 Israelites and make them c clean.
9: 6 day because they were c unclean
9: 13 if anyone who is c clean and not
18: 11 household who is c clean may eat
18: 13 household who is c clean may eat
19: 7 he will be c unclean till evening.
19: 9 in a c clean place outside the camp.
19: 18 a man who is c clean is to take
Dt 12: 15 Both the c unclean and the clean
12: 22 Both the c unclean and the clean
14: 7 they are c unclean for you.
15: 22 Both the c unclean and the clean
1Sa 20: 26 to David to make him c unclean—
2Ch 13: 11 the bread on the c clean table
30: 17 for all those who were not c clean
Ezr 6: 20 themselves and were all c clean.
Ne 12: 30 Levites had purified themselves c,
Isa 66: 20 of the LORD in c clean vessels.
Eze 22: 10 period, when they are c unclean.
Ac 24: 18 I was c clean when they found me
Heb 9: 13 those who are c unclean sanctify
CEREMONY* (CEREMONIAL CEREMONIALLY)
Ge 50: 11 Egyptians are holding a solemn c
Ex 12: 25 you as he promised, observe this c.
12: 26 'What does this c mean to you?'
13: 5 are to observe this c in this month:
CERTAINTY*
Lk 1: 4 you may know the c of the things
Jn 17: 8 They knew with c that I came
CERTIFICATE* (CERTIFIED)
Dt 24: 1 and he writes her a c of divorce,
24: 3 her and writes her a c of divorce,
Isa 50: 1 "Where is your mother's c
Jer 3: 8 I gave faithless Israel her c
Mt 5: 31 divorces his wife must give her a c
19: 7 a man give his wife a c of divorce
Mk 10: 4 a man to write a c of divorce
CERTIFIED* (CERTIFICATE)
Jn 3: 33 Whoever has accepted it has c
CHAFF
Ps 1: 4 They are like c that the wind blows
35: 5 May they be like c before the wind,
Da 2: 35 became like c on a threshing floor
Mt 3: 12 up the c with unquenchable fire."
CHAINED (CHAINS)
2Ti 2: 9 But God's word is not c.
CHAINS (CHAINED)
Eph 6: 20 for which I am an ambassador in c.
Col 4: 18 Remember my c. Grace be
2Ti 1: 16 me and was not ashamed of my c.
Jude : 6 with everlasting c for judgment
CHAMPION
1Sa 17: 4 A c named Goliath, who was from
Ps 19: 5 like a c rejoicing to run his course.
CHANCE
Ecc 9: 11 but time and c happen to them all.
CHANGE (CHANGED)
1Sa 15: 29 being, that he should c his mind."
Ps 110: 4 has sworn and will not c his mind:
Jer 7: 5 If you really c your ways and your
Mal 3: 6 "I the LORD do not c. So you,
Mt 18: 3 unless you c and become like little
Heb 7: 21 has sworn and will not c his mind:
Jas 1: 17 lights, who does not c like shifting
CHANGED (CHANGE)
1Sa 10: 6 will be c into a different person.
Hos 11: 8 My heart is c within me;
1Co 15: 51 not all sleep, but we will all be c—

CHARACTER*
Ru 3: 11 that you are a woman of noble **c**.
Pr 12: 4 of noble **c** is her husband's crown,
31: 10 A wife of noble **c** who can find?
Ac 17: 11 were of more noble **c** than those
Ro 5: 4 perseverance, **c**; and **c**, hope.
1Co 15: 33 "Bad company corrupts good **c**."

CHARGE (CHARGED CHARGES)
Job 34: 13 Who put him in **c** of the whole
Ro 8: 33 will bring any **c** against those
1Co 9: 18 the gospel I may offer it free of **c**,
2Co 11: 7 the gospel of God to you free of **c**?
2Ti 4: 1 and his kingdom, I give you this **c**:
Phm : 18 or owes you anything, **c** it to me.

CHARGED (CHARGE)
Ro 5: 13 sin is not **c** against anyone's

CHARGES (CHARGE)
Isa 50: 8 Who then will bring **c** against me?

CHARIOT (CHARIOTS)
2Ki 2: 11 suddenly a **c** of fire and horses
Ps 104: 3 makes the clouds his **c** and rides
Ac 8: 28 sitting in his **c** reading the Book

CHARIOTS (CHARIOT)
2Ki 6: 17 and **c** of fire all around Elisha.
Ps 20: 7 trust in **c** and some in horses,
68: 17 The **c** of God are tens of thousands

CHARM* (CHARMING)
Pr 17: 8 A bribe is seen as a **c** by the one
31: 30 **C** is deceptive, and beauty is

CHARMING* (CHARM)
Pr 26: 25 Though their speech is **c**, do not
SS 1: 16 Oh, how **c**! And our bed is verdant.

CHASE
Lev 26: 8 Five of you will **c** a hundred,
Pr 12: 11 who **c** fantasies have no sense.
28: 19 those who **c** fantasies will have

CHASM*
Lk 16: 26 you a great **c** has been set in place,

CHASTENS*
Heb 12: 6 and he **c** everyone he accepts as his

CHATTER* (CHATTERING)
1Ti 6: 20 Turn away from godless **c**
2Ti 2: 16 Avoid godless **c**, because those who

CHATTERING* (CHATTER)
Pr 10: 8 but a **c** fool comes to ruin.
10: 10 grief, and a **c** fool comes to ruin.

CHEAT* (CHEATED CHEATING)
Lev 6: 2 stolen, or if they **c** their neighbor,
Mal 1: 14 "Cursed is the **c** who has
1Co 6: 8 you yourselves **c** and do wrong,

CHEATED* (CHEAT)
Ge 31: 7 yet your father has **c** me
1Sa 12: 3 Whom have I **c**? Whom have I
12: 4 "You have not **c** or oppressed us,"
Lk 19: 8 if I have **c** anybody out of anything,
1Co 6: 7 Why not rather be **c**?

CHEATING* (CHEAT)
Am 8: 5 price and **c** with dishonest scales,

CHEEK (CHEEKS)
Mt 5: 39 anyone slaps you on the right **c**, turn to them the other **c** also.
Lk 6: 29 If someone slaps you on one **c**,

CHEEKS (CHEEK)
Isa 50: 6 my **c** to those who pulled out my

CHEERFUL* (CHEERS)
Pr 15: 13 A happy heart makes the face **c**,
15: 15 the **c** heart has a continual feast.
17: 22 A **c** heart is good medicine,
2Co 9: 7 for God loves a **c** giver.

CHEERS (CHEERFUL)
Pr 12: 25 the heart, but a kind word **c** it up.

CHEMOSH
2Ki 23: 13 for **C** the vile god of Moab,

CHERISHED (CHERISHES)
Ps 66: 18 If I had **c** sin in my heart,

CHERISHES* (CHERISHED)
Pr 19: 8 **c** understanding will soon prosper.

CHERUB (CHERUBIM)
Ex 25: 19 Make one **c** on one end
Eze 28: 14 You were anointed as a guardian **c**,

CHERUBIM (CHERUB)
Ge 3: 24 east side of the Garden of Eden **c**
1Sa 4: 4 who is enthroned between the **c**.
2Sa 6: 2 who is enthroned between the **c**
22: 11 He mounted the **c** and flew;
1Ki 6: 23 inner sanctuary he made a pair of **c**
2Ki 19: 15 enthroned between the **c**, you
1Ch 13: 6 who is enthroned between the **c**—
Ps 18: 10 He mounted the **c** and flew;
80: 1 who sit enthroned between the **c**,
99: 1 he sits enthroned between the **c**,
Isa 37: 16 enthroned between the **c**, you
Eze 10: 1 that was over the heads of the **c**.

CHEST
2Ki 12: 9 Jehoiada the priest took a **c**
Da 2: 32 pure gold, its **c** and arms of silver,
Rev 1: 13 with a golden sash around his **c**.

CHEWS
Lev 11: 3 a divided hoof and that **c** the cud.

CHIEF
1Pe 5: 4 And when the **C** Shepherd appears,

CHILD (CHILDBEARING CHILDBIRTH CHILDHOOD CHILDLESS CHILDREN GRANDCHILDREN)
Pr 22: 15 Folly is bound up in the heart of a **c**,
23: 13 Do not withhold discipline from a **c**;
29: 15 but a **c** left undisciplined disgraces
Isa 9: 6 For to us a **c** is born, to us a son is
11: 6 and a little **c** will lead them.
66: 13 As a mother comforts her **c**, so will
Eze 18: 20 The **c** will not share the guilt
Mt 18: 2 He called a little **c** to him,
Lk 1: 42 and blessed is the **c** you will bear!
1: 80 And the **c** grew and became strong
1Co 13: 11 When I was a **c**, I talked like a **c**,
1Jn 5: 1 loves the father loves his **c** as well.

CHILDBEARING (BEAR CHILD)
Ge 3: 16 make your pains in **c** very severe;
1Ti 2: 15 women will be saved through **c**
Heb 11: 11 who was past **c** age, was enabled

CHILDBIRTH (BEAR CHILD)
Gal 4: 19 pains of **c** until Christ is formed

CHILDHOOD (CHILD)
1Co 13: 11 I put the ways of **c** behind me.

CHILDLESS (CHILD)
Ge 11: 30 Now Sarai was **c** because she was
29: 31 to conceive, but Rachel remained **c**.
Ps 113: 9 settles the **c** woman in her home

CHILDREN (CHILD)
Ex 20: 5 punishing the **c** for the sin
Dt 4: 9 Teach them to your **c** and to their **c**
6: 7 Impress them on your **c**.
11: 19 Teach them to your **c**,
14: 1 You are the **c** of the LORD your
24: 16 nor **c** put to death for their parents;
30: 19 life, so that you and your **c** may live
32: 46 you may command your **c** to obey
Job 1: 5 "Perhaps my **c** have sinned
Ps 8: 2 Through the praise of **c** and infants
17: 14 may their **c** gorge themselves on it,
78: 5 our ancestors to teach their **c**,
127: 3 **C** are a heritage from the LORD,
Pr 13: 24 spares the rod hates their **c**,
17: 6 parents are the pride of their **c**.
20: 7 blessed are their **c** after them.
20: 11 Even small **c** are known by their
22: 6 Start **c** off on the way they should
29: 17 Discipline your **c**, and they will
31: 28 Her **c** arise and call her blessed;
Isa 54: 13 All your **c** will be taught
Hos 1: 10 they will be called '**c** of the living
Joel 1: 3 Tell it to your **c**, and let your **c** tell it to their **c**,
Mal 4: 6 the hearts of the parents to their **c**,
4: 6 the hearts of the **c** to their parents;
Mt 5: 9 for they will be called **c** of God.
7: 11 how to give good gifts to your **c**,
11: 25 and revealed them to little **c**.
18: 3 change and become like little **c**,
19: 14 said, "Let the little **c** come to me,
21: 16 "'From the lips of **c** and infants
Mk 9: 37 these little **c** in my name welcomes
10: 14 them, "Let the little **c** come to me,
Mk 10: 16 And he took the **c** in his arms,
13: 12 **C** will rebel against their parents
Lk 6: 35 and you will be **c** of the Most High,
10: 21 and revealed them to little **c**.
18: 16 said, "Let the little **c** come to me,
Jn 1: 12 the right to become **c** of God—
12: 36 so that you may become **c** of light."
Ac 2: 39 your **c** and for all who are far off—
Ro 8: 14 the Spirit of God are the **c** of God.
8: 16 with our spirit that we are God's **c**.
9: 26 there they will be called '**c**
1Co 14: 20 and sisters, stop thinking like **c**.
2Co 12: 14 **c** should not have to save up for
Gal 3: 26 in Christ Jesus you are all **c** of God
Eph 6: 1 **C**, obey your parents in the Lord,
6: 4 Fathers, do not exasperate your **c**;
Col 3: 20 **C**, obey your parents in everything,
3: 21 do not embitter your **c**, or they will
1Th 2: 7 we were like young **c** among you.
2: 7 as a nursing mother cares for her **c**,
1Ti 3: 4 well and see that his **c** obey him,
3: 12 wife and must manage his **c** and
5: 10 such as bringing up **c**,
Heb 2: 13 am I, and the **c** God has given me."
12: 7 God is treating you as his **c**.
1Jn 3: 1 that we should be called **c** of God!

CHOKE
Mk 4: 19 things come in and **c** the word,

CHOOSE (CHOOSES CHOSE CHOSEN)
Dt 30: 19 Now **c** life, so that you and your
Jos 24: 15 **c** for yourselves this day whom you
Pr 8: 10 **C** my instruction instead of silver,
Jn 15: 16 You did not **c** me, but I chose you

CHOOSES (CHOOSE)
Mt 11: 27 to whom the Son **c** to reveal him.
Lk 10: 22 to whom the Son **c** to reveal him."
Jn 7: 17 who **c** to do the will of God

CHORAZIN
Mt 11: 21 "Woe to you, **C**! Woe to you,

CHOSE (CHOOSE)
Ge 13: 11 Lot **c** for himself the whole plain
Ps 33: 12 the people he **c** for his inheritance.
Jn 15: 16 but I **c** you and appointed you so
1Co 1: 27 But God **c** the foolish things
Eph 1: 4 For he **c** us in him before
2Th 2: 13 because God **c** you as firstfruits

CHOSEN (CHOOSE)
Isa 41: 8 whom I have **c**, you descendants
Mt 22: 14 many are invited, but few are **c**."
Lk 10: 42 Mary has **c** what is better, and it
23: 35 if he is God's Messiah, the **C** One."
Jn 1: 34 I testify that this is God's **C** One."
15: 19 but I have **c** you out of the world.
1Pe 1: 20 He was **c** before the creation
2: 9 But you are a **c** people, a royal

CHRIST (CHRIST'S CHRISTIAN CHRISTIANS)
Jn 1: 41 found the Messiah" (that is, the **C**).
Ac 9: 34 said to him, "Jesus **C** heals you.
Ro 1: 4 from the dead: Jesus **C** our Lord.
3: 22 faith in Jesus **C** to all who believe.
5: 1 God through our Lord Jesus **C**,
5: 6 powerless, **C** died for the ungodly.
5: 8 we were still sinners, **C** died for us.
5: 11 in God through our Lord Jesus **C**,
5: 17 life through the one man, Jesus **C**!
6: 4 just as **C** was raised from the dead
6: 9 we know that since **C** was raised
6: 23 is eternal life in **C** Jesus our Lord.
7: 4 to the law through the body of **C**,
8: 1 for those who are in **C** Jesus,
8: 9 does not have the Spirit of **C**, they do not belong to **C**.
8: 17 heirs of God and co-heirs with **C**,
8: 34 **C** Jesus who died—more than that,
8: 35 separate us from the love of **C**?
10: 4 **C** is the culmination of the law so
12: 5 so in **C** we, though many, form one
13: 14 yourselves with the Lord Jesus **C**,
14: 9 **C** died and returned to life so that
15: 3 even **C** did not please himself but,
15: 5 toward each other that **C** Jesus had,
15: 7 then, just as **C** accepted you,
16: 18 people are not serving our Lord **C**,

1Co 1: 2 to those sanctified in **C** Jesus
1: 7 for our Lord Jesus **C** to be revealed.
1: 13 Is **C** divided? Was Paul crucified
1: 17 For **C** did not send me to baptize,
1: 17 lest the cross of **C** be emptied of
1: 23 but we preach **C** crucified:
1: 30 of him that you are in **C** Jesus,
2: 2 while I was with you except Jesus **C**
3: 11 one already laid, which is Jesus **C**.
5: 7 For **C**, our Passover lamb, has been
6: 15 bodies are members of **C** himself?
8: 6 Jesus **C**, through whom all things
8: 12 conscience, you sin against **C**.
10: 4 them, and that rock was **C**.
10: 9 We should not test **C**, as some
11: 1 as I follow the example of **C**.
11: 3 that the head of every man is **C**,
11: 3 and the head of **C** is God.
12: 27 Now you are the body of **C**,
15: 3 **C** died for our sins according
15: 14 And if **C** has not been raised,
15: 22 die, so in **C** all will be made alive.
15: 57 victory through our Lord Jesus **C**.
2Co 1: 5 abundantly in the sufferings of **C**,
1: 5 our comfort abounds through **C**.
3: 3 show that you are a letter from **C**,
3: 14 because only in **C** is it taken away.
4: 4 gospel that displays the glory of **C**,
4: 5 but Jesus **C** as Lord, and ourselves
4: 6 glory displayed in the face of **C**.
5: 10 before the judgment seat of **C**,
5: 17 if anyone is in **C**, the new creation
6: 15 What harmony is there between **C**
10: 1 the humility and gentleness of **C**,
11: 2 to **C**, so that I might present you as
Gal 1: 7 trying to pervert the gospel of **C**.
2: 4 on the freedom we have in **C** Jesus
2: 16 of the law, but by faith in Jesus **C**.
2: 16 we may be justified by faith in **C**
2: 17 that mean that **C** promotes sin?
2: 20 I have been crucified with **C** and I no longer live, but **C** lives in me.
2: 21 the law, **C** died for nothing!"
3: 13 **C** redeemed us from the curse
3: 16 meaning one person, who is **C**.
3: 26 So in **C** Jesus you are all children
4: 19 of childbirth until **C** is formed
5: 1 for freedom that **C** has set us free.
5: 4 law have been alienated from **C**;
5: 24 to **C** Jesus have crucified the flesh
6: 14 in the cross of our Lord Jesus **C**,
Eph 1: 3 with every spiritual blessing in **C**.
1: 10 in heaven and on earth under **C**.
1: 20 when he raised **C** from the dead
2: 5 made us alive with **C** even when
2: 10 created in **C** Jesus to do good
2: 12 time you were separate from **C**,
2: 20 with **C** Jesus himself as the chief
3: 8 Gentiles the boundless riches of **C**,
3: 17 so that **C** may dwell in your hearts
4: 7 has been given as **C** apportioned it.
4: 13 whole measure of the fullness of **C**.
4: 15 of him who is the head, that is, **C**.
4: 32 other, just as in **C** God forgave you.
5: 2 just as **C** loved us and gave himself
5: 21 one another out of reverence for **C**.
5: 23 head of the wife as **C** is the head
5: 25 just as **C** loved the church and gave
Php 1: 18 motives or true, **C** is preached.
1: 21 to live is **C** and to die is gain.
1: 23 I desire to depart and be with **C**,
1: 27 manner worthy of the gospel of **C**.
1: 29 on behalf of **C** not only to believe
2: 5 have the same mindset as **C** Jesus:
3: 7 now consider loss for the sake of **C**.
3: 10 I want to know **C**—yes, to know
3: 18 live as enemies of the cross of **C**.
4: 19 to the riches of his glory in **C** Jesus.
Col 1: 4 have heard of your faith in **C** Jesus
1: 27 which is **C** in you, the hope
1: 28 present everyone fully mature in **C**.
2: 2 the mystery of God, namely, **C**,
2: 6 as you received **C** Jesus as Lord,
2: 9 in **C** all the fullness of the Deity
2: 13 flesh, God made you alive with **C**.
Col 2: 17 the reality, however, is found in **C**.
3: 1 you have been raised with **C**,
3: 1 hearts on things above, where **C** is,
3: 3 your life is now hidden with **C**
3: 15 Let the peace of **C** rule in your
1Th 5: 9 through our Lord Jesus **C**.
2Th 2: 1 the coming of our Lord Jesus **C**
2: 14 in the glory of our Lord Jesus **C**.
1Ti 1: 12 I thank **C** Jesus our Lord, who has
1: 15 **C** Jesus came into the world to save
1: 16 **C** Jesus might display his immense
2: 5 and mankind, the man **C** Jesus,
2Ti 1: 9 us in **C** Jesus before the beginning
1: 10 appearing of our Savior, **C** Jesus,
2: 1 in the grace that is in **C** Jesus.
2: 3 like a good soldier of **C** Jesus.
2: 8 Remember Jesus **C**,
2: 10 the salvation that is in **C** Jesus,
3: 12 life in **C** Jesus will be persecuted,
3: 15 salvation through faith in **C** Jesus.
4: 1 the presence of God and of **C** Jesus,
Titus 2: 13 our great God and Savior, Jesus **C**,
Heb 3: 6 **C** is faithful as the Son over God's
3: 14 We have come to share in **C**,
5: 5 **C** did not take on himself the glory
6: 1 the elementary teachings about **C**
9: 11 when **C** came as high priest
9: 14 will the blood of **C**, who through
9: 15 For this reason **C** is the mediator
9: 24 **C** did not enter a sanctuary made
9: 26 Otherwise **C** would have had
9: 28 so **C** was sacrificed once to take
10: 10 of the body of Jesus **C** once for all.
13: 8 Jesus **C** is the same yesterday
1Pe 1: 2 Spirit, to be obedient to Jesus **C**
1: 3 and Father of our Lord Jesus **C**!
1: 11 Spirit of **C** in them was pointing
1: 19 but with the precious blood of **C**,
2: 21 called, because **C** suffered for you,
3: 15 in your hearts revere **C** as Lord.
3: 18 For **C** also suffered once for sins,
3: 21 you by the resurrection of Jesus **C**,
4: 13 participate in the sufferings of **C**,
4: 14 insulted because of the name of **C**,
2Pe 1: 1 a servant and apostle of Jesus **C**,
1: 16 of our Lord Jesus **C** in power,
1Jn 2: 1 Jesus **C**, the Righteous One.
2: 22 whoever denies that Jesus is the **C**.
3: 16 Jesus **C** laid down his life for us.
3: 23 Jesus **C**, and to love one another as
4: 2 that Jesus **C** has come in the flesh
5: 1 believes that Jesus is the **C** is born
5: 20 is true by being in his Son Jesus **C**.
2Jn : 9 teaching of **C** does not have God;
Jude : 4 deny Jesus **C** our only Sovereign
Rev 1: 1 The revelation from Jesus **C**,
1: 5 and from Jesus **C**, who is
20: 4 reigned with **C** a thousand years.
20: 6 of **C** and will reign with him

CHRISTIAN* (CHRIST)
Ac 26: 28 you can persuade me to be a **C**?"
1Pe 4: 16 if you suffer as a **C**, do not be

CHRISTIANS* (CHRIST)
Ac 11: 26 The disciples were called **C** first

CHRIST'S (CHRIST)
1Co 9: 21 God's law but am under **C** law),
2Co 2: 14 captives in **C** triumphal procession
5: 14 For **C** love compels us, because we
5: 20 We are therefore **C** ambassadors,
5: 20 We implore you on **C** behalf:
12: 9 so that **C** power may rest on me.
Col 1: 22 by **C** physical body through death

CHURCH
Mt 16: 18 and on this rock I will build my **c**,
18: 17 refuse to listen, tell it to the **c**;
18: 17 they refuse to listen even to the **c**,
Ac 20: 28 Be shepherds of the **c** of God,
1Co 5: 12 mine to judge those outside the **c**?
14: 4 one who prophesies edifies the **c**.
14: 12 excel in those that build up the **c**.
14: 26 done so that the **c** may be built up.
15: 9 because I persecuted the **c** of God.
Gal 1: 13 how intensely I persecuted the **c**
Eph 5: 23 wife as Christ is the head of the **c**,
Col 1: 18 he is the head of the body, the **c**;
1: 24 the sake of his body, which is the **c**.

CHURNING
Pr 30: 33 For as **c** cream produces butter,

CIRCLE
Isa 40: 22 enthroned above the **c** of the earth,

CIRCUMCISE (CIRCUMCISED CIRCUMCISION)
Dt 10: 16 **C** your hearts, therefore, and do

CIRCUMCISED (CIRCUMCISE)
Ge 17: 10 Every male among you shall be **c**.
17: 12 who is eight days old must be **c**,
Jos 5: 3 **c** the Israelites at Gibeath
Gal 2: 8 in Peter as an apostle to the **c**,
5: 2 you that if you let yourselves be **c**,

CIRCUMCISION (CIRCUMCISE)
Ro 2: 25 **C** has value if you observe the law,
2: 29 and **c** is **c** of the heart, by the Spirit,
1Co 7: 19 **C** is nothing and uncircumcision is

CIRCUMSTANCES
Php 4: 11 to be content whatever the **c**.
1Th 5: 18 give thanks in all **c**; for this is God's

CITIES (CITY)
Lk 19: 17 small matter, take charge of ten **c**.'
19: 19 'You take charge of five **c**.'

CITIZENS (CITIZENSHIP)
Eph 2: 19 but fellow **c** with God's people

CITIZENSHIP* (CITIZENS)
Ac 22: 28 to pay a lot of money for my **c**."
Eph 2: 12 excluded from **c** in Israel
Php 3: 20 But our **c** is in heaven.

CITY (CITIES)
Ac 18: 10 I have many people in this **c**."
Heb 13: 14 here we do not have an enduring **c**,
Rev 21: 2 I saw the Holy **C**, the new

CIVILIAN*
2Ti 2: 4 a soldier gets entangled in **c** affairs,

CLAIM (CLAIMS RECLAIM)
Pr 25: 6 do not **c** a place among his great
1Jn 1: 6 If we **c** to have fellowship with him
1: 8 If we **c** to be without sin,
1: 10 If we **c** we have not sinned,

CLAIMS (CLAIM)
Jas 2: 14 if someone **c** to have faith but has
1Jn 2: 6 Whoever **c** to live in him must live
2: 9 Anyone who **c** to be in the light

CLANGING*
1Co 13: 1 a resounding gong or a **c** cymbal.

CLAP* (CLAPPED CLAPS)
Job 21: 5 **c** your hand over your mouth.
Ps 47: 1 **C** your hands, all you nations;
98: 8 Let the rivers **c** their hands,
Pr 30: 32 evil, **c** your hand over your mouth!
Isa 55: 12 trees of the field will **c** their hands.
La 2: 15 who pass your way **c** their hands
Na 3: 19 the news about you **c** their hands

CLAPPED* (CLAP)
2Ki 11: 12 and the people **c** their hands
Eze 25: 6 Because you have **c** your hands

CLAPS* (CLAP)
Job 27: 23 It **c** its hands in derision and hisses
34: 37 scornfully he **c** his hands among us

CLASSIFY*
2Co 10: 12 We do not dare to **c** or compare

CLAUDIUS
Ac 11: 28 happened during the reign of **C**.)
18: 2 because **C** had ordered all Jews

CLAY
Isa 45: 9 Does the **c** say to the potter,
64: 8 We are the **c**, you are the potter;
Jer 18: 6 "Like **c** in the hand of the potter,
La 4: 2 are now considered as pots of **c**,
Da 2: 33 of iron and partly of baked **c**.
Ro 9: 21 the same lump of **c** some pottery
2Co 4: 7 this treasure in jars of **c** to show
2Ti 2: 20 and silver, but also of wood and **c**;

CLEAN (CLEANNESS CLEANSE CLEANSED CLEANSING)
Ge 7: 2 pairs of every kind of **c** animal,

Lev 4: 12 the camp to a place ceremonially **c**,
16: 30 you will be **c** from all your sins.
Ps 24: 4 one who has **c** hands and a pure
51: 7 me with hyssop, and I will be **c**;
Pr 20: 9 I am **c** and without sin"?
Eze 36: 25 I will sprinkle **c** water on you, and you will be **c**;
Mt 8: 2 are willing, you can make me **c**."
12: 44 swept **c** and put in order.
23: 25 You **c** the outside of the cup
Mk 7: 19 this, Jesus declared all foods **c**.)
Jn 13: 10 you are **c**, though not every one
15: 3 You are already **c** because
Ac 10: 15 impure that God has made **c**."
Ro 14: 20 All food is **c**, but it is wrong

CLEANNESS (CLEAN)
2Sa 22: 25 according to my **c** in his sight.

CLEANSE (CLEAN)
Ps 51: 2 my iniquity and **c** me from my sin.
51: 7 **C** me with hyssop, and I will be
2Ti 2: 21 Those who **c** themselves
Heb 9: 14 **c** our consciences from acts
10: 22 having our hearts sprinkled to **c** us

CLEANSED (CLEAN)
Mt 11: 5 those who have leprosy are **c**,
Heb 9: 22 nearly everything be **c** with blood,
2Pe 1: 9 they have been **c** from their past

CLEANSING (CLEAN)
Eph 5: 26 **c** her by the washing with water
Heb 6: 2 instruction about **c** rites, the laying

CLEFT*
Ex 33: 22 I will put you in a **c** in the rock

CLEVER (CLEVERNESS)
Isa 5: 21 own eyes and **c** in their own sight.

CLEVERNESS (CLEVER)
Pr 23: 4 get rich; do not trust your own **c**.

CLING
Ps 63: 8 I **c** to you; your right hand upholds
Ro 12: 9 Hate what is evil; **c** to what is good.

CLOAK
Ex 12: 11 with your **c** tucked into your belt,
2Ki 4: 29 "Tuck your **c** into your belt,
9: 1 to him, "Tuck your **c** into your belt,

CLOSE (CLOSER)
2Ki 11: 8 Stay **c** to the king wherever he
Ps 34: 18 The LORD is **c**
148: 14 of Israel, the people **c** to his heart.
Pr 28: 27 but those who **c** their eyes to them
Isa 40: 11 and carries them **c** to his heart;
Jer 30: 21 near and he will come **c** to me—

CLOSER (CLOSE)
Ex 3: 5 "Do not come any **c**," God said.
Pr 18: 24 friend who sticks **c** than a brother.

CLOTHE (CLOTHED CLOTHES CLOTHING CLOTHS)
Ps 45: 3 **c** yourself with splendor
Isa 52: 1 Zion, **c** yourself with strength!
Ro 13: 14 **c** yourselves with the Lord Jesus
Col 3: 12 **c** yourselves with compassion,
1Pe 5: 5 **c** yourselves with humility toward

CLOTHED (CLOTHE)
Ps 30: 11 my sackcloth and **c** me with joy,
104: 1 you are **c** with splendor
Pr 31: 22 she is **c** in fine linen and purple.
31: 25 She is **c** with strength and dignity;
Isa 61: 10 For he has **c** me with garments
Lk 24: 49 the city until you have been **c**
Gal 3: 27 into Christ have **c** yourselves

CLOTHES (CLOTHE)
Dt 8: 4 Your **c** did not wear out and your
Mt 6: 25 food, and the body more than **c**?
6: 28 "And why do you worry about **c**?
27: 35 divided up his **c** by casting lots.
Jn 11: 44 "Take off the grave **c** and let him
19: 24 "They divided my **c** among them

CLOTHING (CLOTHE)
Dt 22: 5 A woman must not wear men's **c**,
22: 5 nor a man wear women's **c**,
Job 29: 14 I put on righteousness as my **c**;
Mt 7: 15 They come to you in sheep's **c**,
1Ti 6: 8 But if we have food and **c**, we will

CLOTHS (CLOTHE)
Lk 2: 12 You will find a baby wrapped in **c**

CLOUD (CLOUDS)
Ex 13: 21 them in a pillar of **c** to guide them
1Ki 18: 44 "A **c** as small as a man's hand is
Pr 16: 15 his favor is like a rain **c** in spring.
Isa 19: 1 the LORD rides on a swift **c** and is
Lk 21: 27 of Man coming in a **c** with power
Heb 12: 1 by such a great **c** of witnesses,
Rev 14: 14 seated on the **c** was one like a son

CLOUDS (CLOUD)
Dt 33: 26 you and on the **c** in his majesty.
Ps 68: 4 extol him who rides on the **c**;
104: 3 makes the **c** his chariot and rides
Pr 25: 14 Like **c** and wind without rain is one
Da 7: 13 man, coming with the **c** of heaven.
Mt 24: 30 of Man coming on the **c** of heaven,
26: 64 and coming on the **c** of heaven."
Mk 13: 26 Man coming in **c** with great power
1Th 4: 17 them in the **c** to meet the Lord
Rev 1: 7 he is coming with the **c**,"

CLUB
Pr 25: 18 a **c** or a sword or a sharp arrow

CO-HEIRS* (INHERIT)
Ro 8: 17 heirs of God and **c** with Christ,

CO-WORKERS (WORK)
Ro 16: 3 Priscilla and Aquila, my **c** in Christ
1Co 3: 9 For we are **c** in God's service;

COALS
Pr 25: 22 will heap burning **c** on his head,
Ro 12: 20 this, you will heap burning **c** on his

COARSE*
Eph 5: 4 foolish talk or **c** joking, which are

COAT
Mt 5: 40 shirt, hand over your **c** as well.

CODE*
Ro 2: 27 even though you have the written **c**
2: 29 by the Spirit, not by the written **c**.
7: 6 not in the old way of the written **c**.

COINS
Mt 18: 28 who owed him a hundred silver **c**.
Mk 12: 42 put in two very small copper **c**,
Lk 15: 8 suppose a woman has ten silver **c**

COLD
Pr 25: 25 Like **c** water to a weary soul is
Mt 10: 42 anyone gives even a cup of **c** water
24: 12 the love of most will grow **c**,

COLLECTION
1Co 16: 1 about the **c** for the Lord's people:

COLT
Zec 9: 9 on a **c**, the foal of a donkey.
Mt 21: 5 a donkey, and on a **c**, the foal

COMFORT* (COMFORTED COMFORTER COMFORTERS COMFORTING COMFORTS)
Ge 5: 29 said, "He will **c** us in the labor
37: 35 sons and daughters came to **c** him,
1Ch 7: 22 and his relatives came to **c** him.
Job 2: 11 sympathize with him and **c** him.
7: 13 When I think my bed will **c** me
16: 5 **c** from my lips would bring you
36: 16 to the **c** of your table laden
Ps 23: 4 your rod and your staff, they **c** me.
71: 21 my honor and **c** me once more.
119: 50 My **c** in my suffering is this:
119: 52 ancient laws, and I find **c** in them.
119: 76 May your unfailing love be my **c**,
119: 82 I say, "When will you **c** me?"
Isa 40: 1 **C**, **c** my people, says your God.
51: 3 The LORD will surely **c** Zion
51: 19 upon you—who can **c** you?—
57: 18 and restore **c** to Israel's mourners,
61: 2 of our God, to **c** all who mourn,
66: 13 comforts her child, so will I **c** you;
Jer 16: 7 offer food to **c** those who mourn
31: 13 I will give them **c** and joy instead
La 1: 2 her lovers there is no one to **c** her.
1: 9 there was none to **c** her.
1: 16 No one is near to **c** me, no one
1: 17 hands, but there is no one to **c** her.
1: 21 but there is no one to **c** me.
La 2: 13 that I may **c** you, Virgin Daughter
Eze 16: 54 all you have done in giving them **c**.
Na 3: 7 Where can I find anyone to **c** you?"
Zec 1: 17 the LORD will again **c** Zion
10: 2 that are false, they give **c** in vain.
Lk 6: 24 you have already received your **c**.
Jn 11: 19 Mary to **c** them in the loss of their
1Co 14: 3 strengthening, encouraging and **c**.
2Co 1: 3 of compassion and the God of all **c**,
1: 4 that we can **c** those in any trouble
1: 4 with the **c** we ourselves receive
1: 5 also our **c** abounds through Christ.
1: 6 it is for your **c** and salvation;
1: 6 it is for your **c**, which produces
1: 7 so also you share in our **c**.
2: 7 you ought to forgive and **c** him,
7: 7 also by the **c** you had given him.
Php 2: 1 Christ, if any **c** from his love, if any
Col 4: 11 and they have proved a **c** to me.

COMFORTED* (COMFORT)
Ge 24: 67 Isaac was **c** after his mother's
37: 35 him, but he refused to be **c**.
2Sa 12: 24 Then David **c** his wife Bathsheba,
Job 42: 11 They **c** and consoled him over all
Ps 77: 2 hands, and I would not be **c**.
86: 17 LORD, have helped me and **c** me.
Isa 12: 1 turned away and you have **c** me.
52: 9 for the LORD has **c** his people,
54: 11 lashed by storms and not **c**, I will
66: 13 and you will be **c** over Jerusalem."
Jer 31: 15 her children and refusing to be **c**,
Mt 2: 18 her children and refusing to be **c**,
5: 4 who mourn, for they will be **c**.
Lk 16: 25 but now he is **c** here and you are
Ac 20: 12 man home alive and were greatly **c**.
2Co 1: 6 If we are **c**, it is for your comfort,
7: 6 **c** us by the coming of Titus,

COMFORTER* (COMFORT)
Ecc 4: 1 and they have no **c**;
4: 1 and they have no **c**.
Jer 8: 18 You who are my **C** in sorrow,

COMFORTERS* (COMFORT)
Job 16: 2 you are miserable **c**, all of you!
Ps 69: 20 was none, for **c**, but I found none.

COMFORTING* (COMFORT)
Isa 66: 11 and be satisfied at her **c** breasts;
Zec 1: 13 **c** words to the angel who talked
Jn 11: 31 with Mary in the house, **c** her,
1Th 2: 12 **c** and urging you to live lives

COMFORTS* (COMFORT)
Job 29: 25 I was like one who **c** mourners.
Isa 49: 13 For the LORD **c** his people
51: 12 "I, even I, am he who **c** you.
66: 13 As a mother **c** her child, so will I
2Co 1: 4 who **c** us in all our troubles,
7: 6 But God, who **c** the downcast,

COMMAND (COMMANDED COMMANDING COMMANDMENT COMMANDMENTS COMMANDS)
Ex 7: 2 You are to say everything I **c** you,
Nu 14: 41 are you disobeying the LORD's **c**?
24: 13 to go beyond the **c** of the LORD—
Dt 4: 2 Do not add to what I **c** you and do
8: 1 to follow every **c** I am giving you
12: 32 See that you do all I **c** you;
15: 11 I **c** you to be openhanded
30: 16 For I **c** you today to love
32: 46 so that you may **c** your children
Ps 91: 11 he will **c** his angels concerning you
148: 5 for at his **c** they were created,
Pr 6: 23 For this **c** is a lamp, this teaching is
13: 13 whoever respects a **c** is rewarded.
Ecc 8: 2 Obey the king's **c**, I say,
Jer 1: 7 you to and say whatever I **c** you.
1: 17 and say to them whatever I **c** you.
7: 23 Walk in obedience to all I **c** you,
11: 4 me and do everything I **c** you,
26: 2 Tell them everything I **c** you;
Joel 2: 11 mighty is the army that obeys his **c**.
Mt 4: 6 "'He will **c** his angels concerning
15: 3 why do you break the **c** of God
Lk 4: 10 "'He will **c** his angels concerning
Jn 13: 34 "A new **c** I give you:
15: 12 My **c** is this: Love each other as I

Jn 15: 14 are my friends if you do what I **c**.
15: 17 This is my **c**: Love each other.
Ro 13: 9 are summed up in this one **c**:
1Co 14: 37 I am writing to you is the Lord's **c**.
Gal 5: 14 is fulfilled in keeping this one **c**:
1Ti 1: 5 The goal of this **c** is love,
1: 18 I am giving you this **c** in keeping
6: 14 keep this **c** without spot or blame
6: 17 **C** those who are rich in this
Heb 9: 19 Moses had proclaimed every **c**
11: 3 the universe was formed at God's **c**,
2Pe 2: 21 on the sacred **c** that was passed
3: 2 and the **c** given by our Lord
1Jn 2: 7 I am not writing you a new **c**
2: 7 This old **c** is the message you have
3: 23 And this is his **c**: to believe
4: 21 And he has given us this **c**:
2Jn : 6 his **c** is that you walk in love.

COMMANDED (COMMAND)
Ge 2: 16 And the LORD God **c** the man,
7: 5 Noah did all that the LORD **c** him.
50: 12 Jacob's sons did as he had **c** them:
Ex 7: 6 did just as the LORD **c** them.
19: 7 all the words the LORD had **c** him
Dt 4: 5 laws as the LORD my God **c** me,
6: 24 The LORD **c** us to obey all these
Jos 1: 9 Have I not **c** you? Be strong
1: 16 "Whatever you have **c** us we will
2Sa 5: 25 So David did as the LORD **c** him,
2Ki 17: 13 entire Law that I **c** your ancestors
21: 8 careful to do everything I **c** them
2Ch 33: 8 do everything I **c** them concerning
Ps 33: 9 came to be; he **c**, and it stood firm.
78: 5 which he **c** our ancestors to teach
Mt 28: 20 to obey everything I have **c** you.
1Co 9: 14 way, the Lord has **c** that those who
1Jn 3: 23 and to love one another as he **c** us.
2Jn : 4 in the truth, just as the Father **c** us.

COMMANDING (COMMAND)
2Ti 2: 4 rather tries to please his **c** officer.

COMMANDMENT* (COMMAND)
Jos 22: 5 be very careful to keep the **c**
Mt 22: 36 which is the greatest **c** in the Law?"
22: 38 This is the first and greatest **c**.
Mk 12: 31 There is no **c** greater than these."
Lk 23: 56 the Sabbath in obedience to the **c**.
Ro 7: 8 the opportunity afforded by the **c**,
7: 9 but when the **c** came, sin sprang
7: 10 that the very **c** that was intended
7: 11 and through the **c** put me to death.
7: 12 and the **c** is holy,
7: 13 that through the **c** sin might
Eph 6: 2 is the first **c** with a promise—

COMMANDMENTS* (COMMAND)
Ex 20: 6 those who love me and keep my **c**.
24: 12 the law and **c** I have written for
34: 28 words of the covenant—the Ten **C**.
Dt 4: 13 the Ten **C**, which he commanded
5: 10 those who love me and keep my **c**.
5: 22 These are the **c** the LORD
6: 6 These **c** that I give you today are
7: 9 those who love him and keep his **c**.
9: 10 On them were all the **c** the LORD
10: 4 Ten **C** he had proclaimed to you
Ne 1: 5 those who love him and keep his **c**,
Pr 19: 16 Whoever keeps **c** keeps their life,
Ecc 12: 13 Fear God and keep his **c**, for this is
Da 9: 4 those who love him and keep his **c**,
Mt 19: 17 you want to enter life, keep the **c**."
22: 40 the Prophets hang on these two **c**."
Mk 10: 19 You know the **c**: 'You shall not
12: 28 "Of all the **c**, which is the most
Lk 18: 20 You know the **c**: 'You shall not
Ro 13: 9 The **c**, "You shall not commit

COMMANDS (COMMAND)
Ex 25: 22 give you all my **c** for the Israelites.
34: 32 gave them all the **c** the LORD had
Lev 22: 31 "Keep my **c** and follow them.
Nu 15: 39 so you will remember all the **c**
Dt 7: 11 take care to follow the **c**,
11: 1 decrees, his laws and his **c** always.
11: 27 you obey the **c** of the LORD your
28: 1 carefully follow all his **c** I give you
30: 10 and keep his **c** and decrees that are
Jos 22: 5 to keep his **c**, to hold fast to him
1Ki 2: 3 keep his decrees and **c**, his laws
8: 58 obedience to him and keep the **c**,
8: 61 live by his decrees and obey his **c**,
1Ch 28: 7 is unswerving in carrying out my **c**
29: 19 devotion to keep your **c**,
2Ch 31: 21 in obedience to the law and the **c**,
Ps 78: 7 his deeds but would keep his **c**.
112: 1 who find great delight in his **c**.
119: 10 do not let me stray from your **c**.
119: 32 I run in the path of your **c**, for you
119: 35 Direct me in the path of your **c**,
119: 47 in your **c** because I love them.
119: 48 I reach out for your **c**, which I love,
119: 73 me understanding to learn your **c**.
119: 86 All your **c** are trustworthy;
119: 96 a limit, but your **c** are boundless.
119: 98 Your **c** are always with me
119:115 that I may keep the **c** of my God!
119:127 I love your **c** more than gold,
119:131 and pant, longing for your **c**.
119:143 but your **c** give me delight.
119:151 and all your **c** are true.
119:172 for all your **c** are righteous.
119:176 I have not forgotten your **c**.
Pr 2: 1 and store up my **c** within you,
3: 1 but keep my **c** in your heart,
10: 8 The wise in heart accept **c**,
Isa 48: 18 you had paid attention to my **c**,
Mt 5: 19 sets aside one of the least of these **c**
5: 19 teaches these **c** will be called great
Mk 7: 8 You have let go of the **c** of God
7: 9 way of setting aside the **c** of God
Lk 1: 6 God, observing all the Lord's **c**
Jn 14: 15 "If you love me, keep my **c**.
14: 21 Whoever has my **c** and keeps them
15: 10 just as I have kept my Father's **c**
Ac 17: 30 now he **c** all people everywhere
1Co 7: 19 Keeping God's **c** is what counts.
Eph 2: 15 aside in his flesh the law with its **c**
1Jn 2: 3 come to know him if we keep his **c**.
2: 4 but does not do what he **c** is a liar,
3: 22 because we keep his **c** and do what
3: 24 The one who keeps God's **c** lives
5: 2 loving God and carrying out his **c**.
5: 3 this is love for God: to keep his **c**.
5: 3 And his **c** are not burdensome,
2Jn : 6 that we walk in obedience to his **c**.
Rev 12: 17 those who keep God's **c** and hold
14: 12 the people of God who keep his **c**

COMMEMORATE
Ex 12: 14 "This is a day you are to **c**;

COMMEND* (COMMENDABLE COMMENDED COMMENDS)
Ecc 8: 15 So I **c** the enjoyment of life,
Ro 16: 1 I **c** to you our sister Phoebe,
2Co 3: 1 we beginning to **c** ourselves again?
4: 2 the truth plainly we **c** ourselves
5: 12 We are not trying to **c** ourselves
6: 4 God we **c** ourselves in every way:
10: 12 with some who **c** themselves.
1Pe 2: 14 wrong and to **c** those who do right.

COMMENDABLE* (COMMEND)
1Pe 2: 19 it is **c** if someone bears up under
2: 20 you endure it, this is **c** before God.

COMMENDED* (COMMEND)
Ne 11: 2 The people **c** all who volunteered
Job 29: 11 of me, and those who saw me **c** me,
Lk 16: 8 "The master **c** the dishonest
Ac 15: 40 **c** by the believers to the grace
Ro 13: 3 do what is right and you will be **c**.
2Co 12: 11 I ought to have been **c** by you, for I
Heb 11: 2 is what the ancients were **c** for.
11: 4 By faith he was **c** as righteous,
11: 5 he was **c** as one who pleased God.
11: 39 These were all **c** for their faith,

COMMENDS* (COMMEND)
Ps 145: 4 One generation **c** your works
2Co 10: 18 not the one who **c** himself who is
10: 18 but the one whom the Lord **c**.

COMMIT (COMMITS COMMITTED)
Ex 20: 14 "You shall not **c** adultery.
Dt 5: 18 "You shall not **c** adultery.
1Sa 7: 3 and **c** yourselves to the LORD
Ps 31: 5 Into your hands I **c** my spirit;
37: 5 **C** your way to the LORD;
Pr 16: 3 **C** to the LORD whatever you do,
Mt 5: 27 was said, 'You shall not **c** adultery.'
19: 18 you shall not **c** adultery, you shall
Mk 10: 19 you shall not **c** adultery, you shall
Lk 18: 20 'You shall not **c** adultery, you shall
23: 46 into your hands I **c** my spirit."
Ac 20: 32 "Now I **c** you to God
Ro 2: 22 should not **c** adultery, do you **c** adultery?
13: 9 "You shall not **c** adultery,"
1Co 10: 8 We should not **c** sexual immorality,
Jas 2: 11 "You shall not **c** adultery,"
1Pe 4: 19 to God's will should **c** themselves
Rev 2: 22 I will make those who **c** adultery

COMMITS* (COMMIT)
Lev 20: 10 man **c** adultery with another man's
Pr 6: 32 a man who **c** adultery has no sense;
29: 22 hot-tempered person **c** many sins.
Ecc 8: 12 a wicked person who **c** a hundred
Eze 18: 12 the poor and needy. He **c** robbery.
18: 14 who sees all the sins his father **c**,
18: 24 from their righteousness and **c** sin
18: 26 from their righteousness and **c** sin,
22: 11 you one man **c** a detestable offense
Mt 5: 32 a divorced woman **c** adultery.
19: 9 marries another woman **c** adultery."
Mk 10: 11 another woman **c** adultery against
10: 12 another man, she **c** adultery."
Lk 16: 18 marries another woman **c** adultery,
16: 18 a divorced woman **c** adultery.
1Co 6: 18 All other sins a person **c** are

COMMITTED (COMMIT)
Nu 5: 7 must confess the sin they have **c**.
1Ki 8: 61 may your hearts be fully **c**
15: 14 Asa's heart was fully **c**
2Ch 16: 9 those whose hearts are fully **c**
Mt 5: 28 lustfully has already **c** adultery
11: 27 "All things have been **c** to me
Lk 10: 22 "All things have been **c** to me
Ac 14: 23 and fasting, **c** them to the Lord,
14: 26 where they had been **c** to the grace
1Co 9: 17 I am simply discharging the trust **c**
2Co 5: 19 And he has **c** to us the message
1Pe 2: 22 "He **c** no sin, and no deceit was
Rev 17: 2 the kings of the earth **c** adultery,
18: 3 of the earth **c** adultery with her,
18: 9 the earth who **c** adultery with her

COMMON
Ge 11: 1 had one language and a **c** speech.
Lev 10: 10 between the holy and the **c**,
Pr 22: 2 Rich and poor have this in **c**:
29: 13 and the oppressor have this in **c**:
Ac 2: 44 together and had everything in **c**.
Ro 9: 21 purposes and some for **c** use?
1Co 10: 13 has overtaken you except what is **c**
2Co 6: 14 and wickedness have in **c**?
2Ti 2: 20 purposes and some for **c** use.

COMMUNITY
Pr 6: 19 who stirs up conflict in the **c**.

COMPANION (COMPANIONS)
Ps 55: 13 like myself, my **c**, my close friend,
55: 20 My **c** attacks his friends;
Pr 13: 20 wise, for a **c** of fools suffers harm.
28: 7 a **c** of gluttons disgraces his father.
29: 3 but a **c** of prostitutes squanders his
Rev 1: 9 your brother and **c** in the suffering

COMPANIONS (COMPANION)
Ps 45: 7 you above your **c** by anointing you
Heb 1: 9 you above your **c** by anointing you

COMPANY
Ps 14: 5 is present in the **c** of the righteous.
Pr 21: 16 comes to rest in the **c** of the dead.
24: 1 the wicked, do not desire their **c**;
Jer 15: 17 I never sat in the **c** of revelers,
1Co 15: 33 "Bad **c** corrupts good character."

COMPARE* (COMPARED COMPARING COMPARISON)
Job 28: 17 Neither gold nor crystal can **c**
28: 19 The topaz of Cush cannot **c** with it;
39: 13 they cannot **c** with the wings
Ps 40: 5 None can **c** with you; were I

Ps 86: 8 no deeds can c with yours.
89: 6 skies above can c with the LORD?
Pr 3: 15 nothing you desire can c with her.
8: 11 nothing you desire can c with her.
Isa 40: 18 With whom, then, will you c God?
40: 25 "To whom will you c me?
46: 5 "With whom will you c me
La 2: 13 With what can I c you,
Eze 31: 8 nor could the plane trees c with its
Da 1: 13 c our appearance
Mt 11: 16 "To what can I c this generation?
Lk 7: 31 then, can I c the people of this
13: 18 of God like? What shall I c it to?
13: 20 shall I c the kingdom of God
2Co 10: 12 or c ourselves with some who
10: 12 and c themselves with themselves,

COMPARED* (COMPARE)
Jdg 8: 2 "What have I accomplished c
8: 3 What was I able to do c to you?"
Isa 46: 5 you liken me that we may be c?
Eze 31: 2 "'Who can be c with you
31: 18 the trees of Eden can be c with you
Ro 5: 16 the gift of God be c with the result

COMPARING* (COMPARE)
Ro 8: 18 present sufferings are not worth c
2Co 8: 8 of your love by c it
Gal 6: 4 without c themselves to someone

COMPARISON* (COMPARE)
2Co 3: 10 was glorious has no glory now in c

COMPASSION* (COMPASSIONATE COMPASSIONS)
Ex 33: 19 I will have c on whom I will have c.
Dt 13: 17 you mercy, and will have c on you.
28: 54 man among you will have no c
30: 3 your fortunes and have c on you
2Ki 13: 23 had c and showed concern for
2Ch 30: 9 your children will be shown c
Ne 9: 19 your great c you did not abandon
9: 27 and in your great c you gave them
9: 28 In your c you delivered them time
Ps 51: 1 to your great c blot out my
77: 9 Has he in anger withheld his c?"
90: 13 will it be? Have c on your servants.
102: 13 You will arise and have c on Zion,
103: 4 pit and crowns you with love and c,
103: 13 As a father has c on his children,
103: 13 so the LORD has c on those who
116: 5 our God is full of c.
119: 77 Let your c come to me that I may
119:156 Your c, LORD, is great;
135: 14 and have c on his servants.
145: 9 he has c on all he has made.
Isa 13: 18 infants, nor will they look with c
14: 1 The LORD will have c on Jacob;
27: 11 so their Maker has no c on them,
30: 18 he will rise up to show you c.
49: 10 He who has c on them will guide
49: 13 will have c on his afflicted ones.
49: 15 and have no c on the child she has
51: 3 will look with c on all her ruins;
54: 7 with deep c I will bring you back.
54: 8 everlasting kindness I will have c
54: 10 says the LORD, who has c on you.
60: 10 you, in favor I will show you c.
63: 7 Israel, according to his c and many
63: 15 and c are withheld from us.
Jer 12: 15 I will again have c and will bring
13: 14 or c to keep me from destroying
21: 7 show them no mercy or pity or c.'
30: 18 tents and have c on his dwellings;
31: 20 I have great c for him,"
33: 26 fortunes and have c on them.'"
42: 12 I will show you c so that he will have c on you
La 3: 32 grief, he will show c, so great is his
Eze 9: 5 and kill, without showing pity or c.
16: 5 or had c enough to do any of these
39: 25 and will have c on all the people
Da 1: 9 to show favor and c to Daniel,
Hos 2: 19 and justice, in love and c.
11: 8 all my c is aroused.
13: 14 "I will have no c,
14: 3 for in you the fatherless find c."
Jnh 3: 9 with c turn from his fierce anger so
Mic 7: 19 You will again have c on us;
Zec 7: 9 show mercy and c to one another.
10: 6 I will restore them because I have c
Mal 3: 17 just as a father has c and spares his
Mt 9: 36 saw the crowds, he had c on them,
14: 14 he had c on them and healed their
15: 32 and said, "I have c for these people;
20: 34 Jesus had c on them and touched
Mk 6: 34 a large crowd, he had c on them,
8: 2 "I have c for these people;
Lk 15: 20 him and was filled with c for him;
Ro 9: 15 I will have c on whom I have c."
2Co 1: 3 the Father of c and the God of all
Php 2: 1 the Spirit, if any tenderness and c,
Col 3: 12 clothe yourselves with c, kindness,
Jas 5: 11 The Lord is full of c and mercy.

COMPASSIONATE* (COMPASSION)
Ex 22: 27 to me, I will hear, for I am c.
34: 6 LORD, the c and gracious God,
2Ch 30: 9 LORD your God is gracious and c.
Ne 9: 17 gracious and c, slow to anger
Ps 86: 15 Lord, are a c and gracious God,
103: 8 The LORD is c and gracious,
111: 4 the LORD is gracious and c.
112: 4 for those who are gracious and c
145: 8 The LORD is gracious and c,
La 4: 10 their own hands c women have
Joel 2: 13 for he is gracious and c,
Jnh 4: 2 that you are a gracious and c God,
Eph 4: 32 Be kind and c to one another,
1Pe 3: 8 love one another, be c and humble.

COMPASSIONS* (COMPASSION)
La 3: 22 not consumed, for his c never fail.

COMPELLED (COMPULSION)
Ac 20: 22 "And now, c by the Spirit, I am
1Co 9: 16 boast, since I am c to preach.

COMPELS (COMPULSION)
Job 32: 18 and the spirit within me c me;
2Co 5: 14 For Christ's love c us, because we

COMPETENCE* (COMPETENT)
2Co 3: 5 but our c comes from God.

COMPETENT* (COMPETENCE)
Ro 15: 14 and c to instruct one another.
1Co 6: 2 are you not c to judge trivial cases?
2Co 3: 5 Not that we are c in ourselves
3: 6 He has made us c as ministers

COMPETES*
1Co 9: 25 Everyone who c in the games goes
2Ti 2: 5 anyone who c as an athlete does

COMPLACENCY* (COMPLACENT)
Pr 1: 32 the c of fools will destroy them;
Eze 30: 9 ships to frighten Cush out of her c.

COMPLACENT* (COMPLACENCY)
Isa 32: 9 You women who are so c,
32: 11 Tremble, you c women;
Am 6: 1 Woe to you who are c in Zion,
Zep 1: 12 lamps and punish those who are c,

COMPLETE (COMPLETENESS)
Dt 16: 15 your hands, and your joy will be c.
Jn 3: 29 That joy is mine, and it is now c.
15: 11 in you and that your joy may be c.
16: 24 will receive, and your joy will be c.
17: 23 they may be brought to c unity.
Ac 20: 24 c the task the Lord Jesus has given
Php 2: 2 then make my joy c by being
Col 4: 17 it that you c the ministry you have
Jas 1: 4 so that you may be mature and c,
2: 22 faith was made c by what he did.
1Jn 1: 4 We write this to make our joy c.
2: 5 for God is truly made c in them.
4: 12 in us and his love is made c in us.
4: 17 is how love is made c among us so
2Jn : 12 to face, so that our joy may be c.

COMPLETENESS* (COMPLETE)
1Co 13: 10 but when c comes, what is in part

COMPLIMENTS*
Pr 23: 8 eaten and will have wasted your c.

COMPREHEND* (COMPREHENDED COMPREHENDS)
Ecc 8: 17 No one can c what goes on under
8: 17 they know, they cannot really c it.

COMPREHENDED* (COMPREHEND)
Job 38: 18 Have you c the vast expanses

COMPREHENDS* (COMPREHEND)
Job 28: 13 No mortal c its worth; it cannot be

COMPULSION (COMPELLED COMPELS)
2Co 9: 7 not reluctantly or under c, for God

CONCEAL (CONCEALED CONCEALS)
Ps 40: 10 I do not c your love and your
Pr 25: 2 It is the glory of God to c a matter;

CONCEALED (CONCEAL)
Jer 16: 17 me, nor is their sin c from my eyes.
Mt 10: 26 there is nothing c that will not be
Mk 4: 22 whatever is c is meant to be
Lk 8: 17 nothing c that will not be known
12: 2 There is nothing c that will not be

CONCEALS* (CONCEAL)
Pr 10: 11 mouth of the wicked c violence.
10: 18 Whoever c hatred with lying lips
28: 13 Whoever c their sins does not

CONCEIT* (CONCEITED)
Isa 16: 6 of her c, her pride and her
Jer 48: 29 her c and the haughtiness of her
Php 2: 3 out of selfish ambition or vain c.

CONCEITED* (CONCEIT)
1Sa 17: 28 I know how c you are and how
Ro 11: 25 sisters, so that you may not be c:
12: 16 of low position. Do not be c.
2Co 12: 7 order to keep me from becoming c,
Gal 5: 26 Let us not become c,
1Ti 3: 6 he may become c and fall under
6: 4 they are c and understand nothing.
2Ti 3: 4 rash, c, lovers of pleasure rather

CONCEIVE (CONCEIVED CONCEIVES)
Isa 7: 14 The virgin will c and give birth
Mt 1: 23 "The virgin will c and give birth
Lk 1: 7 Elizabeth was not able to c,

CONCEIVED (CONCEIVE)
Ps 51: 5 from the time my mother c me.
Mt 1: 20 because what is c in her is
1Co 2: 9 and what no human mind has c"—
Jas 1: 15 after desire has c, it gives birth

CONCEIVES* (CONCEIVE)
Ps 7: 14 is pregnant with evil c trouble

CONCERN* (CONCERNED)
Ge 39: 6 he did not c himself with anything
39: 8 "my master does not c himself
1Sa 23: 21 LORD bless you for your c for me.
2Ki 13: 23 showed c for them because of his
Job 9: 21 blameless, I have no c for myself;
19: 4 my error remains my c alone.
Ps 131: 1 I do not c myself with great matters
Pr 29: 7 but the wicked have no such c.
Eze 36: 21 I had c for my holy name,
Jnh 4: 11 I not have c for the great city
Ac 18: 17 and Gallio showed no c whatever.
1Co 7: 32 I would like you to be free from c.
12: 25 that its parts should have equal c
2Co 7: 7 deep sorrow, your ardent c for me,
7: 11 what c, what readiness to see
8: 16 of Titus the same c I have for you.
11: 28 of my c for all the churches.
Php 2: 20 who will show genuine c for your
4: 10 at last you renewed your c for me.

CONCERNED (CONCERN)
Ex 2: 25 Israelites and was c about them.
Ps 142: 4 my right hand; no one is c for me.
Jnh 4: 10 "You have been c about this plant,
1Co 7: 32 An unmarried man is c
9: 9 Is it about oxen that God is c?
Php 4: 10 Indeed, you were c, but you had no

CONCESSION*
1Co 7: 6 I say this as a c, not as a command.

CONDEMN* (CONDEMNATION CONDEMNED CONDEMNING CONDEMNS)
Job 9: 20 innocent, my mouth would c me;
34: 17 you c the just and mighty One?
34: 29 he remains silent, who can c him?
40: 8 Would you c me to justify yourself?
Ps 94: 21 and c the innocent to death.
109: 7 guilty, and may his prayers c him.

Ps 109: 31 from those who would **c** them.
Isa 50: 9 Who will **c** me? They will all wear
Mt 12: 41 with this generation and **c** it;
12: 42 with this generation and **c** it;
20: 18 of the law. They will **c** him to death
Mk 10: 33 They will **c** him to death and will
Lk 6: 37 Do not **c**, and you will not be
11: 31 of this generation and **c** them,
11: 32 with this generation and **c** it,
Jn 3: 17 Son into the world to **c** the world,
7: 51 "Does our law **c** a man without
8: 11 *"Then neither do I **c** you,"*
12: 48 words I have spoken will **c** them
Ro 2: 27 yet obeys the law will **c** you who,
14: 22 is the one who does not **c** himself
2Co 7: 3 I do not say this to **c** you;
1Jn 3: 20 If our hearts **c** us, we know that
3: 21 if our hearts do not **c** us, we have
Jude : 9 did not himself dare to **c** him

CONDEMNATION* (CONDEMN)
Eze 33: 12 former wickedness will not bring **c**.
Ro 3: 8 good may result"? Their **c** is just!
5: 16 followed one sin and brought **c**,
5: 18 just as one trespass resulted in **c**
8: 1 there is now no **c** for those who are
2Co 3: 9 that brought **c** was glorious,
2Pe 2: 3 Their **c** has long been hanging over
Jude : 4 individuals whose **c** was written

CONDEMNED* (CONDEMN)
Dt 13: 17 none of the **c** things are to be
Job 32: 3 to refute Job, and yet had **c** him.
Ps 34: 21 the foes of the righteous will be **c**.
34: 22 who takes refuge in him will be **c**.
37: 33 let them be **c** when brought to trial.
79: 11 your strong arm preserve those **c**
102: 20 and release those **c** to death."
Mt 12: 7 you would not have **c** the innocent.
12: 37 and by your words you will be **c**."
23: 33 How will you escape being **c**
27: 3 saw that Jesus was **c**, he was seized
Mk 14: 64 They all **c** him as worthy of death.
16: 16 *does not believe will be **c**.*
Lk 6: 37 condemn, and you will not be **c**.
Jn 3: 18 Whoever believes in him is not **c**,
3: 18 not believe stands **c** already
5: 29 done what is evil will rise to be **c**.
8: 10 *Has no one **c** you?"*
16: 11 prince of this world now stands **c**.
Ac 25: 15 against him and asked that he be **c**.
Ro 3: 7 glory, why am I still **c** as a sinner?"
8: 3 And so he **c** sin in the flesh,
14: 23 whoever has doubts is **c** if they eat,
1Co 4: 9 like those **c** to die in the arena.
11: 32 that we will not be finally **c**
Gal 2: 11 him to his face, because he stood **c**.
Col 2: 14 which stood against us and **c** us;
2Th 2: 12 all will be **c** who have not believed
Titus 2: 8 of speech that cannot be **c**,
Heb 11: 7 By his faith he **c** the world
Jas 5: 6 You have **c** and murdered
5: 12 Otherwise you will be **c**.
2Pe 2: 6 if he **c** the cities of Sodom
Rev 19: 2 He has **c** the great prostitute who

CONDEMNING* (CONDEMN)
Dt 25: 1 the innocent and **c** the guilty.
1Ki 8: 32 **c** the guilty by bringing down
2Ch 6: 23 **c** the guilty and bringing down
Pr 17: 15 the guilty and **c** the innocent—
Ac 13: 27 in **c** him they fulfilled the words
Ro 2: 1 you are **c** yourself, because you

CONDEMNS* (CONDEMN)
Job 15: 6 Your own mouth **c** you, not mine;
Pr 12: 2 but he **c** those who devise wicked
14: 34 a nation, but sin **c** any people.
Ro 8: 34 then is the one who **c**? No one.

CONDITION
Pr 27: 23 Be sure you know the **c** of your

CONDUCT (CONDUCTED)
Ps 112: 5 who **c** their affairs with justice.
Pr 20: 11 is their **c** really pure and upright?
21: 8 but the **c** of the innocent is upright.
Ecc 6: 8 how to **c** themselves before others?
Jer 4: 18 "Your own **c** and actions have
17: 10 each person according to their **c**,
Eze 7: 3 I will judge you according to your **c**
Php 1: 27 **c** yourselves in a manner worthy of
1Ti 3: 15 how people ought to **c** themselves
4: 12 believers in speech, in **c**, in love,

CONDUCTED* (CONDUCT)
2Co 1: 12 we have **c** ourselves in the world,

CONFESS* (CONFESSED CONFESSES CONFESSING CONFESSION)
Lev 5: 5 they must **c** in what way they have
16: 21 and **c** over it all the wickedness
26: 40 if they will **c** their sins and the sins
Nu 5: 7 **c** the sin they have committed.
Ne 1: 6 I **c** the sins we Israelites,
Ps 32: 5 "I will **c** my transgressions
38: 18 I **c** my iniquity; I am troubled by
Jn 1: 20 He did not fail to **c**, but confessed
Jas 5: 16 Therefore **c** your sins to each other
1Jn 1: 9 If we **c** our sins, he is faithful

CONFESSED* (CONFESS)
1Sa 7: 6 day they fasted and there they **c**,
Ne 9: 2 in their places and **c** their sins
Da 9: 4 to the LORD my God and **c**:
Jn 1: 20 confess, but **c** freely, "I am not
Ac 19: 18 and openly **c** what they had done.

CONFESSES* (CONFESS)
Pr 28: 13 **c** and renounces them finds mercy.
2Ti 2: 19 "Everyone who **c** the name

CONFESSING* (CONFESS)
Ezr 10: 1 While Ezra was praying and **c**,
Da 9: 20 **c** my sin and the sin of my people
Mt 3: 6 **C** their sins, they were baptized
Mk 1: 5 **C** their sins, they were baptized

CONFESSION* (CONFESS)
Ne 9: 3 and spent another quarter in **c**
2Co 9: 13 accompanies your **c** of the gospel
1Ti 6: 12 when you made your good **c**
6: 13 Pontius Pilate made the good **c**,

CONFIDENCE* (CONFIDENT)
Jdg 9: 26 and its citizens put their **c** in him.
2Ki 18: 19 are you basing this **c** of yours?
2Ch 32: 8 And the people gained **c** from what
32: 10 On what are you basing your **c**,
Job 4: 6 Should not your piety be your **c**
Ps 71: 5 LORD, my **c** since my youth.
Pr 3: 32 but takes the upright into his **c**.
11: 13 A gossip betrays a **c**,
20: 19 A gossip betrays a **c**;
25: 9 to court, do not betray another's **c**,
31: 11 Her husband has full **c** in her
Isa 32: 17 will be quietness and **c** forever.
36: 4 are you basing this **c** of yours?
Jer 17: 7 in the LORD, whose **c** is in him.
49: 31 ease, which lives in **c**,"
Eze 29: 16 will no longer be a source of **c**
Mic 7: 5 put no **c** in a friend.
2Co 2: 3 I had **c** in all of you, that you
3: 4 Such **c** we have through Christ
7: 16 I am glad I can have complete **c**
8: 22 so because of his great **c** in you.
Eph 3: 12 approach God with freedom and **c**.
Php 3: 3 and who put no **c** in the flesh—
3: 4 I myself have reasons for such **c**.
3: 4 have reasons to put **c** in the flesh,
2Th 3: 4 We have **c** in the Lord that you are
Heb 3: 6 if indeed we hold firmly to our **c**
4: 16 God's throne of grace with **c**,
10: 19 since we have **c** to enter the Most
10: 35 So do not throw away your **c**;
11: 1 Now faith is **c** in what we hope for
13: 6 So we say with **c**, "The Lord is my
13: 17 Have **c** in your leaders and submit
1Jn 3: 21 condemn us, we have **c** before God
4: 17 us so that we will have **c** on the day
5: 14 This is the **c** we have

CONFIDENT* (CONFIDENCE)
Job 6: 20 because they had been **c**;
Ps 27: 3 against me, even then I will be **c**.
27: 13 I remain **c** of this: I will see
Lk 18: 9 To some who were **c** of their own
2Co 1: 15 Because I was **c** of this, I wanted
5: 6 Therefore we are always **c**
5: 8 We are **c**, I say, and would prefer
9: 4 be ashamed of having been so **c**.
2Co 10: 7 If anyone is **c** that they belong
Gal 5: 10 I am **c** in the Lord that you will
Php 1: 6 being **c** of this, that he who began
1: 14 sisters have become **c** in the Lord
2: 24 I am **c** in the Lord that I myself will
Phm : 21 **C** of your obedience, I write to
1Jn 2: 28 that when he appears we may be **c**

CONFIDES*
Ps 25: 14 The LORD **c** in those who fear

CONFIRM
2Pe 1: 10 make every effort to **c** your calling

CONFLICT
Pr 6: 14 in his heart—he always stirs up **c**.
6: 19 who stirs up **c** in the community.
10: 12 Hatred stirs up **c**, but love covers
15: 18 A hot-tempered person stirs up **c**,
16: 28 A perverse person stirs up **c**,
28: 25 The greedy stir up **c**, but those who
29: 22 An angry person stirs up **c**, and a
Heb 10: 32 in a great **c** full of suffering.

CONFORM* (CONFORMED CONFORMITY CONFORMS)
Ro 12: 2 not **c** to the pattern of this world,
1Pe 1: 14 do not **c** to the evil desires you had

CONFORMED* (CONFORM)
Eze 5: 7 You have not even **c**
11: 12 but have **c** to the standards
Ac 26: 5 that I **c** to the strictest sect of our
Ro 8: 29 predestined to be **c** to the image

CONFORMITY* (CONFORM)
Eph 1: 11 everything in **c** with the purpose

CONFORMS* (CONFORM)
1Ti 1: 11 that **c** to the gospel concerning

CONQUEROR* (CONQUERORS)
Mic 1: 15 I will bring a **c** against you who live
Rev 6: 2 rode out as a **c** bent on conquest.

CONQUERORS* (CONQUEROR)
Ro 8: 37 are more than **c** through him who

CONSCIENCE* (CONSCIENCE-STRICKEN CONSCIENCES CONSCIENTIOUS)
Ge 20: 5 I have done this with a clear **c**
20: 6 I know you did this with a clear **c**,
1Sa 25: 31 have on his **c** the staggering burden
Job 27: 6 my **c** will not reproach me as long
Ac 23: 1 to God in all good **c** to this day."
24: 16 to keep my **c** clear before God
Ro 9: 1 my **c** confirms it through the Holy
13: 5 but also as a matter of **c**.
1Co 4: 4 My **c** is clear, but that does not
8: 7 a god, and since their **c** is weak,
8: 10 if someone with a weak **c** sees you,
8: 12 this way and wound their weak **c**,
10: 25 without raising questions of **c**,
10: 27 you without raising questions of **c**.
10: 28 who told you and for the sake of **c**.
10: 29 referring to the other person's **c**,
10: 29 being judged by another's **c**?
2Co 1: 12 Our **c** testifies that we have
4: 2 to everyone's **c** in the sight of God.
5: 11 and I hope it is also plain to your **c**.
1Ti 1: 5 and a good **c** and a sincere faith.
1: 19 holding on to faith and a good **c**,
3: 9 truths of the faith with a clear **c**.
2Ti 1: 3 with a clear **c**, as night and day I
Heb 9: 9 able to clear the **c** of the worshiper.
10: 22 to cleanse us from a guilty **c**
13: 18 We are sure that we have a clear **c**
1Pe 3: 16 keeping a clear **c**, so that those who
3: 21 the pledge of a clear **c** toward God.

CONSCIENCES* (CONSCIENCE)
Ro 2: 15 hearts, their **c** also bearing witness,
1Ti 4: 2 whose **c** have been seared as
Titus 1: 15 their minds and **c** are corrupted.
Heb 9: 14 cleanse our **c** from acts that lead

CONSCIENCE-STRICKEN* (CONSCIENCE)
1Sa 24: 5 David was **c** for having cut off
2Sa 24: 10 David was **c** after he had counted

CONSCIENTIOUS* (CONSCIENCE)
2Ch 29: 34 for the Levites had been more **c**

CONSCIOUS*
Ro 3: 20 through the law we become **c** of
1Pe 2: 19 unjust suffering because they are **c**

CONSECRATE (CONSECRATED)
Ex 13: 2 "**C** to me every firstborn male.
40: 9 **c** it and all its furnishings, and it
Lev 20: 7 "'**C** yourselves and be holy,
25: 10 **C** the fiftieth year and proclaim
1Ch 15: 12 fellow Levites are to **c** yourselves

CONSECRATED (CONSECRATE)
Ex 29: 43 and the place will be **c** by my glory.
Lev 8: 30 So he **c** Aaron and his garments
2Ch 7: 16 **c** this temple so that my Name may
Lk 2: 23 male is to be **c** to the Lord"),
1Ti 4: 5 because it is **c** by the word of God

CONSENT
1Co 7: 5 other except perhaps by mutual **c**

CONSIDER (CONSIDERATE CONSIDERED CONSIDERS)
1Sa 12: 24 **c** what great things he has done
16: 7 "Do not **c** his appearance or his
2Ch 19: 6 them, "**C** carefully what you do,
Job 37: 14 stop and **c** God's wonders.
Ps 8: 3 When I **c** your heavens, the work
77: 12 I will **c** all your works and meditate
143: 5 and **c** what your hands have done.
Pr 6: 6 **c** its ways and be wise!
20: 25 and only later to **c** one's vows.
Ecc 7: 13 **C** what God has done:
Lk 12: 24 **C** the ravens: They do not sow
12: 27 "**C** how the wild flowers grow.
Php 3: 8 I **c** everything a loss because
3: 8 I **c** them garbage, that I may gain
Heb 10: 24 And let us **c** how we may spur one
Jas 1: 2 **C** it pure joy, my brothers
1: 26 Those who **c** themselves religious

CONSIDERATE* (CONSIDER)
Titus 3: 2 to be peaceable and **c**, and always
Jas 3: 17 then peace-loving, **c**, submissive,
1Pe 2: 18 only to those who are good and **c**,
3: 7 the same way be **c** as you live

CONSIDERED (CONSIDER)
Job 1: 8 "Have you **c** my servant Job?
2: 3 "Have you **c** my servant Job?
Ps 44: 22 we are **c** as sheep to be slaughtered.
Isa 53: 4 yet we **c** him punished by God,
Ro 8: 36 all day long; we are **c** as sheep to be

CONSIDERS (CONSIDER)
Pr 31: 16 She **c** a field and buys it; out of her
Ro 14: 5 One person **c** one day more sacred
14: 5 another **c** every day alike.

CONSIST (CONSISTS)
Lk 12: 15 life does not **c** in an abundance

CONSISTS (CONSIST)
Eph 5: 9 fruit of the light **c** in all goodness,

CONSOLATION
Ps 94: 19 within me, your **c** brought me joy.

CONSPIRE
Ps 2: 1 Why do the nations **c**

CONSTANT
Dt 28: 66 You will live in **c** suspense,
Pr 19: 13 wife is like the **c** dripping of a leaky
Ac 27: 33 "you have been in **c** suspense
Heb 5: 14 by **c** use have trained themselves

CONSTRUCTIVE*
1Co 10: 23 but not everything is **c**.

CONSULT
Gal 1: 16 was not to **c** any human being.

CONSUME (CONSUMES CONSUMING)
Jn 2: 17 "Zeal for your house will **c** me."

CONSUMES (CONSUME)
Ps 69: 9 for zeal for your house **c** me,

CONSUMING (CONSUME)
Dt 4: 24 For the LORD your God is a **c** fire,
Heb 12: 29 for our "God is a **c** fire."

CONTAIN* (CONTAINED CONTAINS)
1Ki 8: 27 the highest heaven, cannot **c** you.
2Ch 2: 6 the highest heavens, cannot **c** him?
6: 18 the highest heavens, cannot **c** you.
Ecc 8: 8 has power over the wind to **c** it,
2Pe 3: 16 His letters **c** some things that are

CONTAINED (CONTAIN)
Heb 9: 4 This ark **c** the gold jar of manna,

CONTAINS (CONTAIN)
Pr 15: 6 of the righteous **c** great treasure,

CONTAMINATES*
2Co 7: 1 from everything that **c** body

CONTEMPLATE*
2Co 3: 18 unveiled faces **c** the Lord's glory,

CONTEMPT
Pr 14: 31 oppresses the poor shows **c** for
17: 5 Whoever mocks the poor shows **c**
18: 3 so does **c**, and with shame comes
Da 12: 2 others to shame and everlasting **c**.
Mal 1: 6 "It is you priests who show **c**
Ro 2: 4 do you show **c** for the riches of his
14: 3 treat with **c** the one who does not,
Gal 4: 14 did not treat me with **c** or scorn.
1Th 5: 20 Do not treat prophecies with **c**

CONTEND (CONTENDED CONTENDING CONTENTIOUS)
Ge 6: 3 "My Spirit will not **c** with humans
Ps 35: 1 **C**, LORD, with those who **c**
Isa 49: 25 I will **c** with those who **c** with you,
Jude : 3 urge you to **c** for the faith that was

CONTENDED (CONTEND)
Php 4: 3 these women since they have **c**

CONTENDING* (CONTEND)
Col 2: 1 to know how hard I am **c** for you

CONTENT* (CONTENTMENT)
Ge 25: 27 while Jacob was **c** to stay at home
Jos 7: 7 If only we had been **c** to stay
Ps 131: 2 like a weaned child I am **c**.
Pr 13: 25 The righteous eat to their hearts' **c**,
19: 23 then one rests **c**,
Ecc 4: 8 toil, yet his eyes were not **c** with his
Lk 3: 14 be **c** with your pay."
Php 4: 11 to be **c** whatever the circumstances.
4: 12 learned the secret of being **c** in any
1Ti 6: 8 clothing, we will be **c** with that.
Heb 13: 5 and be **c** with what you have,

CONTENTIOUS* (CONTEND)
1Co 11: 16 If anyone wants to be **c** about this,

CONTENTMENT* (CONTENT)
Job 36: 11 in prosperity and their years in **c**.
SS 8: 10 in his eyes like one bringing **c**.
1Ti 6: 6 But godliness with **c** is great gain.

CONTINUAL (CONTINUE)
Pr 15: 15 but the cheerful heart has a **c** feast.

CONTINUE (CONTINUAL CONTINUES CONTINUING)
1Ki 8: 23 servants who **c** wholeheartedly
2Ch 6: 14 servants who **c** wholeheartedly
Ps 36: 10 **C** your love to those who know
Ac 13: 43 them to **c** in the grace of God.
Ro 11: 22 that you **c** in his kindness.
Gal 3: 10 Cursed is everyone who does not **c**
Php 2: 12 **c** to work out your salvation
Col 1: 23 if you **c** in your faith,
2: 6 as Lord, **c** to live your lives in him,
1Ti 2: 15 if they **c** in faith, love and holiness
2Ti 3: 14 **c** in what you have learned and
1Jn 2: 28 dear children, **c** in him,
3: 9 who is born of God will **c** to sin,
5: 18 born of God does not **c** to sin;
2Jn : 9 not **c** in the teaching of Christ
Rev 22: 11 Let the one who does wrong **c** to
22: 11 let the one who does right **c** to do
22: 11 let the holy person **c** to be holy."

CONTINUES (CONTINUE)
Ps 100: 5 his faithfulness **c** through all
119: 90 Your faithfulness **c** through all
2Co 10: 15 is that, as your faith **c** to grow,
1Jn 3: 6 No one who **c** to sin has either seen

CONTINUING (CONTINUE)
Ro 13: 8 except the **c** debt to love one

CONTRIBUTION (CONTRIBUTIONS)
Ro 15: 26 to make a **c** for the poor among

CONTRIBUTIONS (CONTRIBUTION)
2Ch 24: 10 the people brought their **c** gladly,
31: 12 they faithfully brought in the **c**,

CONTRITE*
Ps 51: 17 a broken and **c** heart you, God,
Isa 57: 15 with the one who is **c** and lowly
Isa 57: 15 and to revive the heart of the **c**.
66: 2 who are humble and **c** in spirit,

CONTROL (CONTROLLED CONTROLS SELF-CONTROL SELF-CONTROLLED)
1Co 7: 9 But if they cannot **c** themselves,
7: 37 but has **c** over his own will,
1Th 4: 4 should learn to **c** your own body

CONTROLLED (CONTROL)
Ps 32: 9 understanding but must be **c** by bit

CONTROLS* (CONTROL)
Job 37: 15 you know how God **c** the clouds

CONTROVERSIES*
Ac 26: 3 with all the Jewish customs and **c**.
1Ti 6: 4 have an unhealthy interest in **c**
Titus 3: 9 But avoid foolish **c** and genealogies

CONVERSATION
Col 4: 6 Let your **c** be always full of grace,

CONVERT
1Ti 3: 6 He must not be a recent **c**, or he

CONVICT (CONVICTED CONVICTION)
Pr 24: 25 go well with those who **c** the guilty,
Jude : 15 to **c** all of them of all the ungodly

CONVICTED (CONVICT)
1Co 14: 24 they are **c** of sin and are brought

CONVICTION* (CONVICT)
1Th 1: 5 with the Holy Spirit and deep **c**.
Heb 3: 14 we hold our original **c** firmly

CONVINCED* (CONVINCING)
Ge 45: 28 And Israel said, "I'm **c**!
Lk 16: 31 they will not be **c** even if someone
Ac 19: 26 hear how this fellow Paul has **c**
26: 9 "I too was **c** that I ought to do all
26: 26 am **c** that none of this has escaped
28: 24 Some were **c** by what he said,
Ro 2: 19 if you are **c** that you are a guide
8: 38 I am **c** that neither death nor life,
14: 5 them should be fully **c** in their own
14: 14 I am **c**, being fully persuaded
15: 14 I myself am **c**, my brothers
2Co 5: 14 because we are **c** that one died
Php 1: 25 **C** of this, I know that I will remain,
2Ti 1: 12 am **c** that he is able to guard what I
3: 14 have learned and have become **c** of,
Heb 6: 9 we are **c** of better things in your

CONVINCING* (CONVINCED)
Ac 1: 3 and gave many **c** proofs that he was

COPIES (COPY)
Heb 9: 23 for the **c** of the heavenly things

COPY (COPIES)
Dt 17: 18 himself on a scroll a **c** of this law,
Heb 8: 5 They serve at a sanctuary that is a **c**
9: 24 that was only a **c** of the true one;

CORBAN*
Mk 7: 11 their father or mother is **C** (that is,

CORD (CORDS)
Jos 2: 18 you have tied this scarlet **c**
Ecc 4: 12 A **c** of three strands is not quickly

CORDS (CORD)
Pr 5: 22 the **c** of their sins hold them fast.
Isa 54: 2 lengthen your **c**, strengthen your
Hos 11: 4 I led them with **c** of human

CORINTH
Ac 18: 1 Paul left Athens and went to **C**.
1Co 1: 2 To the church of God in **C**,
2Co 1: 1 To the church of God in **C**,

CORNELIUS*
Roman to whom Peter preached; first Gentile Christian (Ac 10).

CORNER (CORNERS CORNERSTONE)
Ru 3: 9 "Spread the **c** of your garment over
Pr 21: 9 Better to live on a **c** of the roof
25: 24 Better to live on a **c** of the roof
Ac 26: 26 because it was not done in a **c**.

CORNERS (CORNER)
Mt 6: 5 on the street **c** to be seen by others.
22: 9 So go to the street **c** and invite

CORNERSTONE* (CORNER STONE)
Job 38: 6 its footings set, or who laid its **c**—
Ps 118: 22 builders rejected has become the **c**;

Isa 28: 16 a precious **c** for a sure foundation;
Jer 51: 26 rock will be taken from you for a **c**,
Zec 10: 4 From Judah will come the **c**,
Mt 21: 42 builders rejected has become the **c**;
Mk 12: 10 builders rejected has become the **c**;
Lk 20: 17 rejected has become the **c**'?
Ac 4: 11 rejected, which has become the **c**.'
Eph 2: 20 Christ Jesus himself as the chief **c**.
1Pe 2: 6 a chosen and precious **c**, and the
2: 7 rejected has become the **c**,"

CORRECT* (CORRECTED CORRECTING CORRECTION CORRECTS)
Job 6: 26 Do you mean to **c** what I say,
40: 2 contends with the Almighty **c** him?
2Ti 4: 2 **c**, rebuke and encourage—

CORRECTED* (CORRECT)
Pr 29: 19 Servants cannot be **c** by mere

CORRECTING* (CORRECT)
2Ti 3: 16 **c** and training in righteousness,

CORRECTION* (CORRECT)
Lev 26: 23 things you do not accept my **c**
Job 36: 10 He makes them listen to **c**
Pr 5: 12 How my heart spurned **c**!
6: 23 and **c** and instruction are the way
10: 17 but whoever ignores **c** leads others
12: 1 but whoever hates **c** is stupid.
13: 18 but whoever heeds **c** is honored.
15: 5 whoever heeds **c** shows prudence.
15: 10 the one who hates **c** will die.
15: 12 Mockers resent **c**, so they avoid
15: 31 Whoever heeds life-giving **c** will be
15: 32 who heeds **c** gains understanding.
Jer 2: 30 they did not respond to **c**.
5: 3 crushed them, but they refused **c**.
7: 28 LORD its God or responded to **c**.
Zep 3: 2 She obeys no one, she accepts no **c**.
3: 7 you will fear me and accept **c**!'

CORRECTS* (CORRECT)
Job 5: 17 "Blessed is the one whom God **c**;
Pr 9: 7 Whoever **c** a mocker invites insults

CORRUPT (CORRUPTED CORRUPTION CORRUPTS)
Ge 6: 11 Now the earth was **c** in God's sight
Ps 14: 1 They are **c**, their deeds are vile;
14: 3 turned away, all have become **c**;
Pr 4: 24 keep **c** talk far from your lips.
6: 12 who goes about with a **c** mouth,
19: 28 A **c** witness mocks at justice,

CORRUPTED (CORRUPT)
2Co 7: 2 wronged no one, we have **c** no one,
Titus 1: 15 their minds and consciences are **c**.

CORRUPTION (CORRUPT)
2Pe 1: 4 having escaped the **c** in the world
2: 20 have escaped the **c** of the world

CORRUPTS* (CORRUPT)
Ecc 7: 7 into a fool, and a bribe **c** the heart.
1Co 15: 33 "Bad company **c** good character."
Jas 3: 6 It **c** the whole body, sets the whole

COST (COSTS)
Nu 16: 38 who sinned at the **c** of their lives.
Pr 4: 7 Though it **c** all you have,
7: 23 little knowing it will **c** him his life.
Isa 55: 1 milk without money and without **c**.
Lk 14: 28 estimate the **c** to see if you have
Rev 21: 6 thirsty I will give water without **c**

COSTS (COST)
Pr 6: 31 though it **c** him all the wealth of

COUNCIL
Ps 89: 7 the **c** of the holy ones God is
107: 32 praise him in the **c** of the elders.

COUNSEL (COUNSELOR COUNSELS)
1Ki 22: 5 "First seek the **c** of the LORD."
2Ch 18: 4 "First seek the **c** of the LORD."
Ps 73: 24 You guide me with your **c**,
Pr 8: 14 **C** and sound judgment are mine;
15: 22 Plans fail for lack of **c**,
1Ti 5: 14 So I **c** younger widows to marry,
Rev 3: 18 I **c** you to buy from me gold

COUNSELOR (COUNSEL)
Isa 9: 6 And he will be called Wonderful **C**,
Ro 11: 34 Or who has been his **c**?"

COUNSELS* (COUNSEL)
Ps 16: 7 I will praise the LORD, who **c** me;

COUNT (COUNTED COUNTING COUNTS)
Eze 33: 12 former righteousness will **c**
Ro 4: 8 Lord will never **c** against them."
6: 11 **c** yourselves dead to sin but alive

COUNTED (COUNT)
Ac 5: 41 because they had been **c** worthy
2Th 1: 5 as a result you will be **c** worthy

COUNTERFEIT*
1Jn 2: 27 as that anointing is real, not **c**—

COUNTING (COUNT)
2Co 5: 19 not **c** people's sins against them.

COUNTRY
Pr 28: 2 When a **c** is rebellious, it has many
29: 4 By justice a king gives a **c** stability,
Isa 66: 8 Can a **c** be born in a day or
Lk 15: 13 had, set off for a distant **c** and there
Jn 4: 44 prophet has no honor in his own **c**.)
2Co 11: 26 in danger in the **c**, in danger at sea;
Heb 11: 14 are looking for a **c** of their own.

COUNTS (COUNT)
Jn 6: 63 the flesh **c** for nothing.
1Co 7: 19 God's commands is what **c**.
Gal 5: 6 that **c** is faith expressing itself
6: 15 what **c** is the new creation.

COURAGE* (COURAGEOUS)
Jos 2: 11 everyone's **c** failed because of you,
5: 1 they no longer had the **c** to face
2Sa 4: 1 he lost **c**, and all Israel became
7: 27 So your servant has found **c** to pray
1Ch 17: 25 So your servant has found **c** to pray
2Ch 15: 8 of Oded the prophet, he took **c**.
19: 11 Act with **c**, and may the LORD be
Ezr 7: 28 I took **c** and gathered leaders
10: 4 support you, so take **c** and do it."
Ps 107: 26 in their peril their **c** melted away.
Eze 22: 14 Will your **c** endure or your hands
Da 11: 25 and **c** against the king of the South.
Mt 14: 27 immediately said to them: "Take **c**!
Mk 6: 50 he spoke to them and said, "Take **c**!
Ac 4: 13 When they saw the **c** of Peter
23: 11 stood near Paul and said, "Take **c**!
27: 22 now I urge you to keep up your **c**,
27: 25 So keep up your **c**, men, for I have
Php 1: 20 will have sufficient **c** so that now as

COURAGEOUS* (COURAGE)
Dt 31: 6 Be strong and **c**. Do not be afraid
31: 7 "Be strong and **c**, for you must go
31: 23 "Be strong and **c**, for you will bring
Jos 1: 6 Be strong and **c**, because you will
1: 7 "Be strong and very **c**. Be careful
1: 9 Be strong and **c**. Do not be afraid;
1: 18 to death. Only be strong and **c**!"
10: 25 Be strong and **c**. This is what
1Ch 22: 13 Be strong and **c**. Do not be afraid
28: 20 "Be strong and **c**, and do the work.
2Ch 26: 17 eighty other **c** priests of the LORD
32: 7 "Be strong and **c**. Do not be afraid
1Co 16: 13 firm in the faith; be **c**; be strong.

COURSE
Ps 19: 5 a champion rejoicing to run his **c**.
Pr 2: 8 for he guards the **c** of the just
15: 21 understanding keeps a straight **c**.
16: 9 In their hearts humans plan their **c**,
17: 23 in secret to pervert the **c** of justice.
Jas 3: 6 sets the whole **c** of one's life on fire,

COURT (COURTS)
Pr 22: 22 and do not crush the needy in **c**,
25: 8 do not bring hastily to **c**, for what
Mt 5: 25 adversary who is taking you to **c**.
1Co 4: 3 judged by you or by any human **c**;
6: 6 one brother takes another to **c**—

COURTS (COURT)
Ps 84: 10 your **c** than a thousand elsewhere;
100: 4 thanksgiving and his **c** with praise;
Am 5: 15 maintain justice in the **c**.
Zec 8: 16 and sound judgment in your **c**;

COURTYARD
Ex 27: 9 "Make a **c** for the tabernacle.

COUSIN
Est 2: 7 Mordecai had a **c** named Hadassah
Col 4: 10 as does Mark, the **c** of Barnabas.

COVENANT (COVENANTS)
Ge 9: 9 "I now establish my **c** with you
17: 2 I will make my **c** between me
Ex 19: 5 if you obey me fully and keep my **c**,
24: 7 he took the Book of the **C** and read
Dt 4: 13 He declared to you his **c**, the Ten
29: 1 of the **c** the LORD commanded
Jdg 2: 1 'I will never break my **c** with you,
1Sa 23: 18 them made a **c** before the LORD.
1Ki 8: 21 which is the **c** of the LORD that he
8: 23 you who keep your **c** of love
2Ki 23: 2 all the words of the Book of the **C**,
1Ch 16: 15 He remembers his **c** forever,
2Ch 6: 14 you who keep your **c** of love
34: 30 all the words of the Book of the **C**,
Ne 1: 5 who keeps his **c** of love with those
Job 31: 1 "I made a **c** with my eyes not
Ps 105: 8 He remembers his **c** forever,
Pr 2: 17 ignored the **c** she made before God
Isa 42: 6 make you to be a **c** for the people
61: 8 make an everlasting **c** with them.
Jer 11: 2 "Listen to the terms of this **c**
31: 31 I will make a new **c** with the people
31: 32 It will not be like the **c** I made
31: 32 because they broke my **c**, though I
31: 33 "This is the **c** I will make
Eze 37: 26 will make a **c** of peace with them;
37: 26 it will be an everlasting **c**.
Da 9: 27 He will confirm a **c** with many
Hos 6: 7 at Adam, they have broken the **c**;
Mal 2: 14 the wife of your marriage **c**.
3: 1 the messenger of the **c**, whom you
Mt 26: 28 This is my blood of the **c**, which is
Mk 14: 24 "This is my blood of the **c**, which is
Lk 22: 20 "This cup is the new **c** in my blood,
1Co 11: 25 "This cup is the new **c** in my blood;
2Co 3: 6 as ministers of a new **c**—
Gal 4: 24 One **c** is from Mount Sinai
Heb 8: 6 since the new **c** is established
8: 8 I will make a new **c** with the people
9: 15 Christ is the mediator of a new **c**,
12: 24 to Jesus the mediator of a new **c**,

COVENANTS* (COVENANT)
Ro 9: 4 the **c**, the receiving of the law,
Gal 4: 24 The women represent two **c**.
Eph 2: 12 foreigners to the **c** of the promise,

COVER (COVER-UP COVERED COVERING COVERINGS COVERS)
Ex 25: 17 "Make an atonement **c** of pure
25: 21 Place the **c** on top of the ark and
33: 22 and **c** you with my hand until I
Lev 16: 2 of the atonement **c** on the ark,
16: 2 in the cloud over the atonement **c**.
Ps 32: 5 you and did not **c** up my iniquity.
91: 4 He will **c** you with his feathers,
Hos 10: 8 will say to the mountains, "**C** us!"
Lk 23: 30 and to the hills, "**C** us!"'
1Co 11: 6 if a woman does not **c** her head,
11: 6 shaved, then she should **c** her head.
11: 7 A man ought not to **c** his head,
Jas 5: 20 and **c** over a multitude of sins.

COVERED (COVER)
Ps 32: 1 are forgiven, whose sins are **c**.
85: 2 of your people and **c** all their sins.
Isa 6: 2 With two wings they **c** their faces,
51: 16 **c** you with the shadow of my hand
Ro 4: 7 are forgiven, whose sins are **c**.
1Co 11: 4 with his head **c** dishonors his head.

COVERING (COVER)
1Co 11: 15 For long hair is given to her as a **c**.

COVERINGS (COVER)
Ge 3: 7 and made **c** for themselves.
Pr 31: 22 She makes **c** for her bed;

COVERS (COVER)
Pr 10: 12 conflict, but love **c** over all wrongs.
17: 9 would foster love **c** over an offense,
2Co 3: 15 Moses is read, a veil **c** their hearts.
1Pe 4: 8 because love **c** over a multitude

COVER-UP* (COVER)
1Pe 2: 16 do not use your freedom as a **c**

COVET* (COVETED COVETING)
Ex 20: 17 "You shall not **c** your neighbor's
20: 17 You shall not **c** your neighbor's

Ex 34: 24 no one will **c** your land when you
Dt 5: 21 "You shall not **c** your neighbor's
7: 25 Do not **c** the silver and gold
Mic 2: 2 They **c** fields and seize them,
Ro 7: 7 had not said, "You shall not **c**."
13: 9 "You shall not **c**," and whatever
Jas 4: 2 You **c** but you cannot get what you

COVETED* (COVET)
Jos 7: 21 shekels, I **c** them and took them.
Ac 20: 33 I have not **c** anyone's silver or gold

COVETING*
Ro 7: 7 not have known what **c** really was
7: 8 produced in me every kind of **c**.

COWARDLY*
Rev 21: 8 But the **c**, the unbelieving, the vile,

COWS
Ge 41: 2 of the river there came up seven **c**,
1Sa 6: 7 with two **c** that have calved

CRAFTINESS* (CRAFTY)
Job 5: 13 He catches the wise in their **c**,
1Co 3: 19 "He catches the wise in their **c**";
Eph 4: 14 and **c** of people in their deceitful

CRAFTY* (CRAFTINESS)
Ge 3: 1 the serpent was more **c** than any
1Sa 23: 22 They tell me he is very **c**.
Job 5: 12 He thwarts the plans of the **c**,
15: 5 you adopt the tongue of the **c**.
Pr 7: 10 like a prostitute and with **c** intent.
2Co 12: 16 Yet, **c** fellow that I am, I caught you

CRAVE* (CRAVED CRAVES CRAVING CRAVINGS)
Nu 11: 4 with them began to **c** other food,
Dt 12: 20 you, and you **c** meat and say,
Pr 21: 10 The wicked **c** evil;
23: 3 not **c** his delicacies, for that food
23: 6 host, do not **c** his delicacies;
31: 4 drink wine, not for rulers to **c** beer,
Mic 7: 1 eat, none of the early figs that I **c**.
1Pe 2: 2 babies, **c** pure spiritual milk,

CRAVED* (CRAVE)
Nu 11: 34 the people who had **c** other food.
Ps 78: 18 test by demanding the food they **c**.
78: 29 he had given them what they **c**.
78: 30 they turned from what they **c**,

CRAVES* (CRAVES)
Pr 21: 26 All day long he **c** for more,

CRAVING* (CRAVE)
Job 20: 20 he will have no respite from his **c**;
Ps 106: 14 In the desert they gave in to their **c**;
Pr 10: 3 but he thwarts the **c** of the wicked.
21: 25 **c** of a sluggard will be the death
Jer 2: 24 desert, sniffing the wind in her **c**—

CRAVINGS* (CRAVE)
Ps 10: 3 He boasts about the **c** of his heart;
Eph 2: 3 gratifying the **c** of our flesh

CRAWL
Ge 3: 14 You will **c** on your belly and you

CREATE* (CREATED CREATES CREATING CREATION CREATOR)
Ps 51: 10 **C** in me a pure heart, O God,
Isa 4: 5 the LORD will **c** over all of Mount
45: 7 I form the light and **c** darkness,
45: 7 I bring prosperity and **c** disaster;
45: 18 he did not **c** it to be empty,
65: 17 I will **c** new heavens and a new
65: 18 and rejoice forever in what I will **c**,
65: 18 I will **c** Jerusalem to be a delight
Jer 31: 22 The LORD will **c** a new thing
Mal 2: 10 Did not one God **c** us? Why do we
Eph 2: 15 His purpose was to **c** in himself

CREATED* (CREATE)
Ge 1: 1 the beginning God **c** the heavens
1: 21 So God **c** the great creatures
1: 27 So God **c** mankind in his own
1: 27 in the image of God he **c** them; male and female he **c** them.
2: 4 and the earth when they were **c**,
5: 1 When God **c** mankind, he made
5: 2 He **c** them male and female
5: 2 "Mankind" when they were **c**.
6: 7 earth the human race I have **c**—
Dt 4: 32 the day God **c** human beings
Ps 89: 12 You **c** the north and the south;
89: 47 futility you have **c** all humanity!
102: 18 a people not yet **c** may praise
104: 30 they are **c**, and you renew the face
139: 13 For you **c** my inmost being;
148: 5 for at his command they were **c**,
Ecc 7: 29 God **c** mankind upright, but they
Isa 40: 26 to the heavens: Who **c** all these?
41: 20 that the Holy One of Israel has **c** it.
43: 1 he who **c** you, Jacob, he who
43: 7 my name, whom I **c** for my glory,
45: 8 I, the LORD, have **c** it.
45: 12 the earth and **c** mankind on it.
45: 18 he who **c** the heavens, he is God;
48: 7 They are **c** now, and not long ago;
54: 16 it is I who **c** the blacksmith who
54: 16 it is I who have **c** the destroyer
57: 16 the very people I have **c**.
Eze 21: 30 In the place where you were **c**,
28: 13 day you were **c** they were prepared.
28: 15 day you were **c** till wickedness was
Mk 13: 19 when God **c** the world, until now—
Ro 1: 25 and served **c** things rather than
1Co 11: 9 neither was man **c** for woman,
Eph 2: 10 **c** in Christ Jesus to do good works,
3: 9 hidden in God, who **c** all things.
4: 24 the new self, **c** to be like God in
Col 1: 16 For in him all things were **c**:
1: 16 all things have been **c** through him
1Ti 4: 3 which God **c** to be received
4: 4 For everything God **c** is good,
Heb 12: 27 that is, **c** things—so that what
Jas 1: 18 be a kind of firstfruits of all he **c**.
Rev 4: 11 for you **c** all things, and by your will they were **c**
10: 6 who **c** the heavens and all that is

CREATES* (CREATE)
Am 4: 13 the mountains, who **c** the wind,

CREATING* (CREATE)
Ge 2: 3 all the work of **c** that he had done.
Isa 57: 19 **c** praise on their lips.

CREATION* (CREATE)
Ps 96: 13 Let all **c** rejoice before the LORD,
Hab 2: 18 who makes it trusts in his own **c**;
Mt 13: 35 will utter things hidden since the **c**
25: 34 for you since the **c** of the world.
Mk 10: 6 of **c** God 'made them male
16: 15 *preach the gospel to all* **c**.
Jn 17: 24 because you loved me before the **c**
Ro 1: 20 For since the **c** of the world God's
8: 19 For the **c** waits in eager expectation
8: 20 For the **c** was subjected
8: 21 that the **c** itself will be liberated
8: 22 the whole **c** has been groaning as
8: 39 nor anything else in all **c**, will be
2Co 5: 17 is in Christ, the new **c** has come:
Gal 6: 15 what counts is the new **c**.
Eph 1: 4 us in him before the **c** of the world
Col 1: 15 God, the firstborn over all **c**.
Heb 4: 3 have been finished since the **c**
4: 13 Nothing in all **c** is hidden
9: 11 that is to say, is not a part of this **c**.
9: 26 suffer many times since the **c**
1Pe 1: 20 He was chosen before the **c**
2Pe 3: 4 as it has since the beginning of **c**."
Rev 3: 14 true witness, the ruler of God's **c**.
13: 8 was slain from the **c** of the world.
17: 8 book of life from the **c** of the world

CREATOR* (CREATE)
Ge 14: 19 Most High, **C** of heaven and earth.
14: 22 Most High, **C** of heaven and earth,
Dt 32: 6 your **C**, who made you and formed
Ecc 12: 1 Remember your **C** in the days
Isa 27: 11 and their **C** shows them no favor.
40: 28 God, the **C** of the ends of the earth.
42: 5 the **C** of the heavens, who stretches
43: 15 Holy One, Israel's **C**, your King."
Mt 19: 4 at the beginning the **C** 'made them
Ro 1: 25 created things rather than the **C**—
Col 3: 10 in knowledge in the image of its **C**.
1Pe 4: 19 themselves to their faithful **C**

CREATURE (CREATURES)
Lev 17: 11 For the life of a **c** is in the blood,
17: 14 the life of every **c** is its blood.
17: 14 must not eat the blood of any **c**,
Ps 136: 25 He gives food to every **c**.
Eze 1: 15 on the ground beside each **c** with
Rev 4: 7 The first living **c** was like a lion,

CREATURES (CREATURE)
Ge 6: 19 into the ark two of all living **c**,
8: 21 again will I destroy all living **c**, as I
Ps 104: 24 the earth is full of your **c**.
Eze 1: 5 was what looked like four living **c**.

CREDIT (CREDITED CREDITOR CREDITS)
Lk 6: 33 good to you, what **c** is that to you?
Ro 4: 24 whom God will **c** righteousness—
1Pe 2: 20 it to your **c** if you receive a beating

CREDITED (CREDIT)
Ge 15: 6 and he **c** it to him as righteousness.
Ps 106: 31 This was **c** to him as righteousness
Eze 18: 20 of the righteous will be **c** to them,
Ro 4: 3 it was **c** to him as righteousness."
4: 4 wages are not **c** as a gift but as
4: 5 their faith is **c** as righteousness.
4: 9 Abraham's faith was **c** to him as
4: 23 The words "it was **c** to him" were
Gal 3: 6 it was **c** to him as righteousness."
Php 4: 17 is that more be **c** to your account.
Jas 2: 23 it was **c** to him as righteousness,"

CREDITOR (CREDIT)
Dt 15: 2 Every **c** shall cancel any loan they

CREDITS* (CREDIT)
Ro 4: 6 whom God **c** righteousness apart

CRETANS (CRETE)
Titus 1: 12 "**C** are always liars, evil brutes,

CRETE (CRETANS)
Ac 27: 12 This was a harbor in **C**, facing both

CRIED (CRY)
Ex 2: 23 groaned in their slavery and **c** out,
14: 10 terrified and **c** out to the LORD.
Nu 20: 16 but when we **c** out to the LORD,
Jos 24: 7 But they **c** to the LORD for help,
Jdg 3: 9 But when they **c** out to the LORD,
3: 15 Again the Israelites **c**
4: 3 they **c** to the LORD for help.
6: 6 the Israelites that they **c**
10: 12 you and you **c** to me for help, did I
1Sa 7: 9 He **c** out to the LORD on Israel's
12: 8 they **c** to the LORD for help,
12: 10 They **c** out to the LORD and said,
Ps 18: 6 I **c** to my God for help.

CRIMINALS
Lk 23: 32 both **c**, were also led out with him

CRIMSON
Isa 1: 18 though they are red as **c**, they shall
63: 1 with his garments stained **c**?

CRIPPLED
Mk 9: 45 to enter life **c** than to have two feet

CRISIS*
1Co 7: 26 Because of the present **c**, I think

CRITICISM*
2Co 8: 20 want to avoid any **c** of the way we

CROOKED*
Dt 32: 5 are a warped and **c** generation.
Ps 125: 5 to **c** ways the LORD will banish
Pr 2: 15 whose paths are **c** and who are
8: 8 none of them is **c** or perverse.
10: 9 whoever takes **c** paths will be
Ecc 1: 15 What is **c** cannot be straightened;
7: 13 can straighten what he has made **c**?
Isa 59: 8 have turned them into **c** roads;
La 3: 9 he has made my paths **c**.
Lk 3: 5 The **c** roads shall become straight,
Php 2: 15 fault in a warped and **c** generation."

CROP (CROPS)
Mt 13: 8 good soil, where it produced a **c**—
21: 41 his share of the **c** at harvest time."

CROPS (CROP)
Pr 3: 9 with the firstfruits of all your **c**;
10: 5 He who gathers **c** in summer is
28: 3 like a driving rain that leaves no **c**.
2Ti 2: 6 the first to receive a share of the **c**.

CROSS (CROSSED CROSSING)
Dt 4: 21 swore that I would not c the Jordan
12: 10 But you will c the Jordan and settle
Mt 10: 38 Whoever does not take up their c
16: 24 and take up their c and follow me.
Mk 8: 34 and take up their c and follow me.
Lk 9: 23 take up their c daily and follow me.
14: 27 whoever does not carry their c
Jn 19: 17 Carrying his own c, he went
Ac 2: 23 to death by nailing him to the c.
5: 30 you killed by hanging him on a c.
1Co 1: 17 lest the c of Christ be emptied of
1: 18 the message of the c is foolishness
Gal 5: 11 offense of the c has been abolished.
6: 12 persecuted for the c of Christ.
6: 14 in the c of our Lord Jesus Christ,
Eph 2: 16 both of them to God through the c,
Php 2: 8 even death on a c!
3: 18 live as enemies of the c of Christ.
Col 1: 20 through his blood, shed on the c.
2: 14 taken it away, nailing it to the c.
2: 15 triumphing over them by the c.
Heb 12: 2 set before him he endured the c,
1Pe 2: 24 bore our sins" in his body on the c,

CROSSED (CROSS)
Jos 4: 7 When it c the Jordan, the waters
Jn 5: 24 but has c over from death to life.

CROSSING (CROSS)
Ge 48: 14 and c his arms, he put his left hand

CROSSROADS (ROAD)
Jer 6: 16 "Stand at the c and look;

CROUCHING
Ge 4: 7 what is right, sin is c at your door;

CROWD (CROWDS)
Ex 23: 2 pervert justice by siding with the c,

CROWDS (CROWD)
Mt 9: 36 When he saw the c, he had

CROWED (CROWS)
Mt 26: 74 Immediately a rooster c.

CROWN (CROWNED CROWNS)
Pr 4: 9 and present you with a glorious c."
10: 6 Blessings c the head
12: 4 noble character is her husband's c,
16: 31 Gray hair is a c of splendor;
17: 6 Children's children are a c
Isa 35: 10 everlasting joy will c their heads.
51: 11 everlasting joy will c their heads.
61: 3 on them a c of beauty instead
62: 3 You will be a c of splendor
Eze 16: 12 and a beautiful c on your head.
Zec 9: 16 in his land like jewels in a c.
Mt 27: 29 then twisted together a c of thorns
Mk 15: 17 then twisted together a c of thorns
Jn 19: 2 The soldiers twisted together a c
19: 5 came out wearing the c of thorns
1Co 9: 25 do it to get a c that will not last,
9: 25 to get a c that will last forever.
Php 4: 1 joy and c, stand firm in the Lord
1Th 2: 19 the c in which we will glory
2Ti 2: 5 not receive the victor's c except
4: 8 store for me the c of righteousness,
Jas 1: 12 that person will receive the c of life
1Pe 5: 4 you will receive the c of glory
Rev 2: 10 will give you life as your victor's c.
3: 11 so that no one will take your c.
14: 14 of man with a c of gold on his head

CROWNED* (CROWN)
Ps 8: 5 the angels and c them with glory
Pr 14: 18 the prudent are c with knowledge.
SS 3: 11 which his mother c him on the day
Heb 2: 7 you c them with glory and honor
2: 9 now c with glory and honor

CROWNS (CROWN)
Ps 103: 4 from the pit and c you with love
149: 4 he c the humble with victory.
Rev 4: 4 and had c of gold on their heads.
4: 10 They lay their c before the throne
12: 3 ten horns and seven c on its heads.
19: 12 fire, and on his head are many c.

CROWS (CROWED)
Mt 26: 34 night, before the rooster c, you will

CRUCIFIED* (CRUCIFY)
Mt 20: 19 to be mocked and flogged and c.
26: 2 Man will be handed over to be c."
27: 26 and handed him over to be c.
27: 35 When they had c him, they divided
27: 38 Two rebels were c with him,
27: 44 same way the rebels who were c
28: 5 are looking for Jesus, who was c.
Mk 15: 15 and handed him over to be c.
15: 24 And they c him. Dividing up his
15: 25 in the morning when they c him.
15: 27 They c two rebels with him,
15: 32 Those c with him also heaped
16: 6 for Jesus the Nazarene, who was c.
Lk 23: 23 insistently demanded that he be c,
23: 33 called the Skull, they c him there,
24: 7 be c and on the third day be raised
24: 20 to death, and they c him;
Jn 19: 16 handed him over to them to be c.
19: 18 There they c him, and with him
19: 20 where Jesus was c was near the city,
19: 23 When the soldiers c Jesus, they
19: 32 the first man who had been c
19: 41 At the place where Jesus was c,
Ac 2: 36 Jesus, whom you c, both Lord
4: 10 whom you c but whom God raised
Ro 6: 6 that our old self was c with him so
1Co 1: 13 Was Paul c for you?
1: 23 but we preach Christ c:
2: 2 you except Jesus Christ and him c.
2: 8 they would not have c the Lord
2Co 13: 4 to be sure, he was c in weakness,
Gal 2: 20 I have been c with Christ and I no
3: 1 Christ was clearly portrayed as c.
5: 24 have c the flesh with its passions
6: 14 which the world has been c to me,
Rev 11: 8 where also their Lord was c.

CRUCIFY* (CRUCIFIED CRUCIFYING)
Mt 23: 34 Some of them you will kill and c;
27: 22 They all answered, "C him!"
27: 23 shouted all the louder, "C him!"
27: 31 Then they led him away to c him.
Mk 15: 13 "C him!" they shouted.
15: 14 shouted all the louder, "C him!"
15: 20 Then they led him out to c him.
Lk 23: 21 kept shouting, "C him! C him!"
Jn 19: 6 saw him, they shouted, "C! C!"
19: 6 "You take him and c him.
19: 10 either to free you or to c you?"
19: 15 C him!" "Shall I c your king?"

CRUCIFYING* (CRUCIFY)
Heb 6: 6 their loss they are c the Son of God

CRUSH (CRUSHED)
Ge 3: 15 he will c your head, and you will
Isa 53: 10 it was the LORD's will to c him
Ro 16: 20 peace will soon c Satan under your

CRUSHED (CRUSH)
Ps 34: 18 and saves those who are c in spirit.
Pr 17: 22 but a c spirit dries up the bones.
18: 14 but a c spirit who can bear?
Isa 53: 5 he was c for our iniquities;
2Co 4: 8 pressed on every side, but not c;

CRY (CRIED)
Ex 2: 23 their c for help because of their
Ps 5: 2 Hear my c for help, my King
34: 15 and his ears are attentive to their c;
40: 1 he turned to me and heard my c.
130: 1 Out of the depths I c to you,
Pr 21: 13 their ears to the c of the poor will
La 2: 18 The hearts of the people c
Hab 2: 11 The stones of the wall will c out,
Lk 19: 40 keep quiet, the stones will c out."

CULMINATION
Ro 10: 4 Christ is the c of the law so

CUNNING
2Co 11: 3 was deceived by the serpent's c,
Eph 4: 14 by the c and craftiness of people

CUP
Ps 23: 5 my head with oil; my c overflows.
Isa 51: 22 that c, the goblet of my wrath,
Mt 10: 42 anyone gives even a c of cold water
20: 22 "Can you drink the c I am going
23: 25 You clean the outside of the c
23: 26 First clean the inside of the c
26: 27 Then he took a c, and when he had
26: 39 may this c be taken from me.
26: 42 for this c to be taken away unless I
Mk 9: 41 anyone who gives you a c of water
10: 38 "Can you drink the c I drink or be
10: 39 "You will drink the c I drink and
14: 23 Then he took a c, and when he had
14: 36 Take this c from me.
Lk 11: 39 Pharisees clean the outside of the c
22: 17 After taking the c, he gave thanks
22: 20 "This c is the new covenant in my
22: 42 are willing, take this c from me;
Jn 18: 11 Shall I not drink the c the Father
1Co 10: 16 Is not the c of thanksgiving
10: 21 You cannot drink the c of the Lord
and the c of demons too;
11: 25 "This c is the new covenant in my

CUPBEARER
Ge 40: 1 the c and the baker of the king
Ne 1: 11 of this man." I was c to the king.

CURE (CURED)
Jer 17: 9 above all things and beyond c.
30: 15 wound, your pain that has no c?
Hos 5: 13 But he is not able to c you, not able
Lk 9: 1 out all demons and to c diseases,

CURED (CURE)
Lk 6: 18 troubled by impure spirits were c,

CURSE (ACCURSED CURSED CURSES CURSING)
Ge 4: 11 Now you are under a c and driven
8: 21 again will I c the ground because
12: 3 and whoever curses you I will c;
Dt 11: 26 you today a blessing and a c—
11: 28 the c if you disobey the commands
21: 23 is hung on a pole is under God's c.
23: 5 turned the c into a blessing for you,
Job 1: 11 he will surely c you to your face."
2: 5 he will surely c you to your face."
2: 9 C God and die!"
Ps 109: 28 While they c, may you bless;
Pr 3: 33 The LORD's c is on the house
Jer 42: 18 You will be a c and an object
Mal 2: 2 "I will send a c on you, and I will c
your blessings.
Lk 6: 28 bless those who c you,
Ro 12: 14 bless and do not c.
Gal 1: 8 to you, let them be under God's c!
3: 10 the works of the law are under a c,
3: 13 redeemed us from the c of the law
by becoming a c for us,
Jas 3: 9 and with it we c human beings,
Rev 22: 3 No longer will there be any c.

CURSED (CURSE)
Ge 3: 17 "C is the ground because of you;
Dt 27: 15 "C is anyone who makes an idol—
27: 16 "C is anyone who dishonors their
27: 17 "C is anyone who moves their
27: 18 "C is anyone who leads the blind
27: 19 "C is anyone who withholds justice
27: 20 "C is anyone who sleeps with his
27: 21 "C is anyone who has sexual
27: 22 "C is anyone who sleeps with his
27: 23 "C is anyone who sleeps with his
27: 24 "C is anyone who kills their
27: 25 "C is anyone who accepts a bribe
27: 26 "C is anyone who does not uphold
Pr 24: 24 be c by peoples and denounced
Jer 17: 5 "C is the one who trusts in man,
Mal 1: 14 "C is the cheat who has
Ro 9: 3 I could wish that I myself were c
1Co 4: 12 When we are c, we bless;
12: 3 "Jesus be c," and no one can say,
Gal 3: 10 "C is everyone who does not
3: 13 "C is everyone who is hung

CURSES (CURSE)
Ex 21: 17 "Anyone who c their father
Lev 20: 9 "'Anyone who c their father
Nu 5: 23 priest is to write these c on a scroll
Jos 8: 34 the blessings and the c—just as it is
Pr 20: 20 someone c their father or mother,
28: 27 their eyes to them receive many c.
Mt 15: 4 and 'Anyone who c their father
Mk 7: 10 and, 'Anyone who c their father

CURSING (CURSE)
Ps 109: 18 He wore **c** as his garment;
Ro 3: 14 "Their mouths are full of **c**
Jas 3: 10 the same mouth come praise and **c**.

CURTAIN
Ex 26: 31 "Make a **c** of blue,
26: 33 The **c** will separate the Holy Place
Mt 27: 51 that moment the **c** of the temple
Mk 15: 38 The **c** of the temple was torn in
Lk 23: 45 the **c** of the temple was torn in two.
Heb 6: 19 the inner sanctuary behind the **c**,
9: 3 Behind the second **c** was a room
10: 20 way opened for us through the **c**,

CUSTODY
Gal 3: 23 we were held in **c** under the law,

CUSTOM
Job 1: 5 This was Job's regular **c**.
Mk 10: 1 and as was his **c**, he taught them.
Lk 4: 16 into the synagogue, as was his **c**.
Ac 17: 2 As was his **c**, Paul went

CUT
Lev 19: 27 "'Do not **c** the hair at the sides
21: 5 of their beards or **c** their bodies.
1Ki 3: 25 "**C** the living child in two and give
Isa 51: 1 to the rock from which you were **c**
53: 8 For he was **c** off from the land
Da 2: 45 of the vision of the rock **c**
Mt 3: 10 produce good fruit will be **c** down
24: 22 "If those days had not been **c** short,
1Co 11: 6 for a woman to have her hair **c** off

CYMBAL* (CYMBALS)
1Co 13: 1 a resounding gong or a clanging **c**.

CYMBALS (CYMBAL)
1Ch 15: 16 lyres, harps and **c**.
2Ch 5: 12 dressed in fine linen and playing **c**,
Ps 150: 5 praise him with the clash of **c**,
150: 5 praise him with resounding **c**.

CYRUS
Persian king who allowed exiles to return (2Ch 36:22–Ezr 1:8), to rebuild temple (Ezr 5:13—6:14), as appointed by the LORD (Isa 44:28—45:13).

DAGON
Jdg 16: 23 a great sacrifice to **D** their god
1Sa 5: 2 Dagon's temple and set it beside **D**.

DAMASCUS
Ac 9: 3 As he neared **D** on his journey,

DAN
1. Son of Jacob by Bilhah (Ge 30:4–6; 35:25; 46:23). Tribe of blessed (Ge 49:16–17; Dt 33:22), numbered (Nu 1:39; 26:43), allotted land (Jos 19:40–48; Eze 48:1), failed to fully possess (Jdg 1:34–35), failed to support Deborah (Jdg 5:17), possessed Laish/Dan (Jdg 18).
2. Northernmost city in Israel (Ge 14:14; Jdg 18; 20:1).

DANCE (DANCED DANCING)
Ecc 3: 4 a time to mourn and a time to **d**,
Mt 11: 17 the pipe for you, and you did not **d**;

DANCED (DANCE)
Mk 6: 22 of Herodias came in and **d**,

DANCING (DANCE)
2Sa 6: 14 David was **d** before the LORD
Ps 30: 11 You turned my wailing into **d**;
149: 3 Let them praise his name with **d**

DANGER
Pr 22: 3 The prudent see **d** and take refuge,
27: 12 The prudent see **d** and take refuge,
Mt 5: 22 will be in **d** of the fire of hell.
Ro 8: 35 or nakedness or **d** or sword?
2Co 11: 26 bandits, in **d** from my fellow Jews,

DANIEL
1. Hebrew exile to Babylon, name changed to Belteshazzar (Da 1:6–7). Refused to eat unclean food (Da 1:8–21). Interpreted Nebuchadnezzar's dreams (Da 2; 4), writing on the wall (Da 5). Thrown into lion's den (Da 6). Visions of (Da 7–12).
2. Son of David (1Ch 3:1).

DARIUS
1. King of Persia (Ezr 4:5), allowed rebuilding of temple (Ezr 5–6).
2. Mede who conquered Babylon (Da 5:31).

DARK (DARKENED DARKENS DARKEST DARKNESS)
Ps 18: 9 **d** clouds were under his feet.
SS 1: 6 Do not stare at me because I am **d**,
Jn 12: 35 the **d** does not know where they
Ro 2: 19 a light for those who are in the **d**,
2Pe 1: 19 it, as to a light shining in a **d** place,

DARKENED (DARK)
Joel 2: 10 the sun and moon are **d**,
Mt 24: 29 of those days "'the sun will be **d**,
Ro 1: 21 and their foolish hearts were **d**.
Eph 4: 18 They are **d** in their understanding

DARKENS* (DARK)
Am 5: 8 into dawn and **d** day into night,

DARKEST* (DARK)
Ps 23: 4 though I walk through the **d** valley,
88: 6 in the lowest pit, in the **d** depths.

DARKNESS (DARK)
Ge 1: 2 **d** was over the surface of the deep,
1: 4 he separated the light from the **d**.
Ex 10: 22 total **d** covered all Egypt for three
20: 21 approached the thick **d** where God
2Sa 22: 29 the LORD turns my **d** into light.
Ps 18: 28 my God turns my **d** into light.
91: 6 the pestilence that stalks in the **d**,
112: 4 Even in **d** light dawns
139: 12 day, for **d** is as light to you.
Pr 4: 19 way of the wicked is like deep **d**;
Isa 5: 20 who put **d** for light and light for **d**,
42: 16 I will turn the **d** into light before
45: 7 I form the light and create **d**,
58: 10 then your light will rise in the **d**,
61: 1 release from **d** for the prisoners,
Joel 2: 31 The sun will be turned to **d**
Mt 4: 16 living in **d** have seen a great light;
6: 23 If then the light within you is **d**,
Lk 11: 34 your body also is full of **d**.
23: 44 **d** came over the whole land until
Jn 1: 5 The light shines in the **d**, and the **d**
3: 19 but people loved **d** instead of light
Ac 2: 20 The sun will be turned to **d**
2Co 4: 6 "Let light shine out of **d**," made his
6: 14 fellowship can light have with **d**?
Eph 5: 8 For you were once **d**, but now you
5: 11 to do with the fruitless deeds of **d**,
1Pe 2: 9 out of **d** into his wonderful light.
2Pe 2: 17 Blackest **d** is reserved for them.
1Jn 1: 5 in him there is no **d** at all.
2: 9 a brother or sister is still in the **d**.
Jude : 6 these he has kept in **d**,
: 13 whom blackest **d** has been reserved

DASH
Ps 2: 9 you will **d** them to pieces like

DAUGHTER (DAUGHTERS)
Ex 2: 10 she took him to Pharaoh's **d** and he
Jdg 11: 40 commemorate the **d** of Jephthah
Est 2: 7 had taken her as his own **d** when
Ps 9: 14 your praises in the gates of **D** Zion,
137: 8 **D** Babylon, doomed to destruction
Isa 62: 11 "Say to **D** Zion, 'See, your Savior
Zec 9: 9 Rejoice greatly, **D** Zion! Shout,
Mk 5: 34 He said to her, "**D**, your faith has
7: 29 the demon has left your **d**."

DAUGHTERS (DAUGHTER)
Ge 6: 2 the **d** of humans were beautiful,
19: 36 So both of Lot's **d** became pregnant
Nu 36: 10 So Zelophehad's **d** did as
Joel 2: 28 Your sons and **d** will prophesy,

DAVID
Son of Jesse (Ru 4:17–22; 1Ch 2:13–15), ancestor of Jesus (Mt 1:1–17; Lk 3:31). Wives and children (1Sa 18; 25:39–44; 2Sa 3:2–5; 5:13–16; 11:27; 1Ch 3:1–9).
Anointed king by Samuel (1Sa 16:1–13). Musician to Saul (1Sa 16:14–23; 18:10). Killed Goliath (1Sa 17). Relation with Jonathan (1Sa 18:1–4; 19–20; 23:16–18; 2Sa 1). Disfavor of Saul (1Sa 18:6—23:29). Spared Saul's life (1Sa 24; 26). Among Philistines (1Sa 21:10–14; 27–30). Lament for Saul and Jonathan (2Sa 1).
Anointed king of Judah (2Sa 2:1–11). Conflict with house of Saul (2Sa 2–4). Anointed king of Israel (2Sa 5:1–4; 1Ch 11:1–3). Conquered Jerusalem (2Sa 5:6–10; 1Ch 11:4–9). Brought ark to Jerusalem (2Sa 6; 1Ch 13; 15–16). The LORD promised eternal dynasty (2Sa 7; 1Ch 17; Ps 132). Showed kindness to Mephibosheth (2Sa 9). Adultery with Bathsheba, murder of Uriah (2Sa 11–12). Son Amnon raped daughter Tamar; killed by Absalom (2Sa 13). Absalom's revolt (2Sa 14–17); death (2Sa 18). Sheba's revolt (2Sa 20). Victories: Philistines (2Sa 5:17–25; 1Ch 14:8–17; 2Sa 21:15–22; 1Ch 20:4–8), Ammonites (2Sa 10; 1Ch 19), various (2Sa 8; 1Ch 18). Mighty men (2Sa 23:8–39; 1Ch 11–12). Punished for numbering army (2Sa 24; 1Ch 21). Appointed Solomon king (1Ki 1:28—2:9). Prepared for building of temple (1Ch 22–29). Last words (2Sa 23:1–7). Death (1Ki 2:10–12; 1Ch 29:28).
Psalmist (Mt 22:43–45), musician (Am 6:5), prophet (2Sa 23:2–7; Ac 1:16; 2:30).
Psalms of: 2 (Ac 4:25), 3–32, 34–41, 51–65, 68–70, 86, 95 (Heb 4:7), 101, 103, 108–110, 122, 124, 131, 133, 138–145.

DAWN (DAWNED DAWNS)
Ps 37: 6 righteous reward shine like the **d**,
Isa 14: 12 heaven, morning star, son of the **d**!
Am 4: 13 mankind, who turns **d** to darkness,
5: 8 who turns midnight into **d**

DAWNED (DAWN)
Isa 9: 2 land of deep darkness a light has **d**.
Mt 4: 16 the shadow of death a light has **d**."

DAWNS* (DAWN)
Ps 65: 8 where morning **d**, where evening
112: 4 in darkness light **d** for the upright,
Hos 10: 15 When that day **d**, the king of Israel
2Pe 1: 19 the day **d** and the morning star

DAY (DAYS)
Ge 1: 5 God called the light "**d**,"
1: 5 there was morning—the first **d**.
1: 8 there was morning—the second **d**.
1: 13 there was morning—the third **d**.
1: 19 there was morning—the fourth **d**.
1: 23 there was morning—the fifth **d**.
1: 31 there was morning—the sixth **d**.
2: 2 so on the seventh **d** he rested
8: 22 **d** and night will never cease."
Ex 16: 30 the people rested on the seventh **d**.
20: 8 "Remember the Sabbath **d**
Lev 16: 30 on this **d** atonement will be made
23: 28 Do not do any work on that **d**, because it is the **D** of Atonement,
Nu 14: 14 in a pillar of cloud by **d**
Jos 1: 8 meditate on it **d** and night,
2Ki 7: 9 This is a **d** of good news and we
25: 30 **D** by **d** the king gave Jehoiachin
1Ch 16: 23 proclaim his salvation **d** after **d**.
Ne 8: 18 **D** after **d**, from the first **d**
Ps 84: 10 Better is one **d** in your courts than
96: 2 proclaim his salvation **d** after **d**.
118: 24 The LORD has done it this very **d**;
Pr 27: 1 do not know what a **d** may bring.
Isa 13: 9 the **d** of the LORD is coming—
13: 9 a cruel **d**, with wrath and fierce
Jer 46: 10 But that **d** belongs to the Lord,
50: 31 "for your **d** has come, the time
Eze 30: 2 and say, "Alas for that **d**!"
Joel 1: 15 Alas for that **d**! For the **d**
2: 31 great and dreadful **d** of the LORD.
Am 3: 14 "On the **d** I punish Israel for her
5: 20 Will not the **d** of the LORD be
Ob : 15 "The **d** of the LORD is near for all
Zep 1: 14 The great **d** of the LORD is near—
Zec 2: 11 be joined with the LORD in that **d**
14: 1 A **d** of the LORD is coming,
14: 7 a unique **d**—a **d** known only
Mal 4: 5 dreadful **d** of the LORD comes.
Mt 24: 38 up to the **d** Noah entered the ark;
Lk 11: 3 Give us each **d** our daily bread.
17: 24 in his **d** will be like the lightning,
Ac 5: 42 **D** after **d**, in the temple courts

Ac 17: 11 examined the Scriptures every **d**
17: 17 as well as in the marketplace **d** by **d**
Ro 14: 5 considers one **d** more sacred
14: 5 another considers every **d** alike.
1Co 5: 5 may be saved on the **d** of the Lord.
2Co 4: 16 we are being renewed **d** by **d**.
11: 25 a night and a **d** in the open sea,
1Th 5: 2 the **d** of the Lord will come like
5: 4 that this **d** should surprise you like
2Th 2: 2 the **d** of the Lord has already come.
Heb 7: 27 need to offer sacrifices **d** after **d**,
2Pe 3: 8 the Lord a **d** is like a thousand
3: 8 and a thousand years are like a **d**.
3: 10 the **d** of the Lord will come like
Rev 6: 17 great **d** of their wrath has come,
16: 14 on the great **d** of God Almighty.

DAYS (DAY)
Dt 17: 19 he is to read it all the **d** of his life so
32: 7 Remember the **d** of old;
Ps 23: 6 love will follow me all the **d** of my
34: 12 and desires to see many good **d**,
39: 5 You have made my **d** a mere
90: 10 Our **d** may come to seventy years,
90: 12 Teach us to number our **d**, that we
128: 5 of Jerusalem all the **d** of your life.
Pr 31: 12 not harm, all the **d** of her life.
Ecc 9: 9 all the **d** of this meaningless life
12: 1 Creator in the **d** of your youth,
Isa 38: 20 stringed instruments all the **d** of
Da 7: 9 and the Ancient of **D** took his seat.
7: 13 He approached the Ancient of **D**
7: 22 until the Ancient of **D** came
Hos 3: 5 and to his blessings in the last **d**.
Joel 2: 29 I will pour out my Spirit in those **d**.
Mic 4: 1 In the last **d** the mountain
Lk 19: 43 The **d** will come upon you
Ac 2: 17 "'In the last **d**, God says, I will
2Ti 3: 1 will be terrible times in the last **d**.
Heb 1: 2 in these last **d** he has spoken to us
2Pe 3: 3 that in the last **d** scoffers will come,

DAZZLING*
Da 2: 31 an enormous, **d** statue,
Mk 9: 3 His clothes became **d** white,

DEACON* (DEACONS)
Ro 16: 1 a **d** of the church in Cenchreae.
1Ti 3: 12 A **d** must be faithful to his wife

DEACONS* (DEACON)
Php 1: 1 together with the overseers and **d**:
1Ti 3: 8 way, **d** are to be worthy of respect,
3: 10 against them, let them serve as **d**.

DEAD (DIE)
Lev 17: 15 who eats anything found **d** or torn
Dt 18: 11 or spiritist or who consults the **d**.
Job 26: 6 realm of the **d** is naked before God;
Ps 49: 15 me from the realm of the **d**;
Isa 8: 19 Why consult the **d** on behalf
Mt 8: 22 and let the **d** bury their own **d**."
28: 7 'He has risen from the **d** and is
Lk 15: 24 For this son of mine was **d** and is
24: 46 rise from the **d** on the third day,
Ac 2: 27 abandon me to the realm of the **d**,
Ro 6: 11 count yourselves **d** to sin but alive
1Co 15: 29 who are baptized for the **d**?
Eph 2: 1 you were **d** in your transgressions
1Th 4: 16 and the **d** in Christ will rise first.
Jas 2: 17 is not accompanied by action, is **d**.
2: 26 As the body without the spirit is **d**,
so faith without deeds is **d**.
Rev 14: 13 Blessed are the **d** who die
20: 12 The **d** were judged according

DEAR* (DEARER)
2Sa 1: 26 you were very **d** to me.
Ps 102: 14 her stones are **d** to your servants;
Jer 31: 20 Is not Ephraim my **d** son, the child
Ac 15: 25 to you with our **d** friends Barnabas
Ro 12: 19 Do not take revenge, my **d** friends,
16: 5 Greet my **d** friend Epenetus,
16: 8 my **d** friend in the Lord.
16: 9 in Christ, and my **d** friend Stachys.
16: 12 Greet my **d** friend Persis,
1Co 4: 14 but to warn you as my **d** children.
10: 14 Therefore, my **d** friends,
15: 58 my **d** brothers and sisters,
2Co 7: 1 we have these promises, **d** friends,
12: 19 and everything we do, **d** friends,
Gal 4: 19 My **d** children, for whom I am
Eph 6: 21 the **d** brother and faithful servant
Php 2: 12 Therefore, my **d** friends, as you
4: 1 in the Lord in this way, **d** friends!
Col 1: 7 Epaphras, our **d** fellow servant,
4: 7 is a **d** brother, a faithful minister
4: 9 our faithful and **d** brother, who is
4: 14 Our **d** friend Luke, the doctor,
1Ti 6: 2 better because their masters are **d**
2Ti 1: 2 To Timothy, my **d** son:
Phm : 1 To Philemon our **d** friend
: 16 better than a slave, as a **d** brother.
: 16 He is very **d** to me but even dearer
Heb 6: 9 we speak like this, **d** friends,
Jas 1: 16 my **d** brothers and sisters.
1: 19 My **d** brothers and sisters, take
2: 5 Listen, my **d** brothers and sisters:
1Pe 2: 11 **D** friends, I urge you, as foreigners
4: 12 **D** friends, do not be surprised
2Pe 3: 1 **D** friends, this is now my second
3: 8 not forget this one thing, **d** friends:
3: 14 So then, **d** friends, since you are
3: 15 as our **d** brother Paul also wrote
3: 17 Therefore, **d** friends, since you
1Jn 2: 1 My **d** children, I write this to you
2: 7 **D** friends, I am not writing you
2: 12 I am writing to you, **d** children,
2: 14 I write to you, **d** children,
2: 18 **D** children, this is the last hour;
2: 28 And now, **d** children,
3: 2 **D** friends, now we are children
3: 7 **D** children, do not let anyone lead
3: 18 **D** children, let us not love
3: 21 **D** friends, if our hearts do not
4: 1 **D** friends, do not believe every
4: 4 You, **d** children, are from God
4: 7 **D** friends, let us love one another,
4: 11 **D** friends, since God so loved us,
5: 21 **D** children, keep yourselves
2Jn : 5 And now, **d** lady, I am not writing
3Jn : 1 To my **d** friend Gaius, whom I love
: 2 **D** friend, I pray that you may enjoy
: 5 **D** friend, you are faithful in what
: 11 **D** friend, do not imitate what is
Jude : 3 **D** friends, although I was very
: 17 But, **d** friends, remember what
: 20 But you, **d** friends, by building

DEARER* (DEAR)
Phm : 16 very dear to me but even **d** to you,

DEATH (DIE)
Ex 21: 12 with a fatal blow is to be put to **d**.
Nu 35: 16 the murderer is to be put to **d**.
Dt 30: 19 I have set before you life and **d**,
Ru 1: 17 if even **d** separates you and me."
2Ki 4: 40 of God, there is **d** in the pot!"
Ps 44: 22 your sake we face **d** all day long;
89: 48 Who can live and not see **d**, or who
116: 15 of the LORD is the **d** of his faithful
Pr 8: 36 all who hate me love **d**."
11: 19 but whoever pursues evil finds **d**.
14: 12 right, but in the end it leads to **d**.
15: 11 **D** and Destruction lie open before
16: 25 right, but in the end it leads to **d**.
18: 21 tongue has the power of life and **d**,
19: 18 do not be a willing party to their **d**.
23: 14 with the rod and save them from **d**.
Ecc 7: 2 for **d** is the destiny of everyone;
Isa 25: 8 he will swallow up **d** forever.
53: 12 he poured out his life unto **d**,
Eze 18: 23 pleasure in the **d** of the wicked?
18: 32 no pleasure in the **d** of anyone,
33: 11 no pleasure in the **d** of the wicked,
Da 9: 26 the Anointed One will be put to **d**
Hos 13: 14 I will redeem them from **d**.
13: 14 Where, O **d**, are your plagues?
Jn 5: 24 but has crossed over from **d** to life.
Ro 4: 25 He was delivered over to **d** for our
5: 12 and **d** through sin, and in this way **d**
came to all
5: 14 **d** reigned from the time of Adam
6: 3 Jesus were baptized into his **d**?
6: 23 For the wages of sin is **d**,
7: 24 from this body that is subject to **d**?
8: 13 Spirit you put to **d** the misdeeds
Ro 8: 36 your sake we face **d** all day long;
1Co 15: 21 For since **d** came through a man,
15: 26 last enemy to be destroyed is **d**.
15: 31 I face **d** every day—yes, just as
15: 55 "Where, O **d**, is your victory?
2Ti 1: 10 Jesus, who has destroyed **d** and has
Heb 2: 14 by his **d** he might break the power
1Jn 5: 16 a sin that does not lead to **d**,
5: 16 There is a sin that leads to **d**.
Rev 1: 18 I hold the keys of **d** and Hades.
2: 11 not be hurt at all by the second **d**.
20: 6 The second **d** has no power over
20: 14 Then **d** and Hades were thrown
20: 14 The lake of fire is the second **d**.
21: 4 There will be no more **d**'
21: 8 This is the second **d**."

DEBAUCHERY*
Ro 13: 13 not in sexual immorality and **d**,
2Co 12: 21 and **d** in which they have indulged.
Gal 5: 19 sexual immorality, impurity and **d**;
Eph 5: 18 drunk on wine, which leads to **d**.
1Pe 4: 3 living in **d**, lust, drunkenness,

DEBORAH*
1. Prophetess who led Israel to victory over Canaanites (Jdg 4–5).
2. Rebekah's nurse (Ge 35:8).

DEBT* (DEBTOR DEBTORS DEBTS INDEBTEDNESS)
Dt 15: 3 you must cancel any **d** your fellow
24: 6 as security for a **d**,
1Sa 22: 2 or in **d** or discontented gathered
Job 24: 9 infant of the poor is seized for a **d**.
Mt 18: 25 that he had be sold to repay the **d**.
18: 27 canceled the **d** and let him go.
18: 30 prison until he could pay the **d**.
18: 32 said, 'I canceled all that **d** of yours
Lk 7: 43 who had the bigger **d** forgiven."
Ro 13: 8 Let no **d** remain outstanding,
13: 8 the continuing **d** to love one

DEBTOR* (DEBT)
Isa 24: 2 as for lender, for **d** as for creditor.

DEBTORS* (DEBT)
Mt 6: 12 as we also have forgiven our **d**.
Lk 16: 5 called in each one of his master's **d**.

DEBTS* (DEBT)
Dt 15: 1 seven years you must cancel **d**.
15: 2 canceling **d** has been proclaimed.
15: 9 the year for canceling **d**, is near,"
31: 10 in the year for canceling **d**,
2Ki 4: 7 "Go, sell the oil and pay your **d**.
Ne 10: 31 the land and will cancel all **d**.
Pr 22: 26 in pledge or puts up security for **d**;
Mt 6: 12 And forgive us our **d**, as we
Lk 7: 42 back, so he forgave the **d** of both.

DECAY*
Ps 16: 10 will you let your faithful one see **d**.
49: 9 live on forever and not see **d**.
49: 14 Their forms will **d** in the grave,
55: 23 down the wicked into the pit of **d**;
Pr 12: 4 a disgraceful wife is like **d** in his
Isa 5: 24 so their roots will **d** and their
Hab 3: 16 **d** crept into my bones, and my legs
Ac 2: 27 will not let your holy one see **d**.
2: 31 of the dead, nor did his body see **d**.
13: 34 that he will never be subject to **d**.
13: 35 will not let your holy one see **d**.'
13: 37 raised from the dead did not see **d**.
Ro 8: 21 be liberated from its bondage to **d**

DECEIT (DECEIVE)
Isa 53: 9 nor was any **d** in his mouth.
Da 8: 25 He will cause **d** to prosper, and he
Mk 7: 22 greed, malice, **d**, lewdness, envy,
Jn 1: 47 an Israelite in whom there is no **d**."
Ac 13: 10 You are full of all kinds of **d**
Ro 1: 29 envy, murder, strife, **d** and malice.
3: 13 their tongues practice **d**."
1Pe 2: 1 yourselves of all malice and all **d**,
2: 22 and no **d** was found in his mouth."

DECEITFUL (DECEIVE)
Jer 17: 9 The heart is **d** above all things
Hos 10: 2 Their heart is **d**, and now they
Zep 3: 13 A **d** tongue will not be found
2Co 11: 13 are false apostles, **d** workers,

Eph 4: 14 of people in their **d** scheming.
4: 22 is being corrupted by its **d** desires;
1Pe 3: 10 evil and their lips from **d** speech.
Rev 21: 27 who does what is shameful or **d**,

DECEITFULNESS* (DECEIVE)
Mt 13: 22 the **d** of wealth choke the word,
Mk 4: 19 the **d** of wealth and the desires
Heb 3: 13 of you may be hardened by sin's **d**.

DECEIVE (DECEIT DECEITFUL DECEITFULNESS DECEIVED DECEIVER DECEIVERS DECEIVES DECEIVING DECEPTION DECEPTIVE)
Lev 19: 11 "'Do not **d** one another.
Pr 14: 5 An honest witness does not **d**,
Jer 37: 9 Do not **d** yourselves, thinking,
Zec 13: 4 garment of hair in order to **d**.
Mt 24: 5 am the Messiah,' and will **d** many.
24: 11 will appear and **d** many people.
24: 24 great signs and wonders to **d**,
Mk 13: 6 'I am he,' and will **d** many.
13: 22 perform signs and wonders to **d**,
Ro 16: 18 flattery they **d** the minds of naive
1Co 3: 18 Do not **d** yourselves. If any of you
Gal 6: 3 they are not, they **d** themselves.
Eph 5: 6 no one **d** you with empty words,
Col 2: 4 one may **d** you by fine-sounding
2Th 2: 3 Don't let anyone **d** you in any way,
Jas 1: 22 to the word, and so **d** yourselves.
Jas 1: 26 rein on their tongues **d** themselves,
1Jn 1: 8 we **d** ourselves and the truth is not
Rev 20: 8 to **d** the nations in the four corners

DECEIVED (DECEIVE)
Ge 3: 13 said, "The serpent **d** me, and I ate."
Lk 21: 8 "Watch out that you are not **d**.
1Co 6: 9 Do not be **d**: Neither the sexually
2Co 11: 3 just as Eve was **d** by the serpent's
Gal 6: 7 Do not be **d**: God cannot be
1Ti 2: 14 Adam was not the one **d**; it was the woman who was **d**
2Ti 3: 13 to worse, deceiving and being **d**.
Titus 3: 3 **d** and enslaved by all kinds
Jas 1: 16 Don't be **d**, my dear brothers
Rev 13: 14 it **d** the inhabitants of the earth.
20: 10 And the devil, who **d** them,

DECEIVER (DECEIVE)
Mt 27: 63 while he was still alive that **d** said,
2Jn : 7 Any such person is the **d**

DECEIVERS* (DECEIVE)
Job 11: 11 Surely he recognizes **d**; and when
Ps 49: 5 when wicked **d** surround me—
2Jn : 7 I say this because many **d**, who do

DECEIVES* (DECEIVE)
Pr 26: 19 is one who **d** their neighbor
Jer 9: 5 Friend **d** friend, and no one speaks
Mt 24: 4 "Watch out that no one **d** you.
Mk 13: 5 "Watch out that no one **d** you.
Jn 7: 12 replied, "No, he **d** the people."
2Th 2: 10 that wickedness **d** those who are

DECEIVING (DECEIVE)
Lev 6: 2 the Lord by **d** a neighbor
1Ki 22: 22 be a **d** spirit in the mouths of all
1Ti 4: 1 the faith and follow **d** spirits
2Ti 3: 13 to worse, **d** and being deceived.
Rev 20: 3 from **d** the nations anymore until

DECENCY* (DECENTLY)
1Ti 2: 9 modestly, with **d** and propriety,

DECENTLY* (DECENCY)
Ro 13: 13 Let us behave **d**, as in the daytime,

DECEPTION (DECEIVE)
Pr 14: 8 ways, but the folly of fools is **d**.
26: 26 malice may be concealed by **d**,
Mt 27: 64 This last **d** will be worse than
2Co 4: 2 we do not use **d**, nor do we distort
Titus 1: 10 full of meaningless talk and **d**,

DECEPTIVE (DECEIVE)
Pr 11: 18 A wicked person earns **d** wages,
31: 30 Charm is **d**, and beauty is fleeting;
Jer 7: 4 Do not trust in **d** words and say,
Col 2: 8 through hollow and **d** philosophy,

DECIDED (DECISION)
2Co 9: 7 you should give what you have **d**

DECISION (DECIDED)
Ex 28: 29 **d** as a continuing memorial before
Joel 3: 14 multitudes in the valley of **d**!

DECLARE (DECLARED DECLARING)
1Ch 16: 24 **D** his glory among the nations,
Ps 19: 1 The heavens **d** the glory of God;
96: 3 **D** his glory among the nations,
Isa 42: 9 taken place, and new things I **d**;
Ro 10: 9 If you **d** with your mouth, "Jesus is

DECLARED (DECLARE)
Mk 7: 19 saying this, Jesus **d** all foods clean.)
Ro 2: 13 the law who will be **d** righteous.
3: 20 no one will be **d** righteous

DECLARING (DECLARE)
Ps 71: 8 **d** your splendor all day long.
Ac 2: 11 hear them **d** the wonders of God

DECREE (DECREED DECREES)
1Ch 16: 17 He confirmed it to Jacob as a **d**,
Ps 2: 7 I will proclaim the Lord's **d**:
7: 6 Awake, my God; **d** justice.
81: 4 this is a **d** for Israel, an ordinance
148: 6 he issued a **d** that will never pass
Da 4: 24 and this is the **d** the Most High has
Lk 2: 1 days Caesar Augustus issued a **d**
Ro 1: 32 they know God's righteous **d**

DECREED (DECREE)
Ps 78: 5 He **d** statutes for Jacob
Jer 40: 2 Lord your God **d** this disaster
La 3: 37 it happen if the Lord has not **d** it?
Da 9: 24 "Seventy 'sevens' are **d** for your
9: 26 end, and desolations have been **d**.
Lk 22: 22 Son of Man will go as it has been **d**.

DECREES (DECREE)
Ge 26: 5 my **d** and my instructions."
Ex 15: 26 his commands and keep all his **d**,
18: 16 and inform them of God's **d**
18: 20 Teach them his **d** and instructions,
Lev 10: 11 Israelites all the **d** the Lord has
10: 4 laws and be careful to follow my **d**.
18: 5 Keep my **d** and laws, for the person
18: 26 you must keep my **d** and my laws.
Ps 119: 12 to you, Lord; teach me your **d**.
119: 16 I delight in your **d**; I will not
119: 48 that I may meditate on your **d**.
119:112 on keeping your **d** to the very end.

DEDICATE (DEDICATED DEDICATION REDEDICATE)
Pr 20: 25 It is a trap to **d** something rashly

DEDICATED (DEDICATE)
Lev 21: 12 it, because he has been **d**
Nu 18: 6 **d** to the Lord to do the work
1Ki 8: 63 all the Israelites **d** the temple
2Ch 29: 31 "You have now **d** yourselves
Ne 3: 1 They **d** it and set its doors in

DEDICATION (DEDICATE)
Nu 6: 2 a vow of **d** to the Lord as
6: 9 the hair that symbolizes their **d**,
6: 19 the hair that symbolizes their **d**,
Jn 10: 22 the Festival of **D** at Jerusalem.
1Ti 5: 11 sensual desires overcome their **d**

DEED (DEEDS)
Jer 32: 10 I signed and sealed the **d**, had it
32: 16 I had given the **d** of purchase
Col 3: 17 whether in word or **d**, do it all
2Th 2: 17 strengthen you in every good **d**

DEEDS (DEED)
Dt 3: 24 or on earth who can do the **d**
4: 34 or by great and awesome **d**, like all
34: 12 or performed the awesome **d**
1Sa 2: 3 knows, and by him **d** are weighed.
1Ch 16: 24 his marvelous **d** among all peoples.
Job 34: 25 Because he takes note of their **d**,
Ps 26: 7 and telling of all your wonderful **d**.
45: 4 right hand achieve awesome **d**.
65: 5 us with awesome and righteous **d**,
66: 3 to God, "How awesome are your **d**!
66: 5 done, his awesome **d** for mankind!
71: 17 day I declare your marvelous **d**.
72: 18 who alone does marvelous **d**.
73: 28 I will tell of all your **d**.
75: 1 people tell of your wonderful **d**.
77: 11 I will remember the **d**
Ps 77: 12 and meditate on all your mighty **d**."
78: 4 next generation the praiseworthy **d**
78: 7 would not forget his **d** but would
86: 8 no **d** can compare with yours.
86: 10 you are great and do marvelous **d**;
88: 12 or your righteous **d** in the land
90: 16 May your **d** be shown to your
92: 4 For you make me glad by your **d**,
96: 3 his marvelous **d** among all peoples.
107: 8 and his wonderful **d** for mankind,
107: 15 and his wonderful **d** for mankind,
107: 21 and his wonderful **d** for mankind.
107: 24 his wonderful **d** in the deep.
107: 31 and his wonderful **d** for mankind.
107: 43 ponder the loving **d** of the Lord.
111: 3 Glorious and majestic are his **d**,
145: 6 and I will proclaim your great **d**.
Jer 32: 19 conduct and as their **d** deserve.
Hab 3: 2 I stand in awe of your **d**, Lord.
Mt 5: 16 that they may see your good **d**
11: 19 wisdom is proved right by her **d**."
Lk 1: 51 He has performed mighty **d** with
23: 41 we are getting what our **d** deserve.
Ac 26: 20 their repentance by their **d**.
1Ti 6: 18 good, to be rich in good **d**,
Heb 10: 24 on toward love and good **d**,
Jas 2: 14 claims to have faith but has no **d**?
2: 18 Show me your faith without **d**, and I will show you my faith by my **d**.
2: 20 that faith without **d** is useless?
2: 26 is dead, so faith without **d** is dead.
1Pe 2: 12 they may see your good **d**
Rev 2: 19 I know your **d**, your love and faith,
2: 23 each of you according to your **d**.
3: 1 I know your **d**; you have
3: 2 I have found your **d** unfinished
3: 8 I know your **d**. See, I have placed
3: 15 I know your **d**, that you are neither
14: 13 labor, for their **d** will follow them."
15: 3 "Great and marvelous are your **d**,

DEEP (DEPTH DEPTHS)
Ge 1: 2 was over the surface of the **d**,
8: 2 Now the springs of the **d**
Job 34: 22 There is no **d** shadow, no utter
Ps 42: 7 **D** calls to **d** in the roar of your
Pr 25: 27 search out matters that are too **d**.
Lk 5: 4 "Put out into **d** water, and let down
1Co 2: 10 things, even the **d** things of God.
1Ti 3: 9 must keep hold of the **d** truths

DEER
Ps 42: 1 As the **d** pants for streams of water,

DEFAMED*
Isa 48: 11 How can I let myself be **d**?

DEFEATED
1Co 6: 7 have been completely **d** already.

DEFEND (DEFENDED DEFENDER DEFENDING DEFENDS DEFENSE)
Ps 72: 4 May he **d** the afflicted among
74: 22 Rise up, O God, and **d** your cause;
82: 2 "How long will you **d** the unjust
82: 3 **D** the weak and the fatherless;
119:154 **D** my cause and redeem me;
Pr 31: 9 **d** the rights of the poor and needy.
Isa 1: 17 seek justice. **D** the oppressed.
1: 23 They do not **d** the cause
Jer 5: 28 they do not **d** the just cause
50: 34 He will vigorously **d** their cause so

DEFENDED (DEFEND)
Jer 22: 16 He **d** the cause of the poor

DEFENDER (DEFEND)
Ex 22: 2 the **d** is not guilty of bloodshed;
Ps 68: 5 to the fatherless, a **d** of widows,
Pr 23: 11 for their **D** is strong; he will take

DEFENDING (DEFEND)
Ps 10: 18 **d** the fatherless and the oppressed,
Ro 2: 15 and at other times even **d** them.)
Php 1: 7 and, whether I am in chains or **d**

DEFENDS* (DEFEND)
Dt 10: 18 He **d** the cause of the fatherless
33: 7 With his own hands he **d** his cause.
Isa 51: 22 says, your God, who **d** his people:

DEFENSE (DEFEND)
Ex 15: 2 Lord is my strength and my **d**;

Ps 35: 23 Awake, and rise to my **d**!
Php 1: 16 am put here for the **d** of the gospel.

DEFERRED*
Pr 13: 12 Hope **d** makes the heart sick,

DEFIED
1Sa 17: 45 armies of Israel, whom you have **d**.
1Ki 13: 26 is the man of God who **d** the word

DEFILE (DEFILED)
Da 1: 8 Daniel resolved not to **d** himself
Mt 15: 11 someone's mouth does not **d** them,
Rev 14: 4 are those who did not **d** themselves

DEFILED (DEFILE)
Isa 24: 5 The earth is **d** by its people;

DEFRAUD
Lev 19: 13 "'Do not **d** or rob your neighbor.
Mk 10: 19 you shall not **d**, honor your father

DEITY*
Col 2: 9 Christ all the fullness of the **D** lives

DELAY
Ecc 5: 4 a vow to God, do not **d** to fulfill it.
Isa 48: 9 my own name's sake I **d** my wrath;
Heb 10: 37 coming will come and will not **d**."
Rev 10: 6 and said, "There will be no more **d**!

DELIBERATE*
Ac 2: 23 over to you by God's **d** plan

DELICACIES
Ps 141: 4 do not let me eat their **d**.
Pr 23: 3 Do not crave his **d**, for that food is
23: 6 host, do not crave his **d**;

DELICIOUS*
Pr 9: 17 food eaten in secret is **d**!"

DELIGHT* (DELIGHTED DELIGHTFUL DELIGHTING DELIGHTS)
Lev 26: 31 and I will take no **d** in the pleasing
Dt 30: 9 The LORD will again **d** in you
1Sa 2: 1 for I **d** in your deliverance.
15: 22 "Does the LORD **d** in burnt
Ne 1: 11 of your servants who **d** in revering
Job 22: 26 you will find **d** in the Almighty
27: 10 Will they find **d** in the Almighty?
Ps 1: 2 but whose **d** is in the law
16: 3 noble ones in whom is all my **d**."
35: 9 the LORD and **d** in his salvation.
35: 27 those who **d** in my vindication
37: 4 Take **d** in the LORD, and he will
43: 4 of God, to God, my joy and my **d**.
51: 16 You do not **d** in sacrifice, or I
51: 19 you will **d** in the sacrifices
62: 4 my lofty place; they take **d** in lies.
68: 30 Scatter the nations who **d** in war.
111: 2 are pondered by all who **d** in them.
112: 1 who find great **d** in his commands.
119: 16 I **d** in your decrees; I will not
119: 24 Your statutes are my **d**; they are my
119: 35 your commands, for there I find **d**.
119: 47 for I **d** in your commands because
119: 70 and unfeeling, but I **d** in your law.
119: 77 I may live, for your law is my **d**.
119: 92 If your law had not been my **d**,
119:143 but your commands give me **d**.
119:174 LORD, and your law gives me **d**.
147: 10 his **d** in the legs of the warrior;
149: 4 the LORD takes **d** in his people;
Pr 1: 22 How long will mockers **d**
2: 14 who **d** in doing wrong and rejoice
8: 30 I was filled with **d** day after day,
18: 2 but **d** in airing their own opinions.
23: 26 and let your eyes **d** in my ways,
Ecc 2: 10 My heart took **d** in all my labor,
SS 1: 4 We rejoice and **d** in you;
2: 3 I **d** to sit in his shade, and his fruit
Isa 11: 3 he will **d** in the fear of the LORD.
13: 17 for silver and have no **d** in gold.
32: 14 forever, the **d** of donkeys,
42: 1 my chosen one in whom I **d**;
55: 2 you will **d** in the richest of fare.
58: 13 if you call the Sabbath a **d**
61: 10 I **d** greatly in the LORD;
62: 4 for the LORD will take **d** in you,
65: 18 for I will create Jerusalem to be a **d**
65: 19 Jerusalem and take **d** in my people;
66: 3 and they **d** in their abominations;
Isa 66: 11 **d** in her overflowing abundance."
Jer 9: 24 earth, for in these I **d**,"
15: 16 they were my joy and my heart's **d**,
31: 20 dear son, the child in whom I **d**?
49: 25 abandoned, the town in which I **d**?
Eze 24: 16 away from you the **d** of your eyes.
24: 21 you take pride, the **d** of your eyes,
24: 25 joy and glory, the **d** of their eyes,
Hos 7: 3 "They **d** the king with their
Mic 1: 16 for the children in whom you **d**;
7: 18 angry forever but **d** to show mercy.
Zep 3: 17 He will take great **d** in you;
Mt 12: 18 the one I love, in whom I **d**;
Mk 12: 37 large crowd listened to him with **d**.
Lk 1: 14 He will be a joy and **d** to you,
Ro 7: 22 in my inner being I **d** in God's law;
1Co 13: 6 Love does not **d** in evil but rejoices
2Co 12: 10 for Christ's sake, I **d** in weaknesses,
Col 2: 5 and **d** to see how disciplined you

DELIGHTED (DELIGHT)
2Sa 22: 20 he rescued me because he **d** in me.
1Ki 10: 9 who has **d** in you and placed you
2Ch 9: 8 who has **d** in you and placed you
Ps 18: 19 he rescued me because he **d** in me.
Isa 5: 7 of Judah are the vines he **d** in.
Lk 13: 17 but the people were **d** with all

DELIGHTFUL* (DELIGHT)
Ps 16: 6 surely I have a **d** inheritance.
SS 1: 2 for your love is more **d** than wine.
4: 10 How **d** is your love, my sister,
Mal 3: 12 for yours will be a **d** land,"

DELIGHTING* (DELIGHT)
Pr 8: 31 his whole world and **d** in mankind.

DELIGHTS (DELIGHT)
Est 6: 6 for the man the king **d** to honor?"
Ps 22: 8 deliver him, since he **d** in him."
35: 27 who **d** in the well-being of his
36: 8 them drink from your river of **d**.
37: 23 the steps of the one who **d** in him;
147: 11 the LORD **d** in those who fear
Pr 3: 12 loves, as a father the son he **d** in.
10: 23 of understanding **d** in wisdom.
11: 20 but he **d** in those whose ways are
12: 22 **d** in people who are trustworthy.
14: 35 A king **d** in a wise servant,
29: 17 will bring you the **d** you desire.
Col 2: 18 Do not let anyone who **d** in false

DELILAH*
Woman who betrayed Samson (Jdg 16:4–22).

DELIVER (DELIVERANCE DELIVERED DELIVERER DELIVERS)
Dt 32: 39 and no one can **d** out of my hand.
Ps 22: 8 Let him **d** him, since he delights
72: 12 he will **d** the needy who cry out,
79: 9 **d** us and forgive our sins for your
109: 21 of the goodness of your love, **d** me.
119:170 **d** me according to your promise.
Isa 50: 2 Was my arm too short to **d** you?
Eze 7: 19 gold will not be able to **d** them
Da 3: 17 the God we serve is able to **d** us
Hos 13: 14 will **d** this people from the power
Mt 6: 13 but **d** us from the evil one.'
2Co 1: 10 hope that he will continue to **d** us,

DELIVERANCE (DELIVER)
1Sa 2: 1 my enemies, for I delight in your **d**.
Ps 3: 8 From the LORD comes **d**.
32: 7 and surround me with songs of **d**.
33: 17 A horse is a vain hope for **d**;
Ob : 17 But on Mount Zion will be **d**;

DELIVERED (DELIVER)
Job 33: 28 God has **d** me from going down
Ps 34: 4 he **d** me from all my fears.
71: 23 praise to you—I whom you have **d**.
107: 6 and he **d** them from their distress.
116: 8 LORD, have **d** me from death,
Da 7: 25 The holy people will be **d** into his
12: 1 written in the book—will be **d**.
Ro 4: 25 He was **d** over to death for our sins

DELIVERER* (DELIVER)
Jdg 3: 9 he raised up for them a **d**,
3: 15 the LORD, and he gave them a **d**—
2Sa 22: 2 is my rock, my fortress and my **d**;
2Ki 13: 5 The LORD provided a **d** for Israel,
Ps 18: 2 is my rock, my fortress and my **d**;
40: 17 You are my help and my **d**;
70: 5 You are my help and my **d**;
140: 7 my strong **d**, you shield my head
144: 2 stronghold and my **d**, my shield,
Ac 7: 35 their ruler and **d** by God himself,
Ro 11: 26 "The **d** will come from Zion;

DELIVERS (DELIVER)
Ps 34: 17 he **d** them from all their troubles.
34: 19 the LORD **d** him from them all;
37: 40 The LORD helps them and **d** them;

DELUSION* (DELUSIONS)
2Th 2: 11 God sends them a powerful **d** so

DELUSIONS (DELUSION)
Ps 119:118 for their **d** come to nothing.

DEMAND (DEMANDED)
Lk 6: 30 belongs to you, do not **d** it back.

DEMANDED (DEMAND)
Lk 12: 20 This very night your life will be **d**
12: 48 been given much, much will be **d**;

DEMETRIUS
Ac 19: 24 A silversmith named **D**, who made
3Jn : 12 **D** is well spoken of by everyone—

DEMON* (DEMON-POSSESSED DEMONIC DEMONS)
Mt 9: 33 And when the **d** was driven out,
11: 18 drinking, and they say, 'He has a **d**.'
17: 18 Jesus rebuked the **d**, and it came
Mk 7: 26 She begged Jesus to drive the **d**
7: 29 the **d** has left your daughter."
7: 30 lying on the bed, and the **d** gone.
Lk 4: 33 there was a man possessed by a **d**,
4: 35 the **d** threw the man down before
7: 33 wine, and you say, 'He has a **d**.'
8: 29 driven by the **d** into solitary places.
9: 42 the **d** threw him to the ground
11: 14 was driving out a **d** that was mute.
11: 14 When the **d** left, the man who had
Jn 8: 49 "I am not possessed by a **d**,"
10: 21 sayings of a man possessed by a **d**.
Can a **d** open the eyes

DEMON-POSSESSED* (DEMON)
Mt 4: 24 pain, the **d**, those having seizures,
8: 16 many who were **d** were brought
8: 28 two **d** men coming from the tombs
8: 33 what had happened to the **d** men.
9: 32 man who was **d** and could not talk
12: 22 they brought him a **d** man who
15: 22 My daughter is **d** and suffering
Mk 1: 32 brought to Jesus all the sick and **d**.
5: 16 what had happened to the **d** man—
5: 18 the man who had been **d** begged
Lk 8: 27 he was met by a **d** man
8: 36 the people how the **d** man had
Jn 7: 20 "You are **d**," the crowd answered.
8: 48 that you are a Samaritan and **d**?"
8: 52 "Now we know that you are **d**!
10: 20 said, "He is **d** and raving mad.
Ac 19: 13 Lord Jesus over those who were **d**.

DEMONIC* (DEMON)
Jas 3: 15 but is earthly, unspiritual, **d**.
Rev 16: 14 They are **d** spirits that perform

DEMONS* (DEMON)
Mt 7: 22 and in your name drive out **d**
8: 31 The **d** begged Jesus, "If you drive
9: 34 by the prince of **d** that he drives out **d**."
10: 8 who have leprosy, drive out **d**.
12: 24 the prince of **d**, that this fellow drives out **d**."
12: 27 And if I drive out **d** by Beelzebul,
12: 28 the Spirit of God that I drive out **d**,
Mk 1: 34 He also drove out many **d**, but he
1: 34 not let the **d** speak because they
1: 39 synagogues and driving out **d**.
3: 15 to have authority to drive out **d**.
3: 22 the prince of **d** he is driving out **d**."
5: 12 The **d** begged Jesus, "Send us
5: 15 been possessed by the legion of **d**,
6: 13 They drove out many **d**
9: 38 "we saw someone driving out **d**
16: 9 *of whom he had driven seven **d**.*

Mk 16: 17 *they will drive out **d**;*
Lk 4: 41 **d** came out of many people,
8: 2 from whom seven **d** had come out;
8: 30 many **d** had gone into him.
8: 32 The **d** begged Jesus to let them go
8: 33 When the **d** came out of the man,
8: 35 from whom the **d** had gone out,
8: 38 man from whom the **d** had gone
9: 1 authority to drive out all **d**
9: 49 "we saw someone driving out **d**
10: 17 even the **d** submit to us in your
11: 15 the prince of **d**, he is driving out **d**."
11: 18 that I drive out **d** by Beelzebul.
11: 19 Now if I drive out **d** by Beelzebul,
11: 20 I drive out **d** by the finger of God,
13: 32 'I will keep on driving out **d**
Ro 8: 38 life, neither angels nor **d**,
1Co 10: 20 of pagans are offered to **d**,
10: 20 want you to be participants with **d**.
10: 21 of the Lord and the cup of **d** too;
10: 21 the Lord's table and the table of **d**.
1Ti 4: 1 spirits and things taught by **d**.
Jas 2: 19 Good! Even the **d** believe that—
Rev 9: 20 they did not stop worshiping **d**,
18: 2 She has become a dwelling for **d**

DEMONSTRATE* (DEMONSTRATES DEMONSTRATION)
Ac 26: 20 **d** their repentance by their deeds.
Ro 3: 25 He did this to **d** his righteousness,
3: 26 he did it to **d** his righteousness

DEMONSTRATES* (DEMONSTRATE)
Ro 5: 8 God **d** his own love for us in this:

DEMONSTRATION* (DEMONSTRATE)
1Co 2: 4 but with a **d** of the Spirit's power,

DEN (DENS)
Da 6: 16 and threw him into the lions' **d**.
Mt 21: 13 but you are making it 'a **d**
Mk 11: 17 But you have made it 'a **d**
Lk 19: 46 but you have made it 'a **d**

DENARII* (DENARIUS)
Lk 7: 41 One owed him five hundred **d**,
10: 35 he took out two **d** and gave them

DENARIUS (DENARII)
Mt 20: 2 agreed to pay them a **d** for the day
Mk 12: 15 "Bring me a **d** and let me look

DENIED (DENY)
Mt 26: 70 But he **d** it before them all.
Mk 14: 68 But he **d** it. "I don't know
Lk 22: 57 But he **d** it. "Woman, I don't know
Jn 18: 25 He **d** it, saying, "I am not."
1Ti 5: 8 has **d** the faith and is worse than
Rev 3: 8 my word and have not **d** my name.

DENIES* (DENY)
Job 34: 5 am innocent, but God **d** me justice.
1Jn 2: 22 It is whoever **d** that Jesus is
2: 23 No one who **d** the Son has

DENS (DEN)
Mt 8: 20 "Foxes have **d** and birds have nests,

DENY (DENIED DENIES DENYING SELF-DENIAL)
Ex 23: 6 "Do not **d** justice to your poor
Job 27: 5 till I die, I will not **d** my integrity.
Isa 5: 23 bribe, but **d** justice to the innocent.
La 3: 35 **d** people their rights before the
Am 2: 7 and **d** justice to the oppressed.
Mt 16: 24 be my disciple must **d** themselves
Mk 8: 34 be my disciple must **d** themselves
Lk 9: 23 be my disciple must **d** themselves
22: 34 you will **d** three times that you
Ac 4: 16 a notable sign, and we cannot **d** it.
Titus 1: 16 but by their actions they **d** him.
Jas 3: 14 not boast about it or **d** the truth.
Jude : 4 **d** Jesus Christ our only Sovereign

DENYING* (DENY)
Eze 22: 29 the foreigner, **d** them justice.
2Ti 3: 5 a form of godliness but **d** its power.
2Pe 2: 1 even **d** the sovereign Lord who
1Jn 2: 22 **d** the Father and the Son.

DEPART (DEPARTED DEPARTURE)
Ge 49: 10 The scepter will not **d** from Judah,
Job 1: 21 mother's womb, and naked I will **d**.
Ecc 5: 15 and as everyone comes, so they **d**.
Mt 25: 41 to those on his left, '**D** from me,
Php 1: 23 I desire to **d** and be with Christ,

DEPARTED (DEPART)
1Sa 4: 21 "The Glory has **d** from Israel"—
Ps 119:102 I have not **d** from your laws,
2Ti 2: 18 who have **d** from the truth.

DEPARTURE (DEPART)
Lk 9: 31 They spoke about his **d**, which he
2Ti 4: 6 and the time for my **d** is near.
2Pe 1: 15 after my **d** you will always be able

DEPEND
Ps 62: 7 salvation and my honor **d** on God;
Jer 49: 11 Your widows too can **d** on me.'"

DEPOSES*
Da 2: 21 he **d** kings and raises up others.

DEPOSIT
Mt 25: 27 should have put my money on **d**
Lk 19: 23 didn't you put my money on **d**,
2Co 1: 22 put his Spirit in our hearts as a **d**,
5: 5 who has given us the Spirit as a **d**,
Eph 1: 14 who is a **d** guaranteeing our
2Ti 1: 14 Guard the good **d** that was

DEPRAVED* (DEPRAVITY)
Eze 16: 47 soon became more **d** than they.
23: 11 she was more **d** than her sister.
Ro 1: 28 God gave them over to a **d** mind,
2Ti 3: 8 They are men of **d** minds, who,
2Pe 2: 2 Many will follow their **d** conduct
2: 7 was distressed by the **d** conduct

DEPRAVITY* (DEPRAVED)
Ro 1: 29 of wickedness, evil, greed and **d**.
2Pe 2: 19 they themselves are slaves of **d**—

DEPRIVE
Dt 24: 17 Do not **d** the foreigner
Pr 18: 5 and so **d** the innocent of justice.
31: 5 **d** all the oppressed of their rights.
Isa 10: 2 to **d** the poor of their rights
29: 21 with false testimony **d** the innocent
La 3: 36 to **d** them of justice—would not
1Co 7: 5 Do not **d** each other except
9: 15 die than allow anyone to **d** me

DEPTH (DEEP)
Ro 8: 39 neither height nor **d**, nor anything
11: 33 the **d** of the riches of the wisdom

DEPTHS (DEEP)
Ps 130: 1 Out of the **d** I cry to you, LORD;

DERIDES*
Pr 11: 12 Whoever **d** their neighbor has no

DERIVES*
Eph 3: 15 in heaven and on earth **d** its name.

DESCEND (DESCENDANTS DESCENDED DESCENDING)
Ro 10: 7 "or 'Who will **d** into the deep?'"

DESCENDANTS (DESCEND)
Jer 31: 17 So there is hope for your **d**,"

DESCENDED (DESCEND)
Eph 4: 9 except that he also **d** to the lower,
Heb 7: 14 clear that our Lord **d** from Judah,

DESCENDING (DESCEND)
Ge 28: 12 of God were ascending and **d** on it.
Mt 3: 16 saw the Spirit of God **d** like a dove
Mk 1: 10 and the Spirit **d** on him like a dove.
Jn 1: 51 and **d** on' the Son of Man."

DESECRATING*
Ne 13: 17 you are doing—**d** the Sabbath day?
13: 18 against Israel by **d** the Sabbath."
Isa 56: 2 keeps the Sabbath without **d** it,
56: 6 who keep the Sabbath without **d** it
Eze 44: 7 **d** my temple while you offered me

DESERT
Pr 21: 19 live in a **d** than with a quarrelsome
Isa 32: 2 like streams of water in the **d**
32: 15 and the **d** becomes a fertile field,
35: 6 wilderness and streams in the **d**.

DESERTED (DESERTS)
Mt 26: 56 all the disciples **d** him and fled.
2Ti 1: 15 in the province of Asia has **d** me,

DESERTING (DESERTS)
Gal 1: 6 you are so quickly **d** the one who

DESERTS (DESERTED DESERTING)
Zec 11: 17 shepherd, who **d** the flock!

DESERVE* (DESERVED DESERVES)
Ge 40: 15 I have done nothing to **d** being put
Lev 26: 21 seven times over, as your sins **d**.
Jdg 20: 10 can give them what they **d** for this
1Ki 2: 26 You **d** to die, but I will not put you
Ps 28: 4 bring back on them what they **d**.
94: 2 pay back to the proud what they **d**.
103: 10 he does not treat us as our sins **d**
Ecc 8: 14 who get what the wicked **d**,
8: 14 who get what the righteous **d**.
Isa 66: 6 repaying his enemies all they **d**.
Jer 14: 16 out on them the calamity they **d**.
17: 10 according to what their deeds **d**."
21: 14 I will punish you as your deeds **d**,
32: 19 their conduct and as their deeds **d**.
49: 12 who do not **d** to drink the cup
La 3: 64 Pay them back what they **d**,
Eze 16: 59 I will deal with you as you **d**,
Zec 1: 6 us what our ways and practices **d**,
Mt 8: 8 I do not **d** to have you come under
22: 8 those I invited did not **d** to come.
Lk 7: 6 I do not **d** to have you come under
23: 15 he has done nothing to **d** death.
23: 41 we are getting what our deeds **d**.
Ro 1: 32 those who do such things **d** death,
1Co 15: 9 and do not even **d** to be called
16: 18 Such men **d** recognition.
2Co 11: 15 end will be what their actions **d**.
Rev 16: 6 them blood to drink as they **d**."

DESERVED* (DESERVE)
2Sa 19: 28 descendants **d** nothing
Ezr 9: 13 punished us less than our sins **d**
Job 33: 27 is right, but I did not get what I **d**.
Ac 23: 29 no charge against him that **d** death

DESERVES* (DESERVE)
Nu 35: 31 the life of a murderer, who **d** to die.
Dt 25: 2 If the guilty person **d** to be beaten,
25: 2 the number of lashes the crime **d**,
Jdg 9: 16 Have you treated him as he **d**?
Job 34: 11 on them what their conduct **d**.
Jer 51: 6 he will repay her what she **d**.
Lk 7: 4 "This man **d** to have you do this,
10: 7 for the worker **d** his wages.
Ac 26: 31 is not doing anything that **d** death
1Ti 1: 15 saying that **d** full acceptance:
4: 9 saying that **d** full acceptance.
5: 18 and "The worker **d** his wages."
Heb 10: 29 severely do you think someone **d**

DESIGNATED
Lk 6: 13 of them, whom he also **d** apostles:
Heb 5: 10 was **d** by God to be high priest

DESIRABLE* (DESIRE)
Ge 3: 6 and also **d** for gaining wisdom,
Pr 22: 1 name is more **d** than great riches;

DESIRE* (DESIRABLE DESIRED DESIRES)
Ge 3: 16 Your **d** will be for your husband,
Dt 5: 21 You shall not set your **d** on your
1Sa 9: 20 whom is all the **d** of Israel turned,
2Sa 19: 38 anything you **d** from me I will do
23: 5 salvation and grant me my every **d**.
2Ki 9: 15 "If you **d** to make me king,
1Ch 28: 9 and understands every **d** and every
2Ch 1: 11 "Since this is your heart's **d**
9: 8 and his **d** to uphold them forever,
Job 13: 3 But I **d** to speak to the Almighty
21: 14 We have no **d** to know your ways.
Ps 10: 17 LORD, hear the **d** of the afflicted;
20: 4 he give you the **d** of your heart
21: 2 You have granted him his heart's **d**
27: 12 turn me over to the **d** of my foes,
40: 6 and offering you did not **d**—
40: 8 I **d** to do your will, my God;
40: 14 may all who **d** my ruin be turned
41: 2 them over to the **d** of their foes.
70: 2 may all who **d** my ruin be turned
73: 25 earth has nothing I **d** besides you.
Pr 3: 15 nothing you **d** can compare
8: 11 and nothing you **d** can compare
10: 24 what the righteous **d** will be
11: 23 The **d** of the righteous ends only
12: 12 The wicked **d** the stronghold
19: 2 **D** without knowledge is not good

Pr 24: 1 wicked, do not **d** their company;
29: 17 will bring you the delights you **d**.
Ecc 6: 2 they lack nothing their hearts **d**,
12: 5 along and **d** no longer is stirred.
SS 6: 12 it, my **d** set me among the royal
7: 10 to my beloved, and his **d** is for me.
Isa 26: 8 and renown are the **d** of our hearts.
53: 2 appearance that we should **d** him.
55: 11 but will accomplish what I **d**
Eze 24: 25 their heart's **d**, and their sons
Hos 6: 6 For I **d** mercy, not sacrifice,
Mic 7: 3 the powerful dictate what they **d**—
Mal 3: 1 covenant, whom you **d**, will come,"
Mt 9: 13 'I **d** mercy, not sacrifice.'
12: 7 what these words mean, 'I **d** mercy,
Ro 7: 18 For I have the **d** to do what is good,
9: 16 depend on human **d** or effort,
10: 1 my heart's **d** and prayer to God
1Co 12: 31 Now eagerly **d** the greater gifts.
14: 1 and eagerly **d** gifts of the Spirit,
2Co 8: 10 give but also to have the **d** to do so.
8: 13 Our **d** is not that others might be
Php 1: 23 I **d** to depart and be with Christ,
4: 17 Not that I **d** your gifts; what I **d** is
2Th 1: 11 fruition your every **d** for goodness
Heb 10: 5 and offering you did not **d**,
10: 8 and sin offerings you did not **d**,
13: 18 **d** to live honorably in every way.
Jas 1: 14 dragged away by their own evil **d**
1: 15 after **d** has conceived, it gives birth
4: 2 You **d** but do not have, so you kill.
2Pe 2: 10 of those who follow the corrupt **d**

DESIRED (DESIRE)
Ps 51: 6 Yet you **d** faithfulness even
Hag 2: 7 what is **d** by all nations will come,
Lk 22: 15 them, "I have eagerly **d** to eat this

DESIRES* (DESIRE)
Ge 4: 7 it **d** to have you, but you must rule
41: 16 will give Pharaoh the answer he **d**."
2Sa 3: 21 rule over all that your heart **d**."
14: 14 But that is not what God **d**;
1Ki 11: 37 will rule over all that your heart **d**;
1Ch 29: 18 keep these **d** and thoughts
Job 17: 11 Yet the **d** of my heart
31: 16 "If I have denied the **d** of the poor
Ps 34: 12 life and **d** to see many good days,
37: 4 will give you the **d** of your heart.
103: 5 who satisfies your **d** with good
140: 8 Do not grant the wicked their **d**,
145: 16 satisfy the **d** of every living thing.
145: 19 He fulfills the **d** of those who fear
Pr 11: 6 the unfaithful are trapped by evil **d**.
13: 4 but the **d** of the diligent are fully
19: 22 What a person **d** is unfailing love;
SS 2: 7 arouse or awaken love until it so **d**.
3: 5 arouse or awaken love until it so **d**.
8: 4 arouse or awaken love until it so **d**.
Hab 2: 4 puffed up; his **d** are not upright—
Mk 4: 19 and the **d** for other things come
Jn 8: 44 want to carry out your father's **d**.
Ro 1: 24 over in the sinful **d** of their hearts
6: 12 body so that you obey its evil **d**.
8: 5 their minds set on what the flesh **d**;
8: 5 minds set on what the Spirit **d**.
13: 14 how to gratify the **d** of the flesh.
Gal 5: 16 and you will not gratify the **d**
5: 17 For the flesh **d** what is contrary
5: 24 the flesh with its passions and **d**.
Eph 2: 3 and following its **d** and thoughts.
4: 22 being corrupted by its deceitful **d**;
Col 3: 5 lust, evil **d** and greed, which is
1Ti 3: 1 to be an overseer **d** a noble task.
5: 11 when their sensual **d** overcome
6: 9 harmful **d** that plunge people
2Ti 2: 22 Flee the evil **d** of youth and pursue
3: 6 are swayed by all kinds of evil **d**,
4: 3 to suit their own **d**, they will gather
Jas 1: 20 the righteousness that God **d**.
4: 1 from your **d** that battle within you?
1Pe 1: 14 do not conform to the evil **d** you
2: 11 to abstain from sinful **d**,
4: 2 their earthly lives for evil human **d**,
2Pe 1: 4 in the world caused by evil **d**.
2: 18 to the lustful **d** of the flesh,
3: 3 and following their own evil **d**.
1Jn 2: 17 The world and its **d** pass away,
Jude : 16 they follow their own evil **d**;
: 18 will follow their own ungodly **d**."

DESOLATE (DESOLATION)
Isa 54: 1 the children of the **d** woman than
Gal 4: 27 the children of the **d** woman than

DESOLATION (DESOLATE)
Da 11: 31 up the abomination that causes **d**.
12: 11 abomination that causes **d** is set
Mt 24: 15 'the abomination that causes **d**,'

DESPAIR (DESPAIRED)
Isa 61: 3 of praise instead of a spirit of **d**.
2Co 4: 8 perplexed, but not in **d**;

DESPAIRED* (DESPAIR)
2Co 1: 8 to endure, so that we **d** of life itself.

DESPERATE*
2Sa 12: 18 He may do something **d**."
Job 6: 26 say, and treat my **d** words as wind?
Ps 60: 3 have shown your people **d** times;
79: 8 to meet us, for we are in **d** need.
142: 6 to my cry, for I am in **d** need;

DESPISE (DESPISED DESPISES)
2Sa 12: 9 Why did you **d** the word
Job 5: 17 so do not **d** the discipline
42: 6 Therefore I **d** myself and repent
Ps 51: 17 contrite heart you, God, will not **d**.
102: 17 he will not **d** their plea.
Pr 1: 7 fools **d** wisdom and instruction.
3: 11 do not **d** the LORD's discipline,
6: 30 People do not **d** a thief if he steals
14: 21 It is a sin to **d** one's neighbor,
15: 32 disregard discipline **d** themselves,
23: 22 do not **d** your mother when she is
Jer 14: 21 the sake of your name do not **d** us;
Am 5: 21 "I hate, I **d** your religious festivals;
Zec 4: 10 "Who dares **d** the day of small
Mt 6: 24 devoted to the one and **d** the other.
18: 10 do not **d** one of these little ones.
Lk 16: 13 devoted to the one and **d** the other.
1Co 11: 22 Or do you **d** the church of God
Titus 2: 15 Do not let anyone **d** you.
2Pe 2: 10 desire of the flesh and **d** authority.

DESPISED (DESPISE)
Ge 25: 34 and left. So Esau **d** his birthright.
Ps 22: 6 by everyone, **d** by the people.
Pr 12: 8 and one with a warped mind is **d**.
Isa 53: 3 He was **d** and rejected by mankind,
1Co 1: 28 of this world and the **d** things—

DESPISES (DESPISE)
Job 36: 5 "God is mighty, but **d** no one;
Pr 15: 20 but a foolish man **d** his mother.

DESTINED (DESTINY)
Lk 2: 34 "This child is **d** to cause the falling
1Co 2: 7 God **d** for our glory before time
Col 2: 22 things that are all **d** to perish
1Th 3: 3 quite well that we are **d** for them.
Heb 9: 27 Just as people are **d** to die once,
1Pe 2: 8 which is also what they were **d** for.

DESTINY* (DESTINED PREDESTINED)
Job 8: 13 Such is the **d** of all who forget God;
Ps 73: 17 then I understood their final **d**.
Ecc 7: 2 for death is the **d** of everyone;
9: 2 All share a common **d**—
9: 3 The same **d** overtakes all.
Isa 65: 11 and fill bowls of mixed wine for **D**,
Php 3: 19 Their **d** is destruction, their god is

DESTITUTE
Ps 102: 17 will respond to the prayer of the **d**;
Pr 31: 8 for the rights of all who are **d**.
Heb 11: 37 in sheepskins and goatskins, **d**,

DESTROY (DESTROYED DESTROYING DESTROYS DESTRUCTION DESTRUCTIVE)
Ge 6: 17 to **d** all life under the heavens,
9: 11 will there be a flood to **d** the earth."
Pr 1: 32 complacency of fools will **d** them;
11: 9 the godless **d** their neighbors,
Mt 10: 28 of the One who can **d** both soul
Mk 14: 58 say, 'I will **d** this temple made
Lk 4: 34 Have you come to **d** us?
Jn 10: 10 comes only to steal and kill and **d**;
Ac 8: 3 But Saul began to **d** the church.
Rev 11: 18 destroying those who **d** the earth."

DESTROYED (DESTROY)
Dt 8: 19 you today that you will surely be **d**.
Job 19: 26 And after my skin has been **d**,
Pr 6: 15 he will suddenly be **d**—
11: 3 but the unfaithful are **d** by their
29: 1 many rebukes will suddenly be **d**—
Da 2: 44 up a kingdom that will never be **d**,
6: 26 his kingdom will not be **d**,
1Co 8: 11 died, is **d** by your knowledge.
15: 24 Father after he has **d** all dominion,
15: 26 The last enemy to be **d** is death.
2Co 4: 9 struck down, but not **d**.
5: 1 if the earthly tent we live in is **d**,
Gal 5: 15 out or you will be **d** by each other.
Eph 2: 14 groups one and has **d** the barrier,
2Ti 1: 10 who has **d** death and has brought
Heb 10: 39 those who shrink back and are **d**,
2Pe 2: 12 born only to be caught and **d**,
3: 10 the elements will be **d** by fire,
3: 11 Since everything will be **d** in this
Jude : 5 later **d** those who did not believe.
: 11 they have been **d** in Korah's

DESTROYING (DESTROY)
Jer 23: 1 "Woe to the shepherds who are **d**

DESTROYS (DESTROY)
Pr 6: 32 whoever does so **d** himself.
18: 9 his work is brother to one who **d**.
28: 24 wrong," is partner to one who **d**.
Ecc 9: 18 war, but one sinner **d** much good.
1Co 3: 17 If anyone **d** God's temple, God will

DESTRUCTION (DESTROY)
Nu 32: 15 you will be the cause of their **d**."
Ps 1: 6 the way of the wicked leads to **d**.
Pr 16: 18 Pride goes before **d**, a haughty
17: 19 builds a high gate invites **d**.
24: 22 for those two will send sudden **d**
Hos 13: 14 Where, O grave, is your **d**?
Mt 7: 13 broad is the road that leads to **d**,
Lk 6: 49 collapsed and its **d** was complete."
Jn 17: 12 lost except the one doomed to **d** so
Ro 9: 22 of his wrath—prepared for **d**?
1Co 5: 5 over to Satan for the **d** of the flesh,
Gal 6: 8 flesh, from the flesh will reap **d**;
Php 3: 19 Their destiny is **d**, their god is their
1Th 5: 3 **d** will come on them suddenly,
2Th 1: 9 will be punished with everlasting **d**
2: 3 is revealed, the man doomed to **d**.
1Ti 6: 9 that plunge people into ruin and **d**.
2Pe 2: 1 bringing swift **d** on themselves.
2: 3 and their **d** has not been sleeping.
3: 7 of judgment and **d** of the ungodly.
3: 12 bring about the **d** of the heavens
3: 16 other Scriptures, to their own **d**.
Rev 17: 8 up out of the Abyss and go to its **d**.
17: 11 to the seven and is going to his **d**.

DESTRUCTIVE (DESTROY)
2Pe 2: 1 will secretly introduce **d** heresies,

DETERMINED (DETERMINES)
Job 14: 5 A person's days are **d**;
Isa 14: 26 This is the plan **d** for the whole
Da 11: 36 what has been **d** must take place.

DETERMINES* (DETERMINED)
Ps 147: 4 He **d** the number of the stars
1Co 12: 11 them to each one, just as he **d**.

DETEST (DETESTABLE DETESTED DETESTS)
Dt 7: 26 Regard it as vile and utterly **d** it,
Ps 119:163 I hate and **d** falsehood
Pr 8: 7 is true, for my lips **d** wickedness.
13: 19 soul, but fools **d** turning from evil.
16: 12 Kings **d** wrongdoing, for a throne
24: 9 are sin, and people **d** a mocker.
29: 27 The righteous **d** the dishonest;
29: 27 the wicked **d** the upright.
Am 5: 10 and **d** the one who tells the truth.

DETESTABLE (DETEST)
Pr 6: 16 hates, seven that are **d** to him:
21: 27 The sacrifice of the wicked is **d**—
28: 9 even their prayers are **d**.
Isa 1: 13 Your incense is **d** to me.
41: 24 whoever chooses you is **d**.
44: 19 Shall I make a **d** thing from what is
Jer 44: 4 'Do not do this **d** thing that I hate!'
Eze 8: 13 doing things that are even more **d**."

Lk 16: 15 What people value highly is **d**
Titus 1: 16 They are **d**, disobedient and unfit
1Pe 4: 3 orgies, carousing and **d** idolatry.

DETESTED* (DETEST)
Zec 11: 8 The flock **d** me, and I grew weary

DETESTS* (DETEST)
Dt 22: 5 the LORD your God **d** anyone who
23: 18 the LORD your God **d** them both.
25: 16 the LORD your God **d** anyone who
Pr 3: 32 For the LORD **d** the perverse
11: 1 The LORD **d** dishonest scales,
11: 20 The LORD **d** those whose hearts
12: 22 The LORD **d** lying lips, but he
15: 8 The LORD **d** the sacrifice
15: 9 The LORD **d** the way
15: 26 The LORD **d** the thoughts
16: 5 The LORD **d** all the proud
17: 15 the LORD **d** them both.
20: 10 the LORD **d** them both.
20: 23 The LORD **d** differing weights,

DEVIATE*
2Ch 8: 15 They did not **d** from the king's

DEVICES
Ps 81: 12 hearts to follow their own **d**.

DEVIL* (DEVIL'S)
Mt 4: 1 wilderness to be tempted by the **d**.
4: 5 the **d** took him to the holy city
4: 8 the **d** took him to a very high
4: 11 Then the **d** left him, and angels
13: 39 the enemy who sows them is the **d**.
25: 41 the eternal fire prepared for the **d**
Lk 4: 2 forty days he was tempted by the **d**.
4: 3 The **d** said to him, "If you are
4: 5 The **d** led him up to a high place
4: 9 The **d** led him to Jerusalem and
4: 13 **d** had finished all this tempting,
8: 12 then the **d** comes and takes away
Jn 6: 70 Yet one of you is a **d**!"
8: 44 the **d**, and you want to carry
13: 2 the **d** had already prompted Judas,
Ac 10: 38 were under the power of the **d**,
13: 10 "You are a child of the **d**
Eph 4: 27 and do not give the **d** a foothold.
1Ti 3: 6 under the same judgment as the **d**.
2Ti 2: 26 and escape from the trap of the **d**,
Heb 2: 14 power of death—that is, the **d**—
Jas 4: 7 Resist the **d**, and he will flee
1Pe 5: 8 Your enemy the **d** prowls around
1Jn 3: 8 does what is sinful is of the **d**,
3: 8 because the **d** has been sinning
3: 10 and who the children of the **d** are:
Jude : 9 disputing with the **d** about the
Rev 2: 10 **d** will put some of you in prison
12: 9 that ancient serpent called the **d**,
12: 12 sea, because the **d** has gone down
20: 2 serpent, who is the **d**, or Satan,
20: 10 And the **d**, who deceived them,

DEVIL'S* (DEVIL)
Eph 6: 11 your stand against the **d** schemes.
1Ti 3: 7 into disgrace and into the **d** trap.
1Jn 3: 8 was to destroy the **d** work.

DEVIOUS*
2Sa 22: 27 to the **d** you show yourself shrewd.
Ps 18: 26 to the **d** you show yourself shrewd.
Pr 2: 15 and who are **d** in their ways.
14: 2 who despise him are **d** in their
21: 8 The way of the guilty is **d**,

DEVISED
2Pe 1: 16 we did not follow cleverly **d** stories

DEVOTE* (DEVOTED DEVOTING DEVOTION DEVOUT)
1Ch 22: 19 Now **d** your heart and soul
2Ch 31: 4 Levites so they could **d** themselves
Job 11: 13 "Yet if you **d** your heart to him
Jer 30: 21 who is he who will **d** himself to be
Mic 4: 13 You will **d** their ill-gotten gains
1Co 7: 5 you may **d** yourselves to prayer.
Col 4: 2 **D** yourselves to prayer,
1Ti 1: 4 or to **d** themselves to myths
4: 13 **d** yourself to the public reading
Titus 3: 8 may be careful to **d** themselves
3: 14 people must learn to **d** themselves

DEVOTED (DEVOTE)
1Ki 11: 4 and his heart was not fully **d**
Ezr 7: 10 For Ezra had **d** himself to the study
Mt 6: 24 or you will be **d** to the one
Mk 7: 11 is Corban (that is, **d** to God)—
Ac 2: 42 They **d** themselves to the apostles'
18: 5 Paul **d** himself exclusively
Ro 12: 10 Be **d** to one another in love.
1Co 7: 34 Her aim is to be **d** to the Lord
16: 15 and they have **d** themselves
2Co 7: 12 for yourselves how **d** to us you are.

DEVOTING* (DEVOTE)
1Ti 5: 10 **d** herself to all kinds of good deeds.

DEVOTION* (DEVOTE)
2Ki 20: 3 with wholehearted **d** and have
1Ch 28: 9 serve him with wholehearted **d**
29: 3 in my **d** to the temple of my God I
29: 19 son Solomon the wholehearted **d**
2Ch 32: 32 acts of **d** are written in the vision
35: 26 and his acts of **d** in accordance
Job 15: 4 piety and hinder **d** to God.
Isa 38: 3 wholehearted **d** and have done
Jer 2: 2 "'I remember the **d** of your
1Co 7: 35 way in undivided **d** to the Lord.
2Co 11: 3 your sincere and pure **d** to Christ.

DEVOUR (DEVOURED DEVOURS)
2Sa 2: 26 to Joab, "Must the sword **d** forever?
Mk 12: 40 They **d** widows' houses
Gal 5: 15 If you bite and **d** each other,
1Pe 5: 8 lion looking for someone to **d**.

DEVOURED (DEVOUR)
Jer 30: 16 all who devour you will be **d**;

DEVOURS (DEVOUR)
2Sa 11: 25 the sword **d** one as well as another.

DEVOUT* (DEVOTE)
1Ki 18: 3 (Obadiah was a **d** believer
Isa 57: 1 the **d** are taken away, and no one
Lk 2: 25 Simeon, who was righteous and **d**.
Ac 10: 2 He and all his family were **d**
10: 7 and a **d** soldier who was one of his
13: 43 **d** converts to Judaism followed
22: 12 He was a **d** observer of the law

DEW
Jdg 6: 37 If there is **d** only on the fleece

DICTATED
Jer 36: 4 while Jeremiah **d** all the words

DIE (DEAD DEATH DIED DIES DYING)
Ge 2: 17 eat from it you will certainly **d**."
3: 3 must not touch it, or you will **d**.'"
3: 4 "You will not certainly **d**,"
Ex 11: 5 Every firstborn son in Egypt will **d**,
Ru 1: 17 Where you **d** I will **d**, and there I
2Ki 14: 6 each will **d** for their own sin."
Job 2: 9 Curse God and **d**!"
Pr 5: 23 For lack of discipline they will **d**,
10: 21 many, but fools **d** for lack of sense.
11: 7 placed in mortals **d** with them;
15: 10 one who hates correction will **d**.
23: 13 them with the rod, they will not **d**.
Ecc 3: 2 a time to be born and a time to **d**,
Isa 22: 13 you say, "for tomorrow we **d**!"
66: 24 the worms that eat them will not **d**,
Jer 31: 30 everyone will **d** for their own sin;
Eze 3: 18 wicked person will **d** for their sin,
3: 19 ways, they will **d** for their sin;
3: 20 them, they will **d** for their sin.
18: 4 one who sins is the one who will **d**.
18: 20 who sins is the one who will **d**.
18: 31 Why will you **d**, people of Israel?
33: 8 wicked person will **d** for their sin,
Mt 26: 52 all who draw the sword will **d**
Mk 9: 48 worms that eat them do not **d**,
Jn 8: 21 for me, and you will **d** in your sin.
11: 25 will live, even though they **d**;
11: 26 by believing in me will never **d**.
Ro 5: 7 Very rarely will anyone **d**
14: 8 if we **d**, we **d** for the Lord.
1Co 15: 22 For as in Adam all **d**, so in Christ
15: 32 eat and drink, for tomorrow we **d**."
Php 1: 21 to live is Christ and to **d** is gain.
Heb 9: 27 as people are destined to **d** once,
1Pe 2: 24 so that we might **d** to sins and live
Rev 14: 13 Blessed are the dead who **d**

DIED (DIE)
1Ki 16: 18 palace on fire around him. So he **d**,
1Ch 1: 51 Hadad also **d**. The chiefs of Edom
10: 13 Saul **d** because he was unfaithful
Lk 16: 22 rich man also **d** and was buried.
Ro 5: 6 Christ **d** for the ungodly.
5: 8 were still sinners, Christ **d** for us.
6: 2 We are those who have **d** to sin;
6: 7 anyone who has **d** has been set free
6: 8 Now if we **d** with Christ, we believe
6: 10 The death he **d**, he **d** to sin once
14: 9 Christ **d** and returned to life so
14: 15 someone for whom Christ **d**.
1Co 8: 11 for whom Christ **d**, is destroyed
15: 3 that Christ **d** for our sins according
2Co 5: 14 we are convinced that one **d** for all, and therefore all **d**.
5: 15 he **d** for all, that those who live
Col 2: 20 Since you **d** with Christ
3: 3 For you **d**, and your life is now
1Th 4: 14 we believe that Jesus **d** and rose
5: 10 He **d** for us so that, whether we are
2Ti 2: 11 If we **d** with him, we will also live
Heb 9: 15 that he has **d** as a ransom to set
9: 17 force only when somebody has **d**;
Rev 2: 8 Last, who **d** and came to life again.

DIES (DIE)
Job 14: 14 If someone **d**, will they live again?
Pr 26: 20 without a gossip a quarrel **d** down.
Jn 12: 24 But if it **d**, it produces many seeds.
Ro 7: 2 if her husband **d**, she is released
14: 7 none of us **d** for ourselves alone.
1Co 7: 39 But if her husband **d**, she is free
15: 36 does not come to life unless it **d**.

DIFFERENCE* (DIFFERENT)
2Sa 19: 35 Can I tell the **d** between what is
2Ch 12: 8 learn the **d** between serving me
Eze 22: 26 there is no **d** between the unclean
44: 23 my people the **d** between the holy
Ro 3: 22 There is no **d** between Jew
10: 12 For there is no **d** between Jew
Gal 2: 6 whatever they were makes no **d**

DIFFERENCES* (DIFFERENT)
1Co 11: 19 there have to be **d** among you

DIFFERENT* (DIFFERENCE DIFFERENCES DIFFERING DIFFERS)
Lev 19: 19 "'Do not mate **d** kinds
Nu 14: 24 my servant Caleb has a **d** spirit
1Sa 10: 6 will be changed into a **d** person.
Est 1: 7 of gold, each one **d** from the other,
3: 8 Their customs are **d** from those
Eze 15: 2 how is the wood of a vine **d**
Da 7: 3 beasts, each **d** from the others,
7: 7 It was **d** from all the former beasts,
7: 19 which was **d** from all the others
7: 23 It will be **d** from all the other
7: 24 will arise, **d** from the earlier ones;
11: 29 this time the outcome will be **d**
Mk 16: 12 *Jesus appeared in a d form*
Ro 12: 6 We have **d** gifts,
1Co 4: 7 makes you **d** from anyone else?
12: 4 There are **d** kinds of gifts,
12: 5 There are **d** kinds of service,
12: 6 There are **d** kinds of working,
12: 10 to another speaking in **d** kinds
12: 28 and of **d** kinds of tongues.
2Co 11: 4 receive a **d** spirit from the Spirit
11: 4 or a **d** gospel from the one you
Gal 1: 6 and are turning to a **d** gospel—
4: 1 underage, he is no **d** from a slave,
Heb 7: 13 are said belonged to a **d** tribe,
Jas 2: 25 and sent them off in a **d** direction?

DIFFERING* (DIFFERENT)
Dt 25: 13 Do not have two **d** weights in your
25: 14 Do not have two **d** measures in
Pr 20: 10 **D** weights and **d** measures—
20: 23 The LORD detests **d** weights,

DIFFERS* (DIFFERENT)
1Co 15: 41 and star **d** from star in splendor.

DIFFICULT (DIFFICULTIES)
Ex 18: 22 but have them bring every **d** case
Dt 30: 11 commanding you today is not too **d**
2Ki 2: 10 "You have asked a **d** thing,"
Ac 15: 19 that we should not make it **d**

DIFFICULTIES* (DIFFICULT)
2Co 12: 10 in hardships, in persecutions, in **d**.

DIGNITY
Pr 31: 25 She is clothed with strength and **d**;

DIGS
Pr 26: 27 Whoever **d** a pit will fall into it;

DILIGENCE (DILIGENT)
Ezr 5: 8 work is being carried on with **d**
Heb 6: 11 show this same **d** to the very end,

DILIGENT* (DILIGENCE)
2Ch 24: 13 men in charge of the work were **d**,
Pr 10: 4 poverty, but **d** hands bring wealth.
12: 24 **D** hands will rule, but laziness ends
12: 27 **d** feed on the riches of the hunt.
13: 4 desires of the **d** are fully satisfied.
21: 5 The plans of the **d** lead to profit as
1Ti 4: 15 Be **d** in these matters;

DINAH*
Only daughter of Jacob, by Leah (Ge 30:21; 46:15). Raped by Shechem; avenged by Simeon and Levi (Ge 34).

DINE
Pr 23: 1 When you sit to **d** with a ruler,

DIOTREPHES*
3Jn : 9 but **D**, who loves to be first,

DIRECT (DIRECTED DIRECTIVES DIRECTS)
Ge 18: 19 so that he will **d** his children and
Ps 119: 35 **D** me in the path of your
119:133 **D** my footsteps according to your
Jer 10: 23 it is not for them to **d** their steps.
2Th 3: 5 May the Lord **d** your hearts
1Ti 5: 17 The elders who **d** the affairs

DIRECTED (DIRECT)
Ge 24: 51 master's son, as the LORD has **d**."
Nu 16: 40 as the LORD **d** him through
Dt 2: 1 Red Sea, as the LORD had **d** me.
6: 1 laws the LORD your God **d** me
Jos 11: 9 did to them as the LORD had **d**:
11: 23 just as the LORD had **d** Moses,
Pr 20: 24 A person's steps are **d**
Jer 13: 2 as the LORD **d**, and put it around
Ac 7: 44 It had been made as God **d** Moses,
Titus 1: 5 elders in every town, as I **d** you.

DIRECTIVES* (DIRECT)
1Co 11: 17 In the following **d** I have no praise

DIRECTS* (DIRECT)
Ps 42: 8 By day the LORD **d** his love,
Isa 48: 17 who **d** you in the way you should

DIRGE*
Mt 11: 17 we sang a **d**, and you did not
Lk 7: 32 we sang a **d**, and you did not cry.'

DISABLED*
2Sa 4: 4 to leave, he fell and became **d**.
Jn 5: 3 a great number of **d** people used
Heb 12: 13 so that the lame may not be **d**,

DISAGREEMENT*
Ac 15: 39 They had such a sharp **d** that they

DISAPPEAR (DISAPPEARED DISAPPEARS)
Mt 5: 18 until heaven and earth **d**,
5: 18 by any means **d** from the Law until
Lk 16: 17 earth to **d** than for the least stroke
Heb 8: 13 obsolete and outdated will soon **d**.
2Pe 3: 10 The heavens will **d** with a roar;

DISAPPEARED (DISAPPEAR)
1Ki 20: 40 busy here and there, the man **d**."

DISAPPEARS (DISAPPEAR)
1Co 13: 10 comes, what is in part **d**.

DISAPPROVE*
Pr 24: 18 the LORD will see and **d** and turn

DISARMED*
Col 2: 15 And having **d** the powers

DISASTER
Ex 32: 12 and do not bring **d** on your people.
Ps 57: 1 your wings until the **d** has passed.
Pr 1: 26 turn will laugh when **d** strikes you;
3: 25 Have no fear of sudden **d**
6: 15 Therefore **d** will overtake him
16: 4 even the wicked for a day of **d**.
17: 5 whoever gloats over **d** will not go
27: 10 house when **d** strikes you—
Isa 45: 7 I bring prosperity and create **d**;
Jer 17: 17 you are my refuge in the day of **d**.
Eze 7: 5 Unheard-of **d**! See, it comes!

DISCERN (DISCERNED DISCERNING DISCERNMENT)
Ps 19: 12 But who can **d** their own errors?
139: 3 You **d** my going out and my lying
Php 1: 10 you may be able to **d** what is best

DISCERNED* (DISCERN)
1Co 2: 14 because they are **d** only through

DISCERNING (DISCERN)
1Ki 3: 9 So give your servant a **d** heart
3: 12 I will give you a wise and **d** heart,
Pr 1: 5 and let the **d** get guidance—
8: 9 To the **d** all of them are right;
10: 13 is found on the lips of the **d**,
14: 6 knowledge comes easily to the **d**.
14: 33 reposes in the heart of the **d**
15: 14 The **d** heart seeks knowledge,
16: 21 The wise in heart are called **d**,
17: 10 A rebuke impresses a **d** person
17: 24 A **d** person keeps wisdom in view,
17: 28 and **d** if they hold their tongues.
18: 15 heart of the **d** acquires knowledge,
19: 25 rebuke the **d**, and they will gain
28: 7 A **d** son heeds instruction,
28: 11 and **d** sees how deluded they are.
1Co 11: 31 if we were more **d** with regard

DISCERNMENT (DISCERN)
Ps 119:125 give me **d** that I may understand

DISCHARGED (DISCHARGING)
Ecc 8: 8 As no one is **d** in time of war,

DISCHARGING* (DISCHARGED)
1Co 9: 17 I am simply **d** the trust committed

DISCIPLE (DISCIPLES DISCIPLES')
Mt 10: 42 of these little ones who is my **d**,
Mt 13: 52 of the law who has become a **d**
Lk 14: 26 such a person cannot be my **d**.
14: 27 and follow me cannot be my **d**.
Jn 13: 23 of them, the **d** whom Jesus loved,
19: 26 and the **d** whom he loved standing
21: 7 the **d** whom Jesus loved said
21: 20 that the **d** whom Jesus loved was

DISCIPLES (DISCIPLE)
Mt 10: 1 Jesus called his twelve **d** to him
26: 56 Then all the **d** deserted him
28: 19 go and make **d** of all nations,
Mk 3: 7 withdrew with his **d** to the lake,
16: 20 *Then the **d** went out and*
Lk 6: 13 he called his **d** to him and chose
14: 33 you have cannot be my **d**.
Jn 2: 11 and his **d** believed in him.
6: 66 time many of his **d** turned back
8: 31 my teaching, you are really my **d**.
12: 16 At first his **d** did not understand all
13: 35 will know that you are my **d**, if you
15: 8 showing yourselves to be my **d**.
20: 20 The **d** were overjoyed when they
Ac 6: 1 the number of **d** was increasing,
11: 26 The **d** were called Christians first
14: 22 strengthening the **d** and
18: 23 Phrygia, strengthening all the **d**.

DISCIPLES'* (DISCIPLE)
Jn 13: 5 basin and began to wash his **d** feet,

DISCIPLINE* (DISCIPLINED DISCIPLINES SELF-DISCIPLINE)
Dt 4: 36 made you hear his voice to **d** you.
11: 2 experienced the **d** of the LORD
21: 18 listen to them when they **d** him,
Job 5: 17 so do not despise the **d**
Ps 6: 1 your anger or **d** me in your wrath.
38: 1 your anger or **d** me in your wrath.
39: 11 rebuke and **d** anyone for their sin,
94: 12 Blessed is the one you **d**, LORD,
Pr 3: 11 do not despise the LORD's **d**,
5: 12 You will say, "How I hated **d**!
5: 23 For lack of **d** they will die,
10: 17 Whoever heeds **d** shows the way
12: 1 Whoever loves **d** loves knowledge,
13: 18 Whoever disregards **d** comes
13: 24 their children is careful to **d** them.
15: 5 A fool spurns a parent's **d**,
15: 10 Stern **d** awaits anyone who leaves
Pr 15: 32 disregard **d** despise themselves,
19: 18 **D** your children, for in that there is
19: 20 Listen to advice and accept **d**,
22: 15 the rod of **d** will drive it far away.
23: 13 Do not withhold **d** from a child;
29: 17 **D** your children, and they will give
Jer 10: 24 **D** me, LORD, but only in due
17: 23 would not listen or respond to **d**.
30: 11 I will **d** you but only in due
32: 33 would not listen or respond to **d**.
46: 28 I will **d** you but only in due
Hos 5: 2 I will **d** all of them.
1Co 4: 21 Shall I come to you with a rod of **d**,
Heb 12: 5 do not make light of the Lord's **d**,
12: 7 Endure hardship as **d**;
12: 8 and everyone undergoes **d**—
12: 11 No **d** seems pleasant at the time,
Rev 3: 19 Those whom I love I rebuke and **d**.

DISCIPLINED* (DISCIPLINE)
Isa 26: 16 when you **d** them, they could
Jer 31: 18 'You **d** me like an unruly calf, and I have been **d**.
1Co 11: 32 we are being **d** so that we will not
Col 2: 5 delight to see how **d** you are
Titus 1: 8 upright, holy and **d**.
Heb 12: 7 For what children are not **d** by
12: 8 If you are not **d**—
12: 9 all had human fathers who **d** us
12: 10 They **d** us for a little while as they

DISCIPLINES* (DISCIPLINE)
Dt 8: 5 as a man **d** his son, so the LORD your God **d** you.
Ps 94: 10 Does he who **d** nations not punish?
Pr 3: 12 because the LORD **d** those he
Heb 12: 6 the Lord **d** the one he loves,
12: 10 God **d** us for our good, in order

DISCLOSED
Lk 8: 17 nothing hidden that will not be **d**,
Col 1: 26 but is now **d** to the Lord's people.
Heb 9: 8 had not yet been **d** as long as

DISCORD
Gal 5: 20 hatred, **d**, jealousy, fits of rage,

DISCOURAGED* (DISCOURAGEMENT)
Nu 32: 9 they **d** the Israelites from entering
Dt 1: 21 Do not be afraid; do not be **d**."
31: 8 Do not be afraid; do not be **d**."
Jos 1: 9 do not be **d**, for the LORD your
8: 1 "Do not be afraid; do not be **d**.
10: 25 "Do not be afraid; do not be **d**.
1Ch 22: 13 Do not be afraid or **d**.
28: 20 Do not be afraid or **d**,
2Ch 20: 15 or **d** because of this vast army.
20: 17 Do not be afraid; do not be **d**.
32: 7 or **d** because of the king of Assyria
Job 4: 5 comes to you, and you are **d**;
Isa 42: 4 or be **d** till he establishes justice
Eph 3: 13 not to be **d** because of my
Col 3: 21 children, or they will become **d**.

DISCOURAGEMENT* (DISCOURAGED)
Ex 6: 9 not listen to him because of their **d**

DISCOVERED
2Ki 23: 24 that Hilkiah the priest had **d**

DISCREDIT* (DISCREDITED)
Ne 6: 13 give me a bad name to **d** me.
Job 40: 8 "Would you **d** my justice?

DISCREDITED (DISCREDIT)
2Co 6: 3 so that our ministry will not be **d**.

DISCRETION*
1Ch 22: 12 May the LORD give you **d**
Pr 1: 4 knowledge and **d** to the young—
2: 11 **D** will protect you,
3: 21 preserve sound judgment and **d**;
5: 2 that you may maintain **d** and your
8: 12 I possess knowledge and **d**.
11: 22 beautiful woman who shows no **d**.

DISCRIMINATE* (DISCRIMINATED)
Ac 15: 9 He did not **d** between us and them,

DISCRIMINATED* (DISCRIMINATE)
Jas 2: 4 have you not **d** among yourselves

DISEASE (DISEASES)
Nu 12: 10 saw that she had a defiling skin **d**,
Mt 4: 23 healing every **d** and sickness

Mt 9: 35 and healing every **d** and sickness.
10: 1 and to heal every **d** and sickness.

DISEASES (DISEASE)
Ps 103: 3 all your sins and heals all your **d**,
Mt 8: 17 up our infirmities and bore our **d**."
Mk 3: 10 those with **d** were pushing forward
Lk 9: 1 drive out all demons and to cure **d**,

DISFIGURE* (DISFIGURED)
Mt 6: 16 they **d** their faces to show others

DISFIGURED (DISFIGURE)
Isa 52: 14 his appearance was so **d** beyond

DISGRACE (DISGRACEFUL DISGRACES)
Ps 44: 15 I live in **d** all day long, and my face
52: 1 who are a **d** in the eyes of God?
74: 21 not let the oppressed retreat in **d**;
Pr 6: 33 Blows and **d** are his lot, and his
11: 2 then comes **d**, but with humility
19: 26 is a child who brings shame and **d**.
Mt 1: 19 not want to expose her to public **d**,
Ac 5: 41 of suffering **d** for the Name.
1Co 11: 6 if it is a **d** for a woman to have her
11: 14 man has long hair, it is a **d** to him,
1Ti 3: 7 so that he will not fall into **d**
Heb 6: 6 and subjecting him to public **d**.
11: 26 regarded **d** for the sake of Christ
13: 13 the camp, bearing the **d** he bore.

DISGRACEFUL* (DISGRACE)
Pr 10: 5 sleeps during harvest is a **d** son.
12: 4 a **d** wife is like decay in his bones.
17: 2 servant will rule over a **d** son
Hos 4: 7 glorious God for something **d**.
1Co 14: 35 for it is **d** for a woman to speak

DISGRACES (DISGRACE)
Pr 28: 7 companion of gluttons **d** his father.
29: 15 left undisciplined **d** its mother.

DISGUISE
Pr 26: 24 Enemies **d** themselves with their

DISH
Pr 19: 24 sluggard buries his hand in the **d**;
Mt 23: 25 clean the outside of the cup and **d**,

DISHEARTENED
1Th 5: 14 encourage the **d**, help the weak,

DISHONEST*
Ex 18: 21 trustworthy men who hate **d** gain
Lev 19: 35 "'Do not use **d** standards
1Sa 8: 3 They turned aside after **d** gain
Pr 11: 1 The LORD detests **d** scales,
13: 11 **D** money dwindles away,
20: 23 and **d** scales do not please him.
29: 27 The righteous detest the **d**;
Jer 22: 17 your heart are set only on **d** gain,
Eze 28: 18 **d** trade you have desecrated your
Hos 12: 7 The merchant uses **d** scales
Am 8: 5 price and cheating with **d** scales,
Mic 6: 11 I acquit someone with **d** scales,
Lk 16: 8 commended the **d** manager
16: 10 whoever is **d** with very little will also be **d** with much.
1Ti 3: 8 wine, and not pursuing **d** gain.
Titus 1: 7 not violent, not pursuing **d** gain.
1: 11 and that for the sake of **d** gain.
1Pe 5: 2 not pursuing **d** gain, but eager

DISHONOR* (DISHONORED DISHONORS)
Lev 18: 7 "'Do not **d** your father by having
18: 8 that would **d** your father.
18: 10 that would **d** you.
18: 14 "'Do not **d** your father's brother
18: 16 that would **d** your brother.
20: 19 for that would **d** a close relative;
Dt 22: 30 he must not **d** his father's bed.
Pr 30: 9 and so **d** the name of my God.
Jer 14: 21 do not **d** your glorious throne.
20: 11 their **d** will never be forgotten.
La 2: 2 princes down to the ground in **d**.
Eze 22: 10 are those who **d** their father's bed;
Jn 8: 49 I honor my Father and you **d** me.
Ro 2: 23 do you **d** God by breaking the law?
1Co 13: 5 It does not **d** others, it is not
15: 43 it is sown in **d**, it is raised in glory;
2Co 6: 8 through glory and **d**, bad report

DISHONORED* (DISHONOR)
Lev 20: 11 his father's wife, he has **d** his father.
20: 17 He has **d** his sister and will be held
20: 20 with his aunt, he has **d** his uncle.
20: 21 of impurity; he has **d** his brother.
Dt 21: 14 her as a slave, since you have **d** her.
Ezr 4: 14 not proper for us to see the king **d**,
1Co 4: 10 You are honored, we are **d**!
Jas 2: 6 But you have **d** the poor. Is it not

DISHONORS* (DISHONOR)
Dt 27: 16 is anyone who **d** their father
27: 20 wife, for he **d** his father's bed."
Job 20: 3 I hear a rebuke that **d** me, and my
Mic 7: 6 For a son **d** his father, a daughter
1Co 11: 4 with his head covered **d** his head.
11: 5 her head uncovered **d** her head—

DISILLUSIONMENT*
Ps 7: 14 trouble and gives birth to **d**.

DISMAYED
Isa 41: 10 do not be **d**, for I am your God.

DISOBEDIENCE* (DISOBEY)
Jos 22: 22 in rebellion or **d** to the LORD,
Jer 43: 7 So they entered Egypt in **d**
Ro 5: 19 as through the **d** of the one man
11: 30 mercy as a result of their **d**,
11: 32 has bound everyone over to **d** so
2Co 10: 6 be ready to punish every act of **d**,
Heb 2: 2 and **d** received its just punishment,
4: 6 did not go in because of their **d**,
4: 11 by following their example of **d**.

DISOBEDIENT* (DISOBEY)
Ne 9: 26 they were **d** and rebelled against
Lk 1: 17 and the **d** to the wisdom
Ac 26: 19 I was not **d** to the vision
Ro 10: 21 I have held out my hands to a **d**
11: 30 at one time **d** to God have now
11: 31 so they too have now become **d**
Eph 2: 2 is now at work in those who are **d**.
5: 6 wrath comes on those who are **d**.
5: 12 to mention what the **d** do in secret.
2Ti 3: 2 proud, abusive, **d** to their parents,
Titus 1: 6 to the charge of being wild and **d**.
1: 16 **d** and unfit for doing anything
3: 3 At one time we too were foolish, **d**,
Heb 11: 31 not killed with those who were **d**.
1Pe 3: 20 to those who were **d** long ago

DISOBEY* (DISOBEDIENCE DISOBEDIENT DISOBEYED DISOBEYING DISOBEYS)
Dt 11: 28 the curse if you **d** the commands
2Ch 24: 20 'Why do you **d** the LORD's
Est 3: 3 "Why do you **d** the king's
Jer 42: 13 and so **d** the LORD your God,
Ro 1: 30 of doing evil; they **d** their parents;
1Pe 2: 8 because they **d** the message—

DISOBEYED* (DISOBEY)
Nu 14: 22 in the wilderness but who **d** me
27: 14 Zin, both of you **d** my command
Jdg 2: 2 Yet you have **d** me. Why have you
Ne 9: 29 arrogant and **d** your commands.
Isa 24: 5 they have **d** the laws,
Jer 43: 4 and all the people **d** the LORD's
Lk 15: 29 for you and never **d** your orders.
Heb 3: 18 enter his rest if not to those who **d**?

DISOBEYING* (DISOBEY)
Nu 14: 41 said, "Why are you **d** the LORD's

DISOBEYS* (DISOBEY)
Eze 33: 12 'If someone who is righteous **d**,

DISORDER*
Job 10: 22 of utter darkness and **d**, where
1Co 14: 33 For God is not a God of **d**
2Co 12: 20 slander, gossip, arrogance and **d**.
Jas 3: 16 there you find **d** and every evil

DISOWN (DISOWNS)
Pr 30: 9 I may have too much and **d** you
Mt 10: 33 will **d** before my Father in heaven.
26: 35 to die with you, I will never **d** you."
2Ti 2: 12 If we **d** him, he will also **d** us;

DISOWNS (DISOWN)
Lk 12: 9 whoever **d** me before others will be

DISPENSATION See ADMINISTRATION, TRUST

DISPLACES*
Pr 30: 23 and a servant who **d** her mistress.

DISPLAY (DISPLAYED DISPLAYS)
Ps 22: 17 All my bones are on **d**;
Eze 39: 21 "I will **d** my glory among
Ro 9: 17 that I might **d** my power in you
1Co 4: 9 God has put us apostles on **d**
1Ti 1: 16 Christ Jesus might **d** his immense

DISPLAYED (DISPLAY)
Jn 9: 3 works of God might be **d** in him.

DISPLAYS (DISPLAY)
Isa 44: 23 Jacob, he **d** his glory in Israel.
2Th 2: 9 He will use all sorts of **d** of power

DISPLEASE (DISPLEASED)
1Th 2: 15 They **d** God and are hostile

DISPLEASED (DISPLEASE)
2Sa 11: 27 thing David had done **d** the LORD.

DISPUTABLE* (DISPUTE)
Ro 14: 1 without quarreling over **d** matters.

DISPUTE (DISPUTABLE DISPUTES DISPUTING)
Pr 17: 14 the matter before a **d** breaks out.
1Co 6: 1 If any of you has a **d** with another,

DISPUTES (DISPUTE)
Pr 18: 18 Casting the lot settles **d** and keeps

DISPUTING (DISPUTE)
1Ti 2: 8 up holy hands without anger or **d**.

DISQUALIFY* (DISQUALIFIED)
Col 2: 18 and the worship of angels **d** you.

DISQUALIFIED* (DISQUALIFY)
1Co 9: 27 I myself will not be **d** for the prize.

DISREGARD (DISREGARDS)
Pr 15: 32 Those who **d** discipline despise

DISREGARDS* (DISREGARD)
Pr 13: 18 Whoever **d** discipline comes

DISREPUTE*
2Pe 2: 2 will bring the way of truth into **d**.

DISRUPTING*
Titus 1: 11 they are **d** whole households

DISSENSION* (DISSENSIONS)
Ro 13: 13 debauchery, not in **d** and jealousy.

DISSENSIONS* (DISSENSION)
Gal 5: 20 of rage, selfish ambition, **d**,

DISTINGUISH (DISTINGUISHING)
1Ki 3: 9 and to **d** between right and wrong.
Heb 5: 14 have trained themselves to **d** good

DISTINGUISHING
1Co 12: 10 to another **d** between spirits,

DISTORT
Ac 20: 30 **d** the truth in order to draw away
2Co 4: 2 nor do we **d** the word of God.
2Pe 3: 16 ignorant and unstable people **d**,

DISTRACTED*
Lk 10: 40 Martha was **d** by all the

DISTRESS (DISTRESSED)
2Ch 15: 4 in their **d** they turned to the LORD,
Ps 18: 6 In my **d** I called to the LORD;
81: 7 In your **d** you called and I rescued
86: 7 When I am in **d**, I call to you,
116: 3 I was overcome by **d** and sorrow.
120: 1 I call on the LORD in my **d**,
Jnh 2: 2 "In my **d** I called to the LORD,
Mt 24: 21 For then there will be great **d**,
Jas 1: 27 and widows in their **d** and to keep

DISTRESSED (DISTRESS)
Ro 14: 15 sister is **d** because of what you eat,

DIVIDE (DIVIDED DIVIDING DIVISION DIVISIONS DIVISIVE)
Ps 22: 18 They **d** my clothes among them

DIVIDED (DIVIDE)
Mt 12: 25 "Every kingdom **d** against itself
Lk 23: 34 **d** up his clothes by casting lots.
1Co 1: 13 Is Christ **d**? Was Paul crucified

DIVIDING (DIVIDE)
Eph 2: 14 the barrier, the **d** wall of hostility,
Heb 4: 12 it penetrates even to **d** soul

DIVINATION
Lev 19: 26 "'Do not practice **d** or seek

DIVINE
Ro 1: 20 his eternal power and **d** nature—
2Co 10: 4 they have **d** power to demolish
2Pe 1: 4 may participate in the **d** nature,

DIVISION (DIVIDE)
Lk 12: 51 on earth? No, I tell you, but **d**.
1Co 12: 25 there should be no **d** in the body,

DIVISIONS (DIVIDE)
Ro 16: 17 to watch out for those who cause **d**
1Co 1: 10 and that there be no **d** among you,
11: 18 as a church, there are **d** among you,

DIVISIVE* (DIVIDE)
Titus 3: 10 Warn a **d** person once,

DIVORCE* (DIVORCED DIVORCES)
Dt 22: 19 he must not **d** her as long as he
22: 29 He can never **d** her as long as he
24: 1 and he writes her a certificate of **d**,
24: 3 and writes her a certificate of **d**,
Isa 50: 1 is your mother's certificate of **d**
Jer 3: 8 faithless Israel her certificate of **d**
Mt 1: 19 he had in mind to **d** her quietly.
5: 31 must give her a certificate of **d**.'
19: 3 for a man to **d** his wife for any
19: 7 man give his wife a certificate of **d**
19: 8 **d** your wives because your hearts
Mk 10: 2 it lawful for a man to **d** his wife?"
10: 4 a man to write a certificate of **d**
1Co 7: 11 a husband must not **d** his wife.
7: 12 to live with him, he must not **d** her.
7: 13 live with her, she must not **d** him.

DIVORCED* (DIVORCE)
Lev 21: 7 or **d** from their husbands,
21: 14 not marry a widow, a **d** woman,
22: 13 daughter becomes a widow or is **d**,
Nu 30: 9 or **d** woman will be binding on her.
Dt 24: 4 then her first husband, who **d** her,
1Ch 8: 8 after he had **d** his wives Hushim
Eze 44: 22 not marry widows or **d** women;
Mt 5: 32 who marries a **d** woman commits
Lk 16: 18 who marries a **d** woman commits

DIVORCES* (DIVORCE)
Jer 3: 1 "If a man **d** his wife and she leaves
Mal 2: 16 man who hates and **d** his wife,"
Mt 5: 31 'Anyone who **d** his wife must give
5: 32 tell you that anyone who **d** his wife,
19: 9 tell you that anyone who **d** his wife,
Mk 10: 11 "Anyone who **d** his wife
10: 12 if she **d** her husband and marries
Lk 16: 18 "Anyone who **d** his wife

DOCTOR
Mt 9: 12 "It is not the healthy who need a **d**,
Col 4: 14 Our dear friend Luke, the **d**,

DOCTRINE* (DOCTRINES)
1Ti 1: 10 else is contrary to the sound **d**
4: 16 Watch your life and **d** closely.
2Ti 4: 3 will not put up with sound **d**.
Titus 1: 9 can encourage others by sound **d**
2: 1 what is appropriate to sound **d**.

DOCTRINES* (DOCTRINE)
1Ti 1: 3 not to teach false **d** any longer

DOEG*
Edomite; Saul's head shepherd; responsible for murder of priests at Nob (1Sa 21:7; 22:6–23; Ps 52).

DOG (DOGS)
Pr 26: 11 As a **d** returns to its vomit, so fools
Ecc 9: 4 even a live **d** is better off than
2Pe 2: 22 "A **d** returns to its vomit," and,

DOGS (DOG)
Mt 7: 6 "Do not give **d** what is sacred;
15: 26 bread and toss it to the **d**."

DOMINION
Job 25: 2 "**D** and awe belong to God;
Ps 22: 28 for **d** belongs to the LORD and he

DONKEY
Nu 22: 30 The **d** said to Balaam, "Am I not
Zec 9: 9 lowly and riding on a **d**, on a colt,
Mt 21: 5 gentle and riding on a **d**,
2Pe 2: 16 rebuked for his wrongdoing by a **d**

DOOR (DOORS)
Job 31: 32 for my **d** was always open
Ps 141: 3 keep watch over the **d** of my lips.
Mt 6: 6 close the **d** and pray to your Father,
7: 7 and the **d** will be opened to you.
Ac 14: 27 how he had opened a **d** of faith
1Co 16: 9 because a great **d** for effective work
2Co 2: 12 the Lord had opened a **d** for me,
Rev 3: 20 I stand at the **d** and knock.

DOORFRAMES
Dt 6: 9 Write them on the **d** of your

DOORKEEPER
Ps 84: 10 I would rather be a **d** in the house

DOORS (DOOR)
Ps 24: 7 ancient **d**, that the King of glory

DORCAS
Ac 9: 36 Tabitha (in Greek her name is **D**);

DOUBLE
2Ki 2: 9 "Let me inherit a **d** portion of your
1Ti 5: 17 church well are worthy of **d** honor,

DOUBLE-EDGED (EDGE)
Heb 4: 12 Sharper than any **d** sword,
Rev 1: 16 of his mouth was a sharp, **d** sword.
2: 12 of him who has the sharp, **d** sword.

DOUBLE-MINDED* (MIND)
Ps 119:113 I hate **d** people, but I love your law.
Jas 1: 8 Such a person is **d** and unstable
4: 8 and purify your hearts, you **d**.

DOUBT (DOUBTING DOUBTS)
Mt 14: 31 faith," he said, "why did you **d**?"
21: 21 if you have faith and do not **d**,
Mk 11: 23 and does not **d** in their heart
Jas 1: 6 you must believe and not **d**,
Jude : 22 Be merciful to those who **d**;

DOUBTING* (DOUBT)
Jn 20: 27 it into my side. Stop **d** and believe."

DOUBTS* (DOUBT)
Lk 24: 38 and why do **d** rise in your minds?
Ro 14: 23 whoever has **d** is condemned if
Jas 1: 6 because the one who **d** is like

DOVE (DOVES)
Ge 8: 8 he sent out a **d** to see if the water
Mt 3: 16 Spirit of God descending like a **d**

DOVES (DOVE)
Lev 12: 8 she is to bring two **d** or two young
Mt 10: 16 as snakes and as innocent as **d**.
Lk 2: 24 "a pair of **d** or two young pigeons."

DOWNCAST
Ps 42: 5 Why, my soul, are you **d**?
2Co 7: 6 who comforts the **d**, comforted us

DOWNFALL
Hos 14: 1 Your sins have been your **d**!

DRAGON
Rev 12: 7 and his angels fought against the **d**,
13: 2 The **d** gave the beast his power
20: 2 He seized the **d**, that ancient

DRAW (DRAWING DRAWS)
Mt 26: 52 "for all who **d** the sword will die
Jn 12: 32 earth, will **d** all people to myself."
Heb 10: 22 let us **d** near to God with a sincere

DRAWING (DRAW)
Lk 21: 28 your redemption is **d** near."

DRAWS (DRAW)
Jn 6: 44 the Father who sent me **d** them,

DREAD (DREADFUL)
Ps 53: 5 overwhelmed with **d**, where there was nothing to **d**.

DREADFUL (DREAD)
Mt 24: 19 How **d** it will be in those days
Heb 10: 31 It is a **d** thing to fall into the hands

DREAM
Joel 2: 28 your old men will **d** dreams,
Ac 2: 17 your old men will **d** dreams.

DRESS
1Ti 2: 9 want the women to **d** modestly,

DRIFT
Heb 2: 1 heard, so that we do not **d** away.

DRINK (DRINKING DRINKS DRUNK DRUNKARD DRUNKARD'S DRUNKARDS DRUNKENNESS)
Ex 29: 40 of a hin of wine as a **d** offering.
Nu 6: 3 from wine or other fermented **d**.
6: 3 They must not **d** grape juice or eat
Jdg 7: 5 from those who kneel down to **d**."
2Sa 23: 15 someone would get me a **d** of water
Pr 5: 15 **D** water from your own cistern,
Mt 20: 22 "Can you **d** the cup I am going to **d**?"
26: 27 saying, "**D** from it, all of you.
Mk 16: 18 *when they **d** deadly poison,*
Lk 12: 19 eat, **d** and be merry."'
Jn 7: 37 who is thirsty come to me and **d**.
18: 11 Shall I not **d** the cup the Father has
1Co 10: 4 and drank the same spiritual **d**;
12: 13 were all given the one Spirit to **d**.
Php 2: 17 like a **d** offering on the sacrifice
2Ti 4: 6 being poured out like a **d** offering,
Rev 14: 10 too, will **d** the wine of God's fury,

DRINKING (DRINK)
Ro 14: 17 is not a matter of eating and **d**,

DRINKS (DRINK)
Isa 5: 22 wine and champions at mixing **d**,
Jn 4: 13 "Everyone who **d** this water will be
6: 54 and **d** my blood has eternal life,
1Co 11: 27 bread or **d** the cup of the Lord

DRIPPING
Pr 19: 13 wife is like the constant **d** of a leaky
27: 15 A quarrelsome wife is like the **d**

DRIVE (DRIVES)
Ex 23: 30 little I will **d** them out before you,
Nu 33: 52 **d** out all the inhabitants of the land
Jos 13: 13 But the Israelites did not **d**
23: 13 LORD your God will no longer **d**
Pr 22: 10 **D** out the mocker, and out goes
Mt 10: 1 them authority to **d** out impure
Jn 6: 37 comes to me I will never **d** away.

DRIVES (DRIVE)
Mt 12: 26 If Satan **d** out Satan, he is divided
1Jn 4: 18 But perfect love **d** out fear,

DROP (DROPS)
Pr 17: 14 so **d** the matter before a dispute
Isa 40: 15 Surely the nations are like a **d**

DROPS (DROP)
Lk 22: 44 his sweat was like **d** of blood falling

DROSS
Ps 119:119 of the earth you discard like **d**;
Pr 25: 4 Remove the **d** from the silver,
26: 23 silver **d** on earthenware are fervent

DROUGHT
Jer 17: 8 It has no worries in a year of **d**

DROWNED
Ex 15: 4 Pharaoh's officers are **d** in the Red
Mt 18: 6 to be **d** in the depths of the sea.
Heb 11: 29 tried to do so, they were **d**.

DROWSINESS*
Pr 23: 21 poor, and **d** clothes them in rags.

DRUNK (DRINK)
1Sa 1: 13 Eli thought she was **d**
Ac 2: 15 These people are not **d**, as you
Eph 5: 18 Do not get **d** on wine, which leads

DRUNKARD (DRINK)
Mt 11: 19 'Here is a glutton and a **d**, a friend
1Co 5: 11 or slanderer, a **d** or swindler.

DRUNKARD'S* (DRINK)
Pr 26: 9 thornbush in a **d** hand is a proverb

DRUNKARDS (DRINK)
Pr 23: 21 for **d** and gluttons become poor,
1Co 6: 10 the greedy nor **d** nor slanderers

DRUNKENNESS (DRINK)
Lk 21: 34 **d** and the anxieties of life,
Ro 13: 13 in carousing and **d**, not in sexual
Gal 5: 21 and envy; **d**, orgies, and the like.
1Ti 3: 3 not given to **d**, not violent
1Pe 4: 3 living in debauchery, lust, **d**, orgies,

DRY
Ge 1: 9 place, and let **d** ground appear."
Ex 14: 16 go through the sea on **d** ground.
Jos 3: 17 the Jordan and stood on **d** ground,
Isa 53: 2 and like a root out of **d** ground.
Eze 37: 4 bones and say to them, '**D** bones,

DUE
Pr 3: 27 good from those to whom it is **d**,

DULL
Isa 6: 10 make their ears **d** and close their
2Co 3: 14 But their minds were made **d**,

DUST
Ge 2: 7 a man from the **d** of the ground
3: 19 for **d** you are and to **d** you will
Job 42: 6 myself and repent in **d** and ashes."
Ps 22: 15 you lay me in the **d** of death.
103: 14 he remembers that we are **d**.
Ecc 3: 20 come from **d**, and to **d** all return.
Mt 10: 14 town and shake the **d** off your feet.
1Co 15: 47 first man was of the **d** of the earth;

DUTIES (DUTY)
2Ti 4: 5 all the **d** of your ministry.

DUTY (DUTIES)
Ecc 12: 13 for this is the **d** of all mankind.
Ac 23: 1 I have fulfilled my **d** to God in all
1Co 7: 3 husband should fulfill his marital **d**

DWELL (DWELLING DWELLINGS DWELLS DWELT)
Ex 25: 8 for me, and I will **d** among them.
2Sa 7: 5 one to build me a house to **d** in?
1Ki 8: 27 "But will God really **d** on earth?
Ps 23: 6 I will **d** in the house of the LORD
37: 3 **d** in the land and enjoy safe
61: 4 I long to **d** in your tent forever
Pr 8: 12 wisdom, **d** together with prudence;
Isa 33: 14 can **d** with everlasting burning?"
43: 18 do not **d** on the past.
Jn 5: 38 nor does his word **d** in you, for
Ro 7: 18 that good itself does not **d** in me,
Eph 3: 17 Christ may **d** in your hearts
Col 1: 19 to have all his fullness **d** in him,
3: 16 Christ **d** among you richly as you

DWELLING (DWELL)
Lev 26: 11 I will put my **d** place among you,
Dt 26: 15 your holy **d** place, and bless your
Ps 90: 1 been our **d** place throughout all
2Co 5: 2 instead with our heavenly **d**,
Eph 2: 22 built together to become a **d**

DWELLINGS (DWELL)
Lk 16: 9 will be welcomed into eternal **d**.

DWELLS (DWELL)
Ps 46: 4 holy place where the Most High **d**.
91: 1 Whoever **d** in the shelter
1Co 3: 16 that God's Spirit **d** in your midst?

DWELT (DWELL)
Dt 33: 16 of him who **d** in the burning bush.

DYING (DIE)
Ro 7: 6 now, by **d** to what once bound us,
2Co 6: 9 **d**, and yet we live on;

EAGER
Pr 31: 13 and flax and works with **e** hands.
Ro 8: 19 the creation waits in **e** expectation
1Co 14: 12 Since you are **e** for gifts
14: 39 sisters, be **e** to prophesy, and do
Titus 2: 14 his very own, **e** to do what is good.
1Pe 5: 2 dishonest gain, but **e** to serve;

EAGLE (EAGLE'S EAGLES)
Dt 32: 11 like an **e** that stirs up its nest
Eze 1: 10 each also had the face of an **e**.
Rev 4: 7 man, the fourth was like a flying **e**.
12: 14 given the two wings of a great **e**,

EAGLE'S (EAGLE)
Ps 103: 5 your youth is renewed like the **e**.

EAGLES (EAGLE)
Isa 40: 31 They will soar on wings like **e**;

EAR (EARS)
Ex 21: 6 and pierce his **e** with an awl.
Pr 2: 2 turning your **e** to wisdom
1Co 2: 9 eye has seen, what no **e** has heard,
12: 16 And if the **e** should say, "Because I

EARN (EARNINGS)
2Th 3: 12 down and **e** the food they eat.

EARNESTNESS
2Co 7: 11 what **e**, what eagerness to clear
8: 7 in complete **e** and in the love we

EARNINGS (EARN)
Pr 31: 16 out of her **e** she plants a vineyard.

EARRING (EARRINGS)
Pr 25: 12 Like an **e** of gold or an ornament

EARRINGS (EARRING)
Ex 32: 2 them, "Take off the gold **e** that

EARS (EAR)
Job 42: 5 My **e** had heard of you but now my
Ps 34: 15 and his **e** are attentive to their cry;
Pr 21: 13 Whoever shuts their **e** to the cry
26: 17 dog by the **e** is someone who
Isa 6: 10 make their **e** dull and close their
Mt 11: 15 Whoever has **e**, let them hear.
2Ti 4: 3 to say what their itching **e** want
1Pe 3: 12 his **e** are attentive to their prayer,
Rev 2: 7 Whoever has **e**, let them hear what

EARTH (EARTH'S EARTHLY)
Ge 1: 1 God created the heavens and the **e**.
1: 2 Now the **e** was formless and empty,
7: 24 The waters flooded the **e**
14: 19 High, Creator of heaven and **e**.
1Ki 8: 27 "But will God really dwell on **e**?
Job 26: 7 he suspends the **e** over nothing.
Ps 24: 1 The **e** is the LORD's,
46: 6 he lifts his voice, the **e** melts.
97: 5 before the Lord of all the **e**.
102: 25 you laid the foundations of the **e**,
108: 5 let your glory be over all the **e**.
Pr 8: 26 its fields or any of the dust of the **e**.
Isa 6: 3 the whole **e** is full of his glory."
24: 20 The **e** reels like a drunkard,
37: 16 You have made heaven and **e**.
40: 22 enthroned above the circle of the **e**,
51: 6 the **e** will wear out like a garment
54: 5 he is called the God of all the **e**.
55: 9 the heavens are higher than the **e**,
65: 17 create new heavens and a new **e**.
66: 1 throne, and the **e** is my footstool.
Jer 10: 10 When he is angry, the **e** trembles;
23: 24 "Do not I fill heaven and **e**?"
33: 25 the laws of heaven and **e**,
Hab 2: 20 let all the **e** be silent before him.
Zep 1: 18 sudden end of all who live on the **e**.
Mt 5: 5 meek, for they will inherit the **e**.
5: 35 or by the **e**, for it is his footstool;
6: 10 will be done, on **e** as it is in heaven.
16: 19 you bind on **e** will be bound
16: 19 you loose on **e** will be loosed
24: 35 Heaven and **e** will pass away,
28: 18 and on **e** has been given to me.
Lk 2: 14 on **e** peace to those on whom his
Jn 12: 32 when I am lifted up from the **e**,
Ac 4: 24 the heavens and the **e** and the sea,
7: 49 throne, and the **e** is my footstool.
1Co 10: 26 for, "The **e** is the Lord's,
Eph 3: 15 heaven and on **e** derives its name.
Php 2: 10 heaven and on **e** and under the **e**,
Heb 1: 10 you laid the foundations of the **e**,
2Pe 3: 13 to a new heaven and a new **e**,
Rev 8: 7 and it was hurled down on the **e**.
12: 12 But woe to the **e** and the sea,
20: 11 The **e** and the heavens fled from
21: 1 I saw "a new heaven and a new **e**,"
21: 1 and the first **e** had passed away,

EARTH'S (EARTH)
Job 38: 4 you when I laid the **e** foundation?

EARTHENWARE*
Pr 26: 23 of silver dross on **e** are fervent lips

EARTHLY (EARTH)
Ro 1: 3 as to his **e** life was a descendant
Eph 4: 9 descended to the lower, **e** regions?
Php 3: 19 Their mind is set on **e** things.
Col 3: 2 on things above, not on **e** things.
3: 5 whatever belongs to your **e** nature:

EARTHQUAKE (EARTHQUAKES)
Eze 38: 19 time there shall be a great **e**
Mt 28: 2 There was a violent **e**, for an angel
Rev 6: 12 There was a great **e**. The sun

EARTHQUAKES (EARTHQUAKE)
Mt 24: 7 be famines and **e** in various places.

EASE
Ru 2: 13 put me at **e** by speaking kindly
Pr 1: 33 will live in safety and be at **e**,

EASIER (EASY)
Lk 16: 17 It is **e** for heaven and earth
18: 25 it is **e** for a camel to go through

EAST
Ge 2: 8 God had planted a garden in the **e**,
Ps 103: 12 as far as the **e** is from the west,
Eze 43: 2 God of Israel coming from the **e**.
Mt 2: 1 Magi from the **e** came to Jerusalem

EASY (EASIER)
Mt 11: 30 For my yoke is **e** and my burden is

EAT (ATE EATEN EATER EATING EATS)
Ge 2: 16 "You are free to **e** from any tree
2: 17 you must not **e** from the tree
3: 19 you will **e** your food until you
Ex 12: 11 **E** it in haste; it is the LORD's
Lev 11: 2 land, these are the ones you may **e**:
17: 12 "None of you may **e** blood,
Dt 8: 16 He gave you manna to **e**
14: 4 These are the animals you may **e**:
Jdg 14: 14 "Out of the eater, something to **e**;
2Sa 9: 7 and you will always **e** at my table."
Pr 31: 27 does not **e** the bread of idleness.
Isa 55: 1 have no money, come, buy and **e**!
65: 25 the lion will **e** straw like the ox,
Eze 3: 1 "Son of man, **e** what is before you, **e** this scroll;
Mt 14: 16 You give them something to **e**."
15: 2 wash their hands before they **e**!"
26: 26 his disciples, saying, "Take and **e**;
Mk 14: 14 where I may **e** the Passover with
Lk 10: 8 welcomed, **e** what is offered to you.
12: 19 **e**, drink and be merry."'
12: 22 about your life, what you will **e**;
Jn 4: 32 "I have food to **e** that you know
6: 31 them bread from heaven to **e**.'"
6: 52 can this man give us his flesh to **e**?"
Ac 10: 13 him, "Get up, Peter. Kill and **e**."
Ro 14: 2 faith allows them to **e** anything,
14: 15 is distressed because of what you **e**,
14: 20 a person to **e** anything that causes
14: 21 It is better not to **e** meat or drink
14: 23 has doubts is condemned if they **e**,
1Co 5: 11 Do not even **e** with such people.
8: 13 if what I **e** causes my brother
10: 25 **E** anything sold in the meat market
10: 27 to go, **e** whatever is put before you
10: 31 So whether you **e** or drink
11: 26 For whenever you **e** this bread
2Th 3: 10 is unwilling to work shall not **e**."
Rev 2: 7 I will give the right to **e**
3: 20 come in and **e** with that person,

EATEN (EAT)
Ge 3: 11 Have you **e** from the tree that I
Ac 10: 14 "I have never **e** anything impure
Rev 10: 10 but when I had **e** it, my stomach

EATER (EAT)
Isa 55: 10 for the sower and bread for the **e**,

EATING (EAT)
Ex 34: 28 and forty nights without **e** bread
Ro 14: 15 Do not by your **e** destroy someone
14: 17 of God is not a matter of **e**
14: 23 because their **e** is not from faith;
1Co 8: 4 about **e** food sacrificed to idols:
8: 10 knowledge, **e** in an idol's temple,
Jude : 12 **e** with you without the slightest

EATS (EAT)
1Sa 14: 24 be anyone who **e** food before
Lk 15: 2 sinners and **e** with them."
Jn 6: 51 Whoever **e** this bread will live
6: 54 Whoever **e** my flesh and drinks my
Ro 14: 2 faith is weak, **e** only vegetables.
14: 3 one who **e** everything must not
Ro 14: 6 Whoever **e** meat does so to
1Co 11: 27 whoever **e** the bread or drinks

EBAL
Dt 11: 29 and on Mount **E** the curses.
Jos 8: 30 Joshua built on Mount **E** an altar

EBENEZER
1Sa 7: 12 He named it **E**, saying, "Thus far

EDEN
Ge 2: 8 planted a garden in the east, in **E**;
Eze 28: 13 You were in **E**, the garden of God;

EDGE (DOUBLE-EDGED)
Mt 9: 20 him and touched the **e** of his cloak.

EDICT
Heb 11: 23 they were not afraid of the king's **e**.

EDIFICATION* (EDIFIED EDIFIES)
Ro 14: 19 leads to peace and to mutual **e**.

EDIFIED* (EDIFICATION)
1Co 14: 5 so that the church may be **e**.
14: 17 well enough, but no one else is **e**.

EDIFIES* (EDIFICATION)
1Co 14: 4 speaks in a tongue **e** themselves,
14: 4 one who prophesies **e** the church.

EDOM
Ge 36: 1 the family line of Esau (that is, **E**).
Isa 63: 1 Who is this coming from **E**,
Ob : 1 Sovereign LORD says about **E**—

EDUCATED*
Ac 7: 22 Moses was **e** in all the wisdom

EFFECT* (EFFECTIVE)
Job 41: 26 The sword that reaches it has no **e**,
Isa 32: 17 its **e** will be quietness
Zep 2: 2 before the decree takes **e**
1Co 15: 10 his grace to me was not without **e**.
Eph 1: 10 be put into **e** when the times reach
Heb 9: 17 it never takes **e** while the one who
9: 18 was not put into **e** without blood.

EFFECTIVE* (EFFECT)
Phm : 6 in the faith may be **e** in deepening
1Co 16: 9 a great door for **e** work has opened
Jas 5: 16 righteous person is powerful and **e**.

EFFORT*
Ecc 2: 19 toil into which I have poured my **e**
Da 6: 14 every **e** until sundown to save
Lk 13: 24 "Make every **e** to enter through
Ro 9: 16 depend on human desire or **e**,
14: 19 Let us therefore make every **e** to do
Eph 4: 3 Make every **e** to keep the unity
1Th 2: 16 in their **e** to keep us from speaking
2: 17 intense longing we made every **e**
Heb 4: 11 make every **e** to enter that rest,
12: 14 Make every **e** to live in peace
2Pe 1: 5 make every **e** to add to your faith
1: 15 I will make every **e** to see
1: 10 make every **e** to confirm your
3: 14 make every **e** to be found spotless,

EGG*
Lk 11: 12 Or if he asks for an **e**, will give him

EGLON
1. Fat king of Moab killed by Ehud (Jdg 3:12–30).
2. City in Canaan (Jos 10).

EGYPT (EGYPTIANS)
Ge 12: 10 Abram went down to **E** to live
37: 28 Ishmaelites, who took him to **E**.
42: 3 went down to buy grain from **E**.
45: 20 the best of all **E** will be yours.'"
46: 6 and all his offspring went to **E**,
47: 27 Now the Israelites settled in **E**
Ex 3: 11 and bring the Israelites out of **E**?"
12: 40 people lived in **E** was 430 years.
12: 41 all the LORD's divisions left **E**.
32: 1 Moses who brought us up out of **E**,
Nu 11: 18 We were better off in **E**!"
14: 4 choose a leader and go back to **E**."
24: 8 "God brought them out of **E**;
Dt 6: 21 "We were slaves of Pharaoh in **E**,
6: 21 us out of **E** with a mighty hand.
1Ki 4: 30 greater than all the wisdom of **E**.
10: 28 horses were imported from **E**
11: 40 but Jeroboam fled to **E**, to Shishak
14: 25 king of **E** attacked Jerusalem.
2Ch 35: 20 Necho king of **E** went up to fight
36: 3 The king of **E** dethroned him
Isa 19: 23 there will be a highway from **E**
Hos 11: 1 him, and out of **E** I called my son.
Mt 2: 15 "Out of **E** I called my son."
Heb 11: 27 By faith he left **E**, not fearing
Rev 11: 8 figuratively called Sodom and **E**—

EGYPTIANS (EGYPT)
Nu 14: 13 "Then the **E** will hear about it!

EHUD
Left-handed judge who delivered Israel from Moabite king, Eglon (Jdg 3:12–30).

EKRON
1Sa 5: 10 So they sent the ark of God to **E**.

ELABORATE*
1Ti 2: 9 not with **e** hairstyles or gold
1Pe 3: 3 as **e** hairstyles and the wearing

ELAH
Son of Baasha; king of Israel (1Ki 16:6–14).

ELATION*
Pr 28: 12 righteous triumph, there is great **e**;

ELDER* (ELDERLY ELDERS)
Isa 3: 2 the prophet, the diviner and the **e**,
1Ti 5: 19 accusation against an **e** unless it is
Titus 1: 6 An **e** must be blameless,
1Pe 5: 1 I appeal as a fellow **e** and a witness
2Jn : 1 The **e**, To the lady chosen by God
3Jn : 1 The **e**, To my dear friend Gaius,

ELDERLY* (ELDER)
Lev 19: 32 show respect for the **e** and revere
2Ch 36: 17 young women, the **e** or the infirm.

ELDERS (ELDER)
1Ki 12: 8 rejected the advice the **e** gave him
Mt 15: 2 break the tradition of the **e**?
Mk 7: 3 holding to the tradition of the **e**.
7: 5 to the tradition of the **e** instead
Ac 11: 30 their gift to the **e** by Barnabas
14: 23 Barnabas appointed **e** for them
15: 2 apostles and **e** about this question.
15: 4 the church and the apostles and **e**,
15: 6 **e** met to consider this question.
15: 22 Then the apostles and **e**,
15: 23 The apostles and **e**, your brothers,
16: 4 and **e** in Jerusalem for the people
20: 17 to Ephesus for the **e** of the church.
21: 18 James, and all the **e** were present.
23: 14 the chief priests and the **e** and said,
24: 1 to Caesarea with some of the **e**
1Ti 4: 14 the body of **e** laid their hands
5: 17 The **e** who direct the affairs
Titus 1: 5 and appoint **e** in every town, as I
Jas 5: 14 Let them call the **e** of the church
1Pe 5: 1 To the **e** among you, I appeal as
Rev 4: 4 seated on them were twenty-four **e**.
4: 10 the twenty-four **e** fall down before

ELEAZAR
Third son of Aaron (Ex 6:23–25). Succeeded Aaron as high priest (Nu 20:26; Dt 10:6). Allotted land to tribes (Jos 14:1). Death (Jos 24:33).

ELECT* (ELECTION)
Mt 24: 22 the **e** those days will be shortened.
24: 24 to deceive, if possible, even the **e**.
24: 31 they will gather his **e** from the four
Mk 13: 20 But for the sake of the **e**, whom he
13: 22 to deceive, if possible, even the **e**.
13: 27 gather his **e** from the four winds,
Ro 11: 7 The **e** among them did,
1Ti 5: 21 and Christ Jesus and the **e** angels,
2Ti 2: 10 everything for the sake of the **e**,
Titus 1: 1 to further the faith of God's **e**
1Pe 1: 1 Christ, To God's **e**, exiles scattered

ELECTION* (ELECT)
Ro 9: 11 God's purpose in **e** might stand:
11: 28 but as far as **e** is concerned, they
2Pe 1: 10 to confirm your calling and **e**.

ELEMENTARY* (ELEMENTS)
Heb 5: 12 to teach you the **e** truths of God's
6: 1 let us move beyond the **e** teachings

ELEMENTS* (ELEMENTARY)
2Pe 3: 10 the **e** will be destroyed by fire,
3: 12 fire, and the **e** will melt in the heat.

ELEVATE*
2Co 11: 7 in order to **e** you by preaching

ELI
High priest in youth of Samuel (1Sa 1–4). Blessed Hannah (1Sa 1:12–18); raised Samuel (1Sa 2:11–26). Prophesied against because of wicked sons (1Sa 2:27–36). Death of Eli and sons (1Sa 4:11–22).
Mt 27: 46 in a loud voice, ***"E, E,***

ELIHU
One of Job's friends (Job 32–37).

ELIJAH
Prophet; predicted famine in Israel (1Ki 17:1; Jas 5:17). Fed by ravens (1Ki 17:2–6). Raised Sidonian widow's son (1Ki 17:7–24). Defeated prophets of Baal at Carmel (1Ki 18:16–46). Ran from Jezebel (1Ki 19:1–9). Prophesied death of Azariah (2Ki 1). Succeeded by Elishah (1Ki 19:19–21; 2Ki 2:1–18). Taken to heaven in whirlwind (2Ki 2:11–12).
Return prophesied (Mal 4:5–6); equated with John the Baptist (Mt 17:9–13; Mk 9:9–13; Lk 1:17). Appeared with Moses in transfiguration of Jesus (Mt 17:1–8; Mk 9:1–8).

ELIMELEK
Ru 1: 3 Now **E**, Naomi's husband, died,

ELIPHAZ
1. Firstborn of Esau (Ge 36).
2. One of Job's friends (Job 4–5; 15; 22).

ELISHA
Prophet; successor of Elijah (1Ki 19:16–21); inherited his cloak (2Ki 2:1–18). Purified bad water (2Ki 2:19–22). Cursed young men (2Ki 2:23–25). Aided Israel's defeat of Moab (2Ki 3). Provided widow with oil (2Ki 4:1–7). Raised Shunammite woman's son (2Ki 4:8–37). Purified food (2Ki 4:38–41). Fed 100 men (2Ki 4:42–44). Healed Naaman's leprosy (2Ki 5). Made axhead float (2Ki 6:1–7). Captured Arameans (2Ki 6:8–23). Political adviser to Israel (2Ki 6:24—8:6; 9:1–3; 13:14–19), Damascus (2Ki 8:7–15). Death (2Ki 13:20).

ELIZABETH*
Mother of John the Baptist, relative of Mary (Lk 1:5–58).

ELKANAH
Husband of Hannah, father of Samuel (1Sa 1–2).

ELOI*
Mk 15: 34 in a loud voice, ***"E, E,***

ELOQUENCE* (ELOQUENT)
1Co 1: 17 gospel—not with wisdom and **e**,
1Co 2: 1 I did not come with **e** or human

ELOQUENT* (ELOQUENCE)
Ex 4: 10 I have never been **e**,
Pr 17: 7 **E** lips are unsuited to a godless

ELYMAS
Ac 13: 8 **E** the sorcerer (for that is what his

EMBEDDED*
Ecc 12: 11 sayings like firmly **e** nails—

EMBERS
Pr 26: 21 As charcoal to **e** and as wood

EMBITTER* (BITTER)
Col 3: 21 Fathers, do not **e** your children,

EMBODIMENT* (BODY)
Ro 2: 20 have in the law the **e** of knowledge

EMPEROR
1Pe 2: 13 whether to the **e**, as the supreme
2: 17 of believers, fear God, honor the **e**.

EMPTIED (EMPTY)
1Co 1: 17 cross of Christ be **e** of its power.

EMPTY (EMPTIED)
Ge 1: 2 Now the earth was formless and **e**,
Job 26: 7 out the northern skies over **e** space;
Isa 45: 18 he did not create it to be **e**,
55: 11 It will not return to me **e**, but will
Jer 4: 23 earth, and it was formless and **e**;
Mt 12: 36 for every **e** word they have spoken.
Lk 1: 53 things but has sent the rich away **e**.
Eph 5: 6 no one deceive you with **e** words,
1Pe 1: 18 you were redeemed from the **e** way
2Pe 2: 18 For they mouth **e**, boastful words

ENABLE* (ABLE)
Lk 1: 74 to **e** us to serve him without fear
Ac 4: 29 **e** your servants to speak your word

ENABLED (ABLE)
Lev 26: 13 **e** you to walk with heads held high.
Ru 4: 13 her, the LORD **e** her to conceive,
Jn 6: 65 me unless the Father has **e** them."

Ac 2: 4 other tongues as the Spirit **e** them.
7: 10 and **e** him to gain the goodwill
Heb 11: 11 was **e** to bear children because she

ENABLES* (ABLE)
Hab 3: 19 he **e** me to tread on the heights.
Php 3: 21 by the power that **e** him to bring

ENABLING* (ABLE)
Ac 14: 3 grace by **e** them to perform signs

ENCAMPS* (CAMP)
Ps 34: 7 the LORD **e** around those who fear

ENCOURAGE* (ENCOURAGED ENCOURAGEMENT ENCOURAGES ENCOURAGING)
Dt 1: 38 **E** him, because he will lead Israel
3: 28 Joshua, and **e** and strengthen him,
2Sa 11: 25 and destroy it.' Say this to **e** Joab."
19: 7 Now go out and **e** your men.
Job 16: 5 But my mouth would **e** you;
Ps 10: 17 you **e** them, and you listen to their
64: 5 They **e** each other in evil plans,
Jer 29: 8 to the dreams you **e** them to have.
Ac 15: 32 said much to **e** and strengthen
Ro 12: 8 if it is to **e**, then give
2Co 13: 11 for full restoration, **e** one another,
Eph 6: 22 how we are, and that he may **e** you.
Col 4: 8 and that he may **e** your hearts.
1Th 3: 2 strengthen and **e** you in your faith,
4: 18 Therefore **e** one another with these
5: 11 Therefore **e** one another and build
5: 14 and disruptive, **e** the disheartened,
2Th 2: 17 **e** your hearts and strengthen you
2Ti 4: 2 correct, rebuke and **e**—
Titus 1: 9 he can **e** others by sound doctrine
2: 6 Similarly, **e** the young men to be
2: 15 **E** and rebuke with all authority.
Heb 3: 13 But **e** one another daily, as long as

ENCOURAGED* (ENCOURAGE)
Jdg 7: 11 you will be **e** to attack the camp."
20: 22 But the Israelites **e** one another
2Ch 22: 3 his mother **e** him to act wickedly.
32: 6 gate and **e** them with these words:
35: 2 and **e** them in the service
Eze 13: 22 and because you **e** the wicked not
Ac 9: 31 the Lord and **e** by the Holy Spirit,
11: 23 **e** them all to remain true to the
16: 40 brothers and sisters and **e** them.
18: 27 the brothers and sisters **e** him
27: 36 They were all **e** and ate some food
28: 15 Paul thanked God and was **e**.
Ro 1: 12 I may be mutually **e** by each other's
1Co 14: 31 everyone may be instructed and **e**.
2Co 7: 4 I am greatly **e**; in all our troubles
7: 13 By all this we are **e**. In addition
Col 2: 2 goal is that they may be **e** in heart
1Th 3: 7 persecution we were **e** about you
Heb 6: 18 hope set before us may be greatly **e**.

ENCOURAGEMENT* (ENCOURAGE)
Ac 4: 36 (which means "son of **e**"),
20: 2 speaking many words of **e**
Ro 12: 8 if it is to encourage, then give **e**;
15: 4 the **e** they provide we might have
15: 5 **e** give you the same attitude of
2Co 7: 13 In addition to our own **e**, we were
Php 2: 1 you have any **e** from being united
2Th 2: 16 by his grace gave us eternal **e**
Phm : 7 love has given me great joy and **e**,
Heb 12: 5 completely forgotten this word of **e**

ENCOURAGES* (ENCOURAGE)
Isa 41: 7 The metalworker **e** the goldsmith,

ENCOURAGING* (ENCOURAGE)
Ac 14: 22 **e** them to remain true to the faith.
15: 31 it and were glad for its **e** message.
20: 1 after **e** them, said goodbye and set
1Co 14: 3 their strengthening, **e** and comfort.
1Th 2: 12 **e**, comforting and urging you to
Heb 10: 25 habit of doing, but **e** one another—
1Pe 5: 12 **e** you and testifying that this is

ENCROACH
Pr 23: 10 or **e** on the fields of the fatherless,

END (ENDS)
Ps 119: 33 that I may follow it to the **e**.
119:112 keeping your decrees to the very **e**.
Pr 5: 4 but in the **e** she is bitter as gall,
5: 11 At the **e** of your life you will groan,
14: 12 right, but in the **e** it leads to death.
14: 13 ache, and rejoicing may **e** in grief.
16: 25 right, but in the **e** it leads to death.
19: 20 the **e** you will be counted among
20: 21 soon will not be blessed at the **e**.
23: 32 In the **e** it bites like a snake
25: 8 do in the **e** if your neighbor puts
28: 23 the **e** gain favor rather than one
Ecc 3: 11 God has done from beginning to **e**.
7: 8 The **e** of a matter is better than its
12: 12 making many books there is no **e**,
Eze 7: 2 to the land of Israel: "'The **e**!
Mt 10: 22 stands firm to the **e** will be saved.
24: 13 stands firm to the **e** will be saved.
24: 14 nations, and then the **e** will come.
Lk 21: 9 but the **e** will not come right away."
Jn 13: 1 the world, he loved them to the **e**.
1Co 15: 24 Then the **e** will come, when he
Rev 21: 6 Omega, the Beginning and the **E**.
22: 13 the Last, the Beginning and the **E**.

ENDS (END)
Ps 19: 4 their words to the **e** of the world.
Pr 20: 17 but one **e** up with a mouth full
Isa 49: 6 may reach to the **e** of the earth."
62: 11 proclamation to the **e** of the earth:
Ac 13: 47 salvation to the **e** of the earth.'"
Ro 10: 18 their words to the **e** of the world."

ENDURANCE* (ENDURE)
Ro 15: 4 so that through the **e** taught
15: 5 May the God who gives **e**
2Co 1: 6 you patient **e** of the same sufferings
6: 4 in great **e**; in troubles,
Col 1: 11 might so that you may have great **e**
1Th 1: 3 **e** inspired by hope in our Lord
1Ti 6: 11 faith, love, **e** and gentleness.
2Ti 3: 10 my purpose, faith, patience, love, **e**,
Titus 2: 2 and sound in faith, in love and in **e**.
Rev 1: 9 and patient **e** that are ours in Jesus,
13: 10 This calls for patient **e**
14: 12 This calls for patient **e** on the part

ENDURE (ENDURANCE ENDURED ENDURES ENDURING)
Ps 72: 17 May his name **e** forever;
Pr 12: 19 Truthful lips **e** forever, but a lying
27: 24 for riches do not **e** forever,
Ecc 3: 14 everything God does will **e** forever;
Isa 55: 13 sign, that will **e** forever."
Da 2: 44 to an end, but it will itself **e** forever.
Mal 3: 2 who can **e** the day of his coming?
1Co 4: 12 when we are persecuted, we **e** it;
10: 13 a way out so that you can **e** it.
2Co 1: 8 far beyond our ability to **e**,
2Ti 2: 10 Therefore I **e** everything
2: 12 if we **e**, we will also reign with him.
4: 5 head in all situations, **e** hardship,
Heb 12: 7 **E** hardship as discipline;
1Pe 2: 20 suffer for doing good and you **e** it,
Rev 3: 10 kept my command to **e** patiently,

ENDURED* (ENDURE)
Ps 123: 3 for we have **e** no end of contempt.
123: 4 We have **e** no end of ridicule
Ac 13: 18 forty years he **e** their conduct
2Ti 3: 11 and Lystra, the persecutions I **e**.
Heb 10: 32 when you **e** in a great conflict full
12: 2 joy set before him he **e** the cross,
12: 3 him who **e** such opposition
Rev 2: 3 and have **e** hardships for my name,

ENDURES (ENDURE)
Ps 102: 12 your renown **e** through all
112: 9 poor, their righteousness **e** forever;
136: 1 *His love **e** forever.*
Pr 12: 12 but the root of the righteous **e**.
Isa 40: 8 but the word of our God **e** forever."
Da 9: 15 yourself a name that **e** to this day,
2Co 9: 9 their righteousness **e** forever."
1Pe 1: 25 but the word of the Lord **e** forever."

ENDURING (ENDURE)
2Th 1: 4 persecutions and trials you are **e**.
1Pe 1: 23 the living and **e** word of God.

ENEMIES (ENEMY)
Ps 23: 5 before me in the presence of my **e**.
110: 1 until I make your **e** a footstool
Pr 16: 7 he causes their **e** to make peace
26: 24 **E** disguise themselves with their
29: 24 of thieves are their own **e**;
Isa 59: 18 so will he repay wrath to his **e**
Mic 7: 6 a man's **e** are the members of his
Mt 5: 44 love your **e** and pray for those who
10: 36 a man's **e** will be the members
Lk 6: 27 Love your **e**, do good to those who
6: 35 But love your **e**, do good to them,
20: 43 until I make your **e** a footstool
Ro 5: 10 if, while we were God's **e**, we were
1Co 15: 25 he has put all his **e** under his feet.
Php 3: 18 tears, many live as **e** of the cross
Heb 1: 13 until I make your **e** a footstool
10: 13 for his **e** to be made his footstool.

ENEMY (ENEMIES ENMITY)
Pr 24: 17 Do not gloat when your **e** falls;
25: 21 If your **e** is hungry, give him food
27: 6 trusted, but an **e** multiplies kisses.
Lk 10: 19 to overcome all the power of the **e**;
Ro 12: 20 "If your **e** is hungry, feed him;
1Co 15: 26 The last **e** to be destroyed is death.
1Ti 5: 14 and to give the **e** no opportunity
1Pe 5: 8 Your **e** the devil prowls around like

ENERGY*
Col 1: 29 the **e** Christ so powerfully works

ENGRAVED
Isa 49: 16 I have **e** you on the palms of my
2Co 3: 7 which was **e** in letters on stone,

ENHANCES*
Ro 3: 7 my falsehood **e** God's truthfulness

ENJOY (JOY)
Dt 6: 2 and so that you may **e** long life.
Est 5: 14 king to the banquet and **e** yourself."
Ps 37: 3 in the land and **e** safe pasture.
Pr 28: 16 ill-gotten gain will **e** a long reign.
Ecc 3: 22 for a person than to **e** their work,
Eph 6: 3 and that you may **e** long life
Heb 11: 25 than to **e** the fleeting pleasures
3Jn : 2 I pray that you may **e** good health

ENJOYMENT (JOY)
Ecc 4: 8 why am I depriving myself of **e**?"
1Ti 6: 17 us with everything for our **e**.

ENLARGE (ENLARGES)
2Co 9: 10 seed and will **e** the harvest of your

ENLARGES (ENLARGE)
Dt 33: 20 is he who **e** Gad's domain!

ENLIGHTENED* (LIGHT)
Eph 1: 18 eyes of your heart may be **e** in order
Heb 6: 4 for those who have once been **e**,

ENMITY (ENEMY)
Ge 3: 15 I will put **e** between you
Jas 4: 4 the world means **e** against God?

ENOCH
1. Son of Cain (Ge 4:17–18).
2. Descendant of Seth; walked with God and taken by him (Ge 5:18–24; Heb 11:5). Prophet (Jude 14).

ENSLAVED (SLAVE)
Gal 4: 9 to be **e** by them all over again?
Titus 3: 3 and **e** by all kinds of passions

ENSNARE (SNARE)
Pr 5: 22 evil deeds of the wicked **e** them;
Ecc 7: 26 her, but the sinner she will **e**.

ENSNARED* (SNARE)
Dt 7: 25 or you will be **e** by it, for it is
12: 30 be careful not to be **e** by inquiring
Ps 9: 16 the wicked are **e** by the work
Pr 6: 2 said, **e** by the words of your mouth.
22: 25 learn their ways and get yourself **e**.

ENTANGLED (ENTANGLES)
2Ti 2: 4 No one serving as a soldier gets **e**
2Pe 2: 20 Jesus Christ and are again **e** in it

ENTANGLES* (ENTANGLED)
Heb 12: 1 hinders and the sin that so easily **e**.

ENTER (ENTERED ENTERING ENTERS ENTRANCE)
Ps 95: 11 'They shall never **e** my rest.'"
100: 4 **E** his gates with thanksgiving
Pr 2: 10 For wisdom will **e** your heart,

Mt 5: 20 will certainly not **e** the kingdom
7: 13 "**E** through the narrow gate.
7: 21 will **e** the kingdom of heaven,
18: 3 you will never **e** the kingdom
18: 8 It is better for you to **e** life maimed
19: 17 If you want to **e** life,
19: 23 who is rich to **e** the kingdom
Mk 9: 43 you to **e** life maimed than with two
9: 45 you to **e** life crippled than to have
9: 47 for you to **e** the kingdom of God
10: 15 like a little child will never **e** it."
10: 23 the rich to **e** the kingdom of God!"
Lk 13: 24 to **e** through the narrow door,
18: 17 like a little child will never **e** it."
18: 24 the rich to **e** the kingdom of God!
Jn 3: 5 no one can **e** the kingdom of God
Heb 3: 11 'They shall never **e** my rest.'"
4: 11 make every effort to **e** that rest,

ENTERED (ENTER)
Ps 73: 17 till I **e** the sanctuary of God;
Eze 4: 14 impure meat has ever **e** my mouth."
Ac 11: 8 or unclean has ever **e** my mouth.'
Ro 5: 12 just as sin **e** the world through one
Heb 9: 12 he **e** the Most Holy Place once

ENTERING (ENTER)
Mt 21: 31 the prostitutes are **e** the kingdom
Lk 11: 52 have hindered those who were **e**."
Heb 4: 1 promise of **e** his rest still stands,

ENTERS (ENTER)
Mk 7: 18 that nothing that **e** a person
Jn 10: 2 The one who **e** by the gate is

ENTERTAIN* (ENTERTAINMENT)
Jdg 16: 25 "Bring out Samson to **e** us."
Mt 9: 4 "Why do you **e** evil thoughts
1Ti 5: 19 Do not **e** an accusation against

ENTERTAINMENT* (ENTERTAIN)
Da 6: 18 without any **e** being brought to

ENTHRALLED*
Ps 45: 11 Let the king be **e** by your beauty;

ENTHRONED* (THRONE)
1Sa 4: 4 who is **e** between the cherubim.
2Sa 6: 2 who is **e** between the cherubim
2Ki 19: 15 of Israel, **e** between the cherubim,
1Ch 13: 6 who is **e** between the cherubim—
Ps 2: 4 The One **e** in heaven laughs;
7: 7 while you sit **e** over them on high.
9: 4 sitting **e** as the righteous judge.
9: 11 praises of the LORD, **e** in Zion;
22: 3 Yet you are **e** as the Holy One;
29: 10 The LORD sits **e** over the flood;
29: 10 the LORD is **e** as King forever.
55: 19 God, who is **e** from of old,
61: 7 May he be **e** in God's presence
80: 1 You who sit **e** between
99: 1 he sits **e** between the cherubim,
102: 12 But you, LORD, sit **e** forever;
113: 5 God, the One who sits **e** on high,
123: 1 to you, to you who sit **e** in heaven.
132: 14 here I will sit **e**, for I have desired
Isa 14: 13 I will sit **e** on the mount
37: 16 of Israel, **e** between the cherubim,
40: 22 He sits **e** above the circle
52: 2 rise up, sit **e**, Jerusalem.
Rev 18: 7 heart she boasts, 'I sit **e** as queen.

ENTHRONES* (THRONE)
Job 36: 7 he **e** them with kings and exalts

ENTHUSIASM*
2Co 8: 17 he is coming to you with much **e**
9: 2 your **e** has stirred most of them

ENTICE (ENTICED ENTICES)
Pr 1: 10 if sinful men **e** you, do not give
2Pe 2: 18 they **e** people who are just escaping
Rev 2: 14 who taught Balak to **e** the Israelites

ENTICED (ENTICE)
Dt 4: 19 do not be **e** into bowing down
11: 16 or you will be **e** to turn away
2Ki 17: 21 Jeroboam **e** Israel away
Job 31: 9 my heart has been **e** by a woman,
31: 27 so that my heart was secretly **e**
Jas 1: 14 by their own evil desire and **e**.

ENTICES* (ENTICE)
Dt 13: 6 your closest friend secretly **e** you,
Job 36: 18 careful that no one **e** you by riches;
Pr 16: 29 A violent person **e** their neighbor

ENTIRE
Gal 5: 14 For the **e** law is fulfilled in keeping

ENTRANCE (ENTER)
Mt 27: 60 stone in front of the **e** to the tomb
Mk 15: 46 he rolled a stone against the **e**
16: 3 away from the **e** of the tomb?"
Jn 11: 38 cave with a stone laid across the **e**.
20: 1 had been removed from the **e**.

ENTRUST (TRUST)
Ps 143: 8 I should go, for to you I **e** my life.
Jn 2: 24 Jesus would not **e** himself to them,
2Ti 2: 2 many witnesses **e** to reliable people

ENTRUSTED (TRUST)
Jer 13: 20 is the flock that was **e** to you,
Jn 5: 22 but has **e** all judgment to the Son,
Ro 3: 2 the Jews have been **e** with the very
1Co 4: 1 as those **e** with the mysteries God
1Th 2: 4 by God to be **e** with the gospel.
1Ti 1: 11 the blessed God, which he **e** to me.
6: 20 guard what has been **e** to your care.
2Ti 1: 12 to guard what I have **e** to him until
1: 14 good deposit that was **e** to you—
Titus 1: 3 through the preaching **e** to me
1Pe 2: 23 he **e** himself to him who judges
5: 3 not lording it over those **e** to you,
Jude : 3 once for all **e** to God's holy people.

ENVIOUS (ENVY)
Dt 32: 21 I will make them **e** by those who
Pr 24: 19 of evildoers or be **e** of the wicked,
Ro 10: 19 "I will make you **e** by those who

ENVOY
Pr 13: 17 but a trustworthy **e** brings healing.

ENVY (ENVIOUS ENVYING)
Pr 3: 31 Do not **e** the violent or choose any
14: 30 to the body, but **e** rots the bones.
23: 17 Do not let your heart **e** sinners,
24: 1 Do not **e** the wicked, do not desire
Mk 7: 22 malice, deceit, lewdness, **e**, slander,
Ro 1: 29 They are full of **e**, murder, strife,
11: 14 arouse my own people to **e** and
1Co 13: 4 It does not **e**, it does not boast, it is
Gal 5: 21 and **e**; drunkenness, orgies,
Php 1: 15 that some preach Christ out of **e**
1Ti 6: 4 about words that result in **e**,
Titus 3: 3 We lived in malice and **e**,
Jas 3: 14 if you harbor bitter **e** and selfish
3: 16 For where you have **e** and selfish
1Pe 2: 1 hypocrisy, **e**, and slander of every

ENVYING* (ENVY)
Gal 5: 26 provoking and **e** each other.

EPHAH
Lev 19: 36 an honest **e** and an honest hin.
Eze 45: 10 use accurate scales, an accurate **e**

EPHESUS
Ac 18: 19 They arrived at **E**, where Paul left
19: 1 the interior and arrived at **E**.
Eph 1: 1 God, To God's holy people in **E**,
Rev 2: 1 the angel of the church in **E** write:

EPHRAIM

1. Second son of Joseph (Ge 41:52; 46:20). Blessed as firstborn by Jacob (Ge 48). Tribe of numbered (Nu 1:33; 26:37), blessed (Dt 33:17), allotted land (Jos 16:4–9; Eze 48:5), failed to fully possess (Jos 16:10; Jdg 1:29).

2. Synonymous with northern kingdom (Isa 7:17; Hos 5).

EQUAL (EQUALITY EQUITY)
Dt 33: 25 and your strength will **e** your days.
Isa 40: 25 Or who is my **e**?" says the Holy
46: 5 you compare me or count me **e**?
Da 1: 19 and he found none **e** to Daniel,
Jn 5: 18 Father, making himself **e** with God.
1Co 12: 25 its parts should have **e** concern
2Co 2: 16 And who is **e** to such a task?

EQUALITY* (EQUAL)
2Co 8: 13 pressed, but that there might be **e**.
8: 14 what you need. The goal is **e**,
Php 2: 6 God, did not consider **e** with God

EQUIP* (EQUIPPED)
Eph 4: 12 to **e** his people for works of service,
Heb 13: 21 **e** you with everything good

EQUIPPED (EQUIP)
2Ti 3: 17 God may be thoroughly **e** for every

EQUITY* (EQUAL)
Ps 9: 8 and judges the peoples with **e**.
58: 1 Do you judge people with **e**?
67: 4 for you rule the peoples with **e**
75: 2 it is I who judge with **e**.
96: 10 he will judge the peoples with **e**.
98: 9 and the peoples with **e**.
99: 4 you have established **e**; in Jacob

ERODES*
Job 14: 18 "But as a mountain **e** and crumbles

ERROR (ERRORS)
Ro 1: 27 the due penalty for their **e**.
Jas 5: 20 the **e** of their way will save them
2Pe 2: 18 escaping from those who live in **e**.

ERRORS* (ERROR)
Ps 19: 12 But who can discern their own **e**?

ESAU

Firstborn of Isaac, twin of Jacob (Ge 25:21–26). Also called Edom (Ge 25:30). Sold Jacob his birthright (Ge 25:29–34); lost blessing (Gen 27). Married Hittites (Ge 26:34), Ishmaelites (Ge 28:6–9). Reconciled to Jacob (Gen 33). Genealogy (Ge 36). The LORD chose Jacob over Esau (Mal 1:2–3), but gave Esau land (Dt 2:2–12). Descendants eventually obliterated (Ob 1–21; Jer 49:7–22).

ESCAPE (ESCAPED ESCAPING)
Ps 68: 20 the Sovereign LORD comes **e**
89: 48 who can **e** the power of the grave?
Pr 11: 9 knowledge the righteous **e**.
12: 13 talk, and so the innocent **e** trouble.
Ro 2: 3 think you will **e** God's judgment?
1Th 5: 3 woman, and they will not **e**.
2Ti 2: 26 and **e** from the trap of the devil,
Heb 2: 3 how shall we **e** if we ignore so great
12: 25 If they did not **e** when they refused

ESCAPED (ESCAPE)
2Pe 1: 4 **e** the corruption in the world
2: 20 If they have **e** the corruption

ESCAPING (ESCAPE)
1Co 3: 15 only as one **e** through the flames.
2Pe 2: 18 they entice people who are just **e**

ESTABLISH (ESTABLISHED ESTABLISHES)
Ge 6: 18 But I will **e** my covenant with you,
17: 21 my covenant I will **e** with Isaac,
2Sa 7: 11 the LORD himself will **e** a house
1Ki 9: 5 will **e** your royal throne over Israel
1Ch 28: 7 I will **e** his kingdom forever if he is
Ps 90: 17 **e** the work of our hands for us—
Pr 16: 3 you do, and he will **e** your plans.
Isa 26: 12 LORD, you **e** peace for us;
Ro 10: 3 of God and sought to **e** their own,
16: 25 Now to him who is able to **e** you
Heb 10: 9 sets aside the first to **e** the second.

ESTABLISHED (ESTABLISH)
Ge 9: 17 the covenant I have **e** between me
Ex 6: 4 **e** my covenant with them to give
Ps 8: 2 infants you have **e** a stronghold
111: 8 They are **e** for ever and ever,
Pr 16: 12 throne is **e** through righteousness.
20: 18 Plans are **e** by seeking advice;
Jer 33: 25 night and **e** the laws of heaven
Heb 8: 6 one, since the new covenant is **e**

ESTABLISHES (ESTABLISH)
Job 25: 2 he **e** order in the heights of heaven.
Pr 16: 9 course, but the LORD **e** their steps.
Isa 42: 4 or be discouraged till he **e** justice

ESTATE
Ps 136: 23 He remembered us in our low **e**

ESTEEM (ESTEEMED)
Isa 53: 3 and we held him in low **e**.
Gal 2: 6 those who were held in high **e**—

ESTEEMED (ESTEEM)
Pr 22: 1 to be **e** is better than silver or gold.

ESTHER

Jewess, originally named Hadassah, who

lived in Persia; cousin of Mordecai (Est 2:7). Chosen queen of Xerxes (Est 2:8–18). Persuaded by Mordecai to foil Haman's plan to exterminate the Jews (Est 3–4). Revealed Haman's plans to Xerxes, resulting in Haman's death (Est 7), the Jews' preservation (Est 8–9), Mordecai's exaltation (Est 8:15; 9:4; 10). Decreed celebration of Purim (Est 9:18–32).

ETERNAL* (ETERNITY)

Ge 21: 33 the name of the LORD, the **E** God.
Dt 33: 27 The **e** God is your refuge,
1Ki 10: 9 of the LORD's **e** love for Israel,
Ps 16: 11 with **e** pleasures at your right hand.
111: 10 To him belongs **e** praise.
119: 89 Your word, LORD, is **e**;
119:160 all your righteous laws are **e**.
Ecc 12: 5 Then people go to their **e** home
Isa 26: 4 the LORD himself, is the Rock **e**.
47: 7 said, 'I am forever—the **e** queen!'
Jer 10: 10 he is the living God, the **e** King.
Da 4: 3 His kingdom is an **e** kingdom;
4: 34 His dominion is an **e** dominion;
Mt 18: 8 two feet and be thrown into **e** fire.
19: 16 good thing must I do to get **e** life?"
19: 29 as much and will inherit **e** life.
25: 41 the **e** fire prepared for the devil
25: 46 they will go away to **e** punishment,
25: 46 but the righteous to **e** life."
Mk 3: 29 they are guilty of an **e** sin."
10: 17 "what must I do to inherit **e** life?"
10: 30 and in the age to come **e** life.
Lk 10: 25 "what must I do to inherit **e** life?"
16: 9 will be welcomed into **e** dwellings.
18: 18 what must I do to inherit **e** life?"
18: 30 age, and in the age to come **e** life."
Jn 3: 15 who believes may have **e** life
3: 16 him shall not perish but have **e** life.
3: 36 believes in the Son has **e** life,
4: 14 of water welling up to **e** life."
4: 36 wage and harvests a crop for **e** life,
5: 24 believes him who sent me has **e** life
5: 39 think that in them you have **e** life.
6: 27 but for food that endures to **e** life,
6: 40 believes in him shall have **e** life,
6: 47 the one who believes has **e** life.
6: 54 and drinks my blood has **e** life,
6: 68 You have the words of **e** life.
10: 28 I give them **e** life, and they shall
12: 25 in this world will keep it for **e** life.
12: 50 that his command leads to **e** life.
17: 2 he might give **e** life to all those you
17: 3 Now this is **e** life: that they know
Ac 13: 46 yourselves worthy of **e** life,
13: 48 were appointed for **e** life believed.
Ro 1: 20 his **e** power and divine nature—
2: 7 and immortality, he will give **e** life.
5: 21 bring **e** life through Jesus Christ
6: 22 to holiness, and the result is **e** life.
6: 23 of God is **e** life in Christ Jesus our
16: 26 by the command of the **e** God,
2Co 4: 17 for us an **e** glory that far outweighs
4: 18 temporary, but what is unseen is **e**.
5: 1 from God, an **e** house in heaven,
Gal 6: 8 from the Spirit will reap **e** life.
Eph 3: 11 according to his **e** purpose that he
2Th 2: 16 his grace gave us **e** encouragement
1Ti 1: 16 believe in him and receive **e** life.
1: 17 Now to the King **e**, immortal,
6: 12 Take hold of the **e** life to which you
2Ti 2: 10 that is in Christ Jesus, with **e** glory.
Titus 1: 2 in the hope of **e** life, which God,
3: 7 heirs having the hope of **e** life.
Heb 5: 9 he became the source of **e** salvation
6: 2 of the dead, and **e** judgment.
9: 12 thus obtaining **e** redemption.
9: 14 who through the **e** Spirit offered
9: 15 receive the promised **e** inheritance
13: 20 of the **e** covenant brought back
1Pe 5: 10 who called you to his **e** glory
2Pe 1: 11 a rich welcome into the **e** kingdom
1Jn 1: 2 and we proclaim to you the **e** life,
2: 25 this is what he promised us—**e** life.
3: 15 no murderer has **e** life residing
5: 11 God has given us **e** life, and this life
5: 13 you may know that you have **e** life.
5: 20 He is the true God and **e** life.
Jude : 7 suffer the punishment of **e** fire.
: 21 Jesus Christ to bring you to **e** life.
Rev 14: 6 he had the **e** gospel to proclaim

ETERNITY* (ETERNAL)

Ps 93: 2 you are from all **e**.
Ecc 3: 11 has also set **e** in the human heart;

ETHIOPIAN*

Jer 13: 23 Can an **E** change his skin
Ac 8: 27 on his way he met an **E** eunuch,

EUNUCH (EUNUCHS)

Ac 8: 27 on his way he met an Ethiopian **e**,

EUNUCHS (EUNUCH)

Isa 56: 4 "To the **e** who keep my Sabbaths,
Mt 19: 12 For there are **e** who were born
19: 12 choose to live like **e** for the sake

EUTYCHUS*

Ac 20: 9 was a young man named **E**,

EVANGELIST* (EVANGELISTS)

Ac 21: 8 stayed at the house of Philip the **e**,
2Ti 4: 5 do the work of an **e**, discharge all

EVANGELISTS* (EVANGELIST)

Eph 4: 11 the **e**, the pastors and teachers,

EVE*

Ge 3: 20 Adam named his wife **E**,
4: 1 Adam made love to his wife **E**,
2Co 11: 3 afraid that just as **E** was deceived
1Ti 2: 13 For Adam was formed first, then **E**.

EVEN-TEMPERED* (TEMPER)

Pr 17: 27 whoever has understanding is **e**.

EVENING

Ge 1: 5 And there was **e**, and there was

EVER (EVERLASTING FOREVER FOREVERMORE)

Ex 15: 18 "The LORD reigns for **e** and **e**."
Dt 8: 19 you **e** forget the LORD your God
1Ki 3: 12 like you, nor will there **e** be.
Job 4: 7 being innocent, has **e** perished?
Ps 5: 11 you be glad; let them **e** sing for joy.
10: 16 The LORD is King for **e** and **e**;
21: 4 length of days, for **e** and **e**.
25: 3 one who hopes in you will **e** be put
25: 15 My eyes are **e** on the LORD,
45: 6 O God, will last for **e** and **e**;
45: 17 will praise you for **e** and **e**.
48: 14 this God is our God for **e** and **e**;
52: 8 unfailing love for **e** and **e**.
61: 8 I will **e** sing in praise of your name
71: 6 I will **e** praise you.
84: 4 they are **e** praising you.
89: 33 nor will I **e** betray my faithfulness.
111: 8 They are established for **e** and **e**,
119: 44 always obey your law, for **e** and **e**.
132: 12 sit on your throne for **e** and **e**."
145: 1 praise your name for **e** and **e**.
145: 2 and extol your name for **e** and **e**.
145: 21 praise his holy name for **e** and **e**.
Pr 4: 18 shining **e** brighter till the full light
5: 19 may you **e** be intoxicated with her
Isa 66: 8 Who has **e** heard of such things?
Jer 7: 7 the land I gave your ancestors for **e**
25: 5 you and your ancestors for **e** and **e**.
31: 36 "will Israel **e** cease being a nation
Da 2: 20 "Praise be to the name of God for **e**
7: 18 possess it forever—yes, for **e** and **e**.'
12: 3 like the stars for **e** and **e**.
Mic 4: 5 the LORD our God for **e** and **e**.
Mt 13: 14 "'You will be **e** hearing but never
13: 14 you will be **e** seeing but never
Mk 4: 12 "'they may be **e** seeing but never
Jn 1: 18 No one has **e** seen God, but the
Gal 1: 5 to whom be glory for **e** and **e**.
Eph 3: 21 all generations, for **e** and **e**! Amen.
Php 4: 20 and Father be glory for **e** and **e**.
1Ti 1: 17 be honor and glory for **e** and **e**.
2Ti 4: 18 To him be glory for **e** and **e**. Amen.
Heb 1: 8 throne, O God, will last for **e** and **e**;
13: 21 to whom be glory for **e** and **e**.
1Pe 4: 11 glory and the power for **e** and **e**.
5: 11 To him be the power for **e** and **e**.
1Jn 4: 12 No one has **e** seen God; but if we
Rev 1: 6 be glory and power for **e** and **e**!
1: 18 now look, I am alive for **e** and **e**!
21: 27 Nothing impure will **e** enter it,
22: 5 And they will reign for **e** and **e**.

EVER-INCREASING* (INCREASE)

Ro 6: 19 to impurity and to **e** wickedness,
2Co 3: 18 into his image with **e** glory,

EVERLASTING (EVER)

Ge 9: 16 remember the **e** covenant between
17: 7 covenant as an **e** covenant between
17: 8 I will give as an **e** possession to you
17: 13 in your flesh is to be an **e** covenant.
17: 19 with him as an **e** covenant for his
48: 4 give this land as an **e** possession
Nu 18: 19 It is an **e** covenant of salt before
Dt 33: 15 and the fruitfulness of the **e** hills;
33: 27 and underneath are the **e** arms.
2Sa 23: 5 have made with me an **e** covenant,
1Ch 16: 17 a decree, to Israel as an **e** covenant:
16: 36 the God of Israel, from **e** to **e**.
29: 10 of our father Israel, from **e** to **e**.
Ezr 9: 12 your children as an **e** inheritance.'
Ne 9: 5 your God, who is from **e** to **e**."
Ps 41: 13 the God of Israel, from **e** to **e**.
52: 5 God will bring you down to **e** ruin:
74: 3 your steps toward these **e** ruins,
78: 66 he put them to **e** shame.
90: 2 world, from **e** to **e** you are God.
103: 17 But from **e** to **e** the LORD's love is
105: 10 a decree, to Israel as an **e** covenant:
106: 48 the God of Israel, from **e** to **e**.
119:142 Your righteousness is **e** and your
139: 24 and lead me in the way **e**.
145: 13 Your kingdom is an **e** kingdom,
Isa 9: 6 Mighty God, **E** Father,
24: 5 statutes and broken the **e** covenant,
30: 8 to come it may be an **e** witness.
33: 14 of us can dwell with **e** burning?"
35: 10 **e** joy will crown their heads.
40: 28 The LORD is the **e** God,
45: 17 by the LORD with an **e** salvation;
45: 17 to shame or disgraced, to ages **e**.
51: 11 **e** joy will crown their heads.
54: 8 **e** kindness I will have compassion
55: 3 I will make an **e** covenant with you,
55: 13 for an **e** sign, that will endure
56: 5 I will give them an **e** name that will
60: 15 I will make you the **e** pride
60: 19 for the LORD will be your **e** light,
60: 20 the LORD will be your **e** light,
61: 7 your land, and **e** joy will be yours.
61: 8 make an **e** covenant with them.
63: 12 them, to gain for himself **e** renown,
Jer 5: 22 the sea, an **e** barrier it cannot cross.
23: 40 I will bring on you **e** disgrace—
23: 40 I will bring on you **e** disgrace—
25: 9 of horror and scorn, and an **e** ruin.
31: 3 "I have loved you with an **e** love;
32: 40 I will make an **e** covenant
50: 5 to the LORD in an **e** covenant
Eze 16: 60 I will establish an **e** covenant
37: 26 it will be an **e** covenant.
Da 7: 14 His dominion is an **e** dominion
7: 27 His kingdom will be an **e** kingdom,
9: 24 to bring in **e** righteousness, to seal
12: 2 some to **e** life, others to shame and **e** contempt.
Mic 6: 2 you **e** foundations of the earth.
Hab 1: 12 LORD, are you not from **e**?
2Th 1: 9 will be punished with **e** destruction
Jude : 6 bound with **e** chains for judgment

EVER-PRESENT*

Ps 46: 1 and strength, an **e** help in trouble.

EVERYONE

Ps 11: 4 He observes **e** on earth;
Eze 18: 4 For **e** belongs to me, the parent as
Lk 6: 26 to you when **e** speaks well of you,
Jn 13: 35 By this **e** will know that you are my
1Ti 5: 20 sinning you are to reprove before **e**,

EVIDENCE (EVIDENT)

Jn 14: 11 on the **e** of the works themselves.
2Th 1: 5 All this is **e** that God's judgment is
Jas 2: 20 do you want **e** that faith without

EVIDENT (EVIDENCE)

Php 4: 5 Let your gentleness be **e** to all.

EVIL (EVILDOER EVILDOERS EVILS)
Ge 2: 9 of the knowledge of good and **e**.
3: 5 be like God, knowing good and **e**."
6: 5 heart was only **e** all the time.
Ex 32: 22 how prone these people are to **e**.
Jdg 2: 11 the Israelites did **e** in the eyes
3: 7 The Israelites did **e** in the eyes
3: 12 the Israelites did **e** in the eyes
4: 1 the Israelites did **e** in the eyes
6: 1 The Israelites did **e** in the eyes
10: 6 the Israelites did **e** in the eyes
13: 1 the Israelites did **e** in the eyes
1Ki 11: 6 So Solomon did **e** in the eyes
16: 25 But Omri did **e** in the eyes
2Ki 15: 24 Pekahiah did **e** in the eyes
Job 1: 1 he feared God and shunned **e**.
1: 8 a man who fears God and shuns **e**."
34: 10 Far be it from God to do **e**,
36: 21 Beware of turning to **e**, which you
Ps 5: 4 you, **e** people are not welcome.
23: 4 will fear no **e**, for you are with me;
34: 13 keep your tongue from **e** and your
34: 14 Turn from **e** and do good;
34: 16 LORD is against those who do **e**,
37: 1 not fret because of those who are **e**
37: 8 do not fret—it leads only to **e**.
37: 27 Turn from **e** and do good;
49: 5 should I fear when **e** days come,
51: 4 and done what is **e** in your sight;
97: 10 those who love the LORD hate **e**,
101: 4 have nothing to do with what is **e**.
141: 4 drawn to what is **e** so that I take
Pr 4: 27 or the left; keep your foot from **e**.
8: 13 To fear the LORD is to hate **e**;
11: 19 but whoever pursues **e** finds death.
11: 27 **e** comes to one who searches for it.
14: 16 wise fear the LORD and shun **e**,
17: 13 **E** will never leave the house of one who pays back **e** for good.
20: 30 Blows and wounds scrub away **e**,
26: 23 are fervent lips with an **e** heart.
Ecc 12: 14 thing, whether it is good or **e**.
Isa 5: 20 who call **e** good and good **e**,
13: 11 I will punish the world for its **e**,
Jer 4: 14 wash the **e** from your heart and be
18: 8 nation I warned repents of its **e**,
18: 11 So turn from your **e** ways, each one
Eze 33: 11 Turn from your **e** ways!
33: 13 will die for the **e** they have done.
33: 15 that give life, and do no **e**—
Am 5: 13 in such times, for the times are **e**.
Hab 1: 13 Your eyes are too pure to look on **e**;
Zec 8: 17 do not plot **e** against each other,
Mt 5: 45 He causes his sun to rise on the **e**
6: 13 but deliver us from the **e** one.'
7: 11 though you are **e**, know how to
12: 34 you who are **e** say anything good?
12: 35 an **e** man brings **e** things out of the **e** stored up
15: 19 out of the heart come **e** thoughts—
Mk 7: 21 heart, that **e** thoughts come—
Lk 6: 45 an **e** man brings **e** things out of the **e** stored up
11: 13 though you are **e**, know how to
Jn 3: 19 of light because their deeds were **e**.
3: 20 Everyone who does **e** hates
17: 15 you protect them from the **e** one.
Ro 1: 30 they invent ways of doing **e**;
2: 8 who reject the truth and follow **e**,
2: 9 for every human being who does **e**:
3: 8 "Let us do **e** that good may
6: 12 body so that you obey its **e** desires.
7: 19 do, but the **e** I do not want to do—
7: 21 do good, **e** is right there with me.
12: 9 Hate what is **e**; cling to what is
12: 17 Do not repay anyone **e** for **e**.
12: 21 Do not be overcome by **e**, but overcome **e** with good.
14: 16 know is good be spoken of as **e**.
16: 19 and innocent about what is **e**.
1Co 13: 6 Love does not delight in **e**
14: 20 In regard to **e** be infants, but in
Eph 5: 16 because the days are **e**.
6: 12 against the spiritual forces of **e**
6: 16 all the flaming arrows of the **e** one.
Col 3: 5 lust, **e** desires and greed, which is
1Th 5: 22 reject every kind of **e**.
2Th 3: 3 and protect you from the **e** one.
1Ti 6: 10 of money is a root of all kinds of **e**.
2Ti 2: 22 Flee the **e** desires of youth
3: 6 are swayed by all kinds of **e** desires,
Heb 5: 14 to distinguish good from **e**.
Jas 1: 13 For God cannot be tempted by **e**,
1: 21 filth and the **e** that is so prevalent
3: 6 a world of **e** among the parts
3: 8 It is a restless **e**, full of deadly
1Pe 2: 16 your freedom as a cover-up for **e**;
3: 9 Do not repay **e** with **e** or
3: 9 contrary, repay **e** with blessing,
3: 10 days must keep their tongue from **e**
3: 17 for doing good than for doing **e**.
1Jn 2: 13 you have overcome the **e** one.
2: 14 and you have overcome the **e** one.
3: 12 Cain, who belonged to the **e** one
5: 18 and the **e** one cannot harm them.
5: 19 is under the control of the **e** one.
3Jn : 11 do not imitate what is **e** but what

EVILDOER* (EVIL)
2Sa 3: 39 the LORD repay the **e** according
Ps 10: 15 call the **e** to account for his
101: 8 I will cut off every **e** from the city
Pr 24: 20 for the **e** has no future hope,
Mal 4: 1 and every **e** will be stubble,

EVILDOERS (EVIL)
1Sa 24: 13 'From **e** come evil deeds,' so my
Job 8: 20 or strengthen the hands of **e**.
34: 8 He keeps company with **e**;
34: 22 utter darkness, where **e** can hide.
Ps 14: 4 Do all these **e** know nothing?
14: 6 You **e** frustrate the plans
26: 5 I abhor the assembly of **e** and
36: 12 See how the **e** lie fallen—
53: 4 Do all these **e** know nothing?
59: 2 Deliver me from **e** and save me
64: 2 of the wicked, from the plots of **e**.
92: 7 up like grass and all **e** flourish,
92: 9 all **e** will be scattered.
94: 4 all the **e** are full of boasting.
94: 16 will take a stand for me against **e**?
119:115 Away from me, you **e**, that I may
125: 5 the LORD will banish with the **e**.
141: 5 still be against the deeds of **e**.
141: 9 safe from the traps set by **e**,
Pr 21: 15 to the righteous but terror to **e**.
24: 19 Do not fret because of **e** or be
28: 5 **E** do not understand what is right,
29: 6 **E** are snared by their own sin,
Isa 1: 4 great, a brood of **e**, children given
31: 2 nation, against those who help **e**.
Jer 23: 14 They strengthen the hands of **e**,
Hos 10: 9 Will not war again overtake the **e**
Mal 3: 15 Certainly **e** prosper, and even
Mt 7: 23 Away from me, you **e**!'
Lk 13: 27 Away from me, all you **e**!'
18: 11 robbers, **e**, adulterers—
2Ti 3: 13 while **e** and impostors will go

EVILS* (EVIL)
Mk 7: 23 All these **e** come from inside

EWE
2Sa 12: 3 except one little **e** lamb he had

EXACT*
Ge 43: 21 us found his silver—the **e** weight—
Est 4: 7 including the **e** amount of money
Pr 22: 23 up their case and will **e** life for life.
Mt 2: 7 from them the **e** time the star had
Jn 4: 53 realized that this was the **e** time
Heb 1: 3 the **e** representation of his being,

EXALT* (EXALTED EXALTS)
Ex 15: 2 my father's God, and I will **e** him.
Jos 3: 7 "Today I will begin to **e** you
1Sa 2: 10 and **e** the horn of his anointed."
1Ch 25: 5 the promises of God to **e** him.
29: 12 power to **e** and give strength to all.
Job 19: 5 If indeed you would **e** yourselves
Ps 30: 1 I will **e** you, LORD, for you lifted
34: 3 let us **e** his name together.
35: 26 may all who **e** themselves over me
37: 34 He will **e** you to inherit the land;
38: 16 **e** themselves over me when my feet
Ps 75: 6 from the desert can **e** themselves.
89: 17 and by your favor you **e** our horn.
99: 5 **E** the LORD our God and worship
99: 9 **E** the LORD our God and worship
107: 32 Let them **e** him in the assembly
118: 28 you are my God, and I will **e** you.
145: 1 I will **e** you, my God the King;
Pr 4: 8 Cherish her, and she will **e** you;
25: 6 Do not **e** yourself in the king's
30: 32 "If you play the fool and **e** yourself,
Isa 24: 15 **e** the name of the LORD, the God
25: 1 I will **e** you and praise your name,
Eze 29: 15 will never again **e** itself
Da 4: 37 praise and **e** and glorify the King
11: 36 He will **e** and magnify himself
11: 37 but will **e** himself above them all.
Hos 11: 7 High, I will by no means **e** them.
Mt 23: 12 For those who **e** themselves will be
Lk 14: 11 all those who **e** themselves will be
Lk 18: 14 all those who **e** themselves will be
2Th 2: 4 will **e** himself over everything

EXALTED* (EXALT)
Ex 15: 1 to the LORD, for he is highly **e**.
15: 21 to the LORD, for he is highly **e**.
Nu 24: 7 their kingdom will be **e**.
Jos 4: 14 day the LORD **e** Joshua
2Sa 5: 12 had **e** his kingdom for the sake
22: 47 **E** be my God, the Rock, my Savior!
22: 49 You **e** me above my foes;
23: 1 of the man **e** by the Most High,
1Ch 14: 2 his kingdom had been highly **e**
17: 17 me as though I were the most **e**
29: 11 you are **e** as head over all.
29: 25 The LORD highly **e** Solomon
Ne 9: 5 and may it be **e** above all blessing
Job 24: 24 For a little while they are **e**,
36: 22 "God is **e** in his power. Who is
37: 23 beyond our reach and **e** in power;
Ps 18: 46 to my Rock! **E** be God my Savior!
18: 48 You **e** me above my foes;
21: 13 Be **e** in your strength, LORD;
27: 6 Then my head will be **e**
35: 27 "The LORD be **e**, who delights
46: 10 I will be **e** among the nations, I will be **e** in the earth."
47: 9 belong to God; he is greatly **e**.
57: 5 Be **e**, O God, above the heavens;
57: 11 Be **e**, O God, above the heavens;
89: 13 hand is strong, your right hand **e**.
89: 24 my name his horn will be **e**.
89: 27 the most **e** of the kings of the earth.
89: 42 You have **e** the right hand of his
92: 8 But you, LORD, are forever **e**.
92: 10 You have **e** my horn like
97: 9 you are **e** far above all gods.
99: 2 he is **e** over all the nations.
108: 5 Be **e**, O God, above the heavens;
113: 4 The LORD is **e** over all
138: 2 you have so **e** your solemn decree
138: 6 Though the LORD is **e**, he looks
148: 13 the LORD, for his name alone is **e**;
Pr 11: 11 blessing of the upright a city is **e**,
Isa 2: 2 it will be **e** above the hills, and all
2: 11 the LORD alone will be **e**
2: 12 for all that is **e** (and they will be
2: 17 the LORD alone will be **e**
5: 16 the LORD Almighty will be **e**
6: 1 high and **e**, seated on a throne;
12: 4 and proclaim that his name is **e**.
33: 5 The LORD is **e**, for he dwells
33: 10 "Now will I be **e**; now will I be
52: 13 raised and lifted up and highly **e**.
57: 15 is what the high and **e** One says—
Jer 17: 12 throne, **e** from the beginning,
La 2: 17 you, he has **e** the horn of your foes.
Eze 21: 26 The lowly will be **e** and the **e** will be brought low.
Hos 13: 1 he was **e** in Israel.
Mic 4: 1 it will be **e** above the hills,
6: 6 and bow down before the **e** God?
Mt 23: 12 who humble themselves will be **e**.
Lk 14: 11 who humble themselves will be **e**."
18: 14 who humble themselves will be **e**."
Ac 2: 33 **E** to the right hand of God, he has
5: 31 God **e** him to his own right hand

Php 1: 20 now as always Christ will be **e**
2: 9 Therefore God **e** him to the highest
Heb 7: 26 from sinners, **e** above the heavens.

EXALTS* (EXALT)
1Sa 2: 7 he humbles and he **e**.
Job 36: 7 with kings and **e** them forever.
Ps 75: 7 He brings one down, he **e** another.
Pr 14: 34 Righteousness **e** a nation, but sin

EXAMINE (EXAMINED EXAMINES)
Ps 11: 4 everyone on earth; his eyes **e** them.
17: 3 though you **e** me at night and test
26: 2 try me, **e** my heart and my mind;
Jer 17: 10 search the heart and **e** the mind,
20: 12 you who **e** the righteous and probe
La 3: 40 Let us **e** our ways and test them,
1Co 11: 28 to **e** themselves before they eat
2Co 13: 5 **E** yourselves to see whether you

EXAMINED (EXAMINE)
Job 13: 9 Would it turn out well if he **e** you?
Ac 17: 11 **e** the Scriptures every day to see

EXAMINES (EXAMINE)
Ps 11: 5 The LORD **e** the righteous,
Pr 5: 21 the LORD, and he **e** all your paths.

EXAMPLE* (EXAMPLES)
2Ki 14: 3 everything he followed the **e** of his
Ecc 9: 13 saw under the sun this **e** of wisdom
Eze 14: 8 and make them an **e** and a byword.
Jn 13: 15 I have set you an **e** that you should
Ro 6: 19 I am using an **e** from everyday life
7: 2 For **e**, by law a married woman is
1Co 11: 1 Follow my **e**, as I follow the **e** of Christ.
Gal 3: 15 let me take an **e** from everyday life.
Eph 5: 1 Follow God's **e**, therefore, as dearly
Php 3: 17 Join together in following my **e**,
2Th 3: 7 how you ought to follow our **e**.
1Ti 1: 16 his immense patience as an **e**
4: 12 set an **e** for the believers in speech,
Titus 2: 7 everything set them an **e** by doing
Heb 4: 11 following their **e** of disobedience.
Jas 3: 4 Or take ships as an **e**.
5: 10 as an **e** of patience in the face
1Pe 2: 21 leaving you an **e**, that you should
2Pe 2: 6 made them an **e** of what is going
Jude : 7 They serve as an **e** of those who

EXAMPLES* (EXAMPLE)
1Co 10: 6 Now these things occurred as **e**
10: 11 things happened to them as **e**
1Pe 5: 3 to you, but being **e** to the flock.

EXASPERATE*
Eph 6: 4 Fathers, do not **e** your children;

EXCEL* (EXCELLENT)
Ge 49: 4 you will no longer **e**, for you went
1Co 14: 12 try to **e** in those that build
2Co 8: 7 But since you **e** in everything—
8: 7 also **e** in this grace of giving.

EXCELLENT (EXCEL)
1Co 12: 31 yet I will show you the most **e** way.
Php 4: 8 if anything is **e** or praiseworthy—
1Ti 3: 13 have served well gain an **e** standing
Titus 3: 8 These things are **e** and profitable

EXCESSIVE
2Co 2: 7 not be overwhelmed by **e** sorrow.

EXCHANGE (EXCHANGED)
Mt 16: 26 what can anyone give in **e** for their
Mk 8: 37 what can anyone give in **e** for their
2Co 6: 13 As a fair **e**—I speak as to my

EXCHANGED (EXCHANGE)
Ps 106: 20 They **e** their glorious God
Jer 2: 11 people have **e** their glorious God
Hos 4: 7 they **e** their glorious God
Ro 1: 23 **e** the glory of the immortal God
1: 25 **e** the truth about God for a lie,
1: 26 Even their women **e** natural sexual

EXCLAIM
Ps 35: 10 My whole being will **e**, "Who is

EXCUSE* (EXCUSES)
Lk 14: 18 I must go and see it. Please **e** me.'
14: 19 way to try them out. Please **e** me.'
Jn 15: 22 now they have no **e** for their sin.
Ro 1: 20 made, so that people are without **e**.
2: 1 have no **e**, you who pass judgment

EXCUSES* (EXCUSE)
Lk 14: 18 "But they all alike began to make **e**.

EXERTED*
Eph 1: 20 he **e** when he raised Christ

EXHORT* (EXHORTATION)
1Ti 5: 1 but **e** him as if he were your father.

EXHORTATION (EXHORT)
Ac 13: 15 have a word of **e** for the people,

EXILE (EXILES)
2Ki 17: 23 their homeland into **e** in Assyria,
25: 11 into **e** the people who remained

EXILES (EXILE)
1Pe 2: 11 as foreigners and **e**, to abstain

EXISTS
Heb 2: 10 and through whom everything **e**,
11: 6 to him must believe that he **e**

EXPECT (EXPECTATION EXPECTED EXPECTING)
Mt 24: 44 at an hour when you do not **e** him.
Lk 12: 40 at an hour when you do not **e** him."
Php 1: 20 I eagerly **e** and hope that I will in

EXPECTATION (EXPECT)
Ro 8: 19 waits in eager **e** for the children
Heb 10: 27 but only a fearful **e** of judgment

EXPECTED (EXPECT)
Hag 1: 9 "You **e** much, but see, it turned

EXPECTING (EXPECT)
Lk 6: 35 to them without **e** to get anything

EXPEL* (EXPELLED)
1Co 5: 13 "**E** the wicked person from among

EXPELLED (EXPEL)
Eze 28: 16 God, and I **e** you, guardian cherub,

EXPENSE (EXPENSIVE)
1Co 9: 7 serves as a soldier at his own **e**?

EXPENSIVE* (EXPENSE)
Mt 26: 7 an alabaster jar of very **e** perfume,
Mk 14: 3 an alabaster jar of very **e** perfume,
Lk 7: 25 No, those who wear **e** clothes
Jn 12: 3 a pint of pure nard, an **e** perfume;
1Ti 2: 9 or gold or pearls or **e** clothes,

EXPLAINING (EXPLAINS)
Ac 17: 3 **e** and proving that the Messiah had
1Co 2: 13 the Spirit, **e** spiritual realities

EXPLAINS* (EXPLAINING)
Ac 8: 31 said, "unless someone **e** it to me?"

EXPLOIT* (EXPLOITED EXPLOITING EXPLOITS)
Pr 22: 22 Do not **e** the poor because they are
Isa 58: 3 you please and **e** all your workers.
2Co 12: 17 Did I **e** you through any of the
12: 18 Titus did not **e** you, did he?
2Pe 2: 3 greed these teachers will **e** you

EXPLOITED* (EXPLOIT)
2Co 7: 2 no one, we have **e** no one.

EXPLOITING* (EXPLOIT)
Jas 2: 6 Is it not the rich who are **e** you?

EXPLOITS (EXPLOIT)
2Co 11: 20 anyone who enslaves you or **e** you

EXPLORE
Nu 13: 2 "Send some men to **e** the land

EXPOSE (EXPOSED)
1Co 4: 5 and will **e** the motives of the heart.
Eph 5: 11 of darkness, but rather **e** them.

EXPOSED (EXPOSE)
Jn 3: 20 for fear that their deeds will be **e**.
Eph 5: 13 everything **e** by the light becomes

EXPRESSING*
Gal 5: 6 counts is faith **e** itself through love.

EXTENDS
Pr 31: 20 poor and **e** her hands to the needy.
Lk 1: 50 His mercy **e** to those who fear him,

EXTINGUISH* (EXTINGUISHED)
Eph 6: 16 you can **e** all the flaming arrows

EXTINGUISHED (EXTINGUISH)
2Sa 21: 17 the lamp of Israel will not be **e**."

EXTOL*
1Ch 16: 4 the ark of the LORD, to **e**, thank,
Job 36: 24 Remember to **e** his work,
Ps 34: 1 I will **e** the LORD at all times;
68: 4 **e** him who rides on the clouds;
95: 2 thanksgiving and **e** him with music
109: 30 mouth I will greatly **e** the LORD;
111: 1 I will **e** the LORD with all my
115: 18 it is we who **e** the LORD,
117: 1 **e** him, all you peoples.
145: 2 you and **e** your name for ever
145: 10 your faithful people **e** you.
147: 12 **E** the LORD, Jerusalem;
Ro 15: 11 let all the peoples **e** him."

EXTORT* (EXTORTION)
Eze 22: 12 **e** unjust gain from your neighbors.
Lk 3: 14 "Don't **e** money and don't accuse

EXTORTION (EXTORT)
Pr 28: 16 A tyrannical ruler practices **e**,

EXTRAORDINARY*
Ac 19: 11 God did **e** miracles through Paul,

EXTREME (EXTREMES)
2Co 8: 2 their **e** poverty welled up in rich

EXTREMES* (EXTREME)
Ecc 7: 18 Whoever fears God will avoid all **e**.

EYE (EYES)
Ge 3: 6 for food and pleasing to the **e**,
Ex 21: 24 **e** for **e**, tooth for tooth,
Dt 19: 21 life for life, **e** for **e**, tooth for tooth,
2Ki 9: 30 about it, she put on **e** makeup,
Ps 94: 9 Does he who formed the **e** not see?
Am 9: 4 "I will keep my **e** on them for harm
Mt 5: 29 If your right **e** causes you
5: 38 have heard that it was said, '**E** for **e**,
6: 22 "The **e** is the lamp of the body.
7: 3 of sawdust in your brother's **e**
1Co 2: 9 "What no **e** has seen, what no ear
12: 16 "Because I am not an **e**, I do not
15: 52 in the twinkling of an **e**, at the last
Eph 6: 6 to win their favor when their **e** is
Col 3: 22 not only when their **e** is on you
Rev 1: 7 and "every **e** will see him,

EYES (EYE)
Nu 15: 39 the lusts of your own hearts and **e**.
33: 55 remain will become barbs in your **e**
Dt 11: 12 the **e** of the LORD your God are
12: 25 what is right in the **e** of the LORD.
16: 19 for a bribe blinds the **e** of the wise
Jos 23: 13 your backs and thorns in your **e**,
1Sa 15: 17 you were once small in your own **e**,
1Ki 10: 7 I came and saw with my own **e**.
2Ch 16: 9 For the **e** of the LORD range
Job 31: 1 "I made a covenant with my **e** not
36: 7 not take his **e** off the righteous;
Ps 25: 15 My **e** are ever on the LORD,
36: 1 is no fear of God before their **e**.
101: 6 My **e** will be on the faithful
118: 23 this, and it is marvelous in our **e**.
119: 18 Open my **e** that I may see
119: 37 Turn my **e** away from worthless
121: 1 I lift up my **e** to the mountains—
123: 1 I lift up my **e** to you, to you who sit
139: 16 Your **e** saw my unformed body;
141: 8 But my **e** are fixed on you,
Pr 3: 7 Do not be wise in your own **e**;
4: 25 Let your **e** look straight ahead;
15: 3 The **e** of the LORD are
15: 30 Light in a messenger's **e** brings joy
17: 24 a fool's **e** wander to the ends
Isa 6: 5 and my **e** have seen the King,
33: 17 Your **e** will see the king in his
42: 7 to open **e** that are blind, to free
Jer 24: 6 My **e** will watch over them for their
Hab 1: 13 Your **e** are too pure to look on evil;
Mt 6: 22 If your **e** are healthy, your whole
21: 42 this, and it is marvelous in our **e**'?
Lk 16: 15 justify yourselves in the **e** of others,
24: 31 Then their **e** were opened and they
Jn 4: 35 open your **e** and look at the fields!
Ac 1: 9 was taken up before their very **e**,
4: 19 replied, "Which is right in God's **e**:
2Co 4: 18 So we fix our **e** not on what is seen,
8: 21 not only in the **e** of the Lord
Eph 1: 18 pray that the **e** of your heart may
Php 3: 17 keep your **e** on those who live as

Heb 12: 2 fixing our **e** on Jesus, the pioneer
Jas 2: 5 who are poor in the **e** of the world
1Pe 3: 12 For the **e** of the Lord are
Rev 7: 17 away every tear from their **e**."
21: 4 will wipe every tear from their **e**.

EYEWITNESSES* (WITNESS)
Lk 1: 2 by those who from the first were **e**
2Pe 1: 16 but we were **e** of his majesty.

EZEKIEL*
Priest called to be prophet to the exiles (Eze 1–3). Symbolically acted out destruction of Jerusalem (Eze 4–5; 12; 24).

EZRA*
Priest and teacher of the Law who led a return of exiles to Israel to reestablish temple and worship (Ezr 7–8). Corrected intermarriage of priests (Ezr 9–10). Read Law at celebration of Festival of Tabernacles (Ne 8). Participated in dedication of Jerusalem's walls (Ne 12).

FACE (FACES)
Ge 32: 30 "It is because I saw God **f** to **f**,
Ex 3: 6 Moses hid his **f**, because he was
33: 11 would speak to Moses **f** to **f**, as one
33: 20 "you cannot see my **f**, for no one
34: 29 that his **f** was radiant because he
Nu 6: 25 the LORD make his **f** shine on you
12: 8 With him I speak **f** to **f**,
14: 14 LORD, have been seen **f** to **f**,
Dt 5: 4 The LORD spoke to you **f** to **f**
31: 17 I will hide my **f** from them, and
34: 10 whom the LORD knew **f** to **f**,
Jdg 6: 22 the angel of the LORD **f** to **f**!"
2Ki 14: 8 let us **f** each other in battle."
1Ch 16: 11 and his strength; seek his **f** always.
2Ch 7: 14 and seek my **f** and turn from their
25: 17 let us **f** each other in battle."
Ezr 9: 6 to lift up my **f** to you, because our
Ps 4: 6 Let the light of your **f** shine on us.
27: 8 My heart says of you, "Seek his **f**!"
31: 16 Let your **f** shine on your servant;
44: 3 the light of your **f**, for you loved
44: 22 your sake we **f** death all day long;
51: 9 Hide your **f** from my sins and blot
67: 1 bless us and make his **f** shine on us
80: 3 make your **f** shine on us, that we
105: 4 and his strength; seek his **f** always.
119:135 Make your **f** shine on your servant
SS 2: 14 voice is sweet, and your **f** is lovely.
Isa 50: 7 Therefore have I set my **f** like flint,
50: 8 Let us **f** each other!
54: 8 surge of anger I hid my **f** from you
Jer 32: 4 will speak with him **f** to **f**
34: 3 he will speak with you **f** to **f**.
Eze 1: 10 four had the **f** of a human being,
20: 35 of the nations and there, **f** to **f**,
Mt 17: 2 His **f** shone like the sun, and his
18: 10 in heaven always see the **f** of my
Lk 9: 29 the appearance of his **f** changed,
Ro 8: 36 your sake we **f** death all day long;
1Co 13: 12 in a mirror; then we shall see **f** to **f**.
2Co 3: 7 steadily at the **f** of Moses because
4: 6 glory displayed in the **f** of Christ.
10: 1 who am "timid" when **f** to **f**
1Pe 3: 12 the **f** of the Lord is against those
2Jn : 12 to visit you and talk with you **f** to **f**,
3Jn : 14 you soon, and we will talk **f** to **f**.
Rev 1: 16 His **f** was like the sun shining in all
22: 4 They will see his **f**, and his name

FACES (FACE)
2Co 3: 18 unveiled **f** contemplate the Lord's

FACTIONS
Gal 5: 20 selfish ambition, dissensions, **f**

FADE
Dt 4: 9 or let them **f** from your heart as
Jas 1: 11 the rich will **f** away even while they
1Pe 5: 4 of glory that will never **f** away.

FAIL (FAILED FAILING FAILINGS FAILS)
Lev 26: 15 **f** to carry out all my commands
1Ki 2: 4 you will never **f** to have a successor
1Ch 28: 20 He will not **f** you or forsake you
2Ch 34: 33 they did not **f** to follow the LORD,
Ps 89: 28 my covenant with him will never **f**.
Pr 15: 22 Plans **f** for lack of counsel,
Isa 51: 6 my righteousness will never **f**.
Jer 14: 6 their eyes **f** for lack of food."
La 3: 22 for his compassions never **f**.
Lk 1: 37 For no word from God will ever **f**."
22: 32 Simon, that your faith may not **f**.
2Co 13: 5 unless, of course, you **f** the test?

FAILED (FAIL)
Jos 23: 14 has been fulfilled; not one has **f**.
1Ki 8: 56 Not one word has **f** of all the good
Ps 77: 8 Has his promise **f** for all time?
Ro 9: 6 is not as though God's word had **f**.
2Co 13: 6 discover that we have not **f** the test.

FAILING (FAIL)
1Sa 12: 23 I should sin against the LORD by **f**

FAILINGS* (FAIL)
Ro 15: 1 to bear with the **f** of the weak

FAILS (FAIL)
Ps 143: 7 me quickly, LORD; my spirit **f**.
Joel 1: 10 wine is dried up, the olive oil **f**.
1Co 13: 8 Love never **f**. But where there are

FAINT
Isa 40: 31 weary, they will walk and not be **f**.

FAINTHEARTED* (HEART)
Dt 20: 3 Do not be **f** or afraid; do not panic
20: 8 shall add, "Is anyone afraid or **f**?

FAIR (FAIRNESS)
Pr 1: 3 doing what is right and just and **f**;
Col 4: 1 your slaves with what is right and **f**,

FAIRNESS* (FAIR)
Pr 29: 14 If a king judges the poor with **f**,

FAITH* (FAITHFUL FAITHFULLY FAITHFULNESS FAITHLESS)
Ex 21: 8 because he has broken **f** with her.
Dt 32: 51 because both of you broke **f** with
Jos 22: 16 'How could you break **f**
Jdg 9: 16 good **f** by making Abimelek king?
9: 19 in good **f** toward Jerub-Baal and
1Sa 14: 33 "You have broken **f**," he said.
2Ch 20: 20 Have **f** in the LORD your God
20: 20 have **f** in his prophets and you
Isa 7: 9 If you do not stand firm in your **f**,
26: 2 may enter, the nation that keeps **f**.
Mt 6: 30 more clothe you—you of little **f**?
8: 10 anyone in Israel with such great **f**.
8: 26 "You of little **f**, why are you so
9: 2 When Jesus saw their **f**, he said
9: 22 he said, "your **f** has healed you."
9: 29 "According to your **f** let it be done
13: 58 there because of their lack of **f**.
14: 31 "You of little **f**," he said, "why did
15: 28 to her, "Woman, you have great **f**!
16: 8 "You of little **f**, why are you talking
17: 20 "Because you have so little **f**.
17: 20 you have **f** as small as a mustard
21: 21 if you have **f** and do not doubt,
24: 10 many will turn away from the **f**
Mk 2: 5 When Jesus saw their **f**, he said
4: 40 Do you still have no **f**?"
5: 34 "Daughter, your **f** has healed you.
6: 6 He was amazed at their lack of **f**.
10: 52 said Jesus, "your **f** has healed you."
11: 22 "Have **f** in God," Jesus answered.
16: 14 *rebuked them for their lack of* ***f***
Lk 5: 20 When Jesus saw their **f**, he said,
7: 9 I have not found such great **f** even
7: 50 the woman, "Your **f** has saved you;
8: 25 "Where is your **f**?" he asked his
8: 48 "Daughter, your **f** has healed you.
12: 28 will he clothe you—you of little **f**!
17: 5 said to the Lord, "Increase our **f**!"
17: 6 "If you have **f** as small as a mustard
17: 19 your **f** has made you well."
18: 8 comes, will he find **f** on the earth?"
18: 42 your **f** has healed you."
22: 32 Simon, that your **f** may not fail.
Jn 12: 42 not openly acknowledge their **f**
Ac 3: 16 By **f** in the name of Jesus, this man
3: 16 the **f** that comes through him
6: 5 a man full of **f** and of the Holy
6: 7 of priests became obedient to the **f**.
11: 24 full of the Holy Spirit and **f**,
13: 8 to turn the proconsul from the **f**.
Ac 14: 9 him, saw that he had **f** to be healed
14: 22 them to remain true to the **f**.
14: 27 how he had opened a door of **f**
15: 9 for he purified their hearts by **f**.
16: 5 were strengthened in the **f**
20: 21 and have **f** in our Lord Jesus.
24: 24 him as he spoke about **f** in Christ
26: 18 those who are sanctified by **f**
27: 25 men, for I have **f** in God that it will
Ro 1: 5 comes from **f** for his name's sake.
1: 8 because your **f** is being reported all
1: 12 encouraged by each other's **f**.
1: 17 righteousness that is by **f** from first
1: 17 "The righteous will live by **f**."
3: 22 righteousness is given through **f**
3: 25 of his blood—to be received by **f**.
3: 26 one who justifies those who have **f**
3: 27 because of the law that requires **f**.
3: 28 a person is justified by **f** apart
3: 30 will justify the circumcised by **f**
3: 30 uncircumcised through that same **f**.
3: 31 we, then, nullify the law by this **f**?
4: 5 their **f** is credited as righteousness.
4: 9 that Abraham's **f** was credited
4: 11 **f** while he was still uncircumcised.
4: 12 of the **f** that our father Abraham
4: 13 the righteousness that comes by **f**.
4: 14 **f** means nothing and the promise
4: 16 the promise comes by **f**, so that it
4: 16 those who have the **f** of Abraham.
4: 19 Without weakening in his **f**,
4: 20 was strengthened in his **f** and gave
5: 1 we have been justified through **f**,
5: 2 whom we have gained access by **f**
9: 30 it, a righteousness that is by **f**;
9: 32 Because they pursued it not by **f**
10: 6 the righteousness that is by **f** says:
10: 8 the message concerning **f** that we
10: 10 your mouth that you profess your **f**
10: 17 **f** comes from hearing the message,
11: 20 of unbelief, and you stand by **f**.
12: 3 with the **f** God has distributed
12: 6 prophesy in accordance with your **f**;
14: 1 Accept the one whose **f** is weak,
14: 2 One person's **f** allows them to eat
14: 2 but another, whose **f** is weak,
14: 23 because their eating is not from **f**;
14: 23 that does not come from **f** is sin.
16: 26 the obedience that comes from **f**—
1Co 2: 5 so that your **f** might not rest
7: 22 who was a slave when called to **f**
12: 9 to another **f** by the same Spirit,
13: 2 have a **f** that can move mountains,
13: 13 three remain: **f**, hope and love.
15: 14 is useless and so is your **f**.
15: 17 has not been raised, your **f** is futile;
16: 13 stand firm in the **f**; be courageous;
2Co 1: 24 Not that we lord it over your **f**,
1: 24 because it is by **f** you stand firm.
4: 13 Since we have that same spirit of **f**,
5: 7 For we live by **f**, not by sight.
8: 7 in **f**, in speech, in knowledge,
10: 15 is that, as your **f** continues to grow,
13: 5 to see whether you are in the **f**;
Gal 1: 23 now preaching the **f** he once tried
2: 16 the law, but by **f** in Jesus Christ.
2: 16 have put our **f** in Christ Jesus
2: 16 we may be justified by **f** in Christ
2: 20 body, I live by **f** in the Son of God,
3: 7 that those who have **f** are children
3: 8 would justify the Gentiles by **f**,
3: 9 who rely on **f** are blessed along with Abraham, the man of **f**.
3: 11 "the righteous will live by **f**."
3: 12 The law is not based on **f**;
3: 14 by **f** we might receive the promise
3: 22 being given through **f** in Jesus
3: 23 Before the coming of this **f**,
3: 23 law, locked up until the **f** that was
3: 24 that we might be justified by **f**.
3: 25 Now that this **f** has come, we are
3: 26 are all children of God through **f**,
5: 5 eagerly await by **f** the righteousness
5: 6 counts is **f** expressing itself through
Eph 1: 15 heard about your **f** in the Lord

Eph 2: 8 you have been saved, through **f**—
3: 12 through **f** in him we may approach
3: 17 may dwell in your hearts through **f**.
4: 5 one Lord, one **f**, one baptism;
4: 13 until we all reach unity in the **f**
6: 16 take up the shield of **f**,
6: 23 love with **f** from God the Father
Php 1: 25 for your progress and joy in the **f**,
1: 27 as one for the **f** of the gospel
2: 17 and service coming from your **f**,
3: 9 that which is through **f** in Christ—
3: 9 comes from God on the basis of **f**.
Col 1: 4 have heard of your **f** in Christ Jesus
1: 5 the **f** and love that spring
1: 23 if you continue in your **f**,
2: 5 and how firm your **f** in Christ is.
2: 7 in the **f** as you were taught,
2: 12 him through your **f** in the working
1Th 1: 3 Father your work produced by **f**,
1: 8 your **f** in God has become known
3: 2 and encourage you in your **f**,
3: 5 I sent to find out about your **f**.
3: 6 brought good news about your **f**
3: 7 about you because of your **f**.
3: 10 supply what is lacking in your **f**.
5: 8 be sober, putting on **f** and love as
2Th 1: 3 because your **f** is growing more
1: 4 and **f** in all the persecutions
1: 11 your every deed prompted by **f**.
3: 2 evil people, for not everyone has **f**.
1Ti 1: 2 To Timothy my true son in the **f**:
1: 4 which is by **f**.
1: 5 a good conscience and a sincere **f**.
1: 14 along with the **f** and love that are
1: 19 holding on to **f** and a good
1: 19 shipwreck with regard to the **f**.
2: 15 if they continue in **f**,
3: 9 of the **f** with a clear conscience.
3: 13 assurance in their **f** in Christ Jesus.
4: 1 later times some will abandon the **f**
4: 6 nourished on the truths of the **f**
4: 12 conduct, in love, in **f** and in purity.
5: 8 has denied the **f** and is worse than
6: 10 have wandered from the **f**
6: 11 righteousness, godliness, **f**, love,
6: 12 Fight the good fight of the **f**.
6: 21 so doing have departed from the **f**.
2Ti 1: 5 I am reminded of your sincere **f**,
1: 13 with **f** and love in Christ Jesus.
2: 18 and they destroy the **f** of some.
2: 22 youth and pursue righteousness, **f**,
3: 8 who, as far as the **f** is concerned,
3: 10 way of life, my purpose, **f**, patience,
3: 15 salvation through **f** in Christ Jesus.
4: 7 finished the race, I have kept the **f**.
Titus 1: 1 to further the **f** of God's elect
1: 4 my true son in our common **f**:
1: 13 so that they will be sound in the **f**
2: 2 and sound in **f**, in love
3: 15 Greet those who love us in the **f**.
Phm : 5 and your **f** in the Lord Jesus.
: 6 with us in the **f** may be effective
Heb 4: 2 because they did not share the **f**
4: 14 us hold firmly to the **f** we profess.
6: 1 that lead to death, and of **f** in God,
6: 12 to imitate those who through **f**
10: 22 the full assurance that **f** brings,
10: 38 my righteous one will live by **f**.
10: 39 to those who have **f** and are saved.
11: 1 Now **f** is confidence in what we
11: 3 By **f** we understand that the
11: 4 **f** Abel brought God a better
11: 4 By **f** he was commended as
11: 4 And by **f** Abel still speaks,
11: 5 By **f** Enoch was taken from this
11: 6 without **f** it is impossible to please
11: 7 By **f** Noah, when warned
11: 7 By his **f** he condemned the world
11: 7 that is in keeping with **f**.
11: 8 By **f** Abraham, when called to go
11: 9 By **f** he made his home
11: 11 And by **f** even Sarah, who was past
11: 13 these people were still living by **f**
11: 17 By **f** Abraham, when God tested
11: 20 By **f** Isaac blessed Jacob and Esau
Heb 11: 21 By **f** Jacob, when he was dying,
11: 22 By **f** Joseph, when his end was
11: 23 By **f** Moses' parents hid him
11: 24 By **f** Moses, when he had grown
11: 27 By **f** he left Egypt, not fearing
11: 28 By **f** he kept the Passover
11: 29 **f** the people passed through the
11: 30 By **f** the walls of Jericho fell,
11: 31 By **f** the prostitute Rahab,
11: 33 through **f** conquered kingdoms,
11: 39 were all commended for their **f**,
12: 2 the pioneer and perfecter of **f**.
13: 7 their way of life and imitate their **f**.
Jas 1: 3 of your **f** produces perseverance.
2: 5 the eyes of the world to be rich in **f**
2: 14 if someone claims to have **f** but has
2: 14 Can such **f** save them?
2: 17 In the same way, **f** by itself, if
2: 18 But someone will say, "You have **f**;
2: 18 Show me your **f** without deeds,
2: 18 I will show you my **f** by my deeds.
2: 20 that **f** without deeds is useless?
2: 22 You see that his **f** and his actions
2: 22 his **f** was made complete by what
2: 24 by what they do and not by **f** alone.
2: 26 is dead, so **f** without deeds is dead.
5: 15 in **f** will make the sick person well;
1Pe 1: 5 through **f** are shielded by God's
1: 7 the proven genuineness of your **f**—
1: 9 receiving the end result of your **f**,
1: 21 and so your **f** and hope are in God.
5: 9 standing firm in the **f**, because you
2Pe 1: 1 have received a **f** as precious as
1: 5 effort to add to your **f** goodness;
1Jn 5: 4 overcome the world, even our **f**.
Jude : 3 contend for the **f** that was once
: 20 yourselves up in your most holy **f**
Rev 2: 13 You did not renounce your **f** in me,
2: 19 your love and **f**, your service

FAITHFUL (FAITH)
Nu 12: 7 he is **f** in all my house.
Dt 7: 9 he is the **f** God, keeping his
32: 4 A **f** God who does no wrong,
1Sa 2: 35 I will raise up for myself a **f** priest,
2Sa 20: 19 We are the peaceful and **f** in Israel.
22: 26 "To the **f** you show yourself **f**,
1Ki 3: 6 David, because he was **f** to you
2Ch 31: 18 For they were **f** in consecrating
31: 20 and **f** before the LORD his God.
Ne 9: 8 You found his heart **f** to you,
Ps 4: 3 LORD has set apart his **f** servant
12: 1 LORD, for no one is **f** anymore;
16: 10 will you let your **f** one see decay.
18: 25 To the **f** you show yourself **f**,
25: 10 and **f** toward those who keep
31: 5 deliver me, LORD, my **f** God.
31: 23 Love the LORD, all his **f** people!
33: 4 right and true; he is **f** in all he does.
37: 28 just and will not forsake his **f** ones.
78: 8 whose spirits were not **f** to him.
78: 37 they were not **f** to his covenant.
86: 2 Guard my life, for I am **f** to you;
89: 19 a vision, to your **f** people you said:
89: 24 My **f** love will be with him,
89: 37 the moon, the **f** witness in the sky."
97: 10 for he guards the lives of his **f** ones
101: 6 eyes will be on the **f** in the land,
111: 7 The works of his hands are **f**
145: 13 all he promises and **f** in all he does.
145: 17 in all his ways and **f** in all he does.
146: 6 he remains **f** forever.
Pr 2: 8 and protects the way of his **f** ones.
20: 6 love, but a **f** person who can find?
28: 20 A **f** person will be richly blessed,
31: 26 and **f** instruction is on her tongue.
Isa 1: 21 See how the **f** city has become
1: 26 City of Righteousness, the **F** City."
49: 7 who is **f**, the Holy One of Israel,
55: 3 you, my **f** love promised to David.
Jer 3: 12 for I am **f**,' declares the LORD,
42: 5 **f** witness against us if we do not act
Eze 43: 11 so that they may be **f** to its design
48: 11 who were **f** in serving me and did
Hos 11: 12 God, even against the **f** Holy One.
Zec 8: 3 Jerusalem will be called the **F** City,
Zec 8: 8 I will be **f** and righteous to them as
Mt 24: 45 then is the **f** and wise servant,
25: 21 'Well done, good and **f** servant!
25: 21 You have been **f** with a few things;
25: 23 'Well done, good and **f** servant!
25: 23 You have been **f** with a few things;
Lk 12: 42 then is the **f** and wise manager,
Ro 12: 12 patient in affliction, **f** in prayer.
1Co 1: 9 God is **f**, who has called you
4: 2 been given a trust must prove **f**.
4: 17 whom I love, who is **f** in the Lord.
10: 13 And God is **f**; he will not let you be
2Co 1: 18 But as surely as God is **f**,
Eph 1: 1 in Ephesus, the **f** in Christ Jesus:
6: 21 brother and **f** servant in the Lord,
Col 1: 2 the **f** brothers and sisters in Christ:
1: 7 who is a **f** minister of Christ on our
4: 7 a **f** minister and fellow servant
4: 9 Onesimus, our **f** and dear brother,
1Th 5: 24 The one who calls you is **f**, and he
2Th 3: 3 But the Lord is **f**, and he will
1Ti 2: 7 a true and **f** teacher of the Gentiles.
3: 2 to be above reproach, **f** to his wife,
3: 12 A deacon must be **f** to his wife
5: 9 sixty, has been **f** to her husband,
2Ti 2: 13 he remains **f**, for he cannot disown
Titus 1: 6 must be blameless, **f** to his wife,
Heb 2: 17 and **f** high priest in service to God,
3: 2 He was **f** to the one who appointed
3: 2 just as Moses was **f** in all God's
3: 5 "Moses was **f** as a servant in all
3: 6 Christ is **f** as the Son over God's
8: 9 because they did not remain **f** to
10: 23 profess, for he who promised is **f**.
11: 11 she considered him **f** who had
1Pe 4: 10 as **f** stewards of God's grace in its
4: 19 themselves to their **f** Creator
5: 12 whom I regard as a **f** brother,
1Jn 1: 9 he is **f** and just and will forgive us
3Jn : 5 you are **f** in what you are doing
Rev 1: 5 who is the **f** witness, the firstborn
2: 10 Be **f**, even to the point of death,
2: 13 the days of Antipas, my **f** witness,
3: 14 the Amen, the **f** and true witness,
14: 12 commands and remain **f** to Jesus.
17: 14 his called, chosen and **f** followers."
19: 11 whose rider is called **F** and True.

FAITHFULLY (FAITH)
Dt 11: 13 So if you **f** obey the commands I
Jos 2: 14 and **f** when the LORD gives us
1Sa 12: 24 and serve him **f** with all your heart;
1Ki 2: 4 if they walk **f** before me with all
2Ki 20: 3 how I have walked before you **f**
2Ch 19: 9 "You must serve **f**
31: 12 they **f** brought in the contributions,
31: 15 and Shekaniah assisted him **f**
32: 1 all that Hezekiah had so **f** done,
34: 12 The workers labored **f**. Over them
Ne 9: 33 you have acted **f**, while we acted
13: 14 what I have so **f** done for the house
Isa 38: 3 how I have walked before you **f**
Jer 23: 28 one who has my word speak it **f**.
Eze 18: 9 my decrees and **f** keeps my laws.

FAITHFULNESS* (FAITH)
Ge 24: 27 his kindness and **f** to my master.
24: 49 show kindness and **f** to my master,
32: 10 **f** you have shown your servant.
47: 29 you will show me kindness and **f**.
Ex 34: 6 to anger, abounding in love and **f**,
Jos 24: 14 the LORD and serve him with all **f**.
1Sa 26: 23 for their righteousness and **f**.
2Sa 2: 6 now show you kindness and **f**,
15: 20 LORD show you kindness and **f**."
Ps 26: 3 have lived in reliance on your **f**.
30: 9 Will it proclaim your **f**?
36: 5 to the heavens, your **f** to the skies.
40: 10 I speak of your **f** and your saving
40: 10 and your **f** from the great assembly.
40: 11 your love and **f** always protect me.
51: 6 you desired **f** even in the womb;
54: 5 in your **f** destroy them.
57: 3 God sends forth his love and his **f**.
57: 10 your **f** reaches to the skies.
61: 7 your love and **f** to protect him.
71: 22 praise you with the harp for your **f**,

Ps 85: 10 Love and **f** meet together;
85: 11 **F** springs forth from the earth,
86: 11 LORD, that I may rely on your **f**;
86: 15 to anger, abounding in love and **f**.
88: 11 in the grave, your **f** in Destruction?
89: 1 make your **f** known through all
89: 2 that you have established your **f**
89: 5 LORD, your **f** too, in the assembly
89: 8 mighty, and your **f** surrounds you.
89: 14 love and **f** go before you.
89: 33 him, nor will I ever betray my **f**.
89: 49 in your **f** you swore to David?
91: 4 his **f** will be your shield
92: 2 in the morning and your **f** at night,
96: 13 and the peoples in his **f**.
98: 3 his love and his **f** to Israel;
100: 5 his **f** continues through all
108: 4 your **f** reaches to the skies.
111: 8 ever, enacted in **f** and uprightness.
115: 1 glory, because of your love and **f**.
117: 2 the **f** of the LORD endures forever.
119: 30 I have chosen the way of **f**;
119: 75 and that in **f** you have afflicted me.
119: 90 Your **f** continues through all
138: 2 for your unfailing love and your **f**,
143: 1 in your **f** and righteousness come
Pr 3: 3 Let love and **f** never leave you;
14: 22 plan what is good find love and **f**.
16: 6 Through love and **f** sin is atoned
20: 28 Love and **f** keep a king safe;
Isa 11: 5 and **f** the sash around his waist.
16: 5 in **f** a man will sit on it—
25: 1 perfect **f** you have done wonderful
38: 18 to the pit cannot hope for your **f**.
38: 19 tell their children about your **f**.
40: 6 all their **f** is like the flowers
42: 3 In **f** he will bring forth justice;
61: 8 In my **f** I will reward my people
La 3: 23 new every morning; great is your **f**.
Hos 2: 20 I will betroth you in **f**, and you will
4: 1 "There is no **f**, no love,
Hab 2: 4 righteous person will live by his **f**—
Mt 23: 23 of the law—justice, mercy and **f**.
Ro 3: 3 their unfaithfulness nullify God's **f**?
Gal 5: 22 forbearance, kindness, goodness, **f**,
3Jn : 3 testified about your **f** to the truth,
Rev 13: 10 and **f** on the part of God's people.

FAITHLESS* (FAITH)
Ps 78: 57 ancestors they were disloyal and **f**,
101: 3 I hate what **f** people do; I will have
119:158 I look on the **f** with loathing,
Pr 14: 14 The **f** will be fully repaid for their
Jer 3: 6 you seen what **f** Israel has done?
3: 8 I gave **f** Israel her certificate
3: 11 "**F** Israel is more righteous than
3: 12 "'Return, **f** Israel,'
3: 14 "Return, **f** people,"
3: 22 "Return, **f** people; I will cure you
12: 1 Why do all the **f** live at ease?
2Ti 2: 13 if we are **f**, he remains faithful,

FALL (FALLEN FALLS)
Ps 37: 24 he will not **f**, for the LORD
69: 9 of those who insult you **f** on me.
145: 14 The LORD upholds all who **f**
Pr 11: 28 who trust in their riches will **f**,
Isa 40: 7 The grass withers and the flowers **f**,
Mt 7: 25 yet it did not **f**, because it had its
13: 21 of the word, they quickly **f** away.
Lk 10: 18 "I saw Satan **f** like lightning
11: 17 a house divided against itself will **f**.
23: 30 say to the mountains, "**F** on us!"
Jn 16: 1 you so that you will not **f** away.
Ro 3: 23 and **f** short of the glory of God,
14: 4 own master, servants stand or **f**.

FALLEN (FALL)
2Sa 1: 19 How the mighty have **f**!
Isa 14: 12 How you have **f** from heaven,
1Co 11: 30 and a number of you have **f** asleep.
15: 6 living, though some have **f** asleep.
15: 18 have **f** asleep in Christ are lost.
15: 20 of those who have **f** asleep.
Gal 5: 4 you have **f** away from grace.
1Th 4: 15 precede those who have **f** asleep.
Heb 6: 6 and who have **f** away, to be brought

FALLS (FALL)
Pr 11: 14 For lack of guidance a nation **f**,
24: 17 Do not gloat when your enemy **f**;
28: 14 whoever hardens their heart **f**
Mt 21: 44 Anyone who **f** on this stone will be
Jn 12: 24 a kernel of wheat **f** to the ground
Heb 12: 15 it that no one **f** short of the grace

FALSE (FALSEHOOD FALSELY)
Ex 20: 16 shall not give **f** testimony against
23: 1 "Do not spread **f** reports.
23: 7 Have nothing to do with a **f** charge
Dt 5: 20 shall not give **f** testimony against
Pr 12: 17 the truth, but a **f** witness tells lies.
13: 5 The righteous hate what is **f**,
14: 5 but a **f** witness pours out lies.
14: 25 lives, but a **f** witness is deceitful.
19: 5 A **f** witness will not go unpunished,
19: 9 A **f** witness will not go unpunished,
21: 28 A **f** witness will perish, but a
25: 18 one who gives **f** testimony against
Isa 44: 25 who foils the signs of **f** prophets
Jer 23: 16 they fill you with **f** hopes.
Mt 7: 15 "Watch out for **f** prophets.
15: 19 theft, **f** testimony, slander.
19: 18 steal, you shall not give **f** testimony,
24: 11 and many **f** prophets will appear
24: 24 For **f** messiahs and **f** prophets will
Mk 10: 19 you shall not give **f** testimony,
13: 22 For **f** messiahs and **f** prophets will
Lk 6: 26 ancestors treated the **f** prophets.
18: 20 steal, you shall not give **f** testimony,
1Co 15: 15 found to be **f** witnesses about God,
2Co 11: 13 For such people are **f** apostles,
11: 26 and in danger from **f** believers.
Gal 2: 4 arose because some **f** believers had
Php 1: 18 whether from **f** motives or true,
Col 2: 18 anyone who delights in **f** humility
2: 23 their **f** humility and their harsh
1Ti 1: 3 not to teach **f** doctrines any longer
2Pe 2: 1 also **f** prophets among the people,
2: 1 there will be **f** teachers among you.
1Jn 4: 1 because many **f** prophets have gone
Rev 16: 13 out of the mouth of the **f** prophet.
19: 20 the **f** prophet who had performed
20: 10 the **f** prophet had been thrown.

FALSEHOOD* (FALSE)
Job 21: 34 is left of your answers but **f**!"
31: 5 "If I have walked with **f** or my foot
Ps 52: 3 **f** rather than speaking the truth.
119:163 and detest **f** but I love your law.
Pr 30: 8 Keep **f** and lies far from me;
Isa 28: 15 our refuge and **f** our hiding place."
Ro 3: 7 my **f** enhances God's truthfulness
Eph 4: 25 each of you must put off **f**
1Jn 4: 6 Spirit of truth and the spirit of **f**.
Rev 22: 15 everyone who loves and practices **f**.

FALSELY (FALSE)
Lev 19: 12 "'Do not swear **f** by my name
Isa 59: 3 Your lips have spoken **f**, and your
Mt 5: 11 **f** say all kinds of evil against you
Lk 3: 14 money and don't accuse people **f**—
1Ti 6: 20 ideas of what is **f** called knowledge,

FALTER*
Pr 24: 10 If you **f** in a time of trouble,
Isa 42: 4 he will not **f** or be discouraged till

FAME
Jos 9: 9 of the **f** of the LORD your God.
Isa 66: 19 islands that have not heard of my **f**
Hab 3: 2 LORD, I have heard of your **f**;

FAMILIES (FAMILY)
Ps 68: 6 God sets the lonely in **f**, he leads

FAMILY (FAMILIES)
Pr 31: 15 she provides food for her **f**
Lk 9: 61 go back and say goodbye to my **f**."
12: 52 in one **f** divided against each other,
Ac 10: 2 He and all his **f** were devout
1Ti 3: 4 He must manage his own **f** well
3: 5 know how to manage his own **f**,
5: 4 practice by caring for their own **f**

FAMINE
Ge 12: 10 Now there was a **f** in the land,
26: 1 Now there was a **f** in the land—
41: 30 seven years of **f** will follow them.
Ru 1: 1 ruled, there was a **f** in the land.
1Ki 18: 2 Now the **f** was severe in Samaria,
Am 8: 11 I will send a **f** through the land—
8: 11 but a **f** of hearing the words
Ro 8: 35 or persecution or **f** or nakedness

FAN*
2Ti 1: 6 this reason I remind you to **f**

FANTASIES*
Ps 73: 20 Lord, you will despise them as **f**.
Pr 12: 11 those who chase **f** have no sense.
28: 19 who chase **f** will have their fill

FASHIONED
Ps 94: 9 Does he who **f** the ear not hear?

FAST (FASTING)
Dt 10: 20 Hold **f** to him and take your oaths
11: 22 to him and to hold **f** to him—
13: 4 serve him and hold **f** to him.
30: 20 to his voice, and hold **f** to him.
Jos 22: 5 to hold **f** to him and to serve him
23: 8 to hold **f** to the LORD your God,
2Ki 18: 6 He held **f** to the LORD and did not
Ps 119: 31 I hold **f** to your statutes, LORD;
139: 10 me, your right hand will hold me **f**.
Mt 6: 16 "When you **f**, do not look somber
1Pe 5: 12 the true grace of God. Stand **f** in it.

FASTING (FAST)
Ps 35: 13 and humbled myself with **f**.
Ac 13: 2 were worshiping the Lord and **f**,
14: 23 with prayer and **f**, committed them

FATAL
Ex 21: 12 who strikes a person with a **f** blow

FATHER (FATHER'S FATHERLESS FATHERS)
Ge 2: 24 That is why a man leaves his **f**
17: 4 You will be the **f** of many nations.
Ex 20: 12 "Honor your **f** and your mother,
21: 15 "Anyone who attacks their **f**
21: 17 "Anyone who curses their **f**
Lev 18: 7 "'Do not dishonor your **f**
19: 3 must respect your mother and **f**,
20: 9 "'Anyone who curses their **f**
Dt 1: 31 carried you, as a **f** carries his son,
5: 16 "Honor your **f** and your mother,
21: 18 son who does not obey his **f**
32: 6 Is he not your **F**, your Creator,
2Sa 7: 14 I will be his **f**, and he will be my
1Ch 17: 13 I will be his **f**, and he will be my
22: 10 will be my son, and I will be his **f**.
28: 6 to be my son, and I will be his **f**.
Job 38: 28 Does the rain have a **f**?
Ps 2: 7 today I have become your **f**.
27: 10 Though my **f** and mother forsake
68: 5 A **f** to the fatherless, a defender
89: 26 out to me, 'You are my **F**, my God,
103: 13 As a **f** has compassion on his
Pr 3: 12 loves, as a **f** the son he delights in.
10: 1 A wise son brings joy to his **f**,
17: 25 A foolish son brings grief to his **f**
23: 22 Listen to your **f**, who gave you life,
23: 24 The **f** of a righteous child has great
28: 7 of gluttons disgraces his **f**.
28: 24 Whoever robs their **f** or mother
29: 3 loves wisdom brings joy to his **f**,
Isa 9: 6 Everlasting **F**, Prince of Peace.
45: 10 Woe to the one who says to a **f**,
63: 16 our **F**, our Redeemer from of old
Jer 2: 27 wood, 'You are my **f**,' and to stone,
3: 19 I thought you would call me '**F**'
31: 9 because I am Israel's **f**,
Eze 18: 19 the son not share the guilt of his **f**?'
Mic 7: 6 a son dishonors his **f**, a daughter
Mal 1: 6 If I am a **f**, where is the honor due
2: 10 Do we not all have one **F**?
Mt 3: 9 'We have Abraham as our **f**.'
5: 16 deeds and glorify your **F** in heaven.
6: 9 "'Our **F** in heaven, hallowed be
6: 26 yet your heavenly **F** feeds them.
10: 37 "Anyone who loves their **f**
11: 27 one knows the Son except the **F**,
11: 27 no one knows the **F** except the Son
15: 4 said, 'Honor your **f** and mother'
15: 4 and 'Anyone who curses their **f**
18: 10 see the face of my **F** in heaven.
19: 5 this reason a man will leave his **f**

Mt 19: 19 honor your **f** and mother,' and 'love
19: 29 brothers or sisters or **f** or mother
23: 9 do not call anyone on earth '**f**,' for you have one **F**,
Mk 7: 10 said, 'Honor your **f** and mother,'
Lk 9: 59 first let me go and bury my **f**."
12: 53 **f** against son and son against **f**,
14: 26 and does not hate **f** and mother,
18: 20 honor your **f** and mother.'"
23: 34 Jesus said, "**F**, forgive them,
Jn 3: 35 The **F** loves the Son and has placed
4: 21 you will worship the **F** neither
5: 17 "My **F** is always at his work to this
5: 18 he was even calling God his own **F**,
5: 20 For the **F** loves the Son and shows
6: 44 unless the **F** who sent me draws
6: 46 from God; only he has seen the **F**.
8: 19 "You do not know me or my **F**,"
8: 28 just what the **F** has taught me.
8: 41 "The only **F** we have is God
8: 42 "If God were your **F**, you would
8: 44 You belong to your **f**, the devil,
8: 44 he is a liar and the **f** of lies.
10: 17 The reason my **F** loves me is that I
10: 30 I and the **F** are one."
10: 38 that the **F** is in me, and I in the **F**."
14: 6 comes to the **F** except through me.
14: 9 who has seen me has seen the **F**.
14: 28 for the **F** is greater than I.
15: 9 "As the **F** has loved me, so have I
15: 23 hates me hates my **F** as well.
20: 17 I have not yet ascended to the **F**.
20: 17 ascending to my **F** and your **F**,
Ac 13: 33 today I have become your **f**.'
Ro 4: 11 he is the **f** of all who believe
4: 16 He is the **f** of us all.
8: 15 And by him we cry, *"Abba*, **F**."
1Co 4: 15 became your **f** through the gospel.
2Co 6: 18 And, "I will be a **F** to you, and you
Eph 5: 31 this reason a man will leave his **f**
6: 2 "Honor your **f** and mother"—
Php 2: 11 is Lord, to the glory of God the **F**.
Heb 1: 5 today I have become your **F**"?
12: 7 are not disciplined by their **f**?
1Jn 1: 3 our fellowship is with the **F**
2: 15 world, love for the **F** is not in them.
2: 22 denying the **F** and the Son.

FATHER'S (FATHER)
Pr 13: 1 A wise son heeds his **f** instruction,
19: 13 A foolish child is a **f** ruin,
Mt 16: 27 come in his **F** glory with his angels,
Lk 2: 49 know I had to be in my **F** house?"
Jn 2: 16 Stop turning my **F** house
10: 29 can snatch them out of my **F** hand.
14: 2 My **F** house has many rooms;
15: 8 This is to my **F** glory, that you bear

FATHERLESS (FATHER)
Ex 22: 22 advantage of the widow or the **f**.
Dt 10: 18 He defends the cause of the **f**
14: 29 the **f** and the widows who live
24: 17 the foreigner or the **f** of justice,
24: 19 the foreigner, the **f** and the widow,
26: 12 the foreigner, the **f** and the widow,
Ps 68: 5 A father to the **f**, a defender
82: 3 Defend the weak and the **f**;
Pr 23: 10 or encroach on the fields of the **f**,

FATHERS (FATHER)
Lk 11: 11 "Which of you **f**, if your son asks
1Co 4: 15 you do not have many **f**,
Eph 6: 4 **F**, do not exasperate your children;
Col 3: 21 **F**, do not embitter your children,
Heb 12: 9 all had human **f** who disciplined us

FATHOM* (FATHOMED)
Job 11: 7 "Can you **f** the mysteries of God?
Ps 145: 3 his greatness no one can **f**.
Ecc 3: 11 no one can **f** what God has done
Isa 40: 13 Who can **f** the Spirit of the LORD,
40: 28 his understanding no one can **f**.
1Co 13: 2 of prophecy and can **f** all mysteries

FATHOMED* (FATHOM)
Job 5: 9 performs wonders that cannot be **f**,
9: 10 performs wonders that cannot be **f**,

FATTENED
Pr 15: 17 with love than a **f** calf with hatred.
Lk 15: 23 Bring the **f** calf and kill it.

FAULT (FAULTS)
1Sa 29: 3 now, I have found no **f** in him."
Mt 18: 15 sins, go and point out their **f**,
Php 2: 15 of God without **f** in a warped
Jas 1: 5 generously to all without finding **f**,
Jude : 24 his glorious presence without **f**

FAULTFINDERS*
Jude : 16 These people are grumblers and **f**;

FAULTLESS*
Php 3: 6 righteousness based on the law, **f**.
Jas 1: 27 Father accepts as pure and **f** is this:

FAULTS* (FAULT)
Job 10: 6 that you must search out my **f**
Ps 19: 12 Forgive my hidden **f**.

FAVOR (FAVORITISM)
Ge 4: 4 The LORD looked with **f** on Abel
6: 8 But Noah found **f** in the eyes
Ex 33: 12 and you have found **f** with me.'
34: 9 "if I have found **f** in your eyes,
Lev 26: 9 "'I will look on you with **f**
Nu 11: 15 if I have found **f** in your eyes—
Jdg 6: 17 "If now I have found **f** in your eyes,
1Sa 2: 26 in stature and in **f** with the LORD
2Sa 2: 6 you the same **f** because you have
2Ki 13: 4 Jehoahaz sought the LORD's **f**,
2Ch 33: 12 In his distress he sought the **f**
Est 7: 3 "If I have found **f** with you,
Ps 90: 17 May the **f** of the Lord our God rest
Pr 3: 34 mockers but shows **f** to the humble
8: 35 life and receive **f** from the LORD.
10: 32 of the righteous know what finds **f**,
11: 1 accurate weights find **f** with him.
18: 22 and receives **f** from the LORD.
19: 6 Many curry **f** with a ruler,
Isa 61: 2 proclaim the year of the LORD's **f**
Zec 11: 7 called one **F** and the other Union,
Lk 1: 30 you have found **f** with God.
2: 14 to those on whom his **f** rests."
2: 52 and in **f** with God and man.
4: 19 proclaim the year of the Lord's **f**."
2Co 6: 2 "In the time of my **f** I heard you,
1Pe 5: 5 proud but shows **f** to the humble."

FAVORITISM* (FAVOR)
Ex 23: 3 do not show **f** to a poor person
Lev 19: 15 to the poor or **f** to the great,
Ac 10: 34 true it is that God does not show **f**
Ro 2: 11 For God does not show **f**.
Gal 2: 6 God does not show **f**—
Eph 6: 9 heaven, and there is no **f** with him.
Col 3: 25 for their wrongs, and there is no **f**.
1Ti 5: 21 and to do nothing out of **f**.
Jas 2: 1 Lord Jesus Christ must not show **f**.
2: 9 But if you show **f**, you sin and are

FEAR (AFRAID FEARED FEARS FRIGHTENED GOD-FEARING)
Dt 6: 13 **F** the LORD your God, serve him
10: 12 you but to **f** the LORD your God,
31: 12 learn to **f** the LORD your God
31: 13 to **f** the LORD your God as long as
Jos 4: 24 that you might always **f** the LORD
24: 14 "Now **f** the LORD and serve him
1Sa 12: 14 If you **f** the LORD and serve
12: 24 be sure to **f** the LORD and serve
2Sa 23: 3 when he rules in the **f** of God,
2Ch 19: 7 Now let the **f** of the LORD be
26: 5 instructed him in the **f** of God.
Job 1: 9 "Does Job **f** God for nothing?"
Ps 2: 11 Serve the LORD with **f**
19: 9 The **f** of the LORD is pure,
23: 4 the darkest valley, I will **f** no evil,
27: 1 and my salvation—whom shall I **f**?
33: 8 Let all the earth **f** the LORD;
34: 7 encamps around those who **f** him,
34: 9 **F** the LORD, you his holy people,
46: 2 Therefore we will not **f**,
86: 11 heart, that I may **f** your name.
90: 11 Your wrath is as great as the **f** that
91: 5 You will not **f** the terror of night,
111: 10 The **f** of the LORD is
112: 1 are those who **f** the LORD,
118: 4 Let those who **f** the LORD say:
128: 1 Blessed are all who **f** the LORD,
145: 19 the desires of those who **f** him;
147: 11 LORD delights in those who **f** him,
Pr 1: 7 The **f** of the LORD is
1: 33 and be at ease, without **f** of harm."
8: 13 To **f** the LORD is to hate evil;
9: 10 The **f** of the LORD is
10: 27 The **f** of the LORD adds length
14: 16 The wise **f** the LORD and shun
14: 27 The **f** of the LORD is a fountain
15: 33 instruction is to **f** the LORD,
16: 6 through the **f** of the LORD evil is
19: 23 The **f** of the LORD leads to life;
22: 4 Humility is the **f** of the LORD;
29: 25 **F** of man will prove to be a snare,
31: 21 she has no **f** for her household;
Ecc 3: 14 does it so that people will **f** him.
5: 7 Therefore **f** God.
8: 12 go better with those who **f** God,
12: 13 of the matter: **F** God and keep his
Isa 11: 3 will delight in the **f** of the LORD.
33: 6 the **f** of the LORD is the key to this
35: 4 fearful hearts, "Be strong, do not **f**;
41: 10 So do not **f**, for I am with you;
41: 13 and says to you, Do not **f**;
43: 1 "Do not **f**, for I have redeemed
51: 7 Do not **f** the reproach of mere
54: 14 you will have nothing to **f**.
Jer 10: 7 Who should not **f** you,
17: 8 It does not **f** when heat comes;
Lk 12: 5 show you whom you should **f**:
2Co 5: 11 we know what it is to **f** the Lord,
Php 2: 12 to work out your salvation with **f**
1Jn 4: 18 There is no **f** in love.
4: 18 But perfect love drives out **f**,
Jude : 23 others show mercy, mixed with **f**—
Rev 14: 7 voice, "**F** God and give him glory,

FEARED (FEAR)
Job 1: 1 he **f** God and shunned evil.
Ps 76: 7 It is you alone who are to be **f**.
Mal 3: 16 those who **f** the LORD talked

FEARS (FEAR)
Job 1: 8 a man who **f** God and shuns evil."
2: 3 a man who **f** God and shuns evil.
Ps 34: 4 he delivered me from all my **f**.
Pr 14: 26 Whoever **f** the LORD has a secure
31: 30 a woman who **f** the LORD is to be
2Co 7: 5 conflicts on the outside, **f** within.
1Jn 4: 18 The one who **f** is not made perfect

FEAST (FEASTING FEASTS)
Pr 15: 15 the cheerful heart has a continual **f**.
2Pe 2: 13 in their pleasures while they **f**

FEASTING (FEAST)
Pr 17: 1 and quiet than a house full of **f**,

FEASTS (FEAST)
Jude : 12 people are blemishes at your love **f**,

FEATHERS
Ps 91: 4 He will cover you with his **f**,

FEEBLE
Job 4: 3 you have strengthened **f** hands.
Isa 35: 3 Strengthen the **f** hands,
Heb 12: 12 strengthen your **f** arms and weak

FED (FEED)
Ps 105: 40 he **f** them well with the bread

FEED (FED FEEDS)
Jn 21: 15 Jesus said, "**F** my lambs."
21: 17 Jesus said, "**F** my sheep.
Ro 12: 20 "If your enemy is hungry, **f** him;
Jude : 12 shepherds who **f** only themselves.

FEEDS (FEED)
Pr 15: 14 but the mouth of a fool **f** on folly.
Mt 6: 26 yet your heavenly Father **f** them.
Jn 6: 57 so the one who **f** on me will live

FEEL
Jdg 16: 26 "Put me where I can **f** the pillars
Ps 115: 7 They have hands, but cannot **f**,

FEET (FOOT)
Ru 3: 8 there was a woman lying at his **f**!
Ps 8: 6 you put everything under their **f**:
22: 16 they pierce my hands and my **f**.
40: 2 he set my **f** on a rock and gave me
56: 13 death and my **f** from stumbling,
66: 9 lives and kept our **f** from slipping.
73: 2 as for me, my **f** had almost slipped;
110: 1 enemies a footstool for your **f**."

Ps 119:105 Your word is a lamp to my **f**
Pr 4: 26 thought to the paths for your **f**
Isa 52: 7 the mountains are the **f** of those
Da 2: 33 iron, its **f** partly of iron and partly
Na 1: 15 the **f** of one who brings good news,
Mt 10: 14 town and shake the dust off your **f**.
22: 44 put your enemies under your **f**."'
Lk 1: 79 death, to guide our **f** into the path
20: 43 enemies a footstool for your **f**."'
24: 39 Look at my hands and my **f**. It is I
Jn 13: 5 and began to wash his disciples' **f**,
13: 14 also should wash one another's **f**.
Ro 3: 15 "Their **f** are swift to shed blood;
10: 15 "How beautiful are the **f** of those
16: 20 will soon crush Satan under your **f**.
1Co 12: 21 And the head cannot say to the **f**,
15: 25 has put all his enemies under his **f**.
Eph 1: 22 God placed all things under his **f**
1Ti 5: 10 washing the **f** of the Lord's people,
Heb 1: 13 enemies a footstool for your **f**"?
2: 8 and put everything under their **f**."
12: 13 "Make level paths for your **f**,"
Rev 1: 15 His **f** were like bronze glowing

FELIX

Governor before whom Paul was tried (Ac 23:23–24:27).

FELLOWSHIP
Ex 20: 24 burnt offerings and **f** offerings,
Lev 3: 1 "'If your offering is a **f** offering,
1Co 1: 9 who has called you into **f** with his
5: 2 put out of your **f** the man who has
2Co 6: 14 **f** can light have with darkness?
13: 14 the **f** of the Holy Spirit be with you
Gal 2: 9 Barnabas the right hand of **f**
1Jn 1: 3 that you also may have **f** with us.
1: 3 And our **f** is with the Father
1: 6 If we claim to have **f** with him
1: 7 light, we have **f** with one another,

FEMALE
Ge 1: 27 male and **f** he created them.
5: 2 He created them male and **f**
Mt 19: 4 Creator 'made them male and **f**,'
Mk 10: 6 God 'made them male and **f**.'
Gal 3: 28 nor is there male and **f**, for you are

FEROCIOUS
Mt 7: 15 but inwardly they are **f** wolves.

FERTILE (FERTILIZE)
Isa 32: 15 and the desert becomes a **f** field,
Jer 2: 7 I brought you into a **f** land to eat

FERTILIZE* (FERTILE)
Lk 13: 8 year, and I'll dig around it and **f** it.

FERVOR*
Ac 18: 25 he spoke with great **f** and taught
Ro 12: 11 but keep your spiritual **f**,

FESTIVAL (FESTIVALS)
1Co 5: 8 Therefore let us keep the **F**,
Col 2: 16 or with regard to a religious **f**,

FESTIVALS (FESTIVALS)
Am 5: 21 "I hate, I despise your religious **f**;

FESTUS

Successor of Felix; sent Paul to Caesar (Ac 25–26).

FEVER
Job 30: 30 my body burns with **f**.
Mt 8: 14 lying in bed with a **f**.
Lk 4: 38 was suffering from a high **f**,
Jn 4: 52 in the afternoon, the **f** left him."
Ac 28: 8 suffering from **f** and dysentery.

FIDELITY*
Ro 1: 31 no understanding, no **f**, no love,
16: 10 **f** to Christ has stood the test.

FIELD (FIELDS)
Ge 4: 8 Abel, "Let's go out to the **f**."
Lev 19: 9 not reap to the very edges of your **f**
19: 19 "'Do not plant your **f** with two
Pr 31: 16 She considers a **f** and buys it;
Isa 40: 6 is like the flowers of the **f**.
Mt 6: 28 See how the flowers of the **f** grow.
6: 30 how God clothes the grass of the **f**,
13: 38 The **f** is the world, and the good
13: 44 is like treasure hidden in a **f**.
Lk 14: 18 'I have just bought a **f**, and I must
1Co 3: 9 you are God's **f**, God's building.
1Pe 1: 24 glory is like the flowers of the **f**;

FIELDS (FIELD)
Ru 2: 2 "Let me go to the **f** and pick
Lk 2: 8 shepherds living out in the **f**
Jn 4: 35 open your eyes and look at the **f**!

FIERY (FIRE)
1Pe 4: 12 do not be surprised at the **f** ordeal

FIG (FIGS SYCAMORE-FIG)
Ge 3: 7 so they sewed **f** leaves together
Jdg 9: 10 the trees said to the **f** tree,
1Ki 4: 25 vine and under their own **f** tree.
Pr 27: 18 one who guards a **f** tree will eat its
Mic 4: 4 vine and under their own **f** tree,
Zec 3: 10 to sit under your vine and **f** tree,'
Mt 21: 19 Seeing a **f** tree by the road, he went
Lk 13: 6 "A man had a **f** tree growing in his
Jas 3: 12 and sisters, can a **f** tree bear olives,
Rev 6: 13 as figs drop from a **f** tree

FIGHT (FIGHTING FIGHTS FOUGHT)
Ex 14: 14 The LORD will **f** for you;
Dt 1: 30 is going before you, will **f** for you,
3: 22 the LORD your God himself will **f**
1Sa 25: 28 because you **f** the LORD's battles,
Ne 4: 20 Our God will **f** for us!"
Ps 35: 1 **f** against those who **f** against me.
Jn 18: 36 my servants would **f** to prevent my
1Co 9: 26 I do not **f** like a boxer beating
2Co 10: 4 The weapons we **f** with are not
1Ti 1: 18 them you may **f** the battle well,
6: 12 **F** the good **f** of the faith.
2Ti 4: 7 I have fought the good **f**, I have

FIGHTING (FIGHT)
Jos 10: 14 Surely the LORD was **f** for Israel!

FIGHTS (FIGHT)
Jos 23: 10 because the LORD your God **f**
Jas 4: 1 What causes **f** and quarrels among

FIGS (FIG)
Lk 6: 44 People do not pick **f**
Jas 3: 12 bear olives, or a grapevine bear **f**?

FILL (FILLED FILLING FILLS FULL FULLNESS FULLY)
Ge 1: 28 **f** the earth and subdue it.
Ps 16: 11 you will **f** me with joy in your
81: 10 wide your mouth and I will **f** it.
Pr 28: 19 chase fantasies will have their **f**
Hag 2: 7 and I will **f** this house with glory,'
Jn 6: 26 you ate the loaves and had your **f**.
Ac 2: 28 you will **f** me with joy in your
Ro 15: 13 May the God of hope **f** you with all

FILLED (FILL)
Ex 31: 3 I have **f** him with the Spirit of God,
35: 31 he has **f** him with the Spirit of God,
Dt 34: 9 son of Nun was **f** with the spirit
1Ki 8: 10 Place, the cloud **f** the temple
8: 11 glory of the LORD **f** his temple.
2Ch 5: 14 the glory of the LORD **f** the temple
7: 1 glory of the LORD **f** the temple.
Ps 72: 19 may the whole earth be **f** with his
119: 64 The earth is **f** with your love,
Isa 6: 4 and the temple was **f** with smoke.
11: 9 for the earth will be **f**
Eze 10: 3 in, and a cloud **f** the inner court.
10: 4 The cloud **f** the temple,
43: 5 glory of the LORD **f** the temple.
Hab 2: 14 For the earth will be **f**
3: 3 heavens and his praise **f** the earth.
Mt 5: 6 for righteousness, for they will be **f**.
Lk 1: 15 he will be **f** with the Holy Spirit
1: 41 Elizabeth was **f** with the Holy Spirit
1: 67 His father Zechariah was **f**
2: 40 was **f** with wisdom, and the grace
Jn 12: 3 the house was **f** with the fragrance
Ac 2: 2 **f** the whole house where they were
2: 4 of them were **f** with the Holy Spirit
4: 8 Then Peter, **f** with the Holy Spirit,
4: 31 they were all **f** with the Holy Spirit
9: 17 and be **f** with the Holy Spirit."
13: 9 called Paul, **f** with the Holy Spirit,
Eph 5: 18 Instead, be **f** with the Spirit,
Php 1: 11 **f** with the fruit of righteousness
Rev 15: 8 the temple was **f** with smoke

FILLING (FILL)
Eze 44: 4 the glory of the LORD **f** the temple

FILLS (FILL)
Nu 14: 21 of the LORD **f** the whole earth,
Ps 107: 9 and **f** the hungry with good things.
Eph 1: 23 him who **f** everything in every way.

FILTH (FILTHY)
Isa 4: 4 The Lord will wash away the **f**
Jas 1: 21 get rid of all moral **f** and the evil

FILTHY (FILTH)
Isa 64: 6 all our righteous acts are like **f** rags;
Col 3: 8 and **f** language from your lips.

FINAL (FINALITY)
Ps 73: 17 then I understood their **f** destiny.

FINALITY* (FINAL)
Ro 9: 28 on earth with speed and **f**."

FINANCIAL*
1Ti 6: 5 that godliness is a means to **f** gain.

FIND (FINDS FOUND)
Nu 32: 23 be sure that your sin will **f** you out.
Dt 4: 29 you will **f** him if you seek him
1Sa 23: 16 and helped him **f** strength in God.
Job 23: 3 If only I knew where to **f** him;
Ps 62: 5 Yes, my soul, **f** rest in God;
91: 4 under his wings you will **f** refuge;
112: 1 LORD, who **f** great delight in his
Pr 3: 13 Blessed are those who **f** wisdom,
8: 17 me, and those who seek me **f** me.
8: 35 For those who **f** me **f** life
14: 22 those who plan what is good **f** love
20: 6 but a faithful person who can **f**?
24: 14 If you **f** it, there is a future hope
31: 10 wife of noble character who can **f**?
Jer 6: 16 and you will **f** rest for your souls.
29: 13 and **f** me when you seek me with
Mt 7: 7 seek and you will **f**;
11: 29 and you will **f** rest for your souls.
16: 25 loses their life for me will **f** it.
22: 9 invite to the banquet anyone you **f**.'
Lk 11: 9 seek and you will **f**;
18: 8 will he **f** faith on the earth?"
Jn 10: 9 come in and go out, and **f** pasture.

FINDS (FIND)
Ps 62: 1 Truly my soul **f** rest in God;
119:162 promise like one who **f** great spoil.
Pr 11: 27 Whoever seeks good **f** favor,
18: 22 He who **f** a wife **f** what is good
Mt 7: 8 the one who seeks **f**; and to the one
10: 39 Whoever **f** their life will lose it,
Lk 11: 10 the one who seeks **f**; and to the one
12: 37 whose master **f** them watching
12: 43 servant whom the master **f** doing
15: 4 go after the lost sheep until he **f** it?
15: 8 and search carefully until she **f** it?

FINE
Pr 17: 26 imposing a **f** on the innocent is not
Zec 3: 4 and I will put **f** garments on you."

FINE-SOUNDING* (SOUND)
Col 2: 4 may deceive you by **f** arguments.

FINGER
Ex 8: 19 to Pharaoh, "This is the **f** of God."
31: 18 of stone inscribed by the **f** of God.
Dt 9: 10 tablets inscribed by the **f** of God.
Lk 11: 20 I drive out demons by the **f** of God,
16: 24 to dip the tip of his **f** in water
Jn 8: 6 *write on the ground with his **f**.*
20: 25 and put my **f** where the nails were,

FINISH (FINISHED)
Jn 4: 34 who sent me and to **f** his work.
5: 36 that the Father has given me to **f**—
Ac 20: 24 my only aim is to **f** the race
2Co 8: 11 Now **f** the work, so that your eager
Gal 3: 3 are you now trying to **f** by means
Jas 1: 4 Let perseverance **f** its work so

FINISHED (FINISH)
Ge 2: 2 seventh day God had **f** the work he
Jn 19: 30 the drink, Jesus said, "It is **f**."
2Ti 4: 7 the good fight, I have **f** the race,

FIRE (FIERY)
Ex 3: 2 bush was on **f** it did not burn up.
13: 21 in a pillar of **f** to give them light,

Lev 6: 12 The **f** on the altar must be kept
9: 24 **F** came out from the presence
1Ki 18: 38 Then the **f** of the LORD fell
2Ki 2: 11 suddenly a chariot of **f** and horses
Isa 5: 24 as tongues of **f** lick up straw and as
30: 27 and his tongue is a consuming **f**.
Jer 23: 29 "Is not my word like **f**,"
Da 3: 25 four men walking around in the **f**,
Zec 3: 2 stick snatched from the **f**?"
Mal 3: 2 For he will be like a refiner's **f**
Mt 3: 11 you with the Holy Spirit and **f**.
3: 12 up the chaff with unquenchable **f**."
5: 22 will be in danger of the **f** of hell.
18: 8 feet and be thrown into eternal **f**.
25: 41 the eternal **f** prepared for the devil
Mk 9: 43 hell, where the **f** never goes out.
9: 48 not die, and the **f** is not quenched.'
9: 49 Everyone will be salted with **f**.
Lk 3: 16 you with the Holy Spirit and **f**.
12: 49 have come to bring **f** on the earth,
Ac 2: 3 to be tongues of **f** that separated
1Co 3: 13 It will be revealed with **f**, and the **f**
Heb 12: 29 for our "God is a consuming **f**."
Jas 3: 5 what a great forest is set on **f**
3: 6 The tongue also is a **f**, a world
3: 6 and is itself set on **f** by hell.
2Pe 3: 10 the elements will be destroyed by **f**,
Jude : 7 suffer the punishment of eternal **f**.
: 23 by snatching them from the **f**;
Rev 1: 14 and his eyes were like blazing **f**.
20: 14 The lake of **f** is the second death.

FIRM*
Ex 14: 13 Stand **f** and you will see
2Ch 20: 17 stand **f** and see the deliverance
Ezr 9: 8 giving us a **f** place in his sanctuary,
Job 11: 15 you will stand **f** and without fear.
36: 5 he is mighty, and **f** in his purpose.
41: 23 they are **f** and immovable.
Ps 19: 9 The decrees of the LORD are **f**,
20: 8 fall, but we rise up and stand **f**.
30: 7 made my royal mountain stand **f**;
33: 9 he commanded, and it stood **f**.
33: 11 plans of the LORD stand **f** forever,
37: 23 The LORD makes **f** the steps
40: 2 and gave me a **f** place to stand.
75: 3 quake, it is I who hold its pillars **f**.
89: 2 that your love stands **f** forever,
89: 4 and make your throne **f** through all
93: 1 world is established, **f** and secure.
93: 5 Your statutes, LORD, stand **f**;
119: 89 it stands **f** in the heavens.
Pr 10: 25 but the righteous stand **f** forever.
12: 7 the house of the righteous stands **f**.
Isa 7: 9 If you do not stand **f** in your faith,
22: 17 is about to take **f** hold of you
22: 23 drive him like a peg into a **f** place;
22: 25 into the **f** place will give way;
Eze 13: 5 so that it will stand **f** in the battle
Zec 8: 23 nations will take **f** hold of one Jew
Mt 10: 22 the one who stands **f** to the end
24: 13 the one who stands **f** to the end
Mk 13: 13 the one who stands **f** to the end
Lk 21: 19 Stand **f**, and you will win life.
1Co 1: 8 He will also keep you **f** to the end,
10: 12 if you think you are standing **f**,
15: 58 dear brothers and sisters, stand **f**.
16: 13 on your guard; stand **f** in the faith;
2Co 1: 7 And our hope for you is **f**,
1: 21 both us and you stand **f** in Christ.
1: 24 because it is by faith you stand **f**.
Gal 5: 1 Stand **f**, then, and do not let
Eph 6: 14 Stand **f** then, with the belt of truth
Php 1: 27 that you stand **f** in the one Spirit,
4: 1 stand **f** in the Lord in this way,
Col 1: 23 established and **f**, and do not move
2: 5 and how **f** your faith in Christ is.
4: 12 that you may stand **f** in all the will
1Th 3: 8 you are standing **f** in the Lord.
2Th 2: 15 stand **f** and hold fast to the
1Ti 6: 19 themselves as a **f** foundation
2Ti 2: 19 God's solid foundation stands **f**,
Heb 6: 19 anchor for the soul, **f** and secure.
Jas 5: 8 be patient and stand **f**,
1Pe 5: 9 Resist him, standing **f** in the faith,
5: 10 make you strong, **f** and steadfast.

FIRST
Ge 1: 5 and there was morning—the **f** day.
13: 4 and where he had **f** built an altar.
Ex 34: 19 "The **f** offspring of every womb
1Ki 22: 5 of Israel, "**F** seek the counsel
Pr 18: 17 a lawsuit the **f** to speak seems right,
Isa 44: 6 I am the **f** and I am the last;
48: 12 he; I am the **f** and I am the last.
Mt 5: 24 **F** go and be reconciled to them;
6: 33 But seek **f** his kingdom and his
7: 5 **f** take the plank out of your own
19: 30 But many who are **f** will be last,
20: 16 "So the last will be **f**, and the **f** will
20: 27 wants to be **f** must be your slave—
22: 38 This is the **f** and greatest
23: 26 **F** clean the inside of the cup
Mk 9: 35 wants to be **f** must be the very last,
10: 31 are **f** will be last, and the last **f**."
10: 44 wants to be **f** must be slave
13: 10 the gospel must **f** be preached to all
Lk 13: 30 who are last who will be **f**, and **f** who will be last."
Jn 8: 7 *without sin be the **f** to throw*
Ac 11: 26 disciples were called Christians **f**
Ro 1: 16 **f** to the Jew, then to the Gentile.
1: 17 that is by faith from **f** to last, just as
2: 9 **f** for the Jew, then for the Gentile;
2: 10 **f** for the Jew, then for the Gentile.
1Co 12: 28 in the church **f** of all apostles,
15: 45 "The **f** man Adam became a living
2Co 8: 5 They gave themselves **f** of all
Eph 6: 2 which is the **f** commandment
1Th 4: 16 and the dead in Christ will rise **f**.
1Ti 2: 13 For Adam was formed **f**, then Eve.
Heb 10: 9 He sets aside the **f** to establish
Jas 3: 17 comes from heaven is **f** of all pure;
1Jn 4: 19 We love because he **f** loved us.
3Jn : 9 who loves to be **f**, will not welcome
Rev 1: 17 I am the **F** and the Last.
2: 4 have forsaken the love you had at **f**.
22: 13 and the Omega, the **F** and the Last,

FIRSTBORN (BEAR)
Ex 11: 5 Every **f** son in Egypt will die,
34: 20 Redeem all your **f** sons. "No one
Ps 89: 27 And I will appoint him to be my **f**,
Lk 2: 7 and she gave birth to her **f**, a son.
Ro 8: 29 be the **f** among many brothers
Col 1: 15 God, the **f** over all creation.
1: 18 and the **f** from among the dead,
Heb 1: 6 God brings his **f** into the world,
12: 23 the church of the **f**, whose names
Rev 1: 5 witness, the **f** from the dead,

FIRSTFRUITS
Ex 23: 16 with the **f** of the crops you sow
23: 19 "Bring the best of the **f** of your soil
Ro 8: 23 who have the **f** of the Spirit,
1Co 15: 23 Christ, the **f**; then, when he comes,
Rev 14: 4 mankind and offered as **f** to God

FISH
Ge 1: 26 they may rule over the **f** in the sea
Jnh 1: 17 in the belly of the **f** three days
Mt 4: 19 I will send you out to **f** for people."
7: 10 Or if he asks for a **f**, will give him
12: 40 three nights in the belly of a huge **f**,
14: 17 five loaves of bread and two **f**,"
Mk 1: 17 I will send you out to **f** for people."
6: 38 out, they said, "Five—and two **f**."
Lk 5: 6 caught such a large number of **f**
5: 10 from now on you will **f** for people."
9: 13 five loaves of bread and two **f**—
Jn 6: 9 small barley loaves and two small **f**,
21: 5 "Friends, haven't you any **f**?"
21: 11 It was full of large **f**, 153, but even

FISHERMEN
Mk 1: 16 a net into the lake, for they were **f**.

FISHHOOK*
Job 41: 1 "Can you pull in Leviathan with a **f**

FISTS
Mt 26: 67 face and struck him with their **f**.

FIT (FITTING)
Jdg 17: 6 everyone did as they saw **f**.
21: 25 everyone did as they saw **f**.

FITTING* (FIT)
Ps 33: 1 it is **f** for the upright to praise him.
147: 1 how pleasant and **f** to praise him!
Pr 19: 10 It is not **f** for a fool to live
26: 1 in harvest, honor is not **f** for a fool.
1Co 14: 40 everything should be done in a **f**
Col 3: 18 your husbands, as is **f** in the Lord.
Heb 2: 10 to glory, it was **f** that God,

FIX* (FIXED FIXING)
Dt 11: 18 **F** these words of mine in your
Job 14: 3 Do you **f** your eye on them?
Pr 4: 25 **f** your gaze directly before you.
2Co 4: 18 So we **f** our eyes not on what is
Heb 3: 1 calling, **f** your thoughts on Jesus,

FIXED* (FIX)
2Ki 8: 11 him with a **f** gaze until Hazael was
Job 38: 10 when I **f** limits for it and set its
Ps 141: 8 But my eyes are **f** on you,
Pr 8: 28 **f** securely the fountains of the deep

FIXING* (FIX)
Heb 12: 2 **f** our eyes on Jesus, the pioneer

FLAME (FLAMES FLAMING)
2Ti 1: 6 you to fan into **f** the gift of God,

FLAMES (FLAME)
1Co 3: 15 only as one escaping through the **f**.

FLAMING (FLAME)
Eph 6: 16 you can extinguish all the **f** arrows

FLANK
Eze 34: 21 Because you shove with **f**

FLASH
1Co 15: 52 in a **f**, in the twinkling of an eye,

FLATTER* (FLATTERING FLATTERY)
Job 32: 21 no partiality, nor will I **f** anyone;
Ps 12: 2 they **f** with their lips but harbor
36: 2 their own eyes they **f** themselves
78: 36 would **f** him with their mouths,
Pr 29: 5 Those who **f** their neighbors are
Jude : 16 **f** others for their own advantage

FLATTERING* (FLATTER)
Ps 12: 3 May the LORD silence all **f** lips
Pr 26: 28 it hurts, and a **f** mouth works ruin.
28: 23 than one who has a **f** tongue.
Eze 12: 24 or **f** divinations among the people

FLATTERY* (FLATTER)
Job 32: 22 for if I were skilled in **f**, my Maker
Da 11: 32 **f** he will corrupt those who have
Ro 16: 18 **f** they deceive the minds of naive
1Th 2: 5 You know we never used **f**, nor did

FLAWLESS*
2Sa 22: 31 The LORD's word is **f**;
Job 11: 4 'My beliefs are **f** and I am pure
Ps 12: 6 And the words of the LORD are **f**,
18: 30 The LORD's word is **f**;
Pr 30: 5 "Every word of God is **f**; he is
SS 5: 2 my darling, my dove, my **f** one.

FLEE
Ps 139: 7 Where can I **f** from your presence?
Pr 28: 1 The wicked **f** though no one
1Co 6: 18 **F** from sexual immorality.
10: 14 my dear friends, **f** from idolatry.
1Ti 6: 11 man of God, **f** from all this,
2Ti 2: 22 **F** the evil desires of youth
Jas 4: 7 the devil, and he will **f** from you.

FLEECE
Jdg 6: 37 If there is dew only on the **f** and

FLEETING*
Job 14: 2 like **f** shadows, they do not endure.
Ps 39: 4 let me know how **f** my life is.
89: 47 Remember how **f** is my life.
144: 4 their days are like a **f** shadow.
Pr 21: 6 made by a lying tongue is a **f** vapor
31: 30 is deceptive, and beauty is **f**;
Heb 11: 25 than to enjoy the **f** pleasures of sin.

FLESH
Ge 2: 23 bone of my bones and **f** of my **f**;
2: 24 to his wife, and they become one **f**.
2Ch 32: 8 With him is only the arm of **f**,
Job 19: 26 yet in my **f** I will see God;
Eze 11: 19 of stone and give them a heart of **f**.
36: 26 of stone and give you a heart of **f**.
Mt 19: 5 and the two will become one **f**'?
26: 41 spirit is willing, but the **f** is weak."

Mk 10: 8 and the two will become one **f**.’
Jn 1: 14 The Word became **f** and made his
6: 51 This bread is my **f**, which I will
Ro 8: 4 who do not live according to the **f**
8: 5 live according to the **f** have their minds set on what the **f** desires;
8: 7 governed by the **f** is hostile to God;
8: 8 realm of the **f** cannot please God.
8: 13 live according to the **f**, you will die;
13: 14 how to gratify the desires of the **f**.
1Co 5: 5 Satan for the destruction of the **f**,
6: 16 said, "The two will become one **f**."
15: 39 Not all **f** is the same:
Gal 3: 3 trying to finish by means of the **f**?
4: 23 was born according to the **f**,
4: 29 born according to the **f** persecuted
5: 13 use your freedom to indulge the **f**;
5: 16 will not gratify the desires of the **f**.
5: 19 The acts of the **f** are obvious:
5: 24 to Christ Jesus have crucified the **f**
6: 8 Whoever sows to please their **f**, from the **f** will reap destruction;
Eph 5: 31 and the two will become one **f**."
6: 12 For our struggle is not against **f**
Php 3: 2 evildoers, those mutilators of the **f**.
Col 2: 11 self ruled by the **f** was put off
2Pe 2: 18 to the lustful desires of the **f**,
1Jn 4: 2 that Jesus Christ has come in the **f**
Jude : 23 the clothing stained by corrupted **f**.

FLIGHT
Dt 32: 30 or two put ten thousand to **f**,

FLINT
Isa 50: 7 Therefore have I set my face like **f**,
Zec 7: 12 They made their hearts as hard as **f**

FLIRTING*
Isa 3: 16 necks, **f** with their eyes,

FLOCK (FLOCKS)
Ps 77: 20 You led your people like a **f**
78: 52 he brought his people out like a **f**;
95: 7 of his pasture, the **f** under his care.
Isa 40: 11 He tends his **f** like a shepherd:
Jer 10: 21 prosper and all their **f** is scattered.
23: 2 "Because you have scattered my **f**
31: 10 watch over his **f** like a shepherd.'
Eze 34: 2 not shepherds take care of the **f**?
Zec 11: 17 shepherd, who deserts the **f**!
Mt 26: 31 the sheep of the **f** will be scattered.'
Lk 12: 32 little **f**, for your Father has been
Jn 10: 16 and there shall be one **f** and one
Ac 20: 28 all the **f** of which the Holy Spirit
1Co 9: 7 Who tends a **f** and does not drink
1Pe 5: 2 of God's **f** that is under your care,
5: 3 to you, but being examples to the **f**.

FLOCKS (FLOCK)
Lk 2: 8 keeping watch over their **f** at night.

FLOG (FLOGGED FLOGGING)
Pr 19: 25 **F** a mocker, and the simple will
Ac 22: 25 **f** a Roman citizen who hasn't even

FLOGGED (FLOG)
Jn 19: 1 Pilate took Jesus and had him **f**.
Ac 5: 40 the apostles in and had them **f**.
16: 23 After they had been severely **f**,
2Co 11: 23 frequently, been **f** more severely,

FLOGGING (FLOG)
Heb 11: 36 Some faced jeers and **f**, and even

FLOOD (FLOODGATES)
Ge 7: 7 ark to escape the waters of the **f**.
Mal 2: 13 You **f** the LORD's altar with tears.
Mt 24: 38 For in the days before the **f**,
2Pe 2: 5 he brought the **f** on its ungodly

FLOODGATES (FLOOD)
Ge 7: 11 the **f** of the heavens were opened.
Mal 3: 10 will not throw open the **f** of heaven

FLOOR
Jas 2: 3 there" or "Sit on the **f** by my feet,"

FLOUR
Lev 2: 1 their offering is to be of the finest **f**.
Nu 7: 13 the finest **f** mixed with olive oil as
28: 9 of the finest **f** mixed with olive oil.

FLOURISH (FLOURISHING)
Ps 72: 7 In his days may the righteous **f**
92: 7 up like grass and all evildoers **f**,
92: 12 righteous will **f** like a palm tree,
Pr 14: 11 but the tent of the upright will **f**.
Ac 12: 24 of God continued to spread and **f**.

FLOURISHING (FLOURISH)
Ps 52: 8 am like an olive tree **f** in the house

FLOW (FLOWING FLOWS)
Nu 13: 27 and it does **f** with milk and honey!
Jn 7: 38 of living water will **f** from within

FLOWER (FLOWERS)
Ps 103: 15 they flourish like a **f** of the field;
Jas 1: 10 they will pass away like a wild **f**.

FLOWERS (FLOWER)
Job 14: 2 They spring up like **f** and wither
Ps 37: 20 the LORD's enemies are like the **f**
Isa 40: 6 all their faithfulness is like the **f**
40: 7 The grass withers and the **f** fall,
Lk 12: 27 "Consider how the wild **f** grow.
1Pe 1: 24 the grass withers and the **f** fall,

FLOWING (FLOW)
Ex 3: 8 a land **f** with milk and honey—
33: 3 Go up to the land **f** with milk
Nu 16: 14 brought us into a land **f** with milk
Jos 5: 6 us, a land **f** with milk and honey.
Ps 107: 33 **f** springs into thirsty ground,
107: 35 the parched ground into **f** springs;
Jer 32: 22 a land **f** with milk and honey.
Eze 20: 6 a land **f** with milk and honey,
Rev 22: 1 **f** from the throne of God

FLOWS (FLOW)
Pr 4: 23 for everything you do **f** from it.

FOAL*
Zec 9: 9 donkey, on a colt, the **f** of a donkey.
Mt 21: 5 and on a colt, the **f** of a donkey.'"

FOILS*
Ps 33: 10 The LORD **f** the plans
Isa 44: 25 who **f** the signs of false prophets

FOLD (FOLDING)
Ecc 4: 5 Fools **f** their hands and ruin

FOLDING* (FOLD)
Pr 6: 10 a little **f** of the hands to rest—
24: 33 a little **f** of the hands to rest—

FOLLOW (FOLLOWED FOLLOWING FOLLOWS)
Ex 23: 2 "Do not **f** the crowd in doing
Lev 18: 4 laws and be careful to **f** my decrees.
Dt 5: 1 Learn them and be sure to **f** them.
17: 19 **f** carefully all the words of this law
1Ki 11: 6 he did not **f** the LORD completely,
2Ch 34: 33 they did not fail to **f** the LORD,
Ps 23: 6 love will **f** me all the days of my
119:166 LORD, and I **f** your commands.
Mt 4: 19 "Come, **f** me," Jesus said, "and I
8: 19 I will **f** you wherever you go."
8: 22 But Jesus told him, "**F** me, and let
16: 24 and take up their cross and **f** me.
19: 27 "We have left everything to **f** you!
Lk 9: 23 take up their cross daily and **f** me.
9: 61 another said, "I will **f** you, Lord;
Jn 10: 4 his sheep **f** him because they know
10: 5 But they will never **f** a stranger;
10: 27 I know them, and they **f** me.
12: 26 Whoever serves me must **f** me;
21: 19 Then he said to him, "**F** me!"
1Co 1: 12 One of you says, "I **f** Paul";
1: 12 still another, "I **f** Christ."
11: 1 **F** my example, as I **f** the example
14: 1 **F** the way of love and eagerly desire
Eph 5: 1 **F** God's example, therefore,
1Pe 2: 21 that you should **f** in his steps.
Rev 14: 4 They **f** the Lamb wherever he goes.

FOLLOWED (FOLLOW)
Nu 32: 11 they have not **f** me wholeheartedly,
Dt 1: 36 his feet on, because he **f** the LORD
Jos 14: 14 ever since, because he **f** the LORD,
2Ch 10: 14 he **f** the advice of the young men
Mt 4: 20 once they left their nets and **f** him.
9: 9 and Matthew got up and **f** him.
26: 58 But Peter **f** him at a distance,
Lk 18: 43 he received his sight and **f** Jesus,

FOLLOWING (FOLLOW)
Ps 119: 14 in **f** your statutes as one rejoices
Php 3: 17 Join together in **f** my example,

FOLLOWS (FOLLOW)
Jn 8: 12 Whoever **f** me will never walk

FOLLY (FOOL)
Pr 14: 29 who is quick-tempered displays **f**.
19: 3 person's own **f** leads to their ruin,
Ecc 10: 1 so a little **f** outweighs wisdom
Mk 7: 22 envy, slander, arrogance and **f**.
2Ti 3: 9 their **f** will be clear to everyone.

FOOD (FOODS)
Ge 1: 30 I give every green plant for **f**."
Pr 12: 9 to be somebody and have no **f**.
12: 11 their land will have abundant **f**,
20: 13 awake and you will have **f** to spare.
20: 17 **F** gained by fraud tastes sweet,
21: 20 The wise store up choice **f** and
22: 9 for they share their **f** with the poor.
23: 3 delicacies, for that **f** is deceptive.
23: 6 Do not eat the **f** of a begrudging
25: 21 enemy is hungry, give him **f** to eat;
31: 14 ships, bringing her **f** from afar.
31: 15 she provides **f** for her family
Isa 58: 7 not to share your **f** with the hungry
Eze 18: 7 but gives his **f** to the hungry
Da 1: 8 to defile himself with the royal **f**
Mt 3: 4 His **f** was locusts and wild honey.
6: 25 Is not life more than **f**, and the
Jn 4: 32 "I have **f** to eat that you know
4: 34 "My **f**," said Jesus, "is to do
6: 27 Do not work for **f** that spoils,
6: 27 for **f** that endures to eternal life,
6: 55 For my flesh is real **f** and my blood
Ac 15: 20 to abstain from **f** polluted by idols,
1Co 8: 1 Now about **f** sacrificed to idols:
8: 8 **f** does not bring us near to God;
2Co 11: 27 and have often gone without **f**;
1Ti 6: 8 But if we have **f** and clothing,
Heb 5: 14 But solid **f** is for the mature,
Jas 2: 15 sister is without clothes and daily **f**.

FOODS (FOOD)
Mk 7: 19 this, Jesus declared all **f** clean.)

FOOL (FOLLY FOOL'S FOOLISH FOOLISHNESS FOOLS)
1Sa 25: 25 his name means **F**, and folly goes
Ps 14: 1 The **f** says in his heart, "There is
Pr 10: 10 and a chattering **f** comes to ruin.
10: 18 lying lips and spreads slander is a **f**.
14: 16 but a **f** is hotheaded and yet feels
15: 5 A **f** spurns a parent's discipline,
17: 12 of her cubs than a **f** bent on folly.
17: 21 a **f** for a child brings grief;
20: 3 but every **f** is quick to quarrel.
26: 4 not answer a **f** according to his
26: 5 Answer a **f** according to his folly,
26: 7 is a proverb in the mouth of a **f**.
26: 12 There is more hope for a **f** than
27: 22 Though you grind a **f** in a mortar,
29: 20 There is more hope for a **f** than
Mt 5: 22 And anyone who says, 'You **f**!'
Lk 12: 20 "But God said to him, 'You **f**!
2Co 11: 21 I am speaking as a **f**—I also dare

FOOLISH (FOOL)
Pr 10: 1 a **f** son brings grief to his mother.
14: 1 her own hands the **f** one tears hers
15: 20 but a **f** man despises his mother.
17: 25 A **f** son brings grief to his father
19: 13 A **f** child is a father's ruin,
Mt 7: 26 practice is like a **f** man who built
25: 2 Five of them were **f** and five were
Lk 11: 40 You **f** people! Did not the one who
24: 25 He said to them, "How **f** you are,
1Co 1: 20 Has not God made **f** the wisdom
1: 27 God chose the **f** things of the world
Gal 3: 1 You **f** Galatians!
Eph 5: 4 obscenity, **f** talk or coarse joking,
5: 17 Therefore do not be **f**,
Titus 3: 9 But avoid **f** controversies

FOOLISHNESS* (FOOL)
2Sa 15: 31 turn Ahithophel's counsel into **f**."
1Co 1: 18 of the cross is **f** to those who are
1: 21 God was pleased through the **f**
1: 23 block to Jews and **f** to Gentiles,
1: 25 the **f** of God is wiser than human
2: 14 Spirit of God but considers them **f**,
3: 19 of this world is **f** in God's sight.
2Co 11: 1 you will put up with me in a little **f**.

FOOL'S (FOOL)
Pr 12: 23 but a **f** heart blurts out folly.
14: 3 A **f** mouth lashes out with pride,

FOOLS (FOOL)
Pr 1: 7 but **f** despise wisdom
3: 35 inherit honor, but **f** get only shame.
12: 15 The way of **f** seems right to them,
12: 16 **F** show their annoyance at once,
13: 19 soul, but **f** detest turning from evil.
13: 20 for a companion of **f** suffers harm.
14: 9 **F** mock at making amends for sin,
14: 24 crown, but the folly of **f** yields folly.
17: 16 Why should **f** have money in hand
17: 28 Even **f** are thought wise if they
18: 2 **F** find no pleasure in
18: 7 The mouths of **f** are their undoing,
23: 9 Do not speak to **f**, for they will
24: 7 Wisdom is too high for **f**;
26: 11 to its vomit, so **f** repeat their folly.
28: 26 who trust in themselves are **f**,
29: 11 **F** give full vent to their rage,
Ecc 7: 5 than to listen to the song of **f**.
7: 6 the pot, so is the laughter of **f**.
10: 6 **F** are put in many high positions,
Mt 23: 17 You blind **f**! Which is greater:
Ro 1: 22 claimed to be wise, they became **f**
1Co 3: 18 you should become "**f**" so that you
4: 10 We are **f** for Christ, but you are so

FOOT (FEET FOOTHOLD)
Jos 1: 3 every place where you set your **f**,
Ps 121: 3 He will not let your **f** slip—
Pr 3: 23 safety, and your **f** will not stumble.
4: 27 or the left; keep your **f** from evil.
25: 17 Seldom set **f** in your neighbor's
Isa 1: 6 the sole of your **f** to the top of your
Mt 18: 8 or your **f** causes you to stumble,
Lk 4: 11 you will not strike your **f** against
1Co 12: 15 Now if the **f** should say, "Because I
Rev 10: 2 He planted his right **f** on the sea

FOOTHOLD* (FOOT)
Ps 69: 2 miry depths, where there is no **f**.
73: 2 I had nearly lost my **f**.
Eph 4: 27 and do not give the devil a **f**.

FOOTSTEPS (STEP)
Ps 119:133 Direct my **f** according to your

FOOTSTOOL
Ps 99: 5 our God and worship at his **f**;
110: 1 hand until I make your enemies a **f**
Isa 66: 1 is my throne, and the earth is my **f**.
Mt 5: 35 or by the earth, for it is his **f**;
Ac 7: 49 is my throne, and the earth is my **f**.
Heb 1: 13 hand until I make your enemies a **f**
10: 13 for his enemies to be made his **f**.

FORBEARANCE*
Ro 2: 4 of his kindness, **f** and patience,
3: 25 his **f** he had left the sins committed
Gal 5: 22 love, joy, peace, **f**, kindness,

FORBID
1Co 14: 39 and do not **f** speaking in tongues.
1Ti 4: 3 They **f** people to marry and order

FORCE (FORCED FORCEFUL FORCES FORCING)
Jn 6: 15 to come and make him king by **f**,
Ac 26: 11 and I tried to **f** them to blaspheme.
Gal 2: 14 that you **f** Gentiles to follow Jewish

FORCED (FORCE)
Mt 27: 32 and they **f** him to carry the cross.
Phm : 14 any favor you do would not seem **f**

FORCEFUL* (FORCE)
2Co 10: 10 "His letters are weighty and **f**,

FORCES (FORCE)
Mt 5: 41 If anyone **f** you to go one mile,
Eph 6: 12 against the spiritual **f** of evil

FORCING (FORCE)
Lk 16: 16 and everyone is **f** their way into it.

FOREHEAD (FOREHEADS)
Ex 13: 9 a reminder on your **f** that this law
13: 16 your **f** that the LORD brought us
1Sa 17: 49 and struck the Philistine on the **f**.

FOREHEADS (FOREHEAD)
Dt 6: 8 hands and bind them on your **f**.
Rev 9: 4 not have the seal of God on their **f**.
13: 16 on their right hands or on their **f**,
14: 1 Father's name written on their **f**.

FOREIGN (FOREIGNER FOREIGNERS)
Ge 35: 2 "Get rid of the **f** gods you have
2Ch 14: 3 He removed the **f** altars and the
33: 15 He got rid of the **f** gods
Isa 28: 11 with **f** lips and strange tongues

FOREIGNER (FOREIGN)
Ex 22: 21 "Do not mistreat or oppress a **f**,
Lev 24: 22 are to have the same law for the **f**
Ps 146: 9 The LORD watches over the **f**
Lk 17: 18 give praise to God except this **f**?"
1Co 14: 11 is saying, I am a **f** to the speaker,

FOREIGNERS (FOREIGN)
Ex 23: 9 know how it feels to be **f**,
1Co 14: 21 through the lips of **f** I will speak
Eph 2: 12 **f** to the covenants of the promise,
2: 19 you are no longer **f** and strangers,
1Pe 2: 11 urge you, as **f** and exiles, to abstain

FOREKNEW* (KNOW)
Ro 8: 29 those God **f** he also predestined
11: 2 not reject his people, whom he **f**.

FOREKNOWLEDGE* (KNOW)
Ac 2: 23 you by God's deliberate plan and **f**;
1Pe 1: 2 to the **f** of God the Father,

FORESAW*
Gal 3: 8 Scripture **f** that God would justify

FOREST
Jas 3: 5 Consider what a great **f** is set on

FOREVER (EVER)
Ge 3: 22 the tree of life and eat, and live **f**."
6: 3 will not contend with humans **f**,
Ex 3: 15 "This is my name **f**, the name you
2Sa 7: 26 so that your name will be great **f**.
1Ki 2: 33 there be the LORD's peace **f**."
9: 3 built, by putting my Name there **f**.
1Ch 16: 15 He remembers his covenant **f**,
16: 34 for he is good; his love endures **f**.
16: 41 LORD, "for his love endures **f**."
17: 24 and that your name will be great **f**.
2Ch 5: 13 "He is good; his love endures **f**."
20: 21 the LORD, for his love endures **f**."
Ps 9: 7 The LORD reigns **f**;
23: 6 dwell in the house of the LORD **f**.
28: 9 their shepherd and carry them **f**.
29: 10 the LORD is enthroned as King **f**.
33: 11 plans of the LORD stand firm **f**,
44: 8 and we will praise your name **f**.
61: 4 I long to dwell in your tent **f**
72: 19 Praise be to his glorious name **f**;
73: 26 of my heart and my portion **f**.
77: 8 Has his unfailing love vanished **f**?
79: 13 of your pasture, will praise you **f**;
81: 15 and their punishment would last **f**.
86: 12 I will glorify your name **f**.
89: 1 sing of the LORD's great love **f**;
92: 8 But you, LORD, are **f** exalted.
100: 5 is good and his love endures **f**;
102: 12 But you, LORD, sit enthroned **f**;
104: 31 the glory of the LORD endure **f**;
107: 1 for he is good; his love endures **f**.
110: 4 "You are a priest **f**, in the order
111: 3 and his righteousness endures **f**.
112: 6 they will be remembered **f**.
117: 2 of the LORD endures **f**.
118: 1 for he is good; his love endures **f**.
119:111 Your statutes are my heritage **f**;
119:152 that you established them to last **f**.
136: 1 *His love endures **f**.*
146: 6 he remains faithful **f**.
Pr 10: 25 but the righteous stand firm **f**.
27: 24 for riches do not endure **f**,
Isa 25: 8 he will swallow up death **f**.
26: 4 Trust in the LORD **f**,
32: 17 will be quietness and confidence **f**.
40: 8 the word of our God endures **f**."
51: 6 But my salvation will last **f**,
51: 8 But my righteousness will last **f**,
57: 15 he who lives **f**, whose name is holy:
59: 21 from this time on and **f**,"
Jer 33: 11 his love endures **f**."
Eze 37: 26 put my sanctuary among them **f**.
Da 2: 44 to an end, but it will itself endure **f**.
3: 9 "May the king live **f**!
Hab 3: 6 but he marches on **f**.
Jn 6: 51 Whoever eats this bread will live **f**.
14: 16 to help you and be with you **f**—
Ro 9: 5 who is God over all, **f** praised!
16: 27 God be glory **f** through Jesus
1Co 9: 25 do it to get a crown that will last **f**.
1Th 4: 17 And so we will be with the Lord **f**.
Heb 5: 6 "You are a priest **f**, in the order
7: 17 "You are a priest **f**, in the order
7: 24 but because Jesus lives **f**, he has
13: 8 same yesterday and today and **f**.
1Pe 1: 25 the word of the Lord endures **f**."
1Jn 2: 17 does the will of God lives **f**.
2Jn : 2 lives in us and will be with us **f**:

FOREVERMORE (EVER)
Ps 113: 2 LORD be praised, both now and **f**.

FORFEIT
Mk 8: 36 the whole world, yet **f** their soul?
Lk 9: 25 and yet lose or **f** their very self?

FORGAVE* (FORGIVE)
Ps 32: 5 And you **f** the guilt of my sin.
65: 3 by sins, you **f** our transgressions.
78: 38 he **f** their iniquities and did not
85: 2 You **f** the iniquity of your people
Lk 7: 42 him back, so he **f** the debts of both.
Eph 4: 32 other, just as in Christ God **f** you.
Col 2: 13 He **f** us all our sins,
3: 13 Forgive as the Lord **f** you.

FORGET (FORGETS FORGETTING FORGOT FORGOTTEN)
Dt 4: 23 Be careful not to **f** the covenant
6: 12 that you do not **f** the LORD,
2Ki 17: 38 Do not **f** the covenant I have made
Ps 9: 17 the dead, all the nations that **f** God.
10: 12 O God. Do not **f** the helpless.
50: 22 you who **f** God, or I will tear you
78: 7 in God and would not **f** his deeds
103: 2 my soul, and **f** not all his benefits—
119: 93 I will never **f** your precepts,
137: 5 If I **f** you, Jerusalem, may my right hand **f** its skill.
Pr 3: 1 My son, do not **f** my teaching,
4: 5 do not **f** my words or turn away
Isa 49: 15 "Can a mother **f** the baby at her
49: 15 may **f**, I will not **f** you!
51: 13 that you **f** the LORD your Maker,
Jer 2: 32 Does a young woman **f** her jewelry,
23: 39 I will surely **f** you and cast you
Heb 6: 10 will not **f** your work and the love
13: 2 Do not **f** to show hospitality
13: 16 And do not **f** to do good
2Pe 3: 8 But do not **f** this one thing,

FORGETS (FORGET)
Jn 16: 21 is born she **f** the anguish because
Jas 1: 24 immediately **f** what he looks like.

FORGETTING* (FORGET)
Php 3: 13 **F** what is behind and straining
Jas 1: 25 not **f** what they have heard,
2Pe 1: 9 **f** that they have been cleansed

FORGIVE* (FORGAVE FORGIVENESS FORGIVES FORGIVING)
Ge 50: 17 I ask you to **f** your brothers the sins
50: 17 please **f** the sins of the servants
Ex 10: 17 Now **f** my sin once more and pray
23: 21 he will not **f** your rebellion,
32: 32 But now, please **f** their sin—
34: 9 **f** our wickedness and our sin,
Nu 14: 19 great love, **f** the sin of these people,
Dt 29: 20 will never be willing to **f** them;
Jos 24: 19 He will not **f** your rebellion
1Sa 15: 25 **f** my sin and come back with me,
25: 28 "Please **f** your servant's
1Ki 8: 30 place, and when you hear, **f**.
8: 34 and **f** the sin of your people Israel
8: 36 and **f** the sin of your servants,
8: 39 **F** and act; deal with everyone
8: 50 **f** your people, who have sinned
8: 50 **f** all the offenses they have
2Ki 5: 18 may the LORD **f** your servant
5: 18 may the LORD **f** your servant
24: 4 and the LORD was not willing to **f**.

2Ch 6: 21 and when you hear, **f**.
6: 25 and **f** the sin of your people Israel
6: 27 and **f** the sin of your servants,
6: 30 **F**, and deal with everyone
6: 39 **f** your people, who have sinned
7: 14 and I will **f** their sin and will heal
Job 7: 21 pardon my offenses and **f** my sins?
Ps 19: 12 **F** my hidden faults.
25: 11 LORD, **f** my iniquity, though it is
79: 9 and **f** our sins for your name's sake.
Isa 2: 9 do not **f** them.
Jer 5: 1 seeks the truth, I will **f** this city.
5: 7 "Why should I **f** you?
18: 23 Do not **f** their crimes or blot
31: 34 "For I will **f** their wickedness
33: 8 and will **f** all their sins of rebellion
36: 3 then I will **f** their wickedness
50: 20 for I will **f** the remnant I spare.
Da 9: 19 Lord, **f**! Lord, hear and act!
Hos 1: 6 to Israel, that I should at all **f** them.
14: 2 "**F** all our sins and receive us
Am 7: 2 I cried out, "Sovereign LORD, **f**!
Mt 6: 12 And **f** us our debts, as we also have
6: 14 if you **f** other people when they sin
6: 14 heavenly Father will also **f** you.
6: 15 if you do not **f** others their sins,
6: 15 your Father will not **f** your sins.
9: 6 has authority on earth to **f** sins."
18: 21 many times shall I **f** my brother
18: 35 of you unless you **f** your brother
Mk 2: 7 Who can **f** sins but God alone?"
2: 10 has authority on earth to **f** sins."
11: 25 anything against anyone, **f** them,
11: 25 in heaven may **f** you your sins."
Lk 5: 21 Who can **f** sins but God alone?"
5: 24 has authority on earth to **f** sins."
6: 37 **F**, and you will be forgiven.
11: 4 **F** us our sins, for we also **f** everyone
17: 3 and if they repent, **f** them.
17: 4 saying 'I repent,' you must **f** them."
23: 34 "Father, **f** them, for they do not
Jn 20: 23 If you **f** anyone's sins, their sins
20: 23 if you do not **f** them, they are not
Ac 5: 31 to repentance and **f** their sins.
8: 22 that he may **f** you for having such
2Co 2: 7 you ought to **f** and comfort him,
2: 10 Anyone you **f**, I also **f**.
2: 10 if there was anything to **f**—
12: 13 a burden to you? **F** me this wrong!
Col 3: 13 and **f** one another if any of you
3: 13 **F** as the Lord forgave you.
Heb 8: 12 For I will **f** their wickedness
1Jn 1: 9 just and will **f** us our sins and

FORGIVENESS* (FORGIVE)
Ps 130: 4 But with you there is **f**, so that we
Mt 26: 28 out for many for the **f** of sins.
Mk 1: 4 of repentance for the **f** of sins.
Lk 1: 77 through the **f** of their sins,
3: 3 of repentance for the **f** of sins.
24: 47 for the **f** of sins will be preached
Ac 2: 38 Jesus Christ for the **f** of your sins.
10: 43 in him receives **f** of sins through
13: 38 that through Jesus the **f** of sins is
26: 18 so that they may receive **f** of sins
Eph 1: 7 through his blood, the **f** of sins,
Col 1: 14 we have redemption, the **f** of sins.
Heb 9: 22 the shedding of blood there is no **f**.

FORGIVES* (FORGIVE)
Ps 103: 3 who **f** all your sins and heals all
Mic 7: 18 **f** the transgression of the remnant
Lk 7: 49 "Who is this who even **f** sins?"

FORGIVING* (FORGIVE)
Ex 34: 7 **f** wickedness, rebellion and sin.
Nu 14: 18 abounding in love and **f** sin
Ne 9: 17 But you are a **f** God,
Ps 86: 5 Lord, are **f** and good,
99: 8 you were to Israel a **f** God,
Da 9: 9 Lord our God is merciful and **f**,
Eph 4: 32 to one another, **f** each other, just as

FORGOT (FORGET)
Dt 32: 18 you **f** the God who gave you birth.
Ps 78: 11 They **f** what he had done,
106: 13 But they soon **f** what he had done

FORGOTTEN (FORGET)
Job 11: 6 God has even **f** some of your sin.
Ps 44: 20 If we had **f** the name of our God
Isa 17: 10 You have **f** God your Savior;
Hos 8: 14 Israel has **f** their Maker and built
Lk 12: 6 Yet not one of them is **f** by God.

FORM (FORMED)
Isa 52: 14 and his **f** marred beyond human
2Ti 3: 5 having a **f** of godliness but denying

FORMED (FORM)
Ge 2: 7 the LORD God **f** a man
2: 19 Now the LORD God had **f**
Ps 103: 14 for he knows how we are **f**,
Pr 8: 23 I was **f** long ages ago, at the very
Ecc 11: 5 or how the body is **f** in a mother's
Isa 29: 16 Shall what is **f** say to the one who **f**
45: 18 be empty, but **f** it to be inhabited—
49: 5 he who **f** me in the womb to be his
Jer 1: 5 "Before I **f** you in the womb I knew
Ro 9: 20 is **f** say to the one who **f** it,
Gal 4: 19 childbirth until Christ is **f** in you,
1Ti 2: 13 For Adam was **f** first, then Eve.
Heb 11: 3 that the universe was **f** at God's
2Pe 3: 5 and the earth was **f** out of water

FORMLESS*
Ge 1: 2 Now the earth was **f** and empty,
Jer 4: 23 the earth, and it was **f** and empty;

FORSAKE (FORSAKEN)
Dt 31: 6 he will never leave you nor **f** you."
Jos 1: 5 I will never leave you nor **f** you.
24: 16 us to **f** the LORD to serve other
2Ch 15: 2 you, but if you **f** him, he will **f** you.
Ps 27: 10 my father and mother **f** me,
94: 14 he will never **f** his inheritance.
Isa 55: 7 Let the wicked **f** their ways
Heb 13: 5 will I leave you; never will I **f** you."

FORSAKEN (FORSAKE)
Ezr 9: 9 God has not **f** us in our bondage.
Ps 22: 1 God, my God, why have you **f** me?
37: 25 I have never seen the righteous **f**
Mt 27: 46 my God, why have you **f** me?").
Rev 2: 4 You have **f** the love you had at first.

FORTIFIED
Pr 18: 10 name of the LORD is a **f** tower;

FORTRESS
2Sa 22: 2 is my rock, my **f** and my deliverer;
Ps 18: 2 is my rock, my **f** and my deliverer;
31: 2 of refuge, a strong **f** to save me.
59: 16 you are my **f**, my refuge in times
71: 3 me, for you are my rock and my **f**.
Pr 14: 26 fears the LORD has a secure **f**,

FORTUNE-TELLING*
Ac 16: 16 deal of money for her owners by **f**.

FORTY
Ge 7: 4 will send rain on the earth for **f** days and **f** nights,
18: 29 "For the sake of **f**, I will not do it."
Ex 16: 35 The Israelites ate manna **f** years,
24: 18 he stayed on the mountain **f** days
Nu 14: 34 For **f** years—one year for each
Jos 14: 7 I was **f** years old when Moses
1Sa 4: 18 He had led Israel **f** years.
2Sa 5: 4 king, and he reigned **f** years.
1Ki 19: 8 he traveled **f** days and **f** nights until
2Ki 12: 1 he reigned in Jerusalem **f** years.
2Ch 9: 30 in Jerusalem over all Israel **f** years.
Eze 29: 12 cities will lie desolate **f** years
Jnh 3: 4 "**F** more days and Nineveh will be
Mt 4: 2 After fasting **f** days and **f** nights,

FOUGHT (FIGHT)
1Co 15: 32 If I **f** wild beasts in Ephesus with
2Ti 4: 7 I have **f** the good fight, I have

FOUND (FIND)
1Sa 9: 2 young man as could be **f** anywhere
2Ki 22: 8 "I have **f** the Book of the Law
1Ch 28: 9 If you seek him, he will be **f** by you;
2Ch 15: 15 God eagerly, and he was **f** by them.
Isa 55: 6 Seek the LORD while he may be **f**;
65: 1 I was **f** by those who did not seek
Da 5: 27 on the scales and **f** wanting.
Mt 1: 18 she was **f** to be pregnant through
Lk 15: 6 I have **f** my lost sheep.'
15: 9 I have **f** my lost coin.'
15: 24 is alive again; he was lost and is **f**.'
Ac 4: 12 Salvation is **f** in no one else,
Ro 10: 20 "I was **f** by those who did not seek
Jas 2: 8 If you really keep the royal law **f**
Rev 5: 4 no one was **f** who was worthy

FOUNDATION (FOUNDATIONS FOUNDED)
Isa 28: 16 a precious cornerstone for a sure **f**;
Mt 7: 25 fall, because it had its **f** on the rock.
Lk 14: 29 For if you lay the **f** and are not able
Ro 15: 20 be building on someone else's **f**.
1Co 3: 10 me, I laid a **f** as a wise builder,
3: 11 one can lay any **f** other than the
Eph 2: 20 built on the **f** of the apostles
1Ti 3: 15 God, the pillar and **f** of the truth.
2Ti 2: 19 God's solid **f** stands firm,
Heb 6: 1 not laying again the **f** of repentance

FOUNDATIONS (FOUNDATION)
Ps 102: 25 In the beginning you laid the **f**
Heb 1: 10 Lord, you laid the **f** of the earth,

FOUNDED (FOUNDATION)
Jer 10: 12 he **f** the world by his wisdom

FOUNTAIN
Ps 36: 9 For with you is the **f** of life;
Pr 14: 27 The fear of the LORD is a **f** of life,
18: 4 **f** of wisdom is a rushing stream.
Zec 13: 1 that day a **f** will be opened

FOX* (FOXES)
Ne 4: 3 a **f** climbing up on it would break
Lk 13: 32 "Go tell that **f**, 'I will keep

FOXES (FOX)
SS 2: 15 Catch for us the **f**, the little **f**
Mt 8: 20 "**F** have dens and birds have nests,

FRAGRANCE (FRAGRANT)
Ex 30: 38 like it to enjoy its **f** must be cut off
Jn 12: 3 was filled with the **f** of the perfume.

FRAGRANT (FRAGRANCE)
Eph 5: 2 himself up for us as a **f** offering
Php 4: 18 They are a **f** offering, an acceptable

FRANKINCENSE
Mt 2: 11 him with gifts of gold, **f** and myrrh.

FREE (FREED FREEDOM FREELY)
Ge 2: 16 "You are **f** to eat from any tree
Ps 146: 7 The LORD sets prisoners **f**,
Pr 6: 3 to **f** yourself, since you have fallen
Lk 4: 18 for the blind, to set the oppressed **f**,
Jn 8: 32 truth, and the truth will set you **f**."
8: 36 So if the Son sets you **f**, you will be **f** indeed.
Ro 6: 7 anyone who has died has been set **f**
6: 18 You have been set **f** from sin
8: 2 Spirit who gives life has set you **f**
1Co 7: 27 you **f** from such a commitment?
12: 13 Jews or Gentiles, slave or **f**—
Gal 3: 28 neither slave nor **f**, nor is there
5: 1 for freedom that Christ has set us **f**.
1Pe 2: 16 Live as **f** people, but do not use

FREED (FREE)
Ps 116: 16 you have **f** me from my chains.
Rev 1: 5 has **f** us from our sins by his blood,

FREEDOM (FREE)
Ps 119: 45 I will walk about in **f**, for I have
Isa 61: 1 to proclaim **f** for the captives
Lk 4: 18 me to proclaim **f** for the prisoners
Ro 8: 21 brought into the **f** and glory
1Co 7: 21 although if you can gain your **f**,
2Co 3: 17 the Spirit of the Lord is, there is **f**.
Gal 2: 4 spy on the **f** we have in Christ Jesus
5: 13 But do not use your **f** to indulge
Jas 1: 25 into the perfect law that gives **f**,
1Pe 2: 16 do not use your **f** as

FREELY (FREE)
Isa 55: 7 to our God, for he will **f** pardon.
Mt 10: 8 **F** you have received; **f** give.
Ro 3: 24 and all are justified **f** by his grace
Eph 1: 6 which he has **f** given us in the One

FRESH
Jas 3: 11 Can both **f** water and salt water

FRET*
Ps 37: 1 Do not **f** because of those who are
37: 7 do not **f** when people succeed

Ps 37: 8 do not **f**—it leads only to evil.
Pr 24: 19 Do not **f** because of evildoers or be

FRICTION*
1Ti 6: 5 constant **f** between people of

FRIEND (FRIENDS FRIENDSHIP)
Ex 33: 11 face to face, as one speaks to a **f**.
2Ch 20: 7 descendants of Abraham your **f**?
Pr 17: 17 A **f** loves at all times, and a brother
18: 24 there is a **f** who sticks closer than
27: 6 Wounds from a **f** can be trusted,
27: 10 Do not forsake your **f** or a **f** of your
Isa 41: 8 you descendants of Abraham my **f**,
Mt 11: 19 a **f** of tax collectors and sinners.'
Jn 19: 12 this man go, you are no **f** of Caesar.
Ro 16: 8 Ampliatus, my dear **f** in the Lord.
Jas 2: 23 and he was called God's **f**.
4: 4 to be a **f** of the world becomes

FRIENDS (FRIEND)
Pr 16: 28 and a gossip separates close **f**.
17: 9 repeats the matter separates close **f**.
18: 24 who has unreliable **f** soon comes
Zec 13: 6 I was given at the house of my **f**.'
Jn 15: 13 to lay down one's life for one's **f**.
15: 14 You are my **f** if you do what I

FRIENDSHIP (FRIEND)
Lk 11: 8 give you the bread because of **f**,
Jas 4: 4 don't you know that **f**

FRIGHTENED (FEAR)
Php 1: 28 without being **f** in any way by
1Pe 3: 14 not fear their threats; do not be **f**."

FROGS
Ex 8: 2 go, I will send a plague of **f** on your
Rev 16: 13 impure spirits that looked like **f**;

FROLIC
Mal 4: 2 go out and **f** like well-fed calves.

FRUIT (FRUITFUL)
Jdg 9: 11 'Should I give up my **f**, so good
Ps 1: 3 which yields its **f** in season
Pr 11: 30 The **f** of the righteous is a tree
12: 14 the **f** of their lips people are filled
27: 18 who guards a fig tree will eat its **f**,
Isa 11: 1 from his roots a Branch will bear **f**.
27: 6 and fill all the world with **f**.
32: 17 The **f** of that righteousness will be
Jer 17: 8 drought and never fails to bear **f**."
Hos 10: 12 reap the **f** of unfailing love,
14: 2 that we may offer the **f** of our lips.
Am 8: 1 a basket of ripe **f**.
Mt 3: 8 Produce **f** in keeping
3: 10 does not produce good **f** will be cut
7: 16 By their **f** you will recognize them.
7: 17 every good tree bears good **f**, but a bad tree bears bad **f**.
7: 20 by their **f** you will recognize them.
12: 33 a tree good and its **f** will be good,
12: 33 for a tree is recognized by its **f**.
Lk 3: 9 does not produce good **f** will be cut
6: 43 "No good tree bears bad **f**, nor does a bad tree bear good **f**.
13: 6 he went to look for **f** on it but did
Jn 15: 2 every branch in me that bears no **f**,
15: 2 branch that does bear **f** he prunes
15: 16 so that you might go and bear **f**—
Ro 7: 4 order that we might bear **f** for God.
Gal 5: 22 But the **f** of the Spirit is love, joy,
Php 1: 11 filled with the **f** of righteousness
Col 1: 10 bearing **f** in every good work,
Heb 13: 15 the **f** of lips that openly profess his
Jas 3: 17 full of mercy and good **f**,
Jude : 12 trees, without **f** and uprooted—
Rev 22: 2 bearing twelve crops of **f**,

FRUITFUL (FRUIT)
Ge 1: 22 "Be **f** and increase in number
9: 1 "Be **f** and increase in number
35: 11 be **f** and increase in number.
Ex 1: 7 the Israelites were exceedingly **f**;
Ps 128: 3 wife will be like a **f** vine within
Jn 15: 2 so that it will be even more **f**.
Php 1: 22 body, this will mean **f** labor for me.

FRUITLESS*
Eph 5: 11 to do with the **f** deeds of darkness,

FRUSTRATION
Ro 8: 20 For the creation was subjected to **f**,

FUEL
Isa 44: 19 to say, "Half of it I used for **f**;

FULFILL (FULFILLED FULFILLMENT FULFILLS)
Nu 23: 19 Does he promise and not **f**?
Ps 61: 8 name and **f** my vows day after day.
116: 14 I will **f** my vows to the LORD
Ecc 5: 5 vow than to make one and not **f** it.
Isa 46: 11 land, a man to **f** my purpose.
Jer 33: 14 I will **f** the good promise I made
Mt 1: 22 **f** what the Lord had said through
3: 15 us to do this to **f** all righteousness."
4: 14 **f** what was said through the
5: 17 to abolish them but to **f** them.
8: 17 to **f** what was spoken through
12: 17 to **f** what was spoken through
21: 4 to **f** what was spoken through
Jn 12: 38 This was to **f** the word of Isaiah
13: 18 this is to **f** this passage of Scripture:
15: 25 this is to **f** what is written in their
1Co 7: 3 The husband should **f** his marital

FULFILLED (FULFILL)
Jos 21: 45 to Israel failed; every one was **f**.
23: 14 Every promise has been **f**;
Pr 13: 12 sick, but a longing **f** is a tree of life.
13: 19 A longing **f** is sweet to the soul,
Mt 2: 15 so was **f** what the Lord had said
2: 17 the prophet Jeremiah was **f**:
2: 23 So was **f** what was said through
13: 14 In them is **f** the prophecy of Isaiah:
13: 35 So was **f** what was spoken through
26: 54 would the Scriptures be **f** that say it
26: 56 of the prophets might be **f**."
27: 9 by Jeremiah the prophet was **f**:
Mk 13: 4 sign that they are all about to be **f**?"
14: 49 But the Scriptures must be **f**."
Lk 4: 21 "Today this scripture is **f** in your
18: 31 about the Son of Man will be **f**.
24: 44 Everything must be **f** that is
Jn 18: 9 words he had spoken would be **f**:
19: 24 the scripture might be **f** that said,
19: 28 and so that Scripture would be **f**,
19: 36 so that the scripture would be **f**:
Ac 1: 16 the Scripture had to be **f**
Gal 5: 14 the entire law is **f** in keeping this
Ro 13: 8 whoever loves others has **f** the law.
Jas 2: 23 And the scripture was **f** that says,

FULFILLMENT (FULFILL)
Ro 13: 10 Therefore love is the **f** of the law.

FULFILLS (FULFILL)
Ps 145: 19 He **f** the desires of those who fear

FULL (FILL)
2Ch 24: 10 them into the chest until it was **f**.
Ps 127: 5 is the man whose quiver is **f**
Pr 27: 7 One who is **f** loathes honey
31: 11 Her husband has **f** confidence in
Isa 6: 3 the whole earth is **f** of his glory."
Mt 12: 34 speaks what the heart is **f** of.
Lk 4: 1 Jesus, **f** of the Holy Spirit,
6: 45 speaks what the heart is **f** of.
Jn 10: 10 may have life, and have it to the **f**.
Ac 6: 3 who are known to be **f** of the Spirit
6: 5 a man **f** of faith and of the Holy
7: 55 But Stephen, **f** of the Holy Spirit,
11: 24 man, **f** of the Holy Spirit and faith,
Ro 11: 12 riches will their **f** inclusion bring!
Eph 4: 19 of impurity, and they are **f** of greed.

FULL-GROWN* (GROW)
Jas 1: 15 sin, when it is **f**, gives birth to

FULLNESS* (FILL)
Dt 33: 16 its **f** and the favor of him who
Jn 1: 16 of his **f** we have all received grace
Eph 1: 23 the **f** of him who fills everything
3: 19 to the measure of all the **f** of God.
4: 13 whole measure of the **f** of Christ.
Col 1: 19 to have all his **f** dwell in him,
1: 25 to you the word of God in its **f**—
2: 9 in Christ all the **f** of the Deity lives
2: 10 Christ you have been brought to **f**.

FULLY (FILL)
1Ki 8: 61 may your hearts be **f** committed
2Ch 16: 9 whose hearts are **f** committed
Ps 119: 4 precepts that are to be **f** obeyed.
119:138 they are **f** trustworthy.
Pr 13: 4 of the diligent are **f** satisfied.
Lk 6: 40 everyone who is **f** trained will be
Ro 4: 21 being **f** persuaded that God had
14: 5 should be **f** convinced in their
1Co 13: 12 then I shall know **f**, even as I am **f**
15: 58 Always give yourselves **f**
2Ti 4: 17 the message might be **f** proclaimed

FURIOUS (FURY)
Dt 29: 28 In **f** anger and in great wrath
Jer 21: 5 mighty arm in **f** anger and in great
32: 37 where I banish them in my **f** anger

FURNACE
Isa 48: 10 tested you in the **f** of affliction.
Da 3: 6 be thrown into a blazing **f**."
Mt 13: 42 will throw them into the blazing **f**,

FURY (FURIOUS)
Isa 14: 6 in **f** subdued nations with
Am 1: 11 and his **f** flamed unchecked,
Rev 14: 10 too, will drink the wine of God's **f**,
16: 19 with the wine of the **f** of his wrath.
19: 15 the winepress of the **f** of the wrath

FUTILE (FUTILITY)
Mal 3: 14 have said, 'It is **f** to serve God.
1Co 3: 20 that the thoughts of the wise are **f**."

FUTILITY (FUTILE)
Eph 4: 17 do, in the **f** of their thinking.

FUTURE
Ps 37: 37 a **f** awaits those who seek peace.
Pr 23: 18 There is surely a **f** hope for you,
Ecc 7: 14 discover anything about their **f**.
8: 7 Since no one knows the **f**, who can
Jer 29: 11 you, plans to give you hope and a **f**.
Ro 8: 38 neither the present nor the **f**, nor
1Co 3: 22 or death or the present or the **f**—

GABRIEL*
Angel who interpreted Daniel's visions (Da 8:16–26; 9:20–27); announced births of John (Lk 1:11–20), Jesus (Lk 1:26–38).

GAD
1. Son of Jacob by Zilpah (Ge 30:9–11; 35:26; 1Ch 2:2). Tribe of blessed (Ge 49:19; Dt 33:20–21), numbered (Nu 1:25; 26:18), allotted land east of the Jordan (Nu 32; 34:14; Jos 18:7; 22), west (Eze 48:27–28), 12,000 from (Rev 7:5).
2. Prophet; seer of David (1Sa 22:5; 2Sa 24:11–19; 1Ch 29:29).

GAIN (GAINED GAINS)
Ex 14: 17 I will **g** glory through Pharaoh
Ps 60: 12 With God we will **g** the victory,
Pr 3: 13 those who **g** understanding,
4: 1 pay attention and **g** understanding.
8: 5 You who are simple, **g** prudence;
28: 16 who hates ill-gotten **g** will enjoy
28: 23 the end **g** favor rather than one
29: 23 low, but the lowly in spirit **g** honor.
Isa 63: 12 **g** for himself everlasting renown,
Da 2: 8 that you are trying to **g** time,
Mt 16: 26 for someone to **g** the whole world,
Mk 8: 36 for someone to **g** the whole world,
Lk 9: 25 for someone to **g** the whole world,
1Co 13: 3 but do not have love, I **g** nothing.
Php 1: 21 me, to live is Christ and to die is **g**.
3: 8 them garbage, that I may **g** Christ
1Ti 3: 13 have served well **g** an excellent
6: 5 godliness is a means to financial **g**.
6: 6 with contentment is great **g**.
1Pe 5: 2 not pursuing dishonest **g**, but eager

GAINED (GAIN)
Jer 32: 20 **g** the renown that is still yours.
Ro 5: 2 through whom we have **g** access

GAINS (GAIN)
Pr 11: 16 A kindhearted woman **g** honor,
15: 32 heeds correction **g** understanding.
Php 3: 7 But whatever were **g** to me I now

GALILEE
Isa 9: 1 in the future he will honor **G**
Mt 4: 15 the Jordan, **G** of the Gentiles—
26: 32 I will go ahead of you into **G**."
28: 10 Go and tell my brothers to go to **G**;

GALL
Mt 27: 34 Jesus wine to drink, mixed with **g**;

GALLIO
Ac 18: 12 While **G** was proconsul of Achaia,

GAMALIEL
Ac 5: 34 But a Pharisee named **G**, a teacher

GAMES*
1Co 9: 25 who competes in the **g** goes

GAP
Eze 22: 30 stand before me in the **g** on behalf

GARBAGE*
1Co 4: 13 the earth, the **g** of the world—
Php 3: 8 I consider them **g**, that I may gain

GARDEN (GARDENER)
Ge 2: 8 the LORD God had planted a **g**
2: 15 put him in the **G** of Eden to work it
SS 4: 12 You are a **g** locked up, my sister,
Isa 58: 11 You will be like a well-watered **g**,
Jer 31: 12 They will be like a well-watered **g**,
Eze 28: 13 You were in Eden, the **g** of God;
31: 9 the trees of Eden in the **g** of God.

GARDENER (GARDEN)
Jn 15: 1 true vine, and my Father is the **g**.
20: 15 Thinking he was the **g**, she said,

GARLAND*
Pr 1: 9 They are a **g** to grace your head
4: 9 She will give you a **g** to grace your

GARMENT (GARMENTS)
Ps 22: 18 among them and cast lots for my **g**.
102: 26 they will all wear out like a **g**.
Isa 50: 9 They will all wear out like a **g**;
51: 6 the earth will wear out like a **g**
61: 3 a **g** of praise instead of a spirit
Mt 9: 16 patch will pull away from the **g**,
Jn 19: 23 This **g** was seamless, woven in one
Heb 1: 11 they will all wear out like a **g**.

GARMENTS (GARMENT)
Ge 3: 21 The LORD God made **g** of skin
Ex 28: 2 Make sacred **g** for your brother
Lev 16: 23 take off the linen **g** he put on
16: 24 area and put on his regular **g**.
Isa 61: 10 For he has clothed me with **g**
63: 1 with his **g** stained crimson?
Joel 2: 13 Rend your heart and not your **g**.
Zec 3: 4 sin, and I will put fine **g** on you."

GATE (GATES)
Ps 118: 20 This is the **g** of the LORD through
Pr 31: 23 husband is respected at the city **g**,
31: 31 works bring her praise at the city **g**.
Mt 7: 13 "Enter through the narrow **g**.
7: 13 For wide is the **g** and broad is
Jn 10: 1 not enter the sheep pen by the **g**,
10: 2 who enters by the **g** is the shepherd
10: 7 I tell you, I am the **g** for the sheep.
10: 9 I am the **g**; whoever enters through
Heb 13: 12 suffered outside the city **g** to make
Rev 21: 21 each **g** made of a single pearl.

GATES (GATE)
Ps 24: 7 Lift up your heads, you **g**;
24: 9 Lift up your heads, you **g**;
100: 4 Enter his **g** with thanksgiving
118: 19 Open for me the **g** of the righteous;
Isa 60: 11 Your **g** will always stand open,
60: 18 walls Salvation and your **g** Praise.
62: 10 Pass through, pass through the **g**!
Mt 16: 18 **g** of Hades will not overcome it.
Rev 21: 12 high wall with twelve **g**, and with twelve angels at the **g**.
21: 25 On no day will its **g** ever be shut,
22: 14 may go through the **g** into the city.

GATH
1Sa 17: 23 the Philistine champion from **G**,
2Sa 1: 20 "Tell it not in **G**, proclaim it not
Mic 1: 10 Tell it not in **G**; weep not at all.

GATHER (GATHERED GATHERS)
Ps 106: 47 and **g** us from the nations, that we
Isa 11: 12 nations and **g** the exiles of Israel;
Jer 3: 17 all nations will **g** in Jerusalem
23: 3 "I myself will **g** the remnant of my
31: 10 who scattered Israel will **g** them
Zep 2: 1 **G** together, **g** yourselves together,
3: 20 At that time I will **g** you;
Zec 14: 2 I will **g** all the nations to Jerusalem
Mt 12: 30 and whoever does not **g** with me
13: 30 then **g** the wheat and bring it
23: 37 longed to **g** your children together,
24: 31 they will **g** his elect from the four
25: 26 **g** where I have not scattered seed?
Mk 13: 27 **g** his elect from the four winds,
Lk 3: 17 and to **g** the wheat into his barn,
11: 23 and whoever does not **g** with me
13: 34 longed to **g** your children together,

GATHERED (GATHER)
Ex 16: 18 the one who **g** much did not have
16: 18 Everyone had **g** just as much as
Pr 30: 4 Whose hands have **g** up the wind?
Mt 25: 32 the nations will be **g** before him,
2Co 8: 15 "The one who **g** much did not have
2Th 2: 1 Christ and our being **g** to him,
Rev 16: 16 they **g** the kings together

GATHERS (GATHER)
Ps 147: 2 he **g** the exiles of Israel.
Pr 10: 5 He who **g** crops in summer is
Isa 40: 11 He **g** the lambs in his arms
Mt 23: 37 as a hen **g** her chicks under her

GAVE (GIVE)
Ge 2: 20 So the man **g** names to all
3: 6 She also **g** some to her husband,
14: 20 Abram **g** him a tenth of everything.
28: 4 the land God **g** to Abraham."
35: 12 The land I **g** to Abraham and Isaac
39: 23 **g** him success in whatever he did.
47: 11 **g** them property in the best part
Ex 4: 11 him, "Who **g** human beings their
31: 18 he **g** him the two tablets
Dt 2: 12 the land the LORD **g** them as their
2: 36 The LORD our God **g** us all
3: 12 I **g** the Reubenites and the Gadites
3: 13 I **g** to the half-tribe of Manasseh.
3: 15 And I **g** Gilead to Makir.
3: 16 and the Gadites I **g** the territory
8: 16 He **g** you manna to eat
26: 9 us to this place and **g** us this land,
32: 8 the Most High **g** the nations their
Jos 11: 23 he **g** it as an inheritance to Israel
13: 14 tribe of Levi he **g** no inheritance,
14: 13 **g** him Hebron as his inheritance.
21: 44 The LORD **g** them rest on every
24: 13 So I **g** you a land on which you did
1Sa 27: 6 on that day Achish **g** him Ziklag,
2Sa 12: 8 I **g** your master's house to you,
1Ki 4: 29 God **g** Solomon wisdom and very
5: 12 The LORD **g** Solomon wisdom,
Ezr 2: 69 their ability they **g** to the treasury
Ne 9: 15 their hunger you **g** them bread
9: 20 You **g** your good Spirit to instruct
9: 22 "You **g** them kingdoms
9: 27 compassion you **g** them deliverers,
Job 1: 21 The LORD **g** and the LORD has
42: 10 and **g** him twice as much as he had
Ps 69: 21 and **g** me vinegar for my thirst.
135: 12 he **g** their land as an inheritance,
Ecc 12: 7 the spirit returns to God who **g** it.
Eze 3: 2 and he **g** me the scroll to eat.
Mt 1: 25 And he **g** him the name Jesus.
25: 35 and you **g** me something to eat,
25: 42 and you **g** me nothing to drink,
26: 26 he broke it and **g** it to his disciples,
27: 50 in a loud voice, he **g** up his spirit.
Mk 6: 7 and **g** them authority over impure
Jn 1: 12 he **g** the right to become children
3: 16 so loved the world that he **g** his
17: 4 finishing the work you **g** me to do.
17: 6 you to those whom you **g** me
19: 30 bowed his head and **g** up his spirit.
Ac 1: 3 **g** many convincing proofs that he
11: 17 if God **g** them the same gift he **g** us
Ro 1: 24 Therefore God **g** them over
1: 26 God **g** them over to shameful lusts.
1: 28 so God **g** them over to a depraved
8: 32 own Son, but **g** him up for us all—
2Co 5: 18 **g** us the ministry of reconciliation:
8: 3 they **g** as much as they were able,
8: 5 They **g** themselves first of all
Gal 1: 4 **g** himself for our sins to rescue
2: 20 loved me and **g** himself for me.
Eph 4: 8 captives and **g** gifts to his people."
5: 2 **g** himself up for us as a fragrant
5: 25 church and **g** himself up for her
2Th 2: 16 us and by his grace **g** us eternal
1Ti 2: 6 who **g** himself as a ransom for all
Titus 2: 14 who **g** himself for us to redeem us
1Jn 3: 24 We know it by the Spirit he **g** us.

GAZE
Ps 27: 4 to **g** on the beauty of the LORD
Pr 4: 25 fix your **g** directly before you.

GEDALIAH
Governor of Judah appointed by Nebuchadnezzar (2Ki 25:22–26; Jer 39–41).

GEHAZI*
Servant of Elisha (2Ki 4:12—5:27; 8:4–5).

GENEALOGIES
1Ti 1: 4 themselves to myths and endless **g**.
Titus 3: 9 avoid foolish controversies and **g**

GENERATION (GENERATIONS)
Ex 3: 15 name you shall call me from **g** to **g**.
Nu 32: 13 until the whole **g** of those who had
Dt 1: 35 this evil **g** shall see the good land
Jdg 2: 10 another **g** grew up who knew
Job 8: 8 "Ask the former **g** and find
Ps 24: 6 Such is the **g** of those who seek
48: 13 you may tell of them to the next **g**.
71: 18 I declare your power to the next **g**,
78: 4 will tell the next **g** the praiseworthy
102: 18 Let this be written for a future **g**,
112: 2 the **g** of the upright will be blessed.
145: 4 One **g** commends your works
La 5: 19 your throne endures from **g** to **g**.
Da 4: 3 his dominion endures from **g** to **g**.
4: 34 his kingdom endures from **g** to **g**.
Joel 1: 3 and their children to the next **g**.
Mt 12: 39 and adulterous **g** asks for a sign!
17: 17 "You unbelieving and perverse **g**,"
23: 36 tell you, all this will come on this **g**.
24: 34 this **g** will certainly not pass away
Mk 9: 19 "You unbelieving **g**,"
13: 30 this **g** will certainly not pass away
Lk 1: 50 to those who fear him, from **g** to **g**.
11: 29 Jesus said, "This is a wicked **g**.
11: 30 will the Son of Man be to this **g**.
11: 50 Therefore this **g** will be held
21: 32 this **g** will certainly not pass away
Ac 2: 40 yourselves from this corrupt **g**."
Php 2: 15 fault in a warped and crooked **g**."

GENERATIONS (GENERATION)
Ge 9: 12 you, a covenant for all **g** to come:
17: 7 after you for the **g** to come, to be
17: 9 after you for the **g** to come.
Ex 20: 6 a thousand **g** of those who love me
31: 13 me and you for the **g** to come,
Dt 7: 9 thousand **g** of those who love him
32: 7 consider the **g** long past.
1Ch 16: 15 promise he made, for a thousand **g**,
Ps 22: 30 future **g** will be told about the Lord
33: 11 purposes of his heart through all **g**.
45: 17 your memory through all **g**;
89: 1 faithfulness known through all **g**.
90: 1 dwelling place throughout all **g**.
100: 5 faithfulness continues through all **g**
102: 12 renown endures through all **g**.
105: 8 promise he made, for a thousand **g**,
119: 90 faithfulness continues through all **g**
135: 13 renown, LORD, through all **g**.
145: 13 dominion endures through all **g**.
146: 10 your God, O Zion, for all **g**.
Pr 27: 24 and a crown is not secure for all **g**.
Isa 41: 4 through, calling forth the **g**
51: 8 my salvation through all **g**."
Lk 1: 48 now on all **g** will call me blessed,
Eph 3: 5 other **g** as it has now been revealed
3: 21 in Christ Jesus throughout all **g**,
Col 1: 26 been kept hidden for ages and **g**,

GENEROSITY* (GENEROUS)
2Co 8: 2 poverty welled up in rich **g**.
9: 11 and through us your **g** will result
9: 13 for your **g** in sharing with them

GENEROUS* (GENEROSITY)
Ps 37: 26 They are always **g** and lend freely;
112: 5 Good will come to those who are **g**

Pr 11: 25 A **g** person will prosper;
22: 9 The **g** will themselves be blessed,
Mt 20: 15 are you envious because I am **g**?'
Lk 11: 41 be **g** to the poor, and everything
Ac 28: 7 showed us **g** hospitality for three
2Co 9: 5 for the **g** gift you had promised.
9: 5 Then it will be ready as a **g** gift,
9: 11 you can be **g** on every occasion,
1Ti 6: 18 and to be **g** and willing to share.

GENTILE (GENTILES)
Ac 21: 25 As for the **G** believers, we have
Ro 1: 16 first to the Jew, then to the **G**.
2: 9 first for the Jew, then for the **G**;
2: 10 first for the Jew, then for the **G**.
10: 12 no difference between Jew and **G**—
Gal 3: 28 There is neither Jew nor **G**,
Col 3: 11 Here there is no **G** or Jew,

GENTILES (GENTILE)
Isa 42: 6 for the people and a light for the **G**,
49: 6 also make you a light for the **G**,
Lk 2: 32 a light for revelation to the **G**,
21: 24 trampled on by the **G** until the times of the **G** are fulfilled.
Ac 9: 15 to proclaim my name to the **G**
10: 45 had been poured out even on **G**.
11: 18 to **G** God has granted repentance
13: 16 and you **G** who worship God,
13: 46 eternal life, we now turn to the **G**.
13: 47 have made you a light for the **G**,
14: 27 opened a door of faith to the **G**.
15: 14 a people for his name from the **G**.
18: 6 From now on I will go to the **G**."
22: 21 send you far away to the **G**.'"
26: 20 and then to the **G**, I preached
28: 28 salvation has been sent to the **G**,
Ro 2: 14 when **G**, who do not have the law,
3: 9 **G** alike are all under the power
3: 29 Is he not the God of **G** too?
9: 24 from the Jews but also from the **G**?
11: 11 to the **G** to make Israel envious.
11: 12 their loss means riches for the **G**,
11: 13 as I am the apostle to the **G**,
15: 9 that the **G** might glorify God for
15: 9 I will praise you among the **G**;
1Co 1: 23 block to Jews and foolishness to **G**,
Gal 1: 16 I might preach him among the **G**,
2: 2 gospel that I preach among the **G**.
2: 8 work in me as an apostle to the **G**.
2: 9 agreed that we should go to the **G**,
3: 8 God would justify the **G** by faith,
3: 14 to the **G** through Christ Jesus,
Eph 3: 6 the gospel the **G** are heirs together
3: 8 preach to the **G** the boundless
Col 1: 27 known among the **G** the glorious
1Ti 2: 7 a true and faithful teacher of the **G**.
2Ti 4: 17 and all the **G** might hear it.

GENTLE* (GENTLENESS)
Dt 28: 54 Even the most **g** and sensitive man
28: 56 The most **g** and sensitive woman
28: 56 and **g** that she would not venture
2Sa 18: 5 Be **g** with the young man Absalom
1Ki 19: 12 after the fire came a **g** whisper.
Job 41: 3 Will it speak to you with **g** words?
Pr 15: 1 A **g** answer turns away wrath,
25: 15 and a **g** tongue can break a bone.
Jer 11: 19 I had been like a **g** lamb led
Mt 11: 29 for I am **g** and humble in heart,
21: 5 to you, **g** and riding on a donkey,
Ac 27: 13 When a **g** south wind began
1Co 4: 21 I come in love and with a **g** spirit?
Eph 4: 2 Be completely humble and **g**;
1Ti 3: 3 not violent but **g**, not quarrelsome,
Titus 3: 2 always to be **g** toward everyone.
1Pe 3: 4 unfading beauty of a **g** and quiet

GENTLENESS* (GENTLE)
2Co 10: 1 By the humility and **g** of Christ,
Gal 5: 23 **g** and self-control.
Php 4: 5 Let your **g** be evident to all.
Col 3: 12 kindness, humility, **g** and patience.
1Ti 6: 11 faith, love, endurance and **g**.
1Pe 3: 15 But do this with **g** and respect,

GENUINE* (GENUINENESS)
2Co 6: 8 **g**, yet regarded as impostors;
Php 2: 20 who will show **g** concern for your

GENUINENESS* (GENUINE)
1Pe 1: 7 that the proven **g** of your faith—

GERIZIM
Dt 27: 12 on Mount **G** to bless the people:

GERSHOM
Ex 2: 22 and Moses named him **G**, saying,

GETHSEMANE*
Mt 26: 36 his disciples to a place called **G**,
Mk 14: 32 They went to a place called **G**,

GHOST See also SPIRIT
Lk 24: 39 a **g** does not have flesh and bones,

GIBEON
Jos 10: 12 "Sun, stand still over **G**, and you,

GIDEON*
Judge, also called Jerub-Baal; freed Israel from Midianites (Jdg 6–8; Heb 11:32). Given sign of fleece (Jdg 6:36–40).

GIFT (GIFTED GIFTS)
Pr 18: 16 A **g** opens the way and ushers
21: 14 A **g** given in secret soothes anger,
Ecc 3: 13 all their toil—this is the **g** of God.
Mt 5: 23 you are offering your **g** at the altar
Jn 4: 10 "If you knew the **g** of God and who
Ac 1: 4 wait for the **g** my Father promised,
2: 38 you will receive the **g** of the Holy
11: 17 gave them the same **g** he gave us
Ro 6: 23 the **g** of God is eternal life in Christ
12: 6 If your **g** is prophesying,
1Co 7: 7 of you has your own **g** from God;
7: 7 one has this **g**, another has that.
2Co 8: 12 the **g** is acceptable according
9: 15 be to God for his indescribable **g**!
Eph 2: 8 yourselves, it is the **g** of God—
1Ti 4: 14 Do not neglect your **g**, which was
2Ti 1: 6 you to fan into flame the **g** of God,
Heb 6: 4 who have tasted the heavenly **g**,
Jas 1: 17 good and perfect **g** is from above,
1Pe 3: 7 with you of the gracious **g** of life,
4: 10 you should use whatever **g** you
Rev 22: 17 the one who wishes take the free **g**

GIFTED* (GIFT)
1Co 14: 37 or otherwise **g** by the Spirit,

GIFTS (GIFT)
Ps 76: 11 all the neighboring lands bring **g**
112: 9 They have freely scattered their **g**
Pr 25: 14 is one who boasts of **g** never given.
Mt 2: 11 and presented him with **g** of gold,
7: 11 to give good **g** to your children,
7: 11 in heaven give good **g** to those who
Lk 11: 13 to give good **g** to your children,
Ac 10: 4 and **g** to the poor have come up as
Ro 11: 29 for God's **g** and his call are
12: 6 We have different **g**,
1Co 12: 1 Now about the **g** of the Spirit,
12: 4 There are different kinds of **g**,
12: 28 then **g** of healing, of helping,
12: 30 Do all have **g** of healing?
12: 31 Now eagerly desire the greater **g**.
14: 1 and eagerly desire **g** of the Spirit,
14: 12 Since you are eager for **g**
2Co 9: 9 "They have freely scattered their **g**
Eph 4: 8 captives and gave **g** to his people."
Heb 2: 4 by **g** of the Holy Spirit distributed
9: 9 indicating that the **g** and sacrifices

GILEAD
1Ch 27: 21 the half-tribe of Manasseh in **G**:
Jer 8: 22 Is there no balm in **G**? Is there no
46: 11 "Go up to **G** and get balm,

GILGAL
Jos 5: 9 So the place has been called **G**

GIRD*
Ps 45: 3 **G** your sword on your side,

GIRL
2Ki 5: 2 had taken captive a young **g**
Mk 5: 41 (which means "Little **g**, I say

GIVE (GAVE GIVEN GIVER GIVES GIVING LIFE-GIVING)
Ge 28: 4 he **g** you and your descendants
28: 22 that you **g** me I will **g** you a tenth."
Ex 20: 16 "You shall not **g** false testimony
30: 15 the poor are not to **g** less when you
Nu 6: 26 toward you and **g** you peace."'
Dt 5: 20 "You shall not **g** false testimony
15: 10 **G** generously to them and do so
15: 14 **G** to them as the LORD your God
1Sa 1: 11 I will **g** him to the LORD for all
1: 28 So now I **g** him to the LORD.
2Ch 15: 7 be strong and do not **g** up, for your
Pr 21: 26 the righteous **g** without sparing.
23: 26 **g** me your heart and let your eyes
25: 21 enemy is hungry, **g** him food to
25: 26 well are the righteous who **g** way
28: 27 Those who **g** to the poor will lack
30: 8 **g** me neither poverty nor riches,
30: 8 but **g** me only my daily bread.
Ecc 3: 6 a time to search and a time to **g** up,
Eze 36: 26 I will **g** you a new heart and put
Mt 6: 11 **G** us today our daily bread.
7: 11 your Father in heaven **g** good gifts
10: 8 Freely you have received; freely **g**.
16: 19 will **g** you the keys of the kingdom
22: 21 them, "So **g** back to Caesar what is
Mk 8: 37 what can anyone **g** in exchange
10: 19 you shall not **g** false testimony,
Lk 6: 38 **G**, and it will be given to you.
11: 3 **G** us each day our daily bread.
11: 13 Father in heaven **g** the Holy Spirit
14: 33 you who do not **g** up everything
Jn 10: 28 I **g** them eternal life, and they shall
13: 34 "A new command I **g** you:
14: 16 he will **g** you another advocate
14: 27 I leave with you; my peace I **g** you.
14: 27 do not **g** to you as the world gives.
17: 2 people that he might **g** eternal life
Ac 2: 45 possessions to **g** to anyone who
20: 35 'It is more blessed to **g** than
Ro 2: 7 immortality, he will **g** eternal life.
8: 32 him, graciously **g** us all things?
12: 8 if it is giving, then **g** generously;
13: 7 **G** to everyone what you owe them:
14: 12 then, each of us will **g** an account
1Co 13: 3 If I **g** all I possess to the poor and **g**
2Co 9: 7 have decided in your heart to **g**,
Gal 2: 5 We did not **g** in to them
6: 9 reap a harvest if we do not **g** up.
Rev 14: 7 voice, "Fear God and **g** him glory,
21: 6 thirsty I will **g** water without cost

GIVEN (GIVE)
Nu 8: 16 Israelites who are to be **g** wholly
Dt 26: 11 things the LORD your God has **g**
Job 3: 23 Why is life **g** to a man whose way
Ps 115: 16 but the earth he has **g** to mankind.
Isa 9: 6 us a son is **g**, and the government
Mt 6: 33 all these things will be **g** to you as
7: 7 "Ask and it will be **g** to you;
13: 12 Whoever has will be **g** more,
22: 30 people will neither marry nor be **g**
25: 29 For whoever has will be **g** more,
Lk 6: 38 Give, and it will be **g** to you.
8: 10 kingdom of God has been **g** to you,
11: 9 Ask and it will be **g** to you;
22: 19 saying, "This is my body **g** for you;
Jn 3: 27 can receive only what is **g** them
17: 24 glory you have **g** me because you
18: 11 the cup the Father has **g** me?"
Ac 5: 32 God has **g** to those who obey
7: 53 the law that was **g** through angels
20: 24 the task the Lord Jesus has **g** me—
Ro 5: 5 Holy Spirit, who has been **g** to us.
1Co 4: 2 those who have been **g** a trust must
11: 24 when he had **g** thanks, he broke
12: 13 and we were all **g** the one Spirit
2Co 5: 5 has **g** us the Spirit as a deposit,
Gal 3: 19 Why, then, was the law **g** at all?
3: 19 The law was **g** through angels
Eph 1: 6 he has freely **g** us in the One he
4: 7 of us grace has been **g** as Christ
1Ti 4: 14 which was **g** you through prophecy
1Jn 4: 13 he in us: He has **g** us of his Spirit.

GIVER* (GIVE)
Pr 18: 16 ushers the **g** into the presence
2Co 9: 7 for God loves a cheerful **g**.

GIVES (GIVE)
Job 35: 10 Maker, who **g** songs in the night,
Ps 119:130 unfolding of your words **g** light;
Pr 11: 24 One person **g** freely, yet gains even

Pr 14: 30 A heart at peace **g** life to the body,
15: 30 good news **g** health to the bones.
19: 6 is the friend of one who **g** gifts.
29: 4 justice a king **g** a country stability,
Isa 40: 29 He **g** strength to the weary
Hab 2: 15 him who **g** drink to his neighbors,
Mt 10: 42 anyone **g** even a cup of cold water
Jn 5: 21 raises the dead and **g** them life,
6: 63 The Spirit **g** life; the flesh counts
1Co 15: 57 He **g** us the victory through our
2Co 3: 6 the letter kills, but the Spirit **g** life.
1Th 4: 8 the very God who **g** you his Holy
Jas 1: 25 into the perfect law that **g** freedom,
4: 6 But he **g** us more grace. That is

GIVING (GIVE)
Ne 8: 8 **g** the meaning so that the people
Est 9: 19 a day for **g** presents to each other.
Ps 19: 8 are radiant, **g** light to the eyes.
Pr 15: 23 person finds joy in **g** an apt reply—
Mt 6: 4 so that your **g** may be in secret.
24: 38 marrying and **g** in marriage,
Ac 15: 8 accepted them by **g** the Holy Spirit
2Co 8: 7 you also excel in this grace of **g**.
Php 4: 15 shared with me in the matter of **g**
Heb 10: 25 not **g** up meeting together, as some

GLAD* (GLADDENS GLADNESS)
Ex 4: 14 you, and he will be **g** to see you.
Jos 22: 33 They were **g** to hear the report
Jdg 8: 25 "We'll be **g** to give them."
1Sa 19: 5 Israel, and you saw it and were **g**.
2Sa 1: 20 daughters of the Philistines be **g**,
1Ki 8: 66 **g** in heart for all the good things
1Ch 16: 31 heavens rejoice, let the earth be **g**;
2Ch 7: 10 **g** in heart for the good things
Ps 5: 11 let all who take refuge in you be **g**;
9: 2 I will be **g** and rejoice in you;
14: 7 let Jacob rejoice and Israel be **g**!
16: 9 Therefore my heart is **g** and my
21: 6 made him **g** with the joy of your
31: 7 I will be **g** and rejoice in your love,
32: 11 Rejoice in the LORD and be **g**,
40: 16 seek you rejoice and be **g** in you;
45: 8 music of the strings makes you **g**.
46: 4 whose streams make **g** the city
48: 11 of Judah are **g** because of your
53: 6 let Jacob rejoice and Israel be **g**!
58: 10 The righteous will be **g** when they
67: 4 May the nations be **g** and sing
68: 3 may the righteous be **g** and rejoice
69: 32 The poor will see and be **g**—
70: 4 seek you rejoice and be **g** in you;
90: 14 sing for joy and be **g** all our days.
90: 15 Make us **g** for as many days as you
92: 4 For you make me **g** by your deeds,
96: 11 heavens rejoice, let the earth be **g**;
97: 1 LORD reigns, let the earth be **g**;
97: 8 of Judah are **g** because of your
105: 38 Egypt was **g** when they left,
107: 30 They were **g** when it grew calm,
118: 24 let us rejoice today and be **g**.
149: 2 people of Zion be **g** in their King.
Pr 23: 15 then my heart will be **g** indeed;
29: 6 righteous shout for joy and are **g**.
Ecc 8: 15 sun than to eat and drink and be **g**.
Isa 25: 9 rejoice and be **g** in his salvation."
35: 1 and the parched land will be **g**;
65: 18 be **g** and rejoice forever in what I
66: 10 with Jerusalem and be **g** for her,
Jer 20: 15 who made him very **g**, saying,
31: 13 young women will dance and be **g**,
41: 13 who were with him, they were **g**.
50: 11 "Because you rejoice and are **g**,
La 4: 21 Rejoice and be **g**, Daughter Edom,
Joel 2: 21 land of Judah; be **g** and rejoice.
2: 23 Be **g**, people of Zion,
Hab 1: 15 and so he rejoices and is **g**.
Zep 3: 14 Be **g** and rejoice with all your heart
Zec 2: 10 "Shout and be **g**, Daughter Zion.
8: 19 will become joyful and **g** occasions
10: 7 their hearts will be **g** as with wine.
Mt 5: 12 Rejoice and be **g**, because great is
Lk 15: 32 But we had to celebrate and be **g**,
Jn 4: 36 and the reaper may be **g** together.
8: 56 he saw it and was **g**."
11: 15 your sake I am **g** I was not there,
Jn 14: 28 you would be **g** that I am going
Ac 2: 26 Therefore my heart is **g** and my
2: 46 and ate together with **g** and sincere
11: 23 he was **g** and encouraged them all
13: 48 they were **g** and honored the word
15: 3 news made all the believers very **g**.
15: 31 were **g** for its encouraging message.
1Co 16: 17 I was **g** when Stephanas,
2Co 2: 2 who is left to make me **g** but you
7: 16 I am **g** I can have complete
13: 9 We are **g** whenever we are weak
Gal 4: 27 "Be **g**, barren woman, you who
Php 2: 17 I am **g** and rejoice with all of you.
2: 18 So you too should be **g** and rejoice
2: 28 you see him again you may be **g**
Rev 19: 7 and be **g** and give him glory!

GLADDENS* (GLAD)
Ps 104: 15 wine that **g** human hearts,

GLADNESS* (GLAD)
2Ch 29: 30 So they sang praises with **g**
Est 8: 16 of happiness and joy, **g** and honor.
8: 17 was joy and **g** among the Jews,
Job 3: 22 who are filled with **g** and rejoice
Ps 35: 27 my vindication shout for joy and **g**;
45: 15 Led in with joy and **g**, they enter
51: 8 Let me hear joy and **g**; let the
65: 12 the hills are clothed with **g**.
100: 2 Worship the LORD with **g**;
Ecc 5: 20 God keeps them occupied with **g**
9: 7 eat your food with **g**, and drink
Isa 16: 10 **g** are taken away from the
35: 10 **G** and joy will overtake them,
51: 3 Joy and **g** will be found in her,
51: 11 **G** and joy will overtake them,
Jer 7: 34 an end to the sounds of joy and **g**
16: 9 an end to the sounds of joy and **g**
25: 10 from them the sounds of joy and **g**,
31: 13 I will turn their mourning into **g**;
33: 11 the sounds of joy and **g**, the voices
48: 33 and **g** are gone from the orchards
Joel 1: 16 and **g** from the house of our God?

GLEAM*
Da 10: 6 legs like the **g** of burnished bronze,

GLOAT (GLOATS)
Pr 24: 17 Do not **g** when your enemy falls;

GLOATS* (GLOAT)
Pr 17: 5 whoever **g** over disaster will not go

GLORIES* (GLORY)
1Pe 1: 11 and the **g** that would follow.

GLORIFIED* (GLORY)
Isa 66: 5 'Let the LORD be **g**, that we may
Da 4: 34 and **g** him who lives forever.
Jn 7: 39 since Jesus had not yet been **g**.
11: 4 God's Son may be **g** through it."
12: 16 after Jesus was **g** did they realize
12: 23 come for the Son of Man to be **g**.
12: 28 "I have **g** it, and will glorify it
13: 31 "Now the Son of Man is **g** and God
is **g** in him.
13: 32 If God is **g** in him, God will glorify
Jn 14: 13 the Father may be **g** in the Son.
Ac 3: 13 our fathers, has **g** his servant Jesus.
Ro 1: 21 they neither **g** him as God nor gave
8: 30 those he justified, he also **g**.
2Th 1: 10 he comes to be **g** in his holy people
1: 12 of our Lord Jesus may be **g** in you,
1Pe 1: 21 him from the dead and **g** him,

GLORIFIES* (GLORY)
Lk 1: 46 "My soul **g** the Lord
Jn 8: 54 as your God, is the one who **g** me.

GLORIFY* (GLORY)
Ps 34: 3 **G** the LORD with me; let us exalt
63: 3 better than life, my lips will **g** you.
69: 30 song and **g** him with thanksgiving.
86: 12 I will **g** your name forever.
Isa 60: 13 and I will **g** the place for my feet.
Da 4: 37 and exalt and **g** the King of heaven,
Mt 5: 16 deeds and **g** your Father in heaven.
Jn 8: 54 "If I **g** myself, my glory means
12: 28 Father, **g** your name!" Then a voice
12: 28 glorified it, and will **g** it again."
13: 32 God will **g** the Son in himself, and
will **g** him at once.
Jn 16: 14 He will **g** me because it is from me
17: 1 **G** your Son, that your Son may **g**
17: 5 **g** me in your presence
21: 19 death by which Peter would **g** God.
Ro 15: 6 one voice you may **g** the God
15: 9 the Gentiles might **g** God for his
1Pe 2: 12 and **g** God on the day he visits us.
Rev 16: 9 they refused to repent and **g** him.

GLORIFYING* (GLORY)
Lk 2: 20 **g** and praising God for all the

GLORIOUS* (GLORY)
Dt 28: 58 do not revere this **g** and awesome
33: 29 and helper and your **g** sword.
1Ch 29: 13 thanks, and praise your **g** name.
Ne 9: 5 "Blessed be your **g** name, and may
Ps 45: 13 All **g** is the princess within her
66: 2 of his name; make his praise **g**.
72: 19 Praise be to his **g** name forever;
87: 3 **G** things are said of you,
106: 20 They exchanged their **g** God
111: 3 **G** and majestic are his deeds,
145: 5 They speak of the **g** splendor
145: 12 the **g** splendor of your kingdom.
Pr 4: 9 and present you with a **g** crown."
Isa 3: 8 the LORD, defying his **g** presence.
4: 2 the LORD will be beautiful and **g**,
11: 10 him, and his resting place will be **g**.
12: 5 LORD, for he has done **g** things;
28: 1 to the fading flower, his **g** beauty,
28: 4 That fading flower, his **g** beauty,
28: 5 Almighty will be a **g** crown,
42: 21 to make his law great and **g**.
60: 7 altar, and I will adorn my **g** temple.
63: 12 who sent his **g** arm of power to be
63: 14 to make for yourself a **g** name.
63: 15 from your lofty throne, holy and **g**.
64: 11 Our holy and **g** temple, where our
Jer 2: 11 people have exchanged their **g** God
13: 18 for your **g** crowns will fall
14: 21 do not dishonor your **g** throne.
17: 12 A **g** throne,
48: 17 scepter, how broken the **g** staff!'
Hos 4: 7 they exchanged their **g** God
Zec 2: 8 the **G** One has sent me against
Mt 19: 28 Son of Man sits on his **g** throne,
25: 31 him, he will sit on his **g** throne.
Lk 9: 30 and Elijah, appeared in **g** splendor,
Ac 2: 20 of the great and **g** day of the Lord.
2Co 3: 8 of the Spirit be even more **g**?
3: 9 that brought condemnation was **g**,
how much more **g** is the ministry
3: 10 For what was **g** has no glory now
Eph 1: 6 to the praise of his **g** grace,
1: 17 our Lord Jesus Christ, the **g** Father,
1: 18 the riches of his **g** inheritance in
3: 16 his **g** riches he may strengthen you
Php 3: 21 so that they will be like his **g** body.
Col 1: 11 power according to his **g** might so
1: 27 among the Gentiles the **g** riches
Jas 2: 1 in our **g** Lord Jesus Christ must not
1Pe 1: 8 with an inexpressible and **g** joy,
Jude : 24 you before his **g** presence without

GLORY (GLORIES GLORIFIED GLORIFIES GLORIFY GLORIFYING GLORIOUS)
Ex 14: 4 But I will gain **g** for myself through
14: 17 I will gain **g** through Pharaoh
15: 11 awesome in **g**, working wonders?
16: 10 and there was the **g** of the LORD
24: 16 and the **g** of the LORD settled
33: 18 said, "Now show me your **g**."
40: 34 and the **g** of the LORD filled
Nu 14: 21 and as surely as the **g** of the LORD
Dt 5: 24 LORD our God has shown us his **g**
Jos 7: 19 "My son, give **g** to the LORD,
1Sa 4: 21 "The **G** has departed from Israel"
1Ch 16: 10 **G** in his holy name; let the hearts
16: 24 Declare his **g** among the nations,
16: 28 ascribe to the LORD **g**
29: 11 power and the **g** and the majesty
Ps 8: 1 You have set your **g** in the heavens.
8: 5 crowned them with **g** and honor.
19: 1 The heavens declare the **g** of God;
24: 7 that the King of **g** may come in.
26: 8 live, the place where your **g** dwells.
29: 1 beings, ascribe to the LORD **g**

Ps 29: 9 And in his temple all cry, "**G**!"
34: 2 I will **g** in the LORD;
57: 5 let your **g** be over all the earth.
66: 2 Sing the **g** of his name;
72: 19 the whole earth be filled with his **g**.
96: 3 Declare his **g** among the nations,
102: 15 of the earth will revere your **g**.
108: 5 let your **g** be over all the earth.
149: 9 this is the **g** of all his faithful
Pr 19: 11 is to one's **g** to overlook an offense.
25: 2 It is the **g** of God to conceal
Isa 4: 5 over everything the **g** will be
6: 3 the whole earth is full of his **g**."
24: 16 "**G** to the Righteous One."
24: 23 and before its elders—with great **g**.
26: 15 You have gained **g** for yourself;
35: 2 they will see the **g** of the LORD,
40: 5 And the **g** of the LORD will be
42: 8 I will not yield my **g** to another
42: 12 Let them give **g** to the LORD
43: 7 whom I created for my **g**, whom I
44: 23 Jacob, he displays his **g** in Israel.
48: 11 I will not yield my **g** to another.
66: 18 and they will come and see my **g**.
66: 19 not heard of my fame or seen my **g**.
Eze 1: 28 the likeness of the **g** of the LORD.
10: 4 Then the **g** of the LORD rose
39: 13 and the day I display my **g** will be
43: 2 I saw the **g** of the God of Israel
43: 2 the land was radiant with his **g**.
44: 4 saw the **g** of the LORD filling
Hab 2: 14 of the **g** of the LORD as the waters
3: 3 His **g** covered the heavens and his
Zec 2: 5 LORD, 'and I will be its **g** within.'
Mt 16: 27 in his Father's **g** with his angels,
24: 30 of heaven, with power and great **g**.
25: 31 the Son of Man comes in his **g**,
Mk 8: 38 in his Father's **g** with the holy
13: 26 in clouds with great power and **g**.
Lk 2: 9 and the **g** of the Lord shone around
2: 14 "**G** to God in the highest heaven,
9: 26 of them when he comes in his **g**
9: 26 and in the **g** of the Father
9: 32 they saw his **g** and the two men
19: 38 in heaven and **g** in the highest!"
21: 27 in a cloud with power and great **g**.
24: 26 these things and then enter his **g**?"
Jn 1: 14 We have seen his **g**, the **g** of the
2: 11 through which he revealed his **g**;
5: 44 can you believe since you accept **g**
7: 18 own does so to gain personal **g**,
8: 50 I am not seeking **g** for myself;
8: 54 myself, my **g** means nothing.
11: 4 it is for God's **g** so that God's Son
11: 40 believe, you will see the **g** of God?"
12: 41 said this because he saw Jesus' **g**
15: 8 This is to my Father's **g**, that you
17: 4 I have brought you **g** on earth
17: 5 your presence with the **g** I had
17: 10 **g** has come to me through them.
17: 22 I have given them the **g** that you
17: 24 and to see my **g**, the **g** you have
Ac 7: 2 The God of **g** appeared to our
7: 55 up to heaven and saw the **g** of God,
Ro 1: 23 exchanged the **g** of the immortal
2: 7 persistence in doing good seek **g**,
2: 10 **g**, honor and peace for everyone
3: 7 truthfulness and so increases his **g**,
3: 23 and fall short of the **g** of God,
4: 20 in his faith and gave **g** to God,
8: 17 that we may also share in his **g**.
8: 18 with the **g** that will be revealed
8: 21 and **g** of the children of God.
9: 4 theirs the divine **g**, the covenants,
9: 23 to make the riches of his **g** known
9: 23 he prepared in advance for **g**—
11: 36 To him be the **g** forever! Amen.
15: 17 Therefore I **g** in Christ Jesus in my
16: 27 God be **g** forever through Jesus
1Co 2: 7 for our **g** before time began.
10: 31 do it all for the **g** of God.
11: 7 he is the image and **g** of God;
11: 7 but woman is the **g** of man.
11: 15 a woman has long hair, it is her **g**?
15: 43 sown in dishonor, it is raised in **g**;
2Co 1: 20 is spoken by us to the **g** of God.
3: 7 came with **g**, so that the Israelites
3: 7 the face of Moses because of its **g**,
3: 10 what was glorious has no **g** now
3: 10 comparison with the surpassing **g**.
3: 11 if what was transitory came with **g**,
3: 18 faces contemplate the Lord's **g**,
3: 18 his image with ever-increasing **g**,
4: 4 gospel that displays the **g** of Christ,
4: 6 the knowledge of God's **g** displayed
4: 15 to overflow to the **g** of God.
4: 17 us an eternal **g** that far outweighs
Gal 1: 5 to whom be **g** for ever and ever.
Eph 1: 12 might be for the praise of his **g**.
1: 14 to the praise of his **g**.
3: 13 for you, which are your **g**.
3: 21 to him be **g** in the church
Php 1: 11 to the **g** and praise of God.
2: 11 is Lord, to the **g** of God the Father.
4: 19 the riches of his **g** in Christ Jesus.
4: 20 To our God and Father be **g** for
Col 1: 27 is Christ in you, the hope of **g**.
3: 4 you also will appear with him in **g**.
1Th 2: 12 calls you into his kingdom and **g**.
2: 19 which we will **g** in the presence
2: 20 Indeed, you are our **g** and joy.
2Th 1: 9 Lord and from the **g** of his might
2: 14 in the **g** of our Lord Jesus Christ.
1Ti 1: 11 to the gospel concerning the **g**
1: 17 be honor and **g** for ever and ever.
3: 16 on in the world, was taken up in **g**.
2Ti 2: 10 is in Christ Jesus, with eternal **g**.
4: 18 To him be **g** for ever and ever.
Titus 2: 13 appearing of the **g** of our great God
Heb 1: 3 The Son is the radiance of God's **g**
2: 7 crowned them with **g** and honor
2: 9 now crowned with **g** and honor
2: 10 many sons and daughters to **g**,
5: 5 on himself the **g** of becoming a
9: 5 ark were the cherubim of the **G**,
13: 21 to whom be **g** for ever and ever.
1Pe 1: 7 **g** and honor when Jesus Christ is
1: 24 all their **g** is like the flowers
4: 11 To him be the **g** and the power
4: 13 overjoyed when his **g** is revealed.
4: 14 for the Spirit of **g** and of God rests
5: 1 will share in the **g** to be revealed:
5: 4 you will receive the crown of **g**
5: 10 you to his eternal **g** in Christ,
2Pe 1: 3 of him who called us by his own **g**
1: 17 and **g** from God the Father
1: 17 came to him from the Majestic **G**,
3: 18 To him be **g** both now and forever!
Jude : 25 to the only God our Savior be **g**,
Rev 1: 6 to him be **g** and power for ever
4: 9 the living creatures give **g**,
4: 11 to receive **g** and honor and power,
5: 12 and honor and **g** and praise!"
5: 13 praise and honor and **g** and power,
7: 12 Praise and **g** and wisdom and
11: 13 and gave **g** to the God of heaven.
14: 7 "Fear God and give him **g**,
15: 4 Lord, and bring **g** to your name?
15: 8 with smoke from the **g** of God
19: 1 Salvation and **g** and power belong
19: 7 rejoice and be glad and give him **g**!
21: 11 It shone with the **g** of God, and its
21: 23 for the **g** of God gives it light,
21: 26 The **g** and honor of the nations will

GLOWING
1Sa 16: 12 He was **g** with health and had a
Eze 8: 2 was as bright as **g** metal.
Rev 1: 15 His feet were like bronze **g**

GLUTTONS* (GLUTTONY)
Pr 23: 21 for drunkards and **g** become poor,
28: 7 of **g** disgraces his father.
Titus 1: 12 always liars, evil brutes, lazy **g**."

GLUTTONY* (GLUTTONS)
Pr 23: 2 to your throat if you are given to **g**.

GNASHING
Mt 8: 12 will be weeping and **g** of teeth."

GNAT* (GNATS)
Mt 23: 24 You strain out a **g** but swallow

GNATS (GNAT)
Ex 8: 16 of Egypt the dust will become **g**."

GOADS
Ecc 12: 11 The words of the wise are like **g**,
Ac 26: 14 hard for you to kick against the **g**.'

GOAL*
Lk 13: 32 on the third day I will reach my **g**.'
Ro 9: 31 have not attained their **g**.
2Co 5: 9 So we make it our **g** to please him,
8: 14 what you need. The **g** is equality,
Php 3: 12 or have already arrived at my **g**,
3: 14 on toward the **g** to win the prize
Col 2: 2 **g** is that they may be encouraged
1Ti 1: 5 The **g** of this command is love,

GOAT (GOATS SCAPEGOAT)
Ge 15: 9 "Bring me a heifer, a **g** and a ram,
30: 32 and every spotted or speckled **g**.
37: 31 slaughtered a **g** and dipped the
Ex 26: 7 "Make curtains of **g** hair
Lev 16: 9 shall bring the **g** whose lot falls
Nu 7: 16 one male **g** for a sin offering;
Isa 11: 6 leopard will lie down with the **g**,
Da 8: 5 a **g** with a prominent horn

GOATS (GOAT)
Nu 7: 17 five male **g** and five male lambs
Mt 25: 32 separates the sheep from the **g**.
Heb 10: 4 of bulls and **g** to take away sins.

GOD (GOD'S GODLINESS GODLY GODS)
Ge 1: 1 beginning **G** created the heavens
1: 2 of **G** was hovering over the waters.
1: 3 And **G** said, "Let there be light,"
1: 7 So **G** made the vault and separated
1: 9 And **G** said, "Let the water under
1: 11 Then **G** said, "Let the land produce
1: 20 And **G** said, "Let the water teem
1: 21 And **G** saw that it was good.
1: 25 And **G** saw that it was good.
1: 26 Then **G** said, "Let us make
1: 27 So **G** created mankind in his own
1: 27 in the image of **G** he created them;
1: 31 **G** saw all that he had made, and it
2: 3 Then **G** blessed the seventh day
2: 7 the LORD **G** formed a man
2: 8 Now the LORD **G** had planted
2: 18 The LORD **G** said, "It is not good
2: 22 the LORD **G** made a woman
3: 1 to the woman, "Did **G** really say,
3: 5 and you will be like **G**,
3: 8 of the LORD **G** as he was walking
3: 9 the LORD **G** called to the man,
3: 21 The LORD **G** made garments
3: 22 And the LORD **G** said, "The man
3: 23 So the LORD **G** banished him
5: 1 he made them in the likeness of **G**.
5: 22 walked faithfully with **G** 300 years
5: 24 Enoch walked faithfully with **G**;
6: 2 sons of **G** saw that the daughters
6: 9 and he walked faithfully with **G**.
6: 12 **G** saw how corrupt the earth had
8: 1 But **G** remembered Noah and all
9: 1 Then **G** blessed Noah and his sons,
9: 6 image of **G** has **G** made mankind.
9: 16 everlasting covenant between **G**
14: 18 He was priest of **G** Most High,
14: 19 be Abram by **G** Most High,
16: 13 "You are the **G** who sees me,"
17: 1 to him and said, "I am **G** Almighty;
17: 7 to be your **G** and the **G** of your
21: 4 him, as **G** commanded him.
21: 6 said, "**G** has brought me laughter,
21: 20 **G** was with the boy as he grew up.
21: 22 "**G** is with you in everything you
21: 33 name of the LORD, the Eternal **G**.
22: 1 Some time later **G** tested Abraham.
22: 8 "**G** himself will provide the lamb
22: 12 Now I know that you fear **G**,
25: 11 death, **G** blessed his son Isaac,
28: 12 the angels of **G** were ascending
28: 17 is none other than the house of **G**;
31: 42 But **G** has seen my hardship
31: 50 that **G** is a witness between you
32: 1 way, and the angels of **G** met him.
32: 28 because you have struggled with **G**
32: 30 "It is because I saw **G** face to face,

Ge 33: 11 for **G** has been gracious to me and
35: 1 and build an altar there to **G**,
35: 5 the terror of **G** fell on the towns
35: 10 **G** said to him, "Your name is
35: 11 And **G** said to him, "I am **G**
41: 51 said, "It is because **G** has made me
41: 52 said, "It is because **G** has made me
50: 20 me, but **G** intended it for good
50: 24 But **G** will surely come to your aid
Ex 2: 24 **G** heard their groaning and he
3: 5 "Do not come any closer," **G** said.
3: 6 he said, "I am the **G** of your father,
the **G** of Abraham, the **G** of Isaac and
the **G** of Jacob."
3: 6 because he was afraid to look at **G**.
3: 12 And **G** said, "I will be with you.
3: 14 **G** said to Moses, "I AM WHO I AM.
4: 27 he met Moses at the mountain of **G**
6: 7 know that I am the LORD your **G**,
8: 10 is no one like the LORD our **G**.
10: 16 sinned against the LORD your **G**
13: 18 So **G** led the people around
15: 2 He is my **G**, and I will praise him,
16: 12 that I am the LORD your **G**.'"
17: 9 with the staff of **G** in my hands."
18: 5 camped near the mountain of **G**.
19: 3 Then Moses went up to **G**,
20: 1 And **G** spoke all these words:
20: 2 "I am the LORD your **G**,
20: 5 the LORD your **G**, am a jealous **G**,
20: 7 the name of the LORD your **G**,
20: 10 is a sabbath to the LORD your **G**.
20: 12 the LORD your **G** is giving you.
20: 19 But do not have **G** speak to us or
20: 20 **G** has come to test you,
22: 20 any **g** other than the LORD must
22: 28 "Do not blaspheme **G** or curse
23: 19 to the house of the LORD your **G**.
31: 18 stone inscribed by the finger of **G**.
34: 6 the compassionate and gracious **G**,
34: 14 Do not worship any other **g**,
34: 14 name is Jealous, is a jealous **G**.
Lev 2: 13 the covenant of your **G** out of your
11: 44 I am the LORD your **G**;
18: 21 not profane the name of your **G**.
19: 2 I, the LORD your **G**, am holy.
20: 7 because I am the LORD your **G**.
21: 6 not profane the name of their **G**.
22: 33 you out of Egypt to be your **G**.
26: 12 walk among you and be your **G**,
Nu 15: 40 and will be consecrated to your **G**.
22: 18 the command of the LORD my **G**.
22: 38 I must speak only what **G** puts
23: 19 **G** is not human, that he should lie,
25: 13 was zealous for the honor of his **G**
Dt 1: 17 anyone, for judgment belongs to **G**.
1: 21 LORD, the **G** of your ancestors,
1: 30 The LORD your **G**, who is going
3: 22 the LORD your **G** himself will
3: 24 For what **g** is there in heaven
4: 24 the LORD your **G** is a consuming fire,
a jealous **G**.
4: 29 there you seek the LORD your **G**,
4: 31 the LORD your **G** is a merciful **G**;
4: 39 day that the LORD is **G** in heaven
5: 9 the LORD your **G**, am a jealous **G**,
5: 11 the name of the LORD your **G**,
5: 12 the LORD your **G** has commanded
5: 14 is a sabbath to the LORD your **G**.
5: 15 the LORD your **G** brought you
5: 16 the LORD your **G** is giving you.
5: 24 a person can live even if **G** speaks
5: 26 voice of the living **G** speaking
6: 2 fear the LORD your **G** as long as
6: 4 The LORD our **G**, the LORD is
6: 5 Love the LORD your **G** with all
6: 13 Fear the LORD your **G**, serve him
6: 16 Do not put the LORD your **G**
7: 6 people holy to the LORD your **G**.
7: 6 The LORD your **G** has chosen you
7: 9 that the LORD your **G** is **G**;
7: 12 the LORD your **G** will keep his
7: 19 The LORD your **G** will do
7: 21 is a great and awesome **G**.
8: 5 the LORD your **G** disciplines you.
Dt 8: 11 do not forget the LORD your **G**,
8: 18 But remember the LORD your **G**,
9: 10 tablets inscribed by the finger of **G**.
10: 12 what does the LORD your **G** ask
10: 12 but to fear the LORD your **G**,
10: 12 serve the LORD your **G** with all
10: 14 To the LORD your **G** belong
10: 17 For the LORD your **G** is **G** of gods
10: 21 he is your **G**, who performed
11: 1 Love the LORD your **G** and keep
11: 13 to love the LORD your **G**
12: 12 rejoice before the LORD your **G**—
12: 28 in the eyes of the LORD your **G**.
13: 3 The LORD your **G** is testing you
13: 4 It is the LORD your **G** you must
15: 6 the LORD your **G** will bless you
15: 19 the LORD your **G** every firstborn
16: 11 rejoice before the LORD your **G**
16: 17 the LORD your **G** has blessed you.
18: 13 before the LORD your **G**.
18: 15 The LORD your **G** will raise
19: 9 to love the LORD your **G**
22: 5 the LORD your **G** detests anyone
23: 5 the LORD your **G** loves you.
23: 14 the LORD your **G** moves
23: 21 make a vow to the LORD your **G**,
25: 16 the LORD your **G** detests anyone
26: 5 declare before the LORD your **G**:
29: 13 he may be your **G** as he promised
29: 29 things belong to the LORD our **G**,
30: 2 return to the LORD your **G**
30: 4 the LORD your **G** will gather you
30: 6 The LORD your **G** will circumcise
30: 16 today to love the LORD your **G**,
30: 20 you may love the LORD your **G**,
31: 6 the LORD your **G** goes with you;
32: 3 Oh, praise the greatness of our **G**!
32: 4 A faithful **G** who does no wrong,
33: 27 The eternal **G** is your refuge,
Jos 1: 9 the LORD your **G** will be with you
14: 8 the LORD my **G** wholeheartedly.
14: 9 the LORD my **G** wholeheartedly.'
14: 14 the LORD, the **G** of Israel,
22: 5 to love the LORD your **G**, to walk
22: 22 "The Mighty One, **G**, the LORD!
22: 34 that the LORD is **G**.
23: 8 to hold fast to the LORD your **G**,
23: 11 careful to love the LORD your **G**.
23: 14 the LORD your **G** gave you has
23: 15 the LORD your **G** has promised
24: 19 He is a holy **G**; he is a jealous **G**.
24: 23 to the LORD, the **G** of Israel."
Jdg 5: 3 praise the LORD, the **G** of Israel,
16: 28 Please, **G**, strengthen me just once
Ru 1: 16 be my people and your **G** my **G**.
2: 12 by the LORD, the **G** of Israel,
1Sa 2: 2 there is no Rock like our **G**.
2: 3 for the LORD is a **G** who knows,
2: 25 **G** may mediate for the offender;
10: 26 men whose hearts **G** had touched.
12: 12 the LORD your **G** was your king.
16: 15 evil spirit from **G** is tormenting
17: 26 defy the armies of the living **G**?"
17: 36 defied the armies of the living **G**.
17: 45 the **G** of the armies of Israel,
17: 46 know that there is a **G** in Israel.
23: 16 and helped him find strength in **G**.
28: 15 me, and **G** has departed from me.
30: 6 found strength in the LORD his **G**.
2Sa 7: 22 and there is no **G** but you, as we
7: 23 one nation on earth that **G** went
14: 14 But that is not what **G** desires;
21: 14 **G** answered prayer in behalf
22: 3 my **G** is my rock, in whom I take
22: 31 "As for **G**, his way is perfect:
22: 32 For who is **G** besides the LORD?
22: 33 It is **G** who arms me with strength
22: 47 Exalted be my **G**, the Rock,
1Ki 2: 3 what the LORD your **G** requires:
4: 29 **G** gave Solomon wisdom and very
5: 5 for the Name of the LORD my **G**,
8: 23 there is no **G** like you in heaven
8: 27 "But will **G** really dwell on earth?
8: 60 may know that the LORD is **G**
8: 61 committed to the LORD our **G**,
1Ki 10: 24 to hear the wisdom **G** had put in
15: 30 of the LORD, the **G** of Israel.
18: 21 If the LORD is **G**, follow him;
18: 36 today that you are **G** in Israel
18: 37 are **G**, and that you are turning
20: 28 Arameans think the LORD is a **g**
2Ki 5: 15 no **G** in all the world except
18: 5 in the LORD, the **G** of Israel.
19: 15 you alone are **G** over all
19: 19 that you alone, LORD, are **G**."
1Ch 12: 18 you, for your **G** will help you."
13: 2 if it is the will of the LORD our **G**,
16: 35 Cry out, "Save us, **G** our Savior;
17: 20 and there is no **G** but you, as we
17: 24 Almighty, the **G** over Israel,
21: 8 Then David said to **G**, "I have
22: 1 of the LORD **G** is to be here,
22: 19 the sanctuary of the LORD **G**,
28: 2 for the footstool of our **G**, and I
28: 9 acknowledge the **G** of your father,
28: 20 for the LORD **G**, my **G**,
29: 1 the one whom **G** has chosen,
29: 2 provided for the temple of my **G**—
29: 3 and silver for the temple of my **G**,
29: 10 LORD, the **G** of our father Israel,
29: 13 Now, our **G**, we give you thanks,
29: 16 LORD our **G**, all this abundance
29: 17 my **G**, that you test the heart and
29: 18 the **G** of our fathers Abraham,
2Ch 2: 4 festivals of the LORD our **G**.
5: 14 the LORD filled the temple of **G**.
6: 4 be to the LORD, the **G** of Israel,
6: 14 there is no **G** like you in heaven
6: 18 will **G** really dwell on earth
10: 15 for this turn of events was from **G**,
13: 12 **G** is with us; he is our leader.
15: 3 time Israel was without the true **G**,
15: 12 LORD, the **G** of their ancestors,
15: 15 They sought **G** eagerly, and he was
18: 13 can tell him only what my **G** says."
19: 3 have set your heart on seeking **G**."
19: 7 with the LORD our **G** there is no
20: 6 "LORD, the **G** of our ancestors,
20: 20 Have faith in the LORD your **G**
25: 8 for **G** has the power to help
26: 5 He sought **G** during the days
26: 5 the LORD, **G** gave him success.
30: 9 for the LORD your **G** is gracious
30: 19 sets their heart on seeking **G**—
31: 21 he sought his **G** and worked
32: 31 **G** left him to test him and to know
33: 12 the favor of the LORD his **G**
34: 33 in Israel serve the LORD their **G**.
Ezr 6: 21 to seek the LORD, the **G** of Israel.
7: 18 accordance with the will of your **G**.
7: 23 for the temple of the **G** of heaven.
8: 22 "The gracious hand of our **G** is
8: 31 The hand of our **G** was on us,
9: 6 my **G**, to lift up my face to you,
9: 9 our **G** has not forsaken us in our
9: 13 our **G**, you have punished us less
9: 15 LORD, the **G** of Israel, you are
Ne 1: 5 "LORD, the **G** of heaven,
5: 9 fear of our **G** to avoid the reproach
5: 15 for **G** I did not act like that.
7: 2 feared **G** more than most people
8: 8 from the Book of the Law of **G**,
8: 18 from the Book of the Law of **G**.
9: 5 up and praise the LORD your **G**,
9: 17 But you are a forgiving **G**,
9: 31 you are a gracious and merciful **G**.
9: 32 "Now therefore, our **G**, the great **G**,
10: 29 through Moses the servant of **G**
10: 39 not neglect the house of our **G**."
12: 43 rejoicing because **G** had given
13: 11 is the house of **G** neglected?"
13: 26 was loved by his **G**, and **G** made
13: 31 Remember me with favor, my **G**.
Job 1: 1 he feared **G** and shunned evil.
1: 22 by charging **G** with wrongdoing.
2: 10 Shall we accept good from **G**,
4: 17 mortal be more righteous than **G**?
5: 17 is the one whom **G** corrects;
8: 3 Does **G** pervert justice?
8: 20 "Surely **G** does not reject one who

Job 9: 2 prove their innocence before **G**?
11: 7 you fathom the mysteries of **G**?
12: 13 "To **G** belong wisdom and power;
16: 7 Surely, **G**, you have worn me out;
19: 26 yet in my flesh I will see **G**;
21: 19 '**G** stores up the punishment
21: 22 anyone teach knowledge to **G**,
22: 12 "Is not **G** in the heights of heaven?
22: 13 Yet you say, 'What does **G** know?
22: 21 "Submit to **G** and be at peace
25: 2 "Dominion and awe belong to **G**;
25: 4 a mortal be righteous before **G**?
26: 6 of the dead is naked before **G**;
30: 20 "I cry out to you, **G**, but you do not
31: 6 let **G** weigh me in honest scales
31: 14 will I do when **G** confronts me?
32: 13 let **G**, not a man, refute him.'
33: 14 For **G** does speak—now one way,
33: 26 that person can pray to **G** and find
34: 10 Far be it from **G** to do evil,
34: 12 that **G** would do wrong,
34: 23 **G** has no need to examine people
34: 33 Should **G** then reward you on your
36: 5 "**G** is mighty, but despises no one;
36: 26 How great is **G**—
37: 22 **G** comes in awesome majesty.
Ps 5: 4 you are not a **G** who is pleased
7: 11 **G** is a righteous judge, a **G** who
10: 14 But you, **G**, see the trouble
14: 5 for **G** is present in the company
18: 2 my **G** is my rock, in whom I take
18: 28 my **G** turns my darkness into light.
18: 30 As for **G**, his way is perfect:
18: 31 For who is **G** besides the LORD?
18: 31 who is the Rock except our **G**?
18: 32 It is **G** who arms me with strength
18: 46 Exalted be **G** my Savior!
19: 1 The heavens declare the glory of **G**;
22: 1 My **G**, my **G**, why have you
22: 10 womb you have been my **G**.
27: 9 me or forsake me, **G** my Savior.
29: 3 the **G** of glory thunders, the LORD
31: 5 deliver me, LORD, my faithful **G**.
31: 14 I say, "You are my **G**."
33: 12 the nation whose **G** is the LORD,
35: 24 your righteousness, LORD my **G**;
37: 31 law of their **G** is in their hearts;
40: 3 mouth, a hymn of praise to our **G**.
40: 8 I desire to do your will, my **G**;
42: 1 so my soul pants for you, my **G**.
42: 2 soul thirsts for **G**, for the living **G**.
42: 2 When can I go and meet with **G**?
42: 5 praise him, my Savior and my **G**.
42: 8 a prayer to the **G** of my life.
42: 11 Put your hope in **G**, for I will
43: 4 with the lyre, O **G**, my **G**.
44: 8 **G** we make our boast all day long,
45: 6 O **G**, will last for ever and ever;
45: 7 therefore **G**, your **G**, has set you
46: 1 **G** is our refuge and strength,
46: 5 **G** is within her, she will not fall;
46: 10 "Be still, and know that I am **G**;
47: 1 shout to **G** with cries of joy.
47: 6 Sing praises to **G**, sing praises;
47: 7 For **G** is the King of all the earth;
48: 9 **G**, we meditate on your unfailing
49: 7 or give to **G** a ransom for them—
50: 2 perfect in beauty, **G** shines forth.
50: 3 **G** comes and will not be silent;
51: 1 O **G**, according to your unfailing
51: 10 O **G**, and renew a steadfast spirit
51: 17 sacrifice, O **G**, is a broken spirit;
53: 2 **G** looks down from heaven on all
53: 2 who understand, any who seek **G**.
54: 4 Surely **G** is my help; the Lord is
55: 19 **G**, who is enthroned from of old,
55: 19 because they have no fear of **G**.
56: 4 In **G**, whose word I praise—in **G** I
56: 10 In **G**, whose word I praise,
56: 13 I may walk before **G** in the light
57: 3 **G** sends forth his love and his
57: 7 My heart, O **G**, is steadfast,
59: 17 you, **G**, are my fortress, my **G**
62: 1 Truly my soul finds rest in **G**;
62: 7 and my honor depend on **G**;

Ps 62: 8 hearts to him, for **G** is our refuge.
62: 11 "Power belongs to you, **G**,
63: 1 **G**, are my **G**, earnestly I seek
65: 5 and righteous deeds, **G** our Savior,
66: 1 Shout for joy to **G**, all the earth!
66: 3 Say to **G**, "How awesome are your
66: 5 Come and see what **G** has done,
66: 16 Come and hear, all you who fear **G**;
66: 20 Praise be to **G**, who has not
68: 4 Sing to **G**, sing in praise of his
68: 6 **G** sets the lonely in families,
68: 20 Our **G** is a **G** who saves;
68: 24 the procession of my **G** and King
68: 35 the **G** of Israel gives power
69: 5 You, **G**, know my folly; my guilt is
70: 1 Hasten, O **G**, to save me;
70: 5 come quickly to me, O **G**.
71: 17 my youth, **G**, you have taught
71: 18 my **G**, till I declare your power
71: 19 Who is like you, **G**?
71: 22 harp for your faithfulness, my **G**;
73: 17 till I entered the sanctuary of **G**;
73: 26 but **G** is the strength of my heart
76: 11 Make vows to the LORD your **G**
77: 13 What **g** is as great as our **G**?
77: 14 You are the **G** who performs
78: 19 They spoke against **G**;
79: 9 Help us, **G** our Savior, for the glory
81: 1 Sing for joy to **G** our strength;
82: 1 **G** presides in the great assembly;
84: 2 my flesh cry out for the living **G**.
84: 10 the house of my **G** than dwell
84: 11 For the LORD **G** is a sun
86: 12 you, Lord my **G**, with all my heart;
86: 15 a compassionate and gracious **G**,
87: 3 things are said of you, city of **G**:
89: 7 of the holy ones **G** is greatly feared;
90: 2 to everlasting you are **G**.
91: 2 fortress, my **G**, in whom I trust."
94: 22 and my **G** the rock in whom I take
95: 7 for he is our **G** and we are
99: 8 you were to Israel a forgiving **G**,
99: 9 for the LORD our **G** is holy.
100: 3 Know that the LORD is **G**.
108: 1 My heart, O **G**, is steadfast;
113: 5 Who is like the LORD our **G**,
115: 3 Our **G** is in heaven;
116: 5 our **G** is full of compassion.
123: 2 our eyes look to the LORD our **G**,
136: 2 Give thanks to the **G** of gods.
136: 26 Give thanks to the **G** of heaven.
139: 17 to me are your thoughts, **G**!
139: 23 Search me, **G**, and know my heart;
143: 10 to do your will, for you are my **G**;
144: 2 He is my loving **G** and my fortress,
147: 1 good it is to sing praises to our **G**,
Pr 3: 4 a good name in the sight of **G**
14: 31 is kind to the needy honors **G**.
25: 2 It is the glory of **G** to conceal
28: 14 one who always trembles before **G**,
30: 5 "Every word of **G** is flawless;
Ecc 2: 26 who pleases him, **G** gives wisdom,
3: 11 no one can fathom what **G** has
3: 13 their toil—this is the gift of **G**.
3: 14 that everything **G** does will endure
3: 14 **G** does it so that people will fear
5: 4 When you make a vow to **G**, do
5: 19 when **G** gives someone wealth
8: 12 go better with those who fear **G**,
11: 5 cannot understand the work of **G**,
12: 7 the spirit returns to **G** who gave it.
12: 13 of the matter: Fear **G** and keep his
Isa 5: 16 the holy **G** will be proved holy
9: 6 Mighty **G**, Everlasting Father,
12: 2 **G** is my salvation; I will trust
25: 9 they will say, "Surely this is our **G**;
28: 11 strange tongues **G** will speak to
29: 23 will stand in awe of the **G** of Israel.
30: 18 For the LORD is a **G** of justice.
35: 4 your **G** will come, he will come
37: 16 you alone are **G** over all
40: 1 comfort my people, says your **G**.
40: 3 in the desert a highway for our **G**.
40: 8 the word of our **G** endures forever."
40: 18 whom, then, will you compare **G**?

Isa 40: 28 The LORD is the everlasting **G**,
41: 10 not be dismayed, for I am your **G**.
41: 13 the LORD your **G** who takes hold
43: 10 Before me no **g** was formed,
44: 6 apart from me there is no **G**.
44: 15 also fashions a **g** and worships it;
45: 18 who created the heavens, he is **G**;
48: 17 "I am the LORD your **G**,
52: 7 who say to Zion, "Your **G** reigns!"
52: 12 the **G** of Israel will be your rear
55: 7 and to our **G**, for he will freely
57: 21 says my **G**, "for the wicked."
59: 2 have separated you from your **G**;
60: 19 and your **G** will be your glory.
61: 2 and the day of vengeance of our **G**,
61: 10 my soul rejoices in my **G**.
62: 5 so will your **G** rejoice over you.
Jer 7: 23 I will be your **G** and you will be my
10: 10 But the LORD is the true **G**;
10: 10 he is the living **G**, the eternal
10: 12 **G** made the earth by his power;
23: 23 "Am I only a **G** nearby,"
23: 36 distort the words of the living **G**,
31: 33 I will be their **G**, and they will be
32: 27 the LORD, the **G** of all mankind.
42: 6 we will obey the LORD our **G**,
51: 10 what the LORD our **G** has done.'
51: 56 the LORD is a **G** of retribution;
Eze 28: 13 You were in Eden, the garden of **G**;
34: 31 and I am your **G**,
Da 2: 28 there is a **G** in heaven who reveals
3: 17 the **G** we serve is able to deliver us
3: 29 for no other **g** can save in this
6: 16 "May your **G**, whom you serve
9: 4 the great and awesome **G**,
10: 12 to humble yourself before your **G**,
11: 36 magnify himself above every **g**
11: 36 things against the **G** of gods.
Hos 1: 9 my people, and I am not your **G**.
1: 10 be called 'children of the living **G**.'
4: 6 have ignored the law of your **G**,
6: 6 of **G** rather than burnt offerings.
9: 8 along with my **G**, is the watchman
12: 6 But you must return to your **G**;
Joel 2: 13 Return to the LORD your **G**, for he
2: 23 rejoice in the LORD your **G**, for he
Am 4: 12 Israel, prepare to meet your **G**."
4: 13 the LORD **G** Almighty is his
Jnh 1: 6 Get up and call on your **g**!
4: 2 a gracious and compassionate **G**,
Mic 6: 8 and to walk humbly with your **G**.
7: 7 **G** my Savior; my **G** will hear me.
7: 18 Who is a **G** like you, who pardons
Na 1: 2 is a jealous and avenging **G**;
Hab 3: 18 I will be joyful in **G** my Savior.
Zep 3: 17 The LORD your **G** is with you,
Zec 14: 5 Then the LORD my **G** will come,
Mal 2: 10 Did not one **G** create us?
2: 16 says the LORD, the **G** of Israel,
3: 8 "Will a mere mortal rob **G**?
Mt 1: 23 (which means "**G** with us").
4: 4 comes from the mouth of **G**.'"
4: 7 'Do not put the Lord your **G**
4: 10 'Worship the Lord your **G**,
5: 8 pure in heart, for they will see **G**.
6: 24 You cannot serve both **G**
19: 6 Therefore what **G** has joined
19: 26 but with **G** all things are possible."
22: 21 Caesar's, and to **G** what is God's."
22: 32 'I am the **G** of Abraham,
22: 32 He is not the **G** of the dead
22: 37 "'Love the Lord your **G** with all
27: 46 (which means "My **G**, my **G**,
Mk 2: 7 Who can forgive sins but **G** alone?"
7: 13 Thus you nullify the word of **G**
10: 6 of creation **G** 'made them male
10: 9 Therefore what **G** has joined
10: 18 "No one is good—except **G** alone.
10: 27 impossible, but not with **G**; all things
are possible with **G**."
11: 22 "Have faith in **G**," Jesus answered.
12: 17 Caesar's and to **G** what is God's."
12: 29 The Lord our **G**, the Lord is one.
12: 30 Love the Lord your **G** with all your
15: 34 (which means "My **G**, my **G**,

Mk 16: 19 *sat at the right hand of **G**.*
Lk 1: 30 you have found favor with **G**.
1: 37 For no word from **G** will ever fail."
1: 47 my spirit rejoices in **G** my Savior,
2: 14 "Glory to **G** in the highest heaven,
2: 52 and in favor with **G** and man.
4: 8 'Worship the Lord your **G** and
5: 21 Who can forgive sins but **G** alone?"
8: 39 tell how much **G** has done for you."
10: 9 'The kingdom of **G** has come near
10: 27 "'Love the Lord your **G** with all
13: 18 "What is the kingdom of **G** like?
18: 19 "No one is good—except **G** alone.
18: 27 with man is possible with **G**."
20: 25 Caesar's, and to **G** what is God's."
20: 38 He is not the **G** of the dead,
22: 69 at the right hand of the mighty **G**."
Jn 1: 1 and the Word was with **G**, and the Word was **G**.
1: 18 No one has ever seen **G**, but the
1: 29 the Lamb of **G**, who takes away
3: 16 For **G** so loved the world that he
3: 34 the one whom **G** has sent speaks
3: 34 **G** gives the Spirit without limit.
4: 24 **G** is spirit, and his worshipers must
5: 44 glory that comes from the only **G**?
6: 29 answered, "The work of **G** is this:
7: 17 my teaching comes from **G**
8: 42 "If **G** were your Father, you would
8: 42 not come on my own; **G** sent me.
8: 47 belongs to **G** hears what **G** says.
11: 40 you will see the glory of **G**?"
13: 3 that he had come from **G** and was returning to **G**;
13: 31 glorified and **G** is glorified in him.
14: 1 You believe in **G**;
17: 3 the only true **G**, and Jesus Christ,
20: 17 Father, to my **G** and your **G**.'"
20: 28 said to him, "My Lord and my **G**!"
20: 31 the Son of **G**, and that by believing
Ac 2: 11 them declaring the wonders of **G**
2: 24 But **G** raised him from the dead,
2: 33 Exalted to the right hand of **G**,
2: 36 **G** has made this Jesus, whom you
3: 15 but **G** raised him from the dead.
3: 19 turn to **G**, so that your sins may
4: 31 and spoke the word of **G** boldly.
5: 4 lied just to human beings but to **G**."
5: 29 "We must obey **G** rather than
5: 31 **G** exalted him to his own right
5: 32 whom **G** has given to those who
7: 55 to heaven and saw the glory of **G**,
7: 55 standing at the right hand of **G**.
8: 21 your heart is not right before **G**.
11: 9 impure that **G** has made clean.'
12: 24 the word of **G** continued to spread
13: 32 What **G** promised our ancestors
15: 10 why do you try to test **G** by putting
17: 23 inscription: TO AN UNKNOWN **G**.
17: 30 In the past **G** overlooked such
20: 27 to you the whole will of **G**.
20: 32 "Now I commit you to **G**
24: 16 keep my conscience clear before **G**
Ro 1: 16 because it is the power of **G**
1: 17 righteousness of **G** is revealed—
1: 18 The wrath of **G** is being revealed
1: 24 Therefore **G** gave them over
1: 26 **G** gave them over to shameful
2: 11 For **G** does not show favoritism.
2: 16 **G** judges people's secrets through
3: 4 Let **G** be true, and every human
3: 19 world held accountable to **G**.
3: 23 and fall short of the glory of **G**,
3: 29 Or is **G** the **G** of Jews only?
3: 29 Is he not the **G** of Gentiles too?
4: 3 "Abraham believed **G**, and it was
4: 6 whom **G** credits righteousness
4: 17 the **G** who gives life to the dead
4: 24 whom **G** will credit righteousness
5: 1 **G** through our Lord Jesus Christ,
5: 8 **G** demonstrates his own love for us
6: 22 sin and have become slaves of **G**,
6: 23 the gift of **G** is eternal life in Christ
8: 7 by the flesh is hostile to **G**;
8: 17 heirs of **G** and co-heirs with Christ
Ro 8: 28 in all things **G** works for the good
9: 14 then shall we say? Is **G** unjust?
9: 18 Therefore **G** has mercy on whom
10: 9 in your heart that **G** raised him
11: 2 **G** did not reject his people,
11: 22 the kindness and sternness of **G**:
11: 32 For **G** has bound everyone over
13: 1 that which **G** has established.
14: 12 give an account of ourselves to **G**.
16: 20 The **G** of peace will soon crush
1Co 1: 18 being saved it is the power of **G**.
1: 20 not **G** made foolish the wisdom
1: 25 of **G** is wiser than human wisdom,
1: 25 **G** is stronger than human strength.
1: 27 **G** chose the foolish things
1: 27 **G** chose the weak things
2: 9 the things **G** has prepared for those
2: 11 the thoughts of **G** except the Spirit
3: 6 but **G** has been making it grow.
3: 17 temple, **G** will destroy that person;
6: 20 Therefore honor **G** with your
7: 7 of you has your own gift from **G**;
7: 15 **G** has called us to live in peace.
7: 20 they were in when **G** called them.
7: 24 they were in when **G** called them.
8: 3 whoever loves **G** is known by **G**.
8: 8 food does not bring us near to **G**;
10: 13 And **G** is faithful; he will not let
10: 31 you do, do it all for the glory of **G**.
12: 24 But **G** has put the body together,
14: 33 For **G** is not a **G** of disorder
15: 24 over the kingdom to **G** the Father
15: 28 him, so that **G** may be all in all.
15: 34 are some who are ignorant of **G**—
15: 57 But thanks be to **G**! He gives us
2Co 1: 9 not rely on ourselves but on **G**,
2: 14 But thanks be to **G**, who always
2: 15 we are to **G** the pleasing aroma
2: 17 we do not peddle the word of **G**
2: 17 sincerity, as those sent from **G**.
3: 5 our competence comes from **G**.
4: 2 nor do we distort the word of **G**.
4: 7 this all-surpassing power is from **G**
5: 5 us for this very purpose is **G**,
5: 19 that **G** was reconciling the world
5: 20 Be reconciled to **G**.
5: 21 **G** made him who had no sin to be
5: 21 become the righteousness of **G**.
6: 16 we are the temple of the living **G**.
6: 16 I will be their **G**, and they will
9: 7 for **G** loves a cheerful giver.
9: 8 **G** is able to bless you abundantly,
10: 13 of service **G** himself has assigned
Gal 2: 6 **G** does not show favoritism—
3: 5 does **G** give you his Spirit and
3: 6 So also Abraham "believed **G**,
3: 11 on the law is justified before **G**,
3: 26 are all children of **G** through faith,
6: 7 **G** cannot be mocked.
Eph 1: 22 **G** placed all things under his feet
2: 8 yourselves, it is the gift of **G**—
2: 10 **G** prepared in advance for us
2: 22 in which **G** lives by his Spirit.
4: 6 one **G** and Father of all, who is
4: 24 to be like **G** in true righteousness
6: 6 the will of **G** from your heart.
Php 2: 6 being in very nature **G**, did not consider equality with **G**
2: 9 Therefore **G** exalted him
2: 13 for it is **G** who works in you to will
4: 7 And the peace of **G**,
4: 19 And my **G** will meet all your needs
Col 1: 19 For **G** was pleased to have all his
2: 13 **G** made you alive with Christ.
1Th 2: 4 not trying to please people but **G**,
2: 13 also thank **G** continually because,
3: 9 How can we thank **G** enough
4: 7 For **G** did not call us to be impure,
4: 9 yourselves have been taught by **G**
5: 9 For **G** did not appoint us to suffer
1Ti 2: 5 For there is one **G** and one mediator between **G**
4: 4 For everything **G** created is good,
5: 4 for this is pleasing to **G**.
2Ti 1: 6 you to fan into flame the gift of **G**,
Titus 1: 2 life, which **G**, who does not lie,
2: 13 of the glory of our great **G**
Heb 1: 1 In the past **G** spoke to our
3: 4 but **G** is the builder of everything.
4: 4 the seventh day **G** rested from all
4: 12 For the word of **G** is alive
6: 10 **G** is not unjust; he will not forget
6: 18 it is impossible for **G** to lie,
7: 19 by which we draw near to **G**.
7: 25 those who come to **G** through him,
10: 22 let us draw near to **G** with a sincere
10: 31 fall into the hands of the living **G**.
11: 5 because **G** had taken him away."
11: 5 commended as one who pleased **G**.
11: 6 faith it is impossible to please **G**,
12: 7 **G** is treating you as his children.
12: 10 but **G** disciplines us for our good,
12: 29 for our "**G** is a consuming fire."
13: 15 us continually offer to **G** a sacrifice
Jas 1: 13 For **G** cannot be tempted by evil,
1: 27 that **G** our Father accepts as pure
2: 19 You believe that there is one **G**.
2: 23 "Abraham believed **G**, and it was
4: 4 the world becomes an enemy of **G**.
4: 6 "**G** opposes the proud but shows
4: 8 Come near to **G** and he will come
1Pe 1: 23 the living and enduring word of **G**.
2: 20 it, this is commendable before **G**.
3: 18 the unrighteous, to bring you to **G**.
4: 11 who speaks the very words of **G**.
5: 5 "**G** opposes the proud but shows
2Pe 1: 21 from **G** as they were carried along
2: 4 if **G** did not spare angels when they
1Jn 1: 5 him and declare to you: **G** is light;
2: 5 love for **G** is truly made complete
2: 17 does the will of **G** lives forever.
3: 1 we should be called children of **G**!
3: 9 one who is born of **G** will continue
3: 10 we know who the children of **G** are
3: 20 that **G** is greater than our hearts,
4: 7 another, for love comes from **G**.
4: 8 does not love does not know **G**, because **G** is love.
4: 9 This is how **G** showed his love
4: 11 Dear friends, since **G** so loved us,
4: 12 No one has ever seen **G**; but if we
4: 12 **G** lives in us and his love is made
4: 15 that Jesus is the Son of **G**, **G** lives in them and they in **G**.
4: 16 Whoever lives in love lives in **G**,
4: 20 claims to love **G** yet hates a brother
4: 21 Anyone who loves **G** must also
5: 2 by loving **G** and carrying out his
5: 3 In fact, this is love for **G**:
5: 4 born of **G** overcomes the world.
5: 10 believed the testimony **G** has given
5: 14 we have in approaching **G**:
5: 18 was born of **G** keeps them safe,
Rev 4: 8 holy is the Lord **G** Almighty,'
7: 12 strength be to our **G** for ever
7: 17 **G** will wipe away every tear
11: 16 seated on their thrones before **G**,
15: 3 are your deeds, Lord **G** Almighty.
17: 17 For **G** has put it into their hearts
19: 6 For our Lord **G** Almighty reigns.
21: 3 and **G** himself will be with them and be their **G**.

GOD-BREATHED* (BREATH)
2Ti 3: 16 All Scripture is **G** and is useful

GOD-FEARING* (FEAR)
Ac 2: 5 were staying in Jerusalem **G** Jews
10: 2 all his family were devout and **G**;
10: 22 He is a righteous and **G** man,
13: 26 of Abraham and you **G** Gentiles,
13: 50 leaders incited the **G** women
17: 4 as did a large number of **G** Greeks
17: 17 with both Jews and **G** Greeks,

GOD-HATERS* (HATE)
Ro 1: 30 slanderers, **G**, insolent,

GODLESS
Job 20: 5 the joy of the **g** lasts but a moment.
1Ti 6: 20 Turn away from **g** chatter

GODLINESS (GOD)
1Ti 2: 2 quiet lives in all **g** and holiness.

1Ti 3: 16 mystery from which true **g** springs
4: 8 value, but **g** has value for all things,
6: 5 and who think that **g** is a means
6: 6 **g** with contentment is great gain.
6: 11 and pursue righteousness, **g**, faith,
2Ti 3: 5 a form of **g** but denying its power.
2Pe 1: 6 and to perseverance, **g**;

GODLY (GOD)
2Co 7: 10 **G** sorrow brings repentance
11: 2 jealous for you with a **g** jealousy.
2Ti 3: 12 live a **g** life in Christ Jesus will be
2Pe 3: 11 You ought to live holy and **g** lives

GOD'S (GOD)
2Ch 20: 15 For the battle is not yours, but **G**.
Job 33: 6 I am the same as you in **G** sight;
37: 14 stop and consider **G** wonders.
Ps 52: 8 I trust in **G** unfailing love for ever
69: 30 I will praise **G** name in song
Mk 3: 35 Whoever does **G** will is my brother
Jn 10: 36 because I said, 'I am **G** Son'?
Ro 2: 3 think you will escape **G** judgment?
2: 4 that **G** kindness is intended
3: 3 nullify **G** faithfulness?
5: 5 because **G** love has been poured
7: 22 my inner being I delight in **G** law;
9: 16 desire or effort, but on **G** mercy.
11: 29 for **G** gifts and his call are
12: 2 test and approve what **G** will is—
13: 6 for the authorities are **G** servants,
1Co 7: 19 Keeping **G** commands is what
2Co 6: 2 now is the time of **G** favor, now is
Eph 1: 7 with the riches of **G** grace
5: 1 Follow **G** example, therefore,
1Th 4: 3 It is **G** will that you should be
5: 18 for this is **G** will for you in Christ
1Ti 6: 1 so that **G** name and our teaching
2Ti 2: 19 **G** solid foundation stands firm,
Titus 1: 7 an overseer manages **G** household,
Heb 1: 3 The Son is the radiance of **G** glory
9: 24 to appear for us in **G** presence.
11: 3 was formed at **G** command,
1Pe 2: 15 For it is **G** will that by doing good
3: 4 which is of great worth in **G** sight.

GODS (GOD)
Ex 20: 3 shall have no other **g** before me.
Dt 5: 7 shall have no other **g** before me.
32: 17 They sacrificed to false **g**,
1Ch 16: 26 all the **g** of the nations are idols,
Ps 82: 6 "I said, 'You are "**g**"; you are
106: 37 sons and their daughters to false **g**.
Jn 10: 34 Law, 'I have said you are "**g**"'?
Ac 19: 26 He says that **g** made by human hands are no **g** at all.

GOG
Eze 38: 18 When **G** attacks the land of Israel,
Rev 20: 8 of the earth—**G** and Magog—

GOLD
1Ki 20: 3 'Your silver and **g** are mine,
Job 22: 25 then the Almighty will be your **g**,
23: 10 tested me, I will come forth as **g**.
28: 15 cannot be bought with the finest **g**,
31: 24 "If I have put my trust in **g** or said
Ps 19: 10 They are more precious than **g**,
119:127 more than **g**, more than pure **g**,
Pr 3: 14 and yields better returns than **g**.
22: 1 esteemed is better than silver or **g**.
Hag 2: 8 silver is mine and the **g** is mine,'
Mt 2: 11 and presented him with gifts of **g**,
Rev 3: 18 buy from me **g** refined in the fire,

GOLGOTHA*
Mt 27: 33 a place called **G** (which means
Mk 15: 22 to the place called **G** (which means
Jn 19: 17 (which in Aramaic is called **G**).

GOLIATH
Philistine giant killed by David (1Sa 17; 21:9).

GOMORRAH
Ge 19: 24 burning sulfur on Sodom and **G**—
Mt 10: 15 **G** on the day of judgment than
2Pe 2: 6 and **G** by burning them to ashes,
Jude : 7 Sodom and **G** and the surrounding

GOOD
Ge 1: 4 God saw that the light was **g**,
1: 10 And God saw that it was **g**.
1: 12 And God saw that it was **g**.
1: 18 And God saw that it was **g**.
1: 21 And God saw that it was **g**.
1: 25 And God saw that it was **g**.
1: 31 he had made, and it was very **g**.
2: 9 pleasing to the eye and **g** for food.
2: 9 the tree of the knowledge of **g**
2: 18 "It is not **g** for the man to be alone.
3: 22 like one of us, knowing **g** and evil.
50: 20 God intended it for **g** to
2Ch 7: 3 to the LORD, saying, "He is **g**;
31: 20 doing what was **g** and right
Job 2: 10 Shall we accept **g** from God,
Ps 14: 1 there is no one who does **g**.
34: 8 Taste and see that the LORD is **g**;
34: 14 Turn from evil and do **g**;
37: 3 Trust in the LORD and do **g**;
37: 27 Turn from evil and do **g**;
52: 9 in your name, for your name is **g**.
53: 3 there is no one who does **g**, not
84: 11 no **g** thing does he withhold
86: 5 are forgiving and **g**,
100: 5 For the LORD is **g** and his love
103: 5 your desires with **g** things so
112: 5 **G** will come to those who are
119: 68 You are **g**, and what you do is **g**;
133: 1 How **g** and pleasant it is
145: 9 The LORD is **g** to all;
147: 1 How **g** it is to sing praises to our
Pr 3: 4 and a **g** name in the sight of God
3: 27 Do not withhold **g** from those
11: 27 Whoever seeks **g** finds favor,
13: 21 are rewarded with **g** things.
13: 22 A **g** person leaves an inheritance
14: 22 those who plan what is **g** find love
15: 3 watch on the wicked and the **g**.
15: 23 and how **g** is a timely word!
15: 30 **g** news gives health to the bones.
17: 22 A cheerful heart is **g** medicine,
18: 22 He who finds a wife finds what is **g**
19: 2 Desire without knowledge is not **g**
22: 1 A **g** name is more desirable than
31: 12 She brings him **g**, not harm,
Ecc 12: 14 thing, whether it is **g** or evil.
Isa 5: 20 Woe to those who call evil **g** and **g**
40: 9 You who bring **g** news to Zion,
52: 7 the feet of those who bring **g** news,
61: 1 anointed me to proclaim **g** news
Jer 6: 16 ask where the **g** way is, and walk
13: 23 can you do **g** who are accustomed
Eze 34: 14 will lie down in **g** grazing land,
Mic 6: 8 shown you, O mortal, what is **g**.
Na 1: 15 the feet of one who brings **g** news,
Mt 5: 45 sun to rise on the evil and the **g**,
7: 11 heaven give **g** gifts to those who
7: 17 every **g** tree bears **g** fruit,
7: 18 and a bad tree cannot bear **g** fruit.
12: 35 A **g** man brings **g** things out of the **g** stored up
13: 8 Still other seed fell on **g** soil,
13: 24 is like a man who sowed **g** seed
13: 48 and collected the **g** fish in baskets,
19: 17 "There is only One who is **g**.
22: 10 the bad as well as the **g**,
25: 21 'Well done, **g** and faithful servant!
Mk 1: 15 Repent and believe the **g** news!"
3: 4 to do **g** or to do evil, to save life
4: 8 Still other seed fell on **g** soil.
8: 36 What **g** is it for someone to gain
10: 18 "No one is **g**—except God alone.
Lk 2: 10 I bring you **g** news that will cause
3: 9 does not produce **g** fruit will be cut
6: 27 do **g** to those who hate you,
6: 43 "No **g** tree bears bad fruit, nor
6: 45 A **g** man brings **g** things out of the **g** stored up
8: 8 Still other seed fell on **g** soil.
9: 25 What **g** is it for someone to gain
14: 34 "Salt is **g**, but if it loses its
18: 19 "No one is **g**—except God alone.
19: 17 "'Well done, my **g** servant!'
Jn 10: 11 "I am the **g** shepherd. The **g**
Ro 3: 12 there is no one who does **g**, not
7: 12 is holy, righteous and **g**.
7: 16 want to do, I agree that the law is **g**.
7: 18 I know that **g** itself does not dwell
8: 28 for the **g** of those who love him,
10: 15 feet of those who bring **g** news!"
12: 2 his **g**, pleasing and perfect will.
12: 9 Hate what is evil; cling to what is **g**.
13: 4 is God's servant for your **g**.
16: 19 you to be wise about what is **g**,
1Co 7: 1 "It is **g** for a man not to have sexual
10: 24 No one should seek their own **g**, but the **g** of others.
15: 33 company corrupts **g** character."
2Co 9: 8 you will abound in every **g** work.
Gal 4: 18 provided the purpose is **g**, and to
6: 9 us not become weary in doing **g**,
6: 10 let us do **g** to all people,
Eph 2: 10 in Christ Jesus to do **g** works,
6: 8 each one for whatever **g** they do,
Php 1: 6 he who began a **g** work in you will
Col 1: 10 bearing fruit in every **g** work,
1Th 5: 15 strive to do what is **g** for each other
5: 21 test them all; hold on to what is **g**,
2Th 3: 13 never tire of doing what is **g**.
1Ti 3: 7 have a **g** reputation with outsiders,
4: 4 For everything God created is **g**,
6: 12 Fight the **g** fight of the faith.
6: 18 Command them to do **g**, to be rich in **g** deeds,
2Ti 3: 17 equipped for every **g** work.
4: 7 I have fought the **g** fight, I have
Titus 1: 8 one who loves what is **g**, who is
2: 7 an example by doing what is **g**.
2: 14 his very own, eager to do what is **g**.
Heb 5: 14 to distinguish **g** from evil.
10: 24 on toward love and **g** deeds,
12: 10 but God disciplines us for our **g**,
13: 16 do not forget to do **g** and to share
Jas 4: 17 knows the **g** they ought to do
1Pe 2: 3 you have tasted that the Lord is **g**.
2: 12 Live such **g** lives among the pagans
2: 18 not only to those who are **g**
3: 17 to suffer for doing **g** than for doing

GOODS
Ecc 5: 11 As **g** increase, so do those who

GORGE
Pr 23: 20 wine or **g** themselves on meat,

GOSHEN
Ge 45: 10 You shall live in the region of **G**
Ex 8: 22 deal differently with the land of **G**,

GOSPEL
Mk 16: 15 *preach the **g** to all creation.*
Ac 14: 7 they continued to preach the **g**.
14: 21 They preached the **g** in that city
Ro 1: 16 For I am not ashamed of the **g**,
15: 16 duty of proclaiming the **g** of God,
15: 20 preach the **g** where Christ was not
1Co 1: 17 to baptize, but to preach the **g**—
9: 12 anything rather than hinder the **g**
9: 14 who preach the **g** should receive their living from the **g**.
9: 16 Woe to me if I do not preach the **g**!
15: 1 to remind you of the **g** I preached
15: 2 By this **g** you are saved, if you hold
2Co 4: 4 light of the **g** that displays the glory
9: 13 your confession of the **g** of Christ,
Gal 1: 7 trying to pervert the **g** of Christ.
Eph 6: 15 that comes from the **g** of peace.
Php 1: 27 a manner worthy of the **g** of Christ.
Col 1: 23 This is the **g** that you heard
1Th 2: 4 by God to be entrusted with the **g**.
2Th 1: 8 not obey the **g** of our Lord Jesus.
2Ti 1: 10 immortality to light through the **g**.
Rev 14: 6 he had the eternal **g** to proclaim

GOSSIP* (GOSSIPS)
Pr 11: 13 A **g** betrays a confidence, but a
16: 28 and a **g** separates close friends.
18: 8 of a **g** are like choice morsels;
20: 19 A **g** betrays a confidence;
26: 20 without a **g** a quarrel dies down.
26: 22 of a **g** are like choice morsels;
2Co 12: 20 slander, **g**, arrogance and disorder.

GOSSIPS* (GOSSIP)
Ro 1: 29 deceit and malice. They are **g**,

GOVERN (GOVERN GOVERNMENT)
Ge 1: 16 the greater light to **g** the day
Job 34: 17 Can someone who hates justice **g**?

GOVERNED (GOVERN)
Ro 8: 6 The mind **g** by the flesh is death,
8: 6 the mind **g** by the Spirit is life

GOVERNMENT (GOVERN)
Isa 9: 6 and the **g** will be on his shoulders.

GRACE* (GRACIOUS)
Ps 45: 2 lips have been anointed with **g**,
Pr 1: 9 They are a garland to **g** your head
3: 22 you, an ornament to **g** your neck.
4: 9 give you a garland to **g** your head
22: 11 speaks with **g** will have the king
Isa 26: 10 But when **g** is shown to the wicked,
Zec 12: 10 of Jerusalem a spirit of **g**
Lk 2: 40 and the **g** of God was on him.
Jn 1: 14 from the Father, full of **g** and truth.
1: 16 we have all received **g** in place of **g** already given.
1: 17 **g** and truth came through Jesus
Ac 4: 33 God's **g** was so powerfully at work
6: 8 a man full of God's **g** and power,
11: 23 saw what the **g** of God had done,
13: 43 them to continue in the **g** of God.
14: 3 message of his **g** by enabling them
14: 26 been committed to the **g** of God
15: 11 We believe it is through the **g** of
15: 40 the believers to the **g** of the Lord.
18: 27 to those who by **g** had believed.
20: 24 to the good news of God's **g**.
20: 32 to God and to the word of his **g**,
Ro 1: 5 Through him we received **g**
1: 7 **G** and peace to you from God our
3: 24 by his **g** through the redemption
4: 16 so that it may be by **g** and may be
5: 2 by faith into this **g** in which we
5: 15 how much more did God's **g**
5: 15 came by the **g** of the one man,
5: 17 God's abundant provision of **g**
5: 20 increased, **g** increased all the more,
5: 21 **g** might reign through
6: 1 on sinning so that **g** may increase?
6: 14 are not under the law, but under **g**.
6: 15 are not under the law but under **g**?
11: 5 there is a remnant chosen by **g**.
11: 6 if by **g**, then it cannot be based
11: 6 were, **g** would no longer be **g**.
12: 3 by the **g** given me I say to every
12: 6 according to the **g** given to each
15: 15 because of the **g** God gave me
16: 20 The **g** of our Lord Jesus be
1Co 1: 3 **G** and peace to you from God our
1: 4 you because of his **g** given you
3: 10 By the **g** God has given me, I laid
15: 10 by the **g** of God I am what I am,
15: 10 his **g** to me was not without effect.
15: 10 but the **g** of God that was with me.
16: 23 The **g** of the Lord Jesus be
2Co 1: 2 **G** and peace to you from God our
1: 12 on worldly wisdom but on God's **g**.
4: 15 so that the **g** that is reaching more
6: 1 you not to receive God's **g** in vain.
8: 1 about the **g** that God has given
8: 6 to completion this act of **g** on your
8: 7 you also excel in this **g** of giving.
8: 9 you know the **g** of our Lord Jesus
9: 14 surpassing **g** God has given you.
12: 9 to me, "My **g** is sufficient for you,
13: 14 May the **g** of the Lord Jesus Christ,
Gal 1: 3 **G** and peace to you from God our
1: 6 called you to live in the **g** of Christ
1: 15 womb and called me by his **g**,
2: 9 they recognized the **g** given to me.
2: 21 I do not set aside the **g** of God,
3: 18 God in his **g** gave it to Abraham
5: 4 you have fallen away from **g**.
6: 18 The **g** of our Lord Jesus Christ be
Eph 1: 2 **G** and peace to you from God our
1: 6 to the praise of his glorious **g**,
1: 7 with the riches of God's **g**
2: 5 it is by **g** you have been saved.
2: 7 the incomparable riches of his **g**,
2: 8 For it is by **g** you have been saved,
3: 2 of God's **g** that was given to me
Eph 3: 7 of God's **g** given me through
3: 8 Lord's people, this **g** was given me:
4: 7 of us **g** has been given as Christ
6: 24 **G** to all who love our Lord Jesus
Php 1: 2 **G** and peace to you from God our
1: 7 all of you share in God's **g** with me.
4: 23 The **g** of the Lord Jesus Christ be
Col 1: 2 **G** and peace to you from God our
1: 6 it and truly understood God's **g**.
4: 6 conversation be always full of **g**,
4: 18 **G** be with you.
1Th 1: 1 **G** and peace to you.
5: 28 The **g** of our Lord Jesus Christ be
2Th 1: 2 **G** and peace to you from God
1: 12 according to the **g** of our God
2: 16 **g** gave us eternal encouragement
3: 18 The **g** of our Lord Jesus Christ be
1Ti 1: 2 **G**, mercy and peace from God
1: 14 The **g** of our Lord was poured
6: 21 from the faith. **G** be with you all.
2Ti 1: 2 **G**, mercy and peace from God
1: 9 because of his own purpose and **g**.
1: 9 This **g** was given us in Christ Jesus
2: 1 be strong in the **g** that is in Christ
4: 22 with your spirit. **G** be with you all.
Titus 1: 4 **G** and peace from God the Father
2: 11 For the **g** of God has appeared
3: 7 having been justified by his **g**,
3: 15 us in the faith. **G** be with you all.
Phm : 3 **G** and peace to you from God our
: 25 The **g** of the Lord Jesus Christ be
Heb 2: 9 the **g** of God he might taste death
4: 16 approach God's throne of **g**
4: 16 **g** to help us in our time of need.
10: 29 who has insulted the Spirit of **g**?
12: 15 no one falls short of the **g** of God
13: 9 our hearts to be strengthened by **g**,
13: 25 **G** be with you all.
Jas 4: 6 But he gives us more **g**. That is why
1Pe 1: 2 **G** and peace be yours in
1: 10 spoke of the **g** that was to come
1: 13 set your hope on the **g** to be
4: 10 of God's **g** in its various forms.
5: 10 And the God of all **g**, who called
5: 12 that this is the true **g** of God.
2Pe 1: 2 **G** and peace be yours in
3: 18 grow in the **g** and knowledge of
2Jn : 3 **G**, mercy and peace from God
Jude : 4 who pervert the **g** of our God
Rev 1: 4 **G** and peace to you from him who
22: 21 The **g** of the Lord Jesus be

GRACIOUS (GRACE)
Ex 34: 6 the compassionate and **g** God,
Nu 6: 25 face shine on you and be **g** to you;
Ne 9: 17 God, **g** and compassionate,
Ps 67: 1 May God be **g** to us and bless us
Pr 16: 21 and **g** words promote instruction.
16: 24 **G** words are a honeycomb,
Isa 30: 18 the LORD longs to be **g** to you;

GRAIN
Lev 2: 1 anyone brings a **g** offering
Ecc 11: 1 Ship your **g** across the sea;
Lk 17: 35 women will be grinding **g** together;
1Co 9: 9 an ox while it is treading out the **g**."

GRANDCHILDREN (CHILD)
1Ti 5: 4 But if a widow has children or **g**,

GRANDMOTHER (MOTHER)
2Ti 1: 5 which first lived in your **g** Lois

GRANT (GRANTED)
Ps 20: 5 May the LORD **g** all your
51: 12 salvation and **g** me a willing spirit,

GRANTED (GRANT)
Pr 10: 24 what the righteous desire will be **g**.
Mt 15: 28 Your request is **g**."
Php 1: 29 For it has been **g** to you on behalf

GRAPES
Nu 13: 23 bearing a single cluster of **g**.
Jer 31: 29 'The parents have eaten sour **g**,
Eze 18: 2 "'The parents eat sour **g**,
Mt 7: 16 people pick **g** from thornbushes,
Rev 14: 18 earth's vine, because its **g** are ripe."

GRASS
Ps 103: 15 The life of mortals is like **g**,
Isa 40: 6 "All people are like **g**, and all their
Mt 6: 30 that is how God clothes the **g**
1Pe 1: 24 the **g** withers and the flowers fall,

GRASSHOPPERS
Nu 13: 33 We seemed like **g** in our own eyes,

GRATIFY* (GRATITUDE)
Ro 13: 14 how to **g** the desires of the flesh.
Gal 5: 16 and you will not **g** the desires

GRATITUDE (GRATIFY)
Col 3: 16 to God with **g** in your hearts.

GRAVE (GRAVES)
Nu 19: 16 who touches a human bone or a **g**,
Dt 34: 6 day no one knows where his **g** is.
Ps 5: 9 Their throat is an open **g**;
Pr 7: 27 Her house is a highway to the **g**,
Hos 13: 14 Where, O **g**, is your destruction?
Jn 11: 44 "Take off the **g** clothes and let him

GRAVES (GRAVE)
Eze 37: 12 I am going to open your **g** and
Jn 5: 28 are in their **g** will hear his voice
Ro 3: 13 "Their throats are open **g**;

GRAY
Pr 16: 31 **G** hair is a crown of splendor;
20: 29 **g** hair the splendor of the old.

GREAT (GREATER GREATEST GREATNESS)
Ge 12: 2 "I will make you into a **g** nation,
12: 2 I will make your name **g**, and you
Ex 32: 11 brought out of Egypt with **g** power
Nu 14: 19 In accordance with your **g** love,
Dt 4: 32 Has anything so **g** as this ever
10: 17 gods and Lord of lords, the **g** God,
29: 28 **g** wrath the LORD uprooted them
Jos 7: 9 will you do for your own **g** name?"
Jdg 16: 5 you the secret of his **g** strength
2Sa 7: 22 "How **g** you are,
22: 36 your help has made me **g**.
24: 14 of the LORD, for his mercy is **g**;
1Ch 17: 19 made known all these **g** promises.
Ps 18: 35 your help has made me **g**.
19: 11 in keeping them there is **g** reward.
40: 16 always say, "The LORD is **g**!"
47: 2 the **g** King over all the earth.
57: 10 For **g** is your love,
70: 4 always say, "The LORD is **g**!"
89: 1 sing of the LORD's **g** love forever;
103: 11 so **g** is his love for those who fear
108: 4 For **g** is your love, higher than
117: 2 For **g** is his love toward us,
119:165 **G** peace have those who love your
145: 3 **G** is the LORD and most worthy
Pr 22: 1 is more desirable than **g** riches;
23: 24 of a righteous child has **g** joy;
Isa 42: 21 his righteousness to make his law **g**
Jer 27: 5 With my **g** power and outstretched
32: 19 **g** are your purposes and mighty
La 3: 23 **g** is your faithfulness.
Da 9: 4 "Lord, the **g** and awesome God,
Joel 2: 11 The day of the LORD is **g**;
2: 20 Surely he has done **g** things!
Zep 1: 14 The **g** day of the LORD is near—
Mal 1: 11 name will be **g** among the nations,
4: 5 prophet Elijah to you before that **g**
Mt 20: 26 become **g** among you must be your
Mk 10: 43 become **g** among you must be your
Lk 6: 23 because **g** is your reward in heaven.
6: 35 Then your reward will be **g**, and
21: 27 in a cloud with power and **g** glory.
Eph 1: 19 his incomparably **g** power for us
2: 4 But because of his **g** love for us,
1Ti 6: 6 with contentment is **g** gain.
Titus 2: 13 of the glory of our **g** God
Heb 2: 3 if we ignore so **g** a salvation?
1Jn 3: 1 See what **g** love the Father has
Rev 6: 17 For the **g** day of their wrath has
20: 11 I saw a **g** white throne and him

GREATER (GREAT)
Mt 11: 11 has not risen anyone **g** than John
12: 6 something **g** than the temple is
12: 41 now something **g** than Jonah is
12: 42 now something **g** than Solomon is
Mk 12: 31 is no commandment **g** than these."
Jn 1: 50 You will see **g** things than that."
3: 30 He must become **g**; I must become

Jn 14: 12 will do even **g** things than these,
15: 13 **G** love has no one than this:
1Co 12: 31 Now eagerly desire the **g** gifts.
2Co 3: 11 how much **g** is the glory
Heb 3: 3 worthy of **g** honor than Moses,
7: 7 doubt the lesser is blessed by the **g**.
11: 26 as of **g** value than the treasures
1Jn 3: 20 know that God is **g** than our hearts
4: 4 is in you is **g** than the one who is

GREATEST (GREAT)
Mt 22: 38 is the first and **g** commandment.
23: 11 The **g** among you will be your
Lk 9: 48 least among you all who is the **g**."
1Co 13: 13 But the **g** of these is love.

GREATNESS* (GREAT)
Ex 15: 7 "In the **g** of your majesty you
Dt 3: 24 to show to your servant your **g**
32: 3 Oh, praise the **g** of our God!
1Ch 29: 11 the **g** and the power and the glory
2Ch 9: 6 not even half the **g** of your wisdom
Est 10: 2 a full account of the **g** of Mordecai,
Ps 145: 3 his **g** no one can fathom.
150: 2 praise him for his surpassing **g**.
Isa 9: 7 Of the **g** of his government and
63: 1 forward in the **g** of his strength?
Eze 38: 23 And so I will show my **g** and my
Da 4: 22 your **g** has grown until it reaches
5: 18 Nebuchadnezzar sovereignty and **g**
7: 27 **g** of all the kingdoms under heaven
Mic 5: 4 his **g** will reach to the ends
Lk 9: 43 were all amazed at the **g** of God.

GREED (GREEDY)
Lk 12: 15 your guard against all kinds of **g**;
Ro 1: 29 wickedness, evil, **g** and depravity.
Eph 5: 3 or of **g**, because these are improper
Col 3: 5 desires and **g**, which is idolatry.
2Pe 2: 14 they are experts in **g**—

GREEDY (GREED)
Pr 15: 27 The **g** bring ruin to their
1Co 6: 10 thieves nor the **g** nor drunkards
Eph 5: 5 No immoral, impure or **g** person—

GREEKS
1Co 1: 22 signs and **G** look for wisdom,

GREEN
Ps 23: 2 makes me lie down in **g** pastures,

GREW (GROW)
Lk 1: 80 the child **g** and became strong
2: 52 And Jesus **g** in wisdom and stature,
Ac 16: 5 in the faith and **g** daily in numbers.

GRIEF (GRIEFS GRIEVE GRIEVED)
Ps 10: 14 you consider their **g** and take it
Pr 10: 1 foolish son brings **g** to his mother.
14: 13 ache, and rejoicing may end in **g**.
17: 21 To have a fool for a child brings **g**;
Ecc 1: 18 the more knowledge, the more **g**.
La 3: 32 Though he brings **g**, he will show
Jn 16: 20 grieve, but your **g** will turn to joy.
1Pe 1: 6 have had to suffer **g** in all kinds

GRIEFS* (GRIEF)
1Ti 6: 10 pierced themselves with many **g**.

GRIEVANCE
Col 3: 13 of you has a **g** against someone.

GRIEVE (GRIEF)
Eph 4: 30 do not **g** the Holy Spirit of God,
1Th 4: 13 so that you do not **g** like the rest

GRIEVED (GRIEF)
Isa 63: 10 they rebelled and **g** his Holy Spirit.

GRINDING
Lk 17: 35 women will be **g** grain together;

GROAN (GROANING GROANS)
Ro 8: 23 **g** inwardly as we wait eagerly
2Co 5: 4 in this tent, we **g** and are burdened,

GROANING (GROAN)
Ex 2: 24 God heard their **g** and he
Eze 21: 7 they ask you, 'Why are you **g**?'
Ro 8: 22 the whole creation has been **g** as

GROANS (GROAN)
Ro 8: 26 for us through wordless **g**.

GROUND
Ge 1: 10 God called the dry **g** "land,"
3: 17 it,"Cursed is the **g** because of you;
4: 10 blood cries out to me from the **g**.
Ex 3: 5 where you are standing is holy **g**."
15: 19 walked through the sea on dry **g**.
Isa 53: 2 shoot, and like a root out of dry **g**.
Mt 10: 29 to the **g** outside your Father's care.
25: 25 out and hid your gold in the **g**.
Jn 8: 6 *write on the **g** with his finger.*
Eph 6: 13 you may be able to stand your **g**,

GROW (FULL-GROWN GREW GROWING GROWS)
Pr 13: 11 money little by little makes it **g**.
20: 13 not love sleep or you will **g** poor;
Isa 40: 31 they will run and not **g** weary,
Mt 6: 28 See how the flowers of the field **g**.
1Co 3: 6 it, but God has been making it **g**.
2Pe 3: 18 But **g** in the grace and knowledge

GROWING (GROW)
Lk 13: 6 "A man had a fig tree **g** in his
Col 1: 6 and **g** throughout the whole world
1: 10 work, **g** in the knowledge of God,
2Th 1: 3 so, because your faith is **g** more

GROWS (GROW)
Eph 4: 16 **g** and builds itself up in love,
Col 2: 19 sinews, **g** as God causes it to grow.

GRUMBLE (GRUMBLED GRUMBLERS GRUMBLING)
1Co 10: 10 do not **g**, as some of them did—
Jas 5: 9 Don't **g** against one another,

GRUMBLED (GRUMBLE)
Ex 15: 24 So the people **g** against Moses,
Nu 14: 29 census and who has **g** against me.

GRUMBLERS* (GRUMBLE)
Jude : 16 people are **g** and faultfinders;

GRUMBLING (GRUMBLE)
Jn 6: 43 "Stop **g** among yourselves,"
Php 2: 14 everything without **g** or arguing,
1Pe 4: 9 to one another without **g**.

GUARANTEEING* (GUARANTOR)
2Co 1: 22 as a deposit, **g** what is to come.
5: 5 as a deposit, **g** what is to come.
Eph 1: 14 is deposit **g** our inheritance until

GUARANTOR* (GUARANTEEING)
Heb 7: 22 Jesus has become the **g** of a better

GUARD (GUARDED GUARDIAN-REDEEMER GUARDIAN)
1Sa 2: 9 He will **g** the feet of his faithful
Ps 141: 3 Set a **g** over my mouth, LORD;
Pr 2: 11 you, and understanding will **g** you.
4: 13 let it go; **g** it well, for it is your life.
4: 23 Above all else, **g** your heart,
7: 2 **g** my teachings as the apple of your
13: 3 Those who **g** their lips preserve
21: 23 Those who **g** their mouths and
Isa 52: 12 God of Israel will be your rear **g**.
Mk 13: 33 Be on **g**! Be alert! You do not know
Lk 12: 1 "Be on your **g** against the yeast
12: 15 Be on your **g** against all kinds
Ac 20: 31 So be on your **g**!
1Co 16: 13 Be on your **g**; stand firm
Php 4: 7 will **g** your hearts and your minds
1Ti 6: 20 **g** what has been entrusted to your
2Ti 1: 14 **G** the good deposit that was

GUARDED (GUARD)
Eze 44: 15 and who **g** my sanctuary

GUARDIAN (GUARD)
Eze 28: 14 You were anointed as a **g** cherub,
Gal 3: 24 law was our **g** until Christ came

GUARDIAN-REDEEMER (GUARD)
Ru 3: 9 since you are a **g** of our family."
4: 14 has not left you without a **g**.

GUEST (GUEST)
Lk 2: 7 there was no **g** room available

GUIDANCE (GUIDE)
Pr 1: 5 and let the discerning get **g**—
11: 14 For lack of **g** a nation falls,
24: 6 Surely you need **g** to wage war,
1Co 12: 28 of **g**, and of different kinds

GUIDE (GUIDANCE GUIDED GUIDES)
Ex 13: 21 of cloud to **g** them on their way
15: 13 In your strength you will **g** them
Ne 9: 19 cloud did not fail to **g** them on
Ps 25: 5 **G** me in your truth and teach me,
48: 14 he will be our **g** even to the end.
67: 4 and **g** the nations of the earth.
73: 24 You **g** me with your counsel,
139: 10 even there your hand will **g** me,
Pr 6: 22 When you walk, they will **g** you;
Isa 58: 11 The LORD will **g** you always;
Jn 16: 13 he will **g** you into all the truth.

GUIDED (GUIDE)
Ps 107: 30 he **g** them to their desired haven.

GUIDES (GUIDE)
Ps 23: 3 He **g** me along the right paths
25: 9 He **g** the humble in what is right
Pr 11: 3 integrity of the upright **g** them,
Mt 23: 16 "Woe to you, blind **g**! You say,
23: 24 You blind **g**! You strain out a gnat

GUILT (GUILTY)
Lev 5: 15 It is a **g** offering.
Ps 32: 5 And you forgave the **g** of my sin.
38: 4 My **g** has overwhelmed me like
Isa 6: 7 your **g** is taken away and your sin
Jer 2: 22 stain of your **g** is still before me,"
Eze 18: 19 'Why does the son not share the **g**

GUILTY (GUILT)
Ex 23: 1 Do not help a **g** person by being
34: 7 does not leave the **g** unpunished;
Job 10: 2 Do not declare me **g**, but tell me
Mk 3: 29 they are **g** of an eternal sin."
Jn 8: 46 Can any of you prove me **g** of sin?
1Co 11: 27 in an unworthy manner will be **g**
Heb 10: 2 would no longer have felt **g** for
10: 22 to cleanse us from a **g** conscience
Jas 2: 10 at just one point is **g** of breaking all

GULLIBLE* (GULLIBLE)
2Ti 3: 6 and gain control over **g** women,

GULP*
Pr 21: 20 olive oil, but fools **g** theirs down.

HABAKKUK*
Prophet to Judah (Hab 1:1; 3:1).

HABIT
1Ti 5: 13 they get into the **h** of being idle
Heb 10: 25 as some are in the **h** of doing,

HADAD
Edomite adversary of Solomon (1Ki 11:14–25).

HADES*
Mt 11: 23 No, you will go down to **H**.
16: 18 the gates of **H** will not overcome it.
Lk 10: 15 No, you will go down to **H**.
16: 23 In **H**, where he was in torment,
Rev 1: 18 I hold the keys of death and **H**.
6: 8 **H** was following close behind him.
20: 13 and **H** gave up the dead that were
20: 14 **H** were thrown into the lake of fire.

HAGAR
Servant of Sarah, wife of Abraham, mother of Ishmael (Ge 16:1–6; 25:12). Driven away by Sarah while pregnant (Ge 16:5–16); after birth of Isaac (Ge 21:9–21; Gal 4:21–31).

HAGGAI*
Post-exilic prophet who encouraged rebuilding of the temple (Ezr 5:1; 6:14; Hag 1–2).

HAIL
Ex 9: 19 because the **h** will fall on every
Rev 8: 7 there came **h** and fire mixed

HAIR (HAIRS HAIRY)
Lev 19: 27 "'Do not cut the **h** at the sides
Nu 6: 5 they must let their **h** grow long.
2Sa 18: 9 Absalom's **h** got caught in the tree.
Pr 16: 31 Gray **h** is a crown of splendor;
20: 29 gray **h** the splendor of the old.
Lk 7: 44 tears and wiped them with her **h**.
21: 18 not a **h** of your head will perish.
Jn 11: 2 and wiped his feet with her **h**.)
12: 3 feet and wiped his feet with her **h**.
1Co 11: 6 might as well have her **h** cut off;
11: 14 teach you that if a man has long **h**,
11: 15 but that if a woman has long **h**,
Rev 1: 14 The **h** on his head was white like

HAIRS (HAIR)
Mt 10: 30 even the very **h** of your head are all
Lk 12: 7 the very **h** of your head are all

HAIRY (HAIR)
Ge 27: 11 brother Esau is a **h** man while I

HALF
Ex 30: 13 This **h** shekel is an offering
Jos 8: 33 **h** of them in front of Mount Ebal,
1Ki 3: 25 child in two and give **h** to one and **h** to the other."
10: 7 Indeed, not even **h** was told me;
Est 5: 3 Even up to **h** the kingdom, it will
Da 7: 25 for a time, times and **h** a time.
Mk 6: 23 give you, up to **h** my kingdom."

HALF-TRIBE (TRIBE)
Nu 32: 33 the **h** of Manasseh son of Joseph

HALL
Eze 41: 1 the man brought me to the main **h**

HALLELUJAH*
Rev 19: 1 multitude in heaven shouting: "**H**!
19: 3 And again they shouted: "**H**!
19: 4 And they cried: "Amen, **H**!"
19: 6 peals of thunder, shouting: "**H**!

HALLOWED* (HOLY)
Mt 6: 9 Father in heaven, **h** be your name,
Lk 11: 2 "'Father, **h** be your name,

HALT
Job 38: 11 here is where your proud waves **h**'?

HAM
Son of Noah (Ge 5:32; 1Ch 1:4), father of Canaan (Ge 9:18; 10:6–20; 1Ch 1:8–16). Saw Noah's nakedness (Ge 9:20–27).

HAMAN
Agagite nobleman honored by Xerxes (Est 3:1–2). Plotted to exterminate the Jews because of Mordecai (Est 3:3–15). Forced to honor Mordecai (Est 5–6). Plot exposed by Esther (Est 5:1–8; 7:1–8). Hanged (Est 7:9–10).

HAMPERED*
Pr 4: 12 you walk, your steps will not be **h**;

HAND (HANDED HANDFUL HANDIWORK HANDS OPENHANDED)
Ge 24: 2 had, "Put your **h** under my thigh.
47: 29 eyes, put your **h** under my thigh
Ex 13: 3 you out of it with a mighty **h**.
15: 6 Your right **h**, LORD, was majestic
33: 22 with my **h** until I have passed by.
Dt 12: 7 everything you have put your **h** to,
1Ki 8: 42 mighty **h** and your outstretched
13: 4 stretched out his **h** from the altar
1Ch 29: 14 you only what comes from your **h**.
29: 16 Holy Name comes from your **h**,
2Ch 6: 15 with your **h** you have fulfilled it—
Ne 4: 17 did their work with one **h**
Job 40: 4 I put my **h** over my mouth.
Ps 16: 8 With him at my right **h**, I will not
32: 4 and night your **h** was heavy on me;
37: 24 the LORD upholds him with his **h**.
44: 3 it was your right **h**, your arm,
45: 9 at your right **h** is the royal bride
63: 8 your right **h** upholds me.
75: 8 In the **h** of the LORD is a cup full
91: 7 ten thousand at your right **h**, but it
98: 1 his right **h** and his holy arm have
109: 31 stands at the right **h** of the needy,
110: 1 "Sit at my right **h** until I make your
137: 5 may my right **h** forget its skill.
139: 10 even there your **h** will guide me,
145: 16 You open your **h** and satisfy
Pr 27: 16 the wind or grasping oil with the **h**.
Ecc 9: 10 Whatever your **h** finds to do, do it
Isa 11: 8 child will put its **h** into the viper's
40: 12 the waters in the hollow of his **h**,
40: 12 his **h** marked off the heavens?
41: 13 God who takes hold of your right **h**
44: 5 still others will write on their **h**,
48: 13 my right **h** spread out the heavens;
64: 8 we are all the work of your **h**.
La 3: 3 has turned his **h** against me again
Da 10: 10 A **h** touched me and set me
Jnh 4: 11 who cannot tell their right **h**
Hab 3: 4 rays flashed from his **h**, where his
Mt 5: 30 And if your right **h** causes you
6: 3 not let your left **h** know what your right **h** is doing,
12: 10 a man with a shriveled **h** was there.
18: 8 If your **h** or your foot causes you
22: 44 my right **h** until I put your enemies
26: 64 at the right **h** of the Mighty One
Mk 3: 1 a man with a shriveled **h** was there.
9: 43 If your **h** causes you to stumble,
12: 36 my right **h** until I put your enemies
16: 19 *sat at the right **h** of God.*
Lk 6: 6 there whose right **h** was shriveled.
20: 42 said to my Lord: "Sit at my right **h**
22: 69 at the right **h** of the mighty God."
Jn 10: 28 one will snatch them out of my **h**.
20: 27 Reach out your **h** and put it into
Ac 7: 55 standing at the right **h** of God.
1Co 12: 15 say, "Because I am not a **h**, I do not
Heb 1: 13 "Sit at my right **h** until I make your

HANDED (HAND)
1Ti 1: 20 whom I have **h** over to Satan to be

HANDFUL (HAND)
Ecc 4: 6 Better one **h** with tranquillity than

HANDIWORK (HAND)
Eph 2: 10 For we are God's **h**,

HANDLE (HANDLES)
Col 2: 21 "Do not **h**! Do not taste!

HANDLES (HANDLE)
2Ti 2: 15 who correctly **h** the word of truth.

HANDS (HAND)
Ge 27: 22 Jacob, but the **h** are the **h** of Esau."
Ex 17: 11 As long as Moses held up his **h**,
29: 10 sons shall lay their **h** on its head.
Dt 6: 8 Tie them as symbols on your **h**
Jdg 7: 6 of them drank from cupped **h**,
2Ki 11: 12 and the people clapped their **h**
2Ch 6: 4 **h** has fulfilled what he promised
Ps 22: 16 they pierce my **h** and my feet.
24: 4 The one who has clean **h** and a
31: 5 Into your **h** I commit my spirit;
31: 15 My times are in your **h**;
47: 1 Clap your **h**, all you nations;
63: 4 in your name I will lift up my **h**.
Pr 10: 4 Lazy **h** make for poverty,
21: 25 him, because his **h** refuse to work.
31: 13 and flax and works with eager **h**.
31: 20 and extends her **h** to the needy.
Ecc 5: 15 toil that they can carry in their **h**.
10: 18 because of idle **h**, the house leaks.
Isa 35: 3 Strengthen the feeble **h**,
49: 16 you on the palms of my **h**;
55: 12 trees of the field will clap their **h**.
65: 2 out my **h** to an obstinate people,
La 3: 41 hearts and our **h** to God in heaven,
Lk 18: 15 for him to place his **h** on them.
23: 46 into your **h** I commit my spirit."
Ac 6: 6 prayed and laid their **h** on them.
8: 18 at the laying on of the apostles' **h**,
13: 3 they placed their **h** on them and
19: 6 When Paul placed his **h** on them,
28: 8 placed his **h** on him and healed
1Th 4: 11 business and work with your **h**,
1Ti 2: 8 lifting up holy **h** without anger
4: 14 body of elders laid their **h** on you.
5: 22 not be hasty in the laying on of **h**,
2Ti 1: 6 you through the laying on of my **h**.
Heb 6: 2 the laying on of **h**, the resurrection
Rev 13: 16 to receive a mark on their right **h**

HANDSOME*
Ge 39: 6 Now Joseph was well-built and **h**,
1Sa 9: 2 **h** a young man as could be found
16: 12 a fine appearance and **h** features.
17: 42 glowing with health and **h**, and he
2Sa 14: 25 for his **h** appearance as Absalom.
1Ki 1: 6 also very **h** and was born next
SS 1: 16 How **h** you are, my beloved!
Eze 23: 6 all of them **h** young men,
23: 12 horsemen, all **h** young men.
23: 23 Assyrians with them, **h** young men
Da 1: 4 men without any physical defect, **h**,
Zec 11: 13 **h** price at which they valued me!

HANG (HANGED HANGING HUNG)
Mt 22: 40 and the Prophets **h** on these two

HANGED* (HANG)
2Sa 17: 23 house in order and then **h** himself.
Mt 27: 5 Then he went away and **h** himself.

HANGING (HANG)
Ac 10: 39 They killed him by **h** him

HANNAH*
Wife of Elkanah, mother of Samuel (1Sa 1). Prayer at dedication of Samuel (1Sa 2:1–10). Blessed (1Sa 2:18–21).

HAPPIER* (HAPPY)
Ecc 4: 2 already died, are **h** than the living,
Mt 18: 13 he is **h** about that one sheep than
1Co 7: 40 she is **h** if she stays as she is—

HAPPINESS* (HAPPY)
Dt 24: 5 bring **h** to the wife he has married.
Est 8: 16 For the Jews it was a time of **h**
Job 7: 7 my eyes will never see **h** again.
Ecc 2: 26 knowledge and **h**, but to the sinner
Mt 25: 21 Come and share your master's **h**!'
25: 23 Come and share your master's **h**!'

HAPPY* (HAPPIER HAPPINESS)
Ge 30: 13 Then Leah said, "How **h** I am!
30: 13 The women will call me **h**."
1Ki 4: 20 ate, they drank and they were **h**.
10: 8 How **h** your people must be! How **h** your officials,
2Ch 9: 7 How **h** your people must be! How **h** your officials,
Est 5: 9 Haman went out that day **h**
Ps 68: 3 may they be **h** and joyful.
113: 9 home as a **h** mother of children.
137: 8 **h** is the one who repays you
137: 9 **H** is the one who seizes your
Pr 15: 13 A **h** heart makes the face cheerful,
Ecc 3: 12 better for people than to be **h**
5: 19 their lot and be **h** in their toil—
7: 14 When times are good, be **h**;
11: 9 young, be **h** while you are young,
Jnh 4: 6 Jonah was very **h** about the plant.
Zec 8: 19 occasions and **h** festivals for Judah.
1Co 7: 30 who are **h**, as if they were not;
2Co 7: 9 yet now I am **h**, not because you
7: 13 delighted to see how **h** Titus was,
Jas 5: 13 Is anyone **h**? Let them sing songs

HARD (HARDEN HARDENED HARDENING HARDENS HARDER HARDSHIP HARDSHIPS)
Ge 18: 14 Is anything too **h** for the LORD?
1Ki 10: 1 to test Solomon with **h** questions.
Pr 14: 23 All **h** work brings a profit, but
Jer 32: 17 Nothing is too **h** for you.
Zec 7: 12 They made their hearts as **h** as flint
Mt 19: 23 it is **h** for someone who is rich
Mk 10: 5 "It was because your hearts were **h**
Jn 6: 60 disciples said, "This is a **h** teaching.
Ac 20: 35 of **h** work we must help the weak,
26: 14 It is **h** for you to kick against
Ro 16: 12 those women who work **h**
16: 12 woman who has worked very **h**
1Co 4: 12 We work **h** with our own hands.
2Co 6: 5 in **h** work, sleepless nights
1Th 5: 12 those who work **h** among you,
Rev 2: 2 **h** work and your perseverance.

HARDEN (HARD)
Ex 4: 21 I will **h** his heart so that he will not
Ps 95: 8 "Do not **h** your hearts as you did
Ro 9: 18 he hardens whom he wants to **h**.
Heb 3: 8 do not **h** your hearts as you did

HARDENED (HARD)
Ex 10: 20 But the LORD **h** Pharaoh's heart,
Jn 12: 40 their eyes and **h** their hearts,

HARDENING* (HARD)
Ro 11: 25 Israel has experienced a **h** in part
Eph 4: 18 them due to the **h** of their hearts.

HARDENS* (HARD)
Pr 28: 14 but whoever **h** their heart falls
Ro 9: 18 he **h** whom he wants to harden.

HARDER (HARD)
1Co 15: 10 No, I worked **h** than all of them—
2Co 11: 23 I have worked much **h**,

HARDHEARTED* (HEART)
Dt 15: 7 do not be **h** or tightfisted toward

HARDSHIP (HARD)
Ro 8: 35 Shall trouble or **h** or persecution
1Co 13: 3 give over my body to **h** that I may
2Ti 4: 5 endure **h**, do the work
Heb 12: 7 Endure **h** as discipline;

HARDSHIPS (HARD)
Ac 14: 22 "We must go through many **h**
2Co 6: 4 in troubles, **h** and distresses;
12: 10 in insults, in **h**, in persecutions,
Rev 2: 3 and have endured **h** for my name,

HARM
1Ch 16: 22 do my prophets no **h**."
Ps 105: 15 do my prophets no **h**."
121: 6 the sun will not **h** you by day,
Pr 3: 29 not plot **h** against your neighbor,
8: 36 who fail to find me **h** themselves;
12: 21 No **h** overtakes the righteous,
31: 12 good, not **h**, all the days of her life.
Jer 10: 5 they can do no **h** nor can they do
29: 11 to prosper you and not to **h** you,
Ro 13: 10 Love does no **h** to a neighbor.
1Co 11: 17 meetings do more **h** than good.
1Jn 5: 18 and the evil one cannot **h** them.

HARMONY*
Zec 6: 13 there will be **h** between the two.'
Ro 12: 16 Live in **h** with one another.
2Co 6: 15 What **h** is there between Christ

HARP (HARPS)
Ps 33: 2 Praise the LORD with the **h**;
98: 5 music to the LORD with the **h**,
150: 3 praise him with the **h** and lyre,
Rev 5: 8 Each one had a **h** and they were

HARPS (HARP)
Ps 137: 2 on the poplars we hung our **h**,

HARSH
Pr 15: 1 wrath, but a **h** word stirs up anger.
Col 2: 23 and their **h** treatment of the body,
3: 19 wives and do not be **h** with them.
1Pe 2: 18 but also to those who are **h**.

HARVEST (HARVESTERS)
Ge 8: 22 seedtime and **h**, cold and heat,
Ex 23: 16 "Celebrate the Festival of **H**
Dt 16: 15 God will bless you in all your **h**
Pr 10: 5 sleeps during **h** is a disgraceful
Jer 8: 20 "The **h** is past, the summer has
Joel 3: 13 Swing the sickle, for the **h** is ripe.
Mt 9: 37 "The **h** is plentiful but the workers
Lk 10: 2 He told them, "The **h** is plentiful,
10: 2 send out workers into his **h** field.
Jn 4: 35 'It's still four months until **h**'?
4: 35 the fields! They are ripe for **h**.
1Co 9: 11 if we reap a material **h** from you?
2Co 9: 10 seed and will enlarge the **h** of your
Gal 6: 9 at the proper time we will reap a **h**
Heb 12: 11 it produces a **h** of righteousness
Jas 3: 18 in peace reap a **h** of righteousness.
Rev 14: 15 come, for the **h** of the earth is ripe."

HARVESTERS (HARVEST)
Ru 2: 3 and began to glean behind the **h**.

HASTE (HASTEN HASTY)
Ex 12: 11 Eat it in **h**; it is the LORD's
Pr 21: 5 lead to profit as surely as **h** leads
29: 20 you see someone who speaks in **h**?

HASTEN (HASTE)
Ps 70: 1 **H**, O God, to save me;
119: 60 I will **h** and not delay to obey your

HASTY* (HASTE)
Pr 19: 2 how much more will **h** feet miss
Ecc 5: 2 do not be **h** in your heart to utter
1Ti 5: 22 Do not be **h** in the laying

HATE (GOD-HATERS HATED HATES HATING HATRED)
Lev 19: 17 "'Do not **h** a fellow Israelite
Ps 5: 5 You **h** all who do wrong;
36: 2 too much to detect or **h** their sin.
45: 7 righteousness and **h** wickedness;
97: 10 those who love the LORD **h** evil,
119:104 therefore I **h** every wrong path.
119:163 I **h** and detest falsehood but I love
139: 21 Do I not **h** those who **h** you, LORD,
Pr 8: 13 To fear the LORD is to **h** evil; I **h**
9: 8 rebuke mockers or they will **h** you;
13: 5 The righteous **h** what is false,
25: 17 much of you, and they will **h** you.
29: 10 The bloodthirsty **h** a person
Ecc 3: 8 a time to love and a time to **h**,
Isa 61: 8 I **h** robbery and wrongdoing.
Eze 35: 6 Since you did not **h** bloodshed,
Am 5: 15 **H** evil, love good;
Mt 5: 43 your neighbor and **h** your enemy.'
Lk 6: 22 Blessed are you when people **h**
6: 27 do good to those who **h** you,
14: 26 and does not **h** father and mother,
Ro 12: 9 **H** what is evil; cling to what is

HATED (HATE)
Mal 1: 3 Esau I have **h**, and I have turned
Mt 10: 22 be **h** by everyone because of me,
Jn 15: 18 keep in mind that it **h** me first.
Ro 9: 13 "Jacob I loved, but Esau I **h**."
Eph 5: 29 all, no one ever **h** their own body,
Heb 1: 9 righteousness and **h** wickedness;

HATES (HATE)
Pr 6: 16 There are six things the LORD **h**,
13: 24 spares the rod **h** their children,
15: 27 but the one who **h** bribes will live.
26: 28 A lying tongue **h** those it hurts,
Mal 2: 16 "The man who **h** and divorces his
Jn 3: 20 Everyone who does evil **h** the light,
12: 25 while anyone who **h** their life in
1Jn 2: 9 to be in the light but **h** a brother
4: 20 claims to love God yet **h** a brother

HATING* (HATE)
Titus 3: 3 being hated and **h** one another.
Jude : 23 **h** even the clothing stained

HATRED (HATE)
Pr 10: 12 **H** stirs up conflict, but love covers
15: 17 love than a fattened calf with **h**.

HAUGHTY
Pr 6: 17 **h** eyes, a lying tongue,
16: 18 destruction, a **h** spirit before a fall.
18: 12 Before a downfall the heart is **h**,

HAVEN
Ps 107: 30 he guided them to their desired **h**.

HAY
1Co 3: 12 costly stones, wood, **h** or straw,

HEAD (HEADS HOTHEADED)
Ge 3: 15 he will crush your **h**, and you will
Nu 6: 5 no razor may be used on their **h**.
Jdg 16: 17 If my **h** were shaved, my strength
1Sa 9: 2 he was a **h** taller than anyone else.
Ps 23: 5 You anoint my **h** with oil;
133: 2 is like precious oil poured on the **h**,
Pr 10: 6 Blessings crown the **h**
25: 22 will heap burning coals on his **h**,
Isa 59: 17 the helmet of salvation on his **h**;
Eze 33: 4 their blood will be on their own **h**.
Mt 8: 20 of Man has no place to lay his **h**."
Jn 19: 2 crown of thorns and put it on his **h**
Ro 12: 20 will heap burning coals on his **h**."
1Co 11: 3 the **h** of every man is Christ,
11: 3 and the **h** of the woman is man,
11: 3 and the **h** of Christ is God.
11: 5 her **h** uncovered dishonors her **h**—
12: 21 And the **h** cannot say to the feet,
Eph 1: 22 him to be **h** over everything
5: 23 the husband is the **h** of the wife as Christ is the **h** of the church,
Col 1: 18 And he is the **h** of the body,
2Ti 4: 5 you, keep your **h** in all situations,
Rev 14: 14 man with a crown of gold on his **h**
19: 12 fire, and on his **h** are many crowns.

HEADS (HEAD)
Lev 26: 13 you to walk with **h** held high.
Ps 22: 7 they hurl insults, shaking their **h**.
24: 7 Lift up your **h**, you gates;
Isa 35: 10 everlasting joy will crown their **h**.
51: 11 everlasting joy will crown their **h**.
Mt 27: 39 insults at him, shaking their **h**
Lk 21: 28 stand up and lift up your **h**,
Ac 18: 6 "Your blood be on your own **h**!
Rev 4: 4 and had crowns of gold on their **h**.

HEAL* (HEALED HEALING HEALS)
Nu 12: 13 the LORD, "Please, God, **h** her!"
Dt 32: 39 I have wounded and I will **h**, and
2Ki 20: 5 and seen your tears; I will **h** you.
2Ki 20: 8 the sign that the LORD will **h** me
2Ch 7: 14 their sin and will **h** their land.
Job 5: 18 he injures, but his hands also **h**.
Ps 6: 2 **h** me, LORD, for my bones are
41: 4 **h** me, for I have sinned against
Ecc 3: 3 a time to kill and a time to **h**,
Isa 19: 22 he will strike them and **h** them.
19: 22 respond to their pleas and **h** them.
57: 18 seen their ways, but I will **h** them;
57: 19 "And I will **h** them."
Jer 17: 14 **H** me, LORD, and I will be healed;
30: 17 you to health and **h** your wounds,'
33: 6 I will **h** my people and will let
La 2: 13 as deep as the sea. Who can **h** you?
Hos 5: 13 cure you, not able to **h** your sores.
6: 1 torn us to pieces but he will **h** us;
7: 1 whenever I would **h** Israel, the sins
14: 4 "I will **h** their waywardness
Na 3: 19 Nothing can **h** you; your wound is
Zec 11: 16 **h** the injured, or feed the healthy,
Mt 8: 7 to him, "Shall I come and **h** him?"
10: 1 to **h** every disease and sickness.
10: 8 **H** the sick, raise the dead,
12: 10 "Is it lawful to **h** on the Sabbath?"
13: 15 and turn, and I would **h** them.'
17: 16 but they could not **h** him."
Mk 3: 2 if he would **h** him on the Sabbath.
6: 5 on a few sick people and **h** them.
Lk 4: 23 'Physician, **h** yourself!'
5: 17 Lord was with Jesus to **h** the sick.
6: 7 see if he would **h** on the Sabbath.
7: 3 him to come and **h** his servant.
8: 43 years, but no one could **h** her.
9: 2 kingdom of God and to **h** the sick.
10: 9 **H** the sick who are there and tell
14: 3 "Is it lawful to **h** on the Sabbath
Jn 4: 47 begged him to come and **h** his son,
12: 40 and I would **h** them."
Ac 4: 30 Stretch out your hand to **h**
28: 27 and turn, and I would **h** them.'

HEALED* (HEAL)
Ge 20: 17 and God **h** Abimelek, his wife
Ex 21: 19 see that the victim is completely **h**.
Lev 13: 37 in it, the affected person is **h**.
14: 3 If they have been **h** of their defiling
Jos 5: 8 were in camp until they were **h**.
1Sa 6: 3 Then you will be **h**, and you will
2Ki 2: 21 'I have **h** this water.
2Ch 30: 20 heard Hezekiah and **h** the people.
Ps 30: 2 to you for help, and you **h** me.
107: 20 He sent out his word and **h** them;
Isa 6: 10 their hearts, and turn and be **h**."
53: 5 him, and by his wounds we are **h**.
Jer 14: 19 afflicted us so that we cannot be **h**?
17: 14 Heal me, LORD, and I will be **h**;
51: 8 for her pain; perhaps she can be **h**.
51: 9 "'We would have **h** Babylon, but she cannot be **h**;
Eze 30: 21 It has not been bound up to be **h**
34: 4 the weak or **h** the sick
Hos 11: 3 did not realize it was I who **h** them.
Mt 4: 24 and the paralyzed; and he **h** them.
8: 8 the word, and my servant will be **h**.
8: 13 his servant was **h** at that moment.
8: 16 with a word and **h** all the sick.
9: 21 I only touch his cloak, I will be **h**."
9: 22 he said, "your faith has **h** you."
9: 22 the woman was **h** at that moment.
12: 15 him, and he **h** all who were ill.
12: 22 and Jesus **h** him, so that he could
14: 14 on them and **h** their sick.
14: 36 and all who touched it were **h**.
15: 28 daughter was **h** at that moment.
15: 30 them at his feet; and he **h** them.
17: 18 boy, and he was **h** at that moment.
19: 2 followed him, and he **h** them there.
21: 14 him at the temple, and he **h** them.
Mk 1: 34 and Jesus **h** many who had various
3: 10 For he had **h** many, so that those
5: 23 hands on her so that she will be **h**
5: 28 I just touch his clothes, I will be **h**."
5: 34 "Daughter, your faith has **h** you.
6: 13 sick people with oil and **h** them.
6: 56 and all who touched it were **h**.
10: 52 said Jesus, "your faith has **h** you."

Lk 4: 40 his hands on each one, he **h** them.
5: 15 him and to be **h** of their sicknesses.
6: 18 him and to be **h** of their diseases.
7: 7 the word, and my servant will be **h**.
8: 47 and how she had been instantly **h**.
8: 48 "Daughter, your faith has **h** you.
8: 50 just believe, and she will be **h**."
9: 11 and **h** those who needed healing.
9: 42 **h** the boy and gave him back to his
13: 14 Indignant because Jesus had **h**
13: 14 So come and be **h** on those days,
14: 4 he **h** him and sent him on his way.
17: 15 when he saw he was **h**, came back,
18: 42 your faith has **h** you."
22: 51 touched the man's ear and **h** him.
Jn 5: 10 said to the man who had been **h**,
5: 13 The man who was **h** had no idea
Ac 3: 16 him that has completely **h** him,
4: 9 and are being asked how he was **h**,
4: 10 that this man stands before you **h**.
4: 14 who had been **h** standing there
4: 22 who was miraculously **h** was over
5: 16 spirits, and all of them were **h**.
8: 7 were paralyzed or lame were **h**.
14: 9 him, saw that he had faith to be **h**
28: 8 his hands on him and **h** him.
Heb 12: 13 may not be disabled, but rather **h**.
Jas 5: 16 each other so that you may be **h**.
1Pe 2: 24 "by his wounds you have been **h**."
Rev 13: 3 but the fatal wound had been **h**.
13: 12 whose fatal wound had been **h**.

HEALING* (HEAL)
2Ch 28: 15 food and drink, and **h** balm.
Pr 12: 18 but the tongue of the wise brings **h**.
13: 17 but a trustworthy envoy brings **h**.
16: 24 to the soul and **h** to the bones.
Isa 58: 8 and your **h** will quickly appear;
Jer 8: 15 for a time of **h** but there is only
8: 22 is there no **h** for the wound of my
14: 19 for a time of **h** but there is only
30: 12 is incurable, your injury beyond **h**.
30: 13 remedy for your sore, no **h** for you.
33: 6 I will bring health and **h** to it;
46: 11 there is no **h** for you.
Eze 47: 12 for food and their leaves for **h**."
Mal 4: 2 righteousness will rise with **h** in its
Mt 4: 23 and **h** every disease and sickness
9: 35 of the kingdom and **h** every disease
Lk 6: 19 coming from him and **h** them all.
9: 6 news and **h** people everywhere.
9: 11 and healed those who needed **h**.
13: 32 out demons and **h** people today
Jn 6: 2 he had performed by **h** the sick.
7: 23 me for **h** a man's whole body
Ac 10: 38 **h** all who were under the power
1Co 12: 9 to another gifts of **h** by that one
12: 28 miracles, then gifts of **h**, of helping,
12: 30 Do all have gifts of **h**? Do all speak
Rev 22: 2 the tree are for the **h** of the nations.

HEALS* (HEAL)
Ex 15: 26 for I am the LORD, who **h** you."
Lev 13: 18 has a boil on their skin and it **h**,
Ps 103: 3 your sins and **h** all your diseases,
147: 3 He **h** the brokenhearted and binds
Isa 30: 26 and **h** the wounds he inflicted.
Ac 9: 34 said to him, "Jesus Christ **h** you.

HEALTH* (HEALTHIER HEALTHY)
1Sa 16: 12 He was glowing with **h** and had
17: 42 glowing with **h** and handsome,
25: 6 Good **h** to you and your household
25: 6 And good **h** to all that is yours!
Ps 38: 3 wrath there is no **h** in my body;
38: 7 there is no **h** in my body.
Pr 3: 8 This will bring **h** to your body
4: 22 them and **h** to one's whole body.
15: 30 good news gives **h** to the bones.
Isa 38: 16 You restored me to **h** and let me
Jer 30: 17 I will restore you to **h** and heal
33: 6 I will bring **h** and healing to it;
3Jn : 2 I pray that you may enjoy good **h**

HEALTHIER* (HEALTH)
Da 1: 15 end of the ten days they looked **h**

HEALTHY* (HEALTH)
Ge 41: 5 Seven heads of grain, **h** and good,
41: 7 of grain swallowed up the seven **h**,

Ps 73: 4 their bodies are **h** and strong.
Zec 11: 16 or feed the **h**, but will eat the meat
Mt 6: 22 If your eyes are **h**, your whole body
9: 12 "It is not the **h** who need a doctor,
Mk 2: 17 "It is not the **h** who need a doctor,
Lk 5: 31 "It is not the **h** who need a doctor,
11: 34 When your eyes are **h**, your whole

HEAP
Pr 25: 22 you will **h** burning coals on his
Ro 12: 20 you will **h** burning coals on his

HEAR (HEARD HEARING HEARS)
Ex 15: 14 The nations will **h** and tremble;
22: 27 I will **h**, for I am compassionate.
Nu 14: 13 the Egyptians will **h** about it!
Dt 1: 16 time, "**H** the disputes between your
4: 36 heaven he made you **h** his voice
6: 4 **H**, O Israel: The LORD our God,
19: 20 The rest of the people will **h** of this
31: 13 law, must **h** it and learn to fear
Jos 7: 9 of the country will **h** about this
1Ki 8: 30 **H** from heaven, your dwelling
8: 30 and when you **h**, forgive.
2Ki 19: 16 Give ear, LORD, and **h**;
2Ch 7: 14 then I will **h** from heaven, and I
Job 31: 35 ("Oh, that I had someone to **h** me!
Ps 94: 9 he who fashioned the ear not **h**?
95: 7 if only you would **h** his voice,
Ecc 7: 21 or you may **h** your servant cursing
Isa 21: 3 I am staggered by what I **h**, I am
29: 18 day the deaf will **h** the words
30: 21 your ears will **h** a voice behind you,
51: 7 "**H** me, you who know what is
59: 1 to save, nor his ear too dull to **h**.
65: 24 they are still speaking I will **h**.
Jer 5: 21 see, who have ears but do not **h**:
Eze 33: 7 **h** the word I speak and give them
37: 4 bones, **h** the word of the LORD!
Mt 11: 5 the deaf **h**, the dead are raised,
11: 15 Whoever has ears, let them **h**.
13: 17 to **h** what you **h** but did not **h** it.
Mk 12: 29 Jesus, "is this: '**H**, O Israel:
Lk 7: 22 the deaf **h**, the dead are raised,
Jn 8: 47 The reason you do not **h** is that
Ac 13: 7 because he wanted to **h** the word
13: 44 whole city gathered to **h** the word
17: 32 "We want to **h** you again on this
Ro 2: 13 is not those who **h** the law who are
10: 14 how can they **h** without someone
2Ti 4: 3 what their itching ears want to **h**.
Heb 3: 7 "Today, if you **h** his voice,
Rev 1: 3 blessed are those who **h** it and take

HEARD (HEAR)
Ex 2: 24 God **h** their groaning and he
Dt 4: 32 has anything like it ever been **h** of?
2Sa 7: 22 as we have **h** with our own ears.
Job 42: 5 My ears had **h** of you but now my
Isa 40: 21 Have you not **h**? Has it not been
40: 28 Have you not **h**? The LORD is
66: 8 Who has ever **h** of such things?
Jer 18: 13 Who has ever **h** anything like this?
Da 10: 12 words were **h**, and I have come
12: 8 I **h**, but I did not understand.
Hab 3: 16 I **h** and my heart pounded, my lips
Mt 5: 21 "You have **h** that it was said
5: 27 "You have **h** that it was said,
5: 33 you have **h** that it was said
5: 38 "You have **h** that it was said,
5: 43 "You have **h** that it was said,
Lk 12: 3 the dark will be **h** in the daylight,
Jn 8: 26 what I have **h** from him I tell
Ac 2: 6 because each one **h** their own
1Co 2: 9 what no ear has **h**, and what no
2Co 12: 4 and **h** inexpressible things,
1Th 2: 13 which you **h** from us, you accepted
2Ti 1: 13 What you **h** from me, keep as
Jas 1: 25 not forgetting what they have **h**,
Rev 22: 8 am the one who **h** and saw these

HEARING (HEAR)
Isa 6: 9 "'Be ever **h**, but never
Mt 13: 14 "'You will be ever **h** but never
Mk 4: 12 ever **h** but never understanding;
Ac 28: 26 say, "You will be ever **h** but never
Ro 10: 17 faith comes from **h** the message,
1Co 12: 17 where would the sense of **h** be?

HEARS (HEAR)
Jn 5: 24 whoever **h** my word and believes
1Jn 5: 14 according to his will, he **h** us.
Rev 3: 20 If anyone **h** my voice and opens

HEART (BROKENHEARTED FAINTHEARTED HARDHEARTED HEART'S HEARTACHE HEARTS KINDHEARTED WHOLEHEARTED WHOLEHEARTEDLY)
Ge 6: 5 of the human **h** was only evil all
Ex 4: 21 I will harden his **h** so that he will
25: 2 everyone whose **h** prompts them
35: 21 and whose **h** moved them came
Lev 19: 17 not hate a fellow Israelite in your **h**.
Dt 4: 9 from your **h** as long as you live.
4: 29 him if you seek him with all your **h**
6: 5 LORD your God with all your **h**
10: 12 LORD your God with all your **h**
11: 13 and to serve him with all your **h**
13: 3 you love him with all your **h**
15: 10 and do so without a grudging **h**;
26: 16 observe them with all your **h**
29: 18 you today whose **h** turns away
30: 2 obey him with all your **h**
30: 6 you may love him with all your **h**
30: 10 LORD your God with all your **h**
Jos 22: 5 and to serve him with all your **h**
23: 14 You know with all your **h** and soul
1Sa 10: 9 God changed Saul's **h**, and all these
12: 20 serve the LORD with all your **h**.
12: 24 serve him faithfully with all your **h**;
13: 14 sought out a man after his own **h**
14: 7 I am with you **h** and soul."
16: 7 but the LORD looks at the **h**."
17: 32 "Let no one lose **h** on account
1Ki 2: 4 faithfully before me with all their **h**
3: 9 So give your servant a discerning **h**
3: 12 give you a wise and discerning **h**,
8: 48 turn back to you with all their **h**
9: 3 eyes and my **h** will always be there.
9: 4 me faithfully with integrity of **h**
10: 24 the wisdom God had put in his **h**.
11: 4 his wives turned his **h** after other
11: 4 his **h** was not fully devoted
14: 8 and followed me with all his **h**,
15: 14 Asa's **h** was fully committed
2Ki 22: 19 Because your **h** was responsive
23: 3 decrees with all his **h** and all his
1Ch 28: 9 for the LORD searches every **h**
2Ch 6: 38 turn back to you with all their **h**
7: 16 eyes and my **h** will always be there.
15: 12 ancestors, with all their **h** and soul.
15: 17 Asa's **h** was fully committed
17: 6 His **h** was devoted to the ways
22: 9 sought the LORD with all his **h**."
34: 31 decrees with all his **h** and all his
36: 13 hardened his **h** and would not turn
Ezr 1: 5 everyone whose **h** God had moved
Ne 4: 6 the people worked with all their **h**.
Job 19: 27 How my **h** yearns within me!
22: 22 and lay up his words in your **h**.
37: 1 "At this my **h** pounds and leaps
Ps 9: 1 to you, LORD, with all my **h**;
14: 1 says in his **h**, "There is no God."
16: 9 Therefore my **h** is glad and my
19: 14 this meditation of my **h** be pleasing
20: 4 he give you the desire of your **h**
24: 4 who has clean hands and a pure **h**,
26: 2 me, examine my **h** and my mind;
37: 4 will give you the desires of your **h**.
44: 21 since he knows the secrets of the **h**?
45: 1 My **h** is stirred by a noble theme as
51: 10 Create in me a pure **h**, O God,
51: 17 a broken and contrite **h** you, God,
53: 1 says in his **h**, "There is no God."
66: 18 If I had cherished sin in my **h**,
73: 1 Israel, to those who are pure in **h**.
73: 26 My flesh and my **h** may fail,
86: 11 give me an undivided **h**, that I may
90: 12 that we may gain a **h** of wisdom.
97: 11 and joy on the upright in **h**.
108: 1 My **h**, O God, is steadfast;
109: 22 and my **h** is wounded within me.
111: 1 LORD with all my **h** in the council
119: 2 and seek him with all their **h**—

Ps 119: 10 I seek you with all my **h**; do not let
119: 11 in my **h** that I might not sin against
119: 30 I have set my **h** on your laws.
119: 34 your law and obey it with all my **h**.
119: 36 Turn my **h** toward your statutes
119: 58 sought your face with all my **h**;
119: 69 I keep your precepts with all my **h**.
119:111 they are the joy of my **h**.
119:112 My **h** is set on keeping your
119:145 I call with all my **h**;
125: 4 to those who are upright in **h**.
138: 1 praise you, LORD, with all my **h**;
139: 23 Search me, God, and know my **h**;
Pr 2: 2 applying your **h** to understanding
3: 1 but keep my commands in your **h**,
3: 3 write them on the tablet of your **h**.
3: 5 Trust in the LORD with all your **h**
4: 4 hold of my words with all your **h**;
4: 21 sight, keep them within your **h**;
4: 23 guard your **h**, for everything you
6: 21 Bind them always on your **h**;
7: 3 write them on the tablet of your **h**.
10: 8 The wise in **h** accept commands,
13: 12 Hope deferred makes the **h** sick,
14: 13 Even in laughter the **h** may ache,
14: 30 A **h** at peace gives life to the body,
15: 13 A happy **h** makes the face cheerful,
15: 15 the cheerful **h** has a continual feast.
15: 28 The **h** of the righteous weighs its
15: 30 eyes brings joy to the **h**, and good
17: 22 A cheerful **h** is good medicine,
20: 9 can say, "I have kept my **h** pure;
22: 11 One who loves a pure **h** and who
22: 17 apply your **h** to what I teach,
22: 18 when you keep them in your **h**
23: 15 if your **h** is wise, then my **h** will be
23: 19 and set your **h** on the right path:
23: 26 give me your **h** and let your eyes
24: 17 stumble, do not let your **h** rejoice,
27: 19 the face, so one's life reflects the **h**.
Ecc 3: 11 also set eternity in the human **h**;
5: 2 your **h** to utter anything before God.
8: 5 the wise **h** will know the proper
11: 10 banish anxiety from your **h** and
SS 3: 1 I looked for the one my **h** loves;
4: 9 You have stolen my **h**, my sister,
5: 2 I slept but my **h** was awake. Listen!
5: 4 my **h** began to pound for him.
8: 6 Place me like a seal over your **h**,
Isa 6: 10 the **h** of this people calloused;
40: 11 and carries them close to his **h**;
51: 7 have taken my instruction to **h**:
57: 15 and to revive the **h** of the contrite.
66: 14 your **h** will rejoice and you will
Jer 3: 15 give you shepherds after my own **h**,
4: 14 wash the evil from your **h** and be
9: 26 of Israel is uncircumcised in **h**."
17: 9 The **h** is deceitful above all things
20: 9 his word is in my **h** like a fire, a fire
24: 7 I will give them a **h** to know me,
29: 13 when you seek me with all your **h**.
32: 39 I will give them singleness of **h**
32: 41 them in this land with all my **h**
51: 46 Do not lose **h** or be afraid
Eze 11: 19 I will give them an undivided **h**
11: 19 remove from them their **h** of stone
and give them a **h** of flesh.
18: 31 and get a new **h** and a new spirit.
36: 26 I will give you a new **h** and put
36: 26 remove from you your **h** of stone
and give you a **h** of flesh.
44: 7 foreigners uncircumcised in **h**
Joel 2: 12 "return to me with all your **h**,
2: 13 Rend your **h** and not your
Zep 3: 14 Be glad and rejoice with all your **h**,
Mt 5: 8 Blessed are the pure in **h**, for they
5: 28 adultery with her in his **h**.
6: 21 treasure is, there your **h** will be
11: 29 for I am gentle and humble in **h**,
12: 34 mouth speaks what the **h** is full of.
13: 15 For this people's **h** has become
15: 18 a person's mouth come from the **h**,
15: 19 out of the **h** come evil thoughts—
18: 35 your brother or sister from your **h**."
22: 37 the Lord your God with all your **h**
Mk 7: 21 out of a person's **h**, that evil
11: 23 and does not doubt in their **h**
12: 30 the Lord your God with all your **h**
12: 33 To love him with all your **h**, with
Lk 2: 19 and pondered them in her **h**.
2: 51 treasured all these things in her **h**.
6: 45 out of the good stored up in his **h**,
6: 45 mouth speaks what the **h** is full of.
8: 15 for those with a noble and good **h**,
10: 27 the Lord your God with all your **h**
12: 34 treasure is, there your **h** will be
Ac 1: 24 "Lord, you know everyone's **h**.
2: 37 they were cut to the **h** and said
4: 32 All the believers were one in **h**
8: 21 because your **h** is not right before
15: 8 who knows the **h**, showed that he
16: 14 The Lord opened her **h** to respond
28: 27 For this people's **h** has become
Ro 2: 29 is circumcision of the **h**,
6: 17 to obey from your **h** the pattern
10: 9 in your **h** that God raised him
10: 10 it is with your **h** that you believe
1Co 4: 5 will expose the motives of the **h**.
2Co 2: 4 anguish of **h** and with many tears,
4: 1 this ministry, we do not lose **h**.
4: 16 Therefore we do not lose **h**.
9: 7 you have decided in your **h** to give,
Eph 1: 18 eyes of your **h** may be enlightened
5: 19 music from your **h** to the Lord,
6: 5 and with sincerity of **h**, just as you
6: 6 doing the will of God from your **h**.
Php 1: 7 you, since I have you in my **h** and,
Col 2: 2 that they may be encouraged in **h**
3: 22 with sincerity of **h** and reverence
3: 23 you do, work at it with all your **h**,
1Ti 1: 5 which comes from a pure **h**
2Ti 2: 22 call on the Lord out of a pure **h**.
Phm : 12 who is my very **h**—back to you.
: 20 in the Lord; refresh my **h** in Christ.
Heb 4: 12 the thoughts and attitudes of the **h**.
1Pe 1: 22 one another deeply, from the **h**.

HEARTACHE* (HEART)
Pr 15: 13 cheerful, but **h** crushes the spirit.

HEARTLESS*
La 4: 3 have become **h** like ostriches

HEART'S* (HEART)
2Ch 1: 11 "Since this is your **h** desire and you
Ps 21: 2 You have granted him his **h** desire
Jer 15: 16 they were my joy and my **h** delight,
Eze 24: 25 delight of their eyes, their **h** desire,
Ro 10: 1 my **h** desire and prayer to God

HEARTS (HEART)
Lev 26: 41 their uncircumcised **h** are humbled
Dt 6: 6 give you today are to be on your **h**.
10: 16 Circumcise your **h**, therefore,
11: 18 Fix these words of mine in your **h**
30: 6 your God will circumcise your **h**
Jos 11: 20 himself who hardened their **h**
24: 23 you and yield your **h** to the LORD,
1Sa 7: 3 to the LORD with all your **h**,
10: 26 by valiant men whose **h** God had
2Sa 15: 6 so he stole the **h** of the people
1Ki 8: 39 do, since you know their **h** (for you
8: 61 may your **h** be fully committed
18: 37 you are turning their **h** back again."
1Ch 29: 18 and keep their **h** loyal to you.
2Ch 6: 30 do, since you know their **h** (for you
11: 16 Israel who set their **h** on seeking
29: 31 all whose **h** were willing brought
Ps 7: 9 God who probes minds and **h**.
33: 21 In him our **h** rejoice, for we trust
37: 31 The law of their God is in their **h**;
62: 8 pour out your **h** to him, for God is
95: 8 "Do not harden your **h** as you did
112: 7 their **h** are steadfast,
112: 8 Their **h** are secure, they will have
Pr 16: 23 The **h** of the wise make their
Isa 26: 8 and renown are the desire of our **h**.
29: 13 lips, but their **h** are far from me.
35: 4 say to those with fearful **h**,
63: 17 harden our **h** so we do not revere
65: 14 will sing out of the joy of their **h**,
Jer 4: 4 circumcise your **h**, you people
12: 2 on their lips but far from their **h**.
17: 1 on the tablets of their **h**
31: 33 their minds and write it on their **h**.
Mal 4: 6 He will turn the **h** of the parents
4: 6 **h** of the children to their parents;
Mt 15: 8 lips, but their **h** are far from me.
Mk 6: 52 their **h** were hardened.
7: 6 lips, but their **h** are far from me.
Lk 1: 17 to turn the **h** of the parents to their
16: 15 of others, but God knows your **h**.
24: 32 "Were not our **h** burning within us
Jn 5: 42 not have the love of God in your **h**.
14: 1 "Do not let your **h** be troubled.
14: 27 Do not let your **h** be troubled and
Ac 7: 51 Your **h** and ears are still
11: 23 true to the Lord with all their **h**.
15: 9 for he purified their **h** by faith.
28: 27 understand with their **h** and turn,
Ro 1: 21 and their foolish **h** were darkened.
2: 15 of the law are written on their **h**,
5: 5 into our **h** through the Holy Spirit,
8: 27 searches our **h** knows the mind
1Co 14: 25 the secrets of their **h** are laid bare.
2Co 1: 22 put his Spirit in our **h** as a deposit,
3: 2 written on our **h**, known and read
3: 3 of stone but on tablets of human **h**.
4: 6 shine in our **h** to give us the light
6: 11 and opened wide our **h** to you.
6: 13 open wide your **h** also.
7: 2 Make room for us in your **h**.
Gal 4: 6 the Spirit of his Son into our **h**,
Eph 3: 17 may dwell in your **h** through faith.
Php 4: 7 will guard your **h** and your minds
Col 3: 1 Christ, set your **h** on things above,
3: 15 the peace of Christ rule in your **h**,
3: 16 to God with gratitude in your **h**.
1Th 2: 4 people but God, who tests our **h**.
3: 13 May he strengthen your **h** so
2Th 2: 17 encourage your **h** and strengthen
Phm : 7 have refreshed the **h** of the Lord's
Heb 3: 8 do not harden your **h** as you did
8: 10 minds and write them on their **h**.
10: 16 I will put my laws in their **h**, and I
10: 22 having our **h** sprinkled to cleanse
Jas 4: 8 you sinners, and purify your **h**,
2Pe 1: 19 the morning star rises in your **h**.
1Jn 3: 20 If our **h** condemn us, we know that
God is greater than our **h**,

HEAT
2Pe 3: 12 and the elements will melt in the **h**.

HEAVEN (HEAVENLY HEAVENS HEAVENWARD)
Ge 14: 19 Most High, Creator of **h** and earth.
28: 12 with its top reaching to **h**,
Ex 16: 4 "I will rain down bread from **h**
20: 22 that I have spoken to you from **h**:
Dt 26: 15 Look down from **h**, your holy
30: 12 It is not up in **h**, so that you have
1Ki 8: 27 even the highest **h**, cannot contain
8: 30 Hear from **h**, your dwelling place,
22: 19 multitudes of **h** standing around
2Ki 2: 1 take Elijah up to **h** in a whirlwind,
19: 15 You have made **h** and earth.
2Ch 7: 14 then I will hear from **h**, and I will
Isa 14: 12 How you have fallen from **h**,
66: 1 "**H** is my throne, and the earth is
Da 7: 13 man, coming with the clouds of **h**.
Mt 3: 2 the kingdom of **h** has come near."
3: 16 At that moment **h** was opened,
4: 17 the kingdom of **h** has come near."
5: 12 because great is your reward in **h**,
5: 19 be called least in the kingdom of **h**,
5: 19 called great in the kingdom of **h**.
6: 9 "'Our Father in **h**, hallowed be
6: 10 will be done, on earth as it is in **h**.
6: 20 up for yourselves treasures in **h**,
7: 21 the will of my Father who is in **h**.
16: 19 you the keys of the kingdom of **h**;
18: 3 will never enter the kingdom of **h**.
18: 18 bind on earth will be bound in **h**,
18: 18 loose on earth will be loosed in **h**.
19: 14 the kingdom of **h** belongs to such
19: 21 and you will have treasure in **h**.
19: 23 is rich to enter the kingdom of **h**.
23: 13 the kingdom of **h** in people's faces.
24: 35 **H** and earth will pass away, but my

Mt 24: 30 the sign of the Son of Man in **h**.
26: 64 and coming on the clouds of **h**."
28: 18 "All authority in **h** and on earth has
Mk 1: 10 he saw **h** being torn open
10: 21 and you will have treasure in **h**.
13: 31 **H** and earth will pass away, but my
14: 62 and coming on the clouds of **h**."
16: 19 *he was taken up into **h***
Lk 3: 21 as he was praying, **h** was opened
10: 18 Satan fall like lightning from **h**.
10: 20 that your names are written in **h**."
12: 33 a treasure in **h** that will never fail,
15: 7 **h** over one sinner who repents
18: 22 and you will have treasure in **h**.
21: 33 **H** and earth will pass away, but my
24: 51 left them and was taken up into **h**.
Jn 3: 13 gone into **h** except the one who came from **h**—
6: 38 I have come down from **h** not to
12: 28 Then a voice came from **h**, "I have
Ac 1: 11 has been taken from you into **h**,
7: 49 "'**H** is my throne, and the earth is
7: 55 looked up to **h** and saw the glory
9: 3 a light from **h** flashed around him.
26: 19 disobedient to the vision from **h**.
Ro 10: 6 heart, 'Who will ascend into **h**?'"
1Co 15: 47 the earth; the second man is of **h**.
2Co 5: 1 an eternal house in **h**, not built
12: 2 ago was caught up to the third **h**.
Eph 1: 10 to bring unity to all things in **h**
Php 2: 10 in **h** and on earth and under
3: 20 But our citizenship is in **h**.
Col 1: 16 things in **h** and on earth,
4: 1 that you also have a Master in **h**.
1Th 1: 10 and to wait for his Son from **h**,
4: 16 himself will come down from **h**,
Heb 1: 3 the right hand of the Majesty in **h**.
4: 14 priest who has ascended into **h**,
8: 5 a copy and shadow of what is in **h**.
9: 24 he entered **h** itself, now to appear
12: 23 whose names are written in **h**.
1Pe 1: 4 inheritance is kept in **h** for you,
3: 22 who has gone into **h** and is at God's
2Pe 3: 13 we are looking forward to a new **h**
Rev 5: 13 I heard every creature in **h**
11: 19 God's temple in **h** was opened,
12: 7 Then war broke out in **h**.
15: 5 I looked, and I saw in **h** the temple
19: 1 of a great multitude in **h** shouting:
19: 11 I saw **h** standing open and there
21: 1 I saw "a new **h** and a new earth,"
21: 10 coming down out of **h** from God.

HEAVENLY (HEAVEN)
2Co 5: 2 instead with our **h** dwelling,
Eph 1: 3 who has blessed us in the **h** realms
1: 20 at his right hand in the **h** realms,
2Ti 4: 18 bring me safely to his **h** kingdom.
Heb 12: 22 of the living God, the **h** Jerusalem.

HEAVENS (HEAVEN)
Ge 1: 1 In the beginning God created the **h**
11: 4 with a tower that reaches to the **h**,
Dt 33: 26 who rides across the **h** to help you
1Ki 8: 27 The **h**, even the highest heaven,
2Ch 2: 6 since the **h**, even the highest **h**,
Ezr 9: 6 and our guilt has reached to the **h**.
Ne 9: 6 You made the **h**, even the highest **h**,
Job 11: 8 They are higher than the **h** above—
38: 33 Do you know the laws of the **h**?
Ps 8: 3 When I consider your **h**, the work
19: 1 The **h** declare the glory of God;
33: 6 of the LORD the **h** were made,
57: 5 Be exalted, O God, above the **h**;
71: 19 righteousness, God, reaches to the **h**,
102: 25 the **h** are the work of your hands.
103: 11 high as the **h** are above the earth,
108: 4 is your love, higher than the **h**;
115: 16 The highest **h** belong
119: 89 it stands firm in the **h**.
135: 6 him, in the **h** and on the earth,
139: 8 If I go up to the **h**, you are there;
148: 1 Praise the LORD from the **h**;
Isa 24: 4 the **h** languish with the earth.
40: 26 Lift up your eyes and look to the **h**:
45: 8 "You **h** above, rain down my
51: 6 the **h** will vanish like smoke,
Isa 55: 9 "As the **h** are higher than the earth,
65: 17 will create new **h** and a new earth.
Jer 31: 37 if the **h** above can be measured
32: 17 you have made the **h** and the earth
Eze 1: 1 **h** were opened and I saw visions
Da 12: 3 shine like the brightness of the **h**,
Joel 2: 30 I will show wonders in the **h**
Mt 24: 31 from one end of the **h** to the other.
Mk 13: 27 of the earth to the ends of the **h**.
Eph 4: 10 ascended higher than all the **h**,
Heb 7: 26 from sinners, exalted above the **h**.
2Pe 3: 5 God's word the **h** came into being
3: 10 The **h** will disappear with a roar;
Rev 20: 11 and the **h** fled from his presence,

HEAVENWARD* (HEAVEN)
Php 3: 14 God has called me **h** in Christ

HEAVIER (HEAVY)
Pr 27: 3 a fool's provocation is **h** than both.

HEAVY (HEAVIER)
1Ki 12: 4 "Your father put a **h** yoke on us,
Ecc 1: 13 What a **h** burden God has laid
Isa 47: 6 on the aged you laid a very **h** yoke.
Mt 23: 4 They tie up **h**, cumbersome loads

HEBREW (HEBREWS)
Ge 14: 13 and reported this to Abram the **H**.
2Ki 18: 26 speak to us in **H** in the hearing
Php 3: 5 tribe of Benjamin, a **H** of Hebrews;

HEBREWS (HEBREW)
Ex 9: 1 the LORD, the God of the **H**, says:
2Co 11: 22 Are they **H**? So am I.

HEBRON
Ge 13: 18 near the great trees of Mamre at **H**,
23: 2 (that is, **H**) in the land of Canaan,
Jos 14: 13 and gave him **H** as his inheritance.
20: 7 is, **H**) in the hill country of Judah.
21: 13 Aaron the priest they gave **H**
2Sa 2: 11 in **H** over Judah was seven years

HEDGE
Job 1: 10 "Have you not put a **h** around him

HEED (HEEDS)
Ecc 7: 5 It is better to **h** the rebuke of a wise

HEEDS (HEED)
Pr 10: 17 Whoever **h** discipline shows
13: 1 A wise son **h** his father's
13: 18 whoever **h** correction is honored.
15: 5 but whoever **h** correction shows
15: 31 Whoever **h** life-giving correction
15: 32 but the one who **h** correction gains

HEEL
Ge 3: 15 head, and you will strike his **h**."
25: 26 with his hand grasping Esau's **h**;

HEIGHT (HIGH)
1Sa 17: 4 His **h** was six cubits and a span.

HEIR (INHERIT)
Gal 4: 7 child, God has made you also an **h**.
Heb 1: 2 whom he appointed **h** of all things,

HEIRS (INHERIT)
Ro 8: 17 then we are **h**—**h** of God
Gal 3: 29 and **h** according to the promise.
Eph 3: 6 gospel the Gentiles are **h** together
1Pe 3: 7 as **h** with you of the gracious gift

HELD (HOLD)
Ex 17: 11 As long as Moses **h** up his hands,
Dt 4: 4 you who **h** fast to the LORD your
2Ki 18: 6 He **h** fast to the LORD and did not
SS 3: 4 I **h** him and would not let him go
Isa 65: 2 All day long I have **h** out my hands
Ro 10: 21 says, "All day long I have **h** out my
Col 2: 19 and **h** together by its ligaments

HELL*
Mt 5: 22 will be in danger of the fire of **h**.
5: 29 whole body to be thrown into **h**.
5: 30 for your whole body to go into **h**.
10: 28 destroy both soul and body in **h**.
18: 9 and be thrown into the fire of **h**.
23: 15 as much a child of **h** as you are.
23: 33 you escape being condemned to **h**?
Mk 9: 43 than with two hands to go into **h**,
9: 45 two feet and be thrown into **h**.
9: 47 two eyes and be thrown into **h**,
Lk 12: 5 has authority to throw you into **h**.
Jas 3: 6 on fire, and is itself set on fire by **h**.
2Pe 2: 4 but sent them to **h**, putting them

HELMET
Isa 59: 17 and the **h** of salvation on his head;
Eph 6: 17 Take the **h** of salvation
1Th 5: 8 and the hope of salvation as a **h**.

HELP (HELPED HELPER HELPFUL HELPING HELPLESS HELPS)
Ex 23: 5 be sure you **h** them with it.
Lev 25: 35 **h** them as you would a foreigner
Dt 33: 26 rides across the heavens to **h** you
2Sa 22: 36 your **h** has made me great.
2Ch 16: 12 in his illness he did not seek **h**
Ps 18: 6 I cried to my God for **h**.
30: 2 called to you for **h**, and you healed
33: 20 he is our **h** and our shield.
40: 10 faithfulness and your saving **h**.
40: 16 long for your saving **h** always say,
46: 1 an ever-present **h** in trouble.
70: 4 long for your saving **h** always say,
72: 12 the afflicted who have no one to **h**.
79: 9 **H** us, God our Savior, for the glory
108: 12 enemy, for human **h** is worthless.
115: 9 he is their **h** and shield.
121: 1 where does my **h** come from?
Ecc 4: 10 falls and has no one to **h** them up.
Isa 41: 10 I will strengthen you and **h** you;
Jnh 2: 2 the realm of the dead I called for **h**,
Mk 9: 24 **h** me overcome my unbelief!"
Lk 11: 46 will not lift one finger to **h** them.
Ac 16: 9 over to Macedonia and **h** us."
18: 27 he was a great **h** to those who
20: 35 of hard work we must **h** the weak,
2Co 9: 2 For I know your eagerness to **h**,
1Ti 5: 16 the church can **h** those widows

HELPED (HELP)
1Sa 7: 12 "Thus far the LORD has **h** us."
Ac 26: 22 But God has **h** me to this very day;

HELPER (HELP)
Ge 2: 18 I will make a **h** suitable for him."
Ps 10: 14 you are the **h** of the fatherless.
Heb 13: 6 confidence, "The Lord is my **h**;

HELPFUL (HELP)
Eph 4: 29 only what is **h** for building others

HELPING (HELP)
Ac 9: 36 always doing good and **h** the poor.
1Co 12: 28 gifts of healing, of **h**, of guidance,
1Ti 5: 10 **h** those in trouble and devoting

HELPLESS (HELP)
Ps 10: 12 hand, O God. Do not forget the **h**.
Mt 9: 36 because they were harassed and **h**,

HELPS (HELP)
Ro 8: 26 the Spirit **h** us in our weakness.

HEN*
Zec 6: 14 **H** son of Zephaniah as a memorial
Mt 23: 37 as a **h** gathers her chicks under her
Lk 13: 34 as a **h** gathers her chicks under her

HERALD
1Ti 2: 7 this purpose I was appointed a **h**
2Ti 1: 11 of this gospel I was appointed a **h**

HERBS
Ex 12: 8 along with bitter **h**, and bread

HERITAGE (INHERIT)
Ps 61: 5 you have given me the **h** of those
119:111 Your statutes are my **h** forever;
127: 3 Children are a **h** from the LORD,

HERO
2Sa 23: 1 of Jacob, the **h** of Israel's songs:

HEROD

1. King of Judea who tried to kill Jesus (Mt 2; Lk 1:5).

2. Son of 1. Tetrarch of Galilee who arrested and beheaded John the Baptist (Mt 14:1–12; Mk 6:14–29; Lk 3:1, 19–20; 9:7–9); tried Jesus (Lk 23:6–15).

3. Grandson of 1. King of Judea who killed James (Ac 12:2); arrested Peter (Ac 12:3–19). Death (Ac 12:19–23).

HERODIAS

Wife of Herod the tetrarch who persuaded

her daughter to ask for John the Baptist's head (Mt 14:1–12; Mk 6:14–29).

HEWN*
Isa 51: 1 the quarry from which you were **h**;

HEZEKIAH
King of Judah. Restored the temple and worship (2Ch 29–31). Sought the Lord for help against Assyria (2Ki 18–19; 2Ch 32:1–23; Isa 36–37). Illness healed (2Ki 20:1–11; 2Ch 32:24–26; Isa 38). Judged for showing Babylonians his treasures (2Ki 20:12–21; 2Ch 32:31; Isa 39).

HID (HIDE)
Ge 3: 8 they **h** from the LORD God among
Ex 2: 2 child, she **h** him for three months.
Jos 6: 17 because she **h** the spies we sent.
1Ki 18: 13 I **h** a hundred of the LORD's
2Ch 22: 11 she **h** the child from Athaliah so
Isa 54: 8 In a surge of anger I **h** my face
Mt 13: 44 a man found it, he **h** it again,
25: 25 out and **h** your gold in the ground.
Heb 11: 23 By faith Moses' parents **h** him for

HIDDEN (HIDE)
1Sa 10: 22 "Yes, he has **h** himself among
Job 28: 11 rivers and bring **h** things to light.
Ps 19: 12 Forgive my **h** faults.
119: 11 I have **h** your word in my heart
Pr 2: 4 and search for it as for **h** treasure,
27: 5 Better is open rebuke than **h** love.
Isa 59: 2 your sins have **h** his face from you,
Da 2: 22 He reveals deep and **h** things;
Mt 5: 14 A town built on a hill cannot be **h**.
10: 26 or **h** that will not be made known.
11: 25 because you have **h** these things
13: 35 utter things **h** since the creation
13: 44 heaven is like treasure **h** in a field.
Mk 4: 22 For whatever is **h** is meant to be
Ro 16: 25 of the mystery **h** for long ages past,
1Co 2: 7 a mystery that has been **h**
Eph 3: 9 for ages past was kept **h** in God,
Col 1: 26 that has been kept **h** for ages
2: 3 in whom are **h** all the treasures
3: 3 and your life is now **h** with Christ

HIDE (HID HIDDEN HIDING)
Dt 31: 17 I will **h** my face from them,
Ps 17: 8 **h** me in the shadow of your wings
27: 5 he will **h** me in the shelter of his
143: 9 LORD, for I **h** myself in you.
Isa 53: 3 whom people **h** their faces he was

HIDING (HIDE)
Ps 32: 7 You are my **h** place;
Pr 28: 12 rise to power, people go into **h**.

HIGH (HEIGHT)
Ge 14: 18 He was priest of God Most **H**,
14: 22 God Most **H**, Creator of heaven
Ps 21: 7 the Most **H** he will not be shaken.
82: 6 you are all sons of the Most **H**.'
Isa 14: 14 will make myself like the Most **H**."
Da 4: 17 the Most **H** is sovereign over all
Mk 5: 7 me, Jesus, Son of the Most **H** God?
Heb 7: 1 Salem and priest of God Most **H**.

HIGHWAY
Isa 40: 3 in the desert a **h** for our God.

HILL (HILLS)
Isa 40: 4 every mountain and **h** made low;
Mt 5: 14 town built on a **h** cannot be hidden
Lk 3: 5 every mountain and **h** made low.

HILLS (HILL)
1Ki 20: 23 him, "Their gods are gods of the **h**.
Ps 50: 10 and the cattle on a thousand **h**.
Hos 10: 8 and to the **h**, "Fall on us!"
Lk 23: 30 and to the **h**, "Cover us!'"
Rev 17: 9 The seven heads are seven **h**

HINDER (HINDERED HINDERS)
1Sa 14: 6 Nothing can **h** the LORD
Mt 19: 14 do not **h** them, for the kingdom
1Co 9: 12 anything rather than **h** the gospel
1Pe 3: 7 so that nothing will **h** your prayers.

HINDERED (HINDER)
Lk 11: 52 and you have **h** those who were

HINDERS* (HINDER)
Heb 12: 1 let us throw off everything that **h**

HINT*
Eph 5: 3 you there must not be even a **h**

HIP
Ge 32: 32 of Jacob's **h** was touched near

HIRAM
King of Tyre; helped David build his palace (2Sa 5:11–12; 1Ch 14:1); helped Solomon build the temple (1Ki 5; 2Ch 2) and his navy (1Ki 9:10–27; 2Ch 8).

HIRED
Lk 15: 15 and **h** himself out to a citizen
Jn 10: 12 The **h** hand is not the shepherd

HOARDED* (HOARDS)
Ecc 5: 13 wealth **h** to the harm of its owners,
Isa 23: 18 they will not be stored up or **h**.
Jas 5: 3 You have **h** wealth in the last days.

HOARDS* (HOARDED)
Pr 11: 26 People curse the one who **h** grain,

HOLD (HELD HOLDING)
Ex 20: 7 LORD will not **h** anyone guiltless
Lev 19: 13 "'Do not **h** back the wages
Dt 5: 11 LORD will not **h** anyone guiltless
11: 22 to him and to **h** fast to him—
13: 4 serve him and **h** fast to him.
30: 20 to his voice, and **h** fast to him.
Jos 22: 5 to **h** fast to him and to serve him
2Ki 4: 16 "you will **h** a son in your arms."
Ps 18: 16 from on high and took **h** of me;
73: 23 you **h** me by my right hand.
Pr 4: 4 "Take **h** of my words with all your
10: 19 but the prudent **h** their tongues.
17: 28 discerning if they **h** their tongues.
Isa 41: 13 the LORD your God who takes **h**
54: 2 tent curtains wide, do not **h** back;
Eze 3: 18 I will **h** you accountable for their
3: 20 I will **h** you accountable for their
33: 6 I will **h** the watchman accountable
Zec 8: 23 nations will take firm **h** of one Jew
Mk 11: 25 if you **h** anything against anyone,
Jn 20: 17 Jesus said, "Do not **h** on to me,
Php 2: 16 as you **h** firmly to the word of life.
3: 12 I press on to take **h** of that
Col 1: 17 and in him all things **h** together.
1Th 5: 21 test them all; **h** on to what is good,
1Ti 6: 12 Take **h** of the eternal life
Heb 10: 23 Let us **h** unswervingly to the hope

HOLDING (HOLD)
Jer 15: 6 I am tired of **h** back.

HOLES
Hag 1: 6 to put them in a purse with **h** in it."

HOLINESS* (HOLY)
Ex 15: 11 majestic in **h**, awesome in glory,
Dt 32: 51 you did not uphold my **h** among
1Ch 16: 29 the LORD in the splendor of his **h**.
2Ch 20: 21 the splendor of his **h** as they went
Ps 29: 2 the LORD in the splendor of his **h**.
89: 35 for all, I have sworn by my **h**—
93: 5 **h** adorns your house for endless
96: 9 the LORD in the splendor of his **h**;
Isa 29: 23 they will acknowledge the **h**
35: 8 it will be called the Way of **H**;
Eze 36: 23 I will show the **h** of my great name,
38: 23 I will show my greatness and my **h**,
Am 4: 2 LORD has sworn by his **h**:
Lk 1: 75 in **h** and righteousness before him
Ro 1: 4 Spirit of **h** was appointed the Son
6: 19 to righteousness leading to **h**.
6: 22 the benefit you reap leads to **h**,
1Co 1: 30 righteousness, **h** and redemption.
2Co 7: 1 perfecting **h** out of reverence
Eph 4: 24 God in true righteousness and **h**.
1Ti 2: 2 quiet lives in all godliness and **h**.
2: 15 in faith, love and **h** with propriety.
Heb 12: 10 in order that we may share in his **h**.
12: 14 without **h** no one will see the Lord.

HOLY (HALLOWED HOLINESS)
Ge 2: 3 the seventh day and made it **h**,
Ex 3: 5 you are standing is **h** ground."
16: 23 rest, a **h** sabbath to the LORD.
19: 6 kingdom of priests and a **h** nation.'
20: 8 the Sabbath day by keeping it **h**.
26: 33 curtain will separate the **H** Place from the Most **H** Place.
28: 36 on a seal: H TO THE LORD.
29: 37 Then the altar will be most **h**, and whatever touches it will be **h**.
30: 10 It is most **h** to the LORD."
30: 29 whatever touches them will be **h**.
31: 13 I am the LORD, who makes you **h**.
40: 9 all its furnishings, and it will be **h**.
Lev 10: 3 approach me I will be proved **h**;
10: 10 you can distinguish between the **h**
11: 44 and be **h**, because I am **h**.
11: 45 therefore be **h**, because I am **h**.
19: 2 'Be **h** because I, the LORD your God, am **h**.
19: 8 they have desecrated what is **h**
19: 24 fourth year all its fruit will be **h**,
20: 3 and profaned my **h** name.
20: 7 yourselves and be **h**, because I am
20: 8 I am the LORD, who makes you **h**.
20: 26 You are to be **h** to me because I,
21: 6 They must be **h** to their God
21: 8 Consider them **h**, because I the LORD am **h**—
22: 9 am the LORD, who makes them **h**.
22: 32 Do not profane my **h** name, for I
22: 32 I am the LORD, who made you **h**
25: 12 a jubilee and is to be **h** for you;
27: 9 given to the LORD becomes **h**.
Nu 4: 15 they must not touch the **h** things
6: 5 They must be **h** until the period
20: 12 to honor me as **h** in the sight
20: 13 he was proved **h** among them.
Dt 5: 12 the Sabbath day by keeping it **h**,
23: 14 Your camp must be **h**, so that he
26: 15 heaven, your **h** dwelling place,
33: 2 myriads of **h** ones from the south,
Jos 5: 15 place where you are standing is **h**."
24: 19 He is a **h** God; he is a jealous God.
1Sa 2: 2 "There is no one **h** like the LORD;
6: 20 of the LORD, this **h** God?
21: 5 The men's bodies are **h** even
2Ki 4: 9 often comes our way is a **h** man
1Ch 16: 10 Glory in his **h** name; let the hearts
16: 35 may give thanks to your **h** name,
29: 3 I have provided for this **h** temple:
2Ch 30: 27 heaven, his **h** dwelling place.
Ezr 9: 2 have mingled the **h** race
Ne 11: 1 to live in Jerusalem, the **h** city,
Job 6: 10 denied the words of the **H** One.
Ps 2: 6 my king on Zion, my **h** mountain."
11: 4 The LORD is in his **h** temple;
16: 3 the **h** people who are in the land,
22: 3 you are enthroned as the **H** One;
24: 3 Who may stand in his **h** place?
30: 4 praise his **h** name.
77: 13 Your ways, God, are **h**. What god is
78: 54 them to the border of his **h** land,
99: 3 great and awesome name—he is **h**.
99: 5 worship at his footstool; he is **h**.
99: 9 for the LORD our God is **h**.
105: 3 Glory in his **h** name; let the hearts
111: 9 **h** and awesome is his name.
Pr 9: 10 of the **H** One is understanding.
Isa 5: 16 the **h** God will be proved **h** by his
6: 3 "**H**, **h**, **h** is the LORD Almighty;
8: 13 is the one you are to regard as **h**,
29: 23 hands, they will keep my name **h**;
40: 25 who is my equal?" says the **H** One.
43: 3 your God, the **H** One of Israel,
54: 5 the **H** One of Israel is your
57: 15 "I live in a high and **h** place,
58: 13 and the LORD's **h** day honorable,
Jer 17: 22 but keep the Sabbath day **h**, as I
Eze 20: 41 I will be proved **h** through you
22: 26 to my law and profane my **h** things;
28: 22 and within you am proved to be **h**.
28: 25 I will be proved **h** through them
36: 20 nations they profaned my **h** name,
38: 16 I am proved **h** through you before
44: 23 the difference between the **h**
Da 9: 24 and to anoint the Most **H** Place.
Hab 2: 20 The LORD is in his **h** temple;
Zec 14: 5 come, and all the **h** ones with him.
14: 20 On that day H TO THE LORD

Mt 24: 15 in the **h** place 'the abomination
Mk 1: 24 who you are—the **H** One of God!"
Lk 1: 35 "The **H** Spirit will come on you,
1: 35 So the **h** one to be born will be
1: 49 great things for me—**h** is his name.
4: 34 who you are—the **H** One of God!"
Jn 6: 69 that you are the **H** One of God."
Ac 2: 27 will not let your **h** one see decay.
13: 35 will not let your **h** one see decay.'
Ro 1: 2 his prophets in the **H** Scriptures
7: 12 law is **h**, and the commandment
11: 16 is **h**, then the whole batch is **h**;
12: 1 sacrifice, **h** and pleasing to God—
1Co 1: 2 Jesus and called to be his **h** people,
7: 14 be unclean, but as it is, they are **h**.
Eph 1: 4 the creation of the world to be **h**
2: 21 to become a **h** temple in the Lord.
3: 5 by the Spirit to God's **h** apostles
5: 26 to make her **h**, cleansing her
Col 1: 22 death to present you **h** in his sight,
1Th 2: 10 of how **h**, righteous and blameless
3: 13 Jesus comes with all his **h** ones.
4: 7 us to be impure, but to live a **h** life.
2Th 1: 10 to be glorified in his **h** people
1Ti 2: 8 lifting up **h** hands without anger
2Ti 1: 9 saved us and called us to a **h** life—
2: 21 made **h**, useful to the Master
3: 15 you have known the **H** Scriptures,
Titus 1: 8 upright, **h** and disciplined.
Heb 2: 11 Both the one who makes people **h**
7: 26 one who is **h**, blameless, pure,
10: 10 we have been made **h** through
10: 14 those who are being made **h**.
10: 19 the Most **H** Place by the blood
12: 14 peace with everyone and to be **h**;
13: 12 make the people **h** through his
1Pe 1: 15 as he who called you is **h**, so be **h** in all you do;
1: 16 "Be **h**, because I am **h**."
2: 5 house to be a **h** priesthood,
2: 9 a royal priesthood, a **h** nation,
3: 5 this is the way the **h** women
2Pe 3: 11 You ought to live **h** and godly lives
Jude : 14 upon thousands of his **h** ones
Rev 3: 7 are the words of him who is **h**
4: 8 "'**H**, **h**, **h** is the Lord God
15: 4 For you alone are **h**. All nations
20: 6 **h** are those who share in the first
22: 11 let the **h** person continue to be **h**."

HOME (HOMES)
Dt 6: 7 Talk about them when you sit at **h**
11: 19 about them when you sit at **h**
20: 5 Let him go **h**, or he may die in
24: 5 one year he is to be free to stay at **h**
Ru 1: 11 said, "Return **h**, my daughters.
2Sa 7: 10 that they can have a **h** of their own
1Ch 16: 43 David returned **h** to bless his
Ps 84: 3 Even the sparrow has found a **h**,
113: 9 woman in her **h** as a happy mother
Pr 3: 33 he blesses the **h** of the righteous.
27: 8 its nest is anyone who flees from **h**.
Ecc 12: 5 people go to their eternal **h**
Eze 36: 8 Israel, for they will soon come **h**.
Mt 1: 24 him and took Mary **h** as his wife.
Mk 10: 29 "no one who has left **h** or brothers
Lk 10: 38 named Martha opened her **h**
Jn 14: 23 them and make our **h** with them.
19: 27 on, this disciple took her into his **h**.
Ac 16: 15 baptized, she invited us to her **h**.
Titus 2: 5 pure, to be busy at **h**, to be kind,

HOMELESS*
1Co 4: 11 we are brutally treated, we are **h**.

HOMES (HOME)
Ne 4: 14 daughters, your wives and your **h**."
Isa 32: 18 in secure **h**, in undisturbed places
Mic 2: 2 They defraud people of their **h**,
Mk 10: 30 **h**, brothers, sisters, mothers,
1Ti 5: 14 to manage their **h** and to give

HOMETOWN
Mt 13: 54 to his **h**, he began teaching
Lk 4: 24 "no prophet is accepted in his **h**.

HOMOSEXUALITY*
1Ti 1: 10 for those practicing **h**, for slave

HONEST (HONESTY)
Lev 19: 36 Use **h** scales and **h** weights, an **h** ephah and an **h** hin.
Dt 25: 15 must have accurate and **h** weights
2Ki 22: 7 to them, because they are **h** in their
Job 31: 6 let God weigh me in **h** scales and
Pr 12: 17 An **h** witness tells the truth,
14: 5 An **h** witness does not deceive,
17: 26 to flog **h** officials is not right.
22: 21 teaching you to be **h** and to speak

HONESTY (HONEST)
2Ki 12: 15 they acted with complete **h**.

HONEY (HONEYCOMB)
Ex 3: 8 a land flowing with milk and **h**—
Jdg 14: 8 saw a swarm of bees and some **h**.
1Sa 14: 26 woods, they saw the **h** oozing out;
Ps 19: 10 they are sweeter than **h**, than **h**
119:103 taste, sweeter than **h** to my mouth!
Pr 24: 14 also that wisdom is like **h** for you:
25: 16 If you find **h**, eat just enough—
SS 4: 11 milk and **h** are under your tongue.
Isa 7: 15 **h** when he knows enough to reject
Eze 3: 3 it tasted as sweet as **h** in my mouth.
Mt 3: 4 His food was locusts and wild **h**.
Rev 10: 9 mouth it will be as sweet as **h**.'"

HONEYCOMB (HONEY)
Ps 19: 10 honey, than honey from the **h**.
SS 4: 11 Your lips drop sweetness as the **h**,
5: 1 I have eaten my **h** and my honey;

HONOR (HONORABLE HONORABLY HONORED HONORS)
Ex 20: 12 "**H** your father and your mother,
Nu 20: 12 in me enough to **h** me as holy
25: 13 he was zealous for the **h** of his God
Dt 5: 16 "**H** your father and your mother,
Jdg 4: 9 are taking, the **h** will not be yours,
1Sa 2: 8 and has them inherit a throne of **h**.
2: 30 Those who **h** me I will **h**, but those
1Ch 29: 12 Wealth and **h** come from you;
2Ch 1: 11 possessions or **h**, nor for the death
18: 1 had great wealth and **h**,
Ezr 10: 11 Now **h** the LORD, the God of your
Est 6: 6 the man the king delights to **h**?"
Ps 8: 5 crowned them with glory and **h**.
45: 11 **h** him, for he is your lord.
84: 11 the LORD bestows favor and **h**;
Pr 3: 9 **H** the LORD with your wealth,
3: 35 The wise inherit **h**, but fools get
11: 16 A kindhearted woman gains **h**,
15: 33 and humility comes before **h**.
18: 12 but humility comes before **h**.
20: 3 It is to one's **h** to avoid strife,
31: 31 **H** her for all that her hands have
Isa 29: 13 mouth and **h** me with their lips,
Jer 33: 9 **h** before all nations on earth
Mt 13: 57 "A prophet is not without **h** except
15: 4 '**H** your father and mother'
15: 8 "'These people **h** me with their
19: 19 **h** your father and mother,' and
23: 6 they love the place of **h** at banquets
Mk 6: 4 "A prophet is not without **h** except
Lk 14: 8 do not take the place of **h**,
Jn 5: 23 all may **h** the Son just as they **h**
12: 26 My Father will **h** the one who
Ro 12: 10 **H** one another above yourselves.
1Co 6: 20 Therefore **h** God with your bodies.
Eph 6: 2 "**H** your father and mother"—
1Ti 5: 17 church well are worthy of double **h**,
Heb 2: 7 crowned them with glory and **h**
Rev 4: 9 **h** and thanks to him who sits

HONORABLE (HONOR)
1Th 4: 4 body in a way that is holy and **h**,

HONORABLY (HONOR)
Heb 13: 18 and desire to live **h** in every way.

HONORED (HONOR)
Ps 12: 8 what is vile is **h** by the human race.
Pr 13: 18 but whoever heeds correction is **h**.
Da 4: 34 I **h** and glorified him who lives
1Co 12: 26 if one part is **h**, every part rejoices
Heb 13: 4 Marriage should be **h** by all,

HONORS (HONOR)
Ps 15: 4 but **h** those who fear the LORD;
Pr 14: 31 is kind to the needy **h** God.
3Jn : 6 their way in a manner that **h** God.

HOOF
Ex 10: 26 not a **h** is to be left behind.

HOOKS
Isa 2: 4 and their spears into pruning **h**.
Joel 3: 10 and your pruning **h** into spears.
Mic 4: 3 and their spears into pruning **h**.

HOPE (HOPES)
Job 13: 15 he slay me, yet will I **h** in him;
Ps 33: 17 A horse is a vain **h** for deliverance;
33: 18 on those whose **h** is in his unfailing
42: 5 Put your **h** in God, for I will yet
62: 5 rest in God; my **h** comes from him.
119: 74 for I have put my **h** in your word.
130: 5 waits, and in his word I put my **h**.
130: 7 Israel, put your **h** in the LORD,
146: 5 whose **h** is in the LORD their God.
147: 11 put their **h** in his unfailing love.
Pr 13: 12 **H** deferred makes the heart sick,
23: 18 There is surely a future **h** for you,
23: 18 and your **h** will not be cut off.
Isa 40: 31 but those who **h** in the LORD will
Jer 29: 11 plans to give you **h** and a future.
La 3: 21 call to mind and therefore I have **h**:
Zec 9: 12 to your fortress, you prisoners of **h**;
Ro 5: 4 and character, **h**.
8: 20 of the one who subjected it, in **h**
8: 24 But **h** that is seen is no **h** at all.
8: 25 if we **h** for what we do not yet have,
12: 12 Be joyful in **h**, patient in affliction,
15: 4 they provide we might have **h**.
15: 13 May the God of **h** fill you with all
1Co 13: 13 three remain: faith, **h** and love.
15: 19 for this life we have **h** in Christ,
Eph 2: 12 without **h** and without God
Col 1: 27 is Christ in you, the **h** of glory.
1Th 1: 3 your endurance inspired by **h** in
5: 8 and the **h** of salvation as a helmet.
1Ti 4: 10 because we have put our **h**
6: 17 nor to put their **h** in wealth,
Titus 1: 2 in the **h** of eternal life, which God,
2: 13 while we wait for the blessed **h**—
Heb 6: 19 We have this **h** as an anchor
10: 23 unswervingly to the **h** we profess,
11: 1 faith is confidence in what we **h**
1Jn 3: 3 All who have this **h** in him purify

HOPES (HOPE)
Ps 25: 3 No one who **h** in you will ever be
1Co 13: 7 trusts, always **h**, always perseveres.

HORN (HORNS)
Ex 19: 13 the ram's **h** sounds a long blast
27: 2 Make a **h** at each of the four
Da 7: 8 This **h** had eyes like the eyes

HORNS (HORN)
Da 7: 24 The ten **h** are ten kings who will
Rev 5: 6 The Lamb had seven **h** and seven
12: 3 ten **h** and seven crowns on its
13: 1 It had ten **h** and seven heads,
17: 3 and had seven heads and ten **h**.

HORRIBLE (HORROR)
Jer 5: 30 "A **h** and shocking thing has

HORROR (HORRIBLE)
Jer 2: 12 and shudder with great **h**,"

HORSE
Ps 147: 10 is not in the strength of the **h**,
Pr 26: 3 A whip for the **h**, a bridle
Zec 1: 8 me was a man mounted on a red **h**.
Rev 6: 2 and there before me was a white **h**!
6: 4 another **h** came out, a fiery red
6: 5 and there before me was a black **h**!
6: 8 and there before me was a pale **h**!
19: 11 and there before me was a white **h**,

HOSANNA
Mt 21: 9 shouted, "**H** to the Son of David!"
21: 9 "**H** in the highest heaven!"
Mk 11: 9 those who followed shouted, "**H**!"
Jn 12: 13 out to meet him, shouting, "**H**!"

HOSEA*
Prophet whose wife and family pictured the unfaithfulness of Israel (Hos 1–3; Ro 9:25).

HOSHEA (JOSHUA)
1. Original name of Joshua (Nu 13:16).
2. Last king of Israel (2Ki 15:30; 17:1–6).

HOSPITABLE* (HOSPITALITY)
1Ti 3: 2 respectable, **h**, able to teach,
Titus 1: 8 he must be **h**, one who loves what

HOSPITALITY* (HOSPITABLE)
Ac 28: 7 showed us generous **h** for three
Ro 12: 13 people who are in need. Practice **h**.
16: 23 whose **h** I and the whole church
1Ti 5: 10 showing **h**, washing the feet
Heb 13: 2 not forget to show **h** to strangers,
13: 2 **h** to angels without knowing it.
1Pe 4: 9 Offer **h** to one another without
3Jn : 8 to show **h** to such people so that

HOSTILE (HOSTILITY)
Ro 8: 7 governed by the flesh is **h** to God;

HOSTILITY (HOSTILE)
Eph 2: 14 the barrier, the dividing wall of **h**,
2: 16 by which he put to death their **h**.

HOT
1Ti 4: 2 have been seared as with a **h** iron.
Rev 3: 15 that you are neither cold nor **h**.

HOT-TEMPERED* (TEMPER)
Pr 15: 18 A **h** person stirs up conflict,
19: 19 A **h** person must pay the penalty;
22: 24 not make friends with a **h** person,
29: 22 and a **h** person commits many sins.

HOTHEADED* (HEAD)
Pr 14: 16 but a fool is **h** and yet feels secure.

HOUR
Ecc 9: 12 one knows when their **h** will come:
Mt 6: 27 add a single **h** to your life?
Lk 12: 40 an **h** when you do not expect him."
Jn 2: 4 "My **h** has not yet come."
12: 23 "The **h** has come for the Son
12: 27 'Father, save me from this **h**'?
12: 27 this very reason I came to this **h**.
17: 1 "Father, the **h** has come.

HOUSE (HOUSEHOLD HOUSEHOLDS HOUSES STOREHOUSE)
Ex 12: 22 the door of your **h** until morning.
20: 17 shall not covet your neighbor's **h**.
Nu 12: 7 he is faithful in all my **h**.
Dt 5: 21 your desire on your neighbor's **h**
2Sa 7: 2 living in a **h** of cedar, while the ark
7: 11 LORD himself will establish a **h**
1Ch 17: 23 and his **h** be established forever.
Ne 10: 39 "We will not neglect the **h** of our
Ps 23: 6 in the **h** of the LORD forever.
27: 4 in the **h** of the LORD all the days
69: 9 for zeal for your **h** consumes me,
84: 10 in the **h** of my God than dwell
122: 1 "Let us go to the **h** of the LORD."
127: 1 Unless the LORD builds the **h**,
Pr 7: 27 Her **h** is a highway to the grave,
21: 9 of the roof than share a **h**
Isa 56: 7 for my **h** will be called a **h** of prayer
Jer 7: 11 Has this **h**, which bears my Name,
18: 2 "Go down to the potter's **h**,
Joel 3: 18 will flow out of the LORD's **h**
Hab 2: 9 who builds his **h** by unjust gain,
Zec 13: 6 I was given at the **h** of my friends.'
Mt 7: 24 is like a wise man who built his **h**
10: 11 and stay at their **h** until you leave.
12: 29 can anyone enter a strong man's **h**
21: 13 "'My **h** will be called a **h**
Mk 3: 25 If a **h** is divided against itself,
11: 17 'My **h** will be called a **h** of prayer
Lk 6: 48 They are like a man building a **h**,
10: 7 Do not move around from **h** to **h**.
11: 17 a **h** divided against itself will fall.
11: 24 it says, 'I will return to the **h** I left.'
15: 8 sweep the **h** and search carefully
19: 9 salvation has come to this **h**,
Jn 2: 16 Stop turning my Father's **h**
2: 17 for your **h** will consume me."
12: 3 the **h** was filled with the fragrance
14: 2 My Father's **h** has many rooms;
Ac 20: 20 you publicly and from **h** to **h**.
Ro 16: 5 the church that meets at their **h**.
Heb 3: 3 of a **h** has greater honor than the **h**
1Pe 2: 5 spiritual **h** to be a holy priesthood,

HOUSEHOLD (HOUSE)
Ex 12: 3 lamb for his family, one for each **h**.
Jos 24: 15 But as for me and my **h**, we will
Pr 31: 21 it snows, she has no fear for her **h**;
31: 27 watches over the affairs of her **h**
Mic 7: 6 are the members of his own **h**.
Mt 10: 36 will be the members of his own **h**.'
12: 25 or **h** divided against itself will not
Ac 16: 31 will be saved—you and your **h**."
16: 33 he and all his **h** were baptized.
16: 34 in God—he and his whole **h**.
Eph 2: 19 people and also members of his **h**,
1Ti 3: 12 manage his children and his **h** well.
3: 15 to conduct themselves in God's **h**,
5: 8 and especially for their own **h**,

HOUSEHOLDS (HOUSE)
Pr 15: 27 The greedy bring ruin to their **h**,
Titus 1: 11 they are disrupting whole **h**

HOUSES (HOUSE)
Ex 12: 27 who passed over the **h**
Mt 19: 29 who has left **h** or brothers

HOVERING* (HOVERS)
Ge 1: 2 Spirit of God was **h** over the waters
Isa 31: 5 Like birds **h** overhead, the LORD

HOVERS* (HOVERING)
Dt 32: 11 up its nest and **h** over its young,

HULDAH*
Prophetess inquired by Hilkiah for Josiah (2Ki 22; 2Ch 34:14–28).

HUMAN (HUMANITY HUMANKIND HUMANS MAN)
Ge 6: 6 he had made **h** beings on the earth,
6: 7 earth the **h** race I have created—
9: 6 "Whoever sheds **h** blood,
Lev 24: 17 who takes the life of a **h** being is
1Sa 15: 29 for he is not a **h** being, that he
2Ki 19: 18 and stone, fashioned by **h** hands.
2Ch 32: 19 of the world—the work of **h** hands.
Ps 8: 4 **h** beings that you care for them?
144: 3 what are **h** beings that you care
Isa 52: 14 form marred beyond **h** likeness—
Mk 7: 7 their teachings are merely **h** rules.'
Jn 8: 15 You judge by **h** standards;
Ac 5: 29 obey God rather than **h** beings!
Ro 9: 5 them is traced the **h** ancestry
1Co 1: 25 of God is wiser than **h** wisdom,
1: 25 God is stronger than **h** strength.
1: 26 of you were wise by **h** standards;
2: 5 faith might not rest on **h** wisdom,
2: 13 in words taught us by **h** wisdom
3: 21 no more boasting about **h** leaders!
2Co 3: 3 of stone but on tablets of **h** hearts.
Gal 1: 10 to win the approval of **h** beings,
1Th 2: 13 you accepted it not as a **h** word,
Heb 9: 11 that is not made with **h** hands,
9: 24 a sanctuary made with **h** hands
2Pe 1: 21 never had its origin in the **h** will,

HUMANITY* (HUMAN)
Eph 2: 15 create in himself one new **h**
Heb 2: 14 he too shared in their **h** so

HUMANS (HUMAN)
Ge 6: 3 will not contend with **h** forever,
1Co 3: 3 Are you not acting like mere **h**?

HUMBLE (HUMBLED HUMBLES HUMILIATE HUMILIATED HUMILIATING HUMILITY)
Nu 12: 3 (Now Moses was a very **h** man,
2Ch 7: 14 **h** themselves and pray and seek
Ps 18: 27 You save the **h** but bring low those
25: 9 He guides the **h** in what is right
149: 4 he crowns the **h** with victory.
Pr 3: 34 favor to the **h** and oppressed.
Isa 66: 2 those who are **h** and contrite
Mt 11: 29 for I am gentle and **h** in heart,
23: 12 and those who **h** themselves will be
Lk 14: 11 and those who **h** themselves will be
18: 14 and those who **h** themselves will be
Eph 4: 2 Be completely **h** and gentle;
Jas 4: 6 proud but shows favor to the **h**."
4: 10 **H** yourselves before the Lord,
1Pe 5: 5 proud but shows favor to the **h**."
5: 6 **H** yourselves, therefore,

HUMBLED (HUMBLE)
Mt 23: 12 who exalt themselves will be **h**,
Lk 14: 11 who exalt themselves will be **h**,
Php 2: 8 he **h** himself by becoming obedient

HUMBLES* (HUMBLE)
1Sa 2: 7 he **h** and he exalts.
Isa 26: 5 He **h** those who dwell on high,

HUMILIATE* (HUMBLE)
Pr 25: 7 for him to **h** you before his nobles.

HUMILIATED (HUMBLE)
Jer 31: 19 **h** because I bore the disgrace of my
Lk 14: 9 Then, **h**, you will have to take

HUMILIATING* (HUMBLE)
1Co 11: 22 God by **h** those who have nothing?

HUMILITY* (HUMBLE)
Ps 45: 4 in the cause of truth, **h** and justice;
Pr 11: 2 but with **h** comes wisdom.
15: 33 LORD, and **h** comes before honor.
18: 12 haughty, but **h** comes before honor.
22: 4 **H** is the fear of the LORD;
Zep 2: 3 Seek righteousness, seek **h**;
Ac 20: 19 I served the Lord with great **h**
2Co 10: 1 By the **h** and gentleness of Christ,
Php 2: 3 in **h** value others above yourselves,
Col 2: 18 let anyone who delights in false **h**
2: 23 their false **h** and their harsh
3: 12 kindness, **h**,
Jas 3: 13 deeds done in the **h** that comes
1Pe 5: 5 with **h** toward one another,

HUNG (HANG)
Dt 21: 23 because anyone who is **h** on a pole
Mt 18: 6 a large millstone **h** around their
Lk 19: 48 because all the people **h** on his
Gal 3: 13 "Cursed is everyone who is **h**

HUNGER (HUNGRY)
Ne 9: 15 In their **h** you gave them bread
Pr 6: 30 to satisfy his **h** when he is starving.
Mt 5: 6 Blessed are those who **h** and thirst
Lk 6: 21 Blessed are you who **h** now, for you
2Co 6: 5 hard work, sleepless nights and **h**;
11: 27 I have known **h** and thirst and have
Rev 7: 16 'Never again will they **h**;

HUNGRY (HUNGER)
Job 24: 10 carry the sheaves, but still go **h**.
Ps 107: 9 and fills the **h** with good things.
146: 7 oppressed and gives food to the **h**.
Pr 19: 15 deep sleep, and the shiftless go **h**.
25: 21 If your enemy is **h**, give him food
27: 7 to the **h** even what is bitter tastes
Isa 58: 7 it not to share your food with the **h**
58: 10 spend yourselves in behalf of the **h**
Eze 18: 7 gives his food to the **h** and
18: 16 gives his food to the **h** and
Mt 15: 32 I do not want to send them away **h**,
25: 35 For I was **h** and you gave me
25: 42 For I was **h** and you gave me
Lk 1: 53 has filled the **h** with good things
Jn 6: 35 comes to me will never go **h**,
Ro 12: 20 "If your enemy is **h**, feed him;
1Co 4: 11 To this very hour we go **h**
Php 4: 12 whether well fed or **h**,

HUR
Ex 17: 12 Aaron and **H** held his hands up—

HURL
Mic 7: 19 **h** all our iniquities into the depths

HURT (HURTS)
Ecc 8: 9 lords it over others to his own **h**.
Mk 16: 18 *it will not **h** them at all;*
Rev 2: 11 one who is victorious will not be **h**

HURTS* (HURT)
Ps 15: 4 who keeps an oath even when it **h**,
Pr 26: 28 A lying tongue hates those it **h**,

HUSBAND (HUSBAND'S HUSBANDS)
Pr 31: 11 Her **h** has full confidence in her
31: 23 Her **h** is respected at the city gate,
31: 28 her **h** also, and he praises her:
Isa 54: 5 For your Maker is your **h**—
Jer 3: 14 the LORD, "for I am your **h**.
3: 20 like a woman unfaithful to her **h**,
Jn 4: 17 "I have no **h**," she replied.
Ro 7: 2 bound to her **h** as long as he is
7: 2 but if her **h** dies, she is released
1Co 7: 2 and each woman with her own **h**.
7: 3 The **h** should fulfill his marital
7: 3 and likewise the wife to her **h**.
7: 4 her own body but yields it to her **h**.

1Co 7: 4 the **h** does not have authority over
7: 10 wife must not separate from her **h**.
7: 11 or else be reconciled to her **h**.
7: 11 a **h** must not divorce his wife.
7: 13 And if a woman has a **h** who is not
7: 14 sanctified through her believing **h**.
7: 39 bound to her **h** as long as he lives.
7: 39 But if her **h** dies, she is free
2Co 11: 2 I promised you to one **h**, to Christ,
Gal 4: 27 woman than of her who has a **h**."
Eph 5: 23 For the **h** is the head of the wife as
5: 33 and the wife must respect her **h**.
1Ti 5: 9 sixty, has been faithful to her **h**,

HUSBANDMAN See GARDENER

HUSBAND'S (HUSBAND)
Dt 25: 5 Her **h** brother shall take her
Pr 12: 4 of noble character is her **h** crown,

HUSBANDS (HUSBAND)
Eph 5: 22 yourselves to your own **h** as you do
5: 25 **H**, love your wives, just as Christ
5: 28 **h** ought to love their wives as their
Col 3: 18 submit yourselves to your **h**, as is
3: 19 **H**, love your wives and do not be
Titus 2: 4 the younger women to love their **h**
2: 5 and to be subject to their **h**,
1Pe 3: 1 yourselves to your own **h** so that,
3: 7 **H**, in the same way be considerate

HUSHAI
Wise man of David who frustrated Ahithophel's advice and foiled Absalom's revolt (2Sa 15:32–37; 16:15—17:16; 1Ch 27:33).

HYMN* (HYMNS)
Ps 40: 3 mouth, a **h** of praise to our God.
Mt 26: 30 When they had sung a **h**, they went
Mk 14: 26 When they had sung a **h**, they went
1Co 14: 26 each of you has a **h**, or a word

HYMNS* (HYMN)
Ac 16: 25 were praying and singing **h** to God,
Eph 5: 19 to one another with psalms, **h**,
Col 3: 16 with all wisdom through psalms, **h**,

HYPOCRISY* (HYPOCRITE HYPOCRITES HYPOCRITICAL)
Mt 23: 28 on the inside you are full of **h**
Mk 12: 15 But Jesus knew their **h**.
Lk 12: 1 yeast of the Pharisees, which is **h**.
Gal 2: 13 The other Jews joined him in his **h**,
2: 13 by their **h** even Barnabas was led
1Pe 2: 1 of all malice and all deceit, **h**, envy,

HYPOCRITE* (HYPOCRISY)
Mt 7: 5 You **h**, first take the plank
Lk 6: 42 You **h**, first take the plank

HYPOCRITES* (HYPOCRISY)
Ps 26: 4 deceitful, nor do I associate with **h**.
Mt 6: 2 as the **h** do in the synagogues
6: 5 do not be like the **h**, for they love
6: 16 do not look somber as the **h** do,
15: 7 You **h**! Isaiah was right when he
22: 18 "You **h**, why are you trying to trap
23: 13 of the law and Pharisees, you **h**!
23: 15 of the law and Pharisees, you **h**!
23: 23 of the law and Pharisees, you **h**!
23: 25 of the law and Pharisees, you **h**!
23: 27 of the law and Pharisees, you **h**!
23: 29 of the law and Pharisees, you **h**!
24: 51 and assign him a place with the **h**,
Mk 7: 6 when he prophesied about you **h**;
Lk 12: 56 **H**! You know how to interpret
13: 15 The Lord answered him, "You **h**!

HYPOCRITICAL* (HYPOCRISY)
1Ti 4: 2 teachings come through **h** liars,

HYSSOP
Ex 12: 22 Take a bunch of **h**, dip it
Ps 51: 7 Cleanse me with **h**, and I will be
Jn 19: 29 sponge on a stalk of the **h** plant,

ICHABOD*
1Sa 4: 21 She named the boy **I**, saying,

IDLE* (IDLENESS IDLERS)
Dt 32: 47 They are not just **i** words for you—
Job 11: 3 Will your **i** talk reduce others
Ecc 10: 18 because of **i** hands, the house leaks.
11: 6 at evening let your hands not be **i**,
Isa 58: 13 as you please or speaking **i** words,
Col 2: 18 with **i** notions by their unspiritual
1Th 5: 14 those who are **i** and disruptive,
2Th 3: 6 away from every believer who is **i**
3: 7 We were not **i** when we were
3: 11 We hear that some among you are **i**
1Ti 5: 13 they get into the habit of being **i**

IDLENESS* (IDLE)
Pr 31: 27 and does not eat the bread of **i**.

IDLERS* (IDLE)
1Ti 5: 13 And not only do they become **i**,

IDOL (IDOLATER IDOLATERS IDOLATRY IDOLS)
Ex 32: 4 made it into an **i** cast in the shape
Dt 27: 15 is anyone who makes an **i**—
Isa 40: 19 As for an **i**, a metalworker casts it,
41: 7 other nails down the **i** so it will not
44: 15 he makes an **i** and bows down to it.
44: 17 From the rest he makes a god, his **i**;
Hab 2: 18 "Of what value is an **i** carved
1Co 8: 4 We know that "An **i** is nothing

IDOLATER* (IDOL)
1Co 5: 11 or greedy, an **i** or slanderer,
Eph 5: 5 such a person is an **i**—

IDOLATERS (IDOL)
1Co 5: 10 or the greedy and swindlers, or **i**.
6: 9 immoral nor **i** nor adulterers nor

IDOLATRY (IDOL)
1Sa 15: 23 and arrogance like the evil of **i**.
1Co 10: 14 my dear friends, flee from **i**.
Gal 5: 20 **i** and witchcraft;
Col 3: 5 evil desires and greed, which is **i**.
1Pe 4: 3 orgies, carousing and detestable **i**.

IDOLS (IDOL)
Ex 34: 17 "Do not make any **i**.
Dt 32: 16 angered him with their detestable **i**.
Ps 78: 58 aroused his jealousy with their **i**.
Isa 44: 9 All who make **i** are nothing,
Eze 23: 39 sacrificed their children to their **i**,
Mic 5: 13 I will destroy your **i** and your
Ac 15: 20 to abstain from food polluted by **i**,
21: 25 abstain from food sacrificed to **i**,
1Co 8: 1 Now about food sacrificed to **i**:
1Jn 5: 21 children, keep yourselves from **i**.
Rev 2: 14 so that they ate food sacrificed to **i**

IGNORANT (IGNORE)
1Co 15: 34 there are some who are **i** of God—
Heb 5: 2 to deal gently with those who are **i**
1Pe 2: 15 good you should silence the **i** talk
2Pe 3: 16 **i** and unstable people distort,

IGNORE (IGNORANT IGNORED IGNORES)
Dt 22: 1 not **i** it but be sure to take it back
Ps 9: 12 he does not **i** the cries
Heb 2: 3 escape if we **i** so great a salvation?

IGNORED (IGNORE)
Hos 4: 6 because you have **i** the law of your
1Co 14: 38 this, they will themselves be **i**.

IGNORES* (IGNORE)
Pr 10: 17 whoever **i** correction leads others
1Co 14: 38 But if anyone **i** this, they will

ILL (ILLNESS)
Mt 4: 24 to him all who were **i** with various

ILL-GOTTEN
Pr 1: 19 the paths of all who go after **i** gain;
10: 2 **I** treasures have no lasting value,

ILLNESS (ILL)
2Ki 8: 9 ask, 'Will I recover from this **i**?'"
2Ch 16: 12 even in his **i** he did not seek help
Ps 41: 3 restores them from their bed of **i**.
Isa 38: 9 Hezekiah king of Judah after his **i**

ILLUMINATED*
Eph 5: 13 that is **i** becomes a light.
Rev 18: 1 and the earth was **i** by his splendor.

IMAGE (IMAGES)
Ge 1: 26 "Let us make mankind in our **i**,
1: 27 God created mankind in his own **i**, in the **i** of God
9: 6 for in the **i** of God has God made
Ex 20: 4 make for yourself an **i** in the form
Isa 40: 18 To what **i** will you liken him?
Da 3: 1 King Nebuchadnezzar made an **i**
Lk 20: 24 Whose **i** and inscription are on it?"
Ro 8: 29 to be conformed to the **i** of his Son,
1Co 11: 7 since he is the **i** and glory of God;
2Co 3: 18 his **i** with ever-increasing glory,
4: 4 of Christ, who is the **i** of God.
Col 1: 15 The Son is the **i** of the invisible
3: 10 in knowledge in the **i** of its Creator.
Rev 13: 14 set up an **i** in honor of the beast

IMAGES (IMAGE)
Ps 97: 7 who worship **i** are put to shame,
Jer 10: 14 The **i** he makes are a fraud;
Ro 1: 23 the immortal God for **i** made to

IMAGINATION (IMAGINE)
Eze 13: 2 who prophesy out of their own **i**:

IMAGINE (IMAGINATION)
Eph 3: 20 more than all we ask or **i**,

IMITATE* (IMITATORS)
Dt 18: 9 not learn to **i** the detestable ways
Eze 23: 48 may take warning and not **i** you.
1Co 4: 16 Therefore I urge you to **i** me.
2Th 3: 9 ourselves as a model for you to **i**.
Heb 6: 12 but to **i** those who through faith
13: 7 of their way of life and **i** their faith.
3Jn : 11 do not **i** what is evil but what is

IMITATORS* (IMITATE)
1Th 1: 6 became **i** of us and of the Lord,
2: 14 became **i** of God's churches

IMMANUEL*
Isa 7: 14 birth to a son, and will call him **I**.
8: 8 cover the breadth of your land, **I**!"
Mt 1: 23 they will call him **I**" (which means

IMMENSE
1Ti 1: 16 might display his **i** patience as

IMMORAL* (IMMORALITY)
1Co 5: 9 associate with sexually **i** people—
5: 10 the people of this world who are **i**,
5: 11 or sister but is sexually **i** or greedy,
6: 9 Neither the sexually **i** nor idolaters
Eph 5: 5 No **i**, impure or greedy person—
1Ti 1: 10 for the sexually **i**, for those
Heb 12: 16 See that no one is sexually **i**, or is
13: 4 the adulterer and all the sexually **i**.
Rev 21: 8 the sexually **i**, those who practice
22: 15 arts, the sexually **i**, the murderers,

IMMORALITY* (IMMORAL)
Nu 25: 1 in sexual **i** with Moabite women,
Jer 3: 9 Because Israel's **i** mattered so little
Mt 5: 32 except for sexual **i**, makes her
15: 19 adultery, sexual **i**, theft,
19: 9 except for sexual **i**, and marries
Mk 7: 21 sexual **i**, theft, murder,
Ac 15: 20 from sexual **i**, from the meat
15: 29 animals and from sexual **i**.
21: 25 animals and from sexual **i**."
Ro 13: 13 not in sexual **i** and debauchery,
1Co 5: 1 that there is sexual **i** among you,
6: 13 is not meant for sexual **i**
6: 18 Flee from sexual **i**. All other sins
7: 2 But since sexual **i** is occurring,
10: 8 We should not commit sexual **i**,
Gal 5: 19 sexual **i**, impurity and debauchery;
Eph 5: 3 must not be even a hint of sexual **i**,
Col 3: 5 sexual **i**, impurity, lust, evil desires
1Th 4: 3 that you should avoid sexual **i**;
Jude : 4 of our God into a license for **i**
: 7 gave themselves up to sexual **i**
Rev 2: 14 to idols and committed sexual **i**.
2: 20 misleads my servants into sexual **i**
2: 21 given her time to repent of her **i**,
9: 21 arts, their sexual **i** or their thefts.

IMMORTAL* (IMMORTALITY)
Ro 1: 23 exchanged the glory of the **i** God
1Ti 1: 17 Now to the King eternal, **i**,
6: 16 who alone is **i** and who lives

IMMORTALITY* (IMMORTAL)
Pr 12: 28 there is life; along that path is **i**.
Ro 2: 7 and **i**, he will give eternal life.
1Co 15: 53 and the mortal with **i**.
15: 54 and the mortal with **i**,
2Ti 1: 10 and **i** to light through the gospel.

IMPART
Pr 29: 15 A rod and a reprimand **i** wisdom,

IMPARTIAL*
Jas 3: 17 and good fruit, **i** and sincere.

IMPERISHABLE
1Co 15: 42 is sown is perishable, it is raised **i**;
15: 50 does the perishable inherit the **i**.
1Pe 1: 23 seed, but of **i**, through the living

IMPLORE*
2Co 5: 20 We **i** you on Christ's behalf:

IMPORTANCE* (IMPORTANT)
1Co 15: 3 I passed on to you as of first **i**:

IMPORTANT (IMPORTANCE)
Mt 23: 23 have neglected the more **i** matters
Mk 12: 29 "The most **i** one," answered Jesus,
12: 33 as yourself is more **i** than all burnt
Php 1: 18 The **i** thing is that in every way,

IMPOSSIBLE
Mt 17: 20 Nothing will be **i** for you."
19: 26 "With man this is **i**, but with God
Mk 10: 27 "With man this is **i**, but not
Lk 18: 27 "What is **i** with man is possible
Ac 2: 24 because it was **i** for death to keep
Heb 6: 4 It is **i** for those who have once been
6: 18 in which it is **i** for God to lie,
10: 4 It is **i** for the blood of bulls
11: 6 without faith it is **i** to please God,

IMPOSTORS
2Ti 3: 13 and **i** will go from bad to worse,

IMPRESS* (IMPRESSES)
Dt 6: 7 **I** them on your children.

IMPRESSES* (IMPRESS)
Pr 17: 10 A rebuke **i** a discerning person more

IMPRISONED (PRISON)
1Pe 3: 19 made proclamation to the **i** spirits—

IMPRISONMENT (PRISON)
Heb 11: 36 flogging, and even chains and **i**.

IMPROPER*
Eph 5: 3 because these are **i** for God's holy

IMPURE (IMPURITY)
Mt 12: 43 "When an **i** spirit comes out of a
Ac 10: 15 "Do not call anything **i** that God
Eph 5: 5 No immoral, **i** or greedy person—
1Th 2: 3 not spring from error or **i** motives,
4: 7 For God did not call us to be **i**,
Rev 21: 27 Nothing **i** will ever enter it, nor

IMPURITY (IMPURE)
Ro 1: 24 hearts to sexual **i** for the degrading
Gal 5: 19 immorality, **i** and debauchery;
Eph 4: 19 so as to indulge in every kind of **i**,
5: 3 or of any kind of **i**, or of greed,
Col 3: 5 sexual immorality, **i**, lust,

INCENSE
Ex 30: 1 altar of acacia wood for burning **i**.
40: 5 Place the gold altar of **i** in front
Ps 141: 2 my prayer be set before you like **i**;
Heb 9: 4 which had the golden altar of **i**
Rev 5: 8 were holding golden bowls full of **i**,
8: 4 The smoke of the **i**,

INCLINATION* (INCLINES)
Ge 6: 5 that every **i** of the thoughts
8: 21 every **i** of the human heart is evil

INCLINES* (INCLINATION)
Ecc 10: 2 The heart of the wise **i** to the right,

INCOME
Ecc 5: 10 is never satisfied with their **i**.
1Co 16: 2 of money in keeping with your **i**,

INCOMPARABLE*
Eph 2: 7 ages he might show the **i** riches

INCREASE (EVER-INCREASING INCREASED INCREASING)
Ge 1: 22 "Be fruitful and **i** in number and
8: 17 be fruitful and **i** in number on it."
Ps 62: 10 though your riches **i**, do not set
Pr 22: 16 oppresses the poor to **i** his wealth
Mt 24: 12 Because of the **i** of wickedness,
Lk 17: 5 said to the Lord, "**I** our faith!"
Ro 5: 20 in so that the trespass might **i**.
1Th 3: 12 May the Lord make your love **i**

INCREASED (INCREASE)
Ac 6: 7 of disciples in Jerusalem **i** rapidly,
9: 31 by the Holy Spirit, it **i** in numbers.
Ro 5: 20 where sin **i**, grace **i** all the more,

INCREASING (INCREASE)
Ac 6: 1 the number of disciples was **i**,
2Th 1: 3 all of you have for one another is **i**.
2Pe 1: 8 these qualities in **i** measure,

INCREDIBLE*
Ac 26: 8 you consider it **i** that God raises

INDEBTEDNESS* (DEBT)
Col 2: 14 canceled the charge of our legal **i**,

INDEPENDENT*
1Co 11: 11 in the Lord woman is not **i** of man, nor is man **i** of woman.

INDESCRIBABLE*
2Co 9: 15 Thanks be to God for his **i** gift!

INDESTRUCTIBLE*
Heb 7: 16 the basis of the power of an **i** life.

INDIGNANT
Mk 1: 41 Jesus was **i**. He reached out his
10: 14 When Jesus saw this, he was **i**.

INDISPENSABLE*
1Co 12: 22 body that seem to be weaker are **i**,

INEFFECTIVE*
2Pe 1: 8 they will keep you from being **i**

INEXPRESSIBLE*
2Co 12: 4 up to paradise and heard **i** things,
1Pe 1: 8 are filled with an **i** and glorious joy,

INFANCY* (INFANTS)
2Ti 3: 15 from **i** you have known the Holy

INFANTS (INFANCY)
Ps 8: 2 **i** you have established a stronghold
Mt 21: 16 the lips of children and **i** you, Lord,
1Co 3: 1 are still worldly—mere **i** in Christ.
14: 20 In regard to evil be **i**, but in your
Eph 4: 14 Then we will no longer be **i**,

INFIRMITIES*
Mt 8: 17 "He took up our **i** and bore our

INFLAMED
Ro 1: 27 were **i** with lust for one another.

INFLUENTIAL*
1Co 1: 26 not many were **i**; not many were

INHABITANTS (INHABITED)
Nu 33: 55 do not drive out the **i** of the land,
Rev 8: 13 Woe to the **i** of the earth,

INHABITED (INHABITANTS)
Isa 45: 18 to be empty, but formed it to be **i**—

INHERIT (CO-HEIRS HEIR HEIRS HERITAGE INHERITANCE)
Dt 1: 38 because he will lead Israel to **i** it.
Jos 1: 6 these people to **i** the land I swore
Ps 37: 11 the meek will **i** the land and enjoy
37: 29 The righteous will **i** the land
Zec 2: 12 The LORD will **i** Judah as his
Mt 5: 5 the meek, for they will **i** the earth.
19: 29 as much and will **i** eternal life.
Mk 10: 17 "what must I do to **i** eternal life?"
Lk 10: 25 "what must I do to **i** eternal life?"
18: 18 what must I do to **i** eternal life?"
1Co 6: 9 wrongdoers will not **i** the kingdom
15: 50 cannot **i** the kingdom of God,
Rev 21: 7 who are victorious will **i** all this,

INHERITANCE (INHERIT)
Lev 20: 24 I will give it to you as an **i**, a land
Dt 4: 20 to be the people of his **i**, as you
10: 9 the LORD is their **i**, as the LORD
Jos 14: 3 the Levites an **i** among the rest,
Ps 16: 6 surely I have a delightful **i**.
33: 12 the people he chose for his **i**.
136: 21 and gave their land as an **i**,
Pr 13: 22 A good person leaves an **i** for their
Mt 25: 34 take your **i**, the kingdom prepared
Eph 1: 14 deposit guaranteeing our **i** until
5: 5 has any **i** in the kingdom of Christ
Col 1: 12 share in the **i** of his holy people
3: 24 you will receive an **i** from the Lord
Heb 9: 15 receive the promised eternal **i**—
1Pe 1: 4 into an **i** that can never perish,
1: 4 This **i** is kept in heaven for you,

INIQUITIES (INIQUITY)
Ps 78: 38 he forgave their **i** and did not
103: 10 or repay us according to our **i**.
Isa 53: 5 he was crushed for our **i**;
53: 11 many, and he will bear their **i**.
59: 2 your **i** have separated you from
Mic 7: 19 hurl all our **i** into the depths

INIQUITY (INIQUITIES)
Ps 25: 11 forgive my **i**, though it is great.
32: 5 to you and did not cover up my **i**.
51: 2 Wash away all my **i** and cleanse me
51: 9 from my sins and blot out all my **i**.
Isa 53: 6 has laid on him the **i** of us all.

INJURED
Eze 34: 16 I will bind up the **i** and strengthen
Zec 11: 16 or heal the **i**, or feed the healthy,

INJUSTICE
2Ch 19: 7 the LORD our God there is no **i**

INK
2Co 3: 3 not with **i** but with the Spirit

INN*
Lk 10: 34 brought him to an **i** and took care

INNOCENT
Ex 23: 7 do not put an **i** or honest person
Dt 25: 1 acquitting the **i** and condemning
Pr 6: 17 tongue, hands that shed **i** blood,
17: 26 a fine on the **i** is not good,
Joel 3: 21 I leave their **i** blood unavenged?
Mt 10: 16 shrewd as snakes and as **i** as doves.
27: 4 said, "for I have betrayed **i** blood."
27: 24 "I am **i** of this man's blood,"
Ac 18: 6 be on your own heads! I am **i** of it.
20: 26 you today that I am **i** of the blood
Ro 16: 19 is good, and **i** about what is evil.
1Co 4: 4 clear, but that does not make me **i**.

INQUIRE
Isa 8: 19 should not a people **i** of their God?

INSCRIPTION
Mt 22: 20 image is this? And whose **i**?"
2Ti 2: 19 stands firm, sealed with this **i**:

INSIGHT
1Ki 4: 29 Solomon wisdom and very great **i**,
Ps 119: 99 I have more **i** than all my teachers,
Pr 5: 1 turn your ear to my words of **i**,
7: 4 and to **i**, "You are my relative."
16: 16 gold, to get **i** rather than silver!
20: 5 but one who has **i** draws them out.
21: 30 no **i**, no plan that can succeed
23: 23 wisdom, instruction and **i** as well.
Php 1: 9 more in knowledge and depth of **i**,
2Ti 2: 7 Lord will give you **i** into all this.

INSOLENT
Pr 29: 21 from youth will turn out to be **i**.
Ro 1: 30 **i**, arrogant and boastful;

INSPIRED*
2Sa 23: 1 "The **i** utterance of David son of
Pr 30: 1 Agur son of Jakeh—an **i** utterance.
31: 1 Lemuel—an **i** utterance his mother
Hos 9: 7 a fool, the **i** person a maniac.
1Th 1: 3 your endurance **i** by hope in our

INSTALLED
Ps 2: 6 "I have **i** my king on Zion, my holy

INSTINCT* (INSTINCTS)
2Pe 2: 12 creatures of **i**, born only to be
Jude : 10 things they do understand by **i**—

INSTINCTS* (INSTINCT)
Jude : 19 who follow mere natural **i** and do

INSTITUTED
Ro 13: 2 is rebelling against what God has **i**,

INSTRUCT (INSTRUCTED INSTRUCTION INSTRUCTIONS INSTRUCTOR)
Dt 17: 10 to do everything they **i** you to do.
Ps 32: 8 I will **i** you and teach you
105: 22 to **i** his princes as he pleased
Pr 4: 11 I **i** you in the way of wisdom
9: 9 **I** the wise and they will be wiser
Ro 15: 14 and competent to **i** one another.
1Co 2: 16 mind of the Lord so as to **i** him?"
14: 19 **i** others than ten thousand words

INSTRUCTED (INSTRUCT)
2Ch 26: 5 who **i** him in the fear of God.
Isa 50: 4 my ear to listen like one being **i**.
1Co 14: 31 in turn so that everyone may be **i**
2Ti 2: 25 Opponents must be gently **i**,

INSTRUCTION (INSTRUCT)
Pr 1: 2 for gaining wisdom and **i**;
1: 3 for receiving **i** in prudent behavior,
1: 7 but fools despise wisdom and **i**.
1: 8 your father's **i** and do not forsake
4: 1 Listen, my sons, to a father's **i**;
4: 13 Hold on to **i**, do not let it go;
6: 23 correction and **i** are the way to life,
8: 10 Choose my **i** instead of silver,
8: 33 Listen to my **i** and be wise;
13: 1 A wise son heeds his father's **i**,
13: 13 Whoever scorns **i** will pay for it,
15: 33 Wisdom's **i** is to fear the LORD,
16: 20 Whoever gives heed to **i** prospers,
16: 21 and gracious words promote **i**.
23: 12 Apply your heart to **i** and your ears
23: 23 wisdom, **i** and insight as well.
28: 9 If anyone turns a deaf ear to my **i**,
29: 18 is the one who heeds wisdom's **i**.
Isa 8: 20 Consult God's **i** and the testimony
1Co 14: 6 or prophecy or word of **i**?
14: 26 hymn, or a word of **i**, a revelation,
Eph 6: 4 in the training and **i** of the Lord.
1Th 4: 8 who rejects this **i** does not reject
2Th 3: 14 anyone who does not obey our **i**
1Ti 6: 3 sound **i** of our Lord Jesus Christ
2Ti 4: 2 with great patience and careful **i**.

INSTRUCTIONS (INSTRUCT)
1Ti 3: 14 I am writing you these **i** so that,

INSTRUCTOR (INSTRUCT)
Mt 23: 10 for you have one **I**, the Messiah.
Gal 6: 6 share all good things with their **i**.

INSTRUMENT* (INSTRUMENTS)
Eze 33: 32 beautiful voice and plays an **i** well,
Ac 9: 15 man is my chosen **i** to proclaim
Ro 6: 13 to sin as an **i** of wickedness,
6: 13 to him as an **i** of righteousness.

INSTRUMENTS (INSTRUMENT)
2Ch 23: 13 their **i** were leading the praises.
2Ti 2: 21 from the latter will be **i** for special

INSULT (INSULTED INSULTS)
Pr 12: 16 but the prudent overlook an **i**.
Mt 5: 11 are you when people **i** you,
Lk 6: 22 when they exclude you and **i** you
1Pe 3: 9 not repay evil with evil or **i** with **i**.

INSULTED (INSULT)
Heb 10: 29 and who has **i** the Spirit of grace?
1Pe 4: 14 If you are **i** because of the name

INSULTS (INSULT)
Ps 22: 7 they hurl **i**, shaking their heads.
69: 9 the **i** of those who insult you fall
Pr 9: 7 corrects a mocker invites **i**;
22: 10 quarrels and **i** are ended.
Mk 15: 29 who passed by hurled **i** at him,
Jn 9: 28 Then they hurled **i** at him and said,
Ro 15: 3 "The **i** of those who insult you
2Co 12: 10 in weaknesses, in **i**, in hardships,
1Pe 2: 23 When they hurled their **i** at him,

INTEGRITY*
Dt 9: 5 your **i** that you are going in to take
1Ki 9: 4 walk before me faithfully with **i**
1Ch 29: 17 the heart and are pleased with **i**.
Ne 7: 2 he was a man of **i** and feared God
Job 2: 3 And he still maintains his **i**,
2: 9 "Are you still maintaining your **i**?
6: 29 reconsider, for my **i** is at stake.
27: 5 till I die, I will not deny my **i**.
Ps 7: 8 according to my **i**, O Most High.
25: 21 May **i** and uprightness protect me,
41: 12 Because of my **i** you uphold me
78: 72 David shepherded them with **i**
Pr 10: 9 Whoever walks in **i** walks securely,
11: 3 The **i** of the upright guides them,
13: 6 guards the person of **i**,
29: 10 The bloodthirsty hate a person of **i**
Isa 45: 23 mouth has uttered in all **i** a word
59: 4 no one pleads a case with **i**.
Mt 22: 16 "we know that you are a man of **i**
Mk 12: 14 we know that you are a man of **i**.
2Co 1: 12 you, with **i** and godly sincerity.
Titus 2: 7 In your teaching show **i**,

INTELLIGENCE (INTELLIGENT)
Isa 29: 14 the **i** of the intelligent will vanish."
1Co 1: 19 the **i** of the intelligent I will

INTELLIGENT (INTELLIGENCE)
Isa 29: 14 intelligence of the **i** will vanish."

INTELLIGIBLE*
1Co 14: 9 Unless you speak **i** words with
14: 19 I would rather speak five **i** words

INTENDED
Ge 50: 20 You **i** to harm me, but God **i** it

INTENSE
1Th 2: 17 our **i** longing we made every effort
Rev 16: 9 They were seared by the **i** heat

INTERCEDE (INTERCEDES INTERCEDING INTERCESSION INTERCESSOR)
1Sa 2: 25 sins against the LORD, who will **i**
Heb 7: 25 him, because he always lives to **i**

INTERCEDES* (INTERCEDE)
Ro 8: 26 the Spirit himself **i** for us through
8: 27 Spirit, because the Spirit **i** for God's

INTERCEDING* (INTERCEDE)
Ro 8: 34 hand of God and is also **i** for us.

INTERCESSION* (INTERCEDE)
Isa 53: 12 and made **i** for the transgressors.
1Ti 2: 1 **i** and thanksgiving be made for all

INTERCESSOR* (INTERCEDE)
Job 16: 20 My **i** is my friend as my eyes pour

INTEREST (INTERESTS)
Lev 25: 36 Do not take **i** or any profit
Dt 23: 20 You may charge a foreigner **i**,
Ps 15: 5 lends money to the poor without **i**;
Ne 5: 10 But let us stop charging **i**!
Mt 25: 27 would have received it back with **i**.

INTERESTS (INTEREST)
1Co 7: 34 and his **i** are divided.
Php 2: 4 each of you to the **i** of the others.
2: 21 everyone looks out for their own **i**,

INTERFERE*
2Sa 19: 22 What right do you have to **i**?
Ezr 6: 7 Do not **i** with the work on this

INTERMARRY (MARRY)
Dt 7: 3 Do not **i** with them. Do not give
Ezr 9: 14 **i** with the peoples who commit

INTERPRET (INTERPRETATION INTERPRETER INTERPRETS)
Ge 41: 15 a dream, and no one can **i** it.
Mt 16: 3 cannot **i** the signs of the times.
1Co 12: 30 Do all speak in tongues? Do all **i**?
14: 13 pray that they may **i** what they say.
14: 27 one at a time, and someone must **i**.

INTERPRETATION (INTERPRET)
1Co 12: 10 to still another the **i** of tongues.
14: 26 a revelation, a tongue or an **i**.
2Pe 1: 20 by the prophet's own **i** of things.

INTERPRETER* (INTERPRET)
Ge 42: 23 them, since he was using an **i**.
1Co 14: 28 If there is no **i**, the speaker should

INTERPRETS (INTERPRET)
1Co 14: 5 someone **i**, so that the church

INTERVENED
Ac 15: 14 to us how God first **i** to choose

INTOXICATED
Pr 5: 19 may you ever be **i** with her love.
5: 20 son, be **i** with another man's wife?

INVADED
2Ki 17: 5 king of Assyria **i** the entire land,
24: 1 king of Babylon **i** the land,

INVENT*
Ro 1: 30 they **i** ways of doing evil;

INVESTIGATED
Lk 1: 3 I myself have carefully **i** everything

INVISIBLE*
Ro 1: 20 of the world God's **i** qualities—
Col 1: 15 The Son is the image of the **i** God,
1: 16 visible and **i**, whether thrones
1Ti 1: 17 eternal, immortal, **i**, the only God,
Heb 11: 27 because he saw him who is **i**.

INVITE (INVITED INVITES)
Pr 18: 6 strife, and their mouths **i** a beating.
Mt 22: 9 **i** to the banquet anyone you find.'
25: 38 we see you a stranger and **i** you in,
Lk 14: 12 or dinner, do not **i** your friends,
14: 13 you give a banquet, **i** the poor,

INVITED (INVITE)
Zep 1: 7 he has consecrated those he has **i**.
Mt 22: 14 "For many are **i**, but few are
25: 35 I was a stranger and you **i** me in,
Lk 14: 10 But when you are **i**, take the lowest
Rev 19: 9 Blessed are those who are **i**

INVITES (INVITE)
1Co 10: 27 If an unbeliever **i** you to a meal

IRON
2Ki 6: 6 threw it there, and made the **i** float.
Ps 2: 9 You will break them with a rod of **i**;
Pr 27: 17 As **i** sharpens **i**, so one person
Da 2: 33 its legs of **i**, its feet partly of **i**
1Ti 4: 2 have been seared as with a hot **i**.
Rev 2: 27 'will rule them with an **i** scepter
12: 5 all the nations with an **i** scepter."
19: 15 will rule them with an **i** scepter."

IRRELIGIOUS*
1Ti 1: 9 the unholy and **i**, for those who kill

IRREVOCABLE*
Ro 11: 29 for God's gifts and his call are **i**.

ISAAC
Son of Abraham by Sarah (Ge 17:19; 21:1–7; 1Ch 1:28). Abrahamic covenant perpetuated through (Ge 17:21; 26:2–5). Offered up by Abraham (Ge 22; Heb 11:17–19). Rebekah taken as wife (Ge 24). Inherited Abraham's estate (Ge 25:5). Fathered Esau and Jacob (Ge 25:19–26; 1Ch 1:34). Nearly lost Rebekah to Abimelek (Ge 26:1–11). Covenant with Abimelek (Ge 26:12–31). Tricked into blessing Jacob (Ge 27). Death (Ge 35:27–29). Father of Israel (Ex 3:6; Dt 29:13; Ro 9:10).

ISAIAH
Prophet to Judah (Isa 1:1). Called by the LORD (Isa 6). Announced judgment to Ahaz (Isa 7), deliverance from Assyria to Hezekiah (2Ki 19; Isa 36–37), deliverance from death to Hezekiah (2Ki 20:1–11; Isa 38). Chronicler of Judah's history (2Ch 26:22; 32:32).

ISH-BOSHETH*
Son of Saul who attempted to succeed him as king (2Sa 2:8—4:12; 1Ch 8:33).

ISHMAEL
Son of Abraham by Hagar (Ge 16; 1Ch 1:28). Blessed, but not son of covenant (Ge 17:18–21; Gal 4:21–31). Sent away by Sarah (Ge 21:8–21). Children (Ge 25:12–18; 1Ch 1:29–31). Death (Ge 25:17).

ISLAND
Rev 1: 9 was on the **i** of Patmos because
16: 20 Every **i** fled away

ISRAEL (ISRAEL'S ISRAELITE ISRAELITES)
1. Name given to Jacob (see JACOB).
2. Corporate name of Jacob's descendants; often specifically northern kingdom.
Ex 28: 11 the sons of **I** on the two stones
28: 29 of the sons of **I** over his heart
Nu 24: 17 a scepter will rise out of **I**.
Dt 6: 4 Hear, O **I**: The LORD our God,
10: 12 And now, **I**, what does the LORD
Jos 4: 22 them, '**I** crossed the Jordan on dry
Jdg 17: 6 In those days **I** had no king;
Ru 2: 12 the God of **I**, under whose wings
1Sa 3: 20 And all **I** from Dan to Beersheba
4: 21 "The Glory has departed from **I**"—
14: 23 So on that day the LORD saved **I**,
15: 26 has rejected you as king over **I**!"
17: 46 will know that there is a God in **I**.
18: 16 But all **I** and Judah loved David,
2Sa 5: 2 'You will shepherd my people **I**,
5: 3 they anointed David king over **I**.
14: 25 all **I** there was not a man so highly
1Ki 1: 35 I have appointed him ruler over **I**
10: 9 of the LORD's eternal love for **I**,
12: 1 all **I** had gone there to make him
18: 17 "Is that you, you troubler of **I**?"
19: 18 Yet I reserve seven thousand in **I**—
2Ki 5: 8 know that there is a prophet in **I**."
1Ch 17: 22 made your people **I** your very own
21: 1 Satan rose up against **I** and incited
29: 25 Solomon in the sight of all **I**

2Ch 9: 8 the love of your God for **I** and his
Ps 73: 1 Surely God is good to **I**, to those
81: 8 if you would only listen to me, **I**!
98: 3 his love and his faithfulness to **I**;
99: 8 you were to **I** a forgiving God,
Isa 11: 12 nations and gather the exiles of **I**;
27: 6 **I** will bud and blossom and fill all
44: 21 Jacob, for you, **I**, are my servant.
46: 13 salvation to Zion, my splendor to **I**.
Jer 2: 3 **I** was holy to the LORD,
23: 6 be saved and **I** will live in safety.
31: 2 I will come to give rest to **I**."
31: 10 'He who scattered **I** will gather
31: 31 new covenant with the people of **I**
33: 17 a man to sit on the throne of **I**,
Eze 3: 17 a watchman for the people of **I**;
33: 7 a watchman for the people of **I**;
34: 2 against the shepherds of **I**;
37: 28 that I the LORD make **I** holy,
39: 23 that the people of **I** went into exile
Da 9: 20 the sin of my people **I** and making
Hos 11: 1 "When **I** was a child, I loved him,
Am 4: 12 this is what I will do to you, **I**,
7: 11 and **I** will surely go into exile,
8: 2 "The time is ripe for my people **I**;
9: 14 I will bring my people **I** back
Mic 5: 2 one who will be ruler over **I**,
Zec 11: 14 family bond between Judah and **I**.
Mal 1: 5 even beyond the borders of **I**!'
Mt 2: 6 who will shepherd my people **I**.'"
10: 6 Go rather to the lost sheep of **I**.
15: 24 sent only to the lost sheep of **I**."
Mk 12: 29 'Hear, O **I**: The Lord our God,
Lk 22: 30 judging the twelve tribes of **I**.
Ac 1: 6 going to restore the kingdom to **I**?"
9: 15 their kings and to the people of **I**.
Ro 9: 4 the people of **I**. Theirs is
9: 6 all who are descended from **I** are **I**.
9: 31 but the people of **I**, who pursued
11: 7 of **I** sought so earnestly they did
11: 26 and in this way all **I** will be saved,
Gal 6: 16 follow this rule—to the **I** of God.
Eph 2: 12 excluded from citizenship in **I**
3: 6 Gentiles are heirs together with **I**,
Heb 8: 8 new covenant with the people of **I**
Rev 7: 4 144,000 from all the tribes of **I**.
21: 12 the names of the twelve tribes of **I**.

ISRAELITE (ISRAEL)
Ex 16: 1 The whole **I** community set
35: 29 All the **I** men and women who
Nu 8: 16 offspring from every **I** woman.
20: 1 the whole **I** community arrived
20: 22 The whole **I** community set
Jn 1: 47 "Here truly is an **I** in whom there
Ro 11: 1 I am an **I** myself, a descendant

ISRAELITES (ISRAEL)
Ex 1: 7 but the **I** were exceedingly fruitful;
2: 23 The **I** groaned in their slavery
3: 9 the cry of the **I** has reached me,
12: 35 The **I** did as Moses instructed
12: 37 The **I** journeyed from Rameses
14: 22 the **I** went through the sea on dry
16: 12 have heard the grumbling of the **I**.
16: 35 The **I** ate manna forty years,
24: 17 To the **I** the glory of the LORD
28: 30 for the **I** over his heart before
29: 45 I will dwell among the **I** and be
31: 16 The **I** are to observe the Sabbath,
33: 5 "Tell the **I**, 'You are a stiff-necked
39: 42 The **I** had done all the work just as
Lev 22: 32 be acknowledged as holy by the **I**.
25: 46 rule over your fellow **I** ruthlessly.
25: 55 for the **I** belong to me as servants.
Nu 2: 32 These are the **I**, counted according
6: 23 'This is how you are to bless the **I**.
9: 2 "Have the **I** celebrate the Passover
9: 17 the cloud settled, the **I** encamped.
10: 12 **I** set out from the Desert of Sinai
14: 2 All the **I** grumbled against Moses
20: 12 me as holy in the sight of the **I**,
21: 6 bit the people and many **I** died.
26: 65 had told those **I** they would surely
27: 12 and see the land I have given the **I**.
33: 3 The **I** set out from Rameses
35: 10 "Speak to the **I** and say to them:
Dt 33: 1 on the **I** before his death.
Jos 1: 2 about to give to them—to the **I**.
5: 6 The **I** had moved
7: 1 the **I** were unfaithful in regard
8: 32 in the presence of the **I**,
18: 1 whole assembly of the **I** gathered
21: 3 the **I** gave the Levites the following
22: 9 of Manasseh left the **I** at Shiloh
Jdg 2: 11 Then the **I** did evil in the eyes
3: 12 Again the **I** did evil in the eyes
4: 1 Again the **I** did evil in the eyes
6: 1 The **I** did evil in the eyes
10: 6 because the **I** forsook the LORD
13: 1 Again the **I** did evil in the eyes
1Sa 17: 2 Saul and the **I** assembled
1Ki 8: 63 all the **I** dedicated the temple
9: 22 did not make slaves of any of the **I**;
12: 17 as for the **I** who were living
2Ki 17: 24 towns of Samaria to replace the **I**.
1Ch 9: 2 in their own towns were some **I**,
10: 1 the **I** fled before them, and many
11: 4 all the **I** marched to Jerusalem
2Ch 7: 6 and all the **I** were standing.
Ne 1: 6 I confess the sins we **I**,
Jer 16: 14 who brought the **I** up out of Egypt,'
Hos 1: 10 "Yet the **I** will be like the sand
3: 1 Love her as the LORD loves the **I**,
Am 4: 5 you **I**, for this is what you love
Mic 5: 3 of his brothers return to join the **I**.
Ro 9: 27 number of the **I** be like the sand
10: 1 to God for the **I** is that they may be
10: 16 all the **I** accepted the good news.
2Co 11: 22 So am I. Are they **I**? So am I.

ISRAEL'S (ISRAEL)
Jdg 10: 16 he could bear **I** misery no longer.
2Sa 23: 1 God of Jacob, the hero of **I** songs:
Isa 44: 6 **I** King and Redeemer, the LORD
Jer 3: 9 Because **I** immorality mattered so
31: 9 because I am **I** father, and Ephraim
Jn 3: 10 "You are **I** teacher," said Jesus,

ISSACHAR
Son of Jacob by Leah (Ge 30:18; 35:23; 1Ch 2:1). Tribe of blessed (Ge 49:14–15; Dt 33:18–19), numbered (Nu 1:29; 26:25), allotted land (Jos 19:17–23; Eze 48:25), assisted Deborah (Jdg 5:15), 12,000 from (Rev 7:7).

ITALY
Ac 27: 1 decided that we would sail for **I**,
Heb 13: 24 from **I** send you their greetings.

ITCHING*
2Ti 4: 3 say what their **i** ears want to hear.

ITHAMAR
Son of Aaron (Ex 6:23; 1Ch 6:3). Duties at tabernacle (Ex 38:21; Nu 4:21–33; 7:8).

ITTAI
2Sa 15: 19 The king said to **I** the Gittite,

IVORY
1Ki 10: 22 silver and **i**, and apes and baboons.
22: 39 palace he built and adorned with **i**,

JABBOK
Ge 32: 22 sons and crossed the ford of the **J**.
Dt 3: 16 the border) and out to the **J** River,

JABESH (JABESH GILEAD)
1Sa 31: 12 wall of Beth Shan and went to **J**,
1Ch 10: 12 bones under the great tree in **J**,

JABESH GILEAD (JABESH)
Jdg 21: 8 none of the people of **J** were there.
1Sa 11: 1 Ammonite went up and besieged **J**.
2Sa 2: 4 men from **J** who had buried Saul,

JACOB
Second son of Isaac, twin of Esau (Ge 25:21–26; 1Ch 1:34). Bought Esau's birthright (Ge 25:29–34); tricked Isaac into blessing him (Ge 27:1–37). Fled to Harran (Ge 28:1–5). Abrahamic covenant perpetuated through (Ge 28:13–15; Mal 1:2). Vision at Bethel (Ge 28:10–22). Served Laban for Rachel and Leah (Ge 29:1–30). Children (Ge 29:31—30:24; 35:16–26; 1Ch 2–9). Flocks increased (Ge 30:25–43). Returned to Canaan (Ge 31). Wrestled with God; name changed to Israel (Ge 32:22–32). Reconciled to Esau (Ge 33). Returned to Bethel (Ge 35:1–15). Favored Joseph (Ge 37:3). Sent sons to Egypt during famine (Ge 42–43). Settled in Egypt (Ge 46). Blessed Ephraim and Manasseh (Ge 48). Blessed sons (Ge 49:1–28; Heb 11:21). Death (Ge 49:29–33). Burial (Ge 50:1–14).

JAEL*
Woman who killed Canaanite general, Sisera (Jdg 4:17–22; 5:24–27).

JAIR
Judge from Gilead (Jdg 10:3–5).

JAIRUS*
Synagogue ruler whose daughter Jesus raised (Mk 5:22–43; Lk 8:41–56).

JAMES
1. Apostle; brother of John (Mt 4:21–22; 10:2; Mk 3:17; Lk 5:1–10). At transfiguration (Mt 17:1–13; Mk 9:1–13; Lk 9:28–36). Killed by Herod (Ac 12:2).
2. Apostle; son of Alphaeus (Mt 10:3; Mk 3:18; Lk 6:15).
3. Brother of Jesus (Mt 13:55; Mk 6:3; Lk 24:10; Gal 1:19) and Judas (Jude 1). With believers before Pentecost (Ac 1:13). Leader of church at Jerusalem (Ac 12:17; 15; 21:18; Gal 2:9, 12). Author of epistle (Jas 1:1).

JAPHETH
Son of Noah (Ge 5:32; 1Ch 1:4–5). Blessed (Ge 9:18–28). Sons of (Ge 10:2–5).

JAR (JARS)
Ge 24: 14 'Please let down your **j** that I may
1Ki 17: 14 'The **j** of flour will not be used
Jer 19: 1 "Go and buy a clay **j** from a potter.
Lk 8: 16 hides it in a clay **j** or puts it under

JARS (JAR)
Jn 2: 6 Nearby stood six stone water **j**,
2Co 4: 7 we have this treasure in **j** of clay

JASPER
Ex 28: 20 row shall be topaz, onyx and **j**.
Eze 28: 13 topaz, onyx and **j**, lapis lazuli,
Rev 4: 3 sat there had the appearance of **j**
21: 19 The first foundation was **j**,

JAVELIN
1Sa 17: 45 me with sword and spear and **j**,

JAWBONE
Jdg 15: 15 Finding a fresh **j** of a donkey,

JEALOUS (JEALOUSLY JEALOUSY)
Ex 20: 5 am a **j** God, punishing the children
34: 14 whose name is **J**, is a **j** God.
Dt 4: 24 God is a consuming fire, a **j** God.
6: 15 is a **j** God and his anger will burn
32: 21 They made me **j** by what is no god
Jos 24: 19 He is a holy God; he is a **j** God.
Eze 16: 38 vengeance of my wrath and **j** anger.
16: 42 **j** anger will turn away from you;
23: 25 I will direct my **j** anger against you,
36: 6 in my **j** wrath because you have
Joel 2: 18 Then the LORD was **j** for his land
Na 1: 2 The LORD is a **j** and avenging
Zep 3: 8 consumed by the fire of my **j** anger.
Zec 1: 14 'I am very **j** for Jerusalem and Zion
8: 2 "I am very **j** for Zion;
2Co 11: 2 am **j** for you with a godly jealousy.

JEALOUSLY* (JEALOUS)
Jas 4: 5 says without reason that he **j** longs

JEALOUSY (JEALOUS)
Ps 79: 5 How long will your **j** burn like fire?
Pr 6: 34 For **j** arouses a husband's fury,
27: 4 but who can stand before **j**?
SS 8: 6 death, its **j** unyielding as the grave.
Zep 1: 18 fire of his **j** the whole earth will be
Zec 8: 2 I am burning with **j** for her."
Ro 13: 13 not in dissension and **j**.
1Co 3: 3 For since there is **j** and quarreling
10: 22 we trying to arouse the Lord's **j**?
2Co 11: 2 I am jealous for you with a godly **j**.
12: 20 I fear that there may be discord, **j**,
Gal 5: 20 hatred, discord, **j**, fits of rage,

JEERS*
Heb 11: 36 Some faced **j** and flogging,

JEHOAHAZ
1. Son of Jehu; king of Israel (2Ki 13:1–9).

2. Son of Josiah; king of Judah (2Ki 23:31–34; 2Ch 36:1–4).

JEHOASH

1. See JOASH.

2. Son of Jehoahaz; king of Israel. Defeat of Aram prophesied by Elisha (2Ki 13:10–25). Defeated Amaziah in Jerusalem (2Ki 14:1–16; 2Ch 25:17–24).

JEHOIACHIN

Son of Jehoiakim; king of Judah exiled by Nebuchadnezzar (2Ki 24:8–17; 2Ch 36:8–10; Jer 22:24–30; 24:1). Raised from prisoner status (2Ki 25:27–30; Jer 52:31–34).

JEHOIADA

Priest who sheltered Joash from Athaliah (2Ki 11–12; 2Ch 22:11—24:16).

JEHOIAKIM

Son of Josiah; made king of Judah by Pharaoh Necho (2Ki 23:34—24:6; 2Ch 36:4–8; Jer 22:18–23). Burned scroll of Jeremiah's prophecies (Jer 36).

JEHORAM

1. Son of Jehoshaphat; king of Judah (2Ki 8:16–24). Prophesied against by Elijah; killed by the LORD (2Ch 21).

2. See JORAM.

JEHOSHAPHAT

Son of Asa; king of Judah. Strengthened his kingdom (2Ch 17). Joined with Ahab against Aram (2Ki 22; 2Ch 18). Established judges (2Ch 19). Joined with Joram against Moab (2Ki 3; 2Ch 20).

JEHU

1. Prophet against Baasha (2Ki 16:1–7).

2. King of Israel. Anointed by Elijah to obliterate house of Ahab (1Ki 19:16–17); anointed by servant of Elisha (2Ki 9:1–13). Killed Joram and Ahaziah (2Ki 9:14–29; 2Ch 22:7–9), Jezebel (2Ki 9:30–37), relatives of Ahab (2Ki 10:1–17), ministers of Baal (2Ki 10:18–29). Death (2Ki 10:30–36).

JEPHTHAH

Judge from Gilead who delivered Israel from Ammon (Jdg 10:6—12:7). Made rash vow concerning his daughter (Jdg 11:30–40).

JEREMIAH

Prophet to Judah (Jer 1:1–3). Called by the LORD (Jer 1). Put in stocks (Jer 20:1–3). Threatened for prophesying (Jer 11:18–23; 26). Opposed by Hananiah (Jer 28). Scroll burned (Jer 36). Imprisoned (Jer 37). Thrown into cistern (Jer 38). Forced to Egypt with those fleeing Babylonians (Jer 43).

JERICHO

Nu 22: 1 along the Jordan across from **J**.
Jos 3: 16 the people crossed over opposite **J**.
5: 10 camped at Gilgal on the plains of **J**,
Lk 10: 30 going down from Jerusalem to **J**,
Heb 11: 30 By faith the walls of **J** fell,

JEROBOAM

1. Official of Solomon; rebelled to become first king of Israel (1Ki 11:26–40; 12:1–20; 2Ch 10). Idolatry (1Ki 12:25–33); judgment for (1Ki 13–14; 2Ch 13).

2. Son of Jehoash; king of Israel (1Ki 14:23–29).

JERUSALEM

Jos 10: 1 Now Adoni-Zedek king of **J** heard
15: 8 slope of the Jebusite city (that is, **J**).
Jdg 1: 8 The men of Judah attacked **J**
1Sa 17: 54 Philistine's head and brought it to **J**
2Sa 5: 5 in **J** he reigned over all Israel
5: 6 his men marched to **J** to attack
9: 13 And Mephibosheth lived in **J**,
11: 1 But David remained in **J**.
15: 29 took the ark of God back to **J**
24: 16 stretched out his hand to destroy **J**,
1Ki 3: 1 the LORD, and the wall around **J**.
9: 15 terraces, the wall of **J**, and Hazor,
9: 19 whatever he desired to build in **J**,
10: 26 cities and also with him in **J**.
10: 27 silver as common in **J** as stones,
1Ki 11: 7 On a hill east of **J**, Solomon built
11: 13 my servant and for the sake of **J**,
11: 36 always have a lamp before me in **J**,
11: 42 in **J** over all Israel forty years.
12: 27 at the temple of the LORD in **J**,
14: 21 he reigned seventeen years in **J**,
14: 25 Shishak king of Egypt attacked **J**.
15: 2 and he reigned in **J** three years.
15: 10 and he reigned in **J** forty-one years.
22: 42 he reigned in **J** twenty-five years.
2Ki 8: 17 and he reigned in **J** eight years.
8: 26 king, and he reigned in **J** one year.
12: 1 and he reigned in **J** forty years.
12: 17 Then he turned to attack **J**.
14: 2 he reigned in **J** twenty-nine years.
14: 13 broke down the wall of **J**
15: 2 he reigned in **J** fifty-two years.
15: 33 and he reigned in **J** sixteen years.
16: 2 and he reigned in **J** sixteen years.
16: 5 Israel marched up to fight against **J**
18: 2 he reigned in **J** twenty-nine years.
18: 17 They came up to **J** and stopped
19: 31 For out of **J** will come a remnant,
21: 1 and he reigned in **J** fifty-five years.
21: 12 going to bring such disaster on **J**
21: 19 king, and he reigned in **J** two years.
22: 1 he reigned in **J** thirty-one years.
23: 27 I will reject **J**, the city I chose,
23: 31 and he reigned in **J** three months.
23: 36 and he reigned in **J** eleven years.
24: 8 and he reigned in **J** three months.
24: 10 king of Babylon advanced on **J**
24: 14 He carried all **J** into exile:
24: 18 and he reigned in **J** eleven years.
24: 20 anger that all this happened to **J**
25: 1 Babylon marched against **J** with his
25: 9 royal palace and all the houses of **J**.
1Ch 11: 4 all the Israelites marched to **J**
21: 16 sword in his hand extended over **J**.
2Ch 1: 4 he had pitched a tent for it in **J**.
3: 1 the LORD in **J** on Mount Moriah,
6: 6 now I have chosen **J** for my Name
9: 1 she came to **J** to test him with hard
20: 15 and all who live in Judah and **J**!
20: 27 Judah and **J** returned joyfully to **J**,
29: 8 LORD has fallen on Judah and **J**;
36: 19 and broke down the wall of **J**;
Ezr 1: 2 a temple for him at **J** in Judah.
2: 1 to Babylon (they returned to **J**
3: 1 assembled together as one in **J**.
4: 12 up to us from you have gone to **J**
4: 24 of God in **J** came to a standstill
6: 12 or to destroy this temple in **J**.
7: 8 Ezra arrived in **J** in the fifth month
9: 9 a wall of protection in Judah and **J**.
10: 7 **J** for all the exiles to assemble in **J**.
Ne 1: 2 survived the exile, and also about **J**.
1: 3 The wall of **J** is broken down,
2: 11 I went to **J**, and after staying there
2: 17 let us rebuild the wall of **J**,
2: 20 you have no share in **J** or any claim
3: 8 They restored **J** as far as the Broad
4: 8 fight against **J** and stir up trouble
11: 1 leaders of the people settled in **J**.
12: 27 At the dedication of the wall of **J**,
12: 43 in **J** could be heard far away.
Ps 51: 18 Zion, to build up the walls of **J**.
79: 1 they have reduced **J** to rubble.
122: 2 feet are standing in your gates, **J**.
122: 3 **J** is built like a city that is closely
122: 6 Pray for the peace of **J**:
125: 2 As the mountains surround **J**,
128: 5 see the prosperity of **J** all the days
137: 5 If I forget you, **J**, may my right
147: 2 The LORD builds up **J**;
147: 12 Extol the LORD, **J**;
SS 6: 4 as lovely as **J**, as majestic as troops
Isa 1: 1 and **J** that Isaiah son of Amoz saw
2: 1 Amoz saw concerning Judah and **J**:
3: 1 is about to take from **J** and Judah
3: 8 **J** staggers, Judah is falling;
4: 3 are recorded among the living in **J**.
8: 14 for the people of **J** he will be a trap
27: 13 LORD on the holy mountain in **J**.
31: 5 the LORD Almighty will shield **J**;
Isa 33: 20 your eyes will see **J**, a peaceful
40: 2 Speak tenderly to **J**, and proclaim
40: 9 You who bring good news to **J**,
52: 1 on your garments of splendor, **J**,
52: 2 rise up, sit enthroned, **J**.
62: 6 posted watchmen on your walls, **J**;
62: 7 give him no rest till he establishes **J**
65: 18 for I will create **J** to be a delight
Jer 2: 2 and proclaim in the hearing of **J**:
3: 17 time they will call **J** The Throne
4: 5 in Judah and proclaim in **J** and say:
4: 14 **J**, wash the evil from your heart
5: 1 "Go up and down the streets of **J**,
6: 6 and build siege ramps against **J**.
8: 5 Why does **J** always turn away?
9: 11 "I will make **J** a heap of ruins,
13: 27 Woe to you, **J**! How long will you
23: 14 the people of **J** are like Gomorrah."
24: 1 carried into exile from **J** to Babylon
26: 18 **J** will become a heap of rubble,
32: 2 of Babylon was then besieging **J**,
33: 10 the streets of **J** that are deserted,
39: 1 Babylon marched against **J** with his
51: 50 a distant land, and call to mind **J**."
52: 14 broke down all the walls around **J**.
La 1: 7 and wandering **J** remembers all
Eze 14: 21 I send against **J** my four dreadful
16: 2 man, confront **J** with her detestable
Da 6: 10 the windows opened toward **J**.
9: 2 of **J** would last seventy years.
9: 12 done like what has been done to **J**.
9: 25 rebuild **J** until the Anointed One,
Joel 3: 1 restore the fortunes of Judah and **J**,
3: 16 from Zion and thunder from **J**;
3: 17 **J** will be holy; never again will
Am 2: 5 will consume the fortresses of **J**."
Ob : 11 entered his gates and cast lots for **J**,
Mic 1: 5 is Judah's high place? Is it not **J**?
4: 2 the word of the LORD from **J**.
Zep 3: 16 On that day they will say to **J**,
Zec 1: 14 'I am very jealous for **J** and Zion,
1: 17 comfort Zion and choose **J**.'"
2: 2 me, "To measure **J**, to find out how
2: 4 man, '**J** will be a city without walls
8: 3 **J** will be called the Faithful City,
8: 8 I will bring them back to live in **J**;
8: 15 determined to do good again to **J**
8: 22 powerful nations will come to **J**
9: 9 Shout, Daughter **J**! See, your king
9: 10 Ephraim and the warhorses from **J**,
12: 3 I will make **J** an immovable rock
12: 10 the inhabitants of **J** a spirit of grace
14: 2 I will gather all the nations to **J**
14: 8 living water will flow out from **J**,
14: 16 nations that have attacked **J** will go
Mt 16: 21 to his disciples that he must go to **J**
20: 18 "We are going up to **J**, and the Son
21: 10 When Jesus entered **J**, the whole
23: 37 "**J**, **J**, you who kill the prophets
Mk 10: 33 "We are going up to **J**," he said,
Lk 2: 22 Mary took him to **J** to present him
2: 41 Every year Jesus' parents went to **J**
2: 43 the boy Jesus stayed behind in **J**,
4: 9 The devil led him to **J** and had him
9: 31 about to bring to fulfillment at **J**.
9: 51 Jesus resolutely set out for **J**.
13: 34 "**J**, **J**, you who kill the prophets
18: 31 them, "We are going up to **J**,
19: 41 As he approached **J** and saw
21: 20 "When you see **J** being surrounded
21: 24 **J** will be trampled
24: 47 name to all nations, beginning at **J**.
Jn 4: 20 where we must worship is in **J**."
Ac 1: 4 "Do not leave **J**, but wait
1: 8 and you will be my witnesses in **J**,
6: 7 of disciples in **J** increased rapidly,
20: 22 I am going to **J**, not knowing what
23: 11 As you have testified about me in **J**,
Ro 15: 19 So from **J** all the way around
Gal 4: 25 to the present city of **J**,
4: 26 But the **J** that is above is free,
Heb 12: 22 of the living God, the heavenly **J**.
Rev 3: 12 the new **J**, which is coming down
21: 2 the new **J**, coming down
21: 10 and showed me the Holy City, **J**,

JESSE

Father of David (Ru 4:17–22; 1Sa 16; 1Ch 2:12–17).

JESUS

LIFE: Genealogy (Mt 1:1–17; Lk 3:21–37). Birth announced (Mt 1:18–25; Lk 1:26–45). Birth (Mt 2:1–12; Lk 2:1–40). Escape to Egypt (Mt 2:13–23). As a boy in the temple (Lk 2:41–52). Baptism (Mt 3:13–17; Mk 1:9–11; Lk 3:21–22; Jn 1:32–34). Temptation (Mt 4:1–11; Mk 1:12–13; Lk 4:1–13). Ministry in Galilee (Mt 4:12—18:35; Mk 1:14—9:50; Lk 4:14—13:9; Jn 1:35—2:11; 4; 6), Transfiguration (Mt 17:1–8; Mk 9:2–8; Lk 9:28–36), on the way to Jerusalem (Mt 19–20; Mk 10; Lk 13:10—19:27), in Jerusalem (Mt 21–25; Mk 11–13; Lk 19:28—21:38; Jn 2:12—3:36; 5; 7–12). Last supper (Mt 26:17–35; Mk 14:12–31; Lk 22:1–38; Jn 13–17). Arrest and trial (Mt 26:36—27:31; Mk 14:43—15:20; Lk 22:39—23:25; Jn 18:1—19:16). Crucifixion (Mt 27:32–66; Mk 15:21–47; Lk 23:26–55; Jn 19:28–42). Resurrection and appearances (Mt 28; Mk 16; Lk 24; Jn 20–21; Ac 1:1–11; 7:56; 9:3–6; 1Co 15:1–8; Rev 1:1–20).

MIRACLES. Healings: official's son (Jn 4:43–54), demoniac in Capernaum (Mk 1:23–26; Lk 4:33–35), Peter's mother-in-law (Mt 8:14–17; Mk 1:29–31; Lk 4:38–39), leper (Mt 8:2–4; Mk 1:40–45; Lk 5:12–16), paralytic (Mt 9:1–8; Mk 2:1–12; Lk 5:17–26), cripple (Jn 5:1–9), shriveled hand (Mt 12:10–13; Mk 3:1–5; Lk 6:6–11), centurion's servant (Mt 8:5–13; Lk 7:1–10), widow's son raised (Lk 7:11–17), demoniac (Mt 12:22–23; Lk 11:14), Gerasenes demoniacs (Mt 8:28–34; Mk 5:1–20; Lk 8:26–39), woman's bleeding and Jairus's daughter (Mt 9:18–26; Mk 5:21–43; Lk 8:40–56), blind man (Mt 9:27–31), mute man (Mt 9:32–33), Canaanite woman's daughter (Mt 15:21–28; Mk 7:24–30), deaf man (Mk 7:31–37), blind man (Mk 8:22–26), demoniac boy (Mt 17:14–18; Mk 9:14–29; Lk 9:37–43), ten lepers (Lk 17:11–19), man born blind (Jn 9:1–7), Lazarus raised (Jn 11), crippled woman (Lk 13:11–17), man with abnormal swelling (Lk 14:1–6), two blind men (Mt 20:29–34; Mk 10:46–52; Lk 18:35–43), Malchus's ear (Lk 22:50–51). Other miracles: water to wine (Jn 2:1–11), catch of fish (Lk 5:1–11), storm stilled (Mt 8:23–27; Mk 4:37–41; Lk 8:22–25), 5,000 fed (Mt 14:15–21; Mk 6:35–44; Lk 9:10–17; Jn 6:1–14), walking on water (Mt 14:25–33; Mk 6:48–52; Jn 6:15–21), 4,000 fed (Mt 15:32–39; Mk 8:1–9), money from fish (Mt 17:24–27), fig tree cursed (Mt 21:18–22; Mk 11:12–14), catch of fish (Jn 21:1–14).

MAJOR TEACHING: Sermon on the Mount/Plain (Mt 5–7; Lk 6:17–49), to Nicodemus (Jn 3), to Samaritan woman (Jn 4), Bread of Life (Jn 6:22–59), at Festival of Tabernacles (Jn 7–8), woes to Pharisees (Mt 23; Lk 11:37–54), Good Shepherd (Jn 10:1–18), Olivet Discourse (Mt 24–25; Mk 13; Lk 21:5–36), Upper Room Discourse (Jn 13–16).

PARABLES: Sower (Mt 13:3–23; Mk 4:3–25; Lk 8:5–18), seed's growth (Mk 4:26–29), wheat and weeds (Mt 13:24–30, 36–43), mustard seed (Mt 13:31–32; Mk 4:30–32), yeast (Mt 13:33; Lk 13:20–21), hidden treasure (Mt 13:44), valuable pearl (Mt 13:45–46), net (Mt 13:47–51), house owner (Mt 13:52), good Samaritan (Lk 10:25–37), unmerciful servant (Mt 18:15–35), lost sheep (Mt 18:10–14; Lk 15:4–7), lost coin (Lk 15:8–10), lost son (Lk 15:11–32), shrewd manager (Lk 16:1–13), rich man and Lazarus (Lk 16:19–31), persistent widow (Lk 18:1–8), Pharisee and tax collector (Lk 18:9–14), payment of workers (Mt 20:1–16), tenants and the vineyard (Mt 21:28–46; Mk 12:1–12; Lk 20:9–19), wedding banquet (Mt 22:1–14), faithful servant (Mt 24:45–51), ten virgins (Mt 25:1–13), bags of gold/ten minas (Mt 25:1–30; Lk 19:12–27).

DISCIPLES see APOSTLES. Call of (Jn 1:35–51; Mt 4:18–22; 9:9; Mk 1:16–20; 2:13–14; Lk 5:1–11, 27–28). Named apostles (Mk 3:13–19; Lk 6:12–16). Twelve sent out (Mt 10; Mk 6:7–11; Lk 9:1–5). Seventy-two sent out (Lk 10:1–24). Defection of (Jn 6:60–71; Mt 26:56; Mk 14:50–52). Final commission (Mt 28:16–20; Jn 21:15–23; Ac 1:3–8).

Ac 2: 32 God has raised this J to life, and we
9: 5 Saul asked. "I am J, whom you are
9: 34 said to him, "J Christ heals you.
15: 11 of our Lord J that we are saved,
16: 31 "Believe in the Lord J, and you will
20: 24 the task the Lord J has given me—
Ro 3: 24 redemption that came by Christ J.
5: 17 life through the one man, J Christ!
8: 1 for those who are in Christ J,
1Co 1: 7 our Lord J Christ to be revealed.
2: 2 I was with you except J Christ
6: 11 in the name of the Lord J Christ
8: 6 and there is but one Lord, J Christ,
12: 3 Spirit of God says, "J be cursed,"
12: 3 and no one can say, "J is Lord,"
2Co 4: 5 but J Christ as Lord, and ourselves
13: 5 Do you not realize that Christ J is
Gal 2: 16 the law, but by faith in J Christ.
3: 28 for you are all one in Christ J.
5: 6 in Christ J neither circumcision
6: 17 I bear on my body the marks of J.
Eph 1: 5 to sonship through J Christ,
2: 10 in Christ J to do good works,
2: 20 with Christ J himself as the chief
Php 1: 6 until the day of Christ J.
2: 5 have the same mindset as Christ J:
2: 10 name of J every knee should bow,
Col 3: 17 do it all in the name of the Lord J,
1Th 1: 10 J, who rescues us from the coming
4: 14 with J those who have fallen asleep
5: 23 at the coming of our Lord J Christ.
2Th 1: 7 happen when the Lord J is revealed
2: 1 the coming of our Lord J Christ
1Ti 1: 15 J came into the world to save
2Ti 1: 10 Christ J, who has destroyed death
2: 3 like a good soldier of Christ J.
3: 12 life in Christ J will be persecuted,
Titus 2: 13 our great God and Savior, J Christ,
Heb 2: 9 But we do see J, who was made
2: 11 So J is not ashamed to call them
3: 1 fix your thoughts on J, whom we
3: 3 J has been found worthy of greater
4: 14 into heaven, J the Son of God,
6: 20 our forerunner, J, has entered
7: 22 J has become the guarantor
7: 24 but because J lives forever, he has
8: 6 the ministry J has received is as
12: 2 fixing our eyes on J, the pioneer
12: 24 J the mediator of a new covenant,
1Pe 1: 3 the resurrection of J Christ
2Pe 1: 16 of our Lord J Christ in power,
1Jn 1: 7 and the blood of J, his Son,
2: 1 J Christ, the Righteous One.
2: 6 to live in him must live as J did.
4: 15 acknowledges that J is the Son
Rev 1: 1 The revelation from J Christ,
22: 16 "I, J, have sent my angel to give
22: 20 Amen. Come, Lord J.

JETHRO

Father-in-law and adviser of Moses (Ex 3:1; 18). Also known as Reuel (Ex 2:18).

JEW (JEWS JEWS' JUDAISM)

Est 2: 5 the citadel of Susa a J of the tribe
Zec 8: 23 take firm hold of one J by the hem
Ac 21: 39 "I am a J, from Tarsus in Cilicia,
Ro 1: 16 first to the J, then to the Gentile.
2: 28 A person is not a J who is one only
10: 12 there is no difference between J
1Co 9: 20 To the Jews I became like a J,
Gal 2: 14 all, "You are a J, yet you live like
3: 28 There is neither J nor Gentile,
Col 3: 11 Here there is no Gentile or J,

JEWEL* (JEWELRY JEWELS)

Pr 20: 15 that speak knowledge are a rare j.
SS 4: 9 eyes, with one j of your necklace.
Isa 13: 19 Babylon, the j of kingdoms,
Rev 21: 11 was like that of a very precious j,

JEWELRY (JEWEL)

Ex 35: 22 and brought gold j of all kinds:
Jer 2: 32 Does a young woman forget her j,
Eze 16: 11 I adorned you with j: I put
1Pe 3: 3 wearing of gold j or fine clothes.

JEWELS (JEWEL)

Isa 54: 12 your gates of sparkling j, and all
61: 10 as a bride adorns herself with her j.
Zec 9: 16 in his land like j in a crown.

JEWS (JEW)

Ne 4: 1 He ridiculed the J,
Est 3: 13 kill and annihilate all the J—
4: 14 deliverance for the J will arise
Mt 2: 2 who has been born king of the J?
27: 11 him, "Are you the king of the J?"
Jn 4: 9 (For J do not associate
4: 22 know, for salvation is from the J.
19: 3 saying, "Hail, king of the J!"
Ac 20: 21 I have declared to both J
Ro 3: 29 Or is God the God of J only?
9: 24 not only from the J
1Co 1: 22 J demand signs and Greeks look
9: 20 To the J I became like a Jew, to win the J.
12: 13 whether J or Gentiles,
2Co 11: 26 in danger from my fellow J,
Rev 2: 9 slander of those who say they are J
3: 9 claim to be J though they are not,

JEWS'* (JEW)

Ro 15: 27 shared in the J spiritual blessings,

JEZEBEL

Sidonian wife of Ahab (1Ki 16:31). Promoted Baal worship (1Ki 16:32–33). Killed prophets of the LORD (1Ki 18:4, 13). Opposed Elijah (1Ki 19:1–2). Had Naboth killed (1Ki 21). Death prophesied (1Ki 21:17–24). Killed by Jehu (2Ki 9:30–37).

JEZREEL

2Ki 9: 36 J dogs will devour Jezebel's flesh.
10: 7 baskets and sent them to Jehu in J.
Hos 1: 4 "Call him J, because I will soon

JOAB

Nephew of David (1Ch 2:16). Commander of his army (2Sa 8:16). Victorious over Ammon (2Sa 10; 1Ch 19), Rabbah (2Sa 11; 1Ch 20), Jerusalem (1Ch 11:6), Absalom (2Sa 18), Sheba (2Sa 20). Killed Abner (2Sa 3:22–39), Amasa (2Sa 20:1–13). Numbered David's army (2Sa 24; 1Ch 21). Sided with Adonijah (1Ki 1:17, 19). Killed by Benaiah (1Ki 2:5–6, 28–35).

JOASH

Son of Ahaziah; king of Judah. Sheltered from Athaliah by Jehoiada (2Ki 11; 2Ch 22:10—23:21). Repaired temple (2Ki 12; 2Ch 24).

JOB

Wealthy man from Uz; feared God (Job 1:1–5). Righteousness tested by disaster (Job 1:6–22), personal affliction (Job 2). Maintained innocence in debate with three friends (Job 3–31), Elihu (Job 32–37). Rebuked by the LORD (Job 38–41). Vindicated and restored to greater stature by the LORD (Job 42). Example of righteousness (Eze 14:14, 20).

JOCHEBED*

Mother of Moses and Aaron (Ex 6:20; Nu 26:59).

JOEL

Prophet (Joel 1:1; Ac 2:16).

JOHN

1. Son of Zechariah and Elizabeth (Lk 1). Called the Baptist (Mt 3:1–12; Mk 1:2–8). Witness to Jesus (Mt 3:11–12; Mk 1:7–8; Lk 3:15–18; Jn 1:6–35; 3:27–30; 5:33–36). Doubts about Jesus (Mt 11:2–6; Lk 7:18–23). Arrest (Mt 4:12; Mk 1:14). Execution (Mt 14:1–12; Mk 6:14–29; Lk 9:7–9). Ministry compared to Elijah (Mt 11:7–19; Mk 9:11–13; Lk 7:24–35).

2. Apostle; brother of James (Mt 4:21–22; 10:2; Mk 3:17; Lk 5:1–10). At transfiguration (Mt 17:1–13; Mk 9:1–13; Lk 9:28–36). Desire to be greatest (Mk 10:35–45). Leader of church at Jerusalem (Ac 4:1–3; Gal 2:9). Elder who wrote

epistles (2Jn 1; 3Jn 1). Prophet who wrote Revelation (Rev 1:1; 22:8).

3. Cousin of Barnabas, co-worker with Paul, (Ac 12:12—13:13; 15:37), see MARK.

JOIN (JOINED JOINS)

Ne 10: 29 these now **j** their fellow Israelites
Pr 23: 20 not **j** those who drink too much
24: 21 do not **j** with rebellious officials,
Jer 3: 18 people of Judah will **j** the people
Eze 37: 17 **J** them together into one stick so
Da 11: 34 who are not sincere will **j** them.
Ro 15: 30 to **j** me in my struggle by praying
2Ti 1: 8 **j** with me in suffering
2: 3 **J** with me in suffering, like a good
1Pe 4: 4 you do not **j** them in their reckless,

JOINED (JOIN)

Zec 2: 11 "Many nations will be **j**
Mt 19: 6 Therefore what God has **j** together,
Mk 10: 9 Therefore what God has **j** together,
Ac 1: 14 They all **j** together constantly
Eph 2: 21 the whole building is **j** together
4: 16 body, **j** and held together by every

JOINS (JOIN)

1Co 16: 16 to everyone who **j** in the work

JOINT (JOINTS)

Ps 22: 14 water, and all my bones are out of **j**.

JOINTS* (JOINT)

Heb 4: 12 soul and spirit, **j** and marrow;

JOKING*

Ge 19: 14 his sons-in-law thought he was **j**.
Pr 26: 19 neighbor and says, "I was only **j**!"
Eph 5: 4 foolish talk or coarse **j**, which are

JONAH

Prophet in days of Jeroboam II (2Ki 14:25). Called to Nineveh; fled to Tarshish (Jnh 1:1–3). Cause of storm; thrown into sea (Jnh 1:4–16). Swallowed by fish (Jnh 1:17). Prayer (Jnh 2). Preached to Nineveh (Jnh 3). Attitude reproved by the LORD (Jnh 4). Sign of (Mt 12:39–41; Lk 11:29–32).

JONATHAN

Son of Saul (1Sa 13:16; 1Ch 8:33). Valiant warrior (1Sa 13–14). Relation to David (1Sa 18:1–4; 19–20; 23:16–18). Killed at Gilboa (1Sa 31). Mourned by David (2Sa 1).

JOPPA

Ezr 3: 7 logs by sea from Lebanon to **J**,
Jnh 1: 3 went down to **J**, where he found
Ac 9: 43 Peter stayed in **J** for some time

JORAM

1. Son of Ahab; king of Israel. Fought with Jehoshaphat against Moab (2Ki 3). Killed with Ahaziah by Jehu (2Ki 8:25–29; 9:14–26; 2Ch 22:5–9).

2. See JEHORAM.

JORDAN

Ge 13: 10 **J** toward Zoar was well watered,
Nu 22: 1 and camped along the **J** across
34: 12 boundary will go down along the **J**
Dt 3: 27 you are not going to cross this **J**.
Jos 1: 2 cross the **J** River into the land I am
3: 11 all the earth will go into the **J**
3: 17 stopped in the middle of the **J**
4: 22 'Israel crossed the **J** on dry ground.'
2Ki 2: 7 and Elisha had stopped at the **J**.
2: 13 and stood on the bank of the **J**.
5: 10 wash yourself seven times in the **J**,
6: 4 They went to the **J** and began to
Ps 114: 3 looked and fled, the **J** turned back;
Isa 9: 1 the Way of the Sea, beyond the **J**—
Jer 12: 5 manage in the thickets by the **J**?
Mt 3: 6 baptized by him in the **J** River.
4: 15 the Sea, beyond the **J**,
Mk 1: 9 and was baptized by John in the **J**.

JOSEPH

1. Son of Jacob by Rachel (Ge 30:24; 1Ch 2:2). Favored by Jacob, hated by brothers (Ge 37:3–4). Dreams (Ge 37:5–11). Sold by brothers (Ge 37:12–36). Served Potiphar; imprisoned by false accusation (Ge 39). Interpreted dreams of Pharaoh's servants (Ge 40), of Pharaoh (Ge 41:4–40). Made greatest in Egypt (Ge 41:41–57). Sold grain to brothers (Ge 42–45). Brought Jacob and sons to Egypt (Ge 46–47). Sons Ephraim and Manasseh blessed (Ge 48). Blessed (Ge 49:22–26; Dt 33:13–17). Death (Ge 50:22–26; Ex 13:19; Heb 11:22). 12,000 from (Rev 7:8).

2. Husband of Mary, mother of Jesus (Mt 1:16–24; 2:13–19; Lk 1:27; 2; Jn 1:45).

3. Disciple from Arimathea, who gave his tomb for Jesus' burial (Mt 27:57–61; Mk 15:43–47; Lk 23:50–53).

4. Original name of Barnabas (Ac 4:36).

JOSHUA (HOSHEA)

1. Son of Nun; name changed from Hoshea (Nu 13:8, 16; 1Ch 7:27). Fought Amalekites under Moses (Ex 17:9–14). Servant of Moses on Sinai (Ex 24:13; 32:17). Spied Canaan (Nu 13). With Caleb, allowed to enter land (Nu 14:6, 30). Succeeded Moses (Dt 1:38; 31:1–8; 34:9).

Charged Israel to conquer Canaan (Jos 1). Crossed Jordan (Jos 3–4). Circumcised sons of wilderness wanderings (Jos 5). Conquered Jericho (Jos 6), Ai (Jos 7–8), five kings at Gibeon (Jos 10:1–28), southern Canaan (Jos 10:29–43), northern Canaan (Jos 11–12). Defeated at Ai (Jos 7). Deceived by Gibeonites (Jos 9). Renewed covenant (Jos 8:30–35; 24:1–27). Divided land among tribes (Jos 13–22). Last words (Jos 23). Death (Jos 24:28–31).

2. High priest during rebuilding of temple (Hag 1–2; Zec 3:1–9; 6:11).

JOSIAH

Son of Amon; king of Judah (2Ki 21:26; 1Ch 3:14). Prophesied (1Ki 13:2). Book of Law discovered during his reign (2Ki 22; 2Ch 34:14–31). Reforms (2Ki 23:1–25; 2Ch 34:1–13; 35:1–19). Killed by Pharaoh Necho (2Ki 23:29–30; 2Ch 35:20–27).

JOTHAM

1. Son of Gideon (Jdg 9).

2. Son of Azariah (Uzziah); king of Judah (2Ki 15:32–38; 2Ch 26:21—27:9).

JOURNEY

Dt 1: 33 who went ahead of you on your **j**,
2: 7 watched over your **j** through this
Jdg 18: 6 Your **j** has the LORD's approval."
Ezr 8: 21 ask him for a safe **j** for us and our
Isa 35: 8 The unclean will not **j** on it;
Mt 25: 14 it will be like a man going on a **j**,
Ro 15: 24 have you assist me on my **j** there,

JOY* (ENJOY ENJOYMENT JOYFUL JOYOUS OVERJOYED REJOICE REJOICES REJOICING)

Ge 31: 27 so I could send you away with **j**
Lev 9: 24 saw it, they shouted for **j** and fell
Dt 16: 15 hands, and your **j** will be complete.
Jdg 9: 19 may Abimelek be your **j**, and may
1Ch 12: 40 and sheep, for there was **j** in Israel.
16: 27 and **j** are in his dwelling place.
16: 33 them sing for **j** before the LORD,
29: 17 **j** how willingly your people who
29: 22 drank with great **j** in the presence
2Ch 30: 26 There was great **j** in Jerusalem,
Ezr 3: 12 while many others shouted for **j**.
3: 13 of the shouts of **j** from the sound
6: 16 of the house of God with **j**.
6: 22 they celebrated with **j** the Festival
6: 22 the LORD had filled them with **j**
Ne 8: 10 for the **j** of the LORD is your
8: 12 food and to celebrate with great **j**,
8: 17 And their **j** was very great.
12: 43 God had given them great **j**.
Est 8: 16 it was a time of happiness and **j**,
8: 17 there was **j** and gladness among
9: 17 and made it a day of feasting and **j**.
9: 18 and made it a day of feasting and **j**.
9: 19 of the month of Adar as a day of **j**
9: 22 their sorrow was turned into **j**
9: 22 the days as days of feasting and **j**
Job 3: 7 may no shout of **j** be heard in it.
6: 10 my **j** in unrelenting pain—that I
8: 21 and your lips with shouts of **j**.
9: 25 fly away without a glimpse of **j**.
Job 10: 20 from me so I can have a moment's **j**
20: 5 brief, the **j** of the godless lasts
33: 26 will see God's face and shout for **j**;
38: 7 and all the angels shouted for **j**?
Ps 4: 7 Fill my heart with **j** when their
5: 11 be glad; let them ever sing for **j**.
16: 11 you will fill me with **j** in your
19: 8 are right, giving **j** to the heart.
20: 5 we shout for **j** over your victory
21: 1 How great is his **j** in the victories
21: 6 glad with the **j** of your presence.
27: 6 tent I will sacrifice with shouts of **j**;
28: 7 My heart leaps for **j**, and with my
30: 11 sackcloth and clothed me with **j**,
33: 3 play skillfully, and shout for **j**.
35: 27 in my vindication shout for **j**
42: 4 of the Mighty One with shouts of **j**
43: 4 God, to God, my **j** and my delight.
45: 7 by anointing you with the oil of **j**.
45: 15 Led in with **j** and gladness,
47: 1 shout to God with cries of **j**.
47: 5 God has ascended amid shouts of **j**,
48: 2 loftiness, the **j** of the whole earth,
51: 8 Let me hear **j** and gladness;
51: 12 to me the **j** of your salvation
65: 8 fades, you call forth songs of **j**.
65: 13 they shout for **j** and sing.
66: 1 Shout for **j** to God, all the earth!
67: 4 the nations be glad and sing for **j**,
71: 23 My lips will shout for **j** when I sing
81: 1 Sing for **j** to God our strength;
86: 4 Bring **j** to your servant, Lord, for I
89: 12 Hermon sing for **j** at your name.
90: 14 that we may sing for **j** and be glad
92: 4 I sing for **j** at what your hands have
94: 19 me, your consolation brought me **j**.
95: 1 let us sing for **j** to the LORD;
96: 12 all the trees of the forest sing for **j**.
97: 11 and **j** on the upright in heart.
98: 4 Shout for **j** to the LORD,
98: 6 shout for **j** before the LORD,
98: 8 the mountains sing together for **j**;
100: 1 Shout for **j** to the LORD,
105: 43 his chosen ones with shouts of **j**;
106: 5 I may share in the **j** of your nation
107: 22 tell of his works with songs of **j**.
118: 15 Shouts of **j** and victory resound
119:111 they are the **j** of my heart.
126: 2 our tongues with songs of **j**.
126: 3 and we are filled with **j**.
126: 5 with tears will reap with songs of **j**.
126: 6 to sow, will return with songs of **j**,
132: 9 your faithful people sing for **j**."
132: 16 faithful people will ever sing for **j**.
137: 3 tormentors demanded songs of **j**;
137: 6 consider Jerusalem my highest **j**.
149: 5 and sing for **j** on their beds.
Pr 10: 1 A wise son brings **j** to his father,
10: 28 The prospect of the righteous is **j**,
11: 10 wicked perish, there are shouts of **j**.
12: 20 those who promote peace have **j**.
14: 10 and no one else can share its **j**.
15: 20 A wise son brings **j** to his father,
15: 21 Folly brings **j** to one who has no
15: 23 A person finds **j** in giving an apt
15: 30 in a messenger's eyes brings **j**
17: 21 there is no **j** for the parent
21: 15 brings **j** to the righteous but terror
23: 24 of a righteous child has great **j**;
27: 9 and incense bring **j** to the heart,
27: 11 my son, and bring **j** to my heart;
29: 3 A man who loves wisdom brings **j**
29: 6 but the righteous shout for **j** and
Ecc 8: 15 **j** will accompany them in their toil
11: 9 let your heart give you **j** in the days
Isa 9: 3 the nation and increased their **j**;
12: 3 With **j** you will draw water
12: 6 Shout aloud and sing for **j**,
16: 9 shouts of **j** over your ripened fruit
16: 10 **J** and gladness are taken away
22: 13 But see, there is **j** and revelry,
24: 11 all **j** turns to gloom, all joyful
24: 14 raise their voices, they shout for **j**;
26: 19 the dust wake up and shout for **j**—
35: 2 will rejoice greatly and shout for **j**.

Isa 35: 6 and the mute tongue shout for **j**.
35: 10 everlasting **j** will crown their heads
35: 10 Gladness and **j** will overtake them,
42: 11 Let the people of Sela sing for **j**;
44: 23 Sing for **j**, you heavens,
48: 20 Announce this with shouts of **j**
49: 13 Shout for **j**, you heavens;
51: 3 **J** and gladness will be found in her,
51: 11 everlasting **j** will crown their heads
51: 11 Gladness and **j** will overtake them,
52: 8 together they shout for **j**.
52: 9 Burst into songs of **j** together,
54: 1 shout for **j**, you who were never
55: 12 You will go out in **j** and be led
56: 7 give them **j** in my house of prayer.
58: 14 you will find your **j** in the LORD,
60: 5 heart will throb and swell with **j**;
60: 15 pride and the **j** of all generations.
61: 3 the oil of **j** instead of mourning,
61: 7 and everlasting **j** will be yours.
65: 14 will sing out of the **j** of their hearts,
65: 18 to be a delight and its people a **j**.
66: 5 glorified, that we may see your **j**!'
Jer 7: 34 will bring an end to the sounds of **j**
15: 16 they were my **j** and my heart's
16: 9 will bring an end to the sounds of **j**
25: 10 banish from them the sounds of **j**
31: 7 "Sing with **j** for Jacob;
31: 12 shout for **j** on the heights of Zion;
31: 13 comfort and **j** instead of sorrow.
33: 9 this city will bring me renown, **j**,
33: 11 the sounds of **j** and gladness,
48: 33 **J** and gladness are gone
48: 33 one treads them with shouts of **j**.
48: 33 shouts, they are not shouts of **j**.
51: 48 them will shout for **j** over Babylon,
La 2: 15 of beauty, the **j** of the whole earth?"
5: 15 **J** is gone from our hearts;
Eze 7: 7 is panic, not **j**, on the mountains.
24: 25 their stronghold, their **j** and glory,
Joel 1: 12 Surely the people's **j** is withered
1: 16 **j** and gladness from the house of
Mt 13: 20 word and at once receives it with **j**.
13: 44 in his **j** went and sold all he had
28: 8 afraid yet filled with **j**, and ran
Mk 4: 16 word and at once receive it with **j**.
Lk 1: 14 He will be a **j** and delight to you,
1: 44 the baby in my womb leaped for **j**.
1: 58 great mercy, and they shared her **j**.
2: 10 will cause great **j** for all the people.
6: 23 "Rejoice in that day and leap for **j**,
8: 13 ones who receive the word with **j**
10: 17 The seventy-two returned with **j**
10: 21 full of **j** through the Holy Spirit,
24: 41 still did not believe it because of **j**
24: 52 returned to Jerusalem with great **j**.
Jn 3: 29 and is full of **j** when he hears
3: 29 That **j** is mine, and it is now
15: 11 told you this so that my **j** may be
15: 11 and that your **j** may be complete.
16: 20 grieve, but your grief will turn to **j**.
16: 21 because of her **j** that a child is born
16: 22 and no one will take away your **j**.
16: 24 and your **j** will be complete.
17: 13 full measure of my **j** within them.
Ac 2: 28 you will fill me with **j** in your
8: 8 So there was great **j** in that city.
13: 52 the disciples were filled with **j**
14: 17 of food and fills your hearts with **j**."
16: 34 filled with **j** because he had come
Ro 14: 17 peace and **j** in the Holy Spirit,
15: 13 the God of hope fill you with all **j**
15: 32 so that I may come to you with **j**,
2Co 1: 24 but we work with you for your **j**,
2: 3 you, that you would all share my **j**.
7: 4 troubles my **j** knows no bounds.
7: 7 so that my **j** was greater than ever.
8: 2 trial, their overflowing **j** and their
Gal 4: 27 shout for **j** and cry aloud, you who
5: 22 But the fruit of the Spirit is love, **j**,
Php 1: 4 for all of you, I always pray with **j**
1: 25 for your progress and **j** in the faith,
2: 2 then make my **j** complete by being
2: 29 him in the Lord with great **j**,
4: 1 love and long for, my **j** and crown,
1Th 1: 6 severe suffering with the **j** given
2: 19 our **j**, or the crown in which we
2: 20 Indeed, you are our glory and **j**.
3: 9 in return for all the **j** we have
2Ti 1: 4 you, so that I may be filled with **j**.
Phm : 7 Your love has given me great **j**
Heb 1: 9 by anointing you with the oil of **j**."
12: 2 the **j** set before him he endured
13: 17 this so that their work will be a **j**,
Jas 1: 2 Consider it pure **j**, my brothers
4: 9 to mourning and your **j** to gloom.
1Pe 1: 8 an inexpressible and glorious **j**,
1Jn 1: 4 write this to make our **j** complete.
2Jn : 4 It has given me great **j** to find some
: 12 face, so that our **j** may be complete.
3Jn : 3 It gave me great **j** when some
: 4 I have no greater **j** than to hear
Jude : 24 without fault and with great **j**—

JOYFUL* (JOY)
Dt 16: 14 Be **j** at your festival—
1Sa 18: 6 with **j** songs and with timbrels
1Ki 8: 66 **j** and glad in heart for all the good
1Ch 15: 16 to make a **j** sound with musical
2Ch 7: 10 **j** and glad in heart for the good
Ps 68: 3 may they be happy and **j**.
100: 2 come before him with **j** songs.
Pr 23: 25 may she who gave you birth be **j**!
Ecc 9: 7 and drink your wine with a **j** heart,
Isa 24: 8 The **j** timbrels are stilled,
24: 8 has stopped, the **j** harp is silent.
24: 11 all **j** sounds are banished from the
Jer 31: 4 and go out to dance with the **j**.
Hab 3: 18 I will be **j** in God my Savior.
Zec 8: 19 tenth months will become **j** and
10: 7 Their children will see it and be **j**;
Ro 12: 12 Be **j** in hope, patient in affliction,
Col 1: 12 and giving **j** thanks to the Father,
Heb 12: 22 thousands of angels in **j** assembly,

JOYOUS* (JOY)
Est 8: 15 the city of Susa held a **j** celebration.

JUBILANT
Ps 96: 12 Let the fields be **j**, and everything
98: 4 earth, burst into **j** song with music;

JUBILEE
Lev 25: 11 fiftieth year shall be a **j** for you;

JUDAH (JUDEA)
1. Son of Jacob by Leah (Ge 29:35; 35:23; 1Ch 2:1). Did not want to kill Joseph (Ge 37:26–27). Among Canaanites, fathered Perez by Tamar (Ge 38). Tribe of blessed as ruling tribe (Ge 49:8–12; Dt 33:7), numbered (Nu 1:27; 26:22), allotted land (Jos 15; Eze 48:7), failed to fully possess (Jos 15:63; Jdg 1:1–20).
2. Name used for people and land of southern kingdom.
Ru 1: 7 take them back to the land of **J**.
2Sa 2: 4 David king over the tribe of **J**.
Isa 1: 1 The vision concerning **J**
3: 8 Jerusalem staggers, **J** is falling;
Jer 13: 19 All **J** will be carried into exile,
30: 3 Israel and **J** back from captivity
Hos 1: 7 Yet I will show love to **J**; and I will
Zec 10: 4 From **J** will come the cornerstone,
Mt 2: 6 least among the rulers of **J**;
Heb 7: 14 that our Lord descended from **J**,
8: 8 of Israel and with the people of **J**.
Rev 5: 5 the Lion of the tribe of **J**, the Root

JUDAISM (JEW)
Ac 13: 43 devout converts to **J** followed Paul
Gal 1: 13 of my previous way of life in **J**,
1: 14 I was advancing in **J** beyond many

JUDAS
1. Apostle; son of James (Lk 6:16; Jn 14:22; Ac 1:13). Probably also called Thaddaeus (Mt 10:3; Mk 3:18).
2. Brother of James and Jesus (Mt 13:55; Mk 6:3), also called Jude (Jude 1).
3. Christian prophet (Ac 15:22–32).
4. Apostle, also called Iscariot, who betrayed Jesus (Mt 10:4; 26:14–56; Mk 3:19; 14:10–50; Lk 6:16; 22:3–53; Jn 6:71; 12:4; 13:2–30; 18:2–11). Suicide of (Mt 27:3–5; Ac 1:16–25).

JUDEA (JUDAH)
Mt 2: 1 Jesus was born in Bethlehem in **J**,
24: 16 let those who are in **J** flee
Lk 3: 1 Pontius Pilate was governor of **J**,
Ac 1: 8 and in all **J** and Samaria,
9: 31 Then the church throughout **J**,
1Th 2: 14 imitators of God's churches in **J**,

JUDGE (JUDGED JUDGES JUDGING JUDGMENT JUDGMENTS)
Ge 16: 5 May the LORD **j** between you
18: 25 Will not the **J** of all the earth do
Lev 19: 15 great, but **j** your neighbor fairly.
Dt 1: 16 between your people and **j** fairly,
17: 12 who shows contempt for the **j**
Jdg 2: 18 the LORD raised up a **j** for them,
2: 18 he was with the **j** and saved them
1Sa 2: 10 the LORD will **j** the ends
3: 13 I would **j** his family forever
24: 12 May the LORD **j** between you
1Ki 8: 32 **J** between your servants,
1Ch 16: 33 LORD, for he comes to **j** the earth.
2Ch 6: 23 **J** between your servants,
19: 7 **J** carefully, for with the LORD our
Job 9: 15 only plead with my **J** for mercy.
Ps 7: 8 Let the LORD **j** the peoples.
7: 11 God is a righteous **j**, a God who
9: 4 enthroned as the righteous **j**.
51: 4 verdict and justified when you **j**.
75: 2 it is I who **j** with equity.
76: 9 rose up to **j**, to save all the afflicted
82: 8 up, O God, **j** the earth, for all
94: 2 Rise up, **J** of the earth; pay back
96: 10 he will **j** the peoples with equity.
96: 13 he comes, he comes to **j** the earth.
96: 13 will **j** the world in righteousness
98: 9 LORD, for he comes to **j** the earth.
98: 9 will **j** the world in righteousness
110: 6 He will **j** the nations,
Pr 31: 9 Speak up and **j** fairly;
Isa 2: 4 He will **j** between the nations
3: 13 he rises to **j** the people.
11: 3 He will not **j** by what he sees
33: 22 For the LORD is our **j**, the LORD
Jer 11: 20 who **j** righteously and test the heart
Eze 7: 3 I will **j** you according to your
7: 27 their own standards I will **j** them.
18: 30 I will **j** each of you according
20: 36 Egypt, so I will **j** you,
22: 2 Will you **j** this city of bloodshed?
34: 17 I will **j** between one sheep
Joel 3: 12 there I will sit to **j** all the nations
Mic 3: 11 Her leaders **j** for a bribe, her priests
4: 3 He will **j** between many peoples
Mt 7: 1 "Do not **j**, or you too will be
Lk 6: 37 "Do not **j**, and you will not be
18: 2 there was a **j** who neither feared
Jn 5: 27 authority to **j** because he is the Son
5: 30 I **j** only as I hear, and my judgment
7: 24 but instead **j** correctly."
8: 16 But if I do **j**, my decisions are true,
12: 47 For I did not come to **j** the world,
12: 48 There is a **j** for the one who rejects
Ac 10: 42 the one whom God appointed as **j**
17: 31 set a day when he will **j** the world
Ro 3: 6 so, how could God **j** the world?
14: 10 do you **j** your brother or sister?
1Co 4: 3 indeed, I do not even **j** myself.
4: 5 Therefore **j** nothing before
6: 2 Lord's people will **j** the world?
6: 2 not competent to **j** trivial cases?
Col 2: 16 Therefore do not let anyone **j** you
2Ti 4: 1 who will **j** the living and the dead,
4: 8 the righteous **J**, will award to me
Heb 10: 30 "The Lord will **j** his people."
12: 23 You have come to God, the **J** of all,
13: 4 for God will **j** the adulterer and all
Jas 4: 12 There is only one Lawgiver and **J**,
4: 12 who are you to **j** your neighbor?
1Pe 4: 5 to him who is ready to **j** the living
Rev 20: 4 who had been given authority to **j**.

JUDGED (JUDGE)
Mt 7: 1 "Do not judge, or you too will be **j**.
Jn 5: 24 will not be **j** but has crossed over
1Co 4: 3 I care very little if I am **j** by you
10: 29 For why is my freedom being **j**

Jas 3: 1 who teach will be **j** more strictly.
Rev 20: 12 The dead were **j** according to what

JUDGES (JUDGE)
Jdg 2: 16 Then the LORD raised up **j**,
Job 9: 24 of the wicked, he blindfolds its **j**.
Ps 9: 8 and **j** the peoples with equity.
58: 11 there is a God who **j** the earth."
75: 7 It is God who **j**: He brings one
Pr 29: 14 If a king **j** the poor with fairness,
Jn 5: 22 Moreover, the Father **j** no one,
Ro 2: 16 **j** people's secrets through Jesus
1Co 4: 4 It is the Lord who **j** me.
Heb 4: 12 it **j** the thoughts and attitudes
1Pe 1: 17 a Father who **j** each person's work
2: 23 himself to him who **j** justly.
Rev 19: 11 With justice he **j** and wages war.

JUDGING (JUDGE)
Pr 24: 23 To show partiality in **j** is not good:
Isa 16: 5 one who in **j** seeks justice
Mt 19: 28 **j** the twelve tribes of Israel.
Jn 7: 24 Stop **j** by mere appearances,
2Co 10: 7 You are **j** by appearances.

JUDGMENT (JUDGE)
Nu 33: 4 the LORD had brought **j** on their
Dt 1: 17 of anyone, for **j** belongs to God.
32: 41 sword and my hand grasps it in **j**,
1Sa 25: 33 May you be blessed for your good **j**
Ps 1: 5 the wicked will not stand in the **j**,
9: 7 he has established his throne for **j**.
76: 8 From heaven you pronounced **j**,
82: 1 he renders **j** among the "gods":
119: 66 Teach me knowledge and good **j**,
143: 2 Do not bring your servant into **j**,
Pr 3: 21 preserve sound **j** and discretion;
8: 14 Counsel and sound **j** are mine;
18: 1 against all sound **j** starts quarrels.
Ecc 12: 14 God will bring every deed into **j**,
Isa 3: 14 enters into **j** against the elders
28: 6 of justice to the one who sits in **j**,
53: 8 and **j** he was taken away.
66: 16 his sword the LORD will execute **j**
Jer 2: 35 I will pass **j** on you because you
25: 31 he will bring **j** on all mankind
51: 18 their **j** comes, they will perish.
Eze 11: 10 and I will execute **j** on you
Da 7: 22 pronounced **j** in favor of the holy
Am 7: 4 Sovereign LORD was calling for **j**
Zec 8: 16 true and sound **j** in your courts;
Mt 5: 21 who murders will be subject to **j**.'
5: 22 brother or sister will be subject to **j**.
10: 15 Gomorrah on the day of **j** than
11: 24 on the day of **j** than for you."
12: 36 the day of **j** for every empty word
12: 41 up at the **j** with this generation
Jn 5: 22 but has entrusted all **j** to the Son,
5: 30 and my **j** is just, for I seek not
8: 26 "I have much to say in **j** of you.
9: 39 "For **j** I have come into this world,
12: 31 Now is the time for **j** on this world;
16: 8 about sin and righteousness and **j**:
16: 11 and about **j**, because the prince
Ac 24: 25 self-control and the **j** to come,
Ro 2: 1 you who pass **j** do the same
2: 2 God's **j** against those who do such
5: 16 The **j** followed one sin and brought
12: 3 think of yourself with sober **j**,
14: 10 will all stand before God's **j** seat.
14: 13 Therefore let us stop passing **j**
1Co 7: 40 In my **j**, she is happier if she stays
11: 29 eat and drink **j** on themselves.
14: 24 sin and are brought under **j** by all,
2Co 5: 10 we must all appear before the **j** seat
2Th 1: 5 is evidence that God's **j** is right,
1Ti 3: 6 fall under the same **j** as the devil.
5: 12 Thus they bring **j** on themselves,
Heb 6: 2 of the dead, and eternal **j**.
9: 27 to die once, and after that to face **j**,
10: 27 only a fearful expectation of **j**
Jas 2: 13 Mercy triumphs over **j**.
4: 11 not keeping it, but sitting in **j** on it.
1Pe 4: 17 For it is time for **j** to begin
2Pe 2: 9 for punishment on the day of **j**.
3: 7 fire, being kept for the day of **j**
1Jn 4: 17 have confidence on the day of **j**:
Jude : 6 everlasting chains for **j** on the great
Rev 14: 7 because the hour of his **j** has come.

JUDGMENTS (JUDGE)
Jer 1: 16 will pronounce my **j** on my people
Da 9: 11 and sworn **j** written in the Law
Hos 6: 5 then my **j** go forth like the sun.
Ro 11: 33 How unsearchable his **j**, and his
1Co 2: 15 the Spirit makes **j** about all things,
2: 15 is not subject to merely human **j**,
Rev 16: 7 Almighty, true and just are your **j**."

JUG
1Sa 26: 12 spear and water **j** near Saul's head,
1Ki 17: 12 in a jar and a little olive oil in a **j**.

JUST (JUSTICE JUSTIFICATION JUSTIFIED JUSTIFIES JUSTIFY JUSTIFYING JUSTLY)
Ge 18: 19 by doing what is right and **j**,
Dt 2: 12 place, **j** as Israel did in the land
6: 3 milk and honey, **j** as the LORD,
27: 3 milk and honey, **j** as the LORD,
30: 9 **j** as he delighted in your ancestors,
32: 4 are perfect, and all his ways are **j**.
32: 4 does no wrong, upright and **j** is he.
32: 47 They are not **j** idle words for you—
32: 50 **j** as your brother Aaron died
2Sa 8: 15 doing what was **j** and right for all
1Ch 18: 14 doing what was **j** and right for all
2Ch 12: 6 and said, "The LORD is **j**."
Ne 9: 13 and laws that are **j** and right,
Job 34: 17 you condemn the **j** and mighty
35: 2 "Do you think this is **j**? You say,
Ps 37: 28 For the LORD loves the **j** and will
37: 30 and their tongues speak what is **j**.
99: 4 in Jacob you have done what is **j**
111: 7 of his hands are faithful and **j**;
119:121 have done what is righteous and **j**;
Pr 1: 3 doing what is right and **j** and fair;
2: 8 for he guards the course of the **j**
2: 9 will understand what is right and **j**
8: 8 All the words of my mouth are **j**;
8: 15 and rulers issue decrees that are **j**;
12: 5 The plans of the righteous are **j**,
21: 3 **j** is more acceptable to the LORD
Isa 32: 7 when the plea of the needy is **j**.
58: 2 They ask me for **j** decisions
Jer 4: 2 **j** and righteous way you swear,
22: 3 Do what is **j** and right.
22: 15 He did what was right and **j**, so all
23: 5 do what is **j** and right in the land.
33: 15 he will do what is **j** and right
Eze 18: 5 a righteous man who does what is **j**
18: 19 Since the son has done what is **j**
18: 21 and does what is **j** and right,
18: 25 say, 'The way of the Lord is not **j**.'
18: 27 and does what is **j** and right,
18: 29 say, 'The way of the Lord is not **j**.'
33: 14 sin and do what is **j** and right—
33: 16 They have done what is **j** and right;
33: 17 'The way of the Lord is not **j**.' But it is their way that is not **j**.
33: 19 and does what is **j** and right,
33: 20 say, 'The way of the Lord is not **j**.'
45: 9 and do what is **j** and right.
Da 4: 37 does is right and all his ways are **j**.
Jn 5: 30 my judgment is **j**, for I seek not
Ro 3: 8 Their condemnation is **j**!
3: 26 time, so as to be **j** and the one who
2Th 1: 6 God is **j**: He will pay back trouble
Heb 2: 2 received its **j** punishment,
1Jn 1: 9 he is faithful and **j** and will forgive
Rev 15: 3 **J** and true are your ways,
16: 5 "You are **j** in these judgments,
16: 7 true and **j** are your judgments."
19: 2 for true and **j** are his judgments.

JUSTICE* (JUST)
Ge 49: 16 "Dan will provide **j** for his people
Ex 23: 2 do not pervert **j** by siding
23: 6 "Do not deny **j** to your poor people
Lev 19: 15 "'Do not pervert **j**; do not show
Dt 16: 19 Do not pervert **j** or show partiality.
16: 20 Follow **j** and **j** alone, so that you
24: 17 the foreigner or the fatherless of **j**,
27: 19 "Cursed is anyone who withholds **j**
1Sa 8: 3 accepted bribes and perverted **j**.
2Sa 15: 4 and I would see that they receive **j**."
15: 6 who came to the king asking for **j**,
1Ki 3: 11 for discernment in administering **j**,
3: 28 wisdom from God to administer **j**.
7: 7 hall, the Hall of **J**, where he was
10: 9 he has made you king to maintain **j**
2Ch 9: 8 to maintain **j** and righteousness."
Ezr 7: 25 to administer **j** to all the people
Est 1: 13 experts in matters of law and **j**,
Job 8: 3 Does God pervert **j**?
9: 19 And if it is a matter of **j**, who can
19: 7 though I call for help, there is no **j**.
27: 2 has denied me **j**, the Almighty,
29: 14 **j** was my robe and my turban.
31: 13 "If I have denied **j** to any of my
34: 5 am innocent, but God denies me **j**.
34: 12 that the Almighty would pervert **j**.
34: 17 Can someone who hates **j** govern?
36: 3 I will ascribe **j** to my Maker.
36: 17 and **j** have taken hold of you.
37: 23 in his **j** and great righteousness,
40: 8 "Would you discredit my **j**?
Ps 7: 6 Awake, my God; decree **j**.
9: 16 LORD is known by his acts of **j**;
11: 7 the LORD is righteous, he loves **j**;
33: 5 LORD loves righteousness and **j**;
36: 6 your **j** like the great deep.
45: 4 the cause of truth, humility and **j**;
45: 6 a scepter of **j** will be the scepter
50: 6 righteousness, for he is a God of **j**.
72: 1 Endow the king with your **j**,
72: 2 your afflicted ones with **j**.
89: 14 **j** are the foundation of your throne
97: 2 **j** are the foundation of his throne.
99: 4 The King is mighty, he loves **j**—
101: 1 I will sing of your love and **j**;
103: 6 and **j** for all the oppressed.
112: 5 who conduct their affairs with **j**.
140: 12 the LORD secures **j** for the poor
Pr 8: 20 righteousness, along the paths of **j**,
16: 10 and his mouth does not betray **j**.
17: 23 in secret to pervert the course of **j**.
18: 5 and so deprive the innocent of **j**.
19: 28 A corrupt witness mocks at **j**,
21: 15 When **j** is done, it brings joy
29: 4 By **j** a king gives a country stability,
29: 7 The righteous care about **j**
29: 26 is from the LORD that one gets **j**.
Ecc 3: 16 was there, in the place of **j**—
5: 8 a district, and **j** and rights denied,
Isa 1: 17 Learn to do right; seek **j**.
1: 21 She once was full of **j**;
1: 27 Zion will be delivered with **j**,
5: 7 And he looked for **j**, but saw
5: 16 Almighty will be exalted by his **j**,
5: 23 a bribe, but deny **j** to the innocent.
9: 7 and upholding it with **j**
10: 2 withhold **j** from the oppressed of
11: 4 with **j** he will give decisions
16: 5 one who in judging seeks **j**
28: 6 He will be a spirit of **j** to the one
28: 17 I will make **j** the measuring line
29: 21 deprive the innocent of **j**.
30: 18 For the LORD is a God of **j**.
32: 1 and rulers will rule with **j**.
32: 16 The LORD's **j** will dwell
33: 5 he will fill Zion with his **j**
42: 1 and he will bring **j** to the nations.
42: 3 In faithfulness he will bring forth **j**;
42: 4 be discouraged till he establishes **j**
51: 4 my **j** will become a light
51: 5 my arm will bring **j** to the nations.
56: 1 "Maintain **j** and do what is right,
59: 4 No one calls for **j**; no one pleads
59: 8 there is no **j** in their paths.
59: 9 So **j** is far from us,
59: 11 We look for **j**, but find none;
59: 14 So **j** is driven back,
59: 15 was displeased that there was no **j**.
61: 8 "For I, the LORD, love **j**;
Jer 5: 28 have no limit; they do not seek **j**.
9: 24 **j** and righteousness on earth,
12: 1 would speak with you about your **j**:
21: 12 "'Administer **j** every morning;
La 3: 36 to deprive them of **j**—would not
Eze 22: 29 the foreigner, denying them **j**.
34: 16 I will shepherd the flock with **j**.
Hos 2: 19 betroth you in righteousness and **j**,
12: 6 maintain love and **j**, and wait

Am 2: 7 and deny **j** to the oppressed.
5: 7 There are those who turn **j**
5: 10 who hate the one who upholds **j** in
5: 12 deprive the poor of **j** in the courts.
5: 15 maintain **j** in the courts.
5: 24 But let **j** roll on like a river,
6: 12 But you have turned **j** into poison
Mic 3: 1 Should you not embrace **j**,
3: 8 and with **j** and might, to declare
3: 9 who despise **j** and distort all that is
Hab 1: 4 is paralyzed, and **j** never prevails.
1: 4 the righteous, so that **j** is perverted.
Zep 3: 5 by morning he dispenses his **j**,
Zec 7: 9 'Administer true **j**; show mercy
Mal 2: 17 them" or "Where is the God of **j**?"
3: 5 the foreigners among you of **j**,
Mt 12: 18 he will proclaim **j** to the nations.
12: 20 out, till he has brought **j** through
23: 23 **j**, mercy and faithfulness.
Lk 11: 42 you neglect **j** and the love of God.
18: 3 'Grant me **j** against my adversary.'
18: 5 I will see that she gets **j**, so that she
18: 7 will not God bring about **j** for his
18: 8 you, he will see that they get **j**,
Ac 8: 33 humiliation he was deprived of **j**.
17: 31 he will judge the world with **j**
28: 4 the goddess **J** has not allowed him
2Co 7: 11 what readiness to see **j** done.
Heb 1: 8 a scepter of **j** will be the scepter
11: 33 administered **j**, and gained what
Rev 19: 11 With **j** he judges and wages war.

JUSTIFICATION* (JUST)
Eze 16: 52 you have furnished some **j** for your
Ac 13: 39 sin, a **j** you were not able to obtain
Ro 4: 25 sins and was raised to life for our **j**.
5: 16 many trespasses and brought **j**.
5: 18 one righteous act resulted in **j**

JUSTIFIED* (JUST)
Ps 51: 4 your verdict and **j** when you judge.
Lk 18: 14 the other, went home **j** before God
Ro 3: 24 all are **j** freely by his grace through
3: 28 that a person is **j** by faith apart
4: 2 in fact, Abraham was **j** by works,
5: 1 since we have been **j** through faith,
5: 9 Since we have now been **j** by his
8: 30 those he called, he also **j**; those he **j**, he also glorified.
10: 10 heart that you believe and are **j**,
1Co 6: 11 you were **j** in the name of the Lord
Gal 2: 16 that a person is not **j** by the works
2: 16 Jesus that we may be **j** by faith
2: 16 works of the law no one will be **j**.
2: 17 seeking to be **j** in Christ, we Jews
3: 11 relies on the law is **j** before God,
3: 24 came that we might be **j** by faith.
5: 4 be **j** by the law have been alienated
Titus 3: 7 so that, having been **j** by his grace,

JUSTIFIES* (JUST)
Ro 3: 26 the one who **j** those who have faith
4: 5 but trusts God who **j** the ungodly,
8: 33 God has chosen? It is God who **j**.

JUSTIFY* (JUST)
Est 7: 4 such distress would **j** disturbing
Job 40: 8 you condemn me to **j** yourself?
Isa 53: 11 my righteous servant will **j** many,
Lk 10: 29 But he wanted to **j** himself, so he
16: 15 "You are the ones who **j** yourselves
Ro 3: 30 who will **j** the circumcised by faith
Gal 3: 8 that God would **j** the Gentiles

JUSTIFYING* (JUST)
Job 32: 2 Job for **j** himself rather than God.

JUSTLY* (JUST)
Ps 58: 1 Do you rulers indeed speak **j**?
106: 3 Blessed are those who act **j**,
Jer 7: 5 actions and deal with each other **j**,
Mic 6: 8 To act **j** and to love mercy
Lk 23: 41 We are punished **j**, for we are
1Pe 2: 23 himself to him who judges **j**.

KADESH (KADESH BARNEA)
Nu 20: 1 Desert of Zin, and they stayed at **K**.
Dt 1: 46 so you stayed in **K** many days—

KADESH BARNEA (KADESH)
Nu 32: 8 I sent them from **K** to look over

KEBAR
Eze 1: 1 among the exiles by the **K** River,

KEDORLAOMER
Ge 14: 17 Abram returned from defeating **K**

KEEP (KEEPER KEEPING KEEPS KEPT)
Ge 31: 49 "May the LORD **k** watch between
Ex 15: 26 commands and **k** all his decrees,
20: 6 love me and **k** my commandments.
Lev 15: 31 "'You must **k** the Israelites
Nu 6: 24 LORD bless you and **k** you;
Dt 4: 2 **k** the commands of the LORD your
6: 17 Be sure to **k** the commands
7: 9 love him and **k** his commandments.
7: 12 your God will **k** his covenant
11: 1 your God and **k** his requirements,
13: 4 **K** his commands and obey him;
30: 10 your God and **k** his commands
30: 16 and to **k** his commands,
Jos 22: 5 careful to **k** the commandment
1Ki 8: 58 to him and **k** the commands,
2Ki 17: 19 Judah did not **k** the commands
23: 3 the LORD and **k** his commands,
1Ch 29: 18 and **k** their hearts loyal to you.
2Ch 6: 14 you who **k** your covenant of love
34: 31 the LORD and **k** his commands,
Ne 1: 5 love him and **k** his commandments,
Job 14: 16 my steps but not **k** track of my sin.
Ps 18: 28 You, LORD, **k** my lamp burning;
19: 13 **K** your servant also from willful
78: 10 they did not **k** God's covenant
119: 2 Blessed are those who **k** his statutes
121: 7 The LORD will **k** you from all
141: 3 **k** watch over the door of my lips.
Pr 4: 21 sight, **k** them within your heart;
4: 24 **K** your mouth free of perversity;
12: 23 The prudent **k** their knowledge
17: 28 are thought wise if they **k** silent,
30: 8 **K** falsehood and lies far from me;
Ecc 3: 6 up, a time to **k** and a time to throw
12: 13 Fear God and **k** his commandments,
Isa 26: 3 You will **k** in perfect peace those
42: 6 I will **k** you and will make you to
46: 8 "Remember this, **k** it in mind,
58: 13 "If you **k** your feet from breaking
Jer 16: 11 forsook me and did not **k** my law.
Eze 20: 19 and be careful to **k** my laws.
Da 9: 4 love him and **k** his commandments,
Am 5: 13 Therefore the prudent **k** quiet
Mt 10: 10 staff, for the worker is worth his **k**.
19: 17 enter life, **k** the commandments."
Lk 12: 35 service and **k** your lamps burning,
17: 33 tries to **k** their life will lose it,
Jn 10: 24 saying, "How long will you **k** us
12: 25 this world will **k** it for eternal life.
14: 15 "If you love me, **k** my commands.
15: 10 If you **k** my commands, you will
Ac 2: 24 for death to **k** its hold on him.
18: 9 **k** on speaking, do not be silent.
Ro 7: 19 not want to do—this I **k** on doing.
12: 11 but **k** your spiritual fervor,
14: 22 these things **k** between yourself
16: 17 **K** away from them.
1Co 1: 8 He will also **k** you firm to the end,
2Co 12: 7 in order to **k** me from becoming
Gal 5: 25 let us **k** in step with the Spirit.
Eph 4: 3 Make every effort to **k** the unity
2Th 3: 6 to **k** away from every believer who
1Ti 5: 22 the sins of others. **K** yourself pure.
2Ti 4: 5 you, **k** your head in all situations,
Heb 9: 20 God has commanded you to **k**."
13: 5 **K** your lives free from the love
Jas 1: 26 yet do not **k** a tight rein on their
2: 8 If you really **k** the royal law found
3: 2 to **k** their whole body in check.
2Pe 1: 8 they will **k** you from being
1Jn 5: 3 love for God: to **k** his commands.
Jude : 21 **k** yourselves in God's love as you
: 24 To him who is able to **k** you
Rev 3: 10 **k** you from the hour of trial that is
12: 17 those who **k** God's commands
14: 12 of God who **k** his commands
22: 9 with all who **k** the words of this

KEEPER (KEEP)
Ge 4: 9 "Am I my brother's **k**?"

KEEPING (KEEP)
Ex 20: 8 the Sabbath day by **k** it holy.
Dt 5: 12 the Sabbath day by **k** it holy,
13: 18 your God by **k** all his commands
Ps 19: 11 in **k** them there is great reward.
119:112 My heart is set on **k** your decrees
Pr 15: 3 **k** watch on the wicked and the good.
Mt 3: 8 Produce fruit in **k** with repentance.
Lk 2: 8 **k** watch over their flocks at night.
1Co 7: 19 **K** God's commands is what counts.
Jas 4: 11 law, you are not **k** it, but sitting
1Pe 3: 16 **k** a clear conscience, so that those
2Pe 3: 9 Lord is not slow in **k** his promise,

KEEPS (KEEP)
Ne 1: 5 who **k** his covenant of love
Ps 15: 4 who **k** an oath even when it hurts,
Pr 15: 21 has understanding **k** a straight
19: 16 Whoever **k** commandments **k** their life,
Isa 56: 2 **k** their hands from doing any evil."
Da 9: 4 who **k** his covenant of love
Jn 7: 19 Yet not one of you **k** the law.
14: 21 **k** them is the one who loves me.
1Co 13: 5 angered, it **k** no record of wrongs.
Jas 2: 10 For whoever **k** the whole law
1Jn 3: 24 The one who **k** God's commands
Rev 22: 7 Blessed is the one who **k** the words

KEILAH
1Sa 23: 13 that David had escaped from **K**,

KEPT (KEEP)
Ex 12: 42 Because the LORD **k** vigil
Dt 7: 8 and **k** the oath he swore to your
2Ki 18: 6 he **k** the commands the LORD had
Ne 9: 8 You have **k** your promise because
Ps 130: 3 LORD, **k** a record of sins, Lord,
Isa 38: 17 In your love you **k** me from the pit
Mt 19: 20 "All these I have **k**," the young
Jn 15: 10 as I have **k** my Father's commands
2Co 11: 9 have **k** myself from being a burden
2Ti 4: 7 finished the race, I have **k** the faith.
1Pe 1: 4 This inheritance is **k** in heaven

KERNEL*
Mk 4: 28 head, then the full **k** in the head.
Jn 12: 24 you, unless a **k** of wheat falls

KEY (KEYS)
Isa 33: 6 the LORD is the **k** to this treasure.
Rev 20: 1 having the **k** to the Abyss

KEYS* (KEY)
Mt 16: 19 will give you the **k** of the kingdom
Rev 1: 18 And I hold the **k** of death

KICK*
Ac 26: 14 hard for you to **k** against the goads.'

KILL (KILLED KILLS)
Ecc 3: 3 a time to **k** and a time to heal,
Mt 10: 28 those who **k** the body but cannot **k** the soul.
17: 23 They will **k** him, and on the third
Mk 9: 31 will **k** him, and after three days
10: 34 spit on him, flog him and **k** him.

KILLED (KILL)
Ge 4: 8 his brother Abel and **k** him.
Ex 2: 12 he **k** the Egyptian and hid him
13: 15 the LORD **k** the firstborn of both
Nu 35: 11 who has **k** someone accidentally
1Sa 17: 50 down the Philistine and **k** him.
Ne 9: 26 They **k** your prophets, who had
Hos 6: 5 I **k** you with the words of my
Lk 11: 48 they **k** the prophets, and you build
Ac 3: 15 You **k** the author of life, but God

KILLS (KILL)
Lev 24: 21 whoever **k** a human being is to be
2Co 3: 6 the letter **k**, but the Spirit gives

KIND (KINDNESS KINDNESSES KINDS)
Ge 1: 24 animals, each according to its **k**."
2Ch 10: 7 "If you will be **k** to these people
Pr 11: 17 who are **k** benefit themselves,
12: 25 the heart, but a **k** word cheers it up.
14: 21 blessed is the one who is **k**
14: 31 whoever is **k** to the needy honors
19: 17 Whoever is **k** to the poor lends
Da 4: 27 by being **k** to the oppressed.

Lk 6: 35 because he is **k** to the ungrateful
1Co 13: 4 Love is patient, love is **k**.
15: 35 what **k** of body will they come?"
Eph 4: 32 Be **k** and compassionate to one
2Ti 2: 24 but must be **k** to everyone,
Titus 2: 5 to be **k**, and to be subject to their

KINDHEARTED* (HEART)
Pr 11: 16 A **k** woman gains honor,

KINDNESS (KIND)
Ge 24: 12 show **k** to my master Abraham.
32: 10 I am unworthy of all the **k**
39: 21 he showed him **k** and granted him
Ru 2: 20 "He has not stopped showing his **k**
2Sa 9: 3 to whom I can show God's **k**?"
22: 51 he shows unfailing **k** to his
Job 6: 14 "Anyone who withholds **k**
Ps 141: 5 that is a **k**; let him rebuke me—
Isa 54: 8 with everlasting **k** I will have
Jer 9: 24 who exercises **k**,
31: 3 I have drawn you with unfailing **k**.
Hos 11: 4 I led them with cords of human **k**,
Ac 14: 17 He has shown **k** by giving you rain
Ro 11: 22 but **k** to you, provided that you continue in his **k**.
2Co 6: 6 understanding, patience and **k**;
Gal 5: 22 peace, forbearance, **k**, goodness,
Eph 2: 7 expressed in his **k** to us in Christ
Col 3: 12 yourselves with compassion, **k**,
Titus 3: 4 But when the **k** and love of God

KINDNESSES* (KIND)
Ps 106: 7 did not remember your many **k**,
Isa 63: 7 I will tell of the **k** of the LORD,
63: 7 to his compassion and many **k**.

KINDS (KIND)
Ge 1: 12 bearing seed according to their **k**
1Co 12: 4 There are different **k** of gifts,
1Ti 6: 10 of money is a root of all **k** of evil.
1Pe 1: 6 had to suffer grief in all **k** of trials.

KING (KING'S KINGDOM KINGDOMS KINGS)

1. Kings of Judah and Israel: see Saul, David, Solomon.

2. Kings of Judah: see Rehoboam, Abijah, Asa, Jehoshaphat, Jehoram, Ahaziah, Athaliah (Queen), Joash, Amaziah, Azariah (Uzziah), Jotham, Ahaz, Hezekiah, Manasseh, Amon, Josiah, Jehoahaz, Jehoiakim, Jehoiachin, Zedekiah.

3. Kings of Israel: see Jeroboam I, Nadab, Baasha, Elah, Zimri, Tibni, Omri, Ahab, Ahaziah, Joram, Jehu, Jehoahaz, Jehoash, Jeroboam II, Zechariah, Shallum, Menahem, Pekah, Pekahiah, Hoshea.

Ex 1: 8 Then a new **k**, to whom Joseph
Dt 17: 14 "Let us set a **k** over us like all
Jdg 17: 6 In those days Israel had no **k**;
1Sa 8: 5 now appoint a **k** to lead us, such as
11: 15 made Saul **k** in the presence
12: 12 we want a **k** to rule over us'—
12: 12 the LORD your God was your **k**.
2Sa 2: 4 anointed David **k** over the tribe
1Ki 1: 30 Solomon your son shall be **k**
Ps 2: 6 "I have installed my **k** on Zion,
24: 7 that the **K** of glory may come in.
44: 4 You are my **K** and my God,
47: 7 For God is the **K** of all the earth;
Isa 32: 1 a **k** will reign in righteousness
Jer 30: 9 their God and David their **k**,
Hos 3: 5 their God and David their **k**.
Mic 2: 13 Their **K** will pass through before
Zec 9: 9 See, your **k** comes to you,
Mt 2: 2 is the one who has been born **k**
27: 11 him, "Are you the **k** of the Jews?"
Lk 19: 38 "Blessed is the **k** who comes
23: 3 Jesus, "Are you the **k** of the Jews?"
23: 38 THIS IS THE **K** OF THE
Jn 1: 49 you are the **k** of Israel."
12: 13 "Blessed is the **k** of Israel!"
Ac 17: 7 saying that there is another **k**,
1Ti 1: 17 Now to the **K** eternal, immortal,
6: 15 the **K** of kings and Lord of lords,
Heb 7: 1 This Melchizedek was **k** of Salem
Rev 15: 3 are your ways, **K** of the nations.
17: 14 is Lord of lords and **K** of kings—
19: 16 this name written: **K** OF KINGS

KINGDOM (KING)
Ex 19: 6 you will be for me a **k** of priests
Dt 17: 18 When he takes the throne of his **k**,
2Sa 7: 12 blood, and I will establish his **k**.
1Ki 11: 31 'See, I am going to tear the **k**
1Ch 17: 11 own sons, and I will establish his **k**.
29: 11 Yours, LORD, is the **k**;
Ps 45: 6 justice will be the scepter of your **k**.
103: 19 in heaven, and his **k** rules over all.
145: 11 They tell of the glory of your **k**
Eze 29: 14 There they will be a lowly **k**.
Da 2: 39 "After you, another **k** will arise,
4: 3 His **k** is an eternal **k**;
7: 27 His **k** will be an everlasting **k**,
Ob : 21 And the **k** will be the LORD's.
Mt 3: 2 for the **k** of heaven has come near."
4: 17 for the **k** of heaven has come near."
4: 23 the good news of the **k**,
5: 3 spirit, for theirs is the **k** of heaven.
5: 10 for theirs is the **k** of heaven.
5: 19 be called least in the **k** of heaven,
5: 19 be called great in the **k** of heaven.
5: 20 you will certainly not enter the **k**
6: 10 your **k** come, your will be done,
6: 33 But seek first his **k** and his
7: 21 Lord,' will enter the **k** of heaven,
8: 11 Isaac and Jacob in the **k** of heaven.
8: 12 of the **k** will be thrown outside,
9: 35 the good news of the **k**
10: 7 'The **k** of heaven has come near.'
11: 11 the **k** of heaven is greater than he.
11: 12 the **k** of heaven has been subjected
12: 25 "Every **k** divided against itself will
12: 26 How then can his **k** stand?
12: 28 the **k** of God has come upon you.
13: 11 of the **k** of heaven has been given
13: 19 hears the message about the **k**
13: 24 "The **k** of heaven is like a man who
13: 31 "The **k** of heaven is like a mustard
13: 33 "The **k** of heaven is like yeast
13: 38 seed stands for the people of the **k**.
13: 41 of his **k** everything that causes sin
13: 43 like the sun in the **k** of their Father.
13: 44 "The **k** of heaven is like treasure
13: 45 the **k** of heaven is like a merchant
13: 47 the **k** of heaven is like a net that
13: 52 in the **k** of heaven is like the owner
16: 19 you the keys of the **k** of heaven;
16: 28 the Son of Man coming in his **k**."
18: 1 is the greatest in the **k** of heaven?"
18: 3 will never enter the **k** of heaven.
18: 4 is the greatest in the **k** of heaven.
18: 23 the **k** of heaven is like a king who
19: 12 for the sake of the **k** of heaven.
19: 14 for the **k** of heaven belongs to such
19: 23 is rich to enter the **k** of heaven.
19: 24 who is rich to enter the **k** of God."
20: 1 the **k** of heaven is like a landowner
20: 21 the other at your left in your **k**."
21: 31 the prostitutes are entering the **k**
21: 43 the **k** of God will be taken away
22: 2 "The **k** of heaven is like a king who
23: 13 shut the door of the **k** of heaven
24: 7 rise against nation, and **k** against **k**.
24: 14 gospel of the **k** will be preached
25: 1 the **k** of heaven will be like ten
25: 34 the **k** prepared for you since
26: 29 it new with you in my Father's **k**."
Mk 1: 15 "The **k** of God has come near.
3: 24 If a **k** is divided against itself, that **k**
4: 11 of the **k** of God has been given
4: 26 "This is what the **k** of God is like.
4: 30 "What shall we say the **k** of God is
6: 23 I will give you, up to half my **k**."
9: 1 see that the **k** of God has come
9: 47 you to enter the **k** of God with one
10: 14 for the **k** of God belongs to such as
10: 15 anyone who will not receive the **k**
10: 23 for the rich to enter the **k** of God!"
10: 24 hard it is to enter the **k** of God!
10: 25 who is rich to enter the **k** of God."
11: 10 "Blessed is the coming **k** of our
12: 34 are not far from the **k** of God."
13: 8 rise against nation, and **k** against **k**.
14: 25 I drink it new in the **k** of God."
Mk 15: 43 himself waiting for the **k** of God,
Lk 1: 33 his **k** will never end."
4: 43 the good news of the **k** of God
6: 20 are poor, for yours is the **k** of God.
7: 28 in the **k** of God is greater than he."
8: 1 the good news of the **k** of God.
8: 10 of the **k** of God has been given
9: 2 them out to proclaim the **k** of God
9: 11 spoke to them about the **k** of God,
9: 27 taste death before they see the **k**
9: 60 you go and proclaim the **k** of God."
9: 62 is fit for service in the **k** of God."
10: 9 'The **k** of God has come near
10: 11 The **k** of God has come near.'
11: 2 be your name, your **k** come.
11: 17 "Any **k** divided against itself will
11: 18 himself, how can his **k** stand?
11: 20 the **k** of God has come upon you.
12: 31 But seek his **k**, and these things
12: 32 has been pleased to give you the **k**.
13: 18 asked, "What is the **k** of God like?
13: 20 What shall I compare the **k** of God
13: 28 all the prophets in the **k** of God,
13: 29 places at the feast in the **k** of God.
14: 15 eat at the feast in the **k** of God."
16: 16 of the **k** of God is being preached,
17: 20 when the **k** of God would come,
17: 20 the **k** of God is not something
17: 21 is,' because the **k** of God is in your
18: 16 for the **k** of God belongs to such as
18: 17 anyone who will not receive the **k**
18: 24 for the rich to enter the **k** of God!
18: 25 who is rich to enter the **k** of God."
18: 29 for the sake of the **k** of God
19: 11 that the **k** of God was going
21: 10 rise against nation, and **k** against **k**.
21: 31 you know that the **k** of God is near.
22: 16 it finds fulfillment in the **k** of God."
22: 18 the vine until the **k** of God comes."
22: 29 And I confer on you a **k**, just as my
22: 30 drink at my table in my **k** and sit
23: 42 me when you come into your **k**."
23: 51 was waiting for the **k** of God.
Jn 3: 3 no one can see the **k** of God unless
3: 5 no one can enter the **k** of God
18: 36 said, "My **k** is not of this world.
Ac 1: 3 days and spoke about the **k** of God.
1: 6 going to restore the **k** to Israel?"
8: 12 the good news of the **k** of God
14: 22 hardships to enter the **k** of God,"
19: 8 persuasively about the **k** of God.
20: 25 preaching the **k** will ever see me
28: 23 explaining about the **k** of God,
28: 31 He proclaimed the **k** of God
Ro 14: 17 For the **k** of God is not a matter
1Co 4: 20 For the **k** of God is not a matter
6: 9 wrongdoers will not inherit the **k**
6: 10 nor swindlers will inherit the **k**
15: 24 when he hands over the **k** to God
15: 50 blood cannot inherit the **k** of God,
Gal 5: 21 live like this will not inherit the **k**
Eph 2: 2 and of the ruler of the **k** of the air,
5: 5 any inheritance in the **k** of Christ
Col 1: 12 of his holy people in the **k** of light.
1: 13 us into the **k** of the Son he loves,
4: 11 my co-workers for the **k** of God,
1Th 2: 12 who calls you into his **k** and glory.
2Th 1: 5 be counted worthy of the **k** of God,
2Ti 4: 1 in view of his appearing and his **k**,
4: 18 bring me safely to his heavenly **k**.
Heb 1: 8 justice will be the scepter of your **k**.
12: 28 since we are receiving a **k**
Jas 2: 5 inherit the **k** he promised those
2Pe 1: 11 into the eternal **k** of our Lord
Rev 1: 6 has made us to be a **k** and priests
1: 9 companion in the suffering and **k**
5: 10 You have made them to be a **k**
11: 15 the world has become the **k** of our
12: 10 the power and the **k** of our God,
16: 10 its **k** was plunged into darkness.
17: 12 who have not yet received a **k**,

KINGDOMS (KING)
2Ki 19: 15 you alone are God over all the **k**
19: 19 all the **k** of the earth may know
2Ch 20: 6 You rule over all the **k**

Ps 68: 32 Sing to God, you **k** of the earth,
Isa 37: 16 you alone are God over all the **k**
37: 20 all the **k** of the earth may know
Eze 29: 15 It will be the lowliest of **k** and will
37: 22 nations or be divided into two **k**.
Da 4: 17 Most High is sovereign over all **k**
Zep 3: 8 to gather the **k** and to pour out my

KING'S (KING)
Pr 21: 1 the LORD's hand the **k** heart is
Ecc 8: 3 in a hurry to leave the **k** presence.

KINGS (KING)
Ps 2: 2 The **k** of the earth rise
47: 9 the **k** of the earth belong to God;
68: 29 at Jerusalem **k** will bring you gifts.
72: 11 May all **k** bow down to him and all
110: 5 he will crush **k** on the day of his
149: 8 to bind their **k** with fetters,
Pr 16: 12 **K** detest wrongdoing, for a throne
Isa 24: 21 and the **k** on the earth below.
52: 15 **k** will shut their mouths because
60: 11 their **k** led in triumphal procession.
Da 2: 21 he deposes **k** and raises up others.
7: 17 'The four great beasts are four **k**
7: 24 ten horns are ten **k** who will come
Lk 21: 12 you will be brought before **k**
1Ti 2: 2 for **k** and all those in authority,
6: 15 the King of **k** and Lord of lords,
Rev 1: 5 and the ruler of the **k** of the earth.
17: 14 he is Lord of lords and King of **k**—
19: 16 this name written: KING OF K

KISS (KISSED KISSES)
Ps 2: 12 **K** his son, or he will be angry
Pr 24: 26 An honest answer is like a **k**
SS 1: 2 Let him **k** me with the kisses of his
8: 1 I would **k** you, and no one would
Lk 22: 48 the Son of Man with a **k**?"
Ro 16: 16 Greet one another with a holy **k**.
1Co 16: 20 Greet one another with a holy **k**.
2Co 13: 12 Greet one another with a holy **k**.
1Th 5: 26 all God's people with a holy **k**.
1Pe 5: 14 Greet one another with a **k** of love.

KISSED (KISS)
Mk 14: 45 Judas said, "Rabbi!" and **k** him.
Lk 7: 38 hair, **k** them and poured perfume

KISSES* (KISS)
Pr 27: 6 trusted, but an enemy multiplies **k**.
SS 1: 2 kiss me with the **k** of his mouth—

KNEE (KNEES)
Isa 45: 23 Before me every **k** will bow;
Ro 14: 11 Lord, 'every **k** will bow before me;
Php 2: 10 name of Jesus every **k** should bow,

KNEEL (KNELT)
Est 3: 2 Mordecai would not **k** down or pay
Ps 95: 6 let us **k** before the LORD our
Eph 3: 14 this reason I **k** before the Father,

KNEES (KNEE)
1Ki 19: 18 all whose **k** have not bowed down
Isa 35: 3 hands, steady the **k** that give way;
Da 6: 10 times a day he got down on his **k**
Lk 5: 8 saw this, he fell at Jesus' **k** and said,
Heb 12: 12 your feeble arms and weak **k**.

KNELT* (KNEEL)
2Ch 6: 13 **k** down before the whole assembly
7: 3 they **k** on the pavement with their
29: 29 everyone present with him **k** down
Est 3: 2 officials at the king's gate **k** down
Mt 8: 2 leprosy came and **k** before him
9: 18 leader came and **k** before him
15: 25 woman came and **k** before him.
17: 14 approached Jesus and **k** before him
27: 29 Then they **k** in front of him
Lk 22: 41 beyond them, **k** down and prayed,
Ac 20: 36 he **k** down with all of them
21: 5 there on the beach we **k** to pray.

KNEW (KNOW)
2Ch 33: 13 Manasseh **k** that the LORD is God.
Job 23: 3 If only I **k** where to find him;
Pr 24: 12 say, "But we **k** nothing about this,"
Jer 1: 5 I formed you in the womb I **k** you,
Jnh 4: 2 I **k** that you are a gracious
Mt 7: 23 tell them plainly, 'I never **k** you.
12: 25 Jesus **k** their thoughts and said
Jn 2: 24 to them, for he **k** all people.

KNIFE
Ge 22: 10 hand and took the **k** to slay his son.
Pr 23: 2 put a **k** to your throat if you are

KNOCK* (KNOCKS)
Mt 7: 7 **k** and the door will be opened
Lk 11: 9 **k** and the door will be opened
Rev 3: 20 I stand at the door and **k**.

KNOCKS (KNOCK)
Mt 7: 8 and to the one who **k**, the door will
Lk 11: 10 and to the one who **k**, the door will

KNOW (FOREKNEW FOREKNOWLEDGE KNEW KNOWING KNOWLEDGE KNOWN KNOWS)
Ge 22: 12 Now I **k** that you fear God,
Ex 6: 7 you will **k** that I am the LORD
14: 4 the Egyptians will **k** that I am
33: 13 teach me your ways so I may **k** you
Dt 7: 9 **K** therefore that the LORD your
18: 21 "How can we **k** when a message
Jos 4: 24 of the earth might **k** that the hand
23: 14 You **k** with all your heart and soul
1Sa 17: 46 the whole world will **k** that there is
1Ki 8: 39 you alone **k** every human heart),
Job 11: 6 **K** this: God has even forgotten
19: 25 I **k** that my redeemer lives,
42: 3 things too wonderful for me to **k**.
Ps 9: 10 Those who **k** your name trust
46: 10 says, "Be still, and **k** that I am God;
73: 11 Does the Most High **k** anything?"
100: 3 **K** that the LORD is God. It is he
139: 1 me, LORD, and you **k** me.
139: 23 Search me, God, and **k** my heart;
145: 12 all people may **k** of your mighty
Pr 27: 1 you do not **k** what a day may bring.
30: 4 the name of his son? Surely you **k**!
Ecc 8: 5 wise heart will **k** the proper time
8: 17 Even if the wise claim they **k**,
Isa 29: 15 think, "Who sees us? Who will **k**?"
29: 16 say to the potter, "You **k** nothing"?
40: 21 Do you not **k**? Have you not heard?
Jer 6: 15 they do not even **k** how to blush.
9: 24 have the understanding to **k** me,
22: 16 Is that not what it means to **k** me?"
24: 7 I will give them a heart to **k** me,
31: 34 say to one another, '**K** the LORD,'
31: 34 because they will all **k** me,
33: 3 unsearchable things you do not **k**.'
Eze 2: 5 they will **k** that a prophet has been
6: 10 they will **k** that I am the LORD;
Da 11: 32 but the people who **k** their God
Mt 6: 3 let your left hand **k** what your right
7: 11 **k** how to give good gifts to your
9: 6 want you to **k** that the Son of Man
22: 29 you do not **k** the Scriptures
24: 42 because you do not **k** on what day
26: 74 to them, "I don't **k** the man!"
Mk 12: 24 you do not **k** the Scriptures
Lk 1: 4 so that you may **k** the certainty
11: 13 **k** how to give good gifts to your
12: 48 the one who does not **k** and does
13: 25 'I don't **k** you or where you come
21: 31 you **k** that the kingdom of God is
23: 34 they do not **k** what they are doing."
Jn 1: 26 stands one you do not **k**.
3: 11 we speak of what we **k**, and we
4: 22 worship what you do not **k**; we worship what we do **k**,
4: 42 and we **k** that this man really is
6: 69 to **k** that you are the Holy One
7: 28 you **k** me, and you **k** where I
8: 14 valid, for I **k** where I came
8: 19 "You do not **k** me or my Father,"
8: 32 Then you will **k** the truth,
9: 25 One thing I do **k**. I was blind
10: 4 him because they **k** his voice.
10: 14 I **k** my sheep and my sheep **k** me—
10: 27 I **k** them, and they follow me.
12: 35 the dark does not **k** where they are
13: 17 Now that you **k** these things,
13: 35 this everyone will **k** that you are
14: 7 If you really **k** me, you will **k** my
14: 17 But you **k** him, for he lives with
15: 21 they do not **k** the one who sent me.
16: 30 we can see that you **k** all things
17: 3 that they **k** you, the only true God,
Jn 17: 23 the world will **k** that you sent me
21: 15 he said, "you **k** that I love you."
21: 24 We **k** that his testimony is true.
Ac 1: 7 "It is not for you to **k** the times
1: 24 "Lord, you **k** everyone's heart.
Ro 3: 17 the way of peace they do not **k**."
6: 3 don't you **k** that all of us who were
6: 6 we **k** that our old self was crucified
6: 16 Don't you **k** that when you offer
7: 14 We **k** that the law is spiritual;
7: 18 I **k** that good itself does not dwell
8: 22 We **k** that the whole creation has
8: 26 We do not **k** what we ought to pray
8: 28 we **k** that in all things God works
1Co 1: 21 through its wisdom did not **k** him,
2: 2 I resolved to **k** nothing while I was
3: 16 Don't you **k** that you yourselves are
5: 6 Don't you **k** that a little yeast
6: 2 do you not **k** that the Lord's people
6: 15 Do you not **k** that your bodies are
6: 16 Do you not **k** that he who unites
6: 19 Do you not **k** that your bodies are
7: 16 How do you **k**, wife, whether you
7: 16 Or, how do you **k**, husband,
8: 2 think they **k** something do not
9: 13 Don't you **k** that those who serve
9: 24 Do you not **k** that in a race all
13: 9 For we **k** in part and we prophesy
13: 12 Now I **k** in part; then I shall **k** fully,
14: 16 since they do not **k** what you are
15: 58 because you **k** that your labor
2Co 5: 1 For we **k** that if the earthly tent we
5: 11 we **k** what it is to fear the Lord,
8: 9 For you **k** the grace of our Lord
Gal 1: 11 want you to **k**, brothers and sisters,
2: 16 **k** that a person is not justified
Eph 1: 17 so that you may **k** him better.
1: 18 in order that you may **k** the hope
6: 8 because you **k** that the Lord will
6: 9 since you **k** that he who is both
Php 3: 10 I want to **k** Christ—yes, to **k**
4: 12 I **k** what it is to be in need, and I **k**
Col 2: 2 order that they may **k** the mystery
4: 1 because you **k** that you also have
4: 6 may **k** how to answer everyone.
1Th 3: 3 For you **k** quite well that we are
5: 2 for you **k** very well that the day
2Th 1: 8 punish those who do not **k** God
1Ti 1: 7 they do not **k** what they are talking
3: 5 anyone does not **k** how to manage
3: 15 you will **k** how people ought
2Ti 1: 12 because I **k** whom I have believed,
2: 23 because you **k** they produce
3: 14 because you **k** those from whom
Heb 8: 11 say to one another, '**K** the Lord,'
8: 11 because they will all **k** me,
11: 8 though he did not **k** where he was
Jas 1: 3 because you **k** that the testing
3: 1 because you **k** that we who teach
4: 4 don't you **k** that friendship
4: 14 do not even **k** what will happen
1Pe 1: 18 For you **k** that it was not
2Pe 1: 12 even though you **k** them and are
1Jn 2: 3 We **k** that we have come to **k** him
2: 4 Whoever says, "I **k** him," but does
2: 5 This is how we **k** we are in him:
2: 11 do not **k** where they are going,
2: 20 One, and all of you **k** the truth.
2: 29 If you **k** that he is righteous, you **k**
3: 1 reason the world does not **k** us is that it did not **k** him.
3: 2 But we **k** that when Christ appears,
3: 10 This is how we **k** who the children
3: 14 We **k** that we have passed
3: 16 This is how we **k** what love is:
3: 19 This is how we **k** that we belong
3: 24 this is how we **k** that he lives in us:
3: 24 We **k** it by the Spirit he gave us.
4: 8 does not love does not **k** God,
4: 13 This is how we **k** that we live in
4: 16 so we **k** and rely on the love God
5: 2 This is how we **k** that we love
5: 13 may **k** that you have eternal life.
5: 15 And if we **k** that he hears us—
5: 18 We **k** that anyone born of God

1Jn 5: 20 so that we may **k** him who is true.
Rev 2: 2 I **k** your deeds, your hard work
2: 9 I **k** your afflictions and your
2: 19 I **k** your deeds, your love and faith,
3: 3 you will not **k** at what time I will
3: 15 I **k** your deeds, that you are neither

KNOWING (KNOW)
Ge 3: 5 will be like God, **k** good and evil."
3: 22 like one of us, **k** good and evil.
Jn 19: 28 **k** that everything had now been
Php 3: 8 worth of **k** Christ Jesus my Lord,
Phm : 21 **k** that you will do even more than I
Heb 13: 2 hospitality to angels without **k** it.

KNOWLEDGE (KNOW)
Ge 2: 9 the tree of the **k** of good and evil.
2: 17 eat from the tree of the **k** of good
2Ch 1: 10 Give me wisdom and **k**, that I may
Job 21: 22 "Can anyone teach **k** to God,
38: 2 my plans with words without **k**?
42: 3 that obscures my plans without **k**?'
Ps 19: 2 night after night they reveal **k**.
94: 10 he who teaches mankind lack **k**?
119: 66 Teach me **k** and good judgment,
139: 6 Such **k** is too wonderful for me,
Pr 1: 4 **k** and discretion to the young—
1: 7 of the LORD is the beginning of **k**,
2: 5 the LORD and find the **k** of God.
2: 6 from his mouth come **k**
2: 10 and **k** will be pleasant to your soul.
3: 20 by his **k** the watery depths were
8: 10 of silver, **k** rather than choice gold,
8: 12 I possess **k** and discretion.
9: 10 **k** of the Holy One is understanding
10: 14 The wise store up **k**, but the mouth
12: 1 Whoever loves discipline loves **k**,
12: 23 The prudent keep their **k**
13: 16 All who are prudent act with **k**,
14: 6 **k** comes easily to the discerning.
15: 7 The lips of the wise spread **k**,
15: 14 The discerning heart seeks **k**,
17: 27 The one who has **k** uses words
18: 15 heart of the discerning acquires **k**,
19: 2 Desire without **k** is not good—
19: 25 discerning, and they will gain **k**.
20: 15 lips that speak **k** are a rare jewel.
23: 12 and your ears to words of **k**.
24: 4 through **k** its rooms are filled
Ecc 7: 12 but the advantage of **k** is this:
Isa 11: 2 the Spirit of the **k** and fear
11: 9 the **k** of the LORD as the waters
40: 14 Who was it that taught him **k**,
Jer 3: 15 heart, who will lead you with **k**
Hos 4: 6 are destroyed from lack of **k**.
Hab 2: 14 will be filled with the **k** of the glory
Mal 2: 7 lips of a priest ought to preserve **k**,
Mt 13: 11 "Because the **k** of the secrets
Lk 8: 10 He said, "The **k** of the secrets
11: 52 you have taken away the key to **k**.
Ac 18: 24 a thorough **k** of the Scriptures.
Ro 1: 28 worthwhile to retain the **k** of God,
10: 2 but their zeal is not based on **k**.
11: 33 riches of the wisdom and **k** of God!
1Co 8: 1 But **k** puffs up while love builds up.
8: 11 Christ died, is destroyed by your **k**.
12: 8 to another a message of **k** by means
13: 2 can fathom all mysteries and all **k**,
13: 8 where there is **k**, it will pass away.
2Co 2: 14 aroma of the **k** of him everywhere.
4: 6 of the **k** of God's glory displayed
8: 7 in **k**, in complete earnestness
11: 6 as a speaker, but I do have **k**.
Eph 3: 19 know this love that surpasses **k**—
4: 13 and in the **k** of the Son of God
Php 1: 9 and more in **k** and depth of insight,
Col 1: 9 with the **k** of his will through all
1: 10 work, growing in the **k** of God,
2: 3 all the treasures of wisdom and **k**.
3: 10 is being renewed in **k** in the image
1Ti 2: 4 and to come to a **k** of the truth.
6: 20 ideas of what is falsely called **k**,
Titus 1: 1 and their **k** of the truth that leads
Heb 10: 26 we have received the **k** of the truth,
2Pe 1: 5 and to goodness, **k**;
3: 18 in the grace and **k** of our Lord

KNOWN (KNOW)
Ex 6: 3 I did not make myself fully **k**
Ps 16: 11 You make **k** to me the path of life;
89: 1 make your faithfulness **k** through
98: 2 LORD has made his salvation **k**
105: 1 make **k** among the nations what he
119:168 for all my ways are **k** to you.
Pr 20: 11 Even small children are **k** by their
Isa 12: 4 make **k** among the nations what he
46: 10 I make **k** the end
61: 9 descendants will be **k** among
Eze 38: 23 I will make myself **k** in the sight
39: 7 "'I will make **k** my holy name
Mt 10: 26 or hidden that will not be made **k**.
24: 43 of the house had **k** at what time
Lk 19: 42 had only **k** on this day what would
Jn 15: 15 my Father I have made **k** to you.
16: 14 he will receive what he will make **k**
17: 26 I have made you **k** to them,
Ac 2: 28 You have made **k** to me the paths
Ro 1: 19 since what may be **k** about God is
3: 21 of God has been made **k**,
9: 22 his wrath and make his power **k**,
11: 34 "Who has **k** the mind of the Lord?
15: 20 the gospel where Christ was not **k**,
16: 26 and made **k** through the prophetic
1Co 2: 16 "Who has **k** the mind of the Lord
8: 3 whoever loves God is **k** by God.
13: 12 know fully, even as I am fully **k**.
2Co 3: 2 our hearts, **k** and read by everyone.
Gal 4: 9 or rather are **k** by God—how is it
Eph 3: 5 which was not made **k** to people
6: 19 I will fearlessly make **k** the mystery
2Ti 3: 15 from infancy you have **k** the Holy
2Pe 2: 21 than to have **k** it and then to turn

KNOWS (KNOW)
1Sa 2: 3 for the LORD is a God who **k**,
Est 4: 14 who **k** but that you have come
Job 23: 10 But he **k** the way that I take;
Ps 44: 21 since he **k** the secrets of the heart?
94: 11 The LORD **k** all human plans; he **k**
103: 14 for he **k** how we are formed,
Ecc 8: 7 Since no one **k** the future, who can
9: 12 one **k** when their hour will come:
Mt 6: 8 Father **k** what you need before
11: 27 one **k** the Son except the Father,
11: 27 no one **k** the Father except the Son
24: 36 about that day or hour no one **k**,
Lk 12: 47 "The servant who **k** the master's
16: 15 of others, but God **k** your hearts.
Ac 15: 8 God, who **k** the heart,
Ro 8: 27 searches our hearts **k** the mind
1Co 2: 11 who **k** a person's thoughts except
2Ti 2: 19 "The Lord **k** those who are his,"
Jas 4: 17 **k** the good they ought to do
1Jn 4: 6 and whoever **k** God listens to us;
4: 7 has been born of God and **k** God.

KOHATHITE (KOHATHITES)
Nu 3: 29 The **K** clans were to camp

KOHATHITES (KOHATHITE)
Nu 3: 28 The **K** were responsible for the
4: 15 The **K** are to carry those things

KORAH

Levite who led rebellion against Moses and Aaron (Nu 16; Jude 11).

LABAN

Brother of Rebekah (Ge 24:29), father of Rachel and Leah (Ge 29:16). Received Abraham's servant (Ge 24:29–51). Provided daughters as wives for Jacob in exchange for Jacob's service (Ge 29:1–30). Provided flocks for Jacob's service (Ge 30:25–43). After Jacob's departure, pursued and covenanted with him (Ge 31).

LABOR (LABORING)
Ex 1: 11 to oppress them with forced **l**,
20: 9 Six days you shall **l** and do all your
Dt 5: 13 Six days you shall **l** and do all your
Ps 127: 1 the house, the builders **l** in vain.
128: 2 You will eat the fruit of your **l**;
Pr 12: 24 rule, but laziness ends in forced **l**.
Isa 54: 1 for joy, you who were never in **l**;
55: 2 your **l** on what does not satisfy?
Mt 6: 28 They do not **l** or spin.
Jn 4: 38 have reaped the benefits of their **l**."
1Co 3: 8 rewarded according to their own **l**.
15: 58 know that your **l** in the Lord is not
Gal 4: 27 cry aloud, you who were never in **l**;
Php 2: 16 that I did not run or **l** in vain.
Rev 14: 13 "they will rest from their **l**, for their

LABORING* (LABOR)
2Th 3: 8 **l** and toiling so that we would not

LACK (LACKED LACKING LACKS)
Ps 34: 9 for those who fear him **l** nothing.
Pr 5: 23 For **l** of discipline they will die,
10: 21 many, but fools die for **l** of sense.
11: 14 For **l** of guidance a nation falls,
15: 22 Plans fail for **l** of counsel,
28: 27 who give to the poor will **l** nothing,
Mk 6: 6 He was amazed at their **l** of faith.
16: 14 *rebuked them for their **l** of faith*
1Co 1: 7 you do not **l** any spiritual gift
7: 5 because of your **l** of self-control.
Col 2: 23 but they **l** any value in restraining

LACKED (LACK)
Dt 2: 7 you, and you have not **l** anything.
Ne 9: 21 they **l** nothing, their clothes did
1Co 12: 24 greater honor to the parts that **l** it,

LACKING (LACK)
Ro 12: 11 Never be **l** in zeal, but keep your
Jas 1: 4 and complete, not **l** anything.

LACKS (LACK)
Pr 25: 28 is a person who **l** self-control.
31: 11 in her and **l** nothing of value.
Eze 34: 8 because my flock **l** a shepherd
Jas 1: 5 If any of you **l** wisdom, you should

LAID (LAY)
Isa 53: 6 and the LORD has **l** on him
Mk 6: 29 took his body and **l** it in a tomb.
Lk 6: 48 deep and **l** the foundation on rock.
Ac 6: 6 prayed and **l** their hands on them.
1Co 3: 11 other than the one already **l**,
1Ti 4: 14 the body of elders **l** their hands
1Jn 3: 16 Jesus Christ **l** down his life for us.

LAKE
Mt 8: 24 a furious storm came up on the **l**,
14: 25 went out to them, walking on the **l**.
Mk 4: 1 Again Jesus began to teach by the **l**.
Lk 8: 33 down the steep bank into the **l**
Jn 6: 25 him on the other side of the **l**,
Rev 19: 20 into the fiery **l** of burning sulfur.
20: 14 were thrown into the **l** of fire.
20: 14 The **l** of fire is the second death.

LAMB (LAMB'S LAMBS)
Ge 22: 8 "God himself will provide the **l**
Ex 12: 21 and slaughter the Passover **l**.
Nu 9: 11 They are to eat the **l**,
2Sa 12: 4 he took the ewe **l** that belonged
Isa 11: 6 The wolf will live with the **l**,
53: 7 he was led like a **l** to the slaughter,
Mk 14: 12 to sacrifice the Passover **l**,
Jn 1: 29 "Look, the **L** of God, who takes
Ac 8: 32 as a **l** before its shearer is silent,
1Co 5: 7 our Passover **l**, has been sacrificed.
1Pe 1: 19 a **l** without blemish or defect.
Rev 5: 6 The **L** had seven horns and seven
5: 12 "Worthy is the **L**, who was slain,
7: 14 them white in the blood of the **L**.
14: 4 They follow the **L** wherever he
15: 3 God's servant Moses and of the **L**:
17: 14 They will wage war against the **L**, but the **L** will triumph
19: 9 to the wedding supper of the **L**!"
21: 23 gives it light, and the **L** is its lamp.

LAMB'S* (LAMB)
Rev 13: 8 been written in the **L** book of life,
21: 27 names are written in the **L** book

LAMBS (LAMB)
Lk 10: 3 you out like **l** among wolves.
Jn 21: 15 Jesus said, "Feed my **l**."

LAME
2Sa 9: 3 he is **l** in both feet."
Isa 33: 23 even the **l** will carry off plunder.
35: 6 Then will the **l** leap like a deer,
Mt 11: 5 The blind receive sight, the **l** walk,
15: 31 the **l** walking and the blind seeing.
Lk 14: 21 the crippled, the blind and the **l**.'

LAMENT
2Sa 1: 17 took up this **l** concerning Saul
Eze 19: 1 a **l** concerning the princes

LAMP (LAMPS LAMPSTAND LAMPSTANDS)
2Sa 22: 29 You, LORD, are my **l**;
Ps 18: 28 You, LORD, keep my **l** burning;
119:105 Your word is a **l** to my feet
132: 17 set up a **l** for my anointed one.
Pr 6: 23 For this command is a **l**,
20: 27 The human spirit is the **l**
31: 18 and her **l** does not go out at night.
Mt 6: 22 "The eye is the **l** of the body.
Lk 8: 16 "No one lights a **l** and hides it
Rev 21: 23 gives it light, and the Lamb is its **l**.
22: 5 They will not need the light of a **l**

LAMPS (LAMP)
Mt 25: 1 be like ten virgins who took their **l**
Lk 12: 35 service and keep your **l** burning,
Rev 4: 5 of the throne, seven **l** were blazing.

LAMPSTAND (LAMP)
Ex 25: 31 "Make a **l** of pure gold.
Zec 4: 2 "I see a solid gold **l** with a bowl
4: 11 on the right and the left of the **l**?"
Heb 9: 2 In its first room were the **l**
Rev 2: 5 and remove your **l** from its place.

LAMPSTANDS (LAMP)
2Ch 4: 7 He made ten gold **l** according
Rev 1: 12 when I turned I saw seven golden **l**,
1: 20 the seven **l** are the seven churches.

LAND (LANDS)
Ge 1: 10 God called the dry ground "**l**,"
1: 11 said, "Let the **l** produce vegetation:
1: 24 "Let the **l** produce living creatures
12: 1 household to the **l** I will show you.
12: 7 your offspring I will give this **l**."
13: 15 All the **l** that you see I will give
15: 18 "To your descendants I give this **l**,
50: 24 this **l** to the **l** he promised on oath
Ex 3: 8 a **l** flowing with milk and honey
6: 8 I will bring you to the **l** I swore
33: 3 Go up to the **l** flowing with milk
Lev 25: 23 you reside in my **l** as foreigners
Nu 14: 8 he will lead us into that **l**,
35: 33 not pollute the **l** where you are.
35: 33 Bloodshed pollutes the **l**,
Dt 1: 8 See, I have given you this **l**.
8: 7 God is bringing you into a good **l**
11: 10 is not like the **l** of Egypt,
28: 21 you from the **l** you are entering
29: 19 on the watered **l** as well as the dry.
34: 1 LORD showed him the whole **l**—
Jos 13: 2 "This is the **l** that remains:
14: 4 Levites received no share of the **l**
14: 9 me, 'The **l** on which your feet have
2Sa 21: 14 answered prayer in behalf of the **l**.
2Ki 17: 5 of Assyria invaded the entire **l**,
24: 1 king of Babylon invaded the **l**,
25: 21 into captivity, away from her **l**.
2Ch 7: 14 their sin and will heal their **l**.
7: 20 then I will uproot Israel from my **l**,
36: 21 The **l** enjoyed its sabbath rests;
Ezr 9: 11 entering to possess is a **l** polluted
Ne 9: 36 the **l** you gave our ancestors so
Ps 37: 11 meek will inherit the **l** and enjoy
37: 29 The righteous will inherit the **l**
136: 21 and gave their **l** as an inheritance,
142: 5 my portion in the **l** of the living."
Pr 2: 21 For the upright will live in the **l**,
12: 11 work their **l** will have abundant
Isa 6: 13 seed will be the stump in the **l**."
53: 8 was cut off from the **l** of the living;
Jer 2: 7 came and defiled my **l** and made
Eze 36: 24 bring you back into your own **l**.

LANDS (LAND)
Ps 111: 6 giving them the **l** of other nations.
Eze 20: 6 honey, the most beautiful of all **l**.
Zec 10: 9 in distant **l** they will remember me.

LANGUAGE (LANGUAGES)
Ge 11: 1 Now the whole world had one **l**
11: 9 there the LORD confused the **l**
Jn 8: 44 speaks his native **l**, for he is a liar
Ac 2: 6 Sheard their own **l** being spoken.
Col 3: 8 slander, and filthy **l** from your lips.

Rev 5: 9 God persons from every tribe and **l**
7: 9 people and **l**, standing before
14: 6 to every nation, tribe, **l** and people.

LANGUAGES (LANGUAGE)
Isa 66: 18 the people of all nations and **l**,
Zec 8: 23 "In those days ten people from all **l**

LAODICEA
Rev 3: 14 the angel of the church in **L** write:

LAP
Jdg 7: 5 "Separate those who **l** the water

LASHES
Pr 17: 10 more than a hundred **l** a fool.
2Co 11: 24 the Jews the forty **l** minus one.

LAST (LASTING LASTS LATTER)
Ex 14: 24 During the **l** watch of the night
2Sa 23: 1 These are the **l** words of David:
Isa 2: 2 In the **l** days the mountain
41: 4 the first of them and with the **l**—
44: 6 I am the first and I am the **l**;
48: 12 I am the first and I am the **l**.
Hos 3: 5 and to his blessings in the **l** days.
Mic 4: 1 In the **l** days the mountain
Mt 19: 30 are first will be **l**, and many who are **l** will be first.
20: 8 beginning with the **l** ones hired
21: 37 **L** of all, he sent his son to them.
Mk 9: 35 wants to be first must be the very **l**,
10: 31 But many who are first will be **l**,
15: 37 a loud cry, Jesus breathed his **l**.
Jn 6: 40 I will raise them up at the **l** day."
15: 16 fruit that will **l**—and so
Ac 2: 17 "'In the **l** days, God says, I will
Ro 1: 17 is by faith from first to **l**, just as
1Co 15: 26 The **l** enemy to be destroyed is
15: 52 of an eye, at the **l** trumpet.
2Ti 3: 1 will be terrible times in the **l** days.
2Pe 3: 3 in the **l** days scoffers will come,
Jude : 18 "In the **l** times there will be scoffers
Rev 1: 17 I am the First and the **L**.
22: 13 the First and the **L**, the Beginning

LASTING (LAST)
Ex 12: 14 to the LORD—a **l** ordinance.
Lev 24: 8 of the Israelites, as a **l** covenant.
Nu 25: 13 have a covenant of a **l** priesthood,
Heb 10: 34 had better and **l** possessions.

LASTS (LAST)
Ps 30: 5 For his anger **l** only a moment, but his favor **l** a lifetime;
2Co 3: 11 greater is the glory of that which **l**!

LATTER (LAST)
Job 42: 12 The LORD blessed the **l** part
Mt 23: 23 You should have practiced the **l**,
Php 1: 16 The **l** do so out of love,

LAUGH (LAUGHED LAUGHS LAUGHTER)
Ps 59: 8 But you **l** at them, LORD;
Pr 31: 25 she can **l** at the days to come.
Ecc 3: 4 a time to weep and a time to **l**,
Lk 6: 21 you who weep now, for you will **l**.
6: 25 Woe to you who **l** now, for you will

LAUGHED (LAUGH)
Ge 17: 17 **l** and said to himself, "Will a son
18: 12 So Sarah **l** to herself as she thought,

LAUGHS (LAUGH)
Ps 2: 4 The One enthroned in heaven **l**;
37: 13 but the Lord **l** at the wicked, for he

LAUGHTER (LAUGH)
Ge 21: 6 said, "God has brought me **l**,
Ps 126: 2 Our mouths were filled with **l**,
Pr 14: 13 Even in **l** the heart may ache,
Jas 4: 9 Change your **l** to mourning and

LAVISHED
Eph 1: 8 that he **l** on us. With all wisdom
1Jn 3: 1 See what great love the Father has **l**

LAW (LAWFUL LAWGIVER LAWS)
Ex 31: 18 the two tablets of the covenant **l**,
Lev 24: 22 to have the same **l** for the foreigner
Nu 6: 13 "'Now this is the **l** of the Nazirite
Dt 1: 5 Moses began to expound this **l**,
6: 25 to obey all this **l** before the LORD
27: 26 of this **l** by carrying them out."
31: 11 you shall read this **l** before them

Dt 31: 26 "Take this Book of the **L** and place
Jos 1: 7 to obey all the **l** my servant Moses
1: 8 Keep this Book of the **L** always
22: 5 the **l** that Moses the servant
2Ki 22: 8 the Book of the **L** in the temple
2Ch 6: 16 walk before me according to my **l**,
17: 9 the Book of the **L** of the LORD;
34: 14 the Book of the **L** of the LORD
Ezr 7: 6 well versed in the **L** of Moses,
Ne 8: 2 the priest brought the **L** before
8: 8 from the Book of the **L** of God,
Ps 1: 2 delight is in the **l** of the LORD,
19: 7 The **l** of the LORD is perfect,
37: 31 The **l** of their God is in their hearts
40: 8 your **l** is within my heart."
119: 18 may see wonderful things in your **l**.
119: 70 unfeeling, but I delight in your **l**.
119: 72 The **l** from your mouth is more
119: 77 I may live, for your **l** is my delight.
119: 97 Oh, how I love your **l**! I meditate
119:163 detest falsehood but I love your **l**.
119:165 peace have those who love your **l**,
Isa 2: 3 The **l** will go out from Zion,
42: 21 righteousness to make his **l** great
Jer 2: 8 deal with the **l** did not know me;
8: 8 for we have the **l** of the LORD,"
31: 33 "I will put my **l** in their minds
Mic 4: 2 The **l** will go out from Zion,
Hab 1: 7 they are a **l** to themselves
Zec 7: 12 would not listen to the **l**
Mt 5: 17 that I have come to abolish the **L**
7: 12 you, for this sums up the **L**
22: 36 greatest commandment in the **L**?"
22: 40 All the **L** and the Prophets hang
23: 23 more important matters of the **l**—
Lk 11: 52 "Woe to you experts in the **l**,
16: 17 of a pen to drop out of the **L**.
24: 44 about me in the **L** of Moses,
Jn 1: 17 For the **l** was given through Moses;
Ac 13: 39 able to obtain under the **l** of Moses.
Ro 2: 12 sin apart from the **l** will also perish apart from the **l**,
2: 12 under the **l** will be judged by the **l**.
2: 15 requirements of the **l** are written
2: 20 you have in the **l** the embodiment
2: 25 has value if you observe the **l**,
3: 19 it says to those who are under the **l**,
3: 20 through the **l** we become conscious
3: 21 apart from the **l** the righteousness
3: 28 faith apart from the works of the **l**.
3: 31 nullify the **l** by this faith?
3: 31 Not at all! Rather, we uphold the **l**.
4: 13 It was not through the **l**
4: 15 because the **l** brings wrath.
4: 16 not only to those who are of the **l**
5: 13 account where there is no **l**.
5: 20 The **l** was brought in so
6: 14 because you are not under the **l**,
6: 15 sin because we are not under the **l**
7: 1 the **l** has authority over someone
7: 4 died to the **l** through the body
7: 5 passions aroused by the **l** were
7: 6 we have been released from the **l** so
7: 7 Is the **l** sinful? Certainly not!
7: 8 For apart from the **l**, sin was dead.
7: 12 So then, the **l** is holy,
7: 14 We know that the **l** is spiritual;
7: 22 my inner being I delight in God's **l**;
7: 25 in my mind am a slave to God's **l**,
8: 2 has set you free from the **l** of sin
8: 3 For what the **l** was powerless to do
8: 4 of the **l** might be fully met in us,
8: 7 it does not submit to God's **l**,
9: 4 the receiving of the **l**, the temple
9: 31 who pursued the **l** as the way
10: 4 Christ is the culmination of the **l**
13: 8 loves others has fulfilled the **l**.
13: 10 love is the fulfillment of the **l**.
1Co 9: 9 For it is written in the **L** of Moses:
9: 20 those under the **l** I became like one
9: 21 I am not free from God's **l** but am under Christ's **l**),
15: 56 is sin, and the power of sin is the **l**.
Gal 2: 16 not justified by the works of the **l**,
2: 19 "For through the **l** I died to the **l** so

Gal 3: 2 the Spirit by the works of the **l**,
3: 5 among you by the works of the **l**,
3: 10 works of the **l** are under a curse,
3: 11 on the **l** is justified before God,
3: 13 curse of the **l** by becoming a curse
3: 17 The **l**, introduced 430 years later,
3: 19 The **l** was given through angels
3: 21 Is the **l**, therefore, opposed
3: 23 were held in custody under the **l**,
3: 24 So the **l** was our guardian until
4: 21 you who want to be under the **l**,
5: 3 he is obligated to obey the whole **l**.
5: 4 by the **l** have been alienated
5: 14 For the entire **l** is fulfilled
5: 18 the Spirit, you are not under the **l**.
6: 2 in this way you will fulfill the **l**
Eph 2: 15 his flesh the **l** with its commands
Php 3: 6 as for righteousness based on the **l**,
3: 9 of my own that comes from the **l**,
1Ti 1: 8 We know that the **l** is good if one
Heb 7: 12 the **l** must be changed also.
7: 19 (for the **l** made nothing perfect),
10: 1 The **l** is only a shadow of the good
Jas 1: 25 the perfect **l** that gives freedom,
2: 8 you really keep the royal **l** found
2: 10 For whoever keeps the whole **l**
4: 11 When you judge the **l**, you are not
1Jn 3: 4 Everyone who sins breaks the **l**;

LAWFUL (LAW)
Mt 12: 12 Therefore it is **l** to do good

LAWGIVER* (LAW)
Isa 33: 22 the LORD is our **l**, the LORD is
Jas 4: 12 There is only one **L** and Judge,

LAWLESS (LAWLESSNESS)
2Th 2: 8 then the **l** one will be revealed,
Heb 10: 17 **l** acts I will remember no more."

LAWLESSNESS* (LAWLESS)
2Th 2: 3 occurs and the man of **l** is revealed,
2: 7 the secret power of **l** is already
1Jn 3: 4 sins breaks the law; in fact, sin is **l**.

LAWS (LAW)
Ex 21: 1 "These are the **l** you are to set
Lev 25: 18 and be careful to obey my **l**,
Dt 4: 1 and **l** I am about to teach you.
30: 16 keep his commands, decrees and **l**;
Ps 119: 30 I have set my heart on your **l**.
119: 43 for I have put my hope in your **l**.
119:120 fear of you; I stand in awe of your **l**.
119:164 I praise you for your righteous **l**.
119:175 and may your **l** sustain me.
Eze 36: 27 and be careful to keep my **l**.
Heb 8: 10 I will put my **l** in their minds
10: 16 I will put my **l** in their hearts, and I

LAWSUIT (LAWSUIT)
Pr 18: 17 In a **l** the first to speak seems right,

LAWSUITS (LAWSUITS)
Hos 10: 4 **l** spring up like poisonous weeds
1Co 6: 7 you have **l** among you means you

LAY (LAID LAYING LAYS)
Ex 29: 10 his sons shall **l** their hands on its
Lev 1: 4 You are to **l** your hand on the head
4: 15 the community are to **l** their hands
Nu 8: 10 the Israelites are to **l** their hands
27: 18 and **l** your hand on him.
1Sa 26: 9 Who can **l** a hand on the LORD's
Job 1: 12 the man himself do not **l** a finger."
22: 22 and **l** up his words in your heart.
Ecc 10: 4 calmness can **l** great offenses
Isa 28: 16 "See, I **l** a stone in Zion, a tested
Mt 8: 20 of Man has no place to **l** his head."
28: 6 Come and see the place where he **l**.
Mk 6: 5 except **l** his hands on a few sick
Lk 9: 58 of Man has no place to **l** his head."
Jn 10: 15 and I **l** down my life for the sheep.
10: 18 I have authority to **l** it down
15: 13 to **l** down one's life for one's
Ac 8: 19 whom I **l** my hands may receive
Ro 9: 33 I **l** in Zion a stone that causes
1Co 3: 11 no one can **l** any foundation other
1Pe 2: 6 "See, I **l** a stone in Zion, a chosen
1Jn 3: 16 we ought to **l** down our lives for
Rev 4: 10 They **l** their crowns before

LAYING* (LAY)
2Ch 32: 9 and all his forces were **l** siege
Job 34: 30 ruling, from **l** snares for the people.
Lk 4: 40 and **l** his hands on each one,
Ac 8: 18 the Spirit was given at the **l**
1Ti 5: 22 not be hasty in the **l** on of hands,
2Ti 1: 6 is in you through the **l** on of my
Heb 6: 1 not **l** again the foundation
6: 2 cleansing rites, the **l** on of hands,

LAYS (LAY)
Jn 10: 11 The good shepherd **l** down his life

LAZARUS
1. Poor man in Jesus' parable (Lk 16:19–31).
2. Brother of Mary and Martha whom Jesus raised from the dead (Jn 11:1—12:19).

LAZINESS* (LAZY)
Pr 12: 24 will rule, but **l** ends in forced labor.
19: 15 **L** brings on deep sleep,
Ecc 10: 18 Through **l**, the rafters sag;

LAZY* (LAZINESS)
Ex 5: 8 They are **l**; that is why they are
5: 17 "**L**, that's what you are—**l**!
Pr 10: 4 **L** hands make for poverty,
12: 27 The **l** do not roast any game,
26: 15 he is too **l** to bring it back to his
Mt 25: 26 replied, 'You wicked, **l** servant!
Titus 1: 12 always liars, evil brutes, **l** gluttons."
Heb 6: 12 We do not want you to become **l**,

LEAD (LEADER LEADERS LEADERSHIP LEADS LED)
Ex 15: 13 love you will **l** the people you have
Nu 14: 8 with us, he will **l** us into that land,
Dt 31: 2 and I am no longer able to **l** you.
Jos 1: 6 because you will **l** these people
1Sa 8: 5 now appoint a king to **l** us, such as
2Ch 1: 10 that I may **l** this people, for who is
Ps 27: 11 **l** me in a straight path because
43: 3 your faithful care, let them **l** me;
61: 2 **l** me to the rock that is higher than
139: 24 and **l** me in the way everlasting.
143: 10 may your good Spirit **l** me on level
Pr 4: 11 and **l** you along straight paths.
20: 7 The righteous **l** blameless lives;
Ecc 5: 6 Do not let your mouth **l** you
Isa 11: 6 and a little child will **l** them.
49: 10 and **l** them beside springs of water.
Da 12: 3 those who **l** many to righteousness,
Mt 6: 13 And **l** us not into temptation,
15: 14 If the blind **l** the blind, both will
Lk 11: 4 And **l** us not into temptation.'"
Ro 12: 8 if it is to **l**, do it diligently; if it is
1Th 4: 11 it your ambition to **l** a quiet life:
1Jn 3: 7 do not let anyone **l** you astray.
Rev 7: 17 'he will **l** them to springs of living

LEADER (LEAD)
1Sa 7: 6 Now Samuel was serving as **l**
7: 15 continued as Israel's **l** all the days
12: 2 Now you have a king as your **l**.

LEADERS (LEAD)
Heb 13: 7 Remember your **l**, who spoke
13: 17 Have confidence in your **l**

LEADERSHIP* (LEAD)
Nu 27: 18 a man in whom is the spirit of **l**,
33: 1 by divisions under the **l** of Moses
Ps 109: 8 may another take his place of **l**.
Ac 1: 20 another take his place of **l**.'

LEADS (LEAD)
Dt 27: 18 is anyone who **l** the blind astray
Ps 23: 2 he **l** me beside quiet waters,
37: 8 do not fret—it **l** only to evil.
68: 6 he **l** out the prisoners with singing;
Pr 2: 18 Surely her house **l** down to death
10: 17 ignores correction **l** others astray.
14: 23 but mere talk **l** only to poverty.
16: 25 right, but in the end it **l** to death.
19: 23 The fear of the LORD **l** to life;
21: 5 as surely as haste **l** to poverty.
Isa 40: 11 he gently **l** those that have young.
Mt 7: 13 gate and broad is the road that **l**
Jn 10: 3 sheep by name and **l** them out.
Ro 6: 16 slaves to sin, which **l** to death,
6: 22 the benefit you reap **l** to holiness,
14: 19 every effort to do what **l** to peace

2Co 2: 14 God, who always **l** us as captives
7: 10 sorrow brings repentance that **l**
Titus 1: 1 of the truth that **l** to godliness—

LEAH
Wife of Jacob (Ge 29:16–30); bore six sons and one daughter (Ge 29:31—30:21; 34:1; 35:23).

LEAN (LEANED)
Pr 3: 5 **l** not on your own understanding;

LEANED (LEAN)
Ge 47: 31 Israel worshiped as he **l** on the top
Jn 21: 20 one who had **l** back against Jesus
Heb 11: 21 worshiped as he **l** on the top of his

LEAP (LEAPED LEAPS)
Isa 35: 6 Then will the lame **l** like a deer,
Lk 6: 23 "Rejoice in that day and **l** for joy,

LEAPED (LEAP)
Lk 1: 41 greeting, the baby **l** in her womb,

LEAPS (LEAP)
Ps 28: 7 My heart **l** for joy, and with my

LEARN (LEARNED LEARNING)
Dt 4: 10 they may **l** to revere me as long as
5: 1 **L** them and be sure to follow them.
31: 12 and **l** to fear the LORD your God
Ps 119: 7 heart as I **l** your righteous laws.
Isa 1: 17 **L** to do right; seek justice.
26: 9 of the world **l** righteousness.
Mt 11: 29 my yoke upon you and **l** from me,
Jn 14: 31 that the world may **l** that I love
1Th 4: 4 you should **l** to control your own
1Ti 2: 11 A woman should **l** in quietness
5: 4 should **l** first of all to put their

LEARNED (LEARN)
Ps 119:152 Long ago I **l** from your statutes
Mt 11: 25 these things from the wise and **l**,
Jn 6: 45 and **l** from him comes to me.
Php 4: 9 Whatever you have **l** or received
4: 11 I have **l** to be content whatever
2Ti 3: 14 continue in what you have **l**
Heb 5: 8 he was, he **l** obedience from what

LEARNING (LEARN)
Pr 1: 5 the wise listen and add to their **l**,
9: 9 and they will add to their **l**.
Isa 44: 25 who overthrows the **l** of the wise
Jn 7: 15 man get such **l** without having
2Ti 3: 7 always **l** but never able to come

LEATHER
Nu 4: 6 cover the curtain with a durable **l**,
2Ki 1: 8 and had a **l** belt around his waist."
Mt 3: 4 he had a **l** belt around his waist.

LEAVES
Ge 3: 7 so they sewed fig **l** together
Eze 47: 12 Their **l** will not wither, nor will
47: 12 for food and their **l** for healing."
Rev 22: 2 **l** of the tree are for the healing

LEBANON
Dt 11: 24 will extend from the desert to **L**,
1Ki 4: 33 from the cedar of **L** to the hyssop

LED (LEAD)
Ex 3: 1 he **l** the flock to the far side
Dt 8: 2 the LORD your God **l** you all
1Ki 11: 3 and his wives **l** him astray.
2Ch 26: 16 his pride **l** to his downfall.
Ne 13: 26 even he was **l** into sin by foreign
Ps 78: 52 he **l** them like sheep through
Pr 7: 21 persuasive words she **l** him astray;
20: 1 whoever is **l** astray by them is not
Isa 53: 7 he was **l** like a lamb
Jer 11: 19 I had been like a gentle lamb **l**
Am 2: 10 I **l** you forty years in the wilderness
Mt 4: 1 Jesus was **l** by the Spirit
27: 31 they **l** him away to crucify him.
Lk 4: 1 and was **l** by the Spirit
Ac 8: 32 "He was **l** like a sheep
Ro 8: 14 For those who are **l** by the Spirit
2Co 7: 9 but because your sorrow **l** you
Gal 5: 18 But if you are **l** by the Spirit,

LEEKS*
Nu 11: 5 melons, **l**, onions and garlic.

LEFT
Dt 28: 14 to the right or to the **l**,

Jos 1: 7 turn from it to the right or to the **l**,
23: 6 aside to the right or to the **l**.
2Ki 22: 2 aside to the right or to the **l**.
Pr 4: 27 Do not turn to the right or the **l**;
Isa 30: 21 you turn to the right or to the **l**,
Mt 6: 3 do not let your **l** hand know what
25: 33 on his right and the goats on his **l**.

LEGAL
Col 2: 14 the charge of our **l** indebtedness,

LEGION
Mk 5: 9 "My name is **L**," he replied,

LEGITIMATE*
Heb 12: 8 then you are not **l**, not true sons

LEND (LENDER LENDS MONEYLENDER)
Ex 22: 25 "If you **l** money to one of my
Lev 25: 37 You must not **l** them money
Dt 15: 8 freely **l** them whatever they need.
Ps 37: 26 are always generous and **l** freely;
112: 5 who are generous and **l** freely,
Eze 18: 8 He does not **l** to them at interest
Lk 6: 34 Even sinners **l** to sinners,

LENDER* (LEND)
Pr 22: 7 and the borrower is slave to the **l**.
Isa 24: 2 for borrower as for **l**, for debtor as

LENDS (LEND)
Ps 15: 5 who **l** money to the poor without
Pr 19: 17 is kind to the poor **l** to the LORD,

LENGTH (LONG)
Pr 10: 27 fear of the LORD adds **l** to life,

LENGTHY* (LONG)
Mk 12: 40 and for a show make **l** prayers.
Lk 20: 47 and for a show make **l** prayers.

LEOPARD
Isa 11: 6 the **l** will lie down with the goat,
Da 7: 6 beast, one that looked like a **l**.
Rev 13: 2 The beast I saw resembled a **l**,

LEPROSY (LEPROUS)
2Ki 5: 1 was a valiant soldier, but he had **l**.
7: 3 Now there were four men with **l**
2Ch 26: 21 King Uzziah had **l** until the day he
Mt 11: 5 those who have **l** are cleansed,
Lk 17: 12 ten men who had **l** met him.

LEPROUS (LEPROSY)
Ex 4: 6 he took it out, the skin was **l**—

LETTER (LETTERS)
Mt 5: 18 not the smallest **l**, not the least
2Co 3: 2 You yourselves are our **l**,
3: 6 not of the **l** but of the Spirit; for the **l** kills,
2Th 3: 14 not obey our instruction in this **l**.

LETTERS (LETTER)
2Co 3: 7 which was engraved in **l** on stone,
10: 10 "His **l** are weighty and forceful,
2Pe 3: 16 His **l** contain some things that are

LEVEL
Ps 143: 10 good Spirit lead me on **l** ground.
Isa 26: 7 The path of the righteous is **l**;
40: 4 the rough ground shall become **l**,
Jer 31: 9 **l** path where they will not stumble,
Heb 12: 13 "Make **l** paths for your feet,"

LEVI (LEVITE LEVITES LEVITICAL)
1. Son of Jacob by Leah (Ge 29:34; 46:11; 1Ch 2:1). With Simeon avenged rape of Dinah (Ge 34). Tribe of blessed (Ge 49:5–7; Dt 33:8–11), chosen as priests (Nu 3–4), numbered (Nu 3:39; 26:62), allotted cities, but not land (Nu 18; 35; Dt 10:9; Jos 13:14; 21), land (Eze 48:8–22), 12,000 from (Rev 7:7).
2. See MATTHEW.

LEVIATHAN
Job 41: 1 "Can you pull in **L** with a fishhook
Ps 74: 14 you who crushed the heads of **L**
Isa 27: 1 **L** the gliding serpent, **L** the coiling

LEVITE (LEVI)
Dt 26: 12 tithe, you shall give it to the **L**,
Jdg 19: 1 a **L** who lived in a remote area

LEVITES (LEVI)
Nu 1: 53 The **L** are to be responsible
3: 12 The **L** are mine,
8: 6 "Take the **L** from among all
Nu 18: 21 "I give to the **L** all the tithes
35: 7 must give the **L** forty-eight towns,
2Ch 31: 2 to their duties as priests or **L**—
Mal 3: 3 will purify the **L** and refine them

LEVITICAL (LEVI)
Heb 7: 11 attained through the **L** priesthood

LEVY
Am 5: 11 You **l** a straw tax on the poor

LEWDNESS
Mk 7: 22 malice, deceit, **l**, envy, slander,

LIAR* (LIE)
Dt 19: 18 and if the witness proves to be a **l**,
Job 34: 6 I am right, I am considered a **l**;
Ps 116: 11 my alarm I said, "Everyone is a **l**."
Pr 17: 4 a **l** pays attention to a destructive
19: 22 better to be poor than a **l**.
30: 6 will rebuke you and prove you a **l**.
Mic 2: 11 If a **l** and deceiver comes and says,
Jn 8: 44 for he is a **l** and the father of lies.
8: 55 I would be a **l** like you, but I do
Ro 3: 4 be true, and every human being a **l**.
1Jn 1: 10 we make him out to be a **l** and his
2: 4 not do what he commands is a **l**,
2: 22 Who is the **l**? It is whoever denies
4: 20 yet hates a brother or sister is a **l**.
5: 10 God has made him out to be a **l**,

LIARS* (LIE)
Ps 63: 11 the mouths of **l** will be silenced.
Isa 57: 4 brood of rebels, the offspring of **l**?
Mic 6: 12 your inhabitants are **l** and their
1Ti 1: 10 for slave traders and **l**
4: 2 come through hypocritical **l**,
Titus 1: 12 "Cretans are always **l**, evil brutes,
Rev 3: 9 Jews though they are not, but are **l**
21: 8 magic arts, the idolaters and all **l**—

LIBERATED*
Ro 8: 21 the creation itself will be **l** from its

LICENSE*
Jude : 4 of our God into a **l** for immorality

LICK
Ps 72: 9 him and his enemies **l** the dust.
Isa 49: 23 they will **l** the dust at your feet.
Mic 7: 17 They will **l** dust like a snake,

LIE (LIAR LIARS LIED LIES LYING)
Lev 6: 3 find lost property and **l** about it,
19: 11 "'Do not **l**. "'Do not deceive
Nu 23: 19 he should **l**, not a human being,
Dt 6: 7 when you **l** down and when you
25: 2 the judge shall make them **l** down
1Sa 15: 29 is the Glory of Israel does not **l**
Ps 4: 8 In peace I will **l** down and sleep,
23: 2 He makes me **l** down in green
89: 35 and I will not **l** to David—
Pr 3: 24 when you **l** down, your sleep will
Isa 11: 6 the leopard will **l** down
28: 15 for we have made a **l** our refuge
Jer 9: 5 have taught their tongues to **l**;
23: 14 They commit adultery and live a **l**.
Eze 13: 6 are false and their divinations a **l**.
34: 14 There they will **l** down in good
Ro 1: 25 the truth about God for a **l**,
Col 3: 9 Do not **l** to each other, since you
2Th 2: 9 signs and wonders that serve the **l**,
2: 11 so that they will believe the **l**
Titus 1: 2 who does not **l**, promised before
Heb 6: 18 which it is impossible for God to **l**,
1Jn 2: 21 because no **l** comes from the truth.
Rev 14: 5 No **l** was found in their mouths;

LIED (LIE)
Ac 5: 4 have not **l** just to human beings

LIES (LIE)
Ps 5: 6 you destroy those who tell **l**.
5: 9 with their tongues they tell **l**.
10: 7 His mouth is full of **l** and threats;
12: 2 Everyone **l** to their neighbor;
34: 13 evil and your lips from telling **l**.
58: 3 they are wayward, spreading **l**.
144: 8 whose mouths are full of **l**,
Pr 6: 19 a false witness who pours out **l**
12: 17 the truth, but a false witness tells **l**.
19: 5 pours out **l** will not go free.
19: 9 whoever pours out **l** will perish.
Pr 29: 12 If a ruler listens to **l**, all his officials
30: 8 Keep falsehood and **l** far from me;
Jer 5: 31 prophets prophesy **l**, the priests
9: 3 their tongue like a bow, to shoot **l**;
14: 14 "The prophets are prophesying **l**
Hos 11: 12 has surrounded me with **l**,
Jn 8: 44 he is a liar and the father of **l**.

LIFE (LIVE)
Ge 1: 30 that has the breath of **l** in it—
2: 7 into his nostrils the breath of **l**,
2: 9 of the garden were the tree of **l**
6: 17 to destroy all **l** under the heavens,
9: 5 for the **l** of another human being.
9: 11 Never again will all **l** be destroyed
Ex 21: 6 Then he will be his servant for **l**.
21: 23 you are to take **l** for **l**,
23: 26 I will give you a full **l** span.
Lev 17: 14 the **l** of every creature is its
24: 17 "'Anyone who takes the **l**
24: 18 make restitution—**l** for **l**.
Nu 35: 31 a ransom for the **l** of a murderer,
Dt 4: 42 one of these cities and save their **l**.
12: 23 because the blood is the **l**,
12: 23 must not eat the **l** with the meat.
19: 21 **l** for **l**, eye for eye, tooth for
30: 15 See, I set before you today **l**
30: 19 Now choose **l**, so that you and your
30: 20 For the LORD is your **l**, and he
32: 39 I put to death and I bring to **l**,
32: 47 words for you—they are your **l**.
1Sa 19: 5 He took his **l** in his hands when he
Job 2: 6 but you must spare his **l**."
33: 4 breath of the Almighty gives me **l**.
33: 30 the light of **l** may shine on them.
Ps 16: 11 make known to me the path of **l**;
17: 14 world whose reward is in this **l**.
23: 6 will follow me all the days of my **l**,
27: 1 LORD is the stronghold of my **l**—
34: 12 Whoever of you loves **l** and desires
36: 9 For with you is the fountain of **l**;
39: 4 let me know how fleeting my **l** is.
49: 7 No one can redeem the **l** of
49: 8 the ransom for a **l** is costly,
63: 3 Because your love is better than **l**,
69: 28 they be blotted out of the book of **l**
91: 16 With long **l** I will satisfy him
103: 15 The **l** of mortals is like grass,
104: 33 I will sing to the LORD all my **l**;
119: 25 preserve my **l** according to your
Pr 1: 19 it takes away the **l** of those who get
3: 2 will prolong your **l** many years
3: 18 She is a tree of **l** to those who take
6: 23 and instruction are the way to **l**,
6: 26 man's wife preys on your very **l**.
7: 23 little knowing it will cost him his **l**.
8: 35 For those who find me find **l**
10: 11 of the righteous is a fountain of **l**,
10: 27 fear of the LORD adds length to **l**,
11: 30 fruit of the righteous is a tree of **l**,
13: 12 but a longing fulfilled is a tree of **l**.
13: 14 of the wise is a fountain of **l**,
14: 27 of the LORD is a fountain of **l**,
15: 4 The soothing tongue is a tree of **l**,
16: 22 Prudence is a fountain of **l**
19: 23 The fear of the LORD leads to **l**;
21: 21 righteousness and love finds **l**,
22: 5 who would preserve their **l** stay far
22: 23 up their case and will exact **l** for **l**.
Isa 53: 10 the LORD makes his **l** an offering
53: 11 he will see the light of **l** and be
53: 12 he poured out his **l** unto death,
La 3: 58 up my case; you redeemed my **l**.
Eze 18: 27 and right, they will save their **l**.
37: 5 enter you, and you will come to **l**.
Da 12: 2 some to everlasting **l**,
Jnh 2: 6 God, brought my **l** up from the pit.
Mal 2: 5 him, a covenant of **l** and peace,
Mt 6: 25 do not worry about your **l**,
6: 25 Is not **l** more than food,
7: 14 narrow the road that leads to **l**,
10: 39 Whoever finds their **l** will lose it,
10: 39 whoever loses their **l** for my sake
16: 21 and on the third day be raised to **l**.
16: 25 wants to save their **l** will lose it,
16: 25 but whoever loses their **l** for me

Mt 18: 8 is better for you to enter l maimed
19: 16 thing must I do to get eternal l?"
19: 29 as much and will inherit eternal l.
20: 28 to give his l as a ransom for many."
25: 46 but the righteous to eternal l."
Mk 8: 35 wants to save their l will lose it,
8: 35 but whoever loses their l for me
9: 43 to enter l maimed than with two
10: 17 must I do to inherit eternal l?"
10: 30 and in the age to come eternal l.
10: 45 to give his l as a ransom for many."
Lk 6: 9 do evil, to save l or to destroy it?"
9: 22 and on the third day be raised to l."
9: 24 wants to save their l will lose it,
9: 24 but whoever loses their l for me
12: 15 l does not consist in an abundance
12: 22 not worry about your l, what you
12: 25 can add a single hour to your l?
14: 26 yes, even their own l—
17: 33 tries to keep their l will lose it,
17: 33 whoever loses their l will preserve
21: 19 Stand firm, and you will win l.
Jn 1: 4 In him was l, and that l was the light
3: 15 who believes may have eternal l
3: 36 believes in the Son has eternal l,
4: 14 of water welling up to eternal l."
5: 21 even so the Son gives l to whom he
5: 24 has crossed over from death to l.
5: 26 For as the Father has l in himself,
5: 39 that in them you have eternal l.
5: 40 you refuse to come to me to have l.
6: 27 for food that endures to eternal l,
6: 33 heaven and gives l to the world."
6: 35 Jesus declared, "I am the bread of l.
6: 40 believes in him shall have eternal l,
6: 47 the one who believes has eternal l.
6: 48 I am the bread of l.
6: 51 I will give for the l of the world."
6: 53 his blood, you have no l in you.
6: 63 The Spirit gives l; the flesh
6: 68 You have the words of eternal l.
8: 12 but will have the light of l."
10: 10 I have come that they may have l,
10: 15 and I lay down my l for the sheep.
10: 17 loves me is that I lay down my l—
10: 28 I give them eternal l, and they shall
11: 25 "I am the resurrection and the l.
12: 25 who loves their l will lose it,
12: 25 will keep it for eternal l.
12: 50 his command leads to eternal l.
13: 37 I will lay down my l for you."
14: 6 am the way and the truth and the l.
15: 13 lay down one's l for one's friends.
17: 2 he might give eternal l to all those
17: 3 this is eternal l: that they know
20: 31 by believing you may have l in his
Ac 2: 32 God has raised this Jesus to l,
3: 15 You killed the author of l, but God
11: 18 granted repentance that leads to l."
13: 48 appointed for eternal l believed.
Ro 2: 7 immortality, he will give eternal l.
4: 25 was raised to l for our justification.
5: 10 shall we be saved through his l!
5: 18 in justification and l for all people.
5: 21 bring eternal l through Jesus Christ
6: 4 the Father, we too may live a new l.
6: 13 have been brought from death to l;
6: 22 holiness, and the result is eternal l.
6: 23 God is eternal l in Christ Jesus our
8: 6 the mind governed by the Spirit is l
8: 11 give l to your mortal bodies
8: 38 convinced that neither death nor l,
1Co 15: 19 If only for this l we have hope
15: 36 does not come to l unless it dies.
2Co 2: 16 to the other, an aroma that brings l.
3: 6 the letter kills, but the Spirit gives l.
4: 10 so that the l of Jesus may also be
5: 4 mortal may be swallowed up by l.
Gal 2: 20 The l I now live in the body, I live
3: 21 had been given that could impart l,
6: 8 from the Spirit will reap eternal l.
Eph 4: 1 to live a l worthy of the calling you
Php 2: 16 as you hold firmly to the word of l.
4: 3 whose names are in the book of l.
Col 1: 10 you may live a l worthy of the Lord
Col 3: 3 your l is now hidden with Christ
1Th 4: 12 your daily l may win the respect
1Ti 1: 16 believe in him and receive eternal l.
4: 8 promise for both the present l and the l to come.
4: 16 Watch your l and doctrine closely.
6: 12 Take hold of the eternal l
6: 19 take hold of the l that is truly l.
2Ti 1: 9 saved us and called us to a holy l—
1: 10 and has brought l and immortality
3: 12 live a godly l in Christ Jesus will be
Titus 1: 2 the hope of eternal l, which God,
3: 7 heirs having the hope of eternal l.
Heb 7: 16 of the power of an indestructible l.
Jas 1: 12 person will receive the crown of l
3: 13 Let them show it by their good l,
1Pe 3: 7 with you of the gracious gift of l,
3: 10 "Whoever would love l and see
2Pe 1: 3 a godly l through our knowledge
1Jn 1: 1 proclaim concerning the Word of l.
2: 25 is what he promised us—eternal l.
3: 14 we have passed from death to l,
3: 16 Jesus Christ laid down his l for us.
5: 11 God has given us eternal l, and this l
5: 20 He is the true God and eternal l.
Jude : 21 Christ to bring you to eternal l.
Rev 2: 7 the right to eat from the tree of l,
2: 8 Last, who died and came to l again.
2: 10 and I will give you l as your victor's
3: 5 of that person from the book of l,
13: 8 written in the Lamb's book of l,
17: 8 in the book of l from the creation
20: 12 was opened, which is the book of l.
20: 15 in the book of l was thrown
21: 6 from the spring of the water of l.
21: 27 are written in the Lamb's book of l.
22: 1 me the river of the water of l,
22: 2 side of the river stood the tree of l,
22: 14 may have the right to the tree of l
22: 17 take the free gift of the water of l.
22: 19 person any share in the tree of l

LIFE-GIVING* (GIVE LIVE)
Pr 15: 31 Whoever heeds l correction will be
1Co 15: 45 the last Adam, a l spirit.

LIFETIME (LIVE)
Ps 30: 5 a moment, but his favor lasts a l;
Lk 16: 25 in your l you received your good

LIFT (LIFTED LIFTING LIFTS)
Ps 28: 2 as I l up my hands toward your
63: 4 in your name I will l up my hands.
91: 12 they will l you up in their hands,
121: 1 I l up my eyes to the mountains—
123: 1 I l up my eyes to you, to you who
134: 2 L up your hands in the sanctuary
Isa 40: 9 l up your voice with a shout, l it up,
La 2: 19 L up your hands to him for the
3: 41 Let us l up our hearts and our
Mt 4: 6 they will l you up in their hands,
Lk 21: 28 stand up and l up your heads,
Jas 4: 10 the Lord, and he will l you up.
1Pe 5: 6 that he may l you up in due time.

LIFTED (LIFT)
Ne 8: 6 and all the people l their hands
Ps 24: 7 be l up, you ancient doors,
40: 2 He l me out of the slimy pit,
Isa 52: 13 he will be raised and l up and
63: 9 he l them up and carried them all
Jn 3: 14 Just as Moses l up the snake
3: 14 so the Son of Man must be l up,
8: 28 "When you have l up the Son
12: 32 I, when I am l up from the earth,
12: 34 'The Son of Man must be l up'?

LIFTING* (LIFT)
Ps 141: 2 may the l up of my hands be like
Eze 31: 14 l their tops above the thick foliage.
1Ti 2: 8 l up holy hands without anger

LIFTS (LIFT)
Ps 3: 3 glory, the One who l my head high.
113: 7 and l the needy from the ash heap;

LIGAMENT* (LIGAMENTS)
Eph 4: 16 together by every supporting l,

LIGAMENTS* (LIGAMENT)
Col 2: 19 held together by its l and sinews,

LIGHT (ENLIGHTENED LIGHTS)
Ge 1: 3 "Let there be l," and there was l.
Ex 13: 21 in a pillar of fire to give them l,
25: 37 so that they l the space in front
2Sa 22: 29 LORD turns my darkness into l.
Job 38: 19 "What is the way to the abode of l?
Ps 4: 6 Let the l of your face shine on us.
18: 28 my God turns my darkness into l.
19: 8 are radiant, giving l to the eyes.
27: 1 The LORD is my l and my
36: 9 fountain of life; in your l we see l.
56: 13 walk before God in the l of life.
76: 4 You are radiant with l,
89: 15 who walk in the l of your presence,
104: 2 The LORD wraps himself in l as
119:105 to my feet and a l for my path.
119:130 unfolding of your words gives l;
139: 12 for darkness is as l to you.
Pr 4: 18 shining ever brighter till the full l
15: 30 L in a messenger's eyes brings joy
Isa 2: 5 let us walk in the l of the LORD.
9: 2 in darkness have seen a great l;
42: 6 the people and a l for the Gentiles,
45: 7 I form the l and create darkness,
49: 6 also make you a l for the Gentiles,
53: 11 he will see the l of life and be
60: 1 for your l has come, and the glory
60: 19 The sun will no more be your l
60: 19 LORD will be your everlasting l,
Eze 1: 27 and brilliant l surrounded him.
Mic 7: 8 darkness, the LORD will be my l.
Mt 4: 16 in darkness have seen a great l;
5: 14 "You are the l of the world.
5: 15 Neither do people l a lamp and put
5: 16 way, let your l shine before others,
6: 22 your whole body will be full of l.
11: 30 yoke is easy and my burden is l."
17: 2 clothes became as white as the l.
24: 29 and the moon will not give its l;
Mk 13: 24 and the moon will not give its l;
Lk 2: 32 a l for revelation to the Gentiles,
8: 16 those who come in can see the l.
11: 33 those who come in may see the l.
Jn 1: 4 that life was the l of all mankind.
1: 5 The l shines in the darkness,
1: 7 witness to testify concerning that l,
1: 9 The true l that gives l to everyone
3: 19 L has come into the world,
3: 20 Everyone who does evil hates the l,
8: 12 he said, "I am the l of the world.
9: 5 the world, I am the l of the world."
12: 35 Walk while you have the l,
12: 46 I have come into the world as a l,
Ac 13: 47 "'I have made you a l
Ro 13: 12 darkness and put on the armor of l.
2Co 4: 6 made his l shine in our hearts
6: 14 Or what fellowship can l have
11: 14 masquerades as an angel of l.
Eph 5: 8 now you are l in the Lord. Live as children of l
1Th 5: 5 You are all children of the l
1Ti 6: 16 and who lives in unapproachable l,
1Pe 2: 9 of darkness into his wonderful l.
2Pe 1: 19 it, as to a l shining in a dark place,
1Jn 1: 5 God is l; in him there is no
1: 7 But if we walk in the l, as he is
2: 9 Anyone who claims to be in the l
Rev 21: 23 for the glory of God gives it l,
22: 5 They will not need the l of a lamp
22: 5 for the Lord God will give them l.
22: 5 They will not need the l of a lamp

LIGHTNING
Ex 9: 23 and l flashed down to the ground.
20: 18 the people saw the thunder and l
Ps 18: 12 with hailstones and bolts of l.
Eze 1: 13 it was bright, and l flashed out of it.
Da 10: 6 his face like l, his eyes like flaming
Mt 24: 27 For as l that comes from the east is
28: 3 His appearance was like l, and his
Lk 10: 18 replied, "I saw Satan fall like l
Rev 4: 5 From the throne came flashes of l,

LIGHTS (LIGHT)
Ge 1: 14 "Let there be l in the vault
Lk 8: 16 "No one l a lamp and hides it

LIKE-MINDED* (MIND)
Php 2: 2 make my joy complete by being **l**,
1Pe 3: 8 all of you, be **l**, be sympathetic,
LIKENESS
Ge 1: 26 in our **l**, so that they may rule over
Ps 17: 15 will be satisfied with seeing your **l**.
Isa 52: 14 form marred beyond human **l**—
Ro 8: 3 his own Son in the **l** of sinful flesh
Php 2: 7 a servant, being made in human **l**.
Jas 3: 9 who have been made in God's **l**.
LILY
SS 2: 1 a rose of Sharon, a **l** of the valleys.
2: 2 a **l** among thorns is my darling
LIMIT (LIMITATIONS)
Ps 147: 5 his understanding has no **l**.
Jn 3: 34 for God gives the Spirit without **l**.
LIMITATIONS* (LIMIT)
Ro 6: 19 life because of your human **l**.
LINEN
Lev 16: 4 is to put on the sacred **l** tunic,
16: 4 him and put on the **l** turban.
Pr 31: 22 she is clothed in fine **l** and purple.
31: 24 She makes **l** garments and sells
Mk 15: 46 wrapped it in the **l**, and placed it
Jn 20: 6 He saw the strips of **l** lying there,
Rev 15: 6 shining **l** and wore golden sashes
19: 8 (Fine **l** stands for the righteous acts
LINGER
Hab 2: 3 Though it **l**, wait for it;
LION (LION'S LIONS')
Jdg 14: 6 he tore the **l** apart with his bare
1Sa 17: 34 a **l** or a bear came and carried
Isa 11: 7 and the **l** will eat straw like the ox.
65: 25 and the **l** will eat straw like the ox,
Eze 1: 10 right side each had the face of a **l**,
10: 14 the third the face of a **l**,
Da 7: 4 "The first was like a **l**, and it had
1Pe 5: 8 around like a roaring **l** looking
Rev 4: 7 first living creature was like a **l**
5: 5 See, the **L** of the tribe of Judah,
LION'S (LION)
Ge 49: 9 You are a **l** cub, Judah;
LIONS' (LION)
Da 6: 7 shall be thrown into the **l** den.
Rev 9: 8 and their teeth were like **l** teeth.
LIPS
Jos 1: 8 Book of the Law always on your **l**;
Ps 34: 1 his praise will always be on my **l**.
40: 9 I do not seal my **l**, LORD, as you
63: 3 than life, my **l** will glorify you.
119:171 May my **l** overflow with praise,
140: 3 the poison of vipers is on their **l**.
141: 3 keep watch over the door of my **l**.
Pr 10: 13 is found on the **l** of the discerning,
10: 18 conceals hatred with lying **l**
10: 32 The **l** of the righteous know what
12: 22 The LORD detests lying **l**, but he
13: 3 who guard their **l** preserve their
14: 7 will not find knowledge on their **l**.
24: 26 answer is like a kiss on the **l**.
26: 23 on earthenware are fervent **l**
27: 2 an outsider, and not your own **l**.
Isa 6: 5 For I am a man of unclean **l**, and I live among a people of unclean **l**,
28: 11 with foreign **l** and strange tongues
29: 13 mouth and honor me with their **l**,
Mal 2: 7 "For the **l** of a priest ought
Mt 15: 8 people honor me with their **l**,
21: 16 read, "'From the **l** of children
Lk 4: 22 words that came from his **l**.
Ro 3: 13 "The poison of vipers is on their **l**."
Col 3: 8 and filthy language from your **l**.
Heb 13: 15 the fruit of **l** that openly profess his
1Pe 3: 10 and their **l** from deceitful speech.
LISTEN (LISTENED LISTENING LISTENS)
Dt 18: 15 You must **l** to him.
30: 20 LORD your God, **l** to his voice,
1Ki 4: 34 From all nations people came to **l**
2Ki 21: 9 But the people did not **l**.
Ps 5: 1 **L** to my words, LORD,
Pr 1: 5 let the wise **l** and add to their
12: 15 to them, but the wise **l** to advice.
Ecc 5: 1 Go near to **l** rather than to offer
Eze 2: 5 And whether they **l** or fail to **l**—
Mt 12: 42 the earth to **l** to Solomon's wisdom,
Mk 9: 7 is my Son, whom I love. **L** to him!"
Jn 10: 27 My sheep **l** to my voice;
Ac 3: 22 you must **l** to everything he tells
Jas 1: 19 Everyone should be quick to **l**,
1: 22 Do not merely **l** to the word, and
1Jn 4: 6 is not from God does not **l** to us.
LISTENED (LISTEN)
Ne 8: 3 all the people **l** attentively
Isa 66: 4 answered, when I spoke, no one **l**.
Da 9: 6 We have not **l** to your servants
LISTENING (LISTEN)
1Sa 3: 9 LORD, for your servant is **l**.'"
Pr 18: 13 To answer before **l**—that is folly
Lk 10: 39 at the Lord's feet **l** to what he said.
LISTENS (LISTEN)
Lk 10: 16 "Whoever **l** to you **l** to me;
1Jn 4: 6 and whoever knows God **l** to us;
LIVE (ALIVE LIFE LIFE-GIVING LIFETIME LIVES LIVING)
Ge 3: 22 tree of life and eat, and **l** forever."
Ex 20: 12 that you may **l** long in the land
33: 20 face, for no one may see me and **l**."
Nu 21: 8 who is bitten can look at it and **l**."
Dt 5: 24 a person can **l** even if God speaks
6: 2 LORD your God as long as you **l**
8: 3 that man does not **l** on bread alone
Job 14: 14 If someone dies, will they **l** again?
Ps 15: 1 may **l** on your holy mountain?
24: 1 in it, the world, and all who **l** in it;
26: 8 I love the house where you **l**,
119:175 Let me **l** that I may praise you,
Pr 21: 9 Better to **l** on a corner of the roof
21: 19 Better to **l** in a desert than
Ecc 9: 4 a **l** dog is better off than a dead
Isa 26: 19 But your dead will **l**, LORD;
55: 3 come to me; listen, that you may **l**.
Eze 17: 19 As surely as I **l**, I will repay him
20: 11 the person who obeys them will **l**.
37: 3 "Son of man, can these bones **l**?"
Am 5: 6 Seek the LORD and **l**, or he will
Hab 2: 4 the righteous person will **l** by his
Zec 2: 11 I will **l** among you and you will
Mt 4: 4 'Man shall not **l** on bread alone,
Lk 4: 4 'Man shall not **l** on bread
Jn 14: 19 Because I **l**, you also will **l**.
Ac 17: 24 not **l** in temples built by human
17: 28 'For in him we **l** and move and
Ro 1: 17 "The righteous will **l** by faith."
2Co 5: 7 For we **l** by faith, not by sight.
6: 16 "I will **l** with them and walk among
Gal 2: 20 with Christ and I no longer **l**,
3: 11 because "the righteous will **l**
5: 25 Since we **l** by the Spirit, let us keep
Eph 4: 17 must no longer **l** as the Gentiles
Php 1: 21 me, to **l** is Christ and to die is gain.
Col 1: 10 so that you may **l** a life worthy
1Th 4: 1 we instructed you how to **l** in order
5: 13 **L** in peace with each other.
1Ti 2: 2 that we may **l** peaceful and quiet
2Ti 3: 12 who wants to **l** a godly life
Titus 2: 12 and to **l** self-controlled,
Heb 10: 38 my righteous one will **l** by faith.
12: 14 Make every effort to **l** in peace
1Pe 1: 17 **l** out your time as foreigners here
LIVES (LIVE)
Ge 45: 7 save your **l** by a great deliverance.
Job 19: 25 I know that my redeemer **l**,
Pr 11: 30 and the one who is wise saves **l**.
13: 3 guard their lips preserve their **l**,
Isa 57: 15 he who **l** forever, whose name is
Jer 10: 23 that people's **l** are not their own;
Da 3: 28 to give up their **l** rather than serve
Jn 14: 17 he **l** with you and will be in you.
Ro 6: 10 but the life he **l**, he **l** to God.
8: 9 if indeed the Spirit of God **l** in you.
14: 7 none of us **l** for ourselves alone,
Gal 2: 20 I no longer live, but Christ **l** in me.
1Th 2: 8 the gospel of God but our **l** as well.
1Ti 2: 2 peaceful and quiet **l** in all godliness
Titus 2: 12 and godly **l** in this present age,
Heb 7: 24 but because Jesus **l** forever, he has
Heb 13: 5 Keep your **l** free from the love
1Pe 3: 2 the purity and reverence of your **l**.
4: 2 rest of their earthly **l** for evil
2Pe 3: 11 You ought to live holy and godly **l**
1Jn 3: 16 to lay down our **l** for our brothers
4: 16 Whoever **l** in love **l** in God,
LIVING (LIVE)
Ge 2: 7 life, and the man became a **l** being.
1Sa 17: 26 defy the armies of the **l** God?"
Isa 53: 8 was cut off from the land of the **l**;
Jer 2: 13 the spring of **l** water, and have dug
Eze 1: 5 what looked like four **l** creatures.
Zec 14: 8 On that day **l** water will flow
Mt 22: 32 the God of the dead but of the **l**."
Jn 4: 10 he would have given you **l** water."
6: 51 I am the **l** bread that came down
7: 38 said, rivers of **l** water will flow
Ro 8: 11 Jesus from the dead is **l** in you,
12: 1 to offer your bodies as a **l** sacrifice,
1Co 9: 14 the gospel should receive their **l**
Heb 10: 20 and **l** way opened for us through
10: 31 to fall into the hands of the **l** God.
1Pe 1: 23 through the **l** and enduring word
Rev 1: 18 I am the **L** One; I was dead,
4: 6 were four **l** creatures, and they
7: 17 will lead them to springs of **l** water.'
LOAD (LOADS)
Gal 6: 5 each one should carry their own **l**.
LOADS (LOAD)
Mt 23: 4 cumbersome **l** and put them
LOAF (LOAVES)
Hos 7: 8 Ephraim is a flat **l** not turned over.
1Co 10: 17 one body, for we all share the one **l**.
LOAVES (LOAF)
Mk 6: 41 he gave thanks and broke the **l**.
8: 6 When he had taken the seven **l**
Lk 11: 5 'Friend, lend me three **l** of bread;
LOCKED
Jn 20: 26 Though the doors were **l**,
Gal 3: 22 Scripture has **l** up everything
3: 23 **l** up until the faith that was to
LOCUSTS
Ex 10: 4 I will bring **l** into your country
Joel 2: 25 for the years the **l** have eaten—
Mt 3: 4 His food was **l** and wild honey.
Rev 9: 3 of the smoke **l** came down
LOFTY
Ps 139: 6 for me, too **l** for me to attain.
LONELY
Ps 68: 6 God sets the **l** in families, he leads
Lk 5: 16 Jesus often withdrew to **l** places
LONG (LENGTH LENGTHY LONGED LONGING LONGINGS LONGS)
Ex 17: 11 As **l** as Moses held up his hands,
Nu 6: 5 they must let their hair grow **l**.
1Ki 18: 21 "How **l** will you waver between
Ps 40: 16 may those who **l** for your saving
70: 4 may those who **l** for your saving
119: 97 I meditate on it all day **l**.
119:174 I **l** for your salvation, LORD,
Hos 7: 13 I **l** to redeem them but they speak
Am 5: 18 Woe to you who **l** for the day
Mt 25: 5 The bridegroom was a **l** time
Jn 9: 4 As **l** as it is day, we must do
1Co 11: 14 teach you that if a man has **l** hair,
Eph 3: 18 to grasp how wide and **l** and high
Php 1: 8 God can testify how I **l** for all
1Pe 1: 12 Even angels **l** to look into these
LONGED (LONG)
Mt 13: 17 righteous people **l** to see what you
23: 37 how often I have **l** to gather your
Lk 13: 34 how often I have **l** to gather your
2Ti 4: 8 to all who have **l** for his appearing.
LONGING* (LONG)
Dt 28: 65 eyes weary with **l**, and a despairing
Job 7: 2 Like a slave **l** for the evening
Ps 119: 20 My soul is consumed with **l** for
119: 81 My soul faints with **l** for your
119:131 and pant, **l** for your commands.
Pr 13: 12 sick, but a **l** fulfilled is a tree of life.
13: 19 A **l** fulfilled is sweet to the soul,
Eze 23: 27 will not look on these things with **l**

Lk 16: 21 and **l** to eat what fell from the rich
Ro 15: 23 since I have been **l** for many years
2Co 5: 2 **l** to be clothed instead with our
7: 7 He told us about your **l** for me,
7: 11 what alarm, what **l**, what concern,
1Th 2: 17 our intense **l** we made every effort
Heb 11: 16 they were **l** for a better country—

LONGINGS* (LONG)
Ps 38: 9 All my **l** lie open before you, Lord;
112: 10 the **l** of the wicked will come

LONGS* (LONG)
Ps 63: 1 for you, my whole being **l** for you,
Isa 26: 9 in the morning my spirit **l** for you.
30: 18 Yet the LORD **l** to be gracious
Php 2: 26 For he **l** for all of you and is
Jas 4: 5 he jealously **l** for the spirit he has

LOOK (LOOKED LOOKING LOOKS)
Ge 19: 17 Don't **l** back, and don't stop
Ex 3: 6 because he was afraid to **l** at God.
Nu 21: 8 anyone who is bitten can **l** at it
32: 8 Kadesh Barnea to **l** over the land.
1Sa 16: 7 The LORD does not **l** at the things people **l** at.
Job 31: 1 my eyes not to **l** lustfully at a young
Ps 34: 5 Those who **l** to him are radiant;
105: 4 **L** to the LORD and his strength;
113: 6 who stoops down to **l**
123: 2 so our eyes **l** to the LORD our
Pr 1: 28 they will **l** for me but will not find
4: 25 Let your eyes **l** straight ahead;
Isa 17: 7 day people will **l** to their Maker
31: 1 do not **l** to the Holy One of Israel,
40: 26 up your eyes and **l** to the heavens:
60: 5 Then you will **l** and be radiant,
Jer 3: 3 Yet you have the brazen **l**
6: 16 "Stand at the crossroads and **l**;
Eze 34: 11 for my sheep and **l** after them.
34: 12 them, so will I **l** after my sheep.
Hab 1: 13 Your eyes are too pure to **l** on evil;
Zec 12: 10 They will **l** on me, the one they
Mt 18: 12 go to **l** for the one that wandered
23: 27 which **l** beautiful on the outside
Mk 13: 21 the Messiah!' or, '**L**, there he is!'
Lk 6: 41 "Why do you **l** at the speck
24: 39 **L** at my hands and my feet. It is I
Jn 1: 36 by, he said, "**L**, the Lamb of God!"
4: 35 open your eyes and **l** at the fields!
19: 37 "They will **l** on the one they have
1Ti 4: 12 Don't let anyone **l** down on you
Jas 1: 27 to **l** after orphans and widows
1Pe 1: 12 Even angels long to **l** into these
2Pe 3: 12 as you **l** forward to the day of God

LOOKED (LOOK)
Ge 19: 26 But Lot's wife **l** back, and she
Ex 2: 25 So God **l** on the Israelites and was
1Sa 6: 19 to death because they **l** into the ark
SS 3: 1 I **l** for him but did not find him.
Eze 22: 30 "I **l** for someone among them who
34: 6 and no one searched or **l** for them.
44: 4 I **l** and saw the glory of the LORD
Da 7: 9 "As I **l**, "thrones were set in place,
10: 5 I **l** up and there before me was
Hab 3: 6 he **l**, and made the nations tremble.
Mt 25: 36 I was sick and you **l** after me, I was
Lk 18: 9 and **l** down on everyone else,
22: 61 Lord turned and **l** straight at Peter.
1Jn 1: 1 which we have **l** at and our hands

LOOKING (LOOK)
Ps 69: 3 My eyes fail, **l** for my God.
119: 82 My eyes fail, **l** for your promise;
119:123 My eyes fail, **l** for your salvation,
Mk 16: 6 "You are **l** for Jesus the Nazarene,
Php 2: 4 not **l** to your own interests but each
1Th 2: 6 We were not **l** for praise
2Pe 3: 13 his promise we are **l** forward
Rev 5: 6 a Lamb, **l** as if it had been slain,

LOOKS (LOOK)
1Sa 16: 7 but the LORD **l** at the heart."
Ezr 8: 22 God is on everyone who **l** to him,
Ps 104: 32 he who **l** at the earth, and it
138: 6 is exalted, he **l** kindly on the lowly;
Mt 5: 28 anyone who **l** at a woman lustfully
16: 4 adulterous generation **l** for a sign,
Lk 9: 62 and **l** back is fit for service
Jn 6: 40 is that everyone who **l** to the Son
12: 45 The one who **l** at me is seeing
Php 2: 21 For everyone **l** out for their own
Jas 1: 25 whoever **l** intently into the perfect

LOOSE
Isa 33: 23 Your rigging hangs **l**: The mast is
Mt 16: 19 and whatever you **l** on earth will be
18: 18 and whatever you **l** on earth will be

LORD (LORD'S LORDED LORDING)
Ge 18: 27 been so bold as to speak to the **L**,
Ex 15: 17 the sanctuary, **L**, your hands
Nu 16: 13 now you also want to **l** it over us!
Dt 10: 17 God is God of gods and **L** of lords,
Jos 3: 13 the **L** of all the earth—
1Ki 3: 10 The **L** was pleased that Solomon
Ne 4: 14 Remember the **L**, who is great
Job 28: 28 human race, "The fear of the **L**—
Ps 37: 13 but the **L** laughs at the wicked,
38: 22 to help me, my **L** and my Savior.
54: 4 the **L** is the one who sustains me.
62: 12 and with you, **L**, is unfailing love";
69: 6 **L**, the LORD Almighty, may those
86: 5 You, **L**, are forgiving and good,
86: 8 the gods there is none like you, **L**;
89: 49 **L**, where is your former great love,
110: 1 The LORD says to my **l**:
110: 5 The **L** is at your right hand;
130: 3 kept a record of sins, **L**, who could
135: 5 that our **L** is greater than all gods.
136: 3 Give thanks to the **L** of lords:
147: 5 Great is our **L** and mighty in
Isa 6: 1 died, I saw the **L**, high and exalted,
Da 2: 47 the God of gods and the **L** of kings
9: 4 "**L**, the great and awesome God,
9: 7 "**L**, you are righteous, but this day
9: 9 The **L** our God is merciful
9: 19 **L**, listen! **L**, forgive! **L**, hear and act!
Mt 3: 3 'Prepare the way for the **L**,
4: 7 'Do not put the **L** your God
4: 10 'Worship the **L** your God, and
7: 21 "Not everyone who says to me, '**L**,
9: 38 Ask the **L** of the harvest, therefore,
12: 8 Son of Man is **L** of the Sabbath."
20: 25 rulers of the Gentiles **l** it over them
21: 9 who comes in the name of the **L**!"
22: 37 "'Love the **L** your God with all
22: 44 "'The **L** said to my **L**: "Sit at my
23: 39 comes in the name of the **L**.'"
Mk 1: 3 'Prepare the way for the **L**,
12: 11 the **L** has done this, and it is
12: 29 The **L** our God, the **L** is one.
12: 30 Love the **L** your God with all your
Lk 2: 9 angel of the **L** appeared to them,
6: 5 Son of Man is **L** of the Sabbath."
6: 46 "Why do you call me, '**L**, **L**,'
10: 27 "'Love the **L** your God with all
11: 1 one of his disciples said to him, "**L**,
24: 34 The **L** has risen and has appeared
Jn 1: 23 straight the way for the **L**.'"
Ac 2: 21 on the name of the **L** will be saved.'
2: 25 "'I saw the **L** always before me.
2: 34 yet he said, "'The **L** said to my **L**:
8: 16 baptized in the name of the **L**
9: 5 "Who are you, **L**?" Saul asked.
10: 36 Jesus Christ, who is **L** of all.
11: 23 true to the **L** with all their hearts.
16: 31 "Believe in the **L** Jesus, and you
Ro 4: 24 him who raised Jesus our **L**
5: 11 in God through our **L** Jesus Christ,
6: 23 is eternal life in Christ Jesus our **L**.
8: 39 of God that is in Christ Jesus our **L**.
10: 9 "Jesus is **L**," and believe in your
10: 13 the name of the **L** will be saved."
10: 16 For Isaiah says, "**L**, who has
11: 34 has known the mind of the **L**?
12: 11 your spiritual fervor, serving the **L**.
13: 14 yourselves with the **L** Jesus Christ,
14: 4 the **L** is able to make them stand.
14: 8 live or die, we belong to the **L**.
1Co 1: 31 the one who boasts boast in the **L**."
3: 5 as the **L** has assigned to each his
4: 5 wait until the **L** comes.
6: 13 sexual immorality but for the **L**,
6: 14 his power God raised the **L**
7: 32 how he can please the **L**.
1Co 7: 34 to be devoted to the **L** in both body
7: 35 in undivided devotion to the **L**.
7: 39 but he must belong to the **L**.
8: 6 and there is but one **L**, Jesus Christ,
11: 23 The **L** Jesus, on the night he was
12: 3 "Jesus is **L**," except by the Holy
15: 57 victory through our **L** Jesus Christ.
15: 58 your labor in the **L** is not in vain.
16: 22 let that person be cursed! Come, **L**!
2Co 1: 24 Not that we **l** it over your faith,
2: 12 that the **L** had opened a door
3: 17 Now the **L** is the Spirit,
4: 5 but Jesus Christ as **L**,
5: 6 the body we are away from the **L**.
8: 5 gave themselves first of all to the **L**,
8: 21 not only in the eyes of the **L**
10: 17 the one who boasts boast in the **L**."
10: 18 the one whom the **L** commends.
13: 10 the authority the **L** gave me
Gal 6: 14 in the cross of our **L** Jesus Christ,
Eph 4: 5 one **L**, one faith, one baptism;
5: 8 but now you are light in the **L**.
5: 10 and find out what pleases the **L**.
5: 19 music from your heart to the **L**,
5: 22 own husbands as you do to the **L**.
6: 1 obey your parents in the **L**, for this
6: 7 as if you were serving the **L**,
6: 8 that the **L** will reward each one
6: 10 strong in the **L** and in his mighty
Php 2: 11 acknowledge that Jesus Christ is **L**,
3: 1 and sisters, rejoice in the **L**!
3: 8 of knowing Christ Jesus my **L**,
4: 1 stand firm in the **L** in this way,
4: 4 Rejoice in the **L** always. I will say it
4: 5 be evident to all. The **L** is near.
Col 1: 10 you may live a life worthy of the **L**
2: 6 as you received Christ Jesus as **L**,
3: 13 Forgive as the **L** forgave you.
3: 17 do it all in the name of the **L** Jesus,
3: 18 husbands, as is fitting in the **L**.
3: 20 everything, for this pleases the **L**.
3: 23 working for the **L**, not for human
3: 24 inheritance from the **L** as a reward.
3: 24 It is the **L** Christ you are serving.
4: 17 you have received in the **L**."
1Th 3: 8 you are standing firm in the **L**.
3: 12 May the **L** make your love increase
4: 1 urge you in the **L** Jesus to do this
4: 6 The **L** will punish all those who
4: 15 are left until the coming of the **L**,
5: 2 day of the **L** will come like a thief
5: 23 at the coming of our **L** Jesus Christ.
2Th 1: 7 when the **L** Jesus is revealed
1: 12 of our **L** Jesus may be glorified
2: 1 the coming of our **L** Jesus Christ
2: 8 whom the **L** Jesus will overthrow
3: 3 But the **L** is faithful, and he will
3: 5 May the **L** direct your hearts
1Ti 6: 15 the King of kings and **L** of lords,
2Ti 1: 8 of the testimony about our **L**
2: 19 "The **L** knows those who are his,"
4: 8 which the **L**, the righteous Judge,
4: 17 the **L** stood at my side and gave
Heb 1: 10 "In the beginning, **L**, you laid
10: 30 "The **L** will judge his people."
12: 14 holiness no one will see the **L**.
13: 6 confidence, "The **L** is my helper;
Jas 1: 12 of life that the **L** has promised
3: 9 With the tongue we praise our **L**
4: 10 Humble yourselves before the **L**,
5: 11 The **L** is full of compassion
1Pe 1: 25 the word of the **L** endures forever."
2: 3 you have tasted that the **L** is good.
3: 12 **L** is against those who do evil."
3: 15 in your hearts revere Christ as **L**.
2Pe 1: 11 into the eternal kingdom of our **L**
1: 16 the coming of our **L** Jesus Christ
2: 1 sovereign **L** who bought them—
2: 9 then the **L** knows how to rescue
3: 9 The **L** is not slow in keeping his
3: 18 and knowledge of our **L** and Savior
Jude : 14 the **L** is coming with thousands
Rev 4: 8 holy is the **L** God Almighty,'
4: 11 "You are worthy, our **L** and God,
11: 15 has become the kingdom of our **L**

Rev 17: 14 triumph over them because he is **L**
19: 16 KING OF KINGS AND **L** OF LORDS.
22: 5 for the **L** God will give them light.
22: 20 Amen. Come, **L** Jesus.

LORD'S (LORD)
Lk 1: 38 "I am the **L** servant,"
Ac 11: 21 The **L** hand was with them,
21: 14 up and said, "The **L** will be done."
Ro 12: 13 Share with the **L** people who are
1Co 7: 32 is concerned about the **L** affairs—
10: 26 "The earth is the **L**, and everything
11: 26 you proclaim the **L** death until he
2Co 3: 18 faces contemplate the **L** glory,
Eph 5: 17 but understand what the **L** will is.
2Ti 2: 24 And the **L** servant must not be
Heb 12: 5 not make light of the **L** discipline,
Jas 4: 15 "If it is the **L** will, we will live
5: 8 firm, because the **L** coming is near.
1Pe 2: 13 Submit yourselves for the **L** sake

LORDED (LORD)
Ne 5: 15 assistants also **l** it over the people.

LORDING (LORD)
1Pe 5: 3 not **l** it over those entrusted to you,

LORD† (LORD'S†)
Ge 2: 4 when the **L** God made the earth
2: 7 the **L** God formed a man
2: 22 the **L** God made a woman
3: 21 The **L** God made garments of skin
3: 23 So the **L** God banished him
4: 4 The **L** looked with favor on Abel
4: 26 began to call on the name of the **L**.
6: 7 So the **L** said, "I will wipe
7: 16 Then the **L** shut him in.
9: 26 "Praise be to the **L**, the God
11: 9 because there the **L** confused
12: 1 The **L** had said to Abram,
15: 6 Abram believed the **L**, and he
15: 18 that day the **L** made a covenant
17: 1 the **L** appeared to him and said,
18: 1 The **L** appeared to Abraham near
18: 14 Is anything too hard for the **L**?
18: 19 way of the **L** by doing what is right
21: 1 Now the **L** was gracious to Sarah as
22: 14 that place The **L** Will Provide.
24: 1 the **L** had blessed him in every
26: 2 The **L** appeared to Isaac and said,
28: 13 There above it stood the **L**, and he
31: 49 "May the **L** keep watch between
39: 2 The **L** was with Joseph so that he
39: 21 the **L** was with him; he showed
Ex 3: 2 There the angel of the **L** appeared
4: 11 them blind? Is it not I, the **L**?
4: 31 heard that the **L** was concerned
6: 2 also said to Moses, "I am the **L**.
9: 12 But the **L** hardened Pharaoh's heart
12: 27 the Passover sacrifice to the **L**,
12: 43 The **L** said to Moses and Aaron,
13: 9 the **L** brought you out of Egypt
13: 21 By day the **L** went ahead of them
14: 13 deliverance the **L** will bring you
14: 30 That day the **L** saved Israel
15: 3 The **L** is a warrior; the **L** is his
15: 11 among the gods is like you, **L**?
15: 26 for I am the **L**, who heals you."
16: 12 know that I am the **L** your God.'"
16: 23 rest, a holy sabbath to the **L**.
17: 15 and called it The **L** is my Banner.
19: 8 will do everything the **L** has said."
19: 20 The **L** descended to the top
20: 2 "I am the **L** your God, who
20: 5 for I, the **L** your God, am a jealous
20: 7 misuse the name of the **L** your God
20: 10 day is a sabbath to the **L** your God.
20: 11 in six days the **L** made the heavens
20: 11 the **L** blessed the Sabbath
20: 12 the land the **L** your God is giving
23: 25 Worship the **L** your God, and his
24: 3 "Everything the **L** has said we will
24: 12 The **L** said to Moses,
24: 16 the glory of the **L** settled on Mount
25: 1 The **L** said to Moses,
28: 36 on it as on a seal: HOLY TO THE **L**.
30: 11 Then the **L** said to Moses,
31: 13 so you may know that I am the **L**,
Ex 31: 18 When the **L** finished speaking
33: 11 The **L** would speak to Moses face
33: 19 my name, the **L**, in your presence.
34: 1 The **L** said to Moses,
34: 6 proclaiming, "The **L**, the **L**,
34: 10 work that I, the **L**, will do for you.
34: 29 because he had spoken with the **L**.
40: 34 glory of the **L** filled the tabernacle.
40: 38 of the **L** was over the tabernacle
Lev 8: 36 did everything the **L** commanded
9: 23 the glory of the **L** appeared to all
10: 2 them, and they died before the **L**.
19: 2 'Be holy because I, the **L** your God,
20: 8 I am the **L**, who makes you holy.
20: 26 to me because I, the **L**, am holy,
23: 40 rejoice before the **L** your God
Nu 6: 24 "'"The **L** bless you and keep
8: 5 The **L** said to Moses:
11: 1 fire from the **L** burned among
14: 18 'The **L** is slow to anger,
14: 21 glory of the **L** fills the whole earth,
21: 6 the **L** sent venomous snakes among
22: 31 Then the **L** opened Balaam's eyes,
23: 12 "Must I not speak what the **L** puts
30: 2 When a man makes a vow to the **L**
32: 12 followed the **L** wholeheartedly.'
Dt 1: 21 take possession of it as the **L**,
2: 7 forty years the **L** your God has
4: 29 there you seek the **L** your God,
5: 6 am the **L** your God, who brought
5: 9 for I, the **L** your God, am a jealous
6: 4 The **L** our God, the **L** is one.
6: 5 Love the **L** your God with all your
6: 16 Do not put the **L** your God
6: 25 all this law before the **L** our God,
7: 1 When the **L** your God brings you
7: 6 The **L** your God has chosen you
7: 8 it was because the **L** loved you
7: 9 that the **L** your God is God; he is
7: 12 then the **L** your God will keep his
8: 5 so the **L** your God disciplines you.
9: 10 The **L** gave me two stone tablets
10: 12 but to fear the **L** your God,
10: 12 serve the **L** your God with all
10: 14 **L** your God belong the heavens,
10: 17 For the **L** your God is God of gods
10: 20 Fear the **L** your God and serve
10: 22 now the **L** your God has made you
11: 1 Love the **L** your God and keep his
11: 13 to love the **L** your God and to serve
16: 1 the Passover of the **L** your God,
17: 15 you a king the **L** your God chooses.
28: 1 If you fully obey the **L** your God
28: 15 if you do not obey the **L** your God
29: 1 covenant the **L** commanded Moses
29: 29 things belong to the **L** our God,
30: 4 there the **L** your God will gather
30: 6 The **L** your God will circumcise
30: 10 if you obey the **L** your God
30: 16 today to love the **L** your God,
30: 16 the **L** your God will bless you
30: 20 you may love the **L** your God,
30: 20 For the **L** is your life,
31: 6 for the **L** your God goes with you;
34: 5 the servant of the **L** died there
Jos 10: 14 the **L** was fighting for Israel!
22: 5 to love the **L** your God, to walk
23: 11 careful to love the **L** your God.
24: 15 household, we will serve the **L**."
24: 18 We too will serve the **L**, because
Jdg 2: 12 They forsook the **L**, the God of
Ru 1: 8 May the **L** show you kindness,
4: 13 her, the **L** enabled her to conceive,
1Sa 1: 11 give him to the **L** for all the days
1: 15 I was pouring out my soul to the **L**.
1: 28 So now I give him to the **L**.
2: 2 "There is no one holy like the **L**;
2: 25 but if anyone sins against the **L**,
2: 26 favor with the **L** and with people.
3: 9 say, 'Speak, **L**, for your servant is
3: 19 The **L** was with Samuel as he grew
7: 12 "Thus far the **L** has helped us."
9: 17 sight of Saul, the **L** said to him,
11: 15 fellowship offerings before the **L**,
12: 18 Then Samuel called on the **L**,
1Sa 12: 18 the people stood in awe of the **L**
12: 22 his great name the **L** will not reject
12: 24 be sure to fear the **L** and serve him
13: 14 the **L** has sought out a man after
14: 6 Nothing can hinder the **L**
15: 22 as much as in obeying the **L**?
16: 13 the Spirit of the **L** came powerfully
17: 45 you in the name of the **L** Almighty,
2Sa 6: 14 David was dancing before the **L**
7: 22 "How great you are, Sovereign **L**!
8: 6 The **L** gave David victory wherever
12: 7 This is what the **L**, the God
22: 2 "The **L** is my rock, my fortress
22: 29 You, **L**, are my lamp; the **L** turns
1Ki 1: 30 day what I swore to you by the **L**,
2: 3 and observe what the **L** your God
3: 7 "Now, **L** my God, you have made
5: 5 for the Name of the **L** my God,
5: 12 The **L** gave Solomon wisdom,
8: 11 the glory of the **L** filled his temple.
8: 23 "**L**, the God of Israel, there is no
8: 61 fully committed to the **L** our God,
9: 3 The **L** said to him: "I have heard
10: 9 Praise be to the **L** your God,
15: 14 fully committed to the **L** all his life.
18: 21 If the **L** is God, follow him;
18: 36 "**L**, the God of Abraham,
18: 39 **L**—he is God! The **L**—he is God!"
21: 23 also concerning Jezebel the **L** says:
2Ki 13: 23 But the **L** was gracious to them
17: 18 So the **L** was very angry with Israel
18: 5 Hezekiah trusted in the **L**, the God
19: 1 and went into the temple of the **L**.
20: 11 the **L** made the shadow go back
21: 12 Therefore this is what the **L**,
22: 2 what was right in the eyes of the **L**
22: 8 of the Law in the temple of the **L**."
23: 3 to follow the **L** and keep his
23: 21 the Passover to the **L** your God, as
23: 25 who turned to the **L** as he did—
24: 2 The **L** sent Babylonian, Aramean,
24: 4 the **L** was not willing to forgive.
1Ch 10: 13 he did not keep the word of the **L**
11: 3 as the **L** had promised through
11: 9 because the **L** Almighty was
13: 6 up from there the ark of God the **L**,
16: 8 Give praise to the **L**, proclaim his
16: 11 Look to the **L** and his strength;
16: 14 He is the **L** our God;
16: 23 Sing to the **L**, all the earth;
17: 1 covenant of the **L** is under a tent."
21: 24 not take for the **L** what is yours,
22: 5 be built for the **L** should be of great
22: 11 build the house of the **L** your God,
22: 13 and laws that the **L** gave Moses
22: 16 the work, and the **L** be with you."
22: 19 build the sanctuary of the **L** God,
25: 7 and skilled in music for the **L**—
28: 9 for the **L** searches every heart
28: 20 the temple of the **L** is finished.
29: 1 is not for man but for the **L** God.
29: 11 Yours, **L**, is the kingdom;
29: 18 **L**, the God of our fathers Abraham,
29: 25 The **L** highly exalted Solomon
2Ch 1: 1 for the **L** his God was with him
5: 13 the temple of the **L** was filled
5: 14 the glory of the **L** filled the temple
6: 16 "Now, **L**, the God of Israel,
6: 41 "Now arise, **L** God, and come
6: 42 **L** God, do not reject your anointed
7: 1 the glory of the **L** filled the temple.
7: 12 the **L** appeared to him at night
7: 21 'Why has the **L** done such a thing
9: 8 king to rule for the **L** your God.
13: 12 do not fight against the **L**, the God
14: 2 right in the eyes of the **L** his God.
15: 14 to the **L** with loud acclamation,
16: 9 the **L** range throughout the earth
17: 9 them the Book of the Law of the **L**;
18: 13 "As surely as the **L** lives, I can tell
19: 6 for mere mortals but for the **L**,
19: 9 wholeheartedly in the fear of the **L**.
20: 15 This is what the **L** says to you:
20: 20 Have faith in the **L** your God
26: 5 As long as he sought the **L**,

2Ch 26: 16 was unfaithful to the **L** his God,
29: 30 to praise the **L** with the words
30: 9 for the **L** your God is gracious
31: 20 and faithful before the **L** his God.
32: 8 with us is the **L** our God to help us
34: 14 taken into the temple of the **L**,
34: 31 covenant in the presence of the **L**—
Ezr 3: 10 foundation of the temple of the **L**,
7: 6 the hand of the **L** his God was
7: 10 observance of the Law of the **L**,
9: 5 hands spread out to the **L** my God
9: 8 the **L** our God has been gracious
9: 15 **L**, the God of Israel, you are
Ne 1: 5 "**L**, the God of heaven, the great
8: 1 which the **L** had commanded
9: 6 You alone are the **L**. You made
Job 1: 6 to present themselves before the **L**,
1: 21 The **L** gave and the **L** has taken
1: 21 may the name of the **L** be praised."
38: 1 the **L** spoke to Job out of the storm.
42: 9 what the **L** told them; and the **L**
42: 12 **L** blessed the latter part of Job's
Ps 1: 2 whose delight is in the law of the **L**,
1: 6 For the **L** watches over the way
4: 6 Many, **L**, are asking, "Who will
4: 8 for you alone, **L**, make me dwell
5: 3 In the morning, **L**, you hear my
6: 1 **L**, do not rebuke me in your anger
8: 1 **L**, our Lord, how majestic is your
9: 9 The **L** is a refuge for the oppressed,
9: 19 Arise, **L**, do not let mortals
10: 16 The **L** is King for ever and ever;
12: 6 the words of the **L** are flawless,
16: 5 **L**, you alone are my portion and
16: 8 I keep my eyes always on the **L**.
18: 1 I love you, **L**, my strength.
18: 6 In my distress I called to the **L**;
19: 7 The law of the **L** is perfect,
19: 14 heart be pleasing in your sight, **L**,
20: 5 May the **L** grant all your requests.
20: 7 trust in the name of the **L** our God.
22: 8 they say, "let the **L** rescue him.
23: 1 The **L** is my shepherd, I lack
23: 6 dwell in the house of the **L** forever.
24: 3 may ascend the mountain of the **L**?
24: 8 The **L** strong and mighty, the **L**
25: 10 All the ways of the **L** are loving
27: 1 The **L** is the stronghold of my life
27: 4 to gaze on the beauty of the **L**
27: 6 will sing and make music to the **L**.
29: 1 Ascribe to the **L**, you heavenly
29: 4 The voice of the **L** is powerful;
30: 4 Sing the praises of the **L**, you his
31: 5 deliver me, **L**, my faithful God.
32: 2 one whose sin the **L** does not count
33: 1 Sing joyfully to the **L**,
33: 6 of the **L** the heavens were made,
33: 12 is the nation whose God is the **L**,
33: 18 the eyes of the **L** are on those who
34: 1 I will extol the **L** at all times;
34: 3 Glorify the **L** with me; let us exalt
34: 4 sought the **L**, and he answered me;
34: 7 the **L** encamps around those who
34: 8 Taste and see that the **L** is good;
34: 9 Fear the **L**, you his holy people,
34: 15 The eyes of the **L** are
34: 18 The **L** is close to the brokenhearted
37: 4 Take delight in the **L**, and he will
37: 5 Commit your way to the **L**;
39: 4 "Show me, **L**, my life's end
40: 1 I waited patiently for the **L**;
40: 5 Many, **L** my God, are the wonders
46: 8 Come and see what the **L** has done,
47: 2 For the **L** Most High is awesome,
48: 1 Great is the **L**, and most worthy
50: 1 the **L**, speaks and summons
55: 22 Cast your cares on the **L** and he
59: 8 But you laugh at them, **L**;
68: 4 his name is the **L**.
68: 18 that you, **L** God, might dwell there.
68: 20 from the Sovereign **L** comes escape
69: 31 This will please the **L** more than
70: 4 help always say, "The **L** is great!"
72: 18 Praise be to the **L** God, the God
75: 8 In the hand of the **L** is a cup full
Ps 78: 4 the praiseworthy deeds of the **L**,
84: 8 Hear my prayer, **L** God Almighty;
84: 11 the **L** God is a sun and shield;
85: 7 Show us your unfailing love, **L**,
86: 11 Teach me your way, **L**, that I may
87: 2 The **L** loves the gates of Zion more
89: 5 heavens praise your wonders, **L**,
89: 8 Who is like you, **L** God Almighty?
91: 2 I will say of the **L**, "He is my
92: 1 It is good to praise the **L** and make
92: 4 make me glad by your deeds, **L**;
92: 13 planted in the house of the **L**,
93: 1 The **L** reigns, he is robed in
93: 5 Your statutes, **L**, stand firm;
94: 1 The **L** is a God who avenges.
94: 12 Blessed is the one you discipline, **L**,
94: 18 your unfailing love, **L**,
95: 1 Come, let us sing for joy to the **L**;
95: 3 the **L** is the great God, the great
95: 6 kneel before the **L** our Maker;
96: 1 Sing to the **L** a new song;
96: 5 idols, but the **L** made the heavens.
96: 8 to the **L** the glory due his name;
96: 9 Worship the **L** in the splendor of
96: 13 Let all creation rejoice before the **L**,
97: 1 The **L** reigns, let the earth be glad;
97: 9 For you, **L**, are the Most High over
98: 1 Sing to the **L** a new song, for he has
98: 2 The **L** has made his salvation
98: 4 Shout for joy to the **L**, all the earth,
99: 1 The **L** reigns, let the nations
99: 2 Great is the **L** in Zion; he is exalted
99: 5 Exalt the **L** our God and worship
100: 1 Shout for joy to the **L**, all the earth.
100: 2 Worship the **L** with gladness;
100: 3 Know that the **L** is God. It is he
100: 5 For the **L** is good and his love
101: 1 to you, **L**, I will sing praise.
102: 12 But you, **L**, sit enthroned forever;
103: 1 Praise the **L**, my soul; all my
103: 8 The **L** is compassionate
103: 19 The **L** has established his throne
104: 1 Praise the **L**, my soul. **L** my God,
104: 24 How many are your works, **L**!
104: 33 I will sing to the **L** all my life;
105: 4 Look to the **L** and his strength;
105: 7 He is the **L** our God;
106: 2 proclaim the mighty acts of the **L**
107: 1 thanks to the **L**, for he is good;
107: 8 thanks to the **L** for his unfailing
107: 21 thanks to the **L** for his unfailing
107: 43 ponder the loving deeds of the **L**.
108: 3 I will praise you, **L**,
109: 26 Help me, **L** my God;
110: 1 The **L** says to my lord: "Sit at my
110: 4 The **L** has sworn and will not
111: 2 Great are the works of the **L**;
111: 4 the **L** is gracious
111: 10 The fear of the **L** is the beginning
112: 1 Blessed are those who fear the **L**,
113: 1 praise the name of the **L**.
113: 2 Let the name of the **L** be praised,
113: 4 The **L** is exalted over all the
113: 5 Who is like the **L** our God, the One
115: 1 Not to us, **L**, not to us but to your
116: 12 return to the **L** for all his goodness
116: 15 the sight of the **L** is the death of his
117: 1 Praise the **L**, all you nations;
118: 1 thanks to the **L**, for he is good;
118: 5 hard pressed, I cried to the **L**;
118: 8 to take refuge in the **L** than to trust
118: 18 The **L** has chastened me severely,
118: 23 the **L** has done this, and it is
118: 24 The **L** has done it this very day;
118: 26 who comes in the name of the **L**.
119: 1 walk according to the law of the **L**.
119: 64 earth is filled with your love, **L**;
119: 89 Your word, **L**, is eternal;
119:126 It is time for you to act, **L**;
119:159 preserve my life, **L**, in accordance
120: 1 I call on the **L** in my distress,
121: 2 My help comes from the **L**,
121: 5 The **L** watches over you—the **L** is
your shade
121: 8 the **L** will watch over your coming
Ps 122: 1 "Let us go to the house of the **L**."
123: 2 our eyes look to the **L** our God,
124: 1 If the **L** had not been on our side—
124: 8 Our help is in the name of the **L**,
125: 2 so the **L** surrounds his people
126: 3 The **L** has done great things for us,
126: 4 Restore our fortunes, **L**,
127: 1 Unless the **L** builds the house,
127: 3 Children are a heritage from the **L**,
128: 1 Blessed are all who fear the **L**,
130: 1 Out of the depths I cry to you, **L**;
130: 3 If you, **L**, kept a record of sins,
130: 5 I wait for the **L**,
131: 3 Israel, put your hope in the **L**
132: 1 **L**, remember David and all his
132: 13 For the **L** has chosen Zion,
133: 3 there the **L** bestows his blessing,
134: 3 May the **L** bless you from Zion,
135: 4 For the **L** has chosen Jacob
135: 6 The **L** does whatever pleases him,
136: 1 Give thanks to the **L**,
137: 4 How can we sing the songs of the **L**
138: 1 I will praise you, **L**, with all
138: 8 The **L** will vindicate me;
139: 1 You have searched me, **L**,
140: 1 Rescue me, **L**, from evildoers;
141: 1 I call to you, **L**, come quickly
141: 3 Set a guard over my mouth, **L**;
142: 5 I cry to you, **L**; I say,
143: 9 Rescue me from my enemies, **L**,
144: 3 **L**, what are human beings that you
145: 3 Great is the **L** and most worthy
145: 8 **L** is gracious and compassionate,
145: 9 The **L** is good to all;
145: 17 The **L** is righteous in all his ways
145: 18 The **L** is near to all who call
146: 5 whose hope is in the **L** their God.
146: 7 The **L** sets prisoners free,
147: 2 The **L** builds up Jerusalem;
147: 7 Sing to the **L** with grateful praise;
147: 11 **L** delights in those who fear him,
147: 12 Extol the **L**, Jerusalem;
148: 1 Praise the **L** from the heavens;
148: 7 Praise the **L** from the earth,
149: 4 **L** takes delight in his people;
150: 1 Praise the **L**. Praise God
150: 6 that has breath praise the **L**.
Pr 1: 7 The fear of the **L** is the beginning
1: 29 and did not choose to fear the **L**.
2: 5 will understand the fear of the **L**
2: 6 For the **L** gives wisdom;
3: 5 Trust in the **L** with all your heart
3: 7 fear the **L** and shun evil.
3: 9 Honor the **L** with your wealth,
3: 12 because the **L** disciplines those he
3: 19 By wisdom the **L** laid the earth's
5: 21 your ways are in full view of the **L**,
6: 16 There are six things the **L** hates,
8: 13 To fear the **L** is to hate evil;
9: 10 The fear of the **L** is the beginning
10: 27 fear of the **L** adds length to life,
11: 1 The **L** detests dishonest scales,
12: 22 The **L** detests lying lips, but he
14: 2 fears the **L** walks uprightly,
14: 26 Whoever fears the **L** has a secure
14: 27 The fear of the **L** is a fountain
15: 3 The eyes of the **L** are everywhere,
15: 16 the fear of the **L** than great wealth
15: 33 instruction is to fear the **L**,
16: 2 but motives are weighed by the **L**.
16: 3 Commit to the **L** whatever you do,
16: 4 The **L** works out everything to its
16: 5 The **L** detests all the proud of heart
16: 9 but the **L** establishes their steps.
16: 33 but its every decision is from the **L**.
18: 10 name of the **L** is a fortified tower;
18: 22 and receives favor from the **L**.
19: 14 but a prudent wife is from the **L**.
19: 17 is kind to the poor lends to the **L**,
19: 23 The fear of the **L** leads to life;
20: 10 the **L** detests them both.
21: 2 right, but the **L** weighs the heart.
21: 3 acceptable to the **L** than sacrifice.
21: 30 plan that can succeed against the **L**.
21: 31 battle, but victory rests with the **L**.

Pr 22: 2 The **L** is the Maker of them all.
22: 23 for the **L** will take up their case
23: 17 be zealous for the fear of the **L**.
24: 18 or the **L** will see and disapprove
24: 21 Fear the **L** and the king, my son,
25: 22 head, and the **L** will reward you.
29: 26 is from the **L** that one gets justice.
30: 7 "Two things I ask of you, **L**;
31: 30 a woman who fears the **L** is to be
Isa 2: 3 the word of the **L** from Jerusalem.
2: 10 from the fearful presence of the **L**
3: 17 the **L** will make their scalps bald."
4: 2 Branch of the **L** will be beautiful
5: 16 the **L** Almighty will be exalted
6: 3 holy, holy is the **L** Almighty;
9: 7 of the **L** Almighty will accomplish
11: 2 Spirit of the **L** will rest on him—
11: 9 of the **L** as the waters cover the sea.
12: 2 The **L**, the **L** himself, is my strength
18: 7 of the Name of the **L** Almighty.
24: 1 the **L** is going to lay waste the earth
25: 1 **L**, you are my God; I will exalt you
25: 6 this mountain the **L** Almighty will
25: 8 The Sovereign **L** will wipe away
26: 4 the **L** himself, is the Rock
26: 8 Yes, **L**, walking in the way of your
26: 13 **L** our God, other lords besides you
26: 21 the **L** is coming out of his dwelling
27: 1 the **L** will punish with his sword—
27: 12 that day the **L** will thresh
28: 5 In that day the **L** Almighty will be
29: 6 the **L** Almighty will come
29: 15 to hide their plans from the **L**,
30: 18 For the **L** is a God of justice.
30: 26 when the **L** binds up the bruises
30: 27 the Name of the **L** comes from afar,
30: 30 The **L** will cause people to hear his
33: 2 **L**, be gracious to us; we long
33: 6 the fear of the **L** is the key to
33: 22 our lawgiver, the **L** is our king;
34: 2 The **L** is angry with all nations;
35: 2 they will see the glory of the **L**,
35: 10 those the **L** has rescued will return.
38: 7 **L** will do what he has promised:
40: 3 prepare the way for the **L**;
40: 5 glory of the **L** will be revealed,
40: 7 because the breath of the **L** blows
40: 10 the Sovereign **L** comes with power,
40: 14 Whom did the **L** consult
40: 28 The **L** is the everlasting God,
40: 31 in the **L** will renew their strength.
41: 14 declares the **L**, your Redeemer,
41: 20 the hand of the **L** has done this,
42: 6 "I, the **L**, have called you
42: 8 "I am the **L**; that is my name!
42: 13 The **L** will march out like
42: 21 It pleased the **L** for the sake of his
43: 3 For I am the **L** your God, the Holy
43: 11 am the **L**, and apart from me there
44: 6 and Redeemer, the **L** Almighty:
44: 24 the **L**, the Maker of all things,
45: 5 I am the **L**, and there is no other;
45: 7 I, the **L**, do all these things.
45: 21 Was it not I, the **L**?
48: 17 the **L** your God, who teaches
50: 4 The Sovereign **L** has given me
50: 10 Who among you fears the **L**
51: 1 righteousness and who seek the **L**:
51: 11 the **L** has rescued will return.
51: 15 the **L** Almighty is his name.
53: 1 has the arm of the **L** been revealed?
53: 6 the **L** has laid on him the iniquity
53: 10 the will of the **L** will prosper
54: 5 the **L** Almighty is his name—
55: 6 Seek the **L** while he may be found;
55: 7 Let them turn to the **L**, and he
56: 6 to love the name of the **L**,
58: 8 of the **L** will be your rear guard.
58: 11 The **L** will guide you always;
59: 1 the arm of the **L** is not too short
60: 1 the glory of the **L** rises upon you.
60: 16 know that I, the **L**, am your Savior,
60: 20 the **L** will be your everlasting light,
61: 1 because the **L** has anointed me
61: 3 a planting of the **L** for the display
Isa 61: 10 I delight greatly in the **L**;
61: 11 grow, so the Sovereign **L** will make
62: 4 for the **L** will take delight in you,
63: 7 tell of the kindnesses of the **L**,
64: 8 Yet you, **L**, are our Father.
66: 15 See, the **L** is coming with fire,
Jer 1: 9 Then the **L** reached out his hand
2: 19 when you forsake the **L** your God
3: 25 have not obeyed the **L** our God."
4: 4 Circumcise yourselves to the **L**,
8: 7 know the requirements of the **L**.
9: 24 these I delight," declares the **L**.
10: 6 No one is like you, **L**; you are great,
10: 10 But the **L** is the true God; he is
12: 1 You are always righteous, **L**, when I
14: 7 us, do something, **L**, for the sake
14: 20 acknowledge our wickedness, **L**,
16: 15 said, 'As surely as the **L** lives,
16: 19 **L**, my strength and my fortress,
17: 7 is the one who trusts in the **L**,
17: 10 "I the **L** search the heart
20: 11 But the **L** is with me like a mighty
23: 6 The **L** Our Righteous Savior.
24: 7 heart to know me, that I am the **L**.
28: 9 as one truly sent by the **L** only if
31: 11 For the **L** will deliver Jacob
31: 22 The **L** will create a new thing
31: 34 'Know the **L**,' because they will
32: 27 "I am the **L**, the God of all
33: 16 The **L** Our Righteous Savior.'
36: 6 the **L** that you wrote as I dictated.
40: 3 now the **L** has brought it about;
42: 3 the **L** your God will tell us where
42: 4 pray to the **L** your God as you have
42: 6 we will obey the **L** our God,
50: 4 in tears to seek the **L** their God.
51: 10 "'The **L** has vindicated us;
51: 56 For the **L** is a God of retribution;
La 3: 24 to myself, "The **L** is my portion;
3: 25 The **L** is good to those whose hope
3: 40 them, and let us return to the **L**.
Eze 1: 3 the hand of the **L** was on him.
1: 28 the likeness of the glory of the **L**.
4: 14 I said, "Not so, Sovereign **L**!
10: 4 the glory of the **L** rose
15: 7 you will know that I am the **L**.
30: 3 is near, the day of the **L** is near—
36: 23 nations will know that I am the **L**,
37: 4 'Dry bones, hear the word of the **L**!
43: 4 the **L** entered the temple through
44: 4 the glory of the **L** filling the temple
Da 9: 2 the word of the **L** given to Jeremiah
Hos 1: 7 but I, the **L** their God, will save
2: 20 and you will acknowledge the **L**.
3: 1 as the **L** loves the Israelites,
3: 5 They will come trembling to the **L**
6: 1 "Come, let us return to the **L**.
6: 3 Let us acknowledge the **L**;
10: 12 for it is time to seek the **L**, until he
12: 5 the **L** God Almighty, the **L** is his
14: 1 Return, Israel, to the **L** your God.
Joel 1: 1 The word of the **L** that came to Joel
1: 15 For the day of the **L** is near;
2: 1 for the day of the **L** is coming.
2: 11 The day of the **L** is great;
2: 13 Return to the **L** your God, for he is
2: 23 rejoice in the **L** your God, for he
2: 31 the great and dreadful day of the **L**.
2: 32 on the name of the **L** will be saved;
2: 32 the survivors whom the **L** calls.
3: 14 day of the **L** is near in the valley
3: 16 The **L** will roar from Zion
Am 4: 13 the **L** God Almighty is his name.
5: 6 Seek the **L** and live, or he will
5: 15 Perhaps the **L** God Almighty will
5: 18 who long for the day of the **L**!
7: 15 But the **L** took me from tending
8: 12 searching for the word of the **L**,
9: 5 The Lord, the **L** Almighty—
Ob : 15 "The day of the **L** is near for all
Jnh 1: 3 But Jonah ran away from the **L**
1: 4 the **L** sent a great wind on the sea,
1: 17 Now the **L** provided a huge fish
2: 9 'Salvation comes from the **L**.'"
4: 2 He prayed to the **L**, "Isn't this
4: 6 the **L** God provided a leafy plant
Mic 1: 1 The word of the **L** that came
4: 2 the word of the **L** from Jerusalem.
5: 4 his flock in the strength of the **L**,
6: 2 the **L** has a case against his people;
6: 8 what does the **L** require of you?
7: 7 I watch in hope for the **L**, I wait
Na 1: 2 The **L** is a jealous and avenging
1: 3 The **L** is slow to anger but great
Hab 2: 14 the **L** as the waters cover the sea.
2: 20 The **L** is in his holy temple;
3: 2 **L**, I have heard of your fame;
Zep 1: 1 The word of the **L** that came
1: 7 Be silent before the Sovereign **L**,
3: 17 The **L** your God is with you,
Hag 1: 1 of the **L** came through the prophet
1: 8 in it and be honored," says the **L**.
Zec 1: 1 the word of the **L** came
1: 17 and the **L** will again comfort Zion
3: 1 standing before the angel of the **L**,
4: 6 by my Spirit,' says the **L** Almighty.
6: 12 and build the temple of the **L**.
8: 21 'Let us go at once to entreat the **L**
9: 16 **L** their God will save his people
14: 5 Then the **L** my God will come,
14: 9 On that day there will be one **L**,
14: 16 worship the King, the **L** Almighty,
Mal 1: 1 of the **L** to Israel through Malachi.
3: 6 "I the **L** do not change. So you,
4: 5 and dreadful day of the **L** comes.

LORD'S† (LORD†)
Ex 4: 14 the **L** anger burned against Moses
12: 11 Eat it in haste; it is the **L** Passover.
34: 34 he entered the **L** presence to speak
Lev 23: 4 These are the **L** appointed festivals,
Nu 9: 23 At the **L** command they encamped,
14: 41 you disobeying the **L** command?
32: 13 The **L** anger burned against Israel
Dt 6: 18 is right and good in the **L** sight,
10: 13 to observe the **L** commands and
32: 9 For the **L** portion is his people,
Jos 21: 45 Not one of all the **L** good promises
1Sa 24: 10 lord, because he is the **L** anointed.'
2Sa 22: 31 is perfect: The **L** word is flawless;
1Ki 10: 9 of the **L** eternal love for Israel,
Ps 18: 30 is perfect: The **L** word is flawless;
24: 1 The earth is the **L**, and everything
32: 10 the **L** unfailing love surrounds the
89: 1 I will sing of the **L** great love forever;
103: 17 **L** love is with those who fear him,
118: 15 "The **L** right hand has done mighty
Pr 3: 11 do not despise the **L** discipline,
19: 21 but it is the **L** purpose that prevails.
Isa 24: 14 west they acclaim the **L** majesty.
30: 9 to listen to the **L** instruction.
49: 4 Yet what is due me is in the **L** hand,
53: 10 Yet it was the **L** will to crush him
55: 13 This will be for the LORD's **r**,
61: 2 to proclaim the year of the **L** favor
62: 3 a crown of splendor in the **L** hand,
Jer 25: 17 So I took the cup from the **L** hand
48: 10 who is lax in doing the **L** work!
51: 7 was a gold cup in the **L** hand;
La 3: 22 Because of the **L** great love we are
Eze 7: 19 them in the day of the **L** wrath.
Joel 3: 18 A fountain will flow out of the **L**
Ob : 21 And the kingdom will be the **L**.
Mic 4: 1 the **L** temple will be established as
6: 2 you mountains, the **L** accusation;
Hab 2: 16 The cup from the **L** right hand is
Zep 2: 3 sheltered on the day of the **L** anger.

LOSE (LOSES LOSS LOST)
1Sa 17: 32 "Let no one **l** heart on account
Isa 7: 4 Do not **l** heart because of these two
Mt 10: 39 Whoever finds their life will **l** it,
Lk 9: 25 and yet **l** or forfeit their very self?
Jn 6: 39 that I shall **l** none of all those he
2Co 4: 1 this ministry, we do not **l** heart.
4: 16 Therefore we do not **l** heart.
Heb 12: 3 will not grow weary and **l** heart.
12: 5 not **l** heart when he rebukes you,
2Jn : 8 you do not **l** what we have worked

LOSES (LOSE)
Mt 5: 13 But if the salt **l** its saltiness,
Lk 15: 4 a hundred sheep and **l** one of them.
15: 8 has ten silver coins and **l** one.

LOSS (LOSE)
Ro 11: 12 l means riches for the Gentiles,
1Co 3: 15 the builder will suffer l but yet will
Php 3: 8 I consider everything a l because

LOST (LOSE)
Ps 73: 2 I had nearly l my foothold.
Jer 50: 6 "My people have been l sheep;
Eze 34: 4 the strays or searched for the l.
34: 16 I will search for the l and bring
Lk 15: 4 after the l sheep until he finds it?
15: 6 I have found my l sheep.'
15: 9 I have found my l coin.'
15: 24 he was l and is found.'
19: 10 came to seek and to save the l."
Php 3: 8 for whose sake I have l all things.

LOT (LOTS)
Nephew of Abraham (Ge 11:27; 12:5). Chose to live in Sodom (Ge 13). Rescued from four kings (Ge 14). Rescued from Sodom (Ge 19:1–29; 2Pe 2:7). Fathered Moab and Ammon by his daughters (Ge 19:30–38).
Est 3: 7 the l) was cast in the presence
9: 24 the l) for their ruin and
Pr 16: 33 The l is cast into the lap, but its
18: 18 Casting the l settles disputes
Ecc 3: 22 their work, because that is their l.
Ac 1: 26 cast lots, and the l fell to Matthias;

LOTS (LOT)
Jos 18: 10 then cast l for them in Shiloh
Ps 22: 18 them and cast l for my garment.
Joel 3: 3 They cast l for my people
Ob : 11 his gates and cast l for Jerusalem,
Mt 27: 35 divided up his clothes by casting l.
Ac 1: 26 Then they cast l, and the lot fell

LOVE* (BELOVED BELOVED'S LOVED LOVELY LOVER LOVERS LOVES LOVING)
Ge 4: 1 Adam made l to his wife Eve,
4: 17 Cain made l to his wife, and she
4: 25 Adam made l to his wife again,
20: 13 'This is how you can show your l
22: 2 son, your only son, whom you l—
29: 18 Jacob was in l with Rachel and
29: 20 days to him because of his l for her.
29: 21 and I want to make l to her."
29: 23 to Jacob, and Jacob made l to her.
29: 30 Jacob made l to Rachel also, and
29: 30 his l for Rachel was greater than his l for Leah.
29: 32 Surely my husband will l me now."
38: 2 He married her and made l to her;
Ex 15: 13 In your unfailing l you will lead
20: 6 showing l to a thousand generations of those who l me
21: 5 'I l my master and my wife
34: 6 abounding in l and faithfulness,
34: 7 maintaining l to thousands,
Lev 19: 18 but l your neighbor as yourself.
19: 34 L them as yourself, for you were
Nu 14: 18 abounding in l and forgiving sin
14: 19 In accordance with your great l,
Dt 5: 10 showing l to a thousand generations of those who l me
6: 5 L the LORD your God with all
7: 9 God, keeping his covenant of l
7: 9 generations of those who l him
7: 12 God will keep his covenant of l
7: 13 He will l you and bless you
10: 12 to l him, to serve the LORD your
10: 19 are to l those who are foreigners,
11: 1 L the LORD your God and keep
11: 13 to l the LORD your God
11: 22 to l the LORD your God, to walk
13: 3 whether you l him with all your
13: 6 or the wife you l, or your closest
19: 9 to l the LORD your God
21: 15 is the son of the wife he does not l,
21: 16 the son of the wife he does not l.
30: 6 you may l him with all your heart
30: 16 today to l the LORD your God,
30: 20 you may l the LORD your God,
33: 3 Surely it is you who l the people;
Jos 22: 5 to l the LORD your God, to walk
23: 11 careful to l the LORD your God.
Jdg 5: 31 may all who l you be like the sun
Jdg 14: 16 You don't really l me.
16: 4 he fell in l with a woman
16: 15 "How can you say, 'I l you,'
Ru 4: 13 When he made l to her, the LORD
1Sa 1: 19 Elkanah made l to his wife Hannah
18: 20 Saul's daughter Michal was in l
18: 22 you, and his attendants all l you;
20: 17 reaffirm his oath out of l for him,
2Sa 1: 26 Your l for me was wonderful,
7: 15 my l will never be taken away
11: 11 and drink and make l to my wife?
12: 24 he went to her and made l to her.
13: 1 son of David fell in l with Tamar,
13: 4 said to him, "I'm in l with Tamar,
16: 17 "So this is the l you show your
19: 6 You l those who hate you and hate those who l you.
1Ki 3: 3 Solomon showed his l
3: 26 deeply moved out of l for her son
8: 23 you who keep your covenant of l
10: 9 of the LORD's eternal l for Israel,
11: 2 Solomon held fast to them in l.
1Ch 2: 21 He made l to her, and she bore him
7: 23 Then he made l to his wife again,
16: 34 he is good; his l endures forever.
16: 41 "for his l endures forever."
17: 13 I will never take my l away
2Ch 5: 13 his l endures forever."
6: 14 you who keep your covenant of l
6: 42 Remember the great l promised
7: 3 his l endures forever."
7: 6 saying, "His l endures forever."
9: 8 Because of the l of your God
19: 2 and l those who hate the LORD?
20: 21 LORD, for his l endures forever."
Ezr 3: 11 his l toward Israel endures forever."
Ne 1: 5 who keeps his covenant of l with those who l him
9: 17 slow to anger and abounding in l.
9: 32 who keeps his covenant of l, do not
13: 22 to me according to your great l.
Job 15: 34 the tents of those who l bribes.
19: 19 those I l have turned against me.
37: 13 to water his earth and show his l.
Ps 4: 2 How long will you l delusions
5: 7 by your great l, can come into your
5: 11 those who l your name may rejoice
6: 4 me because of your unfailing l.
11: 5 those who l violence, he hates
13: 5 But I trust in your unfailing l;
17: 7 me the wonders of your great l,
18: 1 I l you, LORD, my strength.
18: 50 shows unfailing l to his anointed,
21: 7 through the unfailing l of the Most
23: 6 l will follow me all the days of my
25: 6 your great mercy and l, for they are
25: 7 according to your l remember me,
26: 3 been mindful of your unfailing l
26: 8 I l the house where you live,
31: 7 I will be glad and rejoice in your l,
31: 16 save me in your unfailing l.
31: 21 me the wonders of his l when I was
31: 23 L the LORD, all his faithful
32: 10 LORD's unfailing l surrounds
33: 5 the earth is full of his unfailing l.
33: 18 whose hope is in his unfailing l,
33: 22 May your unfailing l be with us,
36: 5 Your l, LORD,
36: 7 How priceless is your unfailing l,
36: 10 Continue your l to those who
40: 10 I do not conceal your l and your
40: 11 may your l and faithfulness always
42: 8 By day the LORD directs his l,
44: 26 us because of your unfailing l.
45: 7 You l righteousness and hate
48: 9 we meditate on your unfailing l.
51: 1 God, according to your unfailing l;
52: 3 You l evil rather than good,
52: 4 You l every harmful word,
52: 8 I trust in God's unfailing l for ever
57: 3 God sends forth his l and his
57: 10 For great is your l,
59: 16 in the morning I will sing of your l;
60: 5 that those you l may be delivered.
61: 7 appoint your l and faithfulness
Ps 62: 12 and with you, Lord, is unfailing l";
63: 3 Because your l is better than life,
66: 20 prayer or withheld his l from me!
69: 13 in your great l, O God, answer me
69: 16 out of the goodness of your l;
69: 36 those who l his name will dwell
77: 8 his unfailing l vanished forever?
85: 7 Show us your unfailing l, LORD,
85: 10 L and faithfulness meet together;
86: 5 abounding in l to all who call
86: 13 For great is your l toward me;
86: 15 abounding in l and faithfulness.
88: 11 Is your l declared in the grave,
89: 1 sing of the LORD's great l forever;
89: 2 that your l stands firm forever,
89: 14 l and faithfulness go before you.
89: 24 My faithful l will be with him,
89: 28 I will maintain my l to him forever,
89: 33 but I will not take my l from him,
89: 49 where is your former great l,
90: 14 the morning with your unfailing l,
92: 2 proclaiming your l in the morning
94: 18 slipping," your unfailing l, LORD,
97: 10 Let those who l the LORD hate
98: 3 He has remembered his l and his
100: 5 is good and his l endures forever;
101: 1 I will sing of your l and justice;
103: 4 crowns you with l and compassion,
103: 8 slow to anger, abounding in l.
103: 11 so great is his l for those who fear
103: 17 to everlasting the LORD's l is
106: 1 for he is good; his l endures forever.
106: 45 and out of his great l he relented.
107: 1 he is good; his l endures forever.
107: 8 to the LORD for his unfailing l
107: 15 to the LORD for his unfailing l
107: 21 to the LORD for his unfailing l
107: 31 to the LORD for his unfailing l
108: 4 For great is your l, higher than
108: 6 that those you l may be delivered.
109: 21 out of the goodness of your l,
109: 26 me according to your unfailing l.
115: 1 because of your l and faithfulness.
116: 1 I l the LORD, for he heard my
117: 2 For great is his l toward us,
118: 1 he is good; his l endures forever.
118: 2 "His l endures forever."
118: 3 "His l endures forever."
118: 4 "His l endures forever."
118: 29 he is good; his l endures forever.
119: 41 May your unfailing l come to me,
119: 47 your commands because I l them.
119: 48 which I l, that I may meditate
119: 64 The earth is filled with your l,
119: 76 May your unfailing l be my
119: 88 In your unfailing l preserve my life,
119: 97 Oh, how I l your law! I meditate
119:113 people, but I l your law.
119:119 therefore I l your statutes.
119:124 your servant according to your l
119:127 Because I l your commands more
119:132 do to those who l your name.
119:149 voice in accordance with your l;
119:159 See how I l your precepts;
119:159 LORD, in accordance with your l.
119:163 detest falsehood but I l your law.
119:165 peace have those who l your law,
119:167 your statutes, for I l them greatly.
122: 6 "May those who l you be secure.
130: 7 for with the LORD is unfailing l
136: 1 *His l endures forever.*
136: 2 *His l endures forever.*
136: 3 *His l endures forever.*
136: 4 *His l endures forever.*
136: 5 *His l endures forever.*
136: 6 *His l endures forever.*
136: 7 *His l endures forever.*
136: 8 *His l endures forever.*
136: 9 *His l endures forever.*
136: 10 *His l endures forever.*
136: 11 *His l endures forever.*
136: 12 *His l endures forever.*
136: 13 *His l endures forever.*
136: 14 *His l endures forever.*
136: 15 *His l endures forever.*

Ps 136: 16 *His **l** endures forever.*
136: 17 *His **l** endures forever.*
136: 18 *His **l** endures forever.*
136: 19 *His **l** endures forever.*
136: 20 *His **l** endures forever.*
136: 21 *His **l** endures forever.*
136: 22 *His **l** endures forever.*
136: 23 *His **l** endures forever.*
136: 24 *His **l** endures forever.*
136: 25 *His **l** endures forever.*
136: 26 *His **l** endures forever.*
138: 2 your name for your unfailing **l**
138: 8 your **l**, LORD, endures forever—
143: 8 bring me word of your unfailing **l**,
143: 12 In your unfailing **l**, silence my
145: 8 slow to anger and rich in **l**.
145: 20 watches over all who **l** him,
147: 11 their hope in his unfailing **l**.
Pr 1: 22 who are simple **l** your simple ways?
3: 3 Let **l** and faithfulness never leave
4: 6 **l** her, and she will watch over you.
5: 19 you ever be intoxicated with her **l**.
7: 18 let's drink deeply of **l** till morning;
7: 18 let's enjoy ourselves with **l**!
8: 17 I **l** those who **l** me, and those who
8: 21 rich inheritance on those who **l** me
8: 36 all who hate me **l** death."
9: 8 rebuke the wise and they will **l** you.
10: 12 but **l** covers over all wrongs.
14: 22 those who plan what is good find **l**
15: 17 with **l** than a fattened calf
16: 6 Through **l** and faithfulness sin is
17: 9 Whoever would foster **l** covers
18: 21 and those who **l** it will eat its fruit.
19: 22 a person desires is unfailing **l**;
20: 6 Many claim to have unfailing **l**,
20: 13 Do not **l** sleep or you will grow
20: 28 **L** and faithfulness keep a king safe;
20: 28 through **l** his throne is made
21: 21 righteousness and **l** finds life,
27: 5 is open rebuke than hidden **l**.
Ecc 3: 8 a time to **l** and a time to hate,
9: 1 no one knows whether **l** or hate
9: 6 Their **l**, their hate and their
9: 9 whom you **l**, all the days of this
SS 1: 2 your **l** is more delightful than wine.
1: 3 wonder the young women **l** you!
1: 4 will praise your **l** more than wine.
1: 7 you whom I **l**, where you graze
2: 4 and let his banner over me be **l**.
2: 5 with apples, for I am faint with **l**.
2: 7 or awaken **l** until it so desires.
3: 5 or awaken **l** until it so desires.
3: 10 purple, its interior inlaid with **l**.
4: 10 How delightful is your **l**, my sister,
4: 10 more pleasing is your **l** than wine,
5: 1 drink your fill of **l**.
5: 8 Tell him I am faint with **l**.
7: 6 pleasing, my **l**, with your delights!
7: 12 there I will give you my **l**.
8: 4 or awaken **l** until it so desires.
8: 6 for **l** is as strong as death,
8: 7 Many waters cannot quench **l**;
8: 7 the wealth of one's house for **l**,
Isa 1: 23 they all **l** bribes and chase
8: 3 Then I made **l** to the prophetess,
5: 1 sing for the one I **l** a song about his
16: 5 In **l** a throne will be established;
38: 17 In your **l** you kept me from the pit
43: 4 and because I **l** you, I will give
54: 10 yet my unfailing **l** for you will not
55: 3 my faithful **l** promised to David.
56: 6 to him, to **l** the name of the LORD,
56: 10 around and dream, they **l** to sleep.
57: 8 a pact with those whose beds you **l**,
61: 8 "For I, the LORD, **l** justice;
63: 9 In his **l** and mercy he redeemed
66: 10 be glad for her, all you who **l** her;
Jer 2: 25 I **l** foreign gods, and I must go
2: 33 How skilled you are at pursuing **l**!
5: 31 and my people **l** it this way.
12: 7 I will give the one I **l** into the hands
14: 10 "They greatly **l** to wander;
16: 5 my **l** and my pity from this people,"
31: 3 loved you with an everlasting **l**;
Jer 32: 18 You show **l** to thousands but bring
33: 11 his **l** endures forever."
La 3: 22 of the LORD's great **l** we are not
3: 32 so great is his unfailing **l**.
Eze 16: 8 saw that you were old enough for **l**,
23: 17 to the bed of **l**, and in their lust
33: 31 Their mouths speak of **l**, but their
33: 32 more than one who sings **l** songs
Da 9: 4 who keeps his covenant of **l** with
those who **l** him
Hos 1: 6 for I will no longer show **l** to Israel,
1: 7 Yet I will show **l** to Judah;
2: 4 will not show my **l** to her children,
2: 19 and justice, in **l** and compassion.
2: 23 I will show my **l** to the one I called
3: 1 show your **l** to your wife again,
3: 1 **L** her as the LORD loves
3: 1 and **l** the sacred raisin cakes."
4: 1 no **l**, no acknowledgment of God
4: 18 their rulers dearly **l** shameful ways.
6: 4 Your **l** is like the morning mist,
9: 1 you **l** the wages of a prostitute
9: 15 I will no longer **l** them;
10: 12 reap the fruit of unfailing **l**,
11: 4 of human kindness, with ties of **l**.
12: 6 maintain **l** and justice, and wait
14: 4 waywardness and **l** them freely,
Joel 2: 13 slow to anger and abounding in **l**,
Am 4: 5 for this is what you **l** to do,"
5: 15 Hate evil, **l** good; maintain justice
Jnh 2: 8 turn away from God's **l** for them.
4: 2 slow to anger and abounding in **l**,
Mic 3: 2 you who hate good and **l** evil;
6: 8 to **l** mercy and to walk humbly
7: 20 and show **l** to Abraham, as you
Zep 3: 17 his **l** he will no longer rebuke you,
Zec 8: 17 other, and do not **l** to swear falsely.
8: 19 Therefore **l** truth and peace."
Mt 3: 17 said, "This is my Son, whom I **l**;
5: 43 said, '**L** your neighbor and hate
5: 44 **l** your enemies and pray for those
5: 46 If you **l** those who **l** you,
6: 5 for they **l** to pray standing
6: 24 will hate the one and **l** the other,
12: 18 the one I **l**, in whom I delight;
17: 5 said, "This is my Son, whom I **l**;
19: 19 '**l** your neighbor as yourself.'"
22: 37 "'**L** the Lord your God with all
22: 39 '**L** your neighbor as yourself.'
23: 6 they **l** the place of honor at
23: 7 they **l** to be greeted with respect
24: 12 the **l** of most will grow cold,
Mk 1: 11 "You are my Son, whom I **l**;
9: 7 "This is my Son, whom I **l**.
12: 30 **L** the Lord your God with all your
12: 31 '**L** your neighbor as yourself.'
12: 33 To **l** him with all your heart,
12: 33 **l** your neighbor as yourself is more
Lk 3: 22 "You are my Son, whom I **l**;
6: 27 **L** your enemies, do good to those
6: 32 "If you **l** those who **l** you,
6: 32 Even sinners **l** those who **l** them.
6: 35 But **l** your enemies, do good
7: 42 which of them will **l** him more?"
7: 47 as her great **l** has shown.
10: 27 "'**L** the Lord your God with all
10: 27 '**L** your neighbor as yourself.'"
11: 42 neglect justice and the **l** of God.
11: 43 because you **l** the most important
16: 13 will hate the one and **l** the other,
20: 13 I will send my son, whom I **l**;
20: 46 **l** to be greeted with respect
Jn 5: 42 that you do not have the **l** of God
8: 42 you would **l** me, for I have come
11: 3 Jesus, "Lord, the one you **l** is sick."
13: 34 I give you: **L** one another.
13: 34 so you must **l** one another.
13: 35 my disciples, if you **l** one another."
14: 15 "If you **l** me, keep my commands.
14: 21 I too will **l** them and show myself
14: 23 My Father will **l** them, and we will
14: 24 Anyone who does not **l** me will not
14: 31 world may learn that I **l** the Father
15: 9 I loved you. Now remain in my **l**.
15: 10 you will remain in my **l**, just as
Jn 15: 10 commands and remain in his **l**.
15: 12 **L** each other as I have loved you.
15: 13 Greater **l** has no one than this:
15: 17 This is my command: **L** each other.
15: 19 world, it would **l** you as its own.
17: 26 that the **l** you have for me may
21: 15 do you **l** me more than these?"
21: 15 he said, "you know that I **l** you."
21: 16 son of John, do you **l** me?"
21: 16 Lord, you know that I **l** you."
21: 17 son of John, do you **l** me?"
21: 17 the third time, "Do you **l** me?"
21: 17 you know that I **l** you."
Ro 1: 31 no fidelity, no **l**, no mercy.
5: 5 because God's **l** has been poured
5: 8 God demonstrates his own **l** for us
8: 28 for the good of those who **l** him,
8: 35 separate us from the **l** of Christ?
8: 39 separate us from the **l** of God that
12: 9 **L** must be sincere. Hate what is evil
12: 10 Be devoted to one another in **l**.
13: 8 continuing debt to **l** one another,
13: 9 "**L** your neighbor as yourself."
13: 10 **L** does no harm to a neighbor.
13: 10 Therefore **l** is the fulfillment
14: 15 eat, you are no longer acting in **l**.
15: 30 Christ and by the **l** of the Spirit,
1Co 2: 9 prepared for those who **l** him—
4: 17 my son whom I **l**, who is faithful
4: 21 shall I come in **l** and with a gentle
8: 1 puffs up while **l** builds up.
13: 1 but do not have **l**, I am only
13: 2 but do not have **l**, I am nothing.
13: 3 but do not have **l**, I gain nothing.
13: 4 **L** is patient, **l** is kind. It does not
13: 6 **L** does not delight in evil
13: 8 **L** never fails. But where there are
13: 13 three remain: faith, hope and **l**.
13: 13 But the greatest of these is **l**.
14: 1 Follow the way of **l** and eagerly
16: 14 Do everything in **l**.
16: 22 If anyone does not **l** the Lord,
16: 24 My **l** to all of you in Christ Jesus.
2Co 2: 4 know the depth of my **l** for you.
2: 8 to reaffirm your **l** for him.
5: 14 For Christ's **l** compels us,
6: 6 in the Holy Spirit and in sincere **l**;
8: 7 in the **l** we have kindled in you—
8: 8 sincerity of your **l** by comparing it
8: 24 show these men the proof of your **l**
11: 11 Because I do not **l** you?
12: 15 If I **l** you more, will you **l** me less?
13: 11 the God of **l** and peace will be
13: 14 the **l** of God, and the fellowship
Gal 5: 6 is faith expressing itself through **l**.
5: 13 serve one another humbly in **l**.
5: 14 "**L** your neighbor as yourself."
5: 22 But the fruit of the Spirit is **l**, joy,
Eph 1: 4 holy and blameless in his sight. In **l**
1: 15 and your **l** for all God's people,
2: 4 But because of his great **l** for us,
3: 17 being rooted and established in **l**,
3: 18 high and deep is the **l** of Christ,
3: 19 and to know this **l** that surpasses
4: 2 bearing with one another in **l**.
4: 15 speaking the truth in **l**, we will
4: 16 grows and builds itself up in **l**,
5: 2 and walk in the way of **l**, just as
5: 25 Husbands, **l** your wives, just as
5: 28 to **l** their wives as their own bodies.
5: 33 must **l** his wife as he loves himself,
6: 23 **l** with faith from God the Father
6: 24 to all who **l** our Lord Jesus Christ
with an undying **l**.
Php 1: 9 that your **l** may abound more
1: 16 The latter do so out of **l**,
2: 1 if any comfort from his **l**, if any
2: 2 having the same **l**, being one
4: 1 sisters, you whom I **l** and long for,
Col 1: 4 and of the **l** you have for all God's
1: 5 **l** that spring from the hope stored
1: 8 also told us of your **l** in the Spirit.
2: 2 in heart and united in **l**,
3: 14 And over all these virtues put on **l**,
3: 19 **l** your wives and do not be harsh

1Th 1: 3 your labor prompted by l, and your
3: 6 good news about your faith and l.
3: 12 May the Lord make your l increase
4: 9 your l for one another we do not
4: 9 taught by God to l each other.
4: 10 in fact, you do l all of God's family
5: 8 on faith and l as a breastplate,
5: 13 in the highest regard in l because
2Th 1: 3 l all of you have for one another
2: 10 because they refused to l the truth
3: 5 Lord direct your hearts into God's l
1Ti 1: 5 The goal of this command is l,
1: 14 faith and l that are in Christ Jesus.
2: 15 faith, l and holiness with propriety.
4: 12 conduct, in l, in faith and in purity.
6: 10 For the l of money is a root of all
6: 11 faith, l, endurance and gentleness.
2Ti 1: 7 us power, l and self-discipline.
1: 13 with faith and l in Christ Jesus.
2: 22 faith, l and peace, along with those
3: 3 without l, unforgiving, slanderous,
3: 10 faith, patience, l, endurance,
Titus 2: 2 in faith, in l and in endurance.
2: 4 women to l their husbands
3: 4 and l of God our Savior appeared,
3: 15 Greet those who l us in the faith.
Phm : 5 about your l for all his holy people
: 7 Your l has given me great joy
: 9 to appeal to you on the basis of l.
Heb 6: 10 the l you have shown him as you
10: 24 may spur one another on toward l
13: 5 your lives free from the l of money
Jas 1: 12 has promised to those who l him.
2: 5 he promised those who l him?
2: 8 "L your neighbor as yourself,"
1Pe 1: 8 you have not seen him, you l him;
1: 22 you have sincere l for each other,
2: 17 everyone, l the family of believers,
3: 8 be sympathetic, l one another,
3: 10 For, "Whoever would l life and see
4: 8 Above all, l each other deeply,
4: 8 because l covers over a multitude
5: 14 Greet one another with a kiss of l.
2Pe 1: 7 and to mutual affection, l.
1: 17 saying, "This is my Son, whom I l;
1Jn 2: 5 l for God is truly made complete
2: 15 Do not l the world or anything
2: 15 l for the Father is not in them.
3: 1 See what great l the Father has
3: 10 who does not l their brother
3: 11 We should l one another.
3: 14 life, because we l each other.
3: 14 Anyone who does not l remains
3: 16 This is how we know what l is:
3: 17 them, how can the l of God be
3: 18 let us not l with words or speech
3: 23 l one another as he commanded
4: 7 Dear friends, let us l one another, for l comes from God.
4: 8 Whoever does not l does not know God, because God is l.
4: 9 is how God showed his l among us:
4: 10 This is l: not that we loved God,
4: 11 us, we also ought to l one another.
4: 12 but if we l one another, God
4: 12 and his l is made complete in us.
4: 16 and rely on the l God has for us.
4: 16 God is l. Whoever lives in l
4: 17 This is how l is made complete
4: 18 There is no fear in l. But perfect l
4: 18 fears is not made perfect in l.
4: 19 We l because he first loved us.
4: 20 claims to l God yet hates a brother
4: 20 whoever does not l their brother
4: 20 they have seen, cannot l God,
4: 21 loves God must also l their brother
5: 2 we know that we l the children
5: 3 this is l for God: to keep his
2Jn : 1 whom I l in the truth—
: 3 Son, will be with us in truth and l.
: 5 I ask that we l one another.
: 6 And this is l: that we walk
: 6 command is that you walk in l.
3Jn : 1 friend Gaius, whom I l in the truth.
: 6 have told the church about your l.
Jude : 2 peace and l be yours in abundance.
: 12 are blemishes at your l feasts,
: 21 yourselves in God's l as you wait
Rev 2: 4 You have forsaken the l you had
2: 19 know your deeds, your l and faith,
3: 19 Those whom I l I rebuke
12: 11 they did not l their lives so much

LOVED* (LOVE)
Ge 24: 67 she became his wife, and he l her;
25: 28 l Esau, but Rebekah l Jacob.
29: 31 the LORD saw that Leah was not l,
29: 33 the LORD heard that I am not l,
34: 3 he l the young woman and spoke
37: 3 Now Israel l Joseph more than any
37: 4 that their father l him more than
Dt 4: 37 Because he l your ancestors
7: 8 it was because the LORD l you
10: 15 on your ancestors and l them,
1Sa 1: 5 a double portion because he l her,
18: 1 David, and he l him as himself.
18: 3 David because he l him as himself.
18: 16 But all Israel and Judah l David,
18: 28 that his daughter Michal l David,
20: 17 because he l him as he l himself.
2Sa 1: 23 in life they were l and admired,
12: 24 The LORD l him;
12: 25 and because the LORD l him,
13: 15 hated her more than he had l her.
1Ki 11: 1 l many foreign women besides
2Ch 11: 21 Rehoboam l Maakah daughter
26: 10 in the fertile lands, for he l the soil.
Ne 13: 26 He was l by his God, and God
Ps 44: 3 light of your face, for you l them.
47: 4 us, the pride of Jacob, whom he l.
78: 68 of Judah, Mount Zion, which he l.
109: 17 He l to pronounce a curse—
Isa 5: 1 My l one had a vineyard on a
Jer 2: 2 youth, how as a bride you l me
8: 2 which they have l and served
31: 3 "I have l you with an everlasting
Eze 16: 37 those you l as well as those you
Hos 1: 6 (which means "not l"),
2: 1 and of your sisters, 'My l one.'
2: 23 to the one I called 'Not my l one.'
3: 1 though she is l by another man
9: 10 became as vile as the thing they l.
11: 1 "When Israel was a child, I l him,
Mal 1: 2 "I have l you," says the LORD.
1: 2 "But you ask, 'How have you l us?'
1: 2 "Yet I have l Jacob,
Mk 10: 21 Jesus looked at him and l him.
12: 6 one left to send, a son, whom he l.
Lk 16: 14 The Pharisees, who l money,
Jn 3: 16 For God so l the world that he gave
3: 19 people l darkness instead of light
11: 5 Now Jesus l Martha and her sister
11: 36 the Jews said, "See how he l him!"
12: 43 for they l human praise more than
13: 1 Having l his own who were
13: 1 he l them to the end.
13: 23 the disciple whom Jesus l,
13: 34 As I have l you, so you must love
14: 21 The one who loves me will be l
14: 28 If you l me, you would be glad
15: 9 "As the Father has l me, so have I l you.
15: 12 Love each other as I have l you.
16: 27 loves you because you have l me
17: 23 have l them even as you have l me.
17: 24 me because you l me before
19: 26 disciple whom he l standing
20: 2 disciple, the one Jesus l, and said,
21: 7 the disciple whom Jesus l said
21: 20 whom Jesus l was following them.
Ro 1: 7 To all in Rome who are l by God
8: 37 conquerors through him who l us.
9: 13 "Jacob I l, but Esau I hated."
9: 25 I will call her 'my l one' who is not my l one,"
11: 28 they are l on account
Gal 2: 20 who l me and gave himself for me.
Eph 5: 1 therefore, as dearly l children
5: 2 just as Christ l us and gave himself
5: 25 just as Christ l the church and gave
Col 3: 12 holy and dearly l, clothe yourselves
1Th 1: 4 brothers and sisters l by God,
2: 8 Because we l you so much, we were
2Th 2: 13 brothers and sisters l by the Lord,
2: 16 who l us and by his grace gave us
2Ti 4: 10 for Demas, because he l this world,
Heb 1: 9 You have l righteousness and hated
2Pe 2: 15 who l the wages of wickedness.
1Jn 4: 10 not that we l God, but that he l us
4: 11 since God so l us, we also ought
4: 19 We love because he first l us.
Jude : 1 who are l in God the Father
Rev 3: 9 and acknowledge that I have l you.

LOVELY* (LOVE)
Ge 29: 17 but Rachel had a l figure and was
Est 1: 11 and nobles, for she was l to look at.
2: 7 had a l figure and was beautiful.
Ps 84: 1 How l is your dwelling place,
SS 1: 5 am l, yet l, daughters of Jerusalem,
2: 14 voice is sweet, and your face is l.
4: 3 a scarlet ribbon; your mouth is l.
5: 16 sweetness itself; he is altogether l.
6: 4 my darling, as l as Jerusalem,
Am 8: 13 "In that day "the l young women
Php 4: 8 is pure, whatever is l, whatever is

LOVER* (LOVE)
Isa 47: 8 listen, you l of pleasure,
1Ti 3: 3 not quarrelsome, not a l of money.

LOVERS* (LOVE)
Jer 3: 1 lived as a prostitute with many l—
3: 2 the roadside you sat waiting for l,
4: 30 Your l despise you; they want to
La 1: 2 Among all her l there is no one
Eze 16: 33 gifts, but you give gifts to all your l,
16: 36 in your promiscuity with your l,
16: 37 I am going to gather all your l,
16: 39 you into the hands of your l,
16: 41 and you will no longer pay your l.
23: 5 and she lusted after her l,
23: 9 her into the hands of her l,
23: 20 There she lusted after her l,
23: 22 I will stir up your l against you,
Hos 2: 5 'I will go after my l, who give me
2: 7 She will chase after her l but not
2: 10 lewdness before the eyes of her l;
2: 12 she said were her pay from her l;
2: 13 and went after her l, but me she
8: 9 Ephraim has sold herself to l.
2Ti 3: 2 will be l of themselves, l of money,
3: 3 brutal, not l of the good,
3: 4 l of pleasure rather than l of God—

LOVES* (LOVE)
Ge 44: 20 sons left, and his father l him.'
Dt 10: 18 l the foreigner residing among you,
15: 16 because he l you and your family
21: 15 and he l one but not the other,
21: 16 son of the wife he l in preference
23: 5 the LORD your God l you.
28: 54 or the wife he l or his surviving
28: 56 will begrudge the husband she l
33: 12 one the LORD l rests between his
Ru 4: 15 who l you and who is better to you
2Ch 2: 11 "Because the LORD l his people,
Ps 11: 7 LORD is righteous, he l justice;
33: 5 The LORD l righteousness
34: 12 Whoever of you l life and desires
37: 28 For the LORD l the just and will
87: 2 The LORD l the gates of Zion
91: 14 "Because he l me,"
99: 4 The King is mighty, he l justice—
119:140 tested, and your servant l them.
127: 2 he grants sleep to those he l.
146: 8 the LORD l the righteous.
Pr 3: 12 the LORD disciplines those he l,
12: 1 Whoever l discipline l knowledge,
13: 24 but the one who l their children is
15: 9 wicked, but he l those who pursue
17: 17 A friend l at all times, and a
17: 19 Whoever l a quarrel l sin;
19: 8 The one who gets wisdom l life;
21: 17 Whoever l pleasure will become
21: 17 whoever l wine and olive oil will
22: 11 One who l a pure heart and who
29: 3 A man who l wisdom brings joy
Ecc 5: 10 l money never has enough;

Ecc 5: 10 whoever **l** wealth is never
SS 3: 1 I looked for the one my heart **l**;
3: 2 will search for the one my heart **l**.
3: 3 you seen the one my heart **l**?"
3: 4 when I found the one my heart **l**.
Hos 3: 1 her as the LORD **l** the Israelites,
10: 11 Ephraim is a trained heifer that **l**
12: 7 dishonest scales and **l** to defraud.
Mal 2: 11 the sanctuary the LORD **l**
Mt 10: 37 "Anyone who **l** their father
10: 37 who **l** their son or daughter
Lk 7: 5 he **l** our nation and has built
7: 47 has been forgiven little **l** little."
Jn 3: 35 The Father **l** the Son and has
5: 20 For the Father **l** the Son and shows
10: 17 The reason my Father **l** me is that I
12: 25 Anyone who **l** their life will lose it,
14: 21 keeps them is the one who **l** me.
14: 21 The one who **l** me will be loved
14: 23 "Anyone who **l** me will obey my
16: 27 the Father himself **l** you because
Ro 13: 8 for whoever **l** others has fulfilled
1Co 8: 3 whoever **l** God is known by God.
2Co 9: 7 for God **l** a cheerful giver.
Eph 1: 6 has freely given us in the One he **l**.
5: 28 He who **l** his wife **l** himself.
5: 33 must love his wife as he **l** himself,
Col 1: 13 into the kingdom of the Son he **l**,
Titus 1: 8 hospitable, one who **l** what is good,
Heb 12: 6 the Lord disciplines the one he **l**,
1Jn 2: 10 Anyone who **l** their brother
2: 15 If anyone **l** the world, love for
4: 7 Everyone who **l** has been born
4: 21 Anyone who **l** God must also love
5: 1 who **l** the father **l** his child
3Jn : 9 but Diotrephes, who **l** to be first,
Rev 1: 5 To him who **l** us and has freed us
20: 9 camp of God's people, the city he **l**.
22: 15 and everyone who **l** and practices

LOVING* (LOVE)
Ps 25: 10 All the ways of the LORD are **l**
32: 8 I will counsel you with my **l** eye
107: 43 ponder the **l** deeds of the LORD.
144: 2 He is my **l** God and my fortress,
Pr 5: 19 A **l** doe, a graceful deer—
Heb 13: 1 Keep on **l** one another as brothers
1Jn 5: 2 by **l** God and carrying out his

LOW (LOWER LOWLY)
Ps 116: 6 when I was brought **l**, he saved me.

LOWER (LOW)
Ps 8: 5 made them a little **l** than the angels
2Co 11: 7 it a sin for me to **l** myself in order
Heb 2: 7 them a little **l** than the angels;

LOWING
1Sa 15: 14 What is this **l** of cattle that I hear?"

LOWLY (LOW)
Job 5: 11 The **l** he sets on high, and those
Ps 138: 6 is exalted, he looks kindly on the **l**;
Pr 29: 23 low, but the **l** in spirit gain honor.
Isa 57: 15 one who is contrite and **l** in spirit,
57: 15 to revive the spirit of the **l**
Eze 21: 26 The **l** will be exalted and the
Zec 9: 9 **l** and riding on a donkey,
Mt 18: 4 takes the **l** position of this child is
1Co 1: 28 God chose the **l** things of this

LOYAL (LOYALTY)
1Ch 29: 18 and keep their hearts **l** to you.
Ps 78: 8 whose hearts were not **l** to God,

LOYALTY (LOYAL)
Jdg 8: 35 failed to show any **l** to the family

LUKE*
Co-worker with Paul (Col 4:14; 2Ti 4:11; Phm 24).

LUKEWARM*
Rev 3: 16 So, because you are **l**—

LUST (LUSTED LUSTS)
Pr 6: 25 Do not **l** in your heart after her
Eze 20: 30 did and **l** after their vile images?
Col 3: 5 impurity, **l**, evil desires and greed,
1Th 4: 5 not in passionate **l** like the pagans,
1Pe 4: 3 living in debauchery, **l**,
1Jn 2: 16 the **l** of the flesh, the **l** of the eyes,

LUSTED (LUST)
Eze 23: 5 and she **l** after her lovers,

LUSTS* (LUST)
Nu 15: 39 after the **l** of your own hearts
Ro 1: 26 God gave them over to shameful **l**.

LUXURY
Jas 5: 5 You have lived on earth in **l**

LYDIA'S*
Ac 16: 40 they went to **L** house, where they

LYING (LIE)
Pr 6: 17 haughty eyes, a **l** tongue,
12: 22 The LORD detests **l** lips, but he
21: 6 by a **l** tongue is a fleeting vapor
26: 28 A **l** tongue hates those it hurts,

LYRE (LYRE)
1Sa 16: 23 David would take up his **l** and play.

MACEDONIA
Ac 16: 9 a vision of a man of **M** standing

MAD
Dt 28: 34 sights you see will drive you **m**.

MADE (MAKE)
Ge 1: 7 So God **m** the vault and separated
1: 16 God **m** two great lights—
1: 16 He also **m** the stars.
1: 25 God **m** the wild animals according
1: 31 God saw all that he had **m**, and it
2: 22 the LORD God **m** a woman
6: 6 that he had **m** human beings
9: 6 of God has God **m** mankind.
15: 18 day the LORD **m** a covenant
Ex 20: 11 six days the LORD **m** the heavens
20: 11 the Sabbath day and **m** it holy.
24: 8 that the LORD has **m** with you
32: 4 **m** it into an idol cast in the shape
Lev 16: 34 Atonement is to be **m** once a year
Dt 32: 6 who **m** you and formed you?
Jos 24: 25 that day Joshua **m** a covenant
2Ki 19: 15 You have **m** heaven and earth.
2Ch 2: 12 of Israel, who **m** heaven and earth!
Ne 9: 6 You **m** the heavens,
9: 10 You **m** a name for yourself,
Ps 33: 6 of the LORD the heavens were **m**,
95: 5 for he **m** it, and his hands formed
96: 5 but the LORD **m** the heavens.
100: 3 It is he who **m** us, and we are his;
136: 7 who **m** the great lights—
139: 14 I am fearfully and wonderfully **m**;
Ecc 3: 11 He has **m** everything beautiful in
Isa 43: 7 my glory, whom I formed and **m**."
45: 12 It is I who **m** the earth and created
45: 18 he who fashioned and **m** the earth,
66: 2 not my hand **m** all these things,
Jer 10: 12 But God **m** the earth by his power;
27: 5 outstretched arm I **m** the earth
32: 17 you have **m** the heavens
33: 2 LORD says, he who **m** the earth,
51: 15 "He **m** the earth by his power;
Eze 3: 17 I have **m** you a watchman
33: 7 I have **m** you a watchman
Am 5: 8 He who **m** the Pleiades and Orion,
Jnh 1: 9 who **m** the sea and the dry land."
Mk 2: 27 "The Sabbath was **m** for man,
Jn 1: 3 Through him all things were **m**;
Ac 17: 24 "The God who **m** the world
Heb 1: 2 whom also he **m** the universe.
Jas 3: 9 who have been **m** in God's likeness.
Rev 14: 7 Worship him who **m** the heavens,

MAGDALENE
Lk 8: 2 Mary (called **M**) from whom seven

MAGI
Mt 2: 1 **M** from the east came to Jerusalem

MAGIC (MAGICIANS)
Eze 13: 20 I am against your **m** charms
Rev 21: 8 those who practice **m** arts,
22: 15 dogs, those who practice **m** arts,

MAGICIANS (MAGIC)
Ex 7: 11 the Egyptian **m** also did the same
Da 2: 2 So the king summoned the **m**,

MAGNIFICENCE* (MAGNIFICENT)
1Ch 22: 5 for the LORD should be of great **m**

MAGNIFICENT (MAGNIFICENCE)
1Ki 8: 13 I have indeed built a **m** temple
Isa 28: 29 is wonderful, whose wisdom is **m**.
Mk 13: 1 What **m** buildings!"

MAGOG
Eze 38: 2 of the land of **M**, the chief prince
39: 6 I will send fire on **M** and on those
Rev 20: 8 Gog and **M**—and to gather them

MAIMED
Mt 18: 8 It is better for you to enter life **m**

MAINTAIN (MAINTAINING)
Hos 12: 6 **m** love and justice, and wait
Am 5: 15 **m** justice in the courts.
Ro 3: 28 For we **m** that a person is justified

MAINTAINING (MAINTAIN)
Ex 34: 7 **m** love to thousands, and forgiving

MAJESTIC* (MAJESTY)
Ex 15: 6 hand, LORD, was **m** in power.
15: 11 **m** in holiness, awesome in glory,
Job 37: 4 he thunders with his **m** voice.
Ps 8: 1 **m** is your name in all the earth!
8: 9 **m** is your name in all the earth!
29: 4 the voice of the LORD is **m**.
68: 15 Mount Bashan, **m** mountain,
76: 4 more **m** than mountains rich
111: 3 Glorious and **m** are his deeds,
SS 6: 4 as **m** as troops with banners.
6: 10 sun, **m** as the stars in procession?
Isa 30: 30 cause people to hear his **m** voice
Eze 31: 7 It was **m** in beauty, with its
2Pe 1: 17 came to him from the **M** Glory,

MAJESTY (MAJESTIC)
Ex 15: 7 your **m** you threw down those who
Dt 5: 24 has shown us his glory and his **m**,
11: 2 his **m**, his mighty hand,
33: 17 In **m** he is like a firstborn bull;
33: 26 you and on the clouds in his **m**.
1Ch 16: 27 Splendor and **m** are before him;
29: 11 glory and the **m** and the splendor,
Est 1: 4 the splendor and glory of his **m**.
7: 3 you, Your **M**, and if it pleases you,
Job 37: 22 God comes in awesome **m**.
40: 10 clothe yourself in honor and **m**.
Ps 21: 5 bestowed on him splendor and **m**.
45: 3 yourself with splendor and **m**.
45: 4 In your **m** ride forth victoriously
68: 34 of God, whose **m** is over Israel,
93: 1 LORD reigns, he is robed in **m**;
96: 6 Splendor and **m** are before him;
104: 1 are clothed with splendor and **m**.
145: 5 the glorious splendor of your **m**—
Isa 2: 10 LORD and the splendor of his **m**!
2: 19 LORD and the splendor of his **m**,
2: 21 LORD and the splendor of his **m**,
24: 14 west they acclaim the LORD's **m**.
26: 10 do not regard the **m** of the LORD.
53: 2 beauty or **m** to attract us to him,
Eze 31: 2 can be compared with you in **m**?
31: 18 with you in splendor and **m**?
Da 4: 30 power and for the glory of my **m**?"
Mic 5: 4 in the **m** of the name of the LORD
Zec 6: 13 he will be clothed with **m** and will
Ac 19: 27 will be robbed of her divine **m**."
25: 26 to write to His **M** about him.
Heb 1: 3 the right hand of the **M** in heaven.
8: 1 of the throne of the **M** in heaven,
2Pe 1: 16 but we were eyewitnesses of his **m**.
Jude : 25 only God our Savior be glory, **m**,

MAKE (MADE MAKER MAKERS MAKES MAKING)
Ge 1: 26 "Let us **m** mankind in our image,
2: 18 I will **m** a helper suitable for him."
6: 14 So **m** yourself an ark of cypress
12: 2 "I will **m** you into a great nation,
Ex 22: 3 steals must certainly **m** restitution,
25: 9 **M** this tabernacle and all its
25: 40 See that you **m** them according
Nu 6: 25 the LORD **m** his face shine on you
2Sa 7: 9 Now I will **m** your name great,
Job 7: 17 is mankind that you **m** so much
Ps 4: 8 LORD, **m** me dwell in safety.
20: 4 heart and **m** all your plans succeed.
108: 1 sing and **m** music with all my soul.

Ps 110: 1 right hand until I **m** your enemies
119:165 and nothing can **m** them stumble.
Pr 3: 6 and he will **m** your paths straight.
16: 23 the wise **m** their mouths prudent,
Isa 14: 14 I will **m** myself like the Most
29: 16 formed it, "You did not **m** me"?
55: 3 I will **m** an everlasting covenant
61: 8 and **m** an everlasting covenant
Jer 31: 31 "when I will **m** a new covenant
Eze 37: 26 I will **m** a covenant of peace
Mt 3: 3 Lord, **m** straight paths for him.'"
28: 19 go and **m** disciples of all nations,
Lk 13: 24 "**M** every effort to enter through
Ro 14: 19 Let us therefore **m** every effort to
2Co 5: 9 So we **m** it our goal to please him,
Eph 4: 3 **M** every effort to keep the unity
Col 4: 5 **m** the most of every opportunity.
1Th 4: 11 **m** it your ambition to lead a quiet
2Th 1: 11 our God may **m** you worthy of his
Heb 4: 11 **m** every effort to enter that rest,
8: 5 it that you **m** everything according
12: 14 **M** every effort to live in peace
2Pe 1: 5 **m** every effort to add to your faith
3: 14 **m** every effort to be found spotless,

MAKER* (MAKE)
Job 4: 17 man be more pure than his **M**?
9: 9 He is the **M** of the Bear and Orion,
32: 22 my **M** would soon take me away.
35: 10 'Where is God my **M**, who gives
36: 3 I will ascribe justice to my **M**.
40: 19 yet its **M** can approach it with his
Ps 95: 6 us kneel before the LORD our **M**;
115: 15 LORD, the **M** of heaven and earth.
121: 2 LORD, the **M** of heaven and earth.
124: 8 LORD, the **M** of heaven and earth.
134: 3 he who is the **M** of heaven
146: 6 He is the **M** of heaven and earth,
149: 2 Let Israel rejoice in their **M**;
Pr 14: 31 poor shows contempt for their **M**,
17: 5 poor shows contempt for their **M**;
22: 2 The LORD is the **M** of them all.
Ecc 11: 5 work of God, the **M** of all things.
Isa 17: 7 that day people will look to their **M**
27: 11 so their **M** has no compassion
44: 24 I am the LORD, the **M** of all things,
45: 9 to those who quarrel with their **M**,
45: 11 the Holy One of Israel, and its **M**:
51: 13 that you forget the LORD your **M**,
54: 5 For your **M** is your husband—
Jer 10: 16 these, for he is the **M** of all things,
51: 19 these, for he is the **M** of all things,
Hos 8: 14 Israel has forgotten their **M**

MAKERS* (MAKE)
Isa 45: 16 All the **m** of idols will be put

MAKES (MAKE)
Ps 23: 2 **m** me lie down in green pastures,
Pr 13: 12 Hope deferred **m** the heart sick,
1Co 3: 7 but only God, who **m** things grow.

MAKING (MAKE)
Ps 19: 7 are trustworthy, **m** wise the simple.
Ecc 12: 12 Of **m** many books there is no end,
Jn 5: 18 Father, **m** himself equal with God.
1Co 3: 6 it, but God has been **m** it grow.
Eph 5: 16 **m** the most of every opportunity,

MALACHI*
Mal 1: 1 of the LORD to Israel through **M**.

MALE
Ge 1: 27 **m** and female he created them.
Ex 13: 2 to me every firstborn **m**.
Nu 8: 16 the first **m** offspring from every
Mt 19: 4 the Creator 'made them **m**
Gal 3: 28 nor free, nor is there **m** and female,

MALICE (MALICIOUS)
Mk 7: 22 greed, **m**, deceit, lewdness,
Ro 1: 29 envy, murder, strife, deceit and **m**.
1Co 5: 8 with the old bread leavened with **m**
Eph 4: 31 along with every form of **m**.
Col 3: 8 anger, rage, **m**, slander, and filthy
1Pe 2: 1 rid yourselves of all **m** and all

MALICIOUS (MALICE)
1Ti 3: 11 not **m** talkers but temperate
6: 4 envy, strife, **m** talk, evil suspicions

MALIGN
Titus 2: 5 no one will **m** the word of God.

MAN (HUMAN MANKIND MEN WOMAN WOMEN)
Ge 2: 7 the LORD God formed a **m**
2: 7 and the **m** became a living being.
2: 8 there he put the **m** he had formed.
2: 15 The LORD God took the **m**
2: 18 is not good for the **m** to be alone.
2: 20 So the **m** gave names to all
2: 23 The **m** said, "This is now bone
2: 23 for she was taken out of **m**."
3: 9 the LORD God called to the **m**,
3: 22 "The **m** has now become like one
4: 1 LORD I have brought forth a **m**."
Dt 8: 3 **m** does not live on bread alone
1Sa 13: 14 sought out a **m** after his own heart
Ps 127: 5 Blessed is the **m** whose quiver is
Pr 30: 19 way of a **m** with a young woman.
Isa 53: 3 by mankind, a **m** of suffering,
Jer 17: 5 "Cursed is the one who trusts in **m**,
Mt 4: 4 '**M** shall not live on bread alone,
19: 5 this reason a **m** will leave his father
Lk 4: 4 '**M** shall not live on bread alone.'"
Ro 5: 12 entered the world through one **m**,
1Co 7: 1 "It is good for a **m** not to have
7: 2 **m** should have sexual relations
11: 3 the head of every **m** is Christ,
11: 3 and the head of the woman is **m**,
13: 11 When I became a **m**, I put the ways
15: 21 For since death came through a **m**,
15: 47 The first **m** was of the dust
15: 47 the second **m** is of heaven.
2Co 12: 2 I know a **m** in Christ who fourteen
Eph 5: 31 this reason a **m** will leave his father
Php 2: 8 being found in appearance as a **m**,
1Ti 2: 12 or to assume authority over a **m**;
Heb 2: 6 a son of **m** that you care for him?

MANAGE* (MANAGER MANAGES)
Jer 12: 5 how will you **m** in the thickets
1Ti 3: 4 He must **m** his own family well
3: 5 not know how to **m** his own family,
3: 12 to his wife and must **m** his children
5: 14 to **m** their homes and to give

MANAGER (MANAGE)
Lk 12: 42 then is the faithful and wise **m**,
16: 1 a rich man whose **m** was accused

MANAGES* (MANAGE)
Titus 1: 7 an overseer **m** God's household,

MANASSEH
1. Firstborn of Joseph (Ge 41:51; 46:20). Blessed by Jacob but not firstborn (Ge 48). Tribe of blessed (Dt 33:17), numbered (Nu 1:35; 26:34), half allotted land east of Jordan (Nu 32; Jos 13:8–33), half west (Jos 17; Eze 48:4), failed to fully possess (Jos 17:12–13; Jdg 1:27), 12,000 from (Rev 7:6).
2. Son of Hezekiah; king of Judah (2Ki 21:1–18; 2Ch 33:1–20). Judah exiled for his detestable sins (2Ki 21:10–15). Repentance (2Ch 33:12–19).

MANDRAKES
Ge 30: 14 give me some of your son's **m**."

MANGER
Lk 2: 12 in cloths and lying in a **m**."

MANIFESTATION*
1Co 12: 7 one the **m** of the Spirit is given

MANKIND (MAN)
Ge 1: 26 said, "Let us make **m** in our image,
Ps 8: 4 what is **m** that you are mindful of
33: 13 LORD looks down and sees all **m**;
Pr 8: 31 whole world and delighting in **m**.
Ecc 7: 29 God created **m** upright, but they
Isa 45: 12 the earth and created **m** on it.
Jer 32: 27 "I am the LORD, the God of all **m**.
Zec 2: 13 Be still before the LORD, all **m**,
Jn 1: 4 that life was the light of all **m**.
Heb 2: 6 "What is **m** that you are mindful of
1Ti 2: 5 one mediator between God and **m**,

MANNA
Ex 16: 31 people of Israel called the bread **m**.
Dt 8: 16 He gave you **m** to eat
Jn 6: 49 Your ancestors ate the **m**
Rev 2: 17 I will give some of the hidden **m**.

MANNER
1Co 11: 27 in an unworthy **m** will be guilty
Php 1: 27 conduct yourselves in a **m** worthy

MANSIONS*
Ps 49: 14 grave, far from their princely **m**.
Isa 5: 9 the fine **m** left without occupants.
Am 3: 15 and the **m** will be demolished,"
5: 11 though you have built stone **m**,

MARCH
Jos 6: 4 day, **m** around the city seven times,
Isa 42: 13 The LORD will **m** out like

MARITAL* (MARRY)
Ex 21: 10 of her food, clothing and **m** rights.
1Co 7: 3 husband should fulfill his **m** duty

MARK (MARKED MARKS)
Cousin of Barnabas (Col 4:10; 2Ti 4:11; Phm 24; 1Pe 5:13), see JOHN.
Ge 4: 15 the LORD put a **m** on Cain so
Rev 13: 16 to receive a **m** on their right hands

MARKED (MARK)
Ac 17: 26 he **m** out their appointed times

MARKET (MARKETPLACE MARKETPLACES)
Jn 2: 16 my Father's house into a **m**!"

MARKETPLACE (MARKET)
Lk 7: 32 are like children sitting in the **m**

MARKETPLACES (MARKET)
Mt 23: 7 to be greeted with respect in the **m**

MARKS (MARK)
Jn 20: 25 "Unless I see the nail **m** in his
Gal 6: 17 I bear on my body the **m** of Jesus.

MARRED
Isa 52: 14 and his form **m** beyond human

MARRIAGE (MARRY)
Mt 22: 30 neither marry nor be given in **m**;
24: 38 marrying and giving in **m**,
Heb 13: 4 **M** should be honored by all,
13: 4 and the **m** bed kept pure,

MARRIED (MARRY)
Dt 24: 5 happiness to the wife he has **m**.
Ezr 10: 10 you have **m** foreign women,
Pr 30: 23 contemptible woman who gets **m**,
Mt 1: 18 was pledged to be **m** to Joseph,
Mk 12: 23 be, since the seven were **m** to her?"
Ro 7: 2 by law a **m** woman is bound to her
1Co 7: 33 But a **m** man is concerned
7: 36 is not sinning. They should get **m**.

MARRIES (MARRY)
Mt 5: 32 anyone who **m** a divorced woman
19: 9 and **m** another woman commits
Lk 16: 18 the man who **m** a divorced woman

MARROW
Heb 4: 12 soul and spirit, joints and **m**;

MARRY (INTERMARRY MARITAL MARRIAGE MARRIED MARRIES)
Dt 25: 5 brother shall take her and **m** her
Mt 22: 30 people will neither **m** nor be given
1Co 7: 9 they should **m**, for it is better to **m**
7: 28 But if you do **m**, you have not
1Ti 4: 3 They forbid people to **m** and order
5: 14 So I counsel younger widows to **m**,

MARTHA*
Sister of Mary and Lazarus (Lk 10:38–42; Jn 11; 12:2).

MARVELED* (MARVELOUS)
Lk 2: 33 mother **m** at what was said
2Th 1: 10 to be **m** at among all those who

MARVELING* (MARVELOUS)
Lk 9: 43 While everyone was **m** at all

MARVELOUS* (MARVELED MARVELING)
1Ch 16: 24 his **m** deeds among all peoples.
Job 37: 5 God's voice thunders in **m** ways;
Ps 71: 17 to this day I declare your **m** deeds.
72: 18 of Israel, who alone does **m** deeds.
86: 10 For you are great and do **m** deeds;
96: 3 his **m** deeds among all peoples.
98: 1 song, for he has done **m** things;
118: 23 done this, and it is **m** in our eyes.
Zec 8: 6 "It may seem **m** to the remnant

Zec 8: 6 time, but will it seem **m** to me?"
Mt 21: 42 done this, and it is **m** in our eyes'?
Mk 12: 11 done this, and it is **m** in our eyes'?"
Rev 15: 1 heaven another great and **m** sign:
15: 3 "Great and **m** are your deeds,

MARY

1. Mother of Jesus (Mt 1:16–25; Lk 1:27–56; 2:1–40). With Jesus at temple (Lk 2:41–52), at wedding in Cana (Jn 2:1–5), questioning his sanity (Mk 3:21), at the cross (Jn 19:25–27). Among disciples after Jesus' ascension (Ac 1:14).

2. Magdalene; former demoniac (Lk 8:2). Helped support Jesus' ministry (Lk 8:1–3). At the cross (Mt 27:56; Mk 15:40; Jn 19:25), burial (Mt 27:61; Mk 15:47). Saw angel after resurrection (Mt 28:1–10; Mk 16:1–9; Lk 24:1–12); also saw Jesus (Jn 20:1–18).

3. Sister of Martha and Lazarus (Jn 11). Washed Jesus' feet (Jn 12:1–8).

MASQUERADES*
2Co 11: 14 for Satan himself **m** as an angel

MASTER (MASTER'S MASTERED MASTERS MASTERY)
Pr 25: 13 he refreshes the spirit of his **m**.
Hos 2: 16 you will no longer call me 'my **m**.'
Mal 1: 6 If I am a **m**, where is the respect
Mt 10: 24 teacher, nor a servant above his **m**.
24: 46 servant whose **m** finds him doing
25: 21 "His **m** replied, 'Well done,
25: 23 "His **m** replied, 'Well done,
Ro 6: 14 For sin shall no longer be your **m**,
14: 4 To their own **m**, servants stand
Col 4: 1 that you also have a **M** in heaven.
2Ti 2: 21 useful to the **M** and prepared to do

MASTERED* (MASTER)
1Co 6: 12 but I will not be **m** by anything.
2Pe 2: 19 are slaves to whatever has **m** them."

MASTER'S (MASTER)
Mt 25: 21 and share your **m** happiness!'

MASTERS (MASTER)
Mt 6: 24 "No one can serve two **m**.
Lk 16: 13 "No one can serve two **m**.
Eph 6: 5 obey your earthly **m** with respect
6: 9 **m**, treat your slaves in the same
Col 3: 22 obey your earthly **m** in everything;
4: 1 **M**, provide your slaves with what is
1Ti 6: 1 should consider their **m** worthy
6: 2 who have believing **m** should not
Titus 2: 9 be subject to their **m** in everything,
1Pe 2: 18 God submit yourselves to your **m**,

MASTERY* (MASTER)
Ro 6: 9 death no longer has **m** over him.

MAT
Mk 2: 9 'Get up, take your **m** and walk'?
Ac 9: 34 Get up and roll up your **m**."

MATCHED*
2Co 8: 11 do it may be **m** by your completion

MATTHEW*

Apostle; former tax collector (Mt 9:9–13; 10:3; Mk 3:18; Lk 6:15; Ac 1:13). Also called Levi (Mk 2:14–17; Lk 5:27–32).

MATTHIAS
Ac 1: 26 they cast lots, and the lot fell to **M**;

MATURE* (MATURITY)
Lk 8: 14 and pleasures, and they do not **m**.
1Co 2: 6 message of wisdom among the **m**,
Eph 4: 13 of the Son of God and become **m**,
4: 15 in every respect the **m** body of him
Php 3: 15 who are **m** should take such a view
Col 1: 28 we may present everyone fully **m**
4: 12 will of God, **m** and fully assured.
Heb 5: 14 But solid food is for the **m**,
Jas 1: 4 its work so that you may be **m**

MATURITY* (MATURE)
Heb 6: 1 Christ and be taken forward to **m**,

MEAL
1Co 10: 27 If an unbeliever invites you to a **m**
Heb 12: 16 single **m** sold his inheritance rights

MEANING
Ne 8: 8 and giving the **m** so that the people

MEANINGLESS
Ecc 1: 2 "**M**! **M**!" says the Teacher.
1Ti 1: 6 these and have turned to **m** talk.

MEANS
1Co 9: 22 all possible **m** I might save some.

MEASURE (MEASURED MEASURES)
Jer 10: 24 me, LORD, but only in due **m**—
30: 11 discipline you but only in due **m**;
46: 28 discipline you but only in due **m**;
Eze 45: 3 **m** off a section 25,000 cubits long
Zec 2: 2 "To **m** Jerusalem, to find out how
Lk 6: 38 For with the **m** you use, it will be
Eph 3: 19 be filled to the **m** of all the fullness
4: 13 to the whole **m** of the fullness
Rev 11: 1 "Go and **m** the temple of God

MEASURED (MEASURE)
Isa 40: 12 has **m** the waters in the hollow
Jer 31: 37 if the heavens above can be **m**

MEASURES (MEASURE)
Dt 25: 14 Do not have two differing **m** in
Pr 20: 10 Differing weights and differing **m**

MEAT
Pr 23: 20 wine or gorge themselves on **m**,
Ro 14: 6 eats **m** does so to the Lord,
14: 21 It is better not to eat **m** or drink
1Co 8: 13 I will never eat **m** again, so that I
10: 25 sold in the **m** market without

MEDDLER*
1Pe 4: 15 kind of criminal, or even as a **m**.

MEDIATE* (MEDIATOR)
1Sa 2: 25 God may **m** for the offender;
Job 9: 33 If only there were someone to **m**

MEDIATOR* (MEDIATE)
Gal 3: 19 angels and entrusted to a **m**.
3: 20 A **m**, however, implies more than
1Ti 2: 5 one God and one **m** between God
Heb 8: 6 which he is **m** is superior to the old
9: 15 this reason Christ is the **m** of a new
12: 24 to Jesus the **m** of a new covenant,

MEDICINE*
Pr 17: 22 A cheerful heart is good **m**,

MEDITATE* (MEDITATED MEDITATES MEDITATION)
Ge 24: 63 out to the field one evening to **m**,
Jos 1: 8 **m** on it day and night, so that you
Ps 48: 9 God, we **m** on your unfailing love.
77: 3 I **m**, and my spirit grew faint.
77: 6 My heart **m** and my spirit asked:
77: 12 and **m** on all your mighty deeds."
119: 15 I **m** on your precepts and consider
119: 23 servant will **m** on your decrees.
119: 27 I may **m** on your wonderful deeds.
119: 48 love, that I may **m** on your decrees.
119: 78 but I will **m** on your precepts.
119: 97 I **m** on it all day long.
119: 99 teachers, for I **m** on your statutes.
119:148 that I may **m** on your promises.
143: 5 I **m** on all your works
145: 5 I will **m** on your wonderful works.

MEDITATED* (MEDITATE)
Ps 39: 3 While I **m**, the fire burned;

MEDITATES* (MEDITATE)
Ps 1: 2 and who **m** on his law day

MEDITATION* (MEDITATE)
Ps 19: 14 this **m** of my heart be pleasing
49: 3 the **m** of my heart will give you
104: 34 May my **m** be pleasing to him, as I

MEDIUM
Lev 20: 27 or woman who is a **m** or spiritist

MEEK*
Ps 37: 11 But the **m** will inherit the land
Zep 3: 12 I will leave within you the **m**
Mt 5: 5 Blessed are the **m**, for they will

MEET (MEETING MEETINGS MEETS)
Ps 42: 2 When can I go and **m** with God?
85: 10 Love and faithfulness **m** together;
Am 4: 12 Israel, prepare to **m** your God."
1Co 11: 34 you **m** together it may not result
1Th 4: 17 the clouds to **m** the Lord in the air.

MEETING (MEET)
Ex 40: 34 the cloud covered the tent of **m**,
Heb 10: 25 not giving up **m** together, as some

MEETINGS* (MEET)
1Co 11: 17 your **m** do more harm than good.

MEETS (MEET)
Heb 7: 26 a high priest truly **m** our need—

MELCHIZEDEK
Ge 14: 18 **M** king of Salem brought out bread
Ps 110: 4 a priest forever, in the order of **M**."
Heb 7: 11 one in the order of **M**,

MELT (MELTS)
Dt 1: 28 brothers have made our hearts **m**
2Pe 3: 12 the elements will **m** in the heat.

MELTS (MELT)
Am 9: 5 he touches the earth and it **m**,

MEMBER (MEMBERS)
Ro 12: 5 each **m** belongs to all the others.

MEMBERS (MEMBER)
Mic 7: 6 a man's enemies are the **m** of his
Mt 10: 36 man's enemies will be the **m** of his
Ro 12: 4 of us has one body with many **m**,
12: 4 these **m** do not all have the same
1Co 6: 15 bodies are **m** of Christ himself?
Eph 3: 6 Israel, **m** together of one body,
4: 25 for we are all **m** of one body.
5: 30 for we are **m** of his body.
Col 3: 15 since as **m** of one body you were

MEMORABLE* (MEMORY)
Eze 39: 13 I display my glory will be a **m** day

MEMORIES* (MEMORY)
1Th 3: 6 you always have pleasant **m** of us

MEMORY (MEMORABLE MEMORIES)
Mt 26: 13 done will also be told, in **m** of her."

MEN (MAN)
Ge 6: 4 the heroes of old, **m** of renown.
Ro 1: 27 **M** committed shameful acts with other **m**,
1Co 13: 1 in the tongues of **m** or of angels,
16: 18 Such **m** deserve recognition.
Gal 1: 1 Paul, an apostle—sent not from **m**
1Ti 5: 1 Treat younger **m** as brothers,
Heb 7: 28 the law appoints as high priests **m**

MENAHEM*

King of Israel (2Ki 15:17–23).

MENE
Da 5: 25 inscription that was written: M, M,

MEPHIBOSHETH

Son of Jonathan shown kindness by David (2Sa 4:4; 9; 21:7). Accused of siding with Absalom (2Sa 16:1–4; 19:24–30).

MERCHANT
Pr 31: 14 She is like the **m** ships, bringing
Mt 13: 45 heaven is like a **m** looking for fine

MERCIFUL (MERCY)
Dt 4: 31 the LORD your God is a **m** God;
Ne 9: 31 for you are a gracious and **m** God.
Ps 77: 9 Has God forgotten to be **m**?
78: 38 Yet he was **m**; he forgave their
Da 9: 9 The Lord our God is **m**
Mt 5: 7 Blessed are the **m**, for they will be
Lk 1: 54 Israel, remembering to be **m**
6: 36 Be **m**, just as your Father is **m**.
Heb 2: 17 in order that he might become a **m**
Jas 2: 13 to anyone who has not been **m**.
Jude : 22 Be **m** to those who doubt;

MERCY (MERCIFUL)
Ex 33: 19 have **m** on whom I will have **m**,
2Sa 24: 14 of the LORD, for his **m** is great;
1Ch 21: 13 the LORD, for his **m** is very great;
Ne 9: 31 great **m** you did not put an end
Ps 25: 6 LORD, your great **m** and love,
28: 6 for he has heard my cry for **m**.
57: 1 Have **m** on me, my God, have **m**
Pr 28: 13 and renounces them finds **m**.
Isa 63: 9 his love and **m** he redeemed them;
Da 9: 18 but because of your great **m**.
Hos 6: 6 For I desire **m**, not sacrifice,
Am 5: 15 LORD God Almighty will have **m**
Mic 6: 8 to love **m** and to walk humbly

Mic 7: 18 forever but delight to show **m**.
Hab 3: 2 in wrath remember **m**.
Zec 7: 9 show **m** and compassion to one
Mt 5: 7 merciful, for they will be shown **m**.
9: 13 'I desire **m**, not sacrifice.'
12: 7 mean, 'I desire **m**, not sacrifice,'
18: 33 Shouldn't you have had **m** on your
23: 23 justice, **m** and faithfulness.
Lk 1: 50 His **m** extends to those who fear
Ro 1: 31 no fidelity, no love, no **m**.
9: 15 "I will have **m** on whom I have **m**,
9: 18 God has **m** on whom he wants to have **m**,
11: 32 so that he may have **m** on them all.
12: 1 in view of God's **m**, to offer your
12: 8 if it is to show **m**, do it cheerfully.
Eph 2: 4 love for us, God, who is rich in **m**,
1Ti 1: 13 I was shown **m** because I acted
1: 16 very reason I was shown **m** so
Titus 3: 5 we had done, but because of his **m**.
Heb 4: 16 so that we may receive **m** and find
Jas 2: 13 **M** triumphs over judgment.
3: 17 full of **m** and good fruit,
5: 11 Lord is full of compassion and **m**.
1Pe 1: 3 In his great **m** he has given us new
2: 10 once you had not received **m**, but now you have received **m**.
Jude : 23 to others show **m**, mixed with fear

MERRY
Lk 12: 19 eat, drink and be **m**."'

MESHACH
Hebrew exiled to Babylon; name changed from Mishael (Da 1:6–7). Refused defilement by food (Da 1:8–20). Refused to worship idol (Da 3:1–18); saved from furnace (Da 3:19–30).

MESSAGE (MESSENGER)
Isa 53: 1 Who has believed our **m**
Jn 12: 38 who has believed our **m**
Ac 10: 36 You know the **m** God sent
17: 11 for they received the **m** with great
Ro 10: 16 "Lord, who has believed our **m**?"
10: 17 faith comes from hearing the **m**,
1Co 1: 18 the **m** of the cross is foolishness
2: 4 My **m** and my preaching were not
2Co 5: 19 to us the **m** of reconciliation.
Col 3: 16 Let the **m** of Christ dwell among
2Th 3: 1 that the **m** of the Lord may spread
Titus 1: 9 to the trustworthy **m** as it has been
Heb 4: 2 the **m** they heard was of no value
1Pe 2: 8 because they disobey the **m**—
2Pe 1: 19 have the prophetic **m** as something

MESSENGER (MESSAGE)
Pr 25: 13 at harvest time is a trustworthy **m**
Mal 3: 1 "I will send my **m**, who will
Mt 11: 10 "'I will send my **m** ahead of you,
2Co 12: 7 a thorn in my flesh, a **m** of Satan,

MESSIAH (MESSIAHS)
Mt 1: 16 of Jesus who is called the **M**.
16: 16 "You are the **M**, the Son
22: 42 "What do you think about the **M**?
Mk 1: 1 the good news about Jesus the **M**,
8: 29 Peter answered, "You are the **M**."
14: 61 him, "Are you the **M**, the Son
Lk 9: 20 Peter answered, "God's **M**."
Jn 1: 41 "We have found the **M**" (that is,
4: 25 that **M**" (called Christ) "is coming.
20: 31 may believe that Jesus is the **M**,
Ac 2: 36 you crucified, both Lord and **M**."
5: 42 the good news that Jesus is the **M**.
9: 22 by proving that Jesus is the **M**.
17: 3 proving that the **M** had to suffer
18: 28 the Scriptures that Jesus was the **M**.
26: 23 that the **M** would suffer and,
Ro 9: 5 the human ancestry of the **M**,
Rev 11: 15 kingdom of our Lord and of his **M**,

MESSIAHS* (MESSIAH)
Mt 24: 24 For false **m** and false prophets will
Mk 13: 22 For false **m** and false prophets will

METHUSELAH
Ge 5: 27 **M** lived a total of 969 years,

MICAH
1. Idolater from Ephraim (Jdg 17–18).
2. Prophet from Moresheth (Jer 26:18–19; Mic 1:1).

MICAIAH
Prophet of the LORD who spoke against Ahab (1Ki 22:1–28; 2Ch 18:1–27).

MICHAEL
Archangel (Jude 9); warrior in angelic realm, protector of Israel (Da 10:13, 21; 12:1; Rev 12:7).

MICHAL
Daughter of Saul, wife of David (1Sa 14:49; 18:20–28). Warned David of Saul's plot (1Sa 19). Saul gave her to Paltiel (1Sa 25:44); David retrieved her (2Sa 3:13–16). Criticized David for dancing before the ark (2Sa 6:16–23); 1Ch 15:29).

MIDIAN
Ex 2: 15 Pharaoh and went to live in **M**,
Jdg 7: 2 cannot deliver **M** into their hands,

MIDWIVES
Ex 1: 17 The **m**, however, feared God

MIGHT (ALMIGHTY MIGHTIER MIGHTY)
Jdg 16: 30 Then he pushed with all his **m**,
2Sa 6: 5 with all their **m** before the LORD,
6: 14 before the LORD with all his **m**,
2Ch 20: 6 Power and **m** are in your hand,
Ps 21: 13 we will sing and praise your **m**.
54: 1 vindicate me by your **m**.
Isa 11: 2 the Spirit of counsel and of **m**,
63: 15 Where are your zeal and your **m**?
Mic 3: 8 and with justice and **m**, to declare
Zec 4: 6 'Not by **m** nor by power, but by my
Col 1: 11 glorious **m** so that you may have
1Ti 6: 16 To him be honor and **m** forever.

MIGHTIER* (MIGHT)
Ps 93: 4 **M** than the thunder of the great
93: 4 **m** than the breakers of the sea—

MIGHTY (MIGHT)
Ge 49: 24 of the hand of the **M** One of Jacob,
Ex 6: 1 of my **m** hand he will let them go;
13: 3 you out of it with a **m** hand.
Dt 5: 15 you out of there with a **m** hand
7: 8 he brought you out with a **m** hand
10: 17 the great God, **m** and awesome,
34: 12 one has ever shown the **m** power
2Sa 1: 19 How the **m** have fallen!
23: 8 the names of David's **m** warriors:
Ne 9: 32 the great God, **m** and awesome,
Job 36: 5 "God is **m**, but despises no one;
Ps 24: 8 and **m**, the LORD **m** in battle.
45: 3 sword on your side, you **m** one;
50: 1 The **M** One, God, the LORD,
62: 7 he is my **m** rock, my refuge.
68: 11 women who proclaim it are a **m**
68: 33 who thunders with **m** voice.
71: 16 come and proclaim your **m** acts,
77: 12 and meditate on all your **m** deeds."
77: 15 your **m** arm you redeemed your
89: 8 are **m**, and your faithfulness
93: 4 the LORD on high is **m**.
99: 4 The King is **m**, he loves justice—
110: 2 LORD will extend your **m** scepter
118: 15 right hand has done **m** things!
136: 12 a **m** hand and outstretched arm;
145: 4 they tell of your **m** acts.
145: 12 people may know of your **m** acts
147: 5 Great is our Lord and **m** in power;
SS 8: 6 like blazing fire, like a **m** flame.
Isa 9: 6 Wonderful Counselor, **M** God,
60: 16 Redeemer, the **M** One of Jacob.
63: 1 I, proclaiming victory, **m** to save."
Jer 10: 6 and your name is **m** in power.
20: 11 LORD is with me like a **m** warrior;
32: 18 Great and **m** God, whose name is
32: 19 purposes and **m** are your deeds.
Eze 20: 33 I will reign over you with a **m** hand
Zep 3: 17 you, the **M** Warrior who saves.
Mt 26: 64 at the right hand of the **M** One
Eph 1: 19 is the same as the **m** strength
6: 10 in the Lord and in his **m** power.
1Pe 5: 6 under God's **m** hand, that he may

MILE*
Mt 5: 41 If anyone forces you to go one **m**,

MILK
Ex 3: 8 a land flowing with **m** and honey—
23: 19 a young goat in its mother's **m**.
Isa 55: 1 buy wine and **m** without money
1Co 3: 2 I gave you **m**, not solid food,
Heb 5: 12 You need **m**, not solid food!
1Pe 2: 2 crave pure spiritual **m**, so that by it

MILLSTONE (STONE)
Lk 17: 2 with a **m** tied around their neck

MIND (DOUBLE-MINDED LIKE-MINDED MINDFUL MINDS MINDSET)
Nu 23: 19 being, that he should change his **m**.
Dt 28: 65 LORD will give you an anxious **m**,
1Sa 15: 29 does not lie or change his **m**;
1Ch 28: 9 devotion and with a willing **m**,
2Ch 30: 12 to give them unity of **m** to carry
Ps 26: 2 me, examine my heart and my **m**;
110: 4 sworn and will not change his **m**:
Jer 17: 10 the heart and examine the **m**,
Da 7: 4 the **m** of a human was given to it.
Mt 22: 37 all your soul and with all your **m**.'
Mk 12: 30 with all your **m** and with all your
Lk 10: 27 your strength and with all your **m**';
Ac 4: 32 believers were one in heart and **m**.
Ro 1: 28 gave them over to a depraved **m**,
7: 25 then, I myself in my **m** am a slave
8: 6 The **m** governed by the flesh is
8: 6 the **m** governed by the Spirit is
8: 7 The **m** governed by the flesh is
12: 2 by the renewing of your **m**.
14: 13 make up your **m** not to put any
15: 6 so that with one **m** and one voice
1Co 1: 10 that you be perfectly united in **m**
2: 9 what no human **m** has conceived"
14: 14 spirit prays, but my **m** is unfruitful.
2Co 13: 11 another, be of one **m**, live in peace.
Php 2: 2 being one in spirit and of one **m**.
3: 19 Their **m** is set on earthly things.
4: 2 to be of the same **m** in the Lord.
Col 2: 18 idle notions by their unspiritual **m**.
1Th 4: 11 You should **m** your own business
Heb 7: 21 sworn and will not change his **m**:
1Pe 4: 7 of sober **m** so that you may pray.

MINDFUL* (MIND)
Ps 8: 4 is mankind that you are **m** of them,
26: 3 for I have always been **m** of your
Lk 1: 48 he has been **m** of the humble state
Heb 2: 6 is mankind that you are **m** of them,

MINDS (MIND)
Dt 11: 18 of mine in your hearts and **m**;
Ps 7: 9 the righteous God who probes **m**
Isa 26: 3 peace those whose **m** are steadfast,
Jer 31: 33 "I will put my law in their **m**
Lk 24: 38 and why do doubts rise in your **m**?
24: 45 he opened their **m** so they could
Ro 8: 5 the flesh have their **m** set on what
8: 5 the Spirit have their **m** set on what
2Co 4: 4 god of this age has blinded the **m**
Eph 4: 23 new in the attitude of your **m**;
Col 3: 2 Set your **m** on things above,
Heb 8: 10 I will put my laws in their **m**
10: 16 and I will write them on their **m**."
1Pe 1: 13 **m** that are alert and fully sober,
Rev 2: 23 am he who searches hearts and **m**,

MINDSET* (MIND)
Php 2: 5 have the same **m** as Christ Jesus:

MINISTER (MINISTERING MINISTERS MINISTRY)
Ps 101: 6 one whose walk is blameless will **m**
1Ti 4: 6 you will be a good **m** of Christ

MINISTERING (MINISTER)
Heb 1: 14 Are not all angels **m** spirits sent

MINISTERS (MINISTER)
2Co 3: 6 He has made us competent as **m**

MINISTRY (MINISTER)
Ac 6: 4 to prayer and the **m** of the word."
Ro 11: 13 the Gentiles, I take pride in my **m**
2Co 4: 1 God's mercy we have this **m**, we do
5: 18 gave us the **m** of reconciliation:
6: 3 that our **m** will not be discredited.
2Ti 4: 5 discharge all the duties of your **m**.
Heb 8: 6 in fact the **m** Jesus has received is

MIRACLE* (MIRACLES MIRACULOUS)
Ex 7: 9 'Perform a **m**,' then say to Aaron,
Mk 9: 39 no one who does a **m** in my name
Jn 7: 21 them, "I did one **m**, and you are all

MIRACLES* (MIRACLE)
1Ch 16: 12 done, his **m**, and the judgments he
Ne 9: 17 to remember the **m** you performed
Job 5: 9 **m** that cannot be counted.
9: 10 **m** that cannot be counted.
Ps 77: 11 will remember your **m** of long ago.
77: 14 You are the God who performs **m**;
78: 12 He did **m** in the sight of their
105: 5 done, his **m**, and the judgments he
106: 7 they gave no thought to your **m**;
106: 22 **m** in the land of Ham and
Mt 7: 22 in your name perform many **m**?'
11: 20 most of his **m** had been performed,
11: 21 the **m** that were performed in you
11: 23 the **m** that were performed in you
13: 58 did not do many **m** there because
Mk 6: 2 What are these remarkable **m** he is
6: 5 He could not do any **m** there,
Lk 10: 13 the **m** that were performed in you
19: 37 voices for all the **m** they had seen:
Ac 2: 22 accredited by God to you by **m**,
8: 13 by the great signs and **m** he saw.
19: 11 did extraordinary **m** through Paul,
1Co 12: 28 then **m**, then gifts of healing,
12: 29 Are all teachers? Do all work **m**?
2Co 12: 12 including signs, wonders and **m**.
Gal 3: 5 work **m** among you by the works
Heb 2: 4 wonders and various **m**, and by

MIRACULOUS (MIRACLE)
Mt 13: 54 this wisdom and these **m** powers?"
1Co 12: 10 to another **m** powers, to another

MIRE
Ps 40: 2 slimy pit, out of the mud and **m**;
Isa 57: 20 whose waves cast up **m** and mud.

MIRIAM
Sister of Moses and Aaron (Nu 26:59). Led dancing at "Red Sea" (Ex 15:20–21). Struck with leprosy for criticizing Moses (Nu 12). Death (Nu 20:1).

MIRROR*
Job 37: 18 skies, hard as a **m** of cast bronze?
1Co 13: 12 we see only a reflection as in a **m**;
Jas 1: 23 who looks at his face in a **m**

MISDEEDS*
Ps 99: 8 though you punished their **m**.
Ro 8: 13 you put to death the **m** of the body,

MISERY
Ex 3: 7 "I have indeed seen the **m** of my
Jdg 10: 16 he could bear Israel's **m** no longer.
Hos 5: 15 in their **m** they will earnestly seek
Ro 3: 16 ruin and **m** mark their ways,
Jas 5: 1 because of the **m** that is coming

MISFORTUNE
Ob : 12 your brother in the day of his **m**,

MISLEAD (MISLED)
Pr 24: 28 would you use your lips to **m**?
Isa 47: 10 knowledge **m** you when you say

MISLED (MISLEAD)
1Co 15: 33 Do not be **m**:

MISS
Pr 19: 2 more will hasty feet **m** the way!

MIST
Hos 6: 4 Your love is like the morning **m**,
Jas 4: 14 You are a **m** that appears for a little

MISTREAT (MISTREATED)
Ex 22: 21 "Do not **m** or oppress a foreigner,
Eze 22: 29 and needy and **m** the foreigner,
Lk 6: 28 you, pray for those who **m** you.

MISTREATED (MISTREAT)
Eze 22: 7 the foreigner and **m** the fatherless
Heb 11: 25 He chose to be **m** along
11: 37 destitute, persecuted and **m**—
13: 3 and those who are **m** as if you

MISUSE* (MISUSES)
Ex 20: 7 "You shall not **m** the name
Dt 5: 11 "You shall not **m** the name
Ps 139: 20 your adversaries **m** your name.

MISUSES* (MISUSE)
Ex 20: 7 anyone guiltless who **m** his name.
Dt 5: 11 anyone guiltless who **m** his name.

MIXED (MIXING)
Da 2: 41 even as you saw iron **m** with clay.

MIXING (MIXED)
Isa 5: 22 wine and champions at **m** drinks,

MOAB
Ge 19: 37 had a son, and she named him **M**;
Dt 34: 6 He buried him in **M**, in the valley
Ru 1: 1 for a while in the country of **M**.
1: 22 returned from **M** accompanied
Isa 15: 1 A prophecy against **M**: Ar in **M**
Jer 48: 16 "The fall of **M** is at hand;
Am 2: 1 "For three sins of **M**, even for four,

MOAN
Ps 90: 9 we finish our years with a **m**.

MOCK (MOCKED MOCKER MOCKERS MOCKING MOCKS)
Ps 22: 7 All who see me **m** me;
119: 51 The arrogant **m** me unmercifully,
Pr 1: 26 I will **m** when calamity overtakes
14: 9 Fools **m** at making amends for sin,
Mk 10: 34 who will **m** him and spit on him,

MOCKED (MOCK)
Ps 89: 51 have **m**, with which they have **m**
Mt 27: 29 knelt in front of him and **m** him.
27: 41 of the law and the elders **m** him.
Gal 6: 7 not be deceived: God cannot be **m**.

MOCKER (MOCK)
Pr 9: 7 corrects a **m** invites insults;
9: 12 you are a **m**, you alone will suffer.
20: 1 Wine is a **m** and beer a brawler;
22: 10 Drive out the **m**, and out goes

MOCKERS (MOCK)
Ps 1: 1 take or sit in the company of **m**,
Pr 29: 8 **M** stir up a city, but the wise turn

MOCKING (MOCK)
Isa 50: 6 I did not hide my face from **m**

MOCKS (MOCK)
Pr 17: 5 Whoever **m** the poor shows
30: 17 "The eye that **m** a father,

MODEL*
Php 3: 17 and just as you have us as a **m**,
1Th 1: 7 And so you became a **m** to all
2Th 3: 9 to offer ourselves as a **m** for you

MODESTY*
1Co 12: 23 are treated with special **m**,

MOLDED*
Job 10: 9 Remember that you **m** me like clay.

MOLDY
Jos 9: 5 their food supply was dry and **m**.

MOLEK
Lev 20: 2 any of his children to **M** is to be
1Ki 11: 33 and **M** the god of the Ammonites,

MOMENT (MOMENTARY)
Job 20: 5 the joy of the godless lasts but a **m**.
Ps 2: 12 for his wrath can flare up in a **m**.
30: 5 For his anger lasts only a **m**, but his
Pr 12: 19 but a lying tongue lasts only a **m**.
Isa 54: 7 "For a brief **m** I abandoned you,
66: 8 a nation be brought forth in a **m**?
Gal 2: 5 We did not give in to them for a **m**,

MOMENTARY* (MOMENT)
2Co 4: 17 **m** troubles are achieving for us

MONEY
Pr 13: 11 Dishonest **m** dwindles away,
Ecc 5: 10 loves **m** never has enough;
Isa 55: 1 and you who have no **m**, come,
Mt 6: 24 You cannot serve both God and **m**.
27: 5 So Judas threw the **m**
Lk 3: 14 "Don't extort **m** and don't accuse
9: 3 bag, no bread, no **m**, no extra shirt.
16: 13 cannot serve both God and **m**."
Ac 5: 2 kept back part of the **m** for himself,
1Co 16: 2 you should set aside a sum of **m**
1Ti 3: 3 not quarrelsome, not a lover of **m**.
6: 10 the love of **m** is a root of all kinds
2Ti 3: 2 themselves, lovers of **m**, boastful,
Heb 13: 5 your lives free from the love of **m**

MONEYLENDER* (LEND)
Lk 7: 41 people owed money to a certain **m**.

MONTH (MONTHS)
Ex 12: 2 "This **m** is to be for you the first **m**,
Eze 47: 12 Every **m** they will bear fruit,
Rev 22: 2 of fruit, yielding its fruit every **m**.

MONTHS (MONTH)
Gal 4: 10 are observing special days and **m**
Rev 11: 2 trample on the holy city for 42 **m**.
13: 5 its authority for forty-two **m**.

MOON
Jos 10: 13 and the **m** stopped, till the nation
Ps 8: 3 your fingers, the **m** and the stars,
74: 16 you established the sun and **m**.
89: 37 be established forever like the **m**,
104: 19 made the **m** to mark the seasons,
121: 6 you by day, nor the **m** by night.
136: 9 **m** and stars to govern the night;
148: 3 Praise him, sun and **m**;
SS 6: 10 fair as the **m**, bright as the sun,
Joel 2: 31 the **m** to blood before the coming
Hab 3: 11 **m** stood still in the heavens
Mt 24: 29 and the **m** will not give its light;
Ac 2: 20 the **m** to blood before the coming
1Co 15: 41 **m** another and the stars another;
Col 2: 16 a New **M** celebration or a Sabbath
Rev 6: 12 the whole **m** turned blood red,
21: 23 the sun or the **m** to shine on it,

MORAL*
Jas 1: 21 get rid of all **m** filth and the evil

MORDECAI
Benjamite exile who raised Esther (Est 2:5–15). Exposed plot to kill Xerxes (Est 2:19–23). Refused to honor Haman (Est 3:1–6; 5:9–14). Charged Esther to foil Haman's plot against the Jews (Est 4). Xerxes forced Haman to honor Mordecai (Est 6). Mordecai exalted (Est 8–10). Established Purim (Est 9:18–32).

MORIAH*
Ge 22: 2 Isaac—and go to the region of **M**.
2Ch 3: 1 Lord in Jerusalem on Mount **M**,

MORNING
Ge 1: 5 was evening, and there was **m**—
Dt 28: 67 In the **m** you will say, "If only
2Sa 23: 4 he is like the light of **m** at sunrise
Ps 5: 3 In the **m**, Lord, you hear my
Pr 4: 18 of the righteous is like the **m** sun,
27: 14 their neighbor early in the **m**,
Isa 14: 12 have fallen from heaven, **m** star,
La 3: 23 They are new every **m**; great is
2Pe 1: 19 and the **m** star rises in your hearts.
Rev 2: 28 I will also give that one the **m** star.
22: 16 of David, and the bright **M** Star."

MORTAL (MORTALS)
Ge 6: 3 humans forever, for they are **m**;
Job 10: 4 Do you see as a **m** sees?
Ps 9: 20 the nations know they are only **m**.
Ro 8: 11 give life to your **m** bodies because
1Co 15: 53 and the **m** with immortality.
2Co 5: 4 that what is **m** may be swallowed

MORTALS (MORTAL)
Job 14: 1 "**M**, born of woman, are of few
Ps 103: 15 The life of **m** is like grass,

MOSES
Levite; brother of Aaron (Ex 6:20; 1Ch 6:3). Put in basket into Nile; discovered and raised by Pharaoh's daughter (Ex 2:1–10). Fled to Midian after killing Egyptian (Ex 2:11–15). Married to Zipporah, fathered Gershom (Ex 2:16–22).

Called by the Lord to deliver Israel (Ex 3–4). Pharaoh's resistance (Ex 5). Ten plagues (Ex 7–11). Passover and Exodus (Ex 12–13). Led Israel through "Red Sea" (Ex 14). Song of deliverance (Ex 15:1–21). Brought water from rock (Ex 17:1–7). Raised hands to defeat Amalekites (Ex 17:8–16). Delegated judges (Ex 18; Dt 1:9–18).

Received Law at Sinai (Ex 19–23; 25–31; Jn 1:17). Announced Law to Israel (Ex 19:7–8; 24; 35). Broke tablets because of golden calf (Ex 32; Dt 9). Saw glory of the Lord (Ex 33–34). Supervised building of tabernacle (Ex 36–40). Set apart Aaron and priests (Lev 8–9). Numbered tribes (Nu 1–4; 26). Opposed by Aaron and Miriam (Nu 12). Sent spies into Canaan

(Nu 13). Announced forty years of wandering for failure to enter land (Nu 14). Opposed by Korah (Nu 16). Forbidden to enter land for striking rock (Nu 20:1–13; Dt 1:37). Lifted bronze snake for healing (Nu 21:4–9; Jn 3:14). Final address to Israel (Dt 1–33). Succeeded by Joshua (Nu 27:12–23; Dt 34). Death (Dt 34:5–12).

"Law of Moses" (1Ki 2:3; Ezr 3:2; Mk 12:26; Lk 24:44). "Book of Moses" (2Ch 25:12; Ne 13:1). "Song of Moses" (Ex 15:1–21; Rev 15:3). "Prayer of Moses" (Ps 90).

MOTHER (GRANDMOTHER MOTHER-IN-LAW MOTHER'S)
Ge 2: 24 why a man leaves his father and **m**
3: 20 because she would become the **m**
Ex 20: 12 "Honor your father and your **m**,
Lev 20: 9 they have cursed their father or **m**,
Dt 5: 16 "Honor your father and your **m**,
21: 18 does not obey his father and **m**
27: 16 who dishonors their father or **m**."
Jdg 5: 7 arose, until I arose, a **m** in Israel.
1Sa 2: 19 Each year his **m** made him a little
Ps 113: 9 her home as a happy **m** of children.
Pr 10: 1 a foolish son brings grief to his **m**.
23: 22 do not despise your **m** when she is
23: 25 May your father and **m** rejoice;
29: 15 left undisciplined disgraces its **m**.
30: 17 that scorns an aged **m**, will be
31: 1 utterance his **m** taught him.
Isa 49: 15 "Can a **m** forget the baby at her
66: 13 As a **m** comforts her child, so will I
Jer 20: 17 with my **m** as my grave, her womb
Mic 7: 6 a daughter rises up against her **m**,
Mt 10: 35 father, a daughter against her **m**,
10: 37 or **m** more than me is not worthy
12: 48 "Who is my **m**, and who are my
15: 4 said, 'Honor your father and **m**'
19: 5 a man will leave his father and **m**
19: 19 honor your father and **m**,' and 'love
Mk 7: 10 'Honor your father and **m**,' and,
10: 19 honor your father and **m**.'"
Lk 11: 27 "Blessed is the **m** who gave you
12: 53 **m** against daughter and daughter
18: 20 honor your father and **m**.'"
Jn 19: 27 to the disciple, "Here is your **m**."
Gal 4: 26 is above is free, and she is our **m**.
Eph 5: 31 a man will leave his father and **m**
6: 2 "Honor your father and **m**"—
1Th 2: 7 Just as a nursing **m** cares for her
2Ti 1: 5 Lois and in your **m** Eunice and,

MOTHER-IN-LAW (MOTHER)
Ru 2: 19 Ruth told her **m** about the one
Mt 10: 35 a daughter-in-law against her **m**—

MOTHER'S (MOTHER)
Job 1: 21 "Naked I came from my **m** womb,
Pr 1: 8 do not forsake your **m** teaching.
Ecc 5: 15 comes naked from their **m** womb,
11: 5 the body is formed in a **m** womb,
Jn 3: 4 a second time into their **m** womb

MOTHS
Mt 6: 19 where **m** and vermin destroy,

MOTIVES*
Pr 16: 2 but **m** are weighed by the LORD.
1Co 4: 5 and will expose the **m** of the heart.
Php 1: 18 way, whether from false **m** or true,
1Th 2: 3 not spring from error or impure **m**,
Jas 4: 3 because you ask with wrong **m**,

MOUNT (MOUNTAIN MOUNTAINS MOUNTAINTOPS)
Ps 89: 9 its waves **m** up, you still them.
Isa 14: 13 the utmost heights of **M** Zaphon.
Eze 28: 14 You were on the holy **m** of God;
Zec 14: 4 **M** of Olives will be split in two

MOUNTAIN (MOUNT)
Ge 22: 14 "On the **m** of the LORD it will be
Ex 24: 18 he stayed on the **m** forty days
Dt 5: 4 to face out of the fire on the **m**.
Job 14: 18 "But as a **m** erodes and crumbles
Ps 24: 3 Who may ascend the **m**
48: 1 in the city of our God, his holy **m**.
Isa 40: 4 up, every **m** and hill made low;
Mic 4: 2 let us go up to the **m** of the LORD,
Mt 4: 8 devil took him to a very high **m**
17: 20 you can say to this **m**,
Mk 9: 2 him and led them up a high **m**,
Lk 3: 5 every **m** and hill made low.
Jn 4: 21 the Father neither on this **m** nor
2Pe 1: 18 we were with him on the sacred **m**.

MOUNTAINS (MOUNT)
Ps 36: 6 righteousness is like the highest **m**,
46: 2 the **m** fall into the heart of the sea,
90: 2 Before the **m** were born or you
121: 1 I lift up my eyes to the **m**—
Isa 52: 7 beautiful on the **m** are the feet
54: 10 Though the **m** be shaken
55: 12 the **m** and hills will burst into song
Eze 34: 6 My sheep wandered over all the **m**
Mt 24: 16 who are in Judea flee to the **m**.
Lk 23: 30 Then "'they will say to the **m**,
1Co 13: 2 if I have a faith that can move **m**,
Rev 6: 16 They called to the **m** and the rocks,

MOUNTAINTOPS (MOUNT)
Isa 42: 11 let them shout from the **m**.

MOURN (MOURNING MOURNS)
Ecc 3: 4 a time to **m** and a time to dance,
Isa 61: 2 of our God, to comfort all who **m**,
Mt 5: 4 Blessed are those who **m**, for they
Ro 12: 15 **m** with those who **m**.

MOURNING (MOURN)
Isa 61: 3 the oil of joy instead of **m**,
Jer 31: 13 I will turn their **m** into gladness;
Rev 21: 4 There will be no more death' or **m**

MOURNS (MOURN)
Zec 12: 10 for him as one **m** for an only child,

MOUTH (MOUTHS)
Nu 22: 38 only what God puts in my **m**."
Dt 8: 3 comes from the **m** of the LORD.
18: 18 and I will put my words in his **m**.
30: 14 it is in your **m** and in your heart so
2Ki 4: 34 the bed and lay on the boy, **m** to **m**,
Ps 10: 7 His **m** is full of lies and threats;
17: 3 my **m** has not transgressed.
19: 14 May these words of my **m** and this
40: 3 put a new song in my **m**, a hymn
71: 8 My **m** is filled with your praise,
119:103 taste, sweeter than honey to my **m**!
141: 3 Set a guard over my **m**, LORD;
Pr 2: 6 from his **m** come knowledge
4: 24 Keep your **m** free of perversity;
10: 11 but the **m** of the wicked conceals
10: 31 the **m** of the righteous comes
26: 28 and a flattering **m** works ruin.
27: 2 praise you, and not your own **m**;
Ecc 5: 2 Do not be quick with your **m**, do
SS 1: 2 kiss me with the kisses of his **m**—
5: 16 His **m** is sweetness itself;
Isa 29: 13 come near to me with their **m**
40: 5 the **m** of the LORD has spoken."
45: 23 my **m** has uttered in all integrity
51: 16 I have put my words in your **m**
53: 7 silent, so he did not open his **m**.
55: 11 my word that goes out from my **m**:
59: 21 I have put in your **m** will always be
Eze 3: 2 So I opened my **m**, and he gave me
Mal 2: 7 seek instruction from his **m**.
Mt 4: 4 that comes from the **m** of God.'"
12: 34 the **m** speaks what the heart is full
15: 11 someone's **m** does not defile them,
15: 18 a person's **m** come from the heart,
Lk 6: 45 the **m** speaks what the heart is full
Ro 10: 9 If you declare with your **m**,
1Pe 2: 22 and no deceit was found in his **m**."
Rev 1: 16 coming out of his **m** was a sharp,
2: 16 them with the sword of my **m**.
3: 16 I am about to spit you out of my **m**.
19: 15 out of his **m** is a sharp sword

MOUTHS (MOUTH)
Ps 37: 30 The **m** of the righteous utter
78: 36 would flatter him with their **m**,
Pr 16: 23 of the wise make their **m** prudent,
Eze 33: 31 Their **m** speak of love, but their
Ro 3: 14 "Their **m** are full of cursing
Eph 4: 29 talk come out of your **m**, but only
Jas 3: 3 we put bits into the **m** of horses

MOVE (MOVED MOVES)
Dt 19: 14 not **m** your neighbor's boundary
Pr 23: 10 not **m** an ancient boundary stone
Ac 17: 28 'For in him we live and **m** and have
1Co 13: 2 have a faith that can **m** mountains,
15: 58 Let nothing **m** you.
Col 1: 23 do not **m** from the hope held

MOVED (MOVE)
Ex 35: 21 and whose heart **m** them came
1Ki 3: 26 whose son was alive was deeply **m**
2Ch 36: 22 the LORD **m** the heart of Cyrus
Ezr 1: 5 everyone whose heart God had **m**
Jn 11: 33 he was deeply **m** in spirit

MOVES (MOVE)
Dt 23: 14 For the LORD your God **m**

MUD (MUDDIED)
Ps 40: 2 slimy pit, out of the **m** and mire;
Isa 57: 20 whose waves cast up mire and **m**.
Jn 9: 6 made some **m** with the saliva,
2Pe 2: 22 returns to her wallowing in the **m**."

MUDDIED (MUD)
Pr 25: 26 Like a **m** spring or a polluted well
Eze 32: 13 man or **m** by the hooves of cattle.

MULBERRY*
Lk 17: 6 seed, you can say to this **m** tree,

MULTITUDE (MULTITUDES)
Isa 31: 1 who trust in the **m** of their chariots
Jas 5: 20 death and cover over a **m** of sins.
1Pe 4: 8 because love covers over a **m**
Rev 7: 9 there before me was a great **m**
19: 1 of a great **m** in heaven shouting:

MULTITUDES (MULTITUDE)
Ne 9: 6 and the **m** of heaven worship you.
Da 12: 2 **M** who sleep in the dust of the
Joel 3: 14 **M**, **m** in the valley of decision!

MURDER (MURDERED MURDERER MURDERERS)
Ex 20: 13 "You shall not **m**.
Dt 5: 17 "You shall not **m**.
Pr 28: 17 the guilt of **m** will seek refuge
Mt 5: 21 'You shall not **m**, and anyone who
15: 19 **m**, adultery, sexual immorality,
Ro 1: 29 They are full of envy, **m**, strife,
13: 9 "You shall not **m**,"
Jas 2: 11 also said, "You shall not **m**."

MURDERED (MURDER)
Mt 23: 31 of those who **m** the prophets.
Ac 7: 52 you have betrayed and **m** him—
1Jn 3: 12 to the evil one and **m** his brother.

MURDERER (MURDER)
Nu 35: 16 the **m** is to be put to death.
Jn 8: 44 He was a **m** from the beginning,
1Jn 3: 15 hates a brother or sister is a **m**,
3: 15 no **m** has eternal life residing

MURDERERS (MURDER)
1Ti 1: 9 kill their fathers or mothers, for **m**,
Rev 21: 8 vile, the **m**, the sexually immoral,
22: 15 the **m**, the idolaters and everyone

MUSIC (MUSICAL MUSICIAN MUSICIANS)
Ge 31: 27 and singing to the **m** of timbrels
1Ch 6: 31 charge of the **m** in the house
6: 32 with **m** before the tabernacle,
25: 6 their father for the **m** of the temple
25: 7 and skilled in **m** for the LORD—
Ne 12: 27 and with the **m** of cymbals,
Job 21: 12 They sing to the **m** of timbrel
Ps 27: 6 sing and make **m** to the LORD.
33: 2 make **m** to him on the ten-stringed
45: 8 ivory the **m** of the strings makes
57: 7 I will sing and make **m**.
81: 2 Begin the **m**, strike the timbrel,
87: 7 As they make **m** they will sing,
92: 1 LORD and make **m** to your name,
92: 3 to the **m** of the ten-stringed lyre
95: 2 and extol him with **m** and song.
98: 4 burst into jubilant song with **m**;
98: 5 make **m** to the LORD
108: 1 sing and make **m** with all my soul.
144: 9 the ten-stringed lyre I will make **m**
147: 7 make **m** to our God on the harp.
149: 3 and make **m** to him with timbrel
Isa 30: 32 club will be to the **m** of timbrels

La 5: 14 young men have stopped their **m**.
Eze 26: 13 the **m** of your harps will be heard
Da 3: 5 pipe and all kinds of **m**, you must
3: 7 lyre, harp and all kinds of **m**,
3: 10 all kinds of **m** must fall down
3: 15 pipe and all kinds of **m**, if you are
Am 5: 23 not listen to the **m** of your harps.
Hab 3: 19 For the director of **m**.
Lk 15: 25 house, he heard **m** and dancing.
Eph 5: 19 **m** from your heart to the Lord,
Rev 18: 22 The **m** of harpists and musicians,

MUSICAL* (MUSIC)
1Ch 15: 16 a joyful sound with **m** instruments:
23: 5 the **m** instruments I have provided
2Ch 7: 6 with the LORD's **m** instruments,
34: 12 skilled in playing **m** instruments—
Ne 12: 36 with **m** instruments prescribed
Am 6: 5 and improvise on **m** instruments.

MUSICIAN* (MUSIC)
1Ch 6: 33 Heman, the **m**, the son of Joel,

MUSICIANS (MUSIC)
1Ki 10: 12 to make harps and lyres for the **m**.
1Ch 9: 33 Those who were **m**, heads of Levite
15: 19 The **m** Heman, Asaph and Ethan
2Ch 5: 12 All the Levites who were **m**—
9: 11 to make harps and lyres for the **m**.
35: 15 The **m**, the descendants of Asaph,
Ps 68: 25 are the singers, after them the **m**;
Rev 18: 22 The music of harpists and **m**,

MUSTARD
Mt 13: 31 of heaven is like a **m** seed,
17: 20 you have faith as small as a **m** seed,
Mk 4: 31 It is like a **m** seed, which is

MUSTER
Pr 24: 5 have knowledge **m** their strength.

MUTILATORS*
Php 3: 2 evildoers, those **m** of the flesh.

MUTUAL* (MUTUALLY)
Ro 14: 19 leads to peace and to **m** edification
1Co 7: 5 other except perhaps by **m** consent
2Pe 1: 7 and to godliness, **m** affection; and to **m** affection, love.

MUTUALLY* (MUTUAL)
Ro 1: 12 I may be **m** encouraged by each

MUZZLE*
Dt 25: 4 Do not **m** an ox while it is treading
Ps 39: 1 I will put a **m** on my mouth while
1Co 9: 9 Do not **m** an ox while it is treading
1Ti 5: 18 Do not **m** an ox while it is treading

MYRRH
Ps 45: 8 All your robes are fragrant with **m**
SS 1: 13 of **m** resting between my breasts.
Mt 2: 11 gifts of gold, frankincense and **m**.
Mk 15: 23 offered him wine mixed with **m**,
Jn 19: 39 brought a mixture of **m** and aloes,
Rev 18: 13 of incense, **m** and frankincense,

MYSTERIES* (MYSTERY)
Job 11: 7 "Can you fathom the **m** of God?
Da 2: 28 is a God in heaven who reveals **m**.
2: 29 of **m** showed you what is going
2: 47 Lord of kings and a revealer of **m**,
1Co 4: 1 with the **m** God has revealed.
13: 2 fathom all **m** and all knowledge,
14: 2 they utter **m** by the Spirit.

MYSTERY* (MYSTERIES)
Da 2: 18 God of heaven concerning this **m**,
2: 19 During the night the **m** was
2: 27 the king the **m** he has asked about,
2: 30 this **m** has been revealed to me,
2: 47 for you were able to reveal this **m**."
4: 9 and no **m** is too difficult for you.
Ro 11: 25 want you to be ignorant of this **m**,
16: 25 the revelation of the **m** hidden
1Co 2: 7 a **m** that has been hidden
15: 51 Listen, I tell you a **m**: We will not
Eph 1: 9 to us the **m** of his will according
3: 3 that is, the **m** made known to me
3: 4 my insight into the **m** of Christ,
3: 6 This **m** is that through the gospel
3: 9 the administration of this **m**,
5: 32 This is a profound **m**—but I am
6: 19 I will fearlessly make known the **m**
Col 1: 26 the **m** that has been kept hidden
1: 27 the glorious riches of this **m**,
2: 2 that they may know the **m** of God,
4: 3 we may proclaim the **m** of Christ,
1Ti 3: 16 the **m** from which true godliness
Rev 1: 20 The **m** of the seven stars that you
10: 7 the **m** of God will be accomplished,
17: 5 written on her forehead was a **m**:
17: 7 explain to you the **m** of the woman

MYTHS*
1Ti 1: 4 or to devote themselves to **m**
4: 7 Have nothing to do with godless **m**
2Ti 4: 4 from the truth and turn aside to **m**.
Titus 1: 14 will pay no attention to Jewish **m**

NAAMAN
Aramean general whose leprosy was cleansed by Elisha (2Ki 5).

NABAL
Wealthy Carmelite the LORD killed for refusing to help David (1Sa 25). David married Abigail, his widow (1Sa 25:39–42).

NABOTH*
Jezreelite killed by Jezebel for his vineyard (1Ki 21). Ahab's family destroyed for this (1Ki 21:17–24; 2Ki 9:21–37).

NADAB
1. Firstborn of Aaron (Ex 6:23); killed with Abihu for offering unauthorized fire (Lev 10; Nu 3:4).
2. Son of Jeroboam I; king of Israel (1Ki 15:25–32).

NAGGING
Pr 21: 19 with a quarrelsome and **n** wife.

NAHUM
Prophet against Nineveh (Na 1:1).

NAIL* (NAILING)
Jn 20: 25 "Unless I see the **n** marks in his

NAILING* (NAIL)
Ac 2: 23 him to death by **n** him to the cross.
Col 2: 14 has taken it away, **n** it to the cross.

NAIVE*
Ro 16: 18 they deceive the minds of **n** people.

NAKED
Ge 2: 25 Adam and his wife were both **n**,
Job 1: 21 "**N** I came from my mother's womb, and **n** I will depart.
Isa 58: 7 you see the **n**, to clothe them,
2Co 5: 3 are clothed, we will not be found **n**.

NAME (NAMED NAMES)
Ge 2: 19 man to see what he would **n** them;
4: 26 to call on the **n** of the LORD.
11: 4 we may make a **n** for ourselves;
12: 2 I will make your **n** great, and you
32: 29 Jacob said, "Please tell me your **n**."
Ex 3: 15 "This is my **n** forever, the **n** you
20: 7 "You shall not misuse the **n**
34: 14 for the LORD, whose **n** is Jealous,
Lev 24: 11 Israelite woman blasphemed the **N**
Dt 5: 11 "You shall not misuse the **n**
12: 11 choose as a dwelling for his **N**—
18: 5 minister in the LORD's **n** always.
25: 6 carry on the **n** of the dead brother
28: 58 this glorious and awesome **n**—
Jos 7: 9 and wipe out our **n** from the earth.
Jdg 13: 17 "What is your **n**, so that we may
1Sa 12: 22 of his great **n** the LORD will not
2Sa 6: 2 which is called by the **N**, the **n**
7: 9 Now I will make your **n** great,
1Ki 5: 5 will build the temple for my **N**.'
8: 29 you said, 'My **N** shall be there,'
1Ch 17: 8 I will make your **n** like the names
2Ch 7: 14 people, who are called by my **n**,
Ne 9: 10 You made a **n** for yourself,
Ps 8: 1 how majestic is your **n** in all
9: 10 Those who know your **n** trust
20: 7 in the **n** of the LORD our God.
29: 2 to the LORD the glory due his **n**;
34: 3 let us exalt his **n** together.
44: 20 we had forgotten the **n** of our God
66: 2 Sing the glory of his **n**;
68: 4 his **n** is the LORD.
79: 9 our Savior, for the glory of your **n**;
96: 8 to the LORD the glory due his **n**;
Ps 103: 1 my inmost being, praise his holy **n**.
115: 1 not to us but to your **n** be the glory,
138: 2 praise your **n** for your unfailing
145: 1 I will praise your **n** for ever
147: 4 the stars and calls them each by **n**.
Pr 3: 4 and a good **n** in the sight of God
10: 7 The **n** of the righteous is used
10: 7 but the **n** of the wicked will rot.
18: 10 The **n** of the LORD is a fortified
22: 1 A good **n** is more desirable than
30: 4 What is his **n**, and what is the **n**
Ecc 7: 1 A good **n** is better than fine
SS 1: 3 your **n** is like perfume poured out.
Isa 12: 4 and proclaim that his **n** is exalted.
26: 8 your **n** and renown are the desire
40: 26 and calls forth each of them by **n**.
42: 8 "I am the LORD; that is my **n**!
56: 5 I will give them an everlasting **n**
57: 15 who lives forever, whose **n** is holy:
63: 14 to make for yourself a glorious **n**.
Jer 14: 7 LORD, for the sake of your **n**.
15: 16 for I bear your **n**, LORD God
Eze 20: 9 But for the sake of my **n**, I brought
20: 14 of my **n** I did what would keep it
20: 22 of my **n** I did what would keep it
Da 12: 1 everyone whose **n** is found written
Hos 12: 5 God Almighty, the LORD is his **n**!
Joel 2: 32 the **n** of the LORD will be saved;
Mic 5: 4 of the **n** of the LORD his God.
Zep 3: 9 may call on the **n** of the LORD
Zec 6: 12 is the man whose **n** is the Branch,
14: 9 one LORD, and his **n** the only **n**.
Mal 1: 6 who show contempt for my **n**.
Mt 1: 21 you are to give him the **n** Jesus,
6: 9 in heaven, hallowed be your **n**,
18: 20 where two or three gather in my **n**,
24: 5 For many will come in my **n**,
28: 19 baptizing them in the **n** of the
Mk 9: 41 water in my **n** because you belong
Lk 11: 2 hallowed be your **n**, your kingdom
Jn 10: 3 He calls his own sheep by **n**
14: 13 I will do whatever you ask in my **n**,
16: 24 not asked for anything in my **n**.
Ac 2: 21 on the **n** of the Lord will be saved.'
4: 12 is no other **n** under heaven given
Ro 10: 13 on the **n** of the Lord will be saved."
Php 2: 9 gave him the **n** that is above every **n**,
2: 10 at the **n** of Jesus every knee should
Col 3: 17 do it all in the **n** of the Lord Jesus,
Heb 1: 4 the angels as the **n** he has inherited
Jas 5: 14 them with oil in the **n** of the Lord.
1Jn 5: 13 you who believe in the **n** of the Son
Rev 2: 17 stone with a new **n** written on it,
3: 5 I will never blot out the **n** of that
3: 12 write on them the **n** of my God
3: 12 and the **n** of the city of my God,
3: 12 I will also write on them my new **n**.
19: 13 and his **n** is the Word of God.
20: 15 Anyone whose **n** was not found

NAMED (NAME)
Ge 5: 2 And he **n** them "Mankind" when

NAMES (NAME)
Ex 28: 9 engrave on them the **n** of the sons
Lk 10: 20 but rejoice that your **n** are written
Php 4: 3 whose **n** are in the book of life.
Heb 12: 23 whose **n** are written in heaven.
Rev 21: 27 only those whose **n** are written

NAOMI
Wife of Elimelek, mother-in-law of Ruth (Ru 1:2, 4). Left Bethlehem for Moab during famine (Ru 1:1). Returned a widow, with Ruth (Ru 1:6–22). Advised Ruth to seek marriage with Boaz (Ru 2:17—3:4). Cared for Ruth's son Obed (Ru 4:13–17).

NAPHTALI
Son of Jacob by Bilhah (Ge 30:8; 35:25; 1Ch 2:2). Tribe of blessed (Ge 49:21; Dt 33:23), numbered (Nu 1:43; 26:50), allotted land (Jos 19:32–39; Eze 48:3), failed to fully possess (Jdg 1:33), supported Deborah (Jdg 4:10; 5:18), David (1Ch 12:34), 12,000 from (Rev 7:6).

NARROW
Mt 7: 13 "Enter through the **n** gate.
7: 14 and **n** the road that leads to life,

NATHAN
Prophet and chronicler of Israel's history (1Ch 29:29; 2Ch 9:29). Announced the Davidic covenant (2Sa 7; 1Ch 17). Denounced David's sin with Bathsheba (2Sa 12). Supported Solomon (1Ki 1).

NATHANAEL*
Apostle (Jn 1:45–49; 21:2). Probably also called Bartholomew (Mt 10:3).

NATION (NATIONS)
Ge 12: 2 "I will make you into a great **n**,
Ex 19: 6 a kingdom of priests and a holy **n**.'
Dt 4: 7 What other **n** is so great as to have
Jos 5: 8 the whole **n** had been circumcised,
2Sa 7: 23 the one **n** on earth that God went
Ps 33: 12 Blessed is the **n** whose God is
Pr 11: 14 For lack of guidance a **n** falls,
14: 34 Righteousness exalts a **n**, but sin
Isa 2: 4 **N** will not take up sword against **n**,
26: 2 that the righteous **n** may enter,
60: 12 For the **n** or kingdom that will not
65: 1 a **n** that did not call on my name,
66: 8 a **n** be brought forth in a moment?
Mic 4: 3 **N** will not take up sword against **n**,
Mt 24: 7 **N** will rise against **n**, and kingdom
Mk 13: 8 **N** will rise against **n**, and kingdom
1Pe 2: 9 a holy **n**, God's special possession,
Rev 5: 9 and language and people and **n**.
7: 9 could count, from every **n**, tribe,
14: 6 to every **n**, tribe,

NATIONS (NATION)
Ge 17: 4 You will be the father of many **n**.
18: 18 and all **n** on earth will be blessed
Ex 19: 5 of all **n** you will be my treasured
Lev 20: 26 apart from the **n** to be my own.
Dt 7: 1 seven **n** larger and stronger than
15: 6 You will rule over many **n** but none
Jdg 3: 1 These are the **n** the LORD left
2Ch 20: 6 rule over all the kingdoms of the **n**.
Ne 1: 8 I will scatter you among the **n**,
Ps 2: 1 Why do the **n** conspire
2: 8 I will make the **n** your inheritance,
9: 5 You have rebuked the **n**
22: 28 the LORD and he rules over the **n**.
46: 10 I will be exalted among the **n**, I will
47: 8 God reigns over the **n**; God is
66: 7 his power, his eyes watch the **n**—
67: 2 earth, your salvation among all **n**.
68: 30 Scatter the **n** who delight in war.
72: 17 all **n** will be blessed through him,
96: 3 Declare his glory among the **n**,
99: 2 he is exalted over all the **n**.
106: 35 mingled with the **n** and adopted
110: 6 He will judge the **n**,
113: 4 LORD is exalted over all the **n**,
Isa 2: 2 the hills, and all **n** will stream to it.
11: 10 the **n** will rally to him, and his
12: 4 known among the **n** what he has
40: 15 Surely the **n** are like a drop
42: 1 and he will bring justice to the **n**.
49: 22 I will beckon to the **n**, I will lift
51: 4 justice will become a light to the **n**.
52: 15 so he will sprinkle many **n**,
56: 7 called a house of prayer for all **n**."
60: 3 **N** will come to your light,
66: 18 and gather the people of all **n**
Jer 1: 5 you as a prophet to the **n**."
3: 17 and all **n** will gather in Jerusalem
31: 10 the word of the LORD, you **n**;
33: 9 honor before all **n** on earth that
46: 28 completely destroy all the **n** among
Eze 22: 4 you an object of scorn to the **n**
34: 13 I will bring them out from the **n**
36: 23 Then the **n** will know that I am
37: 22 they will never again be two **n** or
39: 21 will display my glory among the **n**,
Hos 7: 8 "Ephraim mixes with the **n**;
Joel 2: 17 of scorn, a byword among the **n**.
3: 2 scattered my people among the **n**
Am 9: 12 and all the **n** that bear my name,"
Zep 3: 8 I have decided to assemble the **n**,
Hag 2: 7 what is desired by all **n** will come,
Zec 8: 13 have been a curse among the **n**,
8: 23 **n** will take firm hold of one Jew
9: 10 He will proclaim peace to the **n**.
14: 2 I will gather all the **n** to Jerusalem
Mt 12: 18 he will proclaim justice to the **n**.
24: 9 you will be hated by all **n** because
24: 14 whole world as a testimony to all **n**,
25: 32 All the **n** will be gathered before
28: 19 go and make disciples of all **n**,
Mk 11: 17 called a house of prayer for all **n**'?
Ac 4: 25 "'Why do the **n** rage
Ro 15: 12 who will arise to rule over the **n**;
Gal 3: 8 "All **n** will be blessed through
1Ti 3: 16 was preached among the **n**,
Rev 15: 3 true are your ways, King of the **n**.
15: 4 All **n** will come and worship before
21: 24 The **n** will walk by its light,
22: 2 the tree are for the healing of the **n**.

NATURAL (NATURE)
1Co 15: 44 it is sown a **n** body, it is raised

NATURE (NATURAL)
Ro 1: 20 his eternal power and divine **n**—
7: 18 dwell in me, that is, in my sinful **n**.
Php 2: 6 Who, being in very **n** God, did not
Col 3: 5 whatever belongs to your earthly **n**:
2Pe 1: 4 may participate in the divine **n**,

NAZARENE* (NAZARETH)
Mt 2: 23 that he would be called a **N**.
Mk 14: 67 "You also were with that **N**,
16: 6 "You are looking for Jesus the **N**,
Ac 24: 5 He is a ringleader of the **N** sect

NAZARETH (NAZARENE)
Mt 4: 13 Leaving **N**, he went and lived
Lk 4: 16 He went to **N**, where he had been
Jn 1: 46 "**N**! Can anything good come

NAZIRITE
Nu 6: 2 of dedication to the LORD as a **N**,
Jdg 13: 7 because the boy will be a **N** of God

NEBO
Dt 34: 1 Moses climbed Mount **N**

NEBUCHADNEZZAR
Babylonian king. Subdued and exiled Judah (2Ki 24–25; 2Ch 36; Jer 39). Dreams interpreted by Daniel (Da 2; 4). Worshiped God (Da 3:28–29; 4:34–37).

NECESSARY*
Ac 1: 21 Therefore it is **n** to choose one
Ro 13: 5 it is **n** to submit to the authorities,
2Co 9: 5 I thought it **n** to urge the brothers
Php 1: 24 it is more **n** for you that I remain
2: 25 I think it is **n** to send back to you
Heb 8: 3 and so it was **n** for this one
9: 16 it is **n** to prove the death of the one
9: 23 It was **n**, then, for the copies
10: 18 sacrifice for sin is no longer **n**.

NECHO
Pharaoh who killed Josiah (2Ki 23:29–30; 2Ch 35:20–22), deposed Jehoahaz (2Ki 23:33–35; 2Ch 36:3–4).

NECK (STIFF-NECKED)
Pr 3: 22 an ornament to grace your **n**.
6: 21 fasten them around your **n**.
Mt 18: 6 millstone hung around their **n**

NEED (NEEDS NEEDY)
1Ki 8: 59 Israel according to each day's **n**,
Ps 79: 8 meet us, for we are in desperate **n**.
142: 6 to my cry, for I am in desperate **n**;
Mt 6: 8 knows what you **n** before you ask
Lk 15: 14 country, and he began to be in **n**.
Ac 2: 45 to give to anyone who had **n**.
Ro 12: 13 the Lord's people who are in **n**.
1Co 12: 21 say to the hand, "I don't **n** you!"
Eph 4: 28 something to share with those in **n**.
1Ti 5: 3 those widows who are really in **n**.
Heb 4: 16 grace to help us in our time of **n**.
1Jn 3: 17 sister in **n** but has no pity on them,

NEEDLE
Mt 19: 24 to go through the eye of a **n** than

NEEDS (NEED)
Isa 58: 11 he will satisfy your **n**
Php 2: 25 you sent to take care of my **n**.
4: 19 God will meet all your **n** according
Jas 2: 16 nothing about their physical **n**,

NEEDY (NEED)
Dt 15: 11 who are poor and **n** in your land.
1Sa 2: 8 and lifts the **n** from the ash heap;
Ps 35: 10 and **n** from those who rob them."
69: 33 The LORD hears the **n** and does
72: 12 he will deliver the **n** who cry out,
140: 12 and upholds the cause of the **n**.
Pr 14: 21 is the one who is kind to the **n**.
14: 31 is kind to the **n** honors God.
22: 22 and do not crush the **n** in court,
31: 9 the rights of the poor and **n**.
31: 20 and extends her hands to the **n**.
Mt 6: 2 "So when you give to the **n**, do not

NEGLECT* (NEGLECTED)
Dt 12: 19 to **n** the Levites as long as you live
14: 27 do not **n** the Levites living in your
Ezr 4: 22 Be careful not to **n** this matter.
Ne 10: 39 "We will not **n** the house of our
Est 6: 10 Do not **n** anything you have
Ps 119: 16 I will not **n** your word.
SS 1: 6 my own vineyard I had to **n**.
Lk 11: 42 but you **n** justice and the love
Ac 6: 2 for us to **n** the ministry of the word
1Ti 4: 14 not **n** your gift, which was given

NEGLECTED (NEGLECT)
Mt 23: 23 But you have **n** the more important

NEHEMIAH
Cupbearer of Artaxerxes (Ne 2:1); governor of Israel (Ne 8:9). Returned to Jerusalem to rebuild walls (Ne 2–6). With Ezra, reestablished worship (Ne 8). Prayer confessing nation's sin (Ne 9). Dedicated wall (Ne 12).

NEIGHBOR (NEIGHBOR'S NEIGHBORS)
Ex 20: 16 give false testimony against your **n**.
20: 17 anything that belongs to your **n**."
Lev 19: 13 "'Do not defraud or rob your **n**.
19: 17 Rebuke your **n** frankly so you will
19: 18 people, but love your **n** as yourself.
Ps 15: 3 who does no wrong to a **n**,
88: 18 have taken from me friend and **n**—
Pr 3: 29 Do not plot harm against your **n**,
11: 12 derides their **n** has no sense,
14: 21 It is a sin to despise one's **n**,
16: 29 A violent person entices their **n**
24: 28 against your **n** without cause—
25: 18 gives false testimony against a **n**.
27: 10 better a **n** nearby than a relative far
27: 14 anyone loudly blesses their **n** early
Jer 31: 34 No longer will they teach their **n**,
Mt 5: 43 'Love your **n** and hate your enemy.'
19: 19 and 'love your **n** as yourself.'"
Mk 12: 31 'Love your **n** as yourself.'
Lk 10: 27 and, 'Love your **n** as yourself.'"
10: 29 asked Jesus, "And who is my **n**?"
Ro 13: 9 "Love your **n** as yourself."
13: 10 Love does no harm to a **n**.
Gal 5: 14 "Love your **n** as yourself."
Eph 4: 25 and speak truthfully to your **n**,
Heb 8: 11 No longer will they teach their **n**,
Jas 2: 8 "Love your **n** as yourself,"

NEIGHBOR'S (NEIGHBOR)
Ex 20: 17 "You shall not covet your **n** house.
Dt 5: 21 "You shall not covet your **n** wife.
19: 14 not move your **n** boundary stone
27: 17 moves their **n** boundary stone."
Pr 25: 17 Seldom set foot in your **n** house—

NEIGHBORS (NEIGHBOR)
Pr 29: 5 who flatter their **n** are spreading
Ro 15: 2 of us should please our **n** for their

NESTS
Mt 8: 20 "Foxes have dens and birds have **n**,

NET (NETS)
Pr 1: 17 spread a **n** where every bird can
Hab 1: 15 he catches them in his **n**,
Mt 13: 47 heaven is like a **n** that was let down
Jn 21: 6 unable to haul the **n** in because

NETS (NET)
Ps 141: 10 the wicked fall into their own **n**,
Mt 4: 20 At once they left their **n**
Lk 5: 4 and let down the **n** for a catch."

NEVER-FAILING*
Am 5: 24 river, righteousness like a **n** stream!

NEW
Ps 40: 3 He put a **n** song in my mouth,

Ps 98: 1 Sing to the LORD a **n** song, for he
Ecc 1: 9 there is nothing **n** under the sun.
Isa 42: 9 taken place, and **n** things I declare;
62: 2 you will be called by a **n** name
65: 17 I will create **n** heavens and a **n**
66: 22 "As the **n** heavens and the **n** earth
Jer 31: 31 I will make a **n** covenant
La 3: 23 They are **n** every morning;
Eze 11: 19 heart and put a **n** spirit in them;
18: 31 and get a **n** heart and a **n** spirit.
36: 26 will give you a **n** heart and put a **n**
Zep 3: 5 and every **n** day he does not fail,
Mt 9: 17 pour **n** wine into **n** wineskins,
Mk 16: 17 *they will speak in **n** tongues;*
Lk 5: 39 drinking old wine wants the **n**,
22: 20 "This cup is the **n** covenant in my
Jn 13: 34 "A **n** command I give you:
Ac 5: 20 tell the people all about this **n** life."
Ro 6: 4 the Father, we too may live a **n** life.
1Co 5: 7 may be a **n** unleavened batch—
11: 25 "This cup is the **n** covenant in my
2Co 3: 6 as ministers of a **n** covenant—
5: 17 in Christ, the **n** creation has come:
5: 17 The old has gone, the **n** is here!
Gal 6: 15 what counts is the **n** creation.
Eph 4: 23 be made **n** in the attitude of your
4: 24 and to put on the **n** self,
Col 3: 10 and have put on the **n** self, which is
Heb 8: 8 I will make a **n** covenant
9: 15 is the mediator of a **n** covenant,
10: 20 a **n** and living way opened for us
12: 24 Jesus the mediator of a **n** covenant,
1Pe 1: 3 great mercy he has given us **n** birth
2Pe 3: 13 looking forward to a **n** heaven and a **n** earth,
1Jn 2: 8 Yet I am writing you a **n** command;
Rev 2: 17 white stone with a **n** name written
3: 12 city of my God, the **n** Jerusalem,
3: 12 will also write on them my **n** name.
21: 1 I saw "a **n** heaven and a **n** earth,"

NEWBORN (BEAR)
1Pe 2: 2 Like **n** babies, crave pure spiritual

NEWS
2Ki 7: 9 This is a day of good **n** and we are
Ps 112: 7 They will have no fear of bad **n**;
Pr 15: 30 good **n** gives health to the bones.
25: 25 to a weary soul is good **n**
Isa 40: 9 You who bring good **n** to Zion,
52: 7 the feet of those who bring good **n**,
61: 1 me to proclaim good **n** to the poor.
Na 1: 15 the feet of one who brings good **n**,
Mt 4: 23 proclaiming the good **n**
9: 35 proclaiming the good **n**
11: 5 and the good **n** is proclaimed
Mk 1: 15 Repent and believe the good **n**!"
Lk 1: 19 to you and to tell you this good **n**.
2: 10 I bring you good **n** that will cause
3: 18 proclaimed the good **n** to them.
4: 43 "I must proclaim the good **n**
8: 1 proclaiming the good **n**
16: 16 the good **n** of the kingdom of God
Ac 5: 42 proclaiming the good **n** that Jesus
10: 36 announcing the good **n** of peace
17: 18 Paul was preaching the good **n**
Ro 10: 15 feet of those who bring good **n**!"

NICODEMUS*
Pharisee who visited Jesus at night (Jn 3). Argued fair treatment of Jesus (Jn 7:50–52). With Joseph, prepared Jesus for burial (Jn 19:38–42).

NIGHT (NIGHTS)
Ge 1: 5 and the darkness he called "**n**."
1: 16 the lesser light to govern the **n**.
Ex 13: 21 by **n** in a pillar of fire to give
14: 24 of the **n** the LORD looked down
Dt 28: 66 filled with dread both **n** and day,
Jos 1: 8 meditate on it day and **n**, so that
Job 35: 10 Maker, who gives songs in the **n**,
Ps 1: 2 meditates on his law day and **n**.
19: 2 **n** after **n** they reveal knowledge.
42: 8 his love, at **n** his song is with me—
63: 6 you through the watches of the **n**.
77: 6 I remembered my songs in the **n**.
90: 4 gone by, or like a watch in the **n**.
Ps 91: 5 You will not fear the terror of **n**,
119:148 open through the watches of the **n**,
121: 6 by day, nor the moon by **n**.
136: 9 moon and stars to govern the **n**;
Pr 31: 15 She gets up while it is still **n**;
31: 18 and her lamp does not go out at **n**.
Isa 21: 11 "Watchman, what is left of the **n**?
58: 10 and your **n** will become like
Jer 33: 20 day and my covenant with the **n**,
Zec 14: 7 no distinction between day and **n**.
Lk 2: 8 watch over their flocks at **n**.
6: 12 and spent the **n** praying to God.
Jn 3: 2 He came to Jesus at **n** and said,
9: 4 **N** is coming, when no one can
1Th 5: 2 Lord will come like a thief in the **n**.
5: 5 We do not belong to the **n**
Rev 21: 25 shut, for there will be no **n** there.

NIGHTS (NIGHT)
Jnh 1: 17 of the fish three days and three **n**.
Mt 4: 2 After fasting forty days and forty **n**,
12: 40 three **n** in the belly of a huge fish,
12: 40 three **n** in the heart of the earth.
2Co 6: 5 hard work, sleepless **n** and hunger;

NIMROD
Ge 10: 9 "Like **N**, a mighty hunter before

NINEVEH
Jnh 1: 2 "Go to the great city of **N**
Na 1: 1 A prophecy concerning **N**.
Mt 12: 41 The men of **N** will stand

NOAH
Righteous man (Eze 14:14, 20) called to build ark (Ge 6–8; Heb 11:7; 1Pe 3:20; 2Pe 2:5). God's covenant with (Ge 9:1–17). Drunkenness of (Ge 9:18–23). Blessed sons, cursed Canaan (Ge 9:24–27).

NOBLE
Ru 3: 11 you are a woman of **n** character.
Ps 16: 3 "They are the **n** ones in whom is
45: 1 by a **n** theme as I recite my verses
Pr 12: 4 **n** character is her husband's crown,
31: 10 wife of **n** character who can find?
31: 29 "Many women do **n** things, but
Isa 32: 8 But the **n** make **n** plans, and by **n**
Lk 8: 15 good soil stands for those with a **n**
Php 4: 8 whatever is **n**, whatever is right,

NOSTRILS
Ge 2: 7 into his **n** the breath of life,
Ex 15: 8 blast of your **n** the waters piled up.
Ps 18: 15 at the blast of breath from your **n**.

NOTE
Ac 4: 13 they took **n** that these men had

NOTHING
2Sa 24: 24 burnt offerings that cost me **n**."
Ne 9: 21 they lacked **n**, their clothes did not
Ps 73: 25 earth has **n** I desire besides you.
Jer 32: 17 **N** is too hard for you.
Jn 15: 5 apart from me you can do **n**.
Ro 14: 14 Jesus, that **n** is unclean in itself.

NOURISH
Pr 10: 21 The lips of the righteous **n** many,

NULLIFY
Mt 15: 6 Thus you **n** the word of God
Ro 3: 31 we, then, **n** the law by this faith?

OATH
Ex 33: 1 go up to the land I promised on **o**
Nu 30: 2 takes an **o** to obligate himself
Dt 6: 18 land the LORD promised on **o**
7: 8 and kept the **o** he swore to your
29: 12 you this day and sealing with an **o**,
Ps 95: 11 So I declared on **o** in my anger,
119:106 I have taken an **o** and confirmed it,
132: 11 The LORD swore an **o** to David, a sure **o** he will not revoke:
Ecc 8: 2 because you took an **o** before God.
Mt 5: 33 'Do not break your **o**, but fulfill
Heb 7: 20 became priests without any **o**,

OBADIAH
1. Believer who sheltered 100 prophets from Jezebel (1Ki 18:1–16).
2. Prophet against Edom (Ob 1).

OBEDIENCE (OBEY)
Ge 49: 10 the **o** of the nations shall be his.
Dt 10: 12 to walk in **o** to him, to love him,
26: 17 and that you will walk in **o** to him,
30: 16 to walk in **o** to him, and to keep his
Jos 22: 5 to walk in **o** to him, to keep his
1Ch 21: 19 So David went up in **o** to the word
2Ch 31: 21 of God's temple and in **o** to the law
Lk 23: 56 rested on the Sabbath in **o**
Ac 21: 24 you yourself are living in **o**
Ro 1: 5 all the Gentiles to the **o** that comes
5: 19 through the **o** of the one man
6: 16 to death, or to **o**, which leads
16: 19 Everyone has heard about your **o**,
16: 26 might come to the **o** that comes
2Co 9: 13 God for the **o** that accompanies
10: 6 once your **o** is complete.
Phm : 21 Confident of your **o**, I write to you,
Heb 5: 8 he learned **o** from what he suffered
2Jn : 6 that we walk in **o** to his commands.

OBEDIENT* (OBEY)
Dt 30: 17 heart turns away and you are not **o**,
Jdg 2: 17 been **o** to the LORD's commands.
Isa 1: 19 If you are willing and **o**, you will
Lk 2: 51 with them and was **o** to them.
Ac 6: 7 of priests became **o** to the faith.
Ro 6: 16 yourselves to someone as **o** slaves,
2Co 2: 9 the test and be **o** in everything.
7: 15 he remembers that you were all **o**,
10: 5 thought to make it **o** to Christ.
Php 2: 8 himself by becoming **o** to death—
Titus 3: 1 to be **o**, to be ready to do whatever
1Pe 1: 2 be **o** to Jesus Christ and sprinkled
1: 14 As **o** children, do not conform

OBEY (OBEDIENCE OBEDIENT OBEYED OBEYING OBEYS)
Ex 12: 24 "**O** these instructions as a lasting
19: 5 Now if you **o** me fully and keep my
24: 7 the LORD has said; we will **o**."
Lev 18: 4 You must **o** my laws and be careful
25: 18 and be careful to **o** my laws,
Nu 15: 40 remember to **o** all my commands
Dt 5: 27 We will listen and **o**."
6: 3 be careful to **o** so that it may go
6: 24 commanded us to **o** all these
11: 13 faithfully **o** the commands I am
12: 28 **o** all these regulations I am giving
13: 4 Keep his commands and **o** him;
21: 18 son who does not **o** his father
28: 1 If you fully **o** the LORD your God
28: 15 you do not **o** the LORD your God
30: 2 God and **o** him with all your heart
30: 10 if you **o** the LORD your God
30: 14 and in your heart so you may **o** it.
32: 46 to **o** carefully all the words
Jos 1: 7 **o** all the law my servant Moses
24: 24 the LORD our God and **o** him."
1Sa 15: 22 To **o** is better than sacrifice,
1Ki 8: 61 his decrees and **o** his commands,
2Ki 17: 13 I commanded your ancestors to **o**
2Ch 34: 31 and to **o** the words of the covenant
Ps 103: 18 and remember to **o** his precepts.
103: 20 do his bidding, who **o** his word.
119: 17 I live, that I may **o** your word.
119: 34 your law and **o** it with all my heart.
119: 57 I have promised to **o** your words.
119: 67 went astray, but now I **o** your word.
119:100 the elders, for I **o** your precepts.
119:129 therefore I **o** them.
119:167 I **o** your statutes, for I love them
Pr 5: 13 I would not **o** my teachers or turn
Jer 7: 23 **O** me, and I will be your God
11: 4 I said, '**O** me and do everything I
11: 7 again and again, saying, "**O** me."
42: 6 we will **o** the LORD our God,
Mt 8: 27 the winds and the waves **o** him!"
28: 20 to **o** everything I have commanded
Lk 11: 28 hear the word of God and **o** it."
Jn 14: 23 who loves me will **o** my teaching.
14: 24 not love me will not **o** my teaching.
Ac 5: 29 must **o** God rather than human
5: 32 has given to those who **o** him."
Ro 2: 13 it is those who **o** the law who will
6: 12 body so that you **o** its evil desires.
6: 16 you are slaves of the one you **o**—
6: 17 have come to **o** from your heart
15: 18 in leading the Gentiles to **o** God

Gal 5: 3 he is obligated to **o** the whole law.
Eph 6: 1 **o** your parents in the Lord, for this
6: 5 **o** your earthly masters with respect
6: 5 just as you would **o** Christ.
Col 3: 20 **o** your parents in everything,
3: 22 Slaves, **o** your earthly masters
2Th 3: 14 who does not **o** our instruction
1Ti 3: 4 and see that his children **o** him,
Heb 5: 9 eternal salvation for all who **o** him
1Pe 4: 17 for those who do not **o** the gospel

OBEYED (OBEY)
Ge 22: 18 blessed, because you have **o** me."
Jos 1: 17 Just as we fully **o** Moses, so we will
Ps 119: 4 precepts that are to be fully **o**.
Da 9: 10 we have not **o** the LORD our God
Jnh 3: 3 Jonah **o** the word of the LORD
Mic 5: 15 on the nations that have not **o** me."
Jn 15: 20 If they **o** my teaching, they will
17: 6 to me and they have **o** your word.
Ac 7: 53 through angels but have not **o** it."
Php 2: 12 friends, as you have always **o**—
Heb 11: 8 as his inheritance, **o** and went,
1Pe 3: 6 who **o** Abraham and called him

OBEYING (OBEY)
1Sa 15: 22 as much as in **o** the LORD?
Ps 119: 5 were steadfast in **o** your decrees!
Gal 5: 7 you to keep you from **o** the truth?
1Pe 1: 22 purified yourselves by **o** the truth

OBEYS (OBEY)
Lev 18: 5 for the person who **o** them will live
Eze 20: 11 the person who **o** them will live.
Jn 8: 51 whoever **o** my word will never see
Ro 2: 27 yet **o** the law will condemn you
1Jn 2: 5 But if anyone **o** his word,

OBLIGATED (OBLIGATION)
Ro 1: 14 I am **o** both to Greeks
Gal 5: 3 that he is **o** to obey the whole law.

OBLIGATION (OBLIGATED)
Ro 8: 12 brothers and sisters, we have an **o**

OBSCENITY*
Eph 5: 4 Nor should there be **o**, foolish talk

OBSCURES*
Job 38: 2 "Who is this that **o** my plans
42: 3 **o** my plans without knowledge?'

OBSERVE
Ex 31: 13 'You must **o** my Sabbaths.
Lev 25: 2 the land itself must **o** a sabbath
Dt 4: 6 **O** them carefully, for this will show
5: 12 "**O** the Sabbath day by keeping it
8: 6 **O** the commands of the LORD
11: 22 you carefully **o** all these commands
26: 16 carefully **o** them with all your heart
Ps 37: 37 the blameless, **o** the upright;

OBSOLETE*
Heb 8: 13 "new," he has made the first one **o**;

OBSTACLE* (OBSTACLES)
Ro 14: 13 block or **o** in the way of a brother

OBSTACLES (OBSTACLE)
Ro 16: 17 put **o** in your way that are contrary

OBSTINATE
Isa 65: 2 held out my hands to an **o** people,
Ro 10: 21 to a disobedient and **o** people."

OBTAIN (OBTAINED OBTAINING)
Pr 12: 2 Good people **o** favor
Ro 11: 7 sought so earnestly they did not **o**.
2Ti 2: 10 they too may **o** the salvation that is

OBTAINED (OBTAIN)
Ro 9: 30 not pursue righteousness, have **o** it,
Php 3: 12 Not that I have already **o** all this,

OBTAINING* (OBTAIN)
Heb 9: 12 blood, thus **o** eternal redemption.

OBVIOUS*
Mt 6: 18 so that it will not be **o** to others
Gal 5: 19 The acts of the flesh are **o**:
1Ti 5: 24 The sins of some are **o**,
5: 25 good deeds are **o**, and even those
5: 25 are not **o** cannot remain hidden

OCCASIONS
Eph 6: 18 the Spirit on all **o** with all kinds

OFFENSE (OFFENSES OFFENSIVE)
Pr 17: 9 would foster love covers over an **o**,
19: 11 it is to one's glory to overlook an **o**.
Gal 5: 11 In that case the **o** of the cross has

OFFENSES (OFFENSE)
Ecc 10: 4 calmness can lay great **o** to rest.
Isa 44: 22 swept away your **o** like a cloud,
59: 12 For our **o** are many in your sight,
Eze 18: 30 Turn away from all your **o**;
33: 10 "Our **o** and sins weigh us down,

OFFENSIVE (OFFENSE)
Ps 139: 24 See if there is any **o** way in me,

OFFER (OFFERED OFFERING OFFERINGS OFFERS)
Ps 4: 5 **O** the sacrifices of the righteous
Ro 6: 13 not **o** any part of yourself to sin
6: 13 rather **o** yourselves to God as those
12: 1 **o** your bodies as a living sacrifice,
Heb 9: 25 he enter heaven to **o** himself again
13: 15 let us continually **o** to God

OFFERED (OFFER)
Isa 50: 6 I **o** my back to those who beat me,
1Co 9: 13 share in what is **o** on the altar?
10: 20 of pagans are **o** to demons,
Heb 7: 27 sins once for all when he **o** himself.
9: 14 Spirit **o** himself unblemished
11: 17 tested him, **o** Isaac as a sacrifice.
Jas 5: 15 the prayer **o** in faith will make

OFFERING (OFFER)
Ge 4: 3 of the soil as an **o** to the LORD.
22: 2 Sacrifice him there as a burnt **o**
22: 8 provide the lamb for the burnt **o**,
Ex 29: 24 before the LORD as a wave **o**.
29: 40 of a hin of wine as a drink **o**.
Lev 1: 3 "'If the **o** is a burnt **o**
2: 4 you bring a grain **o** baked
3: 1 "'If your **o** is a fellowship **o**,
4: 3 young bull without defect as a sin **o**
5: 15 the sanctuary shekel. It is a guilt **o**.
7: 37 are the regulations for the burnt **o**, the grain **o**, the sin **o**,
9: 24 consumed the burnt **o** and the fat
22: 18 to fulfill a vow or as a freewill **o**,
22: 21 a special vow or as a freewill **o**,
1Sa 13: 9 And Saul offered up the burnt **o**.
1Ch 21: 26 heaven on the altar of burnt **o**.
2Ch 7: 1 and consumed the burnt **o**
Ps 40: 6 Sacrifice and **o** you did not desire
116: 17 I will sacrifice a thank **o** to you
Isa 53: 10 the LORD makes his life an **o**
Mt 5: 23 if you are **o** your gift at the altar
Ro 8: 3 likeness of sinful flesh to be a sin **o**.
Eph 5: 2 himself up for us as a fragrant **o**
Php 2: 17 out like a drink **o** on the sacrifice
4: 18 are a fragrant **o**, an acceptable
2Ti 4: 6 being poured out like a drink **o**,
Heb 10: 5 "Sacrifice and **o** you did not desire,
11: 4 God a better **o** than Cain did.
1Pe 2: 5 **o** spiritual sacrifices acceptable

OFFERINGS (OFFER)
1Sa 15: 22 the LORD delight in burnt **o**
2Ch 35: 7 lambs and goats for the Passover **o**,
Isa 1: 13 Stop bringing meaningless **o**!
Hos 6: 6 of God rather than burnt **o**.
Mal 3: 8 we robbing you?' "In tithes and **o**.
Mk 12: 33 is more important than all burnt **o**
Heb 10: 8 "Sacrifices and **o**, burnt **o** and sin **o**

OFFERS (OFFER)
Heb 10: 11 and again he **o** the same sacrifices,

OFFICER (OFFICIALS)
2Ti 2: 4 tries to please his commanding **o**.

OFFICIALS (OFFICER)
Ex 5: 21 his **o** and have put a sword in their
Pr 17: 26 surely to flog honest **o** is not right.
29: 12 to lies, all his **o** become wicked.

OFFSPRING
Ge 3: 15 and between your **o** and hers;
12: 7 "To your **o** I will give this land."
13: 16 I will make your **o** like the dust
26: 4 through your **o** all nations on earth
28: 14 be blessed through you and your **o**.
Ex 13: 2 The first **o** of every womb among
Ru 4: 12 Through the **o** the LORD gives
Isa 44: 3 I will pour out my Spirit on your **o**,
53: 10 he will see his **o** and prolong his
Ac 3: 25 'Through your **o** all peoples
17: 28 own poets have said, 'We are his **o**.'
17: 29 "Therefore since we are God's **o**,
Ro 4: 18 said to him, "So shall your **o** be."
9: 8 who are regarded as Abraham's **o**.

OG
Nu 21: 33 and **O** king of Bashan and his
Ps 136: 20 and **O** king of Bashan—

OIL
Ex 29: 7 Take the anointing **o** and anoint
30: 25 It will be the sacred anointing **o**.
Dt 14: 23 grain, new wine and olive **o**,
1Sa 10: 1 Samuel took a flask of olive **o**
16: 13 So Samuel took the horn of **o**
1Ki 17: 16 up and the jug of **o** did not run dry,
2Ki 4: 6 Then the **o** stopped flowing.
Ps 23: 5 You anoint my head with **o**;
45: 7 by anointing you with the **o** of joy.
104: 15 hearts, **o** to make their faces shine,
133: 2 It is like precious **o** poured
Pr 21: 17 wine and olive **o** will never be rich.
Isa 1: 6 bandaged or soothed with olive **o**.
61: 3 the **o** of joy instead of mourning,
Mt 25: 3 but did not take any **o** with them.
Heb 1: 9 by anointing you with the **o** of joy."

OLIVE (OLIVES)
Ge 8: 11 beak was a freshly plucked **o** leaf!
Jdg 9: 8 They said to the **o** tree, 'Be our
Jer 11: 16 LORD called you a thriving **o** tree
Zec 4: 3 Also there are two **o** trees by it,
Ro 11: 17 though a wild **o** shoot, have been
11: 24 grafted into a cultivated **o** tree,
11: 24 be grafted into their own **o** tree!
Rev 11: 4 They are "the two **o** trees"

OLIVES (OLIVE)
Zec 14: 4 the Mount of **O** will be split in two
Mt 24: 3 was sitting on the Mount of **O**,
Jas 3: 12 can a fig tree bear **o**, or a grapevine

OMEGA*
Rev 1: 8 "I am the Alpha and the **O**,"
21: 6 I am the Alpha and the **O**,
22: 13 I am the Alpha and the **O**, the First

OMENS
Lev 19: 26 not practice divination or seek **o**.

OMIT*
Jer 26: 2 I command you; do not **o** a word.

OMRI
King of Israel (1Ki 16:21–26).

ONESIMUS*
Col 4: 9 He is coming with **O**, our faithful
Phm : 10 that I appeal to you for my son **O**,

ONESIPHORUS*
2Ti 1: 16 show mercy to the household of **O**,
4: 19 Aquila and the household of **O**.

ONIONS*
Nu 11: 5 melons, leeks, **o** and garlic.

ONYX
Ex 28: 9 "Take two **o** stones and engrave
28: 20 row shall be topaz, **o** and jasper.

OPEN (OPENED)
Ps 78: 2 I will **o** my mouth with a parable;

OPENED (OPEN)
Ps 40: 6 but my ears you have **o**—

OPENHANDED* (HAND OPEN)
Dt 15: 8 be **o** and freely lend them whatever
15: 11 be **o** toward your fellow Israelites

OPINIONS*
1Ki 18: 21 will you waver between two **o**?
Pr 18: 2 but delight in airing their own **o**.

OPPONENTS (OPPOSE)
Pr 18: 18 disputes and keeps strong **o** apart.
2Ti 2: 25 **O** must be gently instructed,

OPPORTUNE (OPPORTUNITY)
Lk 4: 13 he left him until an **o** time.

OPPORTUNITY* (OPPORTUNE)
Jdg 9: 33 seize the **o** to attack them."
1Sa 18: 21 "Now you have a second **o**

Jer 46: 17 a loud noise; he has missed his **o**.'
Mt 26: 16 watched for an **o** to hand him over.
Mk 14: 11 watched for an **o** to hand him over.
Lk 22: 6 for an **o** to hand Jesus over
Ac 25: 16 have had an **o** to defend themselves
27: 13 began to blow, they saw their **o**;
Ro 7: 8 sin, seizing the **o** afforded
7: 11 sin, seizing the **o** afforded
1Co 16: 12 but he will go when he has the **o**.
2Co 5: 12 are giving you an **o** to take pride
11: 12 under those who want an **o** to be
Gal 6: 10 as we have **o**, let us do good to all
Eph 5: 16 making the most of every **o**,
Php 4: 10 but you had no **o** to show it.
Col 4: 5 make the most of every **o**.
1Ti 5: 14 to give the enemy no **o** for slander.
Heb 11: 15 they would have had **o** to return.

OPPOSE (OPPONENTS OPPOSED OPPOSES OPPOSING OPPOSITION)
Ex 23: 22 and will **o** those who **o** you.
1Sa 2: 10 those who **o** the LORD will be
Job 23: 13 stands alone, and who can **o** him?
Titus 1: 9 doctrine and refute those who **o** it.
2: 8 those who **o** you may be ashamed

OPPOSED (OPPOSE)
Gal 2: 11 to Antioch, I **o** him to his face,
3: 21 **o** to the promises of God?

OPPOSES (OPPOSE)
Jas 4: 6 "God **o** the proud but shows favor
1Pe 5: 5 "God **o** the proud but shows favor

OPPOSING (OPPOSE)
1Ti 6: 20 the **o** ideas of what is falsely called

OPPOSITION (OPPOSE)
Heb 12: 3 Consider him who endured such **o**

OPPRESS (OPPRESSED OPPRESSES OPPRESSION OPPRESSOR)
Ex 1: 11 slave masters over them to **o** them
22: 21 "Do not mistreat or **o** a foreigner,
Isa 3: 5 People will **o** each other—
Eze 22: 29 they **o** the poor and needy
Da 7: 25 Most High and **o** his holy people
Am 5: 12 are those who **o** the innocent
Zec 7: 10 Do not **o** the widow
Mal 3: 5 wages, who **o** the widows

OPPRESSED (OPPRESS)
Jdg 2: 18 their groaning under those who **o**
Ps 9: 9 The LORD is a refuge for the **o**,
82: 3 the cause of the poor and the **o**.
146: 7 He upholds the cause of the **o**
Pr 16: 19 along with the **o** than to share
31: 5 and deprive all the **o** of their rights.
Isa 1: 17 Defend the **o**. Take up the cause
53: 7 He was **o** and afflicted, yet he did
58: 10 and satisfy the needs of the **o**,
Zec 10: 2 the people wander like sheep **o**
Lk 4: 18 sight for the blind, to set the **o** free,

OPPRESSES* (OPPRESS)
Pr 14: 31 Whoever **o** the poor shows
22: 16 **o** the poor to increase his wealth
28: 3 A ruler who **o** the poor is like
Eze 18: 12 He **o** the poor and needy.

OPPRESSION (OPPRESS)
Ps 72: 14 He will rescue them from **o**
119:134 Redeem me from human **o**, that I
Isa 53: 8 By **o** and judgment he was taken
58: 9 "If you do away with the yoke of **o**,

OPPRESSOR (OPPRESS)
Ps 72: 4 of the needy; may he crush the **o**.
Isa 51: 13 For where is the wrath of the **o**?

ORDAINED
Ps 111: 9 he **o** his covenant forever—
139: 16 all the days **o** for me were written
Eze 28: 14 a guardian cherub, for so I **o** you.
Hab 1: 12 my Rock, have **o** them to punish.

ORDEAL*
1Pe 4: 12 at the fiery **o** that has come on you

ORDER (ORDERLY ORDERS)
Nu 9: 23 They obeyed the LORD'S **o**,
Ps 110: 4 forever, in the **o** of Melchizedek."
Heb 5: 10 high priest in the **o** of Melchizedek.
9: 10 until the time of the new **o**.
Rev 21: 4 for the old **o** of things has passed

ORDERLY* (ORDER)
Lk 1: 3 I too decided to write an **o** account
1Co 14: 40 be done in a fitting and **o** way.

ORDERS (ORDER)
Mk 1: 27 He even gives **o** to impure spirits
3: 12 But he gave them strict **o** not to tell
9: 9 Jesus gave them **o** not to tell

ORDINARY
Ac 4: 13 that they were unschooled, **o** men,

ORGIES*
Gal 5: 21 drunkenness, **o**, and the like.
1Pe 4: 3 lust, drunkenness, **o**,

ORIGIN (ORIGINATE ORIGINS)
2Pe 1: 21 For prophecy never had its **o**

ORIGINATE* (ORIGIN)
1Co 14: 36 did the word of God **o** with you?

ORIGINS* (ORIGIN)
Mic 5: 2 Israel, whose **o** are from of old,

ORNAMENT*
Pr 3: 22 for you, an **o** to grace your neck.
25: 12 an **o** of fine gold is the rebuke

ORNATE
Ge 37: 3 and he made an **o** robe for him.

ORPHANS*
Jn 14: 18 I will not leave you as **o**;
Jas 1: 27 to look after **o** and widows in

OTHERWISE
1Ti 6: 3 If anyone teaches **o** and does not

OTHNIEL
Nephew of Caleb (Jos 15:15–19; Jdg 1:12–15). Judge who freed Israel from Aram (Jdg 3:7–11).

OUTCOME
Heb 13: 7 Consider the **o** of their way of life
1Pe 4: 17 what will the **o** be for those who do

OUTNUMBER
Ps 139: 18 they would **o** the grains of sand

OUTSIDERS*
Col 4: 5 wise in the way you act toward **o**;
1Th 4: 12 daily life may win the respect of **o**
1Ti 3: 7 also have a good reputation with **o**,

OUTSTANDING
SS 5: 10 and ruddy, **o** among ten thousand.
Ro 13: 8 Let no debt remain **o**,

OUTSTRETCHED
Ex 6: 6 I will redeem you with an **o** arm
Dt 4: 34 by a mighty hand and an **o** arm,
5: 15 with a mighty hand and an **o** arm.
1Ki 8: 42 mighty hand and your **o** arm—
Ps 136: 12 with a mighty hand and **o** arm;
Jer 27: 5 power and **o** arm I made the earth
32: 17 by your great power and **o** arm.
Eze 20: 33 with a mighty hand and an **o** arm

OUTWEIGHS (WEIGH)
2Co 4: 17 an eternal glory that far **o** them all.

OUTWIT*
2Co 2: 11 in order that Satan might not **o** us.

OVERAWED* (AWE)
Ps 49: 16 not be **o** when others grow rich,

OVERBEARING*
Titus 1: 7 not **o**, not quick-tempered, not

OVERCOME (OVERCOMES)
Mt 16: 18 and the gates of Hades will not **o** it.
Mk 9: 24 help me **o** my unbelief!"
Lk 10: 19 to **o** all the power of the enemy;
Jn 1: 5 and the darkness has not **o** it.
16: 33 But take heart! I have **o** the world."
Ro 12: 21 Do not be **o** by evil, but **o** evil
2Pe 2: 20 are again entangled in it and are **o**,
1Jn 2: 13 because you have **o** the evil one.
4: 4 are from God and have **o** them,
5: 4 is the victory that has **o** the world,

OVERCOMES* (OVERCOME)
1Jn 5: 4 everyone born of God **o** the world.
5: 5 Who is it that **o** the world?

OVERFLOW (OVERFLOWING OVERFLOWS)
Ps 65: 11 and your carts **o** with abundance.
119:171 May my lips **o** with praise, for you
La 1: 16 I weep and my eyes **o** with tears.
Ro 5: 15 man, Jesus Christ, **o** to the many!
15: 13 so that you may **o** with hope
2Co 4: 15 may cause thanksgiving to **o**
1Th 3: 12 love increase and **o** for each other

OVERFLOWING (OVERFLOW)
Pr 3: 10 then your barns will be filled to **o**,
8: 24 were no springs **o** with water;
2Co 8: 2 trial, their **o** joy and their extreme
9: 12 **o** in many expressions of thanks
Col 2: 7 taught, and **o** with thankfulness.

OVERFLOWS* (OVERFLOW)
Ps 23: 5 anoint my head with oil; my cup **o**.

OVERJOYED* (JOY)
Da 6: 23 The king was **o** and gave orders
Mt 2: 10 they saw the star, they were **o**.
Jn 20: 20 The disciples were **o** when they
Ac 12: 14 she was so **o** she ran back without
1Pe 4: 13 that you may be **o** when his glory

OVERLOOK
Pr 19: 11 it is to one's glory to **o** an offense.

OVERSEER (OVERSEERS)
Pr 6: 7 has no commander, no **o** or ruler,
1Ti 3: 1 to be an **o** desires a noble task.
3: 2 Now the **o** is to be above reproach,
Titus 1: 7 Since an **o** manages God's
1Pe 2: 25 the Shepherd and **O** of your souls.

OVERSEERS (OVERSEER)
Ac 20: 28 the Holy Spirit has made you **o**.
Php 1: 1 together with the **o** and deacons:

OVERSHADOW* (OVERSHADOWING)
1Ch 28: 18 **o** the ark of the covenant of the
Lk 1: 35 power of the Most High will **o** you.

OVERSHADOWING (OVERSHADOW)
Ex 25: 20 upward, **o** the cover with them.
Heb 9: 5 the Glory, **o** the atonement cover.

OVERTAKES
Pr 12: 21 No harm **o** the righteous,

OVERTHROW (OVERTHROWS)
2Th 2: 8 whom the Lord Jesus will **o**

OVERTHROWS (OVERTHROW)
Pr 13: 6 but wickedness **o** the sinner.
Isa 44: 25 who **o** the learning of the wise

OVERWHELMED (OVERWHELMING)
2Sa 22: 5 the torrents of destruction **o** me.
1Ki 10: 5 temple of the LORD, she was **o**.
Ps 38: 4 My guilt has **o** me like a burden
65: 3 When we were **o** by sins,
Mt 26: 38 "My soul is **o** with sorrow
Mk 7: 37 People were **o** with amazement.
9: 15 they were **o** with wonder and ran
2Co 2: 7 so that he will not be **o** by excessive

OVERWHELMING (OVERWHELMED)
Pr 27: 4 Anger is cruel and fury **o**, but who
Isa 10: 22 has been decreed, **o** and righteous.
28: 15 When an **o** scourge sweeps by,

OWE
Ro 13: 7 Give to everyone what you **o** them:
If you **o** taxes, pay taxes;
Phm : 19 that you **o** me your very self.

OWNER'S (OWNERSHIP)
Isa 1: 3 the donkey its **o** manger, but Israel

OWNERSHIP* (OWNER'S)
2Co 1: 22 set his seal of **o** on us, and put his

OX (OXEN)
Dt 25: 4 Do not muzzle an **o** while it is
Isa 11: 7 the lion will eat straw like the **o**.
Eze 1: 10 and on the left the face of an **o**;
Lk 13: 15 of you on the Sabbath untie your **o**
1Co 9: 9 "Do not muzzle an **o** while it is
1Ti 5: 18 "Do not muzzle an **o** while it is
Rev 4: 7 the second was like an **o**, the third

OXEN (OX)
1Ki 19: 20 then left his **o** and ran after Elijah.
Lk 14: 19 'I have just bought five yoke of **o**,

PAGAN (PAGANS)
Isa 2: 6 Philistines and embrace **p** customs.
Mt 18: 17 treat them as you would a **p** or a
Lk 12: 30 For the **p** world runs after all such

PAGANS* (PAGAN)
Mt 5: 47 Do not even **p** do that?

Mt 13: 4 some fell along the **p**, and the birds
Lk 1: 79 guide our feet into the **p** of peace."
2Co 6: 3 no stumbling block in anyone's **p**,

PATHS (PATH)
Ps 23: 3 He guides me along the right **p**
25: 4 ways, LORD, teach me your **p**.
Pr 1: 19 Such are the **p** of all who go
2: 13 who have left the straight **p** to walk
3: 6 and he will make your **p** straight.
4: 11 and lead you along straight **p**.
4: 26 thought to the **p** for your feet
5: 21 and he examines all your **p**.
8: 20 along the **p** of justice,
22: 5 In the **p** of the wicked are snares
Isa 2: 3 so that we may walk in his **p**."
Jer 6: 16 ask for the ancient **p**, ask where
Mic 4: 2 so that we may walk in his **p**."
Mt 3: 3 Lord, make straight **p** for him.'"
Ac 2: 28 made known to me the **p** of life;
Ro 11: 33 and his **p** beyond tracing out!
Heb 12: 13 "Make level **p** for your feet,"

PATIENCE* (PATIENT)
Pr 19: 11 A person's wisdom yields **p**; it is
25: 15 Through **p** a ruler can be
Ecc 7: 8 and **p** is better than pride.
Isa 7: 13 not enough to try the **p** of humans?
7: 13 Will you try the **p** of my God also?
Ro 2: 4 forbearance and **p**, not realizing
9: 22 bore with great **p** the objects of his
2Co 6: 6 understanding, **p** and kindness;
Col 1: 11 may have great endurance and **p**,
3: 12 humility, gentleness and **p**.
1Ti 1: 16 might display his immense **p** as
2Ti 3: 10 of life, my purpose, faith, **p**, love,
4: 2 great **p** and careful instruction.
Heb 6: 12 **p** inherit what has been promised.
Jas 5: 10 as an example of **p** in the face
2Pe 3: 15 that our Lord's **p** means salvation,

PATIENT* (PATIENCE PATIENTLY)
Ne 9: 30 many years you were **p** with them.
Job 6: 11 What prospects, that I should be **p**?
Pr 14: 29 Whoever is **p** has great
15: 18 the one who is **p** calms a quarrel.
16: 32 Better a **p** person than a warrior,
Mt 18: 26 'Be **p** with me,' he begged, 'and I
18: 29 and begged him, 'Be **p** with me,
Ro 12: 12 Be joyful in hope, **p** in affliction,
1Co 13: 4 Love is **p**, love is kind. It does not
2Co 1: 6 produces in you **p** endurance
Eph 4: 2 be **p**, bearing with one another
1Th 5: 14 help the weak, be **p** with everyone.
Jas 5: 7 Be **p**, then, brothers and sisters,
5: 8 You too, be **p** and stand firm,
2Pe 3: 9 Instead he is **p** with you,
Rev 1: 9 **p** endurance that are ours in Jesus,
13: 10 This calls for **p** endurance
14: 12 This calls for **p** endurance

PATIENTLY* (PATIENT)
Ps 37: 7 the LORD and wait **p** for him;
40: 1 I waited **p** for the LORD;
Isa 38: 13 I waited **p** till dawn, but like a lion
Hab 3: 16 Yet I will wait **p** for the day
Ac 26: 3 I beg you to listen to me **p**.
Ro 8: 25 we do not yet have, we wait for it **p**.
Heb 6: 15 And so after waiting **p**,
1Pe 3: 20 ago when God waited **p** in the days
Jas 5: 7 **p** waiting for the autumn and
Rev 3: 10 kept my command to endure **p**,

PATTERN
Ex 25: 40 according to the **p** shown you
Ro 5: 14 who is a **p** of the one to come.
12: 2 not conform to the **p** of this world,
2Ti 1: 13 keep as the **p** of sound teaching,
Heb 8: 5 according to the **p** shown you

PAUL

Also called Saul (Ac 13:9). Pharisee from Tarsus (Ac 9:11; Php 3:5). Apostle (Gal 1). At stoning of Stephen (Ac 8:1). Persecuted church (Ac 9:1–2; Gal 1:13). Vision of Jesus on road to Damascus (Ac 9:4–9; 26:12–18). In Arabia (Gal 1:17). Preached in Damascus; escaped death through the wall in a basket (Ac 9:19–25). In Jerusalem; sent back to Tarsus (Ac 9:26–30).

Brought to Antioch by Barnabas (Ac 11:22–26). First missionary journey to Cyprus and Galatia (Ac 13–14). Stoned at Lystra (Ac 14:19–20). At Jerusalem council (Ac 15). Split with Barnabas over Mark (Ac 15:36–41).

Second missionary journey with Silas (Ac 16–20). Called to Macedonia (Ac 16:6–10). Freed from prison in Philippi (Ac 16:16–40). In Thessalonica (Ac 17:1–9). Speech in Athens (Ac 17:16–33). In Corinth (Ac 18). In Ephesus (Ac 19). Return to Jerusalem (Ac 20). Farewell to Ephesian elders (Ac 20:13–38). Arrival in Jerusalem (Ac 21:1–26). Arrested (Ac 21:27–36). Addressed crowds (Ac 22), Sanhedrin (Ac 23:1–11). Transferred to Caesarea (Ac 23:12–35). Trial before Felix (Ac 24), Festus (Ac 25:1–12). Before Agrippa (Ac 25:13—26:32). Voyage to Rome; shipwreck (Ac 27). Arrival in Rome (Ac 28).

Epistles: Romans, 1 and 2 Corinthians, Galatians, Ephesians, Philippians, Colossians, 1 and 2 Thessalonians, 1 and 2 Timothy, Titus, Philemon.

PAVEMENT
Jn 19: 13 at a place known as the Stone **P**

PAY (PAID PAYMENT PAYS REPAID REPAY REPAYING)
Lev 26: 43 They will **p** for their sins because
Dt 7: 12 If you **p** attention to these laws
Pr 4: 1 **p** attention and gain understanding
4: 20 My son, **p** attention to what I say;
5: 1 My son, **p** attention to my wisdom,
6: 31 must **p** sevenfold, though it costs
19: 19 person must **p** the penalty;
22: 17 **P** attention and turn your ear
24: 29 I'll **p** them back for what they did."
Eze 40: 4 **p** attention to everything I am
Zec 11: 12 "If you think it best, give me my **p**;
Mt 20: 2 He agreed to **p** them a denarius
22: 16 because you **p** no attention to who
22: 17 Is it right to **p** the imperial tax
Lk 3: 14 be content with your **p**."
19: 8 I will **p** back four times
Ro 13: 6 This is also why you **p** taxes,
2Pe 1: 19 you will do well to **p** attention to it,

PAYMENT (PAY)
Ps 49: 8 a life is costly, no **p** is ever enough
Php 4: 18 I have received full **p** and have

PAYS (PAY)
Pr 17: 13 the house of one who **p** back evil
1Th 5: 15 sure that nobody **p** back wrong

PEACE (PEACEABLE PEACEFUL PEACEMAKERS)
Lev 26: 6 "'I will grant **p** in the land,
Nu 6: 26 toward you and give you **p**."'
25: 12 him I am making my covenant of **p**
Dt 20: 10 a city, make its people an offer of **p**.
Jdg 3: 11 So the land had **p** for forty years,
3: 30 and the land had **p** for eighty years.
5: 31 Then the land had **p** forty years.
6: 24 there and called it The LORD Is **P**.
8: 28 lifetime, the land had **p** forty years.
1Sa 7: 14 And there was **p** between Israel
2Sa 10: 19 they made **p** with the Israelites
1Ki 2: 33 there be the LORD's **p** forever."
22: 44 also at **p** with the king of Israel.
2Ki 9: 17 and ask, 'Do you come in **p**?'"
1Ch 19: 19 they made **p** with David and
22: 9 have a son who will be a man of **p**
2Ch 14: 1 his days the country was at **p** for
20: 30 kingdom of Jehoshaphat was at **p**,
Job 3: 26 I have no **p**, no quietness; I have no
22: 21 to God and be at **p** with him;
Ps 29: 11 LORD blesses his people with **p**.
34: 14 and do good; seek **p** and pursue it.
37: 11 land and enjoy **p** and prosperity.
37: 37 a future awaits those who seek **p**.
85: 10 and **p** kiss each other.
119:165 Great **p** have those who love your
120: 7 I am for **p**; but when I speak,
122: 6 Pray for the **p** of Jerusalem:
147: 14 He grants **p** to your borders
Pr 12: 20 but those who promote **p** have joy.
14: 30 A heart at **p** gives life to the body,
16: 7 enemies to make **p** with them.
17: 1 Better a dry crust with **p** and quiet
Ecc 3: 8 a time for war and a time for **p**.
Isa 9: 6 Everlasting Father, Prince of **P**.
14: 7 All the lands are at rest and at **p**;
26: 3 in perfect **p** those whose minds are
32: 17 of that righteousness will be **p**;
48: 18 **p** would have been like a river,
48: 22 "There is no **p**," says the LORD,
52: 7 who proclaim **p**, who bring good
53: 5 that brought us **p** was on him,
54: 10 nor my covenant of **p** be removed,"
55: 12 go out in joy and be led forth in **p**;
57: 2 who walk uprightly enter into **p**;
57: 19 **P**, **p**, to those far and near,"
57: 21 "There is no **p**," says my God,
59: 8 who walks along them will know **p**.
Jer 6: 14 '**P**, **p**,' they say, when there is no **p**.
8: 11 "**P**, **p**," they say, when there is no
30: 10 Jacob will again have **p**
46: 27 Jacob will again have **p**
Eze 13: 10 saying, "**P**," when there is no **p**,
34: 25 "'I will make a covenant of **p**
37: 26 I will make a covenant of **p**
Mic 5: 5 will be our **p** when the Assyrians
Zec 8: 19 Therefore love truth and **p**."
9: 10 He will proclaim **p** to the nations.
Mal 2: 5 a covenant of life and **p**,
2: 6 He walked with me in **p**
Mt 10: 34 have come to bring **p** to the earth.
10: 34 I did not come to bring **p**,
Mk 9: 50 and be at **p** with each other."
Lk 1: 79 guide our feet into the path of **p**."
2: 14 and on earth **p** to those on whom
10: 6 If someone who promotes **p** is there, your **p** will rest on them;
19: 38 "**P** in heaven and glory
Jn 14: 27 **P** I leave with you; my **p** I give you.
16: 33 so that in me you may have **p**.
Ro 1: 7 and **p** to you from God our Father
2: 10 and **p** for everyone who does good:
5: 1 we have **p** with God through our
8: 6 governed by the Spirit is life and **p**.
12: 18 on you, live at **p** with everyone.
14: 19 every effort to do what leads to **p**
1Co 7: 15 God has called us to live in **p**.
14: 33 is not a God of disorder but of **p**—
2Co 13: 11 be of one mind, live in **p**.
13: 11 God of love and **p** will be with you.
Gal 5: 22 Spirit is love, joy, **p**, forbearance,
Eph 2: 14 For he himself is our **p**, who has
2: 15 out of the two, thus making **p**,
2: 17 preached **p** to you who were far
6: 15 that comes from the gospel of **p**.
Php 4: 7 the **p** of God, which transcends
Col 1: 20 by making **p** through his blood,
3: 15 Let the **p** of Christ rule in your
3: 15 of one body you were called to **p**.
1Th 5: 3 people are saying, "**P** and safety,"
5: 13 Live in **p** with each other.
5: 23 the God of **p**, sanctify you through
2Th 3: 16 the Lord of **p** himself give you **p**
2Ti 2: 22 love and **p**, along with those who
Heb 7: 2 of Salem" means "king of **p**."
12: 11 **p** for those who have been trained
12: 14 effort to live in **p** with everyone
13: 20 Now may the God of **p**,
1Pe 3: 11 they must seek **p** and pursue it.
2Pe 3: 14 blameless and at **p** with him.
Rev 6: 4 power to take **p** from the earth

PEACEABLE* (PEACE)
Titus 3: 2 no one, to be **p** and considerate,

PEACEFUL (PEACE)
1Ti 2: 2 that we may live **p** and quiet lives

PEACE-LOVING*
Jas 3: 17 then **p**, considerate, submissive,

PEACEMAKERS* (PEACE)
Mt 5: 9 Blessed are the **p**, for they will be
Jas 3: 18 **P** who sow in peace reap a harvest

PEARL* (PEARLS)
Rev 21: 21 each gate made of a single **p**.

PEARLS (PEARL)
Mt 7: 6 do not throw your **p** to pigs.
13: 45 like a merchant looking for fine **p**.
1Ti 2: 9 or gold or **p** or expensive clothes,
Rev 21: 21 The twelve gates were twelve **p**,

PEDDLE*
2Co 2: 17 we do not **p** the word of God
PEG
Jdg 4: 21 She drove the **p** through his temple
PEKAH
King of Israel (2Ki 15:25–31; Isa 7:1).
PEKAHIAH*
Son of Menahem; king of Israel (2Ki 15:22–26).
PEN
Ps 45: 1 my tongue is the **p** of a skillful
Mt 5: 18 not the least stroke of a **p**,
Jn 10: 1 who does not enter the sheep **p**
PENETRATES*
Heb 4: 12 **p** even to dividing soul and spirit,
PENNIES* (PENNY)
Lk 12: 6 not five sparrows sold for two **p**?
PENNY* (PENNIES)
Mt 5: 26 out until you have paid the last **p**.
10: 29 Are not two sparrows sold for a **p**?
Lk 12: 59 out until you have paid the last **p**."
PENTECOST*
Ac 2: 1 When the day of **P** came, they were
20: 16 if possible, by the day of **P**.
1Co 16: 8 I will stay on at Ephesus until **P**,
PEOPLE (PEOPLE'S PEOPLES)
Ge 11: 6 said, "If as one **p** speaking the same
Ex 5: 1 'Let my **p** go, so that they may hold
6: 7 I will take you as my own **p**, and I
8: 23 make a distinction between my **p** and your **p**.
15: 13 will lead the **p** you have redeemed.
19: 8 The **p** all responded together,
24: 3 told the **p** all the LORD's words
32: 1 When the **p** saw that Moses was so
32: 9 "and they are a stiff-necked **p**.
33: 13 that this nation is your **p**."
Lev 9: 7 atonement for yourself and the **p**;
16: 24 for himself and for the **p**.
26: 12 be your God, and you will be my **p**.
Nu 11: 11 the burden of all these **p** on me?
14: 11 "How long will these **p** treat me
14: 19 forgive the sin of these **p**, just as
22: 5 "A **p** has come out of Egypt;
Dt 4: 6 is a wise and understanding **p**."
4: 20 be the **p** of his inheritance, as you
5: 28 "I have heard what this **p** said
7: 6 you are a **p** holy to the LORD your
26: 18 declared this day that you are his **p**,
31: 7 must go with this **p** into the land
31: 16 and these **p** will soon prostitute
32: 9 For the LORD's portion is his **p**,
32: 43 atonement for his land and **p**.
33: 29 like you, a **p** saved by the LORD?
Jos 1: 6 because you will lead these **p**
24: 24 And the **p** said to Joshua, "We will
Jdg 2: 7 The **p** served the LORD
Ru 1: 16 Your **p** will be my **p** and your God
1Sa 8: 7 to all that the **p** are saying to you;
12: 22 the LORD will not reject his **p**,
16: 7 **P** look at the outward appearance,
2Sa 5: 2 'You will shepherd my **p** Israel,
7: 10 Wicked **p** will not oppress them
1Ki 3: 8 a great **p**, too numerous to count
8: 30 of your **p** Israel when they pray
8: 56 to his **p** Israel just as he promised.
18: 39 When all the **p** saw this, they fell
2Ki 23: 3 all the **p** pledged themselves
1Ch 17: 21 And who is like your **p** Israel—
17: 21 out to redeem a **p** for himself,
29: 17 how willingly your **p** who are here
2Ch 2: 11 "Because the LORD loves his **p**,
7: 5 and all the **p** dedicated the temple
7: 14 if my **p**, who are called by my
30: 6 "**P** of Israel, return to the LORD,
36: 16 LORD was aroused against his **p**
Ezr 2: 1 these are the **p** of the province
3: 1 the **p** assembled together as one
Ne 1: 10 They are your servants and your **p**,
4: 6 the **p** worked with all their heart.
8: 1 all the **p** came together as one
Est 3: 6 a way to destroy all Mordecai's **p**,
Job 12: 2 you are the only **p** who matter,
Ps 29: 11 The LORD gives strength to his **p**;
30: 4 of the LORD, you his faithful **p**;
31: 23 Love the LORD, all his faithful **p**!
33: 12 the **p** he chose for his inheritance.
50: 4 the earth, that he may judge his **p**:
53: 6 When God restores his **p**, let Jacob
81: 13 "If my **p** would only listen to me,
94: 14 For the LORD will not reject his **p**;
95: 7 and we are the **p** of his pasture,
95: 10 said, 'They are a **p** whose hearts go
125: 2 LORD surrounds his **p** both now
133: 1 it is when God's **p** live together
135: 14 For the LORD will vindicate his **p**
144: 15 blessed is the **p** whose God is
149: 1 in the assembly of his faithful **p**.
149: 5 Let his faithful **p** rejoice in this
Pr 14: 34 a nation, but sin condemns any **p**.
29: 2 the righteous thrive, the **p** rejoice;
29: 18 is no revelation, **p** cast off restraint;
Isa 1: 3 know, my **p** do not understand."
1: 4 nation, a **p** whose guilt is great,
5: 13 Therefore my **p** will go into exile
6: 10 Make the heart of this **p** calloused;
9: 2 The **p** walking in darkness have
11: 12 he will assemble the scattered **p**
19: 25 "Blessed be Egypt my **p**,
29: 13 "These **p** come near to me
40: 1 comfort my **p**, says your God.
40: 5 and all **p** will see it together.
40: 7 Surely the **p** are grass.
42: 6 you to be a covenant for the **p**
49: 13 For the LORD comforts his **p**
51: 4 "Listen to me, my **p**; hear me,
52: 6 Therefore my **p** will know my
53: 8 of my **p** he was punished.
60: 21 Then all your **p** will be righteous
62: 12 They will be called the Holy **P**,
65: 23 for they will be a **p** blessed
Jer 2: 11 **p** have exchanged their glorious
2: 13 "My **p** have committed two sins:
2: 32 Yet my **p** have forgotten me,
4: 22 "My **p** are fools; they do not know
5: 14 and these **p** the wood it consumes.
5: 31 and my **p** love it this way.
7: 16 not pray for this **p** nor offer any
7: 23 be your God and you will be my **p**.
18: 15 Yet my **p** have forgotten me;
30: 3 'when I will bring my **p** Israel
Eze 13: 23 I will save my **p** from your hands.
36: 8 branches and fruit for my **p** Israel,
36: 28 you will be my **p**, and I will be your
36: 38 cities be filled with flocks of **p**.
37: 11 these bones are the **p** of Israel.
37: 13 you, my **p**, will know that I am
38: 14 day, when my **p** Israel are living
39: 7 my holy name among my **p** Israel.
Da 7: 18 But the holy **p** of the Most High
7: 27 to the holy **p** of the Most High.
8: 24 those who are mighty, the holy **p**.
9: 19 city and your **p** bear your Name."
9: 24 'sevens' are decreed for your **p**
9: 26 The **p** of the ruler who will come
10: 14 will happen to your **p** in the future,
11: 32 but the **p** who know their God will
12: 1 great prince who protects your **p**,
Hos 1: 10 'You are not my **p**,' they will be
2: 23 say to those called 'Not my **p**,' 'You are my **p**';
4: 14 a **p** without understanding will
Joel 2: 18 for his land and took pity on his **p**.
3: 16 LORD will be a refuge for his **p**,
Am 9: 14 I will bring my **p** Israel back
Mic 6: 2 the LORD has a case against his **p**;
7: 14 Shepherd your **p** with your staff,
Hag 1: 12 And the **p** feared the LORD.
Zec 2: 11 in that day and will become my **p**.
8: 7 "I will save my **p**
13: 9 'They are my **p**,' and they will say,
Mt 4: 19 I will send you out to fish for **p**."
23: 5 "Everything they do is done for **p**
Mk 5: 19 "Go home to your own **p** and tell
7: 6 "'These **p** honor me with their
8: 27 asked them, "Who do **p** say I am?"
Lk 1: 17 to make ready a **p** prepared
1: 68 because he has come to his **p**
Lk 2: 10 will cause great joy for all the **p**.
3: 6 all **p** will see God's salvation.'"
6: 22 Blessed are you when **p** hate you,
21: 23 the land and wrath against this **p**.
Jn 2: 24 himself to them, for he knew all **p**.
3: 19 **p** loved darkness instead of light
11: 50 one man die for the **p** than
12: 32 earth, will draw all **p** to myself."
18: 14 be good if one man died for the **p**.
Ac 15: 14 to choose a **p** for his name
18: 10 because I have many **p** in this city."
Ro 1: 18 godlessness and wickedness of **p**,
5: 12 and in this way death came to all **p**,
8: 27 for God's **p** in accordance
9: 3 from Christ for the sake of my **p**,
9: 25 call them 'my **p**' who are not my **p**;
11: 1 I ask then: Did God reject his **p**?
15: 10 you Gentiles, with his **p**."
1Co 6: 2 the Lord's **p** will judge the world?
9: 22 I have become all things to all **p** so
2Co 6: 16 their God, and they will be my **p**."
Eph 1: 15 Jesus and your love for all God's **p**,
1: 18 glorious inheritance in his holy **p**,
4: 8 captives and gave gifts to his **p**."
5: 3 are improper for God's holy **p**.
6: 18 keep on praying for all the Lord's **p**.
1Th 5: 26 Greet all God's **p** with a holy kiss.
1Ti 2: 4 who wants all **p** to be saved
2: 6 gave himself as a ransom for all **p**.
4: 10 God, who is the Savior of all **p**,
2Ti 2: 2 entrust to reliable **p** who will also
Titus 2: 11 that offers salvation to all **p**.
2: 14 himself a **p** that are his very own,
Phm : 7 refreshed the hearts of the Lord's **p**.
Heb 2: 17 atonement for the sins of the **p**.
4: 9 a Sabbath-rest for the **p** of God;
5: 1 priest is selected from among the **p**
5: 3 sins, as well as for the sins of the **p**.
9: 27 Just as **p** are destined to die once,
10: 30 again, "The Lord will judge his **p**."
11: 25 with the **p** of God rather than
13: 12 make the **p** holy through his own
1Pe 2: 9 But you are a chosen **p**, a royal
2: 10 Once you were not a **p**, but now you are the **p** of God;
2Pe 2: 1 also false prophets among the **p**,
3: 11 what kind of **p** ought you to be?
Rev 5: 8 which are the prayers of God's **p**.
18: 4 my **p**,' so that you will not share
19: 8 the righteous acts of God's holy **p**.)
21: 3 dwelling place is now among the **p**,
21: 3 They will be his **p**, and God
PEOPLE'S (PEOPLE)
Isa 25: 8 he will remove his **p** disgrace
Jer 10: 23 that **p** lives are not their own;
PEOPLES (PEOPLE)
Ge 17: 16 kings of **p** will come from her."
25: 23 and two **p** from within you will be
27: 29 serve you and **p** bow down to you.
28: 3 you become a community of **p**.
48: 4 I will make you a community of **p**,
Dt 14: 2 of all the **p** on the face of the earth,
28: 10 all the **p** on earth will see that you
32: 8 up boundaries for the **p** according
Jos 4: 24 all the **p** of the earth might know
1Ki 8: 43 all the **p** of the earth may know
2Ch 7: 20 an object of ridicule among all **p**.
Ps 9: 8 and judges the **p** with equity.
67: 5 may all the **p** praise you.
87: 6 will write in the register of the **p**:
96: 10 he will judge the **p** with equity.
Isa 2: 4 and will settle disputes for many **p**.
17: 12 Woe to the **p** who roar—
25: 6 a feast of rich food for all **p**,
34: 1 pay attention, you **p**!
55: 4 I have made him a witness to the **p**,
Jer 10: 3 the practices of the **p** are worthless;
Da 7: 14 **p** of every language worshiped him
Mic 4: 1 the hills, and **p** will stream to it.
4: 3 He will judge between many **p**
5: 7 the midst of many **p** like dew
Zep 3: 9 Then I will purify the lips of the **p**,
3: 20 praise among all the **p** of the earth
Zec 8: 20 "Many **p** and the inhabitants
12: 2 all the surrounding **p** reeling.

Rev 10: 11 prophesy again about many **p**,
17: 15 prostitute sits, are **p**, multitudes,

PEOR
Nu 25: 3 yoked themselves to the Baal of **P**.
Dt 4: 3 who followed the Baal of **P**,

PERCEIVE (PERCEIVING)
Ps 139: 2 you **p** my thoughts from afar.
Pr 24: 12 not he who weighs the heart **p** it?

PERCEIVING* (PERCEIVE)
Isa 6: 9 be ever seeing, but never **p**.'
Mt 13: 14 you will be ever seeing but never **p**.
Mk 4: 12 may be ever seeing but never **p**,
Ac 28: 26 will be ever seeing but never **p**."

PERFECT* (PERFECTER PERFECTING PERFECTION)
Dt 32: 4 his works are **p**, and all his ways
2Sa 22: 31 "As for God, his way is **p**:
Job 36: 4 one who has **p** knowledge is
37: 16 of him who has **p** knowledge?
Ps 18: 30 As for God, his way is **p**:
19: 7 The law of the LORD is **p**,
50: 2 Zion, **p** in beauty, God shines
64: 6 say, "We have devised a **p** plan!"
SS 6: 9 but my dove, my **p** one, is unique,
Isa 25: 1 for in **p** faithfulness you have done
26: 3 in **p** peace those whose minds are
Eze 16: 14 had given you made your beauty **p**,
27: 3 say, Tyre, "I am **p** in beauty."
28: 12 full of wisdom and **p** in beauty.
Mt 5: 48 Be **p**, therefore, as your heavenly Father is **p**.
19: 21 answered, "If you want to be **p**, go,
Ro 12: 2 his good, pleasing and **p** will.
2Co 12: 9 my power is made **p** in weakness."
Col 3: 14 binds them all together in **p** unity.
Heb 2: 10 of their salvation **p** through what
5: 9 made **p**, he became the source
7: 19 (for the law made nothing **p**),
7: 28 Son, who has been made **p** forever.
9: 11 more **p** tabernacle that is not made
10: 1 make **p** those who draw near
10: 14 he has made **p** forever those who
11: 40 with us would they be made **p**.
12: 23 the spirits of the righteous made **p**,
Jas 1: 17 good and **p** gift is from above,
1: 25 looks intently into the **p** law
3: 2 never at fault in what they say is **p**,
1Jn 4: 18 But **p** love drives out fear,
4: 18 The one who fears is not made **p**

PERFECTER* (PERFECT)
Heb 12: 2 on Jesus, the pioneer and **p** of faith.

PERFECTING* (PERFECT)
2Co 7: 1 **p** holiness out of reverence for God

PERFECTION* (PERFECT)
Ps 119: 96 To all **p** I see a limit, but your
La 2: 15 city that was called the **p** of beauty,
Eze 27: 4 builders brought your beauty to **p**.
27: 11 they brought your beauty to **p**.
28: 12 "'You were the seal of **p**,
43: 10 Let them consider its **p**,
Heb 7: 11 **p** could have been attained

PERFORM (PERFORMED PERFORMS)
Ex 3: 20 wonders that I will **p** among them.
2Sa 7: 23 to **p** great and awesome wonders
Jn 3: 2 For no one could **p** the signs you

PERFORMED (PERFORM)
Mt 11: 21 that were **p** in you had been **p**
Jn 10: 41 "Though John never **p** a sign,

PERFORMS (PERFORM)
Ps 77: 14 You are the God who **p** miracles;

PERFUME
Ecc 7: 1 A good name is better than fine **p**,
SS 1: 3 your name is like **p** poured out.
Mk 14: 3 jar and poured the **p** on his head.

PERIL
2Co 1: 10 delivered us from such a deadly **p**,

PERISH (PERISHABLE PERISHED PERISHES PERISHING)
Ge 6: 17 in it. Everything on earth will **p**.
Est 4: 16 is against the law. And if I **p**, I **p**."
Ps 37: 20 But the wicked will **p**:
73: 27 Those who are far from you will **p**;
102: 26 They will **p**, but you remain;
Pr 11: 10 the wicked **p**, there are shouts
19: 9 and whoever pours out lies will **p**.
21: 28 A false witness will **p**, but a careful
28: 28 but when the wicked **p**,
Isa 1: 28 who forsake the LORD will **p**.
29: 14 the wisdom of the wise will **p**,
60: 12 that will not serve you will **p**;
Zec 11: 9 the dying die, and the perishing **p**.
Mt 18: 14 any of these little ones should **p**.
Lk 13: 3 you repent, you too will all **p**.
13: 5 you repent, you too will all **p**."
21: 18 But not a hair of your head will **p**.
Jn 3: 16 believes in him shall not **p**
10: 28 eternal life, and they shall never **p**;
Ro 2: 12 law will also **p** apart from the law,
Col 2: 22 that are all destined to **p** with use,
2Th 2: 10 They **p** because they refused to
Heb 1: 11 They will **p**, but you remain;
1Pe 1: 4 an inheritance that can never **p**,
2Pe 3: 9 you, not wanting anyone to **p**,

PERISHABLE (PERISH)
1Co 15: 42 The body that is sown is **p**, it is
1Pe 1: 18 was not with **p** things such as silver
1: 23 not of **p** seed, but of imperishable,

PERISHED (PERISH)
Ps 119: 92 I would have **p** in my affliction.

PERISHES (PERISH)
Job 8: 13 so **p** the hope of the godless.
1Pe 1: 7 which **p** even though refined

PERISHING (PERISH)
1Co 1: 18 is foolishness to those who are **p**,
2Co 2: 15 being saved and those who are **p**.
4: 3 it is veiled to those who are **p**.

PERJURERS* (PERJURY)
Mal 3: 5 adulterers and **p**, against those who
1Ti 1: 10 for slave traders and liars and **p**—

PERJURY* (PERJURERS)
Jer 7: 9 commit adultery and **p**, burn

PERMANENT
Heb 7: 24 lives forever, he has a **p** priesthood.

PERMIT (PERMITTED)
Hos 5: 4 "Their deeds do not **p** them
1Ti 2: 12 I do not **p** a woman to teach

PERMITTED (PERMIT)
Mt 19: 8 "Moses **p** you to divorce your
2Co 12: 4 things that no one is **p** to tell.

PERSECUTE (PERSECUTED PERSECUTION PERSECUTIONS)
Mt 5: 11 **p** you and falsely say all kinds
5: 44 and pray for those who **p** you,
Jn 15: 20 persecuted me, they will **p** you
Ac 9: 4 "Saul, Saul, why do you **p** me?"
Ro 12: 14 Bless those who **p** you; bless and

PERSECUTED (PERSECUTE)
Ps 119: 86 me, for I am being **p** without cause.
Mt 5: 10 Blessed are those who are **p**
5: 12 same way they **p** the prophets who
Jn 15: 20 If they **p** me, they will persecute
1Co 4: 12 when we are **p**, we endure it;
15: 9 because I **p** the church of God.
2Co 4: 9 **p**, but not abandoned;
1Th 3: 4 telling you that we would be **p**.
2Ti 3: 12 godly life in Christ Jesus will be **p**,
Heb 11: 37 destitute, **p** and mistreated—

PERSECUTION (PERSECUTE)
Mt 13: 21 or **p** comes because of the word,
Ro 8: 35 trouble or hardship or **p** or famine

PERSECUTIONS* (PERSECUTE)
Mk 10: 30 along with **p**—and in the age
2Co 12: 10 in hardships, in **p**, in difficulties.
2Th 1: 4 faith in all the **p** and trials you are
2Ti 3: 11 **p**, sufferings—what kinds of things
3: 11 and Lystra, the **p** I endured.

PERSEVERANCE* (PERSEVERE)
Ro 5: 3 we know that suffering produces **p**;
5: 4 **p**, character; and character, hope.
2Th 1: 4 churches we boast about your **p**
3: 5 into God's love and Christ's **p**.
Heb 12: 1 let us run with **p** the race marked
Jas 1: 3 testing of your faith produces **p**.
1: 4 Let **p** finish its work so that you
5: 11 You have heard of Job's **p** and have
2Pe 1: 6 and to self-control, **p**; and to **p**,
Rev 2: 2 deeds, your hard work and your **p**.
2: 19 your service and **p**, and that you

PERSEVERE* (PERSEVERANCE PERSEVERED PERSEVERES PERSEVERING)
1Ti 4: 16 **P** in them, because if you do,
Heb 10: 36 You need to **p** so that when you

PERSEVERED* (PERSEVERE)
2Co 12: 12 I **p** in demonstrating among you
Heb 11: 27 he **p** because he saw him who is
Jas 5: 11 count as blessed those who have **p**.
Rev 2: 3 You have **p** and have endured

PERSEVERES* (PERSEVERE)
1Co 13: 7 trusts, always hopes, always **p**.
Jas 1: 12 one who **p** under trial because,

PERSEVERING* (PERSEVERE)
Lk 8: 15 retain it, and by **p** produce a crop.

PERSIANS
Da 6: 15 law of the Medes and **P** no decree

PERSISTENCE*
Ro 2: 7 those who by **p** in doing good seek

PERSUADE (PERSUADED PERSUASIVE)
Ac 18: 4 trying to **p** Jews and Greeks.
28: 23 the Prophets he tried to **p** them
2Co 5: 11 to fear the Lord, we try to **p** others.

PERSUADED (PERSUADE)
Ro 4: 21 being fully **p** that God had power

PERSUASIVE (PERSUADE)
1Co 2: 4 were not with wise and **p** words,

PERVERSION* (PERVERT)
Lev 18: 23 sexual relations with it; that is a **p**.
20: 12 What they have done is a **p**;
Jude : 7 up to sexual immorality and **p**.

PERVERT (PERVERSION PERVERTED)
Ex 23: 2 do not **p** justice by siding
Dt 16: 19 Do not **p** justice or show partiality.
Job 34: 12 that the Almighty would **p** justice.
Pr 17: 23 in secret to **p** the course of justice.
Gal 1: 7 are trying to **p** the gospel of Christ.

PERVERTED (PERVERT)
1Sa 8: 3 and accepted bribes and **p** justice.

PESTILENCE (PESTILENCES)
Ps 91: 6 the **p** that stalks in the darkness,

PESTILENCES* (PESTILENCE)
Lk 21: 11 famines and **p** in various places,

PETER
Apostle, brother of Andrew, also called Simon (Mt 10:2; Mk 3:16; Lk 6:14; Ac 1:13), and Cephas (Jn 1:42). Confession of Christ (Mt 16:13–20; Mk 8:27–30; Lk 9:18–27). At transfiguration (Mt 17:1–8; Mk 9:2–8; Lk 9:28–36; 2Pe 1:16–18). Caught fish with coin (Mt 17:24–27). Disowning of Jesus predicted (Mt 26:31–35; Mk 14:27–31; Lk 22:31–34; Jn 13:31–38). Disowned Jesus (Mt 26:69–75; Mk 14:66–72; Lk 22:54–62; Jn 18:15–27). Commissioned by Jesus to shepherd his flock (Jn 21:15–23).

Speech at Pentecost (Ac 2). Healed beggar (Ac 3:1–10). Speech at temple (Ac 3:11–26), before Sanhedrin (Ac 4:1–22). In Samaria (Ac 8:14–25). Sent by vision to Cornelius (Ac 10). Announced salvation of Gentiles in Jerusalem (Ac 11; 15). Freed from prison (Ac 12). Inconsistency at Antioch (Gal 2:11–21). At Jerusalem council (Ac 15).

Epistles: 1 and 2 Peter.

PETITION (PETITIONS)
Php 4: 6 by prayer and **p**, with thanksgiving,

PETITIONS (PETITION)
Heb 5: 7 up prayers and **p** with fervent cries

PHANTOM*
Ps 39: 6 goes around like a mere **p**;

PHARAOH (PHARAOH'S)
Ge 12: 15 they praised her to **P**, and she was
41: 14 So **P** sent for Joseph, and he was
Ex 14: 4 gain glory for myself through **P**
14: 17 I will gain glory through **P** and all

PHARAOH'S (PHARAOH)
Ex 7: 3 But I will harden **P** heart,

PHARISEE (PHARISEES)
Jn 3: 1 Now there was a **P**, a man named
Ac 23: 6 am a **P**, descended from Pharisees.
Php 3: 5 in regard to the law, a **P**;

PHARISEES (PHARISEE)
Mt 5: 20 surpasses that of the **P**
16: 6 guard against the yeast of the **P**
23: 13 you, teachers of the law and **P**,

PHILADELPHIA
Rev 3: 7 the angel of the church in **P** write:

PHILEMON*
Phm : 1 To **P** our dear friend and fellow

PHILIP
1. Apostle (Mt 10:3; Mk 3:18; Lk 6:14; Jn 1:43–48; 14:8; Ac 1:13).
2. Deacon (Ac 6:1–7); evangelist in Samaria (Ac 8:4–25), to Ethiopian (Ac 8:26–40).

PHILIPPI
Ac 16: 12 From there we traveled to **P**,
Php 1: 1 holy people in Christ Jesus at **P**,

PHILISTINE (PHILISTINES)
Jos 13: 3 held by the five **P** rulers in Gaza,
1Sa 14: 1 let's go over to the **P** outpost
17: 26 Who is this uncircumcised **P** that
17: 37 rescue me from the hand of this **P**."

PHILISTINES (PHILISTINE)
Jdg 10: 7 sold them into the hands of the **P**
13: 1 the hands of the **P** for forty years.
16: 5 The rulers of the **P** went to her
1Sa 4: 1 went out to fight against the **P**.
5: 8 together all the rulers of the **P**
13: 23 Now a detachment of **P** had gone
17: 1 Now the **P** gathered their forces
23: 1 the **P** are fighting against Keilah
27: 1 do is to escape to the land of the **P**.
31: 1 Now the **P** fought against Israel;
2Sa 5: 17 When the **P** heard that David had
8: 1 David defeated the **P** and subdued
21: 15 with his men to fight against the **P**,
2Ki 18: 8 he defeated the **P**, as far as Gaza
Am 1: 8 till the last of the **P** are dead,"

PHILOSOPHER* (PHILOSOPHY)
1Co 1: 20 Where is the **p** of this age?

PHILOSOPHY* (PHILOSOPHER)
Col 2: 8 through hollow and deceptive **p**,

PHINEHAS
Nu 25: 7 When **P** son of Eleazar, the son
Ps 106: 30 But **P** stood up and intervened,

PHOEBE*
Ro 16: 1 I commend to you our sister **P**,

PHYLACTERIES*
Mt 23: 5 They make their **p** wide

PHYSICAL*
Da 1: 4 young men without any **p** defect,
Ro 2: 28 merely outward and **p**.
9: 8 not the children by **p** descent who
Col 1: 22 by Christ's **p** body through death
1Ti 4: 8 For **p** training is of some value,
Jas 2: 16 does nothing about their **p** needs,

PICK (PICKED)
Mk 16: 18 *they will **p** up snakes with their*

PICKED (PICK)
Lk 14: 7 noticed how the guests **p** the places
Jn 5: 9 he **p** up his mat and walked.

PIECE (PIECES)
Jn 19: 23 in one **p** from top to bottom.

PIECES (PIECE)
Ge 15: 17 and passed between the **p**.
Jer 34: 18 two and then walked between its **p**.
Zec 11: 12 So they paid me thirty **p** of silver.
Mt 14: 20 of broken **p** that were left over.

PIERCE (PIERCED)
Ex 21: 6 doorpost and **p** his ear with an awl.
Ps 22: 16 they **p** my hands and my feet.
Pr 12: 18 words of the reckless **p** like swords,
Lk 2: 35 a sword will **p** your own soul too."

PIERCED (PIERCE)
Isa 53: 5 he was **p** for our transgressions,
Zec 12: 10 the one they have **p**, and they will
Jn 19: 37 will look on the one they have **p**."
Rev 1: 7 see him, even those who **p** him";

PIGEONS
Lev 5: 11 afford two doves or two young **p**,
Lk 2: 24 "a pair of doves or two young **p**."

PIG'S* (PIGS)
Pr 11: 22 in a **p** snout is a beautiful woman
Isa 66: 3 is like one who presents **p** blood,

PIGS (PIG'S)
Mt 7: 6 do not throw your pearls to **p**.
Mk 5: 11 A large herd of **p** was feeding

PILATE
Governor of Judea. Questioned Jesus (Mt 27:1–26; Mk 15:15; Lk 22:66—23:25; Jn 18:28—19:16); sent him to Herod (Lk 23:6–12); consented to his crucifixion when crowds chose Barabbas (Mt 27:15–26; Mk 15:6–15; Lk 23:13–25; Jn 19:1–10).

PILLAR (PILLARS)
Ge 19: 26 back, and she became a **p** of salt.
Ex 13: 21 in a **p** of cloud to guide them
13: 21 by night in a **p** of fire to give
1Ti 3: 15 the **p** and foundation of the truth.
Rev 3: 12 who is victorious I will make a **p**

PILLARS (PILLAR)
Gal 2: 9 those esteemed as **p**, gave me

PIPE
Ps 150: 4 praise him with the strings and **p**,
Mt 11: 17 "'We played the **p** for you,
1Co 14: 7 sounds, such as the **p** or harp,

PISGAH
Dt 3: 27 Go up to the top of **P** and look

PIT
Ps 7: 15 out falls into the **p** they have made.
40: 2 He lifted me out of the slimy **p**,
103: 4 who redeems your life from the **p**
Pr 23: 27 an adulterous woman is a deep **p**,
26: 27 Whoever digs a **p** will fall into it;
Isa 24: 17 Terror and **p** and snare await you,
38: 17 kept me from the **p** of destruction;
Mt 15: 14 the blind, both will fall into a **p**."

PITCH
Ge 6: 14 it and coat it with **p** inside and out.
Ex 2: 3 him and coated it with tar and **p**.

PITIED* (PITY)
1Co 15: 19 we are of all people most to be **p**.

PITY (PITIED)
Ps 72: 13 He will take **p** on the weak
Ecc 4: 10 But **p** anyone who falls and has no
Lk 10: 33 he saw him, he took **p** on him.

PLAGUE (PLAGUED PLAGUES)
2Ch 6: 28 famine or **p** comes to the land,
Ps 91: 6 nor the **p** that destroys at midday.

PLAGUED* (PLAGUE)
Ps 73: 5 they are not **p** by human ills.

PLAGUES (PLAGUE)
Hos 13: 14 Where, O death, are your **p**?
Rev 21: 9 bowls full of the seven last **p** came
22: 18 the **p** described in this scroll.

PLAIN
Isa 40: 4 level, the rugged places a **p**.
Ro 1: 19 be known about God is **p** to them,

PLAN (PLANNED PLANS)
Ex 26: 30 according to the **p** shown you
Pr 14: 22 those who **p** what is good find love
21: 30 no **p** that can succeed against
Isa 28: 29 Almighty, whose **p** is wonderful,
Am 3: 7 nothing without revealing his **p**
Eph 1: 11 to the **p** of him who works

PLANK
Mt 7: 3 attention to the **p** in your own eye?
Lk 6: 41 attention to the **p** in your own eye?

PLANNED (PLAN)
Ps 17: 3 you will find that I have **p** no evil;
40: 5 have done, the things you **p** for us.
Isa 14: 24 "Surely, as I have **p**, so it will be,
23: 9 The LORD Almighty **p** it, to bring
46: 11 what I have **p**, that I will do.
Heb 11: 40 since God had **p** something better

PLANS (PLAN)
Job 38: 2 obscures my **p** with words without
42: 3 obscures my **p** without knowledge?
Ps 20: 4 heart and make all your **p** succeed.
33: 11 But the **p** of the LORD stand firm
94: 11 The LORD knows all human **p**;
107: 11 despised the **p** of the Most High.
Pr 15: 22 **P** fail for lack of counsel,
16: 3 do, and he will establish your **p**.
19: 21 Many are the **p** in a person's heart,
20: 18 **P** are established by seeking advice;
Isa 29: 15 to hide their **p** from the LORD,
30: 1 those who carry out **p** that are not
32: 8 But the noble make noble **p**,
2Co 1: 17 I make my **p** in a worldly manner

PLANT (PLANTED PLANTING PLANTS)
Jnh 4: 6 the LORD God provided a leafy **p**
Am 9: 15 I will **p** Israel in their own land,
Mt 15: 13 "Every **p** that my heavenly Father

PLANTED (PLANT)
Ge 2: 8 the LORD God had **p** a garden
Ps 1: 3 person is like a tree **p** by streams
Jer 17: 8 They will be like a tree **p**
Mt 15: 13 Father has not **p** will be pulled
21: 33 was a landowner who **p** a vineyard.
1Co 3: 6 I **p** the seed, Apollos watered it,
Jas 1: 21 humbly accept the word **p** in you,

PLANTING (PLANT)
Isa 61: 3 a **p** of the LORD for the display

PLANTS (PLANT)
Pr 31: 16 of her earnings she **p** a vineyard.
1Co 3: 7 neither the one who **p** nor the one
9: 7 Who **p** a vineyard and does not eat

PLATTER
Mk 6: 25 head of John the Baptist on a **p**."

PLAY (PLAYED)
1Sa 16: 23 would take up his lyre and **p**.
Isa 11: 8 The infant will **p** near the cobra's

PLAYED (PLAY)
Lk 7: 32 "'We **p** the pipe for you, and you
1Co 14: 7 what tune is being **p** unless there is

PLEA (PLEAD PLEADED PLEADS)
1Ki 8: 28 prayer and his **p** for mercy,
Ps 102: 17 he will not despise their **p**.
La 3: 56 You heard my **p**: "Do not close

PLEAD (PLEA)
Isa 1: 17 **p** the case of the widow.
Mal 1: 9 **p** with God to be gracious to us.

PLEADED (PLEA)
2Co 12: 8 Three times I **p** with the Lord

PLEADS (PLEA)
Job 16: 21 of a man he **p** with God as one **p**

PLEASANT (PLEASE)
Ge 49: 15 resting place and how **p** is his land,
Ps 16: 6 lines have fallen for me in **p** places;
133: 1 and **p** it is when God's people live
135: 3 praise to his name, for that is **p**.
147: 1 how **p** and fitting to praise him!
Pr 2: 10 knowledge will be **p** to your soul.
3: 17 Her ways are **p** ways, and all her
Isa 30: 10 Tell us **p** things, prophesy illusions.
Jer 3: 19 my children and give you a **p** land,
1Th 3: 6 you always have **p** memories of us
Heb 12: 11 No discipline seems **p** at the time,

PLEASANTNESS* (PLEASE)
Pr 27: 9 the **p** of a friend springs from their

PLEASE (PLEASANT PLEASANTNESS PLEASED PLEASES PLEASING PLEASURE PLEASURES)
Ps 69: 31 This will **p** the LORD more than
Pr 20: 23 and dishonest scales do not **p** him.
21: 1 he channels toward all who **p** him.
Isa 46: 10 will stand, and I will do all that I **p**.'
Jer 6: 20 your sacrifices do not **p** me."
27: 5 on it, and I give it to anyone I **p**.
Jn 5: 30 for I seek not to **p** myself but him
Ro 8: 8 realm of the flesh cannot **p** God.
15: 1 of the weak and not to **p** ourselves.
15: 2 Each of us should **p** our neighbors
1Co 7: 32 how he can **p** the Lord.
10: 33 even as I try to **p** everyone in every

2Co 5: 9 So we make it our goal to **p** him,
Gal 1: 10 Or am I trying to **p** people?
6: 8 Whoever sows to **p** their flesh,
6: 8 whoever sows to **p** the Spirit,
Col 1: 10 the Lord and **p** him in every way:
1Th 2: 4 We are not trying to **p** people
4: 1 you how to live in order to **p** God,
2Ti 2: 4 tries to **p** his commanding officer.
Titus 2: 9 to try to **p** them, not to talk back
Heb 11: 6 faith it is impossible to **p** God,

PLEASED (PLEASE)
Dt 28: 63 Just as it **p** the LORD to make you
Jdg 18: 20 The priest was very **p**. He took
1Sa 12: 22 because the LORD was **p** to make
1Ki 3: 10 The Lord was **p** that Solomon had
1Ch 29: 17 the heart and are **p** with integrity.
Ps 5: 4 For you are not a God who is **p**
Mic 6: 7 Will the LORD be **p**
Mal 1: 10 I am not **p** with you,"
Mt 3: 17 with him I am well **p**."
17: 5 whom I love; with him I am well **p**.
Mk 1: 11 with you I am well **p**."
Lk 3: 22 with you I am well **p**."
10: 21 this is what you were **p** to do.
1Co 1: 21 God was **p** through the foolishness
Col 1: 19 God was **p** to have all his fullness
Heb 10: 6 and sin offerings you were not **p**.
10: 8 desire, nor were you **p** with them"
11: 5 commended as one who **p** God.
13: 16 for with such sacrifices God is **p**.
2Pe 1: 17 with him I am well **p**."

PLEASES (PLEASE)
Job 23: 13 He does whatever he **p**.
Ps 115: 3 he does whatever **p** him.
135: 6 The LORD does whatever **p** him,
Pr 15: 8 the prayer of the upright **p** him.
Ecc 2: 26 To the person who **p** him, God
7: 26 The man who **p** God will escape
Da 4: 35 He does as he **p** with the powers
Jn 3: 8 The wind blows wherever it **p**.
8: 29 alone, for I always do what **p** him.
Eph 5: 10 and find out what **p** the Lord.
Col 3: 20 in everything, for this **p** the Lord.
1Ti 2: 3 is good, and **p** God our Savior,
1Jn 3: 22 his commands and do what **p** him.

PLEASING (PLEASE)
Ge 2: 9 trees that were **p** to the eye
Lev 1: 9 offering, an aroma **p** to the LORD.
Ps 19: 14 of my heart be **p** in your sight,
104: 34 May my meditation be **p** to him,
SS 1: 3 **P** is the fragrance of your perfumes
4: 10 How much more **p** is your love
7: 6 How beautiful you are and how **p**,
Ro 12: 1 living sacrifice, holy and **p** to God
14: 18 Christ in this way is **p** to God
Php 4: 18 an acceptable sacrifice, **p** to God.
1Ti 5: 4 grandparents, for this is **p** to God.
Heb 13: 21 he work in us what is **p** to him,

PLEASURE (PLEASE)
Ps 51: 16 do not take **p** in burnt offerings.
147: 10 His **p** is not in the strength
Pr 10: 23 A fool finds **p** in wicked schemes,
16: 7 the LORD takes **p** in anyone's
18: 2 Fools find no **p** in understanding
21: 17 loves **p** will become poor;
Isa 1: 11 I have no **p** in the blood of bulls
Jer 6: 10 they find no **p** in it.
Eze 18: 23 Do I take any **p** in the death
18: 32 For I take no **p** in the death
33: 11 I take no **p** in the death
Eph 1: 5 in accordance with his **p** and will—
1: 9 of his will according to his good **p**,
1Ti 5: 6 for **p** is dead even while she lives.
2Ti 3: 4 lovers of **p** rather than lovers
Heb 10: 38 I take no **p** in the one who shrinks
2Pe 2: 13 Their idea of **p** is to carouse

PLEASURES* (PLEASE)
Ps 16: 11 with eternal **p** at your right hand.
Lk 8: 14 riches and **p**, and they do not
Titus 3: 3 by all kinds of passions and **p**.
Heb 11: 25 than to enjoy the fleeting **p** of sin.
Jas 4: 3 may spend what you get on your **p**.
2Pe 2: 13 reveling in their **p** while they feast

PLEDGE (PLEDGED)
Dt 24: 17 take the cloak of the widow as a **p**.
1Pe 3: 21 the **p** of a clear conscience toward

PLEDGED (PLEDGE)
1Co 7: 27 you **p** to a woman? Do not seek

PLEIADES
Job 38: 31 "Can you bind the chains of the **P**?
Am 5: 8 He who made the **P** and Orion,

PLENTIFUL (PLENTY)
Mt 9: 37 "The harvest is **p** but the workers
Lk 10: 2 "The harvest is **p**, but the workers

PLENTY (PLENTIFUL)
2Co 8: 14 the present time your **p** will supply
Php 4: 12 whether living in **p** or in want.

PLOT (PLOTS)
Est 2: 22 Mordecai found out about the **p**
Ps 2: 1 conspire and the peoples **p** in vain?
Pr 3: 29 Do not **p** harm against your
Zec 8: 17 do not **p** evil against each other,
Ac 4: 25 rage and the peoples **p** in vain?

PLOTS (PLOT)
Pr 6: 14 **p** evil with deceit in his heart—

PLOW (PLOWSHARES)
1Sa 13: 20 Philistines to have their **p** points,
Lk 9: 62 "No one who puts a hand to the **p**

PLOWSHARES* (PLOW)
Isa 2: 4 They will beat their swords into **p**
Joel 3: 10 Beat your **p** into swords and your
Mic 4: 3 They will beat their swords into **p**

PLUCK
Mk 9: 47 eye causes you to stumble, **p** it out.

PLUNDER (PLUNDERED)
Ex 3: 22 And so you will **p** the Egyptians."
Est 3: 13 of Adar, and to **p** their goods.
8: 11 to **p** the property of their enemies.
9: 10 did not lay their hands on the **p**.
Isa 3: 14 the **p** from the poor is in your

PLUNDERED (PLUNDER)
Ps 12: 5 "Because the poor are **p**
Eze 34: 8 so has been **p** and has become food

PLUNGE
1Ti 6: 9 harmful desires that **p** people

PODS
Lk 15: 16 the **p** that the pigs were eating,

POINT
Mt 4: 5 on the highest **p** of the temple.
26: 38 with sorrow to the **p** of death.
Jas 2: 10 yet stumbles at just one **p** is guilty
Rev 2: 10 even to the **p** of death, and I will

POISON
Ps 140: 3 the **p** of vipers is on their lips.
Mk 16: 18 *and when they drink deadly* **p**,
Ro 3: 13 "The **p** of vipers is on their lips."
Jas 3: 8 It is a restless evil, full of deadly **p**.

POLE (POLES)
Nu 21: 8 "Make a snake and put it up on a **p**;
Dt 16: 21 any wooden Asherah **p** beside
21: 23 hung on a **p** is under God's curse.
Est 7: 10 impaled Haman on the **p** he had
Gal 3: 13 is everyone who is hung on a **p**."

POLES (POLE)
Ex 25: 13 Then make **p** of acacia wood

POLISHED
Isa 49: 2 he made me into a **p** arrow

POLLUTE* (POLLUTED POLLUTES)
Nu 35: 33 "'Do not **p** the land where you
Jude : 8 these ungodly people **p** their own

POLLUTED* (POLLUTE)
Ezr 9: 11 is a land **p** by the corruption
Pr 25: 26 a **p** well are the righteous who give
Ac 15: 20 to abstain from food **p** by idols,
Jas 1: 27 oneself from being **p** by the world.

POLLUTES* (POLLUTE)
Nu 35: 33 Bloodshed **p** the land,

PONDER (PONDERED)
Ps 64: 9 of God and **p** what he has done.
107: 43 **p** the loving deeds of the LORD.
119: 95 me, but I will **p** your statutes.

PONDERED (PONDER)
Ps 111: 2 they are **p** by all who delight
Lk 2: 19 things and **p** them in her heart.

POOR (POVERTY)
Lev 19: 10 Leave them for the **p**
23: 22 Leave them for the **p**
27: 8 anyone making the vow is too **p**
Dt 15: 4 need be no **p** people among you,
15: 7 If anyone is **p** among your fellow
15: 11 There will always be **p** people
24: 12 If the neighbor is **p**, do not go
24: 14 of a hired worker who is **p**
Job 5: 16 So the **p** have hope, and injustice
24: 4 and force all the **p** of the land
Ps 14: 6 frustrate the plans of the **p**,
34: 6 This **p** man called, and the LORD
35: 10 You rescue the **p** from those too
40: 17 But as for me, I am **p** and needy;
68: 10 God, you provided for the **p**.
82: 3 uphold the cause of the **p**
112: 9 freely scattered their gifts to the **p**,
113: 7 He raises the **p** from the dust
140: 12 the LORD secures justice for the **p**
Pr 13: 7 another pretends to be **p**, yet has
14: 20 The **p** are shunned even by their
14: 31 oppresses the **p** shows contempt
17: 5 mocks the **p** shows contempt
19: 1 Better the **p** whose walk is
19: 17 Whoever is kind to the **p** lends
19: 22 better to be **p** than a liar.
20: 13 not love sleep or you will grow **p**;
21: 13 their ears to the cry of the **p** will
21: 17 loves pleasure will become **p**;
22: 2 Rich and **p** have this in common:
22: 9 they share their food with the **p**.
22: 22 not exploit the **p** because they are **p**
28: 6 Better the **p** whose walk is
28: 27 who give to the **p** will lack nothing,
29: 7 care about justice for the **p**,
31: 9 the rights of the **p** and needy.
31: 20 She opens her arms to the **p**
Ecc 4: 13 Better a **p** but wise youth than
Isa 3: 14 the plunder from the **p** is in your
10: 2 to deprive the **p** of their rights
14: 30 poorest of the **p** will find pasture,
25: 4 You have been a refuge for the **p**,
32: 7 schemes to destroy the **p** with lies,
61: 1 to proclaim good news to the **p**.
Jer 22: 16 He defended the cause of the **p**
Eze 18: 12 He oppresses the **p** and needy.
Am 2: 7 on the heads of the **p** as on the dust
4: 1 you women who oppress the **p**
5: 11 You levy a straw tax on the **p**
Zec 7: 10 fatherless, the foreigner or the **p**.
Mt 5: 3 "Blessed are the **p** in spirit,
11: 5 good news is proclaimed to the **p**.
19: 21 your possessions and give to the **p**,
26: 11 The **p** you will always have
Mk 12: 42 a **p** widow came and put in two
14: 7 The **p** you will always have
Lk 4: 18 to proclaim good news to the **p**.
6: 20 "Blessed are you who are **p**,
11: 41 generous to the **p**, and everything
14: 13 banquet, invite the **p**, the crippled,
21: 2 also saw a **p** widow put in two very
Jn 12: 8 will always have the **p** among you,
Ac 9: 36 doing good and helping the **p**.
10: 4 and gifts to the **p** have come up as
24: 17 to bring my people gifts for the **p**
Ro 15: 26 for the **p** among the Lord's people
1Co 13: 3 If I give all I possess to the **p**
2Co 6: 10 **p**, yet making many rich;
8: 9 yet for your sake he became **p**,
Gal 2: 10 continue to remember the **p**,
Jas 2: 2 and a **p** man in filthy old clothes
2: 5 not God chosen those who are **p**
2: 6 But you have dishonored the **p**.

POPULATION*
Pr 14: 28 A large **p** is a king's glory,

PORTION
Nu 18: 29 present as the LORD's **p** the best
Dt 32: 9 For the LORD's **p** is his people,
1Sa 1: 5 gave a double **p** because he loved
2Ki 2: 9 "Let me inherit a double **p** of your
Ps 73: 26 of my heart and my **p** forever.

Ps 119: 57 You are my **p**, LORD;
Isa 53: 12 I will give him a **p** among the great,
Jer 10: 16 He who is the **P** of Jacob is not like
La 3: 24 to myself, "The LORD is my **p**;
Zec 2: 12 LORD will inherit Judah as his **p**

PORTRAYED
Gal 3: 1 Christ was clearly **p** as crucified.

POSITION (POSITIONS)
Ro 12: 16 to associate with people of low **p**.
Jas 1: 9 ought to take pride in their high **p**.
2Pe 3: 17 lawless and fall from your secure **p**.

POSITIONS (POSITION)
2Ch 20: 17 Take up your **p**; stand firm and see
Jude : 6 the angels who did not keep their **p**

POSSESS (POSSESSED POSSESSING POSSESSION POSSESSIONS)
Nu 33: 53 for I have given you the land to **p**.
Dt 4: 14 you are crossing the Jordan to **p**.
Pr 8: 12 I **p** knowledge and discretion.

POSSESSED (POSSESS)
Jn 10: 21 the sayings of a man **p** by a demon.

POSSESSING* (POSSESS)
2Co 6: 10 nothing, and yet **p** everything.

POSSESSION (POSSESS)
Ge 15: 7 give you this land to take **p** of it."
Ex 6: 8 I will give it to you as a **p**. I am
19: 5 nations you will be my treasured **p**.
Nu 13: 30 go up and take **p** of the land,
Dt 7: 6 to be his people, his treasured **p**.
Jos 1: 11 take **p** of the land the LORD your
Ps 2: 8 the ends of the earth your **p**.
135: 4 own, Israel to be his treasured **p**.
Eph 1: 14 of those who are God's **p**—
1Pe 2: 9 God's special **p**, that you may

POSSESSIONS (POSSESS)
Mt 19: 21 go, sell your **p** and give to the poor,
Lk 11: 21 his own house, his **p** are safe.
12: 15 not consist in an abundance of **p**."
19: 8 now I give half of my **p** to the poor,
Ac 4: 32 that any of their **p** was their own,
2Co 12: 14 because what I want is not your **p**
Heb 10: 34 yourselves had better and lasting **p**.
1Jn 3: 17 If anyone has material **p** and sees

POSSIBLE
Mt 19: 26 but with God all things are **p**."
26: 39 if it is **p**, may this cup be taken
Mk 9: 23 "Everything is **p** for one who
10: 27 all things are **p** with God."
14: 35 if **p** the hour might pass from him.
Ro 12: 18 If it is **p**, as far as it depends on
1Co 6: 5 Is it **p** that there is nobody among
9: 19 to everyone, to win as many as **p**.
9: 22 by all **p** means I might save some.

POT (POTSHERDS POTTER POTTER'S POTTERY)
2Ki 4: 40 of God, there is death in the **p**!"
Jer 18: 4 the potter formed it into another **p**,

POTIPHAR*
Egyptian who bought Joseph (Ge 37:36), set him over his house (Ge 39:1–6), sent him to prison (Ge 39:7–30).

POTSHERDS (POT)
Isa 45: 9 but **p** among the **p** on the ground.

POTTER (POT)
Isa 29: 16 Can the pot say to the **p**,
45: 9 Does the clay say to the **p**,
64: 8 We are the clay, you are the **p**;
Jer 18: 6 with you, Israel, as this **p** does?"
Zec 11: 13 said to me, "Throw it to the **p**"—
Ro 9: 21 Does not the **p** have the right

POTTER'S (POT)
Mt 27: 7 to buy the **p** field as a burial place

POTTERY (POT)
Ro 9: 21 of clay some **p** for special purposes

POUR (POURED POURS)
Ps 62: 8 **p** out your hearts to him, for God
Isa 44: 3 I will **p** out my Spirit on your
Eze 20: 8 So I said I would **p** out my wrath
39: 29 for I will **p** out my Spirit
Joel 2: 28 I will **p** out my Spirit on all people.
Zec 12: 10 I will **p** out on the house of David
Mal 3: 10 **p** out so much blessing that there
Ac 2: 17 I will **p** out my Spirit on all people.

POURED (POUR)
Ps 22: 14 I am **p** out like water, and all my
Isa 32: 15 till the Spirit is **p** on us
Mt 26: 28 which is **p** out for many
Lk 22: 20 my blood, which is **p** out for you.
Ac 2: 33 and has **p** out what you now see
10: 45 the Holy Spirit had been **p** out
Ro 5: 5 because God's love has been **p**
Php 2: 17 if I am being **p** out like a drink
2Ti 4: 6 am already being **p** out like a drink
Titus 3: 6 whom he **p** out on us generously
Rev 16: 2 and **p** out his bowl on the land,

POURS (POUR)
Lk 5: 37 And no one **p** new wine into old

POVERTY* (POOR)
Dt 28: 48 in nakedness and dire **p**, you will
1Sa 2: 7 The LORD sends **p** and wealth;
Pr 6: 11 and **p** will come on you like a thief
10: 4 Lazy hands make for **p**, but diligent
10: 15 city, but **p** is the ruin of the poor.
11: 24 withholds unduly, but comes to **p**.
13: 18 disregards discipline comes to **p**
14: 23 but mere talk leads only to **p**.
21: 5 profit as surely as haste leads to **p**.
22: 16 gifts to the rich—both come to **p**.
24: 34 and **p** will come on you like a thief
28: 19 fantasies will have their fill of **p**.
28: 22 are unaware that **p** awaits them.
30: 8 give me neither **p** nor riches,
31: 7 forget their **p** and remember their
Ecc 4: 14 born in **p** within his kingdom.
Mk 12: 44 she, out of her **p**, put in everything
Lk 21: 4 she out of her **p** put in all she had
2Co 8: 2 their extreme **p** welled up in rich
8: 9 you through his **p** might become
Rev 2: 9 I know your afflictions and your **p**

POWER (POWERFUL POWERFULLY POWERS)
Ex 15: 6 hand, LORD, was majestic in **p**.
32: 11 brought out of Egypt with great **p**
Dt 8: 17 "My **p** and the strength of my
34: 12 one has ever shown the mighty **p**
1Ch 29: 11 greatness and the **p** and the glory
2Ch 20: 6 **P** and might are in your hand,
32: 7 for there is a greater **p** with us than
Job 9: 4 wisdom is profound, his **p** is vast.
36: 22 "God is exalted in his **p**. Who is
37: 23 beyond our reach and exalted in **p**;
Ps 20: 6 the victorious **p** of his right hand.
62: 11 "**P** belongs to you, God,
63: 2 and beheld your **p** and your glory.
66: 3 great is your **p** that your enemies
68: 34 Proclaim the **p** of God,
77: 14 you display your **p** among
89: 13 Your arm is endowed with **p**;
145: 6 of the **p** of your awesome works—
147: 5 Great is our Lord and mighty in **p**;
150: 2 Praise him for his acts of **p**;
Pr 3: 27 it is due, when it is in your **p** to act.
18: 21 The tongue has the **p** of life
24: 5 The wise prevail through great **p**,
Isa 40: 10 Sovereign LORD comes with **p**,
40: 26 Because of his great **p** and mighty
63: 12 who sent his glorious arm of **p** to
Jer 10: 6 and your name is mighty in **p**.
10: 12 But God made the earth by his **p**;
27: 5 With my great **p** and outstretched
32: 17 and the earth by your great **p**
Hos 13: 14 this people from the **p** of the grave;
Na 1: 3 is slow to anger but great in **p**;
Zec 4: 6 'Not by might nor by **p**, but by my
Mt 22: 29 the Scriptures or the **p** of God.
24: 30 of heaven, with **p** and great glory.
Lk 1: 35 and the **p** of the Most High will
4: 14 to Galilee in the **p** of the Spirit,
9: 1 he gave them **p** and authority
10: 19 to overcome all the **p** of the enemy;
24: 49 until you have been clothed with **p**
Ac 1: 8 you will receive **p** when the Holy
4: 28 They did what your **p** and will had
4: 33 With great **p** the apostles
10: 38 with the Holy Spirit and **p**,
26: 18 and from the **p** of Satan to God,
Ro 1: 16 because it is the **p** of God
1: 20 his eternal **p** and divine nature—
4: 21 that God had **p** to do what he had
9: 17 that I might display my **p** in you
15: 13 hope by the **p** of the Holy Spirit.
15: 19 through the **p** of the Spirit of God.
1Co 1: 17 cross of Christ be emptied of its **p**.
1: 18 us who are being saved it is the **p**
2: 4 a demonstration of the Spirit's **p**,
6: 14 By his **p** God raised the Lord
15: 24 all dominion, authority and **p**.
15: 56 is sin, and the **p** of sin is the law.
2Co 4: 7 this all-surpassing **p** is from God
6: 7 speech and in the **p** of God;
10: 4 they have divine **p** to demolish
12: 9 for you, for my **p** is made perfect
13: 4 yet by God's **p** we will live
Eph 1: 19 his incomparably great **p** for us
3: 16 you with **p** through his Spirit
3: 20 according to his **p** that is at work
6: 10 in the Lord and in his mighty **p**.
Php 3: 10 to know the **p** of his resurrection
3: 21 by the **p** that enables him to bring
Col 1: 11 strengthened with all **p** according
2: 10 He is the head over every **p**
1Th 1: 5 simply with words but also with **p**,
2Ti 1: 7 us timid, but gives us **p**,
3: 5 form of godliness but denying its **p**
Heb 2: 14 by his death he might break the **p** of him who holds the **p** of death—
7: 16 of the **p** of an indestructible life.
1Pe 1: 5 by God's **p** until the coming
2Pe 1: 3 divine **p** has given us everything
Jude : 25 majesty, **p** and authority,
Rev 4: 11 to receive glory and honor and **p**,
5: 12 receive **p** and wealth and wisdom
11: 17 you have taken your great **p**
19: 1 glory and **p** belong to our God,
20: 6 second death has no **p** over them,

POWERFUL (POWER)
2Ch 27: 6 Jotham grew **p** because he walked
Est 9: 4 and he became more and more **p**.
Ps 29: 4 The voice of the LORD is **p**;
Zec 8: 22 **p** nations will come to Jerusalem
Mk 1: 7 me comes the one more **p** than I,
Lk 24: 19 **p** in word and deed before God
2Th 1: 7 in blazing fire with his **p** angels.
Heb 1: 3 sustaining all things by his **p** word.
Jas 5: 16 prayer of a righteous person is **p**

POWERFULLY (POWER)
1Sa 10: 6 Spirit of the LORD will come **p**
10: 10 Spirit of God came **p** upon him,
11: 6 Spirit of God came **p** upon him,
16: 13 of the LORD came **p** upon David.

POWERLESS
Ro 5: 6 when we were still **p**, Christ died
8: 3 what the law was **p** to do because it

POWERS (POWER)
Da 4: 35 as he pleases with the **p** of heaven
Ro 8: 38 present nor the future, nor any **p**,
1Co 12: 10 to another miraculous **p**,
Eph 6: 12 against the **p** of this dark world
Col 1: 16 whether thrones or **p** or rulers
2: 15 And having disarmed the **p**
Heb 6: 5 of God and the **p** of the coming age
1Pe 3: 22 and **p** in submission to him.

PRACTICE (PRACTICED PRACTICES)
Lev 19: 26 "'Do not **p** divination or seek
Ps 119: 56 This has been my **p**: I obey your
Eze 33: 31 but they do not put them into **p**.
Mt 7: 24 **p** is like a wise man who built his
23: 3 for they do not **p** what they preach.
Lk 8: 21 hear God's word and put it into **p**."
Ro 12: 13 who are in need. **P** hospitality.
Php 4: 9 me, or seen in me—put it into **p**.
1Ti 5: 4 put their religion into **p** by caring

PRACTICED (PRACTICE)
Mt 23: 23 You should have **p** the latter,

PRACTICES (PRACTICE)
Ps 101: 7 No one who **p** deceit will dwell
Mt 5: 19 but whoever **p** and teaches these
Col 3: 9 taken off your old self with its **p**

PRAISE (PRAISED PRAISES PRAISEWORTHY PRAISING)
Ex 15: 2 and I will **p** him, my father's God,
Dt 10: 21 is the one you **p**; he is your God,
26: 19 declared that he will set you in **p**,
32: 3 Oh, **p** the greatness of our God!
Ru 4: 14 "**P** be to the LORD, who this day
2Sa 22: 4 who is worthy of **p**, and have been
22: 47 **P** be to my Rock!
1Ki 8: 33 to you and give **p** to your name,
8: 35 this place and give **p** to your name
1Ch 16: 8 Give **p** to the LORD, proclaim his
16: 25 the LORD and most worthy of **p**;
16: 35 holy name, and glory in your **p**."
23: 5 four thousand are to **p** the LORD
29: 10 saying, "**P** be to you, LORD,
2Ch 5: 13 joined in unison to give **p**
6: 24 turn back and give **p** to your name,
6: 26 this place and give **p** to your name
20: 21 to **p** him for the splendor of his
29: 30 ordered the Levites to **p** the LORD
Ezr 3: 10 took their places to **p** the LORD,
Ne 9: 5 be exalted above all blessing and **p**.
Ps 8: 2 Through the **p** of children
16: 7 I will **p** the LORD, who counsels
26: 7 proclaiming aloud your **p**
28: 7 for joy, and with my song I **p** him.
30: 4 faithful people; **p** his holy name.
30: 12 my God, I will **p** you forever.
33: 1 it is fitting for the upright to **p** him.
34: 1 his **p** will always be on my lips.
40: 3 mouth, a hymn of **p** to our God.
42: 5 for I will yet **p** him, my Savior
43: 5 for I will yet **p** him, my Savior
45: 17 therefore the nations will **p** you
47: 7 sing to him a psalm of **p**.
48: 1 and most worthy of **p**, in the city
51: 15 and my mouth will declare your **p**.
56: 4 In God, whose word I **p**—in God I
57: 9 I will **p** you, Lord,
63: 4 I will **p** you as long as I live,
65: 1 **P** awaits you, our God, in Zion;
66: 2 of his name; make his **p** glorious.
66: 8 let the sound of his **p** be heard;
68: 19 **P** be to the Lord, to God our Savior
68: 26 **P** God in the great congregation;
69: 30 I will **p** God's name in song
69: 34 Let heaven and earth **p** him,
71: 8 My mouth is filled with your **p**,
71: 14 I will **p** you more and more.
71: 22 I will **p** you with the harp fo
74: 21 the poor and needy **p** your name.
75: 1 We **p** you, God, we **p** you, for
86: 12 I will **p** you, Lord my God, with all
89: 5 The heavens **p** your wonders,
92: 1 It is good to **p** the LORD and make
96: 2 Sing to the LORD, **p** his name;
100: 4 thanksgiving and his courts with **p**;
101: 1 to you, LORD, I will sing **p**.
102: 18 not yet created may **p** the LORD:
103: 1 **P** the LORD, my soul;
103: 20 **P** the LORD, you his angels,
104: 1 **P** the LORD, my soul.
105: 2 Sing to him, sing **p** to him;
106: 1 **P** the LORD. Give thanks
108: 3 I will **p** you, LORD,
111: 1 **P** the LORD. I will extol
113: 1 **P** the LORD. **P** the LORD,
117: 1 **P** the LORD, all you nations;
118: 28 You are my God, and I will **p** you;
119:175 Let me live that I may **p** you,
135: 1 **P** the LORD. **P** the name of the LORD; **p** him,
135: 20 you who fear him, **p** the LORD.
138: 1 I will **p** you, LORD, with all
139: 14 I **p** you because I am fearfully
144: 1 **P** be to the LORD my Rock,
145: 3 the LORD and most worthy of **p**;
145: 10 All your works **p** you, LORD;
145: 21 every creature **p** his holy name
146: 1 **P** the LORD. **P** the LORD,
147: 1 **P** the LORD. How good it is
148: 1 **P** the LORD. **P** the LORD
148: 13 Let them **p** the name of the LORD,
149: 1 **P** the LORD. Sing to the LORD
Ps 149: 6 the **p** of God be in their mouths
149: 9 his faithful people. **P** the LORD.
150: 2 **p** him for his surpassing greatness.
150: 6 everything that has breath **p** the LORD. **P** the LORD.
Pr 27: 2 Let someone else **p** you, and not
27: 21 but people are tested by their **p**.
31: 31 let her works bring her **p** at the city
SS 1: 4 will **p** your love more than wine.
Isa 12: 1 "I will **p** you, LORD.
42: 10 his **p** from the ends of the earth,
61: 3 a garment of **p** instead of a spirit
Jer 33: 9 **p** and honor before all nations
Da 2: 20 "**P** be to the name of God for ever
4: 37 **p** and exalt and glorify the King
Mt 21: 16 Lord, have called forth your **p**'?"
Lk 19: 37 disciples began joyfully to **p** God
Jn 12: 43 for they loved human **p** more than **p** from God.
Ro 2: 29 Such a person's **p** is not from other
15: 7 you, in order to bring **p** to God.
2Co 1: 3 **P** be to the God and Father of our
Eph 1: 3 **P** be to the God and Father of our
1: 6 to the **p** of his glorious grace,
1: 12 might be for the **p** of his glory.
1: 14 to the **p** of his glory.
1Th 2: 6 We were not looking for **p**
Heb 13: 15 offer to God a sacrifice of **p**—
Jas 3: 9 With the tongue we **p** our Lord
5: 13 Let them sing songs of **p**.
Rev 5: 13 and to the Lamb be **p** and honor
7: 12 **P** and glory and wisdom and

PRAISED (PRAISE)
1Ch 29: 10 David **p** the LORD in the presence
Ne 8: 6 Ezra **p** the LORD, the great God;
Job 1: 21 may the name of the LORD be **p**."
Ps 113: 2 Let the name of the LORD be **p**,
Pr 31: 30 who fears the LORD is to be **p**.
Isa 63: 7 the deeds for which he is to be **p**,
Da 2: 19 Then Daniel **p** the God of heaven
4: 34 Then I **p** the Most High;
Lk 18: 43 the people saw it, they also **p** God.
23: 47 had happened, **p** God and said,
Ro 9: 5 who is God over all, forever **p**!
Gal 1: 24 And they **p** God because of me.
1Pe 4: 11 may be **p** through Jesus Christ.

PRAISES (PRAISE)
2Sa 22: 50 I will sing the **p** of your name.
Ps 18: 49 I will sing the **p** of your name.
47: 6 Sing **p** to God, sing **p**; sing **p** to our King, sing **p**.
147: 1 good it is to sing **p** to our God,
Pr 31: 28 her husband also, and he **p** her:
Ro 15: 9 I will sing the **p** of your name."
1Pe 2: 9 you may declare the **p** of him who

PRAISEWORTHY* (PRAISE)
Ps 78: 4 tell the next generation the **p** deeds
Php 4: 8 if anything is excellent or **p**—

PRAISING (PRAISE)
Lk 2: 13 with the angel, **p** God and saying,
2: 20 **p** God for all the things they had
Ac 2: 47 **p** God and enjoying the favor of all
10: 46 speaking in tongues and **p** God.
1Co 14: 16 when you are **p** God in the Spirit,

PRAY (PRAYED PRAYER PRAYERS PRAYING PRAYS)
Dt 4: 7 our God is near us whenever we **p**
1Sa 12: 23 the LORD by failing to **p** for you.
1Ki 8: 30 when they **p** toward this place.
2Ch 7: 14 will humble themselves and **p**
Ezr 6: 10 and **p** for the well-being of the king
Job 42: 8 My servant Job will **p** for you,
Ps 5: 2 King and my God, for to you I **p**.
32: 6 Therefore let all the faithful **p**
122: 6 **P** for the peace of Jerusalem:
Jer 29: 7 **P** to the LORD for it, because if it
29: 12 call on me and come and **p** to me,
42: 3 **P** that the LORD your God will
Mt 5: 44 and **p** for those who persecute you,
6: 5 "And when you **p**, do not be like
6: 9 "This, then, is how you should **p**:
14: 23 on a mountainside by himself to **p**.
19: 13 his hands on them and **p** for them.
26: 36 here while I go over there and **p**."
Lk 6: 28 you, **p** for those who mistreat you.
11: 1 teach us to **p**, just as John taught
18: 1 them that they should always **p**
22: 40 them, "**P** that you will not fall
Jn 17: 20 I **p** also for those who will believe
Ro 8: 26 not know what we ought to **p** for,
1Co 14: 13 in a tongue should **p** that they may
Eph 1: 18 I **p** that the eyes of your heart may
3: 16 I **p** that out of his glorious riches
6: 18 **p** in the Spirit on all occasions
Col 4: 3 And **p** for us, too, that God may
1Th 5: 17 **p** continually,
2Th 1: 11 in mind, we constantly **p** for you,
1Ti 2: 8 I want the men everywhere to **p**,
Jas 5: 13 Let them **p**. Is anyone happy?
5: 16 **p** for each other so that you may be
1Pe 4: 7 of sober mind so that you may **p**.

PRAYED (PRAY)
1Sa 1: 27 I **p** for this child, and the LORD
1Ki 18: 36 Elijah stepped forward and **p**:
19: 4 under it and **p** that he might die.
2Ki 6: 17 And Elisha **p**, "Open his eyes,
2Ch 30: 18 But Hezekiah **p** for them, saying,
Ne 4: 9 But we **p** to our God and posted
Job 42: 10 After Job had **p** for his friends,
Da 6: 10 he got down on his knees and **p**,
9: 4 I **p** to the LORD my God
Jnh 2: 1 From inside the fish Jonah **p**
Mt 26: 39 with his face to the ground and **p**,
Mk 1: 35 off to a solitary place, where he **p**.
14: 35 **p** that if possible the hour might
Lk 22: 41 beyond them, knelt down and **p**,
Jn 17: 1 he looked toward heaven and **p**:
Ac 4: 31 After they **p**, the place where they
6: 6 **p** and laid their hands on them.
8: 15 they **p** for the new believers there
13: 3 So after they had fasted and **p**,

PRAYER (PRAY)
2Ch 30: 27 for their **p** reached heaven, his holy
Ezr 8: 23 about this, and he answered our **p**.
Ps 4: 1 have mercy on me and hear my **p**.
6: 9 the LORD accepts my **p**.
17: 1 Hear my **p**—it does not rise
17: 6 turn your ear to me and hear my **p**.
65: 2 You who answer **p**, to you all
66: 19 surely listened and has heard my **p**.
66: 20 God, who has not rejected my **p**
86: 6 Hear my **p**, LORD; listen to my
Pr 15: 8 the **p** of the upright pleases him.
15: 29 but he hears the **p** of the righteous.
Isa 56: 7 house will be called a house of **p**
Mt 21: 13 house will be called a house of **p**,'
21: 22 receive whatever you ask for in **p**."
Mk 9: 29 kind can come out only by **p**."
11: 24 whatever you ask for in **p**,
Jn 17: 15 My **p** is not that you take them
Ac 1: 14 all joined together constantly in **p**,
2: 42 to the breaking of bread and to **p**.
6: 4 will give our attention to **p**
10: 31 God has heard your **p**
16: 13 we expected to find a place of **p**.
Ro 12: 12 patient in affliction, faithful in **p**.
1Co 7: 5 you may devote yourselves to **p**.
2Co 13: 9 and our **p** is that you may be fully
Php 1: 9 And this is my **p**: that your love
4: 6 every situation, by **p** and petition,
Col 4: 2 Devote yourselves to **p**,
1Ti 4: 5 by the word of God and **p**.
Jas 5: 15 the **p** offered in faith will make
1Pe 3: 12 and his ears are attentive to their **p**,

PRAYERS (PRAY)
1Ch 5: 20 He answered their **p**, because they
Isa 1: 15 even when you offer many **p**, I am
Mk 12: 40 and for a show make lengthy **p**.
2Co 1: 11 as you help us by your **p**.
Eph 6: 18 on all occasions with all kinds of **p**
1Ti 2: 1 that petitions, **p**,
1Pe 3: 7 so that nothing will hinder your **p**.
Rev 5: 8 which are the **p** of God's people.
8: 3 with the **p** of all God's people,

PRAYING (PRAY)
Ge 24: 45 "Before I finished **p** in my heart,
1Sa 1: 12 As she kept on **p** to the LORD,
Mk 11: 25 And when you stand **p**, if you hold

Lk 3: 21 And as he was **p**, heaven was
6: 12 pray, and spent the night **p** to God.
9: 29 As he was **p**, the appearance of his
Jn 17: 9 I am not **p** for the world,
Ac 9: 11 Tarsus named Saul, for he is **p**.
16: 25 Silas were **p** and singing hymns
Ro 15: 30 join me in my struggle by **p** to God
Eph 6: 18 always keep on **p** for all the Lord's
Jude : 20 holy faith and **p** in the Holy Spirit,

PRAYS (PRAY)
1Co 14: 14 tongue, my spirit **p**, but my mind is

PREACH (PREACHED PREACHING)
Mt 23: 3 they do not practice what they **p**.
Mk 16: 15 *and **p** the gospel to all creation.*
Ac 9: 20 At once he began to **p**
16: 10 God had called us to **p** the gospel
Ro 1: 15 is why I am so eager to **p** the gospel
10: 15 how can anyone **p** unless they are
15: 20 to **p** the gospel where Christ was
1Co 1: 17 to baptize, but to **p** the gospel—
1: 23 but we **p** Christ crucified:
9: 14 that those who **p** the gospel should
9: 16 boast, since I am compelled to **p**.
9: 16 Woe to me if I do not **p** the gospel!
2Co 4: 5 For what we **p** is not ourselves,
10: 16 so that we can **p** the gospel
Gal 1: 8 heaven should **p** a gospel other
2Ti 4: 2 **P** the word; be prepared in season

PREACHED (PREACH)
Mt 24: 14 the kingdom will be **p** in the whole
Mk 6: 12 and **p** that people should repent.
13: 10 the gospel must first be **p** to all
14: 9 the gospel is **p** throughout
Ac 8: 4 who had been scattered **p** the word
1Co 9: 27 so that after I have **p** to others,
15: 1 remind you of the gospel I **p** to you
2Co 11: 4 a Jesus other than the Jesus we **p**,
Gal 1: 8 a gospel other than the one we **p**
Eph 2: 17 **p** peace to you who were far away
Php 1: 18 false motives or true, Christ is **p**.
1Ti 3: 16 angels, was **p** among the nations,
1Pe 1: 25 this is the word that was **p** to you.

PREACHING (PREACH)
Ac 18: 5 devoted himself exclusively to **p**,
Ro 10: 14 can they hear without someone **p**
1Co 2: 4 and my **p** were not with wise
9: 18 in **p** the gospel I may offer it free
Gal 1: 9 anybody is **p** to you a gospel other
1Ti 4: 13 of Scripture, to **p** and to teaching.
5: 17 especially those whose work is **p**

PRECEDE*
1Th 4: 15 will certainly not **p** those who have

PRECEPTS*
Dt 33: 10 He teaches your **p** to Jacob and
Ps 19: 8 The **p** of the LORD are right,
103: 18 and remember to obey his **p**.
105: 45 that they might keep his **p**
111: 7 all his **p** are trustworthy.
111: 10 all who follow his **p** have good
119: 4 You have laid down **p** that are to be
119: 15 I meditate on your **p** and consider
119: 27 to understand the way of your **p**,
119: 40 How I long for your **p**!
119: 45 for I have sought out your **p**.
119: 56 been my practice: I obey your **p**.
119: 63 fear you, to all who follow your **p**.
119: 69 I keep your **p** with all my heart.
119: 78 but I will meditate on your **p**.
119: 87 but I have not forsaken your **p**.
119: 93 I will never forget your **p**,
119: 94 I have sought out your **p**.
119:100 than the elders, for I obey your **p**.
119:104 I gain understanding from your **p**;
119:110 but I have not strayed from your **p**.
119:128 because I consider all your **p** right,
119:134 oppression, that I may obey your **p**.
119:141 despised, I do not forget your **p**.
119:159 See how I love your **p**;
119:168 I obey your **p** and your statutes,
119:173 help me, for I have chosen your **p**.

PRECIOUS
Ps 19: 10 They are more **p** than gold,
72: 14 for **p** is their blood in his sight.
116: 15 **P** in the sight of the LORD is
119: 72 your mouth is more **p** to me than
139: 17 How **p** to me are your thoughts,
Pr 8: 11 for wisdom is more **p** than rubies,
Isa 28: 16 stone, a **p** cornerstone for a sure
1Pe 1: 19 but with the **p** blood of Christ,
2: 4 but chosen by God and **p** to him—
2: 6 a chosen and **p** cornerstone,
2Pe 1: 1 have received a faith as **p** as ours:
1: 4 us his very great and **p** promises,

PREDESTINED* (DESTINY)
Ro 8: 29 **p** to be conformed to the image
8: 30 And those he **p**, he also called;
Eph 1: 5 he **p** us for adoption to sonship
1: 11 been **p** according to the plan

PREDICTED (PREDICTION)
1Sa 28: 17 has done what he **p** through me.
Ac 7: 52 killed those who **p** the coming
1Pe 1: 11 pointing when he **p** the sufferings

PREDICTION* (PREDICTED PREDICTIONS)
Jer 28: 9 LORD only if his **p** comes true."

PREDICTIONS (PREDICTION)
Isa 44: 26 and fulfills the **p** of his messengers,

PREGNANT
Ex 21: 22 hit a **p** woman and she gives birth
Mt 24: 19 will be in those days for **p** women
1Th 5: 3 as labor pains on a **p** woman,

PREPARE (PREPARED)
Ps 23: 5 You **p** a table before me
Isa 25: 6 the LORD Almighty will **p** a feast
40: 3 "In the wilderness **p** the way
Am 4: 12 to you, Israel, **p** to meet your God."
Mal 3: 1 who will **p** the way before me.
Mt 3: 3 wilderness, '**P** the way for the Lord,
Jn 14: 2 that I am going there to **p** a place

PREPARED (PREPARE)
Ex 23: 20 to bring you to the place I have **p**.
Mt 25: 34 the kingdom **p** for you since
Ro 9: 22 of his wrath—**p** for destruction?
1Co 2: 9 the things God has **p** for those who
Eph 2: 10 which God **p** in advance for us
2Ti 2: 21 Master and **p** to do any good work.
4: 2 be **p** in season and out of season;
1Pe 3: 15 Always be **p** to give an answer

PRESCRIBED
Ezr 7: 23 Whatever the God of heaven has **p**,

PRESENCE (PRESENT)
Ex 25: 30 Put the bread of the **P** on this table
33: 14 replied, "My **P** will go with you,
Nu 4: 7 "Over the table of the **P** they are
1Sa 6: 20 can stand in the **p** of the LORD,
21: 6 of the **P** that had been removed
2Sa 22: 13 of the brightness of his **p** bolts
2Ki 17: 23 LORD removed them from his **p**,
23: 27 also from my **p** as I removed Israel,
Ezr 9: 15 not one of us can stand in your **p**."
Ps 16: 11 you will fill me with joy in your **p**,
21: 6 him glad with the joy of your **p**.
23: 5 before me in the **p** of my enemies.
31: 20 the shelter of your **p** you hide them
41: 12 me and set me in your **p** forever.
51: 11 not cast me from your **p** or take
52: 9 in the **p** of your faithful people.
89: 15 who walk in the light of your **p**,
90: 8 secret sins in the light of your **p**.
114: 7 at the **p** of the Lord, at the **p**
139: 7 Where can I flee from your **p**?
Isa 26: 17 pain, so were we in your **p**, LORD.
Jer 5: 22 "Should you not tremble in my **p**?
Eze 38: 20 of the earth will tremble at my **p**.
Hos 6: 2 us, that we may live in his **p**.
Na 1: 5 The earth trembles at his **p**,
Mal 3: 16 his **p** concerning those who feared
Ac 2: 28 you will fill me with joy in your **p**.'
1Th 3: 9 we have in the **p** of our God
3: 13 holy in the **p** of our God and
2Th 1: 9 shut out from the **p** of the Lord
Heb 9: 24 now to appear for us in God's **p**.
1Jn 3: 19 we set our hearts at rest in his **p**:
Jude : 24 before his glorious **p** without fault

PRESENT (PRESENCE)
1Co 3: 22 or death or the **p** or the future—
7: 26 Because of the **p** crisis, I think
2Co 11: 2 that I might **p** you as a pure virgin
Eph 5: 27 and to **p** her to himself as a radiant
1Ti 4: 8 holding promise for both the **p** life
2Ti 2: 15 Do your best to **p** yourself to God
Jude : 24 **p** you before his glorious presence

PRESERVE (PRESERVES)
Pr 19: 16 who would **p** their life stay far
Lk 17: 33 whoever loses their life will **p** it.

PRESERVES (PRESERVE)
Ps 119: 50 Your promise **p** my life.

PRESS (PRESSED PRESSURE)
Php 3: 12 I **p** on to take hold
3: 14 I **p** on toward the goal to win

PRESSED (PRESS)
Ps 118: 5 When hard **p**, I cried to the LORD;
Lk 6: 38 A good measure, **p** down,

PRESSURE (PRESS)
2Co 1: 8 We were under great **p**, far beyond
11: 28 I face daily the **p** of my concern

PRETENDED
1Sa 21: 13 So he **p** to be insane in their

PREVAILS
1Sa 2: 9 "It is not by strength that one **p**;
Pr 19: 21 it is the LORD's purpose that **p**.

PRICE (PRICELESS)
Job 28: 18 the **p** of wisdom is beyond rubies.
1Co 6: 20 you were bought at a **p**.
7: 23 You were bought at a **p**;

PRICELESS* (PRICE)
Ps 36: 7 How **p** is your unfailing love,

PRIDE (PROUD)
Pr 8: 13 I hate **p** and arrogance,
11: 2 When **p** comes, then comes
13: 10 there is **p**, but wisdom is found
16: 18 **P** goes before destruction,
29: 23 **P** brings a person low, but the
Isa 25: 11 will bring down their **p** despite
Da 4: 37 those who walk in **p** he is able
Am 8: 7 sworn by himself, the **P** of Jacob:
2Co 5: 12 an opportunity to take **p** in us,
7: 4 I take great **p** in you.
8: 24 and the reason for our **p** in you,
Gal 6: 4 can take **p** in themselves alone,
Jas 1: 9 to take **p** in their high position.

PRIEST (PRIESTHOOD PRIESTLY PRIESTS)
Ge 14: 18 He was **p** of God Most High,
Nu 5: 10 what they give to the **p** will belong
2Ch 13: 9 seven rams may become a **p** of
Ps 110: 4 "You are a **p** forever, in the order
Heb 2: 17 faithful high **p** in service to God,
3: 1 as our apostle and high **p**.
4: 14 a great high **p** who has ascended
4: 15 do not have a high **p** who is unable
5: 6 "You are a **p** forever, in the order
6: 20 He has become a high **p** forever,
7: 3 Son of God, he remains a **p** forever.
7: 15 **p** like Melchizedek appears,
7: 26 Such a high **p** truly meets our need
8: 1 We do have such a high **p**, who sat
10: 11 Day after day every **p** stands
13: 11 The high **p** carries the blood

PRIESTHOOD (PRIEST)
Heb 7: 24 lives forever, he has a permanent **p**.
1Pe 2: 5 a spiritual house to be a holy **p**,
2: 9 people, a royal **p**, a holy nation,

PRIESTLY (PRIEST)
Ro 15: 16 He gave me the **p** duty

PRIESTS (PRIEST)
Ex 19: 6 you will be for me a kingdom of **p**
Lev 21: 1 "Speak to the **p**, the sons of Aaron,
Eze 42: 13 where the **p** who approach
46: 2 The **p** are to sacrifice his burnt
Mal 1: 6 "It is you **p** who show contempt
Rev 5: 10 a kingdom and **p** to serve our God,
20: 6 but they will be **p** of God

PRIME
Isa 38: 10 the **p** of my life must I go through

PRINCE (PRINCES PRINCESS)
Isa 9: 6 Everlasting Father, **P** of Peace.
Eze 34: 24 David will be **p** among them.
37: 25 my servant will be their **p** forever.

Da 8: 25 and take his stand against the **P**
Jn 12: 31 now the **p** of this world will be
Ac 5: 31 him to his own right hand as **P**

PRINCES (PRINCE)
Ps 118: 9 in the LORD than to trust in **p**.
148: 11 you **p** and all rulers on earth,
Isa 40: 23 He brings **p** to naught and reduces

PRINCESS* (PRINCE)
Ps 45: 13 All glorious is the **p** within her

PRISCILLA*
Wife of Aquila; co-worker with Paul (Ac 18; Ro 16:3; 1Co 16:19; 2Ti 4:19); instructor of Apollos (Ac 18:24–28).

PRISON (IMPRISONED IMPRISONMENT PRISONER PRISONERS)
Ps 66: 11 You brought us into **p** and laid
142: 7 Set me free from my **p**, that I may
Isa 42: 7 blind, to free captives from **p**
Mt 25: 36 I was in **p** and you came to visit
2Co 11: 23 been in **p** more frequently,
Heb 13: 3 remember those in **p** as if you were together with them in **p**,
Rev 20: 7 Satan will be released from his **p**

PRISONER (PRISON)
Ro 7: 23 making me a **p** of the law of sin
Eph 3: 1 the **p** of Christ Jesus for the sake

PRISONERS (PRISON)
Ps 68: 6 he leads out the **p** with singing;
79: 11 groans of the **p** come before you;
107: 10 **p** suffering in iron chains,
146: 7 The LORD sets **p** free,
Zec 9: 12 to your fortress, you **p** of hope;
Lk 4: 18 me to proclaim freedom for the **p**

PRIVILEGE*
2Co 8: 4 for the **p** of sharing in this service

PRIZE*
1Co 9: 24 run, but only one gets the **p**?
9: 24 Run in such a way as to get the **p**.
9: 27 will not be disqualified for the **p**.
Php 3: 14 on toward the goal to win the **p**

PROBE (PROBES)
Job 11: 7 Can you **p** the limits
Ps 17: 3 Though you **p** my heart, though

PROBES* (PROBE)
Ps 7: 9 the righteous God who **p** minds

PROCEDURE
Ecc 8: 6 proper time and **p** for every matter,

PROCESSION
Ps 68: 24 Your **p**, God, has come into view,
118: 27 Join in the festal **p** up to the horns
1Co 4: 9 on display at the end of the **p**,
2Co 2: 14 as captives in Christ's triumphal **p**

PROCLAIM (PROCLAIMED PROCLAIMING PROCLAIMS PROCLAMATION)
Ex 33: 19 and I will **p** my name, the LORD,
Lev 25: 10 **p** liberty throughout the land to all
Dt 30: 12 and **p** it to us so we may obey it?"
2Sa 1: 20 **p** it not in the streets of Ashkelon,
1Ch 16: 8 praise to the LORD, **p** his name;
16: 23 **p** his salvation day after day.
Ne 8: 15 and that they should **p** this word
Ps 2: 7 I will **p** the LORD's decree:
9: 11 **p** among the nations what he has
19: 1 the skies **p** the work of his hands.
22: 31 They will **p** his righteousness,
40: 9 I **p** your saving acts in the great
50: 6 the heavens **p** his righteousness,
64: 9 they will **p** the works of God
68: 11 the women who **p** it are a mighty
68: 34 **P** the power of God, whose majesty
71: 16 I will come and **p** your mighty acts,
71: 16 I will **p** your righteous deeds,
79: 13 to generation we will **p** your praise.
96: 2 **p** his salvation day after day.
97: 6 The heavens **p** his righteousness,
105: 1 praise to the LORD, **p** his name;
106: 2 Who can **p** the mighty acts
118: 17 will **p** what the LORD has done.
145: 6 and I will **p** your great deeds.
Isa 12: 4 praise to the LORD, **p** his name;
12: 4 and **p** that his name is exalted.
42: 12 and **p** his praise in the islands.
52: 7 bring good news, who **p** peace,
61: 1 has anointed me to **p** good news
61: 1 to **p** freedom for the captives
66: 19 They will **p** my glory among
Jer 7: 2 house and there **p** this message:
50: 2 and **p** among the nations,
Hos 5: 9 tribes of Israel I **p** what is certain.
Zec 9: 10 He will **p** peace to the nations.
Mt 10: 7 As you go, **p** this message:
10: 27 in your ear, **p** from the roofs.
12: 18 and he will **p** justice to the nations.
Lk 4: 18 he has anointed me to **p** good news
4: 18 He has sent me to **p** freedom
9: 60 you go and **p** the kingdom of God."
Ac 17: 23 this is what I am going to **p** to you.
20: 27 I have not hesitated to **p** to you
Ro 10: 8 concerning faith that we **p**:
1Co 11: 26 cup, you **p** the Lord's death until he
Col 1: 28 He is the one we **p**,
4: 4 Pray that I may **p** it clearly, as I
1Jn 1: 1 this we **p** concerning the Word

PROCLAIMED (PROCLAIM)
Ex 9: 16 name might be **p** in all the earth.
34: 5 there with him and **p** his name,
Ac 28: 31 He **p** the kingdom of God
Ro 15: 19 I have fully **p** the gospel of Christ.
Col 1: 23 has been **p** to every creature under
2Ti 4: 17 me the message might be fully **p**

PROCLAIMING (PROCLAIM)
Ps 26: 7 **p** aloud your praise and telling of
92: 2 **p** your love in the morning and
92: 15 **p**, "The LORD is upright;
Lk 9: 6 **p** the good news and healing
Ac 5: 42 **p** the good news that Jesus is

PROCLAIMS (PROCLAIM)
Dt 18: 22 If what a prophet **p** in the name

PROCLAMATION (PROCLAIM)
Isa 62: 11 The LORD has made **p** to the ends
1Pe 3: 19 made **p** to the imprisoned spirits—

PRODUCE (PRODUCES)
Mt 3: 8 **P** fruit in keeping with repentance.
3: 10 does not **p** good fruit will be cut

PRODUCES (PRODUCE)
Pr 30: 33 so stirring up anger **p** strife."
Ro 5: 3 that suffering **p** perseverance;
Heb 12: 11 it **p** a harvest of righteousness

PROFANE (PROFANED)
Lev 19: 12 and so **p** the name of your God.
22: 32 Do not **p** my holy name, for I must
Mal 2: 10 Why do we **p** the covenant of our

PROFANED (PROFANE)
Eze 36: 20 the nations they **p** my holy name,

PROFESS*
Ro 10: 10 your mouth that you **p** your faith
1Ti 2: 10 for women who **p** to worship God.
Heb 4: 14 let us hold firmly to the faith we **p**.
10: 23 unswervingly to the hope we **p**,
13: 15 fruit of lips that openly **p** his name.

PROFIT (PROFITABLE)
Pr 14: 23 All hard work brings a **p**, but mere
21: 5 lead to **p** as surely as haste leads
Isa 44: 10 casts an idol, which can **p** nothing?
Eze 18: 8 at interest or take a **p** from them.
2Co 2: 17 not peddle the word of God for **p**.

PROFITABLE* (PROFIT)
Pr 3: 14 for she is more **p** than silver
31: 18 She sees that her trading is **p**,
Titus 3: 8 are excellent and **p** for everyone.

PROFOUND
Job 9: 4 His wisdom is **p**, his power is vast.
Ps 92: 5 LORD, how **p** your thoughts!
Eph 5: 32 This is a **p** mystery—but I am

PROGRESS
Php 1: 25 continue with all of you for your **p**
1Ti 4: 15 so that everyone may see your **p**.

PROLONG*
Dt 5: 33 **p** your days in the land that you
Ps 85: 5 Will you **p** your anger through all
Pr 3: 2 for they will **p** your life many years
Isa 53: 10 see his offspring and **p** his days,
La 4: 22 he will not **p** your exile.

PROMISE (PROMISED PROMISES)
Nu 23: 19 Does he **p** and not fulfill?
Jos 23: 14 Every **p** has been fulfilled;
2Sa 7: 25 keep forever the **p** you have made
1Ki 8: 20 LORD has kept the **p** he made:
8: 24 You have kept your **p** to your
Ne 5: 13 anyone who does not keep this **p**.
9: 8 have kept your **p** because you are
Ps 77: 8 Has his **p** failed for all time?
119: 41 salvation, according to your **p**;
119: 50 Your **p** preserves my life.
119: 58 to me according to your **p**.
119:162 in your **p** like one who finds great
Pr 11: 7 all the **p** of their power comes
Ac 2: 39 The **p** is for you and your children
Ro 4: 13 his offspring received the **p** that he
4: 20 through unbelief regarding the **p**
Gal 3: 14 faith we might receive the **p**
Eph 2: 12 foreigners to the covenants of the **p**
1Ti 4: 8 holding **p** for both the present life
Heb 6: 13 God made his **p** to Abraham,
11: 11 him faithful who had made the **p**.
2Pe 3: 9 Lord is not slow in keeping his **p**,
3: 13 with his **p** we are looking forward

PROMISED (PROMISE)
Ge 21: 1 did for Sarah what he had **p**.
24: 7 spoke to me and **p** me on oath,
Ex 3: 17 I have **p** to bring you up out of
Nu 10: 29 for the LORD has **p** good things
Dt 15: 6 God will bless you as he has **p**,
26: 18 his treasured possession as he **p**,
2Sa 7: 28 and you have **p** these good things
1Ki 9: 5 as I **p** David your father when I
2Ch 6: 15 with your mouth you have **p**
Ps 119: 57 I have **p** to obey your words.
Lk 24: 49 to send you what my Father has **p**;
Ac 1: 4 but wait for the gift my Father **p**,
13: 32 What God **p** our ancestors
Ro 4: 21 had power to do what he had **p**.
Titus 1: 2 lie, **p** before the beginning of time,
Heb 10: 23 we profess, for he who **p** is faithful.
10: 36 you will receive what he has **p**.
Jas 1: 12 the Lord has **p** to those who love
2: 5 the kingdom he **p** those who love
2Pe 3: 4 say, "Where is this 'coming' he **p**?
1Jn 2: 25 And this is what he **p** us—

PROMISES (PROMISE)
Jos 21: 45 of all the LORD's good **p** to Israel
23: 14 all the good **p** the LORD your God
1Ki 8: 56 all the good **p** he gave through his
1Ch 17: 19 and made known all these great **p**.
Ps 85: 8 **p** peace to his people, his faithful
106: 12 they believed his **p** and sang his
119:140 **p** have been thoroughly tested,
119:148 that I may meditate on your **p**.
145: 13 LORD is trustworthy in all he **p**
Ro 9: 4 law, the temple worship and the **p**.
2Co 1: 20 matter how many **p** God has made,
7: 1 since we have these **p**, dear friends,
Heb 8: 6 covenant is established on better **p**.
2Pe 1: 4 us his very great and precious **p**,

PROMOTE
Pr 12: 20 but those who **p** peace have joy.
16: 21 and gracious words **p** instruction.
1Ti 1: 4 Such things **p** controversial

PROMPTED
1Th 1: 3 by faith, your labor **p** by love,
2Th 1: 11 and your every deed **p** by faith.

PRONOUNCE (PRONOUNCED)
1Ch 23: 13 to **p** blessings in his name forever.

PRONOUNCED (PRONOUNCE)
1Ch 16: 12 miracles, and the judgments he **p**,

PROOF (PROVE)
Ac 17: 31 He has given **p** of this to everyone
2Co 8: 24 Therefore show these men the **p**

PROPER
Ps 104: 27 give them their food at the **p** time.
145: 15 give them their food at the **p** time.
Ecc 8: 5 the wise heart will know the **p** time
Mt 24: 45 give them their food at the **p** time?
1Co 11: 13 Is it **p** for a woman to pray to God
Gal 6: 9 at the **p** time we will reap a harvest
1Ti 2: 6 been witnessed to at the **p** time.
1Pe 2: 17 Show **p** respect to everyone,

PROPERTY
Heb 10: 34 the confiscation of your **p**,

PROPHECIES (PROPHESY)
1Co 13: 8 But where there are **p**, they will
1Th 5: 20 Do not treat **p** with contempt

PROPHECY (PROPHESY)
Da 9: 24 seal up vision and **p** and to anoint
1Co 12: 10 powers, to another **p**, to another
13: 2 If I have the gift of **p** and can
14: 1 gifts of the Spirit, especially **p**.
14: 6 or knowledge or **p** or word
14: 22 **p**, however, is not for unbelievers
2Pe 1: 20 that no **p** of Scripture came
Rev 22: 18 the words of the **p** of this scroll:

PROPHESIED (PROPHESY)
Nu 11: 25 the Spirit rested on them, they **p**—
1Sa 19: 24 and he too **p** in Samuel's presence.
Jn 11: 51 that year he **p** that Jesus would die
Ac 19: 6 and they spoke in tongues and **p**.
21: 9 four unmarried daughters who **p**.

PROPHESIES (PROPHESY)
Jer 28: 9 But the prophet who **p** peace will
Eze 12: 27 and he **p** about the distant future.'
1Co 11: 4 **p** with his head covered dishonors
14: 3 the one who **p** speaks to people for

PROPHESY (PROPHECIES PROPHECY PROPHESIED PROPHESIES PROPHESYING PROPHET PROPHET'S PROPHETESS PROPHETIC PROPHETS)
1Sa 10: 6 you, and you will **p** with them;
Eze 13: 2 **p** against the prophets of Israel
13: 17 daughters of your people who **p**
34: 2 **p** against the shepherds of Israel;
37: 4 "**P** to these bones and say to them,
Joel 2: 28 Your sons and daughters will **p**,
Mt 7: 22 did we not **p** in your name
Ac 2: 17 Your sons and daughters will **p**,
1Co 13: 9 we know in part and we **p** in part,
14: 39 be eager to **p**, and do not forbid
Rev 11: 3 and they will **p** for 1,260 days,

PROPHESYING (PROPHESY)
1Ch 25: 1 and Jeduthun for the ministry of **p**,
Ro 12: 6 If your gift is **p**, then prophesy

PROPHET (PROPHESY)
Ex 7: 1 your brother Aaron will be your **p**.
15: 20 Then Miriam the **p**, Aaron's sister,
Nu 12: 6 "When there is a **p** among you, I,
Dt 13: 1 If a **p**, or one who foretells
18: 18 for them a **p** like you from among
18: 22 That **p** has spoken presumptuously,
Jdg 4: 4 Deborah, a **p**, the wife of
1Sa 3: 20 Samuel was attested as a **p**
9: 9 because the **p** of today used to be
1Ki 1: 8 Nathan the **p**, Shimei and Rei
18: 36 the **p** Elijah stepped forward
2Ki 5: 8 know that there is a **p** in Israel."
6: 12 "but Elisha, the **p** who is in Israel,
20: 1 The **p** Isaiah son of Amoz went
2Ch 35: 18 since the days of the **p** Samuel;
36: 12 himself before Jeremiah the **p**,
Ezr 5: 1 Haggai the **p** and Zechariah the **p**,
Eze 2: 5 that a **p** has been among them.
33: 33 that a **p** has been among them."
Hos 9: 7 so great, the **p** is considered a fool,
Am 7: 14 was neither a **p** nor the son of a **p**,
Hab 1: 1 that Habakkuk the **p** received.
Hag 1: 1 LORD came through the **p** Haggai
Zec 1: 1 came to the **p** Zechariah son
13: 4 that day every **p** will be ashamed
Mal 4: 5 "See, I will send the **p** Elijah to you
Mt 10: 41 Whoever welcomes a **p** as a **p** will
11: 9 A **p**? Yes, I tell you, and more than a **p**.
12: 39 it except the sign of the **p** Jonah.
Lk 1: 76 will be called a **p** of the Most High;
2: 36 There was also a **p**, Anna,
4: 24 "no **p** is accepted in his hometown.
7: 16 "A great **p** has appeared among
24: 19 "He was a **p**, powerful in word
Jn 1: 21 "Are you the **P**?"
Ac 7: 37 for you a **p** like me from your own
21: 10 a **p** named Agabus came down
1Co 14: 37 If anyone thinks they are a **p** or
Rev 16: 13 out of the mouth of the false **p**.

PROPHETESS* (PROPHESY)
Isa 8: 3 Then I made love to the **p**, and she

PROPHETIC (PROPHET)
2Pe 1: 19 have the **p** message as something

PROPHET'S (PROPHESY)
2Pe 1: 20 about by the **p** own interpretation

PROPHETS (PROPHESY)
Nu 11: 29 that all the LORD's people were **p**
1Sa 10: 11 Is Saul also among the **p**?"
28: 6 him by dreams or Urim or **p**.
1Ki 19: 10 put your **p** to death with the sword.
1Ch 16: 22 do my **p** no harm."
Ps 105: 15 do my **p** no harm."
Jer 23: 9 Concerning the **p**: My heart is
23: 30 "I am against the **p** who steal
Eze 13: 2 prophesy against the **p** of Israel
Mt 5: 17 come to abolish the Law or the **P**;
7: 12 for this sums up the Law and the **P**.
7: 15 "Watch out for false **p**.
22: 40 Law and the **P** hang on these two
23: 37 you who kill the **p** and stone those
24: 24 messiahs and false **p** will appear
26: 56 of the **p** might be fulfilled."
Lk 10: 24 I tell you that many **p** and kings
11: 49 'I will send them **p** and apostles,
24: 25 believe all that the **p** have spoken!
24: 44 of Moses, the **P** and the Psalms."
Ac 3: 24 all the **p** who have spoken have
10: 43 All the **p** testify about him
13: 1 the church at Antioch there were **p**
26: 22 saying nothing beyond what the **p**
28: 23 from the **P** he tried to persuade
Ro 1: 2 beforehand through his **p**
3: 21 to which the Law and the **P** testify.
11: 3 they have killed your **p** and torn
1Co 12: 28 apostles, second **p**, third teachers,
12: 29 Are all **p**? Are all teachers?
14: 32 The spirits of **p** are subject to the control of **p**.
Eph 2: 20 foundation of the apostles and **p**,
3: 5 Spirit to God's holy apostles and **p**.
4: 11 the apostles, the **p**, the evangelists,
Heb 1: 1 our ancestors through the **p** at
1Pe 1: 10 the **p**, who spoke of the grace
2Pe 3: 2 spoken in the past by the holy **p**
1Jn 4: 1 because many false **p** have gone
Rev 11: 10 because these two **p** had tormented
18: 20 Rejoice, apostles and **p**!

PROPORTION
Dt 16: 10 giving a freewill offering in **p**
16: 17 must bring a gift in **p** to the way

PROPRIETY*
1Ti 2: 9 with decency and **p**,
2: 15 in faith, love and holiness with **p**.

PROSPECT*
Pr 10: 28 The **p** of the righteous is joy,

PROSPER (PROSPERED PROSPERITY PROSPEROUS PROSPERS)
Dt 5: 33 you, so that you may live and **p**
28: 63 pleased the LORD to make you **p**
29: 9 you may **p** in everything you do.
1Ki 2: 3 this so that you may **p** in all you do
Ezr 6: 14 **p** under the preaching of Haggai
Pr 11: 10 When the righteous **p**, the city
11: 25 A generous person will **p**;
17: 20 whose heart is corrupt does not **p**;
19: 8 understanding will soon **p**.
28: 13 conceals their sins does not **p**,
28: 25 who trust in the LORD will **p**.
Isa 53: 10 of the LORD will **p** in his hand.
Jer 12: 1 Why does the way of the wicked **p**?

PROSPERED (PROSPER)
Ge 39: 2 was with Joseph so that he **p**,
2Ch 14: 7 on every side." So they built and **p**.
31: 21 And so he **p**.

PROSPERITY (PROSPER)
Dt 28: 11 LORD will grant you abundant **p**—
30: 15 I set before you today life and **p**,
Job 36: 11 spend the rest of their days in **p**
Ps 73: 3 when I saw the **p** of the wicked.
122: 9 LORD our God, I will seek your **p**.
128: 2 blessings and **p** will be yours.
Pr 3: 2 years and bring you peace and **p**.
21: 21 and love finds life, **p** and honor.
Isa 45: 7 I bring **p** and create disaster;

PROSPEROUS (PROSPER)
Dt 30: 9 your God will make you most **p**
Jos 1: 8 Then you will be **p** and successful.

PROSPERS (PROSPER)
Ps 1: 3 whatever they do **p**.
Pr 16: 20 gives heed to instruction **p**,

PROSTITUTE (PROSTITUTES PROSTITUTION)
Lev 20: 6 and spiritists to **p** themselves
Nu 15: 39 not **p** yourselves by chasing
Jos 2: 1 the house of a **p** named Rahab
Pr 6: 26 For a **p** can be had for a loaf
7: 10 dressed like a **p** and with crafty
Eze 16: 15 and used your fame to become a **p**.
23: 7 She gave herself as a **p** to all
Hos 3: 3 you must not be a **p** or be intimate
1Co 6: 15 of Christ and unite them with a **p**?
6: 16 who unites himself with a **p** is one
Rev 17: 1 you the punishment of the great **p**,

PROSTITUTES (PROSTITUTE)
Pr 29: 3 of **p** squanders his wealth.
Mt 21: 31 the **p** are entering the kingdom
Lk 15: 30 your property with **p** comes home,

PROSTITUTION (PROSTITUTE)
Eze 16: 16 where you carried on your **p**.
23: 3 engaging in **p** from their youth.
Hos 4: 10 they will engage in **p** but not

PROSTRATE
Dt 9: 18 again I fell **p** before the LORD
1Ki 18: 39 saw this, they fell **p** and cried,

PROTECT (PROTECTED PROTECTION PROTECTS)
Dt 23: 14 moves about in your camp to **p**
Ps 25: 21 integrity and uprightness **p** me,
32: 7 you will **p** me from trouble
40: 11 love and faithfulness always **p** me.
91: 14 I will **p** him, for he acknowledges
140: 1 **p** me from the violent,
Pr 2: 11 Discretion will **p** you,
4: 6 wisdom, and she will **p** you;
Jn 17: 11 **p** them by the power of your name,
17: 15 that you **p** them from the evil one.
2Th 3: 3 you and **p** you from the evil one.

PROTECTED (PROTECT)
Jos 24: 17 He **p** us on our entire journey
1Sa 30: 23 He has **p** us and delivered into our
Jn 17: 12 I **p** them and kept them safe

PROTECTION (PROTECT)
Ezr 9: 9 he has given us a wall of **p** in Judah
Ps 5: 11 Spread your **p** over them, that

PROTECTS (PROTECT)
Ps 41: 2 The LORD **p** and preserves them—
116: 6 The LORD **p** the unwary;
Pr 2: 8 **p** the way of his faithful ones.
27: 18 whoever **p** their master will be
1Co 13: 7 It always **p**, always trusts,

PROUD (PRIDE)
Ps 31: 23 him, but the **p** he pays back in full.
101: 5 has haughty eyes and a **p** heart,
Pr 3: 34 He mocks **p** mockers but shows
16: 5 The LORD detests all the **p**
16: 19 than to share plunder with the **p**.
21: 4 Haughty eyes and a **p** heart—
Isa 2: 12 has a day in store for all the **p**
Ro 12: 16 Do not be **p**, but be willing
1Co 13: 4 envy, it does not boast, it is not **p**.
2Ti 3: 2 of money, boastful, **p**, abusive,
Jas 4: 6 "God opposes the **p** but shows
1Pe 5: 5 "God opposes the **p** but shows

PROVE (PROOF PROVED PROVEN PROVING)
Pr 29: 25 Fear of man will **p** to be a snare,
Jn 8: 46 Can any of you **p** me guilty of sin?
16: 8 he will **p** the world to be
1Co 4: 2 been given a trust must **p** faithful.

PROVED (PROVE)
Isa 5: 16 the holy God will be **p** holy by his
Eze 28: 25 I will be **p** holy through them
Mt 11: 19 wisdom is **p** right by her deeds."
Ro 3: 4 may be **p** right when you speak

PROVEN* (PROVE)
1Pe 1: 7 the **p** genuineness of your faith—

PROVIDE (PROVIDED PROVIDES PROVISION)
Ge 22: 8 "God himself will **p** the lamb
22: 14 that place The LORD Will **P**.
Isa 43: 20 because I **p** water in the wilderness
61: 3 and **p** for those who grieve in Zion
1Co 10: 13 **p** a way out so that you can endure
1Ti 5: 8 Anyone who does not **p** for their
Titus 3: 14 in order to **p** for urgent needs

PROVIDED (PROVIDE)
Ps 68: 10 bounty, God, you **p** for the poor.
111: 9 He **p** redemption for his people;
Jnh 1: 17 Now the LORD **p** a huge fish
4: 6 the LORD God **p** a leafy plant
4: 7 dawn the next day God **p** a worm,
4: 8 rose, God **p** a scorching east wind,
Gal 4: 18 be zealous, **p** the purpose is good,
Heb 1: 3 he had **p** purification for sins,

PROVIDES (PROVIDE)
Ps 111: 5 He **p** food for those who fear him;
Pr 31: 15 she **p** food for her family
Eze 18: 7 and **p** clothing for the naked.
1Ti 6: 17 who richly **p** us with everything
1Pe 4: 11 do so with the strength God **p**,

PROVING* (PROVE)
Ac 9: 22 in Damascus by **p** that Jesus is
17: 3 **p** that the Messiah had to suffer
18: 28 **p** from the Scriptures that Jesus

PROVISION (PROVIDE)
Ro 5: 17 who receive God's abundant **p**

PROVOKED
Ecc 7: 9 Do not be quickly **p** in your spirit,
Jer 32: 32 Judah have **p** me by all the evil

PROWLS
1Pe 5: 8 enemy the devil **p** around like

PRUDENCE* (PRUDENT)
Pr 1: 4 giving **p** to those who are simple,
8: 5 You who are simple, gain **p**;
8: 12 "I, wisdom, dwell together with **p**;
12: 8 is praised according to their **p**,
15: 5 whoever heeds correction shows **p**.
16: 22 **P** is a fountain of life to the
19: 25 and the simple will learn **p**;
21: 16 from the path of **p** comes to rest

PRUDENT (PRUDENCE)
Pr 1: 3 receiving instruction in **p** behavior,
12: 16 once, but the **p** overlook an insult.
12: 23 The **p** keep their knowledge
13: 16 All who are **p** act with knowledge,
14: 8 The wisdom of the **p** is to give
14: 15 the **p** give thought to their steps.
14: 18 the **p** are crowned with knowledge.
19: 14 but a **p** wife is from the LORD.
22: 3 The **p** see danger and take refuge,
27: 12 The **p** see danger and take refuge,
Jer 49: 7 Has counsel perished from the **p**?
Am 5: 13 Therefore the **p** keep quiet in such

PRUNES* (PRUNING)
Jn 15: 2 does bear fruit he **p** so that it will

PRUNING (PRUNES)
Isa 2: 4 and their spears into **p** hooks.
Joel 3: 10 and your **p** hooks into spears.

PSALMS
Eph 5: 19 speaking to one another with **p**,
Col 3: 16 with all wisdom through **p**,

PUBERTY*
Eze 16: 7 grew and developed and entered **p**.

PUBLICLY
Ac 20: 20 have taught you **p** and from house

PUFFS*
1Co 8: 1 knowledge **p** up while love builds

PUNISH (PUNISHED PUNISHMENT)
Ge 15: 14 But I will **p** the nation they serve
Ex 32: 34 when the time comes for me to **p**,
Pr 23: 13 if you **p** them with the rod, they
Isa 13: 11 I will **p** the world for its evil,
Jer 2: 19 Your wickedness will **p** you;
21: 14 I will **p** you as your deeds deserve,
Zep 1: 12 and **p** those who are complacent,
Ac 7: 7 But I will **p** the nation they serve as
2Th 1: 8 He will **p** those who do not know
1Pe 2: 14 by him to **p** those who do wrong

PUNISHED (PUNISH)
Ezr 9: 13 you have **p** us less than our sins
Ps 99: 8 God, though you **p** their misdeeds.
Isa 53: 8 of my people he was **p**.
La 3: 39 should the living complain when **p**
Mk 12: 40 men will be **p** most severely."
Lk 23: 41 We are **p** justly, for we are getting
2Th 1: 9 They will be **p** with everlasting
Heb 10: 29 to be **p** who has trampled the Son

PUNISHMENT (PUNISH)
Isa 53: 5 the **p** that brought us peace was
Jer 4: 18 This is your **p**. How bitter it is!
Mt 25: 46 they will go away to eternal **p**,
Lk 12: 48 and does things deserving **p** will be
21: 22 this is the time of **p** in fulfillment
Ro 13: 4 wrath to bring **p** on the wrongdoer.
Heb 2: 2 disobedience received its just **p**,
2Pe 2: 9 to hold the unrighteous for **p**

PURCHASED
Ps 74: 2 the nation you **p** long ago,
Rev 5: 9 your blood you **p** for God persons

PURE (PURIFICATION PURIFIED PURIFIES PURIFY PURITY)
2Sa 22: 27 to the **p** you show yourself **p**,
2Ki 2: 22 the water has remained **p** to this
Job 14: 4 Who can bring what is **p**
Ps 19: 9 The fear of the LORD is **p**,
24: 4 who has clean hands and a **p** heart,
51: 10 Create in me a **p** heart, O God,
Pr 15: 26 gracious words are **p** in his sight.
20: 9 can say, "I have kept my heart **p**;
Isa 52: 11 Come out from it and be **p**, you
Hab 1: 13 Your eyes are too **p** to look on evil;
Mt 5: 8 Blessed are the **p** in heart, for they
2Co 11: 2 I might present you as a **p** virgin
Php 4: 8 whatever is **p**, whatever is lovely,
1Ti 1: 5 which comes from a **p** heart
5: 22 the sins of others. Keep yourself **p**.
2Ti 2: 22 call on the Lord out of a **p** heart.
Titus 1: 15 To the **p**, all things are **p**,
2: 5 to be self-controlled and **p**, to be
Heb 7: 26 **p**, set apart from sinners,
13: 4 all, and the marriage bed kept **p**,
Jas 1: 27 that God our Father accepts as **p**
3: 17 comes from heaven is first of all **p**;
1Jn 3: 3 purify themselves, just as he is **p**.

PURGE
Pr 20: 30 and beatings **p** the inmost being.

PURIFICATION (PURE)
Heb 1: 3 After he had provided **p** for sins,

PURIFIED (PURE)
Ac 15: 9 them, for he **p** their hearts by faith.
1Pe 1: 22 you have **p** yourselves by obeying

PURIFIES* (PURE)
1Jn 1: 7 of Jesus, his Son, **p** us from all sin.

PURIFY (PURE)
Nu 19: 12 They must **p** themselves
2Co 7: 1 let us **p** ourselves from everything
Titus 2: 14 to **p** for himself a people that are
Jas 4: 8 you sinners, and **p** your hearts,
1Jn 1: 9 and **p** us from all unrighteousness.
3: 3 this hope in him **p** themselves,

PURIM
Est 9: 26 these days were called **P**,

PURITY* (PURE)
Ps 119: 9 person stay on the path of **p**?
Hos 8: 5 long will they be incapable of **p**?
2Co 6: 6 in **p**, understanding,
1Ti 4: 12 conduct, in love, in faith and in **p**.
5: 2 women as sisters, with absolute **p**.
1Pe 3: 2 when they see the **p** and reverence

PURPLE
Pr 31: 22 she is clothed in fine linen and **p**.
Mk 15: 17 They put a **p** robe on him,

PURPOSE (PURPOSED PURPOSES)
Ex 9: 16 I have raised you up for this very **p**,
Job 36: 5 he is mighty, and firm in his **p**.
42: 2 no **p** of yours can be thwarted.
Pr 19: 21 it is the LORD's **p** that prevails.
Isa 46: 10 I say, 'My **p** will stand, and I will
55: 11 achieve the **p** for which I sent it.
Ro 8: 28 been called according to his **p**.
9: 11 God's **p** in election might stand:
9: 17 "I raised you up for this very **p**,
1Co 3: 8 the one who waters have one **p**,
2Co 5: 5 fashioned us for this very **p** is God,
Gal 4: 18 be zealous, provided the **p** is good,
Eph 1: 11 conformity with the **p** of his will,
3: 11 his eternal **p** that he accomplished
Php 2: 13 to act in order to fulfill his good **p**.
2Ti 1: 9 because of his own **p** and grace.

PURPOSED (PURPOSE)
Isa 14: 24 and as I have **p**, so it will happen.
14: 27 For the LORD Almighty has **p**,
Eph 1: 9 pleasure, which he **p** in Christ,

PURPOSES (PURPOSE)
Ps 33: 10 he thwarts the **p** of the peoples.
Jer 23: 20 until he fully accomplishes the **p**
32: 19 great are your **p** and mighty are

PURSE (PURSES)
Hag 1: 6 to put them in a **p** with holes in it."
Lk 10: 4 Do not take a **p** or bag or sandals;
22: 36 "But now if you have a **p**, take it,

PURSES (PURSE)
Lk 12: 33 Provide **p** for yourselves that will

PURSUE (PURSUES)
Ps 34: 14 and do good; seek peace and **p** it.
Pr 15: 9 loves those who **p** righteousness.
Ro 9: 30 who did not **p** righteousness,
1Ti 6: 11 and **p** righteousness, godliness,
2Ti 2: 22 of youth and **p** righteousness, faith,
1Pe 3: 11 they must seek peace and **p** it.

PURSUES (PURSUE)
Pr 21: 21 Whoever **p** righteousness and love
28: 1 The wicked flee though no one **p**,

QUAIL
Ex 16: 13 That evening **q** came and covered
Nu 11: 31 and drove **q** in from the sea.

QUALITIES* (QUALITY)
Da 6: 3 by his exceptional **q** that the king
Ro 1: 20 of the world God's invisible **q**—
2Pe 1: 8 if you possess these **q** in increasing

QUALITY (QUALITIES)
1Co 3: 13 and the fire will test the **q** of each

QUARREL (QUARRELING QUARRELS QUARRELSOME)
Pr 15: 18 the one who is patient calms a **q**.
17: 14 Starting a **q** is like breaching a dam
17: 19 Whoever loves a **q** loves sin;
20: 3 strife, but every fool is quick to **q**.
26: 17 who rushes into a **q** not their own.
26: 20 without a gossip a **q** dies down.
Isa 45: 9 to those who **q** with their Maker,
Jas 4: 2 what you want, so you **q** and fight.

QUARRELING (QUARREL)
1Co 3: 3 there is jealousy and **q** among you,
2Ti 2: 14 Warn them before God against **q**

QUARRELS (QUARREL)
2Ti 2: 23 because you know they produce **q**.
Jas 4: 1 causes fights and **q** among you?

QUARRELSOME (QUARREL)
Pr 19: 13 **q** wife is like the constant dripping
21: 9 than share a house with a **q** wife.
26: 21 so is a **q** person for kindling strife.
1Ti 3: 3 gentle, not **q**, not a lover of money.
2Ti 2: 24 the Lord's servant must not be **q**

QUEEN
1Ki 10: 1 When the **q** of Sheba heard
2Ch 9: 1 When the **q** of Sheba heard
Mt 12: 42 The **Q** of the South will rise

QUENCH (QUENCHED)
SS 8: 7 Many waters cannot **q** love;
1Th 5: 19 Do not **q** the Spirit.

QUENCHED (QUENCH)
Isa 66: 24 fire that burns them will not be **q**,
Mk 9: 48 do not die, and the fire is not **q**.'

QUICK-TEMPERED* (TEMPER)
Pr 14: 17 A **q** person does foolish things,
14: 29 but one who is **q** displays folly.
Titus 1: 7 not **q**, not given to drunkenness,

QUIET (QUIETNESS)
Ps 23: 2 he leads me beside **q** waters,
Pr 17: 1 and **q** than a house full of feasting,
Ecc 9: 17 The **q** words of the wise are more
Am 5: 13 Therefore the prudent keep **q**
Lk 19: 40 "if they keep **q**, the stones will cry
1Th 4: 11 it your ambition to lead a **q** life:
1Ti 2: 2 peaceful and **q** lives in all godliness
1Ti 2: 12 over a man; she must be **q**.
1Pe 3: 4 beauty of a gentle and **q** spirit,

QUIETNESS* (QUIET)
Job 3: 26 I have no peace, no **q**; I have no
Isa 30: 15 in **q** and trust is your strength,
32: 17 its effect will be **q** and confidence
1Ti 2: 11 A woman should learn in **q** and

QUIVER
Ps 127: 5 Blessed is the man whose **q** is full

RACE
Ecc 9: 11 The **r** is not to the swift or the
Ac 20: 24 my only aim is to finish the **r**
1Co 9: 24 that in a **r** all the runners run,
Gal 2: 2 had not been running my **r** in vain.
5: 7 You were running a good **r**.
2Ti 4: 7 I have finished the **r**, I have kept
Heb 12: 1 with perseverance the **r** marked

RACHEL
Daughter of Laban (Ge 29:16); wife of Jacob (Ge 29:28); bore two sons (Ge 30:22–24; 35:16–24; 46:19). Stole Laban's gods (Ge 31:19, 32–35). Death (Ge 35:19–20).

RADIANCE (RADIANT)
Eze 1: 28 rainy day, so was the **r** around him.
Heb 1: 3 The Son is the **r** of God's glory

RADIANT (RADIANCE)
Ex 34: 29 that his face was **r** because he had
Ps 34: 5 Those who look to him are **r**;
76: 4 You are **r** with light, more majestic
132: 18 will be adorned with a **r** crown."
SS 5: 10 My beloved is **r** and ruddy,
Isa 60: 5 Then you will look and be **r**,
Eph 5: 27 her to himself as a **r** church,

RAGE
Pr 29: 11 Fools give full vent to their **r**,
Ac 4: 25 "'Why do the nations **r**
Col 3: 8 anger, **r**, malice, slander, and filthy

RAGS
Isa 64: 6 our righteous acts are like filthy **r**;

RAHAB
Prostitute of Jericho who hid Israelite spies (Jos 2; 6:22–25; Heb 11:31; Jas 2:25). Mother of Boaz (Mt 1:5).

RAIN (RAINBOW)
Ge 7: 4 from now I will send **r** on the earth
1Ki 17: 1 there will be neither dew nor **r**
18: 1 and I will send **r** on the land."
Mt 5: 45 and sends **r** on the righteous
Jas 5: 17 earnestly that it would not **r**,
Jude : 12 They are clouds without **r**,

RAINBOW (RAIN)
Ge 9: 13 I have set my **r** in the clouds, and it
Eze 1: 28 Like the appearance of a **r** in the
Rev 4: 3 A **r** that shone like an emerald

RAISE (RISE)
Jn 6: 39 me, but **r** them up at the last day.
1Co 15: 15 he did not **r** him if in fact the dead

RAISED (RISE)
Ps 89: 19 I have **r** up a young man
Isa 52: 13 he will be **r** and lifted up and
Mt 17: 23 the third day he will be **r** to life."
Lk 7: 22 the dead are **r**, and the good news
Ac 2: 24 But God **r** him from the dead,
Ro 4: 25 was **r** to life for our justification.
6: 4 just as Christ was **r** from the dead
8: 11 he who **r** Christ from the dead will
10: 9 your heart that God **r** him
1Co 15: 4 he was **r** on the third day according
15: 20 Christ has indeed been **r**

RALLY*
Isa 11: 10 the nations will **r** to him, and his

RAM (RAMS)
Ge 22: 13 in a thicket he saw a **r** caught
Ex 25: 5 **r** skins dyed red and another type
Da 8: 3 there before me was a **r** with two

RAMPART*
Ps 91: 4 will be your shield and **r**.

RAMS (RAM)
1Sa 15: 22 to heed is better than the fat of **r**.
Mic 6: 7 be pleased with thousands of **r**,

RAN (RUN)
Jnh 1: 3 But Jonah **r** away from the LORD

RANSOM
Mt 20: 28 to give his life as a **r** for many."
Mk 10: 45 to give his life as a **r** for many."
1Ti 2: 6 who gave himself as a **r** for all
Heb 9: 15 he has died as a **r** to set them free

RARE
Pr 20: 15 that speak knowledge are a **r** jewel.

RAVEN (RAVENS)
Ge 8: 7 and sent out a **r**, and it kept flying
Job 38: 41 food for the **r** when its young cry

RAVENS (RAVEN)
1Ki 17: 6 The **r** brought him bread and meat
Ps 147: 9 and for the young **r** when they call.
Lk 12: 24 Consider the **r**: They do not sow

RAYS
Mal 4: 2 will rise with healing in its **r**.

READ (READING READS)
Dt 17: 19 he is to **r** it all the days of his life so
Jos 8: 34 Joshua **r** all the words of the law—
2Ki 23: 2 He **r** in their hearing all the words
Ne 8: 8 They **r** from the Book of the Law
Jer 36: 6 **r** to the people from the scroll
2Co 3: 2 hearts, known and **r** by everyone.

READING (READ)
1Ti 4: 13 to the public **r** of Scripture,

READS (READ)
Rev 1: 3 is the one who **r** aloud the words

REAFFIRM
2Co 2: 8 therefore, to **r** your love for him.

REAL* (REALITIES REALITY)
Jn 6: 55 For my flesh is **r** food and my blood is **r** drink.
1Jn 2: 27 all things and as that anointing is **r**,

REALITIES* (REAL)
1Co 2: 13 the Spirit, explaining spiritual **r**
Heb 10: 1 not the **r** themselves.

REALITY* (REAL)
Col 2: 17 the **r**, however, is found in Christ.

REALMS
Eph 1: 3 the heavenly **r** with every spiritual
2: 6 in the heavenly **r** in Christ Jesus,

REAP (REAPER REAPS)
Job 4: 8 evil and those who sow trouble **r** it.
Ps 126: 5 sow with tears will **r** with songs
Hos 8: 7 sow the wind and **r** the whirlwind.
10: 12 **r** the fruit of unfailing love,
Jn 4: 38 to **r** what you have not worked for.
Ro 6: 22 the benefit you **r** leads to holiness,
2Co 9: 6 sparingly will also **r** sparingly,
9: 6 generously will also **r** generously.
Gal 6: 8 from the flesh will **r** destruction;
6: 8 from the Spirit will **r** eternal life.

REAPER (REAP)
Jn 4: 36 and the **r** may be glad together.

REAPS (REAP)
Pr 11: 18 who sows righteousness **r** a sure
22: 8 Whoever sows injustice **r** calamity,
Gal 6: 7 A man **r** what he sows.

REASON (REASONED)
Mt 19: 5 this **r** a man will leave his father
Jn 12: 27 it was for this very **r** I came to this
15: 25 'They hated me without **r**.'
1Pe 3: 15 asks you to give the **r** for the hope
2Pe 1: 5 For this very **r**, make every effort

REASONED (REASON)
1Co 13: 11 thought like a child, I **r** like a child.

REBEKAH
Sister of Laban, secured as bride for Isaac (Ge 24). Mother of Esau and Jacob (Ge 25:19–26). Taken by Abimelek as sister of Isaac; returned (Ge 26:1–11). Encouraged Jacob to trick Isaac out of blessing (Ge 27:1–17).

REBEL (REBELLED REBELLION REBELS)
Nu 14: 9 Only do not **r** against the LORD.
1Sa 12: 14 do not **r** against his commands,
Mt 10: 21 children will **r** against their parents

REBELLED (REBEL)
Ps 78: 56 test and **r** against the Most High;
Isa 63: 10 Yet they **r** and grieved his Holy

REBELLION (REBEL)
Ex 34: 7 forgiving wickedness, **r** and sin.
Nu 14: 18 in love and forgiving sin and **r**.
1Sa 15: 23 For **r** is like the sin of divination,
2Th 2: 3 will not come until the **r** occurs

REBELS (REBEL)
Mk 15: 27 They crucified two **r** with him,
Ro 13: 2 whoever **r** against the authority is
1Ti 1: 9 but for lawbreakers and **r**,

REBIRTH* (BEAR)
Titus 3: 5 saved us through the washing of **r**

REBUILD (BUILD)
Ezr 5: 2 set to work to **r** the house of God
Ne 2: 17 let us **r** the wall of Jerusalem,
Ps 102: 16 For the LORD will **r** Zion
Da 9: 25 **r** Jerusalem until the Anointed
Am 9: 14 "They will **r** the ruined cities
Ac 15: 16 return and **r** David's fallen tent.

REBUILT (BUILD)
Zec 1: 16 and there my house will be **r**.

REBUKE (REBUKED REBUKES REBUKING)
Lev 19: 17 **R** your neighbor frankly so you
Ps 141: 5 let him **r** me—that is oil on my
Pr 3: 11 discipline, and do not resent his **r**,
9: 8 **r** the wise and they will love you.
17: 10 A **r** impresses a discerning person
19: 25 **r** the discerning, and they will gain
25: 12 of fine gold is the **r** of a wise judge
27: 5 Better is open **r** than hidden love.
30: 6 he will **r** you and prove you a liar.
Ecc 7: 5 to heed the **r** of a wise person than
Isa 54: 9 with you, never to **r** you again.
Jer 2: 19 your backsliding will **r** you.
Zep 3: 17 in his love he will no longer **r** you,
Lk 17: 3 or sister sins against you, **r** them;
1Ti 5: 1 Do not **r** an older man harshly,
2Ti 4: 2 correct, **r** and encourage—
Titus 1: 13 Therefore **r** them sharply,
2: 15 Encourage and **r** with all authority.
Rev 3: 19 Those whom I love I **r**

REBUKED (REBUKE)
Mk 16: 14 *he **r** them for their lack of faith*

REBUKES (REBUKE)
Job 22: 4 "Is it for your piety that he **r** you
Pr 28: 23 Whoever **r** a person will in the end
29: 1 many **r** will suddenly be destroyed
Heb 12: 5 do not lose heart when he **r** you,

REBUKING (REBUKE)
2Ti 3: 16 and is useful for teaching, **r**,

RECALLING
1Ti 1: 18 by **r** them you may fight the battle

RECEIVE (RECEIVED RECEIVES RECEIVING)
Mt 10: 41 a prophet will **r** a prophet's reward,
10: 41 righteous person will **r** a righteous
Mk 10: 15 anyone who will not **r** the kingdom
Jn 1: 12 Yet to all who did **r** him, to those
20: 22 them and said, "**R** the Holy Spirit.
Ac 1: 8 you will **r** power when the Holy
2: 38 will **r** the gift of the Holy Spirit.
19: 2 "Did you **r** the Holy Spirit
20: 35 more blessed to give than to **r**.'"
1Co 9: 14 the gospel should **r** their living
2Co 1: 4 the comfort we ourselves **r**
6: 17 no unclean thing, and I will **r** you."
1Ti 1: 16 believe in him and **r** eternal life.
Jas 1: 7 should not expect to **r** anything
2Pe 1: 11 you will **r** a rich welcome
1Jn 3: 22 and **r** from him anything we ask,
Rev 4: 11 to **r** glory and honor and power,
5: 12 to **r** power and wealth and wisdom

RECEIVED (RECEIVE)
Mt 6: 2 they have **r** their reward in full.

Mt 10: 8 Freely you have **r**; freely give.
Mk 11: 24 believe that you have **r** it, and it
Jn 1: 16 of his fullness we have all **r** grace
Ac 8: 17 them, and they **r** the Holy Spirit.
10: 47 They have **r** the Holy Spirit just as
Ro 8: 15 The Spirit you **r** does not make you
1Co 11: 23 For I **r** from the Lord what I
Col 2: 6 just as you **r** Christ Jesus as Lord,
1Pe 4: 10 should use whatever gift you have **r**

RECEIVES (RECEIVE)
Pr 18: 22 good and **r** favor from the LORD.
Mt 7: 8 For everyone who asks **r**;
Ac 10: 43 who believes in him **r** forgiveness

RECEIVING (RECEIVE)
Pr 1: 3 for **r** instruction in prudent

RECITE
Ps 45: 1 a noble theme as I **r** my verses

RECKLESS
Pr 12: 18 words of the **r** pierce like swords,
1Pe 4: 4 you do not join them in their **r**,

RECKONING
Isa 10: 3 What will you do on the day of **r**,
Hos 9: 7 coming, the days of **r** are at hand.

RECLAIM* (CLAIM)
Isa 11: 11 time to **r** the surviving remnant

RECOGNITION (RECOGNIZE)
1Co 16: 18 yours also. Such men deserve **r**.
1Ti 5: 3 Give proper **r** to those widows who

RECOGNIZE (RECOGNITION RECOGNIZED)
Mt 7: 16 By their fruit you will **r** them.
1Jn 4: 2 This is how you can **r** the Spirit
4: 6 This is how we **r** the Spirit of truth

RECOGNIZED (RECOGNIZE)
Mt 12: 33 be bad, for a tree is **r** by its fruit.
Ro 7: 13 in order that sin might be **r** as sin,

RECOMPENSE*
Isa 40: 10 him, and his **r** accompanies him.
62: 11 and his **r** accompanies him.'"

RECONCILE* (RECONCILED RECONCILIATION RECONCILING)
Ac 7: 26 He tried to **r** them by saying, 'Men,
Eph 2: 16 and in one body to **r** both of them
Col 1: 20 and through him to **r** to himself all

RECONCILED* (RECONCILE)
Mt 5: 24 First go and be **r** to them;
Lk 12: 58 try hard to be **r** on the way, or your
Ro 5: 10 were **r** to him through the death
5: 10 having been **r**, shall we be saved
1Co 7: 11 or else be **r** to her husband.
2Co 5: 18 who **r** us to himself through Christ
5: 20 you on Christ's behalf: Be **r** to God.
Col 1: 22 But now he has **r** you by Christ's

RECONCILIATION* (RECONCILE)
Ro 5: 11 whom we have now received **r**.
11: 15 For if their rejection brought **r**
2Co 5: 18 and gave us the ministry of **r**:
5: 19 committed to us the message of **r**.

RECONCILING* (RECONCILE)
2Co 5: 19 God was **r** the world to himself

RECORD (RECORDED)
Ps 130: 3 you, LORD, kept a **r** of sins, Lord,
Hos 13: 12 is stored up, his sins are kept on **r**.
1Co 13: 5 angered, it keeps no **r** of wrongs.

RECORDED (RECORD)
Job 19: 23 that my words were **r**, that they
Jn 20: 30 which are not **r** in this book.

RECOUNT*
Ps 119: 13 With my lips I **r** all the laws
Jer 23: 28 the prophet who has a dream **r** the

RED
Ex 15: 4 officers are drowned in the **R** Sea.
Ps 106: 9 He rebuked the **R** Sea, and it dried
Pr 23: 31 Do not gaze at wine when it is **r**,
Isa 1: 18 though they are **r** as crimson,

REDEDICATE* (DEDICATE)
Nu 6: 12 They must **r** themselves

REDEEM (REDEEMED REDEEMER REDEEMS REDEMPTION)
Ex 6: 6 I will **r** you with an outstretched
2Sa 7: 23 out to **r** as a people for himself,
Ps 49: 7 No one can **r** the life of another
49: 15 God will **r** me from the realm
130: 8 He himself will **r** Israel from all
Hos 13: 14 I will **r** them from death.
Gal 4: 5 to **r** those under the law, that we
Titus 2: 14 for us to **r** us from all wickedness

REDEEMED (REDEEM)
Ps 107: 2 Let the **r** of the LORD tell their
Isa 35: 9 But only the **r** will walk there,
63: 9 In his love and mercy he **r** them;
Gal 3: 13 **r** us from the curse of the law
1Pe 1: 18 you were **r** from the empty way

REDEEMER (REDEEM)
Job 19: 25 I know that my **r** lives,
Ps 19: 14 sight, LORD, my Rock and my **R**.
Isa 44: 6 Israel's King and **R**, the LORD
48: 17 your **R**, the Holy One of Israel:
59: 20 "The **R** will come to Zion, to those

REDEEMS* (REDEEM)
Ps 103: 4 who **r** your life from the pit

REDEMPTION (REDEEM)
Ps 130: 7 love and with him is full **r**.
Lk 21: 28 because your **r** is drawing near."
Ro 3: 24 by his grace through the **r** that
8: 23 to sonship, the **r** of our bodies.
1Co 1: 30 our righteousness, holiness and **r**.
Eph 1: 7 him we have **r** through his blood,
1: 14 our inheritance until the **r** of those
4: 30 you were sealed for the day of **r**.
Col 1: 14 in whom we have **r**, the forgiveness
Heb 9: 12 blood, thus obtaining eternal **r**.

REED
Isa 42: 3 A bruised **r** he will not break,
Mt 12: 20 A bruised **r** he will not break,

REFINE*
Jer 9: 7 "See, I will **r** and test them,
Zec 13: 9 I will **r** them like silver and test
Mal 3: 3 the Levites and **r** them like gold

REFLECTS*
Pr 27: 19 As water **r** the face, so one's life **r**

REFRESH (REFRESHED REFRESHES REFRESHING)
Phm : 20 in the Lord; **r** my heart in Christ.

REFRESHED (REFRESH)
Pr 11: 25 whoever refreshes others will be **r**.

REFRESHES (REFRESH)
Ps 23: 3 he **r** my soul. He guides me along

REFRESHING* (REFRESH)
Ps 19: 7 of the LORD is perfect, **r** the soul.
Ac 3: 19 of **r** may come from the Lord,

REFUGE
Nu 35: 11 some towns to be your cities of **r**,
Dt 33: 27 The eternal God is your **r**,
Jos 20: 2 to designate the cities of **r**,
Ru 2: 12 wings you have come to take **r**."
2Sa 22: 3 stronghold, my **r** and my savior—
22: 31 he shields all who take **r** in him.
Ps 2: 12 Blessed are all who take **r** in him.
5: 11 let all who take **r** in you be glad;
9: 9 The LORD is a **r**
16: 1 safe, my God, for in you I take **r**.
17: 7 your right hand those who take **r**
18: 2 in whom I take **r**, my shield
31: 2 be my rock of **r**, a strong fortress
34: 8 blessed is the one who takes **r**
36: 7 People take **r** in the shadow of your
46: 1 God is our **r** and strength,
62: 8 hearts to him, for God is our **r**.
71: 1 In you, LORD, I have taken **r**;
91: 2 "He is my **r** and my fortress,
144: 2 in whom I take **r**, who subdues
Pr 14: 26 and for their children it will be a **r**.
30: 5 a shield to those who take **r** in him.
Na 1: 7 is good, a **r** in times of trouble.

REFUSE (REFUSED)
Jn 5: 40 you **r** to come to me to have life.

REFUSED (REFUSE)
2Th 2: 10 They perish because they **r** to love
Rev 16: 9 they **r** to repent and glorify him.

REGARD (REGARDS)
1Th 5: 13 in the highest **r** in love because

REGARDS (REGARD)
Ro 14: 14 if anyone **r** something as unclean,

REGRET
2Co 7: 10 leads to salvation and leaves no **r**,

REHOBOAM
Son of Solomon (1Ki 11:43; 1Ch 3:10). Harsh treatment of subjects caused divided kingdom (1Ki 12:1–24; 14:21–31; 2Ch 10–12).

REIGN (REIGNED REIGNS)
Ps 68: 16 mountain where God chooses to **r**,
Isa 9: 7 He will **r** on David's throne
24: 23 for the LORD Almighty will **r**
32: 1 a king will **r** in righteousness
Jer 23: 5 a King who will **r** wisely and do
Eze 20: 33 will **r** over you with a mighty hand
Lk 1: 33 he will **r** over Jacob's descendants
Ro 6: 12 Therefore do not let sin **r** in your
1Co 4: 8 You have begun to **r**—
4: 8 that we also might **r** with you!
15: 25 For he must **r** until he has put all
2Ti 2: 12 we endure, we will also **r** with him.
Rev 11: 15 and he will **r** for ever and ever."
20: 6 **r** with him for a thousand years.
22: 5 And they will **r** for ever and ever.

REIGNED (REIGN)
Ro 5: 21 so that, just as sin **r** in death,
Rev 20: 4 and **r** with Christ a thousand years.

REIGNS (REIGN)
Ex 15: 18 "The LORD **r** for ever and ever."
Ps 9: 7 The LORD **r** forever;
47: 8 God **r** over the nations;
93: 1 The LORD **r**, he is robed
96: 10 the nations, "The LORD **r**."
97: 1 The LORD **r**, let the earth be glad;
99: 1 The LORD **r**, let the nations
146: 10 The LORD **r** forever, your God,
Isa 52: 7 who say to Zion, "Your God **r**!"
Rev 19: 6 For our Lord God Almighty **r**.

REIN
Jas 1: 26 yet do not keep a tight **r** on their

REJECT (REJECTED REJECTION REJECTS)
Ps 94: 14 the LORD will not **r** his people;
Ro 11: 1 I ask then: Did God **r** his people?
1Th 5: 22 **r** every kind of evil.

REJECTED (REJECT)
1Sa 8: 7 but they have **r** me as their king.
1Ki 19: 10 Israelites have **r** your covenant,
2Ki 17: 15 They **r** his decrees and the
Ps 66: 20 to God, who has not **r** my prayer
118: 22 stone the builders **r** has become
Isa 5: 24 for they have **r** the law
41: 9 chosen you and have not **r** you.
53: 3 was despised and **r** by mankind,
Jer 8: 9 Since they have **r** the word
Mt 21: 42 stone the builders **r** has become
1Ti 4: 4 nothing is to be **r** if it is received
1Pe 2: 4 **r** by humans but chosen by God
2: 7 stone the builders **r** has become

REJECTION* (REJECT)
Ro 11: 15 if their **r** brought reconciliation

REJECTS (REJECT)
Lk 10: 16 whoever **r** me **r** him who sent me."
Jn 3: 36 whoever **r** the Son will not see life,
1Th 4: 8 anyone who **r** this instruction does

REJOICE (JOY)
Dt 12: 7 shall **r** in everything you have put
1Ch 16: 10 of those who seek the LORD **r**.
16: 31 Let the heavens **r**, let the earth be
Ps 5: 11 those who love your name may **r**
9: 14 Zion, and there **r** in your salvation.
34: 2 let the afflicted hear and **r**.
63: 11 But the king will **r** in God;
66: 6 come, let us **r** in him.
68: 3 be glad and **r** before God;
105: 3 of those who seek the LORD **r**.
118: 24 let us **r** today and be glad.
119: 14 I **r** in following your statutes as one
119:162 I **r** in your promise like one who
149: 2 Let Israel **r** in their Maker;
Pr 5: 18 you **r** in the wife of your youth.
23: 25 May your father and mother **r**;
24: 17 stumble, do not let your heart **r**,

Isa 9: 3 as warriors **r** when dividing
35: 1 the wilderness will **r** and blossom.
61: 7 of disgrace you will **r** in your
62: 5 bride, so will your God **r** over you.
Jer 31: 12 they will **r** in the bounty
Zep 3: 17 but will **r** over you with singing."
Zec 9: 9 **R** greatly, Daughter Zion!
Lk 6: 23 "**R** in that day and leap for joy,
10: 20 but **r** that your names are written
15: 6 together and says, '**R** with me;
15: 9 together and says, '**R** with me;
Ro 12: 15 **R** with those who **r**;
16: 19 obedience, so I **r** because of you;
Php 2: 17 I am glad and **r** with all of you.
3: 1 brothers and sisters, **r** in the Lord!
4: 4 **R** in the Lord always. I will say it again: **R**!
1Th 5: 16 **R** always,
1Pe 4: 13 **r** inasmuch as you participate
Rev 19: 7 Let us **r** and be glad and give him

REJOICES (JOY)
Ps 13: 5 my heart **r** in your salvation.
16: 9 my heart is glad and my tongue **r**;
Pr 23: 24 a man who fathers a wise son **r**
Isa 61: 10 my soul **r** in my God.
62: 5 as a bridegroom **r** over his bride,
Lk 1: 47 and my spirit **r** in God my Savior,
Ac 2: 26 my heart is glad and my tongue **r**;
1Co 12: 26 is honored, every part **r** with it.
13: 6 delight in evil but **r** with the truth.

REJOICING (JOY)
2Sa 6: 12 to the City of David with **r**.
Ne 12: 43 The sound of **r** in Jerusalem could
Ps 30: 5 night, but **r** comes in the morning.
Pr 14: 13 may ache, and **r** may end in grief.
Lk 15: 7 the same way there will be more **r**
Ac 5: 41 **r** because they had been counted
2Co 6: 10 sorrowful, yet always **r**;

RELATE*
Ps 71: 15 I know not how to **r** them all.

RELATIONS
Lev 18: 22 "'Do not have sexual **r**
1Co 7: 1 to have sexual **r** with a woman."

RELATIVE (RELATIVES)
Pr 27: 10 neighbor nearby than a **r** far away.

RELATIVES (RELATIVE)
Pr 19: 7 The poor are shunned by all their **r**
Mk 6: 4 among his **r** and in his own home."
Lk 21: 16 brothers and sisters, **r** and friends,
1Ti 5: 8 who does not provide for their **r**,

RELEASE (RELEASED)
Isa 61: 1 **r** from darkness for the prisoners,

RELEASED (RELEASE)
Ro 7: 6 we have been **r** from the law so
1Co 7: 27 Do not seek to be **r**. Are you free
Rev 20: 7 Satan will be **r** from his prison

RELENT (RELENTED RELENTS)
Dt 32: 36 **r** concerning his servants when he
Am 1: 3 even for four, I will not **r**.

RELENTED (RELENT)
Ex 32: 14 the LORD **r** and did not bring
2Sa 24: 16 the LORD **r** concerning the disaster
Jdg 2: 18 for the LORD **r** because of their
Ps 106: 45 and out of his great love he **r**.
Jnh 3: 10 he **r** and did not bring on them

RELENTS* (RELENT)
Joel 2: 13 and he **r** from sending calamity.
Jnh 4: 2 God who **r** from sending calamity.

RELIABLE (RELY)
2Ti 2: 2 entrust to **r** people who will also be
2Pe 1: 19 message as something completely **r**

RELIANCE* (RELY)
Ps 26: 3 have lived in **r** on your faithfulness.
Pr 25: 19 a lame foot is **r** on the unfaithful

RELIED (RELY)
2Ch 13: 18 were victorious because they **r**
16: 8 Yet when you **r** on the LORD,
Ps 71: 6 From birth I have **r** on you;

RELIEF
Job 35: 9 they plead for **r** from the arm
Ps 94: 13 you grant them **r** from days
Ps 143: 1 and righteousness come to my **r**.
La 3: 49 will flow unceasingly, without **r**,
3: 56 not close your ears to my cry for **r**."
2Th 1: 7 and give **r** to you who are troubled,

RELIES* (RELY)
Isa 28: 16 the one who **r** on it will never be
Gal 3: 11 no one who **r** on the law is justified

RELIGION* (RELIGIOUS)
Ac 25: 19 dispute with him about their own **r**
26: 5 to the strictest sect of our **r**,
1Ti 5: 4 of all to put their **r** into practice
Jas 1: 26 and their **r** is worthless.
1: 27 **R** that God our Father accepts as

RELIGIOUS (RELIGION)
Jas 1: 26 Those who consider themselves **r**

RELY (RELIABLE RELIANCE RELIED RELIES)
Ps 59: 10 my God on whom I can **r**.
59: 17 fortress, my God on whom I can **r**.
Isa 50: 10 of the LORD and **r** on their God.
Eze 33: 26 You **r** on your sword, you do
2Co 1: 9 that we might not **r** on ourselves
Gal 3: 10 For all who **r** on the works
1Jn 4: 16 and **r** on the love God has for us.

REMAIN (REMAINS)
Nu 33: 55 you allow to **r** will become barbs
Ps 102: 27 But you **r** the same, and your years
Jn 1: 32 heaven as a dove and **r** on him.
15: 4 **R** in me, as I also **r** in you.
15: 4 by itself; it must **r** in the vine.
15: 7 If you **r** in me and my words **r**
15: 9 have I loved you. Now **r** in my love.
Ro 13: 8 Let no debt **r** outstanding,
1Co 13: 13 And now these three **r**:
Heb 1: 11 They will perish, but you **r**;
1Jn 2: 27 just as it has taught you, **r** in him.

REMAINS (REMAIN)
Ps 146: 6 he **r** faithful forever.
2Ti 2: 13 if we are faithless, he **r** faithful,
Heb 7: 3 Son of God, he **r** a priest forever.

REMEDY
Isa 3: 7 day he will cry out, "I have no **r**.

REMEMBER (REMEMBERED REMEMBERS REMEMBRANCE)
Ge 9: 15 I will **r** my covenant between me
Ex 20: 8 "**R** the Sabbath day by keeping it
33: 13 **R** that this nation is your people."
Dt 5: 15 **R** that you were slaves in Egypt
1Ch 16: 12 **R** the wonders he has done,
Job 36: 24 **R** to extol his work, which people
Ps 25: 6 **R**, LORD, your great mercy
63: 6 On my bed I **r** you; I think of you
74: 2 **R** the nation you purchased long
77: 11 I will **r** your miracles of long ago.
Ecc 12: 1 **R** your Creator in the days of your
Isa 46: 8 "**R** this, keep it in mind, take it
Jer 31: 34 and will **r** their sins no more."
Hab 3: 2 in wrath **r** mercy.
Lk 1: 72 and to **r** his holy covenant,
Gal 2: 10 we should continue to **r** the poor,
Php 1: 3 I thank my God every time I **r** you.
2Ti 2: 8 **R** Jesus Christ, raised from the
Heb 8: 12 and will **r** their sins no more."

REMEMBERED (REMEMBER)
Ex 2: 24 he **r** his covenant with Abraham,
Ps 98: 3 He has **r** his love and his
106: 45 for their sake he **r** his covenant
111: 4 He has caused his wonders to be **r**;
136: 23 He **r** us in our low estate
Isa 65: 17 The former things will not be **r**,
Eze 18: 22 committed will be **r** against them.
33: 13 that person has done will be **r**;

REMEMBERS (REMEMBER)
Ps 103: 14 are formed, he **r** that we are dust.
111: 5 he **r** his covenant forever.
Isa 43: 25 own sake, and **r** your sins no more.

REMEMBRANCE (REMEMBER)
Lk 22: 19 given for you; do this in **r** of me."
1Co 11: 24 is for you; do this in **r** of me."
11: 25 whenever you drink it, in **r** of me."

REMIND
Jn 14: 26 will **r** you of everything I have said
2Pe 1: 12 So I will always **r** you of these

REMNANT
Ezr 9: 8 has been gracious in leaving us a **r**
Isa 11: 11 the surviving **r** of his people
Jer 23: 3 "I myself will gather the **r** of my
Zec 8: 12 inheritance to the **r** of this people.
Ro 11: 5 the present time there is a **r** chosen

REMOVED
Ps 30: 11 you **r** my sackcloth and clothed me
103: 12 so far has he **r** our transgressions
Jn 20: 1 that the stone had been **r**

REND*
Isa 64: 1 you would **r** the heavens and come
Joel 2: 13 **R** your heart and not your

RENEW (RENEWAL RENEWED RENEWING)
Ps 51: 10 and **r** a steadfast spirit within me.
Isa 40: 31 in the LORD will **r** their strength.

RENEWAL (RENEW)
Isa 57: 10 You found **r** of your strength,
Titus 3: 5 of rebirth and **r** by the Holy Spirit,

RENEWED (RENEW)
Ps 103: 5 that your youth is **r** like the eagle's.
2Co 4: 16 yet inwardly we are being **r** day

RENEWING* (RENEW)
Ro 12: 2 transformed by the **r** of your mind.

RENOUNCE (RENOUNCED RENOUNCES)
Da 4: 27 **R** your sins by doing what is right,

RENOUNCED (RENOUNCE)
2Co 4: 2 we have **r** secret and shameful

RENOUNCES* (RENOUNCE)
Pr 28: 13 confesses and **r** them finds mercy.

RENOWN*
Ge 6: 4 were the heroes of old, men of **r**.
Ps 102: 12 your **r** endures through all
135: 13 endures forever, your **r**, LORD,
Isa 26: 8 and **r** are the desire of our hearts.
55: 13 This will be for the LORD's **r**,
63: 12 to gain for himself everlasting **r**,
Jer 13: 11 'to be my people for my **r**
32: 20 have gained the **r** that is still yours.
33: 9 Then this city will bring me **r**, joy,
49: 25 the city of **r** not been abandoned,
Eze 26: 17 of **r**, peopled by men of the sea!

REPAID (PAY)
Lk 6: 34 to sinners, expecting to be **r** in full.
14: 14 you will be **r** at the resurrection
Col 3: 25 Anyone who does wrong will be **r**

REPAY (PAY)
Dt 7: 10 those who hate him he will **r** to
32: 35 It is mine to avenge; I will **r**.
Ru 2: 12 May the LORD **r** you for what you
Ps 103: 10 or **r** us according to our iniquities.
Jer 25: 14 I will **r** them according to their
Ro 12: 17 Do not **r** anyone evil for evil.
12: 19 I will **r**," says the Lord.
1Pe 3: 9 Do not **r** evil with evil or insult
3: 9 contrary, **r** evil with blessing,

REPAYING (PAY)
1Ti 5: 4 own family and so **r** their parents

REPEATED
Heb 10: 1 the same sacrifices **r** endlessly year

REPENT (REPENTANCE REPENTED REPENTS)
1Ki 8: 47 **r** and plead with you in the land
Job 36: 10 commands them to **r** of their evil.
42: 6 I despise myself and **r** in dust
Jer 15: 19 "If you **r**, I will restore you that you
Eze 18: 30 declares the Sovereign LORD. **R**!
18: 32 the Sovereign LORD. **R** and live!
Mt 3: 2 and saying, "**R**, for the kingdom
4: 17 time on Jesus began to preach, "**R**,
Mk 6: 12 and preached that people should **r**.
Lk 13: 3 But unless you **r**, you too will all
17: 3 and if they **r**, forgive them.
Ac 2: 38 Peter replied, "**R** and be baptized,
3: 19 **R**, then, and turn to God,
17: 30 all people everywhere to **r**.
26: 20 I preached that they should **r**
Rev 2: 5 If you do not **r**, I will come to

REPENTANCE (REPENT)
Isa 30: 15 "In **r** and rest is your salvation,
Mt 3: 8 Produce fruit in keeping with **r**.

Mk 1: 4 preaching a baptism of **r**
Lk 3: 8 Produce fruit in keeping with **r**.
5: 32 call the righteous, but sinners to **r**."
24: 47 **r** for the forgiveness of sins will be
Ac 20: 21 that they must turn to God in **r**
26: 20 demonstrate their **r** by their deeds.
Ro 2: 4 is intended to lead you to **r**?
2Co 7: 10 Godly sorrow brings **r** that leads
2Pe 3: 9 perish, but everyone to come to **r**.

REPENTED (REPENT)
Mt 11: 21 they would have **r** long ago

REPENTS (REPENT)
Lk 15: 7 over one sinner who **r** than over
15: 10 of God over one sinner who **r**."

REPORTS
Ex 23: 1 "Do not spread false **r**. Do not help

REPOSES*
Pr 14: 33 Wisdom **r** in the heart

REPRESENTATION*
Heb 1: 3 glory and the exact **r** of his being,

REPRIMAND
Pr 29: 15 A rod and a **r** impart wisdom,

REPROACH
Job 27: 6 conscience will not **r** me as long
Isa 51: 7 Do not fear the **r** of mere mortals
1Ti 3: 2 Now the overseer is to be above **r**,

REPROVE*
1Ti 5: 20 you are to **r** before everyone,

REPUTATION
1Ti 3: 7 also have a good **r** with outsiders,

REQUESTS
Ps 20: 5 May the LORD grant all your **r**.
Php 4: 6 present your **r** to God.

REQUIRE (REQUIRED REQUIRES)
Mic 6: 8 what does the LORD **r** of you?

REQUIRED (REQUIRE)
1Co 4: 2 Now it is **r** that those who have

REQUIRES (REQUIRE)
1Ki 2: 3 what the LORD your God **r**:
Ro 3: 27 because of the law that **r** faith.
Heb 9: 22 the law **r** that nearly everything

RESCUE (RESCUED RESCUES)
Ps 22: 8 they say, "let the LORD **r** him.
31: 2 ear to me, come quickly to my **r**;
34: 22 The LORD will **r** his servants;
44: 26 **r** us because of your unfailing
69: 14 **R** me from the mire, do not let me
91: 14 says the LORD, "I will **r** him;
143: 9 **R** me from my enemies, LORD,
Da 6: 20 been able to **r** you from the lions?"
Ro 7: 24 Who will **r** me from this body
Gal 1: 4 sins to **r** us from the present evil
2Pe 2: 9 the Lord knows how to **r** the godly

RESCUED (RESCUE)
Ps 18: 17 He **r** me from my powerful enemy,
Pr 11: 8 The righteous person is **r**
Isa 35: 10 those the LORD has **r** will return.
Col 1: 13 For he has **r** us from the dominion

RESCUES (RESCUE)
Da 6: 27 He **r** and he saves;
1Th 1: 10 who **r** us from the coming wrath.

RESENT* (RESENTFUL)
Pr 3: 11 discipline, and do not **r** his rebuke,
15: 12 Mockers **r** correction, so they

RESENTFUL* (RESENT)
2Ti 2: 24 to everyone, able to teach, not **r**.

RESERVE (RESERVED)
1Ki 19: 18 Yet I **r** seven thousand in Israel—

RESERVED (RESERVE)
Ro 11: 4 "I have **r** for myself seven thousand

RESIST (RESISTED)
Da 11: 32 know their God will firmly **r** him.
Mt 5: 39 I tell you, do not **r** an evil person.
Lk 21: 15 of your adversaries will be able to **r**
Ro 9: 19 For who is able to **r** his will?"
Jas 4: 7 **R** the devil, and he will flee
1Pe 5: 9 **R** him, standing firm in the faith,

RESISTED (RESIST)
Job 9: 4 Who has **r** him and come

RESOLVED
Da 1: 8 Daniel **r** not to defile himself
1Co 2: 2 For I **r** to know nothing while I

RESOUNDING*
2Ch 30: 21 day with **r** instruments dedicated
Ps 150: 5 cymbals, praise him with **r** cymbals.
1Co 13: 1 I am only a **r** gong or a clanging

RESPECT (RESPECTABLE RESPECTED RESPECTS)
Lev 19: 3 of you must **r** your mother
19: 32 show **r** for the elderly and revere
Mal 1: 6 a master, where is the **r** due me?"
Eph 5: 33 and the wife must **r** her husband.
6: 5 obey your earthly masters with **r**
1Th 4: 12 that your daily life may win the **r**
1Ti 3: 4 do so in a manner worthy of full **r**.
3: 8 way, deacons are to be worthy of **r**,
3: 11 the women are to be worthy of **r**,
6: 1 their masters worthy of full **r**,
Titus 2: 2 worthy of **r**, self-controlled,
1Pe 2: 17 Show proper **r** to everyone,
3: 7 them with **r** as the weaker partner
3: 15 But do this with gentleness and **r**,

RESPECTABLE* (RESPECT)
1Ti 3: 2 self-controlled, **r**, hospitable,

RESPECTED (RESPECT)
Pr 31: 23 Her husband is **r** at the city gate,

RESPECTS (RESPECT)
Pr 13: 13 whoever **r** a command is rewarded.

RESPOND
Ps 102: 17 He will **r** to the prayer
Hos 2: 21 "In that day I will **r**,"

RESPONSIBLE
Nu 1: 53 The Levites are to be **r** for the care
1Co 7: 24 each person, as **r** to God,

REST (RESTED RESTING RESTS SABBATH-REST)
Ex 31: 15 seventh day is a day of sabbath **r**,
33: 14 go with you, and I will give you **r**."
Lev 25: 5 The land is to have a year of **r**.
Dt 31: 16 "You are going to **r** with your
Jos 14: 15 Then the land had **r** from war.
21: 44 The LORD gave them **r** on every
1Ki 5: 4 the LORD my God has given me **r**
1Ch 22: 9 who will be a man of peace and **r**,
Job 3: 17 and there the weary are at **r**.
Ps 16: 9 my body also will **r** secure,
62: 1 Truly my soul finds **r** in God;
62: 5 Yes, my soul, find **r** in God;
90: 17 favor of the Lord our God **r** on us;
91: 1 the Most High will **r** in the shadow
95: 11 'They shall never enter my **r**.'"
Pr 6: 10 a little folding of the hands to **r**—
Isa 11: 2 Spirit of the LORD will **r** on him—
30: 15 repentance and **r** is your salvation,
32: 18 homes, in undisturbed places of **r**.
57: 20 which cannot **r**, whose waves cast
Jer 6: 16 and you will find **r** for your souls.
47: 6 of the LORD, how long till you **r**?
Mt 11: 28 burdened, and I will give you **r**.
2Co 12: 9 that Christ's power may **r** on me.
Heb 3: 11 'They shall never enter my **r**.'"
4: 3 we who have believed enter that **r**,
4: 10 for anyone who enters God's **r**
Rev 14: 13 "they will **r** from their labor,

RESTED (REST)
Ge 2: 2 on the seventh day he **r** from all his
Heb 4: 4 the seventh day God **r** from all his

RESTING (REST)
Isa 11: 10 and his **r** place will be glorious.

RESTITUTION
Ex 22: 3 who steals must certainly make **r**,
Lev 6: 5 must make **r** in full, add a fifth
Nu 5: 8 the **r** belongs to the LORD

RESTORATION (RESTORE)
2Co 13: 11 Strive for full **r**, encourage one

RESTORE (RESTORATION RESTORED)
Ps 51: 12 **R** to me the joy of your salvation
80: 3 **R** us, O God; make your face shine
126: 4 **R** our fortunes, LORD,
Jer 31: 18 **R** me, and I will return, because
La 5: 21 **R** us to yourself, LORD, that we

Da 9: 25 the time the word goes out to **r**
Na 2: 2 The LORD will **r** the splendor
Gal 6: 1 by the Spirit should **r** that person
1Pe 5: 10 will himself **r** you and make you

RESTORED (RESTORE)
Job 42: 10 the LORD **r** his fortunes and gave
2Co 13: 9 prayer is that you may be fully **r**.

RESTRAINED (RESTRAINT)
Ps 78: 38 Time after time he **r** his anger

RESTRAINING (RESTRAINT)
Pr 27: 16 **r** her is like **r** the wind or grasping
Col 2: 23 any value in **r** sensual indulgence.

RESTRAINT (RESTRAINED RESTRAINING)
Pr 17: 27 has knowledge uses words with **r**,
29: 18 is no revelation, people cast off **r**;

RESTS (REST)
Dt 33: 12 one the LORD loves **r** between his
Pr 19: 23 then one **r** content,
Lk 2: 14 to those on whom his favor **r**."

RESULT (RESULTS)
Ro 6: 22 to holiness, and the **r** is eternal life.
11: 31 too may now receive mercy as a **r**
2Co 3: 3 from Christ, the **r** of our ministry,
2Th 1: 5 as a **r** you will be counted worthy
1Pe 1: 7 may **r** in praise, glory and honor
1Pe 1: 9 you are receiving the end **r** of your

RESULTS* (RESULT)
1Th 2: 1 our visit to you was not without **r**.

RESURRECTION*
Mt 22: 23 who say there is no **r**, came to him
22: 28 at the **r**, whose wife will she be
22: 30 the **r** people will neither marry nor
22: 31 But about the **r** of the dead—
27: 53 came out of the tombs after Jesus' **r**
Mk 12: 18 who say there is no **r**, came to him
12: 23 At the **r** whose wife will she be,
Lk 14: 14 be repaid at the **r** of the righteous."
20: 27 who say there is no **r**, came to Jesus
20: 33 at the **r** whose wife will she be,
20: 35 in the **r** from the dead will neither
20: 36 since they are children of the **r**.
Jn 11: 24 rise again in the **r** at the last day."
11: 25 said to her, "I am the **r** and the life.
Ac 1: 22 become a witness with us of his **r**."
2: 31 he spoke of the **r** of the Messiah,
4: 2 in Jesus the **r** of the dead.
4: 33 to testify to the **r** of the Lord Jesus.
17: 18 good news about Jesus and the **r**.
17: 32 they heard about the **r** of the dead,
23: 6 of the hope of the **r** of the dead."
23: 8 Sadducees say that there is no **r**,
24: 15 that there will be a **r** of both
24: 21 'It is concerning the **r** of the dead
Ro 1: 4 in power by his **r** from the dead:
6: 5 be united with him in a **r** like his.
1Co 15: 12 say that there is no **r** of the dead?
15: 13 If there is no **r** of the dead, then
15: 21 the **r** of the dead comes also
15: 29 Now if there is no **r**, what will
15: 42 So will it be with the **r** of the dead.
Php 3: 10 yes, to know the power of his **r**
3: 11 attaining to the **r** from the dead.
2Ti 2: 18 that the **r** has already taken place,
Heb 6: 2 on of hands, the **r** of the dead,
11: 35 they might gain an even better **r**.
1Pe 1: 3 a living hope through the **r** of Jesus
3: 21 It saves you by the **r** of Jesus Christ,
Rev 20: 5 This is the first **r**.
20: 6 are those who share in the first **r**.

RETALIATE*
1Pe 2: 23 their insults at him, he did not **r**;

RETRIBUTION
Ps 69: 22 may it become **r** and a trap.
Jer 51: 56 For the LORD is a God of **r**;
Ro 11: 9 a stumbling block and a **r** for them.

RETURN (RETURNED RETURNS)
Ge 3: 19 you are and to dust you will **r**."
2Sa 12: 23 to him, but he will not **r** to me."
2Ch 30: 9 If you **r** to the LORD, then your
Ne 1: 9 but if you **r** to me and obey my
Job 10: 21 before I go to the place of no **r**,
16: 22 pass before I take the path of no **r**.

Job 22: 23 If you **r** to the Almighty, you will
Ps 80: 14 **R** to us, God Almighty!
116: 12 What shall I **r** to the LORD for all
126: 6 to sow, will **r** with songs of joy,
Isa 10: 21 A remnant will **r**, a remnant
35: 10 the LORD has rescued will **r**.
55: 11 It will not **r** to me empty, but will
Jer 24: 7 for they will **r** to me with all their
31: 8 a great throng will **r**.
31: 22 the woman will **r** to the man."
La 3: 40 them, and let us **r** to the LORD.
Hos 6: 1 "Come, let us **r** to the LORD.
12: 6 But you must **r** to your God;
14: 1 **R**, Israel, to the LORD your God.
Joel 2: 12 "**r** to me with all your heart,
Zec 1: 3 '**R** to me,' declares the LORD
1: 3 'and I will **r** to you,'
10: 9 will survive, and they will **r**.

RETURNED (RETURN)
Ps 35: 13 my prayers **r** to me unanswered,
Am 4: 6 town, yet you have not **r** to me,"
1Pe 2: 25 now you have **r** to the Shepherd

RETURNS (RETURN)
Pr 3: 14 silver and yields better **r** than gold.
Isa 52: 8 When the LORD **r** to Zion,
Mt 24: 46 finds him doing so when he **r**.

REUBEN
Firstborn of Jacob by Leah (Ge 29:32; 46:8; 1Ch 2:1). Attempted to rescue Joseph (Ge 37:21–30). Lost birthright for sleeping with Bilhah (Ge 35:22; 49:4). Tribe of blessed (Ge 49:3–4; Dt 33:6), numbered (Nu 1:21; 26:7), allotted land east of Jordan (Nu 32; 34:14; Jos 13:15), west (Eze 48:6), failed to help Deborah (Jdg 5:15–16), supported David (1Ch 12:37), 12,000 from (Rev 7:5).

REVEAL (REVEALED REVEALS REVELATION REVELATIONS)
Mt 11: 27 to whom the Son chooses to **r** him.
Gal 1: 16 to **r** his Son in me so that I might

REVEALED (REVEAL)
Dt 29: 29 but the things **r** belong to us
Isa 40: 5 the glory of the LORD will be **r**,
43: 12 I have **r** and saved and proclaimed
53: 1 has the arm of the LORD been **r**?
65: 1 "I **r** myself to those who did not
Mt 11: 25 and **r** them to little children.
Jn 12: 38 has the arm of the Lord been **r**?"
17: 6 "I have **r** you to those whom you
Ro 1: 17 the righteousness of God is **r**—
8: 18 with the glory that will be **r** in us.
10: 20 I **r** myself to those who did not ask
16: 26 now **r** and made known through
1Co 2: 10 these are the things God has **r** to us
2Th 1: 7 the Lord Jesus is **r** from heaven
2: 3 and the man of lawlessness is **r**,
1Pe 1: 7 and honor when Jesus Christ is **r**.
1: 20 was **r** in these last times for your
4: 13 be overjoyed when his glory is **r**.

REVEALS* (REVEAL)
Nu 23: 3 Whatever he **r** to me I will tell
Job 12: 22 He **r** the deep things of darkness
Da 2: 22 He **r** deep and hidden things;
2: 28 a God in heaven who **r** mysteries.
Am 4: 13 who **r** his thoughts to mankind,

REVELATION* (REVEAL)
2Sa 7: 17 David all the words of this entire **r**.
1Ch 17: 15 David all the words of this entire **r**.
Pr 29: 18 Where there is no **r**, people cast off
Da 10: 1 a **r** was given to Daniel (who was
Hab 2: 2 "Write down the **r** and make it
2: 3 For the **r** awaits an appointed time;
Lk 2: 32 a light for **r** to the Gentiles,
Ro 16: 25 with the **r** of the mystery hidden
1Co 14: 6 to you, unless I bring you some **r**
14: 26 a **r**, a tongue or an interpretation.
14: 30 And if a **r** comes to someone who
Gal 1: 12 I received it by **r** from Jesus Christ.
2: 2 I went in response to a **r** and,
Eph 1: 17 you the Spirit of wisdom and **r**,
3: 3 mystery made known to me by **r**,
Rev 1: 1 The **r** from Jesus Christ, which

REVELATIONS* (REVEAL)
2Co 12: 1 on to visions and **r** from the Lord.
12: 7 of these surpassingly great **r**.

REVELED* (REVELRY)
Ne 9: 25 they **r** in your great goodness.
Ac 7: 41 **r** in what their own hands had

REVELRY (REVELED)
Ex 32: 6 drink and got up to indulge in **r**.
1Co 10: 7 drink and got up to indulge in **r**."

REVENGE (VENGEANCE)
Lev 19: 18 "'Do not seek **r** or bear a grudge
Ro 12: 19 Do not take **r**, my dear friends,

REVERE* (REVERENCE REVERENT REVERING)
Lev 19: 32 for the elderly and **r** your God.
Dt 4: 10 learn to **r** me as long as they live
13: 4 must follow, and him you must **r**.
14: 23 to **r** the LORD your God always.
17: 19 may learn to **r** the LORD his God
28: 58 book, and do not **r** this glorious
Job 37: 24 Therefore, people **r** him, for does
Ps 22: 23 **R** him, all you descendants
33: 8 all the people of the world **r** him.
102: 15 kings of the earth will **r** your glory.
Isa 25: 3 cities of ruthless nations will **r** you.
59: 19 of the sun, they will **r** his glory.
63: 17 our hearts so we do not **r** you?
Hos 10: 3 because we did not **r** the LORD.
Mal 4: 2 for you who **r** my name, the sun
1Pe 3: 15 But in your hearts **r** Christ as Lord.
Rev 11: 18 and your people who **r** your name,

REVERENCE (REVERE)
Lev 19: 30 and have **r** for my sanctuary.
Ne 5: 15 of **r** for God I did not act like that.
Ps 5: 7 in **r** I bow down toward your holy
Da 6: 26 must fear and **r** the God of Daniel.
2Co 7: 1 holiness out of **r** for God.
Eph 5: 21 to one another out of **r** for Christ.
Col 3: 22 of heart and **r** for the Lord.
1Pe 3: 2 see the purity and **r** of your lives.

REVERENT* (REVERE)
Ecc 8: 12 fear God, who are **r** before him.
Titus 2: 3 women to be **r** in the way they live,
Heb 5: 7 heard because of his **r** submission.
1Pe 1: 17 time as foreigners here in **r** fear.
2: 18 in **r** fear of God submit yourselves

REVERING* (REVERE)
Dt 8: 6 in obedience to him and **r** him.
Ne 1: 11 who delight in **r** your name.

REVERSE*
Isa 43: 13 When I act, who can **r** it?"

REVIVE*
Ps 80: 18 **r** us, and we will call on your name
85: 6 Will you not **r** us again, that your
Isa 57: 15 to **r** the spirit of the lowly and to **r** the heart of the contrite.
Hos 6: 2 After two days he will **r** us;

REVOKED
Isa 45: 23 integrity a word that will not be **r**:

REWARD (REWARDED REWARDING REWARDS)
Ge 15: 1 am your shield, your very great **r**."
1Sa 24: 19 May the LORD **r** you well
Ps 19: 11 in keeping them there is great **r**.
62: 12 "You **r** everyone according to what
127: 3 the LORD, offspring a **r** from him.
Pr 9: 12 are wise, your wisdom will **r** you;
11: 18 sows righteousness reaps a sure **r**.
12: 14 work of their hands brings them **r**.
19: 17 he will **r** them for what they have
25: 22 head, and the LORD will **r** you.
Isa 40: 10 See, his **r** is with him, and his
49: 4 hand, and my **r** is with my God."
61: 8 my faithfulness I will **r** my people
62: 11 See, his **r** is with him, and his
Jer 17: 10 to **r** each person according to their
32: 19 you **r** each person according to
Mt 5: 12 because great is your **r** in heaven,
6: 1 will have no **r** from your Father
6: 5 they have received their **r** in full.
10: 41 prophet will receive a prophet's **r**,
10: 41 will receive a righteous person's **r**.
Mt 16: 27 he will **r** each person according
Lk 6: 23 because great is your **r** in heaven.
6: 35 Then your **r** will be great, and you
1Co 3: 14 the builder will receive a **r**.
Eph 6: 8 that the Lord will **r** each one
Col 3: 24 inheritance from the Lord as a **r**.
Heb 11: 26 he was looking ahead to his **r**.
Rev 22: 12 My **r** is with me, and I will give

REWARDED (REWARD)
Ru 2: 12 May you be richly **r** by the LORD,
2Sa 22: 21 cleanness of my hands he has **r** me.
2Ch 15: 7 give up, for your work will be **r**."
Ps 18: 24 The LORD has **r** me according
Pr 13: 13 whoever respects a command is **r**.
13: 21 righteous are **r** with good things.
14: 14 ways, and the good **r** for theirs.
Jer 31: 16 for your work will be **r**,"
1Co 3: 8 and they will each be **r** according
Heb 10: 35 it will be richly **r**.
2Jn : 8 for, but that you may be **r** fully.

REWARDING* (REWARD)
Rev 11: 18 for **r** your servants the prophets

REWARDS (REWARD)
1Sa 26: 23 The LORD **r** everyone for their
Heb 11: 6 he **r** those who earnestly seek him.

RIBS
Ge 2: 21 he took one of the man's **r**

RICH (RICHES RICHEST)
Job 34: 19 does not favor the **r** over the poor,
Ps 49: 16 be overawed when others grow **r**,
145: 8 slow to anger and **r** in love.
Pr 21: 17 wine and olive oil will never be **r**.
22: 2 **R** and poor have this in common:
23: 4 Do not wear yourself out to get **r**;
28: 6 blameless than the **r** whose ways
28: 20 to get **r** will not go unpunished.
28: 22 The stingy are eager to get **r** and
Ecc 5: 12 but as for the **r**, their abundance
Isa 33: 6 a **r** store of salvation and wisdom
53: 9 and with the **r** in his death,
Jer 9: 23 or the **r** boast of their riches,
Mt 19: 23 for someone who is **r** to enter
Lk 1: 53 but has sent the **r** away empty.
6: 24 "But woe to you who are **r**, for you
12: 21 but is not **r** toward God."
16: 1 There was a **r** man whose manager
21: 1 he saw the **r** putting their gifts
2Co 6: 10 poor, yet making many **r**;
8: 2 poverty welled up in **r** generosity.
8: 9 that though he was **r**, yet for your
Eph 2: 4 love for us, God, who is **r** in mercy,
1Ti 6: 9 Those who want to get **r** fall
6: 17 Command those who are **r** in this
6: 18 to be **r** in good deeds, and to be
Jas 1: 10 But the **r** should take pride in their
2: 5 eyes of the world to be **r** in faith
5: 1 Now listen, you **r** people,
Rev 2: 9 and your poverty—yet you are **r**!
3: 18 in the fire, so you can become **r**;

RICHES (RICH)
Job 36: 18 that no one entices you by **r**;
Ps 49: 6 wealth and boast of their great **r**?
62: 10 though your **r** increase, do not set
119: 14 statutes as one rejoices in great **r**.
Pr 3: 16 in her left hand are **r** and honor.
11: 28 Those who trust in their **r** will fall,
22: 1 is more desirable than great **r**;
22: 4 its wages are **r** and honor and life.
27: 24 for **r** do not endure forever,
30: 8 give me neither poverty nor **r**,
Isa 10: 3 Where will you leave your **r**?
60: 5 you the **r** of the nations will come.
Jer 9: 23 strength or the rich boast of their **r**,
Lk 8: 14 by life's worries, **r** and pleasures,
Ro 9: 23 to make the **r** of his glory known
11: 33 the depth of the **r** of the wisdom
Eph 2: 7 he might show the incomparable **r**
3: 8 to the Gentiles the boundless **r**
Col 1: 27 among the Gentiles the glorious **r**
2: 2 may have the full **r** of complete

RICHEST (RICH)
Isa 55: 2 and you will delight in the **r** of fare.

RID
Ge 21: 10 "Get **r** of that slave woman and her
1Co 5: 7 Get **r** of the old yeast, so that you
Gal 4: 30 "Get **r** of the slave woman and her

RIDE (RIDER RIDING)
Ps 45: 4 In your majesty **r** forth victoriously

RIDER (RIDE)
Rev 6: 2 Its **r** held a bow, and he was given
19: 11 whose **r** is called Faithful and True.

RIDING (RIDE)
Zec 9: 9 lowly and **r** on a donkey, on a colt,
Mt 21: 5 gentle and **r** on a donkey,

RIGGING
Isa 33: 23 Your **r** hangs loose: The mast is not

RIGHT (RIGHTS)
Ge 4: 7 If you do what is **r**, will you not be
18: 19 of the LORD by doing what is **r**
18: 25 not the Judge of all the earth do **r**?"
48: 13 on his **r** toward Israel's left hand
Ex 15: 6 Your **r** hand, LORD, was majestic
15: 26 God and do what is **r** in his eyes,
Dt 5: 32 do not turn aside to the **r**
6: 18 Do what is **r** and good
13: 18 and doing what is **r** in his eyes.
Jos 1: 7 do not turn from it to the **r**
1Sa 12: 23 you the way that is good and **r**.
1Ki 3: 9 distinguish between **r** and wrong.
15: 5 David had done what was **r**
2Ki 7: 9 other, "What we're doing is not **r**.
Ne 9: 13 and laws that are just and **r**,
Ps 16: 8 With him at my **r** hand, I will not
16: 11 eternal pleasures at your **r** hand.
17: 7 your **r** hand those who take refuge
18: 35 and your **r** hand sustains me;
19: 8 The precepts of the LORD are **r**,
23: 3 He guides me along the **r** paths
25: 9 He guides the humble in what is **r**
33: 4 For the word of the LORD is **r**
44: 3 it was your **r** hand, your arm,
45: 4 let your **r** hand achieve awesome
51: 4 so you are **r** in your verdict
63: 8 your **r** hand upholds me.
73: 23 you hold me by my **r** hand.
91: 7 ten thousand at your **r** hand, but it
98: 1 his **r** hand and his holy arm have
106: 3 act justly, who always do what is **r**.
110: 1 "Sit at my **r** hand until I make your
118: 15 "The LORD's **r** hand has done
137: 5 may my **r** hand forget its skill.
139: 10 me, your **r** hand will hold me fast.
Pr 1: 3 doing what is **r** and just and fair;
4: 27 Do not turn to the **r** or the left;
14: 12 There is a way that appears to be **r**,
16: 13 value the one who speaks what is **r**.
18: 17 a lawsuit the first to speak seems **r**,
28: 5 do not understand what is **r**,
Ecc 7: 20 no one who does what is **r**
SS 1: 4 How **r** they are to adore you!
Isa 1: 17 Learn to do **r**; seek justice.
7: 15 reject the wrong and choose the **r**,
30: 10 us no more visions of what is **r**!
30: 21 Whether you turn to the **r**
41: 10 you with my righteous **r** hand.
41: 13 God who takes hold of your **r** hand
48: 13 my **r** hand spread out the heavens;
64: 5 the help of those who gladly do **r**,
Jer 23: 5 do what is just and **r** in the land.
Eze 18: 5 man who does what is just and **r**.
18: 21 decrees and does what is just and **r**,
33: 14 their sin and do what is just and **r**
Hos 14: 9 The ways of the LORD are **r**;
Mt 5: 29 If your **r** eye causes you to stumble,
6: 3 know what your **r** hand is doing,
22: 44 my **r** hand until I put your enemies
25: 33 He will put the sheep on his **r**
Jn 1: 12 he gave the **r** to become children
Ac 2: 34 said to my Lord: "Sit at my **r** hand
7: 55 standing at the **r** hand of God.
Ro 3: 4 that you may be proved **r** when
8: 34 is at the **r** hand of God and is
9: 21 Does not the potter have the **r**
12: 17 careful to do what is **r** in the eyes
1Co 6: 12 "I have the **r** to do anything,"
9: 4 Don't we have the **r** to food
1Co 10: 23 "I have the **r** to do anything,"
2Co 8: 21 we are taking pains to do what is **r**,
Eph 1: 20 and seated him at his **r** hand
6: 1 parents in the Lord, for this is **r**.
Php 4: 8 whatever is **r**, whatever is pure,
Heb 1: 3 he sat down at the **r** hand
Jas 2: 8 as yourself," you are doing **r**.
1Pe 3: 14 if you should suffer for what is **r**,
1Jn 2: 29 who does what is **r** has been born
Rev 2: 7 I will give the **r** to eat from the tree
3: 21 I will give the **r** to sit with me
22: 11 let the one who does **r** continue

RIGHTEOUS (RIGHTEOUSLY RIGHTEOUSNESS)
Ge 6: 9 Noah was a **r** man,
18: 23 "Will you sweep away the **r**
Nu 23: 10 Let me die the death of the **r**,
Ne 9: 8 your promise because you are **r**.
9: 33 to us, you have remained **r**;
Job 36: 7 He does not take his eyes off the **r**;
Ps 1: 5 sinners in the assembly of the **r**.
5: 12 Surely, LORD, you bless the **r**;
9: 4 sitting enthroned as the **r** judge.
11: 7 For the LORD is **r**, he loves
15: 2 who does what is **r**, who speaks
34: 15 eyes of the LORD are on the **r**,
37: 6 will make your **r** reward shine like
37: 16 that the **r** have than the wealth
37: 21 repay, but the **r** give generously;
37: 25 yet I have never seen the **r** forsaken
37: 30 The mouths of the **r** utter wisdom,
55: 22 he will never let the **r** be shaken.
64: 10 The **r** will rejoice in the LORD
65: 5 us with awesome and **r** deeds,
68: 3 But may the **r** be glad and rejoice
71: 15 My mouth will tell of your **r** deeds,
112: 4 gracious and compassionate and **r**.
118: 19 Open for me the gates of the **r**;
118: 20 through which the **r** may enter.
119: 7 upright heart as I learn your **r** laws.
119:137 You are **r**, LORD, and your laws
119:144 Your statutes are always **r**;
140: 13 the **r** will praise your name,
143: 2 no one living is **r** before you.
145: 17 The LORD is **r** in all his ways
Pr 3: 33 but he blesses the home of the **r**.
4: 18 of the **r** is like the morning sun,
10: 7 The name of the **r** is used
10: 11 The mouth of the **r** is a fountain
10: 16 The wages of the **r** is life,
10: 20 The tongue of the **r** is choice silver,
10: 24 what the **r** desire will be granted.
10: 28 The prospect of the **r** is joy,
10: 32 lips of the **r** know what finds favor,
11: 23 The desire of the **r** ends only
11: 30 The fruit of the **r** is a tree of life,
12: 10 The **r** care for the needs of their
12: 21 No harm overtakes the **r**,
13: 9 The light of the **r** shines brightly,
15: 28 heart of the **r** weighs its answers,
15: 29 but he hears the prayer of the **r**.
18: 10 the **r** run to it and are safe.
20: 7 The **r** lead blameless lives;
21: 15 it brings joy to the **r** but terror
23: 24 father of a **r** child has great joy;
28: 1 but the **r** are as bold as a lion.
29: 6 but the **r** shout for joy and are glad.
29: 7 The **r** care about justice
29: 27 The **r** detest the dishonest;
Ecc 7: 20 there is no one on earth who is **r**,
Isa 5: 16 will be proved holy by his **r** acts.
26: 7 The path of the **r** is level;
41: 10 uphold you with my **r** right hand.
45: 21 from me, a **r** God and a Savior;
53: 11 by his knowledge my **r** servant will
64: 6 all our **r** acts are like filthy rags;
Jer 23: 5 I will raise up for David a **r** Branch,
23: 6 The LORD Our **R** Savior.
Eze 3: 20 when a **r** person turns from their
18: 5 "Suppose there is a **r** man who
18: 20 of the **r** will be credited to them,
33: 12 'If someone who is **r** disobeys,
Da 9: 18 requests of you because we are **r**,
Hab 2: 4 but the **r** person will live by his
Zec 9: 9 comes to you, **r** and victorious,
Mal 3: 18 see the distinction between the **r**
Mt 5: 45 and sends rain on the **r**
9: 13 For I have not come to call the **r**,
10: 41 will receive a **r** person's reward.
13: 43 the **r** will shine like the sun
13: 49 and separate the wicked from the **r**
25: 37 "Then the **r** will answer him, 'Lord,
25: 46 but the **r** to eternal life."
Ac 24: 15 will be a resurrection of both the **r**
Ro 1: 17 "The **r** will live by faith."
2: 5 his **r** judgment will be revealed.
2: 13 the law who will be declared **r**.
3: 10 "There is no one **r**, not even one;
3: 20 Therefore no one will be declared **r**
5: 18 one **r** act resulted in justification
5: 19 one man the many will be made **r**.
Gal 3: 11 because "the **r** will live by faith."
1Ti 1: 9 that the law is made not for the **r**
2Ti 4: 8 which the Lord, the **r** Judge,
Titus 3: 5 because of **r** things we had done,
Heb 10: 38 "But my **r** one will live by faith.
Jas 2: 24 is considered **r** by what they do
5: 16 prayer of a **r** person is powerful
1Pe 3: 12 the eyes of the Lord are on the **r**
3: 18 for sins, the **r** for the unrighteous,
4: 18 "If it is hard for the **r** to be saved,
1Jn 2: 1 Jesus Christ, the **R** One.
3: 7 The one who does what is right is **r**, just as he is **r**.
Rev 19: 8 (Fine linen stands for the **r** acts

RIGHTEOUSLY* (RIGHTEOUS)
Isa 33: 15 Those who walk **r** and speak what
Jer 11: 20 who judge **r** and test the heart

RIGHTEOUSNESS (RIGHTEOUS)
Ge 15: 6 and he credited it to him as **r**.
Dt 9: 4 of this land because of my **r**."
1Sa 26: 23 rewards everyone for their **r**
1Ki 10: 9 you king to maintain justice and **r**."
Job 37: 23 in his justice and great **r**, he does
Ps 7: 17 to the LORD because of his **r**;
9: 8 He rules the world in **r** and judges
33: 5 The LORD loves **r** and justice;
35: 28 My tongue will proclaim your **r**,
36: 6 Your **r** is like the highest
45: 7 You love **r** and hate wickedness;
48: 10 your right hand is filled with **r**.
71: 2 In your **r**, rescue me and deliver
71: 19 Your **r**, God,
85: 10 **r** and peace kiss each other.
89: 14 **R** and justice are the foundation
96: 13 He will judge the world in **r**
98: 9 He will judge the world in **r**
103: 6 The LORD works **r** and justice
103: 17 his **r** with their children's children
106: 31 to him as **r** for endless generations
111: 3 deeds, and his **r** endures forever.
132: 9 your priests be clothed with your **r**;
145: 7 and joyfully sing of your **r**.
Pr 11: 5 The **r** of the blameless makes their
11: 18 the one who sows **r** reaps a sure
13: 6 **R** guards the person of integrity,
14: 34 **R** exalts a nation, but sin
16: 8 Better a little with **r** than much
16: 12 a throne is established through **r**.
16: 31 it is attained in the way of **r**.
21: 21 Whoever pursues **r** and love finds
Isa 9: 7 with justice and **r** from that time
11: 4 but with **r** he will judge the needy,
16: 5 justice and speeds the cause of **r**.
26: 9 the people of the world learn **r**.
32: 17 The fruit of that **r** will be peace;
42: 6 the LORD, have called you in **r**;
42: 21 sake of his **r** to make his law great
45: 8 heavens above, rain down my **r**;
51: 1 you who pursue **r** and who seek
51: 6 last forever, my **r** will never fail.
51: 8 But my **r** will last forever,
58: 8 then your **r** will go before you,
59: 17 He put on **r** as his breastplate,
61: 10 and arrayed me in a robe of his **r**,
Jer 9: 24 justice and **r** on earth, for in these I
Eze 3: 20 righteous person turns from their **r**
14: 20 save only themselves by their **r**.
18: 20 The **r** of the righteous will be
33: 12 that person's former **r** will count

Da 9: 24 to bring in everlasting **r**, to seal
12: 3 and those who lead many to **r**,
Hos 10: 12 Sow **r** for yourselves, reap the fruit
Am 5: 24 river, **r** like a never-failing stream!
Mic 7: 9 out into the light; I will see his **r**.
Zep 2: 3 Seek **r**, seek humility;
Mal 4: 2 the sun of **r** will rise with healing
Mt 5: 6 those who hunger and thirst for **r**,
5: 10 who are persecuted because of **r**,
5: 20 you that unless your **r** surpasses
6: 1 not to practice your **r** in front
6: 33 seek first his kingdom and his **r**,
Jn 16: 8 to be in the wrong about sin and **r**
Ac 24: 25 As Paul talked about **r**,
Ro 1: 17 gospel the **r** of God is revealed—
3: 5 brings out God's **r** more clearly,
3: 22 This **r** is given through faith
3: 25 He did this to demonstrate his **r**,
3: 26 he did it to demonstrate his **r** at
4: 3 and it was credited to him as **r**."
4: 5 ungodly, their faith is credited as **r**.
4: 6 to whom God credits **r** apart
4: 9 faith was credited to him as **r**.
4: 13 through the **r** that comes by faith.
4: 22 why "it was credited to him as **r**."
6: 13 to him as an instrument of **r**.
6: 16 or to obedience, which leads to **r**?
6: 18 sin and have become slaves to **r**.
6: 19 yourselves as slaves to **r** leading
8: 10 the Spirit gives life because of **r**.
9: 30 obtained it, a **r** that is by faith;
10: 3 they did not submit to God's **r**.
14: 17 but of **r**, peace and joy in the Holy
1Co 1: 30 is, our **r**, holiness and redemption.
2Co 3: 9 is the ministry that brings **r**!
5: 21 we might become the **r** of God.
6: 7 with weapons of **r** in the right hand
6: 14 For what do **r** and wickedness have
9: 9 their **r** endures forever."
Gal 2: 21 **r** could be gained through the law,
3: 6 and it was credited to him as **r**."
3: 21 **r** would certainly have come
Eph 4: 24 created to be like God in true **r**
5: 9 in all goodness, **r** and truth)
6: 14 with the breastplate of **r** in place,
Php 1: 11 the fruit of **r** that comes through
3: 6 for **r** based on the law, faultless.
3: 9 the **r** that comes from God
1Ti 6: 11 all this, and pursue **r**, godliness,
2Ti 2: 22 evil desires of youth and pursue **r**,
3: 16 correcting and training in **r**,
4: 8 is in store for me the crown of **r**,
Heb 5: 13 with the teaching about **r**.
7: 2 Melchizedek means "king of **r**";
11: 7 and became heir of the **r** that is
12: 11 it produces a harvest of **r** and peace
Jas 2: 23 and it was credited to him as **r**,"
3: 18 sow in peace reap a harvest of **r**.
1Pe 2: 24 we might die to sins and live for **r**;
2Pe 2: 21 not to have known the way of **r**,
3: 13 and a new earth, where **r** dwells.

RIGHTS (RIGHT)
Pr 31: 8 for the **r** of all who are destitute.
Isa 10: 2 to deprive the poor of their **r**
La 3: 35 deny people their **r** before the Most
1Co 9: 18 so not make full use of my **r** as

RING
Pr 11: 22 Like a gold **r** in a pig's snout is
Lk 15: 22 Put a **r** on his finger and sandals

RIOTS
2Co 6: 5 in beatings, imprisonments and **r**;

RIPE
Joel 3: 13 the sickle, for the harvest is **r**.
Am 8: 1 a basket of **r** fruit.
Jn 4: 35 at the fields! They are **r** for harvest.
Rev 14: 15 for the harvest of the earth is **r**."

RISE (RAISE RAISED RISEN ROSE)
Nu 24: 17 a scepter will **r** out of Israel.
Isa 26: 19 their bodies will **r**—let those who
Mal 4: 2 of righteousness will **r** with healing
Mt 27: 63 'After three days I will **r** again.'
Mk 8: 31 killed and after three days **r** again.
Lk 18: 33 On the third day he will **r** again."
Jn 5: 29 who have done what is good will **r**
5: 29 who have done what is evil will **r**
20: 9 that Jesus had to **r** from the dead.)
Ac 17: 3 had to suffer and **r** from the dead.
1Th 4: 16 and the dead in Christ will **r** first.

RISEN (RISE)
Mt 28: 6 is not here; he has **r**, just as he said.
Mk 16: 6 He has **r**! He is not here.
Lk 24: 34 The Lord has **r** and has appeared

RIVER (RIVERS)
Ps 46: 4 There is a **r** whose streams make
Isa 66: 12 "I will extend peace to her like a **r**,
Eze 47: 12 will grow on both banks of the **r**.
Rev 22: 1 the angel showed me the **r**

RIVERS (RIVER)
Ps 137: 1 By the **r** of Babylon we sat
Jn 7: 38 **r** of living water will flow

ROAD (CROSSROADS ROADS)
Mt 7: 13 gate and broad is the **r** that leads

ROADS (ROAD)
Lk 3: 5 The crooked **r** shall become

ROARING
1Pe 5: 8 prowls around like a **r** lion looking

ROB (ROBBERS ROBBERY ROBS)
Mal 3: 8 "Will a mere mortal **r** God?

ROBBERS (ROB)
Jer 7: 11 Name, become a den of **r** to you?
Lk 19: 46 you have made it 'a den of **r**.'"
Jn 10: 8 come before me are thieves and **r**,

ROBBERY (ROB)
Isa 61: 8 I hate **r** and wrongdoing.

ROBE (ROBED ROBES)
Ge 37: 3 and he made an ornate **r** for him.
Isa 6: 1 the train of his **r** filled the temple.
61: 10 me in a **r** of his righteousness,
Rev 6: 11 each of them was given a white **r**,

ROBED (ROBE)
Ps 93: 1 the LORD is **r** in majesty
Isa 63: 1 Who is this, **r** in splendor,

ROBES (ROBE)
Ps 45: 8 All your **r** are fragrant with myrrh
Rev 7: 13 asked me, "These in white **r**—

ROBS* (ROB)
Pr 19: 26 Whoever **r** their father and drives
28: 24 Whoever **r** their father or mother

ROCK
Ge 49: 24 of the Shepherd, the **R** of Israel,
Ex 17: 6 Strike the **r**, and water will come
Nu 20: 8 Speak to that **r** before their eyes
Dt 32: 4 He is the **R**, his works are perfect,
32: 13 him with honey from the **r**,
2Sa 22: 2 "The LORD is my **r**, my fortress
Ps 18: 2 The LORD is my **r**, my fortress
19: 14 LORD, my **R** and my Redeemer.
40: 2 he set my feet on a **r** and gave me
61: 2 me to the **r** that is higher than I.
92: 15 he is my **R**, and there is no
Isa 26: 4 LORD himself, is the **R** eternal.
51: 1 Look to the **r** from which you were
Da 2: 34 you were watching, a **r** was cut out,
Mt 7: 24 man who built his house on the **r**.
16: 18 on this **r** I will build my church,
Ro 9: 33 and a **r** that makes them fall,
1Co 10: 4 them, and that **r** was Christ.
1Pe 2: 8 and a **r** that makes them fall."

ROD (RODS)
2Sa 7: 14 I will punish him with a **r** wielded
Ps 2: 9 will break them with a **r** of iron;
23: 4 your **r** and your staff, they comfort
Pr 13: 24 Whoever spares the **r** hates their
22: 15 the **r** of discipline will drive it far
23: 13 if you punish them with the **r**,
29: 15 A **r** and a reprimand impart
Isa 11: 4 the earth with the **r** of his mouth;

RODS (ROD)
2Co 11: 25 Three times I was beaten with **r**,

ROLL (ROLLED)
Mk 16: 3 "Who will **r** the stone away

ROLLED (ROLL)
Lk 24: 2 They found the stone **r** away

ROMAN
Ac 16: 37 even though we are **R** citizens,
22: 25 to flog a **R** citizen who hasn't even

ROOF (ROOFS)
Pr 21: 9 a corner of the **r** than share a house

ROOFS
Mt 10: 27 in your ear, proclaim from the **r**.

ROOM (ROOMS)
Mt 6: 6 go into your **r**, close the door
Mk 14: 15 He will show you a large **r** upstairs,
Lk 2: 7 there was no guest **r** available
Jn 8: 37 you have no **r** for my word.
21: 25 the whole world would not have **r**
2Co 7: 2 Make **r** for us in your hearts.

ROOMS (ROOM)
Ge 6: 14 ark of cypress wood; make **r** in it
Jn 14: 2 My Father's house has many **r**;

ROOSTER
Mt 26: 34 before the **r** crows, you will disown

ROOT (ROOTED ROOTS)
Isa 11: 10 day the **R** of Jesse will stand as
53: 2 and like a **r** out of dry ground.
Mt 3: 10 ax is already at the **r** of the trees,
13: 21 But since they have no **r**, they last
Ro 11: 16 if the **r** is holy, so are the branches.
15: 12 "The **R** of Jesse will spring up,
1Ti 6: 10 the love of money is a **r** of all kinds
Rev 5: 5 the tribe of Judah, the **R** of David,
22: 16 I am the **R** and the Offspring

ROOTED (ROOT)
Eph 3: 17 being **r** and established in love,
Col 2: 7 **r** and built up in him, strengthened

ROOTS (ROOT)
Isa 11: 1 from his **r** a Branch will bear fruit.

ROSE (RISE)
SS 2: 1 I am a **r** of Sharon, a lily
Mt 2: 2 We saw his star when it **r** and have
1Th 4: 14 believe that Jesus died and **r** again,

ROTS*
Pr 14: 30 to the body, but envy **r** the bones.

ROUGH
Isa 42: 16 and make the **r** places smooth.
Lk 3: 5 straight, the **r** ways smooth.

ROUND
Ecc 1: 6 **r** and **r** it goes, ever returning on

ROYAL
Ps 45: 9 right hand is the **r** bride in gold
Da 1: 8 to defile himself with the **r** food
Jas 2: 8 If you really keep the **r** law found
1Pe 2: 9 are a chosen people, a **r** priesthood,

RUBIES
Job 28: 18 the price of wisdom is beyond **r**.
Pr 3: 15 She is more precious than **r**;
8: 11 wisdom is more precious than **r**,
31: 10 She is worth far more than **r**.

RUDDER*
Jas 3: 4 by a very small **r** wherever the pilot

RUDDY
SS 5: 10 My beloved is radiant and **r**,

RUIN (RUINED RUINS)
Pr 10: 8 but a chattering fool comes to **r**.
10: 10 and a chattering fool comes to **r**.
10: 14 but the mouth of a fool invites **r**.
10: 29 but it is the **r** of those who do evil.
11: 17 the cruel bring **r** on themselves.
11: 29 Whoever brings **r** on their family
15: 27 The greedy bring **r** to their
18: 24 unreliable friends soon comes to **r**,
19: 3 person's own folly leads to their **r**,
19: 13 A foolish child is a father's **r**,
26: 28 and a flattering mouth works **r**.
Ecc 4: 5 fold their hands and **r** themselves.
SS 2: 15 the little foxes that **r** the vineyards,
Eze 21: 27 A **r**! A **r**! I will make it a **r**!
1Ti 6: 9 desires that plunge people into **r**

RUINED (RUIN)
Isa 6: 5 "I am **r**! For I am a man of unclean
Mt 9: 17 out and the wineskins will be **r**.
12: 25 divided against itself will be **r**,

RUINS (RUIN)
2Ti 2: 14 value, and only **r** those who listen.

RULE (RULER RULERS RULES RULING)
Ge 1: 26 so that they may **r** over the fish
3: 16 husband, and he will **r** over you."
4: 7 have you, but you must **r** over it."
Jdg 8: 22 said to Gideon, "**R** over us—
1Sa 12: 12 'No, we want a king to **r** over us'—
Ps 67: 4 for you **r** the peoples with equity
119:133 to your word; let no sin **r** over me.
Pr 17: 2 A prudent servant will **r** over
Isa 28: 10 do that, a **r** for this, a **r** for that;
Zec 6: 13 and will sit and **r** on his throne.
9: 10 His **r** will extend from sea to sea
Ro 15: 12 who will arise to **r** over the nations;
1Co 7: 17 This is the **r** I lay down in all
Gal 6: 16 mercy to all who follow this **r**—
Eph 1: 21 far above all **r** and authority,
Col 3: 15 peace of Christ **r** in your hearts,
2Th 3: 10 were with you, we gave you this **r**:
Rev 2: 27 that one 'will **r** them with an iron
12: 5 who "will **r** all the nations
19: 15 "He will **r** them with an iron

RULER (RULE)
1Sa 10: 1 the LORD anointed you **r** over his
13: 14 and appointed him **r** of his people,
Pr 19: 6 Many curry favor with a **r**,
23: 1 When you sit to dine with a **r**,
25: 15 Through patience a **r** can be
29: 26 Many seek an audience with a **r**,
Isa 60: 17 governor and well-being your **r**.
Da 9: 25 the Anointed One, the **r**, comes,
Mic 5: 2 me one who will be **r** over Israel,
Mt 2: 6 will come a **r** who will shepherd
Eph 2: 2 of the **r** of the kingdom of the air,
1Ti 6: 15 the blessed and only **R**, the King
Rev 1: 5 and the **r** of the kings of the earth.

RULERS (RULE)
Ps 2: 2 and the **r** band together against
8: 6 You made them **r** over the works
119:161 **R** persecute me without cause,
Isa 40: 23 and reduces the **r** of this world
Da 7: 27 and all **r** will worship and obey
Mt 20: 25 the **r** of the Gentiles lord it over
Ac 13: 27 and their **r** did not recognize Jesus,
Ro 13: 3 For **r** hold no terror for those who
1Co 2: 6 of this age or of the **r** of this age,
Eph 3: 10 should be made known to the **r**
6: 12 blood, but against the **r**,
Col 1: 16 or powers or **r** or authorities;

RULES (RULE)
Nu 15: 15 is to have the same **r** for you
2Sa 23: 3 when he **r** in the fear of God,
Ps 22: 28 LORD and he **r** over the nations.
66: 7 He **r** forever by his power, his eyes
103: 19 heaven, and his kingdom **r** over all.
Isa 29: 13 on merely human **r** they have been
40: 10 power, and he **r** with a mighty arm.
Mt 15: 9 teachings are merely human **r**.'"
Lk 22: 26 and the one who **r** like the one who
2Ti 2: 5 by competing according to the **r**.

RULING (RULE)
Ex 15: 25 There the LORD issued a **r**
Pr 25: 11 settings of silver is a **r** rightly given.

RUMORS
Jer 51: 46 or be afraid when **r** are heard
Mt 24: 6 You will hear of wars and **r** of wars,

RUN (RAN RUNNERS RUNNING RUNS)
Ps 19: 5 champion rejoicing to **r** his course.
Pr 4: 12 when you **r**, you will not stumble.
18: 10 the righteous **r** to it and are safe.
Isa 10: 3 To whom will you **r** for help?
40: 31 they will **r** and not grow weary,
Joel 3: 18 ravines of Judah will **r** with water.
Hab 2: 2 so that a herald may **r** with it.
1Co 9: 24 **R** in such a way as to get the prize.
Php 2: 16 on the day of Christ that I did not **r**
Heb 12: 1 let us **r** with perseverance the race

RUNNERS* (RUN)
1Co 9: 24 know that in a race all the **r** run,

RUNNING (RUN)
Ps 133: 2 on the head, **r** down on the beard,
Lk 17: 23 Do not go **r** off after them.
1Co 9: 26 not run like someone **r** aimlessly;
Gal 2: 2 had not been **r** my race in vain.
5: 7 You were **r** a good race. Who cut

RUNS (RUN)
Jn 10: 12 he abandons the sheep and **r** away.

RUSH (RUSHES RUSHING)
Pr 1: 16 for their feet **r** into evil, they are
6: 18 feet that are quick to **r** into evil,
Isa 59: 7 Their feet **r** into sin; they are swift

RUSHES (RUSH)
Pr 26: 17 by the ears is someone who **r**

RUSHING (RUSH)
Pr 18: 4 fountain of wisdom is a **r** stream.

RUTH*
Moabitess; widow who went to Bethlehem with mother-in-law Naomi (Ru 1). Gleaned in field of Boaz; shown favor (Ru 2). Proposed marriage to Boaz (Ru 3). Married (Ru 4:1–12); bore Obed, ancestor of David (Ru 4:13–22), Jesus (Mt 1:5).

RUTHLESS
Pr 11: 16 honor, but **r** men gain only wealth.

SABBATH (SABBATHS)
Ex 20: 8 "Remember the **S** day by keeping it
31: 14 "'Observe the **S**, because it is
Lev 25: 2 the land itself must observe a **s**
Dt 5: 12 "Observe the **S** day by keeping it
Isa 56: 2 keeps the **S** without desecrating
56: 6 keep the **S** without desecrating
58: 13 if you call the **S** a delight
Jer 17: 21 not to carry a load on the **S** day
Mt 12: 1 through the grainfields on the **S**.
Lk 13: 10 On a **S** Jesus was teaching in one
Col 2: 16 New Moon celebration or a **S** day.

SABBATH-REST* (REST)
Heb 4: 9 then, a **S** for the people of God;

SABBATHS (SABBATH)
2Ch 2: 4 morning and evening and on the **S**,
Eze 20: 12 I gave them my **S** as a sign between

SACKCLOTH
Ps 30: 11 you removed my **s** and clothed me
Da 9: 3 in fasting, and in **s** and ashes.
Mt 11: 21 would have repented long ago in **s**

SACRED
Ge 1: 14 as signs to mark **s** times, and days
Lev 23: 2 you are to proclaim as **s** assemblies.
Ps 15: 1 who may dwell in your **s** tent?
Mt 7: 6 "Do not give dogs what is **s**;
Ro 14: 5 one day more **s** than another;
1Co 3: 17 for God's temple is **s**, and you
2Pe 1: 18 were with him on the **s** mountain.
2: 21 turn their backs on the **s** command

SACRIFICE (SACRIFICED SACRIFICES)
Ge 22: 2 **S** him there as a burnt offering
Ex 12: 27 'It is the Passover **s** to the LORD,
1Sa 15: 22 To obey is better than **s**, and to
1Ki 18: 38 the LORD fell and burned up the **s**,
1Ch 21: 24 or **s** a burnt offering that costs me
Ps 40: 6 **S** and offering you did not desire—
50: 14 "**S** thank offerings to God,
51: 16 You do not delight in **s**, or I would
51: 17 My **s**, O God, is a broken spirit;
54: 6 I will **s** a freewill offering to you;
107: 22 Let them **s** thank offerings and tell
141: 2 of my hands be like the evening **s**.
Pr 15: 8 The LORD detests the **s**
21: 3 acceptable to the LORD than **s**.
Da 9: 27 of the 'seven' he will put an end to **s**
12: 11 time that the daily **s** is abolished
Hos 6: 6 not **s**, and acknowledgment of God
Mt 9: 13 'I desire mercy, not **s**.'
Ro 3: 25 God presented Christ as a **s**
12: 1 to offer your bodies as a living **s**,
Eph 5: 2 as a fragrant offering and **s** to God.
Php 4: 18 an acceptable **s**, pleasing to God.
Heb 9: 26 away with sin by the **s** of himself.
10: 5 "**S** and offering you did not desire,
10: 10 have been made holy through the **s**
10: 14 one **s** he has made perfect forever
10: 18 **s** for sin is no longer necessary.
13: 15 offer to God a **s** of praise—
1Jn 2: 2 He is the atoning **s** for our sins,
4: 10 sent his Son as an atoning **s** for our

SACRIFICED (SACRIFICE)
Ac 15: 29 are to abstain from food **s** to idols,
1Co 5: 7 our Passover lamb, has been **s**.
8: 1 Now about food **s** to idols:
Heb 7: 27 He **s** for their sins once for all
9: 28 so Christ was **s** once to take away

SACRIFICES (SACRIFICE)
Mk 12: 33 than all burnt offerings and **s**."
Heb 9: 23 with better **s** than these.
13: 16 for with such **s** God is pleased.
1Pe 2: 5 offering spiritual **s** acceptable

SAD
Lk 18: 23 he became very **s**, because he was

SADDUCEES
Mt 16: 6 the yeast of the Pharisees and **S**."
Mk 12: 18 Then the **S**, who say there is no
Ac 23: 8 (The **S** say that there is no

SAFE (SAVE)
Ps 27: 5 of trouble he will keep me **s** in his
37: 3 in the land and enjoy **s** pasture.
Pr 18: 10 the righteous run to it and are **s**.
28: 26 who walk in wisdom are kept **s**.
29: 25 trusts in the LORD is kept **s**.
Jer 12: 5 If you stumble in **s** country,
Jn 17: 12 kept them **s** by that name you gave
1Jn 5: 18 was born of God keeps them **s**,

SAFETY (SAVE)
Ps 4: 8 alone, LORD, make me dwell in **s**.
Hos 2: 18 land, so that all may lie down in **s**.
1Th 5: 3 "Peace and **s**," destruction will

SAKE
1Sa 12: 22 the **s** of his great name the LORD
Ps 23: 3 the right paths for his name's **s**.
44: 22 your **s** we face death all day long;
106: 8 Yet he saved them for his name's **s**,
Isa 42: 21 for the **s** of his righteousness
43: 25 for my own **s**, and remembers your
48: 9 my own name's **s** I delay my wrath;
48: 11 For my own **s**, for my own **s**, I do
Jer 14: 7 LORD, for the **s** of your name.
14: 21 the **s** of your name do not despise
Eze 20: 9 But for the **s** of my name, I brought
20: 14 the **s** of my name I did what would
20: 22 the **s** of my name I did what would
36: 22 but for the **s** of my holy name,
Da 9: 17 For your **s**, Lord, look with favor
Mt 10: 39 loses their life for my **s** will find
19: 29 my **s** will receive a hundred times
1Co 9: 23 I do all this for the **s** of the gospel,
2Co 8: 9 yet for your **s** he became poor,
12: 10 is why, for Christ's **s**, I delight
Php 3: 7 consider loss for the **s** of Christ.
Heb 11: 26 disgrace for the **s** of Christ as
1Pe 2: 13 for the Lord's **s** to every human
3Jn : 7 It was for the **s** of the Name

SALEM
Ge 14: 18 Melchizedek king of **S** brought
Heb 7: 2 "king of **S**" means "king of peace."

SALT
Ge 19: 26 back, and she became a pillar of **s**.
Nu 18: 19 covenant of **s** before the LORD
Mt 5: 13 "You are the **s** of the earth.
5: 13 But if the **s** loses its saltiness,
Col 4: 6 seasoned with **s**, so that you may
Jas 3: 11 **s** water flow from the same spring?

SALVATION* (SAVE)
Ex 15: 2 he has become my **s**.
2Sa 22: 3 my shield and the horn of my **s**.
23: 5 he would not bring to fruition my **s**
1Ch 16: 23 proclaim his **s** day after day.
2Ch 6: 41 clothed with **s**, may your faithful
Ps 9: 14 Zion, and there rejoice in your **s**.
13: 5 my heart rejoices in your **s**.
14: 7 that **s** for Israel would come
18: 2 my shield and the horn of my **s**,
27: 1 The LORD is my light and my **s**—
28: 8 a fortress of **s** for his anointed one.
35: 3 Say to me, "I am your **s**."
35: 9 in the LORD and delight in his **s**.
37: 39 The **s** of the righteous comes
50: 23 to the blameless I will show my **s**."
51: 12 Restore to me the joy of your **s**
53: 6 that **s** for Israel would come

Ps 62: 1 rest in God; my **s** comes from him.
62: 2 Truly he is my rock and my **s**;
62: 6 Truly he is my rock and my **s**;
62: 7 **s** and my honor depend on God;
67: 2 on earth, your **s** among all nations.
69: 13 God, answer me with your sure **s**.
69: 27 do not let them share in your **s**.
69: 29 may your **s**, God, protect me.
74: 12 he brings **s** on the earth.
85: 7 love, LORD, and grant us your **s**.
85: 9 Surely his **s** is near those who fear
91: 16 satisfy him and show him my **s**."
95: 1 shout aloud to the Rock of our **s**.
96: 2 proclaim his **s** day after day.
98: 1 holy arm have worked **s** for him.
98: 2 The LORD has made his **s** known
98: 3 of the earth have seen the **s** of our
116: 13 I will lift up the cup of **s** and call
118: 14 he has become my **s**.
118: 21 you have become my **s**.
119: 41 your **s**, according to your promise;
119: 81 soul faints with longing for your **s**,
119:123 looking for your **s**, looking for your
119:155 **S** is far from the wicked, for they
119:166 I wait for your **s**, LORD, and I
119:174 I long for your **s**, LORD, and your
132: 16 I will clothe her priests with **s**,
Isa 12: 2 Surely God is my **s**; I will trust
12: 2 he has become my **s**."
12: 3 will draw water from the wells of **s**.
25: 9 let us rejoice and be glad in his **s**."
26: 1 God makes **s** its walls and
26: 18 We have not brought **s** to the earth,
30: 15 "In repentance and rest is your **s**,
33: 2 morning, our **s** in time of distress.
33: 6 a rich store of **s** and wisdom
45: 8 earth open wide, let **s** spring up,
45: 17 the LORD with an everlasting **s**;
46: 13 and my **s** will not be delayed.
46: 13 I will grant **s** to Zion, my splendor
49: 6 that my **s** may reach to the ends
49: 8 and in the day of **s** I will help you;
51: 5 near speedily, my **s** is on the way,
51: 6 But my **s** will last forever,
51: 8 my **s** through all generations."
52: 7 who proclaim **s**, who say to Zion,
52: 10 the earth will see the **s** of our God.
56: 1 for my **s** is close at hand and my
59: 16 so his own arm achieved **s** for him,
59: 17 and the helmet of **s** on his head;
60: 18 you will call your walls **S** and your
61: 10 has clothed me with garments of **s**
62: 1 the dawn, her **s** like a blazing torch.
63: 5 so my own arm achieved **s** for me,
Jer 3: 23 in the LORD our God is the **s**
La 3: 26 wait quietly for the **s** of the LORD.
Jnh 2: 9 '**S** comes from the LORD.'"
Lk 1: 69 He has raised up a horn of **s** for us
1: 71 **s** from our enemies
1: 77 of **s** through the forgiveness of
2: 30 For my eyes have seen your **s**,
3: 6 all people will see God's **s**.'"
19: 9 "Today **s** has come to this house,
Jn 4: 22 we do know, for **s** is from the Jews.
Ac 4: 12 **S** is found in no one else, for there
13: 26 this message of **s** has been sent.
13: 47 that you may bring **s** to the ends
28: 28 know that God's **s** has been sent
Ro 1: 16 brings **s** to everyone who believes:
11: 11 **s** has come to the Gentiles to make
13: 11 because our **s** is nearer now than
2Co 1: 6 it is for your comfort and **s**;
6: 2 and in the day of **s** I helped you."
6: 2 God's favor, now is the day of **s**.
7: 10 brings repentance that leads to **s**
Eph 1: 13 of truth, the gospel of your **s**.
6: 17 Take the helmet of **s** and the sword
Php 2: 12 to work out your **s** with fear
1Th 5: 8 and the hope of **s** as a helmet.
5: 9 to receive **s** through our Lord Jesus
2Ti 2: 10 they too may obtain the **s** that is
3: 15 make you wise for **s** through faith
Titus 2: 11 appeared that offers **s** to all people.
Heb 1: 14 to serve those who will inherit **s**?
2: 3 we escape if we ignore so great a **s**?
Heb 2: 3 This **s**, which was first announced
2: 10 of their **s** perfect through what he
5: 9 of eternal **s** for all who obey him
6: 9 the things that have to do with **s**.
9: 28 to bring **s** to those who are waiting
1Pe 1: 5 the coming of the **s** that is ready
1: 9 of your faith, the **s** of your souls.
1: 10 Concerning this **s**, the prophets,
2: 2 by it you may grow up in your **s**,
2Pe 3: 15 that our Lord's patience means **s**,
Jude : 3 write to you about the **s** we share,
Rev 7: 10 "**S** belongs to our God, who sits
12: 10 "Now have come the **s**
19: 1 **S** and glory and power belong to

SAMARIA (SAMARITAN)
1Ki 16: 24 bought the hill of **S** from Shemer
2Ki 17: 6 the king of Assyria captured **S**
Jn 4: 4 Now he had to go through **S**.
4: 5 came to a town in **S** called Sychar,

SAMARITAN (SAMARIA)
Lk 10: 33 But a **S**, as he traveled, came where
17: 16 and thanked him—and he was a **S**.
Jn 4: 7 When a **S** woman came to draw
Ac 8: 25 the gospel in many **S** villages.

SAMSON

Danite judge. Birth promised (Jdg 13). Married to Philistine, but wife given away (Jdg 14). Vengeance on Philistines (Jdg 15). Betrayed by Delilah (Jdg 16:1–22). Death (Jdg 16:23–31). Feats of strength: killed lion (Jdg 14:6), 30 Philistines (Jdg 14:19), 1,000 Philistines with jawbone (Jdg 15:13–17), carried off gates of Gaza (Jdg 16:3), pushed down temple of Dagon (Jdg 16:25–30).

SAMUEL

Ephraimite judge and prophet (Heb 11:32). Birth prayed for (1Sa 1:10–18). Dedicated to temple by Hannah (1Sa 1:21–28). Raised by Eli (1Sa 2:11, 18–26). Called as prophet (1Sa 3). Led Israel to victory over Philistines (1Sa 7). Asked by Israel for a king (1Sa 8). Anointed Saul as king (1Sa 9–10). Farewell speech (1Sa 12). Rebuked Saul for sacrifice (1Sa 13). Announced rejection of Saul (1Sa 15). Anointed David as king (1Sa 16). Protected David from Saul (1Sa 19:18–24). Death (1Sa 25:1). Returned from dead to condemn Saul (1Sa 28).

SANBALLAT

Led opposition to Nehemiah's rebuilding of Jerusalem (Ne 2:10, 19; 4; 6).

SANCTIFIED* (SANCTIFY)
Jn 17: 19 that they too may be truly **s**.
Ac 20: 32 among all those who are **s**.
26: 18 a place among those who are **s**
Ro 15: 16 to God, **s** by the Holy Spirit.
1Co 1: 2 to those **s** in Christ Jesus and called
6: 11 you were **s**, you were justified
7: 14 husband has been **s** through his
7: 14 wife has been **s** through her
1Th 4: 3 It is God's will that you should be **s**:
Heb 10: 29 blood of the covenant that **s** them,

SANCTIFY* (SANCTIFIED SANCTIFYING)
Jn 17: 17 **S** them by the truth; your word is
17: 19 For them I **s** myself, that they too
1Th 5: 23 peace, **s** you through and through.
Heb 9: 13 are ceremonially unclean **s** them so

SANCTIFYING* (SANCTIFY)
2Th 2: 13 be saved through the **s** work
1Pe 1: 2 through the **s** work of the Spirit,

SANCTUARY
Ex 25: 8 "Then have them make a **s** for me,
Lev 10: 13 Eat it in the **s** area, because it is
19: 30 and have reverence for my **s**.
Ps 63: 2 I have seen you in the **s** and beheld
68: 24 of my God and King into the **s**.
68: 35 You, God, are awesome in your **s**;
73: 17 till I entered the **s** of God;
102: 19 looked down from his **s** on high,
134: 2 Lift up your hands in the **s**
150: 1 Praise God in his **s**; praise him
Eze 37: 26 will put my **s** among them forever.
Da 9: 26 will destroy the city and the **s**.
Heb 6: 19 the inner **s** behind the curtain,
Heb 8: 2 and who serves in the **s**, the true
8: 5 They serve at a **s** that is a copy
9: 24 Christ did not enter a **s** made

SAND
Ge 22: 17 sky and as the **s** on the seashore.
Mt 7: 26 man who built his house on **s**.

SANDAL (SANDALS)
Ru 4: 7 one party took off his **s** and gave it

SANDALS (SANDAL)
Ex 3: 5 "Take off your **s**, for the place
Dt 25: 9 take off one of his **s**, spit in his face
Jos 5: 15 "Take off your **s**, for the place
Mt 3: 11 whose **s** I am not worthy to carry.

SANG (SING)
Ex 15: 1 and the Israelites **s** this song
15: 21 Miriam **s** to them:
Nu 21: 17 Then Israel **s** this song:
Jdg 5: 1 Barak son of Abinoam **s** this song:
1Sa 18: 7 As they danced, they **s**:
2Sa 22: 1 David **s** to the LORD the words
2Ch 5: 13 in praise to the LORD and **s**:
29: 30 So they **s** praises with gladness
Ezr 3: 11 thanksgiving they **s** to the LORD:
Job 38: 7 while the morning stars **s** together
Ps 106: 12 his promises and **s** his praise.
Rev 5: 9 And they **s** a new song, saying:
14: 3 **s** a new song before the throne
15: 3 **s** the song of God's servant Moses

SAP
Ro 11: 17 nourishing **s** from the olive root,

SAPPHIRA*
Ac 5: 1 together with his wife **S**, also sold

SARAH

Wife of Abraham, originally named Sarai; barren (Ge 11:29–31; 1Pe 3:6). Taken by Pharaoh as Abraham's sister; returned (Ge 12:10–20). Gave Hagar to Abraham; sent her away in pregnancy (Ge 16). Name changed; Isaac promised (Ge 17:15–21; 18:10–15; Heb 11:11). Taken by Abimelek as Abraham's sister; returned (Ge 20). Isaac born; Hagar and Ishmael sent away (Ge 21:1–21; Gal 4:21–31). Death (Ge 23).

SARDIS
Rev 3: 1 the angel of the church in **S** write:

SASH (SASHES)
Rev 1: 13 with a golden **s** around his chest.

SASHES (SASH)
Rev 15: 6 wore golden **s** around their chests.

SAT (SIT)
Ps 137: 1 By the rivers of Babylon we **s**
Mk 16: 19 *he **s** at the right hand of God.*
Lk 10: 39 who **s** at the Lord's feet listening
Heb 1: 3 he **s** down at the right hand
8: 1 who **s** down at the right hand
10: 12 **s** down at the right hand of God,
12: 2 and **s** down at the right hand

SATAN
Job 1: 6 and **S** also came with them.
Zec 3: 2 The LORD said to **S**, "The LORD rebuke you, **S**!
Mt 12: 26 If **S** drives out **S**, he is divided
16: 23 said to Peter, "Get behind me, **S**!
Mk 4: 15 **S** comes and takes away the word
Lk 10: 18 "I saw **S** fall like lightning
22: 3 Then **S** entered Judas,
Ro 16: 20 will soon crush **S** under your feet.
1Co 5: 5 hand this man over to **S**
2Co 11: 14 **S** himself masquerades as an angel
12: 7 a messenger of **S**, to torment me.
1Ti 1: 20 I have handed over to **S** to be
Rev 12: 9 or **S**, who leads the whole world
20: 2 **S**, and bound him for a thousand
20: 7 **S** will be released from his prison

SATISFIED (SATISFY)
Ps 17: 15 will be **s** with seeing your likeness.
22: 26 The poor will eat and be **s**;
63: 5 I will be fully **s** as with the richest
104: 28 hand, they are **s** with good things.
Pr 13: 4 desires of the diligent are fully **s**.
30: 15 are three things that are never **s**,
Ecc 5: 10 whoever loves wealth is never **s**

Isa 53: 11 he will see the light of life and be s;
Mt 14: 20 They all ate and were s,
Lk 6: 21 who hunger now, for you will be s.

SATISFIES* (SATISFY)
Ps 103: 5 s your desires with good things
107: 9 for he s the thirsty and fills
147: 14 and s you with the finest of wheat.

SATISFY (SATISFIED SATISFIES)
Ps 90: 14 S us in the morning with your
145: 16 s the desires of every living thing.
Pr 5: 19 may her breasts s you always,
Isa 55: 2 and your labor on what does not s?
58: 10 and s the needs of the oppressed,

SAUL
1. Benjamite; anointed by Samuel as first king of Israel (1Sa 9–10). Defeated Ammonites (1Sa 11). Rebuked for offering sacrifice (1Sa 13:1–15). Defeated Philistines (1Sa 14). Rejected as king for failing to annihilate Amalekites (1Sa 15). Soothed from evil spirit by David (1Sa 16:14–23). Sent David against Goliath (1Sa 17). Jealousy and attempted murder of David (1Sa 18:1–11). Gave David Michal as wife (1Sa 18:12–30). Second attempt to kill David (1Sa 19). Anger at Jonathan (1Sa 20:26–34). Pursued David: killed priests at Nob (1Sa 22), went to Keilah and Ziph (1Sa 23), life spared by David at En Gedi (1Sa 24) and in his tent (1Sa 26). Rebuked by Samuel's spirit for consulting witch at Endor (1Sa 28). Wounded by Philistines; took his own life (1Sa 31; 1Ch 10). Lamented by David (2Sa 1:17–27). Children (1Sa 14:49–51; 1Ch 8).
2. See PAUL

SAVAGE
Ac 20: 29 s wolves will come in among you

SAVE (SAFE SAFETY SALVATION SAVED SAVES SAVIOR)
Ge 45: 5 because it was to s lives that God
1Ch 16: 35 Cry out, "S us, God our Savior;
Job 40: 14 your own right hand can s you.
Ps 17: 7 who s by your right hand those
18: 27 You s the humble but bring low
28: 9 S your people and bless your
31: 16 s me in your unfailing love.
69: 35 for God will s Zion and rebuild
71: 2 turn your ear to me and s me.
72: 13 needy and s the needy from death.
91: 3 Surely he will s you
109: 31 to s their lives from those who
146: 3 in human beings, who cannot s.
Pr 2: 16 Wisdom will s you
Isa 35: 4 retribution he will come to s you."
38: 20 The LORD will s me, and we will
46: 7 cannot s them from their troubles.
59: 1 of the LORD is not too short to s,
63: 1 proclaiming victory, mighty to s."
Jer 17: 14 s me and I will be saved, for you
Eze 3: 18 evil ways in order to s their life,
14: 14 it, they could s only themselves
34: 22 I will s my flock, and they will no
Hos 1: 7 the LORD their God, will s them."
Zep 1: 18 nor their gold will be able to s
Zec 8: 7 "I will s my people
Mt 1: 21 because he will s his people
16: 25 wants to s their life will lose it,
Lk 19: 10 came to seek and to s the lost."
Jn 3: 17 but to s the world through him.
12: 47 judge the world, but to s the world.
Ro 11: 14 people to envy and s some of them.
1Co 7: 16 whether you will s your husband?
7: 16 whether you will s your wife?
1Ti 1: 15 came into the world to s sinners—
Heb 7: 25 to s completely those who come
Jas 5: 20 of their way will s them from death
Jude : 23 s others by snatching them

SAVED (SAVE)
Ps 22: 5 To you they cried out and were s;
33: 16 No king is s by the size of his army;
34: 6 he s him out of all his troubles.
106: 21 They forgot the God who s them,
116: 6 when I was brought low, he s me.
Isa 25: 9 we trusted in him, and he s us.
45: 22 "Turn to me and be s, all you ends
64: 5 How then can we be s?
Jer 4: 14 the evil from your heart and be s.
8: 20 has ended, and we are not s."
Eze 3: 19 but you will have s yourself.
33: 5 they would have s themselves.
Joel 2: 32 the name of the LORD will be s;
Mt 10: 22 stands firm to the end will be s.
24: 13 stands firm to the end will be s.
Mk 13: 13 stands firm to the end will be s.
16: 16 *believes and is baptized will be s,*
Jn 10: 9 enters through me will be s.
Ac 2: 21 on the name of the Lord will be s.'
2: 47 daily those who were being s.
4: 12 mankind by which we must be s."
15: 11 of our Lord Jesus that we are s,
16: 30 "Sirs, what must I do to be s?"
Ro 5: 9 how much more shall we be s
9: 27 the sea, only the remnant will be s.
10: 1 the Israelites is that they may be s.
10: 9 him from the dead, you will be s.
10: 13 on the name of the Lord will be s."
11: 26 and in this way all Israel will be s.
1Co 1: 18 us who are being s it is the power
3: 15 will suffer loss but yet will be s—
5: 5 that his spirit may be s on the day
10: 33 of many, so that they may be s.
15: 2 By this gospel you are s, if you hold
Eph 2: 5 it is by grace you have been s.
2: 8 For it is by grace you have been s,
2Th 2: 13 be s through the sanctifying work
1Ti 2: 4 who wants all people to be s
2: 15 will be s through childbearing—
2Ti 1: 9 He has s us and called us to a holy
Titus 3: 5 He s us through the washing
Heb 10: 39 to those who have faith and are s.

SAVES (SAVE)
Ps 7: 10 High, who s the upright in heart.
68: 20 Our God is a God who s;
145: 19 he hears their cry and s them.
Pr 11: 30 the one who is wise s lives.
Zep 3: 17 you, the Mighty Warrior who s.
1Pe 3: 21 s you by the resurrection of Jesus

SAVIOR* (SAVE)
Dt 32: 15 them and rejected the Rock their S.
2Sa 22: 3 stronghold, my refuge and my s—
22: 47 be my God, the Rock, my S!
1Ch 16: 35 Cry out, "Save us, God our S;
Ps 18: 46 to my Rock! Exalted be God my S!
24: 5 and vindication from God their S.
25: 5 you are God my S, and my hope
27: 9 reject me or forsake me, God my S.
38: 22 to help me, my Lord and my S.
42: 5 yet praise him, my S and my God.
42: 11 yet praise him, my S and my God.
43: 5 yet praise him, my S and my God.
51: 14 you who are God my S, and my
65: 5 God our S, the hope of all the ends
68: 19 to God our S, who daily bears our
79: 9 us, God our S, for the glory of your
85: 4 God our S, and put away your
89: 26 Father, my God, the Rock my S.'
Isa 17: 10 You have forgotten God your S;
19: 20 he will send them a s and defender,
43: 3 the Holy One of Israel, your S;
43: 11 and apart from me there is no s.
45: 15 himself, the God and S of Israel.
45: 21 from me, a righteous God and a S;
49: 26 am your S, your Redeemer,
60: 16 am your S, your Redeemer,
62: 11 Daughter Zion, 'See, your S comes!
63: 8 and so he became their S.
Jer 14: 8 of Israel, its S in times of distress,
23: 6 The LORD Our Righteous S.
33: 16 The LORD Our Righteous S.'
Hos 13: 4 no God but me, no S except me.
Mic 7: 7 the LORD, I wait for God my S;
Hab 3: 18 I will be joyful in God my S.
Lk 1: 47 and my spirit rejoices in God my S,
2: 11 town of David a S has been born
Jn 4: 42 that this man really is the S
Ac 5: 31 and S that he might bring Israel
13: 23 has brought to Israel the S Jesus,
Eph 5: 23 his body, of which he is the S.
Php 3: 20 we eagerly await a S from there,
1Ti 1: 1 by the command of God our S
2: 3 is good, and pleases God our S,
4: 10 God, who is the S of all people,
2Ti 1: 10 through the appearing of our S,
Titus 1: 3 me by the command of God our S,
1: 4 the Father and Christ Jesus our S.
2: 10 about God our S attractive.
2: 13 the glory of our great God and S,
3: 4 and love of God our S appeared,
3: 6 through Jesus Christ our S,
2Pe 1: 1 S Jesus Christ have received a faith
1: 11 of our Lord and S Jesus Christ.
2: 20 our Lord and S Jesus Christ and
3: 2 Lord and S through your apostles.
3: 18 of our Lord and S Jesus Christ.
1Jn 4: 14 his Son to be the S of the world.
Jude : 25 to the only God our S be glory,

SCALE (SCALES)
Ps 18: 29 with my God I can s a wall.

SCALES (SCALE)
Lev 11: 9 may eat any that have fins and s.
19: 36 Use honest s and honest weights,
Pr 11: 1 The LORD detests dishonest s,
Da 5: 27 You have been weighed on the s
Rev 6: 5 Its rider was holding a pair of s

SCAPEGOAT (GOAT)
Lev 16: 10 it into the wilderness as a s.

SCARECROW*
Jer 10: 5 Like a s in a cucumber field,

SCARLET
Jos 2: 21 she tied the s cord in the window.
Isa 1: 18 "Though your sins are like s,
Mt 27: 28 him and put a s robe on him,

SCATTER (SCATTERED SCATTERS)
Dt 4: 27 The LORD will s you among
Ne 1: 8 I will s you among the nations,
Jer 9: 16 I will s them among nations
30: 11 the nations among which I s you,
Zec 10: 9 I s them among the peoples,

SCATTERED (SCATTER)
Isa 11: 12 he will assemble the s people
Jer 31: 10 'He who s Israel will gather them
Zec 2: 6 "for I have s you to the four winds
13: 7 and the sheep will be s, and I will
Mt 26: 31 and the sheep of the flock will be s.'
Jn 11: 52 but also for the s children of God,
Ac 8: 4 who had been s preached the word
Jas 1: 1 To the twelve tribes s among
1Pe 1: 1 exiles s throughout the provinces

SCATTERS (SCATTER)
Mt 12: 30 does not gather with me s.

SCEPTER
Ge 49: 10 The s will not depart from Judah,
Nu 24: 17 a s will rise out of Israel.
Ps 45: 6 a s of justice will be the s of your
Heb 1: 8 a s of justice will be the s of your
Rev 2: 27 one 'will rule them with an iron s
12: 5 rule all the nations with an iron s."
19: 15 "He will rule them with an iron s."

SCHEMES
Pr 6: 18 a heart that devises wicked s,
10: 23 A fool finds pleasure in wicked s,
12: 2 those who devise wicked s.
14: 17 the one who devises evil s is hated.
24: 9 The s of folly are sin, and people
2Co 2: 11 For we are not unaware of his s.
Eph 6: 11 your stand against the devil's s.

SCOFFERS
2Pe 3: 3 that in the last days s will come,

SCORN (SCORNED SCORNING SCORNS)
Ps 69: 7 For I endure s for your sake,
69: 20 S has broken my heart and has left
89: 41 he has become the s of his
109: 25 I am an object of s to my accusers;
119: 22 Remove from me their s
Mic 6: 16 you will bear the s of the nations."

SCORNED (SCORN)
Ps 22: 6 and not a man, s by everyone,

SCORNING* (SCORN)
Heb 12: 2 he endured the cross, s its shame,

SCORNS* (SCORN)
Pr 13: 13 Whoever s instruction will pay
30: 17 that s an aged mother, will be

SCORPION
Lk 11: 12 asks for an egg, will give him a **s**?
Rev 9: 5 of the sting of a **s** when it strikes.

SCOUNDRELS
1Sa 2: 12 Eli's sons were **s**; they had no

SCRIPTURE (SCRIPTURES)
Jn 2: 22 they believed the **s** and the words
7: 42 Does not **S** say that the Messiah
10: 35 and **S** cannot be set aside—
Ac 8: 32 of **S** the eunuch was reading:
1Ti 4: 13 yourself to the public reading of **S**,
2Ti 3: 16 All **S** is God-breathed and is useful
2Pe 1: 20 that no prophecy of **S** came

SCRIPTURES (SCRIPTURE)
Mt 22: 29 because you do not know the **S**
Lk 24: 27 in all the **S** concerning himself.
24: 45 so they could understand the **S**.
Jn 5: 39 You study the **S** diligently because
Ac 17: 11 examined the **S** every day to see
2Ti 3: 15 you have known the Holy **S**,
2Pe 3: 16 as they do the other **S**, to their own

SCROLL
Ps 40: 7 it is written about me in the **s**.
Isa 34: 4 and the heavens rolled up like a **s**;
Eze 3: 1 eat what is before you, eat this **s**;
Heb 10: 7 it is written about me in the **s**—
Rev 6: 14 receded like a **s** being rolled up,
10: 8 the **s** that lies open in the hand
22: 18 the words of the prophecy of this **s**:

SCRUB*
Pr 20: 30 Blows and wounds **s** away evil,

SCUM
1Co 4: 13 We have become the **s** of the earth,

SEA (SEASHORE)
Ex 14: 16 the Israelites can go through the **s**
Dt 30: 13 Nor is it beyond the **s**, so that you
1Ki 7: 23 He made the **S** of cast metal,
Job 11: 9 the earth and wider than the **s**.
Ps 93: 4 mightier than the breakers of the **s**
95: 5 The **s** is his, for he made it, and his
Ecc 1: 7 All streams flow into the **s**, yet the **s** is never full.
11: 1 Ship your grain across the **s**;
Isa 57: 20 the wicked are like the tossing **s**,
Jnh 1: 4 LORD sent a great wind on the **s**,
Mic 7: 19 iniquities into the depths of the **s**.
Hab 2: 14 LORD as the waters cover the **s**.
Zec 9: 10 His rule will extend from **s** to **s**
Mt 18: 6 be drowned in the depths of the **s**.
1Co 10: 1 that they all passed through the **s**.
Jas 1: 6 who doubts is like a wave of the **s**,
Jude : 13 They are wild waves of the **s**,
Rev 10: 2 He planted his right foot on the **s**
13: 1 I saw a beast coming out of the **s**.
20: 13 The **s** gave up the dead that were
21: 1 and there was no longer any **s**.

SEAL (SEALED SEALS)
Ps 40: 9 I do not **s** my lips, LORD, as you
SS 8: 6 Place me like a **s** over your heart,
Eze 28: 12 "'You were the **s** of perfection,
Da 12: 4 **s** the words of the scroll until
Jn 6: 27 God the Father has placed his **s**
1Co 9: 2 For you are the **s** of my apostleship
2Co 1: 22 set his **s** of ownership on us,
Eph 1: 13 you were marked in him with a **s**,
Rev 6: 3 the Lamb opened the second **s**,
6: 5 the Lamb opened the third **s**,
6: 7 the Lamb opened the fourth **s**,
6: 9 When he opened the fifth **s**, I saw
6: 12 I watched as he opened the sixth **s**.
8: 1 When he opened the seventh **s**,
9: 4 people who did not have the **s**
22: 10 me, "Do not **s** up the words

SEALED (SEAL)
Eph 4: 30 with whom you were **s** for the day
2Ti 2: 19 stands firm, **s** with this inscription:
Rev 5: 1 both sides and **s** with seven seals.

SEALS (SEAL)
Rev 5: 2 "Who is worthy to break the **s**
6: 1 opened the first of the seven **s**.

SEAMLESS*
Jn 19: 23 This garment was **s**, woven in one

SEARCH (SEARCHED SEARCHES SEARCHING)
Ps 4: 4 beds, **s** your hearts and be silent.
139: 23 **S** me, God, and know my heart;
Pr 2: 4 and **s** for it as for hidden treasure,
25: 2 to **s** out a matter is the glory
25: 27 nor is it honorable to **s** out matters
SS 3: 2 I will **s** for the one my heart loves.
Jer 17: 10 "I the LORD **s** the heart
Eze 34: 11 I myself will **s** for my sheep
34: 16 I will **s** for the lost and bring back
Lk 15: 8 and **s** carefully until she finds it?

SEARCHED (SEARCH)
Ps 139: 1 You have **s** me, LORD, and you
Ecc 12: 10 The Teacher **s** to find just the right
1Pe 1: 10 **s** intently and with the greatest care

SEARCHES* (SEARCH)
1Ch 28: 9 for the LORD **s** every heart
Job 39: 8 pasture and **s** for any green thing.
Pr 11: 27 evil comes to one who **s** for it.
Ro 8: 27 who **s** our hearts knows the mind
1Co 2: 10 The Spirit **s** all things, even the
Rev 2: 23 know that I am he who **s** hearts

SEARCHING (SEARCH)
Jdg 5: 15 Reuben there was much **s** of heart.
Am 8: 12 east, **s** for the word of the LORD,

SEARED
1Ti 4: 2 whose consciences have been **s** as

SEASHORE (SEA)
Jos 11: 4 as numerous as the sand on the **s**.
1Ki 4: 29 as measureless as the sand on the **s**.

SEASON (SEASONED SEASONS)
Lev 26: 4 I will send you rain in its **s**,
Ps 1: 3 which yields its fruit in **s** and
2Ti 4: 2 be prepared in **s** and out of **s**;

SEASONED* (SEASON)
Col 4: 6 be always full of grace, **s** with salt,

SEASONS (SEASON)
Gal 4: 10 days and months and **s** and years!

SEAT (SEATED SEATS)
Pr 31: 23 he takes his **s** among the elders
Da 7: 9 and the Ancient of Days took his **s**.
Lk 14: 9 to you, 'Give this person your **s**.'
2Co 5: 10 all appear before the judgment **s**

SEATED (SEAT)
Ps 47: 8 God is **s** on his holy throne.
Isa 6: 1 high and exalted, **s** on a throne;
Lk 22: 69 of Man will be **s** at the right hand
Eph 1: 20 and **s** him at his right hand
2: 6 and **s** us with him in the heavenly
Col 3: 1 is, **s** at the right hand of God.
Rev 14: 14 **s** on the cloud was one like a son
20: 11 throne and him who was **s** on it.

SEATS (SEAT)
Lk 11: 43 you love the most important **s**

SECLUSION*
Lk 1: 24 and for five months remained in **s**.

SECRET (SECRETLY SECRETS)
Dt 29: 29 The **s** things belong to the LORD
Jdg 16: 6 "Tell me the **s** of your great
Ps 90: 8 you, our **s** sins in the light of your
139: 15 when I was made in the **s** place,
Pr 11: 13 but a trustworthy person keeps a **s**.
21: 14 A gift given in **s** soothes anger,
Jer 23: 24 Who can hide in **s** places so that I
Mt 6: 4 so that your giving may be in **s**.
6: 18 who sees what is done in **s**,
Mk 4: 11 "The **s** of the kingdom of God has
2Co 4: 2 we have renounced **s** and shameful
Eph 5: 12 what the disobedient do in **s**.
Php 4: 12 have learned the **s** of being content

SECRETLY (SECRET)
2Pe 2: 1 They will **s** introduce destructive
Jude : 4 long ago have **s** slipped in among

SECRETS (SECRET)
Ps 44: 21 since he knows the **s** of the heart?
Ro 2: 16 judges people's **s** through Jesus
1Co 14: 25 as the **s** of their hearts are laid bare.
Rev 2: 24 learned Satan's so-called deep **s**,

SECURE (SECURITY)
Dt 33: 12 beloved of the LORD rest **s** in him,
2Sa 22: 33 with strength and keeps my way **s**.
Ps 16: 5 and my cup; you make my lot **s**.
16: 9 my body also will rest **s**,
18: 32 with strength and keeps my way **s**.
93: 1 the world is established, firm and **s**.
112: 8 Their hearts are **s**, they will have
Pr 14: 26 fears the LORD has a **s** fortress,
Heb 6: 19 an anchor for the soul, firm and **s**.
2Pe 3: 17 and fall from your **s** position.

SECURITY (SECURE)
Job 31: 24 or said to pure gold, 'You are my **s**,'

SEED (SEEDS SEEDTIME)
Ge 1: 11 the land that bear fruit with **s** in it,
Isa 55: 10 so that it yields **s** for the sower
Mt 13: 3 "A farmer went out to sow his **s**.
13: 31 of heaven is like a mustard **s**,
17: 20 have faith as small as a mustard **s**,
Lk 8: 11 The **s** is the word of God.
1Co 3: 6 I planted the **s**, Apollos watered it,
2Co 9: 10 he who supplies **s** to the sower
Gal 3: 29 you are Abraham's **s**, and heirs
1Pe 1: 23 again, not of perishable **s**,
1Jn 3: 9 because God's **s** remains in them;

SEEDS (SEED)
Jn 12: 24 But if it dies, it produces many **s**.
Gal 3: 16 Scripture does not say "and to **s**,"

SEEDTIME* (SEED)
Ge 8: 22 as the earth endures, **s** and harvest,

SEEK (SEEKING SEEKS SELF-SEEKING SOUGHT)
Lev 19: 18 "'Do not **s** revenge or bear
Dt 4: 29 there you **s** the LORD your God,
4: 29 you will find him if you **s** him
1Ki 22: 5 of Israel, "First **s** the counsel
1Ch 28: 9 If you **s** him, he will be found
2Ch 7: 14 pray and **s** my face and turn
15: 2 If you **s** him, he will be found
Ps 34: 10 but those who **s** the LORD lack no
105: 3 of those who **s** the LORD rejoice.
105: 4 and his strength; **s** his face always.
119: 2 and **s** him with all their heart—
119: 10 I **s** you with all my heart; do not let
119:176 **S** your servant, for I have not
Pr 8: 17 me, and those who **s** me find me.
18: 15 for the ears of the wise **s** it out.
28: 5 those who **s** the LORD understand
Isa 55: 6 **S** the LORD while he may be
65: 1 found by those who did not **s** me.
Jer 29: 13 You will **s** me and find me
Hos 10: 12 for it is time to **s** the LORD,
Am 5: 4 says to Israel: "**S** me and live;
Zep 2: 3 **S** the LORD, all you humble
2: 3 **S** righteousness, **s** humility;
Mt 6: 33 But **s** first his kingdom and his
7: 7 given to you; **s** and you will find;
Lk 12: 31 But **s** his kingdom, and these
19: 10 For the Son of Man came to **s**
Jn 5: 30 for I **s** not to please myself but him
5: 44 do not **s** the glory that comes
Ro 10: 20 found by those who did not **s** me;
1Co 7: 27 Do not **s** to be released.
10: 24 No one should **s** their own good,
Heb 11: 6 rewards those who earnestly **s** him.
1Pe 3: 11 they must **s** peace and pursue it.

SEEKING (SEEK)
2Ch 30: 19 who sets their heart on **s** God—
Pr 20: 18 Plans are established by **s** advice;
Mal 3: 1 the Lord you are **s** will come to his
Jn 8: 50 I am not **s** glory for myself;
1Co 10: 33 For I am not **s** my own good

SEEKS (SEEK)
Pr 11: 27 Whoever **s** good finds favor,
Mt 7: 8 the one who **s** finds; and to the one
Jn 4: 23 the kind of worshipers the Father **s**.
Ro 3: 11 there is no one who **s** God.

SEER
1Sa 9: 9 of today used to be called a **s**.)

SELF-CONTROL* (CONTROL)
Pr 16: 32 with **s** than one who takes a city.
25: 28 through is a person who lacks **s**.
Ac 24: 25 **s** and the judgment to come,
1Co 7: 5 you because of your lack of **s**.
Gal 5: 23 gentleness and **s**.

2Ti 3: 3 slanderous, without **s**, brutal,
2Pe 1: 6 to knowledge, **s**; and to **s**, perseverance;

SELF-CONTROLLED* (CONTROL)
1Ti 3: 2 his wife, temperate, **s**, respectable,
Titus 1: 8 what is good, who is **s**, upright,
2: 2 worthy of respect, **s**, and sound
2: 5 to be **s** and pure, to be busy
2: 6 encourage the young men to be **s**.
2: 12 to live **s**, upright and godly lives

SELF-DENIAL* (SELF-DENIAL)
Ps 132: 1 remember David and all his **s**.

SELF-DISCIPLINE* (DISCIPLINE)
2Ti 1: 7 but gives us power, love and **s**.

SELF-INDULGENCE*
Mt 23: 25 inside they are full of greed and **s**.
Jas 5: 5 have lived on earth in luxury and **s**.

SELFISH*
Ps 119: 36 statutes and not toward **s** gain.
Pr 18: 1 unfriendly person pursues **s** ends
2Co 12: 20 **s** ambition, slander, gossip,
Gal 5: 20 fits of rage, **s** ambition, dissensions,
Php 1: 17 preach Christ out of **s** ambition,
2: 3 Do nothing out of **s** ambition
Jas 3: 14 envy and **s** ambition in your hearts,
3: 16 you have envy and **s** ambition,

SELF-SEEKING* (SEEK)
Ro 2: 8 for those who are **s** and who reject
1Co 13: 5 it is not **s**, it is not easily angered,

SELL (SELLING SELLS SOLD)
Ge 25: 31 "First **s** me your birthright."
Mk 10: 21 **s** everything you have and give
Rev 13: 17 buy or **s** unless they had the mark,

SELLING (SELL)
Lk 17: 28 buying and **s**, planting and

SELLS (SELL)
Pr 31: 24 makes linen garments and **s** them,

SEND (SENDING SENDS SENT)
Ps 43: 3 **S** me your light and your faithful
Isa 6: 8 And I said, "Here am I. **S** me!"
Mal 3: 1 "I will **s** my messenger, who will
Mt 9: 38 to **s** out workers into his harvest
24: 31 And he will **s** his angels with a loud
Mk 1: 2 "I will **s** my messenger ahead
1: 17 I will **s** you out to fish for people."
6: 7 he began to **s** them out two by two
Lk 20: 13 I will **s** my son, whom I love;
Jn 3: 17 God did not **s** his Son into the
16: 7 but if I go, I will **s** him to you.
1Co 1: 17 For Christ did not **s** me to baptize,

SENDING (SEND)
Mt 10: 16 "I am **s** you out like sheep among
Jn 20: 21 the Father has sent me, I am **s** you."
Ro 8: 3 God did by **s** his own Son

SENDS (SEND)
Ps 57: 3 He **s** from heaven and saves me,

SENNACHERIB
Assyrian king whose siege of Jerusalem was overthrown by the LORD following prayer of Hezekiah and Isaiah (2Ki 18:13—19:37; 2Ch 32:1–21; Isa 36–37).

SENSE (SENSES)
Pr 6: 32 who commits adultery has no **s**;
10: 21 many, but fools die for lack of **s**.
11: 12 derides their neighbor has no **s**,
12: 11 who chase fantasies have no **s**.
15: 21 brings joy to one who has no **s**,
17: 18 One who has no **s** shakes hands
24: 30 vineyard of someone who has no **s**;

SENSES* (SENSE)
Lk 15: 17 "When he came to his **s**, he said,
1Co 15: 34 Come back to your **s** as you ought,
2Ti 2: 26 that they will come to their **s**

SENSITIVITY*
Eph 4: 19 Having lost all **s**, they have given

SENSUAL* (SENSUALITY)
Col 2: 23 value in restraining **s** indulgence.
1Ti 5: 11 when their **s** desires overcome

SENSUALITY* (SENSUAL)
Eph 4: 19 given themselves over to **s** so as

SENT (SEND)
Ex 3: 14 'I AM has **s** me to you.'"
Isa 55: 11 achieve the purpose for which I **s**
61: 1 He has **s** me to bind
Jer 28: 9 will be recognized as one truly **s**
Mt 10: 40 me welcomes the one who **s** me.
Lk 4: 18 He has **s** me to proclaim freedom
9: 2 and he **s** them out to proclaim
10: 16 rejects me rejects him who **s** me."
Jn 1: 6 There was a man **s** from God
4: 34 "is to do the will of him who **s** me
5: 24 believes him who **s** me has eternal
8: 16 I stand with the Father, who **s** me.
9: 4 do the works of him who **s** me.
16: 5 now I am going to him who **s** me.
17: 3 and Jesus Christ, whom you have **s**.
17: 18 As you **s** me into the world, I have **s** them
20: 21 As the Father has **s** me, I am
Ro 10: 15 anyone preach unless they are **s**?
Gal 4: 4 had fully come, God **s** his Son,
1Jn 4: 10 **s** his Son as an atoning sacrifice

SENTENCE
2Co 1: 9 we felt we had received the **s**

SEPARATE (SEPARATED SEPARATES)
Mt 19: 6 has joined together, let no one **s**."
Ro 8: 35 Who shall **s** us from the love
1Co 7: 10 A wife must not **s** from her
2Co 6: 17 "Come out from them and be **s**,
Eph 2: 12 that time you were **s** from Christ,

SEPARATED (SEPARATE)
Isa 59: 2 your iniquities have **s** you from
Eph 4: 18 **s** from the life of God because

SEPARATES* (SEPARATE)
Ru 1: 17 if even death **s** you and me."
Pr 16: 28 and a gossip **s** close friends.
17: 9 repeats the matter **s** close friends.
Mt 25: 32 another as a shepherd **s** the sheep

SERAPHIM*
Isa 6: 2 Above him were **s**, each with six
6: 6 of the **s** flew to me with a live coal

SERIOUSNESS*
Titus 2: 7 In your teaching show integrity,

SERPENT (SERPENT'S)
Ge 3: 1 the **s** was more crafty than any
Isa 27: 1 Leviathan the gliding **s**,
Rev 12: 9 that ancient **s** called the devil,
20: 2 that ancient **s**, who is the devil,

SERPENT'S (SERPENT)
2Co 11: 3 Eve was deceived by the **s** cunning,

SERVANT (SERVANTS)
Ex 14: 31 trust in him and in Moses his **s**.
21: 2 "If you buy a Hebrew **s**, he is
1Sa 3: 10 "Speak, for your **s** is listening."
2Sa 7: 19 the future of the house of your **s**—
1Ki 20: 40 While your **s** was busy here
Job 1: 8 "Have you considered my **s** Job?
Ps 19: 11 By them your **s** is warned;
19: 13 Keep your **s** also from willful sins;
31: 16 Let your face shine on your **s**;
89: 3 one, I have sworn to David my **s**,
Pr 14: 35 A king delights in a wise **s**,
17: 2 A prudent **s** will rule over
Isa 41: 8 Israel, my **s**, Jacob, whom I have
49: 3 said to me, "You are my **s**, Israel,
53: 11 my righteous **s** will justify many,
Zec 3: 8 I am going to bring my **s**,
Mt 8: 13 his **s** was healed at that moment.
20: 26 great among you must be your **s**,
24: 45 then is the faithful and wise **s**,
25: 21 'Well done, good and faithful **s**!
Lk 1: 38 "I am the Lord's **s**,"
Jn 12: 26 and where I am, my **s** also will be.
Ro 1: 1 Paul, a **s** of Christ Jesus, called
13: 4 authority is God's **s** for your good.
Php 2: 7 by taking the very nature of a **s**,
Col 1: 23 of which I, Paul, have become a **s**.
2Ti 2: 24 And the Lord's **s** must not be
3: 17 the **s** of God may be thoroughly

SERVANTS (SERVANT)
Lev 25: 55 the Israelites belong to me as **s**.
1Sa 2: 9 guard the feet of his faithful **s**,
2Ki 17: 13 to you through my **s** the prophets."
Ezr 5: 11 "We are the **s** of the God of heaven
Ps 34: 22 The LORD will rescue his **s**;
103: 21 hosts, you his **s** who do his will.
104: 4 his messengers, flames of fire his **s**.
Pr 31: 15 and portions for her female **s**.
Isa 44: 26 who carries out the words of his **s**
65: 8 so will I do in behalf of my **s**;
65: 13 my **s** will rejoice, but you will be
Lk 17: 10 do, should say, 'We are unworthy **s**;
Jn 15: 15 I no longer call you **s**,
Ro 13: 6 for the authorities are God's **s**,
1Co 3: 5 Only **s**, through whom you came
Heb 1: 7 spirits, and his **s** flames of fire."

SERVE (SERVED SERVES SERVICE SERVING)
Dt 10: 12 to **s** the LORD your God with all
11: 13 and to **s** him with all your heart
13: 4 **s** him and hold fast to him.
28: 47 you did not **s** the LORD your God
Jos 22: 5 and to **s** him with all your heart
24: 15 household, we will **s** the LORD."
24: 18 We too will **s** the LORD,
1Sa 7: 3 to the LORD and **s** him only,
12: 20 **s** the LORD with all your heart.
12: 24 **s** him faithfully with all your heart;
2Ch 19: 9 "You must **s** faithfully
Job 36: 11 If they obey and **s** him, they will
Ps 2: 11 **S** the LORD with fear
Da 3: 17 the God we **s** is able to deliver us
Mt 4: 10 Lord your God, and **s** him only.'"
6: 24 "No one can **s** two masters.
6: 24 You cannot **s** both God and money.
20: 28 but to **s**, and to give his life as
Ro 12: 7 if it is serving, then **s**; if it is
Gal 5: 13 **s** one another humbly in love.
Eph 6: 7 **S** wholeheartedly, as if you were
1Ti 6: 2 they should **s** them even better
Heb 9: 14 so that we may **s** the living God!
1Pe 4: 10 gift you have received to **s** others,
5: 2 dishonest gain, but eager to **s**;
Rev 5: 10 kingdom and priests to **s** our God,

SERVED (SERVE)
Mt 20: 28 Son of Man did not come to be **s**,
Jn 12: 2 Martha **s**, while Lazarus was
Ac 17: 25 And he is not **s** by human hands,
Ro 1: 25 and **s** created things rather than
1Ti 3: 13 Those who have **s** well gain

SERVES (SERVE)
Lk 22: 26 one who rules like the one who **s**.
22: 27 But I am among you as one who **s**.
Jn 12: 26 Whoever **s** me must follow me;
12: 26 will honor the one who **s** me.
Ro 14: 18 because anyone who **s** Christ in
1Pe 4: 11 If anyone **s**, they should do so

SERVICE (SERVE)
Lk 9: 62 and looks back is fit for **s**
12: 35 "Be dressed ready for **s** and keep
Ro 15: 17 in Christ Jesus in my **s** to God.
1Co 12: 5 There are different kinds of **s**,
16: 15 to the **s** of the Lord's people.
2Co 9: 12 This **s** that you perform is not only
Eph 4: 12 to equip his people for works of **s**,
Rev 2: 19 and faith, your **s** and perseverance,

SERVING (SERVE)
Jos 24: 15 if **s** the LORD seems undesirable
2Ch 12: 8 learn the difference between **s** me
Pr 15: 17 Better a small **s** of vegetables
Ro 12: 7 if it is **s**, then serve;
12: 11 your spiritual fervor, **s** the Lord.
16: 18 people are not **s** our Lord Christ,
Eph 6: 7 as if you were **s** the Lord,
Col 3: 24 It is the Lord Christ you are **s**.
2Ti 2: 4 No one **s** as a soldier gets entangled

SETH
Ge 4: 25 birth to a son and named him **S**,

SETTLE
Isa 1: 18 "Come now, let us **s** the matter,"
Mt 5: 25 "**S** matters quickly with your
2Th 3: 12 in the Lord Jesus Christ to **s** down

SEVEN (SEVENS SEVENTH)
Ge 7: 2 Take with you **s** pairs of every kind
Jos 6: 4 march around the city **s** times,
1Ki 19: 18 Yet I reserve **s** thousand in Israel—

Pr 6: 16 hates, **s** that are detestable to him:
24: 16 though the righteous fall **s** times,
Isa 4: 1 that day **s** women will take hold
Da 9: 25 comes, there will be **s** 'sevens,'
Mt 18: 21 sins against me? Up to **s** times?"
Lk 11: 26 takes **s** other spirits more wicked
Ro 11: 4 for myself **s** thousand who have
Rev 1: 4 To the **s** churches in the province
1: 4 from the **s** spirits before his throne,
6: 1 opened the first of the **s** seals.
8: 2 I saw the **s** angels who stand before
8: 2 and **s** trumpets were given to them.
10: 4 And when the **s** thunders spoke,
15: 7 to the **s** angels **s** golden bowls filled

SEVENS* (SEVEN)
Da 9: 24 "Seventy '**s**' are decreed for your
9: 25 will be seven '**s**,' and sixty-two '**s**.'
9: 26 the sixty-two '**s**,' the Anointed

SEVENTH (SEVEN)
Ge 2: 2 **s** day God had finished the work
2: 2 so on the **s** day he rested from all
Ex 20: 10 the **s** day is a sabbath to the LORD
23: 11 during the **s** year let the land lie
23: 12 but on the **s** day do not work,
Heb 4: 4 "On the **s** day God rested from all

SEVERE
Ge 3: 16 your pains in childbearing very **s**;
2Co 8: 2 In the midst of a very **s** trial,
1Th 1: 6 midst of **s** suffering with the joy

SEWED (SEWS)
Ge 3: 7 so they **s** fig leaves together

SEWS (SEWED)
Mt 9: 16 "No one **s** a patch of unshrunk

SEX* (SEXUAL SEXUALLY)
Ge 19: 5 so that we can have **s** with them."
Jdg 19: 22 so we can have **s** with him."
1Co 6: 9 nor men who have **s** with men

SEXUAL (SEX)
Ex 22: 19 "Anyone who has **s** relations
Lev 18: 6 close relative to have **s** relations.
18: 7 your father by having **s** relations
18: 20 "'Do not have **s** relations
Mt 15: 19 adultery, **s** immorality, theft,
Ac 15: 20 from **s** immorality, from the meat
1Co 5: 1 there is **s** immorality among you,
6: 13 is not meant for **s** immorality
6: 18 Flee from **s** immorality.
10: 8 should not commit **s** immorality,
2Co 12: 21 **s** sin and debauchery in which they
Gal 5: 19 **s** immorality,
Eph 5: 3 not be even a hint of **s** immorality,
Col 3: 5 **s** immorality, impurity, lust,
1Th 4: 3 that you should avoid **s** immorality;

SEXUALLY (SEX)
1Co 5: 9 to associate with **s** immoral people
6: 9 the **s** immoral nor idolaters
6: 18 but whoever sins **s**, sins against
Heb 12: 16 See that no one is **s** immoral, or is
13: 4 the adulterer and all the **s** immoral.
Rev 21: 8 the murderers, the **s** immoral,

SHADE
Ps 121: 5 the LORD is your **s** at your right
Isa 25: 4 the storm and a **s** from the heat.

SHADOW
Ps 17: 8 hide me in the **s** of your wings
36: 7 take refuge in the **s** of your wings.
91: 1 will rest in the **s** of the Almighty.
Isa 51: 16 covered you with the **s** of my hand
Col 2: 17 These are a **s** of the things that
Heb 8: 5 a copy and **s** of what is in heaven.
10: 1 The law is only a **s** of the good

SHADRACH
Hebrew exiled to Babylon; name changed from Hananiah (Da 1:6–7). Refused defilement by food (Da 1:8–20). Refused to worship idol (Da 3:1–18); saved from furnace (Da 3:19–30).

SHAKE (SHAKEN SHAKING)
Ps 10: 6 himself, "Nothing will ever **s** me."
64: 8 all who see them will **s** their heads
99: 1 the cherubim, let the earth **s**.
Hag 2: 6 I will once more **s** the heavens
Heb 12: 26 "Once more I will **s** not only

SHAKEN (SHAKE)
Ps 16: 8 at my right hand, I will not be **s**.
30: 6 I said, "I will never be **s**."
55: 22 he will never let the righteous be **s**.
62: 2 he is my fortress, I will never be **s**.
112: 6 the righteous will never be **s**;
Isa 54: 10 you will not be **s** nor my covenant
Mt 24: 29 and the heavenly bodies will be **s**.'
Lk 6: 38 down, **s** together and running over,
Ac 2: 25 is at my right hand, I will not be **s**.
Heb 12: 27 that what cannot be **s** may remain.

SHAKING* (SHAKE)
Ps 22: 7 they hurl insults, **s** their heads.
Mt 27: 39 hurled insults at him, **s** their heads
Mk 15: 29 at him, **s** their heads and saying,

SHALLUM
King of Israel (2Ki 15:10–16).

SHAME (ASHAMED SHAMED SHAMEFUL)
Ps 22: 5 they trusted and were not put to **s**.
25: 3 hopes in you will ever be put to **s**,
34: 5 faces are never covered with **s**.
69: 6 seek you not be put to **s** because
Pr 13: 18 discipline comes to poverty and **s**,
18: 13 that is folly and **s**.
Jer 8: 9 The wise will be put to **s**;
8: 12 No, they have no **s** at all;
Ro 5: 5 And hope does not put us to **s**,
9: 33 in him will never be put to **s**."
10: 11 in him will never be put to **s**."
1Co 1: 27 things of the world to **s** the wise;
Heb 12: 2 scorning its **s**, and sat down

SHAMED (SHAME)
Jer 10: 14 every goldsmith is **s** by his idols.
Joel 2: 26 never again will my people be **s**.

SHAMEFUL (SHAME)
Ro 1: 27 Men committed **s** acts with other
2Co 4: 2 have renounced secret and **s** ways;
Rev 21: 27 nor will anyone who does what is **s**

SHAMGAR*
Judge; killed 600 Philistines (Jdg 3:31; 5:6).

SHAPE (SHAPES SHAPING)
Job 38: 14 The earth takes **s** like clay under

SHAPES (SHAPE)
Isa 44: 10 Who **s** a god and casts an idol,

SHAPING* (SHAPE)
Jer 18: 4 pot, **s** it as seemed best to him.

SHARE (SHARED SHARERS SHARING)
Ge 21: 10 that woman's son will never **s**
Lev 19: 17 neighbor frankly so you will not **s**
Dt 10: 9 That is why the Levites have no **s**
1Sa 30: 24 to the battle. All will **s** alike."
Pr 22: 9 they **s** their food with the poor.
Eze 18: 20 The child will not **s** the guilt
18: 20 nor will the parent **s** the guilt
Mt 25: 21 and **s** your master's happiness!'
Lk 3: 11 who has two shirts should **s**
Ro 8: 17 if indeed we **s** in his sufferings
8: 17 that we may also **s** in his glory.
12: 13 **S** with the Lord's people who are
1Co 10: 17 body, for we all **s** the one loaf.
2Co 1: 7 just as you **s** in our sufferings,
1: 7 so also you **s** in our comfort.
Gal 4: 30 the slave woman's son will never **s**
6: 6 the word should **s** all good things
Eph 4: 28 they may have something to **s**
Col 1: 12 who has qualified you to **s**
2Th 2: 14 that you might **s** in the glory of our
1Ti 5: 22 and do not **s** in the sins of others.
6: 18 to be generous and willing to **s**.
2Ti 2: 6 the first to receive a **s** of the crops.
Heb 12: 10 order that we may **s** in his holiness.
13: 16 to do good and to **s** with others,
Rev 22: 19 that person any **s** in the tree of life

SHARED (SHARE)
Ps 41: 9 I trusted, one who **s** my bread,
Jn 13: 18 'He who **s** my bread has turned
Ac 4: 32 but they **s** everything they had.
Heb 2: 14 he too **s** in their humanity so

SHARERS* (SHARE)
Eph 3: 6 **s** together in the promise in Christ

SHARING (SHARE)
1Co 9: 10 so in the hope of **s** in the harvest.
2Co 9: 13 for your generosity in **s** with them
Php 2: 1 if any common **s** in the Spirit,

SHARON
SS 2: 1 I am a rose of **S**, a lily

SHARP (SHARPENED SHARPENS SHARPER)
Pr 5: 4 as gall, **s** as a double-edged sword.
Isa 5: 28 Their arrows are **s**, all their bows
Rev 1: 16 coming out of his mouth was a **s**,
19: 15 out of his mouth is a **s** sword

SHARPENED (SHARP)
Eze 21: 9 sword, a sword, **s** and polished—

SHARPENS* (SHARP)
Pr 27: 17 As iron **s** iron, so one person **s** another.

SHARPER* (SHARP)
Heb 4: 12 **S** than any double-edged sword,

SHATTER (SHATTERED SHATTERS)
Jer 51: 20 with you I **s** nations, with you I

SHATTERED (SHATTER)
Job 16: 12 All was well with me, but he **s** me;
17: 11 days have passed, my plans are **s**,
Ecc 12: 6 before the pitcher is **s** at the spring,

SHATTERS (SHATTER)
Ps 46: 9 He breaks the bow and **s** the spear;

SHAVED
Jdg 16: 17 If my head were **s**, my strength
1Co 11: 5 it is the same as having her head **s**.

SHEAF (SHEAVES)
Lev 23: 11 wave the **s** before the LORD so it

SHEARER* (SHEARERS)
Ac 8: 32 and as a lamb before its **s** is silent,

SHEARERS (SHEARER)
Isa 53: 7 and as a sheep before its **s** is silent,

SHEAVES (SHEAF)
Ge 37: 7 while your **s** gathered around mine
Ps 126: 6 songs of joy, carrying **s** with them.

SHEBA
1. Benjamite who rebelled against David (2Sa 20).
2. See QUEEN.

SHECHEM
1. Raped Jacob's daughter Dinah; killed by Simeon and Levi (Ge 34).
2. City where Joshua renewed the covenant (Jos 24).

SHED (SHEDDING SHEDS)
Ge 9: 6 by humans shall their blood be **s**;
Pr 6: 17 hands that **s** innocent blood,
Ro 3: 15 "Their feet are swift to **s** blood;
Col 1: 20 through his blood, **s** on the cross.

SHEDDING (SHED)
Heb 9: 22 without the **s** of blood there is no

SHEDS (SHED)
Ge 9: 6 "Whoever **s** human blood,
Pr 20: 27 of the LORD that **s** light on one's

SHEEP (SHEEP'S SHEEPSKINS)
Nu 27: 17 not be like **s** without a shepherd."
Dt 17: 1 an ox or a **s** that has any defect
1Sa 15: 14 is this bleating of **s** in my ears?
Ps 44: 22 we are considered as **s** to be
78: 52 he led them like **s** through
100: 3 are his people, the **s** of his pasture.
119:176 I have strayed like a lost **s**.
SS 4: 2 teeth are like a flock of **s** just shorn,
Isa 53: 6 We all, like **s**, have gone astray,
53: 7 as a **s** before its shearers is silent,
Jer 50: 6 "My people have been lost **s**;
Eze 34: 11 I myself will search for my **s**
Zec 13: 7 and the **s** will be scattered, and I
Mt 9: 36 helpless, like **s** without a shepherd.
10: 16 you out like **s** among wolves.
12: 11 "If any of you has a **s** and it falls
18: 13 one **s** than about the ninety-nine
25: 32 as a shepherd separates the **s**
Jn 10: 1 who does not enter the **s** pen
10: 3 He calls his own **s** by name
10: 7 I tell you, I am the gate for the **s**.
10: 15 and I lay down my life for the **s**.
10: 27 My **s** listen to my voice;
21: 17 Jesus said, "Feed my **s**.
1Pe 2: 25 For "you were like **s** going astray,"

SHEEP'S* (SHEEP)
Mt 7: 15 They come to you in **s** clothing,
SHEEPSKINS* (SHEEP)
Heb 11: 37 went about in **s** and goatskins,
SHEKEL
Ex 30: 13 This half **s** is an offering
SHELTER
Ps 27: 5 hide me in the **s** of his sacred tent
31: 20 In the **s** of your presence you hide
55: 8 I would hurry to my place of **s**,
61: 4 take refuge in the **s** of your wings.
91: 1 in the **s** of the Most High will rest
Ecc 7: 12 Wisdom is a **s** as money is a **s**,
Isa 4: 6 It will be a **s** and shade
25: 4 a **s** from the storm and a shade
32: 2 Each one will be like a **s**
58: 7 provide the poor wanderer with **s**
SHEM
Son of Noah (Ge 5:32; 6:10). Blessed (Ge 9:26). Descendants (Ge 10:21–31; 11:10–32).
SHEPHERD (SHEPHERDS)
Ge 48: 15 God who has been my **s** all my life
49: 24 because of the **S**, the Rock of Israel,
Nu 27: 17 will not be like sheep without a **s**."
2Sa 7: 7 commanded to **s** my people Israel,
1Ki 22: 17 on the hills like sheep without a **s**,
Ps 23: 1 The LORD is my **s**, I lack nothing.
28: 9 be their **s** and carry them forever.
80: 1 Hear us, **S** of Israel, you who lead
Isa 40: 11 He tends his flock like a **s**:
Jer 31: 10 will watch over his flock like a **s**.'
Eze 34: 5 scattered because there was no **s**,
34: 12 As a **s** looks after his scattered
Zec 11: 4 "**S** the flock marked for slaughter.
11: 9 and said, "I will not be your **s**.
11: 17 "Woe to the worthless **s**,
13: 7 "Strike the **s**, and the sheep will
Mt 2: 6 come a ruler who will **s** my people
9: 36 helpless, like sheep without a **s**.
26: 31 will strike the **s**, and the sheep
Jn 10: 11 "I am the good **s**. The good **s** lays
10: 14 "I am the good **s**; I know my sheep
10: 16 there shall be one flock and one **s**.
Heb 13: 20 Jesus, that great **S** of the sheep,
1Pe 5: 4 And when the Chief **S** appears,
Rev 7: 17 center of the throne will be their **s**;
SHEPHERDS (SHEPHERD)
Jer 23: 1 "Woe to the **s** who are destroying
50: 6 their **s** have led them astray
Eze 34: 2 prophesy against the **s** of Israel;
Lk 2: 8 there were **s** living out in the fields
Ac 20: 28 Be **s** of the church of God, which
1Pe 5: 2 Be **s** of God's flock that is under
Jude : 12 **s** who feed only themselves.
SHIBBOLETH*
Jdg 12: 6 they said, "All right, say '**S**.'"
SHIELD (SHIELDED SHIELDS)
Ge 15: 1 I am your **s**, your very great
2Sa 22: 3 my **s** and the horn of my salvation.
22: 36 You make your saving help my **s**;
Ps 3: 3 you, LORD, are a **s** around me,
5: 12 them with your favor as with a **s**.
7: 10 My **s** is God Most High, who saves
18: 2 my **s** and the horn of my salvation,
28: 7 LORD is my strength and my **s**;
33: 20 he is our help and our **s**.
84: 11 For the LORD God is a sun and **s**;
91: 4 his faithfulness will be your **s**
115: 9 he is their help and **s**.
119:114 You are my refuge and my **s**;
144: 2 my **s**, in whom I take refuge,
Pr 2: 7 he is a **s** to those whose walk is
30: 5 he is a **s** to those who take refuge
Eph 6: 16 take up the **s** of faith,
SHIELDED (SHIELD)
1Pe 1: 5 who through faith are **s** by God's
SHIELDS (SHIELD)
Dt 33: 12 for he **s** him all day long,
SHIFTLESS*
Pr 19: 15 on deep sleep, and the **s** go hungry.
SHIMEI
Cursed David (2Sa 16:5–14); spared (2Sa 19:16–23). Killed by Solomon (1Ki 2:8–9, 36–46).
SHINE (SHINES SHINING SHONE)
Nu 6: 25 the LORD make his face **s** on you
Job 33: 30 that the light of life may **s** on them.
Ps 4: 6 Let the light of your face **s** on us.
37: 6 your righteous reward **s** like
67: 1 bless us and make his face **s** on us
80: 1 between the cherubim, **s** forth
118: 27 and he has made his light **s** on us.
Isa 60: 1 "Arise, **s**, for your light has come,
Da 12: 3 are wise will **s** like the brightness
Mt 5: 16 let your light **s** before others,
13: 43 the righteous will **s** like the sun
2Co 4: 6 made his light **s** in our hearts
Eph 5: 14 the dead, and Christ will **s** on you."
Php 2: 15 you will **s** among them like stars
SHINES (SHINE)
Ps 50: 2 perfect in beauty, God **s** forth.
Pr 13: 9 light of the righteous **s** brightly,
Jn 1: 5 The light **s** in the darkness,
SHINING (SHINE)
Pr 4: 18 **s** ever brighter till the full light
2Pe 1: 19 as to a light **s** in a dark place,
Rev 1: 16 His face was like the sun **s** in all its
SHIP (SHIPS SHIPWRECK SHIPWRECKS)
Ecc 11: 1 **S** your grain across the sea;
SHIPS (SHIP)
Pr 31: 14 She is like the merchant **s**,
SHIPWRECK (SHIP)
1Ti 1: 19 so have suffered **s** with regard
SHIPWRECKED* (SHIP)
2Co 11: 25 three times I was **s**, I spent a night
SHIRT (SHIRTS)
Lk 6: 29 do not withhold your **s** from them.
SHIRTS* (SHIRT)
Lk 3: 11 who has two **s** should share
SHISHAK
1Ki 14: 25 **S** king of Egypt attacked Jerusalem.
2Ch 12: 2 **S** king of Egypt attacked Jerusalem
SHOCKING*
Jer 5: 30 **s** thing has happened in the land:
SHONE (SHINE)
Mt 17: 2 His face **s** like the sun, and his
Lk 2: 9 glory of the Lord **s** around them,
Rev 21: 11 It **s** with the glory of God, and its
SHOOT
Isa 53: 2 grew up before him like a tender **s**,
Ro 11: 17 though a wild olive **s**, have been
SHORE
Lk 5: 3 asked him to put out a little from **s**.
SHORT (SHORTENED)
Nu 11: 23 Moses, "Is the LORD's arm too **s**?
Isa 50: 2 Was my arm too **s** to deliver you?
59: 1 of the LORD is not too **s** to save,
Mt 24: 22 "If those days had not been cut **s**,
Ro 3: 23 and fall **s** of the glory of God,
1Co 7: 29 and sisters, is that the time is **s**.
Heb 4: 1 you be found to have fallen **s** of it.
Rev 20: 3 he must be set free for a **s** time.
SHORTENED (SHORT)
Mt 24: 22 of the elect those days will be **s**.
SHOULDER (SHOULDERS)
Zep 3: 9 of the LORD and serve him **s** to **s**.
SHOULDERS (SHOULDER)
Dt 33: 12 LORD loves rests between his **s**."
Isa 9: 6 the government will be on his **s**.
Lk 15: 5 finds it, he joyfully puts it on his **s**
SHOUT (SHOUTED)
Ps 47: 1 **s** to God with cries of joy.
66: 1 **S** for joy to God, all the earth!
95: 1 let us **s** aloud to the Rock of our
98: 4 **S** for joy to the LORD,
100: 1 **S** for joy to the LORD,
Isa 12: 6 **S** aloud and sing for joy,
26: 19 in the dust wake up and **s** for joy—
35: 6 deer, and the mute tongue **s** for joy.
40: 9 lift up your voice with a **s**, lift it up,
42: 2 He will not **s** or cry out, or raise his
44: 23 **s** aloud, you earth beneath.
Isa 54: 1 burst into song, **s** for joy, you who
Zec 9: 9 **S**, Daughter Jerusalem!
SHOUTED (SHOUT)
Job 38: 7 and all the angels **s** for joy?
SHOW (SHOWED SHOWN SHOWS)
Ex 18: 20 and **s** them the way they are to live
33: 18 said, "Now **s** me your glory."
2Sa 22: 26 the faithful you **s** yourself faithful,
Ps 17: 7 **S** me the wonders of your great
25: 4 **S** me your ways, LORD, teach me
39: 4 "**S** me, LORD, my life's end
85: 7 **S** us your unfailing love, LORD,
143: 8 **S** me the way I should go, for to
SS 2: 14 the mountainside, **s** me your face,
Isa 30: 18 he will rise up to **s** you compassion.
Joel 2: 30 I will **s** wonders in the heavens
Zec 7: 9 **s** mercy and compassion to one
Ac 2: 19 I will **s** wonders in the heavens
10: 34 it is that God does not **s** favoritism
1Co 12: 31 yet I will **s** you the most excellent
Eph 2: 7 ages he might **s** the incomparable
Titus 2: 7 In your teaching **s** integrity,
Jas 2: 18 **S** me your faith without deeds,
2: 18 I will **s** you my faith by my deeds.
Jude : 23 to others **s** mercy, mixed with fear
SHOWED (SHOW)
1Ki 3: 3 Solomon **s** his love for the LORD
Lk 24: 40 this, he **s** them his hands and feet.
Ac 28: 7 **s** us generous hospitality for three
1Jn 4: 9 This is how God **s** his love among
SHOWERS
Eze 34: 26 there will be **s** of blessing.
Hos 10: 12 and **s** his righteousness on you.
SHOWN (SHOW)
Heb 13: 2 some people have **s** hospitality
SHOWS (SHOW)
Pr 3: 34 mockers but **s** favor to the humble
1Pe 5: 5 proud but **s** favor to the humble."
SHREWD
2Sa 22: 27 to the devious you show yourself **s**.
Mt 10: 16 Therefore be as **s** as snakes and as
SHRINK* (SHRINKS)
Heb 10: 39 do not belong to those who **s** back
Rev 12: 11 lives so much as to **s** from death.
SHRINKS* (SHRINK)
Heb 10: 38 no pleasure in the one who **s** back."
SHRIVEL
Isa 64: 6 we all **s** up like a leaf, and like
SHUDDER
Eze 32: 10 and their kings will **s** with horror
SHUHITE
Job 2: 11 Bildad the **S** and Zophar
SHUN* (SHUNS)
Job 28: 28 and to **s** evil is understanding."
Pr 3: 7 fear the LORD and **s** evil.
Pr 14: 16 wise fear the LORD and **s** evil,
SHUNS (SHUN)
Job 1: 8 a man who fears God and **s** evil."
SHUT
Ge 7: 16 Then the LORD **s** him in.
Isa 22: 22 what he opens no one can **s**,
60: 11 they will never be **s**, day or night,
Da 6: 22 and he **s** the mouths of the lions.
Heb 11: 33 who **s** the mouths of lions,
Rev 3: 7 What he opens no one can **s**,
21: 25 On no day will its gates ever be **s**,
SICK (SICKNESS)
Pr 13: 12 Hope deferred makes the heart **s**,
Eze 34: 4 healed the **s** or bound up the
Mt 9: 12 who need a doctor, but the **s**.
10: 8 Heal the **s**, raise the dead,
25: 36 I was **s** and you looked after me,
1Co 11: 30 many among you are weak and **s**,
Jas 5: 14 Is anyone among you **s**?
SICKBED* (BED)
Ps 41: 3 LORD sustains them on their **s**
SICKLE
Joel 3: 13 Swing the **s**, for the harvest is ripe.
Rev 14: 14 his head and a sharp **s** in his hand.

SICKNESS (SICK)
Mt 4: 23 disease and **s** among the people.
SIDE (SIDES)
Ps 91: 7 A thousand may fall at your **s**,
124: 1 the LORD had not been on our **s**—
Pr 3: 26 for the LORD will be at your **s**
Jn 18: 37 Everyone on the **s** of truth listens
20: 20 he showed them his hands and **s**.
2Ti 4: 17 the Lord stood at my **s** and gave
Heb 10: 33 at other times you stood **s** by **s**
SIDES (SIDE)
Nu 33: 55 in your eyes and thorns in your **s**.
SIFT*
Lk 22: 31 Satan has asked to **s** all of you as
SIGHING
Isa 35: 10 and sorrow and **s** will flee away.
SIGHT
Ps 51: 4 and done what is evil in your **s**;
90: 4 years in your **s** are like a day
116: 15 in the **s** of the LORD is the death
Pr 3: 4 a good name in the **s** of God
Mt 11: 5 The blind receive **s**, the lame walk,
1Co 3: 19 this world is foolishness in God's **s**.
2Co 5: 7 For we live by faith, not by **s**.
1Pe 3: 4 which is of great worth in God's **s**.
SIGN (SIGNS)
Ge 9: 12 "This is the **s** of the covenant I am
17: 11 and it will be the **s** of the covenant
Isa 7: 14 the Lord himself will give you a **s**:
55: 13 an everlasting **s**, that will endure
Eze 20: 12 my Sabbaths as a **s** between us,
Mt 12: 38 we want to see a **s** from you."
12: 39 adulterous generation asks for a **s**!
24: 3 what will be the **s** of your coming
24: 30 will appear the **s** of the Son of Man
Lk 2: 12 This will be a **s** to you:
11: 29 It asks for a **s**, but none will be
23: 8 see him perform a **s** of some sort.
Ac 4: 16 they have performed a notable **s**,
Ro 4: 11 he received circumcision as a **s**,
1Co 14: 22 are a **s**, not for believers
SIGNS (SIGN)
Ge 1: 14 let them serve as **s** to mark sacred
Ps 78: 43 the day he displayed his **s** in Egypt,
105: 27 They performed his **s** among them,
Da 6: 27 he performs **s** and wonders
Mt 24: 24 and perform great **s** and wonders
Mk 16: 17 *these **s** will accompany those who*
Jn 2: 11 of Galilee was the first of the **s**
2: 23 saw the **s** he was performing
3: 2 could perform the **s** you are doing
7: 31 he perform more **s** than this man?"
9: 16 can a sinner perform such **s**?"
12: 37 Jesus had performed so many **s**
20: 30 Jesus performed many other **s**
Ac 2: 19 above and **s** on the earth below,
1Co 1: 22 Jews demand **s** and Greeks look
2Co 12: 12 including **s**, wonders and miracles.
2Th 2: 9 of displays of power through **s**
SIHON
Nu 21: 21 to say to **S** king of the Amorites:
Ps 136: 19 **S** king of the Amorites
SILAS*
Prophet (Ac 15:22–32); co-worker with Paul on second missionary journey (Ac 16–18; 2Co 1:19). Co-writer with Paul (1Th 1:1; 2Th 1:1); Peter (1Pe 5:12).
SILENCE (SILENCED SILENT)
1Pe 2: 15 good you should **s** the ignorant
Rev 8: 1 there was **s** in heaven for about half
SILENCED (SILENCE)
Ro 3: 19 so that every mouth may be **s**
Titus 1: 11 They must be **s**, because they are
SILENT (SILENCE)
Est 4: 14 For if you remain **s** at this time,
Ps 30: 12 may sing your praises and not be **s**.
32: 3 When I kept **s**, my bones wasted
39: 2 So I remained utterly **s**, not even
Pr 17: 28 are thought wise if they keep **s**,
Ecc 3: 7 a time to be **s** and a time to speak,
Isa 53: 7 as a sheep before its shearers is **s**,
62: 1 For Zion's sake I will not keep **s**,
Hab 2: 20 let all the earth be **s** before him.
Ac 8: 32 as a lamb before its shearer is **s**,
1Co 14: 34 Women should remain **s**
SILVER
Ps 12: 6 like **s** purified in a crucible,
66: 10 tested us; you refined us like **s**.
Pr 2: 4 if you look for it as for **s** and search
3: 14 for she is more profitable than **s**
8: 10 my instruction instead of **s**,
22: 1 to be esteemed is better than **s**
25: 4 Remove the dross from the **s**,
25: 11 of **s** is a ruling rightly given.
Isa 48: 10 I have refined you, though not as **s**;
Eze 22: 18 They are but the dross of **s**.
Da 2: 32 its chest and arms of **s**, its belly
Hag 2: 8 'The **s** is mine and the gold is
Zec 13: 9 I will refine them like **s** and test
Mt 26: 15 out for him thirty pieces of **s**.
Ac 3: 6 Peter said, "**S** or gold I do not have,
1Co 3: 12 on this foundation using gold, **s**,
1Pe 1: 18 with perishable things such as **s**
SILVERSMITH
Ac 19: 24 A **s** named Demetrius, who made
SIMEON
Son of Jacob by Leah (Ge 29:33; 35:23; 1Ch 2:1). With Levi killed Shechem for rape of Dinah (Ge 34:25–29). Held hostage by Joseph in Egypt (Ge 42:24—43:23). Tribe of blessed (Ge 49:5–7), numbered (Nu 1:23; 26:14), allotted land (Jos 19:1–9; Eze 48:24), 12,000 from (Rev 7:7).
SIMON
1. See PETER.
2. Apostle, called the Zealot (Mt 10:4; Mk 3:18; Lk 6:15; Ac 1:13).
3. Samaritan sorcerer (Ac 8:9–24).
SIMPLE
Ps 19: 7 are trustworthy, making wise the **s**.
119:130 it gives understanding to the **s**.
Pr 8: 5 You who are **s**, gain prudence;
14: 15 The **s** believe anything,
SIN (SINFUL SINNED SINNER SINNERS SINNING SINS)
Ge 4: 7 right, **s** is crouching at your door;
Ex 32: 32 But now, please forgive their **s**—
Nu 5: 7 and must confess the **s** they have
32: 23 sure that your **s** will find you out.
Dt 24: 16 each will die for their own **s**.
1Sa 12: 23 that I should **s** against the LORD
15: 23 rebellion is like the **s** of divination,
1Ki 8: 46 there is no one who does not **s**—
2Ki 14: 6 each will die for their own **s**."
2Ch 7: 14 I will forgive their **s** and will heal
Job 1: 22 Job did not **s** by charging God
Ps 4: 4 Tremble and do not **s**; when you
32: 2 is the one whose **s** the LORD does
32: 5 And you forgave the guilt of my **s**.
36: 2 too much to detect or hate their **s**.
38: 18 I am troubled by my **s**.
39: 1 ways and keep my tongue from **s**;
51: 2 iniquity and cleanse me from my **s**.
66: 18 If I had cherished **s** in my heart,
119: 11 that I might not **s** against you.
119:133 to your word; let no **s** rule over me.
Pr 10: 19 **S** is not ended by multiplying
14: 9 mock at making amends for **s**,
14: 21 It is a **s** to despise one's neighbor,
16: 6 and faithfulness **s** is atoned for;
17: 19 Whoever loves a quarrel loves **s**;
20: 9 I am clean and without **s**"?
Isa 3: 9 they parade their **s** like Sodom;
6: 7 taken away and your **s** atoned for."
64: 5 we continued to **s** against them,
Jer 31: 30 everyone will die for their own **s**;
Eze 3: 18 wicked person will die for their **s**,
18: 26 their righteousness and commits **s**,
Am 4: 4 "Go to Bethel and **s**; go to Gilgal
Mic 6: 7 of my body for the **s** of my soul?
7: 18 you, who pardons **s** and forgives
Zec 3: 4 I have taken away your **s**, and I will
Mk 3: 29 they are guilty of an eternal **s**."
Jn 1: 29 who takes away the **s** of the world!
8: 7 *without **s** be the first to throw*
8: 34 everyone who sins is a slave to **s**.
Jn 8: 46 any of you prove me guilty of **s**?
Ro 2: 12 All who **s** apart from the law will
5: 12 just as **s** entered the world through
5: 20 But where **s** increased,
6: 2 We are those who have died to **s**;
6: 11 count yourselves dead to **s** but alive
6: 14 **s** shall no longer be your master,
6: 23 For the wages of **s** is death,
7: 7 not have known what **s** was had it
7: 25 sinful nature a slave to the law of **s**.
14: 23 that does not come from faith is **s**.
1Co 8: 12 conscience, you **s** against Christ.
14: 24 they are convicted of **s** and are
15: 56 The sting of death is **s**, and the power of **s** is the law.
2Co 5: 21 God made him who had no **s** to be **s** for us,
Gal 6: 1 if someone is caught in a **s**, you
Heb 4: 15 just as we are—yet he did not **s**.
9: 26 to do away with **s** by the sacrifice
11: 25 to enjoy the fleeting pleasures of **s**.
12: 1 and the **s** that so easily entangles.
Jas 1: 15 has conceived, it gives birth to **s**;
4: 17 and doesn't do it, it is **s** for them.
1Pe 2: 22 "He committed no **s**, and no deceit
1Jn 1: 7 his Son, purifies us from all **s**.
1: 8 If we claim to be without **s**,
2: 1 to you so that you will not **s**.
2: 1 But if anybody does **s**, we have
3: 4 in fact, **s** is lawlessness.
3: 5 away our sins. And in him is no **s**.
3: 6 continues to **s** has either seen him
3: 9 is born of God will continue to **s**,
5: 16 commit a **s** that does not lead
5: 16 There is a **s** that leads to death.
5: 17 wrongdoing is **s**, and there is **s**
5: 18 of God does not continue to **s**;
SINAI
Ex 19: 20 descended to the top of Mount **S**
31: 18 speaking to Moses on Mount **S**,
Ps 68: 17 the Lord has come from **S** into his
SINCERE* (SINCERITY)
Da 11: 34 many who are not **s** will join them.
Lk 20: 20 sent spies, who pretended to be **s**.
Ac 2: 46 ate together with glad and **s** hearts,
Ro 12: 9 Love must be **s**. Hate what is evil;
2Co 6: 6 in the Holy Spirit and in **s** love;
11: 3 somehow be led astray from your **s**
1Ti 1: 5 a good conscience and a **s** faith.
3: 8 are to be worthy of respect, **s**,
2Ti 1: 5 I am reminded of your **s** faith,
Heb 10: 22 us draw near to God with a **s** heart
Jas 3: 17 and good fruit, impartial and **s**.
1Pe 1: 22 that you have **s** love for each other,
SINCERITY* (SINCERE)
1Co 5: 8 with the unleavened bread of **s**
2Co 1: 12 you, with integrity and godly **s**.
2: 17 Christ we speak before God with **s**,
8: 8 I want to test the **s** of your love
Eph 6: 5 fear, and with **s** of heart, just as you
Col 3: 22 but with **s** of heart and reverence
SINFUL (SIN)
Ps 51: 5 Surely I was **s** at birth,
Pr 1: 10 if **s** men entice you, do not give
Lk 5: 8 from me, Lord; I am a **s** man!"
Ro 7: 5 the **s** passions aroused by the law
7: 18 dwell in me, that is, in my **s** nature.
7: 25 in my **s** nature a slave to the law
8: 3 in the likeness of **s** flesh to be a sin
Heb 3: 12 sisters, that none of you has a **s**,
1Pe 2: 11 to abstain from **s** desires,
1Jn 3: 8 The one who does what is **s** is
SINFUL NATURE see FLESH
SING (SANG SINGING SINGS SONG SONGS SUNG)
Ex 15: 1 "I will **s** to the LORD, for he is
Jdg 5: 3 I, even I, will **s** to the LORD;
Ps 5: 11 you be glad; let them ever **s** for joy.
13: 6 I will **s** the LORD's praise, for he
30: 4 **S** the praises of the LORD, you his
33: 1 **S** joyfully to the LORD,
47: 6 **S** praises to God, **s** praises;
57: 7 I will **s** and make music.
59: 16 But I will **s** of your strength,

Ps 63: 7 I **s** in the shadow of your wings.
66: 2 **S** the glory of his name;
89: 1 I will **s** of the LORD's great love
95: 1 let us **s** for joy to the LORD;
96: 1 **S** to the LORD a new song;
98: 1 **S** to the LORD a new song, for he
101: 1 I will **s** of your love and justice;
108: 1 I will **s** and make music with all my
137: 3 "**S** us one of the songs of Zion!"
147: 1 How good it is to **s** praises to our
149: 1 **S** to the LORD a new song,
Isa 54: 1 "**S**, barren woman, you who never
1Co 14: 15 I will **s** with my spirit, but I will
Eph 5: 19 **S** and make music from your heart
Jas 5: 13 Let them **s** songs of praise.

SINGING (SING)
Ps 63: 5 **s** lips my mouth will praise you.
68: 6 he leads out the prisoners with **s**;
98: 5 with the harp and the sound of **s**,
Isa 35: 10 They will enter Zion with **s**;
Zep 3: 17 but will rejoice over you with **s**."
Ac 16: 25 were praying and **s** hymns to God,
Col 3: 16 **s** to God with gratitude in your

SINGLE
Ex 23: 29 will not drive them out in a **s** year,
Mt 6: 27 worrying add a **s** hour to your life?

SINGS (SING)
Eze 33: 32 more than one who **s** love songs

SINNED (SIN)
Lev 5: 5 confess in what way they have **s**.
1Sa 15: 24 Saul said to Samuel, "I have **s**.
2Sa 12: 13 "I have **s** against the LORD."
24: 10 "I have **s** greatly in what I have
2Ch 6: 37 'We have **s**, we have done wrong
Job 1: 5 "Perhaps my children have **s**
33: 27 'I have **s**, I have perverted what is
Ps 51: 4 have I **s** and done what is evil
Jer 2: 35 you because you say, 'I have not **s**.'
14: 20 we have indeed **s** against you.
Da 9: 5 we have **s** and done wrong.
Mic 7: 9 Because I have **s** against him, I will
Mt 27: 4 "I have **s**," he said, "for I have
Lk 15: 18 I have **s** against heaven and against
Ro 3: 23 for all have **s** and fall short
5: 12 came to all people, because all **s**—
2Pe 2: 4 did not spare angels when they **s**,
1Jn 1: 10 If we claim we have not **s**, we make

SINNER (SIN)
Ecc 9: 18 war, but one **s** destroys much good.
Lk 15: 7 heaven over one **s** who repents
18: 13 said, 'God, have mercy on me, a **s**.'
Jas 5: 20 Whoever turns a **s** from the error
1Pe 4: 18 become of the ungodly and the **s**?"

SINNERS (SIN)
Ps 1: 1 stand in the way that **s** take or sit
37: 38 But all **s** will be destroyed;
Pr 23: 17 Do not let your heart envy **s**,
Mt 9: 13 come to call the righteous, but **s**."
Ro 5: 8 While we were still **s**, Christ died
Gal 2: 17 find ourselves also among the **s**,
1Ti 1: 15 came into the world to save **s**—
Heb 7: 26 set apart from **s**,

SINNING (SIN)
Ex 20: 20 be with you to keep you from **s**."
1Co 15: 34 senses as you ought, and stop **s**;
1Ti 5: 20 those elders who are **s** you are
Heb 10: 26 If we deliberately keep on **s** after
1Jn 3: 6 one who lives in him keeps on **s**.
3: 9 they cannot go on **s**, because they

SINS (SIN)
Lev 5: 1 "'If anyone **s** because they do not
16: 30 you will be clean from all your **s**.
26: 40 if they will confess their **s** and the **s**
Nu 15: 30 "'But anyone who **s** defiantly,
1Sa 2: 25 but if anyone **s** against the LORD,
Ezr 9: 6 because our **s** are higher than our
9: 13 us less than our **s** deserved
Ne 9: 2 confessed their **s** and the **s** of their
Ps 19: 13 your servant also from willful **s**;
32: 1 are forgiven, whose **s** are covered.
51: 9 Hide your face from my **s** and blot
79: 9 forgive our **s** for your name's sake.
85: 2 your people and covered all their **s**.
Ps 103: 3 forgives all your **s** and heals all
103: 10 does not treat us as our **s** deserve
130: 3 LORD, kept a record of **s**, Lord,
Pr 5: 22 the cords of their **s** hold them fast.
28: 13 Whoever conceals their **s** does not
29: 22 person commits many **s**.
Ecc 7: 20 who does what is right and never **s**.
Isa 1: 18 "Though your **s** are like scarlet,
38: 17 put all my **s** behind your back.
43: 25 and remembers your **s** no more.
59: 2 your **s** have hidden his face
64: 6 like the wind our **s** sweep us away.
Jer 31: 34 will remember their **s** no more."
La 3: 39 when punished for their **s**?
Eze 18: 4 The one who **s** is the one who will
33: 10 offenses and **s** weigh us down,
36: 33 day I cleanse you from all your **s**,
Hos 14: 1 Your **s** have been your downfall!
Mt 1: 21 will save his people from their **s**."
6: 15 your Father will not forgive your **s**.
9: 6 has authority on earth to forgive **s**."
18: 15 "If your brother or sister **s**,
26: 28 for many for the forgiveness of **s**.
Lk 5: 24 has authority on earth to forgive **s**."
11: 4 Forgive us our **s**, for we also forgive
17: 3 your brother or sister **s** against you,
Jn 8: 24 you will indeed die in your **s**."
20: 23 If you forgive anyone's **s**, their **s** are
Ac 2: 38 Christ for the forgiveness of your **s**.
3: 19 so that your **s** may be wiped out,
10: 43 forgiveness of **s** through his name."
22: 16 be baptized and wash your **s** away,
26: 18 they may receive forgiveness of **s**
Ro 4: 7 are forgiven, whose **s** are covered.
4: 25 delivered over to death for our **s**
1Co 15: 3 Christ died for our **s** according
2Co 5: 19 counting people's **s** against them.
Gal 1: 4 gave himself for our **s** to rescue us
Eph 2: 1 dead in your transgressions and **s**,
Col 2: 13 When you were dead in your **s**
2: 13 He forgave us all our **s**,
1Ti 5: 22 and do not share in the **s** of others.
Heb 1: 3 he had provided purification for **s**,
2: 17 atonement for the **s** of the people.
7: 27 sacrificed for their **s** once for all
8: 12 will remember their **s** no more."
9: 28 once to take away the **s** of many;
10: 4 of bulls and goats to take away **s**.
10: 12 for all time one sacrifice for **s**,
10: 26 the truth, no sacrifice for **s** is left,
Jas 5: 16 Therefore confess your **s** to each
5: 20 and cover over a multitude of **s**.
1Pe 2: 24 "He himself bore our **s**" in his
3: 18 For Christ also suffered once for **s**,
4: 8 love covers over a multitude of **s**.
1Jn 1: 9 If we confess our **s**, he is faithful
2: 2 is the atoning sacrifice for our **s**,
3: 5 so that he might take away our **s**.
4: 10 as an atoning sacrifice for our **s**.
Rev 1: 5 freed us from our **s** by his blood,

SISERA
Jdg 4: 2 **S**, the commander of his army,
5: 26 She struck **S**, she crushed his head,

SISTER (SISTERS)
Lev 18: 9 have sexual relations with your **s**,
Mk 3: 35 does God's will is my brother and **s**
1Co 7: 15 or the **s** is not bound in such
2Jn : 13 The children of your **s**, who is

SISTERS (SISTER)
Mt 13: 56 Aren't all his **s** with us?
19: 29 left houses or brothers or **s** or
Jn 11: 3 So the **s** sent word to Jesus, "Lord,
1Ti 5: 2 and younger women as **s**,

SIT (SAT SITS SITTING)
Dt 6: 7 about them when you **s** at home
1Ki 8: 25 have a successor to **s** before me
Ps 1: 1 or **s** in the company of mockers,
26: 5 and refuse to **s** with the wicked.
80: 1 You who **s** enthroned between
110: 1 "**S** at my right hand until I make
139: 2 know when I **s** and when I rise;
SS 2: 3 I delight to **s** in his shade, and his
Isa 16: 5 in faithfulness a man will **s** on it—
Mic 4: 4 Everyone will **s** under their own
Mt 20: 23 but to **s** at my right or left is not
22: 44 "**S** at my right hand until I put
Lk 22: 30 in my kingdom and **s** on thrones,
Heb 1: 13 "**S** at my right hand until I make
Rev 3: 21 I will give the right to **s** with me

SITS (SIT)
Ps 99: 1 he **s** enthroned between
Isa 40: 22 He **s** enthroned above the circle
Mt 19: 28 Son of Man **s** on his glorious
Rev 4: 9 thanks to him who **s** on the throne

SITTING (SIT)
Est 2: 19 Mordecai was **s** at the king's gate.
Mt 26: 64 the Son of Man **s** at the right hand
Rev 4: 2 in heaven with someone **s** on it.

SITUATION (SITUATIONS)
1Co 7: 24 should remain in the **s** they were
Php 4: 12 being content in any and every **s**,

SITUATIONS* (SITUATION)
2Ti 4: 5 you, keep your head in all **s**,

SKIES (SKY)
Ps 19: 1 the **s** proclaim the work of his
108: 4 your faithfulness reaches to the **s**.

SKILL (SKILLED SKILLFUL)
Ps 137: 5 may my right hand forget its **s**.
Ecc 10: 10 is needed, but **s** will bring success.

SKILLED (SKILL)
Pr 22: 29 Do you see someone **s** in their

SKILLFUL (SKILL)
Ps 45: 1 my tongue is the pen of a **s** writer.
78: 72 with **s** hands he led them.

SKIN (SKINS)
Job 19: 20 escaped only by the **s** of my teeth.
19: 26 And after my **s** has been destroyed,
Jer 13: 23 Can an Ethiopian change his **s**

SKINS (SKIN)
Ex 25: 5 ram **s** dyed red and another type
Lk 5: 37 the new wine will burst the **s**;

SKULL
Mt 27: 33 (which means "the place of the **s**").

SKY (SKIES)
Ge 1: 8 God called the vault "**s**."
Pr 30: 19 the way of an eagle in the **s**,
Isa 34: 4 the stars in the **s** will be dissolved
Jer 33: 22 me as countless as the stars in the **s**
Mt 24: 29 the stars will fall from the **s**,
Php 2: 15 among them like stars in the **s**

SLACK*
Pr 18: 9 One who is **s** in his work is brother

SLAIN (SLAY)
1Sa 18: 7 "Saul has **s** his thousands,
Eze 37: 9 winds and breathe into these **s**,
Rev 5: 6 looking as if it had been **s**,
5: 12 who was **s**, to receive power
6: 9 those who had been **s** because

SLANDER (SLANDERED SLANDERER SLANDERERS SLANDEROUS)
Lev 19: 16 spreading **s** among your people.
Ps 15: 3 whose tongue utters no **s**, who
Pr 10: 18 lying lips and spreads **s** is a fool.
Mk 3: 28 their sins and every **s** they utter,
2Co 12: 20 of rage, selfish ambition, **s**, gossip,
Eph 4: 31 brawling and **s**, along with every
1Ti 5: 14 the enemy no opportunity for **s**.
Titus 3: 2 to **s** no one, to be peaceable
1Pe 3: 16 may be ashamed of their **s**.

SLANDERED (SLANDER)
1Co 4: 13 when we are **s**, we answer kindly.

SLANDERER* (SLANDER)
Jer 9: 4 is a deceiver, and every friend a **s**.
1Co 5: 11 immoral or greedy, an idolater or **s**,

SLANDERERS (SLANDER)
Ro 1: 30 **s**, God-haters, insolent,
1Co 6: 10 nor drunkards nor **s** nor swindlers
Titus 2: 3 live, not to be **s** or addicted to much

SLANDEROUS* (SLANDER)
2Ti 3: 3 unforgiving, **s**, without self-control

SLAPS
Mt 5: 39 If anyone **s** you on the right cheek,

SLAUGHTER (SLAUGHTERED)
Isa 53: 7 he was led like a lamb to the **s**,
Jer 11: 19 been like a gentle lamb led to the **s**;
Ac 8: 32 "He was led like a sheep to the **s**,

SLAUGHTERED (SLAUGHTER)
Ps 44: 22 we are considered as sheep to be **s**.
Ro 8: 36 we are considered as sheep to be **s**."

SLAVE (ENSLAVED SLAVERY SLAVES)
Ge 21: 10 "Get rid of that **s** woman and her
Pr 22: 7 and the borrower is **s** to the lender.
Mal 1: 6 his father, and a **s** his master.
Mt 20: 27 wants to be first must be your **s**—
Jn 8: 34 everyone who sins is a **s** to sin.
Ro 7: 14 I am unspiritual, sold as a **s** to sin.
1Co 7: 21 Were you a **s** when you were
12: 13 whether Jews or Gentiles, **s** or free
Gal 3: 28 Jew nor Gentile, neither **s** nor free,
4: 30 "Get rid of the **s** woman and her
4: 7 no longer a **s**, but God's child;
Col 3: 11 **s** or free, but Christ is all,
1Ti 1: 10 for **s** traders and liars and perjurers
Phm : 16 no longer as a **s**, but better than a **s**,

SLAVERY (SLAVE)
Ex 2: 23 The Israelites groaned in their **s**
Gal 4: 3 in **s** under the elemental spiritual
1Ti 6: 1 of **s** should consider their masters

SLAVES (SLAVE)
Ps 123: 2 As the eyes of **s** look to the hand
Ecc 10: 7 I have seen **s** on horseback,
10: 7 while princes go on foot like **s**.
Ro 6: 6 we should no longer be **s** to sin—
6: 16 whether you are **s** to sin,
6: 19 so now offer yourselves as **s**
6: 22 sin and have become **s** of God,
Gal 2: 4 in Christ Jesus and to make us **s**.
4: 8 you were **s** to those who by nature
Eph 6: 5 **S**, obey your earthly masters
Col 3: 22 **S**, obey your earthly masters
4: 1 provide your **s** with what is right
Titus 2: 9 Teach **s** to be subject to their
2Pe 2: 19 for "people are **s** to whatever has

SLAY (SLAIN)
Job 13: 15 Though he **s** me, yet will I hope

SLEEP (ASLEEP SLEEPER SLEEPING SLEEPS)
Ge 2: 21 the man to fall into a deep **s**;
15: 12 Abram fell into a deep **s**,
28: 11 under his head and lay down to **s**.
Ps 4: 8 In peace I will lie down and **s**,
121: 4 Israel will neither slumber nor **s**.
127: 2 for he grants **s** to those he loves.
Pr 6: 9 When will you get up from your **s**?
Ecc 5: 12 The **s** of a laborer is sweet,
1Co 15: 51 We will not all **s**, but we will all be
1Th 4: 13 about those who **s** in death,
5: 7 For those who **s**, **s** at night,

SLEEPER* (SLEEP)
Eph 5: 14 "Wake up, **s**, rise from the dead,

SLEEPING (SLEEP)
Mk 13: 36 do not let him find you **s**.

SLEEPLESS*
2Co 6: 5 in hard work, **s** nights and hunger;

SLEEPS (SLEEP)
Pr 10: 5 son, but he who **s** during harvest is

SLIMY*
Ps 40: 2 He lifted me out of the **s** pit,

SLING
1Sa 17: 50 over the Philistine with a **s**

SLIP (SLIPPING)
Ps 121: 3 He will not let your foot **s**—

SLIPPING (SLIP)
Ps 66: 9 our lives and kept our feet from **s**.

SLOW
Ex 34: 6 and gracious God, **s** to anger,
Jas 1: 19 **s** to speak and **s** to become angry,
2Pe 3: 9 The Lord is not **s** in keeping his

SLUGGARD (SLUGGARD'S SLUGGARDS)
Pr 6: 6 Go to the ant, you **s**;
26: 15 A **s** buries his hand in the dish;

SLUGGARD'S* (SLUGGARD)
Pr 13: 4 A **s** appetite is never filled,

SLUGGARDS (SLUGGARD)
Pr 20: 4 **S** do not plow in season;

SLUMBER
Ps 121: 3 he who watches over you will not **s**;
Pr 6: 10 little **s**, a little folding of the hands
Ro 13: 11 for you to wake up from your **s**,

SLUR*
Ps 15: 3 neighbor, and casts no **s** on others;

SMELL
Ecc 10: 1 As dead flies give perfume a bad **s**,

SMOKE
Ex 19: 18 Mount Sinai was covered with **s**,
Ps 104: 32 touches the mountains, and they **s**.
Isa 6: 4 and the temple was filled with **s**.
Joel 2: 30 blood and fire and billows of **s**.
Ac 2: 19 blood and fire and billows of **s**.
Rev 15: 8 the temple was filled with **s**

SMYRNA
Rev 2: 8 the angel of the church in **S** write:

SNAKE (SNAKES)
Nu 21: 8 "Make a **s** and put it up on a pole;
Pr 23: 32 In the end it bites like a **s**
Jn 3: 14 lifted up the **s** in the wilderness,

SNAKES (SNAKE)
Mt 10: 16 Therefore be as shrewd as **s** and as
Mk 16: 18 *they will pick up **s** with their*

SNARE (ENSNARE ENSNARED SNARED)
Dt 7: 16 gods, for that will be a **s** to you.
Ps 69: 22 table set before them become a **s**;
91: 3 he will save you from the fowler's **s**
Pr 29: 25 Fear of man will prove to be a **s**,
Ro 11: 9 "May their table become a **s**

SNARED (SNARE)
Pr 3: 26 will keep your foot from being **s**.

SNATCH (SNATCHING)
Jn 10: 28 no one will **s** them out of my hand.

SNATCHING* (SNATCH)
Jude : 23 save others by **s** them from the fire;

SNEER
Ps 35: 21 They **s** at me and say, "Aha! Aha!

SNOUT*
Pr 11: 22 a pig's **s** is a beautiful woman who

SNOW
Ps 51: 7 me, and I will be whiter than **s**.
Isa 1: 18 scarlet, they shall be as white as **s**;

SNUFF (SNUFFED)
Isa 42: 3 smoldering wick he will not **s** out.
Mt 12: 20 smoldering wick he will not **s** out,

SNUFFED (SNUFF)
Pr 13: 9 but the lamp of the wicked is **s** out.

SOAP
Mal 3: 2 a refiner's fire or a launderer's **s**.

SOAR (SOARED)
Isa 40: 31 They will **s** on wings like eagles;

SOARED (SOAR)
2Sa 22: 11 he **s** on the wings of the wind.

SOBER*
1Sa 25: 37 Nabal was **s**, his wife told him
Ro 12: 3 think of yourself with **s** judgment,
1Th 5: 6 asleep, but let us be awake and **s**.
5: 8 be **s**, putting on faith and love
1Pe 1: 13 minds that are alert and fully **s**,
4: 7 of **s** mind so that you may pray.
5: 8 Be alert and of **s** mind.

SODOM
Ge 13: 12 plain and pitched his tents near **S**.
19: 24 rained down burning sulfur on **S**
Isa 1: 9 we would have become like **S**,
Lk 10: 12 that day for **S** than for that town.
Ro 9: 29 we would have become like **S**,
Rev 11: 8 which is figuratively called **S**

SOIL
Ge 4: 2 kept flocks, and Cain worked the **s**.
Mt 13: 23 the seed falling on good **s** refers

SOLD (SELL)
1Ki 21: 25 who **s** himself to do evil in the eyes
Mt 10: 29 not two sparrows **s** for a penny?
13: 44 in his joy went and **s** all he had
Ro 7: 14 I am unspiritual, **s** as a slave to sin.

SOLDIER
1Co 9: 7 Who serves as a **s** at his own
2Ti 2: 3 like a good **s** of Christ Jesus.

SOLE
Dt 28: 65 resting place for the **s** of your foot.
Isa 1: 6 From the **s** of your foot to the top

SOLID
2Ti 2: 19 God's **s** foundation stands firm,
Heb 5: 12 You need milk, not **s** food!

SOLOMON
Son of David by Bathsheba; king of Judah (2Sa 12:24; 1Ch 3:5, 10). Appointed king by David (1Ki 1); adversaries Adonijah, Joab, Shimei killed by Benaiah (1Ki 2). Asked for wisdom (1Ki 3; 2Ch 1). Judged between two prostitutes (1Ki 3:16–28). Built temple (1Ki 5–7; 2Ch 2–5); prayer of dedication (1Ki 8; 2Ch 6). Visited by Queen of Sheba (1Ki 10; 2Ch 9). Wives turned his heart from God (1Ki 11:1–13). Jeroboam rebelled against (1Ki 11:26–40). Death (1Ki 11:41–43; 2Ch 9:29–31).
Proverbs of (1Ki 4:32; Pr 1:1; 10:1; 25:1); psalms of (Ps 72; 127); song of (SS 1:1).

SON (SONS SONSHIP)
Ge 17: 19 your wife Sarah will bear you a **s**,
21: 10 rid of that slave woman and her **s**,
22: 2 said, "Take your **s**, your only **s**,
Ex 11: 5 Every firstborn **s** in Egypt will die,
Dt 1: 31 as a father carries his **s**, all the way
6: 20 your **s** asks you, "What is the
8: 5 that as a man disciplines his **s**,
21: 18 rebellious **s** who does not obey his
2Sa 7: 14 be his father, and he will be my **s**.
1Ki 3: 20 and put her dead **s** by my breast.
Ps 2: 7 He said to me, "You are my **s**;
2: 12 Kiss his **s**, or he will be angry
Pr 3: 12 as a father the **s** he delights in.
6: 20 My **s**, keep your father's command
Pr 10: 1 A wise **s** brings joy to his father, but a foolish **s** brings grief
Isa 7: 14 will conceive and give birth to a **s**,
Da 3: 25 and the fourth looks like a **s**
7: 13 there before me was one like a **s**
Hos 11: 1 and out of Egypt I called my **s**.
Am 7: 14 a prophet nor the **s** of a prophet,
Mt 1: 1 Jesus the Messiah the **s** of David, the **s** of Abraham:
1: 21 She will give birth to a **s**,
2: 15 "Out of Egypt I called my **s**."
3: 17 said, "This is my **S**, whom I love;
4: 3 "If you are the **S** of God, tell these
8: 20 the **S** of Man has no place to lay his
11: 27 one knows the **S** except the Father,
11: 27 whom the **S** chooses to reveal him.
12: 8 For the **S** of Man is Lord
12: 32 who speaks a word against the **S**
12: 40 so the **S** of Man will be three days
13: 41 The **S** of Man will send out his
13: 55 "Isn't this the carpenter's **s**?
14: 33 "Truly you are the **S** of God."
16: 16 Messiah, the **S** of the living God."
16: 27 For the **S** of Man is going to come
17: 5 said, "This is my **S**, whom I love;
19: 28 when the **S** of Man sits on his
20: 18 the **S** of Man will be delivered over
20: 28 just as the **S** of Man did not come
21: 9 "Hosanna to the **S** of David!"
22: 42 the Messiah? Whose **s** is he?"
22: 42 "The **s** of David," they replied.
24: 27 will be the coming of the **S** of Man.
24: 30 appear the sign of the **S** of Man
24: 44 because the **S** of Man will come
25: 31 "When the **S** of Man comes in his
26: 63 you are the Messiah, the **S** of God."
27: 54 "Surely he was the **S** of God!"
28: 19 and of the **S** and of the Holy Spirit,
Mk 1: 11 "You are my **S**, whom I love;
2: 28 So the **S** of Man is Lord even
8: 38 the **S** of Man will be ashamed
9: 7 "This is my **S**, whom I love.
10: 45 even the **S** of Man did not come
13: 32 nor the **S**, but only the Father.
14: 62 you will see the **S** of Man sitting
Lk 1: 32 and will be called the **S** of the Most

Lk 2: 7 she gave birth to her firstborn, a s.
3: 22 "You are my S, whom I love;
9: 35 saying, "This is my S, whom I have
9: 58 the S of Man has no place to lay his
12: 8 the S of Man will also acknowledge
15: 20 he ran to his s, threw his arms
18: 8 when the S of Man comes, will he
18: 31 about the S of Man will be fulfilled.
19: 10 For the S of Man came to seek
Jn 3: 14 so the S of Man must be lifted up,
3: 16 that he gave his one and only S,
3: 36 believes in the S has eternal life,
5: 19 the S can do nothing by himself;
6: 40 is that everyone who looks to the S
11: 4 God's S may be glorified through
17: 1 Glorify your S, that your S may
Ac 7: 56 the S of Man standing at the right
13: 33 "'You are my s; today I have
Ro 1: 4 was appointed the S of God
5: 10 to him through the death of his S,
8: 3 sending his own S in the likeness
8: 29 conformed to the image of his S,
8: 32 He who did not spare his own S,
1Co 15: 28 the S himself will be made subject
Gal 2: 20 I live by faith in the S of God,
4: 4 God sent his S, born of a woman,
4: 30 rid of the slave woman and her s,
1Th 1: 10 and to wait for his S from heaven,
Heb 1: 2 days he has spoken to us by his S,
1: 5 did God ever say, "You are my S;
4: 14 into heaven, Jesus the S of God,
5: 5 God said to him, "You are my S;
7: 28 appointed the S, who has been
10: 29 punished who has trampled the S
12: 6 everyone he accepts as his s."
2Pe 1: 17 saying, "This is my S, whom I love;
1Jn 1: 3 is with the Father and with his S,
1: 7 Jesus, his S, purifies us from all sin.
2: 23 who denies the S has the Father;
2: 23 acknowledges the S has the Father
3: 8 The reason the S of God appeared
4: 9 only S into the world that we might
4: 14 the Father has sent his S to be
5: 5 believes that Jesus is the S of God.
5: 11 eternal life, and this life is in his S.
Rev 1: 13 lampstands was someone like a s
14: 14 the cloud was one like a s of man

SONG (SING)
Ps 40: 3 He put a new s in my mouth,
69: 30 I will praise God's name in s
96: 1 Sing to the LORD a new s;
98: 4 burst into jubilant s with music;
119: 54 theme of my s wherever I lodge.
149: 1 Sing to the LORD a new s,
Isa 49: 13 burst into s, you mountains!
55: 12 hills will burst into s before you,
Rev 5: 9 And they sang a new s, saying:
15: 3 sang the s of God's servant Moses

SONGS (SING)
2Sa 23: 1 God of Jacob, the hero of Israel's s:
Job 35: 10 Maker, who gives s in the night,
Ps 100: 2 come before him with joyful s.
126: 6 to sow, will return with s of joy,
137: 3 "Sing us one of the s of Zion!"
Eph 5: 19 hymns, and s from the Spirit.
Jas 5: 13 Let them sing s of praise.

SONS (SON)
Ge 6: 2 the s of God saw that the daughters
10: 20 These are the s of Ham by their
Ru 4: 15 who is better to you than seven s,
Ps 132: 12 their s will sit on your throne
Joel 2: 28 s and daughters will prophesy,
2Co 6: 18 you will be my s and daughters,
Gal 4: 6 Because you are his s, God sent

SONSHIP* (SON)
Ro 8: 15 brought about your adoption to s.
8: 23 wait eagerly for our adoption to s,
9: 4 Israel. Theirs is the adoption to s;
Gal 4: 5 we might receive adoption to s.
Eph 1: 5 adoption to s through Jesus Christ,

SOOTHING
Pr 15: 4 The s tongue is a tree of life,

SORROW
Ps 6: 7 My eyes grow weak with s;
116: 3 I was overcome by distress and s.
Isa 60: 20 light, and your days of s will end.
Jer 31: 12 garden, and they will s no more.
Ro 9: 2 I have great s and unceasing
2Co 7: 10 Godly s brings repentance that
7: 10 regret, but worldly s brings death.

SOUGHT (SEEK)
2Ch 26: 5 He s God during the days
31: 21 he s his God and worked
Ps 34: 4 I s the LORD, and he answered
119: 58 have s your face with all my heart;

SOUL (SOULS)
Dt 6: 5 with all your s and with all your
10: 12 all your heart and with all your s,
30: 6 all your heart and with all your s,
Jos 22: 5 all your heart and with all your s."
2Ki 23: 25 and with all his s and with all his
Ps 23: 3 he refreshes my s. He guides me
42: 1 of water, so my s pants for you,
42: 11 Why, my s, are you downcast?
62: 5 Yes, my s, find rest in God;
103: 1 Praise the LORD, my s;
Pr 13: 19 A longing fulfilled is sweet to the s,
16: 24 sweet to the s and healing
La 3: 20 and my s is downcast within me.
Mt 10: 28 kill the body but cannot kill the s.
16: 26 the whole world, yet forfeit their s?
16: 26 give in exchange for their s?
22: 37 with all your s and with all your
Jn 12: 27 "Now my s is troubled, and what
Heb 4: 12 it penetrates even to dividing s
3Jn : 2 even as your s is getting along well.

SOULS (SOUL)
Jer 6: 16 it, and you will find rest for your s.
Mt 11: 29 and you will find rest for your s.

SOUND (FINE-SOUNDING)
Ge 3: 8 his wife heard the s of the LORD
Pr 3: 21 preserve s judgment and discretion
Eze 3: 12 me a loud rumbling s as the glory
Jn 3: 8 You hear its s, but you cannot tell
Ac 2: 2 Suddenly a s like the blowing
1Co 14: 8 the trumpet does not s a clear call,
15: 52 For the trumpet will s, the dead
1Ti 1: 10 else is contrary to the s doctrine
2Ti 4: 3 will not put up with s doctrine.
Titus 1: 9 can encourage others by s doctrine
2: 1 what is appropriate to s doctrine.

SOUR
Eze 18: 2 "'The parents eat s grapes,

SOURCE
Heb 5: 9 became the s of eternal salvation

SOVEREIGN (SOVEREIGNTY)
Ge 15: 2 But Abram said, "S LORD,
2Sa 7: 18 "Who am I, S LORD, and what is
Ps 71: 16 your mighty acts, S LORD;
Isa 25: 8 The S LORD will wipe away
40: 10 the S LORD comes with power,
50: 4 The S LORD has given me
61: 1 The Spirit of the S LORD is
61: 11 to grow, so the S LORD will make
Jer 32: 17 "Ah, S LORD, you have made
Eze 12: 28 'This is what the S LORD says:
Da 4: 25 Most High is s over all kingdoms
2Pe 2: 1 even denying the s Lord who
Jude : 4 deny Jesus Christ our only S

SOVEREIGNTY (SOVEREIGN)
Da 7: 27 Then the s, power and greatness

SOW (SOWER SOWN SOWS)
Job 4: 8 and those who s trouble reap it.
Ps 126: 5 Those who s with tears will reap
Hos 8: 7 "They s the wind and reap
10: 12 S righteousness for yourselves,
Mt 6: 26 they do not s or reap or store away
13: 3 "A farmer went out to s his seed.
1Co 15: 36 What you s does not come to life
Jas 3: 18 Peacemakers who s in peace reap
2Pe 2: 22 "A s that is washed returns to her

SOWER (SOW)
Isa 55: 10 so that it yields seed for the s
Mt 13: 18 to what the parable of the s means:
Jn 4: 36 so that the s and the reaper may be
2Co 9: 10 Now he who supplies seed to the s

SOWN (SOW)
Mt 13: 8 sixty or thirty times what was s.
Mk 4: 15 along the path, where the word is s.
1Co 15: 42 The body that is s is perishable,

SOWS (SOW)
Pr 11: 18 the one who s righteousness reaps
22: 8 Whoever s injustice reaps calamity,
2Co 9: 6 Whoever s sparingly will also reap
9: 6 and whoever s generously will
Gal 6: 7 A man reaps what he s.

SPARE (SPARES SPARING)
Est 7: 3 And s my people—this is my
Ro 8: 32 He who did not s his own Son,
11: 21 God did not s the natural branches,
he will not s you either.
2Pe 2: 4 if God did not s angels when they
2: 5 if he did not s the ancient world

SPARES (SPARE)
Pr 13: 24 Whoever s the rod hates their

SPARING (SPARE)
Pr 21: 26 but the righteous give without s.

SPARKLE*
Zec 9: 16 They will s in his land like jewels

SPARROW (SPARROWS)
Ps 84: 3 Even the s has found a home,

SPARROWS (SPARROW)
Mt 10: 29 Are not two s sold for a penny?

SPEAR (SPEARS)
1Sa 19: 10 to pin him to the wall with his s,
Ps 46: 9 breaks the bow and shatters the s;

SPEARS (SPEAR)
Isa 2: 4 and their s into pruning hooks.
Joel 3: 10 and your pruning hooks into s.
Mic 4: 3 and their s into pruning hooks.

SPECIAL
Jas 2: 3 If you show s attention to the man

SPECK
Mt 7: 3 do you look at the s of sawdust

SPECTACLE
1Co 4: 9 We have been made a s to the
Col 2: 15 he made a public s of them,

SPEECH
Ps 19: 3 They have no s, they use no words;
2Co 8: 7 in faith, in s, in knowledge,
1Ti 4: 12 an example for the believers in s,
1Jn 3: 18 let us not love with words or s but

SPEND (SPENT)
Pr 31: 3 Do not s your strength on women,
Isa 55: 2 Why s money on what is not bread,
2Co 12: 15 So I will very gladly s for you

SPENT (SPEND)
Mk 5: 26 doctors and had s all she had,
Lk 6: 12 and s the night praying to God.
15: 14 After he had s everything, there

SPIN
Mt 6: 28 They do not labor or s.

SPIRIT (SPIRIT'S SPIRIT-TAUGHT SPIRITS SPIRITUAL)
Ge 1: 2 the S of God was hovering over
6: 3 said, "My S will not contend
Ex 31: 3 I have filled him with the S of God,
Nu 11: 25 power of the S that was on him
Dt 34: 9 the s of wisdom because Moses
Jdg 6: 34 Then the S of the LORD came
11: 29 Then the S of the LORD came
13: 25 the S of the LORD began to stir
1Sa 10: 10 the S of God came powerfully
16: 13 day on the S of the LORD came
16: 14 Saul, and an evil s from the LORD
2Sa 23: 2 "The S of the LORD spoke
2Ki 2: 9 inherit a double portion of your s,"
Ne 9: 20 You gave your good S to instruct
9: 30 By your S you warned them
Job 33: 4 The S of God has made me;
Ps 31: 5 Into your hands I commit my s;
34: 18 saves those who are crushed in s.
51: 10 and renew a steadfast s within me.
51: 11 or take your Holy S from me.
51: 17 My sacrifice, O God, is a broken s;
106: 33 they rebelled against the S of God,
139: 7 Where can I go from your S?

Ps 143: 10 may your good S lead me on level
Isa 11: 2 The S of the LORD will rest
30: 1 but not by my S, heaping sin
32: 15 till the S is poured on us
44: 3 pour out my S on your offspring,
57: 15 to revive the s of the lowly
61: 1 The S of the Sovereign LORD is
63: 10 rebelled and grieved his Holy S.
Eze 11: 19 heart and put a new s in them;
13: 3 prophets who follow their own s
36: 26 a new heart and put a new s in you;
Da 4: 8 the s of the holy gods is in him.)
Joel 2: 28 I will pour out my S on all people.
Zec 4: 6 but by my S,' says the LORD
Mt 1: 18 to be pregnant through the Holy S.
3: 11 He will baptize you with the Holy S
3: 16 saw the S of God descending like
4: 1 led by the S into the wilderness
5: 3 "Blessed are the poor in s, for
10: 20 but the S of your Father speaking
12: 31 blasphemy against the S will not be
26: 41 The s is willing, but the flesh is
28: 19 and of the Son and of the Holy S,
Mk 1: 8 will baptize you with the Holy S."
Lk 1: 35 "The Holy S will come on you,
1: 80 child grew and became strong in s;
3: 16 He will baptize you with the Holy S
4: 18 "The S of the Lord is on me,
11: 13 in heaven give the Holy S to those
23: 46 into your hands I commit my s."
Jn 1: 33 who will baptize with the Holy S.'
3: 5 they are born of water and the S.
4: 24 God is s, and his worshipers must worship in the S
6: 63 The S gives life; the flesh counts
7: 39 that time the S had not been given,
14: 26 the Holy S, whom the Father will
16: 13 But when he, the S of truth, comes,
20: 22 and said, "Receive the Holy S.
Ac 1: 5 will be baptized with the Holy S."
1: 8 when the Holy S comes on you;
2: 4 other tongues as the S enabled
2: 17 I will pour out my S on all people.
2: 38 will receive the gift of the Holy S.
4: 31 they were all filled with the Holy S
5: 3 that you have lied to the Holy S
6: 3 who are known to be full of the S
8: 15 that they might receive the Holy S,
9: 17 and be filled with the Holy S."
11: 16 will be baptized with the Holy S.'
13: 2 the Holy S said, "Set apart for me
19: 2 even heard that there is a Holy S."
Ro 1: 9 in my s in preaching the gospel
8: 4 to the flesh but according to the S.
8: 5 minds set on what the S desires.
8: 9 if indeed the S of God lives in you.
8: 13 but if by the S you put to death
8: 16 The S himself testifies with our s
8: 23 who have the firstfruits of the S,
8: 26 the S helps us in our weakness.
8: 26 the S himself intercedes for us
1Co 2: 10 God has revealed to us by his S.
2: 10 The S searches all things,
2: 14 without the S does not accept
2: 14 are discerned only through the S.
3: 1 as people who live by the S but
5: 3 present, I am with you in s.
6: 19 bodies are temples of the Holy S,
12: 1 Now about the gifts of the S,
12: 13 we were all baptized by one S so as
12: 13 and we were all given the one S
14: 1 and eagerly desire gifts of the S,
2Co 1: 22 put his S in our hearts as a deposit,
3: 3 but with the S of the living God,
3: 6 letter kills, but the S gives life.
3: 17 Now the Lord is the S, and where
5: 5 who has given us the S as a deposit,
7: 1 that contaminates body and s,
Gal 3: 2 Did you receive the S by the works
5: 16 say, walk by the S, and you will not
5: 22 But the fruit of the S is love, joy,
5: 25 Since we live by the S, let us keep
6: 1 who live by the S should restore
6: 8 whoever sows to please the S,
Eph 1: 13 with a seal, the promised Holy S,
2: 22 in which God lives by his S.
Eph 4: 4 There is one body and one S, just
4: 30 do not grieve the Holy S of God,
5: 18 Instead, be filled with the S,
5: 19 hymns, and songs from the S.
6: 17 of salvation and the sword of the S,
Php 2: 2 being one in s and of one mind.
1Th 5: 19 Do not quench the S.
5: 23 May your whole s, soul and body
2Th 2: 13 the sanctifying work of the S
1Ti 3: 16 was vindicated by the S, was seen
2Ti 1: 7 the S God gave us does not make
Heb 2: 4 of the Holy S distributed according
4: 12 even to dividing soul and s,
10: 29 who has insulted the S of grace?
1Pe 3: 4 beauty of a gentle and quiet s,
2Pe 1: 21 were carried along by the Holy S.
1Jn 3: 24 We know it by the S he gave us.
4: 1 do not believe every s, but test
4: 13 he in us: He has given us of his S.
Jude : 20 faith and praying in the Holy S,
Rev 2: 7 let them hear what the S says

SPIRIT'S* (SPIRIT)
1Co 2: 4 a demonstration of the S power,

SPIRITS (SPIRIT)
1Co 12: 10 another distinguishing between s,
14: 32 The s of prophets are subject
Heb 1: 7 "He makes his angels s, and his
1Jn 4: 1 but test the s to see whether they

SPIRIT-TAUGHT* (SPIRIT TEACH)
1Co 2: 13 spiritual realities with S words.

SPIRITUAL (SPIRIT)
Ro 12: 11 but keep your s fervor,
1Co 2: 13 the Spirit, explaining s realities
15: 44 a natural body, it is raised a s body.
Eph 1: 3 realms with every s blessing
6: 12 against the s forces of evil
1Pe 2: 2 crave pure s milk, so that by it you
2: 5 are being built into a s house to be

SPIT
Mt 27: 30 They s on him, and took the staff
Rev 3: 16 I am about to s you out of my

SPLENDOR
1Ch 16: 29 the LORD in the s of his holiness.
29: 11 glory and the majesty and the s,
Job 37: 22 of the north he comes in golden s;
Ps 29: 2 the LORD in the s of his holiness.
45: 3 clothe yourself with s and majesty.
96: 6 S and majesty are before him;
96: 9 the LORD in the s of his holiness;
104: 1 you are clothed with s and majesty.
110: 3 Arrayed in holy s, your young men
145: 5 of the glorious s of your majesty—
145: 12 the glorious s of your kingdom.
148: 13 his s is above the earth
Pr 16: 31 Gray hair is a crown of s;
20: 29 strength, gray hair the s of the old.
Isa 55: 5 for he has endowed you with s."
60: 21 my hands, for the display of my s.
61: 3 the LORD for the display of his s.
63: 1 robed in s, striding forward
Hab 3: 4 His s was like the sunrise;
Mt 6: 29 in all his s was dressed like one
Lk 9: 30 and Elijah, appeared in glorious s,
2Th 2: 8 and destroy by the s of his coming.

SPOIL (SPOILS)
Ps 119:162 promise like one who finds great s.

SPOILS (SPOIL)
Isa 53: 12 he will divide the s with the strong,
Jn 6: 27 Do not work for food that s,

SPOTLESS
2Pe 3: 14 make every effort to be found s,

SPOTS (SPOTTED)
Jer 13: 23 change his skin or a leopard its s?

SPOTTED (SPOTS)
Ge 30: 32 them every speckled or s sheep,

SPREAD (SPREADING SPREADS)
Ps 78: 19 "Can God really s a table
Ac 6: 7 So the word of God s.
12: 24 the word of God continued to s
13: 49 of the Lord s through the whole
19: 20 way the word of the Lord s widely
2Th 3: 1 message of the Lord may s rapidly

SPREADING (SPREAD)
Pr 29: 5 flatter their neighbors are s nets
1Th 3: 2 in God's service in s the gospel

SPREADS (SPREAD)
Pr 10: 18 lying lips and s slander is a fool.

SPRING (SPRINGS)
Jer 2: 13 forsaken me, the s of living water,
Jn 4: 14 in them a s of water welling
Jas 3: 12 can a salt s produce fresh water.

SPRINGS (SPRING)
2Pe 2: 17 These people are s without water

SPRINKLE (SPRINKLED)
Lev 16: 14 with his finger s it on the front

SPRINKLED (SPRINKLE)
Heb 10: 22 having our hearts s to cleanse us
1Pe 1: 2 Jesus Christ and s with his blood:

SPROUT
Pr 23: 5 for they will surely s wings and fly
Jer 33: 15 I will make a righteous Branch s

SPUR*
Heb 10: 24 consider how we may s one

SPURNS*
Pr 15: 5 A fool s a parent's discipline,

SPY
Gal 2: 4 had infiltrated our ranks to s

SQUANDERED (SQUANDERS)
Lk 15: 13 there s his wealth in wild living.

SQUANDERS* (SQUANDERED)
Pr 29: 3 of prostitutes s his wealth.

SQUARE
Rev 21: 16 The city was laid out like a s,

STABILITY*
Pr 29: 4 By justice a king gives a country s,

STAFF
Ge 49: 10 nor the ruler's s from between his
Ex 7: 12 Aaron's s swallowed up their staffs.
Nu 17: 6 and Aaron's s was among them.
Ps 23: 4 your rod and your s, they comfort

STAIN (STAINED)
Eph 5: 27 without s or wrinkle or any other

STAINED (STAIN)
Isa 63: 1 with his garments s crimson?

STAKES
Isa 54: 2 your cords, strengthen your s.

STAND (STANDING STANDS STOOD)
Ex 14: 13 S firm and you will see
Lev 19: 32 "'S up in the presence
Jos 10: 12 "Sun, s still over Gibeon, and you,
2Ch 20: 17 s firm and see the deliverance
Job 19: 25 in the end he will s on the earth.
Ps 1: 1 or s in the way that sinners take
1: 5 Therefore the wicked will not s
24: 3 Who may s in his holy place?
33: 11 plans of the LORD s firm forever,
40: 2 rock and gave me a firm place to s.
76: 7 Who can s before you when you
93: 5 Your statutes, LORD, s firm;
119:120 fear of you; I s in awe of your laws.
130: 3 of sins, Lord, who could s?
Isa 7: 9 If you do not s firm in your faith,
29: 23 will s in awe of the God of Israel.
Eze 22: 30 s before me in the gap on behalf
Hab 3: 2 I s in awe of your deeds, LORD.
Zec 14: 4 day his feet will s on the Mount
Mal 3: 2 Who can s when he appears?
Mt 12: 25 divided against itself will not s.
Lk 21: 19 S firm, and you will win life.
Ac 11: 17 think that I could s in God's way?"
Ro 14: 4 their own master, servants s or fall.
14: 4 for the Lord is able to make them s.
14: 10 we will all s before God's judgment
1Co 15: 58 dear brothers and sisters, s firm.
16: 13 on your guard; s firm in the faith;
Gal 5: 1 S firm, then, and do not let
Eph 6: 14 S firm then, with the belt of truth
2Th 2: 15 s firm and hold fast to the
Jas 5: 8 be patient and s firm,
Rev 3: 20 I s at the door and knock.

STANDING (STAND)
Ex 3: 5 where you are s is holy ground."

Jos 5: 15 the place where you are **s** is holy.”
Ru 2: 1 side, a man of **s** from the clan
4: 11 May you have **s** in Ephrathah
1Ti 3: 13 have served well gain an excellent **s**
1Pe 5: 9 Resist him, **s** firm in the faith,

STANDS (STAND)
Ps 89: 2 that your love **s** firm forever,
119: 89 it **s** firm in the heavens.
Pr 12: 7 the house of the righteous **s** firm.
Mt 10: 22 the one who **s** firm to the end will
2Ti 2: 19 God’s solid foundation **s** firm,

STAR (STARS)
Nu 24: 17 A **s** will come out of Jacob;
Isa 14: 12 morning **s**, son of the dawn!
Mt 2: 2 We saw his **s** when it rose and have
2Pe 1: 19 the morning **s** rises in your hearts.
Rev 2: 28 also give that one the morning **s**.
22: 16 David, and the bright Morning **S**.”

STARS (STAR)
Ge 1: 16 He also made the **s**.
Job 38: 7 while the morning **s** sang together
Da 12: 3 like the **s** for ever and ever.
Php 2: 15 you will shine among them like **s**

STATURE
1Sa 2: 26 boy Samuel continued to grow in **s**
Lk 2: 52 And Jesus grew in wisdom and **s**,

STATUTES
Ps 19: 7 The **s** of the LORD are
93: 5 Your **s**, LORD, stand firm;
119: 2 Blessed are those who keep his **s**
119: 14 in following your **s** as one rejoices
119: 24 Your **s** are my delight; they are my
119: 36 Turn my heart toward your **s**
119: 99 teachers, for I meditate on your **s**.
119:111 Your **s** are my heritage forever;
119:125 that I may understand your **s**.
119:129 Your **s** are wonderful;
119:138 The **s** you have laid down are
119:152 your **s** that you established them
119:167 I obey your **s**, for I love them

STEADFAST*
Ps 51: 10 and renew a **s** spirit within me.
57: 7 My heart, O God, is **s**, my heart is **s**;
108: 1 My heart, O God, is **s**; I will sing
112: 7 their hearts are **s**,
119: 5 my ways were **s** in obeying your
Pr 4: 26 your feet and be **s** in all your ways.
Isa 26: 3 peace those whose minds are **s**,
1Pe 5: 10 and make you strong, firm and **s**.

STEADY
Isa 35: 3 hands, **s** the knees that give way;

STEAL (STOLEN)
Ex 20: 15 “You shall not **s**.
Lev 19: 11 “‘Do not **s**.’ ‘Do not lie.
Dt 5: 19 “You shall not **s**.
Mt 19: 18 you shall not **s**, you shall not give
Ro 13: 9 “You shall not **s**,” “You shall not
Eph 4: 28 has been stealing must **s** no longer,

STEP (FOOTSTEPS STEPS)
Job 34: 21 he sees their every **s**.
Ps 1: 1 is the one who does not walk in **s**
Gal 5: 25 let us keep in **s** with the Spirit.

STEPHEN*
Early church leader (Ac 6:5). Arrested (Ac 6:8–15). Speech to Sanhedrin (Ac 7). Stoned (Ac 7:54–60; 8:2; 11:19; 22:20).

STEPS (STEP)
Ps 37: 23 The LORD makes firm the **s**
Pr 14: 15 the prudent give thought to their **s**.
16: 9 but the LORD establishes their **s**.
20: 24 A person’s **s** are directed
Jer 10: 23 it is not for them to direct their **s**.
1Pe 2: 21 that you should follow in his **s**.

STERN (STERNNESS)
Pr 15: 10 **S** discipline awaits anyone who

STERNNESS* (STERN)
Ro 11: 22 the kindness and **s** of God:
11: 22 **s** to those who fell, but kindness

STICKS
Pr 18: 24 there is a friend who **s** closer than

STIFF-NECKED (NECK)
Ex 34: 9 Although this is a **s** people,
Pr 29: 1 Whoever remains **s** after many

STILL
Jos 10: 13 So the sun stood **s**, and the moon
Ps 37: 7 Be **s** before the LORD and wait
46: 10 “Be **s**, and know that I am God;
89: 9 its waves mount up, you **s** them.
Zec 2: 13 Be **s** before the LORD,
Mk 4: 39 Be **s**!” Then the wind died down

STIMULATE*
2Pe 3: 1 of them as reminders to **s** you

STING
1Co 15: 55 Where, O death, is your **s**?”

STINGY*
Pr 28: 22 The **s** are eager to get rich and are

STIR (STIRRED STIRS)
Pr 28: 25 The greedy **s** up conflict, but those

STIRRED (STIR)
Ps 45: 1 My heart is **s** by a noble theme as I

STIRS (STIR)
Pr 6: 19 a person who **s** up conflict
10: 12 Hatred **s** up conflict, but love
15: 1 but a harsh word **s** up anger.
Pr 15: 18 A hot-tempered person **s** up
16: 28 A perverse person **s** up conflict,
29: 22 An angry person **s** up conflict,

STOLEN (STEAL)
Lev 6: 4 they must return what they have **s**
SS 4: 9 You have **s** my heart, my sister,

STOMACH
1Co 6: 13 “Food for the **s** and the **s** for food,
Php 3: 19 their god is their **s**, and their glory

STONE (CAPSTONE CORNERSTONE MILLSTONE STONES STONING)
Ex 24: 4 up twelve **s** pillars representing
28: 10 six names on one **s**
34: 1 out two **s** tablets like the first ones,
Dt 4: 13 then wrote them on two **s** tablets.
19: 14 your neighbor’s boundary **s** set
1Sa 17: 50 the Philistine with a sling and a **s**;
Ps 91: 12 will not strike your foot against a **s**.
118: 22 The **s** the builders rejected has
Pr 22: 28 not move an ancient boundary **s**
Isa 8: 14 and Judah he will be a **s** that causes
28: 16 “See, I lay a **s** in Zion, a tested **s**,
Eze 11: 19 remove from them their heart of **s**
36: 26 remove from you your heart of **s**
Mt 7: 9 asks for bread, will give him a **s**?
21: 42 “‘The **s** the builders rejected has
24: 2 you, not one **s** here will be left
Mk 16: 3 “Who will roll the **s** away
Lk 4: 3 God, tell this **s** to become bread.”
Jn 8: 7 *first to throw a s at her.”*
Ac 4: 11 Jesus is “‘the **s** you builders
Ro 9: 32 stumbled over the stumbling **s**.
2Co 3: 3 not on tablets of **s** but on tablets
1Pe 2: 6 “See, I lay a **s** in Zion, a chosen
Rev 2: 17 person a white **s** with a new name

STONES (STONE)
Ex 28: 21 There are to be twelve **s**,
Jos 4: 3 take up twelve **s** from the middle
1Sa 17: 40 hand, chose five smooth **s**
Mt 3: 9 these **s** God can raise up children
1Co 3: 12 silver, costly **s**, wood, hay or straw,
2Co 11: 25 once I was pelted with **s**,
1Pe 2: 5 like living **s**, are being built

STONING (STONE)
Heb 11: 37 They were put to death by **s**;

STOOD (STAND)
Jos 10: 13 So the sun **s** still, and the moon
Lk 22: 28 You are those who have **s** by me
2Ti 4: 17 But the Lord **s** at my side and gave
Jas 1: 12 trial because, having **s** the test,

STOOPS
Ps 113: 6 who **s** down to look on the heavens

STOP (STOPPED)
Job 37: 14 **s** and consider God’s wonders.
Isa 1: 13 **S** bringing meaningless offerings!
1: 16 out of my sight; **s** doing wrong.
2: 22 **S** trusting in mere humans,
Jer 32: 40 I will never **s** doing good to them,
Mk 9: 39 “Do not **s** him,” Jesus said.
Jn 6: 43 “**S** grumbling among yourselves,”
7: 24 **S** judging by mere appearances,
20: 27 **S** doubting and believe.”
Ro 14: 13 let us **s** passing judgment
1Co 14: 20 sisters, **s** thinking like children.

STOPPED (STOP)
Jos 3: 17 of the LORD **s** in the middle

STORE (STORED)
Pr 2: 1 **s** up my commands within you,
7: 1 **s** up my commands within you.
10: 14 The wise **s** up knowledge,
Isa 33: 6 a rich **s** of salvation and wisdom
Mt 6: 19 “Do not **s** up for yourselves
6: 26 not sow or reap or **s** away in barns,
2Ti 4: 8 Now there is in **s** for me the crown

STORED (STORE)
Lk 6: 45 out of the good **s** up in his heart,
6: 45 out of the evil **s** up in his heart.
Col 1: 5 spring from the hope **s** up for you

STOREHOUSE (HOUSE)
Mal 3: 10 Bring the whole tithe into the **s**,

STORIES*
2Pe 1: 16 we did not follow cleverly devised **s**
2: 3 will exploit you with fabricated **s**.

STORM
Job 38: 1 LORD spoke to Job out of the **s**.
Ps 107: 29 He stilled the **s** to a whisper;
Lk 8: 24 the **s** subsided, and all was calm.

STRAIGHT
Ps 27: 11 lead me in a **s** path because of my
107: 7 He led them by a **s** way to a city
Pr 2: 13 who have left the **s** paths to walk
3: 6 and he will make your paths **s**.
4: 11 and lead you along **s** paths.
4: 25 Let your eyes look **s** ahead;
11: 5 the blameless makes their paths **s**,
15: 21 understanding keeps a **s** course.
Isa 40: 3 make **s** in the desert a highway
Mt 3: 3 the Lord, make **s** paths for him.’”
Jn 1: 23 ‘Make **s** the way for the Lord.’”
2Pe 2: 15 They have left the **s** way

STRAIN (STRAINING)
Mt 23: 24 You **s** out a gnat but swallow

STRAINING (STRAIN)
Php 3: 13 behind and **s** toward what is ahead,

STRANGE (STRANGER STRANGERS)
Isa 28: 11 and **s** tongues God will speak to
Eze 3: 5 of obscure speech and **s** language,

STRANGER (STRANGE)
Ps 119: 19 I am a **s** on earth; do not hide your
Mt 25: 35 I was a **s** and you invited me in,
Jn 10: 5 But they will never follow a **s**;

STRANGERS (STRANGE)
Heb 13: 2 not forget to show hospitality to **s**,

STRAPS
Mk 1: 7 **s** of whose sandals I am not worthy

STRAW
Isa 11: 7 and the lion will eat **s** like the ox.
1Co 3: 12 silver, costly stones, wood, hay or **s**,

STRAYED (STRAYS)
Ps 119:176 I have **s** like a lost sheep.
Jer 31: 19 After I **s**, I repented; after I came

STRAYS (STRAYED)
Pr 21: 16 Whoever **s** from the path
Eze 34: 16 for the lost and bring back the **s**.

STREAM (STREAMS)
Am 5: 24 righteousness like a never-failing **s**!

STREAMS (STREAM)
Ps 1: 3 person is like a tree planted by **s**
46: 4 a river whose **s** make glad the city
Ecc 1: 7 All **s** flow into the sea, yet the sea

STREET
Mt 6: 5 and on the **s** corners to be seen
22: 9 So go to the **s** corners and invite
Rev 21: 21 The great **s** of the city was of gold,

STRENGTH (STRONG)
Ex 15: 2 “The LORD is my **s** and my

Dt 4: 37 by his Presence and his great **s**,
6: 5 all your soul and with all your **s**.
Jdg 16: 15 told me the secret of your great **s**."
2Sa 22: 33 It is God who arms me with **s**
2Ki 23: 25 with all his soul and with all his **s**,
1Ch 16: 11 Look to the LORD and his **s**;
16: 28 ascribe to the LORD glory and **s**.
29: 12 power to exalt and give **s** to all.
Ne 8: 10 the joy of the LORD is your **s**."
Ps 18: 1 I love you, LORD, my **s**.
21: 13 Be exalted in your **s**, LORD;
28: 7 The LORD is my **s** and my shield;
29: 11 The LORD gives **s** to his people;
33: 16 no warrior escapes by his great **s**.
46: 1 God is our refuge and **s**,
59: 17 You are my **s**, I sing praise to you;
65: 6 having armed yourself with **s**,
73: 26 but God is the **s** of my heart and
84: 5 Blessed are those whose **s** is in you,
96: 7 ascribe to the LORD glory and **s**.
105: 4 Look to the LORD and his **s**;
118: 14 The LORD is my **s** and my
147: 10 pleasure is not in the **s** of the horse,
Pr 24: 5 have knowledge muster their **s**.
30: 25 Ants are creatures of little **s**,
Isa 12: 2 himself, is my **s** and my defense;
31: 1 in the great **s** of their horsemen,
40: 26 of his great power and mighty **s**,
40: 31 in the LORD will renew their **s**.
63: 1 forward in the greatness of his **s**?
Jer 9: 23 strong boast of their **s** or the rich
Mic 5: 4 his flock in the **s** of the LORD,
Hab 3: 19 The Sovereign LORD is my **s**;
Mk 12: 30 all your mind and with all your **s**.'
1Co 1: 25 of God is stronger than human **s**.
Eph 1: 19 power is the same as the mighty **s**
Php 4: 13 this through him who gives me **s**.
Heb 11: 34 whose weakness was turned to **s**;
1Pe 4: 11 do so with the **s** God provides,

STRENGTHEN (STRONG)
2Ch 16: 9 to **s** those whose hearts are fully
Ps 119: 28 **s** me according to your word.
Isa 35: 3 **S** the feeble hands, steady the
41: 10 I will **s** you and help you;
Lk 22: 32 have turned back, **s** your brothers."
Eph 3: 16 of his glorious riches he may **s** you
1Th 3: 13 May he **s** your hearts so that you
2Th 2: 17 and **s** you in every good deed
Heb 12: 12 **s** your feeble arms and weak knees.

STRENGTHENED (STRONG)
Col 1: 11 being **s** with all power according
Heb 13: 9 for our hearts to be **s** by grace,

STRENUOUSLY*
Col 1: 29 To this end I **s** contend with all

STRETCHES
Ps 104: 2 he **s** out the heavens like a tent

STRICKEN (STRIKE)
Isa 53: 4 him punished by God, **s** by him,

STRICT
1Co 9: 25 in the games goes into **s** training.

STRIFE (STRIVE)
Pr 13: 10 Where there is **s**, there is pride,
17: 1 than a house full of feasting, with **s**.
20: 3 It is to one's honor to avoid **s**,
22: 10 out the mocker, and out goes **s**;
30: 33 so stirring up anger produces **s**."
1Ti 6: 4 about words that result in envy, **s**,

STRIKE (STROKE)
Ge 3: 15 your head, and you will **s** his heel."
Zec 13: 7 "**S** the shepherd, and the sheep will
Mt 4: 6 you will not **s** your foot against
26: 31 "'I will **s** the shepherd,
1Co 9: 27 I **s** a blow to my body and make it

STRIPS
Jn 20: 5 in at the **s** of linen lying there

STRIVE* (STRIFE STRIVING)
Ac 24: 16 So I **s** always to keep my
2Co 13: 11 **S** for full restoration, encourage
1Th 5: 15 always **s** to do what is good for
1Ti 4: 10 That is why we labor and **s**,

STRIVING (STRIVE)
Php 1: 27 **s** together as one for the faith

STROKE (STRIKE)
Mt 5: 18 letter, not the least **s** of a pen,

STRONG (STRENGTH STRENGTHEN STRENGTHENED STRONGER)
Dt 3: 24 your greatness and your **s** hand.
31: 6 Be **s** and courageous. Do not be
Jos 1: 6 Be **s** and courageous, because you
Jdg 5: 21 March on, my soul; be **s**!
2Sa 10: 12 Be **s**, and let us fight bravely for
1Ki 2: 2 "So be **s**, act like a man,
1Ch 28: 20 his son, "Be **s** and courageous,
2Ch 32: 7 "Be **s** and courageous. Do not be
Ps 24: 8 The LORD **s** and mighty,
31: 2 of refuge, a **s** fortress to save me.
Pr 31: 17 her arms are **s** for her tasks.
Ecc 9: 11 to the swift or the battle to the **s**,
SS 8: 6 for love is as **s** as death, its jealousy
Isa 35: 4 fearful hearts, "Be **s**, do not fear;
53: 12 he will divide the spoils with the **s**,
Jer 9: 23 or the **s** boast of their strength
50: 34 Yet their Redeemer is **s**;
Hag 2: 4 Be **s**, all you people of the land,'
Mt 12: 29 can anyone enter a **s** man's house
Lk 2: 40 And the child grew and became **s**;
Ro 15: 1 We who are **s** ought to bear
1Co 1: 27 things of the world to shame the **s**.
16: 13 in the faith; be courageous; be **s**.
2Co 12: 10 For when I am weak, then I am **s**.
Eph 6: 10 be **s** in the Lord and in his mighty
2Ti 2: 1 be **s** in the grace that is in Christ
1Pe 5: 10 restore you and make you **s**,

STRONGER (STRONG)
Dt 4: 38 you nations greater and **s** than you
1Co 1: 25 of God is **s** than human strength.

STRONGHOLD (STRONGHOLDS)
2Sa 22: 3 He is my **s**, my refuge and my
Ps 9: 9 oppressed, a **s** in times of trouble.
18: 2 and the horn of my salvation, my **s**.
27: 1 The LORD is the **s** of my life—
144: 2 my fortress, my **s** and my deliverer,

STRONGHOLDS (STRONGHOLD)
Zep 3: 6 their **s** are demolished.
2Co 10: 4 have divine power to demolish **s**.

STRUGGLE (STRUGGLED)
Ro 15: 30 join me in my **s** by praying to God
Eph 6: 12 For our **s** is not against flesh
Heb 12: 4 In your **s** against sin, you have not

STRUGGLED (STRUGGLE)
Ge 32: 28 because you have **s** with God

STUDENT (STUDY)
Lk 6: 40 The **s** is not above the teacher,

STUDY* (STUDENT)
Ezr 7: 10 Ezra had devoted himself to the **s**
Ecc 1: 13 I applied my mind to **s**
12: 12 end, and much **s** wearies the body.
Jn 5: 39 You **s** the Scriptures diligently

STUMBLE (STUMBLES STUMBLING)
Ps 37: 24 though he may **s**, he will not fall,
119:165 and nothing can make them **s**.
Pr 3: 23 in safety, and your foot will not **s**.
24: 17 when they **s**, do not let your heart
Isa 8: 14 be a stone that causes people to **s**
Jer 13: 16 before your feet **s** on the darkening
31: 9 a level path where they will not **s**,
Eze 7: 19 for it has caused them to **s** into sin.
Hos 14: 9 them, but the rebellious **s** in them.
Mal 2: 8 teaching have caused many to **s**;
Mt 18: 6 to **s**, it would be better for them
Mk 9: 43 If your hand causes you to **s**, cut it
Lk 17: 1 that cause people to **s** are bound
Jn 11: 9 walks in the daytime will not **s**,
11: 10 a person walks at night that they **s**,
Ro 9: 33 Zion a stone that causes people to **s**
14: 20 that causes someone else to **s**.
1Co 10: 32 Do not cause anyone to **s**,
Jas 3: 2 We all **s** in many ways.
1Pe 2: 8 "A stone that causes people to **s**
1Jn 2: 10 is nothing in them to make them **s**.

STUMBLES (STUMBLE)
Jas 2: 10 yet **s** at just one point is guilty

STUMBLING (STUMBLE)
Lev 19: 14 put a **s** block in front of the blind,
Ps 56: 13 me from death and my feet from **s**,
Mt 16: 23 You are a **s** block to me; you do not
Ro 9: 32 They stumbled over the **s** stone.
11: 9 a **s** block and a retribution for.
14: 13 your mind not to put any **s** block
1Co 1: 23 a **s** block to Jews and foolishness
8: 9 rights does not become a **s** block
2Co 6: 3 We put no **s** block in anyone's path,
Jude : 24 him who is able to keep you from **s**

STUMP
Isa 6: 13 so the holy seed will be the **s**
11: 1 will come up from the **s** of Jesse;

STUPID
Pr 12: 1 but whoever hates correction is **s**.
2Ti 2: 23 to do with foolish and **s** arguments,

STUPOR
Ro 11: 8 "God gave them a spirit of **s**,

SUBDUE (SUBDUED)
Ge 1: 28 fill the earth and **s** it.

SUBDUED (SUBDUE)
Jos 10: 40 So Joshua **s** the whole region,
Ps 47: 3 He **s** nations under us,

SUBJECT (SUBJECTED)
Mt 5: 22 or sister will be **s** to judgment.
Ro 13: 1 Let everyone be **s** to the governing
1Co 14: 32 of prophets are **s** to the control
15: 28 the Son himself will be made **s**
Titus 2: 5 and to be **s** to their husbands,
2: 9 slaves to be **s** to their masters
3: 1 Remind the people to be **s** to rulers

SUBJECTED (SUBJECT)
Ro 8: 20 the creation was **s** to frustration,

SUBMISSION (SUBMIT)
1Co 14: 34 but must be in **s**, as the law says.
1Ti 2: 11 learn in quietness and full **s**.
Heb 5: 7 heard because of his reverent **s**.
1Pe 3: 22 authorities and powers in **s** to him.

SUBMISSIVE* (SUBMIT)
Jas 3: 17 considerate, **s**, full of mercy

SUBMIT (SUBMISSION SUBMISSIVE SUBMITS)
Pr 3: 6 in all your ways **s** to him, and he
Ro 13: 5 is necessary to **s** to the authorities,
1Co 16: 16 to **s** to such people and to everyone
Eph 5: 21 **S** to one another out of reverence
Col 3: 18 **s** yourselves to your husbands, as is
Heb 12: 9 How much more should we **s**
13: 17 leaders and **s** to their authority,
Jas 4: 7 **S** yourselves, then, to God.
1Pe 2: 18 reverent fear of God **s** yourselves
3: 1 the same way **s** yourselves to your
5: 5 **s** yourselves to your elders.

SUBMITS* (SUBMIT)
Eph 5: 24 Now as the church **s** to Christ,

SUBTRACT*
Dt 4: 2 you and do not **s** from it,

SUCCEED (SUCCESS SUCCESSFUL)
Ps 20: 4 heart and make all your plans **s**.
Pr 15: 22 but with many advisers they **s**.
21: 30 plan that can **s** against the LORD.

SUCCESS (SUCCEED)
Ge 39: 23 and gave him **s** in whatever he did.
1Sa 18: 14 In everything he did he had great **s**,
1Ch 12: 18 **S**, **s** to you, and **s** to those who help
22: 13 you will have **s** if you are careful
2Ch 26: 5 the LORD, God gave him **s**.
Ecc 10: 10 is needed, but skill will bring **s**.

SUCCESSFUL (SUCCEED)
Jos 1: 7 that you may be **s** wherever you go.
2Ki 18: 7 he was **s** in whatever he undertook.
2Ch 20: 20 in his prophets and you will be **s**."

SUFFER (SUFFERED SUFFERING SUFFERINGS SUFFERS)
Job 36: 15 But those who **s** he delivers in their
Isa 53: 10 to crush him and cause him to **s**,
Mk 8: 31 Son of Man must **s** many things
Lk 24: 26 the Messiah have to **s** these things
24: 46 The Messiah will **s** and rise
2Co 1: 6 of the same sufferings we **s**.
Php 1: 29 in him, but also to **s** for him,
Heb 9: 26 to **s** many times since the creation

1Pe 3: 17 to **s** for doing good than for doing
4: 16 if you **s** as a Christian, do not be

SUFFERED (SUFFER)
Isa 53: 11 After he has **s**, he will see the light
Heb 2: 9 and honor because he **s** death,
2: 10 perfect through what he **s**.
2: 18 Because he himself **s** when he was
10: 34 You **s** along with those in prison
1Pe 2: 21 called, because Christ **s** for you,
3: 18 For Christ also **s** once for sins,
4: 1 since Christ **s** in his body,

SUFFERING (SUFFER)
Job 36: 15 who suffer he delivers in their **s**;
Ps 22: 24 scorned the **s** of the afflicted one;
Isa 53: 3 a man of **s**, and familiar with pain.
La 1: 12 Is any **s** like my **s** that was inflicted
Ac 5: 41 been counted worthy of **s** disgrace
Ro 5: 3 that **s** produces perseverance;
2Ti 1: 8 join with me in **s** for the gospel,
2: 3 Join with me in **s**, like a good
Heb 13: 3 as if you yourselves were **s**.

SUFFERINGS (SUFFER)
Ro 5: 3 but we also glory in our **s**,
8: 17 if indeed we share in his **s** in order
8: 18 that our present **s** are not worth
2Co 1: 5 share abundantly in the **s** of Christ,
Php 3: 10 and participation in his **s**,
1Pe 4: 13 you participate in the **s** of Christ,
5: 9 is undergoing the same kind of **s**.

SUFFERS (SUFFER)
Pr 13: 20 for a companion of fools **s** harm.
1Co 12: 26 If one part **s**, every part **s** with it;

SUFFICIENT
2Co 12: 9 said to me, "My grace is **s** for you,

SUITABLE
Ge 2: 18 I will make a helper **s** for him."

SUMMED* (SUMS)
Ro 13: 9 be, are **s** up in this one command:

SUMMONS
Ps 50: 1 **s** the earth from the rising of the
Isa 45: 3 God of Israel, who **s** you by name.

SUMS* (SUMMED)
Mt 7: 12 to you, for this **s** up the Law

SUN (SUNRISE)
Jos 10: 13 So the **s** stood still, and the moon
Jdg 5: 31 may all who love you be like the **s**
Ps 84: 11 For the LORD God is a **s**
121: 6 the **s** will not harm you by day,
136: 8 the **s** to govern the day,
Pr 4: 18 the righteous is like the morning **s**,
Ecc 1: 9 there is nothing new under the **s**.
Isa 60: 19 The **s** will no more be your light
Mal 4: 2 the **s** of righteousness will rise
Mt 5: 45 He causes his **s** to rise on the evil
13: 43 the righteous will shine like the **s**
17: 2 His face shone like the **s**, and his
Lk 23: 45 for the **s** stopped shining.
Eph 4: 26 Do not let the **s** go down while you
Rev 1: 16 His face was like the **s** shining in
21: 23 The city does not need the **s**

SUNG (SING)
Mt 26: 30 When they had **s** a hymn, they

SUNRISE (SUN)
2Sa 23: 4 light of morning at **s** on a cloudless
Hab 3: 4 His splendor was like the **s**;

SUPERIOR
Ro 11: 18 do not consider yourself to be **s** to
Heb 1: 4 as the name he has inherited is **s**
8: 6 ministry Jesus has received is as **s**

SUPPER
Lk 22: 20 after the **s** he took the cup, saying,
1Co 11: 25 way, after **s** he took the cup, saying,
Rev 19: 9 to the wedding **s** of the Lamb!"

SUPPLIED (SUPPLY)
Ac 20: 34 of mine have **s** my own needs
Php 4: 18 I am amply **s**, now that I have

SUPPLY (SUPPLIED SUPPLYING)
2Co 8: 14 your plenty will **s** what they need,
1Th 3: 10 and **s** what is lacking in your faith.

SUPPLYING* (SUPPLY)
2Co 9: 12 you perform is not only **s** the needs

SUPPORT (SUPPORTED SUPPORTING)
Ps 18: 18 disaster, but the LORD was my **s**.
Ro 11: 18 You do not **s** the root, but the root
1Co 9: 12 have this right of **s** from you,

SUPPORTED (SUPPORT)
Ps 94: 18 your unfailing love, LORD, **s** me.
Col 2: 19 **s** and held together by its ligaments

SUPPORTING (SUPPORT)
Eph 4: 16 held together by every **s** ligament,

SUPPRESS*
Ro 1: 18 **s** the truth by their wickedness,

SUPREMACY*
Col 1: 18 in everything he might have the **s**.

SURE
Nu 28: 31 **s** the animals are without defect.
32: 23 you may be **s** that your sin will find
Dt 6: 17 Be **s** to keep the commands
14: 22 Be **s** to set aside a tenth of all
29: 18 make **s** there is no root among you
Jos 23: 13 you may be **s** that the LORD your
1Sa 12: 24 But be **s** to fear the LORD
Ps 132: 11 David, a **s** oath he will not revoke:
Pr 27: 23 Be **s** you know the condition
Isa 28: 16 cornerstone for a **s** foundation;
Eph 5: 5 For of this you can be **s**:

SURPASS* (SURPASSED SURPASSES SURPASSING)
Pr 31: 29 noble things, but you **s** them all."

SURPASSED* (SURPASS)
Jn 1: 15 me has **s** me because he was before
1: 30 me has **s** me because he was before

SURPASSES* (SURPASS)
Ps 138: 2 solemn decree that it **s** your fame.
Pr 8: 19 what I yield **s** choice silver.
Mt 5: 20 that unless your righteousness **s**
Eph 3: 19 know this love that **s** knowledge—

SURPASSING* (SURPASS)
Ps 150: 2 praise him for his **s** greatness.
2Co 3: 10 in comparison with the **s** glory.
9: 14 of the **s** grace God has given you.
Php 3: 8 a loss because of the **s** worth

SURPRISE (SURPRISED)
1Th 5: 4 this day should **s** you like a thief.

SURPRISED (SURPRISE)
1Pe 4: 4 are **s** that you do not join them
4: 12 do not be **s** at the fiery ordeal
1Jn 3: 13 not be **s**, my brothers and sisters,

SURROUND (SURROUNDED SURROUNDS)
Ps 5: 12 you **s** them with your favor as
32: 7 and **s** me with songs of deliverance.
89: 7 more awesome than all who **s** him.
125: 2 As the mountains **s** Jerusalem,

SURROUNDED (SURROUND)
Heb 12: 1 since we are **s** by such a great cloud

SURROUNDS* (SURROUND)
Ps 32: 10 LORD's unfailing love **s** the one
89: 8 and your faithfulness **s** you.
125: 2 so the LORD **s** his people both

SUSA
Ezr 4: 9 and Babylon, the Elamites of **S**,
Ne 1: 1 year, while I was in the citadel of **S**,

SUSPENDS*
Job 26: 7 he **s** the earth over nothing.

SUSPICIONS*
1Ti 6: 4 in envy, strife, malicious talk, evil **s**

SUSTAIN (SUSTAINING SUSTAINS)
Ps 55: 22 on the LORD and he will **s** you;
Isa 46: 4 will **s** you and I will rescue you.

SUSTAINING* (SUSTAIN)
Heb 1: 3 **s** all things by his powerful word.

SUSTAINS (SUSTAIN)
Ps 18: 35 shield, and your right hand **s** me;
146: 9 the foreigner and **s** the fatherless
147: 6 The LORD **s** the humble but casts
Isa 50: 4 to know the word that **s** the weary.

SWALLOW (SWALLOWED)
Isa 25: 8 he will **s** up death forever.
Jnh 1: 17 provided a huge fish to **s** Jonah,
Mt 23: 24 You strain out a gnat but **s** a camel.

SWALLOWED (SWALLOW)
1Co 15: 54 "Death has been **s** up in victory."
2Co 5: 4 so that what is mortal may be **s**

SWAYED
Mt 11: 7 A reed **s** by the wind?
22: 16 You aren't **s** by others, because you
2Ti 3: 6 are **s** by all kinds of evil desires,

SWEAR (SWORE SWORN)
Lev 19: 12 "'Do not **s** falsely by my name
Ps 24: 4 trust in an idol or **s** by a false god.
Isa 45: 23 by me every tongue will **s**.
Mt 5: 34 I tell you, do not **s** an oath at all:
Jas 5: 12 my brothers and sisters, do not **s**—

SWEAT*
Ge 3: 19 the **s** of your brow you will eat
Lk 22: 44 his **s** was like drops of blood falling

SWEET (SWEETER SWEETNESS)
Job 20: 12 "Though evil is **s** in his mouth
Ps 119:103 How **s** are your words to my taste,
Pr 9: 17 "Stolen water is **s**; food eaten
13: 19 A longing fulfilled is **s** to the soul,
16: 24 **s** to the soul and healing
20: 17 Food gained by fraud tastes **s**,
Ecc 5: 12 The sleep of a laborer is **s**,
Isa 5: 20 who put bitter for **s** and **s** for bitter.
Eze 3: 3 tasted as **s** as honey in my mouth.
Rev 10: 10 tasted as **s** as honey in my mouth,

SWEETER (SWEET)
Ps 19: 10 they are **s** than honey, than honey
119:103 taste, **s** than honey to my mouth!

SWEETNESS* (SWEET)
SS 4: 11 Your lips drop **s** as the honeycomb,
5: 16 His mouth is **s** itself;

SWEPT
Mt 12: 44 **s** clean and put in order.

SWIFT
Pr 1: 16 into evil, they are **s** to shed blood.
Ecc 9: 11 The race is not to the **s** or the battle
Isa 59: 7 they are **s** to shed innocent blood.
Ro 3: 15 "Their feet are **s** to shed blood;
2Pe 2: 1 bringing **s** destruction

SWINDLER* (SWINDLERS)
1Co 5: 11 or slanderer, a drunkard or **s**.

SWINDLERS* (SWINDLER)
1Co 5: 10 or the greedy and **s**, or idolaters.
6: 10 nor slanderers nor **s** will inherit

SWORD (SWORDS)
Ge 3: 24 and a flaming **s** flashing back
Dt 32: 41 when I sharpen my flashing **s**
Jos 5: 13 of him with a drawn **s** in his hand.
1Sa 17: 45 "You come against me with **s**
17: 47 here will know that it is not by **s**
31: 4 Saul took his own **s** and fell on it.
2Sa 12: 10 the **s** will never depart from your
Ps 44: 6 my **s** does not bring me victory;
45: 3 Gird your **s** on your side,
Isa 2: 4 will not take up **s** against nation,
Mic 4: 3 will not take up **s** against nation,
Mt 10: 34 not come to bring peace, but a **s**.
26: 52 all who draw the **s** will die by the **s**.
Lk 2: 35 a **s** will pierce your own soul too."
Ro 13: 4 for rulers do not bear the **s** for no
Eph 6: 17 of salvation and the **s** of the Spirit,
Heb 4: 12 Sharper than any double-edged **s**,
Rev 1: 16 was a sharp, double-edged **s**.
19: 15 of his mouth is a sharp **s**

SWORDS (SWORD)
Ps 64: 3 They sharpen their tongues like **s**
Pr 12: 18 words of the reckless pierce like **s**,
Isa 2: 4 They will beat their **s**
Joel 3: 10 Beat your plowshares into **s**

SWORE (SWEAR)
Heb 6: 13 him to swear by, he **s** by himself,

SWORN (SWEAR)
Ps 110: 4 The LORD has **s** and will not
Eze 20: 42 the land I had **s** with uplifted hand
Heb 7: 21 "The Lord has **s** and will not

SYCAMORE-FIG (FIG)
Am 7: 14 and I also took care of **s** trees.
Lk 19: 4 and climbed a **s** tree to see him,

SYMBOLIZES*
Nu 6: 9 the hair that **s** their dedication,
6: 18 off the hair that **s** their dedication.
6: 19 off the hair that **s** their dedication,
1Pe 3: 21 this water **s** baptism that now saves
SYMPATHETIC* (SYMPATHY)
1Pe 3: 8 like-minded, be **s**, love one another
SYMPATHY (SYMPATHETIC)
Ps 69: 20 I looked for **s**, but there was none,
SYNAGOGUE
Lk 4: 16 the Sabbath day he went into the **s**,
Ac 17: 2 Paul went into the **s**, and on three
TABERNACLE (TABERNACLES)
Ex 40: 34 the glory of the LORD filled the **t**.
Heb 8: 2 the true **t** set up by the Lord,
9: 11 more perfect **t** that is not made
9: 21 sprinkled with the blood both the **t**
Rev 15: 5 that is, the **t** of the covenant law—
TABERNACLES (TABERNACLE)
Lev 23: 34 the LORD's Festival of **T** begins,
Dt 16: 16 of Weeks and the Festival of **T**.
Zec 14: 16 and to celebrate the Festival of **T**.
TABLE (TABLES)
Ex 25: 23 "Make a **t** of acacia wood—
Ps 23: 5 You prepare a **t** before me
TABLES (TABLE)
Jn 2: 15 changers and overturned their **t**.
Ac 6: 2 word of God in order to wait on **t**.
TABLET (TABLETS)
Pr 3: 3 write them on the **t** of your heart.
7: 3 write them on the **t** of your heart.
Isa 30: 8 Go now, write it on a **t** for them,
Lk 1: 63 He asked for a writing **t**, and
TABLETS (TABLET)
Ex 31: 18 Mount Sinai, he gave him the two **t**
31: 18 **t** of stone inscribed by the finger
Dt 10: 5 put the **t** in the ark I had made,
2Co 3: 3 not on **t** of stone but on **t** of human
TAKE (TAKEN TAKES TAKING TOOK)
Ge 15: 7 give you this land to **t** possession
22: 17 Your descendants will **t** possession
Ex 3: 5 "**T** off your sandals, for the place
21: 23 injury, you are to **t** life for life,
22: 22 "Do not **t** advantage of the widow
Lev 10: 17 to you to **t** away the guilt
25: 14 do not **t** advantage of each other.
Nu 13: 30 go up and **t** possession of the land,
Dt 1: 8 **t** possession of the land the LORD
12: 32 do not add to it or **t** away from it.
31: 26 "**T** this Book of the Law and place
1Sa 8: 11 He will **t** your sons and make them
1Ch 17: 13 I will never **t** my love away
Job 23: 10 But he knows the way that I **t**;
Ps 2: 12 Blessed are all who **t** refuge in him.
25: 18 my distress and **t** away all my sins.
27: 14 be strong and **t** heart and wait
31: 24 Be strong and **t** heart, all you who
36: 7 People **t** refuge in the shadow
49: 17 for they will **t** nothing with them
51: 11 or **t** your Holy Spirit from me.
73: 24 afterward you will **t** me into glory.
118: 8 It is better to **t** refuge in the LORD
Pr 22: 23 for the LORD will **t** up their case
25: 9 If you **t** your neighbor to court,
Isa 62: 4 for the LORD will **t** delight in you,
Eze 3: 10 **t** to heart all the words I speak
33: 11 I **t** no pleasure in the death
Mt 10: 38 Whoever does not **t** up their cross
11: 29 **T** my yoke upon you and learn
16: 24 themselves and **t** up their cross
26: 26 to his disciples, saying, "**T** and eat;
Mk 14: 36 **T** this cup from me.
1Ti 6: 12 **T** hold of the eternal life
TAKEN (TAKE)
Ge 2: 23 for she was **t** out of man."
Lev 6: 4 they have stolen or **t** by extortion,
Nu 8: 16 I have **t** them as my own in place
19: 3 it is to be **t** outside the camp
Ecc 3: 14 added to it and nothing **t** from it.
Isa 6: 7 your guilt is **t** away and your sin
Zec 3: 4 "See, I have **t** away your sin, and I
Mt 13: 12 even what they have will be **t**
24: 40 one will be **t** and the other left.
Mt 26: 39 may this cup be **t** from me.
Mk 16: 19 *he was **t** up into heaven*
Ac 1: 9 he was **t** up before their very eyes,
1Ti 3: 16 on in the world, was **t** up in glory.
TAKES (TAKE)
1Ki 20: 11 not boast like one who **t** it off.'"
Ps 34: 8 blessed is the one who **t** refuge
Lk 6: 30 if anyone **t** what belongs to you,
Jn 1: 29 who **t** away the sin of the world!
10: 18 No one **t** it from me, but I lay it
Rev 22: 19 if anyone **t** words away from this
TAKING (TAKE)
Php 2: 7 made himself nothing by **t** the very
TALES*
1Ti 4: 7 godless myths and old wives' **t**;
TALL
1Ch 11: 23 an Egyptian who was five cubits **t**.
TAMAR
1. Wife of Judah's sons Er and Onan (Ge 38:1–10). Tricked Judah into fathering children when he refused her his third son (Ge 38:11–30).
2. Daughter of David, raped by Amnon (2Sa 13).
TAME* (TAMED)
Jas 3: 8 no human being can **t** the tongue.
TAMED* (TAME)
Jas 3: 7 creatures are being **t** and have been **t** by mankind,
TARSHISH
Jnh 1: 3 and sailed for **T** to flee
TARSUS
Ac 9: 11 ask for a man from **T** named Saul,
TASK (TASKS)
1Ch 29: 1 The **t** is great, because this palatial
Mk 13: 34 each with their assigned **t**, and tells
Ac 20: 24 complete the **t** the Lord Jesus has
1Co 3: 5 the Lord has assigned to each his **t**.
2Co 2: 16 And who is equal to such a **t**?
1Ti 3: 1 to be an overseer desires a noble **t**.
TASKS (TASK)
Pr 31: 17 her arms are strong for her **t**.
TASTE (TASTED TASTY)
Ps 34: 8 **T** and see that the LORD is good;
119:103 How sweet are your words to my **t**,
Pr 24: 13 from the comb is sweet to your **t**.
SS 2: 3 and his fruit is sweet to my **t**.
Col 2: 21 Do not **t**! Do not touch!"?
Heb 2: 9 God he might **t** death for everyone.
TASTED (TASTE)
Eze 3: 3 it **t** as sweet as honey in my mouth.
1Pe 2: 3 you have **t** that the Lord is good.
Rev 10: 10 It **t** as sweet as honey in my mouth,
TASTY (TASTE)
Ge 27: 4 Prepare me the kind of **t** food I like
TATTOO*
Lev 19: 28 dead or put **t** marks on yourselves.
TAUGHT (TEACH)
2Ki 17: 28 **t** them how to worship the LORD.
2Ch 17: 9 They **t** throughout Judah,
Ps 119:102 laws, for you yourself have **t** me.
Pr 4: 4 Then he **t** me, and he said to me,
31: 1 utterance his mother **t** him.
Isa 29: 13 human rules they have been **t**.
Mt 7: 29 because he **t** as one who had
Ac 20: 20 to you but have **t** you publicly
1Co 2: 13 but in words **t** by the Spirit,
Gal 1: 12 it from any man, nor was I **t** it;
1Ti 1: 20 to Satan to be **t** not to blaspheme.
1Jn 2: 27 just as it has **t** you, remain in him.
TAX (TAXES)
Mt 11: 19 a friend of **t** collectors and sinners.'
17: 24 your teacher pay the temple **t**?"
22: 17 to pay the imperial **t** to Caesar
TAXES (TAX)
Ro 13: 7 you owe them: If you owe **t**, pay **t**;
TEACH (SPIRIT-TAUGHT TAUGHT TEACHER TEACHERS TEACHES TEACHING TEACHINGS)
Ex 4: 12 speak and will **t** you what to say."
Ex 18: 20 **T** them his decrees and
33: 13 **t** me your ways so I may know you
Lev 10: 11 and so you can **t** the Israelites all
Dt 4: 9 **T** them to your children and to
6: 1 your God directed me to **t** you
8: 3 to **t** you that man does not live
11: 19 **T** them to your children,
1Sa 12: 23 I will **t** you the way that is good
1Ki 8: 36 **T** them the right way to live,
Job 12: 7 and they will **t** you, or the birds
Ps 32: 8 **t** you in the way you should go;
34: 11 I will **t** you the fear of the LORD.
51: 13 I will **t** transgressors your ways,
78: 5 our ancestors to **t** their children,
90: 12 **T** us to number our days, that we
119: 33 **T** me, LORD, the way of your
143: 10 **T** me to do your will, for you are
Pr 9: 9 **t** the righteous and they will add
Jer 31: 34 longer will they **t** their neighbor,
Mic 4: 2 He will **t** us his ways, so that we
Lk 11: 1 "Lord, **t** us to pray, just as John
12: 12 for the Holy Spirit will **t** you
Jn 14: 26 **t** you all things and will remind
Ro 2: 21 then, who **t** others, do you not **t**
15: 4 in the past was written to **t** us,
1Ti 2: 12 I do not permit a woman to **t**
3: 2 respectable, hospitable, able to **t**,
2Ti 2: 2 will also be qualified to **t** others.
2: 24 to everyone, able to **t**, not resentful.
Titus 2: 1 **t** what is appropriate to sound
2: 15 then, are the things you should **t**.
Heb 8: 11 longer will they **t** their neighbor,
Jas 3: 1 that we who **t** will be judged more
1Jn 2: 27 you do not need anyone to **t** you.
TEACHER (TEACH)
Ecc 1: 1 The words of the **T**, son of David,
Mt 10: 24 "The student is not above the **t**,
13: 52 "Therefore every **t** of the law who
23: 8 for you have one **T**, and you are all
Lk 6: 40 The student is not above the **t**,
Jn 3: 2 that you are a **t** who has come
13: 14 Lord and **T**, have washed your
1Co 1: 20 Where is the **t** of the law?
TEACHERS (TEACH)
Ps 119: 99 I have more insight than all my **t**,
Pr 5: 13 I would not obey my **t** or turn my
Lk 20: 46 "Beware of the **t** of the law.
1Co 12: 28 prophets, third **t**, then miracles,
Eph 4: 11 the evangelists, the pastors and **t**,
2Ti 4: 3 around them a great number of **t**
Heb 5: 12 by this time you ought to be **t**,
Jas 3: 1 Not many of you should become **t**,
2Pe 2: 1 as there will be false **t** among you.
TEACHES (TEACH)
Ps 25: 9 in what is right and **t** them his way.
94: 10 Does he who **t** mankind lack
Isa 48: 17 who **t** you what is best for you,
Mt 5: 19 and **t** these commands will be
1Ti 6: 3 If anyone **t** otherwise and does not
Titus 2: 12 It **t** us to say "No" to ungodliness
1Jn 2: 27 But as his anointing **t** you about all
TEACHING (TEACH)
Ezr 7: 10 to **t** its decrees and laws in Israel.
Pr 1: 8 and do not forsake your mother's **t**.
3: 1 son, do not forget my **t**, but keep
6: 23 command is a lamp, this **t** is a light,
Mt 28: 20 **t** them to obey everything I have
Lk 4: 15 He was **t** in their synagogues,
Jn 7: 17 out whether my **t** comes from God
8: 31 "If you hold to my **t**, you are really
14: 23 who loves me will obey my **t**.
Ac 2: 42 themselves to the apostles' **t**
Ro 12: 7 if it is **t**, then teach;
Eph 4: 14 there by every wind of **t**
2Th 3: 6 live according to the **t** you received
1Ti 4: 13 of Scripture, to preaching and to **t**.
5: 17 whose work is preaching and **t**.
6: 3 Lord Jesus Christ and to godly **t**,
2Ti 3: 16 is God-breathed and is useful for **t**,
Titus 1: 11 by **t** things they ought not to teach
2: 7 In your **t** show integrity,
Heb 5: 13 with the **t** about righteousness.
2Jn : 9 in the **t** has both the Father

TEACHINGS (TEACH)
Pr 7: 2 my **t** as the apple of your eye.
2Th 2: 15 hold fast to the **t** we passed
Heb 6: 1 us move beyond the elementary **t**

TEAR (TEARS)
Rev 7: 17 God will wipe away every **t**
21: 4 'He will wipe every **t** from their

TEARING
2Co 10: 8 you up rather than **t** you down,

TEARS (TEAR)
Ps 126: 5 Those who sow with **t** will reap
Isa 25: 8 LORD will wipe away the **t**
Jer 31: 16 weeping and your eyes from **t**,
50: 4 Judah together will go in **t** to seek
Lk 7: 38 she began to wet his feet with her **t**.
2Co 2: 4 anguish of heart and with many **t**,
Php 3: 18 and now tell you again even with **t**,

TEETH (TOOTH)
Job 19: 20 escaped only by the skin of my **t**.
Ps 35: 16 they gnashed their **t** at me.
Jer 31: 29 and the children's **t** are set on edge.'
Mt 8: 12 will be weeping and gnashing of **t**."

TEMPER* (EVEN-TEMPERED HOT-TEMPERED QUICK-TEMPERED)
1Sa 20: 7 if he loses his **t**, you can be sure

TEMPERANCE See SELF-CONTROL

TEMPERATE*
1Ti 3: 2 reproach, faithful to his wife, **t**,
3: 11 not malicious talkers but **t**
Titus 2: 2 Teach the older men to be **t**,

TEMPEST
Ps 50: 3 him, and around him a **t** rages.
55: 8 shelter, far from the **t** and storm."

TEMPLE (TEMPLES)
1Ki 6: 1 began to build the **t** of the LORD.
6: 38 the **t** was finished in all its details
8: 10 the cloud filled the **t** of the LORD.
8: 27 How much less this **t** I have built!
2Ch 36: 19 They set fire to God's **t** and broke
36: 23 appointed me to build a **t** for him
Ezr 6: 14 finished building the **t** according
Ps 27: 4 the LORD and to seek him in his **t**.
Isa 6: 1 the train of his robe filled the **t**.
Eze 10: 4 moved to the threshold of the **t**.
43: 4 LORD entered the **t** through
Hab 2: 20 The LORD is in his holy **t**;
Mt 12: 6 greater than the **t** is here.
26: 61 'I am able to destroy the **t** of God
27: 51 the curtain of the **t** was torn
Lk 21: 5 about how the **t** was adorned
Jn 2: 14 the **t** courts he found people selling
1Co 3: 16 that you yourselves are God's **t**
2Co 6: 16 For we are the **t** of the living God.
Rev 21: 22 Almighty and the Lamb are its **t**.

TEMPLES (TEMPLE)
Ac 17: 24 does not live in **t** built by human
1Co 6: 19 your bodies are **t** of the Holy Spirit,

TEMPORARY
2Co 4: 18 since what is seen is **t**, but what is

TEMPT* (TEMPTATION TEMPTED TEMPTER TEMPTING)
1Co 7: 5 Satan will not **t** you because of
Jas 1: 13 by evil, nor does he **t** anyone;

TEMPTATION* (TEMPT)
Mt 6: 13 lead us not into **t**, but deliver us
26: 41 pray so that you will not fall into **t**.
Mk 14: 38 pray so that you will not fall into **t**.
Lk 11: 4 And lead us not into **t**.'"
22: 40 "Pray that you will not fall into **t**."
22: 46 pray so that you will not fall into **t**."
1Co 10: 13 No **t** has overtaken you except
1Ti 6: 9 who want to get rich fall into **t**

TEMPTED* (TEMPT)
Mt 4: 1 the wilderness to be **t** by the devil.
Mk 1: 13 forty days, being **t** by Satan.
Lk 4: 2 for forty days he was **t** by the devil.
1Co 10: 13 not let you be **t** beyond what you
10: 13 But when you are **t**, he will
Gal 6: 1 yourselves, or you also may be **t**.
1Th 3: 5 in some way the tempter had **t** you
Heb 2: 18 he himself suffered when he was **t**,
2: 18 able to help those who are being **t**.
4: 15 but we have one who has been **t**
Jas 1: 13 When **t**, no one should say, "God
1: 13 For God cannot be **t** by evil,
1: 14 but each person is **t** when they are

TEMPTER* (TEMPT)
Mt 4: 3 The **t** came to him and said, "If you
1Th 3: 5 in some way the **t** had tempted you

TEMPTING* (TEMPT)
Lk 4: 13 the devil had finished all this **t**,
Jas 1: 13 no one should say, "God is **t** me."

TEN (TENTH TITHE TITHES)
Ex 34: 28 the **T** Commandments.
Lev 26: 8 of you will chase **t** thousand,
Dt 4: 13 covenant, the **T** Commandments,
10: 4 the **T** Commandments he had
Ps 91: 7 side, **t** thousand at your right hand,
Da 7: 24 The **t** horns are **t** kings who will
Mt 25: 1 will be like **t** virgins who took their
25: 28 give it to the one who has **t** bags.
Lk 15: 8 suppose a woman has **t** silver coins
Rev 12: 3 with seven heads and **t** horns

TENANTS
Mt 21: 34 servants to the **t** to collect his fruit.

TEND
Jer 23: 2 to the shepherds who **t** my people:
Eze 34: 14 I will **t** them in a good pasture,

TENDERNESS*
Isa 63: 15 **t** and compassion are withheld
Php 2: 1 the Spirit, if any **t** and compassion,

TENT (TENTMAKER TENTS)
Ex 27: 21 In the **t** of meeting,
40: 2 up the tabernacle, the **t** of meeting,
Isa 54: 2 "Enlarge the place of your **t**,
2Co 5: 1 that if the earthly **t** we live in is
2Pe 1: 13 long as I live in the **t** of this body,

TENTH (TEN)
Ge 14: 20 Abram gave him a **t** of everything.
Nu 18: 26 you must present a **t** of that tithe as
Dt 14: 22 Be sure to set aside a **t** of all
1Sa 8: 15 He will take a **t** of your grain
Lk 11: 42 because you give God a **t** of your
18: 12 a week and give a **t** of all I get.'
Heb 7: 4 patriarch Abraham gave him a **t**

TENTMAKER* (TENT)
Ac 18: 3 because he was a **t** as they were,

TENTS (TENT)
Ge 13: 12 and pitched his **t** near Sodom.
Ps 84: 10 than dwell in the **t** of the wicked.

TERAH
Ge 11: 31 **T** took his son Abram, his

TERRIBLE (TERROR)
2Ti 3: 1 There will be **t** times in the last

TERRIFIED (TERROR)
Dt 7: 21 Do not be **t** by them, for the LORD
20: 3 do not panic or be **t** by them.
Ps 90: 7 anger and **t** by your indignation.
Mt 14: 26 walking on the lake, they were **t**.
17: 6 they fell facedown to the ground, **t**.
27: 54 they were **t**, and exclaimed,
Mk 4: 41 They were **t** and asked each other,

TERRIFYING (TERROR)
Heb 12: 21 The sight was so **t** that Moses said,

TERRITORY
2Co 10: 16 already done in someone else's **t**.

TERROR (TERRIBLE TERRIFIED TERRIFYING)
Dt 2: 25 very day I will begin to put the **t**
28: 67 of the **t** that will fill your hearts
Job 9: 34 his **t** would frighten me no more.
Ps 91: 5 You will not fear the **t** of night,
Pr 21: 15 to the righteous but **t** to evildoers.
Isa 13: 8 **T** will seize them, pain and anguish
24: 17 **T** and pit and snare await you,
51: 13 live in constant **t** every day because
54: 14 **T** will be far removed; it will not
Lk 21: 26 People will faint from **t**,
Ro 13: 3 rulers hold no **t** for those who do

TEST (TESTED TESTING TESTS)
Dt 6: 16 your God to the **t** as you did
Jdg 3: 1 to **t** all those Israelites who had not
1Ki 10: 1 she came to **t** Solomon with hard
1Ch 29: 17 that you **t** the heart and are pleased
Ps 26: 2 **T** me, LORD, and try me,
78: 18 to the **t** by demanding the food
106: 14 wilderness they put God to the **t**.
139: 23 **t** me and know my anxious
Jer 11: 20 judge righteously and **t** the heart
Lk 4: 12 put the Lord your God to the **t**.'"
Ac 5: 9 could you conspire to **t** the Spirit
Ro 12: 2 you will be able to **t** and approve
1Co 3: 13 the fire will **t** the quality of each
10: 9 We should not **t** Christ, as some
2Co 13: 5 you are in the faith; **t** yourselves.
1Th 5: 21 but **t** them all; hold on to what is
Jas 1: 12 having stood the **t**, that person will
1Pe 4: 12 that has come on you to **t** you,
1Jn 4: 1 **t** the spirits to see whether they are

TESTED (TEST)
Ge 22: 1 Some time later God **t** Abraham.
Job 23: 10 when he has **t** me, I will come forth
34: 36 that Job might be **t** to the utmost
Ps 66: 10 For you, God, **t** us; you refined us
Pr 27: 21 but people are **t** by their praise.
Isa 28: 16 I lay a stone in Zion, a **t** stone,
48: 10 I have **t** you in the furnace
1Ti 3: 10 They must first be **t**;
Heb 11: 17 when God **t** him, offered Isaac as

TESTIFIES (TESTIFY)
Jn 5: 32 There is another who **t** in my favor,
Ro 8: 16 The Spirit himself **t** with our spirit

TESTIFY (TESTIFIES TESTIMONY)
Pr 24: 28 Do not **t** against your neighbor
Jn 1: 7 came as a witness to **t** concerning
1: 34 I **t** that this is God's Chosen One."
5: 39 These are the very Scriptures that **t**
7: 7 hates me because I **t** that its works
15: 26 the Father—he will **t** about me.
Ac 4: 33 power the apostles continued to **t**
10: 43 All the prophets **t** about him
1Jn 4: 14 **t** that the Father has sent his Son
5: 7 For there are three that **t**:

TESTIMONY (TESTIFY)
Ex 20: 16 shall not give false **t** against your
Nu 35: 30 only on the **t** of witnesses.
Dt 19: 18 a liar, giving false **t** against a fellow
Isa 8: 20 instruction and the **t** of warning.
Mt 15: 19 immorality, theft, false **t**, slander.
24: 14 whole world as a **t** to all nations,
Lk 18: 20 you shall not give false **t**,
Jn 2: 25 He did not need any **t**
21: 24 We know that his **t** is true.
2Ti 1: 8 be ashamed of the **t** about our Lord
1Jn 5: 9 We accept human **t**, but God's **t** is
Rev 12: 11 Lamb and by the word of their **t**;

TESTING (TEST)
Lk 8: 13 but in the time of **t** they fall away.
Heb 3: 8 rebellion, during the time of **t**
Jas 1: 3 that the **t** of your faith produces

TESTS (TEST)
Pr 17: 3 for gold, but the LORD **t** the heart.
1Th 2: 4 people but God, who **t** our hearts.

THADDAEUS*
Apostle (Mt 10:3; Mk 3:18); probably also known as Judas son of James (Lk 6:16; Ac 1:13).

THANK (THANKFUL THANKFULNESS THANKS THANKSGIVING)
Php 1: 3 I **t** my God every time I remember
1Th 3: 9 How can we **t** God enough for you

THANKFUL* (THANK)
Col 3: 15 you were called to peace. And be **t**.
4: 2 to prayer, being watchful and **t**.
Heb 12: 28 let us be **t**, and so worship God

THANKFULNESS* (THANK)
Lev 7: 12 they offer it as an expression of **t**,
1Co 10: 30 If I take part in the meal with **t**,
Col 2: 7 taught, and overflowing with **t**.

THANKS (THANK)
Ne 12: 31 assigned two large choirs to give **t**.
Ps 7: 17 will give **t** to the LORD because
9: 1 give **t** to you, LORD, with all
35: 18 I will give you **t** in the great

Ps 100: 4 give **t** to him and praise his name.
107: 1 Give **t** to the LORD, for he is
136: 1 Give **t** to the LORD, for he is
Ro 1: 21 glorified him as God nor gave **t**
1Co 11: 24 when he had given **t**, he broke it
15: 57 But **t** be to God! He gives us
2Co 2: 14 But **t** be to God, who always leads
9: 15 **T** be to God for his indescribable
1Th 5: 18 give **t** in all circumstances;
Rev 4: 9 and **t** to him who sits on the throne

THANKSGIVING (THANK)
Ps 95: 2 Let us come before him with **t**
100: 4 Enter his gates with **t** and his
1Co 10: 16 Is not the cup of **t** for which we
Php 4: 6 **t**, present your requests to God.
1Ti 4: 3 to be received with **t** by those who

THEFT (THIEF)
Mt 15: 19 adultery, sexual immorality, **t**,

THEFTS* (THIEF)
Rev 9: 21 their sexual immorality or their **t**.

THEME*
Ps 22: 25 From you comes the **t** of my praise
45: 1 by a noble **t** as I recite my verses
119: 54 Your decrees are the **t** of my song

THIEF (THEFT THEFTS THIEVES)
Pr 6: 30 do not despise a **t** if he steals
Lk 12: 39 at what hour the **t** was coming,
1Th 5: 2 of the Lord will come like a **t**
1Pe 4: 15 it should not be as a murderer or **t**
Rev 16: 15 "Look, I come like a **t**!

THIEVES (THIEF)
Mt 6: 19 and where **t** break in and steal.
Jn 10: 8 All who have come before me are **t**
1Co 6: 10 nor **t** nor the greedy nor drunkards

THINK (THINKING THOUGHT THOUGHTS)
Ps 63: 6 I **t** of you through the watches
Isa 44: 19 No one stops to **t**, no one has
Mt 22: 42 "What do you **t** about the Messiah?
Ro 12: 3 Do not **t** of yourself more highly
Php 4: 8 **t** about such things.

THINKING (THINK)
Pr 23: 7 of person who is always **t**
1Co 14: 20 be infants, but in your **t** be adults.
2Pe 3: 1 to stimulate you to wholesome **t**.

THIRST (THIRSTS THIRSTY)
Ps 69: 21 food and gave me vinegar for my **t**.
Mt 5: 6 hunger and **t** for righteousness,
Jn 4: 14 the water I give them will never **t**.
2Co 11: 27 I have known hunger and **t** and
Rev 7: 16 never again will they **t**.

THIRSTS* (THIRST)
Ps 42: 2 My soul **t** for God, for the living

THIRSTY (THIRST)
Ps 107: 9 for he satisfies the **t** and fills
Pr 25: 21 if he is **t**, give him water to drink.
Isa 55: 1 all you who are **t**,
Mt 25: 35 I was **t** and you gave me something
Jn 7: 37 "Let anyone who is **t** come to me
Ro 12: 20 if he is **t**, give him something
Rev 21: 6 the **t** I will give water without cost
22: 17 Let the one who is **t** come;

THOMAS*
Apostle (Mt 10:3; Mk 3:18; Lk 6:15; Jn 11:16; 14:5; 21:2; Ac 1:13). Doubted resurrection (Jn 20:24–28).

THORN (THORNBUSHES THORNS)
2Co 12: 7 I was given a **t** in my flesh,

THORNBUSHES (THORN)
Lk 6: 44 People do not pick figs from **t**,

THORNS (THORN)
Ge 3: 18 It will produce **t** and thistles for
Nu 33: 55 in your eyes and **t** in your sides.
Mt 13: 7 seed fell among **t**, which grew
27: 29 twisted together a crown of **t** and
Heb 6: 8 land that produces **t** and thistles is

THOUGHT (THINK)
1Ch 28: 9 every desire and every **t**.
Pr 4: 26 Give careful **t** to the paths for your
14: 15 the prudent give **t** to their steps.
21: 29 but the upright give **t** to their ways.
1Co 13: 11 I talked like a child, I **t** like a child,

THOUGHTS (THINK)
Ps 139: 23 test me and know my anxious **t**.
Isa 55: 8 "For my **t** are not your **t**,
Mt 15: 19 For out of the heart come evil **t**—
1Co 2: 11 knows a person's **t** except their own
Heb 4: 12 it judges the **t** and attitudes

THREATENED
Isa 38: 14 I am being **t**; Lord, come to my

THREE
Ge 6: 10 Noah had **t** sons: Shem,
Ex 23: 14 "**T** times a year you are to celebrate
Dt 19: 15 the testimony of two or **t** witnesses.
2Sa 23: 8 a Tahkemonite, was chief of the **T**;
Pr 30: 15 "There are **t** things that are never
30: 18 "There are **t** things that are too
30: 21 "Under **t** things the earth trembles,
30: 29 "There are **t** things that are stately
Ecc 4: 12 of **t** strands is not quickly broken.
Da 3: 24 "Weren't there **t** men that we tied
Am 1: 3 "For **t** sins of Damascus,
Jnh 1: 17 was in the belly of the fish **t** days
Mt 12: 40 as Jonah was **t** days and **t** nights
12: 40 so the Son of Man will be **t** days
17: 4 If you wish, I will put up **t** shelters
18: 20 where two or **t** gather in my name,
26: 34 you will disown me **t** times."
26: 75 you will disown me **t** times."
27: 63 said, 'After **t** days I will rise again.'
Mk 8: 31 be killed and after **t** days rise again.
9: 5 Let us put up **t** shelters—
14: 30 yourself will disown me **t** times."
Jn 2: 19 and I will raise it again in **t** days."
1Co 13: 13 And now these **t** remain:
14: 27 or at the most—should speak,
2Co 13: 1 testimony of two or **t** witnesses."
1Jn 5: 7 For there are **t** that testify:

THRESHES* (THRESHING)
1Co 9: 10 whoever plows and **t** should be

THRESHING (THRESHES)
Ru 3: 6 So she went down to the **t** floor
2Sa 24: 18 altar to the LORD on the **t** floor
Lk 3: 17 in his hand to clear his **t** floor

THREW (THROW)
Da 6: 16 and **t** him into the lions' den.
Jnh 1: 15 took Jonah and **t** him overboard,

THRIVE
Pr 29: 2 When the righteous **t**, the people

THROAT (THROATS)
Ps 5: 9 Their **t** is an open grave;
Pr 23: 2 put a knife to your **t** if you are

THROATS (THROAT)
Ro 3: 13 "Their **t** are open graves;

THROB*
Isa 60: 5 your heart will **t** and swell with joy;

THRONE (ENTHRONED ENTHRONES THRONES)
2Sa 7: 16 your **t** will be established
1Ch 17: 12 and I will establish his **t** forever.
Ps 11: 4 the LORD is on his heavenly **t**.
45: 6 Your **t**, O God, will last for ever
47: 8 God is seated on his holy **t**.
89: 14 justice are the foundation of your **t**;
Isa 6: 1 high and exalted, seated on a **t**;
66: 1 "Heaven is my **t**, and the earth is
Eze 28: 2 I sit on the **t** of a god in the heart
Da 7: 9 His **t** was flaming with fire, and its
Mt 19: 28 Son of Man sits on his glorious **t**,
Ac 7: 49 "'Heaven is my **t**, and the earth is
Heb 1: 8 the Son he says, "Your **t**, O God,
4: 16 then approach God's **t** of grace
12: 2 at the right hand of the **t** of God.
Rev 3: 21 the right to sit with me on my **t**,
3: 21 sat down with my Father on his **t**.
4: 2 there before me was a **t** in heaven
4: 10 They lay their crowns before the **t**
20: 11 I saw a great white **t** and him who
22: 3 The **t** of God and of the Lamb will

THRONES (THRONE)
Mt 19: 28 me will also sit on twelve **t**,
Rev 4: 4 throne were twenty-four other **t**,

THROW (THREW)
Jn 8: 7 *the first to **t** a stone at her."*

Heb 10: 35 So do not **t** away your confidence;
12: 1 let us **t** off everything that hinders

THUNDER (THUNDERS)
Ps 93: 4 Mightier than the **t** of the great
Mk 3: 17 which means "sons of **t**"),

THUNDERS (THUNDER)
Job 37: 5 God's voice **t** in marvelous ways;
Ps 29: 3 the God of glory **t**, the LORD **t**
Rev 10: 3 the voices of the seven **t** spoke.

THWART* (THWARTED)
Isa 14: 27 has purposed, and who can **t** him?

THWARTED (THWART)
Job 42: 2 no purpose of yours can be **t**.

THYATIRA
Rev 2: 18 the angel of the church in **T** write:

TIBNI
King of Israel (1Ki 16:21–22).

TIDINGS*
Isa 52: 7 who bring good **t**, who proclaim

TIES
Hos 11: 4 of human kindness, with **t** of love.
Mt 12: 29 unless he first **t** up the strong man?

TIGHT*
Jas 1: 26 yet do not keep a **t** rein on their

TIGHTFISTED*
Dt 15: 7 not be hardhearted or **t** toward

TIMBREL
Ps 150: 4 praise him with **t** and dancing,

TIME (TIMES)
Est 4: 14 royal position for such a **t** as this?"
Ecc 3: 1 There is a **t** for everything,
8: 5 wise heart will know the proper **t**
Da 7: 25 hands for a **t**, times and half a **t**.
12: 7 be for a **t**, times and half a **t**.
Hos 10: 12 for it is **t** to seek the LORD,
Ro 9: 9 "At the appointed **t** I will return,
13: 11 this, understanding the present **t**:
1Co 7: 29 and sisters, is that the **t** is short.
2Co 6: 2 you, now is the **t** of God's favor,
2Ti 1: 9 Jesus before the beginning of **t**,
Titus 1: 2 before the beginning of **t**,
Heb 9: 28 and he will appear a second **t**,
10: 12 had offered for all **t** one sacrifice
1Pe 4: 17 For it is **t** for judgment to begin

TIMES (TIME)
Ps 9: 9 a stronghold in **t** of trouble.
31: 15 My **t** are in your hands;
62: 8 Trust in him at all **t**, you people;
Pr 17: 17 A friend loves at all **t**, and
Isa 46: 10 ancient **t**, what is still to come.
Am 5: 13 in such **t**, for the **t** are evil.
Mt 16: 3 cannot interpret the signs of the **t**.
18: 21 how many **t** shall I forgive my
18: 21 sins against me? Up to seven **t**?"
Ac 1: 7 "It is not for you to know the **t**
Rev 12: 14 for a time, **t** and half a time,

TIMID
2Ti 1: 7 God gave us does not make us **t**,

TIMOTHY
Believer from Lystra (Ac 16:1). Joined Paul on second missionary journey (Ac 16–20). Sent to settle problems at Corinth (1Co 4:17; 16:10). Led church at Ephesus (1Ti 1:3). Co-writer with Paul (1Th 1:1; 2Th 1:1; Phm 1).

TIP
Job 33: 2 words are on the **t** of my tongue.

TIRE (TIRED)
2Th 3: 13 never **t** of doing what is good.

TIRED (TIRE)
Ex 17: 12 When Moses' hands grew **t**,
Isa 40: 28 He will not grow **t** or weary, and

TITHE (TEN)
Lev 27: 30 "'A **t** of everything
Dt 12: 17 your own towns the **t** of your grain
Mal 3: 10 Bring the whole **t**

TITHES (TEN)
Nu 18: 21 the Levites all the **t** in Israel as
Mal 3: 8 "In **t** and offerings.

TITUS*
Gentile co-worker of Paul (Gal 2:1–3; 2Ti 4:10); sent to Corinth (2Co 2:13; 7–8; 12:18), Crete (Titus 1:4–5).

TODAY
Ps 2: 7 **t** I have become your father.
95: 7 **T**, if only you would hear his voice,
Mt 6: 11 Give us **t** our daily bread.
Lk 2: 11 **T** in the town of David a Savior has
23: 43 **t** you will be with me in paradise."
Ac 13: 33 **t** I have become your father.'
Heb 1: 5 **t** I have become your Father"?
3: 7 "**T**, if you hear his voice,
3: 13 as long as it is called "**T**,"
5: 5 **t** I have become your Father."
13: 8 Christ is the same yesterday and **t**

TOIL (TOILED TOILING)
Ge 3: 17 through painful **t** you will eat food
Ecc 5: 19 their lot and be happy in their **t**—

TOILED (TOIL)
2Co 11: 27 I have labored and **t** and have often

TOILING (TOIL)
2Th 3: 8 **t** so that we would not be a burden

TOLERATE
Hab 1: 13 you cannot **t** wrongdoing.
Rev 2: 2 that you cannot **t** wicked people,

TOMB
Mt 27: 65 make the **t** as secure as you know
Lk 24: 2 the stone rolled away from the **t**,

TOMORROW
Pr 27: 1 Do not boast about **t**, for you do
Isa 22: 13 drink," you say, "for **t** we die!"
Mt 6: 34 Therefore do not worry about **t**, for **t** will worry
1Co 15: 32 "Let us eat and drink, for **t** we die."
Jas 4: 13 "Today or **t** we will go to this

TONGUE (TONGUES)
Ex 4: 10 I am slow of speech and **t**."
Job 33: 2 my words are on the tip of my **t**.
Ps 34: 13 keep your **t** from evil and your lips
39: 1 my ways and keep my **t** from sin;
51: 14 Savior, and my **t** will sing of your
52: 4 harmful word, you deceitful **t**!
71: 24 My **t** will tell of your righteous acts
119:172 May my **t** sing of your word, for all
137: 6 my **t** cling to the roof of my mouth
139: 4 Before a word is on my **t** you,
Pr 6: 17 a lying **t**, hands that shed innocent
12: 18 but the **t** of the wise brings healing.
15: 4 The soothing **t** is a tree of life,
17: 20 one whose **t** is perverse falls
25: 15 and a gentle **t** can break a bone.
26: 28 A lying **t** hates those it hurts,
28: 23 than one who has a flattering **t**.
31: 26 and faithful instruction is on her **t**.
SS 4: 11 milk and honey are under your **t**.
Isa 32: 4 and the stammering **t** will be fluent
45: 23 by me every **t** will swear.
50: 4 has given me a well-instructed **t**,
59: 3 and your **t** mutters wicked things.
Lk 16: 24 his finger in water and cool my **t**,
Ro 14: 11 every **t** will acknowledge God.'"
1Co 14: 2 who speaks in a **t** does not speak
14: 4 speaks in a **t** edifies themselves,
14: 9 intelligible words with your **t**,
14: 13 one who speaks in a **t** should pray
14: 19 than ten thousand words in a **t**.
14: 26 revelation, a **t** or an interpretation.
14: 27 If anyone speaks in a **t**, two—
Php 2: 11 and every **t** acknowledge that Jesus
Jas 3: 5 the **t** is a small part of the body,
3: 8 no human being can tame the **t**.

TONGUES (TONGUE)
Ps 5: 9 with their **t** they tell lies.
12: 4 who say, "By our **t** we will prevail;
37: 30 and their **t** speak what is just.
126: 2 laughter, our **t** with songs of joy.
Pr 10: 19 words, but the prudent hold their **t**.
21: 23 and their **t** keep themselves
Isa 28: 11 strange **t** God will speak to this
Jer 23: 31 the prophets who wag their own **t**
Mk 16: 17 *they will speak in new* **t**;
Ac 2: 3 saw what seemed to be **t** of fire
2: 4 other **t** as the Spirit enabled them.
Ac 10: 46 For they heard them speaking in **t**
19: 6 they spoke in **t** and prophesied.
Ro 3: 13 their **t** practice deceit."
1Co 12: 10 speaking in different kinds of **t**,
12: 10 another the interpretation of **t**.
12: 28 and of different kinds of **t**.
12: 30 Do all speak in **t**? Do all interpret?
13: 1 If I speak in the **t** of men
13: 8 where there are **t**, they will be
14: 5 than the one who speaks in **t**,
14: 18 I speak in **t** more than all of you.
14: 21 "With other **t** and through the lips
14: 39 and do not forbid speaking in **t**.
Jas 1: 26 rein on their **t** deceive themselves,

TOOK (TAKE)
Ps 68: 18 on high, you **t** many captives;
Isa 53: 4 Surely he **t** up our pain and bore
Mt 8: 17 "He **t** up our infirmities and bore
26: 26 they were eating, Jesus **t** bread,
26: 27 Then he **t** a cup, and when he had
1Co 11: 23 the night he was betrayed, **t** bread,
11: 25 after supper he **t** the cup, saying,
Eph 4: 8 he **t** many captives and gave gifts
Php 3: 12 which Christ Jesus **t** hold of me.

TOOTH (TEETH)
Ex 21: 24 eye for eye, **t** for **t**, hand for hand,
Mt 5: 38 was said, 'Eye for eye, and **t** for **t**.'

TOP
Dt 28: 13 you will always be at the **t**,
Isa 1: 6 foot to the **t** of your head there is
Mt 27: 51 was torn in two from **t** to bottom.

TORMENT (TORMENTED TORMENTORS)
Lk 16: 28 not also come to this place of **t**.'
2Co 12: 7 a messenger of Satan, to **t** me.

TORMENTED (TORMENT)
Rev 20: 10 They will be **t** day and night

TORMENTORS (TORMENT)
Ps 137: 3 our **t** demanded songs of joy;

TORN
Gal 4: 15 you would have **t** out your eyes
Php 1: 23 I am **t** between the two: I desire

TORTURED*
Mt 18: 34 him over to the jailers to be **t**,
Heb 11: 35 There were others who were **t**,

TOSSED (TOSSING)
Eph 4: 14 **t** back and forth by the waves,
Jas 1: 6 the sea, blown and **t** by the wind.

TOSSING (TOSSED)
Isa 57: 20 But the wicked are like the **t** sea,

TOUCH (TOUCHED TOUCHES)
Ge 3: 3 and you must not **t** it, or you will
Ex 19: 12 the mountain or **t** the foot of it.
Ps 105: 15 "Do not **t** my anointed ones;
Mt 9: 21 "If I only **t** his cloak, I will be
Lk 24: 39 **T** me and see; a ghost does not
2Co 6: 17 **T** no unclean thing, and I will
Col 2: 21 Do not taste! Do not **t**!"?

TOUCHED (TOUCH)
1Sa 10: 26 men whose hearts God had **t**.
Isa 6: 7 With it he **t** my mouth and said,
Mt 14: 36 cloak, and all who **t** it were healed.
Lk 8: 45 "Who **t** me?" Jesus asked.
1Jn 1: 1 looked at and our hands have **t**—

TOUCHES (TOUCH)
Ex 19: 12 Whoever **t** the mountain is to be
Zec 2: 8 for whoever **t** you **t** the apple of his

TOWER
Ge 11: 4 a **t** that reaches to the heavens,
Pr 18: 10 name of the LORD is a fortified **t**;

TOWN (TOWNS)
Mt 2: 23 and lived in a **t** called Nazareth.
5: 14 **t** built on a hill cannot be hidden.
13: 57 without honor except in his own **t**

TOWNS (TOWN)
Nu 35: 2 to give the Levites **t** to live in
35: 15 These six **t** will be a place of refuge
Jer 11: 13 have as many gods as you have **t**;
Mt 9: 35 Jesus went through all the **t**

TRACING*
Ro 11: 33 and his paths beyond **t** out!

TRACK
Job 14: 16 my steps but not keep **t** of my sin.

TRADERS (TRADING)
1Ti 1: 10 for slave **t** and liars and perjurers—

TRADING (TRADERS)
1Ki 10: 22 The king had a fleet of **t** ships at
Pr 31: 18 She sees that her **t** is profitable,

TRADITION (TRADITIONS)
Mt 15: 2 "Why do your disciples break the **t**
15: 6 word of God for the sake of your **t**.
Mk 7: 13 your **t** that you have handed down.
Col 2: 8 which depends on human **t**

TRADITIONS (TRADITION)
Mk 7: 8 and are holding on to human **t**."
Gal 1: 14 zealous for the **t** of my fathers.

TRAIL
1Ti 5: 24 the sins of others **t** behind them.

TRAIN* (TRAINED TRAINING)
Isa 2: 4 nor will they **t** for war anymore.
6: 1 the **t** of his robe filled the temple.
Mic 4: 3 nor will they **t** for war anymore.
1Ti 4: 7 rather, **t** yourself to be godly.

TRAINED (TRAIN)
Lk 6: 40 everyone who is fully **t** will be like
Ac 22: 3 was thoroughly **t** in the law of our
Heb 5: 14 by constant use have **t** themselves
12: 11 for those who have been **t** by it.

TRAINING* (TRAIN)
1Co 9: 25 in the games goes into strict **t**.
Eph 6: 4 instead, bring them up in the **t**
1Ti 4: 8 For physical **t** is of some value,
2Ti 3: 16 correcting and **t** in righteousness,

TRAITOR (TRAITORS)
Lk 6: 16 and Judas Iscariot, who became a **t**.
Jn 18: 5 Judas the **t** was standing there

TRAITORS (TRAITOR)
Ps 59: 5 show no mercy to wicked **t**.

TRAMPLE (TRAMPLED)
Joel 3: 13 Come, **t** the grapes,
Am 2: 7 They **t** on the heads of the poor as
8: 4 you who **t** the needy and do away
Mt 7: 6 they may **t** them under their feet,
Lk 10: 19 I have given you authority to **t**

TRAMPLED (TRAMPLE)
Isa 63: 6 I **t** the nations in my anger;
Lk 21: 24 Jerusalem will be **t**
Heb 10: 29 to be punished who has **t** the Son
Rev 14: 20 They were **t** in the winepress

TRANCE*
Ac 10: 10 was being prepared, he fell into a **t**.
11: 5 praying, and in a **t** I saw a vision.
22: 17 praying at the temple, I fell into a **t**

TRANQUILLITY*
Ecc 4: 6 handful with **t** than two handfuls

TRANSACTIONS*
Ru 4: 7 method of legalizing **t** in Israel.)

TRANSCENDS*
Php 4: 7 God, which **t** all understanding,

TRANSFIGURED*
Mt 17: 2 There he was **t** before them.
Mk 9: 2 There he was **t** before them.

TRANSFORM* (TRANSFORMED)
Php 3: 21 will **t** our lowly bodies so that they

TRANSFORMED (TRANSFORM)
Ro 12: 2 be **t** by the renewing of your mind.
2Co 3: 18 are being **t** into his image

TRANSGRESSED* (TRANSGRESSION)
Ps 17: 3 my mouth has not **t**.
Da 9: 11 All Israel has **t** your law and turned

TRANSGRESSION* (TRANSGRESSED TRANSGRESSIONS TRANSGRESSORS)
Ps 19: 13 be blameless, innocent of great **t**.
Isa 53: 8 **t** of my people he was punished.
Da 9: 24 and your holy city to finish **t**,
Mic 1: 5 All this is because of Jacob's **t**,
1: 5 What is Jacob's **t**? Is it not Samaria?
3: 8 to declare to Jacob his **t**, to Israel
6: 7 Shall I offer my firstborn for my **t**,
7: 18 forgives the **t** of the remnant of his

Ro 4: 15 where there is no law there is no **t**.
11: 11 because of their **t**, salvation has
11: 12 their **t** means riches for the world,

TRANSGRESSIONS* (TRANSGRESSION)
Ps 32: 1 is the one whose **t** are forgiven,
32: 5 I said, "I will confess my **t**
39: 8 Save me from all my **t**; do not
51: 1 great compassion blot out my **t**.
51: 3 For I know my **t**, and my sin is
65: 3 by sins, you forgave our **t**.
103: 12 far has he removed our **t** from us.
Isa 43: 25 am he who blots out your **t**, for my
50: 1 your **t** your mother was sent away.
53: 5 But he was pierced for our **t**,
Mic 1: 13 the **t** of Israel were found in you.
Ro 4: 7 are those whose **t** are forgiven,
Gal 3: 19 added because of **t** until the Seed
Eph 2: 1 you were dead in your **t** and sins,
2: 5 even when we were dead in **t**—

TRANSGRESSORS* (TRANSGRESSION)
Ps 51: 13 Then I will teach **t** your ways,
Isa 53: 12 and was numbered with the **t**.
53: 12 and made intercession for the **t**.
Lk 22: 37 'And he was numbered with the **t**';

TRANSITORY*
2Co 3: 7 of its glory, **t** though it was,
3: 11 And if what was **t** came with glory,

TRAP (TRAPPED TRAPS)
Ps 69: 22 may it become retribution and a **t**.
Pr 20: 25 is a **t** to dedicate something rashly
28: 10 evil path will fall into their own **t**,
Isa 8: 14 people of Jerusalem he will be a **t**
Mt 22: 15 laid plans to **t** him in his words.
Lk 21: 34 will close on you suddenly like a **t**.
Ro 11: 9 their table become a snare and a **t**,
1Ti 3: 7 into disgrace and into the devil's **t**.
6: 9 and a **t** and into many foolish
2Ti 2: 26 and escape from the **t** of the devil,

TRAPPED (TRAP)
Pr 6: 2 you have been **t** by what you said,
12: 13 Evildoers are **t** by their sinful talk,

TRAPS (TRAP)
Jos 23: 13 will become snares and **t** for you,
La 4: 20 life breath, was caught in their **t**.

TRAVEL (TRAVELER)
Pr 4: 15 Avoid it, do not **t** on it; turn from it
Mt 23: 15 You **t** over land and sea to win

TRAVELER (TRAVEL)
Job 31: 32 my door was always open to the **t**
Jer 14: 8 like a **t** who stays only a night?

TREACHEROUS (TREACHERY)
Ps 25: 3 on those who are **t** without cause.
Zep 3: 4 unprincipled; they are **t** people.
2Ti 3: 4 **t**, rash, conceited, lovers of

TREACHERY (TREACHEROUS)
Isa 59: 13 rebellion and **t** against the LORD,

TREAD (TREADING TREADS)
Ps 91: 13 will **t** on the lion and the cobra;

TREADING (TREAD)
Dt 25: 4 Do not muzzle an ox while it is **t**
1Co 9: 9 "Do not muzzle an ox while it is **t**
1Ti 5: 18 "Do not muzzle an ox while it is **t**

TREADS (TREAD)
Rev 19: 15 He **t** the winepress of the fury

TREASURE (TREASURED TREASURES TREASURY)
Pr 2: 4 and search for it as for hidden **t**,
Isa 33: 6 of the LORD is the key to this **t**.
Mt 6: 21 where your **t** is, there your heart
13: 44 of heaven is like **t** hidden in a field.
Lk 12: 33 a **t** in heaven that will never fail,
2Co 4: 7 But we have this **t** in jars of clay
1Ti 6: 19 In this way they will lay up **t**

TREASURED* (TREASURE)
Ex 19: 5 you will be my **t** possession.
Dt 7: 6 to be his people, his **t** possession.
14: 2 chosen you to be his **t** possession.
26: 18 his **t** possession as he promised,
Job 23: 12 I have **t** the words of his mouth
Ps 135: 4 own, Israel to be his **t** possession.
Isa 64: 11 fire, and all that we **t** lies in ruins.
Mal 3: 17 "they will be my **t** possession.
Lk 2: 19 But Mary **t** up all these things
2: 51 his mother **t** all these things in her

TREASURES (TREASURE)
1Ch 29: 3 my God I now give my personal **t**
Pr 10: 2 Ill-gotten **t** have no lasting value,
Mt 6: 19 store up for yourselves **t** on earth,
13: 52 his storeroom new **t** as well as old."
Col 2: 3 in whom are hidden all the **t**
Heb 11: 26 of greater value than the **t** of Egypt,

TREASURY (TREASURE)
Mk 12: 43 more into the **t** than all the others.

TREAT (TREATED TREATING TREATMENT)
Lev 22: 2 sons to **t** with respect the sacred
Ps 103: 10 he does not **t** us as our sins deserve
Mt 18: 17 **t** them as you would a pagan
18: 35 how my heavenly Father will **t** each
Eph 6: 9 **t** your slaves in the same way.
1Th 5: 20 Do not **t** prophecies with contempt
1Ti 5: 1 **T** younger men as brothers,
1Pe 3: 7 **t** them with respect as the weaker

TREATED (TREAT)
Lev 19: 34 you must be **t** as your native-born.
25: 40 They are to be **t** as hired workers
1Sa 24: 17 "You have **t** me well, but I have **t**
Heb 10: 29 who has **t** as an unholy thing

TREATING (TREAT)
Ge 18: 25 **t** the righteous and the wicked
Heb 12: 7 God is **t** you as his children.

TREATMENT (TREAT)
Col 2: 23 and their harsh **t** of the body,

TREATY
Ex 34: 12 not to make a **t** with those who live
Dt 7: 2 Make no **t** with them, and show
23: 6 Do not seek a **t** of friendship

TREE (TREES)
Ge 2: 9 of the garden were the **t** of life
2: 9 the **t** of the knowledge of good
2Sa 18: 9 Absalom's hair got caught in the **t**.
1Ki 14: 23 hill and under every spreading **t**.
Ps 1: 3 is like a **t** planted by streams
52: 8 I am like an olive **t** flourishing
92: 12 will flourish like a palm **t**,
Pr 3: 18 She is a **t** of life to those who take
11: 30 fruit of the righteous is a **t** of life,
27: 18 who guards a fig **t** will eat its fruit,
Isa 65: 22 For as the days of a **t**, so will be
Jer 17: 8 They will be like a **t** planted
Eze 17: 24 I the LORD bring down the tall **t**
17: 24 and make the dry **t** flourish.
Da 4: 10 and there before me stood a **t**
Mic 4: 4 vine and under their own fig **t**,
Zec 3: 10 to sit under your vine and fig **t**,'
Mt 3: 10 every **t** that does not produce good
12: 33 "Make a **t** good and its fruit will be
12: 33 for a **t** is recognized by its fruit.
Lk 19: 4 climbed a sycamore-fig **t** to see
Ro 11: 24 an olive **t** that is wild by nature,
11: 24 be grafted into their own olive **t**!
Jas 3: 12 sisters, can a fig **t** bear olives,
Rev 2: 7 the right to eat from the **t** of life,
22: 2 side of the river stood the **t** of life,
22: 2 leaves of the **t** are for the healing
22: 14 may have the right to the **t** of life
22: 19 person any share in the **t** of life

TREES (TREE)
Jdg 9: 8 One day the **t** went out to anoint
Ps 96: 12 let all the **t** of the forest sing for joy.
Isa 55: 12 all the **t** of the field will clap their
Mt 3: 10 ax is already at the root of the **t**,
Mk 8: 24 they look like **t** walking around."
Jude : 12 autumn **t**, without fruit

TREMBLE (TREMBLED TREMBLES TREMBLING)
Ex 15: 14 The nations will hear and **t**;
1Ch 16: 30 **T** before him, all the earth!
Ps 114: 7 **T**, earth, at the presence of the
Isa 66: 2 in spirit, and who **t** at my word.
Jer 5: 22 "Should you not **t** in my presence?
Eze 38: 20 of the earth will **t** at my presence.
Joel 2: 1 Let all who live in the land **t**,
Hab 3: 6 he looked, and made the nations **t**.
Ro 11: 20 Do not be arrogant, but **t**.

TREMBLED (TREMBLE)
Ex 19: 16 Everyone in the camp **t**.
20: 18 in smoke, they **t** with fear.
2Sa 22: 8 they **t** because he was angry.
Ac 7: 32 Moses **t** with fear and did not dare

TREMBLES (TREMBLE)
Ps 97: 4 up the world; the earth sees and **t**.
104: 32 it **t**, who touches the mountains,
Jer 10: 10 When he is angry, the earth **t**;
Na 1: 5 The earth **t** at his presence,

TREMBLING (TREMBLE)
Ps 2: 11 fear and celebrate his rule with **t**.
Da 10: 10 me and set me **t** on my hands
Php 2: 12 out your salvation with fear and **t**,
Heb 12: 21 that Moses said, "I am **t** with fear."

TRESPASS* (TRESPASSES)
Ro 5: 15 But the gift is not like the **t**.
5: 15 many died by the **t** of the one man,
5: 17 if, by the **t** of the one man,
5: 18 just as one **t** resulted
5: 20 in so that the **t** might increase.

TRESPASSES* (TRESPASS)
Ro 5: 16 but the gift followed many **t**

TRIAL (TRIALS)
Ps 37: 33 be condemned when brought to **t**.
Mal 3: 5 "So I will come to put you on **t**.
Mk 13: 11 you are arrested and brought to **t**,
2Co 8: 2 In the midst of a very severe **t**,
Jas 1: 12 who perseveres under **t** because,
Rev 3: 10 you from the hour of **t** that is going

TRIALS* (TRIAL)
Dt 7: 19 saw with your own eyes the great **t**,
29: 3 own eyes you saw those great **t**,
Lk 22: 28 who have stood by me in my **t**.
1Th 3: 3 one would be unsettled by these **t**.
2Th 1: 4 and **t** you are enduring.
Jas 1: 2 whenever you face **t** of many kinds,
1Pe 1: 6 had to suffer grief in all kinds of **t**.
2Pe 2: 9 how to rescue the godly from **t**

TRIBE (HALF-TRIBE TRIBES)
Heb 7: 13 that **t** has ever served at the altar.
Rev 5: 5 the Lion of the **t** of Judah, the Root
5: 9 for God persons from every **t**
11: 9 days some from every people, **t**,
14: 6 to every nation, **t**,

TRIBES (TRIBE)
Ge 49: 28 All these are the twelve **t** of Israel,
Mt 19: 28 judging the twelve **t** of Israel.

TRIBULATION*
Rev 7: 14 who have come out of the great **t**;

TRICKERY*
Ac 13: 10 are full of all kinds of deceit and **t**.
2Co 12: 16 fellow that I am, I caught you by **t**!

TRIED (TRY)
Ps 73: 16 When I **t** to understand all this,
95: 9 they **t** me, though they had seen
Heb 3: 9 your ancestors tested and **t** me,

TRIES (TRY)
Lk 17: 33 Whoever **t** to keep their life will

TRIMMED
Mt 25: 7 virgins woke up and **t** their lamps.

TRIUMPH (TRIUMPHAL TRIUMPHED TRIUMPHING TRIUMPHS)
Ps 25: 2 nor let my enemies **t** over me.
54: 7 and my eyes have looked in **t** on
112: 8 the end they will look in **t** on their
118: 7 I look in **t** on my enemies.
Pr 28: 12 When the righteous **t**, there is great
Isa 42: 13 cry and will **t** over his enemies.
Rev 17: 14 the Lamb will **t** over them because

TRIUMPHAL* (TRIUMPH)
Isa 60: 11 their kings led in **t** procession.
2Co 2: 14 as captives in Christ's **t** procession

TRIUMPHED (TRIUMPH)
Rev 5: 5 of Judah, the Root of David, has **t**.
12: 11 They **t** over him by the blood

TRIUMPHING* (TRIUMPH)
Col 2: 15 of them, **t** over them by the cross.

TRIUMPHS* (TRIUMPH)
Jas 2: 13 Mercy **t** over judgment.

TROUBLE (TROUBLED TROUBLES TROUBLEMAKER)
Ge 41: 51 God has made me forget all my **t**
Jos 7: 25 The LORD will bring **t** on you
Job 2: 10 accept good from God, and not **t**?"
5: 7 to **t** as surely as sparks fly upward.
14: 1 are of few days and full of **t**.
42: 11 him over all the **t** the LORD had
Ps 7: 14 is pregnant with evil conceives **t**
7: 16 The **t** they cause recoils on them;
9: 9 a stronghold in times of **t**.
10: 14 you, God, see the **t** of the afflicted;
22: 11 for **t** is near and there is no one
27: 5 the day of **t** he will keep me safe
32: 7 you will protect me from **t**
37: 39 he is their stronghold in time of **t**.
41: 1 LORD delivers them in times of **t**.
46: 1 strength, an ever-present help in **t**.
50: 15 and call on me in the day of **t**;
59: 16 fortress, my refuge in times of **t**.
66: 14 my mouth spoke when I was in **t**.
91: 15 will be with him in **t**, I will deliver
107: 6 cried out to the LORD in their **t**,
107: 13 they cried to the LORD in their **t**,
119:143 **T** and distress have come upon me,
138: 7 Though I walk in the midst of **t**,
143: 11 righteousness, bring me out of **t**.
Pr 11: 8 righteous person is rescued from **t**,
12: 13 talk, and so the innocent escape **t**.
12: 21 but the wicked have their fill of **t**.
19: 23 one rests content, untouched by **t**.
24: 10 If you falter in a time of **t**,
25: 19 on the unfaithful in a time of **t**.
28: 14 hardens their heart falls into **t**.
Jer 30: 7 It will be a time of **t** for Jacob,
Na 1: 7 is good, a refuge in times of **t**.
Zep 1: 15 and anguish, a day of **t** and ruin,
Mt 6: 34 Each day has enough **t** of its own.
13: 21 When **t** or persecution comes
Jn 16: 33 In this world you will have **t**.
Ro 8: 35 Shall **t** or hardship or persecution
2Co 1: 4 any **t** with the comfort we
2Th 1: 6 He will pay back **t** to those who **t**
Jas 5: 13 Is anyone among you in **t**?

TROUBLED (TROUBLE)
Ge 6: 6 earth, and his heart was deeply **t**.
Ps 38: 18 I am **t** by my sin.
Mk 14: 33 to be deeply distressed and **t**.
Jn 14: 1 "Do not let your hearts be **t**.
14: 27 Do not let your hearts be **t** and do
2Th 1: 7 and give relief to you who are **t**,

TROUBLEMAKER (TROUBLE)
Pr 6: 12 A **t** and a villain, who goes about

TROUBLES (TROUBLE)
Ps 34: 6 he saved him out of all his **t**.
34: 17 he delivers them from all their **t**.
34: 19 righteous person may have many **t**,
40: 12 **t** without number surround me;
54: 7 have delivered me from all my **t**,
1Co 7: 28 those who marry will face many **t**
2Co 1: 4 who comforts us in all our **t**,
4: 17 momentary **t** are achieving for us
6: 4 in **t**, hardships and distresses;
7: 4 all our **t** my joy knows no bounds.
Php 4: 14 it was good of you to share in my **t**.

TRUE (TRULY TRUTH)
Nu 11: 23 not what I say will come **t** for you."
12: 7 this is not **t** of my servant Moses;
Dt 18: 22 does not take place or come **t**,
1Sa 9: 6 and everything he says comes **t**.
1Ki 10: 6 and your wisdom is **t**.
2Ch 6: 17 your servant David come **t**.
15: 3 time Israel was without the **t** God,
Ps 33: 4 word of the LORD is right and **t**;
119:142 is everlasting and your law is **t**.
119:151 and all your commands are **t**.
119:160 All your words are **t**;
Pr 8: 7 My mouth speaks what is **t**, for my
Isa 65: 16 land will swear by the one **t** God.
Jer 10: 10 But the LORD is the **t** God;
28: 9 only if his prediction comes **t**."
Eze 33: 33 "When all this comes **t**—
Lk 16: 11 who will trust you with **t** riches?
Jn 1: 9 The **t** light that gives light
Jn 4: 23 the **t** worshipers will worship
6: 32 Father who gives you the **t** bread
7: 28 authority, but he who sent me is **t**.
15: 1 "I am the **t** vine, and my Father is
17: 3 the only **t** God, and Jesus Christ,
19: 35 testimony, and his testimony is **t**.
21: 24 We know that his testimony is **t**.
Ac 10: 34 "I now realize how **t** it is that God
11: 23 them all to remain **t** to the Lord
14: 22 them to remain **t** to the faith.
17: 11 day to see if what Paul said was **t**.
Ro 3: 4 Let God be **t**, and every human
12: 1 this is your **t** and proper worship.
Php 4: 8 whatever is **t**, whatever is noble,
Col 1: 5 have already heard in the **t** message
Titus 1: 13 This saying is **t**. Therefore rebuke
1Jn 2: 8 and the **t** light is already shining.
5: 20 so that we may know him who is **t**.
5: 20 He is the **t** God and eternal life.
Rev 19: 9 "These are the **t** words of God."
22: 6 These words are trustworthy and **t**.

TRULY (TRUE)
Mt 5: 18 For **t** I tell you, until heaven
5: 26 **T** I tell you, you will not get
6: 2 **T** I tell you, they have received
6: 5 **T** I tell you, they have received
6: 16 **T** I tell you, they have received
8: 10 those following him, "**T** I tell you,
10: 15 **T** I tell you, it will be more
10: 23 **T** I tell you, you will not finish
10: 42 who is my disciple, **t** I tell you,
11: 11 **T** I tell you, among those born
13: 17 For **t** I tell you, many prophets
16: 28 "**T** I tell you, some who are
17: 20 **T** I tell you, if you have faith as
18: 3 "**T** I tell you, unless you change
18: 13 And if he finds it, **t** I tell you, he is
18: 18 "**T** I tell you, whatever you bind
19: 23 said to his disciples, "**T** I tell you,
19: 28 Jesus said to them, "**T** I tell you,
21: 21 Jesus replied, "**T** I tell you, if you
21: 31 Jesus said to them, "**T** I tell you,
23: 36 **T** I tell you, all this will come
24: 2 "**T** I tell you, not one stone here
24: 34 **T** I tell you, this generation will
24: 47 **T** I tell you, he will put him
25: 12 "But he replied, '**T** I tell you,
25: 40 "The King will reply, '**T** I tell you,
25: 45 "He will reply, '**T** I tell you,
26: 13 **T** I tell you, wherever this gospel is
26: 21 he said, "**T** I tell you, one of you
26: 34 "**T** I tell you," Jesus answered,
Mk 3: 28 **T** I tell you, people can be forgiven
8: 12 **T** I tell you, no sign will be given
9: 1 And he said to them, "**T** I tell you,
9: 41 **T** I tell you, anyone who gives you
10: 15 **T** I tell you, anyone who will not
10: 29 "**T** I tell you," Jesus replied,
11: 23 "**T** I tell you, if anyone says to this
12: 43 Jesus said, "**T** I tell you, this poor
13: 30 **T** I tell you, this generation will
14: 9 **T** I tell you, wherever the gospel is
14: 18 he said, "**T** I tell you, one of you
14: 25 "**T** I tell you, I will not drink again
14: 30 "**T** I tell you," Jesus answered,
Lk 4: 24 "**T** I tell you," he continued,
9: 27 "**T** I tell you, some who are
12: 37 **T** I tell you, he will dress himself
12: 44 **T** I tell you, he will put him
18: 17 **T** I tell you, anyone who will not
18: 29 "**T** I tell you," Jesus said to them,
21: 3 "**T** I tell you," he said, "this poor
21: 32 "**T** I tell you, this generation will
23: 43 Jesus answered him, "**T** I tell you,
Jn 1: 51 He then added, "Very **t** I tell you,
3: 3 Jesus replied, "Very **t** I tell you,
3: 5 Jesus answered, "Very **t** I tell you,
3: 11 Very **t** I tell you, we speak of what
5: 19 "Very **t** I tell you, the Son can do
5: 24 "Very **t** I tell you, whoever hears
5: 25 Very **t** I tell you, a time is coming
6: 26 Jesus answered, "Very **t** I tell you,
6: 32 said to them, "Very **t** I tell you, it is
6: 47 Very **t** I tell you, the one who
6: 53 said to them, "Very **t** I tell you,
Jn 8: 34 Jesus replied, "Very **t** I tell you,
8: 51 Very **t** I tell you, whoever obeys my
8: 58 "Very **t** I tell you," Jesus answered,
10: 1 "Very **t** I tell you Pharisees,
10: 7 Jesus said again, "Very **t** I tell you,
12: 24 Very **t** I tell you, unless a kernel
13: 16 Very **t** I tell you, no servant is
13: 20 Very **t** I tell you, whoever accepts
13: 21 and testified, "Very **t** I tell you,
13: 38 Very **t** I tell you, before the rooster
14: 12 Very **t** I tell you, whoever believes
16: 7 But very **t** I tell you, it is for your
16: 20 Very **t** I tell you, you will weep
16: 23 Very **t** I tell you, my Father will
21: 18 Very **t** I tell you, when you were
Col 1: 6 it and **t** understood God's grace.

TRUMPET (TRUMPETS)
Isa 27: 13 in that day a great **t** will sound.
Eze 33: 5 Since they heard the sound of the **t**
Zec 9: 14 Sovereign LORD will sound the **t**;
Mt 24: 31 send his angels with a loud **t** call,
1Co 14: 8 if the **t** does not sound a clear call,
15: 52 twinkling of an eye, at the last **t**.
1Th 4: 16 and with the **t** call of God,
Rev 8: 7 The first angel sounded his **t**,

TRUMPETS (TRUMPET)
Jdg 7: 19 blew their **t** and broke the jars
Rev 8: 2 and seven **t** were given to them.

TRUST (ENTRUST ENTRUSTED TRUSTED TRUSTFULLY TRUSTING TRUSTS TRUSTWORTHY)
Ex 14: 31 the LORD and put their **t** in him
19: 9 and will always put their **t** in you."
Nu 20: 12 "Because you did not **t** in me
Dt 1: 32 you did not **t** in the LORD your
9: 23 You did not **t** him or obey him.
28: 52 walls in which you **t** fall down.
Jdg 11: 20 did not **t** Israel to pass through his
2Ki 17: 14 who did not **t** in the LORD their
18: 30 not let Hezekiah persuade you to **t**
1Ch 9: 22 to their positions of **t** by David
Job 4: 18 If God places no **t** in his servants,
8: 14 What they **t** in is fragile;
15: 15 If God places no **t** in his holy ones,
31: 24 "If I have put my **t** in gold or said
39: 12 Can you **t** it to haul in your grain
Ps 4: 5 the righteous and **t** in the LORD.
9: 10 Those who know your name **t**
13: 5 But I **t** in your unfailing love;
20: 7 Some **t** in chariots and some
20: 7 we **t** in the name of the LORD our
22: 9 you made me **t** in you, even at
22: 4 In you our ancestors put their **t**;
25: 2 I **t** in you; do not let me be put
31: 6 as for me, I **t** in the LORD.
31: 14 But I **t** in you, LORD; I say,
33: 21 rejoice, for we **t** in his holy name.
37: 3 **T** in the LORD and do good;
37: 5 **t** in him and he will do this:
40: 3 the LORD and put their **t** in him.
44: 6 I put no **t** in my bow, my sword
49: 6 those who **t** in their wealth
49: 13 fate of those who **t** in themselves,
52: 8 I **t** in God's unfailing love for ever
55: 23 But as for me, I **t** in you.
56: 3 I am afraid, I put my **t** in you.
56: 4 in God I **t** and am not afraid.
56: 11 in God I **t** and am not afraid.
62: 8 **T** in him at all times, you people;
62: 10 Do not **t** in extortion or put vain
78: 7 they would put their **t** in God
78: 22 in God or **t** in his deliverance.
91: 2 my fortress, my God, in whom I **t**."
115: 8 and so will all who **t** in them.
115: 9 All you Israelites, **t** in the LORD—
115: 10 House of Aaron, **t** in the LORD—
115: 11 who fear him, **t** in the LORD—
118: 8 in the LORD than to **t** in humans.
118: 9 in the LORD than to **t** in princes.
119: 42 taunts me, for I **t** in your word.
125: 1 Those who **t** in the LORD are like
135: 18 and so will all who **t** in them.
143: 8 love, for I have put my **t** in you.
146: 3 Do not put your **t** in princes,
Pr 3: 5 **T** in the LORD with all your heart

Pr 11: 28 who **t** in their riches will fall,
21: 22 the stronghold in which they **t**.
22: 19 So that your **t** may be
28: 25 but those who **t** in the LORD will
28: 26 Those who **t** in themselves are
Isa 8: 17 I will put my **t** in him.
12: 2 I will **t** and not be afraid.
26: 3 are steadfast, because they **t** in you.
26: 4 **T** in the LORD forever,
30: 15 in quietness and **t** is your strength,
31: 1 who **t** in the multitude of their
36: 15 not let Hezekiah persuade you to **t**
42: 17 But those who **t** in idols, who say
50: 10 **t** in the name of the LORD
Jer 2: 37 the LORD has rejected those you **t**;
5: 17 the fortified cities in which you **t**.
7: 4 not **t** in deceptive words and say,
7: 14 temple you **t** in, the place I gave
9: 4 do not **t** anyone in your clan.
12: 6 Do not **t** them, though they speak
28: 15 you have persuaded this nation to **t**
39: 18 with your life, because you **t** in me,
48: 7 Since you **t** in your deeds
49: 4 you **t** in your riches and say,
Eze 33: 13 then they **t** in their righteousness
Mic 7: 5 Do not **t** a neighbor;
Na 1: 7 He cares for those who **t** in him,
Zep 3: 2 She does not **t** in the LORD,
3: 12 remnant of Israel will **t** in the name
Lk 16: 11 who will **t** you with true riches?
Ac 14: 23 in whom they had put their **t**.
Ro 15: 13 all joy and peace as you **t** in him,
1Co 4: 2 been given a **t** must prove faithful.
9: 17 discharging the **t** committed
2Co 13: 6 I **t** that you will discover that we
Heb 2: 13 again, "I will put my **t** in him."

TRUSTED* (TRUST)
1Sa 27: 12 Achish **t** David and said to himself,
2Ki 18: 5 Hezekiah **t** in the LORD, the God
1Ch 5: 20 prayers, because they **t** in him.
Job 12: 20 He silences the lips of **t** advisers
Ps 5: 9 a word from their mouth can be **t**;
22: 4 they **t** and you delivered them.
22: 5 in you they **t** and were not put
26: 1 I have **t** in the LORD and have not
41: 9 someone I **t**, one who shared my
52: 7 stronghold but **t** in his great wealth
116: 10 I **t** in the LORD when I said,
Pr 27: 6 Wounds from a friend can be **t**,
Isa 20: 5 Those who **t** in Cush and boasted
25: 9 we **t** in him, and he saved us.
25: 9 This is the LORD, we **t** in him;
47: 10 You have **t** in your wickedness
Jer 13: 25 forgotten me and **t** in false gods.
38: 22 those **t** friends of yours.
48: 13 ashamed when they **t** in Bethel.
Eze 16: 15 "'But you **t** in your beauty
Da 3: 28 They **t** in him and defied the king's
6: 23 him, because he had **t** in his God.
Lk 11: 22 away the armor in which the man **t**
16: 10 "Whoever can be **t** with very little
can also be **t** with much,
Ac 12: 20 a **t** personal servant of the king,
Titus 2: 10 but to show that they can be fully **t**,
3: 8 those who have **t** in God may be

TRUSTFULLY* (TRUST)
Pr 3: 29 neighbor, who lives **t** near you.

TRUSTING* (TRUST)
Job 15: 31 himself by **t** what is worthless,
Ps 112: 7 hearts are steadfast, **t** in the LORD.
Isa 2: 22 Stop **t** in mere humans, who have
Jer 7: 8 you are **t** in deceptive words that

TRUSTS* (TRUST)
Ps 21: 7 For the king **t** in the LORD;
22: 8 "He **t** in the LORD," they say,
28: 7 heart **t** in him, and he helps me.
32: 10 love surrounds the one who **t**
40: 4 Blessed is the one who **t**
84: 12 blessed is the one who **t** in you.
86: 2 save your servant who **t** in you.
Pr 16: 20 and blessed is the one who **t**
29: 25 whoever **t** in the LORD is kept
Jer 17: 5 "Cursed is the one who **t** in man,
17: 7 "But blessed is the one who **t**
Hab 2: 18 the one who makes it **t** in his own
Mt 27: 43 He **t** in God. Let God rescue him
Ro 4: 5 **t** God who justifies the ungodly,
1Co 13: 7 protects, always **t**, always hopes,
1Pe 2: 6 the one who **t** in him will never be

TRUSTWORTHY* (TRUST)
Ex 18: 21 **t** men who hate dishonest gain—
2Sa 7: 28 Your covenant is **t**, and you have
Ne 13: 13 because they were considered **t**.
Ps 19: 7 The statutes of the LORD are **t**,
111: 7 all his precepts are **t**.
119: 86 All your commands are **t**;
119:138 are righteous; they are fully **t**.
145: 13 The LORD is **t** in all he promises
Pr 8: 6 Listen, for I have **t** things to say;
11: 13 but a **t** person keeps a secret.
12: 22 but he delights in people who are **t**.
13: 17 but a **t** envoy brings healing.
25: 13 harvest time is a **t** messenger
Da 2: 45 is true and its interpretation is **t**."
6: 4 he was **t** and neither corrupt
Lk 16: 11 if you have not been **t** in handling
16: 12 you have not been **t** with someone
19: 17 'Because you have been **t** in a very
Jn 8: 26 But he who sent me is **t**, and what I
1Co 7: 25 one who by the Lord's mercy is **t**.
1Ti 1: 12 that he considered me **t**,
1: 15 Here is a **t** saying that deserves full
3: 1 Here is a **t** saying:
3: 11 but temperate and **t** in everything.
4: 9 This is a **t** saying that deserves full
2Ti 2: 11 Here is a **t** saying: If we died
Titus 1: 9 the **t** message as it has been taught,
3: 8 This is a **t** saying. And I want you
Rev 21: 5 for these words are **t** and true."
22: 6 to me, "These words are **t** and true.

TRUTH* (TRUE TRUTHFUL TRUTHFULNESS TRUTHS)
Ge 42: 16 tested to see if you are telling the **t**.
1Ki 17: 24 LORD from your mouth is the **t**."
22: 16 the **t** in the name of the LORD?"
2Ch 18: 15 the **t** in the name of the LORD?"
Job 42: 7 have not spoken the **t** about me,
42: 8 have not spoken the **t** about me,
Ps 15: 2 who speaks the **t** from their heart;
25: 5 Guide me in your **t** and teach me,
45: 4 forth victoriously in the cause of **t**,
52: 3 rather than speaking the **t**.
119: 43 Never take your word of **t** from my
145: 18 on him, to all who call on him in **t**.
Pr 12: 17 An honest witness tells the **t**,
22: 21 to be honest and to speak the **t**,
23: 23 Buy the **t** and do not sell it—
Isa 45: 19 I, the LORD, speak the **t**;
48: 1 but not in **t** or righteousness—
59: 14 **t** has stumbled in the streets,
59: 15 **T** is nowhere to be found,
Jer 5: 1 who deals honestly and seeks the **t**,
5: 3 do not your eyes look for **t**?
7: 28 **T** has perished; it has vanished
9: 3 it is not by **t** that they triumph
9: 5 friend, and no one speaks the **t**.
26: 15 in **t** the LORD has sent me to you
Da 8: 12 and **t** was thrown to the ground.
9: 13 sins and giving attention to your **t**.
10: 21 what is written in the Book of **T**.
11: 2 "Now then, I tell you the **t**:
Am 5: 10 and detest the one who tells the **t**.
Zec 8: 16 Speak the **t** to each other, and
8: 19 Therefore love **t** and peace."
Mt 22: 16 of God in accordance with the **t**.
Mk 5: 33 with fear, told him the whole **t**.
12: 14 of God in accordance with the **t**.
Lk 20: 21 of God in accordance with the **t**.
Jn 1: 14 from the Father, full of grace and **t**.
1: 17 and **t** came through Jesus Christ.
3: 21 whoever lives by the **t** comes
4: 23 the Father in the Spirit and in **t**,
4: 24 worship in the Spirit and in **t**."
5: 33 John and he has testified to the **t**.
7: 18 the one who sent him is a man of **t**;
8: 32 Then you will know the **t**, and the **t**
8: 40 a man who has told you the **t** that I
8: 44 not holding to the **t**, for there is
no **t** in him.
8: 45 Yet because I tell the **t**, you do not
Jn 8: 46 If I am telling the **t**, why don't you
9: 24 glory to God by telling the **t**,"
14: 6 am the way and the **t** and the life.
14: 17 the Spirit of **t**. The world cannot
15: 26 the Spirit of **t** who goes
16: 13 when he, the Spirit of **t**, comes,
16: 13 he will guide you into all the **t**.
17: 17 Sanctify them by the **t**; your word
is **t**.
18: 23 But if I spoke the **t**, why did you
18: 37 into the world is to testify to the **t**.
18: 37 on the side of **t** listens to me."
18: 38 "What is **t**?" retorted Pilate.
19: 35 He knows that he tells the **t**, and he
Ac 20: 30 distort the **t** in order to draw away
21: 24 everyone will know there is no **t**
21: 34 could not get at the **t** because
24: 8 learn the **t** about all these charges
28: 25 "The Holy Spirit spoke the **t**
Ro 1: 18 people, who suppress the **t** by their
1: 25 They exchanged the **t** about God
2: 2 who do such things is based on **t**.
2: 8 who reject the **t** and follow evil,
2: 20 embodiment of knowledge and **t**—
9: 1 I speak the **t** in Christ—I am not
15: 8 of the Jews on behalf of God's **t**,
1Co 5: 8 bread of sincerity and **t**.
13: 6 in evil but rejoices with the **t**.
2Co 4: 2 by setting forth the **t** plainly we
11: 10 As surely as the **t** of Christ is in me,
12: 6 because I would be speaking the **t**.
13: 8 we cannot do anything against the **t**,
but only for the **t**.
Gal 2: 5 so that the **t** of the gospel might be
2: 14 in line with the **t** of the gospel,
4: 16 your enemy by telling you the **t**?
5: 7 to keep you from obeying the **t**?
Eph 1: 13 when you heard the message of **t**,
4: 15 Instead, speaking the **t** in love,
4: 21 in accordance with the **t** that is
5: 9 all goodness, righteousness and **t**)
6: 14 belt of **t** buckled around your waist
2Th 2: 10 because they refused to love the **t**
2: 12 who have not believed the **t**
2: 13 Spirit and through belief in the **t**.
1Ti 2: 4 to come to a knowledge of the **t**.
2: 7 I am telling the **t**, I am not lying—
3: 15 the pillar and foundation of the **t**.
4: 3 who believe and who know the **t**.
6: 5 who have been robbed of the **t**
2Ti 2: 15 correctly handles the word of **t**.
2: 18 who have departed from the **t**.
2: 25 them to a knowledge of the **t**,
3: 7 to come to a knowledge of the **t**.
3: 8 so also these teachers oppose the **t**.
4: 4 will turn their ears away from the **t**
Titus 1: 1 their knowledge of the **t** that leads
1: 14 of those who reject the **t**.
Heb 10: 26 received the knowledge of the **t**,
Jas 1: 18 give us birth through the word of **t**,
3: 14 do not boast about it or deny the **t**.
5: 19 of you should wander from the **t**
1Pe 1: 22 by obeying the **t** so that you have
2Pe 1: 12 established in the **t** you now have.
2: 2 and will bring the way of **t**
1Jn 1: 6 we lie and do not live out the **t**.
1: 8 ourselves and the **t** is not in us.
2: 4 liar, and the **t** is not in that person.
2: 8 its **t** is seen in him and in you,
2: 20 One, and all of you know the **t**.
2: 21 because you do not know the **t**,
2: 21 because no lie comes from the **t**.
3: 18 or speech but with actions and in **t**.
3: 19 we know that we belong to the **t**
4: 6 is how we recognize the Spirit of **t**
5: 6 testifies, because the Spirit is the **t**.
2Jn : 1 children, whom I love in the **t**—
: 1 but also all who know the **t**—
: 2 because of the **t**, which lives in us
: 3 Son, will be with us in **t** and love.
: 4 of your children walking in the **t**,
3Jn : 1 friend Gaius, whom I love in the **t**.
: 3 about your faithfulness to the **t**,
: 4 my children are walking in the **t**.
: 8 we may work together for the **t**.
: 12 and even by the **t** itself.

TRUTHFUL* (TRUTH)
Pr 12: 19 **T** lips endure forever, but a lying
14: 25 A **t** witness saves lives, but a false
22: 21 you bring back **t** reports to those
Jer 4: 2 and if in a **t**, just and righteous way
Jn 3: 33 it has certified that God is **t**.
2Co 6: 7 **t** speech and in the power of God;

TRUTHFULNESS* (TRUTH)
Ro 3: 7 "If my falsehood enhances God's **t**

TRUTHS* (TRUTH)
1Ti 3: 9 keep hold of the deep **t** of the faith
4: 6 nourished on the **t** of the faith
Heb 5: 12 teach you the elementary **t** of God's

TRY (TRIED TRIES TRYING)
Ps 26: 2 and **t** me, examine my heart and
Isa 7: 13 Will you **t** the patience of my God
Lk 12: 58 **t** hard to be reconciled on the way,
13: 24 will **t** to enter and will not be able
1Co 10: 33 even as I **t** to please everyone
14: 12 **t** to excel in those that build
2Co 5: 11 the Lord, we **t** to persuade others.
Titus 2: 9 in everything, to **t** to please them,

TRYING (TRY)
2Co 5: 12 We are not **t** to commend ourselves
Gal 1: 10 Or am I **t** to please people? If I
1Th 2: 4 We are not **t** to please people
1Pe 1: 11 **t** to find out the time
1Jn 2: 26 those who are **t** to lead you astray.

TUMORS
1Sa 5: 6 on them and afflicted them with **t**.

TUNE
1Co 14: 7 know what **t** is being played

TUNIC
Ex 28: 4 a woven **t**, a turban and a sash.

TURMOIL
Ps 65: 7 waves, and the **t** of the nations.
Pr 15: 16 LORD than great wealth with **t**.

TURN (TURNED TURNING TURNS)
Ex 32: 12 **T** from your fierce anger;
Nu 32: 15 If you **t** away from following him,
Dt 5: 32 do not **t** aside to the right
28: 14 Do not **t** aside from any
30: 10 **t** to the LORD your God with all
Jos 1: 7 do not **t** from it to the right
1Ki 8: 58 May he **t** our hearts to him, to walk
2Ch 7: 14 face and **t** from their wicked ways,
30: 9 He will not **t** his face from you
Job 33: 30 to **t** them back from the pit,
Ps 28: 1 my Rock, do not **t** a deaf ear to me.
34: 14 **T** from evil and do good;
51: 13 so that sinners will **t** back to you.
78: 6 they in **t** would tell their children.
119: 36 **T** my heart toward your statutes
119:132 **T** to me and have mercy on me,
Pr 4: 5 my words or **t** away from them.
4: 27 Do not **t** to the right or the left;
22: 6 they are old they will not **t** from it.
Isa 17: 7 and **t** their eyes to the Holy One
28: 6 to those who **t** back the battle
29: 16 You **t** things upside down,
30: 21 Whether you **t** to the right
45: 22 "**T** to me and be saved, all you ends
55: 7 Let them **t** to the LORD, and he
Jer 31: 13 I will **t** their mourning
Eze 33: 9 do warn the wicked person to **t**
33: 11 they **t** from their ways and live.
Jnh 3: 9 compassion **t** from his fierce anger
Mal 4: 6 He will **t** the hearts of the parents
Mt 5: 39 **t** to them the other cheek also.
10: 35 to **t** "'a man against his father,
Lk 1: 17 to **t** the hearts of the parents to
Jn 12: 40 understand with their hearts, nor **t**
16: 20 grieve, but your grief will **t** to joy.
Ac 3: 19 and **t** to God, so that your sins may
26: 18 and **t** them from darkness to light,
1Co 14: 31 For you can all prophesy in **t** so
15: 23 each in **t**: Christ, the firstfruits;
1Ti 6: 20 **T** away from godless chatter
1Pe 3: 11 must **t** from evil and do good;

TURNED (TURN)
Dt 23: 5 **t** the curse into a blessing for you,
1Ki 11: 4 old, his wives **t** his heart after other
2Ch 15: 4 their distress they **t** to the LORD,
Est 9: 1 now the tables were **t** and the Jews
9: 22 when their sorrow was **t** into joy
Ps 14: 3 All have **t** away, all have become
30: 11 You **t** my wailing into dancing;
40: 1 he **t** to me and heard my cry.
41: 9 shared my bread, has **t** against me.
Isa 9: 12 his anger is not **t** away, his hand is
53: 6 each of us has **t** to our own way;
Hos 7: 8 Ephraim is a flat loaf not **t** over.
Joel 2: 31 The sun will be **t** to darkness
Lk 22: 32 And when you have **t** back,
Jn 13: 18 shared my bread has **t** against me.'
Ro 3: 12 All have **t** away, they have together

TURNING (TURN)
2Ki 21: 13 wiping it and **t** it upside down.
Pr 2: 2 **t** your ear to wisdom and applying
14: 27 **t** a person from the snares of death.

TURNS (TURN)
2Sa 22: 29 the LORD **t** my darkness
Pr 15: 1 A gentle answer **t** away wrath,
Isa 44: 25 of the wise and **t** it into nonsense,
Jas 5: 20 Whoever **t** a sinner from the error

TWELVE
Ge 35: 22 Israel heard of it. Jacob had **t** sons:
49: 28 All these are the **t** tribes of Israel,
Mt 10: 1 Jesus called his **t** disciples to him
Mk 3: 14 He appointed **t** that they might be
Lk 9: 17 the disciples picked up **t** basketfuls
Rev 21: 12 high wall with **t** gates, and with
21: 12 written the names of the **t** tribes
21: 14 wall of the city had **t** foundations,
21: 14 were the names of the **t** apostles

TWIN (TWINS)
Ge 25: 24 there were **t** boys in her womb.

TWINKLING*
1Co 15: 52 a flash, in the **t** of an eye, at the last

TWINS* (TWIN)
Ro 9: 11 before the **t** were born or had done

TWISTING* (TWISTS)
Pr 30: 33 and as **t** the nose produces blood,

TWISTS (TWISTING)
Ex 23: 8 and **t** the words of the innocent.

TYRANNICAL*
Pr 28: 16 A **t** ruler practices extortion, but

TYRE
Eze 28: 12 a lament concerning the king of **T**
Mt 11: 22 it will be more bearable for **T**

UNAPPROACHABLE*
1Ti 6: 16 immortal and who lives in **u** light,

UNASHAMED*
1Jn 2: 28 and **u** before him at his coming.

UNBELIEF* (UNBELIEVER UNBELIEVERS UNBELIEVING)
Mk 9: 24 help me overcome my **u**!"
Ro 4: 20 not waver through **u** regarding
11: 20 they were broken off because of **u**,
11: 23 And if they do not persist in **u**,
1Ti 1: 13 because I acted in ignorance and **u**.
Heb 3: 19 able to enter, because of their **u**.

UNBELIEVER* (UNBELIEF)
1Co 7: 15 But if the **u** leaves, let it be so.
10: 27 If an **u** invites you to a meal
14: 24 if an **u** or an inquirer comes in
2Co 6: 15 have in common with an **u**?
1Ti 5: 8 the faith and is worse than an **u**.

UNBELIEVERS* (UNBELIEF)
Lk 12: 46 and assign him a place with the **u**.
Ro 15: 31 be kept safe from the **u** in Judea
1Co 6: 6 and this in front of **u**!
14: 22 a sign, not for believers but for **u**;
14: 22 is not for **u** but for believers.
14: 23 inquirers or **u** come in, will they
2Co 4: 4 age has blinded the minds of **u**,
6: 14 Do not be yoked together with **u**.

UNBELIEVING* (UNBELIEF)
Mt 17: 17 "You **u** and perverse generation,"
Mk 9: 19 "You **u** generation," Jesus replied,
Lk 9: 41 "You **u** and perverse generation,"
1Co 7: 14 the **u** husband has been sanctified
7: 14 and the **u** wife has been sanctified
Heb 3: 12 **u** heart that turns away
Rev 21: 8 But the cowardly, the **u**, the vile,

UNBLEMISHED*
Heb 9: 14 the eternal Spirit offered himself **u**

UNCEASING
Ro 9: 2 sorrow and **u** anguish in my heart.

UNCERTAIN*
1Ti 6: 17 which is so **u**, but to put their hope

UNCHANGEABLE* (UNCHANGING)
Heb 6: 18 that, by two **u** things in which it is

UNCHANGING* (UNCHANGEABLE)
Heb 6: 17 make the **u** nature of his purpose

UNCIRCUMCISED
Lev 26: 41 when their **u** hearts are humbled
1Sa 17: 26 Who is this **u** Philistine that he
Jer 9: 26 whole house of Israel is **u** in heart."
Ac 7: 51 Your hearts and ears are still **u**.
Ro 4: 11 he had by faith while he was still **u**.
1Co 7: 18 Was a man **u** when he was called?
Col 3: 11 Jew, circumcised or **u**, barbarian,

UNCIRCUMCISION
1Co 7: 19 is nothing and **u** is nothing.
Gal 5: 6 neither circumcision nor **u** has any

UNCLEAN
Ge 7: 2 one pair of every kind of **u** animal,
Lev 10: 10 between the **u** and the clean,
11: 4 it is ceremonially **u** for you.
11: 10 the water—you are to regard as **u**.
17: 15 will be ceremonially **u** till evening;
Isa 6: 5 and I live among a people of **u** lips,
52: 11 Touch no **u** thing! Come out from
Ac 10: 14 never eaten anything impure or **u**."
Ro 14: 14 Jesus, that nothing is **u** in itself.
2Co 6: 17 Touch no **u** thing, and I will

UNCLOTHED*
2Co 5: 4 because we do not wish to be **u**

UNCONCERNED*
Eze 16: 49 were arrogant, overfed and **u**;

UNCOVERED
Ru 3: 7 quietly, **u** his feet and lay down.
1Co 11: 5 her head **u** dishonors her head—
11: 13 to pray to God with her head **u**?
Heb 4: 13 Everything is **u** and laid bare

UNDERGOES* (UNDERGOING)
Heb 12: 8 and everyone **u** discipline—

UNDERGOING* (UNDERGOES)
1Pe 5: 9 the world is **u** the same kind

UNDERSTAND (UNDERSTANDING UNDERSTANDS UNDERSTOOD)
Job 38: 4 Tell me, if you **u**.
42: 3 Surely I spoke of things I did not **u**,
Ps 14: 2 to see if there are any who **u**,
73: 16 I tried to **u** all this, it troubled
119: 27 Cause me to **u** the way of your
119:125 that I may **u** your statutes.
Pr 2: 5 you will **u** the fear of the LORD
2: 9 Then you will **u** what is right
30: 18 for me, four that I do not **u**:
Ecc 7: 25 to **u** the stupidity of wickedness
11: 5 so you cannot **u** the work of God,
Isa 6: 10 with their ears, **u** with their hearts,
44: 18 minds closed so they cannot **u**.
52: 15 they have not heard, they will **u**.
Jer 17: 9 and beyond cure. Who can **u** it?
31: 19 after I came to **u**, I beat my breast.
Da 9: 25 "Know and **u** this: From the time
Hos 14: 9 Let them **u**. The ways
Mt 13: 15 ears, **u** with their hearts and turn,
24: 15 let the reader **u**—
Lk 24: 45 so they could **u** the Scriptures.
Ac 8: 30 "Do you **u** what you are reading?"
Ro 7: 15 I do not **u** what I do. For what I
15: 21 those who have not heard will **u**."
1Co 2: 12 that we may **u** what God has freely
2: 14 and cannot **u** them because they
Eph 5: 17 but **u** what the Lord's will is.
1Ti 6: 4 they are conceited and **u** nothing.
Heb 11: 3 By faith we **u** that the universe was
2Pe 1: 20 all, you must **u** that no prophecy
3: 3 all, you must **u** that in the last days
3: 16 some things that are hard to **u**,

UNDERSTANDING (UNDERSTAND)
1Ki 4: 29 of **u** as measureless as the sand
Job 12: 12 Does not long life bring **u**?
28: 12 Where does **u** dwell?
28: 28 is wisdom, and to shun evil is **u**."
32: 8 of the Almighty, that gives them **u**.
36: 26 How great is God—beyond our **u**!
37: 5 he does great things beyond our **u**.
Ps 111: 10 follow his precepts have good **u**.
119: 32 for you have broadened my **u**.
119: 34 Give me **u**, so that I may keep your
119:100 I have more **u** than the elders,
119:104 I gain **u** from your precepts;
119:130 it gives **u** to the simple.
136: 5 who by his **u** made the heavens,
147: 5 his **u** has no limit.
Pr 2: 2 and applying your heart to **u**—
2: 6 his mouth come knowledge and **u**.
3: 5 heart and lean not on your own **u**;
3: 13 find wisdom, those who gain **u**,
4: 5 Get wisdom, get **u**; do not forget
4: 7 Though it cost all you have, get **u**.
9: 10 knowledge of the Holy One is **u**.
10: 23 a person of **u** delights in wisdom.
11: 12 one who has **u** holds their tongue.
14: 29 Whoever is patient has great **u**,
15: 21 but whoever has **u** keeps a straight
15: 32 one who heeds correction gains **u**.
17: 27 whoever has **u** is even-tempered.
18: 2 Fools find no pleasure in **u**
19: 8 the one who cherishes **u** will soon
Isa 11: 2 the Spirit of wisdom and of **u**,
40: 28 and his **u** no one can fathom.
56: 11 They are shepherds who lack **u**;
Jer 3: 15 lead you with knowledge and **u**.
9: 24 that they have the **u** to know me,
10: 12 stretched out the heavens by his **u**.
Da 5: 12 a keen mind and knowledge and **u**,
10: 12 that you set your mind to gain **u**
Hos 4: 11 and new wine take away their **u**.
Mk 4: 12 and ever hearing but never **u**;
12: 33 with all your **u** and with all your
Lk 2: 47 heard him was amazed at his **u**
2Co 6: 6 in purity, **u**, patience and kindness;
Eph 1: 8 With all wisdom and **u**,
Php 4: 7 which transcends all **u**, will guard
Col 1: 9 wisdom and **u** that the Spirit gives,
2: 2 have the full riches of complete **u**,
1Jn 5: 20 God has come and has given us **u**,

UNDERSTANDS (UNDERSTAND)
1Ch 28: 9 every heart and **u** every desire
Mt 13: 23 who hears the word and **u** it.
Ro 3: 11 there is no one who **u**; there is no

UNDERSTOOD (UNDERSTAND)
Ne 8: 8 the people **u** what was being read.
8: 12 because they now **u** the words
Ps 73: 17 then I **u** their final destiny.
Isa 40: 21 Have you not **u** since the earth was
Ro 1: 20 being **u** from what has been made,

UNDESIRABLE*
Jos 24: 15 serving the LORD seems **u** to you,

UNDIVIDED*
1Ch 12: 33 to help David with **u** loyalty—
Ps 86: 11 give me an **u** heart, that I may fear
Eze 11: 19 I will give them an **u** heart and put
1Co 7: 35 in a right way in **u** devotion

UNDOING
Pr 18: 7 The mouths of fools are their **u**,

UNDYING*
Eph 6: 24 Lord Jesus Christ with an **u** love.

UNENDING
Ps 21: 6 you have granted him **u** blessings

UNEQUALED*
Mt 24: 21 **u** from the beginning of the world
Mk 13: 19 of distress **u** from the beginning,

UNFADING*
1Pe 3: 4 the **u** beauty of a gentle and quiet

UNFAILING
Ex 15: 13 **u** love you will lead the people
1Sa 20: 14 But show me **u** kindness like
2Sa 22: 51 shows **u** kindness to his anointed,
Ps 6: 4 save me because of your **u** love.
Ps 13: 5 But I trust in your **u** love;
18: 50 he shows **u** love to his anointed,
21: 7 the **u** love of the Most High
26: 3 always been mindful of your **u** love
31: 16 save me in your **u** love.
32: 10 the LORD's **u** love surrounds
33: 5 the earth is full of his **u** love.
33: 18 those whose hope is in his **u** love,
33: 22 May your **u** love be with us,
36: 7 How priceless is your **u** love,
44: 26 rescue us because of your **u** love.
48: 9 God, we meditate on your **u** love.
51: 1 O God, according to your **u** love;
52: 8 I trust in God's **u** love for ever
77: 8 Has his **u** love vanished forever?
85: 7 Show us your **u** love, LORD,
90: 14 in the morning with your **u** love,
107: 8 thanks to the LORD for his **u** love
107: 15 thanks to the LORD for his **u** love
107: 21 thanks to the LORD for his **u** love
107: 31 thanks to the LORD for his **u** love
119: 41 May your **u** love come to me,
119: 76 May your **u** love be my comfort,
130: 7 for with the LORD is **u** love
143: 8 bring me word of your **u** love, for I
143: 12 In your **u** love, silence my enemies;
147: 11 who put their hope in his **u** love.
Pr 19: 22 What a person desires is **u** love;
20: 6 Many claim to have **u** love,
Isa 54: 10 yet my **u** love for you will not be
La 3: 32 compassion, so great is his **u** love.
Hos 10: 12 reap the fruit of **u** love, and break

UNFAITHFUL (UNFAITHFULNESS)
Lev 6: 2 is **u** to the LORD by deceiving
Nu 5: 6 and so is **u** to the LORD is guilty
1Ch 10: 13 Saul died because he was **u**
Pr 11: 6 the **u** are trapped by evil desires.
13: 2 the **u** have an appetite for violence.
13: 15 but the way of the **u** leads to their
22: 12 he frustrates the words of the **u**.
23: 28 and multiplies the **u** among men.
25: 19 foot is reliance on the **u** in a time
Jer 3: 20 Israel, have been **u** to me,"
Mal 2: 10 by being **u** to one another?
2: 11 Judah has been **u**. A detestable
2: 14 You have been **u** to her, though she
2: 15 and do not be **u** to the wife of your
2: 16 be on your guard, and do not be **u**.
Ro 3: 3 What if some were **u**?

UNFAITHFULNESS (UNFAITHFUL)
1Ch 9: 1 to Babylon because of their **u**.
Ro 3: 3 Will their **u** nullify God's

UNFIT*
Titus 1: 16 and **u** for doing anything good.

UNFOLDING*
Ps 119:130 The **u** of your words gives light;

UNFORGIVING*
2Ti 3: 3 without love, **u**, slanderous,

UNFRIENDLY*
Pr 18: 1 An **u** person pursues selfish ends

UNFRUITFUL
1Co 14: 14 my spirit prays, but my mind is **u**.

UNGODLINESS (UNGODLY)
Titus 2: 12 It teaches us to say "No" to **u**

UNGODLY (UNGODLINESS)
Ro 4: 5 but trusts God who justifies the **u**,
5: 6 powerless, Christ died for the **u**.
1Ti 1: 9 and rebels, the **u** and sinful,
2Ti 2: 16 in it will become more and more **u**.
2Pe 2: 6 of what is going to happen to the **u**;
Jude : 15 all the defiant words **u** sinners have

UNGRATEFUL*
Lk 6: 35 because he is kind to the **u**
2Ti 3: 2 disobedient to their parents, **u**,

UNHOLY*
1Ti 1: 9 and sinful, the **u** and irreligious,
2Ti 3: 2 to their parents, ungrateful, **u**,
Heb 10: 29 has treated as an **u** thing the blood

UNINTENTIONALLY
Lev 4: 2 'When anyone sins **u** and does
Nu 15: 22 you as a community **u** fail to keep
Dt 4: 42 had **u** killed a neighbor without

UNITE (UNITED UNITY)
1Co 6: 15 and **u** them with a prostitute?

UNITED (UNITE)
Ge 2: 24 and mother and is **u** to his wife,
Mt 19: 5 and mother and be **u** to his wife,
Ro 6: 5 be **u** with him in a resurrection
Eph 5: 31 and mother and be **u** to his wife,
Php 2: 1 from being **u** with Christ, if any
Col 2: 2 encouraged in heart and **u** in love,

UNITY* (UNITE)
2Ch 30: 12 the people to give them **u** of mind
Ps 133: 1 God's people live together in **u**!
Jn 17: 23 may be brought to complete **u**.
Eph 1: 10 to bring **u** to all things in heaven
4: 3 keep the **u** of the Spirit through
4: 13 until we all reach **u** in the faith
Col 3: 14 them all together in perfect **u**.

UNIVERSE*
1Co 4: 9 made a spectacle to the whole **u**,
Eph 4: 10 in order to fill the whole **u**.)
Heb 1: 2 through whom also he made the **u**.
11: 3 understand that the **u** was formed

UNJUST
Ro 3: 5 God is **u** in bringing his wrath
9: 14 shall we say? Is God **u**? Not at all!
1Pe 2: 19 pain of **u** suffering because they

UNKNOWN
Ac 17: 23 with this inscription: TO AN **U** GOD.

UNLEAVENED
Ex 12: 17 "Celebrate the Festival of **U** Bread,
Dt 16: 16 at the Festival of **U** Bread,

UNMARRIED
1Co 7: 8 good for them to stay **u**, as I do.
7: 32 An **u** man is concerned

UNPLOWED
Ex 23: 11 the seventh year let the land lie **u**
Hos 10: 12 love, and break up your **u** ground;

UNPRODUCTIVE
Titus 3: 14 urgent needs and not live **u** lives.
2Pe 1: 8 **u** in your knowledge of our Lord

UNPROFITABLE
Titus 3: 9 because these are **u** and useless.

UNPUNISHED
Ex 34: 7 Yet he does not leave the guilty **u**;
Pr 6: 29 no one who touches her will go **u**.
11: 21 The wicked will not go **u**, but those
19: 5 A false witness will not go **u**,

UNQUENCHABLE
Lk 3: 17 will burn up the chaff with **u** fire."

UNREASONING*
2Pe 2: 12 They are like **u** animals,

UNREPENTANT*
Ro 2: 5 stubbornness and your **u** heart,

UNRIGHTEOUS*
Isa 55: 7 ways and the **u** their thoughts.
Zep 3: 5 not fail, yet the **u** know no shame.
Mt 5: 45 rain on the righteous and the **u**.
1Pe 3: 18 righteous for the **u**, to bring you
2Pe 2: 9 to hold the **u** for punishment

UNSEARCHABLE
Ro 11: 33 How **u** his judgments, and his

UNSEEN*
Mt 6: 6 and pray to your Father, who is **u**.
6: 18 but only to your Father, who is **u**;
2Co 4: 18 but on what is **u**, since what is seen
4: 18 temporary, but what is **u** is eternal.

UNSETTLED*
1Th 3: 3 no one would be **u** by these trials.
2Th 2: 2 not to become easily **u** or alarmed

UNSHRUNK
Mt 9: 16 "No one sews a patch of **u** cloth

UNSPIRITUAL*
Ro 7: 14 but I am **u**, sold as a slave to sin.
Col 2: 18 with idle notions by their **u** mind.
Jas 3: 15 down from heaven but is earthly, **u**,

UNSTABLE*
Jas 1: 8 double-minded and **u** in all they
2Pe 2: 14 they seduce the **u**; they are experts
3: 16 ignorant and **u** people distort,

UNTHINKABLE*
Job 34: 12 It is **u** that God would do wrong,

UNTIE
Mk 1: 7 not worthy to stoop down and **u**.
Lk 13: 15 of you on the Sabbath **u** your ox

UNTRAINED*
2Co 11: 6 I may indeed be **u** as a speaker,

UNVEILED*
2Co 3: 18 with **u** faces contemplate the Lord's

UNWARY*
Ps 116: 6 The LORD protects the **u**;

UNWHOLESOME*
Eph 4: 29 Do not let any **u** talk come

UNWISE
Eph 5: 15 how you live—not as **u** but as wise,

UNWORTHY*
Ge 32: 10 I am **u** of all the kindness
Job 40: 4 "I am **u**—how can I reply to you?
Lk 17: 10 do, should say, 'We are **u** servants;
1Co 11: 27 Lord in an **u** manner will be guilty

UPHOLD (UPHOLDS)
Ps 82: 3 **u** the cause of the poor
Isa 41: 10 I will **u** you with my righteous
Ro 3: 31 Not at all! Rather, we **u** the law.

UPHOLDS* (UPHOLD)
Ps 37: 17 but the LORD **u** the righteous.
37: 24 for the LORD **u** him with his hand.
63: 8 cling to you; your right hand **u** me.
140: 12 poor and **u** the cause of the needy.
145: 14 The LORD **u** all who fall and lifts
146: 7 He **u** the cause of the oppressed
Am 5: 10 hate the one who **u** justice in court
Mic 7: 9 he pleads my case and **u** my cause.

UPRIGHT (UPRIGHTLY)
Dt 32: 4 does no wrong, **u** and just is he.
Job 1: 1 This man was blameless and **u**;
Ps 7: 10 High, who saves the **u** in heart.
11: 7 the **u** will see his face.
25: 8 Good and **u** is the LORD;
33: 1 it is fitting for the **u** to praise him.
64: 10 all the **u** in heart will glory in him!
92: 15 proclaiming, "The LORD is **u**;
97: 11 righteous and joy on the **u** in heart.
119: 7 an **u** heart as I learn your righteous
Pr 2: 7 He holds success in store for the **u**,
3: 32 but takes the **u** into his confidence.
8: 9 they are **u** to those who have found
15: 8 but the prayer of the **u** pleases him.
21: 29 the **u** give thought to their ways.
Isa 26: 7 you, the **U** One, make the way
Titus 1: 8 who is self-controlled, **u**,
2: 12 **u** and godly lives in this present

UPRIGHTLY* (UPRIGHT)
Pr 14: 2 Whoever fears the LORD walks **u**,
Isa 57: 2 who walk **u** enter into peace;

UPROOTED
Dt 28: 63 You will be **u** from the land you are
Jer 31: 40 The city will never again be **u**
Jude : 12 autumn trees, without fruit and **u**

UPSET
Lk 10: 41 worried and **u** about many things,

URGE
Titus 2: 4 they can **u** the younger women

URIAH
Hittite husband of Bathsheba, killed by David's order (2Sa 11).

USEFUL
Eph 4: 28 doing something **u** with their own
2Ti 2: 21 **u** to the Master and prepared to do
3: 16 is God-breathed and is **u** for
Phm : 11 now he has become **u** both to you

USELESS
1Co 15: 14 our preaching is **u** and so is your
Titus 3: 9 these are unprofitable and **u**.
Phm : 11 Formerly he was **u** to you, but now
Heb 7: 18 set aside because it was weak and **u**
Jas 2: 20 that faith without deeds is **u**?

UTMOST
Job 34: 36 the **u** for answering like a wicked

UTTER
Mt 13: 35 I will **u** things hidden since
1Co 14: 2 they **u** mysteries by the Spirit.

UZZIAH
Son of Amaziah; king of Judah also known as Azariah (2Ki 15:1–7; 1Ch 6:24; 2Ch 26). Struck with leprosy because of pride (2Ch 26:16–23).

VAIN
Ps 33: 17 A horse is a **v** hope for deliverance;
73: 13 in **v** I have kept my heart pure
127: 1 the house, the builders labor in **v**.
Isa 65: 23 They will not labor in **v**, nor will
1Co 15: 2 Otherwise, you have believed in **v**.
15: 58 your labor in the Lord is not in **v**.
2Co 6: 1 you not to receive God's grace in **v**.
Gal 2: 2 had not been running my race in **v**.

VALIANT
1Sa 10: 26 by **v** men whose hearts God had

VALID
Jn 8: 14 my testimony is **v**, for I know

VALLEY (VALLEYS)
Ps 23: 4 I walk through the darkest **v**,
Isa 40: 4 Every **v** shall be raised up,
Joel 3: 14 multitudes in the **v** of decision!

VALLEYS (VALLEY)
SS 2: 1 am a rose of Sharon, a lily of the **v**.

VALUABLE (VALUE)
Lk 12: 24 how much more **v** you are than

VALUE (VALUABLE)
Lev 27: 3 the **v** of a male between the ages
Pr 16: 13 they **v** the one who speaks what is
31: 11 in her and lacks nothing of **v**.
Mt 13: 46 When he found one of great **v**,
Lk 16: 15 What people **v** highly is detestable
1Ti 4: 8 physical training is of some **v**, but godliness has **v** for all things,
Php 2: 3 Rather, in humility **v** others
Heb 11: 26 as of greater **v** than the treasures

VANISHES
Jas 4: 14 for a little while and then **v**.

VASHTI*
Queen of Persia replaced by Esther (Est 1–2).

VAST
Ge 2: 1 were completed in all their **v** array.
Dt 1: 19 of the Amorites through all that **v**
8: 15 He led you through the **v**
Ps 139: 17 How **v** is the sum of them!

VAULT
Ge 1: 7 So God made the **v** and separated
1: 8 God called the **v** "sky."

VEGETABLES
Pr 15: 17 a small serving of **v** with love
Ro 14: 2 whose faith is weak, eats only **v**.

VEIL
Ex 34: 33 to them, he put a **v** over his face.
2Co 3: 14 to this day the same **v** remains

VENGEANCE (AVENGE AVENGER AVENGES AVENGING REVENGE)
Nu 31: 3 carry out the LORD's **v** on them.
Isa 34: 8 For the LORD has a day of **v**,
Na 1: 2 The LORD takes **v** on his foes

VERDICT
Ps 51: 4 so you are right in your **v**
Jn 3: 19 This is the **v**: Light has come

VICTORIES* (VICTORY)
Jdg 5: 11 They recite the **v** of the LORD,
5: 11 the **v** of his villagers in Israel.
2Sa 22: 51 "He gives his king great **v**;
Ps 18: 50 He gives his king great **v**;
21: 1 great is his joy in the **v** you give!
21: 5 Through the **v** you gave, his glory
44: 4 my God, who decrees **v** for Jacob.

VICTORIOUS (VICTORY)
Zec 9: 9 comes to you, righteous and **v**,
Rev 2: 7 To the one who is **v**, I will give
2: 11 The one who is **v** will not be hurt
2: 17 To the one who is **v**, I will give
2: 26 To the one who is **v** and does my
3: 5 The one who is **v** will, like them,
3: 12 The one who is **v** I will make
3: 21 To the one who is **v**, I will give
3: 21 just as I was **v** and sat down
21: 7 who are **v** will inherit all this,

VICTORIOUSLY* (VICTORY)
Ps 45: 4 In your majesty ride forth **v**

VICTOR'S* (VICTORY)
2Ti 2: 5 not receive the **v** crown except
Rev 2: 10 give you life as your **v** crown.

VICTORY (VICTOR'S VICTORIES VICTORIOUS VICTORIOUSLY)
2Sa 8: 6 LORD gave David **v** wherever he
Ps 20: 5 May we shout for joy over your **v**
44: 6 my sword does not bring me **v**;
60: 12 With God we will gain the **v**, and
129: 2 have not gained the **v** over me.
Ps 149: 4 he crowns the humble with **v**.
Pr 11: 14 **v** is won through many advisers.
Isa 63: 1 I, proclaiming **v**, mighty to save."
1Co 15: 54 has been swallowed up in **v**."
15: 57 He gives us the **v** through our Lord
1Jn 5: 4 This is the **v** that has overcome

VIEW
Pr 5: 21 ways are in full **v** of the LORD,
2Ti 4: 1 and in **v** of his appearing and his

VILE
Ps 12: 8 is **v** is honored by the human race.

VILLAGE
Mk 6: 6 Jesus went around teaching from **v** to **v**.

VINDICATE (VINDICATED VINDICATES VINDICATION)
Dt 32: 36 The LORD will **v** his people
Ps 138: 8 The LORD will **v** me;

VINDICATED (VINDICATE)
Job 13: 18 my case, I know I will be **v**.
Ps 17: 15 I will be **v** and will see your face;
1Ti 3: 16 in the flesh, was **v** by the Spirit,

VINDICATES (VINDICATE)
Ps 57: 2 Most High, to God, who **v** me.
Isa 50: 8 He who **v** me is near.

VINDICATION (VINDICATE)
Ps 24: 5 and **v** from God their Savior.
37: 6 dawn, your **v** like the noonday sun.

VINE (VINEYARD)
Ps 128: 3 like a fruitful **v** within your house;
Isa 36: 16 you will eat fruit from your own **v**
Jn 15: 1 "I am the true **v**, and my Father is

VINEGAR
Pr 10: 26 As **v** to the teeth and smoke
Mk 15: 36 filled a sponge with wine **v**, put it

VINEYARD (VINE)
1Ki 21: 1 The **v** was in Jezreel,
Pr 31: 16 out of her earnings she plants a **v**.
SS 1: 6 my own **v** I had to neglect.
Isa 5: 1 the one I love a song about his **v**:
1Co 9: 7 Who plants a **v** and does not eat its

VIOLATION
Heb 2: 2 every **v** and disobedience received

VIOLENCE (VIOLENT)
Ge 6: 11 in God's sight and was full of **v**.
Isa 53: 9 though he had done no **v**, nor was
60: 18 No longer will **v** be heard in your
Eze 45: 9 Give up your **v** and oppression
Joel 3: 19 because of **v** done to the people
Jnh 3: 8 give up their evil ways and their **v**.

VIOLENT (VIOLENCE)
Eze 18: 10 "Suppose he has a **v** son, who sheds
Mt 11: 12 and **v** people have been raiding it.
1Ti 1: 13 and a persecutor and a **v** man,
3: 3 to drunkenness, not **v** but gentle,
Titus 1: 7 not **v**, not pursuing dishonest gain.

VIPERS
Ps 140: 3 the poison of **v** is on their lips.
Lk 3: 7 baptized by him, "You brood of **v**!
Ro 3: 13 "The poison of **v** is on their lips."

VIRGIN (VIRGINS)
Dt 22: 15 at the gate proof that she was a **v**.
Isa 7: 14 The **v** will conceive and give birth

Mt 1: 23 "The **v** will conceive and give birth
Lk 1: 34 asked the angel, "since I am a **v**?"
2Co 11: 2 I might present you as a pure **v**

VIRGINS (VIRGIN)
Mt 25: 1 will be like ten **v** who took their
1Co 7: 25 Now about **v**: I have no command

VIRTUES*
Col 3: 14 And over all these **v** put on love,

VISIBLE
Eph 5: 13 exposed by the light becomes **v**—
Col 1: 16 and on earth, **v** and invisible,

VISION (VISIONS)
Da 9: 24 to seal up **v** and prophecy
Ac 26: 19 disobedient to the **v** from heaven.

VISIONS (VISION)
Nu 12: 6 reveal myself to them in **v**, I speak
Joel 2: 28 dreams, your young men will see **v**.
Ac 2: 17 your young men will see **v**,

VOICE
Dt 30: 20 listen to his **v**, and hold fast to him.
Job 40: 9 and can your **v** thunder like his?
Ps 19: 4 Yet their **v** goes out into all
29: 3 The **v** of the LORD is over
95: 7 if only you would hear his **v**,
Pr 8: 1 not understanding raise her **v**?
Isa 30: 21 your ears will hear a **v** behind you,
40: 3 A **v** of one calling:
Mk 1: 3 "a **v** of one calling
Jn 5: 28 are in their graves will hear his **v**
10: 3 him, and the sheep listen to his **v**.
Ro 10: 18 "Their **v** has gone out into all
15: 6 and one **v** you may glorify the God
Heb 3: 7 "Today, if you hear his **v**,
Rev 3: 20 If anyone hears my **v** and opens

VOLUNTARY*
Phm : 14 not seem forced but would be **v**.

VOMIT
Lev 18: 28 it will **v** you out as it vomited
Pr 26: 11 As a dog returns to its **v**, so fools
2Pe 2: 22 "A dog returns to its **v**," and,

VOW (VOWS)
Nu 6: 2 woman wants to make a special **v**,
30: 2 a man makes a **v** to the LORD
Jdg 11: 30 Jephthah made a **v** to the LORD:

VOWS (VOW)
Ps 116: 14 I will fulfill my **v** to the LORD
Pr 20: 25 and only later to consider one's **v**.

VULTURES
Mt 24: 28 is a carcass, there the **v** will gather.

WAGE (WAGES WAGING)
2Co 10: 3 we do not **w** war as the world does.

WAGES (WAGE)
Mal 3: 5 who defraud laborers of their **w**,
Lk 10: 7 you, for the worker deserves his **w**.
Ro 4: 4 **w** are not credited as a gift but as
6: 23 the **w** of sin is death, but the gift
1Ti 5: 18 and "The worker deserves his **w**."

WAGING (WAGE)
Ro 7: 23 **w** war against the law of my mind

WAILING
Ps 30: 11 You turned my **w** into dancing;

WAIST
2Ki 1: 8 had a leather belt around his **w**."
Mt 3: 4 he had a leather belt around his **w**.

WAIT (AWAITS WAITED WAITING WAITS)
Ps 27: 14 **W** for the LORD; be strong
130: 5 I **w** for the LORD, my whole being
Isa 30: 18 Blessed are all who **w** for him!
Ac 1: 4 **w** for the gift my Father promised,
Ro 8: 23 groan inwardly as we **w** eagerly
1Th 1: 10 and to **w** for his Son from heaven,
Titus 2: 13 while we **w** for the blessed hope—

WAITED (WAIT)
Ps 40: 1 I **w** patiently for the LORD;

WAITING (WAIT)
Heb 9: 28 to those who are **w** for him.

WAITS (WAIT)
Ro 8: 19 the creation **w** in eager expectation

WAKE (AWAKE WAKENS)
Eph 5: 14 "**W** up, sleeper, rise from the dead,

WAKENS* (WAKE)
Isa 50: 4 He **w** me morning by morning,
50: 4 He **w** me morning by morning,

WALK (WALKED WALKING WALKS)
Lev 26: 12 I will **w** among you and be your
Dt 5: 33 **W** in obedience to all
6: 7 and when you **w** along the road,
10: 12 God, to **w** in obedience to him,
11: 19 and when you **w** along the road,
11: 22 to **w** in obedience to him and
26: 17 you will **w** in obedience to him,
Jos 22: 5 God, to **w** in obedience to him,
Ps 1: 1 Blessed is the one who does not **w**
15: 2 The one whose **w** is blameless,
23: 4 though I **w** through the darkest
84: 11 from those whose **w** is blameless.
89: 15 **w** in the light of your presence,
119: 45 I will **w** about in freedom, for I
Pr 4: 12 When you **w**, your steps will not be
6: 22 When you **w**, they will guide you;
13: 20 **W** with the wise and become wise,
Isa 2: 3 so that we may **w** in his paths."
2: 5 let us **w** in the light of the LORD.
30: 21 saying, "This is the way; **w** in it."
33: 15 who **w** righteously and speak
40: 31 weary, they will **w** and not be faint.
57: 2 Those who **w** uprightly enter
Jer 6: 16 and **w** in it, and you will find rest
Da 4: 37 those who **w** in pride he is able
Am 3: 3 Do two **w** together unless they
Mic 4: 5 but we will **w** in the name
6: 8 and to **w** humbly with your God.
Mk 2: 9 say, 'Get up, take your mat and **w**'?
Jn 8: 12 Whoever follows me will never **w**
1Jn 1: 6 him and yet **w** in the darkness,
1: 7 But if we **w** in the light, as he is
2Jn : 6 his command is that you **w** in love.

WALKED (WALK)
Ge 5: 24 Enoch **w** faithfully with God;
Jos 14: 9 your feet have **w** will be your
Mt 14: 29 **w** on the water and came toward

WALKING (WALK)
1Ki 3: 3 the LORD by **w** according
Da 3: 25 see four men **w** around in the fire,
2Jn : 4 of your children **w** in the truth,

WALKS (WALK)
Pr 10: 9 Whoever **w** in integrity **w** securely,
Jn 11: 9 Anyone who **w** in the daytime will

WALL (WALLS)
Jos 6: 20 gave a loud shout, the **w** collapsed;
Ne 2: 17 let us rebuild the **w** of Jerusalem,
Eph 2: 14 barrier, the dividing **w** of hostility,
Rev 21: 12 a great, high **w** with twelve gates,

WALLOWING
2Pe 2: 22 returns to her **w** in the mud."

WALLS (WALL)
Isa 58: 12 be called Repairer of Broken **W**,
60: 18 you will call your **w** Salvation
Heb 11: 30 By faith the **w** of Jericho fell,

WANDER (WANDERED)
Nu 32: 13 he made them **w** in the wilderness
Jas 5: 19 one of you should **w** from the truth

WANDERED (WANDER)
Eze 34: 6 My sheep **w** over all the mountains
Mt 18: 12 go to look for the one that **w** off?
1Ti 6: 10 have **w** from the faith and pierced

WANT (WANTED WANTING WANTS)
1Sa 8: 19 they said. "We **w** a king over us.
Mt 19: 21 "If you **w** to be perfect, go,
Lk 19: 14 say, 'We don't **w** this man to be our
Ro 7: 15 For what I **w** to do I do not do,
13: 3 Do you **w** to be free from fear
2Co 12: 14 you, because what I **w** is not your
Php 3: 10 I **w** to know Christ—yes, to know

WANTED (WANT)
1Co 12: 18 of them, just as he **w** them to be.
Heb 6: 17 Because God **w** to make

WANTING (WANT)
Da 5: 27 weighed on the scales and found **w**.
2Pe 3: 9 with you, not **w** anyone to perish,

WANTS (WANT)
Mt 5: 42 from the one who **w** to borrow
20: 26 whoever **w** to become great among
Mk 8: 35 For whoever **w** to save their life
10: 43 whoever **w** to become great among
Ro 9: 18 on whom he **w** to have mercy,
9: 18 he hardens whom he **w** to harden.
1Ti 2: 4 who **w** all people to be saved
1Pe 5: 2 are willing, as God **w** you to be;

WAR (WARRIOR WARS)
Jos 11: 23 Then the land had rest from **w**.
1Sa 15: 18 wage **w** against them until you
Ps 68: 30 the nations who delight in **w**.
120: 7 but when I speak, they are for **w**.
144: 1 who trains my hands for **w**,
Isa 2: 4 nor will they train for **w** anymore.
Da 9: 26 **W** will continue until the end,
Ro 7: 23 me, waging **w** against the law of my
2Co 10: 3 we do not wage **w** as the world
1Pe 2: 11 which wage **w** against your soul.
Rev 12: 7 Then **w** broke out in heaven.
19: 11 justice he judges and wages **w**.

WARN* (WARNED WARNING WARNINGS)
Ex 19: 21 **w** the people so they do not force
Nu 24: 14 let me **w** you of what this people
1Sa 8: 9 but **w** them solemnly and let them
1Ki 2: 42 swear by the LORD and **w** you,
2Ch 19: 10 are to **w** them not to sin against
Ps 81: 8 me, my people, and I will **w** you—
Jer 42: 19 Be sure of this: I **w** you today
Eze 3: 18 you do not **w** them or speak
3: 19 if you do **w** the wicked person
3: 20 Since you did not **w** them, they will
3: 21 if you do **w** the righteous person
33: 3 blows the trumpet to **w** the people,
33: 6 blow the trumpet to **w** the people
33: 9 if you do **w** the wicked person
Lk 16: 28 Let him **w** them, so that they will
Ac 4: 17 must **w** them to speak no longer
1Co 4: 14 but to **w** you as my dear children.
Gal 5: 21 I **w** you, as I did before, that those
1Th 5: 14 **w** those who are idle and
2Th 3: 15 but **w** them as you would a fellow
2Ti 2: 14 **W** them before God against
Titus 3: 10 **W** a divisive person once,
Rev 22: 18 I **w** everyone who hears the words

WARNED (WARN)
2Ki 17: 13 The LORD **w** Israel and Judah
Ps 19: 11 By them your servant is **w**;
Jer 22: 21 I **w** you when you felt secure,
Mt 3: 7 **w** you to flee from the coming
1Th 4: 6 as we told you and **w** you before.
Heb 11: 7 when **w** about things not yet seen,
12: 25 they refused him who **w** them

WARNING (WARN)
Jer 6: 8 Take **w**, Jerusalem, or I will turn
1Ti 5: 20 so that the others may take **w**.

WARNINGS (WARN)
1Co 10: 11 and were written down as **w** for us,

WARRIOR (WAR)
Ex 15: 3 The LORD is a **w**; the LORD is
1Ch 28: 3 because you are a **w** and have shed
Pr 16: 32 Better a patient person than a **w**,

WARS (WAR)
Ps 46: 9 He makes **w** cease to the ends
Mt 24: 6 will hear of **w** and rumors of **w**,

WASH (WASHED WASHING)
Ps 51: 7 **w** me, and I will be whiter than
Jer 4: 14 **w** the evil from your heart and be
Jn 13: 5 and began to **w** his disciples' feet,
Ac 22: 16 be baptized and **w** your sins away,
Jas 4: 8 **W** your hands, you sinners,
Rev 22: 14 are those who **w** their robes,

WASHED (WASH)
Ps 73: 13 have **w** my hands in innocence.
1Co 6: 11 But you were **w**, you were
Heb 10: 22 and having our bodies **w** with pure
2Pe 2: 22 and, "A sow that is **w** returns to her
Rev 7: 14 they have **w** their robes and made

WASHING (WASH)
Eph 5: 26 the **w** with water through the word,
1Ti 5: 10 **w** the feet of the Lord's people,
Titus 3: 5 saved us through the **w** of rebirth

WASTED (WASTING)
Jn 6: 12 are left over. Let nothing be **w**."

WASTING (WASTED)
2Co 4: 16 Though outwardly we are **w** away,

WATCH (WATCHES WATCHING WATCHMAN)
Ge 31: 49 the LORD keep **w** between you
Ps 90: 4 gone by, or like a **w** in the night.
141: 3 keep **w** over the door of my lips.
Pr 4: 6 love her, and she will **w** over you.
6: 22 you sleep, they will **w** over you;
Jer 31: 10 them and will **w** over his flock like
Mic 7: 7 for me, I **w** in hope for the LORD,
Mt 24: 42 "Therefore keep **w**, because you do
26: 41 "**W** and pray so that you will not
Mk 13: 35 "Therefore keep **w** because you do
Lk 2: 8 keeping **w** over their flocks at night
1Ti 4: 16 **W** your life and doctrine closely.
Heb 13: 17 because they keep **w** over you as

WATCHES* (WATCH)
Nu 19: 5 While he **w**, the heifer is to be
Job 24: 15 eye of the adulterer **w** for dusk;
Ps 1: 6 For the LORD **w** over the way
33: 14 his dwelling place he **w** all who live
63: 6 of you through the **w** of the night.
119:148 My eyes stay open through the **w**
121: 3 who **w** over you will not slumber;
121: 4 he who **w** over Israel will neither
121: 5 The LORD **w** over you—
127: 1 Unless the LORD **w** over the city,
145: 20 LORD **w** over all who love him,
146: 9 The LORD **w** over the foreigner
Pr 31: 27 She **w** over the affairs of her
Ecc 11: 4 Whoever **w** the wind will not plant
La 2: 19 night, as the **w** of the night begin;
4: 16 he no longer **w** over them.

WATCHING (WATCH)
Lk 12: 37 whose master finds them **w** when
1Pe 5: 2 is under your care, **w** over them—

WATCHMAN (WATCH)
Eze 3: 17 I have made you a **w** for the people
33: 6 but I will hold the **w** accountable

WATER (WATERED WATERING WATERS WELL-WATERED)
Ex 7: 20 all the **w** was changed into blood.
17: 1 but there was no **w** for the people
Nu 20: 2 Now there was no **w**
Ps 1: 3 like a tree planted by streams of **w**,
22: 14 I am poured out like **w**, and all my
42: 1 As the deer pants for streams of **w**,
Pr 25: 21 if he is thirsty, give him **w** to drink
Isa 12: 3 joy you will draw **w** from the wells
30: 20 of adversity and the **w** of affliction,
32: 2 like streams of **w** in the desert
49: 10 and lead them beside springs of **w**.
Jer 2: 13 spring of living **w**, and have dug
2: 13 broken cisterns that cannot hold **w**.
17: 8 a tree planted by the **w** that sends
31: 9 will lead them beside streams of **w**
Eze 36: 25 I will sprinkle clean **w** on you,
Zec 14: 8 On that day living **w** will flow
Mt 14: 29 walked on the **w** and came toward
Mk 9: 41 anyone who gives you a cup of **w**
Lk 5: 4 "Put out into deep **w**, and let down
Jn 3: 5 of God unless they are born of **w**
4: 10 he would have given you living **w**."
7: 38 rivers of living **w** will flow
Eph 5: 26 washing with **w** through the word,
Heb 10: 22 our bodies washed with pure **w**.
1Pe 3: 21 this **w** symbolizes baptism that
2Pe 2: 17 These people are springs without **w**
1Jn 5: 6 He did not come by **w** only, but by **w** and blood.
5: 8 the Spirit, the **w** and the blood;
Rev 7: 17 lead them to springs of living **w**.'
21: 6 thirsty I will give **w** without cost

WATERED (WATER)
1Co 3: 6 I planted the seed, Apollos **w** it,

WATERING (WATER)
Isa 55: 10 not return to it without **w** the earth

WATERS (WATER)
Ps 23: 2 he leads me beside quiet **w**,
SS 8: 7 Many **w** cannot quench love;
Isa 11: 9 the LORD as the **w** cover the sea.
43: 2 When you pass through the **w**,
55: 1 you who are thirsty, come to the **w**;
58: 11 like a spring whose **w** never fail.
Hab 2: 14 the LORD as the **w** cover the sea.
1Co 3: 7 nor the one who **w** is anything,

WAVE (WAVES)
Lev 23: 11 **w** the sheaf before the LORD so it
Jas 1: 6 the one who doubts is like a **w**

WAVER*
1Ki 18: 21 "How long will you **w** between two
Ro 4: 20 Yet he did not **w** through unbelief

WAVES (WAVE)
Isa 57: 20 whose **w** cast up mire and mud.
Mt 8: 27 the winds and the **w** obey him!"
Eph 4: 14 tossed back and forth by the **w**,

WAY (WAYS)
Ex 13: 21 of cloud to guide them on their **w**
18: 20 show them the **w** they are to live
Dt 1: 33 to show you the **w** you should go.
32: 6 Is this the **w** you repay the LORD,
1Sa 12: 23 I will teach you the **w** that is good
2Sa 22: 31 "As for God, his **w** is perfect:
1Ki 8: 23 wholeheartedly in your **w**.
8: 36 Teach them the right **w** to live,
Job 23: 10 But he knows the **w** that I take;
Ps 1: 1 stand in the **w** that sinners take or
32: 8 teach you in the **w** you should go;
37: 5 Commit your **w** to the LORD;
86: 11 Teach me your **w**, LORD, that I
139: 24 and lead me in the **w** everlasting.
Pr 4: 11 I instruct you in the **w** of wisdom
12: 15 The **w** of fools seems right to them,
14: 12 is a **w** that appears to be right,
16: 7 takes pleasure in anyone's **w**,
19: 2 more will hasty feet miss the **w**!
22: 6 off on the **w** they should go,
30: 19 and the **w** of a man with a young
Isa 30: 21 behind you, saying, "This is the **w**;
35: 8 it will be called the **W** of Holiness;
40: 3 the wilderness prepare the **w**
48: 17 directs you in the **w** you should go.
53: 6 of us has turned to our own **w**;
Jer 5: 31 and my people love it this **w**.
Mal 3: 1 who will prepare the **w** before me.
Mt 3: 3 'Prepare the **w** for the Lord,
Lk 7: 27 will prepare your **w** before you.'
Jn 14: 6 "I am the **w** and the truth
Ac 1: 11 the same **w** you have seen him go
9: 2 any there who belonged to the **W**,
24: 14 ancestors as a follower of the **W**,
1Co 10: 13 provide a **w** out so that you can
12: 31 will show you the most excellent **w**.
14: 1 Follow the **w** of love and eagerly
Col 1: 10 Lord and please him in every **w**:
Titus 2: 10 every **w** they will make the
Heb 4: 15 who has been tempted in every **w**,
9: 8 the **w** into the Most Holy Place had
10: 20 living **w** opened for us through
13: 18 desire to live honorably in every **w**.

WAYS (WAY)
Ex 33: 13 teach me your **w** so I may know
Dt 32: 4 are perfect, and all his **w** are just.
2Ch 11: 17 years, following the **w** of David
Job 34: 21 "His eyes are on the **w** of mortals;
Ps 25: 4 Show me your **w**, LORD, teach me
25: 10 All the **w** of the LORD are loving
37: 7 when people succeed in their **w**,
51: 13 I will teach transgressors your **w**,
77: 13 Your **w**, God, are holy. What god is
119: 59 I have considered my **w** and have
139: 3 you are familiar with all my **w**.
145: 17 The LORD is righteous in all his **w**
Pr 3: 6 in all your **w** submit to him, and he
4: 26 feet and be steadfast in all your **w**.
5: 21 For your **w** are in full view
16: 2 All a person's **w** seem pure to them,
16: 17 who guard their **w** preserve their
Isa 2: 3 He will teach us his **w**, so that we
55: 7 Let the wicked forsake their **w**
55: 8 neither are your **w** my **w**,"
Eze 28: 15 in your **w** from the day you were
33: 8 out to dissuade them from their **w**,
Hos 14: 9 The **w** of the LORD are right;
Ro 1: 30 they invent **w** of doing evil;
Jas 3: 2 We all stumble in many **w**.

WAYWARD
Pr 6: 24 the smooth talk of a **w** woman.

WEAK (WEAKER WEAKNESS WEAKNESSES)
Ps 41: 1 those who have regard for the **w**;
72: 13 He will take pity on the **w**
82: 3 Defend the **w** and the fatherless;
Eze 34: 4 You have not strengthened the **w**
Mt 26: 41 spirit is willing, but the flesh is **w**."
Ac 20: 35 of hard work we must help the **w**,
Ro 14: 1 Accept the one whose faith is **w**,
15: 1 to bear with the failings of the **w**
1Co 1: 27 God chose the **w** things of the
8: 9 a stumbling block to the **w**.
9: 22 To the **w** I became **w**, to win the **w**.
11: 30 is why many among you are **w**
2Co 12: 10 For when I am **w**, then I am strong.
1Th 5: 14 help the **w**, be patient
Heb 12: 12 your feeble arms and **w** knees.

WEAKER* (WEAK)
2Sa 3: 1 the house of Saul grew **w** and **w**.
1Co 12: 22 seem to be **w** are indispensable,
1Pe 3: 7 them with respect as the **w** partner

WEAKNESS* (WEAK)
La 1: 6 **w** they have fled before the pursuer
Ro 8: 26 way, the Spirit helps us in our **w**.
1Co 1: 25 **w** of God is stronger than human
2: 3 I came to you in **w** with great fear
15: 43 is sown in **w**, it is raised in power;
2Co 11: 30 boast of the things that show my **w**.
12: 9 my power is made perfect in **w**."
13: 4 he was crucified in **w**, yet he lives
Heb 5: 2 since he himself is subject to **w**.
7: 28 as high priests men in all their **w**;
11: 34 whose **w** was turned to strength;

WEAKNESSES* (WEAK)
2Co 12: 5 about myself, except about my **w**.
12: 9 all the more gladly about my **w**,
12: 10 sake, I delight in **w**, in insults,
Heb 4: 15 is unable to empathize with our **w**,

WEALTH
Dt 8: 18 gives you the ability to produce **w**,
2Ch 1: 11 and you have not asked for **w**,
Ps 39: 6 up **w** without knowing whose it
49: 12 despite their **w**, do not endure;
Pr 3: 9 Honor the LORD with your **w**,
10: 4 but diligent hands bring **w**.
11: 4 **W** is worthless in the day of wrath,
13: 7 to be poor, yet has great **w**.
15: 16 of the LORD than great **w**
Ecc 5: 10 whoever loves **w** is never satisfied
5: 13 **w** hoarded to the harm of its
SS 8: 7 to give all the **w** of one's house
Mt 13: 22 deceitfulness of **w** choke the word,
Mk 10: 22 away sad, because he had great **w**.
12: 44 They all gave out of their **w**;
Lk 15: 13 and there squandered his **w** in wild
1Ti 6: 17 nor to put their hope in **w**,
Jas 5: 2 Your **w** has rotted, and moths have
5: 3 You have hoarded **w** in the last

WEAPON (WEAPONS)
Ne 4: 17 one hand and held a **w** in the other,

WEAPONS (WEAPON)
Ecc 9: 18 Wisdom is better than **w** of war,
2Co 6: 7 **w** of righteousness in the right
10: 4 The **w** we fight with are not the **w**

WEAR (WEARING)
Dt 8: 4 Your clothes did not **w** out and
22: 5 woman must not **w** men's clothing,
22: 5 nor a man **w** women's clothing,
Ps 102: 26 they will all **w** out like a garment.
Pr 23: 4 Do not **w** yourself out to get rich;
Isa 51: 6 the earth will **w** out like a garment
Heb 1: 11 they will all **w** out like a garment.
Rev 3: 18 and white clothes to **w**, so you can

WEARIES (WEARY)
Ecc 12: 12 end, and much study **w** the body.

WEARING (WEAR)
Jn 19: 5 Jesus came out **w** the crown
Jas 2: 3 attention to the man **w** fine clothes
1Pe 3: 3 hairstyles and the **w** of gold jewelry
Rev 7: 9 They were **w** white robes and were

WEARY (WEARIES)
Isa 40: 28 He will not grow tired or **w**, and
40: 31 they will run and not grow **w**,
50: 4 know the word that sustains the **w**.
Mt 11: 28 all you who are **w** and burdened,
Gal 6: 9 us not become **w** in doing good,
Heb 12: 3 that you will not grow **w** and lose
Rev 2: 3 my name, and have not grown **w**.

WEDDING
Mt 22: 11 who was not wearing **w** clothes.
Rev 19: 7 For the **w** of the Lamb has come,

WEEDS
Mt 13: 25 and sowed **w** among the wheat,

WEEK
Mt 28: 1 at dawn on the first day of the **w**,
1Co 16: 2 On the first day of every **w**,

WEEP (WEEPING WEPT)
Ecc 3: 4 a time to **w** and a time to laugh,
Lk 6: 21 Blessed are you who **w** now,
23: 28 of Jerusalem, do not **w** for me;

WEEPING (WEEP)
Ps 30: 5 **w** may stay for the night,
126: 6 Those who go out **w**, carrying seed
Jer 31: 15 mourning and great **w**, Rachel **w**
Mt 2: 18 Rachel **w** for her children
8: 12 where there will be **w** and gnashing

WEIGH (OUTWEIGHS WEIGHED WEIGHS WEIGHTIER WEIGHTS)
1Co 14: 29 the others should **w** carefully what

WEIGHED (WEIGH)
Job 28: 15 nor can its price be **w** out in silver.
Da 5: 27 You have been **w** on the scales
Lk 21: 34 or your hearts will be **w** down

WEIGHS (WEIGH)
Pr 12: 25 Anxiety **w** down the heart,
15: 28 of the righteous **w** its answers,
21: 2 right, but the LORD **w** the heart.
24: 12 not he who **w** the heart perceive it?

WEIGHTIER* (WEIGH)
Jn 5: 36 "I have testimony **w** than

WEIGHTS (WEIGH)
Lev 19: 36 Use honest scales and honest **w**,
Dt 25: 13 Do not have two differing **w** in
Pr 11: 1 but accurate **w** find favor with him.

WELCOME (WELCOMES)
Mk 9: 37 welcomes me does not **w** me
2Pe 1: 11 you will receive a rich **w**

WELCOMES (WELCOME)
Mt 10: 40 "Anyone who **w** you **w** me,
18: 5 whoever **w** one such child in my name **w** me.
2Jn : 11 Anyone who **w** them shares in

WELL (WELLED WELLING WELLS)
Jer 32: 39 that all will then go **w** for them
Mt 15: 31 the crippled made **w**, the lame
Lk 14: 5 falls into a **w** on the Sabbath day,
17: 19 your faith has made you **w**."
Jas 5: 15 faith will make the sick person **w**;

WELL-WATERED (WATER)
Isa 58: 11 You will be like a **w** garden,

WELLED* (WELL)
2Co 8: 2 their extreme poverty **w** up in rich

WELLING* (WELL)
Jn 4: 14 in them a spring of water **w**

WELLS (WELL)
Isa 12: 3 draw water from the **w** of salvation.

WEPT (WEEP)
Ps 137: 1 and **w** when we remembered Zion.
Lk 22: 62 And he went outside and **w** bitterly.
Jn 11: 35 Jesus **w**.

WEST
Ps 103: 12 as far as the east is from the **w**,
107: 3 from east and **w**, from north

WHEAT
Mt 3: 12 gathering his **w** into the barn
13: 25 and sowed weeds among the **w**,
Lk 22: 31 has asked to sift all of you as **w**.
Jn 12: 24 you, unless a kernel of **w** falls

WHEELS
Eze 1: 16 appearance and structure of the **w**:

WHIRLWIND (WIND)
2Ki 2: 1 to take Elijah up to heaven in a **w**,
Hos 8: 7 sow the wind and reap the **w**.
Na 1: 3 His way is in the **w** and the storm,

WHISPER (WHISPERED)
1Ki 19: 12 And after the fire came a gentle **w**.
Job 26: 14 how faint the **w** we hear of him!
Ps 107: 29 He stilled the storm to a **w**;

WHISPERED (WHISPER)
Mt 10: 27 what is **w** in your ear,

WHITE (WHITER)
Isa 1: 18 scarlet, they shall be as **w** as snow;
Da 7: 9 His clothing was as **w** as snow;
7: 9 hair of his head was **w** like wool.
Mt 28: 3 and his clothes were **w** as snow.
Rev 1: 14 hair on his head was **w** like wool,
3: 4 dressed in **w**, for they are worthy.
6: 2 and there before me was a **w** horse!
7: 13 asked me, "These in **w** robes—
19: 11 and there before me was a **w** horse,
20: 11 I saw a great **w** throne and him

WHITER (WHITE)
Ps 51: 7 me, and I will be **w** than snow.

WHOLE
Ge 1: 29 plant on the face of the **w** earth
2: 6 the **w** surface of the ground.
11: 1 Now the **w** world had one language
Ex 12: 47 The **w** community of Israel must
19: 5 Although the **w** earth is mine,
Lev 16: 17 and the **w** community of Israel.
Nu 14: 21 of the LORD fills the **w** earth,
32: 13 until the **w** generation of those
Dt 13: 16 all its plunder as a **w** burnt offering
19: 8 gives you the **w** land he promised
Jos 2: 3 have come to spy out the **w** land."
1Sa 1: 28 For his **w** life he will be given over
17: 46 the **w** world will know that there is
1Ki 10: 24 The **w** world sought audience
2Ki 21: 8 keep the **w** Law that my servant
Ps 72: 19 may the **w** earth be filled with his
Pr 4: 22 them and health to one's **w** body.
8: 31 rejoicing in his **w** world
Isa 1: 5 Your **w** head is injured, your **w** heart afflicted.
6: 3 the **w** earth is full of his glory."
14: 26 plan determined for the **w** world;
Eze 34: 6 were scattered over the **w** earth,
Da 2: 35 mountain and filled the **w** earth.
Zep 1: 18 of his jealousy the **w** earth will be
Zec 14: 9 will be king over the **w** earth.
Mal 3: 10 Bring the **w** tithe
Mt 5: 29 your body than for your **w** body
6: 22 your **w** body will be full of light.
16: 26 for someone to gain the **w** world,
24: 14 in the **w** world as a testimony to all
Lk 21: 35 who live on the face of the **w** earth.
Jn 12: 19 Look how the **w** world has gone
13: 10 their **w** body is clean.
21: 25 even the **w** world would not have
Ac 17: 26 they should inhabit the **w** earth;
20: 27 proclaim to you the **w** will of God.
Ro 3: 19 and the **w** world held accountable
8: 22 the **w** creation has been groaning
1Co 4: 9 made a spectacle to the **w** universe,
12: 17 If the **w** body were an eye,
Gal 5: 3 he is obligated to obey the **w** law.
Eph 4: 10 in order to fill the **w** universe.)
4: 13 attaining to the **w** measure
1Th 5: 23 May your **w** spirit, soul and body
Jas 2: 10 For whoever keeps the **w** law
1Jn 2: 2 but also for the sins of the **w** world.
Rev 3: 10 to come on the **w** world to test

WHOLEHEARTED* (HEART)
2Ki 20: 3 with **w** devotion and have done
1Ch 28: 9 serve him with **w** devotion
29: 19 my son Solomon the **w** devotion
Isa 38: 3 with **w** devotion and have done

WHOLEHEARTEDLY* (HEART)
Nu 14: 24 a different spirit and follows me **w**,
32: 11 they have not followed me **w**,
32: 12 for they followed the LORD **w**.'
Dt 1: 36 he followed the LORD **w**."
Jos 14: 8 followed the LORD my God **w**.
14: 9 followed the LORD my God **w**.'
14: 14 the LORD, the God of Israel, **w**.
1Ki 8: 23 your servants who continue **w**
1Ch 29: 9 given freely and **w** to the LORD.
2Ch 6: 14 your servants who continue **w**
15: 15 oath because they had sworn it **w**.
19: 9 and **w** in the fear of the LORD.
25: 2 the eyes of the LORD, but not **w**.
31: 21 he sought his God and worked **w**.
Ps 119: 80 May I **w** follow your decrees,
Eph 6: 7 Serve **w**, as if you were serving

WHOLESOME*
2Pe 3: 1 to stimulate you to **w** thinking.

WICK
Isa 42: 3 a smoldering **w** he will not snuff
Mt 12: 20 a smoldering **w** he will not snuff

WICKED (WICKEDNESS)
Ge 13: 13 Now the people of Sodom were **w**
39: 9 could I do such a **w** thing and sin
Nu 14: 35 things to this whole **w** community,
Dt 15: 9 not to harbor this **w** thought:
Jdg 19: 22 some of the **w** men of the city
1Sa 15: 18 completely destroy those **w** people,
25: 17 He is such a **w** man that no one can
2Sa 13: 12 Don't do this **w** thing.
2Ki 17: 11 They did **w** things that aroused
2Ch 7: 14 face and turn from their **w** ways,
19: 2 "Should you help the **w** and love
Ne 13: 17 "What is this **w** thing you are
Ps 1: 1 does not walk in step with the **w**
1: 5 Therefore the **w** will not stand
7: 9 to an end the violence of the **w**
10: 13 Why does the **w** man revile God?
11: 5 but the **w**, those who love violence,
26: 5 and refuse to sit with the **w**.
32: 10 Many are the woes of the **w**,
36: 1 concerning the sinfulness of the **w**:
37: 13 but the Lord laughs at the **w**, for he
49: 5 when **w** deceivers surround me—
50: 16 But to the **w** person, God says:
58: 3 Even from birth the **w** go astray;
73: 3 when I saw the prosperity of the **w**.
82: 2 and show partiality to the **w**?
112: 10 The **w** will see and be vexed,
119: 61 Though the **w** bind me with ropes,
119:155 Salvation is far from the **w**,
140: 8 Do not grant the **w** their desires,
141: 10 Let the **w** fall into their own nets,
146: 9 he frustrates the ways of the **w**.
Pr 2: 12 save you from the ways of **w** men,
4: 14 not set foot on the path of the **w**
6: 18 a heart that devises **w** schemes,
9: 7 rebukes the **w** incurs abuse.
10: 20 the heart of the **w** is of little value.
10: 23 A fool finds pleasure in **w** schemes,
10: 28 hopes of the **w** come to nothing.
11: 5 but the **w** are brought down by
11: 10 when the **w** perish, there are shouts
11: 21 The **w** will not go unpunished,
12: 5 but the advice of the **w** is deceitful.
12: 10 the kindest acts of the **w** are cruel.
14: 19 the **w** at the gates of the righteous.
15: 3 keeping watch on the **w**
15: 26 detests the thoughts of the **w**,
21: 10 The **w** crave evil;
21: 29 The **w** put up a bold front,
28: 1 The **w** flee though no one pursues,
28: 4 forsake instruction praise the **w**,
29: 7 but the **w** have no such concern.
29: 16 When the **w** thrive, so does sin,
29: 27 the **w** detest the upright.
Isa 11: 4 breath of his lips he will slay the **w**.
13: 11 for its evil, the **w** for their sins.
26: 10 But when grace is shown to the **w**,
48: 22 says the LORD, "for the **w**."
53: 9 was assigned a grave with the **w**,
55: 7 Let the **w** forsake their ways
57: 20 But the **w** are like the tossing sea,
Jer 35: 15 of you must turn from your **w** ways
Eze 3: 18 that **w** person will die for their sin,
13: 22 because you encouraged the **w** not
14: 7 put a **w** stumbling block before
18: 21 if a **w** person turns away from all

Eze 18: 23 any pleasure in the death of the **w**?
21: 25 profane and **w** prince of Israel,
33: 8 that **w** person will die for their sin,
33: 11 no pleasure in the death of the **w**,
33: 14 And if I say to a **w** person,
33: 19 if a **w** person turns away from their
Da 12: 10 but the **w** will continue to be **w**.
Mt 12: 39 "A **w** and adulterous generation
12: 45 other spirits more **w** than itself,
12: 45 it will be with this **w** generation."
Lk 6: 35 he is kind to the ungrateful and **w**.
Ac 2: 23 with the help of **w** men, put him
1Co 5: 13 "Expel the **w** person from among
Rev 2: 2 that you cannot tolerate **w** people,

WICKEDNESS (WICKED)
Ge 6: 5 The LORD saw how great the **w**
Ex 34: 7 and forgiving **w**, rebellion and sin.
Lev 16: 21 and confess over it all the **w**
19: 29 prostitution and be filled with **w**.
Dt 9: 4 account of the **w** of these nations
Ps 45: 7 You love righteousness and hate **w**;
92: 15 Rock, and there is no **w** in him."
Pr 13: 6 but **w** overthrows the sinner.
Jer 3: 2 land with your prostitution and **w**.
8: 6 None of them repent of their **w**,
14: 20 We acknowledge our **w**, LORD,
Eze 18: 20 the **w** of the wicked will be charged
28: 15 you were created till **w** was found
33: 19 person turns away from their **w**
Da 4: 27 and your **w** by being kind
9: 24 end to sin, to atone for **w**, to bring
Jnh 1: 2 because its **w** has come up before
Mt 24: 12 Because of the increase of **w**,
Lk 11: 39 inside you are full of greed and **w**.
Ac 1: 18 the payment he received for his **w**,
Ro 1: 18 who suppress the truth by their **w**,
1Co 5: 8 bread leavened with malice and **w**,
2Co 6: 14 and **w** have in common?
2Ti 2: 19 the Lord must turn away from **w**."
Titus 2: 14 for us to redeem us from all **w**
Heb 1: 9 loved righteousness and hated **w**;
8: 12 For I will forgive their **w** and will
2Pe 2: 15 of Bezer, who loved the wages of **w**.

WIDE
Ps 81: 10 Open **w** your mouth and I will fill
Isa 54: 2 stretch your tent curtains **w**, do not
Mt 7: 13 For **w** is the gate and broad is
2Co 6: 13 open **w** your hearts also.
Eph 3: 18 to grasp how **w** and long and high

WIDOW (WIDOWS)
Ex 22: 22 "Do not take advantage of the **w**
Dt 10: 18 cause of the fatherless and the **w**,
Ps 146: 9 sustains the fatherless and the **w**,
Isa 1: 17 plead the case of the **w**.
Lk 21: 2 saw a poor **w** put in two very small
1Ti 5: 4 a **w** has children or grandchildren,

WIDOWS (WIDOW)
Ps 68: 5 a defender of **w**, is God in his holy
Ac 6: 1 Jews because their **w** were being
1Co 7: 8 to the unmarried and the **w** I say:
1Ti 5: 3 to those **w** who are really in need.
Jas 1: 27 orphans and **w** in their distress

WIFE (WIVES WIVES')
Ge 2: 24 and mother and is united to his **w**,
19: 26 But Lot's **w** looked back, and she
24: 67 So she became his **w**, and he loved
Ex 20: 17 shall not covet your neighbor's **w**,
Lev 20: 10 adultery with another man's **w**—
Dt 5: 21 shall not covet your neighbor's **w**.
22: 13 If a man takes a **w** and,
24: 5 happiness to the **w** he has married.
Ru 4: 13 took Ruth and she became his **w**.
Pr 5: 18 you rejoice in the **w** of your youth.
12: 4 A **w** of noble character is her
18: 22 who finds a **w** finds what is good
19: 13 quarrelsome **w** is like the constant
31: 10 A **w** of noble character who can
Hos 1: 2 for like an adulterous **w** this land is
Mal 2: 14 the **w** of your marriage covenant.
Mt 1: 20 to take Mary home as your **w**,
19: 3 for a man to divorce his **w** for any
Lk 17: 32 Remember Lot's **w**!
18: 29 "no one who has left home or **w**
1Co 7: 2 sexual relations with his own **w**,
7: 33 how he can please his **w**—
Eph 5: 23 head of the **w** as Christ is the head
5: 33 must love his **w** as he loves himself,
5: 33 the **w** must respect her husband.
1Ti 3: 2 faithful to his **w**, temperate,
Rev 21: 9 you the bride, the **w** of the Lamb."

WILD
Ge 1: 25 God made the **w** animals
8: 1 all the **w** animals and the livestock
Lk 15: 13 squandered his wealth in **w** living.
Ro 11: 17 and you, though a **w** olive shoot,

WILDERNESS
Nu 32: 13 them wander in the **w** forty years,
Dt 8: 16 He gave you manna to eat in the **w**,
29: 5 years that I led you through the **w**,
Ne 9: 19 did not abandon them in the **w**.
Ps 78: 19 God really spread a table in the **w**?
78: 52 led them like sheep through the **w**.
Isa 43: 20 because I provide water in the **w**
Mk 1: 3 "a voice of one calling in the **w**,
1: 13 and he was in the **w** forty days,
Rev 12: 6 fled into the **w** to a place prepared

WILL (WILLFUL WILLING WILLINGNESS)
Ps 40: 8 I desire to do your **w**, my God;
143: 10 Teach me to do your **w**, for you are
Isa 53: 10 Yet it was the LORD's **w** to crush
53: 10 the **w** of the LORD **w** prosper
Mt 6: 10 kingdom come, your **w** be done,
7: 21 only the one who does the **w** of my
10: 29 Yet not one of them **w** fall
12: 50 whoever does the **w** of my Father
26: 39 Yet not as I **w**, but as you **w**."
26: 42 I drink it, may your **w** be done."
Jn 6: 38 down from heaven not to do my **w**
6: 38 to do the **w** of him who sent me.
7: 17 chooses to do the **w** of God **w** find
Ac 20: 27 to you the whole **w** of God.
Ro 12: 2 test and approve what God's **w** is—
12: 2 his good, pleasing and perfect **w**.
1Co 7: 37 but has control over his own **w**,
Eph 5: 17 understand what the Lord's **w** is.
Php 2: 13 for it is God who works in you to **w**
1Th 4: 3 It is God's **w** that you should be
5: 18 for this is God's **w** for you in Christ
2Ti 2: 26 has taken them captive to do his **w**.
Heb 2: 4 distributed according to his **w**.
9: 16 In the case of a **w**, it is necessary
10: 7 I have come to do your **w**,
13: 21 everything good for doing his **w**,
Jas 4: 15 "If it is the Lord's **w**, we **w** live
1Pe 3: 17 if it is God's **w**, to suffer for doing
4: 2 but rather for the **w** of God.
2Pe 1: 21 had its origin in the human **w**,
1Jn 5: 14 ask anything according to his **w**,
Rev 4: 11 by your **w** they were created

WILLFUL (WILL)
Ps 19: 13 your servant also from **w** sins;

WILLING (WILL)
1Ch 28: 9 devotion and with a **w** mind,
29: 5 who is **w** to consecrate themselves
Ps 51: 12 salvation and grant me a **w** spirit,
Da 3: 28 were **w** to give up their lives rather
Mt 18: 14 Father in heaven is not **w** that any
23: 37 her wings, and you were not **w**.
26: 41 The spirit is **w**, but the flesh is
1Ti 6: 18 and to be generous and **w** to share.
1Pe 5: 2 but because you are **w**, as God

WILLINGNESS* (WILL)
2Co 8: 11 so that your eager **w** to do it may
8: 12 For if the **w** is there, the gift is

WIN (WON)
Lk 21: 19 Stand firm, and you will **w** life.
1Co 9: 19 everyone, to **w** as many as possible.
Php 3: 14 on toward the goal to **w** the prize
1Th 4: 12 your daily life may **w** the respect

WIND (WHIRLWIND WINDS)
Ps 1: 4 like chaff that the **w** blows away.
Ecc 2: 11 meaningless, a chasing after the **w**;
Hos 8: 7 "They sow the **w** and reap
Mk 4: 41 Even the **w** and the waves obey
Jn 3: 8 The **w** blows wherever it pleases.
Eph 4: 14 there by every **w** of teaching
Jas 1: 6 the sea, blown and tossed by the **w**.

WINDOW
Jos 2: 21 she tied the scarlet cord in the **w**.
Ac 20: 9 in a **w** was a young man named
2Co 11: 33 in a basket from a **w** in the wall

WINDS (WIND)
Ps 104: 4 He makes **w** his messengers,
Mt 24: 31 gather his elect from the four **w**,

WINE
Ps 104: 15 **w** that gladdens human hearts,
Pr 20: 1 **W** is a mocker and beer a brawler;
23: 20 join those who drink too much **w**
23: 31 Do not gaze at **w** when it is red,
31: 6 **w** for those who are in anguish!
SS 1: 2 love is more delightful than **w**.
Isa 28: 7 stagger from **w** and reel from beer:
55: 1 buy **w** and milk without money
Mt 9: 17 Neither do people pour new **w**
Lk 23: 36 They offered him **w** vinegar
Jn 2: 9 water that had been turned into **w**
Ro 14: 21 drink **w** or to do anything else
Eph 5: 18 Do not get drunk on **w**, which
1Ti 5: 23 and use a little **w** because of your
Rev 16: 19 the cup filled with the **w** of the fury

WINEPRESS
Isa 63: 2 like those of one treading the **w**?
Rev 19: 15 He treads the **w** of the fury

WINESKINS
Mt 9: 17 people pour new wine into old **w**.
9: 17 they pour new wine into new **w**,

WINGS
Ex 19: 4 how I carried you on eagles' **w**
Ru 2: 12 under whose **w** you have come
Ps 17: 8 hide me in the shadow of your **w**
91: 4 under his **w** you will find refuge;
Isa 6: 2 were seraphim, each with six **w**:
40: 31 They will soar on **w** like eagles;
Eze 1: 6 of them had four faces and four **w**.
Zec 5: 9 women, with the wind in their **w**!
Lk 13: 34 gathers her chicks under her **w**,
Rev 4: 8 the four living creatures had six **w**

WINTER
Mk 13: 18 that this will not take place in **w**,

WIPE (WIPED)
Isa 25: 8 Sovereign LORD will **w** away
Rev 7: 17 God will **w** away every tear
21: 4 'He will **w** every tear from their

WIPED (WIPE)
Lk 7: 38 Then she **w** them with her hair,
Ac 3: 19 so that your sins may be **w** out,

WISDOM (WISE)
Ge 3: 6 and also desirable for gaining **w**,
1Ki 4: 29 God gave Solomon **w** and very
2Ch 1: 10 Give me **w** and knowledge, that I
Ps 51: 6 taught me **w** in that secret place.
111: 10 the LORD is the beginning of **w**;
Pr 2: 6 For the LORD gives **w**;
3: 13 Blessed are those who find **w**,
4: 7 The beginning of **w** is this: Get **w**.
8: 11 for **w** is more precious than rubies,
11: 2 but with humility comes **w**.
13: 10 **w** is found in those who take
23: 23 **w**, instruction and insight as well.
29: 3 A man who loves **w** brings joy
29: 15 A rod and a reprimand impart **w**,
31: 26 She speaks with **w**, and faithful
Isa 11: 2 rest on him—the Spirit of **w**
28: 29 whose **w** is magnificent.
Jer 10: 12 he founded the world by his **w**
Mic 6: 9 and to fear your name is **w**—
Mt 11: 19 **w** is proved right by her deeds."
Lk 2: 52 And Jesus grew in **w** and stature,
Ac 6: 3 to be full of the Spirit and **w**.
Ro 11: 33 the depth of the riches of the **w**
1Co 1: 17 not with **w** and eloquence,
1: 30 has become for us **w** from God—
12: 8 through the Spirit a message of **w**,
Eph 1: 17 may give you the Spirit of **w**
Col 2: 3 are hidden all the treasures of **w**
2: 23 indeed have an appearance of **w**,
Jas 1: 5 If any of you lacks **w**, you should
3: 13 in the humility that comes from **w**.
Rev 5: 12 and wealth and **w** and strength

WISE (WISDOM WISER)
1Ki 3: 12 I will give you a **w** and discerning
Job 5: 13 He catches the **w** in their craftiness,
Ps 19: 7 trustworthy, making **w** the simple.
Pr 3: 7 Do not be **w** in your own eyes;
9: 8 rebuke the **w** and they will love
9: 9 Instruct the **w** and they will be
10: 1 A **w** son brings joy to his father,
11: 30 and the one who is **w** saves lives.
13: 1 A **w** son heeds his father's
13: 20 Walk with the **w** and become **w**,
16: 23 the **w** make their mouths prudent,
17: 28 Even fools are thought **w** if they
Ecc 9: 17 The quiet words of the **w** are more
Jer 9: 23 "Let not the **w** boast of their
Eze 28: 6 think you are **w**, as **w** as a god,
Da 2: 21 He gives wisdom to the **w**
12: 3 Those who are **w** will shine like
Mt 11: 25 hidden these things from the **w**
25: 2 them were foolish and five were **w**.
1Co 1: 19 will destroy the wisdom of the **w**;
1: 27 things of the world to shame the **w**;
3: 10 I laid a foundation as a **w** builder,
3: 19 "He catches the **w** in their
Eph 5: 15 not as unwise but as **w**,
2Ti 3: 15 make you **w** for salvation through
Jas 3: 13 Who is **w** and understanding

WISER (WISE)
Pr 9: 9 the wise and they will be **w** still;
1Co 1: 25 of God is **w** than human wisdom,

WISH (WISHES)
Jn 15: 7 ask whatever you **w**, and it will be
Ro 9: 3 I could **w** that I myself were cursed
Rev 3: 15 I **w** you were either one or the

WISHES (WISH)
Rev 22: 17 let the one who **w** take the free gift

WITCHCRAFT
Dt 18: 10 interprets omens, engages in **w**,
Gal 5: 20 idolatry and **w**;

WITHDREW
Lk 5: 16 But Jesus often **w** to lonely places

WITHER (WITHERS)
Ps 1: 3 season and whose leaf does not **w**
37: 19 In times of disaster they will not **w**;

WITHERS (WITHER)
Isa 40: 7 The grass **w** and the flowers fall,
1Pe 1: 24 the grass **w** and the flowers fall,

WITHHELD (WITHHOLD)
Ge 22: 12 because you have not **w** from me

WITHHOLD (WITHHELD WITHHOLDS)
Ps 84: 11 no good thing does he **w** from
Pr 23: 13 Do not **w** discipline from a child;

WITHHOLDS (WITHHOLD)
Dt 27: 19 "Cursed is anyone who **w** justice

WITNESS (EYEWITNESSES WITNESSES)
Pr 12: 17 An honest **w** tells the truth,
19: 9 A false **w** will not go unpunished,
Jn 1: 8 he came only as a **w** to the light.

WITNESSES (WITNESS)
Dt 19: 15 by the testimony of two or three **w**.
Mt 18: 16 by the testimony of two or three **w**.'
Ac 1: 8 and you will be my **w** in Jerusalem,

WIVES (WIFE)
Eph 5: 22 **W**, submit yourselves to your own
5: 25 love your **w**, just as Christ loved
1Pe 3: 1 **W**, in the same way submit

WIVES'* (WIFE)
1Ti 4: 7 with godless myths and old **w** tales;

WOE
Isa 6: 5 "**W** to me!" I cried. "I am ruined!
Eze 34: 2 **W** to you shepherds of Israel who
Mt 18: 7 **w** to the person through whom
23: 13 "**W** to you, teachers of the law
Jude : 11 **W** to them! They have taken

WOLF (WOLVES)
Isa 65: 25 The **w** and the lamb will feed

WOLVES (WOLF)
Mt 10: 16 you out like sheep among **w**.

WOMAN (MAN)
Ge 2: 22 the LORD God made a **w**
2: 23 she shall be called '**w**,' for she was
3: 6 When the **w** saw that the fruit
3: 12 "The **w** you put here with me—
3: 15 put enmity between you and the **w**,
3: 16 To the **w** he said, "I will make your
12: 11 "I know what a beautiful **w** you are.
20: 3 because of the **w** you have taken;
24: 5 if the **w** is unwilling to come
24: 16 The **w** was very beautiful, a virgin;
Ex 2: 1 tribe of Levi married a Levite **w**,
3: 22 Every **w** is to ask her neighbor
21: 10 If he marries another **w**, he must
21: 22 hit a pregnant **w** and she gives
Lev 12: 2 'A **w** who becomes pregnant
15: 19 "'When a **w** has her regular flow
15: 25 "'When a **w** has a discharge
18: 17 have sexual relations with both a **w**
20: 13 with a man as one does with a **w**,
Nu 5: 29 of jealousy when a **w** goes astray
30: 3 "When a young **w** still living in her
30: 9 divorced **w** will be binding on her.
30: 10 "If a **w** living with her husband
Dt 20: 7 Has anyone become pledged to a **w**
21: 11 among the captives a beautiful **w**
22: 5 A **w** must not wear men's clothing,
Jdg 4: 9 Sisera into the hands of a **w**."
13: 6 Then the **w** went to her husband
14: 2 "I have seen a Philistine **w**
16: 4 love with a **w** in the Valley of Sorek
20: 4 the husband of the murdered **w**,
Ru 3: 11 that you are a **w** of noble character.
1Sa 1: 15 "I am a **w** who is deeply troubled.
25: 3 was an intelligent and beautiful **w**,
28: 7 "Find me a **w** who is a medium,
2Sa 11: 2 From the roof he saw a **w** bathing.
13: 17 "Get this **w** out of my sight and
14: 2 had a wise **w** brought from there.
20: 16 a wise **w** called from the city,
1Ki 3: 18 was born, this **w** also had a baby.
17: 24 Then the **w** said to Elijah, "Now I
2Ki 4: 8 And a well-to-do **w** was there,
8: 1 to the **w** whose son he had restored
9: 34 "Take care of that cursed **w**,"
Job 14: 1 born of **w**, are of few days and full
Pr 11: 16 A kindhearted **w** gains honor,
11: 22 snout is a beautiful **w** who shows
14: 1 The wise **w** builds her house,
23: 27 for an adulterous **w** is a deep pit,
30: 19 the way of a man with a young **w**.
30: 23 contemptible **w** who gets married,
31: 30 a **w** who fears the LORD is to be
Isa 54: 1 barren **w**, you who never bore
62: 5 a young man marries a young **w**,
Jer 2: 32 Does a young **w** forget her jewelry,
Mt 5: 28 a **w** lustfully has already committed
9: 20 then a **w** who had been subject
15: 28 Then Jesus said to her, "**W**,
26: 7 a **w** came to him with an alabaster
Mk 5: 25 a **w** was there who had been
7: 25 him, a **w** whose little daughter was
Lk 7: 39 him and what kind of **w** she is—
10: 38 a village where a **w** named Martha
13: 12 her forward and said to her, "**W**,
15: 8 suppose a **w** has ten silver coins
Jn 2: 4 "**W**, why do you involve me?"
4: 7 a Samaritan **w** came to draw water,
8: 3 *brought in a **w** caught in adultery.*
19: 26 he said to her, "**W**, here is your
20: 15 He asked her, "**W**, why are you
Ac 9: 40 Turning toward the dead **w**, he
16: 14 of those listening was a **w**
Ro 7: 2 by law a married **w** is bound to her
1Co 7: 2 and each **w** with her own husband.
7: 34 An unmarried **w** or virgin is
7: 39 A **w** is bound to her husband as
11: 3 and the head of the **w** is man,
11: 7 but **w** is the glory of man.
11: 13 Is it proper for a **w** to pray to God
Gal 4: 4 born of a **w**, born under the law,
4: 31 we are not children of the slave **w**, but of the free **w**.
1Ti 2: 11 A **w** should learn in quietness
5: 16 any **w** who is a believer has widows
Rev 2: 20 You tolerate that **w** Jezebel,
12: 1 a **w** clothed with the sun,
12: 13 he pursued the **w** who had given
17: 3 There I saw a **w** sitting on a scarlet

WOMB
Job 1: 21 I came from my mother's **w**,
Ps 139: 13 knit me together in my mother's **w**.
Pr 31: 2 Listen, son of my **w**!
Jer 1: 5 I formed you in the **w** I knew you,
Lk 1: 44 the baby in my **w** leaped for joy.
Jn 3: 4 into their mother's **w** to be born!"

WOMEN (MAN)
SS 1: 3 No wonder the young **w** love you!
Mt 11: 11 among those born of **w** there has
28: 5 The angel said to the **w**, "Do not be
Mk 15: 41 In Galilee these **w** had followed
Lk 1: 42 "Blessed are you among **w**,
8: 2 some **w** who had been cured of evil
23: 27 him, including **w** who mourned
24: 11 But they did not believe the **w**,
Ac 1: 14 along with the **w** and Mary
16: 13 to the **w** who had gathered there.
17: 4 and quite a few prominent **w**.
Ro 1: 26 Even their **w** exchanged natural
1Co 14: 34 **W** should remain silent
Php 4: 3 help these **w** since they have
1Ti 2: 9 I also want the **w** to dress modestly,
5: 2 older **w** as mothers, and younger **w**
Titus 2: 3 teach the older **w** to be reverent
2: 4 can urge the younger **w** to love
Heb 11: 35 **W** received back their dead,
1Pe 3: 5 is the way the holy **w** of the past

WON (WIN)
1Pe 3: 1 they may be **w** over without words

WONDER (WONDERFUL WONDERS)
Dt 13: 1 and announces to you a sign or **w**,
SS 1: 3 No **w** the young women love you!

WONDERFUL* (WONDER)
2Sa 1: 26 Your love for me was **w**, more **w** than that of women.
1Ch 16: 9 praise to him; tell of all his **w** acts.
Job 42: 3 things too **w** for me to know.
Ps 9: 1 I will tell of all your **w** deeds.
26: 7 and telling of all your **w** deeds.
75: 1 people tell of your **w** deeds.
105: 2 praise to him; tell of all his **w** acts.
107: 8 love and his **w** deeds for mankind,
107: 15 love and his **w** deeds for mankind,
107: 21 love and his **w** deeds for mankind.
107: 24 LORD, his **w** deeds in the deep.
107: 31 love and his **w** deeds for mankind.
119: 18 that I may see **w** things in your law.
119: 27 I may meditate on your **w** deeds.
119:129 statutes are **w**; therefore I obey
131: 1 matters or things too **w** for me.
139: 6 Such knowledge is too **w** for me,
139: 14 your works are **w**, I know that
145: 5 I will meditate on your **w** works.
Isa 9: 6 he will be called **W** Counselor,
25: 1 you have done **w** things,
28: 29 whose plan is **w**, whose wisdom is
Mt 21: 15 of the law saw the **w** things he did
Lk 13: 17 with all the **w** things he was doing.
1Pe 2: 9 out of darkness into his **w** light.

WONDERS (WONDER)
Ex 3: 20 all the **w** that I will perform among
Dt 10: 21 awesome **w** you saw with your own
2Sa 7: 23 awesome **w** by driving out nations
Job 37: 14 stop and consider God's **w**.
Ps 17: 7 Show me the **w** of your great love,
31: 21 for he showed me the **w** of his love
89: 5 The heavens praise your **w**,
Joel 2: 30 I will show **w** in the heavens
Mt 24: 24 great signs and **w** to deceive,
Mk 13: 22 perform signs and **w** to deceive,
Jn 4: 48 you people see signs and **w**,"
Ac 2: 11 we hear them declaring the **w**
2: 19 I will show **w** in the heavens
2: 43 was filled with awe at the many **w**
5: 12 signs and **w** among the people.
Ro 15: 19 by the power of signs and **w**,
2Co 12: 12 including signs, **w** and miracles.
2Th 2: 9 signs and **w** that serve the lie,
Heb 2: 4 it by signs, **w** and various miracles,

WOOD
Isa 44: 19 Shall I bow down to a block of **w**?"
1Co 3: 12 costly stones, **w**, hay or straw,

WOOL
Pr 31: 13 She selects **w** and flax and works
Isa 1: 18 as crimson, they shall be like **w**.
Da 7: 9 hair of his head was white like **w**.
Rev 1: 14 hair on his head was white like **w**,

WORD (BYWORD WORDLESS WORDS)
Nu 30: 2 must not break his **w** but must do
Dt 8: 3 but on every **w** that comes
2Sa 22: 31 The LORD's **w** is flawless;
Ps 56: 4 In God, whose **w** I praise—in God
119: 9 By living according to your **w**.
119: 11 I have hidden your **w** in my heart
119:105 Your **w** is a lamp to my feet
Pr 12: 25 the heart, but a kind **w** cheers it up.
15: 1 wrath, but a harsh **w** stirs up anger.
30: 5 "Every **w** of God is flawless; he is
Isa 55: 11 so is my **w** that goes out from my
Jer 23: 29 "Is not my **w** like fire,"
Mt 4: 4 but on every **w** that comes
12: 36 every empty **w** they have spoken.
15: 6 Thus you nullify the **w** of God
Mk 4: 14 The farmer sows the **w**.
Jn 1: 1 In the beginning was the **W**,
1: 14 The **W** became flesh and made his
17: 17 them by the truth; your **w** is truth.
Ac 6: 4 prayer and the ministry of the **w**."
2Co 2: 17 we do not peddle the **w** of God
4: 2 nor do we distort the **w** of God.
Eph 6: 17 of the Spirit, which is the **w** of God.
Php 2: 16 as you hold firmly to the **w** of life.
2Ti 2: 15 and who correctly handles the **w**
Heb 4: 12 the **w** of God is alive and active.
Jas 1: 22 Do not merely listen to the **w**,

WORDLESS* (WORD)
Ro 8: 26 intercedes for us through **w** groans.

WORDS (WORD)
Dt 11: 18 Fix these **w** of mine in your hearts
Ps 12: 6 the **w** of the LORD are flawless,
19: 3 have no speech, they use no **w**;
119:103 How sweet are your **w** to my taste,
119:130 unfolding of your **w** gives light;
119:160 All your **w** are true;
Pr 2: 1 if you accept my **w** and store up my
10: 19 Sin is not ended by multiplying **w**,
16: 24 Gracious **w** are a honeycomb,
30: 6 Do not add to his **w**, or he will
Ecc 12: 11 The **w** of the wise are like goads,
Jer 15: 16 When your **w** came, I ate them;
Mt 24: 35 but my **w** will never pass away.
Lk 6: 47 and hears my **w** and puts them
Jn 6: 68 You have the **w** of eternal life.
15: 7 in me and my **w** remain in you,
1Co 2: 13 but in **w** taught by the Spirit,
2: 13 realities with Spirit-taught **w**.
14: 19 rather speak five intelligible **w**
Rev 22: 19 if anyone takes **w** away from this

WORK (CO-WORKERS WORKED WORKER WORKERS WORKING WORKS)
Ge 2: 2 God had finished the **w** he had
2: 2 day he rested from all his **w**.
Ex 23: 12 but on the seventh day do not **w**,
Nu 8: 11 be ready to do the **w** of the LORD.
Dt 5: 14 On it you shall not do any **w**,
Ps 19: 1 the skies proclaim the **w** of his
Jer 48: 10 who is lax in doing the LORD's **w**!
Jn 6: 27 Do not **w** for food that spoils,
9: 4 is coming, when no one can **w**.
Ac 13: 2 and Saul for the **w** to which I have
1Co 3: 13 test the quality of each person's **w**.
4: 12 We **w** hard with our own hands.
Eph 4: 16 up in love, as each part does its **w**.
Php 1: 6 he who began a good **w** in you will
2: 12 continue to **w** out your salvation
Col 3: 23 you do, **w** at it with all your heart,
1Th 4: 11 business and **w** with your hands,
5: 12 those who **w** hard among you,
2Th 3: 10 is unwilling to **w** shall not eat."
2Ti 3: 17 equipped for every good **w**.
Heb 6: 10 he will not forget your **w**
2Jn : 11 them shares in their wicked **w**.
3Jn : 8 we may **w** together for the truth.

WORKED (WORK)
1Co 15: 10 No, I **w** harder than all of them—
2Th 3: 8 the contrary, we **w** night and day,

WORKER (WORK)
Lk 10: 7 for the **w** deserves his wages.
1Ti 5: 18 and "The **w** deserves his wages."
2Ti 2: 15 a **w** who does not need to be

WORKERS (WORK)
Mt 9: 37 is plentiful but the **w** are few.
20: 1 morning to hire **w** for his vineyard.

WORKING (WORK)
Col 3: 23 all your heart, as **w** for the Lord,

WORKS (WORK)
Ps 145: 6 of the power of your awesome **w**—
Pr 8: 22 me forth as the first of his **w**,
31: 31 her **w** bring her praise at the city
Jn 7: 3 there may see the **w** you do.
10: 25 The **w** I do in my Father's name
10: 32 "I have shown you many good **w**
10: 38 believe the **w**, that you may know
14: 11 the evidence of the **w** themselves.
Ro 4: 2 Abraham was justified by **w**,
8: 28 in all things God **w** for the good
Eph 2: 9 not by **w**, so that no one can boast.
4: 12 to equip his people for **w** of service,

WORLD (WORLDLY)
Ps 9: 8 He rules the **w** in righteousness
50: 12 for the **w** is mine, and all that is
90: 2 or you brought forth the whole **w**,
96: 13 will judge the **w** in righteousness
Pr 8: 23 beginning, when the **w** came to be.
Isa 13: 11 I will punish the **w** for its evil,
Mt 5: 14 "You are the light of the **w**.
16: 26 for someone to gain the whole **w**,
Mk 16: 15 *"Go into all the **w** and preach*
Jn 1: 29 who takes away the sin of the **w**!
3: 16 God so loved the **w** that he gave his
8: 12 he said, "I am the light of the **w**.
15: 19 I have chosen you out of the **w**. That is why the **w** hates you.
16: 33 In this **w** you will have trouble.
16: 33 I have overcome the **w**."
17: 5 I had with you before the **w** began.
17: 14 word and the **w** has hated them,
17: 14 not of the **w** any more than I am
18: 36 said, "My kingdom is not of this **w**.
Ac 17: 24 "The God who made the **w**
Ro 3: 19 and the whole **w** held accountable
10: 18 their words to the ends of the **w**."
1Co 1: 27 things of the **w** to shame the wise;
3: 19 the wisdom of this **w** is foolishness
6: 2 the Lord's people will judge the **w**?
2Co 5: 19 that God was reconciling the **w**
10: 3 we do not wage war as the **w** does.
1Ti 6: 7 For we brought nothing into the **w**,
Heb 11: 38 the **w** was not worthy of them.
Jas 2: 5 the eyes of the **w** to be rich in faith
4: 4 the **w** means enmity against God?
1Pe 1: 20 before the creation of the **w**,
1Jn 2: 2 also for the sins of the whole **w**.
2: 15 Do not love the **w** or anything
5: 4 victory that has overcome the **w**,
Rev 13: 8 slain from the creation of the **w**.

WORLDLY (WORLD)
1Co 3: 1 Spirit but as people who are still **w**
Titus 2: 12 to ungodliness and **w** passions,

WORM (WORMS)
Ps 22: 6 I am a **w** and not a man, scorned
Jnh 4: 7 the next day God provided a **w**,

WORMS (WORM)
Isa 66: 24 the **w** that eat them will not die,
Mk 9: 48 "'the **w** that eat them do not

WORRY (WORRYING)
Mt 6: 25 I tell you, do not **w** about your life,
10: 19 do not **w** about what to say or how

WORRYING (WORRY)
Mt 6: 27 you by **w** add a single hour to your

WORSHIP (WORSHIPED WORSHIPS)
Jos 22: 27 that we will **w** the LORD at his
2Ki 17: 36 arm, is the one you must **w**.
1Ch 16: 29 **W** the LORD in the splendor of his
Ps 95: 6 let us bow down in **w**, let us kneel
Ps 100: 2 **W** the LORD with gladness;
Zec 14: 17 go up to Jerusalem to **w** the King,
Mt 2: 2 it rose and have come to **w** him."
4: 9 "if you will bow down and **w** me."
Jn 4: 24 his worshipers must **w** in the Spirit
Ro 12: 1 this is your true and proper **w**.
Heb 10: 1 perfect those who draw near to **w**.

WORSHIPED (WORSHIP)
2Ch 29: 30 gladness and bowed down and **w**.
Mt 28: 9 to him, clasped his feet and **w** him.

WORSHIPS (WORSHIP)
Isa 44: 15 But he also fashions a god and **w** it;

WORTH (WORTHY)
Job 28: 13 No mortal comprehends its **w**;
Pr 31: 10 She is **w** far more than rubies.
Mt 10: 31 you are **w** more than many
Ro 8: 18 sufferings are not **w** comparing
Php 3: 8 surpassing **w** of knowing Christ
1Pe 1: 7 of greater **w** than gold,
3: 4 which is of great **w** in God's sight.

WORTHLESS
Pr 11: 4 Wealth is **w** in the day of wrath,
Jas 1: 26 themselves, and their religion is **w**.

WORTHY (WORTH)
1Ch 16: 25 is the LORD and most **w** of praise;
Mt 10: 37 or mother more than me is not **w**
Lk 15: 19 I am no longer **w** to be called your
Eph 4: 1 live a life **w** of the calling you have
Php 1: 27 in a manner **w** of the gospel
Col 1: 10 you may live a life **w** of the Lord
1Ti 3: 8 way, deacons are to be **w** of respect,
Heb 3: 3 Jesus has been found **w** of greater
Rev 5: 2 "Who is **w** to break the seals

WOUND (WOUNDS)
1Co 8: 12 way and **w** their weak conscience,

WOUNDS (WOUND)
Pr 27: 6 **W** from a friend can be trusted,
Isa 53: 5 him, and by his **w** we are healed.
Zec 13: 6 'What are these **w** on your body?'
1Pe 2: 24 "by his **w** you have been healed."

WRAPS
Ps 104: 2 The LORD **w** himself in light as

WRATH
2Ch 36: 16 at his prophets until the **w**
Ps 2: 5 anger and terrifies them in his **w**,
76: 10 survivors of your **w** are restrained.
Pr 15: 1 A gentle answer turns away **w**,
Isa 13: 13 at the **w** of the LORD Almighty,
51: 17 of the LORD the cup of his **w**,
Jer 25: 15 cup filled with the wine of my **w**
Eze 5: 13 my **w** against them will subside,
20: 8 I would pour out my **w** on them
Na 1: 2 vengeance and is filled with **w**.
1: 2 vents his **w** against his enemies.
Zep 1: 15 That day will be a day of **w**—
Jn 3: 36 life, for God's **w** remains on them.
Ro 1: 18 The **w** of God is being revealed
2: 5 are storing up **w** against yourself
5: 9 saved from God's **w** through him!
9: 22 great patience the objects of his **w**
1Th 5: 9 God did not appoint us to suffer **w**
Rev 6: 16 and from the **w** of the Lamb!
19: 15 the fury of the **w** of God Almighty.

WRESTLED
Ge 32: 24 a man **w** with him till daybreak.

WRITE (WRITER WRITING WRITTEN WROTE)
Dt 6: 9 **W** them on the doorframes of your
10: 2 I will **w** on the tablets the words
Pr 7: 3 **w** them on the tablet of your heart.
Jer 31: 33 minds and **w** it on their hearts.
Heb 8: 10 minds and **w** them on their hearts.
Rev 3: 12 will also **w** on them my new name.

WRITER* (WRITE)
Ps 45: 1 tongue is the pen of a skillful **w**.

WRITING (WRITE)
1Co 14: 37 what I am **w** to you is the Lord's

WRITTEN (WRITE)
Dt 28: 58 which are **w** in this book, and do
Jos 1: 8 be careful to do everything **w** in it.
23: 6 obey all that is **w** in the Book
Ps 40: 7 it is **w** about me in the scroll.

Da 12: 1 everyone whose name is found **w**
Mal 3: 16 remembrance was **w** in his
Lk 10: 20 that your names are **w** in heaven."
24: 44 must be fulfilled that is **w** about me
Jn 20: 31 these are **w** that you may believe
21: 25 for the books that would be **w**.
Ro 2: 15 of the law are **w** on their hearts,
1Co 4: 6 "Do not go beyond what is **w**."
10: 11 were **w** down as warnings for us,
2Co 3: 3 **w** not with ink but with the Spirit
Heb 10: 7 it is **w** about me in the scroll—
12: 23 whose names are **w** in heaven.
Rev 21: 27 only those whose names are **w**

WRONG (WRONGDOERS WRONGDOING WRONGED WRONGS)
Ex 23: 2 not follow the crowd in doing **w**.
Nu 5: 7 for the **w** they have done,
Dt 32: 4 A faithful God who does no **w**,
Job 34: 12 unthinkable that God would do **w**,
Ps 5: 5 You hate all who do **w**;
1Th 5: 15 that nobody pays back **w** for **w**,

WRONGDOERS* (WRONG)
Ps 37: 28 **W** will be completely destroyed;
1Co 6: 9 that **w** will not inherit the kingdom

WRONGDOING (WRONG)
Job 1: 22 not sin by charging God with **w**.
1Jn 5: 17 All **w** is sin, and there is sin

WRONGED (WRONG)
Pr 18: 19 A brother **w** is more unyielding
1Co 6: 7 Why not rather be **w**?

WRONGS (WRONG)
Pr 10: 12 conflict, but love covers over all **w**.
1Co 13: 5 angered, it keeps no record of **w**.

WROTE (WRITE)
Ex 34: 28 he **w** on the tablets the words
Jn 5: 46 believe me, for he **w** about me.
8: 8 *and* **w** *on the ground.*

XERXES
King of Persia, husband of Esther. Deposed Vashti; replaced her with Esther (Est 1–2). Sealed Haman's edict to annihilate the Jews (Est 3). Received Esther without having called her (Est 5:1–8). Honored Mordecai (Est 6). Hanged Haman (Est 7). Issued edict allowing Jews to defend themselves (Est 8). Exalted Mordecai (Est 8:1–2, 15; 9:4; 10).

YEAR (YEARS)
Ex 34: 23 Three times a **y** all your men are
Lev 16: 34 to be made once a **y** for all the sins
25: 4 in the seventh **y** the land is to have a **y** of sabbath rest,
25: 11 The fiftieth **y** shall be a jubilee
Heb 10: 1 same sacrifices repeated endlessly **y**

YEARS (YEAR)
Ge 1: 14 mark sacred times, and days and **y**,
Ex 12: 40 people lived in Egypt was 430 **y**.
16: 35 The Israelites ate manna forty **y**,
Job 36: 26 number of his **y** is past finding out.
Ps 90: 4 A thousand **y** in your sight are like
90: 10 Our days may come to seventy **y**,
Pr 3: 2 they will prolong your life many **y**
Lk 3: 23 Jesus himself was about thirty **y** old
2Pe 3: 8 the Lord a day is like a thousand **y**, and a thousand **y** are like a day.
Rev 20: 2 and bound him for a thousand **y**.

YEAST
Ex 12: 15 are to eat bread made without **y**.
Mt 16: 6 on your guard against the **y**
1Co 5: 6 a little **y** leavens the whole batch

YESTERDAY
Heb 13: 8 Christ is the same **y** and today

YIELD
Isa 42: 8 I will not **y** my glory to another

YOKE (YOKED)
1Ki 12: 4 "Your father put a heavy **y** on us,
Mt 11: 29 Take my **y** upon you and learn
Gal 5: 1 be burdened again by a **y** of slavery.

YOKED (YOKE)
2Co 6: 14 Do not be **y** together

YOUNG (YOUNGER YOUTH)
2Ch 10: 14 he followed the advice of the **y** men
Ps 37: 25 I was **y** and now I am old, yet I
119: 9 can a **y** person stay on the path
Pr 20: 29 glory of **y** men is their strength,
Isa 40: 11 he gently leads those that have **y**.
Joel 2: 28 your **y** men will see visions.
Ac 2: 17 your **y** men will see visions,
7: 58 at the feet of a **y** man named Saul.
1Ti 4: 12 down on you because you are **y**,
Titus 2: 6 encourage the **y** men to be
1Jn 2: 13 I am writing to you, **y** men,

YOUNGER (YOUNG)
1Ti 5: 1 Treat **y** men as brothers,
Titus 2: 4 they can urge the **y** women to love
1Pe 5: 5 you who are **y**, submit yourselves

YOUTH (YOUNG)
Ps 103: 5 your **y** is renewed like the eagle's.
Ecc 12: 1 your Creator in the days of your **y**,
2Ti 2: 22 Flee the evil desires of **y** and

ZACCHAEUS
Lk 19: 2 A man was there by the name of **Z**;

ZEAL (ZEALOUS)
Ps 69: 9 for **z** for your house consumes me,
Isa 59: 17 wrapped himself in **z** as in a cloak.
Jn 2: 17 "**Z** for your house will consume
Ro 10: 2 their **z** is not based on knowledge.
12: 11 Never be lacking in **z**, but keep

ZEALOUS (ZEAL)
Nu 25: 13 because he was **z** for the honor
Pr 23: 17 but always be **z** for the fear
Eze 39: 25 and I will be **z** for my holy name.
Gal 4: 18 It is fine to be **z**,

ZEBULUN
Son of Jacob by Leah (Ge 30:20; 35:23; 1Ch 2:1). Tribe of blessed (Ge 49:13; Dt 33:18–19), numbered (Nu 1:31; 26:27), allotted land (Jos 19:10–16; Eze 48:26), failed to fully possess (Jdg 1:30), supported Deborah (Jdg 4:6–10; 5:14, 18), David (1Ch 12:33), 12,000 from (Rev 7:8).

ZECHARIAH
1. Son of Jeroboam II; king of Israel (2Ki 15:8–12).
2. Post-exilic prophet who encouraged rebuilding of temple (Ezr 5:1; 6:14; Zec 1:1).
3. Father of John the Baptist (Lk 1:13; 3:2).

ZEDEKIAH
1. False prophet (1Ki 22:11–24; 2Ch 18:10–23).
2. Mattaniah, son of Josiah (1Ch 3:15), made king of Judah by Nebuchadnezzar (2Ki 24:17—25:7; 2Ch 36:10–14; Jer 37–39; 52:1–11).

ZEPHANIAH
Prophet; descendant of Hezekiah (Zep 1:1).

ZERUBBABEL
Descendant of David (1Ch 3:19; Mt 1:3). Led return from exile (Ezr 2:2; Ne 7:7). Governor of Israel; helped rebuild altar and temple (Ezr 3; Hag 1–2; Zec 4).

ZILPAH
Servant of Leah, mother of Jacob's sons Gad and Asher (Ge 30:9–12; 35:26, 46:16–18).

ZIMRI
King of Israel (1Ki 16:9–20).

ZION
2Sa 5: 7 David captured the fortress of **Z**—
Ps 2: 6 "I have installed my king on **Z**,
9: 11 of the LORD, enthroned in **Z**;
74: 2 Mount **Z**, where you dwelt.
87: 2 **Z** more than all the other dwellings
102: 13 arise and have compassion on **Z**,
137: 3 "Sing us one of the songs of **Z**!"
Isa 2: 3 The law will go out from **Z**,
28: 16 I lay a stone in **Z**, a tested stone,
51: 11 They will enter **Z** with singing;
52: 8 When the LORD returns to **Z**,
Jer 50: 5 will ask the way to **Z** and turn
Joel 3: 21 The LORD dwells in **Z**!
Am 6: 1 to you who are complacent in **Z**,
Mic 4: 2 The law will go out from **Z**,
Zec 9: 9 Rejoice greatly, Daughter **Z**!
Ro 9: 33 I lay in **Z** a stone that causes people
11: 26 "The deliverer will come from **Z**;
Heb 12: 22 But you have come to Mount **Z**,
Rev 14: 1 standing on Mount **Z**, and with

ZIPPORAH*
Daughter of Reuel; wife of Moses (Ex 2:21–22; 4:20–26; 18:1–6).

ZOPHAR*
One of Job's friends (Job 2:11; 11; 20; 42:9).

INDEX TO MAPS

INDEX TO MAPS

The Index to Maps will lead you to place-names found on the color maps on pp. 2865 – 2880 at the end of this study Bible. References are to the map number and the margin markings.

MAPS

Map 1: **WORLD OF THE PATRIARCHS**

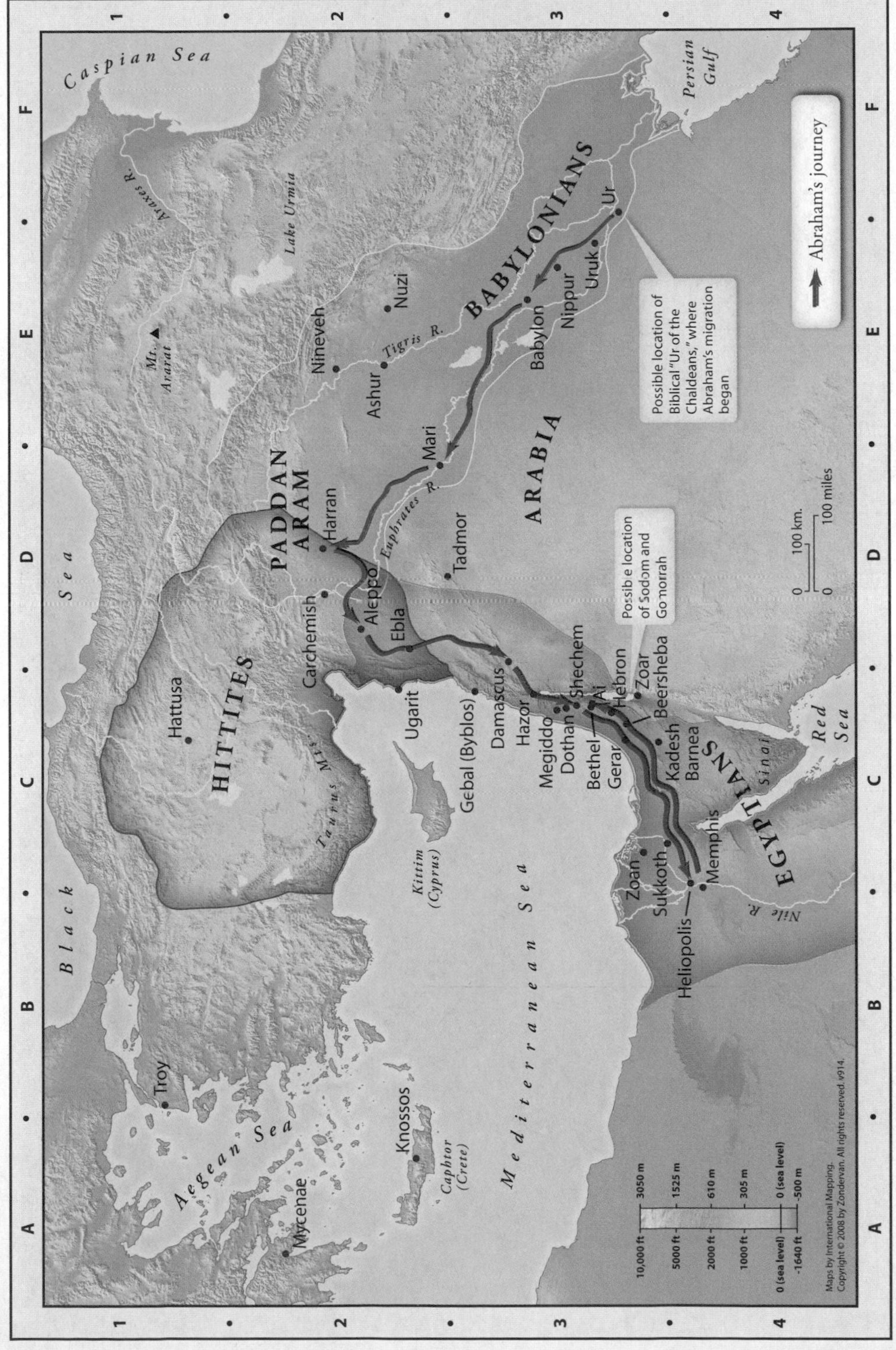
Caspian Sea
Black Sea
Aegean Sea
Mediterranean Sea
Persian Gulf
Red Sea
HITTITES
PADDAN ARAM
BABYLONIANS
ARABIA
EGYPTIANS
Troy
Mycenae
Knossos
Caphtor (Crete)
Kittim (Cyprus)
Hattusa
Taurus Mts.
Carchemish
Harran
Aleppo
Ebla
Ugarit
Gebal (Byblos)
Damascus
Hazor
Megiddo
Dothan
Shechem
Bethel
Ai
Hebron
Gerar
Beersheba
Zoar
Kadesh Barnea
Sinai
Zoan
Sukkoth
Heliopolis
Memphis
Nile R.
Tadmor
Mari
Euphrates R.
Tigris R.
Ashur
Nineveh
Nuzi
Babylon
Nippur
Uruk
Ur
Mt. Ararat
Lake Urmia
Araxes R.
Possible location of Sodom and Gomorrah
Possible location of Biblical "Ur of the Chaldeans," where Abraham's migration began
Abraham's journey
0 100 km.
0 100 miles
10,000 ft 3050 m
5000 ft 1525 m
2000 ft 610 m
1000 ft 305 m
0 (sea level) 0 (sea level)
-1640 ft -500 m
Maps by International Mapping.
Copyright © 2008 by Zondervan. All rights reserved. v914.
A B C D E F
1 2 3 4

Map 2: **HOLY LAND AND SINAI**

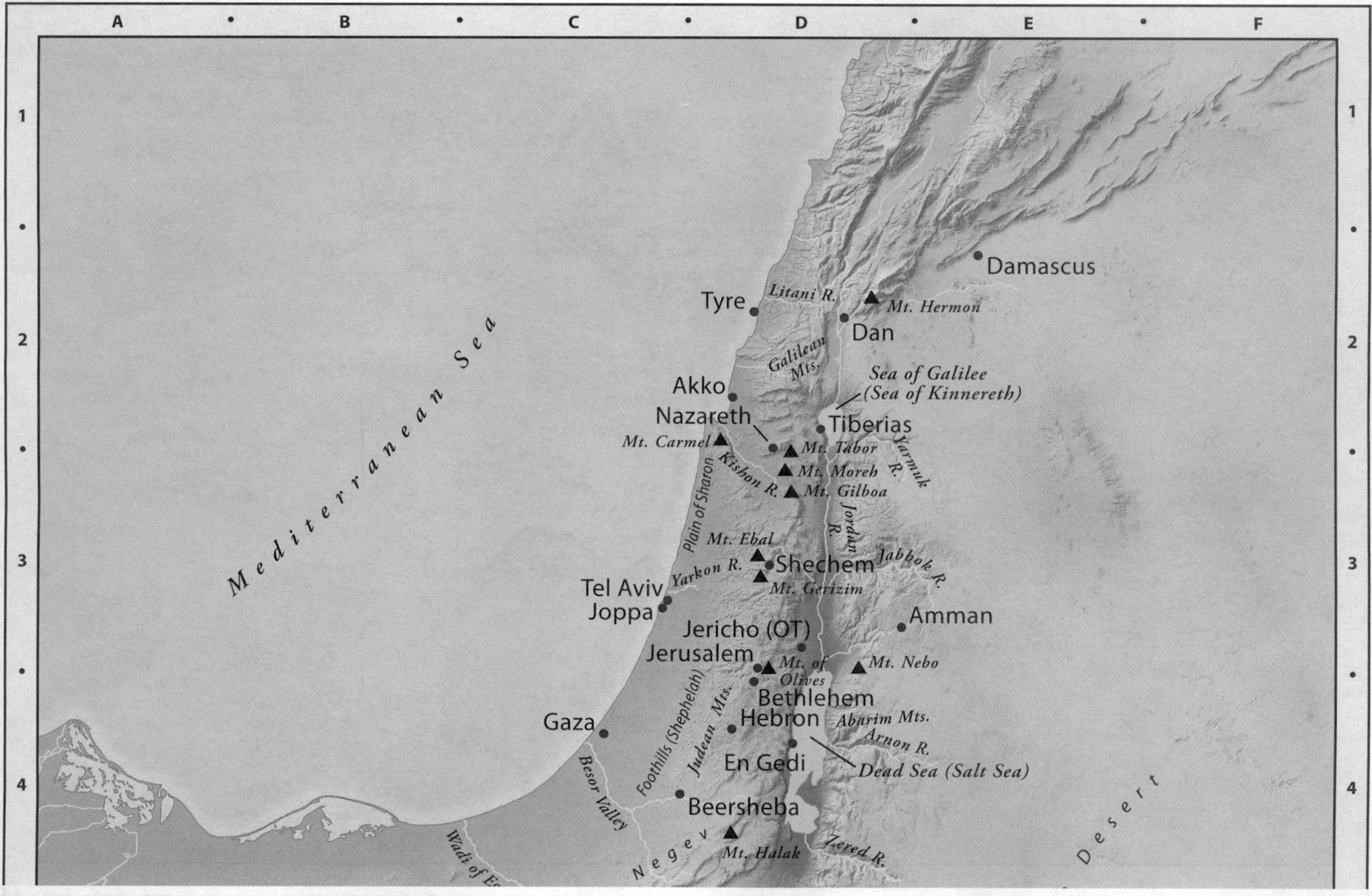

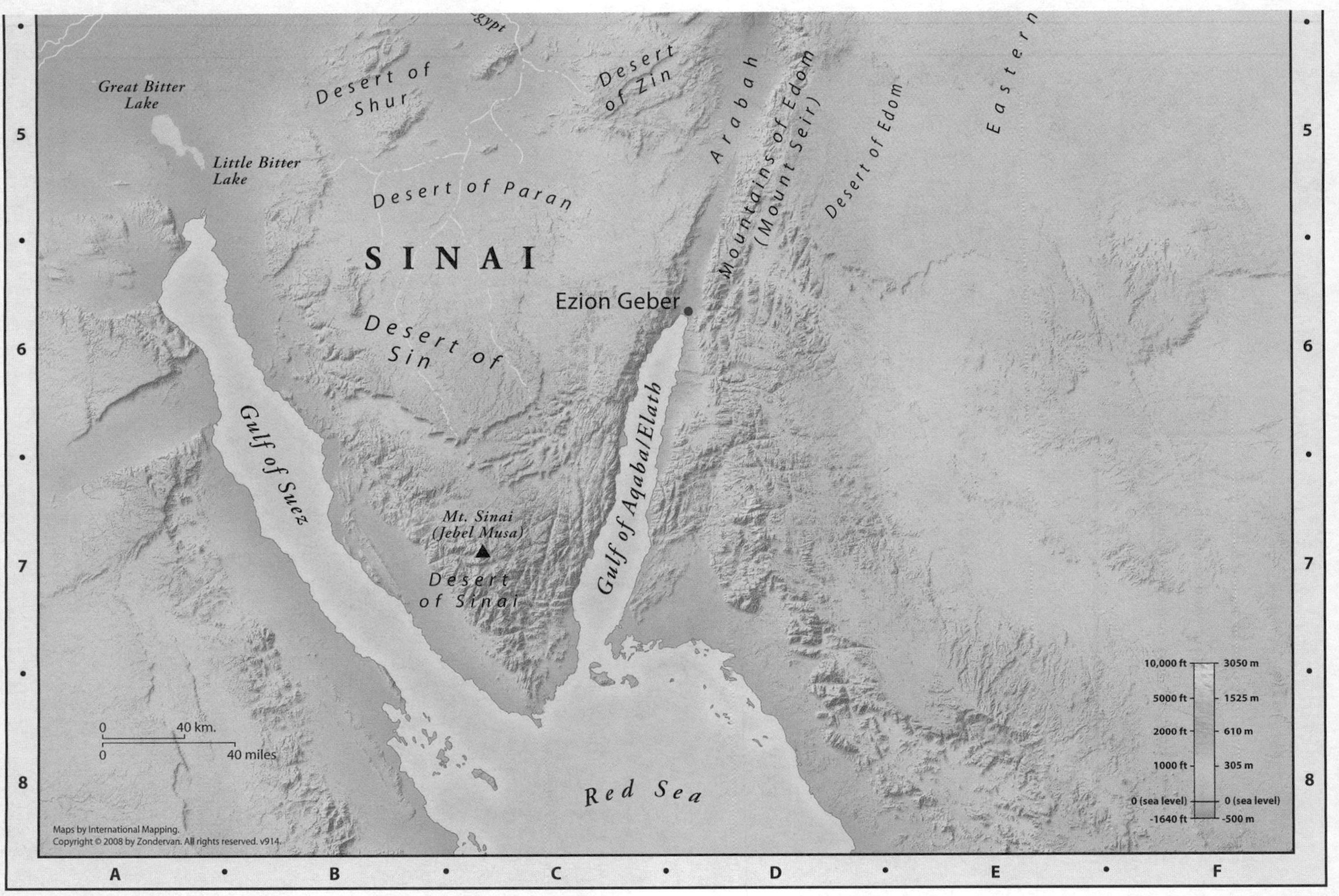
Great Bitter Lake
Little Bitter Lake
Desert of Shur
Desert of Zin
gypt
Arabah
Mountains of Edom (Mount Seir)
Desert of Edom
Eastern
Desert of Paran
SINAI
Ezion Geber
Desert of Sin
Gulf of Suez
Gulf of Aqaba/Elath
Mt. Sinai (Jebel Musa)
Desert of Sinai
Red Sea
0 40 km.
0 40 miles
Maps by International Mapping.
Copyright © 2008 by Zondervan. All rights reserved. v914.
10,000 ft 3050 m
5000 ft 1525 m
2000 ft 610 m
1000 ft 305 m
0 (sea level) 0 (sea level)
-1640 ft -500 m
A B C D E F
5 6 7 8

Map 3: EXODUS AND CONQUEST OF CANAAN

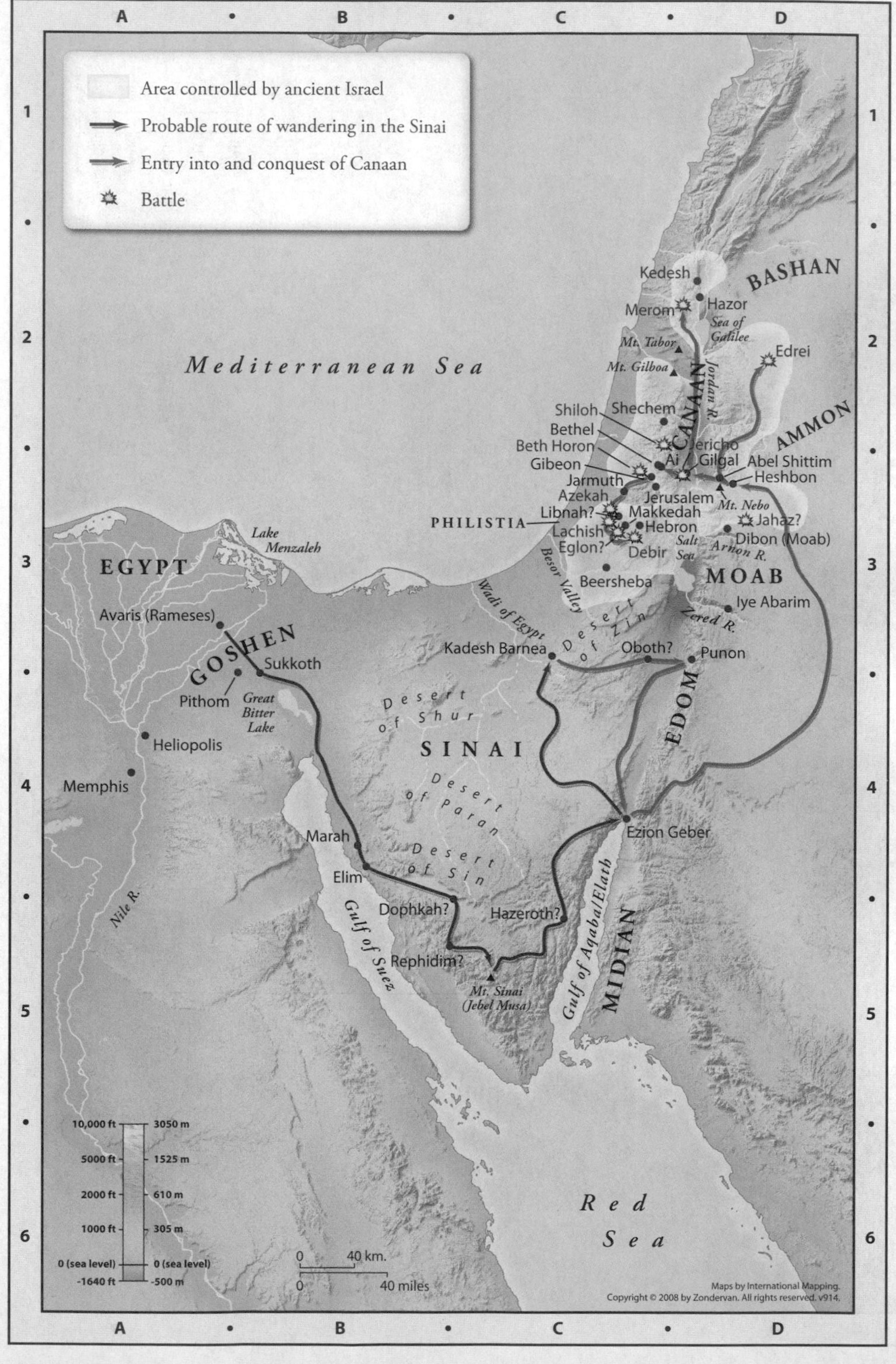

A
B
C
D
1
2
3
4
5
6
Area controlled by ancient Israel
Probable route of wandering in the Sinai
Entry into and conquest of Canaan
Battle
Mediterranean Sea
BASHAN
Kedesh
Hazor
Merom
Sea of Galilee
Mt. Tabor
Mt. Gilboa
Edrei
Jordan R.
CANAAN
Shiloh
Shechem
Bethel
Beth Horon
Gibeon
Jericho
Ai
Gilgal
AMMON
Abel Shittim
Heshbon
Jarmuth
Azekah
Jerusalem
Mt. Nebo
Libnah?
Makkedah
Jahaz?
PHILISTIA
Lachish
Hebron
Dibon (Moab)
Eglon?
Debir
Salt Sea
Arnon R.
MOAB
Beersheba
Besor Valley
Wadi of Egypt
Desert of Zin
Iye Abarim
Zered R.
Kadesh Barnea
Oboth?
Punon
EDOM
Lake Menzaleh
EGYPT
Avaris (Rameses)
GOSHEN
Sukkoth
Pithom
Great Bitter Lake
Heliopolis
Memphis
Desert of Shur
SINAI
Desert of Paran
Ezion Geber
Marah
Desert of Sin
Elim
Dophkah?
Hazeroth?
Nile R.
Gulf of Suez
Rephidim?
Mt. Sinai (Jebel Musa)
Gulf of Aqaba/Elath
MIDIAN
10,000 ft
3050 m
5000 ft
1525 m
2000 ft
610 m
1000 ft
305 m
0 (sea level)
0 (sea level)
-1640 ft
-500 m
0
40 km.
0
40 miles
Red Sea
Maps by International Mapping.
Copyright © 2008 by Zondervan. All rights reserved. v914.

Map 4: **LAND OF THE TWELVE TRIBES**

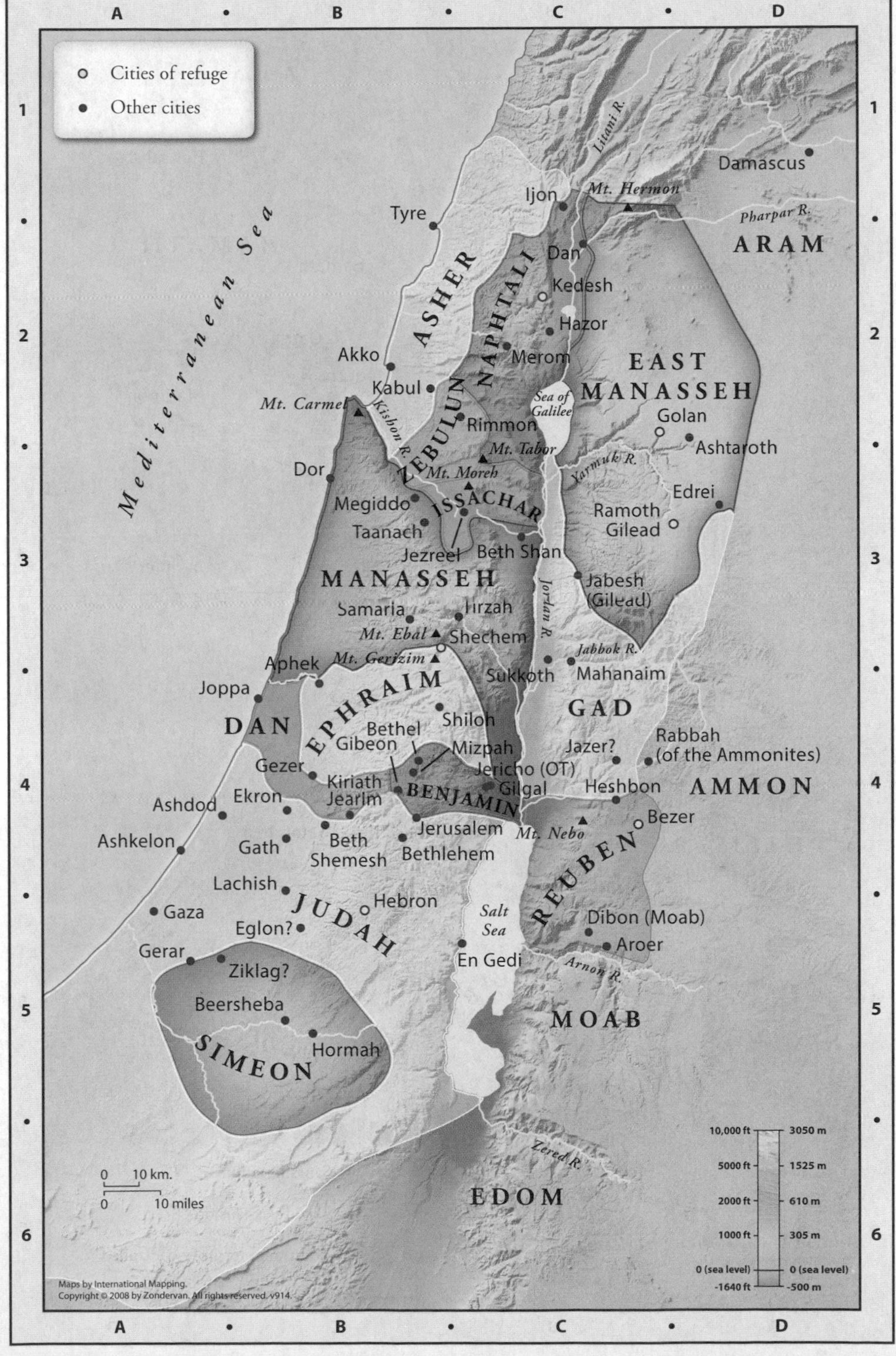

Map 5: **KINGDOM OF DAVID AND SOLOMON**

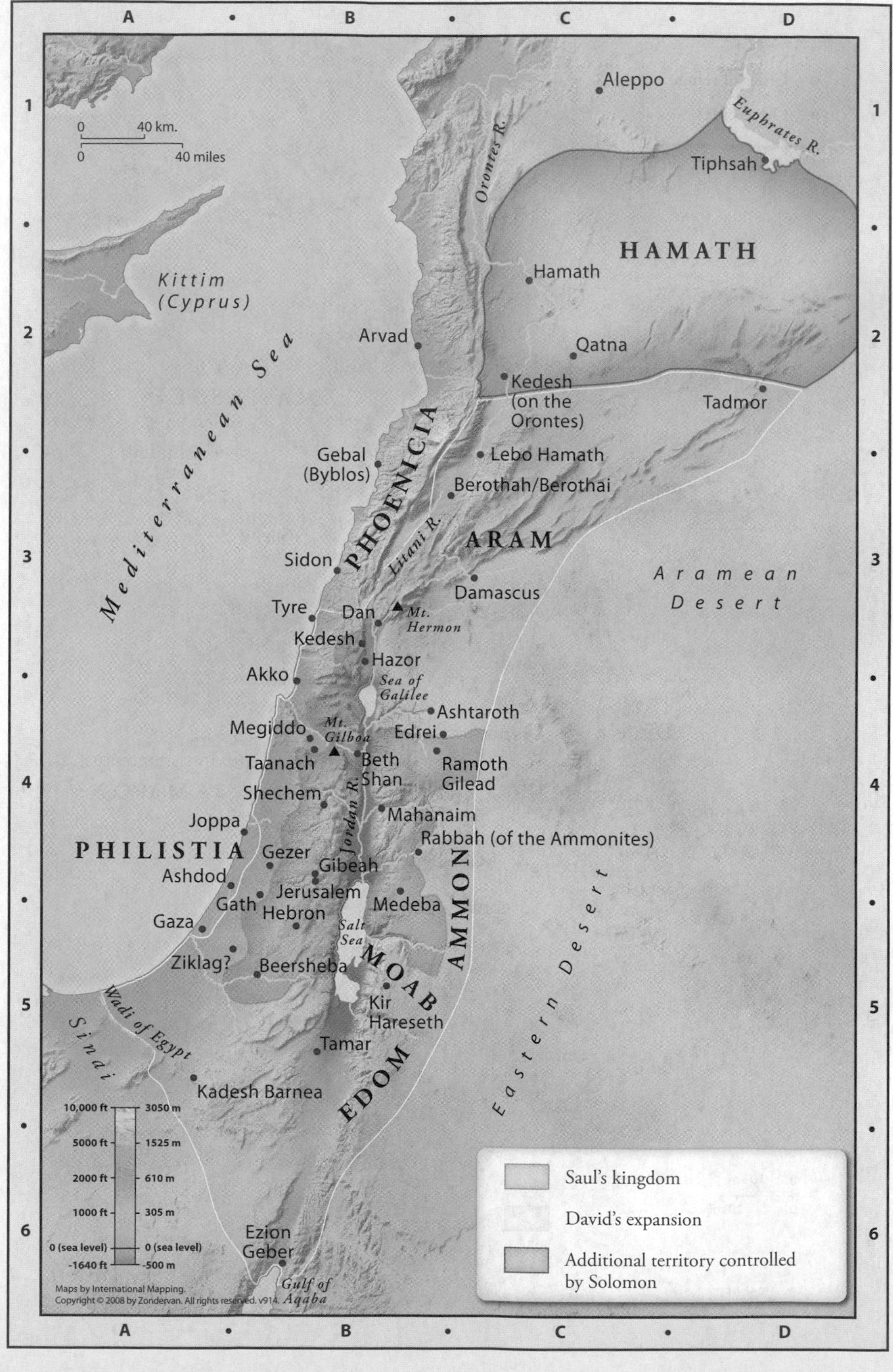
A
B
C
D
1
2
3
4
5
6
0
40 km.
40 miles
Aleppo
Euphrates R.
Tiphsah
Orontes R.
HAMATH
Hamath
Kittim
(Cyprus)
Arvad
Qatna
Mediterranean Sea
Kedesh
(on the
Orontes)
Tadmor
Gebal
(Byblos)
PHOENICIA
Lebo Hamath
Berothah/Berothai
Litani R.
ARAM
Sidon
Damascus
Aramean
Desert
Tyre
Dan
Mt.
Hermon
Kedesh
Hazor
Akko
Sea of
Galilee
Ashtaroth
Megiddo
Mt.
Gilboa
Edrei
Taanach
Beth
Shan
Ramoth
Gilead
Shechem
Jordan R.
Mahanaim
Joppa
Rabbah (of the Ammonites)
PHILISTIA
Gezer
Gibeah
Ashdod
Jerusalem
Gath
Hebron
Medeba
AMMON
Eastern Desert
Gaza
Salt
Sea
Ziklag?
Beersheba
MOAB
Wadi of Egypt
Kir
Hareseth
Sinai
Tamar
EDOM
Kadesh Barnea
10,000 ft
3050 m
5000 ft
1525 m
2000 ft
610 m
1000 ft
305 m
0 (sea level)
0 (sea level)
-1640 ft
-500 m
Ezion
Geber
Gulf of
Aqaba
Saul's kingdom
David's expansion
Additional territory controlled
by Solomon

Map 6: **KINGDOMS OF ISRAEL AND JUDAH**

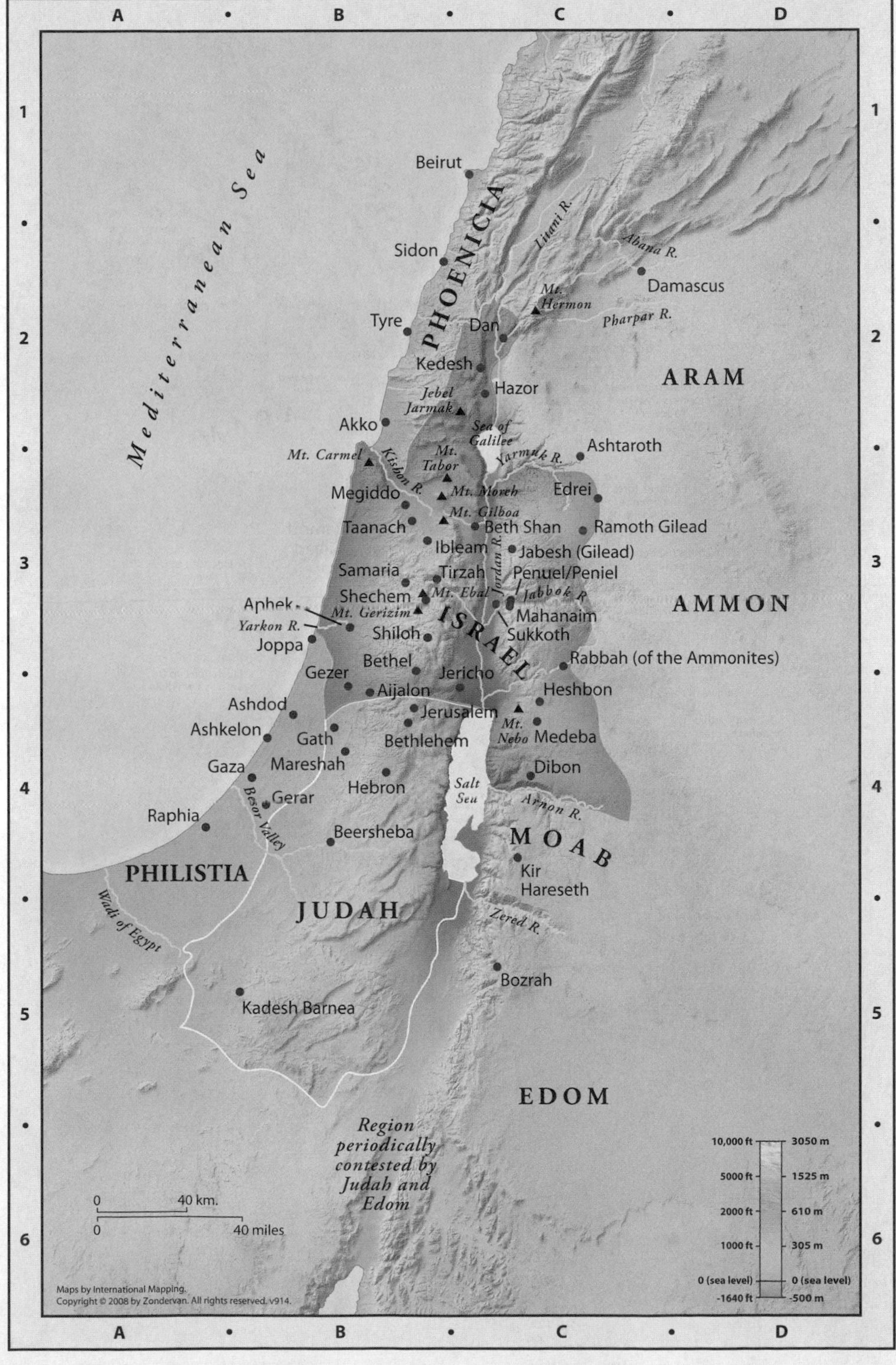
A
B
C
D
1
2
3
4
5
6
Mediterranean Sea
Beirut
PHOENICIA
Sidon
Litani R.
Abana R.
Damascus
Mt. Hermon
Pharpar R.
Tyre
Dan
Kedesh
Hazor
ARAM
Jebel Jarmak
Akko
Sea of Galilee
Mt. Carmel
Kishon R.
Mt. Tabor
Yarmuk R.
Ashtaroth
Megiddo
Mt. Moreh
Edrei
Mt. Gilboa
Taanach
Beth Shan
Ramoth Gilead
Ibleam
Jabesh (Gilead)
Samaria
Tirzah
Jordan R.
Penuel/Peniel
Shechem
Mt. Ebal
Jabbok R.
AMMON
Aphek
Mt. Gerizim
ISRAEL
Mahanaim
Yarkon R.
Shiloh
Sukkoth
Joppa
Bethel
Rabbah (of the Ammonites)
Gezer
Jericho
Aijalon
Heshbon
Ashdod
Jerusalem
Mt. Nebo
Ashkelon
Gath
Bethlehem
Medeba
Gaza
Mareshah
Dibon
Hebron
Salt Sea
Gerar
Besor Valley
Arnon R.
Raphia
Beersheba
MOAB
Kir Hareseth
PHILISTIA
JUDAH
Wadi of Egypt
Zered R.
Bozrah
Kadesh Barnea
EDOM
Region periodically contested by Judah and Edom
0
40 km.
0
40 miles
10,000 ft
3050 m
5000 ft
1525 m
2000 ft
610 m
1000 ft
305 m
0 (sea level)
0 (sea level)
-1640 ft
-500 m

Maps by International Mapping.

Map 7: **PROPHETS IN ISRAEL AND JUDAH**

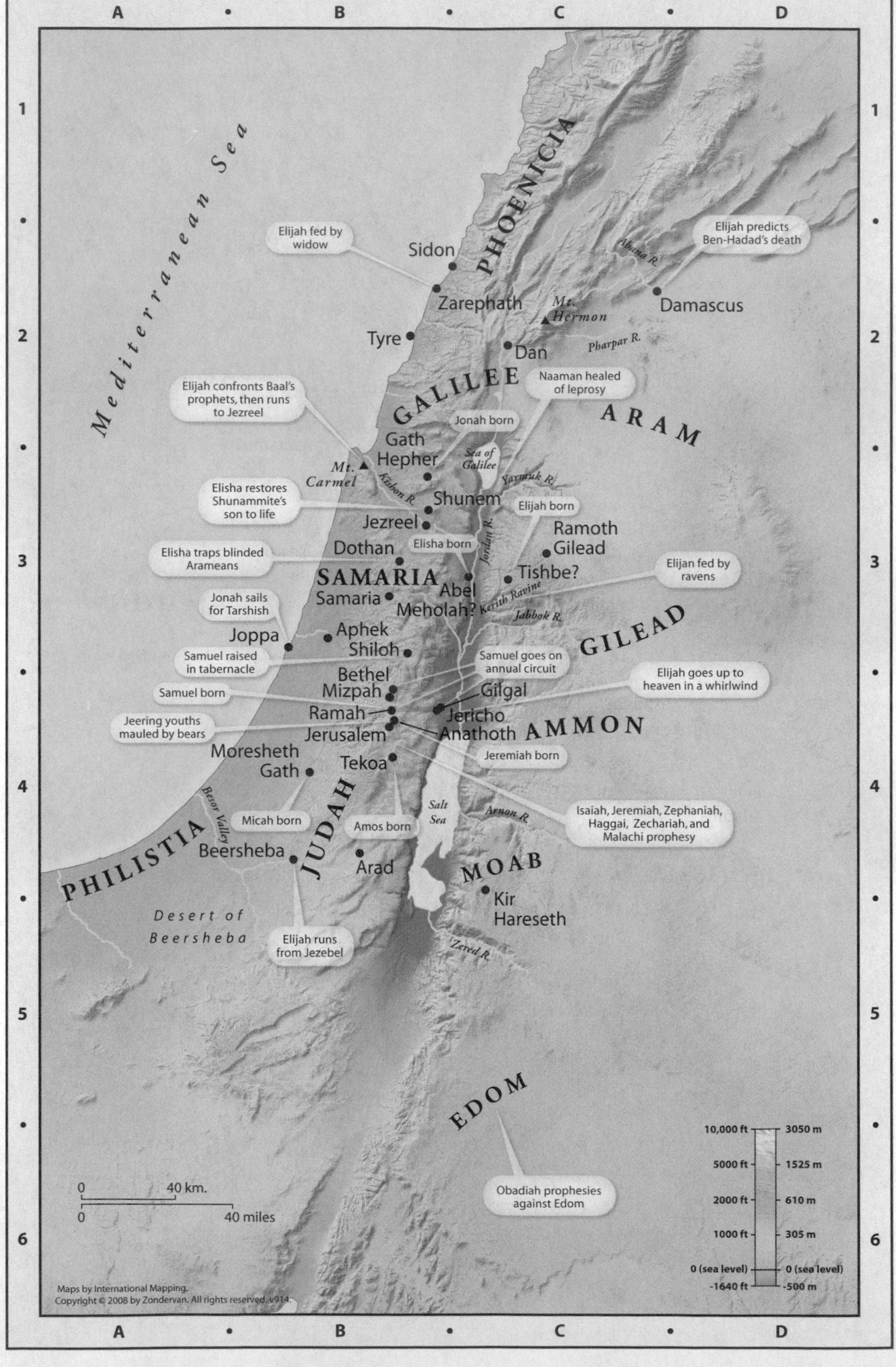

Mediterranean Sea
PHOENICIA
Elijah fed by widow
Sidon
Zarephath
Elijah predicts Ben-Hadad's death
Damascus
Mt. Hermon
Tyre
Dan
Pharpar R.
Abana R.
GALILEE
Naaman healed of leprosy
ARAM
Elijah confronts Baal's prophets, then runs to Jezreel
Jonah born
Gath Hepher
Sea of Galilee
Mt. Carmel
Kishon R.
Yarmuk R.
Elisha restores Shunammite's son to life
Shunem
Elijah born
Jezreel
Ramoth Gilead
Elisha traps blinded Arameans
Dothan
Elisha born
Jordan R.
Tishbe?
Elijah fed by ravens
SAMARIA
Samaria
Abel Meholah?
Kerith Ravine
Jabbok R.
Jonah sails for Tarshish
Joppa
Aphek
Shiloh
GILEAD
Samuel raised in tabernacle
Samuel goes on annual circuit
Bethel
Elijah goes up to heaven in a whirlwind
Samuel born
Mizpah
Gilgal
Ramah
Jericho
Jeering youths mauled by bears
Jerusalem
Anathoth
AMMON
Moresheth Gath
Tekoa
Jeremiah born
Salt Sea
Arnon R.
Isaiah, Jeremiah, Zephaniah, Haggai, Zechariah, and Malachi prophesy
Besor Valley
Micah born
Amos born
JUDAH
PHILISTIA
Beersheba
Arad
MOAB
Kir Hareseth
Desert of Beersheba
Elijah runs from Jezebel
Zered R.
EDOM
Obadiah prophesies against Edom
0 40 km.
0 40 miles
10,000 ft 3050 m
5000 ft 1525 m
2000 ft 610 m
1000 ft 305 m
0 (sea level) 0 (sea level)
-1640 ft -500 m
A B C D
1 2 3 4 5 6

Map 8: ASSYRIAN AND BABYLONIAN EMPIRES

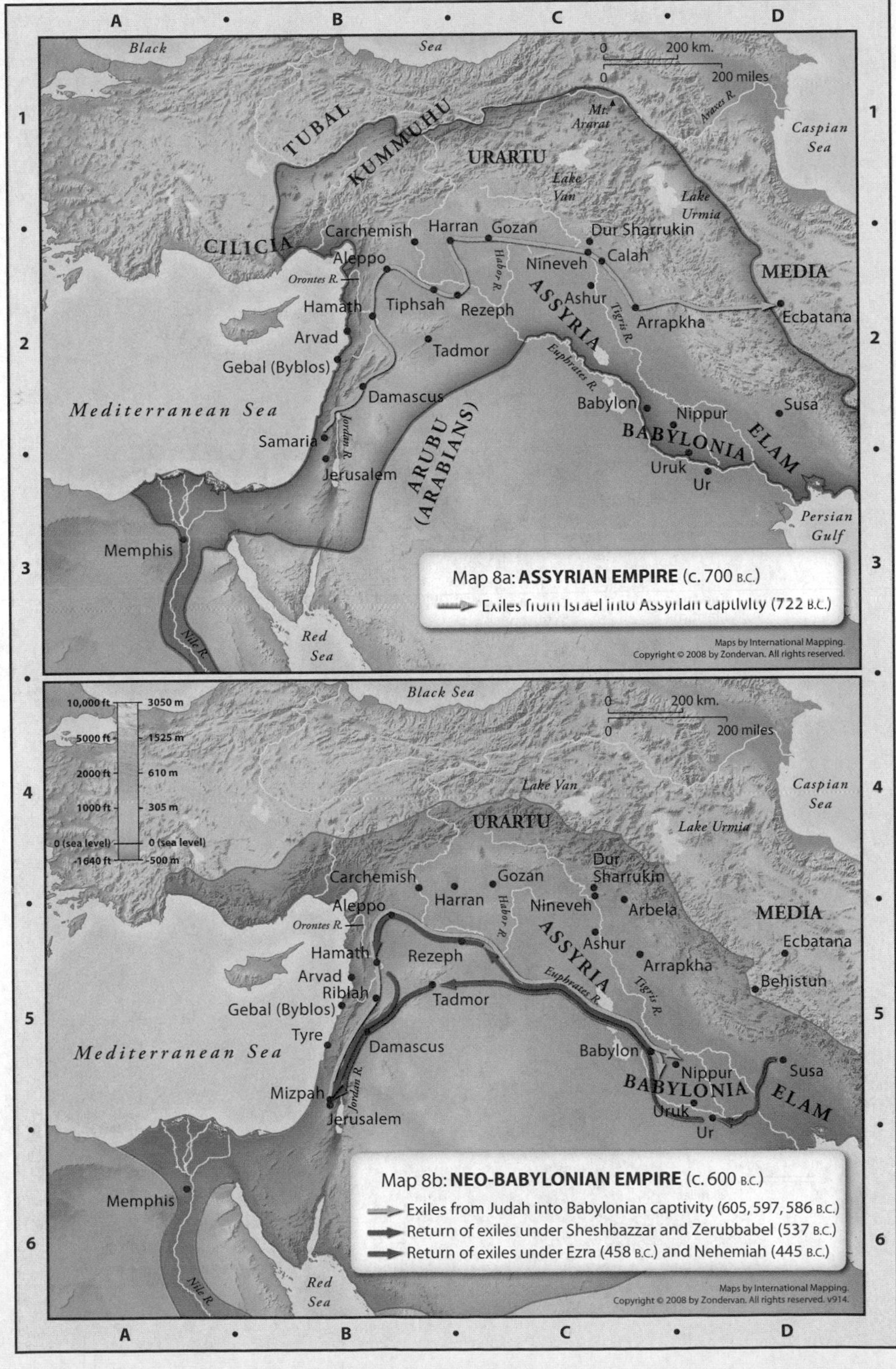

Map 9: **HOLY LAND IN THE TIME OF JESUS**

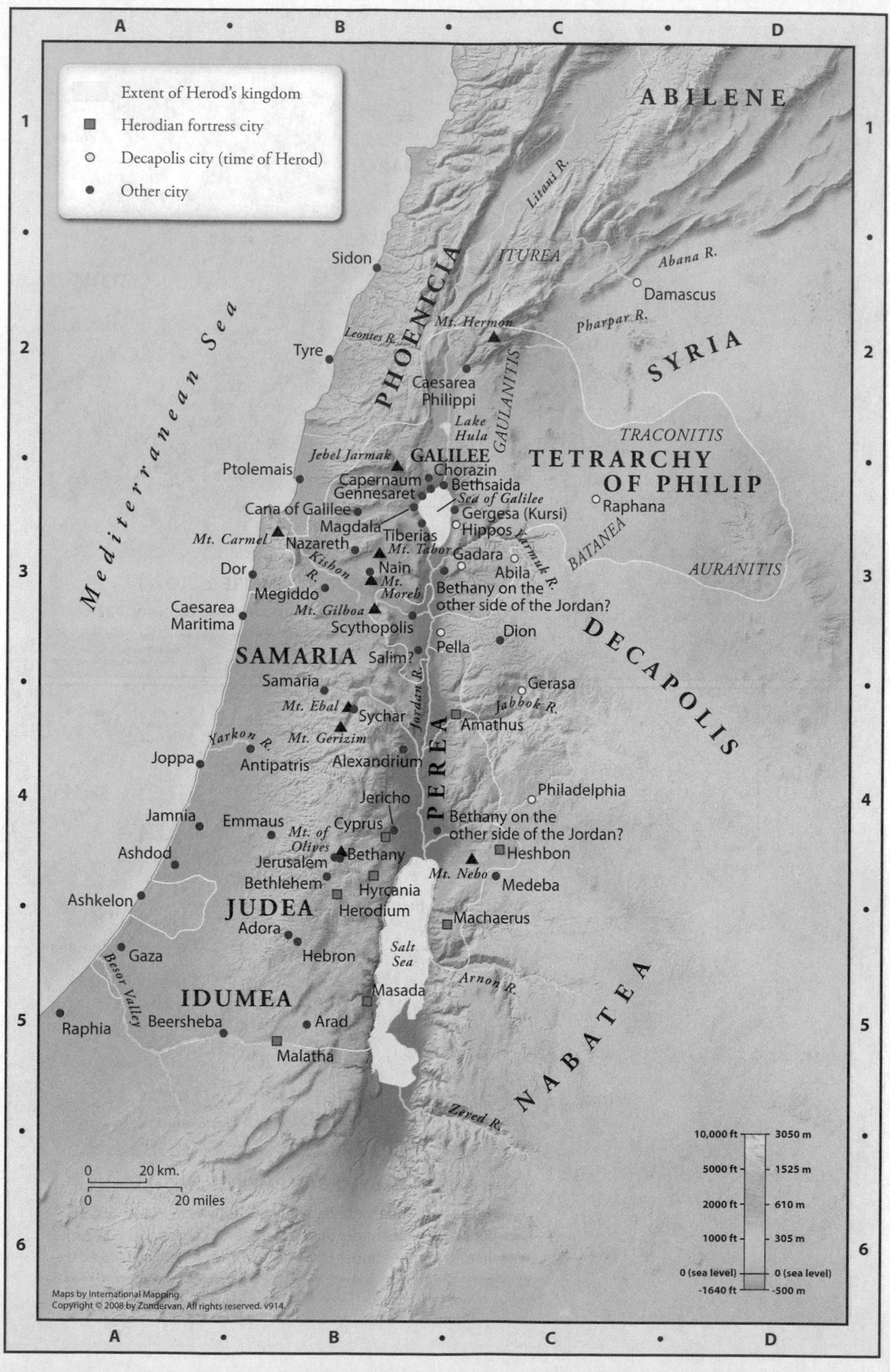

Extent of Herod's kingdom
Herodian fortress city
Decapolis city (time of Herod)
Other city
ABILENE
Litani R.
ITUREA
Abana R.
Damascus
Pharpar R.
SYRIA
Sidon
PHOENICIA
Mt. Hermon
Leontes R.
Tyre
Mediterranean Sea
Caesarea Philippi
GAULANITIS
Lake Hula
TRACONITIS
Jebel Jarmak
GALILEE
TETRARCHY OF PHILIP
Ptolemais
Capernaum
Chorazin
Bethsaida
Gennesaret
Sea of Galilee
Cana of Galilee
Gergesa (Kursi)
Raphana
Magdala
Hippos
Tiberias
BATANEA
Mt. Carmel
Nazareth
Mt. Tabor
Gadara
Yarmuk R.
Kishon R.
Dor
Nain
Abila
AURANITIS
Mt. Moreh
Bethany on the other side of the Jordan?
Megiddo
Caesarea Maritima
Mt. Gilboa
Scythopolis
Dion
DECAPOLIS
Pella
SAMARIA
Salim?
Samaria
Gerasa
Mt. Ebal
Jabbok R.
Sychar
Jordan R.
Amathus
Yarkon R.
Mt. Gerizim
PEREA
Joppa
Antipatris
Alexandrium
Philadelphia
Jericho
Jamnia
Emmaus
Cyprus
Bethany on the other side of the Jordan?
Mt. of Olives
Bethany
Heshbon
Ashdod
Jerusalem
Bethlehem
Mt. Nebo
Medeba
Hyrcania
Ashkelon
JUDEA
Herodium
Machaerus
Adora
Salt Sea
Gaza
Hebron
Besor Valley
Masada
Arnon R.
NABATEA
IDUMEA
Raphia
Beersheba
Arad
Malatha
Zered R.
0 20 km.
0 20 miles
10,000 ft 3050 m
5000 ft 1525 m
2000 ft 610 m
1000 ft 305 m
0 (sea level) 0 (sea level)
-1640 ft -500 m
A B C D
1 2 3 4 5 6
Maps by International Mapping.
Copyright © 2008 by Zondervan. All rights reserved. v914.

Map 10: **JERUSALEM IN THE TIME OF JESUS**

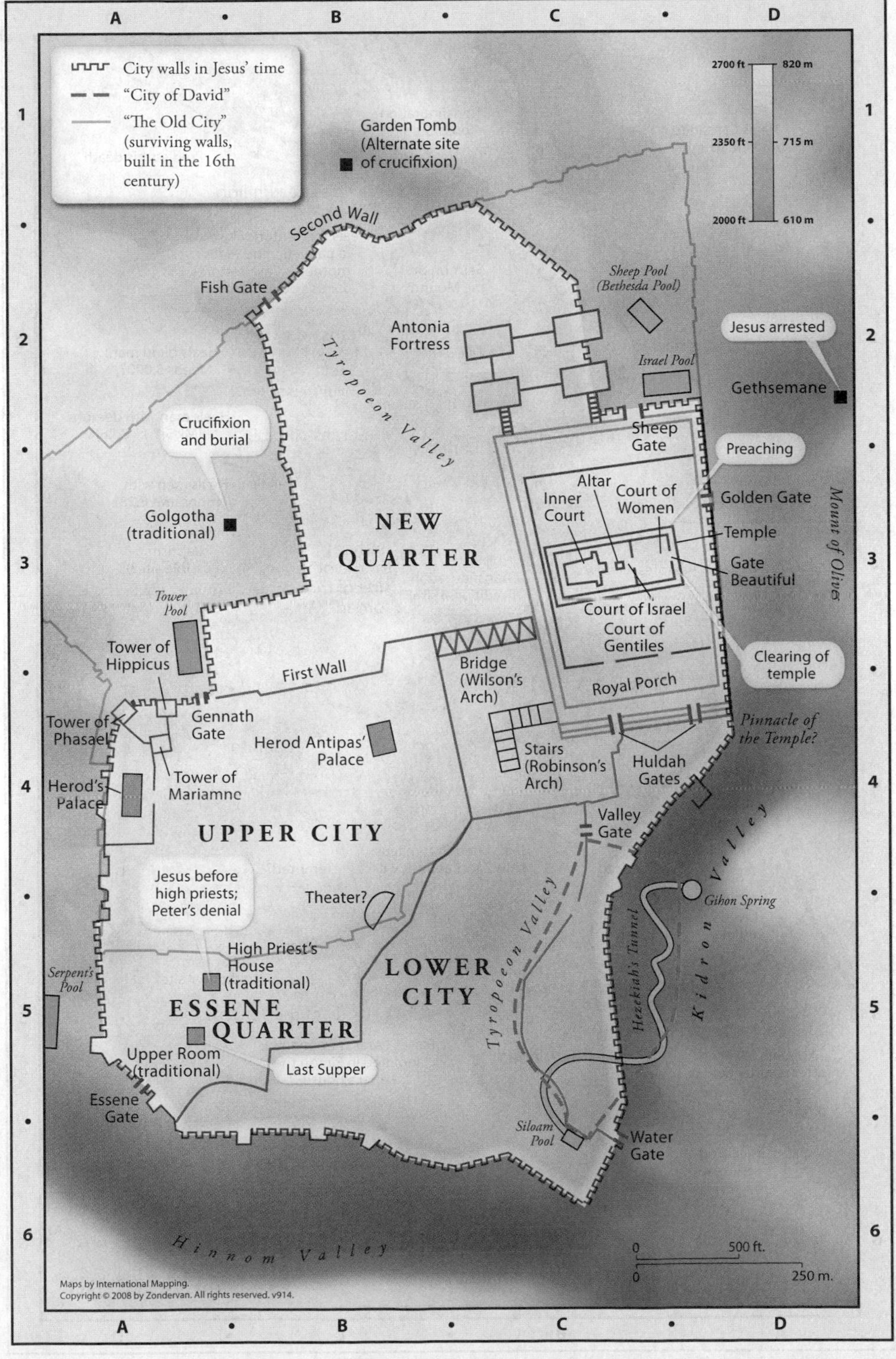

City walls in Jesus' time
"City of David"
"The Old City" (surviving walls, built in the 16th century)
2700 ft
820 m
2350 ft
715 m
2000 ft
610 m
Garden Tomb (Alternate site of crucifixion)
Second Wall
Fish Gate
Antonia Fortress
Tyropoeon Valley
Sheep Pool (Bethesda Pool)
Israel Pool
Jesus arrested
Gethsemane
Crucifixion and burial
Golgotha (traditional)
NEW QUARTER
Sheep Gate
Preaching
Altar
Inner Court
Court of Women
Golden Gate
Temple
Gate Beautiful
Mount of Olives
Court of Israel
Court of Gentiles
Clearing of temple
Tower Pool
Tower of Hippicus
First Wall
Bridge (Wilson's Arch)
Royal Porch
Gennath Gate
Tower of Phasael
Herod Antipas' Palace
Stairs (Robinson's Arch)
Huldah Gates
Pinnacle of the Temple?
Herod's Palace
Tower of Mariamne
Valley Gate
UPPER CITY
Kidron Valley
Jesus before high priests; Peter's denial
Theater?
Gihon Spring
High Priest's House (traditional)
LOWER CITY
Hezekiah's Tunnel
Serpent's Pool
ESSENE QUARTER
Upper Room (traditional)
Last Supper
Essene Gate
Siloam Pool
Water Gate
Hinnom Valley
0 500 ft.
0 250 m.
A B C D
1 2 3 4 5 6

Map 11: JESUS' MINISTRY

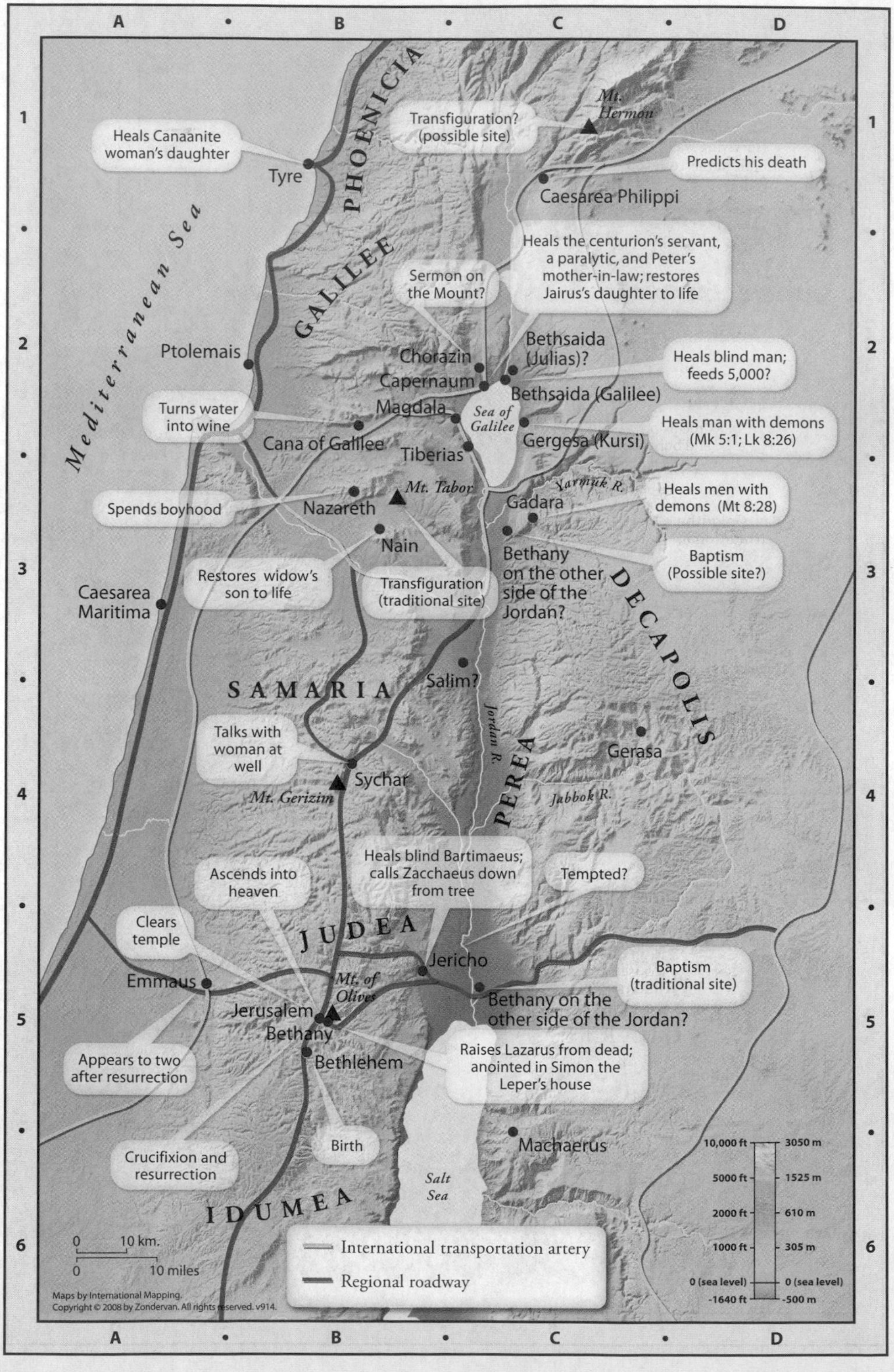

A
B
C
D
1
2
3
4
5
6
PHOENICIA
Mediterranean Sea
GALILEE
SAMARIA
JUDEA
IDUMEA
DECAPOLIS
PEREA
Mt. Hermon
Transfiguration? (possible site)
Heals Canaanite woman's daughter
Tyre
Predicts his death
Caesarea Philippi
Heals the centurion's servant, a paralytic, and Peter's mother-in-law; restores Jairus's daughter to life
Sermon on the Mount?
Ptolemais
Chorazin
Bethsaida (Julias)?
Heals blind man; feeds 5,000?
Capernaum
Bethsaida (Galilee)
Turns water into wine
Magdala
Sea of Galilee
Heals man with demons (Mk 5:1; Lk 8:26)
Cana of Galilee
Gergesa (Kursi)
Tiberias
Yarmuk R.
Mt. Tabor
Heals men with demons (Mt 8:28)
Spends boyhood
Nazareth
Gadara
Nain
Bethany on the other side of the Jordan?
Baptism (Possible site?)
Restores widow's son to life
Transfiguration (traditional site)
Caesarea Maritima
Salim?
Jordan R.
Talks with woman at well
Gerasa
Sychar
Mt. Gerizim
Jabbok R.
Heals blind Bartimaeus; calls Zacchaeus down from tree
Ascends into heaven
Tempted?
Clears temple
Jericho
Baptism (traditional site)
Emmaus
Mt. of Olives
Bethany on the other side of the Jordan?
Jerusalem
Bethany
Appears to two after resurrection
Bethlehem
Raises Lazarus from dead; anointed in Simon the Leper's house
Birth
Machaerus
Crucifixion and resurrection
Salt Sea
0 10 km.
0 10 miles
International transportation artery
Regional roadway
10,000 ft 3050 m
5000 ft 1525 m
2000 ft 610 m
1000 ft 305 m
0 (sea level) 0 (sea level)
-1640 ft -500 m

Map 12: APOSTLES' EARLY TRAVELS

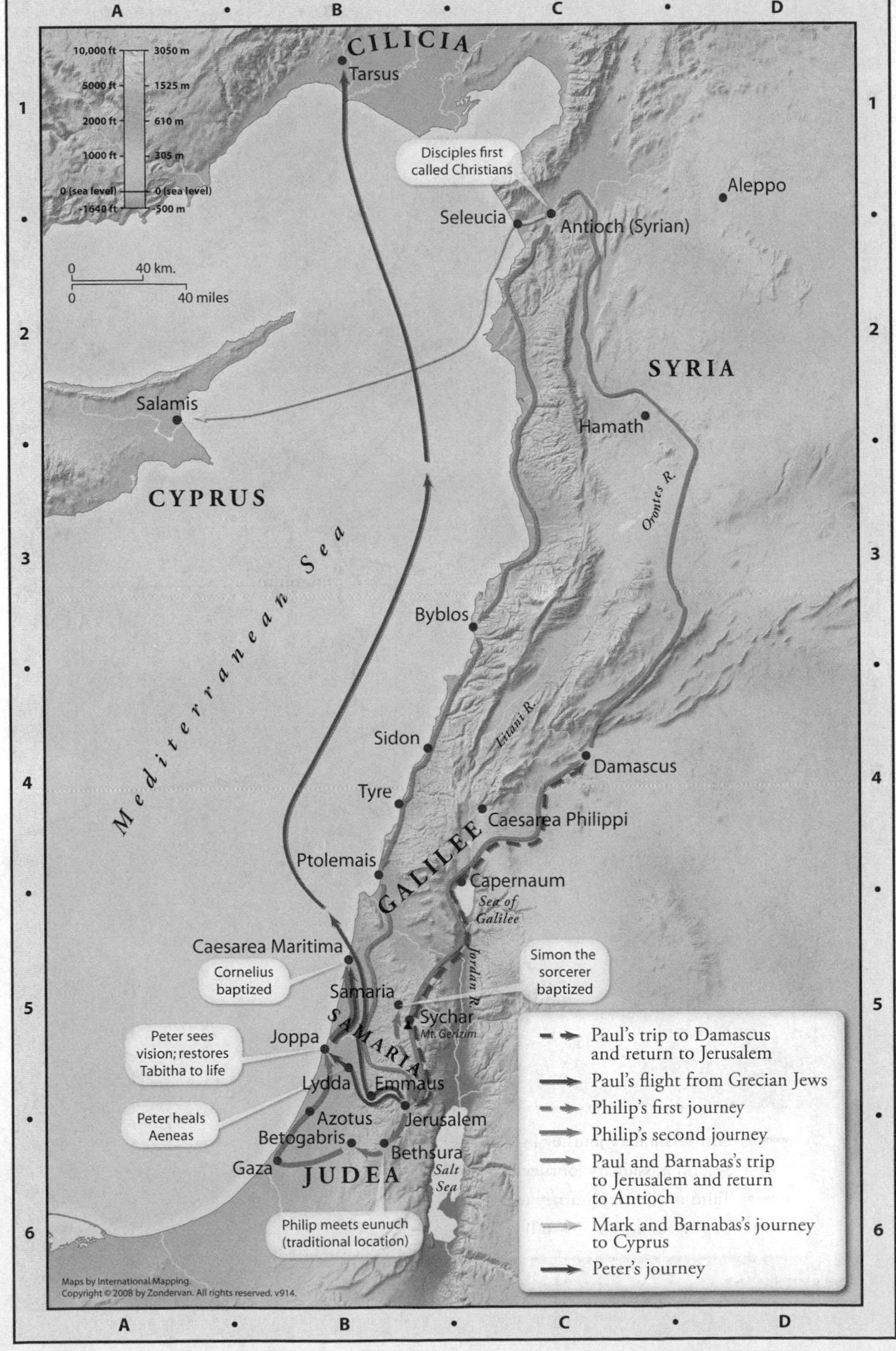
A • B • C • D
1 • 2 • 3 • 4 • 5 • 6
10,000 ft 3050 m
5000 ft 1525 m
2000 ft 610 m
1000 ft 305 m
0 (sea level) 0 (sea level)
-1640 ft -500 m
0 40 km.
0 40 miles
CILICIA
Tarsus
Disciples first called Christians
Aleppo
Seleucia
Antioch (Syrian)
SYRIA
Salamis
Hamath
CYPRUS
Orontes R.
Mediterranean Sea
Byblos
Litani R.
Sidon
Damascus
Tyre
Caesarea Philippi
GALILEE
Ptolemais
Capernaum
Sea of Galilee
Caesarea Maritima
Jordan R.
Cornelius baptized
Simon the sorcerer baptized
Samaria
SAMARIA
Sychar
Mt. Gerizim
Peter sees vision; restores Tabitha to life
Joppa
Lydda
Emmaus
Peter heals Aeneas
Azotus
Jerusalem
Betogabris
Bethsura
Gaza
JUDEA
Salt Sea
Philip meets eunuch (traditional location)
Paul's trip to Damascus and return to Jerusalem
Paul's flight from Grecian Jews
Philip's first journey
Philip's second journey
Paul and Barnabas's trip to Jerusalem and return to Antioch
Mark and Barnabas's journey to Cyprus
Peter's journey

Map 13: **PAUL'S MISSIONARY JOURNEYS**

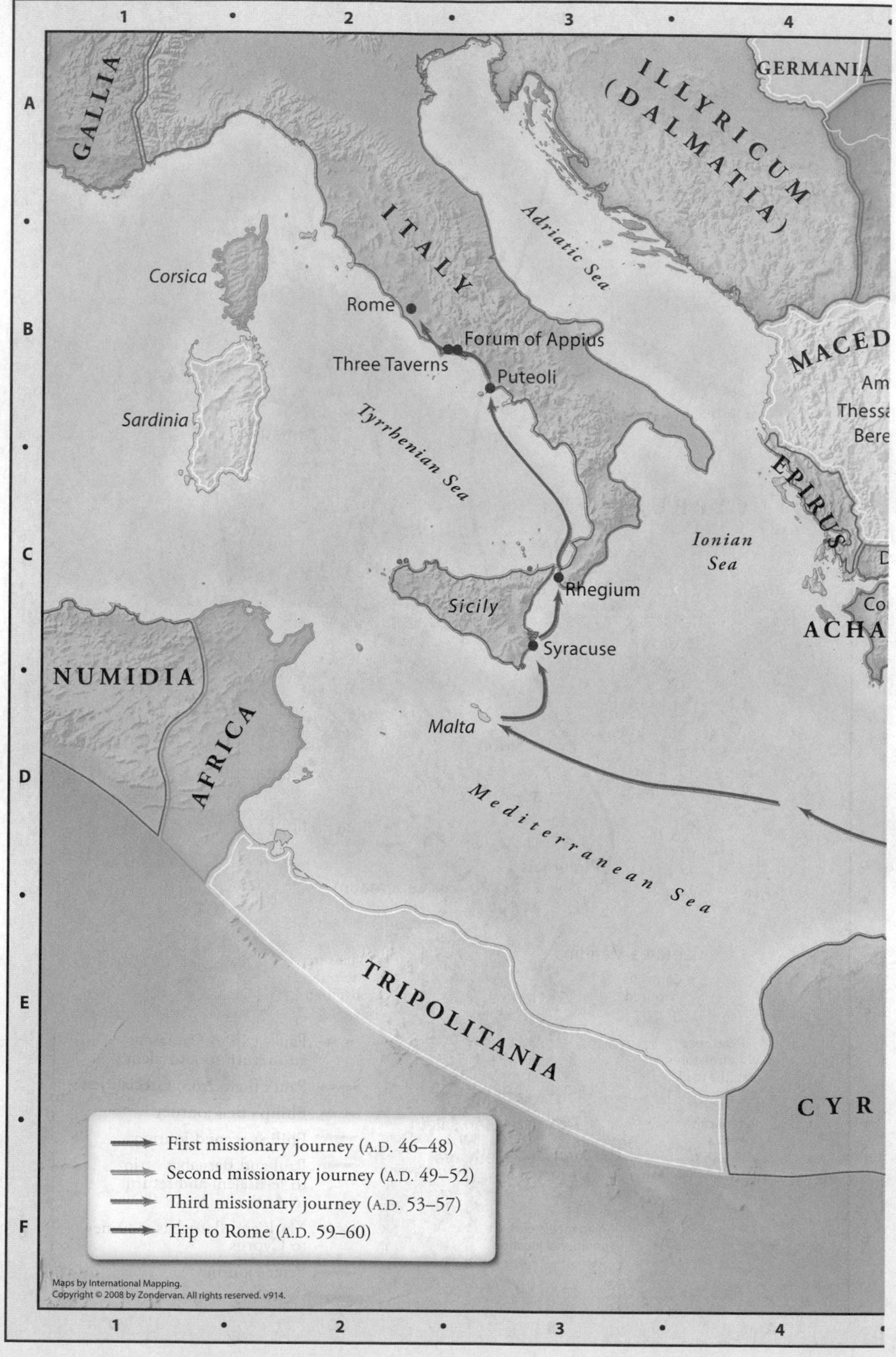
1
2
3
4
A
B
C
D
E
F
GALLIA
GERMANIA
ILLYRICUM (DALMATIA)
ITALY
Adriatic Sea
Corsica
Rome
Forum of Appius
Three Taverns
Puteoli
MACED
Am
Thessa
Bere
Sardinia
Tyrrhenian Sea
EPIRUS
Ionian Sea
Rhegium
Sicily
Syracuse
ACHA
NUMIDIA
AFRICA
Malta
Mediterranean Sea
TRIPOLITANIA
CYR
First missionary journey (A.D. 46–48)
Second missionary journey (A.D. 49–52)
Third missionary journey (A.D. 53–57)
Trip to Rome (A.D. 59–60)
Maps by International Mapping.
Copyright © 2008 by Zondervan. All rights reserved. v914.

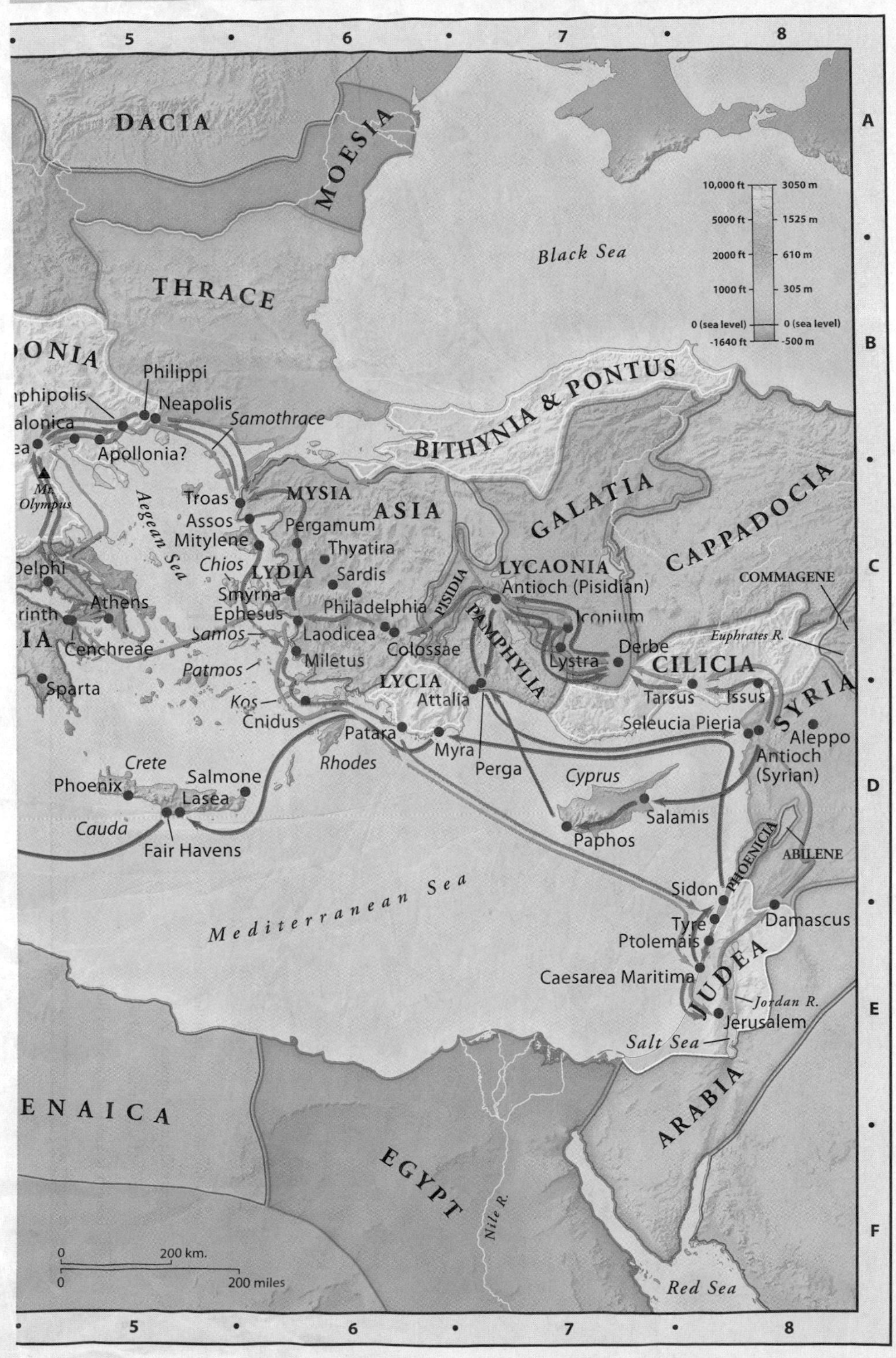
DACIA
MOESIA
THRACE
Black Sea
10,000 ft
5000 ft
2000 ft
1000 ft
0 (sea level)
-1640 ft
3050 m
1525 m
610 m
305 m
0 (sea level)
-500 m
BITHYNIA & PONTUS
GALATIA
CAPPADOCIA
COMMAGENE
Euphrates R.
Philippi
Neapolis
Samothrace
Apollonia?
Mt. Olympus
Aegean Sea
Troas
Assos
Mitylene
Chios
MYSIA
ASIA
Pergamum
Thyatira
LYDIA
Sardis
Smyrna
Ephesus
Samos
Philadelphia
Laodicea
Colossae
Patmos
Miletus
Kos
Cnidus
Delphi
Athens
Cenchreae
Sparta
LYCAONIA
Antioch (Pisidian)
PISIDIA
PAMPHYLIA
Iconium
Lystra
Derbe
CILICIA
Tarsus
Issus
SYRIA
Seleucia Pieria
Aleppo
Antioch (Syrian)
LYCIA
Attalia
Patara
Myra
Perga
Rhodes
Crete
Phoenix
Salmone
Lasea
Cauda
Fair Havens
Cyprus
Salamis
Paphos
PHOENICIA
ABILENE
Sidon
Tyre
Ptolemais
Damascus
Caesarea Maritima
JUDEA
Jordan R.
Jerusalem
Salt Sea
Mediterranean Sea
ARABIA
EGYPT
Nile R.
Red Sea
0
200 km.
0
200 miles
5
6
7
8
A
B
C
D
E
F

Map 14: **ROMAN EMPIRE**

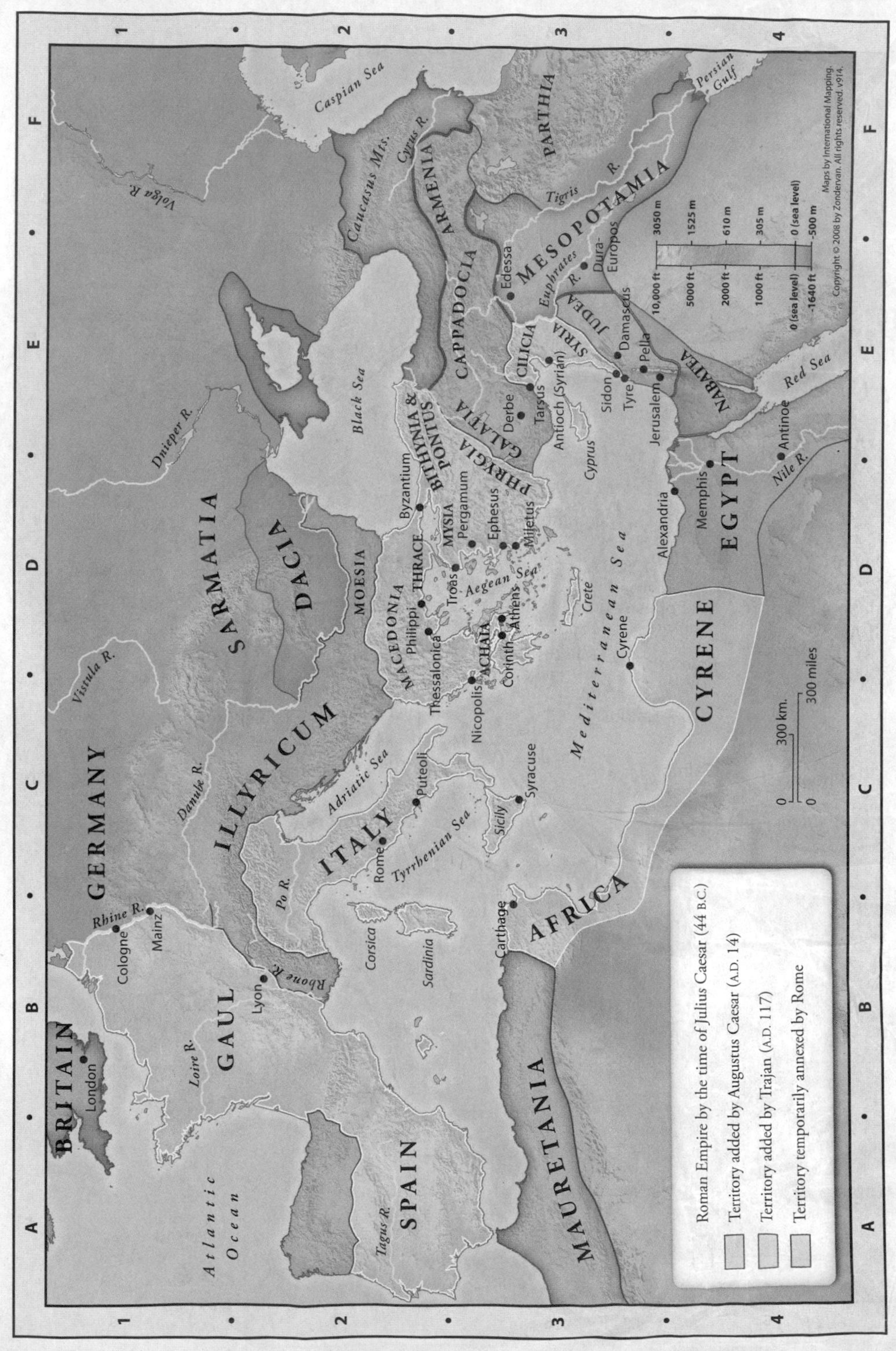
A B C D E F
1 2 3 4
Atlantic Ocean
BRITAIN
London
GAUL
Loire R.
Lyon
Rhone R.
Cologne
Mainz
Rhine R.
GERMANY
Danube R.
Vistula R.
SARMATIA
DACIA
Dnieper R.
Volga R.
Caspian Sea
Caucasus Mts.
Cyrus R.
ARMENIA
PARTHIA
Tigris R.
MESOPOTAMIA
Euphrates R.
Dura-Europos
Edessa
CAPPADOCIA
Black Sea
BITHYNIA & PONTUS
GALATIA
PHRYGIA
CILICIA
SYRIA
JUDEA
NABATEA
Persian Gulf
Red Sea
Damascus
Pella
Jerusalem
Sidon
Tyre
Antioch (Syrian)
Tarsus
Derbe
Cyprus
Byzantium
MYSIA
Pergamum
Ephesus
Miletus
THRACE
Troas
Aegean Sea
MOESIA
MACEDONIA
Philippi
Thessalonica
ACHAIA
Athens
Corinth
Nicopolis
Crete
Mediterranean Sea
Cyrene
CYRENE
EGYPT
Alexandria
Memphis
Antinoe
Nile R.
ILLYRICUM
Adriatic Sea
ITALY
Po R.
Rome
Puteoli
Tyrrhenian Sea
Sicily
Syracuse
Corsica
Sardinia
Carthage
AFRICA
MAURETANIA
SPAIN
Tagus R.
0 300 km.
0 300 miles
10,000 ft 3050 m
5000 ft 1525 m
2000 ft 610 m
1000 ft 305 m
0 (sea level) 0 (sea level)
-1640 ft -500 m
Roman Empire by the time of Julius Caesar (44 B.C.)
Territory added by Augustus Caesar (A.D. 14)
Territory added by Trajan (A.D. 117)
Territory temporarily annexed by Rome
Maps by International Mapping.
Copyright © 2008 by Zondervan. All rights reserved. v914.